## Abbreviations for the States and the District of Columbia

| State Name | Alpha Code | State Name | Alpha Code |
|---|---|---|---|
| Alabama | AL | Montana | MT |
| Alaska | AK | Nebraska | NE |
| Arizona | AZ | Nevada | NV |
| Arkansas | AR | New Hampshire | NH |
| California | CA | New Jersey | NJ |
| Colorado | CO | New Mexico | NM |
| Connecticut | CT | New York | NY |
| Delaware | DE | North Carolina | NC |
| District of Columbia | DC | North Dakota | ND |
| Florida | FL | Ohio | OH |
| Georgia | GA | Oklahoma | OK |
| | HI | Oregon | OR |
| | ID | Pennsylvania | PA |
| | IL | Rhode Island | RI |
| | IN | South Carolina | SC |
| | IA | South Dakota | SD |
| | KS | Tennessee | TN |
| | KY | Texas | TX |
| | LA | Utah | UT |
| | ME | Vermont | VT |
| | MD | Virginia | VA |
| | MA | Washington | WA |
| | MI | West Virginia | WV |
| | MN | Wisconsin | WI |
| | MS | Wyoming | WY |
| | MO | | |



## Abbreviations for the Outlying Areas of the United States

| Area Name | Alpha Code |
|---|---|
| American Samoa | AS |
| Federated States of Micronesia | FM |
| Guam | GU |
| Marshall Islands | MH |
| Northern Mariana Islands | MP |
| Palau | PW |
| Puerto Rico | PR |
| U.S. Minor Outlying Islands | UM |
| Virgin Islands of the U.S. | VI |

## of the
## United States of America

# Omni Gazetteer of the United States of America

Volume 10
National Index

*A Comprehensive Alphabetic List of Nearly 1,500,000 Places throughout the United States, including Populated Places, Structures, Facilities, Locales, Historic Places, and Geographic Features in the Fifty States, the District of Columbia, Puerto Rico, and U.S. Territories, Keyed to the Nine Regional Volumes of the*
**OMNI GAZETTEER**

Frank R. Abate, *Editor*

Omnigraphics, Inc.
Penobscot Building • Detroit, Michigan 48226

## Editorial Staff

*Editor:* Frank R. Abate
*Associate Editors:* Jacquelyn S. Goodwin, Katherine M. Isaacs
*Contributing Editor:* Margaret Mary Missar
*Editorial Assistants:* Caryl Anderson, Elaine Chasse, Elizabeth Jewell, Pamela Korsmeyer, Sue Ellen Thompson, Janene L. Van Ostrand

## Production & Marketing

*Director of Marketing:* Robert R. Tyler
*Production Manager:* Eric F. Berger
*Marketing Associate:* Beth A. Wydra
*Marketing Assistant:* Mary E. Beall
*Graphics Designer:* Richard S. Golobic
*Data Processing and Typesetting:* Shepard Poorman Communications, Inc., Indianapolis, Indiana
*Typographic Consultant:* Otto Barz, Publishing Synthesis, Ltd., New York, New York

## Omnigraphics, Inc.

Laurie Lanzen Harris, *Editorial Director*
Annie M. Brewer, *Vice President, Research*
James A. Sellgren, *Vice President, Operations & Finance*
Peter E. Ruffner, *Vice President, Administration*

Frederick G. Ruffner, Jr., *President and Publisher*



**Library of Congress Cataloging-in-Publication Data**

Omni gazetteer of the United States of America / Frank R. Abate, editor.
p. cm.
Includes indexes.
Summary : v. 1. New England : Connecticut, Maine, Massachusetts, New Hampshire, Rhode Island, Vermont — v. 2. Northeastern states : Delaware, District of Columbia, Maryland, New Jersey, New York, Pennsylvania, West Virginia — v. 3. Southeast : Florida, Georgia, North Carolina, South Carolina, Virginia; Puerto Rico, Virgin Islands — v. 4. South Central states : Alabama, Arkansas, Kentucky, Louisiana, Mississippi, Tennessee — v. 5. Southwestern states : Arizona, New Mexico, Oklahoma, Texas — v. 6. Great Lakes states : Illinois, Indiana, Michigan, Minnesota, Ohio, Wisconsin — v. 7. Plains states : Iowa, Kansas, Missouri, Nebraska, North Dakota, South Dakota — v. 8. Mountain states : Colorado, Idaho, Montana, Nevada, Utah, Wyoming — v. 9. Pacific : Alaska, California, Hawaii, Oregon, Washington; Pacific territories — v. 10. National Index — v. 11. Appendices.
ISBN 1-55888-336-3 (set : lib. bdg.: alk. paper)
1. United States—Gazetteers. I. Abate, Frank R. II. Omnigraphics, Inc.
E154.045 1990 90-7961
917.3'003—dc20 CIP

*The information in this Gazetteer was compiled from the sources cited and from other sources considered reliable. While every possible effort has been made to ensure reliability, the publisher will not assume liability for damages caused by inaccuracies in the data, and makes no warranty, express or implied, on the accuracy of the information contained herein.*

This book is printed on acid-free paper meeting the ANSI Z39.48 Standard. The infinity symbol that appears above indicates that the paper in this book meets that standard.

Printed in the United States of America

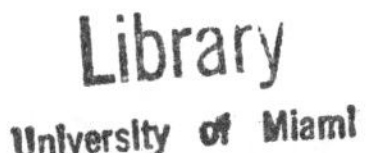

# Contents of the National Index

## Contents of the Complete *Omni Gazetteer of the United States of America*

(*The introductory sections are included in each of the nine regional volumes.*)



### Index and Appendices

# Introduction and How to Use This Index

This National Index lists all text entries from the nine regional volumes of the *Omni Gazetteer of the United States of America* in a single alphabetical sequence. Places from all fifty states, the District of Columbia, Puerto Rico, and all U.S. territories are included.

The total number of places represented here is more than 1,450,000. This includes populated places (cities, towns, counties, villages, etc.), natural features (streams, valleys, summits, lakes, etc.), structures, facilities, historic places—in short, all types of places in the United States that are identified by proper names.

Index entries give name, feature type, state, and *Omni Gazetteer* volume number, as detailed below:

- **Name**: Populated places are in **bold face**, all other types of places in normal type. Variant names appear in italics. Abbreviations used in place names are explained on the **Abbreviations** page, following; and are also printed inside the front cover.

- **Feature type**: This appears in italics after the entry name (except for variant names). All feature types are defined in the **Glossary of Feature Types**, which appears both on the pages that follow and inside the back cover.

  If, in a given state, a place name occurs more than once in connection with a given feature type, the number of such places is given in parentheses after the feature type. Thus, an Index listing such as:

  **Acton**—*pop pl* (2)............................AL-4

  indicates that Acton is a populated place with two entries in Alabama, and can be found in Volume 4 of the *Omni Gazetteer.* The number in parentheses normally indicates that two or more *different places* have the same name.

- **State abbreviation**: The standard two-letter (postal) abbreviation is used to indicate the state or state-equivalent area in which the named feature is located. A table of these abbreviations appears in the pages that follow and also inside the front cover.

- **Volume number**: Following the state abbreviation is the volume number in which the full entry can be found in the main text of the *Omni Gazetteer.*

## Alphabetization and Numerical Entries

Index entries are alphabetized by name, and for items with the same name also by feature type, then state name. Thus, all similarly named places of a given type are grouped together, and appear alphabetically by the *full name* of the state (not by the two-letter state abbreviation). This allows for easy comparison and research of names with the same or very similar form.

Alphabetization is letter-by-letter, following the procedures established and published by the U.S. Board on Geographic Names (see *Principles, Policies, and Procedures: Domestic Geographic Names,* U.S. Geological Survey, Reston, VA, 1989, pp. 31 ff.). Basically, this means that alphabetic order is similar to that used in most dictionaries. The alphabetizing rules may be summarized as follows:

1. **Letter-by-letter order**: Spaces, hyphens, periods, apostrophes, diacritical marks, parentheses, and brackets are disregarded.

2. **Case**: Uppercase and lowercase letters are treated alike.

3. **Numerical Entries**: Numerals (except Roman numerals) are given in numerical order after alphabetic sequence. That is, entries where numerals are initial and not spelled out, such as *1*

*Branch* and *23 River,* follow the *Z* section in this Index. Numerals that occur within place names are also sorted as if the numerals came after *Z.*

4. Names of **populated places** are always listed in reading order; e.g., *Lake Placid, Las Vegas, Mount Airy* (not *Placid, Lake; Vegas, Las; Airy, Mount*).

5. Names of **natural and artificial features** (non-populated places) are listed in reading order, except:

a. The English articles *A, An,* and *The* are transposed to final position if they appear initially in the spoken form of the name:

| | | |
|---|---|---|
| *The Drain* | is sorted as | *Drain, The* |

b. Names in which a generic term precedes the specific term are normally listed with the specific term first, followed by a comma, and then the generic term and any associated preposition or article, e.g.:

| | | |
|---|---|---|
| *Mount Adams* | is sorted as | *Adams, Mount* |
| *Lake Ann* | is sorted as | *Ann, Lake* |
| *Lake of the Woods* | is sorted as | *Woods, Lake of the* |
| *Sierra Nevada* | is sorted as | *Nevada, Sierra* |

c. Non-English initial articles are frequently transposed to final position:

| | | |
|---|---|---|
| *El Capitan* | is sorted as | *Capitan, El* |

## Note: Form and Spelling Variations

With very few exceptions, entries in the *Omni Gazetteer* are printed in the exact form given in the original source. Hence, when there is disagreement between sources regarding the form of the name given for a particular place, there will normally be two separate entries for that place, both in the text and in this Index.

This situation occurs especially with historic places that begin with a person's full name. Entries from one source, the Geographic Names Information System (or GNIS, from the U.S. Geological Survey), generally give these in reading order. Those from the *National Register of Historic Places* consistently list such items by the surname. Thus, an entry such as *John F. Kennedy Memorial* from the GNIS would be sorted under *John F. Kennedy Memorial.* An entry for the same place from the *National Register of Historic Places* would be sorted by the surname: *Kennedy, John F., Memorial.*

Slight spelling variations were occasionally encountered when compiling data from different sources, which can also cause multiple entries for one place. For example:

| | | |
|---|---|---|
| *DeKalb* | spelled | *De Kalb* (in another source) |
| *Cumminsville* | spelled | *Cummingsville* (in another source) |
| *Millers Falls* | spelled | *Miller Falls* (in another source) |

Such variations were generally entered as found in the original source, except for the correction of those determined to be errors.

# Abbreviations Used in the Entries

Abbreviations that are capitalized appear as part of entry names. Other abbreviations are for types of features, especially populated places and facilities.

Items in **boldface type** are defined in the Glossary of Feature Types; see below.

| | |
|---|---|
| Acad | Academy |
| AFB | Air Force Base |
| **Airp** | Airport |
| Ammun | Ammunition |
| Archeol | Archaeological, Archeological |
| Archeol Site # | Archeological Site Number |
| Ave | Avenue |
| **Bldg** | Building |
| Blvd | Boulevard |
| **CDP** | census designated place |
| **Cem** | Cemetery |
| **cens. area** | census area |
| **Ch** | Church |
| **civ. div.** | civil division |
| Coll | College |
| equiv | equivalent |
| Ctr | Center |
| Dist | District |
| E | East |
| Elem Sch | Elementary School |
| fmr. | former |
| **For** | Forest |
| Ft | Fort |
| Hist Dist | Historic District |
| **hist. pl.** | historic place |
| **Hosp** | Hospital |
| HQ | Headquarters |
| HS | High School |
| inact. | inactive |
| ind. city | independent city |
| Ind Res | Indian Reservation |
| **Isl** | Island |
| JHS | Junior High School |
| **MCD** | minor civil division |
| Med Ctr | Medical Center |
| **mil. airp.** | military airport |
| **milit.** | military |
| Mngmt | Management |
| Monmt | Monument |
| Mt | Mount; Mountain |
| Mtn | Mountain |
| Mts | Mountains |
| N | North |
| Nat Pk | National Park |
| Natl | National |
| NE | Northeast |
| No. | Number |
| NW | Northwest |
| **obs. name** | obsolete name |
| **pop. pl.** | populated place |
| **post. sta.** | postal station |
| Rec Area | Recreation(al) Area |
| Ref | Refuge |
| reg. | region |
| **Res** | Reserve |
| RR | Railroad |
| **Rsvr** | Reservoir |
| S | South |
| **Sch** | School |
| Sch Dist | School District |
| SE | Southeast |
| Shop Ctr | Shopping Center |
| St | Saint |
| sta. | station (railroad) |
| SW | Southwest |
| **uninc. pl.** | unincorporated place |
| Univ | University |
| **unorg.** | unorganized region, territory |
| W | West |

# Glossary of Feature Types

The feature types given below are those used to identify each entry in the *National Index*. They appear in italics after each Index entry (except variant names). They identify natural and artificial features and populated places.

Most items in this glossary were developed and defined by Sam Stulberg and Roger L. Payne of the Branch of Geographic Names, U.S. Geological Survey, for use in the Geographic Names Information System. Certain additions and modifications have been made for the *Omni Gazetteer.*

At the end of the definition for many of these types is a list of common generics that are classed under that particular type; these illustrate the range of entities represented by the type. For example, the generic *river* is classed under the feature type **stream**, as are these other generics: *creek, branch, run, slough, bayou, anabranch, distributary, pup, brook, fork, kill, rio.* Thus, all rivers, creeks, branches, runs, etc., are identified with the feature type **stream**.

**Note:** The feature class terms and abbreviations found in this list consist of nine or fewer letters and were chosen in part for computer search and retrieval purposes. They do not necessarily represent balanced, exclusive, or accurate terminology for the identification of all kinds of cultural and natural features. Although some of the terms may agree with dictionary definitions, they represent more generalized categories.

**airport**—facility maintained for the use of aircraft; e.g.: *airfield, airstrip, landing field, landing strip.*

**arch**—natural arch-like opening in a rock mass; e.g.: *bridge, natural bridge, sea arch.*

**area**—any one of several areally extensive natural features not included in other categories; e.g.: *fan, badlands, barren, delta, garden.*

**arroyo**—watercourse or channel through which water may occasionally flow; e.g.: *wash, gulley, coulee, draw.*

**bar**—natural accumulation of sand, gravel, or alluvium forming an underwater or exposed embankment; e.g.: *sandbar, spit, reef, ledge, shoal.*

**basin**—natural depression or relatively low area enclosed by higher land; e.g.: *sink, pit, amphitheater, cirque.*

**bay**—indentation of a coast or shore line enclosing a part of a body of water; a body of water partly surrounded by land; e.g.: *arm, bight, cove, estuary, gulf, inlet, sound.*

**beach**—the sloping shore along a body of water that is washed by waves or tides and is usually covered by sand or gravel; e.g.: *shore, strand, coast.*

**bench**—area of relatively level land on the flank of an elevation such as a hill, ridge, or mountain where the slope of the land rises on one side and descends on the opposite side.

**bend**—a curve in the course of a stream and/or the land within the curve; a curve in a linear body of water; e.g.: *meander, bottom.*

**bridge**—a manufactured structure carrying a trail, road, or other transportation system across a body of water or depression; e.g.: *overpass, trestle.*

**building**—a manufactured structure with walls and a roof for protection of people and/or materials but not including a **church**, **hospital**, or **school**.

**canal**—an artificial waterway used by water craft or for drainage, irrigation, mining, or water power; e.g.: *ditch, lateral.*

**cape**—projection of land extending into a body of water; e.g.: *point, peninsula, neck.*

**cave**—natural underground passageway or chamber, or a hollowed out cavity in the side of a cliff; e.g.: *cavern, grotto.*

**CDP**—census designated place: a populated place that has been delimited by the U.S. Bureau of the Census for statistical purposes. Typically, these are closely settled areas without corporate limits or status as defined by the Bureau of the Census.

**cemetery**—a place or area for burying the dead; e.g.: *burial, grave, burying ground, memorial garden.*

**cens. area**—census area: an area established and defined by the U.S. Bureau of the Census for statistical purposes; typically sparsely populated. These include census county divisions, census subareas (Alaska), and census subdistricts (Virgin Islands).

**channel**—linear deep part of a body of water through which the main volume of water flows and is frequently used as a route for water craft; e.g.: *passage, thoroughfare, thorofare, strait, reach.*

**church**—building used for religious worship; e.g.: *chapel, synagogue, mosque, tabernacle, temple.*

**civil**—a political division formed for administrative purposes; e.g.: *county, borough, town, township.*

**civ. div.**—civil division; see **MCD**.

**cliff**—very steep slope; e.g.: *bluff, crag, precipice, head, headland, nose, palisades, promontory, rim, rimrock.*

**crater**—circular-shaped depression at the summit of a volcanic cone or one on the surface of the land caused by the impact of a meteorite, or a depression created by an explosion.

**crossing**—a place where two or more routes of transportation form a junction or intersection.

**dam**—water barrier or embankment built across the course of a stream or into a body of water to control and/or impound the flow of water.

**falls**—perpendicular or very steep fall of water in the course of a stream; e.g.: *waterfall, cataract, cascade.*

**flat**—relative level area within a region of greater relief; e.g.: *playa, clearing, glade.*

**fmr. MCD**—former MCD, now inactive; see **MCD**.

**forest**—bounded area of woods, forest or grassland under the administration of a political agency (see **woods**); e.g.: *national forest, national grasslands, state forest.*

**gap**—low point or opening between hills or mountains or in a ridge or mountain range; e.g.: *pass, notch, water gap, wind gap, saddle, col.*

**geyser**—eruptive spring from which hot water and/or steam and in some cases mud, are periodically thrown.

**glacier**—body or stream of ice moving outward and downslope from an area of accumulation; an area of relatively permanent snow/ice on the top or side of a mountain or mountainous area; e.g.: *ice patch, snow patch, icefield.*

**gut**—relatively small coastal waterway connecting larger bodies of water or other waterways; e.g.: *slough, creek, inlet.*

**harbor**—sheltered area of water where ships or other water craft can anchor or dock; e.g.: *port, roads, roadstead.*

**hist. pl.**—historic place: one of the districts, sites, buildings, structures, or objects designated by the National Park Service as cultural resources worthy of preservation and listed in the *National Register of Historic Places.* Also identifies areas of natural preservation or of cultural or historical significance listed in the FIPS 55-2 file.

**hospital**—building where the sick or injured may receive medical or surgical attention.

**island**—area of dry or relatively dry land surrounded by water or low wetland; e.g.: *isle, isla, rock, archipelago, atoll, key, cay, hammock, hummock.*

**isthmus**—narrow projection of land in a body of water connecting two larger land areas.

**lake**—natural body of inland water; e.g.: *pond, backwater, lagoon, laguna, pool, resaca, lac, waterhole.*

**lava**—formations resulting from the consolidation of molten rock on the surface of the earth.

**levee**—natural or artificial embankment flanking a stream; e.g.: *bank.*

**locale**—place at which there is or was human activity; it does not include populated places (pop. pl.), mines, and dams; e.g.: *railroad siding, station, junction, site, camp, landing, battlefield, crossroad, ranch, farm, windmill, tower, ruins, ghost town.*

**MCD**—minor civil division: a political or administrative area of a county or county-equivalent, other than an incorporated place, established by appropriate state or local government authorities and adopted as a primary county division (for census purposes); occurs in 29 states and several state-equivalents, e.g., a *township* in Ohio or a *town* in Vermont. Also **civ. div.** (civil division).

**mil. airp.**—military or Coast Guard airport.

**military**—area administered and used by U.S. or State armed forces for military purposes; e.g.: *Air Force Base, air facility, air station, Army post, Marine Corps Base, Naval Base.*

**mine**—place or area from which commercial minerals are or were removed from the earth; not including **oilfield**; e.g.: *shaft, quarry, pit.*

**obs. name**—obsolete name: a former, less preferred, or possibly incorrect name that refers to a place (or part of a place) that is known by another name.

**oilfield**—area where petroleum is or was removed from the earth.

**other**—category for miscellaneous manufactured or constructed named entities that cannot readily be placed in the other feature classes listed here.

**park**—place or area set aside for recreation or preservation of a cultural or natural resource and under some form of governmental administration; not including **forest**; e.g.: *national park, state park, national historical landmark, wilderness.*

**pillar**—vertical-standing, often spire-shaped, natural rock formation; e.g.: *pinnacle, chimney, monument, rock, tower.*

**plain**—a region of general uniform slope, comparatively level and of considerable extent; e.g.: *grassland, highland, upland, plateau.*

**pop. pl.**—populated place; place or area with clustered or scattered buildings and a permanent human population; e.g.: *city, village, settlement, town.*

**post. sta.**—postal station: an office of the U.S. Postal Service.

**range**—chain of hills or mountains; a somewhat linear complex mountainous or hilly area; e.g.: *cordillera, sierra.*

**rapids**—fast-flowing section of a stream, often shallower and with exposed rock or boulders; e.g.: *ripple, riffle.*

**reserve**—a bounded tract of land established as a reserve for a particular purpose (e.g., Indian reservations and Alaska Native villages).

**reservoir**—artificially impounded body of water; e.g.: *tank, lake.*

**ridge**—elevation with a narrow, elongated crest which can be part of a hill or mountain; e.g.: *rim, crest, cuesta, escarpment, hogback, spur.*

**school**—building or group of buildings used as an institution for study, teaching, and learning; e.g.: *academy, high school, college, university.*

**sea**—large body of salt water; e.g.: *gulf, ocean.*

**slope**—a gently inclined part of the earth's surface; e.g.: *pitch, grade.*

**spring**—place where underground water flows naturally to the surface of the Earth; e.g.: *seep.*

**stream**—linear body of water flowing on the Earth's surface; e.g.: *creek, river, anabranch, distributary, branch, run, slough, bayou, pup, brook, fork, kill, rio.*

**summit**—prominent elevation rising above the surrounding level of the Earth's surface; it does not include ridges and ranges; e.g.: *hill, mountain, knob, butte, berg, colina, cone, volcano, cumbre, dome, head, knoll, mesa, meseta, mesita, mound, mount, peak, rock, sugar loaf, table, bald, cerro, horn.*

**swamp**—poorly drained wetland, fresh or saltwater, wooded or grassy, possibly covered with open water; e.g.: *marsh, bog, cienaga, marais, pocosin.*

**tower**—an artificial structure higher than its diameter generally used for observation, storage, or electronic transmission.

**trail**—route for passage from one point to another; it does not include roads or highways (categories of entities not included in this alphabetical list); e.g.: *ski trail, jeep trail, path.*

**tunnel**—linear underground passageway open at both ends.

**uninc. pl.**—unincorporated place: a populated place not possessing, by and for itself, legally defined boundaries and legally constituted governmental functions; may exist as a subpopulation within an incorporated place or census designated place (CDP).

**unorg.**—unorganized region or territory: an area of a county or county-equivalent, not subdivided into minor civil divisions (MCDs) or including any incorporated places, that has been bounded and named for census purposes.

**valley**—linear depression in the Earth's surface that generally slopes from one end to the other; e.g.: *canyon, barranca, chasm, cove, draw, glen, gorge, gulch, gulf, hollow, ravine.*

**well**—an artificial shaft or hole in the Earth's surface used to obtain fluid or gaseous materials.

**woods**—small area covered with a dense growth of trees; does not include an area of trees under the administration of a political agency (see **forest**).

## Abbreviations for the States and the District of Columbia

| State Name | Alpha Code | State Name | Alpha Code |
|---|---|---|---|
| Alabama | AL | Montana | MT |
| Alaska | AK | Nebraska | NE |
| Arizona | AZ | Nevada | NV |
| Arkansas | AR | New Hampshire | NH |
| California | CA | New Jersey | NJ |
| Colorado | CO | New Mexico | NM |
| Connecticut | CT | New York | NY |
| Delaware | DE | North Carolina | NC |
| District of Columbia | DC | North Dakota | ND |
| Florida | FL | Ohio | OH |
| Georgia | GA | Oklahoma | OK |
| Hawaii | HI | Oregon | OR |
| Idaho | ID | Pennsylvania | PA |
| Illinois | IL | Rhode Island | RI |
| Indiana | IN | South Carolina | SC |
| Iowa | IA | South Dakota | SD |
| Kansas | KS | Tennessee | TN |
| Kentucky | KY | Texas | TX |
| Louisiana | LA | Utah | UT |
| Maine | ME | Vermont | VT |
| Maryland | MD | Virginia | VA |
| Massachusetts | MA | Washington | WA |
| Michigan | MI | West Virginia | WV |
| Minnesota | MN | Wisconsin | WI |
| Mississippi | MS | Wyoming | WY |
| Missouri | MO | | |

## Abbreviations for the Outlying Areas of the United States

| Area Name | Alpha Code |
|---|---|
| American Samoa | AS |
| Federated States of Micronesia | FM |
| Guam | GU |
| Marshall Islands | MH |
| Northern Mariana Islands | MP |
| Palau | PW |
| Puerto Rico | PR |
| U.S. Minor Outlying Islands | UM |
| Virgin Islands of the U.S. | VI |

# A

AAA Tank—*reservoir* (3) NM-5
A A A Tank—*reservoir* (2) NM-5
Aaberg Sch (abandoned)—*school* SD-7
A A Call State Park—*park* IA-7
AA Canal—*canal* NV-8
*Aachigan To* MP-9
Aadalen Ch—*church* ND-7
*Aadmalkon Mountain* PW-9
Aa Falls—*falls* HI-9
Aagard Ranch—*locale* UT-8
Aagard Ridge—*ridge* UT-8
A A Helicopters Inc Heliport—*airport* UT-8
A A Hilton Pond—*lake* FL-3
Aahoaka—*summit* HI-9
A A Hopper Pond Dam—*dam* MS-4
Aahuwela—*summit* HI-9
*Aaivonam* AZ-5
Aajker Creek—*stream* MT-8
Aa Junction—*locale* AR-4
Aakakii Gulch—*valley* HI-9
Aaka Ridge—*ridge* HI-9
Aaka Rsvr—*reservoir* HI-9
Aakenson Canyon—*valley* NE-7
*Aakip* PW-9
*Aakukui Gulch* HI-9
Aakukui Valley—*valley* HI-9
Aala Triangle Park—*park* HI-9
Aalberg Siding—*locale* MO-7
Aal Ch—*church* ND-7
Aale Stream—*stream* HI-9
*Aalplaats* NY-2
*Aalplaats Kill* NY-2
*Aalplatts* NY-2
*Aalplatts Kill* NY-2
*Aalplaus* NY-2
*Aalplaus Kill* NY-2
*Aamaka* HI-9
Aamakao—*civil* HI-9
Aamakao Gulch—*valley* HI-9
Aamanu—*civil* HI-9
Aamanu Gulch—*valley* HI-9
A A Miller Dam—*dam* AL-4
*Aammama* MH-9
Aamodt Dairy Rsvr—*reservoir* OR-9
Aamodt Flashboard Dam—*dam* OR-9
Aamodt Park—*park* MI-6
*Aan* MH-9
A and A Acad South—*school* FL-3
A and A Shaft—*mine* AZ-5
A and F Trailer Court—*locale* AZ-5
A and F Trailer Park—*locale* AZ-5
A and G Cafeteria Lake Dam—*dam* MS-4
**A and K Subdivision**—*pop pl* UT-8
A and M Ridge—*ridge* OR-9
A and M Spring—*spring* OR-9
A Andrews Ranch—*locale* NE-7
A and V Lake Dam—*dam* MS-4
*Aaneru* MP-9
Aaneru—*island* MP-9
*Aaneru-To* MP-9
Aang Beach—*beach* GU-9
*Aaniru To* MP-9
Aanonsen Cem—*cemetery* TX-5
Aapueo—*civil* HI-9
Aapuran—*island* MP-9
*Aaraanbiru* MP-9
*Aaraanbiru Island* MP-9
*Aaragan* MH-9
*Aarasnbiru To* MP-9
A A Rauchfuss Lake—*reservoir* NC-3
A A Rauchfuss Lake Dam—*dam* NC-3
Aardahl Ch—*church* MN-6
Aardvark Arch—*arch* UT-8
Aarhus Rsvr—*reservoir* OR-9
Aaron—*locale* GA-3
Aaron—*locale* KY-4
Aaron—*locale* MO-7
**Aaron**—*pop pl* IN-6
Aaron, Lake—*lake* MN-6
Aaron Acad—*school* MS-4
Aaron Branch—*stream* AL-4
Aaron Branch—*stream* AR-4
Aaron Branch—*stream* (3) KY-4
Aaron Branch—*stream* LA-4
Aaron Branch—*stream* NC-3
Aaron Branch—*stream* (3) TN-4
*Aaron Brook* MA-1
*Aaron Cem* AL-4
Aaron Cem—*cemetery* AL-4
Aaron Cem—*cemetery* AR-4
Aaron Cem—*cemetery* OH-6
Aaron Cem—*cemetery* OK-5
Aaron Ch—*church* (2) NC-3
Aaron Chapel—*church* KY-4
Aaron Clark Memorial Cem—*cemetery* MA-1
Aaron Cove—*cape* MD-2
*Aaron Creek* NC-3
*Aaron Creek* VA-3
Aaron Creek—*stream* AK-9
Aaron Creek—*stream* (2) NC-3
Aaron Creek—*stream* OH-6
Aaron Creek—*stream* VA-3
Aaron Creek—*stream* WV-2
Aaron Denny Creek—*stream* NJ-2
Aaron Drain—*stream* ID-8
Aaron Island—*island* AK-9
Aaron Lake—*lake* MS-4
Aaron Ledge—*bench* NH-1
Aaron Mercer Rsvr—*reservoir* OR-9
Aaron Mtn—*summit* GA-3
Aaron Mtn—*summit* VA-3

Aaron Park—*park* AL-4
Aaron Park—*park* TX-5
*Aaron River* MA-1
Aaron River—*stream* MA-1
Aaron River Dam—*dam* MA-1
Aaron Rsvr—*reservoir* CO-8
Aaron Run—*stream* MD-2
Aaron Run—*stream* WV-2
**Aaronsburg**—*pop pl* PA-2
Aaronsburg Hist Dist—*hist pl* PA-2
Aarons Chapel—*church* TN-4
Aarons Corner—*locale* NC-3
Aarons Creek—*locale* VA-3
Aarons Creek—*stream* NC-3
Aarons Creek—*stream* VA-3
Aarons Creek—*stream* (2) WV-2
Aarons Creek Ch—*church* WV-2
Aarons Fork—*stream* WV-2
Aarons Fork Sch—*school* WV-2
Aarons Lake—*lake* OR-9
Aarons Run—*stream* KY-4
Aarons Run—*stream* WV-2
Aarons Temple—*locale* SC-3
Aaron Street Sch—*school* LA-4
Aaron Swamp—*swamp* NC-3
Aaron Tollets Cave—*cave* TN-4
Aarron Mine (underground)—*mine* AL-4
**Aarrons Fork**—*pop pl* WV-2
Aasayii Wash—*valley* AZ-5
A A Scott Sch—*school* HI-9
*Aasgard Pass* WA-9
Aashland State Park—*park* MA-1
Aas Lake—*lake* MN-6
Aastad Ch—*church* MN-6
Aastad State Wildlife Mngmt Area—*park* MN-6
**Aastad (Township of)**—*pop pl* MN-6
Aasu—*hist pl* AS-9
**Aasu**—*pop pl* AS-9
**Aasufou**—*pop pl* AS-9
Aasu Stream—*stream* AS-9
**Aasutuai**—*pop pl* AS-9
A A Tank—*reservoir* AZ-5
A Atkinson or F P Sanchez Grant—*civil* FL-3
Aats Bay—*bay* AK-9
Aats Point—*cape* AK-9
A Ave Sch—*school* AZ-5
A'a Village (AS-34-33)—*hist pl* AS-9
Aawaiki—*island* HI-9
Aawanui—*island* HI-9
Aawela—*summit* HI-9
*Ababais Creek* CA-9
Aba Beach—*beach* GU-9
Abac—*area* GU-9
**Abac (Abraham Baldwin College)**—*pop pl* GA-3
*Abache* IN-6
Abacherli Canyon—*valley* CA-9
Abacoochee (historical)—*locale* AL-4
*Abacotnetic Bog* ME-1
Abacotnetic Stream—*stream* ME-1
*A Bad* PW-9
Abadi Creek—*stream* CA-9
Abadyl—*locale* MO-7
Abagadasset Point—*cape* ME-1
Abagadasset River—*stream* ME-1
*Abagadassett Point* ME-1
*Abagadussett* ME-1
Aba Guadalupe Windmill—*locale* TX-5
Abajo Mtns—*range* UT-8
*Abajona Brook* MA-1
*Abajona Pond* MA-1
*Abajona River* MA-1
*Abajona Road* MA-1
*Abajo Peak* UT-8
Abajo Peak—*summit* UT-8
A B A Lateral—*canal* CO-8
*Abaline* GA-3
Abaline Ch—*church* FL-3
Abalobadiah Creek—*stream* CA-9
Abalone Cove—*bay* CA-9
Abalone Cove—*uninc pl* CA-9
Abalone Island—*island* AK-9
Abalone Point—*cape* (5) CA-9
*Abamgamock Lake* ME-1
**Abanaka**—*pop pl* OH-6
Abanakee, Lake—*reservoir* NY-2
*Abanaugh Canyon* AZ-5
**Abanda**—*pop pl* AL-4
Abanda Cem—*cemetery* AL-4
Abandon Creek—*stream* ID-8
Abandoned Spring—*spring* NV-8
Abandon Mtn—*summit* ID-8
Aband Sch—*school* WA-9
Aband Well—*well* AZ-5
*Abappaomogan Island* PW-9
*Abappaomogan To* PW-9
Abaramiut (Summer Camp)—*locale* AK-9
A Bar A Ranch—*locale* TX-5
A Bar A Ranch—*locale* WY-8
A Bar Draw—*valley* AZ-5
A Bar Draw Tank—*reservoir* AZ-5
A Bar H Ranch Pond—*lake* FL-3
A Barnes—*locale* TX-5
Abarngamook Lake—*lake* ME-1
Abarr—*locale* CO-8
A Bar Ranch—*locale* CO-8
**Abattoir**—*pop pl* NC-3
*Abattpooda Creek* MS-4
*Abay* FM-9
*Abaytche Creek* MS-4

Abba—*locale* GA-3
Abba Ch—*church* GA-3
*Abbajona River* MA-1
Abbapoola Creek—*stream* SC-3
Abba Post Office (historical)—*building* AL-4
Abbaye Peninsula—*cape* MI-6
Abbaye Point—*cape* MI-6
Abb Breland Cem—*cemetery* MS-4
Abbcamp Branch—*stream* WV-2
Abb Creek—*stream* AR-4
Abb Creek—*stream* KY-4
Abb Creek Sch—*school* KY-4
Abbe, Mount—*summit* AK-9
Abbe, Robert, Museum of Stone Antiquities—*hist pl* ME-1
Abbe Creek—*stream* IA-7
Abbe Creek Cem—*cemetery* IA-7
Abbee Pond—*lake* ME-1
Abbe Gulch—*valley* AK-9
Abbe Institute (historical)—*school* TN-4
Abbe Museum—*building* ME-1
*Abbes Brook* CT-1
Abbe Spring—*spring* NM-5
Abbe Spring Canyon—*valley* NM-5
Abbess Island—*island* AK-9
Abbet Place—*locale* CO-8
*Abbett School* IN-6
Abbeville—*hist pl* PA-2
**Abbeville**—*pop pl* AL-4
**Abbeville**—*pop pl* GA-3
**Abbeville**—*pop pl* LA-4
**Abbeville**—*pop pl* MS-4
**Abbeville**—*pop pl* SC-3
Abbeville Canal—*canal* LA-4
Abbeville (CCD)—*cens area* AL-4
Abbeville (CCD)—*cens area* GA-3
Abbeville (CCD)—*cens area* SC-3
Abbeville Cem—*cemetery* AL-4
Abbeville Cem—*cemetery* MS-4
Abbeville Commercial Hist Dist—*hist pl* LA-4
**Abbeville (County)**—*pop pl* SC-3
Abbeville County Courthouse—*hist pl* SC-3
Abbeville Division—*civil* AL-4
Abbeville Hist Dist—*hist pl* SC-3
Abbeville Hist Dist (Boundary Decrease)—*hist pl* SC-3
Abbeville Hist Dist (Boundary Increase)—*hist pl* SC-3
Abbeville HS—*school* AL-4
Abbeville JHS—*school* AL-4
*Abbeville Junction* AL-4
Abbeville Lookout Tower—*locale* AL-4
Abbeville Memorial Library—*building* AL-4
Abbeville Methodist Ch—*church* AL-4
Abbeville Municipal Airp—*airport* AL-4
Abbeville Oil and Gas Field—*oilfield* LA-4
Abbeville Opera House—*hist pl* SC-3
*Abbeville Public Library* AL-4
Abbeville Pumping Station—*other* SC-3
Abbeville Residential Hist Dist—*hist pl* LA-4
Abbeville Sch (historical)—*school* MS-4
*Abbey, The* NY-2
Abbey, The—*hist pl* CA-9
Abbey, The—*hist pl* FL-3
*Abbey Baptist Church* AL-4
Abbey Branch—*stream* KY-4
Abbey Brook—*stream* CT-1
Abbey Brook—*stream* MA-1
Abbey Brook—*stream* VT-1
Abbey Cem—*cemetery* AR-4
Abbey Cem—*cemetery* CO-8
Abbey Cem—*cemetery* KS-7
Abbey Cem—*cemetery* NY-2
*Abbey Church* AL-4
*Abbey Creek* AL-4
Abbey Creek—*stream* MD-2
Abbey Creek—*stream* (2) OR-9
*Abbey Dell* IN-6
**Abbey Dell (Abydel)**—*pop pl* IN-6
Abbey Drain—*canal* MI-6
Abbey Gulf—*valley* NY-2
Abbey Hill—*summit* MA-1
Abbey Hill—*summit* ND-7
Abbey Hill—*summit* TX-5
Abbey Island—*island* WA-9
Abbey Lake—*lake* MN-6
Abbey Lake—*lake* ND-7
Abbey Lake—*reservoir* MA-1
Abbey Lake Dam—*dam* MA-1
Abbey Lane Sch—*school* NY-2
Abbey Of Gethsemani—*other* KY-4
Abbey of Our Lady of Gethsemani (Trappist P.O.)—*church* KY-4
Abbey Plaza—*locale* NC-3
Abbey Point—*cape* MD-2
Abbey Pond—*lake* VT-1
Abbey Pond Trail—*trail* VT-1
Abbey Post Office (historical)—*building* AL-4
Abbey Run—*stream* IN-6
*Abbeys Arch* UT-8
Abbey Sch—*school* CO-8
Abbey Summer Camp—*locale* CO-8
*Abbey Swamp* MA-1
Abbey Swamp—*swamp* MA-1
**Abbeyville**—*pop pl* OH-6
Abbeyville (reduced usage)—*locale* CO-8
Abbie, Mount—*summit* NV-8
*Abbie Baptist Church* AL-4
*Abbie Cemetery* AL-4
Abbie Ch—*church* AL-4
Abbie Creek—*stream* AL-4

Abbie Creek Public Use Area—*park* AL-4
Abbie Lake—*lake* MN-6
Abbie Loveland Tuller School, The—*school* AZ-5
Abbie Pond—*lake* ME-1
*Abbieville* AL-4
Abbie Windmill—*locale* NM-5
*Abbot* TN-4
Abbot—*locale* IL-6
**Abbot**—*pop pl* VA-3
Abbot, Asa and Sylvester, House—*hist pl* MA-1
Abbot, Benjamin, House—*hist pl* MA-1
Abbot, Edwin, House—*hist pl* MA-1
Abbot, J. T., House—*hist pl* MA-1
Abbot, Mount—*summit* CA-9
Abbot Acad—*school* MA-1
Abbot-Baker House—*hist pl* MA-1
Abbot-Battles House—*hist pl* MA-1
Abbot Branch—*stream* MS-4
*Abbot Bute* OR-9
Abbot Butte—*summit* OR-9
Abbot Butte Spring—*spring* OR-9
Abbot Campground—*locale* ID-8
Abbot Canyon—*valley* AZ-5
Abbot Cem—*cemetery* IN-6
Abbot Cem—*cemetery* OH-6
Abbot Cemeteries—*cemetery* ME-1
Abbot Ch—*church* CO-8
Abbot Creek—*stream* AK-9
Abbot Creek—*stream* CO-8
Abbot Creek—*stream* MT-8
Abbot Creek—*stream* NJ-2
Abbot Creek—*stream* OR-9
Abbot Creek Campground—*park* OR-9
Abbot Flat—*flat* MT-8
Abbot Gulch—*valley* ID-8
Abbot Hall—*building* MA-1
Abbot Hall—*hist pl* MA-1
Abbot Hill—*summit* (2) NH-1
Abbot House—*hist pl* NH-1
Abbot Lake—*lake* MT-8
Abbot Lake—*lake* OR-9
Abbot Lake—*reservoir* GA-3
Abbot Lookout Tower—*locale* AR-4
Abbot Mountain—*ridge* AR-4
Abbot Pass—*gap* OR-9
Abbot Ridge—*ridge* PA-2
Abbot Rock—*rock* MA-1
Abbot Row—*hist pl* WI-6
Abbot Rsvr—*reservoir* CO-8
Abbot Run—*stream* PA-2
*Abbot Run Brook* RI-1
*Abbot's Brook* MA-1
*Abbots Butte* OR-9
Abbot Sch—*school* KS-7
*Abbots Creek* CO-8
*Abbots Creek* NC-3
*Abbotsford* MI-6
Abbotsford—*hist pl* MA-1
**Abbotsford**—*pop pl* WI-6
Abbots Fork—*stream* UT-8
*Abbots Lagoon* CA-9
Abbots Lodge—*locale* CO-8
Abbots Meadow—*swamp* NJ-2
Abbot Spring Cave—*cave* AL-4
Abbot Springs—*locale* AL-4
*Abbots River* NC-3
*Abbots Run* MA-1
*Abbots Run* PA-2
*Abbots Run* RI-1
Abbots Swamp—*swamp* NY-2
Abbot Street Sch—*school* MA-1
Abbott—*locale* CA-9
Abbott—*locale* IA-7
Abbott—*locale* PA-2
Abbott—*locale* VA-3
Abbott—*locale* WV-2
**Abbott**—*pop pl* AR-4
**Abbott**—*pop pl* IA-7
**Abbott**—*pop pl* KY-4
**Abbott**—*pop pl* MS-4
**Abbott**—*pop pl* NE-7
**Abbott**—*pop pl* NM-5
**Abbott**—*pop pl* TX-5
Abbott, Ezra, House—*hist pl* MN-6
Abbott, George S., Bldg—*hist pl* CT-1
Abbott, Jacob, House—*hist pl* ME-1
Abbott, John, House—*hist pl* PA-2
Abbott, John II, House—*hist pl* NJ-2
Abbott, Robert S., House—*hist pl* IL-6
Abbott, William Riley, House—*hist pl* NC-3
*Abbott And Dogson Canal* LA-4
*Abbott and Duson Canal* LA-4
Abbot Tavern—*hist pl* MA-1
Abbott Branch—*stream* AL-4
Abbott Branch—*stream* (2) MO-7
Abbott Branch—*stream* TN-4
Abbott Branch—*stream* VA-3
Abbott Branch—*stream* WV-2
Abbott Brook—*stream* (4) ME-1
Abbott Brook—*stream* MA-1
Abbott Brook—*stream* (3) NH-1
Abbott Brook—*stream* VT-1
Abbott Butte—*summit* OR-9
Abbott Canyon—*valley* CA-9
Abbott Cem—*cemetery* AL-4
Abbott Cem—*cemetery* (2) ME-1
Abbott Cem—*cemetery* (2) MS-4
Abbott Cem—*cemetery* MO-7
Abbott Cem—*cemetery* OH-6

Abbott Cem—*cemetery* TN-4
Abbott Cem—*cemetery* TX-5
Abbott Cem—*cemetery* WV-2
Abbott Chapel Cem—*cemetery* AL-4
Abbott Christian Ch (historical)—*church* MS-4
Abbott Coulee—*valley* (2) MT-8
Abbott Cove—*bay* MD-2
*Abbott Creek* OR-9
Abbott Creek—*stream* AK-9
Abbott Creek—*stream* CA-9
Abbott Creek—*stream* KY-4
Abbott Creek—*stream* NM-5
Abbott Creek—*stream* (3) OR-9
Abbott Creek—*stream* TX-5
Abbott Creek—*stream* WV-2
Abbott Crossing—*locale* IA-7
**Abbott Crossing (historical)**—*pop pl* IA-7
Abbott-Decou House—*hist pl* NJ-2
Abbott Ditch—*canal* IL-6
Abbott Drain—*canal* (2) MI-6
Abbott Drain—*stream* MI-6
Abbott Farm Archeol Site—*hist pl* NJ-2
Abbott Fork—*stream* WV-2
Abbott-Fox Camp—*locale* MI-6
*Abbott Gulch* ID-8
Abbott Gulch—*valley* MT-8
Abbott Hill—*summit* (2) ME-1
Abbott Hill—*summit* (2) MA-1
Abbott Hollow—*valley* AL-4
Abbott Hollow—*valley* (3) KY-4
Abbott Hollow—*valley* MO-7
Abbott Hollow—*valley* PA-2
Abbott Hosp—*hospital* MN-6
Abbott House—*school* NY-2
Abbott Island—*island* ME-1
Abbott JHS—*school* IL-6
Abbott JHS—*school* MI-6
Abbott Laboratories—*facility* NC-3
Abbott Laboratories (Abbott Park)—*facility* IL-6
Abbott Laboratories (Warehouse)—*facility* IL-6
Abbott Lake—*lake* (2) CA-9
Abbott Lake—*lake* FL-3
Abbott Lake—*lake* MI-6
Abbott Lake—*lake* MT-8
Abbott Lake—*reservoir* NM-5
Abbott Lake Sch—*school* MT-8
Abbott Lateral—*canal* AZ-5
Abbott Memorial Library—*hist pl* ME-1
Abbott Memorial Sch—*school* MA-1
Abbott Mine—*mine* CA-9
Abbott Missionary Baptist Ch—*church* MS-4
Abbott Mtn—*summit* ME-1
Abbott Oil Field—*oilfield* TX-5
Abbot Top—*summit* NC-3
**Abbot (Town of)**—*pop pl* ME-1
Abbott-Page House—*hist pl* OH-6
Abbott Park—*park* IL-6
Abbott Park—*park* NE-7
**Abbott Park (Industrial Area)**—*pop pl* IL-6
*Abbott Pass* OR-9
Abbott Playground—*park* MA-1
*Abbott Pond* CT-1
Abbott Post Office (historical)—*building* MS-4
Abbott Prairie—*flat* OR-9
Abbott Ranch—*locale* CA-9
Abbott Ridge—*ridge* MT-8
Abbott Ridge—*ridge* VA-3
**Abbott Road**—*pop pl* NY-2
Abbott Road Plaza Shop Ctr—*locale* NY-2
*Abbott Rock* MA-1
**Abbott Run**—*pop pl* RI-1
Abbott Run—*stream* (2) MA-1
Abbott Run—*stream* PA-2
Abbott Run—*stream* RI-1
*Abbott Run Brook* MA-1
*Abbott Run Pond* RI-1
**Abbott Run Valley**—*pop pl* RI-1
**Abbotts**—*pop pl* NY-2
Abbotts Bridge—*bridge* GA-3
**Abbottsburg**—*pop pl* NC-3
Abbott Sch—*school* (2) CA-9
Abbott Sch—*school* IL-6
Abbott Sch—*school* ME-1
Abbott Sch—*school* (3) MI-6
Abbott Sch—*school* MS-4
Abbott Sch Day Care—*school* FL-3
*Abbotts Creek* CO-8
Abbotts Creek—*stream* NC-3
Abbotts Creek Ch—*church* NC-3
Abbott's Creek Primitive Baptist Church Cemetery—*hist pl* NC-3
Abbotts Creek (Township of)—*fmr MCD* (2) NC-3
Abbotts Flats—*flat* MT-8
Abbottsford—*locale* MI-6
**Abbottsford**—*pop pl* GA-3
Abbottsford (CCD)—*cens area* GA-3
Abbotts Fork—*locale* NV-8
Abbotts Island—*island* OH-6
Abbotts Lagoon—*lake* CA-9
Abbott's Mill—*hist pl* DE-2
Abbotts Mill—*locale* DE-2
Abbotts Mill—*locale* ME-1
Abbott's Mill (Boundary Increase)—*hist pl* DE-2
*Abbotts Mills* ME-1
Abbotts Peak—*summit* CA-9
Abbotts Pond—*lake* CT-1
Abbotts Pond—*lake* ME-1
Abbotts Pond—*lake* MA-1

Abbotts Pond—*reservoir* DE-2
Abbotts Pond Dam—*dam* DE-2
Abbott Spring—*spring* AL-4
Abbott Spring—*spring* CA-9
Abbott Spring—*spring* MT-8
Abbott Spring—*spring* TX-5
Abbott Spring—*spring* WA-9
Abbott Springs—*spring* ID-8
Abbott Springs Cem—*cemetery* TX-5
*Abbotts Rock* MA-1
**Abbottstown**—*pop pl* PA-2
Abbottstown Borough—*civil* PA-2
Abbotts (Township of)—*fmr MCD* NC-3
Abbott Street Sch—*hist pl* MA-1
*Abbottsville* MI-6
**Abbottsville**—*pop pl* OH-6
Abbott Tech Sch—*school* CT-1
Abbott Township—*civil* PA-2
**Abbott (Township of)**—*pop pl* PA-2
Abbott Tract Hist Dist—*hist pl* FL-3
Abbott Wash—*stream* NV-8
Abbott Well—*locale* NM-5
**Abbot Village**—*pop pl* ME-1
Abbot Village Station—*locale* ME-1
Abbot Windmill—*locale* AZ-5
Abb Run—*stream* WV-2
Abbs, Walter, House—*hist pl* ID-8
Abbs Branch—*stream* MS-4
Abbs Creek—*stream* NC-3
**Abbs Valley**—*pop pl* VA-3
Abbs Valley—*valley* VA-3
Abbs Valley-Boissevain Sch—*school* VA-3
Abbs Valley Ridge—*ridge* VA-3
Abby, Lake—*reservoir* AR-4
Abby Bend—*bend* TX-5
*Abby Creek* IA-7
Abby Creek—*stream* ID-8
*Abby Leatherman Plantation* MS-4
Abby Lodge Sch—*school* MA-1
Abby Manoc (historical)—*civil* DC-2
**Abby Plantation**—*pop pl* LA-4
**Abbyville**—*pop pl* KS-7
Abbyville Cem—*cemetery* KS-7
A B C Child Care—*school* FL-3
A B C Creek—*stream* TX-5
Abc Dam—*dam* TN-4
ABC Day Care Center—*school* FL-3
A B Chance Company Heliport—*airport* MO-7
A B Church—*church* MO-7
Abc Lake—*reservoir* TN-4
A B C Lateral—*canal* CO-8
**Abco**—*pop pl* AR-4
Ab Cove—*valley* GA-3
ABC Park—*park* TX-5
A B C Post Office (historical)—*building* TN-4
A B Creek—*stream* MO-7
ABC Sch—*school* FL-3
ABC Tanks—*reservoir* TX-5
**Abdal**—*pop pl* NE-7
Abdallah, Mount—*summit* AK-9
**Abdan**—*pop pl* MS-4
Abd Bridge—*bridge* TN-4
**Abdera**—*pop pl* PA-2
*Abdomen Beach* MH-9
*Abdomen District* MH-9
*Abdomen Point* MH-9
Abdou Bldg—*hist pl* TX-5
Abdoul Canyon—*valley* AZ-5
*Abear Creek* SD-7
Abe Branch—*stream* KY-4
Abe Branch—*stream* MS-4
Abe Branch—*stream* TN-4
Abe Burgess Fork—*stream* WV-2
Abe Buzzards Cave—*cave* PA-2
Abe Cem—*cemetery* TN-4
Abe Cem—*cemetery* WV-2
Abe Creek—*stream* KY-4
Abe Creek—*stream* OR-9
Abe Creek—*stream* WA-9
**Abecrumby (historical)**—*pop pl* NC-3
*Abecumbie Creek* AL-4
Abe Duff Sch (abandoned)—*school* MO-7
Abee—*locale* NC-3
Abee Creek—*stream* NC-3
Abees Chapel—*church* NC-3
Abees Grove Ch—*church* NC-3
Abe Fork—*stream* KY-4
**Abegall**—*pop pl* KY-4
Abeg Creek—*stream* AL-4
Abe Hollow—*valley* KY-4
Abe Hollow—*valley* (2) MO-7
*Abeju* MP-9
Abel—*locale* AL-4
Abel—*locale* NE-7
Abel, Dr., House—*hist pl* KY-4
Abel, Elias, House—*hist pl* IN-6
Abe Lake—*lake* MN-6
Abelardo Cabin (Site)—*locale* CA-9
A B E Lateral—*canal* CO-8
Abel Bay—*bay* NC-3
Abel Brook—*stream* NH-1
Abel Camp Spring—*spring* NV-8
Abel Canyon—*valley* CA-9
Abel Canyon—*valley* NV-8
Abel Canyon Campground—*locale* CA-9
Abel Canyon Spring—*spring* CA-9
Abel Cem—*cemetery* AL-4
Abel Cem—*cemetery* (2) TN-4
Abel Cem—*cemetery* TX-5
Abel Creek—*stream* NV-8
Abel Creek—*stream* NC-3

Abel Creek—stream ... WY-8
Abel Dam—dam ... AL-4
Abel Flat—flat ... NV-8
Abel Gap—gap ... AL-4
Abel Hill—summit ... MA-1
Abel (historical)—locale ... MS-4
Abel Holtz Stadium—locale ... FL-3
Abel Horseblock Lookout Tower—tower ... AL-4
Abe Lincoln Mine—mine ... AZ-5
Abe Lincoln Mine—mine ... NV-8
Abe Lincoln Mtn—summit ... MT-8
**Abell**—pop pl ... MD-2
**Abell**—pop pl ... TX-5
Abell, Robert, Round Barn—hist pl ... ND-7
Abel Lake—lake ... MN-6
Abel Lake—lake ... WI-6
Abel Lake—reservoir ... AL-4
Abell Cem—cemetery ... MO-7
Abell Ch—church ... OK-5
Abell City—locale ... TX-5
Abell Clinic—hospital ... TX-5
**Abell Corners**—pop pl ... NY-2
Abell Farmhouse and Barn—hist pl ... NY-2
Abell House—hist pl ... KY-4
Abell Oil And Gas Field—oilfield ... TX-5
Abell Ranch—locale ... CO-8
Abell Sch—school ... MD-2
Abell Sch—school ... SC-3
Abells Millpond—reservoir ... SC-3
Abells Spring Branch—stream ... KY-4
Abells Wharf—locale ... MD-2
Abell Wharf ... MD-2
Abel Mountain ... CA-9
Abe Lord Creek—stream ... NY-2
**Abels Acres**—pop pl ... IN-6
Abels Branch—stream ... MO-7
**Abels Corners**—pop pl ... WI-6
Abels Creek ... NC-3
Abels Point—cliff ... WA-9
Abel Spring—spring (2) ... NV-8
Abels Ranch—locale ... MT-8
Abels Ridge—ridge ... WA-9
Abel Tackett Fork—stream ... KY-4
Abel Valley—valley ... TN-4
Abe Martin Lodge—park ... IN-6
Abe Mills Mtn—summit ... MD-2
Abe Mtn—summit ... GA-3
**Aben**—pop pl ... LA-4
Abenakee Golf Club—other ... ME-1
Abenaki, Lake—lake ... VT-1
Abenaki Brook—stream ... NH-1
Abenicio Salazar Hist Dist—hist pl ... NM-5
Abeniki, Lake—lake ... NH-1
Abeniki Mtn—summit ... NH-1
Aben Mountain ... PW-9
Aber and Haberle Houses—hist pl ... TX-5
Aber Brook—stream ... NY-2
Abercombie Cem—cemetery ... AL-4
Abercombie Ridge—ridge ... ID-8
Abercomby Branch—stream ... AL-4
Abercorn Ch—church ... GA-3
Abercorn Creek—stream ... GA-3
**Abercorn Heights**—pop pl ... GA-3
Aber Creek ... IN-6
Abercrombie—locale ... TX-5
**Abercrombie**—pop pl ... AL-4
**Abercrombie**—pop pl ... ND-7
**Abercrombie**—pop pl ... TX-5
Abercrombie Bald—summit ... GA-3
Abercrombie-Cavanaugh House—hist pl ... TX-5
Abercrombie Creek—stream ... AK-9
Abercrombie Creek—stream ... OR-9
Abercrombie Gulch—valley ... AK-9
Abercrombie Lake—lake ... AK-9
Abercrombie Mtn—summit ... WA-9
Abercrombie Park—park ... FL-3
Abercrombie Peak—summit ... UT-8
Abercrombie Ranch—locale ... NM-5
Abercrombie Ranch—locale ... TX-5
Abercrombie Rapids—rapids ... AK-9
Abercrombie Sch—school ... MA-1
Abercrombies Mill (historical)—locale ... AL-4
**Abercrombie Township**—pop pl ... ND-7
Aberdare Canal—canal ... UT-8
Aberdeen—locale ... CA-9
Aberdeen—locale ... GA-3
Aberdeen—locale ... MT-8
Aberdeen—locale ... TX-5
Aberdeen—locale ... WV-2
**Aberdeen**—pop pl ... AR-4
**Aberdeen**—pop pl ... CA-9
**Aberdeen**—pop pl ... ID-8
**Aberdeen**—pop pl ... IN-6
**Aberdeen**—pop pl ... KY-4
**Aberdeen**—pop pl ... MD-2
**Aberdeen**—pop pl ... MS-4
**Aberdeen**—pop pl ... MT-8
**Aberdeen**—pop pl ... NC-3
**Aberdeen**—pop pl ... OH-6
**Aberdeen**—pop pl (2) ... PA-2
**Aberdeen**—pop pl ... SD-7
**Aberdeen**—pop pl ... WA-9
**Aberdeen, (Township of)**—pop pl ... NJ-2
Aberdeen Assembly of God Ch—church ... MS-4
Aberdeen Canyon—valley ... CA-9
Aberdeen Cem—cemetery ... TX-5
Aberdeen Ch—church ... TX-5
Aberdeen Ch of Christ—church ... MS-4
Aberdeen Ch of God—church ... MS-4
Aberdeen Ch of Jesus Christ (historical)—church ... MS-4
Aberdeen City Hall—hist pl ... MS-4
Aberdeen Commercial Hist Dist—hist pl ... SD-7
Aberdeen Country Club—locale ... SD-7
Aberdeen Creek—bay ... MD-2
Aberdeen Creek—stream ... NC-3
Aberdeen Creek—stream ... VA-3
Aberdeen Ditch—canal ... CA-9
Aberdeen Draw—valley ... NM-5
Aberdeen Elem Sch—school ... MS-4
Aberdeen Elem Sch—school ... NC-3
Aberdeen Filtration Plant—locale ... SD-7
Aberdeen Gardens—locale ... WA-9
**Aberdeen Gardens**—pop pl ... VA-3
Aberdeen Highlands Hist Dist—hist pl ... SD-7
Aberdeen Hist Dist—hist pl ... SD-7
**Aberdeen (historical)**—pop pl ... NC-3
Aberdeen-Hoquiam (CCD)—cens area ... WA-9
Aberdeen HS—school ... MS-4
Aberdeen Junction ... MS-4
Aberdeen Junction—locale ... ID-8
Aberdeen Junction—locale ... MS-4
Aberdeen Junction—locale ... WA-9
Aberdeen Lagoon Dam—dam (2) ... MS-4
Aberdeen Lake—reservoir ... MS-4
**Aberdeen Line Junction**—pop pl ... MN-6
Aberdeen Lock & Dam—dam ... MS-4
Aberdeen Lodge Bay—bay ... ID-8
Aberdeen Mine—mine ... UT-8
Aberdeen-Monroe County Hosp—hospital ... MS-4
Aberdeen Mound—hist pl ... OH-6
Aberdeen MS—school ... MS-4
Aberdeen MS—school ... NC-3
Aberdeen Peak—summit ... NM-5
Aberdeen Post Office—building ... MS-4
Aberdeen-Prairie Sch—school ... MS-4
Aberdeen Proving Ground Military Reservation—other ... MD-2
Aberdeen Proving Ground (U.S. Army)—military ... MD-2
Aberdeen Regional Airp—airport ... SD-7
Aberdeen Rock—bar ... AK-9
Aberdeen Rsvr—reservoir ... WA-9
Aberdeen Sch—school ... IL-6
Aberdeen Sch—school ... MI-6
Aberdeen Sch—school ... VA-3
Aberdeen Springfield Canal—canal (2) ... ID-8
**Aberdeen (subdivision)**—pop pl ... MA-1
Aberdeen Town Lake—reservoir ... NC-3
Aberdeen Town Lake Dam—dam ... NC-3
Aberdeen Township—CDP ... NJ-2
**Aberdeen Township**—pop pl ... SD-7
Aberden, Lake—reservoir ... WA-9
Aberdour Ch—church ... VA-3
**Aberfoil**—pop pl ... AL-4
**Aberfoyle**—pop pl ... TX-5
Aberger Ditch—canal ... IN-6
Aberjona Pond—lake ... MA-1
Aberjona River—stream ... MA-1
**Abernant**—pop pl ... AL-4
Abernant (CCD)—cens area ... AL-4
Abernant Division—civil ... AL-4
Abernanth ... AL-4
Abernath ... AL-4
Abernath City ... AL-4
Abernathy—locale ... AL-4
**Abernathy**—pop pl ... TX-5
Abernathy, Jessie, House—hist pl ... AR-4
Abernathy Bottom—flat ... AL-4
Abernathy Branch—stream ... TN-4
Abernathy Cave ... TN-4
Abernathy (CCD)—cens area ... TX-5
Abernathy Cem—cemetery ... AL-4
Abernathy Cem—cemetery ... MS-4
Abernathy Cem—cemetery (3) ... TN-4
Abernathy Cem—cemetery (2) ... VA-3
Abernathy Cem—cemetery ... WA-9
Abernathy Channel—channel ... MS-4
Abernathy Chapel—church ... MO-7
Abernathy Creek ... WA-9
Abernathy Creek—stream ... AK-9
Abernathy Creek—stream ... SC-3
Abernathy Dam—dam ... SD-7
Abernathy Draw—valley ... NM-5
Abernathy Field (airport)—airport ... TN-4
Abernathy Hill—summit ... TN-4
Abernathy Hill Cave—cave ... TN-4
Abernathy (historical)—locale ... AL-4
**Abernathy (historical)**—pop pl ... MS-4
**Abernathy (historical)**—pop pl ... TN-4
Abernathy Lake ... AL-4
Abernathy Lake—lake ... MI-6
Abernathy Lake—lake ... WA-9
Abernathy Lake—reservoir ... TN-4
Abernathy Landing (historical)—locale ... TN-4
Abernathy Meadow—flat ... CA-9
Abernathy Memorial Hosp—hospital ... AL-4
Abernathy Mill (historical)—locale ... AL-4
Abernathy Mtn—summit ... WA-9
Abernathy Peak—summit ... WA-9
Abernathy Plantation (historical)—locale ... AL-4
Abernathy P.O. (historical)—building ... AL-4
Abernathy Point—cape ... WA-9
Abernathy Post Office (historical)—building ... TN-4
Abernathy Ridge—ridge ... WA-9
Abernathy Run—stream ... WV-2
Abernathy Sch—school ... NC-3
Abernathy Sch (abandoned)—school ... MO-7
Abernathys Mill ... AL-4
Abernathys Mill—locale ... GA-3
Abernathys Mill Creek ... WA-9
Abernathys Mill (historical)—locale ... AL-4
Abernathy Spring—spring ... AR-4
**Abernathy Station (historical)**—pop pl ... OR-9
Abernathy Truck Trail—trail ... WA-9
Abernethy—locale ... OR-9
Abernethy, Edwin and Ethel, House—hist pl ... OR-9
Abernethy Creek—stream ... NC-3
Abernethy Creek—stream ... OR-9
Abernethy Creek—stream ... WA-9
Abernethy Island—island ... OR-9
Abernethy Lake—lake ... OR-9
Abernethy Lake—reservoir ... GA-3
Abernethy Memorial Ch—church ... NC-3
Abernethy Sch—school ... OR-9
Aberque Creek ... OR-9
Abers Creek—stream ... PA-2
Abert—locale ... VA-3
Abert, Lake—lake ... OR-9
Abert Lake Petroglyphs—hist pl ... OR-9
Abertown—locale ... NJ-2
Abert Rim—cliff ... OR-9
Abert Rim Viewpoint—park ... OR-9
Abert Spring—spring ... OR-9
Abe Run—stream ... OH-6
Abes Branch—stream ... IN-6
Abes Branch—stream ... KY-4
Abes Cemetery ... MS-4
Abes Chapel—church ... MS-4
Abes Chapel Cem—cemetery ... MS-4
Abes Creek—stream ... NC-3
Abes Creek—stream ... UT-8
Abes Fork—stream ... IA-7
Abes Fork—stream ... KY-4
Abes Fork—stream ... VA-3
Abes Hill—summit ... NY-2
Abes Knob—summit ... ID-8
Abes Knoll—summit ... UT-8
Abes Knoll Rsvr—reservoir ... UT-8
Abes Lake—reservoir ... UT-8
Abes Lake Dam—dam ... UT-8
Abes Mtn—summit ... NC-3
Abes Mtn—summit ... OR-9
Abe Spring—spring ... NV-8
Abe Spring—spring ... UT-8
Abe Spring Ch—church ... FL-3
Abe Springs—locale ... FL-3
Abe Springs Sch—school ... FL-3
Abes Rsvr—reservoir ... UT-8
Abes Run—stream (2) ... PA-2
Abes Run—stream ... WV-2
Abe Steele Hollow—valley ... AR-4
Abe Stone Park—park ... CT-1
**Abesville**—pop pl ... MO-7
Abets Creek—stream ... NY-2
A B Evans Lake Dam—dam ... MS-4
Abe Wood Brook—stream ... NY-2
Abex Coroporation (Dennison Division)—facility ... OH-6
Abeyabu ... PW-9
Abeyabu Island ... PW-9
Abe Yarbrough—locale ... NM-5
Abeys Lake—lake ... MI-6
Abeyta—locale ... CO-8
Abeyta Arroyo—stream ... NM-5
Abeyta Canyon—valley ... CO-8
Abeyta Canyon—valley (2) ... NM-5
Abeyta Pass ... CO-8
Abeyta Ranch—locale ... NM-5
**Abeytas**—pop pl ... NM-5
Abeytas Cem—cemetery ... NM-5
Abeyta Trujillo Ditch—canal ... NM-5
A B Farris Pond Dam—dam ... MS-4
ABG Mine—mine ... CO-8
Abiaca Creek—stream ... MS-4
Abiaca Watershed Y-34-1 Dam—dam ... MS-4
Abiaca Watershed Y-34-10 Dam—dam ... MS-4
Abiaca Watershed Y-34-11 Dam—dam ... MS-4
Abiaca Watershed Y-34-12 Dam—dam ... MS-4
Abiaca Watershed Y-34-13 Dam—dam ... MS-4
Abiaca Watershed Y-34-14 Dam—dam ... MS-4
Abiaca Watershed Y-34-15 Dam—dam ... MS-4
Abiaca Watershed Y-34-16 Dam—dam ... MS-4
Abiaca Watershed Y-34-2 Dam—dam ... MS-4
Abiaca Watershed Y-34-21 Dam—dam ... MS-4
Abiaca Watershed Y-34-23 Dam—dam ... MS-4
Abiaca Watershed Y-34-25 Dam—dam ... MS-4
Abiaca Watershed Y-34-28 Dam—dam ... MS-4
Abiaca Watershed Y-34-29 Dam—dam ... MS-4
Abiaca Watershed Y-34-3 Dam—dam ... MS-4
Abiaca Watershed Y-34-36 Dam—dam ... MS-4
Abiaca Watershed Y-34-38 Dam—dam ... MS-4
Abiaca Watershed Y-34-4 Dam—dam ... MS-4
Abiaca Watershed Y-34-43 Dam—dam ... MS-4
Abiaca Watershed Y-34-45 Dam—dam ... MS-4
Abiaca Watershed Y-34-5 Dam—dam ... MS-4
Abiaca Watershed Y-34-6 Dam—dam ... MS-4
Abiaca Watershed Y-34-7 Dam—dam ... MS-4
Abiaca Watershed Y-34-8—dam ... MS-4
Abiaca Watershed Y-34-9 Dam—dam ... MS-4
Abiacha Creek ... MS-4
Abiathar Peak—summit ... WY-8
Abide Airp—airport ... MS-4
Abide Airpark—airport ... MS-4
Abiding Love Lutheran Ch—church ... FL-3
Abidoe Hollow—valley ... OK-5
**Abie**—pop pl ... NE-7
Abiel Lake—lake ... WA-9
Abiel Ledge ... MA-1
Abiel Peak—summit ... WA-9
Abiels Ledge—rock ... MA-1
Abiel Smith Sch—school ... MA-1
Abiff—locale ... TN-4
Abigail—locale ... KY-4
Abigail Ch—church ... FL-3
Abigail Gardner Rescue Site—park ... SD-7
Abigale Dam—dam ... SD-7
A Big Childs Place—school ... FL-3
Abijah Creek—stream ... NY-2
Abijah Ledge—bar ... ME-1
Abikakutchee ... AL-4
Abikudshi (historical)—locale ... AL-4
Abilene—locale ... GA-3
Abilene—locale ... VA-3
**Abilene**—pop pl ... KS-7
**Abilene**—pop pl ... TX-5
Abilene, Lake—reservoir ... TX-5
Abilene Airport ... KS-7
Abilene (CCD)—cens area ... TX-5
Abilene Cem—cemetery ... GA-3
Abilene Cem—cemetery ... KS-7
Abilene Ch—church ... GA-3
Abilene Ch—church ... NC-3
Abilene Christian Coll—school ... TX-5
Abilene Christian College Ranch—locale ... TX-5
Abilene Country Club—other ... KS-7
Abilene Country Club—other ... TX-5
Abilene Creek ... KS-7
Abilene Elem Sch—school ... KS-7
Abilene HS—school ... KS-7
Abilene JHS—school ... KS-7
Abilene Municipal Airp—airport ... KS-7
Abilene Municipal Airp—airport ... TX-5
Abilene Speedway—other ... TX-5
Abilene State Hosp—hospital ... TX-5
Abilene State Hospital Cem—cemetery ... TX-5
Abilene State Park—park ... TX-5
Abineau Canyon ... AZ-5
Abingdon—locale ... SC-3
**Abingdon**—pop pl ... IL-6
**Abingdon**—pop pl ... IA-7
**Abingdon**—pop pl ... MD-2
**Abingdon**—pop pl ... NC-3
**Abingdon**—pop pl ... VA-3
Abingdon Bank—hist pl ... VA-3
Abingdon Bible Ch—church ... VA-3
Abingdon Ch—church ... VA-3
Abingdon Church—hist pl ... VA-3
Abingdon Creek—stream ... NC-3
Abingdon Creek—stream ... SC-3
Abingdon Creek Ch—church ... SC-3
Abingdon Gap ... TN-4
Abingdon Glebe House—hist pl ... VA-3
Abingdon Hist Dist—hist pl ... VA-3
Abingdon Hist Dist (Boundary Increase)—hist pl ... VA-3
Abingdon HS—school ... VA-3
Abingdon (Magisterial District)—fmr MCD ... VA-3
Abingdon Sch—school (2) ... VA-3
Abington—locale ... LA-4
Abington—locale ... TX-5
**Abington**—pop pl ... CT-1
**Abington**—pop pl ... IN-6
**Abington**—pop pl ... MA-1
**Abington**—pop pl ... PA-2
Abington, Town of ... MA-1
Abington Ave Sch—school ... NJ-2
Abington Baptist Ch—church ... PA-2
Abington Brook—stream ... CT-1
Abington ( CDP name: Abington Township )—CDP ... PA-2
Abington Cem—cemetery ... TN-4
Abington Center Sch—school ... IL-6
Abington Centre ... MA-1
Abington Congregational Church—hist pl ... CT-1
Abington Cove—bay ... MD-2
Abington Creek ... SC-3
Abington Executive Industrial Park—locale ... PA-2
Abington Farm—hist pl ... MD-2
Abington Friends Cem—cemetery ... PA-2
Abington Friends Sch—school ... PA-2
Abington Heights HS—school ... PA-2
Abington Heights MS—school ... PA-2
Abington Heights South Campus HS—school ... PA-2
Abington Hill Cem—cemetery ... PA-2
Abington (historical P.O.)—locale ... MA-1
Abington HS—school ... MA-1
Abington HS—school ... PA-2
Abington JHS—school ... MA-1
Abington JHS—school ... PA-2
Abington Memorial Hosp—hospital ... PA-2
Abington Senior High School ... PA-2
Abington Shop Ctr—locale ... PA-2
**Abington (subdivision)**—pop pl ... NC-3
**Abington (Town of)**—pop pl ... MA-1
Abington Township—civil (2) ... PA-2
Abington Township HS—hist pl ... PA-2
**Abington (Township of)**—pop pl ... IL-6
**Abington (Township of)**—pop pl ... IN-6
**Abington (Township of)**—pop pl (2) ... PA-2
Abinodji Falls—falls ... MI-6
Abinodji Lake—lake ... MN-6
Abiqua Basin—basin ... OR-9
Abiqua Creek—stream ... OR-9
Abiqua Creek Park—park ... OR-9
Abiqua Falls—falls ... OR-9
Abiqua Lake—lake ... OR-9
**Abiquiu**—pop pl ... NM-5
Abiquiu Creek—stream ... NM-5
Abiquiu Mesa Grid Gardens—hist pl ... NM-5
Abison Branch—stream ... AL-4
Abispa Windmill—locale ... TX-5
Abita Creek—stream ... LA-4
Abita Lake—lake ... MN-6
Abita Lookout Tower—locale ... LA-4
Abita River—stream ... LA-4
**Abita Springs**—pop pl ... LA-4
Abita Springs Hist Dist—hist pl ... LA-4
Abita Springs Pavilion—hist pl ... LA-4
Abitosse Creek—stream ... MI-6
A B Junciton—locale ... TX-5
**A.B. Junction**—pop pl ... TX-5
Abke Sch—school ... MI-6
AB Lake ... IL-6
A B Lateral—canal ... CO-8
Able—locale ... CO-8
Able Area—locale ... UT-8
Able Canal—canal ... FL-3
Able Cem—cemetery ... AL-4
Able Cem—cemetery ... IA-7
Able Cem—cemetery ... TX-5
Able Creek—stream ... VA-3
Ableman ... WI-6
Able Ridge—ridge ... TN-4
Ables Cem—cemetery ... MS-4
Ables Creek—stream ... AR-4
Ables Drain—canal ... CA-9
Able Seep—spring (2) ... NM-5
Ables Island ... PA-2
Ables Point Landing ... MS-4
Ables Pond—reservoir ... SC-3
Able Spring—spring ... CA-9
**Ables Springs**—pop pl ... TX-5
Ables Springs—spring ... TX-5
Ables Springs Cem—cemetery ... TX-5
Ables Well—well ... TX-5
**Ablett Village**—pop pl ... NJ-2
Ablow Post Office (historical)—building ... MS-4
Ablul ... FM-9
A B Mansell Lake Dam—dam ... MS-4
A B Mine—mine ... NV-8
A B Mtn—summit ... AK-9
**Abnaki**—pop pl ... VT-1
Abnecotant's Island ... MA-1
Abnecotants Island—island ... MA-1
Abner—locale ... NC-3
Abner—locale ... TX-5
Abner Branch—stream ... AR-4
Abner Branch—stream (4) ... KY-4
Abner Branch—stream ... VA-3
Abner Branch Chapel—church ... KY-4
Abner Brook—stream ... NY-2
Abner Cem—cemetery ... IL-6
Abner Ch—church ... OK-5
Abner Ch—church ... VA-3
Abner Cloud House—park ... DC-2
Abner Creek—stream ... IN-6
Abner Creek—stream (2) ... SC-3
Abner Creek Cem—cemetery ... IN-6
Abner Creek Ch—church ... SC-3
Abner Fork—stream (3) ... KY-4
Abner Gap—gap ... VA-3
Abner Gap Sch—school ... VA-3
Abner (historical)—locale ... AL-4
Abner Hollow—valley ... KY-4
Abner Mtn—summit ... KY-4
Abner Mtn—summit ... NC-3
Abner Point—cape ... ME-1
Abner Pond—lake ... MA-1
Abner Post Office (historical)—building ... TN-4
Abner Sch—school ... KY-4
Abners Ferry ... AL-4
Abners Fork—stream ... VA-3
Abners Lake—lake ... MN-6
Abners Pond ... MA-1
Abner Tackett Branch—stream ... KY-4
Abney—locale ... MS-4
**Abney**—pop pl ... SC-3
**Abney**—pop pl ... WV-2
Abney Cem—cemetery ... AL-4
Abney Cem—cemetery ... IL-6
Abney Cem—cemetery ... KY-4
Abney Cem—cemetery ... MS-4
Abney Cem—cemetery ... OK-5
Abney Ch—church ... SC-3
**Abney Crossroads**—pop pl ... SC-3
Abney HS—school ... TX-5
Abney Mills—other ... SC-3
**Abney (Phillips)**—pop pl ... WV-2
Abneys Ferry ... AL-4
Abneys Old Ferry ... AL-4
Abneyville Rock—cliff ... IL-6
Abo—hist pl ... NM-5
Abo—locale ... NM-5
**Abo**—pop pl ... MO-7
Abo Arroyo—stream ... NM-5
Abo Canyon—valley ... NM-5
Abo Cove—bay ... GU-9
Abode Creek ... AZ-5
Abo Ditch—canal ... WY-8
Aboit ... IN-6
**Aboite**—pop pl ... IN-6
Aboite Creek—stream ... IN-6
Aboite River ... IN-6
**Aboite (Township of)**—pop pl ... IN-6
Aboit Station ... IN-6
Abol Campsite—locale ... ME-1
Abol Deadwater—channel ... ME-1
Abol Falls—falls ... ME-1
Abol Mtn—summit ... ME-1
Abolochitto ... MS-4
Abol Pond—lake ... ME-1
Abol Stream—stream ... ME-1
Abol Trail—trail ... ME-1
Abo Mine—mine ... NM-5
Abone ... MP-9
Abong Beach—beach ... GU-9
Aboothlacoosta Creek—stream ... GA-3
Aborn, John, House—hist pl ... MA-1
Aborn Brook ... CT-1
Aborn Brook—stream ... CT-1
Aborn Hill—summit ... ME-1
Aborn Sch—school ... MA-1
Abosko Lake—lake ... WY-8
Abo Spring—spring ... NM-5
Abo State Monmt—pillar ... NM-5
Abotcaputa Creek—stream ... MS-4
**Abotts Creek (historical)**—pop pl ... NC-3
Abotts Rock ... MA-1
Abou Ben Adhem Shrine Mosque—hist pl ... MO-7
Aboud Creek—stream ... AK-9
Above All—summit ... CT-1
Above All State Park—park ... CT-1
Abo Well—well ... NM-5
Abra—locale ... AZ-5
Abra—oilfield ... TX-5
Abra de los Cerros—valley ... NM-5
Abraham—locale ... WV-2
**Abraham**—pop pl ... UT-8
Abraham, Mount—summit ... ME-1
Abraham, Mount—summit ... VT-1
Abraham, Plains of—flat ... WA-9
Abraham Baldwin College—other ... GA-3
Abraham Baptist Ch—church ... AL-4
Abraham Baptist Ch (historical)—church ... AL-4
Abraham Baptist Church ... MS-4
Abraham Bay—bay ... AK-9
Abraham Bay—bay ... NC-3
Abraham Canal—canal ... UT-8
Abraham Cem—cemetery ... VA-3
Abraham Ch—church ... MD-2
Abraham Ch—church ... NC-3
Abraham Ch—church ... SC-3
Abraham Chapel—church ... MS-4
Abraham Coulee—valley ... WI-6
Abraham Creek ... PA-2
Abraham Creek ... WV-2
Abraham Creek—stream ... WA-9
Abraham Flat ... WA-9
Abraham Flat—flat ... OR-9
Abraham Islands—area ... AK-9
Abraham Lake—lake ... AK-9
Abraham Lake—lake ... MI-6
Abraham Lake—lake ... SD-7
Abraham Lake—reservoir ... TX-5
Abraham Levitt HS—school ... NJ-2
Abraham Lincoln Birthplace Natl Historic Site—park ... KY-4
Abraham Lincoln Boyhood Home—building ... KY-4
Abraham Lincoln Elementary School ... TN-4
Abraham Lincoln Elem Sch ... PA-2
Abraham Lincoln Elem Sch—school (3) ... IN-6
Abraham Lincoln Elem Sch—school ... PA-2
Abraham Lincoln HS—school ... CA-9
Abraham Lincoln HS—school ... CO-8
Abraham Lincoln HS—school ... NY-2
Abraham Lincoln Sch—school (2) ... IL-6
Abraham Lincoln Sch—school ... NY-2
Abraham Lincoln Sch—school ... PA-2
Abraham Peak—summit ... UT-8
Abraham Plains—plain ... CA-9
Abraham Point—cape ... GA-3
Abraham Point—cape ... ME-1
Abraham Point—cape ... VA-3
Abraham Pond ... ME-1
Abraham Reef—bar ... WI-6
Abraham River—stream ... AK-9
Abraham Rsvr—reservoir ... UT-8
Abrahams—locale ... PA-2
Abrahams Creek ... PA-2
Abrahams Creek—stream ... PA-2
Abrahams Farmhouse—hist pl ... NY-2
Abrahams Hill ... MA-1
Abrahams Knob—summit ... MO-7
Abrahamson Lake—lake ... MN-6
Abrahams Park—park ... WI-6
Abrahams Point—cape ... MD-2
Abrahams Pond ... ME-1
Abraham Spring—spring ... NV-8
Abraham Spring—spring ... OR-9
Abrahams Run—stream ... KY-4
Abrahams Run—stream ... PA-2
**Abrahamsville**—pop pl ... PA-2
Abraham Vinyard Ch of Christ—church ... AL-4
Abrahm Ranch—locale ... NM-5
Abra Honda (Barrio)—fmr MCD ... PR-3
**Abram**—pop pl ... TX-5
Abram, Mount—summit ... ME-1
Abram Branch—stream ... NC-3
Abram Creek ... PA-2
Abram Creek—stream ... OH-6
Abram Creek—stream ... WV-2
Abram Hill ... MA-1
Abram Morris Sch—school ... NJ-2
Abrams—locale ... OR-9
**Abrams**—pop pl ... PA-2
**Abrams**—pop pl ... WI-6
Abrams, H. D., House—hist pl ... NM-5
Abrams Bldg—hist pl ... NY-2
Abrams Branch—stream ... AR-4
Abrams Branch—stream ... SC-3
Abrams Canyon—valley ... CA-9
Abrams Cem—cemetery ... OK-5
Abrams Chapel—church ... TN-4
Abrams CREEK ... PA-2
Abrams Creek ... TN-4
Abrams Creek—stream ... CO-8
Abrams Creek—stream ... GA-3
Abrams Creek—stream ... MA-1
Abrams Creek—stream ... MT-8
Abrams Creek—stream ... NJ-2
Abrams Creek—stream ... OR-9
Abrams Creek—stream ... SC-3
Abrams Creek—stream ... TN-4
Abrams Creek—stream (2) ... VA-3
Abrams Creek Campground—locale ... TN-4
Abrams Creek Forge ... TN-4
Abrams Creek Shoals—bar ... TN-4
Abram's Delight—hist pl ... VA-3
Abrams Falls—falls ... TN-4
Abrams Falls—falls ... VA-3
Abrams Falls Ch—church ... VA-3
Abrams Falls Trail—trail ... TN-4
Abrams Gap—gap ... TN-4
Abrams Hebrew Acad—school ... PA-2
Abrams Height—summit ... ID-8
Abram S Hewitt State For—forest ... NJ-2
Abrams Hill—summit (2) ... MA-1
Abrams HS—school ... AL-4
Abrams HS—school ... VA-3
Abrams Lake—lake ... CA-9
Abrams Landing—locale ... NY-2
Abrams Mtn—summit ... CO-8
Abrams Mtn—summit ... ME-1
Abrams Mtn—summit ... VA-3
Abramson HS—school ... LA-4
Abramson Lake—lake ... AL-4
Abrams Park—park ... WA-9
Abrams Plains—hist pl ... NC-3
Abrams Point—cape ... ME-1
Abrams Point—cape ... MA-1
Abram's Pond ... ME-1
Abrams Pond—lake ... ME-1
Abram Spring—spring ... OR-9
Abrams Ranch—locale ... CO-8
Abrams Ravine—valley ... CA-9
Abrams Ridge—ridge ... TN-4
Abrams Ridge—ridge ... WV-2
Abrams Run—stream ... WV-2
Abrams Sch—school ... LA-4
Abrams Station—building ... PA-2
**Abrams (Town of)**—pop pl ... WI-6
**Abrams Way Subdivision**—pop pl ... UT-8
Abran Spring—spring ... NM-5
Abra Plain, La—plain ... AZ-5
Abraquidassat Point—cape ... ME-1
Abra RR Station—building ... AZ-5
Abras (Barrio)—fmr MCD ... PR-3
Abras Tank—reservoir ... TX-5
Abre Branch—stream ... KY-4
Abreojo Rocks—area ... AK-9
Abresch, Charles, House—hist pl ... WI-6
Abreu Canyon—valley ... NM-5
Abreu Cem—cemetery ... NM-5
Abreys Ferry ... AL-4
Abrhams Lake—lake ... GA-3
Abrigo Canyon—valley ... AZ-5
Abril Mine—mine ... AZ-5
Abron Cem—cemetery ... KY-4
Abroson Park—park ... IA-7
Abrupt End Cave—cave ... AL-4
Absaloka Youth Camp—locale ... MT-8
Absalom Creek—stream ... KY-4
Absalom Doughty Pond Dam—dam ... NJ-2
Absalom Grundy Sch—school ... NJ-2
Absalona Hill—summit ... RI-1
**Absaraka**—pop pl ... ND-7
Absaraka Interchange—crossing ... ND-7
Absaroka-Beartooth Wilderness—park ... WY-8
Absaroka Creek ... WY-8
Absaroka Range—range ... MT-8
Absaroka Range—range ... WY-8
Absaroka Ridge ... WY-8
Absaroka Ridge—ridge ... WY-8
Absaroka Trail—trail ... WY-8
**Absarokee**—pop pl ... MT-8
Absarraca, Lake—lake ... WY-8
Abs Clearing—flat ... UT-8
**Abscota**—pop pl ... MI-6
Abscota Sch—school ... MI-6
Absecom ... NJ-2
Absecom Bay ... NJ-2
Absecombe ... NJ-2
Absecom Inlet ... NJ-2
**Absecon**—pop pl ... NJ-2
Absecon Bay—bay ... NJ-2
Absecon Beach ... NJ-2
Absecon Channel—channel ... NJ-2
Absecon Creek—stream ... NJ-2
Absecon Heights ... NJ-2
**Absecon Heights**—pop pl ... NJ-2
**Absecon Highlands**—pop pl ... NJ-2
Absecon Highland Sch—school ... NJ-2
Absecon Inlet—gut ... NJ-2
Absecon Lighthouse—hist pl ... NJ-2
Absecum Beach ... NJ-2
Absegami, Lake—reservoir ... NJ-2
Abseon Beach ... NJ-2
Abs Gap—gap ... GA-3
Absher ... IL-6
Absher—locale ... KY-4
Absher—other ... IL-6
Absher Cem—cemetery ... IL-6

Aeneas Lake—*lake* MT-8
Aeneas Lake—*lake* WA-9
Aeneas Mtn—*summit* (2) WA-9
Aeneas Spring—*spring* WA-9
Aeneas Valley—*valley* WA-9
Aenemin—*island* MP-9
*Aenemin Island* MP-9
Aennis Coulee—*valley* ND-7
*Aenon* MA-1
Aenon Baptist Ch—*church* FL-3
Aenon Cem—*cemetery* TN-4
Aenon Ch—*church* FL-3
Aenon Ch—*church* NC-3
Aenon Creek—*stream* TN-4
Aeola Landing (historical)—*locale* AL-4
Aeolia Hills—*other* AK-9
Aeolian Buttes—*summit* CA-9
Aeolian Sch—*school* CA-9
Aeolus, Mount—*summit* VT-1
Aeolus Mtn—*summit* AK-9
Aepoalua Rsvr—*reservoir* HI-9
Aepoeha Rsvr—*reservoir* HI-9
Aepoekolu Rsvr—*reservoir* HI-9
Aepo Rsvr—*reservoir* HI-9
Aereboon—*island* MP-9
Aerequus Airp—*airport* PA-2
Aerial—*locale* GA-3
**Aerial Acres**—*pop pl* CA-9
Aerial Furnace (historical)—*locale* TN-4
Aerial Lake—*lake* OR-9
Aerial Lift Bridge—*hist pl* MN-6
Aerie Lake—*lake* MN-6
Aerik Island—*island* MP-9
Aermotor Draw—*valley* TX-5
Aermotor Windmill—*locale* TX-5
**Aero Acres**—*pop pl* MD-2
Aeroacres Airp—*airport* OR-9
Aero Drive Ch—*church* VA-3
**Aero Estates**—*pop pl* IL-6
Aeroflex-Andover—*airport* NJ-2
Aerohaven Sch—*school* CA-9
Aerojet Canal Number C-111—*canal* FL-3
Aerojet General Corporation—*facility* FL-3
Aerojet Wildlife Mngmt Area—*park* FL-3
Aeromotor Windmill—*locale* TX-5
Aeronautical Depot Maintenance Center—*other* TX-5
Aeroplane Island—*island* MN-6
Aeroplane Mesa—*summit* NM-5
Aeroplane Mine—*mine* CA-9
Aero Plantation Airp—*airport* NC-3
Aero Plantation Lake Dam Number One—*dam* NC-3
Aero Plantation Lake Dam Number Two—*dam* NC-3
Aero Plantation Lake Number One—*reservoir* NC-3
Aero Plantation Lake Number Two—*reservoir* NC-3
Aero Plaza Airp—*airport* WA-9
**Aero Vista**—*pop pl* TX-5
Aeschliman Cem—*cemetery* OH-6
*Aestham River* VA-3
Ae Stream—*stream* HI-9
Aethra—*locale* TN-4
*Aetna* AL-4
*Aetna* IL-6
*Aetna* IN-6
*Aetna* MI-6
Aetna—*locale* AR-4
Aetna—*locale* KS-7
Aetna—*locale* MI-6
Aetna—*locale* TN-4
**Aetna**—*pop pl* IN-6
**Aetna**—*pop pl* MI-6
**Aetna**—*pop pl* TN-4
Aetna, Mount—*summit* CO-8
Aetna, Mount—*summit* ME-1
Aetna Brushy Sch—*school* TN-4
Aetna Cem—*cemetery* KS-7
Aetna Cem—*cemetery* (2) MI-6
Aetna Cem—*cemetery* MN-6
Aetna Cem—*cemetery* OH-6
Aetna Cem—*cemetery* TN-4
Aetna Ch—*church* MI-6
Aetna Creek—*stream* MI-6
Aetna-Dell Sch—*school* WV-2
Aetna Earthworks—*hist pl* MI-6
Aetna Elem Sch—*school* IN-6
**Aetna (Ftna)**—*pop pl* IL-6
Aetna Extension Mine—*mine* CA-9
*Aetna Furnace* NJ-2
Aetna Furnace—*locale* KY-4
Aetna Furnace (historical)—*locale* TN-4
Aetna Grove Ch—*church* KY-4
Aetna Hollow—*valley* TN-4
Aetna Hose, Hook and Ladder Company, Fire Station No. 1—*hist pl* DE-2
Aetna Hose, Hook and Ladder Company Fire Station No. 2—*hist pl* DE-2
Aetna Mine—*mine* TN-4
Aetna Mines—*mine* TN-4
Aetna Mtn—*summit* TN-4
*Aetna Peak* UT-8
Aetna Post Office (historical)—*building* TN-4
Aetna Sch—*school* CA-9
Aetna Spring—*spring* TN-4
**Aetna Springs**—*pop pl* CA-9
Aetna Springs Resort—*hist pl* CA-9
Aetna Station No. 5—*hist pl* WI-6
*Aetna Street Baptist Church* AL-4
**Aetna Township**—*pop pl* KS-7
**Aetna (Township of)**—*pop pl* IL-6
**Aetna (Township of)**—*pop pl* (2) MI-6
**Aetna (Township of)**—*pop pl* MN-6
*Aetnaville* OH-6
**Aetnaville**—*pop pl* KY-4
A E Wood Coliseum—*building* MS-4
A E Wood Memorial Library—*building* MS-4
A E Young Lake Dam—*dam* MS-4
*Af* FM-9
**Afami**—*pop pl* GU-9
Afanaoch—*bar* FM-9
Afanasa Creek—*stream* AK-9
*Afanee Creek* AL-4
**Afao**—*pop pl* AS-9
Afarafar—*summit* FM-9
Afarene Island—*island* FM-9
*Afefuniya-saki* MH-9
Afeman—*locale* LA-4
A Fergusen Elem Sch (abandoned)—*school* PA-2
**Afetna**—*pop pl* MH-9
Afetna, Puntan—*cape* MH-9
Afetna, Unai—*beach* MH-9
*Afetna Beach* MH-9
*Afetna Point* MH-9
Affalter Ditch—*canal* WY-8
Affi Falls—*falls* WA-9
Affinity—*locale* WV-2
Affleck, Gregor S. and Elizabeth B., House—*hist pl* MI-6
Affleck Canal—*channel* AK-9
Affleck Cem—*cemetery* TX-5
Affleck Park—*park* UT-8
Affolter Gully—*valley* NY-2
Affolter Park—*park* MI-6
Affonee Creek—*stream* AL-4
**Affton**—*pop pl* MO-7
Afimuao Ridge—*ridge* AS-9
Afimuao Stream—*stream* AS-9
A Fishbach Dam—*dam* SD-7
**Aflex**—*pop pl* KY-4
Afley Peak—*summit* CO-8
**Afognak**—*pop pl* AK-9
Afognak ANV701—*reserve* AK-9
Afognak Bay—*bay* AK-9
Afognak Island—*island* AK-9
Afognak Lake—*lake* AK-9
Afognak Mtn—*summit* AK-9
Afognak Point—*cape* AK-9
Afognak River—*stream* AK-9
Afognak Strait—*channel* AK-9
Afolkey—*locale* IL-6
Afonasi Lake—*lake* AK-9
*Afong* HI-9
*Afong Camp* HI-9
**Afono**—*pop pl* AS-9
Afono Bay—*bay* AS-9
A Four Mtn—*summit* NM-5
*Africa* PA-2
*Africa* TX-5
Africa—*locale* MS-4
**Africa**—*pop pl* IN-6
**Africa**—*pop pl* OH-6
**Africa**—*pop pl* PA-2
Africa Bayou—*stream* FL-3
Africa Cem—*cemetery* OH-6
Africa Cem—*cemetery* TN-4
Africa Ch—*church* AL-4
**Africa (historical)**—*pop pl* MS-4
Africa Inland Mission—*church* FL-3
Africa Lake—*lake* LA-4
Africana Windmill—*locale* TX-5
African Bar (site)—*locale* CA-9
*African Ch* AL-4
African Ch—*church* MS-4
African Ch—*church* TX-5
African Ch (historical)—*church* MS-4
African Church—*hist pl* MO-7
African Hollow—*valley* TN-4
African Island—*island* GA-3
African Jackson Cemetery—*hist pl* OH-6
African Lion (historical)—*ridge* AZ-5
African Meeting House—*building* MA-1
African Meetinghouse—*hist pl* MA-1
African Methodist Ch—*church* AL-4
African Methodist Episcopal Ch—*church* (2) FL-3
African Methodist Episcopal Ch of the Master—*church* FL-3
African Methodist Episcopal Church—*hist pl* MD-2
African Square Park—*park* FL-3
African Zion Baptist Church—*hist pl* WV-2
African Zion Ch—*church* NJ-2
Africa Post Office (historical)—*building* MS-4
Africa-Roundaway Sch—*school* MS-4
*Africky Ch* AL-4
Afro-American Museum—*building* PA-2
Afro Sch (historical)—*school* MS-4
Afrox Mine—*mine* CA-9
A F Siding—*locale* TX-5
Aftano—*area* GU-9
Afterbay Dam—*dam* CA-9
After Bay Rsvr—*reservoir* NC-3
Afterbuffalo Cem—*cemetery* MT-8
Afterglow Lake—*lake* WI-6
Aftermath Ch—*church* FL-3
Aftermath Clubhouse—*hist pl* WA-9
Afternoon Creek—*stream* AK-9
*Afterskut River* NJ-2
Afterthought Mine—*mine* ID-8
*Afton* NJ-2
Afton—*locale* (2) CA-9
Afton—*locale* GA-3
Afton—*locale* LA-4
Afton—*locale* MI-6
Afton—*locale* NM-5
Afton—*locale* VA-3
Afton—*locale* WV-2
**Afton**—*pop pl* DE-2
**Afton**—*pop pl* IA-7
**Afton**—*pop pl* MN-6
**Afton**—*pop pl* NJ-2
**Afton**—*pop pl* NY-2
**Afton**—*pop pl* NC-3
**Afton**—*pop pl* OH-6
**Afton**—*pop pl* OK-5
**Afton**—*pop pl* TN-4
**Afton**—*pop pl* TX-5
**Afton**—*pop pl* WI-6
**Afton**—*pop pl* WY-8
Afton, Lake—*reservoir* IA-7
Afton, Lake—*reservoir* KS-7
Afton Canyon—*valley* CA-9
Afton Cem—*cemetery* IA-7
Afton Cem—*cemetery* KS-7
Afton Cem—*cemetery* TX-5
Afton Cem—*cemetery* WI-6
Afton Cem—*cemetery* WY-8
Afton Center Cem—*cemetery* IL-6
Afton Ch—*church* NE-7
Afton Ch—*church* VA-3
Afton Creek—*stream* KS-7
Afton District Number 12 Sch—*school* SD-7
Afton District Number 13 Sch—*school* SD-7
Afton District Number 14 Sch—*school* SD-7
Afton District Number 15 Sch—*school* SD-7
Afton-Fairland (CCD)—*cens area* OK-5
Afton Grove Ch—*church* TX-5
Afton (historical)—*locale* KS-7
Afton Interchange—*other* OK-5
**Afton Junction (historical)**—*pop pl* IA-7
Afton Lake—*lake* MN-6
Afton Lake—*lake* NY-2
**Afton Lake**—*pop pl* NY-2
Afton-Lakeland Sch—*school* MN-6
Afton Landing Rec Area—*park* OK-5
Afton Overlook—*locale* VA-3
Afton Post Office—*building* TN-4
Afton Post Office (historical)—*building* SD-7
Afton Pumping Station—*other* NM-5
Afton Run—*stream* NC-3
Afton Sch—*school* NE-7
**Afton (Town of)**—*pop pl* NY-2
Afton Township—*fmr MCD* (2) IA-7
**Afton Township**—*pop pl* KS-7
**Afton Township**—*pop pl* ND-7
**Afton Township**—*pop pl* (2) SD-7
Afton Township Hall—*building* SD-7
Afton (Township of)—*fmr MCD* AR-4
Afton (Township of)—*other* MN-6
**Afton (Township of)**—*pop pl* IL-6
Afton United Methodist Ch—*church* TN-4
Afton Villa Ch—*church* LA-4
Afton Villa Gardens—*hist pl* LA-4
A F Traver Ranch—*locale* CA-9
*Afuefuniya Point* MH-9
Afuefuniya Point—*cape* MH-9
Afuelo Stream—*stream* AS-9
Afulei—*locale* AS-9
Afulei Stream—*stream* AS-9
Afuli Cove—*bay* AS-9
Afu Stream—*stream* AS-9
Afutele Stream—*stream* AS-9
Aga—*area* GU-9
Agaak Creek—*stream* AK-9
Aga Bay—*bay* GU-9
Aga Cove—*bay* AK-9
*Agade* PW-9
*A Gadengel* PW-9
**Agafo Gumas**—*pop pl* GU-9
Agaga—*area* GU-9
Agaga—*hist pl* GU-9
Agaga River—*stream* GU-9
*Agag Cliffs* MH-9
Agagrak Creek—*stream* AK-9
**Agagulu**—*pop pl* AS-9
*Agaigan To* MH-9
A G Aiken Lava Bed—*lava* WA-9
Agai Pah Hills—*summit* NV-8
*Aga Island* FM-9
Agalua Rock—*island* AS-9
*Agamak Lake* MN-6
*Agamenticus* ME-1
Agamenticus, Mount—*summit* ME-1
**Agamenticus Station**—*pop pl* ME-1
**Agamenticus Village**—*pop pl* ME-1
Agamgik Bay—*bay* AK-9
Aga Mine—*mine* CA-9
*Agamok Lake* MN-6
Agamok Lake—*lake* MN-6
*Agan* MH-9
**Agana**—*pop pl* GU-9
Agana Bay—*bay* GU-9
Agana Boat Basin—*basin* GU-9
Agana Branch—*stream* TN-4
Agana Channel—*channel* GU-9
Agana (Election District)—*fmr MCD* GU-9
**Agana Heights**—*pop pl* GU-9
Agana Heights (Election District)—*fmr MCD* GU-9
Agana Hist Dist—*hist pl* GU-9
Agana Naval Air Station—*mil airp* GU-9
Agana Powerplant—*other* GU-9
Agana River—*stream* GU-9
Agana Spanish Bridge—*hist pl* GU-9
Agana Springs—*spring* GU-9
Agana Station—*CDP* GU-9
Agana Swamp—*swamp* GU-9
Aganoa—*locale* AS-9
Agaoleatu Point—*cape* AS-9
Agape, Lake—*reservoir* TN-4
Agape Christian Center—*church* AL-4
Agape Christian Sch—*school* FL-3
Agapie Cove—*bay* AS-9
Agapito Windmill—*locale* TX-5
Aga Point—*cape* GU-9
Agaputuputu Stream—*stream* AS-9
*Agar* CA-9
**Agar**—*pop pl* SD-7
Agarak Creek—*stream* AK-9
Agar Cem—*cemetery* SD-7
Agarita Tank—*reservoir* TX-5
Agar Lake Cut-Off—*bend* MS-4
Agasavili Point—*cape* AS-9
Agashashok River—*stream* AK-9
Agasii Stream—*stream* AS-9
**Agasote**—*pop pl* NJ-2
Agassa Lake—*lake* MN-6
Agassiz, Mount—*summit* CA-9
Agassiz, Mount—*summit* NH-1
Agassiz, Mount—*summit* UT-8
Agassiz Bay—*bay* NY-2
Agassiz Col—*gap* CA-9
Agassiz Creek—*stream* MT-8
Agassiz Glacier—*glacier* AK-9
Agassiz Glacier—*glacier* MT-8
Agassiz Lakes—*area* AK-9
Agassiz Mtn—*summit* AK-9
Agassiz Natl Wildlife Ref—*park* MN-6
*Agassiz Needle* CA-9
Agassiz No 1 State Wildlife Mngmt Area—*park* MN-6
Agassiz No 2 State Wildlife Mngmt Area—*park* MN-6
Agassiz Peak—*summit* AK-9
Agassiz Peak—*summit* AZ-5
Agassiz Pool—*reservoir* MN-6
*Agassiz Rock* MA-1
Agassiz Sch—*school* IL-6
Agassiz Sch—*school* IA-7
Agassiz Sch—*school* MA-1
Agassiz Sch—*school* MN-6
Agassiz Sch—*school* ND-7
Agassiz Sch—*school* OH-6
**Agassiz (Township of)**—*pop pl* MN-6
Aga Stream—*stream* AS-9
**Agat**—*pop pl* GU-9
Agatan, Bo'bo'—*spring* MH-9
Agatan, Saddok As—*stream* MH-9
Aga'tasi—*slope* MH-9
Agat Bay—*bay* GU-9
Agat Cem—*cemetery* GU-9
*Agate* GA-3
Agate—*locale* MI-6
Agate—*locale* ND-7
Agate—*locale* UT-8
Agate—*locale* WA-9
**Agate**—*pop pl* CO-8
**Agate**—*pop pl* MN-6
**Agate**—*pop pl* NE-7
**Agate**—*pop pl* ND-7
Agate Basin—*basin* WY-8
Agate Basin Site—*hist pl* WY-8
Agate Bay—*bay* CA-9
Agate Bay—*bay* (2) MN-6
Agate Bay—*bay* WA-9
Agate Bay—*locale* WA-9
Agate Beach—*bay* CA-9
Agate Beach—*beach* CA-9
Agate Beach—*beach* (2) MI-6
Agate Beach—*beach* (2) OR-9
**Agate Beach**—*pop pl* OR-9
**Agate Beach**—*pop pl* WA-9
Agate Beach (CCD)—*cens area* OR-9
Agate Beach County Park—*park* CA-9
Agate Beach County Park—*park* WA-9
Agate Beach Golf Course—*other* OR-9
Agate Beach Wayside—*park* OR-9
Agate Bridge—*arch* AZ-5
Agate Campground—*locale* CO-8
Agate Canyon—*valley* AZ-5
Agate Cave—*cave* AL-4
Agate Cem—*cemetery* MI-6
Agate Ch—*church* MI-6
Agate Creek—*stream* (4) CO-8
Agate Creek—*stream* MT-8
Agate Creek—*stream* OR-9
Agate Creek—*stream* WY-8
Agate Dam—*dam* OR-9
Agate Dam Rsvr—*reservoir* NE-7
Agate Dam 8—*dam* SD-7
Agate Desert—*plain* OR-9
Agate Falls—*falls* MI-6
Agate Flat—*flat* CA-9
Agate Flat—*flat* OR-9
Agate Flats—*flat* WY-8
Agate Fork Susulatna River—*stream* AK-9
Agate Fossil Beds Natl Monmt—*park* NE-7
Agate Harbor—*bay* MI-6
Agate House—*locale* AZ-5
Agate House Pueblo—*hist pl* AZ-5
Agate Lake—*lake* (2) MN-6
Agat (Election District)—*fmr MCD* GU-9
Agate Mound—*summit* CO-8
Agate Mtn—*summit* AZ-5
Agate Oil Field—*oilfield* UT-8
*Agate Pass* CO-8
Agate Pass—*gap* NV-8
Agate Passage—*channel* WA-9
Agate Pass Bridge—*bridge* WA-9
Agate Point—*cape* MI-6
Agate Point—*cape* OR-9
Agate Point—*cape* WA-9
Agate Point—*locale* WA-9
Agate Point—*summit* NV-8
Agate Point—*summit* NM-5
Agate Rapids—*rapids* AZ-5
Agate Rock—*summit* AK-9
Agate Rsvr—*reservoir* OR-9
Agate Springs—*spring* MT-8
Agate Wash—*valley* (2) UT-8
Agate Well—*well* AZ-5
Agatha—*locale* ID-8
**Agatha**—*pop pl* CA-9
Agatha Canal—*canal* CA-9
Agatha Creek—*stream* ID-8
Agatha Gun Club—*other* CA-9
*Aga-thla-Needle* AZ-5
Agathla Peak—*summit* AZ-5
Agat Invasion Beach—*hist pl* GU-9
*A Gatiroir* PW-9
Agat JHS—*school* GU-9
Agatoavalu Rock—*island* AS-9
*Agaton Ravine* MH-9
*Agaton Valley* MH-9
Agat Santa Rita Sch—*school* GU-9
Agattu Island—*island* AK-9
Agattu Strait—*channel* AK-9
*Agawa* MT-8
*Agawam* MA-1
Agawam—*locale* KY-4
Agawam—*locale* MT-8
**Agawam**—*pop pl* MA-1
**Agawam**—*pop pl* OK-5
*Agawam, Town of* MA-1
**Agawam Beach**—*pop pl* MA-1
Agawam Brook—*stream* MA-1
Agawam Canal—*canal* MT-8
Agawam Cem—*cemetery* MA-1
Agawam Lake—*lake* MA-1
Agawam Park—*park* NY-2
Agawam Point—*cape* MA-1
*Agawam River* MA-1
Agawam River—*stream* MA-1
Agawam Sch—*school* OK-5
Agawam Shop Ctr—*locale* MA-1
**Agawam (Town of)**—*pop pl* MA-1
Agawamuck Creek—*stream* NY-2
*Agawam Village* MA-1
Agawan Lake—*lake* NY-2
Agawato Lake—*lake* MN-6
*Agawome* MA-1
Agcklarok—*locale* AK-9
*A G Cox School* NC-3
**Agder (Township of)**—*pop pl* MN-6
A G Despot Sch—*school* VA-3
A G Doss Lake Dam—*dam* MS-4
*Agec* TN-4
Agecroft—*hist pl* VA-3
Agee Branch—*stream* (2) TN-4
Agee Cem—*cemetery* KY-4
Agee Cem—*cemetery* (2) MO-7
Agee Ch—*church* MO-7
Agee Ch—*church* TX-5
Agee Creek—*stream* MO-7
Agee Creek—*stream* WY-8
*Ageegan* MH-9
Agee Gulch—*valley* CO-8
**Agee (historical)**—*pop pl* TN-4
Agee Hollow—*valley* TN-4
Agee House—*hist pl* AL-4
Agee Lake—*lake* MO-7
Agee Post Office (historical)—*building* TN-4
Agee Ridge—*ridge* KY-4
Agee Spring—*spring* NV-8
Age-Herald Bldg—*hist pl* AL-4
*Agekeb* MP-9
Ageklekak—*locale* AK-9
Agency—*locale* OR-9
**Agency**—*pop pl* MO-7
**Agency**—*pop pl* MT-8
**Agency (Agency City Sta)**—*pop pl* IA-7
Agency Bay—*bay* MN-6
Agency Canal—*canal* ID-8
Agency Canal—*canal* MT-8
Agency Canal—*canal* NV-8
Agency Cem—*cemetery* OK-5
Agency Ch—*church* MO-7
Agency Ch—*church* SD-7
*Agency City* IA-7
Agency Coal Mine—*other* NM-5
*Agency Creek* AL-4
Agency Creek—*stream* ID-8
Agency Creek—*stream* (2) MT-8
Agency Creek—*stream* (3) OR-9
Agency Creek—*stream* (2) SD-7
Agency Creek—*stream* TN-4
Agency Creek—*stream* (2) WA-9
Agency Creek Quarry—*mine* OR-9
Agency Creek Rec Area—*park* TN-4
Agency Draw—*valley* UT-8
Agency Draw Oil Field—*oilfield* UT-8
Agency Hill—*summit* OK-5
Agency Hill—*summit* OR-9
Agency (historical)—*locale* MS-4
Agency Lake—*lake* OR-9
**Agency Landing (historical)**—*pop pl* OR-9
Agency Lateral—*canal* ID-8
Agency Mtn—*summit* OR-9
Agency Narrows—*channel* MN-6
Agency Park—*flat* CO-8
Agency Peak—*summit* AZ-5
Agency Peak—*summit* CO-8
Agency Plains—*flat* OR-9
Agency Post Office (historical)—*building* MS-4
Agency Post Office (historical)—*building* TN-4
Agency Spring—*spring* MT-8
Agency Spring—*spring* OR-9
Agency Springs—*spring* MT-8
Agency Tank—*reservoir* (2) AZ-5
Agency Township—*civil* MO-7
Agency Township—*fmr MCD* IA-7
**Agency Township**—*pop pl* KS-7
**Agency Township**—*pop pl* SD-7
Agency Valley—*valley* OR-9
Agency Valley Cem—*cemetery* OR-9
Agency Valley Dam—*dam* OR-9
Agency Village—*post sta* SD-7
**Agenda**—*pop pl* KS-7
Agenda Cem—*cemetery* KS-7
**Agenda (Town of)**—*pop pl* WI-6
Ag Engineering Farm Pond—*dam* AL-4
*Ageni* MP-9
Agent Cem—*cemetery* OK-5
Agenuk Mtn—*summit* AK-9
Ager—*locale* CA-9
Ager Road Sch—*school* MD-2
**Ages**—*pop pl* KY-4
Ages-Brookside—*post sta* KY-4
Ages Creek—*stream* KY-4
Agfa Lake—*lake* NY-2
Agfayan—*area* GU-9
Agfayan Bay—*bay* GU-9
Agfayan Point—*cape* GU-9
Agfayan River—*stream* GU-9
A G Gaston JHS—*school* AL-4
Aggeler HS—*school* CA-9
Agger Rockshelter—*hist pl* WI-6
Aggie, Mount—*summit* CA-9
Aggie Brown Coulee—*stream* ND-7
Aggie Creek—*stream* (2) AK-9
Aggie Creek—*stream* UT-8
Aggie Hollow—*valley* KY-4
Aggieland—*post sta* TX-5
Aggie Run—*stream* NC-3
*Aggie(State University)* AR-4
Aggieville Shop Ctr—*locale* KS-7
Aggipah Mtn—*summit* ID-8
*Aggipah Peak* ID-8
*Aggipan Mountain* ID-8
**Aggregate (Aggregates)**—*pop pl* WV-2
**Aggregates**—*pop pl* WV-2
*Ag-ha-la* AZ-5
Aghaluk Creek—*stream* AK-9
Aghaluk Mtn—*summit* AK-9
Aghik Island—*island* AK-9
Aghileen Pinnacles—*pillar* AK-9
Ag Hill Complex—*hist pl* PA-2
AG Hinton Full Gospel Deliverance Ch—*church* AL-4
Aghiyuk Island—*island* AK-9
Aghnaghak Lagoon—*lake* AK-9
Aghnuk River—*stream* AK-9
A G Holley State Hosp—*hospital* FL-3
Aghsit Point—*cape* AK-9
Agiagiak Creek—*stream* AK-9
*Agiaguano* MH-9
Agiak Creek—*stream* AK-9
Agiak Lagoon—*lake* AK-9
Agiak Lake—*lake* AK-9
Agiak Point—*cape* AK-9
Agiapuk River—*stream* AK-9
*Agidjen* MP-9
*Agidyen Island* MP-9
Agidyen Island—*island* MP-9
*Agigan* MH-9
*Agigan Misaki* MH-9
*Agigan Point* MH-9
*Agiguan* MH-9
*Agiguan Insel* MH-9
*Agiguan Island* MH-9
*Agiigan-Misaki* MH-9
*Agiigan-To* MH-9
*Agiil Island* PW-9
*Agiiru* PW-9
*Agiiru Island* PW-9
*Agiiru To* PW-9
*Agill Island* PW-9
Aginaw Lake—*lake* MI-6
Agingan—*beach* MH-9
Agingan, Laderan—*cliff* MH-9
Agingan, Puntan—*cape* MH-9
*Agingan Cliffs* MH-9
*Agingan Point* MH-9
Agins Run—*stream* OH-6
*Agiochook* NH-1
*Agiqua River* TN-4
Agitator Creek—*stream* AK-9
*Agizen-to* MP-9
Agler-La Follette House—*hist pl* OH-6
**Aglico**—*pop pl* GA-3
Agligadak Island—*island* AK-9
Agligadak Reefs—*bar* AK-9
Aglungak Hills—*other* AK-9
A G McInturff Dam—*dam* MS-4
*Agnanga Mtn* CA-9
Agnayaghit Point—*cape* AK-9
Agnay Swamp—*swamp* SC-3
Agneda Segui Grant—*civil* FL-3
Agner—*locale* MD-2
Agner Mtn—*summit* CO-8
Agnes—*locale* KY-4
Agnes—*locale* MO-7
Agnes—*locale* TX-5
**Agnes**—*pop pl* GA-3
Agnes, Lake—*lake* (2) CO-8
Agnes, Lake—*lake* FL-3
Agnes, Lake—*lake* (3) MN-6
Agnes, Lake—*lake* MT-8
Agnes, Lake—*lake* WA-9
Agnes, Lake—*lake* WI-6
Agnes, Lake—*reservoir* SD-7
*Agnes City* KS-7
Agnes City Cem—*cemetery* KS-7
**Agnes City Township**—*pop pl* KS-7
**Agnes Corners**—*pop pl* NY-2
Agnes Cove—*bay* AK-9
Agnes Creek—*stream* (2) AK-9
Agnes Creek—*stream* CO-8
Agnes Creek—*stream* MT-8
Agnes Creek—*stream* WA-9
Agnes Gorge—*valley* WA-9
Agnes (historical)—*locale* KS-7
Agnes Howard Hall—*hist pl* WV-2
Agnes Island—*island* NY-2
Agnes Island—*island* WA-9
Agnes Lake—*lake* AK-9
Agnes Lake—*lake* (2) MN-6
Agnes McCutchen Park—*park* TN-4
Agnes Mtn—*summit* WA-9
Agnes Pond Brook—*stream* ME-1
Agness—*locale* OR-9
Agness Bar—*bar* OR-9
Agness (CCD)—*cens area* OR-9
Agnes Scott Coll—*school* GA-3
*Agness Lake* MN-6
Agness Pass—*gap* OR-9
Agnes Spring—*spring* OR-9
Agnes Town Hall—*building* ND-7
**Agnes Township**—*pop pl* ND-7
Agnew—*locale* IL-6
Agnew—*locale* WA-9
**Agnew**—*pop pl* CA-9
**Agnew**—*pop pl* MI-6
**Agnew**—*pop pl* NE-7
**Agnew**—*pop pl* WV-2
**Agnew**—*pop pl* WI-6
Agnew, Lake—*reservoir* SD-7
Agnew, Thomas I., House—*hist pl* NJ-2
Agnew Branch—*stream* IN-6
Agnew-Carlsborg (CCD)—*cens area* WA-9
Agnew Cem—*cemetery* FL-3
Agnew Cem—*cemetery* KY-4
Agnew Cem—*cemetery* OK-5
Agnew Corners—*locale* MI-6
Agnew Creek—*stream* TN-4
Agnew Ditch—*canal* IN-6
Agnew Grove—*woods* CA-9
Agnew Gulch—*valley* CO-8
Agnew (historic)—*building* PA-2
*Agnew Hosp* PA-2
Agnew Hosp—*hospital* PA-2
Agnew JHS—*school* TX-5
Agnew Lake—*lake* CA-9
Agnew Meadows—*flat* CA-9
Agnew Pass—*gap* CA-9
Agnew Pond—*lake* PA-2
Agnew Sch—*school* CA-9
Agnew Shaft—*mine* MN-6
Agnews State Hosp (East Area)—*hospital* CA-9
Agnews State Hosp (West Area)—*hospital* CA-9
**Agnewville**—*pop pl* VA-3
Agney Cem—*cemetery* IL-6
Agniels Creek—*stream* KY-4
**Agnos**—*pop pl* AR-4
A Godfrey Bog Rsvr—*reservoir* MA-1
A Godfrey Number 1 Dam—*dam* MA-1
*Agol* PW-9
Agony Hole Cave—*cave* TN-4
Agony Island—*island* MP-9
*Agony islet* MP-9
Agony Point—*cape* AK-9
A Goode Elem Sch—*school* PA-2
Agor Ridge—*ridge* NY-2
Agort Pass—*gap* NV-8
*Agoru* PW-9
*Agosta* OH-6
Agosta—*other* OH-6
Agosta Cem—*cemetery* OH-6
**Agoura**—*pop pl* CA-9
**Agoura Hills**—*pop pl* CA-9
*Agpalomo* MH-9
A G Phelps Dam—*dam* NC-3
Agra—*locale* CA-9
**Agra**—*pop pl* KS-7
**Agra**—*pop pl* (2) OK-5
Agra City Dam—*dam* KS-7
Agram RR Station—*locale* FL-3
**Agram (Township of)**—*pop pl* MN-6
Agrarian Ditch—*canal* (2) WY-8
A Gravos Ranch—*locale* ND-7
Agre Creek—*stream* AK-9
**Agreeable (historical)**—*pop pl* TN-4
*A Grega* MH-9
Agren Creek—*stream* WA-9
Agri Bog—*swamp* ME-1

Aikens Creek—stream CA-9
Aikens Creek—stream MS-4
Aikens Dam—dam SD-7
Aiken Senior HS—school OH-6
Aiken Sewage Disposal—other SC-3
Aiken's Hotel—hist pl ID-8
Aiken Spring—spring NV-8
Aiken's Swamp VA-3
Aiken Stand Complex—hist pl VT-1
Aikens Tank—reservoir AZ-5
Aiken State Park—park SC-3
Aikens Tavern DE-2
Aiken's Tavern Hist Dist—hist pl DE-2
Aiken Summit—locale VA-3
Aiken Summitt VA-3
Aiken Swamp—swamp VA-3
Aiken Swamp-Dutch Gap Cutoff—channel VA-3
Aiken's Wash Natl Register District—hist pl CA-9
**Aikenton**—pop pl GA-3
Aikentown DE-2
Aiken Training Track—hist pl SC-3
Aiken Waterworks—other (2) SC-3
Aiken West—CDP SC-3
Aiken Winter Colony Hist Dist I—hist pl SC-3
Aiken Winter Colony Hist Dist II—hist pl SC-3
Aiken Winter Colony Hist Dist III—hist pl SC-3
Aikers Tank—reservoir NM-5
**Aikin**—pop pl MD-2
Aikin Creek—stream AL-4
Aikin Grove—locale TX-5
Aikin Island—island AL-4
Aikins—locale KS-7
Aikins Cem—cemetery IL-6
Aikinsville—locale MO-7
Aikinsville Cem—cemetery MO-7
Aikio Island—island MN-6
Aikman—locale KS-7
Aikman Ch—church IN-6
Aikman Creek AR-4
Aikman Creek—stream IN-6
Aikman Sch—school TX-5
Aikman Sch—school WY-8
Aikne MP-9
Aikoolua Gulch—valley HI-9
Aiktak Island—island AK-9
Aila—slope MH-9
A Ilagauir Island PW-9
A Ilaguir Island PW-9
Ailanthus AL-4
Ailanthus KS-7
Ailanthus TN-4
Ailanthus VA-3
Ailanthus Grove MO-7
Ail Branch—stream KY-4
Ailemans Creek IN-6
Ailents Cove Branch—stream NC-3
Ailes, William, House—hist pl MS-4
Ailes Point—cape MI-6
**Ailey**—pop pl GA-3
Ailey Branch—stream AL-4
Ailey Chapel—church TN-4
Aileys Chapel Cem—cemetery TN-4
Ailey Sch (historical)—school TN-4
Ailey Spring—spring TN-4
A Ilimalk PW-9
Ailinginae Atoll—island MP-9
Ailinginae (County-equivalent)—civil MP-9
Ailinginae Lagoon (not verified)—lake MP-9
Ailing Jappel—island MP-9
Ailing Jappel (not verified)—island MP-9
Ailinglalap MP-9
Ailinglapalap—island MP-9
Ailinglapalap Anchorage—harbor MP-9
Ailinglapalap Atoll—island MP-9
Ailinglapalap Island—island MP-9
Ailinglapalap Lagoon—lake MP-9
Ailinglap Atoll MP-9
Ailinglap Insel MP-9
Ailinglaplap—island MP-9
Ailinglaplap (County-equivalent)—civil MP-9
Ailmalk PW-9
A Ilmalk Island PW-9
Ailman, H. B., House—hist pl NM-5
Ailol Mountain PW-9
Ailol River PW-9
Ailor Cem—cemetery TN-4
Ailor Gap—gap TN-4
Ailor Hill—summit TX-5
**Allor (historical)**—pop pl TN-4
Ailsa Farms—hist pl NJ-2
Ails Branch—stream TN-4
Ailston—locale PA-2
Ailuk Atoll—island MP-9
Ailuk (County-equivalent)—civil MP-9
Ailuk Island—island MP-9
Alluk Lagoon—lake MP-9
Ailukpebul PW-9
Aily—locale VA-3
Aily Branch—stream VA-3
Aimeliik PW-9
Aimeliik (County-equivalent)—civil PW-9
Aimeliik Municipality PW-9
Aimelik PW-9
Aimelik Mountain PW-9
A Imelogel PW-9
Aimeong PW-9
Aimes Creek—stream VA-3
A Imetang PW-9
A Imeungs PW-9
A Imig PW-9
Aimiliiki PW-9
Aimion PW-9
Aimiriiki PW-9
Aimoch Ch—church LA-4
Aimoo Falls—falls HI-9
**Aims**—pop pl OR-9
Aimuu Gulch—valley HI-9
Aimuul PW-9
**Aimwell**—pop pl AL-4
**Aimwell**—pop pl LA-4
Aimwell Baptist Ch AL-4
Aimwell Baptist Ch—church AL-4
Aimwell Cem—cemetery SC-3
Aim Well Ch AL-4
Aimwell Ch—church (4) AL-4
Aimwell Ch—church GA-3
Aimwell Ch—church (3) LA-4
Aimwell Ch—church SC-3
Aimwell Spring—spring LA-4
Aimy Run PA-2
**Aina Haina**—pop pl HI-9
Aina Haina—post sta HI-9
Aina Haina Sch—school HI-9
Ainahou HI-9
Ainahou—area HI-9
Ainahou—cape HI-9
Ainahou Ranch—locale HI-9
Ainakea—civil HI-9
Ainako—area HI-9
Ainapo—area HI-9
Ainapo—locale HI-9
Ainapo Trail—hist pl HI-9
Ainapo Trail—trail HI-9
Ain Ch—church AR-4
Aineman Island—island MP-9
Aineman-to MP-9
Ainemon MP-9
Ainer Creek TN-4
Ainesworth IN-6
**Ainger**—pop pl MI-6
**Ainger**—pop pl OH-6
Ainger Creek FL-3
Ainger Creek Bridge—bridge FL-3
Ainger Hill—summit NY-2
Ainger Hill Sch—school NY-2
Ainger Lake—lake MT-8
Ainoni Ridge—ridge HI-9
Ainoni Spring—spring HI-9
Ainoni Stream—stream HI-9
Ainshea Butte—locale CA-9
Ainsley Canyon—valley WA-9
Ainsley Lookout Tower—tower FL-3
Ainsleys Cabin—locale TX-5
**Ainsley Woods**—pop pl DE-2
Ainslie Creek WA-9
Ainslie Gulch—valley AK-9
Ainsworth OR-9
**Ainsworth**—pop pl IN-6
**Ainsworth**—pop pl IA-7
**Ainsworth**—pop pl NE-7
**Ainsworth**—pop pl TX-5
Ainsworth, Capt. John C., House—hist pl OR-9
Ainsworth, Lewis, House—hist pl CA-9
Ainsworth, Maud and Belle, House—hist pl OR-9
Ainsworth Brook—stream NY-2
Ainsworth Cem MS-4
Ainsworth Cem—cemetery MS-4
Ainsworth Cem—cemetery NE-7
**Ainsworth Corner**—pop pl CA-9
**Ainsworth Corner**—pop pl OR-9
Ainsworth Creek—stream TX-5
Ainsworth House—hist pl MT-8
Ainsworth House—hist pl WY-8
Ainsworth HS—school MI-6
Ainsworth Junction—locale WA-9
Ainsworth Park—park MN-6
Ainsworth Pumping Station—other WY-8
Ainsworth Sch—school OR-9
Ainsworth Sch—school WI-6
Ainsworth State Forest Park—park VT-1
Ainsworth State Park—park OR-9
Ainsworth Table—summit NE-7
**Ainsworth (Town of)**—pop pl WI-6
Aioi Jima FM-9
Aioi-Shima FM-9
Aip, Dolen—summit FM-9
Aipakapw—summit FM-9
A Ipelau PW-9
Ai Post Office TN-4
Aiqinii MP-9
Air AL-4
Air TX-5
**Air**—pop pl TX-5
Air, Mount—summit TX-5
Air-Ag Airp—airport KS-7
A Irai PW-9
**Airai**—pop pl (2) PW-9
Airai (County-equivalent)—civil PW-9
Airai Elem Sch—school PW-9
Airai Municipality PW-9
Airbase CA-9
Air Base—other AR-4
**Air Base Acres**—pop pl WY-8
**Air Base City**—pop pl NM-5
Airbase East Oil Field—oilfield KS-7
Air Base Elem Sch—school FL-3
Airbase Oil Field—oilfield KS-7
Air Base Road Ch—church LA-4
Air Base Sch—school FL-3
Airbase (siding)—locale CA-9
Airbase Spur—uninc pl KS-7
Air Bellows Dam—dam NC-3
Air Bellows Gap—gap NC-3
Air Bellows Overlook—locale NC-3
Airborne Speedway—other NY-2
**Airboro**—pop pl NC-3
Air Brake—swamp AR-4
Air City NY-2
**Air City**—pop pl NY-2
**Airco**—pop pl KY-4
Aircraft Radio—airport NJ-2
**Aircue**—pop pl MO-7
Airdrie Hill—summit KY-4
Airdrie Iron Furnace—locale KY-4
Airdwood Lake—lake NY-2
Aire, Mount—summit UT-8
Airebon MP-9
Airech FM-9
Airedale—locale KY-4
Airedele—locale MD-2
Airek—island MP-9
**Airek**—pop pl MP-9
Airekku-to MP-9
Aire Libre Mobile Home Park—locale AZ-5
Aires Run PA-2
Aires Run—stream PA-2
Airetj FM-9
**Airey**—pop pl MD-2
**Airey**—pop pl MS-4
**Airey (Aireys)**—pop pl MD-2
Airey Lake Rec Area—park MS-4
Airey Lookout Tower—locale MS-4
Aireys MD-2
Airfield Pond—reservoir VA-3
Airfield Windmill—locale TX-5
Air Force Academy—CDP CO-8
Air Force Academy Rec Area—park CO-8
Air Force Accounting and Finance Center CO-8
Air Force Eastern Test Range (Malabar Annex)—military (2) FL-3
Air Force Electronic Security Command—military TX-5
Air Force Plant No. 36—military OH-6
Air Force Plant No. 4—military TX-5
Air Force Plant No. 44—military AZ-5
Air Force Plant No. 6—military GA-3
Air Force Plant 42—military CA-9
Air Force Well—locale NM-5
Airgate—post sta FL-3
Airglow Observatory—building PA-2
Airground Sch—school NH-1
Air Harbor Airp—airport NC-3
Air Haven Airp—airport PA-2
Air Haven Camp—locale NY-2
A I R Helicopter Sales & Service Airp—airport PA-2
**Airhill**—pop pl OH-6
Air Hill Ch—church PA-2
Air (historical)—locale KS-7
Airhole Lake—lake WI-6
Airie, Mount—summit IN-6
Airiginae-to MP-9
Airik MP-9
Airiken-To MP-9
Airik Island—island MP-9
Airikku Island MP-9
Airikku-to MP-9
Airikuto-To MP-9
Airikuyo MP-9
Airimasuku To PW-9
Air Industrial Park—locale MS-4
Airington Windmill—locale NM-5
Airingurapurapu MP-9
Airingurapurapu-to MP-9
**Airlane Park Subdivision**—pop pl UT-8
Airlawn—uninc pl TX-5
Airlie—hist pl MS-4
Airlie—locale MN-6
Airlie—locale NC-3
Airlie—locale VA-3
**Airlie**—pop pl NC-3
**Airlie**—pop pl OR-9
**Airlie (conference center)**—pop pl VA-3
Airlie Creek—stream OR-9
Airlie Gardens—park NC-3
Air Line—locale GA-3
**Airline**—pop pl GA-3
Air Line—trail NH-1
**Airline Acres**—pop pl MO-7
Airline Canal—canal AZ-5
Airline Ch—church FL-3
Airline Community Coll—school LA-4
Air Line Junction OH-6
Air Line Junction—locale MO-7
Air Line Junction—locale OH-6
Air Line Junction (North Charlotte Yard)—uninc pl NC-3
**Airline Park**—pop pl LA-4
Airline Park Sch—school LA-4
Air Line Sch—school GA-3
Airline Union Ch—church OH-6
Airline Village—uninc pl TX-5
Air Mail Facility—post sta NE-7
Air Mail Facility—post sta NM-5
Air Mail Facility—post sta OR-9
Air Mail Field—post sta IN-6
Airman Peak—summit AZ-5
Air Materiel Command—post sta OH-6
Airmont—locale VA-3
**Airmont**—pop pl NY-2
**Airmont Acres (subdivision)**—pop pl DE-2
**Airmont Heights**—pop pl NY-2
Airmont Sch—school NY-2
Airmount SD-7
Airmount Ch—church AL-4
Airmount Ch—church MS-4
Air Mount (historical)—locale MS-4
Air Mount P. O. (historical)—locale AL-4
Airmount Primitive Baptist Church MS-4
Airmount Sch (historical)—school MS-4
Airola Camp—locale CA-9
Airola Creek—stream CA-9
Airola Peak—summit CA-9
Airoru River PW-9
Airpark—post sta OK-5
Airpark Field Airp—airport IN-6
Airpark Plaza (Shop Ctr)—locale FL-3
Airpark Shop Ctr—locale KS-7
Air Park South—airport MO-7
**Air Park West**—pop pl NE-7
Airplane Canyon—valley WA-9
Airplane Canyon Tank—reservoir AZ-5
Airplane Cave TN-4
Airplane Flat—flat (2) CA-9
Airplane Flat Recreation Site—locale AZ-5
Airplane Hill—summit UT-8
Airplane Hills—ridge NM-5
Airplane Island—island FL-3
Airplane Lake—lake ID-8
Airplane Lake—lake MS-4
Airplane Lake—lake WA-9
Airplane Meadow—flat CA-9
Airplane Prairie—flat FL-3
Airplane Ridge—ridge CA-9
Airplane Ridge—ridge (2) CO-8
Airplane Spring—spring UT-8
Airplane Tank—reservoir AZ-5
Airplane Tank Spring—spring TX-5
Airpoint—locale VA-3
Air Point Sch—school CA-9
**Airport**—pop pl VA-3
Airport—post sta (2) CA-9
Airport—post sta FL-3
Airport—post sta ID-8
Airport—post sta KY-4
Airport—post sta NV-8
Airport—post sta NC-3
Airport—post sta (2) OH-6
Airport—post sta SC-3
Airport—post sta WY-8
Airport Blvd Baptist Ch—church AL-4
Airport Blvd Baptist Ch—church FL-3
Airport Canal—canal FL-3
Airport Cave—cave AL-4
Airport Cave—cave TN-4
Airport Ch—church (2) SC-3
Airport Channel—channel CA-9
**Airport City**—pop pl TX-5
Airport Creek—stream VA-3
Airport Ditch—canal CA-9
**Airport Drive**—pop pl MO-7
**Airport East Business Park (subdivision)**—pop pl UT-8
Airport Estates—uninc pl TN-4
Airport Flats—flat MT-8
Airport For—forest MI-6
**Airport Gardens**—pop pl KY-4
**Airport Heights**—pop pl IL-6
**Airport Highlands**—pop pl AL-4
Airport Hill—summit WV-2
Airport HS—school MI-6
Airport HS—school SC-3
Airport Industrial Park—locale AL-4
Airport Industrial Park—locale MS-4
Airport Interchange—crossing ND-7
Airport JHS—school CA-9
Airport Lake—flat CA-9
Airport Lake—lake MN-6
Airport Lake—lake MO-7
Airport Lake—reservoir OK-5
Airport Lake—reservoir TN-4
Airport Lake Dam—dam TN-4
Airport Mail Facility—post sta CO-8
Airport Mail Facility—post sta FL-3
Airport Mail Facility—post sta GA-3
Airport Mail Facility—post sta MA-1
Airport Mail Facility—post sta (2) TN-4
Airport Mail Facility—post sta TX-5
Airport Park—park CA-9
Airport Park—park ID-8
Airport Park—park OH-6
Airport Playfield—park OH-6
**Airport Plaza**—pop pl TN-4
Airport Plaza Shop Ctr—locale PA-2
Airport Pond—lake NY-2
Airport Ranch—locale WA-9
Airport Ravine—valley AZ-5
**Airport Road**—pop pl WV-2
Airport Road—uninc pl TN-4
Airport Road Lateral—canal CA-9
Airport Rsvr—reservoir MT-8
Airport Sch—school CA-9
Airport Sch—school MO-7
Airport Sch—school NY-2
Airport Sch—school WV-2
Airport School (Abandoned)—locale MO-7
Airport Siding—uninc pl FL-3
**Airport Subdivision**—pop pl GA-3
Airport Tank—reservoir (6) AZ-5
Airport Tank—reservoir NM-5
Airport Tower—pillar UT-8
Airport Township—civil MO-7
**Airport Villa**—pop pl DE-2
**Airport Village**—pop pl AR-4
**Airport Village**—pop pl HI-9
**Airport Village**—pop pl WV-2
Airport Well NV-8
Airport Well—well AZ-5
Airport Windmill—locale NM-5
Airport Windmill—locale (2) TX-5
Air Post Office (historical)—building AL-4
Air Production and Chemicals, Incorporated—facility (2) KY-4
Airrai PW-9
**Air Reserve Personnel Center**—pop pl CO-8
Air Ridge—ridge NC-3
Air Rock Ch—church TN-4
Air Rock Sch (historical)—school TN-4
Air Sailing Gliderport—airport NV-8
Airsdale Sch—school SC-3
Airshaft Hollow—valley TN-4
Air Shaft Number 3—other NY-2
Air Shaft Ridge—ridge NV-8
Airs Hill—summit AK-9
Airs Sch—school MS-4
Airstrip Pond—lake CA-9
Airstrip Pond—reservoir OR-9
Airstrip Rsvr—reservoir OR-9
Air Terminal—post sta TX-5
Airtight Bridge—hist pl IL-6
Airtight Bridge—other IL-6
Air Town NJ-2
Airuken Island—island MP-9
Airukiiji—island MP-9
Airukiji Island, Airukiji—island MP-9
Airukiraru—island MP-9
Airukiraru Island MP-9
Air Univ—school AL-4
A Irur Cave PW-9
Airuss Lake MN-6
**Air View**—pop pl TN-4
Airview Baptist Ch—church AL-4
Airview Cem—cemetery TN-4
Airview Ch—church TN-4
Airview Heights Community Ch of God—church AL-4
Airview Lake—lake WA-9
Airview Ridge WI-6
Airview Tabernacle—church OK-5
Airview Terrace—uninc pl LA-4
Air Village Strip (airport)—airport UT-8
Airville—locale TX-5
**Airville**—pop pl PA-2
Airway Beacon (historical)—tower MO-7
Airway Beacon 212—locale NV-8
Airway Beacon 216—locale NV-8
Airway Beacon 8—other CA-9
Airway Ch—church OH-6
Airway Farms—locale (2) CA-9
**Airway Heights**—pop pl WA-9
Airway Heights (CCD)—cens area WA-9
Airway Park—park ID-8
Airways Ch—church TN-4
Airway Shop Ctr—locale OH-6
Airy MP-9
Airy, Mount—summit NV-8
Airy, Mount—summit NY-2
Airy, Mount—summit OK-5
Airy, Mount—summit (2) PA-2
Airy, Mount—summit VA-3
Airy, Mount—summit WY-8
Airy Castle—hist pl KY-4
**Airydale**—pop pl PA-2
Airy Grove Sch—school NC-3
Airy Hall—locale SC-3
Airy Hill Plantation SC-3
Airy Hill Sch—school PA-2
Airy Ledge—bar ME-1
Airy Mesa, Mount—summit NV-8
Airy Mount—hist pl KY-4
Airy Sch—school OH-6
Airy Spring—spring CO-8
Airy Spring Sch—school SC-3
Airy View Sch—school PA-2
Airy View Sch (abandoned)—school PA-2
Aisemiich PW-9
Aisemith River PW-9
Aisquith Creek MD-2
Aisquith Island MD-2
Ais River FL-3
Aistrop Cem—cemetery VA-3
Aitaburai Point PW-9
Aitaburai Saki PW-9
**Aitch**—pop pl PA-2
**Aitch (Mechanicsburg)**—pop pl OH-6
Aitkan, Robert, Farm House—hist pl MI-6
Aitken Barn—hist pl ID-8
Aitken Cave—cave PA-2
**Aitken (historical)**—pop pl OR-9
Aitken Lake Dam—dam IN-6
Aitken Rsvr—reservoir MT-8
Aitken Spring—spring ID-8
Aitken State For—forest VT-1
**Aitkin**—pop pl MN-6
Aitkin Carnegie Library—hist pl MN-6
**Aitkin (County)**—pop pl MN-6
Aitkin County Courthouse and Jail—hist pl MN-6
Aitkin Lake—lake MN-6
**Aitkin (Township of)**—pop pl MN-6
Ai-to MP-9
Aiton Sch—school DC-2
Aitsu—island MP-9
Aitsu Island MP-9
Aiugnak Columns—bar AK-9
Aiu Jima FM-9
Aiungel PW-9
A Ivegebangel PW-9
Aivichtik River—stream AK-9
**Aix**—pop pl IN-6
Aix, Mount—summit WA-9
**Aix La Chapelle Condominium**—pop pl UT-8
Aiyasu Reef PW-9
Aiyon PW-9
Aiyon Mountain PW-9
Aiyunguru PW-9
Ajalban MP-9
**Ajaltokrok**—pop pl MP-9
Ajanen Island MP-9
Aja Ranch—locale (2) AZ-5
Ajatak MP-9
Ajax—locale LA-4
Ajax—locale PA-2
Ajax—locale SD-7
Ajax—locale VA-3
Ajax—mine UT-8
**Ajax**—pop pl KY-4
**Ajax**—pop pl TX-5
**Ajax**—pop pl WV-2
Ajax Airstrip—airport OR-9
Ajax Bar—bar MS-4
Ajax Branch—stream WV-2
Ajax Cabin—locale MT-8
Ajax Ch—church LA-4
Ajax Field—park CA-9
Ajax Gulch—valley OR-9
Ajax Hill—summit AZ-5
Ajax (historical)—locale OR-9
Ajax Island—island WI-6
Ajax Lake—lake MT-8
Ajax Mine—mine (2) AZ-5
Ajax Mine—mine CO-8
Ajax Mine—mine ID-8
Ajax Mine—mine MN-6
Ajax Mine—mine (3) MT-8
Ajax Mine—mine NV-8
Ajax Mine—mine NM-5
Ajax Mine—mine OR-9
Ajax Mine (abandoned)—mine OR-9
Ajax Mountain ID-8
Ajax Mountain MT-8
**Ajax Park**—pop pl NJ-2
Ajax Peak—summit CO-8
Ajax Peak—summit ID-8
Ajax Peak—summit MT-8
Ajax Peak—summit VI-3
Ajax Ranch—locale MT-8
Ajax Reef—bar AK-9
Ajax Reef—bar FL-3
Ajax Run—stream PA-2
Ajax Station UT-8
Ajayan—valley GU-9
Ajayan Bay—bay GU-9
Ajayan Point—cape GU-9
Ajayan River—stream GU-9
Ajay Lake—lake FL-3
A J Baker Court Drain IN-6
A J Bolon Historic Monmt—park WA-9
A J Camper Park—locale UT-8
Ajeeang—island MP-9
Ajee Spring—spring MO-7
Ajej MP-9
Ajej—island MP-9
Ajejeon MP-9
Ajeleb Island—island MP-9
A Jellesed Ranch—locale ND-7
Ajeltake MP-9
Ajeltokrok MP-9
Ajereppu-to MP-9
Ajibikika Falls—falls MI-6
Ajiddik—island MP-9
Ajiereppu To MP-9
Ajileb MP-9
Ajilien—island MP-9
**Ajiltake**—pop pl MP-9
Ajilwawaen—island MP-9
Ajirik MP-9
Ajirikku Island MP-9
Ajirikku Island—island MP-9
Ajirikku-to MP-9
Ajirrik Island MP-9
Ajjatik—island MP-9
Ajjelaran—island MP-9
Ajjellob MP-9
Ajkadkadebwokwbwokw—island MP-9
Ajkadkadedokake—island MP-9
Ajkan Island MP-9
A J Kennedy Pond One—lake FL-3
A J Kennedy Pond Two—lake FL-3
**Ajlune**—pop pl WA-9
Ajmanol—island MP-9
Ajmo Beach—beach GU-9
**Ajo**—pop pl AZ-5
Ajo, Mount—summit AZ-5
Ajo, Valley of the—valley AZ-5
Ajo (CCD)—cens area AZ-5
Ajo Copper Mines—mine AZ-5
Ajo Country Club—other AZ-5
Ajo HS—school AZ-5
Ajokwola—island MP-9
Ajola MP-9
Ajo Mountains AZ-5
Ajo Municipal Airp—airport AZ-5
A Jones Mill (historical)—locale AL-4
Ajo Peak—summit AZ-5
Ajo Peaks AZ-5
Ajo Range—range AZ-5
Ajo Recreation Center—park AZ-5
Ajo Way Interchange—crossing AZ-5
Ajowean MP-9
Ajowean-To MP-9
A J Siding—locale TX-5
A J Spencer Pond—lake FL-3
AJ Tank—reservoir AZ-5
Ajurolake MP-9
Ajurotaka MP-9
Ajurotake MP-9
Ajwaan—island MP-9
A J West Sch—school WA-9
A J White Dam—dam NC-3
A J White Dam—reservoir NC-3
AJX Bridge over South Fork and Powder River—hist pl WY-8
Akaba, Mount—summit AZ-5
Akaba Tank—reservoir AZ-5
Akabluak Pass—gap AK-9
Akadiken—island MP-9
Akahamut (Site)—locale AK-9
Akahi—summit HI-9
Akahipuu—summit HI-9
Akahk—civil FM-9
Akahk, Dauen—gut FM-9
Akahu Kaimu—bay HI-9
Akain Cem—cemetery TX-5
Akaiyan Falls—falls MT-8
Akaiyan Lake—lake MT-8
Akaka Falls—falls HI-9
Akaka Falls State Park—park HI-9
Akakoa HI-9
Akakoa Point HI-9
Akaku FM-9
Akalak PW-9
Aka Lake—lake AK-9
Akalokul PW-9
Akalokul Point PW-9
Akalolik Creek—stream AK-9
Akaluanui—summit HI-9
Akaluovik Lakes—lake AK-9
Akalura Creek—stream AK-9
Akalura Lake—lake AK-9
Akan Central Sch—school WI-6
Akansa River KS-7
Akansas River KS-7
Akansea River KS-7
**Akan (Town of)**—pop pl WI-6
Akanuklinuk Slough—gut AK-9
Akapilco Creek GA-3
Akarappu PW-9
**Akard Addition**—pop pl TN-4
Akard Cem—cemetery MO-7
Akard Cem—cemetery VA-3
Akard Memorial Elem Sch—school TN-4
Akard Oil Field—oilfield TX-5
Akard Ridge—ridge TN-4
Akard Ridge—ridge VA-3
Akareppu PW-9
Akargichek Mtn—summit AK-9
Akarikiyan MP-9
Akarikiyan-To MP-9
Akarokoro Kaku PW-9
Akarokoro Point PW-9
Akaron PW-9
Akasaki Camp—locale HI-9
**Akaska**—pop pl SD-7
AK Bar Ranch—locale TX-5
A K Bissell Park—park TN-4
Akchin AZ-5
**Ak Chin**—pop pl (2) AZ-5
**Akchin (Ak Chin)**—pop pl AZ-5
Ak Chin Community Airfield—airport AZ-5
Ak Chin Community Center—building AZ-5
**Ak-Chin Ind Res**—pop pl AZ-5
Ak-Chin Reservation AZ-5
Akchin (San Serafin) AZ-5
Ak Chin Wash—stream AZ-5
Akchin Well—well AZ-5
Ak Chut Vaya—locale AZ-5
Ake, F. P., Bldg—hist pl ID-8
Ake Ditch—stream DE-2
Akee-mull AZ-5
Akeftapak—locale AK-9
Akeftapak Bay—bay AK-9
Akeku Point—cape AK-9
Akela—locale NM-5
Akela, Lake—lake PA-2
Akela Flats—flat NM-5
Akela Interchange—other NM-5
Akeley—locale PA-2
**Akeley**—pop pl MN-6
Akeley Cem—cemetery MN-6
Akeley Run—stream PA-2
**Akeley (Township of)**—pop pl MN-6
A Keller Ranch—locale NE-7
Akely Hollow—valley PA-2
Akeman Crossroad—locale TN-4
Akendihdip—swamp FM-9
Akenfonogo GA-3
Akenlian—swamp FM-9
Akens Canyon—valley CA-9
Akens Cem—cemetery MO-7
Akeo—island MP-9
Akeo Island MP-9
Akeonik (Ruins)—locale AK-9
Ake Ranch—locale NM-5
Aker Branch—stream KY-4
Aker Brook—stream ME-1
Aker Cem—cemetery WV-2

Aker Cemetery—hist pl ... MO-7
Aker Creek ... AL-4
Aker Creek ... MS-4
Aker Draw—valley ... CO-8
Aker Hill—summit ... MO-7
Akerlund, August, Photographic Studio—hist pl ... MN-6
**Akerly**—pop pl ... PA-2
Akers ... LA-4
Akers ... PA-2
Akers—locale ... MO-7
**Akers**—pop pl ... CA-9
**Akers**—pop pl ... LA-4
Akers—uninc pl ... KY-4
Akers Branch—stream (4) ... KY-4
Akers Branch—stream ... MS-4
Akers Butte—summit ... OR-9
Akers Canyon Creek—stream ... WY-8
Akers Cem—cemetery ... IN-6
Akers Cem—cemetery (2) ... TX-5
Akers Cem—cemetery ... WI-6
Akers Ch—church ... IL-6
Akers Ch—church ... WV-2
Aker Sch—school ... KS-7
Akers Chapel—church ... TN-4
Akers Ditch—canal ... CO-8
Akers Ditch—canal ... IN-6
Akers Gulch—valley ... ID-8
Akers Lake—reservoir ... TN-4
Akers Lake Dam—dam ... TN-4
Akerson Butte—summit ... OR-9
Akerson Creek ... CA-9
Akers Place Windmill—locale ... NM-5
Akers Pond—lake ... NH-1
Akers Ranch—locale ... MT-8
**Akers (RR name Manchac)**—pop pl ... LA-4
Akers Sch—school (2) ... IL-6
Akers Sch—school ... NC-3
Akers Sch (abandoned)—school ... MO-7
Akers Shop Ctr—locale ... NC-3
Akers Tank—reservoir ... NM-5
Akers Valley—valley ... KY-4
Akersville—locale ... PA-2
**Akersville**—pop pl ... KY-4
Ake Rsvr—reservoir ... CA-9
Akes—locale ... GA-3
Akes (historical)—locale ... AZ-5
Ake Site—hist pl ... NM-5
Ake Well—well ... NM-5
Akey, James, Farm—hist pl ... OH-6
Akey Sch—school ... WI-6
Akfayegak Creek—stream ... AK-9
Akgak, I—slope ... MH-9
Akgak, Laderan I—cliff ... MH-9
A. K. Gulch—valley ... OR-9
**Akhiok**—pop pl ... AK-9
Akhiok Bay—bay ... AK-9
Akhiok Island—island ... AK-9
Akhiok Reef—bar ... AK-9
Akhluaiki—summit ... HI-9
Aki ... FM-9
Aki—civil ... HI-9
**Akiachak**—pop pl ... AK-9
Akiachak ANV704—reserve ... AK-9
**Akiak**—pop pl ... AK-9
Akiak Creek—stream ... AK-9
Akiak Mountains—other ... AK-9
Akiba, Lake—reservoir ... PA-2
Akiba Acad—school ... PA-2
Akihi—summit ... HI-9
Akiknaak Peaks—summit ... AK-9
Akikukchiak Creek—stream ... AK-9
Akillik River—stream ... AK-9
Akimbo Point—cape ... NJ-2
Akin ... NY-2
Akin—locale ... CO-8
Akin—locale ... GA-3
Akin—locale ... OR-9
**Akin**—pop pl ... GA-3
**Akin**—pop pl (2) ... IL-6
Akin, Daniel F., House—hist pl ... MN-6
Akina, As—slope ... MH-9
Akin Airp—airport ... MS-4
Akina Place ... MH-9
Akin Cem ... TN-4
Akin Cem—cemetery (3) ... KY-4
Akin Cem—cemetery ... TN-4
Akin Ch—church ... GA-3
Akin Ch—church ... TN-4
Akin Ch—church ... TX-5
Akin Creek—stream ... IL-6
Akin Dimock Oil Field—oilfield ... TX-5
Akin Ditch—canal ... IN-6
Akin Elementary School ... MS-4
Akin Gap—gap ... GA-3
Akin Hollow—valley ... TN-4
Akin Junction—locale ... IL-6
Akin Knob—summit ... KY-4
Akinkoka Creek—stream ... MT-8
Akinkoka Peak—summit ... MT-8
Akin Landing—locale ... TN-4
Akin Mtn—summit ... GA-3
Akin Park—park ... IN-6
Akin Ranch—locale ... CO-8
Akin Ridge—ridge ... TN-4
Akin Rsvr—reservoir ... CO-8
**Akins**—pop pl ... GA-3
**Akins**—pop pl ... OK-5
Akins, Lyman P., House—hist pl ... NY-2
Akins, Robert, House—hist pl ... NY-2
Akins Bay—swamp ... FL-3
Akins Bay Slough—gut ... FL-3
Akins Branch—stream ... TN-4
Akins Bridge—bridge ... GA-3
Akins Cem—cemetery ... AR-4
Akins Cem—cemetery (2) ... GA-3
Akins Cem—cemetery ... KY-4
Akins Cem—cemetery ... OK-5
Akin Sch—school ... MS-4
Akin Sch—school ... TX-5
Akins Chapel—church ... TN-4
**Akins Chapel**—pop pl ... TN-4
Akins Chapel School ... TN-4
**Akins Corner**—pop pl ... TN-4
Akins Corners—locale ... NY-2
Akins Creek—stream ... AR-4
Akins Creek—stream ... GA-3
Akins Grove Ch—church ... AL-4
Akins Hollow—valley ... OK-5
Akins Lake—lake ... TX-5
Akins Mill—locale ... GA-3
Akins Pond—lake ... FL-3
Akins Pond—lake ... GA-3
Akins Pond—reservoir ... GA-3
Akins Pond Number One—reservoir ... NC-3
Akins Pond Number One Dam—dam ... NC-3
Akins Pond Number Two—reservoir ... NC-3
Akins Pond Number Two Dam—dam ... NC-3
Akins Sawgrass—swamp ... FL-3
Akins Tank—reservoir ... NM-5
Akinsville ... MO-7
Akinsville—locale ... AL-4
Akishima ... FM-9
Aki Sima ... FM-9
Akjemguiga Cove—bay ... AK-9
Akka—locale ... AL-4
Ak Komelik—locale ... AZ-5
A Klbaiel ... PW-9
Aklemeyer Commercial Buildings—hist pl ... OH-6
Akley Run ... PA-2
Aklim Point ... PW-9
Aklis Archeol Site—hist pl ... VI-3
A Kluaiel ... PW-9
Aklue ... MP-9
Aklumayuak Creek—stream ... AK-9
Akmagolik Creek—stream ... AK-9
Akmaktaksrak Bluff—cliff ... AK-9
Akmalik Creek—stream ... AK-9
Akmej—island ... MP-9
Aknerkochik River—stream ... AK-9
Akoakoa Point—cape ... HI-9
Akoddo', As—slope ... MH-9
Akogpak Slough—gut ... AK-9
Akokala Creek—stream ... MT-8
Akokala Lake—lake ... MT-8
Akokala Lake Trail—trail ... MT-8
Akokoa Point ... HI-9
Akoliakatat Pass—channel ... AK-9
Akoliakruich Hills—other ... AK-9
**Akolmiut (includes Nunapitchuk)**—pop pl ... AK-9
Akona—locale ... HI-9
Akoolokok Point—cape ... AK-9
Akorebakissing (historical)—locale ... DE-2
Akoru ... PW-9
Akoswift Creek—stream ... AK-9
Akoviknak Lagoon—bay ... AK-9
Akoviknak Mtn—summit ... AK-9
Akoz Mine—mine ... CA-9
Akpelik Creek—stream ... AK-9
Akporvik Hill—summit ... AK-9
**Akra**—pop pl ... ND-7
A K Ranch—locale ... AZ-5
Akrappu ... PW-9
**Akra Township**—pop pl ... ND-7
Akra Township (historical)—civil ... ND-7
Akridge—locale ... GA-3
Akridge Cem—cemetery ... GA-3
Akridge Number One Mine (underground)—mine ... AL-4
Akron—locale ... IL-6
Akron—locale ... KS-7
Akron—locale ... MS-4
Akron—locale ... NE-7
**Akron**—pop pl ... AL-4
**Akron**—pop pl ... CO-8
**Akron**—pop pl ... IN-6
**Akron**—pop pl ... IA-7
**Akron**—pop pl ... MI-6
**Akron**—pop pl ... MO-7
**Akron**—pop pl ... NY-2
**Akron**—pop pl ... OH-6
**Akron**—pop pl ... PA-2
Akron, Lake—lake ... FL-3
Akron Borough—civil ... PA-2
Akron-Canton Regional Airp—airport ... OH-6
Akron Cem—cemetery ... AR-4
Akron Cem—cemetery ... KS-7
Akron Cem—cemetery ... MO-7
Akron Cem—cemetery ... NE-7
Akron Christian Sch—school ... OH-6
Akron City Rsvr—reservoir ... OH-6
Akron City Sch Of Nursing—school ... OH-6
Akron Community Sch—school ... AL-4
Akron Elem Sch—school ... IN-6
Akron Elem Sch—school ... PA-2
Akron Ford—locale ... AL-4
Akron Hebrew Cem—cemetery ... OH-6
Akron HS—school ... AL-4
Akron Jewish Center—hist pl ... OH-6
Akron Junction ... OH-6
Akron Junction—locale ... NY-2
Akron Mine—mine ... CO-8
Akron New Cem—cemetery ... AL-4
Akron Oil Field—other ... MI-6
Akron Post Office and Federal Bldg—hist pl ... OH-6
Akron Public Library—hist pl ... OH-6
Akron Reservoir ... OH-6
Akron Rsvr—reservoir ... NY-2
Akron Rural Cemetery Buildings—hist pl ... OH-6
Akron Sewage Disposal—other ... OH-6
Akron Spring—spring ... NV-8
Akron Station ... KS-7
**Akron Subdivision**—pop pl ... UT-8
Akron Townhall—building ... MO-7
**Akron (Township of)**—pop pl ... IL-6
**Akron (Township of)**—pop pl ... MI-6
**Akron (Township of)**—pop pl (2) ... MN-6
Akron Y.M.C.A. Bldg—hist pl ... OH-6
Akron Y W C A Camp—locale ... OH-6
Ak Sar Ben Bridge—bridge ... IA-7
Ak Sar Ben Bridge—bridge ... NE-7
Ak Sar Ben Field—park ... NE-7
A. K. Smiley Public Library—hist pl ... CA-9
Aktal—island ... MP-9
Aktjin ... AZ-5
Akukun ... MH-9
Akula Lake—lake ... AK-9
Akularak Pass—gut ... AK-9
Akuliak Lake—lake ... AK-9
Akulik Creek—stream ... AK-9
Akulik River—stream ... AK-9
Akulikutak River—stream ... AK-9
Akuluktok Peak—summit ... AK-9
Akulurak—locale (2) ... AK-9
Akuluwe ... MP-9
Akulwe Islet ... MP-9
Akumsuk—locale ... AK-9
Akumwarvik Bay—bay ... AK-9
Akun Bay—bay ... AK-9
Akun Head—cliff ... AK-9
Akunik Pass—channel ... AK-9
Akun Island—island ... AK-9
Akun Strait—channel ... AK-9
**Akupu**—pop pl ... HI-9
Akurekvik Pass—gap ... AK-9
Akuro ... PW-9
Akuruee ... MP-9
Akuruuee To ... MP-9
Akuruue To ... MP-9
Akuruwe-to ... MP-9
Akusha Island—island ... AK-9
Akushnet River ... MA-1
**Akutan**—pop pl ... AK-9
Akutan Bay—bay ... AK-9
Akutan Harbor—bay ... AK-9
Akutan Island—island ... AK-9
Akutan Pass—channel ... AK-9
Akutan Point—cape ... AK-9
Akutoktak River—stream ... AK-9
Akuyan Creek—stream ... AK-9
Akvalutak Creek—stream ... AK-9
Akvat—locale ... AK-9
Akward Creek—stream ... IL-6
Akwe Lake—lake ... AK-9
Akwe River—stream ... AK-9
Alaalaula Gulch—valley ... HI-9
Alaaloula Gulch ... HI-9
Alaaluala ... HI-9
Alabaha Ch—church ... GA-3
Alabaha River—stream ... GA-3
**Alabam**—pop pl ... AR-4
Alabama ... AL-4
**Alabama**—pop pl ... NY-2
Alabama A and M College ... AL-4
Alabama Acad—school ... AL-4
Alabama Advent Christian Church Campground—locale ... AL-4
Alabama Agricultural and Mechanical Coll—school ... AL-4
Alabama Agricultural and Mechanical Institute ... AL-4
Alabama Agricultural and Mechanical Univ ... AL-4
Alabama Agricultural Center—locale ... AL-4
Alabama Agricultural Experiment Station—locale ... AL-4
Alabama and Coushatta Ind Res—reserve ... TX-5
Alabama Army Ammunition Plant—other ... AL-4
Alabama Ave Baptist Ch—church ... AL-4
Alabama Ave City School ... AL-4
Alabama Ave Methodist Ch—church ... AL-4
Alabama Ave Presbyterian Ch—church ... AL-4
Alabama Ave Sch—school ... AL-4
Alabama Aviation and Technical Coll—school ... AL-4
Alabama Baptist Hosp—hospital ... AL-4
Alabama Bar—bar ... CA-9
Alabama Bayou—stream (2) ... LA-4
Alabama Bend Oil Field—oilfield ... LA-4
Alabama Branch—stream ... TX-5
Alabama Brenau Coll (historical)—school ... AL-4
Alabama Bryce Insane Hospital ... AL-4
Alabama Builders' Hardware Manufacturing Company—hist pl ... AL-4
Alabama Camp ... HI-9
Alabama Caverns ... AL-4
Alabama Caverns—cave ... AL-4
Alabama Cem—cemetery ... NY-2
Alabama Central College ... AL-4
Alabama Central Female Coll (historical)—school ... AL-4
Alabama Ch—church ... LA-4
Alabama Ch—church ... OK-5
Alabama Ch—church ... VA-3
Alabama Christian Coll—school (2) ... AL-4
Alabama Christian Coll (historical)—school ... AL-4
Alabama Christian Youth Camp—locale ... AL-4
Alabama City ... AL-4
**Alabama City**—pop pl ... AL-4
Alabama City Cem—cemetery ... AL-4
Alabama City Ch of God—church ... AL-4
Alabama City Ch of the Nazarene—church ... AL-4
Alabama City Library—hist pl ... AL-4
Alabama City Public Sch (historical)—school ... AL-4
Alabama City United Methodist Ch—church ... AL-4
Alabama College ... AL-4
Alabama Conference Female Coll (historical)—school ... AL-4
Alabama-Coushatta Ind Res—494 (1980) ... TX-5
Alabama Creek ... TX-5
**Alabama Creek**—pop pl ... TX-5
Alabama Creek—stream ... AK-9
Alabama Creek—stream ... OK-5
Alabama Creek—stream ... TX-5
Alabama Creek—stream ... VA-3
Alabama Female Anthenaeum ... AL-4
Alabama Female Coll (historical)—school ... AL-4
Alabama Ferry—locale ... TX-5
Alabama Fork—locale ... AL-4
Alabama Fork Sch (historical)—school ... AL-4
Alabama Furnace ... AL-4
Alabama Girls' Industrial Sch—hist pl ... AL-4
Alabama Graphic Mine (underground)—mine ... AL-4
Alabama Great Southern RR Passenger Depot—hist pl ... AL-4
Alabama Heights—cliff ... AL-4
Alabama Hill—locale ... CA-9
Alabama Hill—locale ... OH-6
Alabama Hill (historical)—summit ... AL-4
Alabama Hills—other ... CA-9
Alabama (historical)—locale ... NV-8
Alabama Hollow—valley ... FL-3
Alabama Home Spur (Partlow State Hospital)—uninc pl ... AL-4
Alabama Industrial Sch—school ... AL-4
Alabama Industrial Sch for Boys—school ... AL-4
Alabama Insane, Hosp—hist pl ... AL-4
Alabama International Motor Speedway ... AL-4
Alabama International Motorsports Hall of Fame Museum—building ... AL-4
Alabama Iron Works—hist pl ... AL-4
Alabama Junction—locale ... GA-3
Alabama Lake—lake ... WI-6
Alabama Landing—locale ... LA-4
**Alabama Landing**—pop pl ... LA-4
Alabama Lutheran Acad ... AL-4
Alabama Marble Quarry—mine ... AL-4
Alabama Masonic Home—building ... AL-4
Alabama Medical College ... AL-4
Alabama Midland Railway Depot—hist pl ... AL-4
Alabama Mine—mine ... AZ-5
Alabama Mine—mine ... CA-9
Alabama Mine—mine ... NV-8
Alabama Mine—mine ... NM-5
Alabama Mine (underground)—mine ... AL-4
Alabama Music Park—park ... AL-4
Alabama Natl Forest ... AL-4
Alabama Normal School ... AL-4
Alabama Ordnance Works—other ... AL-4
Alabama Park—park ... MN-6
Alabama Penny Savings Bank—hist pl ... AL-4
Alabama Plantation—locale ... LA-4
Alabama Point—cape ... AL-4
Alabama Police Acad—school ... AL-4
Alabama Polytechnic Institute ... AL-4
**Alabama Port**—pop pl ... AL-4
Alabama Presbyterian Coll (historical)—school ... AL-4
Alabama River ... GA-3
Alabama River—stream ... AL-4
Alabama River Canal—canal ... AL-4
Alabama River Cutoff—gut ... AL-4
Alabama Sch—school ... WI-6
Alabama Sch for the Blind—school ... AL-4
Alabama Sch for the Deaf—school ... AL-4
Alabama Sch (historical)—school (2) ... AL-4
Alabama Sch (historical)—school ... MS-4
Alabama Sch of Trades ... AL-4
Alabama Sheriffs Boys Ranch—locale (2) ... AL-4
**Alabama Shores**—pop pl ... AL-4
Alabama Short Track Raceway—park ... AL-4
Alabama Slope Mine (underground)—mine ... AL-4
Alabama Space and Rocket Center—military ... AL-4
Alabama State Capitol—building ... AL-4
Alabama State Capitol—hist pl ... AL-4
Alabama State Coll—school ... AL-4
Alabama State Docks—locale ... AL-4
Alabama State Docks Facility—locale ... AL-4
Alabama State Docks Terminal—locale ... AL-4
Alabama State Docks Tuscaloosa-Northport Terminal—locale ... AL-4
Alabama State Fire Coll—school ... AL-4
Alabama State Institute for the Handicapped ... AL-4
Alabama State Normal Sch ... AL-4
Alabama State Penitentiary—hist pl ... AL-4
Alabama State Prison Camp (historical)—locale ... AL-4
Alabama State Teachers College ... AL-4
Alabama State Training Sch—school ... AL-4
Alabama State Training Sch for Girls ... AL-4
Alabama Street Methodist Episcopal Church ... AL-4
Alabama Street Park—park ... MS-4
Alabama Technical Coll—school ... AL-4
Alabama Technical Institute ... AL-4
Alabama Theatre—hist pl ... AL-4
**Alabama (Town of)**—pop pl ... NY-2
Alabama (Township of)—fmr MCD ... AR-4
Alabama Trail—trail ... PA-2
**Alabama Village**—pop pl ... HI-9
Alabama Wildlife Ref—park ... AL-4
Alabam Creek—stream ... AK-9
Alabam Sch—hist pl ... AR-4
Alabam (Township of)—fmr MCD ... AR-4
**Alabaster**—pop pl ... AL-4
**Alabaster**—pop pl ... MI-6
Alabaster Caverns—cave ... OK-5
Alabaster Caverns State Park—park ... OK-5
Alabaster Ch—church ... AL-4
Alabaster-Helena (CCD)—cens area ... AL-4
Alabaster-Helena Division—civil ... AL-4
Alabaster Hist Dist—hist pl ... MI-6
Alabaster Industrial Park—locale ... AL-4
Alabaster Junction—locale ... MI-6
Alabaster Shop Ctr—locale ... AL-4
Alabaster Swamp—swamp ... MI-6
**Alabaster (Township of)**—pop pl ... MI-6
Alabaster Whitney Drain—stream ... MI-6
Alabaugh Canyon—valley ... SD-7
Alabaugh Creek—stream ... MT-8
A La Bonne Veillee—hist pl ... LA-4
Alacan Bay ... TX-5
**Alachua**—pop pl ... FL-3
**Alachua County**—pop pl ... FL-3
Alachua Elem Sch—school ... FL-3
Alachua General Hosp—hospital ... FL-3
Alachua Hillcrest Memorial Park—cemetery ... FL-3
**Alachua II (historical)**—pop pl ... FL-3
Alachua Lake ... FL-3
Alachua Savanna ... FL-3
Alachua Sink—basin ... FL-3
**Alackaway Tolofa (historical)**—pop pl ... FL-3
Alacran Hills—range ... NM-5
Alacran Mtn—summit ... TX-5
Alaculsa Creek ... GA-3
Alaculsy—locale ... GA-3
Alaculsy Gap—gap ... GA-3
Alaculsy Valley—basin ... GA-3
Alaculsy Valley—valley ... TN-4
Aladden Lake ... MN-6
Aladdin ... IN-6
Aladdin ... IA-7
Aladdin—locale ... IL-6
Aladdin—locale ... PA-2
Aladdin—locale ... WA-9
Aladdin—locale ... WY-8
Aladdin Cave—cave ... AL-4
**Aladdin City**—pop pl ... FL-3
Aladdin Mine—mine ... MT-8
Aladdin Mine—mine ... SD-7
Aladdin Mine—mine ... WA-9
Aladdin Mtn—summit ... WA-9
Aladdin Ranch—locale ... CA-9
Aladdins Lamp Arch—arch ... UT-8
Aladdins Lamp Pass—gap ... UT-8
Ala de la Piedra (Barrio)—fmr MCD ... PR-3
Aladocks ... AL-4
Alae—civil ... HI-9
Alae—summit ... HI-9
Alaeakila—civil ... HI-9
Alae Cem—cemetery ... HI-9
Alae Crater—crater ... HI-9
Alaeiki—civil ... HI-9
Alaeli Ridge—ridge ... AS-9
Alaeloa—civil ... HI-9
Alaeloaiki—cape ... HI-9
Alaeloa Point—cape ... HI-9
Alaenui—civil ... HI-9
Alae One-Two—civil (2) ... HI-9
Alae Sch—school ... HI-9
Alae Three-Four—civil ... HI-9
Alae Three-Four Homesteads—civil ... HI-9
**Alafia**—pop pl ... FL-3
Alafia River—stream ... FL-3
Alafiers ... FL-3
Alaflora—locale ... AL-4
**Alaga**—pop pl ... AL-4
Alaganik—locale ... AK-9
Alaganik Slough—gut ... AK-9
Alaga Post Office (historical)—building ... AL-4
Alagnak River—stream ... AK-9
Alagogshak Creek—stream ... AK-9
Alagood Lake—lake ... FL-3
Alaguan—slope ... MH-9
Alahaka, Pali—cliff ... HI-9
Alahaka Bay—bay ... HI-9
Alahkai Wash ... AZ-5
Alai, Mount—summit ... AK-9
Alaialoa Gulch—valley ... HI-9
Alai Creek—stream ... AK-9
Alaid Head—cliff ... AK-9
Alaid Island—island ... AK-9
Alaiedon Sch—school ... MI-6
**Alaiedon (Township of)**—pop pl ... MI-6
Alain L Locke Elem Sch—school ... IN-6
Alajoki Cem—cemetery ... MN-6
Alakaha—cape ... HI-9
Alakaha Point—cape ... HI-9
Alakahi—civil ... HI-9
Alakahi Stream—stream (2) ... HI-9
Alakai Swamp—swamp ... HI-9
Alakai Trail—trail ... HI-9
**Alakanuk**—pop pl ... AK-9
Alakanuk Pass—gut ... AK-9
Alakasoho ... PW-9
A Lake—lake ... TX-5
Alaktak—locale ... AK-9
Alaktak River—stream ... AK-9
Alakuchak River—stream ... AK-9
Alakukui Point—cape ... HI-9
Alalakeiki Channel—channel ... HI-9
Alala Lava Flow—lava ... HI-9
Alala Point—cape ... HI-9
Ala Loa—hist pl ... HI-9
Alamaa Cem—cemetery ... MN-6
Alamacita Creek ... TX-5
Alamaditas Mesa—summit ... CO-8
Alamagan—island ... MH-9
Alamagan Insel ... MH-9
Alamagan Island ... MH-9
Alamaguan ... MH-9
Alamakee Mine—mine ... CO-8
Alamana—locale ... FL-3
**Alamance**—pop pl ... NC-3
**Alamance Acres (subdivision)**—pop pl ... NC-3
Alamance Battleground State Historic Site—hist pl ... NC-3
Alamance Ch—church ... NC-3
Alamance Ch—church ... TX-5
**Alamance County**—pop pl ... NC-3
Alamance County Courthouse—hist pl ... NC-3
Alamance Creek ... NC-3
**Alamance Hills Subdivision**—pop pl ... NC-3
Alamance Hotel—hist pl ... NC-3
Alamance Industrial Park—locale ... NC-3
Alamance Memorial Park—cemetery ... NC-3
Alamance Mine—mine ... ID-8
Alamance Sch—school ... NC-3
Alamanda ... PA-2
Alamanda Park—park ... FL-3
Alamando—locale ... MI-6
Alamar Canyon—valley ... CA-9
Alamar Guard Station—locale ... CA-9
Alamar Hill—summit ... CA-9
Alamar Hill Trail—trail ... CA-9
Alamar Trail—trail ... CA-9
Alambel Alampel ... MP-9
Alambique Creek—stream ... CA-9
Alambre Tank—reservoir ... AZ-5
Alambre Valley—valley ... AZ-5
Alambre Wash—stream ... AZ-5
Alambre Well—well ... AZ-5
Alameda ... CO-8
Alameda ... ID-8
Alameda—hist pl ... IN-6
Alameda—locale ... KS-7
**Alameda**—pop pl (2) ... CA-9
**Alameda**—pop pl ... FL-3
**Alameda**—pop pl ... NM-5
**Alameda**—pop pl ... OR-9
Alameda, Canon de la—valley ... NM-5
Alameda, The—uninc pl ... MD-2
Alameda Administration Center—other ... CA-9
Alameda Apartments—hist pl ... OH-6
Alameda Arroyo—stream ... NM-5
Alameda Bridge—other ... NM-5
Alameda Canyon—valley ... NV-8
Alameda (CCD)—cens area ... CA-9
Alameda Cem—cemetery ... TX-5
Alameda City Hall—hist pl ... CA-9
**Alameda (County)**—pop pl ... CA-9
Alameda County Bldg—building ... CA-9
Alameda County Juvenile Hall—building ... CA-9
Alameda Creek—stream (2) ... AK-9
Alameda Creek—stream ... CA-9
Alameda Creek—stream ... TX-5
Alameda Creek—stream ... WY-8
Alameda Dam—dam ... NM-5
Alameda-Depot Hist Dist—hist pl ... NM-5
Alameda Diversion Tunnel—tunnel ... CA-9
Alameda Drain—canal ... NM-5
Alameda Flat—flat ... WA-9
Alameda Free Library—hist pl ... CA-9
Alameda HS—hist pl ... CA-9
Alameda HS—school ... CA-9
Alameda HS—school ... CO-8
Alameda JHS—school ... CO-8
Alameda JHS—school ... ID-8
Alameda JHS—school ... NM-5
Alameda Lake—lake ... OR-9
Alameda Lateral—canal ... NM-5
Alameda Memorial State Beach—park ... CA-9
Alameda Mine—mine ... MT-8
Alameda Mine (historical)—mine ... SD-7
Alameda Naval Air Station—military ... CA-9
Alameda Oil and Gas Field—oilfield ... KS-7
Alameda Park ... PA-2
Alameda Park—park ... TX-5
Alameda Plaza—park ... CA-9
Alameda Reserve Shipyard—locale ... CA-9
Alameda Sch—school ... CA-9
Alameda Sch—school ... CO-8
Alameda Sch—school ... MI-6
Alameda Sch—school ... NM-5
Alameda Sch—school ... OR-9
Alameda Shop Ctr—locale ... TX-5
Alameda Shop Ctr—other ... CO-8
Alameda Spring—spring ... NM-5
Alameda Tunnel—mine ... CA-9
Alameda Well—well ... CA-9
Alameda Windmill—locale ... TX-5
Alamere Creek—stream ... CA-9
**Alamet**—pop pl ... AL-4
Alamias Creek—stream ... CA-9
Alamicut River ... WA-9
**Alamillo**—pop pl ... NM-5
Alamillo Ditch—canal ... NM-5
Alamine Peak—summit ... CA-9
Alamita Creek ... TX-5
Alamito—locale ... NM-5
Alamito Arroyo—stream (3) ... NM-5
Alamito Camp—locale ... NM-5
Alamito Canyon—valley ... AZ-5
Alamito Creek—stream ... NM-5
Alamito Creek—stream (2) ... TX-5
Alamito Dam—dam ... TX-5
Alamito Picnic Area—park ... NM-5
Alamitos—locale ... CA-9
**Alamitos**—pop pl ... CA-9
Alamitos Bay—bay ... CA-9
Alamitos Canal—canal ... CA-9
Alamitos Canal Lateral Eight—canal ... CA-9
Alamitos Canyon—valley (3) ... NM-5
Alamitos Creek—stream ... CA-9
Alamitos Creek—stream ... NM-5
Alamitos or Juan Salas Grant (as recorded)—civil ... NM-5
Alamito Springs—spring ... NM-5
Alamitos Sch—school ... CA-9
Alamitos Three Drain—canal ... CA-9
Alamito Tank—reservoir ... AZ-5
Alamito Tank—reservoir ... NM-5
Alamito Tank No 16—reservoir ... NM-5
Alamito Wash—stream ... AZ-5
Alamito Well—well ... NM-5
Alamo ... AZ-5
Alamo—locale ... AR-4
Alamo—locale ... CO-8
**Alamo**—pop pl ... CA-9
**Alamo**—pop pl ... GA-3
**Alamo**—pop pl ... IN-6
**Alamo**—pop pl ... KY-4
**Alamo**—pop pl ... MI-6
**Alamo**—pop pl ... NV-8
**Alamo**—pop pl ... NM-5
**Alamo**—pop pl ... ND-7
**Alamo**—pop pl ... TN-4
**Alamo**—pop pl ... TX-5
Alamo, Canal (historical)—canal ... AZ-5
Alamo, The—building ... TX-5
Alamo, The—hist pl ... TX-5
**Alamo Alto**—pop pl ... TX-5
Alamo Alto Drain—canal ... TX-5
Alamo Alto Gaging Station—locale ... TX-5
Ala Moana Park—park ... HI-9
**Alamoar**—pop pl ... FM-9
Alamo Arroyo—stream (2) ... NM-5
Alamo Arroyo—valley ... TX-5
Alamo Beach—locale ... TX-5
Alamo Camp—locale ... CA-9
Alamo Canal—canal ... CA-9
Alamo Canyon—valley (7) ... AZ-5
Alamo Canyon—valley ... CA-9
Alamo Canyon—valley ... CO-8
Alamo Canyon—valley (9) ... NM-5
Alamo Canyon—valley ... TX-5
Alamo Canyon Number One ... AZ-5
Alamo Canyon-Wilkey Ranch Discontiguous Archeol District—hist pl ... TX-5
Alamo (CCD)—cens area ... GA-3
Alamo (CCD)—cens area ... TN-4
Alamo Cem—cemetery ... GA-3
Alamo Cem—cemetery ... NM-5
Alamo Cem—cemetery ... ND-7
Alamo Ch—church ... GA-3
Alamo Ch—church ... TN-4
Alamocita Creek ... TX-5
Alamocita Creek—stream (2) ... NM-5
Alamocito Creek ... TX-5
Alamocitos Camp—locale ... TX-5
Alamocitos Creek—stream ... TX-5
Alamocitos Creek Windmill—locale ... TX-5
Alamocitos Windmill—locale (2) ... TX-5
Alamo Community Coll—school ... TX-5
Alamo Conservation Club—other ... IN-6
Alamo Creek—stream (7) ... CA-9
Alamo Creek—stream ... CO-8
Alamo Creek—stream (4) ... NM-5
Alamo Creek—stream (3) ... TX-5
Alamo Creek—stream ... WY-8
Alamo Crossing (historical)—locale ... AZ-5
Alamo Dam—dam ... AZ-5
Alamo Day Sch—school ... NM-5
Alamo de Cesario Creek—stream ... TX-5
Alamo Ditch—canal ... KS-7
Alamo Division—civil ... TN-4
Alamo Downs Racetrack—other ... TX-5
Alamo Drain—canal ... NM-5
Alamo Draw—valley ... NM-5
Alamo Feeder—canal ... TX-5
Alamo First Baptist Ch—church ... TN-4
Alamo Gas Field—oilfield ... TX-5
**Alamogordo**—pop pl ... NM-5
Alamogordo (CCD)—cens area ... NM-5
Alamogordo Creek—stream ... NM-5
Alamogordo Dam—dam ... NM-5
Alamogordo Rsvr—reservoir ... NM-5
Alamogordo Valley—valley ... NM-5
Alamo Gulch—valley ... OR-9
**Alamo Heights**—pop pl ... TX-5
Alamo Heights Ch—church ... TX-5

Aliceton Town Hall—building ND-7
**Aliceton Township**—pop pl ND-7
Alice Union Cem—cemetery IA-7
*Aliceville* IN-6
Aliceville—locale IL-6
**Aliceville**—pop pl AL-4
**Aliceville**—pop pl KS-7
Aliceville Baptist Ch—church AL-4
Aliceville (CCD)—cens area AL-4
*Aliceville Cemetery* AL-4
Aliceville County Club—locale AL-4
Aliceville Division—civil AL-4
Aliceville Elementary and HS—hist pl AL-4
Aliceville Graded Sch (historical)—school AL-4
Aliceville HS—school AL-4
Aliceville Lake—reservoir AL-4
Aliceville Lake—reservoir MS-4
Aliceville Lock and Dam—dam AL-4
Aliceville Memorial Gardens—cemetery AL-4
Aliceville Presbyterian Ch—church AL-4
**Ali Chuk**—pop pl AZ-5
*Ali Chuk Son* AZ-5
**Ali Chukson**—pop pl AZ-5
Ali Chukson—summit AZ-5
Ali Chuk Valley—valley AZ-5
Ali Chuk Wash—stream AZ-5
*Alicia* PA-2
Alicia—locale MI-6
**Alicia**—pop pl AR-4
**Alicia**—pop pl CA-9
**Alicia**—pop pl (2) PA-2
**Alicia**—pop pl PR-3
Alicia Park—park AZ-5
Alicia Park—park WI-6
Alicia Sch—school CA-9
Alico—locale CA-9
**Alida**—pop pl IN-6
**Alida**—pop pl KS-7
**Alida**—pop pl MN-6
Alida Cem—cemetery MN-6
Alida Ch—church KS-7
Alidade Creek—stream ID-8
Alidade Lake—lake ID-8
Alida Sch—school KS-7
*Alida Station* IN-6
**Alief**—pop pl TX-5
Alief Cem—cemetery TX-5
*Aliej Island* MP-9
Alie Mtn—summit (2) TN-4
Alience Cem—cemetery TX-5
Alien Ridge—ridge KY-4
Alier Hollow—valley VA-3
*Alies* MP-9
Alies Seep Canyon—valley NM-5
Aliet Island—island MP-9
Alifan, Mount—summit GU-9
Aliff Cem—cemetery WV-2
*Alige Lake* MI-6
*Alihahi* MH-9
*Aliia Point* HI-9
*Aliia Stream* HI-9
Alii Fishpond—lake HI-9
Aliiolani Hale—hist pl HI-9
Aliiolani Sch—school HI-9
*Alii Peak* HI-9
Alika—civil HI-9
Alika Bay—bay HI-9
Alika Cone—summit HI-9
Alika Homesteads—civil HI-9
Alika Lava Flow Of 1919—lava HI-9
**Alikanna**—pop pl OH-6
Alikchi—locale OK-5
Aliksemit Island—island AK-9
Aliktongnak Lake—lake AK-9
Alikuld Bay—bay AK-9
Alili—summit HI-9
Alilipali Gulch—valley HI-9
Alili Ridge—ridge AS-9
Alili Spring—spring HI-9
Alili Spring—spring AS-9
*Alimagan Island* MH-9
Alimagnet Lake—lake MN-6
Alimagnet Park—park MN-6
Alimeda—locale IA-7
*Alimo* AZ-5
Ali Molina—locale AZ-5
Ali Molina Canyon—valley AZ-5
Ali Molina Wash—stream AZ-5
Alimony Ridge—ridge CA-9
*Alimuchee* AL-4
Alimuda Bay—bay AK-9
Alinchak Bay—bay AK-9
**Alinda**—pop pl PA-2
Aline—locale PA-2
**Aline**—pop pl GA-3
**Aline**—pop pl OK-5
A Line Canal—canal (2) ID-8
A Line Canal—canal OR-9
Aline (CCD)—cens area GA-3
Aline Ch—church GA-3
Aline Covered Bridge—hist pl PA-2
Aline Creek—stream PA-2
Aline IOOF Lodge No. 263—hist pl OK-5
Alinement Creek—stream AK-9
Ali Oidak—locale AZ-5
Aliomanu—civil HI-9
**Aliquippa**—pop pl PA-2
Aliquippa Borough—civil PA-2
Aliquippa Hosp—hospital PA-2
Aliquippa Hospital Airp—airport PA-2
Aliquippa Shop Ctr—locale PA-2
Alire—locale NM-5
Alires Windmill—locale NM-5
Ali Rsvr—reservoir HI-9
**Alisa Estates (subdivision)**—pop pl DE-2
Alisal—uninc pl CA-9
Alisal Creek—stream (2) CA-9
Alisal HS—school CA-9
Alisal Ranch—locale CA-9
Alisal Sch—school (2) CA-9
Alisal Slough—gut CA-9
*Alisa Pass* AZ-5
Aliso, Canada Del—stream CA-9
Aliso Beach—beach CA-9
Aliso Campground—locale CA-9
Aliso Canal—canal CA-9
Aliso Canyon—valley (2) AZ-5
Aliso Canyon—valley (9) CA-9
*Aliso Canyon Oil Field* CA-9
Aliso Canyon Wash—stream CA-9
*Aliso Creek* AZ-5
*Aliso Creek* CA-9
Aliso Creek—stream (4) CA-9
Alison, Finlay, House—hist pl TN-4
Alison, Jesse, House—hist pl TN-4
Alisons Creek—stream GA-3
*Aliso Pass* AZ-5
Aliso Point—cape CA-9
Aliso Ranch—locale CA-9
Alisos, Canada De Los—valley CA-9
Aliso Sch—school (2) CA-9
Alisos Creek—stream CA-9
Aliso Spring—spring (3) AZ-5
Aliso Spring—spring CA-9
Alisos Well—well AZ-5
Alitak—other AK-9
Alitak Bay—bay AK-9
Alitak Lagoon—bay AK-9
Alitak Shoal—bar AK-9
*Alitjukson* AZ-5
A Little Dude Ranch—school FL-3
Aliulik Peninsula—cape AK-9
Alivio—locale NM-5
Ali Wua Pass—gap AZ-5
**Alix**—pop pl AR-4
Alix Pond—lake AR-4
Alix (Township of)—fmr MCD AR-4
*Aliyir* FM-9
*Aliza Pass* AZ-5
*Aljaltuen'* MP-9
**Aljen Heights**—pop pl CT-1
Aljo Hill—summit NE-7
**Alkabo**—pop pl ND-7
*Alkachuska Creek* AL-4
Alkali—fmr MCD NE-7
Alkali—locale NV-8
**Alkali**—pop pl OH-6
*Alkali Arroyo* CO-8
Alkali Arroyo—stream (2) CO-8
Alkali Arroyo—stream NM-5
Alkali Basin—basin CO-8
Alkali Basin—basin (2) WY-8
Alkali Bog (Mud Springs)—swamp WY-8
Alkali Brook—stream WY-8
Alkali Butte—summit OR-9
Alkali Butte—summit (2) WY-8
Alkali Butte Oil Field—oilfield WY-8
Alkali Buttes—summit OR-9
Alkali Butte Unit—other WY-8
Alkali Camp—park OR-9
*Alkali Canyon* UT-8
Alkali Canyon—valley (3) AZ-5
Alkali Canyon—valley CA-9
Alkali Canyon—valley (3) CO-8
Alkali Canyon—valley (2) NM-5
Alkali Canyon—valley (3) OR-9
Alkali Canyon—valley (2) UT-8
Alkali Canyon—valley WA-9
Alkali Club House—building SD-7
Alkali Coulee—valley (8) MT-8
*Alkali Creek* CO-8
*Alkali Creek* OR-9
*Alkali Creek* UT-8
*Alkali Creek* WY-8
Alkali Creek—stream AK-9
Alkali Creek—stream CA-9
Alkali Creek—stream (7) CO-8
Alkali Creek—stream (5) ID-8
Alkali Creek—stream (23) MT-8
Alkali Creek—stream (2) NE-7
Alkali Creek—stream (2) NV-8
Alkali Creek—stream (6) ND-7
Alkali Creek—stream (6) OR-9
Alkali Creek—stream (5) SD-7
Alkali Creek—stream TX-5
Alkali Creek—stream (2) UT-8
Alkali Creek—stream WA-9
Alkali Creek—stream (27) WY-8
*Alkali Creek Draw* WY-8
Alkali Creek Rsvr No 1—reservoir WY-8
Alkali Creek Rsvr No 2—reservoir WY-8
Alkali Dam—dam SD-7
Alkali Ditch—canal CO-8
Alkali Ditch—canal LA-4
Alkali Ditch No 1—canal CO-8
Alkali Ditch No 2—canal CO-8
Alkali Drain—canal ID-8
*Alkali Draw* CO-8
*Alkali Draw* OR-9
Alkali Draw—valley (2) CO-8
Alkali Draw—valley ID-8
Alkali Draw—valley MT-8
Alkali Draw—valley NM-5
Alkali Draw—valley TX-5
Alkali Draw—valley (6) WY-8
Alkali Draw Pit No 1—reservoir WY-8
Alkali Draw Pit No 2—reservoir WY-8
Alkali Draw Pit No 3—reservoir WY-8
Alkali Draw Pit No 4—reservoir WY-8
Alkali Draw Pit No 5—reservoir WY-8
Alkali Draw Rsvr—reservoir OR-9
*Alkali Flat* NV-8
Alkali Flat—flat (2) CO-8
Alkali Flat—flat ID-8
Alkali Flat—flat (2) NV-8
Alkali Flat—flat OR-9
Alkali Flat—flat WY-8
Alkali Flat Central Hist Dist—hist pl CA-9
Alkali Flat Corrals—locale OR-9
Alkali Flat Creek—stream WA-9
Alkali Flat (historical)—flat SD-7
Alkali Flat North Hist Dist—hist pl CA-9
Alkali Flat Rsvr—reservoir OR-9
*Alkali Flats* AZ-5
Alkali Flats—flat (2) CO-8
Alkali Flats—flat (2) WY-8
Alkali Flat West Hist Dist—hist pl CA-9
*Alkali Gulch* CO-8
Alkali Gulch—valley (4) CO-8
Alkali Gulch—valley OR-9
Alkali Gulch—valley (2) WY-8
Alkali Gulch Rsvr—reservoir OR-9
Alkali (historical)—locale (2) SD-7
Alkali Holes—lake CO-8
Alkali Hollow—valley UT-8
Alkali Hot Spring—spring NV-8
*Alkali Lake* WA-9
*Alkali Lake* WY-8
Alkali Lake—flat NV-8
Alkali Lake—lake CA-9
Alkali Lake—lake (2) CO-8
Alkali Lake—lake MN-6
Alkali Lake—lake (5) MT-8
Alkali Lake—lake (8) NE-7
Alkali Lake—lake (2) NV-8
Alkali Lake—lake (3) NM-5
Alkali Lake—lake (5) ND-7
Alkali Lake—lake (2) OR-9
Alkali Lake—lake (4) SD-7
Alkali Lake—lake TX-5
Alkali Lake—lake UT-8
Alkali Lake—lake (6) WA-9
Alkali Lake—lake WY-8
**Alkali Lake**—pop pl OR-9
Alkali Lake—reservoir WY-8
Alkali Lakebed—flat MN-6
Alkali Lakes—lake NM-5
Alkali Lakes—lake TX-5
Alkali Lakes Coulee—valley MT-8
Alkali Lake State Airp—airport OR-9
Alkali Lake Station—locale OR-9
Alkali Meadows—flat OR-9
Alkaline Ditch—canal CO-8
Alkaline Lake—lake (2) ND-7
Alkaline Seep—spring (2) AZ-5
Alkaline Spring—spring AZ-5
Alkaline Tank—reservoir AZ-5
Alkali Peak—summit NV-8
Alkali Playground—park CA-9
Alkali Point—ridge UT-8
Alkali Pond—lake MT-8
Alkali Pond—lake NE-7
*Alkali Pond Gulch* UT-8
*Alkali Ponds* ND-7
Alkali Ranch—locale NV-8
Alkali Ridge—hist pl UT-8
*Alkali Ridge Historical Landmark* UT-8
Alkali Ridge Historical Marker—park UT-8
Alkali Rsvr—reservoir NV-8
Alkali Rsvr—reservoir (2) OR-9
Alkali Rsvr—reservoir (2) WY-8
Alkali Sch—school OR-9
Alkali Sch—school SD-7
Alkali Seep—spring (2) UT-8
Alkali Siphon—other MT-8
Alkali Slough—stream CO-8
*Alkali Spring* OR-9
Alkali Spring—spring (5) AZ-5
Alkali Spring—spring (2) CO-8
Alkali Spring—spring (2) ID-8
Alkali Spring—spring (2) MT-8
Alkali Spring—spring NV-8
Alkali Spring—spring (5) NM-5
Alkali Spring—spring (5) OR-9
Alkali Spring—spring SD-7
Alkali Spring—spring UT-8
Alkali Spring—spring (3) WY-8
Alkali Springs—spring NV-8
Alkali Springs—spring (2) OR-9
Alkali Springs—spring WY-8
Alkali Springs Coulee—valley MT-8
Alkali Spring 2—spring OR-9
Alkali Tank—reservoir (3) AZ-5
Alkali Tank—reservoir NM-5
Alkali Tank—reservoir TX-5
Alkali Valley—valley AZ-5
Alkali Valley—valley NV-8
Alkali Wash—stream AZ-5
Alkali Wash—stream CA-9
Alkali Wash—valley CO-8
Alkali Wash—valley (2) WY-8
Alkali Well—locale NM-5
Alkali Well—well WY-8
Alkali Wells—well WA-9
Alkali Windmill—locale NV-8
Alkali Windmill—locale NM-5
Alkali Windmill—locale TX-5
Alkalugen Creek—stream AK-9
*Alkau Reservoir* NV-8
*Alkehatchee Creek* AL-4
Alkek Oil Field—oilfield TX-5
*Alken Grove Ch* AL-4
*Alkess Island* PW-9
Alki Beach—beach WA-9
Alki Crest—summit WA-9
Alkins Branch—stream KY-4
Alkinson Cem—cemetery KY-4
Alki Point—cape WA-9
Alkire Cem—cemetery IN-6
Alkire Cem—cemetery OH-6
Alkire Creek—stream ID-8
Alkire Ditch—canal OH-6
Alkire Homestead—locale MT-8
Alkire House—hist pl OH-6
Alkire Lake—lake TX-5
Alkire Park—park AZ-5
*Alkires Mill* WV-2
Alkires Mills—locale WV-2
**Alkol**—pop pl WV-2
Alla—locale CA-9
Allabands Mill Stream—stream DE-2
**Allaben**—pop pl NY-2
**Allagash**—pop pl ME-1
Allagash Brook—stream ME-1
Allagash Falls—falls ME-1
Allagash Inn—locale ME-1
Allagash Lake—lake ME-1
Allagash Mtn—summit ME-1
Allagash Pond—lake ME-1
Allagash River—stream ME-1
Allagash Stream—stream ME-1
Allagash Wilderness State Waterway—park (2) ME-1
*Allaguash River* ME-1
Allah—locale AZ-5
Allah Creek—stream AK-9
Allah Mine—mine UT-8
Allah RR Station—building AZ-5
Allaire—locale NJ-2
Allaire Dam—dam NJ-2
Allaire State Park—park NJ-2
Allaire Village—hist pl NJ-2
Allais—locale KY-4
Alla JHS—school TX-5
**Allakaket**—pop pl AK-9
*Allamah River* GA-3
Allamakee County Courthouse—hist pl IA-7
Allamakee County Home—building IA-7
Allaman, Lake—reservoir MO-7
Allamanda Elem Sch—school FL-3
*Allamead* KS-7
*Allamede* KS-7
Allam Emory Mine—mine CO-8
All America City Park—park IL-6
All American Bank Bldg—hist pl IN-6
All American Canal—canal CA-9
*All American Canal Coachella Branch* CA-9
All American Drain Eight A—canal CA-9
All American Drain Five—canal CA-9
All American Drain Four—canal CA-9
All American Drain Thirteen—canal CA-9
All American Drain Two—canal CA-9
All American Drain Two A—canal CA-9
All American Memorial Ch—church FL-3
All American Memorial Church Sch—school FL-3
All-American Rose Selections Garden—park NC-3
Allamoore—locale TX-5
*Allamore* TX-5
**Allamore (Allamoore)**—pop pl TX-5
**Allamuchy**—pop pl NJ-2
**Allamuchy, (Township of)**—pop pl NJ-2
Allamuchy Mtn—summit NJ-2
Allamuchy Pond—reservoir NJ-2
Allamuchy Pond Dam—dam NJ-2
*Allan Branch* IL-6
Allan Branch—stream (2) MS-4
Allan Branch—stream NC-3
Allan Branch—stream TX-5
Allan B Shepard Sch—school IL-6
Allan Canyon—valley CO-8
Allan Canyon—valley ID-8
Allan Ch—church MD-2
Allan Chapel—church MS-4
*Allanconnie Lake* PA-2
Allan Creek—stream ID-8
Allan Creek—stream MT-8
Allandale—locale VI-3
**Allandale**—pop pl FL-3
**Allandale**—pop pl PA-2
Allandale—uninc pl TX-5
Allandale Mansion—building TN-4
Allandale Market Place Shop Ctr—locale TN-4
Allandale Sch—school CA-9
**Allandale (subdivision)**—pop pl TN-4
Allan Dam—dam AZ-5
All Angels Episcopal Sch—school FL-3
Allan Hancock Coll—school CA-9
Allan Hollow—valley UT-8
Allan Island—island WA-9
Allan JHS—school TX-5
*Allan Key* FL-3
Allan Kirkwood Sch—school WA-9
*Allan Lake* MI-6
Allan Lake—lake ID-8
Allan Lake Landing—locale AZ-5
Allan Lake Tank—reservoir AZ-5
Allan Mtn—summit ID-8
Allan Mtn—summit MT-8
Allan Park—flat MT-8
Allan Pass—channel WA-9
Allan Point—cape AK-9
Allan Pond—swamp TX-5
Allan Richard Brook—stream RI-1
*Allans Creek* AL-4
*Allans Island* VA-3
Allan Spring—spring NV-8
Allan Springs Campground—park OR-9
Allan Tank—reservoir (2) AZ-5
Allanton—locale FL-3
Allan Well—well AZ-5
Allan Well—well NM-5
**Allanwood**—pop pl MD-2
*Allapaha River* FL-3
*Allapaha River* GA-3
*Allapatah* FL-3
**Allapattah**—pop pl FL-3
Allapattah-Comstock Park—park FL-3
Allapattah Flats—flat FL-3
Allapattah JHS—school FL-3
Allapattah Mini Park—park FL-3
Allapattah Neighborhood Service Center—locale FL-3
Allapattah Sch—school FL-3
Allapattah YMCA Day Care—school FL-3
Allapattan Baptist Ch—church FL-3
Allard—locale MT-8
Allard Brook—stream NH-1
Allard Cem—cemetery IL-6
Allard Cem—cemetery NY-2
Allard Cem—cemetery TX-5
Allard Corners—locale NY-2
Allard Creek—stream AK-9
Allard Ditch—canal CO-8
Allard Hill—summit NY-2
Allard Hollow—valley PA-2
Allard Lake—lake IL-6
Allard Mine—mine CO-8
Allard Mtn—summit AR-4
Allard Ranch—locale CO-8
Allard Ranch—locale MT-8
Allard Rsvr—reservoir WY-8
Allard Sch—school SD-7
**Allardt**—pop pl TN-4
Allardt Cem—cemetery TN-4
Allardt Elem Sch—school TN-4
Allardt First Baptist Ch—church TN-4
Allardt Post Office—building TN-4
Allarmarks Oil Field—oilfield TX-5
Allatoona—locale GA-3
Allatoona Creek—stream GA-3
Allatoona Dam—dam GA-3
Allatoona Lake—reservoir GA-3
*Allatoona Rsvr* GA-3
*Allawa* MS-4
*Allawa Landing* MS-4
Allbach House—hist pl TX-5
*Allbee Brook* VT-1
Allbery Cem—cemetery NE-7
Allbery Sch—school NE-7
Allbone Branch—stream NC-3
**Allbright**—pop pl MO-7
All Bright, Lake—lake FL-3
Allbright Cem—cemetery IN-6
Allbright Ch—church IL-6
Allbright Sch (abandoned)—school MO-7
All Bright Shores—locale MI-6
Allbritton Creek—stream MS-4
**Allbrook**—pop pl AR-4
All Cape Shop Ctr Picture Pond Plaza—locale MA-1
All Childrens Hosp—hospital FL-3
Allcock Cem—cemetery KY-4
Allcorn Creek—stream KY-4
Allcorn Creek—stream TX-5
Allcorn Sch—school KY-4
All Creek—stream WA-9
Allday-Jones Cem—cemetery TX-5
Alldis, James, House—hist pl CT-1
Alldredge Cem—cemetery AL-4
Alldredge Cem—cemetery IN-6
Alldredge Spring—spring AL-4
Alldred Spring—spring CO-8
*Allebaugh Creek* MT-8
**Alledonia**—pop pl OH-6
Allee Experiment Farm Iowa University—other IA-7
Allee House—hist pl DE-2
**Alleene**—pop pl AR-4
**Alleene (Allene)**—pop pl AR-4
Alleene Cem—cemetery AR-4
Allee Rsvr—reservoir WY-8
Allee Site—hist pl OK-5
**Allega** Cem—cemetery MO-7
**Allegan**—pop pl MI-6
Allegan, Lake—reservoir MI-6
**Allegan (County)**—pop pl MI-6
Allegan County Park—park MI-6
Allegan (historical)—locale KS-7
Allegan State For—forest MI-6
**Allegan (Township of)**—pop pl MI-6
*Allegany (2)* MD-2
*Allegany* PA-2
**Allegany**—pop pl NY-2
**Allegany**—pop pl OR-9
Allegany Brook—stream NY-2
Allegany Cem—cemetery MD-2
Allegany Cem—cemetery NY-2
Allegany Cem—cemetery OR-9
**Allegany (County)**—pop pl MD-2
**Allegany (County)**—pop pl NY-2
**Allegany Grove**—pop pl MD-2
Allegany HS—school MD-2
Allegany Ind Res—925 (1980) NY-2
Allegany Sch—school OR-9
**Allegany Spring**—pop pl VA-3
Allegany State Park—park NY-2
*Allegany Station* MD-2
**Allegany (Town of)**—pop pl NY-2
*Allegany Township* ND-7
Allegany Township—civil PA-2
**Allegany (Township of)**—pop pl PA-2
*Allegash River* ME-1
*Allegeni* PA-2
Alleghaney HS—school NC-3
*Alleghany* PA-2
Alleghany—other KY-4
**Alleghany**—pop pl CA-9
**Alleghany**—pop pl VA-3
Alleghany Ch—church NC-3
Alleghany Ch—church (3) VA-3
Alleghany Country Club—other VA-3
**Alleghany County**—pop pl NC-3
**Alleghany (County)**—pop pl VA-3
Alleghany County Courthouse—hist pl NC-3
**Alleghany (historical)**—pop pl TN-4
Alleghany (Magisterial District)—fmr MCD VA-3
Alleghany Memorial Park—cemetery VA-3
*Alleghany Post Office* TN-4
*Alleghany River* PA-2
Alleghany Rock—rock MA-1
*Alleghany Spjrings* TN-4
*Alleghany Spring* VA-3
**Alleghany Springs**—pop pl VA-3
Alleghany Springs Post Office (historical)—building TN-4
*Alleghany Station* TN-4
Alleghany Steel Run—stream WV-2
Alleghany Town Hall—building ND-7
**Alleghany Township**—pop pl ND-7
Alleghany (Township of)—fmr MCD NC-3
Allegheny—locale NC-3
**Allegheny Acres**—pop pl PA-2
Allegheny Aqueduct—hist pl PA-2
Allegheny Ave Sch—school NY-2
Allegheny Baptist Church—hist pl PA-2
Allegheny Cem—cemetery PA-2
Allegheny Cem—cemetery TN-4
Allegheny Cemetery—hist pl PA-2
Allegheny Center Mall—locale PA-2
Allegheny Ch—church (2) PA-2
Allegheny Ch—church TN-4
Allegheny Clarion Valley HS—school PA-2
Allegheny Coll—post sta PA-2
Allegheny Country Club—other PA-2
**Allegheny County**—pop pl PA-2
Allegheny County Airp—airport PA-2
Allegheny County Court House—building PA-2
Allegheny County Courthouse and Jail—hist pl PA-2
Allegheny County Jail—building PA-2
*Allegheny county Regional Park* PA-2
Allegheny Creek—stream CA-9
Allegheny Creek—stream NV-8
Allegheny Creek—stream (2) PA-2
Allegheny Fish Hatchery—locale PA-2
Allegheny Freewill Baptist Ch (historical)—church TN-4
*Allegheny Front* WV-2
Allegheny Front—ridge WV-2
**Allegheny Furnace**—pop pl PA-2
Allegheny General Hosp—hospital PA-2
Allegheny General Hospital Airp—airport PA-2
Allegheny Heights—summit MD-2
Allegheny HS—hist pl PA-2
Allegheny HS—school PA-2
Allegheny-Hyde Park Intermediate Sch—school PA-2
**Allegheny Mine**—pop pl KY-4
Allegheny Mines—mine PA-2
Allegheny Mountain Trail—trail VA-3
Allegheny Mountain Trail—trail WV-2
Allegheny Mtn—range WV-2
Allegheny Natl For—forest PA-2
Allegheny (Northside)—uninc pl PA-2
Allegheny Observatory—building PA-2
Allegheny Observatory—hist pl PA-2
Allegheny Portage Creek—stream PA-2
Allegheny Portage RR Natl Historic Site—hist pl PA-2
Allegheny Portage RR Natl Historic Site—park PA-2
*Allegheny Portage Run* PA-2
Allegheny Post Office—hist pl PA-2
Allegheny Ridge—ridge PA-2
Allegheny Ridge—ridge TN-4
Allegheny River—stream NY-2
Allegheny River—stream PA-2
*Allegheny River Dam* PA-2
Allegheny River Lock And Dam Eight—dam PA-2
Allegheny River Lock And Dam Five—dam PA-2
Allegheny River Lock And Dam Four—dam PA-2
Allegheny River Lock And Dam Nine—dam PA-2
Allegheny River Lock And Dam Seven—dam PA-2
Allegheny River Lock And Dam Six—dam PA-2
Allegheny River Lock And Dam Three—dam PA-2
Allegheny River Lock And Dam Two—dam PA-2
Allegheny River Pool Eight—reservoir PA-2
Allegheny River Pool Five—reservoir PA-2
Allegheny River Pool Four—reservoir PA-2
Allegheny River Pool Nine—reservoir PA-2
Allegheny River Pool Seven—reservoir PA-2
Allegheny River Pool Six—reservoir PA-2
Allegheny River Pool Three—reservoir PA-2
Allegheny River Pool Two—reservoir PA-2
*Allegheny River Reservoir* NY-2
*Allegheny River Rsvr* PA-2
Allegheny Rsvr—reservoir NY-2
Allegheny Rsvr—reservoir (2) PA-2
Allegheny Run—stream WV-2
Allegheny Sch—school MI-6
Allegheny Sch—school NV-8
Allegheny Sch (historical)—school TN-4
*Allegheny Spring* VA-3
*Allegheny Springs* VA-3
**Allegheny Springs**—pop pl PA-2
Allegheny Springs—spring TN-4
**Allegheny Springs (historical)**—pop pl TN-4
Allegheny Square—park PA-2
**Allegheny (subdivision)**—pop pl PA-2
*Allegheny Township High School* PA-2
**Allegheny (Township of)**—pop pl (6) PA-2
Allegheny Trail—trail WV-2
Allegheny Tunnel—tunnel PA-2
Allegheny Tunnel—tunnel VA-3
Allegheny Tunnel—tunnel WV-2
Allegheny Valley Camp—locale PA-2
Allegheny Valley Hosp—hospital PA-2
*Allegheny Valley Interchange* PA-2
**Alleghenyville**—pop pl PA-2
Alleghenyville Ch—church PA-2
Allegheny Wesleyan Methodist Ch—church KS-7
Allegheny West Hist Dist—hist pl PA-2
Allegheny 1 Elem Sch—school PA-2
Allegheny 2 Elem Sch—school PA-2
Allegheny County Memorial Park( Cemetery)—cemetery PA-2
Allegood Pond—reservoir VA-3
**Allegre**—pop pl KY-4
*Allegrippes Ridge* PA-2
Allegrippis Ridge—ridge PA-2
Allegrippus—locale PA-2
*Allegripus Ridge* PA-2
Allegros Mtn—summit NM-5
*Allei Reef* FM-9
*Alle Islet* MP-9
**Alleman**—pop pl IA-7
Alleman Creek—stream IA-7
**Allemand**—pop pl LA-4
Allemand Flat—flat WY-8
Allemand Ranch—locale (2) WY-8
*Allemands* LA-4
Allemands, Bayou des—lake LA-4
Allemands, Bayou des—stream LA-4
Allemands, Lac des—lake LA-4
Allemands (census name Des Allemands)—other LA-4
Alleman HS—school IL-6
**Allemania**—pop pl LA-4
Allemania Plantation—locale LA-4
**Allemans**—pop pl PA-2
Allemans Ranch—locale ID-8
Alleman Station—locale SD-7
*Allen* AL-4
*Allen* PA-2
*Allen* WV-2
Allen—fmr MCD (2) NE-7
Allen—locale CA-9
Allen—locale CO-8
Allen—locale IL-6
Allen—locale MS-4
Allen—locale SC-3
Allen—locale SD-7
**Allen**—pop pl FL-3
**Allen**—pop pl IN-6
**Allen**—pop pl IA-7
**Allen**—pop pl KS-7
**Allen**—pop pl LA-4
**Allen**—pop pl MD-2
**Allen**—pop pl MI-6
**Allen**—pop pl (2) MS-4
**Allen**—pop pl NE-7
**Allen**—pop pl NC-3
**Allen**—pop pl OK-5
**Allen**—pop pl (2) PA-2
**Allen**—pop pl TN-4
**Allen**—pop pl TX-5
**Allen**—pop pl WA-9
**Allen**—pop pl WI-6
Allen, Abel, House—hist pl MA-1
Allen, Abram, House—hist pl WI-6
Allen, Bona, House—hist pl GA-3
Allen, Candace, House—hist pl RI-1
Allen, Carter, House—hist pl KY-4
Allen, Charles, House—hist pl DE-2
Allen, Charles, House—hist pl MA-1
Allen, Col. R. T. P., House—hist pl KY-4
Allen, Darlon, House—hist pl OH-6
Allen, Dr. Peter, House—hist pl OH-6

Allison Rsvr—*reservoir* PA-2
Allison Run—*stream* IN-6
Allisons Branch—*stream* SC-3
Allison Sch—*school* (2) CA-9
Allison Sch—*school* FL-3
Allison Sch—*school* IL-6
Allison Sch—*school* IA-7
Allison Sch—*school* OH-6
Allison Sch—*school* TX-5
Allison Sch (historical)—*school* (2) PA-2
Allison School (historical)—*locale* MO-7
*Allison School Number 3* IN-6
Allisons Creek—*stream* GA-3
Allisons Lake—*reservoir* GA-3
*Allison's Pond* CT-1
Allison Spring—*spring* OR-9
Allison Spring—*spring* TN-4
*Allisons Wells* MS-4
Allison Tank—*reservoir* AZ-5
Allison Tank—*reservoir* NM-5
Allison Tiffany Cem—*cemetery* CO-8
Allison Township—*fmr MCD* (2) IA-7
**Allison Township**—*pop pl* KS-7
**Allison Township**—*pop pl* SD-7
Allison Township Hall—*building* SD-7
Allison Township (historical)—*civil* SD-7
**Allison (Township of)**—*pop pl* IL-6
**Allison (Township of)**—*pop pl* PA-2
Allison Trail—*trail* CA-9
*Allisonville* IN-6
**Allisonville**—*pop pl* IN-6
*Allisonville Ch* IN-6
Allisonville Christian Ch—*church* IN-6
Allisonville Elem Sch—*school* IN-6
Allison Well—*well* NM-5
Allison Windmill—*locale* NM-5
Allison Woods—*woods* IL-6
Allison Worcester Camp—*locale* ME-1
Allis Plaza—*park* MO-7
Allis Sch—*school* WI-6
Allis State Forest Park—*park* VT-1
Allister—*locale* WV-2
Allister Ch—*church* TN-4
**Allis (Township of)**—*pop pl* MI-6
**Allman**—*pop pl* IN-6
Allman Branch—*stream* NC-3
Allman Cem—*cemetery* (2) TN-4
Allman Chapel—*church* AL-4
*Allman Chapel Ch* AL-4
Allmand-Archer House—*hist pl* VA-3
Allmandinger Cem—*cemetery* AR-4
Allman Ditch—*canal* IN-6
Allman Hollow—*valley* NC-3
Allman Lake—*lake* AK-9
Allman Run—*stream* OH-6
*Allmans Creek* IN-6
Allmendinger Park—*park* MI-6
Allmon—*locale* TX-5
Allmon Branch—*stream* NC-3
Allmon Camp Branch—*stream* NC-3
Allmon Cem—*cemetery* IL-6
Allmon Cem—*cemetery* OK-5
Allmon Creek—*stream* NC-3
Allmond Cem—*cemetery* TN-4
Allmond Pond—*reservoir* VA-3
**Allmondsville**—*pop pl* VA-3
**Allmondsville (Allmonds Wharf)**—*pop pl* VA-3
*Allmonds Wharf* VA-3
Allmonds Wharf—*other* VA-3
All My Kids Sch—*school* FL-3
All Nations Camp—*locale* CA-9
All Nations Cem—*cemetery* ND-7
All Nations Ch—*church* VA-3
All Nations Temple—*church* MI-6
All Night Creek—*stream* WY-8
Allnight Ridge—*ridge* TN-4
Allnut—*locale* VA-3
Allnutt—*other* VA-3
Allock—*locale* KY-4
**Allodium Township**—*pop pl* KS-7
*Allok* MP-9
Allok—*island* MP-9
Allokkan—*island* MP-9
Allon—*locale* GA-3
Allon—*locale* LA-4
**Allons**—*pop pl* TN-4
Allons Baptist Ch—*church* TN-4
Allons (CCD)—*cens area* TN-4
Allons Cem—*cemetery* TN-4
Allons Division—*civil* TN-4
Allons Post Office (historical)—*building* TN-4
*Allook* MP-9
Al Lopez Field—*park* FL-3
*Allor Creek* MS-4
Allotment Four Rsvr—*reservoir* OR-9
Allotment Rsvr Number Three—*reservoir* OR-9
*Alloues* MI-6
**Allouez**—*pop pl* MI-6
**Allouez**—*pop pl* (3) WI-6
Allouez—*uninc pl* WI-6
Allouez Bay—*bay* WI-6
Allouez Cem—*cemetery* WI-6
Allouez Park—*park* MI-6
Allouez Park—*park* WI-6
*Allouez River* WI-6
**Allouez (Township of)**—*pop pl* MI-6
*Allowance* MA-1
Alloway—*locale* TN-4
**Alloway**—*pop pl* NJ-2
**Alloway**—*pop pl* NY-2
**Alloway, (Township of)**—*pop pl* NJ-2
Alloway Airfield—*airport* NJ-2
Alloway Cem—*cemetery* NC-3
Alloway Ch—*church* TN-4
Alloway Ch of Christ—*church* TN-4
Alloway Creek—*stream* IL-6
Alloway Creek—*stream* IA-7
Alloway Creek—*stream* MD-2
Alloway Creek—*stream* NJ-2
Alloway Creek—*stream* PA-2
Alloway Creek—*stream* TN-4
Alloway Hope Halfway—*stream* NJ-2
Alloway Junction—*locale* NJ-2
Alloway Lake—*reservoir* NJ-2
Alloway Lake Dam—*dam* NJ-2
Alloway Landing—*locale* MS-4
Alloway Oil Field—*oilfield* MS-4
Alloway Sch (historical)—*school* TN-4
*Alloways Creek* NJ-2
*Alloways Creek* PA-2
*Alloways Town* NJ-2
*Allowson Hollow* TN-4
**Alloy**—*pop pl* MT-8
**Alloy**—*pop pl* WV-2
Alloy Creek—*stream* MT-8
Alloy Mtn—*summit* MT-8
All People Ch of God in Christ—*church* FL-3
Allphin Cem—*cemetery* KY-4
Allphin Cem—*cemetery* MO-7
Allphin Cem—*cemetery* OR-9
**Allport**—*pop pl* AR-4
**Allport**—*pop pl* (2) PA-2
Allpress Sch—*school* IL-6
Allread Creek—*stream* TX-5
Allread Spring—*spring* WY-8
Allred—*locale* TX-5
**Allred**—*pop pl* AL-4
**Allred**—*pop pl* TN-4
Allred, Ezra, Bungalow—*hist pl* ID-8
Allred, Ezra, Cottage—*hist pl* ID-8
Allred Canyon—*valley* AZ-5
Allred Canyon—*valley* WY-8
Allred Cem—*cemetery* KY-4
Allred Cem—*cemetery* TN-4
*Allred Cemetery* MS-4
Allred County (historical)—*civil* ND-7
Allred Creek—*stream* AR-4
Allred Creek—*stream* WA-9
Allred Ditch—*canal* (2) UT-8
Allred Flat—*flat* WY-8
Allred Hollow—*valley* TN-4
Allred Lake—*lake* MO-7
Allred Lake—*lake* TX-5
Allred Lake—*lake* UT-8
Allred Memorial Tabernacle—*church* NC-3
Allred Peak—*summit* CO-8
Allred Point—*cape* UT-8
Allred Post Office—*building* TN-4
Allred Ranch—*locale* NM-5
Allreds—*locale* NC-3
Allred Saltpeter Cave—*cave* TN-4
Allred-Sessions Lake—*reservoir* TX-5
Allred Spring—*spring* UT-8
**Allred Subdivision**—*pop pl* (2) UT-8
Allred Well—*well* NM-5
Allright—*locale* IL-6
Allround Point—*bend* FL-3
All Saint Chapel—*church* VT-1
All Saints Acad—*school* TN-4
All Saints Catholic Ch—*church* AL-4
All Saints Cem—*cemetery* CA-9
All Saints Cem—*cemetery* (2) CT-1
All Saints Cem—*cemetery* DE-2
All Saints Cem—*cemetery* FL-3
All Saints Cem—*cemetery* (2) IL-6
All Saints Cem—*cemetery* IN-6
All Saints Cem—*cemetery* KS-7
All Saints Cem—*cemetery* MN-6
All Saints Cem—*cemetery* MO-7
All Saints Cem—*cemetery* (2) NY-2
All Saints Cem—*cemetery* OH-6
All Saints Cem—*cemetery* (2) PA-2
All Saints Cem—*cemetery* SD-7
All Saints Cem—*cemetery* WI-6
All Saints Ch—*church* AL-4
All Saints Ch—*church* (2) DE-2
All Saints Ch—*church* IN-6
All Saints Ch—*church* (5) MD-2
All Saints Ch—*church* MA-1
All Saints Ch—*church* (3) MI-6
All Saints Ch—*church* NJ-2
All Saints Ch—*church* NY-2
All Saints Ch—*church* OH-6
All Saints Ch—*church* (2) SC-3
All Saints Ch—*church* VA-3
All Saint Sch—*school* IA-7
All Saints Ch and Indian Mission (historical)—*church* SD-7
All Saints Chapel—*church* NY-2
All Saints Chapel—*church* WI-6
All Saints' Chapel—*hist pl* NY-2
All Saints Ch (historical)—*church* PA-2
All Saint's Church—*hist pl* AZ-5
All Saints' Church—*hist pl* (2) MD-2
All Saints' Church—*hist pl* MA-1
All Saints' Church—*hist pl* NH-1
All Saints Church-Episcopal—*hist pl* MN-6
All Saints Church of Eben Ezer—*hist pl* CO-8
All Saints Coll—*school* MS-4
All Saints Convent—*church* MD-2
All Saints Early Learning Child Care Sch—*school* FL-3
All Saints Elem Sch—*school* AL-4
All Saints' Episcopal Cathedral Complex—*hist pl* WI-6
All Saints Episcopal Ch—*church* AL-4
All Saints Episcopal Ch—*church* (4) FL-3
All Saints Episcopal Ch—*church* IN-6
All Saints Episcopal Ch—*church* (4) MS-4
All Saints Episcopal Ch—*church* TN-4
All Saints Episcopal Ch—*church* UT-8
All Saints Episcopal Church—*hist pl* CO-8
All Saint's Episcopal Church—*hist pl* FL-3
All Saints Episcopal Church—*hist pl* LA-4
All Saints' Episcopal Church—*hist pl* MI-6
All Saints Episcopal Church—*hist pl* OH-6
All Saints Hist Dist—*hist pl* SD-7
All Saints Hosp—*hospital* PA-2
All Saints Hosp—*hospital* TX-5
All Saints HS—*school* NY-2
All Saints Lutheran Ch—*church* (2) FL-3
All Saints Memorial Church—*hist pl* RI-1
All Saints' Memorial Church Complex—*hist pl* NJ-2
All Saints MS—*school* WA-9
All Saints Roman Catholic Ch—*church* KS-7
All Saints Roman Catholic Church—*hist pl* TX-5
All Saints Sch—*school* AZ-5
All Saints Sch—*school* (2) CA-9
All Saints Sch—*school* CO-8
All Saints Sch—*school* IL-6
All Saints Sch—*school* (2) IA-7
All Saints Sch—*school* KS-7
All Saints Sch—*school* MN-6
All Saints Sch—*school* NY-2
All Saints Sch—*school* OR-9
All Saints Sch—*school* (3) PA-2
All Saints Sch—*school* SD-7
All Saints Sch—*school* (2) TX-5
All Saints Sch—*school* VA-3
All Saints Sch—*school* WA-9
All Saints Sch Main Bldg—*hist pl* SD-7
**All Saints Village**—*pop pl* MO-7
**Allsboro**—*pop pl* AL-4
Allsboro Ch—*church* AL-4
Allsboro JHS—*school* AL-4
*Allsborough* AL-4
**Allsbrook**—*pop pl* SC-3
Allsbrook Ridge—*ridge* KY-4
Allsbrook Sch (historical)—*school* TN-4
Allsbury Sch—*school* ME-1
Alls Cem—*cemetery* VA-3
Alls Fork—*stream* NC-3
Allsop—*locale* AL-4
Allsop Lake—*lake* UT-8
Allsopp Park—*park* AR-4
All Souls Catholic Ch—*church* FL-3
All Souls Cem—*cemetery* CA-9
All Souls Cem—*cemetery* NY-2
All Souls Cem—*cemetery* OH-6
*All Souls Ch* IN-6
All Souls Ch—*church* NY-2
All Souls Ch—*church* NC-3
All Souls Chapel—*church* (2) NY-2
All Soul's Chapel—*hist pl* ME-1
All Souls Church—*hist pl* AR-4
All Souls Episcopal Ch—*church* FL-3
All Souls Episcopal Church and Parish House—*hist pl* NC-3
All Souls Hosp—*hospital* NJ-2
All Souls Rest Cem—*cemetery* AR-4
All Souls Sch—*school* CA-9
All Souls Sch—*school* CO-8
All Souls Sch—*school* FL-3
All Souls Unitarian Ch—*church* DC-2
All Souls Unitarian-Universalist Ch—*church* IN-6
All Souls Unitarian-Universalist Church—*hist pl* OH-6
All Souls Universalist Church—*hist pl* CA-9
Alls Souls Church—*hist pl* ME-1
Allstadt House and Ordinary—*hist pl* WV-2
**All Star Mobile Home Park (subdivision)**—*pop pl* NC-3
All States Ch—*church* PA-2
**Allston**—*pop pl* OR-9
Allston Creek—*stream* SC-3
Allston Station (historical)—*locale* MA-1
**Allston (subdivision)**—*pop pl* MA-1
Allston Township—*civ div* NE-7
*Allstott Creek* IN-6
Allstott Sch—*school* IN-6
*Allsup* AL-4
Allsup, Marion, House—*hist pl* ID-8
Allsup Branch—*stream* KY-4
Allsups Mill (historical)—*locale* AL-4
Allsup Spring—*spring* AL-4
*All Swede Lake* MN-6
*All Tides* FL-3
All Tides Cove—*bay* FL-3
Allton Bldg—*hist pl* ID-8
All Top—*summit* CA-9
Alltop Hollow—*valley* OH-6
Allula (historical)—*locale* AL-4
*Allum Hill* MA-1
Allum Sch—*school* SD-7
Allure, Lake—*lake* NY-2
Allured Mine—*mine* CA-9
*Alluvial* LA-4
*Alluvial City* LA-4
**Alluvial City**—*pop pl* LA-4
**Alluvial City (Yscloskey)**—*pop pl* LA-4
Alluvial Creek—*stream* OR-9
*Alluvial Junction* LA-4
*Alluvian Junction* LA-4
**Alluvium**—*pop pl* NJ-2
Alluvium Creek—*stream* WY-8
**Alluwe**—*pop pl* OK-5
Alluwe (CCD)—*cens area* OK-5
*Alluwe (corporate name New Alluwe)* OK-5
**Allview**—*pop pl* MD-2
**Allview Estates**—*pop pl* MD-2
Allview Golf Course—*other* MD-2
Allwine Creek—*stream* PA-2
Allwington—*uninc pl* VA-3
Allwood—*locale* VA-3
**Allwood**—*pop pl* NJ-2
Ally Gulch—*valley* ID-8
**Allyn**—*pop pl* WA-9
Allyn, A. H., House—*hist pl* WI-6
Allyn, Capt. Benjamin, II, House—*hist pl* CT-1
Allyn, Lake—*lake* OH-6
Allyn Brook—*stream* CT-1
Allyn Brook—*stream* VT-1
Allyn Cem—*cemetery* VT-1
Allyn Finch JHS—*school* TX-5
Allyn Gulch—*valley* CO-8
Allyn House—*hist pl* MA-1
Allyn Millpond—*lake* CT-1
Allyns Bight—*bay* TX-5
Allyn Sch—*school* SD-7
Allyns Lake—*bay* TX-5
Allyns Point—*locale* CT-1
**Allyn Sta**—*pop pl* WA-9
Ally Point—*summit* ID-8
Ally Point Trail—*trail* ID-8
**Allyson Hills (subdivision)**—*pop pl* MS-4
Ally Wash—*stream* AZ-5
*Alma* ND-7
*Alma* WV-2
Alma—*locale* AL-4
Alma—*locale* AZ-5
Alma—*locale* FL-3
Alma—*locale* NM-5
Alma—*locale* OR-9
**Alma**—*pop pl* AR-4
**Alma**—*pop pl* CO-8
**Alma**—*pop pl* GA-3
**Alma**—*pop pl* IL-6
**Alma**—*pop pl* KS-7
**Alma**—*pop pl* LA-4
**Alma**—*pop pl* MI-6
**Alma**—*pop pl* MS-4
**Alma**—*pop pl* MO-7
**Alma**—*pop pl* NE-7
**Alma**—*pop pl* NY-2
**Alma**—*pop pl* NC-3
**Alma**—*pop pl* OH-6
**Alma**—*pop pl* OK-5
**Alma**—*pop pl* TX-5
**Alma**—*pop pl* VA-3
**Alma**—*pop pl* WI-6
Alma, Canal (historical)—*canal* AZ-5
Alma, Lake—*lake* (2) FL-3
Alma, Lake—*lake* MN-6
Alma, Lake—*lake* OH-6
Alma, Lake—*reservoir* AR-4
Alma, Mount—*summit* CA-9
Alma Area Sch—*school* WI-6
Alma (CCD)—*cens area* GA-3
Alma Cem—*cemetery* IL-6
Alma Cem—*cemetery* KS-7
Alma Cem—*cemetery* NE-7
Alma Cem—*cemetery* OK-5
Alma Cem—*cemetery* SD-7
**Alma Center**—*pop pl* WI-6
**Alma (Centerville)**—*pop pl* WV-2
Alma Ch—*church* AR-4
Alma Ch—*church* MN-6
Almacigo Alto (Barrio)—*fmr MCD* PR-3
**Almacigo Bajo**—*pop pl* (2) PR-3
Almacigo Bajo (Barrio)—*fmr MCD* PR-3
**Alma City**—*pop pl* MN-6
Alma City Cem—*cemetery* MN-6
Alma City Dam—*dam* KS-7
Alma City Rsvr—*reservoir* KS-7
Alma Coll—*school* CA-9
Alma Coll—*school* MI-6
*Alma Creek* ID-8
Alma Creek—*stream* (2) AK-9
Alma Creek—*stream* IN-6
Alma Creek—*stream* (2) WA-9
Almadale Christian Sch—*school* FL-3
Almadale (historical)—*locale* MS-4
Almadane—*locale* LA-4
**Alma (Daystrom)**—*pop pl* NC-3
*Almaden* (2) CA-9
**Almaden**—*pop pl* PA-2
Almaden Air Force Station—*military* CA-9
Almaden Canyon—*valley* CA-9
Almaden Country Club—*other* CA-9
Almaden Flats—*flat* CA-9
Almaden Mine—*mine* CA-9
Almaden Rsvr—*reservoir* CA-9
Almaden Union Sch—*school* CA-9
Almaden Valley—*post sta* CA-9
Alma Depot—*hist pl* GA-3
Almadi Mine—*mine* CO-8
Alma Fire Control Station—*locale* CA-9
Alma Fruit Farm—*hist pl* GA-3
*Almagan* MH-9
Alma Gardens (trailer park)—*locale* AZ-5
**Alma Gardens (trailer park)**—*pop pl* AZ-5
Almagosa, Mount—*summit* GU-9
Almagosa River—*stream* GU-9
Almagosa Springs—*spring* GU-9
Almagre Arroyo—*valley* NM-5
Almagre Canyon—*valley* CO-8
Almagre Canyon—*valley* NM-5
Almagre Mtn—*summit* CO-8
**Almagro**—*pop pl* VA-3
*Almaguan* MH-9
Alma Gulch—*valley* AK-9
Alma Hill—*summit* NY-2
Alma Hist Dist—*hist pl* WI-6
Alma (historical)—*locale* AL-4
Alma Hollow—*valley* MO-7
Alma Holt Draw—*valley* WY-8
Alma Island—*island* AK-9
Alma Junction—*locale* CO-8
Al Malaikah Temple—*hist pl* CA-9
Alma Lake—*lake* IN-6
Alma Lake—*lake* (2) MI-6
Alma Lake—*lake* WI-6
**Alma Lake**—*pop pl* IN-6
Alma Lakes—*lake* AK-9
Alma Lincoln Mine—*mine* CO-8
*Alma Martin School* AL-4
Alma Meadows Mobile Home Park—*locale* AZ-5
Alma Mesa—*summit* AZ-5
Alma Mine—*mine* ID-8
Alma Mine—*mine* WA-9
Almanac Mtn—*summit* ME-1
Almanac Pond—*lake* MA-1
Almand Cem—*cemetery* GA-3
Almand Creek—*stream* GA-3
Almani—*island* MP-9
**Almanor**—*pop pl* CA-9
Almanor, Lake—*reservoir* CA-9
Almanor Peninsula—*cape* CA-9
Almanor Ranger Station—*locale* CA-9
Almanor (Siding)—*locale* CA-9
**Almanor (sta.)**—*pop pl* CA-9
Alman Run—*stream* OH-6
Almansor Municipal Golf Course—*locale* CA-9
Almansor Park—*park* CA-9
Alma Park—*park* CA-9
Alma Ranch—*locale* CA-9
Alma Ridge—*ridge* WI-6
Almart—*locale* MT-8
**Almartha**—*pop pl* MO-7
*Almart Mountain Lodge* MT-8
Alma Sch—*school* AL-4
Alma Sch—*school* AZ-5
Alma Sch—*school* OR-9
Alma Sch—*school* SC-3
ALMA (Scow Schooner)—*hist pl* CA-9
Almas Drain—*canal* MI-6
Almasie Creek—*stream* OR-9
*Almaska* PW-9
Alma Tank—*reservoir* NM-5
Alma Taylor Hollow—*valley* UT-8
Alma Taylor Lake—*lake* UT-8
**Alma (Town of)**—*pop pl* NY-2
**Alma (Town of)**—*pop pl* (2) WI-6
**Alma Township**—*pop pl* KS-7
**Alma Township**—*pop pl* NE-7
**Alma Township**—*pop pl* ND-7
Alma (Township of)—*fmr MCD* AR-4
**Alma (Township of)**—*pop pl* IL-6
**Alma (Township of)**—*pop pl* MN-6
**Almaville**—*pop pl* TN-4
Almaville (CCD)—*cens area* TN-4
Almaville Division—*civil* TN-4
Alma Vista Picnic Area—*park* NE-7
Alma Ward Park—*park* AZ-5
Alma White Coll—*school* NJ-2
Alma Young Canyon—*valley* UT-8
*Almeda* TN-4
**Almeda**—*pop pl* SC-3
**Almeda**—*pop pl* TX-5
Almeda Bar—*bar* OR-9
**Almeda Beach**—*pop pl* (2) MI-6
Almeda Gardner Pond Sch (historical)—*school* MS-4
Almeda (historical)—*locale* AL-4
**Almeda (historical)**—*pop pl* OR-9
Almeda Lake—*lake* MT-8
Almeda Mine (abandoned)—*mine* OR-9
Almeda Park—*park* OR-9
**Almeda Plaza**—*pop pl* TX-5
Almeda Post Office (historical)—*building* TN-4
**Almedia**—*pop pl* LA-4
**Almedia**—*pop pl* PA-2
*Almelo* KS-7
*Almelo Township* KS-7
**Almelund**—*pop pl* MN-6
**Almena**—*pop pl* KS-7
**Almena**—*pop pl* MI-6
**Almena**—*pop pl* WI-6
Almena City Lake—*reservoir* KS-7
Almena-District Four Township—*civil* KS-7
Almena Diversion Dam—*dam* KS-7
Almena Diversion Wildlife Area—*park* KS-7
Almena Elem Sch—*school* KS-7
**Almena Jct.**—*pop pl* KS-7
Almena Sch—*school* MI-6
**Almena (Town of)**—*pop pl* WI-6
*Almena Township* KS-7
**Almena (Township of)**—*pop pl* MI-6
*Almeni Islet* MP-9
Almerant Ch—*church* FL-3
Almer Cem—*cemetery* MI-6
Almer Center Sch—*school* MI-6
Almeria—*locale* AL-4
Almeria—*locale* NE-7
Almeria Cem—*cemetery* NE-7
Almeria Ch—*church* AL-4
Almer Store—*hist pl* AR-4
**Almer (Township of)**—*pop pl* MI-6
*Almetonia* PA-2
Almetta Ch—*church* AR-4
Almetta Ch—*church* SC-3
*Almiokan River* PW-9
Almira—*locale* GA-3
Almira—*locale* TX-5
Almira—*locale* VA-3
**Almira**—*pop pl* TN-4
**Almira**—*pop pl* WA-9
Almira Cem—*cemetery* MI-6
Almira Cem—*cemetery* WA-9
Almirante Norte (Barrio)—*fmr MCD* PR-3
Almirante Sur—*post sta* PR-3
Almirante Sur (Barrio)—*fmr MCD* PR-3
Almira Sch—*school* MI-6
Almira Sch—*school* OH-6
**Almira (Township of)**—*pop pl* MI-6
Almlie Cem—*cemetery* ND-7
**Almo**—*pop pl* ID-8
**Almo**—*pop pl* KY-4
Almo Ch—*church* KY-4
Almo Creek—*stream* ID-8
**Almo Heights**—*pop pl* KY-4
**Almolind**—*pop pl* NJ-2
**Almon**—*pop pl* GA-3
**Almon**—*pop pl* MO-7
Almon Branch—*stream* AL-4
Almon Cem—*cemetery* (2) AL-4
*Almond* GA-3
Almond—*locale* AL-4
Almond—*locale* AR-4
**Almond**—*pop pl* NY-2
**Almond**—*pop pl* NC-3
**Almond**—*pop pl* WI-6
**Almondale**—*pop pl* CA-9
Almond Ave Sch—*school* (2) CA-9
Almond Bald—*locale* GA-3
Almond Ch—*church* AL-4
Almond Ch—*church* AR-4
Almond Cove—*valley* CA-9
Almond Creek—*stream* AR-4
Almond Creek—*stream* VA-3
Almond Ditch—*canal* IN-6
Almond Ditch—*canal* UT-8
Almond Hole—*lake* TX-5
*Almond Lake* MN-6
Almond Lake—*reservoir* NY-2
Almond Lookout Tower—*locale* AR-4
Almond Mtn—*summit* CA-9
Almond Park Dock—*locale* NC-3
Almond Ranch—*locale* CA-9
*Almond Rsvr* NY-2
Almond Rsvr—*reservoir* CA-9
Almond Sch—*school* CA-9
Almond Sch—*school* NC-3
*Almondsville* VA-3
*Almonds Wharf* VA-3
**Almond (Town of)**—*pop pl* NY-2
**Almond (Town of)**—*pop pl* WI-6
Almond (Township of)—*fmr MCD* NC-3
**Almond (Township of)**—*pop pl* MN-6
**Almonesson**—*pop pl* NJ-2
Almonesson Creek—*stream* NJ-2
Almonesson Lake—*reservoir* NJ-2
Almonesson Lake Dam—*dam* NJ-2
*Almongui* PW-9
*Almongui Point* PW-9
*Almongui River* PW-9
Almon Knob—*summit* TN-4
*Almonogui* PW-9
Almon Run—*stream* WV-2
Almont—*locale* IA-7
**Almont**—*pop pl* AL-4
**Almont**—*pop pl* CO-8
**Almont**—*pop pl* MI-6
**Almont**—*pop pl* ND-7
**Almont**—*pop pl* PA-2
**Almont**—*pop pl* TX-5
Almont Camp—*locale* MI-6
Almonte—*locale* CA-9
**Almon (Town of)**—*pop pl* WI-6
Almont Post Office (historical)—*building* PA-2
Almont Sch—*school* TX-5
**Almont (Township of)**—*pop pl* MI-6
Almo Park—*park* ID-8
Almora—*locale* IL-6
**Almora**—*pop pl* MN-6
Almoral—*locale* IA-7
Almora Lake—*lake* MN-6
Almoral Branch—*stream* IA-7
Almoral Spring—*locale* IA-7
Almora State Wildlife Mngmt Area—*park* MN-6
Almore Cove—*bay* ME-1
Almores Sch (historical)—*school* TN-4
**Almoris**—*pop pl* WV-2
Almor West Sch—*school* OK-5
Almos Lake—*lake* SD-7
Almost-a-Dog Mtn—*summit* MT-8
Almost Cave—*cave* AL-4
Almota—*locale* WA-9
Almota Creek—*stream* WA-9
Almo Well—*locale* NM-5
Alms and Doepke Dry Goods Company—*hist pl* OH-6
Almshouse—*hist pl* MA-1
Alms House—*locale* DE-2
**Alms House**—*pop pl* MA-1
Almshouse, The—*hist pl* VA-3
Almshouse Branch—*stream* DE-2
Almshouse Creek—*bay* MD-2
Alms House Ditch—*stream* DE-2
*Almshouse Hill* MA-1
Almsted Brothers Bldg—*hist pl* KY-4
Almus Knob—*summit* AR-4
Almwell Ch—*church* SC-3
**Almy**—*pop pl* MS-4
**Almy**—*pop pl* WY-8
Almy Brook—*stream* RI-1
Almy Cem—*cemetery* MA-1
Almy Cem—*cemetery* WY-8
Almy Hill—*summit* RI-1
**Almy Junction**—*pop pl* WY-8
Almy Point—*cape* RI-1
Almy Pond—*lake* RI-1
Almy Post Office (historical)—*building* TN-4
**Almyra**—*pop pl* AR-4
Almyra Cem—*cemetery* AR-4
Almyra Methodist Ch—*church* TN-4
Almyra Sch—*school* TN-4
Almy Reservoir Dam—*dam* RI-1
Almy Rsvr—*reservoir* RI-1
*Almys Beach* RI-1
Almy Sch—*school* TN-4
**Almyville**—*pop pl* CT-1
**Alna**—*pop pl* ME-1
Alna Cem—*cemetery* ME-1
Alna Center—*locale* ME-1
Alna Meetinghouse—*hist pl* ME-1
Alna Sch—*hist pl* ME-1
**Alna (Town of)**—*pop pl* ME-1
Alneta Lake—*reservoir* AR-4
Alney Canyon—*valley* ID-8
Alngaden—*island* MP-9
*Alngarin* MP-9
Alngeeyak Point—*cape* AK-9
*Alnnanack Pond* MA-1
Alnoname Number One Dam—*dam* AL-4
Alnoname Two Dam—*dam* AL-4
Alnus Spring—*spring* WA-9
**Alnwick**—*pop pl* PA-2
**Alnwick**—*pop pl* TN-4
**Alnwick**—*pop pl* WV-2
Alnwick Hall—*hist pl* NJ-2
Alnwick Sch—*school* TN-4
*Aloachulosk* AL-4
*Aloah* MI-6
*Alochaman River* WA-9
*Alochoman River* WA-9
*Alochomin River* WA-9
*Alockaman River* WA-9
*Alocs Creek* NJ-2
Aloe—*locale* MT-8
**Aloe**—*pop pl* TX-5
Aloe, Bayou—*bay* AL-4
Aloe Bay Channel—*channel* AL-4
Aloe Lake—*lake* MT-8
Aloe Sch—*school* MT-8
Alofau—*locale* AS-9
Alofisau Point—*cape* AS-9
*Alog* FM-9
**Aloha**—*pop pl* LA-4
**Aloha**—*pop pl* MI-6
**Aloha**—*pop pl* OR-9
**Aloha**—*pop pl* WA-9
Aloha, Lake—*reservoir* CA-9
Aloha Creek—*stream* AK-9
Aloha HS—*school* OR-9
Aloha-Huber Sch—*school* OR-9
Aloha Plaza (Shop Ctr)—*locale* FL-3
Aloha Sch—*school* CA-9
Aloha State Park—*park* MI-6
Aloha Tower—*hist pl* HI-9
Aloha Tower—*locale* HI-9
**Aloha (Township of)**—*pop pl* MI-6
Alohkapw—*civil* FM-9
Alohkapw—*summit* FM-9
Aloi Crater—*crater* HI-9
*Aloitak* AZ-5
*Alokap* FM-9
*Alokomin River* WA-9
Alolukrok (Site)—*locale* AK-9
**Aloma**—*pop pl* FL-3
Aloma Elem Sch—*school* FL-3
Aloma Methodist Kindergarten—*school* FL-3
**Alomar**—*pop pl* PR-3
*Alomata* KS-7
Alombro Cem—*cemetery* LA-4
Alona Creek—*stream* NM-5
Alonah Mine—*mine* AZ-5
Aloname One Dam—*dam* AL-4
Alona Park—*park* CA-9
**Alondra (census name Alondra Park)**—*pop pl* CA-9
Alondra JHS—*school* CA-9
Alondra Park—*park* CA-9
Alondra Park (census name for Alondra)—*CDP* CA-9
Alone Mill Creek—*stream* VA-3
Along—*island* FM-9
*Alonget* FM-9
Alonso, Frank, House—*hist pl* TX-5
Alonzaville—*locale* VA-3
Alonzo—*locale* IL-6
Alonzo—*locale* MS-4
**Alonzo**—*pop pl* KY-4
*Alonzo McShirley Drain* IN-6
Alonzo Post Office (historical)—*building* MS-4
**Aloquin**—*pop pl* NY-2

Alora Creek—*stream* MT-8
**Alorton**—*pop pl* IL-6
Alo Stream—*stream* HI-9
Alott, Lake—*lake* MN-6
*Aloufa* FL-3
*Alouka* FL-3
Al Owens Spring—*spring* NV-8
**Aloys**—*pop pl* NE-7
**Aloysia**—*pop pl* LA-4
Aloysius Fitzpatrick Sch—*school* PA-2
**Aloysius (historical)**—*pop pl* OR-9
Alparon Park—*park* PA-2
**Alpaugh**—*pop pl* CA-9
Alpaugh Brook—*stream* NJ-2
Alpaugh Irrigation District Canal—*canal* CA-9
Alp Creek—*stream* MT-8
A-L Peak—*summit* NM-5
Alpena—*locale* WV-2
**Alpena**—*pop pl* AR-4
**Alpena**—*pop pl* MI-6
**Alpena**—*pop pl* SD-7
**Alpena (County)**—*pop pl* MI-6
Alpena County Courthouse—*hist pl* MI-6
*Alpena Gap* WV-2
Alpena Gap Rec Area—*park* WV-2
*Alpena Junction* MI-6
**Alpena Junction**—*pop pl* MI-6
Alpena Mine—*mine* MN-6
Alpena State For—*forest* (2) MI-6
Alpena State Park—*park* MI-6
**Alpena Township**—*pop pl* SD-7
**Alpena (Township of)**—*pop pl* MI-6
Alpenglow, Mount—*summit* AK-9
**Alpental**—*pop pl* WA-9
Alpers—*locale* OK-5
Alpers Canyon—*valley* CA-9
Alpert Field—*locale* MA-1
*Alpha* LA-4
Alpha—*locale* AZ-5
Alpha—*locale* AR-4
Alpha—*locale* ID-8
Alpha—*locale* KY-4
Alpha—*locale* MD-2
Alpha—*locale* OK-5
Alpha—*locale* OR-9
Alpha—*locale* TN-4
Alpha—*locale* VA-3
**Alpha**—*pop pl* IL-6
**Alpha**—*pop pl* IA-7
**Alpha**—*pop pl* LA-4
**Alpha**—*pop pl* MI-6
**Alpha**—*pop pl* MN-6
**Alpha**—*pop pl* (2) MO-7
**Alpha**—*pop pl* NV-8
**Alpha**—*pop pl* NJ-2
**Alpha**—*pop pl* OH-6
**Alpha**—*pop pl* WA-9
**Alpha**—*pop pl* WV-2
**Alpha**—*pop pl* WI-6
Alpha and Omega—*church* FL-3
Alpha and Omega Private Sch—*school* FL-3
**Alphaba**—*pop pl* MS-4
Alphaba Post Office (historical)—*building* MS-4
Alphabet Acad—*school* FL-3
Alpha Bradley Branch—*stream* KY-4
Alpha Branch—*stream* KY-4
Alpha Butte—*summit* NV-8
Alpha Cave—*cave* AL-4
Alpha (CCD)—*cens area* TN-4
Alpha Cem—*cemetery* ID-8
Alpha Cem—*cemetery* IL-6
Alpha Cem—*cemetery* IN-6
Alpha Cem—*cemetery* IA-7
Alpha Cem—*cemetery* WA-9
Alpha Center Sch—*school* MS-4
Alpha Ch—*church* GA-3
Alpha Ch—*church* IN-6
Alpha Ch—*church* (2) TN-4
Alpha Coal Mine—*mine* IL-6
Alpha Contaminated Area—*locale* NV-8
Alpha Creek—*stream* (2) AK-9
Alpha Creek—*stream* MI-6
Alpha Creek—*stream* MT-8
Alpha Day Sch—*school* (2) FL-3
Alpha Diggings—*locale* CA-9
Alpha Ditch—*canal* WY-8
Alpha Division—*civil* TN-4
Alpha Elem Sch—*school* TN-4
Alpha Field Outlying—*airport* MS-4
Alpha Grange—*locale* ID-8
Alpha Gulch—*valley* MT-8
**Alpha Heights**—*pop pl* TN-4
Alpha (historical)—*locale* AL-4
Alpha (historical)—*locale* KS-7
Alpha (historical P.O.)—*locale* IN-6
Alpha Key—*island* FL-3
*Alpha Knob* AR-4
*Alpha Lake* PA-2
Alpha Lake—*lake* MN-6
Alpha Lake—*lake* MT-8
Alpha Mine—*mine* AZ-5
Alpha Mine—*mine* (2) CA-9
Alpha Mtn—*summit* NV-8
**Alphano**—*pop pl* NJ-2
Alpha Omega Cem—*cemetery* NC-3
Alpha-Omega Private Sch—*school* FL-3
Alpha Peak—*summit* NV-8
Alpha Pit—*cave* AL-4
Alpha Plastics Corporation—*facility* NC-3
Alpha-Platus Mine (historical)—*mine* SD-7
Alpha Post Office (historical)—*building* SD-7
Alpha Post Office (historical)—*building* TN-4
Alpha Prairie—*flat* WA-9
Alpha Primary Sch—*school* TN-4
Alpha Public Buildings Historic Complex—*hist pl* MI-6
Alpha Ranch—*locale* NV-8
**Alpharetta**—*pop pl* GA-3
Alpharetta, Lake—*lake* FL-3
Alpharetta Cem—*cemetery* GA-3
Alpha Ridge—*ridge* AK-9
Alpha Sch—*school* (2) CA-9
Alpha Sch—*school* NE-7
Alpha Sch—*school* WV-2
Alpha Shaft—*mine* NV-8
*Alphas Pond* PA-2
Alpha Springs—*locale* AL-4
**Alpha Springs**—*pop pl* AL-4
**Alpha (subdivision)**—*pop pl* PA-2
Alpha Tau Omega Fraternity House (Old)—*hist pl* OR-9
Alpha Terrace Hist Dist—*hist pl* PA-2
**Alpha Township**—*pop pl* SD-7
Alphen Hollow—*valley* MO-7
Alphenia Ch—*church* LA-4
Alphenia Landing—*locale* LA-4
Alpheus—*uninc pl* WV-2
Alphia Cem—*cemetery* IN-6
Alphie Canyon—*valley* CA-9
Alphie Spring—*spring* CA-9
Alphin Cem—*cemetery* KY-4
Alphin Cem—*cemetery* TX-5
Alphin Draw—*valley* WY-8
Alphine Campground—*locale* WA-9
Alphin Spring—*spring* WY-8
Alphonse, Bayou—*gut* (2) LA-4
**Alphoretta (Dinwood Station)**—*pop pl* KY-4
Alpica—*other* MS-4
*Alpika* MS-4
*Alpika Post Office* MS-4
Alpina—*locale* NY-2
*Alpine* CA-9
*Al Pine* IN-6
Alpine—*locale* CA-9
Alpine—*locale* CO-8
Alpine—*locale* GA-3
Alpine—*locale* KY-4
Alpine—*locale* OR-9
Alpine—*locale* (2) VA-3
**Alpine**—*pop pl* (2) AL-4
**Alpine**—*pop pl* AZ-5
**Alpine**—*pop pl* AR-4
**Alpine**—*pop pl* CA-9
**Alpine**—*pop pl* CO-8
**Alpine**—*pop pl* FL-3
**Alpine**—*pop pl* ID-8
**Alpine**—*pop pl* IL-6
**Alpine**—*pop pl* IN-6
**Alpine**—*pop pl* MI-6
**Alpine**—*pop pl* MS-4
**Alpine**—*pop pl* MT-8
**Alpine**—*pop pl* NJ-2
**Alpine**—*pop pl* NY-2
**Alpine**—*pop pl* OR-9
**Alpine**—*pop pl* PA-2
**Alpine**—*pop pl* TN-4
**Alpine**—*pop pl* TX-5
**Alpine**—*pop pl* UT-8
**Alpine**—*pop pl* VA-3
**Alpine**—*pop pl* WY-8
Alpine, Lake—*reservoir* AR-4
Alpine, Lake—*reservoir* CA-9
**Alpine Acres**—*pop pl* TN-4
Alpine Acres—*uninc pl* CO-8
Alpine And Blackmore Drain—*canal* MI-6
*Alpine and Black River Ranger Station* AZ-5
*Alpine Baldy* WA-9
Alpine Baldy—*summit* WA-9
Alpine Baptist Ch—*church* AL-4
Alpine Baptist Ch—*church* TN-4
**Alpine Bay**—*pop pl* AL-4
Alpine Beach—*locale* MD-2
Alpine Boat Basin—*harbor* NJ-2
Alpine Brook—*stream* CO-8
Alpine Butte—*summit* CA-9
Alpine Butte—*summit* WA-9
Alpine Camp—*locale* CO-8
Alpine Camp—*locale* NJ-2
Alpine Camp—*locale* WA-9
Alpine Camp for Boys—*locale* AL-4
Alpine Campground—*locale* CA-9
Alpine Campground—*locale* ID-8
Alpine Campground—*locale* WY-8
Alpine Campground—*park* OR-9
Alpine Canyon—*valley* CA-9
Alpine (CCD)—*cens area* CA-9
Alpine (CCD)—*cens area* TN-4
Alpine (CCD)—*cens area* TX-5
Alpine Cem—*cemetery* AR-4
Alpine Cem—*cemetery* KS-7
Alpine Cem—*cemetery* MI-6
Alpine Cem—*cemetery* NJ-2
Alpine Cem—*cemetery* OR-9
Alpine Cem—*cemetery* TX-5
Alpine Cem—*cemetery* UT-8
Alpine Ch—*church* AL-4
Alpine Ch—*church* GA-3
Alpine Ch—*church* NC-3
Alpine Ch—*church* TX-5
Alpine Ch—*church* WV-2
*Alpine City* UT-8
*Alpine City Cemetery* UT-8
Alpine Civilian Conservation Center—*locale* AZ-5
Alpine Col—*gap* CA-9
Alpine Corral—*locale* CO-8
**Alpine (County)**—*pop pl* CA-9
Alpine Court Cabins—*locale* MI-6
Alpine Cove—*bay* AK-9
Alpine Creek—*stream* AL-4
Alpine Creek—*stream* AK-9
Alpine Creek—*stream* AZ-5
Alpine Creek—*stream* (4) CA-9
Alpine Creek—*stream* CO-8
Alpine Creek—*stream* GA-3
Alpine Creek—*stream* (6) ID-8
Alpine Creek—*stream* (2) MT-8
Alpine Creek—*stream* TX-5
Alpine Creek—*stream* (2) WA-9
Alpine Crest Sch—*school* TN-4
Alpine Dam—*dam* CA-9
Alpine Dam—*dam* PA-2
Alpine Divide—*ridge* AZ-5
Alpine Divide Campground—*park* AZ-5
*Alpine Divide Forest Campground* AZ-5
Alpine Division—*civil* TN-4
*Alpine El Capitan* CA-9
Alpine Elem Sch—*school* AZ-5
Alpine Experiment Station—*other* UT-8
Alpine Falls—*falls* MT-8
Alpine Falls—*falls* WA-9
Alpine Forest Camp—*locale* UT-8
Alpine Fort—*locale* UT-8
**Alpine Gardens Subdivision**—*pop pl* UT-8
Alpine Garden Trail—*trail* NH-1
Alpine Golf Course—*other* MI-6
Alpine Guard Station—*locale* CA-9
Alpine Guard Station—*locale* CO-8
Alpine Gulch—*valley* CA-9
Alpine Gulch—*valley* CO-8
Alpine Gulch—*valley* ID-8
Alpine Gulch—*valley* MT-8
**Alpine Heights**—*pop pl* CA-9
**Alpine Heights**—*pop pl* FL-3
**Alpine Heights (subdivision)**—*pop pl* PA-2
**Alpine Heights (subdivision)**—*pop pl* TN-4
Alpine Hill—*summit* MA-1
Alpine Hill—*summit* TX-5
Alpine Hills—*uninc pl* CA-9
Alpine Hills Ch of Christ—*church* AL-4
Alpine Hills Missionary Baptist Ch—*church* AL-4
**Alpine Hills (subdivision)**—*pop pl* (2) AL-4
Alpine (historical)—*locale* NC-3
Alpine Hose Company No. 2—*hist pl* CO-8
Alpine Institute (historical)—*school* TN-4
Alpine Junction—*locale* NY-2
Alpine Junction—*locale* OR-9
Alpine Junction—*locale* WY-8
*Alpine Lake* MT-8
Alpine Lake—*lake* AK-9
Alpine Lake—*lake* (3) CA-9
Alpine Lake—*lake* (3) ID-8
Alpine Lake—*lake* MN-6
Alpine Lake—*lake* (4) MT-8
Alpine Lake—*lake* OR-9
Alpine Lake—*lake* WY-8
Alpine Lake—*reservoir* CA-9
Alpine Lake—*reservoir* CO-8
Alpine Lake—*reservoir* PA-2
Alpine Lakes—*lake* MT-8
Alpine Lakes—*lake* WY-8
Alpine Log Ch—*church* IA-7
Alpine Lookout—*locale* NJ-2
Alpine Lookout—*locale* WA-9
Alpine Lookout Tower—*locale* AR-4
Alpine Meadow—*flat* CA-9
Alpine Meadows—*flat* CA-9
**Alpine Meadows Subdivision**—*pop pl* UT-8
Alpine Mill—*locale* NV-8
Alpine Mine—*mine* (2) CA-9
Alpine Mine—*mine* (2) CO-8
Alpine Mine—*mine* NV-8
*Alpine Mountain* AL-4
*Alpine Mountains* AL-4
Alpine Mountain (ski area)—*locale* PA-2
Alpine Mtn—*summit* TN-4
Alpine Park—*flat* MT-8
Alpine Park—*park* IL-6
Alpine Peak—*summit* CO-8
Alpine Peak—*summit* ID-8
Alpine Plateau—*summit* CO-8
Alpine Pond—*lake* UT-8
Alpine Pond Trail—*trail* UT-8
Alpine Post Office—*building* TN-4
Alpine Post Office (historical)—*building* MS-4
Alpine Ranch—*locale* CO-8
Alpine Ranch—*locale* NV-8
**Alpine Ranchettes Subdivision**—*pop pl* UT-8
**Alpine Ranchettes Subdivision Two**—*pop pl* UT-8
Alpine Ranger Station—*locale* AZ-5
Alpine Rec Area—*park* KY-4
*Alpine Reservoir* CO-8
Alpine Ridge—*ridge* OR-9
Alpine Sch—*school* (2) CA-9
Alpine Sch—*school* IL-6
Alpine Sch—*school* NJ-2
Alpine Sch—*school* UT-8
Alpine Sch (historical)—*school* TN-4
**Alpine Shores**—*pop pl* AL-4
Alpine Ski Club—*other* MI-6
Alpine Ski Trail—*trail* OR-9
Alpines Lakes—*reservoir* AL-4
*Alpine Spring* CA-9
Alpine Spring—*spring* ID-8
Alpine Spring—*spring* OR-9
Alpine Springs Park—*park* CA-9
Alpine Station—*locale* CA-9
Alpine Summer Sch (B Y U)—*school* UT-8
**Alpine Terrace**—*pop pl* OH-6
Alpine Timber Camp—*locale* AZ-5
Alpine Township—*civil* MO-7
**Alpine (Township of)**—*pop pl* MI-6
Alpine Trail—*trail* CO-8
Alpine Trail—*trail* ID-8
Alpine Trail—*trail* MT-8
Alpine Trail—*trail* OR-9
Alpine Union HS—*school* CA-9
Alpine View Point—*cape* TN-4
**Alpine Village**—*pop pl* CA-9
**Alpine Village**—*pop pl* NM-5
**Alpine Village**—*pop pl* VT-1
*Alpine Village (Ski Resort)* OH-6
Alpine Walk Peak—*summit* NV-8
Alp Lake—*lake* MN-6
Alp Lake—*lake* MT-8
**Alplaus**—*pop pl* NY-2
Alplaus Kill—*stream* NY-2
Alplaus Sch—*school* NY-2
Alpoca—*locale* WV-2
Alpowa Creek—*stream* WA-9
Alpowa Ridge—*ridge* WA-9
Alp Rock—*pillar* MT-8
Alps—*locale* GA-3
Alps—*locale* VA-3
**Alps**—*pop pl* NM-5
**Alps**—*pop pl* NY-2
Alps,the—*cliff* NY-2
Alps, The—*summit* VT-1
Alps Gulch—*valley* CO-8
Alps Hill—*summit* CO-8
Alps Mesa—*summit* NM-5
Alps Mine—*mine* MT-8
Alps Mtn—*summit* CO-8
Alps Road—*uninc pl* GA-3
Alps Road Park—*park* NJ-2
Alps Road Sch—*school* GA-3
Alps Road Sch—*school* NJ-2
Alpsville—*locale* PA-2
Alquatka Branch—*stream* NJ-2
**Alquina**—*pop pl* IN-6
Alquina Elem Sch—*school* IN-6
Alrad Canyon—*valley* UT-8
Al Raught Park—*park* WA-9
Alray—*locale* CA-9
Alread—*locale* AR-4
Alread Ch—*church* AR-4
Alread Hill—*summit* AR-4
*Alred* AL-4
**Alred**—*pop pl* AL-4
Al Reddin Dam—*dam* SD-7
Alred Hollow—*valley* MO-7
Alred Marina—*locale* AL-4
Alred Sch—*school* MO-7
Alreds Ranch—*locale* AZ-5
Alridge—*locale* (2) ID-8
*Alrnota Creek* WA-9
Al Rose Canyon—*valley* CA-9
Alruss Lake—*lake* MN-6
Alsace—*locale* CA-9
**Alsace Manor**—*pop pl* PA-2
**Alsace (Township of)**—*pop pl* PA-2
Alsachkee Day Sch—*school* FL-3
Al Sadie Ranch—*locale* ID-8
Alsap Butte—*summit* AZ-5
Al Sarena Buzzard Mine—*mine* OR-9
Alsate Creek—*stream* TX-5
Alsatia—*locale* LA-4
Alsa (Unino)—*locale* TX-5
*Alsboro* AL-4
**Alsco**—*pop pl* CA-9
Als Creek—*stream* MT-8
Alsdorf—*locale* TX-5
**Alsea**—*pop pl* OR-9
Alsea Bay—*bay* OR-9
Alsea Bay - North Bridgehead Wayside—*locale* OR-9
Alsea Cem—*cemetery* OR-9
Alsea Falls—*falls* OR-9
Alsea Falls Recreational Site—*park* OR-9
Alsea Guard Station—*locale* OR-9
Alsea Log Pond—*reservoir* OR-9
Alsea Mountain Roadside Rest Area—*locale* OR-9
*Alsea Peak* OR-9
Alsea Ranger Station—*locale* OR-9
Alsea River—*stream* OR-9
**Alsea Rivera**—*pop pl* OR-9
Alsea Summit—*summit* OR-9
Alsek Glacier—*glacier* AK-9
Alsek River—*stream* AK-9
Alsen—*locale* NY-2
Alsen—*locale* SD-7
**Alsen**—*pop pl* LA-4
**Alsen**—*pop pl* ND-7
Alsen Interchange—*crossing* SD-7
Alsen Oil Field—*oilfield* LA-4
Alsept Fork—*stream* KY-4
**Alsey**—*pop pl* IL-6
*Alseya* OR-9
*Alseya Bay* OR-9
*Alseya River* OR-9
Alsey (Election Precinct)—*fmr MCD* IL-6
Al Shinn Canyon—*valley* CA-9
Als Hollow—*valley* IN-6
Alside, Incorporated (Plant)—*facility* OH-6
Alsike Lake—*lake* MN-6
Alsile Ch—*church* KY-4
**Alsip**—*pop pl* IL-6
Alsip Rsvr—*reservoir* OR-9
*Alsip Woods* IL-6
Als Lake—*lake* AZ-5
Als Lake—*lake* MI-6
Als Lake—*reservoir* OH-6
Als Lake Tank—*reservoir* AZ-5
Als Landing Strip—*airport* NJ-2
Al Slides—*slope* CA-9
*Al Smith Gulch* CA-9
Al Smith Gulch—*valley* CA-9
Als Mtn—*summit* AK-9
*Alsobrook* AL-4
Alsobrook Cem—*cemetery* AL-4
Alsobrook Cem—*cemetery* TN-4
Alsobrook Ch (historical)—*church* AL-4
*Alsobrook Methodist Ch* AL-4
Alsobrook Sch (historical)—*school* AL-4
Alsobrook Slough—*gut* AR-4
Alson (historical)—*locale* SD-7
Alson Spring—*spring* NV-8
Alsop—*locale* VA-3
Alsop, Carroll, House—*hist pl* IA-7
Alsop Cem—*cemetery* MS-4
Alsop Corner—*locale* CT-1
Alsop Ditch No 1—*canal* WY-8
Alsop Ditch No 2—*canal* WY-8
Alsop Drift Mine (underground)—*mine* AL-4
Alsop Hollow—*valley* MO-7
Alsop House—*hist pl* CT-1
Alsop Lake—*lake* WY-8
Alsop Slough—*gut* WY-8
**Alspaugh**—*pop pl* NC-3
A L Spohn Elementary/MS—*school* IN-6
A L Spring—*spring* CO-8
A-L Spring—*spring* NM-5
Al Spring—*spring* WA-9
Als Run—*stream* VA-3
Alstaetter Cem—*cemetery* OH-6
**Alstead**—*pop pl* NH-1
**Alstead Center**—*pop pl* NH-1
Alstead Mine—*mine* MN-6
**Alstead (Town of)**—*pop pl* NH-1
*Alston* AL-4
*Alston* KS-7
Alston—*locale* OK-5
Alston—*locale* SC-3
**Alston**—*pop pl* GA-3
**Alston**—*pop pl* KY-4
**Alston**—*pop pl* MI-6
**Alston**—*pop pl* OR-9
Alston, Emanuel, House—*hist pl* SC-3
Alston Branch—*stream* DE-2
Alston Cem—*cemetery* LA-4
Alston Cem—*cemetery* MI-6
Alston Chapel—*church* (2) NC-3
Alston-Cobb House—*hist pl* AL-4
Alston Creek—*stream* SC-3
Alston-DeGraffenried House—*hist pl* NC-3
Alston Grove Ch—*church* NC-3
Alston House—*hist pl* NC-3
Alston House—*hist pl* SC-3
Alston Ranch—*locale* NM-5
Alston Sch—*school* SC-3
Alston Sch (historical)—*school* TN-4
Alstown—*locale* WA-9
*Alstrom Hollow* UT-8
*Alstrom Point* UT-8
Alstrom Point—*cape* UT-8
Alstrom Spring—*spring* MT-8
**Alsuma**—*pop pl* OK-5
Alsup Cem—*cemetery* TN-4
Alsup Cem—*cemetery* TX-5
Alsup Ch—*church* AR-4
Alsup Creek—*stream* MS-4
Alsup Creek—*stream* OR-9
Alsup Hollow—*valley* (2) TN-4
Alsup Mtn—*summit* OR-9
Alsup Sch—*school* CO-8
Alsups Pond—*reservoir* NC-3
Alsups Pond Dam—*dam* NC-3
Alsup Spring—*spring* OR-9
Alsville—*locale* SD-7
*Alta* KS-7
Alta—*locale* AL-4
Alta—*locale* MT-8
Alta—*locale* WV-2
Alta—*locale* WY-8
**Alta**—*pop pl* CA-9
**Alta**—*pop pl* CO-8
**Alta**—*pop pl* IL-6
**Alta**—*pop pl* IN-6
**Alta**—*pop pl* IA-7
**Alta**—*pop pl* KY-4
**Alta**—*pop pl* OH-6
**Alta**—*pop pl* UT-8
**Alta**—*pop pl* WV-2
Alta, Lake—*lake* CA-9
Alta, Lake—*lake* FL-3
Alta, Lake—*lake* OR-9
Alta, Loma—*summit* (3) TX-5
**Alta Acres Subdivision**—*pop pl* UT-8
Alta Brown Elem Sch—*school* KS-7
Alta Campground—*park* OR-9
Alta Canal—*canal* UT-8
Alta Canyon Baptist Ch—*church* UT-8
**Alta Canyon Village Subdivision**—*pop pl* UT-8
Alta Ch—*church* AL-4
Alta Ch—*church* ND-7
Alta City Cem—*cemetery* UT-8
Alta Coulee—*valley* WA-9
**Alta Cove at Willow Creek PUB Subdivision**—*pop pl* UT-8
Alta Creek—*stream* (2) ID-8
Alta Creek—*stream* NV-8
Alta Creek—*stream* WA-9
Alta Creek—*stream* WY-8
Alta Creek Basin—*basin* NV-8
**Altadena**—*pop pl* CA-9
Altadena Hosp—*hospital* CA-9
Altadena Lake—*reservoir* AL-4
Altadena Lodge—*building* CA-9
Altadena Park—*park* AZ-5
Altadena Sch—*school* CA-9
Altadena Town and Country Club—*other* CA-9
**Altadena Valley**—*pop pl* AL-4
Alta East Branch Canal—*canal* CA-9
Alta E Butler Sch—*school* AZ-5
**Altagracia**—*pop pl* PR-3
Alta Guard Station—*locale* UT-8
Alta Gulch—*valley* MT-8
Alta Heights Sch—*school* CA-9
**Alta Heights Subdivision**—*pop pl* (2) UT-8
**Alta Hill**—*pop pl* CA-9
Alta Hill Rsvr—*reservoir* CA-9
**Alta Hills Subdivision**—*pop pl* UT-8
Alta (historical)—*locale* (2) SD-7
*Al Tahoe* CA-9
**Al Tahoe**—*pop pl* CA-9
*Altahomak Creek* MS-4
Alta Hosp—*hospital* CA-9
Alta HS—*school* UT-8
Altai Hill—*summit* NH-1
**Altair**—*pop pl* KS-7
**Altair**—*pop pl* TX-5
Altaire Camp Grounds—*locale* WA-9
Altaire Ch—*church* MS-4
Alta Lake—*lake* CO-8
Alta Lake—*lake* NY-2
Alta Lake—*lake* WA-9
Alta Lake—*lake* WI-6
Alta Lake Rsvr—*reservoir* CO-8
Alta Lake State Park—*park* WA-9
Alta Lake Trail—*trail* OR-9
Alta la Pita Windmill—*locale* TX-5
*Alta Loma* TX-5
**Alta Loma**—*pop pl* CA-9
Alta Loma—*uninc pl* TX-5
Alta Loma Cem—*cemetery* TX-5
Alta Loma Ch—*church* TN-4
Alta Loma Elem Sch—*school* AZ-5
Alta Loma HS—*school* CA-9
Alta Loma Oil Field—*oilfield* TX-5
Alta Loma Sch—*school* (2) CA-9
Alta Loma Sch—*school* TX-5
Alta Loma Tank—*reservoir* TX-5
Altamaha—*locale* GA-3
Altamaha, Lake—*lake* FL-3
Altamaha Ch—*church* GA-3
**Altamaha Park**—*pop pl* GA-3
Altamaha Plantation—*locale* GA-3
Altamaha River—*stream* GA-3
Altamaha River (CCD)—*cens area* GA-3
Altamaha Sch—*school* (2) GA-3
Altamaha Sound—*bay* GA-3
Altamaha State Waterfowl Mngmt Area—*park* GA-3
**Altamahaw**—*pop pl* NC-3
Altamahaw Mill Office—*hist pl* NC-3
Altamahaw-Ossipee Sch—*school* NC-3
Alta Main Canal—*canal* CA-9
**Alta Manor**—*pop pl* PA-2
Altama Sch—*school* GA-3
Alta Meadow—*flat* CA-9
**Alta Mesa**—*pop pl* CA-9
**Alta Mesa**—*pop pl* TX-5
**Altamesa**—*pop pl* PR-3
Alta Mesa Camp—*locale* TX-5
Alta Mesa Cem—*cemetery* CA-9
Alta Mesa Community Hall—*locale* CA-9
Alta Mesa East Oil Field—*oilfield* TX-5
Alta Mesa Farm Bureau Hall—*hist pl* CA-9
Alta Mesa Gun Club—*other* CA-9
Alta Mesa Oil Field—*oilfield* TX-5
Alta Mesa Sch—*school* CA-9
Alta Mills—*locale* KS-7
*Altamine* SD-7
Alta Mine—*mine* AZ-5
Alta Mine—*mine* CA-9
Alta Mine—*mine* ID-8
Alta Mines—*mine* MT-8
**Altamira**—*pop pl* PR-3
Altamira Canyon—*valley* CA-9
**Alta Mira (subdivision)**—*pop pl* (2) AZ-5
*Altamitcha* AL-4
Altamont—*locale* MD-2
Altamont—*locale* WY-8
**Altamont**—*pop pl* CA-9
**Altamont**—*pop pl* (2) IL-6
**Altamont**—*pop pl* IN-6
**Altamont**—*pop pl* KS-7
**Altamont**—*pop pl* MO-7
**Altamont**—*pop pl* NY-2
**Altamont**—*pop pl* NC-3
**Altamont**—*pop pl* OH-6
**Altamont**—*pop pl* OR-9
**Altamont**—*pop pl* PA-2
**Altamont**—*pop pl* SD-7
**Altamont**—*pop pl* TN-4
**Altamont**—*pop pl* UT-8
Altamont, Lake—*lake* NY-2
Altamont Acad (historical)—*school* TN-4
Altamont Baptist Ch—*church* TN-4
Altamont Campground—*locale* UT-8
Altamont (CCD)—*cens area* TN-4
Altamont Cem—*cemetery* IA-7
Altamont Cem—*cemetery* (2) KS-7
Altamont Cem—*cemetery* TN-4
Altamont Ch—*church* IA-7
Altamont Creek—*stream* KY-4
Altamont Dam—*dam* KS-7
Altamont Division—*civil* TN-4
Altamonte Elem Sch—*school* FL-3
Altamonte Mall—*post sta* FL-3
**Altamonte Springs**—*pop pl* FL-3
Altamonte Springs Sch—*school* FL-3
Altamonte Springs Seventh Day Adventist Ch—*church* FL-3
**Altamont Hills**—*pop pl* OH-6
Altamont Hist Dist—*hist pl* NY-2
Altamont Hotel—*hist pl* WV-2
Altamont HS—*school* UT-8
Altamont Idle Hour Lake—*reservoir* KS-7
*Altamont Lake* SD-7
Altamont Lookout Tower—*locale* TN-4
Altamont Moraine—*range* IA-7
Altamont Moraine—*range* ND-7
Altamont-Mount Emmons Cem—*cemetery* UT-8
*Altamont Park* (2) OH-6
Altamont Park—*park* AL-4
**Altamont Park**—*pop pl* AL-4
Altamont Pass—*gap* CA-9
Altamont Post Office—*building* TN-4
Altamont Rsvr—*reservoir* IL-6
Altamont Rsvr—*reservoir* NY-2
Altamont Sch—*school* UT-8
Altamont Sch—*school* WV-2
Altamont Sch (historical)—*school* TN-4
Altamont Speedway—*other* CA-9
*Altamont Springs* FL-3
Altamont State Public Shooting Areas—*park* SD-7
**Altamont (subdivision)**—*pop pl* AL-4
**Altamont Switch**—*pop pl* IN-6
**Altamont (Town of)**—*pop pl* NY-2
**Altamont Township**—*pop pl* SD-7
Altamont (Township of)—*fmr MCD* NC-3
Altamont Tunnel—*tunnel* WY-8
Alta Morris Lake—*lake* CA-9
*Altamount* AZ-5
*Altamount* UT-8
Alta Mtn—*summit* MT-8
Alta Mtn—*summit* WA-9
Alta Pass—*gap* WA-9
**Altapass**—*pop pl* NC-3
Alta Peak—*summit* (2) CA-9
Alta Plaza—*park* CA-9
Alta Powerhouse—*other* CA-9
**Altara Heights Subdivision**—*pop pl* UT-8
Alta Ranger Station—*hist pl* MT-8
Altara Sch—*school* UT-8
Altar Creek—*stream* IN-6
Altar Hollow—*valley* MO-7
Altarie Ch—*church* MS-4
Altar Mesa—*summit* AZ-5
Altar of Sacrifice—*summit* UT-8
*Altar Of Sacrifice Temple* UT-8
Altar Rock—*summit* MA-1
Altar Temple—*church* GA-3
*Altar Valley* AZ-5
Altar Valley—*valley* AZ-5
*Altar Wash* AZ-5
Altar Wash—*stream* AZ-5
Alta Sch—*school* (2) CA-9
Alta Shaft—*mine* NV-8
Alta Sierra—*CDP* CA-9
**Alta Sierra**—*pop pl* CA-9
**Alta Sierra Estates**—*pop pl* CA-9
Alta Ski Area—*locale* UT-8
Alta Spring—*spring* AZ-5
*Alta Station* AL-4
Altata Mine—*mine* AZ-5
**Alta Township**—*pop pl* KS-7
**Alta Township**—*pop pl* ND-7
Alta Tunnel—*mine* UT-8
*Alta Valley* AZ-5
**Alta View Estates Subdivision**—*pop pl* UT-8
Alta View Hospital Heliport—*airport* UT-8
Alta View Sch—*school* UT-8
**Altavilla Estates Subdivision**—*pop pl* UT-8
**Altaville**—*pop pl* CA-9
Altaville Grammar Sch—*hist pl* CA-9
*Altavista* KS-7
Alta Vista—*locale* CO-8
Alta Vista—*locale* WA-9
**Alta Vista**—*pop pl* CA-9
**Alta Vista**—*pop pl* FL-3
**Alta Vista**—*pop pl* GA-3
**Alta Vista**—*pop pl* IA-7
**Alta Vista**—*pop pl* KS-7
**Alta Vista**—*pop pl* MD-2
**Alta Vista**—*pop pl* SC-3
**Alta Vista**—*pop pl* TN-4
**Altavista**—*pop pl* VA-3
**Altavista**—*pop pl* PR-3
Alta Vista Cem—*cemetery* GA-3
Alta Vista Cem—*cemetery* KS-7

Alta Vista Cem—cemetery MN-6
Alta Vista Ch—church FL-3
Alta Vista Ch—church MO-7
Alta Vista Ch—church TN-4
Alta Vista Cottage Sch—school CO-8
Altavista Country Club—other VA-3
Alta Vista Elem Sch—school FL-3
Alta Vista Elem Sch—school KS-7
**Alta Vista Gardens**—pop pl MD-2
Alta Vista Golf Club—other CA-9
Altavista Memorial Park—cemetery VA-3
Alta Vista Park—park TX-5
Alta Vista Ranch—locale TX-5
Alta Vista Reef—bar TX-5
Alta Vista Sch—school AZ-5
Alta Vista Sch—school (3) CA-9
Alta Vista Sch—school CO-8
Alta Vista Sch—school FL-3
Alta Vista Sch—school MD-2
Alta Vista Sch—school (2) TX-5
Altavista Sch—school WV-2
Alta Vista Sch—school WY-8
Alta Vista Sch (historical)—school MO-7
Alta Vista Shop Ctr—locale AZ-5
**Alta Vista (subdivision)**—pop pl (2) AL-4
**Alta Vista Subdivision**—pop pl (2) UT-8
**Alta Vista Subdivision #1**—pop pl UT-8
**Alta Vista Terrace**—pop pl MD-2
Alta Vista Terrace Hist Dist—hist pl IL-6
**Alta Vista (Township of)**—pop pl MN-6
Alta Vista Windmill—locale (2) TX-5
Alta Well Number 1—well NV-8
Alta West Clark Ditch—canal CA-9
Alta Windmill—locale TX-5
**Altawood Place Subdivision**—pop pl UT-8
Alta Woods Baptist Ch—church MS-4
Alta Woods Presbyterian Ch—church MS-4
**Altawood Subdivision**—pop pl UT-8
**Altawood Subdivision #3**—pop pl UT-8
Alta Woods United Methodist Ch—church MS-4
**Altay**—pop pl NY-2
**Altdorf**—pop pl WI-6
Al Tech County Park—park WI-6
Altemont UT-8
Altemont Mine—mine ID-8
Altenbern Ranch—locale CO-8
**Altenburg**—pop pl MO-7
Altenburg Corners—locale PA-2
Altenburg Hill—summit NV-8
Alten Ditch—canal IN-6
Altenheim Home—locale IL-6
**Altenwald**—pop pl PA-2
Altera Landing (historical)—locale MS-4
Alteration Creek—stream AK-9
Altermatt Lake—lake MN-6
Altermatt Park—park MI-6
Alternative Education Center—school FL-3
Altern Site—hist pl WI-6
Alterton Station (historical)—building PA-2
Altgeld Gardens IL-6
**Altgeld Gardens**—pop pl IL-6
Altgeld Hall, Univ of Illinois—hist pl IL-6
Altgeld Park—park IL-6
Altgeld Sch—school IL-6
**Altha**—pop pl FL-3
Altha (CCD)—cens area FL-3
Altha Grove Ch—church VA-3
Altha Lake—lake CA-9
Altha Public Sch—school FL-3
Althea AL-4
Althea Lake—lake MA-1
Althea Spring—spring MO-7
**Altheim**—pop pl MO-7
**Altheimer**—pop pl AR-4
Althoff HS—school IL-6
**Althom**—pop pl PA-2
Althom Eddy—bay PA-2
Althorp Peninsula—cape AK-9
**Althouse**—pop pl PA-2
Althouse Creek—stream OR-9
**Althouse (historical)**—pop pl OR-9
Althouse Mtn—summit OR-9
Althouse Point—cape AK-9
Althouse Slough—stream OR-9
Althouse Trail—trail OR-9
Althrop, Mount—summit AK-9
Althrop Rock Light—locale AK-9
Altice Cem—cemetery VA-3
Alticrest Post Office (historical)—building TN-4
Alticrest Sch—school TN-4
Altic Sch—school IL-6
Altiers Lake—reservoir OH-6
Altig Bridge—other IL-6
Altiliu FM-9
Altimori Ranch—locale CA-9
Altis Cem—cemetery MO-7
Altison Ranch (historical)—locale SD-7
Altita Creek—stream TX-5
Altitude—locale OH-6
**Altitude**—pop pl MS-4
Altitude Mine—mine NV-8
Altitude Ranch—locale CO-8
Altizer—locale WV-2
Altizer Cem—cemetery VA-3
Altizer Hollow—valley TN-4
Altizer Sch—school WV-2
Altkin Gap—gap PA-2
Altland Ch—church PA-2
Altman—locale CO-8
**Altman**—pop pl GA-3
**Altman**—pop pl PA-2
Altman Branch—stream SC-3
Altman Cem—cemetery GA-3
Altman Cem—cemetery IA-7
Altman Cem—cemetery TX-5
Altman Cem—cemetery WV-2
Altman Dam—dam CO-8
Altman House—hist pl AR-4
Altman Lake—lake MI-6
Altman Lake—lake WI-6
Altman Pond—lake GA-3
Altman Pond—lake SC-3
Altman Rsvr—reservoir CO-8
Altman Run PA-2
Altmans Bay—swamp FL-3
Altmans Corners—locale PA-2
Altmans Run PA-2
Altman Windmill—locale CO-8
Altmar—locale IL-6
**Altmar**—pop pl NY-2
Altmont PA-2
Altner Lake—lake MN-6
Altngot Durchfahrt PW-9
Altngot Einfahrt PW-9
Altngot Passage PW-9
Altnow Dam—dam OR-9
Altnow Ditch—canal OR-9
Altnow Gap—gap OR-9
Altnow Gap Rsvr—reservoir OR-9
Altnow Lake—lake MN-6
Altnow Ranch—locale OR-9
Altnow Rsvr—reservoir OR-9
Altnow Spring—spring (2) OR-9
Alto AL-4
Alto AZ-5
Alto MS-4
Alto—locale AZ-5
Alto—locale NM-5
Alto—locale SD-7
Alto—locale VA-3
Alto—locale WA-9
**Alto**—pop pl AR-4
**Alto**—pop pl CA-9
**Alto**—pop pl GA-3
**Alto**—pop pl IN-6
**Alto**—pop pl LA-4
**Alto**—pop pl MI-6
**Alto**—pop pl TN-4
**Alto**—pop pl TX-5
**Alto**—pop pl WI-6
Alto, Cerro—summit (2) CA-9
Alto, Lake—lake FL-3
Alto, Mount—summit GA-3
Alto, Mount—summit VA-3
Alto Blanco Windmill—locale TX-5
Alto Bonito—locale TX-5
Alto Bonito Well—well (2) TX-5
Alto Bonito Well (Flowing)—well TX-5
Alto Bonito Windmill—locale (3) TX-5
Alto Branch—stream TX-5
Alto (CCD)—cens area TX-5
Alto Cem—cemetery TN-4
Alto Colorado—locale TX-5
Alto Colorado Ranch—locale TX-5
Alto Colorado Well—well TX-5
Alto Creek—stream WI-6
Alto Creek, Rito—stream CO-8
**Alto Crest**—pop pl NM-5
Alto de Hormiga—summit NM-5
Alto de la Bandera—summit PR-3
Alto de la Cruz—summit TX-5
Alto Del Burro Windmill—locale TX-5
Alto del Descanso—summit PR-3
Altoff Sch—school MI-6
Alto Frio Encampment—locale TX-5
**Altoga**—pop pl TX-5
**Alto Grandview Acres**—pop pl PA-2
Alto Group—mine AZ-5
Alto Gulch—valley AZ-5
Alto Hill—summit AZ-5
Alto (historical)—locale SD-7
Altohy Lake WI-6
Altoi Island PW-9
Alto Las Ovejas—summit PR-3
Alto Loma TX-5
Altoman's Run PA-2
Altom Branch—stream (2) TN-4
Altom Cem—cemetery TN-4
Alto Mine—mine AZ-5
Alto Mine—mine CA-9
Alto Mtn GA-3
Alton ND-7
Alton PA-2
Alton—locale FL-3
Alton—locale ID-8
Alton—locale MI-6
Alton—locale ND-7
**Alton**—pop pl AL-4
**Alton**—pop pl CA-9
**Alton**—pop pl IL-6
**Alton**—pop pl IN-6
**Alton**—pop pl IA-7
**Alton**—pop pl KS-7
**Alton**—pop pl (2) KY-4
**Alton**—pop pl LA-4
**Alton**—pop pl ME-1
**Alton**—pop pl MI-6
**Alton**—pop pl MO-7
**Alton**—pop pl NH-1
**Alton**—pop pl NY-2
**Alton**—pop pl NC-3
**Alton**—pop pl OH-6
**Alton**—pop pl PA-2
**Alton**—pop pl RI-1
**Alton**—pop pl TX-5
**Alton**—pop pl UT-8
**Alton**—pop pl VA-3
**Alton**—pop pl WV-2
Alton, Mount—summit NY-2
Altona PA-2
Altona UT-8
Altona—locale CO-8
Altona—locale KY-4
Altona—locale NE-7
Altona—locale OK-5
**Altona**—pop pl IL-6
**Altona**—pop pl IN-6
**Altona**—pop pl MI-6
**Altona**—pop pl MO-7
**Altona**—pop pl (2) NY-2
**Altona**—pop pl (2) VI-3
Altona Cem—cemetery MI-6
Altona Cemetery UT-8
Altona Central Sch—school NY-2
Altona Grange—locale CO-8
**Altonah**—pop pl PA-2
**Altonah**—pop pl UT-8
Altonah Cem—cemetery PA-2
Altonah Cem—cemetery UT-8
Altona Lagoon—bay VI-3
Alton Amphitheater—basin UT-8
Altona State Wildlife Mngmt Area—park MN-6
**Altona (Town of)**—pop pl NY-2
**Altona (Township of)**—pop pl MN-6
Alton Bay—bay NH-1
**Alton Bay**—pop pl NH-1
Alton Bay RR Station—hist pl NH-1
Alton Bench—bench MT-8
Alton Bog—swamp ME-1
Alton Brake—swamp LA-4
Alton Cem—cemetery FL-3
Alton Cem—cemetery IN-6
Alton Cem—cemetery KS-7
Alton Cem—cemetery ME-1
Alton Cem—cemetery OH-6
Alton Cem—cemetery UT-8
Alton Cem—cemetery WV-2
Alton Ch—church KY-4
Alton Ch—church ME-1
Alton Chapter House—hist pl IL-6
Alton Drain—canal MI-6
Alton Elem Sch—school KS-7
Alton Elem Sch (historical)—school AL-4
Altoner IN-6
Alton-Hall Sch—school OH-6
Alton Heights Lookout Tower—locale MN-6
**Alton Hill**—pop pl TN-4
Alton Hill—summit OR-9
Alton Hill Post Office (historical)—building TN-4
**Alton Hospital**—pop pl IL-6
Alton Lake—lake FL-3
Alton Lake—lake MN-6
Alton Lake—reservoir AL-4
Alton Lake—reservoir MO-7
Alton Memorial Hosp—hospital IL-6
Alton Military Prison Site—hist pl IL-6
Alton Mine—mine MT-8
Alton Municipal Golf Course—other IL-6
**Alton North East**—pop pl IL-6
Alton-Osborne JHS—school KS-7
**Alton Park**—pop pl TN-4
Alton Park Ch—church TN-4
Alton Park Ch of Christ—church TN-4
Alton Park JHS—school TN-4
Altonpark Post Office (historical)—building TN-4
**Alton Park (subdivision)**—pop pl PA-2
Alton Plaza—locale MO-7
Alton Pond—lake RI-1
Alton Pond—reservoir RI-1
Alton Pond Dam—dam RI-1
Alton Post Office (historical)—building TN-4
Alton Roberts Cem—cemetery MS-4
Alton Sch—school IA-7
Alton Sch—school MO-7
Alton Siding IL-6
Altons Landing—locale MS-4
Alton Slough—gut MO-7
Alton State Hosp—hospital IL-6
**Alton Station**—pop pl (2) KY-4
Alton Stogner Lake Dam—dam MS-4
Alton Thompson Dam—dam NC-3
**Alton (Town of)**—pop pl NH-1
**Alton Township**—pop pl SD-7
**Alton (Township of)**—pop pl IL-6
**Alton (Township of)**—pop pl MN-6
Alton Tunnel—mine CO-8
**Altonville**—pop pl TN-4
Al-Tony Lake WI-6
Altoona SD-7
Altoona—locale LA-4
Altoona—locale OH-6
**Altoona**—pop pl AL-4
**Altoona**—pop pl FL-3
**Altoona**—pop pl IA-7
**Altoona**—pop pl KS-7
**Altoona**—pop pl PA-2
**Altoona**—pop pl WA-9
**Altoona**—pop pl WI-6
Altoona, Lake—reservoir PA-2
Altoona Area HS—school PA-2
Altoona-Blair County Airp—airport PA-2
Altoona Branch—stream VA-3
Altoona (CCD)—cens area AL-4
Altoona Cem—cemetery AL-4
Altoona Cem—cemetery IA-7
Altoona Cem—cemetery SD-7
Altoona City—civil PA-2
Altoona Coal Mines (underground)—mine AL-4
Altoona Division—civil AL-4
Altoona Elem Sch—school FL-3
Altoona Hill—summit WA-9
Altoona Lake—reservoir WI-6
Altoona Lakes—lake MT-8
Altoona Lower Number Two Dam—dam PA-2
Altoona Mine—mine CA-9
Altoona Mountain—ridge AL-4
Altoona Park—park WI-6
**Altoona Township**—pop pl SD-7
Altoona-Walnut Grove Cem—cemetery AL-4
**Alto Park**—pop pl GA-3
Alto Park Sch—school GA-3
**Alto Pass**—pop pl IL-6
Alto Pass (Election Precinct)—fmr MCD IL-6
Alto Post Office (historical)—building MS-4
Alto Post Office (historical)—building TN-4
**Altor**—pop pl PA-2
Alto Relex—cliff TX-5
Alto Rest Park—park PA-2
**Altorf**—pop pl IL-6
Altorf Sch—school IL-6
Alto Rsvr—reservoir NM-5
Altory KS-7
**Altory Township**—pop pl KS-7
Alto Sano (Barrio)—fmr MCD (2) PR-3
Alto Sch—school CA-9
Alto Sch (historical)—school TN-4
Alto Schumaker Tank—reservoir AZ-5
Altos de la Mesa—range PR-3
Altos Del Mar Park FL-3
Altos de San Luis—range PR-3
Altos Prietos Artesian Well—well TX-5
Alto Spring—spring (2) AZ-5
Alto Spring—spring ID-8
Alto Spring—spring NM-5
Alto Springs—locale TX-5
Altos Windmill—locale TX-5
Alto Tank—reservoir TX-5
**Alto (Town of)**—pop pl WI-6
**Alto Township**—pop pl SD-7
Alto Township Hall—building SD-7
**Alto (Township of)**—pop pl IL-6
Alto Verde Windmill—locale TX-5
Alto Vista Camp—locale TX-5
Alto Vista Tank—reservoir TX-5
Alto Well—well (3) NM-5
Alto Windmill—locale (7) TX-5
**Altro**—pop pl KY-4
Altro (historical)—locale PA-2
Altro Park—park NY-2
Altro Sch—school KY-4
Altruria Post Office (historical)—building SD-7
Altruria School (historical)—building SD-7
Alt Sch—school MO-7
**Altschul**—pop pl FL-3
Altschul RR Station—locale FL-3
Al Tse Toh—spring AZ-5
Altuda—locale TX-5
Altuda Mine—mine CA-9
Altum Cem—cemetery TN-4
Altura CO-8
Altura—locale CO-8
**Altura**—pop pl CO-8
**Altura**—pop pl MN-6
**Altura**—pop pl NJ-2
**Altura**—pop pl PR-3
Altura Annex—post sta CO-8
Altura Blvd Sch—school CO-8
Altura Park—park NM-5
**Alturas**—pop pl CA-9
**Alturas**—pop pl FL-3
Alturas (CCD)—cens area CA-9
Alturas Elem Sch—school FL-3
Alturas Gulch—valley ID-8
Alturas Inlet Campground—locale ID-8
Alturas Lake—lake ID-8
Alturas Lake Creek—stream ID-8
Alturas Number One Mtn—summit MT-8
Alturas Number Two Mtn—summit MT-8
**Alturas Rancheria (Indian Reservation)**—pop pl CA-9
Altur Rock MA-1
Altus—locale MS-4
Altus—locale UT-8
Altus—locale WY-8
**Altus**—pop pl AR-4
**Altus**—pop pl OK-5
Altus, Lake—reservoir OK-5
Altus Air Force Base—military OK-5
Altus Canal—canal OK-5
Altus (CCD)—cens area OK-5
Altus Cem—cemetery OK-5
Altus Dam—dam OK-5
Altus Lake OK-5
Altus-Lugert Lake OK-5
Altus Reservoir OK-5
Altus South (CCD)—cens area OK-5
**Altvan**—pop pl WY-8
Altyn Peak—summit MT-8
Altz Cem—cemetery WV-2
AL-T31/v.1/p.164 AL-4
Aluakpak—hist pl AK-9
Aluck, Dolph, Smokehouse—hist pl KY-4
Aluea HI-9
Aluea Rock HI-9
Aluea Rocks—island HI-9
Alu Insel MP-9
Alu Island—island MP-9
Aluklik Bay—bay AK-9
Alum—locale TX-5
**Aluma**—pop pl ID-8
Aluma, Lake—reservoir OK-5
Alumax Plant—facility SC-3
**Alum Bank**—pop pl PA-2
Alum-Bank Cem—cemetery WV-2
Alum Bank (corporate name Pleasantville) PA-2
Alum Bank Post Office PA-2
Alumbank Post Office (historical)—building PA-2
Alumbaugh—locale KY-4
Alumbaugh Cem—cemetery MO-7
Alumbed Hollow—valley UT-8
Alum Bed Rapids—rapids OR-9
Alum Bluff—cliff FL-3
Alum Bluff—cliff OK-5
Alum Branch—stream (5) TX-5
**Alum Bridge**—pop pl WV-2
Alum Camp—locale NM-5
Alum Canyon UT-8
Alum Canyon—valley AZ-5
Alum Canyon—valley NM-5
Alum Cave—cave AL-4
Alum Cave—cave AR-4
Alum Cave—cave (3) TN-4
Alum Cave Branch—stream (3) KY-4
Alum Cave Canyon—valley AR-4
Alum Cave Creek—stream KY-4
Alum Cave Creek—stream TN-4
Alum Cave Hollow—valley AL-4
Alum Cave Hollow—valley IN-6
Alum Cave Hollow—valley KY-4
Alum Cave Hollow—valley (2) TN-4
Alum Cave Run—stream WV-2
Alum Cliff—cliff OH-6
Alum Cove—valley TN-4
Alum Cove—valley UT-8
Alum Cove Creek TN-4
Alum Creek KS-7
Alum Creek SD-7
Alum Creek WY-8
Alum Creek—locale TX-5
Alum Creek—locale WV-2
Alum Creek—stream AZ-5
Alum Creek—stream CA-9
Alum Creek—stream CO-8
Alum Creek—stream KS-7
Alum Creek—stream KY-4
Alum Creek—stream (3) NV-8
Alum Creek—stream OH-6
Alum Creek—stream SD-7
Alum Creek—stream TN-4
Alum Creek—stream (6) TX-5
Alum Creek—stream VA-3
Alum Creek—stream (2) WV-2
Alum Creek—stream (4) WY-8
Alum Creek Arlington Park—park OH-6
Alum Creek Ch—church OH-6
Alum Creek Lake—reservoir OH-6
Alum Creek Rsvr OH-6
Alum Creek Sch—school WV-2
Alum Creek Station KS-7
Alum Crest Sch—school OH-6
Alum Dirt Branch—stream KY-4
Alum Fork—stream AR-4
Alum Fork—stream (4) WV-2
Alum Fork Saline River—stream AR-4
Alum Gap—gap TN-4
Alum Gulch—valley AZ-5
Alum Gulch—valley CO-8
Alum Gulch—valley ID-8
Alum Hill—summit KY-4
Alum Hill—summit MA-1
Alum Hollow—valley KY-4
Alum Hollow—valley VA-3
Aluminum Company of America (Warwick Works)—facility IN-6
Aluminum Pond—lake NY-2
Aluminum Tank—reservoir NM-5
Alum Knob—summit (2) NC-3
Alum Lick Branch—stream TN-4
Alum Lick Creek—stream KY-4
Alum Lick Fork—stream KY-4
Alum Lick Sch—school KY-4
Alum Mine—mine NV-8
Alum Mountain WV-2
Alum Mtn—summit NM-5
Alumni Field—locale MA-1
Alumni Field Park—park MA-1
Alumni Hall—hist pl IA-7
Alumni Hall—hist pl NY-2
Alumni Memorial Sch—school MI-6
Alum Pond—lake TX-5
Alum Pond—reservoir MA-1
Alum Pond Dam—dam MA-1
Alum Pond Mountain MA-1
Alum Ridge—locale VA-3
Alum Ridge—ridge NC-3
Alum Ridge Ch—church VA-3
Alum Ridge (Magisterial District)—fmr MCD VA-3
Alum Rock—island ME-1
Alum Rock—pillar CA-9
Alum Rock—pillar OH-6
**Alum Rock**—pop pl CA-9
**Alum Rock**—pop pl PA-2
Alum Rock—summit CA-9
Alum Rock—summit PA-2
Alum Rock—summit VA-3
Alum Rock Branch—stream KY-4
Alum Rock Branch—stream WV-2
Alum Rock Canyon—valley CA-9
Alum Rock Hollow—valley WV-2
Alum Rock Park—park CA-9
Alum Rock Post Office (historical)—building PA-2
**Alum Rock (Richmond)**—pop pl PA-2
Alum Rock Ridge—ridge KY-4
Alum Rock Run—stream PA-2
Alumrock Run—stream WV-2
Alum Run PA-2
Alum Run—stream (2) OH-6
Alum Run—stream VA-3
Alum Run Creek OH-6
Alums Park—park OH-6
Alum Spring—spring (3) CO-8
Alum Spring—spring NV-8
Alum Spring—spring NM-5
Alum Spring Hollow—valley VA-3
Alum Springs—locale KY-4
Alum Springs—locale VA-3
Alum Springs Ch—church NC-3
Alum Springs Ch—church VA-3
Alum Spring Sch—school KY-4
Alum Well TN-4
**Alumwell**—pop pl TN-4
Alum Well—well NV-8
Alumwell Acad (historical)—school TN-4
Alum Well Post Office TN-4
Alumwell Post Office (historical)—building TN-4
Alum Wells—locale VA-3
**Alunite**—pop pl UT-8
Alunite Mine—mine NV-8
Alunite Ridge—ridge UT-8
Alunite (site)—locale NV-8
Alupat Island—island GU-9
**Aluta**—pop pl PA-2
Alutom, Mount—summit GU-9
Alutom Island—island GU-9
Alutunitok Hills—summit AK-9
Alva KS-7
Alva—locale WY-8
**Alva**—pop pl FL-3
**Alva**—pop pl KY-4
**Alva**—pop pl MS-4
**Alva**—pop pl MO-7
**Alva**—pop pl OK-5
Alva, Cape—cape WA-9
Alva, Lake—lake MT-8
Alva, Lake—lake WI-6
Alva Armory—hist pl OK-5
Alva B Adams Tunnel—tunnel CO-8
Alva (CCD)—cens area KY-4
Alva (CCD)—cens area OK-5
Alva Chapel—church AL-4
Alva Country Club—other OK-5
Alvada—locale OH-6
Alva Davidson Pond—lake FL-3
**Alvadore**—pop pl OR-9
Alva Elem Sch—school FL-3
Alva Lake—lake WI-6
Alva MS—school FL-3
Alva Municipal Cem—cemetery OK-5
Alvan IL-6
Alvan—locale PA-2
Alva Paul Creek—stream CA-9
Alva Post Office (historical)—building MS-4
Alvarado—locale NM-5
Alvarado—locale VA-3
**Alvarado**—pop pl IN-6
**Alvarado**—pop pl MN-6
**Alvarado**—pop pl TX-5
Alvarado—uninc pl CA-9
Alvarado Canyon—valley CA-9
Alvarado (CCD)—cens area TX-5
Alvarado Cem—cemetery TX-5
Alvarado Creek—stream CO-8
Alvarado Hot Springs—spring CA-9
Alvarado Mine—mine (2) UT-8
Alvarado Park—park CA-9
Alvarado Park—park NM-5
Alvarado Picnic Ground—locale CO-8
Alvarado Sch—school (4) CA-9
Alvarado Sch—school NM-5
Alvarado Tank No 1—reservoir NM-5
Alvarado Tank No 2—reservoir NM-5
Alvarado Terrace Hist Dist—hist pl CA-9
Alvarea Ranch—locale NV-8
Alvares Ferry (historical)—locale AL-4
Alvarez Bridge—bridge AL-4
Alvarez Mountains—range AZ-5
Alvarez Sch—school TX-5
Alva Shelly Rsvr—reservoir AZ-5
Alva Smith Tanks—reservoir NM-5
Alvas Tank—reservoir NM-5
Alvater Corner—locale NJ-2
**Alvaton**—pop pl GA-3
**Alvaton**—pop pl KY-4
Alvaton Sch—school KY-4
Alveda OH-6
Alveda (RR name for Alvada)—other OH-6
**Alverda**—pop pl PA-2
Alverjones Lake—lake CO-8
Alverna Creek—stream IN-6
Alvernia HS—school IL-6
Alvernia Rest Home—building OH-6
Alverno—locale MI-6
Alverno—locale WI-6
Alverno Coll—school WI-6
Alverno Heights Acad—school CA-9
Alvernon Park—park AZ-5
Alvern Pond—reservoir PA-2
Alverson—locale NY-2
Alverson, Mount—summit MT-8
Alverson Ch—church AL-4
Alverson Grove Ch—church SC-3
Alverson Plantation MS-4
Alverstone, Mount—summit AK-9
Alverstone Glacier—glacier AK-9
Alverthorpe Park—park PA-2
**Alverton**—pop pl PA-2
Alverton Sch—school PA-2
Alvery Junction—locale TX-5
Alvey Substation—locale OR-9
Alvey Wash—valley UT-8
Alvia Chase Rsvr—reservoir CT-1
Alvie Ch AL-4
Alvie Cole Ranch—locale TX-5
Alvie Short Hollow—valley KY-4
Alvig Slough—lake MN-6
Alville Cemetery OR-9
Alvin NE-7
Alvin MP-9
Alvin—locale CO-8
Alvin—locale GA-3
Alvin—locale MI-6
**Alvin**—pop pl IL-6
**Alvin**—pop pl KY-4
**Alvin**—pop pl SC-3
**Alvin**—pop pl TX-5
**Alvin**—pop pl WI-6
Alvin, Lake—lake MN-6
Alvin, Lake—reservoir SD-7
Alvina Sch—school CA-9
Alvin Ave Sch—school CA-9
Alvin Bay—bay AK-9
Alvin Branch—stream TN-4
Alvin Branch Workings—mine TN-4
Alvin Callender (New Orleans Naval Air Station)—other LA-4
Alvin Clark (schooner)—hist pl MI-6
Alvin Creek—stream OR-9
Alvin Creek—stream WI-6
Alvin C York Bridge—bridge TN-4
Alvin C York Institute—school TN-4
Alvin Dam—dam SD-7
Alvin Fiske Dam MA-1
Alvin Gulch—valley ID-8
Alvin Hohrman Dam—dam SD-7
Alvin Lake—lake MN-6
Alvin Meadows—flat CA-9
Alvin Mixon Dam—dam AL-4
Alvin Mixon Lake—reservoir AL-4
Alvin-Pearland (CCD)—cens area TX-5
Alvin Point—cape DE-2
Alvin R Bush Reservoir PA-2
Alvins Well—well ID-8
**Alvin (Town of)**—pop pl WI-6
Alvin Wirtz Dam—dam TX-5
Alvin Wirtz Park—park TX-5
Alvira PA-2
**Alvira (historical)**—pop pl PA-2
Alvirez Field—flat CA-9
Alvirne HS—school NH-1
Alvis, James, House—hist pl ID-8
Alvisa Canyon—valley CA-9
Alvis Branch—stream AL-4
Alvis Chapel—church VA-3
Alvis Creek—stream MN-6
Alvise Canyon CA-9
**Alviso**—pop pl CA-9
Alviso Hist Dist—hist pl CA-9
Alviso Ridge—ridge CA-9
Alviso Sch—school CA-9
Alviso Slough—gut CA-9
Alvis Sch—school NM-5
**Al Vita Park Subdivision**—pop pl UT-8
**Al Vi Village Subdivision**—pop pl UT-8
**Alvo**—pop pl NE-7
Alvo Cem—cemetery NE-7
**Alvon**—pop pl WV-2
Alvorado Cem—cemetery CO-8
**Alvord**—pop pl IA-7
**Alvord**—pop pl TX-5
**Alvord**—pop pl WV-2
Alvord Beach—beach CT-1
Alvord (CCD)—cens area TX-5
Alvord Creek OR-9
Alvord Creek—stream OR-9
Alvord Desert—plain OR-9
Alvord Hot Springs—spring OR-9
Alvord House—hist pl NY-2
Alvord Lake—lake OR-9
Alvord Mine—mine CA-9
Alvord Mtn CA-9
Alvord Mtn—summit CA-9
Alvord Oil Field—oilfield TX-5
Alvord Park—park AZ-5
Alvord Peak—summit CA-9
Alvord Peak—summit OR-9
Alvord Sch—school CA-9
Alvord Southeast Bryson Oil Field—oilfield TX-5
**Alvordton**—pop pl OH-6
Alvord Valley—valley OR-9
Alvord Well—well CA-9
Alvord Wildlife Sanctuary—locale NH-1
Alvstad State Wildlife Mngmt Area—park MN-6

**Alvwood**—pop pl ... MN-6
**Alvwood (Township of)**—pop pl ... MN-6
**Alvy**—pop pl ... WV-2
Alvy Creek—stream ... VA-3
Alward Creek—stream ... MI-6
Alward Farmhouse—hist pl ... NJ-2
Alward Lake—lake ... MI-6
Alward Lake Cem—cemetery ... MI-6
Alward Lake Drain—canal ... MI-6
Alward Sch—school ... MI-6
Alwardt Drain—stream ... MI-6
Al White Marsh—swamp ... MD-2
Alwilda (historical)—locale ... SD-7
Al Williams Ridge—ridge ... WA-9
Alwine Civic Center—building ... PA-2
**Alwinn**—pop pl ... OK-5
Alwive Pond ... NY-2
Alwood Cem—cemetery ... MO-7
Alwood HS—school ... IL-6
Alwood JHS—school ... IL-6
Alwood Post Office ... NC-3
Alwood Post Office—locale ... NC-3
Alwood Sch—school ... MI-6
Alworth—locale ... IL-6
Alworth Hill—summit ... CT-1
Alworth Lake—lake ... MN-6
Al Wright Hollow—valley ... PA-2
Alwyn Court Apartments—hist pl ... NY-2
**Aly**—pop pl ... AR-4
Alyasu Reef—bar ... PW-9
Aly Cem—cemetery ... MO-7
**Alyeska**—pop pl ... AK-9
Alyeska, Mount—summit ... AK-9
Alys Drive Sch—school ... NY-2
**Alzada**—pop pl ... MT-8
Alzona Park ... AZ-5
**Ama**—pop pl ... LA-4
Amabel—locale ... OK-5
Amabilis Mtn—summit ... WA-9
Amacarisse ... FL-3
Amachang—locale ... FM-9
Amache Cem—cemetery ... CO-8
Amacher County Park—park ... OR-9
Amacher Hollow—valley ... WI-6
Amacher Strip Airp—airport ... TN-4
Amacker Cem—cemetery ... LA-4
Amacker Ch (historical)—church ... MS-4
Amacker Tippett Oil Field—oilfield ... TX-5
Amacoy Lake—lake ... WI-6
Amada Tank—reservoir ... AZ-5
Amaden Ditch—canal ... OH-6
Amadens Creek—stream ... AK-9
Amader ... KS-7
Amadjang ... FM-9
**Amado**—pop pl ... AZ-5
Amado Mine—mine ... AZ-5
Amadon Pond—lake ... MI-6
Amador ... CA-9
Amador—locale ... NV-8
**Amador**—pop pl ... MI-6
Amador Canal—canal ... CA-9
Amador Canyon—valley ... NV-8
**Amador City**—pop pl ... CA-9
**Amador City (Amador)**—pop pl ... CA-9
Amador Columbia Mine—mine ... CA-9
**Amador (County)**—pop pl ... CA-9
Amador County Hosp Bldg—hist pl ... CA-9
Amador County HS—school ... CA-9
Amador Creek—stream ... CA-9
Amador Creek—stream ... NM-5
Amadore—locale ... MI-6
Amador (historical)—locale ... KS-7
Amador Lake—lake ... NM-5
Amador Mine—mine ... CA-9
Amador Mine—mine ... MT-8
Amador Queen Mine—mine ... CA-9
**Amador (Township of)**—pop pl ... MN-6
Amador Valley ... CA-9
Amador Valley—valley ... CA-9
Amador Valley HS—school ... CA-9
Amado Well—well (2) ... AZ-5
Amado Windmill—locale ... NM-5
**Amagansett**—pop pl ... NY-2
Amagansett Beach—beach ... NY-2
Amagansett Gun Club—other ... NY-2
Amagat Island—island ... AK-9
Amagoalik Creek—stream ... AK-9
**Amagon**—pop pl ... AR-4
Amah Lee, Lake—reservoir ... GA-3
Amaile Ridge—ridge ... AS-9
Amaile Stream—stream ... AS-9
Amakatatee Creek—stream ... AK-9
Amakdedori Creek—stream ... AK-9
Amakdedori (Site)—locale ... AK-9
Amakdedulia Cove—bay ... AK-9
Amaker Pond—reservoir ... SC-3
Amak Island—island ... AK-9
Amaknak Island—island ... AK-9
Amakomanak Creek—stream ... AK-9
Amaktukvik Pass—gap ... AK-9
Amaktusak Creek—stream ... AK-9
Amakuk Arm—bay ... AK-9
Amaladeros Creek—stream ... TX-5
Amalakell ... PW-9
Amalaquel ... PW-9
Amalau—locale ... AS-9
Amalga—locale ... ID-8
**Amalga**—pop pl ... UT-8
Amalga Branch West Cache Canal—canal ... UT-8
Amalga Harbor—bay ... AK-9
Amalgam ... MH-9
Amalgamated Mine—mine ... OR-9
**Amalia**—pop pl ... NM-5
Amalia Mine—mine ... CA-9
Amalia Sch—school ... NM-5
Amalie Mine—mine ... CA-9
Amalik Bay—bay ... AK-9
Amallakell Harbor ... PW-9
**Amaluia**—pop pl ... AS-9
Amalu Stream—stream ... HI-9
**Amana**—pop pl ... IA-7
**Amanave**—pop pl ... AS-9
Amanave Bay—bay ... AS-9
Amana Villages—hist pl ... IA-7
Amanca—locale ... AR-4
Aman Cem—cemetery ... SD-7
Aman Creek—stream ... AK-9
Amanda—locale ... TX-5
Amanda—other ... OH-6
**Amanda**—pop pl ... OH-6
**Amanda**—pop pl ... TN-4
Amanda, Lake—reservoir ... AR-4
Amanda, Lake—reservoir ... OH-6
**Amanda Acres Subdivision**—pop pl ... UT-8
Amanda Bingham Park ... AL-4
Amanda Cem—cemetery ... OH-6
Amanda Ch—church ... OH-6
Amanda Chapel—church ... MS-4
Amanda Clear Creek Sch—school ... OH-6
Amanda Cooley Branch—stream ... KY-4
Amanda Elzy School ... MS-4
Amanda E Stout Sch—school ... PA-2
Amanda Gulch—valley ... AZ-5
Amanda JHS—school ... OH-6
**Amanda Park**—pop pl ... WA-9
Amanda Station—locale ... OH-6
**Amanda (Township of)**—pop pl (3) ... OH-6
Amandaville—locale ... KY-4
**Amandaville**—pop pl ... WV-2
Amanka Lake—lake ... AK-9
Amano Stream—stream ... AS-9
Aman Park—park ... MI-6
Aman Ranch Placer—mine ... OR-9
Amantes Point—summit ... GU-9
**Amantha**—pop pl ... NC-3
Amaouk Creek—stream ... AK-9
Amaqua Center Sch—school ... IA-7
Amaqua Township—fmr MCD ... IA-7
Amara ... FM-9
Amarada Cut—bay ... TX-5
Amarakarakkura ... PW-9
Amaral Spring—spring ... CA-9
Amarante Spring—spring ... NM-5
**Amaranth**—pop pl ... DE-2
**Amaranth**—pop pl ... PA-2
Amaranth Island—island ... MO-7
Amaraw ... FM-9
Amargo—locale ... NM-5
Amargo Canyon—valley ... NM-5
Amargo Creek—stream ... NM-5
Amargo River ... NM-5
Amargosa (2) ... CA-9
Amargosa Cem—cemetery ... TX-5
Amargosa Creek—stream (2) ... CA-9
Amargosa Creek—stream ... TX-5
Amargosa Desert ... CA-9
Amargosa Desert—flat ... NV-8
Amargosa Desert—plain ... CA-9
Amargosa Flat (Alkali)—flat ... NV-8
Amargosa Narrows—gap ... NV-8
Amargosa Oil Field—oilfield ... TX-5
Amargosa River ... TX-5
Amargosa River—stream ... CA-9
Amargosa River—stream ... NV-8
Amargosa Substation—locale ... NV-8
**Amargosa Valley**—pop pl ... NV-8
Amargosa Wash—arroyo ... AZ-5
Amargoso Creek ... TX-5
Amargo Springs—spring ... CA-9
Amarilla Mtn—summit ... TX-5
Amarillo Point—cape ... AK-9
**Amarillo**—pop pl ... TX-5
Amarillo Beach—beach ... CA-9
Amarillo (CCD)—cens area (2) ... TX-5
Amarillo City Lake ... TX-5
Amarillo Coll—school ... TX-5
Amarillo Country Club—other ... TX-5
Amarillo Draw—valley ... NM-5
Amarillo HS—school ... TX-5
Amarillo International Airp—airport ... TX-5
Amarillo Lake (Wild Horse)—lake ... TX-5
Amarillo Osteopathic Hosp—hospital ... TX-5
**Amarillo Park (subdivision)**—pop pl ... NC-3
Amarillo Rifle and Pistol Club Firing
Range—other ... TX-5
Amarillo Speed Bowl—other ... TX-5
Amarillo Well—locale ... NM-5
Amarita Island ... MA-1
Amar Sch—school ... CA-9
Amart Farms Airstrip—airport ... OR-9
Amas—island ... FM-9
Amasa—locale ... PA-2
**Amasa**—pop pl ... MI-6
Amasa Back—ridge ... UT-8
Amasa Historic Business District—hist pl ... MI-6
Amasa Mtn—summit ... NY-2
Amasa Station—locale ... PA-2
Amasa Valley—valley ... UT-8
Amasland Elem Sch—school ... PA-2
Amason Branch—stream ... GA-3
Amason Cem—cemetery ... AR-4
Amason Creek—stream ... AR-4
Amason Creek—stream ... FL-3
**Ama (sta.)**—pop pl ... LA-4
Amatang ... FM-9
Amate Stream—stream ... AS-9
Amateur Spring—spring ... AZ-5
Amatignak Island—island ... AK-9
Amatuli Cove—bay ... AK-9
Amatuli Lighthouse—locale ... AK-9
**Amatus**—pop pl ... PA-2
Amatusuk Creek—stream ... AK-9
Amatusuk Hills—other ... AK-9
Amatusuk Hills—summit ... AK-9
**Amaua**—pop pl ... AS-9
Amaung Lake—lake ... MI-6
Amauulu Camp—locale ... HI-9
**Amauulu Camps**—pop pl ... HI-9
Amavchikilik Pass—gap ... AK-9
**Amawalk**—pop pl ... NY-2
Amawalk Hill Cem—cemetery ... NY-2
Amawalk Rsvr—reservoir ... NY-2
Amawk Creek—stream ... AK-9
Amawk Mtn—summit ... AK-9
Amax, Incorporated—facility ... IA-7
Amax Aluminum (Plant)—facility ... IL-6
Amax Coal Company (Ayrshire
Mine)—facility ... IN-6
Amaya Creek—stream ... CA-9
Amay James Elementary School ... NC-3
Amazeen House—hist pl ... ME-1
Amaziah Cem—cemetery ... MS-4
Amaziah Ch—church ... MS-4
Amazing Ch of God in Christ—church ... MS-4
Amazing Grace Ch—church ... AR-4
Amazing Grace Chapel—church ... TN-4
Amazing Grace Fellowship—church ... FL-3
Amazing Grace Pentecostal Holiness
Ch—church ... MS-4
Amazing Grace Tabernacle—church ... OH-6
Amazon—locale ... MT-8
Amazon Brook—stream ... ME-1
Amazon Creek ... WY-8
Amazon Creek—stream ... AK-9
Amazon Creek—stream ... MT-8
Amazon Creek—stream ... NV-8
Amazon Creek—stream ... OR-9
Amazon Creek—stream ... WA-9
Amazon Creek Diversion Channel—canal ... OR-9
Amazon Ditch—canal ... KS-7
Amazon Ditch Oil Field—oilfield ... KS-7
Amazon Gulch—valley ... AK-9
Amazon Gulch—valley ... AZ-5
Amazon Gulch—valley ... NV-8
Amazon Hollow—valley ... UT-8
Amazon Hosiery Mill—hist pl ... MI-6
**Amazonia**—pop pl ... MO-7
Amazon Lake—lake ... ME-1
Amazon Lake—reservoir ... IN-6
Amazon Lake Dam—dam ... IN-6
Amazon Mine—mine (2) ... NV-8
Amazon Mine—mine ... OR-9
Amazon Mine—mine ... UT-8
Amazon Mine—mine ... WA-9
Amazon Mtn—summit ... ME-1
Amazon Park—park ... OR-9
Amazon Spring—spring ... AZ-5
**Amba**—pop pl ... KY-4
Ambajejus Boom House—hist pl ... ME-1
Ambajejus Camps—locale ... ME-1
Ambajejus Falls—falls ... ME-1
Ambajejus Lake—lake ... ME-1
Ambajejus Point—cape ... ME-1
Ambar—locale ... VA-3
Ambassador—hist pl ... IN-6
Ambassador—uninc pl ... CA-9
Ambassador Apartments—hist pl ... OR-9
Ambassador Bridge—other ... MI-6
Ambassador Coll—school ... CA-9
Ambassador Downs Mobile Home
Park—locale ... AZ-5
Ambassador Hotel Hist Dist—hist pl ... MO-7
Ambassador Mine—mine ... AZ-5
Ambassador Mine—mine ... MT-8
**Ambassador Siding**—pop pl ... OH-6
Ambassador Theater Bldg—hist pl ... MO-7
Ambau—locale ... PA-2
Ambeer Branch ... IL-6
Ambeer Creek—stream ... IL-6
Amber ... AR-4
Amber—locale ... NV-8
**Amber**—pop pl ... IA-7
**Amber**—pop pl ... NY-2
**Amber**—pop pl ... OK-5
**Amber**—pop pl ... WA-9
Amber Bay—bay ... AK-9
Amber Brook—stream ... NY-2
Amber Cem—cemetery ... IA-7
Amber Cem—cemetery ... NY-2
Amber Cem—cemetery ... OK-5
Amber Creek—stream ... KS-7
Amber Creek—stream ... WA-9
Amber Drive Sch—school ... CA-9
Amber Falls ... PA-2
**Amberg**—pop pl ... WI-6
Amber Gap—gap ... TN-4
Amberg Cem—cemetery ... WI-6
Amberger Lake—lake ... MN-6
Amberg State Public Hunting
Grounds—park ... WI-6
Amberg Town Hall—hist pl ... WI-6
**Amberg (Town of)**—pop pl ... WI-6
Amber Gulch—valley ... ID-8
Amber Gulch—valley ... WY-8
Amber Lake—lake ... AK-9
Amber Lake—lake ... MI-6
Amber Lake—lake (2) ... MN-6
Amber Lake—lake (2) ... NY-2
Amber Lake—lake ... WA-9
Amber Lake—reservoir ... NY-2
Amber Lake Park—park ... MN-6
Amber Lakes—lake ... ID-8
**Amberley**—pop pl ... OH-6
Amberley (Township of)—other ... OH-6
**Amberly**—pop pl ... OH-6
Amberly Sch—school ... MI-6
**Amber Meadows**—pop pl (2) ... TN-4
Amber Meadows—uninc pl ... MD-2
Amber Meadows Park—park ... MD-2
Amberon Flat—flat ... AZ-5
Amberon Point—cliff ... AZ-5
Amber-Pocasset (CCD)—cens area ... OK-5
Amber Rsvr—reservoir ... OR-9
Ambers Cem—cemetery ... AL-4
Amber Sch—school ... OK-5
**Amberson**—pop pl ... PA-2
Amberson Creek—stream ... OR-9
Amberson Ridge—ridge ... PA-2
Amberson Trail—trail ... PA-2
Amberson Valley—valley ... PA-2
**Amberson Valley Estates**—pop pl ... PA-2
Amber Spring—spring ... MO-7
Amber Terrace—uninc pl ... NJ-2
**Amber (Township of)**—pop pl ... MI-6
**Amber Valley**—pop pl ... IN-6
**Amber Way Condominium**—pop pl ... UT-8
**Amberwood II (subdivision)**—pop pl
(2) ... AZ-5
**Amberwood North (subdivision)**—pop pl
(2) ... AZ-5
**Amberwood (subdivision)**—pop pl (2) ... AZ-5
**Am-Beth Acres**—pop pl ... OH-6
Ambeto (historical)—locale ... AL-4
Ambia—locale ... TX-5
**Ambia**—pop pl ... IN-6
Ambia Sch—school ... TX-5
**Ambierville**—pop pl ... NY-2
Ambition Lake—lake ... CA-9
Amblard, Emile, Guest House—hist pl ... MN-6
A M B Lateral—canal ... CO-8
**Amble**—pop pl ... MI-6
Amble Cem—cemetery ... MI-6
Ambler ... FL-3
**Ambler**—pop pl ... AK-9
**Ambler**—pop pl ... CA-9
**Ambler**—pop pl ... IN-6
**Ambler**—pop pl ... PA-2
Ambler, Henry, House—hist pl ... IA-7
Ambler, Mount—summit ... TN-4
Ambler Borough—civil ... PA-2
Ambler Ch of the Brethren—church ... PA-2
Ambler Farms—uninc pl ... PA-2
**Ambler Highlands**—pop pl ... PA-2
Ambler Lowland—area ... AK-9
Ambler Park—park ... OH-6
**Ambler Park**—pop pl ... CA-9
Ambler Peak—summit ... AK-9
Ambler Ridge—ridge ... WV-2
Ambler River—stream ... AK-9
**Amblersburg**—pop pl ... WV-2
Ambler Sch—school ... SC-3
Ambler Sch—school ... WV-2
Amblers Crossing—locale ... NY-2
Ambler Spring—spring ... WY-8
**Amblerville**—pop pl ... NY-2
Amble Sch—school ... MI-6
Ambleside Lake—lake ... WI-6
Ambo Channel—channel ... MP-9
Amboirok Island ... MP-9
Amboo ... MP-9
Amboo To ... MP-9
Ambo Point ... NJ-2
Ambo Reef—bar ... MP-9
Ambo-suido ... MP-9
Ambo-to ... MP-9
Amboy ... NJ-2
Amboy ... NC-3
Amboy ... OH-6
Amboy—locale ... NE-7
**Amboy**—pop pl ... AR-4
**Amboy**—pop pl ... CA-9
**Amboy**—pop pl ... GA-3
**Amboy**—pop pl ... IL-6
**Amboy**—pop pl ... IN-6
**Amboy**—pop pl ... IA-7
**Amboy**—pop pl ... MN-6
**Amboy**—pop pl ... NY-2
**Amboy**—pop pl ... OH-6
**Amboy**—pop pl ... WA-9
**Amboy**—pop pl ... WV-2
Amboy Cem—cemetery ... MI-6
**Amboy Center**—pop pl ... NY-2
Amboy Ch—church ... MI-6
Amboy Ch—church ... WV-2
Amboy Crater—summit ... CA-9
Amboy (historical)—locale ... KS-7
Amboy (historical)—locale ... SD-7
Amboy Perth ... NJ-2
Amboy Sch—school ... OH-6
Amboy Station—locale ... NY-2
**Amboy (Town of)**—pop pl ... NY-2
**Amboy (Township of)**—pop pl ... IL-6
**Amboy (Township of)**—pop pl ... MI-6
**Amboy (Township of)**—pop pl ... MN-6
**Amboy (Township of)**—pop pl ... OH-6
Ambraw River ... IL-6
Ambresvajun Lake (Last Lake)—lake ... AK-9
Ambreys Pond—lake ... NY-2
Ambridge ... IN-6
Ambridge—locale ... WI-6
**Ambridge**—pop pl ... PA-2
Ambridge Area Catholic Sch—school ... PA-2
Ambridge Area HS—school ... PA-2
Ambridge Borough—civil ... PA-2
Ambridge Country Club—other ... PA-2
Ambridge Elem Sch—school ... IN-6
**Ambridge Heights**—pop pl (2) ... PA-2
Ambridge Park—park ... PA-2
Ambridge Rsvr—reservoir ... PA-2
Ambridge Woodlawn Bridge—bridge ... PA-2
**Ambro (historical)**—pop pl ... TN-4
Ambroise, Lac—lake ... LA-4
Ambro Post Office (historical)—building ... TN-4
Ambrose—locale ... CA-9
Ambrose—other ... KY-4
**Ambrose**—pop pl ... CA-9
**Ambrose**—pop pl ... GA-3
**Ambrose**—pop pl ... IA-7
**Ambrose**—pop pl ... ND-7
**Ambrose**—pop pl ... PA-2
**Ambrose**—pop pl ... TX-5
Ambrose, H. W., House—hist pl ... SC-3
Ambrose, Lake—lake ... SD-7
Ambrose A Call State Park—park ... IA-7
Ambrose Branch—stream ... VA-3
Ambrose Brook—stream ... NJ-2
Ambrose Canyon—valley ... CA-9
Ambrose (CCD)—cens area ... GA-3
Ambrose Cem—cemetery ... ND-7
Ambrose Cem—cemetery ... OH-6
Ambrose Cem—cemetery ... TN-4
Ambrose Ch—church ... OH-6
Ambrose Channel—channel ... NJ-2
Ambrose Channel—channel ... NY-2
Ambrose Chapel—church ... WV-2
Ambrose Cove—bay ... NH-1
Ambrose Creek—stream ... MT-8
Ambrose Hall—hist pl ... IA-7
Ambrose Hill—summit ... OR-9
Ambrose Hull Grant—civil ... FL-3
Ambrose Lake—lake ... MI-6
Ambrose Lake Dam—dam ... MS-4
AMBROSE (lightship)—hist pl ... NY-2
Ambrose Mine—mine ... CA-9
Ambrose Park—locale ... NV-8
Ambrose Rsvr—reservoir ... CA-9
Ambrose Run—stream ... MD-2
Ambrose Saddle—gap ... MT-8
Ambrose Sch—school ... CA-9
Ambrose Sch (abandoned)—school ... MO-7
Ambrose Sch (historical)—school ... PA-2
Ambrose Spring—spring ... TN-4
Ambrose Station—locale ... CA-9
Ambrose Station—locale ... ND-7
Ambrose Station Pumphouse—other ... CA-9
Ambrose Swamp—swamp ... RI-1
**Ambrose Township**—pop pl ... ND-7
Ambrosetti Pond—lake ... NV-8
Ambrose Valley—valley ... CA-9
Ambrose-Ward Mansion—hist pl ... NJ-2
Ambrose Well—well ... CA-9
Ambrosia—locale ... WV-2
Ambrosia Creek—stream ... IL-6
Ambrosia Lake—locale ... NM-5
Ambrosia Lake—reservoir ... NM-5
Ambrosia Landing Field—airport ... AZ-5
Ambrosia Mill—locale ... AZ-5
Ambrosia Plantation—locale ... LA-4
Ambrosini Ranch—locale ... CA-9
Ambro Slough ... WI-6
Ambrough Slough—gut ... WI-6
Ambrust ... PA-2
Ambuehl Sch—school ... IL-6
Ambulance Butte—summit ... ND-7
Ambulance Butte Sch—school ... ND-7
Ambur Brothers Number 1 Dam—dam ... SD-7
**Amburg**—pop pl ... VA-3
Amburgey—locale ... KY-4
Amburgey Branch—stream ... KY-4
Amburgey Ranch—locale ... TX-5
Amburg Hollow—valley ... KY-4
Amburg Mounds Site (15FU15)—hist pl ... KY-4
Amburn Cem—cemetery ... TN-4
Amburn Mtn—summit ... TN-4
Ambush Lake—lake ... MN-6
Ambush Sch—school ... DC-2
Ambush Water Pocket ... AZ-5
Ambush Water Pocket—reservoir ... AZ-5
**Amby Briggs Subdivision**—pop pl ... UT-8
Amcelle—locale ... MD-2
Amchir—uninc pl ... NY-2
Amchitka Island—island ... AK-9
Amchitka Pass—channel ... AK-9
**Amco**—pop pl ... GA-3
Amco County Park—park ... WI-6
Amc (Township of)—other ... MN-6
Amdur Park Lake—lake ... NY-2
**Ameagle**—pop pl ... WV-2
AME Cem—cemetery ... AL-4
AME Ch—church ... AL-4
Ame Ch—church ... NC-3
AME Ch—church ... OK-5
Ameck Sch—school ... NE-7
Ameda, Lake—lake ... LA-4
Amedee, Lake—lake ... LA-4
Amedee Canyon—valley ... CA-9
Amedee Hot Springs—spring ... CA-9
Amedee Mountains—summit ... CA-9
Amee Bay—bay ... AK-9
Amee Island—island ... AK-9
Amekaud River ... PW-9
Amelbulk—uninc pl ... TX-5
Amelia ... VA-3
Amelia—locale ... NC-3
Amelia—locale ... OR-9
Amelia—locale ... WV-2
**Amelia**—pop pl ... LA-4
**Amelia**—pop pl ... NE-7
**Amelia**—pop pl ... OH-6
**Amelia**—pop pl ... TX-5
**Amelia**—pop pl (2) ... PR-3
Amelia, Lac—lake ... LA-4
Amelia Acad—school (2) ... VA-3
Amelia Beach ... FL-3
Amelia Butte—summit ... CA-9
Amelia Butte—summit ... OR-9
Amelia Ch—church ... FL-3
Amelia Ch—church ... NC-3
Amelia Ch—church ... VA-3
Amelia City—locale ... FL-3
Amelia City Park—park ... AL-4
**Amelia (County)**—pop pl ... VA-3
**Amelia Court House**—pop pl ... VA-3
**Amelia Court House (RR name
Amelia)**—pop pl ... VA-3
Amelia Creek—stream ... OR-9
Amelia Earhart Airp—airport ... KS-7
Amelia Earhart Dam—dam ... MA-1
Amelia Earhart Elem Sch—school ... FL-3
Amelia Earhart JHS—school ... FL-3
Amelia Earhart JHS—school ... MI-6
Amelia Earhart Park—park ... FL-3
Amelia Earhart Peak—summit ... CA-9
Amelia Earhart Stadium—building ... KS-7
Amelia Gas Field—oilfield ... LA-4
Amelia Gayle Gorgas Library—building ... AL-4
Amelia HS—school ... OH-6
Amelia Island—island ... FL-3
Amelia Island Light—locale ... FL-3
Amelia Island Lighthouse—locale ... FL-3
Amelia Island (Shop Ctr)—locale ... FL-3
Amelia Lake—lake (2) ... MN-6
Amelia Oil Field—oilfield ... TX-5
Amelia Plaza (Shop Ctr)—locale ... FL-3
Amelia River—stream ... FL-3
Amelia (RR name for Amelia Court
House)—other ... VA-3
Amelia Spring—spring ... OR-9
Amelia Street Hist Dist—hist pl ... SC-3
Amelia Street Sch—school ... VA-3
**Amelith**—pop pl ... MI-6
Amelius Island—island ... AK-9
Amel Lake—lake ... CA-9
Amelia Wildlife Mngmt Area—park ... VA-3
Amelong Creek—stream ... MT-8
Amelung House and Glassworks—hist pl ... MD-2
Amen Canyon—valley ... NM-5
Amen Corner—bay ... VA-3
**Amend**—pop pl ... PA-2
Amenda Creek—stream ... MN-6
Amended Dobson Estates Three ... AZ-5
Amended Royal Estates West Five ... AZ-5
Amend Ranch—locale ... WY-8
Amenge Field—locale ... MA-1
Amenia—locale ... IL-6
**Amenia**—pop pl ... NY-2
**Amenia**—pop pl ... ND-7
**Amenia (Town of)**—pop pl ... NY-2
**Amenia Township**—pop pl ... ND-7
**Amenia Union**—pop pl ... CT-1
**Amenia Union**—pop pl ... NY-2
Amen Lake—lake ... MN-6
Amen Sch—school ... IL-6
Ament, Lake—reservoir ... TX-5
Ament Cove—cove ... TN-4
Ament Lake—lake ... WI-6
Amerada Camp—locale (3) ... TX-5
Amerada Camp—locale ... WY-8
Amerada Well—well ... NM-5
America ... KS-7
America—hist pl ... MI-6
America—locale ... IL-6
America—locale ... OK-5
**America**—pop pl ... AL-4
**America**—pop pl ... IN-6
America Bottoms ... OR-9
America Branch—stream ... KY-4
America Cem—cemetery ... IN-6
America Cem—cemetery ... MN-6
**America City**—pop pl ... KS-7
America City Cemetery—cemetery ... KS-7
America Creek ... SD-7
America (Election Precinct)—fmr MCD ... IL-6
America Hill—summit ... VI-3
America Junction ... AL-4
America Lake—lake ... SD-7
America Ledge—bench ... RI-1
America Mine—mine (2) ... CA-9
America Mine (underground)—mine ... AL-4
**American**—pop pl ... OR-9
**Americana Apartments**—pop pl ... VA-3
American Acad—school ... FL-3
American Antiquarian Society—building ... MA-1
American Antiquarian Society—hist pl ... MA-1
Americana Preparatory Sch—school ... FL-3
American Association, Limited, Office
Bldg—hist pl ... KY-4
American Association of University
Women—building ... DC-2
Americana Village ... IL-6
American Baptist Ch of
Beautitudes—church ... FL-3
American Baptist Publication
Society—hist pl ... PA-2
American Bar—bar (2) ... CA-9
American Bar—bar ... ID-8
American Bar—bar ... MT-8
American Bar Gulch—valley ... MT-8
American Basin—basin ... CA-9
American Basin—basin ... CO-8
American Bay—bay (2) ... AK-9
American Bay—bay ... LA-4
American Bayou—stream ... LA-4
**American Beach**—pop pl ... FL-3
American Beauty Mine—mine ... NV-8
American Bend—bend ... MS-4
American Bend Lateral—canal ... NM-5
American Boathouse—hist pl ... ME-1
American Borax Company Mines—mine ... NV-8
American Border Peak—summit ... WA-9
American Bottom ... IL-6
American Bottom—flat ... OR-9
American Bottoms—bend ... IL-6
American Bottoms—bend ... IN-6
American Bottoms Sch
(historical)—school ... MO-7
American Boy Mine—mine ... AZ-5
American Brewery—hist pl ... MD-2
American Butte—summit ... WA-9
American Campground—locale ... UT-8
American Camp Lookout—locale ... CA-9
American Campsite—locale ... WA-9
American Camp Station—locale ... CA-9
American Canal—canal ... NV-8
American Canal—canal (2) ... TX-5
American Can Company Dam—dam ... AL-4
American Can Company Lake—reservoir ... AL-4
American Canyon—CDP ... CA-9
American Canyon—valley (3) ... CA-9
American Canyon—valley ... NV-8
American Canyon—valley (2) ... NM-5
American Canyon Campground—locale ... CA-9
American Canyon Creek—stream ... CA-9
American Canyon Spring—spring ... CA-9
American Canyon Spring—spring ... NM-5
American Cem—cemetery ... KS-7
American Cem—cemetery ... NE-7
American Cem—cemetery ... OH-6
American Cement Corporation
Substation—locale ... AZ-5
American Cemetery—hist pl ... AK-9
American Ch—church (2) ... KS-7
American Ch—church ... LA-4
American Ch—church ... MI-6
American Ch—church ... ND-7
American Ch—church ... OH-6
American Ch—church ... TX-5
American Chief Creek ... KS-7
American Christian Acad—school ... AL-4
American Chute—stream ... MS-4
American Cigar Factory—hist pl ... SC-3
American Cities—post sta ... MD-2
American City—locale ... CO-8
American City (historical)—locale ... SD-7
American Club—hist pl ... WI-6
American Colony Canal—canal ... CA-9
American Colony Number Four
Canal—canal ... CA-9
American Colony Number One
Canal—canal ... CA-9
American Colony Number Three
Canal—canal ... CA-9
American Colony Number Two
Canal—canal ... CA-9
American Commercial and Savings
Bank—hist pl ... IA-7
**American Corner**—pop pl ... MD-2
American Corners ... MD-2
**American Corners**—pop pl ... MD-2
American Cove—bay ... ME-1
American Creek—stream (6) ... AK-9
American Creek—stream (2) ... ID-8
American Creek—stream (2) ... MT-8
American Creek—stream (3) ... NM-5
American Creek—stream ... SD-7
American Creek Campground—locale ... AK-9
American Creek Cow Camp—locale ... NM-5
American Creek Rec Area—park ... SD-7
American Crow Creek—stream ... SD-7
American Cutoff—channel ... MS-4
American Cyanamid Company—facility ... MO-7
American Cyanamid Linden—airport ... NJ-2
American Dahk ... AZ-5
**American Dock Terminal**—pop pl ... NY-2
American Eagle Mine—mine (2) ... CA-9
American Eagle Mine—mine (2) ... CO-8
American Eagle Mine—mine ... ID-8
American Eagle Mine—mine ... SD-7
American Eagle School
(Abandoned)—locale ... WI-6
American Eagle Shoal—bar ... OH-6
American Evangelist Day Sch—school ... AZ-5
American Evangelist Lutheran Day Nursery ... AZ-5
American Exchange Bank—hist pl ... WI-6
American Exchange Mine—mine ... CA-9
American Falls—falls ... NY-2
**American Falls**—pop pl ... ID-8
American Falls Dam—dam ... ID-8
American Falls East Shore Power
Plants—hist pl ... ID-8

American Falls Rsvr—*reservoir* ... ID-8
American Federation of Labor Bldg—*hist pl* ... DC-2
American Fine Arts Society—*hist pl* ... NY-2
American Firebrick Company—*hist pl* ... WA-9
American Flag Hill—*summit* ... AZ-5
American Flag Mine—*mine* ... NV-8
American Flag Mtn—*summit* ... CO-8
American Flag Post Office Ranch—*hist pl* ... AZ-5
American Flag Raising Site—*hist pl* ... AK-9
American Flag Ranch—*locale* ... AZ-5
American Flag Shaft—*mine* ... UT-8
American Flag Spring—*spring* ... AZ-5
*American Flag Springs* ... AZ-5
American Flat—*flat* ... CA-9
American Flat—*flat* ... NV-8
American Flat—*locale* ... CA-9
American Flat Canyon—*valley* ... NV-8
American Flats—*flat* (2) ... CO-8
American Forestry Association Bldg—*building* ... DC-2
*American Fork* ... CA-9
**American Fork**—*pop pl* ... UT-8
American Fork—*stream* ... MT-8
American Fork—*stream* ... UT-8
American Fork Big Sheep Creek—*stream* ... WA-9
American Fork Canyon—*valley* ... UT-8
American Fork Canyon Ditch—*canal* ... UT-8
American Fork Cem—*cemetery* ... UT-8
*American Fork Creek* ... UT-8
American Fork Hosp—*hospital* ... UT-8
American Fork Hospital Heliport—*airport* ... UT-8
American Fork HS—*school* ... UT-8
American Fork JHS—*school* ... UT-8
American Fork-Pleasant Grove—*cens area* ... UT-8
American Fork-Pleasant Grove Division—*civil* ... UT-8
American Fork Post Office—*building* ... UT-8
American Fork Presbyterian Church—*hist pl* ... UT-8
American Fork Ranch—*locale* ... MT-8
American Fork Ranch Ditch—*canal* ... MT-8
*American Fork River* ... UT-8
American Forks Campground—*locale* ... WA-9
American Fork Shop Ctr—*locale* ... UT-8
American Fork Training Sch—*school* ... UT-8
American Game Association State Public Shooting Area—*park* ... SD-7
American Girl Gulch—*valley* ... ID-8
American Girl Mine—*mine* ... CA-9
American Girl Mine—*mine* ... CO-8
American Girl Mine—*mine* ... ID-8
American Girl Wash—*stream* ... CA-9
American Gold Mine—*mine* ... MT-8
American Gulch—*valley* ... AK-9
American Gulch—*valley* (2) ... AZ-5
American Gulch—*valley* (3) ... CO-8
American Gulch—*valley* (4) ... MT-8
American Gulch Spring—*spring* ... MT-8
**American Heritage**—*pop pl* ... TN-4
American Heritage Private Sch—*school* ... FL-3
American Heritage Private Sch of Highlands County—*school* ... FL-3
American Heritage Sch—*school* ... FL-3
*American Hill* ... AZ-5
American Hill—*summit* (2) ... CA-9
American Hill Cabin—*locale* ... CA-9
American Hill Lake—*lake* ... ID-8
American Hill Mine—*mine* ... CA-9
American Hill Mine (Inactive)—*mine* ... CA-9
American Hollow—*valley* ... TN-4
American Homes Park—*park* ... FL-3
American Horse Canyon—*valley* ... OK-5
American Horse Creek—*stream* ... SD-7
American Horse Lake—*lake* ... OK-5
American Horse Lake State Hunting And Fishin—*park* ... OK-5
American Hotel—*hist pl* ... NM-5
American Hotel—*hist pl* ... NY-2
American House—*locale* ... CA-9
American House Hotel—*hist pl* ... MN-6
American House Ravine—*valley* ... CA-9
American Indian Mission—*church* ... AZ-5
American Institute for Foreign Trade—*school* ... AZ-5
American Institute of Pharmacy Bldg—*hist pl* ... DC-2
American Insurance Union Citadel—*hist pl* ... OH-6
American International Coll—*school* ... MA-1
*American Island* ... ME-1
American Island—*island* ... LA-4
American Island—*island* ... NY-2
American Island (historical)—*island* ... SD-7
American Knob—*summit* ... TN-4
American Kootenai Mine—*mine* ... MT-8
*American Lake* ... WA-9
American Lake—*lake* ... CA-9
American Lake—*lake* (2) ... CO-8
American Lake—*lake* ... MN-6
American Lake—*lake* (2) ... WA-9
American Lake—*lake* ... WI-6
**American Lake Garden Tract**—*pop pl* ... WA-9
American Lake Seaplane Base—*airport* ... WA-9
American Lake (Veterans Administration Hospital)—*hospital* ... WA-9
American Lead and Zinc Mill—*locale* ... CO-8
American League Park—*park* ... MS-4
American Legion—*reservoir* ... MS-4
American Legion Boys Camp—*locale* ... WI-6
American Legion Cabin—*hist pl* ... ID-8
American Legion Camp—*locale* ... NY-2
American Legion Cem—*cemetery* ... FL-3
American Legion Cem—*cemetery* ... IL-6
American Legion Cem—*cemetery* ... OR-9
American Legion Country Club—*locale* (2) ... PA-2
American Legion Field—*park* ... MO-7
American Legion Forest CCC Shelter—*hist pl* ... CT-1
American Legion Freedom Bell—*park* ... DC-2
American Legion Golf Club—*other* ... GA-3
American Legion Golf Course—*locale* ... NC-3
American Legion Golf Course—*other* (2) ... GA-3
American Legion Golf Course—*other* (2) ... IN-6
American Legion Hall—*hist pl* ... ID-8
American Legion Knoll—*summit* ... KY-4
American Legion Lake—*lake* ... GA-3
American Legion Lake—*lake* ... MS-4
American Legion Lake—*reservoir* ... GA-3
American Legion Lake—*reservoir* (3) ... MS-4
American Legion Lake—*reservoir* ... NC-3
American Legion Lake—*reservoir* ... TX-5
American Legion Lake—*reservoir* ... VA-3
American Legion Lake Dam—*dam* (4) ... MS-4
American Legion Lake Dam—*dam* ... NC-3
American Legion Memorial Bridge—*bridge* ... TN-4
American Legion Memorial Park—*park* ... MI-6
American Legion Memorial Park—*park* ... WA-9
American Legion Memorial Stadium—*locale* ... NC-3
American Legion Mine—*mine* ... AZ-5
American Legion Park—*park* ... CA-9
American Legion Park—*park* ... GA-3
American Legion Park—*park* ... IL-6
American Legion Park—*park* ... MA-1
American Legion Park—*park* ... MI-6
American Legion Park—*park* ... MN-6
American Legion Park—*park* ... MO-7
American Legion Park—*park* ... MT-8
American Legion Park—*park* ... TX-5
American Legion Park—*park* ... WI-6
American Legion Peak—*summit* ... WY-8
American Legion Playground—*park* ... FL-3
American Legion Sch—*school* ... CA-9
American Legion Speedway—*other* ... PA-2
American Legion State For—*forest* ... CT-1
American Legion State For—*forest* ... WI-6
American Linen Company Row Houses—*locale* ... MA-1
American Lutheran Ch—*church* ... FL-3
American Lutheran Sch—*school* ... CA-9
American Luthern Church Dam—*dam* ... SD-7
American Marianas Memorial Park—*locale* ... MH-9
American Martyrs Sch—*school* ... CA-9
American Martyrs Sch—*school* ... MI-6
American Med Ctr—*hospital* ... CO-8
American Mesa—*summit* ... NM-5
American Military Acad—*school* ... PR-3
American Mill—*locale* ... CO-8
American Mills Web Shop—*hist pl* ... CT-1
American Mine—*mine* (3) ... AZ-5
American Mine—*mine* ... CA-9
American Mine—*mine* ... CO-8
American Mine—*mine* ... ID-8
American Mine—*mine* ... MI-6
American Mine—*mine* ... NM-5
American Mine—*mine* ... UT-8
American Mine—*mine* ... WY-8
American Mine Junction—*other* ... MI-6
American Mtn—*summit* ... MT-8
American Museum of Natural History—*building* ... NY-2
American Museum of Natural History—*hist pl* ... NY-2
American Muslim Mission—*church* ... KS-7
American Narrows—*channel* ... NY-2
American Natl Bank Bldg—*hist pl* ... FL-3
American Natl Club—*locale* ... TN-4
American Natl Red Cross Bldg—*hist pl* ... DC-2
American Nature Association Bldg—*building* ... DC-2
American Net and Twine Company Factory—*hist pl* ... MA-1
American Nettie Mine—*mine* ... CO-8
*American Nile River* ... KS-7
Americano, Estero—*stream* ... CA-9
Americano Creek—*stream* ... CA-9
Americanos Tank—*reservoir* ... TX-5
American Park—*flat* ... NM-5
American Park—*park* ... IN-6
American Pass—*gap* ... AK-9
American Pass (Grand Pass)—*channel* ... LA-4
American Peace Society—*hist pl* ... DC-2
American Peak—*summit* ... AZ-5
*American Pharmaceutical Association* ... DC-2
American Pharmaceutical Institute—*building* ... DC-2
American Philosophical Society Hall—*hist pl* ... PA-2
**American Plaza Condominium**—*pop pl* ... UT-8
American Plaza (Shop Ctr)—*locale* ... FL-3
*American Point* ... MN-6
American Point—*cape* (2) ... MN-6
*American Point Island* ... MN-6
American Printing Co. and Metacomet Mill—*hist pl* ... MA-1
American Radiator Bldg—*hist pl* ... NY-2
American Ranch—*locale* ... AZ-5
American Ranch—*locale* ... CA-9
American Ranch Hill—*summit* ... CA-9
American Ravine—*valley* ... NV-8
American Realty Depot Camp—*locale* ... ME-1
*American Red Mountain* ... WA-9
American Revolution Statuary—*hist pl* ... DC-2
American Ridge—*ridge* ... ID-8
American Ridge—*ridge* ... WA-9
American Ridge—*ridge* ... WV-2
American Ridge Cem—*cemetery* ... ID-8
American Ridge Trail—*trail* ... WA-9
*American River* ... ID-8
American River—*stream* (2) ... AK-9
American River—*stream* ... CA-9
American River—*stream* ... ID-8
American River—*stream* ... WA-9
American River Bridge—*bridge* ... CA-9
American River Coll—*school* ... CA-9
American River Flume—*canal* ... CA-9
American River Hosp—*hospital* ... CA-9
American River Parkway—*park* ... CA-9
American River Powerhouse—*other* ... CA-9
American River Trail—*trail* ... CA-9
American Run—*stream* ... IN-6
American Sch—*school* (2) ... IL-6
American Sch—*school* ... PA-2
American Sch for the Deaf—*school* ... CT-1
American Security and Trust Company—*hist pl* ... DC-2
American Senior HS—*school* ... FL-3
American Shoal—*bar* ... FL-3
*American Skyways Airport* ... DE-2
**American Spinning**—*pop pl* ... SC-3
American Spring—*spring* (2) ... NM-5
**American Square**—*pop pl* ... MD-2
American Stock Exchange—*hist pl* ... NY-2
American Street Sch—*hist pl* ... RI-1
American Swedish Historical Museum—*building* ... PA-2
American System Built Homes-Burnham Street District—*hist pl* ... WI-6
American Tank—*reservoir* ... AZ-5
American Tank—*reservoir* ... NM-5
American Telegraph & Telephone Co. Bldg.—*hist pl* ... IA-7
American Telephone & Telegraph Company Airp—*airport* ... NC-3
American Theater—*hist pl* ... MO-7
American Theological Seminary—*school* ... TN-4
American Thread Company Road (historical)—*trail* ... ME-1
*American Tissue Pond* ... MA-1
*American Touladi Brook* ... ME-1
**American Towers Condominium**—*pop pl* ... UT-8
American Towers Heliport—*airport* ... UT-8
**American (Township of)**—*pop pl* ... OH-6
American Trona Corporation Bldg—*hist pl* ... CA-9
*American Trout Lake* ... MN-6
American Trust and Savings Bank (Indiana Bank)—*hist pl* ... IN-6
American Tunnel—*mine* ... UT-8
American Ukranian Camp—*locale* ... WI-6
America Number 3 Mine (underground)—*mine* ... AL-4
America Number 4 Mine (underground)—*mine* ... AL-4
American Union Sch—*school* ... CA-9
American Univ—*school* ... DC-2
American Valley—*flat* ... CA-9
American Valley—*valley* ... WI-6
**American Villa Subdivision**—*pop pl* ... UT-8
American War Mothers Bldg—*building* ... DC-2
American Women's League Chapter House—*hist pl* ... ID-8
*American Woolen Company Dam* ... MA-1
American Woolen Mill Housing District—*hist pl* ... MA-1
American Youth Hostel—*building* ... PA-2
America Point—*cape* ... VI-3
America Post Office (historical)—*building* ... AL-4
America Sch—*school* ... SD-7
America Township—*fmr MCD* ... IA-7
**America Township**—*pop pl* ... SD-7
**Americo**—*pop pl* ... PR-3
Americum Rsvr—*reservoir* ... NV-8
Americus—*locale* ... CO-8
**Americus**—*pop pl* ... GA-3
**Americus**—*pop pl* ... IN-6
**Americus**—*pop pl* ... KS-7
**Americus**—*pop pl* ... MO-7
Americus (CCD)—*cens area* ... GA-3
Americus Cem—*cemetery* ... IN-6
Americus Cem—*cemetery* ... NJ-2
Americus Country Club—*other* ... GA-3
Americus Courthouse (historical)—*locale* ... MS-4
Americus Elem Sch—*school* ... KS-7
Americus Hist Dist—*hist pl* ... GA-3
Americus Hist Dist (Boundary Increase)—*hist pl* ... GA-3
Americus Hotel—*hist pl* ... PA-2
Americus Post Office (historical)—*building* ... MS-4
Americus-Saint Olaf Cem—*cemetery* ... ND-7
Americus Town Hall—*building* ... ND-7
**Americus Township**—*pop pl* ... KS-7
**Americus Township**—*pop pl* ... ND-7
Amerige Field—*locale* ... MA-1
Amerige Park—*park* ... CA-9
Amerina Sch—*school* ... KY-4
Amerine Branch—*stream* ... TN-4
Amerine Cem—*cemetery* ... CO-8
Amerine Cem—*cemetery* ... OH-6
Amerine Cem—*cemetery* ... TN-4
Amerine Park—*park* ... TN-4
Amerines Corner—*locale* ... AL-4
*Amerines Forge* ... TN-4
Amerk Point—*cape* ... AK-9
Amerman Bridge—*other* ... IL-6
Amerman Sch—*school* ... MI-6
Amerone Spring Number One—*spring* ... AZ-5
Amerone Spring Number Two—*spring* ... AZ-5
*Amerong River* ... PW-9
Amerosa Wash—*stream* ... CA-9
Amerotron Mill—*uninc pl* ... NC-3
Amersfort Park—*park* ... NY-2
**Amersham (subdivision)**—*pop pl* ... TN-4
**Amery**—*pop pl* ... WI-6
*Ames* ... IN-6
Ames—*locale* ... AR-4
Ames—*locale* ... CO-8
Ames—*locale* ... NE-7
Ames—*locale* ... SD-7
Ames—*locale* ... TX-5
Ames—*locale* ... WV-2
**Ames**—*pop pl* ... IL-6
**Ames**—*pop pl* ... IN-6
**Ames**—*pop pl* ... IA-7
**Ames**—*pop pl* ... KS-7
**Ames**—*pop pl* ... NE-7
**Ames**—*pop pl* ... NH-1
**Ames**—*pop pl* ... NY-2
**Ames**—*pop pl* ... OK-5
**Ames**—*pop pl* ... TX-5
Ames, Charles Rice, House—*hist pl* ... OH-6
Ames, Henry, House—*hist pl* ... MN-6
Ames, Josiah A., House—*hist pl* ... MA-1
Ames, Lake—*lake* ... NJ-2
*Ames Avenue* ... NE-7
Ames Bldg—*hist pl* ... MA-1
Ames Branch—*stream* ... MO-7
Ames Branch—*stream* ... WI-6
Ames Brook—*stream* ... CT-1
Ames Brook—*stream* (3) ... NH-1
**Amesbury**—*pop pl* ... MA-1
Amesbury, Joe, Place—*hist pl* ... ME-1
Amesbury and Salisbury Mills Village Hist Dist—*hist pl* ... MA-1
Amesbury Cem—*cemetery* ... ME-1
**Amesbury Center**—*pop pl* ... MA-1
Amesbury Country Club—*locale* ... MA-1
Amesbury (historical P.O.)—*locale* ... MA-1
Amesbury HS—*school* ... MA-1
Amesbury MS—*school* ... MA-1
Amesbury Point—*cape* ... ME-1
Amesbury Sch—*school* ... MA-1
Amesbury Town Hall—*building* ... MA-1
**Amesbury (Town of)**—*pop pl* ... MA-1
Ames Canyon—*valley* ... CA-9
Ames Canyon—*valley* ... ID-8
Ames Cem—*cemetery* ... KS-7
Ames Cem—*cemetery* ... ME-1
Ames Cem—*cemetery* ... MI-6
Ames Cem—*cemetery* ... NY-2
Ames Cem—*cemetery* ... OK-5
Ames Cem—*cemetery* ... OR-9
Ames Cem—*cemetery* ... TX-5
Ames Cem—*cemetery* ... VA-3
Ames Ch—*church* ... MD-2
Ames Ch—*church* ... TX-5
Ames Chapel—*church* ... IN-6
Ames Christian Sch—*school* ... IA-7
*Ames Church* ... AL-4
Ames Community Center—*locale* ... TX-5
Ames Country Club—*other* ... IA-7
Ames Cove—*bay* (3) ... ME-1
**Ames Cove (subdivision)**—*pop pl* ... VA-3
Ames Creek—*stream* (2) ... ID-8
Ames Creek—*stream* ... IA-7
Ames Creek—*stream* ... MT-8
Ames Creek—*stream* ... NE-7
Ames Creek—*stream* (2) ... OR-9
Ames Creek—*stream* ... WA-9
Ames Cutoff Ditch—*canal* ... NE-7
Ames Distribution Center—*facility* ... WV-2
Ames Drain—*canal* ... MI-6
Ames Field—*park* ... IN-6
Ames-Florida House—*hist pl* ... MN-6
**Ames Heights**—*pop pl* ... WV-2
**Ames Hill**—*pop pl* ... VT-1
Ames Hill—*summit* (2) ... MA-1
Ames Hill—*summit* ... NH-1
Ames Hill—*summit* ... VT-1
Ames Hill Brook—*stream* ... VT-1
Ames Hill/Crescent Hill District—*hist pl* ... MA-1
*Ameshoak Creek* ... MA-1
Ames Hole—*valley* ... CA-9
Ames Hollow—*valley* ... PA-2
Ames HS—*school* ... MA-1
Ames JHS—*school* ... MA-1
Ames Lake—*lake* (2) ... MI-6
Ames Lake—*lake* ... MN-6
Ames Lake—*lake* (2) ... WA-9
**Ames Lake**—*pop pl* ... WA-9
Ames Lake—*reservoir* ... NC-3
Ames Lake Dam—*dam* ... NC-3
Ames Ledge—*bar* ... ME-1
Ames Long Pond—*lake* ... MA-1
Ames Manufacturing Company—*hist pl* ... MA-1
Ames McDonough Company Plant—*facility* ... WV-2
Ames Monmt—*hist pl* ... WY-8
Ames Monmt—*pillar* ... WY-8
Ames Mtn—*summit* ... ME-1
Ames Mtn—*summit* ... NH-1
Ames Nowell State Park—*park* (2) ... MA-1
Ames Opening—*flat* ... CA-9
Ames Plantation—*locale* ... TN-4
Ames Playground—*park* ... MI-6
Ames Point—*cape* ... ME-1
*Ames Pond* ... MA-1
Ames Pond—*lake* ... ME-1
Ames Pond—*lake* ... MA-1
Ames Pond—*reservoir* (3) ... MA-1
Ames Pond Dam—*dam* (2) ... MA-1
Ames Pond Dike—*dam* ... MA-1
Ames Pond Upper Dam—*dam* ... MA-1
Ames Ranch—*locale* ... WY-8
Ames Research Center—*building* ... CA-9
Ames Research Center (NASA)—*building* ... CA-9
Ames Ridge—*ridge* ... VA-3
Ames Road Ch—*church* ... TX-5
Ames Run—*stream* ... PA-2
Ames Sch—*school* ... CO-8
Ames Sch—*school* (2) ... IL-6
Ames Sch—*school* ... LA-4
Ames Sch—*school* ... MA-1
Ames Sch—*school* ... MI-6
Ames Sch—*school* (2) ... MN-6
Ames Sch (historical)—*school* ... AL-4
Ames Sch (historical)—*school* ... TN-4
Ames Schoolhouse—*hist pl* ... MA-1
Ames Spring—*spring* ... NV-8
Ames Spring—*spring* ... OR-9
Ames Spring Basin—*basin* ... TX-5
Ames State For—*forest* ... NH-1
Amesti Sch—*school* ... CA-9
**Ames (Township of)**—*pop pl* ... OH-6
Amestoy Sch—*school* ... CA-9
*Ames Turnout* ... NC-3
Ames Valley—*valley* ... CA-9
**Amesville**—*pop pl* ... CT-1
**Amesville**—*pop pl* ... OH-6
**Amesville**—*pop pl* ... PA-2
Amesville Mine Station—*locale* ... PA-2
Ames Well—*well* ... CA-9
Amethyst Basin—*basin* ... UT-8
Amethyst Brook—*stream* ... MA-1
Amethyst Creek—*stream* ... CO-8
Amethyst Creek—*stream* ... WY-8
Amethyst Lake—*reservoir* ... UT-8
Amethyst Mine—*mine* ... AZ-5
Amethyst Mine—*mine* ... CO-8
Amethyst Mtn—*summit* ... WY-8
Amethyst Peak—*summit* ... ID-8
Amethyst Peak—*summit* ... NV-8
Amethyst Spring—*spring* ... AZ-5
*Ametoti* ... PW-9
*Ameus* ... TX-5
Amey Brook—*stream* (2) ... NH-1
Amey Cem—*cemetery* ... KY-4
Amey Creek—*stream* ... WA-9
Amey Gap—*gap* ... PA-2
Amey Pond—*lake* ... WI-6
AME Zion Ch—*church* ... AL-4
Amherst—*locale* ... MN-6
Amherst—*locale* ... MT-8
Amherst—*locale* ... NC-3
Amherst—*locale* ... TX-5
Amherst—*other* ... FL-3
**Amherst**—*pop pl* ... CO-8
**Amherst**—*pop pl* ... ME-1
**Amherst**—*pop pl* ... MA-1
**Amherst**—*pop pl* ... NE-7
**Amherst**—*pop pl* ... NH-1
**Amherst**—*pop pl* ... NY-2
**Amherst**—*pop pl* ... OH-6
**Amherst**—*pop pl* ... SD-7
**Amherst**—*pop pl* ... TN-4
**Amherst**—*pop pl* ... TX-5
**Amherst**—*pop pl* (2) ... VA-3
**Amherst**—*pop pl* ... WI-6
Amherst Cem—*cemetery* ... CO-8
Amherst Cem—*cemetery* ... KS-7
Amherst Cem—*cemetery* ... ME-1
Amherst Cem—*cemetery* ... SD-7
Amherst Cem—*cemetery* ... TX-5
Amherst Cem—*cemetery* ... VA-3
Amherst Cem—*cemetery* ... WI-6
Amherst (census name for Amherst Center)—*CDP* ... MA-1
Amherst Center (census name Amherst)—*other* ... MA-1
Amherst Central JHS—*school* ... NY-2
Amherst Ch—*church* ... KS-7
*Amherst Church* ... TN-4
*Amherst City* ... MA-1
Amherst Coll—*school* ... MA-1
*Amherst College* ... NC-3
Amherst Country Club—*other* ... NH-1
**Amherst (County)**—*pop pl* ... VA-3
**Amherstdale**—*pop pl* ... WV-2
Amherstdale-Robinette—*CDP* ... WV-2
Amherst Glacier—*glacier* ... AK-9
**Amherst Heights**—*pop pl* ... OH-6
Amherst (historical)—*locale* ... KS-7
Amherst HS—*school* ... MA-1
Amherst HS—*school* ... NY-2
Amherst H Wilder Day Camp Area—*locale* ... MN-6
Amherst JHS—*school* ... MA-1
**Amherst Junction**—*pop pl* ... WI-6
Amherst Lake—*lake* ... VT-1
Amherst Mtn—*summit* ... CO-8
Amherst Park—*park* ... MI-6
Amherst Park Shop Ctr—*locale* ... OH-6
**Amherst Park Subdivision**—*pop pl* ... UT-8
Amherst Peak—*summit* ... AK-9
*Amherst Post Office* ... NC-3
Amherst Sch—*school* ... CA-9
Amherst Sch—*school* ... TN-4
Amherst Shoppers Park—*locale* ... MA-1
Amherst Street Sch—*school* ... NH-1
**Amherst (subdivision)**—*pop pl* ... NY-2
Amherst Townhall—*building* ... MA-1
Amherst Town Hall—*hist pl* ... OH-6
**Amherst (Town of)**—*pop pl* ... ME-1
**Amherst (Town of)**—*pop pl* ... MA-1
**Amherst (Town of)**—*pop pl* ... NH-1
**Amherst (Town of)**—*pop pl* ... NY-2
**Amherst (Town of)**—*pop pl* ... WI-6
Amherst Township—*fmr MCD* ... IA-7
**Amherst (Township of)**—*pop pl* ... MN-6
**Amherst (Township of)**—*pop pl* ... OH-6
Amherst Training Sch—*school* ... VA-3
*Amherst Village* ... MA-1
Amherst Village Hist Dist—*hist pl* ... NH-1
Amherst Wayside—*locale* ... VA-3
Amiable Ch—*church* ... LA-4
Amicalola—*locale* ... GA-3
Amicalola Ch—*church* ... GA-3
Amicalola Creek—*stream* ... GA-3
Amicalola Falls—*falls* ... GA-3
Amicalola Falls State Park—*park* ... GA-3
Amicalola Lake—*reservoir* ... GA-3
Amicalola Mtn—*summit* ... GA-3
*Amicalola Ridge* ... GA-3
Ami Cem—*cemetery* ... GA-3
Amick Cem—*cemetery* ... WV-2
Amick Grove Ch—*church* ... SC-3
Amick Sch (abandoned)—*school* ... PA-2
Amick Sch (historical)—*school* ... MO-7
*Amicolola* ... GA-3
*Amicolola Creek* ... GA-3
*Amicolola Falls* ... GA-3
Amicus—*locale* ... VA-3
Amicus Mine—*mine* ... ID-8
**Amidon**—*pop pl* ... ND-7
Amidon Pinnacle—*pillar* ... VT-1
Amidon Sch—*school* ... DC-2
Amidon Sch—*school* ... MI-6
Amidon Street Baptist Ch—*church* ... KS-7
Amie No 1—*mine* ... ID-8
Amie No 2—*mine* ... ID-8
**Amigo**—*pop pl* (2) ... WV-2
**Amigo Mine**—*pop pl* ... WV-2
Amigos, Valle De Los—*valley* ... CA-9
Amigo Wash—*stream* ... AZ-5
A M I Kendall Regional Med Ctr—*hospital* ... FL-3
Amik Island—*island* ... AK-9
Amik Island—*island* ... WI-6
Amik Lake—*lake* ... MI-6
Amik Lake—*lake* ... MN-6
Amik Lake—*lake* ... WI-6
Amikopala—*summit* ... HI-9
*Amiko-Zibi* ... MN-6
Amiloyak Lake—*lake* ... AK-9
Amimenipatj (historical)—*locale* ... DE-2
Amimi Lake—*lake* ... MN-6
*Amin* ... FM-9
Amine Canyon—*valley* ... OR-9
Amine Peak—*summit* ... OR-9
*Amiot* ... KS-7
**Amiot**—*pop pl* ... KS-7
**Amiret**—*pop pl* ... MN-6
Amiret Cem—*cemetery* ... MN-6
**Amiret (Township of)**—*pop pl* ... MN-6
Amis—*locale* ... TN-4
Amis, Jonathan, House—*hist pl* ... TN-4
Amis, Rufus, House and Mill—*hist pl* ... NC-3
Amis Branch—*stream* ... KY-4
Amis Cem—*cemetery* ... KY-4
Amis Cem—*cemetery* ... MS-4
Amis Cem—*cemetery* ... TN-4
Amis Chapel—*church* ... NC-3
Amis Chapel—*church* ... TN-4
**Amis Chapel**—*pop pl* ... TN-4
Amis City Park—*park* ... TN-4
Amis-Elder House—*hist pl* ... GA-3
**Amish**—*pop pl* ... IA-7
Amish Cem—*cemetery* ... IA-7
Amish Cem—*cemetery* (4) ... KS-7
Amish Cem—*cemetery* ... MI-6
Amish Cem—*cemetery* ... MO-7
Amish Cem—*cemetery* ... WI-6
Amish Ch—*church* ... KS-7
Amish Farm House—*building* ... PA-2
Amis House—*hist pl* ... AR-4
Amis House—*hist pl* ... TN-4
Amish Sch—*school* (2) ... MI-6
Amish Sch—*school* (2) ... OH-6
Amish Sch—*school* ... WI-6
Amish Village—*locale* ... PA-2
Amison Well—*well* ... NM-5
Amis Post Office (historical)—*building* ... TN-4
*Amisquam* ... MA-1
Amiss Drift Mine (underground)—*mine* ... AL-4
Amissville—*locale* ... VA-3
**Amistad**—*pop pl* ... NM-5
**Amistad**—*pop pl* ... TX-5
**Amistad Acres**—*pop pl* ... TX-5
Amistad Cem—*cemetery* ... NM-5
Amistad Dam—*dam* ... TX-5
Amistad Natl Rec Area—*park* ... TX-5
Amistad Park—*park* (2) ... TX-5
Amistad Tank—*reservoir* ... TX-5
**Amistad Village**—*pop pl* ... TX-5
**Amistead**—*pop pl* ... MS-4
Amitchiak, Lake—*lake* ... AK-9
**Amite**—*pop pl* ... LA-4
Amite Cem—*cemetery* ... LA-4
Amite Ch—*church* ... LA-4
*Amite City* ... LA-4
**Amite City (corporate name for Amite)**—*pop pl* ... LA-4
*Amite (corporate name Amite City)* ... LA-4
**Amite County**—*pop pl* ... MS-4
Amite County Courthouse—*hist pl* ... MS-4
Amite County Training Sch—*school* ... MS-4
*Amite Courthouse* ... MS-4
Amite Female Seminary—*hist pl* ... MS-4
Amite Lookout Tower—*locale* ... MS-4
Amite Memorial Gardens—*cemetery* ... LA-4
Amite River—*stream* ... LA-4
Amite River Cem—*cemetery* ... MS-4
Amite River Ch—*church* ... MS-4
Amite River Diversion Canal—*canal* ... LA-4
Amite River Industries Pond Dam—*dam* ... MS-4
Amite River Sch (historical)—*school* ... MS-4
**Amith**—*pop pl* ... OH-6
*Amith Creek* ... MN-6
*Amiti Church* ... AL-4
*Amity* ... CT-1
*Amity* ... PA-2
Amity—*locale* ... CO-8
Amity—*locale* ... GA-3
Amity—*locale* ... IL-6
Amity—*locale* ... TX-5
**Amity**—*pop pl* ... AR-4
**Amity**—*pop pl* ... IN-6
**Amity**—*pop pl* ... MO-7
**Amity**—*pop pl* ... NY-2
**Amity**—*pop pl* ... NC-3
**Amity**—*pop pl* (4) ... OH-6
**Amity**—*pop pl* ... OR-9
**Amity**—*pop pl* (2) ... PA-2
**Amity**—*pop pl* ... TN-4
Amity Baptist Ch—*church* ... AL-4
Amity Baptist Ch (historical)—*church* ... MS-4
Amity Branch—*stream* ... IN-6
Amity Canal—*canal* ... CO-8
Amity Canal—*canal* ... KS-7
Amity Cem—*cemetery* ... CO-8
Amity Cem—*cemetery* ... IL-6
Amity Cem—*cemetery* ... IA-7
Amity Cem—*cemetery* ... MO-7
Amity Cem—*cemetery* (2) ... NE-7
Amity Cem—*cemetery* (2) ... OH-6
Amity Cem—*cemetery* ... OR-9
Amity Cem—*cemetery* ... TX-5
Amity Ch—*church* (2) ... AL-4
Amity Ch—*church* ... AR-4
Amity Ch—*church* (2) ... IN-6
Amity Ch—*church* ... IA-7
Amity Ch—*church* ... LA-4
Amity Ch—*church* (2) ... MO-7
Amity Ch—*church* ... NY-2
Amity Ch—*church* (5) ... NC-3
Amity Ch—*church* ... OH-6
Amity Ch—*church* ... OK-5
Amity Ch—*church* ... PA-2
Amity Ch—*church* (2) ... TN-4
Amity Ch—*church* (2) ... TX-5
Amity Ch—*church* ... VA-3
Amity Channel—*channel* ... NY-2
Amity Chapel—*church* ... IL-6
Amity Community Hall—*locale* ... MO-7
*Amity Creek* ... OR-9
Amity Creek—*stream* ... MN-6
Amity Creek—*stream* ... OR-9
Amity Ditch—*canal* ... AZ-5
Amity Ditch—*canal* ... IN-6
Amity Drain—*stream* (2) ... ID-8
Amity Gardens—*uninc pl* ... NC-3
Amity Gardens Shop Ctr—*locale* ... NC-3
Amity Hall—*locale* ... PA-2
**Amity Harbor**—*pop pl* ... NY-2
**Amity Heights**—*pop pl* ... TN-4
**Amity Hill**—*pop pl* ... NC-3
Amity Hill Post Office (historical)—*building* ... TN-4
Amity Hills—*summit* ... OR-9
Amity (historical P.O.)—*locale* (2) ... IA-7
Amity HS—*school* ... CT-1
Amity JHS—*school* ... CT-1
Amity Lake—*lake* ... NY-2
Amity Mine—*mine* ... OR-9
Amity Park—*park* ... AL-4
Amity Park—*park* ... MN-6
Amity Regional JHS—*school* ... CT-1
Amity Sch—*school* ... ID-8
Amity Sch—*school* ... IL-6
Amity Sch—*school* ... IA-7
Amity Sch—*school* ... MO-7
Amity Sch—*school* ... NE-7
Amity Sch—*school* ... NC-3
Amity Sch—*school* ... ND-7
Amity Sch—*school* ... OH-6
Amity Sch—*school* ... PA-2
Amity Sch (abandoned)—*school* ... PA-2
Amity Sch (historical)—*school* ... AL-4
Amity Sch (historical)—*school* (2) ... MO-7
Amity Shoal (historical)—*bar* ... NC-3
Amity Shop Ctr—*other* ... CT-1
Amity Spring—*spring* ... CA-9
Amity (Town name for North Amity)—*other* ... ME-1

Anawan Rock—hist pl MA-1
Anaya, Gavino, House—hist pl NM-5
Anayaknaurak Creek—stream AK-9
Anaya Ranch—locale (2) NM-5
Anbalach FM-9
Anblach FM-9
Anboo MP-9
Anboo suido MP-9
Anboo To MP-9
Anbo Pass MP-9
Anbor—island MP-9
Anboru—island MP-9
Anboru-To MP-9
Ancal Cem—cemetery LA-4
Ance Creek MO-7
Ancell MO-7
Ancell Cem—cemetery (2) MO-7
Anceney—locale MT-8
Ancha, Sierra—range AZ-5
Anchard Creek—stream MI-6
Ancheta Canyon—valley NM-5
Ancho—locale NM-5
Ancho, Canal (historical)—canal AZ-5
Ancho Canyon—valley (2) NM-5
Ancho Cem—cemetery NM-5
Ancho Erie Mine—mine CA-9
Ancho Gulch—valley NM-5
Ancho Peak—summit NM-5
Anchor—locale OK-5
Anchor—locale TX-5
**Anchor**—pop pl IL-6
**Anchor**—pop pl LA-4
**Anchor**—pop pl MS-4
**Anchor**—pop pl PA-2
Anchorage IL-6
Anchorage—locale LA-4
Anchorage—locale TX-5
**Anchorage**—pop pl AK-9
**Anchorage**—pop pl KY-4
**Anchorage**—pop pl MD-2
**Anchorage**—pop pl MS-4
**Anchorage**—pop pl NJ-2
**Anchorage**—pop pl UT-8
Anchorage, Point—cape FL-3
Anchorage, The VA-3
Anchorage, The—bay MD-2
Anchorage, The—cove MA-1
Anchorage, The—hist pl KY-4
Anchorage, The—hist pl MD-2
Anchorage, The—hist pl NJ-2
Anchorage, The—hist pl SC-3
**Anchorage, The**—pop pl RI-1
Anchorage Basin—basin TX-5
Anchorage Bay—bay AK-9
Anchorage (Borough) AK-9
Anchorage Cabins—locale MI-6
Anchorage Cem—cemetery WI-6
Anchorage (Census Subarea)—cens area AK-9
Anchorage Channel—channel NJ-2
Anchorage Channel—channel NY-2
Anchorage City Hall—hist pl AK-9
Anchorage Cove—bay (2) AK-9
Anchorage Hist Dist—hist pl KY-4
Anchorage HS—school MS-4
Anchorage Inn—locale NC-3
Anchorage International Airp.—airport AK-9
Anchorage JHS MS-4
Anchorage Oil Field—oilfield MS-4
Anchorage Point—cape AK-9
Anchorage Point—cape NJ-2
Anchorage Yacht Basin—harbor TN-4
Anchor Baptist Ch—church UT-8
Anchor Baptist Church MS-4
Anchor Bay AK-9
Anchor Bay—bay AK-9
Anchor Bay—bay MI-6
Anchor Bay—locale CA-9
**Anchor Bay**—pop pl MI-6
Anchor Bay Gardens MI-6
**Anchor Bay Gardens**—pop pl MI-6
**Anchor Bay Harbor**—pop pl MI-6
Anchor Bay HS—school MI-6
Anchor Bay Sch—school MI-6
**Anchor Bay Shores**—pop pl MI-6
Anchor Boat Dock—locale TN-4
Anchor Canyon—valley NM-5
Anchor Ch—church AR-4
Anchor Ch—church IL-6
Anchor Ch—church MS-4
Anchor Cove—bay (2) AK-9
Anchor Cove—bay NV-8
Anchor Creek—stream CA-9
Anchor Creek—stream (2) ID-8
Anchor Creek—stream IN-6
Anchor Creek—stream MI-6
Anchor Creek—stream MT-8
Anchor Drain—canal MI-6
Anchor D Ranch—locale NM-5
Anchor Gulch—valley CO-8
Anchor High Marina—locale TN-4
Anchor Hill—summit MN-6
Anchor Hill—summit SD-7
**Anchor (historical)**—pop pl OR-9
Anchor HS (historical)—school MS-4
Anchor II (historical)—locale SD-7
Anchor Inn Marina—locale TN-4
Anchor Island—island AK-9
Anchor Island—island WI-6
Anchorite Hills—range NV-8
Anchorite Pass—gap NV-8
Anchor Lake—lake MI-6
Anchor Lake—lake MN-6
Anchor Lake—lake (2) MT-8
Anchor Lake—lake UT-8
Anchor Lake—reservoir MS-4
Anchor Lake—reservoir UT-8
Anchor Lake Dam—dam MS-4
Anchor Lake One—reservoir NJ-2
Anchor Lake Reservoir Dam—dam UT-8
Anchor Lake Two—reservoir NJ-2
Anchor Landing—locale LA-4
Anchor Manufacturing Co.—hist pl AZ-5
Anchor Meadow—flat ID-8
Anchor Mill—locale TN-4
Anchor Mine—mine (2) CO-8
Anchor Mine—mine NV-8
Anchor Mine—mine NM-5
Anchor Mine—mine UT-8
Anchor Mine—mine WA-9
Anchor Mountain Mine—mine SD-7
Anchor Mtn—summit CO-8
Anchor Park—park AK-9
Anchor Park—park FL-3
Anchor Pass—channel AK-9
Anchor Peak—summit NV-8
Anchor Point—cape (3) AK-9
**Anchor Point**—pop pl AK-9
Anchor Post Office (historical)—building MS-4
Anchor Ranch—locale MT-8
Anchor River—stream AK-9
Anchor River Campground—locale AK-9
Anchor Rsvr—reservoir WY-8
Anchor Sch—school OR-9
Anchor Sch—school WY-8
Anchor Sch (historical)—school MO-7
Anchor Spring—spring MT-8
Anchor Spring—spring NM-5
Anchor Spring—spring OR-9
**Anchor (Township of)**—pop pl IL-6
Anchor T Ranch—locale TX-5
Anchor Tunnel—mine UT-8
**Anchorville**—pop pl MI-6
Ancho Valley—valley NM-5
Anchuca—hist pl MS-4
Anchustegui, Pedro, Pelota Court—hist pl ID-8
Anchute Well—well NM-5
Ancient and Accepted Scottish Rite Temple—hist pl KY-4
Ancient and Honorable Artillery Company Museum—building MA-1
Ancient Bristlecone Pine Area—area CA-9
Ancient Burying Ground—hist pl MA-1
Ancient Cem—cemetery MA-1
Ancient City Baptist Ch—church FL-3
Ancient Lake—lake WA-9
**Ancient Oak Estates**—pop pl MD-2
**Ancient Oak North**—pop pl MD-2
**Ancient Oaks**—pop pl PA-2
Ancient Order of Hibernians Hall—hist pl MT-8
Ancient River Warren Channel—channel SD-7
Ancient River Warren Channel (historical)—stream SD-7
Ancient Tank—reservoir AZ-5
Ancient Tree IL-6
Ancil Hoffman Park—park CA-9
Ancilla Domini Coll—school IN-6
Ancilloe Acad—school PA-2
Ancil Rsvr—reservoir CO-8
Ancke Kijhlen DE-2
Anc Lake WI-6
Anclote FL-3
**Anclote**—pop pl FL-3
**Anclote Acres**—pop pl FL-3
Anclote Anchorage—bay FL-3
Anclote Bridge—bridge FL-3
Anclote Key—locale FL-3
Anclote Key Lighthouse—locale FL-3
Anclote Keys—island FL-3
Anclote Keys Lighthouse FL-3
Anclote Key State Preserve FL-3
Anclote Key State Rec Area—park FL-3
Anclote Lighthouse FL-3
Anclote Manor Hosp—hospital FL-3
Anclote Natl Wildlife Ref—park FL-3
Anclote River—stream FL-3
Anclote Sch—school FL-3
Anco—locale KY-4
Ancocas River NJ-2
Ancocus Creek NJ-2
Ancon—locale NM-5
**Ancona**—pop pl IL-6
Ancon Del Gato Ditch—canal NM-5
**Ancones**—pop pl NM-5
Ancones (Barrio)—fmr MCD (2) PR-3
Ancon Mine—mine NM-5
Ancon Peak—summit AK-9
Ancon Rock—other AK-9
Ancoos River NJ-2
Ancor—locale OH-6
Ancora—locale NJ-2
**Ancora (Ancora Psychiatric Hospital)**—pop pl NJ-2
**Ancora (sta.)**—pop pl NJ-2
Ancora State Hosp—hospital NJ-2
**Ancram**—pop pl NY-2
**Ancramdale**—pop pl NY-2
Ancram Old Cem—cemetery NY-2
**Ancram (Town of)**—pop pl NY-2
Ancrumb Swamp SC-3
Ancrum Ferry (Abandoned)—locale SC-3
Ancrum Swamp—swamp SC-3
**Andale**—pop pl KS-7
Andale Elem Sch—school KS-7
Andale HS—school KS-7
Andalucia Sch—school AZ-5
Andalusia—hist pl GA-3
Andalusia—hist pl PA-2
Andalusia—locale FL-3
**Andalusia**—pop pl AL-4
**Andalusia**—pop pl IL-6
**Andalusia**—pop pl PA-2
Andalusia (CCD)—cens area AL-4
Andalusia Cem—cemetery IL-6
Andalusia Country Club—locale AL-4
Andalusia Division—civil AL-4
Andalusia Hosp—hospital AL-4
Andalusia HS—school AL-4
Andalusia Island—island IL-6
Andalusia Memorial Garden—cemetery AL-4
Andalusia Missionary Baptist Ch—church AL-4
Andalusia-Opp Airp—airport AL-4
Andalusia Post Office (historical)—building PA-2
Andalusia Public School AL-4
Andalusia Slough—stream IL-6
**Andalusia (subdivision)**—pop pl (2) AZ-5
**Andalusia (Township of)**—pop pl IL-6
Andanley Branch—stream AL-4
Anda Rsvr—reservoir WY-8
Andazola, Trinidad, House—hist pl NM-5
Andector Oil Field—oilfield TX-5
Andek Lake—lake MN-6
Andeluvia Mtn—summit AL-4
Ander—locale TX-5
Anderberg Ranch—locale NE-7
Anderegg Cem—cemetery TX-5
Anderegg Ranch HQ—locale NM-5
**Anderman Acres**—pop pl IL-6
Anders Branch—stream AL-4
Anders Branch—stream AR-4
Anders Branch—stream KY-4
Anders Branch—stream LA-4
Anders Cave TN-4
Anders Cem—cemetery MO-7
Anders Cem—cemetery (2) NC-3
Anders Cem—cemetery OH-6
Anders Creek OR-9
Anders Creek TX-5
Andersen, Claus P., House—hist pl UT-8
Andersen, Lars S., House—hist pl UT-8
Andersen Air Force Base—military GU-9
Andersen Air Force Base (Communication Annex)—military GU-9
Andersen Air Force Base (Harmon Annex)—military GU-9
Andersen Air Force Base (Marbo Annex)—military GU-9
Andersen Air Force Base (Northwest Field)—military GU-9
Andersen Canyon CA-9
Andersen Creek—stream AK-9
Andersen Island—island AK-9
Andersen Peak CA-9
Andersen Ranch—locale MT-8
Andersen Sch—school IL-6
Andersen Sch—school GU-9
Anders Flat—flat FL-3
Anders Lake AL-4
Anders Lake Dam AL-4
Anders Lake Dam—dam MS-4
Ander Smith Cem—cemetery TN-4
Anderson CO-8
Anderson MI-6
Anderson PA-2
Anderson—locale AR-4
Anderson—locale ID-8
Anderson—locale (2) IL-6
Anderson—locale (2) KY-4
Anderson—locale MI-6
Anderson—locale NV-8
Anderson—locale NC-3
Anderson—locale (2) OK-5
Anderson—locale OR-9
Anderson—locale (2) PA-2
Anderson—locale (2) TN-4
Anderson—locale WI-6
**Anderson**—pop pl (2) AL-4
**Anderson**—pop pl AK-9
**Anderson**—pop pl CA-9
**Anderson**—pop pl IN-6
**Anderson**—pop pl IA-7
**Anderson**—pop pl MO-7
**Anderson**—pop pl NJ-2
**Anderson**—pop pl NY-2
**Anderson**—pop pl NC-3
**Anderson**—pop pl OH-6
**Anderson**—pop pl SC-3
**Anderson**—pop pl (2) TN-4
**Anderson**—pop pl TX-5
Anderson, Andrew G., House—hist pl MN-6
Anderson, Artelia, Hall—hist pl KY-4
Anderson, Capt. R. J., House—hist pl GA-3
Anderson, Clarence, Barn—hist pl AR-4
Anderson, Col. Chap, House—hist pl MS-4
Anderson, D. B., and Company Bldg—hist pl GA-3
Anderson, D. H., Bldg—hist pl IA-7
Anderson, Elijah Teague, House—hist pl MO-7
Anderson, George, House—hist pl AR-4
Anderson, Gustof, House—hist pl MN-6
Anderson, Helen, House—hist pl AZ-5
Anderson, J. A., House—hist pl MN-6
Anderson, James, House—hist pl UT-8
Anderson, James Mechlin, House—hist pl OR-9
Anderson, John F., House—hist pl SD-7
Anderson, John W., House—hist pl TX-5
Anderson, J. S., House—hist pl MN-6
Anderson, Judge Clifford, House—hist pl GA-3
Anderson, Judge William Shaw, House—hist pl OH-6
Anderson, Lake—lake FL-3
Anderson, Lake—lake MI-6
Anderson, Larz, House—hist pl DC-2
Anderson, Larz, Park Hist Dist—hist pl MA-1
Anderson, Levi, House—hist pl OH-6
Anderson, Lewis, House, Barn and Granary—hist pl OR-9
Anderson, Max J., House—hist pl AZ-5
Anderson, Mons, House—hist pl WI-6
Anderson, Mount—summit (2) AK-9
Anderson, Mount—summit NH-1
Anderson, Mount—summit WA-9
Anderson, Neil P., Bldg—hist pl TX-5
Anderson, Niels Ole, House—hist pl UT-8
Anderson, O. G., & Co. Store—hist pl MN-6
Anderson, Oscar, House—hist pl AK-9
Anderson, Peter, House—hist pl CO-8
Anderson, Point—cape MI-6
Anderson, R. L., House—hist pl AZ-5
Anderson, William, General Merchandise Store—hist pl FL-3
Anderson, William, House—hist pl MI-6
Anderson, William Marshall, House—hist pl OH-6
Anderson Acad (historical)—school TN-4
Anderson Airfield—airport OR-9
Anderson Airp—airport (2) TN-4
Anderson Arroyo—stream CO-8
Anderson Bank Bldg—hist pl IN-6
Anderson Bar—bar UT-8
Anderson Bar (inundated)—bar UT-8
Anderson Basin—hist pl NM-5
Anderson Bay AR-4
Anderson Bay—bay (2) AK-9
Anderson Bay—bay LA-4
Anderson Bay—bay MN-6
Anderson Bay—swamp (2) FL-3
Anderson Bay—swamp GA-3
Anderson Bayou—bay FL-3
Anderson Bayou—gut MI-6
Anderson Bayou—gut MS-4
**Anderson Bayview**—pop pl MI-6
Anderson-Bedias (CCD)—cens area TX-5
Anderson-Beletski Prune Farm—hist pl WA-9
Anderson Bend—bend (2) TN-4
Anderson Bend—bend TX-5
Anderson Bend Bridge—bridge TN-4
Anderson Bend Ch—church TN-4
Anderson Bend Mine (surface)—mine TN-4
Anderson Bend Ridge—ridge TN-4
Anderson Bethel Cem—cemetery WV-2
Anderson Bluff—cliff TN-4
Anderson Bluff—cliff TX-5
Anderson Bluff—cliff WI-6
Anderson Bluffs—cliff OR-9
Anderson Boarding House—hist pl AR-4
Anderson Bog—swamp ME-1
Anderson Bottom—bend UT-8
Anderson Branch TN-4
Anderson Branch—stream (3) AL-4
Anderson Branch—stream (2) AR-4
Anderson Branch—stream FL-3
Anderson Branch—stream (2) IL-6
Anderson Branch—stream IN-6
Anderson Branch—stream (7) KY-4
Anderson Branch—stream MS-4
Anderson Branch—stream (2) MO-7
Anderson Branch—stream (4) NC-3
Anderson Branch—stream OK-5
Anderson Branch—stream (2) SC-3
Anderson Branch—stream (10) TN-4
Anderson Branch—stream (4) TX-5
Anderson Branch—stream (4) VA-3
Anderson Branch—stream WV-2
Anderson Branch Ch—church NC-3
Anderson Bridge—bridge MT-8
Anderson Bridge—bridge NE-7
Anderson Bridge—bridge SC-3
Anderson Bridge—bridge TN-4
Anderson Bridge—bridge TX-5
Anderson Bridge—bridge VA-3
Anderson Brook—stream (4) ME-1
Anderson Brook—stream (2) NH-1
Anderson Brook—stream NJ-2
Anderson Brook—stream NY-2
Anderson Brothers Bldg—hist pl VA-3
Anderson Brothers Pond Dam—dam MS-4
Anderson Brothers Rsvr—reservoir CO-8
**Andersonburg**—pop pl PA-2
Anderson Butte—summit AZ-5
Anderson Butte—summit ID-8
Anderson Butte—summit (2) ND-7
Anderson Butte—summit OR-9
Anderson Butte—summit (2) WA-9
Anderson Cabin—locale (2) OR-9
Anderson Camp—locale OR-9
Anderson Camp—locale PA-2
Anderson Camp Ground—hist pl TX-5
Anderson Campground—locale UT-8
Anderson Camp (inundated)—locale UT-8
Anderson Camp Run—stream (2) WV-2
Anderson Canal—canal ID-8
Anderson Canal—canal (2) LA-4
Anderson Canal—canal NV-8
Anderson Canyon ID-8
Anderson Canyon—valley (3) AZ-5
Anderson Canyon—valley (6) CA-9
Anderson Canyon—valley CO-8
Anderson Canyon—valley (2) ID-8
Anderson Canyon—valley (3) NV-8
Anderson Canyon—valley (2) NM-5
Anderson Canyon—valley (3) UT-8
Anderson Canyon—valley WA-9
Anderson Canyon—valley (2) WY-8
Anderson-Capner House—hist pl NJ-2
Anderson Carnegie Memorial Library—hist pl KS-7
Anderson Catfish Pond Dam—dam MS-4
Anderson Cave—cave AL-4
Anderson Cave—cave MO-7
Anderson Cave—cave (2) TN-4
Anderson Cave Branch—stream TN-4
Anderson Cave Spring—spring GA-3
Anderson (CCD)—cens area SC-3
Anderson Cem MS-4
Anderson Cem—cemetery (5) AL-4
Anderson Cem—cemetery (3) AR-4
Anderson Cem—cemetery (2) FL-3
Anderson Cem—cemetery (8) GA-3
Anderson Cem—cemetery (6) IL-6
Anderson Cem—cemetery (4) IN-6
Anderson Cem—cemetery IA-7
Anderson Cem—cemetery (2) KS-7
Anderson Cem—cemetery (4) KY-4
Anderson Cem—cemetery (2) LA-4
Anderson Cem—cemetery (2) MI-6
Anderson Cem—cemetery MN-6
Anderson Cem—cemetery (12) MS-4
Anderson Cem—cemetery (10) MO-7
Anderson Cem—cemetery NE-7
Anderson Cem—cemetery NV-8
Anderson Cem—cemetery (3) NC-3
Anderson Cem—cemetery ND-7
Anderson Cem—cemetery (6) OH-6
Anderson Cem—cemetery (4) OK-5
Anderson Cem—cemetery (2) PA-2
Anderson Cem—cemetery (2) SC-3
Anderson Cem—cemetery SD-7
Anderson Cem—cemetery (21) TN-4
Anderson Cem—cemetery (6) TX-5
Anderson Cem—cemetery (11) VA-3
Anderson Cem—cemetery (8) WV-2
Anderson Cem—cemetery WI-6
Anderson Cem—cemetery WY-8
Anderson Ch AL-4
Anderson Ch—church (2) AL-4
Anderson Ch—church GA-3
Anderson Ch—church IL-6
Anderson Ch—church IN-6
Anderson Ch—church (2) NC-3
Anderson Ch—church TN-4
Anderson Ch—church VA-3
Anderson Chapel MS-4
Anderson Chapel TX-5
Anderson Chapel—church AR-4
Anderson Chapel—church MS-4
Anderson Chapel—church (3) TN-4
Anderson Chapel—church TX-5
Anderson Chapel—church VA-3
Anderson Chapel—hist pl MD-2
Anderson Chapel Cem—cemetery LA-4
Anderson Chapel Cem—cemetery TN-4
Anderson Chapel Cem—cemetery TX-5
Anderson Chapel (historical)—church MS-4
Anderson Chapel (historical)—church TN-4
Anderson Chapel Methodist Ch—church MS-4
Anderson Chapel United Methodist Ch—church TX-5
Anderson-Chappell Ch—church IN-6
Anderson Chute—gut AR-4
Anderson City—locale KY-4
**Anderson City**—pop pl GA-3
**Anderson City (Minton)**—pop pl GA-3
Anderson Cliff—cliff CA-9
Anderson Coll—school IN-6
Anderson Coll—school SC-3
Anderson Cottonwood Canal—canal CA-9
Anderson Coulee—valley (5) MT-8
Anderson Coulee—valley ND-7
Anderson Coulee—valley WI-6
Anderson County—civil KS-7
**Anderson (County)**—pop pl KY-4
**Anderson (County)**—pop pl SC-3
**Anderson County**—pop pl TN-4
**Anderson (County)**—pop pl TX-5
Anderson County Courthouse—building TN-4
Anderson County Courthouse—hist pl KS-7
Anderson County Farm (historical)—locale TN-4
Anderson County High School TN-4
Anderson County Occupational Development Sch—school TN-4
Anderson County Park—park TN-4
Anderson County Sportsmens Club—locale TN-4
Anderson Cove—bay AK-9
Anderson Cove—bay (2) WA-9
Anderson Cove—valley (2) NC-3
Anderson Cove—valley TN-4
Anderson Cove A Campground UT-8
Anderson Cove Campground—locale UT-8
Anderson-Coward House—hist pl TN-4
Anderson Creek AR-4
Anderson Creek IN-6
Anderson Creek MI-6
Anderson Creek NV-8
Anderson Creek NC-3
Anderson Creek—bay MD-2
Anderson Creek—locale PA-2
**Anderson Creek**—pop pl NC-3
Anderson Creek—stream AL-4
Anderson Creek—stream (5) AK-9
Anderson Creek—stream AR-4
Anderson Creek—stream (8) CA-9
Anderson Creek—stream (2) GA-3
Anderson Creek—stream (8) ID-8
Anderson Creek—stream IL-6
Anderson Creek—stream KS-7
Anderson Creek—stream (3) KY-4
Anderson Creek—stream LA-4
Anderson Creek—stream (4) MI-6
Anderson Creek—stream MN-6
Anderson Creek—stream (2) MS-4
Anderson Creek—stream (2) MO-7
Anderson Creek—stream (9) MT-8
Anderson Creek—stream (2) NV-8
Anderson Creek—stream NY-2
Anderson Creek—stream (9) NC-3
Anderson Creek—stream OH-6
Anderson Creek—stream (6) OK-5
Anderson Creek—stream (19) OR-9
Anderson Creek—stream PA-2
Anderson Creek—stream SC-3
Anderson Creek—stream TN-4
Anderson Creek—stream (4) TX-5
Anderson Creek—stream (3) UT-8
Anderson Creek—stream VA-3
Anderson Creek—stream (14) WA-9
Anderson Creek—stream (2) WI-6
Anderson Creek—stream (4) WY-8
Anderson Creek Cem—cemetery TN-4
Anderson Creek Ch—church NC-3
**Anderson Creek Estates (subdivision)**—pop pl AL-4
Anderson Creek Landing—locale MS-4
Anderson Creek Pump Plant—other WA-9
Anderson Creek Sch—school NC-3
Anderson Creek Sch (historical)—school TN-4
**Anderson Creek Subdivision (subdivision)**—pop pl AL-4
Anderson Creek (Township of)—fmr MCD NC-3
Anderson Creek Trail—trail ID-8
Anderson Creek Trail—trail WY-8
Anderson Crossing AL-4
Anderson Crossing—crossing TX-5
Anderson Crossroad AL-4
Anderson Crossroads—locale DE-2
**Anderson Crossroads**—pop pl NC-3
Anderson Dairy—area UT-8
Anderson Dam—dam (2) ND-7
Anderson Dam—dam OR-9
**Anderson Dam**—pop pl ID-8
Anderson Davis Cemetery TN-4
Anderson Ditch—canal CO-8
Anderson Ditch—canal (4) IN-6
Anderson Ditch—canal MT-8
Anderson Ditch—canal OH-6
Anderson Ditch—canal OR-9
Anderson Ditch—canal (3) WY-8
Anderson Ditch No 1—canal CO-8
Anderson Ditch No 2—canal CO-8
Anderson Ditch No 3—canal CO-8
Anderson Dock Hist Dist—hist pl WI-6
Anderson Downtown Hist Dist—hist pl SC-3
Anderson Downtown Hist Dist (Boundary Increase)—hist pl SC-3
Anderson Drain—canal (3) MI-6
Anderson Drain—stream (3) MI-6
Anderson Draw—valley AZ-5
Anderson Draw—valley CO-8
Anderson Draw—valley NM-5
Anderson Draw—valley SD-7
Anderson Draw—valley TX-5
Anderson Draw—valley (4) WY-8
Anderson East Side IN-6
Anderson East Township—civil MO-7
Anderson Elem Sch TN-4
Anderson Elem Sch—school NC-3
Anderson Elem Sch—school PA-2
Anderson-Elwell House—hist pl ID-8
Anderson Extension Ditch—canal CO-8
Anderson Farm—locale AR-4
Anderson Ferry OH-6
Anderson Ferry—hist pl KY-4
Anderson Ferry—hist pl OH-6
Anderson Ferry—locale OH-6
**Anderson Ferry**—pop pl OH-6
Anderson Field—flat AZ-5
Anderson Field—flat NV-8
Anderson Field—flat OR-9
Anderson Field Airp—airport WA-9
Anderson Flat—flat AR-4
Anderson Flat—flat (3) CA-9
Anderson Flat Ch—church AR-4
Anderson Ford—locale CA-9
Anderson Fork WY-8
Anderson Fork—stream CA-9
Anderson Fork—stream WV-2
Anderson-Foster House—hist pl VA-3
Anderson-Frank House—hist pl FL-3
Anderson Gap—gap NC-3
Anderson Gap—gap PA-2
Anderson Gap—gap TN-4
Anderson Gardens—locale NV-8
Anderson Glacier—glacier AK-9
Anderson Glacier—glacier WA-9
Anderson Golf Course—other KY-4
Anderson-Gouffon Cem—cemetery TN-4
Anderson Grammar Sch—school TN-4
Anderson Grove Ch—church MS-4
Anderson Grove Ch—church NE-7
Anderson Grove Ch—church NC-3
Anderson Grove Ch—church TN-4
Anderson Grove Ch—church TX-5
Anderson Grove Elementary School MS-4
Anderson Grove Sch—school MS-4
Anderson Grove Sch—school TN-4
Anderson Gulch CO-8
Anderson Gulch ID-8
Anderson Gulch—valley AK-9
Anderson Gulch—valley (4) CA-9
Anderson Gulch—valley (2) CO-8
Anderson Gulch—valley (4) ID-8
Anderson Gulch—valley (3) MT-8
Anderson Gulch—valley (2) OR-9
Anderson Gulf—valley GA-3
Anderson Gully—valley TX-5
Anderson Hall—hist pl FL-3
Anderson Hall—hist pl KS-7
Anderson Hall—hist pl TN-4
**Anderson Heights**—pop pl TN-4
Anderson Heights Sch—school CA-9
**Anderson Heights (subdivision)**—pop pl NC-3
Anderson Hill—summit GA-3
Anderson Hill—summit IL-6
Anderson Hill—summit KY-4
Anderson Hill—summit ME-1
Anderson Hill—summit MS-4
Anderson Hill—summit MT-8
Anderson Hill—summit TX-5
Anderson Hill—summit UT-8
Anderson Hill—summit VT-1
Anderson Hist Dist—hist pl SC-3
Anderson Hist Dist—hist pl TX-5
Anderson (historical)—locale KS-7
Anderson (historical)—locale (2) MS-4
Anderson Hole—bend CO-8
Anderson Hollow—valley AL-4
Anderson Hollow—valley AR-4
Anderson Hollow—valley (4) KY-4
Anderson Hollow—valley (5) MO-7
Anderson Hollow—valley NY-2
Anderson Hollow—valley OH-6
Anderson Hollow—valley (7) TN-4
Anderson Hollow—valley (2) TX-5
Anderson Hollow—valley (2) UT-8
Anderson Hollow—valley VA-3
Anderson Hollow—valley (2) WV-2
Anderson Hollow Archeol District—hist pl VA-3
Anderson Home—building NY-2
Anderson Homestead—hist pl SD-7
Anderson Homestead—locale (2) NV-8
Anderson Homestead—locale WY-8
Anderson House—hist pl DE-2
Anderson House—hist pl GA-3
Anderson House—hist pl KY-4
Anderson House—hist pl SC-3
Anderson House and Lexington Battlefield—hist pl MO-7
Anderson House and Store—hist pl TX-5
Anderson Howard Canal—canal WY-8
Anderson HS—school IN-6
Anderson HS—school OH-6
Anderson HS—school (2) TX-5
Andersonia—locale CA-9
Anderson Island—island CA-9
Anderson Island—island LA-4
Anderson Island—island MN-6
Anderson Island—island NE-7
Anderson Island—island TN-4
Anderson Island—island WA-9
Anderson Island—island WI-6
**Anderson Island**—pop pl WA-9
Anderson Island Cem—cemetery WA-9
Anderson Island Sch—hist pl WA-9
Anderson JHS—school FL-3
Anderson JHS—school MI-6
Anderson JHS—school OK-5
Anderson-Jones Cem—cemetery TN-4
Anderson Junction—locale UT-8
Anderson-Kerr Oil Field—oilfield TX-5
Anderson Knob—summit AR-4
Anderson Knob—summit GA-3
Anderson Knob—summit TN-4
Anderson Lake MI-6
Anderson Lake MN-6
Anderson Lake TX-5
Anderson Lake WI-6
Anderson Lake—lake AK-9
Anderson Lake—lake AZ-5
Anderson Lake—lake AR-4
Anderson Lake—lake (2) CO-8
Anderson Lake—lake FL-3
Anderson Lake—lake (2) ID-8
Anderson Lake—lake IL-6
Anderson Lake—lake IN-6
Anderson Lake—lake LA-4
Anderson Lake—lake (6) MI-6
Anderson Lake—lake (23) MN-6
Anderson Lake—lake NE-7
Anderson Lake—lake ND-7
Anderson Lake—lake OR-9
Anderson Lake—lake SC-3
Anderson Lake—lake SD-7
Anderson Lake—lake TN-4
Anderson Lake—lake UT-8
Anderson Lake—lake (6) WA-9
Anderson Lake—lake (9) WI-6
Anderson Lake—reservoir CA-9

Anderson Lake—*reservoir* (3) GA-3
Anderson Lake—*reservoir* IL-6
Anderson Lake—*reservoir* IN-6
Anderson Lake—*reservoir* MT-8
Anderson Lake—*swamp* FL-3
Anderson Lake Dam—*dam* (5) MS-4
Anderson Lakes—*lake* MN-6
Anderson Lakes—*lake* WA-9
Anderson Landing—*locale* MS-4
Anderson Landing—*locale* NC-3
Anderson Landing (Abandoned)—*locale* CA-9
Anderson Landing Strip—*airport* NC-3
Anderson Lateral—*canal* ID-8
Anderson Ledge—*bar* NH-1
Anderson Lick Run—*stream* WV-2
Anderson Lodge—*hist pl* WY-8
Anderson Lumber Company—*hist pl* MT-8
Anderson Marsh—*swamp* TX-5
Anderson Marsh Archeol District—*hist pl* CA-9
*Anderson Meadow Campground* UT-8
Anderson Meadow Dam—*dam* UT-8
Anderson Meadow Rsvr—*reservoir* UT-8
Anderson Meadows Cow Camp—*locale* MT-8
Anderson Memorial Ch—*church* GA-3
Anderson Memorial Gardens—*cemetery* TN-4
Anderson Memorial Park—*cemetery* IN-6
Anderson Memorial Playground—*park* CA-9
Anderson Mesa—*summit* (2) AZ-5
Anderson Mesa—*summit* CO-8
*Anderson Mill* AL-4
Anderson Mill—*locale* GA-3
Anderson Mill Canyon—*valley* ID-8
Anderson Mill Creek—*stream* FL-3
Anderson Mill Creek—*stream* GA-3
Anderson Mill Creek—*stream* TN-4
Anderson Mill (historical)—*locale* AL-4
Anderson Mill (historical)—*locale* TN-4
Anderson Millpond—*lake* SC-3
Anderson Mine—*mine* (2) AZ-5
Anderson Mine—*mine* (3) CA-9
Anderson Mine—*mine* CO-8
Anderson Mine—*mine* MT-8
Anderson Mine—*mine* TN-4
Anderson Mine—*mine* (2) UT-8
Anderson Mine—*mine* WA-9
Anderson Mine (surface)—*mine* TN-4
Anderson-Minter Cem—*cemetery* MS-4
Anderson Mound—*hist pl* MS-4
Anderson Mountain—*ridge* GA-3
Anderson Mountain—*ridge* OR-9
Anderson Mountain Trail—*trail* OR-9
Anderson Mtn—*range* NC-3
Anderson Mtn—*summit* AL-4
Anderson Mtn—*summit* AK-9
Anderson Mtn—*summit* (2) AR-4
Anderson Mtn—*summit* (3) CA-9
Anderson Mtn—*summit* CO-8
Anderson Mtn—*summit* ID-8
Anderson Mtn—*summit* MO-7
Anderson Mtn—*summit* NM-5
Anderson Mtn—*summit* NC-3
Anderson Mtn—*summit* OK-5
Anderson Mtn—*summit* (2) OR-9
Anderson Mtn—*summit* (2) TN-4
Anderson Mtn—*summit* TX-5
Anderson Mtn—*summit* UT-8
Anderson Mtn—*summit* WA-9
Anderson Municipal Airp—*airport* IN-6
Anderson Northwest (CCD)—*cens area* KY-4
Anderson Number 1 Dam—*dam* (4) SD-7
Anderson Number 2 Dam—*dam* (2) SD-7
Anderson Oil Field—*other* NM-5
Anderson Outkitchen—*hist pl* NJ-2
Anderson Park—*flat* NM-5
Anderson Park—*park* CA-9
Anderson Park—*park* FL-3
Anderson Park—*park* GA-3
Anderson Park—*park* IN-6
Anderson Park—*park* (4) IA-7
Anderson Park—*park* MA-1
Anderson Park—*park* (2) MN-6
Anderson Park—*park* MS-4
Anderson Park—*park* MT-8
Anderson Park—*park* NJ-2
Anderson Park—*park* NC-3
Anderson Park—*park* OH-6
Anderson Park—*park* SD-7
Anderson Park—*park* TN-4
Anderson Park—*park* (2) TX-5
Anderson Pass—*channel* LA-4
Anderson Pass—*gap* (2) AK-9
Anderson Pass—*gap* UT-8
Anderson Pass—*gap* WA-9
Anderson Peak—*summit* AK-9
Anderson Peak—*summit* (5) CA-9
Anderson Peak—*summit* ID-8
Anderson Peak—*summit* MT-8
Anderson Peak—*summit* NM-5
Anderson Pit—*cave* TN-4
Anderson Pit—*mine* CA-9
Anderson Place—*locale* ID-8
Anderson Place—*locale* NM-5
Anderson Place Hist Dist—*hist pl* AL-4
Anderson Plantation—*locale* AL-4
Anderson Point—*cape* (3) AK-9
Anderson Point—*cape* (2) CA-9
Anderson Point—*cape* ID-8
Anderson Point—*cape* LA-4
Anderson Point—*cape* MI-6
Anderson Point—*cape* OR-9
Anderson Point—*cape* TN-4
Anderson Point—*cape* VA-3
Anderson Point—*cape* (2) WA-9
Anderson Pond—*lake* AL-4
Anderson Pond—*lake* FL-3
Anderson Pond—*lake* GA-3
Anderson Pond—*lake* (2) ME-1
Anderson Pond—*lake* NH-1
Anderson Pond—*lake* WA-9
Anderson Pond—*reservoir* AL-4
Anderson Pond—*reservoir* CT-1
Anderson Pond—*reservoir* FL-3
Anderson Pond—*reservoir* (3) GA-3
Anderson Pond—*reservoir* VA-3
Anderson Post Office—*building* TN-4
Anderson Post Office (historical)—*building* MS-4
Anderson Post Office (historical)—*building* TN-4
Anderson-Price Memorial Library Bldg—*hist pl* FL-3
Anderson Private Airstrip—*airport* SD-7
**Anderson Quarry**—*pop pl* SC-3
Anderson Ranch—*locale* (2) AZ-5
Anderson Ranch—*locale* (2) CO-8
Anderson Ranch—*locale* (4) MT-8
Anderson Ranch—*locale* NE-7
Anderson Ranch—*locale* NV-8
Anderson Ranch—*locale* (3) NM-5
Anderson Ranch—*locale* ND-7
Anderson Ranch—*locale* OR-9
Anderson Ranch—*locale* SD-7
Anderson Ranch—*locale* (2) TX-5
Anderson Ranch—*locale* UT-8
Anderson Ranch—*locale* WA-9
Anderson Ranch—*locale* (3) WY-8
Anderson Ranch Dam—*dam* ID-8
Anderson Ranch Rsvr—*reservoir* ID-8
Anderson Ridge—*ridge* (2) CA-9
Anderson Ridge—*ridge* NV-8
Anderson Ridge—*ridge* SD-7
Anderson Ridge—*ridge* (2) TN-4
Anderson Ridge—*ridge* UT-8
Anderson Ridge—*ridge* WA-9
Anderson Ridge—*ridge* (3) WV-2
Anderson Ridge—*ridge* WI-6
Anderson Ridge—*ridge* WY-8
Anderson Ridge Trail—*trail* OR-9
*Anderson River* IN-6
Anderson River—*stream* IN-6
Anderson Road (RR name for Wireton)—*other* PA-2
Anderson Rock—*bar* ME-1
Anderson-Rose Diversion Dam—*dam* OR-9
Anderson Rosenwald Sch (historical)—*school* AL-4
Anderson-Rose Pool—*reservoir* OR-9
Anderson (RR name for Venetia)—*other* PA-2
Anderson Rsvr—*reservoir* (6) CO-8
Anderson Rsvr—*reservoir* ID-8
Anderson Rsvr—*reservoir* (4) MT-8
Anderson Rsvr—*reservoir* OR-9
Anderson Rsvr—*reservoir* SC-3
Anderson Rsvr—*reservoir* (2) WY-8
Anderson Rsvr No. 1—*reservoir* CO-8
Anderson Rsvr No. 2—*reservoir* CO-8
Anderson Rsvr No. 6—*reservoir* CO-8
Anderson Run—*stream* (3) OH-6
Anderson Run—*stream* (3) PA-2
Anderson Run—*stream* VA-3
Anderson Run—*stream* WV-2
Andersons Airfield—*airport* OR-9
Anderson Sawmill—*locale* WY-8
Andersons Canal Structure Two Dam—*dam* MS-4
Andersons Cem—*cemetery* OK-5
Anderson Sch—*hist pl* MT-8
Anderson Sch—*school* AL-4
Anderson Sch—*school* AR-4
Anderson Sch—*school* (5) CA-9
Anderson Sch—*school* CT-1
Anderson Sch—*school* (3) FL-3
Anderson Sch—*school* (2) IL-6
Anderson Sch—*school* IA-7
Anderson Sch—*school* KY-4
Anderson Sch—*school* ME-1
Anderson Sch—*school* MA-1
Anderson Sch—*school* (6) MI-6
Anderson Sch—*school* (2) MN-6
Anderson Sch—*school* MO-7
Anderson Sch—*school* MT-8
Anderson Sch—*school* NY-2
Anderson Sch—*school* (2) OH-6
Anderson Sch—*school* (2) OK-5
Anderson Sch—*school* PA-2
Anderson Sch—*school* SC-3
Anderson Sch—*school* (2) SD-7
Anderson Sch—*school* (3) TN-4
Anderson Sch—*school* (7) TX-5
Anderson Sch—*school* WA-9
Anderson Sch—*school* WV-2
Anderson Sch—*school* WI-6
Anderson Sch (historical)—*school* (3) AL-4
Anderson Sch (historical)—*school* MS-4
Anderson Sch (historical)—*school* MO-7
Anderson Sch (historical)—*school* SD-7
Anderson Sch (historical)—*school* TN-4
Anderson School—*locale* MI-6
Anderson Schoolhouse—*hist pl* OH-6
Anderson School of Natural History (historical)—*building* MA-1
Andersons Corner—*locale* DE-2
Andersons Corner—*locale* GA-3
Andersons Corner—*locale* PA-2
*Andersons Creek* AL-4
*Andersons Creek* IN-6
Andersons Creek—*stream* VA-3
Andersons Crossing Campground—*locale* MN-6
Andersons Crossroads—*locale* NC-3
Andersons Ferry (historical)—*locale* IN-6
Andersons Ferry (historical)—*locale* TN-4
Anderson-Shaffer House—*hist pl* OH-6
*Andersons Hill* UT-8
Anderson Shoal—*bar* NC-3
Anderson Shoals—*bar* TN-4
Anderson Shopping Plaza Shop Ctr—*locale* MS-4
Andersons Hospital Helipad—*airport* MS-4
Anderson Site—*hist pl* KY-4
Andersons Lake Dam—*dam* MS-4
Andersons Landing (historical)—*locale* TN-4
Anderson Slough—*gut* IL-6
Anderson Slough—*gut* TX-5
Anderson Slough—*lake* SD-7
Andersons Marsh—*lake* MN-6
Anderson's Mill—*hist pl* SC-3
Andersons Mill—*locale* VA-3
Andersons Mill (historical)—*locale* (2) MS-4
Andersons Mill (historical)—*locale* (3) TN-4
Andersons Millpond—*reservoir* SC-3
Anderson-Smith House—*hist pl* KY-4
Anderson Southwest (CCD)—*cens area* KY-4
*Anderson Spring* ID-8
Anderson Spring—*spring* AL-4
Anderson Spring—*spring* (5) AZ-5
Anderson Spring—*spring* FL-3
Anderson Spring—*spring* ID-8
Anderson Spring—*spring* MO-7
Anderson Spring—*spring* (4) OR-9
Anderson Spring—*spring* (2) TN-4
Anderson Spring—*spring* UT-8
Anderson Spring—*stream* ID-8
Anderson Spring Branch—*stream* (2) TN-4
Anderson Spring Number Four—*spring* NV-8
Anderson Spring Number One—*spring* NV-8
Anderson Spring Number Three—*spring* NV-8
Anderson Spring Ridge—*ridge* CA-9
*Anderson Springs* ID-8
**Anderson Springs**—*pop pl* CA-9
Anderson Springs—*spring* CA-9
Anderson Springs—*spring* MT-8
Anderson Springs—*spring* NV-8
Anderson Springs—*spring* OR-9
Anderson Springs—*spring* WI-6
*Andersons Ranch* NV-8
*Andersons River* IN-6
Andersons Rsvr—*reservoir* UT-8
Andersons Run—*stream* OH-6
Andersons Shoals—*bar* TN-4
Andersons Spring—*spring* TN-4
Andersons Store (historical)—*locale* AL-4
Andersons Store Post Office (historical)—*building* TN-4
Anderson State Wildlife Mngmt Area—*park* MN-6
Anderson Station—*locale* OR-9
Anderson Station—*locale* PA-2
Anderson Station (historical)—*locale* AL-4
Anderson Stone House—*building* PA-2
Anderson Street Station—*hist pl* NJ-2
**Anderson Subdivision (subdivision)**—*pop pl* SD-7
**Anderson (subdivsion)**—*pop pl* AL-4
*Anderson Swamp Creek* NC-3
Anderson Tank—*reservoir* (3) AZ-5
Anderson Tank—*reservoir* (3) NM-5
Anderson Tank—*reservoir* TX-5
Anderson Tank Number One—*reservoir* AZ-5
Anderson Tank Number Two—*reservoir* AZ-5
Anderson-Thompson House—*hist pl* IN-6
*Andersonton* IN-6
*Andersontown* IN-6
**Andersontown**—*pop pl* MD-2
**Andersontown**—*pop pl* (2) PA-2
Anderson Town Hall—*building* ND-7
**Anderson (Town of)**—*pop pl* (2) WI-6
Anderson Township—*civil* MO-7
Anderson Township—*fmr MCD* IA-7
**Anderson Township**—*pop pl* (2) NE-7
**Anderson Township**—*pop pl* ND-7
**Anderson Township**—*pop pl* SD-7
Anderson (Township of)—*fmr MCD* AR-4
Anderson (Township of)—*fmr MCD* MO-7
Anderson (Township of)—*fmr MCD* NC-3
**Anderson (Township of)**—*pop pl* IL-6
**Anderson (Township of)**—*pop pl* (4) IN-6
**Anderson (Township of)**—*pop pl* OH-6
*Anderson Trail* UT-8
Anderson Trail—*trail* PA-2
Anderson Trailer Court—*locale* UT-8
Anderson Truck Trail—*trail* CA-9
**Anderson Tully**—*pop pl* AR-4
Anderson-Tully County Airp—*airport* TN-4
Anderson-Tully State Wildlife Mngmt Area—*park* MS-4
Anderson-Tully State Wildlife Mngmt Area—*park* TN-4
Anderson Union HS—*school* CA-9
Anderson United Methodist Ch—*church* MS-4
Anderson Valley—*basin* (2) NE-7
Anderson Valley—*basin* UT-8
Anderson Valley—*valley* (2) CA-9
Anderson Valley—*valley* OR-9
Anderson Valley—*valley* WI-6
Anderson Valley Ch—*church* IN-6
Anderson Valley HS—*school* CA-9
Anderson Valley Sch—*school* CA-9
Anderson-Vickers Cem—*cemetery* VA-3
*Andersonville* IN-6
*Andersonville* NJ-2
Andersonville—*locale* VA-3
Andersonville—*locale* WV-2
Andersonville—*other* KY-4
**Andersonville**—*pop pl* CO-8
**Andersonville**—*pop pl* (2) GA-3
**Andersonville**—*pop pl* (2) IN-6
**Andersonville**—*pop pl* MI-6
**Andersonville**—*pop pl* OH-6
**Andersonville**—*pop pl* TN-4
Andersonville (CCD)—*cens area* GA-3
Andersonville Ch—*church* SC-3
*Andersonville Creek* SC-3
Andersonville Dock—*locale* TN-4
Andersonville Elem Sch—*school* TN-4
Andersonville Institute (historical)—*school* TN-4
Andersonville Natl Historic Site—*hist pl* GA-3
Andersonville Natl Historic Site—*park* GA-3
Anderson Vose Ditch—*canal* MT-8
Anderson Wash—*arroyo* NV-8
Anderson Water Mill (historical)—*locale* MS-4
*Anderson Way* TX-5
**Anderson Ways**—*pop pl* TX-5
Anderson Well—*well* AZ-5
Anderson Well—*well* (2) NV-8
Anderson Well—*well* (3) NM-5
Anderson Well—*well* TX-5
**Anderson West Acres Subdivision**—*pop pl* UT-8
Anderson West Township—*civil* MO-7
Anderson Windmill—*locale* NM-5
Anderson Woods—*woods* WA-9
Anderson Young Ranch—*locale* NM-5
Anderson 1 Dam—*dam* SD-7
Anderson 5 Dam—*dam* SD-7
Anders Ranch—*locale* NE-7
Anders Run—*stream* PA-2
Anders Sch (historical)—*school* MO-7
Anderton Branch—*stream* (2) TN-4
Anderton Branch Public Use Area—*park* TN-4
Anderton Canyon—*valley* UT-8
**Anderton Estates Subdivision**—*pop pl* UT-8
**Anderwood Estates (subdivision)**—*pop pl* NC-3
**Anderwood Estates Subdivision**—*pop pl* UT-8
Andes—*locale* MT-8
**Andes**—*pop pl* NY-2
Andes, Lake—*lake* SD-7
Andes, Riley H., House—*hist pl* TN-4
Andes Cem—*cemetery* KY-4
Andes Creek—*stream* SD-7
Andes Hist Dist—*hist pl* NY-2
Andesite—*locale* CA-9
Andesite Creek—*stream* AK-9
Andesite Lookout Tower—*locale* MT-8
Andesite Peak—*summit* CA-9
Andesite Ridge—*ridge* CA-9
Andesite Ridge—*ridge* NV-8
Andes Mtn—*summit* OK-5
**Andes (Town of)**—*pop pl* NY-2
Andes Windmill—*locale* NM-5
**Andice**—*pop pl* TX-5
Andice Cem—*cemetery* TX-5
Andies Mine—*mine* NV-8
Andies Prairie—*flat* OR-9
Andies Quarry—*mine* TN-4
Andies Ridge—*ridge* OR-9
*Andin Ditch* IN-6
**Anding**—*pop pl* MS-4
Anding Branch—*stream* MS-4
Anding Branch—*stream* TX-5
*Anding Lake* TX-5
Anding Post Office (historical)—*building* MS-4
*Andinosa Creek* TX-5
**Andis**—*pop pl* OH-6
Andis Cem—*cemetery* VA-3
Andis Ditch—*canal* IN-6
Andison Drain—*canal* MI-6
**Andlor Subdivision**—*pop pl* UT-8
**Andora**—*pop pl* MD-2
*Andorinia Creek* NV-8
*Andornia Creek* NV-8
Andorno Creek—*stream* NV-8
Andorno Ranch—*locale* NV-8
Andorra Ch—*church* PA-2
Andorra Springs Golf Club—*other* PA-2
**Andorra Woods**—*pop pl* PA-2
*Andover* SD-7
Andover—*locale* CA-9
Andover—*locale* MO-7
Andover—*locale* PA-2
**Andover**—*pop pl* CT-1
**Andover**—*pop pl* IL-6
**Andover**—*pop pl* IA-7
**Andover**—*pop pl* KS-7
**Andover**—*pop pl* ME-1
**Andover**—*pop pl* MA-1
**Andover**—*pop pl* MN-6
**Andover**—*pop pl* NH-1
**Andover**—*pop pl* NJ-2
**Andover**—*pop pl* NY-2
**Andover**—*pop pl* OH-6
**Andover**—*pop pl* SD-7
**Andover**—*pop pl* VT-1
**Andover**—*pop pl* VA-3
**Andover**—*pop pl* WA-9
*Andover, Town of* MA-1
**Andover, (Township of)**—*pop pl* NJ-2
*Andover Branch* DE-2
Andover Branch—*stream* MD-2
Andover Branch—*stream* VT-1
Andover Cem—*cemetery* (2) KS-7
Andover Cem—*cemetery* MN-6
Andover Cem—*cemetery* MO-7
Andover Cem—*cemetery* SD-7
Andover Central Sch—*school* MA-1
*Andover Centre* MA-1
Andover Ch—*church* KS-7
Andover Chapter House—*hist pl* IL-6
Andover Country Club—*locale* MA-1
**Andover Estates**—*pop pl* MD-2
*Andover Forge* NJ-2
*Andover Furnace* NJ-2
**Andover Golf Estates**—*pop pl* FL-3
Andover HS—*school* KS-7
Andover JHS—*school* KS-7
Andover JHS—*school* MA-1
Andover Junction—*locale* NJ-2
Andover Lake—*reservoir* CT-1
**Andover Lake Estates**—*pop pl* FL-3
Andover Lakes—*lake* FL-3
**Andover Lakes Estates**—*pop pl* FL-3
Andover Natl Bank—*hist pl* MA-1
Andover Newton Theological Sch—*school* MA-1
Andover North Surplus—*unorg* ME-1
Andover Park—*park* FL-3
Andover Park—*park* TX-5
Andover Pond—*lake* NY-2
Andover Ponds—*reservoir* NJ-2
Andover Public Library—*hist pl* ME-1
Andover Road Cem—*cemetery* CT-1
Andover Sch—*school* CT-1
Andover Sch—*school* KS-7
Andover Street Sch—*school* MA-1
Andover Town Hall—*hist pl* MA-1
**Andover (Town of)**—*pop pl* CT-1
**Andover (Town of)**—*pop pl* ME-1
**Andover (Town of)**—*pop pl* MA-1
**Andover (Town of)**—*pop pl* NH-1
**Andover (Town of)**—*pop pl* NY-2
**Andover (Town of)**—*pop pl* VT-1
**Andover Township**—*pop pl* SD-7
Andover Township (historical)—*civil* SD-7
**Andover (Township of)**—*pop pl* IL-6
**Andover (Township of)**—*pop pl* MN-6
**Andover (Township of)**—*pop pl* OH-6
*Andover Village* MA-1
Andover Village Industrial District—*hist pl* MA-1
Andover West Surplus—*unorg* ME-1
Andrada Ranch—*locale* AZ-5
Andrada Tank—*reservoir* AZ-5
**Andrade**—*pop pl* HI-9
Andrade—*post sta* HI-9
Andrade Camp—*locale* HI-9
Andrade Corner—*locale* CA-9
Andrade (Site)—*locale* CA-9
Andraieff Meadows—*flat* OR-9
Andre, Bayou—*channel* LA-4
Andre, Lake—*bay* LA-4
*Andreafski* AK-9
*Andreafsky* AK-9
Andreafsky Hills—*summit* AK-9
Andreafsky(Included In Saint Mary's) ANV721—*reserve* AK-9
Andreafsky Mtn—*summit* AK-9
Andreafsky River—*stream* AK-9
**Andrea Heights**—*pop pl* TN-4
Andre Airp—*airport* PA-2
Andrean HS—*school* IN-6
Andreanof Islands—*island* AK-9
*Andreaoffsky* AK-9
**Andrea Park Estates**—*pop pl* NY-2
Andrea Ranch—*locale* TX-5
**Andreas**—*pop pl* PA-2
Andreas Branch—*stream* NC-3
Andreas Canyon—*hist pl* CA-9
Andreas Canyon—*valley* CA-9
*Andreas Creek* TX-5
Andreas Falls—*falls* CA-9
Andreason Cem—*cemetery* CA-9
Andreason Lake—*lake* MN-6
Andreason Mill (Site)—*locale* CA-9
Andreas Park—*park* NJ-2
**Andrea (Township of)**—*pop pl* MN-6
Andre Bldg—*hist pl* AZ-5
Andre Cem—*cemetery* IA-7
Andrecito Creek—*stream* NM-5
Andre David, Bayou—*stream* LA-4
Andree—*locale* MN-6
Andree Clark Bird Ref—*park* CA-9
Andregg Hollow—*valley* IA-7
Andre Hill—*summit* NJ-2
Andre Hill—*summit* NY-2
Andrei Sakhorov Plaza—*park* DC-2
Andre Island—*island* LA-4
Andreon Bay—*bay* AK-9
**Andrepont**—*pop pl* LA-4
**Andres**—*pop pl* IL-6
Andres Artesian Well—*well* TX-5
Andres Drain—*canal* MI-6
Andresen Coulee—*valley* MT-8
Andres Pond—*bay* LA-4
Andress Cem—*cemetery* AL-4
Andress Cove—*valley* LA-4
Andress Cove Cem—*cemetery* LA-4
Andress Drain—*canal* MI-6
Andress Spring—*spring* CA-9
**Andrew**—*pop pl* FL-3
**Andrew**—*pop pl* IL-6
**Andrew**—*pop pl* IA-7
**Andrew**—*pop pl* LA-4
**Andrew**—*pop pl* WV-2
Andrew, Jesse, House—*hist pl* IN-6
Andrew, Lake—*lake* MN-6
Andrew, Lake—*lake* NY-2
Andrew, Mount—*summit* MA-1
Andrew, Mount—*summit* NY-2
Andrew Acres, Lake—*reservoir* NC-3
Andrew Atkinson Grant—*civil* (2) FL-3
Andrew Bay—*bay* AK-9
Andrew Branch—*stream* GA-3
Andrew Branch—*stream* MS-4
Andrew Brook—*stream* NH-1
Andrew Brook—*stream* NY-2
Andrew Buchanan Elem Sch—*school* PA-2
Andrew Cem—*cemetery* KS-7
Andrew Cem—*cemetery* LA-4
Andrew Cem—*cemetery* NE-7
Andrew Cem—*cemetery* TN-4
Andrew Ch—*church* VA-3
*Andrew Chapel* AL-4
Andrew Chapel—*church* AL-4
Andrew Chapel—*church* GA-3
Andrew Chapel—*church* (3) MS-4
Andrew Chapel—*church* MO-7
Andrew Chapel—*church* NC-3
Andrew Chapel—*church* SC-3
Andrew Chapel—*church* (3) VA-3
Andrew Chapel Cem—*cemetery* MS-4
Andrew Chapel Cem—*cemetery* TX-5
Andrew Chapel Post Office (historical)—*building* TN-4
Andrew Coll—*school* GA-3
Andrew Coll (historical)—*school* TN-4
**Andrew County**—*pop pl* MO-7
Andrew County Courthouse—*hist pl* MO-7
Andrew Cove—*valley* TN-4
Andrew Creek—*stream* (3) AK-9
Andrew Creek—*stream* CA-9
Andrew Creek—*stream* OK-5
Andrew Dairy Canyon—*valley* UT-8
Andrew Dam—*dam* SD-7
Andrew Dewees (Heirs) Grant—*civil* FL-3
Andrew Dickhaut Cottages Hist Dist—*hist pl* RI-1
Andrew Etta Landing (historical)—*locale* TN-4
Andrew Garth Memorial Cem—*cemetery* AL-4
Andrew Gray Creek—*stream* CA-9
**Andrew Guillot Subdivision**—*pop pl* LA-4
Andrew Henry Sch—*school* WI-6
Andrew (historical)—*locale* AL-4
Andrew (historical)—*locale* KS-7
Andrew Hollow—*valley* MO-7
Andrew Hollow—*valley* OH-6
Andrew Hollow—*valley* PA-2
Andrew Island—*island* AK-9
Andrew Island—*island* ME-1
Andrew Jackson—*park* AL-4
Andrew Jackson—*uninc pl* CA-9
Andrew Jackson Boy Scout Lake Dam—*dam* MS-4
Andrew Jackson Camp—*locale* TN-4
Andrew Jackson Elem Sch—*school* TN-4
Andrew Jackson HS—*school* LA-4
Andrew Jackson HS—*school* NY-2
Andrew Jackson HS—*school* SC-3
Andrew Jackson Memorial—*cemetery* NC-3
Andrew Jackson Memorial Park—*park* AL-4
Andrew Jackson Monmt—*park* GA-3
Andrew Jackson MS—*school* FL-3
Andrew Jackson Sch—*school* CA-9
Andrew Jackson Sch—*school* KY-4
Andrew Jackson Sch—*school* PA-2
Andrew Jackson Sch—*school* (2) TN-4
Andrew Jackson Sch—*school* TX-5
Andrew Jackson State Park—*park* SC-3
**Andrew Jackson (subdivision)**—*pop pl* AL-4
Andrew J. Borden House—*building* MA-1
Andrew Johnson Camp—*locale* AK-9
Andrew Johnson Home—*building* TN-4
Andrew Johnson Natl Cem—*cemetery* TN-4
Andrew Johnson Natl Historic Site—*park* TN-4
Andrew Johnson Sch—*school* (2) TN-4
Andrew Johnson Wildlife Mngmt Area—*park* TN-4
Andrew Lake—*lake* (2) AK-9
Andrew Lake—*lake* FL-3
Andrew Lake—*lake* MN-6
Andrew Lake—*lake* WA-9
Andrew Lake—*lake* WI-6
Andrew Lewis HS—*school* VA-3
**Andrew Lewis Place**—*pop pl* VA-3
Andrew Mitchell Grant—*civil* FL-3
Andrew Nelson, Lake—*lake* MN-6
Andrew Norrell Ditch—*canal* CO-8
Andrew Nyman Mtn—*summit* ID-8
Andrew Pass—*gap* WA-9
*Andrew Peak* CA-9
Andrew Peak—*summit* WA-9
Andrew Point—*cape* NJ-2
Andrew Pond—*lake* NY-2
Andrew Pond—*reservoir* MS-4
Andrew Robeson House (Fall River Historical Society)—*building* MA-1
Andrew Run—*stream* PA-2
Andrew-Ryan House—*hist pl* IA-7
*Andrews* MD-2
*Andrews* MN-6
Andrews—*locale* AR-4
Andrews—*locale* FL-3
Andrews—*locale* IA-7
Andrews—*locale* NE-7
Andrews—*locale* NJ-2
Andrews—*locale* OR-9
**Andrews**—*pop pl* IN-6
**Andrews**—*pop pl* MD-2
**Andrews**—*pop pl* NC-3
**Andrews**—*pop pl* SC-3
**Andrews**—*pop pl* TX-5
Andrews, Ebenezer, House—*hist pl* OH-6
Andrews, John R., House—*hist pl* MN-6
Andrews, Josiah, House—*hist pl* IA-7
Andrews, Lake—*lake* ME-1
Andrews, Lake—*lake* WA-9
Andrews, Moses, House—*hist pl* CT-1
Andrews, Mount—*summit* AK-9
Andrews, Sewall, House—*hist pl* WI-6
Andrew-Safford House—*building* MA-1
Andrews Air Force Base—*military* MD-2
Andrews Air Force Hospital—*hospital* MD-2
**Andrews (Andrews University)**—*pop pl* MI-6
Andrews Archeol District—*hist pl* NM-5
Andrews Bald—*summit* NC-3
Andrews Basin—*basin* NV-8
Andrews Bay—*bay* (2) WA-9
Andrews Bayou—*gut* LA-4
Andrews Bayou—*stream* LA-4
Andrews Beach—*beach* ME-1
Andrews Bend—*bend* AR-4
Andrews-Bickam-Quin Cem—*cemetery* MS-4
Andrews Branch—*stream* AL-4
Andrews Branch—*stream* (2) GA-3
Andrews Branch—*stream* (2) KY-4
Andrews Branch—*stream* MD-2
Andrews Branch—*stream* MO-7
Andrews Branch—*stream* (2) TX-5
Andrews Bridge—*bridge* VA-3
Andrews Bridge—*locale* PA-2
Andrews Bridge Hist Dist—*hist pl* PA-2
Andrews Brook—*stream* (2) ME-1
Andrews Camp—*locale* CA-9
Andrews Canyon—*valley* ID-8
Andrews (CCD)—*cens area* SC-3
Andrews Cem—*cemetery* AL-4
Andrews Cem—*cemetery* AR-4
Andrews Cem—*cemetery* CT-1
Andrews Cem—*cemetery* FL-3
Andrews Cem—*cemetery* GA-3
Andrews Cem—*cemetery* IN-6
Andrews Cem—*cemetery* IA-7
Andrews Cem—*cemetery* KY-4
Andrews Cem—*cemetery* (2) MS-4
Andrews Cem—*cemetery* NY-2
Andrews Cem—*cemetery* NC-3
Andrews Cem—*cemetery* OH-6
Andrews Cem—*cemetery* OR-9
Andrews Cem—*cemetery* PA-2
Andrews Cem—*cemetery* (7) TN-4
Andrews Cem—*cemetery* (2) TX-5
Andrews Cem—*cemetery* VA-3
Andrews Cem—*cemetery* WI-6
Andrews Cemeteries—*cemetery* SC-3
Andrews Ch—*church* NC-3
Andrews Ch—*church* TX-5
Andrew Sch—*school* ME-1
*Andrews Chapel* MS-4
*Andrews Chapel* TN-4
Andrews Chapel—*church* (4) AL-4
Andrews Chapel—*church* (3) GA-3
Andrews Chapel—*church* (4) MS-4
Andrews Chapel—*church* (4) NC-3
Andrews Chapel—*church* (3) SC-3
Andrews Chapel—*church* (3) TN-4
**Andrews Chapel**—*pop pl* AL-4
Andrews Chapel Cem—*cemetery* (3) AL-4
Andrews Chapel Cem—*cemetery* (3) MS-4
Andrews Chapel Cem—*cemetery* TX-5
*Andrews Chapel Church* AL-4
Andrews Chapel Church Yard Cem—*cemetery* AL-4
Andrews Chapel (historical)—*church* (2) MS-4
*Andrews Chapel Methodist Ch* MS-4
*Andrews Chapel Methodist Church* AL-4
Andrews Chapel Sch (historical)—*school* AL-4
*Andrews Chapel United Methodist Church* AL-4
Andrews Christian Ch—*church* FL-3
Andrews Corral—*locale* WY-8
Andrews Coulee—*valley* MT-8
**Andrews (County)**—*pop pl* TX-5
*Andrews Creek* CA-9
Andrews Creek—*stream* CA-9
Andrews Creek—*stream* CO-8
Andrews Creek—*stream* FL-3
Andrews Creek—*stream* GA-3
Andrews Creek—*stream* MI-6
Andrews Creek—*stream* MT-8
Andrews Creek—*stream* NV-8
Andrews Creek—*stream* NC-3
Andrews Creek—*stream* ND-7
Andrews Creek—*stream* OH-6
Andrews Creek—*stream* (2) OR-9
Andrews Creek—*stream* TN-4
Andrews Creek—*stream* UT-8
Andrews Creek—*stream* (3) WA-9
Andrews Creek Campground—*locale* WA-9
Andrews Crossroads—*locale* GA-3
Andrews Ditch—*canal* CA-9

Andrews Ditch—*canal* ID-8
Andrews Ditch—*canal* MT-8
Andrews Ditch—*canal* NJ-2
Andrews Draw—*valley* WY-8
Andrews-Duncan House—*hist pl* NC-3
Andrews Elem Sch—*school* IN-6
Andrews Elem Sch—*school* NC-3
**Andrews Estates**—*pop pl* MD-2
Andrews Glacier—*glacier* CO-8
Andrews Grove Cem—*cemetery* NC-3
Andrews Grove Chruch—*church* NC-3
Andrews Gulch—*valley* MT-8
Andrews Harbor—*cove* MA-1
Andrews Heights—*uninc pl* SC-3
Andrews Heights Sch—*school* WV-2
**Andrews Hill**—*pop pl* MD-2
Andrews Hill—*summit* CT-1
Andrews Hill—*summit* (2) MA-1
Andrews Hill—*summit* MT-8
Andrews Hill—*summit* OK-5
Andrews Hill—*summit* RI-1
Andrews Hill—*summit* TX-5
Andrews (historical)—*locale* AL-4
Andrews Hollow—*valley* TN-4
Andrews Hollow—*valley* VA-3
Andrews House—*hist pl* CO-8
Andrews HS—*school* NC-3
*Andrewsia* IN-6
Andrews Institute (historical)—*school* AL-4
Andrews Island—*island* (2) CT-1
Andrews Island—*island* GA-3
Andrews Island—*island* ME-1
Andrews Island—*island* MI-6
*Andrews Lake* ND-7
Andrews Lake—*lake* CA-9
Andrews Lake—*lake* CO-8
Andrews Lake—*lake* (3) FL-3
Andrews Lake—*lake* (2) MN-6
Andrews Lake—*reservoir* DE-2
Andrews Lake—*reservoir* KS-7
Andrews Lake—*reservoir* (2) TX-5
**Andrews Lake Estates (subdivision)**—*pop pl* DE-2
Andrews Lake Sites—*hist pl* TX-5
Andrews Landing—*locale* AR-4
Andrews Landing Gut—*gut* VA-3
Andrews Lateral—*canal* ID-8
Andrews-Leggett House—*hist pl* MI-6
Andrew Slough—*gut* AK-9
Andrews-Luther Farm—*hist pl* RI-1
*Andrews Manor* IN-6
**Andrews Manor**—*pop pl* MD-2
*Andrews Meadow Brook* ME-1
Andrews Memorial Ch—*church* TN-4
Andrews Memorial Chapel—*hist pl* FL-3
Andrews Methodist Church—*hist pl* WV-2
Andrews Mill Creek—*stream* FL-3
Andrews Millpond—*reservoir* SC-3
Andrews Mine—*mine* OR-9
Andrews Mtn—*summit* CA-9
Andrews-Murphy Airp—*airport* NC-3
*Andrews Murphy Airpark* NC-3
Andrews North (CCD)—*cens area* TX-5
Andrews North Oil Field—*oilfield* TX-5
Andrews Nubble—*cape* ME-1
Andrews Oil Field—*oilfield* KS-7
Andrews Oil Field—*oilfield* TX-5
*Andrews Park* PA-2
Andrews Park—*park* IL-6
Andrews Park—*park* OK-5
Andrews Parks—*park* PA-2
Andrews Pass—*gap* CO-8
Andrews Peak—*summit* (2) CA-9
Andrews Peak—*summit* CO-8
Andrews Place—*locale* NM-5
**Andrews Plan**—*pop pl* PA-2
Andrews Plaza (Shop Ctr)—*locale* NC-3
Andrews Point—*cape* MA-1
*Andrews Pond* CT-1
Andrews Pond—*lake* GA-3
Andrews Pond—*lake* MA-1
Andrews Pond—*lake* NC-3
Andrews Pond—*reservoir* GA-3
Andrews Pond—*reservoir* VA-3
Andrew Spring—*spring* NV-8
Andrew Spring—*spring* OR-9
Andrews Ranch—*locale* NM-5
Andrews Reef—*bar* MI-6
Andrews Ridge—*ridge* UT-8
Andrews River—*stream* MA-1
Andrews River East Jetty Light—*locale* MA-1
Andrews Rsvr—*reservoir* CO-8
Andrews Run—*stream* IN-6
Andrews Run—*stream* KY-4
Andrews Run—*stream* OH-6
Andrews Run—*stream* PA-2
Andrews Run Sch (abandoned)—*school* PA-2
Andrews Sch—*school* CA-9
Andrews Sch—*school* LA-4
Andrews Sch—*school* MD-2
Andrews Sch—*school* MI-6
Andrews Sch—*school* NE-7
Andrews Sch—*school* NY-2
Andrews Sch—*school* (2) OH-6
Andrews Sch—*school* TX-5
Andrews Sch (historical)—*school* MS-4
**Andrews Settlement**—*pop pl* PA-2
Andrews South (CCD)—*cens area* TX-5
Andrews South Oil Field—*oilfield* TX-5
Andrews South Tank—*reservoir* NM-5
Andrews Spring—*spring* AZ-5
Andrews Spring—*spring* CA-9
Andrews Spring—*spring* ID-8
Andrews Spring—*spring* TN-4
Andrews Spring Canyon—*valley* UT-8
Andrews Spring Creek—*stream* ID-8
Andrews Store (historical)—*locale* AL-4
Andrews Street Bridge—*hist pl* NY-2
Andrews Tank—*reservoir* NM-5
Andrews Tarn—*lake* CO-8
Andrews Tavern—*hist pl* VA-3
Andrew Storrs Grant—*civil* FL-3
**Andrews Township**—*pop pl* ND-7
Andrews Univ—*school* MI-6
*Andrewsville* PA-2
Andrewsville—*locale* DE-2
Andrews Ward Sch—*school* TX-5
Andrews Well—*well* NM-5
Andrews West Tank—*reservoir* NM-5
Andrews Windmill—*locale* TX-5
Andrew Tank—*reservoir* NM-5
*Andrewville* DE-2
Andrew Warren Hist Dist—*hist pl* WI-6
*Andric Brook* VT-1
Andridge Apartments—*hist pl* IL-6
Andrix—*locale* CO-8
Andrix Cem—*cemetery* CO-8
Andromeda Cone—*summit* AK-9
Andromeda Kindergarten and Day Care—*school* FL-3
Andron—*locale* WA-9
Andronica Island—*island* AK-9
**Androscoggin (County)**—*pop pl* ME-1
Androscoggin County Courthouse and Jail—*hist pl* ME-1
Androscoggin Island—*island* ME-1
Androscoggin Lake—*lake* ME-1
Androscoggin Ranger Station—*locale* NH-1
Androscoggin River—*stream* ME-1
Androscoggin River—*stream* NH-1
*Androvetteville* NY-2
Androy Hotel—*hist pl* MN-6
Andrus, A. J., Duplex—*hist pl* IA-7
*Andrus Canyon* AZ-5
Andrus Canyon—*valley* AZ-5
Andrus Cem—*cemetery* IL-6
Andrus Cem—*cemetery* KY-4
Andrus Creek—*stream* MT-8
Andrus Drain—*canal* MI-6
*Andrus Draw* AZ-5
Andrus Draw—*valley* WY-8
Andrus Hollow—*valley* NY-2
Andrusia—*locale* MN-6
Andrusia Lake—*lake* MN-6
Andrus Island—*island* CA-9
Andrus Lake—*lake* MI-6
Andrus Lake—*lake* MN-6
Andrus Lake—*lake* WI-6
Andrus Memorial Home—*building* NY-2
Andrus Mine—*mine* CO-8
Andrus Peak—*summit* AK-9
Andrus Point—*summit* AZ-5
Andrus Post Office (historical)—*building* SD-7
Andrus Spring—*spring* AZ-5
**Andry**—*pop pl* IN-6
Andstadt Hill—*summit* PA-2
Andvari Cem—*cemetery* ND-7
Andvik Landing Strip—*airport* ND-7
*Andy* AR-4
*Andy* DE-2
**Andy**—*pop pl* KY-4
Andy, Mount—*summit* CA-9
Andy Bowie Park—*park* TX-5
Andy Branch—*stream* AL-4
Andy Branch—*stream* (3) KY-4
Andy Branch—*stream* NC-3
Andy Branch—*stream* (2) TN-4
Andy Branch—*stream* TX-5
Andy Branch—*stream* VA-3
Andy Branch—*stream* WV-2
Andy Branch Hollow—*valley* AL-4
Andy Canyon—*valley* UT-8
Andy Cove—*locale* NC-3
Andy Cove—*valley* NC-3
Andy Creek—*stream* (2) CO-8
Andy Creek—*stream* IL-6
Andy Creek—*stream* MT-8
Andy Creek—*stream* (3) OR-9
Andy Creek—*stream* TN-4
Andy Creek—*stream* WA-9
Andy Crockett Cutoff—*bend* LA-4
Andy Denton Public Access—*locale* MO-7
Andy Dick Creek—*stream* MT-8
Andy Draw—*valley* CO-8
*Andy Fife Spring* OR-9
Andy Five Spring—*spring* OR-9
Andy Gap—*gap* GA-3
Andy Gap—*gap* (2) NC-3
Andy Grant Tank—*reservoir* TX-5
Andy Hill Dam—*dam* OR-9
Andy Hill Rsvr—*reservoir* OR-9
Andy Hollow—*valley* IA-7
Andy Hollow—*valley* (4) TN-4
Andy Jack Hollow—*valley* MO-7
*Andy Lake* AR-4
Andy Lake—*lake* MN-6
Andy Lake—*lake* OR-9
Andylick Branch—*stream* KY-4
Andy Martin Hill—*summit* WY-8
Andy Mason Slough—*gut* CA-9
Andy McCully Branch—*stream* TN-4
Andy McCully Ridge—*ridge* TN-4
Andy Mesa—*summit* UT-8
Andy Miller Flats—*flat* UT-8
Andy Moore Mtn—*summit* TX-5
Andy Mtn—*summit* GA-3
Andy Mtn—*summit* ME-1
Andy Pond—*reservoir* PA-2
Andy Ridge—*ridge* TN-4
Andy Run—*stream* IN-6
Andy Run—*stream* WV-2
**Andys Acres (subdivision)**—*pop pl* SD-7
Andys Branch—*stream* KY-4
Andys Branch—*stream* MO-7
Andys Canyon—*valley* CA-9
Andys Canyon—*valley* NE-7
Andys Cave—*cave* CO-8
Andys Creek—*stream* MO-7
Andys Creek—*stream* NY-2
Andys Creek—*stream* TX-5
Andys Creek—*stream* WY-8
Andys Hole—*bend* AZ-5
Andys Hole—*bend* CO-8
Andys Hump—*summit* ID-8
Andy Simons Mtn—*summit* AK-9
Andys Knob—*summit* MT-8
*Andys Lake* SD-7
Andys Lake—*lake* NE-7
Andys Lakes—*lake* ID-8
Andys Mesa—*summit* CO-8
Andys Place—*locale* NV-8
Andys Point—*cape* MD-2
Andys Pond—*lake* UT-8
Andys Pothole—*lake* AZ-5
Andy Spring—*spring* SD-7
Andys Rapids—*rapids* OR-9
Andys Run—*stream* IL-6
Andys Run—*stream* WV-2
Andys Slough—*stream* AK-9
Andys Spring—*spring* MT-8
Andy Stone Creek—*stream* WY-8
Andy Stone Trail—*trail* WY-8
*Andy Subdivision* AR-4
Andytown—*locale* FL-3
Andy Trent Branch—*stream* KY-4
Andy Trent Branch—*stream* VA-3
Andyville—*locale* KY-4
**Andyville**—*pop pl* MN-6
Andy White Branch—*stream* KY-4
Andy Wilson Rsvr—*reservoir* OR-9
Andy Young Branch—*stream* TX-5
Anea—*island* MP-9
*Aneaidik* MP-9
Aneaitok—*island* MP-9
Aneaitok—*locale* MP-9
Aneal—*island* MP-9
Aneanij—*island* MP-9
*Aneanijna* MP-9
*Aneao* MP-9
Anear—*island* MP-9
Anearemej—*island* MP-9
Anearmej—*island* MP-9
Anearmej—*locale* MP-9
Aneaudik—*island* MP-9
Aneaul—*island* MP-9
Anebaajen—*island* MP-9
Anebaroro—*island* MP-9
Anebdo—*island* MP-9
*Anebin* MP-9
Anebing—*island* MP-9
Anebwilejjairik—*island* MP-9
*Anebwin* MP-9
Anebwubwu—*island* MP-9
Anedik—*island* MP-9
Anedikjaiing—*island* MP-9
Anedikjairik—*island* MP-9
Anedoul—*island* MP-9
*An-e'etseghi* AZ-5
**Anegam**—*pop pl* AZ-5
Anegam Wash—*stream* AZ-5
Anegan Wash—*stream* AZ-5
*Aneja* MP-9
Anejabwaru—*island* MP-9
*Anejabwrok* MP-9
Anejaej—*island* MP-9
*Anejalar* MP-9
Anejamwaden—*island* MP-9
Anejaoeoe—*island* MP-9
**Anejet**—*pop pl* MP-9
*Anejiltak* MP-9
*Ane Jima* FM-9
Anejobwa—*island* MP-9
Aneju—*island* MP-9
*Anejuon* MP-9
Anekaamu—*island* MP-9
Anekaej—*range* MP-9
Anekailik—*island* MP-9
Anekalik—*island* MP-9
*Anekalleb* MP-9
*Anekaron* MP-9
Aneken—*island* MP-9
*Aneken-to* MP-9
Anekijbwar—*island* MP-9
Anekinge—*island* MP-9
Anekinnat—*island* MP-9
Anekio—*island* MP-9
Anekira—*island* MP-9
**Anekirea**—*pop pl* MP-9
*Aneko* MP-9
Anekoble—*island* MP-9
Anekomkwan—*island* MP-9
*Anekonge* MP-9
Anekonno—*island* MP-9
Anekorea—*island* MP-9
Anekotkot—*island* MP-9
*Anel* MP-9
Anelejre—*island* MP-9
Anelijik—*island* MP-9
Anelik—*island* MP-9
Aneloklab—*island* MP-9
**Aneloklab**—*pop pl* MP-9
Anemakij—*island* MP-9
*Aneman* MP-9
Anemaro—*island* MP-9
Anemo—*island* MP-9
Anemone Cave—*cave* ME-1
Anemwaan—*island* MP-9
*Anemwanet* MP-9
Anemwanmwan—*island* MP-9
Anemwanot—*island* (2) MP-9
Anenaan—*island* MP-9
Anenbwubwu—*island* (2) MP-9
*Anenedik* MP-9
Anenedik—*island* MP-9
Anenelibw—*island* (2) MP-9
*Anenemmwaan* MP-9
Anenemmwaan—*island* MP-9
Aneneutejkaan—*island* MP-9
Anengeninon, Unun En—*bar* FM-9
Anengenipuan—*island* FM-9
*Aneniar* MP-9
Anenkinge—*island* MP-9
Anenkora—*island* MP-9
*Anenlik* MP-9
Anenlik—*island* MP-9
Anenoomw—*island* MP-9
Anenuaan—*island* MP-9
Aneraen—*island* MP-9
Anerein—*island* MP-9
Anerkochik River—*stream* AK-9
Aneroid Lake—*lake* OR-9
Aneroid Mtn—*summit* OR-9
Anertz Lake—*lake* AK-9
Anerukkanjaiing—*island* MP-9
Anerukkanjairik—*island* MP-9
**Anes**—*pop pl* TN-4
*Ane Shima* FM-9
Anesi Draw—*valley* WY-8
Aneskett Point—*cape* AK-9
Anes Post Office (historical)—*building* TN-4
**Aneta**—*pop pl* ND-7
Anetatabwuk—*island* MP-9
Aneth—*locale* UT-8
Aneth Oil Field—*oilfield* UT-8
Aneth Point—*ridge* UT-8
Aneth Terrace Archeol District—*hist pl* UT-8
Anewa—*island* MP-9
Anewato—*island* MP-9
Anfinson Lake—*lake* MN-6
Angalls Canyon—*valley* CA-9
*Angarard* PW-9
*Angaur* PW-9
Angaur—*island* PW-9
Angaur (County-equivalent)—*civil* PW-9
Angaur Field—*airport* PW-9
*Angaur Hafen* PW-9
Angaur Harbor—*harbor* PW-9
*Angaur Island* PW-9
*Angaur Ngaurd* PW-9
*Angauru Ko* PW-9
*Angauru-To* PW-9
Angayucham Mountains—*other* AK-9
Angayu Creek—*stream* AK-9
Angayukachak Creek—*stream* AK-9
Angayukak Creek—*stream* AK-9
Angayukak Hill—*summit* AK-9
Angayukalik Hills—*summit* AK-9
Angayukaqsraq, Mount—*summit* AK-9
*Angayukaqsraq Mtn* AK-9
Angayutak Mtn—*summit* AK-9
*A Ngeaur* PW-9
Angel—*locale* OH-6
**Angel**—*pop pl* AL-4
Angel, Arturo, House—*hist pl* NM-5
Angel, Mount—*summit* OR-9
Angel, Myron, House—*hist pl* CA-9
Angela—*locale* MT-8
Angela, Lake—*lake* MI-6
Angela, Lake—*reservoir* CA-9
**Angel Acres**—*pop pl* CO-8
Angela Lake—*lake* FL-3
Angela Merici HS—*school* KY-4
Angela Peak—*summit* TX-5
Angel Arch—*arch* (2) UT-8
Angel Bottom (historical)—*bend* SD-7
Angel Branch—*stream* IL-6
Angel Branch—*stream* TX-5
Angel Branch—*stream* WV-2
Angel Brook—*stream* CT-1
Angel Butte—*summit* ID-8
Angel Butte—*summit* WA-9
Angel Camp—*locale* (2) OR-9
Angel Canyon—*valley* (2) NM-5
Angel Cem—*cemetery* KY-4
Angel Cem—*cemetery* (2) NC-3
Angel Cem—*cemetery* OH-6
Angel City—*locale* TX-5
**Angel City**—*pop pl* FL-3
Angel Cove—*basin* UT-8
Angel Cove—*bay* TX-5
Angel Cove Spring—*spring* UT-8
Angel Creek—*stream* AK-9
Angel Creek—*stream* (4) CA-9
Angel Creek—*stream* CO-8
Angel Creek—*stream* MI-6
Angel Creek—*stream* NV-8
Angel Creek Campground—*locale* NV-8
*Angel Creek Recreation Site* NV-8
Angel Ditch—*canal* IN-6
Angel Draw—*valley* NM-5
Angel Draw—*valley* WY-8
*Angelel* PW-9
Angeles—*locale* TX-5
**Angeles**—*pop pl* (2) PR-3
Angeles, Arroyo de los—*valley* TX-5
Angeles, Lake—*lake* WA-9
Angeles, Mount—*summit* WA-9
Angeles Abbey Mausoleum—*building* CA-9
Angeles (Barrio)—*fmr MCD* PR-3
Angeles Creek—*stream* AK-9
Angeles Crest Station—*locale* CA-9
Angeles Lake—*lake* FL-3
Angeles Mesa Sch—*school* CA-9
Angeles Point—*cape* WA-9
Angeles Tunnel—*tunnel* CA-9
Angeles Wash, Los—*stream* AZ-5
Angel Falls—*falls* NY-2
Angel Falls—*falls* PA-2
Angel Field—*airport* AZ-5
**Angel Fire**—*pop pl* NM-5
Angelfish Creek—*gut* FL-3
Angelfish Key—*island* FL-3
Angel Fork—*stream* WV-2
Angel Gap—*gap* TN-4
*Angel Grove Baptist Church* AL-4
Angel Grove Ch—*church* AL-4
Angel Guardian Orphanage—*building* IL-6
Angel Gulch—*valley* OR-9
Angel Hill—*summit* NY-2
Angel Hill Cem—*cemetery* MD-2
Angel Hollow—*valley* KY-4
Angel Hollow—*valley* MO-7
Angel Hollow—*valley* OH-6
**Angelica**—*pop pl* NY-2
**Angelica**—*pop pl* PA-2
**Angelica**—*pop pl* WI-6
Angelica Branch—*stream* VA-3
Angelica Brook—*stream* MA-1
Angelica Creek—*stream* GA-3
Angelica Creek—*stream* NY-2
Angelica Creek—*stream* PA-2
Angelica Lake—*reservoir* PA-2
Angelica Lake Dam—*dam* PA-2
Angelical Covenant Ch—*church* FL-3
Angelica Park—*park* PA-2
Angelica Park Circle Hist Dist—*hist pl* NY-2
Angelica Point—*cape* MA-1
Angelica Rock—*rock* MA-1
**Angelica (Town of)**—*pop pl* NY-2
**Angelica (Town of)**—*pop pl* WI-6
Angelica Wash—*arroyo* AZ-5
Angelico—*locale* VA-3
Angelico Branch—*stream* FL-3
Angelico Branch—*stream* VA-3
*Angelico Creek* AL-4
*Angelico Creek* VA-3
Angelico Creek—*stream* MT-8
Angelico Creek—*stream* VA-3
Angelico Gap—*gap* NC-3
Angelico Knob—*summit* NC-3
Angelico Mtn—*summit* NC-3
**Angelina**—*pop pl* LA-4
Angelina Club—*other* TX-5
**Angelina (County)**—*pop pl* TX-5
Angelina Natl For—*forest* TX-5
Angelina River—*stream* TX-5
Angelina River Bridge—*hist pl* TX-5
Angelina Spring—*spring* CA-9
Angeline, Lake—*lake* MI-6
Angeline, Lake—*lake* WA-9
Angeline, Lake—*lake* WY-8
Angeline Brook—*stream* MA-1
Angeline Cove—*cove* MA-1
Angeline Hollow—*valley* MO-7
Angeline Lake—*lake* WA-9
Angeline Lemert Ditch—*canal* IN-6
Angeline Trail—*trail* WY-8
*Angel Island* NC-3
Angel Island—*hist pl* CA-9
Angel Island—*island* CA-9
Angel Island—*island* MN-6
Angel Island—*summit* NV-8
Angel Island State Park—*park* CA-9
**Angelita**—*pop pl* TX-5
Angell—*locale* AZ-5
Angell, A. J., House—*hist pl* KS-7
Angell, Daniel, House—*hist pl* RI-1
Angel Lake—*lake* AK-9
Angel Lake—*lake* CA-9
Angel Lake—*lake* (2) MI-6
Angel Lake—*lake* MT-8
Angel Lake—*lake* NV-8
Angel Lake—*lake* WA-9
Angel Lake—*reservoir* CO-8
Angel Lake Recreation Site—*locale* NV-8
Angell Basin—*basin* OR-9
Angell Branch—*stream* VA-3
Angell Brook—*stream* CT-1
Angell Cem—*cemetery* OH-6
Angell Peak—*summit* OR-9
Angell Ranch—*locale* MT-8
Angell RR Station—*building* AZ-5
Angell Sch—*school* (4) MI-6
Angell Sch (abandoned)—*school* MO-7
Angells Corner—*locale* NY-2
Angel Meadow—*flat* CA-9
Angel Meadow Trail—*trail* CA-9
Angel Mill Brook—*stream* NY-2
Angel Moroni Monument—*other* NY-2
Angel Mounds—*hist pl* IN-6
Angel Mounds State Memorial—*park* IN-6
Angel Mtn—*summit* CA-9
Angel Mtn—*summit* KY-4
Angel Mtn—*summit* NC-3
Angelmyer Loucke Ditch—*canal* IN-6
Angelo—*locale* VA-3
**Angelo**—*pop pl* WI-6
Angelo, Lake—*lake* FL-3
Angelo Belli Cabin—*locale* NV-8
Angelo Belli Flat—*flat* NV-8
Angelo Bell Mine—*mine* NV-8
Angelo Cem—*cemetery* WI-6
*Angelo Creek* CA-9
Angelo Ditch—*canal* ID-8
Angelo Heights Hist Dist—*hist pl* TX-5
Angelo Lake—*lake* IL-6
Angelo Lake—*lake* WI-6
Angelo Lake Creek—*stream* WI-6
Angelo Mission Mine—*mine* CA-9
Angelo Pond—*reservoir* WI-6
Angelos Lake—*reservoir* GA-3
*Angelo Slough* CA-9
Angelo's Shop Ctr—*locale* MA-1
Angelo State University—*uninc pl* TX-5
Angelo Towhead—*island* IL-6
**Angelo (Town of)**—*pop pl* WI-6
Angelovie Spring—*spring* WY-8
Angelo Windmill—*locale* NM-5
Angel Park—*park* WI-6
Angel Pass—*gap* CO-8
Angel Pass—*gap* WA-9
Angel Pass—*gap* WY-8
Angel Peak—*summit* NV-8
Angel Peak—*summit* OR-9
Angel Peak—*summit* WY-8
Angel Peak Compression Station—*other* NM-5
Angel Peak Mine—*mine* OR-9
Angel Point—*cape* MT-8
Angel Point—*ridge* UT-8
Angel Point—*summit* AZ-5
Angel Point—*summit* OR-9
Angel Ranch—*locale* CA-9
Angel Ranch—*locale* NM-5
Angel Ridge—*ridge* ID-8
Angel Ridge—*ridge* MO-7
Angel Ridge—*ridge* NC-3
Angel Ridge—*ridge* OH-6
Angel Ridge—*ridge* WV-2
Angel Ridge Cem—*cemetery* ID-8
Angel Ridge Ch—*church* OH-6
Angel Roost—*summit* NM-5
*Angels* CA-9
**Angels**—*pop pl* PA-2
Angels Bathing Pool, The—*lake* MT-8
**Angels Camp**—*pop pl* CA-9
*Angels Camp (corporate name Angels)* CA-9
Angels (CCD)—*cens area* CA-9
Angel Sch—*school* MO-7
Angels Corner Sch—*school* FL-3
**Angels (corporate name for Angels Camp)**—*pop pl* CA-9
Angels Creek—*stream* CA-9
Angels Flight Railway—*locale* CA-9
Angels Gate—*summit* AZ-5
Angels Grove—*locale* UT-8
Angels Gun Club—*other* CA-9
Angel's Hill Hist Dist—*hist pl* MN-6
Angels Hotel—*hist pl* CA-9
Angels Landing—*summit* UT-8
Angels Landing Trail—*trail* UT-8
Angels Landing Trail-West Rim Trail—*hist pl* UT-8
Angel Slough—*stream* CA-9
Angels Mine—*mine* CA-9
Angels Pass—*gap* CA-9
Angels Peak—*summit* NM-5
*Angels Point* UT-8
*Angel Spring* OR-9
Angel Spring—*spring* AZ-5
Angel Spring—*spring* CO-8
Angel Spring—*spring* OR-9
Angel Springs Hollow—*valley* AR-4
Angels Rest—*basin* AL-4
Angels Rest—*summit* OR-9
Angels Rest—*summit* VA-3
Angels Roost—*summit* NM-5
Angels Spring—*spring* AL-4
*Angel Station* AL-4
*Angels Trail* UT-8
Angel Street Cem—*cemetery* OH-6
**Angel Street Subdivision**—*pop pl* UT-8
Angels Window—*arch* AZ-5
**Angeltown**—*pop pl* TN-4
Angel Trail—*trail* UT-8
Angel Trail Spring—*spring* AZ-5
*Angelul* PW-9
**Angelus**—*pop pl* KS-7
**Angelus**—*pop pl* SC-3
Angelus, Lake—*lake* MI-6
Angelus Hill—*summit* CA-9
Angelus Mesa Branch—*hist pl* CA-9
**Angelus Oaks**—*pop pl* CA-9
**Angelus Oaks (Camp Angelus)**—*pop pl* CA-9
Angelus Sch—*school* KS-7
Angelview Ch—*church* VA-3
**Angelview (subdivision)**—*pop pl* NC-3
Angelville—*locale* GA-3
Angel Visit Ch—*church* VA-3
Angel Wells Rsvr—*reservoir* OR-9
Angel Windows—*arch* KY-4
Angel Wing—*summit* MT-8
Angelwing Butte—*summit* MT-8
Angelwing Creek—*stream* FL-3
Angenefan—*bar* FM-9
Angens Pond—*reservoir* NJ-2
Angens Pond Dam—*dam* NJ-2
Angerman Swamp—*swamp* MA-1
Angerona—*locale* WV-2
Anger's Block—*hist pl* MN-6
Angesek, Dauen—*gut* FM-9
Angevine Park Picnic Area—*park* MT-8
Angiaak Pass—*gap* AK-9
**Angie**—*pop pl* LA-4
Angie Canyon—*valley* OR-9
**Angie Circle Condominium**—*pop pl* UT-8
Angie Grant Sch—*school* AR-4
Angie Potholes—*lake* OR-9
**Angier**—*pop pl* NC-3
Angier, John B., House—*hist pl* MA-1
Angier MS—*school* NC-3
Angiers, Point—*cape* NY-2
Angier Sch—*school* CA-9
Angiers Pond—*reservoir* MA-1
Angiola—*locale* CA-9
Angle—*locale* UT-8
**Angle**—*pop pl* WV-2
Angle, D. M., House—*hist pl* TX-5
Angle, The—*locale* PA-2
**Anglea**—*pop pl* TN-4
Angle Canyon—*valley* AZ-5
Angle Canyon—*valley* CA-9
Angle Cem—*cemetery* VA-3
Angle Corners—*locale* PA-2
Anglecot, The—*hist pl* PA-2
*Angle Creek* CA-9
Angle Creek—*stream* AK-9
Angle Creek—*stream* KY-4
Angle Creek—*stream* MT-8
Angle Creek—*stream* NY-2
Angle Ditch Lateral No 4—*canal* AR-4
Angle Farm—*hist pl* PA-2
*Anglefish Creek* FL-3
Angle Fly Brook—*stream* NY-2
Angle Ford—*locale* MO-7
Angle Gulch—*valley* ID-8
Angle Hollow—*valley* WV-2
**Angle Inlet**—*pop pl* MN-6
Angle Inlet Sch—*school* MN-6
Angle Island—*island* MO-7
Angle Lake—*lake* WA-9
Angle Lake—*lake* WI-6
Angle Lakes—*lake* WY-8
Angle Lookout Tower—*locale* LA-4
Anglemeyer Lake—*lake* CO-8
Angle Mtn—*summit* WY-8
Angle Orchard—*locale* AZ-5
Angle Peak—*summit* WA-9
Angle Point—*cape* AK-9
Angle Point—*summit* ID-8
Angle Point—*summit* MT-8
Angle Pond—*lake* NH-1
Angler—*locale* TX-5
Angler Lake—*lake* AK-9
Angle Road Cem—*cemetery* NY-2
Angle Rod Creek—*stream* DE-2
*Angler Park* FL-3
**Angler Park**—*pop pl* FL-3
Anglers Bay—*bay* IA-7
Anglers Cove—*locale* TN-4
Anglers Lake—*lake* FL-3
**Anglers Park**—*pop pl* FL-3
Angle Rsvr—*reservoir* OR-9
Angles, The—*hist pl* KY-4
Angle Sch—*school* MA-1
*Anglesea* NJ-2
**Anglesea**—*pop pl* NJ-2
Anglesea Island—*island* NJ-2
Anglesea Marsh—*swamp* NJ-2
Anglese Sch—*school* IL-6
**Anglesey**—*pop pl* DE-2
Angle Siding—*locale* VA-3
**Angle Siding**—*pop pl* SC-3
**Angleton**—*pop pl* TX-5
Angleton Cem—*cemetery* IL-6
Angleton Lateral—*canal* TX-5
Angleton Oil Field—*oilfield* TX-5
Angleton-Rosharon (CCD)—*cens area* TX-5
**Angleton South**—*pop pl* TX-5
Angle Tree Stone—*hist pl* MA-1
**Angle View Subdivision**—*pop pl* UT-8
**Anglevillas**—*pop pl* FL-3
Anglewood Lake—*reservoir* PA-2
Angleworm Lake—*lake* MI-6
Angleworm Lake—*lake* MN-6
Angleworm Lookout Tower—*locale* MN-6
Angleworm Ranch—*locale* NV-8
Angleworm Spring—*spring* ID-8
Angley Creek—*stream* NC-3
Anglican Ch of the Advent—*church* FL-3
Anglican Ch of the Incarnation—*church* FL-3
Anglim—*locale* MN-6
Anglin—*locale* WA-9
Anglin Branch—*stream* KY-4
Anglin Branch—*stream* NC-3
Anglin Branch—*stream* TN-4
Anglin Branch—*stream* VA-3
Anglin Cem—*cemetery* KY-4
Anglin Cem—*cemetery* LA-4
Anglin Cem—*cemetery* TN-4

Anglin Ch—*church* KY-4
Anglin Creek—*stream* KY-4
Anglin Falls—*falls* KY-4
Anglin Falls Sch—*school* KY-4
Anglin Fork—*stream* KY-4
Angling—*locale* MI-6
Angling Creek—*stream* AR-4
*Angling Fork* TX-5
Angling Hollow—*valley* MO-7
Angling Pinnacle—*summit* AR-4
Angling Road Sch—*school* MI-6
Anglin Knob—*summit* NC-3
Anglin Pond—*lake* KY-4
Anglin Sch—*school* KY-4
Anglins Creek—*stream* WV-2
Anglins Run—*stream* WV-2
Anglo Saxon Mine—*mine* CO-8
Angmakrok Creek—*stream* AK-9
Angmakrok Mtn—*summit* AK-9
*Angola* DE-2
Angola—*locale* VA-3
**Angola**—*pop pl* IN-6
**Angola**—*pop pl* KS-7
**Angola**—*pop pl* LA-4
**Angola**—*pop pl* NY-2
**Angola**—*pop pl* NC-3
**Angola Acres II (trailer park)**—*pop pl* DE-2
**Angola Beach**—*pop pl* DE-2
**Angola Beach Trailer Park**—*pop pl* DE-2
**Angola by the Bay**—*pop pl* DE-2
Angola Creek—*stream* NC-3
Angola Creek—*stream* VA-3
**Angola Crest II (trailer park)**—*pop pl* DE-2
**Angola Crest Trailer Park**—*pop pl* DE-2
Angola Grange—*locale* DE-2
**Angola Lake Shore**—*pop pl* NY-2
**Angola Lake Shore Addition**—*pop pl* NY-2
Angola Landing—*locale* DE-2
Angola Landing—*locale* LA-4
Angola (Louisiana State Penitentiary)—*building* LA-4
Angola Neck—*cape* DE-2
**Angola Neck Park (trailer park)**—*pop pl* DE-2
Angola on the Lake—*CDP* NY-2
Angola Sch—*school* MS-4
Angola Swamp—*swamp* NC-3
Angolian Cem—*cemetery* IL-6
Angolik Creek—*stream* AK-9
*Angomanau* FM-9
*Angonne* IL-6
**Angoon**—*pop pl* AK-9
Angoon (Census Subarea)—*cens area* AK-9
Angora—*locale* CO-8
Angora—*locale* MN-6
**Angora**—*pop pl* NE-7
**Angora**—*pop pl* PA-2
Angora Cem—*cemetery* NE-7
Angora Ch—*church* AR-4
Angora Creek—*stream* (2) CA-9
Angora Creek—*stream* OR-9
**Angora (historical)**—*pop pl* OR-9
Angora Lakes—*lake* CA-9
Angora Lookout—*locale* CA-9
Angora Mtn—*summit* AR-4
Angora Mtn—*summit* CA-9
Angora Peak—*summit* CA-9
Angora Peak—*summit* OR-9
Angora Point—*cape* AK-9
Angora Post Office (historical)—*building* AL-4
**Angora (Township of)**—*pop pl* MN-6
*Angorur Island* PW-9
**Angostura**—*pop pl* (3) NM-5
Angostura Dam—*dam* SD-7
Angostura Drain—*canal* NM-5
Angostura Grant—*civil* NM-5
Angostura Grazing Pond Number 1 Dam—*dam* SD-7
Angostura Grazing Pond Number 2 Dam—*dam* SD-7
Angostura Hill—*summit* NM-5
Angostura Lateral—*canal* NM-5
Angostura Pass—*gap* CA-9
Angostura Ridge—*ridge* NM-5
Angostura Rsvr—*reservoir* SD-7
Angotti Hollow—*valley* AR-4
*Angour* PW-9
Angoyakvik Pass—*gap* AK-9
Angry Mountain Trail—*trail* WA-9
Angry Mtn—*summit* WA-9
*Angstadt Hill* PA-2
*Angston Ditch* UT-8
*Anguijan* MH-9
Anguila, Mesa de—*summit* TX-5
Anguilla—*locale* GA-3
**Anguilla**—*pop pl* MS-4
**Anguilla**—*pop pl* VI-3
Anguilla Baptist Ch—*church* MS-4
Anguilla Bay—*bay* AK-9
Anguilla Brook—*stream* CT-1
Anguilla Elem Sch—*school* MS-4
Anguilla HS—*school* MS-4
Anguilla Island—*island* AK-9
Anguilla Island—*island* ME-1
**Anguilla Junction**—*pop pl* GA-3
*Anguilla Line Consolidated Sch* MS-4
Anguilla Methodist Ch—*church* MS-4
Anguilm Creek—*stream* MI-6
Anguis House (historical)—*locale* AZ-5
Anguk Island—*island* AK-9
*Angulpelu Reef* PW-9
Angunelechak Pass—*gap* AK-9
Angun Lagoon—*bay* AK-9
Angun Point—*cape* AK-9
Angun River—*stream* AK-9
Angus—*locale* MO-7
Angus—*locale* NY-2
**Angus**—*pop pl* IA-7
**Angus**—*pop pl* MN-6
**Angus**—*pop pl* NE-7
**Angus**—*pop pl* OH-6
**Angus**—*pop pl* TX-5
**Angus**—*pop pl* WI-6
Angus Barn Pond—*reservoir* NC-3
Angus Barn Pond Dam—*dam* NC-3
Angus Bell Coulee—*valley* MT-8
Angus Brook—*stream* ME-1
Angus Canyon—*valley* CA-9
Angus Canyon—*valley* NM-5
Angus Cem—*cemetery* AR-4
Angus Cem—*cemetery* NY-2
Angus Creek—*stream* ID-8
Angus Farms Lake Dam—*dam* MS-4
Angus Lake—*lake* MN-6
Angus Lake—*lake* WI-6
Angus Oil Field—*oilfield* TX-5
Angus Park Pond—*lake* CT-1
Angus Rsvr—*reservoir* WY-8
Angus Spring—*spring* MT-8
Angus Spring—*spring* OR-9
*Angustora Creek* CO-8
*Angus Township* ND-7
**Angus (Township of)**—*pop pl* MN-6
Angus Valley Chapel—*church* FL-3
Angus Well—*well* NM-5
Angutikada Peak—*summit* AK-9
Anguvik Island—*island* AK-9
**Angwin**—*pop pl* CA-9
Angwin (CCD)—*cens area* CA-9
Angwin (Pacific Union College)—*CDP* CA-9
*Angyaur* PW-9
Angyoyaravak Bay—*bay* AK-9
Angyuto—*island* MH-9
Anhalt—*locale* TX-5
Anheuser-Busch Beer Depot—*hist pl* NE-7
Anheuser-Busch Brewery—*hist pl* MO-7
Anheuser Busch Heliport—*airport* MO-7
Anheuser-Busch Number Two Heliport—*airport* MO-7
A N Holiday Lake Dam—*dam* MS-4
**Aniak**—*pop pl* AK-9
Aniak Airp—*airport* AK-9
Aniak (Census Subarea)—*cens area* AK-9
Aniakchak Bay—*bay* AK-9
Aniakchak Crater—*crater* AK-9
Aniakchak Natl Monmt and Preserve—*park* AK-9
Aniakchak Peak—*summit* AK-9
Aniakchak River—*stream* AK-9
Aniak Lake—*lake* AK-9
Aniak River—*stream* AK-9
Aniak Slough—*stream* AK-9
Aniakvik Creek—*stream* AK-9
Anianikeha—*cape* HI-9
Anianiku Cove—*bay* HI-9
Aniani Nui Ridge—*ridge* HI-9
Aniceto Spring—*spring* AZ-5
Aniddik—*island* MP-9
*Aniddikan* MP-9
**Anidem (historical)**—*pop pl* OR-9
*Anidik* MP-9
*Anidjek* MP-9
Anidjet Island—*island* MP-9
*Anido Creek* AZ-5
*Anido Creek* UT-8
*Aniej* MP-9
Anielap Island—*island* MP-9
Anient Lake—*lake* WI-6
*Aniere-suido* MP-9
*Aniere-to* MP-9
*Anieru-Suido* MP-9
*Anieru To* MP-9
*Anif* FM-9
*Anigigichaien Island* MP-9
*Anigigichairukku* MP-9
Anigigichairukku Island—*island* MP-9
Anigigichalen Island—*island* MP-9
*Anigiigiichairukku-To* MP-9
**Aniguo**—*pop pl* GU-9
*Aniiru* MP-9
Aniiru Island—*island* MP-9
*Aniiru-to* MP-9
Anikovik River—*stream* AK-9
Aniktun Island—*island* AK-9
Anikunap—*gut* FM-9
*Anil* MP-9
Anil Channel—*channel* MP-9
**Aniline Village (subdivision)**—*pop pl* DE-2
*Anil Insel* MP-9
Anil Island—*island* MP-9
Anillep—*island* MP-9
Anillo Tank—*reservoir* AZ-5
*Anil Passage* MP-9
Anil Passage—*channel* MP-9
Animal Park—*park* CA-9
Animal Science Bldg—*hist pl* CA-9
*Animanete-to* MP-9
Animas—*CDP* PR-3
**Animas**—*pop pl* NM-5
Animas Cem—*cemetery* CO-8
*Animas City* CO-8
Animas City Mtn—*summit* CO-8
Animas Creek—*stream* NM-5
Animas Creek North—*stream* TX-5
Animas Creek South—*stream* TX-5
Animas Forks—*locale* CO-8
Animas Gulch—*valley* NM-5
Animas Island—*island* AK-9
*Animas Mountain* AZ-5
Animas Mountain, Las—*summit* AZ-5
Animas Mountains—*range* NM-5
Animas Mtn—*summit* CO-8
Animas Peak—*summit* (2) NM-5
Animas Ranger Station—*locale* CO-8
Animas River—*stream* CO-8
Animas River—*stream* (2) NM-5
Animas Sch—*school* CO-8
Animas Valley—*valley* NM-5
Animas Valley Consolidated Ditch—*canal* CO-8
*Animiki Lake* MI-6
*Animush Lake* WI-6
Anina Ch—*church* SD-7
**Anina Township**—*pop pl* SD-7
Anine—*island* MP-9
A-ninetyone Spring—*spring* AZ-5
A Ninetysix Spring—*spring* AZ-5
A N Ingram Dam—*dam* AL-4
Anini Beach—*beach* HI-9
Anini Stream—*stream* HI-9
Aninnan Lake—*lake* WI-6
*Anipadsch* FM-9
*Anipaj* FM-9
*Anipas* FM-9
*Anipasu* FM-9
Anipeahi—*area* HI-9
*Anipein Pah* FM-9
*Anipein Powe* FM-9
*Anipen* FM-9
*Anipoas* FM-9
Anirak, Lake—*lake* AK-9
Aniralik Lake—*lake* AK-9
*Aniri* MP-9
Aniri Island—*island* MP-9
*Anirippu* MP-9
Anirippu—*island* MP-9
*Aniri-To* MP-9
Anisak River—*stream* AK-9
Anise—*locale* PA-2
Anisom Point—*cape* AK-9
Anis Post Office (historical)—*building* MS-4
*Anisquam* MA-1
Anita—*locale* AL-4
Anita—*locale* CA-9
Anita—*locale* MT-8
**Anita**—*pop pl* IN-6
**Anita**—*pop pl* IA-7
**Anita**—*pop pl* PA-2
Anita, Lake—*reservoir* IA-7
Anita Artesian Well—*well* TX-5
Anita Bay—*bay* AK-9
Anita Cem—*cemetery* PA-2
*Anita Creek* ID-8
Anita Creek—*stream* (2) AK-9
Anita Creek—*stream* ID-8
Anita Ditch—*canal* WY-8
Anita Gulch—*valley* AK-9
*Anita Lake* MS-4
**Anita Lander Subdivision**—*pop pl* UT-8
Anita Mine—*mine* CA-9
Anita Mine—*mine* NM-5
Anita Park—*gap* AZ-5
Anita Point—*cape* AK-9
Anita Rock—*bar* CA-9
Anita Rsvr—*reservoir* MT-8
Anita Spring—*spring* AZ-5
Anita Station—*locale* AZ-5
Anita Station (historical)—*locale* PA-2
Anita Tank—*reservoir* AZ-5
Anita Tank—*reservoir* TX-5
Anita Well—*well* AZ-5
Anit Lake—*lake* MN-6
Aniuk River—*stream* AK-9
Anivik Creek—*stream* AK-9
Anivik Lake—*lake* AK-9
**Aniwa**—*pop pl* WI-6
Aniwa Lookout Tower—*locale* WI-6
**Aniwa (Town of)**—*pop pl* WI-6
*Aniyaanii Island* MP-9
*Aniyaani Island* MP-9
*Aniyaanii-to* MP-9
*Aniyarappu Inland* MP-9
*Aniyarappu-to* MP-9
*Aniyarapu-to* MP-9
Aniyuyaktuvik Creek—*stream* AK-9
**Anjean**—*pop pl* WV-2
*Anjelab* MP-9
*Anjeni Lake* MI-6
Anka, Lake—*lake* MN-6
Ankau, The—*channel* AK-9
Ankau Head—*cape* AK-9
Ankau Saltchucks—*lake* AK-9
Ankeewinsee Lake—*lake* MN-6
*Ankekejaeon* MP-9
Ankekejairik—*island* MP-9
*Ankekejarak* MP-9
Ankele Lake—*lake* CO-8
Ankele Spring—*spring* CO-8
Ankenbauer Coulee—*valley* ND-7
*Ankenny* IA-7
Ankeny—*locale* WA-9
**Ankeny**—*pop pl* IA-7
**Ankeny**—*pop pl* PA-2
Ankeny Bottom—*flat* OR-9
*Ankeny Bottoms* OR-9
Ankeny Gulch—*valley* CA-9
Ankeny Hill—*ridge* OR-9
*Ankeny Hills* OR-9
Ankeny Memorial Gardens—*cemetery* IA-7
Ankeny Natl Wildlife Ref—*park* OR-9
Ankeny Sch (historical)—*school* PA-2
**Ankenytown**—*pop pl* OH-6
Ankerman Creek—*stream* OH-6
Anker Post Office (historical)—*building* AL-4
Ankle Creek—*stream* OR-9
Anklin Meadows—*flat* CA-9
Anklin Village Archeol Site—*hist pl* CA-9
Ankney Cem—*cemetery* OH-6
Ankodosh Creek—*stream* MI-6
**Ankona**—*pop pl* FL-3
*Ankona* FL-3
Ankony Ranch Dam—*dam* SD-7
*Ankosu Point* PW-9
Ankrom Cem—*cemetery* MO-7
Ankrom Hollow—*valley* OH-6
Ankrum Cem—*cemetery* WV-2
Ankum Creek—*stream* VA-3
**Anlauf**—*pop pl* OR-9
Anlauf Canyon—*valley* CA-9
Anlauf Cem—*cemetery* OR-9
Anlauf Creek—*stream* OR-9
Anlo—*locale* OH-6
*Anman* MP-9
Anman Creek—*stream* AK-9
Anmo (not verified)—*island* MP-9
**Anmoore**—*pop pl* WV-2
Anmwi (not verified)—*island* MP-9
Ann—*locale* MO-7
Ann, Cape—*cape* MA-1
Ann, Lake—*lake* (2) CO-8
Ann, Lake—*lake* (3) FL-3
Ann, Lake—*lake* GA-3
Ann, Lake—*lake* (4) MI-6
Ann, Lake—*lake* (4) MN-6
Ann, Lake—*lake* NY-2
Ann, Lake—*lake* OR-9
Ann, Lake—*lake* (2) WA-9
Ann, Lake—*reservoir* NC-3
Ann, Lake—*reservoir* TN-4
Ann, Lake—*reservoir* VA-3
Ann, Mount—*summit* MA-1
*Anna* KS-7
Anna—*locale* KY-4
**Anna**—*pop pl* IL-6
**Anna**—*pop pl* KS-7
**Anna**—*pop pl* MS-4
**Anna**—*pop pl* OH-6
**Anna**—*pop pl* TX-5
Anna, Lake—*lake* AK-9
Anna, Lake—*lake* CA-9
Anna, Lake—*lake* MN-6
Anna, Lake—*lake* OH-6
Anna, Lake—*lake* WI-6
Anna, Lake—*reservoir* VA-3
Anna, Mount—*summit* NV-8
**Anna Acres**—*pop pl* DE-2
Anna Barre Gas Field—*oilfield* TX-5
Anna Belcher Creek—*stream* CA-9
Annabel Hill—*summit* NY-2
**Annabella**—*pop pl* UT-8
Annabella Canal—*canal* UT-8
Annabella Cem—*cemetery* UT-8
Annabella Dam—*dam* UT-8
Annabella Post Office—*building* UT-8
Annabella Rsvr—*reservoir* UT-8
Annabelle Lake—*lake* (2) WI-6
Annabel Spring—*spring* AZ-5
Annaberg—*locale* (2) VI-3
Annaberg Hist Dist—*hist pl* VI-3
Annaberg Point—*cape* VI-3
Annabessacook Lake—*lake* ME-1
Anna B Lacey Sch—*school* TN-4
Anna Branch—*stream* (2) AL-4
Anna Branch—*stream* AR-4
Anna Brochhausen Elem Sch—*school* IN-6
Anna (CCD)—*cens area* TX-5
*Anna Chapel* AL-4
*Anna Creek* OR-9
*Anna Creek* SD-7
Anna Creek—*stream* MT-8
Anna Creek—*stream* OR-9
**Annada**—*pop pl* MO-7
**Annadale**—*pop pl* LA-4
**Annadale**—*pop pl* NY-2
**Annadale**—*pop pl* TN-4
Annadale Beach—*beach* NY-2
*Anna Dale Landing* MS-4
Anna-Dean Farm—*hist pl* OH-6
Annadel—*locale* TN-4
Annadel Post Office (historical)—*building* TN-4
Anna District No. 1 (Election Precinct)—*fmr MCD* IL-6
Anna District No. 2 (Election Precinct)—*fmr MCD* IL-6
Anna District No. 3 (Election Precinct)—*fmr MCD* IL-6
Anna District No. 4 (Election Precinct)—*fmr MCD* IL-6
Anna District No. 5 (Election Precinct)—*fmr MCD* IL-6
Anna District No. 6 (Election Precinct)—*fmr MCD* IL-6
Anna D Mine—*mine* NV-8
Anna Drain County Park—*park* OR-9
Anna-Edna Cem—*cemetery* MO-7
Anna Ham Branch—*stream* KY-4
Anna Head Sch for Girls—*hist pl* CA-9
*Anna Herman Island* CA-9
Anna Holt Draw—*valley* WY-8
Annahootz Mtn—*summit* AK-9
Anna Howard Branch—*stream* KY-4
Anna Jordan Park—*park* LA-4
*Annalaide Lake* MN-6
Annalaide Lake Ditch—*canal* MN-6
*Anna Lake* CA-9
*Anna Lake* WI-6
Anna Lake—*lake* CA-9
Anna Lake—*lake* (2) MN-6
Annala Ranch—*locale* WY-8
Annala Round Barn—*hist pl* WI-6
Anna Laura Spring—*spring* UT-8
*Anna Lawrence Elementary School* AZ-5
**Annalee Heights**—*pop pl* VA-3
**Annaline Village**—*pop pl* PA-2
*Annaliza* TX-5
**Annalore (historical)**—*pop pl* OR-9
Annaly—*locale* VI-3
Annaly Bay—*bay* VI-3
Anna Lynne—*locale* KY-4
Annamahasung Creek—*stream* MN-6
**Anna Maria**—*pop pl* FL-3
Anna Maria Bridge—*bridge* FL-3
Anna Maria Coll—*school* MA-1
Anna Maria Elem Sch—*school* FL-3
Anna Maria Island—*island* FL-3
*Anna Maria Key* FL-3
Anna Maria Lake—*reservoir* AL-4
Anna Maria Sound—*channel* FL-3
Anna Marie, Lake—*lake* FL-3
Anna Marsh—*lake* MI-6
Anna May Ditch—*canal* WY-8
Annamede—*hist pl* WV-2
*Annamessex Canal* MD-2
Anna Mills, Mount—*summit* CA-9
**Annamoriah**—*pop pl* WV-2
Annamoriah Flats—*flat* WV-2
**Annamoriah Flats**—*pop pl* WV-2
Annamoriah Run—*stream* WV-2
Anna Mounds—*summit* MS-4
*Annandale* NY-2
Annandale—*locale* NC-3
Annandale—*mine* UT-8
**Annandale**—*pop pl* MN-6
**Annandale**—*pop pl* MS-4
**Annandale**—*pop pl* NJ-2
**Annandale**—*pop pl* PA-2
**Annandale**—*pop pl* VA-3
**Annandale Acres**—*pop pl* VA-3
Annandale Cem—*cemetery* PA-2
Annandale Country Club—*other* CA-9
**Annandale Estates**—*pop pl* IN-6
Annandale Estates Lake—*reservoir* IN-6
Annandale Estates Lake Dam—*dam* IN-6
**Annandale Gardens**—*pop pl* VA-3
Annandale Hotel—*hist pl* MN-6
Annandale HS—*school* VA-3
Annandale (Magisterial District)—*fmr MCD* VA-3
**Annandale-on-Hudson**—*pop pl* NY-2
Annandale Plantation—*hist pl* SC-3
Annandale Plantation—*locale* SC-3
Annandale (RR name for Boyers)—*other* PA-2
Annandale Sch—*school* CA-9
Annandale Sch—*school* VA-3
**Annandale Terrace**—*pop pl* VA-3
Annandale Terrace Sch—*school* VA-3
Annan Ranch—*locale* CA-9
Annan Run—*stream* PA-2
Anna Oil Field—*oilfield* MS-4
Anna Point—*cape* VI-3
Annapolis—*locale* CA-9
**Annapolis**—*pop pl* IL-6
**Annapolis**—*pop pl* IN-6
**Annapolis**—*pop pl* MD-2
**Annapolis**—*pop pl* MO-7
**Annapolis**—*pop pl* OH-6
**Annapolis**—*pop pl* WA-9
Annapolis Ave Ch of Christ—*church* AL-4
Annapolis (historical P.O.)—*locale* IN-6
Annapolis HS—*school* MI-6
**Annapolis Junction (Fort Meade Junction)**—*pop pl* MD-2
Annapolis Naval Ship R&D Center—*military* MD-2
**Annapolis Roads**—*pop pl* MD-2
Annapolis Rock—*locale* MD-2
Annapolis Rock—*summit* (2) MD-2
Anna Post Office (historical)—*building* AL-4
Anna Post Office (historical)—*building* MS-4
*Annaquatucket Cove* RI-1
Annaquatucket River—*stream* RI-1
Annaquatucket Rsvr—*reservoir* RI-1
**Ann Arbor**—*pop pl* MI-6
Ann Arbor Central Fire Station—*hist pl* MI-6
Ann Arbor Country Club—*other* MI-6
Ann Arbor Gulch—*valley* MT-8
Ann Arbor Railway Station—*hist pl* MI-6
**Ann Arbor (Township of)**—*pop pl* MI-6
Ann Arbor Trail Sch—*school* MI-6
Annaricken Brook—*stream* NJ-2
Anna River—*stream* MI-6
*Annarosa* TX-5
Anna Rose—*locale* TX-5
**Annarose**—*pop pl* TX-5
Anna R Page Forest Preserve—*park* IL-6
Anna Safley Houston Museum—*building* TN-4
Annas Bay—*bay* WA-9
Annas Chapel Cem—*cemetery* TX-5
Annas Farmhouse—*hist pl* NY-2
**Annas Hope**—*pop pl* VI-3
Anna's Hope Village (Census Subdistrict)—*cens area* VI-3
Annasnappet Brook—*stream* MA-1
Annasnappet Brook Dam—*dam* MA-1
Annasnappet Brook Rsvr—*reservoir* MA-1
*Anna Spring* OR-9
Anna's Retreat—*CDP* VI-3
Anna State Hosp—*hospital* IL-6
Anna Sue Mine—*mine* CA-9
Annata, Lake—*reservoir* PA-2
Anna Tank—*reservoir* NM-5
Anna Thomas Memorial Baptist Ch—*church* AL-4
*Anna T Jeanes School* AL-4
*Annatlylaica* FL-3
**Annaton**—*pop pl* WI-6
Anna Town Hall—*hist pl* OH-6
**Anna Township**—*pop pl* ND-7
Annaville—*locale* TX-5
**Annaville**—*pop pl* TX-5
Annaville Cem—*cemetery* TX-5
Annaville Ch—*church* TX-5
Annawaka P.O. (historical)—*locale* AL-4
*Annawamscot* RI-1
*Annawamscott* RI-1
*Annawamscut Creek* RI-1
**Annawan**—*pop pl* IL-6
Annawan Chapter House—*hist pl* IL-6
Annawan Rock—*summit* MA-1
**Annawan (Township of)**—*pop pl* IL-6
Annawaush Lake—*lake* MN-6
Anna Wilson Elem Sch—*school* IN-6
**Annawomscutt**—*pop pl* RI-1
Annawomscutt Brook—*stream* RI-1
*Annawon Rock* MA-1
*Annawons Rock* MA-1
Annaya Well—*well* NM-5
Anna York Cem—*cemetery* MS-4
Ann Bayou—*stream* MS-4
Anncar—*locale* NE-7
Ann Creek—*stream* AK-9
Ann Creek—*stream* NC-3
Ann Creek—*stream* OR-9
**Anne**—*pop pl* SC-3
Anne, Lake—*lake* FL-3
Anne, Lake—*lake* IN-6
Anne, Lake—*lake* MN-6
Anne, Lake—*reservoir* MO-7
Anne, Lake—*reservoir* NJ-2
Anne, Lake—*reservoir* NC-3
Anne, Lake—*reservoir* TN-4
Anne, Lake—*reservoir* VA-3
**Anne Acres (subdivision)**—*pop pl* DE-2
Annear Copper Mine—*mine* ME-1
**Anne Arundel (County)**—*pop pl* MD-2
Anne Arundel County Free Sch—*hist pl* MD-2
Anne Bates Leach Eye Hosp—*hospital* FL-3
Anne Bee Well—*well* AZ-5
Anne Chapel—*church* AR-4
*Anne Chesnutt Junior High School* NC-3
Anne Creek—*stream* MT-8
Anne Creek—*stream* NE-7
Anneewakee Creek—*stream* GA-3
Anneewakee Hosp—*hospital* FL-3
Anneewakee Treatment Center—*school* FL-3
Annefield—*hist pl* VA-3
Anne Holland Creek—*stream* CO-8
Anne Hollow—*valley* MO-7
Annejaang—*island* MP-9
*Annel* MP-9
Anne Lake—*lake* (2) CA-9
Anne Lake—*lake* WI-6
Annello, Lake—*lake* CO-8
Annelly—*locale* KS-7
Anne Louise, Lake—*lake* MI-6
**Annemanie (Arlington (sta.))**—*pop pl* AL-4
Anne Manie Ch—*church* AL-4
Annemanie Sch—*school* AL-4
Anne Marie Lake—*lake* FL-3
*Annemessex Canal* MD-2
Annemessex Creek—*stream* MD-2
Annen—*locale* MP-9
Annenburg Center—*building* PA-2
*Annenchieen* MP-9
Anner Cem—*cemetery* MS-4
Anner Ch (historical)—*church* MS-4
Annerer Spring—*spring* MT-8
*Annersnack Hill* MA-1
Annesdale—*hist pl* TN-4
Annesdale Park Hist Dist—*hist pl* TN-4
Annesdale-Snowden Hist Dist—*hist pl* TN-4
**Anneslie**—*pop pl* MD-2
Anness—*locale* KS-7
Anness Cem—*cemetery* KY-4
Anneta—*locale* KY-4
**Anneta**—*pop pl* TX-5
**Anneta North**—*pop pl* TX-5
**Anneta South**—*pop pl* TX-5
Annette—*CDP* AK-9
Annette—*locale* CA-9
Annette, Lake—*lake* FL-3
Annette, Mount—*summit* AK-9
Annette Bay—*bay* AK-9
Annette Coast Guard Air Station—*military* AK-9
Annette Island—*island* AK-9
Annette Island—*other* AK-9
**Annette Islands Res (Indian Reservation)**—*pop pl* AK-9
Annette Key—*island* FL-3
Annette Lake—*lake* WA-9
Annette Lake—*reservoir* MS-4
Annette Lake Trail—*trail* WA-9
Annette Workings—*mine* TN-4
Annetts Pond—*reservoir* NC-3
Annetts Pond Dam—*dam* NC-3
Annett State Reservation—*park* NH-1
Anne Valley—*valley* ID-8
Anne Valley Creek—*stream* ID-8
**Anneville**—*pop pl* DE-2
**Anneville**—*pop pl* TX-5
*Annex* AL-4
*Annex* RI-1
**Annex**—*pop pl* OR-9
**Annex**—*pop pl* VA-3
Annex, The—*hist pl* MS-4
Annex Canal—*canal* OR-9
Annex Creek—*stream* AK-9
Annex Creek—*stream* TN-4
Annex III—*post sta* CA-9
Annex Lakes—*lake* AK-9
Annex Peak—*summit* AK-9
Annex Ranch—*locale* CO-8
Annex Ridge—*ridge* AK-9
Annex Sch—*school* OR-9
Annex Spring—*spring* TN-4
Annexstad Lake—*lake* MN-6
Ann Gap—*gap* GA-3
Ann Grubb Hollow—*valley* VA-3
Ann Homer—*ridge* TN-4
Annhurst Coll—*school* CT-1
Annice Creek—*stream* OR-9
Annie, Lake—*lake* AL-4
Annie, Lake—*lake* CA-9
Annie, Lake—*lake* (4) FL-3
Annie, Lake—*lake* MI-6
Annie, Lake—*lake* MN-6
Annie, Lake—*lake* WI-6
Annie, Mount—*summit* NV-8
Annie, Mount—*summit* TX-5
Annie, Mount—*summit* WA-9
Annie Basin—*basin* CO-8
Annie Battle Lake—*lake* MN-6
Annie B Nye Elem Sch—*school* PA-2
Annie Branch—*stream* KY-4
Annie Carter Lake—*lake* MS-4
Annie Creek—*stream* ID-8
Annie Creek—*stream* NV-8
Annie Creek—*stream* (3) OR-9
Annie Creek—*stream* SD-7
Annie Creek (historical)—*locale* SD-7
Annie Creek Slough—*stream* OR-9
Annie Draw—*valley* WY-8
Annie Ellis Elem Sch—*school* MS-4
Annie Falls—*falls* OR-9
Annie Glade Bluff—*cliff* TX-5
Annie Gulch—*valley* CO-8
Annie Gulch—*valley* ID-8
*Annie Hall Lake* MN-6
Annie Hollow—*valley* TN-4
*Annie H Snipes Elementary School* NC-3
Annie Jean Kindergarten—*school* FL-3
Annie Johnson Mine—*mine* CA-9
Annie Lake—*lake* AK-9
Annie Lake—*lake* CO-8
Annie Lake—*lake* MN-6
Annie Lakes—*lake* CO-8
Annie Laurie Ch—*church* SC-3
Annie Mae Creek—*stream* UT-8
Annie Marsh Pond—*lake* FL-3
Annie Mary Ch—*church* GA-3
Annie Mine—*mine* AZ-5
Annie Mtn—*summit* NC-3
Annie Number 1 Lode Mine—*mine* SD-7
*Annie Peak* NV-8
Annie Rooney Creek—*stream* ID-8
Annies Canyon—*valley* UT-8
Annie Spring—*spring* (2) OR-9
Annies Rsvr—*reservoir* OR-9
*Annies Town* AL-4
Annie T Gregory Lake—*reservoir* AL-4
Annie T Gregory Lake Dam—*dam* AL-4
**Annieville**—*pop pl* AR-4
**Annieville**—*pop pl* (2) SC-3
Annieville (Township of)—*fmr MCD* AR-4
Annie Wilder Stratton Sch—*school* TN-4
Annie York Ch—*church* MS-4
Annie York Ch—*church* SC-3
Annin—*unorg reg* SD-7
Annin, Joseph, House—*hist pl* MI-6
Annin Creek—*locale* PA-2
Annin Creek—*stream* PA-2
Annin Creek Sch (historical)—*school* PA-2
Annin Glacier—*glacier* AK-9
Annington—*hist pl* MD-2
Annin Township—*civil* SD-7
**Annin (Township of)**—*pop pl* PA-2
**Annis**—*pop pl* ID-8
Annis Brake—*woods* MS-4
Annis Branch—*stream* KY-4
Annis Brook—*stream* ME-1
Annis Brook—*stream* NH-1
Annis Brook—*stream* VT-1
*Annis Creek* WI-6
Annis Creek—*stream* ID-8
Annis Creek—*stream* WI-6
Anniseta Gulch—*valley* NM-5
Annis Hill—*summit* VT-1
Annis Mound and Village Site (15BT2; 15BT20; 15BT21)—*hist pl* KY-4
Annis Point—*cape* VA-3
**Annisquam**—*pop pl* MA-1

Annisquam Bridge—*hist pl* ... MA-1
*Annisquam Canal* ... MA-1
Annisquam Harbor—*bay* ... MA-1
Annisquam Harbor Light—*locale* ... MA-1
Annisquam Harbor Light Station—*hist pl* ... MA-1
*Annisquam Island* ... MA-1
Annisquam Lighthouse—*locale* ... MA-1
Annisquam River—*gut* ... MA-1
Annisquam River—*stream* ... MA-1
Annisquam River Marshes—*swamp* ... MA-1
Annis Ranch—*locale* ... SD-7
Annis Ridge—*ridge* ... MS-4
Annis Run—*stream* ... NC-3
Annis Sch—*school* ... MI-6
Annis Slough—*stream* ... ID-8
*Annis-squam Village* ... MA-1
**Anniston**—*pop pl* ... AL-4
**Anniston**—*pop pl* ... MO-7
Anniston Acad—*school* ... AL-4
Anniston Area Vocational Technical Sch—*school* ... AL-4
Anniston Army Depot—*military* ... AL-4
Anniston Ave Elem Sch—*school* ... MS-4
Anniston Beach—*locale* ... AL-4
Anniston-Calhoun County Airp—*airport* ... AL-4
Anniston (CCD)—*cens area* ... AL-4
Anniston Cem—*cemetery* ... AL-4
Anniston Cem—*cemetery* ... NM-5
Anniston Center Gadsden State Junior Coll—*school* ... AL-4
Anniston City Hall—*building* ... AL-4
Anniston Coll for Young Ladies (historical)—*school* ... AL-4
Anniston Cotton Manufacturing Company—*hist pl* ... AL-4
Anniston Country Club—*locale* ... AL-4
Anniston Division—*civil* ... AL-4
Anniston HS—*school* ... AL-4
Anniston Inn Kitchen—*hist pl* ... AL-4
*Anniston Memorial Gardens Cemetery* ... AL-4
Anniston Museum of Natural History—*building* ... AL-4
Anniston Negro Sch (historical)—*school* ... AL-4
**Anniston Northwest**—*pop pl* ... AL-4
Anniston Ordnance Depot—*military* ... AL-4
Anniston Plaza Shop Ctr—*locale* ... AL-4
*Anniston Public School* ... AL-4
Anniston Road Ch—*church* ... FL-3
Anniston Speedway—*locale* ... AL-4
Anniston Transfer Company—*hist pl* ... AL-4
Annistown Bridge—*bridge* ... GA-3
**Annisville**—*pop pl* ... PA-2
Anniversary Arch—*arch* ... UT-8
Ann Johnson Mtn—*summit* ... AL-4
Ann Jordan Lake Dam—*dam* ... AL-4
Ann Jordan Resort Area—*park* ... AL-4
Ann Kellogg Sch—*school* ... MI-6
Ann Knudsen Park—*park* ... HI-9
Ann Lake—*lake* (2) ... MN-6
Ann Lake—*lake* ... WA-9
Ann Lake—*lake* ... WY-8
Ann Lake—*reservoir* ... MN-6
Ann Lake State Wildlife Mngmt Area—*park* ... MN-6
**Ann Lake (Township of)**—*pop pl* ... MN-6
Ann Lee Home—*locale* ... NY-2
Ann Lee Mine No 1—*mine* ... NM-5
*Ann Letort Elementary School* ... PA-2
Ann Marguret Beach—*beach* ... NV-8
Ann Mine—*mine* ... MN-6
Ann Moore Run—*stream* ... WV-2
Ann Morrison Park—*park* ... ID-8
Ann Mtn—*summit* ... NC-3
*Annocotuckett River* ... RI-1
*Annogatucket River* ... RI-1
Annokivik Slough—*gut* ... AK-9
Annoksek Creek—*stream* ... AK-9
**Annona**—*pop pl* ... TX-5
Annona-Avery (CCD)—*cens area* ... TX-5
Annoy Rock—*bar* ... AK-9
**Annpere**—*pop pl* ... MI-6
*Ann Pond* ... AL-4
Ann Pond—*reservoir* ... AZ-5
Ann Reno Mobile Home Park—*locale* ... PA-2
Ann River—*stream* ... MN-6
Ann River Logging Company Farm—*hist pl* ... MN-6
Ann Run—*stream* ... WV-2
Ann Rutledge Sch—*school* ... IL-6
Ann Saint Sch—*school* ... CA-9
Anns Butte—*summit* ... OR-9
Anns Cove—*cove* ... MA-1
Anns Creek—*stream* ... OR-9
Anns Lake—*lake* ... ID-8
Anns Point—*cape* ... ME-1
Anns Preschool/Kindergarten—*school* ... FL-3
Anns Run—*stream* ... WV-2
Anns Tabernacle Cem—*cemetery* ... MS-4
Ann Street Baptist Ch—*church* ... AL-4
Ann Street Hist Dist—*hist pl* ... CT-1
**Annsville**—*pop pl* ... NY-2
Annsville Creek—*stream* ... NY-2
**Annsville (Town of)**—*pop pl* ... NY-2
Ann Tormey, Lake—*reservoir* ... WV-2
**Ann (Township of)**—*pop pl* ... MN-6
Ann Tyler Cem—*cemetery* ... MS-4
Annuciation Ukranian Catholic Ch—*church* ... PA-2
Annunciata Sch—*school* ... IL-6
Annunciation Acad—*school* ... AR-4
Annunciation Catholic Ch—*church* ... FL-3
Annunciation Catholic Ch—*church* ... MS-4
Annunciation Ch—*church* ... FL-3
Annunciation Ch—*church* ... MS-4
Annunciation Ch—*church* ... NJ-2
Annunciation Church—*hist pl* ... TX-5
Annunciation Greek Orthodox Ch—*church* ... AL-4
Annunciation Greek Orthodox Church—*hist pl* ... WI-6
Annunciation HS—*school* ... CO-8
Annunciation Priory—*church* ... ND-7
Annunciation Sch—*school* ... CA-9
Annunciation Sch—*school* ... FL-3
Annunciation Sch—*school* (2) ... IL-6
Annunciation Sch—*school* ... LA-4
Annunciation Sch—*school* ... MA-1
Annunciation Sch—*school* ... MI-6
Annunciation Sch—*school* ... MN-6
Annunciation Sch—*school* ... NJ-2
Annunciation Sch—*school* (3) ... NY-2
Annunciation Sch—*school* (2) ... OH-6
Annunciation Sch—*school* (2) ... PA-2
Annunciation Sch—*school* ... WI-6
Annunication Sch—*school* ... TX-5
Annursnac Hill—*summit* ... MA-1
*Annursnack Hill* ... MA-1
*Annursuack Hill* ... MA-1
*Annursuc Hill* ... MA-1
*Annuteliga Hammock* ... FL-3
Annutteliga Hammock—*island* ... FL-3
**Annville**—*pop pl* ... KY-4
**Annville**—*pop pl* ... PA-2
Annville-Cleona HS—*school* ... PA-2
*Annville Cleona Junior Senior HS* ... PA-2
Annville Elem Sch—*school* ... PA-2
Annville Hist Dist—*hist pl* ... PA-2
Annville (historical P.O.)—*locale* ... IA-7
**Annville (Township of)**—*pop pl* ... PA-2
Ann White Cave—*cave* ... TN-4
Ano—*locale* ... KY-4
Anoakia Sch—*school* ... CA-9
Anoatok—*hist pl* ... PA-2
Anodanta Lake—*lake* ... WI-6
Anogok—*locale* ... AK-9
Anohwahk River—*stream* ... AK-9
*Ano Jima* ... FM-9
**Anoka**—*pop pl* ... IN-6
**Anoka**—*pop pl* ... MN-6
**Anoka**—*pop pl* ... NE-7
Anoka, Lake—*lake* ... FL-3
Anoka Ch—*church* ... MN-6
Anoka-Champlin Mississippi River Bridge—*hist pl* ... MN-6
**Anoka (County)**—*pop pl* ... MN-6
**Anoka (historical)**—*pop pl* ... OR-9
Anokaiole—*cape* ... HI-9
Anoka Post Office—*hist pl* ... MN-6
Anoka-Ramsey State Junior Coll—*school* ... MN-6
*Anokeseba* ... MN-6
*Anolani Stream* ... HI-9
*Anolani Tract Storm Drainage* ... HI-9
*Anoma* ... FM-9
Anoma—*summit* ... FM-9
**Anona**—*pop pl* ... FL-3
Anona Lake—*lake* ... CA-9
Anona Lake—*reservoir* ... NJ-2
Anona Sch—*school* ... FL-3
Anon (Barrio)—*fmr MCD* ... PR-3
Anon Ch—*church* ... AL-4
Anones (Barrio)—*fmr MCD* (2) ... PR-3
Anon Grove Ch—*church* ... GA-3
*Anonimo Key* ... FL-3
Anonimo Key—*island* ... FL-3
*Anon Missionary Baptist Ch* ... AL-4
Ano Nuevo Bay—*bay* ... CA-9
Ano Nuevo Creek—*stream* ... CA-9
Ano Nuevo Island—*island* ... CA-9
Ano Nuevo Island State Park—*park* ... CA-9
*Ano Nuevo Point* ... CA-9
Ano Nuevo Windmill—*locale* ... TX-5
Anopia (historical)—*locale* ... AL-4
Anorat Creek—*stream* ... AK-9
*Anorourou* ... HI-9
*Anoth* ... FM-9
Another River—*stream* ... AK-9
Anotleneega Mtn—*summit* ... AK-9
Anoumures—*bar* ... FM-9
Anoway Lake—*lake* ... MN-6
Anowik Island—*island* ... AK-9
*Anoz* ... FM-9
An-qui-ni-gay Indian Burial Ground—*cemetery* ... ND-7
*Anrana Creek* ... TX-5
*Anrania Creek* ... TX-5
Anrbwilejaiing—*island* ... MP-9
Anrook Park—*park* ... MI-6
Ansaldo Lake—*lake* ... WA-9
Ansberry Bird Ditch—*canal* ... IN-6
**Anse**—*pop pl* ... MS-4
Anse Branch—*stream* ... TN-4
Ansel—*locale* ... CA-9
Ansel—*locale* ... CO-8
Ansel—*locale* ... KY-4
**Ansel**—*pop pl* ... SC-3
Anse La Butte—*locale* ... LA-4
Anse La Butte Oil and Gas Field—*oilfield* ... LA-4
Ansel Adams, Mount—*summit* ... CA-9
Ansel Cem—*cemetery* ... KY-4
Ansel Ch—*church* ... KY-4
Ansel Lake—*lake* ... CA-9
Ansell Run—*stream* ... PA-2
**Anselm**—*pop pl* ... ND-7
Anselma—*locale* ... PA-2
Anselm Coulee—*stream* ... LA-4
**Anselmo**—*pop pl* ... NE-7
Anselmo, Fortunato, House—*hist pl* ... UT-8
Anselmo Bench—*bench* ... NM-5
Anselmo Mine—*mine* ... MT-8
Ansel Pond—*lake* ... VT-1
Ansel Prewitt Cem—*cemetery* ... MS-4
Ansels Point—*cape* ... MI-6
Ansel Spring—*spring* ... AZ-5
**Ansel (Township of)**—*pop pl* ... MN-6
Ansel Watrous Campground—*locale* ... CO-8
Ansgaar Cem—*cemetery* ... WI-6
Anshe Chesed Cem—*cemetery* ... MS-4
Anshe Emeth Cem—*cemetery* ... OH-6
Ansley—*locale* ... LA-4
**Ansley**—*pop pl* ... AL-4
**Ansley**—*pop pl* ... MS-4
**Ansley**—*pop pl* ... NE-7
**Ansley Acres**—*pop pl* ... IN-6
Ansley Cem—*cemetery* ... NE-7
Ansley Ch—*church* ... AL-4
**Ansley Heights**—*pop pl* ... NC-3
Ansley Hollow—*valley* ... PA-2
Ansley Island—*island* ... AK-9
Ansley Mill—*locale* ... GA-3
Ansley Park—*park* ... OK-5
Ansley Park Golf Course—*other* ... GA-3
Ansley Park Hist Dist—*hist pl* ... GA-3
Ansley Place—*locale* ... TX-5
Ansley Sch—*school* ... AL-4
**Ansley Township**—*pop pl* ... NE-7
Anson—*locale* ... MO-7
**Anson**—*pop pl* ... KS-7
**Anson**—*pop pl* ... ME-1
**Anson**—*pop pl* ... TX-5
**Anson**—*pop pl* ... WI-6
Anson Branch—*stream* ... IN-6
Anson Cabin—*locale* ... UT-8
Anson (CCD)—*cens area* ... TX-5
Anson Cem—*cemetery* ... MO-7
Anson Cem—*cemetery* ... PA-2
*Anson County* ... NC-3
**Anson County**—*pop pl* ... NC-3
*Anson County Airp* ... NC-3
Anson County Airp—*airport* ... NC-3
Anson County Hosp—*hospital* ... NC-3
Anson Creek—*stream* ... IA-7
Ansones Creek—*stream* ... NM-5
*Anson Harbor* ... MH-9
*Ansonia* ... TN-4
Ansonia—*locale* ... PA-2
**Ansonia**—*pop pl* ... CT-1
**Ansonia**—*pop pl* ... OH-6
Ansonia—*uninc pl* ... NY-2
Ansonia Cem—*cemetery* ... OH-6
Ansonia Depot (historical)—*locale* ... TN-4
Ansonia Hotel—*hist pl* ... NY-2
Ansonia Library—*hist pl* ... CT-1
Ansonia Mills (historical)—*locale* ... TN-4
Ansonia Rsvr—*reservoir* ... CT-1
Ansonia Station—*locale* ... PA-2
Ansonia (Town of)—*civ div* ... CT-1
Anson JHS—*school* ... NC-3
Anson Jones—*uninc pl* ... TX-5
Anson Jones JHS—*school* ... TX-5
Anson Jones Sch—*school* (2) ... TX-5
Anson Lake—*lake* ... UT-8
Anson North Lake—*reservoir* ... TX-5
Anson Oil Field—*oilfield* ... KS-7
Anson Oil Field—*oilfield* ... TX-5
Anson Park—*park* ... WI-6
Anson Park JHS—*school* ... IA-7
Anson Point—*cape* ... MO-7
Anson Point—*cape* ... NC-3
*Anson Reede* ... MH-9
*Anson Road* ... MH-9
*Anson Roads* ... MH-9
Anson Southeast Oil Field—*oilfield* ... KS-7
Anson South Lake—*reservoir* ... TX-5
Anson Spring—*spring* ... TX-5
Anson (Station)—*locale* ... WI-6
**Anson (Town of)**—*pop pl* ... ME-1
**Anson (Town of)**—*pop pl* ... WI-6
**Ansonville**—*pop pl* ... NC-3
**Ansonville**—*pop pl* ... PA-2
Ansonville Sch—*school* ... NC-3
Ansonville (Township of)—*fmr MCD* ... NC-3
Anson Wright Memorial Park—*park* ... OR-9
Ansorge Hotel—*hist pl* ... WA-9
Anspaugh Bridge—*bridge* ... IN-6
Anspaugh Ditch—*canal* ... IN-6
Anspaugh Flats—*flat* ... IN-6
Anstead Bridge—*bridge* ... NY-2
**Ansted**—*pop pl* ... WV-2
**Anstine**—*pop pl* ... PA-2
Anstine Windmill—*locale* ... CO-8
Anstis Ditch—*canal* ... IN-6
Anstis Lake—*reservoir* ... TN-4
**Anston**—*pop pl* ... WI-6
Ansul Islands—*island* ... WI-6
Answer Creek—*stream* ... AK-9
*Answorth* ... IN-6
Answorth Branch—*stream* ... TX-5
*Antajan* ... MH-9
*Antalaunee Creek* ... PA-2
Antares—*locale* ... AZ-5
*Antassawamoc Beach* ... MA-1
**Antassawamock**—*pop pl* ... MA-1
**Antassawamock Beach**—*pop pl* ... MA-1
Ant Atoll—*island* ... FM-9
Ant Bar—*locale* ... MD-2
Ant Basin—*basin* ... ID-8
Ant Basin Creek—*stream* ... ID-8
Ant Bed Well—*well* ... TX-5
Ant Branch—*stream* ... LA-4
Ant Butte—*summit* (3) ... ID-8
*Ant Canyon* ... ID-8
Ant Canyon—*valley* (2) ... CA-9
Ant Creek—*stream* (2) ... CO-8
Ant Creek—*stream* ... ID-8
Ant Creek—*stream* ... OR-9
Ante—*locale* ... VA-3
Antediluvian Pond—*lake* ... NY-2
*Antelauna Creek* ... PA-2
*Antelawney Creek* ... PA-2
*Antelawny Creek* ... PA-2
Antelm Gay Grant—*civil* (2) ... FL-3
*Antelope* ... ND-7
Antelope—*fmr MCD* (5) ... NE-7
Antelope—*locale* ... CA-9
Antelope—*locale* ... NV-8
Antelope—*locale* ... WY-8
**Antelope**—*pop pl* ... ID-8
**Antelope**—*pop pl* ... KS-7
**Antelope**—*pop pl* ... MT-8
**Antelope**—*pop pl* ... ND-7
**Antelope**—*pop pl* ... OR-9
**Antelope**—*pop pl* ... SD-7
**Antelope**—*pop pl* (2) ... TX-5
**Antelope Acres**—*pop pl* ... CA-9
Antelope Basin—*basin* (2) ... ID-8
Antelope Basin—*basin* (3) ... MT-8
Antelope Basin—*basin* ... NV-8
Antelope Basin—*basin* (3) ... WY-8
Antelope Basin Ditch—*canal* ... MT-8
Antelope Bridge—*bridge* ... WY-8
*Antelope Butte* ... WY-8
Antelope Butte—*summit* ... CO-8
Antelope Butte—*summit* (2) ... ID-8
Antelope Butte—*summit* (10) ... MT-8
Antelope Butte—*summit* ... NV-8
Antelope Butte—*summit* ... ND-7
Antelope Butte—*summit* (2) ... OR-9
Antelope Butte—*summit* ... SD-7
Antelope Butte—*summit* (4) ... WY-8
Antelope Butte Creek—*stream* ... WY-8
Antelope Buttes—*summit* (2) ... CA-9
Antelope Canal—*canal* ... CA-9
*Antelope Canyon* ... UT-8
Antelope Canyon—*valley* (3) ... AZ-5
Antelope Canyon—*valley* (2) ... CA-9
Antelope Canyon—*valley* ... ID-8
Antelope Canyon—*valley* (3) ... NV-8
Antelope Canyon—*valley* (6) ... NM-5
Antelope Canyon—*valley* ... OR-9
Antelope Canyon—*valley* ... SD-7
Antelope Canyon—*valley* (2) ... UT-8
Antelope Cave—*hist pl* ... AZ-5
Antelope (CCD)—*cens area* ... OR-9
Antelope Cem—*cemetery* ... CA-9
Antelope Cem—*cemetery* ... ID-8
Antelope Cem—*cemetery* (2) ... NE-7
Antelope Cem—*cemetery* (2) ... ND-7
Antelope Cem—*cemetery* (2) ... OR-9
Antelope Cem—*cemetery* (2) ... TX-5
**Antelope Center**—*pop pl* ... CA-9
Antelope Ch—*church* ... TX-5
**Antelope Commercial Park Subdivision**—*pop pl* ... UT-8
Antelope Corral—*locale* ... NM-5
Antelope Corral—*other* ... NM-5
Antelope Coulee—*valley* (9) ... MT-8
Antelope Coulee Sch—*school* ... MT-8
Antelope Country Club—*other* ... NE-7
Antelope County Courthouse—*hist pl* ... NE-7
Antelope County Lake—*reservoir* ... KS-7
Antelope County Park—*park* ... KS-7
Antelope Cow Camp—*locale* ... OR-9
*Antelope Creek* ... AZ-5
*Antelope Creek* ... CA-9
*Antelope Creek* ... CO-8
*Antelope Creek* ... ID-8
*Antelope Creek* ... MT-8
*Antelope Creek* ... NE-7
*Antelope Creek* ... NV-8
*Antelope Creek* ... ND-7
*Antelope Creek* ... OR-9
*Antelope Creek* ... WY-8
Antelope Creek—*stream* ... AK-9
Antelope Creek—*stream* (4) ... AZ-5
Antelope Creek—*stream* (10) ... CA-9
Antelope Creek—*stream* (14) ... CO-8
Antelope Creek—*stream* (5) ... ID-8
Antelope Creek—*stream* (12) ... KS-7
Antelope Creek—*stream* (28) ... MT-8
Antelope Creek—*stream* (6) ... NE-7
Antelope Creek—*stream* (5) ... NV-8
Antelope Creek—*stream* ... NM-5
Antelope Creek—*stream* (6) ... ND-7
Antelope Creek—*stream* (2) ... OK-5
Antelope Creek—*stream* (14) ... OR-9
Antelope Creek—*stream* (8) ... SD-7
Antelope Creek—*stream* (12) ... TX-5
Antelope Creek—*stream* ... UT-8
Antelope Creek—*stream* ... WA-9
Antelope Creek—*stream* (19) ... WY-8
Antelope Creek Archeol District—*hist pl* ... TX-5
Antelope Creek Lakes—*lake* ... CA-9
Antelope Creek Ranch—*locale* ... ID-8
Antelope Creek Rec Area—*park* ... SD-7
Antelope Creek Sch—*school* ... NE-7
Antelope Creek Sch—*school* ... WY-8
Antelope Creek Site (39ST55)—*hist pl* ... SD-7
Antelope Creek State Game Mngmt Area—*park* ... ND-7
Antelope Creek Summer Camp—*locale* ... WY-8
**Antelope Creek Township**—*pop pl* ... ND-7
Antelope Crossing—*locale* ... TX-5
Antelope Dam—*dam* ... AZ-5
Antelope Dam—*dam* ... NM-5
Antelope Dam—*dam* (2) ... OR-9
Antelope Dam—*dam* ... SD-7
Antelope Desert—*plain* ... OR-9
Antelope Detention Dam—*dam* ... AZ-5
**Antelope Development Area (subdivision)**—*pop pl* ... SD-7
Antelope Ditch—*canal* ... CO-8
Antelope Ditch—*canal* ... UT-8
Antelope Ditch—*canal* ... WY-8
*Antelope Draw* ... TX-5
*Antelope Draw* ... WY-8
Antelope Draw—*valley* ... AZ-5
Antelope Draw—*valley* (4) ... CO-8
Antelope Draw—*valley* (6) ... NM-5
Antelope Draw—*valley* ... SD-7
Antelope Draw—*valley* (5) ... TX-5
Antelope Draw—*valley* ... UT-8
Antelope Draw—*valley* (12) ... WY-8
Antelope Draw Tank—*reservoir* ... AZ-5
Antelope Feeder Canal—*canal* ... OR-9
Antelope Fire Control Station—*other* ... CA-9
*Antelope Flat* ... ID-8
*Antelope Flat* ... OR-9
*Antelope Flat* ... WY-8
Antelope Flat—*flat* ... AZ-5
Antelope Flat—*flat* (4) ... ID-8
Antelope Flat—*flat* (2) ... MT-8
Antelope Flat—*flat* ... NV-8
Antelope Flat—*flat* ... NM-5
Antelope Flat—*flat* ... OK-5
Antelope Flat—*flat* (7) ... OR-9
Antelope Flat—*flat* ... TX-5
Antelope Flat—*flat* (2) ... UT-8
Antelope Flat—*flat* ... WY-8
Antelope Flat Campground—*locale* ... UT-8
Antelope Flat Dam—*dam* ... OR-9
Antelope Flat Development—*locale* ... UT-8
*Antelope Flat Rsvr* ... OR-9
Antelope Flat Rsvr—*reservoir* ... ID-8
Antelope Flat Rsvr—*reservoir* ... OR-9
Antelope Flat Rsvr Number One—*reservoir* ... OR-9
Antelope Flat Rsvr Number Two—*reservoir* ... OR-9
*Antelope Flats* ... OR-9
Antelope Flats—*flat* ... AZ-5
Antelope Flats—*flat* ... CO-8
Antelope Flats—*flat* (2) ... NM-5
Antelope Flats—*flat* (2) ... TX-5
Antelope Flats—*flat* (3) ... WY-8
Antelope Forest Camp—*locale* ... OR-9
Antelope Gap—*gap* ... CO-8
Antelope Gap—*gap* ... TX-5
Antelope Gap—*gap* ... WY-8
Antelope Gap—*locale* ... TX-5
**Antelope Gap**—*pop pl* ... TX-5
Antelope Gorge—*valley* ... MT-8
Antelope Grange Hall—*locale* ... WY-8
Antelope Grocery—*hist pl* ... NE-7
Antelope Guard Station—*locale* ... ID-8
*Antelope Gulch* ... CO-8
Antelope Gulch—*valley* (2) ... CO-8
Antelope Gulch—*valley* ... MT-8
Antelope Gulch—*valley* ... TX-5
Antelope Gulch—*valley* ... WY-8
Antelope Gulch Sch—*school* ... WY-8
*Antelope Hill* ... AZ-5
*Antelope Hill* ... TX-5
Antelope Hill—*summit* (3) ... AZ-5
Antelope Hill—*summit* (2) ... CO-8
Antelope Hill—*summit* ... ID-8
Antelope Hill—*summit* ... MT-8
Antelope Hill—*summit* ... NV-8
Antelope Hill—*summit* (2) ... NM-5
Antelope Hill—*summit* ... TX-5
Antelope Hill Highway Bridge—*hist pl* ... AZ-5
*Antelope Hills* ... AZ-5
Antelope Hills—*hist pl* ... OK-5
Antelope Hills—*other* ... CA-9
Antelope Hills—*range* ... AZ-5
Antelope Hills—*ridge* ... WY-8
Antelope Hills—*summit* (3) ... AZ-5
Antelope Hills—*summit* ... MN-6
Antelope Hills—*summit* ... OK-5
Antelope Hills—*summit* ... TX-5
Antelope Hills Ch—*church* ... MN-6
Antelope Hills Golf Course—*other* ... AZ-5
*Antelope Hills Oil Field* ... CA-9
*Antelope Hills Stage Station* ... AZ-5
Antelope Hollow—*valley* ... SD-7
Antelope Hollow—*valley* ... UT-8
Antelope House Ruins—*locale* ... AZ-5
Antelope Island—*island* ... AZ-5
Antelope Island—*island* ... SD-7
Antelope Island—*island* (2) ... UT-8
Antelope Island Bar—*bar* ... UT-8
Antelope Island Campground—*locale* ... UT-8
Antelope Knoll—*summit* ... AZ-5
Antelope Knoll—*summit* ... WY-8
Antelope Knoll Pond—*reservoir* ... AZ-5
Antelope Knolls—*summit* ... UT-8
*Antelope Lake* ... NE-7
Antelope Lake—*flat* ... OR-9
Antelope Lake—*lake* ... AZ-5
Antelope Lake—*lake* ... CA-9
Antelope Lake—*lake* (2) ... ID-8
Antelope Lake—*lake* ... MT-8
Antelope Lake—*lake* ... NV-8
Antelope Lake—*lake* (3) ... NM-5
Antelope Lake—*lake* (2) ... OR-9
Antelope Lake—*lake* (2) ... SD-7
Antelope Lake—*lake* ... TX-5
Antelope Lake—*reservoir* ... CA-9
Antelope Lake—*reservoir* ... KS-7
Antelope Lake—*reservoir* ... SD-7
Antelope Lake Campground—*park* ... AZ-5
*Antelope Lake Dam* ... KS-7
Antelope Lakes—*lake* ... ID-8
Antelope Lakes—*lake* ... ND-7
Antelope Lake Tank—*reservoir* ... TX-5
**Antelope Lake Township**—*pop pl* ... ND-7
Antelope Lateral—*canal* ... SD-7
Antelope Line Camp—*locale* ... TX-5
Antelope Lookout Mesa—*summit* ... NM-5
Antelope Meadow—*flat* ... NV-8
Antelope Mesa—*summit* (3) ... AZ-5
Antelope Mesa—*summit* ... CO-8
Antelope Mesa—*summit* ... NM-5
Antelope Mesa (reduced usage)—*summit* ... TX-5
Antelope Mine—*mine* ... AZ-5
Antelope Mine—*mine* ... CA-9
Antelope Mine—*mine* (2) ... NV-8
Antelope Mine—*mine* ... UT-8
Antelope Mine—*mine* ... WY-8
Antelope Mound—*summit* ... TX-5
*Antelope Mountain* ... UT-8
Antelope Mountain—*ridge* ... OR-9
*Antelope Mountains* ... NV-8
*Antelope Mountains* ... UT-8
Antelope Mtn—*summit* ... AZ-5
Antelope Mtn—*summit* (5) ... CA-9
Antelope Mtn—*summit* (2) ... CO-8
Antelope Mtn—*summit* ... ID-8
Antelope Mtn—*summit* ... MT-8
Antelope Mtn—*summit* ... NV-8
Antelope Mtn—*summit* ... OR-9
Antelope Mtn—*summit* ... TX-5
Antelope Mtn—*summit* (3) ... UT-8
Antelope Mtn—*summit* ... WY-8
Antelope Oil Field—*oilfield* ... ND-7
Antelope Oil Field—*oilfield* ... TX-5
Antelope Park—*flat* ... AZ-5
Antelope Park—*flat* (4) ... CO-8
Antelope Park—*flat* ... ID-8
Antelope Park—*park* ... NE-7
Antelope Park Tank—*reservoir* ... AZ-5
*Antelope Pass* ... UT-8
Antelope Pass—*gap* ... AZ-5
Antelope Pass—*gap* ... CO-8
Antelope Pass—*gap* ... ID-8
Antelope Pass—*gap* (3) ... NV-8
Antelope Pass—*gap* (2) ... NM-5
*Antelope Peak* ... AZ-5
Antelope Peak—*summit* (4) ... AZ-5
Antelope Peak—*summit* ... MT-8
Antelope Peak—*summit* ... NE-7
Antelope Peak—*summit* (4) ... NV-8
Antelope Peak—*summit* ... OR-9
Antelope Peak—*summit* (2) ... TX-5
Antelope Peak—*summit* (2) ... UT-8
*Antelope Peak Mountains* ... NV-8
Antelope Plain—*plain* ... CA-9
*Antelope Plains* ... UT-8
Antelope Plains—*flat* ... CA-9
Antelope Pocket—*basin* ... ID-8
*Antelope Point* ... MI-6
Antelope Point—*cliff* (2) ... AZ-5
Antelope Point—*summit* (2) ... MT-8
Antelope Point (historical)—*cape* ... SD-7
Antelope Point Sch—*school* ... MT-8
Antelope Pond—*lake* ... MT-8
Antelope Prairie—*flat* ... AZ-5
Antelope Prong—*bay* ... MT-8
Antelope Pumping Station—*other* ... CA-9
Antelope Quarries—*other* ... AZ-5
Antelope Ranch—*locale* ... AZ-5
Antelope Ranch—*locale* ... OR-9
Antelope Ranch Airp—*airport* ... AZ-5
Antelope Range—*range* (2) ... NV-8
Antelope Range—*range* ... UT-8
Antelope Range—*summit* ... UT-8
Antelope Ravine—*valley* ... AZ-5
Antelope (reduced usage)—*locale* ... NM-5
Antelope Reservoir—*lake* ... ID-8
*Antelope Ridge* ... OR-9
Antelope Ridge—*ridge* ... AZ-5
Antelope Ridge—*ridge* (2) ... ID-8
Antelope Ridge—*ridge* ... MT-8
Antelope Ridge—*ridge* (2) ... NM-5
Antelope Ridge—*ridge* ... SD-7
Antelope Ridge—*ridge* ... UT-8
Antelope Ridge—*ridge* ... WY-8
*Antelope Rsvr* ... CA-9
*Antelope Rsvr* ... OR-9
Antelope Rsvr—*reservoir* ... CA-9
Antelope Rsvr—*reservoir* ... CO-8
Antelope Rsvr—*reservoir* (2) ... ID-8
Antelope Rsvr—*reservoir* ... MT-8
Antelope Rsvr—*reservoir* ... NV-8
Antelope Rsvr—*reservoir* (5) ... OR-9
Antelope Rsvr—*reservoir* (4) ... WY-8
Antelope Rsvr No 4—*reservoir* ... WY-8
Antelope Rsvr No 5—*reservoir* ... WY-8
Antelope Rsvr No 7—*reservoir* ... WY-8
Antelope Sch—*school* ... CA-9
Antelope Sch—*school* ... CO-8
Antelope Sch—*school* ... ID-8
Antelope Sch—*school* ... NE-7
Antelope Sch—*school* ... ND-7
Antelope Sch—*school* ... SD-7
Antelope Sch—*school* ... UT-8
Antelope School—*locale* ... MT-8
Antelope School—*locale* ... WY-8
Antelope School—*spring* ... CO-8
Antelope School (Abandoned)—*locale* ... NE-7
Antelope School (abandoned)—*locale* ... OR-9
*Antelope Siding* ... NV-8
Antelope Sink—*basin* ... CA-9
Antelope Sink—*basin* ... NM-5
Antelope Slough—*gut* ... NE-7
Antelope Spring—*mine* ... AZ-5
Antelope Spring—*spring* (4) ... AZ-5
Antelope Spring—*spring* (5) ... CA-9
Antelope Spring—*spring* (6) ... CO-8
Antelope Spring—*spring* (11) ... ID-8
Antelope Spring—*spring* (3) ... MT-8
Antelope Spring—*spring* (19) ... NV-8
Antelope Spring—*spring* ... NM-5
Antelope Spring—*spring* ... OK-5
Antelope Spring—*spring* (16) ... OR-9
Antelope Spring—*spring* ... TX-5
Antelope Spring—*spring* (4) ... UT-8
Antelope Spring—*spring* (4) ... WY-8
Antelope Spring Creek—*stream* ... TX-5
Antelope Spring Draw—*valley* ... UT-8
Antelope Spring Lake—*lake* ... NM-5
Antelope Spring Ranch—*locale* ... ID-8
Antelope Spring Rsvr—*reservoir* ... OR-9
Antelope Spring Rsvr—*reservoir* ... UT-8
*Antelope Springs* ... NV-8
*Antelope Springs* ... UT-8
Antelope Springs—*locale* ... CO-8
Antelope Springs—*locale* ... NM-5
Antelope Springs—*spring* ... AZ-5
Antelope Springs—*spring* (2) ... CO-8
Antelope Springs—*spring* ... MT-8
Antelope Springs—*spring* (3) ... NV-8
Antelope Springs—*spring* ... OR-9
Antelope Springs—*spring* ... SD-7
Antelope Springs—*spring* (3) ... UT-8
Antelope Springs—*spring* (4) ... WY-8
Antelope Springs Camp—*locale* ... CO-8
Antelope Springs Ch—*church* ... CO-8
Antelope Springs Creek—*stream* ... OR-9
Antelope Springs Creek—*stream* ... WY-8
Antelope Springs Draw—*valley* ... WY-8
Antelope Springs Ranch—*locale* ... WY-8
Antelope Springs Rsvr—*reservoir* ... WY-8
Antelope Stage Station—*hist pl* ... MT-8
Antelope Station—*other* ... CA-9
Antelope Station (historical)—*locale* ... NV-8
Antelope Substation—*other* ... CA-9
Antelope Summit—*gap* ... NV-8
Antelope Swale—*basin* ... ID-8
Antelope Swale—*basin* (2) ... OR-9
Antelope Swale Rsvr—*reservoir* (2) ... OR-9
Antelope Swale Spring—*spring* ... OR-9
*Antelope Tank* ... AZ-5
Antelope Tank—*lake* ... NM-5
Antelope Tank—*locale* ... NM-5
Antelope Tank—*reservoir* (33) ... AZ-5
Antelope Tank—*reservoir* (17) ... NM-5
Antelope Tank—*reservoir* (12) ... TX-5
Antelope Tanks—*lake* ... TX-5
Antelope Town Hall—*building* ... ND-7
*Antelope Township* ... ND-7
Antelope Township—*civil* ... SD-7
**Antelope Township**—*pop pl* (3) ... NE-7
**Antelope Township**—*pop pl* ... ND-7
**Antelope Township**—*pop pl* (3) ... SD-7
Antelope Township (historical)—*civil* (2) ... SD-7
Antelope Trail—*trail* ... AZ-5
Antelope Trail—*trail* ... ID-8
Antelope Trail Spring—*spring* ... AZ-5
Antelope Tub—*well* ... NM-5
Antelope Union HS—*school* ... AZ-5
*Antelope Valley* ... AZ-5
*Antelope Valley* ... OR-9
*Antelope Valley* ... UT-8
Antelope Valley—*basin* (2) ... NE-7
Antelope Valley—*basin* (4) ... NV-8
Antelope Valley—*flat* ... NV-8
Antelope Valley—*valley* ... AZ-5
Antelope Valley—*valley* (7) ... CA-9
Antelope Valley—*valley* (3) ... ID-8
Antelope Valley—*valley* (2) ... NE-7
Antelope Valley—*valley* (2) ... NV-8
Antelope Valley—*valley* ... ND-7
Antelope Valley—*valley* (3) ... OR-9
Antelope Valley—*valley* ... SD-7
Antelope Valley—*valley* (5) ... UT-8
Antelope Valley Cem—*cemetery* ... NE-7
Antelope Valley Cem—*cemetery* (2) ... SD-7
Antelope Valley Ch—*church* ... NE-7
Antelope Valley Ch—*church* ... ND-7
Antelope Valley Ch—*church* ... OK-5
Antelope Valley Ch—*church* ... SD-7
Antelope Valley Coll—*school* (2) ... CA-9
Antelope Valley Corral—*locale* ... UT-8
Antelope Valley Country Club—*other* ... CA-9
Antelope Valley Dam—*dam* ... CA-9
Antelope Valley Detention Dam—*dam* ... AZ-5
Antelope Valley Indian Museum—*building* ... CA-9
Antelope Valley Indian Museum—*hist pl* ... CA-9
Antelope Valley Number Three Reservior—*reservoir* ... UT-8
Antelope Valley Ranch—*locale* ... UT-8
*Antelope Valley Reservoir* ... CA-9

Antelope Valley Sch—*school* (2) NE-7
Antelope Valley Sch (historical)—*school* SD-7
*Antelope Valley School* SD-7
*Antelope Valley Township* SD-7
**Antelope Valley Township**—*pop pl* SD-7
Antelope Valley Wash—*stream* NV-8
Antelope Valley Wash—*stream* UT-8
Antelope Valley Wash—*valley* UT-8
Antelope View Mine—*mine* NV-8
*Antelope Wash* AZ-5
Antelope Wash—*arroyo* NV-8
Antelope Wash—*stream* (5) AZ-5
Antelope Wash—*stream* CA-9
Antelope Wash—*stream* NV-8
Antelope Wash—*valley* UT-8
Antelope Wash—*valley* WY-8
Antelope Waterhole—*lake* OR-9
Antelope Well—*locale* NM-5
Antelope Well—*well* (6) AZ-5
Antelope Well—*well* CA-9
Antelope Well—*well* MT-8
Antelope Well—*well* (10) NM-5
Antelope Well—*well* OR-9
Antelope Well—*well* TX-5
Antelope Wells—*locale* NM-5
Antelope Wells—*well* NM-5
Antelope Windmill—*locale* CO-8
Antelope Windmill—*locale* (5) NM-5
Antelope Windmill—*locale* (8) TX-5
Antenna Hill—*summit* NM-5
Antenna Ridge—*ridge* CA-9
**Antepast**—*pop pl* KY-4
Antepast Sch—*school* KY-4
Anterior Sch—*school* IL-6
Antero, Mount—*summit* CO-8
Antero Feeder Ditch—*canal* CO-8
**Antero Junction**—*pop pl* CO-8
*Antero Meadows* CO-8
*Antero Mountain* CO-8
*Antero Peak* CO-8
Antero Rsvr—*reservoir* CO-8
Antes—*locale* CA-9
Antes—*locale* PA-2
Antes, Henry, House—*hist pl* PA-2
*Antes Creek* PA-2
Antes Creek—*stream* PA-2
Antes Drain—*stream* MI-6
**Antes Fort**—*pop pl* PA-2
**Antes Fort (RR name Jersey Shore (sta.))**—*pop pl* PA-2
Ant Flat—*flat* CA-9
Ant Flat—*flat* OR-9
Ant Flat—*flat* WA-9
Ant Flat—*locale* MT-8
Anthelm Gay Grant—*civil* FL-3
Anthem—*locale* WV-2
Anthem Creek—*stream* WA-9
Anthem Post Office (historical)—*building* TN-4
Anthemusia Plantation (historical)—*locale* AL-4
Ant Hill—*summit* CA-9
Ant Hill—*summit* (2) ID-8
Ant Hill—*summit* MT-8
Ant Hill—*summit* OK-5
Ant Hill—*summit* (2) OR-9
Ant Hill—*summit* WY-8
Ant Hill, The—*summit* CO-8
Ant Hill, The—*summit* UT-8
Anthill Creek—*stream* MT-8
Anthill Knob—*summit* WY-8
*Ant Hill Oil Field* CA-9
Anthill Rsvr—*reservoir* WY-8
Ant Hills—*range* CO-8
Anthill Spring—*spring* MT-8
Anthill Trail—*trail* PA-2
Ant Hill Well—*well* ID-8
Anthis Park—*park* OK-5
Anthoine Creek—*stream* ME-1
Anthom Cem—*cemetery* TX-5
Anthon—*locale* OK-5
**Anthon**—*pop pl* IA-7
Anthonie Cem—*cemetery* MO-7
Anthonies Mill—*locale* MO-7
Anthon Ranch—*locale* TX-5
Anthon Sch—*school* TX-5
Anthony—*locale* MD-2
Anthony—*locale* MN-6
Anthony—*locale* NV-8
Anthony—*locale* NJ-2
Anthony—*locale* TX-5
**Anthony** *pop pl* AR-4
**Anthony**—*pop pl* FL-3
**Anthony**—*pop pl* IN-6
**Anthony**—*pop pl* KS-7
**Anthony**—*pop pl* NM-5
**Anthony**—*pop pl* OH-6
**Anthony**—*pop pl* RI-1
**Anthony**—*pop pl* TX-5
**Anthony**—*pop pl* WV-2
**Anthony**—*pop pl* WI-6
Anthony, David M., House—*hist pl* MA-1
Anthony, David Rinehart, House—*hist pl* AL-4
Anthony, Herman, Farm—*hist pl* OR-9
Anthony, John, House—*hist pl* OR-9
Anthony, Lake—*lake* SC-3
Anthony, Levi, Bldg—*hist pl* NY-2
Anthony, Mount—*summit* NY-2
Anthony, Mount—*summit* VT-1
Anthony, Susan B., House—*hist pl* NY-2
Anthony Airp—*airport* PA-2
Anthony Bolick Branch—*stream* NC-3
Anthony Brake—*bend* AR-4
Anthony Branch—*stream* AR-4
Anthony Branch—*stream* MS-4
Anthony Branch—*stream* (2) MO-7
Anthony Branch—*stream* (2) NC-3
Anthony Branch—*stream* (4) TN-4
Anthony Branch—*stream* (3) TX-5
Anthony Bridge—*bridge* TN-4
Anthony Brook—*stream* MA-1
Anthony-Buckley House—*hist pl* OR-9
Anthony Butte—*summit* OR-9
Anthony (CCD)—*cens area* NM-5
Anthony Cem—*cemetery* AL-4
Anthony Cem—*cemetery* (2) AR-4
Anthony Cem—*cemetery* GA-3
Anthony Cem—*cemetery* LA-4
Anthony Cem—*cemetery* NY-2
Anthony Cem—*cemetery* PA-2
Anthony Cem—*cemetery* (4) TN-4
Anthony Cem—*cemetery* TX-5
Anthony Ch—*church* GA-3
Anthony Ch—*church* LA-4
Anthony Ch—*church* OK-5
Anthony Ch—*church* PA-2
Anthony Chapel Cem—*cemetery* AL-4
Anthony Chapel Methodist Ch (historical)—*church* AL-4
Anthony City Dam—*DAM* KS-7
Anthony Collins Cem—*cemetery* AL-4
Anthony Correctional Center—*other* WV-2
Anthony C Ranch—*locale* TX-5
*Anthony Creek* MA-1
*Anthony Creek* NC-3
*Anthony Creek* TN-4
Anthony Creek—*stream* CA-9
Anthony Creek—*stream* ID-8
Anthony Creek—*stream* IL-6
Anthony Creek—*stream* IN-6
Anthony Creek—*stream* NY-2
Anthony Creek—*stream* (3) NC-3
Anthony Creek—*stream* (2) OR-9
Anthony Creek—*stream* TN-4
Anthony Creek—*stream* (2) WV-2
Anthony Creek (Magisterial District)—*fmr MCD* WV-2
Anthony Creek Sch—*school* WV-2
Anthony Creek Trail—*trail* TN-4
Anthony Cut—*canal* NY-2
*Anthony Dam* RI-1
Anthony Ditch—*canal* (2) IN-6
Anthony Drain—*canal* NM-5
Anthony Drain—*canal* TX-5
Anthony Drive Ch—*church* TX-5
Anthony Elem Sch—*school* FL-3
Anthony Elem Sch—*school* IN-6
Anthony Elem Sch—*school* KS-7
Anthony Flat—*flat* UT-8
Anthony Ford—*locale* PA-2
Anthony Fork—*stream* WV-2
*Anthony Fork North Powder River* OR-9
Anthony Gap—*gap* NM-5
Anthony Gorge—*valley* OR-9
Anthony Grove Ch—*church* NC-3
Anthony Gulch—*valley* WY-8
Anthony Gulf—*valley* NY-2
*Anthony Hill* RI-1
**Anthony Hill**—*pop pl* TN-4
Anthony Hill—*summit* WV-2
Anthony Hill Cem—*cemetery* TN-4
Anthony Hill Ch—*church* TN-4
Anthony Hill Sch (historical)—*school* TN-4
Anthony Hollow—*valley* MO-7
Anthony House—*hist pl* MA-1
Anthony Island—*island* WI-6
Anthony JHS—*school* MN-6
Anthony Kill—*stream* NY-2
Anthony Knobs—*summit* VA-3
Anthony Lake—*lake* (2) AR-4
Anthony Lake—*lake* OR-9
Anthony Lake—*reservoir* GA-3
Anthony Lakes—*lake* OR-9
Anthony Lakes Ski Area—*park* OR-9
Anthony Lateral—*canal* NM-5
*Anthony Left Prong* TN-4
Anthony Mill Ruins—*locale* CA-9
Anthony Milne Camp—*locale* CA-9
Anthony Mtn—*summit* NC-3
Anthony Municipal Airp—*airport* KS-7
Anthony Municipal Lake—*reservoir* KS-7
*Anthony Nose* TX-5
Anthony Park—*park* MI-6
Anthony Peak—*summit* CA-9
Anthony Peak—*summit* ID-8
Anthony Pecos Ditch—*canal* NM-5
Anthony Point—*cape* NY-2
Anthony Point—*cape* RI-1
Anthony Pond—*lake* MA-1
Anthony Ponds—*lake* NY-2
Anthony Public Carnegie Library—*hist pl* KS-7
Anthony Ranch—*locale* NM-5
Anthony Ridge—*ridge* CA-9
Anthony Ridge—*ridge* MD-2
Anthony Ridge—*ridge* NC-3
Anthony Ridge—*ridge* TN-4
Anthony Rsvr No. 2—*reservoir* CO-8
Anthony Run—*stream* OH-6
Anthony Run—*stream* PA-2
Anthony Run—*stream* (2) WV-2
Anthony Sch—*school* (3) CA-9
Anthony Sch—*school* IL-6
Anthony Sch—*school* MA-1
Anthony Sch—*school* NJ-2
Anthony Sch—*school* WI-6
Anthony Sch (historical)—*school* TN-4
Anthonys Corners—*locale* DE-2
Anthonys Ferry (historical)—*locale* MS-4
Anthonys (historical)—*locale* SD-7
Anthony Shoals—*bar* GA-3
*Anthonys Location* IN-6
*Anthony's Nose* NY-2
Anthonys Nose—*cliff* (2) NY-2
Anthonys Nose—*summit* TX-5
Anthony Spring—*spring* TN-4
Anthony Springs—*spring* OR-9
Anthony Square—*park* NY-2
*Anthonys Quarters* AR-4
*Anthonys Run* PA-2
**Anthony (subdivision)**—*pop pl* AR-4
Anthony Switch—*locale* AR-4
Anthony Terrace—*uninc pl* GA-3
*Anthony Township* KS-7
Anthony Township—*civil* KS-7
**Anthony (Township of)**—*pop pl* MN-6
**Anthony (Township of)**—*pop pl* (2) PA-2
Anthony United Methodist Ch—*church* FL-3
Anthonyville—*uninc pl* MD-2
Anthony Wash—*stream* NM-5
Anthony Wash—*stream* TX-5
Anthony Wayne Bridge—*bridge* OH-6
Anthony Wayne Elem Sch—*school* PA-2
Anthony Wayne HS—*school* OH-6
Anthony Wayne Rec Area—*park* NY-2
Anthony Wayne Sch—*school* IN-6
Anthony Wayne Sch—*school* (3) OH-6
Anthony Wayne Trail—*trail* OH-6
*Anthony Wayne Village* IN-6
**Anthony Wayne Village**—*pop pl* IN-6
**Anthoston**—*pop pl* KY-4
**Anthracite**—*pop pl* PA-2
Anthracite Bag Plant Station—*locale* PA-2
Anthracite Bank Bldg—*hist pl* PA-2
Anthracite Creek—*stream* CO-8
Anthracite Creek—*stream* WA-9
Anthracite Creek Guard Station—*locale* CO-8
Anthracite Mesa—*summit* CO-8
*Anthracite Mountain* CO-8
Anthracite Park and Museum—*park* PA-2
Anthracite Pass—*gap* CO-8
Anthracite Range—*range* CO-8
Anthracite Ridge—*ridge* AK-9
Anthracite Ridge—*ridge* CO-8
**Anthras**—*pop pl* TN-4
Anthras Baptist Ch—*church* TN-4
Anthras Post Office (historical)—*building* TN-4
Anthras Slope Mine (surface)—*mine* TN-4
*Anthro Mountain* UT-8
Anthro Mtns—*summit* UT-8
*Antiarch Church* AL-4
Antibust Creek—*stream* TX-5
Antice Creek—*stream* MT-8
Antice Knob—*summit* MT-8
Antice Point—*cape* MT-8
Anticline Campground—*locale* UT-8
Anticline Overlook—*locale* UT-8
Anticline Ridge—*ridge* CA-9
Anticoch Ch—*church* IL-6
**Antietam**—*pop pl* MD-2
Antietam Ch—*church* MD-2
Antietam Cove—*valley* PA-2
Antietam Creek—*stream* MD-2
Antietam Creek—*stream* (2) PA-2
Antietam Dam—*dam* PA-2
Antietam Furnace Complex Archeol Site—*hist pl* MD-2
Antietam Hall—*hist pl* MD-2
Antietam Iron Furnace Site and Antietam Village—*hist pl* MD-2
Antietam Natl Battlefield—*hist pl* MD-2
Antietam Natl Battlefield—*park* MD-2
Antietam Natl Battlefield Site—*park* MD-2
Antietam Natl Cem—*cemetery* MD-2
Antietam Rsvr—*reservoir* PA-2
Antietam Sch—*school* MD-2
Antietam Sch (abandoned)—*school* PA-2
**Antietam (sta.)**—*pop pl* MD-2
*Antietum* MD-2
**Antigo**—*pop pl* WI-6
Antigo Cem—*cemetery* WI-6
Antigo Island—*island* WI-6
Antigo Lake—*reservoir* WI-6
Antigo Opera House—*hist pl* WI-6
Antigo Public Library and Deleglise Cabin—*hist pl* WI-6
**Antigo (Town of)**—*pop pl* WI-6
Antiguo Casino Camuyano—*hist pl* PR-3
Antiguo Casino de Puerto Rico—*hist pl* PR-3
Antiguo Cuartel Militar Espanol de Ponce—*hist pl* PR-3
Antiguo Hosp Militar Espanol de Ponce—*hist pl* PR-3
*Antila Lake* MN-6
Antilla Ditch—*canal* MT-8
Antill Cem—*cemetery* WV-2
Antilles Military Acad—*school* PR-3
Antillian Coll—*school* PR-3
Antilon Creek—*stream* WA-9
Antilon Lake—*reservoir* WA-9
Antilope Peak—*summit* CA-9
Anti Mason Drain—*canal* MI-6
**Antimony**—*pop pl* UT-8
Antimony Bench—*bench* UT-8
Antimony Camp—*locale* ID-8
Antimony Canyon—*valley* CA-9
Antimony Canyon—*valley* UT-8
Antimony Cem—*cemetery* UT-8
Antimony Creek—*stream* (2) AK-9
Antimony Creek—*stream* (2) MT-8
Antimony Creek—*stream* UT-8
Antimony Flat—*flat* CA-9
Antimony Gulch—*valley* CA-9
Antimony King Mine—*mine* (2) NV-8
Antimony Knoll—*summit* UT-8
Antimony Lake—*lake* UT-8
Antimony Mine—*mine* CA-9
Antimony Mine—*mine* ID-8
Antimony Peak—*summit* (3) CA-9
Antimony Ridge—*ridge* (2) CA-9
Antimony Ridge—*ridge* ID-8
Antimony Rsvr—*reservoir* NV-8
Antimony Sch—*school* UT-8
Antingmiut Creek—*stream* AK-9
Antioca Cem—*cemetery* AR-4
*Antioch* IN-6
*Antioch* MS-4
*Antioch* MO-7
*Antioch* TN-4
Antioch—*locale* AL-4
Antioch—*locale* (2) AR-4
Antioch—*locale* FL-3
Antioch—*locale* (2) GA-3
Antioch—*locale* KY-4
Antioch—*locale* (2) NC-3
Antioch—*locale* (5) TN-4
Antioch—*locale* (8) TX-5
Antioch—*locale* (2) VA-3
Antioch—*locale* (2) WV-2
**Antioch**—*pop pl* (6) AL-4
**Antioch**—*pop pl* (2) AR-4
**Antioch**—*pop pl* CA-9
**Antioch**—*pop pl* GA-3
**Antioch**—*pop pl* IL-6
**Antioch**—*pop pl* (4) IN-6
**Antioch**—*pop pl* KS-7
**Antioch**—*pop pl* KY-4
**Antioch**—*pop pl* (2) LA-4
**Antioch**—*pop pl* (3) MS-4
**Antioch**—*pop pl* MO-7
**Antioch**—*pop pl* NE-7
**Antioch**—*pop pl* (3) NC-3
**Antioch**—*pop pl* (2) OH-6
**Antioch**—*pop pl* (2) OK-5
**Antioch**—*pop pl* (3) SC-3
**Antioch**—*pop pl* (7) TN-4
**Antioch**—*pop pl* (2) TX-5
**Antioch**—*pop pl* WV-2
Antioch African Methodist Episcopal Ch—*church* DE-2
*Antioch African Methodist Episcopal Church* AL-4
*Antioch Assembly of God Church* MS-4
*Antioch Baptist Ch* AL-4
*Antioch Baptist Ch* MS-4
*Antioch Baptist Ch* TN-4
Antioch Baptist Ch—*church* (5) AL-4
Antioch Baptist Ch—*church* (2) FL-3
Antioch Baptist Ch—*church* KS-7
Antioch Baptist Ch—*church* (4) MS-4
Antioch Baptist Ch—*church* TN-4
Antioch Baptist Ch (historical)—*church* AL-4
Antioch Baptist Ch Number 2—*church* AL-4
Antioch Baptist Church—*hist pl* LA-4
Antioch Bend—*bend* KY-4
Antioch Boat Harbor—*locale* TN-4
Antioch Branch—*stream* (2) AL-4
Antioch Branch—*stream* TX-5
Antioch Branch—*stream* VA-3
Antioch Bridge—*bridge* CA-9
Antioch Bridge—*bridge* TN-4
Antioch Bridge—*other* MO-7
Antioch Campground—*locale* GA-3
Antioch Cem—*cemetery* (23) AL-4
Antioch Cem—*cemetery* (8) AR-4
Antioch Cem—*cemetery* CO-8
Antioch Cem—*cemetery* (3) FL-3
Antioch Cem—*cemetery* (10) GA-3
Antioch Cem—*cemetery* (8) IL-6
Antioch Cem—*cemetery* (4) IN-6
Antioch Cem—*cemetery* IA-7
Antioch Cem—*cemetery* (2) KS-7
Antioch Cem—*cemetery* KY-4
Antioch Cem—*cemetery* (7) LA-4
Antioch Cem—*cemetery* (26) MS-4
Antioch Cem—*cemetery* (15) MO-7
Antioch Cem—*cemetery* NE-7
Antioch Cem—*cemetery* NM-5
Antioch Cem—*cemetery* (3) NC-3
Antioch Cem—*cemetery* (6) OH-6
Antioch Cem—*cemetery* (5) OK-5
Antioch Cem—*cemetery* OR-9
Antioch Cem—*cemetery* (4) SC-3
Antioch Cem—*cemetery* (11) TN-4
Antioch Cem—*cemetery* (16) TX-5
Antioch Cem—*cemetery* VA-3
Antioch Cem Number One—*cemetery* AL-4
*Antioch Cem Number Two* AL-4
Antioch Cem Number 2—*cemetery* AL-4
*Antioch Ch* AL-4
*Antioch Ch* DE-2
*Antioch Ch* GA-3
*Antioch Ch* IN-6
*Antioch Ch* MS-4
*Antioch Ch* TN-4
Antioch Ch—*church* (98) AL-4
Antioch Ch—*church* (25) AR-4
Antioch Ch—*church* (10) FL-3
Antioch Ch—*church* (83) GA-3
Antioch Ch—*church* (14) IL-6
Antioch Ch—*church* (12) IN-6
Antioch Ch—*church* (3) IA-7
Antioch Ch—*church* (3) KS-7
Antioch Ch—*church* (33) KY-4
Antioch Ch—*church* (23) LA-4
Antioch Ch—*church* (2) MD-2
Antioch Ch—*church* (3) MI-6
Antioch Ch—*church* (53) MS-4
Antioch Ch—*church* (27) MO-7
Antioch Ch—*church* NM-5
Antioch Ch—*church* (57) NC-3
Antioch Ch—*church* (9) OH-6
Antioch Ch—*church* (13) OK-5
Antioch Ch—*church* (2) PA-2
Antioch Ch—*church* (36) SC-3
Antioch Ch—*church* (49) TN-4
Antioch Ch—*church* (34) TX-5
Antioch Ch—*church* (33) VA-3
Antioch Ch—*church* (5) WV-2
Antioch Chapel—*church* MD-2
Antioch Chapel—*church* NC-3
Antioch Chapel (historical)—*church* TN-4
Antioch Ch (historical)—*church* (9) AL-4
Antioch Ch (historical)—*church* (3) MS-4
Antioch Ch (historical)—*church* (5) MO-7
Antioch Ch (historical)—*church* (3) TN-4
Antioch Ch Number 1—*church* MS-4
Antioch Ch Number 2—*church* (2) MS-4
*Antioch Ch of Christ* AL-4
Antioch Ch of Christ—*church* MS-4
*Antioch Ch of God* MS-4
Antioch Christian Ch—*church* KS-7
Antioch Christian Church—*hist pl* KY-4
Antioch Christian Church—*hist pl* MO-7
Antioch Christian Church—*hist pl* SC-3
Antioch Church Cem—*cemetery* AL-4
Antioch City Park—*park* CA-9
Antioch Coll—*school* OH-6
Antioch Community Center—*building* FL-3
Antioch Creek—*stream* AR-4
Antioch Creek—*stream* GA-3
Antioch Creek—*stream* IN-6
Antioch Creek—*stream* KY-4
Antioch Creek—*stream* LA-4
Antioch Creek—*stream* MO-7
Antioch Creek—*stream* TN-4
Antioch Cumberland Ch—*church* AL-4
*Antioch Cumberland Presbyterian Ch* AL-4
Antioch East Cem—*cemetery* AL-4
Antioch East Ch—*church* AL-4
**Antioch Estates (subdivision)**—*pop pl* AL-4
Antioch Fork—*locale* VA-3
*Antioch Free Will Baptist Ch* MS-4
Antioch Free Will Baptist Ch—*church* FL-3
*Antioch Freewill Baptist Church* AL-4
**Antioch Grange**—*pop pl* IN-6
Antioch Hall, North And South Halls—*hist pl* OH-6
**Antioch Harbor Resort**—*pop pl* TN-4
Antioch Hill—*summit* MS-4
Antioch (historical)—*locale* (2) AL-4
Antioch (historical)—*locale* MS-4
Antioch (historical)—*locale* SD-7
**Antioch (historical)**—*pop pl* (2) MS-4
**Antioch (historical)**—*pop pl* TX-5
Antiochia Ch—*church* ND-7
Antioch Independent Christian Ch—*church* IN-6
Antioch JHS—*school* MO-7
Antioch Lake—*lake* IL-6
Antioch Landing—*locale* TN-4
Antioch-McCrae Sch—*school* VA-3
*Antioch Methodist Ch* AL-4
Antioch Methodist Ch—*church* AL-4
Antioch Methodist Ch (historical)—*church* AL-4
*Antioch Methodist Church* MS-4
**Antioch Mills**—*pop pl* KY-4
Antioch Mission—*church* NC-3
*Antioch Missionary Baptist Ch* AL-4
*Antioch Missionary Baptist Ch* MS-4
Antioch Missionary Baptist Ch—*church* FL-3
Antioch Missionary Baptist Ch—*church* IN-6
Antioch Missionary Baptist Ch—*church* (2) KS-7
Antioch Missionary Baptist Ch—*church* (4) MS-4
Antioch Missionary Baptist Ch (historical)—*church* TN-4
Antioch Missionary Baptist Church—*hist pl* TX-5
Antioch Missionary Ch—*church* MS-4
Antioch Municipal Rsvr—*reservoir* CA-9
Antioch Number One Ch—*church* AL-4
Antioch Number Two Ch—*church* GA-3
Antioch Number 2 Ch—*church* AL-4
Antiocho Cem—*cemetery* MS-4
Antioch Park—*park* KS-7
Antioch-Pittsburg (CCD)—*cens area* CA-9
Antioch P. O. (historical)—*locale* AL-4
Antioch Point—*cape* CA-9
Antioch Post Office (historical)—*building* AL-4
Antioch Post Office (historical)—*building* TX-5
Antioch Potash Plants—*hist pl* NE-7
Antioch Presbyterian Ch (historical)—*church* AL-4
Antioch Primitive Baptist Ch—*church* (2) AL-4
Antioch Primitive Baptist Ch (historical)—*church* AL-4
Antioch Primitive Baptist Ch (historical)—*church* TX-5
*Antioch Primitive Baptist Church* MS-4
Antioch Primitive Baptist Church Historical Marker—*park* TX-5
Antioch Rest Cem—*cemetery* TX-5
*Antioch Sch* TN-4
Antioch Sch—*hist pl* NE-7
Antioch Sch—*school* (2) AL-4
Antioch Sch—*school* AR-4
Antioch Sch—*school* FL-3
Antioch Sch—*school* (3) GA-3
Antioch Sch—*school* (4) IL-6
Antioch Sch—*school* IA-7
Antioch Sch—*school* (4) KY-4
Antioch Sch—*school* (3) LA-4
Antioch Sch—*school* MS-4
Antioch Sch—*school* (3) MO-7
Antioch Sch—*school* (3) SC-3
Antioch Sch—*school* TN-4
Antioch Sch—*school* (2) TX-5
Antioch Sch—*school* VA-3
Antioch Sch (abandoned)—*school* MO-7
Antioch Sch (historical)—*school* (9) AL-4
Antioch Sch (historical)—*school* (5) MS-4
Antioch Sch (historical)—*school* (2) MO-7
Antioch Sch (historical)—*school* (8) TN-4
Antioch School Cave—*cave* TN-4
Antioch Second Cumberland Presbyterian Ch—*church* AL-4
Antioch Shop Ctr—*other* MO-7
Antioch Spring—*spring* MO-7
Antioch Swamp—*stream* VA-3
Antioch (Township of)—*fmr MCD* (3) AR-4
Antioch (Township of)—*fmr MCD* (2) NC-3
**Antioch (Township of)**—*pop pl* IL-6
**Antioch (Township of)**—*pop pl* MI-6
**Antioch (Turnerville)**—*pop pl* MS-4
*Antioch United Methodist Ch* AL-4
Antioch West Cem—*cemetery* AL-4
Antioch West Ch—*church* AL-4
Antioch West Ch—*church* AR-4
*Antiock* NC-3
Antiock Dam—*dam* AL-4
Antiock Lake—*reservoir* AL-4
Antiocn Cem—*cemetery* KY-4
*Antioine Butte* MT-8
Antionette Mine (underground)—*mine* AL-4
Antipatr Lake—*lake* AK-9
Antipch Cem—*cemetery* MO-7
Antipoison Creek—*stream* VA-3
Antipoison Neck—*cape* VA-3
Antiqua Residencia de la Familia Nadal—*hist pl* PR-3
Antique Lake—*lake* SC-3
Antique Store—*hist pl* AL-4
Antique Well—*well* NM-5
**Antiquity**—*pop pl* (2) OH-6
Antire Creek—*stream* MO-7
Antis—*locale* PA-2
Antis Cem—*cemetery* PA-2
*Antis Creek* PA-2
Ant Island—*island* ME-1
*Antis Run* PA-2
Antis Run—*stream* PA-2
*Antisteven Canyon* CO-8
**Antis (Township of)**—*pop pl* PA-2
Antitonnie Creek—*stream* AK-9
**Antiville**—*pop pl* IN-6
Antiville Ditch—*canal* IN-6
*Antiville Drain* IN-6
Ant Knob—*summit* WV-2
Ant Knoll—*summit* UT-8
Ant Knolls—*arch* UT-8
Ant Knolls—*summit* (2) UT-8
Antl Bay—*bay* MN-6
Antle Cem—*cemetery* IA-7
Antlen River—*stream* AK-9
*Antlens Park* MN-6
Antler—*locale* WV-2
**Antler**—*pop pl* ND-7
Antler-Burlington Mine—*mine* SD-7
*Antler Canal* WY-8
Antler Canyon—*valley* NM-5
Antler Cem—*cemetery* ND-7
Antler Creek—*stream* (3) AK-9
Antler Creek—*stream* MI-6
Antler Creek—*stream* (3) OR-9
Antler Creek—*stream* WY-8
Antler Creek Dam—*dam* ND-7
Antler Dam—*dam* SD-7
Antler Glacier—*glacier* AK-9
Antler Hill—*summit* ME-1
**Antler (historical)**—*pop pl* OR-9
Antler Lake—*lake* (2) AK-9
Antler Lake—*lake* MN-6
Antler Lake—*lake* NY-2
Antler Lake—*lake* WI-6
Antler Lake—*reservoir* PA-2
Antler Mine—*mine* (2) AZ-5
Antler Peak—*summit* NV-8
Antler Peak—*summit* WA-9
Antler Peak—*summit* WY-8
Antler Peaks—*summit* AK-9
Antler Pit—*cave* AL-4
Antler Point—*cape* OR-9
Antler Prairie—*flat* OR-9
Antler Ridge—*bridge* ID-8
Antler Ridge—*ridge* ID-8
Antler River—*stream* AK-9
Antler Rsvr—*reservoir* WY-8
Antlers—*locale* CA-9
Antlers—*locale* CO-8
Antlers—*locale* MI-6
Antlers—*locale* VA-3
**Antlers**—*pop pl* OK-5
Antlers Cabins, The—*locale* MI-6
Antlers Campground—*locale* CA-9
*Antlers Canal* WY-8
Antlers (CCD)—*cens area* OK-5
Antlers Forest Service Station—*locale* OR-9
Antlers Frisco Depot and Antlers Spring—*hist pl* OK-5
Antlers Hotel—*hist pl* OH-6
*Antlers Park* MN-6
Antlers Park—*flat* CO-8
Antlers Park—*park* MN-6
**Antlers Park**—*pop pl* MN-6
*Antlers Peak* NV-8
Antlers Point—*cape* NY-2
Antler Spring—*spring* AZ-5
Antler Spring—*spring* (2) OR-9
Antler Springs—*spring* OR-9
Antler Spring Trail (pack)—*trail* OR-9
Antlers Waterworks—*other* OK-5
**Antler Township**—*pop pl* ND-7
Antler Valley Creek—*stream* AK-9
Antley Branch—*stream* WV-2
Antley Creek—*stream* MT-8
Antley Knob—*summit* WV-2
Antley Spring—*spring* SC-3
Antley Spring Branch—*stream* SC-3
Ant Mount Trail—*trail* PA-2
Ant Mtn—*summit* AR-4
Ant Mtn—*summit* WA-9
*Antoine* MI-6
**Antoine**—*pop pl* AR-4
**Antoine**—*pop pl* MI-6
Antoine, Bayou—*stream* LA-4
Antoine, Lake—*lake* MI-6
Antoine Butte—*summit* MT-8
Antoine Canyon—*valley* CA-9
Antoine Collins Grant—*civil* FL-3
*Antoine Creek* AR-4
Antoine Creek—*stream* LA-4
Antoine Creek—*stream* (2) MI-6
Antoine Creek—*stream* MT-8
Antoine Creek—*stream* (2) WA-9
Antoine LeClair—*locale* IA-7
Antoine LeClaires Reservation—*reserve* IA-7
Antoine LeClair Park—*park* IA-7
Antoine Leroux—*civil* NM-5
Antoine Peak—*summit* WA-9
Antoine Plante Ferry Site Park—*park* WA-9
Antoine River—*stream* AR-4
*Antoines Cabin Creek* CO-8
*Antoine Spring* CO-8
Antoine (Township of)—*fmr MCD* AR-4
Antoine Trail—*trail* WA-9
Antoinette Peak—*summit* WY-8
Antoinette Post Office (historical)—*building* TN-4
Antoine Valley—*valley* WA-9
Antoken Creek—*stream* OR-9
Antolini Hill—*summit* AZ-5
Anton—*locale* KY-4
Anton—*locale* WI-6
**Anton**—*pop pl* CO-8
**Anton**—*pop pl* TX-5
*Anton Billard Lake* WI-6
Anton (CCD)—*cens area* TX-5
Anton Cem—*cemetery* IA-7
Anton Cem—*cemetery* TX-5
Anton Chico—*civil* (2) NM-5
**Anton Chico**—*pop pl* NM-5
Anton Chico de Abajo Hist Dist—*hist pl* NM-5
Anton Creek—*stream* MT-8
Antone—*locale* OR-9
Antone Basin—*basin* CA-9
*Antone Butte* MT-8
Antone Butte—*summit* (2) OR-9
Antone Canyon—*valley* (2) CA-9
Antone Canyon—*valley* CO-8
Antone Canyon—*valley* NV-8
Antone Canyon—*valley* TX-5
Antone Canyon—*valley* UT-8
Antone Creek—*stream* (2) CA-9
Antone Creek—*stream* MT-8
Antone Creek—*stream* (2) NV-8
Antone Creek—*stream* (3) OR-9
Antone Creek—*stream* UT-8
Antone Dike—*dam* WY-8
Antone Flat—*flat* UT-8
Antone Gap—*gap* CO-8
Antone Guard Station—*locale* MT-8
Antone Hollow—*valley* TX-5
Antone Hollow—*valley* UT-8
Antone Lake—*lake* CA-9
Antone Meadows—*flat* CA-9
Antone Mtn—*summit* VT-1
Antone Pass—*gap* MT-8
Antone Pass—*gap* NV-8
*Antone Peak* MT-8
Antone Peak—*summit* MT-8
Antone Rsvr—*reservoir* MT-8
Antones Cabin Creek—*stream* CO-8
Antones Island—*island* AK-9
Antone Spring—*spring* (2) CO-8
Antone Spring—*spring* NV-8
Antones Spring—*spring* CO-8
Antone Station (Site)—*locale* NV-8
Antone Trail—*trail* CO-8
Antone Wash—*stream* NV-8
Antone Wash—*valley* UT-8
Antone Windmill—*locale* TX-5
Anton Hill—*summit* WA-9
Anton Hollow—*valley* (2) TX-5

*Aquia Station* ... VA-3
*Aquibinocket Island* ... RI-1
*Aquidneck Bay* ... MA-1
*Aquidneck Bay* ... RI-1
*Aquidneck Island* ... RI-1
*Aquidnesuc Island* ... RI-1
*Aquidnick Island* ... RI-1
**Aqui Esta**—*pop pl* ... FL-3
Aqui Esta Center (Shop Ctr)—*locale* ... FL-3
Aquila Canyon—*valley* ... NM-5
Aquila Court Bldg—*hist pl* ... NE-7
Aquila Mine—*mine* ... WA-9
Aquila Park—*park* ... MN-6
Aquila Sch—*school* ... MN-6
**Aquilino**—*pop pl* ... PR-3
*Aquilla* ... MS-4
Aquilla—*locale* ... AL-4
**Aquilla**—*pop pl* ... AL-4
**Aquilla**—*pop pl* ... MO-7
**Aquilla**—*pop pl* ... OH-6
**Aquilla**—*pop pl* ... TX-5
Aquilla, Lake—*lake* ... OH-6
Aquilla Cem—*cemetery* ... SD-7
Aquilla Ch—*church* ... AL-4
Aquilla Creek—*stream* (2) ... TX-5
Aquilla JHS (historical)—*school* ... AL-4
Aquilla Lake Wildlife Area—*park* ... OH-6
Aquilla Lookout Tower—*locale* ... AL-4
Aquilla P.O. (historical)—*locale* ... AL-4
Aquilla Run—*stream* ... WV-2
*Aquilla United Methodist church* ... AL-4
*Aqui Mountains* ... UT-8
Aquinaldo Flat—*flat* ... ID-8
Aquinas Acad—*school* ... KY-4
Aquinas Acad—*school* ... WA-9
Aquinas Coll—*school* ... MI-6
Aquinas HS—*school* ... IA-7
Aquinas HS—*school* ... MI-6
Aquinas HS—*school* ... NE-7
Aquinas HS—*school* ... NY-2
Aquinas HS—*school* ... WI-6
Aquinas Institute—*school* ... NY-2
Aquinas Junior Coll—*school* ... TN-4
Aquinas Memorial Stadium—*other* ... NY-2
Aquinas Sch—*school* ... NV-8
*Aquiniuh* ... MA-1
Aquinius Sch—*school* ... CA-9
Aquirre Spring—*spring* ... NM-5
*Aquirre Valley* ... AZ-5
*Aqula Creek* ... TX-5
**Aquone**—*pop pl* ... NC-3
*Aquone Lake* ... NC-3
*Aquone Reservoir* ... NC-3
*Ara'* ... FM-9
Ara—*locale* ... CO-8
**Ara**—*pop pl* ... LA-4
*Araahbiru* ... MP-9
*Araahbiru Island* ... MP-9
Arab—*locale* ... MO-7
**Arab**—*pop pl* ... AL-4
*Arabaketsu* ... PW-9
*Arabaru-to* ... MP-9
Arab (CCD)—*cens area* ... AL-4
Arab City Cem—*cemetery* ... AL-4
Arab Country Club—*other* ... AL-4
Arab Division—*civil* ... AL-4
**Arabela**—*pop pl* ... NM-5
Arab Elem Sch—*school* ... AL-4
Arabella—*locale* ... NM-5
Arabella Mine—*mine* ... CO-8
Arabella Mtn—*summit* ... TX-5
Arabella Windmill—*locale* ... NM-5
Arab Hill—*summit* (2) ... NY-2
Arab Hosp—*hospital* ... AL-4
Arab HS—*school* ... AL-4
**Arabi**—*pop pl* ... GA-3
**Arabi**—*pop pl* ... LA-4
*Arabia* ... KY-4
Arabia—*locale* ... NE-7
Arabia—*locale* ... NV-8
Arabia—*locale* (2) ... NY-2
**Arabia**—*pop pl* ... IN-6
**Arabia**—*pop pl* ... NC-3
**Arabia**—*pop pl* ... OH-6
Arabia Cem—*cemetery* ... GA-3
Arabia Cem—*cemetery* ... IN-6
Arabia Lake—*reservoir* ... GA-3
Arabia (local name for South
Fork)—*other* ... KY-4
Arabia Mtn—*summit* ... GA-3
**Arabian Acres**—*pop pl* ... CO-8
**Arabian Acres (subdivision)**—*pop pl* ... DE-2
Arabian Cem—*cemetery* ... OH-6
Arabian Farm Airp—*airport* ... PA-2
Arabian Mine—*mine* ... AZ-5
Arabi-Antioch Cem—*cemetery* ... GA-3
Arabia Swamp—*swamp* ... GA-3
Arabi (CCD)—*cens area* ... GA-3
Arab JHS—*school* ... AL-4
Arab Mtn—*summit* ... NY-2
Arab Primary Sch—*school* ... AL-4
Arab Sch (abandoned)—*school* ... PA-2
Arabs Fork—*stream* ... KY-4
Arab Tank—*reservoir* ... AZ-5
Araby—*hist pl* ... MD-2
Araby—*locale* ... AZ-5
Araby Road Overpass—*crossing* ... AZ-5
*Aracalong* ... PW-9
**Aracoma**—*pop pl* ... WV-2
Aracoma Park—*park* ... OH-6
*Arad* ... AL-4
Aradojairen—*island* ... MP-9
*Aradojairen Island* ... MP-9
*Aradojairen-to* ... MP-9
Aradojairik—*island* ... MP-9
*Aradojairik Island* ... MP-9
*Aradojairiku-to* ... MP-9
*Araga* ... MH-9
*Aragamae* ... PW-9
*Aragamaye* ... PW-9
Arago—*fmr MCD* ... NE-7
**Arago**—*pop pl* ... MN-6
**Arago**—*pop pl* ... OR-9
Arago, Cape—*cape* ... OR-9
Arago Cem—*cemetery* ... NE-7
Arago Center Sch—*school* ... NE-7
Arago Light—*locale* ... OR-9
Aragon—*locale* ... NM-5
**Aragon**—*pop pl* ... GA-3
**Aragon**—*pop pl* (2) ... NM-5

Aragona Acres—*uninc pl* ... VA-3
Aragona Sch—*school* ... VA-3
Aragon Ave Sch—*school* ... CA-9
**Aragona Village**—*pop pl* ... VA-3
**Aragona Village (subdivision)**—*pop pl* ... NC-3
Aragon (CCD)—*cens area* ... GA-3
Aragon Cem—*cemetery* ... WY-8
Aragon Creek—*stream* (2) ... NM-5
Aragon Ditch—*canal* ... WY-8
Aragon Hill—*summit* (2) ... NM-5
Aragon House—*hist pl* ... NM-5
Aragon HS—*school* ... CA-9
Aragonite—*locale* ... UT-8
**Aragon Mills**—*pop pl* (2) ... SC-3
Aragon Mine—*mine* ... MI-6
**Aragon Park**—*pop pl* ... GA-3
Aragon Place—*locale* ... AZ-5
Aragon Ranch—*locale* ... NM-5
Aragon Spring—*spring* (4) ... NM-5
Aragon Tank—*reservoir* ... NM-5
Aragon Wash—*stream* ... NM-5
Arago Sch—*school* ... NE-7
**Arago (Township of)**—*pop pl* ... MN-6
**Araguey Park**—*pop pl* ... FL-3
Arah—*locale* ... TX-5
*Arahburg* ... AL-4
*Araka* ... MH-9
*Arakabesan* ... PW-9
*Arakabesan Island* ... PW-9
*Arakabesan To* ... PW-9
*Arakalong Cape* ... PW-9
*Arakaso* ... PW-9
*Arakasoaol* ... PW-9
*Arakbesan Island* ... PW-9
*Araktcheef* ... MP-9
*Araktcheeff Island* ... MP-9
*Araktschejeff* ... MP-9
*Arakucheeff Islands* ... MP-9
Aral (historical)—*locale* ... KS-7
*Aramagan* ... MH-9
*Aramagan-To* ... MH-9
*Aramanchy River* ... NC-3
*Aramancy River* ... NC-3
*Aramarakarakkura* ... PW-9
*Aramarakarakkuru* ... PW-9
*Aramarakarakura* ... PW-9
Arambarri, Galo, Boarding House—*hist pl* ... ID-8
Arambel Ranch—*locale* ... WY-8
*Arambiru* ... MP-9
Arambiru—*island* ... MP-9
*Arambiru Island* ... MP-9
*Arambiru-to* ... MP-9
Aramburu Canyon—*valley* ... CA-9
*Aramilog* ... FM-9
Aramuskeet—*area* ... NC-3
*Aran* ... MP-9
Arana Creek —*stream* ... TX-5
Arana Gulch—*valley* ... CA-9
Arana Lake —*lake* ... TX-5
*Aranaypa Canyon* ... AZ-5
Aranbee—*other* ... CA-9
Aranda Tank—*reservoir* ... NM-5
Arand Sch—*school* ... KS-7
*Aranewse Creek* ... NC-3
Aranga—*swamp* ... FM-9
Aranga, Oror En—*locale* ... FM-9
Aranga, Unun En—*bar* ... FM-9
Arange Creek—*stream* ... ID-8
Arange Peak—*summit* ... ID-8
*Aranit* ... MP-9
*Aransas Bay* ... TX-5
Aransas Bay—*bay* ... TX-5
Aransas Channel—*channel* ... TX-5
**Aransas (County)**—*pop pl* ... TX-5
Aransas Creek—*stream* ... TX-5
Aransas Natl Wildlife Ref—*park* ... TX-5
Aransas Pass—*channel* ... TX-5
**Aransas Pass**—*pop pl* (2) ... TX-5
Aransas Pass-Ingleside (CCD)—*cens area* ... TX-5
Aransas Pass Lighthouse—*locale* ... TX-5
Aransas Pass Light Station—*hist pl* ... TX-5
*Aransas River* ... TX-5
Aransas River—*stream* ... TX-5
Arant Branch—*stream* ... SC-3
Arant Creek—*stream* ... TX-5
Arant Point—*summit* ... OR-9
**Arapaho**—*pop pl* ... OK-5
Arapaho Basin Ski Area—*other* ... CO-8
Arapaho Bay—*bay* ... CO-8
Arapaho Cem—*cemetery* ... OK-5
Arapaho Creek—*stream* (3) ... CO-8
Arapaho Creek—*stream* ... OK-5
Arapaho Creek—*stream* ... WY-8
Arapaho Creek Trail—*trail* ... CO-8
Arapaho Ditch—*canal* ... CO-8
*Arapahoe* ... CO-8
**Arapahoe**—*pop pl* ... CO-8
**Arapahoe**—*pop pl* ... NE-7
**Arapahoe**—*pop pl* ... NC-3
**Arapahoe**—*pop pl* ... WY-8
Arapahoe Butte—*summit* ... WY-8
Arapahoe Canal—*canal* ... CO-8
Arapahoe Catholic Cem—*cemetery* ... WY-8
Arapahoe Cem—*cemetery* ... CO-8
Arapahoe Cem—*cemetery* ... WY-8
Arapahoe County Airp—*airport* ... CO-8
Arapahoe Creek—*stream* ... MO-7
Arapahoe Creek—*stream* ... WY-8
Arapahoe Ditch—*canal* ... WY-8
Arapahoe East—*post sta* ... CO-8
Arapahoe Elem Sch—*school* ... NC-3
Arapahoe HS—*school* ... CO-8
Arapahoe Natl Wildlife Ref—*park* ... CO-8
Arapahoe Park—*park* ... CO-8
*Arapahoe Peak* ... CO-8
Arapahoe Power Plant—*other* ... CA-9
Arapahoe Pumping Station—*other* ... CO-8
Arapahoe Ranch—*locale* (2) ... WY-8
Arapahoe Rock—*pillar* ... CO-8
Arapahoe Rsvr—*reservoir* ... WY-8
Arapahoe Sch—*school* ... CO-8
Arapahoe Sch (historical)—*school* ... MO-7
*Arapahoe Township* ... KS-7
Arapaho Glacier—*glacier* ... CO-8
Arapaho Lake—*lake* ... NJ-2
Arapaho Lakes—*lake* (2) ... CO-8
Arapaho Moraine—*ridge* ... CO-8
Arapaho Natl For—*forest* ... CO-8
Arapaho Pass—*gap* (2) ... CO-8
Arapaho Pass Trail—*trail* ... CO-8

*Arapaho Peak* ... CO-8
Arapaho Point—*summit* ... OK-5
Arapaho Ridge—*ridge* ... CO-8
Arapaho Valley Ranch—*locale* ... CO-8
Araphoe and Lost Creek Site
(48SW4882)—*hist pl* ... WY-8
Arapho Glacier Trail—*trail* ... CO-8
Arapien Valley—*valley* ... UT-8
*Arappu Point* ... PW-9
Arappu Point—*cape* ... PW-9
Arapwa—*locale* ... FM-9
**Araquey**—*pop pl* ... FL-3
*Ararat* ... PA-2
**Ararat**—*pop pl* ... AL-4
**Ararat**—*pop pl* ... LA-4
**Ararat**—*pop pl* ... NC-3
**Ararat**—*pop pl* ... PA-2
**Ararat**—*pop pl* ... SC-3
**Ararat**—*pop pl* ... VA-3
Ararat, Mount—*summit* (5) ... CA-9
Ararat, Mount—*summit* ... CT-1
Ararat, Mount—*summit* (3) ... MA-1
Ararat, Mount—*summit* (2) ... PA-2
Ararat, Mount—*summit* ... TX-5
Ararat, Mount—*summit* ... WA-9
Ararat Cem—*cemetery* ... NC-3
Ararat Cem—*cemetery* ... SC-3
Ararat Ch—*church* ... NC-3
Ararat Ch—*church* ... PA-2
Ararat Ch—*church* ... SC-3
Ararat Ch—*church* ... TN-4
Ararat Ch—*church* ... VA-3
*Ararat Creek* ... NC-3
Ararat Mtn—*summit* ... NV-8
*Ararat Peak* ... PA-2
Ararat River—*stream* ... NC-3
Ararat River—*stream* ... VA-3
*Ararat Summit* ... PA-2
**Ararat (Township of)**—*pop pl* ... PA-2
*Arare Jima* ... FM-9
*Arare-Shima* ... FM-9
Arasta Creek—*stream* (2) ... MT-8
Arasta Gulch—*valley* ... WY-8
*Araster Lake* ... WY-8
Araster Spring—*spring* ... AZ-5
*Arastor Spring* ... AZ-5
*Arastra Creek* ... ID-8
*Arastra Creek* ... MT-8
Arastra Creek—*stream* ... CA-9
Arastra Creek—*stream* ... MT-8
Arastradero Creek—*stream* ... CA-9
*Arastra Gulch* ... ID-8
Arastra Gulch—*valley* ... OR-9
Arastraville—*locale* ... CA-9
Arastraville Sch—*school* ... CA-9
*Arastre Creek* ... MT-8
Arat—*locale* ... KY-4
Arata Creek—*stream* ... OR-9
Aratama Maru—*hist pl* ... GU-9
Arathlatuluk, Mount—*summit* ... AK-9
*Aratojaiing* ... MP-9
*Aratojairik* ... MP-9
Arat Sch—*school* ... KY-4
*Arattau* ... PW-9
*Arattsu River* ... PW-9
**Aravaipa**—*pop pl* ... AZ-5
Aravaipa Canyon—*valley* ... AZ-5
Aravaipa Canyon Primitive Area—*park* ... AZ-5
Aravaipa Canyon Primitive Area East
Entrance—*locale* ... AZ-5
Aravaipa Creek—*stream* ... AZ-5
Aravaipa Farms—*locale* ... AZ-5
*Aravaipa Primitive Area* ... AZ-5
Aravaipa Ranger Station—*locale* ... AZ-5
Aravaipa Sch—*school* ... AZ-5
*Aravaipa Valley* ... AZ-5
*Aravapai* ... AZ-5
*Aravapai Canyon* ... AZ-5
*Aravapai Creek* ... AZ-5
*Aravaypa* ... AZ-5
*Aravaypa Creek* ... AZ-5
*Arawana River* ... CT-1
*Arayaipa* ... AZ-5
*Arayaipa Canyon* ... AZ-5
*Arayaipa Creek* ... AZ-5
Araya Well—*locale* ... NM-5
*Arayonzet* ... PW-9
Araz Junction—*locale* ... CA-9
Araz (Site)—*locale* ... CA-9
Araz Wash—*stream* ... CA-9
Arba—*island* ... MP-9
**Arba**—*pop pl* ... IN-6
**Arba**—*pop pl* ... NC-3
Arbacoochee—*locale* ... AL-4
*Arbacoochee River* ... AL-4
*Arbacoohee* ... AL-4
Arbagast's Ranch—*locale* ... MT-8
*Arbajona River* ... MA-1
Arbala—*locale* ... TX-5
Arballo, Ramon, House—*hist pl* ... AZ-5
*Arbaney Creek* ... CO-8
Arbaney Ditch—*canal* ... CO-8
Arbaney Gulch—*valley* ... CO-8
Arbanna Ch—*church* ... AR-4
Arbar—*island* (2) ... MP-9
*Arbar Island* ... MP-9
Arbaugh—*locale* ... AR-4
Arbaugh—*locale* ... OH-6
Arbaugh Cem—*cemetery* ... OH-6
Arbaugh Hollow—*valley* ... OH-6
Arbaugh Ranch—*locale* ... ID-8
Arbeau Point—*cape* ... FL-3
Arbeca Creek—*stream* ... OK-5
Arbee—*locale* ... CA-9
Arbeka Ch—*church* (2) ... OK-5
Arbeka Junior Ch—*church* ... OK-5
**Arbela**—*pop pl* ... MO-7
**Arbela**—*pop pl* ... PR-3
Arbela Cem—*cemetery* ... MI-6
**Arbela (Township of)**—*pop pl* ... MI-6
*Arbell Creek* ... MO-7
Arbery Branch—*stream* ... TX-5
*Arbie Lake* ... MI-6
Arbin Landing—*locale* ... MS-4
Arbios—*locale* ... CA-9
Arbo—*locale* ... MS-4
Arbo Brook—*stream* ... ME-1
Arbo Creek—*stream* ... MT-8
**Arbocrest Acres**—*pop pl* ... OH-6
Arbo Flats—*flat* ... ME-1

**Arboga**—*pop pl* ... CA-9
Arbogas Flats—*flat* ... CO-8
Arbogast Ch—*church* ... PA-2
**Arbolada**—*pop pl* ... CA-9
Arbo Lake—*lake* ... MN-6
**Arboles**—*pop pl* ... CO-8
Arboles Island—*island* ... AK-9
Arbolita Sch—*school* ... CA-9
Arbo Mtn—*summit* ... MT-8
**Arbon**—*pop pl* ... ID-8
**Arbona**—*pop pl* (2) ... PR-3
Arbon Cem—*cemetery* ... PA-2
Arbon Ch—*church* ... VA-3
Arbon Crossing—*locale* ... ID-8
Arbondale Sch—*school* ... MS-4
Arbon PO—*locale* ... ID-8
Arbon Sch—*school* ... ID-8
Arbon Valley—*valley* ... ID-8
Arbo Post Office (historical)—*building* ... MS-4
Arbor—*locale* ... NE-7
Arbor—*locale* (2) ... TX-5
**Arbor**—*pop pl* ... KY-4
**Arbor**—*pop pl* ... MO-7
**Arbor**—*pop pl* ... NJ-2
**Arbor**—*pop pl* ... PA-2
Arbor, Lake—*reservoir* ... IA-7
Arbor Acres—*uninc pl* ... AL-4
**Arbor Acres (subdivision)**—*pop pl* ... NC-3
**Arbor (Adamsville)**—*pop pl* ... PA-2
Arbor Baptist Ch—*church* ... AL-4
Arbor Bush Branch—*stream* ... FL-3
Arbor Camp Ridge—*ridge* ... CA-9
Arbor Cem—*cemetery* (2) ... AL-4
Arbor Cem—*cemetery* ... GA-3
Arbor Cem—*cemetery* ... MS-4
Arbor Cem—*cemetery* ... NE-7
Arbor Ch—*church* ... GA-3
Arbor Ch—*church* ... TN-4
Arbor Ch—*church* (2) ... VA-3
Arbor Chapel—*church* ... GA-3
Arbor Chapel—*church* ... TX-5
Arbor Ch (historical)—*church* ... AL-4
Arbor Ch (historical)—*church* ... TN-4
Arbor Creek—*stream* ... OR-9
*Arborcrest Acres* ... OH-6
Arbor Dale Ch—*church* ... NC-3
Arbordale Sch—*school* ... NE-7
Arbor Day Grove—*woods* ... CA-9
Arbor Estates—*uninc pl* ... VA-3
**Arbor Estates Condominium**—*pop pl* ... UT-8
**Arbor Estates Subdivision**—*pop pl* ... UT-8
Arborest Cem—*cemetery* ... MI-6
Arboretum Sewer Trestle—*hist pl* ... WA-9
Arboretum Tank—*reservoir* ... AZ-5
*Arboretum Villages* ... IL-6
Arbor Grove—*locale* ... AR-4
*Arbor Grove Baptist Church* ... MS-4
Arbor Grove Cem—*cemetery* ... MO-7
Arbor Grove Cem—*cemetery* ... OK-5
Arbor Grove Ch—*church* ... MS-4
Arbor Grove Ch—*church* (2) ... NC-3
**Arbor Heights**—*pop pl* ... WA-9
**Arbor Heights (subdivision)**—*pop pl* ... TN-4
Arbor Hill—*locale* ... IA-7
Arbor Hill—*locale* ... VA-3
**Arborhill**—*pop pl* ... VA-3
Arbor Hill Ch—*church* (2) ... GA-3
Arbor Hill Ch—*church* ... TN-4
Arbor Hill Ch—*church* ... VA-3
Arbor Hill (historical P.O.)—*locale* ... IA-7
Arbor Hill Historic District-Ten Broeck
Triangle—*hist pl* ... NY-2
Arbor Hill Historic District-Ten Broeck Triangle
(Boundary Increase)—*hist pl* ... NY-2
Arbor Hills Country Club—*other* ... MI-6
**Arbor Hills (subdivision)**—*pop pl* ... NC-3
Arbor Island—*island* ... AK-9
Arbor Lake—*lake* ... MN-6
Arbor Lake—*lake* ... WA-9
**Arborland Acres**—*pop pl* ... WV-2
Arbor Lodge—*hist pl* ... NE-7
Arbor Lodge Park—*park* ... OR-9
Arbor Lodge State Park—*park* ... NE-7
**Arbor Meadows (subdivision)**—*pop pl* ... VA-3
Arbor Mine—*mine* ... CA-9
Arbor Park—*park* ... NE-7
Arbor Park Sch—*school* ... IL-6
**Arbor Pointe Apartments**—*pop pl* ... DE-2
**Arbors**—*pop pl* ... NJ-2
Arbor Sch—*school* ... MI-6
Arbor Sch—*school* ... NJ-2
Arbor Sch (historical)—*school* (2) ... TN-4
Arbor Sch (historical)—*school* ... TX-5
*Arbor Springs Baptist Ch* ... AL-4
Arbor Springs Cem—*cemetery* (3) ... AL-4
Arbor Springs Ch—*church* (3) ... AL-4
Arbor Springs Ch (historical)—*church* ... AL-4
Arbor Spring Sch (historical)—*school* ... AL-4
Arbor Springs Sch (historical)—*school* ... AL-4
*Arbor Terrace* ... MO-7
**Arbor Terrace**—*pop pl* ... MO-7
*Arbor Township* ... KS-7
*Arbor Trails* ... IL-6
*Arborvale* ... WV-2
Arbor Villa Park—*park* ... MO-7
Arborville—*locale* ... NE-7
**Arborville**—*pop pl* ... SC-3
Arborville Cem—*cemetery* ... NE-7
**Arbor Vitae**—*pop pl* ... WI-6
Arbor Vitae Cem—*cemetery* ... CA-9
**Arbor Vitae (Town of)**—*pop pl* ... WI-6
Arbor Windmill—*locale* ... TX-5
**Arborwood Park Subdivision**—*pop pl* ... UT-8
**Arboth**—*pop pl* ... LA-4
Arbothknott Canyon—*valley* ... WA-9
**Arbo (Township of)**—*pop pl* ... MN-6
**Arbour Park**—*pop pl* ... DE-2
*Arbour Springs Baptist Ch* ... MS-4
**Arbovale**—*pop pl* ... WV-2
**Arbre Park (trailer park)**—*pop pl* ... DE-2
**Arbroth**—*pop pl* ... LA-4
Arbs Basin—*basin* ... UT-8
Arbter Lake—*lake* ... WI-6
**Arbuckle**—*pop pl* ... CA-9
**Arbuckle**—*pop pl* ... FL-3
**Arbuckle**—*pop pl* ... PA-2
**Arbuckle**—*pop pl* ... WV-2
Arbuckle, Alexander W., I,
House—*hist pl* ... WV-2
Arbuckle, George, House—*hist pl* ... UT-8

Arbuckle, Lake—*lake* ... FL-3
Arbuckle Acres Park—*park* ... IN-6
Arbuckle Basin—*basin* ... CA-9
Arbuckle Branch—*stream* ... FL-3
Arbuckle Branch—*stream* ... WV-2
Arbuckle Canyon—*valley* ... UT-8
Arbuckle Cem—*cemetery* ... AR-4
Arbuckle Cem—*cemetery* ... MO-7
Arbuckle Cem—*cemetery* ... OH-6
Arbuckle Ch—*church* ... WV-2
Arbuckle Corral—*locale* ... OR-9
Arbuckle Creek—*stream* ... CA-9
Arbuckle Creek—*stream* ... FL-3
Arbuckle Creek—*stream* ... KY-4
Arbuckle Creek—*stream* ... VA-3
Arbuckle Creek—*stream* (3) ... WV-2
Arbuckle Dam—*dam* ... OK-5
Arbuckle Ditch—*canal* ... IN-6
Arbuckle Draw—*valley* ... WA-9
Arbuckle Flat—*flat* ... CA-9
Arbuckle Flats—*flat* ... WA-9
Arbuckle Golf Club—*other* ... CA-9
*Arbuckle Gulch* ... MT-8
Arbuckle Gulch—*valley* ... CA-9
Arbuckle Gulch—*valley* ... CO-8
Arbuckle Gulch—*valley* ... MT-8
Arbuckle Hill—*summit* ... OK-5
Arbuckle Hill Cem—*cemetery* ... VA-3
Arbuckle Hollow—*valley* ... NY-2
Arbuckle Island—*island* ... AR-4
Arbuckle Island Cutoff—*channel* ... AR-4
Arbuckle Landing—*locale* ... VA-3
Arbuckle (Magisterial District)—*fmr MCD* ... WV-2
Arbuckle Mountains—*range* ... OK-5
Arbuckle Mtn—*summit* ... CA-9
Arbuckle Mtn—*summit* ... OR-9
Arbuckle Mtn—*summit* ... WA-9
Arbuckle Neck—*cape* ... VA-3
Arbuckle Place—*hist pl* ... VA-3
Arbuckle Pond—*lake* ... NY-2
*Arbuckle Reservoir* ... OK-5
Arbuckles, Lake of the—*reservoir* ... OK-5
*Arbuckle's Bay* ... VA-3
Arbuckle Sch—*school* ... CA-9
Arbuckle Sch—*school* (2) ... WV-2
Arbuckle Ski Area—*area* ... OR-9
Arbuckle Spring—*spring* ... OR-9
Arburua Ranch—*locale* ... CA-9
*Arbury Canyon* ... CO-8
**Arbury Hills**—*pop pl* ... IL-6
Arbury Hills Sch—*school* ... IL-6
Arbuthnet Lake—*lake* ... WA-9
Arbuthnots Store (historical)—*locale* ... FL-3
Arbutus—*locale* ... MN-6
**Arbutus**—*pop pl* ... MD-2
Arbutus, Lake—*reservoir* ... WI-6
**Arbutus Beach**—*pop pl* ... MI-6
Arbutus Branch—*stream* ... TN-4
Arbutus Cem—*cemetery* ... MI-6
Arbutus (census name for
Halethorpe)—*CDP* ... MD-2
Arbutus Ch—*church* ... PA-2
Arbutus Ch—*church* ... WI-6
Arbutus Glen—*valley* ... OH-6
Arbutus Lake—*lake* (2) ... MI-6
Arbutus Lake—*lake* ... NY-2
Arbutus Lake—*lake* (2) ... WI-6
Arbutus Memorial Park Cem—*cemetery* ... MD-2
Arbutus Park—*park* ... WI-6
**Arbutus Park**—*pop pl* ... WV-2
Arbutus Peak—*summit* ... PA-2
Arbutus Pond—*lake* ... NY-2
Arbutus Ridge—*ridge* ... TN-4
**Arbutus (sta.)**—*pop pl* ... MD-2
Arbutus Trail—*trail* ... TN-4
*Arbwa Island* ... MP-9
*Arbwar* ... MP-9
**Arbyrd**—*pop pl* ... MO-7
*Arcada* ... TX-5
Arcada Rock—*island* ... AK-9
**Arcada (Township of)**—*pop pl* ... MI-6
*Arcade* ... WI-6
Arcade—*locale* ... CA-9
Arcade—*locale* ... TX-5
**Arcade**—*pop pl* ... DC-2
**Arcade**—*pop pl* ... GA-3
**Arcade**—*pop pl* ... NY-2
**Arcade**—*pop pl* ... WI-6
Arcade—*post sta* ... MI-6
Arcade—*uninc pl* (2) ... CA-9
Arcade, The—*hist pl* ... RI-1
Arcade, The—*hist pl* ... TN-4
**Arcade Acres**—*pop pl* ... WI-6
Arcade and Attica RR—*hist pl* ... NY-2
Arcade Bldg—*hist pl* ... MA-1
Arcade Bldg—*hist pl* ... NC-3
Arcade Bldg—*hist pl* ... SC-3
Arcade Cem—*cemetery* ... OR-9
Arcade Center—*locale* ... NY-2
Arcade Creek—*stream* ... CA-9
Arcade Drift Mine (underground)—*mine* ... AL-4
Arcade Glen—*valley* ... WI-6
Arcade Hosp—*hospital* ... CA-9
Arcade Hotel—*hist pl* ... FL-3
Arcade Hotel—*hist pl* ... OH-6
Arcade Hotel—*hist pl* ... SC-3
Arcade Junction—*uninc pl* ... NY-2
Arcade Mine—*mine* ... CA-9
Arcade Numbers 1 and 2 Lodes
Mine—*mine* ... SD-7
Arcade Pond—*lake* ... MA-1
Arcade Sch—*school* ... CA-9
Arcade Theater—*hist pl* ... LA-4
**Arcade (Town of)**—*pop pl* ... NY-2
**Arcade Township**—*pop pl* ... KS-7
**Arcade Township**—*pop pl* ... SD-7
*Arcadia* ... IL-6
*Arcadia* ... IN-6
*Arcadia* ... MD-2
*Arcadia* ... TX-5
Arcadia—*hist pl* ... KY-4
Arcadia—*hist pl* ... MD-2
Arcadia—*locale* ... AR-4
Arcadia—*locale* ... OR-9
Arcadia—*locale* ... TN-4
Arcadia—*locale* ... TX-5
Arcadia—*locale* ... UT-8
Arcadia—*locale* (2) ... VA-3
Arcadia—*locale* ... WA-9
**Arcadia**—*pop pl* ... CA-9

**Arcadia**—*pop pl* ... FL-3
**Arcadia**—*pop pl* ... IL-6
**Arcadia**—*pop pl* ... IN-6
**Arcadia**—*pop pl* ... IA-7
**Arcadia**—*pop pl* ... KS-7
**Arcadia**—*pop pl* ... LA-4
**Arcadia**—*pop pl* ... MI-6
**Arcadia**—*pop pl* ... MO-7
**Arcadia**—*pop pl* ... NE-7
**Arcadia**—*pop pl* (2) ... NC-3
**Arcadia**—*pop pl* ... OH-6
**Arcadia**—*pop pl* ... OK-5
**Arcadia**—*pop pl* (2) ... PA-2
**Arcadia**—*pop pl* ... RI-1
**Arcadia**—*pop pl* ... SC-3
**Arcadia**—*pop pl* ... TX-5
**Arcadia**—*pop pl* ... WI-6
**Arcadia**—*pop pl* ... PR-3
Arcadia—*uninc pl* ... AZ-5
Arcadia Beach—*beach* ... OR-9
*Arcadia Bible Camp* ... MO-7
Arcadia Brook—*stream* ... VT-1
Arcadia Campground—*park* ... AZ-5
Arcadia Canal—*canal* ... ID-8
Arcadia Cem—*cemetery* ... IA-7
Arcadia Cem—*cemetery* ... WI-6
Arcadia Ch—*church* ... TN-4
Arcadia Ch—*church* ... TX-5
Arcadia Christian Sch—*school* ... CA-9
Arcadia Country Club—*other* ... WI-6
Arcadia County Park—*park* ... CA-9
Arcadia Creek—*stream* ... MI-6
Arcadia East (CCD)—*cens area* ... FL-3
Arcadia (Election Precinct)—*fmr MCD* ... IL-6
*Arcadia Elementary School* ... AL-4
Arcadia Golf Course—*other* ... CA-9
**Arcadia Heights**—*pop pl* ... SC-3
Arcadia Hills—*CDP* ... NY-2
Arcadia Hills Golf Club—*other* ... MI-6
Arcadia Hist Dist—*hist pl* ... FL-3
Arcadia (historical)—*locale* ... AL-4
**Arcadia (historical)**—*pop pl* ... MS-4
**Arcadia (historical)**—*pop pl* ... OR-9
Arcadia HS—*school* ... CA-9
Arcadia Island—*island* ... NY-2
Arcadia Lake—*lake* ... MA-1
Arcadia Lake—*lake* ... MI-6
Arcadia Lake—*reservoir* ... OR-9
**Arcadia Lakes**—*pop pl* ... SC-3
Arcadia Landing—*locale* ... MS-4
Arcadia (Mayfair Mill)—*CDP* ... SC-3
Arcadia Mine—*mine* ... CA-9
Arcadia Mine (underground)—*mine* ... AL-4
*Arcadia Mountain* ... ME-1
Arcadia MS—*school* ... WA-9
Arcadian Bottling Works—*hist pl* ... WI-6
Arcadian Hill—*summit* ... MI-6
**Arcadian Park Subdivision**—*pop pl* ... UT-8
Arcadia Park—*park* ... TX-5
**Arcadia Park**—*pop pl* ... TX-5
**Arcadia Park Condominium**—*pop pl* ... UT-8
Arcadia Plantation—*hist pl* ... SC-3
Arcadia Plantation—*locale* ... SC-3
Arcadia Plantation (historical)—*locale* ... MS-4
Arcadia Plaza Shop Ctr—*locale* ... AZ-5
Arcadia Point—*cape* ... MS-4
Arcadia Post Office (historical)—*building* ... TN-4
Arcadia Rec Area—*park* ... AZ-5
Arcadia Reef—*bar* ... TX-5
Arcadia Ridge—*ridge* ... WI-6
Arcadia Round Barn—*hist pl* ... OK-5
Arcadia Sanctuary—*park* ... MA-1
Arcadia Sawmill and Arcadia Cotton
Mill—*hist pl* ... FL-3
Arcadia Sch—*school* ... AL-4
Arcadia Sch—*school* ... IL-6
Arcadia Sch—*school* ... NC-3
Arcadia Sch—*school* ... OR-9
Arcadia Sch—*school* ... TN-4
Arcadia Sch—*school* ... UT-8
Arcadia Shopping Plaza—*locale* ... FL-3
**Arcadia Shores**—*pop pl* ... TN-4
**Arcadia (subdivision)**—*pop pl* ... AL-4
**Arcadia Subdivision**—*pop pl* ... UT-8
**Arcadia (Town of)**—*pop pl* ... NY-2
**Arcadia (Town of)**—*pop pl* ... WI-6
Arcadia Township—*civil* ... MO-7
Arcadia Township—*fmr MCD* ... IA-7
**Arcadia Township**—*pop pl* ... NE-7
Arcadia (Township of)—*fmr MCD* ... NC-3
**Arcadia (Township of)**—*pop pl* (2) ... MI-6
*Arcadia (Upperco)* ... MD-2
Arcadia Valley Bible Camp—*locale* ... MO-7
Arcadia Valley Cem—*cemetery* ... MO-7
Arcadia Valley Golf Club—*other* ... MO-7
Arcadia Valley Sch—*school* ... MO-7
Arcadia Village Shop Ctr—*locale* ... AZ-5
Arcadia Wash—*stream* ... CA-9
Arcadia West (CCD)—*cens area* ... FL-3
Arcadia Wilderness Park—*park* ... CA-9
Arcady Country Club—*other* ... NY-2
**Arcana**—*pop pl* ... IN-6
Arcana Creek—*stream* ... AK-9
Arcane Meadows—*flat* ... CA-9
Arcane Sch—*school* ... CA-9
*Arcansas River* ... KS-7
**Arcanum**—*pop pl* ... OH-6
Arcanum Greenlawn Cem—*cemetery* ... OH-6
**Arcata**—*pop pl* ... CA-9
Arcata Airp—*airport* ... CA-9
*Arcata And Mad River* ... CA-9
Arcata Bay—*bay* ... CA-9
Arcata Bottoms—*flat* ... CA-9
Arcata (CCD)—*cens area* ... CA-9
Arcata Channel—*channel* ... CA-9
Arc Corner—*locale* ... DE-2
Arc Dome—*summit* ... NV-8
Arceneaux—*locale* ... LA-4
Arceneaux, Bayou—*stream* ... LA-4
Arceneaux Cem—*cemetery* ... LA-4
Arcente Canyon—*valley* ... NM-5
Arch—*locale* ... KY-4
Arch—*locale* ... OK-5
**Arch**—*pop pl* ... NM-5
**Arch**—*pop pl* ... UT-8
Arch, The—*arch* ... ID-8
Arch, The—*arch* ... MT-8
Arch, The—*arch* ... NV-8
Arch, The—*arch* ... WY-8
Arch, The—*locale* ... WY-8

Archabal—*locale* ID-8
Archaeological Cave—*cave* UT-8
Archaeol Site No. 21SL82—*hist pl* MN-6
Archaeol Site 15 BE 36—*hist pl* KY-4
Archaeol Site 15 McL 18—*hist pl* KY-4
Archaeol Site 15 Mi 109—*hist pl* KY-4
Archambault Creek—*stream* SD-7
Archambault House—*hist pl* MO-7
*Archambeau Branch* OR-9
*Archambeau Creek* OR-9
Archambeau Creek—*stream* MI-6
Archambeault Flats—*flat* MT-8
Archambeault Ranch—*locale* MT-8
Archambeault Retention Rsvr—*reservoir* MT-8
Arch and Ridge Streets Hist Dist—*hist pl* MI-6
Archangel Creek—*stream* AK-9
Arch Apex Gas Field—*area* MT-8
Archawat Creek—*stream* WA-9
Archawat Peak—*summit* WA-9
Archawat (Site)—*locale* WA-9
**Archbald**—*pop pl* PA-2
Archbald Borough—*civil* PA-2
*Archbald Point* NC-3
Archbald Pothole State Park—*park* PA-2
Archbald Shaft—*mine* PA-2
Archbald Township—*civil* PA-2
Arch Beach—*beach* CA-9
Arch Beach Heights—*uninc pl* CA-9
Archbell Gut—*stream* NC-3
Archbell Point—*cape* (2) NC-3
Archbishop Alter HS—*school* OH-6
Archbishop Carroll HS—*school* DC-2
Archbishop Carroll HS—*school* PA-2
Archbishop Chapelle HS—*school* LA-4
Archbishop Curley-Notre Dame HS—*school* FL-3
Archbishop Curley Sch—*school* FL-3
Archbishop Hoban Sch—*school* OH-6
Archbishop Lamy's Chapel—*hist pl* NM-5
Archbishop Murray Sch—*school* MN-6
Archbishop Neale Sch—*school* MD-2
Archbishop Pendergast HS—*school* PA-2
Archbishop R Ryan Memorial Sch—*school* GA-3
Archbishop Stepinac HS—*school* NY-2
Archbishop Williams HS—*school* MA-1
Archbishop Wood HS—*school* PA-2
Archbold—*locale* FL-3
**Archbold**—*pop pl* OH-6
Archbold Biological Station—*locale* FL-3
Archbold Cem—*cemetery* OH-6
Archbold Cem—*cemetery* WV-2
Archbold Memorial Hosp—*hospital* GA-3
Archbold Pothole—*basin* PA-2
Archbold Stadium—*other* NY-2
Archbold Tower—*tower* FL-3
Arch Branch—*stream* OK-5
Arch Bridge—*bridge* TN-4
Arch Canyon—*valley* AZ-5
Arch Canyon—*valley* ID-8
Arch Canyon—*valley* NV-8
Arch Canyon—*valley* (2) UT-8
Arch Canyon Overlook—*locale* UT-8
Arch Cape—*cape* OR-9
**Arch Cape**—*pop pl* OR-9
Arch Cape Creek—*stream* OR-9
Arch Cave—*cave* AL-4
Arch Cave—*cave* (2) MO-7
Arch Cave—*cave* TN-4
Arch Cave Hollow—*valley* MO-7
Arch Chapel Cem—*cemetery* TX-5
**Arch City**—*pop pl* GA-3
*Arch Coulee* MT-8
Arch Coulee—*valley* (2) MT-8
Arch Creek—*other* FL-3
Arch Creek—*stream* AK-9
Arch Creek—*stream* CA-9
Arch Creek—*stream* FL-3
Arch Creek—*stream* MT-8
Arch Creek—*stream* TX-5
Arch Creek—*stream* (2) UT-8
Arch Creek—*stream* (2) WY-8
Arch Creek Cem—*cemetery* VA-3
Arch Creek Historic and Archeol Site—*hist pl* FL-3
Arch Creek Memorial Park—*park* FL-3
Arch Creek Petroglyphs (48CK41)—*hist pl* WY-8
Archdale—*locale* NY-2
Archdale—*locale* NC-3
**Archdale**—*pop pl* NC-3
Archdale Creek—*stream* MT-8
Archdale Elem Sch—*school* NC-3
Archdale-Trinity MS—*school* NC-3
Arch Dam Campground—*locale* UT-8
*Arch Dam Group Area* UT-8
Archdeacons Tower—*summit* AK-9
Arch de Triumphe—*arch* UT-8
*Arche Creek* UT-8
*Archeculs Bay* NJ-2
Arched Rock—*island* (2) CA-9
Arched Rock—*island* HI-9
Arched Rock Beach—*beach* CA-9
*Archeland Hill* MA-1
Archelaus Hill—*summit* MA-1
Archelogical Site HU189—*hist pl* SD-7
Archeogical Site 39JE10—*hist pl* SD-7
Archeol Site CA SBR 3186—*hist pl* CA-9
Archeol Site FS-18, LA-5920—*hist pl* NM-5
Archeol Site FS-199, LA-135—*hist pl* NM-5
Archeol Site FS-3—*hist pl* NM-5
Archeol Site FS-535, LA-385—*hist pl* NM-5
Archeol Site FS-554, LA-386—*hist pl* NM-5
Archeol Site FS-574—*hist pl* NM-5
Archeol Site FS-575—*hist pl* NM-5
Archeol Site FS-580, LA-137—*hist pl* NM-5
Archeol Site FS-647, LA-128—*hist pl* NM-5
Archeol Site FS-688—*hist pl* NM-5
Archeol Site FS-689, LA-403—*hist pl* NM-5
Archeol Site FS-8—*hist pl* NM-5
Archeol Site KHC-3 (15HE635)—*hist pl* KY-4
Archeol Site KHC-4 (15HE580)—*hist pl* KY-4
Archeol Site KHC-6 (15OH97)—*hist pl* KY-4
Archeol Site K-873 (7K-D-35/A, B and D)—*hist pl* DE-2
Archeol Site K-875 (7K-D-37/C)—*hist pl* DE-2
Archeol Site K-876 (7K-D-38/C)—*hist pl* DE-2
Archeol Site K-880 (7K-D-42/F)—*hist pl* DE-2
Archeol Site K-891 (7K-D-45/A and B)—*hist pl* DE-2
Archeol Site K-913 (7K-D-47/C, D and E)—*hist pl* DE-2
Archeol Site K-914 (7K-D-48/F and G)—*hist pl* DE-2
Archeol Site K-915 (7K-D-86/C)—*hist pl* DE-2
Archeol Site K-916 (7K-D-49/C)—*hist pl* DE-2
Archeol Site K-920 (7K-D-52/A and C)—*hist pl* DE-2
Archeol Site LA 12151—*hist pl* NM-5
Archeol Site # LA 15278 (Reservoir Site; CM 100)—*hist pl* NM-5
Archeol Site # LA 45,780—*hist pl* NM-5
Archeol Site # LA 45,781—*hist pl* NM-5
Archeol Site # LA 45,782—*hist pl* NM-5
Archeol Site # LA 45,784—*hist pl* NM-5
Archeol Site # LA 45,785—*hist pl* NM-5
Archeol Site # LA 45,786—*hist pl* NM-5
Archeol Site # LA 45,789—*hist pl* NM-5
Archeol Site # LA 50,000—*hist pl* NM-5
Archeol Site # LA 50,001—*hist pl* NM-5
Archeol Site # LA 50,013 (CM101)—*hist pl* NM-5
Archeol Site # LA 50,014 (CM 102)—*hist pl* NM-5
Archeol Site # LA 50,015 (CM 102A)—*hist pl* NM-5
Archeol Site # LA 50,016 (CM 103)—*hist pl* NM-5
Archeol Site # LA 50,017 (CM 104)—*hist pl* NM-5
Archeol Site # LA 50,018—*hist pl* NM-5
Archeol Site # LA 50,019 (CM 105)—*hist pl* NM-5
Archeol Site # LA 50,020 (CM 106)—*hist pl* NM-5
Archeol Site # LA 50,021—*hist pl* NM-5
Archeol Site # LA 50,022 (CM 107)—*hist pl* NM-5
Archeol Site # LA 50,023 (CM 118)—*hist pl* NM-5
Archeol Site # LA 50,024 (CM 108)—*hist pl* NM-5
Archeol Site # LA 50,025 (CM 109)—*hist pl* NM-5
Archeol Site # LA 50,026 (CM 108)—*hist pl* NM-5
Archeol Site # LA 50,027 (CM 111)—*hist pl* NM-5
Archeol Site # LA 50,028 (CM 112)—*hist pl* NM-5
Archeol Site # LA 50,030 (CM 114)—*hist pl* NM-5
Archeol Site # LA 50,031 (CM 115)—*hist pl* NM-5
Archeol Site # LA 50,033 (CM 117)—*hist pl* NM-5
Archeol Site # LA 50,034—*hist pl* NM-5
Archeol Site # LA 50,036—*hist pl* NM-5
Archeol Site # LA 50,037—*hist pl* NM-5
Archeol Site # LA 50,038—*hist pl* NM-5
Archeol Site # LA 50,044—*hist pl* NM-5
Archeol Site # LA 50,071 (CM 148)—*hist pl* NM-5
Archeol Site # LA 50,072 (CM 94)—*hist pl* NM-5
Archeol Site # LA 50,074 (CM 181)—*hist pl* NM-5
Archeol Site # LA 50,077—*hist pl* NM-5
Archeol Site # LA 50,080—*hist pl* NM-5
Archeol Site LA 61201—*hist pl* NM-5
Archeol Site LA 61204—*hist pl* NM-5
Archeol Site LA 61206—*hist pl* NM-5
Archeol Site LA 61208—*hist pl* NM-5
Archeol Site LA 61210—*hist pl* NM-5
Archeol Site LA 61211—*hist pl* NM-5
Archeol Site No. AU-154—*hist pl* VA-3
Archeol Site No. Ca-Lak-711—*hist pl* CA-9
Archeol Site No. D-4—*hist pl* CA-9
Archeol Site No. E-21—*hist pl* CA-9
Archeol Site No. LA 50,035—*hist pl* NM-5
Archeol Site No. 1LA102—*hist pl* AL-4
Archeol Site No. 1MC110—*hist pl* AL-4
Archeol Site No. 1WI50—*hist pl* AL-4
Archeol Site No. 1-18th Century Vessel (28ME196)—*hist pl* NJ-2
Archeol Site No. 133.7—*hist pl* ME-1
Archeol Site No. 133.8—*hist pl* ME-1
Archeol Site No. 15HR4—*hist pl* KY-4
Archeol Site No. 15McL16—*hist pl* KY-4
Archeol Site No. 15McL17—*hist pl* KY-4
Archeol Site No. 29-64—*hist pl* ME-1
Archeol Site No. 42Md300—*hist pl* UT-8
Archeol Site No. 7K F 4 and 23—*hist pl* DE-2
Archeol Site OCA-CGP-56—*hist pl* NM-5
Archeol Site SMA-151—*hist pl* CA-9
Archeol Site (T-10) 50-60-04-702—*hist pl* HI-9
Archeol Site (T-108) 50-60-03-713—*hist pl* HI-9
Archeol Site (T-111-116; T-182) 50-60-04-710—*hist pl* HI-9
Archeol Site (T-12) 50-60-04-704—*hist pl* HI-9
Archeol Site (T-125-6; T-181) 50-60-03-714—*hist pl* HI-9
Archeol Site (T-134) 5060-03-718—*hist pl* HI-9
Archeol Site (T-135-6) 50-60-03-719—*hist pl* HI-9
Archeol Site (T-155, -158) 50-60-03-721—*hist pl* HI-9
Archeol Site (T-165-6) 50-60-03-727—*hist pl* HI-9
Archeol Site (T-19) 50-60-04-705—*hist pl* HI-9
Archeol Site (T-5, T-122, T-178) 50-60-04-142—*hist pl* HI-9
Archeol Site (T-57) 50-60-03-720—*hist pl* HI-9
Archeol Site (T-6 complex) 50-60-04-700—*hist pl* HI-9
Archeol Site (T-76) 50-60-03-724—*hist pl* HI-9
Archeol Site (T-78) 50-60-03-723—*hist pl* HI-9
Archeol Site (T-79) 50-60-03-726—*hist pl* HI-9
Archeol Site (T-81, -100, -101, -105, -142) 50-60-03-717—*hist pl* HI-9
Archeol Site (T-88) 50-60-04-707—*hist pl* HI-9
Archeol Site (T-92) 50-60-04-708—*hist pl* HI-9
Archeol Site # 14CM305—*hist pl* KS-7
Archeol Site # 14EW14—*hist pl* KS-7
Archeol Site # 14EW17—*hist pl* KS-7
Archeol Site # 14EW303—*hist pl* KS-7
Archeol Site # 14EW33—*hist pl* KS-7
Archeol Site # 14EW401—*hist pl* KS-7
Archeol Site # 14EW403—*hist pl* KS-7
Archeol Site # 14EW404—*hist pl* KS-7
Archeol Site # 14EW405—*hist pl* KS-7
Archeol Site # 14EW406—*hist pl* KS-7
Archeol Site # 14GR320—*hist pl* KS-7
Archeol Site # 14KW301—*hist pl* KS-7
Archeol Site # 14KW302—*hist pl* KS-7
Archeol Site # 14LC306—*hist pl* KS-7
Archeol Site # 14MY1—*hist pl* KS-7
Archeol Site # 14MY1320—*hist pl* KS-7
Archeol Site # 14MY1385—*hist pl* KS-7
Archeol Site # 14MY365—*hist pl* KS-7
Archeol Site # 14OT4—*hist pl* KS-7
Archeol Site # 14RC10—*hist pl* KS-7
Archeol Site # 14RC11—*hist pl* KS-7
Archeol Site # 14RU10—*hist pl* KS-7
Archeol Site # 14RU313—*hist pl* KS-7
Archeol Site # 14RU314—*hist pl* KS-7
Archeol Site # 14RU315—*hist pl* KS-7
Archeol Site # 14RU316—*hist pl* KS-7
Archeol Site # 14RU324—*hist pl* KS-7
Archeol Site # 14RU5—*hist pl* KS-7
Archeol Site 15 Ad 33—*hist pl* KY-4
Archeol Site 15 Ad 36—*hist pl* KY-4
Archeol Site 15 Ad 54—*hist pl* KY-4
Archeol Site 15CW64—*hist pl* KY-4
Archeol Site 15 Da 39—*hist pl* KY-4
Archeol Site 15 Fr 26—*hist pl* KY-4
Archeol Site 15 Fr 34—*hist pl* KY-4
Archeol Site 15 FR 368—*hist pl* KY-4
Archeol Site 15 Fr 52—*hist pl* KY-4
Archeol Site 15 Hk 46 and 47—*hist pl* KY-4
Archeol Site 15 HK 79—*hist pl* KY-4
Archeol Site 15 Hk 8—*hist pl* KY-4
Archeol Site 15 Ma 24—*hist pl* KY-4
Archeol Site 15McN51—*hist pl* KY-4
Archeol Site 15ME15—*hist pl* KY-4
Archeol Site 15MF355—*hist pl* KY-4
Archeol Site 15 Ne 3—*hist pl* KY-4
Archeol Site 15Wd61—*hist pl* KY-4
Archeol Site 16.175—*hist pl* ME-1
Archeol Site 16.198—*hist pl* ME-1
Archeol Site 16.20—*hist pl* ME-1
Archeol Site 16.21—*hist pl* ME-1
Archeol Site 16.37 Area I and II—*hist pl* ME-1
Archeol Site 16.38—*hist pl* ME-1
Archeol Site 16.47—*hist pl* ME-1
Archeol Site 16.68—*hist pl* ME-1
Archeol Site 16.73—*hist pl* ME-1
Archeol Site 16.8—*hist pl* ME-1
Archeol Site 21SL141—*hist pl* MN-6
Archeol Site 21SL35—*hist pl* MN-6
Archeol Site 21SL55—*hist pl* MN-6
Archeol Site 26.27—*hist pl* ME-1
Archeol Site 36 LY 37—*hist pl* PA-2
Archeol Site 38CK1—*hist pl* SC-3
Archeol Site 38CK44—*hist pl* SC-3
Archeol Site 38CK45—*hist pl* SC-3
Archeol Site 38SP11—*hist pl* SC-3
Archeol Site 38SP12—*hist pl* SC-3
Archeol Site 38SP13—*hist pl* SC-3
Archeol Site 38SP17—*hist pl* SC-3
Archeol Site 38SP18—*hist pl* SC-3
Archeol Site 38SP19—*hist pl* SC-3
Archeol Site 38SP20—*hist pl* SC-3
Archeol Site 38SP21—*hist pl* SC-3
Archeol Site 38SP23—*hist pl* SC-3
Archeol Site 38SP52—*hist pl* SC-3
Archeol Site 38SP53—*hist pl* SC-3
Archeol Site 38SP54—*hist pl* SC-3
Archeol Site 38SP57—*hist pl* SC-3
Archeol Site 39HD22—*hist pl* SD-7
Archeol Site 39HU201—*hist pl* SD-7
Archeol Site 39HU66—*hist pl* SD-7
Archeol Site 39JE11—*hist pl* SD-7
Archeol Site 39TU5—*hist pl* SD-7
Archeol Site 4 SLO 834—*hist pl* CA-9
Archeol Site 41 CH 110—*hist pl* TX-5
Archeol Site 49 AF 3—*hist pl* AK-9
Archeol Site 49 MK 10—*hist pl* AK-9
Archeol Site 5EA484—*hist pl* CO-8
Archeol Site 50-60-04-140—*hist pl* HI-9
Archeol Site 50-60-04-144—*hist pl* HI-9
*Archer* OH-6
Archer—*locale* CA-9
Archer—*locale* IL-6
Archer—*locale* WV-2
Archer—*locale* WY-8
**Archer**—*pop pl* AL-4
**Archer**—*pop pl* FL-3
**Archer**—*pop pl* ID-8
**Archer**—*pop pl* IA-7
**Archer**—*pop pl* MT-8
**Archer**—*pop pl* NE-7
**Archer**—*pop pl* TN-4
Archer, Lake—*lake* MA-1
Archer, Mount—*summit* CT-1
Archer, William, House—*hist pl* NY-2
**Archer (Archer Lodge)**—*pop pl* NC-3
Archer Baptist Ch—*church* FL-3
Archer Branch—*stream* TN-4
Archer Bridge—*bridge* TX-5
Archer Brook—*stream* ME-1
Archer Camp—*locale* CA-9
Archer (CCD)—*cens area* TX-5
Archer Cem—*cemetery* (2) IN-6
Archer Cem—*cemetery* (2) OH-6
Archer Cem—*cemetery* OR-9
Archer Cem—*cemetery* (2) TN-4
Archer Cem—*cemetery* VA-3
Archer Cem—*cemetery* WV-2
Archer Center Sch—*school* TN-4
Archer Chapel—*church* TN-4
Archer Ch of the Nazarene—*church* FL-3
**Archer City**—*pop pl* TX-5
Archer Community Sch—*school* FL-3
**Archer (County)**—*pop pl* TX-5
Archer County Courthouse and Jail—*hist pl* TX-5
Archer County Regular Oil Field—*oilfield* TX-5
*Archer Creek* SC-3
Archer Creek—*stream* IL-6
Archer Creek—*stream* MO-7
Archer Creek—*stream* NC-3
Archer Creek—*stream* VA-3
Archer Creek—*stream* (2) WA-9
Archer Fork—*stream* WV-2
Archer Grove Ch—*church* GA-3
**Archer Heights**—*pop pl* WV-2
Archer Hill—*summit* SD-7
Archer House Hotel—*hist pl* IL-6
Archer Island—*island* AR-4
Archer Key—*island* FL-3
Archer Knob—*summit* VA-3
**Archer Kullak Subdivision**—*pop pl* UT-8
Archer Lake—*lake* AR-4
Archer Lake—*lake* MI-6
Archer Lake—*lake* TX-5
Archerletti Landing (historical)—*locale* MS-4
*Archer Lodge* NC-3
Archer Lodge—*other* NC-3
Archer Memorial Ch—*church* CT-1
Archer Mine—*mine* CA-9
Archer Mine—*mine* OR-9
Archer Mtn—*summit* ID-8
Archer Mtn—*summit* VA-3
Archer Mtn—*summit* WA-9
Archer Park—*park* AL-4
Archer Park—*park* IL-6
Archer Park—*park* KY-4
Archer Park—*park* MS-4
Archer Playground—*park* OK-5
Archer Point—*cape* NC-3
Archer Point—*summit* ID-8
Archer Post Office (historical)—*building* TN-4
Archer Ranch—*locale* NE-7
Archer Ridge—*ridge* TN-4
Archer Rock—*rock* MA-1
Archer Run—*stream* VA-3
Archer Saddle—*gap* ID-8
Archers Canyon—*valley* UT-8
Archer Sch—*school* SC-3
Archer Sch—*school* VA-3
*Archers Chapel* AL-4
Archers Chapel—*church* WV-2
Archer Sch (historical)—*school* MS-4
**Archers Corner**—*pop pl* NJ-2
Archers Corners—*locale* ME-1
Archers Creek—*channel* SC-3
Archers Creek—*stream* KY-4
Archers Fork—*locale* OH-6
Archers Fork—*stream* OH-6
*Archers Fork Little Red River* AR-4
*Archer's Grove* IA-7
Archers Island—*island* MS-4
Archers Island—*island* MT-8
Archers Lakes—*reservoir* GA-3
**Archers Lodge**—*pop pl* NC-3
*Archers Pond* MA-1
Archers Pond—*lake* GA-3
Archers Pond—*lake* NH-1
Archer Square Center (Shop Ctr)—*locale* FL-3
Archers Ridge Ch—*church* OH-6
Archer Street Sch—*school* NY-2
Archer Tank—*reservoir* NM-5
Archer Tower—*tower* FL-3
**Archertown**—*pop pl* NJ-2
Archertown Brook—*stream* NH-1
**Archer (Township of)**—*pop pl* OH-6
Archer Valley Sch—*school* AR-4
Archer Vly—*lake* NY-2
Archery—*locale* GA-3
Arches, Point Of—*cape* WA-9
Arches, The—*locale* MN-6
Arches Branch—*stream* KY-4
Arches Fork—*stream* WV-2
*Arches Natl Monument* UT-8
Arches Natl Park—*park* UT-8
Arches Natl Park Visitor Center—*locale* UT-8
*Archette* UT-8
Archey Creek—*stream* AR-4
*Archey Fork Little Red River* AR-4
*Archeys Fork* AR-4
Archey Valley (Township of)—*fmr MCD* AR-4
Arch Falls—*falls* MT-8
Arch Hill—*summit* NC-3
Arch Hollow—*valley* TN-4
*Archibald* OH-6
**Archibald**—*pop pl* LA-4
Archibald, Edward T., House—*hist pl* MN-6
Archibald-Adams House—*hist pl* ME-1
Archibald Cem—*cemetery* LA-4
Archibald Corral—*locale* AZ-5
Archibald Creek—*stream* AK-9
Archibald Creek—*stream* CA-9
Archibald Creek—*stream* MT-8
Archibald Creek—*stream* OR-9
*Archibald Institute* AL-4
Archibald Lake—*lake* WI-6
Archibald Lookout Tower—*locale* WI-6
Archibald Memorial Home—*locale* IN-6
Archibald Mill—*hist pl* MN-6
Archibald Murphy Elem Sch—*school* NC-3
*Archibald Point* NC-3
Archibald Ranch—*locale* NV-8
Archibald Tank—*reservoir* AZ-5
Archibald Tower Springs—*lake* WI-6
Archibald-Vroom House—*hist pl* NJ-2
Archie—*locale* IL-6
Archie—*locale* LA-4
**Archie**—*pop pl* MO-7
Archie Barr Hollow—*valley* PA-2
Archie Branch—*swamp* GA-3
Archie Coulee—*valley* MT-8
Archie Cove—*bay* VA-3
Archie Creek—*stream* AL-4
Archie Creek—*stream* FL-3
Archie Creek—*stream* ID-8
Archie Creek—*stream* (2) IL-6
Archie Creek—*stream* MS-4
Archie Creek—*stream* OR-9
Archie Creek—*stream* UT-8
Archie Creek—*stream* WY-8
Archie Draw—*valley* WY-8
*Archie Duncan Cemetery* MS-4
Archie Ellis Pond—*reservoir* NC-3
Archie Ellis Pond Dam—*dam* NC-3
Archie Institute Sch (historical)—*school* AL-4
Archie Lake—*lake* MN-6
Archie McDuffie Dam—*dam* NC-3
Archie Millard Number 1 Dam—*dam* SD-7
Archie Mtn—*summit* ID-8
Archie Pond—*lake* MI-6
Archie Pond—*lake* WY-8
Archie Rsvr—*reservoir* MT-8
Archies Branch—*stream* KY-4
Archies Chapel—*church* AL-4
*Archies Creek* NC-3
Archies Creek—*stream* VA-3
*Archies Fork* AR-4
Archies Knob—*summit* NC-3
Archie Spring—*spring* NV-8
Archies Spring—*spring* NV-8
Archies Tank—*reservoir* AZ-5
Archie Tank—*reservoir* AZ-5
Archimandritof Shoals—*bar* AK-9
Archimedes Ridge—*ridge* AK-9
*Arch-in-the-Making* UT-8
Arch in the Town of Marshall—*hist pl* IN-6
Arch Irrigation Ditch—*canal* CO-8
*Arch Island* WA-9
Arch Island—*island* FL-3
Arch Island—*island* MI-6
Arch Island Bay—*swamp* FL-3
Architects and Engineers Bldg—*hist pl* MN-6
Architecture of Henry K. Holsman Historic Campus District—*hist pl* IA-7
Architillery Ch—*church* FL-3
Archives Metro Station—*locale* DC-2
Arch Lake—*lake* MN-6
Arch Lake—*lake* MT-8
Arch Lateral—*canal* (2) ID-8
Archmere Acad—*school* DE-2
*Archmere Preparatory Sch* DE-2
Arch Mesa—*summit* NM-5
**Arch Mills**—*pop pl* VA-3
Arch Mtn—*summit* AZ-5
Arch Mtn—*summit* TN-4
Arch of the Navarro—*island* CA-9
**Archongelungel**—*pop pl* PW-9
Arch Point—*cape* AK-9
Arch Point—*cape* CA-9
Arch Pond—*lake* NH-1
Arch Prospect—*mine* AK-9
Arch Redd Canyon—*valley* NM-5
Arch Ridge—*ridge* NC-3
Arch Rock—*bar* CA-9
Arch Rock—*island* AK-9
Arch Rock—*island* (3) CA-9
Arch Rock—*island* (2) OR-9
Arch Rock—*locale* CA-9
Arch Rock—*pillar* (2) CA-9
Arch Rock—*pillar* MI-6
Arch Rock—*pillar* OR-9
Arch Rock—*pillar* (2) TN-4
**Arch Rock**—*pop pl* PA-2
Arch Rock—*ridge* PA-2
Arch Rock—*summit* WA-9
Arch Rock Canyon—*valley* NM-5
Arch Rock Entrance Station—*locale* CA-9
Arch Rocks—*pillar* CO-8
Arch Rock Sch (abandoned)—*school* PA-2
Arch Rock Shelter—*locale* WA-9
Archs Grove Ch—*church* NC-3
Arch Slough—*reservoir* CO-8
**Arch Spring**—*pop pl* PA-2
Arch Spring—*spring* PA-2
*Arch Spring Church* PA-2
Arch Street Meetinghouse—*hist pl* PA-2
Arch Street Opera House—*hist pl* PA-2
Arch Street Presbyterian Church—*hist pl* PA-2
Arch Table—*summit* ID-8
Arch Tank—*reservoir* AZ-5
Archuelinguk River—*stream* AK-9
Archula Landing (historical)—*locale* MS-4
*Archuleta* NM-5
Archuleta, Arroyo—*stream* NM-5
Archuleta, Mount—*summit* NM-5
Archuleta Arroyo—*stream* NM-5
Archuleta Canyon—*valley* CO-8
Archuleta Canyon—*valley* (2) NM-5
*Archuleta Creek* CO-8
Archuleta Creek—*stream* (3) CO-8
Archuleta Creek—*stream* (2) NM-5
Archuleta Lake—*lake* CO-8
Archuleta Mesa—*summit* CO-8
Archuleta Mesa—*summit* NM-5
Archuleta (navajo Dam Post Office)—*locale* NM-5
Archuleta Ranch—*locale* (2) NM-5
Archuleta Tank—*reservoir* NM-5
Archuleta Windmill—*locale* NM-5
Archusa Creek—*stream* MS-4
Archusa Creek Water Park—*park* MS-4
Archusa Creek Water Park Lake Dam—*dam* MS-4
Archusa Memorial Gardens—*cemetery* MS-4
Archusa Springs—*spring* MS-4
Archview Ch—*church* AR-4
**Archville**—*pop pl* NY-2
**Archville**—*pop pl* TN-4
Archville Post Office (historical)—*building* TN-4
Archwood—*building* TN-4
Archwood Ave Hist Dist—*hist pl* OH-6
Archy Bench—*bench* UT-8
Archy Branch—*stream* KY-4
Arcilla—*locale* CA-9
Arciniega Cem—*cemetery* TX-5
Arc Lake—*lake* MI-6
Arc Lake—*lake* MN-6
Arc Lateral—*canal* ID-8
Arc Mtn—*summit* AK-9
Arco—*locale* VA-3
**Arco**—*pop pl* GA-3
**Arco**—*pop pl* ID-8
**Arco**—*pop pl* MN-6
**Arco**—*pop pl* TN-4
Arco Canal—*canal* ID-8
*Arco Church* MS-4
Arco Grove of the Giants—*area* CA-9
Arcohe Union Sch—*school* CA-9
Arco Hills—*range* ID-8
*Arcola* IN-6
Arcola—*locale* AL-4
Arcola—*locale* IA-7
Arcola—*locale* MN-6
Arcola—*locale* NJ-2
Arcola—*locale* WV-2
Arcola—*locale* WY-8
**Arcola**—*pop pl* GA-3
**Arcola**—*pop pl* IL-6
**Arcola**—*pop pl* IN-6
**Arcola**—*pop pl* KS-7
**Arcola**—*pop pl* LA-4
**Arcola**—*pop pl* MD-2
**Arcola**—*pop pl* MS-4
**Arcola**—*pop pl* MO-7
**Arcola**—*pop pl* NC-3
**Arcola**—*pop pl* PA-2
**Arcola**—*pop pl* TX-5
**Arcola**—*pop pl* VA-3
Arcola, Lake—*lake* (2) FL-3
Arcola Cem—*cemetery* MS-4
Arcola Creek—*stream* IA-7
Arcola Creek—*stream* OH-6
Arcola Drainage Ditch No 4—*canal* IL-6
*Arcola Elementary School* MS-4
Arcola Elem Sch—*school* IN-6
Arcola Ferry (historical)—*locale* AL-4
Arcola-Fresno Cem—*cemetery* TX-5
Arcola Golf Club—*other* NJ-2
Arcola (historical P.O.)—*locale* IA-7
Arcola Junction—*locale* TX-5
Arco Lake—*lake* MN-6
Arcola Lake Elem Sch—*school* FL-3
Arcola Lakes Community Park—*park* FL-3
Arcola Landing (historical)—*locale* MS-4
Arcola Oil Field—*oilfield* TX-5
Arcola Park—*park* FL-3
Arcola Plantation—*locale* LA-4
Arcola Pool—*other* NJ-2
Arcola Post Office (historical)—*building* AL-4
Arcola Presbyterian Church—*hist pl* LA-4
Arcola Public Use Area—*park* AL-4
Arcola Sch—*school* MD-2
Arcola Sch (historical)—*school* AL-4
**Arcola (Township of)**—*pop pl* IL-6
Arcole Cem—*cemetery* MS-4
Arcole Ch—*church* MS-4
Arcole Plantation (historical)—*locale* MS-4
Arco Mine—*mine* MN-6
Arco Peak—*summit* ID-8
**Arco-Plaza**—*pop pl* CA-9
**Arcosanti**—*pop pl* AZ-5
Arco Sch—*school* GA-3
*Arcos River* KS-7
Arcot Ch of Christ—*church* TN-4
Arcot Post Office (historical)—*building* TN-4
Arcot Sch (historical)—*school* TN-4
Arcott—*locale* TN-4
*Arcott School* TN-4
Arc Pass—*gap* CA-9
Arc Ridge Sch—*school* TX-5
**Arctander (Township of)**—*pop pl* MN-6
*Arctic* IN-6
*Arctic* WA-9
Arctic—*locale* NY-2
**Arctic**—*pop pl* RI-1
Arctic Bldg—*hist pl* WA-9
Arctic Canyon—*valley* CA-9
Arctic Canyon Pit—*mine* CA-9
Arctic Cem—*cemetery* NY-2
Arctic Creek—*stream* (3) AK-9
Arctic Creek—*stream* ID-8
Arctic Creek—*stream* WA-9
Arctic Dam—*dam* RI-1
Arctic Dome—*summit* AK-9
Arctic Island—*island* AK-9
Arctic Lagoon—*bay* AK-9
Arctic Lake—*lake* (2) CA-9
Arctic Lake—*lake* MN-6
Arctic Mine—*mine* (3) CA-9
Arctic Ocean—*sea* AK-9
Arctic Point—*cliff* ID-8
Arctic River—*stream* AK-9
**Arctic Springs**—*pop pl* IN-6
Arctic Springs—*spring* PA-2
Arctic Springs Park—*park* PA-2
**Arctic Village**—*pop pl* AK-9
Arctic Village ANV727—*reserve* AK-9
*Arcturus* MN-6
**Arcturus**—*pop pl* VA-3
Arcturus Mine—*mine* CO-8
Arcturus Mine—*mine* MN-6
Arcturus Mine—*mine* NV-8
Arcularius Ranch—*locale* CA-9
**Arcus**—*pop pl* AL-4
**Ard**—*pop pl* AR-4
**Arda**—*pop pl* IN-6
*Ardale* KS-7
Ardans Ranch—*locale* NV-8
Ardans Tanks—*reservoir* NM-5
Ardans Well—*well* NV-8
**Ardara**—*pop pl* PA-2
Ardath—*locale* MO-7
Ard Branch—*stream* MS-4
Ard Cem—*cemetery* AR-4
Ard Cem—*cemetery* (2) MS-4
Ard Ch—*church* AR-4
Ard Chapel—*church* LA-4
Ard Creek—*stream* AL-4
**Ard Crossroads**—*pop pl* SC-3
**Ardee (historical)**—*pop pl* TN-4
Ardee Post Office (historical)—*building* TN-4
Ardel—*locale* WV-2
Ardela (historical)—*locale* AL-4
Ardell—*locale* AL-4
Ardell—*locale* KS-7
Ardella Ch—*church* FL-3
Ardell Post Office (historical)—*building* AL-4
Ardell Sch (historical)—*school* AL-4
*Ardelollec* PW-9
*Arden* CA-9
*Arden* DE-2
Arden—*hist pl* MA-1
Arden—*hist pl* NY-2
Arden—*locale* MO-7
Arden—*locale* NY-2
Arden—*locale* PA-2
Arden—*locale* TN-4
Arden—*locale* TX-5
Arden—*locale* WA-9
**Arden**—*pop pl* AR-4
**Arden**—*pop pl* DE-2
**Arden**—*pop pl* IL-6
**Arden**—*pop pl* MI-6
**Arden**—*pop pl* NV-8
**Arden**—*pop pl* NC-3
**Arden**—*pop pl* SC-3
**Arden**—*pop pl* (2) WV-2

Arden—*uninc pl* CA-9
Arden, Lake—*lake* WY-8
**Ardena**—*pop pl* NJ-2
Ardena Brook—*stream* NJ-2
*Arden-Arcade* CA-9
Arden-Arcade—*CDP* CA-9
Arden Brook—*stream* (2) NY-2
Arden Cem—*cemetery* MO-7
Arden Cem—*cemetery* TX-5
Arden Ch—*church* MI-6
*Arden Croft* DE-2
**Ardencroft**—*pop pl* DE-2
*Ardencroft Village* DE-2
*Arden Draw* TX-5
Arden Fairgrounds—*locale* PA-2
Arden Fair Shop Ctr—*locale* CA-9
**Ardenheim**—*pop pl* PA-2
**Arden Hills**—*pop pl* MN-6
Arden Hills Sch—*school* MN-6
**Arden House (Columbia University Extension)**—*pop pl* NY-2
**Ardenhurst (Township of)**—*pop pl* MN-6
Arden Island—*island* MN-6
Arden Lake—*lake* MT-8
Arden (Magisterial District)—*fmr MCD* WV-2
Arden Mill Dam—*dam* MA-1
**Arden Mines**—*pop pl* PA-2
*Ardenmoor* IL-6
**Ardenmoor**—*pop pl* IL-6
**Ardennes (subdivision)**—*pop pl* NC-3
Arden on the Severn (Sunrise Beach)—*CDP* MD-2
Arden Park—*park* MN-6
Arden Park-East Boston Hist Dist—*hist pl* MI-6
Arden Point—*cape* AK-9
Arden Point—*cape* NY-2
Arden Post Office (historical)—*building* AL-4
Arden Quarries—*mine* NV-8
Arden Sch—*school* CA-9
*Arden School* DE-2
Arden School, The—*school* DE-2
*Arden Shores* IL-6
Arden Station—*locale* DE-2
Arden Station—*locale* MD-2
**Arden Town**—*pop pl* CA-9
**Ardentown**—*pop pl* DE-2
Arden (Township of)—*fmr MCD* AR-4
*Ardentown Village* DE-2
Arden Trolley Museum—*building* PA-2
*Arden Village* DE-2
**Ardenvoir**—*pop pl* WA-9
**Ardenwald**—*pop pl* OR-9
Ardenwald Sch—*school* OR-9
**Ardeola**—*pop pl* MO-7
Ardery Hollow—*valley* PA-2
Ardeth Lake—*lake* CA-9
Ardeth Lake—*lake* ID-8
Ard-Field Ch—*church* FL-3
Ardgour—*locale* OR-9
Ardick—*locale* GA-3
Ardie Ditch—*canal* WY-8
*Ardila* AL-4
**Ardilla**—*pop pl* (2) AL-4
Ardilla Post Office (historical)—*building* AL-4
Ardilla Sch (historical)—*school* AL-4
Ardis—*uninc pl* LA-4
Ardis Furnace—*hist pl* MI-6
**Ardis Heights**—*pop pl* TX-5
*Ardis Island* LA-4
Ardis Pond—*lake* SC-3
**Arditta**—*pop pl* MO-7
Ardivey, Mount—*summit* NV-8
Ard Lake—*lake* TX-5
**Ardley**—*pop pl* FL-3
Ard-Menteer Cem—*cemetery* MO-7
Ardmore—*locale* GA-3
**Ardmore**—*pop pl* AL-4
**Ardmore**—*pop pl* IN-6
**Ardmore**—*pop pl* MD-2
**Ardmore**—*pop pl* MO-7
**Ardmore**—*pop pl* NC-3
**Ardmore**—*pop pl* OK-5
**Ardmore**—*pop pl* PA-2
**Ardmore**—*pop pl* SD-7
**Ardmore**—*pop pl* TN-4
**Ardmore**—*pop pl* VA-3
Ardmore—*uninc pl* CA-9
Ardmore—*uninc pl* SC-3
Ardmore, Lake—*lake* OK-5
Ardmore Airp—*airport* AL-4
Ardmore Ave Elem Sch—*school* PA-2
Ardmore Ave Train Station—*hist pl* IL-6
Ardmore (CCD)—*cens area* OK-5
Ardmore Ch—*church* TN-4
**Ardmore Estates**—*pop pl* NJ-2
**Ardmore Estates (subdivision)**—*pop pl* AL-4
Ardmore Highway—*uninc pl* AL-4
Ardmore Historic Commercial District—*hist pl* OK-5
Ardmore HS—*school* AL-4
**Ardmore Manor**—*pop pl* PA-2
Ardmore Mine—*mine* AZ-5
Ardmore North (CCD)—*cens area* OK-5
Ardmore Park—*park* NV-8
**Ardmore Park**—*pop pl* PA-2
Ardmore Post Office—*building* TN-4
Ardmore Presbyterian Church Sch—*school* PA-2
Ardmore Recreation Center—*park* CA-9
Ardmore Sch—*school* IL-6
Ardmore Sch—*school* MD-2
Ardmore Sch—*school* MI-6
Ardmore Sch—*school* NC-3
Ardmore Sch—*school* WA-9
Ardmore Shop Ctr—*locale* AL-4
**Ardoch**—*pop pl* ND-7
Ardoch, Lake—*reservoir* ND-7
Ardoch Natl Wildlife Ref—*park* ND-7
**Ardoch Township**—*pop pl* ND-7
Ardoin Cem—*cemetery* LA-4
*Ardololok* PW-9
Ardon—*locale* IA-7
Ardon Cem—*cemetery* IA-7
**Ardonia**—*pop pl* NY-2
**Ardoyne**—*pop pl* LA-4
Ardoyne Plantation (historical)—*locale* LA-4
Ardoyne Plantation House—*hist pl* LA-4
Ardoyne Sch—*school* LA-4
Ard Ridge—*ridge* KY-4
Ards Creek—*stream* LA-4
Ards Crossroads—*locale* FL-3
**Ardsley**—*pop pl* NY-2
**Ardsley**—*pop pl* PA-2
Ardsley Burial Park Cem—*cemetery* PA-2
Ardsley Country Club—*other* NY-2
Ardsley HS—*school* NY-2
**Ardsley-on-Hudson**—*pop pl* NY-2
Ardsley Park—*park* GA-3
Ardsley Park-Chatham Crescent Hist Dist—*hist pl* GA-3
Ardsley Sch—*school* PA-2
Ardsley Station—*building* PA-2
**Ardulusa**—*pop pl* NC-3
*Ardway Hollow* MO-7
**Ardwick**—*pop pl* MD-2
Area A Recreation Site—*locale* UT-8
Area B Recreation Site—*locale* UT-8
Area Career Center—*school* IN-6
Area C Recreation Site—*locale* UT-8
Area Creek—*stream* MT-8
Area de Recreo El Yunque—*park* PR-3
Areadia Sch—*school* MI-6
Areadia Sch—*school* OR-9
Area D Recreation Site—*locale* UT-8
A Real Ranch—*locale* TX-5
Areanum—*locale* VA-3
**Areanum**—*pop pl* OH-6
Area One Vocational Technical Sch—*school* IA-7
Area Recreativa El Canuelo—*park* PR-3
Area 1 Shaker Plant—*locale* NV-8
Area 10 Coll—*school* IA-7
**Area 12 Camp**—*pop pl* NV-8
Area 2 Support Facility—*locale* NV-8
**Arecibo**—*pop pl* PR-3
Arecibo (Municipio)—*civil* PR-3
Arecibo (Pueblo)—*fmr MCD* PR-3
*Arecifos Atoll* MP-9
**Aredale**—*pop pl* IA-7
Areford Sch—*school* PA-2
Aregua Gulch—*valley* CO-8
A Reids Mill (historical)—*locale* AL-4
*Areifos* MP-9
Arej—*island* MP-9
*Areka* PW-9
*Arekalong Peninsula* PW-9
*Arekalong* PW-9
*Arekalong Halbinsel* PW-9
*Are Kalong Peninsula* PW-9
*Arekalong Point* PW-9
*Arekamae* PW-9
*Arekw* CA-9
**Arell**—*pop pl* OR-9
Arellano Canyon—*valley* NM-5
*Aremanalungi Passage* PW-9
Arena—*locale* AL-4
Arena—*locale* NM-5
**Arena**—*pop pl* CA-9
**Arena**—*pop pl* CO-8
**Arena**—*pop pl* NY-2
**Arena**—*pop pl* ND-7
**Arena**—*pop pl* WI-6
Arena, Canada—*valley* CA-9
Arena (Barrio)—*fmr MCD* PR-3
**Arenac**—*pop pl* MI-6
Arena Canal—*canal* CA-9
Arena Canal—*canal* ID-8
Arena Case Drain—*stream* ID-8
**Arenac (County)**—*pop pl* MI-6
Arena Cem—*cemetery* WI-6
Arena Cove—*bay* AK-9
Arena Cove—*bay* CA-9
*Arena Creek* CO-8
Arena Creek—*stream* CO-8
**Arenac (Township of)**—*pop pl* MI-6
Arena (historical)—*locale* MS-4
**Arenal**—*pop pl* NM-5
**Arenal**—*pop pl* PR-3
Arena Lake—*lake* MN-6
Arena Lake—*reservoir* TX-5
Arena Lake Drain—*stream* ID-8
Arenal Ditch—*canal* NM-5
Arenalejos (Barrio)—*fmr MCD* PR-3
**Arenales**—*pop pl* PR-3
Arenales Altos (Barrio)—*fmr MCD* PR-3
Arenales Bajos (Barrio)—*fmr MCD* PR-3
Arenales (Barrio)—*fmr MCD* PR-3
Arenal Main Canal—*canal* NM-5
Arena Park—*park* MO-7
Arena Prairie—*flat* WI-6
Arena Rock—*island* CA-9
Arena Rock—*locale* NV-8
Arena Rsvr—*reservoir* NY-2
*Arenas* CA-9
**Arenas**—*pop pl* (2) PR-3
Arenas (Barrio)—*fmr MCD* (2) PR-3
Arena Sch—*school* SD-7
Arena State Game Mngmt Area—*park* ND-7
**Arenas Valley**—*pop pl* NM-5
**Arenas Valley (Whiskey Creek)**—*pop pl* NM-5
**Arena (Town of)**—*pop pl* WI-6
Arena Township—*civil* (2) SD-7
**Arena (Township of)**—*pop pl* MN-6
Arena Valley—*valley* ID-8
Arena Valley Cem—*cemetery* SD-7
Aren Beshears Dam—*dam* NC-3
**Arendahl**—*pop pl* MN-6
Arendahl Cem—*cemetery* MN-6
**Arendahl (Township of)**—*pop pl* MN-6
**Arendtsville**—*pop pl* PA-2
Arendtsville Borough—*civil* PA-2
Arendtsville Elem Sch—*school* PA-2
Areneuse Creek—*stream* NC-3
*Arenosa Creek* TX-5
Arenosa Creek—*stream* (2) TX-5
Arenosa Oil Field—*oilfield* TX-5
Arenosa Sch—*school* TX-5
Arenosa Spring—*spring* NM-5
Arenosa Tank—*reservoir* TX-5
Arenoso, Arroyo—*valley* TX-5
Arenoso Arroyo—*valley* TX-5
*Arenoso Creek* TX-5
Arenot Homestead—*locale* ID-8
**Arensberg**—*pop pl* PA-2
Arensburg—*locale* PA-2
Arens Corners—*locale* PA-2
Arensdorf Ranch—*locale* NE-7
Arens Field Airp—*airport* IN-6
Arens Lake—*reservoir* IN-6
Arens Lake Dam—*dam* IN-6
*Arensville* IL-6
Arent Ranch—*locale* NE-7
Arentson Gulch—*valley* ID-8
Arenz Sch—*school* IL-6
**Arenzville**—*pop pl* IL-6
**Arenzville (Township of)**—*pop pl* IL-6
Arequipa Sanatorium—*hospital* CA-9
*Aresapa* DE-2
*Areskond Creek* NY-2
Areskonk Creek—*stream* NY-2
Ares Peak—*summit* NM-5
*Arès River* KS-7
Arethusa Falls—*falls* NH-1
Aretz Airp—*airport* IN-6
Areu—*civil* FM-9
Areu Point—*cape* FM-9
Arevalo Sch—*school* TN-4
Arevalos Sch—*school* CA-9
Arey—*locale* ME-1
Arey Cove—*bay* (2) ME-1
Arey Creek—*stream* AK-9
Arey Glacier—*glacier* AK-9
Arey Island—*island* AK-9
Arey Lagoon—*bay* AK-9
Arey Ledges—*bar* ME-1
Arey Neck—*cape* ME-1
Areys Corners—*locale* ME-1
*Areys Cove* ME-1
Areys Pond—*lake* MA-1
Arfelin, Lake—*lake* MI-6
Arflack Hill—*summit* KY-4
Argabright Hollow—*valley* KY-4
Argall Creek—*stream* MT-8
**Argand**—*pop pl* IA-7
Arganbright Hill—*summit* IN-6
*Arge Creek* AL-4
*Argen* MH-9
Argenta—*locale* TX-5
**Argenta**—*pop pl* IL-6
**Argenta**—*pop pl* MI-6
**Argenta**—*pop pl* MT-8
**Argenta**—*pop pl* NV-8
Argenta Butte—*summit* NV-8
Argenta Cave—*cave* MT-8
Argenta Cem—*cemetery* MT-8
Argenta Falls—*falls* CO-8
Argenta Flats—*flat* MT-8
Argenta Guard Station—*locale* MT-8
Argenta Lake—*lake* FL-3
Argenta Mine—*mine* CA-9
Argenta Mine—*mine* (2) MT-8
Argenta Mine—*mine* NV-8
Argent Apartments—*hist pl* NY-2
Argenta Point—*summit* NV-8
Argenta Ranch—*locale* NV-8
Argenta Rim—*cliff* NV-8
Argenta Sch—*school* AR-4
Argenta Siding—*locale* NV-8
Argenta (siding)—*locale* NV-8
Argenta Spring—*spring* MT-8
Argenta Township—*inact MCD* NV-8
Argent Cem—*cemetery* MO-7
Argentena Mine—*mine* NV-8
Argentina Canyon—*valley* NM-5
Argentina Well—*well* AZ-5
*Argentine* SD-7
**Argentine**—*pop pl* KS-7
**Argentine**—*pop pl* MI-6
**Argentine**—*pop pl* PA-2
Argentine—*uninc pl* KS-7
Argentine, Mount—*summit* CO-8
Argentine Carnegie Library—*hist pl* KS-7
Argentine Cem—*cemetery* MI-6
Argentine Creek—*stream* ID-8
Argentine Creek—*stream* MI-6
Argentine Embassy Bldg—*building* DC-2
Argentine HS—*school* KS-7
Argentine Mine—*mine* CO-8
Argentine Mine (historical)—*mine* ID-8
Argentine North Fork Trail—*trail* CO-8
Argentine Pass—*gap* CO-8
Argentine Peak—*summit* CO-8
Argentine Rock—*summit* CA-9
**Argentine Township**—*pop pl* SD-7
**Argentine (Township of)**—*pop pl* MI-6
Argenti Spring—*spring* OR-9
Argentite Canyon—*valley* NV-8
Argent Slough—*stream* MO-7
**Argentum**—*pop pl* KY-4
Argentum Mine—*mine* NV-8
Argentville—*locale* MO-7
*Argeutel* PW-9
*Argigan Island* MH-9
Argillite—*locale* KY-4
Argillite Lookout Tower—*locale* KY-4
Argillite Wash—*stream* NV-8
Argland (historical)—*locale* IA-7
*Argo* DE-2
*Argo* (2) IL-6
Argo—*locale* AL-4
Argo—*locale* MO-7
Argo—*locale* NV-8
Argo—*locale* TX-5
**Argo**—*pop pl* AL-4
**Argo**—*pop pl* IA-7
**Argo**—*pop pl* KY-4
**Argo**—*pop pl* LA-4
**Argo**—*pop pl* MO-7
Argo—*uninc pl* WA-9
Argo Bill Lake—*lake* AK-9
Argobright Sch—*school* IL-6
Argo Butte—*summit* WY-8
Argo Cave—*cave* AL-4
Argo Cem—*cemetery* AL-4
Argo Cem—*cemetery* IL-6
Argo Cem—*cemetery* MN-6
Argo Cem—*cemetery* NE-7
Argo Ch—*church* (4) AL-4
Argo Chapel—*church* AR-4
*Argo Corinth Ch* AL-4
**Argo Corners**—*pop pl* DE-2
Argo Creek—*stream* OR-9
Argo District Number 24 Sch—*school* SD-7
Argo District Number 25 Sch—*school* SD-7
Argo District Number 26 Sch—*school* SD-7
Argo District Number 27 Sch—*school* SD-7
Argo District Number 53 Sch—*school* SD-7
*Argo Falls* OR-9
*Argo-Fay* IL-6
**Argo (Fay)**—*pop pl* IL-6
Argo Gulch—*valley* AK-9
**Argo Heights (Argo)**—*pop pl* AL-4
Argo Hill—*summit* NE-7
Argo (historical)—*locale* MS-4
Argo (historical)—*locale* NC-3
Argo (historical)—*locale* SD-7
Argo HS—*school* IL-6
Argo Island—*island* AK-9
Argola Ch—*church* LA-4
Argo Lake—*lake* MN-6
Argo Mill—*locale* CO-8
Argo Mine—*mine* CA-9
Argo Mine—*mine* CO-8
Argo Mine—*mine* (2) MT-8
Argonaut Mine—*mine* (2) CA-9
Argonaut Mine—*mine* OR-9
Argonaut Peak—*summit* WA-9
Argonaut Sch—*school* (2) CA-9
**Argonia**—*pop pl* KS-7
Argonia Cem—*cemetery* KS-7
Argonia Creek—*stream* KS-7
*Argonne* MN-6
Argonne—*locale* SD-7
**Argonne**—*pop pl* MN-6
**Argonne**—*pop pl* WV-2
**Argonne**—*pop pl* WI-6
**Argonne (Argonne Natl Laboratory)**—*pop pl* IL-6
Argonne Cem—*cemetery* WI-6
*Argonne Farm* MN-6
Argonne For—*woods* WA-9
*Argonne Forest Preserve* IL-6
Argonne Hill—*summit* MI-6
**Argonne Hills**—*pop pl* MD-2
Argonne HS—*school* WA-9
Argonne Industrial District—*facility* IL-6
Argonne Island—*island* AK-9
Argonne Mesa—*summit* NM-5
Argonne Mine—*mine* MN-6
*Argonne Natl Laboratory* IL-6
Argonne Natl Laboratory—*other* IL-6
Argonne Natl Laboratory Reservation—*other* IL-6
Argonne Park—*park* NJ-2
**Argonne Park Subdivision**—*pop pl* UT-8
Argonne Playground—*park* CA-9
Argonne Point—*cape* AK-9
Argonne Sch—*school* (2) CA-9
**Argonne (Town of)**—*pop pl* WI-6
Argonne Township—*obs name* ND-7
Argonne West—*locale* ID-8
Argon Rsvr—*reservoir* NV-8
Argo Number One Mine (underground)—*mine* AL-4
Argo Park—*park* CO-8
Argo Point—*cape* ME-1
Argo Point—*cape* UT-8
**Argora**—*pop pl* ID-8
Argo Rec Area—*park* OR-9
Argo Riffle—*rapids* OR-9
Argos—*locale* CA-9
**Argos**—*pop pl* IN-6
Argo Sch—*school* IL-6
Argo Sch—*school* IA-7
Argo Sch—*school* MO-7
Argo Sch (historical)—*school* AL-4
**Argos Choice (subdivision)**—*pop pl* DE-2
Argos Community Elem Sch—*school* IN-6
Argos Community Junior-Senior HS—*school* IN-6
*Argos Corner* DE-2
Argo Slough—*stream* IA-7
Argos Mtn—*summit* CA-9
Argo Station (historical)—*locale* AL-4
Argosy Creek—*stream* ID-8
Argosy Creek—*stream* MT-8
Argosy Mtn—*summit* MT-8
**Argo Township**—*pop pl* SD-7
Argo Tunnel and Mill—*hist pl* CO-8
**Argo Village**—*pop pl* NY-2
Argo Well—*well* AZ-5
Argue Creek—*stream* OR-9
*Arguelia* CA-9
*Arguello* CA-9
Arguello—*locale* CA-9
Arguello Island—*island* AK-9
*Arguello Mountain* CA-9
Arguement Creek—*stream* ID-8
Argument Ridge—*ridge* ID-8
**Argura**—*pop pl* NC-3
Argus—*locale* PA-2
**Argus**—*pop pl* CA-9
Argus Gulch—*valley* CA-9
Argus Hollow—*valley* WV-2
Argus Mill (Site)—*locale* NV-8
Argus Mine—*mine* NV-8
*Argus Mountains* CA-9
Argus Peak—*summit* CA-9
Argus P. O. (historical)—*locale* AL-4
Argus Post Office (historical)—*building* PA-2
Argus Range—*range* CA-9
Argus Sch—*school* WI-6
Argus Sterling Mine—*mine* CA-9
**Argusville**—*pop pl* NY-2
**Argusville**—*pop pl* ND-7
Argusville Cem—*cemetery* ND-7
Arguta—*locale* ND-7
Arguta Hunting Club—*locale* AL-4
*Argyle* SD-7
Argyle—*locale* KY-4
Argyle—*locale* LA-4
Argyle—*locale* SD-7
Argyle—*locale* WA-9
Argyle—*other* SC-3
**Argyle**—*pop pl* FL-3
**Argyle**—*pop pl* GA-3
**Argyle**—*pop pl* IL-6
**Argyle**—*pop pl* IA-7
**Argyle**—*pop pl* LA-4
**Argyle**—*pop pl* ME-1
**Argyle**—*pop pl* MI-6
**Argyle**—*pop pl* MN-6
**Argyle**—*pop pl* MO-7
**Argyle**—*pop pl* NY-2
**Argyle**—*pop pl* TX-5
**Argyle**—*pop pl* WV-2
**Argyle**—*pop pl* WI-6
Argyle Canyon—*valley* SD-7
Argyle Canyon—*valley* UT-8
Argyle Cem—*cemetery* MI-6
Argyle Cem—*cemetery* NY-2
Argyle Cem—*cemetery* TX-5
Argyle Ch—*church* FL-3
Argyle Ch—*church* IL-6
Argyle Country Club—*other* MD-2
Argyle Creek—*stream* KS-7
Argyle Creek—*stream* UT-8
Argyle Dam—*dam* SD-7
Argyle Drain—*stream* MI-6
Argyle Flats—*hist pl* IA-7
**Argyle Heights**—*pop pl* VA-3
Argyle Howey Drain—*stream* MI-6
Argyle Island—*island* GA-3
Argyle Lake—*reservoir* IL-6
Argyle Lake State Park—*park* IL-6
Argyle Mine—*mine* AZ-5
*Argyle Park* IL-6
**Argyle Park**—*pop pl* MD-2
Argyle Plantation (historical)—*locale* MS-4
Argyle Ridge—*ridge* UT-8
Argyle Sch—*school* MI-6
Argyle Sch—*school* SD-7
**Argyle (Town of)**—*pop pl* NY-2
**Argyle (Town of)**—*pop pl* WI-6
**Argyle (Township of)**—*pop pl* MI-6
Argyle (Township of)—*unorg* ME-1
Argyle Village Square (Shop Ctr)—*locale* FL-3
Arhelger Ranch—*locale* TX-5
*Arhno Atoll* MP-9
Arhold Cem—*cemetery* TN-4
Arhymot Lake—*lake* AK-9
**Ari**—*pop pl* (2) IN-6
Ariadne Cove—*bay* AK-9
Ariadne Island—*island* AK-9
Ariadne Post Office (historical)—*building* TN-4
*Ariail* SC-3
Ariail (census name for Arial)—*CDP* SC-3
*Ariail Mountain* SC-3
**Arial**—*pop pl* SC-3
Aria Lake—*lake* MN-6
Arial (census name Ariail)—*uninc pl* SC-3
*Arial Cross Roads* SC-3
Arial Mtn—*summit* SC-3
*Arials Crossroads* SC-3
Ariana, Lake—*lake* FL-3
Ariana Creek—*stream* MT-8
*Ariara Creek* MT-8
Arica Mountains—*range* CA-9
*Arichi To* MP-9
Arickaree—*locale* CO-8
Arickaree Point (historical)—*cape* SD-7
*Arickaree River* CO-8
*Arickaree River* KS-7
Arickaree Sch—*school* CO-8
*Arickarie River* KS-7
Arick Hollow—*valley* TN-4
Arid Cave—*cave* AL-4
Arido, Monte—*summit* CA-9
*Arido Creek* AZ-5
*Arido Creek* UT-8
Arid Peak—*summit* ID-8
Arid Ridge Trail—*trail* ID-8
Arie Crown Sch—*school* IL-6
Ariedna Mine—*mine* CO-8
*Ariel* PA-2
Ariel—*locale* FL-3
Ariel—*locale* WA-9
Ariel—*other* PA-2
**Ariel**—*pop pl* MS-4
Ariel, Lake—*lake* PA-2
Ariel Ch—*church* MO-7
Ariel Ch—*church* SC-3
Ariel Creek—*stream* PA-2
*Ariel Cross Roads* SC-3
**Ariel Cross Roads**—*pop pl* SC-3
*Ariel Cross RoA VAR Arial Cross Roads* SC-3
Ariel Point—*cliff* AZ-5
*Ariens Kill* DE-2
Aries Caddo Oil Field—*oilfield* TX-5
Aries Park—*park* PA-2
**Arietta**—*pop pl* NY-2
Arietta, Lake—*lake* FL-3
**Arietta (Town of)**—*pop pl* NY-2
*Ariettsu* MP-9
Ariettsu—*island* MP-9
*Ariettsu Island* MP-9
*Ariettsu-to* MP-9
*Ariichi* MP-9
*Ariichi-to* MP-9
*Ariikan Island* MP-9
*Ariikan Pass* MP-9
*Arijia* MH-9
Arikara, Lake—*reservoir* SD-7
Arikara Bay—*bay* ND-7
Arikara Dam—*dam* SD-7
*Arikara Lake* SD-7
*Arikara Peak* CO-8
Arikaree Peak—*summit* CO-8
Arikaree River—*stream* CO-8
Arikaree River*—*stream* KS-7
Arikaree River—*stream* NE-7
*Arikumu Point* PW-9
Arilsen, Ole, House—*hist pl* UT-8
*Arimasuku* PW-9
*Arimasuku Island* PW-9
*Arimesuku* PW-9
*Arimesuku Island* PW-9
**Arimo**—*pop pl* ID-8
Arimo Ditch—*canal* ID-8
Arimount Cem—*cemetery* MS-4
Arimount Creek—*stream* MS-4
*Arinel* FM-9
*Aringach* FM-9
*Aringel* FM-9
*Aringell* FM-9
*Aringeru* FM-9
*Aringiru* FM-9
*Arington* KS-7
Arington Cem—*cemetery* AL-4
Arington Mtn—*summit* CA-9
Arington Ridge—*ridge* TN-4
Arinosa—*locale* UT-8
*Ariola* TX-5
**Ariola**—*pop pl* TX-5
Ariola Lookout Tower—*locale* TX-5
Ariola Oil Field—*oilfield* TX-5
**Arion**—*pop pl* IA-7
**Arion**—*pop pl* OH-6
Arion Mtn—*summit* TN-4
**Arion Township**—*pop pl* KS-7
**Ariosa**—*pop pl* PA-2
**Aripeka**—*pop pl* FL-3
Aripine—*locale* AZ-5
Aripine Post Office—*building* AZ-5
*Arirudo* PW-9
*Arirudo Island* PW-9
*Arirudo To* PW-9
*Arispe* KS-7
Arispe—*locale* TX-5
**Arispe**—*pop pl* IA-7
Arispie, Lake—*lake* IL-6
Arispie (historical)—*locale* KS-7
**Arispie (Township of)**—*pop pl* IL-6
Arista—*locale* KY-4
**Arista**—*pop pl* WV-2
Arista Cotton Mill Complex—*hist pl* NC-3
**Aristes**—*pop pl* PA-2
*Aristide* LA-4
Aristine Creek—*stream* WA-9
**Aristocrat Ranchettes**—*pop pl* CO-8
Aristocrat Trailer Park—*locale* AZ-5
Aristotle—*locale* NY-2
Aristuc—*uninc pl* AZ-5
*Arita Lake* MN-6
**Ariton**—*pop pl* AL-4
**Arivaca**—*pop pl* AZ-5
Arivaca-Amado Interchange—*crossing* AZ-5
Arivaca (CCD)—*cens area* AZ-5
Arivaca Coop Water Wells—*well* AZ-5
Arivaca Creek—*stream* (2) AZ-5
Arivaca Dam—*dam* AZ-5
**Arivaca Junction**—*pop pl* AZ-5
Arivaca King Mine—*mine* AZ-5
Arivaca Lake—*reservoir* AZ-5
Arivaca Ranch—*locale* AZ-5
Arivaca Tank—*reservoir* AZ-5
*Arivaca Valley* AZ-5
*Arivaca Wash* AZ-5
Arivaca Wash—*stream* AZ-5
*Arivaipa* AZ-5
*Arivaipa Canyon* AZ-5
*Arivaipa Creek* AZ-5
*Arivaipa Mountains* AZ-5
*Arivaipa Valley* AZ-5
*Arivapah* AZ-5
*Arivapah Canyon* AZ-5
*Arivapah Creek* AZ-5
*Arivapai* AZ-5
*Arivapai Canyon* AZ-5
*Arivapai Creek* AZ-5
*Arivaypa* AZ-5
*Arivaypa Creek* AZ-5
*Arivaypa Mountains* AZ-5
**Arizola**—*pop pl* AZ-5
Arizola (historical)—*locale* AL-4
Arizola Interchange—*crossing* AZ-5
*Arizola Mountains* AZ-5
*Arizona* AZ-5
Arizona—*locale* LA-4
Arizona—*locale* NE-7
Arizona—*locale* TX-5
Arizona Acad—*school* AZ-5
Arizona Acres Mobile Home Resort—*locale* AZ-5
Arizona Agricultural Inspection Station—*locale* AZ-5
Arizona Air Natl Guard—*military* (2) AZ-5
Arizona Bank and Trust—*hist pl* AZ-5
Arizona Bible Sch—*school* AZ-5
Arizona Biltmore Golf Course—*other* AZ-5
Arizona Boys Ranch—*school* AZ-5
Arizona Canal—*canal* AZ-5
Arizona Cem—*cemetery* NE-7
Arizona Center for Women (prison)—*locale* AZ-5
Arizona Childrens Colony—*locale* AZ-5
Arizona Citrus Growers Association Warehouse—*hist pl* AZ-5
*Arizona City* AZ-5
**Arizona City**—*pop pl* AZ-5
Arizona Coll of Technology—*school* AZ-5
Arizona Compress & Warehouse Co. Warehouse—*hist pl* AZ-5
Arizona Correctional Training Facility—*locale* AZ-5
Arizona Council of American Youth Hostel—*building* AZ-5
Arizona Country Club—*other* AZ-5
Arizona Creek—*stream* (2) AK-9
Arizona Creek—*stream* OR-9
Arizona Creek—*stream* TX-5
Arizona Creek—*stream* WY-8
Arizona Creek Trail—*trail* WY-8
Arizona Cross Cut Canal—*canal* AZ-5
Arizona Dam Butte—*summit* AZ-5
*Arizona Department of Corrections Alpine Conservation Center* AZ-5
Arizona Desert Sch—*school* AZ-5
Arizona Ditch—*canal* CA-9
Arizona Divide—*ridge* AZ-5
Arizona Falls Power House—*locale* AZ-5
Arizona Fish and Game Department—*building* AZ-5
Arizona Game and Fish Department—*building* AZ-5
Arizona Game and Fish Region Number Seven Office—*building* AZ-5
Arizona Game and Fish Region One Office—*building* AZ-5
Arizona Game & Fish Region IV Office—*building* AZ-5
Arizona Girls Ranch—*locale* AZ-5
Arizona Gulch—*valley* AZ-5
Arizona Highway Department—*building* AZ-5
Arizona Highway Department—*other* AZ-5
Arizona Highway Department and Highway Patrol—*other* AZ-5
Arizona Highway Department and Maintenance Yard—*other* AZ-5
Arizona Highway Department - Claypool—*other* AZ-5
Arizona Highway Department Devils Canyon Maintenance Camp—*other* AZ-5
Arizona Highway Department Florence Junction Maintenance Camp—*other* AZ-5
Arizona Highway Department Maintenance Yard—*other* (2) AZ-5
Arizona Highway Department Oil Storage Tanks—*other* AZ-5

Arizona Highway Department Rest Area—other AZ-5
Arizona Highway Maintenance Beeline Yard—other AZ-5
Arizona Highway Maintenance Chino Valley Yard—other AZ-5
Arizona Highway Maintenance Durango Yard—other AZ-5
Arizona Highway Maintenance Fish Creek Yard—other AZ-5
Arizona Highway Maintenance Gila Bend Yard—other AZ-5
Arizona Highway Maintenance Mingus Mountain Yard—other AZ-5
Arizona Highway Maintenance Peeples Valley Yard—other AZ-5
Arizona Highway Maintenance Wickenburg Yard—other AZ-5
Arizona Highway Maintenance Yard—other (4) AZ-5
Arizona Highway Maintenance Yard (Flagstaff)—other AZ-5
Arizona Highway Maintenance Yard (Quartzsite)—other AZ-5
Arizona Highway Patrol—other AZ-5
Arizona Highway Patrol HQ—other AZ-5
Arizona Inn—hist pl AZ-5
Arizona Inspection Station—other (3) AZ-5
Arizona Inspection Station, Gripe—other AZ-5
Arizona Island—island WY-8
Arizona Job Coll—school AZ-5
Arizona Lake—lake WY-8
Arizona Lumber and Timber Company Office—hist pl AZ-5
Arizona Magma Mine—mine AZ-5
Arizona Mall of Tempe—locale AZ-5
Arizona Methodist Church—hist pl LA-4
Arizona Mine—mine CA-9
Arizona Mine—mine (2) NV-8
Arizona Montana Mine—mine AZ-5
Arizona Mountains AZ-5
Arizona Mtn—summit CO-8
Arizona Natl Guard Airfield AZ-5
Arizona Natl Guard Armory—military (3) AZ-5
Arizona Natl Guard Arsenal—military AZ-5
Arizona Peak NV-8
Arizona Peak—summit NV-8
Arizona Pioneer Historical Society—building AZ-5
Arizona Pioneers Home—building AZ-5
Arizona Pioneers Home Cem—cemetery AZ-5
Arizona Pittsburg Mine—mine AZ-5
Arizona Plateau AZ-5
Arizona Public Service Salome Substation—locale AZ-5
Arizona Sch—school CA-9
**Arizona Shores (Trailer Park)**—pop pl AZ-5
Arizona Snow Bowl—locale AZ-5
Arizona-Sonora Desert Museum—building AZ-5
Arizona-Sonora Manufacturing Company Machine Shop—hist pl AZ-5
Arizona Spring—spring AZ-5
Arizona Spring—spring NV-8
Arizona State Capitol Bldg—hist pl AZ-5
Arizona State Coll—school AZ-5
Arizona State Coll at Tempe—school AZ-5
Arizona State Fairgrounds—locale AZ-5
Arizona State Farm Labor Camp—locale AZ-5
Arizona State Highway Patrol—building AZ-5
Arizona State Highway Patrol Tower—tower AZ-5
Arizona State Hosp—hospital AZ-5
Arizona State Hosp Farm—hospital AZ-5
Arizona State Inspection Station—other (3) AZ-5
Arizona State Prison—locale AZ-5
Arizona State Sanatorium—hospital AZ-5
Arizona State Sch—school AZ-5
Arizona State Teachers College—uninc pl AZ-5
Arizona State University Farm Laboratory—building AZ-5
Arizona Substation—locale AZ-5
Arizona Sunshine Sch—school AZ-5
**Arizona Sun Sites**—pop pl AZ-5
**Arizona Township**—pop pl NE-7
Arizona Victory Mine—mine AZ-5
Arizona Western Coll—school AZ-5
Arizona Youth Center—building AZ-5
Arizona Yucca Mine—mine AZ-5
Arizonia LA-4
Arjal—island MP-9
**Arjay**—pop pl KY-4
**Arjay**—pop pl MS-4
Arjel MP-9
Ark—locale VA-3
**Ark**—pop pl KY-4
Ark, The—island ME-1
**Arkabutla**—pop pl MS-4
Arkabutla Baptist Ch—church MS-4
Arkabutla Cem—cemetery MS-4
Arkabutla Consolidated HS (historical)—school MS-4
Arkabutla Creek—stream MS-4
Arkabutla Dam—dam MS-4
Arkabutla Dam—facility MS-4
Arkabutla Lake—reservoir MS-4
Arkabutla Rsvr MS-4
Arkabutla State Waterfowl Ref—park MS-4
**Arkadelphia**—pop pl AL-4
**Arkadelphia**—pop pl AR-4
Arkadelphia Baptist Church MS-4
Arkadelphia Cem—cemetery (2) AL-4
Arkadelphia Cem—cemetery AR-4
Arkadelphia Cem—cemetery MS-4
Arkadelphia Cem—cemetery MO-7
Arkadelphia Ch—church (3) AL-4
Arkadelphia Ch—church (2) LA-4
Arkadelphia Ch—church MS-4
Arkadelphia Community Center—building AL-4
Arkadelphia Elem Sch (historical)—school AL-4
Arkadelphia Mine (surface)—mine AL-4
Arkadelphia Missionary Baptist Church AL-4
Arkadelphia Mtn—summit AL-4
Arkadelphia Post Office—building AL-4
Arkadelphia Sch—school TX-5
Arkadelphia Sch (historical)—school MS-4
**Arkalite**—pop pl AR-4
Arkalon—locale KS-7
Arkalon Cem—cemetery KS-7
**Arkamais**—pop pl PW-9
Arkana—locale AR-4
Arkana—locale LA-4
**Arkana**—pop pl AR-4
Arkana Cem—cemetery AR-4
Arkanas Cem—cemetery TX-5
Arkana Station—locale AR-4
Arkansas—locale KY-4
Arkansas—locale WV-2
Arkansas, Mount—summit CO-8
**Arkansas A and M College**—pop pl AR-4
Arkansas AM Coll—school AR-4
Arkansas Ave Elem Sch—school KS-7
Arkansas Bank & Trust Company—hist pl AR-4
Arkansas Baptist Camp—locale AR-4
Arkansas Baptist Coll—school AR-4
Arkansas Basin—basin WY-8
Arkansas Bend—bend TX-5
Arkansas Boys State Industrial Sch—school AR-4
Arkansas Branch—stream KY-4
Arkansas Branch—stream LA-4
Arkansas Branch—stream TN-4
Arkansas Branch—stream WV-2
Arkansas Canyon—valley (2) CA-9
Arkansas Canyon—valley ID-8
Arkansas Canyon—valley NM-5
Arkansas Childrens Home—building AR-4
Arkansas City—locale TX-5
**Arkansas City**—pop pl AR-4
**Arkansas City**—pop pl KS-7
Arkansas City Commercial Hist Dist—hist pl KS-7
Arkansas City Country Club Site—hist pl KS-7
Arkansas City HS—hist pl AR-4
Arkansas City HS—school KS-7
Arkansas Coll—school AR-4
**Arkansas (County)**—pop pl AR-4
Arkansas Creek ID-8
Arkansas Creek WY-8
Arkansas Creek—stream AK-9
Arkansas Creek—stream (3) CA-9
Arkansas Creek—stream CO-8
Arkansas Creek—stream GA-3
Arkansas Creek—stream ID-8
Arkansas Creek—stream KY-4
Arkansas Creek—stream (2) MT-8
Arkansas Creek—stream NM-5
Arkansas Creek—stream TN-4
Arkansas Creek—stream TX-5
Arkansas Creek—stream WA-9
Arkansas Creek—stream (4) WY-8
**Arkansas Creek (Arkansas)**—pop pl KY-4
Arkansas Dam—dam OR-9
Arkansas Department of Corrections Prison Farm—locale AR-4
Arkansas Ditch—canal AR-4
Arkansas Flat—flat OR-9
Arkansas Flats—flat WY-8
**Arkansas Fuel Oil Company Village**—pop pl AR-4
Arkansas Gasoline Plant—oilfield TX-5
Arkansas Gulch—valley AZ-5
Arkansas Gulch—valley (3) CO-8
Arkansas Hill—summit VA-3
Arkansas Hollow—valley KY-4
Arkansas Hollow—valley OR-9
Arkansas Hollow—valley TN-4
Arkansas Industrial Sch—school AR-4
**Arkansas Junction**—pop pl NM-5
Arkansas Meadow—flat CA-9
Arkansas Mechanical and Normal Coll—school AR-4
Arkansas Mesa—summit TX-5
Arkansas Mtn—summit AZ-5
Arkansas Mtn—summit (4) CO-8
Arkansas Polytechnic Coll—school AR-4
Arkansas Polytechnic College AR-4
Arkansas Post—locale AR-4
Arkansas Post Canal—canal AR-4
Arkansas Post Natl Memorial—hist pl AR-4
Arkansas Post Natl Memorial—park AR-4
Arkansas Ranch—locale AZ-5
Arkansas Ravine—valley CA-9
Arkansas River—stream AR-4
Arkansas River—stream CO-8
Arkansas River*—stream KS-7
Arkansas River—stream OK-5
Arkansas River Canyon—valley CO-8
Arkansas Rsvr—reservoir OR-9
Arkansas Sch—school MO-7
Arkansas Sch for Deaf and Blind—school AR-4
Arkansas School (Abandoned)—locale MO-7
Arkansas Sheriffs Boys Ranch—locale AR-4
Arkansas Spring—spring ID-8
Arkansas Spring—spring MT-8
Arkansas Spring—spring OR-9
Arkansas Spring—spring WA-9
Arkansas State Capitol—hist pl AR-4
Arkansas State Coll—school AR-4
Arkansas State Junior Coll—school AR-4
Arkansas State Teachers College AR-4
Arkansas Tank—reservoir (2) AZ-5
Arkansas (Township of)—fmr MCD AR-4
Arkansas Valley—basin NE-7
Arkansas Valley—valley WA-9
Arkansas Valley Canal—canal CO-8
Arkansas Valley Christian Ch—church KS-7
Arkansas Valley Conduit—canal CO-8
Arkansas Valley Lodge No. 21, Prince Hall Masons—hist pl KS-7
Arkansas Valley Natl Bank—hist pl OK-5
Arkansas Vocational-technical Sch—school AR-4
Arkansaw MS-4
**Arkansaw**—pop pl WI-6
Arkansaw Creek WA-9
Arkansaw Creek—stream WI-6
Arkansaw Riv KS-7
Arkapola Bluff—cliff AR-4
Arkaqua Creek—stream GA-3
Arkaquia Creek GA-3
Arkarik MP-9
**Arkawana**—pop pl AR-4
Ark Bayou—stream MS-4
Ark Cem—cemetery OH-6
Ark Ch—church OH-6
Ark Christian Sch—school FL-3
**Arkdale**—pop pl WI-6
Arkdale Lake—reservoir WI-6
Arkdale Mill Pond WI-6
Arkdale Sch—school MI-6
Arkdell—locale AL-4
Arkdell P.O. (historical)—locale AL-4
Arkdell Sch (historical)—school AL-4
Arke Dam—dam SD-7
Arkeketa Creek—stream NE-7
Arkendale—locale VA-3
Arken Lake—lake MN-6
Arker Mine (underground)—mine AL-4
Arkin, Lake—reservoir NY-2
**Arkinda**—pop pl AR-4
Arkinda (Township of)—fmr MCD AR-4
**Arkland**—pop pl TN-4
**Arklatex**—pop pl LA-4
Arkle—locale KY-4
Arklet (historical)—locale MS-4
**Arkmo**—pop pl MO-7
Arkoal AR-4
**Arkoal**—pop pl AR-4
Arkoe—locale OH-6
**Arkoe**—pop pl MO-7
Arkoe Cem—cemetery OH-6
**Arko (historical)**—pop pl OR-9
**Arkola**—pop pl AR-4
**Arkoma**—pop pl AR-4
**Arkoma**—pop pl OK-5
Arkoma (CCD)—cens area OK-5
Arkoma HS—school OK-5
Arkoma Sch—hist pl OK-5
Arkoma Sch—school OK-5
Arkoosh Wendell Well—well ID-8
Arkose Lake—lake MN-6
Arkose Ridge—ridge AK-9
**Arkport**—pop pl NY-2
Arkport Dam—dam NY-2
Ark Post Office (historical)—building TN-4
Arkright AL-4
Arkright Flat—flat CA-9
Ark Sch—school AR-4
Arksill Run—stream PA-2
Ark Slough Ditch—canal AR-4
Ark Springs Ch—church OH-6
**Ark Subdivision**—pop pl UT-8
Arkton—locale VA-3
**Arkville**—pop pl NY-2
Arkville Cem—cemetery NY-2
Arkwild Camp—locale AR-4
Arkwright—locale AL-4
Arkwright—locale NY-2
**Arkwright**—pop pl GA-3
**Arkwright**—pop pl RI-1
**Arkwright**—pop pl SC-3
Arkwright Bridge—hist pl RI-1
Arkwright Cem—cemetery AL-4
Arkwright Ch—church AL-4
Arkwright Falls—falls NY-2
**Arkwright (Holton)**—pop pl GA-3
Arkwright Summit Cem—cemetery NY-2
**Arkwright (Town of)**—pop pl NY-2
Arlabesan Anchorage PW-9
Arlam—locale TX-5
**Arland**—pop pl WI-6
Arland D Williams DC-2
**Arlandria**—pop pl VA-3
Arland Sch—school MI-6
**Arland (Town of)**—pop pl WI-6
**Arlanza**—pop pl CA-9
Arlanza Sch—school CA-9
Arlanza Village—uninc pl CA-9
Arlap—island MP-9
Arlberg—locale AR-4
Arlberg—locale MN-6
Arlecho Creek—stream WA-9
Arledge Cem—cemetery TN-4
Arledge Mounds I and II—hist pl OH-6
Arledge Ranch—locale (2) TX-5
Arledge Ridge—locale TX-5
**Arlee**—pop pl MT-8
**Arlee**—pop pl WV-2
Arlee Peak MT-8
Arlen TX-5
Arlena Ch—church AL-4
Arlene—locale MI-6
Arlene Tank—reservoir AZ-5
Arlen Gulch—valley CO-8
Arles—locale GA-3
**Ar'les Acres**—pop pl IN-6
**Arleta**—pop pl OR-9
Arleta—uninc pl CA-9
Arleta Park—park MO-7
Arleta Sch—school OR-9
**Arletta**—pop pl WA-9
Arletta Sch—hist pl WA-9
Arley—locale MO-7
**Arley**—pop pl AL-4
Arley Ch AL-4
Arley Ch—church AL-4
Arley Landing—locale (2) AL-4
Arlie—locale TX-5
Arlie, Lake—lake FL-3
Arlie Canyon—valley OR-9
Arlie Cem—cemetery TX-5
Arlight—locale CA-9
Arlin Brook—stream NH-1
Arline—locale TN-4
Arline Cem—cemetery GA-3
Arline Ch—church GA-3
Arling—locale ID-8
Arlingdale IL-6
**Arlingham**—pop pl PA-2
**Arlingham Hills**—pop pl PA-2
Arlingtion Oaks Sch—school CA-9
Arlington KS-7
Arlington NJ-2
Arlington NC-3
Arlington RI-1
Arlington SC-3
Arlington—CDP VA-3
Arlington—hist pl AL-4
Arlington—hist pl KY-4
Arlington—hist pl MS-4
Arlington—hist pl WY-8
Arlington—locale CO-8
Arlington—locale FL-3
Arlington—locale MS-4
Arlington—locale VA-3
**Arlington**—pop pl AL-4
**Arlington**—pop pl AZ-5
**Arlington**—pop pl CA-9
**Arlington**—pop pl FL-3
**Arlington**—pop pl GA-3
**Arlington**—pop pl IL-6
**Arlington**—pop pl (2) IN-6
**Arlington**—pop pl IA-7
**Arlington**—pop pl KS-7
**Arlington**—pop pl (2) KY-4
**Arlington**—pop pl LA-4
**Arlington**—pop pl MD-2
**Arlington**—pop pl MA-1
**Arlington**—pop pl MN-6
**Arlington**—pop pl MS-4
**Arlington**—pop pl MO-7
**Arlington**—pop pl NE-7
**Arlington**—pop pl NJ-2
**Arlington**—pop pl (2) NY-2
**Arlington**—pop pl NC-3
**Arlington**—pop pl (3) OH-6
**Arlington**—pop pl OK-5
**Arlington**—pop pl OR-9
**Arlington**—pop pl (2) PA-2
**Arlington**—pop pl SD-7
**Arlington**—pop pl (3) TN-4
**Arlington**—pop pl TX-5
**Arlington**—pop pl VT-1
**Arlington**—pop pl VA-3
**Arlington**—pop pl WA-9
**Arlington**—pop pl (3) WV-2
**Arlington**—pop pl WI-6
**Arlington**—pop pl WY-8
Arlington—uninc pl NC-3
Arlington, Lake—reservoir TX-5
Arlington, Mount—summit NJ-2
Arlington Acres IL-6
Arlington Alliance Ch—church FL-3
Arlington Apartments—hist pl WI-6
Arlington (Appalachie) SC-3
Arlington Assembly of God Ch—church FL-3
Arlington Ave Baptist Ch—church IN-6
Arlington Ave Ch IN-6
Arlington Ave Ch—church IN-6
Arlington Ave District—hist pl OH-6
Arlington Ave Sch—school NJ-2
Arlington Baptist Ch—church FL-3
Arlington Baptist Ch—church MS-4
Arlington Baptist Ch—church TN-4
Arlington-Basswood Hist Dist—hist pl MA-1
**Arlington Beach**—pop pl SD-7
Arlington Bridge—bridge CA-9
Arlington Burial Park—cemetery OH-6
Arlington Canal—canal AZ-5
Arlington Canyon—valley CA-9
Arlington (CCD)—cens area GA-3
Arlington (CCD)—cens area KY-4
Arlington (CCD)—cens area OR-9
Arlington (CCD)—cens area TN-4
Arlington (CCD)—cens area TX-5
Arlington (CCD)—cens area WA-9
Arlington Cem—cemetery CO-8
Arlington Cem—cemetery FL-3
Arlington Cem—cemetery GA-3
Arlington Cem—cemetery IL-6
Arlington Cem—cemetery (3) IA-7
Arlington Cem—cemetery LA-4
Arlington Cem—cemetery MD-2
Arlington Cem—cemetery MN-6
Arlington Cem—cemetery NE-7
Arlington Cem—cemetery NJ-2
Arlington Cem—cemetery OH-6
Arlington Cem—cemetery OK-5
Arlington Cem—cemetery (2) PA-2
Arlington Cem—cemetery SD-7
Arlington Cem—cemetery TN-4
Arlington Cem—cemetery VA-3
Arlington Cem—cemetery (2) WI-6
**Arlington Center**—pop pl VT-1
Arlington Center Hist Dist—hist pl MA-1
Arlington Center Hist Dist (Boundary Increase)—hist pl MA-1
Arlington Center Sch—school MI-6
Arlington Ch—church GA-3
Arlington Ch—church MS-4
Arlington Ch—church (2) NC-3
Arlington Ch—church (2) TN-4
Arlington Channel—channel AL-4
Arlington Christian Ch—church FL-3
Arlington Coal & Lumber—hist pl MA-1
Arlington Coll—school CA-9
Arlington Country Day Sch—school FL-3
Arlington Countryside IL-6
**Arlington (County)**—pop pl VA-3
Arlington Creek—stream ID-8
Arlington Ditch—canal CO-8
Arlington Division—civil TN-4
Arlington Downs—uninc pl TX-5
**Arlington Drive (subdivision)**—pop pl AL-4
Arlington Elementary School NC-3
Arlington Elementry Sch—school KS-7
Arlington Elem Sch—school AZ-5
Arlington Elem Sch—school FL-3
Arlington Elem Sch—school IN-6
Arlington Elem Sch—school PA-2
Arlington Farms IL-6
**Arlington Forest**—pop pl VA-3
Arlington Gaslight Company—hist pl MA-1
Arlington Golf Club—other IL-6
Arlington Green—uninc pl FL-3
Arlington Green Covered Bridge—hist pl VT-1
Arlington Greens Park—park IL-6
**Arlington Hall**—pop pl VA-3
Arlington Hall Station—military VA-3
Arlington Height Elem Sch—school FL-3
Arlington Heights FL-3
**Arlington Heights**—pop pl (2) IL-6
**Arlington Heights**—pop pl OH-6
**Arlington Heights**—pop pl PA-2
**Arlington Heights**—pop pl TX-5
**Arlington Heights**—pop pl VA-3
**Arlington Heights**—pop pl WA-9
Arlington Heights—summit CA-9
Arlington Heights—uninc pl FL-3
Arlington Heights—uninc pl KY-4
Arlington Heights—uninc pl (2) TX-5
Arlington Heights—uninc pl VA-3
Arlington Heights Baptist Ch—church IN-6
Arlington Heights Baptist Ch—church MS-4
Arlington Heights Ch IN-6
Arlington Heights Christian Ch—church IN-6
Arlington Heights Elementary School MS-4
Arlington Heights Elem Sch—school (2) IN-6
Arlington Heights Garden IL-6
Arlington Heights Hills—summit MA-1
Arlington Heights HS—school TX-5
Arlington Heights JHS West—school MA-1
Arlington Heights Sch—school (2) CA-9
Arlington Heights Sch—school MI-6
Arlington Heights Sch—school MS-4
Arlington Heights Sch—school TX-5
Arlington Heights Sch—school WI-6
**Arlington Heights (subdivision)**—pop pl MA-1
**Arlington Heights (subdivision)**—pop pl UT-8
Arlington Heights (Township of)—other OH-6
Arlington Hills Library—hist pl MN-6
**Arlington Hills Subdivision**—pop pl UT-8
Arlington Hist Dist—hist pl TN-4
Arlington Hosp—hospital VA-3
Arlington Hotel—hist pl NY-2
Arlington Hotel—hist pl OH-6
Arlington House,The Robert E Lee Memorial—park VA-3
Arlington HS—school IN-6
Arlington HS—school MA-1
Arlington Industrial Arts JHS—school MA-1
Arlington Industrial School AL-4
Arlington JHS—school FL-3
Arlington JHS—school NC-3
Arlington JHS West—school MA-1
Arlington Junction—locale WA-9
Arlington Kindergarten and Private Sch—school FL-3
**Arlington Knolls**—pop pl PA-2
Arlington Lake—reservoir MO-7
Arlington Lake—reservoir PA-2
Arlington Lake Dam—dam PA-2
Arlington Memorial Bridge—hist pl DC-2
Arlington Memorial Cem—cemetery CA-9
Arlington Memorial Gardens Cem—cemetery OH-6
Arlington Memorial Gardens (Cemetery)—cemetery WV-2
Arlington Memorial Park Cem—cemetery IL-6
Arlington Memorial Park Cem—cemetery OK-5
Arlington Memorial Park (Cemetery)—cemetery NJ-2
Arlington Mesa—summit AZ-5
Arlington Mill Rsvr—reservoir NH-1
Arlington Mills Hist Dist—hist pl MA-1
Arlington Mine—mine CA-9
Arlington Muni Airp—airport WA-9
Arlington Municipal Airp—airport OR-9
Arlington Municipal Airp—airport SD-7
Arlington Municipal Airp—airport TN-4
Arlington Natl Cem—cemetery VA-3
Arlington Pack Trail—trail WY-8
Arlington Park CO-8
Arlington Park—park CO-8
Arlington Park—park FL-3
Arlington Park—park NJ-2
**Arlington Park**—pop pl FL-3
**Arlington Park**—pop pl IN-6
**Arlington Park**—pop pl NH-1
**Arlington Park**—pop pl (2) PA-2
Arlington Park—uninc pl GA-3
Arlington Park Racetrack—other IL-6
Arlington Park Sch—school OH-6
**Arlington Park Subdivision**—pop pl (2) UT-8
Arlington Pier—locale AL-4
Arlington Plantation—hist pl LA-4
Arlington Plantation House—hist pl (2) LA-4
Arlington Playground—park MN-6
Arlington Playground—park PA-2
Arlington Plaza OH-6
Arlington Plaza—other CA-9
Arlington Plaza (Shop Ctr)—locale FL-3
Arlington Plaza (Shop Ctr)—locale NC-3
Arlington Post Office—building AZ-5
Arlington Prairie Cem—cemetery WI-6
Arlington Prairie Ch—church WI-6
Arlington Preschool and Kindergarten—school FL-3
Arlington Pumping Station—hist pl MA-1
Arlington Reach—channel NJ-2
Arlington Reservoir—hist pl MA-1
Arlington Ridge IL-6
Arlington Ridge—ridge ID-8
Arlington Ridge—ridge TN-4
Arlington Ridge Sch—school IL-6
Arlington River—stream FL-3
Arlington Rsvr MO-7
Arlington Rsvr—reservoir MA-1
Arlington Run—stream IN-6
Arlington Sch—school (2) AL-4
Arlington Sch—school AZ-5
Arlington Sch—school CA-9
Arlington Sch—school CO-8
Arlington Sch—school IL-6
Arlington Sch—school KY-4
Arlington Sch—school ME-1
Arlington Sch—school MN-6
Arlington Sch—school (2) OH-6
Arlington Sch—school TN-4
Arlington Sch—school VA-3
Arlington Sch—school (2) WA-9
Arlington Sch (abandoned)—school PA-2
Arlington Sch (historical)—school MS-4
Arlington Sch (historical)—school MO-7
Arlington Sch (historical)—school TN-4
Arlington Sewage Disposal—other TX-5
Arlington Speedway—other NY-2
Arlington (sta.) (Annemanie)—locale AL-4
Arlington State Coll—school TX-5
Arlington State For—forest VT-1
Arlington State Wildlife Area—park AZ-5
Arlington Station—locale NJ-2
**Arlington Station**—pop pl AZ-5
**Arlington Station**—pop pl CA-9
Arlington Street Baptist Ch—church NC-3
Arlington Street Ch—church MA-1
Arlington Street Church—hist pl MA-1
Arlington Street Sch—school MA-1
Arlington Street Sch—school NH-1
**Arlington (subdivision)**—pop pl AL-4
**Arlington (subdivision)**—pop pl NC-3
Arlington Substation—locale AZ-5
Arlington Temple—church TX-5
Arlington Towers—uninc pl FL-3
Arlington Townhall—building MA-1
**Arlington (Town of)**—pop pl MA-1
**Arlington (Town of)**—pop pl VT-1
**Arlington (Town of)**—pop pl WI-6
Arlington Township—civil MO-7
Arlington Township—fmr MCD IA-7
**Arlington Township**—pop pl KS-7
Arlington Township (historical)—civil SD-7
**Arlington (Township of)**—pop pl MI-6
**Arlington (Township of)**—pop pl MN-6
Arlington Valley—valley AZ-5
Arlington Valley Channel—canal CA-9
**Arlington Village**—pop pl VA-3
Arlington Wharf—locale VA-3
Arlington Yards—locale NY-2
Arlington Yards—locale PA-2
Arling Trail—trail ID-8
Arlingwood—locale VA-3
Arlingwood—uninc pl FL-3
Arlingwood Playground—park FL-3
Arlin Post Office (historical)—building MS-4
Arlip Lake—lake MN-6
Arlise Gulch—valley ID-8
Arlo (historical)—locale AL-4
**Arlone (Township of)**—pop pl MN-6
Arlt Spring—spring KY-4
**Arlynda Corners**—pop pl CA-9
**Arlyn Oaks**—pop pl NY-2
**Arm**—pop pl MS-4
Arm, Mount—summit NY-2
Arm, The—bay ME-1
Arm, The—bay WA-9
Arm, The—lake MA-1
**Arma**—pop pl KS-7
Armachey Creek GA-3
Armacolola GA-3
Armacolola Creek GA-3
Armacolola Falls GA-3
Armacost—locale MD-2
**Armada**—pop pl MI-6
Armada And Ray Drain—stream MI-6
Armada Cem—cemetery NE-7
Armadale—locale OH-6
Armadale Grove—area SD-7
Armadale (historical)—locale SD-7
Armadale Park—park SD-7
Armadale Township (historical)—civil SD-7
Armada Mine—mine AZ-5
Armada Sch—school CA-9
**Armada Township**—pop pl NE-7
**Armada (Township of)**—pop pl MI-6
Armadillo Draw—valley TX-5
Armadillo Hollow—valley TX-5
Armadillo Tank—reservoir TX-5
Arma Elem Sch—school KS-7
**Armagh**—pop pl MD-2
**Armagh**—pop pl PA-2
Armagh Borough—civil PA-2
Armagh Cem—cemetery PA-2
Armagh Township Elem Sch—school PA-2
**Armagh (Township of)**—pop pl PA-2
**Armaglas**—pop pl TX-5
Armagosa Creek TX-5
**Armah**—pop pl IA-7
Armah Ch—church IA-7
Armalege Drain—stream MI-6
Armament Development and Test Center (U.S.A.F.)—other FL-3
Armanda Cem—cemetery MN-6
Armand Bayou—stream TX-5
Armand Bayou Archeol District—hist pl TX-5
Arm and Hammer Branch—stream WV-2
Armand Larve JHS—school OR-9
Armands Bay NY-2
Arman Ridge—ridge OH-6
**Armant**—pop pl LA-4
**Armar**—pop pl WA-9
Armatage Park—park MN-6
Armatage Sch—school MN-6
Armathwaite—locale TN-4
Armathwaite Post Office (historical)—building TN-4
Armawaithe Sch (historical)—school TN-4
Armawalk—locale NY-2
**Armboy**—pop pl GA-3
Armbrester Cem—cemetery AL-4
Armbrester Sch (historical)—school AL-4
Arm Brook—stream MA-1
Arm Brook Dam—dam MA-1
Arm Brook Rsvr—reservoir MA-1
**Armbrust**—pop pl PA-2
Armbruster School (historical) locale MO-7
Armbrust Sch—school PA-2
**Armbrust (Weavers Old Stand)**—pop pl PA-2
Armbuster Drain—canal MI-6
Arm Campsite, The—locale ME-1
**Armco**—pop pl NC-3
**Armco**—pop pl TX-5
Armco Country Club—other PA-2
Armco Dam PA-2
Armco Park—park (2) OH-6
Armco Park Mound I—hist pl OH-6
Armco Park Mound II—hist pl OH-6
Armed Forces Staff Coll—school VA-3
Armedio Riffle—rapids OR-9
Armeigh Run PA-2
Armel—locale CO-8
Armel—locale VA-3
Armel Cem—cemetery CO-8
Armel Ch—church CO-8
Armelise Canal—canal LA-4
Armells Creek—stream (2) MT-8
Armel Sch—school CO-8
Armel Sch—school VA-3
**Armen**—pop pl WV-2
Armena—locale GA-3
Armenco Branch Canal—canal LA-4
**Armenia**—pop pl GA-3
**Armenia**—pop pl SC-3
Armenia Ch—church NC-3
Armenia Ch—church PA-2
Armenia Ch—church SC-3
Armenia Mtn—summit PA-2
Armenian Ch—church MI-6
Armenian Ch of America—church PA-2
Armenia Shop Ctr—locale FL-3
**Armenia (Town of)**—pop pl WI-6
**Armenia (Township of)**—pop pl PA-2
Armenta Canyon—valley NM-5
Armenta Plaza Cem—cemetery NM-5
Armenta Ranch—locale AZ-5
Armenta Well—well AZ-5

Armentrout Cem—*cemetery* IL-6
Armentrout Dredge Ditch—*canal* IN-6
Armentrout Flat—*flat* CA-9
*Armentrout Mountain* WV-2
Armentrout Sch (historical)—*school* MO-7
Armentrout Spring—*spring* CA-9
Armer Gulch—*valley* AZ-5
Armeria Bay—*bay* AK-9
Armeria Point—*cape* AK-9
Armer Mtn—*summit* AZ-5
Armer Oil Field—*oilfield* TX-5
Armer Tank—*reservoir* AZ-5
*Armes Chapel* TN-4
Armes Gap—*gap* TN-4
Armet Creek—*stream* OR-9
*Armetts Creek* MT-8
*Armey Ditch* IN-6
Armey Ditch—*canal* IN-6
Armfield Bluff—*cliff* TN-4
Armfield Bluff Horror Hole—*cave* TN-4
*Armid* PW-9
**Armiesburg**—*pop pl* IN-6
Armiesburg Cem—*cemetery* IN-6
*Armiesburg Mills* IN-6
**Armiger**—*pop pl* MD-2
**Armijo**—*pop pl* NM-5
Armijo, Juan Cristobal, Homestead—*hist pl* NM-5
Armijo, Lake—*reservoir* NM-5
Armijo, Nestor, House—*hist pl* NM-5
Armijo, Salvador, House—*hist pl* NM-5
Armijo Canyon—*valley* NM-5
Armijo Creek—*stream* NM-5
Armijo Drain—*canal* NM-5
Armijo Draw—*valley* (2) NM-5
Armijo HS—*school* CA-9
Armijo Lake—*lake* NM-5
Armijo Lateral—*canal* NM-5
Armijo Park—*park* TX-5
Armijo Peak—*summit* NM-5
Armijo Rsvr—*reservoir* NM-5
Armijo Sch—*school* NM-5
Armijo Spring—*spring* NM-5
Armijo Tank—*reservoir* NM-5
Armijo Well—*well* NM-5
Armilda—*locale* WV-2
*Armilog* FM-9
Armil Park—*park* IA-7
Arminda—*locale* TN-4
Arminda Sch—*school* TN-4
Armine Branch—*stream* KY-4
**Armington**—*pop pl* IL-6
**Armington**—*pop pl* MT-8
Armington, Lake—*lake* NH-1
*Armington Corner* RI-1
**Armington Corner**—*pop pl* RI-1
Armington Coulee—*valley* MT-8
Armington Junction—*locale* MT-8
Armington Lake—*reservoir* OH-6
**Armin (historical)**—*pop pl* OR-9
Arminius Hotel—*hist pl* OR-9
Arminta Street Sch—*school* CA-9
**Arminto**—*pop pl* WY-8
Arminto Draw—*valley* WY-8
Armison Gulch—*valley* ID-8
*Armistead* VA-3
**Armistead**—*pop pl* CA-9
**Armistead**—*pop pl* LA-4
**Armistead**—*pop pl* MS-4
Armistead, Lake—*lake* FL-3
Armistead, Peter F., Sr., House—*hist pl* AL-4
Armistead Branch—*stream* LA-4
Armistead Branch—*stream* VA-3
Armistead Cem—*cemetery* KY-4
Armistead Cem—*cemetery* MS-4
Armistead Ch—*church* MS-4
Armistead CME Ch—*church* MS-4
**Armistead Forest**—*pop pl* VA-3
**Armistead Forest (subdivision)**—*pop pl* VA-3
**Armistead Gardens**—*pop pl* MD-2
Armistead Gardens Sch—*school* MD-2
Armistead (historical)—*locale* KS-7
*Armistead Sch* AL-4
Armisteads Mine (underground)—*mine* AL-4
Armitage—*hist pl* LA-4
**Armitage**—*pop pl* OH-6
**Armitage**—*pop pl* OR-9
Armitage And Artman Delmont Airp—*airport* PA-2
Armitage Bridge—*bridge* NY-2
Armitage Ditch—*canal* MT-8
Armitage Golf Course—*locale* (2) PA-2
**Armitage (historical)**—*pop pl* MS-4
Armitage Island—*island* WA-9
Armitage Newmansville Airp—*airport* PA-2
Armitage Pond—*reservoir* CT-1
Armitage Post Office (historical)—*building* MS-4
Armitage Ranch—*locale* MT-8
Armitage Sch (historical)—*school* PA-2
Armitage Springs—*spring* CO-8
Armitage State Park—*park* OR-9
Armknecht Creek—*stream* CO-8
*Arm Lake* MN-6
Arm Lake—*lake* AR-4
Arm Lake—*lake* TX-5
Armlin Cem—*cemetery* NY-2
Armlin Hill—*summit* NY-2
Arm Mtn—*summit* AK-9
Arm Number Two Ditch—*canal* IN-6
Arm Oak Cem—*cemetery* SC-3
Arm Oak Ch—*church* SC-3
Arm of Chamberlain—*bay* ME-1
Arm Of Fulkerson Ditch—*canal* KY-4
**Armona**—*pop pl* CA-9
**Armona**—*pop pl* TN-4
Armona Baptist Ch—*church* TN-4
Armona Cem—*cemetery* TN-4
Armona Sch (historical)—*school* TN-4
Armona Union Acad—*school* CA-9
Armond Hill Cem—*cemetery* MS-4
Armon Drain—*stream* MI-6
Armond Run—*stream* PA-2
**Armonk**—*pop pl* NY-2
**Armor**—*pop pl* NY-2
Armor Center (Headquarters), The—*other* KY-4
Armor Creek—*stream* MT-8
**Armorel**—*pop pl* AR-4
Armore United Methodist Ch—*church* TN-4
Armor (historical)—*locale* AL-4
Armor Lake—*lake* LA-4
Armor Mine (underground)—*mine* AL-4
*Armor Mountain* AZ-5
Armory—*uninc pl* MA-1
Armory, The—*hist pl* FL-3
Armory, The—*hist pl* WI-6
Armory Block—*hist pl* MA-1
Armory Creek—*stream* GA-3
Armory Hall, Fraternal Hall—*hist pl* CO-8
Armory Hughes Sch—*school* MS-4
Armory-Latisona Bldg—*hist pl* OH-6
Armory of the First Corps of Cadets—*hist pl* MA-1
Armory of the Kentish Guards—*hist pl* RI-1
Armory Park—*park* IN-6
Armory Park Historic Residential District—*hist pl* AZ-5
Armory Square—*park* MA-1
Armory Square Hist Dist—*hist pl* NY-2
Armory Street Park—*park* MA-1
*Armory village* MA-1
Armour—*locale* (2) IA-7
**Armour**—*pop pl* FL-3
**Armour**—*pop pl* MO-7
**Armour**—*pop pl* NC-3
**Armour**—*pop pl* SD-7
**Armour**—*pop pl* TN-4
Armour, J. Ogden, House—*hist pl* IL-6
Armour, Lester, House—*hist pl* IL-6
Armour, Mount—*summit* AK-9
Armour and Jacobson Bldg—*hist pl* AZ-5
Armour Branch—*stream* MS-4
Armour Cem—*cemetery* GA-3
Armour Cem—*cemetery* MO-7
Armour Cem—*cemetery* TX-5
Armour Company Smokehouse and Distribution Plant—*hist pl* MS-4
*Armour Creek* NC-3
Armour Creek—*stream* TN-4
Armour Creek—*stream* WV-2
Armourdale—*uninc pl* KS-7
Armourdale Dam—*dam* ND-7
Armourdale (historical)—*locale* ND-7
Armourdale Lake—*reservoir* ND-7
Armourdale Lake State Game Mngmt Area—*park* ND-7
**Armourdale Township**—*pop pl* ND-7
Armour Draw—*valley* WA-9
Armour Grocery Products Company—*facility* IL-6
Armour Hist Dist—*hist pl* SD-7
Armour Island—*island* KY-4
Armour Lake—*lake* WI-6
**Armour Number Two Mine**—*pop pl* MN-6
Armour Oil Field—*oilfield* TX-5
Armour Park—*park* IL-6
Armour Pond—*reservoir* SC-3
Armour RR Station—*locale* FL-3
Armour Sch—*school* IL-6
Armour Spring—*spring* AZ-5
Armour-Stiner House—*hist pl* NY-2
Armour Valley—*valley* WI-6
Armour Village—*locale* TN-4
Arm Pond, The—*reservoir* MA-1
Arm Pond Dam, The—*dam* MA-1
Arm Post Office (historical)—*building* MS-4
Arm Prairie Ch—*church* IL-6
Arms Brook—*stream* MA-1
Armsby Block—*hist pl* MA-1
Armsby Cem—*cemetery* MA-1
Arms Canyon—*valley* UT-8
Arms Cem—*cemetery* KY-4
Arms Cem—*cemetery* MA-1
Arms Cem—*cemetery* TN-4
Arms Creek—*stream* MI-6
Arms Creek—*stream* TN-4
Arms Creek—*stream* TX-5
Arms House Pond—*reservoir* MA-1
Arms House Pond Dam—*dam* MA-1
*Arms Knob* KY-4
Arms Lake—*lake* MI-6
Arms Lake—*lake* TX-5
Armsmear—*hist pl* CT-1
Arms Mill (historical)—*locale* TN-4
Arms Mtn—*summit* AR-4
*Armstead* MS-4
**Armstead**—*pop pl* AL-4
*Armstead Branch* VA-3
Armstead Cem—*cemetery* WV-2
Armstead Ch—*church* AL-4
Armstead Chapel CME Ch—*church* AL-4
Armstead Creek—*stream* MS-4
Armstead Dowdy Cem—*cemetery* MO-7
Armstead Hollow—*valley* WV-2
Armstead Memorial—*other* OR-9
Armstead Mine (underground)—*mine* AL-4
Armstead Mtn—*summit* AR-4
Armstead Spring—*spring* NM-5
**Armston**—*pop pl* FL-3
*Armstong Gulch* CO-8
*Armstrong* IN-6
Armstrong—*locale* AR-4
Armstrong—*locale* CA-9
Armstrong—*locale* DE-2
Armstrong—*locale* MN-6
Armstrong—*locale* NJ-2
Armstrong—*locale* PA-2
Armstrong—*locale* (2) TX-5
Armstrong—*locale* VA-3
Armstrong—*locale* WA-9
Armstrong—*locale* WI-6
**Armstrong**—*pop pl* AL-4
**Armstrong**—*pop pl* FL-3
**Armstrong**—*pop pl* GA-3
**Armstrong**—*pop pl* IL-6
**Armstrong**—*pop pl* IN-6
**Armstrong**—*pop pl* IA-7
**Armstrong**—*pop pl* MN-6
**Armstrong**—*pop pl* MO-7
**Armstrong**—*pop pl* OH-6
**Armstrong**—*pop pl* OK-5
Armstrong, A., Farm—*hist pl* DE-2
Armstrong, Francis, House—*hist pl* UT-8
Armstrong, George and Susan Guiberson, House—*hist pl* IA-7
Armstrong, John M., House—*hist pl* MN-6
Armstrong, Joseph, Farm—*hist pl* OH-6
Armstrong, Joseph, House—*hist pl* MI-6
Armstrong, Lake—*lake* (2) WA-9
Armstrong, Louis, House—*hist pl* NY-2
Armstrong, W. J., Company Wholesale Grocers—*hist pl* MN-6
Armstrong Academy Cem—*cemetery* OK-5
Armstrong Acad Site—*hist pl* OK-5
Armstrong-Adams House—*hist pl* TX-5
Armstrong and Armstrong Ranch—*locale* NM-5
Armstrong And Beighley Ditch—*canal* OH-6
Armstrong Anderson Ditch—*canal* IN-6
Armstrong Basin—*basin* NM-5
Armstrong Bay—*bay* MN-6
Armstrong Bend—*bend* TN-4
Armstrong Branch—*stream* (4) AL-4
Armstrong Branch—*stream* GA-3
Armstrong Branch—*stream* KS-7
Armstrong Branch—*stream* (2) MS-4
Armstrong Branch—*stream* NC-3
Armstrong Branch—*stream* OK-5
Armstrong Branch—*stream* SC-3
Armstrong Branch—*stream* (3) TN-4
Armstrong Bridge—*bridge* PA-2
*Armstrong Brook* MI-6
Armstrong Brook—*stream* CT-1
Armstrong Brook—*stream* ME-1
Armstrong-Buckley Cem—*cemetery* MS-4
Armstrong Cabin—*locale* WY-8
Armstrong Camp—*locale* AL-4
Armstrong Camp—*locale* NM-5
Armstrong Camp—*locale* OR-9
Armstrong Canal—*canal* MS-4
Armstrong Canyon—*valley* CA-9
Armstrong Canyon—*valley* (2) CO-8
Armstrong Canyon—*valley* (2) NM-5
Armstrong Canyon—*valley* (3) OR-9
Armstrong Canyon—*valley* UT-8
Armstrong Canyon Rsvr—*reservoir* OR-9
Armstrong Cave—*cave* AL-4
Armstrong Cem—*cemetery* (6) AL-4
Armstrong Cem—*cemetery* AR-4
Armstrong Cem—*cemetery* (2) IL-6
Armstrong Cem—*cemetery* (3) IN-6
Armstrong Cem—*cemetery* (2) IA-7
Armstrong Cem—*cemetery* KY-4
Armstrong Cem—*cemetery* (4) MS-4
Armstrong Cem—*cemetery* MO-7
Armstrong Cem—*cemetery* NY-2
Armstrong Cem—*cemetery* NC-3
Armstrong Cem—*cemetery* (5) OH-6
Armstrong Cem—*cemetery* (2) OK-5
Armstrong Cem—*cemetery* OR-9
Armstrong Cem—*cemetery* (7) TN-4
Armstrong Cem—*cemetery* TX-5
Armstrong Ch—*church* AL-4
Armstrong Ch—*church* IL-6
Armstrong Ch—*church* MS-4
Armstrong Ch—*church* TN-4
*Armstrong Chapel* MS-4
Armstrong Chapel—*church* IN-6
Armstrong Chapel—*church* OH-6
Armstrong Community Center—*building* TX-5
*Armstrong Corners* DE-2
Armstrong Corners—*locale* MI-6
Armstrong Corners—*locale* NY-2
Armstrong Coulee—*valley* MT-8
**Armstrong County**—*pop pl* PA-2
**Armstrong (County)**—*pop pl* TX-5
Armstrong County Courthouse and Jail—*hist pl* PA-2
Armstrong Cove—*bay* NC-3
*Armstrong Creek* DE-2
*Armstrong Creek* MS-4
Armstrong Creek—*bay* GA-3
**Armstrong Creek**—*pop pl* WI-6
Armstrong Creek—*stream* (3) AL-4
Armstrong Creek—*stream* CA-9
Armstrong Creek—*stream* CO-8
Armstrong Creek—*stream* ID-8
Armstrong Creek—*stream* IN-6
Armstrong Creek—*stream* (3) MI-6
Armstrong Creek—*stream* (2) MN-6
Armstrong Creek—*stream* MT-8
Armstrong Creek—*stream* (2) NC-3
Armstrong Creek—*stream* (2) OK-5
Armstrong Creek—*stream* OR-9
Armstrong Creek—*stream* PA-2
Armstrong Creek—*stream* SC-3
Armstrong Creek—*stream* TN-4
Armstrong Creek—*stream* (5) TX-5
Armstrong Creek—*stream* (2) WA-9
Armstrong Creek—*stream* WV-2
Armstrong Creek—*stream* (2) WI-6
**Armstrong Creek (Town of)**—*pop pl* WI-6
Armstrong Dam—*dam* AZ-5
Armstrong Ditch—*canal* (2) IN-6
Armstrong Ditch—*canal* MT-8
Armstrong Dock—*locale* NC-3
Armstrong Draw—*valley* KS-7
Armstrong Eddy Park—*park* WI-6
Armstrong Elem Sch—*school* MS-4
Armstrong Farm—*hist pl* OH-6
Armstrong Ferry (historical)—*locale* TN-4
Armstrong Ferry Rec Area—*park* TN-4
Armstrong Field—*park* TX-5
**Armstrong Gardens**—*pop pl* VA-3
Armstrong Grove (historical P.O.)—*locale* IA-7
Armstrong Grove Township—*fmr MCD* IA-7
Armstrong Gulch—*valley* ID-8
Armstrong Gulch—*valley* MT-8
Armstrong Gulch—*valley* (2) OR-9
Armstrong Hill—*summit* AL-4
Armstrong Hill—*summit* CA-9
Armstrong Hill—*summit* KY-4
Armstrong Hill—*summit* NY-2
Armstrong Hill—*summit* VT-1
Armstrong (historical)—*locale* AL-4
Armstrong Hollow—*valley* TN-4
Armstrong Hollow—*valley* WV-2
Armstrong House—*hist pl* GA-3
Armstrong House—*hist pl* MA-1
Armstrong House—*hist pl* WV-2
Armstrong House-Allen Acad—*hist pl* TX-5
Armstrong HS—*school* DC-2
Armstrong HS—*school* VA-3
*Armstrong Island* IL-6
*Armstrong Island* TN-4
Armstrong Island—*island* (2) TN-4
Armstrong Junior Coll—*school* GA-3
Armstrong Knitting Factory—*hist pl* VA-3
Armstrong Lake—*lake* (2) MI-6
Armstrong Lake—*lake* (4) MN-6
Armstrong Lake—*lake* NE-7
Armstrong Lake—*lake* TX-5
Armstrong Lake—*lake* WI-6
Armstrong Lake—*reservoir* IN-6
Armstrong Lake Dam—*dam* IN-6
Armstrong Lake Dam—*dam* (2) MS-4
Armstrong Landing—*locale* TX-5
Armstrong Lateral—*canal* ID-8
Armstrong-Lee House—*hist pl* MS-4
Armstrong Lookout—*locale* ID-8
Armstrong Meadow—*flat* WA-9
Armstrong Meadows—*flat* ID-8
*Armstrong Methodist Church* AL-4
**Armstrong Mills**—*pop pl* OH-6
Armstrong Mine—*mine* UT-8
Armstrong Mine (underground)—*mine* (2) AL-4
*Armstrong-Moore Cemetery* TN-4
Armstrong MS—*school* MS-4
Armstrong Mtn—*summit* GA-3
Armstrong Mtn—*summit* MT-8
Armstrong Mtn—*summit* (2) NY-2
Armstrong Mtn—*summit* TX-5
Armstrong Mtn—*summit* WA-9
Armstrong Mtn—*summit* WV-2
Armstrong Oil Field—*oilfield* MS-4
Armstrong Oil Field—*oilfield* TX-5
Armstrong Park—*park* AZ-5
Armstrong Park—*park* NC-3
Armstrong Park—*park* OH-6
Armstrong Park—*park* WI-6
Armstrong Pass—*gap* CA-9
Armstrong Playground—*park* PA-2
Armstrong Point—*cape* AK-9
Armstrong Pond—*lake* FL-3
Armstrong Pond—*lake* TN-4
Armstrong Pond—*reservoir* MS-4
Armstrong Post Office—*building* AL-4
Armstrong Prong Bitter Creek—*stream* WY-8
Armstrong Ranch—*locale* (2) CA-9
Armstrong Ranch—*locale* CO-8
Armstrong Ranch—*locale* (2) MT-8
Armstrong Ranch—*locale* NM-5
Armstrong Ranch—*locale* TX-5
Armstrong Ranch HQ—*locale* NM-5
Armstrong Ranch HQ—*locale* TX-5
Armstrong Redwoods State Res—*park* CA-9
Armstrong Ridge—*ridge* OH-6
Armstrong River—*stream* MN-6
Armstrong Row—*hist pl* KY-4
Armstrong Run—*stream* IL-6
Armstrong Run—*stream* (2) OH-6
Armstrong Run—*stream* PA-2
Armstrong Run—*stream* WV-2
Armstrongs Cem—*cemetery* OH-6
Armstrong Sch—*school* (3) IL-6
Armstrong Sch—*school* KY-4
Armstrong Sch—*school* MA-1
Armstrong Sch—*school* MN-6
Armstrong Sch—*school* (2) MS-4
Armstrong Sch—*school* NC-3
Armstrong Sch—*school* OK-5
Armstrong Sch—*school* SC-3
Armstrong Sch—*school* TX-5
Armstrong Sch—*school* (2) VA-3
Armstrong Sch (historical)—*school* (2) AL-4
Armstrong Sch (historical)—*school* MS-4
Armstrong Sch (historical)—*school* TN-4
*Armstrongs Ferry* TN-4
Armstrongs Ford—*crossing* TN-4
Armstrongs Ford—*locale* NC-3
Armstrong Site (22RA576)—*hist pl* MS-4
Armstrong Slough—*bay* TN-4
Armstrong Slough—*lake* MN-6
**Armstrongs Mills**—*pop pl* OH-6
Armstrong Spring—*spring* (2) TN-4
Armstrong Spring—*spring* (2) UT-8
*Armstrong Springs* AR-4
*Armstrong Springs (Crosby)* AR-4
Armstrong State Coll—*school* GA-3
Armstrong Street Ch of God—*church* MS-4
Armstrong Tank—*reservoir* (2) AZ-5
Armstrong-Toro House—*hist pl* PR-3
**Armstrong (Town of)**—*pop pl* WI-6
**Armstrong (Township of)**—*pop pl* IN-6
**Armstrong (Township of)**—*pop pl* (2) PA-2
Armstrong Tunnel—*hist pl* PA-2
Armstrong Tunnel—*mine* UT-8
Armstrong Tunnel—*tunnel* PA-2
Armstrong Valley Bible Ch—*church* PA-2
Armstrong-Walker House—*hist pl* DE-2
*Armstrong Waterhole* AZ-5
Armstrong Well—*well* AZ-5
Armstrong Well—*well* (2) NM-5
*Armucha Creek* GA-3
*Armuche Creek* GA-3
**Armuchee**—*pop pl* GA-3
Armuchee (CCD)—*cens area* GA-3
Armuchee Ch—*church* GA-3
*Armuchee Creek* GA-3
Armuchee Creek—*stream* GA-3
**Armuth Acres**—*pop pl* IN-6
*Armuth Ditch* IN-6
Armuth Ditch—*canal* (2) IN-6
Armwood HS—*school* FL-3
Army and Navy Acad—*school* CA-9
Army And Navy Country Club—*other* VA-3
Army and Navy YMCA—*hist pl* RI-1
Army Aviation Support Facility Airp—*airport* IN-6
Army Branch—*stream* IN-6
*Army Chemical Center* MD-2
Army Creek—*stream* DE-2
Army Dock—*locale* AK-9
Army Drain—*canal* (2) NV-8
Army Guard Helipad Airp—*airport* TN-4
Army Hill—*summit* OR-9
Army Lake—*lake* WI-6
Army Materials and Mechanics Research Center—*military* MA-1
Army Medical Museum and Library (historical)—*hist pl* DC-2
Army Navy Country Club—*other* VA-3
Army-Navy Museum—*building* PA-2
Army Park—*park* TN-4
Army Pass—*gap* CA-9
Army Peak—*summit* AK-9
Army Pictorial Center—*building* NY-2
Army Point—*cape* CA-9
*Army Point (Benicia Arsenal)* CA-9
*Army Terminal (Oakland Army Base)* CA-9
Army Theatre—*hist pl* NE-7
Army Trail Sch—*school* IL-6
Army Well Number 1—*well* NV-8
Arnada Park Annex—*uninc pl* WA-9
Arnak Creek—*stream* AK-9
*Arnald Bend* AR-4
Arnall Lake—*reservoir* GA-3
Arna Meadow Brook—*stream* ME-1
Arnar HS—*school* CA-9
**Arna (Township of)**—*pop pl* MN-6
**Arnaud**—*pop pl* OR-9
**Arnaudville**—*pop pl* LA-4
Arnault Branch—*stream* MO-7
Arnault Ch—*church* MO-7
*Arnault Creek* MO-7
Arnault Sch (historical)—*school* MO-7
**Arna Valley**—*pop pl* VA-3
**Arnaz**—*pop pl* CA-9
Arnco Ch—*church* GA-3
**Arnco Mills**—*pop pl* GA-3
Arnco-Sargent Sch—*school* GA-3
Arndahl Ch—*church* MN-6
Arndt—*locale* ND-7
Arndt, Rufus, House—*hist pl* WI-6
*Arndt and Wessinger Cemetery* PA-2
Arndt Drain—*stream* MI-6
Arndt Draw—*valley* WY-8
Arndt Lake—*lake* CA-9
Arndt Prune Dryer—*hist pl* WA-9
Arndt Ranch—*locale* WY-8
Arndts—*locale* PA-2
Arndts and Messinger Cem—*cemetery* PA-2
Arndts Ch—*church* PA-2
Arndt Sch (abandoned)—*school* PA-2
Arneckeville Gas Field—*oilfield* TX-5
**Arneckville**—*pop pl* TX-5
Arnedra, Lake—*reservoir* AL-4
**Arnegard**—*pop pl* ND-7
Arnegard Cem—*cemetery* ND-7
Arnegard Dam—*dam* ND-7
Arnegard Dam—*reservoir* ND-7
**Arnegard Township**—*pop pl* ND-7
Arnell Creek—*stream* DE-2
*Arnells Creek* DE-2
Arnells Mill (historical)—*locale* MS-4
Arne Sch—*school* ND-7
**Arnesen**—*pop pl* MN-6
*Arnes Lake* CO-8
Arneson Creek—*stream* WI-6
Arneson Ditch—*canal* MT-8
Arneson Lake—*lake* WI-6
Arneson Slough—*lake* SD-7
Arnesons Peak—*summit* WA-9
**Arnessen**—*pop pl* MN-6
Arnested Lake—*lake* MI-6
Arnet Gap—*gap* OK-5
**Arne Township**—*pop pl* ND-7
Arnett—*locale* AR-4
Arnett—*locale* KY-4
Arnett—*locale* TX-5
Arnett—*locale* WV-2
**Arnett**—*pop pl* NY-2
**Arnett**—*pop pl* (2) OK-5
**Arnett**—*pop pl* TX-5
**Arnett**—*pop pl* WV-2
Arnett Branch—*stream* (3) KY-4
Arnett Branch—*stream* NC-3
Arnett Canyon—*valley* AZ-5
Arnett Cem—*cemetery* AL-4
Arnett Cem—*cemetery* GA-3
Arnett Cem—*cemetery* (2) IN-6
Arnett Cem—*cemetery* KY-4
Arnett Cem—*cemetery* MO-7
Arnett Cem—*cemetery* OH-6
Arnett Cem—*cemetery* (2) TN-4
Arnett Cem—*cemetery* TX-5
Arnett Ch—*church* OK-5
Arnett Creek—*stream* AZ-5
Arnett Creek—*stream* ID-8
Arnett Creek—*stream* SD-7
**Arnette (Arnett)**—*pop pl* WV-2
Arnette Cem—*cemetery* SC-3
Arnette Chapel—*church* WV-2
Arnett Field Drain—*swamp* GA-3
Arnett Hollow—*valley* KY-4
Arnett Lake—*reservoir* TX-5
Arnett Meadows—*flat* ID-8
Arnett Mine (underground)—*mine* TN-4
Arnett Mtn—*summit* MO-7
Arnett Ranch—*locale* NE-7
Arnett Run—*stream* WV-2
Arnetts Cem—*cemetery* KY-4
Arnett Sch—*school* GA-3
Arnett Sch—*school* IL-6
Arnett Sch—*school* TX-5
Arnetts Fork—*stream* KY-4
Arnett Spring—*spring* (2) CA-9
**Arnettsville**—*pop pl* WV-2
Arnettsville Sch—*school* WV-2
Arnett Well—*well* AZ-5
Arney—*locale* TX-5
**Arney**—*pop pl* IN-6
*Arney Branch* TN-4
Arney Canyon—*valley* MT-8
Arney Cem—*cemetery* TN-4
Arney Hollow—*valley* VA-3
Arney Run—*stream* OH-6
**Arneys Mount**—*pop pl* NJ-2
Arney's Mount Friends Meetinghouse and Burial Ground—*hist pl* NJ-2
Arneys Store—*locale* NC-3
*Arneys Town* NJ-2
**Arneytown**—*pop pl* NJ-2
Arneytown Hist Dist—*hist pl* NJ-2
*Arngach* FM-9
Arnhart Cem—*cemetery* AR-4
Arnheim—*locale* MI-6
**Arnheim**—*pop pl* OH-6
*Arnho Island* MP-9
Arnhold Ridge—*ridge* MO-7
**Arnica**—*pop pl* MO-7
Arnica Bay—*lake* AL-4
Arnica Creek—*stream* WY-8
Arnica Sink—*basin* CA-9
Arnica Spring—*spring* OR-9
Arnie Ch—*church* GA-3
Arniel—*island* MP-9
*Arniel Island* MP-9
Arnie Shore Lake—*reservoir* NC-3
Arnie Shore Lake Dam—*dam* NC-3
Arnika Ranch Airp—*airport* MO-7
Arnkil Island—*island* AK-9
Arno—*island* MP-9
Arno—*locale* TN-4
Arno—*locale* TX-5
**Arno**—*pop pl* FL-3
**Arno**—*pop pl* MO-7
**Arno**—*pop pl* VA-3
**Arno**—*pop pl* WY-8
Arno Apartments—*hist pl* CO-8
Arno Atoll—*island* MP-9
Arno (County-equivalent)—*civil* MP-9
Arno Draw—*valley* WY-8
*Arno Island* MP-9
*Arnola* PA-2
Arno Lagoon—*lake* MP-9
*Arnold* IN-6
*Arnold* KS-7
*Arnold* MS-4
Arnold—*locale* CA-9
Arnold—*locale* (2) IL-6
Arnold—*locale* IA-7
Arnold—*locale* KS-7
Arnold—*locale* (2) KY-4
Arnold—*locale* MI-6
Arnold—*locale* MT-8
Arnold—*locale* NV-8
Arnold—*locale* TX-5
Arnold—*locale* (2) WV-2
Arnold—*locale* WI-6
**Arnold**—*pop pl* (2) CA-9
**Arnold**—*pop pl* MD-2
**Arnold**—*pop pl* MN-6
**Arnold**—*pop pl* MO-7
**Arnold**—*pop pl* NE-7
**Arnold**—*pop pl* NC-3
**Arnold**—*pop pl* ND-7
**Arnold**—*pop pl* OH-6
**Arnold**—*pop pl* PA-2
Arnold—*uninc pl* MA-1
Arnold, Adam C., Block—*hist pl* MI-6
Arnold, Benjamin Walworth, House and Carriage House—*hist pl* NY-2
Arnold, Capt. Alexander A., Farm—*hist pl* WI-6
Arnold, Dexter, Farmstead—*hist pl* RI-1
Arnold, Earnest, House—*hist pl* OR-9
Arnold, Eleazer, House—*hist pl* RI-1
Arnold, George, House—*hist pl* DE-2
Arnold, Israel, House—*hist pl* RI-1
Arnold, John, House—*hist pl* KY-4
Arnold, John, House—*hist pl* RI-1
Arnold, John Waterman, House—*hist pl* RI-1
Arnold, Lake—*lake* FL-3
Arnold, Lake—*reservoir* NY-2
Arnold, Peleg, Tavern—*hist pl* RI-1
Arnold, Philip, House—*hist pl* KY-4
Arnold, Thomas P., House—*hist pl* GA-3
Arnold AFS Airp—*airport* TN-4
Arnold Air Force Station—*military* TN-4
Arnold Airp—*airport* PA-2
Arnold Airstrip—*airport* OR-9
Arnold and Harriman Ranch—*locale* CO-8
Arnold Arboretum—*hist pl* MA-1
Arnold Arboretum—*park* MA-1
Arnold Ave Sch—*school* NY-2
Arnold Bay—*bay* NY-2
Arnold Bay—*bay* VT-1
**Arnold Bay**—*pop pl* VT-1
Arnold Bend—*bend* AR-4
Arnold Bend—*bend* CA-9
Arnold Bottoms—*bend* KY-4
Arnold Bottoms—*bend* SD-7
Arnold Branch—*stream* (2) AL-4
Arnold Branch—*stream* AR-4
Arnold Branch—*stream* (2) GA-3
Arnold Branch—*stream* KY-4
Arnold Branch—*stream* MS-4
Arnold Branch—*stream* MO-7
Arnold Branch—*stream* NJ-2
Arnold Branch—*stream* (2) NC-3
Arnold Branch—*stream* (8) TN-4
Arnold Branch—*stream* TX-5
Arnold Branch—*stream* WV-2
Arnold Brook—*stream* ME-1
Arnold Brook—*stream* NY-2
Arnold Brook—*stream* VT-1
Arnold B. Sanford House—*building* MA-1
Arnold-Callaway Plantation—*hist pl* GA-3
*Arnold Camp* NE-7
Arnold Camps—*locale* ME-1
Arnold Canal—*canal* OR-9
Arnold Canyon—*valley* AZ-5
Arnold Cave—*cave* PA-2
*Arnold Cave Branch* MO-7
Arnold Cem—*cemetery* (2) AL-4
Arnold Cem—*cemetery* (4) AR-4
Arnold Cem—*cemetery* (2) GA-3
Arnold Cem—*cemetery* (2) IL-6
Arnold Cem—*cemetery* (3) IN-6
Arnold Cem—*cemetery* KS-7
Arnold Cem—*cemetery* (2) KY-4
Arnold Cem—*cemetery* LA-4
Arnold Cem—*cemetery* (3) MO-7
Arnold Cem—*cemetery* NE-7
Arnold Cem—*cemetery* NY-2
Arnold Cem—*cemetery* OH-6
Arnold Cem—*cemetery* (11) TN-4
Arnold Cem—*cemetery* (2) TX-5
Arnold Cem—*cemetery* VA-3
Arnold Cem—*cemetery* (2) WV-2
Arnold Ch—*church* AR-4
Arnold Ch—*church* GA-3
Arnold Ch—*church* IN-6
Arnold Chapel—*church* GA-3
Arnold Chapel—*church* TN-4
Arnold City—*civil* PA-2
**Arnold City**—*pop pl* PA-2
Arnold Club—*other* CA-9
Arnold Corner—*locale* ME-1
Arnold Coulee—*valley* (2) MT-8
Arnold Coulee—*valley* ND-7
*Arnold Creek* DE-2
*Arnold Creek* MT-8
*Arnold Creek* VA-3
Arnold Creek—*stream* (3) AR-4
Arnold Creek—*stream* (2) CA-9
Arnold Creek—*stream* GA-3
Arnold Creek—*stream* (2) IN-6
Arnold Creek—*stream* LA-4

Arrow Lake—*lake* (2) ... MN-6
Arrow Lake—*lake* (2) ... MT-8
Arrow Lake—*lake* ... OR-9
Arrow Lake—*lake* ... WA-9
Arrow Lake—*reservoir* ... CO-8
Arrow Lake—*reservoir* ... TN-4
Arrow Lake Dam—*dam* ... TN-4
Arrow Lateral—*canal* ... ID-8
Arrow Lookout Tower—*locale* ... MN-6
Arrowmakers Ridge—*ridge* ... CA-9
Arrowmink Creek—*stream* ... PA-2
Arrow Mtn—*summit* ... WY-8
**Arrowood**—*pop pl* ... KY-4
**Arrowood**—*pop pl* ... MD-2
Arrowood Acad—*school* ... VA-3
Arrowood Baptist Ch—*church* ... MS-4
Arrowood Branch—*stream* ... NC-3
Arrowood Branch—*stream* ... SC-3
Arrowood Ch—*church* ... SC-3
**Arrowood (Industrial Park)**—*pop pl* ... NC-3
*Arrowood Lake* ... ND-7
Arrowood Sch—*school* ... KY-4
Arrowood Southern—*locale* ... NC-3
**Arrowood (subdivision)**—*pop pl* ... NC-3
Arrow Peak—*summit* ... CA-9
Arrow Peak—*summit* ... CO-8
Arrow Peak—*summit* (2) ... MT-8
Arrow Point—*cape* ... CA-9
Arrow Point—*cape* ... CT-1
Arrow Point—*cape* ... ID-8
Arrow Point—*cape* ... TX-5
Arrow Point—*cape* ... WA-9
Arrow Point Rsvr—*reservoir* ... ID-8
Arrow Press Square Shop Ctr—*locale* ... UT-8
Arrow Ridge—*ridge* ... CA-9
*Arrow River* ... MT-8
Arrow Rock—*hist pl* ... MO-7
**Arrow Rock**—*pop pl* ... MO-7
Arrowrock Dam—*dam* ... ID-8
Arrowrock Dam—*hist pl* ... ID-8
*Arrow Rock Reservoir* ... ID-8
Arrowrock Rsvr—*reservoir* ... ID-8
Arrow Rock State Historic Site Bridge—*hist pl* ... MO-7
Arrow Rock State Historic Site Grave Shelter—*hist pl* ... MO-7
Arrow Rock State Historic Site Lookout Shelter—*hist pl* ... MO-7
Arrow Rock State Historic Site Open Shelter—*hist pl* ... MO-7
Arrow Rock State Park—*park* ... MO-7
Arrow Rock Tavern—*hist pl* ... MO-7
Arrow Rock Township—*civil* ... MO-7
Arrow Run—*stream* ... IN-6
*Arrowseag* ... ME-1
Arrowshead, Lake—*reservoir* ... KS-7
Arrowsic—*locale* ... ME-1
Arrowsic Island—*island* ... ME-1
**Arrowsic (Town of)**—*pop pl* ... ME-1
*Arrowsike* ... ME-1
**Arrowsmith**—*pop pl* (2) ... IL-6
*Arrowsmith Atoll* ... MP-9
*Arrowsmith Island* ... MP-9
**Arrowsmith (Township of)**—*pop pl* ... IL-6
Arrow Spring—*spring* ... CO-8
Arrow Spring—*spring* ... ID-8
Arrowston—*hist pl* ... OH-6
Arrow Swamp—*swamp* ... RI-1
Arrowtail Ranch—*locale* ... WY-8
Arrow Tank—*reservoir* ... AZ-5
Arrow Tank—*reservoir* ... TX-5
Arrow Tunnel—*tunnel* ... CO-8
Arrowview JHS—*school* ... CA-9
Arrowweed Canyon—*valley* ... AZ-5
Arrowweed Spring—*spring* ... AZ-5
Arrowweed Springs—*spring* ... AZ-5
Arrow Well—*well* ... CO-8
**Arrow Wood**—*pop pl* ... IL-6
Arrowwood—*uninc pl* ... AL-4
Arrowwood Creek—*stream* ... NC-3
Arrowwood Creek—*stream* ... WV-2
Arrowwood Dam—*dam* ... ND-7
Arrowwood Glade Rearing Pools—*locale* ... NC-3
*Arrow-wood Lake* ... ND-7
Arrowwood Lake—*reservoir* ... ND-7
Arrowwood Natl Wildlife Ref—*park* ... ND-7
*Arrow Wood Point* ... OR-9
Arrowwood Point—*summit* ... OR-9
Arrowwood Sch—*school* ... ND-7
**Arrow Wood (subdivision)**—*pop pl* ... AL-4
Arrow Wood Township (historical)—*civil* ... ND-7
*Arroyo* ... CO-8
Arroyo—*locale* ... PA-2
Arroyo—*locale* ... TX-5
Arroyo—*locale* ... WV-2
**Arroyo**—*pop pl* ... PR-3
Arroyo Acequias—*stream* ... NM-5
Arroyo Aguague—*stream* ... CA-9
Arroyo Aguaje de la Petaca—*stream* ... NM-5
*Arroyo Agua Poquito* ... TX-5
Arroyo Agua Sarca—*stream* ... NM-5
Arroyo Alamillo—*stream* ... NM-5
Arroyo Alamito—*stream* (3) ... NM-5
Arroyo Alamo—*stream* (4) ... NM-5
Arroyo Alamocito—*stream* ... NM-5
Arroyo Alfredo Padilla—*stream* ... NM-5
Arroyo Ancho—*stream* ... CA-9
Arroyo Ancho—*stream* ... NM-5
Arroyo Angostura—*stream* ... NM-5
Arroyo Arana—*stream* ... NM-5
Arroyo Arenoso—*stream* ... NM-5
Arroyo Armiento—*stream* ... NM-5
Arroyo Armijo—*stream* ... NM-5
Arroyo Balcon—*stream* ... NM-5
Arroyo Banco Quemado—*valley* ... NM-5
Arroyo Barranca—*valley* ... NM-5
Arroyo Benavidez—*stream* ... NM-5
Arroyo Bernalillito—*stream* ... NM-5
Arroyo Bernardo—*stream* ... NM-5
Arroyo Blanco—*stream* (2) ... NM-5
Arroyo Blanco—*valley* ... NM-5
*Arroyo Burro* ... CA-9
Arroyo Burro Beach Park—*park* ... CA-9
*Arroyo Burro Creek* ... CA-9
Arroyo Burro Trail—*trail* ... CA-9
Arroyo Cachulie—*stream* ... NM-5
*Arroyo Calabaces* ... CA-9
Arroyo Calabasas—*valley* ... NM-5
*Arroyo Calabazas* ... CA-9
Arroyo Calaveras—*valley* ... NM-5
Arroyo Calladito—*stream* ... NM-5
Arroyo Canal—*canal* ... CA-9
Arroyo Canamo—*stream* ... NM-5
Arroyo Canoneros—*stream* ... NM-5
*Arroyo Cantua* ... CA-9
Arroyo Carreras—*stream* ... NM-5
*Arroyo Casa Blancas* ... TX-5
*Arroyo Cavelano* ... CA-9
Arroyo Cerro Negro—*stream* ... NM-5
Arroyo Chamisa—*stream* ... NM-5
Arroyo Chanthe—*stream* ... NM-5
Arroyo Chavez—*stream* (2) ... NM-5
Arroyo Chico—*civil* ... CA-9
Arroyo Chico—*stream* ... NM-5
Arroyo Chijuilito—*stream* ... NM-5
Arroyo Chijuilla—*stream* ... NM-5
Arroyo Chijuillita—*stream* ... NM-5
Arroyo Chimaja—*valley* ... NM-5
Arroyo Chinchonte—*stream* ... NM-5
Arroyo Chorro—*stream* (2) ... NM-5
*Arroyo Cibola* ... NM-5
Arroyocita Creek—*stream* ... TX-5
*Arroyo Colorado* ... TX-5
Arroyo Colorado—*stream* (5) ... NM-5
*Arroyo Colorado Floodway* ... TX-5
Arroyo Comanche—*stream* ... NM-5
Arroyo Companero—*valley* ... NM-5
*Arroyo Concepcion* ... TX-5
Arroyo Conchas—*stream* ... NM-5
Arroyo Copita—*stream* ... NM-5
Arroyo Corrales—*stream* ... NM-5
Arroyo Corrales Tierra—*stream* ... NM-5
*Arroyo Covelano* ... CA-9
Arroyo Coyote—*stream* (2) ... NM-5
*Arroyo Creek* ... MT-8
Arroyo Cuchillo—*stream* ... NM-5
Arroyo Cucho—*stream* ... NM-5
Arroyo Cuervo—*stream* (2) ... NM-5
Arroyo Cuervo—*valley* ... NM-5
Arroyo Cuevitas—*stream* ... NM-5
Arroyo Cuma—*valley* ... NM-5
Arroyo Cuyamungue—*stream* ... NM-5
Arroyo de Agua—*stream* ... NM-5
Arroyo de Anil—*stream* ... NM-5
Arroyo de Chamizal—*stream* ... NM-5
*Arroyo de Chilili* ... NM-5
Arroyo de Chilili—*arroyo* ... NM-5
Arroyo de Chinguague—*stream* ... NM-5
Arroyo de Comales—*stream* ... NM-5
Arroyo de Domingo Baca—*stream* ... NM-5
Arroyo Dedos Gordos—*stream* ... NM-5
Arroyo Degollado—*stream* ... CA-9
Arroyo de Gonzalez—*stream* ... NM-5
Arroyo de Guachupangue—*stream* ... NM-5
Arroyo De La Alameda—*civil* ... CA-9
Arroyo de la Anima—*stream* ... NM-5
Arroyo de la Baranca—*stream* ... NM-5
Arroyo de la Canada Ancha—*stream* ... NM-5
Arroyo de la Cejita—*stream* ... NM-5
Arroyo de la Cruz—*stream* ... NM-5
*Arroyo De La Cruz Creek* ... CA-9
Arroyo de la Cuesta Colorada—*stream* ... NM-5
Arroyo de la Cuesta de los Vaqueros—*stream* ... NM-5
Arroyo de la Cueva—*stream* ... NM-5
**Arroyo del Agua**—*pop pl* ... NM-5
Arroyo de la Guaje—*stream* ... NM-5
Arroyo de la Jara—*stream* (2) ... NM-5
Arroyo de la Jara—*valley* ... NM-5
Arroyo De La Laguna—*civil* ... CA-9
Arroyo de la Laguna—*stream* ... CA-9
Arroyo del Alamo—*stream* ... NM-5
Arroyo de la Maestas—*stream* ... NM-5
Arroyo de la Manga—*stream* ... NM-5
Arroyo de la Matanza—*valley* ... NM-5
Arroyo de la Miga—*stream* ... NM-5
Arroyo de la Mora—*stream* ... NM-5
Arroyo de la Morada—*stream* ... NM-5
Arroyo de la Parida—*stream* ... NM-5
Arroyo de la Piedra—*valley* ... NM-5
Arroyo de la Plaza—*stream* ... NM-5
Arroyo de la Plaza Larga—*stream* ... NM-5
Arroyo de la Presa—*stream* (2) ... NM-5
Arroyo de la Presilla—*valley* ... NM-5
*Arroyo de las Benditas Animas* ... TX-5
Arroyo de las Calabacillas—*stream* ... NM-5
Arroyo de las Canas—*locale* ... NM-5
Arroyo de las Canas—*stream* ... NM-5
Arroyo de las Canobitas—*stream* ... NM-5
*Arroyo De Las Garzas* ... CA-9
Arroyo de las Lemitas—*stream* ... NM-5
*Arroyo de las Lomatas Negros* ... NM-5
Arroyo de las Mulas—*stream* ... NM-5
Arroyo De Las Nueces Y Bolbones—*civil* ... CA-9
*Arroyo De Las Ortegas* ... CA-9
Arroyo de las Palomas—*stream* ... NM-5
Arroyo de las Trampas—*valley* ... NM-5
Arroyo de la Vaca—*stream* ... NM-5
Arroyo de la Vega de los Tanos—*stream* ... NM-5
Arroyo del Camino—*stream* ... CA-9
Arroyo del Carrizo—*stream* ... NM-5
Arroyo del Cerrito—*stream* ... NM-5
Arroyo del Cerrito Negro—*stream* ... NM-5
Arroyo del Chamiso—*stream* ... NM-5
Arroyo del Cobre—*stream* ... NM-5
Arroyo del Corral de Piedra—*stream* ... NM-5
Arroyo del Coyote—*stream* ... NM-5
Arroyo del Coyote—*valley* ... NM-5
Arroyo del Cuervo—*stream* (2) ... NM-5
Arroyo del Embudo—*stream* ... NM-5
Arroyo Del Gato—*stream* ... NM-5
Arroyo del Gaucho—*stream* ... NM-5
Arroyo del Guique—*stream* ... NM-5
*Arroyo Del La Campana* ... CA-9
Arroyo del Llano—*stream* ... NM-5
Arroyo del Macho—*stream* ... NM-5
Arroyo del Macho—*valley* ... NM-5
Arroyo del Mesteno—*stream* ... NM-5
*Arroyo Del Montecito* ... CA-9
Arroyo del Ojitos—*stream* ... NM-5
Arroyo del Ojo del Orno—*stream* ... NM-5
Arroyo del Ojo Negro—*stream* ... NM-5
Arroyo de los Ajuelos—*stream* ... NM-5
*Arroyo De Los Alamos* ... CA-9
Arroyo de los Alamos—*stream* ... NM-5
Arroyo de los Angeles—*stream* ... NM-5
Arroyo de los Borregos—*stream* ... NM-5
*Arroyo De Los Capitancillos* ... CA-9
Arroyo de los Cerritos—*valley* ... NM-5
Arroyo de los Cerros Colorados—*stream* ... NM-5
Arroyo de los Chamisos—*valley* ... NM-5
Arroyo de los Chavez—*stream* ... NM-5
Arroyo de los Diegos—*stream* ... NM-5
Arroyo de los Encinos—*stream* ... NM-5
Arroyo de los Frijoles—*stream* ... NM-5
Arroyo de los Frijoles—*valley* ... NM-5
Arroyo De Los Frijoles Beach—*beach* ... CA-9
Arroyo de los Galves—*stream* ... NM-5
Arroyo de los Guardunos—*stream* ... NM-5
Arroyo de los Lovatos—*valley* ... NM-5
Arroyo de los Martinez—*stream* ... NM-5
Arroyo de los Montoyas—*stream* ... NM-5
Arroyo del Oso—*stream* ... NM-5
*Arroyo de los Olmos* ... TX-5
*Arroyo De Los Padres* ... CA-9
Arroyo de los Penita—*stream* ... NM-5
Arroyo de los Pinavetes—*stream* ... NM-5
Arroyo de los Pinos—*stream* ... NM-5
Arroyo de los Pinos—*valley* ... NM-5
Arroyo de los Tanques—*stream* ... NM-5
Arroyo del Palacio—*stream* (2) ... NM-5
*Arroyo Del Pedregoso* ... CA-9
Arroyo del Perro—*stream* ... NM-5
Arroyo del Perro del Oest—*stream* ... NM-5
Arroyo del Perro del Oeste—*stream* ... NM-5
Arroyo del Pino—*stream* ... NM-5
Arroyo del Plomo—*stream* ... NM-5
Arroyo del Pueblito—*stream* ... NM-5
Arroyo del Pueblo—*stream* ... NM-5
Arroyo del Pueblo—*valley* ... NM-5
Arroyo del Puertecito—*stream* ... NM-5
Arroyo del Puerto—*stream* (2) ... NM-5
Arroyo del Puerto Chiquito—*stream* ... NM-5
Arroyo del Rancho—*stream* ... NM-5
Arroyo del Rosario—*valley* ... NM-5
Arroyo del Tajo—*valley* ... NM-5
*Arroyo del Tigre* ... TX-5
Arroyo del Toro—*stream* ... NM-5
Arroyo del Tuerto—*stream* ... NM-5
*Arroyo Del Tulare* ... CA-9
Arroyo del Valle—*stream* ... NM-5
*Arroyo del Vegosa* ... NM-5
*Arroyo del Vegoso* ... NM-5
Arroyo del Veranito—*stream* ... NM-5
Arroyo del Yeso—*stream* ... NM-5
Arroyo de Manzano—*stream* ... NM-5
Arroyo de Miranda—*stream* ... NM-5
Arroyo de Piedra Lumbre—*stream* ... NM-5
Arroyo de Quarteles—*stream* ... NM-5
Arroyo de Ranchitos—*stream* ... NM-5
Arroyo de Rosendo—*stream* ... NM-5
*Arroyo De San Augustin* ... CA-9
Arroyo de San Francisco—*stream* ... NM-5
Arroyo de San Jose—*stream* ... NM-5
Arroyo de Soldados—*stream* ... NM-5
Arroyo Destierro—*stream* ... NM-5
Arroyo de Tajique—*stream* ... NM-5
Arroyo de Tio Bartolo—*valley* ... NM-5
Arroyo de Trujillos—*stream* ... NM-5
Arroyo de Vayarequa—*stream* ... NM-5
Arroyo de Yrisarri—*valley* ... NM-5
*Arroyo Dulce* ... TX-5
Arroyo Dunes Golf Course—*other* ... AZ-5
Arroyo Eighteen—*stream* ... NM-5
*Arroyo El Begoso* ... NM-5
Arroyo el Ojito—*stream* ... NM-5
Arroyo El Rito—*stream* ... NM-5
*Arroyo El Salado* ... TX-5
Arroyo Empedrado—*stream* ... NM-5
Arroyo Escondido—*stream* ... CO-8
Arroyo Gallina—*stream* ... NM-5
Arroyo Gallinas—*valley* ... NM-5
*Arroyo Garcia* ... TX-5
Arroyo Garcia—*stream* ... NM-5
Arroyo Gato—*stream* ... NM-5
Arroyo Gavilan—*stream* ... NM-5
Arroyo Gigante—*stream* (2) ... NM-5
Arroyo Grande—*civil* ... CA-9
**Arroyo Grande**—*pop pl* ... CA-9
Arroyo Grande—*stream* ... NM-5
Arroyo Grande (CCD)—*cens area* ... CA-9
Arroyo Grande Station—*locale* ... CA-9
Arroyo Griego—*stream* ... NM-5
Arroyo Guajalote—*valley* ... NM-5
**Arroyo Heights**—*pop pl* ... WA-9
Arroyo Hermanos—*stream* ... NM-5
Arroyo Hernandez—*stream* ... NM-5
Arroyo Honda—*stream* ... NM-5
Arroyo Hondo—*civil* ... NM-5
**Arroyo Hondo**—*pop pl* ... NM-5
Arroyo Hondo—*stream* ... CO-8
Arroyo Hondo—*stream* (6) ... NM-5
Arroyo Hondo—*valley* (2) ... NM-5
Arroyo Hondo (CCD)—*cens area* ... NM-5
Arroyo HS—*school* (2) ... CA-9
Arroyo Jacona—*stream* ... NM-5
Arroyo Jaconito—*stream* ... NM-5
Arroyo Jaralosa—*stream* ... NM-5
Arroyo Jarido—*stream* ... NM-5
Arroyo Jarosa—*stream* ... NM-5
Arroyo Jaspe—*stream* (2) ... NM-5
Arroyo Jaspe—*valley* ... NM-5
Arroyo la Azabache—*stream* ... NM-5
Arroyo La Jara—*stream* ... NM-5
Arroyo la Joya—*stream* ... NM-5
Arroyo La Manga—*stream* ... NM-5
Arroyo la Mesilla—*stream* ... NM-5
Arroyo la Mina—*stream* ... NM-5
Arroyo Landavaso—*stream* ... NM-5
Arroyo Largo—*stream* ... NM-5
Arroyo las Jollas—*stream* ... NM-5
Arroyo las Lagunitas—*stream* ... NM-5
Arroyo las Tunas—*stream* ... NM-5
*Arroyo Lavacita* ... NM-5
Arroyo Leguino—*stream* ... NM-5
Arroyo Leon—*stream* ... NM-5
Arroyo Lopez—*stream* ... NM-5
Arroyo los Alamos—*stream* ... NM-5
Arroyo los Barrancos—*stream* ... NM-5
Arroyo Lucero—*stream* (2) ... NM-5
Arroyo Lyman—*stream* ... NM-5
Arroyo Madrid—*stream* ... NM-5
Arroyo Manuela—*stream* ... NM-5
Arroyo Maria Chavez—*stream* ... NM-5
*Arroyo Martenas* ... TX-5
Arroyo Mascaras—*valley* ... NM-5
Arroyo Milagro—*stream* ... NM-5
*Arroyo Minitas* ... TX-5
*Arroyo Minito* ... TX-5
Arroyo Miranda—*stream* ... NM-5
Arroyo Mocho—*stream* ... CA-9
*Arroyo Monias* ... TX-5
Arroyo Monte Belen—*valley* ... NM-5
Arroyo Monte Largo—*stream* ... NM-5
Arroyo Montosa—*stream* ... NM-5
Arroyo Montoso—*stream* ... NM-5
Arroyo Montoya—*valley* ... NM-5
Arroyo Moquino—*stream* ... NM-5
Arroyo Mora—*valley* ... NM-5
Arroyo (Municipio)—*civil* ... PR-3
Arroyo Naranjo—*stream* ... NM-5
Arroyo Needam—*stream* ... NM-5
Arroyo Nine—*stream* ... NM-5
*Arroyo Nobre de Dios* ... TX-5
Arroyo Noria—*stream* ... NM-5
Arroyo Ocole—*stream* ... NM-5
Arroyo Ojito—*stream* (2) ... NM-5
Arroyo Ojitos—*stream* ... NM-5
Arroyo Ojo Verde—*stream* ... NM-5
Arroyo Padre Flat—*flat* ... CA-9
*Arroyo Pagosa* ... NM-5
Arroyo Pajarito—*stream* ... NM-5
*Arroyo Palo Alto* ... TX-5
Arroyo Pantadeleon—*stream* ... NM-5
*Arroyo Parida* ... CA-9
*Arroyo Parida Creek* ... CA-9
Arroyo Park—*park* ... AZ-5
*Arroyo Pasajero* ... CA-9
Arroyo Pato—*stream* ... NM-5
Arroyo Pecos—*stream* ... NM-5
Arroyo Pelon—*stream* ... NM-5
Arroyo Penasco—*stream* ... NM-5
Arroyo Piedra Lumbre—*stream* (2) ... NM-5
Arroyo Piedra Parada—*stream* ... NM-5
*Arroyo Piedras Pintos* ... TX-5
Arroyo Pino—*stream* ... NM-5
Arroyo Ponil—*stream* ... NM-5
*Arroyo Poso De Chane* ... CA-9
Arroyo Potrillo—*stream* ... NM-5
Arroyo (Pueblo)—*fmr MCD* ... PR-3
Arroyo Pueblo Alto—*stream* ... NM-5
Arroyo Puertacito de los Salado—*stream* ... NM-5
Arroyo Puertecita—*stream* ... NM-5
Arroyo Puerto—*stream* ... NM-5
Arroyo Punche—*stream* ... NM-5
Arroyo Ranchito—*valley* ... NM-5
Arroyo Rancho—*stream* ... NM-5
Arroyo Rendia—*stream* ... NM-5
Arroyo Rendija—*stream* ... NM-5
Arroyo Rico—*stream* ... NM-5
*Arroyo Rodriquez* ... TX-5
Arroyo Rosa de Castillo—*stream* ... NM-5
Arroyo Saiz—*valley* ... NM-5
*Arroyo Salada Wash* ... CA-9
Arroyo Saladito—*stream* ... NM-5
Arroyo Salado—*stream* (2) ... NM-5
Arroyo Salado—*valley* (2) ... NM-5
Arroyo Salitre—*stream* ... NM-5
*Arroyo San Antonio* ... CA-9
Arroyo San Antonio—*stream* (2) ... NM-5
Arroyo San Antonio—*valley* ... NM-5
*Arroyo San Augustin* ... CA-9
*Arroyo San Augustine* ... CA-9
*Arroyo San Caropforo* ... CA-9
*Arroyo San Carpojo* ... CA-9
Arroyo Sanchez—*valley* ... NM-5
Arroyo Sandoval—*stream* ... NM-5
Arroyo San Jose—*stream* ... NM-5
Arroyo San Juan de Dios—*stream* ... NM-5
Arroyo San Lazaro—*stream* ... NM-5
*Arroyo Santana* ... TX-5
*Arroyo San Ysidro* ... CA-9
Arroyo Sarcio—*stream* ... NM-5
*Arroyo Sauce* ... TX-5
*Arroyo Sausal* ... CA-9
Arroyo Sch—*school* ... AZ-5
Arroyo Sch—*school* (2) ... CA-9
Arroyos Ditch—*canal* ... NM-5
Arroyo Seccion—*stream* ... NM-5
*Arroyo Seco* ... CA-9
Arroyo Seco—*civil* (2) ... CA-9
**Arroyo Seco**—*pop pl* ... NM-5
Arroyo Seco—*stream* (2) ... CA-9
Arroyo Seco—*stream* (8) ... NM-5
Arroyo Seco—*valley* ... NM-5
*Arroyo Seco De Los Capitancillos* ... CA-9
Arroyo Seco Ditch—*canal* ... NM-5
Arroyo Seco Park—*park* ... CA-9
Arroyo Seco Recreation Center—*park* ... CA-9
Arroyo Seco Sch—*school* ... CA-9
Arroyo Seco Tank—*reservoir* ... AZ-5
Arroyo Seco Trail—*trail* ... CA-9
Arroyo Sejitas—*stream* ... NM-5
Arroyo Semilla—*stream* ... NM-5
Arroyo Serrano—*valley* ... NM-5
*Arroyo Siquis* ... CA-9
*Arroyo Siquit* ... CA-9
Arroyo Six—*stream* ... NM-5
Arroyos Ranch—*locale* ... TX-5
Arroyo Suela—*stream* ... NM-5
Arroyo Tank—*reservoir* ... NM-5
Arroyo Techillas—*stream* ... NM-5
Arroyo Tenorio—*valley* ... NM-5
Arroyo Tetilla—*stream* ... NM-5
Arroyo Tierra Blanca—*stream* (2) ... NM-5
Arroyo Tierra Blanca—*valley* ... NM-5
*Arroyo Tigre Grande* ... TX-5
Arroyo Tinaja—*stream* ... NM-5
Arroyo Tinajas—*stream* ... NM-5
Arroyo Tio Lino—*stream* ... NM-5
Arroyo Tonque—*stream* ... NM-5
Arroyo Torreon—*valley* ... NM-5
Arroyo Trujillo—*stream* ... NM-5
Arroyo Tuerto—*stream* ... NM-5
Arroyo Una de Gato—*stream* ... NM-5
Arroyo Valles—*stream* ... NM-5
Arroyo Val Verde—*stream* ... NM-5
Arroyo Veguita Blanca—*stream* ... NM-5
Arroyo Venada—*stream* ... NM-5
*Arroyo Verde* ... AZ-5
Arroyo Viejo—*stream* ... NM-5
Arroyo Viejo Recreation Center—*park* ... CA-9
Arroyo Windmill—*locale* ... TX-5
Arroyo Yeso—*stream* ... NM-5
Arroyo Yupa—*stream* ... NM-5
Arroyo Zia—*stream* ... NM-5
Arroz—*locale* ... CA-9
Arrozal (Barrio)—*fmr MCD* ... PR-3
Arrs Mtn—*summit* ... TX-5
*Arruu-Hana* ... FM-9
Arrwood Mill—*locale* ... NC-3
Arsco—*locale* ... NM-5
Arsenal—*locale* ... UT-8
Arsenal—*uninc pl* ... PA-2
Arsenal (CCD)—*cens area* ... AL-4
Arsenal Division—*civil* ... AL-4
Arsenal Hill—*hist pl* ... SC-3
**Arsenal Hill**—*pop pl* ... NY-2
Arsenal Hill—*summit* ... MO-7
Arsenal House—*hist pl* ... NY-2
Arsenal Island—*island* ... IL-6
Arsenal JHS—*hist pl* ... PA-2
Arsenal JHS—*school* ... PA-2
Arsenal (Joliet Army Ammunition Plant)—*other* ... IL-6
Arsenal Park—*park* ... LA-4
Arsenal Sch—*school* ... CT-1
Arsenal Station—*locale* ... IA-7
Arsenal Street Cem—*cemetery* ... NY-2
Arsenal Technical HS—*school* ... IN-6
**Arsenal Villa**—*pop pl* ... UT-8
Arsenault Creek—*stream* ... MI-6
Arsenault Lake—*lake* ... MI-6
Arsenic Bank—*bar* ... FL-3
Arsenic Canyon—*valley* ... OR-9
Arsenic Cave—*cave* ... AZ-5
Arsenic Creek—*stream* ... AK-9
Arsenic Creek—*stream* ... MT-8
Arsenic Gulch—*valley* ... UT-8
Arsenicker Key—*island* ... FL-3
*Arsenic Lake* ... ID-8
Arsenic Lake—*lake* ... CO-8
Arsenic Mtn—*summit* ... MT-8
*Arsenic Peak* ... MT-8
Arsenic Spring—*spring* ... CA-9
Arsenic Tank—*reservoir* ... AZ-5
Arsenic Tubs—*locale* ... AZ-5
**Arshamonaque**—*pop pl* ... NY-2
Arson Creek—*stream* ... ID-8
Arsons Garden—*flat* ... UT-8
Arsperdell Ch—*church* ... LA-4
Arstell Creek—*stream* ... OR-9
A Rsvr—*reservoir* ... OR-9
Art—*locale* ... TX-5
**Art**—*pop pl* ... IN-6
*Arta* ... AL-4
Arta Lake—*lake* ... UT-8
**Artanna**—*pop pl* ... OH-6
Art Annex—*hist pl* ... NM-5
Arta P.O. (historical)—*locale* ... AL-4
**Artas**—*pop pl* ... SD-7
Artas Cem—*cemetery* ... SD-7
Artas Township (historical)—*civil* ... SD-7
**Artau**—*pop pl* ... PR-3
Art Canyon—*valley* ... UT-8
Art Center Sch—*school* ... CA-9
Art City Sch—*school* ... UT-8
Art Creek—*stream* ... WA-9
Art Creek—*stream* ... WY-8
Arteburn Point—*summit* ... TX-5
Art Ekland Draw—*valley* ... WY-8
*Artemagan* ... MH-9
**Artemas**—*pop pl* ... PA-2
**Artemus**—*pop pl* ... KY-4
Artemus Ward Sch—*school* ... OH-6
Arter, Mount—*summit* ... WY-8
Arter, Solomon, House—*hist pl* ... MD-2
Arterberry Cem—*cemetery* ... IL-6
Arterberry Cove—*bay* ... TX-5
Arterburn Branch—*stream* ... TN-4
Arterburn Lake—*reservoir* ... NE-7
Arterial Canyon—*valley* ... NV-8
Arters Branch—*stream* ... NC-3
Arters Mill—*locale* ... MD-2
Artesa—*locale* ... AZ-5
*Artesa Mount* ... AZ-5
Artesa Mountains—*summit* ... AZ-5
*Artesa Ranch* ... AZ-5
*Artesa Range* ... AZ-5
*Artesia* ... AZ-5
*Artesia* ... CO-8
*Artesia* ... FL-3
Artesia—*cens area* ... CO-8
Artesia—*locale* ... AZ-5
Artesia—*other* ... FL-3
**Artesia**—*pop pl* ... CA-9
**Artesia**—*pop pl* ... MS-4
**Artesia**—*pop pl* ... NM-5
**Artesia**—*pop pl* ... NC-3
Artesia, Lake—*lake* ... NC-3
**Artesia Beach**—*pop pl* ... MI-6
**Artesia Beach**—*pop pl* ... WI-6
**Artesia Camp**—*pop pl* ... NM-5
Artesia (CCD)—*cens area* ... NM-5
Artesia Cem—*cemetery* ... AZ-5
Artesia Cem—*cemetery* ... CA-9
Artesia Christian Sch—*school* ... CA-9
Artesia Country Club—*other* ... NM-5
Artesia Creek—*stream* ... TX-5
*Artesia Depot* ... MS-4
*Artesia Heights* ... NV-8
Artesia HS—*school* ... CA-9
Artesia Lake—*lake* ... NV-8
*Artesia Mountains* ... AZ-5
Artesian—*locale* ... IA-7
**Artesian**—*pop pl* ... AR-4
**Artesian**—*pop pl* ... SD-7
*Artesian Beach* ... WI-6
Artesian Beach, The—*beach* ... OK-5
Artesian Branch—*stream* ... MO-7
Artesian Cem—*cemetery* ... AR-4
*Artesian Cemetery* ... SD-7
*Artesian City* ... SD-7
Artesian City—*locale* ... ID-8
Artesian Coulee—*valley* ... WA-9
*Artesian Creek* ... WY-8
Artesian Creek—*stream* (2) ... TX-5
Artesian Draw—*valley* ... WY-8
Artesian Hollow—*valley* ... AL-4
Artesian Lake—*lake* ... WA-9
Artesian Lake—*reservoir* ... IA-7
Artesian Lake—*reservoir* ... MO-7
Artesian Lake County Park—*park* ... IA-7
Artesian Manufacturing and Bottling Company Bldg—*hist pl* ... TX-5
Artesiano Windmill—*locale* ... TX-5
Artesian Park—*locale* ... TX-5
Artesian Park—*park* ... IL-6
Artesian Park—*park* ... TX-5
Artesian Pasture—*flat* ... KS-7
Artesian Pen Windmill—*locale* ... TX-5
Artesian Presbyterian Ch—*church* ... SD-7
Artesian Slough—*gut* ... TX-5
Artesian Spring Campgrounds—*locale* ... CA-9
Artesian Tank—*reservoir* ... TX-5
Artesian Valley—*valley* ... KS-7
**Artesian Village**—*pop pl* ... AK-9
Artesian Water Co. Pumphouse and Wells—*hist pl* ... ID-8
Artesian Well—*well* ... CA-9
Artesian Well Park—*park* ... UT-8
Artesian Wesleyan Methodist Ch—*church* ... SD-7
Artesian Windmill—*locale* ... NM-5
Artesia Oil Field—*other* ... NM-5
Artesia Park—*park* ... CA-9
Artesia Ranch—*locale* ... NV-8
Artesia Sch—*school* ... AZ-5
Artesia Sch—*school* ... CA-9
Artesia Sch—*school* ... NC-3
Artesia Tank—*reservoir* ... NM-5
**Artesia (Township of)**—*pop pl* ... IL-6
**Artesia Wells**—*pop pl* ... TX-5
Artesia Windmill—*locale* ... NM-5
Artex—*locale* ... AR-4
Art Gallery—*hist pl* ... ME-1
Art Gallery Bldg—*hist pl* ... MI-6
Artherholt Cem—*cemetery* ... OH-6
Artheusa Springs Park—*park* ... OH-6
Art Hill—*ridge* ... AZ-5
Arthington Branch—*stream* ... IN-6
Arth Pasture—*flat* ... UT-8
Arthun Ditch—*canal* ... MT-8
Arthun Ranch—*locale* ... MT-8
*Arthur* ... AL-4
*Arthur* ... SC-3
Arthur—*locale* ... KY-4
Arthur—*locale* ... UT-8
Arthur—*locale* ... WV-2
**Arthur**—*pop pl* ... AR-4
**Arthur**—*pop pl* ... IL-6
**Arthur**—*pop pl* ... IN-6
**Arthur**—*pop pl* ... IA-7
**Arthur**—*pop pl* ... MI-6
**Arthur**—*pop pl* ... MO-7
**Arthur**—*pop pl* ... NE-7
**Arthur**—*pop pl* ... NV-8
**Arthur**—*pop pl* ... NY-2
**Arthur**—*pop pl* ... ND-7
**Arthur**—*pop pl* ... OH-6
**Arthur**—*pop pl* ... OK-5
**Arthur**—*pop pl* ... TN-4
**Arthur**—*pop pl* ... VA-3
**Arthur**—*pop pl* ... WI-6
Arthur, Charles and Lewis, E. N. House—*hist pl* ... NM-5
Arthur, Chester A., House—*hist pl* ... NY-2
Arthur, Lake—*lake* ... FL-3
Arthur, Lake—*lake* ... LA-4
Arthur, Lake—*lake* ... MN-6
Arthur, Lake—*reservoir* ... AL-4
Arthur, Lake—*reservoir* ... CA-9
Arthur, Lake—*reservoir* ... PA-2
Arthur, L. J., House—*hist pl* ... WI-6
Arthur, Mount—*summit* ... CO-8
Arthur, Thomas, House—*hist pl* ... IA-7
Arthur Airp—*airport* ... PA-2
Arthur Bay—*bay* ... MI-6
Arthur Bay—*bay* ... NE-7
Arthur Bay—*locale* ... MI-6
Arthur Canyon—*valley* ... NV-8
Arthur Cem—*cemetery* ... AL-4
Arthur Cem—*cemetery* ... IN-6
Arthur Cem—*cemetery* ... KY-4
Arthur Cem—*cemetery* ... MI-6
Arthur Cem—*cemetery* ... MS-4
Arthur Cem—*cemetery* ... MO-7
Arthur Cem—*cemetery* ... NY-2
Arthur Cem—*cemetery* ... ND-7
Arthur Cem—*cemetery* ... OH-6
Arthur Cem—*cemetery* ... TN-4
Arthur Cem—*cemetery* ... WV-2
Arthur Cem Number Two—*cemetery* ... AL-4
Arthur Center Ch—*church* ... MI-6
Arthur Chapel—*church* ... VA-3
Arthur Circle Sch—*school* ... LA-4
**Arthur City**—*pop pl* ... TX-5
Arthur C Newby Elem Sch—*school* ... IN-6
*Arthur Concentration Mill* ... UT-8
*Arthur Cook School* ... AL-4
Arthur Cove—*bay* ... VA-3
*Arthur Creek* ... TX-5
Arthur Creek—*stream* ... AL-4
Arthur Creek—*stream* ... LA-4
Arthur Creek—*stream* ... MO-7
Arthur Creek Sch—*school* ... MO-7
**Arthurdale**—*pop pl* ... WV-2
Arthurdale Cem—*cemetery* ... WV-2
Arthurdale Sch—*school* ... WV-2
Arthur Dall Lake—*lake* ... AK-9
Arthur Dam—*dam* ... TN-4
Arthur Ditch—*canal* ... IN-6
Arthur Drain—*canal* ... MI-6
Arthur Dunlap Farm Cem—*cemetery* ... OH-6
Arthur Dunn Airpark—*airport* ... FL-3
Arthur Field—*airport* ... ND-7
Arthur Gates Sch—*school* ... NY-2
*Arthur Goodman Memorial Park* ... NC-3
**Arthur Heights**—*pop pl* ... KS-7
Arthur (historical)—*locale* ... KS-7
Arthur (historical)—*locale* ... MS-4
**Arthur (historical)**—*pop pl* (2) ... OR-9
*Arthur Island* ... MP-9
Arthur Island—*island* ... AK-9
Arthur Jones Creek—*stream* ... OR-9
**Arthur Jones Estate Subdivision**—*pop pl* ... UT-8
Arthur Kill—*stream* ... NJ-2
Arthur Kill—*stream* ... NY-2
*Arthur Koll* ... NJ-2
*Arthur Kull* ... NJ-2
*Arthur Lake* ... PA-2
Arthur Lake—*lake* ... CA-9
Arthur Lake—*lake* ... MN-6
Arthur Lake—*reservoir* ... NC-3
Arthur Lake—*reservoir* ... TN-4
Arthurmabel—*locale* ... KY-4
**Arthurmable**—*pop pl* ... KY-4
**Arthur Manor**—*pop pl* ... NY-2
*Arthur McGill Elementary School* ... PA-2
Arthur McGill Sch—*school* ... PA-2

Arthur Municipal Airp—airport IN-6
Arthur Owens Mine (underground)—mine AL-4
Arthur Pack Desert Golf Course AZ-5
Arthur Pack Regional Park—park AZ-5
Arthur Peak—summit AK-9
Arthur Peak—summit WA-9
Arthur Peak—summit WY-8
Arthur Playground—park MI-6
Arthur P Melton Elem Sch—school IN-6
Arthur P.O. (historical)—locale AL-4
Arthur Point—cape AK-9
Arthur Posey Pit—cave AL-4
Arthur Post Office—building TN-4
Arthur Ranch—locale WY-8
Arthur Reeves Branch—stream TX-5
Arthur Ridge—ridge KY-4
Arthur (RR name for Bellarthur)—other NC-3
Arthurs—locale PA-2
Arthur Saltpeter Cave—cave TN-4
**Arthursburg**—pop pl NY-2
Arthur Sch—school AL-4
Arthur Sch—school IA-7
Arthur Sch—school MI-6
Arthur Sch—school OH-6
Arthur Sch—school OK-5
Arthur Sch—school PA-2
Arthur Sch (historical)—school TN-4
Arthurs Creek—stream NC-3
Arthur Seat MA-1
Arthurs Fork—stream UT-8
Arthurs Island IN-6
Arthur S Kingman Lake—reservoir IN-6
Arthur S Kingman Lake Dam—dam IN-6
Arthurs Knob Sch—school VA-3
Arthurs Lake—lake TX-5
Arthur Slough—gut LA-4
Arthur Slough—stream LA-4
Arthurs Meadow Draw—valley AZ-5
Arthur Smith Covered Bridge—bridge MA-1
Arthur Smith Sch—school WA-9
Arthurs Pond—reservoir NY-2
Arthur Spring—spring CO-8
Arthur Spring—spring MO-7
Arthur Spring Ford—locale MO-7
Arthurs Rock—pillar CO-8
Arthurs Rock Gulch—valley CO-8
Arthurs Rsvr—reservoir CO-8
Arthurs Seat—summit MA-1
Arthurstown SC-3
Arthursville DE-2
Arthur Swamp—stream VA-3
Arthur Tank—reservoir TX-5
Arthur T Howells MS—school PA-2
**Arthurtown**—pop pl SC-3
**Arthur (Town of)**—pop pl WI-6
**Arthur Township**—pop pl ND-7
Arthur (Township of)—fmr MCD NC-3
**Arthur (Township of)**—pop pl MI-6
**Arthur (Township of)**—pop pl (2) MN-6
Arthur United Methodist Ch—church TN-4
Arthurville DE-2
Arthur Von Briesen Park—park NY-2
Arthur V Watkins Dam—dam UT-8
Arthur Wellborn Sch (historical)—school AL-4
Arthur W Holzwarth Dam—dam SD-7
Arthur Williams and Son Number One Dam—dam NC-3
Arthur Williams and Son Number Two Dam—dam NC-3
Arthur Williams and Sons Dam Number Three—dam NC-3
Arthur Williams Dam—dam NC-3
Arthur Williams Dam Number Two—dam NC-3
Arthur W Spalding Sch—school TN-4
Arthur W Way County Memorial Park—park CA-9
Arthus FM-9
Arthyde—locale MN-6
Arthyde Stone House—hist pl MN-6
Artic—locale WA-9
**Artic**—pop pl IN-6
Artic Center RI-1
Artic Farm—locale ND-7
Artichoke—locale MN-6
Artichoke Brook MA-1
Artichoke Butte—summit SD-7
Artichoke Creek—stream MN-6
Artichoke Creek—stream SD-7
Artichoke Lake—lake (2) MN-6
**Artichoke Lake**—pop pl MN-6
Artichoke Lake Cem—cemetery MN-6
Artichoke Lake Ch—church MN-6
Artichoke Post Office (historical)—building SD-7
Artichoke River—stream MA-1
Artichoke River—stream MN-6
Artichoke River Dam—dam MA-1
Artichoke River Rsvr—reservoir MA-1
Artichoke River Upper Rsvr MA-1
Artichoke Township—civil SD-7
**Artichoke (Township of)**—pop pl MN-6
Artic Inn Lake IL-6
**Artie**—pop pl IN-6
**Artie**—pop pl WV-2
Artie Cem—cemetery WV-2
Artie Hollow Trail—trail TN-4
Arties Pond—lake GA-3
Artificial Island—island DE-2
Artificial Island—island NJ-2
Artificial Lake—reservoir AR-4
Artigas Statue—park DC-2
Artigotrat—cliff AK-9
Artillery, Lake—lake FL-3
Artillery Bay—bay NV-8
Artillery Creek—stream ID-8
Artillery Dome—summit ID-8
Artillery Hill—summit CA-9
Artillery Hill—summit CT-1
Artillery Hill—summit KS-7
Artillery Lake—lake ID-8
Artillery Lake—lake LA-4
Artillery Mountains—range AZ-5
Artillery Mtn—summit OK-5
Artillery Park—hist pl RI-1
Artillery Peak—summit AZ-5
Artillery Peaks AZ-5
Artillery Ridge—ridge OK-5
Artillery Ridge—summit VA-3
Artillery Spring—spring WY-8
**Artillery Village**—pop pl OK-5
Artimus Owens Dam—dam NC-3
Artingall PW-9
Art Institute—school MO-7
Art Institute of Fort Lauderdale—school FL-3
Art Institute Of Pittsburgh—school PA-2
Artisan's House—hist pl MD-2
Artis Cem—cemetery NC-3
Artist Brook—stream NH-1
Artist Creek—stream CA-9
Artist Glen—valley WI-6
**Artistic Subdivision**—pop pl UT-8
**Artistic Terrace Subdivision**—pop pl UT-8
Artist Island—island OH-6
Artist Lake—lake NY-2
Artist Point WA-9
Artist Point—cape ME-1
Artist Point—cape WY-8
Artist Point—locale AR-4
Artist Point—locale CA-9
**Artist Point**—pop pl IN-6
Artist Point—summit CA-9
Artist Rock—summit NH-1
Artists Bluff—cliff NH-1
Artists Falls—falls NY-2
Artists Glen—valley CO-8
Artists Paintpots—spring WY-8
Artists Palette—summit CA-9
Artists Point—cliff CO-8
Artists Rock—cliff NY-2
**Artists View Heights Subdivision**—pop pl UT-8
Artists Vista Point—locale MT-8
Art Lake—lake (2) WA-9
Artleborough PA-2
Art Lewis Glacier—glacier AK-9
Artman Basin—basin OR-9
Artman Ditch—canal IN-6
Artman Sch—school PA-2
Art McKay Dam—dam OR-9
Art McKay Rsvr—reservoir OR-9
Art Moore Ranch—locale OR-9
**Artois**—pop pl CA-9
Artois Cem—cemetery CA-9
Artomagan MH-9
**Artondale**—pop pl WA-9
Artondale Creek—stream WA-9
Artonish—locale MS-4
Artonish Lake—lake MS-4
Artonish Landing—locale MS-4
Artonish Plantation (historical)—locale MS-4
Artonish Post Office (historical)—building MS-4
Artonish Sch (historical)—school MS-4
Artray Creek—stream CA-9
**Artrip**—pop pl VA-3
Artrip Branch—stream WV-2
Artrip Cem—cemetery (3) VA-3
Artrip Cem—cemetery WV-2
Arts and Industries Bldg—hist pl DC-2
Arts and Science Museum—locale NC-3
Art's Auto—hist pl RI-1
Arts Canyon—valley UT-8
Arts Club of Washington—hist pl DC-2
Arts HS—school NJ-2
Arts Knoll—summit WA-9
Arts of Peace Statue—park DC-2
Arts of War Statue—park DC-2
Arts Pasture UT-8
Arts Peak—summit CA-9
Arts Spring—spring AZ-5
Arts Tank—reservoir AZ-5
Art Stewart Ridge—ridge NC-3
Arts Trail—trail PA-2
Art Tank—reservoir NM-5
**Arturo Lluberas**—pop pl PR-3
Artus Creek—stream WI-6
Artussee Indian Ch—church OK-5
**Art Village**—pop pl NY-2
Artville—locale KY-4
Artz, John, Farmhouse—hist pl OH-6
Artz Cem—cemetery IL-6
Artz Coulee—valley MT-8
Artz House—hist pl OH-6
Artz Sch—school WA-9
Artz-Wenzel Cem—cemetery MO-7
Aru FM-9
Arubai Island MP-9
Arubai-to MP-9
Arubaketsu PW-9
Arubaru MP-9
Arubaru Island MP-9
Arubaru-to MP-9
Aruba To MP-9
Arubodoru PW-9
Aruboe—island MP-9
Aruboe Island MP-9
Aruboe-To MP-9
Arubon Mountain PW-9
Arucenas, Point—cape AK-9
Aru Channel FM-9
Arudowaishi Point—cape PW-9
Arue MP-9
Aru Einfahrt Channel FM-9
Aru Einfarht FM-9
Aruen MP-9
Arugaren Island—island (2) MP-9
Arugaren-To MP-9
Aruguru To PW-9
Aru Hafen FM-9
Aru-Hana FM-9
Aru Harbor FM-9
Aruh Passage—channel FM-9
Arujerii Island MP-9
Arujerii Island—island MP-9
Arujerii-to MP-9
Arukanui Island—island FM-9
Arukaron Point—cape PW-9
Arukeshi PW-9
Arukeshi To PW-9
Arukodorokkoru PW-9
Arukuson River PW-9
Arumaska PW-9
Arumaten Hana PW-9
Arumaten Head PW-9
Arumaten Point PW-9
Arumenii Island MP-9
Arumenii Island—island MP-9
Arumeni Island MP-9
Arumeni-to MP-9
Arumizu PW-9
Arumizu Bay PW-9
Arumizu Wan PW-9
Arumongui PW-9
Arumongui Point PW-9
Arumongui River PW-9
Arumonogui PW-9
Arumukudeu To PW-9
Arumuzu PW-9
Aruna MP-9
Arunasat—spring FM-9
Arunasat—well FM-9
Arunaten Head PW-9
Arunde—locale MS-4
Arundel—locale FL-3
**Arundel**—pop pl DE-2
**Arundel**—pop pl ME-1
**Arundel**—pop pl MD-2
Arundel, Cape—cape ME-1
**Arundel Beach**—pop pl MD-2
Arundel Cem—cemetery ME-1
Arundel Ch—church MD-2
Arundel Cove—bay MD-2
Arundel Cove Archaeol Site—hist pl MD-2
**Arundel Gardens**—pop pl MD-2
Arundel HS—school MD-2
Arundel Lateral—canal CA-9
Arundell Barranca—valley CA-9
Arundell Peak—summit CA-9
Arundell Spring—spring CA-9
Arundel on the Bay—bay MD-2
**Arundel on the Bay**—pop pl MD-2
Arundel Plantation—locale SC-3
**Arundel Plaza**—pop pl MD-2
Arundel Ridge—ridge MD-2
Arundel Sch—school CA-9
Arundel Spring—spring MS-4
Arundel Swamp—swamp ME-1
Arundel Swamp Brook—stream ME-1
**Arundel (Town of)**—pop pl ME-1
**Arundel View**—pop pl MD-2
**Arundel Village**—pop pl PA-2
**Arundel Village (subdivision)**—pop pl MD-2
Aruno MP-9
Aruno Island MP-9
Aruno-to MP-9
Arunoto To MP-9
Aru Point FM-9
Arurakku MP-9
Arurukoku San PW-9
**Arus**—pop pl (2) PR-3
Aru Spitz FM-9
Aru Spitze FM-9
Arusuk ME-1
Arutoerruru Reef PW-9
Arutoeruru Reef PW-9
Arutoeruru Sho PW-9
Aruu FM-9
Aruusuido FM-9
Aruwol FM-9
Arva, Mount—summit AR-4
**Arvada**—pop pl CO-8
**Arvada**—pop pl WY-8
Arvada Cem—cemetery WY-8
Arvada Filtration Plant—other CO-8
Arvada Flour Mill—hist pl CO-8
Arvada Heights CO-8
Arvada Plaza—locale CO-8
Arvada Square—locale CO-8
Arvada West HS—school CO-8
Arvado CO-8
Arvana—locale TX-5
**Arvard (historical)**—pop pl OR-9
Arvel—locale KY-4
Arver Glacier OR-9
**Arverne**—pop pl NY-2
**Arveson (Township of)**—pop pl MN-6
Arvesta Creek—stream (2) AK-9
Arvid, Lake—lake MI-6
Arvida JHS—school FL-3
Arvida Park—park FL-3
Arvid Sch—school ND-7
Arvig Creek—stream MN-6
**Arvilla**—pop pl ND-7
**Arvilla**—pop pl WV-2
Arvilla, Lake—lake MN-6
Arvilla Cem—cemetery ND-7
Arvilla Lookout Station—locale MT-8
**Arvilla Township**—pop pl ND-7
**Arvin**—pop pl CA-9
Arvin Cem—cemetery KY-4
**Arvin Farm Labor Center**—pop pl CA-9
Arvin Farm Labor Supply Center—locale CA-9
Arvin-Lamont (CCD)—cens area CA-9
Arvin Ranch Airp—airport MO-7
Arvin Sch—school NH-1
Arvin Tanks—reservoir NM-5
Arvison Flat—flat CA-9
Arvizu's El Fresnal Grocery Store—hist pl AZ-5
Arvola Gulch—valley CA-9
Arvon VA-3
Arvon Ch—church VA-3
Arvondale—locale WV-2
Arvondale Junction WV-2
Arvondor Apartments—hist pl UT-8
**Arvonia**—pop pl KS-7
**Arvonia**—pop pl VA-3
Arvonia Cem—cemetery KS-7
Arvonia (historical)—locale KS-7
Arvonia Station KS-7
**Arvonia Township**—pop pl KS-7
Arvon Lookout Tower—locale MI-6
**Arvon (Township of)**—pop pl MI-6
A R Windmill—locale TX-5
Arwine Cem—cemetery TX-5
Arwine Ford (historical)—crossing TN-4
Arwirnuk Rock—island AK-9
**Arwold**—pop pl OH-6
Arwood Cem—cemetery NC-3
Arwood Cem—cemetery TN-4
Arwood Hollow—valley VA-3
Arwood Sch (historical)—school AL-4
**Ary**—pop pl KY-4
Ary Cem—cemetery KY-4
Ary Cem—cemetery TN-4
Aryins Store—locale VA-3
Ary Post Office—locale KY-4
Arystown NJ-2
Arytown Ch—church MO-7
Arzberger Site—hist pl SD-7
Arzina—locale WA-9
**Arzina**—pop pl WA-9
Arzt State Wildlife Mngmt Area—park MN-6
Asa—locale KY-4
**Asa**—pop pl MS-4
**Asa**—pop pl TX-5
Asa, Lake—lake GA-3
Asa B Douglas Lake—reservoir TN-4
Asa B Douglas Lake Dam—dam TN-4
Asa Bean Flat—flat CA-9
Asa Bean Ridge—ridge CA-9
Asa Bear Crossing—locale CA-9
Asabeth River MA-1
Asa Breland Cem—cemetery MS-4
Asa Cove—bay GA-3
Asa Cove—valley NC-3
Asa Creek LA-4
Asa Creek—stream IL-6
Asa Creek—stream KY-4
Asa Creek Ch—church LA-4
Asadores Cem—cemetery TX-5
Asafan—area GU-9
Asa Flats Ch—church KY-4
**Asagas**—pop pl GU-9
Asaga Strait—channel AS-9
Asagatai Point—cape AS-9
Asaguero—area GU-9
Asahel—locale AL-4
Asa Island—island ME-1
Asakina MH-9
Asa Lake—lake CA-9
Asalonso—area GU-9
Asalonso River—stream GU-9
Asalonso Spring—spring GU-9
Asamam MH-9
Asa Moore Canyon—valley NV-8
A Samuelson Number 1 Dam—dam SD-7
**Asan**—pop pl GU-9
Asanap—bar FM-9
Asanario—area GU-9
Asan Bay—bay GU-9
Asander—other TX-5
Asan (Election District)—fmr MCD GU-9
Asan Invasion Beach—hist pl GU-9
Asanite Bay—bay GU-9
Asanite Cave—cave GU-9
Asanite Point—cape GU-9
Asan Point—cape GU-9
Asan Ridge Battle Area—hist pl GU-9
Asan River—stream GU-9
Asan Spring—spring GU-9
Asa Packer Elem Sch—school PA-2
Asaph—locale PA-2
Asaph Peak—summit PA-2
Asaph Run—stream PA-2
Asaph Run Picnic Area—area PA-2
Asaph Run Picnic Area—park PA-2
Asa Pond—lake RI-1
**Asarco Mill**—pop pl NM-5
Asasama Point—cape AS-9
Asas Island ME-1
Asas Island—island NY-2
Asa Spring—spring AZ-5
Asatdas—locale GU-9
Asa Township (historical)—civil SD-7
Asa Wood JHS—school MT-8
Asay Bench—bench UT-8
Asay Creek UT-8
Asay Creek—stream UT-8
Asay Knoll—summit UT-8
Asay Ranch—locale ID-8
Asay Spring—spring UT-8
Asays Rsvr—reservoir WY-8
Asay Town—locale UT-8
Asbahr Lake—lake OR-9
ASB Bridge—other MO-7
**Asbeco**—pop pl GU-9
Asbell Cem—cemetery IL-6
Asbell Cem—cemetery MO-7
Asbell Creek Bridge—bridge FL-3
Asbell Homestead Site—locale WY-8
Asbell Sch—school AR-4
Asberded MH-9
Asberry—locale AL-4
Asberry Baptist Ch—church AL-4
Asberry Cem—cemetery FL-3
Asberry Cem—cemetery MS-4
Asberry Cem—cemetery OH-6
Asberry Cem—cemetery TX-5
Asberry Cem—cemetery WV-2
Asberry Ch—church MD 2
Asberry Ch—church MS-4
Asberry Ch (historical)—church AL-4
Asberry Ch (historical)—church MS-4
Asberry Methodist Ch (historical)—church AL-4
Asberrys—locale VA-3
Asberry Sch—school TX-5
Asbery Ch AL-4
Asbery Mine—mine TN-4
Asbestos Canyon—valley AZ-5
Asbestos Ch—church GA-3
Asbestos Creek—stream AK-9
Asbestos Creek—stream ID-8
Asbestos Creek—stream MT-8
Asbestos Creek—stream WA-9
Asbestos Falls—falls WA-9
Asbestos Gulch—valley CA-9
**Asbestos (historical)**—pop pl OR-9
Asbestos Mine—mine CA-9
Asbestos Mtn—summit AK-9
Asbestos Mtn—summit CA-9
Asbestos Peak AZ-5
Asbestos Peak—summit ID-8
Asbestos Point—locale ID-8
Asbestos Point—summit AZ-5
Asbestos Ridge Mine—mine CA-9
Asbestos Spring—spring AZ-5
Asbestos Spring—spring CA-9
Asbestos Spring—spring (2) WY-8
Asbestos Tank—reservoir AZ-5
Asbill Cem—cemetery SC-3
Asbill Creek—stream (2) CA-9
Asbill Pond—reservoir SC-3
Asbridge Cem—cemetery KY-4
Asbridge Hollow—valley MO-7
Asburn Creek Sch (historical)—school TN-4
Asbury NJ-2
Asbury WV-2
Asbury—locale MN-6
Asbury—locale NJ-2
Asbury—locale NY-2
Asbury—locale (3) NC-3
Asbury—locale OH-6
Asbury—locale (4) TN-4
**Asbury**—pop pl (3) AL-4
**Asbury**—pop pl IA-7
**Asbury**—pop pl MO-7
**Asbury**—pop pl NJ-2
**Asbury**—pop pl NY-2
**Asbury**—pop pl (2) NC-3
**Asbury**—pop pl (2) PA-2
**Asbury**—pop pl SC-3
**Asbury**—pop pl (3) TN-4
**Asbury**—pop pl WV-2
Asbury, Henry, House—hist pl GA-3
Asbury, Lake—lake FL-3
Asbury Acres (Home for Retired)—building TN-4
Asbury Cem AL-4
Asbury Cem MS-4
Asbury Cem—cemetery (3) AL-4
Asbury Cem—cemetery DE-2
Asbury Cem—cemetery GA-3
Asbury Cem—cemetery (2) IL-6
Asbury Cem—cemetery (5) IN-6
Asbury Cem—cemetery (3) IA-7
Asbury Cem—cemetery (2) KY-4
Asbury Cem—cemetery (2) MS-4
Asbury Cem—cemetery NC-3
Asbury Cem—cemetery (5) OH-6
Asbury Cem—cemetery PA-2
Asbury Cem—cemetery (3) TN-4
Asbury Cem—cemetery (2) TX-5
Asbury Cem—cemetery VA-3
Asbury Cem—cemetery (3) WV-2
Asbury Cem—cemetery WI-6
Asbury Ch AL-4
Asbury Ch IN-6
Asbury Ch—church (6) AL-4
Asbury Ch—church DE-2
Asbury Ch—church (4) GA-3
Asbury Ch—church (7) IL-6
Asbury Ch—church (3) IN-6
Asbury Ch—church KY-4
Asbury Ch—church LA-4
Asbury Ch—church (7) MD-2
Asbury Ch—church MS-4
Asbury Ch—church (3) MO-7
Asbury Ch—church (4) NJ-2
Asbury Ch—church NM-5
Asbury Ch—church (3) NY-2
Asbury Ch—church (9) NC-3
Asbury Ch—church (6) OH-6
Asbury Ch—church OK-5
Asbury Ch—church (2) PA-2
Asbury Ch—church (3) SC-3
Asbury Ch—church (4) TN-4
Asbury Ch—church TX-5
Asbury Ch—church (9) VA-3
Asbury Ch—church WV-2
Asbury Ch—church WI-6
Asbury Chapel PA-2
Asbury Chapel—church IL-6
Asbury Chapel—church (3) IN-6
Asbury Chapel—church KY-4
Asbury Chapel—church MO-7
Asbury Chapel—church (2) OH-6
Asbury Chapel—church (2) TN-4
Asbury Chapel AME Zion Ch—church MS-4
Asbury Chapel Cem—cemetery OH-6
Asbury Chapel Cem—cemetery PA-2
Asbury Chapel Cem—cemetery TX-5
Asbury Chapel (historical)—church TN-4
Asbury Ch (historical)—church MS-4
Asbury Ch (historical)—church TN-4
Asbury Christian Sch—school FL-3
Asbury Church WV-2
**Asbury Church**—pop pl WV-2
Asbury Church—reservoir PA-2
Asbury Clark Memorial Ch—church SC-3
Asbury College Administration Bldg—hist pl KY-4
Asbury Congregational Methodist Ch—church MS-4
Asbury Creek—stream (2) CA-9
Asbury Creek—stream CO-8
Asbury Creek—stream OH-6
Asbury Creek—stream OR-9
Asbury Creek—stream TN-4
Asbury Dam—dam AL-4
Asbury Elementary School NC-3
Asbury Elementary School PA-2
Asbury Elem Sch—school TN-4
**Asbury Estates**—pop pl TN-4
Asbury Gap—gap VA-3
**Asbury Gardens**—pop pl NJ-2
**Asbury Grove**—pop pl MA-1
Asbury Hollow—valley WV-2
Asbury Home—building MD-2
Asbury Hosp—hospital MN-6
Asbury Knob—summit WV-2
Asbury Lake WI-6
Asbury Lake—CDP FL-3
Asbury Lake—reservoir WV-2
Asbury Lookout Tower—locale AL-4
Asbury Memorial Ch—church NC-3
Asbury Memorial Methodist Church TN-4
Asbury Methodist Ch MS-4
Asbury Methodist Ch—church DE-2
Asbury Methodist Ch—church (2) MS-4
Asbury Methodist Ch (historical)—church AL-4
Asbury Methodist Church AL-4
Asbury Methodist Church TN-4
Asbury Methodist Home—post sta MD-2
Asbury Methodist Kindergarten—school DE-2
Asbury Mission Ch—church SC-3
Asbury Mtn—summit NC-3
Asbury Park—park AL-4
Asbury Park—park IA-7
Asbury Park—park OH-6
**Asbury Park**—pop pl NJ-2
**Asbury Park Addition (subdivision)**—pop pl UT-8
Asbury Park Convention Hall—hist pl NJ-2
Asbury Park Lake—reservoir AL-4
Asbury Peak CA-9
Asbury Pipe—other CA-9
Asbury P.O. (historical—locale AL-4
Asbury Post Office (historical)—building TN-4
Asbury Quarry—mine TN-4
Asbury Ridge—ridge OH-6
Asbury Ridge—ridge WV-2
Asbury Ridge—ridge (2) WI-6
**Asbury (RR name Ludlow-Asbury)**—pop pl NJ-2
Asbury Sch—school AL-4
Asbury Sch—school CO-8
Asbury Sch—school FL-3
Asbury Sch—school IA-7
Asbury Sch—school LA-4
Asbury Sch—school NC-3
Asbury Sch—school PA-2
Asbury Sch—school SD-7
Asbury Sch—school (2) VA-3
Asbury Sch—school WV-2
Asbury Sch (historical)—school AL-4
Asbury Sch (historical)—school (4) TN-4
Asbury School MS-4
Asbury School TN-4
**Asbury (subdivision)**—pop pl AL-4
**Asbury (Township of)**—pop pl IL-6
Asbury Trail—trail NC-3
Asbury United Methodist Ch—church AL-4
Asbury United Methodist Ch—church (2) DE-2
Asbury United Methodist Ch—church FL-3
Asbury United Methodist Ch—church IN-6
Asbury United Methodist Ch—church (3) TN-4
Asbury United Methodist Church—hist pl DC-2
Asbury United Methodist Church—hist pl NH-1
Ascalmore, Lake—reservoir MS-4
Ascalmore Creek—stream MS-4
Ascalmore Creek Structure YO-30-15 Dam—dam MS-4
Ascalmore Creek Structure Yo-30-22 Dam—dam MS-4
Ascalmore Creek Structure YO-30-3 Dam—dam MS-4
Ascalmore Creek Structure YO-30-4 Dam—dam MS-4
Ascalmore Creek Structure Yo-30-6 Dam—dam MS-4
Ascalmore Creek Structure Yo-30-7 Dam—dam MS-4
Ascalmore Creek Structure Yo-30-8 Dam—dam MS-4
Ascalmore Creek Structure Y-17a-1 Dam—dam MS-4
Ascalmore Creek Structure Y-17a-11 Dam—dam MS-4
Ascalmore Creek Structure Y-17a-2 Dam—dam MS-4
Ascalmore Creek Structure Y-17a-5 Dam—dam MS-4
Ascalmore Creek Structure Y-17a-71 Dam—dam MS-4
Ascalmore Creek Structure Y-17a-72 Dam—dam MS-4
Ascalmore Creek Structure Y-17a-73 Dam—dam MS-4
Ascalmore Creek Structure Y-17a-76 Dam—dam MS-4
Ascalmore Creek Structure Y-17a-9 Dam—dam MS-4
Ascalmore Creek Y-17a-75 Dam—dam MS-4
Ascalmore Watershed Y-17a-72 Dam—dam MS-4
**Ascalon**—pop pl MO-7
Ascalon Sch—school GA-3
Ascarate—uninc pl TX-5
Ascarate Lake—lake TX-5
Ascarate Park—park TX-5
Ascauga Lake—lake SC-3
Ascensin, Mount—summit MT-8
Ascension IN-6
Ascension, Mount—summit AK-9
Ascension Acad—school VA-3
Ascension Brook PA-2
Ascension Cem—cemetery CA-9
Ascension Cem—cemetery IL-6
Ascension Ch—church IA-7
Ascension Ch—church LA-4
Ascension Ch—church MD-2
Ascension Ch—church (2) MI-6
Ascension Ch—church NJ-2
Ascension Ch—church NY-2
Ascension Ch—church (2) NC-3
Ascension Ch—church ND-7
Ascension Ch—church PA-2
Ascension Ch—church (2) SD-7
Ascension Ch—church WI-6
Ascension Ch (historical)—church SD-7
Ascension Child Care Center—school FL-3
Ascension Church Cem—cemetery NY-2
Ascension Day Care Center—school FL-3
Ascension Episcopal Church and Rectory—hist pl OR-9
Ascension HS—school LA-4
Ascension Island FM-9
Ascension Lutheran Ch—church AL-4
Ascension Lutheran Ch—church KS-7
Ascension Lutheran Ch—church MS-4
Ascension Lutheran Ch—church (2) UT-8
Ascension Lutheran Ch (ALC)—church FL-3
Ascension Lutheran Ch (Missouri Synod)—church FL-3
Ascension Mtn—summit CA-9
Ascension of Our Lord Catholic Church—hist pl TX-5
Ascension of Our Lord Chapel—hist pl AK-9
**Ascension Parish**—pop pl LA-4
Ascension Sch—school (2) CA-9
Ascension Sch—school (2) IL-6
Ascension Sch—school MI-6
Ascension Sch—school MN-6
Ascension Sch—school NJ-2
Ascension Sch—school NY-2
Ascension Sch—school (2) OH-6
Ascension Sch—school OR-9
Ascension Sch—school PA-2
Ascent Creek—stream ID-8
Ascequia CO-8
A Schletze—locale (2) TX-5
Aschman Pond NY-2
Aschoff Buttes—summit OR-9
Aschoff Buttes Trail—trail OR-9
Asco—locale CA-9
Asco—locale WV-2
Ascola Sito Creek—stream GU-9
Ascombs Island MD-2
**Ascot**—pop pl IA-7
Ascot, Point—cape MS-4
Ascot Ave Sch—school CA-9

**Ascot II (subdivision)**—*pop pl* NC-3
Ascot Park—*park* CA-9
Ascot Park—*park* OH-6
Ascot Park—*park* OR-9
Ascot Rsvr—*reservoir* CA-9
Asculano—*area* GU-9
*Ascuncion* MH-9
Ascutino—*area* GU-9
**Ascutney**—*pop pl* VT-1
Ascutney, Mount—*summit* VT-1
*Ascutney Mtn* VT-1
Ascutney Notch—*gap* VT-1
Ascutney State Park—*park* VT-1
*Ascutneyville* VT-1
Asdigues—*cliff* GU-9
*As Dodo'* MH-9
Asdonao Hill—*summit* GU-9
Asdonlucas—*basin* GU-9
*Asdudo* MH-9
*As Dudu* MH-9
Asdulili—*area* GU-9
Asebuches Arroyo—*valley* TX-5
*Ase Creek* LA-4
Asemblea de Dios—*church* UT-8
Aserdaten—*locale* NJ-2
A Seventy-three, Lateral—*canal* AZ-5
Asfaja—*locale* GU-9
*As Falipi* MH-9
*As Fantango* MH-9
Asgadao—*ridge* GU-9
Asgadao Bay—*bay* GU-9
Asgadao Creek—*stream* GU-9
Asgadao Island—*island* GU-9
*Asgard Pass* WA-9
*Asgawan* MH-9
Asgini Branch—*stream* NC-3
Asgini Ridge—*ridge* NC-3
*Asgonno* MH-9
*Asgono* MH-9
Asgon Point—*island* GU-9
*Asgurome* MH-9
Ash—*locale* MO-7
Ash—*locale* NC-3
Ash—*locale* OH-6
Ash—*locale* OR-9
Ash—*locale* TX-5
Ash—*locale* WA-9
**Ash**—*pop pl* OH-6
**Ash**—*pop pl* TX-5
**Ash Acres**—*pop pl* MI-6
**Ashaha**—*pop pl* OR-9
*Ashahr Lake* OR-9
*Ashakasengu* PW-9
*Ashakasengu Island* PW-9
*Ashakasenguru To* PW-9
A Shanholtzer Ranch—*locale* MT-8
**Ashantee**—*pop pl* NY-2
**Asharoken**—*pop pl* NY-2
Asharoken Beach—*beach* NY-2
*Asharoken Beach Sand Cove* NY-2
*Asharoken Beach Sand Hole* NY-2
*Ashauge River* RI-1
Ashawa—*locale* IA-7
*Ashawauge River* RI-1
**Ashaway**—*pop pl* RI-1
Ashaway River—*stream* CT-1
Ashaway River—*stream* RI-1
*Ashawog River* RI-1
Ashbacker Windmill—*locale* NM-5
*Ashbank* AL-4
**Ashbank**—*pop pl* (2) AL-4
*Ashbant* AL-4
Ashbaugh Airp—*airport* KS-7
Ashbaugh Creek—*stream* MT-8
Ashbaugh Hill—*summit* NY-2
Ashbaugh Lake—*lake* TN-4
Ashbaugh Park—*park* NM-5
Ash Bayou—*gut* LA-4
Ash Bayou—*stream* LA-4
Ash Bayou—*stream* MS-4
Ash Bayou—*stream* TN-4
Ash Bear Pen Dam—*dam* NC-3
Ash Bearpen Knob—*summit* NC-3
Ashbee Harbor—*bay* NC-3
Ash Beetree Hollow—*valley* WV-2
Ashbell Brook—*stream* NY-2
Ashbel Smith Bldg—*hist pl* TX-5
Ash Bend—*bend* AR-4
*Ashbent* AL-4
*Ashberry Branch* VA-3
Ashberry Branch—*stream* AL-4
Ashberry Cem—*cemetery* AR-4
Ash Bog Stream—*stream* ME-1
**Ashboro**—*pop pl* IN-6
Ashbough Canyon—*valley* (2) MT-8
Ashbough Spring—*spring* MT-8
*Ashbourn* PA-2
Ashbourne—*hist pl* KY-4
**Ashbourne**—*pop pl* PA-2
Ashbourne Country Club—*other* PA-2
**Ashbourne Hills**—*pop pl* DE-2
**Ashbourne Hills (subdivision)**—*pop pl* DE-2
Ashbox—*locale* MD-2
Ash Brake Bottom—*bend* LA-4
Ash Branch—*stream* AR-4
Ash Branch—*stream* GA-3
Ash Branch—*stream* IA-7
Ash Branch—*stream* (2) KY-4
Ash Branch—*stream* (2) NC-3
Ash Branch—*stream* WV-2
Ash Branch Ch—*church* GA-3
Ashbridge, David, Log House—*hist pl* PA-2
Ashbridge Spring—*spring* MT-8
**Ashbrook**—*pop pl* KY-4
Ash Brook—*stream* CT-1
Ash Brook—*stream* ME-1
Ash Brook—*stream* (2) NH-1
Ash Brook—*stream* NY-2
Ashbrook Cem—*cemetery* VA-3
Ashbrook Chapel (historical)—*church* MO-7
**Ashbrook Condominium**—*pop pl* UT-8
Ashbrook Creek—*stream* CA-9
Ashbrook Cutoff—*channel* MS-4
Ash Brook Golf Course—*other* NJ-2
Ashbrook HS—*school* NC-3
Ashbrook Neck—*cape* MS-4
Ashbrook Point—*cape* MS-4
Ash Brook Swamp—*swamp* NJ-2
Ash Brook Swamp Reservation—*park* NJ-2
Ash Brook Swimming Club—*other* NJ-2
Ashbrook Wash—*arroyo* AZ-5
Ashburger Lake—*lake* (2) NE-7
**Ashburk (subdivision)**—*pop pl* NC-3
*Ashburn* IL-6
**Ashburn**—*pop pl* GA-3
**Ashburn**—*pop pl* MO-7
**Ashburn**—*pop pl* TN-4
**Ashburn**—*pop pl* VA-3
Ashburn, W. W., House—*hist pl* GA-3
Ashburnam Center (census name Ashburham)—*other* MA-1
Ashburn Branch—*stream* GA-3
Ashburn Bridge—*other* MO-7
Ashburn (CCD)—*cens area* GA-3
Ashburn Cem—*cemetery* AL-4
Ashburn Cem—*cemetery* AR-4
Ashburn Cem—*cemetery* (2) MO-7
Ashburn Ch—*church* GA-3
*Ashburn Cove* VA-3
Ashburn Creek—*stream* TN-4
Ashburn Ford—*locale* TN-4
Ashburn Hall—*hist pl* NC-3
**Ashburnham**—*pop pl* MA-1
**Ashburnham (census name for Ashburnham Center)**—*pop pl* MA-1
*Ashburnham Centre* MA-1
*Ashburnham Junction* MA-1
Ashburnham State For—*forest* MA-1
Ashburnham Street Sch—*school* MA-1
**Ashburnham (Town of)**—*pop pl* MA-1
Ashburn (historical)—*locale* AZ-5
Ashburn Junction—*locale* VA-3
Ashburn Mtn—*summit* AZ-5
Ashburn Park—*park* IL-6
Ashburn Post Office (historical)—*building* TN-4
Ashburns Creek Ch of Christ (historical)—*church* TN-4
*Ashburns Creek School* TN-4
Ashburn Spring—*spring* AL-4
**Ashburton**—*pop pl* MD-2
Ashburton, Lake—*reservoir* MD-2
Ashburton House—*hist pl* DC-2
Ashburton Sch—*school* MD-2
**Ashbury**—*pop pl* PA-2
**Ashbury**—*pop pl* TN-4
Ashbury Arroyo—*stream* NM-5
*Ashbury Branch* SC-3
Ashbury Branch—*stream* SC-3
*Ashbury Cemetery* TX-5
Ashbury Ch—*church* (2) MD-2
Ashbury Ch—*church* OH-6
Ashbury Ch—*church* SC-3
Ashbury Chapel—*church* MO-7
Ashbury Ch (historical)—*church* AL-4
Ashbury Gulch—*valley* CA-9
Ashbury Sch (historical)—*school* MS-4
Ashbury Spring—*spring* ID-8
Ash Butte—*summit* CA-9
Ash Butte—*summit* OR-9
Ashby—*hist pl* IN-6
Ashby—*locale* AL-4
Ashby—*locale* (2) VA-3
Ashby—*locale* WA-9
**Ashby**—*pop pl* IN-6
**Ashby**—*pop pl* MA-1
**Ashby**—*pop pl* (2) MN-6
**Ashby**—*pop pl* NE-7
**Ashby**—*pop pl* TX-5
Ashby, Lake—*lake* FL-3
**Ashby (Bayard)**—*pop pl* VA-3
Ashby Branch—*stream* SC-3
Ashby Branch—*stream* TX-5
**Ashbyburg**—*pop pl* KY-4
Ashby Cem—*cemetery* AR-4
Ashby Cem—*cemetery* IN-6
Ashby Cem—*cemetery* MD-2
Ashby Cem—*cemetery* (2) TN-4
Ashby Cem—*cemetery* TX-5
*Ashby Centre* MA-1
Ashby Ch—*church* AL-4
Ashby Ch—*church* IN-6
Ashby Ch—*church* TX-5
Ashby Creek—*stream* IA-7
Ashby Creek—*stream* (2) MT-8
Ashby Creek—*stream* OR-9
Ashby Creek—*stream* TX-5
Ashby Gap—*gap* VA-3
**Ashby (historical)**—*pop pl* TN-4
Ashby Hollow—*valley* TN-4
Ashby Hollow—*valley* VA-3
Ashby Lake—*reservoir* TX-5
Ashby Lane Ch—*church* KY-4
Ashby Lookout Tower—*tower* FL-3
Ashby (Magisterial District)—*fmr MCD* (2) VA-3
Ashby Monmt—*pillar* VA-3
Ashby Park—*park* CA-9
Ashby Park—*park* IA-7
Ashby Reservoir Dam—*dam* MA-1
Ash by Ridge—*ridge* WV-2
Ashby Rsvr—*reservoir* MA-1
Ashby Sch—*school* WV-2
Ashby Sch (historical)—*school* TN-4
Ashbys Corner—*locale* VA-3
Ashbys Fork—*stream* KY-4
*Ashbys Harbor* NC-3
Ashbys Pinnacle—*summit* NY-2
Ashby Spring—*spring* AZ-5
**Ashby (Town of)**—*pop pl* MA-1
**Ashby Township**—*pop pl* ND-7
Ashby Tunnel—*mine* CO-8
Ashby Yards—*locale* IN-6
Ash Cabin Hollow—*valley* TN-4
Ash Cabin Hollow—*valley* VA-3
Ashcabin Run—*stream* WV-2
Ashcake—*locale* VA-3
Ashcake Creek—*stream* VA-3
Ash Camp—*locale* CA-9
Ash Camp—*locale* WV-2
**Ashcamp**—*pop pl* KY-4
Ashcamp Branch—*stream* KY-4
Ash Camp Branch—*stream* TN-4
Ashcamp Branch—*stream* WV-2
Ash Camp Canyon—*valley* NE-7
Ashcamp (CCD)—*cens area* KY-4
Ash Camp Ch—*church* VA-3
Ash Camp Creek—*stream* NC-3
Ash Camp Creek—*stream* VA-3
Ash Camp Hollow—*valley* TN-4
Ashcamp Hollow—*valley* WV-2
Ashcamp Run—*stream* (3) WV-2
Ash Canyon—*valley* (2) AZ-5
Ash Canyon—*valley* (2) NE-7
Ash Canyon—*valley* (2) NV-8
Ash Canyon—*valley* (6) NM-5
Ash Canyon Creek—*stream* NV-8
Ash Canyon Sch—*school* NE-7
Ash Canyon Spring—*spring* AZ-5
Ash Canyon Trail One Hundred Four—*trail* AZ-5
Ash Cave—*cave* MO-7
Ash Cave—*cave* OH-6
Ash Cave Lookout Tower—*locale* OH-6
Ash Cem—*cemetery* GA-3
Ash Cem—*cemetery* NC-3
Ash Cem—*cemetery* VA-3
Ash Center Cem—*cemetery* MI-6
Ash Ch—*church* TX-5
Ash Ch—*church* WV-2
Ash Clove Brook—*stream* NY-2
Ashcom—*locale* PA-2
Ash Coulee—*stream* (2) ND-7
Ash Coulee—*valley* (2) MT-8
Ash Coulee—*valley* ND-7
Ash Coulee—*valley* SD-7
*Ash Cove* ME-1
Ash Cove—*bay* NH-1
Ash Cove—*bay* TX-5
Ash Cove—*valley* (2) NC-3
Ash Cove Creek—*stream* NC-3
Ashcraft Baptist Ch (historical)—*church* MS-4
Ashcraft Branch—*stream* KY-4
Ash Craft Brook—*stream* NY-2
Ashcraft Cem—*cemetery* AR-4
Ashcraft Cem—*cemetery* MO-7
Ashcraft Cem—*cemetery* NY-2
Ashcraft Ch—*church* AL-4
Ashcraft Chapel—*church* IN-6
**Ashcraft Corner**—*pop pl* AL-4
*Ashcraft Corner Baptist Church* AL-4
Ashcraft Ditch—*canal* IN-6
Ashcraft Flume—*canal* OR-9
Ashcraft Ford—*locale* OH-6
Ashcraft Mtn—*summit* MS-4
Ash Craft Pond—*lake* NY-2
Ashcraft Pond—*lake* (2) NY-2
Ashcraft Ridge—*ridge* OH-6
Ashcraft Run—*stream* PA-2
Ashcraft Sch (historical)—*school* MS-4
*Ash Creek* AZ-5
*Ash Creek* AR-4
*Ash Creek* CA-9
*Ash Creek* NE-7
*Ash Creek* NY-2
*Ash Creek* OR-9
*Ash Creek* UT-8
*Ash Creek* VA-3
**Ash Creek**—*pop pl* MN-6
Ash Creek—*stream* (2) AK-9
Ash Creek—*stream* (22) AZ-5
Ash Creek—*stream* AR-4
Ash Creek—*stream* (7) CA-9
Ash Creek—*stream* CT-1
Ash Creek—*stream* GA-3
Ash Creek—*stream* (3) ID-8
Ash Creek—*stream* (2) IL-6
Ash Creek—*stream* (8) KS-7
Ash Creek—*stream* MI-6
Ash Creek—*stream* MN-6
Ash Creek—*stream* (3) MS-4
Ash Creek—*stream* (17) MT-8
Ash Creek—*stream* (9) NE-7
Ash Creek—*stream* NV-8
Ash Creek—*stream* (2) NM-5
Ash Creek—*stream* NY-2
Ash Creek—*stream* ND-7
Ash Creek—*stream* (3) OK-5
Ash Creek—*stream* (8) OR-9
Ash Creek—*stream* PA-2
Ash Creek—*stream* (12) SD-7
Ash Creek—*stream* (7) TX-5
Ash Creek—*stream* UT-8
Ash Creek—*stream* WI-6
Ash Creek—*stream* WY-8
**Ashcreek (Ash Creek)**—*pop pl* MN-6
Ash Creek Black Hills—*summit* AZ-5
Ash Creek Box—*valley* NM-5
Ash Creek Butte—*summit* CA-9
Ash Creek Camp—*locale* NM-5
Ash Creek Campground—*locale* CA-9
Ash Creek Canyon—*valley* AZ-5
Ash Creek Cem—*cemetery* NE-7
Ash Creek Ch—*church* AL-4
Ash Creek Ch—*church* OK-5
Ash Creek Ch—*church* TX-5
Ash Creek Ch—*church* WI-6
Ash Creek Corral Spring—*spring* AZ-5
Ash Creek Dam—*dam* AZ-5
Ash Creek Dam—*dam* UT-8
Ash Creek Falls—*falls* AZ-5
Ash Creek Junction—*locale* CA-9
Ash Creek Oil Field—*oilfield* KS-7
Ash Creek Ranch—*locale* AZ-5
Ash Creek Ridge—*ridge* (2) AZ-5
Ash Creek Rsvr—*reservoir* MT-8
Ash Creek Rsvr—*reservoir* UT-8
Ash Creek Rsvr Number Two—*reservoir* MT-8
Ash Creek Sch—*hist pl* OK-5
Ash Creek Sch—*school* AZ-5
Ash Creek Sch—*school* MT-8
Ash Creek Sch—*school* (2) NE-7
Ash Creek Sch (historical)—*school* SD-7
Ash Creek Sink—*basin* CA-9
Ash Creek Spring—*spring* (3) AZ-5
Ash Creek Spring—*spring* NV-8
Ash Creek Station—*locale* CA-9
Ash Creek Tank—*reservoir* AZ-5
**Ash Creek Township**—*pop pl* KS-7
Ash Creek Township (historical)—*civil* SD-7
Ash Creek Trail Three Hundred Seven—*trail* AZ-5
Ash Creek Trough—*reservoir* AZ-5
Ash Creek Well—*well* (2) AZ-5
Ash Creek Windmill—*locale* TX-5
Ashcroft—*hist pl* NY-2
Ashcroft—*locale* CO-8
**Ashcroft**—*pop pl* MA-1
Ashcroft, Colorado—*hist pl* CO-8
Ashcroft, Thomas, Ranch—*hist pl* SD-7
Ashcroft Butte—*summit* SD-7
Ashcroft Draw—*valley* CO-8
Ashcroft (historical)—*locale* SD-7
Ashcroft Mtn—*summit* CO-8
Ashcroft Sch—*school* MI-6
Ashcroft-Sherwood Drain—*stream* MI-6
**Ashcroft Subdivision**—*pop pl* TN-4
**Ashdale**—*pop pl* ME-1
**Ashdale**—*pop pl* OR-9
Ashdale Cem—*cemetery* AL-4
Ashdale Junction (reduced usage)—*locale* IL-6
Ashdale Ranger Station—*locale* AZ-5
Ash Dale Sch—*school* MN-6
Ashdick Lake—*lake* MN-6
Ash Disposal Pond—*reservoir* AL-4
Ash Disposal Pond Dam—*dam* AL-4
Ash Ditch—*canal* MO-7
**Ashdod**—*pop pl* MA-1
**Ashdown**—*pop pl* AR-4
Ashdown Canyon—*valley* UT-8
Ashdown Creek—*stream* UT-8
Ashdown Mine—*mine* NV-8
Ash Drain—*canal* CA-9
Ash Drain—*stream* MI-6
Ash Drain Thirtyseven—*canal* CA-9
Ash Draw—*valley* MT-8
Ash Draw—*valley* SD-7
Ash Draw—*valley* (5) WY-8
Ash Drift Mine (underground)—*mine* AL-4
Ashe, Lake—*lake* NC-3
**Asheboro**—*pop pl* NC-3
Asheboro City Hall—*building* NC-3
Asheboro Country Club—*locale* NC-3
Asheboro Country Club Lake Dam—*dam* NC-3
Asheboro County Club Lake—*reservoir* NC-3
Asheboro HS—*school* NC-3
Asheboro JHS—*school* NC-3
Asheboro Municipal Airp—*airport* NC-3
Asheboro Post Office—*building* NC-3
Asheboro South—*CDP* NC-3
Asheboro (Township of)—*fmr MCD* NC-3
Asheboro West—*CDP* NC-3
**Ashebrook Park**—*pop pl* NC-3
Ashe Cem—*cemetery* NC-3
Ashe Central Sch—*school* NC-3
Ashe Cottage—*hist pl* AL-4
*Ashe County* NC-3
**Ashe County**—*pop pl* NC-3
Ashe County Airp—*airport* NC-3
Ashe County Courthouse—*hist pl* NC-3
Ashe Creek—*stream* SC-3
Ashegon Lake—*lake* WI-6
Ashegun Lake—*lake* MI-6
Ashe House—*hist pl* KY-4
Asheim Cem—*cemetery* ND-7
Ashe Island—*island* NC-3
Ashe Island—*island* SC-3
Ashe Knob—*summit* NC-3
Ashe Lake—*lake* TX-5
Ashe Lake—*reservoir* MS-4
Ashe Lake—*reservoir* NC-3
Ashe Lake Dam—*dam* MS-4
Ashe Lake Dam—*dam* NC-3
Ashe Lake Rec Area—*park* MS-4
Ashelawn Gardens—*cemetery* NC-3
Ashelawn Memorial Gardens—*cemetery* NC-3
Ashelman Run—*stream* PA-2
Ashe Mine (underground)—*mine* AL-4
Ashenbrenner Lake—*lake* MN-6
Ashenfelder Canyon—*valley* NM-5
Ashenfelder Creek—*stream* WY-8
Ashenfelter Creek—*stream* ID-8
**Ashepoo**—*pop pl* SC-3
Ashepoo Coosaw Cutoff—*channel* SC-3
**Ashepoo Crossing**—*pop pl* SC-3
Ashepoo River—*stream* SC-3
*Ashepoo Siding* SC-3
**Ashepoo Siding**—*pop pl* SC-3
Asher—*locale* AZ-5
Asher—*locale* AR-4
Asher—*locale* KY-4
**Asher**—*pop pl* OK-5
Asher—*uninc pl* AR-4
Asher Branch—*stream* IN-6
Asher Branch—*stream* (3) KY-4
Asher Branch—*stream* MO-7
Asher Branch—*stream* (2) TN-4
Asherbraner Cem—*cemetery* AL-4
Asher Bridge—*other* MO-7
Asher Canyon—*valley* WA-9
Asher Cem—*cemetery* (2) IN-6
Asher Cem—*cemetery* (3) KY-4
Asher Cem—*cemetery* (2) MO-7
Asher Creek—*stream* CO-8
Asher Creek—*stream* ID-8
Asher Creek—*stream* IA-7
Asher Creek—*stream* KS-7
Asher Creek—*stream* (3) MO-7
*Asher Fork* KY-4
Asher Fork—*stream* TN-4
Asher Glade—*locale* MD-2
Asher Gulch—*valley* CO-8
Asher Hill—*summit* KY-4
Asher Hill—*summit* OH-6
Asher Hills—*summit* AZ-5
Asher Hollow—*valley* MO-7
Asher Knob—*summit* KY-4
Asher Lake—*lake* OH-6
Asher Lookout Tower—*locale* MO-7
Asher Oil Field—*oilfield* OK-5
Asher Run—*stream* OH-6
Asher's Cabin—*hist pl* MS-4
Asher Sch—*school* IL-6
Ashers Fork—*locale* KY-4
Ashers Fork—*stream* KY-4
Ashers Fork (CCD)—*cens area* KY-4
Ashers Fork Sch—*school* KY-4
Ashers Run—*stream* KY-4
*Ashers Spring* AL-4
Asher State Wildlife Mngmt Area—*park* MO-7
**Asherton**—*pop pl* PA-2
**Asherton**—*pop pl* TX-5
Asherton (CCD)—*cens area* TX-5
**Asherville**—*pop pl* IN-6
**Asherville**—*pop pl* KS-7
**Asherville**—*pop pl* MO-7
Asherville Cem—*cemetery* KS-7
**Asherville Township**—*pop pl* KS-7
Asherwood Branch—*stream* MD-2
*Asherwood Swamp* MD-2
Asherwood Swamp—*swamp* MD-2
Ashery Creek—*stream* MI-6
*Ashes Creek* KY-4
Ashes Creek—*stream* KY-4
Ashes Creek—*stream* NC-3
Ashes Creek Ch—*church* KY-4
Ashes Lake—*lake* WA-9
*Ashettimoyawk Lake* MI-6
*Asheville* PA-2
**Asheville**—*pop pl* NC-3
Asheville Airpark—*airport* NC-3
Asheville Biltmore Coll—*school* NC-3
Asheville City Hall—*hist pl* NC-3
Asheville Country Day Sch—*school* NC-3
Asheville Municipal Airp—*airport* NC-3
Asheville Recreation Park—*park* NC-3
Asheville Recreation Park Lake—*reservoir* NC-3
*Asheville Rsvr* NC-3
Asheville Sch for Boys—*school* NC-3
Asheville Steam Plant—*locale* NC-3
Asheville (Township of)—*fmr MCD* NC-3
Asheville Transfer and Storage Company Bldg—*hist pl* NC-3
Asheville Watershed—*ridge* NC-3
*Asheville Water Supply* NC-3
Asheville-Weaverville Speedway—*locale* NC-3
*Ashewage River* RI-1
Asheworth Branch—*stream* NC-3
*Ashfield* MT-8
Ashfield—*locale* MT-8
Ash Field—*other* IA-7
**Ashfield**—*pop pl* MA-1
**Ashfield**—*pop pl* PA-2
Ashfield Butte—*summit* CA-9
*Ashfield Plain* MA-1
Ashfield Plain Cem—*cemetery* MA-1
Ashfield Pond—*reservoir* MA-1
Ashfield Pond Dam—*dam* MA-1
Ashfield Ridge—*ridge* CA-9
**Ashfield (Town of)**—*pop pl* MA-1
Ash Fifteen Drain—*canal* CA-9
Ash Flat—*flat* AZ-5
Ash Flat—*flat* OR-9
Ash Flat—*flat* TX-5
**Ash Flat**—*pop pl* AR-4
Ash Flat—*stream* AR-4
Ash Flat—*swamp* AR-4
Ash Flat Branch—*stream* NC-3
Ash Flat Lake—*swamp* AR-4
Ash Flats—*flat* WV-2
Ashford—*locale* CT-1
Ashford—*locale* WV-2
**Ashford**—*pop pl* AL-4
**Ashford**—*pop pl* NY-2
**Ashford**—*pop pl* NC-3
**Ashford**—*pop pl* WA-9
**Ashford**—*pop pl* WI-6
Ashford Acad—*hist pl* CT-1
Ashford Acad—*school* AL-4
**Ashford Acres**—*pop pl* UT-8
Ashford Assembly of God Ch—*church* AL-4
Ashford Ave Sch—*school* NY-2
Ashford Brook—*stream* ME-1
Ashford Canyon—*valley* CA-9
Ashford Canyon—*valley* CO-8
Ashford Cem—*cemetery* (2) AL-4
Ashford Cem—*cemetery* LA-4
Ashford Ch—*church* TX-5
**Ashford Hollow**—*pop pl* NY-2
Ashford House—*hist pl* WA-9
Ashford HS—*school* AL-4
Ashford Junction—*locale* CA-9
Ashford Lake—*lake* MI-6
**Ashford Lake**—*pop pl* CT-1
Ashford Lake—*reservoir* CT-1
Ashford Mill—*locale* CA-9
Ashford Mine—*mine* CA-9
**Ashford Park**—*pop pl* GA-3
Ashford Peak—*summit* OK-5
Ashford Plaza Shop Ctr—*locale* AL-4
Ashford Post Office—*building* AL-4
Ashford Sch—*school* CT-1
Ashford Spring—*spring* MT-8
Ashford Street Sch—*school* MA-1
Ashford Tank—*reservoir* MT-8
**Ashford (Town of)**—*pop pl* CT-1
**Ashford (Town of)**—*pop pl* NY-2
**Ashford (Town of)**—*pop pl* WI-6
Ashfordville Sch (historical)—*school* MS-4
*Ashfork* AZ-5
**Ash Fork**—*pop pl* AZ-5
Ash Fork—*stream* WV-2
Ashfork (CCD)—*cens area* AZ-5
Ash Fork Cem—*cemetery* AZ-5
*Ashfork Draw* AZ-5
Ash Fork Draw—*valley* AZ-5
Ash Fork Elem Sch—*school* AZ-5
Ash Fork HS—*school* AZ-5
*Ashfork Lake* MI-6
Ash Fork Landing Strip—*airport* AZ-5
Ash Fork Post Office—*building* AZ-5
Ash Fork RR Station—*building* AZ-5
Ash Fork Santa Fe RR Company Water Tank—*reservoir* AZ-5
Ash Fork Steel Dam—*hist pl* AZ-5
Ash Fork Substation—*locale* AZ-5
*Ash Fort, Town of* MA-1
Ash Four Drain—*canal* CA-9
Ash Gap—*gap* NC-3
Ash Gap—*gap* TN-4
Ash Ground Branch—*stream* KY-4
*Ashgrove* MO-7
Ash Grove—*locale* NY-2
**Ash Grove**—*pop pl* IN-6
**Ash Grove**—*pop pl* IA-7
**Ash Grove**—*pop pl* KS-7
**Ash Grove**—*pop pl* MO-7
**Ash Grove**—*pop pl* NY-2
Ash Grove Cem—*cemetery* AR-4
Ash Grove Cem—*cemetery* IL-6
Ash Grove Cem—*cemetery* (2) NE-7
Ash Grove Cem—*cemetery* OH-6
Ash Grove Cem—*cemetery* SD-7
Ash Grove Ch—*church* AR-4
Ash Grove Ch—*church* IL-6
Ash Grove Ch—*church* OH-6
Ash Grove Ch—*church* PA-2
Ash Grove Ch—*church* SD-7
Ash Grove Ch—*church* VA-3
Ash Grove Ch (historical)—*church* TN-4
Ash Grove Plantation (historical)—*locale* AL-4
Ash Grove Sch—*school* CO-8
Ash Grove Sch—*school* (3) IL-6
Ash Grove Sch—*school* (2) NE-7
Ash Grove Sch—*school* OK-5
Ashgrove Sch—*school* PA-2
Ash Grove Sch—*school* SD-7
Ash Grove Sch—*school* WI-6
Ashgrove Sch—*school* WY-8
Ash Grove Sch (historical)—*school* TN-4
Ash Grove School*—*school* NE-7
Ashgrove School (abandoned)—*building* SD-7
Ash Grove Spring—*spring* UT-8
**Ash Grove Township**—*pop pl* NE-7
**Ash Grove (Township of)**—*pop pl* (2) IL-6
Ash Gulch—*valley* AZ-5
Ash Gulch—*valley* OR-9
Ash Gut—*stream* DE-2
Ash Gut Branch—*stream* KY-4
Ash Hill—*hist pl* MD-2
Ash Hill—*locale* CA-9
Ash Hill—*locale* TN-4
**Ash Hill**—*pop pl* MO-7
**Ash Hill**—*pop pl* NC-3
Ash Hill—*summit* CA-9
Ash Hill—*summit* ME-1
Ash Hill Cumberland Presbyterian Ch—*church* TN-4
Ash Hills—*other* MO-7
Ash Hill Sch (historical)—*school* TN-4
*Ash Hill Terrace* AZ-5
Ash Hill Township—*civil* MO-7
Ash Hollow—*valley* CA-9
Ash Hollow—*valley* KY-4
Ash Hollow—*valley* NE-7
Ash Hollow—*valley* PA-2
Ash Hollow—*valley* TN-4
Ash Hollow—*valley* TX-5
Ash Hollow—*valley* WA-9
Ash Hollow Cave—*cave* NE-7
Ash Hollow Cave—*hist pl* NE-7
Ash Hollow Cem—*cemetery* NE-7
Ash Hollow Country Club—*other* NE-7
Ash Hollow Creek—*stream* NE-7
Ash Hollow Hist Dist—*hist pl* NE-7
Ash Hollow Run—*stream* VA-3
Ash Hollow Sch—*school* NE-7
Ash Hollow State Historical Park—*park* NE-7
Ash Hollow Trail—*trail* PA-2
Ash Homestead—*locale* OR-9
Ashhopper Branch—*stream* (2) KY-4
Ash Hopper Branch—*stream* TN-4
*Ash Hopper Hollow* TN-4
Ashhopper Hollow—*valley* TN-4
Ash House Branch—*stream* IN-6
Ashhurst Point—*summit* AZ-5
Ashigan Lake—*lake* MN-6
Ashiiak Island—*island* AK-9
*Ashi Jima* MP-9
Ashimuit (historical)—*locale* MA-1
Ashinger Branch—*stream* MO-7
**Ashintilly**—*pop pl* GA-3
*Ashippun* WI-6
**Ashippun**—*pop pl* WI-6
Ashippun Cem—*cemetery* WI-6
Ashippun Lake—*reservoir* WI-6
Ashippun River—*stream* WI-6
*Ashippun Station* WI-6
**Ashippun (Town of)**—*pop pl* WI-6
**Ash Iron Springs**—*pop pl* IN-6
Ashishik Point—*cape* AK-9
*Ashishima* MP-9
Ash Island—*island* (2) ME-1
Ash Island—*island* NE-7
Ash Island—*island* OR-9
Ash Island Ledge—*bar* ME-1
Ash Knob—*summit* NC-3
**Ashkum**—*pop pl* IL-6
**Ashkum (Township of)**—*pop pl* IL-6
*Ash Lake* MI-6
Ash Lake—*lake* MI-6
Ash Lake—*lake* (4) MN-6
Ash Lake—*lake* (2) TX-5
**Ash Lake**—*pop pl* MN-6
Ash Lake—*reservoir* NE-7
Ash Lake State Wildlife Mngmt Area—*park* MN-6
**Ash Lake (Township of)**—*pop pl* MN-6
*Ashland* IN-6
*Ashland* KS-7
*Ashland* LA-4
*Ashland* MD-2
*Ashland* MS-4
*Ashland* PA-2
Ashland—*fmr MCD* NE-7
Ashland—*hist pl* KY-4
Ashland—*hist pl* LA-4
Ashland—*hist pl* NC-3
Ashland—*locale* DE-2
Ashland—*locale* GA-3
Ashland—*locale* IA-7
Ashland—*locale* MS-4
Ashland—*locale* NC-3
Ashland—*locale* TN-4
Ashland—*locale* TX-5
**Ashland**—*pop pl* AL-4
**Ashland**—*pop pl* CA-9
**Ashland**—*pop pl* IL-6
**Ashland**—*pop pl* IN-6
**Ashland**—*pop pl* (2) KS-7
**Ashland**—*pop pl* KY-4
**Ashland**—*pop pl* (3) LA-4
**Ashland**—*pop pl* ME-1
**Ashland**—*pop pl* MD-2
**Ashland**—*pop pl* MA-1
**Ashland**—*pop pl* (2) MI-6
**Ashland**—*pop pl* (2) MS-4
**Ashland**—*pop pl* MO-7
**Ashland**—*pop pl* MT-8
**Ashland**—*pop pl* NE-7
**Ashland**—*pop pl* NH-1
**Ashland**—*pop pl* NJ-2
**Ashland**—*pop pl* (2) NY-2
**Ashland**—*pop pl* NC-3
**Ashland**—*pop pl* OH-6
**Ashland**—*pop pl* OK-5
**Ashland**—*pop pl* OR-9
**Ashland**—*pop pl* (2) PA-2
**Ashland**—*pop pl* SC-3
**Ashland**—*pop pl* VA-3
**Ashland**—*pop pl* WV-2
**Ashland**—*pop pl* WI-6

Ashland Acad (historical)—*school* ... MS-4
Ashland Agronomy Farm—*locale* ... KS-7
Ashland Anticline—*summit* ... PA-2
Ashland Archeol Site—*hist pl* ... NE-7
Ashland Area Elem Sch—*school* ... PA-2
Ashland Ave Baptist Church—*hist pl* ... OH-6
Ashland Ave Sch—*school* ... NY-2
*Ashland Baptist Ch* ... MS-4
Ashland Baptist Ch—*church* ... MS-4
*Ashland Baptist Church* ... AL-4
*Ashland Bay* ... WI-6
Ashland Borough—*civil* (2) ... PA-2
Ashland Bottoms—*bend* ... KS-7
Ashland Brake—*swamp* ... MS-4
Ashland Branch—*stream* ... TN-4
Ashland Bridge—*hist pl* ... DE-2
Ashland Canal—*canal* ... LA-4
Ashland (CCD)—*cens area* ... AL-4
Ashland (CCD)—*cens area* ... KY-4
Ashland (CCD)—*cens area* ... OR-9
Ashland Cem—*cemetery* ... KS-7
Ashland Cem—*cemetery* ... LA-4
Ashland Cem—*cemetery* (3) ... MS-4
Ashland Cem—*cemetery* ... MO-7
Ashland Cem—*cemetery* ... NY-2
Ashland Cem—*cemetery* ... OH-6
Ashland Cem—*cemetery* ... OR-9
Ashland Cem—*cemetery* ... PA-2
Ashland Cem—*cemetery* ... TX-5
Ashland Center—*locale* ... MI-6
*Ashland Centre* ... MA-1
Ashland Ch—*church* ... IL-6
Ashland Ch—*church* ... KY-4
Ashland Ch—*church* ... MS-4
Ashland Ch—*church* ... MO-7
Ashland Ch—*church* ... PA-2
Ashland Ch—*church* ... SC-3
Ashland Ch—*church* ... VA-3
Ashland Ch—*church* ... WV-2
Ashland Chemical Company—*facility* ... OH-6
Ashland Ch of Christ—*church* ... MS-4
**Ashland City**—*pop pl* ... TN-4
Ashland City (CCD)—*cens area* ... TN-4
Ashland City Division—*civil* ... TN-4
Ashland City Dock—*locale* ... TN-4
Ashland City Elem Sch—*school* ... TN-4
Ashland City First Baptist Ch—*church* ... TN-4
Ashland City Post Office—*building* ... TN-4
Ashland Coal and Iron RR Office—*hist pl* ... KY-4
Ashland Coal and Iron RR Store—*hist pl* ... KY-4
Ashland Coll—*school* ... OH-6
**Ashland Compact (census name Ashland)**—*pop pl* ... NH-1
Ashland Country Club—*other* ... KS-7
Ashland Country Club—*other* ... NE-7
Ashland Country Club—*other* ... OH-6
**Ashland (County)**—*pop pl* ... OH-6
**Ashland (County)**—*pop pl* ... WI-6
Ashland County Courthouse—*hist pl* ... OH-6
Ashland County Courthouse—*hist pl* ... WI-6
*Ashland Coutre* ... MA-1
Ashland Creek—*stream* ... AK-9
Ashland Creek—*stream* ... AR-4
Ashland Creek—*stream* ... CA-9
Ashland Creek—*stream* ... OR-9
Ashland Division—*civil* ... AL-4
Ashland Elem Sch—*school* ... AL-4
Ashland Elem Sch—*school* ... MS-4
**Ashland Estates (subdivision)**—*pop pl* ... MS-4
Ashland Farm—*hist pl* ... GA-3
Ashland Ford—*locale* ... TN-4
Ashland Furnace (historical)—*locale* ... TN-4
Ashland Gristmill and Dam—*hist pl* ... NH-1
Ashland Gulch—*valley* ... CO-8
**Ashland Hills**—*pop pl* ... TN-4
Ashland Hist Dist—*hist pl* ... VA-3
**Ashland (historical)**—*pop pl* ... MS-4
**Ashland (historical)**—*pop pl* ... RI-1
Ashland Hollow—*valley* ... VA-3
Ashland HS—*school* ... KS-7
Ashland HS—*school* ... MA-1
Ashland HS—*school* ... MS-4
Ashland JHS—*hist pl* ... NH-1
Ashland JHS—*school* ... AL-4
Ashland JHS—*school* ... MA-1
Ashland Junction—*locale* ... WI-6
Ashland Lakes—*lake* ... WA-9
*Ashland Landing* ... MS-4
Ashland Landing *locale* ... MD-2
Ashland Lateral—*canal* ... OR-9
Ashland/Lineville Airp—*airport* ... AL-4
Ashland (Magisterial District)—*fmr MCD* ... VA-3
Ashland Middle School—*hist pl* ... WI-6
Ashland Mill—*locale* ... VA-3
Ashland Mine—*mine* ... OR-9
Ashland Mount—*summit* ... OR-9
Ashland Mountian—*summit* ... PA-2
Ashland MS—*school* ... MS-4
Ashland MS—*school* ... PA-2
Ashland Municipal Powerhouse—*hist pl* ... OR-9
Ashland Municipal-Summer Parker Field—*airport* ... OR-9
Ashland Oil Field—*oilfield* ... KS-7
Ashland Oil Field—*oilfield* ... LA-4
Ashland Oregon Natl Guard Armory—*hist pl* ... OR-9
Ashland Park—*park* (2) ... IL-6
**Ashland Park**—*pop pl* ... KY-4
Ashland Park Hist Dist—*hist pl* ... KY-4
Ashland Pinnacle—*pillar* ... NY-2
Ashland Place Hist Dist—*hist pl* ... AL-4
Ashland Place Methodist Ch—*church* ... AL-4
Ashland Plantation (historical)—*locale* ... MS-4
*Ashland Point* ... WI-6
Ashland Pond—*reservoir* ... CT-1
Ashland Public Library—*hist pl* ... NE-7
Ashland Reservoir Dam—*dam* ... MA-1
Ashland Reservoir Dam—*dam* ... PA-2
Ashland Ridge—*ridge* ... WV-2
Ashland RR Station—*hist pl* ... NH-1
Ashland Rsvr—*reservoir* ... CO-8
Ashland Rsvr—*reservoir* ... MA-1
Ashland Rsvr—*reservoir* ... OH-6
Ashland Rsvr—*reservoir* ... PA-2
Ashland Rural (CCD)—*cens area* ... KY-4
Ashland Sch—*school* ... CA-9
Ashland Sch—*school* ... CO-8
Ashland Sch—*school* (2) ... IL-6
Ashland Sch—*school* ... IN-6
Ashland Sch—*school* ... KY-4
Ashland Sch—*school* ... MA-1
Ashland Sch—*school* (2) ... MO-7
Ashland Sch—*school* ... NE-7
Ashland Sch—*school* (2) ... NJ-2
Ashland Sch—*school* (3) ... PA-2
Ashland Sch (historical)—*school* ... MS-4
Ashland Sch (historical)—*school* ... TN-4
Ashland School (abandoned)—*locale* ... MO-7
Ashland Square—*park* ... MO-7
Ashland State General Hospital Airp—*airport* ... PA-2
Ashland State Park—*park* ... MA-1
**Ashland (subdivision)**—*pop pl* ... AL-4
Ashland Terrace Christian Ch—*church* ... TN-4
Ashland Towhead—*area* ... MO-7
Ashland Town Hall—*hist pl* ... NH-1
**Ashland (Town of)**—*pop pl* ... ME-1
**Ashland (Town of)**—*pop pl* ... MA-1
**Ashland (Town of)**—*pop pl* ... NH-1
**Ashland (Town of)**—*pop pl* (2) ... NY-2
**Ashland (Town of)**—*pop pl* ... WI-6
**Ashland Township**—*pop pl* ... KS-7
**Ashland Township**—*pop pl* ... NE-7
**Ashland Township**—*pop pl* ... ND-7
**Ashland (Township and Rural Br. P.O. name Voorhees)**—*3pop pl* ... NJ-2
Ashland (Township of)—*fmr MCD* ... AR-4
**Ashland (Township of)**—*pop pl* ... IL-6
**Ashland (Township of)**—*pop pl* ... IN-6
**Ashland (Township of)**—*pop pl* ... MI-6
**Ashland (Township of)**—*pop pl* ... MN-6
**Ashland (Township of)**—*pop pl* ... PA-2
Ashland Vocational Sch—*school* (2) ... KY-4
**Ashlan Park**—*pop pl* ... CA-9
Ashlan Substation—*other* ... CA-9
Ashlar Hall—*hist pl* ... TN-4
Ashlar Pond—*bay* ... MD-2
Ash Lateral—*canal* ... ID-8
Ash Lateral Fifteen—*canal* ... CA-9
Ash Lateral Forty—*canal* ... CA-9
Ash Lateral Fortyfive—*canal* ... CA-9
Ash Lateral Fortyone—*canal* ... CA-9
Ash Lateral Fortysix—*canal* ... CA-9
Ash Lateral Fortytwo—*canal* ... CA-9
Ash Lateral Nine—*canal* ... CA-9
Ash Lateral Six—*canal* ... CA-9
Ash Lateral Thirteen—*canal* ... CA-9
Ash Lateral Thirty—*canal* ... CA-9
Ash Lateral Thirtyeight—*canal* ... CA-9
Ash Lateral Thirtyfour—*canal* ... CA-9
Ash Lateral Thirtynine—*canal* ... CA-9
Ash Lateral Thirtyseven—*canal* ... CA-9
Ash Lateral Thirtysix—*canal* ... CA-9
Ash Lateral Thirtythree—*canal* ... CA-9
Ash Lateral Tweleve—*canal* ... CA-9
Ash Lateral Twentyfive—*canal* ... CA-9
Ashlawn—*hist pl* ... CT-1
Ash Lawn—*locale* ... VA-3
Ashlawn Airp—*airport* ... PA-2
Ashlawn Park—*park* ... VA-3
Ashlawn Plantation (historical)—*locale* ... TN-4
Ashlawn Sch—*school* ... VA-3
Ashleigh—*hist pl* ... VA-3
**Ashleigh**—*pop pl* ... MD-2
**Ashleigh**—*pop pl* ... SC-3
Ashleigh Ch—*church* ... SC-3
Ashler Cem—*cemetery* ... AR-4
*Ashley* ... MS-4
*Ashley* ... UT-8
Ashley—*locale* ... MS-4
Ashley—*locale* ... OK-5
Ashley—*locale* ... WI-6
**Ashley**—*pop pl* ... DE-2
**Ashley**—*pop pl* ... IL-6
**Ashley**—*pop pl* ... IN-6
**Ashley**—*pop pl* ... LA-4
**Ashley**—*pop pl* ... MI-6
**Ashley**—*pop pl* ... MO-7
**Ashley**—*pop pl* ... ND-7
**Ashley**—*pop pl* ... OH-6
**Ashley**—*pop pl* ... PA-2
**Ashley**—*pop pl* ... TX-5
**Ashley**—*pop pl* ... WV-2
Ashley, Col. John, House—*hist pl* ... MA-1
Ashley, Col. John, House (Boundary Increase)—*hist pl* ... MA-1
Ashley, Dr. George, House—*hist pl* ... ID-8
Ashley, George, Sr., House—*hist pl* ... ID-8
Ashley, Mark A. M., House—*hist pl* ... OR-9
Ashley, Mount—*summit* ... MA-1
Ashley Acad—*school* ... TN-4
Ashley-Alexander House—*hist pl* ... AR-4
Ashley and Bailey Silk Mill—*hist pl* ... PA-2
Ashley and Jays Watermill (historical)—*locale* ... AL-4
Ashley Bay—*swamp* ... FL-3
Ashley Bayou—*gut* ... AR-4
Ashley Beaver Dam—*dam* ... MS-4
Ashley Borough—*civil* ... PA-2
Ashley Branch—*stream* (2) ... MO-7
Ashley Branch—*stream* (2) ... NC-3
Ashley Branch—*stream* ... TN-4
Ashley Bridge—*bridge* ... SC-3
Ashley Brook—*stream* (2) ... MA-1
Ashleycamp Run—*stream* ... WV-2
Ashley Cem—*cemetery* ... GA-3
Ashley Cem—*cemetery* (2) ... KY-4
Ashley Cem—*cemetery* (2) ... MA-1
Ashley Cem—*cemetery* ... MS-4
Ashley Cem—*cemetery* ... NY-2
Ashley Cem—*cemetery* ... NC-3
Ashley Cem—*cemetery* ... WV-2
Ashley Central Canal—*canal* ... UT-8
Ashley Ch—*church* ... MI-6
Ashley Ch—*church* ... MO-7
Ashley Ch—*church* (2) ... SC-3
Ashley Chapel—*church* (3) ... NC-3
Ashley Chapel Sch—*school* ... NC-3
**Ashley Corner**—*pop pl* ... OH-6
**Ashley (County)**—*pop pl* ... AR-4
Ashley Cove—*bay* ... VA-3
*Ashley Creek* ... UT-8
Ashley Creek—*gut* ... GA-3
Ashley Creek—*locale* ... MO-7
Ashley Creek—*stream* ... AR-4
Ashley Creek—*stream* (2) ... GA-3
Ashley Creek—*stream* ... MN-6
Ashley Creek—*stream* (2) ... MS-4
Ashley Creek—*stream* ... MO-7
Ashley Creek—*stream* (4) ... MT-8
Ashley Creek—*stream* ... UT-8
Ashley Creek—*stream* ... WY-8
Ashley Creek Ch—*church* ... MO-7
Ashley Creek Ditch—*canal* ... MT-8
Ashley Creek Rec Area—*locale* ... AR-4
Ashley Creek Recreation Site—*locale* ... UT-8
Ashley Creek Sch—*school* ... MT-8
Ashley Crossing—*locale* ... MS-4
Ashley Cutoff—*reservoir* ... MA-1
*Ashley Dam* ... AL-4
Ashley Ditch—*canal* ... IN-6
Ashley Divide—*ridge* ... MT-8
Ashley Divide Trail—*trail* ... MT-8
Ashley Elem Sch—*school* ... IN-6
Ashley Falls—*falls* ... UT-8
**Ashley Falls**—*pop pl* ... MA-1
Ashley Field—*park* ... OH-6
**Ashley Forest (subdivision)**—*pop pl* ... NC-3
Ashley Gorge—*valley* ... UT-8
Ashley Grove Ch—*church* (3) ... NC-3
Ashley Grove Ch—*church* ... SC-3
Ashley Hall—*locale* ... SC-3
**Ashley Hall Manor**—*pop pl* ... SC-3
*Ashley Hall Plantation* ... SC-3
Ashley Hall Plantation—*hist pl* ... SC-3
Ashley Hall Sch—*school* ... SC-3
Ashley Hammock—*island* ... MS-4
**Ashley Heights**—*pop pl* ... MA-1
**Ashley Heights**—*pop pl* ... NC-3
**Ashley Heights**—*pop pl* ... SC-3
**Ashley Heights (subdivision)**—*pop pl* ... DE-2
*Ashley Hill* ... MA-1
Ashley Hill—*summit* ... NY-2
Ashley Hill Brook—*stream* ... MA-1
Ashley (historical)—*locale* ... AL-4
Ashley Hollow—*valley* ... AR-4
Ashley Hollow—*valley* ... TN-4
Ashley Hot Spring—*spring* ... CA-9
Ashley House—*hist pl* ... MA-1
Ashley HS—*school* ... NC-3
*Ashley-Hudson* ... IN-6
Ashley-Hudson Ch—*church* ... IN-6
Ashley-Hudson (RR name for Ashley)—*other* ... IN-6
Ashley Island (historical)—*island* ... SD-7
*Ashley JHS* ... NC-3
**Ashley Junction**—*pop pl* ... SC-3
*Ashley Lake* ... UT-8
*Ashley Lake* ... WY-8
Ashley Lake—*lake* ... CA-9
Ashley Lake—*lake* ... IL-6
Ashley Lake—*lake* ... MS-4
Ashley Lake—*lake* ... MT-8
Ashley Lake—*lake* ... ND-7
Ashley Lake—*reservoir* ... MA-1
Ashley Lakes—*lake* ... MT-8
Ashley Lateral—*canal* ... CA-9
Ashley Lookout Tower—*locale* ... MS-4
Ashley Mill (historical)—*locale* ... MS-4
Ashley Mtn—*summit* ... MT-8
Ashley Municipal Airfield—*airport* ... ND-7
Ashley Natl For—*forest* ... UT-8
**Ashley Oaks**—*pop pl* ... TN-4
**Ashley Oaks (subdivision)**—*pop pl* ... AL-4
Ashley Oil and Gas Field—*oilfield* ... CO-8
Ashley Oil Field—*other* ... IL-6
Ashley Park—*park* ... MA-1
Ashley Park Sch—*school* ... NC-3
**Ashley Park (subdivision)**—*pop pl* (2) ... NC-3
**Ashley Park Subdivision**—*pop pl* ... UT-8
Ashley Phosphate—*locale* ... SC-3
**Ashley Place (subdivision)**—*pop pl* ... NC-3
Ashley Planes—*hist pl* ... PA-2
Ashley Point—*area* ... AR-4
Ashley Point Lodge—*locale* ... AR-4
Ashley Pond—*reservoir* ... MA-1
Ashley Pond Dam—*dam* ... MA-1
*Ashley Post Office* ... MS-4
Ashley Post Office (historical)—*building* ... MS-4
Ashley Prairie—*lake* ... FL-3
Ashley Ridge—*ridge* ... CO-8
*Ashley River* ... MN-6
*Ashley River* ... SC-3
Ashley River—*stream* ... SC-3
Ashley River Ch—*church* ... SC-3
Ashley River Memorial Bridge—*bridge* ... SC-3
Ashley River Road—*hist pl* ... SC-3
*Ashley Rsvr* ... MA-1
Ashley Rsvr—*reservoir* ... MA-1
Ashleys Branch—*stream* ... LA-4
Ashleys Camp—*locale* ... KY-4
Ashley Sch—*school* ... CO-8
Ashley Sch—*school* ... IL-6
Ashley Sch—*school* (2) ... MA-1
Ashley Sch—*school* ... MO-7
Ashley Sch—*school* (2) ... NC-3
Ashley Sch—*school* ... UT-8
*Ashleys Chapel* ... AL-4
Ashley Sch (historical)—*school* ... TN-4
Ashleys Lake—*reservoir* ... NC-3
Ashleys Lake Dam—*dam* ... NC-3
*Ashleys Landing* ... MS-4
*Ashleys Pond* ... MA-1
Ashley Spring—*spring* ... TN-4
Ashley Spring—*spring* ... UT-8
Ashley Substation—*other* ... UT-8
Ashley Township—*civil* ... MO-7
Ashley (Township of)—*fmr MCD* ... AR-4
**Ashley (Township of)**—*pop pl* ... IL-6
**Ashley (Township of)**—*pop pl* ... MN-6
Ashley Twin Lakes—*reservoir* ... UT-8
Ashley Twin Lakes Dam—*dam* ... UT-8
Ashley Union Cem—*cemetery* ... OH-6
Ashley Upper Canal—*canal* ... UT-8
Ashley Valley—*valley* (2) ... UT-8
Ashley Valley Hospital Heliport—*airport* ... UT-8
Ashley Valley JHS—*school* ... UT-8
Ashley Valley Med Ctr—*hospital* ... UT-8
Ashley Valley Med Ctr Chapel—*church* ... UT-8
Ashley Village (Township of)—*other* ... OH-6
**Ashleyville**—*pop pl* ... MA-1
*Ashley Waterhole* ... OR-9
Ashley Wolf Ditch—*canal* ... WY-8
Ash Lick—*stream* ... WV-2
Ash Lick Fork—*stream* ... KY-4
Ash Lick Run—*stream* ... WV-2
*Ashlito* ... MH-9
Ashlock—*locale* ... KY-4
Ashlock Cem—*cemetery* ... KY-4
Ashlock Cem—*cemetery* ... MO-7
Ashlock Creek—*stream* ... MO-7
Ashlock Gulch—*valley* ... ID-8
Ashlock Hill—*summit* ... AR-4
Ashlock Hollow—*valley* ... KY-4
Ashlock Ridge—*ridge* ... KY-4
Ash Log Bayou—*gut* ... MS-4
Ashlog Branch—*stream* (2) ... KY-4
Ashlog Creek—*stream* ... MS-4
Ash Log Gap—*gap* ... TN-4
Ash Log Mtn—*summit* ... TN-4
**Ashly**—*pop pl* ... LA-4
Ash Main Canal—*canal* ... CA-9
*Ashman Draw* ... UT-8
Ashman Island—*island* ... MI-6
Ashman Sch—*school* ... MI-6
Ashman Sch—*school* ... UT-8
*Ashmead* ... KS-7
Ashmead Draw—*valley* ... CO-8
Ash Meadow—*flat* ... CA-9
Ash Meadows—*basin* ... NV-8
Ash Meadows—*flat* ... CA-9
Ash Meadows Natl Wildlife Ref—*park* ... NV-8
Ash Meadows Natl Wildlife Refuge Office—*locale* ... NV-8
Ash Meadows Rancho—*locale* ... NV-8
Ashmead Village—*locale* ... PA-2
Ashmere Lake—*reservoir* ... MA-1
Ashmere Lake Dam—*dam* ... MA-1
*Ashmere Reservoir* ... MA-1
Ash Mesa—*summit* ... CO-8
Ash Mesa Cem—*cemetery* ... CO-8
**Ashmont**—*pop pl* ... NC-3
Ashmont Station—*locale* ... MA-1
**Ashmont (subdivision)**—*pop pl* ... MA-1
Ashmore—*locale* ... FL-3
Ashmore—*locale* ... TX-5
**Ashmore**—*pop pl* ... IL-6
**Ashmore**—*pop pl* ... MI-6
**Ashmore**—*pop pl* ... PA-2
Ashmore Branch—*stream* ... TX-5
Ashmore Business Coll—*school* ... NC-3
Ashmore Cove—*valley* ... AL-4
Ashmore Creek—*stream* ... IL-6
*Ashmore Lake* ... MA-1
Ashmore Ridge—*ridge* ... CA-9
Ashmore Station—*locale* ... PA-2
**Ashmore (Township of)**—*pop pl* ... IL-6
Ashmore Yards—*locale* ... PA-2
Ash Mountain Entrance Sign—*hist pl* ... CA-9
Ash Mountain Natl Park HQ—*locale* ... CA-9
Ash Mountain Trail—*trail* ... MT-8
Ash Mtn—*summit* ... AZ-5
Ash Mtn—*summit* ... GA-3
Ash Mtn—*summit* ... ME-1
Ash Mtn—*summit* ... MT-8
Ash Mtn—*summit* ... NM-5
Ash Mtn—*summit* ... WY-8
Ashmun, Mount—*summit* ... AK-9
Ashmun Bay—*bay* ... MI-6
Ashmun Creek—*stream* ... MI-6
*Ash Neck* ... ME-1
Ash Nine A Drain—*canal* ... CA-9
Ashnoca, Lake—*reservoir* ... NC-3
Ashnola Mtn—*summit* ... WA-9
Ashnola Pass—*gap* ... WA-9
Ashnola River—*stream* ... WA-9
Ash No. 16 Township—*civ div* ... SD-7
*Ashod* ... MA-1
**Ashokan**—*pop pl* ... NY-2
Ashokan Dam—*dam* ... NY-2
Ashokan Reservoir Aerator—*other* ... NY-2
Ashokan Rsvr—*reservoir* ... NY-2
Ashon Gut—*gut* ... NC-3
Ashpan Butte—*summit* ... CA-9
Ashpan Flat—*flat* ... CA-9
*Ash Peak* ... AZ-5
Ash Peak—*summit* ... AZ-5
Ash Peak Canyon—*valley* ... AZ-5
Ash Peak Mine—*mine* ... AZ-5
Ash Peaks—*summit* ... CA-9
A S H Personal—*airport* ... NJ-2
Ashpile Creek—*stream* ... ID-8
Ashpile Peak—*summit* ... ID-8
Ash Point—*cape* (3) ... ME-1
Ash Point—*cape* ... MI-6
Ash Point—*cape* ... TX-5
**Ash Point**—*pop pl* ... ME-1
Ash Point Cove—*bay* ... ME-1
Ashpole Center Ch—*church* ... NC-3
*Ashpole Center Sch* ... NC-3
Ashpole Center Sch—*school* ... NC-3
Ashpole Ch—*church* ... NC-3
Ashpole Creek—*stream* ... GA-3
Ashpole Presbyterian Church—*hist pl* ... NC-3
Ashpole Run—*stream* ... WV-2
Ashpole Swamp—*swamp* ... NC-3
Ashpole Swamp—*swamp* ... SC-3
Ash Pond—*lake* ... MA-1
Ash Pond—*lake* (2) ... NY-2
Ash Pond—*reservoir* ... GA-3
Ash Pond—*reservoir* ... NC-3
Ash Pond—*swamp* ... TX-5
Ash Pond Number Three—*dam* ... PA-2
Ash Pond Number Two—*dam* ... PA-2
Ash Pond Trail—*trail* ... NY-2
*Ash Port* ... TN-4
**Ashport**—*pop pl* ... TN-4
Ashport Bar—*bar* ... AR-4
Ashport Bend—*bend* ... TN-4
Ashport Cem—*cemetery* ... TN-4
Ashport Ch—*church* (2) ... TN-4
Ashport Ferry (historical)—*crossing* ... TN-4
Ashport Keyes Point Revetment—*levee* ... TN-4
Ashport Landing—*locale* ... TN-4
Ashport Post Office (historical)—*building* ... TN-4
Ashport Revetment—*levee* ... TN-4
Ashport Sch (historical)—*school* ... TN-4
Ashport-Three Point (CCD)—*cens area* ... TN-4
Ashport-Three Point Division—*civil* ... TN-4
Ashport Towhead—*island* ... TN-4
*Ashquoach* ... MA-1
Ashrama—*locale* ... CA-9
Ashrama Ranch—*locale* ... AZ-5
*Ashridge* ... WI-6
Ash Ridge—*locale* ... WI-6
**Ashridge**—*pop pl* ... AL-4
**Ash Ridge**—*pop pl* ... OH-6
Ash Ridge—*ridge* ... GA-3
Ash Ridge—*ridge* ... NY-2
Ash Ridge—*ridge* ... WI-6
Ashridge Ch—*church* ... AL-4
Ash Ridge Ch—*church* ... OH-6
Ash Ridge Ch—*church* ... WI-6
Ash Ridge Spur—*trail* ... PA-2
Ash River—*stream* ... MN-6
Ash River Campground—*locale* ... MN-6
Ash River Falls—*falls* ... MN-6
Ash River Lookout Tower—*locale* ... MN-6
Ash River Trail—*trail* ... MN-6
Ash Rock Ch—*church* ... KS-7
Ash Rock Sch—*school* ... KS-7
*Ash Rock Township* ... KS-7
Ashroe, Lake—*reservoir* ... NJ-2
Ash Run—*stream* ... IN-6
Ash Run—*stream* ... KY-4
Ash Run—*stream* ... NY-2
Ash Run—*stream* (2) ... OH-6
Ash Run—*stream* ... WV-2
Ash Sch—*school* (2) ... TX-5
Ash Sch (abandoned)—*school* (2) ... PA-2
Ash Slash—*gut* ... AR-4
Ash Slough—*gut* ... CA-9
Ash Slough—*gut* (2) ... LA-4
Ash Slough—*gut* ... OR-9
Ash Slough—*stream* ... AR-4
Ash Slough—*stream* ... CA-9
Ash Slough—*stream* ... FL-3
Ash Slough—*stream* (2) ... LA-4
Ash Slough—*stream* ... MO-7
Ash Slough—*stream* ... TN-4
Ash Slough Bypass Canal—*canal* ... CA-9
Ash Slough Ditch—*canal* ... MO-7
*Ash Slough Ditch - in part* ... MO-7
Ash Spread—*stream* ... AR-4
Ash Spread Ditch—*canal* ... AR-4
*Ash Spring* ... AZ-5
Ash Spring—*spring* (11) ... AZ-5
Ash Spring—*spring* ... NV-8
Ash Spring—*spring* (3) ... NM-5
Ash Spring—*spring* (3) ... TX-5
Ash Spring Branch—*stream* ... TN-4
Ash Spring Canyon—*valley* ... AZ-5
Ash Spring Canyon—*valley* ... NV-8
Ash Spring Canyon—*valley* ... NM-5
Ash Spring Creek—*stream* ... AZ-5
Ash Spring Exclosure—*locale* ... NV-8
Ash Spring Hollow—*valley* ... MO-7
Ash Spring Mtn—*summit* ... CA-9
Ash Spring Run—*stream* ... WV-2
Ash Springs—*locale* ... NV-8
Ash Springs—*spring* ... NV-8
Ash Spring Tank—*reservoir* ... AZ-5
Ash Spring Wash—*stream* ... AZ-5
Ash Street Hist Dist—*hist pl* ... MA-1
Ash Street Sch—*hist pl* ... MA-1
Ash Street Sch—*hist pl* ... NH-1
Ash Swale—*basin* ... OR-9
Ash Swale—*gut* ... IL-6
Ash Swale—*stream* ... OR-9
*Ash Swamp* ... NJ-2
Ash Swamp—*swamp* (2) ... CT-1
Ash Swamp—*swamp* (2) ... MA-1
Ash Swamp—*swamp* ... NY-2
Ash Swamp—*swamp* ... NC-3
Ash Swamp—*swamp* ... OR-9
Ash Swamp—*swamp* ... RI-1
Ash Swamp Brook—*stream* (3) ... NH-1
Ash Swamp Brook—*stream* ... RI-1
Ashs West Branch—*stream* ... PA-2
Ashtabula—*hist pl* ... SC-3
**Ashtabula**—*pop pl* ... OH-6
Ashtabula, Lake—*reservoir* ... ND-7
Ashtabula Bridge—*bridge* ... ND-7
Ashtabula Buffalo Dock—*locale* ... OH-6
**Ashtabula (County)**—*pop pl* ... OH-6
Ashtabula County Courthouse Group—*hist pl* ... OH-6
Ashtabula Creek—*stream* ... OH-6
Ashtabula Creek—*stream* ... PA-2
Ashtabula Harbor Light—*hist pl* ... OH-6
Ashtabula Harbor (RR name for Harbor)—*other* ... OH-6
Ashtabula Harbour Commercial District—*hist pl* ... OH-6
**Ashtabula (historical)**—*pop pl* ... ND-7
Ashtabula River—*stream* ... OH-6
Ashtabula Town Hall—*building* ... ND-7
**Ashtabula Township**—*pop pl* ... ND-7
**Ashtabula (Township of)**—*pop pl* ... OH-6
Ash Tank—*reservoir* (2) ... AZ-5
Ash Thirty A Drain—*canal* ... CA-9
Ash Thirty B Drain—*canal* ... CA-9
Ash Thirty Drain—*canal* ... CA-9
Ash Thirtyfour Drain—*canal* ... CA-9
Ash Three Drain—*canal* ... CA-9
Ash Timber Spring—*spring* ... AZ-5
**Ashtola**—*pop pl* ... PA-2
**Ashtola**—*pop pl* ... TX-5
Ashtola Sch (abandoned)—*school* ... PA-2
*Ashton* (2) ... IN-6
*Ashton* ... PA-2
Ashton—*locale* ... AR-4
Ashton—*locale* ... FL-3
Ashton—*locale* ... GA-3
Ashton—*locale* ... IA-7
Ashton—*locale* ... MD-2
Ashton—*locale* ... NV-8
Ashton—*locale* ... NC-3
Ashton—*locale* ... OH-6
**Ashton**—*pop pl* ... ID-8
**Ashton**—*pop pl* ... IL-6
**Ashton**—*pop pl* ... IA-7
**Ashton**—*pop pl* ... KS-7
**Ashton**—*pop pl* ... LA-4
**Ashton**—*pop pl* ... MD-2
**Ashton**—*pop pl* ... MI-6
**Ashton**—*pop pl* ... MO-7
**Ashton**—*pop pl* ... NE-7
**Ashton**—*pop pl* ... RI-1
**Ashton**—*pop pl* ... SC-3
**Ashton**—*pop pl* ... SD-7
**Ashton**—*pop pl* ... WV-2
**Ashton**—*pop pl* ... WI-6
Ashton Branch—*stream* ... TN-4
Ashton Bridge—*bridge* ... LA-4
Ashton Canyon—*valley* ... UT-8
Ashton Cem—*cemetery* ... KS-7
Ashton Cem—*cemetery* ... MI-6
Ashton Cem—*cemetery* ... PA-2
Ashton Cem—*cemetery* ... SD-7
Ashton Cem—*cemetery* (2) ... TX-5
Ashton Ch—*church* ... IL-6
Ashton Ch—*church* ... IA-7
Ashton Ch—*church* ... MO-7
Ashton Community Hall—*building* ... KS-7
Ashton Corners—*locale* ... PA-2
**Ashton Corners**—*pop pl* ... WI-6
Ashton Creek—*stream* ... IA-7
Ashton Creek—*stream* ... VA-3
Ashton Creek—*stream* ... WA-9
Ashton Dam—*dam* ... ID-8
Ashton Dam—*dam* ... RI-1
Ashton Dead River—*lake* ... FL-3
Ashton Draw—*valley* ... UT-8
Ashton-Driggs House—*hist pl* ... UT-8
Ashton Elem Sch—*school* ... FL-3
Ashton Fish Hatchery—*locale* ... ID-8
**Ashton Forrest**—*pop pl* ... NC-3
**Ashton Glen**—*pop pl* ... VA-3
Ashton Gulch—*valley* ... ID-8
**Ashton Heights**—*pop pl* ... VA-3
Ashton Hist Dist—*hist pl* ... DE-2
Ashton Hist Dist—*hist pl* ... RI-1
Ashton Hollow—*valley* ... UT-8
Ashton Lake—*lake* ... LA-4
Ashton Lake—*lake* ... MN-6
Ashton Lake—*lake* ... TX-5
Ashton Landing (historical)—*locale* ... MS-4
Ashton Methodist Church—*hist pl* ... SD-7
Ashton Northwest Oil Field—*oilfield* ... KS-7
Ashton Park—*park* ... MI-6
Ashton Pits State Public Hunting Area—*park* ... IA-7
*Ashton Plantation* ... MS-4
**Ashton Pond**—*pop pl* ... MD-2
Ashton Rsvr—*reservoir* ... ID-8
Ashton-Sandy Springs—*CDP* ... MD-2
Ashton Sch—*school* ... CO-8
Ashton School (Abandoned)—*locale* ... TX-5
Ashton Township—*civ div* ... NE-7
Ashton Township—*fmr MCD* ... IA-7
Ashton Township (historical)—*civil* ... SD-7
**Ashton (Township of)**—*pop pl* ... IL-6
Ashton Villa—*hist pl* ... TX-5
Ashton Wildwood County Park—*park* ... IA-7
Ashtown Pond—*swamp* ... AL-4
Ash Township—*civil* ... MO-7
Ash Township—*civil* ... SD-7
**Ash Township**—*pop pl* ... SD-7
Ash Township (historical)—*civil* ... SD-7
**Ash (Township of)**—*pop pl* ... MI-6
Ashtree—*locale* ... PA-2
Ash Tree Hollow—*valley* ... PA-2
Ash Tree Rsvr—*reservoir* ... SD-7
Ash Tree Spring—*spring* ... NV-8
Ashturn Creek—*stream* ... NC-3
Ash Two Drain—*canal* ... CA-9
Ashue—*locale* ... WA-9
Ashuela Brook—*stream* ... MA-1
Ashuelot—*locale* ... MT-8
**Ashuelot**—*pop pl* ... NH-1
*Ashuelot Bench* ... MT-8
Ashuelot Bench—*bench* ... MT-8
Ashuelot Cem—*cemetery* ... MA-1
Ashuelot Covered Bridge—*hist pl* ... NH-1
*Ashuelot Equivalent Plantation* ... MA-1
Ashuelot Pond—*reservoir* ... NH-1
Ashuelot River—*stream* ... NH-1
Ashumet Holl Reservation—*park* ... MA-1
Ashumet Pond—*lake* ... MA-1
*Ashunet Pond* ... MA-1
Ashur Flat—*flat* ... OR-9
Ashurot Mill (historical)—*locale* ... AL-4
**Ashurst**—*pop pl* ... AZ-5
Ashurst, Craig, House—*hist pl* ... KY-4
Ashurst Cem—*cemetery* ... AL-4
Ashurst Cem—*cemetery* ... AZ-5
Ashurst Creek—*stream* ... AZ-5
Ashurst Hayden Dam—*dam* ... AZ-5
Ashurst House—*hist pl* ... AZ-5
Ashurst Lake—*lake* ... AZ-5
Ashurst Lake—*lake* ... CA-9
Ashurst Lake Campground—*park* ... AZ-5
Ashurst Lake Dam—*dam* ... AZ-5
Ashurst Mtn—*summit* ... CA-9
Ashurst Ranch—*locale* ... CA-9
Ashurst Run—*stream* ... AZ-5
Ashurst Sch—*school* ... VA-3
Ashurst Spring—*spring* ... AZ-5
Ashurst Spring—*spring* ... CA-9
Ashurst Tank—*reservoir* ... AZ-5
Ashurst Well—*well* ... CA-9
**Ash Valley**—*pop pl* ... KS-7
Ash Valley—*valley* ... CA-9
Ash Valley—*valley* ... OR-9
Ash Valley Cem—*cemetery* ... KS-7
Ash Valley Grange Hall—*building* ... KS-7
**Ash Valley Township**—*pop pl* ... KS-7
Ashview Canal—*canal* ... CA-9
Ashview Lateral A—*canal* ... CA-9
Ashview Sch—*school* ... CA-9
*Ashville* ... PA-2
*Ashville* ... RI-1
Ashville—*locale* ... AL-4
Ashville—*locale* ... FL-3
Ashville—*locale* ... VA-3
**Ashville**—*pop pl* ... AL-4
**Ashville**—*pop pl* ... KY-4
**Ashville**—*pop pl* ... ME-1
**Ashville**—*pop pl* ... NY-2
**Ashville**—*pop pl* ... OH-6
**Ashville**—*pop pl* ... PA-2
Ashville Acad (historical)—*school* ... AL-4
Ashville Bay—*bay* ... NY-2
**Ashville Bay**—*pop pl* ... NY-2
Ashville Borough—*civil* ... PA-2
Ashville Bridge Creek—*stream* ... VA-3
Ashville (CCD)—*cens area* ... AL-4
Ashville Depot—*hist pl* ... OH-6
Ashville Division—*civil* ... AL-4
Ashville (historical)—*locale* ... MS-4
Ashville HS—*school* ... AL-4
Ashville Lookout Tower—*tower* ... FL-3
Ashville Pond—*lake* ... RI-1
Ashville Pond Dam—*dam* ... RI-1
Ashville Post Office (historical)—*building* ... PA-2
*Ashville Reservoir Dam* ... NC-3
Ashville Sch—*school* ... MA-1
**Ashville (sta.) (Boomertown)**—*pop pl* ... NY-2

Ashwabay, Mount—*summit* WI-6
Ash Wash—*stream* AZ-5
**Ashwaubenon**—*pop pl* (2) WI-6
Ashwaubenon Creek—*stream* WI-6
Ashway Ch—*church* TN-4
Ashwillet Brook—*stream* CT-1
Ash Windmill—*locale* TX-5
Ashwith Pond—*reservoir* MA-1
Ashwood—*locale* MS-4
Ashwood—*locale* NC-3
Ashwood—*locale* TX-5
**Ashwood**—*pop pl* NY-2
**Ashwood**—*pop pl* OH-6
**Ashwood**—*pop pl* OR-9
**Ashwood**—*pop pl* SC-3
**Ashwood**—*pop pl* TN-4
**Ashwood**—*pop pl* TX-5
**Ashwood**—*pop pl* VA-3
Ashwood Branch—*stream* WV-2
Ashwood (CCD)—*cens area* OR-9
Ashwood (CCD)—*cens area* SC-3
Ashwood Cem—*cemetery* MN-6
Ashwood Ch—*church* MS-4
Ashwood Ch—*church* NC-3
Ashwood Ch—*church* SC-3
**Ashwood (historical)**—*pop pl* MS-4
Ashwood Lake—*reservoir* SC-3
Ashwood Landing—*locale* MS-4
Ashwood Landing (historical)—*locale* MS-4
Ashwood Raceway—*other* SC-3
Ashwood Rsvr—*reservoir* CO-8
Ashwood Sch—*school* WA-9
*Ashwood Station* MS-4
Ashwood Station Post Office
(historical)—*building* MS-4
**Ashwood (Zion Acres)**—*pop pl* TN-4
Ashworth, John, House—*hist pl* UT-8
Ashworth and Jones Factory—*hist pl* MA-1
Ashworth Archaeol Site (12 Po
7)—*hist pl* IN-6
Ashworth Brook—*stream* ME-1
**Ashworth (Cedarvale)**—*pop pl* TX-5
Ashworth Cem—*cemetery* TN-4
Ashworth Creek—*stream* (2) NC-3
Ashworth Creek—*stream* SC-3
Ashworth Creek—*stream* WY-8
Ashworth Dam—*dam* MA-1
Ashworth Hill—*summit* AR-4
Ashworth Hollow—*valley* TN-4
Ashworth Park—*park* IA-7
Ashworth Pond—*lake* MA-1
Ashworth-Remillard House—*hist pl* CA-9
Ashworth Rock Shelters Site—*hist pl* KY-4
Ashworth Sch—*school* MO-7
Ashworth Slough—*gut* LA-4
Ashworth Trail—*trail* PA-2
Asia—*locale* TX-5
**Asia**—*pop pl* TN-4
**Asia**—*pop pl* TX-5
Asia Cem—*cemetery* MS-4
Asia Cem—*cemetery* TN-4
Asia Plantation (historical)—*locale* MS-4
Asia Point—*cliff* AR-4
*Asias* PW-9
Asias Branch—*stream* SC-3
Asia Sch (historical)—*school* TN-4
Asiatic Creek—*stream* CO-8
*Asiga* MH-9
Asiga—*area* GU-9
Asiga, Puntan—*cape* MH-9
Asiga, Sabanetan—*slope* MH-9
Asiga, Unai—*beach* MH-9
Asiga Beach—*beach* GU-9
Asiga Cave—*cave* GU-9
*Asiga Point* MH-9
Asiga Point—*summit* GU-9
Asigyukpak Spit—*bar* AK-9
Asik Mtn—*summit* AK-9
Asikpak Lagoon—*lake* AK-9
Asikpak Mtn—*summit* AK-9
Asikpak River—*stream* AK-9
Asiksat Creek—*stream* AK-9
**Asili**—*pop pl* AS-9
Asili Point—*cape* AS-9
Asili Stream—*stream* AS-9
Asilo De Pobres—*hist pl* PR-3
Asilomar Conference Grounds—*hist pl* CA-9
Asilomar State Beach—*park* CA-9
Asilomar (YMCA)—*other* CA-9
A Simons Dam—*dam* SD-7
Asinan—*bend* GU-9
Asiniak Point—*cape* AK-9
Asinine Bridge—*bridge* OR-9
Asistencia de Las Flores (Ruins)—*locale* CA-9
Asistencia de San Antonio de
Pala—*church* CA-9
Asistencia de Santa Margarita
(Ruins)—*locale* CA-9
Asi-va—*spring* AZ-5
*Asi-va Spring* AZ-5
A Six Lateral—*canal* MT-8
Aska—*locale* GA-3
*Askakerson* DE-2
*Askakeson Branch* DE-2
**Askam**—*pop pl* PA-2
Askea Grove—*locale* AL-4
Askeaton—*locale* WI-6
Askecksy (historical)—*area* DE-2
*Askeeksky* DE-2
**Askel**—*pop pl* MI-6
Askel Cem—*cemetery* MI-6
Asker Creek—*stream* OR-9
Asketum Branch—*stream* DE-2
*Askew* TX-5
**Askew**—*pop pl* MS-4
**Askew**—*pop pl* TX-5
Askew Branch—*stream* IL-6
Askew Bridge—*bridge* MS-4
Askew Bridge—*hist pl* PA-2
Askew Cem—*cemetery* NC-3
Askew Cem—*cemetery* TN-4
Askew Field—*park* AL-4
Askew Grove Ch—*church* MS-4
Askew Hollow—*valley* OK-5
Askew Hollow—*valley* TN-4
Askew Lakes—*reservoir* GA-3
Askew Landing (historical)—*locale* TN-4
Askew Pond—*lake* MS-4
Askew Pond Dam—*dam* MS-4
Askew Ref—*park* MS-4
Askew Ridge—*ridge* NC-3
*Askews Bluff* MS-4
Askew Sch—*school* MO-7
**Askewville**—*pop pl* NC-3
Askewville Sch—*school* NC-3
Askew Windmill—*locale* NM-5
Askey Cem—*cemetery* PA-2
Askey Cem—*cemetery* TX-5
Askey Creek—*stream* TX-5
Askey Ranch—*locale* TX-5
**Askin**—*pop pl* (2) KY-4
**Askin**—*pop pl* NC-3
*As Kina* MH-9
Asking Lake—*lake* IL-6
Askins Cem—*cemetery* MO-7
*Askins Creek* GA-3
Askins Creek—*stream* NC-3
Askins Well—*well* NM-5
Askinuk Mountains—*range* AK-9
Ask Lake—*lake* MN-6
As Knob—*summit* GA-3
*As Kokorocho* MH-9
Askon Hollow—*valley* PA-2
Askon Hollow Dam—*dam* PA-2
*Askonno* MH-9
Askoti, Lake—*reservoir* NY-2
**Askov**—*pop pl* MN-6
Askov Lookout Tower—*locale* MN-6
*Askquexence* DE-2
Askren Cem—*cemetery* KS-7
Askren Ditch—*canal* IN-6
Askue Run—*stream* OH-6
*Askuras* MH-9
*Askwalli Glacier* WA-9
*Askwalli River* WA-9
Aslebe Hill—*summit* MA-1
*Asleet* MH-9
**Asleigh**—*pop pl* MD-2
Aslemon—*other* GU-9
Aslinger Hollow—*valley* TN-4
Aslinger Slough—*bay* TN-4
Aslinget—*area* GU-9
Aslinget River—*stream* GU-9
*Aslito* MH-9
Aslucos—*area* GU-9
Asmafines River—*stream* GU-9
*As Mahalang* MH-9
*As Mahetog* MH-9
*Asmahettog* MH-9
Asmaile—*ridge* GU-9
Asmaile Point—*cape* GU-9
Asmaile Point—*hist pl* GU-9
*Asmalan* MH-9
*As Manila* MH-9
*Asmappo* MH-9
*As Matmus* MH-9
Asmey Drain—*stream* MI-6
**Asmisen**—*pop pl* GU-9
Asmulato Hill—*summit* GU-9
Asmun Brook—*stream* CT-1
**Asmuyao**—*pop pl* GU-9
Asnacomet Pond—*reservoir* MA-1
Asnacomet Pond Dam—*dam* MA-1
*Asnaconcomick Pond* MA-1
*Asnaconet Pond* MA-1
Asnaki—*area* GU-9
*Asnebumsket Hill* MA-1
Asnebumskit Brook—*stream* MA-1
Asnebumskit Hill—*summit* MA-1
Asnebumskit Pond—*reservoir* MA-1
Asnebumskit Pond Dam—*dam* MA-1
*Asnecomomet Pond* MA-1
*Asneconick Pond* MA-1
*Asneconic Pond* MA-1
*Asnuntuck* CT-1
*Asnybumskit Brook* MA-1
*Asnybumskit Hill* MA-1
*Asnybumskit Pond* MA-1
*Asnycomet Pond* MA-1
*Asnyconic Pond* MA-1
Asolido Wash—*stream* AZ-5
**Asomante**—*pop pl* (2) PR-3
Asomante—*post sta* PR-3
Asomante (Barrio)—*fmr MCD* (2) PR-3
*Asomson* MH-9
*As Onaan* MH-9
*Asonan* MH-9
*Asoncon* MH-9
*Asoncun* MH-9
*Asongsong* MH-9
*Asonson* MH-9
Aso Number Two Tank—*reservoir* AZ-5
Aso Pass—*gap* AZ-5
Asor—*island* FM-9
Aso Ranch (historical)—*locale* AZ-5
*Asoscong Creek* NJ-2
*Asotan* WA-9
*Asotan Creek* WA-9
Aso Tank—*reservoir* AZ-5
**Asotin**—*pop pl* WA-9
Asotin (CCD)—*cens area* WA-9
**Asotin County**—*pop pl* WA-9
Asotin Creek—*stream* WA-9
**Asp**—*pop pl* OK-5
Aspaas Lake—*reservoir* CO-8
*As Palacias* MH-9
Aspalaga Landing—*locale* FL-3
*As Palamo* MH-9
*Aspaparkas* MH-9
Asparagus Point—*cape* NC-3
Asparagus Point—*cape* VA-3
*Asparenda* MH-9
Aspatuck River—*stream* NY-2
**Aspel**—*pop pl* AL-4
Aspel Branch—*stream* AL-4
**Aspelund**—*pop pl* MN-6
Aspelund Cem—*cemetery* MN-6
Aspelund Ch—*church* MN-6
Aspen—*locale* VA-3
**Aspen**—*pop pl* CO-8
**Aspen**—*pop pl* NC-3
**Aspen**—*pop pl* WY-8
Aspen, Lake—*lake* NM-5
Aspen Acres Golf Club—*other* ID-8
Aspen Basin—*basin* NM-5
Aspen Brook—*stream* CO-8
*Aspen Butte* CA-9
Aspen Butte—*summit* AZ-5
Aspen Butte—*summit* ID-8
Aspen Butte—*summit* (2) OR-9
Aspen Butte—*summit* WY-8
Aspen Cabin—*locale* NM-5
Aspen Cabin—*locale* OR-9
Aspen Campground—*locale* CA-9
Aspen Campground—*locale* CO-8
Aspen Campground—*locale* (2) MT-8
Aspen Campground—*locale* UT-8
Aspen Campground—*park* AZ-5
Aspen Campground—*park* OR-9
Aspen Canyon—*valley* (2) AZ-5
Aspen Canyon—*valley* NM-5
Aspen-Cloud Rock Shelters—*hist pl* UT-8
Aspen Community Church—*hist pl* CO-8
Aspen Corral—*other* NM-5
*Aspen Creek* MT-8
*Aspen Creek* OR-9
Aspen Creek—*stream* (2) AK-9
Aspen Creek—*stream* AZ-5
Aspen Creek—*stream* CA-9
Aspen Creek—*stream* (8) CO-8
Aspen Creek—*stream* (6) ID-8
Aspen Creek—*stream* MT-8
Aspen Creek—*stream* (4) OR-9
Aspen Creek—*stream* (2) UT-8
Aspen Creek—*stream* (8) WY-8
Aspen Creek Siphon—*canal* CO-8
Aspen Creek Spring—*spring* AZ-5
Aspendale—*hist pl* DE-2
Aspendale Community Hall—*locale* ID-8
**Aspendell**—*pop pl* CA-9
Aspend Hill—*summit* WA-9
Aspen Ditch—*canal* CO-8
Aspen Draw—*valley* ID-8
**Aspen East Subdivision**—*pop pl* UT-8
Aspen Flat—*flat* (3) CA-9
Aspen Flat—*flat* ID-8
Aspen Flat—*flat* UT-8
Aspen Forest Camp—*park* AZ-5
Aspen Fork—*stream* OR-9
**Aspen-Gerbaz**—*pop pl* CO-8
*Aspen Giants Scenic Area, The* UT-8
Aspen Glade Campground—*locale* CO-8
Aspenglen Campground—*locale* CO-8
**Aspen Glen Condominium**—*pop pl* UT-8
Aspen Glen Picnic Area—*park* CA-9
**Aspengo**—*pop pl* GU-9
Aspen Grove—*locale* KY-4
**Aspen Grove**—*pop pl* UT-8
Aspen Grove—*woods* CA-9
Aspen Grove Cabin—*locale* MT-8
*Aspen Grove Campground* UT-8
Aspen Grove Campground—*locale* MT-8
Aspen Grove Campground—*locale* UT-8
Aspen Grove Cem—*cemetery* CO-8
Aspen Grove Cem—*cemetery* IA-7
Aspen Grove Cem—*cemetery* MA-1
Aspen Grove Ch—*church* NC-3
Aspen Grove Sch—*school* CO-8
Aspen Grove Spring—*spring* OR-9
Aspen Grove Wash—*valley* AZ-5
*Aspen Guard Station* OR-9
Aspen Guard Station—*locale* CO-8
Aspen Gulch—*valley* (2) CO-8
Aspen Gulch—*valley* (2) ID-8
Aspen Hall—*hist pl* NC-3
**Aspen Heart and Lakeview Recreation
Residences**—*pop pl* UT-8
**Aspen Heights Subdivision**—*pop pl*
(2) UT-8
Aspen-Highland Sch—*school* OR-9
Aspen Hill—*hist pl* WV-2
**Aspen Hill**—*pop pl* MD-2
**Aspen Hill**—*pop pl* TN-4
Aspen Hill—*summit* AZ-5
Aspen Hill—*summit* NH-1
Aspen Hill—*summit* NM-5
Aspen Hill Cem—*cemetery* TN-4
Aspen Hill Cem—*cemetery* WY-8
Aspen Hill Ch—*church* VA-3
**Aspen Hill Park**—*pop pl* MD-2
*Aspen Hill Post Office* TN-4
Aspenhill Post Office (historical)—*building* TN-4
Aspen Hill Sch—*school* MD-2
Aspen Hill Sch (historical)—*school* (2) TN-4
**Aspenhoff**—*pop pl* MO-7
Aspen Hollow—*valley* ID-8
Aspen Hollow—*valley* (2) UT-8
Aspen Hollow—*valley* WY-8
*Aspen Junction* CO-8
Aspen Knoll—*summit* CO-8
**Aspen Knolls**—*pop pl* MD-2
Aspen Lake—*lake* AK-9
Aspen Lake—*lake* (2) AZ-5
Aspen Lake—*lake* CA-9
Aspen Lake—*lake* (2) MN-6
Aspen Lake—*lake* OR-9
Aspen Lake—*lake* (2) UT-8
Aspen Lake—*lake* WA-9
Aspen Lake—*lake* WI-6
Aspen Lake—*reservoir* CO-8
Aspen Leaf Rsvr—*reservoir* CO-8
Aspen Meadow—*flat* (2) CA-9
**Aspen Meadows (subdivision)**—*pop pl* DE-2
Aspen Mine—*mine* CO-8
Aspen Mine—*mine* ID-8
*Aspen Mirror Lake* UT-8
Aspen-Mirror Lake—*lake* UT-8
Aspen Mountain—*locale* NM-5
Aspen Mtn—*summit* CO-8
Aspen Mtn—*summit* NM-5
Aspen Mtn—*summit* WY-8
**Aspen Park**—*pop pl* CO-8
Aspen Park Campground—*locale* CO-8
**Aspen Park Condo**—*pop pl* UT-8
Aspen Patch—*woods* UT-8
Aspen Peak—*summit* (2) NM-5
Aspen-Pitkin County Airport—*airport* CO-8
Aspen Point—*summit* UT-8
Aspen Point Campground—*park* OR-9
Aspen Point Picnic Area—*locale* CO-8
Aspen Ranch—*locale* NM-5
Aspen Range—*range* ID-8
Aspen Rec Area—*park* AZ-5
*Aspen Ridge* ID-8
Aspen Ridge—*ridge* AZ-5
Aspen Ridge—*ridge* CO-8
Aspen Ridge—*ridge* (2) WY-8
Aspen Ridge Pit Rsvr—*reservoir* WY-8
Aspen Rsvr—*reservoir* (2) CO-8
Aspen Rsvr—*reservoir* (3) OR-9
Aspen Run—*stream* (2) MD-2
Aspen Sch—*school* UT-8
*Aspen Slough* SD-7
*Aspen Spring* AZ-5
*Aspen Spring* NV-8
*Aspen Spring* OR-9
Aspen Spring—*spring* (7) AZ-5
Aspen Spring—*spring* CO-8
Aspen Spring—*spring* (3) ID-8
Aspen Spring—*spring* MT-8
Aspen Spring—*spring* (4) NV-8
Aspen Spring—*spring* (2) NM-5
Aspen Spring—*spring* (8) OR-9
Aspen Spring—*spring* (6) UT-8
Aspen Spring Ranch—*locale* AZ-5
Aspen Springs—*spring* NV-8
Aspen Springs Trail Camp—*locale* NM-5
Aspen Spring Tank—*reservoir* AZ-5
Aspen State Wildlife Mngmt Area—*park* MN-6
*Aspen Tank* AZ-5
Aspen Tank—*locale* AZ-5
Aspen Tank—*reservoir* (4) AZ-5
Aspen Trail—*trail* PA-2
Aspen Tunnel—*tunnel* WY-8
*Aspen Tunnels* WY-8
Aspenvale Cem—*cemetery* VA-3
Aspenvale Cemetery—*hist pl* VA-3
Aspen Valley—*basin* CA-9
**Aspen Valley**—*pop pl* CA-9
Aspen Valley Ranch—*locale* CO-8
Aspenwall—*locale* VA-3
Aspen Wash—*valley* (2) AZ-5
Aspen Well—*well* CA-9
**Aspen West Subdivision**—*pop pl* UT-8
*Asperdido* MH-9
Asperin Butte—*summit* CA-9
**Aspermont**—*pop pl* TX-5
Aspermont Cem—*cemetery* TX-5
Aspermont Lake—*reservoir* TX-5
Aspermont Lake Oil Field—*oilfield* TX-5
Aspermont North (CCD)—*cens area* TX-5
Aspermont South (CCD)—*cens area* TX-5
Aspero Peak—*summit* AK-9
Asperos Canyon—*valley* NM-5
**Aspers**—*pop pl* PA-2
Asper Sch—*school* PA-2
Asper School (Abandoned)—*locale* MO-7
**Aspers (RR name Bendersville
(sta.))**—*pop pl* PA-2
Aspetong, Mount—*summit* NY-2
Aspetuck—*locale* CT-1
Aspetuck Cem—*cemetery* CT-1
Aspetuck Hill—*summit* CT-1
Aspetuck River—*stream* CT-1
Aspetuck Rsvr—*reservoir* CT-1
Asp Gulch—*valley* MT-8
Asphalt—*locale* KY-4
**Asphalt Belt Junction (A.B.
Junction)**—*pop pl* TX-5
*Asphalt Canyon* UT-8
*Asphalt Creek* UT-8
Asphalt Lake—*lake* AL-4
Asphalt Mtn—*summit* TX-5
Asphalt Ridge—*ridge* UT-8
*Asphalt Rock Baptist Church* AL-4
Asphalt Rock Ch—*church* AL-4
Asphaltum—*locale* OK-5
Asphaltum—*locale* UT-8
**Asphaltum**—*pop pl* IN-6
Asphaltum Ch—*church* OK-5
Asphaltum Creek—*stream* CA-9
Asphaltum Mine—*mine* CA-9
Asphalt Wash—*valley* UT-8
Asphodel Plantation and
Cemetery—*hist pl* LA-4
Asphult Ch—*church* MN-6
Aspid, Mount—*summit* AK-9
Aspid Bay—*bay* AK-9
Aspid Cape—*cape* (2) AK-9
*Aspik Lake* MN-6
Aspinall—*locale* WV-2
Aspinall Run—*stream* WV-2
Aspinook Pond—*reservoir* CT-1
Aspinwall—*locale* GA-3
**Aspinwall**—*pop pl* IA-7
**Aspinwall**—*pop pl* PA-2
Aspinwall Airp—*airport* PA-2
Aspinwall Borough—*civil* PA-2
Aspinwall Cem—*cemetery* (2) GA-3
Aspinwall Corners—*locale* NY-2
Aspinwall Corners—*locale* PA-2
Aspinwall Hill—*summit* MA-1
Aspinwall Lake—*lake* (2) MN-6
Aspinwall Seaplane Base
(historical)—*airport* PA-2
*Aspirin Creek* WY-8
Aspirin Pond—*lake* OR-9
Aspitarte Lake—*lake* ID-8
*Aspiwall Lake* MN-6
Asp Lake—*lake* MN-6
Asplin Cem—*cemetery* MO-7
Asplund Field Airp—*airport* WA-9
Asplundh Airp—*airport* PA-2
Asplund Lake—*lake* MI-6
*Aspoeyano* MH-9
Aspualas—*area* GU-9
*As Pupoenge* MH-9
Aspupong—*area* GU-9
Asputlon—*area* GU-9
Aspy Ditch—*canal* IN-6
Asquamchumauke Ridge Trail—*trail* NH-1
Asquede—*area* GU-9
Asquidachay—*area* GU-9
Asquiroga Cave—*hist pl* GU-9
Asquiroga Cliff—*cliff* GU-9
Asquith Creek—*stream* MD-2
Asquith Island—*island* MD-2
*As Rapugau* MH-9
*Asrokayano* MH-9
*Asrosariya* MH-9
*Assabet* MA-1
Assabet, Mount—*summit* MA-1
*Assabet Brook* MA-1
*Assabet Flow* MA-1
Assabet Flow Augmentation
Pond—*reservoir* MA-1
*Assabeth Brook* MA-1
*Assabeth River* MA-1
Assabet Plaza—*locale* MA-1
Assabet River—*stream* MA-1
Assabet River At High Street Dam—*dam* MA-1
Assabet River Dam—*dam* MA-1
Assabet River Rsvr—*reservoir* (2) MA-1
Assacorkin Island—*island* MD-2
Assacorkin Thorofare—*channel* MD-2
Assaguam Brook—*stream* NH-1
*Assaida* MH-9
Assalie—*area* GU-9
Assam Dam—*dam* SD-7
*Assameekig* MA-1
*Assamoosick Creek* VA-3
Assamoosick Swamp—*stream* VA-3
*Assamoosic Swamp* VA-3
*Assamp* AZ-5
*Assamp River* AZ-5
Assan Dechali Spring—*spring* AZ-5
Assapumpset Brook—*stream* RI-1
*Assapumsick Brook* RI-1
*Assapumsik Brook* RI-1
*Assaquakin Island* MD-2
**Assaria**—*pop pl* KS-7
*Assateague Anchorage* VA-3
Assateague Bay—*bay* VA-3
Assateague Beach U S Coast Guard
Station—*locale* VA-3
Assateague Channel—*channel* VA-3
*Assateague Cove* VA-3
Assateague Island—*island* MD-2
Assateague Island—*island* VA-3
Assateague Island Natl Seashore (Also
MD)—*park* VA-3
Assateague Island Natl Seashore (Also
VA)—*park* MD-2
Assateague Island State Park—*park* MD-2
Assateague Lighthouse—*hist pl* VA-3
Assateague Point—*cape* VA-3
*Assateague Sound* DE-2
*Assawaman* VA-3
*Assawaman Creek* VA-3
*Assawaman Inlet* VA-3
*Assawaman Island* VA-3
*Assawampset Pond* MA-1
*Assawampsett Pond* MA-1
*Assawamset Pond* MA-1
*Assawamsett Pond* MA-1
Assawan Lake—*lake* MN-6
Assawoman—*locale* VA-3
Assawoman Bay—*bay* DE-2
Assawoman Bay—*bay* MD-2
*Assawoman Beach* DE-2
Assawoman Canal—*canal* DE-2
Assawoman Creek—*stream* VA-3
Assawoman Inlet—*bay* VA-3
Assawoman Island—*island* VA-3
Assawoman Wildlife Area—*park* DE-2
*Assawomit* MA-1
Assawompset Pond—*lake* MA-1
Assawompset Sch—*school* MA-1
*Assawompsett Pond* MA-1
*Assay Creek* UT-8
Assay Creek—*stream* ID-8
Assay Office—*hist pl* ID-8
Assay Office—*hist pl* WA-9
Assekonk Brook—*stream* CT-1
Assekonk Swamp—*swamp* CT-1
Assemble Ch—*church* TX-5
Assemblies of God Conference
Grounds—*locale* NE-7
**Assembly**—*pop pl* NC-3
Assembly Ch—*church* OK-5
*Assembly Church* TN-4
Assembly Full Gospel Ch—*church* KS-7
Assembly Hall—*hist pl* MS-4
Assembly Hall Peak—*summit* UT-8
Assembly Lake—*reservoir* NC-3
Assembly of Exempt Firemen
Bldg—*hist pl* NJ-2
Assembly of God Campground—*locale* KS-7
Assembly of God Ch—*church* (4) AL-4
Assembly of God Ch—*church* (3) AR-4
Assembly of God Ch—*church* DE-2
Assembly of God Ch—*church* (3) FL-3
Assembly of God Ch—*church* IL-6
Assembly of God Ch—*church* IN-6
Assembly of God Ch—*church* (2) LA-4
Assembly of God Ch—*church* (2) MI-6
Assembly of God Ch—*church* (2) MN-6
Assembly of God Ch—*church* (3) MS-4
Assembly of God Ch—*church* (9) MO-7
Assembly of God Ch—*church* MT-8
Assembly of God Ch—*church* NC-3
Assembly of God Ch—*church* (3) OK-5
Assembly of God Ch—*church* (2) SD-7
Assembly of God Ch—*church* TX-5
Assembly of God Ch—*church* (6) UT-8
Assembly of God Ch—*church* VA-3
Assembly of God Ch
(abandoned)—*church* MO-7
Assembly of God Ch Bethel
Temple—*church* FL-3
Assembly of God Ch Glad Tidings—*church* FL-3
Assembly of God Ch Northside—*church* FL-3
Assembly of God Ch of Oakland
Park—*church* FL-3
Assembly of God-Evangel Ch—*church* FL-3
Assembly of God-Heritage—*church* FL-3
Assembly of God Tabernacle Ch—*church* AL-4
Assembly of God Treasure Coast
Cathedral—*church* FL-3
Assembly of Jesus Christ—*church* UT-8
Assembly of Jesus Christ Ch—*church* AL-4
Assembly of Yahweh—*church* AL-4
**Assembly Park**—*pop pl* NY-2
Assembly Point—*cape* NY-2
**Assembly Point**—*pop pl* NY-2
Assembly Sch (historical)—*school* AL-4
Assembly Training Sch—*school* VA-3
Asses Ears—*summit* AK-9
Assessor Draw—*valley* NV-8
*Assias* PW-9
*Assibuche Draw* TX-5
Assignation Creek—*stream* CO-8
Assignation Ridge—*ridge* CO-8
*Assilly River* FL-3
*Assimippi Village* MA-1
Assington—*hist pl* MA-1
Assiniboine Creek—*stream* MT-8
Assinika Creek—*stream* MN-6
Assinika Lake—*lake* MN-6
Assinins—*hist pl* MI-6
**Assinins**—*pop pl* MI-6
**Assinippi**—*pop pl* MA-1
Assiscong Creek—*stream* NJ-2
Assiscunk Branch—*stream* NJ-2
Assiscunk Creek—*stream* NJ-2
Asslinger Cem—*cemetery* TN-4
Assman Number 1 Dam—*dam* SD-7
Assoc Canal—*canal* TX-5
*Associate Ch* MS-4
*Associated* CA-9
Associated Oil Camp—*locale* CA-9
Associated Reformed Presbyterian Ch of
Covington—*church* TN-4
Associated Reformed Presbyterian
Church—*hist pl* AR-4
Associated Reform Presbyterian
Cem—*cemetery* MS-4
**Association Camp**—*pop pl* CO-8
Association Corral—*locale* OR-9
Association Ditch—*canal* NM-5
Association Gulch—*valley* CO-8
Association Island—*island* NY-2
**Association Island**—*pop pl* NY-2
Association of Oldest Inhabitants
Bldg—*building* DC-2
Association of the Bar of the City of New
York—*hist pl* NY-2
Association Residence Nursing
Home—*hist pl* NY-2
Association Rsvr—*reservoir* OR-9
Association Rsvr—*reservoir* UT-8
Association Spring—*spring* CO-8
Association Tank—*reservoir* (2) AZ-5
Association Well—*well* ID-8
*Assomption* MH-9
*Assonate Bay* MA-1
**Assonet**—*pop pl* MA-1
*Assonet, Town of* MA-1
Assonet Bay—*basin* MA-1
**Assonet Bay Shores**—*pop pl* MA-1
Assonet Burying Ground—*cemetery* MA-1
Assonet Neck—*cape* MA-1
Assonet River—*stream* MA-1
Assonet River Rsvr—*reservoir* MA-1
Assonet Station (historical)—*locale* MA-1
*Assonett* MA-1
*Assonett River* MA-1
*Assonet Village* MA-1
*Assongsong* MH-9
*Assongsong Insel* MH-9
*Assongsong Island* MH-9
*Assongson Island* MH-9
*Assonguson* MH-9
*Assopumsett Brook* RI-1
*Assotan* WA-9
*Assotan Creek* WA-9
*Assowamsoo* MA-1
*Assowompset Pond* MA-1
*Assowompsett Pond* MA-1
*Assumption* AZ-5
**Assumption**—*pop pl* IL-6
**Assumption**—*pop pl* (2) MN-6
**Assumption**—*pop pl* NE-7
**Assumption**—*pop pl* OH-6
Assumption Abbey—*church* MO-7
Assumption Abbey—*church* ND-7
Assumption Abbey Dam—*dam* ND-7
Assumption Acad—*school* NE-7
Assumption Catholic Ch—*church* KS-7
*Assumption Catholic Church* MS-4
Assumption Cem—*cemetery* IL-6
Assumption Cem—*cemetery* MI-6
Assumption Cem—*cemetery* (2) MN-6
Assumption Cem—*cemetery* (3) MO-7
Assumption Cem—*cemetery* (3) NY-2
Assumption Cem—*cemetery* (2) PA-2
Assumption Cem—*cemetery* (2) TX-5
Assumption Ch—*church* FL-3
Assumption Ch—*church* IA-7
Assumption Ch—*church* MI-6
Assumption Ch—*church* MS-4
Assumption Ch—*church* NE-7
Assumption Ch—*church* OH-6
Assumption Chapel—*church* MN-6
Assumption Ch School—*church* IA-7
Assumption Coll—*school* MA-1
Assumption Greek Orthodox
Church—*hist pl* MO-7
Assumption HS—*school* IA-7
Assumption HS—*school* KY-4
Assumption HS—*school* OK-5
Assumptionist Fathers Monastery—*church* NY-2
Assumption Lake—*lake* MN-6
Assumption of Mary Sch—*school* NY-2
**Assumption Parish**—*pop pl* LA-4
Assumption Preparatory Sch—*school* MA-1
Assumption Roman Catholic Ch—*church* AL-4
Assumption Sch—*hist pl* MN-6
Assumption Sch—*school* AL-4
Assumption Sch—*school* (2) CA-9
Assumption Sch—*school* CO-8
Assumption Sch—*school* (2) CT-1
Assumption Sch—*school* DC-2
Assumption Sch—*school* FL-3
Assumption Sch—*school* (3) IL-6
Assumption Sch—*school* KS-7
Assumption Sch—*school* (2) MA-1
Assumption Sch—*school* MI-6
Assumption Sch—*school* MO-7
Assumption Sch—*school* (3) NJ-2
Assumption Sch—*school* (2) OH-6
Assumption Sch—*school* OR-9
Assumption Sch—*school* (5) PA-2
Assumption Sch—*school* (2) WA-9
Assumption Seminary—*school* MN-6
Assumption Seminary—*school* TX-5
**Assumption (Township of)**—*pop pl* IL-6
Assumption Vale Novitiate—*church* PA-2
Assunpink Creek—*stream* NJ-2
Assunpink Creek Fish and Wildlife Mngmt
Area—*park* NJ-2
Assunpink Park—*park* NJ-2
Assupian—*area* GU-9
*Assuption* AZ-5
Assurance—*locale* WV-2
*Assylum* PA-2
**Assyria**—*pop pl* MI-6
Assyrian Cem—*cemetery* MI-6
**Assyria (Township of)**—*pop pl* MI-6
Astaban—*area* GU-9

**Atkinson**—*pop pl* KY-4
**Atkinson**—*pop pl* MN-6
**Atkinson**—*pop pl* NE-7
**Atkinson**—*pop pl* NH-1
**Atkinson**—*pop pl* NC-3
Atkinson, W. H., House—*hist pl* OR-9
Atkinson Acad—*school* NH-1
Atkinson Acad Sch—*hist pl* NH-1
Atkinson And Gilmanton Academy Grant—*civil* NH-1
Atkinson Bay—*bay* WI-6
Atkinson Bldg—*hist pl* ME-1
Atkinson Branch—*stream* AR-4
Atkinson Branch—*stream* SC-3
Atkinson Branch—*stream* (2) TN-4
Atkinson Breaks—*summit* CO-8
Atkinson Bridge—*bridge* GA-3
Atkinson Brook—*stream* ME-1
Atkinson Canal—*canal* CO-8
Atkinson Canyon—*valley* NM-5
Atkinson Cave—*cave* PA-2
Atkinson Cem—*cemetery* IL-6
Atkinson Cem—*cemetery* IN-6
Atkinson Cem—*cemetery* KY-4
Atkinson Cem—*cemetery* MN-6
Atkinson Cem—*cemetery* MS-4
Atkinson Cem—*cemetery* MO-7
Atkinson Cem—*cemetery* (4) NC-3
Atkinson Cem—*cemetery* OH-6
Atkinson Cem—*cemetery* (2) TN-4
Atkinson Cem—*cemetery* (3) TX-5
Atkinson Cem—*cemetery* VA-3
Atkinson Ch—*church* WV-2
Atkinson Chapel—*church* IN-6
Atkinson Chapel—*church* NC-3
Atkinson Common—*park* MA-1
**Atkinson Corner**—*pop pl* ME-1
Atkinson Corners—*locale* ME-1
**Atkinson (County)**—*pop pl* GA-3
Atkinson County Courthouse—*hist pl* GA-3
Atkinson Creek—*stream* (2) CO-8
Atkinson Creek—*stream* IN-6
Atkinson Creek—*stream* MI-6
Atkinson Creek—*stream* MS-4
Atkinson Creek—*stream* OH-6
Atkinson Depot—*locale* NH-1
Atkinson Ditch—*canal* CA-9
Atkinson Ditch—*canal* CO-8
Atkinson Elem Sch—*school* NC-3
Atkinson Flat—*flat* CA-9
Atkinson Flat—*flat* MT-8
Atkinson Flat Campground—*locale* WA-9
Atkinson Flats—*flat* NM-5
Atkinson Hall, Georgia College—*hist pl* GA-3
*Atkinson-Harlow Cemetery* AL-4
**Atkinson Heights**—*pop pl* NH-1
Atkinson House—*hist pl* TX-5
Atkinson Island—*island* NC-3
Atkinson Island—*island* TX-5
Atkinson-Koskinen Site 45.13—*hist pl* ME-1
Atkinson Lake—*lake* GA-3
Atkinson Lake—*lake* MN-6
Atkinson Lake—*lake* NE-7
Atkinson Lake—*reservoir* NC-3
Atkinson Lake Dam—*dam* MS-4
Atkinson Lake Dam—*dam* NC-3
Atkinson Lake Rec Area—*park* NE-7
Atkinson Landing—*locale* NC-3
Atkinson Landing (historical)—*locale* AL-4
Atkinson Lookout Tower—*locale* OH-6
Atkinson Mesa—*summit* CO-8
Atkinson Mill Pond—*reservoir* NC-3
Atkinson Mill Pond Dam—*dam* NC-3
Atkinson Mills—*locale* ME-1
Atkinson Mills—*locale* PA-2
Atkinson Mills Ch—*church* PA-2
Atkinson-Morris House—*hist pl* TX-5
Atkinson MS—*school* NC-3
Atkinson Mtn—*summit* NH-1
Atkinson Municipal Airp—*airport* KS-7
Atkinson Park—*park* KY-4
Atkinson Park—*park* MI-6
Atkinson Peak—*summit* ID-8
Atkinson Ranch—*locale* NE-7
Atkinson Ranch—*locale* NM-5
Atkinson Ranch—*locale* TX-5
Atkinson Ranch—*locale* (2) WY-8
Atkinson Ridge—*ridge* OH-6
Atkinson Ridge—*ridge* TN-4
Atkinson Rsvr—*reservoir* CO-8
Atkinson Sch—*school* AR-4
Atkinson Sch—*school* (2) GA-3
Atkinson Sch—*school* KY-4
Atkinson Sch—*school* MA-1
Atkinson Sch—*school* MI-6
Atkinson Sch—*school* NY-2
Atkinson Sch—*school* NC-3
Atkinson Sch—*school* OH-6
Atkinson Sch—*school* OR-9
Atkinson Sch (abandoned)—*school* MO-7
Atkinson Slough—*gut* KY-4
Atkinsons Mill (historical)—*locale* AL-4
**Atkinsons Mills**—*pop pl* PA-2
Atkinson-Smith House—*hist pl* NC-3
Atkinson Station (historical)—*locale* AL-4
Atkinson Tank—*reservoir* TX-5
**Atkinson (Town of)**—*pop pl* ME-1
**Atkinson (Town of)**—*pop pl* NH-1
**Atkinson Township**—*pop pl* NE-7
**Atkinson (Township of)**—*pop pl* IL-6
**Atkinson (Township of)**—*pop pl* MN-6
**Atkinsonville**—*pop pl* IN-6
Atkinson Well—*well* NM-5
Atkinson-Williams Warehouse—*hist pl* AR-4
Atkinson Windmill—*locale* CO-8
Atkins Park District—*hist pl* GA-3
Atkins Peak—*summit* WY-8
Atkins Pond—*lake* ME-1
Atkins Pond—*reservoir* AR-4
Atkins Porter Sch—*school* TN-4
Atkins Post Office (historical)—*building* TN-4
Atkin Spring—*spring* AZ-5
Atkins Ranch—*locale* CA-9
Atkins Ridge—*ridge* ME-1
Atkins Rsvr—*reservoir* MA-1
Atkins Run—*stream* IN-6
*Atkins Sch* TN-4
Atkins Sch—*school* AR-4
Atkins Sch—*school* LA-4
Atkins Sch—*school* TN-4
Atkins Sch (historical)—*school* MS-4
Atkins Sch (historical)—*school* TN-4
Atkins Slough—*stream* AR-4
Atkins Spring—*spring* UT-8
Atkinstown—*locale* KY-4
**Atkins Township**—*pop pl* ND-7
*Atkinsville Wash* AZ-5
Atkinsville Wash—*valley* UT-8
Atkins Well—*well* (2) AZ-5
*Atkin Tank* AZ-5
Atkinville—*locale* UT-8
Atkinville Wash—*valley* AZ-5
*Atkison* ND-7
Atkisson Rsvr—*reservoir* MD-2
Atkulik Island—*island* AK-9
Atla Creek—*stream* AK-9
Atlakumtsitak Mtn—*summit* AK-9
*Atlan* NC-3
*Atlanta* KS-7
Atlanta—*fmr MCD* NE-7
Atlanta—*locale* AR-4
Atlanta—*locale* CO-8
Atlanta—*locale* DE-2
Atlanta—*locale* IA-7
Atlanta—*locale* KY-4
Atlanta—*locale* (2) NV-8
**Atlanta**—*pop pl* CA-9
**Atlanta**—*pop pl* GA-3
**Atlanta**—*pop pl* ID-8
**Atlanta**—*pop pl* IL-6
**Atlanta**—*pop pl* IN-6
**Atlanta**—*pop pl* KS-7
**Atlanta**—*pop pl* LA-4
**Atlanta**—*pop pl* MI-6
**Atlanta**—*pop pl* MS-4
**Atlanta**—*pop pl* MO-7
**Atlanta**—*pop pl* NE-7
**Atlanta**—*pop pl* NY-2
**Atlanta**—*pop pl* OH-6
**Atlanta**—*pop pl* TX-5
Atlanta, Mount—*summit* WI-6
Atlanta and West Point RR Freight Depot—*hist pl* GA-3
Atlanta Army Depot—*other* GA-3
**Atlanta Baptist College**—*pop pl* GA-3
Atlanta Biltmore Hotel and Biltmore Apartments—*hist pl* GA-3
Atlanta (CCD)—*cens area* GA-3
Atlanta (CCD)—*cens area* TX-5
Atlanta Cem—*cemetery* IL-6
Atlanta Cem—*cemetery* NE-7
Atlanta Ch—*church* MN-6
Atlanta Christian Coll—*school* GA-3
Atlanta City Hall—*hist pl* GA-3
Atlanta City Lake—*reservoir* MO-7
Atlanta Colored Sch (historical)—*school* MS-4
*Atlanta Creek* MT-8
Atlanta Creek—*stream* MT-8
Atlanta Dam and Power Plant—*hist pl* ID-8
Atlanta-Decatur (CCD)—*cens area* GA-3
**Atlanta Estates**—*pop pl* DE-2
Atlanta General Depot—*other* GA-3
Atlanta Hist Dist—*hist pl* ID-8
Atlanta Hot Springs—*spring* ID-8
Atlanta International Raceway—*other* GA-3
Atlanta Junction—*locale* GA-3
Atlanta Lookout Tower—*locale* MI-6
Atlanta Marsh—*swamp* NE-7
Atlanta Marsh Natl Wildlife Mngmt Area—*park* NE-7
Atlanta Memorial Park—*park* GA-3
Atlanta Methodist Ch (historical)—*church* MS-4
Atlanta Mine—*mine* CA-9
Atlanta Mine—*mine* NV-8
Atlanta Naval Air Station—*military* GA-3
Atlanta Oil And Gas Field—*oilfield* AR-4
Atlanta Peak—*summit* NV-8
Atlanta Post Office (historical)—*building* MS-4
Atlanta Power Station—*locale* ID-8
Atlanta Public Library—*hist pl* IL-6
Atlanta Sch (historical)—*school* MS-4
Atlanta State Park—*park* TX-5
Atlanta State Wildlife Area—*park* MO-7
Atlanta State Wildlife Mngmt Area—*park* MN-6
Atlanta Stockade—*hist pl* GA-3
Atlanta Summit—*gap* NV-8
**Atlanta (Town of)**—*pop pl* WI-6
**Atlanta Township**—*pop pl* KS-7
**Atlanta (Township of)**—*pop pl* IL-6
**Atlanta (Township of)**—*pop pl* MN-6
Atlanta Univ—*school* GA-3
Atlanta Univ Center District—*hist pl* GA-3
Atlanta Waterworks Hemphill Ave Station—*hist pl* GA-3
Atlanta Women's Club—*hist pl* GA-3
Atlantic—*locale* PA-2
Atlantic—*other* MI-6
**Atlantic**—*pop pl* IA-7
**Atlantic**—*pop pl* ME-1
**Atlantic**—*pop pl* MA-1
**Atlantic**—*pop pl* NH-1
**Atlantic**—*pop pl* NC-3
**Atlantic**—*pop pl* (4) PA-2
**Atlantic**—*pop pl* VA-3
Atlantic—*post sta* VA-3
Atlantic—*uninc pl* NY-2
Atlantic and Pacific Mine—*reservoir* MT-8
Atlantic Ave Control House—*hist pl* NY-2
Atlantic Ave Park—*park* CA-9
Atlantic Ave Sch—*school* (2) NY-2
Atlantic Bank and Trust Company Bldg—*hist pl* NC-3
Atlantic Basin—*harbor* NY-2
Atlantic Beach—*beach* NY-2
**Atlantic Beach**—*pop pl* FL-3
**Atlantic Beach**—*pop pl* NY-2
**Atlantic Beach**—*pop pl* NC-3
**Atlantic Beach**—*pop pl* RI-1
**Atlantic Beach**—*pop pl* SC-3
Atlantic Beach Assembly of God Ch—*church* FL-3
Atlantic Beach Bridge—*bridge* NY-2
Atlantic Beach Sch—*school* FL-3
Atlantic Blvd Estates—*uninc pl* FL-3
Atlantic Blvd Plaza (Shop Ctr)—*locale* FL-3
Atlantic Camp—*locale* TX-5
Atlantic Camp Ground Spring—*spring* FL-3
Atlantic Canyon—*valley* WY-8
Atlantic Cem—*cemetery* IA-7
Atlantic Channel—*channel* TX-5
Atlantic Christian Acad—*school* FL-3
Atlantic Christian Coll—*school* NC-3
*Atlantic City* NC-3
Atlantic City—*airport* NJ-2
**Atlantic City**—*pop pl* NJ-2
**Atlantic City**—*pop pl* WY-8
Atlantic City Airp—*airport* NJ-2
Atlantic City Cem—*cemetery* NJ-2
Atlantic City Convention Hall—*hist pl* NJ-2
Atlantic City Country Club—*other* NJ-2
Atlantic City Girl Scout Camp—*locale* NJ-2
Atlantic City Mercantile—*hist pl* WY-8
Atlantic City Park—*park* WA-9
Atlantic City Racetrack—*other* NJ-2
Atlantic City Rsvr—*reservoir* NJ-2
Atlantic City Speedway—*other* NJ-2
Atlantic Coast Line Passenger Depot—*hist pl* FL-3
Atlantic Coast Line RR Station—*hist pl* NC-3
Atlantic Community Coll—*school* NJ-2
Atlantic Country Club—*other* IA-7
**Atlantic County**—*pop pl* NJ-2
Atlantic Creek—*stream* MT-8
Atlantic Creek—*stream* (2) WY-8
Atlantic Cut—*channel* TX-5
Atlantic Drain—*stream* AZ-5
Atlantic Dunes Park—*park* FL-3
Atlantic Falls—*falls* MT-8
Atlantic Gas Station—*hist pl* FL-3
*Atlantic Heights* (2) NH-1
**Atlantic Heights**—*pop pl* FL-3
**Atlantic Heights**—*pop pl* NH-1
**Atlantic Highlands**—*pop pl* NJ-2
Atlantic Highlands Yacht Harbor—*bay* NJ-2
Atlantic Hill—*summit* MA-1
Atlantic Hill—*summit* SD-7
Atlantic (historical P.O.)—*locale* MA-1
Atlantic House—*hist pl* ME-1
Atlantic HS—*school* FL-3
Atlantic HS—*school* VA-3
Atlantic Island—*island* FL-3
Atlantic Lake—*lake* WY-8
Atlantic (Magisterial District)—*fmr MCD* VA-3
**Atlantic Mine**—*pop pl* MI-6
Atlantic Ocean—*sea* ME-1
Atlantic Ocean—*sea* MD-2
Atlantic Ocean—*sea* NJ-2
Atlantic Ocean—*sea* (2) NC-3
Atlantic Ocean—*sea* SC-3
Atlantic Ocean—*sea* PR-3
Atlantic Ocean—*sea* VI-3
Atlantic Pacific Creek Trail—*trail* WY-8
**Atlantic Park**—*pop pl* VA-3
Atlantic Peak—*summit* WY-8
Atlantic Plaza—*locale* MA-1
Atlantic Plaza Center (Shop Ctr)—*locale* FL-3
Atlantic Plaza (Shop Ctr)—*locale* FL-3
Atlantic Point—*cape* ME-1
Atlantic Pompano Bridge—*bridge* FL-3
Atlantic Power Systems—*facility* NC-3
Atlantic Richfield Plaza—*post sta* CA-9
Atlantic Rim—*cliff* WY-8
Atlantic Rural Exposition Grounds—*locale* VA-3
Atlantic Sch—*school* NC-3
Atlantic Sch—*school* PA-2
Atlantic Spring—*spring* AZ-5
Atlantic Square (Shop Ctr)—*locale* FL-3
*Atlantic Station* MA-1
Atlantic Station (historical)—*locale* MA-1
**Atlantic (subdivision)**—*pop pl* MA-1
Atlantic Temple Ch of God in Christ—*church* TN-4
Atlantic Terminal—*uninc pl* NY-2
*Atlantic Township* NJ-2
Atlantic (Township of)—*fmr MCD* (2) NC-3
Atlantic Union Coll—*school* MA-1
Atlantic View Cem—*cemetery* NJ-2
Atlantic Village Shop Ctr—*locale* FL-3
Atlantic Vocational Center—*school* FL-3
Atlantic West Elem Sch—*school* FL-3
Atlantic Yacht Basin—*harbor* VA-3
Atlantic Yacht Club—*other* GA-3
**Atlantique**—*pop pl* NY-2
Atlantique Beach—*beach* NY-2
**Atlantis**—*pop pl* FL-3
Atlantis Acad—*school* (2) FL-3
Atlantis (historical)—*locale* SD-7
Atlantis Island—*island* NY-2
Atlantis Plaza (Shop Ctr)—*locale* FL-3
Atlantis Private Sch—*school* FL-3
Atlantis Sch—*school* FL-3
*Atlas* OH-6
Atlas—*locale* CA-9
Atlas—*locale* ID-8
Atlas—*locale* IL-6
Atlas—*locale* KS-7
Atlas—*locale* WV-2
**Atlas**—*pop pl* CA-9
**Atlas**—*pop pl* KY-4
**Atlas**—*pop pl* MI-6
**Atlas**—*pop pl* MO-7
**Atlas**—*pop pl* OH-6
**Atlas**—*pop pl* PA-2
**Atlas**—*pop pl* TX-5
**Atlas**—*pop pl* WI-6
Atlas, Mount—*summit* VA-3
**Atlas (Boston)**—*pop pl* OH-6
**Atlasburg**—*pop pl* PA-2
Atlasburg Elem Sch—*school* PA-2
Atlas Ch—*church* AL-4
Atlas Ch—*church* MO-7
Atlas Ch—*church* TX-5
Atlas Colliery Station—*locale* PA-2
Atlas Creek—*stream* AK-9
Atlas Creek—*stream* IL-6
Atlas Grange Hall—*hist pl* MI-6
**Atlas Hills Subdivision**—*pop pl* UT-8
Atlas (historical)—*locale* AL-4
Atlas Millpond—*reservoir* MI-6
Atlas Mill (Site)—*locale* ID-8
Atlas Mine—*mine* CO-8
Atlas Mine—*mine* ID-8
Atlas Mine—*mine* KY-4
Atlas Mine—*mine* NV-8
Atlas Mine—*mine* UT-8
Atlas Mineral Plant—*locale* UT-8
Atlas Mineral Tailings Pond Dam—*dam* UT-8
Atlas Mineral Tailings Rsvr—*reservoir* UT-8
Atlas Mines (underground)—*mine* AL-4
Atlas Park—*park* PA-2
Atlas Peak—*summit* CA-9
Atlas Peak Sch—*school* CA-9
*Atlas P.O.* AL-4
**Atlas Point**—*pop pl* DE-2
Atlas Quarry—*mine* TN-4
Atlas Road Sch—*school* SC-3
*Atlas School* AL-4
Atlasta Creek—*stream* AK-9
Atlasta House—*locale* AK-9
Atlas Theatre—*hist pl* WY-8
**Atlas (Township of)**—*pop pl* IL-6
**Atlas (Township of)**—*pop pl* MI-6
Atlas Tract—*civil* CA-9
At Last Ranch—*locale* CO-8
Atlas Valley Country Club—*other* MI-6
Atlatl Rock—*pillar* NV-8
Atlee—*locale* OK-5
Atlee—*locale* VA-3
**Atlee**—*pop pl* TX-5
Atlee Cem—*cemetery* OK-5
**Atlee Ogles**—*pop pl* IL-6
Atlee Siding—*locale* TX-5
*Atley* VA-3
Atlik Hill—*summit* AK-9
*Atlirow* FM-9
*Atliw* FM-9
*Atliyrow* FM-9
**Atmautluak**—*pop pl* AK-9
*A Tmegerur* PW-9
Atmo Mtn—*summit* AK-9
**Atmore**—*pop pl* AL-4
Atmore (CCD)—*cens area* AL-4
Atmore City Cem—*cemetery* AL-4
Atmore Country Club—*locale* AL-4
Atmore Division—*civil* AL-4
Atmore Health Center—*hospital* AL-4
Atmore Meadows—*flat* CA-9
Atmore Mine (underground)—*mine* AL-4
Atmore Municipal Airp—*airport* AL-4
Atmore Plaza Shop Ctr—*locale* AL-4
Atmore Ranch—*locale* NM-5
Atmore State Prison Farm—*other* AL-4
Atmore State Technical Coll—*school* AL-4
Atmugiak Creek—*stream* AK-9
*Atna Coal Mines* TN-4
Atna Peaks—*summit* AK-9
Atneerich Creek—*stream* AK-9
Atnip Bluff Cabin Colony—*locale* TN-4
Atnip Hollow—*valley* TN-4
*Ato* OK-5
Atoah Ch—*church* NC-3
Atoah Creek—*stream* NC-3
Atoah Gap—*gap* NC-3
Ato Cha—*post sta* PR-3
*Atoches* AL-4
*Atodd Lake* MI-6
Atodd Lake—*lake* MI-6
Atoka—*locale* KY-4
Atoka—*locale* NM-5
Atoka—*locale* VA-3
**Atoka**—*pop pl* OK-5
**Atoka**—*pop pl* TN-4
Atoka Armory—*hist pl* OK-5
Atoka Cem—*cemetery* TX-5
Atoka City Hall—*building* TN-4
Atoka Community Bldg—*hist pl* OK-5
**Atoka (County)**—*pop pl* OK-5
Atokad Park—*park* NE-7
Atoka Lake—*lake* (2) OK-5
Atoka Post Office—*building* TN-4
Atoka State Game Ref—*park* OK-5
Atoka Station (historical)—*locale* AL-4
*Atokin* FM-9
Atoko Point—*cliff* AZ-5
*Atolak Island* MP-9
Atole Windmill—*locale* (2) TX-5
Atolia—*locale* CA-9
*Atomic Caverns* TN-4
**Atomic City**—*pop pl* ID-8
*Atomic Energy Commission Building* DC-2
Atomic Energy Commission Mound Laboratory—*building* OH-6
Atomic Energy Museum—*building* TN-4
Atomic Rock—*pillar* UT-8
Atomic Sch—*school* TN-4
Atomic Speedway—*other* OH-6
Atonap—*bar* FM-9
Atonement Ch—*church* FL-3
Atonement Ch—*church* KS-7
Atonement Ch—*church* NC-3
Atonement Ch—*church* OH-6
Atonement Episcopal Ch—*church* FL-3
Atonement Lutheran Ch—*church* UT-8
Atonement Lutheran Ch (ALC)—*church* FL-3
Atonement Methodist Ch—*church* DE-2
Atonement Sch—*school* LA-4
Atonement United Methodist Ch (Cont)—*church* UT-8
Atongarak Creek—*stream* AK-9
Aton Jones Ranch—*locale* NM-5
*Atonkin To* FM-9
Atonkis—*bar* FM-9
*Atooi* HI-9
Ator Creek—*stream* MT-8
*Atoscaceta Spring* AZ-5
*Atoscacita Spring* AZ-5
*Atoscos Mountains* AZ-5
Atosik Lagoon—*bay* AK-9
Atot—*other* GU-9
Atotak—*island* MP-9
*Atouai Island* HI-9
*Atoui* HI-9
Atoy—*locale* TX-5
Atoy Creek—*stream* TX-5
*Atpontley* TN-4
Atpontley—*other* TN-4
Atpontley Post Office (historical)—*building* TN-4
Atpontly Mine (underground)—*mine* TN-4
**Atqasuk**—*pop pl* AK-9
Atravasada Windmill—*locale* TX-5
Atravesada Artesian Well—*well* TX-5
Atravesada Canyon, Canada —*valley* AZ-5
*Atreca* TX-5
Atreco—*locale* TX-5
A-Tree, The—*locale* CA-9
Atrevida Glacier—*glacier* AK-9
**Atrisco**—*pop pl* NM-5
Atrisco Ditch—*canal* NM-5
Atrisco Drain—*canal* NM-5
Atrisco Riverside Drain—*canal* NM-5
Atrisco Sch—*school* NM-5
*Atrium* IL-6
Atrnak Point—*cape* AK-9
Atrypa Peak—*summit* NV-8
Atsadahsidahi—*summit* AZ-5
Atsaksovluk Creek—*stream* AK-9
Atsena Otie Cem—*cemetery* FL-3
Atsena Otie Key—*island* FL-3
AT & SF Locomotive—*hist pl* AZ-5
AT & SF Roundhouse—*hist pl* NM-5
*Atshi* PW-9
Atshichlut Mtn—*summit* AK-9
Atsina Falls—*falls* MT-8
Atsina Lake—*lake* MT-8
**Atsion**—*pop pl* NJ-2
Atsion Helistop—*airport* NJ-2
Atsion Lake—*reservoir* NJ-2
Atsion Lake Dam—*dam* NJ-2
*Atsion River* NJ-2
Atsion Village—*hist pl* NJ-2
*Atsurii To* MP-9
Attack Hill—*summit* NM-5
*Attakadokoru Island* PW-9
*Attakadokoru To* PW-9
**Attakapas Canal**—*pop pl* LA-4
**Attakapas Landing**—*pop pl* LA-4
*Attala* MS-4
*Attalabul* PW-9
**Attala County**—*pop pl* MS-4
Attala County Agricultural HS (historical)—*school* MS-4
Attala County Coliseum—*building* MS-4
Attala County Courthouse—*building* MS-4
Attala County Library—*building* MS-4
Attala Male and Female Acad (historical)—*school* MS-4
Attala Memory Gardens—*cemetery* MS-4
**Attalaville (historical)**—*pop pl* MS-4
Attalaville Post Office (historical)—*building* MS-4
Attalia—*locale* WA-9
**Attalla**—*pop pl* AL-4
Attalla Ch of Christ—*church* AL-4
Attalla City Park—*park* AL-4
Attalla Country Club—*locale* AL-4
Attalla Elem Sch—*school* AL-4
Attalla Grammar Sch (historical)—*school* AL-4
Attalla Public Sch (historical)—*school* AL-4
Attalla Sch—*school* AL-4
Attalla Speedway—*locale* AL-4
Attalla Spring—*spring* AL-4
*At-tan-gee* AL-4
**Attapulgas (historical)**—*pop pl* FL-3
**Attapulgus**—*pop pl* GA-3
Attapulgus (CCD)—*cens area* GA-3
*Attapulgus Creek* GA-3
Attapulgus Creek—*stream* FL-3
Attapulgus Creek—*stream* GA-3
Attapulgus (Station)—*locale* GA-3
*At-tau-gee Creek* AL-4
**Attawan Beach**—*pop pl* CT-1
**Attawaugan**—*pop pl* CT-1
Attawaugan Brook—*stream* CT-1
**Attaway**—*pop pl* SC-3
Attaway Spring—*spring* OK-5
AT & T Bldg—*hist pl* AZ-5
Attean Falls—*falls* ME-1
Attean (historical)—*locale* ME-1
Attean Landing—*locale* ME-1
Attean Mtn—*summit* ME-1
Attean Pond—*lake* ME-1
Attean (Township of)—*unorg* ME-1
Atteberry, Lake—*reservoir* TX-5
Atteberry Cem—*cemetery* (2) IL-6
Atteberry Cem—*cemetery* MO-7
Attebery Cem—*cemetery* KS-7
Attebery-Fort Cem—*cemetery* MO-7
Attebury Rsvr—*reservoir* WY-8
Attek—*gap* FM-9
Atteles Cem—*cemetery* LA-4
Attell Lateral—*canal* ID-8
Attention Peak—*summit* ID-8
**Atterberry**—*pop pl* IL-6
Atterberry Canyon—*valley* WY-8
Atterberry Cem—*cemetery* IL-6
Atterberry Cem—*cemetery* (2) MO-7
Atterberry (Election Precinct)—*fmr MCD* IL-6
Atterberry Sch (historical)—*school* MO-7
**Atterbury (Atterberry)**—*pop pl* IL-6
Atterbury Creek—*stream* SD-7
Atterbury Dam East—*dam* IN-6
Atterbury Rsvr—*reservoir* OR-9
Atterbury Spring—*spring* SD-7
Atterbury State Fish and Wildlife Area—*park* IN-6
Atterbury Wash—*arroyo* AZ-5
Atterson—*locale* KY-4
Atterson Sch—*school* KY-4
Atteza Ch—*church* SC-3
At the End of the Trail Cem—*cemetery* WV-2
*Attica* KS-7
Attica—*locale* GA-3
**Attica**—*pop pl* AR-4
**Attica**—*pop pl* IN-6
**Attica**—*pop pl* IA-7
**Attica**—*pop pl* KS-7
**Attica**—*pop pl* MI-6
**Attica**—*pop pl* NY-2
**Attica**—*pop pl* OH-6
**Attica**—*pop pl* WI-6
Attica Cem—*cemetery* KS-7
Attica Cem—*cemetery* NE-7
**Attica Center**—*pop pl* NY-2
Attica City Wells—*well* KS-7
Attica Hill—*summit* AR-4
**Attica Junction**—*pop pl* OH-6
Attica Landing Field—*airport* KS-7
Attica Rsvr—*reservoir* (2) NY-2
Attica State Prison—*other* NY-2
**Attica (Town of)**—*pop pl* NY-2
**Attica Township**—*pop pl* KS-7
**Attica (Township of)**—*pop pl* MI-6
*Attico* WI-6
**Attila**—*pop pl* IL-6
Attilla—*locale* KY-4
*Attines Ferry* PA-2
*Attins Island* PA-2
Attins Islands—*island* PA-2
**Attitash**—*pop pl* MA-1
Attitash, Lake—*reservoir* MA-1
*Attitash Lake* MA-1
Attiunik Channel—*stream* AK-9
Attiunik Point—*cape* AK-9
Attix, Thomas, House—*hist pl* DE-2
Attix Lake Dam—*dam* MS-4
*Attleboro* PA-2
**Attleboro**—*pop pl* MA-1
Attleboro, City of—*civil* MA-1
*Attleboro, Town of* MA-1
*Attleboro City* MA-1
Attleboro City Hall—*building* MA-1
**Attleboro Falls**—*pop pl* MA-1
Attleboro HS—*school* MA-1
Attleboro Mtn—*summit* NH-1
Attleboro Rod and Gun Club—*locale* MA-1
Attleboro Sewage Disposal—*other* MA-1
*Attleborough* MA-1
*Attleborough* PA-2
*Attleborough, Town of* MA-1
**Attleborough City**—*pop pl* MA-1
*Attleborough Falls* MA-1
*Attlebury* PA-2
**Attlebury**—*pop pl* NY-2
Attlebury Creek—*stream* MT-8
Attlebury Glade—*flat* CA-9
AT&T Micro Wave Tower—*tower* MO-7
Attmore-Oliver House—*hist pl* NC-3
Attners Bluffs—*cliff* MO-7
Attoney Mtn—*summit* NM-5
Attongtonganebwokwbwokw—*island* MP-9
Attongtonganedokake—*island* MP-9
Attooga Branch—*stream* NC-3
Attowa Mine—*mine* MT-8
**Attoway**—*pop pl* VA-3
Attoyac—*locale* TX-5
*Attoyac Bayou* TX-5
Attoyac Ch—*church* TX-5
Attoyac River—*stream* TX-5
AT T Road Rsvr—*reservoir* UT-8
Attschul Pond—*lake* CT-1
Attu—*locale* AK-9
Attu Battlefield and U.S. Army and Navy Airfields on Attu—*hist pl* AK-9
Attuck Sch—*school* OK-5
*Attucks High School* IN-6
Attucks HS—*school* FL-3
Attucks JHS—*school* TX-5
Attucks Park—*park* IL-6
Attucks Sch—*school* IL-6
Attucks Sch—*school* KS-7
Attucks Sch—*school* MO-7
Attucks Sch—*school* OH-6
Attucks Theatre—*hist pl* VA-3
Attu Island—*island* AK-9
Attu Island—*other* AK-9
Attu Mtn—*summit* AK-9
Attway Branch—*stream* TX-5
*Attwood* KS-7
Attwood Beach—*beach* MI-6
*Attwood Lake* IN-6
Attwood Sch—*school* MI-6
Atuk Lake—*lake* AK-9
Atuk Mtn—*summit* AK-9
Atutsak River—*stream* AK-9
**Atuu**—*pop pl* AS-9
**Atu'u**—*pop pl* AS-9
Atward Run—*stream* WV-2
Atwater—*locale* IL-6
Atwater—*locale* WI-6
**Atwater**—*pop pl* (2) CA-9
**Atwater**—*pop pl* GA-3
**Atwater**—*pop pl* MN-6
**Atwater**—*pop pl* NY-2
**Atwater**—*pop pl* OH-6
Atwater Bay—*bay* VT-1
Atwater Canal—*canal* CA-9
Atwater (CCD)—*cens area* CA-9
Atwater Cem—*cemetery* KS-7
Atwater Cem—*cemetery* NY-2
Atwater Cem—*cemetery* OH-6
**Atwater Center**—*pop pl* OH-6
Atwater Congregational Church—*hist pl* OH-6
Atwater Creek—*stream* AK-9
Atwater Creek—*stream* NY-2
Atwater Ditch—*canal* OH-6
Atwater Drain—*canal* CA-9
Atwater (historical)—*locale* KS-7
Atwater Kent Museum—*building* PA-2
Atwater Lake—*lake* ID-8
Atwater Manufacturing Company—*hist pl* CT-1
Atwater Memorial Ch—*church* NY-2
Atwater Millpond—*lake* MI-6
Atwater Park—*park* MA-1
*Atwater Pond* MI-6
Atwater Pond—*reservoir* MA-1
Atwater Pond Dam—*dam* MA-1
**Atwaters**—*pop pl* NY-2
Atwater Sch—*school* GA-3
Atwater Sch—*school* OH-6
Atwater Sch—*school* WI-6
Atwater-Stone House—*hist pl* NY-2
**Atwater (Township of)**—*pop pl* OH-6
Atway—*locale* MS-4
Atway Post Office (historical)—*building* MS-4
Atway Sch (historical)—*school* MS-4
Atwell—*locale* MO-7
Atwell—*locale* TX-5
**Atwell**—*pop pl* GA-3
**Atwell**—*pop pl* NY-2
**Atwell**—*pop pl* WV-2
Atwell Branch—*stream* WV-2
Atwell Brook—*stream* ME-1
Atwell Brook—*stream* (2) NH-1
Atwell Cem—*cemetery* (2) KY-4
Atwell Cem—*cemetery* WV-2
**Atwell Corners**—*pop pl* NY-2
Atwell Creek—*stream* (2) CA-9
Atwell Creek—*stream* MO-7
Atwell Drain—*stream* MI-6
Atwell Grove—*woods* CA-9
Atwell Gulch—*valley* CO-8
Atwell Hill—*summit* NH-1
Atwell Hockett Trail—*trail* CA-9
Atwell Homestead—*locale* CO-8
Atwell Mill Ranger Station—*locale* CA-9
Atwell Park—*park* WI-6
Atwell Point—*cape* IA-7
Atwell Pond—*lake* FL-3

Austin Gap—gap (2) ... VA-3
Austin Gap—gap ... WV-2
Austin Gap Branch—stream ... VA-3
Austin Gas Storage Field—other ... MI-6
Austin Glen—valley ... NY-2
Austin Grove Ch—church ... NC-3
Austin Hall—hist pl ... MA-1
Austin Hall—hist pl ... OH-6
Austin Hank Lake—reservoir ... TN-4
Austin Hank Lake Dam—dam ... TN-4
**Austin Heights**—pop pl ... PA-2
Austin-Hennessey Homestead—hist pl ... ME-1
Austin Hill—summit (2) ... MA-1
Austin Hill—summit ... PA-2
Austin Hill—summit (2) ... VT-1
**Austin Hill (subdivision)**—pop pl ... AL-4
Austin Hist Dist—hist pl ... IL-6
Austin Hist Dist—hist pl ... NV-8
Austin (historical)—locale ... KS-7
Austin (historical P.O.)—locale ... IA-7
Austin Hollow—valley (2) ... IL-6
Austin Hollow—valley ... MO-7
Austin Hollow—valley (2) ... PA-2
Austin Hollow—valley ... RI-1
Austin Hollow—valley (4) ... TN-4
Austin Hollow—valley ... VA-3
Austin Hollow—valley ... WV-2
Austin Hot Spring—spring ... OR-9
Austin House—hist pl ... AR-4
Austin HS—school ... AL-4
Austin HS—school ... IL-6
Austin HS—school ... IN-6
Austin HS—school ... MI-6
Austin HS—school ... TN-4
Austin HS—school (3) ... TX-5
Austin JHS—school (3) ... TX-5
Austin Junction ... MN-6
Austin Junction—locale ... OR-9
**Austin Junction**—pop pl ... ME-1
Austin Junior and Senior HS—school ... TX-5
Austin Lake ... MI-6
Austin Lake—lake (4) ... MI-6
Austin Lake—lake ... MN-6
Austin Lake—lake ... MT-8
Austin Lake—lake ... OH-6
Austin Lake—lake ... OK-5
Austin Lake—lake ... WI-6
Austin Lincoln Park—park ... NY-2
Austin-Magie Farm and Mill District—hist pl ... OH-6
Austin-McDonald House—hist pl ... NM-5
Austin Meadow—flat ... CA-9
Austin Meadow—swamp ... OR-9
Austin Memorial Park (Cemetery)—cemetery ... TX-5
Austin Mill Brook—stream ... NH-1
Austin Mills—locale ... NC-3
Austin Mountain Trail—trail ... VA-3
Austin MS—school ... IN-6
Austin Mtn—summit ... NC-3
Austin Mtn—summit ... VA-3
Austin Number One Mine—mine ... MI-6
Austin Number Two Mine—mine ... MI-6
Austin Olds Cem—cemetery ... AL-4
Austin Park ... IL-6
Austin Park—park (2) ... IL-6
Austin Park—park ... NY-2
Austin Park—park ... TX-5
Austin Pass—gap ... WA-9
Austin Peak—summit ... AZ-5
Austin Peak—summit ... CA-9
Austin Peay Rec Area—park ... TN-4
Austin Peay State Coll—school ... TN-4
Austin Peay State Univ—post sta ... TN-4
**Austin Pines (subdivision)**—pop pl ... NC-3
Austin Point ... OR-9
Austin Point—cape ... AL-4
Austin Point—cape ... NC-3
Austin Point—cape ... OR-9
Austin Point—cape ... WA-9
Austin Point—summit ... OR-9
Austin Point Cave—cave ... AL-4
Austin Pond—lake (2) ... ME-1
Austin Pond—lake ... NY-2
Austin Pond—lake ... VT-1
Austin Pond—reservoir ... NC-3
Austin Pond Mtn—summit ... NY-2
Austin Post Office ... CO-8
Austin Post Office ... TN-4
Austin Raceway Park—park ... TX-5
Austin Ranch—locale ... ID-8
Austin Ranch—locale ... NM-5
Austin Ranch—locale ... ND-7
Austin Ranch—locale ... OR-9
Austin Ranch—locale ... WY-8
Austin Ravine—valley ... CA-9
Austin Reef—bar ... NC-3
Austin Ridge—ridge ... AR-4
Austin Ridge—ridge ... ID-8
Austin Ridge—ridge ... OK-5
Austin Ridge—ridge ... TN-4
Austin R Meadows Library—building ... AL-4
Austin Rsvr—reservoir (2) ... WY-8
Austin Run—stream ... IN-6
Austin Run—stream ... VA-3
Austin Sch—school ... AL-4
Austin Sch—school ... AR-4
Austin Sch—school (2) ... IL-6
Austin Sch—school ... KY-4
Austin Sch—school ... MA-1
Austin Sch—school (2) ... MI-6
Austin Sch—school ... MN-6
Austin Sch—school ... MS-4
Austin Sch—school ... NE-7
Austin Sch—school ... SD-7
Austin Sch—school (21) ... TX-5
Austin Sch (abandoned)—school ... PA-2
Austins Corner ... NH-1
Austins Corners—locale (2) ... NY-2
Austins Dam—dam ... ME-1
Austin's Glen ... NY-2
Austins Grove Ch—church ... VA-3
Austin Shoal ... NC-3
Austins Hollow ... RI-1
Austin Site (15McL15)—hist pl ... KY-4
**Austins Mill**—pop pl ... NC-3
**Austins Mill**—pop pl ... TN-4
Austins Mill Post Office ... TN-4
Austins Mill Post Office (historical)—building ... TN-4
Austins Pond Dam—dam ... NC-3
Austin Spring—spring ... AL-4
Austin Spring—spring ... MT-8
Austin Spring—spring (2) ... NV-8
Austin Spring—spring (2) ... WY-8
Austin Spring Cave—cave ... AL-4
**Austin Springs**—pop pl (2) ... TN-4
Austin Springs Elem Sch—school ... TN-4
**Austin Springs (Unity)**—pop pl ... TN-4
Austins Run ... VA-3
Austins Shoal ... NC-3
Austins Springs ... TN-4
Austins Springs Post Office (historical)—building ... TN-4
Austin State Hosp—hospital ... TX-5
Austin State Sch—school ... TX-5
Austin State Sch (Annex)—school ... TX-5
Austin Station ... AR-4
Austin-Straubel Field (Airport)—airport ... WI-6
Austin Stream—stream ... ME-1
**Austin Subdivision**—pop pl ... AL-4
Austin Summit—gap ... NV-8
Austin Terrace—uninc pl ... TX-5
**Austintown**—pop pl ... OH-6
Austintown Log House—hist pl ... OH-6
Austin Township—civil ... MO-7
Austin Township—inact MCD ... NV-8
**Austin Township**—pop pl ... ND-7
Austin (Township of)—fmr MCD ... AR-4
**Austin (Township of)**—pop pl ... IL-6
**Austin (Township of)**—pop pl (2) ... MI-6
**Austin (Township of)**—pop pl ... MN-6
**Austintown (Township of)**—pop pl ... OH-6
Austin-Tracy Sch—school ... KY-4
Austin-Travis County Tuberculosis Sanatorium—hospital ... TX-5
**Austin View**—pop pl ... IL-6
**Austin Village**—pop pl ... OH-6
**Austin Village (subdivision)**—pop pl ... TN-4
**Austinville**—pop pl ... AL-4
**Austinville**—pop pl ... IA-7
**Austinville**—pop pl ... PA-2
**Austinville**—pop pl ... VA-3
Austinville Ch of Christ—church ... AL-4
Austinville Ch of God—church ... AL-4
Austinville Elem Sch—school ... AL-4
Austinville Methodist Ch—church ... AL-4
Austinville Post Office (historical)—building ... AL-4
Austin Wash—basin ... WY-8
Austin Well—locale ... NM-5
Austin Well—well ... NV-8
Austin-Wherritt House—hist pl ... UT-8
Austin-Whittemore House—hist pl ... SD-7
Auston Ch—church ... GA-3
Austonia Cem—cemetery ... TX-5
Austonia Ch—church ... TX-5
**Austonio**—pop pl ... TX-5
Auston Well—well ... UT-8
Austral—locale ... TN-4
Australia Gulch—valley (2) ... CO-8
Australia Gulch—valley ... MT-8
Australia Island—island ... LA-4
Australia Island Number Onehundred and One—island ... LA-4
Australia Landing—locale ... MS-4
Australian Mine—mine ... MT-8
Austral Post Office (historical)—building ... TN-4
Austria ... MO-7
Austrian Bayou—gut ... LA-4
Austrian Central Cem—cemetery ... UT-8
Austrian Creek—stream ... CO-8
Austrian Dam—dam ... CA-9
Austrian Gulch—valley (2) ... CA-9
Austrian Legation Bldg—building ... DC-2
**Austwell**—pop pl (2) ... TX-5
Austwell Cem—cemetery ... TX-5
Austwell-Tivoli (CCD)—cens area ... TX-5
Auszen-Hafen ... FM-9
Auszenn Wafen ... FM-9
**Autapini**—pop pl ... AS-9
Autauga Acad—school ... AL-4
**Autauga County**—pop pl ... AL-4
Autauga County Airp—airport ... AL-4
Autauga County Courthouse—building ... AL-4
Autauga County HS—school ... AL-4
Autauga County Med Ctr—hospital ... AL-4
Autauga Creek—stream ... AL-4
Autauga Heights Baptist Ch—church ... AL-4
Autauga Hill Ch—church ... AL-4
Autauga Hill Sch—school ... AL-4
Autauga (historical)—locale ... AL-4
Autauga Landing—locale ... AL-4
**Autaugaville**—pop pl ... AL-4
Autaugaville (CCD)—cens area ... AL-4
Autaugaville Division—civil ... AL-4
Autaugaville Elem Sch—school ... AL-4
Autaugaville HS—school ... AL-4
Autauga Vocational Sch—school ... AL-4
**Auter**—pop pl ... MS-4
Auter Windmill—locale ... TX-5
Authen Ditch—canal ... IN-6
Authon—locale ... TX-5
Authon Cem—cemetery ... TX-5
Authors Ridge—ridge ... MA-1
Author Well—well ... NM-5
Authur Cem—cemetery ... MO-7
**Auth Village**—pop pl ... MD-2
Autin Cem—cemetery ... OH-6
Autio Lake—lake ... MI-6
Autle—island ... MP-9
Auto—locale ... WV-2
Auto—locale ... AS-9
Autobi ... AL-4
Auto City Speedway—other ... MI-6
Auto Club ... MN-6
Auto Club—locale ... MN-6
Autograph Cliff—cliff ... OK-5
Auto Hill—summit ... NV-8
Auto Hotel Bldg—hist pl ... IN-6
Automatic Creek—stream ... AK-9
Automatic Creek—stream ... ID-8
Automatic Creek—stream ... MT-8
Automba—locale ... MN-6
Automba Ch—church ... MN-6
**Automba (Township of)**—pop pl ... MN-6
Automobile Draw—valley ... NM-5
Automobile Lake—lake ... NM-5
Automobile Water Tank—other ... NM-5
Automw—island ... MP-9
Autore ... MP-9
Autore Island ... MP-9
Autore Island—island ... MP-9
Autore-To ... MP-9
Autori ... MP-9
Autori-To ... MP-9
Autossee (historical)—locale ... AL-4
Auto Storage Dam Number One—dam ... NC-3
Auto Storage Dam Number Two—dam ... NC-3
Auto Storage Lake Number One—reservoir ... NC-3
Auto Storage Lake Number Two—reservoir ... NC-3
Auto Tank ... AZ-5
**Au Train**—pop pl ... MI-6
Au Train Bay—bay ... MI-6
Au Train Falls—falls ... MI-6
Au Train Island—island ... MI-6
Au Train Lake—lake ... MI-6
Au Train Point—cape ... MI-6
Au Train River—stream ... MI-6
**Au Train (Township of)**—pop pl ... MI-6
Autrey Cem—cemetery ... NC-3
Autrey Cem—cemetery ... TN-4
Autrey Cem—cemetery ... WA-9
Autrey Creek ... NC-3
Autrey Creek—stream ... AL-4
Autrey House—hist pl ... LA-4
Autrey Park—uninc pl ... MD-2
Autrey Rsvr—reservoir ... CO-8
Autreys Gap ... AL-4
Autreys (historical)—locale ... AL-4
Autreys Store ... AL-4
**Autreyville**—pop pl ... GA-3
**Autry**—pop pl ... GA-3
Autry, James L., House—hist pl ... TX-5
Autry Branch—stream ... MS-4
Autry Branch—stream ... TX-5
Autry Cem—cemetery ... NC-3
Autry Lake—reservoir ... MS-4
**Autryville**—pop pl ... NC-3
Auts Canyon ... UT-8
Autsidy Smith Well—well ... AZ-5
**Autumn Acres**—pop pl ... OH-6
Autumn Creek—stream ... AK-9
Autumn Creek—stream ... ID-8
Autumn Creek—stream ... MT-8
Autumn Creek Trail—trail ... MT-8
**Autumn Hill**—pop pl ... MD-2
Autumn Hill Park—park ... NJ-2
**Autumn Hills**—pop pl ... NE-7
**Autumn Hills Subdivision**—pop pl ... UT-8
Autumn Island ... FM-9
Autumn Lake—reservoir ... IN-6
Autumn Lake Dam—dam ... IN-6
Autumn Lane Sch—school ... NY-2
Autumn Leaves—locale ... PA-2
Autumn Point—cape ... TX-5
**Autumn Ridge (subdivision)**—pop pl (2) ... AZ-5
**Autumn Wood Circle Subdivision**—pop pl ... UT-8
**Autumnwood (subdivision)**—pop pl ... NC-3
**Autumn Wood Subdivision**—pop pl ... UT-8
Autun—hist pl ... PA-2
Autwine—locale ... OK-5
Autwine Oil Field—oilfield ... OK-5
Autzen Stadium—other ... OR-9
Auun ... FM-9
Auvaiola Stream—stream ... AS-9
Auvaipe Stream—stream ... AS-9
Auvai Stream—stream ... AS-9
Auvase Creek—stream ... MI-6
**Auvergne**—pop pl ... AR-4
Auvil—locale ... WV-2
Auville—uninc pl ... WV-2
Auvinen Corner—locale ... MI-6
Auwae—cape ... HI-9
Auwahi—civil ... HI-9
Auwaiakeakua Gulch—valley ... HI-9
Auwalolimu Playground—park ... HI-9
Auwater Ditch—canal ... MT-8
Aux Bec Scies ... MI-6
Aux Buscies ... MI-6
Auxelia Creek ... TX-5
**Auxier**—pop pl ... KY-4
Auxier Branch—stream (2) ... KY-4
Auxier Branch Trail—trail ... KY-4
Auxier Creek—stream ... IL-6
Auxier Creek Drain—canal ... IL 6
Auxier Ridge—ridge ... KY-4
Auxier Ridge Trail—trail ... KY-4
Auxiliary Field No. 9 (Hurlburt Field)—other ... FL-3
Auxiliary Landing Field Bonham—military ... HI-9
Auxiliary Point—cape ... NV-8
Auxiliary Reservoir Dam—dam ... NJ-2
Auxiliary Rsvr—reservoir ... NJ-2
Auxiliary Supply Canal—canal ... AZ-5
Auxillary Landing Field (Reese AFB)—military ... TX-5
Auxor Basin—basin ... ID-8
Auxor Mine—mine ... ID-8
**Aux Sable**—pop pl ... IL-6
Aux Sable Cem—cemetery ... IL-6
Aux Sable Ch—church ... IL-6
Aux Sable Creek—stream ... IL-6
Aux Sable Island—island ... IL-6
Aux Sable Lock—other ... IL-6
Aux Sable Sch—school ... IL-6
**Aux Sable (Township of)**—pop pl ... IL-6
Aux-um-ne ... CA-9
Aux-um-nes ... CA-9
**Auxvasse**—pop pl ... MO-7
Auxvasse Brook ... MO-7
Auxvasse Cem—cemetery ... MO-7
Auxvasse Creek—stream ... MO-7
Auxvasse Township—civil ... MO-7
Auza Tanks—reservoir ... AZ-5
Au 7 Ranch—locale ... WY-8
**Ava**—pop pl ... AL-4
**Ava**—pop pl ... IL-6
**Ava**—pop pl ... MO-7
**Ava**—pop pl ... NY-2
**Ava**—pop pl ... OH-6
Ava, Mount—summit ... AK-9
Ava Brook—stream ... NY-2
Ava Cem—cemetery ... NY-2
Ava Ch—church ... AL-4
Avaco, Lake—lake ... FL-3
Avagatatau Rock—island ... AS-9
Avaio—locale ... AS-9
Avak Bay—bay ... AK-9
Avak Creek—stream ... AK-9
Avak Inlet—channel ... AK-9
Avak Point—cape ... AK-9
Avak River—stream ... AK-9
Avak Test Hole—bend ... AK-9
Avalanch ... WI-6
**Avalanche**—pop pl ... WI-6
Avalanche Basin—basin ... MT-8
Avalanche Brook—stream ... ME-1
Avalanche Brook—stream (2) ... NH-1
Avalanche Butte—summit ... MT-8
Avalanche Campground—locale ... CO-8
Avalanche Campground—locale ... MT-8
Avalanche Canyon—valley ... AK-9
Avalanche Canyon—valley ... WY-8
Avalanche Cave—cave ... UT-8
Avalanche Creek—stream (2) ... CA-9
Avalanche Creek—stream ... CO-8
Avalanche Creek—stream ... ID-8
Avalanche Creek—stream (2) ... MT-8
Avalanche Creek—stream ... OR-9
Avalanche Creek—stream (2) ... WY-8
Avalanche Glacier—glacier ... WA-9
Avalanche Gorge—valley ... WA-9
Avalanche Gulch—valley ... CA-9
Avalanche Gulch—valley ... CO-8
Avalanche Lake—lake (3) ... CA-9
Avalanche Lake—lake (3) ... MT-8
Avalanche Lake—lake ... NY-2
Avalanche Lake—lake ... OR-9
Avalanche Lake—lake ... WA-9
Avalanche Lake—reservoir ... CO-8
Avalanche Lakes ... MT-8
Avalanche Meadow—flat ... CA-9
Avalanche Mtn—summit ... MI-6
Avalanche Mtn—summit ... NY-2
Avalanche Pass—gap ... CA-9
Avalanche Pass—gap ... CO-8
Avalanche Pass—gap ... NY-2
Avalanche Peak ... CA-9
Avalanche Peak—summit ... CA-9
Avalanche Peak—summit ... CO-8
Avalanche Peak—summit ... NM-5
Avalanche Peak—summit ... WY-8
Avalanche Ranch—locale ... CO-8
Avalanche Ravine ... CA-9
Avalanche Ridge—ridge ... ID-8
Avalanche Spire—pillar ... AK-9
Avalanche-Spire Rock Camp—locale ... MT-8
Avalanche Trail—trail ... MT-8
Avalanche Valley—valley ... WA-9
Avalik River—stream ... AK-9
Avalitkok Creek—stream ... AK-9
Avalitkuk—hist pl ... AK-9
Avalo—locale ... CO-8
Avaloa Point—cape ... AS-9
Avalon ... IN-6
Avalon ... OH-6
Avalon ... SD-7
Avalon—hist pl ... AL-4
Avalon—hist pl ... MD-2
Avalon—locale ... NM-5
Avalon—locale ... VA-3
**Avalon**—pop pl ... CA-9
**Avalon**—pop pl ... DE-2
**Avalon**—pop pl ... GA-3
**Avalon**—pop pl ... IN-6
**Avalon**—pop pl ... LA-4
**Avalon**—pop pl (2) ... MD-2
**Avalon**—pop pl ... MS-4
**Avalon**—pop pl ... MO-7
**Avalon**—pop pl ... NJ-2
**Avalon**—pop pl (2) ... OH-6
**Avalon**—pop pl ... PA-2
**Avalon**—pop pl ... TX-5
**Avalon**—pop pl ... VA-3
**Avalon**—pop pl ... WI-6
Avalon—uninc pl ... GA-3
Avalon, Bayou—gut ... AL-4
Avalon, Lake—lake ... FL-3
Avalon, Lake—reservoir ... AR-4
Avalon, Lake—reservoir ... MO-7
Avalon, Lake—reservoir ... NM-5
Avalon, Mount—summit ... NH-1
Avalon Bay—bay ... CA-9
Avalon Beach—locale ... FL-3
**Avalon Beach**—pop pl (2) ... MI-6
**Avalon Beach**—pop pl ... VT-1
**Avalon Bench**—pop pl ... NC-3
Avalon Borough—civil ... PA-2
Avalon Cem—cemetery ... MO-7
Avalon Cem—cemetery ... UT-8
Avalon Ch—church (2) ... AL-4
Avalon Ch—church ... GA-3
Avalon Ch—church ... NC-3
Avalon Cut-Off—bend ... MS-4
Avalon Dam—dam ... NC-3
Avalon Drain—stream ... AZ-5
Avalon Elem Sch—school ... FL-3
Avalon Elem Sch—school ... PA-2
**Avalon Estates Subdivision**—pop pl ... UT-8
Avalon Farm Pond—reservoir ... CT-1
Avalon Gardens Sch—school ... CA-9
**Avalon Heights**—pop pl ... OH-6
**Avalon Heights (subdivision)**—pop pl ... TN-4
Avalon Hills ... IN-6
**Avalon Hills**—pop pl ... IN-6
**Avalon Hills**—pop pl ... VA-3
Avalon Hills—range ... NM-5
**Avalon Hills Subdivision**—pop pl ... UT-8
Avalon Hotel—hist pl ... MN-6
Avalon Lake—lake ... MI-6
**Avalon Lake**—pop pl ... MI-6
Avalon Life Saving Station—hist pl ... NJ-2
Avalon Lookout Tower—tower ... FL-3
Avalon Memorial Hosp—hospital ... CA-9
Avalon MS—school ... AL-4
Avalon Park ... IL-6
Avalon Park—park ... AL-4
Avalon Park—park ... CA-9
Avalon Park—park ... IL-6
Avalon Park—park ... TX-5
**Avalon Park**—pop pl ... AL-4
Avalon Park Sch—school ... IL-6
**Avalon Park (trailer park)**—pop pl ... DE-2
Avalon Point—cape ... MA-1
Avalon Sch—school ... CA-9
Avalon Sch—school ... MD-2
Avalon Sch—school ... MA-1
Avalon Sch—school ... MI-6
**Avalon Shores**—pop pl ... MD-2
Avalon State Park—park ... TX-5
**Avalon Terrace**—pop pl ... VA-3
Avalon Trails ... IL-6
**Avalon Valley (subdivision)**—pop pl ... NC-3
**Avalon Village**—pop pl ... CA-9
**Avalon Village Subdivision**—pop pl ... UT-8
Avalon Yacht Club—other ... NJ-2
Avals Beach—beach ... CA-9
**Avance**—pop pl ... SD-7
Avance Township (historical)—civil ... SD-7
Avandale ... LA-4
**Avandale**—pop pl ... LA-4
Avandale Spring—spring ... ID-8
Avanelle ... MS-4
Avan Hills ... AK-9
Avan River ... AK-9
**Avans**—pop pl ... GA-3
Avans Ch—church ... GA-3
**Avant**—pop pl ... AL-4
**Avant**—pop pl ... AR-4
**Avant**—pop pl ... OK-5
Avantaquin Campground ... UT-8
Avant Cave—cave ... TN-4
Avant Cem—cemetery ... GA-3
Avant Cem—cemetery ... OK-5
Avant Cemetary—cemetery ... AR-4
Avant Landing—locale ... AR-4
Avant Oil Field—oilfield ... OK-5
Avant Prairie—locale ... TX-5
Avant Ranch—locale ... NM-5
Avants—locale ... GA-3
Avant Sch (historical)—school ... MS-4
Avanzino Ranch—locale ... CA-9
Avanzino Rsvr—reservoir ... CA-9
Av-a-pa ... UT-8
Ava Point—cape ... AS-9
Ava Post Office (historical)—building ... TN-4
Avapui Ridge—ridge ... AS-9
Avaraart Lake—lake ... AK-9
Avarado Gulch—valley ... CO-8
A VAR Arrowhead River ... MN-6
A VAR Balden Lake ... MN-6
**Avard**—pop pl ... OK-5
Avard Lake—reservoir ... OK-5
Avary Canyon ... TX-5
Avatanak Bight—bay (2) ... AK-9
Avatanak Island—island ... AK-9
Avatanak Point—cape ... AK-9
Avatanak Strait—channel ... AK-9
Avatele Cove—bay ... AS-9
Avatele Passage—channel ... AS-9
Avatele Point—cape ... AS-9
Avation HS—school ... NY-2
**Ava (Town of)**—pop pl ... NY-2
Avau—locale ... AS-9
Avau Stream—stream ... AS-9
Avavick Knoll—summit ... UT-8
**Avawam**—pop pl ... KY-4
Avawam Sch—school ... KY-4
Avawatz Mountains—other ... CA-9
Avawatz Pass—gap ... CA-9
Ave Ditch—canal ... MS-4
Avelan Apartments—hist pl ... UT-8
Avelene Creek—stream ... ID-8
**Avella**—pop pl ... PA-2
**Avella Highlands**—pop pl ... PA-2
Ave Maria Grotto—cave ... AL-4
Ave Maria Grotto—hist pl ... AL-4
Ave Maria Shrine—church ... CO-8
Avena—locale ... CA-9
Avena—locale ... IL-6
Avena—locale ... KY-4
Avenak Mtn—summit ... AK-9
**Avenal**—pop pl ... CA-9
Avenal Canyon—valley ... CA-9
Avenal Canyon Mine—mine ... CA-9
Avenal (CCD)—cens area ... CA-9
Avenal Creek—stream ... CA-9
Avenales Observation—locale ... CA-9
Avenales Ranch—locale ... CA-9
Avenales Station—locale ... CA-9
Avenal Gap—gap ... CA-9
Avenaloca Mesa—summit ... CA-9
Avenal Ridge—ridge ... CA-9
**Avena (Township of)**—pop pl ... IL-6
Avendale—locale ... PA-2
**Avendale**—pop pl ... PA-2
Avendale Creek ... CA-9
Avenel—locale ... MD-2
**Avenel**—pop pl ... NJ-2
**Avenel-Hillandale**—pop pl ... MD-2
Avenell ... MS-4
Avenel Station—locale ... NJ-2
Avenenti, Encarnacion, House—hist pl ... AZ-5
**Avenger Village**—pop pl ... TX-5
Aven Lateral—canal ... ID-8
Avens Bridge—bridge ... VA-3
**Avenstoke**—pop pl ... KY-4
Avent ... MS-4
**Avent**—pop pl (2) ... MS-4
Avent Cem—cemetery ... NC-3
Avent Cemetary—cemetery ... TN-4
Avent Chapel ... MS-4
Avent Ditch—canal ... WY-8
Avent Ferry Rd—post sta ... NC-3
Aventine Cem—cemetery ... MI-6
Aventine Hall—hist pl ... VA-3
Avent Lake Dam—dam ... MS-4
Aventon—locale ... NC-3
Avent Park—park ... MS-4
Avent Sch—school ... WY-8
Avents Creek—stream ... NC-3
Avent Station ... MS-4
Aventura—CDP ... FL-3
Aventura Mall—locale ... FL-3
Avenue ... OH-6
**Avenue**—pop pl ... MD-2
**Avenue, The**—pop pl ... OH-6
Avenue A Elem Sch—school ... KS-7
Avenue Branch—bay ... MD-2
Avenue B Sch—school ... IA-7
**Avenue City**—pop pl ... MO-7
Avenue Creek—stream ... OR-9
Avenue E Elem Sch—school ... AZ-5
Avenue Lake—lake ... MN-6
Avenue Landing ... AR-4
Avenue Martin Lateral—canal ... CA-9
Avenue Pond—lake ... FL-3
Avenue Revetment—levee ... AR-4
Avenue Sch—school ... CA-9
**Avenues Condominium, The**—pop pl ... UT-8
Avenues Condominiums ... UT-8
**Avenues Heritage Condominium, The**—pop pl ... UT-8
Avenues Hist Dist—hist pl ... UT-8
Avenue United Methodist Ch—church ... DE-2
Avera—locale ... MS-4
**Avera**—pop pl ... GA-3
Avera Cem—cemetery (2) ... MS-4
Avera Ch—church ... MS-4
Avera Chapel Cem—cemetery ... MS-4
Avera Creek ... GA-3
Averasboro ... NC-3
**Averasboro**—pop pl ... NC-3
Averasboro Battleground Monmt—park ... NC-3
Averasboro Cem—cemetery ... NC-3
Averasboro (Township of)—fmr MCD ... NC-3
Avere Creek ... GA-3
Averell Cem—cemetery ... VT-1
Averell Hill—summit ... NY-2
Averell Hill Cem—cemetery ... NY-2
Averett—locale ... VA-3
Averett Branch—stream ... AL-4
Averett Canyon—valley (2) ... UT-8
Averett Cem—cemetery ... TN-4
Averett-Cliatt Cem—cemetery ... AL-4
Averett Coll—school ... VA-3
Averetts Pond—reservoir ... GA-3
Averia Creek—stream ... TX-5
Averic, Lake—lake ... MA-1
Averick Lake ... MA-1
Averies Island ... MA-1
Averiett, Benjamin H., House—hist pl ... AL-4
Averiett, William, House—hist pl ... AL-4
Averill—locale ... SC-3
**Averill**—pop pl ... MI-6
**Averill**—pop pl ... MN-6
**Averill**—pop pl ... VT-1
Averill, A. T., House—hist pl ... IA-7
Averill Blvd Park—park ... NY-2
Averill Canyon—valley ... CA-9
Averill Cem—cemetery ... MO-7
Averill Ch—church ... MI-6
Averill Creek—stream ... MI-6
Averill Creek—stream ... VT-1
Averill Creek—stream ... WI-6
Averill Drain—canal ... MI-6
Averill Lake ... VT-1
Averill Lake—lake ... MI-6
Averill Lake—lake ... OR-9
Averill Lake—lake ... WI-6
Averill Mtn—summit ... VT-1
Averill Park—park ... CA-9
**Averill Park**—pop pl ... NY-2
Averill Peak—summit ... NY-2
Averill Sch—school ... MI-6
Averill Sch—school ... TX-5
Averills Island—island ... MA-1
Averill (Town of)—fmr MCD ... VT-1
Averitt Branch ... AL-4
Averitt Branch—stream ... TN-4
Averitt Cem—cemetery ... TN-4
Averittes Spring—spring ... AL-4
Averitt Hollow—valley ... TN-4
Averitts Ferry ... AL-4
Avero House—hist pl ... FL-3
Aversboro Elem Sch—school ... NC-3
Avers Mill (historical)—locale ... MS-4
Averson Canyon—valley ... CO-8
Averson Spring—spring ... CO-8
**Avert**—pop pl ... MO-7
**Avert Acres**—pop pl ... GA-3
Avertt Rsvr—reservoir ... NV-8
Avery—locale ... AR-4
Avery—locale ... MD-2
Avery—locale ... OR-9
Avery—locale ... PA-2
Avery—other ... LA-4
**Avery**—pop pl (2) ... AL-4
**Avery**—pop pl ... CA-9
**Avery**—pop pl ... GA-3
**Avery**—pop pl ... ID-8
**Avery**—pop pl ... IN-6
**Avery**—pop pl ... IA-7
**Avery**—pop pl (2) ... MI-6
**Avery**—pop pl ... MO-7
**Avery**—pop pl ... NE-7
**Avery**—pop pl ... OH-6
**Avery**—pop pl ... OK-5
**Avery**—pop pl ... TX-5
Avery—uninc pl ... AL-4
Avery, Alphonse Calhoun, House—hist pl ... NC-3
Avery, Carlos, House—hist pl ... OH-6
Avery, Mount—summit ... OR-9
Avery, Thomas, House—hist pl ... CT-1
Avery Ave Hist Dist—hist pl ... NC-3
Avery Ave Sch—hist pl ... NC-3
Avery Bayou—gut ... FL-3
Avery Bldg—hist pl ... OK-5
Avery Brake—swamp ... AR-4
Avery Branch—stream ... AR-4
Avery Branch—stream (2) ... IL-6
Avery Branch—stream (2) ... TN-4
Avery Branch—stream ... TX-5
Avery Bridges—hist pl ... CO-8
Avery Brook ... CT-1
Avery Brook—stream ... CT-1
Avery Brook—stream (2) ... ME-1
Avery Brook—stream (2) ... MA-1
Avery Brook—stream ... NH-1
Avery Brook—stream ... VT-1
Avery Camp—locale ... NE-7
Avery Canal ... LA-4
Avery Canal—canal ... LA-4
Avery Canyon—valley ... CA-9
Avery Canyon—valley ... TX-5
Avery Cem—cemetery (2) ... AL-4
Avery Cem—cemetery ... AR-4
Avery Cem—cemetery (2) ... CT-1
Avery Cem—cemetery (2) ... IN-6
Avery Cem—cemetery ... MI-6
Avery Cem—cemetery ... MS-4
Avery Cem—cemetery (2) ... MO-7
Avery Cem—cemetery ... OK-5
Avery Cem—cemetery ... TN-4
Avery Cem—cemetery ... TX-5

Aycock Millpond Dam—*dam* NC-3
Aycock Mine (underground)—*mine* AL-4
Aycock Park—*park* TN-4
*Aycock Point* WA-9
*Aycock Pond* AL-4
*Aycock Sch* NC-3
Aycock Sch—*school* (4) NC-3
Aycock Sch—*school* TX-5
Aycocks Creek—*stream* GA-3
*Aycocks Pond* NC-3
Aycock Swamp—*stream* NC-3
Aycrigg Mansion—*hist pl* NJ-2
Aydelette Lake—*reservoir* NC-3
Aydelette Lake Dam—*dam* NC-3
**Aydelotte**—*pop pl* OK-5
Aydelotte—*stream* MD-2
*Aydelotte Branch* MD-2
*Aydelotte Creek* MD-2
Aydelotte Point—*cape* DE-2
Aydelotte Washer—*locale* AR-4
Aydelott House—*hist pl* KY-4
**Ayden**—*pop pl* NC-3
Ayden Elem Sch—*school* NC-3
Ayden Golf and Country Club—*locale* NC-3
Ayden-Grifton HS—*school* NC-3
Ayden MS—*school* NC-3
Ayden Post Office—*building* NC-3
Ayden (Township of)—*fmr MCD* NC-3
Ayding Brook—*stream* NH-1
**Aydlett**—*pop pl* NC-3
*Aydylotte Branch* MD-2
*Ayebukuru* PW-9
*Ayeng* FM-9
Ayer—*locale* CO-8
Ayer—*locale* WA-9
**Ayer**—*pop pl* MA-1
**Ayer Center**—*pop pl* MA-1
Ayer Creek—*stream* GA-3
Ayer Creek—*stream* MD-2
*Ayer Groton Junction* MA-1
Ayer Hall—*hist pl* MS-4
Ayer Hill—*summit* CT-1
Ayer HS—*school* MA-1
Ayer Island—*island* MD-2
*Ayer Junction* MA-1
Ayer Mission Site—*hist pl* MN-6
Ayer Park—*park* CA-9
Ayer Park—*park* IL-6
Ayer Point—*cliff* AZ-5
Ayer Pond—*reservoir* CT-1
Ayer Ranch—*locale* CO-8
Ayers—*locale* FL-3
Ayers—*locale* IL-6
Ayers—*locale* KY-4
Ayers—*locale* ME-1
Ayers—*locale* WV-2
Ayers—*locale* WY-8
**Ayers**—*pop pl* TN-4
Ayers-Allen House—*hist pl* NJ-2
Ayers Bank Bldg—*hist pl* IL-6
Ayers Branch—*stream* LA-4
Ayers Branch—*stream* MI-6
Ayers Branch—*stream* NH-1
Ayers Brook—*stream* CT-1
Ayers Brook—*stream* ME-1
Ayers Brook—*stream* VT-1
*Ayersburgh* KS-7
Ayers Cabin Ruins—*locale* NV-8
Ayers Canyon—*valley* MT-8
Ayers Canyon—*valley* OR-9
Ayers Canyon Spring—*spring* MT-8
Ayers Cem—*cemetery* AR-4
Ayers Cem—*cemetery* GA-3
Ayers Cem—*cemetery* (2) MS-4
Ayers Cem—*cemetery* NY-2
Ayers Cem—*cemetery* OH-6
Ayers Cem—*cemetery* (2) TN-4
Ayers Cem—*cemetery* VA-3
Ayers Cem—*cemetery* WV-2
Ayers Chapel—*church* MD-2
Ayers Chapel—*church* TX-5
Ayers Chapel (historical)—*church* MS-4
*Ayers City* MA-1
Ayers Creek—*stream* CA-9
Ayers Creek—*stream* ID-8
Ayers Creek—*stream* MS-4
Ayers Creek—*stream* NY-2
Ayers Creek—*stream* OH-6
Ayers Creek—*stream* (4) OR-9
Ayers Crossroads—*locale* PA-2
Ayers Ditch—*canal* IN-6
Ayers Draw—*valley* WY-8
Ayers Falls—*falls* OR-9
Ayers Gap—*gap* CT-1
*Ayers Grove* PA-2
Ayers Gulch—*valley* MT-8
Ayers Gulch—*valley* WA-9
Ayer-Shea House—*hist pl* OR-9
Ayers Hill—*locale* PA-2
Ayers Hill—*summit* MA-1
Ayers Hill—*summit* VT-1
*Ayers Hill Branch* PA-2
Ayers Hill Cem—*cemetery* PA-2
Ayers Hollow—*valley* PA-2
Ayers Hollow—*valley* (2) TN-4
Ayers Hollow—*valley* VA-3
Ayers House—*hist pl* MT-8
Ayers Island—*island* ME-1
Ayers Island Dam—*dam* NH-1
*Ayers Junction* ME-1
**Ayers Junction**—*pop pl* ME-1
Ayers Knob—*summit* TN-4
Ayers Lake—*lake* MI-6
Ayers Lake—*lake* NY-2
Ayers Lake—*reservoir* MS-4
Ayers Landing—*locale* TN-4
Ayers Meadows—*flat* ID-8
Ayers Mtn—*summit* CT-1
Ayers Point—*cape* NH-1
Ayers Pond—*lake* (2) NH-1
Ayers Pond—*reservoir* (2) GA-3
Ayers Pond—*reservoir* NH-1
Ayers Pond (historical)—*reservoir* MO-7
Ayers Post Office (historical)—*building* TN-4
Ayers (reduced usage)—*locale* IL-6
Ayers Ridge—*ridge* TN-4
Ayers Rips—*rapids* ME-1
Ayers Rsvr—*reservoir* MT-8
Ayers Shanty Run—*stream* PA-2
*Ayers Shop* MS-4
Ayers State For—*forest* NH-1
*Ayers State Technical College* AL-4
*Ayers State Trade School* AL-4
**Ayers (Township of)**—*pop pl* IL-6
**Ayers Village**—*pop pl* MA-1
Ayersville—*locale* GA-3
**Ayersville**—*pop pl* NC-3
**Ayersville**—*pop pl* OH-6
Ayers Watershed UT-4-1 Dam—*dam* MS-4
**Ayer (Town of)**—*pop pl* MA-1
*Aye Spur* OR-9
Ayford Ditch—*canal* IN-6
*Ayirech* FM-9
Ayish Bayou—*stream* TX-5
Ayiyak Mesa—*summit* AK-9
Ayiyak River—*stream* AK-9
Ayles Creek—*stream* NC-3
**Aylesworth**—*pop pl* (2) IN-6
**Aylesworth**—*pop pl* OK-5
Aylesworth, Mount—*summit* AK-9
Aylesworth Apartments—*hist pl* RI-1
Aylesworth Branch—*stream* IL-6
Aylesworth Creek—*stream* PA-2
Aylesworth Creek Dam—*dam* PA-2
Aylesworth Creek Lake—*reservoir* PA-2
Aylesworth Oil Field—*oilfield* OK-5
Aylesworth Park—*locale* PA-2
*Aylesworth School* IN-6
**Aylett**—*pop pl* VA-3
Aylett Creek—*stream* VA-3
Aylett Mill—*locale* VA-3
Aylett Pond—*reservoir* VA-3
*Aylett's* VA-3
Ayletts Ferry (historical)—*crossing* TN-4
**Aylmer**—*pop pl* ND-7
Aylmer Lake—*lake* ND-7
Aylor—*locale* VA-3
Aylor Cem—*cemetery* KY-4
Aylor Mtn—*summit* VA-3
Aylors Caballo Camp—*locale* AZ-5
Aylworth Creek—*stream* OH-6
Aymett Cem—*cemetery* TN-4
Aymett Ridge—*ridge* TN-4
Aymett Town—*locale* TN-4
*Aymett Town School* TN-4
*Aymine Peak* OR-9
Aynesworth Sch—*school* CA-9
Aynesworth-Wright House—*hist pl* TX-5
**Aynor**—*pop pl* SC-3
Aynor (CCD)—*cens area* SC-3
Ayock Point—*cape* WA-9
*Ayong* FM-9
Ayotte Ditch—*canal* MT-8
*Ayr* KS-7
Ayr—*locale* MI-6
**Ayr**—*pop pl* IN-6
**Ayr**—*pop pl* NE-7
**Ayr**—*pop pl* ND-7
*Ayrach* FM-9
Ayr Cem—*cemetery* MI-6
*Ayrech* FM-9
*Ayre City* MA-1
Ayre Ditch—*stream* OH-6
*Ayrehall Branch* VA-3
*Ayres* MS-4
*Ayres* NJ-2
Ayres—*locale* AL-4
Ayres, Bucher, Farm—*hist pl* PA-2
Ayres, John, House—*hist pl* PA-2
Ayres, L. S. Annex Warehouse—*hist pl* IN-6
Ayres, Nathan, House—*hist pl* MI-6
Ayres Airstrip—*airport* OR-9
Ayres Bay—*bay* TX-5
*Ayres Branch* OR-9
Ayres Branch—*stream* NE-7
Ayres Brook—*stream* ME-1
Ayres Cabin—*locale* CA-9
Ayres Cem—*cemetery* NC-3
**Ayres City (subdivision)**—*pop pl* MA-1
Ayres Creek—*stream* KS-7
Ayres Creek—*stream* MT-8
Ayres Creek—*stream* NE-7
Ayres Creek—*stream* NJ-2
Ayres Ditch—*canal* IN-6
Ayres Dugout—*channel* TX-5
**Ayres Estates (subdivision)**—*pop pl* AL-4
Ayres-Ferrell Cem—*cemetery* MS-4
Ayres Hollow—*valley* (2) TN-4
Ayres Island—*island* TX-5
Ayres Lateral—*canal* WA-9
Ayres Memorial Ch—*church* GA-3
Ayres Park—*park* ID-8
Ayres Park—*park* TX-5
Ayres Peak—*summit* MT-8
Ayres Point—*cape* FL-3
Ayres Point—*cape* TX-5
Ayres Point—*cape* WA-9
*Ayres Pond* MA-1
Ayres Reef—*bar* TX-5
Ayres Sch—*school* MI-6
**Ayres Siding**—*pop pl* IL-6
Ayres Spring—*spring* WY-8
**Ayresville**—*pop pl* IA-7
*Ayreville Branch* VA-3
*Ayr Hill* VA-3
Ayr Interchange—*crossing* ND-7
Ayr Junction—*locale* NE-7
Ayr Lake—*swamp* NE-7
**Ayrlawn**—*pop pl* MD-2
Ayrlawn Sch—*school* MD-2
Ayr Mount—*hist pl* NC-3
**Ayrshire**—*pop pl* (2) IN-6
**Ayrshire**—*pop pl* IA-7
Ayrshire Colleries Corporation—*facility* IN-6
*Ayrstown* NJ-2
**Ayr Township**—*pop pl* NE-7
**Ayr Township**—*pop pl* ND-7
**Ayr (Township of)**—*pop pl* PA-2
Ayr-Way East Shop Ctr—*locale* IN-6
Ayr-Way Lafayette Shop Ctr—*locale* IN-6
**Ayr-Way Northeast**—*pop pl* IN-6
Ayr-Way Northwest Shop Ctr—*locale* IN-6
**Ayr-Way South**—*pop pl* IN-6
**Ayr-Way Washington West**—*pop pl* IN-6
Ayr-Way West Shop Ctr—*locale* IN-6
Ayscues Pond—*reservoir* NC-3
Ayscues Pond Dam—*dam* NC-3
Aysees Peak—*summit* NV-8
Ayson Hotel—*hist pl* AK-9
A-Y Spring—*spring* OR-9
AYS Youth Camp—*locale* AL-4
Aytes Branch—*stream* TX-5
Ayugadak Point—*cape* AK-9
Ayugatak Creek—*stream* AK-9
Ayugatak Hills—*summit* AK-9
Ayugatak Lagoon—*lake* AK-9
Ayuja—*locale* GU-9
Azacharum Slough—*gut* AK-9
Azachorok Hill—*summit* AK-9
*Azalea* MI-6
Azalea—*locale* CA-9
**Azalea**—*pop pl* NC-3
**Azalea**—*pop pl* OR-9
Azalea—*post sta* TX-5
Azalea—*uninc pl* NC-3
Azalea, Lake—*lake* FL-3
**Azalea Acres**—*pop pl* VA-3
Azalea Baptist Ch—*church* AL-4
Azalea Baptist Ch—*church* FL-3
Azalea Campground—*locale* CA-9
Azalea Canyon—*valley* CA-9
Azalea Center (Shop Ctr)—*locale* FL-3
Azalea Ch—*church* NC-3
Azalea City Golf Club—*locale* AL-4
**Azalea Court**—*pop pl* VA-3
Azalea Court Apartments—*hist pl* AL-4
Azalea Creek—*stream* (2) CA-9
Azalea Creek—*stream* OR-9
Azalea Gardens—*uninc pl* VA-3
**Azalea Gardens Mobile Home Park (subdivision)**—*pop pl* NC-3
Azalea Gardens Sch—*school* VA-3
Azalea Hills Christian Ch—*church* AL-4
Azalea JHS—*school* AL-4
Azalea Lake—*lake* (2) CA-9
Azalea Lake—*lake* OR-9
Azalea Mine—*mine* CA-9
Azalea MS—*school* FL-3
Azalea Oil Field—*oilfield* TX-5
Azalea Park—*park* FL-3
**Azalea Park**—*pop pl* FL-3
Azalea Park—*uninc pl* GA-3
Azalea Park Baptist Sch—*school* FL-3
Azalea Park Ch of Christ—*church* FL-3
Azalea Park Sch—*school* FL-3
Azalea Plaza (Shop Ctr)—*locale* FL-3
Azalea Plaza Shop Ctr—*locale* VA-3
Azalea Rest Cem—*cemetery* LA-4
Azalea Road Shop Ctr—*locale* AL-4
Azalea Sch—*school* FL-3
Azalea Spring—*spring* CA-9
Azalea Spring—*spring* OR-9
Azalea State Park—*park* OR-9
Azalea State Res—*reserve* CA-9
**Azalea Terrace (subdivision)**—*pop pl* FL-3
Azalea Trail—*trail* TN-4
Azalea Wash—*stream* CA-9
*Azalea Wood* AL-4
**Azalea Woods Estates (subdivision)**—*pop pl* AL-4
**Azalia**—*pop pl* IN-6
**Azalia**—*pop pl* MI-6
Azalia Garden Cem—*cemetery* NC-3
Azamis Cove—*bay* AK-9
*Azan-sosi Mesa* AZ-5
Azansosi Mesa—*summit* AZ-5
*Azantsosi Mesa* AZ-5
Azbeth Ch—*church* AL-4
Azbil Flat—*flat* CA-9
Azcuenaga Meadows—*flat* OR-9
Azelea Spring—*spring* OR-9
Azelle Creek—*stream* CA-9
Azelta—*locale* PA-2
Azen—*locale* MO-7
Azen Ch—*church* VA-3
*Azesko Lake* ME-1
*Azeyan* MP-9
*Azeyan-To* MP-9
Aziak Island—*island* AK-9
*Aziamp River* AZ-5
Azimuth Point—*cape* AK-9
Azion Lake—*lake* MN-6
Aziscohos Dam—*dam* ME-1
Aziscohos Lake—*reservoir* ME-1
Aziscohos Mtn—*summit* ME-1
Aziscohos Pond—*lake* ME-1
*Aziscoos Lake* ME-1
*Aziscoos Mountain* ME-1
**Azle**—*pop pl* TX-5
Azley Acton Cow Camp—*locale* OR-9
A Z Minerals Corporation Airp—*airport* UT-8
Aznoe Sch—*school* MT-8
*Azoin Lake* MN-6
*Azoiquoneset Island* RI-1
*Azoir Lake* MN-6
Azor—*locale* AR-4
Azotea Mesa—*summit* NM-5
Azotus Ch—*church* IL-6
Azotus Ch—*church* TN-4
A-Z Shop Ctr—*locale* MA-1
Aztalan—*hist pl* WI-6
**Aztalan**—*pop pl* WI-6
Aztalan Cem—*cemetery* WI-6
Aztalan State Park—*park* WI-6
**Aztalan (Town of)**—*pop pl* WI-6
AZ Tank—*reservoir* AZ-5
Aztec—*locale* AZ-5
**Aztec**—*pop pl* NM-5
Aztec, The—*locale* AZ-5
Aztec Amphitheater—*basin* AZ-5
Aztec Butte—*summit* UT-8
Aztec Camp—*locale* UT-8
*Aztec Canyon* CO-8
Aztec Canyon—*valley* TX-5
Aztec Canyon—*valley* (2) UT-8
Aztec (CCD)—*cens area* NM-5
Aztec Ch—*church* OK-5
Aztec Cleaners and Laundry Bldg—*hist pl* TX-5
Aztec Creek—*stream* AZ-5
Aztec Creek—*stream* UT-8
Aztec Creek—*stream* WY-8
Aztec Ditch—*canal* NM-5
Aztec Divide—*ridge* CO-8
Aztec Group Mines—*mine* AZ-5
Aztec Gulch—*valley* AZ-5
Aztec Gulch—*valley* CO-8
Aztec Hills—*summit* AZ-5
Aztec (historical)—*locale* SD-7
Aztec Hotel—*hist pl* CA-9
Aztec Interchange—*crossing* AZ-5
**Aztec Lodge**—*pop pl* AZ-5
Aztec Main Street Hist Dist—*hist pl* NM-5
Aztec Mill (historical)—*mine* AZ-5
Aztec Mine—*mine* (2) CO-8
Aztec Mine—*mine* ID-8
Aztec Mine—*mine* NM-5
Aztec Mines—*mine* CA-9
Aztec Motor Company Bldg—*hist pl* NM-5
*Aztec Mountains* AZ-5
Aztec Mtn—*summit* CO-8
Aztec Pass—*valley* AZ-5
Aztec Peak—*summit* AZ-5
Aztec Rapids (inundated)—*rapids* UT-8
Aztec Ruins—*other* NM-5
Aztec Ruins Natl Monmt—*hist pl* NM-5
Aztec Ruins Natl Monmt—*park* NM-5
Aztec Sch—*school* CA-9
Aztec Sch—*school* NM-5
Aztec Spring—*spring* CA-9
Aztec Spring—*spring* UT-8
Aztec Springs Creek—*stream* NM-5
Aztec Tank—*reservoir* (2) AZ-5
Aztec Tank—*reservoir* NV-8
Aztec Wash—*stream* CO-8
Aztec Wash—*stream* NV-8
Aztec Well—*well* CA-9
A-Z Trail—*trail* NH-1
*Azucar* FL-3
Azucar Mine—*mine* CA-9
Azucar Windmill—*locale* TX-5
Azucena—*locale* LA-4
**Azul**—*pop pl* NM-5
Azul, Canada—*valley* CA-9
Azul, Charco—*lake* PR-3
Azul, Rito—*stream* CO-8
Azul, Sierra—*range* CA-9
**Azundel Gardens**—*pop pl* MD-2
Azun River—*stream* AK-9
*Azuranfauro* MH-9
Azure—*locale* CO-8
Azure Cave—*cave* MT-8
*Azure Cliffs* CO-8
Azure Cove—*bay* NV-8
Azure Dam—*dam* ND-7
Azure Hills Golf Course—*other* MO-7
Azure Lake—*lake* CA-9
Azure Lake—*lake* CO-8
Azure Lake—*lake* ID-8
Azure Lake—*lake* UT-8
Azure Lake—*lake* (2) WA-9
Azure Mtn—*summit* NY-2
Azure Ridge—*ridge* NV-8
Azure Ridge Draw—*valley* AZ-5
Azure Ridge Draw—*valley* NV-8
Azure Ridge Mine—*mine* NV-8
**Azure Vista**—*pop pl* CA-9
Azurite Lake—*lake* WA-9
Azurite Mine—*mine* AZ-5
Azurite Mine—*mine* WA-9
Azurite Pass—*gap* WA-9
Azurite Peak—*summit* WA-9
**Azusa**—*pop pl* CA-9
Azusa (Dalton)—*civil* CA-9
Azusa (Duarte)—*civil* CA-9
Azusa Greens Public Golf Course—*other* CA-9
Azusa Grotto Lake—*lake* NC-3
Azusa Pacific Coll—*school* CA-9
Azusa Powerplant Conduit—*other* CA-9
Azusa-Valley Sanitarium—*hospital* CA-9
**Azwell**—*pop pl* WA-9
AZ Well—*well* AZ-5
Azzens Run—*stream* WV-2
A 1 Canal—*canal* ID-8
*A 1 Ch* AL-4
A 1 Mtn—*summit* AZ-5
A-1 Peak—*summit* UT-8
A-1 Trailer Park—*locale* AZ-5
A-3 Canal—*canal* ID-8
A-4 Canal—*canal* ID-8
A 4 Canal—*canal* MT-8
A-5 Canal—*canal* ID-8
A 8.4 Lateral—*canal* AZ-5
A 8.9 Lateral—*canal* AZ-5
A 8.9 N Lateral—*canal* AZ-5
A 9.4 Lateral—*canal* AZ-5

# B

B—valley MT-8
B, Lateral—canal AZ-5
B, Pond—reservoir ND-7
Baack School—locale MT-8
Baadah Point WA-9
Baada Point—cape WA-9
Baaddah Point WA-9
Baah Lokaa Ridge—ridge AZ-5
Baaki AZ-5
Baamcheenungamook Lake ME-1
Baanimaut FM-9
Baanimut FM-9
Baanimuut FM-9
Baanmaut FM-9
Baarstad Cem—cemetery MN-6
Baas Cem—cemetery AL-4
Baasen House-German YMCA—hist pl WI-6
Baathbakdizuni Creek—stream AK-9
Baba'—slope MH-9
Babahatchie River TN-4
Babantaltlin Creek—stream AK-9
Babantaltlin Hills—other AK-9
Babays Lake—lake LA-4
Babb—locale WA-9
**Babb**—pop pl MT-8
**Babbatasset Village**—pop pl MA-1
Babb Branch—stream (2) MS-4
Babb Brook—stream NH-1
Babb Camp—locale TX-5
Babb Canyon—valley TX-5
Babb Cem—cemetery IL-6
Babb Cem—cemetery KY-4
Babb Cem—cemetery MS-4
Babb Cem—cemetery NE-7
Babb Cem—cemetery SC-3
Babb Cem—cemetery (2) TN-4
Babb Cem—cemetery TX-5
Babb Cem—cemetery WI-6
**Babb Corner**—pop pl ME-1
Babb Creek CA-9
Babb Creek—stream CA-9
Babb Creek—stream PA-2
Babb Creek—stream TN-4
Babb Creek—stream WI-6
Babbe Pond NY-2
Babb Ford (historical)—locale TN-4
Babb Hill—summit MA-1
Babb Hollow—valley WI-6
Babbidge Island—island ME-1
Babbidge Reservoir—lake NH-1
**Babbie**—pop pl AL-4
Babbie Sch (historical)—school AL-4
Babbington Creek—stream ID-8
Babbington Spring #2—spring ID-8
Babbish Gulch—valley CO-8
Babb Island SC-3
Babbitasset MA-1
Babbit Cem—cemetery IL-6
Babbit Cem—cemetery MA-1
Babbit Hill—summit NH-1
Babbits Corners—locale NY-2
Babbit Shanty Hill—summit UT-8
Babbit Spring—spring AZ-5
Babbitt—locale NJ-2
**Babbitt**—pop pl MN-6
**Babbitt**—pop pl NV-8
Babbit Tank—reservoir (3) AZ-5
Babbitt Bay—bay NC-3
Babbitt Corner—locale (2) NY-2
Babbitt Hill—summit MA-1
Babbitt Lake—lake AZ-5
Babbitt Mtn—summit MA-1
Babbitt Peak—summit CA-9
Babbitt Ridge—ridge ME-1
Babbitt Sch—school MN-6
Babbitts Chapel—church NC-3
Babbitt Tank—reservoir (4) AZ-5
Babbitt Tank Canyon—valley AZ-5
Babbitt Wash—stream AZ-5
Babbitt Water Catchment—basin AZ-5
Babbitt Winter—locale AZ-5
Babbitz Lake—lake WA-9
Babb Lake—lake AR-4
Babble Brook—stream ME-1
Babble Brook—stream OH-6
Babble Brook Deadwater—swamp ME-1
Babble Lake—lake MN-6
Babbler Point—cape AK-9
Babbling Brook MA-1
Babb Mine—mine KY-4
Babb Ranch—locale TX-5
Babb Ridge—ridge WI-6
Babbs—locale OK-5
Babbs Beach—beach CT-1
Babbs Canyon—valley CA-9
Babbs Cem—cemetery AR-4
Babb Ch—church GA-3
Babb Sch—school MT-8
Babbs Creek PA-2
Babbs Creek WI-6
Babbs Grove Cem—cemetery IL-6
Babbs Hollow—valley IL-6
Babbs Island—island WV-2
Babbs Island—island WI-6
Babbs Knob—summit TN-4
Babb Slough—lake IL-6
Babbs Mill—locale TN-4
Babbs Mine—mine WY-8
Babb-Smith Cem—cemetery TN-4
Babbs Mtn—summit VA-3
Babbs Run VA-3
Babbs Run—stream VA-3
Babbs Valley—valley TN-4
Babb Swamp—swamp NH-1
Babb Tank—reservoir TX-5
Babbtown—locale MO-7
**Babbtown**—pop pl SC-3
Babbut's Narrows ME-1
Babby Pond NY-2
Bab Cem—cemetery OH-6
Babcock FL-3
Babcock KS-7
Babcock—locale PA-2
Babcock—locale WA-9
Babcock—locale WV-2
**Babcock**—pop pl GA-3
**Babcock**—pop pl IL-6
**Babcock**—pop pl IN-6
**Babcock**—pop pl IA-7
**Babcock**—pop pl MI-6
**Babcock**—pop pl WV-2
**Babcock**—pop pl WI-6
Babcock, Charles C., House—hist pl OR-9
Babcock, Havilah, House—hist pl WI-6
Babcock, Lake—reservoir NE-7
Babcock Basin—basin TX-5
Babcock Bench—bench WA-9
Babcock Block—hist pl MA-1
Babcock Branch—stream AL-4
Babcock Branch—stream IN-6
Babcock Brook—stream ME-1
Babcock Brook—stream (2) MA-1
Babcock Brook—stream VT-1
Babcock Building, South Carolina State Hosp—hist pl SC-3
Babcock Cabin—locale OR-9
Babcock Canyon—valley AZ-5
Babcock Canyon—valley CO-8
Babcock Cem—cemetery MI-6
Babcock Cem—cemetery NY-2
Babcock Cem—cemetery VT-1
Babcock Cem—cemetery VA-3
Babcock Cem—cemetery WI-6
Babcock Corners—locale PA-2
Babcock Cove—bay RI-1
Babcock Creek—stream AK-9
Babcock Creek—stream (2) MT-8
Babcock Creek—stream (2) NJ-2
Babcock Creek—stream OR-9
Babcock Creek—stream PA-2
Babcock Creek—stream WA-9
Babcock Crossing—locale CA-9
Babcock Ditch—canal CA-9
Babcock Drain—canal (2) MI-6
**Babcock Hill**—pop pl NY-2
Babcock Hill—summit CT-1
Babcock Hill—summit VT-1
Babcock Hole—ridge CO-8
Babcock Hollow—valley (2) NY-2
Babcock Hollow—valley TN-4
Babcock Hollow Cem—cemetery NY-2
Babcock House—hist pl RI-1
Babcock Lake—lake CA-9
**Babcock Lake**—pop pl NY-2
Babcock Lake—reservoir NC-3
Babcock Lake Dam—dam NC-3
Babcock Meadow CA-9
Babcock Meadows—flat CA-9
Babcock Mtn—summit MT-8
Babcock Overmyer Ditch—canal IN-6
Babcock Park—park WI-6
Babcock Peak—summit CA-9
Babcock Peak—summit CO-8
Babcock Picnic Area—area PA-2
Babcock Pond MA-1
Babcock Pond RI-1
Babcock Pond—lake CT-1
Babcock Pumping Station—other WA-9
Babcock Ranch—locale FL-3
Babcock Ridge WA-9
Babcock Ridge—ridge WA-9
Babcock Ridge Lake—lake WA-9
Babcock Run—stream NY-2
Babcock Run—stream PA-2
Babcocks Airp—airport IN-6
Babcock Sch—school CA-9
Babcock Sch—school MI-6
Babcock Sch—school WI-6
Babcock Site—hist pl MO-7
Babcock-Smith House—hist pl RI-1
Babcocks Point—cape ME-1
Babcocks Pond—lake MI-6
Babcock Spring—spring AZ-5
Babcocks Ranch (historical)—locale SD-7
Babcock State For—forest PA-2
Babcock State Park—park WV-2
Babcock Swamp—swamp CT-1
Babcock Swamp—swamp NJ-2
Babcock Tank—reservoir AZ-5
Babcock Trestle—bridge TN-4
Babcock & Wilcox Company—facility IN-6
Babeck Sch—school OH-6
Babe Collins Cem—cemetery AR-4
Babe Creek—stream AK-9
Babe Creek—stream (2) OR-9
Babe Island—area AK-9
Babe Island—island MN-6
Babe Island—island GU-9
Babel, Tower of—summit UT-8
Babe Lake—lake OR-9
Babel Brook—stream ME-1
Babel Creek—stream TX-5
Babeldaob PW-9
Babeldaob PW-9
Babeldzuap PW-9
Babel (historical)—locale NV-8
Babelhoup Island PW-9
Babel Mine—mine NV-8
Babel River—stream (2) AK-9
Babel Rock—summit MA-1
Babel Slough—gut CA-9
Babeltaob PW-9
Bab-el-Thaob PW-9
Babelthaub PW-9
Babelthaup PW-9
Babelthouap PW-9
Babelthuab PW-9
Babelthuap—island PW-9
Babelthuap Village PW-9
**Baber**—pop pl WV-2
Baber, Ambrose, House—hist pl GA-3
Baber, Dr. Calvin M., House—hist pl GA-3
Baber, Granville H., House—hist pl OR-9
Baber, Mount—summit AL-4
Baber Branch—stream WV-2
Baber Cem—cemetery TN-4
Baber Cem—cemetery WV-2
Baber Creek—stream AR-4
Baber Lookout—locale OR-9
Baber Point—cape VA-3
Baberry Hill MA-1
Babers Tank—reservoir NM-5
Babe Ruth Field—park CA-9
Babe Ruth Mine—mine CO-8
Babe Ruth Park—park IN-6
Babe Ruth Park—park MS-4
Babe Ruth Park—park NM-5
Babe Ruth Playground—park MA-1
Baber Well—well NM-5
Babery Hill MA-1
Babery Hill Brook MA-1
Babes Canyon—valley OR-9
Babes Canyon Spring—spring OR-9
Babes Hill—summit CT-1
Babes Hole AZ-5
Babes Hole Spring—spring AZ-5
Babes Pond—reservoir AL-4
Babe Thorpe Hollow—valley TN-4
Babgy Memorial Ch—church VA-3
Babies Gulch—valley CA-9
Babin Canal—canal LA-4
Babington, Robert H., House—hist pl LA-4
**Babington (historical)**—pop pl MS-4
Babins Junction—locale ID-8
Babione Creek—stream WY-8
Babion Mine—mine WY-8
Babit Creek—stream WI-6
Babiteoida Arronyo AZ-5
Bablens Fork ID-8
Babler Spring—spring MO-7
Babler State Park—park MO-7
Bablin—locale WV-2
Bablin Hollow—valley WV-2
Bablomekang—island PW-9
Babmore Branch—stream MS-4
Babocomari Ranch—locale AZ-5
Babocomari River—stream AZ-5
Baboon Creek ID-8
Baboon Creek—stream ID-8
Baboon Creek—stream (2) OR-9
Baboon Gulch—valley ID-8
Baboon Gulch—valley MT-8
Baboon Lake WI-6
Baboon Lake—lake MT-8
Baboon Lakes—lake CA-9
Baboon Mtn—summit MT-8
Baboon Peak—summit UT-8
Baboon Seep—spring UT-8
Baboosic Brook—stream NH-1
Baboosic Lake—lake NH-1
**Baboosic Lake**—pop pl NH-1
Baboquerque Fields AZ-5
Baboquivari Canyon—valley AZ-5
Baboquivari HS—school AZ-5
Baboquivari Mountains—range AZ-5
Baboquivari Peak—summit AZ-5
Baboquivari Valley—valley AZ-5
Baboquivari Wash—stream AZ-5
Baboquivavari Range AZ-5
Baboquivarai Peak AZ-5
Baboquivera Plain AZ-5
Baboquiveri Mountains AZ-5
Baboquiveri Peak AZ-5
Baboquiveri Range AZ-5
Baboquivori Paek AZ-5
Babry Hill Brook MA-1
Babs Branch—stream KY-4
Babs Creek—stream AK-9
Babs Flat—flat ID-8
Babs Fork—stream CA-9
**Babsit Estates (subdivision)**—pop pl MS-4
Babs Lake—lake CA-9
Babson IL-6
Babson Coll—school MA-1
Babson Island—island ME-1
Babson Ledge—rock ME-1
**Babson Park**—pop pl FL-3
**Babson Park**—pop pl MA-1
Babson Park Elem Sch—school FL-3
Babson Point—cape MA-1
Babson Pond—lake WI-6
Babson Reservoir Dam—dam MA-1
Babson Rsvr—reservoir MA-1
Babson Sch—school MA-1
Babtist Pond NH-1
Babui, Sabanetan Unai—slope MH-9
Babui, Unai—beach MH-9
Babuquiburi Peak AZ-5
Babuquivari Plain AZ-5
Baby Antelope Rsvr—reservoir WY-8
Baby Arch UT-8
Babybasket Hill—summit AK-9
Baby Brook—stream NY-2
Baby Canyon—valley AZ-5
Baby Capulin—summit NM-5
Baby Cave—cave TN-4
Baby Creek—gut MI-6
Baby Creek—stream (3) AK-9
Baby Creek—stream ID-8
Baby Creek—stream IN-6
Baby Creek Spring—spring ID-8
Baby Doe Campground—locale CO-8
Baby Eddie Tunnel—mine CO-8
Babyfoot Creek—stream OR-9
Babyfoot Lake—lake OR-9
Baby Fourmile Island—island WI-6
Baby Gator Child Care—school FL-3
Baby Glacier—glacier AK-9
Baby Glacier—glacier MT-8
Baby Glacier—glacier WY-8
Baby Grand Lake—lake MN-6
Baby Grand Mtn—summit ID-8
Baby Head—locale TX-5
Babyhead Creek—stream TX-5
Babyhead Mtn—summit TX-5
Baby Hollow—valley IL-6
Baby Hollow—valley WV-2
Baby Island WA-9
Baby Island—island (2) WA-9
**Baby Island Heights**—pop pl WA-9
Baby Islands—island AK-9
Baby Jesus Ridge—ridge AZ-5
Baby Joe Gulch—valley ID-8
Baby King Canyon—valley CA-9
Baby King Creek—stream CA-9
Baby Lake—lake CA-9
Baby Lake—lake MI-6
Baby Lake—lake MN-6
Baby Lake—lake NY-2
Baby Lake—lake WY-8
Baby Lake Creek—stream WY-8
Babylon—locale IL-6
**Babylon**—pop pl NY-2
Babylon Bend Bridge—hist pl IL-6
Babylon Cove—bay NY-2
Babylon Hill—summit MA-1
Babylon Hill—summit PA-2
Babylon Industrial Complex—locale PA-2
Babylon Pasture—flat UT-8
Babylon Post Office (historical)—building TN-4
Babylon Ridge—ridge NV-8
Babylon Run—stream PA-2
Babylon Sch—school MI-6
Babylon Tank—reservoir AZ-5
Babylon Townhall—building NY-2
**Babylon (Town of)**—pop pl NY-2
Babylon Yacht Club—other NY-2
Baby McKee Mine—mine OR-9
Baby McKee Mine—mine UT-8
Baby Mine—mine OR-9
Baby Mtn—summit IN-6
Baby Pass—channel AK-9
Baby Peak—summit CA-9
Baby Rack Cove MA-1
Baby Rock—locale AZ-5
Baby Rock—pillar OR-9
Baby Rocks AZ-5
Baby Rocks—cliff AZ-5
Baby Rocks Mesa—summit AZ-5
Baby Rsvr—reservoir WY-8
Baby Run—stream IN-6
Baby Run—stream PA-2
Baby Rush Island—island IA-7
Babyshoe Ridge—ridge WA-9
Baby Springs Draw—valley WY-8
Baby Stark Mtn—summit VT-1
Baby Stocking Ridge—ridge KY-4
Baby Twin Trail—trail NH-1
Baby Wagon Creek—stream WY-8
Baca NM-5
Baca, Miguel E., House—hist pl NM-5
Baca Arroyo—valley NM-5
Bacabi AZ-5
Baca Canyon—valley AZ-5
Baca Canyon—valley CO-8
Baca Canyon—valley (3) NM-5
Baca Cem—cemetery AZ-5
Baca Dam—dam AL-4
Baca Homestead—locale NM-5
Baca House—building NM-5
Baca House and Outbuilding—hist pl CO-8
Baca-Korte House—hist pl NM-5
Baca Lake—lake (2) AZ-5
Baca Lake—lake OR-9
Baca Lake—reservoir AL-4
Baca Location No 1—civil (2) NM-5
Baca Location No 2—civil NM-5
Baca Mesa—summit NM-5
Baca Ranch—locale AZ-5
Baca Ranch—locale (2) NM-5
Baca Siding—locale NM-5
Baca Spring—spring NM-5
Baca Spring Creek—stream NM-5
Baca Tank—reservoir (2) AZ-5
Baca Tank—reservoir (2) NM-5
**Bacavi**—pop pl AZ-5
**Bacaville**—pop pl NM-5
Baca Well—well NM-5
Baccala Cabin—locale CA-9
Baccala Ranch—locale CA-9
Bacchi Ranch—locale CA-9
Bacchus—locale NC-3
Bacchus—locale TN-4
Bacchus—locale UT-8
Bacchus Branch—stream AL-4
**Bacchus Heights Subdivision**—pop pl UT-8
Bacchus Hollow—valley TN-4
Bacchus Post Office (historical)—building TN-4
Bacchus Sch (historical)—school TN-4
Baccoon Hollow—valley TN-4
Baccus (2) AL-4
Baccus Cem—cemetery TX-5
Baccus Corner CT-1
**Baccus Corner**—pop pl CT-1
Bacera Windmill—locale TX-5
Bac Grove—locale IA-7
**Bach**—pop pl ID-8
**Bach**—pop pl MI-6
Bach, Emil, House—hist pl IL-6
Bachanan Cem—cemetery IN-6
Bachanan Dam TX-5
Bachand Sch—school SD-7
Bachathaiva Spring AZ-5
Bachatna Creek—stream AK-9
Bachatna Flats—flat AK-9
Bachaus Creek—stream WY-8
Bachaus Pasture—flat WY-8
Bach Cem—cemetery KY-4
Bach Cem—cemetery WI-6
Bachcha Chuko AL-4
Bach Drain—canal MI-6
**Bache**—pop pl OK-5
Bache, Alexander Dallas, Sch—hist pl PA-2
Bacheld Creek MO-7
Bachelder—locale TN-4
Bachelder Brook—stream ME-1
Bachelder Brook—stream MA-1
Bachelder Canyon—valley MT-8
Bachelder Cem—cemetery KS-7
Bachelder Hill—summit NH-1
Bachelder Spring—spring MT-8
Bachelers Brook MA-1
Bacheller KS-7
Bachellor KS-7
Bachellor Brook MA-1
Bachellors Brook MA-1
Bachelor KS-7
Bachelor—locale CO-8
Bachelor—locale MO-7
Bachelor—locale NC-3
Bachelor, Mount—summit OR-9
Bachelor Apartment House—hist pl DC-2
Bachelor Basin—basin UT-8
Bachelor Bay NC-3
Bachelor Bend—bend MS-4
Bachelor Bend—bend TN-4
Bachelor Branch—stream MO-7
Bachelor Branch—stream NE-7
Bachelor Branch—stream NC-3
Bachelor Branch—stream TX-5
Bachelor Brook MA-1
Bachelor Brook—stream ME-1
Bachelor Brook Dam—dam MA-1
Bachelor Brook Rsvr—reservoir MA-1
Bachelor Butte OR-9
Bachelor Butte—summit OR-9
Bachelor Camp—locale CO-8
Bachelor Canyon—valley MT-8
Bachelor Canyon—valley OR-9
Bachelor Canyon—valley UT-8
Bachelor Cem—cemetery NY-2
Bachelor Chapel—church AL-4
Bachelor Cove Area—bay AZ-5
Bachelor Creek KS-7
Bachelor Creek MO-7
Bachelor Creek MT-8
Bachelor Creek TX-5
Bachelor Creek—stream AK-9
Bachelor Creek—stream IN-6
Bachelor Creek—stream (6) KS-7
Bachelor Creek—stream MD-2
Bachelor Creek—stream MO-7
Bachelor Creek—stream MT-8
Bachelor Creek—stream NE-7
Bachelor Creek—stream (2) NC-3
Bachelor Creek—stream OK-5
Bachelor Creek—stream (4) OR-9
Bachelor Creek—stream SC-3
Bachelor Creek—stream SD-7
Bachelor Creek—stream TX-5
Bachelor Creek—stream (2) WA-9
Bachelor Creek—stream (2) WY-8
Bachelor Creek Ch—church IN-6
Bachelor Creek Reservoir KS-7
Bachelor Draw—valley CO-8
Bachelor Draw—valley NM-5
Bachelor Field—park AL-4
Bachelor Flat Sch—school OR-9
Bachelor Grove—woods IL-6
Bachelor Grove Cem—cemetery IL-6
Bachelor Gulch—valley CO-8
Bachelor Gulch—valley MT-8
Bachelor Gulch—valley WA-9
Bachelor Hill—summit TX-5
Bachelor Hill Ch—church SC-3
Bachelor Hollow—valley KY-4
Bachelor Island—island MA-1
Bachelor Island—island WA-9
Bachelor Island Point WA-9
Bachelor Island Shoal—bar WA-9
Bachelor Island Slough—gut WA-9
Bachelor Lake MI-6
Bachelor Lake—lake FL-3
Bachelor Lake—lake (2) MN-6
Bachelor Lake—reservoir CO-8
Bachelor Mine—mine (3) CO-8
Bachelor Mountain ID-8
Bachelor Mountain Trail—trail OR-9
Bachelor Mountan—summit MT-8
Bachelor Mtn—summit CA-9
Bachelor Mtn—summit CO-8
Bachelor Mtn—summit ID-8
Bachelor Mtn—summit OR-9
Bachelor Mtn—summit TX-5
Bachelor Peak—summit (2) TX-5
Bachelor Pit—mine CA-9
Bachelor Point—cape MD-2
Bachelor Point—cape VA-3
Bachelor Point—cape WA-9
Bachelor Pond—lake FL-3
Bachelor Prairie—flat WA-9
Bachelor Prong—stream TX-5
Bachelor Run—stream IN-6
Bachelor Run Ch—church IN-6
Bachelors Branch—stream MD-2
Bachelors Brook MA-1
Bachelors Chapel AL-4
**Bachelors Chapel**—pop pl AL-4
Bachelors Chapel Church AL-4
Bachelors Delight Swamp—stream NC-3
**Bachelors Hall**—pop pl VA-3
Bachelor Shoal WA-9
Bachelor's Hope—hist pl (2) MD-2
Bachelors Hope Point—cape MD-2
Bachelors Island WA-9
Bachelors Island Point WA-9
Bachelor Ski Lift—other OR-9
Bachelors Landing AL-4
Bachelor Spring—spring OR-9
Bachelor Springs—spring OK-5
Bachelors Rest—locale KY-4
Bachelors Run—stream IN-6
Bachelors Run—stream KS-7
**Bachelor Township**—pop pl KS-7
Bachelor Valley—flat CA-9
Bachelor Valley—valley CA-9
Bacher Creek—stream OR-9
Bacher Creek Rsvr—reservoir OR-9
Bacher Ditch—canal OH-6
Bache Rock—bar ME-1
Bacher Spring—spring OR-9
Bachert Creek—stream OR-9
Bache Sch—school PA-2
Bache Shoal—bar FL-3
Bachford Sch—school WI-6
Bach Grove (historical P.O.)—locale IA-7
Bach Hollow—valley PA-2
Bachicha Canyon—valley CO-8
Bachicha Creek—stream CO-8
Bachichi Spring—spring CO-8
Bachin Dam—dam SD-7
Bachin Lake Dam SD-7
Bachlador Pond—reservoir AL-4
Bachlott Ch—church GA-3
**Bachman**—pop pl OH-6
**Bachman**—pop pl WV-2
Bachman and Forry Tobacco Warehouse—hist pl PA-2
Bachman Branch—stream TX-5
Bachman Cem—cemetery NY-2
Bachman Cem—cemetery TX-5
**Bachman Chapel**—pop pl SC-3
Bachman Filtration Plant—other TX-5
Bachman Ford (historical)—locale TN-4
Bachman Hollow—valley PA-2
Bachman Junction PA-2
Bachman Lake—reservoir TX-5
Bachman Lake—swamp MN-6
Bachman Lake Park—park TX-5
Bachman Memorial Childrens Home—building TN-4
Bachman Mills—locale MD-2
Bachman Ponds—reservoir SC-3
Bachman Run—stream (2) PA-2
Bachman Tavern PA-2
Bachman Tubes—tunnel TN-4
**Bachmanville**—pop pl PA-2
Bachman Wash—stream AZ-5
Bach Memorial Ch—church KY-4
Bachrach, David, House—hist pl MD-2
Bachrodt Sch—school CA-9
Bach Sch—school MI-6
Bachs Creek—stream CA-9
Bachs Creek Ridge—ridge CA-9
Bach Slough—gut IL-6
Bachs Ridge Trail—trail CA-9
Bachus Pond—lake NY-2
Bach Well—well NV-8
Back—locale TX-5
Backachers Ranch Airstrip—airport OR-9
Back Acres Country Club—locale MS-4
Back Allegheny Mountain—ridge WV-2
Back and Forth Slough—stream MO-7
Back Bay—bay AK-9
Back Bay—bay FL-3
Back Bay—bay (2) ME-1

Back Bay—*bay* MI-6
Back Bay—*bay* MN-6
Back Bay—*bay* NC-3
Back Bay—*bay* TX-5
Back Bay—*bay* VA-3
Back Bay—*locale* VA-3
Backbay—*uninc pl* VA-3
Back Bay Annex—*uninc pl* MA-1
**Back Bay Beach**—*pop pl* MD-2
Back Bay Fens—*swamp* MA-1
Back Bay Hist Dist—*hist pl* MA-1
Back Bay (historical P.O.)—*locale* MA-1
Back Bay Mission United Ch of Christ—*church* MS-4
Back Bay Natl Wildlife Ref—*park* VA-3
Back Bay Of Biloxi—*bay* MS-4
Back Bayou—*gut* (2) MS-4
Back Bay Park—*park* MS-4
Back Bay Social Hall Community Center—*building* MS-4
**Back Bay (subdivision)**—*pop pl* MA-1
*Back Beach* MA-1
Back Beach—*beach* MA-1
Backbone—*locale* VA-3
Backbone—*ridge* MO-7
Backbone, The—*bend* IA-7
Backbone, The—*ridge* AL-4
Backbone, The—*ridge* (2) AR-4
Backbone, The—*ridge* GA-3
Backbone, The—*ridge* TN-4
Backbone, The—*ridge* TX-5
Backbone, The—*ridge* UT-8
Backbone, The—*summit* KY-4
Backbone Bluff—*cape* AR-4
*Backbone Branch* AL-4
Backbone Branch—*stream* KY-4
Backbone Branch—*stream* TN-4
Backbone Branch Public Area—*park* AL-4
Backbone Cem—*cemetery* AL-4
Backbone Cem—*cemetery* IL-6
Backbone Cem—*cemetery* TX-5
Backbone Creek—*stream* AL-4
Backbone Creek—*stream* (4) CA-9
Backbone Creek—*stream* KY-4
Backbone Creek—*stream* OH-6
Backbone Creek—*stream* TX-5
Backbone Creek Inlet—*bay* CA-9
Backbone Dam—*dam* AZ-5
Backbone Ford—*locale* MO-7
Backbone Ford—*locale* TN-4
Backbone Hill—*summit* KY-4
Backbone Hill—*summit* MD-2
Backbone Hill—*summit* TX-5
Backbone Hollow—*valley* AL-4
Backbone Hollow—*valley* KY-4
Backbone Hollow—*valley* MO-7
Backbone Hollow—*valley* (2) TN-4
Backbone Lake—*lake* CA-9
Backbone Lake—*lake* MS-4
Backbone Lake—*lake* MO-7
Backbone Lake—*lake* WA-9
Backbone Lake—*reservoir* IA-7
Backbone Mine—*mine* AZ-5
Backbone Mountain—*ridge* AL-4
Backbone Mountain—*ridge* AR-4
Backbone Mountain—*ridge* WV-2
Backbone Mtn—*summit* (2) AL-4
Backbone Mtn—*summit* AK-9
Backbone Mtn—*summit* AR-4
Backbone Mtn—*summit* CA-9
Backbone Mtn—*summit* MD-2
Backbone Mtn—*summit* OK-5
Backbone Mtn—*summit* (2) TX-5
Backbone Narrows—*gap* AR-4
Backbone Park—*park* AL-4
Backbone Point—*cliff* TN-4
*Backbone Ridge* AL-4
*Backbone Ridge* AR-4
Backbone Ridge—*ridge* (3) AL-4
Backbone Ridge—*ridge* (4) AR-4
Backbone Ridge—*ridge* (3) CA-9
Backbone Ridge—*ridge* GA-3
Backbone Ridge—*ridge* IL-6
Backbone Ridge—*ridge* IN-6
Backbone Ridge—*ridge* (5) KY-4
Backbone Ridge—*ridge* LA-4
Backbone Ridge—*ridge* MS-4
Backbone Ridge—*ridge* MO-7
Backbone Ridge—*ridge* NC-3
Backbone Ridge—*ridge* OR-9
Backbone Ridge—*ridge* PA-2
Backbone Ridge—*ridge* (6) TN-4
Backbone Ridge—*ridge* (2) TX-5
Backbone Ridge—*ridge* (3) VA-3
Backbone Ridge—*ridge* WA-9
Backbone Ridge Lookout—*locale* CA-9
Backbone Ridge Trail—*trail* WA-9
Backbone Rock—*pillar* TN-4
Backbone Rock Rec Area—*park* TN-4
*Backbone Siding* VA-3
Backbone State For—*forest* IA-7
Backbone State Park—*park* IA-7
Backbone Tank—*reservoir* TX-5
Backbone Valley—*basin* TX-5
Back Branch—*stream* GA-3
Back Branch—*stream* IL-6
Back Branch—*stream* KY-4
Back Branch—*stream* MD-2
Back Branch—*stream* (2) NC-3
Back Branch—*stream* VA-3
Back Brook—*stream* (2) ME-1
Back Brook—*stream* NH-1
Back Brook—*stream* (2) NJ-2
*Back Canyon* WY-8
Back Canyon—*valley* CA-9
Back Cave—*cave* TN-4
Back Cem—*cemetery* (2) KY-4
Back Channel—*channel* MD-2
Back Channel—*channel* NJ-2
Back Channel—*channel* PA-2
Back Chuck—*bay* AK-9
Back Coulee—*valley* MT-8
Back Cove—*bay* (6) ME-1
Back Cove—*bay* (2) MD-2
Back Cove—*bay* (2) VA-3
*Back Creek* AL-4
*Back Creek* MD-2
*Back Creek* VA-3
Back Creek—*bay* ME-1
Back Creek—*bay* (5) MD-2
Back Creek—*bay* (2) NC-3
Back Creek—*channel* NJ-2
Back Creek—*stream* CA-9
Back Creek—*stream* DE-2
Back Creek—*stream* ID-8
Back Creek—*stream* IL-6
Back Creek—*stream* (3) IN-6
Back Creek—*stream* (2) KY-4
Back Creek—*stream* (14) MD-2
Back Creek—*stream* MO-7
Back Creek—*stream* MT-8
Back Creek—*stream* NH-1
Back Creek—*stream* (2) NJ-2
Back Creek—*stream* (9) NC-3
Back Creek—*stream* OR-9
Back Creek—*stream* (3) PA-2
Back Creek—*stream* SC-3
Back Creek—*stream* (5) TN-4
Back Creek—*stream* (19) VA-3
Back Creek—*stream* (5) WV-2
Back Creek Ch—*church* IN-6
Back Creek Ch—*church* (2) NC-3
Back Creek Ch—*church* (2) VA-3
Back Creek Chapel—*church* NC-3
Back Creek Farm—*hist pl* VA-3
Back Creek Island—*island* VA-3
Back Creek Lake—*reservoir* NC-3
Back Creek (Magisterial District)—*fmr MCD* VA-3
*Back Creek Mooring Basin* MD-2
Back Creek Mtn—*summit* NC-3
Back Creek Mtn—*summit* (2) VA-3
Back Creek Neck—*cape* MD-2
Back Creek Point—*cape* MD-2
Back Creek Point—*cape* NJ-2
Back Creek Presbyterian Church and Ceneterey—*hist pl* NC-3
Back Creek Sch—*school* VA-3
Back Creek Sch (historical)—*school* TN-4
Back Creek Tabernacle—*church* VA-3
Back Creek (Township of)—*fmr MCD* NC-3
Back Creek Valley Sch—*school* WV-2
Back Dam—*dam* SC-3
Back District Ch—*church* ME-1
Back Ditch—*canal* NJ-2
Backdoor Cave—*cave* PA-2
Back Door Gulch—*valley* CO-8
Back Draft—*stream* WV-2
Back Draft—*valley* (2) VA-3
**Backems Crossroads**—*pop pl* AL-4
Backer Hollow—*valley* AR-4
Backer Ranch—*locale* NM-5
Backers Landing—*locale* AL-4
*Backers Mill Run* PA-2
*Backers Run* PA-2
Backes Lake—*lake* MN-6
Backesto Park—*park* CA-9
Backfield Brook—*stream* NH-1
*Back Fork* KY-4
*Back Fork* WV-2
Back Fork—*stream* KY-4
Back Fork—*stream* VA-3
Back Fork—*stream* (7) WV-2
Back Fork Elk River—*stream* WV-2
*Back Fork Hurricane Creek* VA-3
Back Fork Mtn—*summit* WV-2
Back Fox Ditch—*canal* NV-8
*Back Garden Creek* MD-2
Backgarden Creek—*stream* MD-2
*Back Garden Pond* MD-2
Backgarden Pond—*lake* MD-2
**Back Gate**—*pop pl* AR-4
*Background Creek* SC-3
Back Harbor—*cove* MA-1
Back Hollow—*valley* AL-4
Back Hollow—*valley* OH-6
Back Hollow—*valley* PA-2
Back Hollow—*valley* TN-4
Back Hollow—*valley* VA-3
Back Hollow—*valley* WV-2
*Backhouse* PA-2
Back House—*hist pl* AR-4
Back Island—*island* AK-9
Back Island—*island* SC-3
Back Lake—*lake* IL-6
Back Lake—*lake* MI-6
Back Lake—*lake* (2) MN-6
Back Lake—*lake* NH-1
Back Lake—*lake* NC-3
Back Lake—*lake* TX-5
Back Lake—*lake* WA-9
Back Lake—*lake* WI-6
Back Lake Brook—*stream* NH-1
Back Landing—*locale* NC-3
Back Landing—*locale* VA-3
**Back Landing**—*pop pl* GA-3
Back Landing Bay—*bay* NC-3
Back Landing Creek—*stream* MD-2
Backlanding Creek—*stream* NC-3
Back Levee Canal—*canal* LA-4
Backlick Run—*stream* VA-3
Backman Creek—*stream* WA-9
Backman Flat Spring—*spring* AZ-5
Backman Lake—*lake* MN-6
Backman Sch—*school* UT-8
Back Meadow—*flat* ME-1
Back Meadow Brook—*stream* ME-1
Back Meadows—*flat* CA-9
Back Meadows Creek—*stream* CA-9
**Back Narrows**—*pop pl* ME-1
Back Neck—*cape* NJ-2
*Back of Beyond* TN-4
Back Of Howells Pond—*reservoir* OH-6
**Backoo**—*pop pl* ND-7
Backoo Field (airport)—*airport* ND-7
*Back O' Th' Sound* NJ-2
Back o'th' Sound—*bay* NJ-2
Backout Creek—*stream* OR-9
Backpackers Campground—*locale* CA-9
Backpackers Pass—*gap* WY-8
*Backpasture Gulch* OR-9
Back Pasture Windmill—*locale* TX-5
Back Point—*cape* AK-9
Back Point No 1—*other* AK-9
Back Pond—*lake* (2) NH-1
Back Pond—*lake* VT-1
Back Protection Levee—*levee* LA-4
Back Range—*ridge* AK-9
Back Ridge—*ridge* (3) LA-4
Back Ridge—*ridge* WV-2
Back Ridge Canal—*canal* LA-4
Back Ridge Cem—*cemetery* ME-1
Back Ridge Trail—*trail* WV-2
*Back River* GA-3
*Back River* ME-1
*Back River* MA-1
*Back River* VA-3
Back River—*bay* FL-3
Back River—*bay* MA-1
Back River—*channel* CT-1
Back River—*channel* (2) GA-3
Back River—*gut* ME-1
Back River—*gut* VA-3
Back River—*locale* MD-2
**Back River**—*pop pl* VA-3
Back River—*stream* CT-1
Back River—*stream* FL-3
Back River—*stream* (2) GA-3
Back River—*stream* (4) ME-1
Back River—*stream* MD-2
Back River—*stream* (4) MA-1
Back River—*stream* (2) NH-1
Back River—*stream* (2) SC-3
Back River—*stream* VA-3
Back River Cove—*bay* ME-1
Back River Creek—*stream* ME-1
Back River Farm—*hist pl* NH-1
**Back River Highlands**—*pop pl* MD-2
Back River Marsh—*swamp* VA-3
Back River Marshes—*swamp* MA-1
Back River Neck—*cape* MD-2
Back River Sch—*school* MD-2
*Back Run* OH-6
Back Run—*stream* KY-4
Back Run—*stream* NJ-2
Back Run—*stream* (3) OH-6
Back Run—*stream* PA-2
Back Run—*stream* VA-3
Back Run—*stream* (3) WV-2
Backs, Ferdinand, House—*hist pl* CA-9
Backs Branch—*stream* KY-4
Back Sch—*school* KY-4
Back Scratcher Rsvr—*reservoir* WY-8
Back Scuttle Drift Mine (underground)—*mine* AL-4
Back Settlement—*locale* (2) ME-1
Back Settlement Pond—*lake* ME-1
Back Shore—*beach* ME-1
Backside Inn—*hist pl* NH-1
*Back Slack Reach* SC-3
Back Slack Reach—*channel* SC-3
Back Slough—*gut* FL-3
Back Slough—*gut* KY-4
Back Slough—*stream* KY-4
Back Sound—*bay* NC-3
Back Spur—*ridge* TN-4
Backston Cem—*cemetery* MS-4
Backstop Ridge—*cliff* KS-7
*Back Swamp* VA-3
**Back Swamp**—*pop pl* SC-3
Back Swamp—*stream* (4) NC-3
Back Swamp—*stream* (2) SC-3
Back Swamp—*swamp* GA-3
Back Swamp—*swamp* (4) SC-3
Back Swamp Ch—*church* (3) NC-3
*Back Swamp Creek* SC-3
Back Swamp Creek—*stream* NC-3
Back Swamp (Township of)—*fmr MCD* NC-3
Back Swimmer Spring—*spring* OR-9
Backswitch, The—*locale* UT-8
Back Tank—*reservoir* (2) AZ-5
Back Tank—*reservoir* NM-5
Back Tank—*reservoir* TX-5
**Backup Corners**—*pop pl* PA-2
Backus—*locale* NY-2
Backus—*locale* PA-2
Backus—*locale* WV-2
**Backus**—*pop pl* MN-6
Backus, E. M., Lodge—*hist pl* NC-3
Backus, Nathaniel, House—*hist pl* CT-1
**Backus Beach**—*pop pl* MI-6
Backus Branch—*stream* (2) WV-2
Backusburg—*locale* KY-4
Backus Corners—*locale* PA-2
Backus Creek—*stream* (2) MI-6
Backus Creek—*stream* MT-8
Backus Creek—*stream* WA-9
Backus Creek Flooding—*reservoir* MI-6
Backus Creek State Game Area—*park* MI-6
Backus Hill—*summit* NY-2
Backus Hosp—*hospital* CT-1
Backus Island—*island* MN-6
Backus JHS—*school* DC-2
Backus Knob—*summit* OH-6
Backus Lake—*lake* MI-6
Backus Lake—*lake* MN-6
Backus Lake Flooding—*reservoir* MI-6
Backus Mtn—*summit* WV-2
**Backus (Township of)**—*pop pl* MI-6
Backus Windmill—*locale* NM-5
Back Valley—*basin* (3) VA-3
Back Valley—*stream* GA-3
Back Valley—*valley* AL-4
Back Valley—*valley* AR-4
Back Valley—*valley* GA-3
Back Valley—*valley* (3) TN-4
Back Valley—*valley* (3) VA-3
Back Valley—*valley* WV-2
Back Valley Creek—*stream* GA-3
Back Valley Ridge—*ridge* AL-4
Back Valley Ridge—*ridge* GA-3
Backward Cave—*cave* AL-4
Backward Tank—*reservoir* AZ-5
Backwater Brook—*stream* CT-1
*Backwater Creek* MI-6
*Backwater Pond* MA-1
Backwaters, The—*lake* IN-6
Back Way Gut—*gut* VA-3
Backway Hollow—*valley* VA-3
Backwood Mtn—*summit* ME-1
Backwoods—*locale* TN-4
Backwoods Post Office (historical)—*building* TN-4
Backwoods Sch (historical)—*school* TN-4
*Backworth Island* WA-9
*Back Wye River* MD-2
Back Yukon Slough—*stream* AK-9
Bacliff—*CDP* TX-5
**Bacliff**—*pop pl* TX-5
*Bacobi* AZ-5
**Bacobi**—*pop pl* AZ-5
Bacobi Community Bldg—*building* AZ-5
*Baco Creek* MI-6
Bacom Point—*cape* FL-3
*Bacon* DE-2
Bacon—*locale* MO-7
Bacon—*locale* TX-5
Bacon—*locale* WA-9
**Bacon**—*pop pl* DE-2
**Bacon**—*pop pl* IN-6
Bacon—*post sta* IN-6
Bacon, Bayou—*stream* MS-4
Bacon, George H., House—*hist pl* WA-9
Bacon, Hillary, Store (Woolworth's)—*hist pl* IN-6
Bacon, Jabez, House—*hist pl* CT-1
Bacon, Lake—*lake* MI-6
Bacon, Warren and Myrta, House—*hist pl* TX-5
Bacon Acad—*hist pl* CT-1
Bacon and Kenney Ditch—*canal* DE-2
Bacon and Tomlin, Inc.—*hist pl* FL-3
Bacon Bend—*bend* TN-4
Bacon Branch—*stream* IL-6
Bacon Branch—*stream* KY-4
Bacon Branch—*stream* LA-4
Bacon Branch—*stream* (2) TN-4
Bacon Branch—*stream* VA-3
Bacon Branch—*stream* WI-6
Bacon Bridge—*bridge* SC-3
Bacon Brook—*stream* ME-1
Bacon Brook—*stream* MA-1
Bacon Brook—*stream* NY-2
Bacon Brook Sch—*school* NY-2
Bacon Camp—*locale* OR-9
Bacon Camp Draw—*valley* OR-9
Bacon Camp Lake Waterhole—*reservoir* OR-9
Bacon Camp Waterhole—*reservoir* OR-9
Bacon Canyon—*valley* CA-9
Bacon Canyon—*valley* NV-8
Bacon Cem—*cemetery* GA-3
Bacon Cem—*cemetery* (2) IL-6
Bacon Cem—*cemetery* IN-6
Bacon Cem—*cemetery* (2) KY-4
Bacon Cem—*cemetery* MO-7
Bacon Cem—*cemetery* (4) TN-4
Bacon Cem—*cemetery* (3) TX-5
Bacon Ch—*church* GA-3
Bacon Chapel—*church* MO-7
**Bacon (County)**—*pop pl* GA-3
Bacon County Courthouse—*hist pl* GA-3
*Bacon Creek* CA-9
*Bacon Creek* ID-8
*Bacon Creek* IN-6
Bacon Creek—*stream* AK-9
Bacon Creek—*stream* AR-4
Bacon Creek—*stream* (2) CA-9
Bacon Creek—*stream* (6) ID-8
Bacon Creek—*stream* IN-6
Bacon Creek—*stream* (2) IA-7
Bacon Creek—*stream* KS-7
Bacon Creek—*stream* (4) KY-4
Bacon Creek—*stream* MI-6
Bacon Creek—*stream* ND-7
Bacon Creek—*stream* OR-9
Bacon Creek—*stream* (2) TN-4
Bacon Creek—*stream* TX-5
Bacon Creek—*stream* (3) WA-9
Bacon Creek—*stream* (2) WY-8
Bacon Creek Campground—*locale* WA-9
Bacon Creek Ch—*church* KY-4
Bacon Creek Siding—*locale* WA-9
Bacon District Sch—*school* VA-3
Bacon Ditch—*canal* MT-8
Bacon Draw—*valley* TX-5
**Bacone**—*pop pl* OK-5
Bacone Coll—*school* OK-5
Bacon Family Homestead—*hist pl* GA-3
Bacon Ferry—*locale* TN-4
Bacon Flat—*bend* OR-9
Bacon Flat—*flat* (2) CA-9
Bacon Flat—*flat* NV-8
Bacon Flat—*locale* OH-6
Bacon Flat Riffle—*rapids* OR-9
Bacon Flats—*flat* CA-9
*Bacon Forks* PA-2
Bacon-Fraser House—*hist pl* GA-3
Bacon Gap—*gap* TN-4
**Bacon Gap**—*pop pl* TN-4
Bacon Glacier—*glacier* AK-9
Bacon-Gleason-Blodgett Homestead—*hist pl* MA-1
Bacon Gulch—*valley* CA-9
Bacon Hall—*locale* MD-2
Bacon Hill—*locale* MD-2
**Bacon Hill**—*pop pl* NY-2
Bacon Hill—*summit* CA-9
Bacon Hill—*summit* ME-1
Bacon Hill—*summit* MD-2
Bacon Hill—*summit* NY-2
Bacon Hills—*other* CA-9
Bacon Hills Area—*area* CA-9
Bacon (historical)—*locale* KS-7
**Bacon (historical)**—*pop pl* MS-4
Bacon Hollow—*locale* VA-3
Bacon Hollow—*valley* MO-7
Bacon Hollow—*valley* OH-6
Bacon Hollow—*valley* VA-3
Bacon Hollow—*valley* WV-2
Bacon Hollow Overlook—*locale* VA-3
Bacon Hosp—*hospital* TN-4
Bacon HS—*school* OH-6
*Baconia* MS-4
*Bacon Island* DE-2
Bacon Island—*island* CA-9
Bacon Island—*island* ME-1
Bacon Island—*island* MI-6
Bacon Island Creek—*stream* DE-2
Bacon Island (historical)—*island* TN-4
Bacon JHS—*school* CA-9
Bacon Lake—*lake* (2) AR-4
Bacon Lake—*lake* (2) ID-8
Bacon Lake—*lake* MI-6
Bacon Lake—*lake* ND-7
Bacon Lake—*reservoir* CO-8
Bacon Ledge—*summit* NH-1
Bacon Level—*locale* AL-4
Bacon (Magisterial District)—*fmr MCD* VA-3
Bacon Meadow—*flat* CA-9
Bacon Memorial Park—*park* MO-7
Bacon Mill—*locale* PA-2
Bacon Park—*park* GA-3
Bacon Peak—*summit* ID-8
Bacon Peak—*summit* WA-9
Bacon Point—*summit* WA-9
*Bacon Pond* RI-1
Bacon Pond—*lake* GA-3
Bacon Pond—*lake* NH-1
Bacon Pond—*lake* NY-2
Bacon Prairie Creek—*stream* IN-6
Bacon Ranch—*locale* CA-9
Bacon Ranch—*locale* MT-8
Bacon Reservoir Ranch—*locale* ID-8
Bacon Ridge—*ridge* IN-6
Bacon Ridge—*ridge* ME-1
Bacon Ridge—*ridge* MD-2
Bacon Ridge—*ridge* TN-4
Bacon Ridge—*ridge* WY-8
Bacon Ridge Branch—*stream* MD-2
Bacon Rind Campground—*locale* CA-9
Bacon Rind Canyon—*valley* UT-8
Bacon Rind Creek—*stream* MT-8
Baconrind Creek—*stream* OK-5
Bacon Rind Creek Road Camp—*locale* MT-8
Bacon Rind Flat—*flat* NV-8
Bacon Rind Gate—*locale* ID-8
Bacon Rind Ridge—*ridge* UT-8
Bacon Run—*stream* LA-4
Bacon Run—*stream* OH-6
Bacon Run—*stream* (2) PA-2
Bacons—*locale* DE-2
Bacons Branch—*stream* LA-4
*Bacons Bridge* SC-3
Bacon's Castle—*hist pl* VA-3
Bacons Castle—*locale* VA-3
Bacon Sch—*school* MI-6
Bacon Sch—*school* NJ-2
Bacon Sch—*school* OH-6
Bacon Sch—*school* VA-3
Bacon Sch (abandoned)—*school* (2) MO-7
Bacons Fork—*locale* VA-3
Bacon Shoals—*bar* TN-4
Bacon Siphon—*locale* WA-9
Bacon Slide—*slope* UT-8
Bacons Neck—*cape* NJ-2
**Bacons Neck**—*pop pl* NJ-2
Bacons Neck Sch—*school* NJ-2
Bacon Spring—*spring* MO-7
Bacon Spring—*spring* OR-9
Bacon Spring—*spring* TN-4
**Bacon Springs**—*pop pl* MS-4
Bacon Springs—*spring* NV-8
Bacons Run—*stream* NJ-2
*Bacon Station* DE-2
Bacon-Stickney House—*hist pl* NY-2
*Baconsville* MA-1
Bacon Swamp—*swamp* IN-6
Bacon Tank—*reservoir* AZ-5
**Baconton**—*pop pl* GA-3
Baconton (CCD)—*cens area* GA-3
Baconton Commercial Hist Dist—*hist pl* GA-3
**Bacon Township**—*pop pl* MO-7
Bacon Tunnel—*tunnel* WA-9
**Baconville**—*pop pl* MA-1
Baconville (historical)—*locale* ND-7
Bacot Cem—*cemetery* SC-3
Bacote Cem—*cemetery* SC-3
Bacotes Windmill—*locale* TX-5
Bacot Park—*park* MS-4
**Bacots**—*pop pl* MS-4
**Bacova**—*pop pl* VA-3
Bacova, Lake—*lake* VA-3
Bacova Junction—*locale* VA-3
*Bacovi* AZ-5
**Bacton**—*pop pl* PA-2
Bactrian Point—*cape* AK-9
Baculite Mesa—*summit* CO-8
**Bacuna**—*pop pl* GU-9
Bacus Creek—*stream* OR-9
Bacus Ditch—*canal* WY-8
Bad, Turangel—*cape* PW-9
**Bad Axe**—*pop pl* MI-6
Bad Axe Cem—*cemetery* WI-6
Bad Axe Ch—*church* WI-6
Bad Axe Creek—*stream* MI-6
Bad Axe Drain—*canal* MI-6
Bad Axe Lake—*lake* MN-6
Bad Axe River—*stream* WI-6
Badbaby Coulee—*valley* MT-8
Bad Banks Creek—*stream* OR-9
Bad Bayou—*stream* LA-4
Bad Bear Campground—*locale* ID-8
Bad Bear Creek—*stream* (2) ID-8
Bad Bear Peak—*summit* ID-8
Bad Bottom Tank—*reservoir* TX-5
Badboy Creek—*stream* MN-6
Bad Boy Lake—*lake* MN-6
*Bad Branch* MS-4
Bad Branch—*stream* (2) AL-4
Bad Branch—*stream* AR-4
Bad Branch—*stream* (2) GA-3
Bad Branch—*stream* KY-4
Bad Branch—*stream* MO-7
Bad Branch—*stream* NC-3
Bad Branch—*stream* OK-5
Bad Branch—*stream* (3) VA-3
Bad Branch Creek—*stream* MS-4
Bad Bug Butte—*summit* AZ-5
Bad Canyon—*valley* CA-9
Bad Canyon—*valley* CO-8
Bad Canyon—*valley* MT-8
Bad Canyon Creek—*stream* MT-8
Bad Creek—*stream* CA-9
Bad Creek—*stream* GA-3
Bad Creek—*stream* MI-6
Bad Creek—*stream* (2) NC-3
Bad Creek—*stream* OH-6
Bad Creek—*stream* OK-5
Bad Creek—*stream* (4) SC-3
Bad Creek—*stream* SD-7
Bad Creek—*stream* (2) VA-3
Bad Creek—*stream* WY-8
Bad Creek Cem—*cemetery* NC-3
Bad Creek Sch—*school* KY-4
Baddacook Brook—*stream* MA-1
Baddacook Pond—*lake* MA-1
*Bad Dad* TN-4
*Bad Dad Post Office* TN-4
Badders Creek—*stream* AR-4
Baddie Creek—*stream* MS-4
Bade—*locale* OR-9
Bad East Gully—*valley* TX-5
*Badeau Bayou* AR-4
*Badeau Bayou* LA-4
Badeau Hill—*summit* NY-2
Badeaux Coulee—*stream* LA-4
Badebei—*island* PW-9
Bade Cem—*cemetery* MO-7
Badechamelei—*summit* PW-9
Bade Coulee—*valley* MN-6
Bade Creek—*stream* NV-8
*Baden* MO-7
*Baden* NC-3
Baden—*locale* IA-7
Baden—*locale* MD-2
Baden—*locale* (2) MN-6
Baden—*locale* ND-7
Baden—*locale* VA-3
Baden—*locale* WV-2
**Baden**—*pop pl* GA-3
**Baden**—*pop pl* MO-7
**Baden**—*pop pl* PA-2
**Baden**—*pop pl* TX-5
Baden—*uninc pl* CA-9
Badenaugh Canyon—*valley* CA-9
**Baden Baden**—*pop pl* IL-6
Baden Borough—*civil* PA-2
Baden Cem—*cemetery* IA-7
Baden Ch—*church* WV-2
Baden Coulee—*valley* ND-7
*Baden Creek* WA-9
Baden (historical)—*locale* KS-7
Badenhop Well—*well* TX-5
Badeno Windmill—*locale* TX-5
Baden-Powell, Mount—*summit* CA-9
Baden-Powell Sch—*school* CA-9
Baden-Powell Scout Reservation—*locale* FL-3
**Baden Siding**—*pop pl* WV-2
Baden Springs Cem—*cemetery* MO-7
**Baden Township**—*pop pl* ND-7
Bader—*locale* TX-5
**Bader**—*pop pl* IL-6
Bader Bar—*bar* TN-4
Bader Creek—*stream* TX-5
Bader Drain—*canal* MI-6
Bader Draw—*valley* WY-8
Bader Field—*airport* NJ-2
Bader Gulch—*valley* WY-8
Bader Homestead—*locale* WY-8
Bade Rotor And Wing Svc. Heliport—*airport* WA-9
Bader Sch—*school* MI-6
Baders Hollow—*valley* PA-2
*Badersville* MO-7
**Baderville**—*pop pl* MO-7
*Badfish Creek* WI-6
Badfish Creek—*stream* WI-6
Bad Fork—*stream* KY-4
Bad Fork—*stream* (2) NC-3
*Badger* IN-6
*Badger* WI-6
Badger—*locale* KS-7
Badger—*locale* KY-4
Badger—*locale* NE-7
Badger—*locale* TX-5
Badger—*locale* WA-9
**Badger**—*pop pl* CA-9
**Badger**—*pop pl* IA-7
**Badger**—*pop pl* MN-6
**Badger**—*pop pl* SD-7
Badger—*post sta* AK-9
Badger, Lake—*lake* SD-7
Badger, Rev. Stephen, House—*hist pl* MA-1
Badger Army Ammun Plant—*military* WI-6
Badger Basin—*basin* (2) ID-8
Badger Basin—*basin* WY-8
Badger Basin—*locale* WY-8
Badger Bay—*bay* AK-9
Badger Bay—*bay* ND-7
Badger Bay—*bay* WI-6
Badger Bldg—*hist pl* WI-6
Badger Branch—*stream* MO-7
Badger Branch—*stream* NE-7
Badger Branch—*stream* WY-8
Badger Brook—*stream* (2) ME-1
Badger Brook—*stream* NH-1
Badger Brook—*stream* VT-1
*Badger Butte* AZ-5
Badger Butte—*summit* NM-5
Badger Butte—*summit* (3) OR-9
Badger Cabin—*locale* NV-8
Badger Cabin—*locale* OR-9
*Badger Canal* CO-8
Badger Canyon—*valley* AZ-5
Badger Canyon—*valley* (3) CA-9
Badger Canyon—*valley* ID-8
Badger Canyon—*valley* NV-8
Badger Canyon—*valley* (2) OR-9
Badger Canyon—*valley* UT-8
Badger Canyon—*valley* WA-9
Badger Cem—*cemetery* IN-6
Badger Cem—*cemetery* MN-6
Badger Cem—*cemetery* SD-7
Badger Cem—*cemetery* WI-6
**Badger Corner**—*pop pl* OR-9
Badger Coulee—*valley* MT-8
Badger Cove—*bay* AZ-5
*Badger Creek* ID-8
*Badger Creek* KS-7
*Badger Creek* MN-6
*Badger Creek* NV-8
*Badger Creek* OR-9
Badger Creek—*stream* AZ-5
Badger Creek—*stream* (3) CA-9
Badger Creek—*stream* (4) CO-8
Badger Creek—*stream* (10) ID-8
Badger Creek—*stream* IL-6
Badger Creek—*stream* IN-6
Badger Creek—*stream* (5) IA-7
Badger Creek—*stream* (6) KS-7
Badger Creek—*stream* (3) MN-6
Badger Creek—*stream* MO-7
Badger Creek—*stream* (9) MT-8
Badger Creek—*stream* NE-7
Badger Creek—*stream* (9) NV-8
Badger Creek—*stream* NY-2
Badger Creek—*stream* ND-7
Badger Creek—*stream* (8) OR-9
Badger Creek—*stream* TN-4
Badger Creek—*stream* UT-8
Badger Creek—*stream* (2) WA-9

Badger Creek—*stream* WI-6
Badger Creek—*stream* (9) WY-8
Badger Creek Bar—*bar* ID-8
Badger Creek Basin—*basin* WY-8
Badger Creek Cem—*cemetery* KS-7
Badger Creek Cem—*cemetery* MN-6
Badger Creek (historical)—*locale* KS-7
Badger Creek Oil Field—*oilfield* KS-7
Badger Creek Rapids—*rapids* AZ-5
Badger Creek State Rec Area—*park* IA-7
Badger Creek Trail—*trail* OR-9
Badger Creek Trail—*trail* WY-8
Badger Dam—*dam* NM-5
Badger Den Well—*well* AZ-5
*Badger Din Well* AZ-5
Badger Ditch—*canal* CO-8
Badger Drain—*canal* MI-6
Badger Draw—*valley* OR-9
Badger Draw Rsvr—*reservoir* OR-9
Badger Draw Rsvr—*reservoir* WY-8
Badger East Lateral—*canal* WA-9
Badger Field—*park* TN-4
Badger Fire Control Station—*locale* CA-9
Badger Fisher Main Canal—*canal* MT-8
Badger Flat—*flat* AZ-5
Badger Flat—*flat* (3) CA-9
Badger Flat—*flat* CO-8
Badger Flat—*flat* (2) NV-8
Badger Flat—*flat* (2) OR-9
Badger Flats Airstrip—*airport* CO-8
Badger Flat Tank—*reservoir* AZ-5
Badger Flat Windmill—*well* AZ-5
Badger Gap—*gap* CA-9
Badger Gap—*gap* WA-9
**Badger Grove**—*pop pl* IN-6
Badger Guard Station—*locale* MT-8
*Badger Gulch* ID-8
Badger Gulch—*valley* (3) CO-8
Badger Gulch—*valley* (4) ID-8
Badger Gulch—*valley* (5) MT-8
Badger Gulch—*valley* NV-8
Badger Gulch—*valley* WA-9
Badger Gulch—*valley* WY-8
Badger Gulch Spring—*spring* ID-8
Badger Hill—*summit* AK-9
Badger Hill—*summit* (2) CA-9
Badger Hill—*summit* MA-1
Badger Hill—*summit* NH-1
Badger Hill—*summit* OK-5
Badger Hill Cem—*cemetery* IA-7
Badger Hill Diggings—*locale* CA-9
Badger Hill (historical)—*locale* IA-7
Badger Hill (historical P.O.)—*locale* IA-7
Badger Hill Mine—*mine* CA-9
Badger Hills—*range* CO-8
Badger Hills—*range* WY-8
Badger Hills—*spring* MT-8
Badger Hole—*hist pl* SD-7
Badger Hole—*other* OR-9
Badger Hole Coulee—*valley* MT-8
*Badger Hole Draw* OR-9
Badger Hole Flat—*flat* OR-9
Badger Hole Spring—*spring* ID-8
Badger Hole Spring—*spring* NV-8
Badger Hole Spring—*spring* OR-9
Badger Hole Tank—*reservoir* NM-5
Badger Hole Tank—*reservoir* TX-5
*Badger Hollow* WA-9
Badger Hollow—*valley* TN-4
Badger Hollow—*valley* (2) UT-8
Badger Hollow—*valley* WA-9
Badger Hollow—*valley* WI-6
Badger HS—*school* OH-6
Badger HS—*school* WI-6
Badger Island—*island* NH-1
Badger Island—*island* UT-8
Badger Island—*island* WA-9
Badger Island—*island* WY-8
Badger Knolls—*summit* UT-8
Badger Lake—*lake* AK-9
Badger Lake—*lake* IA-7
Badger Lake—*lake* MI-6
Badger Lake—*lake* MN-6
Badger Lake—*lake* NE-7
Badger Lake—*lake* NM-5
Badger Lake—*lake* (2) WA-9
Badger Lake—*lake* WI-6
Badger Lake—*lake* WY-8
Badger Lake—*reservoir* IA-7
Badger Lake—*reservoir* OR-9
Badger Lake—*swamp* AZ-5
Badger Lake Campground—*park* OR-9
Badger Lake Dam—*dam* OR-9
Badger Lakes—*lake* CA-9
Badger Lake State Wildlife Mngmt Area—*park* IA-7
Badger Lake State Wildlife Mngmt Area—*park* MN-6
Badger Lee Ch—*church* OK-5
Badger Meadows—*flat* ID-8
Badger Mill Creek—*stream* WI-6
Badger Mine—*mine* AZ-5
Badger Mine—*mine* CO-8
Badger Mine—*mine* ID-8
Badger Mine—*mine* MT-8
Badger Mine—*mine* (2) NV-8
Badger Mine—*mine* TN-4
Badger Mine—*mine* WY-8
*Badger Mountain* ID-8
Badger Mountain (CCD)—*cens area* OR-9
Badger Mountain Cem—*cemetery* WA-9
Badger Mountain Community Hall—*building* WA-9
Badger Mountain Lookout Tower—*locale* WA-9
Badger Mountain Spring—*spring* ID-8
Badger Mtn—*summit* AZ-5
Badger Mtn—*summit* (2) CA-9
Badger Mtn—*summit* CO-8
Badger Mtn—*summit* (3) ID-8
Badger Mtn—*summit* (2) NV-8
Badger Mtn—*summit* OK-5
Badger Mtn—*summit* OR-9
Badger Mtn—*summit* RI-1
Badger Mtn—*summit* VT-1
Badger Mtn—*summit* (2) WA-9
Badger Nest Tank—*reservoir* TX-5
Badgero Creek—*stream* CO-8
Badgero Drain—*canal* MI-6
Badgero Extension Drain—*canal* MI-6
Badgerow Bldg—*hist pl* IA-7
Badger Park—*park* AZ-5
Badger Park—*park* WI-6
Badger Pass—*gap* CA-9
Badger Pass—*gap* (2) MT-8
Badger Pass Ski Area—*locale* CA-9
Badger Peak—*summit* CA-9
Badger Peak—*summit* ID-8
Badger Peak—*summit* MT-8
Badger Peak—*summit* UT-8
Badger Peak—*summit* WA-9
Badger Pocket—*valley* WA-9
Badger Point Campground—*locale* UT-8
Badger Pond—*lake* ME-1
Badger Pond—*lake* (2) NH-1
Badger Ridge—*ridge* MT-8
Badger Road Baptist Ch—*church* AK-9
Badger Rsvr—*reservoir* ID-8
Badger Rsvr—*reservoir* MT-8
Badger Rsvr—*reservoir* OR-9
Badger Rsvr—*reservoir* WY-8
Badger Run—*stream* MN-6
Badger Run—*stream* OH-6
Badger Run—*stream* WV-2
Badger Sch—*school* MO-7
Badger Sch—*school* NE-7
Badger Sch—*school* (6) WI-6
Badger Sch—*school* WY-8
Badger School—*bar* ND-7
Badgers Island—*island* ME-1
Badger Spring—*spring* (4) AZ-5
Badger Spring—*spring* CA-9
Badger Spring—*spring* CO-8
Badger Spring—*spring* (4) NV-8
Badger Spring—*spring* (2) NM-5
Badger Spring—*spring* (4) OR-9
Badger Spring—*spring* UT-8
Badger Spring—*spring* (2) WA-9
Badger Spring—*spring* (2) WY-8
Badger Spring Gulch—*valley* ID-8
Badger Spring Interchange—*crossing* AZ-5
*Badger Spring Lake* TN-4
Badger Spring Lake—*reservoir* TN-4
Badger Spring Ranch—*locale* CO-8
Badger Springs—*spring* OR-9
Badger Spring Wash—*stream* AZ-5
Badgers Rock—*rock* MA-1
*Badgers Rocks* MA-1
Badger Stadium—*other* TX-5
Badger State Ditch—*canal* CO-8
Badger State Mine—*mine* CO-8
Badger State Mine—*mine* MT-8
Badger Tank—*reservoir* (5) AZ-5
Badger Tank—*reservoir* TX-5
*Badger Teeth* WY-8
*Badger Teeth Mountain* WY-8
**Badgertown**—*pop pl* OH-6
Badger Township—*fmr MCD* IA-7
**Badger Township**—*pop pl* MO-7
**Badger Township**—*pop pl* ND-7
**Badger Township**—*pop pl* (2) SD-7
**Badger (Township of)**—*pop pl* MN-6
Badger Valley—*basin* NV-8
Badger Valley—*valley* WA-9
Badger Valley—*valley* WI-6
Badger Wash—*stream* AZ-5
Badger Wash—*stream* CO-8
Badger Wasteway—*canal* WY-8
Badger Well—*locale* (2) NM-5
Badger Well—*well* CA-9
Badger Wells—*locale* WA-9
Badger Windmill—*locale* (5) NM-5
Badget Ranch—*locale* SD-7
Badget Spring—*spring* MT-8
Badgett Canyon—*valley* TX-5
*Badgett Cemetery* AL-4
Badgett Hollow—*valley* TN-4
Badgett Post Office (historical)—*building* TN-4
Badgetts Bar—*bar* TN-4
Badgett Sch—*school* AR-4
Badgley Coulee—*valley* MT-8
Badgley Fork—*stream* WV-2
Badgley House and Site—*hist pl* NJ-2
Badgley Spring—*spring* WA-9
Bad Gulch—*valley* CA-9
Bad Gully—*stream* LA-4
**Badham**—*pop pl* SC-3
Bad Hand Creek—*stream* SD-7
Bad Hill—*summit* PA-2
*Bad Hollow* SD-7
Bud Hollow—*valley* IN-6
Bad Horse Creek—*stream* SD-7
*Bad Humoured Island* SD-7
Badillo Sch—*school* CA-9
**Badin**—*pop pl* NC-3
Badin Air Natl Guard Station—*building* NC-3
*Badin Dam* NC-3
Badin Dam—*dam* NC-3
Bad Indian Swamp—*swamp* NY-2
Bading Cem—*cemetery* TX-5
Bading Hill—*summit* TX-5
Badin Hist Dist—*hist pl* NC-3
Badin Lake—*reservoir* NC-3
Badin-Roque House—*hist pl* LA-4
*Badin Rsvr* NC-3
Badin Sch—*school* NC-3
Badin Waterworks—*locale* NC-3
Bad Island—*island* OK-5
Badito—*locale* CO-8
Badito Cone—*summit* CO-8
*Badka Creek* MS-4
Bad Knob—*summit* NC-3
Badland Butte—*summit* MT-8
Bad Land Cliffs—*cliff* UT-8
*Badland Coulee* MT-8
Badland Coulee—*valley* (3) MT-8
Badland Creek—*stream* OR-9
Badland Draw—*valley* WY-8
Bad Land Gulch—*valley* MT-8
Badland Hills—*other* NM-5
Badland Hills—*summit* WY-8
Badland Pond—*lake* NM-5
Badland Pond—*reservoir* SD-7
*Badland Region* SD-7
*Bad Lands* SD-7
Badlands—*area* (2) AZ-5
Badlands—*area* CA-9
Bad Lands—*area* NM-5
Badlands—*area* OR-9
Bad Lands—*area* OR-9
Badlands—*area* SD-7
Badlands—*area* UT-8
Badlands—*flat* MT-8
Bad Lands—*summit* MA-1
Bad Lands—*summit* OK-5
Badlands—*summit* SD-7
Badlands—*unorg reg* SD-7
Badlands, The—*area* CA-9
Badlands, The—*area* MT-8
Badlands, The—*area* NM-5
Badlands, The—*area* WA-9
Badlands, The—*flat* TX-5
Badlands, The—*locale* WA-9
Badlands, The—*other* ID-8
Badlands Airfield—*airport* SD-7
Badlands Canyon—*valley* NM-5
*Bad Lands Cliffs* UT-8
Badlands Coulee—*valley* MT-8
Badlands Creek—*stream* (3) SD-7
Badlands Draw—*valley* IA-7
Badlands Draw—*valley* ND-7
Badlands Hills—*range* WY-8
Badlands Lakes—*lake* WA-9
*Badlands Natl Monument* SD-7
Badlands Natl Park—*park* SD-7
*Badlands of the Little Missouri* ND-7
Badlands Rsvr—*reservoir* WY-8
Badlands Tank—*reservoir* AZ-5
Badlands Tank—*reservoir* NM-5
Badland Tank—*reservoir* AZ-5
Badley Gulch—*valley* OR-9
Badley Ranch—*locale* ID-8
Bad Luck Branch—*stream* VA-3
*Badluck Brook* MA-1
Bad Luck Brook—*stream* MA-1
Bad Luck Creek—*stream* AL-4
Bad Luck Creek—*stream* AR-4
Bad Luck Creek—*stream* (2) ID-8
Bad Luck Creek—*stream* MT-8
Bad Luck Creek—*stream* TX-5
*Badluck Lake* MA-1
Bad Luck Lookout Tower—*locale* ID-8
*Bad-luck Mtn* MA-1
Bad Luck Mtn—*summit* MA-1
Bad Luck Mtn—*summit* NY-2
Badluck Pond—*lake* MA-1
*Bad Luck Pond Bad-luck Pond* MA-1
*Badluck Pond:Laurel Lake* MA-1
Bad Luck Spring—*spring* AZ-5
*Badluck Swamp* MA-1
Bad Luck Swamp—*swamp* MA-1
Bad Marriage Mtn—*summit* MT-8
Bad Medicine Butte—*summit* AZ-5
Bad Mtn—*summit* ME-1
Bad Name Spring—*spring* CA-9
Badnation—*locale* SD-7
**Bad Nation Township**—*pop pl* SD-7
Bad News Camp—*locale* MT-8
Bado—*locale* MO-7
Bado—*locale* OK-5
Badon Cem—*cemetery* LA-4
*Bado Shima* MH-9
Badoura—*locale* MN-6
Badoura Lookout Tower—*locale* MN-6
Badoura State For—*forest* MN-6
Badoura State Nursery—*locale* MN-6
**Badoura (Township of)**—*pop pl* MN-6
Bad Pass Trail—*hist pl* MT-8
Bad Pass Trail—*hist pl* WY-8
Bad Point—*ridge* CO-8
Bad Prong—*stream* GA-3
Badrbaren—*island* MP-9
Bad Ridge—*ridge* VA-3
*Bad River* MI-6
*Bad River* SD-7
Bad River—*stream* ID-8
Bad River—*stream* MI-6
Bad River—*stream* SD-7
Bad River—*stream* WI-6
Bad River Cattle Company Number 1 Dam—*dam* SD-7
Bad River Cattle Company Number 2 Dam—*dam* SD-7
**Bad River Ind Res**—*pop pl* WI-6
*Bad River Slough* WI-6
Bad River Slough—*gut* WI-6
Badrock Canyon—*valley* MT-8
Bad Rock-Columbia Heights—*cens area* MT-8
Bad Route Creek—*stream* MT-8
Badrulchau—*locale* PW-9
**Badrulchau**—*pop pl* PW-9
Badsky Pond—*lake* OR-9
Bad Spring—*spring* AZ-5
Bad Stone Ditch—*canal* KY-4
Bad Tom Mtn—*summit* ID-8
Bad Tom Trail—*trail* ID-8
Badu Bldg—*hist pl* TX-5
Badus, Lake—*reservoir* SD-7
Badus Post Office (historical)—*building* SD-7
**Badus Township**—*pop pl* SD-7
Badwater—*locale* CA-9
Badwater—*locale* WY-8
Badwater Creek—*stream* MI-6
Bad Water Creek—*stream* WY-8
Badwater Creek—*stream* WY-8
Badwater Lake—*lake* MI-6
Badwater Springs—*spring* CA-9
Bad Water Well—*well* TX-5
Badway Branch—*stream* WV-2
*Badwish'a* CA-9
Body Creek—*stream* ID-8
Baechtel Creek—*stream* CA-9
Baecker Cem—*cemetery* (2) MO-7
Bae Creek—*stream* ID-8
**Baederwood**—*pop pl* PA-2
Baederwood Park—*park* PA-2
Baederwood Shop Ctr—*locale* PA-2
Baehr Branch—*stream* IL-6
Baehr Creek—*stream* KS-7
*Baeijuande Zuyt Revier* DE-2
*Baeij Vande Zuyt Revier* DE-2
*Baeij Vande Zuyt Revier* NJ-2
Baekos Creek—*stream* WA-9
Bael—*bar* FM-9
Bael Sch—*school* FM-9
Baenen Ranch—*locale* MT-8
Baer, Albert R., House—*hist pl* WI-6
*Baer Creek* UT-8
*Baer Field* IN-6
Baer Field—*airport* IN-6
*Baergarden Ridge* VA-3
*Baergarden Ridge* WV-2
Baer German Lutheran Ch (historical)—*church* SD-7
Baer House—*hist pl* AR-4
*Baer Lake* WA-9
*Baer Lakes* WY-8
Baer Lakes—*lake* WY-8
Baer Park—*park* CA-9
Baer Park—*park* PA-2
Baer Ridge—*ridge* VA-3
Baers Ferry (historical)—*locale* TX-5
*Baers Rocks* PA-2
Baerthel Canyon—*valley* WY-8
**Baer Township**—*pop pl* ND-7
Baerwolf Drain—*canal* MI-6
Baesemann Cem—*cemetery* WI-6
Baetcke Lake—*lake* MI-6
Baethke Cem—*cemetery* IA-7
Baff Cem—*cemetery* MS-4
Baffin Bay—*bay* TX-5
Baffin Brook—*stream* NJ-2
*Baffin's Bay* TX-5
*Baffle* VA-3
Baffle Point—*cape* TX-5
**Bafrick (historical)**—*pop pl* MS-4
Bagaduce River—*stream* ME-1
Bagan—*locale* WY-8
Bagasha Creek—*stream* MS-4
Bagby—*locale* TX-5
Bagby—*locale* VA-3
**Bagby**—*pop pl* CA-9
Bagby, Alexander, House—*hist pl* KY-4
Bagby Branch—*stream* MO-7
Bagby Cem—*cemetery* KY-4
Bagby Cem—*cemetery* MS-4
Bagby Cem—*cemetery* MO-7
Bagby Ch—*church* VA-3
Bagby Creek—*stream* MO-7
Bagby Hill—*summit* CA-9
Bagby-Hossler House—*hist pl* OH-6
Bagby Hot Springs—*spring* OR-9
Bagby Hot Springs Guard Station—*locale* OR-9
Bagby Ranch—*locale* AZ-5
Bagby Sch—*school* CA-9
Bagby Sch—*school* KS-7
Bagby Sch—*school* MO-7
Bagby Stationhouse, Water Tanks and Turntable—*hist pl* CA-9
Bagby Trail—*trail* OR-9
*Bagdad* CA-9
Bagdad—*locale* LA-4
Bagdad—*locale* (2) PA-2
Bagdad—*locale* VA-3
**Bagdad**—*pop pl* AZ-5
**Bagdad**—*pop pl* CA-9
**Bagdad**—*pop pl* CO-8
**Bagdad**—*pop pl* FL-3
**Bagdad**—*pop pl* KY-4
**Bagdad**—*pop pl* NY-2
**Bagdad**—*pop pl* TX-5
Bagdad Airp—*airport* AZ-5
Bagdad Cem—*cemetery* LA-4
Bagdad Cem—*cemetery* TX-5
Bagdad Ch—*church* TN-4
Bagdad Chase Mine—*mine* CA-9
Bagdad Elem Sch—*school* AZ-5
Bagdad Elem Sch—*school* FL-3
**Bagdad (historical)**—*pop pl* TN-4
Bagdad Hosp—*hospital* AZ-5
Bagdad HS—*school* AZ-5
Bagdad Junction—*locale* WA-9
**Bagdad Junction**—*pop pl* FL-3
Bagdad Open Pit Mine—*mine* AZ-5
Bagdad Post Office—*building* AZ-5
Bagdad Post Office (historical)—*building* TN-4
Bagdad Sch—*school* IL-6
Bagdad Sch—*school* PA-2
Bagdad Tailings Dam—*dam* AZ-5
Bagdad Village Hist Dist—*hist pl* FL-3
Bagely Creek—*stream* ID-8
*Bager Creek* NV-8
Baget Creek—*stream* LA-4
Baggage Branch—*stream* LA-4
**Baggaley**—*pop pl* PA-2
Baggaley Dam—*dam* PA-2
Baggaley Elem Sch—*school* PA-2
*Baggaley Sch* PA-2
Bagga Marsh—*swamp* WI-6
Bagg Bonanza Farm District—*hist pl* ND-7
Bagg Brook—*stream* MA-1
*Bagg Creek* GA-3
Bagg Creek—*stream* SC-3
Baggers Ferry (historical)—*locale* AL-4
*Baggers Point* FL-3
Bagget, Lake—*reservoir* NC-3
Bagget Hollow—*valley* AR-4
Bagget Lake—*lake* FL-3
Bagget Mtn—*summit* TX-5
Baggett and Pickett Mines (underground)—*mine* TN-4
Baggett Branch—*stream* AL-4
Baggett Branch—*stream* (2) TN-4
Baggett Branch—*stream* TX-5
Baggett Cem—*cemetery* AL-4
Baggett Cem—*cemetery* (4) TN-4
Baggett Cem—*cemetery* TX-5
Baggett Creek—*stream* FL-3
Baggett Creek—*stream* TX-5
Baggett Creek Ch—*church* TX-5
Baggett Dam—*dam* AL-4
Baggett Draw—*valley* TX-5
Baggette Crossroads—*locale* SC-3
Baggett Gulch—*valley* CA-9
Baggett Hollow—*valley* (2) TN-4
Baggett Lake—*reservoir* AL-4
Baggett Lake Dam—*dam* MS-4
Baggett Mill Creek—*stream* AL-4
Baggett Pond—*reservoir* AL-4
Baggett Ranch—*locale* (2) TX-5
Baggetts Chapel—*church* AL-4
*Baggetts Chapel Ch* AL-4
Baggett Sch (historical)—*school* AL-4
Baggetts Creek—*stream* NC-3
Baggetts Lake—*reservoir* AL-4
*Baggetts Lake Dam* AL-4
**Baggettsville**—*pop pl* TN-4
Baggettsville Post Office (historical)—*building* TN-4
Bagg Hill—*summit* MA-1
Bagg Ledges—*summit* MA-1
Baggot Rocks—*summit* WY-8
**Baggs**—*pop pl* WY-8
Baggs Branch—*stream* GA-3
Baggs Cem—*cemetery* GA-3
Baggs Cem—*cemetery* NY-2
Baggs Cem—*cemetery* WY-8
Baggs Corner—*locale* NY-2
*Baggs Creek* GA-3
Baggs Creek—*stream* MT-8
Baggs Creek Gap—*gap* GA-3
Baggs Ditch—*canal* WY-8
*Baggs Hill* MA-1
Baggs Lake—*lake* WI-6
*Baggs Reservoir* AZ-5
Baggs Trail—*trail* OK-5
Baggy Branch—*stream* TX-5
Baghdad Run—*stream* PA-2
Bag Hill—*summit* NH-1
Bag Lake—*lake* (2) MN-6
Bagland Memorial Ch—*church* VA-3
**Baglett Grove**—*pop pl* NH-1
**Bagley**—*pop pl* AL-4
**Bagley**—*pop pl* IA-7
**Bagley**—*pop pl* MD-2
**Bagley**—*pop pl* MI-6
**Bagley**—*pop pl* MN-6
**Bagley**—*pop pl* NH-1
**Bagley**—*pop pl* NC-3
**Bagley**—*pop pl* WI-6
Bagley, John A., House—*hist pl* ID-8
Bagley, John N., House—*hist pl* MI-6
Bagley Bend Cem—*cemetery* AL-4
Bagley Bend North Mine (surface)—*mine* AL-4
Bagley Branch—*stream* TN-4
Bagley Brook—*stream* ME-1
Bagley Brook—*stream* NH-1
Bagley Brook—*stream* NY-2
Bagley-Cater Bldg—*hist pl* AL-4
Bagley Cem—*cemetery* GA-3
Bagley Cem—*cemetery* MN-6
Bagley Cem—*cemetery* MS-4
Bagley Cem—*cemetery* ND-7
Bagley Cem—*cemetery* TX-5
Bagley Cem—*cemetery* VA-3
Bagley Cem—*cemetery* WI-6
Bagley Country Club—*other* MN-6
Bagley Cove—*bay* FL-3
Bagley Creek—*stream* CO-8
Bagley Creek—*stream* (2) GA-3
Bagley Creek—*stream* MI-6
Bagley Creek—*stream* MS-4
Bagley Creek—*stream* OR-9
Bagley Creek—*stream* (2) WA-9
Bagley Creek—*stream* WI-6
Bagley Creek Sch—*school* MS-4
Bagley Dam—*dam* ND-7
Bagley Ditch—*canal* OR-9
Bagley Flat—*flat* AZ-5
Bagley Flat—*flat* CA-9
Bagley Flat Recreation Site—*park* AZ-5
Bagley Gap—*gap* TN-4
Bagley Gulch—*valley* UT-8
Bagley Hollow—*valley* AR-4
Bagley Hollow—*valley* ID-8
Bagley Hollow—*valley* (2) TN-4
Bagley Ice Field—*glacier* AK-9
Bagley Island—*island* LA-4
*Bagley JHS* AL-4
Bagley Junction—*locale* WA-9
Bagley Junction—*locale* WI-6
Bagley Lake—*lake* MI-6
Bagley Lake—*lake* MN-6
Bagley Lake—*lake* MO-7
Bagley Lake—*reservoir* MS-4
Bagley Lakes—*lake* WA-9
Bagley Lake State Wildlife Mngmt Area—*park* MN-6
*Bagley Lookout Fire Tower* MS-4
Bagley Lookout Tower—*locale* MS-4
Bagley Lookout Tower—*locale* WI-6
Bagley Meadows—*flat* UT-8
Bagley Memorial Fountain—*hist pl* MI-6
Bagley Mtn—*summit* CA-9
Bagley Mtn—*summit* ME-1
Bagley North Oil Field—*other* NM-5
Bagley Oil Field—*other* NM-5
Bagley Park—*park* GA-3
Bagley Park—*park* OR-9
Bagley Pass—*gap* CA-9
Bagley Pond—*lake* (2) NH-1
Bagley Pond—*reservoir* LA-4
Bagley Rapids—*rapids* WI-6
Bagley Rapids Campground—*locale* WI-6
Bagley Ridge—*ridge* AL-4
Bagley Sch—*school* AL-4
Bagley Sch—*school* (2) MI-6
Bagley Sch—*school* MT-8
Bagley Sch—*school* NM-5
Bagley Sch—*school* WA-9
Bagley Slough—*gut* MN-6
Bagleys Mills—*locale* VA-3
Bagley Spring—*spring* OR-9
Bagleys Ranch—*locale* NM-5
Bagley Swamp—*stream* NC-3
Bagley Tank—*reservoir* AZ-5
**Bagley (Town of)**—*pop pl* WI-6
**Bagley (Township of)**—*pop pl* MI-6
Bagley Valley—*valley* CA-9
Bagley West Oil Field—*other* NM-5
Bagnal Draw—*valley* AZ-5
Bagnall Corral—*locale* UT-8
Bagnalle Branch—*stream* VA-3
*Bagnall Hollow* AZ-5
Bagnall Sch—*school* MA-1
Bagnal Tank—*reservoir* AZ-5
Bagnal Wash—*stream* AZ-5
**Bagnell**—*pop pl* MO-7
Bagnell Cem—*cemetery* ND-7
Bagnell Dam—*dam* MO-7
**Bagnell Ferry**—*pop pl* OR-9
Bagnell Seaplane Base—*airport* MO-7
Bago, Mount—*summit* CA-9
Bagoon Brook—*stream* NH-1
Bagot, Mount—*summit* AK-9
Bagot Ranch—*locale* TX-5
Bagpipe Butte—*summit* UT-8
Bagpipe Butte Overlook—*locale* UT-8
Bag Pond—*lake* ME-1
Bag Pond Mtn—*summit* ME-1
*Bagsby Springs* OR-9
Bags Ditch Cave—*cave* AL-4
Bagshaw Field—*park* WA-9
Bagshaw Swamp—*swamp* SC-3
Bagstevold Cem—*cemetery* MN-6
**Bagtown**—*pop pl* MD-2
**Bagwell**—*pop pl* TX-5
Bagwell Branch—*stream* AL-4
Bagwell Branch—*stream* TN-4
Bagwell Cem—*cemetery* IN-6
Bagwell Cem—*cemetery* NC-3
Bagwell Cem—*cemetery* SC-3
Bagwell Cove—*bay* VA-3
Bagwell Creek—*stream* VA-3
Bagwell Island—*island* MA-1
Bagwell Lake—*lake* FL-3
Bagwell Lake—*reservoir* AL-4
Bagwell Lake Dam—*dam* AL-4
Bagwell Lake Dam—*dam* MS-4
Bagwell Landing—*locale* FL-3
Bagwell Pond—*reservoir* NC-3
Bagwell Pond Dam—*dam* NC-3
Bagwell Ranch—*locale* AZ-5
Bagwell Rsvr—*reservoir* CA-9
Baha Diversion Dam—*dam* AZ-5
Bahai Center Ch—*church* MS-4
Bahai Faith—*church* FL-3
Bahai Faith Ch—*church* FL-3
*Bahai Fanunchuluyan* MH-9
Bahai Temple—*church* IL-6
Bahai Temple—*hist pl* IL-6
*Bahala* MS-4
*Bahala Ch* MS-4
Bahala Chapel—*church* MS-4
Bahala Creek—*stream* MS-4
Bahala Creek Bridge—*hist pl* MS-4
Bahala Creek Watershed Structure 1 Dam—*dam* MS-4
Bahala Creek Watershed Structure 2 Dam—*dam* MS-4
Bahala Creek Watershed Structure 3 Dam—*dam* MS-4
Bahala Creek Watershed Structure 4 Dam—*dam* MS-4
Bahala Creek Watershed Structure 5 Dam—*dam* MS-4
*Bahala P.O.* MS-4
Bahaloa (historical)—*locale* MS-4
**Bahama**—*pop pl* NC-3
Bahama Beach—*beach* FL-3
**Bahama Beach**—*pop pl* FL-3
*Bahama Channel* FL-3
**Bahama Park (subdivision)**—*pop pl* NC-3
Bahama Swamp—*swamp* SC-3
Baham Cem—*cemetery* LA-4
Bahannan Brook—*stream* VT-1
Baha Ranch—*locale* AZ-5
Baha Spring—*spring* AZ-5
Baha Spring Number Two—*spring* AZ-5
Baha Tank—*reservoir* AZ-5
Ba Ha Zohnnie Betoh—*spring* AZ-5
Bahda Hollow—*valley* MO-7
Bahe Adakai Well—*well* AZ-5
Bahia—*locale* CA-9
Bahia Algodones—*bay* PR-3
Bahia Beach—*beach* FL-3
**Bahia Beach**—*pop pl* FL-3
Bahia Bramadero—*bay* PR-3
Bahia Corcho—*bay* PR-3
Bahia de Almodovar—*bay* PR-3
Bahia de Fajardo—*bay* PR-3
Bahia de Jauca—*bay* PR-3
Bahia de la Ballena—*bay* PR-3
Bahia de la Chiva—*bay* PR-3
*Bahia del Espiritu Santo* AL-4
*Bahia del Espiritu Santo* FL-3
*Bahia De Los Tremboles* CA-9
Bahia Demajagua—*bay* PR-3
*Bahia de Ochuse* AL-4
Bahia de Puerca—*bay* PR-3
Bahia de Puerto Nuevo—*bay* PR-3
Bahia de Rincon—*bay* PR-3
Bahia de Sardinas—*bay* PR-3
Bahia de Tallaboa—*bay* PR-3
Bahia de Toa—*bay* PR-3
Bahia Fanduca—*bay* PR-3
Bahia Fosforescente—*bay* PR-3
Bahia Grande—*lake* TX-5
*Bahia Honda* FL-3
*Bahia Honda Channel* FL-3
Bahia Honda Channel—*channel* FL-3
Bahia Honda Key—*island* FL-3
Bahia Honda State Park—*park* FL-3
Bahia Icacos—*bay* PR-3
Bahia Jalova—*bay* PR-3
*Bahia Laulau* MH-9
Bahia Lima—*bay* PR-3
**Bahia Mar**—*pop pl* TX-5
Bahia-mar—*uninc pl* FL-3
Bahia Mar Shop Ctr—*locale* FL-3
Bahia-Mar Yacht Center—*locale* FL-3
Bahia Montalva—*bay* PR-3
Bahia Noroeste—*bay* PR-3
**Bahia Oaks**—*pop pl* FL-3
Bahia Playa Blanca—*bay* PR-3
Bahia Point—*cape* CA-9
Bahia Salina del Sur—*bay* PR-3
Bahia Salinas—*bay* PR-3
**Bahia Shores**—*pop pl* FL-3
**Bahia Subdivision**—*pop pl* FL-3
Bahia Sucia—*bay* PR-3
Bahia Tapon—*bay* PR-3
Bahia Vista Sch—*school* CA-9
Bahia Yoye—*bay* PR-3
*Bahki* AZ-5
Bah Lakes—*lake* MN-6
Bahle Lake—*lake* MN-6
*Bahler Brook* CT-1
Bahlers Brook—*stream* CT-1
Bahlert Lake—*lake* WI-6
Bahlman Lake—*reservoir* AL-4
Bahlman Lake Dam—*dam* AL-4
Bahm Basa Pond—*reservoir* NV-8
Bahm Cem—*cemetery* LA-4
**Bahner**—*pop pl* MO-7
Bahnfieth Park—*park* CA-9
Bahobohosh Point—*cape* WA-9
*Bahokus Hill* WA-9
Bahokus Peak—*summit* WA-9
Bahoma—*locale* FL-3
Bahomamey (Barrio)—*fmr MCD* PR-3

Bain High School NC-3
Bain Hill—summit MO-7
Bain Place—locale WY-8
Bain Ranch—locale CA-9
Bains—pop pl LA-4
Bains Bend—bend AL-4
Bains Branch—stream IN-6
Bains Bridge—bridge AL-4
Bains Bridge Dam AL-4
Bain Sch—school NC-3
Bain Sch—school WI-6
Bain Sch—school WY-8
Bains Chapel—church MS-4
Bain Sch (historical)—school MO-7
Bain Sch (historical)—school TN-4
Bains Corner—pop pl NY-2
Bains Creek TX-5
Bains Creek—stream OR-9
Bains Hollow—valley TN-4
Bain Slough—gut OR-9
Bains Meeting House (historical)—church TN-4
Bain Spring—spring AZ-5
Bain Spring—spring WY-8
Bain Springs—spring MT-8
Bains Sch—school LA-4
Bain Station—locale OR-9
Bainsville Sch (historical)—school MS-4
Bainter Canyon—valley CA-9
Bainter Spring—spring CA-9
Bainter Town—pop pl IN-6
Bain-Thomas Ditch—canal CO-8
Bain (Township of)—fmr MCD AR-4
Bainum Cem—cemetery KS-7
Bainville MS-4
Bainville—locale TX-5
Bainville—pop pl MT-8
Bainwend Kill DE-2
Bair—pop pl PA-2
Bair, Jacob H., House—hist pl OH-6
Bair, Oliver, H., Funeral Home—hist pl PA-2
Bai Ra Irrai—hist pl PW-9
Bairakaseru Island PW-9
Bair Canyon—valley UT-8
Bair Cem—cemetery TN-4
Bair Coulee—valley MT-8
Bair Creek—stream UT-8
Baird PA-2
Baird—locale FL-3
Baird—locale MO-7
Baird—pop pl IA-7
Baird—pop pl MS-4
Baird—pop pl TX-5
Baird—pop pl WA-9
Baird, E. J., House—hist pl IA-7
Baird, F. S., Machine Shop—hist pl AZ-5
Baird, George W., House—hist pl MN-6
Baird, Matthew, Mansion—hist pl PA-2
Baird, Mount—summit ID-8
Baird Branch—stream TX-5
Baird Canyon—valley AK-9
Baird Canyon—valley CA-9
Baird Canyon—valley NM-5
Baird (CCD)—cens area TX-5
Baird Cem—cemetery AL-4
Baird Cem—cemetery (2) KS-7
Baird Cem—cemetery NC-3
Baird Cem—cemetery (6) TN-4
Baird Cem—cemetery VT-1
Baird Corners—locale NY-2
Baird Corners—pop pl NY-2
Baird Cove—bay WA-9
Baird Cove—valley NC-3
Baird Creek—stream FL-3
Baird Creek—stream (2) MI-6
Baird Creek—stream NC-3
Baird Creek—stream TN-4
Baird Creek—stream WA-9
Baird Creek—stream (2) WI-6
Baird Creek Cem—cemetery TN-4
Baird Creek Ch—church NC-3
Baird Ditch—canal IN-6
Baird Drain—stream MI-6
Baird-Dulany Hosital (historical)—hospital TN-4
Baird Field—park NJ-2
Bairdford—pop pl PA-2
Baird Four Corners—pop pl MA-1
Baird Glacier—glacier AK-9
Baird Hardware Company
Warehouse—hist pl FL-3
Baird (historical)—pop pl NC-3
Baird (historical)—pop pl OR-9
Baird Hollow—valley TN-4
Baird House—hist pl FL-3
Baird House—hist pl MA-1
Baird Inlet—bay AK-9
Baird Island—island AK-9
Bair Ditch IN-6
Bair Ditch—canal IN-6
Baird Lake MN-6
Baird Lake—lake AK-9
Baird Lake—lake MN-6
Baird Lake—lake TX-5
Baird Lake—lake WI-6
Baird Lake—reservoir (2) TX-5
Baird Lake Dam—dam MS-4
Baird Landing—locale VA-3
Baird Law Office—hist pl WI-6
Baird Memorial Cem—cemetery TN-4
Baird Millpond—lake CT-1
Baird Mine (surface)—mine TN-4
Baird Mountains—range AK-9
Baird Mtn—summit MO-7
Baird Mtn—summit (2) NC-3
Baird Mtn—summit WA-9
Baird Municipal Park—park TN-4
Baird Park—park WI-6
Baird Peak—summit (2) AK-9
Baird Place—locale OR-9
Baird Point—cape NY-2
Baird Ranch—locale CA-9
Baird Ranch—locale NM-5
Baird Reservoir—lake ID-8
Baird Road Sch—school NY-2
Baird Rsvr—reservoir CO-8
Baird Run—stream PA-2
Bairds Bayou—swamp TX-5
Bairds Ch—church GA-3
Baird Sch—school CA-9
Baird Sch—school IL-6
Baird Sch—school NE-7
Bairds Chapel—church TN-4
Baird Sch (historical)—school MS-4
Baird Sch (historical)—school SD-7
Bairds Creek NC-3
Bairds Creek—stream NY-2
Bairds Furnace Junction—other OH-6
Bairds Gulch—valley ID-8
Bairds Mill—pop pl TN-4
Bairds Mill Ch of Christ—church TN-4
Bairds Mill Post Office
(historical)—building TN-4
Bairds Mills—pop pl TN-4
Baird Spring—spring NE-7
Baird Springs—spring CA-9
Baird Springs—spring WA-9
Bairds Ranch—locale NM-5
Bairds Run PA-2
Bairds Store (historical)—locale AL-4
Bairdstown—pop pl (2) GA-3
Bairdstown—pop pl OH-6
Bairdstown—pop pl (2) PA-2
Bairdstown Ch—church MO-7
Bairdsville—pop pl NJ-2
Baird-Welch House—hist pl TN-4
Baird Windmill—locale (3) TX-5
Baire Lake—reservoir IN-6
Bair Estates Subdivision—pop pl UT-8
Bair Island—island CA-9
Bair Island—island PA-2
Bair Lake—lake MI-6
Bair Lake—lake ND-7
Bair Lateral IN-6
Bair MS—school FL-3
Bairoa—pop pl PR-3
Bairoa (Barrio)—fmr MCD (2) PR-3
Bairo Creek—stream AK-9
Bairoil—pop pl WY-8
Bair Rsvr—reservoir MT-8
Bairs Cove—bay FL-3
Bairs Creek—stream CA-9
Bairs Den—locale FL-3
Bair Slough—lake ND-7
Bair Spring—spring MT-8
Baisdell Hill—summit NH-1
Baisden—pop pl (2) WV-2
Baisden Branch—stream WV-2
Baisden Cem—cemetery (4) WV-2
Baisden Ch—church WV-2
Baisden Fork—stream (2) WV-2
Baisdentown Ch—church WV-2
Baise Chapel—church KY-4
Baiseley Creek—stream OR-9
Baish Oil Field—other NM-5
Baisley Cem—cemetery TN-4
Baisley Creek—stream CA-9
Baisley Pond—lake NY-2
Baisley Pond Park—park NY-2
Baisman Run—stream MD-2
Bais Yaakov Sch for Girls—school MD-2
Bait Creek—stream ID-8
Baitenger Lake—lake WI-6
Baiter Swamp—swamp SC-3
Baiting Brook MA-1
Baiting Brook—stream MA-1
Baiting Hollow—pop pl NY-2
Baiting Pond MA-1
Bait Lake—lake FL-3
Bait Pond FL-3
Bait Pond—lake FL-3
Bait Pond—lake ME-1
Bait Tank—reservoir TX-5
Baitter Branch—stream IL-6
Baituk Creek—stream AK-9
Baity Hall—hist pl MO-7
Baity Sch (historical)—school PA-2
Baizetown—locale KY-4
Baizetown Cem—cemetery KY-4
Bajadero—pop pl PR-3
Baja Karakakooa HI-9
Bajandas—pop pl PR-3
Bajar Quemazon—area NM-5
Bajillo de los Chivas—flat AZ-5
Bajillo Draw—valley NM-5
Bajillo Tank—reservoir NM-5
Bajillo Well—well NM-5
Bajios Largo—area NM-5
Bajios Redondos—area NM-5
Bajo (Barrio)—fmr MCD PR-3
Bajo Casabe—bar PR-3
Bajo Enmedio—bar PR-3
Bajo Palo—bar PR-3
Bajo Ramito—bar PR-3
Bajo Roman—bar PR-3
Bajos Resuello—bar PR-3
Bajura Adentro (Barrio)—fmr MCD PR-3
Bajura Afuera (Barrio)—fmr MCD PR-3
Bajura (Barrio)—fmr MCD (3) PR-3
Bakabi AZ-5
Bak Acad—school FL-3
Bakalar Air Force Base—pop pl IN-6
Bakarich-McCool Ranch—locale AZ-5
Bakariki MP-9
Bakatigikh Mtn—summit AK-9
Bakbuk Creek—stream AK-9
Bake MH-9
Bake, As—slope MH-9
Bake Cave—cave AL-4
Baked Mtn—summit AK-9
Bakekana Lake—lake MN-6
Bakelite Park—park NJ-2
Bakeman Beach—beach ME-1
Bakeman Cove—bay ME-1
Bakemans Run—stream PA-2
Bakenbaker Flats MT-8
Baken Creek—stream PA-2
Baken Park Shop Ctr—locale SD-7
Bakeoven—locale OR-9
Bakeoven Cem—cemetery OR-9
Bakeoven Creek—stream NV-8
Bakeoven Creek—stream OR-9
Bake Oven Flat—flat TX-5
Bakeoven Flats—flat WA-9
Bake Oven Knob—summit PA-2
Bake Oven Knob—summit WV-2
Bakeoven Meadows—flat CA-9
Bake Oven Mtn—summit PA-2
Bakeoven Pass—gap CA-9
Bakeoven Point—cape DE-2
Bake Oven Ridge—ridge CA-9
Bake Oven (Site)—locale CA-9
Bake Oven Trail—trail PA-2
Baker CA-9
Baker MS-4
Baker—fmr MCD NE-7
Baker—hist pl IN-6
Baker—locale AK-9
Baker—locale (2) AR-4
Baker—locale MO-7
Baker—locale NV-8
Baker—locale NY-2
Baker—locale PA-2
Baker—locale (2) TX-5
Baker—locale WV-2
Baker—other TN-4
Baker—pop pl AR-4
Baker—pop pl CA-9
Baker—pop pl (3) FL-3
Baker—pop pl ID-8
Baker—pop pl IL-6
Baker—pop pl IN-6
Baker—pop pl KS-7
Baker—pop pl LA-4
Baker—pop pl MN-6
Baker—pop pl MS-4
Baker—pop pl MO-7
Baker—pop pl MT-8
Baker—pop pl ND-7
Baker—pop pl OH-6
Baker—pop pl OK-5
Baker—pop pl OR-9
Baker—pop pl PA-2
Baker, Benjamin, Jr., House—hist pl MA-1
Baker, Capt. Seth, Jr., House—hist pl MA-1
Baker, Cecil, Round Barn—hist pl ND-7
Baker, Charles H. and Catherine B.,
House—hist pl TX-5
Baker, Frank J., House—hist pl IL-6
Baker, George F., Jr. and Sr.,
Houses—hist pl NY-2
Baker, George Washington,
House—hist pl UT-8
Baker, Henry W., House—hist pl MI-6
Baker, Horace, Log Cabin—hist pl OR-9
Baker, I. G., House—hist pl MT-8
Baker, James B., House—hist pl MD-2
Baker, Jim, Cabin—hist pl WY-8
Baker, John S., House—hist pl OH-6
Baker, Joseph, House—hist pl SD-7
Baker, Lake—lake MT-8
Baker, Laura, Sch—hist pl MN-6
Baker, Maj. John C., House—hist pl OH-6
Baker, Mount—summit AK-9
Baker, Mount—summit WA-9
Baker, Nathaniel, House—hist pl MA-1
Baker, Newton D., House—hist pl DC-2
Baker, O. T., House—hist pl OH-6
Baker, Paschal Todd, House—hist pl KY-4
Baker, Point—cape AK-9
Baker, Samuel, House—hist pl UT-8
Baker, Sarah J., Sch—hist pl MA-1
Baker, Sinks of—basin NV-8
Baker, William, House—hist pl SC-3
Baker Acad—school (2) GA-3
Baker Airp—airport PA-2
Baker and Green Drain—stream MI-6
Baker and Lovering Store—hist pl MT-8
Baker and Maxie Mill (historical)—locale MS-4
Baker And May Drain—stream MI-6
Baker and Nolan Cem—cemetery TX-5
Baker and West Ditch—canal DE-2
Baker Area—locale UT-8
Baker Arm—canal IN-6
Baker Arroyo—stream NM-5
Baker Bar—island MT-8
Baker Bay—bay OR-9
Baker Bay—bay WA-9
Baker Bay—swamp FL-3
Baker Bayou FL-3
Baker Bayou—stream FL-3
Baker Bay Park—park OR-9
Baker Beach—beach CA-9
Baker Beach—beach OR-9
Baker Beach Rec Area—park OR-9
Baker Beach State Park—park CA-9
Baker Bench—bench UT-8
Baker Bench Petroglyphs—other UT-8
Baker Bend—bend AR-4
Baker Bend—bend MO-7
Baker Bldg—hist pl NJ-2
Baker Bluff—cliff AR-4
Baker Bluff—cliff MO-7
Baker Bluff—cliff (2) TN-4
Baker Bluff Subdivision—locale TN-4
Baker Bog ME-1
Baker Bogs—swamp ME-1
Baker Brake LA-4
Baker Branch AL-4
Baker Branch ME-1
Baker Branch—gut FL-3
Baker Branch—pop pl KY-4
Baker Branch—stream (4) AL-4
Baker Branch—stream (3) AR-4
Baker Branch—stream (2) FL-3
Baker Branch—stream (9) GA-3
Baker Branch—stream (2) IN-6
Baker Branch—stream KS-7
Baker Branch—stream (10) KY-4
Baker Branch—stream (7) MO-7
Baker Branch—stream (3) NC-3
Baker Branch—stream (3) OK-5
Baker Branch—stream PA-2
Baker Branch—stream SC-3
Baker Branch—stream (9) TN-4
Baker Branch—stream (3) TX-5
Baker Branch—stream (4) VA-3
Baker Branch—stream WV-2
Baker Branch Ch—church KY-4
Baker Branch Saint John River—stream ME-1
Baker-Brearley House—hist pl NJ-2
Baker Bridge—bridge TN-4
Baker Bridge—other IL-6
Baker Bridge—pop pl MA-1
Baker Brook CT-1
Baker Brook—stream (2) CT-1
Baker Brook—stream (10) ME-1
Baker Brook—stream (6) MA-1
Baker Brook—stream (3) NH-1
Baker Brook—stream (4) NY-2
Baker Brook—stream RI-1
Baker Brook—stream (5) VT-1
Baker Brook Cove—bay ME-1
Baker Brook Point—cape ME-1
Baker Brown Cabin—locale WA-9
Baker Bubbling Spring—spring AL-4
Baker Butte—summit AZ-5
Baker Cabin—locale (2) CA-9
Baker Cabin—locale CO-8
Baker Cabin—locale MT-8
Baker Cabin—locale OR-9
Baker Campground—locale CA-9
Baker Camp Run—stream WV-2
Baker Canal—canal LA-4
Baker Canal East—canal LA-4
Baker Canal North—canal LA-4
Baker Canal South—canal LA-4
Baker Canyon CO-8
Baker Canyon—valley (3) AZ-5
Baker Canyon—valley (3) CA-9
Baker Canyon—valley (2) CO-8
Baker Canyon—valley KS-7
Baker Canyon—valley (2) MT-8
Baker Canyon—valley (3) NM-5
Baker Canyon—valley (5) OR-9
Baker Canyon—valley (5) UT-8
Baker Canyon—valley (2) WY-8
Baker Cave—cave (2) TN-4
Baker Caverns—cave PA-2
Baker (CCD)—cens area FL-3
Baker (CCD)—cens area OR-9
Baker Cem—cemetery (6) AL-4
Baker Cem—cemetery (7) AR-4
Baker Cem—cemetery CT-1
Baker Cem—cemetery FL-3
Baker Cem—cemetery (4) GA-3
Baker Cem—cemetery (10) IL-6
Baker Cem—cemetery (4) IN-6
Baker Cem—cemetery (3) IA-7
Baker Cem—cemetery (4) KS-7
Baker Cem—cemetery (7) KY-4
Baker Cem—cemetery MD-2
Baker Cem—cemetery MI-6
Baker Cem—cemetery (7) MS-4
Baker Cem—cemetery (15) MO-7
Baker Cem—cemetery (7) NY-2
Baker Cem—cemetery NC-3
Baker Cem—cemetery (3) OH-6
Baker Cem—cemetery (3) OK-5
Baker Cem—cemetery PA-2
Baker Cem—cemetery (2) SC-3
Baker Cem—cemetery (25) TN-4
Baker Cem—cemetery (9) TX-5
Baker Cem—cemetery VT-1
Baker Cem—cemetery (8) VA-3
Baker Cem—cemetery (2) WV-2
Baker Cem—cemetery WY-8
Baker Ch—church AR-4
Baker Ch—church GA-3
Baker Ch—church IA-7
Baker Ch—church KY-4
Baker Ch—church NE-7
Baker Ch—church NC-3
Baker Ch—church WV-2
Baker Chapel—church AL-4
Baker Chapel—church AR-4
Baker Chapel—church IN-6
Baker Chapel—church LA-4
Baker Chapel—church NC-3
Baker Chapel—church TN-4
Baker Chapel Cem—cemetery (3) TN-4
Baker Chapel Methodist Ch
(historical)—church TN-4
Baker City OR-9
Baker City Canyon—valley OR-9
Baker City Draw—valley OR-9
Baker City Gulch—valley OR-9
Baker City Springs—spring OR-9
Baker Coll—school OR-9
Baker Corner—locale NH-1
Baker Corner—locale NY-2
Baker Corner—pop pl ME-1
Baker Corners—pop pl NY-2
Baker Coulee—valley (2) MT-8
Baker County AL-4
Baker County—pop pl FL-3
Baker (County)—pop pl GA-3
Baker County—pop pl OR-9
Baker County Adult Center—school FL-3
Baker County Courthouse—hist pl GA-3
Baker County MS—school FL-3
Baker County Senior HS—school FL-3
Baker Cove—bay AK-9
Baker Cove—bay CT-1
Baker Cove—bay ME-1
Baker Cove—bay MD-2
Baker Creek AR-4
Baker Creek CA-9
Baker Creek GA-3
Baker Creek KS-7
Baker Creek MS-4
Baker Creek MT-8
Baker Creek VA-3
Baker Creek WY-8
Baker Creek—pop pl MT-8
Baker Creek—stream (6) AL-4
Baker Creek—stream (3) AK-9
Baker Creek—stream AR-4
Baker Creek—stream (7) CA-9
Baker Creek—stream CO-8
Baker Creek—stream (2) FL-3
Baker Creek—stream (2) GA-3
Baker Creek—stream (4) ID-8
Baker Creek—stream IL-6
Baker Creek—stream IN-6
Baker Creek—stream IA-7
Baker Creek—stream KS-7
Baker Creek—stream (2) KY-4
Baker Creek—stream (2) LA-4
Baker Creek—stream (5) MI-6
Baker Creek—stream (4) MS-4
Baker Creek—stream (3) MO-7
Baker Creek—stream (4) MT-8
Baker Creek—stream NE-7
Baker Creek—stream (2) NV-8
Baker Creek—stream (3) NY-2
Baker Creek—stream (2) NC-3
Baker Creek—stream OH-6
Baker Creek—stream OK-5
Baker Creek—stream (14) OR-9
Baker Creek—stream (2) PA-2
Baker Creek—stream RI-1
Baker Creek—stream (3) SC-3
Baker Creek—stream (3) TN-4
Baker Creek—stream (4) TX-5
Baker Creek—stream UT-8
Baker Creek—stream VA-3
Baker Creek—stream (5) WA-9
Baker Creek—stream (2) WI-6
Baker Creek—stream (2) WY-8
Baker Creek Campground—locale ID-8
Baker Creek Campground—locale WA-9
Baker Creek Cem—cemetery IN-6
Baker Creek Ch—church TN-4
Baker Creek Ditch—canal IL-6
Baker Creek Forest Service Administrative
Site—locale NV-8
Baker Creek Forest Service Recreation
Site—locale NV-8
Baker Creek Inlet—bay TN-4
Baker Creek Lagoon—reservoir AL-4
Baker Creek Lagoon Dam—dam AL-4
Baker Creek Park—park NC-3
Baker Creek Picnic Area—park ID-8
Baker Creek Sch—school (2) MT-8
Baker Creek Sch—school NC-3
Baker Creek Spring—spring TN-4
Baker Crossroads—locale (2) SC-3
Baker Crossroads—locale TN-4
Baker Crossroads—pop pl NC-3
Baker Cut—channel FL-3
Baker Dam—dam AL-4
Baker Dam—dam PA-2
Baker Dam—dam WA-9
Baker Dam Campground UT-8
Baker Den Creek—stream AR-4
Baker Den Hill—summit AR-4
Baker Ditch—canal CO-8
Baker Ditch—canal (6) IN-6
Baker Ditch—canal OH-6
Baker Ditch—canal WY-8
Baker Divide—ridge CA-9
Baker Draft—valley VA-3
Baker Drain—canal (2) MI-6
Baker Drain—canal NE-7
Baker Draw MT-8
Baker Draw—valley (2) CO-8
Baker Draw—valley ID-8
Baker Draw—valley MT-8
Baker Draw—valley NM-5
Baker Draw—valley (2) TX-5
Baker Draw—valley WY-8
Baker Drift Mine (underground)—mine AL-4
Baker Dry Fork WY-8
Baker Elementary School MS-4
Baker Elementary School PA-2
Baker Elem Sch—school TN-4
Baker Falls—falls TN-4
Baker Farm—hist pl MD-2
Baker Farm—hist pl NC-3
Baker Farm—locale WA-9
Baker Field—park AL-4
Baker Field—park NY-2
Baker Field Ch—church GA-3
Baker Fire Control HQ—tower FL-3
Baker Fire Control Station—locale CA-9
Baker Fish Hole—bend TX-5
Baker Flat—flat (2) CA-9
Baker Flat—flat OR-9
Baker Flat Creek—stream CA-9
Baker Flat Picnic Area—park NM-5
Baker Flats—flat WA-9
Baker Flowage—lake ME-1
Baker Ford—locale AR-4
Baker Forge Memorial Cem—cemetery TN-4
Baker Fork—stream (2) KY-4
Baker Fork—stream (2) OH-6
Baker Fork—stream UT-8
Baker Fork—stream WV-2
Baker Fork Sch—school KY-4
Baker Forty Creek—stream CA-9
Baker Free Public Library—building FL-3
Baker Gap—gap NC-3
Baker Gap—gap TN-4
Baker Gap Ch—church TN-4
Baker Gap Sch—school KY-4
Baker Gardens—area OR-9
Baker Glacier—glacier AK-9
Baker Grove Cem—cemetery AL-4
Baker Grove Ch—church AL-4
Baker Guard Station—locale UT-8
Baker Gulch—valley AK-9
Baker Gulch—valley (6) CA-9
Baker Gulch—valley (4) CO-8
Baker Gulch—valley (3) ID-8
Baker Gulch—valley MT-8
Baker Gulch—valley OR-9
Baker-Hawkins House—hist pl KY-4
Baker Heights—locale WA-9
Baker Heights—pop pl WV-2
Baker Heights (subdivision)—pop pl UT-8
Baker High School AL-4
Bakerhill AL-4
Baker Hill MA-1
Baker Hill NY-2
Baker Hill—pop pl AL-4
Baker Hill—pop pl SC-3
Baker Hill—summit (3) AL-4
Baker Hill—summit AZ-5
Baker Hill—summit AR-4
Baker Hill—summit CT-1
Baker Hill—summit IN-6
Baker Hill—summit (5) ME-1
Baker Hill—summit (3) MA-1
Baker Hill—summit MI-6
Baker Hill—summit MO-7
Baker Hill—summit (2) NH-1
Baker Hill—summit (6) NY-2
Baker Hill—summit (2) PA-2
Baker Hill—summit TN-4
Baker Hill—summit VT-1
Baker Hill (Bakerhill)—pop pl AL-4
Bakerhill (CCD)—cens area AL-4
Baker Hill Cuesta—ridge AL-4
Bakerhill Division—civil AL-4
Baker Hills—summit UT-8
Baker Hill Sch—school AL-4
Baker Hill Sch—school NY-2
Baker Hill Sch (historical)—school MO-7
Baker Hills Rsvr—reservoir UT-8
Baker Hist Dist—hist pl OR-9
Baker (historical P.O.)—locale IA-7
Baker Hollow—basin CA-9
Baker Hollow—locale AR-4
Baker Hollow—valley AR-4
Baker Hollow—valley IL-6
Baker Hollow—valley IN-6
Baker Hollow—valley (4) KY-4
Baker Hollow—valley (5) MO-7
Baker Hollow—valley OK-5
Baker Hollow—valley (4) PA-2
Baker Hollow—valley (10) TN-4
Baker Hollow—valley TX-5
Baker Hollow—valley (4) VA-3
Baker Hollow—valley (5) WV-2
Baker Hollow Prospect—mine TN-4
Baker Horse Mtn AZ-5
Baker Hosp—hospital SC-3
Baker Hotel—hist pl TX-5
Baker Hot Spring—spring WA-9
Baker Hot Springs—spring UT-8
Baker House—hist pl AR-4
Baker House—hist pl CO-8
Baker House—hist pl MA-1
Baker House—hist pl SD-7
Baker Hubbard Pond NH-1
Baker Island CT-1
Baker Island MA-1
Baker Island—island AK-9
Baker Island—island GA-3
Baker Island—island (2) ME-1
Baker Island—island NC-3
Baker Island—island OR-9
Baker Island—island PA-2
Baker Island—island VA-3
Baker Island—island WV-2
Baker Island—island WI-6
Baker Island Bar—bar ME-1
Baker Island Light Station—hist pl ME-1
Baker JHS—school CO-8
Baker JHS—school MI-6
Baker JHS—school (2) OH-6
Baker JHS—school WA-9
Baker Junior High—school TX-5
Baker Knob—summit AR-4
Baker Knob—summit GA-3
Baker Knob—summit TN-4
Baker Knoll—summit UT-8
Baker Lain Cem—cemetery TX-5
Baker Lake MN-6
Baker Lake NC-3
Baker Lake WI-6
Baker Lake—lake AK-9
Baker Lake—lake AZ-5
Baker Lake—lake CA-9
Baker Lake—lake CO-8
Baker Lake—lake (2) ID-8
Baker Lake—lake IL-6
Baker Lake—lake ME-1
Baker Lake—lake (7) MI-6
Baker Lake—lake (6) MN-6
Baker Lake—lake MS-4
Baker Lake—lake (2) MT-8
Baker Lake—lake NV-8
Baker Lake—lake (3) NM-5
Baker Lake—lake OH-6
Baker Lake—lake (2) OR-9
Baker Lake—lake SC-3
Baker Lake—lake (2) UT-8
Baker Lake—lake (4) WA-9
Baker Lake—lake (9) WI-6
Baker Lake—lake WY-8
Baker Lake—reservoir (2) AL-4
Baker Lake—reservoir CO-8
Baker Lake—reservoir IN-6
Baker Lake—reservoir OK-5
Baker Lake—reservoir TX-5
Baker Lake Campground—locale MN-6
Baker Lake Dam—dam IN-6
Baker Lake Dam—dam MS-4
Baker Lake Glacier WY-8
Baker Lake Guard Station—locale WA-9
Baker Lake Lookout—locale WA-9
Baker Lake North Campsite—locale ME-1
Baker Lake South Campsite—locale ME-1
Baker Landing Strip—airport MO-7
Baker-Langdon—pop pl WA-9
Baker Lateral—canal AZ-5
Baker Lateral—canal CA-9
Baker Lateral—canal ID-8
Baker Lateral—canal NM-5
Baker Lateral—canal TX-5
Baker Lily Pond NJ-2
Baker Mansion—hist pl PA-2
Baker McPherson Drain—canal MI-6
Baker Meadow—flat CA-9
Baker Meadow Reservation—park MA-1
Baker Memorial Ch—church VA-3
Baker Memorial Park—cemetery GA-3
Baker Mill—locale TN-4
Baker Mill Branch—stream DE-2
Baker Mill Pond—reservoir NJ-2
Baker Mills NY-2
Baker Mine—mine (2) AZ-5
Baker Mine—mine (3) CA-9
Baker Mine—mine IL-6
Baker Mine—mine MO-7
Baker Mine—mine (2) NV-8
Baker Mine—mine OR-9
Baker Mine—mine (2) UT-8
Baker Monmt—pillar MT-8
Baker Mound—hist pl MS-4
Baker Mountain CO-8
Baker Mountain Brook—stream ME-1
Baker Mountain Ch—church NC-3
Baker Mtn—summit (2) AZ-5
Baker Mtn—summit AR-4
Baker Mtn—summit (3) CO-8
Baker Mtn—summit GA-3
Baker Mtn—summit (3) ME-1
Baker Mtn—summit MT-8
Baker Mtn—summit NY-2
Baker Mtn—summit NC-3
Baker Mtn—summit OK-5
Baker Mtn—summit (2) TN-4
Baker Mtn—summit UT-8
Baker Mtn—summit VA-3
Baker Mtn—summit WV-2
Baker Municipal Airp—airport OR-9
Baker Municipal Aqueduct—canal OR-9
Baker Municipal Natatorium—hist pl OR-9
Baker Natl Forest, Mount—forest WA-9

Balden Pond—*lake* GA-3
Balder—*locale* WA-9
Balderas Altas Windmill—*locale* TX-5
Balderas Windmill—*locale* TX-5
Balderson Drain—*canal* MI-6
Balderson Hollow—*valley* WV-2
**Balderson Station**—*pop pl* CA-9
**Balderson Township**—*pop pl* KS-7
Balders Pond—*lake* DE-2
Baldface Brook—*stream* NH-1
Baldface Circle Trail—*trail* NH-1
Baldface Creek—*stream* OR-9
Baldface Hill—*summit* NY-2
Baldface Lake—*lake* OR-9
Bald Face Mountain Overlook—*locale* VA-3
Baldface Mtn—*summit* (6) NY-2
Bald Face Sch—*school* IA-7
Baldface Trail—*trail* NH-1
Bald Fork—*stream* NC-3
Bald Friar—*summit* MD-2
Bald Gap—*gap* (2) NC-3
Bald Gap—*gap* OR-9
Bald Glade Hollow—*valley* MO-7
*Bald Head* ME-1
*Baldhead* MI-6
Bald Head—*cape* (3) ME-1
Bald Head—*cape* NC-3
**Bald Head**—*pop pl* ME-1
Bald Head—*summit* AK-9
Bald Head—*summit* (2) ME-1
Baldhead—*summit* MA-1
Bald Head—*summit* UT-8
Baldhead, Mount—*summit* MI-6
*Bald Head Bluff* ME-1
Bald Head Chris Island—*island* AK-9
Bald Head Cliff—*cliff* ME-1
**Bald Head Cliff**—*pop pl* ME-1
*Bald Head Cliffs* ME-1
Bald Head Cove—*bay* ME-1
Bald Head Creek—*stream* NC-3
Baldhead Creek—*stream* SD-7
Bald Head Creek—*stream* UT-8
Bald Headed Camp—*locale* OR-9
Bald Headed Cove—*bay* AK-9
Bald Head Hollow—*valley* KY-4
*Bald Head Island* NC-3
Bald Head Island—*island* NC-3
**Bald Head Island**—*pop pl* NC-3
Bald Head Island Lighthouse—*hist pl* NC-3
*Baldhead Islands* NC-3
Bald Head Ledge—*bar* ME-1
Bald Head Lighthouse—*tower* NC-3
Baldhead Mtn—*summit* AK-9
Baldhead Mtn—*summit* MT-8
Baldhead Mtn—*summit* NH-1
Baldhead Mtn—*summit* NY-2
*Bald Head Peak* MI-6
*Bald Hill* AZ-5
*Bald Hill* MA-1
*Bald Hill* PA-2
Bald Hill—*locale* (2) KY-4
Bald Hill—*locale* OK-5
Bald Hill—*locale* TX-5
**Bald Hill**—*pop pl* AL-4
**Bald Hill**—*pop pl* MS-4
**Baldhill**—*pop pl* OK-5
**Bald Hill**—*pop pl* (2) PA-2
Bald Hill—*summit* AL-4
Bald Hill—*summit* AK-9
Bald Hill—*summit* (5) AZ-5
Bald Hill—*summit* (3) AR-4
Bald Hill—*summit* (17) CA-9
Bald Hill—*summit* (2) CO-8
Bald Hill—*summit* (5) CT-1
Bald Hill—*summit* (2) ID-8
Bald Hill—*summit* (2) IN-6
Bald Hill—*summit* (4) KY-4
Bald Hill—*summit* LA-4
Bald Hill—*summit* (5) ME-1
Bald Hill—*summit* (11) MA-1
Bald Hill—*summit* (2) MI-6
Bald Hill—*summit* (3) MS-4
Bald Hill—*summit* (5) MO-7
Bald Hill—*summit* (2) MT-8
Bald Hill—*summit* (10) NH-1
Bald Hill—*summit* NJ-2
Bald Hill—*summit* (2) NM-5
Bald Hill—*summit* (6) NY-2
Bald Hill—*summit* NC-3
Bald Hill—*summit* OH-6
Bald Hill—*summit* (2) OK-5
Bald Hill—*summit* (6) OR-9
Bald Hill—*summit* (9) PA-2
Bald Hill—*summit* (4) RI-1
Bald Hill—*summit* SD-7
Bald Hill—*summit* (3) TN-4
Bald Hill—*summit* (4) TX-5
Bald Hill—*summit* (2) UT-8
Bald Hill—*summit* (7) VT-1
Bald Hill—*summit* (3) VA-3
Bald Hill—*summit* (4) WA-9
Bald Hill—*summit* WI-6
Bald Hill—*summit* WY-8
*Bald Hill, The* UT-8
Bald Hill Bay—*bay* NC-3
Bald Hill Branch—*stream* MD-2
Bald Hill Canyon—*valley* CA-9
Bald Hill Cem—*cemetery* AR-4
Bald Hill Cem—*cemetery* CT-1
Bald Hill Cem—*cemetery* IL-6
Bald Hill Cem—*cemetery* KY-4
Bald Hill Cem—*cemetery* OK-5
Baldhill Ch—*church* NC-3
Bald Hill Ch—*church* OK-5
Bald Hill Ch—*church* PA-2
Bald Hill Ch (historical)—*church* TN-4
**Bald Hill Church**—*pop pl* PA-2
Bald Hill Cove—*bay* ME-1
Bald Hill Creek—*stream* CA-9
Bald Hill Creek—*stream* IL-6
Baldhill Creek—*stream* ND-7
Baldhill Creek Dam—*dam* ND-7
**Bald Hill Crossing**—*pop pl* ME-1
*Baldhill Dam* ND-7
Baldhill Dam—*dam* ND-7
Bald Hill Ditch—*canal* CA-9
**Bald Hill (historical)**—*pop pl* TN-4
Bald Hill Hunting Club—*other* PA-2
*Bald Hill Lake* FL-3
Bald Hill Lake—*lake* WA-9
Bald Hill Lead—*ridge* TN-4
Baldhill Park—*park* ND-7
Bald Hill Pond—*lake* VT-1
Bald Hill Range—*range* CT-1
*Baldhill Reservoir* ND-7
Bald Hill Ridge—*ridge* IN-6
Bald Hill Rsvr—*reservoir* CO-8
Baldhill Rsvr—*reservoir* ND-7
Bald Hill Run—*stream* (2) PA-2
Bald Hills—*range* (3) CA-9
Bald Hills—*range* (3) SD-7
Bald Hills—*ridge* CA-9
Bald Hills—*ridge* NM-5
Bald Hills—*summit* CA-9
Bald Hills—*summit* MT-8
Bald Hills—*summit* OR-9
Bald Hills, The—*summit* UT-8
Bald Hills Archeol District—*hist pl* CA-9
Bald Hills Archeol District Extension (Boundary Increase)—*hist pl* CA-9
Bald Hill Sch—*school* MI-6
Bald Hill Sch—*school* MS-4
Bald Hill Sch (historical)—*school* (2) MS-4
Bald Hill Schoolhouse—*hist pl* NY-2
Bald Hill Ski Bowl—*other* NY-2
Bald Hill Spring—*spring* NM-5
Bald Hill Spring No 1—*spring* ID-8
Bald Hill Spring No 2—*spring* ID-8
Bald Hills Sch—*school* CA-9
Bald Hill Station (historical)—*locale* PA-2
Bald Hill Swamp—*swamp* PA-2
Bald Hill Tank—*reservoir* AZ-5
Bald Hill Tank Number Five—*reservoir* AZ-5
Bald Hill Tank Number Four—*reservoir* AZ-5
Bald Hill Tank Number One—*reservoir* (2) AZ-5
Bald Hill Tank Number Three—*reservoir* AZ-5
Bald Hill Tank Number Two—*reservoir* (2) AZ-5
**Bald Hill (Township of)**—*pop pl* IL-6
Bald Hill Trail—*trail* (2) PA-2
Bald Hill Well—*well* AZ-5
Bald Hill Windmill—*locale* NM-5
Bald Hollow—*valley* AL-4
Bald Hollow—*valley* TX-5
Bald Hornet—*summit* AL-4
Bald Hornet Creek—*stream* CA-9
Bald Hornet Creek—*stream* WY-8
Baldie Pond—*lake* GA-3
Baldies, The—*summit* NV-8
*Baldina Chapel* NC-3
Baldin Branch—*stream* NC-3
Baldin Branch Ch—*church* NC-3
Baldin Brook—*stream* VT-1
Balding Ave Hist Dist—*hist pl* NY-2
Balding Chapel—*church* NC-3
Balding Knob—*summit* TN-4
*Bald Island* WA-9
Bald Island—*island* ME-1
Bald Island—*island* MI-6
Bald Island—*island* WA-9
Bald Island (historical)—*island* TN-4
Bald Jess—*summit* MO-7
Bald Jesse—*summit* AR-4
Bald Jesse—*summit* CA-9
*Bald Knob* AL-4
*Bald Knob* ME-1
*Bald Knob* UT-8
*Bald Knob* VA-3
**Bald Knob**—*pop pl* AR-4
**Bald Knob**—*pop pl* WV-2
Bald Knob—*summit* (7) AL-4
Bald Knob—*summit* AZ-5
Bald Knob—*summit* (9) AR-4
Bald Knob—*summit* (4) CA-9
Bald Knob—*summit* (2) CO-8
Bald Knob—*summit* ID-8
Bald Knob—*summit* (4) IL-6
Bald Knob—*summit* (2) IN-6
Bald Knob—*summit* (14) KY-4
Bald Knob—*summit* (2) MD-2
Bald Knob—*summit* MA-1
Bald Knob—*summit* MI-6
Bald Knob—*summit* MS-4
Bald Knob—*summit* (7) MO-7
Bald Knob—*summit* (2) MT-8
Bald Knob—*summit* (3) NH-1
Bald Knob—*summit* (9) NC-3
Bald Knob—*summit* (5) OH-6
Bald Knob—*summit* (5) OK-5
Bald Knob—*summit* (3) OR-9
Bald Knob—*summit* (3) PA-2
Bald Knob—*summit* (10) TN-4
Bald Knob—*summit* (7) TX-5
Bald Knob—*summit* VT-1
Bald Knob—*summit* (12) VA-3
Bald Knob—*summit* (3) WA-9
Bald Knob—*summit* (13) WV-2
Bald Knob—*summit* (2) WI-6
Bald Knob—*summit* WY-8
Bald Knob, Lake—*reservoir* AR-4
Bald Knobber Cave—*cave* MO-7
Bald Knobbers Cave—*cave* MO-7
Bald Knob Branch—*stream* NC-3
Bald Knob (CCD)—*cens area* KY-4
Bald Knob Cem—*cemetery* AR-4
Bald Knob Cem—*cemetery* (2) OH-6
Bald Knob Cem—*cemetery* OK-5
Bald Knob Ch—*church* AL-4
Bald Knob Ch—*church* AR-4
Bald Knob Ch—*church* (2) KY-4
Bald Knob Ch—*church* (2) MO-7
Bald Knob Ch—*church* OH-6
Bald Knob Creek—*stream* (2) IN-6
Bald Knob Creek—*stream* NC-3
Bald Knob Hollow—*valley* MO-7
Baldknob Hollow—*valley* MO-7
Bald Knob Hollow—*valley* (2) TN-4
Bald Knob HS—*school* KY-4
Bald Knob Ridge—*ridge* (3) NC-3
Bald Knob Run—*stream* OH-6
Bald Knobs—*locale* OH-6
**Bald Knobs**—*pop pl* IN-6
Bald Knobs—*summit* CO-8
Bald Knobs—*summit* IN-6
Bald Knob Sch—*school* KY-4
Bald Knob Sch (historical)—*school* TN-4
Bald Knob (Township of)—*fmr MCD* AR-4
Bald Knob Trail—*trail* VA-3
Bald Knob Tunnel—*tunnel* VA-3
*Bald Knoll* UT-8
Bald Knoll—*summit* NM-5
Bald Knoll—*summit* (9) UT-8
Bald Knoll—*summit* (2) WY-8
Bald Knoll Canyon—*valley* UT-8
Bald Knoll Hollow—*valley* UT-8
Bald Knoll Rsvr—*reservoir* UT-8
Bald Knolls—*range* UT-8
*Bald Lake* OR-9
Bald Lake—*lake* MN-6
Bald Lake—*lake* UT-8
Bald Lake—*lake* (2) WA-9
Bald Lake—*reservoir* NE-7
Bald Land Trail—*trail* NH-1
Bald Ledge—*bench* (2) NH-1
Bald Ledge—*bench* NY-2
Bald Ledge—*summit* (2) ME-1
Bald Lick—*stream* OH-6
Baldlick Fork—*stream* WV-2
Bald Mesa—*bench* UT-8
Bald Mesa—*flat* AZ-5
Bald Mesa—*summit* NM-5
Bald Mesa Tank—*reservoir* AZ-5
Bald Mill Creek—*stream* (2) CA-9
**Bald Mound**—*pop pl* IL-6
Bald Mound—*summit* KS-7
Bald Mound—*summit* TX-5
Bald Mound Cem—*cemetery* MO-7
*Bald Mountain* CO-8
*Bald Mountain* ME-1
*Bald Mountain* MT-8
*Bald Mountain* NV-8
*Bald Mountain* NC-3
*Bald Mountain* WY-8
Bald Mountain—*cens area* CO-8
**Bald Mountain**—*pop pl* ME-1
**Bald Mountain**—*pop pl* NY-2
**Bald Mountain**—*pop pl* NC-3
Bald Mountain—*ridge* AL-4
Bald Mountain—*ridge* AR-4
Bald Mountain—*ridge* (2) CA-9
Bald Mountain—*ridge* NV-8
Bald Mountain—*ridge* OR-9
Bald Mountain Basin—*basin* CO-8
Bald Mountain Basin—*basin* WY-8
Bald Mountain Brook—*stream* (2) ME-1
Bald Mountain Brook—*stream* NY-2
Bald Mountain Brook—*stream* VT-1
Bald Mountain Camp—*locale* OR-9
Bald Mountain Campground—*locale* ID-8
Bald Mountain Campground—*locale* UT-8
Bald Mountain Campground—*locale* WY-8
Bald Mountain Canyon—*valley* (3) CA-9
Bald Mountain Canyon—*valley* ID-8
Bald Mountain Canyon—*valley* (2) NV-8
Bald Mountain Cem—*cemetery* CO-8
Bald Mountain Ch—*church* (3) NC-3
Bald Mountain City ( Site)—*locale* WY-8
Bald Mountain Creek—*stream* (2) CA-9
Bald Mountain Creek—*stream* (2) ID-8
Bald Mountain Creek—*stream* NV-8
Bald Mountain Creek—*stream* NC-3
Bald Mountain Creek—*stream* OK-5
Bald Mountain Creek—*stream* OR-9
Bald Mountain Creek—*stream* WY-8
Bald Mountain Draw—*valley* CO-8
Bald Mountain Flat—*flat* CA-9
Bald Mountain Gate House—*locale* CO-8
Bald Mountain Golf Club—*other* MI-6
Bald Mountain Guard Station—*locale* ID-8
Bald Mountain Gulch—*valley* CO-8
Bald Mountain Gulch—*valley* ID-8
Bald Mountain (historical)—*locale* SD-7
Bald Mountain Hollow—*valley* TX-5
Bald Mountain Hot Springs—*hist pl* ID-8
Bald Mountain Lake—*lake* ID-8
Bald Mountain Lake—*lake* NV-8
Bald Mountain Lake—*reservoir* NC-3
Bald Mountain Lake Dam—*dam* NC-3
Bald Mountain Lookout—*locale* OR-9
*Bald Mountain Mine* SD-7
Bald Mountain Mine—*mine* MT-8
Bald Mountain Mine—*mine* OR-9
Bald Mountain Mine—*mine* SD-7
Bald Mountain Overlook—*locale* UT-8
Bald Mountain Overlook—*locale* VA-3
Bald Mountain Pass—*gap* UT-8
Bald Mountain Pond—*lake* ME-1
Bald Mountain Pond—*lake* NY-2
Bald Mountain Prairie—*area* OR-9
Bald Mountain Ranch—*locale* CA-9
Bald Mountain Ridge—*ridge* AK-9
Bald Mountain Ridge—*ridge* OR-9
Bald Mountain Rsvr—*reservoir* (2) CA-9
Bald Mountain Rsvr—*reservoir* CO-8
Bald Mountain Rsvr—*reservoir* ID-8
Bald Mountain Rsvr—*reservoir* OR-9
*Bald Mountains* NV-8
Bald Mountains—*other* TN-4
Bald Mountains—*range* NC-3
Bald Mountains—*range* SD-7
Bald Mountains—*summit* TN-4
Bald Mountain Sch—*school* CA-9
Bald Mountain Shelter—*locale* OR-9
Bald Mountain Sink—*basin* CA-9
Bald Mountain Spring—*spring* AZ-5
Bald Mountain Spring—*spring* (2) CA-9
Bald Mountain Spring—*spring* (2) ID-8
Bald Mountain Spring—*spring* NV-8
Bald Mountain Spring—*spring* OR-9
Bald Mountain Spring—*spring* WY-8
Bald Mountain State Rec Area—*park* MI-6
Bald Mountain Station—*locale* ME-1
Bald Mountain Stream—*stream* ME-1
Bald Mountain (Township of)—*fmr MCD* NC-3
Bald Mountain (Township of) (T2r3)—*unorg* ME-1
Bald Mountain (Township of) (T4r3)—*unorg* ME-1
Bald Mountain Trail—*trail* ME-1
Bald Mountain Trail—*trail* NC-3
Bald Mountain Trail—*trail* TN-4
Bald Mountain Trail—*trail* VT-1
Bald Mountain Tunnel—*tunnel* CO-8
Bald Mountain Wash—*stream* NV-8
Bald Mountain Well—*well* NV-8
Bald Mountain Wildlife Mngmt Area—*park* UT-8
*Bald Mountian* NV-8
*Bald Mtn* AZ-5
*Bald Mtn* NY-2
*Bald Mtn* OR-9
*Bald Mtn* WA-9
Bald Mtn—*summit* (2) AL-4
Bald Mtn—*summit* (5) AK-9
Bald Mtn—*summit* (5) AZ-5
Bald Mtn—*summit* (2) AR-4
Bald Mtn—*summit* (50) CA-9
Bald Mtn—*summit* (15) CO-8
Bald Mtn—*summit* (4) CT-1
Bald Mtn—*summit* (2) GA-3
Bald Mtn—*summit* (18) ID-8
Bald Mtn—*summit* (17) ME-1
Bald Mtn—*summit* (5) MA-1
Bald Mtn—*summit* (2) MI-6
Bald Mtn—*summit* MO-7
Bald Mtn—*summit* (5) MT-8
Bald Mtn—*summit* (15) NV-8
Bald Mtn—*summit* (10) NH-1
Bald Mtn—*summit* NJ-2
Bald Mtn—*summit* NM-5
Bald Mtn—*summit* (17) NY-2
Bald Mtn—*summit* (8) NC-3
Bald Mtn—*summit* (4) OK-5
Bald Mtn—*summit* (25) OR-9
Bald Mtn—*summit* (4) PA-2
Bald Mtn—*summit* (3) SD-7
Bald Mtn—*summit* TN-4
Bald Mtn—*summit* (7) TX-5
Bald Mtn—*summit* (11) UT-8
Bald Mtn—*summit* (9) VT-1
Bald Mtn—*summit* (4) VA-3
Bald Mtn—*summit* (13) WA-9
Bald Mtn—*summit* (10) WY-8
Bald Mtn Range—*range* CA-9
Bald Mtns—*summit* NV-8
*Baldo* AL-4
*Baldoc* SC-3
Baldock—*locale* SC-3
Baldock Chapel—*church* KY-4
Baldock Ditch—*canal* OR-9
Baldock Farm Airp—*airport* KS-7
Baldock Safety Rest Area—*locale* OR-9
Baldock Slough—*stream* OR-9
Bald of Gilead Campground—*locale* CA-9
Baldon Branch—*stream* AR-4
Baldoo Hills Country Club—*other* PA-2
**Baldorioty de Castro**—*pop pl* PR-3
*Bald Pate* MA-1
Baldpate—*summit* ME-1
Bald Pate—*summit* ME-1
Bald Pate—*summit* (2) NY-2
Bald Pate Creek—*gut* FL-3
Baldpate Creek—*stream* MN-6
*Baldpate Hill* MA-1
Bald Pate Hill—*summit* MA-1
Baldpate Hill—*summit* MA-1
Baldpate Lake—*lake* MN-6
*Baldpate Mtn* ME-1
Bald Pate Mtn—*summit* ME-1
Baldpate Mtn—*summit* ME-1
Baldpate Mtn—*summit* (2) NJ-2
*Bald Pate Pond* MA-1
Baldpate Pond—*reservoir* MA-1
Baldpate Pond Dam—*dam* MA-1
*Bald Peak* CA-9
*Bald Peak* MA-1
*Bald Peak* TX-5
*Bald Peak* WA-9
Bald Peak—*summit* AK-9
Bald Peak—*summit* (4) CA-9
Bald Peak—*summit* CT-1
Bald Peak—*summit* ID-8
Bald Peak—*summit* (2) ME-1
Bald Peak—*summit* MA-1
Bald Peak—*summit* MT-8
Bald Peak—*summit* NE-7
Bald Peak—*summit* (2) NV-8
Bald Peak—*summit* NH-1
Bald Peak—*summit* (4) NY-2
Bald Peak—*summit* OR-9
Bald Peak—*summit* VT-1
Bald Peak—*summit* WA-9
Bald Peak—*summit* WI-6
Bald Peak—*summit* WY-8
Bald Peak Colony Club—*other* NH-1
Bald Peaks—*summit* CA-9
Bald Peaks of Plummer—*summit* CA-9
Bald Peak State Park—*park* OR-9
*Bald Peter* OR-9
Bald Peter—*summit* (2) OR-9
Bald Peter Butte—*summit* OR-9
Bald Peter Creek—*stream* OR-9
Bald Peter Pasture Spring—*spring* OR-9
*Bald Point* WA-9
Bald Point—*cape* FL-3
Bald Point—*cape* NC-3
Bald Point—*cape* OR-9
Bald Point—*cape* TN-4
Bald Point—*cliff* IA-7
Bald Point—*locale* TN-4
Bald Point—*summit* AZ-5
Bald Point—*summit* KY-4
Bald Point Hollow—*valley* AL-4
Bald Point Hollow—*valley* TN-4
Bald Point Post Office (historical)—*building* TN-4
Bald Porcupine Island—*island* ME-1
Bald Prairie—*area* MS-4
Bald Prairie—*flat* (2) MS-4
Bald Prairie—*flat* TX-5
Bald Prairie—*locale* TX-5
Bald Range—*range* UT-8
Bald Range—*range* WY-8
**Baldrich**—*pop pl* PR-3
Bald Ridge—*cliff* OK-5
Baldridge—*locale* OK-5
Baldridge—*locale* TX-5
**Baldridge**—*pop pl* IN-6
Bald Ridge—*ridge* AL-4
Bald Ridge—*ridge* AK-9
Bald Ridge—*ridge* AZ-5
Bald Ridge—*ridge* (4) CA-9
Bald Ridge—*ridge* (2) CO-8
Bald Ridge—*ridge* GA-3
Bald Ridge—*ridge* MO-7
Bald Ridge—*ridge* MT-8
Bald Ridge—*ridge* NC-3
Bald Ridge—*ridge* (3) OR-9
Bald Ridge—*ridge* (2) PA-2
Bald Ridge—*ridge* (2) UT-8
Bald Ridge—*ridge* VA-3
Bald Ridge—*ridge* (2) WA-9
Bald Ridge—*ridge* (4) WY-8
Baldridge Branch—*stream* TX-5
Baldridge Canyon—*valley* NM-5
Baldridge Cem—*cemetery* KY-4
Baldridge Cem—*cemetery* OK-5
Baldridge Cem—*cemetery* TN-4
Baldridge Creek—*stream* GA-3
Bald Ridge Creek—*stream* MO-7
Baldridge Creek—*stream* NJ-2
Baldridge Creek—*stream* TX-5
Baldridge Lake—*reservoir* CO-8
Baldridge Marina—*other* GA-3
Baldridge Mtn—*summit* OK-5
Bald Ridge Number One Tank—*reservoir* AZ-5
Bald Ridge Number Two Tank—*reservoir* AZ-5
Baldridge Point—*summit* CO-8
Baldridge Reservation—*reserve* AL-4
Bald Ridges—*ridge* UT-8
Baldridge Sch—*school* MO-7
Baldridge Tank—*reservoir* AZ-5
Baldridge Well—*well* NM-5
Baldrige Cem—*cemetery* TN-4
Bald River—*stream* TN-4
Bald River Falls—*falls* TN-4
Bald River Falls Rec Area—*park* TN-4
Bald River Trail—*trail* TN-4
*Bald Rock* AL-4
*Bald Rock* MA-1
Bald Rock—*island* (2) ME-1
Baldrock—*locale* KY-4
Bald Rock—*locale* SC-3
Bald Rock—*pillar* CA-9
Bald Rock—*pillar* WA-9
Bald Rock—*summit* AL-4
Bald Rock—*summit* (2) CA-9
Bald Rock—*summit* KY-4
Bald Rock—*summit* ME-1
Bald Rock—*summit* MT-8
Bald Rock—*summit* (3) NC-3
Bald Rock—*summit* SC-3
Bald Rock—*summit* (4) VA-3
*Bald Rock Branch* AL-4
*Bald Rock Canyon* UT-8
Bald Rock Canyon—*valley* CA-9
Bald Rock Canyon—*valley* UT-8
Bald Rock Cem—*cemetery* KY-4
Bald Rock Ch—*church* VA-3
Bald Rock Dome—*summit* CA-9
Bald Rock Fork—*stream* KY-4
Bald Rock Ledge—*bar* ME-1
Bald Rock Lookout Tower—*locale* KY-4
*Bald Rock Mtn* NC-3
Bald Rock Mtn—*summit* AL-4
Bald Rock Mtn—*summit* CA-9
Bald Rock Mtn—*summit* ME-1
Bald Rock Mtn—*summit* (2) NC-3
Bald Rock Point—*cape* MN-6
Bald Rock Ridge—*ridge* VA-3
Bald Rocks—*bar* MA-1
Baldry Creek—*stream* AK-9
Baldry Mtn—*summit* AK-9
*Bald School* KS-7
Bald Scrappy—*summit* AR-4
Bald Sister, The—*summit* NV-8
Bald Spring—*spring* AR-4
Bald Spring Hollow—*valley* AR-4
Bald Springs Branch—*stream* NC-3
Bald Spur—*ridge* TN-4
Balds Run—*stream* VA-3
Bald Sunapee—*summit* NH-1
Baldton—*uninc pl* DE-2
Bald Top—*summit* (2) CA-9
Bald Top—*summit* GA-3
Bald Top—*summit* MA-1
Bald Top—*summit* NC-3
Bald Top—*summit* OR-9
Bald Top—*summit* PA-2
Bald Top—*summit* VT-1
Baldtop—*summit* VA-3
Bald Top Mtn—*summit* MT-8
Bald Top Mtn—*summit* NC-3
Bald Top Ridge—*ridge* TN-4
Balduck Memorial Park—*park* MI-6
Balduini Park—*park* NM-5
*Baldwin* KS-7
*Baldwin* MN-6
Baldwin—*locale* MD-2
Baldwin—*locale* OH-6
Baldwin—*locale* PA-2
Baldwin—*locale* TX-5
Baldwin—*locale* VA-3
Baldwin—*other* PA-2
**Baldwin**—*pop pl* AL-4
**Baldwin**—*pop pl* (2) AR-4
**Baldwin**—*pop pl* CO-8
**Baldwin**—*pop pl* FL-3
**Baldwin**—*pop pl* GA-3
**Baldwin**—*pop pl* IL-6
**Baldwin**—*pop pl* IA-7
**Baldwin**—*pop pl* KY-4
**Baldwin**—*pop pl* LA-4
**Baldwin**—*pop pl* MI-6
**Baldwin**—*pop pl* (2) NY-2
**Baldwin**—*pop pl* (2) NC-3
**Baldwin**—*pop pl* ND-7
**Baldwin**—*pop pl* (2) PA-2
**Baldwin**—*pop pl* WV-2
**Baldwin**—*pop pl* WI-6
Baldwin, Benjamin and Adelaide, House—*hist pl* TX-5
Baldwin, Caleb, House—*hist pl* UT-8
Baldwin, Charles, House—*hist pl* UT-8
Baldwin, Charles H., House—*hist pl* RI-1
Baldwin, David, House—*hist pl* NJ-2
Baldwin, George, House—*hist pl* CT-1
Baldwin, Hiram, House—*hist pl* IL-6
Baldwin, Joseph W., House—*hist pl* OH-6
Baldwin, Loammi, Mansion—*hist pl* MA-1
Baldwin, Maria, House—*hist pl* MA-1
Baldwin, Mount—*summit* AK-9
Baldwin, Mount—*summit* CA-9
Baldwin, Nathaniel, House—*hist pl* UT-8
Baldwin, Thomas M., House—*hist pl* OR-9
Baldwin, Timothy, House—*hist pl* CT-1
Baldwin, Zaccheus, House—*hist pl* CT-1
Baldwin Airp—*airport* MO-7
Baldwin And Muskrat Drain—*canal* MI-6
Baldwin Area—*basin* OR-9
Baldwin Assembly of God Ch—*church* FL-3
Baldwin Baptist Camp—*locale* AL-4
Baldwin Bay—*bay* NY-2
Baldwin Bay—*swamp* FL-3
Baldwin Beach—*locale* CA-9
**Baldwin Beach**—*pop pl* IL-6
Baldwin Borough—*civil* PA-2
*Baldwin Branch* KY-4
Baldwin Branch—*stream* AL-4
Baldwin Branch—*stream* IL-6
Baldwin Branch—*stream* KY-4
Baldwin Branch—*stream* NY-2
Baldwin Branch—*stream* NC-3
Baldwin Branch—*stream* OK-5
Baldwin Branch—*stream* PA-2
Baldwin Branch—*stream* (2) VA-3
Baldwin Branch—*stream* (2) WV-2
Baldwin Brook—*stream* CT-1
Baldwin Brook—*stream* ME-1
Baldwin Brook—*stream* MA-1
Baldwin Brook—*stream* NY-2
Baldwin Brook—*stream* VT-1
Baldwin Cabin—*locale* NM-5
Baldwin Camp—*locale* NE-7
Baldwin Canyon—*valley* NV-8
Baldwin Cave—*cave* CT-1
Baldwin (CCD)—*cens area* GA-3
Baldwin Cem—*cemetery* AL-4
Baldwin Cem—*cemetery* CT-1
Baldwin Cem—*cemetery* (2) IL-6
Baldwin Cem—*cemetery* IN-6
Baldwin Cem—*cemetery* (2) IA-7
Baldwin Cem—*cemetery* KS-7
Baldwin Cem—*cemetery* MN-6
Baldwin Cem—*cemetery* (2) MO-7
Baldwin Cem—*cemetery* (2) NY-2
Baldwin Cem—*cemetery* (2) NC-3
Baldwin Cem—*cemetery* ND-7
Baldwin Cem—*cemetery* (2) OH-6
Baldwin Cem—*cemetery* OK-5
Baldwin Cem—*cemetery* (2) PA-2
Baldwin Cem—*cemetery* SD-7
Baldwin Cem—*cemetery* (2) TN-4
Baldwin Cem—*cemetery* TX-5
Baldwin Cem—*cemetery* VT-1
Baldwin Cem—*cemetery* (4) VA-3
Baldwin Cem—*cemetery* (2) WV-2
Baldwin Cem—*cemetery* (2) WI-6
Baldwin (census name Baldwin Mills)—*other* SC-3
Baldwin Ch—*church* AL-4
Baldwin Ch—*church* GA-3
Baldwin Ch—*church* IN-6
Baldwin Ch—*church* MS-4
Baldwin Ch—*church* NC-3
Baldwin Ch—*church* WV-2
Baldwin Chapel—*church* LA-4
Baldwin Chapel Ch—*church* AL-4
Baldwin Christian Sch—*school* WI-6
**Baldwin City**—*pop pl* KS-7
Baldwin City Cem—*cemetery* KS-7
*Baldwin City Cemetery* MS-4
Baldwin City Dam—*dam* KS-7
Baldwin City Lake—*reservoir* KS-7
Baldwin Coll—*school* GA-3
Baldwin Corner—*locale* NY-2
**Baldwin Corner**—*pop pl* NY-2
Baldwin Corners—*locale* NY-2
Baldwin Corners—*locale* OH-6
**Baldwin Corners**—*pop pl* ME-1
**Baldwin County**—*pop pl* AL-4
**Baldwin (County)**—*pop pl* GA-3
*Baldwin County Baptist Church Camp* AL-4
Baldwin County Courthouse—*building* AL-4
Baldwin County HS—*school* AL-4
*Baldwin County Park* AL-4
Baldwin County Training Sch—*school* AL-4
Baldwin Cove—*valley* (2) NC-3
*Baldwin Creek* NV-8
*Baldwin Creek* NY-2
*Baldwin Creek* OR-9
Baldwin Creek—*stream* AR-4
Baldwin Creek—*stream* (2) CA-9
Baldwin Creek—*stream* CO-8
Baldwin Creek—*stream* GA-3
Baldwin Creek—*stream* ID-8
Baldwin Creek—*stream* (2) KS-7
Baldwin Creek—*stream* KY-4
Baldwin Creek—*stream* NY-2
Baldwin Creek—*stream* OH-6
Baldwin Creek—*stream* (2) OR-9
Baldwin Creek—*stream* (3) PA-2
Baldwin Creek—*stream* TX-5
Baldwin Creek—*stream* VT-1
Baldwin Creek—*stream* (2) WI-6
Baldwin Creek—*stream* (2) WY-8
Baldwin Creek Rec Area—*park* KS-7
Baldwin Creek School—*locale* WY-8
Baldwin Dam—*dam* AL-4
Baldwin Dam—*dam* OR-9
Baldwin Ditch—*canal* (2) OR-9
Baldwin Drain—*stream* MI-6
Baldwin Draw—*valley* AZ-5
Baldwin Drive Sch—*school* NY-2
Baldwin Dudley Pond—*lake* CT-1
Baldwin (Election Precinct)—*fmr MCD* IL-6
Baldwin Estate—*hist pl* CA-9
Baldwin Family Cem—*cemetery* MS-4
Baldwin Farms (historical)—*locale* AL-4
Baldwin Field Branch—*stream* NC-3
Baldwin Fish Lake Dam—*dam* MS-4
Baldwin Flats—*flat* PA-2
Baldwin Ford—*locale* KY-4
Baldwin Ford—*locale* TN-4
Baldwin Fork—*stream* WV-2
Baldwin Furnace—*locale* PA-2
Baldwin Gap—*gap* (3) NC-3
Baldwin Gap—*gap* TN-4
Baldwin Gap—*gap* VA-3
Baldwin Gap—*summit* NC-3
Baldwin Glacier—*glacier* AK-9
Baldwin Grade Canyon—*valley* CA-9
Baldwin Grade Sch—*school* KS-7
Baldwin Gulch—*valley* (2) CO-8
Baldwin Gulch—*valley* (2) OR-9
**Baldwin Harbor**—*pop pl* NY-2
Baldwin Harbor JHS—*school* NY-2
Baldwin Head—*summit* ME-1
**Baldwin Heights**—*pop pl* IL-6

**Baldwin Heights**—pop pl ... IN-6
**Baldwin Heights**—pop pl ... NY-2
Baldwin Heights Ch—church ... AL-4
Baldwin Heights Elem Sch—school ... IN-6
Baldwin Heights Sch—school ... MI-6
Baldwin Hill—ridge ... TN-4
Baldwin Hill—summit ... AL-4
Baldwin Hill—summit ... AR-4
Baldwin Hill—summit (2) ... CT-1
Baldwin Hill—summit ... ME-1
Baldwin Hill—summit (3) ... MA-1
Baldwin Hill—summit ... NY-2
Baldwin Hill—summit ... VT-1
Baldwin Hill Cem—cemetery ... AR-4
Baldwin Hills—other ... CA-9
Baldwin Hills—range ... CA-9
Baldwin Hills—summit ... OR-9
Baldwin Hill Sch (historical)—school ... TN-4
Baldwin Hill School (Abandoned)—locale ... WI-6
Baldwin Hills Hosp—hospital ... CA-9
Baldwin Hills Recreation Center—park ... CA-9
Baldwin Hills Sch—school ... CA-9
Baldwin (historical)—locale ... MS-4
Baldwin Hollow—valley ... MO-7
Baldwin Hollow—valley ... PA-2
Baldwin Hollow—valley ... UT-8
Baldwin Hollow—valley (2) ... VA-3
Baldwin Hotel—hist pl ... OR-9
Baldwin House—hist pl ... MT-8
Baldwin HS—school ... HI-9
Baldwin HS—school (2) ... KS-7
Baldwin HS—school ... NY-2
Baldwin HS—school ... PA-2
Baldwin Island—island ... MN-6
Baldwin Island—island ... NY-2
Baldwin JHS—school ... KS-7
Baldwin JHS—school ... NY-2
Baldwin Junior-Senior HS—school ... FL-3
Baldwin Kiln Lake—lake ... MI-6
Baldwin Lake ... MI-6
Baldwin Lake—lake ... CA-9
Baldwin Lake—lake ... ID-8
Baldwin Lake—lake (3) ... MI-6
Baldwin Lake—lake (2) ... MN-6
Baldwin Lake—lake ... OH-6
**Baldwin Lake**—pop pl ... CA-9
**Baldwin Lake**—pop pl ... MO-7
Baldwin Lake—reservoir ... MO-7
Baldwin Lake—reservoir ... TX-5
Baldwin Lakes—lake ... MO-7
Baldwin Lateral—canal ... SD-7
Baldwin Lodge (historical)—locale ... MS-4
Baldwin Mason Creek—stream ... IA-7
Baldwin Memorial Cem—cemetery ... AL-4
Baldwin Memorial Gardens—cemetery ... GA-3
Baldwin Memorial Home—locale ... HI-9
Baldwin Mill Pond—reservoir ... NC-3
Baldwin Millpond Dam—dam ... NC-3
**Baldwin Mills (census name for Baldwin)**—pop pl ... SC-3
Baldwin Mine—mine ... CO-8
Baldwin Mine—mine ... NV-8
Baldwin Monument—other ... HI-9
Baldwin Mtn—summit (2) ... NY-2
Baldwin Mtn—summit ... VA-3
Baldwin Oil Field—oilfield ... TX-5
Baldwin Park—park ... HI-9
Baldwin Park—park ... MO-7
Baldwin Park—park ... NJ-2
Baldwin Park—park ... NY-2
Baldwin Park—park ... TX-5
**Baldwin Park**—pop pl ... CA-9
**Baldwin Park**—pop pl ... MO-7
Baldwin Park Christian Sch—school ... CA-9
Baldwin Park HS—school ... CA-9
Baldwin Peninsula—cape ... AK-9
Baldwin Place—locale ... AZ-5
**Baldwin Place**—pop pl ... NY-2
Baldwin Plaza (Shop Ctr)—locale ... FL-3
Baldwin Point—cape ... AL-4
Baldwin Point—cape ... WA-9
Baldwin Point Trail—trail ... PA-2
Baldwin Pond—lake ... MA-1
Baldwin Pond—lake ... NY-2
Baldwin Pond—lake ... VT-1
Baldwin Pond—reservoir ... MA-1
Baldwin Pond—reservoir ... NC-3
Baldwin Pond Dam—dam ... MA-1
Baldwin Pond Dam—dam ... NC-3
Baldwin Post Office (historical)—building ... PA-2
Baldwin Prairie—flat ... OK-5
Baldwin Ranch—locale ... MT-8
Baldwin-Reynolds House—hist pl ... PA-2
Baldwin Ridge—ridge ... CA-9
Baldwin Ridge—ridge ... UT-8
Baldwin Ridge—ridge ... VA-3
Baldwin River—stream ... MI-6
Baldwin Rsvr—reservoir ... CA-9
Baldwin Rsvr—reservoir ... CO-8
Baldwin Rsvr—reservoir ... NE-7
Baldwin Rsvr—reservoir ... OH-6
Baldwin Run—stream ... OH-6
Baldwin Run—stream (2) ... PA-2
Baldwin's Arcade—hist pl ... ND-7
Baldwin Sch—school (2) ... AL-4
Baldwin Sch—school (2) ... CA-9
Baldwin Sch—school (2) ... CT-1
Baldwin Sch—school ... GA-3
Baldwin Sch—school ... MA-1
Baldwin Sch—school (4) ... MI-6
Baldwin Sch—school ... NJ-2
Baldwin Sch—school (2) ... PA-2
Baldwin Sch—school ... SD-7
Baldwin Sch—school ... VT-1
Baldwin Sch—school ... VA-3
Baldwin Sch (abandoned)—school ... PA-2
Baldwin Sch (historical)—school ... AL-4
Baldwin Sch (historical)—school ... MS-4
Baldwin School—locale ... IL-6
Baldwin School, The—school ... PR-3
Baldwins Corner—locale ... NJ-2
Baldwin's Creek ... NY-2
Baldwins Creek—stream ... NJ-2
Baldwins Crossing—locale ... AZ-5
Baldwins Crossing—locale ... CT-1
Baldwins Ferry (historical)—locale ... MS-4
Baldwin Shop Ctr—locale ... FL-3
Baldwins Lake—lake ... MI-6
Baldwins Lake—reservoir ... AL-4
Baldwins Landing (historical)—locale ... MS-4
Baldwin Slough—stream ... AL-4
Baldwin Slough—stream ... KY-4
Baldwin Slough—stream ... WA-9
Baldwin's Mill—hist pl ... NC-3
Baldwins Mill Cem—cemetery ... WI-6
Baldwins Pond ... MA-1
Baldwins Pond—lake ... CT-1
Baldwins Pond—reservoir ... NC-3
Baldwin Spring—spring ... AZ-5
Baldwin Spring—spring ... OR-9
Baldwin Spring—spring ... SD-7
Baldwin Square Shop Ctr—locale ... AL-4
Baldwin State Wildlife Area—park ... MO-7
Baldwin Station ... CT-1
Baldwin Station—locale ... MD-2
Baldwin Station—locale ... PA-2
Baldwin Stocker Sch—school ... CA-9
Baldwinsville ... MA-1
**Baldwinsville**—pop pl ... NY-2
Baldwinsville (census name Baldwinville)—other ... MA-1
Baldwin Swamp—swamp ... CT-1
Baldwin Swamp—swamp ... NC-3
Baldwin Tank—reservoir (3) ... AZ-5
Baldwin Terrace—hist pl ... NE-7
**Baldwin (Town of)**—pop pl ... ME-1
**Baldwin (Town of)**—pop pl ... NY-2
**Baldwin (Town of)**—pop pl ... WI-6
**Baldwin Township**—pop pl ... ND-7
Baldwin (Township of)—fmr MCD ... NC-3
**Baldwin (Township of)**—pop pl (2) ... MI-6
**Baldwin (Township of)**—pop pl ... MN-6
**Baldwin (Township of)**—pop pl ... PA-2
Baldwin Trail—trail ... PA-2
Baldwin Trick Tank—reservoir ... AZ-5
Baldwinville—locale ... GA-3
**Baldwinville**—pop pl ... MA-1
Baldwinville (census name for Baldwinsville)—CDP ... MA-1
Baldwinville Village Hist Dist—hist pl ... MA-1
Baldwin Vocational Sch—school ... GA-3
Baldwin-Wallace Coll—school ... OH-6
Baldwin Water Supply Pond Dam—dam ... MA-1
Baldwin-Whitehall School ... PA-2
**Baldwin Woods**—pop pl ... NC-3
**Baldwin Woods (subdivision)**—pop pl ... NC-3
**Baldwyn**—pop pl ... MS-4
Baldwyn Ch of Christ—church ... MS-4
Baldwyn Elem Sch—school ... MS-4
Baldwyn Hosp—hospital ... MS-4
Baldwyn HS—school ... MS-4
Baldwyn MS—school ... MS-4
Baldwyn Presbyterian Ch—church ... MS-4
Baldy ... AZ-5
Baldy ... CA-9
Baldy ... CO-8
Baldy ... MT-8
Baldy—summit ... CA-9
Baldy—summit (2) ... CO-8
Baldy—summit ... ID-8
Baldy—summit ... ME-1
Baldy—summit (2) ... MI-6
Baldy—summit (3) ... MT-8
Baldy—summit ... NM-5
Baldy—summit ... NY-2
Baldy—summit (4) ... OR-9
Baldy—summit (3) ... WA-9
Baldy—summit ... WY-8
Baldy, Mount—summit ... AZ-5
Baldy, Mount—summit ... CA-9
Baldy, Mount—summit ... CO-8
Baldy, Mount—summit ... ID-8
Baldy, Mount—summit (5) ... MT-8
Baldy, Mount—summit ... NV-8
Baldy, Mount—summit ... NY-2
Baldy, Mount—summit (2) ... OR-9
Baldy, Mount—summit (5) ... UT-8
Baldy, Mount—summit (2) ... WA-9
Baldy, Mount—summit (2) ... WY-8
Baldy (Abandoned)—locale ... NM-5
Baldy Alto—summit ... CO-8
Baldy Basin—basin ... AZ-5
Baldy Basin—basin ... ID-8
Baldy Bay—bay ... AK-9
Baldy Bear Creek—stream ... ID-8
Baldy Bear Creek—stream ... MT-8
Baldy Bill Point—cliff ... AZ-5
Baldy Blue Lake—lake ... NM-5
Baldy Branch—stream ... CO-8
Baldy Butte ... OR-9
Baldy Butte—summit (3) ... MT-8
Baldy Butte—summit ... ND-7
Baldy Butte—summit ... OR-9
Baldy Butte—summit ... WY-8
Baldy Cabin—locale ... NM-5
Baldy Canyon—valley ... AZ-5
Baldy Canyon—valley ... CO-8
Baldy Canyon—valley ... ID-8
Baldy Chato—summit ... CO-8
Baldy Cinco—summit ... CO-8
Baldy Coal Mine—mine ... CO-8
Baldy Creek ... MN-6
Baldy Creek—stream ... AK-9
Baldy Creek—stream ... CA-9
Baldy Creek—stream (3) ... CO-8
Baldy Creek—stream (4) ... ID-8
Baldy Creek—stream ... IN-6
Baldy Creek—stream ... MT-8
Baldy Creek—stream (5) ... OR-9
Baldy Creek—stream (4) ... WA-9
Baldy Creek—stream ... WY-8
Baldy Gap—gap ... CA-9
Baldy Gulch—valley ... MT-8
Baldy Gulch—valley ... OR-9
Baldy Hill—summit ... NE-7
Baldy Hill—summit (2) ... NM-5
Baldy Hill—summit ... ND-7
Baldy Hill—summit ... WA-9
Baldy Hill—summit ... WI-6
Baldy Hollow—valley ... PA-2
Baldy Knoll—summit (2) ... ID-8
Baldy Knoll—summit ... WY-8
Baldy Lake—lake ... AK-9
Baldy Lake—lake (2) ... CO-8
Baldy Lake—lake ... ID-8
Baldy Lake—lake ... MI-6
Baldy Lake—lake ... MN-6
Baldy Lake—lake (2) ... MT-8
Baldy Lake—lake ... OR-9
Baldy Lakes—lake ... WY-8
Baldy Mesa—summit ... CA-9
Baldy Mount ... MT-8
Baldy Mount ... WA-9
Baldy Mountain ... CO-8
Baldy Mountain ... ID-8
Baldy Mountain ... MT-8
Baldy Mountain Ridge—ridge ... CA-9
Baldy Mtn ... AZ-5
Baldy Mtn ... TX-5
Baldy Mtn ... WA-9
Baldy Mtn—summit ... AK-9
Baldy Mtn—summit (2) ... AZ-5
Baldy Mtn—summit (5) ... CA-9
Baldy Mtn—summit (9) ... CO-8
Baldy Mtn—summit (5) ... ID-8
Baldy Mtn—summit ... MA-1
Baldy Mtn—summit (11) ... MT-8
Baldy Mtn—summit ... NV-8
Baldy Mtn—summit (4) ... NM-5
Baldy Mtn—summit ... NY-2
Baldy Mtn—summit (5) ... OR-9
Baldy Mtn—summit (2) ... TX-5
Baldy Mtn—summit ... UT-8
Baldy Mtn—summit (4) ... WA-9
Baldy Mtn—summit ... WI-6
Baldy Mtn—summit (3) ... WY-8
Baldy Peak ... CA-9
Baldy Peak ... CO-8
Baldy Peak ... TX-5
Baldy Peak—summit (2) ... AZ-5
Baldy Peak—summit ... CA-9
Baldy Peak—summit (5) ... CO-8
Baldy Peak—summit (2) ... MT-8
Baldy Peak—summit ... NV-8
Baldy Peak—summit (2) ... NM-5
Baldy Peak—summit ... OR-9
Baldy Peak—summit ... SD-7
Baldy Peak—summit ... TX-5
Baldy Peak—summit ... UT-8
Baldy Peak—summit ... WA-9
Baldy Peak—summit ... WY-8
Baldy Peak Big Baldy Peak ... MT-8
Baldy Peak Mtn ... AZ-5
Baldy Pit—basin ... MT-8
Baldy Point—cliff ... OK-5
Baldy Point—summit ... WY-8
Baldy Ridge ... CO-8
Baldy Ridge—ridge ... OR-9
Baldy Ridge—ridge (2) ... UT-8
Baldy Ridge—ridge ... WA-9
Baldy Ridge—ridge ... WY-8
Baldy Rsvr ... OR-9
Baldy Rsvr—reservoir ... CA-9
Baldy Ryan Canyon—valley ... CA-9
Baldys, The—summit ... UT-8
Baldy Saddle—gap ... AZ-5
Baldy Spring—spring ... AZ-5
Baldy Spring—spring ... NM-5
Baldy Spring No 1—spring ... WA-9
Baldy Spring No 2—spring ... WA-9
Baldy Tank—reservoir ... AZ-5
Baldy Tank—reservoir ... TX-5
Baldy Trail—trail ... AZ-5
Baldy Trail—trail (2) ... CA-9
Baldy Trail—trail ... WA-9
Baldy Trap—gap ... AZ-5
Baldy Tunnel Spring—spring ... AZ-5
Baldy Valley—basin ... NE-7
Baldy View Sch—school ... CA-9
Baldy Wilderness, Mount—summit ... AZ-5
Baldy Windmill—locale (2) ... TX-5
**Baleabaat'**—pop pl ... FM-9
Balebat' ... FM-9
Balebatt ... FM-9
Bale Brown Branch—stream ... AR-4
Baleebaat ... FM-9
Baleful Peak—summit ... AK-9
Bale Mill—hist pl ... CA-9
Bale Mill Historical Monument—locale ... CA-9
Balentine ... SC-3
Balentine Cem—cemetery ... TN-4
Bale Playground—park ... MI-6
Baler Gulch—valley ... CO-8
Balerma Ch—church ... GA-3
Bales Canyon—valley ... NM-5
Bales Canyon—valley ... OR-9
Bales Cem—cemetery ... IN-6
Bales Cem—cemetery ... TN-4
Bales Cem—cemetery ... VA-3
Bales Ch—church ... NC-3
Bales Chapel—church ... TN-4
Bales Creek—stream ... MS-4
Bales Creek—stream (2) ... MT-8
Bales Creek—stream (2) ... OR-9
Bales Creek—stream ... TN-4
Bales Ditch—canal ... IN-6
Bales Ditch—canal ... OH-6
Bales Ford—locale ... TN-4
Bales Gap—gap ... TN-4
Baleshed Landing—locale ... MS-4
Bales Hollow—valley ... IN-6
Bales Lake—lake ... MO-7
Bales Lake—reservoir ... NM-5
**Bales Lake (Bayles Lake)**—pop pl ... IL-6
Bale Slough—stream ... CA-9
Bales Mill Pond—reservoir ... NJ-2
Bales Mtn—summit ... CA-9
Bales Sch (historical)—school ... MO-7
Bales Seep—spring ... NM-5
Bales Spring—spring ... AL-4
Bales Spring Branch—stream ... VA-3
Balesville—locale ... NJ-2
Balesville Dam—dam ... NJ-2
**Bale Township**—pop pl ... ND-7
**Baleville**—pop pl ... NJ-2
Baley Hotel—hist pl ... CA-9
Baley Reservoir ... CA-9
Balford—locale ... WA-9
Balfore Lake Dam—dam ... AL-4
Balfour ... NC-3
Balfour ... PA-2
Balfour—locale ... CO-8
Balfour—locale ... IA-7
**Balfour**—pop pl ... NC-3
**Balfour**—pop pl ... ND-7
Balfour Brake—swamp ... LA-4
Balfour Cem—cemetery ... MI-6
Balfour Cem—cemetery ... MS-4
Balfour Cem—cemetery ... NC-3
Balfour Creek—stream ... MS-4
Balfour House—hist pl ... MS-4
Balfour Lake—lake ... NY-2
Balfour Lake Camp—locale ... NY-2
Balfour Mtn—summit ... NY-2
Balfour Park—park ... WA-9
Balfour (RR name Smyth)—CDP ... NC-3
Balfours (census name North Asheboro)—other ... NC-3
Balfour Sch—school ... GA-3
Balfour Sch—school (2) ... NC-3
**Balfour Township**—pop pl ... ND-7
Balgaard State Wildlife Mngmt Area—park ... MN-6
Bal Harbor ... FL-3
**Bal Harbour**—pop pl ... FL-3
Bal Harbour Shops—locale ... FL-3
Baliff Well—locale ... NM-5
Balif Lake—lake ... MN-6
**Bali Hai Subdivision**—pop pl (2) ... UT-8
Balika Basin—bay ... AK-9
Balika Cove—bay ... AK-9
Baliston ... MS-4
Balitas, Cerro—summit ... NM-5
Balitmore—locale ... MI-6
Balk, Point—cape ... NY-2
Balkan—locale ... KY-4
**Balkan**—pop pl ... MN-6
Balkan Cem—cemetery ... KY-4
Balkan Lake—lake ... MN-6
**Balkan (Township of)**—pop pl ... MN-6
Balke Cabin—locale ... AZ-5
Balke Lake—lake ... MN-6
Balke Tank—reservoir ... NM-5
Balk Mountain ... MT-8
**Balko**—pop pl ... OK-5
Balko Sch—school (2) ... OK-5
Balkovetz Giem Standvich Whiting Ditch—canal ... MT-8
**Balkum**—pop pl ... AL-4
Balkum Baptist Church ... AL-4
Balkum Cem—cemetery ... AL-4
Balkum Chapel—church ... AL-4
Balkum Post Office (historical)—building ... AL-4
Balky Horse Canyon—valley ... CA-9
Balky Spring—spring ... AZ-5
Balky Tank—reservoir ... AZ-5
**Ball**—pop pl ... LA-4
**Ball**—pop pl ... NC-3
Ball, Billy, House—hist pl ... KY-4
Ball, D. C., House—hist pl ... NM-5
Ball, J., House—hist pl ... NY-2
Ball, Judge Cyrus, House—hist pl ... IN-6
Ball, Levi, House—hist pl ... NY-2
Ball, Parks E., House—hist pl ... AL-4
Ball, Stephen, House—hist pl ... NY-2
Ball, The—summit ... VT-1
Ball, W. C., House—hist pl ... IA-7
Ballahack, Bayou—stream ... LA-4
Ballahack Canal—canal ... NC-3
Ballah Ch—church ... WV-2
Ballaine House—hist pl ... AK-9
Ballaine Lake—lake ... AK-9
Ball Airp—airport ... MS-4
Ball Airp—airport ... NC-3
**Ballaja**—pop pl (3) ... PR-3
Ball Alley—ridge ... NC-3
Ball Alley Creek—stream ... NC-3
Ball Alley Run—stream ... OH-6
Ballance Cem—cemetery ... KY-4
Ball and Moore Rsvr—reservoir ... UT-8
Ballandock Structure—canal ... LA-4
Ball And Patterson Drain—canal ... MI-6
Ballanfant Cem—cemetery ... TN-4
Ballanger Creek ... TX-5
**Ballantine**—pop pl ... MT-8
Ballantine, James, House—hist pl ... WI-6
Ballantine, John, House—hist pl ... NJ-2
Ballantine Canyon—valley ... AZ-5
Ballantine Manor—other ... FL-3
Ballantine Spring—spring ... UT-8
Ballantyne Bridge—bridge ... NY-2
Ballantyne Cem—cemetery ... TX-5
Ballantyne Lake—lake ... MN-6
Ballantyne Sch—school ... CA-9
Ballantyne Sch—school ... NY-2
Ballarach Cove—cove ... MA-1
Ballarat—locale ... CA-9
Ballarat Canyon—valley ... CA-9
Ballarat Creek—stream ... AK-9
Ballarat Creek—stream ... MT-8
Ballard ... TN-4
Ballard—locale ... AR-4
Ballard—locale ... KY-4
Ballard—locale ... NC-3
**Ballard**—pop pl ... CA-9
**Ballard**—pop pl ... FL-3
**Ballard**—pop pl ... IL-6
**Ballard**—pop pl ... MD-2
**Ballard**—pop pl ... MS-4
**Ballard**—pop pl ... MO-7
**Ballard**—pop pl ... OK-5
**Ballard**—pop pl ... UT-8
**Ballard**—pop pl ... WA-9
**Ballard**—pop pl ... WV-2
Ballard, John W., House—hist pl ... IA-7
Ballard, Levi, House—hist pl ... GA-3
Ballard, Mount—summit ... AZ-5
Ballard, Mount—summit ... WA-9
Ballard, Rogers Clark, Memorial Sch—hist pl ... KY-4
Ballard, William H., House—hist pl ... KY-4
Ballard Ave Hist Dist—hist pl ... WA-9
**Ballard Avenues Subdivision**—pop pl ... UT-8
Ballard Bay—bay ... ME-1
Ballard Branch ... AR-4
Ballard Branch—stream ... AR-4
Ballard Branch—stream (3) ... KY-4
Ballard Branch—stream ... MS-4
Ballard Branch—stream ... TN-4
Ballard Branch—stream ... TX-5
Ballard Branch—stream ... WV-2
Ballard Bridge—bridge ... AL-4
Ballard Bridge—bridge ... WA-9
Ballard Bridge—hist pl ... WA-9
Ballard Brook—stream ... NH-1
Ballard Camp—locale ... TX-5
Ballard Campground—locale ... CA-9
Ballard Campground—locale ... WA-9
Ballard Canyon ... CA-9
Ballard Canyon—valley ... CA-9
Ballard Carnegie Library—hist pl ... WA-9
Ballard Cem—cemetery (3) ... AL-4
Ballard Cem—cemetery (4) ... LA-4
Ballard Cem—cemetery ... MS-4
Ballard Cem—cemetery ... MO-7
Ballard Cem—cemetery (2) ... NC-3
Ballard Cem—cemetery ... OK-5
Ballard Cem—cemetery ... PA-2
Ballard Cem—cemetery (2) ... WV-2
Ballard Ch—church ... AL-4
Ballard Ch—church ... OK-5
Ballard Ch—church ... WV-2
Ballard Chapel—church ... TN-4
Ballard Corners—locale ... NY-2
**Ballard Corners**—pop pl ... NY-2
Ballard Country Club—other ... IA-7
**Ballard (County)**—pop pl ... KY-4
Ballard County Courthouse—hist pl ... KY-4
Ballard Cove—bay ... FL-3
Ballard Cove—valley (2) ... NC-3
Ballard Creek ... CA-9
Ballard Creek ... TX-5
Ballard Creek—gut ... TX-5
Ballard Creek—stream ... AL-4
Ballard Creek—stream (2) ... AR-4
Ballard Creek—stream ... CA-9
Ballard Creek—stream ... GA-3
Ballard Creek—stream ... IN-6
Ballard Creek—stream (3) ... IA-7
Ballard Creek—stream ... MS-4
Ballard Creek—stream (3) ... NC-3
Ballard Creek—stream ... OK-5
Ballard Creek—stream ... OR-9
Ballard Creek—stream ... SC-3
Ballard Creek—stream ... TX-5
Ballard Creek—stream (2) ... VA-3
Ballard Crossing—locale ... TX-5
Ballard Crossroads—locale ... NC-3
Ballard Ditch—canal ... ID-8
Ballard Drain—canal ... MI-6
Ballard Draw—valley ... UT-8
Ballard Falls (historical)—locale ... KS-7
Ballard Flat—flat ... CA-9
Ballard Fork—stream ... WV-2
Ballard Freewill Baptist Church ... AL-4
Ballard Gap—gap ... GA-3
Ballard Gap—gap (2) ... NC-3
**Ballard Gardens**—pop pl ... MD-2
Ballard Harmon Branch—stream ... WV-2
Ballard-Harvey Cem—cemetery ... WV-2
Ballard Hill—ridge ... NM-5
Ballard Hill—summit ... AR-4
Ballard Hill—summit (3) ... MA-1
Ballard Hill—summit ... MT-8
Ballard Hollow—valley ... MO-7
Ballard Hollow—valley (2) ... TN-4
Ballard-Howe House—hist pl ... WA-9
Ballard HS—school ... MO-7
Ballard HS—school ... WA-9
Ballard-Hudson HS—school ... GA-3
Ballard JHS—school ... MI-6
Ballard Junction—locale ... UT-8
Ballard Lake ... WI-6
Ballard Lake—lake ... MN-6
Ballard Lake—lake ... NM-5
Ballard Lake—lake ... WI-6
Ballard Lake—reservoir ... NY-2
Ballard Lake Dam—dam ... MS-4
Ballard Landing—locale ... AR-4
Ballard Marsh ... NE-7
Ballard Marsh—swamp ... VA-3
Ballard-Marshall House—hist pl ... VA-3
Ballard Memorial HS—school ... KY-4
Ballard Memorial Sch—school ... KY-4
Ballard Mill Lead Mine Pond—reservoir ... TN-4
Ballard Mill Settlement Dam—dam ... TN-4
Ballard Mine—mine ... MT-8
Ballard Mine—mine ... SD-7
Ballard Mine (underground)—mine ... AL-4
Ballard Mountain—ridge ... GA-3
Ballard Mtn—summit ... CO-8
Ballard Mtn—summit ... WV-2
Ballard Park—park ... GA-3
Ballard Park—park ... MS-4
Ballard Park—park ... NE-7
Ballard Peak ... CO-8
**Ballard Pines**—pop pl ... FL-3
Ballard Playground—park ... WA-9
Ballard Point—cape ... TN-4
Ballard Pond—lake ... ME-1
Ballard Pond—lake ... NH-1
Ballard Pond—reservoir ... GA-3
Ballard Pond—reservoir ... NY-2
Ballard Pond Dam—dam (2) ... MS-4
Ballard Pumping Station—other ... NM-5
Ballard Ranch—locale (2) ... MT-8
Ballard Ranch—locale (2) ... WY-8
Ballard Ravine—valley ... CA-9
Ballard Ridge—ridge ... CA-9
Ballard Ridge—ridge ... NH-1
Ballard Road Covered Bridge—hist pl ... OH-6
Ballard Rsvr—reservoir (2) ... CA-9
Ballard Run—stream ... WV-2
Ballards ... MI-6
**Ballards**—pop pl ... MI-6
Ballards Bridge—bridge ... NC-3
Ballards Bridge Ch—church ... NC-3
Ballard Sch—school ... FL-3
Ballard Sch—school (3) ... IL-6
Ballard Sch—school ... KY-4
Ballard Sch—school ... ME-1
Ballard Sch—school ... MA-1
Ballard Sch—school ... MO-7
Ballard Sch—school ... NY-2
Ballard Sch (abandoned)—school ... MO-7
Ballards Channel—channel ... MI-6
Ballards Chapel—church ... MS-4
Ballards Chapel Baptist Church ... TN-4
Ballards Chapel Cem—cemetery ... TN-4
Ballards Chapel (historical)—church ... TN-4
Ballard Sch (historical)—school ... AL-4
Ballard Sch (historical)—school ... MS-4
**Ballards Corners**—pop pl ... MI-6
Ballards Creek—stream ... AL-4
Ballards Crossraods—locale ... VA-3
**Ballards Crossroad**—pop pl ... NC-3
Ballards Crossroads ... NC-3
**Ballards Crossroads**—pop pl ... NC-3
**Ballards Crossroads**—pop pl ... VA-3
Ballards Grove Ch—church ... NC-3
Ballards Hill ... MA-1
Ballard's Island ... IL-6
Ballard Slough—gut ... TN-4
Ballards Marsh—swamp ... NE-7
Ballard Spring—spring ... TX-5
Ballard Spring Branch—stream ... TN-4
Ballards Rock (not verified)—bar ... MP-9
Ballards Store ... AR-4
Ballard State Waterfowl Mngmt Area—park ... KY-4
Ballard Station—other ... WV-2
**Ballard Subdivision**—pop pl ... UT-8
Ballardsville—locale ... KY-4
**Ballardsville**—pop pl ... KY-4
**Ballardsville**—pop pl ... MS-4
Ballardsville Post Office (historical)—building ... MS-4
Ballard Swamp—swamp ... MI-6
Ballard Tank—reservoir (2) ... AZ-5
Ballard Vale ... MA-1
**Ballardvale**—pop pl ... MA-1
Ballardvale District—hist pl ... MA-1
Ballardville ... MA-1
Ballard Well—well ... CO-8
Ballard Well—well ... NM-5
Ballard Wildlife Mngmt Area—park ... KY-4
Ballard Windmill—locale ... NM-5
Ballard Windmill—locale ... TX-5
Ball Arroyo—stream ... CO-8
Ballast Bank—locale ... NC-3
Ballast Bay—bay ... NC-3
Ballast Bluff—cliff ... GA-3
Ballast Creek—gut ... SC-3
Ballast Island—island ... AK-9
Ballast Island—island ... ME-1
Ballast Island—island ... OH-6
Ballast Island Ledge—beach ... ME-1
Ballast Key—island ... FL-3
Ballast Narrows—gut ... VA-3
**Ballaston**—pop pl ... MS-4
Ballast Pit Lake—lake ... MO-7
Ballast Point—cape (2) ... CA-9
Ballast Point—cape ... DE-2
Ballast Point—cape ... FL-3
Ballast Point—cape ... NC-3
Ballast Point—uninc pl ... FL-3
Ballast Point Baptist Ch—church ... FL-3
Ballast Point Christian Sch—school ... FL-3
Ballast Point Exceptional Center—school ... FL-3
Ballast Point Park—park ... FL-3
Ballast Point Sch—school ... FL-3
Ballast Reef—bar ... CT-1
Ballast Reef—bar ... OH-6
Ballast Ridge—ridge ... SC-3
Ballaststone Ledges—bar ... ME-1
Ballast Tump—island ... VA-3
Ballawe Creek ... VA-3
Ball Bay—bay ... OR-9
Ball Bearing Hill—summit ... OR-9
Ball Bluff—cliff ... AL-4
Ball Bluff—locale ... MN-6
Ball Bluff—summit ... WI-6
Ball Bluff Lake—lake ... MN-6
Ball Bluff Lookout Tower—locale ... MN-6
Ball Bluff Park—park ... MN-6
**Ball Bluff (Township of)**—pop pl ... MN-6
Ball Branch ... KY-4
Ball Branch ... TX-5
Ball Branch—stream ... AR-4
Ball Branch—stream (2) ... GA-3
Ball Branch—stream (4) ... KY-4
Ball Branch—stream ... LA-4
Ball Branch—stream (2) ... MO-7
Ball Branch—stream ... NC-3
Ball Branch—stream ... SC-3
Ball Branch—stream (2) ... TN-4
Ball Branch—stream ... TX-5
Ball Branch Sch—school ... KY-4
Ball Brook ... CT-1
Ball Brook ... MA-1
Ball Brook—stream (2) ... CT-1
Ball Brook—stream ... MA-1
Ball Butte—summit ... ID-8
Ball Butte—summit ... OR-9
**Ball Camp**—pop pl ... TN-4
Ball Camp Baptist Ch—church ... TN-4
Ball Camp Elem Sch—school ... TN-4
Ball Camp Park—park ... TN-4
Ball Camp Post Office (historical)—building ... TN-4
Ball Camp Quarry Cave—cave ... TN-4
Ball Cem—cemetery ... AL-4
Ball Cem—cemetery ... IL-6
Ball Cem—cemetery ... IN-6
Ball Cem—cemetery (2) ... KY-4
Ball Cem—cemetery ... LA-4
Ball Cem—cemetery (4) ... MS-4
Ball Cem—cemetery ... NE-7
Ball Cem—cemetery ... NY-2
Ball Cem—cemetery ... NC-3
Ball Cem—cemetery ... OK-5
Ball Cem—cemetery ... OR-9
Ball Cem—cemetery (5) ... TN-4
Ball Cem—cemetery ... VT-1
Ball Cem—cemetery (7) ... VA-3
Ball Cem—cemetery (3) ... WV-2
Ball Cem—cemetery ... WY-8
Ball Cemeteries—cemetery ... WV-2
Ball Ch—church ... AR-4
Ball Ch—church ... GA-3
Ball Ch—church ... MO-7
Ball Chapel—church ... AR-4
Ball Chapel—church ... VA-3
Ball Chapel—church (2) ... WV-2
Ball City Ch—church ... NC-3
**Ball Club**—pop pl ... MN-6
Ball Club Creek—stream ... MN-6
Ball Club Lake—lake (2) ... MN-6
Ball Club River—stream ... MN-6
Ball Coulee—valley ... MT-8
Ball Court Wash—stream ... AZ-5
Ball Crag—pillar ... NH-1
Ball Creek ... NC-3
Ball Creek ... PA-2
Ball Creek ... SD-7
Ball Creek ... TX-5
Ball Creek ... VA-3
Ball Creek ... WY-8
Ball Creek—stream ... AK-9
Ball Creek—stream ... AR-4

Ball Creek—stream (2) GA-3
Ball Creek—stream (2) ID-8
Ball Creek—stream MI-6
Ball Creek—stream MS-4
Ball Creek—stream MT-8
Ball Creek—stream NY-2
Ball Creek—stream (2) NC-3
Ball Creek—stream OR-9
Ball Creek—stream (2) TN-4
Ball Creek—stream (2) VA-3
Ball Creek—stream WV-2
Ball Creek Ch—church GA-3
Ball Creek Ch—church WV-2
Ball Creek Sch (historical)—school TN-4
Ball Creek Spring—spring TN-4
Ball Ditch—canal WY-8
Ball Dome—summit CA-9
Ballejas Creek—stream NM-5
Ballena Bay—harbor CA-9
Ballena Islands—area AK-9
Ballena Island Shoal—bar AK-9
Ballenas CA-9
Ballenas Bay CA-9
Ballena Valley—valley CA-9
**Ballengee**—pop pl (2) WV-2
Ballengee Knob—summit WV-2
Ballenger Bend—bend TX-5
Ballenger Cem—cemetery MS-4
Ballenger Creek VA-3
Ballenger Creek—stream MD-2
Ballenger Ditch—canal OH-6
Ballenger Draw—valley WY-8
Ballenger Jones Ditch—canal OH-6
Ballenger Park—park MI-6
Ballengers Creek VA-3
**Ballentine**—pop pl MS-4
**Ballentine**—pop pl SC-3
Ballentine Bluff—cliff TN-4
Ballentine-Bryant House—hist pl MS-4
Ballentine Canal—canal ID-8
Ballentine Creek—stream AK-9
Ballentine Hollow—valley TN-4
Ballentine Landing—locale SC-3
**Ballentine Manor**—pop pl FL-3
**Ballentine Place**—pop pl VA-3
Ballentine Post Office (historical)—building MS-4
Ballentine Sch—school VA-3
Ballentine Sch (historical)—school AL-4
Ballentine-Seay House—hist pl MS-4
Ballentine-Shealy House—hist pl SC-3
Ballentyne Creek—stream ID-8
**Ballester**—pop pl PR-3
Ballestone Mansion—hist pl MD-2
Ballet Cem (historical)—cemetery MO-7
Ballet Spring—spring OR-9
Ballew Cave—cave AL-4
Ballew Cem—cemetery AR-4
Ballew Cem—cemetery NC-3
Ballew Ch—church AR-4
Ballew Creek—stream NC-3
Ballew Hollow—valley MO-7
Ballew Lake—flat OR-9
Ballew Lake Spring—spring OR-9
Ballew Mill—locale GA-3
Ballew Mine (underground)—mine AL-4
Ballew Point—cliff AL-4
Ballew Ranch—locale NM-5
Ballew Ridge—ridge OK-5
Ballew Ridge Public Use Area—park OK-5
Ballew Rsvr—reservoir (2) OR-9
Ballew Sch—school MO-7
Ballews Chapel—church AR-4
Ballew Springs Cem—cemetery TX-5
Ballew Springs Ch—church TX-5
Ballew Store—locale NC-3
Ballfield Landing—locale AL-4
Ball Flat—flat CA-9
Ball Flat—locale AL-4
Ball Flat Post Office (historical)—building AL-4
Ball Fork—stream KY-4
Ball Fork—stream WV-2
Ball Free Ch—church MI-6
Ball Gap WV-2
Ball Gap—gap NC-3
Ball Gap—other WV-2
Ball Grey Landing—locale NC-3
Ball Ground—flat TN-4
**Ball Ground**—pop pl (2) GA-3
**Ballground**—pop pl MS-4
Ball Ground (CCD)—cens area GA-3
Ball Ground Ch—church GA-3
Ball Ground Creek—stream MS-4
Ballground Creek—stream MS-4
Ball Ground Creek Landing (historical)—locale MS-4
Ball Ground Mtn—summit NC-3
Ballground Post Office (historical)—building MS-4
Ball Gulch—valley (2) CO-8
Ball Gulf—valley NY-2
Ball Head NC-3
Ball Hill AL-4
Ball Hill MA-1
**Ball Hill**—pop pl MS-4
Ball Hill—summit CT-1
Ball Hill—summit (3) MA-1
Ball Hill—summit MO-7
Ball Hill—summit NH-1
Ball Hill—summit VT-1
Ball Hill Cem—cemetery NY-2
Ball Hill Cem—cemetery TN-4
Ball Hill Ch—church AL-4
Ball Hill Ch—church KY-4
Ball Hill Ch—church MS-4
Ball Hill Reed Brake—stream MS-4
Ball Hill Sch—school IL-6
Ball Hill Sch (historical)—school AL-4
Ball Hill Town Hall—building ND-7
**Ball Hill Township**—pop pl ND-7
Ball (historical)—locale MS-4
Ball Hollow—valley (3) AR-4
Ball Hollow—valley (2) TN-4
Ball Hollow—valley VA-3
Ball Hollow—valley WV-2
Ballhoot Scar Overlook—locale NC-3
Ball Hornet AL-4
Ball HS—school (2) TX-5
Balliard Creek—stream PA-2
Ballibay Cem—cemetery PA-2
Ballibay Sch (historical)—school PA-2
Balli Cem—cemetery TX-5
**Ballico**—pop pl CA-9
Balliet—locale PA-2
Balliet Run—stream PA-2
Balliets Furnace PA-2
Ballietsville PA-2
**Balliettsville**—pop pl PA-2
**Ballina**—pop pl NY-2
**Ballinger**—pop pl TX-5
Ballinger, Lake—lake WA-9
Ballinger, Richard A., House—hist pl WA-9
Ballinger Branch—stream AR-4
Ballinger Canyon—valley CA-9
Ballinger Canyon Wash—stream CA-9
Ballinger Carnegie Library—hist pl TX-5
Ballinger (CCD)—cens area TX-5
Ballinger Cem—cemetery AL-4
Ballinger Cem—cemetery TN-4
Ballinger City Lake—reservoir TX-5
Ballinger Creek—stream ID-8
Ballinger Creek—stream IA-7
Ballinger Creek—stream NJ-2
Ballinger Creek—stream (2) VA-3
Ballinger Draw—valley CO-8
Ballinger Flat—flat ID-8
Ballinger Lake—lake WA-9
Ballinger Point—cliff ID-8
Ballinger Ranch—locale TX-5
Ballinger Rsvr—reservoir CO-8
Ballinger Run—stream OH-6
Ballinger Sch—school TX-5
Ballinger Sch—school WA-9
Ballingers Lake—reservoir NJ-2
Ballingers Mill—locale NJ-2
Ballingers Mill Pond Dam—dam NJ-2
Ballinger Valley—basin NE-7
Ballingo Ranch—locale NM-5
Ballington Pond—reservoir SC-3
Balliots Furnace PA-2
Balliotsville PA-2
Ballis Beach—beach RI-1
Ball Island—island LA-4
Ball Island—island NC-3
Ball Island—island SC-3
Ball Island—island VT-1
Ball Island—island WY-8
Ballistics Missile Defense Advanced Technical Ctr.—other AL-4
Balliston Point—cape MD-2
Ballit Mine—mine AZ-5
Ballixburg Spring—spring CO-8
Ball JHS—school CA-9
Ball Jim Branch—stream KY-4
Ball Knob—summit AL-4
Ball Knob—summit IN-6
Ball Knob—summit (2) KY-4
Ball Knob—summit OH-6
Ball Knob—summit WV-2
Ball Knob Cem—cemetery TX-5
Ball Knob Hill—summit TX-5
Ball Kuehn Oil Field—oilfield TX-5
Ball Lake—lake AR-4
Ball Lake—lake CO-8
Ball Lake—lake IN-6
Ball Lake—lake MI-6
Ball Lake—lake PA-2
Ball Lake—lake SC-3
Ball Lake Dam—dam MS-4
Ball Lakes—lake ID-8
Ballman Sch—school AR-4
Ball Meadow—flat CA-9
Ball Memorial Hosp—hospital IN-6
Ball Mill Bridge—other MO-7
Ball Mill Creek CA-9
Ball Mill Creek—stream GA-3
Ball Mill Creek—stream MS-4
Ball Mill Resurgence—spring MO-7
Ball Mine—mine CA-9
Ball Mountain ID-8
Ball Mountain Brook—stream VT-1
Ball Mtn CA-9
Ball Mtn—summit (5) CA-9
Ball Mtn—summit CO-8
Ball Mtn—summit (2) GA-3
Ball Mtn—summit (2) MA-1
Ball Mtn—summit NC-3
Ball Mtn—summit OR-9
Ball Mtn—summit TX-5
Ball Mtn—summit VT-1
Ball Mtn—summit VA-3
Ball Neck—cape VA-3
Ballo, Loma del—summit TX-5
Ballock—locale NH-1
Ballona—civil CA-9
Ballona Creek—stream CA-9
Ballona Lagoon—lake CA-9
Ballon Creek—stream WA-9
Ballon Lake—lake MN-6
Balloon Cabin Spring—spring AZ-5
Balloon Dome—summit CA-9
Balloon Hill—summit (2) NV-8
Balloon Lake—lake SC-3
Balloon Ridge—ridge CA-9
Balloon Rock—pillar WA-9
Balloon Spring—spring CA-9
Ballou—locale CA-9
Ballou—locale IL-6
Ballou—locale OH-6
Ballou—locale WI-6
Ballou Branch—stream OK-5
Ballou Brook CT-1
Ballou Brook MA-1
Ballou Cem—cemetery (2) NY-2
Ballou Ch—church OK-5
Ballou Creek—stream GA-3
Ballou Creek—stream NY-2
Ballou Creek—stream WI-6
Ballou Dam MA-1
Ballou House—hist pl RI-1
Ballou HS—school DC-2
Ballou-Newbegin House—hist pl NH-1
Ballou Park—park VA-3
Ballou Park Shop Ctr—locale VA-3
Ballou Ranch—locale WY-8
Balloursa Sch—school NE-7
Ballous Creek—stream VA-3
**Ballouville**—pop pl CT-1
Ballou & Wright Company Bldg—hist pl OR-9
Ballow—locale WA-9
Ballowe Cem—cemetery LA-4
Ballowe Ch—church IL-6
Ballowe Creek—stream VA-3
Ballo Windmill—locale TX-5
Ball Park—park MA-1
Ball Park Ch—church AL-4
Ball Place—locale MT-8
Ball Play TN-4
**Ballplay**—pop pl AL-4
**Ball Play**—pop pl TN-4
**Ballplay**—pop pl TN-4
Ball Play Bank Mine—mine TN-4
Ballplay Bend—bend AL-4
Ballplay Ch TN-4
Ball Play Ch—church TN-4
Ballplay Creek—stream (3) AL-4
Ballplay Creek—stream GA-3
Ballplay Creek—stream TN-4
Ball Play Creek—stream TN-4
Ball Play Furnace (historical)—locale TN-4
Ball Playground—park CA-9
Ballplay P.O. (historical)—building AL-4
Ball Play Post Office TN-4
Ballplay Post Office (historical)—building TN-4
Ballplay Rec Area—park TN-4
Ballplay Sch—school TN-4
Ball Pocosin—swamp NC-3
Ball Point RI-1
Ball Point—cape AR-4
Ball Point—cape MD-2
Ball Point—cape (2) OR-9
Ball Point—cape VA-3
Ball Point—cape WI-6
Ball Point Post Office TN-4
Ball Point Trail—trail OR-9
Ball Pond—lake CT-1
Ball Pond—lake MI-6
**Ball Pond**—pop pl CT-1
Ball Pond Brook—stream CT-1
Ball Pond Hollow—valley MO-7
Ball Ranch—locale CA-9
Ball Ranch—locale MT-8
Ball Ranch—locale NM-5
Ball Ranch—locale TX-5
Ball Richard Ditch—canal IN-6
Ball Ridge—ridge PA-2
Ball Ridge—ridge VA-3
Ball Ridge Hollow—valley PA-2
**Ballroad**—pop pl CA-9
Ball Road Ch—church TN-4
Ball Road Tabernacle—church MI-6
Ball Rock—pillar NV-8
Ball Rock—summit CA-9
Ball Rock Ch—church GA-3
Ballrock Sch—school AL-4
Ball Rsvr—reservoir CO-8
Ball Rsvr No. 1—reservoir CO-8
Ball Run—stream (3) IN-6
Ball Run—stream OH-6
Ball Run—stream (2) PA-2
Balls—other CA-9
Balls Bluff AL-4
Balls Bluff—cliff LA-4
Balls Bluff—cliff MT-8
Balls Bluff—cliff WI-6
Ball's Bluff Battlefield and Natl Cemetery—hist pl VA-3
Balls Bluff Natl Cem—cemetery VA-3
Balls Branch—stream (3) KY-4
Balls Branch—stream MS-4
Balls Branch—stream (4) NE-7
Balls Branch—stream VA-3
Balls Branch—stream WV-2
Balls Branch—swamp GA-3
Balls Branch Sch—school KY-4
Balls Camp (Site)—locale CA-9
Balls Canyon—valley (2) CA-9
Ball Sch—school IL-6
Ball Sch—school (2) KY-4
Ball Sch—school LA-4
Ball Sch—school ME-1
Ball Sch—school MA-1
Ball Sch—school OR-9
Ball Sch—school TX-5
Ball Sch—school WI-6
Ball School IN-6
Ball School (historical)—locale MO-7
Balls Cliff—cliff KY-4
Balls Cove—bay RI-1
Balls Creek KS-7
Balls Creek—bay MD-2
Balls Creek—stream NC-3
Balls Creek—stream OR-9
Balls Creek—stream PA-2
Balls Creek—stream (2) VA-3
Balls Creek Campground—locale NC-3
Balls Creek Sch—school NC-3
**Balls Crossing**—pop pl MT-8
Balls Cross Roads VA-3
Balls Eddy—locale PA-2
Ball-Sellers House—hist pl VA-3
Balls Ferry—locale CA-9
Balls Ferry Bridge—bridge GA-3
Balls Ferry (CCD)—cens area GA-3
Balls Ford—locale VA-3
Balls Fork—stream KY-4
Balls Fork—stream VA-3
Balls Fork Ch—church KY-4
Balls Gap—locale WV-2
**Balls Gap (Ball Gap)**—pop pl WV-2
Balls Gap Sch—school WV-2
Ball Shanty Cove—valley TN-4
Balls Hill MA-1
Balls Hill—locale VA-3
Balls Hill—summit KY-4
Balls Hill—summit MA-1
Balls Hill—summit NH-1
**Balls Hills**—pop pl VA-3
Balls Hollow—valley AL-4
Balls Island—island NY-2
Balls Knob—summit WV-2
Balls Lake—flat OR-9
Balls Lake (historical)—lake IA-7
Balls Landing KY-4
Balls Landing—other KY-4
Balls Mill—locale VA-3
Balls Mill Creek—stream MS-4
Balls Millpond—reservoir VA-3
**Balls Mills**—pop pl PA-2
Balls Mtn—summit AL-4
Balls North Point—cape RI-1
Balls Point (2) RI-1
Balls Point—cape MD-2
Balls Point—cape VA-3
Balls Pond—reservoir VA-3
Ball Spring—spring (2) AR-4
Ball Spring—spring MO-7
Ball Spring—spring TN-4
Ball Square—park MA-1
Balls Ranch—locale CA-9
Balls Road—locale MD-2
Balls Run PA-2
Balls Store (historical)—locale TN-4
**Ballstaedt Estates Subdivision**—pop pl UT-8
Ball State Univ—school IN-6
Balls Temple African Methodist Episcopal Ch—church MS-4
Ballston MS-4
Ballston NY-2
**Ballston**—pop pl OR-9
**Ballston**—pop pl VA-3
Ballston Beach—beach MA-1
**Ballston Center**—pop pl NY-2
Ballston Lake—lake NY-2
**Ballston Lake**—pop pl NY-2
**Ballston Spa**—pop pl NY-2
Ballston Spa Rsvr—reservoir NY-2
**Ballston (Town of)**—pop pl NY-2
**Ballstown**—pop pl IN-6
**Ballsville**—pop pl VA-3
Ball Swamp—swamp MA-1
Ball Tank—reservoir AZ-5
Ball Tavern Cem—cemetery WI-6
Ball Town PA-2
Ball Town SC-3
Balltown—locale CO-8
Balltown—locale PA-2
**Balltown**—pop pl IA-7
**Balltown**—pop pl (2) KY-4
**Balltown**—pop pl NY-2
**Balltown**—pop pl SC-3
**Balltown**—pop pl TN-4
Balltown Branch—stream VA-3
Balltown Cem—cemetery MO-7
Balltown Ridge—summit IA-7
Ball (Township of)—fmr MCD AR-4
**Ball (Township of)**—pop pl IL-6
Balluco, Arroyo—valley TX-5
Balluff (historical)—locale IA-7
Ballview Cem—cemetery LA-4
**Ballville**—pop pl OH-6
Ballville (historical)—locale MA-1
**Ballville (Township of)**—pop pl OH-6
Ballwall Brook—stream CT-1
Ball-Waterman House—hist pl IA-7
**Ballwin**—pop pl MO-7
Ballwin Plaza Danny Boy—locale MO-7
**Ballwood (historical)**—pop pl OR-9
**Bally**—pop pl PA-2
Bally—summit CA-9
Bally Blacksmith Shop—hist pl MN-6
Bally Borough—civil PA-2
Ballybridge Creek NJ-2
Bally Buck Canyon—valley UT-8
Bally Camp—locale OR-9
Bally Canyon—valley OR-9
Bally Claugh IA-7
**Ballyclough**—pop pl IA-7
Bally Creek MN-6
Bally Creek—stream MN-6
Ballyhac Cove—bay ME-1
Ballyhack, The—cliff CT-1
Ballyhack Creek—stream NY-2
Ballyhoo Lake—lake MN-6
Bally Knolls—summit NV-8
**Ballylynn Shores**—pop pl VA-3
Ballymahack Brook—stream CT-1
Ballymere—airport NJ-2
Bally Mountain UT-8
Bally Mountain Spring—spring OR-9
Bally Mtn—summit CA-9
Bally Mtn—summit ID-8
Bally Mtn—summit OK-5
Bally Mtn—summit OR-9
Bally Mtns—range ID-8
Bally Mtns—range UT-8
Bally Peak—summit CA-9
Ballys Hole—basin ID-8
Dally Watts Creek—stream UT-8
Ballywick Airp—airport PA-2
Balm—locale FL-3
Balm—locale TX-5
**Balm**—pop pl NC-3
Balman Rsvr—reservoir CO-8
**Balmat**—pop pl NY-2
Balm Canyon—valley OR-9
Balm Creek—stream (4) OR-9
Balm Creek Dam—dam OR-9
Balm Creek Gilead Creek CO-8
Balm Creek Rsvr—reservoir OR-9
Balm Creek Shaft—mine OR-9
Balmer Ditch—canal MT-8
Balmer Ranch—locale MT-8
Balmers Canyon—valley WA-9
Balmer Sch—school MA-1
Balm Fork OR-9
Balm Fork—stream OR-9
Balm Fork Sch—school OR-9
Balm Grove—locale OR-9
Balm Grove Ch—church NC-3
**Balm (historical)**—pop pl OR-9
Balm Hollow—valley OR-9
Balm Lake—lake MN-6
Balm Mtn—summit OR-9
Balm of Gilead Brook—stream ME-1
Balm of Gilead Brook—stream NY-2
Balm of Gilead Canyon—valley NV-8
Balm of Gilead Ch—church AL-4
Balm of Gilead Ch—church VA-3
Balm of Gilead Creek—stream CA-9
Balm of Gilead Creek—stream CO-8
Balm of Gilead Creek—stream MT-8
Balm of Gilead Creek—stream WY-8
Balm of Gilead Mtn—summit NY-2
Balm of Gilead Point—cape VT-1
Balm of Gilead Spring—spring NV-8
Balm of Gilead Spring—spring WY-8
Balm of Gilead Swamp—swamp RI-1
Balmont—locale MT-8
**Balmoral**—pop pl LA-4
**Balmoral**—pop pl MN-6
**Balmoral**—pop pl TN-4
Balmoral Farm Pond—lake CT-1
Balmoral (historical)—locale SD-7
**Balmorhea**—pop pl TX-5
Balmorhea (CCD)—cens area TX-5
Balmorhea Cem—cemetery TX-5
Balmorhea Lake—reservoir TX-5
Balmorhea State Park—park TX-5
Balmorhia TX-5
Balm Tank—reservoir NM-5
**Balmville**—pop pl NY-2
Balmy Lake—lake MN-6
Balneario de Arroyo—beach PR-3
Balneario de Cana Gorda—beach PR-3
**Balneario de Cana Gorda**—pop pl PR-3
Balneario Isla Verde—beach PR-3
Balneario Luquillo—beach PR-3
Balneario Publico de Humacao—beach PR-3
Balon, Lake de—lake WA-9
Baloney Cave—cave TN-4
Baloon Cabin Spring AZ-5
Baloun Creek—stream SD-7
Baloun Lake—lake SD-7
Balsac Basin—basin NV-8
Balsam—locale MI-6
Balsam—locale MN-6
Balsam—locale PA-2
**Balsam**—pop pl NC-3
Balsam Basin—basin UT-8
Balsam Bench—bench UT-8
Balsam Branch—stream WI-6
Balsam Branch State Wildlife Area—park WI-6
Balsam Brook—stream (4) NY-2
Balsam Campground—locale UT-8
Balsam Canyon—valley NV-8
Balsam Cap—summit NY-2
Balsam Cem—cemetery MN-6
Balsam Ch—church WI-6
Balsam Chapel—church MN-6
Balsam Cone NC-3
Balsam Cone—summit NC-3
Balsam Corner—summit NC-3
Balsam Corner Creek—stream NC-3
Balsam Creek—stream CA-9
Balsam Creek—stream (2) MN-6
Balsam Creek—stream MT-8
Balsam Creek—stream (2) NY-2
Balsam Creek—stream UT-8
Balsam Creek—stream WI-6
Balsam Draw—valley (2) WY-8
**Balsam Estates (subdivision)**—pop pl TN-4
Balsam Flat—flat CA-9
Balsam Flats—flat NY-2
Balsam Gap—gap (2) NC-3
Balsam Glade Picnic Area—locale NM-5
**Balsam Grove**—pop pl NC-3
Balsam Grove Ch—church NC-3
Balsam Grove Ridge—ridge UT-8
Balsam High Top—summit NC-3
Balsam Hollow—valley ID-8
Balsam Hollow—valley (3) UT-8
Balsam Lake—lake CO-8
Balsam Lake—lake FL-3
Balsam Lake—lake (3) MN-6
Balsam Lake—lake (3) NY-2
Balsam Lake—lake (5) WI-6
**Balsam Lake**—pop pl WI-6
Balsam Lake Cem—cemetery WI-6
Balsam Lake Chapel—church MN-6
Balsam Lake Mtn—summit NY-2
Balsam Lake Sch—school MN-6
**Balsam Lake (Town of)**—pop pl WI-6
Balsamlund Ch—church MN-6
Balsam Mountain Campground—locale NC-3
Balsam Mountain Inn—hist pl NC-3
Balsam Mountains NC-3
Balsam Mtn—summit (2) NY-2
Balsam Mtn—summit NC-3
Balsam Mtn—summit VA-3
Balsam Picnic Area—locale UT-8
Balsam Point—summit TN-4
Balsam Pond—lake (2) NY-2
Balsam Pond—lake WI-6
Balsam Pond—reservoir PA-2
Balsam Ranch—locale MT-8
Balsam Ridge—ridge (2) NC-3
Balsam River WI-6
Balsam Root Rsvr—reservoir WY-8
Balsam Round Top NY-2
Balsam Spring—spring (2) ID-8
Balsam Spring—spring MT-8
Balsam Spring—spring NV-8
Balsam Spring—spring UT-8
Balsam Swamp—swamp NY-2
Balsam Swamp—swamp (3) PA-2
**Balsam (Township of)**—pop pl (2) MN-6
Balsbaugh Ch—church PA-2
Balser Ranch—locale CO-8
Balsh Windmill—locale NM-5
**Balsinger**—pop pl PA-2
Balsinger Creek—stream MT-8
Balsinger Prairie—flat OR-9
Balsley Cem—cemetery IN-6
Balsome Point TN-4
Balsom Gap NC-3
Balson Point—cape NJ-2
Balsora—locale TX-5
Balsora Cem—cemetery NE-7
Bals Sch (abandoned)—school MO-7
Balster Brook—stream MA-1
Balster Sch—school SD-7
Balsters Creek MI-6
Bals-Wocher House—hist pl IN-6
Balsz House—hist pl AZ-5
Balsz Sch—school AZ-5
Balta—locale KS-7
**Balta**—pop pl ND-7
**Balta**—pop pl TN-4
Balta Dam—dam ND-7
Balta Post Office (historical)—building TN-4
**Balta Township**—pop pl ND-7
Baltazar Tank—reservoir TX-5
Baltazor Hot Spring—spring NV-8
Balter Creek—stream OR-9
Balthrop Branch—stream TN-4
Balthrop Cem—cemetery (2) TN-4
Balthrop Hollow—valley TN-4
Baltic—locale AL-4
**Baltic**—pop pl CT-1
**Baltic**—pop pl MI-6
**Baltic**—pop pl NC-3
**Baltic**—pop pl OH-6
**Baltic**—pop pl SD-7
Baltic Canyon—valley ID-8
Baltic Ch—church OH-6
Baltic Creek—stream (2) CA-9
Baltic Gulch—valley WY-8
Baltic Hist Dist—hist pl CT-1
Baltic Lake—lake MN-6
Baltic Mine—mine CA-9
Baltic Peak—summit CA-9
Baltic Ridge—ridge CA-9
Baltic Rsvr—reservoir CT-1
Baltimore AL-4
Baltimore KS-7
Baltimore ND-7
Baltimore—locale CO-8
Baltimore—locale KY-4
Baltimore—locale TN-4
**Baltimore**—pop pl MD-2
**Baltimore**—pop pl MI-6
**Baltimore**—pop pl NY-2
**Baltimore**—pop pl NC-3
**Baltimore**—pop pl OH-6
**Baltimore**—pop pl VT-1
Baltimore—uninc pl GA-3
Baltimore Acad of Visitation—school MD-2
Baltimore and Ohio and Related Industries Hist Dist—hist pl WV-2
Baltimore and Ohio RR Depot—hist pl WV-2
Baltimore and Ohio RR Freight Station—locale DC-2
Baltimore and Ohio RR Station, Oakland—hist pl MD-2
Baltimore and Ohio RR Terminal—building PA-2
Baltimore and Ohio Transportation Museum and Mount Clare Station—hist pl MD-2
Baltimore Approach Channel VA-3
Baltimore Ave Sch—school VA-3
Baltimore Bay—bay MI-6
Baltimore Block—hist pl GA-3
Baltimore Branch—stream NC-3
Baltimore Branch—stream TN-4
Baltimore Canyon—valley CA-9
Baltimore Cem—cemetery IL-6
Baltimore Cem—cemetery IN-6
Baltimore Cem—cemetery MD-2
Baltimore Ch—church KY-4
Baltimore Ch—church (3) NC-3
Baltimore Channel VA-3
Baltimore Channel—channel MI-6
Baltimore City Coll—school MD-2
Baltimore City College—hist pl MD-2
Baltimore City Hall—hist pl MD-2
Baltimore City Hospitals—hospital MD-2
Baltimore College of Dental Surgery—hist pl MD-2
Baltimore Corner—locale MD-2
Baltimore Corner—locale VA-3
Baltimore Country Club—other MD-2
**Baltimore (County)**—pop pl MD-2
Baltimore County Courthouse—hist pl MD-2
Baltimore Creek—stream MO-7
Baltimore Creek—stream OR-9
Baltimore Ditch—canal OR-9
Baltimore Equitable Society—hist pl MD-2
Baltimore Ferry (historical)—locale AL-4
Baltimore Ford—locale AL-4
Baltimore General Dispensary—hist pl MD-2
Baltimore Glacier—glacier AK-9
Baltimore Gulch—valley UT-8
Baltimore Hebrew Cem—cemetery MD-2
Baltimore Hebrew Congregation Synagogue—hist pl MD-2
**Baltimore Highlands**—pop pl MD-2
Baltimore Highway—channel MI-6
Baltimore Hill—locale AL-4
Baltimore Hill—summit NH-1
Baltimore (historical)*—locale KS-7
Baltimore (historical)—locale SD-7
**Baltimore (historical)**—pop pl IA-7
Baltimore Hundred—civil DE-2
Baltimore Island—island MO-7
Baltimore Lake—lake CA-9
Baltimore Landing—locale NC-3
Baltimore Lighthouse—locale MD-2
Baltimore Mill—locale NV-8
Baltimore Mine—mine CA-9
Baltimore Mine—mine CO-8
Baltimore Mine (historical)—mine SD-7
Baltimore Museum of Art—building MD-2
Baltimore Natl Cem—cemetery MD-2
Baltimore & Ohio RR Terminal—hist pl OH-6
Baltimore Park—park AL-4
**Baltimore Park**—pop pl CA-9
Baltimore Pike Cem—cemetery OH-6
Baltimore Ravine—valley CA-9
Baltimore Ridge—ridge CO-8
Baltimore River—stream MI-6
Baltimore Rock—island OR-9
Baltimore Run WV-2
Baltimore Run—stream WV-2
Baltimore Sch—school AL-4
Baltimore Sch—school IL-6
Baltimore Sch—school LA-4
Baltimore Shaft—mine NV-8
Baltimore Ship Channel VA-3
Baltimore Spring—spring AZ-5
Baltimore Town—locale CA-9
**Baltimore (Town of)**—pop pl VT-1
Baltimore Township—fmr MCD IA-7
**Baltimore (Township of)**—pop pl MI-6
Baltimore-Washington Int. Airp—airport MD-2
Baltimore Yacht Club—other MD-2
Balto Creek—stream AK-9
Balton Crossing VA-3
Baltusrol—locale NJ-2
Baltusrol Golf Course—other NJ-2
Baltusrol Station—locale NJ-2
Balty—locale VA-3
Baltzar Peak—summit NM-5
Baltz Cem—cemetery IL-6
Baltzell—locale AL-4
Baltzell Cem—cemetery VA-3
Baltzell Mountains—summit AL-4
**Baltzer**—pop pl MS-4
Baltzer Post Office (historical)—building MS-4

Baltzley Valley—*valley* ... OH-6
Baltzly Spring—*spring* ... SD-7
Baluarte, Arroyo—*stream* ... TX-5
*Baluarte Creek* ... TX-5
Baluarte Ranch—*locale* ... TX-5
Balucta Creek—*stream* ... MS-4
Balucta (historical)—*locale* ... MS-4
*Balukai Mesa* ... AZ-5
*Balukai Point* ... AZ-5
*Balukai Wash* ... AZ-5
Balup Cem—*cemetery* ... MS-4
Balus Creek—*stream* ... GA-3
Balus Creek Access Point—*locale* ... GA-3
*Baluxy Creek* ... TX-5
Balwearie—*hist pl* ... SC-3
Balyeat Cem—*cemetery* ... OH-6
Balyeat Ditch—*canal* ... OH-6
*Balyss Creek* ... MS-4
Balzac—*locale* ... CO-8
Balzac Gulch—*valley* ... CO-8
**Bama**—*pop pl* ... AL-4
**Bama**—*pop pl* ... KY-4
**Bama Dale (subdivision)**—*pop pl* ... AL-4
Bama Mall Shop Ctr—*locale* ... AL-4
**Bama Park**—*pop pl* ... AL-4
Bama Rock Garden—*locale* ... AL-4
Bama Theatre-City Hall Bldg—*hist pl* ... AL-4
*Bamber* ... NJ-2
Bamber—*other* ... NJ-2
Bamber Cem—*cemetery* ... OH-6
Bamber Creek—*stream* ... MI-6
Bamber Creek—*stream* ... WA-9
**Bamberg**—*pop pl* ... SC-3
Bamberg, Gen. Francis Marion, House—*hist pl* ... SC-3
Bamberg (CCD)—*cens area* ... SC-3
**Bamberg (County)**—*pop pl* ... SC-3
Bamberg County Memory Gardens—*cemetery* ... SC-3
Bamberg Ehrhardt HS—*school* ... SC-3
Bamberger, Simon, House—*hist pl* ... UT-8
**Bamberger Addition Subdivision**—*pop pl* ... UT-8
Bamberger Hill—*summit* ... UT-8
Bamberger Monmt—*park* ... UT-8
Bamberg Hist Dist—*hist pl* ... SC-3
Bamber Lake—*lake* ... MN-6
**Bamber Lake**—*pop pl* ... NJ-2
Bamber Lake—*reservoir* ... NJ-2
Bamber Lake Dam—*dam* ... NJ-2
Bamber Mtn—*summit* ... WA-9
**Bamberry Estates**—*pop pl* ... NJ-2
Bamber Valley Sch—*school* ... MN-6
Bambi Lake—*lake* ... MI-6
Bambi Lake—*lake* ... WI-6
Bamblett Cem—*cemetery* ... IL-6
Bamboo—*locale* ... FL-3
Bamboo—*locale* ... NC-3
**Bamboo**—*pop pl* ... WV-2
Bamboo Banks—*bar* (2) ... FL-3
Bamboo Branch—*stream* ... NC-3
Bamboo Cave—*cave* ... AL-4
Bamboo Creek—*stream* ... TN-4
Bamboo Gulch—*valley* ... OR-9
*Bamboo Island* ... FM-9
Bamboo Island—*island* ... VA-3
Bamboo Key—*island* ... FL-3
Bamboo Mound—*summit* ... FL-3
Bam Boo Ranch—*locale* ... AZ-5
*Bamboo Road* ... MH-9
Bamboos, The—*locale* ... FL-3
Bamboo Strand—*swamp* ... FL-3
*Bambo Wash* ... AZ-5
*Bam Bridge* ... AL-4
Bambrough Canal—*canal* ... UT-8
Bamburg—*locale* ... GA-3
Bamdoroshni Island—*island* ... AK-9
*Bamesberger Lake* ... TX-5
Bamfield Creek—*stream* ... MI-6
*Bamfield Dam Pond* ... MI-6
*Bamfield Pond* ... MI-6
Bamford—*locale* ... AL-4
**Bamford**—*pop pl* ... PA-2
Bamford Slope Mine (underground)—*mine* ... AL-4
Bamfords Ridge—*ridge* ... ME-1
Bamfords Ridge—*summit* ... ME-1
*Bamfordville* ... PA-2
Bamforth Lake—*lake* ... WY-8
*Bamforth Lakes* ... WY-8
Bamforth Natl Wildlife Ref—*park* ... WY-8
**Bammel**—*pop pl* ... TX-5
Bammer Lake—*lake* ... MI-6
*Bamonemanganook Lake* ... ME-1
Bams Butte—*summit* ... SD-7
Banadad Creek—*stream* ... MN-6
Banadad Lake—*lake* ... MN-6
Banada Ridge—*ridge* ... CA-9
*Banadel* ... MH-9
*Banadero* ... MH-9
*Banadero Cliffs* ... MH-9
Banaderu—*cape* ... MH-9
Banaderu, Laderan—*cliff* ... MH-9
Banai Faith—*church* ... FL-3
**Banalsburg (historical)**—*pop pl* ... NC-3
Banan, Bayou—*gut* ... LA-4
Banana Branch—*stream* ... FL-3
Banana Branch Bridge—*bridge* ... FL-3
Banana Canyon—*valley* ... CO-8
*Banana Cave* ... AL-4
Banana Creek—*stream* (2) ... FL-3
*Banana Gulch* ... ID-8
Banana Gulch—*valley* ... ID-8
Banana Hill—*summit* ... MS-4
Banana Island—*island* ... FL-3
**Banana Junction**—*pop pl* ... TX-5
Banana Lake—*lake* (2) ... FL-3
Banana Lake—*lake* ... MI-6
Banana Lake—*lake* ... MN-6
Banana Lake—*lake* ... MT-8
Banana Mtn—*summit* ... CO-8
Banana Point—*cape* ... VI-3
Banana Pond—*lake* ... NV-8
Banana Ridge—*ridge* ... NM-5
Banana Ridge Wash—*stream* ... NM-5
Banana River—*gut* ... FL-3
Banana River—*lake* ... FL-3
Banana River Aquatic Preserve—*park* ... FL-3
Banana Spring—*spring* ... AZ-5
*Banard* ... NJ-2
**Banard Town**—*pop pl* ... PA-2
**Banat**—*pop pl* ... MI-6
*Banberia Point* ... TX-5
Banberry Golf and Country Club—*locale* ... TN-4
Banbury Natatorium—*other* ... ID-8
Banbury Springs—*spring* ... ID-8
Bancas Point—*cape* ... AK-9
Bancert Cem—*cemetery* ... MO-7
Banchero Rock—*summit* ... CA-9
Bancker—*locale* ... LA-4
Bancker Canal—*canal* ... LA-4
Bancker Cem—*cemetery* ... LA-4
Banco—*locale* ... VA-3
Banco—*locale* ... WV-2
Banco Aragon—*area* ... NM-5
Banco Bonito—*bench* ... NM-5
Banco Bonito Campground—*locale* ... NM-5
Banco Credito y Ahorro Ponceno—*hist pl* ... PR-3
Banco de la Casa—*summit* ... NM-5
Banco del Encierro—*other* ... NM-5
Banco de Ponce—*hist pl* ... PR-3
Banco Isidro—*other* ... NM-5
Banco Julian—*summit* ... NM-5
Banco Largo—*ridge* ... NM-5
Banco Lona—*summit* ... NM-5
Banco Redondo—*area* ... NM-5
Banco Ridge—*ridge* (2) ... AZ-5
Bancos Cow Camp—*locale* ... CO-8
Bancos Lake—*reservoir* ... NM-5
Bancos Mesa—*summit* ... NM-5
Bancroft—*locale* ... GA-3
Bancroft—*locale* ... KY-4
Bancroft—*locale* ... MN-6
Bancroft—*locale* ... MO-7
Bancroft—*locale* ... OR-9
**Bancroft**—*pop pl* ... CA-9
**Bancroft**—*pop pl* ... ID-8
**Bancroft**—*pop pl* ... IA-7
**Bancroft**—*pop pl* ... KS-7
**Bancroft**—*pop pl* ... KY-4
**Bancroft**—*pop pl* ... LA-4
**Bancroft**—*pop pl* ... ME-1
**Bancroft**—*pop pl* ... MA-1
**Bancroft**—*pop pl* ... MI-6
**Bancroft**—*pop pl* ... NE-7
**Bancroft**—*pop pl* ... SD-7
**Bancroft**—*pop pl* ... TX-5
**Bancroft**—*pop pl* ... WV-2
**Bancroft**—*pop pl* ... WI-6
Bancroft, A. A., House—*hist pl* ... OH-6
Bancroft, Hubert H., Ranchhouse—*hist pl* ... CA-9
Bancroft, Joseph, House—*hist pl* ... MA-1
Bancroft, Lake—*lake* ... MI-6
Bancroft, Mount—*summit* ... CO-8
Bancroft, Samuel, House—*hist pl* ... MA-1
Bancroft, Timothy, House—*hist pl* ... NH-1
Bancroft, Wendell, House—*hist pl* ... MA-1
Bancroft and Sons Cotton Mills—*hist pl* ... DE-2
Bancroft Brook—*stream* ... CT-1
Bancroft Brook—*stream* ... MA-1
Bancroft Canal—*canal* ... LA-4
Bancroft Cem—*cemetery* ... NE-7
Bancroft Cem—*cemetery* ... TN-4
Bancroft Ch—*church* ... TN-4
Bancroft Chapel—*church* ... TN-4
Bancroft Creek—*stream* ... MI-6
Bancroft Creek—*stream* ... MN-6
Bancroft Elem Sch—*school* ... DE-2
Bancroft Elem Sch—*school* ... PA-2
Bancroft Hill—*summit* ... AR-4
Bancroft Hills Sch—*school* ... OH-6
Bancroft Hotel—*hist pl* ... MA-1
*Bancroft JHS* ... DE-2
Bancroft JHS—*school* (3) ... CA-9
Bancroft Lake (historical)—*lake* ... IA-7
Bancroft Landing—*locale* ... MA-1
BANCROFT (motor vessel)—*hist pl* ... MD-2
Bancroft Noles Drain—*stream* ... MI-6
Bancroft Oil Field—*oilfield* ... LA-4
Bancroft Park—*park* ... MI-6
**Bancroft Point**—*pop pl* ... CA-9
Bancroft Pond—*lake* ... VT-1
Bancroft Ranch—*locale* ... CO-8
Bancroft Ranch House—*building* ... CA-9
Bancroft Reservoir—*lake* ... NH-1
*Bancroft River* ... MN-6
Bancroft Sch—*school* (2) ... CA-9
Bancroft Sch—*school* ... CO-8
Bancroft Sch—*school* ... DC-2
Bancroft Sch—*school* (2) ... IA-7
Bancroft Sch—*school* (2) ... MA-1
Bancroft Sch—*school* ... MN-6
Bancroft Sch—*school* ... MO-7
Bancroft Sch—*school* ... NE-7
Bancroft Sch—*school* ... NJ-2
Bancroft Sch—*school* ... OH-6
Bancroft Sch—*school* ... SD-7
Bancroft Sch—*school* ... TX-5
Bancroft Sch—*school* ... WA-9
Bancroft Spring—*spring* ... UT-8
Bancroft Springs—*spring* ... ID-8
Bancroft Tabernacle—*church* ... TN-4
Bancroft Tower—*hist pl* ... MA-1
**Bancroft (Town of)**—*pop pl* ... ME-1
**Bancroft Township**—*pop pl* ... NE-7
**Bancroft (Township of)**—*pop pl* ... MN-6
Bancshares Helistop—*airport* ... NJ-2
B and A Lake—*lake* ... IL-6
Bandana—*locale* ... NC-3
Bandana—*other* ... PA-2
**Bandana**—*pop pl* ... KY-4
Bandana Lake—*lake* ... MN-6
Bandana Lake—*lake* ... WA-9
**Bandanna (Pleasant Hill)**—*pop pl* ... PA-2
Bandanna Point—*summit* ... NM-5
Bandarita Mine—*mine* ... CA-9
Bandarita Ridge—*ridge* ... CA-9
Bandarito Canyon—*valley* ... CO-8
B And B Atwood Bog Dam—*dam* ... MA-1
B and B Chemical Company—*hist pl* ... MA-1
B and B Duck Club—*other* ... CA-9
**B and B Estates (subdivision)**—*pop pl* ... UT-8
B and B Fishpond—*reservoir* ... MT-8
B and B Marina—*locale* ... TN-4
Band Box Butte—*summit* ... UT-8
*Band Box Mountain* ... MT-8
Bandbox Mtn—*summit* ... MT-8
Band Branch—*stream* ... VA-3
**B and B Subdivision**—*pop pl* ... UT-8
Band Cove—*bay* ... AK-9
B and C Spring—*spring* ... NV-8
Banddana Creek—*stream* ... AK-9
Bandeau Bay (Carolina Bay)—*swamp* ... NC-3
Bandeau Creek—*stream* ... NC-3
Banded Glacier—*glacier* ... WA-9
*Banded Mountain* ... CO-8
Banded Mtn—*summit* (2) ... AK-9
Banded Mtn—*summit* ... NV-8
Banded Peak—*summit* ... CO-8
Banded Peak Ranch—*locale* ... CO-8
Banded Pigeon Dam—*dam* ... CO-8
Banded Ridge—*ridge* ... NV-8
Bandeera—*summit* ... MH-9
*Bandeera Rock* ... MH-9
Bandeja Well—*well* ... AZ-5
Bandel Airp—*airport* ... PA-2
Bandelier CCC Hist Dist—*hist pl* ... NM-5
Bandelier Ditch—*canal* ... IN-6
Bandelier Ditch Number Two—*canal* ... IN-6
Bandelier Natl Monument—*hist pl* ... NM-5
Bandelier Sch—*school* ... NM-5
Bandel Sch—*school* ... MN-6
Bandera—*locale* ... WA-9
**Bandera**—*pop pl* ... TX-5
Bandera (CCD)—*cens area* ... TX-5
**Bandera (County)**—*pop pl* ... TX-5
Bandera County Courthouse and Jail—*hist pl* ... TX-5
Bandera Crater—*crater* ... NM-5
Bandera Creek—*stream* (2) ... TX-5
**Bandera Falls**—*pop pl* ... TX-5
Bandera Mesa—*summit* ... TX-5
Bandera Mtn—*summit* ... WA-9
Bandera Pass—*gap* ... TX-5
Bandera Shop Ctr—*locale* ... TX-5
Bandera State Airp—*airport* ... WA-9
Banderia Point—*cape* ... TX-5
Banderitas Artesian Well—*well* ... TX-5
Banderitas Creek—*stream* ... NM-5
*Banderson Sch* ... PA-2
Banderson Sch—*school* ... PA-2
*Banderu* ... MH-9
B and G—*locale* ... UT-8
**B And G**—*pop pl* ... WA-9
B And G—*post sta* ... WA-9
B and H Mine—*mine* ... MT-8
B and H Rsvr—*reservoir* ... MT-8
Bandi County Park—*park* ... WI-6
Bandido Tank—*reservoir* ... TX-5
Bandini—*locale* ... CA-9
**Bandini**—*pop pl* ... CA-9
Bandini Sch—*school* (2) ... CA-9
Bandit Pass—*gap* ... CA-9
Bandit Peak—*summit* ... CO-8
Bandit Rock—*hist pl* ... CA-9
Bandit Spring—*spring* ... OR-9
Bandits Roost Park—*park* ... NC-3
Bandit Tank—*reservoir* ... AZ-5
B And M—*post sta* ... WA-9
Bandmann Bridge—*bridge* ... MT-8
Bandmann Flats—*flat* ... MT-8
Bandman Park—*park* ... KY-4
*Bandmill* ... TN-4
**Band Mill**—*pop pl* ... AR-4
**Bandmill**—*pop pl* ... IN-6
**Band Mill**—*pop pl* ... TN-4
**Band Mill**—*pop pl* ... VA-3
Band Mill Creek—*stream* ... AR-4
Bandmill Hollow—*valley* (2) ... TN-4
Band Mill Hollow—*valley* ... VA-3
Bandmill Hollow—*valley* ... WV-2
Bandmill Junction—*locale* ... WV-2
**Band Mill Junction**—*pop pl* ... WV-2
Bandmill Post Office (historical)—*building* ... TN-4
Band Mill Spring—*spring* ... AL-4
Band M Ledge—*bench* ... NH-1
B and M Placers—*mine* ... NV-8
B And M Ranch Airp—*airport* ... WA-9
Band of Hope Ch—*church* ... WV-2
**Bandon**—*pop pl* ... IN-6
**Bandon**—*pop pl* ... OR-9
Bandon Beach—*beach* ... OR-9
Bandon (CCD)—*cens area* ... OR-9
Bandon Gun Club—*other* ... OR-9
Bandon Ocean State Wayside—*park* ... OR-9
Bandon Rsvr—*reservoir* ... OR-9
Bandon State Airp—*airport* ... OR-9
Bandon State Park—*park* ... OR-9
**Bandon (Township of)**—*pop pl* ... MN-6
Bandora Mine—*mine* ... CO-8
Bandora Springs Sch—*school* ... NC-3
B and O Terminal—*locale* ... PA-2
Band Rock—*summit* ... PA-2
Band Rock Vista—*locale* ... PA-2
*Bands Pond* ... ME-1
Band Spring—*spring* ... NV-8
Band Springs Sch (historical)—*school* ... TN-4
*Bandstand Rock* ... PA-2
B And S Trail—*trail* ... PA-2
Band Valley—*valley* ... AZ-5
Band Wheel Oil Field—*oilfield* ... OK-5
B and W Junction Station—*locale* ... PA-2
Bandy—*locale* ... VA-3
**Bandy**—*pop pl* ... KY-4
**Bandy**—*pop pl* ... NC-3
Bandy, Dr. Robert W., House—*hist pl* ... TN-4
Bandy Branch—*stream* (2) ... AR-4
Bandy Branch—*stream* ... FL-3
Bandy Branch—*stream* ... KY-4
Bandy Branch—*stream* ... WV-2
Bandy Canyon—*valley* ... CA-9
Bandy Cem—*cemetery* ... KY-4
Bandy Cem—*cemetery* ... VA-3
Bandy Cove Mtn—*summit* ... NC-3
Bandy Creek—*stream* ... AR-4
Bandy Creek—*stream* ... OK-5
Bandy Creek—*stream* ... TN-4
Bandy Creek Campground—*locale* ... TN-4
Bandy Hollow—*valley* ... OH-6
Bandy Lake—*lake* ... FL-3
Bandy Ranch—*locale* ... NV-8
Bandy Rsvr—*reservoir* ... MT-8
**Bandy's**—*pop pl* ... NC-3
Bandy Sch—*school* ... NE-7
Bandys Chapel—*church* ... TN-4
Bandys Pit—*cave* ... TN-4
Bandy's (Township of)—*fmr MCD* ... NC-3
Bandy Tank—*reservoir* ... AZ-5
**Bandytown**—*pop pl* ... WV-2
Bandy Valley—*basin* ... NE-7
Bane—*locale* ... VA-3
Bane—*locale* ... WV-2
Bane, Warren, Site—*hist pl* ... IL-6
**Baneberry**—*pop pl* ... TN-4
Bane Cem—*cemetery* ... NC-3
Bane Cem—*cemetery* ... OH-6
Bane Cem—*cemetery* ... TX-5
Bane Creek—*stream* ... AR-4
Bane Creek—*stream* ... ID-8
Bane Creek—*stream* ... PA-2
*Banegas Spring* ... AZ-5
Banegas Well—*well* ... AZ-5
Bane Hill—*summit* ... TN-4
Bane Hollow—*valley* ... AR-4
Bane Hollow—*valley* ... IN-6
Banek Number 1 Dam—*dam* ... SD-7
Baner Creek—*stream* ... ID-8
Bane Sch—*school* ... IL-6
Bane Sch—*school* ... PA-2
Bane Sch—*school* ... TX-5
Bane Sch—*school* ... VA-3
Banes Chapel—*church* ... AR-4
Banetown—*locale* ... PA-2
Baney Canyon—*valley* ... NM-5
Baney Coulee—*valley* ... MT-8
Baney Lake—*lake* (2) ... MT-8
Baney Park Canyon—*valley* ... NM-5
Baney Park Tank—*reservoir* ... NM-5
Baney Post Office (historical)—*building* ... AL-4
**Baney Settlement**—*pop pl* ... PA-2
**Banfield**—*pop pl* ... MI-6
**Banfield**—*pop pl* ... PA-2
Banfield Brook—*stream* ... NH-1
Banfield Cem—*cemetery* ... MI-6
Banfield Creek—*stream* ... NY-2
Banfield Mtn—*summit* ... AZ-5
Banfield Mtn—*summit* ... MT-8
Banfield Saddle—*gap* ... WI-6
Banfield Sch—*school* ... MI-6
Banfield Sch—*school* ... MN-6
Banfield Spring—*spring* ... AZ-5
Banfield Tank—*reservoir* ... AZ-5
Banfill Island—*island* ... MN-6
Banfill Tavern—*hist pl* ... MN-6
Banfill Turn—*locale* ... CA-9
**Bangall**—*pop pl* (2) ... NY-2
Bangall Sch—*school* ... VT-1
Bang-Bang Hill—*summit* ... NM-5
*Bang Bayou* ... MS-4
Bang Cem—*cemetery* ... SD-7
Bang Ch—*church* ... ND-7
Bang Creek—*stream* ... WY-8
Bangdoodle Branch—*stream* ... AL-4
*Banger* ... KS-7
Banger Branch—*stream* ... KY-4
Bangert—*locale* ... MO-7
**Bangert**—*pop pl* ... MO-7
**Bangerter Subdivision**—*pop pl* ... UT-8
Bangert Park—*park* ... MO-7
**Bangham**—*pop pl* ... TN-4
Bangham Ch (historical)—*church* ... TN-4
Bangham Heights Baptist Ch—*church* ... TN-4
Bangham Sch—*school* ... TN-4
**Bangham Village**—*pop pl* ... TN-4
Bangi Island—*island* ... GU-9
Bangi Point—*cape* ... GU-9
*Bang Island* ... MS-4
*Bang Lake* ... MS-4
Bang Lake—*lake* ... MN-6
Bangle Cem—*cemetery* ... IN-6
Bangle Hill—*summit* ... NY-2
Bango—*locale* ... NV-8
Bangookbit Dunes—*beach* ... AK-9
Bangookthleet Dunes—*beach* ... AK-9
*Bangor* ... KS-7
Bangor—*locale* ... KS-7
Bangor—*locale* ... KY-4
Bangor—*locale* ... VA-3
**Bangor**—*pop pl* ... AL-4
**Bangor**—*pop pl* ... CA-9
**Bangor**—*pop pl* ... IA-7
**Bangor**—*pop pl* ... ME-1
**Bangor**—*pop pl* ... MI-6
**Bangor**—*pop pl* ... NY-2
**Bangor**—*pop pl* ... PA-2
**Bangor**—*pop pl* ... VA-3
**Bangor**—*pop pl* ... WA-9
**Bangor**—*pop pl* ... WI-6
Bangor Annex Cave—*cave* ... AL-4
Bangor Borough—*civil* ... PA-2
Bangor Cave—*cave* ... AL-4
Bangor Cem—*cemetery* ... IA-7
Bangor Cem—*cemetery* ... NY-2
Bangor Cem—*cemetery* (2) ... SD-7
Bangor Center Sch—*school* ... MI-6
Bangor Central Sch—*school* ... MI-6
Bangor Children's Home—*hist pl* ... ME-1
Bangor Creek—*stream* ... AK-9
Bangor Dam Cave—*cave* ... AL-4
Bangor Ditch—*canal* ... CA-9
Bangor Edison Sch—*school* ... MI-6
Bangor Elem Sch—*school* ... PA-2
Bangor Episcopal Church—*hist pl* ... PA-2
Bangor Fire Engine House No. 6—*hist pl* ... ME-1
**Bangor Heights**—*pop pl* ... MI-6
Bangor Hill—*summit* ... ME-1
Bangor (historical)—*locale* ... SD-7
Bangor House—*hist pl* ... ME-1
Bangor International Airp—*airport* ... ME-1
Bangor JHS—*school* ... MI-6
Bangor Junior-Senior HS—*school* ... PA-2
Bangor-Lincoln Sch—*school* ... MI-6
Bangor Mental Health Institute—*hist pl* ... ME-1
Bangor Naval Submarine Base—*military* ... WA-9
Bangor North Central Sch—*school* ... MI-6
Bangor Sch—*school* ... OR-9
Bangor South Central Sch—*school* ... MI-6
Bangor Standpipe—*hist pl* ... ME-1
Bangor State Hosp—*hospital* ... ME-1
Bangor State Wildlife Mngmt Area—*park* ... MN-6
Bangor Station—*locale* ... NY-2
Bangor Station—*locale* ... WA-9
Bangor Theological Seminary Hist Dist—*hist pl* ... ME-1
**Bangor (Town of)**—*pop pl* ... NY-2
**Bangor (Town of)**—*pop pl* ... WI-6
Bangor Township—*civil* ... SD-7
Bangor Township—*fmr MCD* ... IA-7
**Bangor Township**—*pop pl* ... MI-6
**Bangor Township**—*pop pl* ... SD-7
**Bangor (Township of)**—*pop pl* (2) ... MI-6
**Bangor (Township of)**—*pop pl* ... MN-6
**Bangorville**—*pop pl* ... OH-6
**Bangs**—*pop pl* ... OH-6
**Bangs**—*pop pl* ... TX-5
Bangs, Algernon, House—*hist pl* ... ME-1
Bangs, Benjamin, House—*hist pl* ... MI-6
Bangs, Mount—*summit* ... AZ-5
Bangs Bayou—*gut* ... MS-4
**Bangs Beach**—*pop pl* ... ME-1
Bangs Block—*hist pl* ... MA-1
Bangs Bog—*swamp* ... MA-1
Bangs Brook—*stream* ... MN-6
Bangs Canyon—*valley* ... CO-8
Bangs (CCD)—*cens area* ... TX-5
*Bangs Creek* ... WI-6
*Bang's Island* ... ME-1
Bangs Island—*island* ... ME-1
Bangs Island—*island* ... MS-4
Bangs Lake—*lake* ... IL-6
Bangs Lake—*lake* ... MS-4
Bangs Landing—*locale* ... AR-4
Bangs Mtn—*summit* ... WA-9
*Bangs Pond* ... MA-1
Bangs Slough—*gut* ... AR-4
Bangs-Wineman Block—*hist pl* ... ND-7
Bang Tail Canyon—*valley* ... NM-5
Bangtail Creek—*stream* (2) ... MT-8
Bangtail Ranger Station—*locale* ... MT-8
Bangtail Trail—*trail* ... MT-8
*Banham* ... MP-9
*Ban Hill* ... MA-1
Bani Amoona Sch—*school* ... MO-7
Banian Junction—*locale* ... PA-2
Banian Run—*stream* ... PA-2
**Banida**—*pop pl* ... ID-8
Banie Canyon—*valley* ... CA-9
Ban Island—*island* ... AK-9
*Banister* ... VA-3
Banister—*locale* ... VA-3
Banister Branch—*stream* ... MO-7
Banister Cem—*cemetery* ... AL-4
Banister Cem—*cemetery* ... LA-4
Banister Ch—*church* ... VA-3
Banister Creek—*stream* ... LA-4
Banister Drain—*stream* ... MI-6
Banister Hill Ch—*church* ... VA-3
Banister Lake—*reservoir* ... VA-3
Banister (Magisterial District)—*fmr MCD* ... VA-3
Banister River—*stream* ... VA-3
Banisters Chapel—*church* ... NC-3
Banister Springs Ch—*church* ... VA-3
Banjo, The—*summit* ... NV-8
Banjo Bill Campground—*park* ... AZ-5
Banjo Branch—*stream* ... KY-4
Banjo Branch—*stream* (3) ... NC-3
Banjo Branch—*stream* ... TN-4
Banjo Canyon—*valley* ... AZ-5
Banjo Canyon—*valley* ... NM-5
Banjo Flats—*flat* ... WY-8
Banjo Lake—*lake* ... CO-8
Banjo Lake—*lake* ... FL-3
Banjo Point—*cape* ... AK-9
Banjo Ranch—*locale* ... WY-8
Banjo Spring—*spring* ... OR-9
Banjo Spring—*spring* (2) ... UT-8
Banjo Tank—*reservoir* ... AZ-5
*Bank* ... RI-1
**Bank**—*pop pl* ... NH-1
Bankard-Gunther Mansion—*hist pl* ... MD-2
Bank Bldg—*hist pl* ... MA-1
Bank Bldg—*hist pl* ... VA-3
Bank Block—*building* ... MA-1
Bank Branch—*stream* ... MO-7
Bank Branch Sch (abandoned)—*school* ... MO-7
Bank Ch—*church* ... VA-3
*Bank Channel* ... NC-3
Bank Channel—*channel* ... NC-3
*Bank Creek* ... MT-8
*Bank Creek* ... ND-7
*Bank Creek* ... OR-9
Bank Creek—*stream* ... SC-3
Bank Ditch—*canal* ... DE-2
Banker Cave—*locale* ... MO-7
Banker Cem—*cemetery* ... MI-6
Banker Creek—*stream* ... WA-9
**Banker Heights**—*pop pl* ... OH-6
Banker Hollow—*valley* ... MO-7
Banker Mine—*mine* (2) ... CO-8
Banker Pass—*gap* ... WA-9
**Banker Plantation**—*pop pl* ... LA-4
Banker Pond—*lake* ... NY-2
Bankers—*locale* ... LA-4
**Bankers**—*pop pl* (2) ... MI-6
Bankers Cem—*cemetery* ... MI-6
*Bankers Harbor* ... ME-1
Banker's House—*hist pl* ... NC-3
Bankers Lake—*lake* ... MI-6
Bankers Loan and Trust Company Bldg—*hist pl* ... KS-7
Bankersmith—*locale* ... TX-5
Bankers Tunnel—*mine* ... CO-8
**Bank Harbor Retreat (subdivision)**—*pop pl* ... DE-2
Bankhead—*locale* ... AL-4
**Bankhead**—*pop pl* ... AL-4
Bankhead, James Greer, House—*hist pl* ... AL-4
Bankhead Canyon—*valley* ... UT-8
Bankhead Cem—*cemetery* (2) ... AL-4
Bankhead Cove—*bay* ... MD-2
Bankhead Creek—*stream* ... AR-4
Bankhead Creek—*stream* ... CA-9
Bankhead Dam—*facility* ... AL-4
Bankhead Draw—*valley* ... TX-5
Bankhead Farmstead Sch—*school* ... AL-4
Bankhead Highway—*hist pl* ... AZ-5
Bankhead House—*hist pl* ... AL-4
Bankhead Lake—*reservoir* ... AL-4
*Bankhead Lock and Dam* ... AL-4
Bankhead Lookout Tower—*tower* ... AL-4
*Bankhead Middle School* ... AL-4
Bankhead Mound—*summit* ... TX-5
*Bankhead Natl Forest* ... AL-4
Bankhead Point—*cape* ... MD-2
Bankhead Post Office (historical)—*building* ... AL-4
Bankhead Sch—*school* ... AL-4
Bankhead Shaft Mine (underground)—*mine* ... AL-4
Bankhead Spring—*spring* ... CA-9
**Bankhead Springs**—*pop pl* ... CA-9
Bankhead Tank—*reservoir* ... AZ-5
Bankhead Tunnel—*tunnel* ... AL-4
Bankhead Well—*well* ... UT-8
Bankhead Windmill—*locale* ... TX-5
**Bank (historical)**—*pop pl* ... TN-4
Bank Hotel—*hist pl* ... AZ-5
Bank House—*hist pl* ... DE-2
Bankier Ranch—*locale* ... TX-5
Banking Grounds—*cliff* ... AL-4
Bank Island—*island* ... OH-6
Bank Lake, The—*flat* ... WY-8
Bank Lateral—*canal* ... WY-8
Banklick—*locale* ... IL-6
Bank Lick—*locale* ... KY-4
Banklick Ch—*church* ... KY-4
Banklick Creek—*stream* ... KY-4
Banklick Creek—*stream* ... OH-6
Bankline Owens Oil Field—*oilfield* ... TX-5
Bank Mine—*mine* ... NM-5
Bank Mtn—*summit* ... NC-3
Bank of Alamo—*hist pl* ... TN-4
Bank of Alexandria—*hist pl* ... VA-3
Bank of Anniston—*hist pl* ... AL-4
Bank of Arizona Bldg—*hist pl* ... AZ-5
Bank of Balboa-Bank of America—*hist pl* ... CA-9
Bank of Bigheart—*hist pl* ... OK-5
Bank of Booneville Bldg—*hist pl* ... AR-4
Bank of Bowdle—*hist pl* ... SD-7
Bank of Burbank—*hist pl* ... OK-5
Bank of California Bldg—*hist pl* ... OR-9
Bank of Carthage—*hist pl* ... AR-4
Bank of Clarendon—*hist pl* ... AR-4
Bank of College Grove, The—*hist pl* ... TN-4
Bank of Commerce—*hist pl* ... AR-4
Bank of Commerce and Trust Company Bldg—*hist pl* ... TN-4
Bank of Dyersburg—*hist pl* ... TN-4
Bank of Echo Bldg—*hist pl* ... OR-9
Bank of Ensley—*hist pl* ... AL-4
Bank of Eureka Bldg—*hist pl* ... CA-9
Bank of Fairhope—*hist pl* ... AL-4
Bank of Florence—*hist pl* ... NE-7
Bank of Gage—*hist pl* ... OK-5
Bank of Gentry—*hist pl* ... AR-4
Bank of Glen Jean—*hist pl* ... WV-2
Bank of Grand Cane—*hist pl* ... LA-4
Bank of Hartland—*hist pl* ... WI-6
Bank of Hominy—*hist pl* ... OK-5
Bank of Hunter—*hist pl* ... OK-5
Bank of Italy—*hist pl* (4) ... CA-9
Bank of Italy Bldg—*hist pl* ... CA-9
Bank of Jersey—*hist pl* ... GA-3
Bank of Kingston—*hist pl* ... AR-4
Bank of Lafourche Bldg—*hist pl* ... LA-4
Bank of Loleta—*hist pl* ... CA-9
Bank of Long Prairie—*hist pl* ... MN-6
Bank of Los Banos Bldg—*hist pl* ... CA-9
Bank of Louisiana—*hist pl* ... LA-4
Bank of Magdalena—*hist pl* ... NM-5
Bank of Malvern—*hist pl* ... AR-4
Bank of Middletown—*hist pl* ... KY-4
Bank of Midland Bldg—*hist pl* ... SD-7
Bank of Minden—*hist pl* ... LA-4
Bank of Newark Bldg—*hist pl* ... DE-2
Bank of Nolensville—*hist pl* ... TN-4
Bank of Osceola—*hist pl* ... AR-4
Bank of Pee Dee Bldg—*hist pl* ... NC-3
Bank of Portales—*hist pl* ... NM-5
Bank of Redwood Falls Bldg—*hist pl* ... MN-6
Bank of Rogers Bldg—*hist pl* ... AR-4
Bank of Santa Cruz County—*hist pl* ... CA-9
Bank of Simpsonville—*hist pl* ... KY-4
Bank of St. Albans Bldg—*hist pl* ... WV-2
Bank of Starbuck—*hist pl* ... WA-9
Bank of Summit—*hist pl* ... MS-4
Bank of the Commonwealth—*hist pl* ... KY-4
Bank of Tracy—*hist pl* ... CA-9
Bank of Waldo—*hist pl* ... AR-4
Bank of Washburn—*hist pl* ... WI-6
Bank of Washington—*hist pl* ... MS-4
Bank of Washington, West End Branch—*hist pl* ... NC-3
Bank of Webster—*hist pl* ... LA-4
Bank of Western Carolina—*hist pl* ... SC-3
Bank of Winchester Bldg—*hist pl* ... TN-4
Bank Of Xenia—*hist pl* ... OH-6
**Bank Plaza**—*pop pl* ... NY-2
Bank Point—*cape* ... NC-3
Bank Post Office (historical)—*building* ... TN-4
Bank Ranch—*locale* ... NV-8
Bank Ranch Ditch—*canal* ... MT-8
Bank Run—*stream* ... PA-2
*Banks* ... ND-7
Banks—*locale* ... KY-4
Banks—*locale* ... ND-7
**Banks**—*pop pl* ... AL-4
**Banks**—*pop pl* ... AR-4
**Banks**—*pop pl* ... ID-8
**Banks**—*pop pl* ... IL-6
**Banks**—*pop pl* ... LA-4
**Banks**—*pop pl* ... MS-4
**Banks**—*pop pl* ... NC-3
**Banks**—*pop pl* ... OR-9
**Banks**—*pop pl* ... WA-9
Banks, Col. J. A., House—*hist pl* ... SC-3
Banks, Ralph, Place—*hist pl* ... GA-3
**Banks Acres (subdivision)**—*pop pl* ... DE-2
Bank Saloon—*hist pl* ... NV-8
**Bank Sand**—*pop pl* ... MI-6
Banks Bayou—*gut* ... TX-5
Banks-Bennett Ditch—*canal* ... DE-2
Banks Branch—*stream* ... AL-4
Banks Branch—*stream* ... GA-3
Banks Branch—*stream* (3) ... KY-4
Banks Brothers Lake—*reservoir* ... NC-3
Banks Canyon—*valley* ... CA-9
Banks Cave—*cave* ... TN-4
Banks Cem—*cemetery* (2) ... AL-4
Banks Cem—*cemetery* (3) ... AR-4
Banks Cem—*cemetery* ... DE-2
Banks Cem—*cemetery* (2) ... GA-3
Banks Cem—*cemetery* (2) ... MS-4
Banks Cem—*cemetery* ... MO-7
Banks Cem—*cemetery* ... NY-2
Banks Cem—*cemetery* ... NC-3
Banks Cem—*cemetery* (3) ... OH-6
Banks Cem—*cemetery* ... SC-3

Banks Cem—cemetery TN-4
Banks Cem—cemetery VA-3
Banks Ch—church AR-4
Banks Ch—church (3) NC-3
Banks Ch—church ND-7
Banks Ch—church TN-4
Banks Channel—channel (4) NC-3
Banks Chapel—church (2) AL-4
Banks Chapel—church GA-3
Banks Chapel Ch AL-4
Banks Church KS-7
**Banks (County)**—pop pl GA-3
Banks County Courthouse—hist pl GA-3
Banks County Jail—hist pl GA-3
Banks County Speedway—other GA-3
Banks Cove—bay ME-1
Banks Covered Bridge—hist pl PA-2
**Banks Creek**—pop pl NC-3
Banks Creek—stream AL-4
Banks Creek—stream GA-3
Banks Creek—stream ID-8
Banks Creek—stream MS-4
Banks Creek—stream NJ-2
Banks Creek—stream (2) NC-3
Banks Creek—stream OR-9
Banks Creek—stream TX-5
Banks Creek—stream WA-9
Banks Creek Ch—church GA-3
Banks Creek Ch—church NC-3
Banks Creek Church Cem—cemetery GA-3
Banks Creek Sch—school NC-3
**Banks Development (subdivision)**—pop pl DE-2
Banks Ditch—canal CA-9
Banks Ditch—canal OR-9
Banks Draw—valley MT-8
Banks Elem Sch NC-3
Banks Fork—stream KY-4
Banks Gulch—valley ID-8
Banks Hill—summit NH-1
Banks (historical)—locale KS-7
Banks Hollow—valley NY-2
Banks Hollow—valley TN-4
Banks House—hist pl AR-4
Banks HS—school AL-4
Banksia Hall—hist pl SC-3
Banks Island—island FL-3
Banks Island—island ID-8
Banks-Jackson-Commerce Hosp—hospital GA-3
Banks-Josie (CCD)—cens area AL-4
Banks-Josie Division—civil AL-4
Banks Knob—summit KY-4
Banks Lake NC-3
Banks Lake—lake FL-3
Banks Lake—lake GA-3
Banks Lake—lake LA-4
Banks Lake—lake (2) MI-6
Banks Lake—lake WA-9
Banks Lake—lake WI-6
Banks Lake—reservoir AL-4
Banks Lake—reservoir GA-3
Banks Lake—reservoir IN-6
Banks Lake—reservoir NC-3
Banks Lake—reservoir WA-9
Banks Lake Dam—dam IN-6
Banks Land and Cattle Company Pond Dam—dam MS-4
Banks Landing—locale NC-3
Banks Lookout Tower—locale AR-4
Banks (Magisterial District)—fmr MCD WV-2
Banks Mine (underground)—mine AL-4
Banks Mtn—summit (2) VA-3
Banks O'Dee—locale MD-2
Banks-Ogg House—hist pl TX-5
Bankson Lake—lake MI-6
**Banksons Lake**—pop pl MI-6
Banks Park—park AL-4
Banks Pinnacle—pillar NH-1
Banks Pond—lake (2) CT-1
Banks Post Office (historical)—building MS-4
Bank Spring—spring NV-8
Banks Ranch—locale AZ-5
Banks Ridge—ridge VA-3
Banks Rock—bar ME-1
Banks Sch AL-4
Banks Sch—school (3) AL-4
Banks Sch—school (3) GA-3
Banks Sch—school KS-7
Banks Sch—school LA-4
Banks Sch—school MA-1
Banks Sch—school NC-3
Banks Sch (historical)—school MS-4
Banks Spring—spring ID-8
Banks Spring—spring UT-8
**Banks Springs**—pop pl LA-4
Banks State Wildlife Mngmt Area—park MN-6
Banks Stop—locale TX-5
Banks Tank—reservoir (3) AZ-5
**Bankston**—pop pl AL-4
**Bankston**—pop pl IA-7
Bankston Baptist Ch—church AL-4
Bankston Cem—cemetery (5) LA-4
Bankston Cem—cemetery MS-4
Bankston Ch of Christ—church AL-4
Bankston Elementary School MS-4
Bankston Fork—stream IL-6
Bankston Fork Ch—church IL-6
Bankston (historical)—locale MS-4
Bankston JHS—school AL-4
Bankston Lake—reservoir GA-3
Bankston Pond Dam—dam MS-4
Bankston Post Office (historical)—building MS-4
Bankston Post Office (historical)—building TN-4
Bankston Sch—school AL-4
Bankston Sch—school IA-7
Bankston Sch—school MS-4
Bankston Sch (historical)—school MS-4
Bankston Spring—spring CO-8
Bankstons Spring—spring AL-4
Banks Township—fmr MCD IA-7
**Banks (Township of)**—pop pl MI-6
**Banks (Township of)**—pop pl (2) PA-2
Bank Street Hist Dist—hist pl AL-4
Bank Street Hist Dist—hist pl CT-1
Bank Street-Old Decatur Hist Dist (Boundary Increase)—hist pl AL-4
Banks Valley—valley ID-8
**Banks Villa East (subdivision)**—pop pl AL-4
**Banksville**—pop pl CT-1
**Banksville**—pop pl NY-2
**Banksville**—pop pl PA-2
**Banksville Park (subdivision)**—pop pl DE-2
Banksville Sch—school NE-7
Banks Windmill—locale NV-8
Banks Windmill—locale TX-5
Bankton Cem—cemetery MN-6
**Bank Village**—pop pl NH-1
Banky Branch—stream TX-5
Ban Lake—lake MN-6
**Bannack**—pop pl MT-8
Bannack Bench Windmill—locale MT-8
Bannack Cem—cemetery MT-8
Bannack City MT-8
Bannack Hist Dist—hist pl MT-8
Bannack Pass ID-8
Bannack Pass MT-8
Bannack Pass—gap ID-8
Bannack Pass—gap MT-8
Bannahassee River—stream FL-3
Bannamon Creek—stream IN-6
Bannan Run—stream PA-2
Bannan Swamp—swamp NY-2
Bannard Pup—stream AK-9
Banna Sch—school CA-9
**Bannas Junction**—pop pl TX-5
Banneker JHS—school DC-2
Banneker Recreation Center—hist pl DC-2
Banneker Sch—school IL-6
Banneker Sch—school KY-4
Banneker Sch—school (2) MD-2
Banneker Sch—school MO-7
Banneker Sch—school VA-3
Banneker School IN-6
Bannen—locale WV-2
Bannen Meadow Brook—stream NJ-2
Banner KS-7
Banner—locale AK-9
Banner—locale CA-9
Banner—locale KY-4
Banner—locale WA-9
Banner—locale WI-6
Banner—locale WY-8
**Banner**—pop pl AR-4
**Banner**—pop pl IL-6
**Banner**—pop pl MS-4
**Banner**—pop pl MO-7
**Banner**—pop pl OK-5
**Banner**—pop pl TN-4
**Banner**—pop pl VA-3
**Banner**—pop pl WY-8
Banner—unorg reg SD-7
Banner Baptist Ch—church MS-4
Banner Bay—bay AK-9
Banner Branch—stream NC-3
Banner Canyon AZ-5
Banner Canyon—valley CA-9
Banner Canyon—valley NM-5
Banner Canyon Windmill—locale TX-5
Banner Cem—cemetery IA-7
Banner Cem—cemetery KS-7
Banner Cem—cemetery KY-4
Banner Cem—cemetery MS-4
Banner Cem—cemetery MO-7
Banner Cem—cemetery NE-7
Banner Cem—cemetery (2) NC-3
Banner Cem—cemetery (4) OK-5
Banner Cem—cemetery TN-4
Banner Cem—cemetery (5) VA-3
Banner Ch—church (2) AR-4
Banner Ch—church ND-7
Banner Ch—church (3) OK-5
Banner Ch—church TN-4
Banner Ch—church WV-2
Banner Chapel—church NC-3
Banner City KS-7
Banner Community Center—building MS-4
Banner Compressor Station—other MS-4
Banner Creek—stream (3) AK-9
Banner Creek—stream CA-9
Banner Creek—stream (3) ID-8
Banner Creek—stream KS-7
Banner Creek—stream MI-6
Banner Creek—stream MT-8
Banner Creek Rest Area—locale ID-8
Banner Draw—valley WY-8
**Banner Elk**—pop pl NC-3
Banner Elk Creek NC-3
Banner Elk Creek TN-4
Banner Elk Elem Sch—school NC-3
Banner Elk (Township of)—fmr MCD NC-3
Banner Fork—stream KY-4
Banner Grange—locale CA-9
Banner Gulch—valley SD-7
**Banner Hill**—pop pl TN-4
Banner Hill—summit MA-1
**Banner Hill Estates Subdivision**—pop pl UT-8
Banner Hill Spring—spring TN-4
Banner (historical)—locale (2) AL-4
Banner (historical)—locale KS-7
Banner Hollow—valley WV-2
Banner Lake MN-6
Banner Lake—lake AK-9
Banner Lake—lake FL-3
Banner Lake—lake MI-6
Banner Lakes—reservoir CO-8
Banner Lookout Tower—locale MS-4
Bannerman—locale WI-6
Bannerman Cem—cemetery NC-3
Bannerman House—hist pl NC-3
Bannerman Lookout Tower—tower NC-3
Bannermans Island NY-2
Bannerman's Island Arsenal—hist pl NY-2
**Banner Mills**—pop pl IN-6
Banner Mine—mine (2) AZ-5
Banner Mine—mine (3) CA-9
Banner Mine—mine (3) ID-8
Banner Mine—mine MT-8
Banner Mine—mine NM-5
Banner Mine—mine OR-9
Banner Mine (Inactive)—mine CA-9
Banner Mine State Wildlife Mgt Area—park IA-7
Banner Mines (underground)—mine AL-4
Banner Mine (underground)—mine AL-4
Banner Mountain Mine (Inactive)—mine CA-9
Banner Mtn—summit AR-4
Banner Mtn—summit CA-9
Banner Mtn—summit NV-8
Banner Mtn—summit WY-8
Banner New Mine (underground)—mine AL-4
Banner Peak—summit AK-9
Banner Peak—summit CA-9
Banner Peak—summit CO-8
Banner P.O. AL-4
Banner Point—cape AK-9
Banner Queen Mine—mine CA-9
Banner Queen Trading Post—locale CA-9
Banner Ranch—locale WY-8
**Banner Ridge**—pop pl PA-2
Banner Ridge—ridge CA-9
Banner Ridge—ridge CO-8
Banner Ridge—ridge ID-8
Banner Ridge Ch—church PA-2
Banner Roslin School TN-4
Banner Rsvr—reservoir CA-9
Banner Rsvr—reservoir ID-8
Banner Sch—school CO-8
Banner Sch—school (3) IL-6
Banner Sch—school IA-7
Banner Sch—school KS-7
Banner Sch—school MI-6
Banner Sch—school MS-4
Banner Sch—school (2) MO-7
Banner Sch—school (4) NE-7
Banner Sch—school (2) OK-5
Banner Sch—school SD-7
Banner Sch—school WV-2
Banner Sch—school WI-6
Banner Sch (abandoned)—school (4) MO-7
Banner Sch Number 14—school ND-7
Banner Sch Number 4—school ND-7
Banner School (Abandoned)—locale MO-7
**Banners Corner**—pop pl VA-3
Banners Elk NC-3
Banners Elk Creek NC-3
Banners Elk Creek TN-4
Banner Shaft Mine (underground)—mine AL-4
**Banner Springs**—pop pl TN-4
Banner Springs—spring CA-9
Banner Springs Freewill Baptist Ch—church TN-4
Banner Springs Post Office (historical)—building TN-4
Banner Station NE-7
Banner Summit—summit ID-8
Banner Town NC-3
**Bannertown**—pop pl (2) NC-3
Banner Township KS-7
Banner Township—civil (2) KS-7
Banner Township—civil (2) SD-7
Banner Township—fmr MCD IA-7
**Banner Township**—pop pl (3) KS-7
**Banner Township**—pop pl (2) ND-7
**Banner Township**—pop pl (2) SD-7
Banner (Township of)—fmr MCD (2) AR-4
Banner (Township of)—fmr MCD NC-3
**Banner (Township of)**—pop pl (2) IL-6
Banner Trap Windmill—locale TX-5
Banner Valley—valley WI-6
**Bannerville**—pop pl PA-2
Banner Wash—stream AZ-5
Banneshee Creek NY-2
Bann Fork MO-7
Bannick Lake—lake MN-6
Bannie Mine—mine AZ-5
Bannie Mine Dump—mine AZ-5
Bannie Tank Number One—reservoir AZ-5
Bannie Tank Number Two—reservoir AZ-5
Bannihoff Lake MI-6
Banning—locale GA-3
Banning—locale MN-6
**Banning**—pop pl CA-9
**Banning**—pop pl PA-2
Banning, Mount—summit CA-9
Banning Bench—bench CA-9
Banning Cabin Gulch—valley CO-8
Banning Canyon—valley CA-9
Banning Cem—cemetery DE-2
**Banning Corner**—pop pl IN-6
Banning Cove—bay CT-1
Banning Creek—stream AZ-5
Banning Creek—stream OR-9
Banning House—hist pl CA-9
Banning HS—school CA-9
Banning Lake—lake IN-6
Banning Lewis Ranch—locale CO-8
Banning Mills—locale GA-3
Banning Park—park CA-9
Banning Park—park DE-2
Banning Place—locale NM-5
Banning Ranch—locale WA-9
Banning Ranger Station—locale CA-9
Bannings Beach—beach CA-9
Banning Sch—school CA-9
Banning Toll Station—locale AZ-5
Banning Wash—stream AZ-5
Bannion Cemetery MO-7
Bannion Spring—spring UT-8
Bannister—locale CA-9
Bannister—locale MO-7
**Bannister**—pop pl AR-4
**Bannister**—pop pl IL-6
**Bannister**—pop pl MI-6
**Bannister**—pop pl WA-9
Bannister, Emory, House—hist pl MA-1
Bannister Basin—basin ID-8
Bannister Bay—bay NY-2
Bannister Brook MA-1
Bannister Brook—stream MA-1
Bannister Creek—stream GA-3
Bannister Creek—stream NY-2
Bannister Creek—stream (3) OR-9
Bannister Ditch—canal OH-6
Bannister Ford—locale MO-7
Bannister Hall—locale DE-2
Bannister Hall and Baynard House—hist pl DE-2
Bannister Hollow—valley MO-7
Bannister Hollow—valley TX-5
Bannister Lake—reservoir TX-5
Bannister Landing (historical)—locale TN-4
Bannister River VA-3
Bannister Ruin—locale UT-8
Bannister Spring—spring UT-8
Bannock MT-8
Bannock—locale CA-9
Bannock—locale ID-8
Bannock—locale NV-8
**Bannock**—pop pl OH-6
Bannock—uninc pl ID-8
Bannockburn—locale GA-3
**Bannockburn**—pop pl IL-6
**Bannockburn**—pop pl MD-2
**Bannock Burn**—pop pl SC-3
**Bannockburn Estates**—pop pl MD-2
**Bannockburn Estates**—pop pl VA-3
**Bannockburn Heights**—pop pl MD-2
Bannockburn Sch—school IL-6
Bannockburn Sch—school MD-2
Bannock Canal—canal ID-8
Bannock City MT-8
Bannock Corral Spring—spring OR-9
Bannock Creek—stream (2) ID-8
Bannock Drain—canal ID-8
Bannock Falls—falls WY-8
Bannock Ford—locale WY-8
Bannock Guard Station—locale ID-8
Bannock Gulch—valley OR-9
Bannock Gulch Spring—spring OR-9
Bannock Hill—summit NH-1
Bannock Jim Slough—stream ID-8
Bannock Lakes—lake WA-9
Bannock Lateral—canal NM-5
Bannock Memorial Hosp—hospital ID-8
Bannock Mtn—summit AK-9
Bannock Mtn—summit ME-1
Bannock Mtn—summit WA-9
Bannock Pass—gap ID-8
Bannock Pass—gap MT-8
Bannock Peak—summit ID-8
Bannock Peak—summit WY-8
Bannock Pumping Station—other ID-8
Bannock Range—range ID-8
Bannock Ridge—ridge OR-9
Bannock Shoals Run—stream WV-2
Bannock Spring—spring ID-8
Bannock Spring—spring OR-9
Bannon OH-6
Bannon—locale OH-6
Bannon, Patrick, House—hist pl KY-4
Bannon Cem—cemetery MO-7
Bannon Cem—cemetery WV-2
Bannon Creek—stream AZ-5
Bannon Creek—stream WA-9
Bannon Hill—summit MA-1
Bannon Island—island FL-3
Bannon Mtn—summit WA-9
Bannon Park—park OH-6
Bannon Point—cape SC-3
Bannon (Site)—locale AZ-5
Bannon Spring—spring ID-8
Bannowsky Cem—cemetery TX-5
Bann Substation—other TX-5
**Banoak**—pop pl NC-3
Banoak Elem Sch—school NC-3
Banock—locale KY-4
Banos de Coamo—locale PR-3
**Banos de Coamo**—pop pl PR-3
Banos Well—well AZ-5
Bano Tank—reservoir NM-5
Bano Windmill—locale TX-5
Banqueros Windmill—locale TX-5
**Banquete**—pop pl TX-5
Banquete Creek—stream TX-5
**Banquo**—pop pl IN-6
Bans Branch—stream WV-2
Bans Creek MO-7
Banser Run OH-6
Bansfield MI-6
Banshee Creek—stream AK-9
**Ban Spur**—pop pl OR-9
Bansterdown SC-3
**Banta**—pop pl CA-9
**Banta**—pop pl IN-6
Banta, Derick, House—hist pl NJ-2
Banta, John, House—hist pl NJ-2
Banta, J. V., House—hist pl IA-7
Banta Beatty Park—park CA-9
Banta Branch—stream TX-5
Banta Carbona Canal—canal CA-9
Banta Cem—cemetery IA-7
Banta-Coe House—hist pl NJ-2
Banta Creek—stream IN-6
Banta Drain—stream MI-6
Banta Flats Rsvr—reservoir CO-8
Banta Gulch—valley CO-8
Banta Hill—summit CO-8
Banta House—hist pl TX-5
Banta Lakes—lake IL-6
**Bantam**—pop pl CT-1
**Bantam**—pop pl OH-6
Bantam Lake—lake CT-1
Bantam Ledge—bar ME-1
Bantam Mine—mine OR-9
Bantam Ridge Sch—hist pl OH-6
Bantam Ridge Sch—school OH-6
Bantam River—stream CT-1
Bantam Rock—bar ME-1
Banta Park—park IL-6
Banta Point—cliff AZ-5
Banta Ridge—ridge CO-8
Banta Sch—school IN-6
Bantas Fork—stream KY-4
Bantas Fork—stream OH-6
Banta Shut-In—summit TX-5
Banta Spring—spring CA-9
Banta Spring—spring NM-5
Banta Spring Creek—stream CO-8
Bante Mine—mine NV-8
Banton, Dr. B. M., House—hist pl SD-7
Banton Branch—stream NC-3
Banton Creek—stream OR-9
**Bantry**—pop pl ND-7
**Bantry Township**—pop pl ND-7
Banty—locale OK-5
Banty Creek—stream (2) AZ-5
Banty Gulch—valley NV-8
Banty Point—summit CO-8
Banty Saunders Bridge—bridge FL-3
Banty Spring—spring OK-5
Bantywater Pond NY-2
Bantz Park—park PA-2
Banyan Drive Park—park FL-3
Banyan Elem Sch—school (2) FL-3
Banyan Park—park FL-3
Banyan Post Office (historical)—building AL-4
Banyan Sch—school FL-3
Banyan Sch—school KY-4
Banyard—locale AR-4
Banyon Creek—stream AL-4
Banyon Swamp Creek—stream AL-4
Banzai Cliff—hist pl MH-9
Banzer Creek—stream AK-9
Banzet—locale OK-5
Banzhof Ranch—locale WY-8
Baoba—locale PA-2
Baojan—island MP-9
Baojen MP-9
Baojen—island MP-9
Baojen Island MP-9
**Bapchule**—pop pl AZ-5
Bapchule Community Center—building AZ-5
Bap Church SD-7
Bapot, Laderan—cliff MH-9
Bapot, Puntan—cape MH-9
Bapot Beach MH-9
Bapot Point MH-9
Baptic Lake ID-8
Baptie Lake—lake ID-8
Baptish Hosp—hospital FL-3
Baptising Pond—lake (2) FL-3
Baptism Branch—stream MS-4
Baptism Crossing—locale MN-6
Baptism Hole—lake TX-5
Baptism Hole, The—lake TX-5
Baptism Pond—lake GA-3
Baptism River MN-6
Baptism River—stream MN-6
Baptism River State Park—park MN-6
Baptist MS-4
Baptist—locale KY-4
**Baptist**—pop pl LA-4
Baptist—uninc pl TN-4
Baptist Acad—school TX-5
Baptist Bible College PA-2
Baptist Bible Institute—school FL-3
Baptist Branch DE-2
Baptist Branch—stream GA-3
Baptist Branch—stream MS-4
Baptist Branch—stream (2) TN-4
Baptist Branch—stream (2) TX-5
Baptist Brook—stream CT-1
Baptist Camp—locale AL-4
Baptist Camp—locale CA-9
Baptist Camp Lake—reservoir AL-4
Baptist Cem—cemetery CT-1
Baptist Cem—cemetery (5) KS-7
Baptist Cem—cemetery MS-4
Baptist Cem—cemetery MO-7
Baptist Cem—cemetery NE-7
Baptist Cem—cemetery ND-7
Baptist Cem—cemetery OH-6
Baptist Cem—cemetery SD-7
Baptist Cem—cemetery VA-3
Baptist Cem of Bellflower—cemetery MO-7
Baptist Center—church MS-4
Baptist Center Ch—church AL-4
Baptist Ch—church GA-3
Baptist Ch—church (2) KS-7
Baptist Ch—church ME-1
Baptist Ch—church (3) MO-7
Baptist Ch—church OK-5
Baptist Chapel Church and Cemetery—hist pl NC-3
Baptist Ch First—church FL-3
Baptist Ch (historical)—church SD-7
Baptist Childrens Home—building (2) AL-4
Baptist Childrens Village—locale MS-4
Baptist Ch of Atlantic Beach—church FL-3
Baptist Ch of Estero—church FL-3
Baptist Ch of Palm Valley—church FL-3
Baptist Church—hist pl ID-8
Baptist Church—hist pl IA-7
Baptist Church Branch—stream SC-3
Baptist Church Camp—locale OK-5
Baptist Church in Exeter—hist pl RI-1
Baptist Church of Chitty at Adoniram AL-4
Baptist Church of Chitty at Yatta Abbey AL-4
Baptist Church of Christ at Bulluctah MS-4
Baptist Church of Christ in Denham MS-4
Baptist Cluster Church AL-4
**Baptist College**—pop pl SC-3
Baptist Collegiate Institute (historical)—school AL-4
Baptist Community Bible Ch—church UT-8
**Baptist Corner**—pop pl MA-1
**Baptist Corners**—pop pl MA-1
**Baptist Corners**—pop pl NY-2
Baptist Corners Cem—cemetery NY-2
Baptist Creek—stream GA-3
Baptist Creek—stream IL-6
Baptist Creek—stream SD-7
Baptist Day Sch—school CA-9
Baptist Draw—valley UT-8
Baptiste, Mount—summit MT-8
Baptiste Collette Bayou—channel LA-4
Baptiste Creek—stream LA-4
Baptiste Creek—stream MT-8
Baptiste Creek—stream WY-8
Baptiste Graye—cemetery MT-8
Baptiste JHS—school MO-7
Baptiste Lake—lake WY-8
Baptiste Lookout—locale MT-8
Baptiste Lookout Trail—trail MT-8
Baptiste Orchard—locale CA-9
Baptist Female College-Adams House—hist pl TN-4
Baptist Female Coll (historical)—school AL-4
Baptist Female Coll (historical)—school MS-4
Baptist Female Institute TN-4
Baptist Fork—stream KY-4
Baptist Freewill Orphanage—building TN-4
Baptist Gap—gap TN-4
Baptist Grove Ch—church AL-4
Baptist Grove Ch—church (2) MS-4
Baptist Grove Missionary Baptist Ch MS-4
**Baptist Hill**—pop pl SC-3
Baptist Hill—summit MA-1
Baptist Hill—summit (2) NY-2
Baptist Hill—summit TN-4
Baptist Hill—summit VT-1
Baptist Hill Assembly—other MO-7
Baptist Hill Baptist Ch—church AL-4
Baptist Hill Cem—cemetery AL-4
Baptist Hill Cem—cemetery MS-4
Baptist Hill Cem—cemetery TN-4
Baptist Hill Cem—cemetery (2) TX-5
Baptist Hill Cem—cemetery VT-1
Baptist Hill Ch—church AL-4
Baptist Hill Ch—church IN-6
Baptist Hill Ch—church MS-4
Baptist Hill Ch—church MO-7
Baptist Hill Ch—church OH-6
Baptist Hill Ch—church PA-2
Baptist Hill Ch—church TN-4
Baptist Hills Ch MS-4
Baptist Hill Sch—school AL-4
Baptist Hill Sch—school VT-1
**Baptist Hill (subdivision)**—pop pl AL-4
Baptist Hollow—valley MO-7
Baptist Hollow—valley TN-4
Baptist Hollow Branch—stream TN-4
Baptist Home—building AL-4
Baptist Home Ch—church NC-3
Baptist Hosp—hospital AL-4
Baptist Hosp—hospital AR-4
Baptist Hosp—hospital MS-4
Baptist Hosp—hospital MO-7
Baptist Hosp—hospital NC-3
Baptist Hospital Airp—airport TN-4
Baptist Hospital of Scottsdale AZ-5
Baptist Hosp of Miami—hospital FL-3
Baptist Institute—school PA-2
Baptist Institute for Christian Workers—hist pl PA-2
Baptist Lake—lake FL-3
Baptist Lake—lake MI-6
Baptist Lake Dam—dam AL-4
Baptist Lake Sch—school MI-6
Baptist Med Ctr—hospital FL-3
Baptist Med Ctr Airp—airport AL-4
Baptist Med Ctr De Kalb—hospital AL-4
Baptist Med Ctr Princeton—hospital AL-4
Baptist Medical Hosp—hospital AL-4
Baptist Memorial Hosital—hospital TN-4
Baptist Memorial Hosp—hospital AL-4
Baptist Memorial Hosp—hospital MS-4
Baptist Memorial Hosp—hospital (2) TN-4
Baptist Memorial Hosp Tipton—hospital TN-4
Baptist Mission—church MI-6
Baptist Mission Camp—locale AL-4
Baptist Mission (historical)—locale KS-7
**Baptistown**—pop pl NJ-2
Baptist Parish MA-1
Baptist Parsonage, Old—hist pl OH-6
Baptist Pond MA-1
Baptist Pond—lake AK-9
Baptist Pond—lake MA-1
Baptist Pond—lake NH-1
Baptist Post Office (historical)—building TN-4
Baptist Rest Primitive Baptist Ch (historical)—church AL-4
Baptist Retreat Ch—church AL-4
Baptist Ridge—locale TN-4
Baptist Ridge—ridge OH-6
Baptist Ridge—ridge TN-4
Baptist Ridge Baptist Ch—church TN-4
Baptist Ridge Sch (historical)—school TN-4
Baptist River Access—locale MO-7
Baptist Run—stream VA-3
Baptists Creek SD-7
Baptist Shed Cem—cemetery MO-7
Baptist Society Meeting House—hist pl MA-1
Baptist Spanish Mission—church FL-3
Baptist State Convention Center—building AL-4
Baptist Street Sch—school VT-1
Baptist Student Center—church AL-4
Baptist Tabernacle Ch—church AL-4
Baptist Temple—church (2) FL-3
Baptist Temple—church MI-6
Baptist Temple—church MO-7
Baptist Temple, The AL-4
Baptist Temple Church, The—church AL-4
Baptist Temple Sch—school FL-3
Baptist Theological Seminary—school CA-9
Baptisttown NJ-2
Baptist Valley—valley VA-3
**Baptist Village**—pop pl MA-1
Baptist Village Lake—reservoir GA-3
Baptist Village Nursing Home—building GA-3
Baptist Youth Camp—locale MO-7
Baptize Lake—lake GA-3
Baptizing Branch—stream (3) AL-4
Baptizing Branch—stream LA-4
Baptizing Creek—stream AL-4
Baptizing Creek—stream OK-5
Baptizing Hole—bar MO-7
Baptizing Hole—lake FL-3
Baptizing Hole—locale TN-4
Baptizing Lake FL-3
Baptizing Pond—lake FL-3
Baptizing Pond—lake GA-3
Baptizing Slough—gut MS-4
Baptizing Spring—spring FL-3
Bapt Rsvr—reservoir NV-8
Baput, Unai—beach MH-9
Baqanimaqut—locale FM-9
Bar, The—bar AR-4
Bar, The—bar CT-1
Bar, The—bay CT-1
Bar, The—cape ME-1
Bar, The—ridge MT-8
Barabado FM-9
Barabara Cove—bay AK-9
Barabara Creek—stream (2) AK-9
Barabara Island—island AK-9
Barabara Point—cape AK-9
Barabaras—other AK-9
Barabato FM-9
**Baraboo**—pop pl WI-6
Baraboo Creek MT-8
Baraboo Public Library—hist pl WI-6
Baraboo River WI-6
Baraboo River—stream WI-6
**Baraboo (Town of)**—pop pl WI-6
**Barachias**—pop pl AL-4
Baracos Creek—stream NM-5
Bar A Creek—stream UT-8
**Barada**—pop pl NE-7
Barado—locale TX-5
**Baraga**—pop pl MI-6
**Baraga (County)**—pop pl MI-6
Baraga Creek—stream MI-6
Baragan Mountains AZ-5
Baragan Mtn—summit AZ-5
Baragan Wash—stream AZ-5

Baragan Well—*well* ... AZ-5
Baraga Plains—*flat* ... MI-6
Baraga Sch—*school* ... MI-6
Baraga State For—*forest* ... MI-6
**Baraga (Township of)**—*pop pl* ... MI-6
*Barager Creek* ... MI-6
Barager Creek—*stream* ... OR-9
Barager Sch—*school* ... MI-6
*Baragon Mountains* ... AZ-5
Barahona—*CDP* ... PR-3
Barahona (Barrio)—*fmr MCD* ... PR-3
Bara Industrial Park Subdivision—*locale* ... UT-8
Barajita Valley—*valley* ... AZ-5
Barajita Well—*well* ... AZ-5
*Barajito Valley* ... AZ-5
Barales School (Abandoned)—*locale* ... NM-5
Baralock Hill—*summit* ... MA-1
Baralof Bay—*bay* ... AK-9
**Baralto**—*pop pl* ... KY-4
*Baranailingin* ... MP-9
Barangka—*slope* ... MH-9
Barangka, Puntan—*cape* ... MH-9
**Baranof**—*pop pl* ... AK-9
Baranof Island—*island* ... AK-9
Baranof Lake—*lake* ... AK-9
Baranof River—*stream* ... AK-9
Baran Park—*park* ... WI-6
Baranski Drain—*canal* ... MI-6
Barasco Gulch—*valley* ... CA-9
**Barataria**—*pop pl* ... LA-4
Barataria, Bayou—*canal* ... LA-4
Barataria Bay—*bay* ... LA-4
*Barataria Bay Waterway* ... LA-4
Barataria Creek—*stream* ... SC-3
Barataria Island—*island* ... SC-3
Barataria Oil and Gas Field—*oilfield* ... LA-4
Barataria Pass—*channel* ... LA-4
Barataria Unit of Jean Lafitte Historical Park Hist Dist—*hist pl* ... LA-4
Barataria Waterway—*channel* ... LA-4
Barat Coll—*school* ... IL-6
Baratta Airp—*airport* ... PA-2
Bar A-3 Ranch—*locale* ... NV-8
Barbacoas Oil Field—*oilfield* ... TX-5
Barbacoa Windmill—*locale* ... TX-5
*Barbadoes* ... DC-2
Barbadoes Basin—*bay* ... NY-2
Barbadoes Island—*island* ... PA-2
*Barbadoes Neck* ... NJ-2
Barbadoes Pond—*lake* ... MD-2
Barbadoes Pond—*lake* ... NH-1
*Barbara* ... PA-2
Barbara—*locale* ... MS-4
Barbara, Lake—*lake* ... AK-9
Barbara, Lake—*lake* ... FL-3
Barbara, Lake—*lake* ... TX-5
Barbara, Lake—*lake* ... WI-6
Barbara, Lake—*reservoir* ... IN-6
Barbara Ann Mine—*mine* ... MT-8
Barbara Budd Ditch—*canal* ... WY-8
*Barbara Creek* ... AK-9
Barbara Creek—*stream* ... AK-9
Barbara Creek—*stream* ... CO-8
Barbara Gulch—*valley* ... CO-8
Barbara J No 1 Mine—*mine* ... NM-5
Barbara Kay Mine—*mine* ... IL-6
Barbara Lake—*lake* ... AK-9
Barbara Lake—*lake* ... FL-3
Barbara Lake—*lake* ... WY-8
Barbara Mine—*mine* ... MN-6
Barbara Mines—*mine* ... PA-2
Barbara Oil Field—*oilfield* ... TX-5
Barbara Point—*cape* ... AK-9
Barbara Rock—*island* ... AK-9
Barbaras Point—*cape* ... TX-5
**Barbara Terrace**—*pop pl* ... CA-9
Barbara Webster Sch—*school* ... CA-9
Barbara Well—*well* ... AZ-5
Barbara Well—*well* ... NM-5
Barbara Worth Country Club—*other* ... CA-9
Barbara Worth Drain—*canal* ... CA-9
Barbara Worth Spring—*spring* ... NV-8
Barbara Worth Well—*well* ... NV-8
Barbaree Branch—*stream* ... AR-4
Barbaree Creek—*stream* ... AL-4
Barbarees Pond—*reservoir* ... AL-4
*Bar-Bar-En* ... MP-9
**Barbarosa**—*pop pl* ... TX-5
Barbarossa Mines—*mine* ... CA-9
Barbarossa Ridge—*ridge* ... CA-9
*Bar-Barry Heights* ... IN-6
**Bar-Barry Heights**—*pop pl* ... IN-6
Barbars Landing (historical)—*locale* ... AL-4
Barbary, Bayou—*stream* ... LA-4
Barbashela Creek—*stream* ... GA-3
*Bar Basin* ... AZ-5
Barb Cem—*cemetery* ... WV-2
Bar B C Ranch—*locale* ... WY-8
Bar B Creek—*stream* ... WY-8
Bar Beach—*beach* ... NY-2
Barbeau—*locale* ... MI-6
Barbeau Hollow—*valley* ... IL-6
Barbeau Point—*cape* ... MI-6
Barbeau Tower—*locale* ... MI-6
**Barbecue**—*pop pl* ... NC-3
Barbecue Branch—*stream* ... FL-3
Barbecue Branch—*stream* (2) ... KY-4
Barbecue Branch—*stream* ... SC-3
Barbecue Branch—*stream* ... VA-3
Barbecue Creek—*stream* ... NC-3
Barbecue Run—*stream* (2) ... WV-2
*Barbecue Swamp* ... NC-3
Barbecue Terrace—*bench* ... CA-9
Barbecue (Township of)—*fmr MCD* ... NC-3
Barbed Point—*cape* ... MI-6
Barbed Wire Cave—*cave* ... AL-4
**Barbee**—*pop pl* ... IN-6
**Barbee**—*pop pl* ... MS-4
Barbee, John, House—*hist pl* ... KY-4
Barbee-Berry Mercantile Bldg—*hist pl* ... TX-5
Barbee Cem—*cemetery* ... AL-4
Barbee Cem—*cemetery* ... AR-4
Barbee Cem—*cemetery* ... IL-6
Barbee Cem—*cemetery* ... MS-4
Barbee Cem—*cemetery* ... TN-4
Barbee Cem—*cemetery* (2) ... TX-5
Barbee Ch—*church* ... NC-3
Barbee Creek—*stream* ... AL-4
Barbee Draw—*valley* ... NM-5
Barbee Field—*park* ... TX-5
*Barbee Flat* ... MS-4
*Barbee Lake* ... IN-6
Barbees Ch—*church* ... NC-3
Barbee Sch—*school* ... NC-3
Barbee Sch (historical)—*school* ... AL-4
Barbees Pond—*reservoir* ... NC-3
Barbees Pond Dam—*dam* ... NC-3
Barbee Tank—*reservoir* (2) ... NM-5
Barbeeue Bay—*swamp* ... NC-3
Barbee Windmill—*locale* ... CO-8
Bar-Bel Lake—*reservoir* ... CO-8
Bar Below Benton—*bar* ... AL-4
Bar Below Gause Bar (historical)—*bar* ... AL-4
Barbenceta Butte—*summit* ... AZ-5
*Barbencita Butte* ... AZ-5
*Barbeneeta Butte* ... AZ-5
Barbeque Point—*cape* ... MD-2
Barbeque Swamp—*stream* ... NC-3
*Barber* ... LA-4
*Barber* ... VA-3
Barber—*locale* ... CA-9
Barber—*locale* (2) ... ID-8
Barber—*locale* ... KS-7
Barber—*locale* ... NJ-2
Barber—*locale* ... NC-3
Barber—*locale* ... OK-5
Barber—*other* ... LA-4
**Barber**—*pop pl* ... AL-4
**Barber**—*pop pl* ... AR-4
**Barber**—*pop pl* ... MD-2
**Barber**—*pop pl* ... MT-8
**Barber**—*pop pl* ... NC-3
Barber—*uninc pl* ... MA-1
Barber, Charles A., Farmstead—*hist pl* ... SD-7
Barber, Giles, House—*hist pl* ... CT-1
Barber, Henry D., House—*hist pl* ... IL-6
Barber, James, House—*hist pl* ... WI-6
Barber, Lake—*lake* ... FL-3
Barber, O. C., Barn No. 1—*hist pl* ... OH-6
Barber, O. C., Colt Barn—*hist pl* ... OH-6
Barber, O. C., Creamery—*hist pl* ... OH-6
Barber, O. C., Machine Barn—*hist pl* ... OH-6
Barber, O. C., Piggery—*hist pl* ... OH-6
Barber Airp—*airport* ... MO-7
Barber Airstrip—*airport* ... SD-7
Barber Ave Sch—*school* ... NJ-2
Barber-Barbour House—*hist pl* ... KY-4
Barber Basin—*basin* ... CO-8
Barber Bay—*bay* ... NY-2
Barber Bay—*swamp* ... FL-3
Barber Block—*hist pl* ... OR-9
*Barber Branch* ... GA-3
Barber Branch—*stream* ... FL-3
Barber Branch—*stream* ... GA-3
Barber Branch—*stream* ... KY-4
Barber Branch—*stream* ... MS-4
Barber Branch—*stream* (2) ... MO-7
Barber Branch—*stream* (4) ... TN-4
Barber Branch—*stream* ... TX-5
Barber Bridge—*other* ... MI-6
*Barber Brook* ... RI-1
Barber Brook—*stream* ... NY-2
Barber Butte—*summit* ... MT-8
Barber Cabin—*locale* ... ID-8
Barber Camp—*locale* ... MA-1
Barber Canyon—*valley* (2) ... CA-9
Barber Canyon—*valley* (2) ... NV-8
Barber Canyon—*valley* ... OR-9
Barber Cem—*cemetery* ... AR-4
Barber Cem—*cemetery* (2) ... FL-3
Barber Cem—*cemetery* ... IL-6
Barber Cem—*cemetery* ... IN-6
Barber Cem—*cemetery* ... KY-4
Barber Cem—*cemetery* ... LA-4
Barber Cem—*cemetery* ... ME-1
Barber Cem—*cemetery* ... MI-6
Barber Cem—*cemetery* ... MS-4
Barber Cem—*cemetery* ... MO-7
Barber Cem—*cemetery* ... NJ-2
Barber Cem—*cemetery* (2) ... NY-2
Barber Cem—*cemetery* ... OH-6
Barber Cem—*cemetery* ... OK-5
Barber Cem—*cemetery* ... PA-2
Barber Cem—*cemetery* (3) ... TN-4
Barber Cem—*cemetery* (2) ... TX-5
Barber Cem—*cemetery* ... VT-1
Barber Ch—*church* ... OK-5
Barber Chapel—*church* ... NC-3
**Barber City**—*pop pl* ... CA-9
Barber City Channel—*canal* ... CA-9
Barber Corners—*locale* ... NY-2
Barber Coulee—*valley* (2) ... MT-8
Barber County—*civil* ... KS-7
Barber County State Lake—*reservoir* ... KS-7
Barber County State Lake Dam—*dam* ... KS-7
Barber Creek—*stream* ... AR-4
Barber Creek—*stream* (2) ... CA-9
Barber Creek—*stream* ... GA-3
Barber Creek—*stream* (2) ... IA-7
Barber Creek—*stream* (2) ... LA-4
Barber Creek—*stream* (2) ... MI-6
Barber Creek—*stream* ... MN-6
Barber Creek—*stream* ... MS-4
Barber Creek—*stream* ... MO-7
Barber Creek—*stream* (2) ... MT-8
Barber Creek—*stream* ... NV-8
Barber Creek—*stream* ... NC-3
Barber Creek—*stream* (2) ... OR-9
Barber Creek—*stream* ... WI-6
Barber Creek—*stream* ... WY-8
Barber Creek Ch—*church* ... GA-3
Barber Creek Oil Field—*oilfield* ... WY-8
Barber Creek West Oil Field—*oilfield* ... WY-8
Barber Crossing—*locale* ... NM-5
Barber Dam—*dam* ... ID-8
Barber Dam and Lumber Mill—*hist pl* ... ID-8
Barber Drain—*canal* ... MI-6
Barber Draw—*valley* ... MT-8
Barber Falls—*falls* ... TX-5
Barber Flat—*flat* (2) ... ID-8
Barber Flat—*flat* ... OR-9
Barber Flat Forest Service Station—*locale* ... ID-8
Barber Gene Mine—*mine* ... AZ-5
Barber Gulch—*valley* ... CA-9
Barber Gulch—*valley* ... MT-8
Barber Gulf—*stream* ... NY-2
*Barber Heights* ... RI-1
Barber Heights—*other* ... RI-1
Barber Heights—*summit* ... RI-1
Barber Hill—*summit* (3) ... MA-1
Barber Hill—*summit* ... TN-4
Barber Hill—*summit* ... VT-1
*Barber Hill Canal* ... TX-5
Barber Hills—*summit* ... NY-2
**Barber (historical)**—*pop pl* ... OR-9
Barber Hollow—*valley* ... MO-7
Barber Hollow—*valley* ... PA-2
Barber Hollow—*valley* (4) ... TN-4
Barber House—*hist pl* ... SC-3
Barber House—*hist pl* ... TX-5
Barberie Cem—*cemetery* ... WV-2
Barber Island—*island* ... NY-2
Barber Lake—*lake* ... AZ-5
Barber Lake—*lake* (2) ... MI-6
Barber Lake—*lake* ... MN-6
Barber Lake—*lake* ... MO-7
Barber Lake—*lake* ... WI-6
Barber Lake—*lake* ... WY-8
Barber Lake—*reservoir* ... TX-5
Barber Lake (historical)—*lake* ... MS-4
Barber Lakes—*lake* ... MI-6
Barber Landing—*locale* ... NC-3
Barber Landing Field—*airport* ... SD-7
Barber Ledge—*cliff* ... VT-1
Barber (Maurer)—*uninc pl* ... NJ-2
Barber Memorial Sch for Negro Girls (historical)—*school* ... AL-4
*Barber Mill Reservoir* ... RI-1
Barber Mine (underground)—*mine* ... AL-4
Barber Mtn—*summit* ... CA-9
Barber Mtn—*summit* (2) ... NH-1
Barber Mtn—*summit* ... NY-2
Barber Mtn—*summit* ... TX-5
Barber Mtn—*summit* ... VT-1
Barber Mtn—*summit* ... WA-9
Barber-Mulligan Farm—*hist pl* ... NY-2
Barbero Canyon—*valley* ... NM-5
Barbero Tank—*reservoir* ... NM-5
Barber Peak—*summit* ... NM-5
Barber-Pittman House—*hist pl* ... GA-3
Barber Point—*cape* ... MD-2
Barber Point—*cape* (2) ... NY-2
Barber Pole Butte—*summit* ... OR-9
Rarher Pond—*lake* ... CT-1
Barber Pond—*lake* ... RI-1
Barber Pond—*lake* ... VT-1
Barber Pond—*lake* ... WI-6
Barber Prairie—*area* ... CA-9
**Barber Quarters**—*pop pl* ... FL-3
Barberra Hollow—*valley* ... UT-8
Barber Ranch—*locale* ... MT-8
Barber Ranch—*locale* ... NV-8
Barber Ridge—*ridge* ... AR-4
Barber Ridge—*ridge* ... CA-9
Barber Ridge—*ridge* ... NM-5
Barber Ridge—*ridge* ... OH-6
Barber Rsvr—*reservoir* ... OR-9
Barber Rsvr—*reservoir* ... WY-8
Barber Run—*stream* ... PA-2
Barberry Creek—*stream* ... AR-4
Barberry Creek—*stream* ... ME-1
**Barberry Heights (subdivision)**—*pop pl* ... NC-3
Barberry Spring—*spring* ... CA-9
Barbers—*locale* ... GA-3
Barbers Bay—*bay* ... WI-6
Barbers Branch—*stream* ... TN-4
Barbers Branch Sch—*school* ... SC-3
*Barbers Brook* ... RI-1
*Barbers Cap* ... HI-9
Barber Sch—*school* (2) ... MI-6
Barber Sch—*school* ... NJ-2
Barber Sch—*school* ... OH-6
Barber Sch—*school* ... VT-1
Barber Sch—*school* ... WI-6
Barber Sch (historical)—*school* ... AL-4
Barber School—*locale* ... MI-6
Barbers Corners—*locale* ... NY-2
**Barbers Corners**—*pop pl* ... IL-6
Barbers Corners Cem—*cemetery* ... IL-6
Barber-Scotia Coll—*school* ... NC-3
Barber-Scotia College—*hist pl* ... NC-3
Barbers Creek—*stream* ... GA-3
Barbers Creek—*stream* ... MO-7
Barbers Creek—*stream* ... SC-3
Barbers Crossing Station (historical)—*locale* ... MA-1
*Barbers Crossroads* ... AL-4
Barbers Flat—*flat* ... WA-9
Barbers Gulch—*valley* ... CO-8
Barber Shaft Ridge—*ridge* ... TN-4
*Barbers Heights* ... RI-1
*Barber'S Hill* ... MA-1
Barbers Hill—*summit* ... TX-5
Barbers Hill Canal—*canal* ... TX-5
Barbers Hill Oil Field—*oilfield* ... TX-5
Barbers Hollow—*valley* ... OH-6
Barbershop Canyon—*valley* ... AZ-5
Barbershop Spring—*spring* ... AZ-5
Barbers Lake—*lake* ... AR-4
Barbers Lake Slough—*stream* ... AR-4
Barbers Landing—*locale* ... GA-3
Barbers Mill (historical)—*locale* ... AL-4
*Barbers Mill Reservoir* ... RI-1
*Barbers Mills* ... IN-6
*Barber's Point* ... NY-2
*Barbers Point* ... TX-5
Barbers Point—*cape* ... HI-9
Barbers Point—*cliff* ... WY-8
Barbers Point Harbor—*harbor* ... HI-9
Barbers Point Housing—*CDP* ... HI-9
Barbers Point Naval Air Station—*military* ... HI-9
Barbers Point Sch—*school* ... HI-9
Barbers Pole—*channel* ... NH-1
*Barbers Pond* ... RI-1
Barbers Pond—*lake* ... CT-1
Barber Spring—*spring* ... CO-8
Barber Spring—*spring* ... NM-5
Barber Springs—*spring* ... WA-9
Barber Springs Trail (Pack)—*trail* ... NM-5
Barber Spring Trail (Pack)—*trail* ... NM-5
Barber Spur—*locale* ... LA-4
Barbers Run—*stream* ... GA-3
**Barbers Subdivision**—*pop pl* ... UT-8
Barber State Fishing Lake And Wildlife Area—*park* ... KS-7
**Barbersville**—*pop pl* ... IN-6
Barber Tank—*reservoir* ... NM-5
**Barberton**—*pop pl* ... OH-6
**Barberton**—*pop pl* ... WA-9
Barberton Church Camp—*locale* ... OH-6
Barberton Rsvr—*reservoir* ... OH-6
Barberton Speedway—*other* ... OH-6
Barberton Stadium—*other* ... OH-6
Barberton (Township of)—*other* ... OH-6
*Barbertown* ... PA-2
**Barbertown**—*pop pl* ... NJ-2
Barber (Township of)—*fmr MCD* ... AR-4
**Barber (Township of)**—*pop pl* ... MN-6
Barber Valley—*basin* ... NE-7
**Barberville**—*pop pl* ... FL-3
**Barberville**—*pop pl* ... NY-2
**Barberville**—*pop pl* ... RI-1
Barberville Ch—*church* ... NC-3
Barber Well—*well* ... CA-9
Barber Wheatfield Overlook—*locale* ... NY-2
Barber-Whitticar House—*hist pl* ... OH-6
Barber Windmill—*locale* ... CO-8
Barbe Sch—*school* ... LA-4
Barbe Sch—*school* ... WV-2
Barbettini Ranch—*locale* ... CA-9
*Barbett Knob* ... VA-3
Barb Fork—*stream* ... KY-4
Barb Gap—*gap* ... VA-3
Barbham Cem—*cemetery* ... OH-6
Barb Hollow—*valley* ... TN-4
Barb Hollow—*valley* ... VA-3
Barbie Lakes—*lake* ... OR-9
Barbieri Dam—*dam* ... MA-1
Barbieri Rsvr—*reservoir* ... MA-1
Barbier Ridge—*ridge* ... MO-7
Barbin Branch—*stream* ... MO-7
Barbizon Hotel for Women—*hist pl* ... NY-2
Barb Lake—*lake* ... MI-6
Barb Lake—*lake* ... MT-8
Barbless Pond—*lake* ... ME-1
Barb Mtn—*summit* ... MT-8
Barbo Lake—*lake* ... WI-6
Barbone Creek—*stream* ... TX-5
Bar Boot Ranch—*locale* ... AZ-5
*Barbor Creek* ... MI-6
Barbos Lake—*lake* ... VT-1
Bar Bottom Hollow—*valley* ... PA-2
Barbour, Lucius, House—*hist pl* ... CT-1
Barbour Brook—*stream* ... CT-1
Barbour Brook—*stream* ... NY-2
Barbour Cem—*cemetery* ... IN-6
Barbour Cem—*cemetery* ... KY-4
Barbour Cem—*cemetery* ... WV-2
Barbour Ch—*church* ... WV-2
**Barbour County**—*pop pl* ... AL-4
**Barbour (County)**—*pop pl* ... WV-2
Barbour County Courthouse—*building* ... AL-4
Barbour County Courthouse—*hist pl* ... WV-2
*Barbour County High School* ... AL-4
*Barbour County Public Lake* ... AL-4
Barbour County Public Lake Dam—*dam* ... AL-4
Barbour County State Wildlife Mngmt Area—*park* ... AL-4
Barbour County Training Sch—*school* ... AL-4
*Barbour Creek* ... AL-4
Barbour Creek—*stream* ... AL-4
Barbour Creek—*stream* ... ID-8
Barbour Creek—*stream* ... WA-9
Barbour Creek Landing Recreational Facility—*park* ... AL-4
Barbour Ditch—*canal* ... MT-8
Barbour-Estes House—*hist pl* ... MS-4
Barbour Fork—*stream* ... CO-8
Barbour Fork Picnic Ground—*locale* ... CO-8
Barbour Gulch—*valley* ... MT-8
Barbour Hill—*summit* ... MT-8
Barbour Hill—*summit* ... NY-2
Barbour HS—*school* ... WV-2
Barbour Island—*island* ... GA-3
Barbour Island River—*stream* ... GA-3
Barbour Lake—*lake* ... MI-6
Barbour Lake—*lake* ... MN-6
Barbour (Magisterial District)—*fmr MCD* ... VA-3
**Barbourmeade**—*pop pl* ... KY-4
Barbour Mill Dam—*dam* ... NJ-2
Barbour Pond—*lake* ... NJ-2
Barbour Pond—*reservoir* ... NJ-2
Barbour Pond Park—*park* ... NJ-2
Barbour Rock—*summit* ... PA-2
Barbour Ruins—*locale* ... VA-3
Barbour Run—*stream* ... VA-3
Barbours—*locale* ... PA-2
Barbour Sch—*school* ... CT-1
Barbour Sch—*school* ... IL-6
Barbour Sch—*school* ... MI-6
Barbours Creek—*locale* ... VA-3
Barbours Creek—*stream* ... VA-3
Barbours Creek Sch—*school* ... VA-3
Barbours Cut—*channel* ... TX-5
*Barbours Island* ... GA-3
Barbours Lake—*reservoir* ... NC-3
Barbours Lake Dam—*dam* ... NC-3
*Barbours Mill Pond* ... NJ-2
*Barbours Mills* ... PA-2
*Barbours Pond* ... NJ-2
Barbour Spring—*spring* ... ID-8
*Barboursville* ... AL-4
*Barboursville* ... IN-6
Barboursville—*hist pl* ... VA-3
**Barboursville**—*pop pl* ... VA-3
**Barboursville**—*pop pl* ... WV-2
Barboursville (Magisterial District)—*fmr MCD* ... WV-2
Barbourton Ch—*church* ... NC-3
Barbourville—*locale* ... NY-2
**Barbourville**—*pop pl* ... KY-4
Barbourville (CCD)—*cens area* ... KY-4
Barbourville Cem—*cemetery* ... KY-4
*Barbourville City* ... KY-4
Barbourville Commercial District—*hist pl* ... KY-4
*Barbourville P.O.* ... AL-4
**Barbra (historical)**—*pop pl* ... OR-9
Bar B Ranch—*locale* (2) ... CA-9
Bar B Ranch—*locale* ... NM-5
Bar Branch—*stream* ... AL-4
Bar Branch—*stream* ... VA-3
**Barbreck**—*pop pl* ... LA-4
Barbree Island—*island* ... FL-3
Barb Ridge—*ridge* ... CA-9
Barbrook Park—*park* ... TX-5
Barb Run—*stream* ... VA-3
Barbs Hill—*summit* ... RI-1
*Bar B Tank* ... NM-5
Bar B Tank—*reservoir* ... NM-5
Barbue, Bayou—*stream* (2) ... LA-4
Barbwood Branch—*stream* ... TN-4
Barb Wood Spring—*spring* ... MT-8
Barby Creek—*stream* ... OK-5
Barcal Site—*hist pl* ... NE-7
*Barcamt Creek* ... GA-3
Bar Canyon—*valley* (2) ... NM-5
Bar Canyon—*valley* ... TX-5
Bar C Bar Ranch—*locale* ... NM-5
Bar C Creek—*stream* ... WY-8
Bar C Draw—*valley* ... WY-8
**Barce**—*pop pl* ... IN-6
Barcelona—*locale* ... AR-4
Barcelona—*locale* ... LA-4
**Barcelona**—*pop pl* ... NY-2
Barcelona Lighthouse and Keeper's Cottage—*hist pl* ... NY-2
Barcelona Mine—*mine* ... NV-8
Barcelona Neck—*cape* ... NY-2
Barcelona North Sch—*school* ... AZ-5
Barcelona Point—*cape* ... NY-2
Barcelona Sch—*school* ... AZ-5
Barcelona Sch—*school* ... NM-5
Barcelona South Sch—*school* ... AZ-5
Barcelona Summit—*gap* ... NV-8
**Barceloneta**—*pop pl* ... PR-3
Barceloneta (Municipio)—*civil* ... PR-3
Barceloneta (Pueblo)—*fmr MCD* ... PR-3
Barcer Run—*stream* ... OH-6
*Barcer Run Creek* ... OH-6
Bar C Gap—*gap* ... WY-8
Bar Channel—*bay* ... CA-9
Bar Channel—*channel* ... VA-3
Barchard Lake—*lake* ... MI-6
Barchas Ranch—*locale* ... AZ-5
Barcheers Post Office (historical)—*building* ... TN-4
Barch Hill Ch (historical)—*church* ... MS-4
*Barckley Brook* ... NJ-2
Bar C Lake—*lake* ... NM-5
Barclay—*locale* ... AL-4
Barclay—*locale* ... OH-6
Barclay—*locale* ... PA-2
**Barclay**—*pop pl* ... IL-6
**Barclay**—*pop pl* ... KS-7
**Barclay**—*pop pl* ... MD-2
**Barclay**—*pop pl* ... NV-8
**Barclay**—*pop pl* ... OR-9
**Barclay**—*pop pl* ... TX-5
**Barclay**—*pop pl* ... WV-2
Barclay, Dr. Forbes, House—*hist pl* ... OR-9
Barclay Bay Picnic Area—*park* ... ID-8
Barclay Branch—*stream* ... AL-4
Barclay Branch—*stream* ... MO-7
*Barclay Bridge* ... AL-4
Barclay Brook—*stream* ... NH-1
Barclay Brook—*stream* ... NJ-2
Barclay-Bryan House—*hist pl* ... TX-5
Barclay Cave—*cave* ... AL-4
Barclay Cem—*cemetery* ... AL-4
Barclay Cem—*cemetery* ... FL-3
Barclay Cem—*cemetery* ... IA-7
Barclay Cem—*cemetery* ... KS-7
Barclay Cem—*cemetery* ... MO-7
Barclay Cem—*cemetery* (2) ... TX-5
Barclay Ch—*church* ... IA-7
Barclay Court—*hist pl* ... NJ-2
*Barclay Creek* ... MI-6
Barclay Creek—*stream* ... ID-8
Barclay Creek—*stream* ... OR-9
Barclay Creek—*stream* ... WA-9
**Barclay Downs (subdivision)**—*pop pl* (2) ... NC-3
Barclay Draw—*valley* ... NM-5
**Barclay Farm**—*pop pl* ... NJ-2
Barclay Farm House—*hist pl* ... NJ-2
Barclay Heights—*uninc pl* ... NY-2
Barclay Hills Sch—*school* ... MI-6
**Barclay Hills (subdivision)**—*pop pl* ... NC-3
Barclay House—*hist pl* ... PA-2
Barclay Island—*island* ... TX-5
*Barclay Lake* ... MI-6
Barclay Lake—*lake* ... MI-6
Barclay Lake—*lake* ... WA-9
Barclay Lake—*reservoir* ... TX-5
*Barclay Landing Field* ... OR-9
Barclay Meadows—*flat* ... OR-9
**Barclay (Merrickton)**—*pop pl* ... MD-2
Barclay Pond—*lake* ... MI-6
Barclay Run—*stream* ... WV-2
Barclay Sch—*school* ... NJ-2
Barclay Sch—*school* ... NY-2
Barclay Sch—*school* ... OR-9
Barclay Sch—*school* ... PA-2
*Barclays Ferry* ... AL-4
Barclay Spring—*spring* ... MO-7
*Barclay Station* ... AL-4
Barclay Station—*locale* ... PA-2
**Barclaysville**—*pop pl* ... NC-3
Barclay-Teney Cem—*cemetery* ... AL-4
Barclay Townhall—*building* ... IA-7
Barclay Township—*fmr MCD* ... IA-7
**Barclay Township**—*pop pl* ... KS-7
Barclay (Township of)—*civil* ... PA-2
**Barclay (Township of)**—*pop pl* ... MN-6
Barclay Well—*well* ... NV-8
Barcley Sch—*school* ... IL-6
Barco—*locale* ... WA-9
**Barco**—*pop pl* ... IL-6
**Barco**—*pop pl* ... NC-3
Barco, Lake—*lake* ... FL-3
**Barcola**—*pop pl* ... FL-3
Barco Mine—*mine* ... CO-8
Bar Coulee—*valley* ... MT-8
Bar C Ranch—*locale* ... WY-8
*Bar Creek* ... CA-9
*Bar Creek* ... MI-6
*Bar Creek* ... WA-9
Barcreek—*locale* ... KY-4
Bar Creek—*stream* ... AK-9
Bar Creek—*stream* (2) ... CA-9
Bar Creek—*stream* ... CO-8
Bar Creek—*stream* (4) ... ID-8
Bar Creek—*stream* ... MT-8
Bar Creek—*stream* (3) ... OR-9
Bar Creek—*stream* ... UT-8
Bar Creek—*stream* ... WA-9
**Barcroft**—*pop pl* ... VA-3
**Barcroft, Lake**—*pop pl* ... VA-3
Barcroft, Lake—*reservoir* ... VA-3
Barcroft, Mount—*summit* ... CA-9
Barcroft Airp—*airport* ... DE-2
**Barcroft Hill**—*pop pl* ... VA-3
**Barcroft Woods**—*pop pl* ... VA-3
Bar Cross Basin Rsvr—*reservoir* ... OR-9
Bar Cross Ranch—*locale* ... WY-8
Bar Cross Tank—*reservoir* ... AZ-5
Barcus Creek—*stream* ... CO-8
Barcus Creek—*stream* ... WY-8
Barcus Ditch—*canal* ... CA-9
Barcus Peak—*summit* ... WY-8
Bard—*locale* ... NV-8
**Bard**—*pop pl* ... AR-4
**Bard**—*pop pl* ... CA-9
**Bard**—*pop pl* ... IA-7
**Bard**—*pop pl* ... NM-5
**Bard**—*pop pl* ... PA-2
**Bard**—*pop pl* ... WV-2
Bard, Elizabeth, Memorial Hosp—*hist pl* ... CA-9
**Bardane**—*pop pl* ... WV-2
Bard Branch—*stream* ... NJ-2
Bard Coll—*school* ... NY-2
Bar D Corral—*locale* ... AZ-5
Bard Creek—*stream* ... CO-8
Bard Creek Mine—*mine* ... CO-8
Bardeaux, Bayou—*channel* ... LA-4
**Bar Dee Homes**—*pop pl* ... FL-3
**Bardeen Corners**—*pop pl* ... NY-2
Bardees Bar—*bar* ... CA-9
Bardel—*locale* ... LA-4
Bardel State Wildlife Mngmt Area—*park* ... MN-6
*Barden* ... MN-6
Barden—*locale* ... MN-6
Barden Bay—*swamp* ... NC-3
Barden Branch—*stream* ... MI-6
Barden Brook—*stream* ... PA-2
Barden Cem—*cemetery* ... NC-3
Barden Cem—*cemetery* ... VT-1
Barden Creek—*stream* ... IL-6
Barden Hills—*summit* ... MA-1
Barden Inlet—*channel* ... NC-3
Barden Memorial Cem—*cemetery* ... OK-5
Barden-O'Connor House—*hist pl* ... TX-5
Barden Park—*park* ... MN-6
Barden Pond—*lake* ... NH-1
Barden Ranch—*locale* ... CO-8
Barden Reservoir—*dam* ... RI-1
Barden Rsvr—*reservoir* ... RI-1
Barden Sch—*school* ... GA-3
Barden Sch—*school* ... VA-3
*Bardens Inlet* ... NC-3
Barde Park—*park* ... CO-8
Barder, Byron R., House—*hist pl* ... OH-6
Bar-Dew Lake—*reservoir* ... OK-5
Bard (historical)—*locale* ... SD-7
Bardi—*locale* ... CA-9
Bardill Branch—*stream* ... TN-4
Bardin—*locale* ... FL-3
Bardin Cem—*cemetery* ... NY-2
Bardin Sch—*school* ... CA-9
Bard Lake—*lake* ... CA-9
Bard Lake—*lake* ... WY-8
**Bardley**—*pop pl* ... MO-7
Bardley Ch—*church* (2) ... MO-7
Bardman Canyon—*valley* ... AZ-5
Bardman Grove Ch—*church* ... GA-3
Bardman Hill—*summit* ... GA-3
Bardmoor Sch—*school* ... FL-3
Bardmoor Village Center (Shop Ctr)—*locale* ... FL-3
**Bardo**—*pop pl* ... KY-4
Bardo Cem—*cemetery* ... MN-6
**Bardolph**—*pop pl* ... IL-6
*Bardon* ... MN-6
Bardon Cem—*cemetery* ... IL-6
Bardon Creek—*stream* ... WI-6
Bar Doney Tank—*reservoir* ... AZ-5
Bar Doney Well—*well* ... AZ-5
**Bardonia**—*pop pl* ... NY-2
Bardon Lake—*lake* ... WI-6
Bardonner Lake—*reservoir* ... IN-6
Bardonner Lake Dam—*dam* ... IN-6
Bardon Park—*park* ... WI-6
Bardon Peak—*summit* ... MN-6
Bar Double 9 Ranch—*locale* ... NV-8
Bardow Shoal—*bar* ... MA-1
Bard Peak—*summit* ... CO-8
Bard Ranch—*locale* ... AZ-5
Bar D Ranch—*locale* ... CO-8
Bard Ranch—*locale* ... WY-8
Bard Rock—*cliff* ... NY-2
Bard Rock Creek—*stream* ... NY-2
Bard Sanitarium—*hospital* ... CA-9
Bard Sch—*school* ... MI-6
Bard Sch—*school* ... SD-7
Bards Creek—*stream* ... TN-4
**Bardsdale**—*pop pl* ... CA-9
Bardsdale Cem—*cemetery* ... CA-9
Bardsdale Methodist Episcopal Church—*hist pl* ... CA-9
Bards Dam—*dam* ... TN-4
Bard's Field—*hist pl* ... MD-2
Bardshare Spring—*spring* ... AZ-5
Bards Hill Ch—*church* ... KY-4
Bards Lake—*lake* ... IA-7
Bards Lake—*reservoir* ... TN-4
Bardsley, Joseph, House—*hist pl* ... NJ-2
*Bardsley Branch* ... MO-7
Bardsley Spring—*spring* ... UT-8
Bardsly Gulch Drain—*canal* ... ID-8
Bards Point—*cape* ... MD-2
Bard Spring—*spring* ... AZ-5
Bard Spring—*spring* ... WY-8
**Bardstown**—*pop pl* ... AR-4
**Bardstown**—*pop pl* ... KY-4
Bardstown Bayou—*stream* ... LA-4
Bardstown (CCD)—*cens area* ... KY-4
Bardstown Cem—*cemetery* ... KY-4
Bardstown Hist Dist—*hist pl* ... KY-4
**Bardstown Junction**—*pop pl* ... KY-4
Bar D Tank—*reservoir* ... AZ-5
Bardwell—*locale* ... WI-6
**Bardwell**—*pop pl* ... KY-4
**Bardwell**—*pop pl* (2) ... MA-1
**Bardwell**—*pop pl* ... OH-6
**Bardwell**—*pop pl* ... PA-2
**Bardwell**—*pop pl* ... TX-5
Bardwell Branch—*stream* ... TN-4
Bardwell (CCD)—*cens area* ... KY-4
Bardwell Cem—*cemetery* ... KY-4

Bardwell Cem—*cemetery* TX-5
Bardwell Dam—*dam* TX-5
Bardwell-Ferrant House—*hist pl* MN-6
Bardwell Island—*island* IL-6
*Bardwell Lake* MN-6
Bardwell Lake—*reservoir* TX-5
Bardwell Mill—*locale* NY-2
*Bardwell Rsvr* TX-5
Bardwell Sch—*school* IL-6
*Bardwells Ferry* MA-1
*Bardwell Village* MA-1
*Barea* KY-4
*Bare Beach* FL-3
**Bare Beach**—*pop pl* FL-3
**Bare Beach (sta.)**—*pop pl* FL-3
Bare Bone Bay—*swamp* SC-3
Barebone Creek—*stream* AL-4
Barebone Creek—*stream* KY-4
Barebottom Park—*flat* CO-8
Bare Branch—*stream* GA-3
Bare Branch—*stream* TN-4
Bare Branch—*stream* TX-5
Bare Branch Ch—*church* TX-5
*Bare Butte* SD-7
Bare Butte—*summit* TX-5
Bare Canyon—*valley* ID-8
Bare Cem—*cemetery* TN-4
Bar-E Club Lake—*reservoir* OH-6
Bare Cone—*summit* MT-8
Bare Cove—*bay* ME-1
*Barecove, Town of* MA-1
*Bare Creek* WY-8
Bare Creek—*stream* CA-9
Bare Creek—*stream* IL-6
Bare Creek—*stream* (2) WY-8
Bare Creek Ditch—*canal* CA-9
Barecroft Sch—*school* VA-3
Bare Drain—*canal* MI-6
Bar Ed Ranch—*locale* WY-8
Baree Creek—*stream* MT-8
Baree Lake—*lake* MT-8
Baree Mtn—*summit* MT-8
Bareface Bluff—*cliff* AK-9
Bareface Butte—*summit* OR-9
Bare Field Branch—*stream* AL-4
Barefield Crossroads—*locale* AL-4
Barefield Landing (historical)—*locale* AL-4
Bare Flat—*flat* OR-9
Barefoot—*locale* KY-4
Barefoot—*locale* TN-4
Barefoot Bay Commercial Center (Shop Ctr)—*locale* FL-3
**Barefoot Bay (Mobile Home Park)**—*pop pl* FL-3
Barefoot Beach State Preserve—*park* FL-3
Barefoot Branch—*stream* TX-5
Barefoot Bridge—*bridge* NC-3
Barefoot Brook—*stream* MA-1
Barefoot Brook Dam—*dam* MA-1
*Barefoot Cave* AL-4
Barefoot Cem—*cemetery* NC-3
*Barefoot Ch* MS-4
Barefoot Creek—*stream* ID-8
Barefoot Hill—*summit* MA-1
Barefoot Hollow—*valley* KY-4
Barefoot Lake—*lake* TX-5
Barefoot Mountains—*summit* TX-5
Barefoot Mtn—*summit* AL-4
Barefoot Nation Hills—*summit* IN-6
Barefoot Run—*stream* PA-2
Barefoot Sch (historical)—*school* MS-4
Barefoot Spring—*spring* AL-4
Barefoot Spring—*spring* MS-4
*Barefoot Springs Baptist Church* MS-4
Barefoot Springs Cem—*cemetery* MS-4
Barefoot Springs Ch—*church* MS-4
*Barefoot Swamp* NC-3
Bare-Garver Cem—*cemetery* PA-2
Baregrass Island—*island* NC-3
Bare Gulch—*valley* AK-9
Bare Gulch—*valley* ID-8
Barehead Branch—*stream* TN-4
*Bare Hill* CT-1
*Bare Hill* MA-1
*Bare Hill* RI-1
Bare Hill—*summit* CT-1
Bare Hill—*summit* ID-8
Bare Hill—*summit* (7) MA-1
Bare Hill—*summit* MT-8
Bare Hill—*summit* (2) NY-2
Bare Hill—*summit* NC-3
Bare Hill—*summit* VT-1
Bare Hill—*summit* WA-9
*Bare-hill Pond* MA-1
Bare Hill Pond—*reservoir* MA-1
Bare Hill Pond Dam—*dam* MA-1
**Bare Hills**—*pop pl* MD-2
Bare Hills—*range* CO-8
Bare Hills House—*hist pl* MD-2
Bare Hill Springs—*spring* ID-8
Bare Hole—*basin* WY-8
*Bare Island* MN-6
Bare Island—*island* (3) AK-9
Bare Island—*island* (2) ME-1
Bare Island—*island* OR-9
Bare Island—*island* WA-9
Bare Island Lake—*lake* CA-9
*Bare Islands* PA-2
Barekneed Rocks—*bar* MA-1
Bare Knob—*summit* TN-4
Bare Knob—*summit* WY-8
Bare Knoll—*summit* MA-1
Barela—*locale* CO-8
Barela, Adrian, House—*hist pl* NM-5
Barela-Bledsoe House—*hist pl* NM-5
Barela Canyon—*valley* (2) NM-5
Barela Cem—*cemetery* CO-8
Barela Creek—*stream* NM-5
Bare Lake—*lake* OR-9
Barela Lake—*lake* NM-5
Barela Mesa—*summit* CO-8
Barela Mesa—*summit* NM-5
Barela Mtn—*summit* NM-5
Barela-Reynolds House—*hist pl* NM-5
**Barelas**—*pop pl* NM-5
Barelas Bridge—*other* NM-5
Barelas Ditch—*canal* NM-5
Barela Spring—*spring* NM-5
Barela Springs—*spring* NM-5
Barelas Windmill—*locale* NM-5
Barela Well—*well* NM-5
Bare Ledges, The—*bar* ME-1
Bar Eleven Well—*well* AZ-5
*Barello Mountains* TX-5
*Barem* FM-9
*Bare Market* NY-2
Bare Marsh—*swamp* MD-2
*Baremeadow Brook* MA-1
Bare Meadow Brook—*stream* MA-1
Baremore Quarters—*bay* NJ-2
*Bare Mountain* UT-8
Bare Mountain Canyon—*valley* CA-9
Bare Mtn—*summit* (2) CA-9
Bare Mtn—*summit* MA-1
Bare Mtn—*summit* MT-8
Bare Mtn—*summit* NV-8
Bare Mtn—*summit* (3) NY-2
Bare Mtn—*summit* (2) TX-5
Bare Mtn—*summit* (3) WA-9
Bare Mtn—*summit* WY-8
Bareneaus Landing (historical)—*locale* MS-4
*Bare Neck Island* ME-1
Bareneck Island—*island* ME-1
Bare Neck Shore—*beach* MD-2
Barents Bay—*bay* VI-3
Barentsen, Andrew, House—*hist pl* UT-8
Barent Valley—*basin* NE-7
Bare Pass—*gap* NV-8
Bare Pass—*gap* WY-8
Bare Peak—*summit* MT-8
Bare Plain Cem—*cemetery* CT-1
Bare Point—*cape* ME-1
Bare Point—*cape* MI-6
Bare Point—*cape* TN-4
Bare Point—*cape* VA-3
Bare Ranch—*locale* CA-9
Bare Ridge—*ridge* WV-2
Bare Ring Butte—*summit* WY-8
Bare Ring Slough—*stream* WY-8
Bare Rock—*other* AK-9
Bare Rock—*pillar* CA-9
Bare Rock—*summit* PA-2
Bare Rock—*summit* RI-1
Bare Rock Mtn—*summit* NY-2
Bare Sand Beach—*beach* NC-3
Bares Brook—*stream* MA-1
Bares Cem—*cemetery* LA-4
Bare Spot—*flat* UT-8
Bare Spot Spring—*spring* UT-8
Bare Spring—*spring* ID-8
Bares Run—*stream* (2) OH-6
**Baresville**—*pop pl* PA-2
Baret Creek—*stream* AL-4
Baret Island—*island* MA-1
*Bare Top Mountain* UT-8
Bare Top Mtn—*summit* NY-2
Bare Top Mtn—*summit* UT-8
Bare Top Number 2 Lode Mine—*mine* SD-7
*Baretown* PA-2
Bare Tree Spring (Dry)—*spring* CA-9
*Baretto's Point* NY-2
Bare Valley—*basin* UT-8
**Bareville**—*pop pl* PA-2
Bareville Post Office (historical)—*building* PA-2
*Bare Wall Canyon* ID-8
Barewire Pond—*reservoir* UT-8
Bar F Bar Detention—*reservoir* AZ-5
Bar F Bar Detention Dam—*dam* AZ-5
Bar F Bar Ranch—*locale* AZ-5
Bar F Canyon—*valley* AZ-5
*Barfelden* PA-2
*Barfeldon* PA-2
Barfield—*locale* AR-4
Barfield—*locale* NC-3
**Barfield**—*pop pl* AL-4
**Barfield**—*pop pl* TN-4
Barfield Bar—*bar* TN-4
Barfield Bay—*bay* FL-3
Barfield Bend—*bend* TN-4
Barfield Cem—*cemetery* (2) FL-3
Barfield Cem—*cemetery* MO-7
Barfield Cem—*cemetery* NC-3
Barfield Cem—*cemetery* TX-5
Barfield Creek—*stream* GA-3
Barfield Ferry (historical)—*locale* NC-3
Barfield JHS—*school* AL-4
Barfield Knobs—*summit* TN-4
Barfield Lake—*reservoir* AL-4
Barfield Lakes—*lake* MI-6
Barfield Mill—*locale* SC-3
Barfield Mill Creek—*stream* SC-3
Barfield Point—*cape* AR-4
Barfield Ponds—*reservoir* AL-4
Barfield Sch—*school* FL-3
Barfields Old Mill Creek—*stream* SC-3
Barfield-Staples House—*hist pl* WI-6
Bar-Fly Corporation Airp—*airport* NC-3
Barfoot—*locale* MS-4
Barfoot—*locale* VA-3
*Barfoot Church* MO-7
Barfoot Lookout—*locale* AZ-5
Barfoot Lookout Complex—*hist pl* AZ-5
Barfoot Park—*flat* AZ-5
Barfoot Peak—*summit* AZ-5
Barfoot Post Office (historical)—*building* MS-4
Barfoot Spring—*spring* AZ-5
Barford Ch—*church* FL-3
Barfoth-Blood Mound Group (47 WK 63)—*hist pl* WI-6
Bar Four Pocket—*summit* CO-8
Bar F Ranch—*locale* TX-5
Bar F Ranch—*locale* UT-8
**Bargaintown**—*pop pl* NJ-2
Bargaintown Pond—*lake* NJ-2
Bargaman Draw—*valley* AZ-5
Bargaman Park—*flat* AZ-5
Bargaman Park Tank—*reservoir* AZ-5
Bargamin Bar—*bar* ID-8
Bargamin Bar Campsite—*locale* ID-8
Bargamin Creek—*stream* (2) ID-8
*Bargamot* AL-4
Barganier—*locale* AL-4
Barganier Hill—*summit* AL-4
Barganier Lookout Tower—*locale* AL-4
Barganier Slough—*stream* TX-5
Barge, Bayou—*gut* LA-4
*Barge Canal* NY-2
Barge Cem—*cemetery* TX-5
Barge Channel—*channel* FL-3
Barge Creek—*stream* KY-4
Bargee Creek—*stream* WY-8
Bargee Ranch—*locale* WY-8
Bargee Rsvr—*reservoir* WY-8
Bargee Sch—*school* WY-8
Barge Lake—*reservoir* MS-4
Barge Lookout Tower—*locale* MS-4
Barge Mountain, La—*summit* AZ-5
Bargen, Isaac, House—*hist pl* MN-6
Barge Point—*cape* VA-3
Barger Branch—*stream* (2) KY-4
Barger Branch—*stream* NC-3
Barger Branch—*stream* (2) TN-4
Barger Branch—*stream* TX-5
Barger Brook—*stream* NY-2
*Barger Canyon* CA-9
Barger Canyon—*valley* CA-9
Barger Cem—*cemetery* AR-4
Barger Cem—*cemetery* (2) IL-6
Barger Cem—*cemetery* MO-7
Barger Cem—*cemetery* (2) OH-6
Barger Cem—*cemetery* PA-2
Barger Cem—*cemetery* (2) TN-4
Barger Ch—*church* TN-4
*Barger Creek* PA-2
Barger Creek—*stream* MI-6
Barger Gulch—*valley* CO-8
Barger Hill—*other* WV-2
Barger Hollow—*valley* (3) TN-4
Barger Knob—*summit* TN-4
Barger Lake—*lake* NC-3
Bargeron Ch—*church* GA-3
Barger Pond—*lake* NY-2
Barger Pond—*lake* VA-3
Barger Ridge—*ridge* AR-4
Barger Ridge—*ridge* OH-6
Barger Run—*stream* PA-2
Bargers Branch—*stream* VA-3
Barger Sch (historical)—*school* MO-7
Bargers Run—*stream* PA-2
**Bargers Springs**—*pop pl* WV-2
**Bargersville**—*pop pl* IN-6
Bargersville Cem—*cemetery* IN-6
**Bargerton**—*pop pl* TN-4
**Bargerville**—*pop pl* IL-6
Barges—*locale* GA-3
Barge Sch—*school* WA-9
Barge Slough—*gut* AK-9
Barges P. O. (historical)—*locale* AL-4
Barge's Tavern—*hist pl* NC-3
Bargfeld Creek—*stream* OR-9
*Bargh Reservoir* CT-1
*Bargh Reservoir* NY-2
*Barg Lake* MN-6
Bargman Tank—*reservoir* AZ-5
Bar G O Ranch—*locale* CA-9
Bargo Sch—*school* KY-4
Bar Gulch—*valley* CA-9
Bar Gulch—*valley* CO-8
Bar Gulch—*valley* MT-8
Barham—*locale* AR-4
Barham—*locale* VA-3
Barham—*locale* WA-9
**Barham**—*pop pl* NC-3
Barham Branch—*stream* (2) AR-4
Barham Branch—*stream* TN-4
Barham Cem—*cemetery* GA-3
Barham Cem—*cemetery* NC-3
Barham Cem—*cemetery* TN-4
Barham Hollow—*valley* TN-4
Barham Lake—*reservoir* AR-4
Barham Ranch—*locale* CA-9
**Barhamsville**—*pop pl* VA-3
Barham (Township of)—*fmr MCD* AR-4
Bar Harbor—*bay* (2) ME-1
**Bar Harbor**—*pop pl* ME-1
**Bar Harbor**—*pop pl* MD-2
Bar Harbor Center (Census name Bar Harbor)—*other* ME-1
Bar Harbor Ferry Terminal—*locale* ME-1
**Bar Harbor (Town of)**—*pop pl* ME-1
Bar Harbor Yarmouth Nova Scotia Ferry—*locale* ME-1
Barhaven Creek—*stream* OR-9
Bar H Creek—*stream* AZ-5
Bar H Creek—*stream* SD-7
Bar Head—*cliff* MA-1
Bar Heart Ranch—*locale* AZ-5
Bar Heart Ranch Landing Strip—*airport* AZ-5
Bar Heart Rsvr—*reservoir* OR-9
Bar H Farm—*locale* NM-5
Bar Hill—*summit* AL-4
Bar Hill—*summit* MT-8
Barhite Lake—*lake* MI-6
Barhitte Sch—*school* MI-6
Bar H L Guard Station—*locale* CO-8
Bar H L Park—*flat* CO-8
Bar Hole Lake—*lake* GA-3
*Bar H Park* CO-8
Bar H Spring—*spring* AZ-5
Bar H Spring—*spring* SD-7
Barich Block—*hist pl* MT-8
**Barichs Subdivision**—*pop pl* UT-8
Barigan Stringer—*stream* CA-9
Bar II Ranch—*locale* WY-8
*Barilla Draw* TX-5
*Barilla Mesa* CO-8
*Barilla Mesa* NM-5
*Barilla Mountains* TX-5
Barillas Creek—*stream* NM-5
Barillas Peak—*summit* NM-5
Barillas Spring—*spring* NM-5
Barillos Creek—*stream* TX-5
*Barillo Valley* CA-9
Bar I-L Wash—*stream* AZ-5
Barin—*uninc pl* GA-3
Barina (Barrio)—*fmr MCD* PR-3
**Barinas**—*pop pl* PR-3
**Barinces**—*pop pl* PR-3
**Baring**—*pop pl* ME-1
**Baring**—*pop pl* MO-7
**Baring**—*pop pl* WA-9
Baring, Otto H., House—*hist pl* TX-5
*Baringate Bay* NJ-2
*Baring Atoll* MP-9
Baring Creek—*stream* MT-8
Baring Falls—*falls* MT-8
*Baring Inseln* MP-9
*Baring Island* MP-9
*Baring Islands* MP-9
Baring Lake—*lake* WA-9
Baring Mtn—*summit* WA-9
Baring (Plantation of)—*civ div* ME-1
Baring Sch—*school* AR-4
Baring Spring—*spring* WA-9
*Barings River* OR-9
*Barington Hills* NC-3
*Bar Insel* MP-9
Bar in Well—*well* AZ-5
BARISH Lake—*lake* MN-6
*Bar Island* ME-1
*Bar Island* MP-9
Bar Island—*island* (16) ME-1
Bar Island Ledge—*bar* ME-1
*Barite* VA-3
Barite—*locale* ID-8
Barite—*locale* MT-8
**Barite (historical)**—*pop pl* OR-9
Baritoe Campground—*locale* ID-8
*Baritoe Island* ID-8
*Baritts Pond* MA-1
Barium Queen Mine—*mine* CA-9
Barium Spring Orphanage Dam—*dam* NC-3
**Barium Springs**—*pop pl* NC-3
Bar J G Windmill—*locale* TX-5
Bar J H Ranch—*locale* CO-8
Barkaboom Mtn—*summit* NY-2
Barkaboom Stream—*stream* NY-2
Barkada—*locale* AR-4
Barkadare Sch (abandoned)—*school* MO-7
*Barkadaro Sch* MO-7
Barkalow Hollow—*valley* NY-2
Barka Slough—*swamp* CA-9
*Barkay Bayou* MS-4
Bark Basin—*basin* CO-8
Bark Bay—*bay* NV-8
Bark Bay—*bay* WI-6
Bark Branch—*stream* KY-4
Bark Cabin—*locale* WA-9
Bark Cabin Creek—*stream* MT-8
Bark Cabin Creek—*stream* OR-9
Bark Cabin Natural Area—*area* PA-2
Bark Cabin Run—*stream* PA-2
Bark Camp—*locale* GA-3
Bark Camp—*locale* ID-8
Bark Camp—*locale* KY-4
*Bark Camp Branch* GA-3
Barkcamp Branch—*stream* (4) KY-4
Barkcamp Branch—*stream* TN-4
Barkcamp Branch—*stream* VA-3
Bark Camp Branch—*stream* (3) VA-3
Barkcamp Branch—*stream* (2) WV-2
Bark Camp Branch—*stream* WV-2
Bark Camp Ch—*church* GA-3
Bark Camp Ch—*church* MO-7
Bark Camp Creek—*stream* GA-3
Bark Camp Creek—*stream* ID-8
Bark Camp Creek—*stream* KY-4
Barkcamp Creek—*stream* OH-6
Barkcamp Creek—*stream* TN-4
Bark Camp Fork—*stream* TN-4
Bark Camp Island—*island* AR-4
Bark Camp Lake—*reservoir* VA-3
Bark Camp Ridge—*ridge* NC-3
Bark Camp Run—*stream* PA-2
Bark Camp Run—*stream* TN-4
Bark Camp Run—*stream* WV-2
Bark Camp Sch (abandoned)—*school* MO-7
*Bark Creek* WA-9
Bark Creek—*stream* MI-6
Bark Creek—*stream* OH-6
Bark Creek—*stream* OR-9
Barkdoll Coulee—*valley* MT-8
*Barkdol Spring* AZ-5
Bark Drain—*stream* MI-6
Barkdull Prairie—*flat* CA-9
Barkdull Ranch—*locale* ID-8
Barkdull Sch—*school* LA-4
**Barke Circle Subdivision**—*pop pl* UT-8
Barkelew Draw—*valley* CO-8
Barkeley Ridge—*ridge* GA-3
Barkely Cabin Gulch—*valley* CO-8
Barkenberger Creek—*stream* OR-9
*Barker* ND-7
*Barker* PA-2
Barker—*locale* WA-9
**Barker**—*pop pl* MT-8
**Barker**—*pop pl* NY-2
**Barker**—*pop pl* OH-6
**Barker**—*pop pl* TX-5
**Barker**—*pop pl* WV 2
Barker—*uninc pl* KS-7
Barker, Benjamin, House—*hist pl* RI-1
Barker, Clarence, Memorial Hosp—*hist pl* NC-3
Barker, Col. Joseph, House—*hist pl* OH-6
Barker, John, House—*hist pl* CT-1
Barker, John H., Mansion—*hist pl* IN-6
Barker, Judge Joseph, Jr., House—*hist pl* OH-6
Barker, Mount—*summit* TX-5
Barker, Richard, Octagon House—*hist pl* MA-1
Barker, Stephen, House—*hist pl* MA-1
Barker, William, Residence—*hist pl* OH-6
Barker Airp—*airport* WA-9
Barker Arroyo—*stream* CO-8
Barker Arroyo—*stream* NM-5
Barker Bluff—*cliff* IL-6
Barker Branch—*stream* AL-4
Barker Branch—*stream* (4) KY-4
Barker Branch—*stream* NC-3
Barker Branch—*stream* TN-4
Barker Branch—*stream* (2) TX-5
Barker Branch—*stream* WV-2
Barker Branch (historical)—*stream* TN-4
Barker Brook—*stream* (4) ME-1
Barker Brook—*stream* RI-1
Barker Brook—*stream* (2) VT-1
Barker Butt—*summit* NC-3
Barker Camp—*locale* CA-9
*Barker Canyon* CO-8
Barker Canyon—*valley* WA-9
Barker Canyon Lake—*lake* WA-9
Barker Cem—*cemetery* AL-4
Barker Cem—*cemetery* GA-3
Barker Cem—*cemetery* IL-6
Barker Cem—*cemetery* (3) KY-4
Barker Cem—*cemetery* ME-1
Barker Cem—*cemetery* MS-4
Barker Cem—*cemetery* (2) MO-7
Barker Cem—*cemetery* MT-8
Barker Cem—*cemetery* OH-6
Barker Cem—*cemetery* (4) TN-4
Barker Cem—*cemetery* (3) TX-5
Barker Cem—*cemetery* VT-1
Barker Cem—*cemetery* (5) VA-3
Barker Cem—*cemetery* (3) WV-2
Barker Central Sch—*school* NY-2
Barker Ch—*church* IL-6
Barker Ch—*church* IN-6
Barker Ch—*church* NC-3
Barker Ch—*church* WV-2
Barker Coulee—*valley* MT-8
Barker Cove—*cove* MA-1
Barker Cove—*valley* TN-4
*Barker Creek* CO-8
Barker Creek—*locale* MI-6
Barker Creek—*stream* AR-4
Barker Creek—*stream* (4) CA-9
Barker Creek—*stream* ID-8
Barker Creek—*stream* IL-6
Barker Creek—*stream* IA-7
Barker Creek—*stream* MD-2
Barker Creek—*stream* (2) MI-6
Barker Creek—*stream* MN-6
Barker Creek—*stream* MO-7
Barker Creek—*stream* MT-8
Barker Creek—*stream* (2) NV-8
Barker Creek—*stream* NC-3
Barker Creek—*stream* OR-9
Barker Creek—*stream* VA-3
Barker Creek—*stream* WA-9
Barker Creek—*stream* WI-6
Barker Crossroads—*locale* VA-3
Barker-Cypress Archeol Site (41HR436)—*hist pl* TX-5
Barker Dam—*dam* CA-9
Barker Dam—*dam* KS-7
Barker Dam—*dam* TX-5
Barker Dam—*dam* UT-8
Barker Dam—*hist pl* CA-9
Barker Ditch—*canal* IN-6
Barker Dome—*summit* CO-8
Barker Dome—*summit* NM-5
Barker Draw—*valley* (2) WY-8
Barker Fork—*stream* WV-2
Barker Fork Ch—*church* WV-2
Barker Gap—*gap* AR-4
Barker Gap—*gap* WV-2
*Barker Gap Hollow* AR-4
Barker Gulch—*valley* CA-9
Barker Gulch—*valley* ID-8
**Barker Heights**—*pop pl* NC-3
Barker Hill—*summit* (2) MA-1
Barker Hill—*summit* TX-5
Barker Hill—*summit* VT-1
Barker Hollow—*valley* KY-4
Barker Hollow—*valley* (2) MO-7
Barker Hollow—*valley* OH-6
Barker Hollow—*valley* TN-4
Barker Hollow—*valley* TX-5
Barker Hollow—*valley* UT-8
Barker Hollow—*valley* (2) WV-2
Barker House—*building* NC-3
Barker House—*hist pl* CO-8
Barker House—*hist pl* NC-3
Barker House—*hist pl* TX-5
Barker Island—*island* FL-3
Barker Island—*island* RI-1
Barker Island—*island* TN-4
Barker JHS—*school* IN-6
Barker Knob—*summit* AR-4
Barker Knob—*summit* KY-4
Barker Lake—*lake* GA-3
Barker Lake—*lake* MI-6
Barker Lake—*lake* (2) MN-6
Barker Lake—*lake* WI-6
Barker Lakes—*lake* MT-8
Barker Meadow—*flat* CA-9
*Barker Meadow Reservoir* CO-8
Barker Mill—*hist pl* ME-1
Barker Mill—*locale* VA-3
Barker Mill Creek—*stream* AL-4
Barker Mill Creek—*stream* GA-3
Barker Mill Creek—*stream* TN-4
Barker Mtn—*summit* AL-4
Barker Mtn—*summit* CA-9
Barker Mtn—*summit* ME-1
Barker Mtn—*summit* MT-8
Barker Mtn—*summit* NY-2
Barker Mtn—*summit* OK-5
Barker Mtn—*summit* VT-1
Barker Mtn—*summit* WA-9
Barker Park—*park* AL-4
Barker Pass—*gap* CA-9
Barker Peak—*summit* (2) CA-9
Barker Plaza—*locale* KS-7
Barker Point—*cape* NY-2
Barker Point—*summit* KY-4
*Barker Pond* NY-2
Barker Pond—*lake* (2) ME-1
Barker Pond—*lake* NY-2
Barker Pond—*reservoir* ME-1
Barker Post Office (historical)—*building* AL-4
Barker Pounds—*summit* TN-4
Barker Rapids—*rapids* WA-9
Barker Reservoir Campground—*locale* UT-8
*Barker Ridge* WV-2
Barker Ridge—*ridge* ME-1
Barker Ridge—*ridge* TN-4
Barker Ridge—*ridge* (2) WV-2
Barker Ridge Ch—*church* WV-2
Barker Road Gap—*gap* NC-3
Barker Road Sch—*school* NY-2
Barker Rockhouse Branch—*stream* KY-4
Barker Rsvr—*reservoir* CO-8
Barker Rsvr—*reservoir* TX-5
Barker Rsvr—*reservoir* (2) UT-8
Barker Rsvr—*reservoir* WY-8
Barker Run—*stream* NY-2
Barker Run—*stream* WV-2
*Barkers* RI-1
Barkers Branch—*stream* NC-3
Barkers Branch—*stream* VA-3
Barkers Brook—*stream* (3) ME-1
Barkers Brook—*stream* NJ-2
Barkers Cabin—*locale* CA-9
Barker Sch—*hist pl* OH-6
Barker Sch—*school* KS-7
Barker Sch—*school* MA-1
Barker Sch—*school* NE-7
Barker Sch—*school* OH-6
Barker Sch—*school* (2) SD-7
Barker Sch—*school* TN-4
Barker Sch—*school* VA-3
Barker Sch—*school* (2) WV-2
Barkers Chapel—*church* TN-4
Barkers Chapel—*church* VA-3
Barker School (historical)—*locale* MO-7
**Barkers Corner**—*pop pl* NJ-2
**Barkers Creek**—*pop pl* NC-3
Barkers Creek—*stream* GA-3
Barkers Creek—*stream* (3) NC-3
Barkers Creek—*stream* SC-3
Barkers Creek—*stream* WV-2
Barkers Creek Ch—*church* SC-3
Barkers Creek (Township of)—*fmr MCD* NC-3
Barkers Crossroads—*locale* VA-3
**Barkers Crossroads**—*pop pl* GA-3
Barkers Ditch Cove—*bay* FL-3
Barkers Ferry (historical)—*locale* AL-4
Barkers Field—*airport* OR-9
**Barkers Grove**—*pop pl* NY-2
Barker Sheep Camp—*locale* WY-8
Barkers High Ledge—*summit* ME-1
Barkers Hill—*summit* NH-1
Barkers Island—*island* (2) WI-6
Barkers Landing—*locale* DE-2
Barkers Landing Bridge—*bridge* DE-2
Barker Slough—*stream* CA-9
Barkers Mill—*locale* KY-4
Barkers Mill—*locale* VA-3
*Barker's Point* NY-2
Barkers Pond—*lake* AL-4
Barkers Pond—*lake* MA-1
Barker Spring—*locale* GA-3
Barker Spring—*spring* TN-4
Barker Spring—*spring* UT-8
Barker Springs—*spring* NV-8
Barkers Ridge—*ridge* WV-2
Barkers Ridge Ch—*church* WV-2
Barkers Ridge (Magisterial District)—*fmr MCD* WV-2
Barkers Sch (historical)—*school* AL-4
*Barkers Slough* WA-9
*Barkers Station* ND-7
Barkers Store (historical)—*locale* AL-4
Barkers Swamp—*swamp* GA-3
Barker Store—*locale* FL-3
Barker Stream—*stream* ME-1
**Barker Subdivision**—*pop pl* UT-8
**Barkersville**—*pop pl* NY-2
**Barkersville**—*pop pl* SC-3
*Barkersville Brook* MA-1
Barkersville Cem—*cemetery* NY-2
Barkersville Ch—*church* MO-7
Barker Tank—*reservoir* TX-5
Barker Tenmile Sch—*school* NC-3
Barkertown—*locale* NY-2
Barkertown—*locale* TN-4
**Barker (Town of)**—*pop pl* NY-2
Barker Trailer Court—*locale* UT-8
Barker Valley—*valley* CA-9
Barker Valley Spur—*trail* CA-9
Barker Village Site—*hist pl* OH-6
Barkerville—*locale* AZ-5
Barkerville—*locale* CA-9
**Barkerville**—*pop pl* AZ-5
**Barkerville**—*pop pl* MA-1
*Barkerville Brook* MA-1
Barker Windmill—*locale* NM-5
Barkey Ditch—*canal* IN-6
Barkey Ditch—*canal* WY-8
**Barkeyville**—*pop pl* PA-2
Barkeyville Borough—*civil* PA-2
Barkhampsted Cem—*cemetery* CT-1
Barkhampsted Center—*locale* CT-1
Barkhamsted—*locale* CT-1
Barkhamsted Rsvr—*reservoir* CT-1
**Barkhamsted (Town of)**—*pop pl* CT-1
**Bark Hill**—*pop pl* MD-2
Bark Hill—*summit* PA-2
*Bark Hollow* UT-8
Bark Hollow—*valley* KY-4
Bark Hollow—*valley* UT-8
Barkhouse Branch—*stream* VA-3
Barkhouse Creek—*stream* CA-9
Barkhouse Picnic Area—*locale* NC-3
**Barking**—*pop pl* PA-2
Barking Dog—*rock* MT-8
Barking Dog Spring—*spring* CO-8
Barking Fox Lake—*lake* ID-8
*Barking Sands* HI-9
Barking Sands—*beach* HI-9
Barking Sands (not verified)—*island* MP-9
Barking Sch—*school* KY-4
Barkis Island—*island* IL-6
Bark Island—*island* SC-3
Bark Island Slough—*stream* SC-3
Bark Lake—*lake* WI-6
Bark Landing River—*stream* LA-4
*Barklay* TX-5
Barklay Creek—*stream* CO-8
*Barklays Bayou* MS-4
Bark Legging Lead—*ridge* TN-4
*Barklegging Trail* TN-4
**Barkley**—*pop pl* DE-2
Barkley, Isaac, House—*hist pl* KY-4
Barkley, Lake—*reservoir* KY-4
Barkley, Lake—*reservoir* TN-4
Barkley, Levi, House—*hist pl* MO-7
Barkley Bayou—*stream* MS-4
Barkley Branch—*stream* AR-4
Barkley Branch—*stream* MD-2
Barkley Branch—*stream* (2) TN-4
Barkley Bridge—*bridge* AL-4
*Barkley Brook* NJ-2
Barkley Canal—*canal* KY-4
Barkley Cem—*cemetery* AL-4
Barkley Cem—*cemetery* (2) MO-7
Barkley Cem—*cemetery* PA-2
Barkley Cem—*cemetery* TN-4
Barkley Ch—*church* IN-6
Barkley Ch—*church* PA-2
Barkley Coulee—*valley* WI-6
Barkley Creek—*stream* MI-6
Barkley Creek—*stream* OR-9
Barkley Creek—*stream* TX-5
Barkley Dam—*dam* AL-4
Barkley Dam—*dam* KY-4
Barkley-Floyd House—*hist pl* TX-5
**Barkley (historical)**—*pop pl* OR-9
Barkley House—*hist pl* KY-4

Barkley Lake—*lake* AK-9
Barkley Lake—*lake* NM-5
Barkley Lake—*lake* PA-2
Barkley Lake—*reservoir* AL-4
Barkley Lateral—*canal* AZ-5
Barkley Memorial State Park—*park* IA-7
Barkley Mtn—*summit* AL-4
Barkley Mtn—*summit* CA-9
Barkley Mtn—*summit* NY-2
Barkley Park—*park* KY-4
Barkley Pond—*lake* NY-2
Barkley Regional Airp—*airport* KY-4
Barkley Ridge—*ridge* AK-9
Barkley Ridge—*ridge* PA-2
*Barkleys Brook* NJ-2
Barkley Sch—*school* NE-7
Barkley Sch—*school* PA-2
Barkley Sch—*school* TX-5
Barkley Sch (historical)—*school* MO-7
Barkley Shores—*locale* KY-4
Barkley Spring—*spring* AL-4
Barkley Spring—*spring* OR-9
Barkley Store (historical)—*locale* MS-4
**Barkley (Township of)**—*pop pl* IN-6
Barkley Waterfowl Mngmt Area—*park* TN-4
Barklie Sch (abandoned)—*school* PA-2
Barklow Mountain Campground—*park* OR-9
Barklow Mtn—*summit* OR-9
Barkly Ranch—*locale* TX-5
Barkman—*locale* TX-5
Barkman, James E. M., House—*hist pl* AR-4
Barkman Cem—*cemetery* IN-6
Barkman Creek—*stream* TX-5
Barkman Sch (abandoned)—*school* PA-2
Bark Meadow Brook—*stream* CT-1
Barkmill Brook—*stream* VT-1
Bark Point—*cape* WI-6
Bark Point—*locale* WI-6
*Bark Point Bay* WI-6
Bark Pond—*reservoir* DE-2
Bar K Ranch—*locale* SD-7
Bark Ridge—*ridge* KY-4
Bark Ridge—*ridge* PA-2
Barkridge Sch (abandoned)—*school* PA-2
**Bark River**—*pop pl* MI-6
Bark River—*stream* MI-6
Bark River—*stream* (2) WI-6
Bark River Cem—*cemetery* MI-6
Bark River Ch—*church* MI-6
Bark River-Harris Sch—*school* MI-6
Bark River Park—*park* WI-6
Bark River Sch—*school* WI-6
**Bark River (Township of)**—*pop pl* MI-6
Bark Road Ch—*church* KY-4
Bark Road Sch—*school* KY-4
Barks—*locale* MO-7
Barks Canyon—*valley* (2) AZ-5
Barks Cem—*cemetery* MO-7
Barks Ch—*church* MO-7
Bark Sch—*school* MA-1
Barks Chapel—*church* MO-7
*Barksdale* MS-4
Barksdale—*locale* MD-2
Barksdale—*locale* WV-2
**Barksdale**—*pop pl* GA-3
**Barksdale**—*pop pl* MS-4
**Barksdale**—*pop pl* SC-3
**Barksdale**—*pop pl* TX-5
**Barksdale**—*pop pl* WI-6
Barksdale AFB—*military* LA-4
*Barksdale-Aldridge Cemetery* MS-4
Barksdale Bend (historical)—*bend* TN-4
Barksdale Branch—*stream* LA-4
Barksdale Bridge—*bridge* NC-3
Barksdale Cem—*cemetery* AR-4
Barksdale Cem—*cemetery* (2) MS-4
Barksdale Cem—*cemetery* SC-3
*Barksdale Creek* TX-5
*Barksdale Elementary School* TN-4
Barksdale Hollow—*valley* KY-4
Barksdale Lake—*reservoir* AL-4
Barksdale Ridge—*ridge* TN-4
*Barksdale School* MS-4
Barksdales Ferry (historical)—*crossing* TN-4
Barksdale Tank—*reservoir* AZ-5
Barksdale Tank—*reservoir* NM-5
**Barksdale (Town of)**—*pop pl* WI-6
Bark Shanty Camp—*locale* CA-9
Bark Shanty Creek—*stream* (2) CA-9
Bark Shanty Creek—*stream* (2) OR-9
Bark Shanty Gulch—*valley* CA-9
Bark Shanty Hollow—*valley* (2) PA-2
Bark Shanty Lake—*lake* AR-4
Bark Shanty Prairie—*flat* OR-9
Bark Shanty Shelter—*locale* WA-9
Bark Sharrly Canyon—*valley* CA-9
Barkshed Branch—*stream* SC-3
Barkshed Creek—*stream* AR-4
Barkshed Opening—*flat* CA-9
Barkshed Picnic Area—*locale* AR-4
Barkshed Run—*stream* PA-2
Bark Shed Trail—*trail* PA-2
Bark Slide Trail—*trail* PA-2
Bark Spring—*spring* CA-9
Barks Spur—*locale* ND-7
*Barks Station* AZ-5
Barktable Creek—*stream* MT-8
Barkwill Sch—*school* OH-6
**Barkwood (subdivision)**—*pop pl* TN-4
Bark Works Cem—*cemetery* IN-6
*Bar Lake* MI-6
Bar Lake—*lake* AR-4
Bar Lake—*lake* (2) LA-4
Bar Lake—*lake* (3) MI-6
**Bar Lake**—*pop pl* MI-6
Bar Lake Swamp—*swamp* MI-6
Barland—*locale* MS-4
Barland Cem—*cemetery* MS-4
Barland Creek—*stream* MS-4
Barland Post Office (historical)—*building* MS-4
*Barlay Cabin Gulch* CO-8
Barlean Creek—*stream* IA-7
Bar Ledge—*bar* (3) ME-1
Bar Ledges—*bar* ME-1
Barler Cem—*cemetery* OK-5
Barles Sch (historical)—*school* AL-4
Barlett—*locale* VA-3
Barlett Bench—*bench* OR-9
Barlett Canyon—*valley* KS-7
Barlett Canyon—*valley* NE-7
Barlett Cem—*cemetery* ME-1
Barlett Cem—*cemetery* MD-2
Barlett Country Club—*other* NY-2
Barlett Creek—*stream* CA-9
Barlett Hosp—*hospital* OK-5
Barlett JHS—*school* PA-2
Barlett Mtn—*summit* NH-1
Barlett Pond—*lake* ME-1
Barlett Run—*stream* PA-2
Barlett Sch—*school* WI-6
Barletts Ferry Dam—*dam* AL-4
*Barletts Pond* MA-1
**Barlett Springs**—*pop pl* CA-9
Barley—*fmr MCD* NE-7
Barley—*locale* VA-3
Barley Barber Swamp—*swamp* FL-3
Barley Beach—*beach* OR-9
Barley Bend Sch (historical)—*school* TN-4
Barley Branch—*stream* AL-4
Barley Branch—*stream* MO-7
Barley Branch—*stream* (2) TN-4
Barley Camp—*locale* OR-9
Barley Camp Creek—*stream* OR-9
Barley Canyon—*valley* (2) NM-5
Barley Cem—*cemetery* KS-7
Barley Cem—*cemetery* WV-2
Barley Ch—*church* PA-2
Barley Coulee—*valley* MT-8
Barley Cove—*basin* AL-4
Barley Creek—*stream* KY-4
Barley Creek—*stream* MT-8
Barley Creek—*stream* NV-8
Barley Creek—*stream* TN-4
Barley Creek Forest Service
Facility—*locale* NV-8
Barley Creek Ranch—*locale* NV-8
Barleyfield Cove—*bay* NY-2
Barleyfield Creek—*stream* CA-9
Barleyfield Peak—*summit* CA-9
Barley Flat—*flat* CA-9
Barley Flats—*flat* CA-9
Barley Ford—*locale* TN-4
Barley Hill—*summit* ME-1
*Barley Hollow* AL-4
Barley Hollow—*valley* KY-4
Barley Lake—*lake* CA-9
Barley Lake—*reservoir* MS-4
Barley Ledge—*bar* ME-1
Barley Mouth Branch—*stream* TN-4
Barley Neck—*cape* ME-1
Barley Neck—*cape* MA-1
Barley Patch Tank—*reservoir* AZ-5
Barley Point—*cape* NJ-2
Barley Point Reach—*channel* NJ-2
Barley Post Office (historical)—*building* TN-4
Barley Ranch—*locale* MT-8
Barley Reservoirs—*reservoir* MT-8
Barley Ridge—*ridge* MT-8
Barley Road—*trail* NV-8
*Barleys Creek* NC-3
Barley Sheaf—*locale* NJ-2
Barley Sheaf Inn—*hist pl* PA-2
Barley Slough—*stream* OR-9
**Barleytown**—*pop pl* NY-2
**Barley Woods (subdivision)**—*pop pl* DE-2
Barlietz Sch (abandoned)—*school* PA-2
Barlin Acres—*hist pl* MA-1
**Barling**—*pop pl* AR-4
Barling Bay—*bay* AK-9
Barling Cem—*cemetery* AR-4
Barling City Hall—*building* AR-4
Barling Post Office—*building* AR-4
Barling Sch—*school* AR-4
Barlous Lake—*lake* MN-6
Barlow—*locale* CA-9
Barlow—*locale* ID-8
Barlow—*locale* PA-2
**Barlow**—*pop pl* AL-4
**Barlow**—*pop pl* KY-4
**Barlow**—*pop pl* MS-4
**Barlow**—*pop pl* MO-7
**Barlow**—*pop pl* NJ-2
**Barlow**—*pop pl* ND-7
**Barlow**—*pop pl* OH-6
**Barlow**—*pop pl* OR-9
**Barlow**—*pop pl* WV-2
Barlow, Aaron, House—*hist pl* CT-1
Barlow, Lake—*lake* FL-3
Barlow, Smith H., House—*hist pl* NY-2
Barlow, William, House—*hist pl* OR-9
Barlow, William V. N., House—*hist pl* NY-2
*Barlow AME Church* MS-4
Barlow Basin—*basin* NM-5
Barlow Basin Tank—*reservoir* NM-5
Barlow Bay—*bay* WA-9
Barlow Bend—*locale* AL-4
Barlow Bottoms—*bend* KY-4
Barlow Branch—*stream* AR-4
Barlow Branch—*stream* DE-2
Barlow Branch—*stream* KY-4
Barlow Branch—*stream* LA-4
Barlow Branch—*stream* (2) MS-4
Barlow Branch—*stream* TN-4
*Barlow Butte* OR-9
Barlow Butte—*summit* (2) OR-9
*Barlow Buttes* OR-9
Barlow Campground—*park* OR-9
Barlow Canyon—*valley* CA-9
Barlow Canyon—*valley* UT-8
Barlow Canyon—*valley* WY-8
Barlow Canyon Sch—*school* WY-8
Barlow (CCD)—*cens area* KY-4
Barlow Cem—*cemetery* AR-4
Barlow Cem—*cemetery* CT-1
Barlow Cem—*cemetery* (2) KY-4
Barlow Cem—*cemetery* MA-1
Barlow Cem—*cemetery* (2) MS-4
Barlow Cem—*cemetery* MO-7
Barlow Cem—*cemetery* ND-7
Barlow Cem—*cemetery* OR-9
Barlow Cem—*cemetery* TN-4
Barlow Cem—*cemetery* TX-5
*Barlow Ch* AL-4
Barlow Ch—*church* AL-4
Barlow Ch—*church* KY-4
Barlow Ch—*church* MS-4
Barlow Channel—*channel* OR-9
Barlow Chapel—*church* AL-4
Barlow Chapel—*church* TX-5
*Barlow Chapel Methodist Ch* AL-4
Barlow Christian Mtn—*summit* AR-4
Barlow-Coolidge House—*hist pl* AR-4
**Barlow Corners**—*pop pl* VA-3
Barlow Cove—*bay* AK-9
*Barlow Creek* NC-3
Barlow Creek—*stream* AR-4
Barlow Creek—*stream* CO-8
Barlow Creek—*stream* ID-8
Barlow Creek—*stream* MO-7
Barlow Creek—*stream* MT-8
Barlow Creek—*stream* (2) OR-9
Barlow Creek—*stream* UT-8
Barlow Creek—*stream* VA-3
Barlow Creek—*stream* WA-9
Barlow Creek—*stream* WY-8
Barlow Creek Forest Camp—*locale* OR-9
Barlow Crossing Forest Camp—*locale* OR-9
Barlow Cutoff—*trail* OR-9
Barlow Drain—*canal* MI-6
**Barlowes**—*pop pl* NC-3
Barlow Flat Camp—*locale* CA-9
Barlow Flats—*flat* OR-9
Barlow Gap—*gap* WY-8
Barlow Guard Station—*locale* OR-9
Barlow Gulch—*valley* CA-9
**Barlow Heights**—*pop pl* PA-2
**Barlow Heights Subdivision**—*pop pl* UT-8
Barlow High Top—*summit* NC-3
Barlow Hill—*summit* PA-2
Barlow Hollow—*valley* PA-2
Barlow Hollow—*valley* UT-8
Barlow Hollow—*valley* WV-2
Barlow House—*hist pl* KY-4
Barlow HS—*school* CT-1
Barlow Island—*island* WA-9
Barlow Islands—*island* AK-9
Barlow Knoll—*locale* PA-2
Barlow Lake—*lake* IL-6
Barlow Lake—*lake* MI-6
Barlow Lake—*lake* TX-5
Barlow Lake—*lake* WI-6
Barlow Lake—*reservoir* CO-8
Barlow Lake Drain*—*stream* IA-7
*Barlow Landing* MA-1
Barlow Landing—*locale* AL-4
Barlow Mine (Inactive)—*mine* GA-3
*Barlow Mountain Campground* OR-9
Barlow Notch—*gap* NY-2
Barlow Park—*locale* IL-6
Barlow Park—*park* WI-6
Barlow Pass—*gap* AZ-5
Barlow Pass—*gap* OR-9
Barlow Pass—*gap* WA-9
Barlow Peak—*summit* WY-8
Barlow Point—*cape* AK-9
Barlow Point—*cape* WA-9
Barlow Point—*summit* WA-9
Barlow Point Channel—*channel* WA-9
*Barlow Pond* NY-2
Barlow Pond—*lake* NY-2
Barlow Ranch—*locale* CA-9
Barlow Ranch—*locale* WY-8
Barlow Ridge—*ridge* KY-4
Barlow Ridge—*ridge* OR-9
Barlow Rsvr—*reservoir* OR-9
Barlow Saint Sch—*school* VT-1
Barlow Sanatorium—*hospital* CA-9
Barlow Sch—*school* MN-6
Barlow Sch—*school* OR-9
Barlow Sch (historical)—*school* MO-7
Barlow Sch (historical)—*school* PA-2
Barlows Corner—*locale* VA-3
Barlows Corners—*locale* NY-2
**Barlows Landing**—*pop pl* MA-1
*Barlows Point* WA-9
Barlows Point—*cape* RI-1
Barlows Pond—*reservoir* VA-3
Barlows Pond Dam—*dam* MS-4
Barlow Springs—*spring* WY-8
Barlow Springs Draw—*valley* WY-8
*Barlows River* MA-1
**Barlow Subdivision**—*pop pl* UT-8
Barlow Top—*summit* (2) WV-2
**Barlow (Township of)**—*pop pl* OH-6
Barlow-Vincent Sch—*school* OH-6
Barlow Vista Ch—*church* NC-3
Barlow Well—*well* OR-9
Barloy Canyon—*valley* CA-9
Bar L Ranch—*locale* OK-5
Bar-L Ranch Country Club—*other* MN-6
Bar L Y Ranch—*locale* AZ-5
**Barmac**—*pop pl* NC-3
Bar Mac Ramp Station—*locale* PA-2
Bar M Canyon—*valley* AZ-5
Bar M Creek—*stream* WY-8
Barmen—*locale* LA-4
Barmes Pond—*reservoir* AR-4
*Barmgate Beach* NJ-2
*Barmgate Inlet* NJ-2
**Bar Mills**—*pop pl* ME-1
**Bar Mine**—*pop pl* FL-3
Bar Mine RR Station—*building* FL-3
Bar M Mtn—*summit* WY-8
Barmore Lake—*reservoir* PA-2
Barmore Lake Dam—*dam* PA-2
Barmore Run—*stream* PA-2
**Barmouth**—*pop pl* PA-2
Barmouth Station—*building* PA-2
Barmouth Station—*locale* PA-2
Bar M Ranch—*locale* OR-9
Bar M Slough—*stream* UT-8
Bar M Spring—*spring* UT-8
Barn—*locale* WV-2
*Barn, The* NC-3
Barn, The—*basin* UT-8
Barnabas Rock—*bar* AK-9
Barnabas (RR name for
Barnabus)—*other* WV-2
Barnabas Sch—*school* CA-9
Barnabe Creek—*stream* CA-9
Barnabee, Lake—*lake* NY-2
Barnabe Mtn—*summit* CA-9
Barnabie Point—*cape* WA-9
Barnabite Fathers Seminary—*school* NY-2
Barnable Sch (abandoned)—*school* MO-7
Barnabless Ch—*church* NC-3
Barnaboo Creek—*stream* MT-8
**Barnabus**—*pop pl* WV-2
**Barnabus (RR name**
**Barnabas)**—*pop pl* WV-2
Barnaby, Mount—*summit* MT-8
**Barnaby Acres**—*pop pl* IN-6
Barnaby Buttes—*summit* WA-9
Barnaby Creek—*stream* WA-9
Barnaby Drain—*stream* MI-6
Barnaby Island—*island* WA-9
Barnaby Lake—*lake* MT-8
**Barnaby Manor Oaks**—*pop pl* MD-2
Barnaby Rapids—*rapids* WI-6
Barnaby Run—*stream* DC-2
Barnaby Run—*stream* MD-2
Barnaby Sch—*school* NE-7
Barnaby Slough—*gut* WA-9
**Barnaby Terrace**—*pop pl* DC-2
**Barnaby Village**—*pop pl* MD-2
**Barnaby Woods**—*pop pl* DC-2
Barnacle Rock—*island* OR-9
Barnacle Rock—*other* AK-9
Barnacle State Historic Site,
The—*building* FL-3
*Barnard* KS-7
*Barnard* ME-1
Barnard—*locale* ME-1
Barnard—*locale* MI-6
Barnard—*locale* NJ-2
**Barnard**—*pop pl* IN-6
**Barnard**—*pop pl* KS-7
**Barnard**—*pop pl* MO-7
**Barnard**—*pop pl* NY-2
**Barnard**—*pop pl* NC-3
**Barnard**—*pop pl* SD-7
**Barnard**—*pop pl* VT-1
Barnard, Henry, House—*hist pl* CT-1
Barnard, J. T., Shell Midden (KHC-
1)—*hist pl* KY-4
Barnard, Mount—*summit* AK-9
Barnard, Mount—*summit* CA-9
Barnard, Parson, House—*hist pl* MA-1
Barnard, William J., Residence—*hist pl* PA-2
Barnard Bldg—*building* NC-3
Barnard Block—*hist pl* MA-1
Barnard Bridge—*bridge* NC-3
Barnard Bridge—*bridge* OR-9
Barnard Brook—*stream* (2) ME-1
Barnard Brook—*stream* NH-1
Barnard Brook—*stream* (2) VT-1
Barnard Buttes—*spring* MT-8
Barnard Canyon—*valley* WY-8
Barnard (CCD)—*cens area* TN-4
Barnard Cem—*cemetery* GA-3
Barnard Cem—*cemetery* IL-6
Barnard Cem—*cemetery* KY-4
Barnard Cem—*cemetery* MD-2
Barnard Cem—*cemetery* (2) MO-7
Barnard Cem—*cemetery* (3) TN-4
Barnard Corner—*locale* ME-1
*Barnard Creek* NE-7
*Barnard Creek* NC-3
Barnard Creek—*stream* CO-8
Barnard Creek—*stream* ID-8
Barnard Creek—*stream* MI-6
Barnard Creek—*stream* NY-2
Barnard Creek—*stream* OR-9
Barnard Creek—*stream* UT-8
Barnard Creek—*stream* VA-3
Barnard Creek—*stream* WA-9
Barnard Creek—*stream* WY-8
*Barnard Ditch* IN-6
Barnard Division—*civil* TN-4
Barnard Glacier—*glacier* AK-9
Barnard Gulch—*valley* OR-9
Barnard Hill—*summit* IN-6
Barnard Hill—*summit* (2) MA-1
Barnard Hill—*summit* NH-1
Barnard Hill Park—*park* DC-2
Barnard Hollow—*valley* AR-4
Barnard Hollow—*valley* TN-4
Barnard JHS—*school* CT-1
Barnard Knob—*summit* NC-3
Barnard Knob—*summit* TX-5
Barnard Lake—*lake* (3) MI-6
Barnard Lake—*reservoir* OK-5
Barnard Mill (Big) Branch—*stream* GA-3
Barnard Mills—*hist pl* MA-1
Barnard Mortuary—*hist pl* MN-6
Barnard Mountains—*summit* ME-1
Barnard Mtn—*summit* ME-1
Barnard Narrows—*gap* TN-4
Barnard Narrows Branch—*stream* TN-4
Barnard Observatory—*hist pl* MS-4
Barnard Park—*park* IL-6
Barnard Pond—*lake* ME-1
Barnard Pond—*lake* MI-6
Barnard Post Office (historical)—*building* PA-2
Barnard Ranch—*locale* MT-8
Barnard Ridge—*ridge* MT-8
Barnard Rsvr—*reservoir* CO-8
**Barnards**—*pop pl* (2) PA-2
Barnard Saddle—*gap* WA-9
Barnard Sch—*school* (2) CT-1
Barnard Sch—*school* DC-2
Barnard Sch—*school* IL-6
Barnard Sch—*school* ME-1
Barnard Sch—*school* (2) NY-2
Barnard Sch—*school* OK-5
Barnard Sch (abandoned)—*school* MO-7
Barnards Creek—*stream* (2) NC-3
Barnards Diggings—*mine* CA-9
Barnards Grove Ch—*church* TN-4
*Barnards Hill* MA-1
*Barnards Island* MS-4
Barnard's Mill—*hist pl* TX-5
Barnards Point—*cape* NY-2
Barnard Spring—*spring* AL-4
Barnard Spring—*spring* TN-4
*Barnardstones Grant* MA-1
**Barnardsville**—*pop pl* NC-3
**Barnardsville**—*pop pl* TN-4
Barnardsville Ch—*church* NC-3
Barnardsville Elem Sch—*school* NC-3
Barnardsville Post Office
(historical)—*building* TN-4
**Barnard (Town of)**—*pop pl* VT-1
Barnard Trail—*trail* VT-1
Barnard (Unorganized Territory
of)—*unorg* ME-1
Barn at Lucerne (Shop Ctr), The—*locale* MO-7
Barn at Oxford Horse Ranch—*hist pl* WY-8
Barn at 4277 Irish Road—*hist pl* MI-6
Barn Bluff—*cliff* MN-6
Barn Branch—*stream* (6) KY-4
Barn Branch—*stream* (2) NC-3
Barn Branch—*stream* SC-3
Barn Branch—*stream* (2) VA-3
Barn Branch—*stream* WV-2
Barn Brook—*stream* PA-2
Barn Butte—*summit* NE-7
Barn Canyon—*valley* CA-9
Barn Canyon—*valley* ID-8
Barn Canyon—*valley* (3) UT-8
Barncastle—*hist pl* ME-1
Barn Cove—*bay* MD-2
*Barn Creek* IN-6
*Barn Creek* MT-8
Barn Creek—*channel* GA-3
Barn Creek—*stream* AL-4
Barn Creek—*stream* CA-9
Barn Creek—*stream* ID-8
Barn Creek—*stream* KY-4
Barn Creek—*stream* MT-8
Barn Creek—*stream* OR-9
Barn Creek—*stream* TN-4
Barn Creek—*stream* VA-3
Barn Creek Ch—*church* AL-4
Barnd, John, House—*hist pl* NE-7
Barn Dam—*dam* SD-7
*Barndegat* NJ-2
Barndollar-Gann House—*hist pl* CO-8
Barn Door Gap—*gap* NH-1
Barndoor Hills—*range* CT-1
Barndoor Island—*island* NH-1
Barn Draw—*valley* MT-8
Barn Draw—*valley* NM-5
Bar N Draw—*valley* WY-8
*Barndtsville* PA-2
Barneburg Hill—*summit* OR-9
Barne Cem—*cemetery* TN-4
Bar Neck—*cape* (2) MD-2
Bar Neck—*cape* VA-3
**Bar Neck**—*pop pl* MD-2
*Barne Creek* IN-6
Barnegat—*airport* NJ-2
Barnegat—*locale* NY-2
**Barnegat**—*pop pl* NJ-2
Barnegat, Lake—*reservoir* NJ-2
**Barnegat, (Township of)**—*pop pl* NJ-2
Barnegat Bay—*bay* NJ-2
**Barnegat Bay**—*pop pl* NJ-2
**Barnegat Bay Estates**—*pop pl* NJ-2
**Barnegat Beach**—*pop pl* NJ-2
*Barnegat City* NJ-2
**Barnegat Estates**—*pop pl* NJ-2
**Barnegat (historical)**—*pop pl* OR-9
Barnegat Inlet—*gut* NJ-2
**Barnegat Light**—*pop pl* NJ-2
Barnegat Lighthouse—*hist pl* NJ-2
Barnegat Lighthouse State Park—*park* NJ-2
Barnegat Light Public Sch—*hist pl* NJ-2
BARNEGAT (lightship)—*hist pl* PA-2
Barnegat Natl Wildlife Ref—*park* NJ-2
Barnegat Pier—*locale* NJ-2
**Barnegat Pines**—*pop pl* NJ-2
Barneich Ranch—*locale* CA-9
Barnell Creek—*stream* WA-9
Barnell Meadow—*flat* WA-9
Barner Branch—*stream* AL-4
Barner Cem—*cemetery* (2) TN-4
Barner Cem—*cemetery* VA-3
Barner Gap—*gap* PA-2
Barner Hollow—*valley* AL-4
Barner Hollow—*valley* TX-5
Barner Run—*stream* PA-2
Barners Ch—*church* PA-2
Barners Creek—*stream* CA-9
**Barners Hill**—*pop pl* PA-2
Barner Site (22CO542)—*hist pl* MS-4
Barners Sch (abandoned)—*school* PA-2
Barnert Hosp—*hospital* NJ-2
**Barnerville**—*pop pl* NY-2
*Barnes* OH-6
Barnes—*locale* AL-4
Barnes—*locale* AR-4
Barnes—*locale* IL-6
Barnes—*locale* LA-4
Barnes—*locale* TX-5
Barnes—*locale* UT-8
Barnes—*locale* WY-8
**Barnes**—*pop pl* AL-4
**Barnes**—*pop pl* KS-7
**Barnes**—*pop pl* MS-4
**Barnes**—*pop pl* (3) PA-2
**Barnes**—*pop pl* SC-3
**Barnes**—*pop pl* (2) TN-4
**Barnes**—*pop pl* VA-3
Barnes, Andrew, House—*hist pl* WI-6
Barnes, Charles, House—*hist pl* UT-8
Barnes, Charles W., House—*hist pl* TX-5
Barnes, Frank C., House—*hist pl* OR-9
Barnes, Gen. Joshua, House—*hist pl* NC-3
Barnes, James B., House—*hist pl* MA-1
Barnes, John George Moroni,
House—*hist pl* UT-8
Barnes, John R., House—*hist pl* UT-8
Barnes, Jonathan, House—*hist pl* NH-1
Barnes, Mount—*summit* WA-9
Barnes, Tom, Barn—*hist pl* ID-8
Barnes, W. C., House—*hist pl* TX-5
Barnes and Hecker Mine—*mine* MI-6
Barnes Area County Park—*park* IA-7
Barnes Ave Sch—*school* MI-6
Barnes Bay—*bay* AR-4
Barnes Bay—*bay* VT-1
Barnes Bay Cem—*cemetery* NY-2
Barnes Bayou Landing
(historical)—*locale* MS-4
Barnes Bend—*bend* AL-4
Barnes Bend Access Area—*park* AL-4
Barnes Bldg—*hist pl* WA-9
Barnes Block—*hist pl* WI-6
Barnes Bluff—*cliff* KY-4
Barnes Bluff—*cliff* TX-5
**Barnes Bluff**—*pop pl* NC-3
Barnes Bluff Waterhole—*lake* TX-5
*Barnesboro* NJ-2
**Barnesboro**—*pop pl* PA-2
Barnesboro Borough—*civil* PA-2
*Barnesborough* NJ-2
Barnes Branch—*stream* AL-4
Barnes Branch—*stream* (2) AR-4
Barnes Branch—*stream* IN-6
Barnes Branch—*stream* KY-4
Barnes Branch—*stream* MO-7
Barnes Branch—*stream* (4) NC-3
Barnes Branch—*stream* (4) TN-4
Barnes Branch—*stream* TX-5
Barnes Bridge—*bridge* AL-4
Barnes Bridge—*bridge* WY-8
*Barnes Brook* NH-1
Barnes Brook—*stream* (2) ME-1
Barnes Brook—*stream* NH-1
Barnes Brook—*stream* NY-2
Barnes Brook—*stream* PA-2
Barnes Brook—*stream* (2) VT-1
Barnes Brothers Rsvr—*reservoir* OR-9
Barnes Brothers Rsvr Dam—*dam* OR-9
Barnesburg—*locale* KY-4
**Barnesburg**—*pop pl* OH-6
*Barnesbury* OH-6
Barnes Butte—*ridge* OR-9
Barnes Butte—*summit* AZ-5
Barnes Butte—*summit* WA-9
Barnes Butte Dam—*dam* OR-9
Barnes Butte Rsvr—*reservoir* OR-9
Barnes Cabin—*locale* WA-9
Barnes Camp—*locale* VT-1
Barnes Canyon—*valley* (2) CO-8
Barnes Canyon—*valley* NV-8
Barnes Cem—*cemetery* (4) AL-4
Barnes Cem—*cemetery* (5) AR-4
Barnes Cem—*cemetery* (5) IL-6
Barnes Cem—*cemetery* (5) IN-6
Barnes Cem—*cemetery* KS-7
Barnes Cem—*cemetery* (5) KY-4
Barnes Cem—*cemetery* LA-4
Barnes Cem—*cemetery* MI-6
Barnes Cem—*cemetery* (7) MS-4
Barnes Cem—*cemetery* (9) MO-7
Barnes Cem—*cemetery* (4) NY-2
Barnes Cem—*cemetery* (3) NC-3
Barnes Cem—*cemetery* OH-6
Barnes Cem—*cemetery* (8) TN-4
Barnes Cem—*cemetery* (4) TX-5
Barnes Cem—*cemetery* (3) VA-3
Barnes Cem—*cemetery* WV-2
Barnes Cem—*cemetery* WI-6
Barnes Ch—*church* AL-4
Barnes Ch—*church* GA-3
Barnes Ch—*church* VA-3
Barnes Chapel—*church* AR-4
Barnes Chapel—*church* GA-3
Barnes Chapel—*church* MO-7
Barnes Chapel—*church* (2) NC-3
Barnes Chapel—*church* VA-3
Barnes Chapel Sch (historical)—*school* MS-4
**Barnes City**—*pop pl* IA-7
**Barnes Corner**—*pop pl* MD-2
Barnes Corners—*locale* (3) NY-2
**Barnes Corners**—*pop pl* NY-2
Barnes County—*civil* ND-7
Barnes County Courthouse—*hist pl* ND-7
Barnes County Municipal Airp—*airport* ND-7
Barnes Cove—*bay* AK-9
Barnes Cove—*bay* MD-2
*Barnes Creek* MT-8
*Barnes Creek* SC-3
*Barnes Creek* UT-8
Barnes Creek—*gut* FL-3
Barnes Creek—*stream* AL-4
Barnes Creek—*stream* AK-9
Barnes Creek—*stream* (2) AR-4
Barnes Creek—*stream* (2) CA-9
Barnes Creek—*stream* (3) GA-3
Barnes Creek—*stream* (2) ID-8
Barnes Creek—*stream* IL-6
Barnes Creek—*stream* IN-6
Barnes Creek—*stream* KS-7
Barnes Creek—*stream* KY-4
Barnes Creek—*stream* (2) LA-4
Barnes Creek—*stream* MS-4
Barnes Creek—*stream* (2) MO-7
Barnes Creek—*stream* MT-8
Barnes Creek—*stream* NE-7
Barnes Creek—*stream* NY-2
Barnes Creek—*stream* (3) NC-3
Barnes Creek—*stream* (2) OH-6
Barnes Creek—*stream* (2) OR-9
Barnes Creek—*stream* (2) TN-4
Barnes Creek—*stream* (2) TX-5
Barnes Creek—*stream* UT-8
Barnes Creek—*stream* (3) VA-3
Barnes Creek—*stream* (2) WA-9
Barnes Creek—*stream* (3) WI-6
Barnes Creek Rsvr—*reservoir* TX-5
Barnes Creek Site—*hist pl* WI-6
*Barnes Crossroads* AL-4
Barnes Crossroads—*locale* GA-3
**Barnes Crossroads**—*pop pl* NC-3
Barnesdale—*locale* OR-9
**Barnesdale**—*pop pl* GA-3
Barnes Ditch—*canal* (2) IN-6
Barnes Draw—*valley* WY-8
*Barnese Lake* WI-6
**Barnes Estates Subdivision**—*pop pl* UT-8
*Barnes Ferry* TN-4
Barnes Field House—*building* AZ-5
Barnes Ford—*locale* TN-4
Barnes Fork—*stream* TN-4
Barnes Gap—*gap* GA-3
Barnes Gap—*gap* TX-5
**Barnes Gap**—*pop pl* PA-2
Barnes General Hosp—*hospital* WA-9
Barnes Gin Bar—*bar* AL-4
Barnes Gin (historical)—*locale* AL-4
Barnes Graves—*cemetery* TN-4
Barnes Gulch—*valley* ID-8
Barnes Gulch—*valley* MT-8
Barnes Gully—*valley* NY-2
Barnes Hill—*summit* (2) CT-1
Barnes Hill—*summit* KY-4
Barnes Hill—*summit* (2) MA-1
Barnes Hill—*summit* (3) NY-2
Barnes Hill—*summit* VT-1
Barnes Hill Ch—*church* NC-3
**Barnes (historical)**—*pop pl* OR-9
**Barnes Hole**—*pop pl* NY-2
Barnes Hollow—*valley* AL-4
Barnes Hollow—*valley* AR-4
Barnes Hollow—*valley* KY-4
Barnes Hollow—*valley* MS-4
Barnes Hollow—*valley* (3) MO-7

Barnes Hollow—valley (2) OH-6
Barnes Hollow—valley PA-2
Barnes Hollow—valley (6) TN-4
Barnes Hollow—valley TX-5
Barnes Hollow—valley VA-3
Barnes Hollow Branch—stream TN-4
Barnes Hosp—hospital MO-7
Barnes Hosp—hospital PA-2
Barnes-Hunter Cem—cemetery AL-4
Barnes Island—island ME-1
Barnes Island—island TX-5
Barnes Island—island WA-9
Barnes JHS—school TX-5
Barnes JHS—school WV-2
Barnes Joy Point MA-1
Barnes Junction—locale VA-3
Barnes Key—island FL-3
Barnes Knob—summit KY-4
Barnes Knob—summit WV-2
Barnes-Laird House—hist pl TX-5
Barnes Lake—lake (2) AK-9
Barnes Lake—lake (2) AR-4
Barnes Lake—lake GA-3
Barnes Lake—lake (2) MI-6
Barnes Lake—lake (2) MN-6
Barnes Lake—lake (3) MS-4
Barnes Lake—lake (2) NY-2
Barnes Lake—lake ND-7
Barnes Lake—lake SC-3
Barnes Lake—lake (2) TX-5
Barnes Lake—lake WA-9
Barnes Lake—lake (3) WI-6
Barnes Lake—lake WY-8
Barnes Lake—reservoir (2) GA-3
Barnes Lake—reservoir IN-6
Barnes Lake—reservoir NC-3
Barnes Lake—reservoir PA-2
Barnes Lake—reservoir (2) TX-5
Barnes Lake Dam—dam IN-6
Barnes Lake Dam—dam MS-4
Barnes Lake Dam—dam NC-3
Barnes Landing—locale MD-2
**Barnes Landing**—pop pl NY-2
Barnes Landing Creek—stream MD-2
Barnes Lick Run—stream WV-2
Barnes Meadow Rsvr—reservoir CO-8
Barnes Memorial Cem—cemetery FL-3
Barnes Memorial Park—park AL-4
Barnes Mill—locale WV-2
Barnes Mill Creek—stream (2) AL-4
Barnes Mill Creek—stream NC-3
Barnes Mill (historical)—locale AL-4
Barnes Mill (historical)—locale MS-4
Barnes Mill Rsvr—reservoir CO-8
Barnes Mine (underground)—mine AL-4
Barnes Mine (underground)—mine TN-4
Barnes Mission AL-4
Barnes Mountain Ch—church KY-4
Barnes Mtn MA-1
Barnes Mtn—summit AK-9
Barnes Mtn—summit CA-9
Barnes Mtn—summit CO-8
Barnes Mtn—summit KY-4
Barnes Mtn—summit TN-4
Barnes Mtn—summit TX-5
Barnes No 2 Cem—cemetery OH-6
Barnes Park—park CA-9
Barnes Park—park IN-6
Barnes Park—park MI-6
Barnes Park—park MN-6
Barnes Peak—summit AZ-5
Barnes Pinnacle—summit NY-2
Barnes Point VA-3
Barnes Point—cape AK-9
Barnes Point—cape (2) FL-3
Barnes Point—cape ME-1
Barnes Point—cape TN-4
Barnes Point—cape VA-3
Barnes Point—cape WA-9
Barnes Pond—lake (2) NY-2
Barnes Prairie—flat MS-4
Barnes Prairie—locale MS-4
Barnes Private Sch (historical)—school AL-4
Barnes Ranch—locale AZ-5
Barnes Ranch—locale (2) CA-9
Barnes Ranch—locale MT-8
Barnes Ranch—locale NE-7
Barnes Ranch—locale NV-8
Barnes Ranch—locale NM-5
Barnes Ranch—locale OR-9
Barnes Ranch—locale SD-7
Barnes Rancher Cem—cemetery AL-4
Barnes Ranch (Headquarters)—locale TX-5
Barnes Reservoir Dam—dam UT-8
Barnes Ridge—ridge MO-7
Barnes Ridge—ridge MT-8
Barnes Ridge—ridge OH-6
Barnes Ridge—ridge SC-3
Barnes Ridge—ridge TN-4
Barnes Ridge Ch—church MO-7
Barnes Rim—cliff OR-9
**Barnes Road**—pop pl OR-9
Barnes Rsvr—reservoir CO-8
Barnes Rsvr—reservoir CT-1
Barnes Rsvr—reservoir OR-9
Barnes Rsvr—reservoir UT-8
Barnes Run PA-2
Barnes Run—stream (3) OH-6
Barnes Run—stream PA-2
Barnes Run—stream (5) WV-2
Barnes Run Sch—school WV-2
Barness, Mount—summit AK-9
Barnes Sch AL-4
Barnes Sch—school AL-4
Barnes Sch—school AR-4
Barnes Sch—school CT-1
Barnes Sch—school (2) KY-4
Barnes Sch—school MA-1
Barnes Sch—school (3) MI-6
Barnes Sch—school NC-3
Barnes Sch—school ND-7
Barnes Sch—school OK-5
Barnes Sch—school OR-9
Barnes Sch—school SD-7
Barnes Sch (abandoned)—school MO-7
Barnes Sch (historical)—school AL-4
Barnes Sch (historical)—school MS-4
Barnes Sch (historical)—school (2) MO-7
Barnes Sch (historical)—school (2) TN-4
Barnes Shaft—mine NM-5
Barnes Shop Ctr—locale FL-3
Barnes Slough—stream OR-9
Barnes Slough—stream TX-5
Barnes Sound FL-3
Barnes Sound—bay FL-3
Barnes Southwest Oil Field—oilfield KS-7
Barness Point—cape MN-6
Barnes Spring—spring AZ-5
Barnes Spring—spring CO-8
Barnes Spring—spring (2) OR-9
Barnes Spring—spring TN-4
Barnes Spring Ch—church TN-4
**Barnes (sta.)**—pop pl OR-9
Barnes State Park—park WA-9
Barnes Station—locale NY-2
**Barnes Station**—pop pl SC-3
Barnes-Steverson House—hist pl OK-5
Barnes Store—locale TN-4
**Barnes Store**—pop pl KY-4
Barnes Store (historical P.O.)—locale MS-4
Barnes Strand—swamp FL-3
Barnes Swamp—stream VA-3
Barnes Swamp—swamp IN-6
Barneston—locale PA-2
**Barneston**—pop pl NE-7
**Barneston**—pop pl WA-9
Barneston Cem—cemetery NE-7
Barneston Junction WA-9
Barneston Site—hist pl NE-7
**Barneston Township**—pop pl NE-7
**Barnes (Town of)**—pop pl WI-6
Barnestown Post Office
(historical)—building PA-2
Barnes Township—fmr MCD IA-7
**Barnes Township**—pop pl KS-7
**Barnes Township**—pop pl ND-7
Barnes Township Cem—cemetery IA-7
Barnes (Township of)—fmr MCD AR-4
Barnes Tunnel—cave AZ-5
Barnes United Methodist Ch—church IN-6
Barnes Valley—valley OR-9
Barnes Valley Creek—stream OR-9
Barnes Valley Guard Station—locale OR-9
Barnes Valley Sch—school TN-4
Barnesville MD-2
Barnesville VA-3
Barnesville—locale AL-4
Barnesville—locale KS-7
Barnesville—locale (2) MO-7
**Barnesville**—pop pl AL-4
**Barnesville**—pop pl CO-8
**Barnesville**—pop pl GA-3
**Barnesville**—pop pl MD-2
**Barnesville**—pop pl MN-6
**Barnesville**—pop pl MS-4
**Barnesville**—pop pl NC-3
**Barnesville**—pop pl OH-6
**Barnesville**—pop pl PA-2
**Barnesville**—pop pl TN-4
**Barnesville**—pop pl VA-3
Barnesville Acad—school GA-3
Barnesville Baltimore and Ohio RR
Depot—hist pl OH-6
Barnesville Baptist Ch—church TN-4
Barnesville (CCD)—cens area GA-3
Barnesville Cem—cemetery AL-4
Barnesville Cem—cemetery KS-7
Barnesville Cem—cemetery NC-3
Barnesville Cem—cemetery TN-4
Barnesville Cem—cemetery TX-5
Barnesville Ch—church TX-5
Barnesville City Hall and Jail—hist pl MN-6
Barnesville Creek—stream AL-4
Barnesville Depot—hist pl GA-3
Barnesville Hist Dist—hist pl OH-6
Barnesville Methodist Ch—church TN-4
Barnesville Petroglyph—hist pl OH-6
Barnesville Rsvr—reservoir GA-3
Barnesville Rsvr—reservoir OH-6
Barnesville Sch—school CO-8
Barnesville (sta.) (Sellman) MD-2
Barnesville Station—locale CO-8
Barnesville Station—locale MD-2
**Barnesville (Township of)**—pop pl MN-6
Barnes Wash—stream AZ-5
Barnes Well—locale NM-5
Barnes Well—well NM-5
Barnes-Wellford House—hist pl WV-2
Barnes Woods Nature Preserve—park DE-2
Barnes Yard—locale OR-9
**Barnet**—pop pl VT-1
Barnet Canyon—valley OR-9
Barnet Center—locale VT-1
Barnet Center Hist Dist—hist pl VT-1
Barnet Creek AR-4
Barnet-Fisher Cem—cemetery OK-5
Barnet-Hoover Log House—hist pl OH-6
Barnet Mtn—summit VT-1
Barnet Mtn—summit VA-3
Barnet Run PA-2
**Barnet Run**—pop pl WV-2
Barnet Run—stream WV-2
Barnet Sch—school NJ-2
Barnets Cutoff—bend IA-7
Barnets Island—island IA-7
Barnet Spring—spring KY-4
**Barnet Springs**—pop pl LA-4
Barnet Springs Creek—stream LA-4
Barnett—locale GA-3
Barnett—locale (2) IL-6
Barnett—locale MS-4
Barnett—locale OR-9
Barnett—other PA-2
**Barnett**—pop pl CO-8
**Barnett**—pop pl MO-7
**Barnett**—pop pl VA-3
Barnett, R. T., and Company
Bldg—hist pl MT-8
Barnett, Thompson, House—hist pl IN-6
Barnet Tank—reservoir NM-5
Barnett-Attwood House—hist pl AR-4
Barnett Bay—bay KY-4
Barnett Bend—bend AR-4
Barnett Bend—bend KY-4
Barnett Branch—stream (3) AL-4
Barnett Branch—stream (4) KY-4
Barnett Branch—stream MS-4
Barnett Branch—stream (5) NC-3
Barnett Branch—stream (3) TN-4
Barnett Branch—stream (2) TX-5
Barnett Branch—stream WV-2
Barnett Bridge—other IL-6
Barnett Camp—locale AZ-5
Barnett Cem—cemetery (5) AL-4
Barnett Cem—cemetery (3) AR-4
Barnett Cem—cemetery (3) IL-6
Barnett Cem—cemetery (4) IN-6
Barnett Cem—cemetery (9) KY-4
Barnett Cem—cemetery LA-4
Barnett Cem—cemetery MN-6
Barnett Cem—cemetery (4) MS-4
Barnett Cem—cemetery MO-7
Barnett Cem—cemetery (2) OH-6
Barnett Cem—cemetery OK-5
Barnett Cem—cemetery (2) TN-4
Barnett Cem—cemetery (2) TX-5
Barnett Cem—cemetery (2) VA-3
Barnett Cem—cemetery WV-2
Barnett Chapel—church (2) AL-4
Barnett Chapel—church AR-4
Barnett Chapel—church KY-4
**Barnett Chapel**—pop pl (2) AL-4
Barnett Chapel Cem—cemetery AR-4
Barnett Community Chapel—church WV-2
Barnett Creek AL-4
Barnett Creek CO-8
Barnett Creek GA-3
**Barnett Creek**—pop pl KY-4
Barnett Creek—stream AR-4
Barnett Creek—stream FL-3
Barnett Creek—stream (3) KY-4
Barnett Creek—stream MS-4
Barnett Creek—stream MT-8
Barnett Creek—stream NC-3
Barnett Creek—stream (4) TX-5
Barnett Creek Ch—church (2) KY-4
Barnett Creek Landing—locale NC-3
Barnett-Criss House—hist pl OH-6
Barnett Crossroads—locale AL-4
Barnett Ditch—canal IN-6
Barnett Ditch—canal MT-8
Barnett Draw—valley WY-8
Barnette Cem—cemetery AL-4
Barnette Cem—cemetery SD-7
Barnette Cem—cemetery WV-2
Barnette Creek—stream AK-9
Barnette Ditch—canal IN-6
Barnette Hill—summit WV-2
Barnettes TN-4
Barnette Sch—school AK-9
Barnetteville Ch—church SC-3
Barnett Ferry (historical)—locale AL-4
Barnett Fork—stream WV-2
Barnett Grove Ch—church SC-3
Barnett Gut—stream NC-3
Barnett Hill—summit NH-1
Barnett Hill—summit TX-5
Barnett Hills—summit NV-8
Barnett Hollow—valley (3) MO-7
Barnett Hollow—valley (3) TN-4
Barnett Hollow—valley VA-3
Barnett Island—island SC-3
Barnett Knob—summit MS-4
Barnett Knob—summit NC-3
Barnett Knob—summit TX-5
Barnett Knoll—summit OR-9
Barnett Lake—lake AR-4
Barnett Lake—lake FL-3
Barnett Lake—lake KY-4
Barnett Lake—lake LA-4
Barnett Lake—lake SC-3
Barnett Lake—lake TX-5
Barnett Lake—reservoir (2) AL-4
Barnett Lake—reservoir GA-3
Barnett Lake Dam—dam AL-4
Barnett Lake Dam—dam MS-4
Barnett Landing—locale TN-4
Barnett Lookout Tower—locale GA-3
Barnett Marsh—swamp NY-2
Barnett Meadows—flat MT-8
Barnett Memorial Garden—cemetery MS-4
Barnett Mill Creek FL-3
Barnett Mill Hollow—valley AL-4
Barnett Mine—mine CA-9
Barnett Mtn—summit MO-7
Barnett Mtn—summit NY-2
Barnett Mtn—summit NC-3
Barnett Mtn—summit SC-3
Barnett Mtn—summit TN-4
Barnett Oil Field—oilfield MS-4
**Barnettown**—pop pl WV-2
**Barnet (Town of)**—pop pl VT-1
Barnett Pond—lake ME-1
Barnett Pond Dam—dam AL-4
Barnett Prong MO-7
Barnett Ridge—ridge KY-4
Barnett Ridge—ridge OH-6
Barnett Ridge Ch—church (2) OH-6
Barnett Run PA-2
Barnett Run—stream (2) WV-2
Barnetts—locale VA-3
**Barnetts**—pop pl TN-4
Barnett Sch—school (3) IL-6
Barnett Sch—school OH-6
Barnett Sch—school TN-4
Barnett Sch—school UT-8
Barnett Sch—school WV-2
Barnett Sch (abandoned)—school (2) MO-7
Barnetts Chapel—church IN-6
Barnetts Chapel—church KY-4
Barnett Sch (historical)—school (2) AL-4
Barnett Sch (historical)—school MO-7
Barnett Sch (historical)—school TN-4
Barnett School (abandoned)—locale MO-7
Barnett School (historical)—locale MO-7
Barnetts Creek GA-3
Barnetts Creek—locale KY-4
Barnetts Creek—stream GA-3
Barnetts Creek—stream KY-4
Barnetts Creek—stream MI-6
Barnetts Creek Ch—church GA-3
Barnetts Creek Ch—church KY-4
Barnett-Seawright-Wilson House—hist pl IN-6
Barnetts Field—airport CO-8
Barnett Shoals—locale GA-3
Barnett Shoals Dam—dam GA-3
Barnett Siding IL-6
Barnetts Knob Cem—cemetery KY-4
Barnetts Lake AL-4
Barnetts Lick Ch—church KY-4
Barnett Spring—spring AZ-5
Barnett Spring—spring KY-4
Barnett Spring—spring MO-7
Barnett Spring—spring OR-9
Barnett Spring—spring (2) TX-5
Barnett Spring Draw—valley TX-5
Barnett Springs—locale KY-4
Barnett Springs Creek—stream TX-5
Barnetts Run—stream PA-2
Barnetts Run—stream VA-3
Barnetts Store AL-4
Barnetts Store TN-4
**Barnettstown**—pop pl PA-2
Barnett Tank—reservoir AZ-5
Barnett-Tiner Hill Cem—cemetery TN-4
Barnett (Township of)—fmr MCD AR-4
**Barnett (Township of)**—pop pl IL-6
**Barnett (Township of)**—pop pl MN-6
**Barnett (Township of)**—pop pl (2) PA-2
Barnett Valley—valley KY-4
Barnett Well—well NM-5
**Barneveld**—pop pl NY-2
**Barneveld**—pop pl WI-6
Barneveld Station—locale NY-2
Barney—locale AR-4
Barney—locale IA-7
Barney—locale OR-9
**Barney**—pop pl AL-4
**Barney**—pop pl GA-3
**Barney**—pop pl ND-7
Barney, Commodore Joshua,
House—hist pl MD-2
Barney, Freeland T., House—hist pl OH-6
Barney, H. S., Bldg—hist pl NY-2
Barney, Lake—lake WI-6
Barney, Mount—summit WA-9
Barney Backup—gut IL-6
**Barney (Barney Mines)**—pop pl AL-4
Barney Bird Rsvr No 1—reservoir CO-8
Barney Bluff—cliff GA-3
Barney Branch LA-4
Barney Branch WV-2
Barney Branch—stream KY-4
Barney Branch—stream MS-4
Barney Branch—stream NC-3
Barney Brook—stream ME-1
Barney Brook—stream NY-2
Barney Brook—stream VT-1
Barney Canyon—valley AZ-5
Barney Canyon—valley WY-8
Barney Carrier Corners—locale PA-2
Barney Cavanah Ridge—ridge CA-9
Barney (CCD)—cens area GA-3
Barney Cem—cemetery IA-7
Barney Cem—cemetery WI-6
Barney Chute—gut TN-4
Barney Chute—stream (2) AR-4
Barney Circle—locale DC-2
Barney Coker Canyon—valley WA-9
Barney Convalescent Hosp—hospital OH-6
Barney Cove—valley UT-8
Barney Creek—stream AL-4
Barney Creek—stream AK-9
Barney Creek—stream CA-9
Barney Creek—stream FL-3
Barney Creek—stream (2) ID-8
Barney Creek—stream MO-7
Barney Creek—stream (2) MT-8
Barney Creek—stream NE-7
Barney Creek—stream OK-5
Barney Creek—stream OR-9
Barney Creek—stream TN-4
Barney Creek—stream WA-9
Barney Draw—valley AZ-5
Barney Dry Dam—dam AZ-5
Barney Flat—flat AZ-5
Barney Ford—locale IL-6
Barney Ford Hill—summit CO-8
Barney Fork—stream OH-6
Barney Fry Creek—stream MN-6
Barney Gulch—valley CA-9
Barney Gulch—valley MT-8
Barney Hill—summit CO-8
Barney Hill—summit CT-1
Barney Hill—summit NY-2
Barney Hill—summit PA-2
Barney Hollow—valley AR-4
Barney Hollow—valley KY-4
Barney Hollow—valley NY-2
Barney Hollow—valley UT-8
Barney Hot Springs—spring ID 8
Barney Island—island IL-6
Barney Kerr Canyon—valley NM-5
Barney Knob—summit CA-9
Barney Knoll—summit AZ-5
Barney Lake MI-6
Barney Lake—lake (2) CA-9
Barney Lake—lake MI-6
Barney Lake—lake MN-6
Barney Lake—lake UT-8
Barney Lake—lake WA-9
Barney Lake—reservoir GA-3
Barney Lake—reservoir UT-8
Barney Lake Reservoir Dam—dam UT-8
Barney Lakes—lake MN-6
Barney Meadow—flat CA-9
Barney Meadows—flat NV-8
Barney Meadows—flat WY-8
Barney Meadows Creek—stream NV-8
Barney Meadows Spring—spring NV-8
Barney Meadows Spring—spring WY-8
Barney Mills—locale NY-2
Barney Mine AL-4
Barney Mines AL-4
Barney Mound—summit CA-9
Barney Pacific Lateral—canal WA-9
Barney Pasture—area AZ-5
Barney Pasture Burn—area AZ-5
Barney Pinnacle—summit MT-8
Barney Pits—mine CA-9
Barney Point MA-1
Barney Point—cape ME-1
Barney Point—cape VT-1
Barney Pond—lake NH-1
Barney Pond—lake NY-2
Barney Pond—reservoir RI-1
Barney Pond Dam—dam RI-1
Barney Ranch—locale AZ-5
Barney Ranch—locale OR-9
Barney Reevey Gulch—valley UT-8
Barney Ridge—ridge AZ-5
Barney Ridge—ridge CA-9
Barney Riley Creek—stream CA-9
Barney Riley (Site)—locale CA-9
Barney Rsvr—reservoir CO-8
Barney Rsvr—reservoir OR-9
Barney Rsvr—reservoir UT-8
Barney Run—stream OH-6
Barney Run—stream PA-2
Barney Run—stream VA-3
Barneys Battery Site—locale DC-2
Barneys Branch—stream NE-7
Barneys Butte—summit OR-9
Barneys Butte Waterhole—lake OR-9
Barneys Canyon—valley UT-8
Barney Sch—school FL-3
Barney Sch—school IL-6
Barney Sch—school KY-4
Barney Sch—school MI-6
Barneys Coulee—valley MT-8
Barneys Creek—stream UT-8
Barneys Fork MS-4
Barneys Hill—summit PA-2
Barneys Hollow—valley UT-8
Barneys Joy MA-1
Barneys Joy Point—cape MA-1
Barneys Lake—lake MI-6
Barneys Lake—lake WI-6
Barneys Little Island—island ME-1
Barneys Lower Landing—locale AL-4
Barney Slue Beacon (C)—tower NC-3
Barneys Peak—summit UT-8
Barney's Point ME-1
Barneys Point—cape MA-1
Barneys Pond RI-1
Barneys Prairie Ch—church IL-6
Barney Spring—spring AZ-5
Barney Spring—spring WI-6
Barney Spring Canyon—valley AZ-5
Barneys Ridge—ridge PA-2
Barneys Run—stream (2) PA-2
Barneys Shoals—bar AL-4
Barney Stage Station (Site)—locale NM-5
Barney Station ND-7
Barneys Upper Landing
(historical)—locale AL-4
Barneys Wall—summit VA-3
Barney Swamp ME-1
Barney Swamp—swamp WI-6
Barneys Wash—stream UT-8
Barney Tank—reservoir (2) AZ-5
Barney Tank—reservoir NM-5
Barney Top—summit UT-8
Barneytown PA-2
**Barneytown (Latta Grove)**—pop pl PA-2
**Barney Township**—pop pl ND-7
**Barneyville**—pop pl GA-3
**Barneyville**—pop pl MA-1
Barneyville Sch (historical)—school PA-2
Barney Waterhole—lake OR-9
Barney Well—well (2) AZ-5
Barney White Ranch—locale WA-9
Barney Williams Dam Tank—reservoir AZ-5
Barney Zell Ridge—ridge WA-9
Barn Fork MO-7
Barn Fork—stream MO-7
Barngrover Creek—stream NE-7
Barn Gulch—valley CA-9
Barn Gulch—valley MT-8
Barn Gulch—valley NV-8
Barnhard Creek—stream AK-9
Barnhard Sch—school CA-9
Barnhard Sch—school MN-6
Barnhardt Canyon—valley AZ-5
Barnhardt Ch—church VA-3
Barnhardt Creek—stream MI-6
Barnhardt Creek—stream TX-5
Barnhardt Creek—stream VA-3
Barnhardt Mesa—summit AZ-5
Barnhardt Mesa Tank—reservoir AZ-5
Barnhardt Pond—lake NY-2
Barnhardt Tank—reservoir AZ-5
Barnhardt Trail—trail AZ-5
Barnhardy—locale OR-9
Barnhart—locale OR-9
**Barnhart**—pop pl MO-7
**Barnhart**—pop pl TX-5
Barnhart Apartments—hist pl UT-8
Barnhart Boles Cem—cemetery TX-5
Barnhart Canyon—valley CO-8
Barnhart Cem—cemetery IN-6
Barnhart Cem—cemetery (2) MO-7
Barnhart Coulee—valley MT-8
Barnhart Creek TX-5
Barnhart Creek—stream AR-4
Barnhart Hollow—valley OH-6
Barnhart Island—island NY-2
Barnhart Island Beach—beach NY-2
Barnhart Island Bridge—bridge NY-2
Barnhart Island Dyke—levee NY-2
Barnhart Oil Field—oilfield TX-5
Barnhart Sch—school MI-6
Barnhart Strip Airp—airport IN-6
**Barnhart Town**—pop pl IN-6
Barnhart Trail—trail PA-2
Barnhart Windmill—locale CO-8
Barnhart Windmill—locale TX-5
Barnheisel Hollow—valley IN-6
Barnhill—locale GA-3
Barnhill—locale SC-3
**Barnhill**—pop pl IL-6
**Barnhill**—pop pl OH-6
Barn Hill—summit AR-4
Barn Hill—summit CT-1
Barn Hill—summit KY-4
Barn Hill—summit TN-4
Barnhill Airp—airport NC-3
Barnhill Branch—stream TN-4
Barnhill Bridge—bridge KS-7
Barnhill Cem—cemetery NC-3
Barnhill Cem—cemetery OH-6
Barn Hill Ch—church AR-4
Barn Hill Ch—church TN-4
Barn Hill Creek—stream AR-4
Barnhill Mtn—summit NC-3
Barnhill Oil Field—other IL-6
Barn Hill (RR name for Barnhill)—other IL-6
Barn Hills—summit UT-8
Barn Hills Sch (abandoned)—school PA-2
**Barnhill (Township of)**—pop pl IL-6
Barnhill Windmill—locale NM-5
Barnhisel, Henry II, House—hist pl OH-6
Barnholdt Ditch—canal NE-7
Barn Hollow—basin CA-9
Barn Hollow—valley AL-4
Barn Hollow—valley AR-4
Barn Hollow—valley (5) KY-4
Barn Hollow—valley (9) MO-7
Barn Hollow—valley (5) TN-4
Barn Hollow—valley (8) WV-2
Barn Hollow Float Camp—locale MO-7
Barn Hollow Natural Area—park MO-7
Barnhouse Cem—cemetery WV-2
Barnhouse Hill—summit MO-7
Barnhouse Spring—spring OR-9
Barnhurst Ridge UT-8
Barnhurst Ridge—ridge UT-8
Barnical Chapel MO-7
Barnicle Ch—church MO-7
Barnigate Inlet NJ-2
**Barnisdale Forest**—pop pl AL-4
Barnishaw Cem—cemetery AR-4
Barnishee Bayou—gut TN-4
Barnisky Cem—cemetery OK-5
Barn Island—island CT-1
Barn Island Hunting Area—park CT-1
**Barnitz**—pop pl PA-2
Barnitz Creek—stream OK-5
Barnitz Park—park MO-7
Barnitz Prong—stream MO-7
Barnjum—locale ME-1
Barn Lake AL-4
Barn Lake Dam AL-4
Barn Lick Branch—stream VA-3
Bar NL Mesa—summit NM-5
Barnlog Hollow—valley MO-7
Bar NL Tank—reservoir NM-5
Barn Meadow—flat CA-9
Barn Mtn—summit GA-3
Bar None Ranch—locale MN-6
Barn Opening—flat CA-9
Barn Pass, The—gap UT-8
Barn Point VA-3
Barn Point—cape ME-1
Barn Point—cape VA-3
Barn Point Windmill—locale NM-5
Barn Pole Hollow—valley NV-8
Barn Pond AL-4
Barn Pond Dam AL-4
Barn Ridge—ridge KY-4
Barn Ridge—ridge MO-7
Barn Ridge—ridge NC-3
Barn Ridge—ridge VA-3
Barn Ridge—ridge WV-2
Barn River—stream MO-7
Barn Rock—cape NY-2
**Barnrock**—pop pl KY-4
Barn Rock Bay—bay NY-2
Barnrock Branch—stream KY-4
Barn Rocks—bar MA-1
Barnroof Point—cliff CO-8
Barn Run—stream IN-6
Barn Run—stream PA-2
Barn Run—stream (2) WV-2
Barns, Acors, House—hist pl CT-1
**Barnsboro**—pop pl NJ-2
Barnsboro Ch—church NJ-2
Barnsboro Hotel—hist pl NJ-2
Barns Branch—stream AR-4
Barns-Brinton House—hist pl PA-2
Barnsburg OH-6
Barns Canyon—valley WY-8
Barns Cem—cemetery KY-4
Barns Cem—cemetery VA-3
Barns Chapel GA-3
Barns Cove—valley NC-3
Barns Creek AR-4
Barnsdale GA-3
**Barnsdall**—pop pl LA-4
**Barnsdall**—pop pl OK-5
Barnsdall (CCD)—cens area OK-5
Barnsdall Oil Field—oilfield OK-5
Barnsdall Park—hist pl CA-9
Barnsdall Park—park CA-9
Barnsdall Sch—school OK-5
Barns Ferry (historical)—locale TN-4
Barns Hill—summit CT-1
Barns JHS—school OH-6
Barns Lake AR-4
Barns Lake—reservoir AL-4
Barnsley GA-3
Barnsley—locale PA-2
**Barnsley**—pop pl GA-3
**Barnsley**—pop pl KY-4
Barnsley Cem—cemetery KY-4
Barnsley Ch—church GA-3
Barnsley Creek GA-3
Barnsley Gardens—locale GA-3
Barnsley Hills—range KY-4
Barnsley Lake—lake WA-9
Barnsleys Ford PA-2
Barns Mill Branch—stream AL-4
Barns Mtn KY-4
Barns Pond—lake MI-6
Barns Pond—lake NY-2
Barns Pond—reservoir AL-4
Barn Spring—spring CA-9
Barn Spring—spring UT-8
**Barnstable**—pop pl MA-1
Barnstable (census name for Barnstable
Center)—CDP MA-1
Barnstable Center (census name
Barnstable)—other MA-1
**Barnstable County**—pop pl MA-1
Barnstable County Court House—building MA-1
Barnstable County Courthouse—hist pl MA-1
Barnstable County Fairgrounds—locale MA-1
Barnstable County Hosp—hospital MA-1
Barnstable Harbor—harbor MA-1
Barnstable HS—school MA-1
Barnstable Municipal Airp—airport MA-1
Barnstable Municipal Airport Aero
Light—locale MA-1
Barnstable Public Lands—park Town of MA-1
**Barnstable (Town of)**—pop pl MA-1
Barnstable Village MA-1
Barnstaple MA-1
Barnstaple, Town of MA-1
Barnstaple Harbor MA-1
**Barnstead**—pop pl NH-1
**Barnstead (Town of)**—pop pl NH-1

Barrett Springs Well—*well* ... NV-8
Barrett Springs Windmill—*locale* ... NV-8
Barrett Spur—*ridge* ... OR-9
Barretts Range Channel—*channel* ... OR-9
Barretts Store—*locale* ... VA-3
Barrett Stadium—*other* ... KY-4
Barretts Tunnels—*hist pl* ... MO-7
**Barrett Superette**—*pop pl* ... IA-7
Barrettsville—*locale* ... GA-3
**Barrett Township**—*pop pl* ... KS-7
**Barrett Township**—*pop pl* (2) ... SD-7
**Barrett (Township of)**—*pop pl* ... PA-2
Barrett 3School—*school* ... MA-1
**Barretville**—*pop pl* ... TN-4
**Barreville**—*pop pl* ... IL-6
Barr Gap—*gap* ... PA-2
Barr Gap—*gap* ... TX-5
Barr Gulch—*valley* ... ID-8
Barr Hill—*summit* ... ME-1
Barr Hill—*summit* ... NY-2
Barr Hill—*summit* ... VT-1
Barr Hollow—*valley* ... AL-4
Barr Hollow—*valley* ... PA-2
Barr Hollow—*valley* ... TN-4
Barr Hollow Branch—*stream* ... TN-4
Barr Hotel—*hist pl* ... OH-6
Barr House—*hist pl* (2) ... OH-6
**Barriada Jaime L Drew**—*pop pl* ... PR-3
**Barriada Monte Santo**—*pop pl* ... PR-3
Barrial Lateral—*canal* ... TX-5
*Barriar Peak* ... WA-9
**Barrick**—*pop pl* ... OH-6
Barrick Airp—*airport* ... PA-2
**Barrick Corner**—*pop pl* ... IN-6
**Barrick Corners**—*pop pl* ... OH-6
Barrick Field—*park* ... OR-9
Barrick Sch—*school* ... TX-5
Barricks Dam—*dam* ... NC-3
Barricks Hill—*summit* ... KY-4
Barricks Lake—*reservoir* ... NC-3
Barricks Millpond—*reservoir* ... VA-3
Barriclause Canyon—*valley* ... CO-8
**Barridge**—*pop pl* ... KY-4
Bar Ridge Ch—*church* ... MS-4
**Barrie**—*pop pl* ... ND-7
Barrie, Point—*cape* ... AK-9
Barrie Church*—*church* ... ND-7
*Barrie Crossing* ... ND-7
Barrie Island—*island* ... AK-9
Barrie Island—*island* ... AZ-5
Barrie Lake—*lake* ... AK-9
Barrie Park—*park* ... WI-6
**Barrier**—*pop pl* ... KY-4
Barrier, The—*ridge* (2) ... WA-9
Barrier Buttes—*summit* ... MT-8
Barrier Cem—*cemetery* ... KY-4
Barrier Cem—*cemetery* ... TX-5
Barrier Creek—*stream* ... AK-9
Barrier Creek—*stream* ... UT-8
Barrier Dunes—*summit* ... MA-1
Barriere, Bayou—*gut* ... LA-4
Barrier Falls—*falls* ... MT-8
Barrier Field (airport)—*airport* ... MS-4
Barrier Glacier—*glacier* ... AK-9
Barrier Islands—*area* ... AK-9
Barrier Islands—*island* ... AK-9
Barrier Peak—*summit* ... WA-9
Barrier Range—*range* ... AK-9
Barriers Mill—*locale* ... NC-3
**Barrier's Mill**—*pop pl* ... NC-3
Barries Bay—*bay* ... CA-9
Barrie Sch—*school* ... WI-6
Barries Gin Landing (historical)—*locale* ... AL-4
Barriet Canyon—*valley* ... CO-8
Barrie Town Hall—*building* ... ND-7
**Barrie Township**—*pop pl* ... ND-7
Barriet Spring—*spring* ... CO-8
**Barrigada**—*pop pl* ... GU-9
Barrigada, Mount—*summit* ... GU-9
Barrigada (Election District)—*fmr MCD* ... GU-9
Barrigada Heights—*CDP* ... GU-9
Barrigan Coulee—*valley* ... MT-8
Barriles Ranch—*locale* ... AZ-5
Barriles Tank—*reservoir* ... AZ-5
Barrilla Bluff—*cliff* ... TX-5
Barrilla Draw—*valley* (2) ... TX-5
Barrilla Mountains—*range* ... TX-5
Barrilla Spring—*spring* ... TX-5
Barrilla Windmill—*locale* ... TX-5
Barrille, Mount—*summit* ... AK-9
*Barrillo Mountains* ... TX-5
*Barrillo Spring* ... TX-5
*Barril Valley* ... CA-9
Barrinaga Corrals—*locale* ... ID-8
*Barrineau* ... FL-3
**Barrineau**—*pop pl* ... SC-3
Barrineau Cem—*cemetery* ... FL-3
**Barrineau Crossroads**—*pop pl* ... SC-3
Barrineau Park—*locale* ... FL-3
Barrineau Park Sch—*school* ... FL-3
Barringer—*locale* ... AR-4
*Barringer Crater* ... AZ-5
Barringer Ditch—*canal* ... IN-6
Barringer Ditch—*canal* ... MT-8
Barringer Farmhouse—*hist pl* ... NY-2
Barringer HS—*school* ... NJ-2
Barringer Incline—*mine* ... NM-5
Barringer Mansion—*hist pl* ... VA-3
Barringer Mtn—*summit* ... VA-3
Barringer Ridge—*ridge* ... OH-6
Barringer Sch—*school* ... NC-3
Barringer Slough—*gut* ... IA-7
Barringer Slough State Game Mgt
Area—*park* ... IA-7
Barringers Mill (historical)—*locale* ... AL-4
Barringer Tank—*reservoir* ... NM-5
Barringer (Township of)—*fmr MCD* ... NC-3
**Barrington**—*pop pl* ... IL-6
**Barrington**—*pop pl* ... NH-1
**Barrington**—*pop pl* ... NJ-2
**Barrington**—*pop pl* ... NY-2
**Barrington**—*pop pl* ... RI-1
Barrington—*uninc pl* ... CA-9
Barrington, Lake—*lake* ... IL-6
Barrington Beach—*beach* ... RI-1
Barrington Cem—*cemetery* ... NY-2
Barrington Cem—*cemetery* ... NC-3
*Barrington Center* ... IL-6
*Barrington Center* ... RI-1
Barrington Center—*locale* ... IL-6
Barrington Civic Center—*hist pl* ... RI-1
Barrington Creek—*stream* ... CA-9
Barrington Creek—*stream* ... OR-9
Barrington Hall—*hist pl* ... GA-3
Barrington Helena Crusade for Christ
Ch—*church* ... FL-3
**Barrington Highlands**—*pop pl* ... IL-6
Barrington Hill—*summit* ... NY-2
**Barrington Hills**—*pop pl* (2) ... IL-6
**Barrington Hills (subdivision)**—*pop pl* ... NC-3
Barrington Hist Dist—*hist pl* ... IL-6
Barrington House—*hist pl* ... TX-5
Barrington Lake—*lake* ... GA-3
Barrington Manor—*uninc pl* ... NJ-2
**Barrington Park**—*pop pl* ... UT-8
Barrington Recreation Center—*park* ... CA-9
Barrington River—*stream* ... RI-1
Barrington Run—*stream* ... IN-6
Barrington Sch—*school* ... OH-6
Barrington Spring—*spring* ... CA-9
*Barrington Square* ... IL-6
**Barrington (Town of)**—*pop pl* ... NH-1
**Barrington (Town of)**—*pop pl* ... NY-2
**Barrington (Town of)**—*pop pl* ... RI-1
**Barrington (Township of)**—*pop pl* ... IL-6
**Barrington Woods**—*pop pl* ... IL-6
Barr Interior Drain—*canal* ... NM-5
Barrio Cortes—*post sta* ... PR-3
Barrio de Analco Hist Dist—*hist pl* ... NM-5
Barrio Ditch—*canal* ... MI-6
Barrio Espinar—*post sta* ... PR-3
**Barrio Indios**—*pop pl* ... PR-3
Barrio Libre—*hist pl* ... AZ-5
**Barrio Nuevo**—*pop pl* ... PR-3
**Barrio Obrero**—*pop pl* ... PR-3
Barris Chapel Sch (historical)—*school* ... TN-4
Barris Creek—*stream* ... NC-3
Barris Hill—*summit* ... CA-9
Barris Lake—*lake* ... MI-6
*Barr Island* ... MP-9
**Barrisville**—*pop pl* ... PA-2
Barritt Sch—*school* ... IL-6
*Barritts Pond* ... MA-1
Barr JHS—*school* ... NE-7
Barr Lake—*lake* ... GA-3
Barr Lake—*lake* (2) ... IN-6
Barr Lake—*lake* ... MN-6
Barr Lake—*lake* (2) ... WI-6
**Barr Lake**—*pop pl* ... CO-8
Barr Lake—*reservoir* ... CO-8
Barr Lake—*reservoir* ... NC-3
Barr Lake—*reservoir* ... SC-3
*Barr Lake Reservoir* ... CO-8
Barr Landing—*locale* ... TN-4
**Barr (local name Barrs Mills)**—*pop pl* ... OH-6
Barr Mine—*mine* ... OR-9
Barr Mine—*mine* ... WY-8
Barr Mtn—*summit* ... AR-4
Barro—*locale* ... CA-9
Barro—*locale* ... UT-8
Barro, Canada Del—*valley* ... CA-9
Barro Canyon—*valley* ... NM-5
Barrocito Creek—*stream* ... TX-5
Bar Rock—*rock* (2) ... MA-1
*Bar Rocks* ... MA-1
Barroll—*cape* ... MD-2
*Barron* ... MS-4
Barron—*locale* ... LA-4
Barron—*locale* ... MO-7
Barron—*locale* ... WA-9
**Barron**—*pop pl* ... MS-4
**Barron**—*pop pl* ... WI-6
Barron, E.R., Bldg—*hist pl* ... WI-6
Barron, J. C., Flour Mill—*hist pl* ... WA-9
Barron, Martin Van Buren, House—*hist pl* ... WI-6
Barron, Thomas, House—*hist pl* ... NY-2
Barron Branch—*stream* ... TN-4
*Barron Cem* ... MS-4
Barron Cem—*cemetery* ... AR-4
Barron Cem—*cemetery* ... GA-3
Barron Cem—*cemetery* ... LA-4
Barron Cem—*cemetery* (2) ... MS-4
Barron Cem—*cemetery* ... TN-4
Barron Cem—*cemetery* ... TX-5
Barron Cem—*cemetery* ... VA-3
Barron Ch (historical)—*church* ... PA-2
Barron Collier Bridge—*bridge* ... FL-3
Barron Collier HS—*school* ... FL-3
Barron Corner—*locale* ... ME-1
**Barron (County)**—*pop pl* ... WI-6
Barron County Park—*park* ... WI-6
Barron County Pipestone Quarry—*hist pl* ... WI-6
*Barron Creek* ... AR-4
Barron Creek—*stream* ... AL-4
Barron Creek—*stream* ... AR-4
Barron Creek—*stream* (2) ... CA-9
Barron Creek—*stream* ... CO-8
Barron Creek—*stream* ... MS-4
Barron Creek—*stream* ... MT-8
Barron Creek—*stream* ... OH-6
Barron Creek—*stream* ... OR-9
Barron Creek—*stream* ... TX-5
Barron Creek—*stream* ... WA-9
*Barron Creek Point* ... MD-2
Barronena Ranch—*locale* ... TX-5
**Barronett**—*pop pl* ... WI-6
Barronette Peak—*summit* ... WY-8
**Barronett (Township of)**—*pop pl* ... WI-6
Barron Flats—*flat* ... WY-8
*Barron Fork* ... AR-4
*Barron Fork* ... OK-5
Barron-Gatlin Cem—*cemetery* ... MS-4
Barron Hill—*summit* ... TN-4
Barron Hill—*summit* ... VT-1
Barron Island—*island* ... WI-6
Barron Junction—*uninc pl* ... WI-6
Barron Lake—*lake* ... MI-6
**Barron Lake**—*pop pl* ... MI-6
Barron Lake Cem—*cemetery* ... MI-6
Barron Lake Dam—*dam* ... MS-4
Barron-Latham-Hopkins Gate
Lodge—*hist pl* ... CA-9
Barron Library—*hist pl* ... NJ-2
Barron Mtn—*summit* ... NH-1
*Barron Neck* ... MD-2
Barron Park—*uninc pl* ... CA-9
Barron Park Sch—*school* ... CA-9
Barron Point—*cape* ... AL-4
Barron Point—*locale* ... MS-4
Barron Ranch—*locale* ... CA-9
Barron Ranch—*locale* ... TX-5
Barron River—*stream* ... FL-3
Barrons Cabin (historical)—*locale* ... AZ-5
Barron Sch—*school* ... LA-4
Barron Sch—*school* ... MN-6
Barron Sch—*school* ... VA-3
**Barrons Corner**—*pop pl* ... TN-4
*Barrons Creek* ... TX-5
Barrons Lake—*reservoir* ... TX-5
Barrons Landing—*locale* ... AL-4
Barrons Lane—*locale* ... GA-3
Barron Spring—*spring* ... TN-4
Barron Springs Sch (historical)—*school* ... TN-4
*Barrons River* ... FL-3
*Barrontown* ... MS-4
**Barrontown**—*pop pl* ... MS-4
**Barron (Town of)**—*pop pl* ... WI-6
**Barronvale**—*pop pl* ... PA-2
Barronvale Bridge—*hist pl* ... PA-2
Barron-Wells Cem—*cemetery* ... AL-4
Barroom, The—*locale* ... AL-4
Barroom Bay—*bay* ... TX-5
*Barrosa* ... TX-5
*Barrosa Creek* ... TX-5
Barros (Barrio)—*fmr MCD* ... PR-3
*Barroso* ... TX-5
Barroso Camp—*locale* ... TX-5
Barroso Pasture—*flat* ... TX-5
Barroso Trap—*summit* ... TX-5
Barrot Spring—*spring* ... MT-8
Barrow—*locale* ... IL-6
**Barrow**—*pop pl* ... AK-9
Barrow, Dr. William, Mansion—*hist pl* ... NJ-2
Barrow, Mount—*summit* ... CA-9
Barrow, Point—*cape* ... TX-5
Barrow Bend—*bend* ... AR-4
Barrow Branch—*stream* ... OK-5
Barrow Cave—*cave* ... AL-4
Barrow Cem—*cemetery* ... IL-6
Barrow Cem—*cemetery* ... LA-4
Barrow Cem—*cemetery* (3) ... TN-4
Barrow Cem—*cemetery* (3) ... TX-5
Barrow Cem—*cemetery* ... VA-3
Barrow Ch—*church* ... GA-3
**Barrow (County)**—*pop pl* ... GA-3
Barrow County Courthouse—*hist pl* ... GA-3
*Barrow Creek* ... AL-4
Barrow Creek—*stream* ... AL-4
Barrow Creek—*stream* ... GA-3
Barrow Creek—*stream* ... MS-4
Barrow Creek—*stream* ... OR-9
Barrow Fork—*stream* ... LA-4
**Barrow Heights**—*pop pl* ... GA-3
Barrow Hill—*summit* ... GA-3
Barrow Hill Cem—*cemetery* ... FL-3
*Barrow Lake* ... MN-6
Barrow Lake—*lake* ... MN-6
Barrow Lake—*lake* ... TX-5
*Barrow Memorial Elementary School* ... MS-4
Barrow Memorial Gardens—*cemetery* ... GA-3
Barrow Mesa—*summit* ... CO-8
Barrow Mtn—*summit* ... CT-1
Barrow Park—*park* ... TX-5
Barrow Point—*cape* ... NC-3
Barrow Pond—*reservoir* ... AL-4
Barrow Post Office (historical)—*building* ... TN-4
Barrow-Pt. Hope (Census
Subarea)—*cens area* ... AK-9
Barrow Rsvr—*reservoir* ... CO-8
*Barrows* ... ME-1
*Barrows* ... MA-1
**Barrows**—*pop pl* ... MN-6
Barrows, Edward S., House—*hist pl* ... IA-7
*Barrows Brook* ... MA-1
Barrows Brook—*stream* ... MA-1
Barrows Brook—*stream* ... VT-1
Barrows Camp—*locale* ... VT-1
Barrows Cem—*cemetery* ... KY-4
Barrows Cem—*cemetery* ... OH-6
Barrow Sch—*school* (2) ... MI-6
Barrow Sch—*school* ... MS-4
Barrows Cove—*bay* ... ME-1
Barrows Creek—*stream* ... MT-8
Barrows Creek—*stream* ... VA-3
Barrows Grove Ch—*church* ... GA-3
Barrows Lake—*lake* ... ME-1
Barrows Lake—*swamp* ... MN-6
Barrows Lake (historical)—*lake* ... MS-4
Barrow Slough—*bay* ... TX-5
Barrows Millpond—*lake* ... NC-3
Barrows Playground—*locale* ... MA-1
Barrows Point—*cape* ... ME-1
Barrows Sch—*school* (2) ... MA-1
Barrows Sch—*school* ... MI-6
Barrows-Scribner Mill—*hist pl* ... ME-1
Barrows-Steadman Homestead—*hist pl* ... ME-1
Barrows Stream—*stream* ... ME-1
Barrow Street Sch—*school* ... GA-3
**Barrowsville**—*pop pl* ... MA-1
Barrowsville Pond—*lake* ... MA-1
Barrow Tank—*reservoir* ... AZ-5
**Barrow (Utkiavi)**—*pop pl* ... AK-9
Barrowville—*hist pl* ... GA-3
Barrow Windmill—*locale* (2) ... NM-5
Barr Post Office (historical)—*building* ... MS-4
Barr Post Office (historical)—*building* ... TN-4
Barr Ranch—*locale* ... OR-9
Barr Ranch—*locale* ... TX-5
Barr Ridge—*ridge* ... TN-4
*Barr Rocks* ... MA-1
*Barr Run* ... PA-2
Barr Run—*stream* ... OH-6
Barr Run—*stream* (2) ... PA-2
*Barrs* ... OH-6
*Barrs* ... PA-2
**Barrs**—*pop pl* ... WV-2
Barr Sch—*school* ... IL-6
Barr Sch—*school* ... IA-7
Barr Sch—*school* ... MS-4
Barr Sch—*school* ... OH-6
Barr Sch—*school* ... WI-6
Barrs Chapel—*church* ... SC-3
Barrs Chapel—*church* ... TN-4
Barrs Chapel—*church* ... WV-2
Barr Sch (historical)—*school* ... MO-7
Barr Sch (historical)—*school* ... TN-4
**Barrs Corners**—*pop pl* ... PA-2
Barrs Creek—*stream* ... WY-8
Barrs Lake—*lake* ... MN-6
Barrs Landing—*locale* ... FL-3
**Barr Slope**—*pop pl* ... PA-2
**Barrs Mill**—*pop pl* ... MS-4
**Barrs Mills**—*pop pl* ... OH-6
Barrs Pond—*reservoir* ... AL-4
Barrs Ponds—*reservoir* ... SC-3
Barr Spring—*spring* ... CA-9
Barrs Run—*stream* (2) ... PA-2
Barrs Run—*stream* ... WV-2
Barrs Sch (abandoned)—*school* ... PA-2
Barr (Station)—*locale* ... IL-6
Barr Street—*post sta* ... KY-4
Barr Street Sch—*school* ... SC-3
Barr Terrace—*hist pl* ... NE-7
**Barr (Township of)**—*pop pl* ... IL-6
**Barr (Township of)**—*pop pl* ... IN-6
**Barr (Township of)**—*pop pl* ... PA-2
Barr Trail—*trail* ... CO-8
Bar Run—*stream* (2) ... WV-2
**Barrville**—*pop pl* ... PA-2
Barrville Cave—*cave* ... PA-2
Barrville Sch—*school* ... PA-2
**Barry**—*pop pl* ... AL-4
**Barry**—*pop pl* ... IL-6
**Barry**—*pop pl* ... MN-6
**Barry**—*pop pl* ... MO-7
**Barry**—*pop pl* ... TX-5
Barry, George J., House—*hist pl* ... UT-8
Barry, Gov. John S., House—*hist pl* ... MI-6
Barry Arm—*bay* ... AK-9
Barry Babcock and Baker Drain—*stream* ... MI-6
Barry Bay—*bay* ... NC-3
Barry Branch—*gut* ... TX-5
Barry Branch—*stream* ... TN-4
*Barry Brook* ... MA-1
Barry Brook—*stream* ... MA-1
Barry Cabin—*locale* ... OR-9
Barry Cem—*cemetery* ... KS-7
Barry Cem—*cemetery* ... MO-7
Barry Cem—*cemetery* ... TN-4
Barry Cem—*cemetery* ... TX-5
*Barry College* ... FL-3
Barry College—*uninc pl* ... FL-3
Barry Corner—*locale* ... WI-6
**Barry (County)**—*pop pl* ... MI-6
**Barry County**—*pop pl* ... MO-7
Barry County Courthouse
Complex—*hist pl* ... MI-6
*Barry Creek* ... OR-9
Barry Creek—*stream* (2) ... CA-9
Barry Creek—*stream* ... IA-7
Barry Creek Mine—*mine* ... CA-9
Barry Creek Trail—*trail* ... CA-9
Barrydale Ch—*church* ... IN-6
Barry Dam—*dam* ... SD-7
Barry Farm (historical)—*locale* ... DC-2
Barry Field—*park* ... TX-5
Barry Glacier—*glacier* ... AK-9
Barry Gold Sch—*school* ... NC-3
Barry Heights—*uninc pl* ... PA-2
Barry Hill—*summit* ... MA-1
Barry Hist Dist—*hist pl* ... IL-6
Barry (historical)—*locale* ... KS-7
Barry Island—*island* ... IL-6
Barry Lagoon—*lake* ... AK-9
Barry Lake—*lake* ... MN-6
Barry Lakes—*lake* ... NJ-2
Barrylum (historical)—*locale* ... AL-4
Barry Memorial Ch—*church* ... MI-6
**Barry Mine**—*pop pl* ... WV-2
Barrymore—*locale* ... ID-8
Barrymore Creek—*stream* ... ID-8
Barry Oil Field—*oilfield* ... KS-7
Barry Oil Field—*oilfield* ... TX-5
Barry Park—*park* ... ID-8
Barry Park—*park* ... MA-1
Barry Point—*cape* ... AL-4
Barry Point—*cape* ... OR-9
*Barry Pond* ... NH-1
Barry Ranch—*locale* (2) ... OR-9
Barry Ridge—*ridge* ... CA-9
Barry (RR name for Platter)—*other* ... OK-5
*Barry Rsvr* ... OR-9
Barry Rsvr—*reservoir* ... OR-9
Barry Run—*stream* ... NY-2
*Barrys Bay* ... NC-3
Barry Sch—*school* ... CT-1
Barry Sch—*school* ... IL-6
Barry Sch—*school* ... NE-7
Barry Sch—*school* ... PA-2
Barry Sch—*school* ... SD 7
Barry Sch—*school* ... WI-6
Barry School (Abandoned)—*locale* ... WA-9
Barrys Creek—*stream* ... VA-3
Barrys Island—*summit* ... MT-8
Barrys Landing (historical)—*locale* ... MS-4
Barry Southeast Oil Field—*oilfield* ... KS-7
*Barrys Point* ... AL-4
Barry Spring—*spring* ... OR-9
*Barry Square* ... CT-1
Barrys Ridge Ch—*church* ... OH-6
**Barry (sta.)**—*pop pl* ... IL-6
Barry State Game Area—*park* ... MI-6
Barry Substation—*other* ... CA-9
Barry Tank—*reservoir* ... CA-9
*Barryton* ... AL-4
**Barryton**—*pop pl* ... MI-6
**Barrytown**—*pop pl* ... AL-4
**Barrytown**—*pop pl* ... NY-2
*Barrytown Ch* ... AL-4
Barrytown Ch—*church* ... AL-4
*Barrytown Ch of God* ... AL-4
*Barrytown Methodist Episcopal Ch* ... AL-4
**Barry (Township of)**—*pop pl* ... IL-6
**Barry (Township of)**—*pop pl* ... MI-6
**Barry (Township of)**—*pop pl* ... MN-6
**Barry (Township of)**—*pop pl* ... PA-2
*Barrytown United Methodist Ch* ... AL-4
Barry Union Sch—*school* ... CA-9
Barry Univ—*school* ... FL-3
*Barryvilla* ... NH-1
**Barry Village**—*pop pl* ... AL-4
**Barryville**—*pop pl* ... NY-2
Barryville Sch—*school* ... MI-6
Bars, The—*bar* ... MT-8
Bars, The—*flat* ... MA-1
Bars Branch—*stream* ... MS-4
Bars Canyon—*valley* ... AZ-5
Bar Sch—*school* ... OH-6
Bar Sch (historical)—*school* ... TN-4
Bars Creek—*stream* ... CA-9
Barse Mine—*mine* ... NV-8
*Barshas-piss Brook* ... MA-1
Barsher Cem—*cemetery* ... MO-7
Barshinger Creek—*stream* ... PA-2
Bar Six Canyon—*valley* ... NM-5
Bar S Lake—*reservoir* ... MS-4
Bars Leak, Lake—*lake* ... MI-6
Bar Slough—*stream* ... IA-7
*Barslow Rock* ... MA-1
Barsness Ch—*church* ... MN-6
*Barsness Lake* ... MN-6
Barsness Lake—*lake* ... MN-6
Barsness Park—*park* ... MN-6
**Barsness (Township of)**—*pop pl* ... MN-6
Barso—*locale* ... LA-4
Barsola Ch—*church* ... TX-5
Barson—*locale* ... AR-4
Barsotti Cem—*cemetery* ... MO-7
Bar Spring—*spring* ... WY-8
Bar Springs Cem—*cemetery* ... TN-4
Bar S Ranch—*locale* ... NM-5
Bar S Ranch (Headquarters)—*locale* ... TX-5
Bar S Rsvr—*reservoir* ... OR-9
Barstow—*locale* ... CA-9
Barstow—*locale* ... WA-9
**Barstow**—*pop pl* ... CA-9
**Barstow**—*pop pl* ... IL-6
**Barstow**—*pop pl* ... MD-2
**Barstow**—*pop pl* ... TX-5
Barstow Brook—*stream* ... ME-1
Barstow Canal—*canal* ... TX-5
Barstow Cem—*cemetery* ... ME-1
Barstow Cem—*cemetery* ... TX-5
Barstow Coll—*school* ... CA-9
**Barstow Colony**—*pop pl* ... CA-9
Barstow Dam—*dam* ... TX-5
Barstow Heights Park—*park* ... CA-9
Barstow HS—*school* ... MO-7
Barstow Marine Corps Logistics
Base—*military* ... CA-9
Barstow Mine—*mine* ... CO-8
Barstow Point—*cape* ... ME-1
Barstow-Pyote (CCD)—*cens area* ... TX-5
Barstow Rock—*rock* ... MA-1
Barstow Sch—*school* ... CA-9
Barstow Sch—*school* ... VT-1
Barstow Sch—*school* (2) ... WI-6
Barstows Pond—*reservoir* ... MA-1
Barstows Pond Dam—*dam* ... MA-1
*Barstows Rock* ... MA-1
Barstow Tank—*reservoir* ... TX-5
Barstow-Victorville (CCD)—*cens area* ... CA-9
Barstow Water Tank—*reservoir* ... TX-5
Barstow Well—*well* ... TX-5
Barstow Woods—*woods* ... MI-6
Barsug—*locale* ... CA-9
Bar Swamp Creek—*stream* ... VA-3
*Bart* ... PA-2
**Bart**—*pop pl* ... MI-6
**Bart**—*pop pl* ... PA-2
Barta Crooked Dam—*dam* ... SD-7
**Bartahatchie**—*pop pl* ... MS-4
*Bartahatchie Baptist Church* ... MS-4
Bartahatchie Ch—*church* ... MS-4
*Bartahatchie River* ... MS-4
Barta Sch—*school* ... ND-7
Bartash Lake—*lake* ... WI-6
Bar T Bar Ranch—*locale* ... AZ-5
Bart Branch—*stream* ... NC-3
Bart Chapel—*church* ... PA-2
Bart Cove—*valley* ... NC-3
Bart Creek—*stream* ... MI-6
Bar T Cross Camp—*locale* ... NM-5
Barteau House—*hist pl* ... MO-7
Bartee Branch—*stream* ... AL-4
Bartee Branch—*stream* (2) ... TN-4
Bartee Cave—*cave* ... AL-4
Bartee Ditch—*canal* ... IN-6
Bartees Bar—*bar* ... AL-4
Bartees Bluff Landing (historical)—*locale* ... AL-4
Bartees Point—*cape* ... AL-4
Bartel Bend—*bend* ... MO-7
*Bartel Canyon* ... ID-8
Bartel Canyon—*valley* ... ID-8
Bartel Cem—*cemetery* ... NE-7
Bartell, Fred, House—*hist pl* ... AR-4
Bartell Bay—*bay* ... FL-3
Bartell Creek—*stream* ... AK-9
Bartell Crossroads—*locale* ... SC-3
Bartell House—*hist pl* ... KS-7
Bartell Island—*island* ... TX-5
Bartell Pass—*channel* ... TX-5
**Bartelme (Town of)**—*pop pl* ... WI-6
Bartel Rsvr—*reservoir* ... CO-8
Bartels Dam—*dam* ... SD-7
Bartels Hollow—*valley* ... TN-4
Bartels Lake—*lake* ... MN-6
**Bartelso**—*pop pl* ... IL-6
Bartelso East Oil Field—*other* ... IL-6
Bartelso Oil Field—*other* ... IL-6
Bartelso West Oil Field—*other* ... IL-6
Bartemus Brook—*stream* ... NH-1
Bartenbach, H. J., House—*hist pl* ... NE-7
Barten Ditch—*canal* ... IN-6
Barterbrook—*locale* ... VA-3
Barter Brook—*stream* ... ME-1
Barterbrook Branch—*stream* ... VA-3
Barter Cem—*cemetery* ... IL-6
Barter Creek—*stream* ... NY-2
Barter Hill—*summit* ... NY-2
*Barter Island* ... ME-1
Barter Island—*island* ... AK-9
Barter Island—*island* ... ME-1
Barter Island (airline name for
Kaktovik)—*other* ... AK-9
Barter Island DEW Station—*mil airp* ... AK-9
Barter Lake—*lake* ... MN-6
Barter Ranch—*locale* ... MT-8
*Barters* ... AL-4
Barter Sch—*school* ... SC-3
Barters Creek—*bay* ... ME-1
Barter Shoal—*bar* ... ME-1
Barters Island—*island* ... ME-1
**Barterville**—*pop pl* ... KY-4
Bartesta Branch—*stream* ... KY-4
Barth—*locale* ... NV-8
**Barth**—*pop pl* ... FL-3
**Barth**—*pop pl* ... MS-4
Barth, Peter, Farm—*hist pl* ... KY-4
Barth Cem—*cemetery* (2) ... IL-6
*Barth Elementary School* ... PA-2
Barthelia—*locale* ... TN-4
**Barthelia**—*pop pl* ... TN-4
Barthell—*locale* ... KY-4
Barthel Pigeonnier—*hist pl* ... LA-4
Barthels Pond—*lake* ... MN-6
*Bartheney* ... TN-4
Bartheney Post Office
(historical)—*building* ... TN-4
Barth Falls—*falls* ... OR-9
Barth Hot Springs—*spring* ... ID-8
Bart Hill—*summit* ... MS-4
Bar Thirtyseven Ranch—*locale* ... AZ-5
Bar Thirty Seven Tank—*reservoir* ... AZ-5
Barth Lake—*lake* ... AZ-5
Barth Lateral—*canal* ... CA-9
Barth Lateral—*canal* ... ID-8
Barth Mine—*mine* ... NV-8
Barth Mtn—*summit* ... CA-9
Bartho, Lake—*swamp* ... FL-3
Barthold Flat—*flat* ... SD-7
*Bartholdi* ... KS-7
Bartholdi Fountain—*park* ... DC-2
Bartholdi (historical)—*locale* ... SD-7
Bartholf, John, House—*hist pl* ... NJ-2
Bart Hollow—*valley* ... TN-4
Bartholomaus Canyon—*valley* ... CA-9
Bartholomew, Bayou—*gut* ... LA-4
Bartholomew, Bayou—*stream* ... LA-4
Bartholomew, Lake—*lake* ... MI-6
Bartholomew, Riley Lucas,
House—*hist pl* ... MN-6
*Bartholomew Baptist Church* ... MS-4
*Bartholomew Bayou* ... LA-4
Bartholomew Canyon—*valley* ... UT-8
Bartholomew Ch—*church* ... AL-4
Bartholomew Ch—*church* ... LA-4
Bartholomew Ch—*church* ... MS-4
**Bartholomew County**—*pop pl* ... IN-6
Bartholomew County Courthouse—*hist pl* ... IN-6
Bartholomew County Hospital
Airp—*airport* ... IN-6
*Bartholomew Creek* ... PA-2
Bartholomew Creek—*stream* ... AK-9
Bartholomew Creek—*stream* ... MI-6
Bartholomew Crossing—*locale* ... TX-5
Bartholomew Fork—*stream* ... WV-2
Bartholomew Hill—*summit* ... CT-1
Bartholomew Hill—*summit* ... MA-1
Bartholomew Hill—*summit* ... NY-2
Bartholomew Oil Field—*oilfield* ... KS-7
Bartholomew Park—*park* ... TX-5
*Bartholomew Pond Reservoir* ... MA-1
Bartholomew Run—*stream* ... OH-6
*Bartholomews Canyon* ... UT-8
Bartholomews Cobble—*park* ... MA-1
*Bartholomews Pond* ... MA-1
Bartholomew (Township of)—*fmr MCD*
(2) ... AR-4
*Bartholow* ... MD-2
**Bartholow**—*pop pl* ... MD-2
Bartholowmew Pond—*lake* ... MA-1
**Bartholows**—*pop pl* ... MD-2
Barth Pit—*cave* ... AL-4
Barth Ridge—*ridge* ... MT-8
Barths Butte—*summit* ... ND-7
Barths Creek—*stream* ... CA-9
Barths Lake—*reservoir* ... IL-6
Barth Spring—*spring* ... MD-2
Barth Spring—*spring* ... MT-8
Barths Retreat—*locale* ... CA-9
Barth Well—*well* ... AZ-5
Barth Well—*well* ... CA-9
*Bartietts Pond* ... NC-3
Bartig Lake—*lake* ... MI-6
Bartine Ranch—*locale* ... NV-8
Bartinger Ditch—*canal* ... IN-6
Bartish Park—*park* ... OH-6
Bart Island—*island* ... AK-9
Bartizan, The—*summit* ... UT-8
Bart Lake—*lake* ... AK-9
Bart Lake—*reservoir* ... TX-5
Bartle—*locale* ... CA-9
**Bartle**—*pop pl* ... IN-6
**Bartlebaugh**—*pop pl* ... TN-4
Bartlebaugh Baptist Ch—*church* ... TN-4
**Bartlebaugh Subdivision**—*pop pl* ... TN-4
Bartle Creek—*stream* ... CA-9
Bartle Gap—*gap* ... CA-9
Bartle Knob Run—*stream* ... IN-6
Bartle Knobs—*ridge* ... IN-6
**Bartles**—*pop pl* ... OH-6
Bartles, Mount—*summit* ... UT-8
*Bartles Branch* ... WI-6
**Bartles Corners**—*pop pl* ... NJ-2
Bartleson Hill—*summit* ... KY-4
Bartleson Peak—*summit* ... MT-8
**Bartlesville**—*pop pl* ... OK-5
Bartlesville (CCD)—*cens area* ... OK-5
Bartlet Lake—*lake* (2) ... MN-6
*Bartlet Peak* ... NV-8
*Bartlett* ... IN-6
Bartlett—*locale* ... CO-8
Bartlett—*locale* ... MN-6
Bartlett—*locale* ... MS-4
Bartlett—*locale* ... MO-7
Bartlett—*locale* ... OR-9
Bartlett—*other* ... OK-5
**Bartlett**—*pop pl* ... CA-9
**Bartlett**—*pop pl* ... GA-3
**Bartlett**—*pop pl* ... IL-6
**Bartlett**—*pop pl* ... IA-7
**Bartlett**—*pop pl* ... KS-7
**Bartlett**—*pop pl* ... NE-7
**Bartlett**—*pop pl* ... NH-1
**Bartlett**—*pop pl* ... NY-2
**Bartlett**—*pop pl* ... NC-3
**Bartlett**—*pop pl* ... ND-7
**Bartlett**—*pop pl* ... OH-6
**Bartlett**—*pop pl* ... TN-4
**Bartlett**—*pop pl* ... TX-5
**Bartlett**—*pop pl* ... VA-3
Bartlett, Francis H., House—*hist pl* ... MN-6
Bartlett, Frank, House—*hist pl* ... WA-9
Bartlett, George A., House—*hist pl* ... NV-8
Bartlett, J.C., House—*hist pl* ... MA-1
Bartlett, Josiah, House—*hist pl* ... NH-1
Bartlett, L. L., House—*hist pl* ... SD-7
Bartlett, Robert Rensselaer,
House—*hist pl* ... OR-9

Bartlett Airp—airport ... IN-6
Bartlett Ave Sch—school ... WI-6
Bartlett Beach—locale ... WA-9
Bartlett Bench—bench ... OR-9
Bartlett Blacksmith Shop-Scandinavian Hotel—hist pl ... WI-6
Bartlett Bog—swamp ... ME-1
Bartlett Branch ... VA-3
Bartlett Branch—stream (2) ... GA-3
Bartlett Branch—stream ... MS-4
Bartlett Branch—stream ... TN-4
Bartlett Branch - in part ... TN-4
Bartlett Brook ... ME-1
Bartlett Brook—stream ... CT-1
Bartlett Brook—stream (3) ... ME-1
Bartlett Brook—stream (3) ... MA-1
Bartlett Brook—stream (4) ... NH-1
Bartlett Brook—stream ... NY-2
Bartlett Brook—stream (2) ... VT-1
Bartlett Butte ... NV-8
Bartlett Canal—canal ... MT-8
Bartlett Canyon—valley ... CA-9
Bartlett Cave—cave ... AL-4
Bartlett Cave—cave ... TN-4
Bartlett Cem—cemetery ... IL-6
Bartlett Cem—cemetery ... IN-6
Bartlett Cem—cemetery ... ME-1
Bartlett Cem—cemetery ... MS-4
Bartlett Cem—cemetery ... MO-7
Bartlett Cem—cemetery ... NE-7
Bartlett Cem—cemetery ... NH-1
Bartlett Cem—cemetery ... OH-6
Bartlett Cem—cemetery ... OR-9
Bartlett Cem—cemetery (2) ... TN-4
Bartlett Cem—cemetery ... TX-5
Bartlett Chapel—church ... IN-6
Bartlett Chapel—church ... TN-4
Bartlett Chapel Cem—cemetery ... TN-4
Bartlett Commercial Hist Dist—hist pl ... TX-5
Bartlett Corners—locale ... CT-1
Bartlett Corners—locale ... NY-2
Bartlett Corners—locale ... OH-6
**Bartlett Corners**—pop pl ... NY-2
Bartlett Cove—bay ... AK-9
Bartlett Cove—bay ... CT-1
Bartlett Cove—bay ... ME-1
**Bartlett Cove**—pop pl ... AK-9
Bartlett Cove—valley ... AR-4
Bartlett Creek—stream ... CA-9
Bartlett Creek—stream (2) ... ID-8
Bartlett Creek—stream ... KS-7
Bartlett Creek—stream ... MO-7
Bartlett Creek—stream (2) ... MT-8
Bartlett Creek—stream ... NV-8
Bartlett Creek—stream ... NC-3
Bartlett Creek—stream ... SD-7
Bartlett Creek—stream ... TN-4
Bartlett Creek—stream ... WA-9
Bartlett Creek—stream ... WY-8
Bartlett Crossroads (historical)—locale ... AL-4
Bartlett Dam—dam ... AZ-5
Bartlett Dam—dam ... KS-7
Bartlett Drain—canal ... MI-6
Bartlett Earth Station—locale ... AK-9
Bartlett Elem Sch—school (2) ... KS-7
Bartlett Flat—flat ... CA-9
Bartlett Flat—flat ... UT-8
Bartlett Ford Cem—cemetery ... MS-4
Bartlett Fork—stream ... KY-4
Bartlett Fork Little Kentucky River ... KY-4
Bartlett Glacier—glacier ... AK-9
Bartlett Gulch—valley ... CO-8
Bartlett Harbor—bay ... ME-1
Bartlett-Hawkes Farm—hist pl ... MA-1
Bartlett Haystack—summit ... NH-1
**Bartlett Heights Subdivision**—pop pl ... UT-8
Bartlett Hill—summit (3) ... ME-1
Bartlett Hill—summit ... MD-2
Bartlett Hill—summit ... MA-1
Bartlett Hill—summit ... NH-1
Bartlett Hill—summit ... NY-2
Bartlett Hill—summit (2) ... VT-1
Bartlett Hill—summit ... WA-9
Bartlett Hills—other ... AK-9
Bartlett Hills Lake—reservoir ... IA-7
Bartlett Hills Lake Dam—dam ... IA-7
Bartlett (historical)—locale ... AL-4
**Bartlett Hollow**—pop pl ... NY-2
Bartlett Hollow—valley ... IN-6
Bartlett Hollow—valley ... TN-4
Bartlett Hollow—valley ... UT-8
Bartlett Hollow—valley ... WY-8
Bartlett HS—school ... MA-1
Bartlett Island—island ... AK-9
Bartlett Island—island ... ME-1
Bartlett Island—island ... NY-2
Bartlett Jackson Creek ... KY-4
Bartlett Lake ... MN-6
Bartlett Lake—lake ... AK-9
Bartlett Lake—lake ... ID-8
Bartlett Lake—lake ... MI-6
Bartlett Lake—lake ... MN-6
Bartlett Lake—lake ... NM-5
Bartlett Lake Public Hunting Area—park ... IA-7
Bartlett Lake Recreation Site—park ... AZ-5
Bartlett Landing—locale ... OR-9
Bartlett Memorial Historical Museum—hist pl ... WI-6
Bartlett Mesa—summit ... CO-8
Bartlett Mesa—summit ... NM-5
**Bartlett Mills**—pop pl ... ME-1
Bartlett Mine—mine ... MT-8
Bartlett Mine—mine (2) ... NV-8
Bartlett Mine—mine ... NM-5
Bartlett Mountain Summit—gap ... CA-9
Bartlett Mtn—summit ... AZ-5
Bartlett Mtn—summit ... CA-9
Bartlett Mtn—summit ... CO-8
Bartlett Mtn—summit ... ME-1
Bartlett Mtn—summit ... MT-8
Bartlett Mtn—summit ... NY-2
Bartlett Mtn—summit ... NC-3
Bartlett Mtn—summit ... OR-9
Bartlett Mtn—summit ... PA-2
Bartlett Mtn—summit ... VT-1
Bartlett Narrows—channel ... ME-1
Bartlett Oil Field—oilfield ... TX-5
Bartlett Park—park ... CA-9
Bartlett Park—park ... FL-3
Bartlett Park—park ... MO-7
Bartlett Park—park ... NY-2
Bartlett Peak—summit ... CA-9
Bartlett Peak—summit ... NV-8
Bartlett Peak—summit ... TX-5
Bartlett Pit—cave ... TN-4
Bartlett Point—cape ... AK-9
Bartlett Point—cape ... CT-1
Bartlett Point—cape (2) ... ME-1
Bartlett Point—cape ... NY-2
Bartlett Point—cliff ... ID-8
Bartlett Point—summit ... ID-8
Bartlett Pond—lake (2) ... CT-1
Bartlett Pond—lake (2) ... ME-1
Bartlett Pond—lake (4) ... MA-1
Bartlett Pond—lake (2) ... NY-2
Bartlett Pond—reservoir ... AL-4
Bartlett Pond—reservoir (2) ... MA-1
Bartlett Pond—reservoir ... NY-2
Bartlett Pond Brook—stream ... MA-1
Bartlett Pond Dam—dam (2) ... MA-1
Bartlett Post Office (historical)—building ... MS-4
Bartlett Ranch—locale ... WY-8
Bartlett Reef—bar ... CT-1
Bartlett Ridge—ridge ... NY-2
Bartlett River—stream ... AK-9
Bartlett Rock—rock (2) ... MA-1
Bartlett Rsvr—reservoir ... AZ-5
Bartlett Run—stream ... OH-6
Bartlett Run—stream (2) ... WV-2
Bartlett-Russell-Hedge House—hist pl ... MA-1
Bartlett's ... CT-1
Bartletts Bar—bar ... TN-4
Bartletts Branch—stream ... NJ-2
Bartletts Bridge—bridge ... NJ-2
Bartletts Brook ... MA-1
Bartletts Brook ... NH-1
Bartletts Carry—locale ... NY-2
Bartlett Sch—hist pl ... PA-2
Bartlett Sch—school ... CA-9
Bartlett Sch—school ... GA-3
Bartlett Sch—school (2) ... MA-1
Bartlett Sch—school ... MO-7
Bartlett Sch—school (2) ... NH-1
Bartlett Sch—school ... WV-2
Bartlett Sch—school ... WI-6
Bartlett School—locale ... MI-6
Bartletts Corner—locale ... NY-2
**Bartletts Ferry**—pop pl ... GA-3
Bartletts Ferry Dam—dam ... GA-3
Bartletts Ferry Lake ... AL-4
Bartletts Ferry Lake ... GA-3
Bartletts Fort (historical)—locale ... TN-4
Bartlett Shaft—mine ... CO-8
Bartletts Island—island ... MA-1
Bartlett Slough—stream ... ID-8
Bartlett Slough—stream ... WY-8
Bartletts Marsh (historical)—swamp ... MA-1
Bartlett Springs—locale ... CA-9
Bartletts Reservoir ... GA-3
Bartletts Run—stream ... WV-2
Bartletts Switch ... TN-4
Bartlett Stream—stream (2) ... ME-1
**Bartlettsville**—pop pl ... IN-6
Bartlett Swamp—swamp ... MA-1
Bartlett Tower—locale ... NH-1
**Bartlett (Town of)**—pop pl ... NH-1
Bartlett Township—civil ... MO-7
**Bartlett Township**—pop pl ... ND-7
Bartlett Township (historical)—civil ... SD-7
**Bartlett (Township of)**—pop pl ... MN-6
Bartlett Trail—trail ... CO-8
Bartlett Tunnel—mine ... CO-8
Bartlett Wash—valley ... UT-8
Bartlett Windmills—locale ... TX-5
Bartlett Yancey Elem Sch—school ... NC-3
Bartlett Yancey HS ... NC-3
Bartley ... PA-2
Bartley ... WV-2
Bartley—locale ... NJ-2
**Bartley**—pop pl ... IL-6
**Bartley**—pop pl ... IN-6
**Bartley**—pop pl ... NE-7
**Bartley**—pop pl ... WV-2
Bartley Branch ... GA-3
Bartley Branch—stream ... SC-3
Bartley Branch—stream ... TX-5
Bartley Branch—stream ... VA-3
Bartley Bridge—bridge ... TN-4
Bartley Canal—canal ... NE-7
Bartley Cem—cemetery ... NE-7
Bartley Cem—cemetery ... SC-3
Bartley Cem—cemetery ... TN-4
Bartley Creek ... MO-7
Bartley Creek—stream ... WV-2
**Bartley Estates**—pop pl ... OH-6
Bartley Gap—gap ... PA-2
Bartley Gap Trail ... PA-2
Bartley Gulch—valley ... OR-9
Bartley Hollow—valley ... AR-4
Bartley Hollow—valley ... TN-4
Bartley HQ (site)—locale ... OR-9
Bartley Island—island ... NC-3
Bartley Lake—lake ... IN-6
Bartley Mtn—summit ... PA-2
Bartley Ranch—locale ... MT-8
Bartley Ridge—ridge ... IN-6
Bartley Ridge—ridge ... KY-4
Bartley Run—stream (2) ... PA-2
Bartleys Lake—reservoir ... KY-4
Bartley Town Hall—building ... ND-7
**Bartley Township**—pop pl ... ND-7
Bartley Trail—trail ... PA-2
Bartley-Tweed Farm—hist pl ... DE-2
Bartleyville ... NJ-2
Bartley Woods—locale ... TX-5
Bartlick—locale ... VA-3
Bartlick Lookout Tower—locale ... VA-3
Bartlick Sch—school ... VA-3
**Bartlow (Township of)**—pop pl ... OH-6
Bartman Elementary School ... PA-2
Bartman Hill—summit ... MD-2
Bartman Sch—school ... PA-2
Bartmess Cem—cemetery ... IL-6
Bartmess Lake—reservoir ... IN-6
Bartmess Lake Dam—dam ... IN-6
Bartmess Sch—school ... IL-6
Barto—locale ... MS-4
Barto—locale ... PA-2
Barto Bridge—hist pl ... PA-2
Barto Creek—stream ... MN-6
Bartoff Hollow—valley ... PA-2
Barto Hill—summit ... NY-2
Barto Lake—lake ... MN-6
Barto Lake—lake ... NY-2
Bartolas Country—flat ... CA-9
Bartolas Creek—stream ... CA-9
Bartoldus Ranch—locale ... CA-9
Bartol Hill ... ME-1
Bartol Island—island ... ME-1
Bartolo—locale ... CA-9
**Bartolo**—pop pl ... PR-3
Bartolo (Barrio)—fmr MCD ... PR-3
Bartolo Canyon—valley ... AZ-5
Bartolome Fernandez—civil ... NM-5
Bartolomeo de Castro Y Ferro Grant—civil ... FL-3
Bartolome Sanchez Grant—civil ... NM-5
Bartolo Mtn—summit ... AZ-5
Bartol Spring—spring ... AZ-5
Bartome Knoll—summit ... NV-8
Bartomes Creek—stream ... NV-8
Bartomes Spring—spring ... NV-8
Barton ... IN-6
Barton ... OK-5
Barton—locale ... CA-9
Barton—locale ... CO-8
Barton—locale ... ID-8
Barton—locale ... KS-7
Barton—locale ... MS-4
Barton—locale ... NE-7
Barton—locale ... NM-5
Barton—locale ... PA-2
Barton—locale ... TX-5
**Barton**—pop pl ... AL-4
**Barton**—pop pl ... AR-4
**Barton**—pop pl ... LA-4
**Barton**—pop pl ... MD-2
**Barton**—pop pl ... MS-4
**Barton**—pop pl ... NY-2
**Barton**—pop pl ... ND-7
**Barton**—pop pl ... OH-6
**Barton**—pop pl ... OR-9
**Barton**—pop pl ... SC-3
**Barton**—pop pl ... UT-8
**Barton**—pop pl ... VT-1
**Barton**—pop pl ... WI-6
Barton—uninc pl ... CA-9
Barton—uninc pl ... WI-6
Barton, Abraham, House—hist pl ... KY-4
Barton, Clara, Homestead—hist pl ... MA-1
Barton, Clara, Sch—hist pl ... PA-2
Barton, Guy C., House—hist pl ... NE-7
Barton, Lake—lake ... FL-3
Barton, Mount—summit ... MS-4
Barton, William, House—hist pl ... UT-8
Barton Acad—hist pl ... AL-4
Barton Acad—school ... AL-4
Barton Arroyo—stream ... NM-5
Barton Ave Sch—school ... NY-2
Barton Baptist Ch—church ... MS-4
Barton Bend—bend ... AL-4
Barton Branch ... AL-4
Barton Branch—stream (2) ... AL-4
Barton Branch—stream ... GA-3
Barton Branch—stream ... MO-7
Barton Branch—stream ... TN-4
Barton Branch—stream (3) ... TX-5
Barton Branch—stream ... VA-3
Barton Bridge—bridge ... OR-9
Barton Brook ... MN-6
Barton Brook—stream ... ME-1
Barton Brook—stream ... MA-1
Barton Brook—stream ... NH-1
Barton Brook—stream (2) ... NY-2
Barton Cabin ... CA-9
Barton Cabin—locale ... CA-9
Barton Cabin—locale ... ID-8
Barton Camp—locale ... CO-8
Barton Canal—canal ... CA-9
Barton Canyon—valley ... CA-9
Barton Canyon—valley ... NV-8
Barton Canyon—valley ... UT-8
Barton Cave—cave ... PA-2
Barton Cem—cemetery (2) ... AL-4
Barton Cem—cemetery (2) ... FL-3
Barton Cem—cemetery ... ID-8
Barton Cem—cemetery (2) ... IL-6
Barton Cem—cemetery (2) ... IN-6
Barton Cem—cemetery ... KY-4
Barton Cem—cemetery (2) ... MS-4
Barton Cem—cemetery (2) ... MO-7
Barton Cem—cemetery ... NY-2
Barton Cem—cemetery (5) ... OH-6
Barton Cem—cemetery (4) ... TN-4
Barton Cem—cemetery (2) ... TX-5
Barton Cem—cemetery (2) ... VA-3
Barton Cem—cemetery (2) ... WV-2
Barton Cemetery ... SD-7
Barton Center Cem—cemetery ... NY-2
Barton Ch—church ... AL-4
Barton Ch—church (2) ... MS-4
Barton Chapel—church ... AR-4
Barton Chapel—church ... KY-4
Barton Chapel—church ... PA-2
Barton Chapel—church ... SC-3
Barton Chapel—church ... WV-2
Barton Chapel—hist pl ... TN-4
**Barton City**—pop pl ... MI-6
Barton City Cem—cemetery ... MO-7
**Barton City Township**—pop pl ... MO-7
Barton Coliseum—other ... AR-4
Barton Compressor Station—other ... AL-4
Barton Corners—locale (2) ... NY-2
Barton Corners—locale ... TX-5
Barton County—civil ... KS-7
**Barton County**—pop pl ... MO-7
Barton County Fairgrounds—locale ... KS-7
Barton County Park—park (2) ... OR-9
Barton Cove—cove ... MA-1
Barton Creek ... TX-5
Barton Creek—stream (2) ... AL-4
Barton Creek—stream (2) ... CA-9
Barton Creek—stream ... MT-8
Barton Creek—stream (2) ... NV-8
Barton Creek—stream (3) ... SC-3
Barton Creek—stream ... TN-4
Barton Creek—stream (4) ... TX-5
Barton Creek—stream ... WA-9
Barton Crossroad—locale ... VA-3
Bartondale ... PA-2
Bartondale Ditch—canal ... IN-6
Bartondale (historical)—locale ... KS-7
Barton Dam One ... AL-4
Barton Depot ... AL-4
Barton Ditch—canal ... UT-8
Barton Elem Sch—school ... AL-4
**Bartonette**—pop pl ... CA-9
Barton Ferry Cutoff—channel ... MS-4
Barton Ferry Marina—locale ... MS-4
Barton Ferry Rec Area—park ... MS-4
Barton Field—park ... TN-4
Barton Fishing Lake Dam Two—dam ... AL-4
Barton Flats—flat ... CA-9
Barton Flats—flat ... ID-8
Barton Flats Campground—locale ... CA-9
Barton Flats Forest Service Station—locale ... CA-9
Barton Fork—stream ... VA-3
Barton Gap—gap ... VA-3
**Barton Glen**—pop pl ... PA-2
Barton Grove Ch—church ... AL-4
Barton Gulch—valley ... CA-9
Barton Gulch—valley (2) ... ID-8
Barton Gulch—valley ... MT-8
Barton Hall—hist pl ... AL-4
**Barton Heights**—pop pl ... OR-9
Barton Heights—uninc pl ... TN-4
Barton Heights Ch—church ... TN-4
Barton Hill—summit (2) ... CA-9
Barton Hill—summit ... ME-1
Barton Hill—summit ... MD-2
Barton Hill—summit (3) ... NH-1
Barton Hill—summit ... NY-2
Barton Hill—summit ... TX-5
Barton Hill Cem—cemetery ... NY-2
**Barton Hills**—pop pl ... MI-6
Barton Hill Sch—school ... CA-9
Barton Hill Sch—school ... NY-2
Barton Hills Sch—school ... TX-5
Barton (historical)—locale ... MS-4
Barton Hollow—valley ... AL-4
Barton Hollow—valley ... MO-7
Barton Hollow—valley ... PA-2
Barton Hollow—valley (?) ... TN-4
Barton Hollow—valley ... WI-6
Barton House—hist pl ... MO-7
Barton House—hist pl ... TX-5
Barton Hump—summit ... ID-8
**Bartonia**—pop pl ... IN-6
Bartonia Cem—cemetery ... IN-6
Bartonia Run—stream ... IN-6
Barton Island—island ... AL-4
Barton Island—island ... ME-1
Barton Island—island ... MA-1
Barton JHS—school ... MI-6
**Barton Junction**—pop pl ... AR-4
Barton Knob—summit ... WV-2
Barton-Lackey Cabin—hist pl ... CA-9
Barton Lake—lake ... AR-4
Barton Lake—lake ... FL-3
Barton Lake—lake ... IN-6
Barton Lake—lake ... KY-4
Barton Lake—lake ... MI-6
Barton Lake—lake ... MN-6
**Barton Lake**—pop pl ... MI-6
Barton Lake—reservoir ... AL-4
Barton Lake—reservoir ... KS-7
Barton Lake—reservoir ... OR-9
Barton Lake—reservoir ... TX-5
Barton Lake Ranch Airstrip—airport ... OR-9
Barton Lake Rsvr ... OR-9
Barton Lakes ... OR-9
Barton Lake Well—well ... OR-9
Barton Landing ... VT-1
Barton Landing—locale ... TN-4
Barton Ledge—bar ... ME-1
**Barton Manor Subdivision One**—pop pl ... UT-8
**Barton Manor Subdivision Three**—pop pl ... UT-8
**Barton Manor Subdivision Two**—pop pl ... UT-8
Barton Memorial Hosp—hospital ... CA-9
**Barton Mill**—pop pl ... TN-4
Barton Mtn—summit ... AR-4
Barton Mtn—summit (3) ... NY-2
Barton Mtn—summit ... VT-1
Barton Mtn—summit ... VA-3
Barton Number 1 Dam—dam ... SD-7
Barton Number 2 Dam—dam ... SD-7
Barton Number 3 Dam—dam ... SD-7
Barton Oil Field—oilfield ... WY-8
Barton Park—park ... OR-9
Barton Peak ... CA-9
Barton Peak—summit ... CA-9
Barton Peak—summit ... UT-8
Barton Point—cape ... AL-4
Barton Pond—lake ... IL-6
Barton Pond—reservoir ... MI-6
Barton Ponds Park—park ... UT-8
Barton Ranch—locale ... OR-9
Barton Ranch—locale ... WY-8
Barton Range Canyon—valley ... UT-8
Barton Reservation—reserve ... MD-2
Barton River—stream ... VT-1
Barton (RR name for Curtin)—other ... WV-2
Barton Rsvr—reservoir ... ID-8
Barton Rsvr—reservoir (2) ... OR-9
Barton Run—stream (2) ... KY-4
Barton Run—stream ... NJ-2
Barton Run—stream (2) ... PA-2
Bartons ... AL-4
Bartons Bluff—cliff ... MS-4
Bartons Brook—stream ... MA-1
Bartons Brook—stream ... MN-6
Barton Sch—school ... AL-4
Barton Sch—school (2) ... CA-9
Barton Sch—school ... CO-8
Barton Sch—school ... ID-8
Barton Sch—school (3) ... IL-6
Barton Sch—school (2) ... MI-6
Barton Sch—school ... MN-6
Barton Sch—school ... NH-1
Barton Sch—school (2) ... ND-7
Barton Sch—school ... OH-6
Barton Sch—school ... OR-9
Barton Sch—school ... TN-4
Barton Sch—school ... TX-5
Barton Sch—school ... WI-6
Barton Sch—school ... WY-8
Barton Sch (abandoned)—school ... PA-2
Bartons Chapel—church ... AL-4
Bartons Chapel—church ... GA-3
Bartons Chapel—church ... TX-5
**Bartons Chapel**—pop pl ... TX-5
Bartons Chapel Cem—cemetery ... TX-5
Bartons Chapel Ch ... AL-4
Barton Sch (historical)—school ... MS-4
Barton Sch (historical)—school ... MO-7
Barton Sch No 1—school ... KY-4
Barton Sch No 2—school ... KY-4
Barton School (abandoned)—locale ... MO-7
Bartons Church ... AL-4
Bartons Corner—locale ... RI-1
Bartons Corners—locale ... WI-6
Bartons Creek ... MD-2
Bartons Creek—stream (2) ... TN-4
Bartons Creek—stream ... TX-5
Bartons Creek—stream ... VA-3
Bartons Creek Ch—church ... TN-4
Bartons Creek Ch—church ... TX-5
Bartons Creek (Township of)—fmr MCD ... NC-3
Bartons Crossroad—other ... VA-3
Bartons Crossroads ... VA-3
Bartons Ferry (historical)—locale ... MS-4
Bartons Fishing Lake Dam—dam ... AL-4
Bartons Ford ... PA-2
Bartons Hollow—valley ... PA-2
Bartons Hollow—valley ... UT-8
Barton Shores Baptist Ch—church ... FL-3
Bartons Island—island ... NY-2
Bartons Lake ... ND-7
Bartons Lake—lake ... MI-6
Bartons Lake—lake ... ND-7
Bartons Landing ... AL-4
**Bartons Location**—pop pl ... IN-6
Bartons Mine—mine ... NY-2
Bartons Peak—summit ... UT-8
Barton Spring—spring ... MT-8
Barton Spring—spring (2) ... NV-8
Barton Spring—spring (2) ... TN-4
Barton Spring—spring ... TX-5
Barton Spring Public Use Area—park ... TN-4
Barton Springs ... TN-4
Barton Springs—hist pl ... TN-4
Barton Springs—locale ... TN-4
**Barton Springs**—pop pl ... TN-4
Barton Springs—spring ... NV-8
Barton Springs—spring ... TX-5
Barton Springs Archeol and Historical District—hist pl ... TX-5
Barton Spur—ridge ... VA-3
Bartons Resort—locale ... CA-9
Bartons Spring ... NV-8
Bartons Springs ... NV-8
Barton Station ... AL-4
Barton Store—locale ... OK-5
**Barton Subdivision**—pop pl ... UT-8
Bartonsville ... VA-3
Bartonsville—locale ... NC-3
**Bartonsville**—pop pl ... MD-2
**Bartonsville**—pop pl ... PA-2
**Bartonsville**—pop pl ... VT-1
Bartonsville Covered Bridge—hist pl ... VT-1
Bartonsville Sch (abandoned)—school ... PA-2
Barton Tank—reservoir ... NM-5
Barton Tebbs LaFevre Canal—canal ... UT-8
**Barton-Thompson Subdivision**—pop pl ... UT-8
**Barton (Town of)**—pop pl ... NY-2
**Barton (Town of)**—pop pl ... VT-1
**Barton (Town of)**—pop pl ... WI-6
Bartontown Sch—school ... VA-3
Barton Township—fmr MCD ... IA-7
Barton (Township of)—fmr MCD ... AR-4
**Barton (Township of)**—pop pl ... IN-6
**Barton (Township of)**—pop pl ... MI-6
Barton Trail—trail ... PA-2
Barton Village Site—hist pl ... MD-2
Bartonville ... NY-2
Bartonville—locale ... VA-3
**Bartonville**—pop pl ... AL-4
**Bartonville**—pop pl ... IL-6
**Bartonville**—pop pl ... TX-5
Bartonville Ch—church ... TX-5
Bartonville Mtn—summit ... NY-2
Bartonville Post Office (historical)—building ... AL-4
Barton Windmill—locale ... NM-5
Barton Windmill—locale ... TX-5
**Bartonwoods**—pop pl ... GA-3
Bartoo Island—island ... ID-8
Barto Post Office (historical)—building ... MS-4
**Barto (Township of)**—pop pl ... MN-6
Bartow—locale ... GA-3
**Bartow**—pop pl ... FL-3
**Bartow**—pop pl ... GA-3
**Bartow**—pop pl ... WV-2
Bartow (CCD)—cens area ... FL-3
Bartow Cem—cemetery ... FL-3
Bartow Cem—cemetery ... GA-3
**Bartow (County)**—pop pl ... GA-3
Bartow County Courthouse—hist pl ... GA-3
Bartow Elem Sch—school ... FL-3
Bartow JHS—school ... FL-3
Bartow Mall—locale ... FL-3
Bartow Memorial Hosp—hospital ... FL-3
Bartown ... PA-2
Bartow Pell Mansion—building ... NY-2
Bartow-Pell Mansion and Carriage House—hist pl ... NY-2
Bartow Senior HS—school ... FL-3
Bartram, Isaac, House—hist pl ... MI-6
Bartram, John, House—hist pl ... PA-2
Bartram, John, HS—hist pl ... PA-2
Bartram Branch—stream ... WV-2
Bartram Cem—cemetery ... WV-2
Bartram Chapel—church ... WV-2
Bartram Gardens Park—park ... PA-2
Bartram HS—school ... PA-2
Bartram Island—island ... FL-3
Bartram Sch—school ... FL-3
Bartram's Covered Bridge—hist pl ... PA-2
**Bartramville**—pop pl ... OH-6
Bartrand Spring—spring ... WY-8
Bartron Pond—lake ... PA-2
Bartron Site—hist pl ... MN-6
Bart Royce Hill—summit ... NY-2
Bartrug Cem—cemetery ... WV-2
Bartrums Rock—summit ... OR-9
Barts Ch—church ... PA-2
Bart Sch—school ... PA-2
Bartsch Ranch—locale ... CA-9
Barts Creek—stream ... CA-9
Barts Crossing ... AZ-5
Barts Crossing—locale ... AZ-5
Bartsdale Tank—reservoir ... NM-5
Barts Lick ... VA-3
Barts Lick Creek—stream ... VA-3
Bart Spring—spring ... NV-8
Barts Valley—valley ... CA-9
Bartsville ... IN-6
Bart Top—summit ... GA-3
**Bart (Township of)**—pop pl ... PA-2
Bartville—locale ... PA-2
Bartville Post Office (historical)—building ... PA-2
Bartville Sch—school ... MO-7
Bar Twenty Ranch—locale ... MT-8
Bartz Spring Creek ... TX-5
Baru ... MP-9
Bar U Bar Ranch—locale (2) ... AZ-5
Bar U Bar Tank—reservoir ... AZ-5
Baruch—uninc pl ... NY-2
Baruch Statue—park ... DC-2
Barum Branch—stream ... AR-4
Barum Ch—church ... WI-6
Barum Creek—stream ... TN-4
Barurukan ... MP-9
Barus Cem—cemetery ... NH-1
Baruth Sch (historical)—school ... SD-7
Bar View ... OR-9
**Barview**—pop pl (2) ... OR-9
Barview District ... OR-9
Barview State Wayside—park ... OR-9
Barville ... PA-2
Barville Pond—lake ... NH-1
Barvo Oil Field—oilfield ... TX-5
Bar V Ranch—locale ... CA-9
Bar V Ranch—locale ... MT-8
Bar V Ranch—locale ... WY-8
Bar V Tank—reservoir ... NM-5
**Barwal**—pop pl ... FL-3
**Bar Wayne Circle (subdivision)**—pop pl ... AL-4
Barweis Cem—cemetery ... MO-7
Barwell (historical)—locale ... AL-4
Barwell Island—island ... AK-9
Barwell Lake—reservoir ... IL-6
Barwick—locale ... KY-4
**Barwick**—pop pl ... GA-3
**Barwick**—pop pl ... MO-7
Barwick, Bayou—stream ... LA-4
Barwick-Pavo (CCD)—cens area ... GA-3
Barwick Sch—school ... MO-7
Barwiler Ditch ... IN-6
Barwise—locale ... TX-5
Barwise JHS—school ... TX-5
Barwise Lake—lake ... MN-6
**Barwood**—pop pl ... PA-2
Barwood Park—park ... FL-3
Bar W W Ranch—locale ... CO-8
**Barwyn Acres**—pop pl ... OH-6
Bar X Canyon—valley ... AZ-5
Bar X Canyon—valley ... UT-8
Bar X Gas Field—oilfield ... CO-8
Bar X Gas Field—oilfield ... UT-8
Bar X Mine—mine ... UT-8
Bar X Ranch—locale ... WY-8
Bar X Tank—reservoir (2) ... AZ-5
Bar X Tank—reservoir ... NM-5
Barxtel Hollow—valley ... MO-7
Bar X Trick Tank—reservoir ... AZ-5
Bar X Wash—stream ... AZ-5
Bar X Wash—valley ... UT-8
Bar Y Dome—summit ... NM-5
Baryeta Cabins—locale ... CO-8
Bar Y Ranch—locale ... NM-5
Bar Y Tank—reservoir ... NM-5
**Barytes**—pop pl ... AR-4
**Barytes**—pop pl ... VA-3
**Baryties**—pop pl ... MO-7
Baryties Sch—school ... MO-7
Bar Z F Ranch—locale ... MT-8
Bar Z Peak—summit ... MT-8
Bar Z Trail—trail ... MT-8
Bar 44 Well—well ... NM-5
Bar 74 Ranch—locale ... CO-8
Basaham Creek ... AR-4
Basal Creek—stream ... NC-3
Basal Creek Ch—church ... NC-3
Basalt—locale ... NV-8
**Basalt**—pop pl ... CO-8
**Basalt**—pop pl ... ID-8
Basalt Butte—summit ... NV-8
Basalt Canyon—valley ... AZ-5
Basalt Cem—cemetery ... ID-8
Basalt Cliff—cliff ... WA-9
Basalt Cliffs—cliff ... AZ-5
Basalt Cobblestone Quarries District—hist pl ... WA-9
Basalt Creek—stream ... AZ-5
Basalt Creek—stream ... CA-9
Basalt Creek—stream ... OR-9
Basalt Creek—stream ... WA-9
Basalte Hill ... CO-8
Basalt Hill—summit ... CA-9
Basalt Hill—summit ... ID-8
Basalt Hill—summit ... NV-8
Basalt Hill—summit ... WA-9
Basaltic Falls—falls ... WA-9
Basaltic Hills—range ... CO-8
Basaltic Mountain ... CO-8
Basalt Knob—summit ... AK-9
Basalt Lake—lake ... AK-9
Basalt Mesa—summit ... NV-8
Basalt Mtn—summit ... CO-8
Basalt Peak—summit ... NV-8
Basalt Peak—summit ... WA-9
Basalt Point—cape ... WA-9
Basalt Ridge—ridge ... NV-8
Basalt Rock—island ... AK-9
Basalt Rsvr—reservoir ... OR-9
Basalt Spring—spring ... WA-9
Basargin, Mount—summit ... AK-9
Basche Ditch—canal ... OR-9
Baschor ... KS-7
**Basco**—pop pl ... IL-6
**Basco**—pop pl ... WI-6
Basco Canyon—valley ... NV-8
Basco Creek—stream (2) ... WY-8
Basco Field—flat ... NV-8

Basco Island—island AK-9
Basco Lake—lake ID-8
Bascom IN-6
Bascom—locale GA-3
Bascom—locale KY-4
Bascom—locale MT-8
**Bascom**—pop pl FL-3
**Bascom**—pop pl OH-6
**Bascom**—pop pl TX-5
Bascomb Ch—church GA-3
**Bascomb Church**—pop pl VA-3
Bascomb Eldrige Creek—stream TN-4
Bascombe Reef (not verified)—bar MP-9
Bascom Brook—stream NY-2
Bascom Brook—stream VT-1
Bascombs Female Acad (historical)—school MS-4
Bascom Camp—locale NM-5
Bascom Canyon—valley ID-8
Bascom Cem—cemetery AL-4
Bascom Cem—cemetery GA-3
Bascom Cem—cemetery TN-4
Bascom Cem—cemetery VT-1
Bascom Ch—church FL-3
Bascom Ch—church OK-5
Bascom Ch—church (3) TN-4
Bascom Ch—church TX-5
Bascom Ch—church VA-3
Bascom Chapel—church AL-4
**Bascom Corner**—pop pl IN-6
Bascom Hill—summit MA-1
Bascom Hill Hist Dist—hist pl WI-6
Bascom Irvin Knob—summit TN-4
Bascom Lookout Tower—tower FL-3
Bascom Oil Field—oilfield MT-8
Bascom Pens—locale NM-5
Bascoms Chapel—church NC-3
Bascom Sch (historical)—school TN-4
Bascom Spring—spring OR-9
Bascom Tank Canyon AZ-5
**Bascomville**—pop pl SC-3
Basco Spring—spring NV-8
Basco Spring—spring (2) OR-9
Basco Spring Rsvr—reservoir OR-9
Basco Spring 3 NV-8
Basco Tank—reservoir AZ-5
Bascule Bridge AL-4
Bascule Bridge—bridge CA-9
Bascule Bridge—bridge FL-3
Bascule Bridge—bridge NJ-2
Bascule Drawbridge—other CA-9
Basden Cem—cemetery AL-4
Base Administration Bldg—hist pl TX-5
Baseball Flat—flat UT-8
Baseball Park—park IA-7
Baseball Park—park WY-8
Baseball Pond—reservoir UT-8
Baseball Rsvr—reservoir CA-9
Baseball Spring—spring UT-8
Baseball Tank—reservoir TX-5
Base Campground—locale CO-8
Base Camp One—locale MS-4
Base Camp Two—locale MS-4
Base Chapel—church GA-3
Base Chapel—church OH-6
Base Creek—stream MT-8
Base Creek—stream TX-5
Base Crossroads—locale PA-2
Base Hill—summit VI-3
**Basehor**—pop pl KS-7
Base Island—island AK-9
Basel KS-7
Base Lake MI-6
Base Line MI-6
Baseline—locale MT-8
**Base Line**—pop pl AR-4
**Base Line**—pop pl OR-9
Base Line—uninc pl CA-9
Baseline, Canal (historical)—canal AZ-5
Base Line Bridge—other IL-6
Base Line Camp—locale CA-9
Base Line Ch—church MI-6
Base Line Creek—stream MI-6
Baseline Flat—flat WY-8
Base Line JHS—school CO-8
Base Line Lake CO-8
Base Line Lake—lake (2) MI-6
**Base Line Lake**—pop pl MI-6
Baseline Mesa—summit NV-8
Baseline Ridge—ridge OR-9
Base Line Ridge—ridge WY-8
Base Line Rsvr—reservoir CO-8
Base Line Sch—school CO-8
Base Line Sch—school MI-6
Base Line Sch—school MT-8
Baseline Sch—school OR-9
Baseline Substation—locale AZ-5
Baseline Tank—reservoir AZ-5
Baseline Tank Number Two—reservoir AZ-5
Baseline Village Shop Ctr—locale AZ-5
Basement Point—cape AR-4
Base of Mount Mazama—area OR-9
**Base (of Mount Washington)**—pop pl NH-1
Base Rock Quarry—mine PA-2
Baser Wash—valley UT-8
Base Spring Chapel—church GA-3
Base Trail—trail NM-5
Base (Trailer Park) IL-6
Baseview Ch—church ND-7
Basey Canyon—valley OR-9
Basey Ch—church MN-6
Basford Bayou—stream TX-5
Basford Falls—falls NY-2
Basford Lake—lake MI-6
Basgalore, Lake—lake NJ-2
Basgalore Lake NJ-2
Basgal Place—locale NM-5
Bash, Henry, House—hist pl WA-9
Basha Elem Sch—school AZ-5
Bashai Creek AL-4
Basham—locale AL-4
Basham—locale VA-3
Basham Branch—stream WV-2
Basham Cem—cemetery VA-3
Basham Ch—church AL-4
Basham Ch—church VA-3
Basham Chapel Methodist Church AL-4
Basham Creek—stream AR-4
Basham Gap—gap AL-4
Basham (historical)—locale KS-7
Basham Hollow—valley AL-4
Basham Hollow—valley TX-5
Basham Lake CT-1
Basham Lake—lake MT-8
Basham Memorial Cem—cemetery AR-4
Basham Post Office (historical)—building AL-4
Bashams Gap AL-4
Bashams Gap Post Office (historical)—building AL-4
Bashan—locale CT-1
Bashan—locale OH-6
**Bashan**—pop pl SC-3
Bashan Brook—stream VT-1
Bashan Ch—church AL-4
Bashan Ch—church NC-3
Bashan Hill—summit MA-1
Bashan Lake—lake CT-1
Bashan Lake Cem—cemetery CT-1
Bashapish MA-1
Bashapish Brook MA-1
Bashapish Brook NY-2
Bashapish Falls MA-1
Bashapish Mtn MA-1
Bashavia Creek—stream NC-3
**Bashaw**—pop pl WI-6
Bashaway Creek—stream LA-4
Bashaw Bridge—bridge TN-4
Bashaw Brook—stream WI-6
Bashaw Brook Sch—school WI-6
Bashaw Creek—stream OR-9
Bashaw Creek—stream TN-4
Bashaw Ford—locale TN-4
Bashaw Lake—lake WI-6
Bashaw Mountain—ridge AR-4
Bashaw State Wildlife Mngmt Area—park MN-6
**Bashaw (Town of)**—pop pl WI-6
**Bashaw (Township of)**—pop pl MN-6
Bashaw Trout Springs—reservoir WI-6
Bash Bish MA-1
Bashbish Brook MA-1
Bashbish Brook NY-2
Bash Bish Brook—stream MA-1
Bash Bish Brook—stream NY-2
Bashbish Falls MA-1
Bash Bish Falls—falls MA-1
Bashbish Falls State For—forest MA-1
Bashbish Mtn MA-1
Bash Bish Mtn—summit MA-1
Bashem Cem—cemetery MO-7
Bash Creek IA-7
**Bashe**—pop pl AR-4
**Bashe**—pop pl OK-5
**Basher**—pop pl MO-7
Basher Kill—stream NY-2
Basher's Kill NY-2
Bashes Creek—stream NJ-2
Bashford, Robert M., House—hist pl WI-6
Bashford Cem—cemetery KY-4
Bashford Manor Sch—school KY-4
Bashful Peak—summit AK-9
Bash Hollow—valley TN-4
**Bashi**—pop pl (2) AL-4
Bashi Acad—school AL-4
Bashi Ch—church (2) AL-4
Bashi Creek—stream AL-4
Bashi Creek Landing and Rec Area AL-4
Bashi Creek Public Use Area—park AL-4
Bashitanakueb Lake MN-6
Bashitanaqueb Lake MN-6
Bashi United Methodist Church AL-4
Bashmair Bayou LA-4
Bashman Bayou—gut LA-4
Bash Mtn—summit AL-4
Bashon Hill—summit CT-1
Bashop Creek OR-9
Bashor Childrens Home—school IN-6
Bashore Boy Scout Camp—park PA-2
Bashore Island—island PA-2
Bashore Sch—school IL-6
Bashore Scout Reservation PA-2
Bashor Mill—hist pl TN-4
Bashors Mill (historical)—locale TN-4
Bashors Mill Post Office (historical)—building TN-4
Bashville Post Office (historical)—building TN-4
**Basic**—pop pl MS-4
Basic—uninc pl VA-3
**Basic (Basic City)**—pop pl MS-4
Basic City MS-4
Basic City—other MS-4
Basic Creek—stream AK-9
Basic Creek—stream NY-2
Basic Creek Rsvr—reservoir NY-2
Basic HS—school NV-8
Basic Sch—school NV-8
Basidonia Cem—cemetery AL-4
Basie Branch—stream MS-4
Basil OH-6
Basil—locale KS-7
**Basil**—pop pl KY-4
**Basil**—pop pl OH-6
Basil Chapel—church KY-4
Basil Corners—locale PA-2
**Basile**—pop pl LA-4
Basile, Lake—reservoir CT-1
Basil Gap—gap TN-4
Basil Hollow—valley TN-4
Basilica of St. Mary-Catholic—hist pl MN-6
Basilica Sch—school MN-6
Basil Oil and Gas Field—oilfield KS-7
Basilone Bridge—bridge NJ-2
Basils Ch—church MD-2
Basin—locale MS-4
Basin—locale MT-8
Basin—locale WV-2
**Basin**—pop pl AL-4
**Basin**—pop pl CA-9
**Basin**—pop pl CO-8
**Basin**—pop pl ID-8
**Basin**—pop pl ME-1
**Basin**—pop pl TX-5
**Basin**—pop pl WY-8
Basin, The AZ-5
Basin, The UT-8
Basin, The—basin AL-4
Basin, The—basin AK-9
Basin, The—basin (3) AZ-5
Basin, The—basin AR-4
Basin, The—basin (3) CA-9
Basin, The—basin (2) CO-8
Basin, The—basin FL-3
Basin, The—basin GA-3
Basin, The—basin ID-8
Basin, The—basin (2) LA-4
Basin, The—basin (3) ME-1
Basin, The—basin MA-1
Basin, The—basin MS-4
Basin, The—basin (4) MT-8
Basin, The—basin (2) NH-1
Basin,the—basin NY-2
Basin, The—basin (4) OR-9
Basin, The—basin (2) TN-4
Basin, The—basin TX-5
Basin, The—basin (4) UT-8
Basin, The—basin (2) VT-1
Basin, The—basin WY-8
Basin, The—bay (2) ME-1
Basin, The—bay (2) NH-1
Basin, The—bay NC-3
Basin, The—cove MA-1
Basin, The—flat AZ-5
Basin, The—gut ME-1
Basin, The—lake AR-4
Basin, The—lake IN-6
Basin, The—lake ME-1
Basin, The—lake MI-6
Basin, The—lake TX-5
Basin, The—slope PA-2
Basin, The—swamp CA-9
Basin, The—valley MA-1
Basin A—harbor CA-9
Basin B—harbor CA-9
Basin Bay—bay NY-2
Basin Bayou—bay FL-3
Basin Bayou—stream FL-3
Basin Bayou State Rec Area—park FL-3
Basin Beaver Ponds—lake UT-8
Basin Branch—stream NC-3
Basin Branch—stream TN-4
Basin Branch—stream VA-3
Basin Brook MA-1
Basin Brook—stream (2) ME-1
Basin Brook—stream MA-1
Basin Brook—stream NH-1
Basin Brook—stream NY-2
Basin Brook—stream (5) VT-1
Basin Butte—summit CO-8
Basin Butte—summit ID-8
Basin Butte—summit OR-9
Basin C—harbor CA-9
Basin Cabin—locale NV-8
Basin Cabin Spring—spring MT-8
Basin Camp—locale OR-9
Basin Campground—locale MT-8
Basin Canyon—valley AZ-5
Basin Canyon—valley (3) NV-8
Basin Canyon—valley NM-5
Basin Canyon—valley (4) UT-8
Basin Canyon Picnic Ground—locale MT-8
Basin Cascade Trail—trail NH-1
Basin Cave—cave TN-4
Basin Cedar CA-9
Basin Cem—cemetery ID-8
Basin Cem—cemetery WY-8
Basin Ch—church AL-4
Basin Ch—church AR-4
Basin Chapel—church MS-4
**Basin City**—pop pl WA-9
Basin City Airfield Airp—airport WA-9
Basin Clove—valley NY-2
Basin Corner—locale DE-2
Basin Coulee—valley MT-8
Basin Cove—bay AK-9
Basin Cove—bay ME-1
Basin Cove—bay OR-9
Basin Cove—valley AL-4
Basin Coves Overlook—locale NC-3
Basin Creek CA-9
Basin Creek CO-8
Basin Creek ID-8
Basin Creek TN-4
Basin Creek—stream AL-4
Basin Creek—stream (3) AK-9
Basin Creek—stream (2) AR-4
Basin Creek—stream (7) CA-9
Basin Creek—stream (3) CO-8
Basin Creek—stream FL-3
Basin Creek—stream GA-3
Basin Creek—stream (13) ID-8
Basin Creek—stream (24) MT-8
Basin Creek—stream NV-8
Basin Creek—stream NC-3
Basin Creek—stream (15) OR-9
Basin Creek—stream (2) TN-4
Basin Creek—stream (4) UT-8
Basin Creek—stream (3) WA-9
Basin Creek—stream (5) WY-8
Basin Creek Campground—locale ID-8
Basin Creek Guard Station—locale MT-8
Basin Creek Lake—lake MT-8
Basin Creek Lake—lake WY-8
Basin Creek Meadows—flat WY-8
Basin Creek Park—locale MT-8
Basin Creek Rsvr—reservoir MT-8
Basin Creek Trail—trail OR-9
Basin D—harbor CA-9
Basin Draw—valley MT-8
Basin Draw—valley (4) WY-8
Basin E—harbor CA-9
Basin-Elba Pass—gap ID-8
Basin F—harbor CA-9
Basin Falls—falls ME-1
Basin Falls—falls TN-4
Basin Falls Brook—stream ME-1
Basin Flats—flat UT-8
Basin Flats—flat WY-8
Basin Fork—stream MO-7
Basin G—harbor CA-9
Basin Gap—gap KY-4
Basin Gap—gap TN-4
Basin Gap Trail—trail TN-4
Basinger—locale FL-3
Basinger Canyon—valley ID-8
Basinger Cem—cemetery FL-3
Basinger Cem—cemetery OH-6
Basinger Sch—school FL-3
Basin Gulch MT-8
Basin Gulch—valley (2) CA-9
Basin Gulch—valley CO-8
Basin Gulch—valley ID-8
Basin Gulch—valley MT-8
Basin Gulch—valley OR-9
Basin Gulch Creek CA-9
Basin H—harbor CA-9
Basin Harbor—bay NY-2
Basin Harbor—bay VT-1
**Basin Harbor**—pop pl VT-1
Basin Harbor Sch—school VT-1
Basin Hill Cem—cemetery CT-1
Basin Hill Light Number 31—locale FL-3
Basin Hills—summit FL-3
Basin Hole—basin VT-1
Basin Hollow—valley AR-4
Basin Hollow—valley MO-7
Basin Hollow—valley TN-4
Basin Hollow—valley (2) UT-8
Basin Hollow—valley VA-3
Basin Hollow Creek—stream CA-9
Basin Island WI-6
Basin Island—island FL-3
Basin Junction—locale TX-5
Basin Knob Cem—cemetery MO-7
Basin Lake—lake AK-9
Basin Lake—lake AZ-5
Basin Lake—lake GA-3
Basin Lake—lake (2) ID-8
Basin Lake—lake IN-6
Basin Lake—lake (2) MI-6
Basin Lake—lake MT-8
Basin Lake—lake (2) TX-5
Basin Lake—lake (2) WA-9
Basin Lake—lake WI-6
Basin Lake—reservoir ID-8
Basin Lakes—lake WY-8
Basin Lateral—canal ID-8
Basin Lead—ridge TN-4
Basin Lead Trail—trail TN-4
Basin Meadows—flat MT-8
Basin Mills—locale ME-1
Basin Mine—mine AZ-5
Basin Mine—mine CA-9
Basin Mine—mine OR-9
Basin Mtn—summit CA-9
Basin Mtn—summit CO-8
Basin Mtn—summit KY-4
Basin Mtn—summit ME-1
Basin Mtn—summit MT-8
Basin Mtn—summit NY-2
Basin Mtn—summit TN-4
Basin Oil Field—oilfield WY-8
Basin Oil Field Tipi Rings (48CA1667)—hist pl WY-8
Basin Patch Spring—spring ID-8
Basin Peak—summit CA-9
Basin Peak—summit MT-8
Basin Point ME-1
Basin Point—cape (2) ME-1
Basin Point—summit OR-9
Basin Pond MA-1
Basin Pond—lake GA-3
Basin Pond—lake (4) ME-1
Basin Pond—lake MA-1
Basin Pond—swamp NY-2
Basin-pond Brook MA-1
Basin Pond Brook—stream MA-1
Basin Post Office (historical)—building MS-4
Basin Ranch—locale (2) WY-8
Basin Ranger Station—locale MT-8
Basin Republican-Rustler Printing Bldg—hist pl WY-8
Basin Ridge—ridge CA-9
Basin Rim Trail—trail NH-1
Basin Rock—pillar TN-4
Basin Rsvr—reservoir (3) CO-8
Basin Rsvr—reservoir MT-8
Basin Rsvr—reservoir OR-9
Basin Rsvr—reservoir WY-8
Basin Rsvr No. 1—reservoir CO-8
Basin Rsvr No 1—reservoir WY-8
Basin Rsvr No. 2—reservoir CO-8
Basin Rsvr No 2—reservoir WY-8
Basin Run—stream MD-2
Basin Run—stream PA-2
Basin Sch—school AL-4
Basin Sch—school CO-8
Basin Sch—school MS-4
Basin Sch—school NE-7
Basin Sch—school WY-8
Basin School, The—school ME-1
Basin Six—harbor CA-9
Basin Spring—locale KY-4
Basin Spring—spring (4) AZ-5
Basin Spring—spring AR-4
Basin Spring—spring (2) ID-8
Basin Spring—spring (7) NV-8
Basin Spring—spring (2) OR-9
Basin Spring—spring TN-4
Basin Spring Branch—stream TX-5
Basin Spring Post Office TN-4
Basinspring Post Office (historical)—building TN-4
Basin Springs—locale TX-5
**Basin Springs**—pop pl KY-4
Basin Springs Draw—valley CO-8
Basin Swamp—swamp FL-3
Basin Tank—reservoir (10) AZ-5
Basin Tank—reservoir (5) NM-5
Basin Tank—reservoir TX-5
Basin Township—civ div NE-7
Basin Trail—trail CO-8
Basin Trail—trail NH-1
Basin Trail Tank—reservoir NM-5
Basin Trail Two Hundred Fortyseven—trail AZ-5
Basin View Dam—dam MT-8
Basin Well—well (2) AZ-5
Basin Well—well NM-5
Basin Well—well (2) TX-5
Basin Well—well WY-8
Basin Windmill—locale NM-5
Basis FM-9
Basis Insel FM-9
Basis Island FM-9
Baskahegan Lake—lake ME-1
Baskahegan Stream—stream (2) ME-1
Baskatong Lake—lake MN-6
Baskens Hollow—valley AL-4
Baskeridge NJ-2
Baskerville—locale VA-3
Baskerville Apartment Bldg—hist pl WI-6
Baskerville Cem—cemetery TN-4
Baskerville Mill—locale VA-3
Baskerville Sch—school NC-3
Baskerville Spring—spring HI-9
Basket—locale NY-2
Basket—locale PA-2
Basket Bar—bar AR-4
Basket Bay—bay AK-9
Basket Burn AZ-5
Basket Butte—summit OR-9
Basket Cave—cave AL-4
Basket Cem—cemetery TN-4
Basket Creek—stream (2) AK-9
Basket Creek—stream AR-4
Basket Creek—stream GA-3
Basket Creek—stream KS-7
Basket Creek—stream MS-4
Basket Creek—stream NY-2
Basket Creek—stream WA-9
Basket Creek Ch—church GA-3
Basket Dome—summit CA-9
Basket Farm—hist pl KY-4
Basket Flat—flat CA-9
Basket Flat—flat NJ-2
Basket Gulch—valley WY-8
Basket Island—island (2) ME-1
Basket Lake—lake AK-9
Basket Lake—lake FL-3
Basket Lake—lake NY-2
Basketmakers Cave No 1—cave OK-5
Basket Mtn—summit OR-9
Basket Pass—gap CA-9
Basket Peak—summit CA-9
Basket Pond—lake NY-2
Basket Reservoir WA-9
Basket Ridge—ridge CA-9
Basket Spring—spring CA-9
Basket Spring—spring OR-9
Basket Springs Creek—stream ID-8
Basket Swamp—swamp RI-1
Basket Switch—locale MD-2
**Baskett**—pop pl KY-4
Baskett Cabin—locale WY-8
Baskett Cem—cemetery KY-4
Baskett Cem—cemetery MO-7
Baskett Point—bend OR-9
Baskett Ridge—ridge TN-4
Baskett Slough—stream OR-9
Baskett Slough Natl Wildlife Ref—park OR-9
Basket Valley—valley NV-8
**Baskin**—pop pl FL-3
**Baskin**—pop pl LA-4
**Baskin**—pop pl UT-8
Baskin, William, House—hist pl NM-5
Baskin Branch—stream SC-3
Baskin Chapel—church LA-4
Baskin Creek—stream AR-4
Baskin Ferry—locale AL-4
Baskingridge NJ-2
**Basking Ridge**—pop pl NJ-2
Basking Ridge—ridge ME-1
Basking Ridge Classical Sch—hist pl NJ-2
**Basking Ridge (subdivision)**—pop pl (2) AZ-5
Basking Rsvr—reservoir NJ-2
Baskin HS Bldg—hist pl LA-4
Baskin Point—cape NY-2
Baskin Rsvr—reservoir UT-8
Baskin Run—stream PA-2
Baskins Cem—cemetery GA-3
Baskin Sch—school TX-5
Baskins Chapel—church AL-4
Baskins Creek IA-7
Baskins Creek—stream SC-3
Baskins Creek—stream TN-4
Baskins Mill Creek—stream AL-4
Baskin Spring—spring OR-9
Baskin Spring—spring UT-8
Baskins Run PA-2
Baskins Run—stream IA-7
Baskin Tank—reservoir AZ-5
Baskin Tank Canyon—valley AZ-5
**Baskinton**—pop pl LA-4
Baski Windmill—locale CO-8
Bask Pond MA-1
Basle Brook MA-1
Baslee Branch—stream MO-7
Basler Hollow—valley MO-7
Baslington, George, Farmhouse—hist pl MN-6
**Basnesville**—pop pl AL-4
**Basnettville**—pop pl WV-2
Basnight Canal—canal NC-3
Baso Found—mine NM-5
**Basom**—pop pl NY-2
Basonia Ch—church MO-7
Basore—locale WV-2
Basque—locale OR-9
Basque Canyon—valley (2) NV-8
Basque Canyon—valley OR-9
Basque Creek—stream ID-8
Basque Creek—stream OR-9
Basque Flat—flat OR-9
Basque Flat Well—well OR-9
Basque Hills—summit OR-9
Basque Mine—mine NV-8
Basque Pit Rsvr—reservoir OR-9
Basque Spring—spring (2) ID-8
Basque Summit—summit NV-8
Basque Well—well NV-8
Basque Well Number 2—well NV-8
Basquez Creek CA-9
Basrah Brook MA-1
Bas Rsvr—reservoir OR-9
Bass AL-4
Bass—locale AL-4
Bass—locale FL-3
Bass—locale KY-4
Bass—locale OR-9
Bass—locale WV-2
**Bass**—pop pl AR-4
**Bass**—pop pl IN-6
**Bass**—pop pl MT-8
Bass, John H., Mansion—hist pl IN-6
Bass, Raymond, Site (22HR636)—hist pl MS-4
Bassa Basso—locale LA-4
Bassa Basso Bay—bay LA-4
Bassam Creek—stream CO-8
Bassam Guard Station—locale CO-8
Bassam Park—flat CO-8
Bassam Spring—spring CO-8
Bassards Corners PA-2
**Bassards Corners**—pop pl PA-2
Bassarisc Tank—reservoir AZ-5
Bass Bay—bay MN-6
Bass Bay—bay NY-2
Bass Bay—bay TN-4
Bass Bay—bay TX-5
Bass Bay—bay WI-6
Bass Bay—locale TN-4
Bass Bay—uninc pl WI-6
Bass Baygall—swamp TX-5
Bass Bay Marina—harbor TN-4
Bass Bay Resort—locale TN-4
Bass Bay Resort Dock—locale TN-4
Bass Beach—beach NH-1
Bassbish Brook MA-1
Bass Bldg—hist pl NV-8
Bass Boarding House—hist pl ME-1
Bass Branch—stream FL-3
Bass Branch—stream GA-3
Bass Branch—stream MO-7
Bass Branch—stream NC-3
Bass Branch—stream TN-4
Bass Brinks Creek—stream FL-3
Bass Brook—stream CT-1
Bass Brook—stream (2) ME-1
Bass Brook—stream MN-6
**Bass Brook (Township of)**—pop pl MN-6
Bass Camp—locale MN-6
Bass Canyon—valley (3) AZ-5
Bass Canyon—valley CO-8
Bass Canyon—valley TX-5
Bass Cem—cemetery (2) AL-4
Bass Cem—cemetery AR-4
Bass Cem—cemetery (2) GA-3
Bass Cem—cemetery IN-6
Bass Cem—cemetery KY-4
Bass Cem—cemetery (2) MS-4
Bass Cem—cemetery MO-7
Bass Cem—cemetery NM-5
Bass Cem—cemetery NY-2
Bass Cem—cemetery (2) NC-3
Bass Cem—cemetery OH-6
Bass Cem—cemetery SC-3
Bass Cem—cemetery SD-7
Bass Cem—cemetery (4) TN-4
Bass Cemeteries—cemetery NC-3
Bass Ch—church GA-3
Bass Channel—channel LA-4
Bass Chapel—church NC-3
Bass Chapel—church TN-4
Bass Cove—bay MI-6
Bass Cove—cove MA-1
Bass Creek MA-1
Bass Creek MI-6
Bass Creek TX-5
Bass Creek WI-6
Bass Creek—cove MA-1
Bass Creek—stream (2) AR-4
Bass Creek—stream ID-8
Bass Creek—stream (2) IA-7
Bass Creek—stream (3) MA-1
Bass Creek—stream (3) MI-6
Bass Creek—stream (2) MN-6
Bass Creek—stream MO-7
Bass Creek—stream MT-8
Bass Creek—stream NC-3
Bass Creek—stream (4) SC-3
Bass Creek—stream WI-6
**Bass Crossroads**—pop pl GA-3
**Bass Crossroads**—pop pl NC-3
**Bass Crossroads**—pop pl SC-3
Bass Ditch—canal IN-6
Bass Draw—valley NM-5
Bass Draw—valley WY-8
Basse, Pointe—cape LA-4
**Bassel Addition (subdivision)**—pop pl TN-4
Basselin Cem—cemetery NY-2
Bassella Creek—stream CA-9
Bassel Sch—school TN-4
Bassendorf Beach OR-9
Bassenger FL-3
Basses Bay—bay NJ-2
Basses Choice-Days Point Archeol District—hist pl VA-3
Basses Creek—stream TN-4
Basset PA-2
Basset Branch—stream FL-3
Basset Branch—stream TX-5
Basset Brook—stream CT-1
Basset Brook—stream NY-2
Basset Cabin—locale CO-8
Basset Cabin—locale WY-8
Basset Cem—cemetery IN-6
Basset Cem—cemetery OH-6
Basset Cem—cemetery VA-3
Basset Creek TX-5
Basset Creek—stream TX-5
Basset Dam—dam PA-2
Basset Island MA-1
Basset Island—island AK-9
Basset Lake MI-6
Basset Pond PA-2
Basset Pond—lake CT-1
Basset Sch—school IL-6
**Bassets Corner**—pop pl MA-1
Basset Slough MN-6
Bassett—locale ID-8
**Bassett**—pop pl AR-4
**Bassett**—pop pl CA-9
**Bassett**—pop pl IA-7
**Bassett**—pop pl KS-7
**Bassett**—pop pl MN-6
**Bassett**—pop pl NE-7
**Bassett**—pop pl TX-5
**Bassett**—pop pl VA-3
**Bassett**—pop pl WI-6
Bassett, C.J.H., House—hist pl MA-1
Bassett, Edwin, House—hist pl MA-1
Bassett, Maria, House—hist pl MA-1
Bassett, O. T., Tower—hist pl TX-5
Bassett and Bassett Banking House—hist pl TX-5
Bassett Branch—stream VA-3
Bassett Bridge—bridge CT-1
Bassett Brook—stream ME-1
Bassett Brook—stream (4) MA-1
Bassett Brook—stream VT-1
Bassett Cave—cave AR-4

Bassett Cem—cemetery AR-4
Bassett Cem—cemetery CO-8
Bassett Cem—cemetery MN-6
Bassett Cem—cemetery OH-6
Bassett Cem—cemetery TN-4
Bassett Ch—church MN-6
Bassett Country Club—other VA-3
Bassett Creek—stream (2) AL-4
Bassett Creek—stream ME-1
Bassett Creek—stream MD-2
Bassett Creek—stream MI-6
Bassett Creek—stream MN-6
Bassett Creek—stream MT-8
Bassett Creek—stream NV-8
Bassett Creek—stream TX-5
Bassett Creek—stream UT-8
Bassett Creek—stream WI-6
Bassett Creek Ch—church AL-4
Bassett Creek Park—park MN-6
Bassett Ditch IN-6
Bassett Ditch—canal IN-6
Bassett Forks—locale VA-3
Bassett Grove Ceremonial Grounds—hist pl OK-5
Bassett Gulch—valley ID-8
Bassett Hill—summit MA-1
Bassett Hill—summit NH-1
Bassett Hot Springs—spring CA-9
Bassett House—hist pl NC-3
Bassett HS—school CA-9
Bassett Island MA-1
Bassett JHS—school CT-1
Bassett Junction—locale WA-9
Bassett Lake—lake MI-6
Bassett Lake—lake MN-6
Bassett Lake—lake NM-5
Bassett Lake—reservoir AL-4
Bassett Lake—reservoir NV-8
Bassett Lake—reservoir NM-5
Bassett Lakes—lake MN-6
Bassett Meadow—flat MA-1
Bassett Memorial Park—cemetery NE-7
Bassett Millpond—swamp MD-2
Bassett Mtn—summit NY-2
Bassett Park—park CT-1
Bassett Park—park (3) MI-6
Bassett Park—park NY-2
Bassett Peak—summit AZ-5
Bassett Pond MA-1
Bassett Pond—lake MA-1
Bassett Pond—lake PA-2
Bassett Ranch—locale CA-9
Bassett Ranch—locale (2) NE-7
Bassett Ranch—locale NV-8
Bassett Ranch—locale NM-5
Bassett Reservoir Dam—dam MA-1
Bassett Rsvr—reservoir MA-1
Bassetts VA-3
Bassetts—locale CA-9
Bassetts Brook MA-1
Bassett Sch—school CA-9
Bassett Sch—school MN-6
Bassett Sch—school NC-3
Bassett's Creek MN-6
Bassetts Creek—locale AL-4
Bassetts Creek—stream AL-4
Bassetts Creek—stream NY-2
Bassetts Field—locale AL-4
Bassetts Field Landing AL-4
Bassetts Island—island MA-1
Bassetts Lot Pond—lake MA-1
Bassett Slough—lake MN-6
Bassetts Pond MA-1
Bassett Spring—spring CO-8
Bassett Spring—spring NM-5
Bassett Spring—spring UT-8
Bassett Spring—spring WA-9
Bassett Street Sch—school CA-9
Bassett Tank—reservoir AZ-5
**Bassett (Township of)**—pop pl MN-6
Bassett Valley—basin NE-7
Bassettville Cem—cemetery KS-7
**Bassettville Township**—pop pl KS-7
Bassetville (historical)—locale KS-7
Bass Everett Cem—cemetery MS-4
Bassey Creek—stream OR-9
**Bassfield**—pop pl MS-4
Bassfield Baptist Ch—church MS-4
Bassfield Ch—church MS-4
Bassfield Elem Sch—school MS-4
Bassfield HS—school MS-4
Bassfield Sewage Lagoon Dam—dam MS-4
Bass Flat—flat NV-8
Bass Flats NV-8
Bass Flats—flat FL-3
Bassfold Creek—stream MD-2
Bass Fox Ditch—canal IN-6
Bass Furniture Bldg—hist pl GA-3
Bass Gap—gap AR-4
Bass Haines Place—locale OR-9
Bassham Branch—stream TN-4
Bassham Ch (historical)—church AL-4
Bass Harbor—bay AK-9
Bass Harbor—bay ME-1
Bass Harbor—bay NJ-2
**Bass Harbor**—pop pl ME-1
Bass Harbor Head—cliff ME-1
Bass Harbor Head Light Station—hist pl ME-1
Bass Harbor Marsh—swamp ME-1
Bass Hatchery WI-6
Bass Head—cape SC-3
Bass Hill—summit CA-9
Bass Hill—summit NH-1
Bass Hill—summit VT-1
Bass Hill Lookout Tower—locale IL-6
Bass Hole—cove MA-1
Bass Hole—lake IN-6
Bass Hole—lake TX-5
Bass Hole Bay—bay SC-3
Bass Hole Cove—bay FL-3
Bass Hole Creek—gut SC-3
Bass Hole Marshes—swamp MA-1
Bass Hole River MA-1
Bass Hollow—valley AL-4
Bass Hollow—valley TN-4
Bass Hollow—valley WI-6
Bass Hollow County Rec Area—park WI-6
Bass HS—school GA-3
Bassick HS—school CT-1
Bassick Mine—mine CO-8
Bassickville Hist Dist—hist pl CT-1
Bassie, Mount—summit AK-9
Bassie Canyon—valley NV-8
Bassi Falls—falls CA-9
Bassi Fork—stream CA-9
Bassing Beach—beach MA-1
Bassinger FL-3
Bassinger Corner—locale MO-7
Bassinger Ditch—canal OH-6
Bassinger Mountain AR-4
Bassinger Pond—reservoir GA-3
Bassinger Union Memorial Chapel—church MO-7
Bassing Harbor—cove MA-1
Bass Island—island GA-3
Bass Island—island IL-6
Bass Island—island (2) ME-1
Bass Island—island MO-7
Bass Island—island NH-1
Bass Island—island (2) NY-2
Bass Island—island OH-6
Bass Island—island SC-3
Bass Island—island TX-5
Bass Island—island WI-6
Bass Island Brownstone Company Quarry—hist pl WI-6
Bassit Field—flat NV-8
Bass JHS—school MS-4
Bass JHS—school TN-4
Bass Lake IL-6
Bass Lake IN-6
Bass Lake MI-6
Bass Lake MN-6
Bass Lake NC-3
Bass Lake WI-6
Bass Lake—island MN-6
Bass Lake—lake CA-9
Bass Lake—lake (7) FL-3
Bass Lake—lake (3) IN-6
Bass Lake—lake LA-4
Bass Lake—lake (48) MI-6
Bass Lake—lake (56) MN-6
Bass Lake—lake (2) NM-5
Bass Lake—lake (3) NY-2
Bass Lake—lake (2) OH-6
Bass Lake—lake SC-3
Bass Lake—lake TX-5
Bass Lake—lake (4) WA-9
Bass Lake—lake WV-2
Bass Lake—lake (66) WI-6
**Bass Lake**—pop pl CA-9
**Bass Lake**—pop pl IN-6
**Bass Lake**—pop pl MI-6
**Bass Lake**—pop pl OH-6
Bass Lake—reservoir (3) CA-9
Bass Lake—reservoir MN-6
Bass Lake—reservoir MO-7
Bass Lake—reservoir MT-8
Bass Lake—reservoir NJ-2
Bass Lake—reservoir (2) NC-3
Bass Lake—swamp MN-6
Bass Lake Cabins—locale MI-6
Bass Lake Ch—church IN-6
Bass Lake Country Club—other WI-6
Bass Lake Dam NC-3
Bass Lake Dam—dam MS-4
Bass Lake Dam—dam NJ-2
Bass Lake Dam—dam NC-3
Bass Lake Drain—canal MI-6
Bass Lake Falls—falls NJ-2
Bass Lake (historical)—lake IA-7
Bass Lake Lookout Tower—locale MN-6
Bass Lake Number Three WI-6
Bass Lake Number Two WI-6
Bass Lakes—lake ID-8
Bass Lakes—lake MN-6
Bass Lakes—lake OH-6
Bass Lakes—lake (2) WI-6
Bass Lake Sch—school CA-9
Bass Lake Sch—school (2) WI-6
**Bass Lake (sta.)**—pop pl IN-6
Bass Lake State Beach—beach IN-6
Bass Lake State Fish Hatchery—other IN-6
Bass Lake Station IN-6
**Bass Lake (subdivision)**—pop pl NC-3
**Bass Lake (subdivision)**—pop pl PA-2
**Bass Lake (Town of)**—pop pl (2) WI-6
Bass Landing NC-3
Bass Landing—locale MS-4
Bass Landing—locale NC-3
Bass Landing (historial)—locale AL-4
Bass Landing Post Office (historical)—building TN-4
Bass Ledge—rock MA-1
Bass Little (Township of)—fmr MCD AR-4
Basslot Pond MA-1
Bass Mansion—hist pl MT-8
Bass Memorial Acad—school MS-4
Bass Memorial Cemetery AL-4
Bass Memorial Park—park IA-7
Bass Mill (historical)—locale TN-4
Bass-Morrell House—hist pl TN-4
Bass Mountain Marker—other CA-9
Bass Mtn—summit AR-4
Bass Mtn—summit CA-9
Bass Mtn—summit NC-3
Bass Mtn—summit TX-5
Bass Museum of Art—building FL-3
Bassnet Homestead—locale CO-8
Bassnet Point—cliff CO-8
Basso Bridge—bridge CA-9
Bassola, Lake—lake KS-7
Basso Lake WI-6
Bassoo Creek—stream MT-8
Bassoo Peak—summit MT-8
Bassout Pond—lake NY-2
Bass Park—park ME-1
Bass Peak—summit MT-8
Bass Pecan Plant Pond Dam—dam MS-4
Bass-Perry House—hist pl AL-4
Bass Playground—park OH-6
Bass Point—cape AK-9
Bass Point—cape AZ-5
Bass Point—cape (3) MA-1
Bass Point—cape NJ-2
Bass Point—cape (2) WA-9
Bass Point—cliff AZ-5
**Bass Point**—pop pl MA-1
Bass Point Cem—cemetery IA-7
Bass Point Creek—stream IA-7
Bass Pond—lake MA-1
Bass Pond—lake MN-6
Bass Pond—reservoir (2) NC-3
Bass Pond—reservoir VA-3
Bass Pond Dam—dam NC-3
Bass Pond Site—hist pl SC-3
Bass Pond Tank—reservoir AZ-5
Bass Post Office (historical)—building AL-4
Bass Post Office (historical)—building TN-4
Bass Ranch—locale NM-5
Bass Ranch—locale WY-8
Bass Ranch (historical)—locale MO-7
Bass Rapids—rapids AZ-5
Bass Reef Island—island MI-6
Bass reeftied Island MP-9
Bass Ridge—ridge KY-4
Bass Rip—bar MA-1
Bass River MA-1
Bass River MI-6
Bass River—locale NJ-2
**Bass River**—pop pl MA-1
Bass River—stream (2) MA-1
Bass River—stream MI-6
Bass River—stream NJ-2
Bass River, Town of MA-1
**Bass River, (Township of)**—pop pl NJ-2
Bass River Beach—beach MA-1
Bass River Breakwater—dam MA-1
Bass River Golf Club—locale MA-1
Bass River Neck—cape NJ-2
Bass River Sch—school MA-1
**Bass River (sta.)**—pop pl MA-1
Bass River State For—forest NJ-2
Bass River West Jetty Light—locale MA-1
Bass Rock MA-1
Bass Rock—locale CA-9
Bass Rock—pillar (2) RI-1
Bass Rock—rock (3) MA-1
Bass Rocks—cliff MA-1
**Bass Rocks**—pop pl MA-1
Bass Rocks Country Club—locale MA-1
Bass Rsvr—reservoir MT-8
Bass Rsvr—reservoir WY-8
Bass Run—gut IL-6
Bass Run—stream NJ-2
Bass Sch—school AR-4
Bass Sch—school CA-9
Bass Sch—school IL-6
Bass Sch—school VA-3
Bass Sch (historical)—school AL-4
Bass School MS-4
Bass Site (47Gt25)—hist pl WI-6
Bass Slough—stream FL-3
Bass Spring—spring AZ-5
**Bass Station**—pop pl IN-6
Bass Station (historical)—locale AL-4
Bass Swamp—swamp MA-1
Bass Tank—reservoir (3) AZ-5
Bass Tank—reservoir TX-5
Bass Tomb AZ-5
Basstown Creek GA-3
Basstown Creek NC-3
Bass Trail—trail AZ-5
Bassuot Cabin—locale OR-9
**Bassville**—pop pl MO-7
**Bassville Park**—pop pl FL-3
Bass-Walters Cem—cemetery NC-3
Bass Well—well NM-5
Bass Windmill—locale CO-8
Basswood—locale MI-6
Basswood—locale MN-6
Basswood—locale WI-6
Basswood Baptist Ch—church TN-4
Basswood Cem—cemetery WI-6
Basswood Ch—church IL-6
Basswood Corner Sch—school IL-6
Basswood Creek—stream IA-7
Basswood Creek—stream MN-6
Basswood Creek—stream TN-4
Basswood Creek—stream WI-6
**Basswood Estates**—pop pl FL-3
Basswood Falls—falls MN-6
Basswood Grove—locale MN-6
Basswood Hollow—valley PA-2
Basswood Island—island WI-6
Basswood Lake—lake MN-6
Basswood Lake—lake MO-7
Basswood Lake—lake ND-7
Basswood Lake—lake (2) WI-6
Basswood Pond—lake MI-6
Basswood River MN-6
Basswood River—stream MN-6
Basswood Run—stream PA-2
Basswood Sch—school WI-6
Bastain-Haralson, Ed, House—hist pl TX-5
Bastard Butte—summit WY-8
Bastard Butte Well—well WY-8
Bastard Canyon—valley CA-9
Bastard Creek MD-2
Bastard Creek—stream OR-9
Bastard Spring—spring OR-9
Bast Creek—stream TX-5
Bastc Rips—rapids ME-1
Basteen Creek—stream WI-6
B A Steinhagen Lake—reservoir TX-5
Bastendorf Beach OR-9
Bastendorff Beach—beach OR-9
**Bastian**—pop pl VA-3
Bastian Bay—bay LA-4
Bastian Bay Oil and Gas Field—oilfield LA-4
Bastian Creek—stream NV-8
Bastian Creek Ranch—locale NV-8
Bastian Elementary School NC-3
Bastian Island—island LA-4
Bastian Lake—bay LA-4
Bastian Pass—channel LA-4
Bastian Peak NV-8
Bastian Ranch—locale SD-7
Bastian Rsvr—reservoir UT-8
Bastian Rsvr No 1—reservoir WY-8
Bastian Sch—school TX-5
Bastian Site—hist pl IA-7
Bastian Spring—spring NV-8
Bastic Creek—stream AL-4
Bastile Glacier—glacier WA-9
Bastile Lake—lake WI-6
Bastile Ridge—ridge WA-9
Bastille, Mount—summit AK-9
Bastin Bend—bend TN-4
Bastin Cem—cemetery KY-4
Bastin Cem—cemetery TN-4
Bastin (RR name for Thornton)—other KY-4
Bastion Peak—summit WY-8
Bastion Ranch—locale NM-5
Bastion Ranch—locale UT-8
Basto Cem—cemetery ND-7
**Bastogne Gables (subdivision)**—pop pl NC-3
Baston TX-5
Baston Brook—stream ME-1
Baston Cem—cemetery TN-4
Baston Creek—stream ID-8
Baston Hollow—valley TN-4
Baston Sch—school MN-6
Baston Spring—spring NM-5
Bastonville—locale GA-3
Bastow, Lake—lake WY-8
**Bastress**—pop pl PA-2
**Bastress (Township of)**—pop pl PA-2
Bastron Lake—reservoir NE-7
**Bastrop**—pop pl LA-4
**Bastrop**—pop pl TX-5
Bastrop Bay—bay TX-5
**Bastrop Bayou**—pop pl TX-5
Bastrop Bayou—stream TX-5
**Bastrop Beach**—pop pl TX-5
Bastrop (CCD)—cens area TX-5
Bastrop Commercial District—hist pl TX-5
**Bastrop (County)**—pop pl TX-5
Bastrop County Courthouse and Jail Complex—hist pl TX-5
Bastrop State Park—park TX-5
Baswell Cave—cave AL-4
Baswell Dam—dam AL-4
Baswell Lake—reservoir AL-4
Baswell Sch (historical)—school AL-4
Basye—locale VA-3
Basye, T. D., House—hist pl KY-4
**Bat**—pop pl LA-4
Bat, The—summit AK-9
Bataan Lodge—locale NM-5
Bataan Memorial Hosp—hospital NM-5
Bataan Memorial Sch—school OH-6
Bataan Mine—mine NV-8
Bataan Park—park NM-5
**Bataan (subdivision)**—pop pl NC-3
Batamote Hills—summit AZ-5
Batamote Mountains—summit AZ-5
Batamote Mtn AZ-5
Batamote Pasture Tank—reservoir AZ-5
Batamote Ranch—locale AZ-5
Batamote Tank—reservoir (2) AZ-5
Batamote Wash—stream (2) AZ-5
Batamote Well—well (2) AZ-5
Bata Mtn—summit MT-8
Batan, Point—cape AK-9
**Batan (historical)**—pop pl OR-9
Batarora—locale NC-3
Batarora Branch—stream NC-3
Bataupan River Bogue MS-4
Batavia—locale CA-9
**Batavia**—pop pl AR-4
**Batavia**—pop pl IL-6
**Batavia**—pop pl IA-7
**Batavia**—pop pl MI-6
**Batavia**—pop pl NY-2
**Batavia**—pop pl OH-6
**Batavia**—pop pl WI-6
Batavia Cem—cemetery NY-2
**Batavia Center**—pop pl MI-6
Batavia Ch—church (2) MI-6
Batavia Ch—church MN-6
Batavia Club—hist pl NY-2
Batavia Creek—stream WI-6
Batavia Downs—area NY-2
Batavia Golf Club—other NY-2
Batavia Highlands IL-6
Batavia House—hist pl OH-6
Batavia Institute—hist pl IL-6
Batavia Kill—stream (2) NY-2
Batavia Peoples Ch—church IA-7
Batavia Sch—school MT-8
**Batavia (Town of)**—pop pl NY-2
Batavia (Township of)—fmr MCD AR-4
**Batavia (Township of)**—pop pl IL-6
**Batavia (Township of)**—pop pl MI-6
**Batavia (Township of)**—pop pl OH-6
Batawpan Bogue MS-4
Bat Branch—stream IN-6
Bat Branch—stream WV-2
Bat Butte—summit CA-9
Bat Canyon—valley (4) AZ-5
Bat Canyon—valley NM-5
Bat Canyon—valley WA-9
Bat Cave AL-4
Bat Cave—cave (2) AL-4
Bat Cave—cave (2) AZ-5
Bat Cave—cave (2) AR-4
Bat Cave—cave CA-9
Bat Cave—cave (8) MO-7
Bat Cave—cave OK-5
Bat Cave—cave (3) TN-4
Bat Cave—cave (2) TX-5
Bat Cave—hist pl NM-5
**Bat Cave**—pop pl NC-3
Bat Cave Archeol Site—hist pl OK-5
Bat Cave Canyon—valley NM-5
Bat Cave Canyon—valley TX-5
Bat Cave Draw—valley NM-5
Bat Cave (Frio Cave)—cave TX-5
Bat Cave Hollow—valley AR-4
Bat Cave Hollow—valley MO-7
Bat Cave Mtn—summit OK-5
Bat Cave Ridge—ridge MO-7
Bat Caves—cave NC-3
Bat Caves Buttes—summit CA-9
Bat Cave Tank—reservoir AZ-5
Bat Cave Wash—stream CA-9
Bat Cave Windmill—locale TX-5
Batcha Chukka AL-4
Batch Brook—stream ME-1
Batch Cem—cemetery TN-4
Batch Creek—stream KS-7
Batchelder, Alden, House—hist pl MA-1
Batchelder, George, House—hist pl MA-1
Batchelder, Nathaniel, House—hist pl MA-1
Batchelder Brook—stream NH-1
Batchelder Brook—stream VT-1
Batchelder Column—pillar WY-8
Batchelder Creek NC-3
Batchelder Hill—summit ME-1
Batchelder House—hist pl CA-9
Batchelder House—hist pl MA-1
Batchelder Pond—lake NH-1
Batchelder Sch—school CT-1
Batchelder Sch—school MA-1
Batchelders Crossing—locale ME-1
Batchelders Grant—unorg ME-1
Batcheller KS-7
Batcheller Creek—stream NY-2
Batcheller Hill—summit MA-1
Batcheller Lake—lake MI-6
Batcheller School—locale MI-6
Batchellers Hill MA-1
Batchellers Landing AL-4
**Batchellerville**—pop pl NY-2
Batchellor Brook—stream VT-1
**Batchelor**—pop pl LA-4
Batchelor, Thomas, House—hist pl MS-4
Batchelor Bay—bay NC-3
Batchelor Branch—stream SC-3
Batchelor Brook—stream MA-1
Batchelor Creek MT-8
Batchelor Creek NC-3
Batchelor Creek—stream MS-4
**Batchelor Crossroads**—pop pl NC-3
Batchelor Gulch—valley MT-8
Batchelor Lake MI-6
Batchelor Point—cape CA-9
Batchelors Bay NC-3
Batchelors Brook MA-1
Batchelor Sch—school MI-6
Batchelors Hill MA-1
Batchelors Island—island MI-6
Batchelors Landing—locale AL-4
**Batchelor Subdivision**—pop pl AL-4
Batch Head—summit ME-1
Batch Lake—lake OR-9
Batchler Cem—cemetery AL-4
Batchlers Creek KS-7
Batchlet Run—stream OH-6
Batch Pond—lake ME-1
**Batchtown**—pop pl IL-6
Batcom Pond CT-1
Bat Creek—gut AL-4
Bat Creek—stream (3) ID-8
Bat Creek—stream MD-2
Bat Creek—stream TN-4
Bat Creek Knobs—summit TN-4
Bate, John Leslie, House—hist pl KY-4
Bate, S. A., Barn and Chicken House—hist pl ID-8
Batea MH-9
Bat East Creek—stream KY-4
Bateau Pond—lake GA-3
Bateau Pond—swamp FL-3
Bateha—slope MH-9
Bateham—locale KS-7
Bate Hollow—valley TN-4
Bate Lick Branch—stream KY-4
Bateman—locale TX-5
**Bateman**—pop pl WI-6
Bateman Bend—bend AR-4
Bateman Bottom—flat TN-4
Bateman Branch—stream NC-3
Bateman Branch—stream (3) TN-4
Bateman Brook—stream NH-1
Bateman Canyon—valley NV-8
Bateman Cem—cemetery (2) AR-4
Bateman Cem—cemetery MN-6
Bateman Cem—cemetery TN-4
Bateman Cem—cemetery TX-5
Bateman Cem—cemetery WI-6
Bateman Coulee—valley MT-8
Bateman Creek—stream CA-9
Bateman Creek—stream MT-8
Bateman Creek—stream NC-3
Bateman Creek—stream OR-9
Bateman Gap—gap NC-3
Bateman-Griffith House—hist pl AR-4
Bateman Hollow—valley (2) TN-4
Bateman Hollow—valley VA-3
Bateman Island—island LA-4
Bateman Island—island WA-9
Bateman Lake—lake LA-4
Bateman Lake—reservoir GA-3
Bateman Lake—reservoir MS-4
Bateman Lake Gas and Oil Field—oilfield LA-4
Bateman Lake Gas And Oil Field—oilfield LA-4
Bateman Oil Field—oilfield (2) TX-5
Bateman Pond MA-1
Bateman Ranch—locale TX-5
Bateman Ridge—ridge CA-9
Bateman Rsvr—reservoir OR-9
Batemans Beach—beach NC-3
Bateman Sch—school IL-6
Bateman Sch—school IN-6
Bateman Sch—school KS-7
Bateman Sch—school MN-6
Bateman Sch (historical)—school TN-4
Bateman Slough—stream TN-4
Batemans Pond—reservoir MA-1
Batemans Pond Dam—dam MA-1
Batemans Pond Swamp—swamp MA-1
Bateman Spring—spring AZ-5
Bateman Spring—spring (2) NV-8
**Batemantown**—pop pl OH-6
Bateman (Township of)—fmr MCD AR-4
Bateman Woods—flat OK-5
Batemote Mountain AZ-5
Bate Pond—lake NH-1
Bates—locale ID-8
Bates—locale IL-6
Bates—locale LA-4
Bates—locale MI-6
Bates—locale NY-2
Bates—locale TN-4
Bates—locale WA-9
**Bates**—pop pl AR-4
**Bates**—pop pl CO-8
**Bates**—pop pl KY-4
**Bates**—pop pl NY-2
**Bates**—pop pl OH-6
**Bates**—pop pl OR-9
Bates, Daniel V., House—hist pl AR-4
Bates, John, House—hist pl KY-4
Bates, Levin, House—hist pl KY-4
Bates, William, House—hist pl SC-3
Bates and Powers Reservoir MA-1
Bates Bar—bar AL-4
Bates Battlefield—hist pl WY-8
Bates Battlefield—locale WY-8
Bates Bend—bend TN-4
Bates Bldg—hist pl OH-6
Bates Branch AR-4
Bates Branch—stream AL-4
Bates Branch—stream (2) GA-3
Bates Branch—stream (3) KY-4
Bates Branch—stream LA-4
Bates Branch—stream MO-7
Bates Branch—stream NE-7
Bates Branch—stream (2) NC-3
Bates Branch—stream SC-3
Bates Branch—stream (5) TN-4
Bates Branch—stream TX-5
Bates Branch—stream WV-2
Bates Bridge—bridge MA-1
Bates Brook—stream (2) CT-1
Bates Brook—stream ME-1
Bates Brook—stream MA-1
**Batesburg**—pop pl SC-3
Batesburg (CCD)—cens area SC-3
Batesburg Commercial Hist Dist—hist pl SC-3
Batesburg-Leesville (CCD)—cens area SC-3
Batesburg-Leesville Country Club—other SC-3
Batesburg Rsvr—reservoir SC-3
Bates Butte—summit OR-9
Bates Cabin Hollow—valley KY-4
Bates Canyon CA-9
Bates Canyon—valley AZ-5
Bates Canyon—valley CA-9
Bates Canyon—valley NM-5
Bates Canyon—valley UT-8
Bates Canyon Campground—locale CA-9
Bates Cem—cemetery AL-4
Bates Cem—cemetery (2) AR-4
Bates Cem—cemetery CT-1
Bates Cem—cemetery (3) GA-3
Bates Cem—cemetery ID-8
Bates Cem—cemetery LA-4
Bates Cem—cemetery ME-1
Bates Cem—cemetery (2) MI-6
Bates Cem—cemetery (2) MS-4
Bates Cem—cemetery (2) MO-7
Bates Cem—cemetery (2) NY-2
Bates Cem—cemetery OH-6
Bates Cem—cemetery (2) SC-3
Bates Cem—cemetery (5) TN-4
Bates Cem—cemetery VA-3
Bates Ch—church OH-6
**Bates City**—pop pl MO-7
Bates City Cem—cemetery MO-7
Bates-Cockrem House—hist pl OH-6
Bates Coll—school ME-1
Bates Corner—locale MO-7
**Bates County**—pop pl MO-7
Bates County Drainage Ditch—canal MO-7
Bates County Hospital Heliport—airport MO-7
Bates Cove—cove MA-1
Bates Creek GA-3
Bates Creek WY-8
**Bates Creek**—pop pl NC-3
Bates Creek—stream (3) AL-4
Bates Creek—stream (2) AK-9
Bates Creek—stream AR-4
Bates Creek—stream CA-9
Bates Creek—stream (2) ID-8
Bates Creek—stream (3) MS-4
Bates Creek—stream MO-7
Bates Creek—stream NC-3
Bates Creek—stream (2) OH-6
Bates Creek—stream TN-4
Bates Creek—stream TX-5
Bates Creek—stream (3) WY-8
**Bates Creek Camp**—pop pl MO-7
Bates Creek Rsvr—reservoir WY-8
Bates Creek Sch—school WY-8
Bates Dam—dam AL-4
Bates Dam—dam OR-9
Bates Drain—canal MI-6
Bates Draw—valley AZ-5
Bates Draw—valley (3) WY-8
Batese Lake—lake LA-4
Batesell Landing—locale MO-7
Bates-Felder Cem—cemetery MS-4
Bates Ferry Crossing TX-5
Bates Ferry (historical)—locale TX-5
Bates Field (Airport)—airport AL-4
Bates Field (airport)—airport AL-4
Bates Field Assembly of God Ch—church AL-4
Bates-Finch-Muse Cem—cemetery TN-4
Bates Fire Tower—locale MI-6
Bates Fork—stream (2) KY-4
Bates Fork—stream PA-2
Bates Fork Cem—cemetery PA-2
Bates Gap—gap NC-3
Bates-Geers House—hist pl MO-7
Bates Gulch—valley CO-8
Bates Gulch—valley ID-8
Bates Gulch—valley UT-8
Bates-Hendricks House—hist pl IN-6
Bates Hill—locale TN-4
Bates Hill—summit CO-8
Bates Hill—summit CT-1
Bates Hill—summit MA-1
Bates Hill—summit VT-1
Bates Hill Cem—cemetery IN-6
Bates Hill Ch—church OH-6
Bates Hill Cumberland Presbyterian Ch—church TN-4
Bates Hill Plantation—locale SC-3
Bates (historical)—locale AL-4
Bates (historical)—locale KS-7
Bates (historical)—locale SD-7
Bates Hole—bend (2) WY-8
Bates Hole Rsvr—reservoir WY-8
Bates Hole Stock Trail—trail WY-8
Bates Hollow AL-4
Bates Hollow TN-4
Bates Hollow—valley AL-4
Bates Hollow—valley AR-4
Bates Hollow—valley KY-4
Bates Hollow—valley (4) MO-7
Bates Hollow—valley (2) PA-2
Bates Hollow—valley (3) TN-4
Bates Hollow—valley WI-6
Bates House—hist pl KY-4
Bates HS—school MD-2
Bates Island MO-7

Bates Island—island ME-1
Bates Island—island MA-1
Bates Junction—locale MI-6
Bates Knob—summit KY-4
Bates Knolls—summit UT-8
Bates Lake—lake AL-4
Bates Lake—lake CO-8
Bates Lake—lake (3) MI-6
Bates Lake—lake PA-2
Bates Lake—reservoir AL-4
Bates Lake—reservoir CO-8
Bates Lake—reservoir TX-5
Bates Lake Arroyo—stream CO-8
Bates Lakes—lake CO-8
**Batesland**—pop pl (2) SD-7
**Bates Location**—pop pl MI-6
Bates Log House—hist pl KY-4
Bates Memorial Hosp—hospital AR-4
Bates Memorial State Park—park MA-1
Bates Mill—locale NJ-2
Bates Mill Branch NJ-2
Bates Mill Bridge (historical)—bridge MS-4
Bates Mill Creek—stream SC-3
Bates Mill Sch—school NJ-2
Bates Mine—mine MI-6
Bates Mountain MT-8
Bates Mountains AZ-5
Bates Mountains—summit AZ-5
Bates Mountain Spring—spring NV-8
Bates Mtn—summit AL-4
Bates Mtn—summit AR-4
Bates Mtn—summit NV-8
Bates Mtn—summit NC-3
Bates Mtn—summit OK-5
Bates Mtn—summit TN-4
Bates Old River—stream SC-3
**Bates Park (subdivision)**—pop pl MS-4
Bates Park Tank—reservoir NM-5
Bates Place—locale NM-5
Bates Point—cape MA-1
Bates Pond OR-9
Bates Pond—lake (3) CT-1
Bates Pond—lake MA-1
Bates Pond—lake NY-2
Bates Pond (historical)—lake AL-4
**Bates (Power Plant)**—pop pl TX-5
Bates Power Reservoir MA-1
Bates Power Reservoir Dam—dam MA-1
Bates Powers Rsvr—reservoir MA-1
Bates Ramp—locale TX-5
Bates Ranch—locale NE-7
Bates Ranch—locale NM-5
Bates Ranch—locale UT-8
Bates Ridge—ridge IN-6
Bates Ridge—ridge (2) ME-1
Bates Ridge—ridge NC-3
Bates Road Cem—cemetery NY-2
Bates Rock CT-1
Bates Rock—rock MA-1
Bates Rocks—summit CT-1
Bates Round Barn—hist pl NY-2
Bates (RR name for West Paris)—other ME-1
Bates Rsvr—reservoir CO-8
Bates Rsvr—reservoir OR-9
Bates Run—stream (2) PA-2
Bates Sch—school AR-4
Bates Sch—school IL-6
Bates Sch—school KS-7
Bates Sch—school KY-4
Bates Sch—school (3) MA-1
Bates Sch—school (3) MI-6
Bates Sch—school MO-7
Bates Sch—school OH-6
Bates Sch—school (2) SC-3
Bates Sch—school UT-8
Bates Sch (historical)—school MS-4
Bates Sch (historical)—school (2) TN-4
Bates-Seller House—hist pl OR-9
Bates Shaft—mine UT-8
Bates-Sheppard House—hist pl TX-5
Bates Slough—gut MO-7
Bates Slough—stream CA-9
Bates Slough Ditch—canal CA-9
Bates Spring—spring TN-4
Bates Spring—spring WY-8
Bates Spring Branch—stream TN-4
Bates Station—locale CA-9
Bates Store—locale SC-3
Bates Store (historical)—locale TN-4
Bates Swamp—swamp PA-2
Bates Tank—reservoir (2) AZ-5
Bates Tank—reservoir NM-5
Bates Tank—reservoir TX-5
**Batestown**—pop pl IL-6
Batestown Bridge—bridge AL-4
**Bates Township**—pop pl (2) SD-7
**Bates (Township of)**—pop pl MI-6
Bates Union Sch—school CA-9
Bates Ville IN-6
Batesville—locale AL-4
Batesville—locale (2) GA-3
Batesville—locale KS-7
Batesville—locale ME-1
**Batesville**—pop pl AR-4
**Batesville**—pop pl IN-6
**Batesville**—pop pl MS-4
**Batesville**—pop pl MO-7
**Batesville**—pop pl NJ-2
**Batesville**—pop pl OH-6
**Batesville**—pop pl SC-3
**Batesville**—pop pl TX-5
**Batesville**—pop pl VA-3
Batesville (CCD)—cens area TX-5
Batesville Ch of God—church MS-4
Batesville City Hall—building MS-4
Batesville Commercial Hist Dist—hist pl AR-4
Batesville Country Club—locale SD-7
Batesville Creek—stream AR-4
Batesville East Main Hist Dist—hist pl AR-4
Batesville Elem Sch—school MS-4
Batesville Hill—summit TX-5
Batesville Intermediate Sch—school MS-4
Batesville JHS—school AR-4
Batesville JHS—school MS-4
Batesville Lookout Tower—tower MS-4
Batesville Mounds (22Pa500)—hist pl MS-4
Batesville Mtn—summit AR-4
Batesville Presbyterian Ch—church MS-4
Batesville Senior HS—school AR-4
Batesville Shoal—bar AR-4
Batesville Water Carnival Stadium—park AR-4
Bates Wash AZ-5
Bates Well—locale AZ-5
Bates Well—well AZ-5
Bates Well—well NM-5
Bates Well Mountains AZ-5
Bates Windmill—locale (2) NM-5
Bates Woods Park—park CT-1
Batey Branch—stream NC-3
Batey Branch—stream TN-4
Batey Cem—cemetery TN-4
Bateyes (Barrio)—fmr MCD PR-3
Batey Ridge IN-6
Bat Fork—stream NC-3
Bat Guano Arch—arch UT-8
Bath IN-6
Bath KS-7
Bath WV-2
Bath—locale KY-4
Bath—locale MN-6
Bath—locale TX-5
**Bath**—pop pl GA-3
**Bath**—pop pl IL-6
**Bath**—pop pl IN-6
**Bath**—pop pl ME-1
**Bath**—pop pl MI-6
**Bath**—pop pl NH-1
**Bath**—pop pl NY-2
**Bath**—pop pl NC-3
**Bath**—pop pl OH-6
**Bath**—pop pl PA-2
**Bath**—pop pl SC-3
**Bath**—pop pl SD-7
**Bath Addition**—pop pl PA-2
Bath Alum—locale VA-3
Batham Drain—stream MI-6
**Bat Harbor**—pop pl TN-4
Bat Harbor Ch—church TN-4
Bat Harris Brook—stream VT-1
Bath Ave Hist Dist—hist pl KY-4
**Bath Beach**—pop pl NY-2
Bath Bend—bend TX-5
Bath Borough—civil PA-2
Bath Branch—stream GA-3
Bath Brothers Ranch—locale WY-8
Bath Canyon—valley OR-9
Bath Cem—cemetery GA-3
Bath Cem—cemetery SC-3
**Bath Center**—pop pl OH-6
Bath Ch—church OH-6
Bath Corner—locale SD-7
**Bath (corporate name for Berkeley Springs)**—pop pl WV-2
**Bath (County)**—pop pl KY-4
**Bath (County)**—pop pl VA-3
Bath Covered Bridge—hist pl NH-1
Bath Creek—stream ID-8
Bath Creek—stream IN-6
Bath Creek—stream NC-3
Bath Creek—stream (2) WA-9
Bath Creek Gorge—valley ID-8
Bathel Ch—church KS-7
Bathelhem Cem—cemetery AR-4
**Bathgate**—pop pl ND-7
Bathgate Cem—cemetery ND-7
Bathgate Drain—stream MI-6
**Bathgate Township**—pop pl ND-7
Bath Hist Dist—hist pl ME-1
Bath Hist Dist—hist pl NC-3
Bathhouse Creek ID-8
Bathhouse Creek—stream MT-8
Bathhouse Island—island FL-3
Bathhouse Key FL-3
Bathhouse Ravine—valley CA-9
Bathhouse Row—hist pl AR-4
Bath HS—school OH-6
Bathing Beach Park—park MI-6
Bathing Tank—reservoir TX-5
Bath Junction—locale PA-2
Bath Lake—lake FL-3
Bath Lake—lake IL-6
Bath Lake—lake MN-6
Bath Lakes—lake WA-9
Bath Lookout—locale TX-5
Bath (Magisterial District)—fmr MCD WV-2
**Bath Manor**—pop pl PA-2
Bath Mills Sch—school MI-6
Bath Mtn—summit CA-9
Bat Hollow—valley TN-4
Bat Hot Spring—spring ID-8
Bat House Branch—stream AR-4
Bat House Cove—cave AR-4
Bathouse Ditch—canal CO-8
Bath Pass CO-8
Bath Pond—lake OH-6
Bath Ranch—hist pl WY-8
Bath Ranch—locale (2) WY-8
Bath Rock—pillar ID-8
Bath Row—hist pl WY-8
Baths—uninc pl CA-9
Bath Sch—school NC-3
Bath Sch—school OH-6
Bath Sch—school OK-5
Bath Sch No 9—school IA-7
Bathsheba Creek NC-3
Bath Spring—spring CA-9
Bath Springs—locale AL-4
**Bath Springs**—pop pl TN-4
Bath Springs Baptist Ch—church TN-4
Bath Springs Ch TN-4
Bath Springs Post Office—building TN-4
Bath Springs Sch (historical)—school TN-4
Bath Springs School TN-4
**Bath (Town of)**—pop pl NH-1
**Bath (Town of)**—pop pl NY-2
Bath Township—fmr MCD IA-7
**Bath Township**—pop pl SD-7
Bath Township Consolidated Sch—hist pl OH-6
Bath Township Hall—hist pl OH-6
Bath (Township of)—fmr MCD NC-3
**Bath (Township of)**—pop pl IL-6
**Bath (Township of)**—pop pl IN-6
**Bath (Township of)**—pop pl MI-6
**Bath (Township of)**—pop pl MN-6
**Bath (Township of)**—pop pl (3) OH-6
Bath Township Sch—hist pl OH-6
Bathtub Creek—stream ID-8
Bathtub Creek—stream OR-9
Bathtub Draw—valley NM-5
Bathtub Forest Camp—park AZ-5
Bathtub Lake—lake (2) CA-9
Bathtub Lake—lake WA-9
Bathtub Lakes—lake WA-9
Bathtub Meadows—flat ID-8
Bathtub Mtn—summit ID-8
Bathtub Spring—spring AZ-5
Bath Tub Spring—spring AZ-5
Bathtub Spring—spring (3) CA-9
Bathtub Spring—spring CO-8
Bathtub Spring—spring MT-8
Bath Tub Spring—spring NV-8
Bathtub Spring—spring (2) NV-8
Bathtub Spring—spring (3) OR-9
Bathtub Spring (hot)—spring OR-9
Bath Tub Tank—reservoir AZ-5
Bathtub Trough—valley UT-8
Bathtub Water—lake AZ-5
Batick Mtn—summit VA-3
Batie Creek—stream VA-3
Batie Sch—school MI-6
Batina Branch—stream LA-4
Batin Cem—cemetery NE-7
Bating Brook—stream MA-1
Bating Pond—lake MA-1
Batiquitos Lagoon—bay CA-9
Batise Springs ID-8
Bat Island—island AK-9
Bat Island—island MI-6
Batista Lake—lake MN-6
Batiste, Bay—bay LA-4
Batiste Canyon—valley CA-9
Batiste Creek—stream LA-4
Batiste Creek—stream TX-5
Batiste Prairie—flat TX-5
Batiste Springs—spring ID-8
Batiste Woods—woods TX-5
**Batiz**—pop pl PR-3
Bat Knob Hill—summit AR-4
Batko, I—slope MH-9
Bat Lake MN-6
Bat Lake—lake MI-6
Bat Lake—lake (2) MN-6
Batley—locale TN-4
Batley Baptist Church TN-4
Batley Ch—church TN-4
Batlick Mtn—summit WV-2
Batloon, The—locale CA-9
Batman Cem—cemetery AR-4
Batman Cem—cemetery TN-4
Batman Sch (historical)—school MO-7
Batman Spring—spring MO-7
Bat Mtn—summit CA-9
Batna—locale VA-3
Bato MH-9
Batoff Creek—stream WV-2
Batoff Mtn—summit WV-2
Batola, Bayou—gut (2) LA-4
Batola, Lake—lake LA-4
**Baton**—pop pl NC-3
Baton Cem—cemetery MI-6
Baton Elem Sch—school NC-3
Baton Flat—flat CA-9
Baton Lake FL-3
Baton Pilon, Bayou—stream LA-4
**Baton Rouge**—pop pl LA-4
**Baton Rouge**—pop pl SC-3
Baton Rouge, Bayou—stream LA-4
Baton Rouge Country Club—other LA-4
Baton Rouge Depot—locale LA-4
Baton Rouge Harbor—harbor LA-4
Baton Rouge HS—hist pl LA-4
Baton Rouge HS—school LA-4
Baton Rouge JHS—hist pl LA-4
Baton Rouge JHS—school LA-4
Baton Rouge Metropolitan Airp (Ryan Field)—airport LA-4
Baton Rouge Waterworks Company Standpipe—hist pl LA-4
Bat Point—cape AK-9
Bat Point—summit ID-8
Bat Ranch Spring—spring NM-5
Batre, Bayou la—stream AL-4
**Batree**—pop pl LA-4
**Batree (Baytree)**—pop pl LA-4
Batree Community Drainage Canal—canal LA-4
Bat Ridge—ridge VA-3
Bat Rock—pillar CA-9
Bat Rock—summit AZ-5
Batron Elem Sch—school FL-3
Bat Roost Branch—stream AL-4
Batrum Gap—gap WY-8
Bat Run—stream IN-6
Bat Run—stream WV-2
Batsaw Branch—stream NC-3
Batsells Landing MO-7
Bats Grave NC-3
Bats Grocery Store—hist pl CO-8
Batsmith Creek—stream TX-5
Bats Neck MD-2
Batson—locale AR-4
Batson—locale MS-4
**Batson**—pop pl OH-6
**Batson**—pop pl TX-5
Batson Bay—swamp MS-4
Batson Branch—stream DE-2
Batson Cem MS-4
Batson Cem—cemetery IN-6
Batson Cem—cemetery MS-4
Batson Cem—cemetery MO-7
Batson Cem—cemetery (2) TN-4
Batson Ch—church AR-4
Batson Ch—church TN-4
Batson Creek—stream (2) GA-3
Batson Drain—stream IN-6
Batson Hill—summit NH-1
Batson Hollow—valley TN-4
Batson Lake—lake AL-4
Batson Lake—lake MN-6
Batson Lake Dam—dam MS-4
Batson Ledges—island ME-1
Batson Memorial Sanitarium—hospital AL-4
Batson Oil Field—oilfield TX-5
Batson Pond—lake NH-1
Batson Post Office (historical)—building MS-4
Batson Prairie—flat TX-5
Batson Prairie Baptist Ch—church TX-5
Batson River—stream ME-1
Batson Sch (historical)—school MO-7
Batsons Mill (historical)—locale TN-4
Batson (Township of)—fmr MCD AR-4
Bat Spring—spring AZ-5
Bat Spring—spring ID-8
**Batsto**—pop pl NJ-2
Batsto Dam—dam NJ-2
Batsto Furnace NJ-2
Batsto Historical Area NJ-2
Batsto Lake—reservoir NJ-2
Batston NJ-2
Batsto River—stream NJ-2
Batsto Village—hist pl NJ-2
Batsto Village Restoration NJ-2
Batt—locale VA-3
Battaille Sch—school MS-4
Battalina Creek—bay NC-3
Battalina Point—cape NC-3
Battalion Creek—stream WA-9
Battalion Lake—lake CA-9
Battalion Lake—lake WA-9
Battalion Pass—gap CA-9
Battaman Wash NV-8
Bat Tank—reservoir AZ-5
Battan Lodge NM-5
Battan Pond—lake NM-5
Batt Cem—cemetery TN-4
Batt Ch—church OK-5
Batt Creek TN-4
Batte Cem—cemetery TX-5
Batteese Creek—stream MI-6
Batteese Lake—lake MI-6
Battees Point—cape MD-2
Battelle—locale AL-4
Battelle Institute—school OH-6
Battell Elem Sch—school IN-6
Battelle Memorial Institute—school OH-6
Battelle Mines (underground)—mine AL-4
Battelle Sch—school MI-6
Battell House—hist pl MA-1
Battell Mtn—summit VT-1
Battell Park—park IN-6
Battell Shelter—locale VT-1
Battell Trail—trail VT-1
Battema Lake—lake ND-7
**Batten**—pop pl NC-3
Batten Bay—bay VA-3
Batten Branch—stream IA-7
Batten Cem—cemetery (2) NC-3
Batten Ditch—canal CO-8
Battendorf Canyon—valley KS-7
Batten Hollow—valley AL-4
Battenhouse Ditch—canal OH-6
Batten Island—island FL-3
Batten Kill—stream NY-2
Batten Kill—stream VT-1
Batten Kill Country Club—other NY-2
Batten Knob—summit TN-4
Batten Round Hollow—valley TN-4
Batten Run—stream (2) WV-2
Battens Ch—church AL-4
Batten Sch—school MI-6
**Battens Crossroads**—pop pl AL-4
Battentown—uninc pl NJ-2
**Battenville**—pop pl NY-2
Batterbee Branch—stream GA-3
Battered Rock Mtn—summit SC-3
Battern Fork—stream WV-2
Batterno Canyon—valley NV-8
Batter Park—park OH-6
Battersby Field—park WA-9
Battersea—hist pl VA-3
**Battersea**—pop pl VA-3
**Batterson**—pop pl OR-9
Batterson Block—hist pl CT-1
Batterson Cem—cemetery OH-6
Batterson Creek—stream OR-9
Batterson Park Pond—lake CT-1
Batter Street Cem—cemetery NY-2
Battery NY-2
Battery—locale VA-3
Battery, The—cape NY-2
Battery, The—cape SC-3
Battery A (historical)—locale MS-4
Battery Bay WI-6
Battery Bayou—gut LA-4
Battery B (historical)—locale MS-4
Battery Bienvenue Ruins—locale LA-4
Battery Buchanan (historical)—locale AL-4
Battery Cameron—military DC-2
Battery Ch—church GA-3
Battery Cheves—hist pl SC-3
Battery C (historical)—locale MS-4
Battery Creek—stream AK-9
Battery Creek—stream KY-4
Battery Creek—stream MT-8
Battery Creek—stream SC-3
Battery Creek—stream VA-3
Battery Creek Sch—school SC-3
Battery C Site—hist pl AR-4
Battery D—hist pl AR-4
Battery DeGolyer (historical)—locale MS-4
Battery D (historical)—locale MS-4
Battery Dillon (historical)—locale MS-4
Battery E (historical)—locale MS-4
Battery F (historical)—locale MS-4
Battery Gadsden—hist pl SC-3
Battery Gladden—locale AL-4
Battery Gut—stream VI-3
Battery Hasebrouck—hist pl HI-9
Battery Hawkins—hist pl HI-9
Battery Hawkins Annex—hist pl HI-9
Battery Heights—summit VA-3
**Battery Heights (subdivision)**—pop pl MS-4
**Battery Heights (subdivision)**—pop pl TN-4
**Battery Hill**—pop pl AL-4
Battery Hill—summit KS-7
Battery Hollow—valley TN-4
Battery Huger AL-4
Battery Island—island ME-1
Battery Island—island NC-3
Battery Island—other AK-9
Battery Islets—area AK-9
Battery Jackson—hist pl HI-9
Battery John Barlow and Saxton—hist pl CA-9
Battery Kemble (historical)—military DC-2
Battery Kemble Park—park DC-2
Battery Knob—summit TN-4
Battery Lake—lake AK-9
Battery Lathrop (historical)—locale MS-4
Battery LeRoy—hist pl SC-3
Battery Mackintosh AL-4
Battery Madison (historical)—locale MS-4
Battery Mahon (historical)—military DC-2
Battery Martin Scott (historical)—military DC-2
Battery Maury—locale VA-3
Battery McIntosh—locale AL-4
Battery Missouri (historical)—locale AL-4
Battery Morris (historical)—military DC-2
Battery Mountain Trail—trail MT-8
Battery Mtn—summit MT-8
Battery No. 1—hist pl SC-3
Battery No. 5—hist pl SC-3
Battery Osgood-Farley—hist pl CA-9
Battery Park—park DE-2
Battery Park—park KS-7
Battery Park—park NY-2
Battery Park—park VA-3
**Battery Park**—pop pl MD-2
**Battery Park**—pop pl (2) VA-3
Battery Park Cem—cemetery VA-3
Battery Park Control House—hist pl NY-2
Battery Park Hotel—hist pl NC-3
Battery Park Sch—school SC-3
Battery Parrott (historical)—military DC-2
Battery Phillips (historical)—locale MS-4
Battery Point WA-9
Battery Point—cape (2) AK-9
Battery Point—cape CA-9
Battery Point—cape GA-3
Battery Point—cape ME-1
Battery Point—cape (2) MD-2
Battery Point—cape NH-1
**Battery Point**—pop pl GA-3
Battery Point State Rec Area—area AK-9
Battery Power (historical)—locale MS-4
Battery Randolph—hist pl HI-9
Battery Robinett—locale MS-4
Battery Rock—cliff IL-6
Battery Rock (Election Precinct)—fmr MCD IL-6
**Battery Russell (historical)**—pop pl OR-9
Battery Selfridge—hist pl HI-9
Battery Selfridge—locale MS-4
Battery Sill (historical)—military DC-2
Battery Street Hist Dist—hist pl VT-1
Battery Street Hist Dist (Boundary Increase)—hist pl VT-1
Battery Street Subway—tunnel WA-9
Battery Tank—reservoir TX-5
Battery Tannrath (historical)—locale MS-4
Battery Thomson—hist pl SC-3
Battery Tracy AL-4
Battery Tynes—hist pl SC-3
Battery Vermont—military DC-2
Battery Weed—hist pl NY-2
Battery Wharf—locale MA-1
Battery White—hist pl SC-3
Battery Wilkes—hist pl SC-3
Battery Williams (historical)—locale MS-4
Battey, Dr. Robert, House—hist pl GA-3
Battey-Barden House—hist pl RI-1
Battey State Hosp—hospital GA-3
Batt Hill—summit MA-1
Battie, Mount—summit ME-1
**Battiest**—pop pl OK-5
**Battin**—pop pl OR-9
Battin Brook Pond MA-1
Battin Chapel—church IA-7
Battin Ditch—canal WY-8
Battine Lake—lake WI-6
Battin HS—school NJ-2
Battin Mill Pond MA-1
Battin Mine—mine MT-8
Battin Sch—school OR-9
Battjes Park—park MI-6
Battle—locale KY-4
Battle—locale LA-4
Battle—locale WY-8
**Battle**—pop pl TX-5
Battle Abbey—church VA-3
Battle Ax—summit OR-9
Battle Ax Ch—church TX-5
Battle Ax Creek—stream OR-9
Battle Axe Bend—bend AR-4
Battle Axe Mine SD-7
Battleaxe Mtn—summit ID-8
Battle-axe Ranch—locale NM-5
Battleaxe Ridge—ridge MO-7
Battle-axe West Windmill—locale NM-5
Battle Bar—bar OR-9
Battle Bar Riffle—rapids OR-9
Battle Beach—locale VA-3
Battle Bend Sch—school NE-7
**Battle Bluff**—pop pl MS-4
**Battleboro**—pop pl NC-3
Battle Branch NC-3
Battle Branch—stream AL-4
Battle Branch—stream (3) GA-3
Battle Branch—stream KY-4
Battle Branch—stream MD-2
Battle Branch—stream MS-4
Battle Branch—stream (2) NC-3
Battle Branch Ch—church GA-3
Battle Bridge Brook—stream ME-1
Battle Brook—stream IN-6
Battle Brook—stream (2) ME-1
Battle Brook—stream MN-6
Battle Butte WA-9
Battle Butte—summit (2) MT-8
Battle Butte—summit WA-9
Battle Butte Creek—stream MT-8
Battle Butte Mine—mine MT-8
Battle Butte Sch—school MT-8
Battle Butte School—locale MT-8
Battle Canyon—valley CO-8
Battle Canyon—valley KS-7
Battle Canyon Creek—stream WA-9
Battle Cem—cemetery (2) AL-4
Battle Cem—cemetery NY-2
Battle Cem—cemetery NC-3
Battle Cem—cemetery TN-4
Battle Cem—cemetery WY-8
Battle Center Ch—church IA-7
Battle Chapel—church LA-4
Battlecock Hill—summit MA-1
Battle Community Building—locale NC-3
Battle Coulee—valley MT-8
Battle Cove—valley NC-3
Battle Cove Ruins—locale AZ-5
Battle Creek AL-4
Battle Creek CA-9
Battle Creek NV-8
Battle Creek TX-5
Battle Creek WY-8
Battle Creek—gut FL-3
Battle Creek—locale CO-8
Battle Creek—locale SC-3
Battle Creek—locale VA-3
**Battle Creek**—pop pl IA-7
**Battle Creek**—pop pl MI-6
**Battle Creek**—pop pl NE-7
Battle Creek—stream AL-4
Battle Creek—stream (2) AK-9
Battle Creek—stream AR-4
Battle Creek—stream (5) CA-9
Battle Creek—stream (4) CO-8
Battle Creek—stream FL-3
Battle Creek—stream GA-3
Battle Creek—stream (3) ID-8
Battle Creek—stream IL-6
Battle Creek—stream IN-6
Battle Creek—stream (2) IA-7
Battle Creek—stream (6) KS-7
Battle Creek—stream KY-4
Battle Creek—stream MD-2
Battle Creek—stream (2) MI-6
Battle Creek—stream MN-6
Battle Creek—stream (2) MO-7
Battle Creek—stream (5) MT-8
Battle Creek—stream NE-7
Battle Creek—stream (3) NV-8
Battle Creek—stream NY-2
Battle Creek—stream (2) NC-3
Battle Creek—stream ND-7
Battle Creek—stream (2) OK-5
Battle Creek—stream (12) OR-9
Battle Creek—stream SC-3
Battle Creek—stream (5) SD-7
Battle Creek—stream (2) TN-4
Battle Creek—stream (5) TX-5
Battle Creek—stream UT-8
Battle Creek—stream (2) WI-6
Battle Creek—stream (4) WY-8
Battle Creek Acad—school MI-6
Battle Creek Burial Ground Historical Marker—locale TX-5
Battle Creek Butte—summit SD-7
Battle Creek Camp—locale OR-9
Battle Creek Campground—locale WY-8
Battle Creek Canal—canal AZ-5
Battle Creek Canal—canal ID-8
Battle Creek Canyon—valley SD-7
Battle Creek Cave Number One—cave TN-4
Battle Creek Cem—cemetery KS-7
Battle Creek Cem—cemetery TN-4
Battle Creek Cem—cemetery TX-5
Battle Creek Ch—church GA-3
Battle Creek Ch—church TN-4
Battle Creek City Hall—hist pl MI-6
Battle Creek Country Club—other MI-6
Battle Creek Country Club—other OR-9
Battle Creek Crossing Waterhole No 1—spring ID-8
Battle Creek Crossing Waterhole No 2—spring ID-8
Battle Creek Debris Basin Dam—dam UT-8
Battle Creek Debris Basin Rsvr—reservoir UT-8
Battle Creek Fort—locale UT-8
Battle Creek Guard Station—locale OR-9
Battle Creek Horror Hole—cave TN-4
Battle Creek Institute—school TN-4
Battle Creek Lake—lake MN-6
Battle Creek Lakes—lake ID-8
Battle Creek Meadows—flat CA-9
Battle Creek Mines—mine NV-8
Battle Creek Mines (underground)—mine TN-4
Battle Creek Mountain Rsvr—reservoir OR-9
Battle Creek Mtn—summit OR-9
Battle Creek Park—park MN-6
Battle Creek Post Office—hist pl MI-6
Battle Creek Public Farm Sch—school MI-6
Battle Creek Ranch—locale CA-9
Battle Creek Ranch—locale ID-8
Battle Creek Ranch—locale NV-8
Battle Creek Ridge—ridge ID-8
Battle Creek Rod and Gun Club—other CA-9
Battle Creek Sch—school MN-6
Battle Creek Sch—school (2) WI-6
Battle Creek Sch (historical)—school MO-7
Battle Creek Sch (historical)—school SD-7
Battle Creek Shelter—locale OR-9
Battle Creek Slough—stream OR-9
**Battle Creek Township**—pop pl KS-7
Battle Creek (Township of) MI-6
Battle Creek Trail—trail OR-9
Battle Creek Well—well ID-8
Battleday Ditch—canal IN-6
Battle Ditch—canal MT-8
Battledore Island LA-4
Battledore Reef—bar LA-4
Battle Drain—canal MI-6
Battle Ewing Catfish Ponds Dam—dam MS-4
Battlefield—locale AR-4
**Battle Field**—pop pl MS-4
**Battlefield**—pop pl MO-7
**Battlefield**—pop pl TN-4
Battlefield—uninc pl MS-4
**Battlefield Acres**—pop pl VA-3
Battlefield Airp—airport PA-2
Battlefield Cem—cemetery KS-7
**Battlefield Farms**—pop pl VA-3
Battlefield Golf Club and Estates—other GA-3
**Battlefield (historical)**—pop pl MS-4
**Battlefield Junction**—pop pl TN-4
Battlefield Mall Shop Ctr—other MO-7
Battlefield Of The Brandywine—park PA-2
Battlefield Park—park MS-4
**Battlefield Park**—pop pl VA-3
Battlefield Park Sch—school VA-3
Battlefield Plaza—locale MO-7
Battlefield Post Office (historical)—building MS-4
Battlefield Sch (historical)—school MS-4
Battlefield Shop Ctr—locale MS-4
Battle Flag MS-4
Battle Flat—flat AZ-5
Battle Ford Creek—stream IL-6
**Battle Forest (subdivision)**—pop pl NC-3
Battle-Friedman House—hist pl AL-4
Battle Gap—gap AL-4
Battlegin Bar—bar AL-4
Battle Glacier—glacier (2) AK-9

Battleground IN-6
Battleground NV-8
**Battleground**—pop pl AL-4
**Battle Ground**—pop pl IN-6
**Battleground**—pop pl NC-3
**Battle Ground**—pop pl WA-9
Battle Ground—summit ID-8
Battle Ground—uninc pl NC-3
Battle Ground Acad—school TN-4
Battleground Bay LA-4
Battle Ground Bay—bay LA-4
Battleground Buttes—summit OR-9
Battle Ground Campground—park IN-6
Battle Ground (CCD)—cens area WA-9
Battleground Cem—cemetery ID-8
Battle Ground Cem—cemetery IN-6
Battleground Creek—stream AZ-5
Battleground Creek—stream GA-3
Battleground Creek—stream TX-5
Battleground Elementary School NC-3
Battle Ground Elem Sch—school IN-6
Battle Ground Forks—locale FL-3
Battle Ground Hist Dist—hist pl IN-6
Battle Ground JHS—school IN-6
Battle Ground Lake—lake WA-9
Battleground Monument UT-8
Battleground Natl Cemetery—hist pl DC-2
Battleground Number One Tank—reservoir AZ-5
Battleground Point—summit NV-8
Battleground Plantation—hist pl LA-4
Battleground Post Office (historical)—building AL-4
Battleground Ridge—ridge AZ-5
Battleground Road Ch—church NC-3
Battleground Sch—school AL-4
Battleground Sch—school NC-3
Battleground State For—forest MN-6
Battleground Tank—reservoir AZ-5
**Battle Grove**—pop pl MD-2
Battle Grove Cem—cemetery KY-4
Battle Grove Sch—school MD-2
Battle Gulch valley UT-8
Battle Hall—hist pl TX-5
Battleham Gap—gap TN-4
Battle Hill NJ-2
Battle Hill—summit CT-1
Battle Hill—summit IA-7
Battle Hill—summit (2) NY-2
Battle Hill Ch (historical)—church AL-4
Battle Hill Haven—locale GA-3
Battle Hill JHS—school NY-2
Battle Hill Sch—school PA-2
**Battle Hill Township**—pop pl KS-7
Battle Hollow—locale PA-2
Battle Hollow—valley AL-4
Battle Hollow—valley TN-4
Battle Hollow—valley WI-6
Battle Hollow Sch (historical)—school PA-2
Battle House Royale—hist pl AL-4
Battle Island—island ME-1
Battle Island—island MN-6
Battle Island—island NY-2
Battle Island—island (2) WI-6
Battle Island Monmt—park OH-6
Battle Island State Park—park NY-2
Battle Knob—summit VA-3
Battle Lake MN-6
Battle Lake WI-6
Battle Lake—lake AK-9
Battle Lake—lake AR-4
Battle Lake—lake ID-8
Battle Lake—lake (3) MN-6
Battle Lake—lake ND-7
Battle Lake—lake OR-9
Battle Lake—lake WY-8
**Battle Lake**—pop pl MN-6
Battle Lake—reservoir TX-5
Battlement Cem—cemetery CO-8
Battlement Creek—stream CO-8
Battlement Mesa—area CO-8
Battlement Mesa Schoolhouse—hist pl CO-8
Battlement Mtn—summit MT-8
Battlement Mtn—summit WY-8
Battlement Reservoirs—reservoir CO-8
Battlement Ridge—ridge WA-9
Battlement Sch—school CO-8
Battlement Trail—trail CO-8
Battle Monmt—hist pl MD-2
Battle Monument Sch—school MD-2
**Battle Mountain**—pop pl NV-8
Battle Mountain Creek—stream MT-8
Battle Mountain HS—school CO-8
**Battle Mountain Indian Colony**—pop pl NV-8
Battle Mountain Ind Res NV-8
Battle Mountain Ind Res—reserve NV-8
Battle Mountain Natl Sanitarium—hospital SD-7
Battle Mountain Radio Range Station—locale NV-8
Battle Mountain Res—reserve SD-7
Battle Mountain State Park—park OR-9
Battle Mountain to Austin Stage Route—trail NV-8
Battle Mtn—summit AZ-5
Battle Mtn—summit (3) CA-9
Battle Mtn—summit (3) CO-8
Battle Mtn—summit (2) MT-8
Battle Mtn—summit (2) NV-8
Battle Mtn—summit (4) OR-9
Battle Mtn—summit SD-7
Battle Mtn—summit UT-8
Battle Mtn—summit VA-3
Battle Mtn—summit WA-9
Battle Mtn—summit (4) WY-8
Battle Mtn Summit—summit OR-9
Battle of Big Dry Wash Historical Marker—park AZ-5
Battle of Big Dry Wash Historical Monmt—park AZ-5
Battle of Blackstock's Historic Site—hist pl SC-3
Battle of Corinth, Confederate Assault Position—hist pl MS-4
Battle of Dry Lake 1873 (Site)—locale CA-9
Battle of Dry Plaines OR-9
Battle of Hanging Rock Historic Site—hist pl SC-3
Battle of Kepaniwai Historical Marker—locale HI-9
Battle of Killdeer Mountain Historical Monmt Park—park ND-7
Battle of Lands Ranch (Site)—locale CA-9
Battle of Milk River Site—hist pl CO-8
Battle of Mine Creek Site—hist pl KS-7
Battle of Old Wells OR-9
Battle of Palmito Hill (historical monument)—park TX-5
Battle of Rhode Island Site—hist pl RI-1
Battle of Scorpion Point (Site)—locale CA-9
Battle of the Rosebud Site—hist pl MT-8
Battle Oil Field—oilfield TX-5
Battle Park—area WY-8
Battle Park—flat CO-8
Battle Park—park GA-3
**Battle Park**—pop pl VA-3
Battle Peak—summit OR-9
Battle Plain (Township of)—civ div MN-6
Battle Point—cape (4) MN-6
Battle Point—cape WA-9
Battle Point—locale WA-9
Battle Point—summit IN-6
Battle Point Flowage—reservoir WI-6
Battle Point Site—hist pl MI-6
Battle Pond—lake FL-3
Battle Ranch—locale MT-8
Battle Ridge—ridge CO-8
Battle Ridge—ridge ID-8
Battle Ridge—ridge ME-1
Battle Ridge—ridge MT-8
Battle Ridge—ridge OR-9
Battle Ridge—ridge SD-7
Battle Ridge Campground—locale MT-8
Battle Ridge Cem—cemetery ID-8
Battle Ridge Pass—gap MT-8
Battle Ridge Ranger Station—locale (2) MT-8
Battle Ridge Rsvr—reservoir OR-9
**Battle River**—pop pl MN-6
Battle River—stream MN-6
Battle Road Visitor Center—building MA-1
Battle Rock—island OR-9
Battle Rock—summit CO-8
Battle Rock Sch—school CO-8
Battle Rock Wayside Park—park OR-9
**Battle Run**—pop pl KY-4
Battle Run—stream IA-7
Battle Run—stream NC-3
Battle Run—stream OH-6
Battle Run—stream VA-3
Battle Run—stream (2) WV-2
Battle Run Ch—church VA-3
Battles AL-4
Battles—locale CA-9
Battles—locale MS-4
Battles Branch—stream AR-4
Battles Branch—stream NC-3
Battles Branch—stream TN-4
Battles Bridge—bridge NC-3
Battles Brook—stream VT-1
**Battlesburg**—pop pl OH-6
Battlesburg Cem—cemetery OH-6
Battle Sch—school NC-3
Battles Chapel—church AR-4
Battle Sch (historcal)—school AL-4
Battles Gin Bar AL-4
Battles Hill MA-1
Battleship MH-9
Battleship—summit NM-5
Battleship, The AZ-5
Battleship, The—summit (2) AZ-5
Battleship Butte—summit AZ-5
Battleship Butte—summit (2) MT-8
Battleship Butte—summit UT-8
Battleship Causeway AL-4
Battleship Cove—bay MA-1
Battleship Iowa, The AZ-5
Battleship Island MH-9
Battleship Island—island AK-9
Battleship Island—island MI-6
Battleship Island—island MN-6
Battleship Island—island WA-9
Battleship Maine Memorial—park NJ-2
Battleship Mtn AZ-5
Battleship Mtn—summit (2) AZ-5
Battleship Mtn—summit (2) WY-8
Battleship Oil Field—oilfield CO-8
Battleship Peak—summit AZ-5
Battleship Reef—bar AK-9
Battleship Rock—island NV-8
Battleship Rock—pillar CO-8
Battleship Rock—pillar KY-4
Battleship Rock—pillar SD-7
Battleship Rock—summit CO-8
Battleship Rock—summit NM-5
Battleship Rock—summit UT-8
Battleship Texas—other TX-5
Battleship Wash—stream NV-8
Battles Hollow—valley TN-4
Battlesite Monmt—park MA-1
Battle Slough—gut WI-6
Battle Slough—swamp FL-3
Battle Slough—swamp WI-6
Battles Memorial Sch—school PA-2
Battles Mill—locale ID-8
Battles Post Office—locale AR-4
Battle Spring—spring WY-8
Battle Spring Draw—valley WY-8
Battle Spring Flat—flat WY-8
Battle Spring Number One—spring NV-8
Battle Spring Number Three—spring NV-8
Battle Spring Number Two—spring NV-8
Battle Springs—spring AR-4
Battle Springs (historical)—locale MS-4
Battle Springs Lake—reservoir OK-5
Battles Sch—school VT-1
Battles Spring—spring AL-4
Battle Swamp Brook—stream CT-1
Battles Wells NV-8
**Battles Wharf**—pop pl AL-4
Battles Wharf Hist Dist—hist pl AL-4
Battle Tank—reservoir AZ-5
Battletown PA-2
**Battletown**—pop pl KY-4
Battletown (Magisterial District)—fmr MCD VA-3
Battletown-Payneville (CCD)—cens area KY-4
Battle Township—fmr MCD IA-7
**Battle (Township of)**—pop pl MN-6
**Battleview**—pop pl ND-7
**Battleview Township**—pop pl ND-7
**Battlewood Estates**—pop pl TN-4
**Battlewood Forest**—pop pl TN-4
Battley Pond—reservoir NC-3
Battley Pond Dam—dam NC-3
Batto—locale CA-9
Batto Creek—stream AK-9
Batton Cem—cemetery MS-4
Batton Gulch—canal CO-8
Bat Tower-Sugarloaf Key—hist pl FL-3
Battown Cem—cemetery TN-4
Bat Town Cove—valley TN-4
Batt Place—locale MS-4
Battrum Mtn—summit WY-8
Batts, Judge R., House—hist pl TX-5
Batts, Judge Robert Lynn, House—hist pl TX-5
Batts Camp Lake—lake OR-9
Batts Cem—cemetery (2) TN-4
Batts Chapel—church NC-3
**Batts Court (subdivision)**—pop pl NC-3
Batts Creek—stream MO-7
Batts Creek—stream WY-8
Batts Crossroads—locale NC-3
Batts Grove NC-3
Batts Grove Ch—church GA-3
**Batts Heights (subdivision)**—pop pl AL-4
Batts Hill MA-1
Batts Island (historical)—island NC-3
Batt Slough—gut WA-9
Batts Meadow—flat OR-9
Batts Mill TN-4
Batts Mill Creek—stream NC-3
Batts Neck—cape MD-2
Batts Neck Sch—school MD-2
Battson Cem—cemetery MS-4
Batts Pond—reservoir NC-3
Batt Spring—spring SD-7
Battsville School (historical)—locale MO-7
Batts-Ward Cem—cemetery AL-4
Batt Tank—reservoir AZ-5
Batt Trail—trail ID-8
Batty Doe Lake—lake MI-6
Batty Pass—gap UT-8
Batty Pass Caves—cave UT-8
Batty Sch—school IL-6
Batty Sch—school OR-9
Batum—locale WA-9
Batupan Bogue MS-4
Batupan Bogue—stream MS-4
Batupan Bogue Creek MS-4
Batupon Bogue MS-4
Baturin Lake—lake AK-9
Batway Drain—stream MI-6
Bat Well—well AZ-5
Baty Branch MO-7
Baty Butte—summit OR-9
Baty-Plummer House—hist pl TX-5
Baty Silver King Trail—trail OR-9
Batys Mtn—summit PA-2
Batza River—stream AK-9
Batza Slough—stream AK-9
Batz Ditch IN-6
Batz Draw—valley WY-8
Batzka Ditch IN-6
Batztoa Lake—lake AK-9
Batzulnetas—locale AK-9
Baubaugo IN-6
Baublitz Airp—airport PA-2
Bauchmanns Pony Express Station Historical Marker—park UT-8
Bauch Ranch—locale CO-8
Bauck Cem—cemetery MN-6
Bauckman Creek MS-4
**Baucom**—pop pl TN-4
Baucom Cypress Strand—swamp FL-3
Baucom Hollow—valley TN-4
Baucom Lake—reservoir NC-3
Baucom Lake Dam—dam NC-3
Baucom Post Office (historical)—building AK-9
Baucoms Cem—cemetery NC-3
Baucom Sch—school NC-3
**Baucum**—pop pl AR-4
Baucumbrig Creek DE-2
Baucum Cem—cemetery AR-4
Baucum Cem—cemetery TN-4
Baucum Hill—summit OK-5
Baudendistel Sch—school MO-7
Bauder Sch—school (2) FL-3
Bauder Sch (abandoned)—school PA-2
**Baudette**—pop pl MN-6
Baudette Air Force Station—other MN-6
Baudette River—stream MN-6
Baudino Ranch—locale UT-8
Bauds Pond—lake ME-1
Bauduit Sch—school LA-4
Bauejin Island MP-9
Bauejin Island—island MP-9
Bauer—locale KY-4
**Bauer**—pop pl IA-7
**Bauer**—pop pl MI-6
**Bauer**—pop pl UT-8
Bauer Apartments—hist pl OH-6
Bauer Branch—stream MO-7
Bauer Canyon—valley UT-8
Bauer Cem—cemetery KS-7
Bauer Cem—cemetery MT-8
Bauer Cem—cemetery TX-5
Bauer Coulee—valley WA-9
Bauer Creek OR-9
Bauer Creek—stream IN-6
Bauer Creek—stream OR-9
Bauer Creek—stream PA-2
Bauer Creek—stream WA-9
Bauer Dam—dam OR-9
Bauer Drain—canal MI-6
Bauer Drive Hammock—island FL-3
Bauerfeind Cem—cemetery NY-2
Bauer Hollow—valley PA-2
Bauer Lake—lake MN-6
Bauer Lake—reservoir CO-8
Bauerlein Cem—cemetery TX-5
Bauerlein Creek—stream TX-5
Bauerman Ridge—ridge WA-9
Bauer Mine (Inactive)—mine CA-9
Bauern Freund Print Shop—hist pl PA-2
Bauer Park—park TX-5
Bauer Pgi Airp—airport MO-7
Bauer Point—cape UT-8
Bauer Pond—lake CT-1
Bauer Ranch—locale CA-9
Bauer Ranch—locale TX-5
Bauer Ranch—locale WY-8
Bauer Rock—pillar PA-2
Bauer Rsvr—reservoir CO-8
Bauer Rsvr—reservoir OR-9
Bauer Sch—school SD-7
Bauer School (Abandoned)—locale IL-6
Bauers Creek—stream OR-9
Bauers Creek—stream WI-6
Bauers Knoll—summit UT-8
Bauers Knolls UT-8
Bauers Rock PA-2
**Bauerstown**—pop pl PA-2
Bauer Township—civil SD-7
Bauer Valley—valley WI-6
Baugass Cem—cemetery TX-5
**Baugh**—pop pl OK-5
**Baugh**—pop pl TN-4
Baugh, W. H., House—hist pl ID-8
Baughaman Lookout—locale OR-9
Baugham Branch—stream MS-4
Baugham Lake—reservoir MS-4
BaughanStrozier Cem—cemetery GA-3
Baugh Bend—bend TN-4
Baugh Branch—stream KY-4
Baugh Branch—stream MO-7
Baugh Canyon—valley KS-7
Baugh Cem—cemetery IL-6
Baugh Cem—cemetery MO-7
Baugh Cem—cemetery (3) TN-4
Baugh Cem—cemetery VA-3
Baugh Chapel—church AR-4
**Baugh City**—pop pl IN-6
Baugh Creek—stream AL-4
Baugh Creek—stream ID-8
Baugh Creek—stream MN-6
Baugher Cem—cemetery MO-7
Baugher Cem—cemetery (2) OH-6
Baugher Lake—reservoir IN-6
Baugher Run PA-2
Baugher Run—stream PA-2
Baugh Gachter Drain—canal MI-6
**Baugh (historical)**—pop pl MS-4
Baugh Hollow—valley TN-4
**Baughman**—pop pl KY-4
Baughman, John, House—hist pl KY-4
Baughman Branch—stream IL-6
Baughman Branch—stream LA-4
Baughman Canal—canal CA-9
Baughman Cem—cemetery (2) IL-6
Baughman Cem—cemetery LA-4
Baughman Cem—cemetery OH-6
Baughman Cem—cemetery (2) PA-2
Baughman Ch—church (2) PA-2
Baughman Ch—church WV-2
Baughman Creek—stream CO-8
Baughman Creek—stream KY-4
Baughman Creek—stream MS-4
Baughman Creek—stream OH-6
Baughman Ditch—canal OH-6
Baughman Draft—valley WV-2
Baughman Drain—canal CA-9
Baughman Drain Number One—canal CA-9
Baughman Farm Strip—airport KS-7
Baughman Field—airport KS-7
Baughman Fork—stream KY-4
**Baughman Heights**—pop pl KY-4
Baughman Hill—summit IN-6
Baughman Hollow—valley PA-2
Baughman Lake—lake MS-4
Baughman Memorial Park—hist pl OH-6
Baughman Park—park SD-7
Baughman Rocks—summit PA-2
Baughman Run—stream (2) OH-6
Baughman Run—stream WV-2
Baughman Sch—school OH-6
Baughmans Creek—stream IA-7
Baughman Settlement—locale WV-2
Baughman Slough—stream TX-5
Baughman's Mill and Stanford RR Depot—hist pl KY-4
Baughmans Pond—reservoir SC-3
Baughman Spring—spring CA-9
Baughman Spring—spring PA-2
Baughmans Slough TX-5
**Baughman (Township of)**—pop pl OH-6
Baughmanville Ch—church SC-3
Baugh Mine (underground)—mine AL-4
Baugh Mtn—summit GA-3
Baughn Cem—cemetery OH-6
Baughner Lake MI-6
Baugh Sch—school IL-6
Baugh Post Office (historical)—building TN-4
Baugh Ranch—locale TX-5
Baugh Rsvr—reservoir CO-8
Baugh Sch—school MO-7
Baugh Sch (historical)—school (2) MS-4
Baughs Crossroads—locale GA-3
Baughs Landing (historical)—locale AL-4
**Baugh Spring**—pop pl TN-4
Baugh Spring—spring TN-4
Baughville—locale GA-3
Baugo Bay—bay IN-6
Baugo Creek—stream IN-6
**Baugo (Township of)**—pop pl IN-6
Bauguess Cem—cemetery NC-3
Baugus Branch—stream (2) TN-4
Baugus Cave—cave TN-4
Baugus Chapel—church TN-4
Baugus Hollow—valley (2) TN-4
Baugus Spring—spring TN-4
Bauhoff Park—park OH-6
Bauldree Branch—stream FL-3
Baulenas CA-9
Baulenas Bay CA-9
Bauler Well—well NM-5
Baullies—area UT-8
Baultoff Creek—stream AK-9
Baultoff Lakes—lake AK-9
Baum PA-2
Baum—locale FL-3
Baum—locale IL-6
**Baum**—pop pl OK-5
**Baum**—pop pl OR-9
Baum, Howard, Site (33RO270)—hist pl OH-6
Bauman Branch TX-5
Bauman Draw—valley OR-9
Bauman Hall—hist pl MN-6
Baumann Branch—stream TX-5
Baumann Bump—summit AK-9
Baumann Farm Inc. Airp—airport WA-9
Baumann House—hist pl KY-4
Baumann Lake Dam—dam MS-4
Baumann Ranch—locale NE-7
Baumann Ranch—locale NV-8
Baumann Sch—school TX-5
Baumann Trail—trail CA-9
Baumann Well—well NV-8
Bauman Ranch NV-8
Bauman Rsvr—reservoir OR-9
Baumans Pond Park—park AL-4
Baumans Ranch—locale WY-8
Baumbach Bldg—hist pl WI-6
Baumbach Lake—lake MN-6
Baum Bay NC-3
Baum Bay—bay ME-1
Baum Bay—bay NC-3
**Baumberg**—pop pl CA-9
Baumberger Ditch—canal OH-6
Baum Branch—stream IL-6
Baum Ch—church OK-5
Baum Creek—stream NC-3
Baum Drain—canal MI-6
Baum Drain—stream MI-6
Baumert Springs—spring CA-9
Baumfalk Mine—mine WY-8
Baumfalk Rsvr—reservoir WY-8
Baumgard Creek—stream WA-9
Baumgard Hill—summit WA-9
Baumgardner—locale PA-2
Baumgardner, William, House and Farm Buildings—hist pl OH-6
Baumgardner Cem—cemetery OR-9
Baumgardner's Mill Covered Bridge—hist pl PA-2
Baumgardner Tank—reservoir NM-5
Baumgardner Windmill—locale TX-5
Baumgarten Oil Field—oilfield KS-7
Baumgartner Campground—locale ID-8
Baumgartner Lake—lake MN-6
Baumgartner Lake—lake ND-7
Baumgartner Park—park MI-6
Baumgartner Sch—school IL-6
Baumgartner Tank—reservoir NM-5
Baumhauer Park—park AL-4
Baum Hill Cem—cemetery OH-6
Baumhoer Sch (abandoned)—school MO-7
Baumhoff Lake—lake MI-6
Baum Hollow—valley IN-6
Baumkirchner Mine—mine AZ-5
Baum Lake—lake CA-9
Baum Lake—lake NM-5
Baum Lake—lake UT-8
Baummer Pond—lake CT-1
Baum Mine—mine CO-8
Baum North Oil Field—other NM-5
Baum Oil Field—other NM-5
Baumont Sch—school MI-6
Baum Point—cape NC-3
Baum Point Island—island NC-3
Baum Pond—lake NJ-2
Baum Ranch—locale UT-8
Baumrucker Dam—dam NC-3
Baumrucker Lake—reservoir NC-3
Baum Sch—school IL-6
Baum Sch (abandoned)—school PA-2
Baums Corners—locale PA-2
Baums Creek—stream NC-3
Baum Site—hist pl NC-3
Baums Lead NC-3
Baum Slough—stream OR-9
Baumstown—locale PA-2
Baumtown PA-2
**Baumtown**—pop pl NC-3
**Bauneg Beg**—pop pl ME-1
Bauneg Beg Mtn—summit ME-1
Bauneg Beg Pond—lake ME-1
Baunin, Baldomero, Residence—hist pl PR-3
Baures Creek OR-9
Baur Ranch—locale WY-8
Baur Sch—school TX-5
Baursville Cem—cemetery TX-5
Bausch Creek—stream OR-9
Bausch Sch (abandoned)—school PA-2
**Bausman**—pop pl PA-2
Bauta Abajo (Barrio)—fmr MCD PR-3
Bauta Arriba (Barrio)—fmr MCD PR-3
Bautch Valley—valley WI-6
Bautista—locale TX-5
Bautista Cem—cemetery TX-5
Bautista Creek—stream CA-9
Bautista Emmanuel Mission—church TX-5
Bautista Guard Station—locale CA-9
Bautista Peak—summit AK-9
Bautista Wash—stream CA-9
Bauxite—locale AL-4
**Bauxite**—pop pl AR-4
Bauxite Cem—cemetery AR-4
Bauxite Hollow—valley TN-4
Bauxite Junction—locale AR-4
Bauxite Post Office (historical)—building AL-4
Bauxite Ridge—ridge TN-4
Bauxite Sch—school AR-4
Bauxite (Township of)—fmr MCD AR-4
Baux Mountain Ch—church NC-3
Baux Mtn—summit NC-3
Bavar Creek—stream AL-4
Bavar Creek Ch—church AL-4
Bavaria—locale WI-6
**Bavaria**—pop pl KS-7
Bavaria, Lake—lake MN-6
Bavarian Brewery—hist pl OH-6
Bavarla Lake MN-6
Bave Creek—stream OR-9
Baver Drain—canal MI-6
Baver Lake—reservoir IN-6
Baver Lake Dam—dam IN-6
**Bavington**—pop pl PA-2
Baviza, Arroyo—valley TX-5
Bavley Tank—reservoir CA-9
**Bavon**—pop pl VA-3
Baw Beese Lake—lake MI-6
**Baw Beese Lake**—pop pl MI-6
Bawcom Cem—cemetery TN-4
Bawcom Tank—reservoir AZ-5
**Bawcomville**—pop pl LA-4
Bawcum Cem—cemetery TN-4
Bawdy Creek NC-3
Bawdy Swamp—stream NC-3
Bawker Lake—lake MI-6
Bawley Branch—stream VA-3
Bawling Calf Rsvr—reservoir NV-8
Baxendale Sch—school MT-8
Baxiron Landing MD-2
**Baxley**—pop pl GA-3
Baxley (CCD)—cens area GA-3
Baxley Cem—cemetery AR-4
Baxley Hill—summit AL-4
Baxley Hill (historical)—locale AL-4
Baxley Sch—school GA-3
Baxman Sch—school MI-6
Baxter SC-3
Baxter—locale AL-4
Baxter—locale FL-3
Baxter—locale GA-3
Baxter—locale MI-6
Baxter—locale MS-4
Baxter—locale MT-8
Baxter—locale NE-7
Baxter—locale NC-3
Baxter—locale TX-5
Baxter—locale WV-2
Baxter—locale WY-8
**Baxter**—pop pl AR-4
**Baxter**—pop pl CA-9
**Baxter**—pop pl CO-8
**Baxter**—pop pl IA-7
**Baxter**—pop pl KY-4
**Baxter**—pop pl MN-6
**Baxter**—pop pl MO-7
**Baxter**—pop pl PA-2
**Baxter**—pop pl TN-4
**Baxter**—pop pl WV-2
Baxter—post sta KY-4
Baxter, Capt. Rodney J., House—hist pl MA-1
Baxter, Capt. Sylvester, House—hist pl MA-1
Baxter, Charles L., House—hist pl MA-1
Baxter, H. H., Memorial Library—hist pl VT-1
Baxter, Mount—summit CA-9
Baxter, Shubael, House—hist pl MA-1
Baxter and Martin Cow Camp—locale CO-8
Baxter Ave—uninc pl KY-4
Baxter Basin—basin CO-8
Baxter Basin—basin ID-8
Baxter Bay—swamp FL-3
Baxter Bayou—stream LA-4
Baxter Bay Pond—lake FL-3
Baxter Bottom—basin TN-4
Baxter Branch NC-3
Baxter Branch TN-4
Baxter Branch—stream GA-3
Baxter Branch—stream IN-6
Baxter Branch—stream (2) KY-4
Baxter Branch—stream NC-3
Baxter Branch—stream OK-5
Baxter Branch—stream TN-4
Baxter Bridge—other MI-6
Baxter Brook—stream ME-1
Baxter Brook—stream NY-2
Baxter Camp—locale CO-8
Baxter Camp—locale NV-8
Baxter Canyon—valley WA-9
Baxter (CCD)—cens area TN-4
Baxter Cem—cemetery IL-6
Baxter Cem—cemetery (2) IN-6
Baxter Cem—cemetery (8) TN-4
Baxter Cem—cemetery TX-5
Baxter Cem—cemetery (2) WV-2
Baxter Center—locale KS-7
Baxter Ch—church FL-3
Baxter Ch—church TX-5
Baxter City Hall—building TN-4
Baxter Cliff—cliff NC-3
Baxter Clock—hist pl NC-3
**Baxter (County)**—pop pl AR-4
Baxter Creek CA-9
Baxter Creek—stream (2) CA-9
Baxter Creek—stream (2) CO-8
Baxter Creek—stream GA-3
Baxter Creek—stream ID-8
Baxter Creek—stream MS-4
Baxter Creek—stream MT-8
Baxter Creek—stream NV-8
Baxter Creek—stream (2) NC-3
Baxter Creek—stream (3) OR-9
Baxter Creek—stream WA-9
Baxter Creek Rsvr—reservoir OR-9
Baxter Creek Trail—trail NC-3
Baxter Ditch—canal CO-8
Baxter Division—civil TN-4
Baxter Draw—valley WY-8
Baxter Elem Sch—school TN-4
**Baxter Estates**—pop pl NY-2
Baxter First Baptist Ch—church TN-4
Baxter Forks—locale SC-3
Baxter Game Preserve—park ME-1
Baxter Grist Mill Dam—dam MA-1
Baxter Gulch—valley (2) CA-9
Baxter Gulch—valley CO-8
Baxter Gulch—valley (2) MT-8
Baxter High School TN-4
Baxter Hill—summit AR-4
Baxter Hill—summit TN-4
Baxter Hollow—valley (2) TN-4
Baxter Hosp—hospital AR-4
Baxter House—hist pl CO-8
Baxter House—hist pl ME-1
Baxter House—hist pl OR-9
Baxter House—hist pl VA-3
Baxter HS—hist pl PA-2
Baxter Island—island TX-5
Baxter Island—swamp FL-3
Baxter Junction—locale KS-7
Baxter Lake—lake GA-3
Baxter Lake—lake MN-6
Baxter Lake—lake NH-1
Baxter Lake—reservoir CO-8
Baxter Lake—reservoir KY-4
Baxter Lake—reservoir NY-2
Baxter Lakes—lake CA-9
Baxter Lookout Tower—locale MS-4
Baxter Memorial Gardens—cemetery AR-4
Baxter Mill—hist pl MA-1
Baxter Mine—mine AK-9
Baxter Mine—mine CA-9
Baxter Mine—mine IL-6
Baxter Mountain AR-4
Baxter Mtn—summit CO-8
Baxter Mtn—summit NM-5
Baxter Mtn—summit (2) NY-2

Bayou Boeuf - Cocodrie Diversion Channel—*canal* LA-4
*Bayou Boeuf Cocoorie Diversion Channel* LA-4
**Bayou Boeuf (Kraemer Post Office)**—*pop pl* (2) LA-4
*Bayou Bois Connie* LA-4
*Bayou Bois Connue* LA-4
*Bayou Bois Courier* LA-4
*Bayou Bouillion* LA-4
Bayou Bouillon Oil and Gas Field—*oilfield* LA-4
*Bayou Boullion* LA-4
*Bayou Bourbeau* LA-4
*Bayou Bourbeaux* LA-4
Bayou Branch—*stream* FL-3
*Bayou Buckhorn* LA-4
*Bayou Butte* LA-4
*Bayou Cache* LA-4
Bayou Caddy Sch (historical)—*school* MS-4
*Bayou Cadet* LA-4
*Bayou Camitte* LA-4
Bayou Cane—*CDP* LA-4
*Bayou Carlin* LA-4
Bayou Carlin Oil and Gas Field—*oilfield* LA-4
*Bayou Cascas* LA-4
*Bayou Casotte Sch* MS-4
Bayou Cassotte Channel—*channel* MS-4
*Bayou Casta* LA-4
*Bayou Caster* LA-4
*Bayou Castor* LA-4
*Bayou Caucheon* LA-4
Bayou Cem—*cemetery* IL-6
Bayou Ch—*church* TX-5
*Bayou Chameau* MS-4
*Bayou Chamier* MS-4
Bayou Chantilly—*uninc pl* TX-5
Bayou Chauvin Oil and Gas Field—*oilfield* LA-4
*Bayou Chegley* LA-4
*Bayou Chene* LA-4
**Bayou Chene**—*pop pl* LA-4
*Bayou Cheniere* LA-4
*Bayou Cherovem* LA-4
*Bayou Chevereux* LA-4
Bayou Chico—*bay* FL-3
*Bayou Chicot* MS-4
**Bayou Chicot**—*pop pl* LA-4
*Bayou Chien* LA-4
*Bayou Chien Blanc* LA-4
Bayou Choctan Oil Field—*oilfield* LA-4
*Bayou Choctaw* LA-4
*Bayou Choctaw* MS-4
*Bayou Choupique* LA-4
Bayou Choupique Oil and Gas Field—*oilfield* LA-4
*Bayou Clear* LA-4
Bayou Coco Cem—*cemetery* MS-4
Bayou Cocodrie Oil Field—*oilfield* LA-4
*Bayou Combest* MS-4
*Bayou Comitte* LA-4
*Bayou Corne* LA-4
**Bayou Corne**—*pop pl* LA-4
*Bayou Corps Mourant* LA-4
Bayou Couba Oil and Gas Field—*oilfield* LA-4
Bayou Country Club—*other* LA-4
Bayou Country Club—*other* UT-8
*Bayou Cowan* MS-4
**Bayou Crab**—*pop pl* LA-4
Bayou Creek—*stream* FL-3
Bayou Creek—*stream* IL-6
Bayou Creek—*stream* IN-6
Bayou Creek—*stream* (3) KY-4
*Bayou Creole* MS-4
Bayou Crossing—*locale* FL-3
**Bayou Current**—*pop pl* LA-4
*Bayou Cypre-mort* LA-4
*Bayou Cypres* LA-4
*Bayou Cypres Mort* LA-4
*Bayou Cypress* LA-4
Bayou Dan Hills—*summit* LA-4
Bayou D'Arbonne Lake—*reservoir* LA-4
*Bayou Dauchite* AR-4
*Bayou Dauchite* LA-4
Bayou de Butte—*stream* LA-4
Bayou De Cade—*stream* LA-4
Bayou Deception Island—*island* LA-4
Bayou de Chene—*gut* LA-4
Bayou deChene—*stream* LA-4
Bayou de Chien—*stream* KY-4
Bayou de Chien Ch—*church* KY-4
Bayou De Fleur Oil and Gas Field—*oilfield* LA-4
Bayou de Glaize—*stream* LA-4
*Bayou Deipuent* LA-4
Bayou de la Baie Sec—*stream* LA-4
Bayou de la Gauche—*gut* LA-4
*Bayou de Lassaire* LA-4
Bayou de la Valle—*gut* (2) LA-4
*Bayou de Lesiare* LA-4
*Bayou de Lessaire* LA-4
Bayou de L'Isle—*stream* LA-4
Bayou de Log—*stream* LA-4
*Bayou De L'Outre* LA-4
Bayou de Loutre—*stream* AR-4
Bayou Del Puent—*stream* LA-4
Bayou de Muse—*stream* LA-4
Bayou De Plomb—*stream* LA-4
*Bayou de Roche* AR-4
*Bayou des Acadiens* LA-4
Bayou des Acadiens—*stream* LA-4
Bayou Des Allemands Oil And Gas Field—*oilfield* LA-4
Bayou Des Amoreux—*gut* (2) LA-4
*Bayou desArc Bayou* AR-4
Bayou Des Arc State Game Area—*park* AR-4
Bayou de Sauce—*gut* LA-4
Bayou Des Cannes—*stream* LA-4
Bayou des Cyprairres—*stream* LA-4
*Bayou des Cypress* LA-4
Bayou des Familles—*stream* LA-4
Bayou Des Glaises—*stream* LA-4
Bayou des Glaises—*stream* LA-4
Bayou Des Glaises Diversion Channel—*canal* LA-4
Bayou Des Glaises Oil and Gas Field—*oilfield* LA-4
Bayou des Glaizes—*gut* LA-4
Bayou De Siard Country Club—*other* LA-4
Bayou deSiard Dam—*dam* LA-4
Bayou des Illettes—*gut* LA-4
*Bayou des Lance* LA-4
Bayou Des Oies—*gut* LA-4
Bayou De Soto—*gut* LA-4
Bayou des Ourses—*stream* LA-4
Bayou des Plantins—*gut* LA-4
Bayou des Saules—*gut* LA-4
Bayou des Saules—*stream* LA-4
Bayou Des Sot—*stream* LA-4
Bayou des Sots, Lac—*swamp* LA-4
Bayou de Suite—*gut* LA-4
Bayou DeView Public Hunting Area—*park* AR-4
Bayou De West—*gut* LA-4
Bayou De Zaire—*stream* LA-4
Bayou d'Inde—*stream* LA-4
Bayou Din Golf Club—*other* TX-5
Bayou Ditch—*canal* MO-7
*Bayou Dorcheat* AR-4
Bayou Drain—*stream* IN-6
*Bayou Dubrock* LA-4
*Bayou Du Chien* TN-4
Bayou du Chien—*stream* LA-4
Bayou du Cougrant—*gut* LA-4
Bayou du Lac—*lake* LA-4
Bayou Dulac—*stream* LA-4
Bayou Du Large Ch—*church* LA-4
Bayou du Nord—*gut* LA-4
*Bayou Du Pre* LA-4
*Bayou du Prince Noir* LA-4
*Bayou Durazno* TX-5
Bayou du Rosset—*gut* LA-4
*Bayou Enceinte* MS-4
*Bayou Eugene* LA-4
*Bayou Falia* MS-4
*Bayou False* LA-4
*Bayou False River* LA-4
Bayou Fordoche Oil Field—*oilfield* LA-4
*Bayou Fourchon* LA-4
*Bayou Fredrick* LA-4
*Bayou Fria* AL-4
Bayou Garcon—*bay* FL-3
*Bayou Gaspergou* LA-4
**Bayou Gauche**—*pop pl* LA-4
Bayou Gauche Cem—*cemetery* LA-4
Bayou Gauche Ch—*church* LA-4
**Bayou Geneve**—*pop pl* LA-4
*Bayou George* FL-3
Bayou George—*bay* FL-3
Bayou George—*locale* FL-3
Bayou George—*swamp* FL-3
Bayou George Assembly of God Ch—*church* FL-3
Bayou George Ch—*church* FL-3
Bayou George Creek—*stream* FL-3
*Bayou Goddet* LA-4
*Bayou Godell* LA-4
*Bayou Godelle* LA-4
*Bayou-Go-To-Hell* LA-4
**Bayou Goula**—*pop pl* LA-4
Bayou Goula Towhead—*island* LA-4
*Bayou Grand* LA-4
*Bayou Grande* LA-4
Bayou Grande—*bay* FL-3
*Bayou Grandecore* LA-4
*Bayou Grand Marais* LA-4
*Bayou Grand Sale* LA-4
*Bayou Grosbeak* LA-4
Bayou Grove Ch—*church* FL-3
Bayou Gulch—*valley* CO-8
Bayou Henry Gas Field—*oilfield* LA-4
Bayou Heron Channel—*channel* AL-4
Bayou Hill Cem—*cemetery* MS-4
*Bayou Ile des Cannes* LA-4
*Bayou Ipois Chines* MS-4
Bayou Island—*island* LA-4
*Bayou Isle Aux Pois* MS-4
*Bayou Jack* LA-4
Bayou Jack—*locale* LA-4
Bayou Jack Bend—*bay* LA-4
Bayou Jack Canal—*canal* LA-4
Bayou Jack Ch—*church* LA-4
Bayou Jacque Ch—*church* LA-4
*Bayou Jaque* LA-4
*Bayou Jasmin* LA-4
Bayou Jasmine Archeol Site—*hist pl* LA-4
*Bayou Jason* LA-4
*Bayou Jean et Pierre* MS-4
Bayou Jean Lacroix Oil and Gas Field—*oilfield* LA-4
*Bayou Jeansonne* LA-4
*Bayou Joson* LA-4
*Bayou Jumonville de Villers* LA-4
*Bayou Labatra* AL-4
*Bayou Labatre* AL-4
**Bayou La Batre**—*pop pl* AL-4
Bayou La Batre (CCD)—*cens area* AL-4
Bayou La Batre Division—*civil* AL-4
*Bayou La Bove* LA-4
*Bayou la Branche* LA-4
*Bayou La Butte* LA-4
*Bayou La Carpe* LA-4
*Bayou Lacasine* LA-4
*Bayou Lacassine* LA-4
*Bayou Lacere* LA-4
Bayou la Chape—*gut* LA-4
*Bayou la Cheniere* LA-4
Bayou La Chute—*gut* LA-4
*Bayou Lacombe* LA-4
Bayou la Croix—*gut* LA-4
Bayou La Fee—*gut* LA-4
*Bayou La Fleur* LA-4
Bayou la Fleur—*gut* LA-4
*Bayou La Fourche* LA-4
Bayou LaFourche Acad—*school* LA-4
Bayou La Fourche Bay—*bay* AL-4
Bayou La Glaise—*gut* LA-4
*Bayou Lagroulle* TX-5
Bayou Lake—*lake* FL-3
Bayou La Launch—*lake* AL-4
*Bayou La Loutre* LA-4
Bayou la Loutre—*stream* LA-4
Bayou la Mer—*gut* LA-4
Bayou La Nana—*stream* LA-4
*Bayou la Rompe* LA-4
Bayou La Rose—*stream* (2) LA-4
Bayou Lasseigne—*bay* LA-4
Bayou La Terre—*stream* MS-4
Bayou La Tour—*gut* LA-4
Bayou La Trainasse—*stream* LA-4
Bayou la Ville—*stream* LA-4
Bayou Lawrence—*stream* LA-4
Bayou L'Eau Bleu—*stream* LA-4
*Bayou L'eau Noir* LA-4
*Bayou le Batre* AL-4
Bayou Leche—*gut* LA-4
Bayou L' Embarras—*stream* LA-4
*Bayou Le Noir* LA-4
*Bayou Little Caillou* LA-4
Bayou L'Ivrogne—*stream* LA-4
*Bayou Long* LA-4
Bayou Long—*gut* LA-4
Bayou Long Gas Field—*oilfield* LA-4
*Bayou L'Ours* LA-4
Bayou l'Ours—*gut* LA-4
Bayou L'Ours—*stream* LA-4
*Bayou l'Ourse* LA-4
*Bayou Machey* AL-4
Bayou Macon Ch—*church* AR-4
Bayou Macon Ch—*church* (2) LA-4
Bayou Macon Cutoff Number One—*canal* LA-4
*Bayou Mallet* LA-4
Bayou Mallet Oil and Gas Field—*oilfield* LA-4
Bayou Marcus—*bay* FL-3
Bayou Maria Basin—*lake* LA-4
*Bayou Marie Croquant* LA-4
Bayou Marron, Lakes of—*lake* LA-4
*Bayou Marron L'anse aux Pailles* LA-4
*Bayou Matagua* AL-4
*Bayou McCall* LA-4
*Bayou McCutchon* LA-4
*Bayou McNeely* LA-4
Bayou Mercier—*gut* LA-4
**Bayou Meto**—*pop pl* AR-4
Bayou Meto Cem—*cemetery* AR-4
Bayou Meto Ch—*church* (2) AR-4
Bayou Meto Public Use Area—*park* AR-4
Bayou Meto Sch—*school* AR-4
Bayou Meto State Game Area—*park* AR-4
Bayou Meto (Township of)—*fmr MCD* AR-4
**Bayou Metro**—*pop pl* AR-4
Bayou Milligan Oil Field—*oilfield* LA-4
Bayou Missionary Ch—*church* AR-4
Bayou Mtn—*summit* AR-4
*Bayou Na Bonchasse* LA-4
*Bayou Nantachie* LA-4
Bayou Narrow—*basin* AR-4
*Bayou Oscar* LA-4
*Bayou Pass des Ilettes* LA-4
*Bayou Patout* LA-4
**Bayou Paul**—*pop pl* LA-4
*Bayou Pelton* LA-4
Bayou Penchant Oil and Gas Field—*oilfield* LA-4
Bayou Perot Oil and Gas Field—*oilfield* LA-4
*Bayou Perrault* LA-4
*Bayou Peru* LA-4
*Bayou Petit Amite* LA-4
*Bayou Petit Chevreau* LA-4
*Bayou Pierre Church* MS-4
*Bayou Pierre Creek* MS-4
Bayou Pierre Mounds—*summit* MS-4
Bayou Pierre Site—*hist pl* MS-4
**Bayou Pigeon**—*pop pl* LA-4
Bayou Pigeon Mission—*church* LA-4
Bayou Pigeon Oil and Gas Field—*oilfield* LA-4
*Bayou Pilicox* MS-4
*Bayou Pisana* LA-4
*Bayou Pistache* MS-4
Bayou Plantation (historical)—*locale* MS-4
Bayou Plaquemine Ch—*church* LA-4
Bayou Plaquemine Lock—*hist pl* LA-4
Bayou Plaza (Shop Ctr)—*locale* FL-3
Bayou Poignard Gas Field—*oilfield* LA-4
Bayou Point—*cape* AK-9
Bayou Point—*cape* MS-4
*Bayou Point aux Chien* LA-4
Bayou Point Public Use Area—*park* MS-4
*Bayou Poito* MS-4
*Bayou Portico* MS-4
Bayou Portuguese—*gut* LA-4
Bayou Postillion Oil Field—*oilfield* LA-4
*Bayou Pusilier* LA-4
*Bayou Rageet* AL-4
Bayou Rambio Oil and Gas Field—*oilfield* LA-4
*Bayou Razzi* AL-4
*Bayou Regault* LA-4
*Bayou Rigault* LA-4
*Bayou Rigolets* LA-4
*Bayou Rosean* LA-4
*Bayou Rouge* LA-4
Bayou Rouge Baptist Church—*hist pl* LA-4
Bayous Adois—*stream* LA-4
Bayou Saint John—*lake* AL-4
Bayou Saint Vincent Gas Field—*oilfield* LA-4
**Bayou Sale**—*pop pl* LA-4
Bayou Sale Bay—*bay* LA-4
Bayou Sale Oil and Gas Field—*oilfield* LA-4
Bayou San Patricio—*stream* LA-4
*Bayou Sapata* LA-4
Bayou Sara—*locale* LA-4
Bayou Sara Baptist Ch—*church* AL-4
Bayou Sara Bridge (historical)—*bridge* AL-4
Bayou Scie Ch—*church* LA-4
Bayou Sec—*valley* LA-4
*Bayou Segge* LA-4
Bayou Segnette Oil Field—*oilfield* LA-4
*Bayou Segur* LA-4
Bayou Sel—*hist pl* AR-4
Bayouside—*hist pl* LA-4
*Bayou Siepe* TX-5
*Bayou Sigur* LA-4
**Bayou Sorrel**—*pop pl* LA-4
Bayou Sorrel Locks—*dam* LA-4
Bayou Sorrel Oil and Gas Field—*oilfield* LA-4
Bayou Springs Creek—*stream* TX-5
*Bayou Step* TX-5
Bayou Talla Ch—*church* MS-4
*Bayou Teche* LA-4
*Bayou Terblanc* LA-4
Bayou Texter—*bay* FL-3
*Bayou Tortillon* LA-4
Bayou Township—*civil* MO-7
Bayou (Township of)—*fmr MCD* (2) AR-4
*Bayou Train* LA-4
*Bayou Trois Chenes* MS-4
*Bayou Trove* LA-4
*Bayou Tuntier* LA-4
*Bayou Vermilion* LA-4
*Bayou Verrett* LA-4
*Bayou Verrette* LA-4
Bayou Vicknair—*stream* LA-4
Bayou View Elem Sch—*school* MS-4
Bayou View Golf Course—*locale* MS-4
Bayou View JHS—*school* MS-4
Bayou Villars Oil Field—*oilfield* LA-4
Bayouville—*locale* MO-7
*Bayou Villere* LA-4
**Bayou Vista**—*pop pl* LA-4
**Bayou Vista**—*pop pl* TX-5
Bayou Vista (RR name Lagonda)—*CDP* LA-4
Bayou White Oil Field—*oilfield* LA-4
**Bayo Vista**—*pop pl* CA-9
Bay Park—*park* MN-6
Bay Park—*park* NY-2
**Bay Park**—*pop pl* CA-9
**Bay Park**—*pop pl* MI-6
**Bay Park**—*pop pl* NY-2
**Bay Park**—*pop pl* OR-9
Bay Park Sch—*school* CA-9
Bay Path Cem—*cemetery* (2) MA-1
Bay Path Junior Coll—*school* MA-1
**Bay Pines**—*pop pl* FL-3
Bay Pines Ch—*church* FL-3
Bay Pines Site (8Pi64)—*hist pl* FL-3
Bay Pines Station RR Station—*locale* FL-3
Bay Pines (Veterans' Administration Hospital)—*hospital* FL-3
Bay Pines Veterans Hosp—*hospital* FL-3
Bay Plaza—*uninc pl* TX-5
Bay Plaza at Bird Bay Village—*locale* FL-3
Bay Plaza (Shop Ctr)—*locale* (2) FL-3
*Bay Point* CA-9
*Baypoint* ME-1
*Bay Point* MI-6
Bay Point—*cape* (2) AK-9
Bay Point—*cape* CA-9
Bay Point—*cape* CT-1
Bay Point—*cape* (5) FL-3
Bay Point—*cape* LA-4
Bay Point—*cape* (3) MD-2
Bay Point—*cape* MA-1
Bay Point—*cape* MT-8
Bay Point—*cape* NH-1
Bay Point—*cape* NJ-2
Bay Point—*cape* (5) NC-3
Bay Point—*cape* OH-6
Bay Point—*cape* (2) SC-3
**Bay Point**—*pop pl* FL-3
**Bay Point**—*pop pl* ME-1
**Bay Point**—*pop pl* NY-2
Bay Point Ch—*church* GA-3
Bay Point Christian Ch—*church* FL-3
Bay Pointe Golf Club—*other* MI-6
Bay Point Elem Sch—*school* FL-3
Bay Pointe Plaza (Shop Ctr)—*locale* FL-3
Bay Point Island—*island* SC-3
Bay Point Knoll—*summit* AK-9
Bay Point Marina—*locale* OH-6
Bay Point MS—*school* FL-3
Bay Point Park—*park* MN-6
Bay Pole Branch—*stream* (2) GA-3
Bay Pole Sink—*basin* GA-3
Bay Pomme d'Or—*lake* LA-4
Bay Pond—*lake* DE-2
Bay Pond—*lake* NY-2
Bay Pond—*locale* NY-2
Bay Pond—*swamp* GA-3
Bay Pond Hill—*summit* NY-2
Bay Ponds—*lake* NJ-2
*Bay Port* FL-3
*Bay Port* VA-3
Bayport—*locale* FL-3
Bayport—*locale* VA-3
**Bay Port**—*pop pl* MI-6
**Bayport**—*pop pl* MN-6
**Bayport**—*pop pl* NY-2
Bay Port Cem—*cemetery* MI-6
Bay Port Historic Commercial Fishing District—*hist pl* MI-6
**Bayport (Industrial Area)**—*pop pl* TX-5
**Bayport Park**—*pop pl* MI-6
*Bayport Wharf* VA-3
Bay Post Office (historical)—*building* AL-4
Bay Pumpkin—*lake* LA-4
Bay Quarter Neck—*cape* VA-3
Bay Rambo—*bay* LA-4
Bay Ranch—*locale* WY-8
*Bayridge* RI-1
Bay Ridge—*locale* FL-3
**Bayridge**—*pop pl* FL-3
**Bay Ridge**—*pop pl* MD-2
**Bay Ridge**—*pop pl* NY-2
Bay Ridge Beach—*beach* MD-2
Bay Ridge Cem—*cemetery* FL-3
Bay Ridge Ch—*church* FL-3
Bay Ridge Channel—*channel* NY-2
Bay Ridge Flats—*bar* NY-2
Bay Ridge Hosp—*hospital* NY-2
Bay Ridge HS—*school* NY-2
Bay Ridge HS Annex—*school* NY-2
**Bay Ridge Junction**—*pop pl* MD-2
Bay Ridge Sch—*school* MS-4
Bay River—*stream* NC-3
*Bay River Point* NC-3
Bay Road—*hist pl* MA-1
Bay Road Ch—*church* AR-4
Bay Road Ch—*church* NY-2
Bay Road Sch—*school* NY-2
*Bay Ronde* LA-4
Bay Ronfleur—*bay* LA-4
Bay Ronquille—*bay* LA-4
Bayroot Slough—*swamp* (2) FL-3
*Bays* KS-7
Bays—*locale* KY-4
Bays—*locale* WV-2
**Bays**—*pop pl* OH-6
Bays, The—*canal* LA-4
*Baysag Point* AZ-5
Bay Sainte Elaine—*bay* LA-4
Bay Sainte Elaine Oil and Gas Field—*oilfield* LA-4
Bay Saint Honore—*bay* LA-4
**Bay Saint Louis**—*pop pl* MS-4
Bay Saint Louis Bridge—*bridge* MS-4
Bay Saint Louis Catholic Elem Sch—*school* MS-4
Bay Saint Louis Ch of Christ—*church* MS-4
Bay Saint Louis City Hall—*building* MS-4
Bay Saint Louis Post Office—*building* MS-4
Bay Sale—*lake* LA-4
Bay San Blas—*bay* FL-3
Bay Sansbois—*lake* LA-4
*Bays Branch* IA-7
Bays Branch—*locale* KY-4
Bays Branch—*stream* (3) KY-4
Bays Branch—*stream* MO-7
Bays Branch Lake—*reservoir* IA-7
Bays Branch Lake Dam—*dam* IA-7
Bays Branch State Wildlife Area—*park* IA-7
*Bay's Brook* MN-6
Bays Cem—*cemetery* (2) KY-4
Bays Cem—*cemetery* VA-3
Bays Cem—*cemetery* (4) WV-2
Bay Sch—*school* (3) CA-9
Bay Sch—*school* ND-7
Bays Chapel—*church* TX-5
Bays Chapel—*church* (2) WV-2
Bays Chapel Cem—*cemetery* TX-5
Bay Schayot—*lake* LA-4
**Bays Cove (subdivision)**—*pop pl* TN-4
Bays Creek—*stream* OR-9
Baysden Chapel—*church* NC-3
Bay Sec—*bay* LA-4
Bayse Cem—*cemetery* TN-4
Baysenburgs Lake Dam—*dam* MS-4
Bay Senior HS—*school* MS-4
Bayse Point—*cape* VA-3
**Bay Settlement**—*pop pl* WI-6
Bay Settlement Church and Monmt—*hist pl* IA-7
Bay Sevin—*lake* LA-4
Bays Fork—*stream* KY-4
Bays Fork—*stream* WV-2
Bays Fork Ch—*church* KY-4
Bay Shallow—*lake* LA-4
**Bays Heights**—*pop pl* WV-2
Bay Sherman—*bay* LA-4
Bays Hollow—*valley* KY-4
*Bay Shore* MI-6
*Bayshore* MO-7
*Bayshore* NJ-2
**Bayshore**—*pop pl* (2) CA-9
**Bayshore**—*pop pl* (2) FL-3
**Bayshore**—*pop pl* MI-6
**Bay Shore**—*pop pl* NJ-2
**Bay Shore**—*pop pl* NY-2
**Bayshore**—*pop pl* OH-6
**Bay Shore**—*pop pl* OH-6
**Bayshore**—*pop pl* WA-9
**Bay Shore Acres**—*pop pl* MD-2
Bayshore Baptist Ch—*church* FL-3
Bayshore Baptist Kindergarden—*school* FL-3
Bayshore Cem—*cemetery* TX-5
Bayshore Ch—*church* TX-5
Bay Shore Channel—*channel* NJ-2
Bayshore Chapel—*church* FL-3
Bayshore Ch of God—*church* FL-3
Bayshore Christian Sch—*school* FL-3
Bayshore Community Chapel—*church* FL-3
Bayshore County Park—*park* WI-6
Bayshore Elem Sch—*school* FL-3
Bay Shore Estates—*uninc pl* FL-3
**Bayshore Gardens**—*pop pl* FL-3
Bayshore Golf Course—*locale* FL-3
**Bay Shore Hills (subdivision)**—*pop pl* DE-2
Bayshore JHS—*school* FL-3
Bayshore Lagoon—*lake* NJ-2
Bay Shore Landing—*locale* NC-3
**Bayshore Manor**—*pop pl* FL-3
Bay Shore Marina—*other* NY-2
Bayshore Mennonite Ch—*church* FL-3
Bay Shore MS—*school* NY-2
*Bay Shore Park* NJ-2
**Bayshore Park**—*pop pl* FL-3
**Bayshore Park (subdivision)**—*pop pl* NC-3
Bay Shore Point—*cape* VA-3
**Bayshore (RR name Bay Shore)**—*pop pl* MI-6
Bay Shore (RR name for Bayshore)—*other* MI-6
**Bay Shores**—*pop pl* NY-2
Bayshore Sch—*school* FL-3
Bayshore Shop Ctr—*locale* (2) FL-3
Bay Shore (Siding)—*locale* WA-9
Bayshore (sta.)—*uninc pl* CA-9
**Bayshore (subdivision)**—*pop pl* NC-3
**Bayshore (subdivision)**—*pop pl* OR-9
**Bay Shore (trailer park)**—*pop pl* DE-2
Bayshore Union Ch—*church* ME-1
**Bay Shore West**—*pop pl* NJ-2
*Bayside* MI-6
*Bayside* NC-3
*Bay Side* RI-1
*Bayside* RI-1
*Bayside* VT-1
*Bayside* VA-3
Bayside—*hist pl* LA-4
Bayside—*locale* ME-1
Bay Side—*locale* NJ-2
Bayside—*locale* VA-3
Bayside—*other* MI-6
Bayside—*other* TX-5
**Bayside**—*pop pl* (2) AL-4
**Bayside**—*pop pl* CA-9
**Bayside**—*pop pl* ME-1
**Bayside**—*pop pl* NH-1
**Bay Side**—*pop pl* NJ-2
**Bayside**—*pop pl* NY-2
**Bayside**—*pop pl* RI-1
**Bayside**—*pop pl* TN-4
**Bayside**—*pop pl* TX-5
**Bayside**—*pop pl* VT-1
**Bayside**—*pop pl* VA-3
**Bayside**—*pop pl* WI-6
Bayside—*uninc pl* VA-3
Bayside Baptist Ch—*church* AL-4
Bayside Baptist Ch—*church* TN-4
**Bayside Beach**—*pop pl* MD-2
**Bayside Beach**—*pop pl* MA-1
**Bayside Beach**—*pop pl* NJ-2
Bayside Cem—*cemetery* LA-4
Bayside Cem—*cemetery* NH-1
Bayside Cem—*cemetery* (2) NY-2
Bayside Cem—*cemetery* WI-6
Bayside Ch—*church* (2) NC-3
*Bayside Channel* NJ-2
Bayside Dock—*locale* TN-4
Bayside Exposition Center—*building* MA-1
**Bayside Garden**—*pop pl* OR-9
**Bayside Gardens**—*pop pl* OR-9
Bayside Golf Course—*other* CA-9
**Bayside Hamlet (subdivision)**—*pop pl* DE-2
Bayside HS—*school* VA-3
*Bayside Marina* TN-4
Bay Side Park—*park* MD-2
Bayside Park—*park* NJ-2
**Bayside Park**—*pop pl* MI-6
**Bayside Park**—*pop pl* MS-4
**Bayside Park**—*pop pl* VA-3
Bayside Sch—*school* (3) CA-9
Bayside Sch—*school* FL-3
Bayside Sch—*school* NJ-2
Bayside Sch—*school* NC-3
Bayside Sch—*school* VA-3
Bayside Sch—*school* WI-6
Bayside Shopping Mall—*locale* FL-3
*Bayside Station* NH-1
Bayside Station—*locale* NY-2
Bay Side Station (historical)—*locale* MA-1
**Bayside (subdivision)**—*pop pl* MA-1
**Bayside Terrace**—*pop pl* TX-5
*Bayside Wharf* VA-3
Baysinger Drain—*stream* AZ-5
Baysinger Hollow—*valley* TN-4
Bay Sirius—*swamp* LA-4
*Bays Lake* AL-4
Bays Lake—*lake* OR-9
*Bays Lake Dam* AL-4
Bay Slough—*gut* CA-9
Bays Mills Ind Res—*reserve* MI-6
Bays Mountain Ch—*church* TN-4
Bays Mountain Dam—*dam* TN-4
**Bays Mountain Estates**—*pop pl* TN-4
Bays Mountain Park—*park* TN-4
Bays Mountain Rsvr—*reservoir* TN-4
Bays Mountains—*ridge* TN-4
Bays Mountains—*summit* TN-4
Bays Mtn—*range* TN-4
*Bayspring* MS-4
Bay Spring—*church* LA-4
**Bay Spring**—*pop pl* RI-1
Bay Spring—*spring* AL-4
Bay Spring—*spring* WI-6
Bay Spring Bayou—*stream* LA-4
Bay Spring Cem—*cemetery* LA-4
*Bay Spring Ch* AL-4
Bay Spring Ch—*church* (2) AL-4
Bay Spring Ch—*church* (2) GA-3
Bay Spring Lookout Tower—*locale* LA-4
*Bayspring Post Office* MS-4
Bay Spring Post Office (historical)—*building* AL-4
Bay Springs—*locale* SC-3
**Bay Springs**—*pop pl* AL-4
**Bay Springs**—*pop pl* FL-3
**Bay Springs**—*pop pl* MS-4
**Bay Springs**—*pop pl* SC-3
*Bay Springs Baptist Ch* MS-4
Bay Springs Baptist Ch—*church* MS-4
Bay Springs Branch—*stream* MS-4
Bay Springs Branch—*stream* SC-3
Bay Springs Cem—*cemetery* MS-4
Bay Springs Cem—*cemetery* TX-5
*Bay Springs Ch* AL-4
Bay Springs Ch—*church* AL-4
Bay Springs Ch—*church* (3) GA-3
Bay Springs Ch—*church* (2) MS-4
Bay Springs Ch—*church* MO-7
Bay Spring Sch—*school* FL-3
Bay Springs Ch (historical)—*church* MS-4
Bay Springs Ch of Christ—*church* MS-4
*Bay Spring School* MS-4
Bay Springs Country Club—*other* MS-4
Bay Springs Creek—*stream* GA-3
Bay Springs Elem Sch—*school* MS-4
Bay Springs (historical)—*locale* MS-4
Bay Springs HS—*school* MS-4
Bay Springs Lagoon Dam—*dam* MS-4
Bay Springs Lake—*reservoir* MS-4
Bay Springs Lock and Dam—*dam* MS-4
Bay Springs Marina—*locale* AL-4
Bay Springs Methodist Ch—*church* MS-4
Bay Springs MS—*school* MS-4
Bay Springs Oil And Gas Field—*oilfield* MS-4
Bay Springs Post Office—*building* MS-4
Bay Springs Presbyterian Ch—*church* MS-4
Bay Springs Sch (abandoned)—*school* MO-7
Bay Springs Sch (historical)—*school* (3) MS-4
*Bay St. Armand* NY-2
**Bay State**—*pop pl* MA-1
Bay State Brook—*stream* NY-2
Bay State Company Bog Rsvr—*reservoir* MA-1
Bay State Company Dam—*dam* MA-1
Baystate Corset Block—*hist pl* MA-1
Bay State Creek—*stream* MT-8
Bay State Mine—*mine* NV-8
Bay State Raceway—*park* MA-1
Bay State Tunnel—*mine* UT-8
Bay Steer Creek—*stream* OR-9
**Bay St. Louis**—*pop pl* MS-4
Bay Street Presbyterian Ch—*church* MS-4
Bay Street Rsvr—*reservoir* CA-9
Bay Stud Coulee—*valley* MT-8
Bay Stud Rsvr—*reservoir* OR-9
**Bay Subdivision**—*pop pl* UT-8
Baysville Ch—*church* NC-3
Baysville Sch—*school* NC-3
Bay Swamp—*swamp* FL-3
Bay Swamp—*swamp* SC-3
Bays Windmill—*locale* NM-5
Bay Sylvester—*bay* LA-4
Bay Tambour—*bay* (2) LA-4
Bay Tartellon—*lake* LA-4
Bay Terrace—*uninc pl* (2) NY-2
Bay Toni—*lake* LA-4
Bay Touch-me-not—*lake* LA-4
*Baytown* IL-6
Baytown—*other* IL-6
**Baytown**—*pop pl* TX-5
Baytown (CCD)—*cens area* TX-5
Baytown Memorial Cem—*cemetery* TX-5
**Bay (Township of)**—*pop pl* MI-6
**Bay (Township of)**—*pop pl* OH-6
Baytown Site—*hist pl* AR-4
**Baytown (Township of)**—*pop pl* MN-6
Baytown Tunnel—*tunnel* TX-5
Bay Trail JHS—*school* NY-2
Bay Tree—*island* NC-3
Bay Tree Creek—*stream* VA-3
Bay Tree Lake—*lake* NC-3
Bay Tree Point—*cape* VA-3

Beacon Street Baptist Ch—*church* ... MS-4
Beacon Street Firehouse—*hist pl* ... MA-1
Beacon Street Hist Dist—*hist pl* ... MA-1
Beacon Street Station (historical)—*locale* ... MA-1
Beacon Tank—*reservoir* ... AZ-5
Beacon Theater and Hotel—*hist pl* ... NY-2
Beacon Trotting Park (historical)—*park* ... MA-1
**Beacon View**—*pop pl* ... NE-7
Beacon Well—*locale* ... AZ-5
Beacon Well—*well* (2) ... AZ-5
Beacon Windmill—*locale* ... TX-5
Beacon Yards—*locale* ... MA-1
Bea Creek—*stream* ... OR-9
Beacrofts Hole—*basin* ... TX-5
Beacroft Trail—*trail* ... CA-9
Bead and Lace Falls—*falls* ... NC-3
Bead Creek—*stream* ... CO-8
Beadens Creek—*stream* ... IN-6
Beader Branch—*stream* ... AL-4
*Beader Church* ... AL-4
**Beades Estate (subdivision)**—*pop pl* ... DE-2
Bead Lake—*lake* ... WA-9
Bead Lake Peak—*summit* ... WA-9
Bead Lakes—*lake* ... ID-8
**Beadle**—*pop pl* ... TX-5
Beadle County—*civil* ... SD-7
Beadle Hill—*summit* ... NY-2
Beadle Lake—*lake* ... MI-6
**Beadle Lake**—*pop pl* ... MI-6
Beadle Lake Sch—*school* ... MI-6
Beadle Park—*park* ... SD-7
Beadle Point—*cape* ... NY-2
Beadle Run—*stream* ... WV-2
Beadles Bayou—*stream* ... LA-4
Beadles Cem—*cemetery* ... IN-6
Beadle Sch—*school* (5) ... SD-7
Beadles Cove—*bay* ... VT-1
Beadles Creek—*stream* ... NV-8
Beadles Rocks—*bar* ... MA-1
Beadleston Cem—*cemetery* ... SD-7
Beadle Tank—*reservoir* ... NM-5
**Beadling**—*pop pl* ... PA-2
Beadling Chapel—*church* ... PA-2
Bead Mountain Creek—*stream* ... TX-5
Bead Mtn—*summit* ... TX-5
Beadon Cove—*bay* ... NJ-2
Beadon Creek—*stream* ... NJ-2
Beadon Point—*cape* ... NJ-2
*Beadons Cove* ... NJ-2
*Beadons Creek* ... NJ-2
*Beadons Point* ... NJ-2
Beadow Creek—*stream* ... NE-7
Bead Park—*flat* ... CO-8
Beads Creek—*stream* ... SD-7
Bead Spring—*spring* ... NM-5
Bead Wreck Site—*hist pl* ... NJ-2
**Beagle**—*pop pl* ... KS-7
Beagle Creek—*stream* ... ID-8
Beagle Creek—*stream* (2) ... OR-9
Beagle Gap—*gap* ... VA-3
Beagle Gap Overlook—*locale* ... VA-3
Beagle Gulch—*valley* ... ID-8
**Beagle (historical)**—*pop pl* ... OR-9
Beagle Hole Swamp—*swamp* ... PA-2
Beagle Pond—*reservoir* ... MA-1
Beagle Pond Dam—*dam* ... MA-1
Beagles Island—*island* ... IL-6
Beagle Sky Ranch Airp—*airport* ... OR-9
Beagley-Stinson Archeol Site—*hist pl* ... OK-5
Beaglin Branch—*stream* ... MD-2
Beahms Chapel—*church* ... VA-3
Beahms Gap—*gap* ... VA-3
Beahms Gap Trail—*trail* ... VA-3
Beaird Cem—*cemetery* ... TX-5
Beaird Spring—*spring* ... WY-8
Beakban Island—*island* ... CA-9
Be Akeghalchee—*lake* ... AZ-5
Beakley Hollow—*valley* ... TN-4
Beakleyville Ch—*church* ... PA-2
Beakman Lake—*lake* ... FL-3
Beakman Lake Rec Area—*park* ... FL-3
Beak Point—*cape* ... AK-9
Beal—*locale* ... MO-7
Beal—*locale* ... OR-9
**Beal**—*pop pl* ... IN-6
Beal, Mattie, House—*hist pl* ... OK-5
Beal, Persia, House—*hist pl* ... NH-1
Beal Branch—*stream* ... IN-6
Beal Branch—*stream* ... TX-5
Beal Cabin—*locale* ... ID-8
Beal Cem—*cemetery* ... FL-3
Beal Cem—*cemetery* ... IL-6
Beal Cem—*cemetery* ... IA-7
Beal Cem—*cemetery* ... MA-1
Beal Cem—*cemetery* (2) ... TN-4
**Beal City**—*pop pl* ... MI-6
Beal Coll—*school* ... ME-1
Beal Cove—*cove* ... MA-1
*Beal Creek* ... OR-9
*Beal Creek* ... TX-5
Beal Creek—*stream* (2) ... CA-9
Beal Creek—*stream* ... MI-6
Beal Creek—*stream* ... MS-4
Beal Creek—*stream* ... OR-9
Beal Crossing—*locale* ... LA-4
Beal Dam—*dam* ... SD-7
Beal Ditch—*canal* ... AZ-5
Beale, Joseph, House—*hist pl* ... DC-2
Beale AFB—*military* ... CA-9
Beale Air Force Base East—*CDP* ... CA-9
Beale Branch—*stream* ... TX-5
Beale Canyon—*valley* ... OR-9
Beale Cem—*cemetery* ... GA-3
Beale Cem—*cemetery* ... TN-4
Beale Cem—*cemetery* ... TX-5
Beale Chapel—*church* ... WV-2
Beale Creek—*stream* ... FL-3
**Beale East**—*pop pl* ... CA-9
**Beale (historical)**—*pop pl* ... TN-4
*Beale Island* ... ME-1
Beale Lake—*lake* ... MT-8
Beale Lake—*lake* ... OR-9
Beale Mtn—*summit* ... AZ-5
Beale Park—*park* ... CA-9
Beale Point—*cliff* ... AZ-5
Beale Post Office (historical)—*building* ... TN-4
Beale Queen Ranch—*locale* ... TX-5
Beale Ranch—*locale* ... SD-7
Bealer Branch—*stream* ... TN-4
Bealer Sch—*school* ... SD-7
**Bealers Knob**—*pop pl* ... KY-4
Beales—*locale* ... VA-3
Beales Branch—*stream* ... VA-3
Beales Brook—*stream* ... ME-1
Beales Butte—*summit* ... OR-9
Beale Sch—*school* ... CA-9
Beale Sch—*school* ... IL-6
Beale Sch—*school* ... WV-2
Beales Crossing—*locale* ... AZ-5
Beales Millpond—*reservoir* ... VA-3
Beales Mill Run—*stream* ... VA-3
Beales Pond—*lake* ... NY-2
Beale Spring—*spring* (2) ... AZ-5
Beale Street Hist Dist—*hist pl* ... TN-4
Beales Wharf—*locale* ... VA-3
**Bealeton**—*pop pl* ... VA-3
**Beale (Township of)**—*pop pl* ... PA-2
**Beale West**—*pop pl* ... CA-9
Beal-Gaillard House—*hist pl* ... AL-4
Beal Heights Ch—*church* ... OK-5
Beal Hill—*summit* ... KY-4
Beal Hill—*summit* ... WA-9
Beal Hollow—*valley* ... TX-5
Beal HS—*school* ... MA-1
*Beal Island* ... ME-1
Beal Island—*island* ... ME-1
Beal Knob—*summit* ... NC-3
Beall—*locale* ... GA-3
Beall, Gen. Reasin, House—*hist pl* ... OH-6
Beall, Robert Vinton, House—*hist pl* ... OR-9
Beall-Air—*hist pl* ... WV-2
*Beal Lake* ... AZ-5
Beal Lake—*lake* ... AZ-5
Beal Lake—*lake* ... OR-9
Beal Lake—*reservoir* ... OH-6
Beal Landing—*locale* ... MO-7
Beal Lateral—*canal* ... ID-8
Beal Lateral—*canal* ... SD-7
Beall Ave Sch—*school* ... OH-6
Beall Cem—*cemetery* ... MD-2
Beall Cem—*cemetery* (2) ... MS-4
Beall Chapel—*church* ... IN-6
*Beall Creek* ... MS-4
Beall Creek—*stream* ... CO-8
Beall Creek—*stream* ... MT-8
Beall-Dawson House—*hist pl* ... MD-2
*Beal Ledge* ... MA-1
Beall (historical)—*locale* ... MS-4
Beall Lake—*lake* ... MT-8
*Beall-McGehee Cemetery* ... MS-4
Beallmont—*hist pl* ... NC-3
Beallmore—*hist pl* ... WV-2
Beall Park Community Center—*hist pl* ... MT-8
Beall Place (Site)—*locale* ... CA-9
Beall Sch—*school* ... MD-2
Beall Sch—*school* ... TX-5
Bealls Island—*island* ... MD-2
Bealls Levels (historical)—*civil* ... DC-2
Bealls Mill Cem—*cemetery* ... WV-2
Bealls Mills—*locale* ... WV-2
Beall's Pleasure—*hist pl* ... MD-2
Bealls Pond—*reservoir* ... AL-4
*Bealls Pond Dam* ... AL-4
Beall Springs—*locale* ... GA-3
Beall-Stigler Cem—*cemetery* ... MS-4
**Beallsville**—*pop pl* ... MD-2
**Beallsville**—*pop pl* ... OH-6
**Beallsville**—*pop pl* ... PA-2
Beallsville Borough—*civil* ... PA-2
Beallwood—*uninc pl* ... GA-3
*Beal Mountain* ... OR-9
Beal Place—*locale* ... CA-9
*Beal Point* ... ME-1
Beal Pond—*lake* ... ME-1
Beal Pond—*lake* ... TN-4
Beal Prairie—*flat* ... OR-9
Beal Ranch—*locale* ... NM-5
Beal Ridge—*ridge* ... NC-3
Beal Run—*stream* ... OH-6
Beals—*locale* ... MT-8
**Beals**—*pop pl* ... KY-4
**Beals**—*pop pl* ... ME-1
**Beals**—*pop pl* ... OH-6
Beals and Torrey Shoe Co. Bldg—*hist pl* ... WI-6
Beals Bar—*bar* ... AL-4
*Beals Branch* ... TX-5
Beals Brook—*stream* ... ME-1
Beals Butte—*summit* ... ID-8
Beals Cem—*cemetery* ... OH-6
Beals Cem—*cemetery* ... TN-4
Beal Sch—*school* ... FL-3
Beals Chapel—*church* ... NC-3
Beals Chapel—*church* ... TN-4
*Beals Cove* ... MA-1
Beals Cove—*bay* ... ME-1
Beals Creek—*stream* ... OR-9
Beals Creek—*stream* ... TX-5
Beals Creek Tank—*reservoir* ... TX-5
Beals Fork—*stream* ... KY-4
Beals Frizzle Drain—*canal* ... MI-6
Beals Harbor—*bay* ... ME-1
Beals Hill—*summit* ... MT-8
Beals Hill—*summit* ... NY-2
*Beal's Island* ... ME-1
Beals Island—*island* ... ME-1
Beals Lake—*lake* ... MI-6
Beals Landing—*locale* ... AL-4
Beals Ledge—*ridge* ... MA-1
Beal Slough*—*stream* ... NE-7
*Beal Slough Creek* ... NE-7
Beals Mill—*locale* ... NJ-2
*Beals Mountain* ... ID-8
Beals Mtn—*summit* ... MT-8
Beals Mtn—*summit* ... OR-9
Beals Mtn—*summit* ... TX-5
Beals Park—*park* ... MA-1
Beals Point—*cape* ... CA-9
Beals Run—*stream* ... KY-4
Beals Run—*stream* ... OH-6
Beals Sch—*school* ... NE-7
Beal State For—*forest* ... MO-7
Beal Stockwater Dam—*dam* ... SD-7
**Beals (Town of)**—*pop pl* ... ME-1
**Bealsville**—*pop pl* ... FL-3
Beal Tank—*reservoir* ... AZ-5
Beal Taylor Ditch—*canal* ... IN-6
Bealton Ditch—*canal* ... IN-6
Bealville—*locale* ... CA-9
Beal Well—*well* ... CA-9
Bealwood Cem—*cemetery* ... GA-3
Bealwood Sch—*school* ... GA-3
**Beam**—*pop pl* ... KY-4
Beam, Joshua, House—*hist pl* ... NC-3
Beam, T. Jeremiah, House—*hist pl* ... KY-4
*Beaman* ... VA-3
**Beaman**—*pop pl* ... IA-7
**Beaman**—*pop pl* ... MO-7
Beaman Branch—*stream* ... GA-3
Beaman Branch—*stream* ... NC-3
Beaman Branch—*stream* (3) ... SC-3
Beaman Brook—*stream* ... MA-1
Beaman Cem—*cemetery* ... PA-2
*Beaman Crossrads* ... NC-3
*Beaman Crossroad* ... NC-3
**Beaman Crossroads**—*pop pl* ... NC-3
Beaman Ditch—*canal* ... IN-6
Beaman Hill—*summit* ... MA-1
Beaman Hill—*summit* ... NH-1
Beaman Hill—*summit* ... NY-2
Beaman Lake—*reservoir* ... NC-3
Beaman Lake—*reservoir* ... TN-4
Beaman Lake Dam—*dam* ... TN-4
Beaman Lakes—*lake* ... NV-8
Beaman Ledge Mine—*mine* ... CA-9
*Beaman Pond* ... MA-1
Beaman Pond—*lake* ... CT-1
Beaman Pond—*lake* ... MA-1
Beaman Run—*stream* ... NC-3
Beamans Brook—*stream* ... CT-1
Beamans Crossroads—*locale* ... NC-3
Beaman Tank—*reservoir* ... NM-5
**Beamantown**—*pop pl* ... VA-3
Beam Branch—*stream* ... AL-4
Beam Brook—*stream* ... ME-1
Beam Cem—*cemetery* ... ME-1
Beam Cem—*cemetery* ... MS-4
Beam Cem—*cemetery* ... NC-3
Beam Ch—*church* ... PA-2
*Beam Creek* ... OR-9
Beam Creek—*stream* ... MT-8
Beam Creek—*stream* ... OR-9
Beam Creek—*stream* ... TN-4
Beame Mine—*mine* ... CA-9
**Beamer**—*pop pl* ... IN-6
Beamer, R. H., House—*hist pl* ... CA-9
Beamer Cem—*cemetery* (2) ... VA-3
Beamer Creek—*stream* ... GA-3
Beamer Creek—*stream* ... OR-9
Beamer-Davis Cem—*cemetery* ... TX-5
Beamer Ditch—*canal* ... IN-6
Beamer Flat—*flat* ... OR-9
Beamer Hollow—*valley* ... OK-5
Beamer Knob—*summit* ... VA-3
Beamer Park—*park* ... CA-9
Beamer Ranch—*locale* ... OR-9
Beamers Head—*summit* ... VA-3
Beamer Well—*well* ... AZ-5
Beames Cem—*cemetery* ... IL-6
Beames School (Abandoned)—*locale* ... OK-5
Beam Flat—*flat* ... CA-9
Beam Flat—*flat* ... MT-8
Beam Hill—*summit* (2) ... NY-2
Beamington—*locale* ... IL-6
Beam Lake—*lake* ... MN-6
Beam Lake—*lake* ... MT-8
Beam Lake—*reservoir* ... NC-3
Beam Lake Dam—*dam* ... NC-3
**Beam Mill**—*pop pl* ... NC-3
Beamon—*locale* ... VA-3
**Beamon**—*pop pl* ... AL-4
Beamon Creek—*stream* ... CT-1
Beamon Creek—*stream* ... IA-7
Beamon Pond—*reservoir* ... VA-3
Beam Pond—*lake* ... ME-1
Beam Rocks—*cliff* ... PA-2
Beam Run—*stream* (2) ... PA-2
Beams Cem—*cemetery* ... KY-4
Beam Sch—*school* ... SC-3
Beams Lake—*reservoir* ... NC-3
Beams Mill (historical)—*locale* ... NC-3
**Beams Mills**—*pop pl* ... NC-3
*Beams Run* ... PA-2
Beams Store (historical)—*locale* ... MS-4
**Beamsville**—*pop pl* ... OH-6
*Bean* ... ND-7
Bean, Daniel V., House—*hist pl* ... MT-8
Bean Belly Well—*well* ... AZ-5
*Bean Blossom* ... IN-6
**Bean Blossom**—*pop pl* ... IN-6
**Beanblossom**—*pop pl* ... IN-6
*Bean Blossom Creek* ... IN-6
Beanblossom Creek—*stream* ... IN-6
Bean Blossom Creek—*stream* ... MT-8
Bean Blossom Creek—*stream* ... SD-7
*Bean Blossom Creek North Fork* ... IN-6
Bean Blossom Dam—*dam* ... IN-6
*Bean Blossom Lake* ... IN-6
Beanblossom Lake—*reservoir* ... IN-6
Bean Blossom (Township of)—*civ div* ... IN-6
Bean Bluff—*cliff* ... AR-4
Bean Branch—*stream* (2) ... KY-4
Bean Branch—*stream* ... LA-4
Bean Branch—*stream* ... MS-4
Bean Branch—*stream* (2) ... MO-7
Bean Branch—*stream* ... TN-4
Bean Branch—*stream* ... TX-5
Bean Bridge—*bridge* ... AL-4
Bean Brook—*stream* (4) ... ME-1
Bean Brook—*stream* ... MN-6
Bean Brook—*stream* (2) ... NH-1
Bean Brook—*stream* ... VT-1
Bean Brook—*stream* ... WI-6
Bean Brook Mtn—*summit* ... ME-1
Bean Brook Spring—*lake* ... WI-6
Bean Brook State Wildlife Mngmt Area—*park* ... WI-6
*Beancamp Branch* ... WV-2
Bean Canyon—*valley* ... AZ-5
Bean Canyon—*valley* (3) ... CA-9
Bean Canyon—*valley* ... CO-8
Bean Canyon—*valley* ... UT-8
Bean Canyon—*valley* ... WA-9
Bean Cem—*cemetery* (2) ... AL-4
Bean Cem—*cemetery* ... AR-4
Bean Cem—*cemetery* ... IL-6
Bean Cem—*cemetery* ... KS-7
Bean Cem—*cemetery* (2) ... KY-4
Bean Cem—*cemetery* ... ME-1
Bean Cem—*cemetery* ... MS-4
Bean Cem—*cemetery* ... MO-7
Bean Cem—*cemetery* ... MT-8
Bean Cem—*cemetery* ... NH-1
Bean Cem—*cemetery* ... OH-6
Bean Cem—*cemetery* (2) ... TN-4
Bean Cem—*cemetery* ... TX-5
Bean Cem—*cemetery* ... WV-2
**Bean City**—*pop pl* ... FL-3
*Bean Creek* ... AR-4
*Bean Creek* ... MI-6
*Bean Creek* ... MT-8
*Bean Creek* ... OH-6
*Bean Creek* ... OR-9
Bean Creek—*stream* ... AK-9
Bean Creek—*stream* ... AR-4
Bean Creek—*stream* (5) ... CA-9
Bean Creek—*stream* (3) ... ID-8
Bean Creek—*stream* ... IL-6
Bean Creek—*stream* ... IN-6
Bean Creek—*stream* ... KS-7
Bean Creek—*stream* (2) ... MI-6
Bean Creek—*stream* (2) ... MS-4
Bean Creek—*stream* (3) ... MO-7
Bean Creek—*stream* (3) ... MT-8
Bean Creek—*stream* (2) ... NE-7
Bean Creek—*stream* (2) ... OH-6
Bean Creek—*stream* (3) ... OR-9
Bean Creek—*stream* ... TN-4
Bean Creek—*stream* (2) ... TX-5
Bean Creek—*stream* (3) ... WA-9
Bean Creek—*stream* (2) ... WY-8
Bean Creek Cem—*cemetery* ... MO-7
Bean Creek Ch—*church* ... GA-3
*Bean Creek Ditch* ... IL-6
*Bean Creek Ditch* ... MI-6
*Bean Creek Ditch* ... OH-6
Bean Creek Ditch—*canal* ... IL-6
Bean Creek Saddle—*gap* ... ID-8
Bean Creek Trail—*trail* ... WA-9
Bean Dam State Wildlife Mngmt Area—*park* ... MN-6
Bean Dam Tank—*reservoir* ... AZ-5
Bean Ditch—*canal* ... CA-9
Bean Draw—*valley* ... TX-5
Bean Draw—*valley* ... UT-8
Bean Draw—*valley* ... WY-8
Beane Cem—*cemetery* ... WV-2
*Beane Creek* ... AR-4
*Beane Creek* ... TX-5
Beane Creek—*stream* ... WA-9
Bean Embody Ditch—*canal* ... MT-8
Beane Mtn—*summit* ... VT-1
Beaner Lake—*lake* ... WA-9
Beanes Corners—*locale* ... VA-3
Beane Trail—*trail* ... VT-1
Bean Factory Spring—*spring* ... MO-7
Bean Flat—*flat* ... NV-8
*Bean Fork* ... KY-4
Bean Fork—*stream* ... KY-4
*Bean Gap* ... TN-4
Bean Gap—*gap* ... VA-3
Bean Gap—*gap* ... WV-2
Bean Glade—*flat* ... CA-9
Bean Gulch—*valley* (4) ... CA-9
Bean Gulch—*valley* ... CO-8
Bean Gulch—*valley* ... OR-9
Bean Hill—*summit* ... CA-9
Bean Hill—*summit* ... KY-4
Bean Hill—*summit* (2) ... ME-1
Bean Hill—*summit* (3) ... NH-1
Bean Hill—*summit* (3) ... NY-2
Bean Hill—*summit* ... PA-2
Bean Hill—*summit* (2) ... UT-8
Bean Hill Crossing—*locale* ... NY-2
Bean Hill Hist Dist—*hist pl* ... CT-1
Bean Hills—*summit* ... TX-5
Beanhole Lake—*lake* ... MT-8
Bean Hole Mtn—*summit* ... ME-1
Bean Hole Pond—*lake* ... ME-1
Bean Hole Ranch—*locale* ... AZ-5
Bean Hollow—*valley* ... OH-6
Bean Hollow—*valley* (3) ... TN-4
Bean Hollow—*valley* ... VA-3
Bean Hollow—*valley* ... WV-2
Bean Hollow—*valley* (2) ... WI-6
Beanies Hole—*basin* ... UT-8
Bean Island—*island* ... AK-9
Bean Island—*island* (3) ... ME-1
Bean Island—*island* (2) ... NC-3
**Bean Island**—*pop pl* ... NH-1
*Bean Lake* ... MN-6
Bean Lake—*lake* ... AK-9
Bean Lake—*lake* ... AR-4
Bean Lake—*lake* (3) ... MN-6
Bean Lake—*lake* ... MO-7
Bean Lake—*lake* ... MT-8
Bean Lake—*lake* ... NE-7
Bean Lake—*lake* (2) ... WI-6
**Bean Lake**—*pop pl* ... MO-7
Bean Lake Airp—*airport* ... MO-7
Bean Lake Islands Archeol District—*hist pl* ... WI-6
Bean Lake Slough—*stream* ... TX-5
*Bean Mtn* ... TN-4
Bean Mtn—*summit* ... AL-4
Bean Mtn—*summit* ... AR-4
Bean Mtn—*summit* (3) ... ME-1
Bean Mtn—*summit* (2) ... NH-1
Bean Mtn—*summit* ... TN-4
Bean Mtn—*summit* ... VT-1
Bean-Newlee House—*hist pl* ... NM-5
Bean Pass—*gap* ... AZ-5
Bean Patch—*flat* ... AZ-5
Bean Patch Creek—*stream* ... MS-4
Beanpatch Hollow—*valley* ... WV-2
Bean Patch Tank—*reservoir* ... AZ-5
Bean Patch Well—*well* ... AZ-5
Bean Peaks—*summit* ... AZ-5
Bean Point—*cape* ... AR-4
Bean Point—*cape* ... FL-3
Bean Point—*cape* (2) ... ME-1
Bean Pond—*lake* (2) ... ME-1
Bean Pond—*lake* ... NH-1
Bean Pond—*lake* (2) ... VT-1
Bean Pond Ch—*church* ... SC-3
Bean Ponds—*lake* ... ME-1
*Bean Porridge Hill* ... MA-1
Bean Porridge Hill—*summit* ... MA-1
Bean Pot Pond—*lake* ... ME-1
Bean Pott Cliff—*cliff* ... TX-5
*Bean Ranch* ... TX-5
Bean Ranch—*locale* ... CA-9
Bean Ranch—*locale* (2) ... MT-8
Bean Ranch—*locale* ... TX-5
Bean Ranch—*locale* (2) ... WY-8
Bean Ridge—*ridge* ... AK-9
Bean Ridge—*ridge* ... MT-8
Bean Ridge—*ridge* ... OH-6
Bean Ridge—*ridge* (2) ... TN-4
Bean Ridge—*ridge* ... UT-8
Bean Ridge—*ridge* ... WV-2
Bean Riffle—*rapids* ... OR-9
*Bean River* ... OH-6
Bean River—*stream* ... AL-4
Bean River—*stream* ... NH-1
Bean River—*stream* ... NY-2
*Bean River Branch* ... MS-4
Bean Rock—*locale* ... AL-4
Bean Rock—*pillar* ... CA-9
Bean Rock Bluff—*cliff* ... AL-4
Bean Rock Creek—*stream* ... AL-4
Bean Rock Ferry (historical)—*locale* ... AL-4
Bean Rock Landing (historical)—*locale* ... AL-4
Bean Rock Sch—*school* ... AL-4
Bean Rsvr—*reservoir* ... CO-8
Bean Run—*stream* ... IN-6
Bean Run—*stream* ... PA-2
Bean Run—*stream* ... VA-3
*Beans* ... NY-2
**Beans**—*pop pl* ... TN-4
Bean Salinas Tank—*reservoir* ... TX-5
*Beans Branch* ... NJ-2
Beans Camp—*locale* ... CA-9
Beans Canyon—*valley* ... NE-7
Bean Sch—*school* (2) ... IL-6
Bean Sch—*school* ... MI-6
Bean Sch—*school* ... TX-5
Bean Sch—*school* ... VT-1
Beans Corner—*locale* ... ME-1
Beans Corner—*locale* ... PA-2
**Beans Corner**—*pop pl* ... ME-1
Beans Cove—*bay* ... PA-2
Beans Cove—*locale* ... PA-2
Beans Cove Ch—*church* ... PA-2
Beans Cove Post Office (historical)—*building* ... PA-2
Beans Creek—*locale* ... TN-4
**Beans Creek**—*pop pl* ... TN-4
**Beans Creek**—*pop pl* ... TX-5
Beans Creek—*stream* ... NC-3
Beans Creek—*stream* (2) ... TN-4
Beans Creek—*stream* (3) ... TX-5
Beans Creek Cave Number 1—*cave* ... TN-4
Beans Creek Cave Number 2—*cave* ... TN-4
Beans Creek Ch—*church* ... NC-3
Beans Creek Ch—*church* (2) ... TN-4
Beans Creek Ch (historical)—*church* ... TN-4
*Beanscreek Post Office* ... TN-4
Beans Creek Post Office (historical)—*building* ... TN-4
Beans Creek Sch—*school* ... TN-4
Beans Crossroads—*locale* ... AL-4
Bean Settlement—*locale* ... WV-2
**Beans Ferry**—*pop pl* ... MS-4
Beans Ferry Ch of Christ—*church* ... MS-4
Beans Fork—*stream* ... KY-4
Beans Fork Sch—*school* ... KY-4
*Beans Gap* ... TN-4
Beans Grant—*civil* ... NH-1
Beans Gulch—*valley* ... CA-9
Beans Hill—*summit* ... VA-3
*Beanshuttle Lakes* ... MI-6
Beanshuttle Lakes—*lake* ... MI-6
*Beans Island* ... ME-1
**Beans Island**—*pop pl* ... NH-1
Beans Knob—*summit* ... VA-3
Beans Lake—*lake* ... WI-6
Beans Mill—*locale* ... AL-4
Beans Mill—*locale* ... WV-2
*Beans Mountain* ... TN-4
Beansnapper Creek—*stream* ... ID-8
Bean Soup Lake—*lake* ... NE-7
Beans Pit—*cave* ... AL-4
*Beans Point* ... ME-1
Beans Point—*cape* ... VT-1
Beans Point—*cape* ... WA-9
Bean Spring—*spring* ... AZ-5
Bean Spring—*spring* ... CA-9
Bean Spring—*spring* ... OR-9
*Beans Purchase* ... NH-1
Beans Purchase—*civil* ... NH-1
*Beans Ridge* ... UT-8
Beans Ridge—*ridge* ... CA-9
Beans Spring—*spring* ... WY-8
Beans Spring Creek—*stream* ... WY-8
Beans Spur—*ridge* ... KY-4
*Beans Station* ... TN-4
Beans Station—*locale* ... NY-2
Bean Stack Creek—*stream* ... AL-4
*Bean Station* ... TN-4
**Bean Station**—*pop pl* ... TN-4
Bean Station (CCD)—*cens area* ... TN-4
Bean Station Cem—*cemetery* ... TN-4
Bean Station Ch—*church* ... TN-4
Bean Station Division—*civil* ... TN-4
Bean Station Post Office—*building* ... TN-4
Bean Station Sch—*school* ... TN-4
Bean Tank—*reservoir* ... TX-5
Beantown—*locale* ... MD-2
Beantown—*locale* ... NY-2
**Beantown**—*pop pl* ... MD-2
Beantown Creek—*stream* ... NC-3
*Beanville* ... AL-4
Beanville—*locale* ... VT-1
**Beanville**—*pop pl* ... VT-1
Beanville Creek—*stream* ... CA-9
Beanville Sch—*school* ... VT-1
Beanwallow Gap—*gap* ... TN-4
Bean Well—*well* ... TX-5
Beany Creek—*stream* ... MN-6
Beany Pond—*lake* ... FL-3
*Bea Ogwa Canyon* ... WY-8
*Beap Inseln* ... PW-9
Bear—*locale* ... DE-2
Bear—*locale* ... ID-8
Bear—*locale* ... WA-9
**Bear**—*pop pl* ... AR-4
Bear, Mount—*summit* ... AK-9
*Bear, The* ... WY-8
Bear, The—*rock* ... MT-8
Bear and Rabbit Summit—*summit* ... UT-8
Bear Arroyo—*stream* ... NM-5
*Bear Banks* ... NC-3
Bear Bar—*bar* (2) ... ID-8
Bear Basin—*basin* ... AZ-5
Bear Basin—*basin* (3) ... CA-9
Bear Basin—*basin* (2) ... CO-8
Bear Basin—*basin* ... ID-8
Bear Basin—*basin* ... MT-8
Bear Basin—*basin* ... UT-8
Bear Basin—*basin* (2) ... WY-8
Bear Basin Butte—*summit* ... CA-9
Bear Basin Camp—*locale* ... CA-9
Bear Basin Creek—*stream* ... CA-9
Bear Basin Creek—*stream* ... ID-8
*Bear Bay* ... FL-3
Bear Bay—*bay* (3) ... AK-9
Bear Bay—*bay* ... NC-3
Bear Bay—*stream* ... MS-4
Bear Bay—*swamp* ... AL-4
Bear Bay—*swamp* (11) ... FL-3
Bear Bay—*swamp* (2) ... GA-3
Bear Bay—*swamp* ... NC-3
Bear Bay Branch—*stream* (3) ... FL-3
Bear Bay Creek—*stream* ... FL-3
Bear Bay Island—*island* ... AK-9
Bear Bayou—*gut* ... AR-4
Bear Bayou—*stream* (4) ... AR-4
Bear Bayou—*stream* (4) ... LA-4
Bear Bayou—*stream* (3) ... MS-4
Bear Bayou—*stream* ... TX-5
Bear Bay Sch—*school* ... SC-3
Bear Bay Sink—*basin* ... FL-3
Bear Bay Swamp—*swamp* ... FL-3
Bear Beaver Ridge—*ridge* ... AZ-5
Bear Belly Strand—*stream* ... GA-3
Bear Bench Ridge—*ridge* ... TN-4
Bearberry Hill—*summit* ... MA-1
Bear Blanket Slough—*stream* ... AK-9
Bear Bluff—*cliff* ... AK-9
Bear Bluff—*cliff* ... OR-9
Bear Bluff—*cliff* (2) ... SC-3
Bear Bluff—*summit* (2) ... WI-6
Bear Bluff Lodge—*locale* ... SC-3
Bear Bluff Station—*locale* ... WI-6
**Bear Bluff (Town of)**—*pop pl* ... WI-6
Bear Bone Cave—*cave* ... AL-4
*Bear Bones Mtn* ... OR-9
Bearbones Mtn—*summit* ... OR-9
*Bear Brake* ... AR-4
Bear Brake—*swamp* ... AR-4
Bear Brake (historical)—*swamp* ... LA-4
*Bear Branch* ... GA-3
*Bear Branch* ... LA-4
*Bear Branch* ... NC-3
*Bear Branch* ... TN-4
*Bear Branch* ... TX-5
*Bear Branch* ... WV-2
Bear Branch—*locale* ... KY-4
**Bear Branch**—*pop pl* ... IN-6
Bear Branch—*stream* (14) ... AL-4
Bear Branch—*stream* (7) ... AR-4
Bear Branch—*stream* (8) ... FL-3
Bear Branch—*stream* (13) ... GA-3
Bear Branch—*stream* (3) ... IL-6
Bear Branch—*stream* (3) ... IN-6
Bear Branch—*stream* ... IA-7
Bear Branch—*stream* (42) ... KY-4
Bear Branch—*stream* (6) ... LA-4
Bear Branch—*stream* (5) ... MD-2
Bear Branch—*stream* (2) ... MS-4
Bear Branch—*stream* (11) ... MO-7
Bear Branch—*stream* ... NJ-2
Bear Branch—*stream* (21) ... NC-3
Bear Branch—*stream* (2) ... OR-9
Bear Branch—*stream* ... PA-2
Bear Branch—*stream* (7) ... SC-3
Bear Branch—*stream* (27) ... TN-4
Bear Branch—*stream* (12) ... TX-5
Bear Branch—*stream* (12) ... VA-3
Bear Branch—*stream* ... WA-9
Bear Branch—*stream* (12) ... WV-2
Bear Branch—*stream* ... WI-6
Bear Branch Access Area—*park* ... TN-4
Bear Branch Bridge—*bridge* ... NC-3
Bear Branch Cem—*cemetery* ... KY-4
Bear Branch Cem—*cemetery* ... NC-3
Bear Branch Cem—*cemetery* ... WV-2
Bear Branch Ch—*church* ... MO-7
Bear Branch Ch—*church* ... NC-3
Bear Branch Ch—*church* ... VA-3
Bear Branch Ch—*church* ... WV-2
**Bear Branch (historical)**—*pop pl* ... TN-4
Bear Branch Post Office (historical)—*building* ... TN-4
Bear Branch Sch—*school* (2) ... KY-4
Bear Branch Sch—*school* ... WV-2
Bear Branch Sch (abandoned)—*school* ... MO-7
Bear Branch Sch (historical)—*school* ... PA-2
*Bear Branch School* ... TX-5
Bear Brook—*stream* (30) ... ME-1
Bear Brook—*stream* ... MN-6
Bear Brook—*stream* (4) ... NH-1
Bear Brook—*stream* (4) ... NJ-2
Bear Brook—*stream* (10) ... NY-2
Bear Brook—*stream* (2) ... PA-2
Bear Brook—*stream* ... RI-1
Bear Brook—*stream* (2) ... VT-1
Bear Brook Bog—*lake* ... ME-1
Bear Brook Campsite—*locale* ... ME-1
Bear Brook Cove—*bay* (2) ... ME-1
Bear Brook Pond—*lake* ... NH-1
Bear Brook State Park—*park* ... NH-1
Bear Brook Trail—*trail* ... NH-1
*Bear Butte* ... OR-9
Bear Butte—*hist pl* ... SD-7
Bear Butte—*locale* ... SD-7
Bear Butte—*summit* ... CA-9
Bear Butte—*summit* ... ID-8
Bear Butte—*summit* ... ND-7
Bear Butte—*summit* (5) ... OR-9
Bear Butte—*summit* ... SD-7
Bear Butte Creek—*stream* ... SD-7
Bear Butte (historical)—*locale* ... SD-7
Bear Butte Lake—*reservoir* ... SD-7
Bear Butte Natl Wildlife Ref—*park* ... SD-7
Bear Buttes—*summit* ... CA-9
Bear Buttes—*summit* ... NV-8
Bear Butte Tank—*reservoir* ... AZ-5
Bear Cabin Branch—*stream* ... MD-2
Bear Cabin Creek—*stream* ... WY-8

Beardsley's Brook ... CT-1
Beardsley Sch—school ... CA-9
Beardsley Sch—school ... CT-1
Beardsley Sch—school ... PA-2
Beardsley Substation—locale ... AZ-5
Beardsley Wash—stream ... CA-9
Beardsley Weir—dam ... CA-9
Beards Marsh—swamp ... TX-5
Beards Mill—locale ... AL-4
Beards Mine (underground)—mine ... AL-4
Beards Mountain Ford Trail—trail ... VA-3
Beards Mtn—summit ... VA-3
Beards Plaisance—park ... MN-6
Beards Point—cape ... MD-2
Beard Spring—spring ... AZ-5
Beard Spring—spring ... MS-4
Beard Spring—spring ... TX-5
Beards Reef—bar ... AL-4
Beards Run—stream ... OH-6
Beards Run—stream ... WV-2
Beards Sch—school ... PA-2
Beardstey Sch—school ... TN-4
Beards Town ... IN-6
**Beardstown**—pop pl ... IL-6
**Beardstown**—pop pl ... IN-6
**Beardstown**—pop pl ... TN-4
Beardstown Post Office (historical)—building ... TN-4
Beardstown Sch (historical)—school ... TN-4
**Beardstown (Township of)**—pop pl ... IL-6
Beard Valley—valley ... TN-4
Beard Windmill—locale ... TX-5
Beardy Branch ... AR-4
Beardy Branch—stream ... AR-4
Beardy Gulch—valley ... ID-8
Bear Ears ... CO-8
Bear Ears Mountain ... CO-8
Beare Glacier—glacier ... AK-9
Bear Fall Point—cliff ... AZ-5
Bear Falls—falls ... NY-2
Bear Falls—falls ... OK-5
Bearfence Mountain Shelter—locale ... VA-3
Bearfence Mtn—summit ... VA-3
Bearfield Branch—stream ... TX-5
Bearfield Hollow—valley ... PA-2
Bearfield Run—stream ... PA-2
Bearfield Sch—school ... OH-6
**Bearfield (Township of)**—pop pl ... OH-6
Bearfite Creek—stream ... MT-8
Bear Flag Sch—school ... CA-9
Bear Flat ... CA-9
Bear Flat—flat (2) ... AZ-5
Bear Flat—flat (10) ... CA-9
Bear Flat—flat ... ID-8
Bear Flat—flat (7) ... OR-9
Bear Flat—flat (5) ... UT-8
Bear Flat Campground—park ... AZ-5
Bear Flat Creek—stream ... AZ-5
Bear Flat Creek—stream ... ID-8
Bear Flat Draw—valley ... OR-9
Bear Flat Guard Station ... OR-9
Bear Flat Meadow ... OR-9
Bear Flat Pleasant Valley Trail—trail ... AZ-5
Bear Flat Springs—spring ... OR-9
Bear Flat Station—other ... OR-9
Bear Flat Swamp—swamp ... FL-3
Bear Flat Trail Tank—reservoir ... AZ-5
Bearfoot Branch—stream ... MS-4
Bearfoot Canyon—valley ... TX-5
Bearfoot Hill ... MA-1
Bearfoot Lake ... FL-3
Bearfoot Lake ... MI-6
Bearfoot Lake—lake ... MI-6
Bearfoot Mountain ... NJ-2
Bear Ford—flat ... NC-3
Bear Ford Mountain ... NJ-2
Bear Ford Swamp—stream ... NC-3
Bear Fork—stream (7) ... KY-4
Bear Fork—stream ... UT-8
Bear Fork—stream (2) ... VA-3
Bear Fork—stream (10) ... WV-2
Bear Fork Bayou—stream ... LA-4
Bear Fork Ch—church ... KY-4
Bear Fork Sch—school ... KY-4
Bearfort Lake ... NJ-2
Bearfort Mtn—summit ... NJ-2
Bearfort Waters—lake ... NJ-2
Bearfort Waters Lake ... NJ-2
Bear Frap Landing—locale ... ME-1
Bear Gap—gap (2) ... GA-3
Bear Gap—gap (4) ... NC-3
Bear Gap—gap (4) ... PA-2
Bear Gap—gap ... WA-9
Bear Gap—locale ... PA-2
Bear Gap Branch—stream ... AL-4
Bear Gap Branch—stream ... KY-4
Bear Gap Number Six Dam—dam ... PA-2
Bear Gap Number Two Dam—dam ... PA-2
Bear Gap Picnic Area—area ... PA-2
Bear Gap Run—stream ... PA-2
Bear Gap Tabernacle—church ... PA-2
Bear Gap Trail—trail (2) ... PA-2
Bear Garden—locale ... MS-4
Bear Garden Bay—swamp ... NC-3
Bear Garden Creek ... MD-2
Bear Garden Creek—stream ... VA-3
Beargarden Knob—summit ... WV-2
Bear Garden Mtn—summit ... VA-3
Bear Garden Mtn—summit ... WV-2
Beargarden Pocosin—swamp ... NC-3
Bear Garden Point—cape ... NC-3
Bear Garden Pond ... MD-2
Bear Garden Run—stream ... VA-3
Bear Garden Swamp—swamp ... GA-3
Bear Glacier—glacier ... AK-9
Bear Glacier Point—cape ... AK-9
Bear Grap ... PA-2
**Beargrass**—pop pl ... NC-3
**Bear Grass**—pop pl ... NC-3
**Bear Grass**—pop pl ... TX-5
Bear Grass—uninc pl ... KY-4
Beargrass Basin—basin ... AZ-5
Beargrass Butte—summit ... WA-9
Bear Grass Creek ... AL-4
Bear-Grass Creek ... IN-6
Beargrass Creek ... WI-6
Beargrass Creek—stream ... AL-4
Beargrass Creek—stream ... IN-6
Beargrass Creek—stream ... KY-4
Bear Grass Draw—valley ... NM-5
Beargrass Flat—flat ... AZ-5
Bear Grass Hill—summit ... NM-5
Bear Grass HS—school ... NC-3
Beargrass Mountain ... ID-8
Beargrass Point—cape ... NC-3
Bear Grass Ridge—ridge ... ID-8
Bear Grass Ridge—ridge ... TX-5
Bear Grass Swamp—stream ... NC-3
Bear Grass Tank—reservoir (3) ... AZ-5
Bear Grass Tank—reservoir ... TX-5
Beargrass (Township of)—fmr MCD ... NC-3
Beargrease Island—island ... MN-6
Bearground Gulch—valley ... CA-9
Bearground Spring—spring ... CA-9
Bear Grove—locale ... IA-7
Bear Grove Cem—cemetery ... IA-7
Bear Grove Township—fmr MCD (2) ... IA-7
**Bear Grove (Township of)**—pop pl ... IL-6
Bear Guard Station—locale ... ID-8
Bear Gulch ... CA-9
Bear Gulch ... MT-8
Bear Gulch ... WY-8
Bear Gulch—stream (2) ... MT-8
Bear Gulch—stream ... OR-9
Bear Gulch—stream ... WA-9
Bear Gulch—valley ... AK-9
Bear Gulch—valley ... AZ-5
Bear Gulch—valley (28) ... CA-9
Bear Gulch—valley (16) ... CO-8
Bear Gulch—valley (22) ... ID-8
Bear Gulch—valley (35) ... MT-8
Bear Gulch—valley ... NY-2
Bear Gulch—valley ... OK-5
Bear Gulch—valley (17) ... OR-9
Bear Gulch—valley (4) ... SD-7
Bear Gulch—valley ... TX-5
Bear Gulch—valley (3) ... UT-8
Bear Gulch—valley (3) ... WA-9
Bear Gulch—valley (12) ... WY-8
Bear Gulch Camp—locale ... CA-9
Bear Gulch Camp—locale ... WA-9
Bear Gulch Campground—locale (2) ... ID-8
Bear Gulch Creek—stream ... MT-8
Bear Gulch Gravel Pit—mine ... ID-8
Bear Gulch I (historical)—locale ... SD-7
Bear Gulch II (historical)—locale ... SD-7
Bear Gulch Pond—reservoir ... NY-2
Bear Gulch Rsvr—reservoir (2) ... CA-9
Bear Gulch Rsvr—reservoir ... CO-8
Bear Gulch Sch—school ... MT-8
Bear Gulch Ski Area—other ... ID-8
Bear Gulch Spring—spring ... ID-8
Bear Gulch Trail—trail ... MT-8
Bear Gulch Trail—trail ... SD-7
Bear Gulf—valley ... NY-2
Bear Gully Canal—canal ... FL-3
Bear Gully Creek—stream ... FL-3
Bear Gully Lake—lake ... FL-3
Bear Gut Bayou—stream ... MS-4
Bear Gutter Creek—stream ... NY-2
Bear Hallow Creek ... CA-9
Bear Hammock—island (2) ... FL-3
Bear Hammock—island ... NC-3
Bear Hammock Lake—lake ... FL-3
Bear Hammock Lakes—lake ... FL-3
Bear Hammock Ponds ... FL-3
Bear Harbor—bay ... AK-9
Bear Harbor Lake—lake ... FL-3
Bear Harbor Ranch—locale ... CA-9
Bearhat Mtn—summit ... MT-8
Bear Haven Creek—stream ... CA-9
Bearhead—island ... NC-3
**Bear Head**—pop pl ... FL-3
Bear Head—summit ... ME-1
Bear Head—summit ... VT-1
Bear Head Bay—bay ... MN-6
Bearhead Branch—stream ... AR-4
Bear Head Canyon—valley ... AZ-5
Bearhead Cem—cemetery ... MN-6
Bear Head Cem—cemetery ... TX-5
Bear Head Creek ... AR-4
Bear Head Creek—stream ... AL-4
Bear Head Creek—stream ... LA-4
Bearhead Creek—stream ... NC-3
Bear Head Creek—stream ... TX-5
Bear Head Creek Oil Field—oilfield ... LA-4
Bear Head Lake—lake ... FL-3
Bear Head Lake—lake ... MN-6
Bear Head Lake State Park—park ... MN-6
Bear Headland—cliff ... AZ-5
Bear Head Mountain ... WY-8
Bear Head Mtn ... AZ-5
Bear Head Mtn—summit ... AZ-5
Bear Head Mtn—summit ... AR-4
Bearhead Mtn—summit ... MT-8
Bearhead Mtn—summit ... WA-9
Bear Head Mtn—summit ... WY-8
Bearhead Peak—summit ... NM-5
Bearhead Ridge—ridge ... NM-5
Bear Head Spring—spring ... AZ-5
Bear Heaven—area ... CA-9
Bear Heaven Rec Area—park ... WV-2
Bear Heels Ranch—locale ... SD-7
Bearhide Canyon—valley ... AZ-5
Bear Hide Lake—reservoir ... CA-9
Bearhide Spring—spring ... AZ-5
Bear Hill ... AZ-5
Bear Hill ... MA-1
Bear Hill—ridge ... MA-1
Bear Hill—summit ... CA-9
Bear Hill—summit (6) ... CT-1
Bear Hill—summit ... IN-6
Bear Hill—summit ... IA-7
Bear Hill—summit (3) ... ME-1
Bear Hill—summit ... MD-2
Bear Hill—summit (13) ... MA-1
Bear Hill—summit ... MN-6
Bear Hill—summit ... NE-7
Bear Hill—summit (5) ... NH-1
Bear Hill—summit (5) ... NY-2
Bear Hill—summit ... OR-9
Bear Hill—summit ... PA-2
Bear Hill—summit ... RI-1
Bear Hill—summit (6) ... VT-1
Bear Hill Cem—cemetery ... MA-1
Bearhill Creek—stream ... ID-8
Bear Hill Golf Club—locale ... MA-1
Bear Hill Hollow—valley ... AR-4
Bear Hill HS—school ... MA-1
Bear Hill Mine—mine ... AR-4
Bear Hill Pond—lake ... NH-1
Bear Hill Pond Camp—locale ... NH-1
Bear Hills—ridge ... AZ-5
Bear Hill Sch—school ... ME-1
Bear Hill Sch—school ... MD-2
Bear Hill Sch—school ... VT-1
**Bear (historical)**—pop pl ... TN-4
Bear Hole ... MA-1
Bear Hole ... NJ-2
Bear Hole—basin ... MT-8
Bear Hole—basin (3) ... UT-8
Bear Hole—bay ... FL-3
Bear Hole—cave ... TN-4
Bear Hole Bend—bend ... TN-4
Bear Hole Brook—stream ... NY-2
Bearhole Creek—stream ... AK-9
Bear Hole Creek—stream ... ID-8
Bearhole Creek—stream ... WY-8
Bear Hole Ditch ... DE-2
Bearhole Ditch—stream ... DE-2
Bearhole Fork—stream ... WV-2
Bear Hole Hollow—valley ... AR-4
Bearhole Hollow—valley ... TN-4
Bear Hole Hollow—valley ... UT-8
Bear Hole Island—island ... TN-4
Bear Hole Lake—lake ... MI-6
Bearhole Reservoir Dam—dam ... MA-1
Bearhole Ridge—ridge ... WV-2
Bearhole Rsvr—reservoir ... MA-1
Bear Hole Run—stream ... OH-6
Bear Hole Run—stream ... PA-2
Bear Hole Run—stream ... VA-3
Bear Hole Trail—trail ... ID-8
Bear Hollow ... PA-2
Bear Hollow—basin ... UT-8
**Bear Hollow**—pop pl ... FL-3
Bear Hollow—valley (2) ... AL-4
Bear Hollow—valley (13) ... AR-4
Bear Hollow—valley ... CA-9
Bear Hollow—valley (6) ... ID-8
Bear Hollow—valley ... IL-6
Bear Hollow—valley (2) ... IN-6
Bear Hollow—valley (6) ... KY-4
Bear Hollow—valley ... MD-2
Bear Hollow—valley (6) ... MO-7
Bear Hollow—valley (2) ... NY-2
Bear Hollow—valley (2) ... OH-6
Bear Hollow—valley ... OR-9
Bear Hollow—valley (8) ... PA-2
Bear Hollow—valley (15) ... TN-4
Bear Hollow—valley (8) ... TX-5
Bear Hollow—valley (14) ... UT-8
Bear Hollow—valley (7) ... VA-3
Bear Hollow—valley (7) ... WV-2
Bear Hollow Creek ... TN-4
Bear Hollow Creek—stream (2) ... CA-9
Bear Hollow Creek—stream ... PA-2
Bear Hollow Creek—stream ... WV-2
Bear Hollow Mtn—summit ... TN-4
Bear Hollow Sch (abandoned)—school ... MO-7
**Bear Hollow Village**—pop pl ... AR-4
Bear Hollow Windmill—locale ... TX-5
Bearhouse Creek—stream ... AR-4
Bear House Run ... PA-2
Bearhouse (Township of)—fmr MCD (2) ... AR-4
Bear Hug Ridge—ridge ... NC-3
Bear Hunt Gulch—valley ... OR-9
Bearing Cove—bay ... NV-8
Bearinger Bldg—hist pl ... MI-6
Bearinger Ch—church ... MI-6
**Bearinger Corners**—pop pl ... MI-6
**Bearinger (Township of)**—pop pl ... MI-6
Bearing Island ... ME-1
Bearing Peak—summit ... NV-8
Bearing Point—cape ... NV-8
Bear Inlet—bay ... NC-3
Bear In Middle Creek ... MT-8
Bear-in-Middle Creek—stream ... MT-8
Bear-in-the-Lodge Creek—stream ... SD-7
Bear Island—area ... LA-4
Bear Island—island (6) ... AK-9
Bear Island—island ... AR-4
Bear Island—island ... CT-1
Bear Island—island (9) ... FL-3
Bear Island—island (4) ... GA-3
Bear Island—island ... ID-8
Bear Island—island (2) ... LA-4
Bear Island—island (7) ... ME-1
Bear Island—island ... MD-2
Bear Island—island (2) ... MA-1
Bear Island—island (2) ... MI-6
Bear Island—island (6) ... MN-6
Bear Island—island (3) ... NH-1
Bear Island—island ... NJ-2
Bear Island—island ... NY-2
Bear Island—island (2) ... NC-3
Bear Island—island ... ND-7
Bear Island—island ... OR-9
Bear Island—island ... SC-3
Bear Island—island ... VA-3
Bear Island—island (2) ... WI-6
**Bear Island**—pop pl ... NH-1
Bear Island Creek—stream ... SC-3
Bear Island Game Mngmt Area—park ... SC-3
Bear Island (historical)—island ... ND-7
Bear Island Lake—lake ... AK-9
Bear Island Lake—lake ... MN-6
Bear Island Light Station—hist pl ... ME-1
Bear Island River—stream ... MN-6
Bear Island Shoal—bar ... WI-6
Bear Island State For—forest ... MN-6
Bear Island Strand—swamp ... FL-3
Bear Island Swamp—swamp ... GA-3
Bear Jaw Canyon—valley ... AZ-5
Bear Jaw Creek—stream ... MT-8
Bear Jaw Windmill—locale ... MT-8
Bear Jump—cliff ... NM-5
Bear Keg Spring—spring ... CO-8
Bear Key—island ... FL-3
Bear Kill—stream (2) ... NY-2
Bear Knob—summit ... KY-4
Bear Knob—summit (3) ... NC-3
Bear Knob—summit ... PA-2
Bear Knob—summit (2) ... TN-4
Bear Knob—summit ... TX-5
Bear Knob—summit (2) ... VA-3
Bear Knob—summit (3) ... WV-2
Bear Knob Cem—cemetery ... WV-2
Bear Knob Lookout Tower—locale ... AR-4
Bear Knot Island—island ... SC-3
Bear Lake ... CA-9
Bear Lake ... CO-8
Bear Lake ... MI-6
Bear Lake ... MN-6
Bear Lake ... MT-8
Bear Lake ... NJ-2
Bear Lake ... WI-6
Bear Lake ... WY-8
Bear Lake—bay ... LA-4
Bear Lake—bay ... WI-6
Bear Lake—lake ... AL-4
Bear Lake—lake (7) ... AK-9
Bear Lake—lake ... AZ-5
Bear Lake—lake (4) ... AR-4
Bear Lake—lake (11) ... CA-9
Bear Lake—lake (7) ... CO-8
Bear Lake—lake (5) ... FL-3
Bear Lake—lake ... GA-3
Bear Lake—lake (6) ... ID-8
Bear Lake—lake ... IL-6
Bear Lake—lake ... IN-6
Bear Lake—lake ... LA-4
Bear Lake—lake (28) ... MI-6
Bear Lake—lake (18) ... MN-6
Bear Lake—lake (5) ... MS-4
Bear Lake—lake (6) ... MT-8
Bear Lake—lake (3) ... NM-5
Bear Lake—lake (4) ... NY-2
Bear Lake—lake ... ND-7
Bear Lake—lake (6) ... OR-9
Bear Lake—lake ... PA-2
Bear Lake—lake (2) ... TX-5
Bear Lake—lake (3) ... UT-8
Bear Lake—lake (12) ... WA-9
Bear Lake—lake (20) ... WI-6
Bear Lake—lake (5) ... WY-8
Bear Lake—locale ... WI-6
**Bear Lake**—pop pl ... FL-3
**Bear Lake**—pop pl ... IN-6
**Bear Lake**—pop pl ... MI-6
**Bear Lake**—pop pl (2) ... PA-2
Bear Lake—reservoir ... AL-4
Bear Lake—reservoir ... CO-8
Bear Lake—reservoir ... FL 3
Bear Lake—reservoir ... ID-8
Bear Lake—reservoir (2) ... IN-6
Bear Lake—reservoir ... NM-5
Bear Lake—reservoir ... PA-2
Bear Lake—reservoir ... UT-8
Bear Lake—stream (2) ... MS-4
Bear Lakebed—flat ... MN-6
Bear Lake Bible Chapel—church ... FL-3
Bear Lake Borough—civil ... PA-2
Bear Lake Camp—locale ... CA-9
Bear Lake Campground—locale ... CO-8
Bear Lake Campground—locale ... WI-6
Bear Lake Cem—cemetery ... PA-2
Bear Lake Ch—church ... MN-6
Bear Lake Chapel—church ... IN-6
Bear Lake Comfort Station—hist pl ... CO-8
Bear Lake County Courthouse—hist pl ... ID-8
Bear Lake Creek ... MT-8
Bear Lake Creek—stream ... ID-8
Bear Lake Creek—stream ... OR-9
Bear Lake Dam ... NJ-2
Bear Lake Dam—dam ... IN-6
Bear Lake Elem Sch—school ... FL-3
Bear Lake Glacier—glacier ... AK-9
Bear Lake (historical)—lake ... IA-7
Bear Lake Hot Springs—locale ... ID-8
Bear Lake Inlet ... ID-8
Bear Lake JHS—school ... ID-8
Bear Lake KOA Campground—locale ... UT-8
Bear Lake Marina Campground—locale ... UT-8
Bear Lake Marina State Park ... UT-8
Bear Lake Market—hist pl ... ID-8
Bear Lake Mound—summit ... FL-3
Bear Lake Natl Wildlife Ref—park ... ID-8
Bear Lake Outlet—canal ... ID-8
Bear Lake Outlet—stream ... NY-2
Bear Lake Overlook—locale ... UT-8
Bear Lake Plateau—area ... ID-8
Bear Lake Ranger Station—hist pl ... CO-8
Bear Lake Rendezvous Beach Campground—locale ... UT-8
Bear Lake Rendezvous Beach State Park ... UT-8
Bear Lakes ... WY-8
Bear Lakes—lake ... CO-8
Bear Lakes—lake (2) ... MT-8
Bear Lakes—lake ... PA-2
Bear Lakes—lake ... WA-9
**Bear Lake Sands**—pop pl ... ID-8
Bear Lake Sch—school (2) ... MN-6
Bear Lake Slough—stream ... AR-4
Bear Lake Stake Tabernacle—hist pl ... ID-8
Bear Lake State Park—park ... UT-8
Bear Lake State Rec Area ... UT-8
Bear Lake State Wildlife Area—park ... WI-6
Bear Lakes Trail—trail ... MT-8
Bear Lake Summit—gap ... UT-8
**Bear Lake (Town of)**—pop pl ... WI-6
**Bear Lake (Township of)**—pop pl (2) ... MI-6
Bear Lake Trail—trail ... CO-8
Bear Lake Trail—trail ... FL-3
Bear Lake Valley—valley ... ID-8
Bear Lick—locale ... PA-2
Bear Lick Hollow—valley ... NY-2
Bearlick Knob—summit ... WV-2
Bearlick Run—stream ... WV-2
Bear Lithia Ch—church ... VA-3
Bear Lithia Spring—spring ... VA-3
Bear Lodge—locale ... WY-8
Bear Lodge Campground—locale ... WY-8
Bear Lodge Lake—reservoir ... IN-6
Bear Lodge Lake Dam—dam ... IN-6
Bear Lodge Mtns—range ... WY-8
Bear Lodge Ranch—locale ... WY-8
Bear Lodge Trail—trail ... PA-2
Bearlog Hollow—valley ... TN-4
**Bear Loop**—pop pl ... PA-2
Bear Loop Branch—stream ... VA-3
Bear Loop Run—stream ... PA-2
Bearman Creek—stream ... FL-3
Bearman Creek—stream ... MS-4
Bearman Creek—stream ... TN-4
Bearman Lake—lake ... AK-9
Bear Mans Bluff—cliff ... TX-5
Bear Mans Lake—lake ... TX-5
Bear Market ... NY-2
Bear Market Corner ... NY-2
Bear Marsh—stream ... LA-4
Bear Marsh Branch—stream ... NC-3
Bear Marsh Ch—church ... NC-3
Bear Meadow—flat (8) ... CA-9
Bear Meadow—flat ... ID-8
Bear Meadow—flat ... OR-9
Bear Meadow—flat ... WA-9
Bear Meadow—swamp ... MA-1
Bear Meadow Brook ... MA-1
Bear Meadow Brook—stream (2) ... MA-1
Bear Meadow Brook—stream ... NH-1
Bear Meadow Creek ... CA-9
Bear Meadow Creek ... MA-1
Bear Meadow Creek—stream (2) ... CA-9
Bear Meadow Run ... PA-2
Bear Meadows—flat ... OR-9
Bear Meadows—swamp ... PA-2
Bear Meadows Natural Area—park ... PA-2
Bearmeat Branch—stream ... NC-3
Bearmeat Creek—stream ... GA-3
Bearmeat Gap—gap ... GA-3
Bear Mine—mine ... AZ-5
Bear Mine—mine ... CO-8
Bear Mine—mine ... OR-9
**Bear Mine**—pop pl ... CO-8
Bear Mound ... FL-3
Bear Mound ... WI-6
Bear Mount—summit ... VT-1
Bear Mountain ... CO-8
Bear Mountain ... MS-4
Bear Mountain ... NV-8
Bear Mountain ... UT-8
Bear Mountain—locale ... NY-2
**Bear Mountain**—pop pl ... CA-9
**Bear Mountain**—pop pl ... WV-2
Bear Mountain—ridge (2) ... AR-4
Bear Mountain—ridge ... NH-1
Bear Mountain Basin—basin ... SD-7
Bear Mountain Branch—stream ... AL-4
Bear Mountain Bridge—bridge ... NY-2
Bear Mountain Bridge and Toll House—hist pl ... NY-2
Bear Mountain Bridge Rd.—hist pl ... NY-2
Bear Mountain Cem—cemetery ... ME-1
Bear Mountain Creek—stream ... AK-9
Bear Mountain Creek—stream ... ID-8
Bear Mountain Flow—bay ... NY-2
Bear Mountain Gap—gap ... NC-3
Bear Mountain Hollow—valley ... MO-7
Bear Mountain Lake—lake ... AK-9
Bear Mountain Lookout Complex—hist pl ... AZ-5
**Bear Mountain Mine (Brown Mines)**—pop pl ... WV-2
Bear Mountain Point—cliff ... MT-8
Bear Mountain Pond—lake ... ME-1
Bear Mountain Ranch—locale ... CA-9
Bear Mountain Ranch—locale ... CO-8
Bear Mountains—other ... CA-9
Bear Mountains—ridge ... NM-5
Bear Mountain Ski Trail—trail ... NH-1
Bear Mountain Swamp—swamp ... NY-2
Bear Mountain Trail—trail ... NH-1
Bear Mountain Trail—trail ... OR-9
Bear Mountain Trail—trail ... WA-9
Bearmouth—locale ... MT-8
Bear Mouth—summit ... NM-5
Bearmouth Run—stream ... PA-2
Bearmouth Spring—spring ... MT-8
Bear Mtn ... CA-9
Bear Mtn ... MA-1
Bear Mtn ... NY-2
Bear Mtn ... PA-2
Bear Mtn ... WV-2
Bear Mtn—summit ... AL-4
Bear Mtn—summit (5) ... AK-9
Bear Mtn—summit (4) ... AZ-5
Bear Mtn—summit (5) ... AR-4
Bear Mtn—summit (14) ... CA-9
Bear Mtn—summit (11) ... CO-8
Bear Mtn—summit (2) ... CT-1
Bear Mtn—summit ... GA-3
Bear Mtn—summit (3) ... ID-8
Bear Mtn—summit ... KY-4
Bear Mtn—summit (11) ... ME-1
Bear Mtn—summit (2) ... MA-1
Bear Mtn—summit ... MI-6
Bear Mtn—summit (2) ... MO-7
Bear Mtn—summit (5) ... MT-8
Bear Mtn—summit ... NV-8
Bear Mtn—summit (3) ... NH-1
Bear Mtn—summit (6) ... NM-5
Bear Mtn—summit (10) ... NY-2
Bear Mtn—summit (2) ... NC-3
Bear Mtn—summit (2) ... OK-5
Bear Mtn—summit (7) ... OR-9
Bear Mtn—summit (6) ... PA-2
Bear Mtn—summit ... SD-7
Bear Mtn—summit (7) ... TX-5
Bear Mtn—summit (6) ... VT-1
Bear Mtn—summit (3) ... VA-3
Bear Mtn—summit (7) ... WA-9
Bear Mtn—summit ... WV-2
Bear Mtn—summit (5) ... WY-8
Bear Mtn Canyon ... CA-9
Bearneck Cove—valley ... TN-4
Bear Neck Creek ... MD-2
Bear Neck Creek—stream ... MD-2
Bearneck Gap ... TN-4
Bear Neck Gap—gap ... TN-4
Bear Neck Marsh—swamp ... MD-2
Bear North Brook—stream ... VT-1
Bearnose Hill—summit ... AK-9
Bear Notch—gap ... VT-1
Bear Notch—summit ... NH-1
Bear Number One Spring ... AZ-5
Bear Oil Field—oilfield ... LA-4
Bear Pan ... OR-9
Bear Pan Creek ... OR-9
Bear Pan Creek—stream ... OR-9
Bear Pan Ridge—ridge ... TN-4
Bear Pan Spring—spring ... OR-9
Bear Park ... AL-4
Bear Park—flat ... AZ-5
Bear Park—flat (3) ... CO-8
Bear Park—flat ... ID-8
Bear Park—flat (3) ... MT-8
Bear Park—flat (2) ... UT-8
Bear Park—flat ... WA-9
Bear Park—flat ... WY-8
Bear Park—park ... WY-8
Bear Park Creek—stream ... CO-8
Bear Park Rsvr—reservoir ... CO-8
**Bear Park (Township of)**—pop pl ... MN-6
Bear Pass—gap ... OR-9
Bear Pass—gap (3) ... WA-9
Bear Pass—gap ... WY-8
Bear Pass Mtn—summit ... AK-9
Bear Pasture—flat ... WA-9
Bear Path Bay—swamp ... NC-3
Bear Path Sch—school ... CT-1
Bear Path Trail—trail ... PA-2
Bearpaw—locale ... AK-9
Bear Paw—locale ... NC-3
Bearpaw Bay—bay ... WY-8
Bear Paw Branch—stream ... GA-3
Bearpaw Butte—summit ... CA-9
Bearpaw Butte—summit ... WA-9
Bear Paw Camp—locale ... WI-6
Bear Paw Campground—locale ... MN-6
Bearpaw Ch—church ... NC-3
Bearpaw Country Club—other ... MT-8
Bearpaw Creek—stream ... AK-9
Bear Paw Creek—stream ... ID-8
Bear Paw Creek—stream ... MN-6
Bearpaw Creek—stream ... MT-8
Bear Paw Creek—stream ... NY-2
Bear Paw Creek—stream ... WA-9
Bear Paw Forest Camp—locale ... OR-9
Bear Paw Fork—stream ... WY-8
Bear Paw Lake ... MI-6
Bear Paw Lake ... WI-6
Bear Paw Lake—lake ... AK-9
Bearpaw Lake—lake ... CA-9
Bearpaw Lake—lake ... MI-6
Bear Paw Lake—lake ... WI-6
Bearpaw Lake—lake ... WY-8
Bearpaw Lake—reservoir ... MT-8
Bearpaw Meadow—flat ... CA-9
Bear Paw Meadow—flat ... MT-8
Bear Paw Meadow—flat ... OR-9
Bearpaw Meadow Ranger Station—locale ... CA-9
Bear Paw Mountain ... MT-8
Bear Paw Mountain ... NV-8
Bearpaw Mountain Lake—lake ... WA-9
Bear Paw Mountains ... MT-8
Bearpaw Mtn—summit ... AK-9
Bearpaw Mtn—summit ... NV-8
Bearpaw Mtn—summit ... WA-9
Bear Paw Mtns—range ... MT-8
Bear Paw Point—cape ... MN-6
Bear Paw Resort Dock—locale ... NC-3
Bear Paw Ridge—ridge ... WA-9
Bearpaw River—stream ... AK-9
Bear Paw Sch—school ... MT-8
Bearpaws Peaks—summit ... CO-8
Bear Paw Spring—spring ... AZ-5
Bear Paw Spring—spring ... OR-9
Bear Paw Trail—trail ... MT-8
Bear Peak ... MT-8
Bear Peak—summit (2) ... CA-9
Bear Peak—summit (2) ... CO-8
Bear Peak—summit ... ID-8
Bear Peak—summit ... MT-8
Bear Peak—summit ... NM-5
Bear Peak—summit ... WY-8
Bear Peak Trail—trail ... CO-8
Bearpen ... NY-2
Bearpen ... NC-3
Bear Pen Airp—airport ... NC-3
Bearpen Bend—bend ... FL-3
Bear Pen Branch—stream ... AL-4
Bearpen Branch—stream ... GA-3
Bearpen Branch—stream (2) ... KY-4
Bearpen Branch—stream (13) ... NC-3
Bearpen Branch—stream (3) ... TN-4
Bearpen Branch—stream (3) ... VA-3
Bearpen Branch—stream ... WV-2
Bear Pen Canal—canal ... MS-4
Bear Pen Canyon—valley ... CA-9
Bearpen Coulee—valley ... WI-6
Bear Pen Creek—stream (2) ... AR-4
Bear Pen Creek—stream (4) ... CA-9
Bearpen Creek—stream ... CA-9
Bear Pen Creek—stream ... CA-9
Bearpen Creek—stream ... CA-9
Bear Pen Creek—stream ... ID-8
Bear Pen Creek—stream ... KY-4
Bearpen Creek—stream ... MI-6
Bear Pen Creek—stream ... MT-8
Bearpen Creek—stream (5) ... NC-3
Bear Pen Creek—stream ... OR-9
Bear Pen Creek—stream ... TX-5
Bearpen Creek—stream ... TX-5
Bearpen Creek—stream ... VA-3
Bear Pen Falls—falls ... AR-4
Bear Pen Flat—flat ... CA-9
Bearpen Fork ... WV-2
Bearpen Fork—stream (2) ... WV-2
Bear Pen Gap ... TN-4
Bear Pen Gap—gap ... GA-3
Bearpen Gap—gap (14) ... NC-3
Bearpen Gap—gap (2) ... TN-4
Bearpen Gap—gap (2) ... VA-3
Bearpen Gap Tunnel—tunnel ... VA-3
Bear Pen Gulch—valley ... CO-8
Bearpen Gulf—valley ... TN-4
Bearpen Gut—gut ... AL-4
Bearpen Hill—summit ... TN-4
Bear Pen Hollow—valley ... AR-4
Bearpen Hollow—valley ... KY-4
Bearpen Hollow—valley ... MO-7
Bear Pen Hollow—valley ... MO-7
Bearpen Hollow—valley ... NY-2
Bear Pen Hollow—valley (2) ... PA-2
Bearpen Hollow—valley ... PA-2
Bear Pen Hollow—valley ... PA-2
Bearpen Hollow—valley ... PA-2
Bear Pen Hollow—valley ... PA-2
Bearpen Hollow—valley (2) ... PA-2
Bearpen Hollow—valley ... TN-4
Bear Pen Hollow—valley ... VA-3
Bearpen Hollow—valley (2) ... WV-2
Bear Pen Hollow Trail—trail ... PA-2
Bear Pen Island—island ... FL-3
Bearpen Island—island ... GA-3
Bear Pen Islands—island ... NC-3
Bear Pen Islands Swamp—swamp ... NC-3
Bearpen Knob—summit ... NC-3
Bearpen Landing—locale ... FL-3
Bearpen Lead—ridge ... TN-4

Bear Pen Mission—church ..... KY-4
Bearpen Mountain ..... GA-3
Bear Pen Mtn—summit ..... AL-4
Bearpen Mtn—summit ..... NY-2
Bearpen Mtn—summit (4) ..... NC-3
Bear Pen Park—park ..... MS-4
Bearpen Peak—summit ..... NY-2
Bearpen Ridge ..... NC-3
Bearpen Ridge ..... TN-4
Bear Pen Ridge—ridge ..... CA-9
Bearpen Ridge—ridge ..... GA-3
Bearpen Ridge—ridge (7) ..... NC-3
Bearpen Ridge—ridge (3) ..... TN-4
Bearpen Ridge—ridge (2) ..... VA-3
Bearpen Ridge—ridge ..... WV-2
Bearpen Rock—summit ..... NC-3
Bearpen Rough—valley ..... TN-4
Bear Pen Run ..... PA-2
Bearpen Run ..... WV-2
Bear Pen Run—stream ..... MD-2
Bear Pen Run—stream ..... PA-2
Bear Pen Run—stream ..... PA-2
Bearpen Run—stream ..... PA-2
Bearpen Run—stream ..... WV-2
Bear Pen Run Trail—trail ..... WV-2
Bear Pen Springs—spring ..... CA-9
Bear Pen Trail—trail ..... PA-2
Bear Pete Lake—lake ..... ID-8
Bear Pete Mtn—summit ..... ID-8
Bear Playground Spring—spring ..... AZ-5
Bear Pocket—valley ..... WY-8
Bear Pocosin—swamp ..... NC-3
Bear Point—cape ..... AL-4
Bear Point—cape (2) ..... AK-9
Bear Point—cape (3) ..... FL-3
Bear Point—cape ..... ID-8
Bear Point—cape ..... MD-2
Bear Point—cape ..... MI-6
Bear Point—cape ..... NY-2
Bear Point—cape ..... NC-3
Bear Point—cape ..... OR-9
Bear Point—cape ..... RI-1
Bear Point—cape ..... WI-6
Bear Point—cliff ..... CO-8
Bear Point—summit ..... MT-8
Bear Point—summit ..... OR-9
Bear Point Cem—cemetery ..... IL-6
Bear Point Ch—church ..... IL-6
Bear Point Cove—bay (2) ..... FL-3
Bear Point Marina—locale ..... AL-4
Bear Pond—lake ..... AR-4
Bear Pond—lake (2) ..... FL-3
Bear Pond—lake (14) ..... ME-1
Bear Pond—lake (3) ..... MA-1
Bear Pond—lake (5) ..... NH-1
Bear Pond—lake ..... NJ-2
Bear Pond—lake (10) ..... NY-2
Bear Pond—lake (2) ..... PA-2
Bear Pond—lake ..... VT-1
Bear Pond—lake ..... WI-6
**Bear Pond**—pop pl ..... NC-3
**Bearpond**—pop pl ..... NC-3
Bear Pond—swamp ..... FL-3
Bear Pond—swamp ..... NC-3
Bear Pond Branch—stream ..... MS-4
Bear Pond Brook—stream (2) ..... ME-1
Bear Pond Cem—cemetery ..... ME-1
Bear Pond Dam—dam ..... AL-4
Bear Pond (historical)—lake ..... MA-1
Bear Pond (historical)—lake ..... MS-4
Bear Pond Hollow—valley ..... MD-2
Bear Pond Hollow—valley (2) ..... PA-2
Bear Pond Ledge—bench ..... ME-1
Bear Pond Mountains—range ..... MD-2
Bear Pond Mountains—range ..... PA-2
Bear Pond Mtn—summit ..... NY-2
Bear Ponds—swamp ..... TX-5
Bear Pond Trail—trail ..... NY-2
Bear Pond Trail—trail ..... PA-2
**Bear Poplar**—pop pl ..... NC-3
Bearport Mountain ..... NJ-2
Bear Post Office (historical)—building ..... TN-4
Bear Prairie—area ..... CA-9
Bear Prairie—flat ..... FL-3
Bear Prairie—flat ..... MT-8
Bear Prairie—flat (2) ..... WA-9
Bear Prong—stream ..... NC-3
Bear Puddles—lake ..... PA-2
Bear Rabbit ..... UT-8
Bear Ranch Creek—stream ..... CA-9
Bear Ranch Hill—summit ..... CA-9
Bear Ravine—valley ..... CA-9
Bear Rear Creek ..... SC-3
Bear Ridge ..... CA-9
Bear Ridge—ridge ..... AZ-5
Bear Ridge—ridge ..... AR-4
Bear Ridge—ridge (4) ..... CA-9
Bear Ridge—ridge ..... ME-1
Bear Ridge—ridge (2) ..... NY-2
Bear Ridge—ridge (2) ..... NC-3
Bear Ridge—ridge (6) ..... OR-9
Bear Ridge—ridge ..... PA-2
Bear Ridge—ridge (2) ..... TN-4
Bear Ridge—ridge ..... UT-8
Bear Ridge—ridge (4) ..... VA-3
Bear Ridge—ridge (2) ..... WV-2
Bear Ridge—summit ..... FL-3
Bear Ridge Cem—cemetery ..... NY-2
Bear Ridge Lake—lake ..... NY-2
Bear Ridge Sch—school ..... NY-2
Bear Ridge Sch—school ..... VA-3
Bear Ridge School—locale ..... MO-7
Bear Ridge Well—well ..... OR-9
Bear Riffle—rapids ..... OR-9
Bear River ..... AL-4
Bear River ..... CO-8
Bear River ..... MS-4
Bear River—locale ..... AK-9
Bear River—locale ..... CO-8
**Bear River**—pop pl ..... CA-9
**Bear River**—pop pl ..... MN-6
Bear River—stream (2) ..... AK-9
Bear River—stream (3) ..... CA-9
Bear River—stream ..... CO-8
Bear River—stream ..... GA-3
Bear River—stream (2) ..... ID-8
Bear River—stream (2) ..... ME-1
Bear River—stream ..... MA-1
Bear River—stream ..... MI-6
Bear River—stream (3) ..... MN-6
Bear River—stream (2) ..... UT-8
Bear River—stream ..... WA-9
Bear River—stream ..... WI-6
Bear River—stream (2) ..... WY-8
Bear River Battleground—hist pl ..... ID-8
Bear River Bay—bay ..... UT-8
Bear River Campground—locale ..... UT-8
Bear River Canal—canal ..... CA-9
Bear River Canal—canal ..... UT-8
Bear River Canal—canal ..... WY-8
Bear River Cem—cemetery ..... UT-8
**Bear River City**—pop pl ..... UT-8
Bear River City Sch—school ..... UT-8
Bear River Creek—stream ..... MN-6
Bear River Divide—ridge ..... WY-8
Bear River Duck Club—other ..... UT-8
Bear River HS—school ..... UT-8
Bear River HS Science Bldg—hist pl ..... UT-8
**Bear River Lake**—pop pl ..... CA-9
Bear River Migratory Bird Ref—park ..... UT-8
Bear River Mountains ..... UT-8
Bear River MS—school ..... UT-8
Bear River Natl Migratory Bird Refuge HQ (inundated—locale ..... UT-8
Bear River Natl Wildlife Refuge ..... UT-8
**Bear River Pines**—pop pl ..... CA-9
Bear River Range—range ..... ID-8
Bear River Range—range ..... UT-8
Bear River Ranger Station—locale ..... UT-8
Bear River Ridge—ridge ..... CA-9
Bear River Ridge—ridge ..... WA-9
Bear River Rsvr—reservoir ..... CA-9
Bear River Sch—school ..... CA-9
Bear River Shitecap ..... ME-1
Bear River Smiths Fork Trail—trail ..... UT-8
Bear River Valley—valley ..... UT-8
Bear River Valley Heliport—airport ..... UT-8
Bear River Valley Hosp—hospital ..... UT-8
Bear Road Sch—school ..... NY-2
Bear Rock ..... RI-1
Bear Rock—bar ..... AK-9
Bear Rock—pillar ..... CT-1
Bear Rock—summit ..... PA-2
Bear Rock—summit ..... WY-8
Bear Rock Bog—swamp ..... NH-1
Bear Rock Dam One—dam ..... PA-2
Bear Rock Dam Two—dam ..... PA-2
Bear Rock Falls—falls ..... MA-1
Bear Rock Lakes State Rec Area—park ..... WV-2
Bear Rock Pond—reservoir ..... CT-1
Bearrock Run ..... PA-2
Bear Rock Run—stream ..... PA-2
Bear Rocks ..... PA-2
Bear Rocks—pillar ..... VA-3
Bear Rocks—pillar ..... WV-2
**Bear Rocks**—pop pl ..... PA-2
Bear Rocks—ridge ..... WY-8
Bear Rocks—summit (2) ..... PA-2
Bear Rock Sch—school ..... NH-1
Bear Rock Sch (historical)—school ..... PA-2
Bear Rock Stream—stream ..... MA-1
Bear Rock Swamp—swamp ..... PA-2
Bear Rock Trail—trail ..... VA-3
Bear Rough Lake—lake ..... TX-5
Bear RR Station—building ..... AZ-5
Bear Rsvr—reservoir ..... CA-9
Bear Run ..... PA-2
Bear Run—stream ..... CO-8
Bear Run—stream ..... ID-8
Bear Run—stream ..... IN-6
Bear Run—stream (4) ..... KY-4
Bear Run—stream (9) ..... OH-6
Bear Run—stream (27) ..... PA-2
Bear Run—stream ..... SD-7
Bear Run—stream (2) ..... VA-3
Bear Run—stream (27) ..... WV-2
Bear Run—stream ..... WY-8
Bear Run Camp—locale ..... PA-2
Bear Run Ch—church ..... OH-6
Bear Run Ch—church ..... PA-2
Bear Run Ch—church ..... WV-2
Bear Run Creek—stream ..... MT-8
Bear Run Dam—dam ..... PA-2
Bear Run Junction—locale ..... PA-2
**Bear Run Mine**—pop pl ..... OH-6
Bear Run Ridge—ridge ..... PA-2
Bear Run Rsvr—reservoir ..... PA-2
Bear Run Sch—school ..... WV-2
Bear Run Trail—trail ..... PA-2
Bear Run Trail—trail ..... WV-2
Bear Saddle—gap ..... AZ-5
Bear Saddle—gap ..... ID-8
Bear Saint Sch—school ..... CA-9
Bear Sand Ridges—ridge ..... SC-3
Bears Bluff—locale ..... SC-3
Bears Branch ..... IN-6
Bears Breast Mtn—summit ..... WA-9
Bear Sch—school ..... AL-4
Bear Sch—school ..... OH-6
Bear Sch (abandoned)—school ..... MO-7
Bears Claw—ridge ..... UT-8
Bears Creek ..... AL-4
Bears Creek ..... MS-4
**Bears Crossroads**—pop pl ..... PA-2
Bearsdale—locale ..... IL-6
Bearsdale Creek—stream ..... WI-6
Bearsdale Springs—spring ..... WI-6
Bears Den—basin ..... CO-8
Bears Den—basin ..... MT-8
Bears Den—cave ..... NH-1
Bears Den—summit ..... MA-1
Bears Den, The—gap ..... MA-1
Bears Den Hill—summit ..... VT-1
Bears Den Hillock—summit ..... ND-7
Bears Den Oil and Gas Field—oilfield ..... MT-8
Bears Den Run—stream ..... OH-6
Bearsden Waterhole—lake ..... ID-8
Bearse, Capt. Allen H., House—hist pl ..... MA-1
Bearse, Capt. Oliver, House—hist pl ..... MA-1
Bears Ears—summit ..... UT-8
Bears Ears, The—summit ..... CO-8
Bears Ears Mountain ..... CO-8
Bears Ears Mtn—summit ..... WY-8
Bears Ears Peak ..... CO-8
Bears Ears Peaks—summit ..... CO-8
Bear's Ears Plateau ..... UT-8
Bears Ears Trail—trail ..... CO-8
Bears Ears Trail—trail ..... WY-8
Bearse Brook—stream ..... ME-1
Bear Seep—spring ..... UT-8
Bear Seep Tank—reservoir ..... AZ-5
Bears Element Creek—stream ..... VA-3
Bearse Pond—lake ..... MA-1
Bearse Rock—rock ..... MA-1
Bearse Shoal—bar ..... MA-1
Bearse's Pond ..... MA-1
Bearses Rock ..... MA-1
Bearses Shoal ..... MA-1
Bears Foot Creek—stream ..... TX-5
Bears Glen—valley ..... OK-5
Bears Grass Creek—stream ..... WI-6
Bears Gulch—valley ..... CO-8
Bears Ham Sch (historical)—school ..... AL-4
Bears Head—summit ..... CO-8
Bears Head—summit ..... PA-2
Bears Head Branch—stream ..... NJ-2
Bears Hell—ridge ..... WV-2
Bears Hell Run—stream ..... WV-2
Bear Sign Branch—stream ..... TN-4
Bear Sign Canyon—valley ..... AZ-5
Bear Sign Tank—reservoir ..... AZ-5
**Bear Skin**—pop pl ..... LA-4
**Bearskin**—pop pl ..... NC-3
Bear Skin Bayou—stream ..... LA-4
Bearskin Branch—stream ..... KY-4
Bearskin Canyon—valley ..... CA-9
Bearskin Creek—stream ..... AK-9
Bearskin Creek—stream ..... CA-9
Bearskin Creek—stream ..... ID-8
Bearskin Creek—stream (2) ..... NC-3
Bearskin Creek—stream ..... VA-3
Bearskin Creek—stream ..... WI-6
Bearskin Flat—flat ..... UT-8
Bearskin Grove—woods ..... CA-9
Bearskin Gulch—valley ..... AK-9
Bearskin Hollow—valley ..... KY-4
Bearskin Lake ..... MN-6
Bearskin Lake—lake ..... AR-4
Bearskin Lake—lake (2) ..... MN-6
Bearskin Lake—lake ..... WI-6
Bearskin Lookout Tower—locale ..... MN-6
Bearskin Meadow—flat ..... CA-9
Bearskin Meadows—flat ..... ID-8
Bearskin Mtn—summit ..... UT-8
Bearskin Neck—cape ..... MA-1
Bearskin River ..... MN-6
Bearskin Swamp—stream ..... NC-3
Bear Skull—summit ..... ID-8
Bear Skull—summit ..... OR-9
Bear Skull Camp—locale ..... CA-9
Bearskull Creek ..... MT-8
Bear Skull Creek—stream ..... CA-9
Bearskull Creek—stream ..... GA-3
Bear Skull Creek—stream ..... ID-8
Bear Skull Creek—stream ..... MS-4
Bear Skull Creek—stream ..... MT-8
Bearskull Creek—stream ..... MT-8
Bearskull Lake—lake ..... WI-6
Bear Skull Mtn—summit ..... MT-8
Bear Skull Rims—ridge ..... OR-9
Bear Skull Rock—pillar ..... WI-6
Bear Skull Shelter—locale ..... WA-9
Bear Skull Spring—spring ..... OR-9
Bearslee Lake—lake ..... MI-6
Bearsley Brook—stream ..... ME-1
Bear Slide Creek—stream ..... IN-6
**Bearslide (subdivision)**—pop pl ..... NC-3
Bear Slough ..... AR-4
Bear Slough—gut (2) ..... AR-4
Bear Slough—gut (2) ..... CA-9
Bear Slough—gut ..... TX-5
Bear Slough—stream (4) ..... AR-4
Bear Slough—stream ..... LA-4
Bear Slough—stream ..... MI-6
Bear Slough—stream ..... MO-7
Bear's Mill—hist pl ..... OH-6
**Bears Mill**—pop pl ..... OH-6
Bears Mountain ..... MA-1
Bear's Paw Mountain ..... MT-8
Bears Paw Mtns—range ..... MT-8
Bears Plaza (Shop Ctr)—locale ..... FL-3
Bear Spring ..... NM-5
Bear Spring—locale ..... VA-3
**Bear Spring**—pop pl ..... MT-8
**Bear Spring**—pop pl ..... TN-4
Bear Spring—spring (29) ..... AZ-5
Bear Spring—spring ..... AR-4
Bear Spring—spring (14) ..... CA-9
Bear Spring—spring (3) ..... CO-8
Bear Spring—spring ..... FL-3
Bear Spring—spring (2) ..... ID-8
Bear Spring—spring ..... MO-7
Bear Spring—spring (2) ..... MT-8
Bear Spring—spring ..... NV-8
Bear Spring—spring (7) ..... NM-5
Bear Spring—spring (9) ..... OR-9
Bear Spring—spring (2) ..... PA-2
Bear Spring—spring ..... SD-7
Bear Spring—spring ..... TN-4
Bear Spring—spring (2) ..... TX-5
Bear Spring—spring (5) ..... UT-8
Bear Spring—spring (3) ..... WA-9
Bear Spring—spring (5) ..... WY-8
Bear Spring Branch ..... TX-5
Bear Spring Branch—stream ..... VA-3
Bear Spring Branch—stream ..... WV-2
Bear Spring Brook—stream ..... NH-1
Bear Spring Canyon—valley (3) ..... AZ-5
Bear Spring Creek—stream ..... ID-8
Bear Spring Creek—stream ..... SD-7
Bear Spring Creek—stream ..... TX-5
Bear Spring Creek—stream ..... WY-8
Bear Spring Flat ..... CA-9
Bear Spring Flats—flat ..... CA-9
Bear Spring Furnace (historical)—locale ..... TN-4
Bear Spring Gap—gap ..... AR-4
Bear Spring Hollow—valley ..... AR-4
Bear Spring Hollow—valley ..... MO-7
Bear Spring Hollow—valley ..... TN-4
Bear Spring House, Guardhouse, and Spring—hist pl ..... AZ-5
Bear Spring Mountain Game Mngmt Area—park ..... NY-2
Bear Spring Mtn—summit ..... NY-2
Bear Spring Number One—spring ..... AZ-5
Bear Spring Pass—gap ..... AZ-5
Bearspring Post Office ..... TN-4
Bear Spring Post Office (historical)—building ..... TN-4
Bear Spring Ranch—locale ..... AZ-5
Bear Springs—spring (3) ..... AZ-5
Bear Springs—spring (2) ..... CA-9
Bear Springs—spring ..... ID-8
Bear Springs—spring ..... MT-8
Bear Springs—spring (2) ..... NM-5
Bear Springs—spring ..... NY-2
Bear Springs—spring ..... TX-5
Bear Springs—spring ..... UT-8
Bear Springs—spring ..... WI-6
Bear Springs—spring ..... WY-8
Bear Springs Arroyo—stream ..... CO-8
Bear Springs Bench—bench ..... MT-8
Bear Springs Branch ..... TX-5
Bear Springs Canyon—valley ..... AZ-5
Bear Springs Canyon—valley (3) ..... NM-5
Bear Springs Ch—church ..... TX-5
Bear Springs Coulee—valley ..... MT-8
Bear Springs Creek—stream ..... CA-9
Bear Springs Creek—stream ..... MT-8
Bear Springs Creek—stream ..... TX-5
Bear Springs Draw—valley ..... AZ-5
Bear Springs Flat—flat ..... AZ-5
Bear Springs Forest Camp—locale ..... OR-9
Bear Springs Guard Station—locale ..... NM-5
Bear Springs Gulch—valley ..... CO-8
Bear Springs Hills—range ..... CO-8
Bear Springs Knoll—summit ..... AZ-5
Bear Springs Landing—locale ..... TN-4
Bear Springs Peak—summit ..... NM-5
Bear Springs Ranch—locale ..... NM-5
Bear Springs Ranger Station—locale ..... OR-9
Bear Springs Rsvr—reservoir ..... CO-8
Bear Springs Tank—reservoir ..... AZ-5
Bear Springs Trail One Hundred Ten—trail ..... AZ-5
Bear Springs Wash—stream ..... AZ-5
Bear Springs Windmill—locale ..... NM-5
Bear's River ..... MT-8
Bears Rocks—summit ..... PA-2
Bears Run ..... PA-2
Bears Acad—school ..... MS-4
Bears Sch—school ..... PA-2
Bears Sch (abandoned)—school ..... PA-2
Bearss Drain—canal ..... MI-6
Bearss Plaza—post sta ..... FL-3
Bear Stand—locale ..... TN-4
Bear Station ..... DE-2
Bear Still Cove—cave ..... AL-4
Bears Tooth—peak ..... WY-8
Bear Suck Knob—summit ..... OK-5
Bearsville—locale ..... WV-2
**Bearsville**—pop pl ..... NY-2
Bear Swamp ..... NC-3
Bear Swamp ..... PA-2
Bear Swamp—lake ..... NY-2
Bear Swamp—locale ..... PA-2
Bear Swamp—stream (4) ..... NC-3
Bear Swamp—stream (2) ..... SC-3
Bear Swamp—swamp ..... AL-4
Bear Swamp—swamp (3) ..... CT-1
Bear Swamp—swamp ..... DE-2
Bear Swamp—swamp ..... FL-3
Bear Swamp—swamp ..... MD-2
Bear Swamp—swamp (7) ..... MA-1
Bear Swamp—swamp (3) ..... MI-6
Bear Swamp—swamp (5) ..... NJ-2
Bear Swamp—swamp (11) ..... NY-2
Bear Swamp—swamp (3) ..... NC-3
Bear Swamp—swamp (13) ..... PA-2
Bear Swamp—swamp (3) ..... RI-1
Bear Swamp—swamp (2) ..... SC-3
Bear Swamp—swamp (2) ..... VT-1
Bear Swamp—swamp ..... WA-9
Bear Swamp Bridge—bridge ..... NC-3
Bear Swamp Brook—stream ..... CT-1
Bear Swamp Brook—stream ..... MA-1
Bear Swamp Brook—stream (2) ..... NJ-2
Bear Swamp (CCD)—cens area ..... SC-3
Bear Swamp Ch—church (2) ..... NC-3
Bear Swamp Ch—church ..... SC-3
Bear Swamp Creek—stream ..... MI-6
Bear Swamp Creek—stream ..... NJ-2
Bear Swamp Creek—stream ..... NY-2
Bear Swamp Creek—stream ..... NC-3
Bear Swamp Creek—stream ..... PA-2
Bear Swamp Ditch—canal ..... MI-6
Bear Swamp Drain—canal (2) ..... MI-6
Bear Swamp Hill—summit ..... NJ-2
Bear Swamp Lake—reservoir (2) ..... NJ-2
Bear Swamp Lake Dam—dam ..... NJ-2
Bear Swamp Lake Dam One—dam ..... NJ-2
Bear Swamp Lake Dam Two—dam ..... NJ-2
Bear Swamp Pond ..... NJ-2
Bear Swamp Pond—lake ..... NY-2
Bear Swamp Pond—reservoir ..... CT-1
Bear Swamp Pool—reservoir ..... DE-2
Bear Swamp Pool Dam—dam ..... DE-2
Bear Swamp Pumped Storage Lower Dam—dam ..... MA-1
Bear Swamp Pumped Storage - Upper Dam—dam ..... MA-1
Bear Swamp River—stream ..... NJ-2
Bear Swamp Run—stream ..... PA-2
Bear Swamp Sch (historical)—school ..... PA-2
Bear Swamp State For—forest ..... NY-2
Bear Swamp Upper Rsvr—reservoir ..... MA-1
Bear Tail Creek ..... MS-4
Beartail Creek—stream ..... MS-4
Bear Tank—reservoir (15) ..... AZ-5
Bear Tank—reservoir (4) ..... NM-5
Bear Tank Canyon—valley ..... AZ-5
Bear Tank Number Two—reservoir ..... AZ-5
Bear Tavern—locale ..... NJ-2
Bearthick Branch—stream ..... AL-4
Bear Thicket Ch—church ..... MO-7
Bear Thicket Creek—stream ..... AZ-5
Bear Thicket Sch (abandoned)—school ..... MO-7
Bearthick Swamp—swamp ..... FL-3
Bear Tooth—pillar ..... MT-8
Beartooth Butte—summit ..... WY-8
Beartooth Creek—stream ..... MT-8
Beartooth Creek—stream ..... NM-5
Beartooth Creek—stream ..... WY-8
Beartooth Falls—falls ..... WY-8
Beartooth Glacier—glacier ..... MT-8
Beartooth Lake—lake ..... WY-8
Beartooth Lake Campground—locale ..... WY-8
Beartooth Mountain ..... CO-8
Beartooth Mtn—summit ..... CA-9
Beartooth Mtn—summit (2) ..... MT-8
Beartooth Mtns—range ..... MT-8
Beartooth Pass—gap ..... WY-8
Beartooth Plateau ..... MT-8
Beartooth Plateau—area ..... WY-8
Beartooth Ranch—locale (3) ..... MT-8
Beartooth Range ..... MT-8
Beartop Lookout—locale ..... MT-8
Beartoter Hollow—valley ..... OK-5
Beartown ..... PA-2
Beartown—locale ..... CO-8
Beartown—locale ..... KY-4
Bear Town—locale ..... MI-6
Beartown—locale ..... MT-8
Beartown—locale (3) ..... NY-2
Beartown—locale ..... TN-4
Beartown—locale ..... VT-1
Beartown—locale ..... WV-2
Beartown—locale ..... WY-8
**Bear Town**—pop pl ..... MS-4
**Beartown**—pop pl (2) ..... OH-6
**Beartown**—pop pl (2) ..... PA-2
Beartown Branch—stream ..... VA-3
Beartown Branch—stream ..... WV-2
Beartown Brook—stream ..... MA-1
Beartown Brook—stream ..... NY-2
Bear Town (census name for McComb South)—CDP ..... MS-4
Beartown Ch—church ..... KY-4
Beartown Ch—church ..... WV-2
Beartown Ch (abandoned)—church ..... PA-2
Beartown Fork—stream ..... WV-2
Beartown Hill—summit ..... SD-7
Beartown Lake—reservoir ..... OH-6
Beartown Mtn—summit ..... MA-1
Beartown Mtn—summit ..... NC-3
Beartown Mtn—summit ..... TN-4
Beartown Mtn—summit ..... VA-3
Beartown Post Office (historical)—building ..... PA-2
Beartown Ridge—ridge ..... NC-3
Beartown Ridge—ridge ..... VA-3
Beartown Ridge—ridge ..... WV-2
Beartown Rocks—locale ..... PA-2
Beartown Rocks—summit ..... PA-2
Beartown Rocks Vista—locale ..... PA-2
**Beartown (RR name Gluck)**—pop pl ..... WV-2
Beartown Sch—school ..... KY-4
Bear Town Slough—gut ..... MI-6
Beartown State For—forest ..... MA-1
Beartown State Park—park ..... WV-2
Beartown Swamp—swamp ..... NY-2
Bear Track Canyon—valley ..... AZ-5
Beartrack Canyon—valley ..... TX-5
Beartrack Cove—bay ..... AK-9
Beartrack Creek—stream ..... AK-9
Bear Track Creek—stream ..... CO-8
Beartrack Creek—stream ..... ID-8
Bear Track Creek—stream ..... WY-8
Beartrack Hollow—valley ..... IL-6
Beartrack Island—island ..... AK-9
Beartrack Lake—lake ..... MN-6
Beartrack Lake—lake ..... WI-6
Beartrack Lakes—lake ..... CO-8
Bear Track Lookout Tower—locale ..... KY-4
Bear Track Mission Sch—school ..... KY-4
Beartrack River—stream ..... AK-9
Bear Track Run—stream ..... WV-2
Beartracks Rsvr—reservoir ..... MT-8
Bear Track Tank—reservoir (2) ..... AZ-5
Bear Trail—trail (3) ..... PA-2
Bear Trail Canyon—valley ..... AZ-5
Bear Trail Creek ..... AR-4
Beartrail Creek—stream ..... AK-9
Bear Trail Ridge—ridge ..... TN-4
Beartrail Ridge Gap—gap ..... NC-3
Bear Trap—flat ..... WY-8
**Bear Trap**—pop pl ..... WI-6
Bear Trap, The—ridge ..... CA-9
Beartrap, The—summit ..... CA-9
Bear Trap Basin—basin ..... CA-9
Beartrap Bay—bay ..... AK-9
Beartrap Brook—stream ..... ME-1
Bear Trap Brook—stream ..... NY-2
Bear Trap Cabin—locale ..... CA-9
Beartrap Canyon ..... UT-8
Bear Trap Canyon—valley ..... CA-9
Beartrap Canyon—valley ..... CA-9
Bear Trap Canyon—valley (2) ..... CA-9
Beartrap Canyon—valley (2) ..... CA-9
Bear Trap Canyon—valley (3) ..... CA-9
Beartrap Canyon—valley ..... CA-9
Bear Trap Canyon—valley ..... CO-8
Beartrap Canyon—valley ..... ID-8
Beartrap Canyon—valley ..... MT-8
Bear Trap Canyon—valley (2) ..... NM-5
Bear Trap Canyon—valley ..... OR-9
Bear Trap Canyon—valley (3) ..... UT-8
Bear Trap Canyon—valley ..... WA-9
Bear Trap Cave—cave ..... ID-8
Beartrap Cave—cave ..... SD-7
Beartrap Creek ..... MT-8
Beartrap Creek—stream (2) ..... CA-9
Bear Trap Creek—stream ..... CA-9
Beartrap Creek—stream (5) ..... CA-9
Bear Trap Creek—stream ..... CA-9
Beartrap Creek—stream ..... CO-8
Bear Trap Creek—stream ..... ID-8
Beartrap Creek—stream ..... ID-8
Beartrap Creek—stream ..... MN-6
Beartrap Creek—stream ..... MT-8
Bear Trap Creek—stream ..... MT-8
Beartrap Creek—stream ..... MT-8
Beartrap Creek—stream ..... NY-2
Beartrap Creek—stream ..... OR-9
Bear Trap Creek—stream ..... UT-8
Beartrap Creek—stream ..... WI-6
Beartrap Creek—stream ..... WY-8
Bear Trap Creek—stream (2) ..... WY-8
Beartrap Draw—valley ..... MT-8
Beartrap Falls—falls ..... WI-6
Beartrap Flat—flat ..... CA-9
Beartrap Flat—flat ..... UT-8
Beartrap Fork—stream ..... MT-8
Beartrap Fork—stream ..... UT-8
Bear Trap Gap—gap ..... CA-9
Beartrap Gulch—summit ..... CO-8
Bear Trap Gulch—valley ..... CA-9
Beartrap Gulch—valley ..... CA-9
Bear Trap Gulch—valley ..... CO-8
Beartrap Gulch—valley ..... ID-8
Bear Trap Gulch—valley ..... MT-8
Beartrap Gulch—valley (2) ..... MT-8
Bear Trap Gulch—valley ..... WY-8
Beartrap Hollow—valley ..... PA-2
Bear Trap Hollow—valley (2) ..... PA-2
Beartrap Hollow—valley ..... PA-2
Beartrap Island—island ..... NC-3
Beartrap Island—island ..... VT-1
Beartrap Junction—gap ..... WY-8
Beartrap Knob—summit ..... NC-3
Bear Trap Knoll—summit ..... UT-8
Beartrap Lake—lake (2) ..... CA-9
Beartrap Lake—lake ..... MN-6
Bear Trap Lake—lake ..... WI-6
Beartrap Lake—lake ..... WI-6
Bear Trap Lava Tube—lava ..... ID-8
Beartrap Lookout—locale ..... ID-8
Beartrap Meadow—flat ..... CA-9
Bear Trap Meadow—flat ..... CA-9
Beartrap Meadow—flat (2) ..... CA-9
Beartrap Meadow—flat ..... OR-9
Beartrap Meadow County Park—park ..... WY-8
Beartrap Meadows ..... OR-9
Beartrap Meadows—flat ..... WY-8
Bear Trap Mountain—summit ..... PA-2
Beartrap Mtn—summit ..... CA-9
Beartrap Mtn—summit ..... MT-8
Beartrap Peak—summit ..... MT-8
Bear Trap Ridge—ridge ..... CA-9
Beartrap Ridge—ridge ..... CA-9
Bear Trap Ridge—ridge ..... CA-9
Beartrap Ridge—ridge ..... ID-8
Beartrap Ridge—ridge ..... NC-3
Bear Trap Ridge—ridge ..... UT-8
Bear Trap River ..... MN-6
Beartrap River—stream ..... MN-6
Beartrap Saddle—gap (2) ..... ID-8
Bear Trap Saddle—gap ..... ID-8
Bear Trap Saddle Trail—trail ..... ID-8
Bear Trap Spring—spring ..... AZ-5
Bear Trap Spring—spring ..... CA-9
Beartrap Spring—spring ..... CA-9
Bear Trap Spring—spring ..... CA-9
Beartrap Spring—spring ..... CA-9
Bear Trap Spring—spring ..... CA-9
Beartrap Spring—spring ..... CA-9
Bear Trap Spring—spring (2) ..... CA-9
Beartrap Spring—spring ..... ID-8
Bear Trap Spring—spring ..... NV-8
Beartrap Spring—spring ..... OR-9
Bear Trap Spring—spring ..... OR-9
Bear Trap Swamp—swamp ..... NY-2
Beartrap Trail—trail ..... OR-9
Bear Trap Trail—trail ..... PA-2
Beartree Branch—stream ..... KY-4
Beartree Branch—stream ..... WV-2
Bear Tree Brook—stream ..... RI-1
Beartree Canyon—valley ..... CA-9
Beartree Creek—stream ..... OR-9
Beartree Fork—stream ..... KY-4
Beartree Gap—gap ..... KY-4
Bear Tree Gap—gap ..... VA-3
Bear Tree Guard Station—locale ..... OR-9
Beartree Hollow—valley ..... TN-4
Bear Tree Meadow—flat ..... CA-9
Beartree Run—stream (2) ..... WV-2
Beartree Sch—school ..... KY-4
Bear Tree Spring—spring ..... OR-9
Bear Twin Lakes—lake ..... CA-9
Bea Run—stream ..... IN-6
Bearup Lake—lake ..... CA-9
Bearup Mine—mine ..... NM-5
Bearup Spring—spring ..... NM-5
Bearup Well—well ..... NM-5
Bear Valley—basin ..... AZ-5
Bear Valley—basin (4) ..... CA-9
Bear Valley—basin (3) ..... OR-9
Bear Valley—flat ..... WA-9
Bear Valley—locale ..... MN-6
**Bear Valley**—pop pl (2) ..... CA-9
**Bear Valley**—pop pl ..... PA-2
**Bear Valley**—pop pl ..... WI-6
Bear Valley—post sta ..... CO-8
Bear Valley—valley (2) ..... AK-9
Bear Valley—valley ..... AZ-5
Bear Valley—valley (16) ..... CA-9
Bear Valley—valley ..... CO-8
Bear Valley—valley ..... ID-8
Bear Valley—valley ..... MN-6
Bear Valley—valley ..... NM-5
Bear Valley—valley ..... NY-2
Bear Valley—valley (2) ..... OR-9
Bear Valley—valley (3) ..... PA-2
Bear Valley—valley (2) ..... UT-8
Bear Valley—valley ..... WI-6
Bear Valley Archeol Site—hist pl ..... CA-9
Bear Valley Buttes—summit ..... CA-9
Bear Valley Campground—locale ..... ID-8
Bear Valley Canyon—valley ..... OR-9
Bear Valley Cem—cemetery ..... CO-8
Bear Valley Creek ..... OR-9
Bear Valley Creek ..... PA-2
Bear Valley Creek—stream (4) ..... CA-9
Bear Valley Creek—stream (2) ..... ID-8
Bear Valley Creek—stream ..... OR-9
Bear Valley Dam—dam ..... PA-2
Bear Valley Draw—valley ..... CO-8
Bear Valley Fire Control Station—locale ..... CA-9
Bear Valley Guard Station—locale ..... OR-9
Bear Valley Guard Station—locale ..... UT-8
Bear Valley Gulch—valley ..... OR-9
Bear Valley High Line Aqueduct—canal ..... CA-9
Bear Valley Junction—locale ..... UT-8
Bear Valley Lakes—reservoir ..... ID-8
Bear Valley Lutheran Cem—cemetery ..... SD-7
Bear Valley Lutheran Church ..... SD-7
Bear Valley Meadows Camp—locale ..... CA-9
Bear Valley Mountains ..... AZ-5
Bear Valley Mtn—summit ..... ID-8
Bear Valley Natl Wildlife Ref—reserve ..... OR-9
Bear Valley Peak ..... UT-8
Bear Valley Picnic Area—area ..... PA-2
Bear Valley Ranch—locale ..... AZ-5
Bear Valley Ranch—locale (2) ..... CA-9
Bear Valley Ranger Station ..... UT-8
Bear Valley Ridge—ridge ..... CO-8
Bear Valley Rsvr—reservoir ..... CA-9
Bear Valley Rsvr—reservoir ..... UT-8
Bear Valley Sch—school (2) ..... CA-9
Bear Valley Sch—school ..... CO-8

Beaumont Ch (historical)—church ... AL-4
Beaumont Ch of God—church ... MS-4
Beaumont Commercial District—hist pl ... TX-5
Beaumont Country Club—other ... TX-5
Beaumont Creek—stream ... TX-5
Beaumont Elementary School ... PA-2
Beaumont Elem Sch—school ... MS-4
Beaumont Fire Tower—locale ... MS-4
Beaumont Hop House—hist pl ... WI-6
Beaumont Hosp—hospital ... MI-6
Beaumont Hotel—hist pl ... CO-8
Beaumont Hotel—hist pl ... WI-6
Beaumont Hotel Airp—airport ... KS-7
Beaumont HS—school ... MS-4
Beaumont HS—school ... MO-7
Beaumont HS—school ... OH-6
Beaumont JHS—school ... KY-4
**Beaumont Learning Center**—pop pl ... VA-3
Beaumont Medical Bldg—hist pl ... MO-7
Beaumont MS—school ... FL-3
Beaumont Oil Field—oilfield ... KS-7
Beaumont Park—park ... NC-3
**Beaumont Park**—pop pl ... KY-4
**Beaumont Park**—pop pl ... MD-2
**Beaumont Place**—pop pl ... TX-5
Beaumont Pond—lake ... MA-1
Beaumont Sch—school ... CA-9
Beaumont Sch—school ... OH-6
Beaumont Sch—school ... OR-9
Beaumont Sch—school ... PA-2
Beaumont Sch—school ... TN-4
Beaumont Sch—school ... WI-6
Beaumont South Oil Field—oilfield ... KS-7
**Beaumont (subdivision)**—pop pl ... NC-3
Beaumont-Tyson Quarry District—hist pl ... MO-7
Beaumont Water Canal ... TX-5
Beaumont Y.M.C.A.—hist pl ... TX-5
Beaumount—locale ... GA-3
Beauna Vista Plantation—locale ... LA-4
Beauport—hist pl ... MA-1
Beauport Museum—building ... MA-1
Beaupre Coulee—valley ... MT-8
Beaupre Sch—school ... IL-6
Beaupre Springs—spring ... WI-6
Beauprey Lake—lake ... WI-6
Beauprey Springs—lake ... WI-6
**Beauregard**—pop pl ... AL-4
**Beauregard**—pop pl ... MS-4
Beauregard, Bayou—gut ... LA-4
Beauregard Bay—bay ... VI-3
Beauregard Cem—cemetery ... MS-4
Beauregard Creek—stream ... CA-9
Beauregard Island—island ... LA-4
Beauregard JHS—school ... LA-4
Beauregard Lake—lake ... WI-6
Beauregard-Marvyn (CCD)—cens area ... AL-4
Beauregard-Marvyn Division—civil ... AL-4
**Beauregard Parish**—pop pl ... LA-4
Beauregard Parish Courthouse—hist pl ... LA-4
Beauregard Parish Jail—hist pl ... LA-4
Beauregard Post Office (historical)—building ... MS-4
Beauregard Sch—school ... AL-4
Beauregard Sch—school ... LA-4
Beauregard Tower—pillar ... LA-4
Beauregard Town Hist Dist—hist pl ... LA-4
Beauregard Town Hist Dist (Boundary Increase)—hist pl ... LA-4
Beaureguard Creek ... CA-9
Beauridell Sch—school ... WA-9
Beaurline Gas Field—oilfield ... TX-5
Beaus Creek ... AL-4
Beausite Lake—lake ... WA-9
**Beautancus**—pop pl ... NC-3
Beautiful ... MN-6
Beautiful—other ... PA-2
Beautiful, Lake—lake ... MN-6
Beautiful, Mount—summit ... AZ-5
Beautiful Ch (historical)—church ... MS-4
Beautiful Creek—stream ... MN-6
Beautiful Gate Ch—church ... SC-3
Beautiful Hammock—island ... FL-3
Beautiful Island—island ... AK-9
Beautiful Island—island ... FL-3
Beautiful Lake—lake ... AR-4
Beautiful Lake—lake ... WI-6
Beautiful Ligh Ch—church ... GA-3
Beautiful Mtn—summit ... CO-8
Beautiful Mtn—summit ... NM-5
Beautiful Pond ... VT-1
Beautiful Ridge—ridge ... OH-6
Beautiful Run—stream ... VA-3
Beautiful Savior Ch—church ... MI-6
Beautiful Saviour Evangelical Lutheran Ch—church ... KS-7
Beautiful Star Ch—church ... MS-4
Beautiful Valley—valley ... AZ-5
Beautiful Valley Ch—church ... NC-3
Beautiful Valley Well—well ... AZ-5
Beautiful View Cem—cemetery ... MD-2
Beautiful Zion AME Zion Church ... AL-4
Beautiful Zion Cem—cemetery ... AL-4
Beautiful Zion Cem—cemetery ... GA-3
Beautiful Zion Ch ... MS-4
Beautiful Zion Ch—church (2) ... AL-4
Beautiful Zion Ch—church ... GA-3
Beautiful Zion Ch—church (3) ... MS-4
Beautiful Zion Ch—church ... NC-3
Beautiful Zion Ch—church ... VA-3
Beautiful Zion Ch (historical)—church ... MS-4
Beautiful Zion Ch Number Two—church ... MS-4
**Beauty**—pop pl ... KY-4
**Beauty**—pop pl ... WV-2
Beauty, Lake—lake ... FL-3
Beauty, Lake—lake ... WA-9
Beauty Bay—bay ... AK-9
Beauty Bay—bay ... ID-8
Beauty Camp—locale ... PA-2
Beauty Camp—locale ... WA-9
Beauty Cave—cave ... ID-8
Beauty Cove—bay ... MO-7
Beauty Creek—stream ... AK-9
Beauty Creek—stream ... ID-8
Beauty Creek—stream ... IN-6
Beauty Creek—stream ... MT-8
Beauty Creek—stream ... NY-2
Beauty Creek—stream ... WA-9
Beauty Flat—flat ... CA-9
Beauty Grove Ch—church ... GA-3
**Beauty Hill**—pop pl ... TN-4
Beauty Hill—summit (3) ... NH-1
Beauty Hill Cem—cemetery ... TN-4
Beauty Hill Ch—church ... SC-3
Beauty Hill Ch—church ... TN-4
Beauty Lake ... MN-6
Beauty Lake—lake (2) ... CA-9
Beauty Lake—lake (7) ... MN-6
Beauty Lake—lake ... WI-6
Beauty Lake—lake (2) ... WY-8
Beauty Lakebed—flat ... MN-6
Beauty Mine—mine ... CA-9
Beauty Mountain Ch—church ... WV-2
Beauty Mtn—summit ... CA-9
Beauty Mtn—summit ... WA-9
Beauty Park—flat ... WY-8
Beauty Park Creek—stream ... WY-8
Beauty Peak—summit (3) ... CA-9
Beauty Peak—summit ... NV-8
Beauty Peak—summit ... WA-9
Beauty Ridge—ridge ... KY-4
Beauty Run—stream ... PA-2
Beauty Shore Lake—lake ... MN-6
Beauty Spot—summit ... NC-3
Beauty Spot—summit ... TN-4
Beauty Spot Cem—cemetery ... SC-3
Beauty Spot Ch—church ... NC-3
Beauty Spot Gap—gap ... NC-3
Beauty Spot Gap—gap ... TN-4
Beauty Spot Sch—school ... SC-3
Beauty Spring ... TN-4
Beauty Spring—spring ... CA-9
Beauty Spring—spring ... TX-5
Beauty Springs—spring ... AZ-5
Beautys Run—stream ... PA-2
Beauty Valley—valley ... ND-7
Beauty Valley Cem—cemetery ... ND-7
Beauvais Canyon—valley ... NE-7
Beauvais Creek ... MT-8
Beauvais Creek—stream ... MT-8
Beauvais' Ranche Archeol Site—hist pl ... NE-7
Beauvais Township—civil ... MO-7
Beauvis Creek ... MT-8
Beauvoir—hist pl ... MS-4
**Beauvoir**—pop pl ... MS-4
Beauvoir Elem Sch—school ... MS-4
Beauvois Creek ... MT-8
Beauvue—locale ... MD-2
**Beauxart Gardens**—pop pl ... TX-5
**Beaux Arts**—pop pl ... WA-9
Beaux Arts Park Hist Dist—hist pl ... NY-2
**Beaux Arts Village**—pop pl ... WA-9
Beauyan Lake—lake ... MI-6
Beavais Creek ... MT-8
**Beavan**—pop pl ... OH-6
BeA VAR Beaver ... MN-6
Beaven Ch ... AL-4
Beaven Mountain ... ID-8
Beaver ... KS-7
Beaver ... MN-6
Beaver ... NE-7
Beaver—fmr MCD (6) ... NE-7
Beaver—locale ... MI-6
Beaver—locale ... MN-6
Beaver—locale ... WV-2
**Beaver**—pop pl ... AK-9
**Beaver**—pop pl ... AR-4
**Beaver**—pop pl ... IA-7
**Beaver**—pop pl ... KS-7
**Beaver**—pop pl ... KY-4
**Beaver**—pop pl ... LA-4
**Beaver**—pop pl ... MA-1
**Beaver**—pop pl ... MI-6
**Beaver**—pop pl ... OH-6
**Beaver**—pop pl ... OK-5
**Beaver**—pop pl ... OR-9
**Beaver**—pop pl ... PA-2
**Beaver**—pop pl ... TN-4
**Beaver**—pop pl ... UT-8
**Beaver**—pop pl ... WA-9
**Beaver**—pop pl ... WV-2
**Beaver**—pop pl ... WI-6
Beaver, John, House—hist pl ... VA-3
Beaver, Thomas, Free Library and Danville YMCA—hist pl ... PA-2
Beaver Acad (historical)—school ... TN-4
**Beaver Acres**—pop pl ... PA-2
Beaver Acres Sch—school ... OR-9
Beaver-Adams Sch—school ... PA-2
Beaver Airstrip—airport ... IN-6
Beaver and Belfast Mine—mine ... CO-8
Beaver ANV733—reserve ... AK-9
Beaver Area Junior Senior HS—school ... PA-2
Beaver Army Terminal—other ... OR-9
Beaver Ball Creek—stream ... MT-8
Beaverball Creek—stream ... MT-8
Beaver Baptist Ch—church ... TN-4
Beaver Basin—basin ... CA-9
Beaver Basin—basin ... CO-8
Beaver Basin—basin ... MT-8
Beaver Basin—basin ... UT-8
Beaver Bay—bay ... AK-9
Beaver Bay—bay ... MI-6
Beaver Bay—bay ... MN-6
Beaver Bay—bay ... MT-8
Beaver Bay—bay ... NY-2
Beaver Bay—bay ... WI-6
Beaver Bay—bay ... WY-8
Beaver Bay—other ... MN-6
**Beaver Bay**—pop pl ... MN-6
Beaver Bay—swamp ... FL-3
Beaver Bayou ... AR-4
Beaver Bayou—stream ... AR-4
Beaver Bayou—stream ... LA-4
Beaver Bayou—stream (2) ... MS-4
Beaver Bayou Ditch—canal ... AR-4
Beaver Bayou Ditch—gut ... AR-4
Beaver Bay River ... MN-6
**Beaver (Beaver City)**—pop pl ... OK-5
Beaver Bend Sch—school ... OK-5
Beaver Bill Creek—stream ... WA-9
Beaver Blockade Lake ... MI-6
Beaver Bog—lake ... ME-1
Beaver Bog—swamp ... CT-1
Beaver Bog—swamp ... ME-1
Beaver Bog Brook—stream ... ME-1
Beaver Bog Ch—church ... CT-1
Beaver Bog Mtn—summit ... CT-1
Beaver Bogs—swamp ... ME-1
Beaver Borough—civil ... PA-2
Beaver Bottom—bend ... UT-8
**Beaver Bottom**—pop pl ... KY-4
Beaver Bottoms—bend ... UT-8
Beaver Box ... UT-8
Beaver Brake—stream ... AR-4
Beaver Branch ... DE-2
Beaver Branch ... VA-3
Beaver Branch—gut ... TN-4
Beaver Branch—stream (6) ... AL-4
Beaver Branch—stream ... DE-2
Beaver Branch—stream ... FL-3
Beaver Branch—stream ... GA-3
Beaver Branch—stream ... IA-7
Beaver Branch—stream ... KY-4
Beaver Branch—stream (3) ... LA-4
Beaver Branch—stream ... ME-1
Beaver Branch—stream ... MD-2
Beaver Branch—stream (5) ... MS-4
Beaver Branch—stream ... MO-7
Beaver Branch—stream ... NJ-2
Beaver Branch—stream (4) ... NC-3
Beaver Branch—stream ... OK-5
Beaver Branch—stream ... PA-2
Beaver Branch—stream ... SC-3
Beaver Branch—stream ... TX-5
Beaver Branch—stream (3) ... VA-3
Beaver Branch—stream ... WV-2
Beaver Branch—stream ... WI-6
Beaver Branch Oil Field—oilfield ... MS-4
Beaver Brook ... CT-1
Beaverbrook ... CT-1
Beaver Brook ... MA-1
Beaver Brook ... MN-6
Beaver Brook ... NH-1
Beaver Brook ... NY-2
Beaver Brook ... RI-1
Beaver Brook ... VT-1
Beaver Brook ... WI-6
Beaver Brook—locale ... WI-6
**Beaverbrook**—pop pl ... CT-1
**Beaver Brook**—pop pl ... DE-2
**Beaverbrook**—pop pl ... MD-2
**Beaver Brook**—pop pl ... MA-1
**Beaver Brook**—pop pl ... NY-2
**Beaverbrook**—pop pl ... NC-3
**Beaver Brook**—pop pl ... PA-2
Beaver Brook—stream (3) ... CO-8
Beaver Brook—stream (8) ... CT-1
Beaver Brook—stream (31) ... ME-1
Beaver Brook—stream (19) ... MA-1
Beaver Brook—stream (2) ... MN-6
Beaver Brook—stream (15) ... NH-1
Beaver Brook—stream (6) ... NJ-2
Beaver Brook—stream (20) ... NY-2
Beaver Brook—stream (12) ... VT-1
Beaver Brook—stream (2) ... WI-6
Beaver Brook—uninc pl ... MA-1
**Beaver Brook Apartments**—pop pl ... DE-2
Beaver Brook Canyon—valley ... CO-8
Beaver Brook Cem—cemetery ... NY-2
Beaver Brook Corners—locale ... NY-2
Beaver Brook Country Club—locale ... TN-4
Beaver Brook Creek ... CO-8
Beaver Brook Falls—falls (2) ... NH-1
Beaver Brook Flowed Meadow ... MA-1
Beaver Brook Lake—lake ... ME-1
Beaver Brook Lodge—locale ... CO-8
**Beaver Brook Manor (subdivision)**—pop pl ... PA-2
Beaver Brook Meadow—swamp ... CT-1
Beaver Brook Mtn—summit ... CT-1
Beaver Brook Park—park ... MA-1
Beaver Brook Ranch—locale ... CO-8
Beaver Brook Rec Area—park ... NH-1
Beaver Brook Reservation—park ... MA-1
Beaver Brook Rsvr—reservoir ... MA-1
Beaver Brook Sch—school ... GA-3
Beaver Brook Sch (abandoned)—school ... PA-2
Beaver Brook State Wildlife Area—park ... WI-6
Beaver Brook Station ... MA-1
**Beaver Brook Station**—pop pl ... MA-1
Beaver Brook Station (historical)—locale ... MA-1
**Beaver Brook (subdivision)**—pop pl ... MA-1
**Beaver Brook (Town of)**—pop pl ... WI-6
Beaver Brook Trail—trail ... CO-8
Beaver Brook Trail—trail ... NH-1
Beaver Butte ... MT-8
Beaver Butte—summit ... ID-8
Beaver Butte—summit ... OR-9
Beaver Butte Creek—stream ... OR-9
Beaver Cabin (historical)—locale ... ID-8
Beaver Camp—locale ... WY-8
Beaver Camp Cabin—locale ... AK-9
Beaver Canyon ... AZ-5
Beaver Canyon ... UT-8
Beaver Canyon—valley (4) ... AZ-5
Beaver Canyon—valley ... CA-9
Beaver Canyon—valley ... CO-8
Beaver Canyon—valley ... ID-8
Beaver Canyon—valley (4) ... NM-5
Beaver Canyon—valley ... TX-5
Beaver Canyon—valley (4) ... UT-8
Beaver Canyon Campground—locale ... UT-8
Beaver Cave—cave (2) ... AL-4
Beaver (CCD)—cens area ... KY-4
Beaver (CCD)—cens area ... OR-9
Beaver Cem—cemetery ... AR-4
Beaver Cem—cemetery (3) ... IL-6
Beaver Cem—cemetery (2) ... IA-7
Beaver Cem—cemetery ... LA-4
Beaver Cem—cemetery ... MA-1
Beaver Cem—cemetery ... MI-6
Beaver Cem—cemetery (2) ... MN-6
Beaver Cem—cemetery ... MS-4
Beaver Cem—cemetery (2) ... MO-7
Beaver Cem—cemetery ... NY-2
Beaver Cem—cemetery (2) ... OK-5
Beaver Cem—cemetery ... PA-2
Beaver Cem—cemetery ... TN-4
Beaver Cem—cemetery ... VT-1
Beaver Cem—cemetery ... WA-9
Beaver Cem—cemetery (2) ... WI-6
**Beaver Center**—pop pl ... PA-2
Beaver Center Sch—school ... IN-6
Beaver Center Sch—school ... WI-6
**Beaver Center (Township name Beaver)**—pop pl ... PA-2
Beaver Ch—church ... IL-6
Beaver Ch—church ... KY-4
Beaver Ch—church ... MN-6
Beaver Ch—church ... OH-6
Beaver Ch—church ... OK-5
Beaver Ch—church ... WI-6
Beaver Chapel—church (3) ... OH-6
Beaver Charlie Rsvr ... OR-9
Beaver Chief Falls—falls ... MT-8
Beaver City ... OK-5
Beaver City—other ... OK-5
**Beaver City**—pop pl ... IN-6
**Beaver City**—pop pl ... NE-7
**Beaver City**—pop pl ... PA-2
Beaver City Cem—cemetery ... IN-6
Beaver City Cem—cemetery ... UT-8
Beaver City Library—hist pl ... UT-8
Beaver Coll—school ... PA-2
Beaver Coulee—valley (2) ... MT-8
Beaver County—civil ... UT-8
**Beaver (County)**—pop pl ... OK-5
**Beaver County**—pop pl ... PA-2
Beaver County Airp—airport ... PA-2
Beaver County Courthouse—hist pl ... OK-5
Beaver County Courthouse—hist pl ... UT-8
Beaver County Home and Hosp—hospital ... PA-2
Beaver County Sanitarium—hospital ... PA-2
Beaver Cove—bay ... ME-1
**Beaver Cove (Town of)**—pop pl ... ME-1
Beaver Creek ... AL-4
Beaver Creek ... AZ-5
Beaver Creek ... AR-4
Beaver Creek ... CA-9
Beaver Creek ... CO-8
Beaver Creek ... GA-3
Beaver Creek ... ID-8
Beaver Creek ... IL-6
Beaver Creek ... IN-6
Beaver Creek ... IA-7
Beaver Creek ... KS-7
Beaver Creek ... KY-4
Beaver Creek ... LA-4
Beaver Creek ... MI-6
Beaver Creek ... MN-6
Beaver Creek ... MS-4
Beaver Creek ... MO-7
Beaver Creek ... MT-8
Beaver Creek ... NE-7
Beaver Creek ... NV-8
Beaver Creek ... NY-2
Beaver Creek ... NC-3
Beaver Creek ... ND-7
Beaver Creek ... OH-6
Beaver Creek ... OK-5
Beaver Creek ... OR-9
Beaver Creek ... PA-2
Beaver Creek ... SC-3
Beaver Creek ... SD-7
Beaver Creek ... TN-4
Beaver Creek ... TX-5
Beaver Creek ... UT-8
Beaver Creek ... VA-3
Beaver Creek ... WA-9
Beaver Creek ... WV-2
Beaver Creek ... WI-6
Beaver Creek ... WY-8
Beaver Creek—area ... NC-3
Beaver Creek—locale ... FL-3
Beaver Creek—locale ... WY-8
**Beaver Creek**—pop pl ... MD-2
**Beaver Creek**—pop pl ... MN-6
**Beaver Creek**—pop pl (2) ... NC-3
**Beavercreek**—pop pl ... OH-6
**Beaver Creek**—pop pl ... OR-9
Beaver Creek—stream (26) ... AL-4
Beaver Creek—stream (11) ... AK-9
Beaver Creek—stream (3) ... AZ-5
Beaver Creek—stream (8) ... AR-4
Beaver Creek—stream (10) ... CA-9
Beaver Creek—stream (27) ... CO-8
Beaver Creek—stream ... DE-2
Beaver Creek—stream (2) ... FL-3
Beaver Creek—stream (11) ... GA-3
Beaver Creek—stream (35) ... ID-8
Beaver Creek—stream (6) ... IL-6
Beaver Creek—stream (4) ... IN-6
Beaver Creek—stream (20) ... IA-7
Beaver Creek—stream (15) ... KS-7
Beaver Creek—stream (8) ... KY-4
Beaver Creek—stream (15) ... LA-4
Beaver Creek—stream ... ME-1
Beaver Creek—stream ... MD-2
Beaver Creek—stream ... MA-1
Beaver Creek—stream (18) ... MI-6
Beaver Creek—stream (8) ... MN-6
Beaver Creek—stream (14) ... MS-4
Beaver Creek—stream (5) ... MO-7
Beaver Creek—stream (40) ... MT-8
Beaver Creek—stream (10) ... NE-7
Beaver Creek—stream (3) ... NV-8
Beaver Creek—stream ... NJ-2
Beaver Creek—stream (5) ... NM-5
Beaver Creek—stream (12) ... NY-2
Beaver Creek—stream (15) ... NC-3
Beaver Creek—stream (12) ... ND-7
Beaver Creek—stream (11) ... OH-6
Beaver Creek—stream (12) ... OK-5
Beaver Creek—stream (57) ... OR-9
Beaver Creek—stream (18) ... PA-2
Beaver Creek—stream (4) ... SC-3
Beaver Creek—stream (12) ... SD-7
Beaver Creek—stream (6) ... TN-4
Beaver Creek—stream (14) ... TX-5
Beaver Creek—stream (16) ... UT-8
Beaver Creek—stream (13) ... VA-3
Beaver Creek—stream (28) ... WA-9
Beaver Creek—stream (8) ... WV-2
Beaver Creek—stream (30) ... WI-6
Beaver Creek—stream (33) ... WY-8
Beaver Creek Access Point—park ... IA-7
Beaver Creek Bay—bay ... ND-7
Beaver Creek Boat Ramp—other ... KY-4
Beaver Creek Bridge—hist pl ... SD-7
Beaver Creek Cabin—locale ... NM-5
Beaver Creek Camp—locale ... SD-7
Beaver Creek Camp—locale ... WA-9
Beaver Creek Campground ... OR-9
Beaver Creek Campground—locale ... CA-9
Beaver Creek Campground—locale (2) ... CO-8
Beaver Creek Campground—locale (4) ... ID-8
Beaver Creek Campground—locale ... MT-8
Beaver Creek Campground—locale ... UT-8
Beaver Creek Campground—park ... AZ-5
Beaver Creek Canal—canal ... TN-4
Beaver Creek (CCD)—cens area ... OR-9
Beaver Creek Cem ... AL-4
Beaver Creek Cem—cemetery ... AL-4
Beaver Creek Cem—cemetery ... MI-6
Beaver Creek Cem—cemetery ... MT-8
Beaver Creek Cem—cemetery (2) ... NE-7
Beaver Creek Cem—cemetery ... ND-7
Beaver Creek Cem—cemetery (3) ... OH-6
Beaver Creek Cem—cemetery ... TX-5
Beaver Creek Cem—cemetery ... WA-9
Beaver Creek Cem—cemetery ... WV-2
Beaver Creek Cemetery—cemetery (2) ... OR-9
Beaver Creek Ch—church (3) ... AL-4
Beaver Creek Ch—church ... FL-3
Beaver Creek Ch—church (2) ... IA-7
Beaver Creek Ch—church (2) ... KY-4
Beaver Creek Ch—church (5) ... NC-3
Beaver Creek Ch—church (2) ... ND-7
Beavercreek Ch—church ... OH-6
Beaver Creek Ch—church ... PA-2
Beaver Creek Ch—church (5) ... SC-3
Beaver Creek Ch—church ... SD-7
Beaver Creek Ch—church (4) ... TN-4
Beaver Creek Ch—church (2) ... VA-3
Beaver Creek Ch—church (2) ... WV-2
Beaver Creek Ch (historical)—church ... AL-4
Beaver Creek Church Camp—locale ... OH-6
Beaver Creek Counting Pens—locale ... WY-8
Beaver Creek Dam—dam ... NC-3
Beaver Creek Dam—dam ... ND-7
Beaver Creek Dam—dam ... PA-2
Beaver Creek Ditch—canal ... CO-8
Beaver Creek Ditch—canal ... WY-8
Beaver Creek Driveway—trail ... OR-9
Beaver Creek East—stream ... MN-6
Beaver Creek Edmonds Creek Kelcey Creek ... NY-2
Beaver Creek Elem Sch—school ... PA-2
Beaver Creek Flats—flat ... AK-9
Beaver Creek Forest Camp—locale ... OR-9
Beaver Creek Forest Service Station—locale ... ID-8
Beaver Creek Hills—range ... WY-8
Beaver Creek Hills—summit (2) ... WY-8
Beaver Creek HS—school ... NC-3
Beaver Creek Knobs—summit ... TN-4
Beaver Creek Lake—reservoir ... IN-6
Beaver Creek Lake—reservoir ... VA-3
Beaver Creek Lake Dam—dam ... IN-6
Beaver Creek Landing (historical)—locale ... AL-4
Beaver Creek Lookout Tower—locale ... AL-4
Beaver Creek Lower Forge (historical)—locale ... TN-4
Beaver Creek Massacre Site—hist pl ... CO-8
Beaver Creek Mine—mine ... MO-7
Beaver Creek Mountains—ridge ... AL-4
Beaver Creek Mtn—summit ... VA-3
Beaver Creek Oil And Gas Field—oilfield ... WY-8
Beaver Creek Oil Field—other ... IL-6
Beaver Creek Park—park ... MT-8
Beaver Creek Pasture—flat ... CA-9
Beaver Creek Plantation—hist pl ... VA-3
Beaver Creek Pond—reservoir ... NC-3
Beaver Creek Prairie—flat ... OR-9
Beaver Creek Public Use Area—locale ... MO-7
Beaver Creek (Public Use Area)—park ... MO-7
Beaver Creek Public Use Area—park ... ND-7
Beaver Creek Ranch—locale ... AZ-5
Beaver Creek Ranch—locale ... CO-8
Beaver Creek Ranch—locale ... WY-8
Beaver Creek Ranger Station—locale ... AZ-5
Beaver Creek Ranger Station—locale ... MT-8
Beaver Creek Recreation Site—locale ... UT-8
Beaver Creek Reservoir ... IN-6
Beaver Creek Rim—cliff ... CA-9
Beaver Creek Roadhouse—locale ... AK-9
Beaver Creek Rsvr—reservoir ... CO-8
Beaver Creek Rsvr—reservoir ... OR-9
Beaver Creek Rsvr—reservoir ... VA-3
Beaver Creek Rsvr—reservoir ... WY-8
Beaver Creek Sch—school ... AZ-5
Beaver Creek Sch—school ... CO-8
Beaver Creek Sch—school ... IL-6
Beaver Creek Sch—school ... KS-7
Beaver Creek Sch—school ... KY-4
Beaver Creek Sch—school (2) ... MI-6
Beaver Creek Sch—school (5) ... MT-8
Beavercreek Sch—school ... OH-6
Beaver Creek Sch—school (2) ... OR-9
Beaver Creek Sch—school ... SC-3
Beaver Creek Sch—school (2) ... SD-7
Beaver Creek Sch—school ... WI-6
Beaver Creek Sch—school ... WY-8
Beaver Creek Sch (abandoned)—school (2) ... PA-2
Beavercreek Sch (historical)—school ... MS-4
Beaver Creek Sewage Treatment Plant—locale ... AL-4
Beaver Creek Shoals—bar ... TN-4
Beaver Creek South Oil And Gas Field—other ... IL-6
Beaver Creek Spring—spring ... MT-8
Beaver Creek Spring—spring ... WI-6
Beaver Creek Springs—spring ... ID-8
Beaver Creek Spruce Pine Supply Dam—dam ... NC-3
Beaver Creek State For—forest ... OH-6
Beaver Creek State Game Mngmt Area—park ... ND-7
Beaver Creek State Public Hunting Grounds—park ... WI-6
Beaver Creek Stump Park Trail—trail ... CO-8
**Beaver Creek (subdivision)**—pop pl ... MS-4
Beaver Creek Summit—summit ... ID-8
Beaver Creek Swamp—swamp ... LA-4
Beaver Creek Town Hall—building ... ND-7
**Beaver Creek Township**—pop pl ... ND-7
**Beaver Creek Township**—pop pl ... SD-7
Beaver Creek Township Hall—locale ... MI-6
Beaver Creek (Township of)—civ div ... IL-6
Beaver Creek (Township of)—civ div ... MI-6
Beaver Creek (Township of)—civ div ... MN-6
Beaver Creek (Township of)—civ div ... OH-6
Beaver Creek (Township of)—fmr MCD ... NC-3
Beaver Creek Trail—trail ... CO-8
Beaver Creek Trail—trail ... ID-8
Beaver Creek Trail—trail ... WV-2
Beaver Creek Trail—trail ... WY-8
Beaver Creek Upper Forge (historical)—locale ... TN-4
Beaver Creek Valley—valley ... AL-4
Beavercreek Valley Sch—school ... OH-6
Beaver Creek Valley State Park—park ... MN-6
Beaver Creek Well—well ... MT-8
Beaver Creek West—stream ... MN-6
Beaver Creek Wildlife Area—park ... OH-6
**Beaver Creek (Wisetown)**—pop pl ... IL-6
Beaver Creek Youth Camp—locale ... CO-8
Beaver Cross ... AL-4
Beaver Crossing—locale ... MN-6
Beaver Crossing—locale ... SD-7
**Beaver Crossing**—pop pl ... NE-7
Beaverdale ... IA-7
Beaverdale—locale ... GA-3
**Beaverdale**—pop pl ... IA-7
**Beaverdale**—pop pl (2) ... PA-2
Beaver Dale Ch—church ... TN-4
Beaverdale Ditch—canal ... CO-8
**Beaverdale Heights**—pop pl ... IA-7
Beaverdale-Lloydell—CDP ... PA-2
Beaverdale Memorial Park (Cemetery)—cemetery ... CT-1
Beaverdale Mine—mine ... WA-9
Beaverdale Park—park ... IA-7
Beaverdale Post Office (historical)—building ... AL-4
Beaverdale Rsvr—reservoir ... PA-2
Beaverdale Sportsmans Lodge—building ... PA-2
Beaverdam ... AZ-5
Beaverdam (2) ... MD-2
Beaver Dam ... MA-1
Beaverdam ... MS-4
Beaver Dam ... NC-3
Beaver Dam ... PA-2
Beaver Dam ... UT-8
Beaver Dam—dam ... AR-4
Beaver Dam—dam ... NJ-2
Beaver Dam—dam ... OR-9
Beaver Dam—dam ... PA-2
Beaver Dam—dam ... SD-7
Beaver Dam—dam ... UT-8
Beaver Dam—hist pl ... NC-3
Beaver Dam—locale ... AZ-5
Beaver Dam—locale ... ME-1
Beaver Dam—locale ... MD-2
Beaverdam—locale ... MS-4
Beaver Dam—locale ... NJ-2
Beaver Dam—locale ... NY-2
Beaver Dam—locale ... NC-3
Beaverdam—locale ... PA-2
Beaver Dam—locale ... UT-8
Beaverdam—locale ... WV-2
**Beaver Dam**—pop pl ... IN-6
**Beaver Dam**—pop pl ... KY-4
**Beaverdam**—pop pl ... MI-6
**Beaver Dam**—pop pl ... NJ-2
**Beaverdam**—pop pl (3) ... NC-3
**Beaverdam**—pop pl ... OH-6
**Beaver Dam**—pop pl ... PA-2
**Beaver Dam**—pop pl ... TX-5
**Beaverdam**—pop pl ... UT-8
**Beaverdam**—pop pl ... VA-3
**Beaver Dam**—pop pl ... WI-6
Beaver Dam—stream ... NC-3
Beaver Dam—swamp ... AZ-5
Beaver Dam, The—dam ... NY-2
**Beaver Dam Acres (subdivision)**—pop pl ... DE-2
Beaverdam Bald—summit ... NC-3
Beaverdam Bald—summit ... TN-4
Beaverdam Bay—swamp ... GA-3
Beaverdam Bay—swamp ... NC-3
Beaver Dam Bay—swamp (2) ... NC-3
Beaverdam Bayou—gut ... MS-4
Beaver Dam Bayou—stream ... AR-4
Beaverdam Bayou—stream ... AR-4
Beaverdam Bayou—stream ... MS-4
Beaver Dam Bayou—stream (2) ... MS-4
**Beaver Dam (Beaverdam)**—pop pl ... MD-2
Beaver Dam Bend—bend ... KY-4
Beaver Dam Brake—swamp ... MS-4
Beaver Dam Branch ... AL-4
Beaverdam Branch ... DE-2
Beaver Dam Branch ... GA-3
Beaver Dam Branch ... NC-3
Beaverdam Branch—stream ... AL-4
Beaver Dam Branch—stream ... AL-4
Beaverdam Branch—stream (3) ... AL-4
Beaver Dam Branch—stream ... AL-4
Beaverdam Branch—stream (3) ... DE-2
Beaver Dam Branch—stream ... DE-2
Beaverdam Branch—stream (3) ... DE-2
Beaverdam Branch—stream ... GA-3
Beaverdam Branch—stream ... KY-4
Beaverdam Branch—stream (3) ... MD-2
Beaver Dam Branch—stream (3) ... MS-4
Beaverdam Branch—stream ... MS-4
Beaverdam Branch—stream ... NJ-2
Beaver Dam Branch—stream ... NC-3
Beaverdam Branch—stream (14) ... NC-3
Beaverdam Branch—stream ... OR-9
Beaverdam Branch—stream ... PA-2
Beaverdam Branch—stream (6) ... SC-3
Beaverdam Branch—stream (2) ... TN-4
Beaver Dam Branch—stream ... TX-5
Beaverdam Branch—stream ... VA-3
Beaverdam Branch Beaver Creek ... PA-2
Beaver Dam Branch North Fork Mesa Creek—stream ... CO-8
Beaverdam Bridge—bridge ... DE-2
Beaverdam Bridge—bridge ... TN-4
Beaver Dam Brook ... CT-1
Beaver-dam Brook ... MA-1
Beaverdam Brook—stream (2) ... CT-1
Beaver Dam Brook—stream ... CT-1
Beaverdam Brook—stream ... ME-1
Beaver Dam Brook—stream ... ME-1
Beaverdam Brook—stream ... ME-1
Beaver Dam Brook—stream ... MA-1
Beaverdam Brook—stream (5) ... MA-1
Beaverdam Brook—stream ... NH-1
Beaverdam Brook—stream (2) ... NJ-2
Beaverdam Brook—stream (4) ... NY-2
Beaverdam Buttes—summit ... OR-9
Beaver Dam Cabin—locale ... CA-9
Beaver Dam Campground—locale ... UT-8
Beaver Dam Campground—park ... OR-9
Beaver Dam Canyon—valley ... ID-8
Beaverdam Canyon—valley ... NM-5
Beaver Dam Canyon—valley ... WY-8
Beaver Dam (CCD)—cens area ... KY-4

Beaverdam Cem—*cemetery* (2) AL-4
Beaverdam Cem—*cemetery* DE-2
Beaverdam Cem—*cemetery* GA-3
Beaverdam Cem—*cemetery* MS-4
Beaverdam Cem—*cemetery* NH-1
Beaverdam Cem—*cemetery* NC-3
Beaverdam Cem—*cemetery* SC-3
Beaver Dam Cem—*cemetery* TN-4
Beaverdam Cem—*cemetery* TN-4
Beaver Dam Cem—*cemetery* TX-5
Beaver Dam Cem—*cemetery* UT-8
*Beaverdam Ch* AL-4
Beaver Dam Ch—*church* AL-4
Beaverdam Ch—*church* (2) AL-4
Beaverdam Ch—*church* (3) GA-3
Beaver Dam Ch—*church* KY-4
Beaver Dam Ch—*church* (2) MD-2
Beaver Dam Ch—*church* MS-4
Beaverdam Ch—*church* MS-4
Beaver Dam Ch—*church* MO-7
Beaverdam Ch—*church* MO-7
Beaverdam Ch—*church* NC-3
Beaver Dam Ch—*church* NC-3
Beaverdam Ch—*church* NC-3
Beaver Dam Ch—*church* NC-3
Beaverdam Ch—*church* (7) NC-3
Beaverdam Ch—*church* (9) SC-3
Beaverdam Ch—*church* (2) TN-4
Beaver Dam Ch—*church* TN-4
Beaverdam Ch—*church* (4) VA-3
Beaver Dam Chapel—*church* KY-4
Beaverdam Ch (historical)—*church* AL-4
Beaverdam Ch (historical)—*church* TN-4
Beaver Dam Club—*other* MI-6
*Beaver Dam Creek* AL-4
*Beaver Dam Creek* AZ-5
*Beaver Dam Creek* CO-8
*Beaverdam Creek* DE-2
*Beaverdam Creek* IA-7
*Beaverdam Creek* MD-2
*Beaver Dam Creek* MS-4
*Beaver Dam Creek* NV-8
*Beaverdam Creek* NC-3
*Beaver Dam Creek* OR-9
*Beaver Dam Creek* PA-2
*Beaver Dam Creek* SC-3
*Beaver Dam Creek* SD-7
*Beaver Dam Creek* TN-4
*Beaver Dam Creek* UT-8
Beaverdam Creek—*stream* (2) AL-4
Beaver Dam Creek—*stream* AL-4
Beaverdam Creek—*stream* (4) AL-4
Beaver Dam Creek—*stream* AL-4
Beaverdam Creek—*stream* (5) AL-4
Beaver Dam Creek—*stream* AL-4
Beaverdam Creek—*stream* (6) AL-4
Beaver Dam Creek—*stream* AK-9
Beaverdam Creek—*stream* AR-4
Beaver Dam Creek—*stream* CO-8
Beaverdam Creek—*stream* CO-8
Beaver Dam Creek—*stream* (2) CO-8
Beaverdam Creek—*stream* DE-2
Beaverdam Creek—*stream* DC-2
Beaverdam Creek—*stream* (2) FL-3
Beaverdam Creek—*stream* (20) GA-3
Beaver Dam Creek—*stream* GA-3
Beaverdam Creek—*stream* (4) GA-3
Beaverdam Creek—*stream* ID-8
Beaver Dam Creek—*stream* (3) ID-8
Beaverdam Creek—*stream* ID-8
Beaverdam Creek—*stream* IN-6
Beaverdam Creek—*stream* IA-7
Beaverdam Creek—*stream* (2) KY-4
Beaver Dam Creek—*stream* KY-4
Beaverdam Creek—*stream* KY-4
Beaver Dam Creek—*stream* LA-4
Beaverdam Creek—*stream* (9) MD-2
Beaver Dam Creek—*stream* MD-2
Beaverdam Creek—*stream* MA-1
Beaver Dam Creek—*stream* MI-6
Beaverdam Creek—*stream* MI-6
Beaver Dam Creek—*stream* (2) MI-6
Beaverdam Creek—*stream* MN-6
Beaverdam Creek—*stream* MS-4
Beaverdam Creek—*stream* (2) MS-4
Beaver Dam Creek—*stream* MS-4
Beaverdam Creek—*stream* (2) MS-4
Beaver Dam Creek—*stream* MS-4
Beaverdam Creek—*stream* (2) MS-4
Beaverdam Creek—*stream* (3) MS-4
Beaver Dam Creek—*stream* (2) MS-4
Beaverdam Creek—*stream* (3) MO-7
Beaver Dam Creek—*stream* MT-8
Beaverdam Creek—*stream* (2) NJ-2
Beaverdam Creek—*stream* (4) NY-2
Beaver Dam Creek—*stream* NC-3
Beaverdam Creek—*stream* (13) NC-3
Beaver Dam Creek—*stream* NC-3
Beaver Dam Creek—*stream* (3) NC-3
Beaver Dam Creek—*stream* NC-3
Beaverdam Creek—*stream* (3) NC-3
Beaver Dam Creek—*stream* NC-3
Beaver Dam Creek—*stream* (9) NC-3
Beaver Dam Creek—*stream* NC-3
Beaverdam Creek—*stream* (11) NC-3
Beaverdam Creek—*stream* OH-6
Beaverdam Creek—*stream* (2) OK-5
Beaverdam Creek—*stream* OR-9
Beaver Dam Creek—*stream* (2) OR-9
Beaverdam Creek—*stream* (2) OR-9
Beaver Dam Creek—*stream* OR-9
Beaver Dam Creek—*stream* (5) OR-9
Beaverdam Creek—*stream* (5) PA-2
Beaverdam Creek—*stream* (27) SC-3
Beaver Dam Creek—*stream* SD-7
Beaverdam Creek—*stream* (2) TN-4
Beaver Dam Creek—*stream* TN-4
Beaver Dam Creek—*stream* (4) TN-4
Beaverdam Creek—*stream* TX-5
Beaver Dam Creek—*stream* TX-5
Beaver Dam Creek—*stream* UT-8
Beaverdam Creek—*stream* (21) VA-3
Beaver Dam Creek—*stream* WA-9
Beaver Dam Creek—*stream* WI-6
Beaver Dam Creek—*stream* WY-8
Beaverdam Creek—*stream* (2) WY-8
Beaver Dam Creek—*stream* (2) WY-8
Beaverdam Creek Cabin Area—*locale* TN-4
Beaver Dam Creek Springs—*spring* AL-4
**Beaverdam Creek Subdivision**—*pop pl* TN-4
Beaverdam Depot—*hist pl* VA-3
*Beaverdam Ditch* DE-2
Beaver Dam Ditch—*canal* AR-4
Beaver Dam Ditch—*canal* DE-2
Beaverdam Ditch—*canal* GA-3
Beaverdam Ditch—*canal* MD-2
Beaverdam Ditch—*canal* OH-6
Beaver Dam Ditch—*canal* (2) WY-8
Beaverdam Drain—*stream* (2) MI-6
Beaver Dam Draw—*valley* SD-7
Beaver Dam Draw—*valley* WY-8
**Beaverdam Estates**—*pop pl* MD-2
Beaverdam Falls—*falls* VA-3
Beaver Dam Fire Control Station—*locale* CA-9
Beaver Dam Flat—*flat* NV-8
Beaver Dam Flat—*flat* OR-9
Beaver Dam Forest Camp—*locale* AZ-5
*Beaverdam Fork* MS-4
*Beaver Dam Fork* SC-3
Beaverdam Gap—*gap* (3) NC-3
Beaverdam Gap—*gap* VA-3
Beaver Dam Gulch—*valley* CO-8
Beaverdam Gulch—*valley* ID-8
Beaver Dam Gulch—*valley* MT-8
Beaver Dam Heath—*swamp* ME-1
**Beaver Dam Heights**—*pop pl* DE-2
Beaverdam Hill—*summit* CT-1
Beaverdam Hill—*summit* MA-1
**Beaver Dam (historical)**—*pop pl* TN-4
Beaver Dam Hollow—*valley* UT-8
Beaver Dam Hollow—*valley* WY-8
Beaverdam Island—*island* AR-4
Beaver Dam Junction—*uninc pl* WI-6
*Beaverdam Lake* WI-6
Beaverdam Lake—*CDP* NY-2
Beaverdam Lake—*lake* AK-9
Beaver Dam Lake—*lake* (2) AR-4
Beaver Dam Lake—*lake* CT-1
Beaverdam Lake—*lake* FL-3
Beaver Dam Lake—*lake* IL-6
Beaver Dam Lake—*lake* IN-6
Beaverdam Lake—*lake* IN-6
Beaverdam Lake—*lake* KY-4
Beaver Dam Lake—*lake* MI-6
Beaver Dam Lake—*lake* (2) MN-6
Beaverdam Lake—*lake* (3) MS-4
Beaver Dam Lake—*lake* NY-2
Beaverdam Lake—*lake* WA-9
Beaver Dam Lake—*lake* WI-6
Beaverdam Lake—*lake* WI-6
Beaver Dam Lake—*lake* WI-6
Beaverdam Lake—*lake* WI-6
Beaver Dam Lake—*reservoir* IL-6
Beaverdam Lake—*reservoir* NJ-2
Beaverdam Lake—*reservoir* NY-2
Beaverdam Lake—*reservoir* NC-3
Beaver Dam Lake—*reservoir* WI-6
Beaver Dam Lake—*swamp* AL-4
Beaverdam Lake—*swamp* OR-9
Beaverdam Lake—*swamp* TN-4
Beaverdam Lake Dam—*dam* NJ-2
Beaverdam Lake Dam—*dam* NC-3
Beaver Dam Lodge—*locale* UT-8
Beaverdam (Magisterial District)—*fmr MCD* VA-3
Beaverdam Marsh—*swamp* CT-1
Beaver Dam Marsh—*swamp* TX-5
Beaverdam Millpond—*reservoir* SC-3
Beaver Dam Mountains—*range* AZ-5
Beaver Dam Mtns—*range* UT-8
Beaver Dam Park—*flat* AZ-5
Beaver Dam Park—*park* WI-6
Beaver Dam Park—*park* WY-8
Beaverdam Pass—*gap* ID-8
Beaverdam Pass Spring—*spring* ID-8
Beaverdam Peak—*summit* ID-8
Beaver Dam Picnic Ground—*park* OR-9
Beaver Dam Plantation House—*hist pl* NC-3
Beaver Dam Pocosin—*swamp* NC-3
Beaverdam Point—*cape* ME-1
*Beaver Dam Pond* CT-1
*Beaverdam Pond* MA-1
Beaverdam Pond—*lake* CT-1
Beaver Dam Pond—*lake* ME-1
Beaver Dam Pond—*lake* (2) MD-2
Beaver Dam Pond—*lake* MA-1
Beaver Dam Pond—*lake* MI-6
Beaver Dam Pond—*lake* NH-1
Beaverdam Pond—*lake* (5) NY-2
Beaverdam Pond—*lake* OR-9
Beaver Dam Pond—*lake* PA-2
Beaver Dam Pond—*reservoir* GA-3
Beaver Dam Pond—*reservoir* MA-1
Beaverdam Pond—*reservoir* NY-2
Beaverdam Pond—*reservoir* NC-3
Beaverdam Pond—*reservoir* SC-3
Beaverdam Pond—*reservoir* VA-3
Beaver Dam Pond Dam—*dam* MA-1
*Beaverdam Primitive Baptist Church* AL-4
Beaver Dam Rapids—*rapids* WI-6
Beaver Dam Rec Area—*park* ID-8
*Beaver Dam Reservoir* PA-2
Beaverdam Ridge—*ridge* NC-3
Beaverdam Ridge—*ridge* WV-2
*Beaverdam River* WI-6
Beaver Dam River—*stream* WI-6
**Beaverdam (RR name Beaver Dam)**—*pop pl* VA-3
Beaver Dam (RR name for Beaverdam)—*other* OH-6
Beaver Dam (RR name for Beaverdam)—*other* VA-3
Beaver Dam (RR name for Beaver Dams)—*other* NY-2
Beaver Dam Rsvr—*reservoir* CO-8
Beaver Dam Rsvr—*reservoir* (2) OR-9
Beaver Dam Rsvr—*reservoir* UT-8
Beaverdam Rsvr—*reservoir* VA-3
*Beaver Dam Run* DE-2
*Beaver Dam Run* PA-2
*Beaver Dam Run* VA-3
Beaverdam Run—*stream* MD-2
Beaverdam Run—*stream* (2) NC-3
Beaverdam Run—*stream* OH-6
Beaverdam Run—*stream* (10) PA-2
Beaverdam Run—*stream* (5) VA-3
Beaverdam Run—*stream* (3) WV-2
Beaverdam Run Dam—*dam* PA-2
Beaver Dams—*area* UT-8
Beaver Dams—*dam* UT-8
**Beaver Dams**—*pop pl* NY-2
Beaver Dam Saddle—*gap* ID-8
Beaverdam Sch—*school* KY-4
Beaver Dam Sch—*school* MI-6
Beaver Dam Sch—*school* MN-6
Beaverdam Sch—*school* (2) NC-3
Beaver Dam Sch—*school* NC-3
Beaver Dam Sch—*school* VA-3
Beaverdam Sch—*school* WV-2
Beaverdam Sch (abandoned)—*school* PA-2
Beaverdam Sch (historical)—*school* AL-4
Beaverdam Sch (historical)—*school* MS-4
Beaver Dams Creek—*stream* CO-8
Beaver Dam Shoals—*bar* TN-4
Beaver Dam Site—*hist pl* MS-4
Beaverdam Slough—*gut* (2) KY-4
Beaverdam Slough—*gut* LA-4
Beaver Dam Slough—*stream* AR-4
Beaverdam Slough—*stream* KY-4
Beaverdam Spring—*spring* AL-4
Beaver Dam Spring—*spring* OR-9
Beaverdam Spring—*spring* WY-8
Beaverdam Springs—*locale* TN-4
Beaverdam Springs—*spring* OR-9
Beaverdam Springs—*spring* TN-4
**Beaverdam Springs (Nacome)**—*pop pl* TN-4
Beaverdam Springs Sch—*school* TN-4
*Beaver Dams Reservoir* UT-8
**Beaver Dams (RR name Beaver Dam)**—*pop pl* NY-2
**Beaver Dams Summer Homes Area**—*pop pl* UT-8
Beaver Dam State Park—*park* IL-6
Beaver Dam State Park—*park* NV-8
**Beaver Dam Station**—*pop pl* OH-6
Beaverdam Stream—*stream* ME-1
*Beaver Dam Swamp* MA-1
*Beaverdam Swamp* NC-3
Beaverdam Swamp—*stream* (3) NC-3
Beaver Dam Swamp—*stream* NC-3
Beaverdam Swamp—*stream* (12) NC-3
Beaverdam Swamp—*stream* SC-3
Beaverdam Swamp—*stream* (2) VA-3
Beaverdam Swamp—*swamp* AL-4
Beaverdam Swamp—*swamp* GA-3
Beaver Dam Swamp—*swamp* GA-3
Beaverdam Swamp—*swamp* (2) MA-1
Beaver Dam Swamp—*swamp* NC-3
Beaver Dam Swamp—*swamp* PA-2
Beaver Dam Swamp—*swamp* SC-3
Beaverdam Swamp Canal—*canal* NC-3
Beaver Dam Tank—*reservoir* AZ-5
**Beaver Dam (Town of)**—*pop pl* WI-6
Beaver Dam Township—*civil* MO-7
Beaver Dam Township (historical)—*civil* SD-7
Beaverdam (Township of)—*fmr MCD* (3) NC-3
Beaver Dam (Township of)—*fmr MCD* NC-3
Beaverdam (Township of)—*fmr MCD* NC-3
Beaver Dam Trail—*trail* CO-8
Beaverdam Trail—*trail* OR-9
Beaverdam Valley—*valley* TN-4
*Beaver Dam Wash* NV-8
*Beaver Dam Wash* UT-8
Beaver Dam Wash—*stream* AZ-5
Beaver Dam Wash—*stream* NV-8
Beaver Dam Wash—*valley* AZ-5
Beaver Dam Wash—*valley* UT-8
Beaver Dam Wash Bridge—*bridge* AZ-5
Beaver Dam Wash Well—*well* AZ-5
Beaverdam Wildlife Restoration Area—*park* NC-3
Beaver Dasm Rsvr—*reservoir* UT-8
Beaver Dick Cem—*cemetery* ID-8
*Beaver Ditch* IN-6
Beaver Ditch—*canal* CO-8
Beaver Ditch—*canal* IN-6
Beaver Ditch—*canal* WY-8
Beaver Ditch No 1—*canal* IL-6
Beaver Ditch No 2—*canal* IL-6
*Beaver Divide* WY-8
Beaver Division—*civil* UT-8
Beaver Drain—*canal* (2) MI-6
Beaver Drain—*stream* MI-6
Beaver Eddy—*rapids* OR-9
**Beaver Edge**—*pop pl* WI-6
Beaver Falls—*falls* AK-9
Beaver Falls—*falls* AZ-5
Beaver Falls—*falls* OR-9
Beaver Falls—*falls* WA-9
**Beaver Falls**—*pop pl* MN-6
**Beaver Falls**—*pop pl* NY-2
**Beaver Falls**—*pop pl* PA-2
Beaver Falls Cem—*cemetery* MN-6
Beaver Falls City—*civil* PA-2
Beaver Falls Creek—*stream* AK-9
*Beaver Falls High School* PA-2
Beaver Falls MS—*school* PA-2
Beaver Falls MS (historical)—*school* PA-2
Beaver Falls Power House—*locale* AK-9
Beaver Falls Senior HS—*school* PA-2
Beaver Falls (Township of)—*civ div* MN-6
Beaver Farm Creek—*stream* MI-6
Beaver Fish Hatchery—*locale* UT-8
Beaver Flat—*flat* ID-8
Beaver Flat—*flat* WA-9
Beaver Flats—*flat* MT-8
Beaver Flats Elem Sch—*school* KS-7
Beaver Flat Tops—*summit* CO-8
Beaver Flow—*lake* NY-2
Beaver Flowage—*reservoir* WI-6
Beaver Ford—*crossing* TN-4
Beaver Fork—*stream* AR-4
Beaver Fork—*stream* KY-4
Beaver Fork—*stream* OR-9
Beaver Fork Lake—*reservoir* AR-4
*Beaver Fork Pickle Gap Creek* AR-4
*Beaver Furnace Creek* IN-6
Beaver Gap—*gap* KY-4
Beaver Gap—*gap* NC-3
Beaver Glade Station—*locale* CA-9
**Beaver Grove**—*pop pl* MI-6
Beaver Grove Cem—*cemetery* IA-7
Beaver Grove Sch—*school* MI-6
Beaver Gulch—*valley* (2) CO-8
Beaver Gulch—*valley* ID-8
Beaver Gulch—*valley* MT-8
Beaver Gulch—*valley* SD-7
Beaver Gut Ditch—*stream* DE-2
*Beaver Harbor* MI-6
Beaver Harbor Lighthouse—*locale* MI-6
Beaver-Harrison Mine—*mine* (2) UT-8
*Beaver Head* RI-1
Beaverhead—*cape* RI-1
Beaverhead—*cliff* AZ-5
Beaverhead Canyon Gateway—*gap* MT-8
Beaver Head Corner—*locale* CT-1
Beaverhead Flat—*flat* AZ-5
Beaverhead Mtn—*summit* MT-8
Beaverhead Mtns—*range* (2) ID-8
Beaverhead Mtns—*range* MT-8
Beaverhead Natl For—*forest* MT-8
*Beaverhead Range* ID-8
*Beaverhead Range* MT-8
Beaverhead Ranger Station—*locale* NM-5
Beaverhead River—*stream* MT-8
Beaverhead Rock—*summit* MT-8
Beaverhead Rock-Lewis and Clark Expedition—*hist pl* MT-8
Beaverhead Rsvr—*reservoir* MT-8
Beaver Head Swamp—*swamp* CT-1
Beaverhead Tank—*reservoir* AZ-5
Beaverhead Tank Number One—*reservoir* AZ-5
Beaverhead Tank Number Two—*reservoir* AZ-5
Beaverhead Water Company Ditch—*canal* MT-8
**Beaver Heights**—*pop pl* MD-2
Beaver Heights Sch—*school* MD-2
*Beaver Hill* WY-8
Beaver Hill—*locale* TN-4
**Beaver Hill**—*pop pl* MT-8
Beaver Hill—*summit* CO-8
Beaver Hill—*summit* CT-1
Beaver Hill—*summit* ME-1
Beaver Hill—*summit* MD-2
Beaver Hill—*summit* MT-8
Beaver Hill—*summit* (2) NY-2
Beaver Hill—*summit* OR-9
Beaver Hill—*summit* WA-9
Beaver Hill Cem—*cemetery* NC-3
Beaverhill Cem—*cemetery* TN-4
Beaverhill Ch—*church* TN-4
Beaver Hill Country Club—*other* IA-7
Beaver Hill Pond—*lake* ME-1
*Beaver Hill Post Office* TN-4
Beaverhill Post Office (historical)—*building* TN-4
Beaverhill Sch (historical)—*school* TN-4
*Beaver Hill School* TN-4
Beaver Hills Hist Dist—*hist pl* CT-1
Beaver Hill Siding—*locale* MT-8
Beaver Hill (site)—*locale* OR-9
Beaver (historical)—*locale* SD-7
Beaver Hole—*basin* UT-8
Beaver Hole—*bay* MD-2
Beaver Hole—*bay* MO-7
Beaverhole—*bay* WV-2
*Beaver Hole Brook* MA-1
Beaver Hole Draw—*valley* WY-8
Beaver Holes Creek—*stream* ND-7
Beaver Hole Swamp—*stream* SC-3
Beaver Hollow—*valley* CA-9
Beaver Hollow—*valley* (2) PA-2
Beaver Hollow—*valley* (2) VA-3
**Beaver Homes**—*pop pl* OR-9
Beaverhouse Hill—*summit* AK-9
Beaverhouse Hole—*lake* KY-4
Beaverhouse Lake—*lake* AK-9
Beaverhouse Lake—*lake* MI-6
Beaver HS—*hist pl* UT-8
Beaver HS—*school* OH-6
Beaver HS—*school* UT-8
Beaver Hut Lake—*lake* MN-6
Beaver II (Boston Tea Party Ship)—*park* MA-1
Beaver Inlet—*bay* AK-9
*Beaver Interchange* PA-2
*Beaver Island* AZ-5
Beaver Island—*flat* OR-9
Beaver Island—*island* AZ-5
Beaver Island—*island* CA-9
Beaver Island—*island* ID-8
Beaver Island—*island* (2) IL-6
Beaver Island—*island* IA-7
Beaver Island—*island* (2) ME-1
Beaver Island—*island* MA-1
Beaver Island—*island* (2) MI-6
Beaver Island—*island* (2) MN-6
Beaver Island—*island* NH-1
Beaver Island—*island* NY-2
Beaver Island—*island* OK-5
Beaver Island Campground—*locale* MI-6
Beaver Island Ch—*church* NC-3
*Beaver Island Creek* NC-3
*Beaver Island Harbor* MI-6
Beaver Island Light Station—*hist pl* MI-6
Beaver Island Lookout Tower—*locale* MI-6
*Beaver Islands* MN-6
Beaver Islands—*island* MN-6
Beaver Island State Park—*park* NY-2
Beaver Island (Township of)—*fmr MCD* NC-3
Beaver Jack Mtn—*summit* ID-8
Beaver Jimmy Creek—*stream* WY-8
**Beaver Junction**—*pop pl* KY-4
Beaver Jungle—*swamp* CO-8
*Beaver Kill* NY-2
**Beaverkill**—*pop pl* NY-2
Beaver Kill—*stream* (3) NY-2
Beaverkill Campground—*locale* NY-2
Beaver Kill Range—*range* NY-2
*Beaverkill River* NY-2
Beaverkill Valley Ch—*church* NY-2
Beaverkill Valley Inn—*hist pl* NY-2
Beaver Knob—*summit* GA-3
Beaver Knob—*summit* KY-4
Beaver KOA—*locale* UT-8
*Beaver Lake* AL-4
*Beaver Lake* MI-6
*Beaver Lake* MN-6
*Beaver Lake* MS-4
*Beaver Lake* WI-6
Beaver Lake—*lake* (9) AK-9
Beaver Lake—*lake* (5) AR-4
Beaver Lake—*lake* CA-9
Beaver Lake—*lake* (6) CO-8
Beaver Lake—*lake* (5) ID-8
Beaver Lake—*lake* IL-6
Beaver Lake—*lake* LA-4
Beaver Lake—*lake* ME-1
Beaver Lake—*lake* (14) MI-6
Beaver Lake—*lake* (18) MN-6
Beaver Lake—*lake* (2) MS-4
Beaver Lake—*lake* (4) MT-8
Beaver Lake—*lake* (2) NE-7
Beaver Lake—*lake* NH-1
Beaver Lake—*lake* NJ-2
Beaver Lake—*lake* (3) NM-5
Beaver Lake—*lake* (8) NY-2
Beaver Lake—*lake* (3) ND-7
Beaver Lake—*lake* OH-6
Beaver Lake—*lake* OK-5
Beaver Lake—*lake* (3) OR-9
Beaver Lake—*lake* (2) PA-2
Beaver Lake—*lake* SD-7
Beaver Lake—*lake* TN-4
Beaver Lake—*lake* (3) UT-8
Beaver Lake—*lake* (11) WA-9
Beaver Lake—*lake* (21) WI-6
Beaver Lake—*lake* (2) WY-8
Beaver Lake—*locale* MI-6
Beaver Lake—*locale* NJ-2
Beaver Lake—*locale* PA-2
**Beaver Lake**—*pop pl* NH-1
Beaver Lake—*reservoir* (2) AL-4
Beaver Lake—*reservoir* AR-4
Beaver Lake—*reservoir* (4) CO-8
Beaver Lake—*reservoir* GA-3
Beaver Lake—*reservoir* IL-6
Beaver Lake—*reservoir* KY-4
Beaver Lake—*reservoir* LA-4
Beaver Lake—*reservoir* MA-1
Beaver Lake—*reservoir* MI-6
Beaver Lake—*reservoir* (2) MS-4
Beaver Lake—*reservoir* MO-7
Beaver Lake—*reservoir* NJ-2
Beaver Lake—*reservoir* NY-2
Beaver Lake—*reservoir* NC-3
Beaver Lake—*reservoir* OH-6
Beaver Lake—*reservoir* (5) PA-2
Beaver Lake—*reservoir* SD-7
Beaver Lake—*reservoir* TN-4
Beaver Lake—*reservoir* TX-5
Beaver Lake—*swamp* CA-9
Beaver Lake—*swamp* MI-6
Beaver Lake Campground—*locale* CO-8
Beaver Lake Cem—*cemetery* MI-6
Beaver Lake Ch—*church* MI-6
Beaver Lake Club—*other* WA-9
Beaver Lake Country Club—*other* GA-3
Beaver Lake Creek—*stream* CO-8
Beaver Lake Creek—*stream* WI-6
Beaver Lake Dam—*dam* MA-1
Beaver Lake Dam—*dam* MS-4
Beaver Lake Dam—*dam* NC-3
Beaver Lake Dam—*dam* ND-7
Beaver Lake Dam—*dam* (3) PA-2
Beaver Lake Dam—*dam* TN-4
Beaver Lake Ditch—*canal* IN-6
Beaver Lake Flooding—*reservoir* MI-6
Beaver Lake Golf Course—*locale* NC-3
Beaver Lake (historical)—*lake* AL-4
Beaver Lake Lodge Dam—*dam* PA-2
Beaver Lake Mtns—*summit* UT-8
Beaver Lake Park—*park* MN-6
Beaver Lake Prairie Chicken Ref—*park* IN-6
Beaver Lake Ranch—*locale* ID-8
Beaver Lake Ranch—*locale* TX-5
Beaver Lake Rec Area—*park* MS-4
Beaver Lakes—*area* AK-9
Beaver Lakes—*lake* OR-9
Beaver Lakes—*lake* WY-8
Beaver Lake Sch—*school* MN-6
Beaver Lake Sch—*school* OR-9
Beaver Lakes Loop Trail—*trail* MT-8
Beaver Lakes Loop Trail—*trail* WY-8
Beaver Lake Trail—*trail* ID-8
Beaver Lake Trail—*trail* WA-9
Beaver Lodge Pass—*gap* ID-8
**Beaverlett**—*pop pl* VA-3
*Beaverley Beach* MD-2
**Beaverlick**—*pop pl* KY-4
Beaverlick Ch—*church* KY-4
Beaver Lick Mountain—*ridge* WV-2
Beaver Lick Mountain Trail—*trail* WV-2
Beaver Lodge—*locale* CO-8
Beaver Lodge Dam Number One—*dam* NC-3
Beaver Lodge Lake Number One—*reservoir* NC-3
Beaver Lodge Oil and Gas Field—*oilfield* ND-7
Beaver Lodge Pond—*spring* WI-6
Beaverlog Lakes—*lake* AK-9
Beaver Lookout—*locale* OR-9
Beaver Lookout Tower—*locale* GA-3
Beaver Lookout Tower—*locale* LA-4
Beaver Lookout Tower—*locale* MI-6
Beaver Lookout Tower—*locale* OK-5
Beaver Lookout Tower—*locale* WI-6
Beaver (Magisterial District)—*fmr MCD* WV-2
Beaverman Lake—*lake* NY-2
*Beaver Marsh* OR-9
**Beaver Marsh**—*pop pl* OR-9
Beaver Marsh—*swamp* MI-6
Beaver Marsh—*swamp* NY-2
Beaver Marsh—*swamp* (4) OR-9
Beaver Marsh—*swamp* (2) TX-5
Beaver Marsh Airp—*airport* OR-9
Beaver Marsh Guard Station—*locale* OR-9
Beaver Marsh Safety Rest Area—*locale* OR-9
Beaver Marsh State Airp—*airport* OR-9
*Beaver Meadow* MI-6
*Beaver Meadow* OR-9
*Beaver Meadow* PA-2
Beaver Meadow—*flat* CA-9
Beaver Meadow—*flat* CO-8
Beaver Meadow—*flat* MA-1
Beaver Meadow—*flat* (2) NY-2
Beaver Meadow—*flat* OR-9
Beaver Meadow—*flat* PA-2
Beaver Meadow—*flat* (6) VT-1
Beaver Meadow—*flat* WA-9
**Beaver Meadow**—*pop pl* NY-2
Beaver Meadow—*stream* ME-1
Beaver Meadow—*swamp* NY-2
Beaver Meadow—*swamp* VT-1
*Beaver Meadow Branch* PA-2
*Beaver Meadow Brook* CT-1
Beaver Meadow Brook—*stream* CT-1
Beaver Meadow Brook—*stream* ME-1
Beaver Meadow Brook—*stream* (2) MA-1
Beaver Meadow Brook—*stream* NH-1
Beaver Meadow Brook—*stream* (8) NY-2
Beaver Meadow Brook—*stream* (12) VT-1
Beaver Meadow Cem—*cemetery* PA-2
Beaver Meadow Ch—*church* MS-4
Beaver Meadow Colliery—*building* PA-2
Beaver Meadow Colliery (RR name for Beaver Meadows)—*other* PA-2
Beaver Meadow Complex Prehistoric Archeol District—*hist pl* CT-1
Beaver Meadow Creek—*stream* IN-6
Beaver Meadow Creek—*stream* MI-6
Beaver Meadow Creek—*stream* (4) NY-2
Beaver Meadow Creek—*stream* PA-2
*Beaver Meadow Dam* PA-2
Beaver Meadow Dam—*dam* UT-8
Beaver Meadow Drain—*stream* MI-6
Beaver Meadow Hill—*summit* NY-2
Beaver Meadow (historical)—*locale* AL-4
Beaver Meadow (historical)—*locale* MA-1
Beaver Meadow Marsh—*swamp* NY-2
Beaver Meadow Pond—*lake* NY-2
Beaver Meadow Pond—*lake* (2) PA-2
Beaver Meadow Rsvr—*reservoir* (2) UT-8
Beaver Meadow Run—*stream* PA-2
*Beaver Meadows* NY-2
Beaver Meadows—*flat* (3) CO-8
Beaver Meadows—*flat* ID-8
Beaver Meadows—*flat* (2) MT-8
Beaver Meadows—*flat* NY-2
Beaver Meadows—*flat* (3) OR-9
Beaver Meadows—*flat* VT-1
**Beaver Meadows**—*pop pl* PA-2
Beaver Meadows—*swamp* (3) NY-2
Beaver Meadows—*swamp* (2) VT-1
Beaver Meadows Borough—*civil* PA-2
Beaver Meadows Cem—*cemetery* NY-2
Beaver Meadow Sch—*school* NY-2
Beaver Meadows County Park—*park* IA-7
Beaver Meadows Creek—*stream* (2) NY-2
Beaver Meadows Dam—*dam* PA-2
Beaver Meadows Entrance—*locale* CO-8
Beaver Meadows Falls—*falls* NY-2
Beaver Meadows Lake—*reservoir* PA-2
Beaver Meadow Spring—*spring* CO-8
**Beaver Meadows (RR name Beaver Meadow Colliery)**—*pop pl* PA-2
Beaver Meadows Trail—*trail* OR-9
Beaver Meadow Swamp—*swamp* NY-2
Beaver Meadow Swamp—*swamp* PA-2
Beaver Meadow Trail—*trail* VT-1
Beaver Medicine Falls—*falls* MT-8
Beaver Mesa—*summit* CO-8
Beaver Milit Reservation—*military* OR-9
*Beaver Mill* PA-2
Beaver Mill—*hist pl* MA-1
**Beaver Mill**—*pop pl* OH-6
**Beaver Mills**—*pop pl* PA-2
Beaver Mine—*mine* CO-8
Beaver Mine—*mine* MT-8
*Beaver Mount* MT-8
*Beaver Mountain* AL-4
Beaver Mountain Rsvr—*reservoir* CA-9
*Beaver Mountains* AL-4
*Beaver Mountains* UT-8
Beaver Mountains—*other* AK-9
Beaver Mountain Ski Area—*park* UT-8
*Beaver Mtn* OK-5
Beaver Mtn—*summit* (2) AK-9
Beaver Mtn—*summit* CA-9
Beaver Mtn—*summit* (4) CO-8
Beaver Mtn—*summit* GA-3
Beaver Mtn—*summit* ID-8
Beaver Mtn—*summit* ME-1
Beaver Mtn—*summit* MT-8
Beaver Mtn—*summit* NY-2
Beaver Mtn—*summit* (2) OK-5
Beaver Mtn—*summit* OR-9
Beaver Mtn—*summit* TX-5
Beaver Mtn—*summit* UT-8
Beaver Mtn—*summit* (2) WA-9
Beaver Mtn—*summit* (2) WY-8
Beaver Municide Power Plant—*other* UT-8
Beaver Municipal Airp—*airport* UT-8
Beaver North Oil Field—*oilfield* KS-7
Beaver Oil Field—*oilfield* KS-7
Beaver Opera House—*hist pl* UT-8
*Beaver Park* OH-6
*Beaver Park* UT-8
Beaver Park—*flat* AZ-5
Beaver Park—*flat* CO-8
Beaver Park—*flat* WY-8
Beaver Park—*locale* CO-8
Beaver Park—*park* IA-7
Beaver Park—*park* ME-1
**Beaver Park**—*pop pl* OH-6
**Beaver Park**—*pop pl* VA-3
Beaver Park Ditch—*canal* CO-8
Beaver Parks—*flat* UT-8
Beaver Pass—*gap* ID-8
Beaver Pass—*gap* WA-9
Beaver Pass Shelter—*locale* WA-9
Beaver Peak—*summit* AK-9
Beaver Peak—*summit* (2) ID-8
Beaver Peak—*summit* (2) MT-8
Beaver Peak—*summit* NV-8
Beaver Placer Mine—*mine* MT-8
Beaver Point—*cape* AK-9
Beaver Point—*cape* ID-8
Beaver Point—*cape* MT-8
Beaver Point—*cape* (2) NY-2
Beaver Point—*cliff* AZ-5
**Beaver Point**—*pop pl* CO-8
Beaver Point Rsvr—*reservoir* CO-8
Beaver Points—*summit* NM-5
*Beaver Pond* CO-8
*Beaver Pond* ME-1
*Beaver Pond* NH-1
*Beaver Pond* WI-6
Beaver Pond—*lake* (2) AL-4
Beaver Pond—*lake* (4) AR-4
Beaver Pond—*lake* CT-1
Beaver Pond—*lake* FL-3
Beaver Pond—*lake* GA-3
Beaver Pond—*lake* ID-8
Beaver Pond—*lake* (2) IL-6
Beaver Pond—*lake* (21) ME-1
Beaver Pond—*lake* (5) MA-1
Beaver Pond—*lake* (4) MI-6
Beaver Pond—*lake* (4) MN-6
Beaver Pond—*lake* (4) MS-4

**Beech**—pop pl KY-4
**Beech**—pop pl NC-3
Beech Aircraft Field KS-7
Beecham AL-4
Beecham Bayou—stream LA-4
Beecham Bayou—stream MS-4
Beecham Branch—stream MO-7
Beecham Cem—cemetery OK-5
Beecham Cem—cemetery (3) TN-4
Beecham Gap—gap TX-5
Beecham Hollow TN-4
Beecham Lake—lake AL-4
Beechatuda Draw—valley NM-5
Beech Ave Houses—hist pl OH-6
Beech Ave Sch—school NY-2
Beech Bay—bay VT-1
Beech Bay—swamp FL-3
Beech Bayou—stream LA-4
Beech Bayou—stream MS-4
Beech Bend—bend (2) TN-4
Beech Bend Park—park KY-4
Beech Bend Rec Area—park TN-4
Beech Bethany Ch—church TN-4
Beech Bethany Sch (historical)—school TN-4
Beech Bingham Branch—stream KY-4
Beech Bluff AL-4
Beech Bluff—cliff IL-6
**Beech Bluff**—pop pl TN-4
Beech Bluff—stream TN-4
Beech Bluff Cem—cemetery TN-4
Beech Bluff Ch—church TN-4
Beech Bluff Elem Sch—school TN-4
Beechbluff Post Office TN-4
Beech Bluff Post Office—building TN-4
Beech Bluff Sch—school TN-4
Beechbottom WV-2
Beech Bottom—basin AL-4
Beech Bottom—bend GA-3
Beech Bottom—bend KY-4
Beech Bottom—bend (2) TN-4
Beech Bottom—locale KY-4
Beech Bottom—locale TN-4
**Beech Bottom**—pop pl NC-3
**Beech Bottom**—pop pl WV-2
Beechbottom Branch—stream KY-4
Beech Bottom Branch—stream KY-4
Beech Bottom Branch—stream WV-2
Beech Bottom Ch—church KY-4
Beech Bottom Hollow—valley PA-2
Beech Bottom Mtn—summit TN-4
Beech Bottom Natural Area—area PA-2
Beech Bottom Run—stream PA-2
Beech Bottoms—bend TN-4
Beech Bottoms—flat TN-4
Beech Bottom Sch—school KY-4
Beech Bottom School TN-4
Beech Branch WV-2
Beech Branch—stream (4) AL-4
Beech Branch—stream (2) AR-4
Beech Branch—stream FL-3
Beech Branch—stream GA-3
Beech Branch—stream (7) KY-4
Beech Branch—stream LA-4
Beech Branch—stream MS-4
Beech Branch—stream (2) NC-3
Beech Branch—stream (2) SC-3
Beech Branch—stream (6) TN-4
Beech Branch—stream (2) TX-5
Beech Branch—stream (2) VA-3
Beech Branch—stream (3) WV-2
Beech Branch Cem—cemetery GA-3
Beech Branch Ch—church SC-3
Beech Brook CT-1
**Beech Brook**—pop pl IN-6
Beech Brook—stream (2) NJ-2
Beech Brook—stream NY-2
Beechbrook Cem—cemetery MA-1
Beechbrook Orphanage—school OH-6
**Beech Brook (subdivision)**—pop pl NC-3
Beechburg—locale KY-4
Beech Canal—canal CA-9
Beech Cem—cemetery IN-6
Beech Cem—cemetery MI-6
Beech Cem—cemetery MS-4
Beech Cem—cemetery OH-6
Beech Ch—church IN-6
Beech Ch—church (2) OH-6
Beech Chapel—church (2) TN-4
Beech Chapel Cem—cemetery TN-4
Beech Cliff ME-1
**Beechcliff**—pop pl PA-2
Beech Cliff Church—cemetery TN-4
**Beechcliff Estates (subdivision)**—pop pl TN-4
Beech Corner Sch (abandoned)—school MO-7
Beech Cove Branch—stream NC-3
Beech Cove Cem—cemetery TN-4
Beech Cove Knob—summit NC-3
Beech Cove Vista—locale GA-3
Beech Creek AR-4
Beech Creek NJ-2
Beech Creek NY-2
Beech Creek OR-9
Beech Creek PA-2
Beech Creek TN-4
Beech Creek TX-5
Beech Creek—locale NC-3
Beech Creek—locale OR-9
**Beech Creek**—pop pl AR-4
**Beech Creek**—pop pl KY-4
**Beech Creek**—pop pl PA-2
**Beech Creek**—pop pl WV-2
Beech Creek—stream (3) AL-4
Beech Creek—stream (18) AR-4
Beech Creek—stream (5) GA-3
Beech Creek—stream (5) IN-6
Beech Creek—stream (6) KY-4
Beech Creek—stream (2) LA-4
Beech Creek—stream MT-8
Beech Creek—stream NY-2
Beech Creek—stream (8) NC-3
Beech Creek—stream OH-6
Beech Creek—stream OK-5
Beech Creek—stream OR-9
Beech Creek—stream PA-2
Beech Creek—stream (3) SC-3
Beech Creek—stream (8) TN-4
Beech Creek—stream (9) TX-5
Beech Creek—stream (3) VA-3
Beech Creek—stream (2) WV-2
Beech Creek Baptist Church TN-4
Beech Creek Borough—civil PA-2
Beech Creek (CCD)—cens area TN-4
Beech Creek Cem—cemetery AR-4
Beech Creek Cem—cemetery KY-4
Beech Creek Cem—cemetery NC-3
Beech Creek Cem—cemetery TN-4
Beech Creek Cem—cemetery TX-5
Beech Creek Ch—church (2) AR-4
Beech Creek Ch—church GA-3
Beech Creek Ch—church LA-4
Beech Creek Ch—church NC-3
Beech Creek Ch—church TN-4
Beech Creek Ch—church (2) TX-5
Beech Creek Ch (historical)—church AL-4
Beech Creek Ch (historical)—church TN-4
Beech Creek Crossing—locale AR-4
Beech Creek Division—civil TN-4
Beech Creek Forest Camp—locale OR-9
Beech Creek Gap—gap PA-2
**Beech Creek (historical)**—pop pl FL-3
Beech Creek Island—island TN-4
Beech Creek Junction (RR name for Beechmont)—other KY-4
Beech Creek Lodge—locale PA-2
Beech Creek Marina—locale AL-4
Beech Creek Mountain Ch—church NC-3
Beech Creek Oil Field—oilfield (2) TX-5
Beech Creek Post Office (historical)—building TN-4
Beech Creek Ridge—ridge NC-3
**Beech Creek (RR name Wright)**—pop pl KY-4
Beech Creek Sch—school WV-2
Beech Creek Station—locale PA-2
Beech Creek Swamp—swamp AL-4
Beech Creek Tower—tower PA-2
Beech Creek (Township of)—fmr MCD AR-4
**Beech Creek (Township of)**—pop pl IN-6
**Beech Creek (Township of)**—pop pl PA-2
Beech Creek Valley—valley TN-4
**Beechcrest**—pop pl OH-6
**Beechcroft (subdivision)**—pop pl NC-3
Beech Cumberland Presbyterian Church TN-4
Beechdale Bridge—hist pl PA-2
Beechdale Sch—school MI-6
Beech Dam—dam (2) TN-4
Beech Drain—canal CA-9
Beech Draw—valley WY-8
Beecher—locale OR-9
**Beecher**—pop pl IL-6
**Beecher**—pop pl MI-6
**Beecher**—pop pl WI-6
Beecher, Lake—lake WA-9
Beecher, Lucas, House—hist pl OH-6
Beecher Bible and Rifle Church—hist pl KS-7
Beecher Branch—stream KY-4
Beecher Branch—stream VA-3
Beecher Brook—stream NY-2
Beecher Canyon—valley AZ-5
Beecher Canyon—valley CA-9
Beecher Ch—church WI-6
**Beecher City**—pop pl IL-6
Beecher Corners—locale NY-2
Beecher Creek NJ-2
Beecher Creek—stream MT-8
Beecher Creek—stream NY-2
Beecher Creek—stream (2) OR-9
Beecher Creek—stream WI-6
Beecher Creek—stream WY-8
Beecher Ditch—canal IN-6
Beecher Ditch—canal OH-6
Beecher Draw—valley WY-8
**Beecher Falls**—pop pl VT-1
Beecher Flat Canyon—valley OR-9
Beecher Flats—flat OR-9
Beecher Gulch—valley CO-8
Beecher Hall, Illinois College—hist pl IL-6
Beecher Heights MI-6
Beecher Hill—summit MI-6
Beecher Hill—summit PA-2
Beecher Hollow—valley IN-6
Beecher Hollow—valley PA-2
Beecher Hollow Trail PA-2
Beecher HS—school MI-6
Beecher Island—island NY-2
Beecher Island—locale CO-8
Beecher Island Battleground—hist pl CO-8
Beecher JHS—school (2) MI-6
Beecher Lake—lake WI-6
Beecher Lake—locale WI-6
Beecher Lake—reservoir NY-2
Beecher-McFadden Estate—hist pl NY-2
Beecher Number Two Mine—mine SD-7
Beecher Park—park NY-2
Beecher Pass—channel AK-9
Beecher Peak—summit MT-8
Beecher Playground—park KY-4
Beecher Point—cape FL-3
Beecher Pond—lake VT-1
Beecher Ridge—ridge UT-8
Beecher Ridge—ridge VA-3
Beecher Ridge Trail—trail VA-3
Beecher Road Sch—school CT-1
Beecher Rock—pillar SD-7
Beecher Run—stream FL-3
Beechers Bay CA-9
Beechers Bay—bay CA-9
Beecher Sch—school CT-1
Beecher Sch—school NY-2
Beechers Corners (2) CA-9
Beecher's Creek NY-2
**Beechers Lot (subdivision)**—pop pl DE-2
Beecher Smith Dam—dam TN-4
Beecher Smith Lake—reservoir TN-4
Beechers Pillar SD-7
Beecher Spring—spring AZ-5
Beecher Spring—spring FL-3
Beecher Street Sch—school CT-1
**Beechersville**—pop pl PA-2
Beecher Tank—reservoir AZ-5
Beechertown—locale NY-2
**Beechertown**—pop pl NC-3
**Beecher (Town of)**—pop pl WI-6
Beecherville—locale NY-2
Beeches—hist pl KY-4
Beeches, The AL-4
Beeches, The—hist pl TN-4
Beeches, The—hist pl WV-2
Beeches, The—uninc pl DE-2
Beechey Mound—summit AK-9
Beechey Point—cape AK-9
**Beechey Point**—pop pl AK-9
Beechey Ridge—ridge NC-3
Beech Factory Airport KS-7
Beech Factory Landing Field—airport KS-7
Beech Farm—locale KY-4
Beechflat Creek—stream NC-3
Beech Flat Knob—summit WV-2
Beech Flats—flat GA-3
Beech Flats—flat OH-6
Beech Flats—flat TN-4
Beech Flats—locale PA-2
Beech Flats Branch—stream GA-3
Beech Flats Branch—stream NC-3
Beech Flats Cem—cemetery PA-2
Beech Flats Ch—church OH-6
Beech Flats Creek—stream PA-2
Beech Flats Prong—stream NC-3
Beech Flats Run—stream PA-2
**Beechford**—pop pl NY-2
Beech Fork OH-6
Beech Fork—locale TN-4
**Beech Fork**—pop pl KY-4
Beech Fork—stream AR-4
Beech Fork—stream (7) KY-4
Beech Fork—stream (2) OH-6
Beech Fork—stream (2) TN-4
Beech Fork—stream VA-3
Beech Fork—stream (10) WV-2
Beech Fork Buffalo Creek—stream OH-6
Beech Fork Cem—cemetery OH-6
Beech Fork Cem—cemetery (2) TN-4
Beech Fork Ch—church KY-4
Beech Fork Ch—church OH-6
Beech Fork Ch—church TN-4
Beech Fork Ch—church WV-2
Beech Fork Creek—stream KY-4
Beech Fork Creek—stream TN-4
Beech Fork Lake—reservoir WV-2
Beech Fork Lookout Tower—locale KY-4
Beech Fork Rsvr WV-2
Beech Fork Sch—school (3) KY-4
Beech Fork Sch—school WV-2
Beech Gap—gap KY-4
Beech Gap—gap (4) NC-3
Beech Gap—gap (2) TN-4
Beech Glen—locale NC-3
Beech Glen—locale PA-2
**Beech Glen**—pop pl WV-2
Beech Ground Swamp—swamp MD-2
Beech Grove IN-6
Beech Grove KS-7
Beech Grove TN-4
Beech Grove—locale KY-4
Beech Grove—locale MS-4
Beechgrove—locale OH-6
Beech Grove—locale (2) PA-2
Beech Grove—locale (6) TN-4
Beech Grove—locale TX-5
Beech Grove—locale WV-2
**Beech Grove**—pop pl (2) AR-4
**Beech Grove**—pop pl (2) IN-6
**Beech Grove**—pop pl (2) KY-4
**Beech Grove**—pop pl PA-2
**Beechgrove**—pop pl TN-4
**Beech Grove**—pop pl (4) TN-4
**Beech Grove**—pop pl VA-3
**Beechgrove**—pop pl WV-2
Beech Grove—uninc pl VA-3
Beech Grove Baptist Ch TN-4
Beech Grove Baptist Ch—church TN-4
Beech Grove Baptist Church MS-4
Beech Grove Branch—stream MO-7
Beech Grove Branch—stream TX-5
Beech Grove Branch—stream VA-3
Beech Grove Cabin Area—locale TN-4
Beech Grove Campground—locale TX-5
Beech Grove (CCD)—cens area TN-4
Beech Grove Cem—cemetery AL-4
Beech Grove Cem—cemetery AR-4
Beech Grove Cem—cemetery (4) IN-6
Beech Grove Cem—cemetery KY-4
Beech Grove Cem—cemetery (2) LA-4
Beech Grove Cem—cemetery (2) MA-1
Beech Grove Cem—cemetery (2) MS-4
Beech Grove Cem—cemetery (3) OH-6
Beech Grove Cem—cemetery (10) TN-4
Beech Grove Cem—cemetery WV-2
Beech Grove Ch—church (5) AL-4
Beech Grove Ch—church (2) IL-6
Beech Grove Ch—church (9) IN-6
Beech Grove Ch—church (20) KY-4
Beech Grove Ch—church (6) LA-4
Beech Grove Ch—church (2) MS-4
Beech Grove Ch—church MO-7
Beech Grove Ch—church NC-3
Beech Grove Ch—church (3) OH-6
Beech Grove Ch—church (25) TN-4
Beech Grove Ch—church (6) VA-3
Beech Grove Ch—church (3) WV-2
Beechgrove Ch—church WV-2
Beech Grove Ch—church WV-2
Beech Grove Chapel—church KY-4
Beech Grove Ch (historical)—church MS-4
Beech Grove Ch (historical)—church (3) TN-4
Beech Grove Ch Number 1—church LA-4
Beech Grove Ch Number 2—church LA-4
Beech Grove Ch of Christ—church AL-4
Beech Grove Ch of God—church IN-6
Beechgrove Coll (historical)—school TN-4
Beech Grove Cumberland Presbyterian Church TN-4
Beech Grove Division—civil TN-4
Beech Grove Farm IN-6
Beech Grove Fork—stream TN-4
Beech Grove Freewill Baptist Ch AL-4
Beech Grove High School IN-6
Beech Grove Landing—locale MS-4
Beech Grove Lateral AR-4
Beech Grove Methodist Ch—church TN-4
Beech Grove Mine—mine TN-4
Beech Grove Mine (underground)—mine AL-4
Beech Grove MS—school IN-6
Beechgrove Post Office TN-4
Beech Grove Post Office—building TN-4
Beech Grove Post Office (historical)—building AL-4
Beech Grove Ridge—ridge KY-4
Beech Grove Run—stream IN-6
Beech Grove Sch TN-4
Beech Grove Sch—school AR-4
Beech Grove Sch—school FL-3
Beech Grove Sch—school IL-6
Beech Grove Sch—school (7) KY-4
Beech Grove Sch—school OH-6
Beech Grove Sch—school TN-4
Beech Grove Sch—school TX-5
Beech Grove Sch—school (3) VA-3
Beech Grove Sch—school WV-2
Beech Grove Sch (abandoned)—school (2) PA-2
Beech Grove Sch (historical)—school (2) AL-4
Beech Grove Sch (historical)—school MS-4
Beech Grove Sch (historical)—school (14) TN-4
Beech Grove Senior HS—school IN-6
Beech Grove United Methodist Ch—church IN-6
Beech Grove United Methodist Ch—church TN-4
Beech Grove Wesleyan Ch—church IN-6
Beech Haven—locale DE-2
Beech Haven Ch—church GA-3
**Beechhaven (subdivision)**—pop pl DE-2
Beech Hill MA-1
Beech Hill—hist pl NH-1
Beech Hill—locale GA-3
Beech Hill—locale TN-4
**Beech Hill**—pop pl DE-2
**Beech Hill**—pop pl NY-2
**Beech Hill**—pop pl (2) TN-4
**Beech Hill**—pop pl WV-2
Beech Hill—ridge (2) NH-1
Beech Hill—summit CO-8
Beech Hill—summit (2) CT-1
Beech Hill—summit (12) ME-1
Beech Hill—summit (6) MA-1
Beech Hill—summit (11) NH-1
Beech Hill—summit (9) NY-2
Beech Hill—summit PA-2
Beech Hill—summit SC-3
Beech Hill Brook—stream ME-1
Beech Hill Brook—stream NH-1
Beech Hill Cem—cemetery (2) MS-4
Beech Hill Cem—cemetery (2) NY-2
Beech Hill Cem—cemetery SC-3
Beech Hill Cem—cemetery (3) TN-4
Beech Hill Ch—church (2) AR-4
Beech Hill Ch—church GA-3
Beech Hill Ch—church MS-4
Beech Hill Ch—church (3) TN-4
Beech Hill Ch—church VA-3
Beech Hill Ch of Christ MS-4
Beech Hill Heath—swamp ME-1
**Beech Hill (historical)**—pop pl TN-4
Beech Hill Lookout Tower—locale MI-6
Beech Hill Meadow MA-1
Beech Hill Pond—lake ME-1
Beech Hill Pond—reservoir NY-2
Beech Hills—range IN-6
Beech Hill Sch—school LA-4
Beech Hill Sch—school NY-2
Beech Hill Sch—school TN-4
Beech Hill Sch (historical)—school MS-4
Beech Hill Sch (historical)—school (4) TN-4
**Beech Hills (subdivision)**—pop pl AL-4
Beech Hill State For—forest NH-1
Beech Hill Summer Home District—hist pl NH-1
Beech Hill Swamp—swamp MA-1
Beech Hill Trail—trail NH-1
Beech Hollow—basin MD-2
Beech Hollow—valley (2) IL-6
Beech Hollow—valley (3) KY-4
Beech Hollow—valley PA-2
Beech Hollow—valley (6) TN-4
Beech Hollow—valley VA-3
Beech Hollow Sch (abandoned)—school PA-2
Beech HS—school TN-4
Beech Hurricane Creek—stream AR-4
**Beechhurst**—pop pl NY-2
Beech Island ME-1
Beech Island—island AR-4
Beech Island—island FL-3
Beech Island—island GA-3
Beech Island—island MD-2
Beech Island—island NH-1
Beech Island—island (2) NC-3
Beech Island—island PA-2
Beech Island—island SC-3
Beech Island—island TN-4
**Beech Island**—pop pl SC-3
Beech Island (CCD)—cens area SC-3
Beech Island Ch—church AL-4
Beech Island Ch—church SC-3
Beech Island Creek—stream MD-2
Beech Island Pond—lake ME-1
**Beech Junction**—pop pl WV-2
Beech Knob—summit NC-3
Beech Knob—summit (2) WV-2
Beech Lake—lake ID-8
Beech Lake—lake PA-2
Beech Lake—reservoir KS-7
Beech Lake—reservoir NC-3
Beech Lake—reservoir (2) TN-4
Beech Lake And Park Dam—dam KS-7
Beech Lake Dam—dam NC-3
Beechland—hist pl (2) KY-4
Beechland—hist pl MS-4
Beechland—locale (2) KY-4
**Beechland Beach**—pop pl KY-4
Beechland Ch—church KY-4
Beechland Ch—church MS-4
Beech Landing—locale IL-6
Beech Landing Field KS-7
Beechland Park—park CT-1
Beech Lateral One—canal CA-9
Beech Lateral Two—canal CA-9
Beech Lawn—hist pl KY-4
Beechlawn—hist pl TN-4
Beechler Cem—cemetery MI-6
Beech Lick—stream PA-2
Beech Lick—stream (2) WV-2
Beech Lick Branch—stream AL-4
Beech Lick Knob—summit VA-3
Beech Lick Run—stream VA-3
Beechlick Run—stream WV-2
Beech Lick Run—stream WV-2
Beechlick Run—stream (2) WV-2
Beech Log Creek—stream TN-4
Beechman Branch—stream TX-5
**Beech-Mar**—pop pl OH-6
**Beechmont**—pop pl (2) KY-4
**Beechmont**—pop pl NY-2
**Beechmont**—pop pl PA-2
**Beechmont**—pop pl VA-3
Beechmont Country Club—other OH-6
Beechmont Lake—reservoir NY-2
**Beechmont (RR name Beach Creek Junction)**—pop pl KY-4
Beechmont Sch—school KY-4
**Beechmont Woods**—pop pl NY-2
**Beech Mountain**—pop pl NC-3
Beech Mountain Airp—airport NC-3
Beech Mountain Ch—church (2) NC-3
Beech Mountain Sch—school NC-3
Beech Mountain (Township of)—fmr MCD NC-3
Beech Mtn—summit ME-1
Beech Mtn—summit (2) NY-2
Beech Mtn—summit (2) NC-3
Beech Mtn—summit (2) VA-3
Beech Mtn—summit (2) WV-2
Beech Nursery Creek—stream NC-3
Beech Nursery Gap—gap NC-3
**Beechnut**—pop pl TN-4
Beechnut—post sta TX-5
Beechnut City—locale TN-4
Beechnut Fork—stream KY-4
Beechnut Gap—gap NC-3
Beechnut Gap—gap TN-4
Beechnut Lake—lake MI-6
Beechnut Ridge—ridge PA-2
Beechnut Ridge—ridge VT-1
**Beechnut Subdivision**—pop pl TN-4
Beech Oak Branch—stream KY-4
Beech Park Baptist Ch—church TN-4
Beech Pen Ridge—ridge WV-2
Beech Plain Cem—cemetery MA-1
Beech P O—locale KY-4
Beech Point TN-4
Beech Point—cape VA-3
Beech Pond PA-2
Beech Pond—lake ME-1
Beech Pond—swamp FL-3
**Beech Ridge**—pop pl ME-1
Beech Ridge—ridge GA-3
Beech Ridge—ridge (5) ME-1
Beech Ridge—ridge MD-2
Beech Ridge—ridge MS-4
Beech Ridge—ridge (4) NY-2
Beech Ridge—ridge (3) NC-3
Beech Ridge—ridge TN-4
Beech Ridge—ridge VT-1
Beech Ridge—ridge (2) WV-2
Beech Ridge—summit NY-2
Beech Ridge Brook—stream ME-1
Beech Ridge Brook—stream NY-2
Beech Ridge Cem—cemetery NY-2
Beech Ridge Ch—church KY-4
Beech Ridge Ch—church ME-1
Beech Ridge Ch—church OH-6
Beech Ridge Sch (historical)—school MO-7
Beech Ridge Speedway—other ME-1
Beech Ridge Trail—trail WV-2
Beech River—stream NH-1
Beech River—stream TN-4
Beech River Landing—locale TN-4
Beech River Sch—school TN-4
Beech River Slough—stream TN-4
Beech Road Sch—school MI-6
Beech Rock—locale CT-1
Beech Rock Branch—stream KY-4
Beechroot Branch—stream KY-4
Beech Run—stream MA-1
Beech Run—stream OH-6
Beech Run—stream (3) PA-2
Beech Run—stream (12) WV-2
Beech Run Cem—cemetery (2) WV-2
Beech Run Ch—church PA-2
Beech Run Ch—church (3) WV-2
**Beech Run Junction**—pop pl WV-2
Beech Run Sch—school WV-2
Beech Sch—school TN-4
Beech Sch (abandoned)—school (2) PA-2
Beech Sch (historical)—school MS-4
Beech Spring—spring (2) AL-4
Beech Spring—spring AZ-5
Beech Spring—spring (4) TN-4
Beech Spring—spring VA-3
Beech Spring Cem—cemetery AL-4
Beech Spring Cem—cemetery OH-6
Beech Spring Ch—church AL-4
Beech Spring Ch—church GA-3
Beech Spring Ch—church KY-4
Beech Spring Ch—church LA-4
Beech Spring Ch—church TN-4
Beech Spring Ch—church VA-3
Beech Spring Gap—gap NC-3
Beech Spring Hollow—valley AL-4
Beech Spring Hollow—valley VA-3
Beech Springs MS-4
**Beech Springs**—pop pl LA-4
**Beech Springs**—pop pl MS-4
**Beech Springs**—pop pl TN-4
**Beech Springs**—pop pl VA-3
Beech Springs Branch—stream TN-4
Beech Springs Camp—locale AR-4
Beech Springs (CCD)—cens area TN-4
Beech Springs Cem—cemetery (2) MS-4
Beech Springs Cem—cemetery (2) TN-4
Beech Springs Ch—church GA-3
Beech Springs Ch—church MS-4
Beech Springs Ch—church SC-3
Beech Springs Ch—church (2) TN-4
Beech Springs Division—civil TN-4
Beech Springs Freewill Baptist Ch—church MS-4
Beech Springs (historical)—locale MS-4
Beech Springs Sch (historical)—school (2) MS-4
Beech Springs Sch (historical)—school TN-4
Beech Springs School MS-4
Beech Stand Fork—stream KY-4
Beech Street Ch of Christ—church AL-4
Beech Street Hist Dist—hist pl AR-4
Beech Street Sch—school NJ-2
Beech Street Sch—school VT-1
Beech Swamp—stream VA-3
Beech Swamp—swamp MD-2
Beech Swamp—swamp NC-3
Beech Tank—reservoir NM-5
Beechton—locale PA-2
Beechtown WV-2
Beechtown Cem—cemetery WV-2
Beech (Township of)—fmr MCD AR-4
Beechtree—locale PA-2
Beech Tree Branch—stream AL-4
Beech Tree Branch—stream NC-3
Beechtree Cem—cemetery OK-5
Beech Tree Creek—stream FL-3
Beechtree Creek—stream GA-3
Beechtree Creek—stream VA-3
**Beechtree (subdivision)**—pop pl NC-3
Beechurst—uninc pl NY-2
Beech Valley—valley KY-4
Beech Valley Cem—cemetery PA-2
Beech Valley Ch—church KY-4
Beech Valley Ch—church NC-3
Beech Valley Ch—church TN-4
Beech Valley Mills TN-4
Beech Valley Mine—mine TN-4
Beech Valley Sch—school PA-2
**Beechview**—pop pl PA-2
Beechview Estates OH-6
**Beechview Estates**—pop pl OH-6
Beechview Sch—school MI-6
Beechville TN-4
Beechville—locale IL-6
Beechville—locale KY-4
Beechville Sch—school NE-7
Beechwell Ch (abandoned)—church MO-7
Beechwold OH-6
Beechwold—hist pl KY-4
**Beechwold (subdivision)**—pop pl DE-2
Beechwood LA-4
Beechwood MI-6
Beechwood OH-6
Beechwood PA-2
Beechwood—CDP MI-6
Beechwood—hist pl VA-3
Beechwood—locale AR-4
Beechwood—locale GA-3
Beechwood—locale KY-4
Beechwood—locale MI-6
Beechwood—locale (2) MS-4
Beechwood—locale TN-4
Beechwood—locale (2) VA-3
Beechwood—locale WV-2
**Beechwood**—pop pl AL-4
**Beechwood**—pop pl IN-6
**Beechwood**—pop pl MA-1
**Beechwood**—pop pl MI-6
**Beechwood**—pop pl NE-7
**Beechwood**—pop pl (2) OH-6
**Beechwood**—pop pl (2) PA-2
**Beechwood**—pop pl TN-4
**Beechwood**—pop pl (2) VA-3
**Beechwood**—pop pl (3) WV-2
**Beechwood**—pop pl WI-6
Beechwood—uninc pl KS-7
Beechwood—uninc pl NY-2
**Beechwood Acres**—pop pl AL-4
**Beechwood Acres**—pop pl PA-2
Beechwood Airp—airport AL-4
**Beechwood (Beechwood Park)**—pop pl PA-2
Beechwood Branch—stream AL-4
Beechwood Camp—locale PA-2
Beechwood Camp—locale VT-1
Beechwood Cem—cemetery MA-1
Beechwood Cem—cemetery MI-6
Beechwood Cem—cemetery NC-3
Beechwood Cem—cemetery (3) OH-6
Beechwood Cem—cemetery VA-3
Beechwood Cem—cemetery WV-2
Beechwood Ch—church AL-4
Beechwood Ch—church GA-3
Beechwood Ch—church LA-4
Beechwood Ch—church MI-6
Beechwood Ch—church TN-4
Beechwood Corners—locale NH-1
Beechwood Country Club—locale NC-3
**Beechwood Court (subdivision)**—pop pl TN-4
Beechwood Elem Sch—hist pl PA-2
Beechwood Elem Sch—school PA-2
Beechwood Greens Golf Club—other MI-6
Beechwood Hall—hist pl TN-4
Beechwood Hall Female Acad (historical)—school MS-4
**Beechwood Heights**—pop pl NJ-2
**Beechwood Hills**—pop pl (2) VA-3
Beechwood Hills—summit VA-3
Beechwood Hills—uninc pl GA-3
Beechwood Home—building NY-2
Beechwood (Isaac Kinsey House)—hist pl IN-6
Beechwood Lake—lake PA-2
Beechwood Lake—reservoir IN-6
Beechwood Lake—reservoir NC-3
Beechwood Lake—reservoir WI-6
Beechwood Lake Dam—dam IN-6
**Beechwood Manor**—pop pl VA-3
Beechwood on the Burley—locale MD-2
Beechwood Park—locale PA-2
Beechwood Park—other PA-2
Beechwood Park—park MD-2
Beechwood Park—park MI-6
Beechwood Park—park OH-6
**Beechwood Park**—pop pl VA-3
Beechwood Playground—park OH-6
Beechwood River MA-1
Beechwoods—locale PA-2
Beechwoods Cem—cemetery NY-2
Beechwoods Cem—cemetery PA-2
Beechwood Sch—school AR-4
Beechwood Sch—school GA-3
Beechwood Sch—school (2) MI-6
Beechwood Sch—school NY-2
Beechwood Sch—school OH-6
Beechwood Sch—school WV-2
Beechwood Sch (historical)—school MS-4
Beechwood Sch (historical)—school TN-4
Beechwood Seminary (historical)—school MS-4
Beechwood Shop Ctr—locale GA-3
**Beechwood Shores**—pop pl NC-3
Beechwoods Sch—school OH-6
Beechwoods Schools (abandoned)—school PA-2
Beechwood Store—hist pl MI-6
**Beechwood (subdivision)**—pop pl AL-4
Beechwood Swamp—swamp GA-3
Beechwood Trail—trail PA-2
**Beechwood Village**—pop pl KY-4

**Beechwood Village**—*pop pl* TN-4
Beechy—*locale* KY-4
Beechy Bottom Brook—*stream* NY-2
Beechy Branch—*stream* WV-2
Beechy Ch—*church* OH-6
Beechy Creek—*stream* (3) KY-4
Beechy Creek—*stream* TN-4
Beechy Creek—*stream* WV-2
Beechy Fork—*stream* KY-4
Beechy Hollow—*valley* (2) KY-4
Beechy Mire (historical P.O.)—*locale* IN-6
Beechy Run—*stream* WV-2
Beechy Sch—*school* KY-4
Bee Cienega—*flat* AZ-5
Bee Cistern—*well* AZ-5
Bee Cliff—*cliff* TN-4
Bee Cliff Hollow—*valley* TN-4
Beecn Cliff Ch—*church* TN-4
Beecomb Branch—*stream* AL-4
**Bee (County)**—*pop pl* TX-5
Bee Cove—*valley* NC-3
Bee Cove Branch—*stream* TN-4
*Bee Cove Creek* TX-5
Bee Cove Creek—*stream* TN-4
Bee Cove Creek—*stream* TX-5
Bee Cove Knob—*summit* NC-3
Bee Cove Lead—*ridge* NC-3
Bee Cove Tank—*reservoir* TX-5
*Bee Creek* MT-8
Bee Creek—*locale* MO-7
**Bee Creek**—*pop pl* IL-6
**Beecreek**—*pop pl* IL-6
Bee Creek—*stream* AL-4
Bee Creek—*stream* (3) AR-4
Bee Creek—*stream* (2) CA-9
Bee Creek—*stream* ID-8
Bee Creek—*stream* IL-6
Bee Creek—*stream* (3) IN-6
Bee Creek—*stream* IA-7
Bee Creek—*stream* KS-7
Bee Creek—*stream* (5) KY-4
Bee Creek—*stream* MN-6
Bee Creek—*stream* (6) MO-7
Bee Creek—*stream* MT-8
Bee Creek—*stream* (2) NC-3
Bee Creek—*stream* (3) OK-5
Bee Creek—*stream* (3) OR-9
Bee Creek—*stream* SC-3
Bee Creek—*stream* (3) TN-4
Bee Creek—*stream* (18) TX-5
Bee Creek—*stream* (2) WA-9
Bee Creek—*stream* WV-2
Bee Creek Cem—*cemetery* MO-7
Bee Creek Cem—*cemetery* TX-5
Bee Creek Lake—*reservoir* KS-7
Bee Creek Mtn—*summit* OK-5
Bee Creek Oil Field—*oilfield* TX-5
*Bee Creek Post Office* TN-4
Bee Dam—*dam* AZ-5
Beede Bay—*swamp* GA-3
Beede Brook—*stream* NY-2
Beede Desert—*plain* OR-9
Bee Dee Creek—*stream* TX-5
Beede Falls—*falls* NH-1
Beede Hill—*summit* NH-1
Beede Hill—*summit* NY-2
Beede Lake—*lake* WI-6
Beede Ledge—*bench* NY-2
Beedell Cem—*cemetery* IN-6
Beede Mtn—*summit* NH-1
Beede North Dam—*dam* OR-9
Beede South Dam—*dam* OR-9
**Beedeville**—*pop pl* AR-4
Bee Ditch—*canal* MT-8
*Beedle Point* ID-8
Beedle Point—*cape* ID-8
Beedle Road Ch—*church* ME-1
Beedles Station—*locale* OH-6
Bee Draw—*valley* SD-7
Beeds Lake—*reservoir* IA-7
Beeds Lake State Park—*park* IA-7
Beedy Branch—*stream* GA-3
Beedy Ditch—*canal* IN-6
Beedy Lake—*reservoir* IN-6
Beedy Lake Dam—*dam* IN-6
Beef Acre—*basin* WY-8
Beef Basin—*basin* UT-8
Beef Basin Spring—*spring* UT-8
Beef Basin Wash—*valley* UT-8
Beef Bayou—*stream* TX-5
Beef Boeuf Lock—*dam* LA-4
Beef Branch—*stream* LA-4
Beef Branch—*stream* MO-7
Beef Branch Ch—*church* MO-7
Beef Camp Branch—*stream* FL-3
Beef Canyon—*valley* CO-8
Beef Canyon—*valley* (2) TX-5
Beef Corral Bottom—*bend* ND-7
Beef Corral Dam—*dam* AZ-5
Beef Corral Draw—*valley* AZ-5
Beef Corral Gulch—*valley* CA-9
Beef Corral Tank—*reservoir* AZ-5
Beef Corral Wash—*stream* ND-7
*Beef Creek* OK-5
Beef Creek—*stream* (2) OK-5
Beef Creek—*stream* (2) SD-7
Beef Creek—*stream* (2) TX-5
Beef Draw—*valley* CO-8
Beef Draw—*valley* SD-7
Beef Eater Canyon—*valley* AZ-5
Beef Flats—*flat* OK-5
Beef Gap—*gap* TX-5
Beef Gap—*gap* WY-8
Beef Head Creek—*stream* TX-5
*Beefhead Slough* TX-5
Beefhide—*locale* KY-4
Beefhide Creek—*stream* KY-4
Beef Hollow—*valley* OR-9
Beef Hollow—*valley* (2) TX-5
Beef Hollow—*valley* (2) UT-8
Beef Hollow Creek—*stream* TX-5
Beef Hollow Rsvr—*reservoir* UT-8
Beef Island—*flat* TN-4
Beef Island—*island* RI-1
Bee Flat—*flat* (2) CA-9
Bee Flat—*flat* OR-9
Bee Flat—*flat* WA-9
Beef Market Top—*summit* NC-3
Beef Meadows—*flat* UT-8
Bee Fork—*stream* (2) KY-4
Bee Fork—*stream* (2) MO-7
Bee Fork—*stream* TN-4
Bee Fork—*stream* (2) WV-2
Bee Fork Ch—*church* MO-7
Bee Fork Creek—*stream* MO-7
Beef Pass—*gap* NV-8
Beef Pasture—*area* UT-8
Beef Pasture—*flat* CO-8
Beef Pasture Cabin—*locale* WA-9
Beef Pasture Gap—*gap* TX-5
Beef Pasture Point—*summit* CO-8
Beef Pasture Tank—*reservoir* (3) TX-5
Beefpen Gully—*stream* LA-4
Beef Pen Spring—*spring* TX-5
*Beef Ridge* LA-4
Beef Ridge—*ridge* (2) LA-4
Beef Rock—*island* ME-1
Beef Slide Canyon—*valley* UT-8
*Beef Slough* WI-6
Beef Slough—*stream* MT-8
Beefsteak Gulch—*valley* CO-8
Beefsteak Hollow—*valley* MO-7
Beef Steer Creek—*stream* WY-8
Beef Steer Spring—*spring* WY-8
Beefstraight Creek—*stream* (2) MT-8
Beef Tank—*reservoir* OK-5
Beef Tank—*reservoir* TX-5
Beef Trail, The (pack)—*trail* OR-9
Beef Trail Campground—*locale* TX-5
Beef Trail Rsvr—*reservoir* CO-8
Beef Trap Windmill—*locale* TX-5
Beef Well—*well* TX-5
Beefwood Branch—*stream* FL-3
Bee Gap—*gap* GA-3
Bee Gap—*gap* NC-3
Beeghly Heights—*locale* FL-3
**Beegleton**—*pop pl* PA-2
Bee Grove Sch—*school* IL-6
Bee Gulch—*valley* CA-9
Beegum—*locale* CA-9
Beegum Basin—*basin* CA-9
Beegum Branch—*stream* GA-3
Bee Gum Branch—*stream* GA-3
Bee Gum Branch—*stream* (2) NC-3
Bee Gum Branch—*stream* WV-2
Bee Gum Creek—*stream* AL-4
Beegum Creek—*stream* CA-9
Beegum Gap—*gap* (2) GA-3
Beegum Gorge—*valley* CA-9
Bee Gum Hollow—*valley* AR-4
Bee Gum Lake—*lake* FL-3
Bee Gum Lake—*lake* GA-3
Beegum Peak—*summit* CA-9
Bee Gum Point—*cape* FL-3
Bee Gum Prairie—*swamp* GA-3
Bee Gum Ridge—*ridge* MO-7
Bee Gum Tank—*reservoir* TX-5
Beegum Union Ch—*church* WV-2
Beeham Run—*stream* OH-6
Bee Haven Bay—*swamp* FL-3
Beehbito Spring—*spring* AZ-5
*Bee Hill* MA-1
Bee Hill—*summit* AL-4
Bee Hill—*summit* (2) MA-1
Bee Hill—*summit* MO-7
Beehive—*locale* AL-4
Beehive—*pillar* AZ-5
**Beehive**—*pop pl* MT-8
Beehive—*summit* ID-8
Beehive—*summit* PA-2
Beehive, The—*pillar* WA-9
Beehive, The—*summit* AK-9
Beehive, The—*summit* CA-9
Beehive, The—*summit* CO-8
Beehive, The—*summit* UT-8
Beehive Acres Commercial Subdivision—*locale* UT-8
Beehive Arch—*arch* (2) UT-8
Beehive Basin—*basin* MT-8
Beehive Beach—*locale* MD-2
Beehive Bend—*bend* CA-9
Beehive Branch—*stream* KY-4
Beehive Butte—*summit* UT-8
Beehive Canyon—*valley* AZ-5
Beehive Canyon—*valley* CO-8
Beehive Canyon—*valley* UT-8
Beehive Cave—*cave* NM-5
Bee Hive Cem—*cemetery* GA-3
Beehive Ch—*church* LA-4
Beehive Cove—*bay* MD-2
Beehive Creek—*stream* (2) ID-8
Beehive Crossing—*locale* NY-2
**Beehive Crossing**—*pop pl* NY-2
Beehive Dam—*dam* AZ-5
Beehive Dome—*summit* UT-8
Beehive Flat—*flat* CA-9
Beehive Hollow—*valley* VA-3
Beehive House—*hist pl* UT-8
Beehive Island—*island* (2) AK-9
Beehive Knob—*summit* MO-7
Beehive Lake—*lake* IL-6
Beehive Lake—*lake* MT-8
Beehive Lakes—*lake* ID-8
Beehive Mine—*mine* AZ-5
Beehive Mine—*mine* CA-9
*Beehive Mountain* UT-8
Beehive Mtn—*summit* TX-5
Beehive Mtn—*summit* (2) WA-9
Beehive Peak—*summit* AZ-5
Bee Hive Peak—*summit* UT-8
Beehive Peak—*summit* UT-8
Beehive Point—*cape* UT-8
Beehive Ridge—*ridge* UT-8
Beehive Rock—*pillar* AZ-5
Beehive Rock—*summit* MT-8
Beehive Rock—*summit* NV-8
Beehive Rsvr—*reservoir* WA-9
Beehive Ruins—*locale* AZ-5
Bee Hives—*summit* UT-8
*Beehives, The* UT-8
Beehive Sch—*hist pl* OH-6
Bee Hive Sch—*school* IL-6
Beehive Sch—*school* IL-6
Beehive Sch—*school* IA-7
Beehive Sch—*school* KY-4
Beehive Sch—*school* MT-8
Beehive Sch—*school* OH-6
Beehive Sch—*school* UT-8
Beehive Sch (historical)—*school* AL-4
Beehive Spring—*spring* AZ-5
Beehive Spring—*spring* NM-5
Beehive Spring—*spring* WA-9
Beehive Spring Campground—*locale* WA-9
Beehive Tank—*reservoir* (3) AZ-5
Beehive Trail—*trail* PA-2
Beehive Well—*well* AZ-5
Bee Hole Brook—*stream* NH-1
Beehole Hollow—*valley* MO-7
Bee Hollow—*valley* (3) AR-4
Bee Hollow—*valley* (2) KY-4
Bee Hollow—*valley* (2) MO-7
Bee Hollow—*valley* NY-2
Bee Hollow—*valley* (2) PA-2
Bee Hollow—*valley* (2) TN-4
Bee Hollow—*valley* TX-5
Bee Hollow—*valley* (3) WV-2
Bee Hollow—*valley* WI-6
Bee House—*locale* TX-5
Beehouse Canyon—*valley* AZ-5
*Bee House Creek* TX-5
Bee House Creek—*stream* TX-5
Beehouse Spring—*spring* AZ-5
Beehouse Tank—*reservoir* AZ-5
Beehr Drain—*canal* MI-6
**Beehunter**—*pop pl* IN-6
*Bee Hunter (Beehunter)* IN-6
Beehunter Creek—*stream* NY-2
Beehunter Ditch—*canal* IN-6
Bee Hunt Hollow—*valley* ID-8
Bee Island—*island* (2) FL-3
Bee Island Bay—*swamp* NC-3
*Beek Creek* MT-8
Beeken Ranch—*locale* NE-7
Beeker Ranch—*locale* WA-9
Beekid Halani Tank—*reservoir* AZ-5
Beekin Ranch—*locale* NE-7
Beekins Ranch—*locale* NE-7
**Beekman**—*pop pl* LA-4
**Beekman**—*pop pl* NY-2
Beekman, James William, House—*hist pl* NY-2
Beekman Beach—*beach* NY-2
Beekman Cem—*cemetery* IL-6
Beekman Cem—*cemetery* (2) NY-2
Beekman Cem—*cemetery* OH-6
Beekman Ch—*church* NY-2
Beekman Corners—*locale* (2) NY-2
Beekman Creek—*stream* TX-5
Beekman Flat—*flat* OR-9
Beekman Gas and Oil Field—*oilfield* LA-4
Beekman Hosp—*hospital* NY-2
Beekman Lookout Tower—*locale* LA-4
Beekman Ridge—*ridge* OH-6
Beekman Ridge—*ridge* OR-9
Beekman Sch—*school* (2) NY-2
Beekman Spring—*spring* TX-5
**Beekmantown**—*pop pl* NY-2
**Beekman (Town of)**—*pop pl* NY-2
**Beekmantown (Town of)**—*pop pl* NY-2
Bee Knob—*summit* AR-4
Bee Knob—*summit* GA-3
Bee Knob—*summit* (2) NC-3
Bee Knob—*summit* (4) WV-2
Bee Knob Gap—*gap* GA-3
Bee Knob Hill—*summit* KY-4
Bee Knobs—*summit* NC-3
Bee Knoll—*summit* (2) CA-9
Beeks, Silas Jacob N., House—*hist pl* OR-9
Beeks Bight—*bay* CA-9
Beeks Canyon—*valley* WA-9
Beeks Cem—*cemetery* MS-4
**Beeks (historical)**—*pop pl* MS-4
Beeks Place—*locale* CA-9
*Beek Spring* WA-9
Beek Spring—*spring* TX-5
Beeks Sch—*school* VA-3
Beeks Spring—*spring* WA-9
*Beelake* MS-4
Bee Lake—*lake* CA-9
Bee Lake—*lake* (2) LA-4
Bee Lake—*lake* MI-6
Bee Lake—*lake* MN-6
Bee Lake—*lake* (4) MS-4
Bee Lake—*lake* TN-4
Bee Lake—*lake* WA-9
**Bee Lake**—*pop pl* MS-4
Bee Lake—*swamp* AR-4
Bee Lake Landing (historical)—*locale* MS-4
*Bee Lake Plantation* MS-4
**Beelake (RR name Bee Lake)**—*pop pl* MS-4
Bee Lake (RR name for Beelake)—*other* MS-4
Bee Lake Rsvr No. 5—*reservoir* CO-8
Bee Lake State Wildlife Mngmt Area—*park* MN-6
**Beeler**—*pop pl* KS-7
Beeler Branch—*stream* MO-7
Beeler Branch—*stream* TN-4
Beeler Canyon—*valley* CA-9
Beeler Cem—*cemetery* IA-7
Beeler Cem—*cemetery* KS-7
Beeler Cem—*cemetery* MO-7
Beeler Cem—*cemetery* OH-6
Beeler Cem—*cemetery* (6) TN-4
Beeler Ch—*church* TN-4
Beeler Chapel—*church* TN-4
Beeler Creek—*stream* AZ-5
Beeler Creek—*stream* CA-9
Beeler Creek—*stream* OR-9
Beeler Ditch—*canal* IN-6
Beeler Fork—*stream* TN-4
*Beeler Fork Branch* TN-4
Beeler Gap—*gap* TN-4
Beeler Gulch—*valley* CO-8
Beeler Hollow—*valley* TN-4
Beeler Island—*island* KY-4
Beeler Lake—*lake* LA-4
Beeler Mill—*locale* TN-4
Beeler Ridge—*ridge* OR-9
Beeler Ridge—*ridge* TN-4
Beeler Rsvr—*reservoir* CA-9
Beeler Sch—*school* NJ-2
Beelers Ford—*locale* VA-3
Beeler Spring—*spring* OR-9
Beeler Spring—*spring* TN-4
Beeler Spring—*spring* UT-8
*Beelers Station* IN-6
Beelers Station—*locale* WV-2
Beelers Summit—*locale* MD-2
**Beeler's Summit**—*pop pl* MD-2
Beelerton—*locale* KY-4
*Beelerville* KS-7
Beeler-Vittitow Cem—*cemetery* KY-4
Bee Lick—*locale* KY-4
Bee Lick—*stream* KY-4
*Beelick Branch* WV-2
Beelick Branch—*stream* WV-2
Bee Lick Creek—*stream* (5) KY-4
*Bee Lick Hollow* OH-6
**Beelick Knob**—*pop pl* WV-2
Beelick Knob—*summit* WV-2
Beelick Run—*stream* WV-2
*Beeline Creek* NY-2
Beeline Dragway—*other* AZ-5
Beeline Rsvr—*reservoir* NM-5
Beeline Tank—*reservoir* (3) AZ-5
Bee Line Trail—*trail* NH-1
**Bee Log**—*pop pl* NC-3
Bee Log Elem Sch—*school* NC-3
Beel Ranch—*locale* NE-7
Beelzebub—*summit* NM-5
Beeman—*locale* PA-2
Beeman Acad—*school* VT-1
Beeman Branch—*stream* TX-5
*Beeman Branch Hollow* MO-7
*Beeman Brook* CT-1
Beeman Canyon—*valley* CA-9
Beeman Canyon—*valley* NM-5
Beeman Canyon—*valley* OR-9
Beeman Cem—*cemetery* MS-4
Beeman Cem—*cemetery* NY-2
Beeman Creek—*stream* AL-4
Beeman Creek—*stream* NE-7
Beeman Creek—*stream* NY-2
Beeman Creek—*stream* OK-5
Beeman Creek—*stream* OR-9
Beeman Creek—*stream* WI-6
Beeman Ditch—*canal* CO-8
Beeman Hollow—*valley* MO-7
Beeman Hollow—*valley* NY-2
Beeman Junkens Trail—*trail* OR-9
Beeman Memorial Sch—*school* MA-1
Beeman Park Montessori Sch—*school* FL-3
Beeman Ridge—*ridge* OH-6
Beemans Brook—*stream* CT-1
Beeman Sch—*school* WA-9
*Beemans Creek* AL-4
*Beemans Creek* MO-7
Beeman Tank—*reservoir* NM-5
Beeman Tank—*reservoir* TX-5
Beem Cem—*cemetery* IN-6
Bee Meadow Pond—*lake* NJ-2
**Beemer**—*pop pl* NE-7
*Beemer Ditch* OH-6
Beemer Drain—*canal* MI-6
*Beemersville* NJ-2
**Beemer Township**—*pop pl* NE-7
Beemerville—*locale* NJ-2
Bee Mesa—*summit* AZ-5
Beemguiga Creek—*stream* AK-9
Beem Gulch—*valley* WY-8
Beemis Creek—*stream* IA-7
**Beemont**—*pop pl* MO-7
Beemont Ch—*church* MO-7
Bee Mountain—*ridge* AL-4
Bee Mountain Lookout Tower—*locale* AR-4
Beemouth Branch—*stream* LA-4
Beem Ranch—*locale* NE-7
Bee Mtn—*summit* AL-4
Bee Mtn—*summit* AZ-5
Bee Mtn—*summit* (3) AR-4
Bee Mtn—*summit* CA-9
Bee Mtn—*summit* CT-1
Bee Mtn—*summit* GA-3
Bee Mtn—*summit* MS-4
Bee Mtn—*summit* (2) NC-3
Bee Mtn—*summit* (3) TX-5
Bee Mtn—*summit* VA-3
Bee Mtn—*summit* WV-2
Beene Branch—*stream* TX-5
Beene Cem—*cemetery* (2) TN-4
Beene Cove—*valley* (2) TN-4
Beene Cove Branch—*stream* TN-4
Beene Creek—*stream* AR-4
Beene Creek—*stream* LA-4
Beene-Pearson Memorial Library—*building* TN-4
Beenes Ferry (historical)—*locale* MS-4
Beene Stadium—*park* TN-4
Beenham—*locale* NM-5
Beenik—*locale* FM-9
Been Mtn—*summit* AR-4
Bee Oak Trail—*trail* MD-2
Bee Pond—*swamp* (2) FL-3
Bee Pond Flats—*swamp* GA-3
Bee Ponds—*lake* FL-3
Bee Press Ridge—*ridge* MO-7
Beer, Judge Thomas, House—*hist pl* OH-6
Beer, William F., Estate—*hist pl* UT-8
Bee Ranch—*locale* NV-8
Bee Ranch—*locale* OR-9
Bee Ranch Trail—*trail* CA-9
Beer Bottle Creek—*stream* CA-9
Beer Bottle Crossing—*locale* ID-8
Beer Bottle Pass—*gap* NV-8
Beer Bottle Spring—*spring* UT-8
Beer Bottle Wash—*stream* AZ-5
Beer Bottle Well—*well* AZ-5
Beerbower Ditch—*canal* OH-6
Beer Bum Hill—*summit* ND-7
Beer Can Pond—*lake* FL-3
Beer Cem—*cemetery* IL-6
*Beer Creek* ID-8
*Beer Creek* TX-5
Beer Creek—*stream* CA-9
Beer Creek—*stream* UT-8
Beeres Pond—*lake* OR-9
Beer Garden Creek—*stream* SC-3
Beer Garden Gulch—*valley* WY-8
*Beer Garden Ridge* VA-3
*Beer Garden Ridge* WV-2
Beer Garden Spring—*spring* OR-9
Beergerson Slough—*swamp* MN-6
*Beer Gulch* CA-9
Beer Hollow—*valley* UT-8
Beer Hollow Trail—*trail* PA-2
**Bee Ridge**—*pop pl* FL-3
**Bee Ridge**—*pop pl* IN-6
Bee Ridge—*ridge* AL-4
Bee Ridge—*ridge* (2) AR-4
Bee Ridge—*ridge* IL-6
Bee Ridge—*ridge* (5) NC-3
Bee Ridge—*ridge* TN-4
Bee Ridge—*ridge* (3) WV-2
Bee Ridge Baptist Ch—*church* FL-3
Bee Ridge Ch—*church* MO-7
Bee Ridge Fire Tower—*tower* FL-3
Bee Ridge Hollow—*valley* TN-4
Bee Ridge Park—*park* FL-3
Bee Ridge Sch—*school* IN-6
Bee Ridge Square (Shop Ctr)—*locale* FL-3
Bee Ridge Township—*civil* MO-7
Beer Keg Hollow—*valley* PA-2
Beer Keg Meadow—*flat* CA-9
Beer Keg Spring—*spring* CO-8
Beer Kill—*stream* NY-2
Beerline Canal—*canal* NE-7
Beer Logan—*swamp* ME-1
Beerman Creek—*stream* OR-9
Beerman Creek—*stream* WY-8
Beermug Dam—*dam* SD-7
Beermug Lake—*reservoir* SD-7
Beer Mug Mtn—*summit* WY-8
Beer Mug Ranch—*locale* WY-8
Beer Mug Spring—*spring* ID-8
Bee Rock—*island* CA-9
Bee Rock—*locale* CA-9
Bee Rock—*pillar* AR-4
Bee Rock—*pillar* (2) CA-9
**Bee Rock**—*pop pl* CA-9
Bee Rock—*summit* CA-9
Bee Rock—*summit* CO-8
Bee Rock—*summit* TN-4
Bee Rock Canyon—*valley* (3) CA-9
Bee Rock Creek—*stream* NC-3
Bee Rock Flats—*flat* TX-5
Bee Rock Hollow—*valley* MO-7
Bee Rock Mtn—*summit* TX-5
Bee Rock Ridge—*ridge* TN-4
Bee Rocks—*area* AK-9
Beeroth Canal—*canal* ID-8
Beer Pond—*lake* CT-1
Beer Run—*stream* PA-2
**Beers**—*pop pl* ID-8
Beers, Oliver, House—*hist pl* OR-9
Beers, Samuel, House—*hist pl* OH-6
Beers, William, House—*hist pl* VA-3
Beers Brook—*stream* (2) NY-2
*Beers Creek* NJ-2
Beers Creek—*stream* IA-7
Beers Dam—*dam* OR-9
Beers Ditch—*canal* OR-9
Beers Farm Airp—*airport* PA-2
Beersheba Cem—*cemetery* AL-4
Beersheba Cem—*cemetery* TN-4
Beersheba Ch—*church* (2) GA-3
Beersheba Ch—*church* TN-4
*Beersheba Church* MS-4
Beersheba Cumberland Ch—*church* MS-4
**Beersheba Springs**—*pop pl* TN-4
Beersheba Springs Cem—*cemetery* TN-4
Beersheba Springs Hist Dist—*hist pl* TN-4
Beersheba Springs Post Office—*building* TN-4
Beersheba Springs Sch (historical)—*school* TN-4
Beershebas Spring—*spring* TN-4
Beers Hill—*summit* NY-2
Beers Hollow—*valley* (2) PA-2
Beers Island—*island* CT-1
Beers Island—*island* LA-4
Beerskill—*stream* NJ-2
Beers Lake—*lake* MN-6
Beers Lake—*reservoir* IN-6
Beers Lake—*reservoir* MO-7
Beer Slough—*stream* NE-7
Beers Mtn—*summit* MA-1
Beers Pass—*gap* UT-8
Beers Plain—*bench* MA-1
Beer Spring—*spring* UT-8
Beers Rocks—*island* CT-1
Beers Rsvr—*reservoir* NV-8
Beers Run—*stream* PA-2
Beers Sch—*school* DC-2
Beers Sch—*school* NJ-2
Beers Sch—*school* NC-3
Beers Spring—*spring* OR-9
Beers Street Sch—*school* NJ-2
Beerston—*locale* NY-2
Beer Straight Gulch—*valley* MT-8
Beers Trail—*trail* PA-2
Beers Tunnel Spring—*spring* UT-8
**Beersville**—*pop pl* PA-2
Bee Rsvr—*reservoir* OR-9
Beers Well—*well* AZ-5
Bee Run—*stream* IN-6
Bee Run—*stream* KY-4
Bee Run—*stream* MO-7
Bee Run—*stream* (5) OH-6
Bee Run—*stream* VA-3
Bee Run—*stream* (18) WV-2
Bee Run Campsite—*locale* WV-2
Bee Run Ch—*church* VA-3
Bee Run Hollow—*valley* AR-4
Bee Run Picnic Area—*locale* WV-2
Bee Run Trail—*trail* WV-2
Beerwagon Spring—*spring* SD-7
Beery, John K., Farm—*hist pl* VA-3
*Beery Ch* MS-4
Bees Branch—*stream* NJ-2
Bees Creek—*stream* SC-3
Bee Seep Tank—*reservoir* AZ-5
Bee Sellers Hollow—*valley* PA-2
*Bees Hill* MA-1
Bee Shoals—*bar* KY-4
Bee Shoals Creek—*stream* KY-4
Beeshsikad Spring—*spring* AZ-5
Bee Sinkhole Cave—*cave* AL-4
Beeskove Creek—*stream* MT-8
Beesley, Ebenezer, House—*hist pl* UT-8
Beesley Farms Airp—*airport* KS-7
**Beesleys Point**—*pop pl* NJ-2
Beeslick Brook—*stream* CT-1
Beeslick Pond—*lake* CT-1
Bee Slough—*gut* KY-4
Bees Mill—*locale* WA-9
*Beeson* IN-6
Beeson—*locale* WV-2
Beeson—*uninc pl* KS-7
Beeson, Col. Isaac, House—*hist pl* NC-3
Beeson Branch—*stream* AL-4
Beeson Bridge—*hist pl* IN-6
Beeson Cem—*cemetery* AR-4
Beeson Cem—*cemetery* CA-9
Beeson Chapel—*church* WV-2
Beeson Covered Bridge—*bridge* IN-6
*Beeson Creek* TX-5
**Beeson Crossroads**—*pop pl* NC-3
Beeson Field—*park* CA-9
Beeson Gap—*gap* AL-4
Beeson P.O. (historical)—*locale* AL-4
Beeson Pond—*swamp* TX-5
Beeson Run—*stream* WV-2
**Beesons**—*pop pl* IN-6
**Beesons**—*pop pl* PA-2
Beeson Sch—*school* MI-6
Beeson's Crossroad—*other* NC-3
Beeson Slough—*gut* AK-9
Beeson Station—*locale* NM-5
**Bee Spring**—*pop pl* KY-4
Bee Spring—*spring* (4) AZ-5
Bee Spring—*spring* NM-5
Bee Spring—*spring* OR-9
Bee Spring—*spring* TN-4
Bee Spring Branch—*stream* AL-4
Bee Spring Branch—*stream* TN-4
Bee Spring Camp—*locale* KY-4
Bee Spring Cem—*cemetery* TN-4
Bee Spring Ch—*church* TN-4
Bee Spring Hill—*summit* TN-4
Bee Spring Memorial Ch—*church* TN-4
Bee Spring Point—*cliff* AZ-5
Bee Springs—*spring* AZ-5
Bee Springs—*spring* CA-9
Bee Springs Canyon—*valley* CA-9
Bee Springs Tank—*reservoir* AZ-5
*Bees River* MA-1
*Beestick Brook* CT-1
*Beestick Pond* CT-1
Bee Sting Cave—*cave* AL-4
Beeston Hill—*locale* VI-3
Bee Suck Branch—*stream* TN-4
Bee Suck Creek—*stream* AR-4
Bee Suck Mountain—*ridge* AR-4
Beesum Lake Dam—*dam* MS-4
Bees Wax Bay—*basin* SC-3
Beeswax Branch—*stream* AL-4
Beeswax Canyon—*valley* CA-9
Beeswax Creek—*stream* AL-4
Bee Tank—*reservoir* (2) AZ-5
*Beetem Hollow* PA-2
Beetems Ch—*church* PA-2
Beeterman Chapel—*church* OH-6
Beetham Swale—*basin* ME-1
Beethoven Sch—*school* (2) MA-1
Beethoven Street Sch—*school* CA-9
Beet Island—*island* SC-3
Beetison, Israel, House—*hist pl* NE-7
**Beetland**—*pop pl* CO-8
Beetle—*locale* KY-4
Beetle Bluff—*cliff* OK-5
*Beetle Branch* NC-3
Beetle Brook—*stream* VT-1
Beetlebug Lake—*lake* CA-9
Beetle Bung Pond—*lake* CT-1
Beetle Butte—*summit* CA-9
Beetle Creek—*stream* ID-8
Beetle Creek—*stream* (2) MT-8
Beetle Creek—*stream* OH-6
Beetle Creek—*stream* OR-9
Beetle Creek—*stream* UT-8
Beetle Creek—*stream* WA-9
Beetle Creek—*stream* WI-6
Beetle Gulch—*valley* MT-8
Beetle Hill—*summit* MT-8
Beetle Hump—*summit* ID-8
Beetle Lake—*lake* MN-6
Beetle Mtn—*summit* ME-1
Beetle Run—*stream* VA-3
Beetle Spring—*spring* OR-9
Beetles Rest Rsvr—*reservoir* OR-9
Beetle Swamp—*swamp* MA-1
Beeton—*locale* UT-8
Bee Top Mtn—*summit* ID-8
**Beetown**—*pop pl* WI-6
Beetown Branch—*stream* WI-6
Beetown Cem—*cemetery* WI-6
**Beetown (Town of)**—*pop pl* WI-6
Beetrace (historical P.O.)—*locale* IA-7
Bee Trail—*trail* PA-2
Bee Trail—*trail* WV-2
Bee Tree—*locale* CA-9
Beetree—*locale* MD-2
Bee Tree Bay—*swamp* NC-3
Bee Tree Bay—*swamp* (2) SC-3
Bee Tree Bayou—*stream* LA-4
Bee Tree Brake—*stream* MS-4
Bee Tree Branch—*stream* AL-4
Bee Tree Branch—*stream* FL-3
Bee Tree Branch—*stream* GA-3
Bee Tree Branch—*stream* KY-4
Beetree Branch—*stream* (3) KY-4
Beetree Branch—*stream* LA-4
Beetree Branch—*stream* MS-4
Bee Tree Branch—*stream* (2) NC-3
Beetree Branch—*stream* NC-3
Bee Tree Branch—*stream* SC-3
Bee Tree Branch—*stream* TN-4
Beetree Branch—*stream* TN-4
Beetree Branch—*stream* VA-3
Bee Tree Branch—*stream* VA-3
Beetree Branch—*stream* (2) WV-2
Bee Tree Canal—*canal* NC-3
*Bee Tree Ch* NC-3
Beetree Ch—*church* NC-3
Beetree Creek—*stream* AL-4
Bee Tree Creek—*stream* CA-9
Beetree Creek—*stream* MS-4
Beetree Creek—*stream* (4) NC-3
Bee Tree Creek—*stream* (2) NC-3
Beetree Creek—*stream* NC-3
*Bee Tree Dam* NC-3
Beetree Ditch—*canal* MD-2
Bee Tree Draft—*valley* PA-2
Bee Tree Flat—*flat* CA-9
Beetree Ford—*locale* FL-3
Beetree Fork—*stream* (2) KY-4
Beetree Fork—*stream* NC-3
Bee Tree Gap—*gap* CA-9
Beetree Gap—*gap* (2) NC-3
Beetree Hill—*summit* NY-2
Beetree Hollow—*valley* KY-4
Bee Tree Hollow—*valley* MD-2

Bee Tree Hollow—valley (3) ... PA-2
Beetree Hollow—valley ... TN-4
Bee Tree Hollow—valley ... WV-2
Bee Tree Island (historical)—island ... AL-4
Beetree Knob—summit ... NC-3
Bee Tree Knob—summit ... NC-3
Beetree Knob—summit ... TN-4
Beetree Knob Prospect—mine ... TN-4
Bee Tree Lake—lake ... MN-6
Bee Tree Lake—lake ... SC-3
Bee Tree Lake Dam—dam ... NC-3
Bee Tree Overlook—locale ... NC-3
Beetree Pond—lake ... FL-3
Bee Tree Pond—lake ... FL-3
Bee Tree Pond—lake ... TN-4
Bee Tree Ridge ... CA-9
Bee Tree Ridge—ridge ... GA-3
Beetree Ridge—ridge ... NC-3
Bee Tree Ridge—ridge ... NC-3
Beetree Ridge—ridge ... NC-3
Bee Tree Ridge—ridge (2) ... NC-3
Beetree Ridge—ridge ... NC-3
Bee Tree Ridge—ridge ... TN-4
Bee Tree Ridge—ridge ... WV-2
Bee Tree Rsvr—reservoir ... NC-3
Beetree Run—stream ... IN-6
Beetree Run—stream ... MD-2
Beetree Run—stream ... OH-6
Beetree Run—stream ... PA-2
Bee Tree Run—stream ... WV-2
Beetree Run—stream ... WV-2
Bee Tree Sch—school ... WA-9
Bee Tree Shoals ... AL-4
Bee Tree Slough—gut (2) ... AR-4
Beetree Slough—gut ... FL-3
Bee Tree Slough—gut ... TN-4
Bee Tree Slough—stream ... AR-4
Bee Tree Spring—spring ... AZ-5
Bee Tree Spring—spring ... CA-9
Bee Tree Swamp—swamp ... FL-3
Bee Tree Swamp—swamp ... NC-3
Bee Tree Swamp—swamp ... TX-5
Bee Tree Tank—reservoir ... AZ-5
Bee Tree Tanks—reservoir ... AZ-5
Beets Cave—cave ... AL-4
Beets Cem—cemetery ... TN-4
Beetso Well—well ... AZ-5
Beets Run ... NC-3
Beet Sugar Factory—hist pl ... AZ-5
Beetville—locale ... ID-8
Beevale Flat—flat ... OK-5
Bee Valley—valley ... CA-9
Beevers Cem—cemetery ... NM-5
**Beeville**—pop pl ... TX-5
Beeville (CCD)—cens area ... TX-5
Beeville Country Club—other ... TX-5
Beeville Memorial Park (Cemetery)—cemetery ... TX-5
Beeville Post Office (historical)—building ... TN-4
Bee Wash—stream ... CA-9
Bee Waterhole Windmill—locale ... TX-5
Bee Well—well ... AZ-5
Beezer Creek ... CO-8
Beezley Hills—range ... WA-9
Bega Cem—cemetery ... NE-7
Began ... MP-9
Begashi-bito Canyon ... AZ-5
Begashibito Canyon—valley ... AZ-5
Begashibito Creek ... AZ-5
Begashibito Wash—valley ... AZ-5
Begashinitoni Canyon—valley ... AZ-5
Begay Well—well (2) ... AZ-5
Begay Windmill—locale ... AZ-5
Beg Creek Cem—cemetery ... MS-4
Begef—island ... FM-9
Begeman Cem—cemetery ... IN-6
Begeman Cem—cemetery ... MO-7
Begeman State Public Shooting Area—park ... SD-7
Begen—island ... MP-9
Begeraburappu—island ... MP-9
Begeraburappu Island ... MP-9
Beggar Run—stream ... OH-6
Beggars Bridge Creek—stream ... VA-3
Beggar's Neck ... MD-2
Beggarstown Sch—hist pl ... PA-2
Beggenadick ... MP-9
**Beggs**—pop pl ... LA-4
**Beggs**—pop pl ... OK-5
Beggs, Ellsworth J., House—hist pl ... UT-8
Beggs, Lake—lake ... FL-3
Beggs (CCD)—cens area ... OK-5
Beggs Cem—cemetery ... OK-5
Begg Sch—school ... CA-9
Beggs Fork ... WV-2
Beggs Island—island ... WI-6
Beggs Lake—reservoir ... OK-5
Beggs Ranch—locale (2) ... TX-5
Beggs Sch (historical)—school ... MO-7
Beggs Vocational Sch—school ... FL-3
Beghtol Cem—cemetery ... IL-6
Beghto Ridge—ridge ... KY-4
Begin Channel—channel ... MP-9
Begin Island—island ... MP-9
Beginnigar Island ... MP-9
Beginning Branch—stream ... KY-4
Beginning Point of the U.S. Public Land Survey—hist pl ... OH-6
Beginning Point of the U.S. Public Land Survey—hist pl ... PA-2
Begin Pass ... MP-9
Begin-sand ... MP-9
Begin-suido ... MP-9
Begin-to ... MP-9
Begley Branch—stream ... KY-4
Begley Branch—stream ... TN-4
Begley Cem—cemetery ... KY-4
Begley Creek—stream ... AR-4
Begley Hollow—valley ... KY-4
Begley Hollow—valley ... VA-3
Begnard Bay—bay ... LA-4
Begole Sch—school ... MI-6
**Begonia (historical)**—pop pl ... NC-3
Begonia Park—park ... CA-9
Begsley Lane Ch—church ... TN-4
Beguin Cem—cemetery ... NE-7
Begum Cem—cemetery ... AR-4
Begunn Creek—stream ... MI-6
**Beham**—pop pl ... PA-2
Beham Knob Sch (abandoned)—school ... PA-2
Beham Run—stream ... PA-2
Behan Brook—stream ... NY-2
Behanin Creek—stream ... UT-8
Behannon-Kenley House—hist pl ... TX-5
Beheaiaha Creek ... MS-4
Beheimer Well—well ... NM-5
Be He Lini Spring—spring ... AZ-5
Behemotosh Mountain ... CA-9
Behe Point Sch—school ... AR-4
Behestian (Township of)—fmr MCD ... AR-4
Behihlih—area ... AZ-5
Behiliper Island—island ... FM-9
Behind Horse Pasture Tank—reservoir ... TX-5
Behind Nazareth ... PA-2
Behind Rock Cave—cave ... AL-4
Behind the Rocks—area ... UT-8
**Beh Lake Estates**—pop pl ... IL-6
**Behlen**—pop pl ... NE-7
Behler—locale ... WV-2
Behler Creek—stream ... CO-8
Behler Creek—stream ... MN-6
Behler Swamp—swamp ... PA-2
**Behlmer Corner**—pop pl ... IN-6
Behlow Lake—lake ... MI-6
Behm Canal—channel ... AK-9
Behme Cem—cemetery ... IL-6
Behmes Windmill—locale ... TX-5
Behm Mesa—summit ... AZ-5
Behm Mesa Tank—reservoir ... AZ-5
Behm Mtn—summit ... AK-9
Behm Mtn—summit ... OH-6
Behm Narrows—channel ... AK-9
Behm Run—stream ... PA-2
Behner Brook—stream ... IN-6
Behning Creek—stream ... WI-6
Behning Creek State Public Fishing Area—park ... WI-6
Behnke Brook—stream ... NJ-2
Behorn Cem—cemetery ... AR-4
Behrend Campus Pennsylvania State Univ—school ... PA-2
Behren Pond—reservoir ... PA-2
Behrens Cem—cemetery ... TX-5
Behrens Hosp—hospital ... CA-9
Behrens Pond ... PA-2
Behrens Rsvr—reservoir ... CO-8
Behringer Canyon—valley ... NM-5
Behringer Creek—stream ... WI-6
Behringer Park—park ... CA-9
Behringer Spring—spring ... NM-5
**Behring Store**—pop pl ... TX-5
Behr Lake—lake ... WI-6
Behrman ... AL-4
Behrman HS—school ... LA-4
Behrman Park—park ... LA-4
Behrns Creek ... TX-5
Behtlehem Lutheran Ch—church ... TN-4
Behunin Canyon—valley ... UT-8
Behunin Rsvr—reservoir ... WY-8
Beibersteine Cem—cemetery ... IN-6
Beicegel Creek—stream ... ND-7
Beidell Creek ... CO-8
Beiderbecke, Leon Bismark, House—hist pl ... IA-7
Beiderman, Ed, Fish Camp—hist pl ... AK-9
Beidleman Ch—church ... TN-4
Beidleman Creek—stream ... TN-4
Beidleman Mill (historical)—locale ... TN-4
**Beidlemans (historical)**—pop pl ... TN-4
Beidler Cem—cemetery ... OH-6
Beidler Sch—school ... IL-6
Beidler Sch—school ... OH-6
Beidler Trail—trail ... PA-2
Beierle Cem—cemetery ... TX-5
Bei Eten Ankerplatz ... FM-9
Beiger Elementary and JHS—school ... IN-6
Beiger House—hist pl ... IN-6
Beiger Sch ... IN-6
Beigh Lake—lake ... IN-6
Beigh Sch—school ... MI-6
Beightol Run ... PA-2
Beigle Mtn—summit ... WA-9
Beiler Airp—airport ... PA-2
Beiler Cem—cemetery ... PA-2
Beilfuss Park—park ... IL-6
Beim Lake—lake ... MN-6
Beiningen Lake—lake ... MN-6
Beir, Anna, House—hist pl ... OH-6
Beirdneau Campground—locale ... UT-8
Beirdneau Canyon ... UT-8
Beirdneau Hollow—valley ... UT-8
Beirdneau Peak—summit ... UT-8
Beirges Hill—summit ... CT-1
Beirman Spring—spring ... OR-9
**Beirne**—pop pl ... AR-4
Beirnes Ave Holiness Ch—church ... AL-4
Beisecker Sch (historical)—school ... PA-2
Beiseker Mansion—hist pl ... ND-7
Beiser Branch—stream ... AL-4
Beiser Drain—canal ... MI-6
Beiser Lake—swamp ... MN-6
Beisers Pond—lake ... NJ-2
Beisigl Sch—school ... ND-7
**Beisigl Township**—pop pl ... ND-7
Beisler Lake—reservoir ... NJ-2
Beisman Ranch—locale ... NM-5
Beismeir Beach ... NV-8
Beissner, Henry, House—hist pl ... TX-5
Beitel Creek—stream ... TX-5
Be-ite-Lini Spring—spring ... AZ-5
Beitel Memorial Cem—cemetery ... TX-5
Beitel Sch—school ... WY-8
Beitey Lake—lake ... WA-9
Beith, William, House—hist pl ... IL-6
Beitiu ... FM-9
Beitner Lake—lake ... MI-6
Beitner School—locale ... MI-6
Beiton Range ... CA-9
**Beixedon Estates**—pop pl ... NY-2
Bejao—area ... GU-9
Bejikobowa ... MP-9
**Bejou**—pop pl ... MN-6
Bejou Cem—cemetery ... MN-6
Bejou State Wildlife Mngmt Area—park ... MN-6
**Bejou (Township of)**—pop pl ... MN-6
Bejucos (Barrio)—fmr MCD ... PR-3
Bekanare ... MP-9
Bekebrede Draw—valley ... WY-8
Bekefos—island ... FM-9
Bekerappu ... MP-9
Bekerappu Island—island ... MP-9
Bekerappu-to ... MP-9
Beketei—summit ... PW-9
Bek-i hatso ... AZ-5
Bekihatso—lake ... AZ-5
Bekihatso Wash—stream ... AZ-5
Bekishi-bito Canyon ... AZ-5
Bekja—island ... MP-9
Bekken, J. H., House—hist pl ... TX-5
Bekke Post Office (historical)—building ... TN-4
Bekkie Creek ... NC-3
**Bekkvar**—pop pl ... WA-9
Beklabito ... NM-5
**Beklabito**—pop pl ... NM-5
Bekrak Islet ... MP-9
Beks Bay—swamp ... NC-3
Bel—locale ... LA-4
Bela—locale ... PA-2
Bela Brook—stream ... NH-1
Bela Creek—stream ... MI-6
Belafonte Tacolcy Center Preschool—school ... FL-3
Belah Ch—church ... LA-4
Belah Lookout Tower—locale ... LA-4
Belair—hist pl ... MD-2
Belair—hist pl ... TN-4
Bel Air—hist pl ... VA-3
Belair—locale ... GA-3
Belair—locale ... LA-4
**Bel Air**—pop pl ... AL-4
**Bel Air**—pop pl ... CA-9
**Bel-Air**—pop pl ... FL-3
**Belair**—pop pl ... FL-3
**Bel Air**—pop pl ... KY-4
**Bel Air**—pop pl (2) ... MD-2
**Bel Air**—pop pl ... TN-4
**Bel Air**—pop pl ... TX-5
**Bel Air**—pop pl (2) ... VA-3
Bel Air—uninc pl ... AL-4
Bel Air—uninc pl ... FL-3
Bel-air—uninc pl ... KY-4
Belair—uninc pl ... MD-2
Bel Air, Lake—lake ... RI-1
**Bel Air Acres**—pop pl (2) ... MD-2
Bel Air Armory—hist pl ... MD-2
Bel Air Assembly of God Ch—church ... AL-4
Bel Air Baptist Ch ... AL-4
Belair Baptist Ch—church ... AL-4
Belair Beach ... FL-3
**Bel Air Beach**—pop pl ... IA-7
Belair Buckingham—uninc pl ... MD-2
Belair Canal—canal ... LA-4
Belair Cem—cemetery ... LA-4
Bel Air Ch—church ... AL-4
Bel Air Ch—church ... SC-3
Bel Air Ch—church ... TX-5
Belair Chapel Forge—uninc pl ... MD-2
Bel Air Country Club—locale ... MS-4
Bel Air Country Club—other ... CA-9
Bel Air Courthouse Hist Dist—hist pl ... MD-2
**Belair Cove**—pop pl ... LA-4
Bel Air Dam—dam ... MA-1
Bel Aire ... AL-4
Belaire ... CA-9
Bel Aire ... KS-7
**Bel Aire**—pop pl ... KS-7
**Bel Aire**—pop pl ... TN-4
**Bel-Aire**—pop pl ... TN-4
**Bel-Aire**—pop pl ... VA-3
Bel Aire—uninc pl ... TN-4
Belaire—uninc pl ... VA-3
Bel Aire Canal Number C 1-N—canal ... FL-3
Belaire Ch—church ... MS-4
Bel Aire Ch—church ... NM-5
Bel Aire Ch of Christ—church ... TN-4
Bel Aire Ch of the Nazarene—church ... KS-7
**Bel-Aire Condominium**—pop pl ... UT-8
Bel-Aire Elem Sch—school ... FL-3
Bel Aire Elem Sch—school ... TN-4
**Bel Aire Estates**—pop pl ... CT-1
Bel Aire Estates—uninc pl ... CA-9
**Belaire Estates (subdivision)**—pop pl ... MS-4
**Bel-Aire Heights**—pop pl ... TN-4
Belaire Manor (trailer park)—locale ... AZ-5
**Belaire Manor (trailer park)**—pop pl ... AZ-5
Bel Aire Park—park ... FL-3
Bel-Aire Park—park ... MI-6
Bel-aire Rearing Station—locale ... CO-8
Bel Aire Sch—school (2) ... CA-9
Bel Aire Sch—school ... FL-3
Belaire Sch—school ... TX-5
Bel Aire Shop Ctr—locale ... AL-4
Bel Aire Shop Ctr—locale ... MS-4
Bel-aire Shop Ctr—locale ... MO-7
Bel Aire Shop Ctr—other ... NM-5
**Bel-Air Estates**—pop pl ... TN-4
**Bel Air Estates (subdivision)**—pop pl ... AL-4
**Belair Estates (subdivision)**—pop pl ... NC-3
**Belaire (subdivision)**—pop pl ... MS-4
Bel-Aire Trailer Park—locale ... AZ-5
**Bel-Air Forest (subdivision)**—pop pl ... NC-3
Belair Foxhill—uninc pl ... MD-2
Bel Air Gardens ... IL-6
Belair Golf Club—other ... MD-2
Belair Heather Hills—uninc pl ... MD-2
Belair Idlewild—uninc pl ... MD-2
Belair JHS—school ... MD-2
Belair Kenilworth—uninc pl ... MD-2
Bel-Air Lake—lake ... FL-3
Bel-Air Lake—reservoir ... PA-2
Bel-Air Lake Dam—dam ... PA-2
Belair Longridge—uninc pl ... MD-2
Bel Air Mall Shop Ctr—locale ... AL-4
Bel Air Memorial Gardens—cemetery ... MD-2
Bel Air Memorial Hosp—hospital ... CA-9
Bel-Air Mission—church ... NM-5
Bel Air North—CDP ... MD-2
**Bel Air One (subdivision)**—pop pl ... TN-4
Belair Overbrook—uninc pl ... MD-2
Bel Air Park—park ... TN-4
**Belair Park**—pop pl ... PA-2
Bel Air Plaza Shop Ctr—locale ... AZ-5
Bel-Air Pond—reservoir ... NC-3
Bel-Air Pond Dam—dam ... NC-3
Bel-Air Ranch Health Camp—locale ... NY-2
Belair Road—uninc pl ... NY-2
Belair Rockledge—uninc pl ... MD-2
Bel Air Rsvr—reservoir ... MD-2
Bel Air Sch—school ... CA-9
Bel Air Sch—school ... MN-6
Belair Sch—school ... MO-7
Bel-Air Sch—school ... NM-5
Bel Air Sch—school ... ND-7
Bel-Air Shop Ctr—locale ... FL-3
Bel Air Shop Ctr—locale ... MS-4
Bel-Air Shopping Plaza—locale ... PA-2
Belair Somerset—uninc pl ... MD-2
Bel Air South—CDP ... MD-2
Belair Springs—locale ... VA-3
Belair Stables—hist pl ... MD-2
**Bel Air (subdivision)**—pop pl ... AL-4
**Bel Air (subdivision)**—pop pl ... NC-3
**Belair (subdivision)**—pop pl ... NC-3
**Bel-Air (subdivision)**—pop pl ... NC-3
**Belair (subdivision)**—pop pl ... TN-4
**Bel Air Subdivision**—pop pl ... UT-8
Belair Tulip Grove—uninc pl ... MD-2
**Bel Air Two (subdivision)**—pop pl ... TN-4
Bel Air Village Shop Ctr—locale ... AL-4
Belair White Hall—uninc pl ... MD-2
Belair Yorktown—uninc pl ... MD-2
Bela Lake—lake ... MI-6
**Bel Alton**—pop pl ... MD-2
**Bel Alton (Cox)**—pop pl ... MD-2
**Bel Alton (Cox Station)**—pop pl ... MD-2
Beland—locale ... OK-5
Beland Petree Pond Dam—dam ... MS-4
Beland Sch—school ... IL-6
Belandville—locale ... FL-3
Belanger Pass—gap ... AK-9
Belanger Point—cape ... ME-1
Belangers Creek—stream ... MI-6
Belanger Settlement—locale ... ME-1
Belanger Sugar Camp—locale ... ME-1
Belaoto Reef ... PW-9
Belardes Potrero—area ... CA-9
**Belardley**—pop pl ... PA-2
**Belardy**—pop pl ... PA-2
Belas Lake—lake ... MI-6
Belates Cem—cemetery ... TN-4
Belau, Toachel—channel ... PW-9
Belau International Airp—airport ... PW-9
Belau Mission Academy ... PW-9
**Belcamp**—pop pl ... MD-2
Belcamp Beach ... MD-2
Belcamp Beach—beach ... MD-2
Belcaro—hist pl ... CO-8
Belcaro Shop Ctr—other ... CO-8
Belch Branch—stream ... NC-3
Belcher—locale ... AR-4
**Belcher**—pop pl ... KY-4
**Belcher**—pop pl ... LA-4
**Belcher**—pop pl ... NY-2
Belcher, Jonathan, House—hist pl ... MA-1
Belcher Airp—airport ... KS-7
Belcher Basin—basin ... NV-8
Belcher Bethel Ch—church ... AL-4
Belcher Branch—stream ... GA-3
Belcher Branch—stream ... MO-7
Belcher Branch—stream ... VA-3
Belcher Branch—stream (4) ... WV-2
Belcher Brook—stream ... CT-1
Belcher Canal—canal ... FL-3
Belcher Canyon—valley ... NV-8
Belcher Cem—cemetery (2) ... AR-4
Belcher Cem—cemetery (2) ... KY-4
Belcher Cem—cemetery ... TN-4
Belcher Cem—cemetery (2) ... TX-5
Belcher Cem—cemetery (3) ... VA-3
Belcher Cem—cemetery (3) ... WV-2
Belcher Cemetery ... AL-4
Belcher Chapel—church ... AL-4
Belcher Chapel—church ... LA-4
Belcher Chapel—church ... VA-3
Belcher Cove—bay ... RI-1
Belcher Creek—stream ... AL-4
Belcher Creek—stream (2) ... KY-4
Belcher Creek—stream ... NJ-2
Belcher Creek—stream ... TN-4
Belcher Creek—stream ... TX-5
Belcher Crossroads—locale ... SC-3
Belcher Ditch—canal ... IN-6
Belcher Divide Mine—mine ... NV-8
Belcher Draw—valley ... SD-7
Belcher Elem Sch—school ... FL-3
Belcher Family Homestead and Farm—hist pl ... NY-2
Belcher Fork—stream ... KY-4
Belcher Fork—stream ... VA-3
Belcher Gap—gap ... AL-4
Belcher Gap—gap ... TN-4
Belcher Hill—summit ... CO-8
Belcher Hill—summit ... VT-1
Belcher Hole—lake ... FL-3
Belcher Hollow—valley ... TN-4
Belcher Hollow—valley (2) ... WV-2
Belcher Lake—lake ... AR-4
Belcher Lake—reservoir ... AL-4
Belcher Lake Dam—dam ... AL-4
Belcher Lumber Company Dam—dam ... AL-4
Belcher Mine—mine ... CO-8
Belcher Mine—mine ... OR-9
Belcher Mtn—summit ... MT-8
Belcher Mtn—summit ... WA-9
Belcher Mtn—summit ... WV-2
Belcher-Ogden House—hist pl ... NJ-2
Belcher-Ogden Mansion-Price, Benjamin-Price-Brittan Houses Dist—hist pl ... NJ-2
Belcher Park—park ... MA-1
Belcher Ridge—ridge ... IL-6
Belcher-Rowe House—hist pl ... MA-1
Belchers—locale ... AL-4
Belchers Bluff—cliff ... TN-4
Belchers Cem—cemetery ... AL-4
Belcher Sch—school (2) ... MA-1
Belcher Sch (abandoned)—school ... MO-7
Belchers Chapel ... AL-4
**Belchers Corner (historical)**—pop pl ... MA-1
Belchers Cove ... RI-1
Belchers Creek ... AL-4
Belchers Ferry ... TN-4
Belchers Gap Ch—church ... AL-4
Belchers Shafts—mine ... NV-8
Belchers Hole ... FL-3
Belchers Mound ... SD-7
**Belcher Square**—pop pl ... MA-1
Belchers Rsvr—reservoir ... OR-9
Belchers Town ... MA-1
Belchers Town, Town of ... MA-1
**Belchertown**—pop pl ... MA-1
Belchertown (census name for Belchertown Center)—CDP ... MA-1
Belchertown Center (census name Belchertown)—other ... MA-1
Belchertown Center Hist Dist—hist pl ... MA-1
Belchertown HS—school ... MA-1
Belcher (Township of)—fmr MCD ... AR-4
Belchertown State Sch—school ... MA-1
**Belchertown (Town of)**—pop pl ... MA-1
Belchertown Village ... MA-1
**Belcherville**—pop pl ... TX-5
Belcherville Cem—cemetery ... TX-5
Belcher Wells—well ... NM-5
Belches Bayou—stream ... MS-4
Belci (historical)—locale ... MS-4
**Bel-Clear Heights**—pop pl ... SC-3
Bel-Clear Heights Ch—church ... SC-3
Belco—locale ... TX-5
**Belcoda**—pop pl ... NY-2
Belcoe Lake—lake ... AR-4
**Belcourt**—pop pl ... KY-4
**Belcourt**—pop pl ... ND-7
Belcourt Lake—lake ... MN-6
Belcourt Lake—lake ... ND-7
**Belcoville**—pop pl ... NJ-2
**Belcraft**—pop pl ... KY-4
**Belcrest**—pop pl ... WI-6
Belcrest Hotel—hist pl ... MI-6
Belcrest Memorial Park—cemetery ... OR-9
Bel-Crest Shop Ctr—locale ... FL-3
**Belcross**—pop pl ... NC-3
Belcross Lookout Tower—tower ... NC-3
Beldelin HS—school ... OR-9
Belden ... CT-1
Belden—locale ... CO-8
Belden—locale ... IL-6
Belden—locale ... MN-6
**Belden**—pop pl ... CA-9
**Belden**—pop pl ... MS-4
**Belden**—pop pl ... NE-7
**Belden**—pop pl ... NY-2
**Belden**—pop pl ... ND-7
**Belden**—pop pl ... OH-6
**Belden**—pop pl ... PA-2
Belden, C. A., House—hist pl ... CA-9
Belden Attendance Center—school ... MS-4
Belden Baptist Ch—church ... MS-4
Belden Brook—stream (3) ... CT-1
Belden Brook—stream ... NY-2
Belden Cem—cemetery ... MS-4
Belden Ditch—canal ... MT-8
Belden Dugout—channel ... TX-5
Belden Field—airport ... ND-7
Belden Forebay—reservoir ... CA-9
Belden Hill—summit ... CT-1
Belden Hill—summit ... MA-1
Belden Hill—summit ... NY-2
Belden Hill—summit ... VT-1
Belden Hill Brook—stream ... CT-1
Belden Hill Golf Course—other ... NY-2
Belden-Horne House—hist pl ... NC-3
Belden Island—island ... CT-1
Belden Lake—lake ... NY-2
Belden Lake—swamp ... MN-6
Belden Mine—mine ... CA-9
Belden Point—cape ... NY-2
Belden Pond—lake ... ME-1
Belden Ranch—locale ... NM-5
Belden Ravine—valley ... CA-9
Beldens—locale ... VT-1
Belden Sch—school ... CA-9
Belden Sch—school ... OH-6
Belden Spring—spring ... AR-4
Belden Swamp—swamp ... WI-6
**Beldenville**—pop pl ... WI-6
Beldenville Cem—cemetery ... WI-6
Belden Vly—swamp ... NY-2
Belding—locale ... OR-9
**Belding**—pop pl ... MI-6
**Belding**—pop pl ... TX-5
Belding Brook—stream ... CT-1
Belding Cem—cemetery ... ME-1
Belding Creek ... MI-6
Belding Creek—stream ... OR-9
Belding Draw—valley ... TX-5
Belding House Branch—stream ... NC-3
Belding Lake—lake ... WI-6
Belding Lateral—canal ... CA-9
Belding Oil And Gas Field—oilfield ... TX-5
Belding Oil Field—oilfield ... TX-5
Belding Point—summit ... OR-9
Belding Pond—lake ... VT-1
Belding Pond Brook—stream ... VT-1
Belding Ranch—locale ... TX-5
Beldings Brook ... CT-1
Belding Sch—school ... CA-9
Belding Sch—school ... IL-6
**Beldingville**—pop pl ... MA-1
Beldin Hollow—valley ... PA-2
Beldoc ... SC-3
Beldoc (Beldock) ... SC-3
Beldock ... SC-3
Beldon ... TN-4
Beldon—other ... TN-4
Beldon Hollow—valley ... TX-5
Beldons Landing—locale ... CA-9
Beldor—locale ... VA-3
Beldorah Cem—cemetery ... MS-4
Beldor Ch—church ... VA-3
Beldor Hollow Overlook—locale ... VA-3
Beldor Ridge Trail—trail ... VA-3
Beleden House—hist pl ... CT-1
Belefont Church ... NC-3
Belegante ... MS-4
**Belen**—pop pl ... MS-4
**Belen**—pop pl ... NM-5
**Belen**—pop pl ... TX-5
Belen Baptist Ch—church ... MS-4
Belen (CCD)—cens area ... NM-5
Belen Grant—civil ... NM-5
Belen Grant Lateral No 1—canal ... NM-5
Belen Highline Canal—canal ... NM-5
Belen Hotel—hist pl ... NM-5
Belen Jesuit Preparatory Sch—school ... FL-3
Belen Jesuit Sch—school ... FL-3
Belen Waste Ditch—canal ... NM-5
Belew Cem—cemetery ... AL-4
Belew Cem—cemetery (2) ... TN-4
Belew Creek ... MO-7
Belew Creek ... NC-3
Belew (historical)—locale ... AL-4
Belew Hollow—valley ... MO-7
Belew Hollow—valley ... NC-3
Belew Hollow—valley ... TN-4
Belew Landing (historical)—locale ... AL-4
Belew P.O. ... AL-4
Belew Ridge School ... TN-4
Belews ... TN-4
Belews Ch—church ... TN-4
Belews Chapel Cem—cemetery ... TN-4
**Belews Creek**—pop pl ... MO-7
**Belews Creek**—pop pl ... NC-3
Belews Creek—stream ... MO-7
Belews Creek—stream (2) ... NC-3
Belews Creek Dam—dam ... NC-3
Belews Creek (Township of)—fmr MCD ... NC-3
Belews Lake—reservoir (2) ... NC-3
Belew Springs—spring ... TN-4
Beley Ditch—canal ... MT-8
Beley Homestead—locale ... MT-8
Beley Lakes—lake ... MT-8
Beley Pond—reservoir ... MT-8
Beley Ranch—locale ... MT-8
Belfair—locale ... WA-9
**Belfair**—pop pl ... WA-9
Belfair (CCD)—cens area ... WA-9
Belfair Crossroads—locale ... VA-3
Belfair Sch—school ... LA-4
Belfair Sch—school ... WA-9
Belfair State Park—park ... WA-9
**Belfalls**—pop pl ... TX-5
Belfast—locale ... AR-4
Belfast—locale ... CA-9
Belfast—locale ... VA-3
**Belfast**—pop pl ... GA-3
**Belfast**—pop pl ... IN-6
**Belfast**—pop pl ... ME-1
**Belfast**—pop pl ... MD-2
**Belfast**—pop pl ... MO-7
**Belfast**—pop pl ... NE-7
**Belfast**—pop pl ... NY-2
**Belfast**—pop pl ... NC-3
**Belfast**—pop pl (2) ... OH-6
**Belfast**—pop pl ... PA-2
**Belfast**—pop pl ... TN-4
Belfast Bar—bar ... AL-4
Belfast Bay—bay ... ME-1
Belfast Cem—cemetery ... OH-6
Belfast Ch—church ... MO-7
Belfast Ch—church ... VA-3
Belfast Commercial Hist Dist—hist pl ... ME-1
Belfast Creek—stream ... TN-4
Belfast Creek—stream ... VA-3
Belfast Elem Sch—school ... NC-3
Belfast Hist Dist—hist pl ... ME-1
Belfast (historical)—locale ... KS-7
**Belfast (historical)**—pop pl ... IA-7
**Belfast Junction**—pop pl ... PA-2
Belfast Meadows—flat ... CA-9
**Belfast Mills**—pop pl ... VA-3
Belfast Natl Bank—hist pl ... ME-1
Belfast Number 2 Mine Station—locale ... PA-2
Belfast Post Office—building ... TN-4
Belfast River ... ME-1
Belfast River—stream ... GA-3
Belfast RR Depot—hist pl ... TN-4
Belfast Rsvr Number One—reservoir ... ME-1
Belfast Rsvr Number Two—reservoir ... ME-1
Belfast Sch—school ... NC-3
Belfast Sch—school ... VA-3
Belfast Sch (historical)—school ... TN-4
Belfast School—locale ... WA-9
**Belfast (Town of)**—pop pl ... NY-2
**Belfast (Township of)**—pop pl ... MN-6
**Belfast (Township of)**—pop pl ... PA-2
Belfast Trail—trail ... VA-3
Belfield—locale ... LA-4
**Belfield**—pop pl ... ND-7
Belfield Creek—stream ... VA-3
Belfield (historical)—locale ... KS-7
Belfield (Magisterial District)—fmr MCD ... VA-3
Belfield Recreation Center—park ... PA-2
Belfield Sch—school ... VA-3
Belfield Sch Number 1—school ... ND-7
Belfield Sch Number 4—school ... ND-7
Belfont—locale ... WV-2
Belfont Plantation House—hist pl ... NC-3
Belfont Sch—school ... OK-5
Belfo Park—park ... CA-9
Belford—locale ... PA-2
**Belford**—pop pl ... NJ-2
Belford, Mount—summit ... CO-8
Belford Ch—church ... NC-3
Belford Gulch—valley ... CO-8
Belford Harbor—bay ... NJ-2
Belford Hist Dist—hist pl ... TX-5
Belford (historical)—locale ... NC-3
Belford Lake—lake ... WY-8
**Belford Manor**—pop pl ... DE-2
Belford Number 3 Mine Station—locale ... PA-2
Belford Sch—school ... SD-7
Belford Spring—spring ... KY-4
**Belford Township**—pop pl ... ND-7
**Belford Township**—pop pl ... SD-7
Belford Township (historical)—civil ... ND-7
**Belforest**—pop pl ... AL-4
Belforest Cem—cemetery ... AL-4
Belforest Ch—church ... AL-4
Belforest Sch—school ... AL-4
Belfort—locale ... CA-9
Belfort—locale ... NY-2
Belfort—locale ... OR-9
**Belfort**—pop pl ... OH-6
Belfort Creek—stream ... OR-9
Belfort Pond—reservoir ... NY-2
**Belfountain**—pop pl ... AL-4
Belfrin Extension Mine—mine ... CA-9
Belfrin Mine—mine ... CA-9
**Belfry**—pop pl ... KY-4
**Belfry**—pop pl ... MT-8
**Belfry**—pop pl ... PA-2
Belfry Cem—cemetery ... MT-8
Belfry Hill—summit ... MA-1
Belfry Mtn—summit ... NY-2
Belfry Station—locale ... PA-2
**Belgacia**—pop pl ... PR-3
Belgard Cem—cemetery ... LA-4
Belger-Cahill Lime Kiln—hist pl ... TX-5
Belgian Ch—church ... MT-8

Belgian Embassy Bldg—*building* ... DC-2
*Belgian Gulch* ... OR-9
Belgian Gulch—*valley* ... MT-8
Belgian Gulch—*valley* ... OR-9
Belgian Lake—*lake* ... WI-6
Belgian Sch—*school* ... MT-8
**Belgie**—*pop pl* ... PR-3
**Belgique**—*pop pl* ... MO-7
Belgium—*locale* ... WV-2
**Belgium**—*pop pl* ... IL-6
**Belgium**—*pop pl* ... NY-2
**Belgium**—*pop pl* ... WI-6
Belgium Branch—*stream* ... VA-3
*Belgium Lake* ... MN-6
Belgium Ridge—*ridge* ... WI-6
Belgium Ridge Cem—*cemetery* ... WI-6
Belgium Row—*locale* ... IL-6
**Belgium (Town of)**—*pop pl* ... WI-6
**Belgium (Township of)**—*pop pl* ... MN-6
**Belgodere**—*pop pl* ... PR-3
Belgrade—*locale* ... ME-1
**Belgrade**—*pop pl* (2) ... MN-6
**Belgrade**—*pop pl* ... MO-7
**Belgrade**—*pop pl* ... MT-8
**Belgrade**—*pop pl* ... NE-7
**Belgrade**—*pop pl* ... NC-3
**Belgrade**—*pop pl* ... TX-5
Belgrade and St. David's Church—*hist pl* ... NC-3
Belgrade Cave—*reservoir* ... MN-6
Belgrade Cem—*cemetery* ... MN-6
Belgrade Cem—*cemetery* ... TX-5
Belgrade Central Sch—*school* ... ME-1
Belgrade City Hall and Jail—*hist pl* ... MT-8
Belgrade Junction—*locale* ... MT-8
**Belgrade Lakes**—*pop pl* ... ME-1
Belgrade Sch—*school* ... MO-7
Belgrade Sch (historical)—*school* ... TN-4
Belgrade Stream—*stream* ... ME-1
**Belgrade (Town of)**—*pop pl* ... ME-1
Belgrade Township—*civil* ... MO-7
**Belgrade (Township of)**—*pop pl* ... MN-6
**Belgravia**—*pop pl* ... MD-2
Belgravia Hotel—*hist pl* ... PA-2
**Belgreen**—*pop pl* ... AL-4
Belgreen Cave—*cave* ... AL-4
Belgreen Cem—*cemetery* ... AL-4
Belgreen HS—*school* ... AL-4
Belgreen Spring Branch—*stream* ... AL-4
Belgrove—*locale* ... WV-2
Belgrove Sch—*school* ... WV-2
Belgum Lake—*lake* ... MN-6
**Belhaven**—*pop pl* ... NC-3
Belhaven City Hall—*hist pl* ... NC-3
Belhaven Coll—*school* ... MS-4
Belhaven Elem Sch—*school* ... NC-3
*Belhaven Female Coll* ... MS-4
Belhaven Heights Hist Dist—*hist pl* ... MS-4
Belhaven Memorial Museum—*building* ... NC-3
Belhurst Castle—*hist pl* ... NY-2
**Belian Village**—*pop pl* ... PA-2
Belicum Peak—*summit* ... WA-9
Belieu Creek—*stream* ... OR-9
Believers Bible Ch—*church* ... KS-7
Believers Fellowship Ch—*church* ... MS-4
Beli Island—*island* ... FL-3
Beliliou—*civil* ... PW-9
Beliliou—*island* ... PW-9
*Beliliou Air Field* ... PW-9
Belin—*locale* ... SC-3
Belinda—*locale* ... VA-3
**Belinda**—*pop pl* ... IA-7
**Belinda City**—*pop pl* ... TN-4
Belinda Creek—*stream* ... AK-9
Belinda (historical P.O.)—*locale* ... IA-7
Belinda Sch—*school* ... IA-7
Belinder Elem Sch—*school* ... KS-7
**Belington**—*pop pl* ... WV-2
*Belinsgate* ... MA-1
*Belinsgate Point* ... MA-1
Belisle Sch—*school* ... MA-1
Belix Trail—*trail* ... CA-9
Beljica, Mount—*summit* ... WA-9
Beljica Meadows—*flat* ... WA-9
Belk—*locale* ... TN-4
**Belk**—*pop pl* ... AL-4
**Belk**—*pop pl* ... TX-5
Belk Branch—*stream* ... SC-3
Belk Cem—*cemetery* ... AR-4
*Belk Cemetery* ... AL-4
Belk Corner—*locale* ... AR-4
Belk Floor Covering Company—*facility* ... NC-3
Belk Hall—*building* ... NC-3
*Belkhers Creek* ... NJ-2
Belk JHS—*school* ... AL-4
Belknap—*cens area* ... MT-8
Belknap—*locale* ... KY-4
Belknap—*locale* ... MT-8
Belknap—*locale* ... UT-8
**Belknap**—*pop pl* ... AL-4
**Belknap**—*pop pl* ... IL-6
**Belknap**—*pop pl* (2) ... IN-6
**Belknap**—*pop pl* ... IA-7
**Belknap**—*pop pl* ... MI-6
**Belknap**—*pop pl* ... OH-6
**Belknap**—*pop pl* ... PA-2
Belknap, Gen. William Worth,
House—*hist pl* ... IA-7
Belknap, Mount—*summit* ... UT-8
Belknap, Willam R., Sch—*hist pl* ... KY-4
**Belknap Beach**—*pop pl* ... KY-4
Belknap Branch—*stream* ... TX-5
Belknap Bridge—*hist pl* ... OR-9
Belknap Camp—*locale* ... OR-9
Belknap Camp Grove—*woods* ... CA-9
Belknap Cem—*cemetery* ... IA-7
Belknap Cem—*cemetery* ... NY-2
Belknap Cem—*cemetery* ... TX-5
Belknap Ch—*church* ... KS-7
Belknap Ch—*church* ... KY-4
Belknap Corner—*other* ... MI-6
**Belknap County**—*pop pl* ... NH-1
Belknap Crater—*crater* ... OR-9
Belknap Creek—*stream* ... CA-9
Belknap Creek—*stream* (2) ... OR-9
Belknap Creek—*stream* ... TX-5
Belknap Creek—*stream* ... WY-8
Belknap Crossing—*locale* ... NY-2
Belknap Gulch—*valley* ... OR-9
Belknap Hills—*range* ... TX-5
Belknap Hollow—*valley* ... WV-2
Belknap Hot Spring—*spring* ... OR-9
Belknap-Icarus Acres Airp—*airport* ... IN-6
*Belknap Island* ... WY-8
Belknap Islands—*area* ... AK-9
Belknap Mine Number 1—*mine* ... TX-5
Belknap Mine Number 2—*mine* ... TX-5
Belknap Mine Number 3—*mine* ... TX-5
Belknap Mine Number 4—*mine* ... TX-5
Belknap Mine Number 5—*mine* ... TX-5
Belknap Mountains—*range* ... TX-5
Belknap Mountains—*summit* ... NH-1
Belknap Mtn—*summit* ... NH-1
Belknap Park—*park* ... MI-6
Belknap Point—*cape* ... NH-1
Belknap Ranch—*locale* ... WY-8
Belknap Ranger Station—*locale* ... UT-8
Belknap Sch—*school* ... KS-7
Belknap Sch—*school* ... KY-4
Belknap Sch—*school* ... MI-6
Belknap Sch—*school* ... NY-2
Belknap Sch—*school* ... UT-8
**Belknap Springs**—*pop pl* ... OR-9
Belknap Springs—*spring* ... OR-9
*Belknaps Springs* ... OR-9
Belknap State Reservation—*park* ... NH-1
*Belknap Station* ... IN-6
Belknap-Sulloway Mill—*hist pl* ... NH-1
Belknap Tank—*reservoir* ... AZ-5
Belknap Township—*fmr MCD* ... IA-7
**Belknap (Township of)**—*pop pl* ... MI-6
Belkofski—*locale* ... AK-9
Belkofski Bay—*bay* ... AK-9
**Belkofski (Belkofsky)**—*pop pl* ... AK-9
Belkofski Point—*cape* ... AK-9
Belkofsky (Belkofski) ANV735—*reserve* ... AK-9
Belk Park—*park* ... IL-6
Belk Post Office (historical)—*building* ... TN-4
Belk Sch (historical)—*school* ... TN-4
Belk Store (historical)—*locale* ... TN-4
Belk Tower—*tower* ... NC-3
Bell—*locale* ... AL-4
Bell—*locale* ... AZ-5
Bell—*locale* ... GA-3
Bell—*locale* ... IL-6
Bell—*locale* ... OK-5
**Bell**—*pop pl* ... CA-9
**Bell**—*pop pl* ... FL-3
**Bell**—*pop pl* ... IA-7
**Bell**—*pop pl* ... MD-2
**Bell**—*pop pl* ... MI-6
**Bell**—*pop pl* ... OR-9
Bell, Alvin Bushnell, House—*hist pl* ... IA-7
Bell, Bayou—*stream* ... LA-4
Bell, C.S., Foundry and
Showroom—*hist pl* ... OH-6
Bell, Dr. James, House—*hist pl* ... OH-6
Bell, George and Annie, House—*hist pl* ... KS-7
Bell, Hill McClelland, House—*hist pl* ... IA-7
Bell, Isaac, House—*hist pl* ... RI-1
Bell, James George, House—*hist pl* ... CA-9
Bell, Jasper Newton, House—*hist pl* ... NE-7
Bell, John, Farm—*hist pl* ... PA-2
Bell, John, House—*hist pl* ... KY-4
Bell, John C., House—*hist pl* ... PA-2
Bell, John Y., House—*hist pl* ... TX-5
Bell, Lake—*lake* (2) ... FL-3
Bell, Marcus Sears, Farm—*hist pl* ... WI-6
Bella, Lake—*reservoir* ... MN-6
Bella Creek—*gut* ... SC-3
Bella Creek—*stream* ... AK-9
**Bell Acres**—*pop pl* ... PA-2
Bell Acres Borough—*civil* ... PA-2
Bellagio Road Sch—*school* ... CA-9
Bellah Cem—*cemetery* ... AR-4
Bellah Creek—*stream* ... AR-4
Bellah Hills—*summit* ... AR-4
*Bellair* ... FL-3
Bellair—*hist pl* ... NC-3
Bellair—*locale* ... MO-7
Bellair—*locale* ... NC-3
**Bellair**—*pop pl* ... FL-3
**Bellair**—*pop pl* ... IL-6
**Bellair**—*pop pl* ... VA-3
**Bell Air**—*pop pl* ... VA-3
Bellair Cove (Shop Ctr)—*locale* ... FL-3
**Bellaire**—*pop pl* ... AR-4
**Bellaire**—*pop pl* ... CA-9
**Bellaire**—*pop pl* (2) ... KS-7
**Bellaire**—*pop pl* ... MI-6
**Bellaire**—*pop pl* ... MN-6
**Bellaire**—*pop pl* ... NY-2
**Bellaire**—*pop pl* (2) ... OH-6
**Bellaire**—*pop pl* ... PA-2
**Bellaire**—*pop pl* ... TX-5
Bellaire, Lake—*lake* ... MI-6
**Bellaire Addition**—*pop pl* ... TX-5
Bellaire Cem—*cemetery* ... OH-6
Bellaire Ch—*church* ... AR-4
Bellaire Country Club—*other* ... MI-6
Bellaire Ditch—*canal* ... CO-8
Bellaire Elem Sch—*school* ... PA-2
**Bellaire Gardens**—*pop pl* ... OH-6
Bellaire Junction—*locale* ... TX-5
Bellaire Lake—*lake* ... CO-8
Bellaire Park—*park* (2) ... TX-5
Bellaire Sch—*school* ... MN-6
Bellaire Sch—*school* ... NE-7
Bellaire Sch—*school* ... TX-5
**Bellaire West**—*pop pl* ... TX-5
Bellair Golf Course—*other* ... AZ-5
**Bellair (historical)**—*pop pl* ... IA-7
Bellair-Meadowbrook Terrace—*CDP* ... FL-3
Bellair Oil Field—*other* ... IL-6
Bell Airp—*airport* ... MS-4
Bellair Plaza (Shop Ctr)—*locale* ... FL-3
Bellair Shop Ctr—*locale* ... FL-3
Bellair Township—*fmr MCD* ... IA-7
**Bellair West**—*pop pl* ... FL-3
Bella Lake—*lake* ... MI-6
Bella Mara Estates—*locale* ... TN-4
Bella May Mine—*mine* ... WA-9
Bellamy—*locale* (2) ... VA-3
**Bellamy**—*pop pl* ... AL-4
**Bellamy**—*pop pl* ... MO-7
**Bellamy**—*pop pl* ... NC-3
Bellamy, Edward, House—*hist pl* ... MA-1
Bellamy, Joseph, House—*hist pl* ... CT-1
Bellamy Bay—*swamp* ... FL-3
**Bellamy (Belroi)**—*pop pl* ... VA-3
Bellamy Branch—*stream* ... AL-4
Bellamy Branch—*stream* (2) ... KY-4
Bellamy Branch—*stream* ... SC-3
Bellamy Bridge—*bridge* ... FL-3
Bellamy Cave—*cave* ... TN-4
Bellamy Cem—*cemetery* ... FL-3
Bellamy Cem—*cemetery* (2) ... KY-4
Bellamy Cem—*cemetery* ... MS-4
Bellamy Cem—*cemetery* ... NY-2
Bellamy Cem—*cemetery* ... NC-3
Bellamy Cem—*cemetery* ... TN-4
Bellamy Cem—*cemetery* (2) ... VA-3
Bellamy Ch—*church* ... VA-3
Bellamy Chapel—*cemetery* ... MS-4
Bellamy Chapel—*church* ... MS-4
**Bellamy Court (subdivision)**—*pop pl* ... TN-4
*Bellamy Creek* ... AL-4
Bellamy Creek—*stream* ... MI-6
Bellamy Creek—*stream* ... MS-4
Bellamy Creek—*stream* ... VA-3
Bellamy Ditch—*canal* (2) ... WY-8
Bellamy Ditch No 1—*canal* ... WY-8
Bellamy Ditch No 2—*canal* ... WY-8
Bellamy Elem Sch—*school* ... FL-3
Bellamy Gap—*gap* ... TN-4
**Bellamy (historical)**—*pop pl* ... TN-4
Bellamy Hollow—*valley* ... OH-6
Bellamy Hollow—*valley* ... VA-3
Bellamy Lake—*lake* ... WY-8
Bellamy Lake—*reservoir* ... NC-3
Bellamy Landing—*locale* ... NC-3
Bellamy Park—*park* ... NH-1
Bellamy Park—*park* ... NY-2
Bellamy-Philips House—*hist pl* ... NC-3
Bellamy Pond—*swamp* ... FL-3
Bellamy Post Office (historical)—*building* ... TN-4
Bellamy River—*stream* ... NH-1
*Bellamy Run Hollow* ... OH-6
*Bellamys* ... DE-2
Bellamys Bridge—*bridge* ... NC-3
Bellamy Sch—*school* ... MA-1
Bellamy Sch—*school* ... OH-6
*Bellamy School Number 102* ... IN-6
Bellamys Lake—*reservoir* ... NC-3
Bellamys Lake Dam—*dam* ... NC-3
Bellamy's Mill—*hist pl* ... NC-3
Bellamytown—*locale* ... VA-3
*Bellanca Beach* ... DE-2
Bellan Ledge—*bench* ... NY-2
Bell Anne Sch—*school* ... MI-6
**Bellany Manor**—*pop pl* ... VA-3
Bella Oak Mine—*mine* ... CA-9
Bell Apartments—*hist pl* ... WA-9
Bel La Pass—*channel* ... LA-4
Bell Arm—*bay* ... AK-9
Bellarmine Coll—*school* ... KY-4
Bellarmine Coll Preparatory—*school* ... CA-9
Bellarmine Hall—*locale* ... IL-6
Bellarmine HS—*school* ... WA-9
Bellarmine-Jefferson HS—*school* ... CA-9
Bellarmine Sch—*school* ... CA-9
**Bell Arthur**—*pop pl* ... NC-3
**Bellarthur (RR name Arthur)**—*pop pl* ... NC-3
Bellas Brook—*stream* ... PA-2
Bellas Canyon—*valley* ... ID-8
Bellas Canyon—*valley* ... UT-8
Bellas Creek—*stream* ... CA-9
Bellas Flat—*flat* ... CA-9
Bellas Hess Shop Ctr—*locale* ... AL-4
Bellas Lakes—*reservoir* ... ID-8
**Bellasylva**—*pop pl* ... PA-2
*Bella Sylvia* ... PA-2
Bellatre Park—*park* ... WI-6
Bella Union Ravine—*valley* ... CA-9
Bell Ave Ch—*church* (2) ... TN-4
Bell Ave Elem Sch—*school* ... PA-2
Bell Ave Sch—*school* ... CA-9
Bell Ave Sch—*school* ... PA-2
**Bella Villa**—*pop pl* ... MO-7
*Bella Vista* ... AL-4
**Bella Vista**—*pop pl* (2) ... AR-4
**Bella Vista**—*pop pl* (3) ... CA-9
**Bella Vista**—*pop pl* ... DE-2
**Bella Vista**—*pop pl* ... PA-2
Bella Vista—*uninc pl* ... CA-9
**Bella Vista Acres**—*pop pl* ... TN-4
Bella Vista Bay—*bay* ... FL-3
Bella Vista Country Club—*locale* ... TN-4
Bella Vista Country Club—*other* ... AR-4
Bella Vista Estates—*uninc pl* ... AZ-5
Bellavista Farms—*locale* ... AZ-5
Bella Vista HS—*school* ... CA-9
Bella Vista Island—*island* ... FL-3
Bella Vista Lake—*reservoir* ... AR-4
Bella Vista Neighborhood Park—*park* ... AZ-5
Bella Vista Park—*park* ... CA-9
Bella Vista Ranch—*locale* ... NM-5
Bella Vista Sch—*school* ... AZ-5
Bella Vista Sch—*school* (2) ... CA-9
Bella Vista Sch—*school* ... UT-8
Bella Vista Windmill—*locale* ... TX-5
Bell Band Park—*park* ... IN-6
Bell Baptist Ch—*church* ... AL-4
Bell Bar Creek—*stream* ... CA-9
*Bell Bay* ... NC-3
Bell Bay—*bay* ... ID-8
Bell Bay—*bay* ... NC-3
Bell Bay—*swamp* ... FL-3
Bell Bay Branch—*stream* (2) ... FL-3
Bell Bayou—*gut* (2) ... LA-4
Bell Bayou—*stream* (2) ... LA-4
Bell Bend—*bend* ... PA-2
Bell Bldg—*hist pl* ... AL-4
Bell Bluff—*cliff* ... AL-4
Bell Bluff—*cliff* ... AR-4
Bell Bluff—*cliff* ... CA-9
Bell Bluff—*cliff* (2) ... MO-7
**Bellbluff**—*pop pl* ... VA-3
Bell Bluff Cem—*cemetery* ... AR-4
**Bellbluff (sta.)**—*pop pl* ... VA-3
Bell Bottom Creek—*stream* ... TX-5
Bell Bottoms—*bend* ... MT-8
Bellboy Mine—*mine* ... NM-5
*Bell Branch* ... SC-3
*Bell Branch* ... VA-3
Bell Branch—*locale* ... TX-5
Bell Branch—*stream* (3) ... AL-4
Bell Branch—*stream* (4) ... AR-4
Bell Branch—*stream* (2) ... FL-3
Bell Branch—*stream* (2) ... GA-3
Bell Branch—*stream* ... IL-6
Bell Branch—*stream* ... IN-6
Bell Branch—*stream* (2) ... KS-7
Bell Branch—*stream* (3) ... KY-4
Bell Branch—*stream* (3) ... LA-4
Bell Branch—*stream* ... MD-2
Bell Branch—*stream* ... MI-6
Bell Branch—*stream* (5) ... MS-4
Bell Branch—*stream* (5) ... MO-7
Bell Branch—*stream* (4) ... NC-3
Bell Branch—*stream* ... PA-2
Bell Branch—*stream* (6) ... SC-3
Bell Branch—*stream* (11) ... TN-4
Bell Branch—*stream* (9) ... TX-5
Bell Branch—*stream* ... VA-3
Bell Branch Ch—*church* ... TX-5
Bell Branch Sch (historical)—*school* ... TN-4
Bell Branch Trail—*trail* ... PA-2
Bell Bridge—*bridge* ... FL-3
Bell Bridge—*bridge* ... TN-4
Bell Bridge—*bridge* ... TX-5
Bell Bridge—*other* ... MO-7
**Bell Bridge**—*pop pl* ... TN-4
**Bellbrook**—*pop pl* ... OH-6
Bell Brook—*stream* ... ME-1
Bell Brook—*stream* ... MA-1
Bell Brook—*stream* ... NH-1
Bell Brook—*stream* (6) ... NY-2
Bell Brook—*stream* ... VT-1
Bellbrook HS—*school* ... OH-6
Bell Brook Pond—*reservoir* ... NY-2
*Bellbuckle* ... TN-4
**Bell Buckle**—*pop pl* ... TN-4
Bell Buckle (CCD)—*cens area* ... TN-4
Bell Buckle Creek—*stream* ... TN-4
Bell Buckle Division—*civil* ... TN-4
Bell Buckle First Baptist Ch—*church* ... TN-4
Bell Buckle Hist Dist—*hist pl* ... TN-4
*Bellbuckle Post Office* ... TN-4
Bell Buckle Post Office—*building* ... TN-4
Bell Buckle Sch (historical)—*school* ... TN-4
**Bellburn**—*pop pl* ... WV-2
Bell Butte—*summit* (3) ... AZ-5
Bell Butte—*summit* ... ND-7
Bell Butte—*summit* ... UT-8
Bell Butte—*summit* ... WA-9
Bell Butte—*summit* (2) ... WY-8
Bell Butte Spring—*spring* ... AZ-5
Bellcalf Creek—*stream* ... OK-5
**Bell Campground**—*pop pl* ... TN-4
Bell Camp Meadow—*flat* ... CA-9
Bellcamp Ridge—*ridge* ... GA-3
Bell Camp Spring—*spring* ... OR-9
Bell Canton Shoals—*bar* ... TN-4
Bell Canyon—*valley* ... AZ-5
Bell Canyon—*valley* (6) ... CA-9
Bell Canyon—*valley* (2) ... CO-8
Bell Canyon—*valley* (2) ... ID-8
Bell Canyon—*valley* ... MT-8
Bell Canyon—*valley* (3) ... NV-8
Bell Canyon—*valley* (4) ... NM-5
Bell Canyon—*valley* ... OR-9
Bell Canyon—*valley* ... TX-5
Bell Canyon—*valley* (3) ... UT-8
Bell Canyon—*valley* ... WA-9
**Bell Canyon Acres
Subdivision**—*pop pl* ... UT-8
Bell Canyon Creek—*stream* ... WA-9
Bell Canyon Dam—*dam* ... CA-9
**Bell Canyon Estates**—*pop pl* ... UT-8
Bell Canyon Rsvr—*reservoir* ... CA-9
Bell Canyon Rsvr—*reservoir* ... CO-8
Bell Canyon Shop Ctr—*locale* ... UT-8
Bell Canyon Tank—*reservoir* ... AZ-5
Bell Catfish Ponds Dam—*dam* ... MS-4
Bell Cave—*cave* ... AL-4
Bell Cave—*cave* ... MO-7
Bell (CCD)—*cens area* ... FL-3
Bell Cedar Swamp—*swamp* ... CT-1
*Bell Cem* ... MS-4
*Bell Cem* ... TN-4
Bell Cem—*cemetery* (4) ... AL-4
Bell Cem—*cemetery* (5) ... AR-4
Bell Cem—*cemetery* ... CT-1
Bell Cem—*cemetery* (2) ... FL-3
Bell Cem—*cemetery* (3) ... GA-3
Bell Cem—*cemetery* (4) ... IL-6
Bell Cem—*cemetery* (4) ... IN-6
Bell Cem—*cemetery* ... KS-7
Bell Cem—*cemetery* (5) ... KY-4
Bell Cem—*cemetery* (3) ... LA-4
Bell Cem—*cemetery* ... MA-1
Bell Cem—*cemetery* ... MI-6
Bell Cem—*cemetery* ... MN-6
Bell Cem—*cemetery* (4) ... MS-4
Bell Cem—*cemetery* (8) ... MO-7
Bell Cem—*cemetery* (3) ... NC-3
Bell Cem—*cemetery* (2) ... OH-6
Bell Cem—*cemetery* ... OK-5
Bell Cem—*cemetery* ... SC-3
Bell Cem—*cemetery* (15) ... TN-4
Bell Cem—*cemetery* (5) ... TX-5
Bell Cem—*cemetery* (6) ... WV-2
Bell Cem—*cemetery* (2) ... WI-6
Bell Cemeteries—*cemetery* ... AL-4
*Bellcenter* ... WI-6
Bell Center—*locale* ... OH-6
**Bell Center**—*pop pl* ... IN-6
**Bell Center**—*pop pl* ... WI-6
Bell Center Cem—*cemetery* ... IN-6
Bell Ch—*church* ... AL-4
Bell Ch—*church* ... FL-3
Bell Ch—*church* ... IL-6
Bell Ch—*church* ... LA-4
Bell Ch—*church* ... MO-7
Bell Ch—*church* ... NY-2
Bell Ch—*church* ... OH-6
Bell Ch—*church* ... TX-5
*Bell Chapel* ... AL-4
Bell Chapel—*church* ... AR-4
Bell Chapel—*church* (2) ... MS-4
Bell Chapel—*church* ... NC-3
Bell Chapel—*church* ... TN-4
Bell Chapel—*church* ... TX-5
Bell Chapel—*church* ... VA-3
Bell Chapel—*church* ... WV-2
Bell Chapel Cem—*cemetery* ... TX-5
*Bellches Pond* ... VA-3
Bell Chute Public Access—*locale* ... MO-7
Bell City—*locale* ... AR-4
Bell City—*locale* ... KY-4
**Bell City**—*pop pl* ... KY-4
**Bell City**—*pop pl* ... LA-4
**Bell City**—*pop pl* ... MO-7
Bell City Cem—*cemetery* ... MO-7
Bell City Drainage Canal—*canal* ... LA-4
Bell City Gas Field—*oilfield* ... LA-4
Bell City (historical)—*locale* ... AL-4
Bell Cliff—*cliff* ... KY-4
Bellco—*locale* ... TX-5
Bell Collar Cove—*valley* ... NC-3
Bellcollar Gap—*gap* ... NC-3
Bell Coney Branch—*stream* ... NC-3
Bell Coney Mtn—*summit* ... NC-3
Bell Conservation Lake—*reservoir* ... IN-6
Bell Conservation Lake Dam—*dam* ... IN-6
Bell Corral—*locale* ... WY-8
Bell Coulee—*valley* ... MT-8
Bell Coulee—*valley* ... WI-6
Bell Coulee Ch—*church* ... WI-6
Bell Coulee Sch—*school* ... WI-6
**Bell (County)**—*pop pl* ... KY-4
**Bell (County)**—*pop pl* ... TX-5
Bell County Courthouse—*hist pl* ... TX-5
Bell County Sportsmans Club—*other* ... TX-5
Bell Court Neighborhood Hist
Dist—*hist pl* ... KY-4
Bell Cove—*valley* ... TN-4
Bell Cove Branch—*stream* ... TN-4
Bell Cow Canyon—*valley* ... AZ-5
Bellcow Creek—*stream* ... OK-5
Bell Cow Creek—*stream* ... OR-9
Bell Cow Lake—*basin* ... MS-4
Bellcow Mtn—*summit* ... TN-4
Bell Cow Tank—*reservoir* ... AZ-5
**Bellcraft**—*pop pl* ... GA-3
**Bellcraft**—*pop pl* ... KY-4
*Bell Creek* ... AL-4
*Bell Creek* ... GA-3
*Bell Creek* ... ID-8
*Bell Creek* ... LA-4
*Bell Creek* ... MT-8
*Bell Creek* ... NC-3
*Bell Creek* ... TX-5
*Bell Creek* ... VA-3
Bell Creek—*bay* ... NC-3
Bell Creek—*stream* (3) ... AL-4
Bell Creek—*stream* ... AK-9
Bell Creek—*stream* (2) ... AR-4
Bell Creek—*stream* (5) ... CA-9
Bell Creek—*stream* (2) ... CO-8
Bell Creek—*stream* (3) ... FL-3
Bell Creek—*stream* (3) ... GA-3
Bell Creek—*stream* (5) ... ID-8
Bell Creek—*stream* (3) ... IN-6
Bell Creek—*stream* (2) ... IA-7
Bell Creek—*stream* (3) ... LA-4
Bell Creek—*stream* (2) ... MD-2
Bell Creek—*stream* ... MI-6
Bell Creek—*stream* (4) ... MS-4
Bell Creek—*stream* (2) ... MO-7
Bell Creek—*stream* ... MT-8
Bell Creek—*stream* (2) ... NE-7
Bell Creek—*stream* ... NV-8
Bell Creek—*stream* ... NY-2
Bell Creek—*stream* (5) ... NC-3
Bell Creek—*stream* ... OH-6
Bell Creek—*stream* (2) ... OK-5
Bell Creek—*stream* (3) ... OR-9
Bell Creek—*stream* (2) ... PA-2
Bell Creek—*stream* (2) ... SC-3
Bell Creek—*stream* ... TN-4
Bell Creek—*stream* (6) ... TX-5
Bell Creek—*stream* (2) ... VA-3
Bell Creek—*stream* (4) ... WA-9
Bell Creek—*stream* ... WI-6
Bell Creek—*stream* (6) ... WY-8
Bell Creek Community Building—*locale* ... CO-8
Bell Creek County Park—*park* ... MI-6
Bell Creek Springs—*spring* ... CO-8
Bell Creek Swamp—*swamp* ... FL-3
**Bell Creek Township**—*pop pl* ... NE-7
**Bellcrest Park**—*pop pl* ... NJ-2
Bell Crossing—*locale* ... MT-8
Bell Dam—*dam* ... AL-4
*Bell Ditch* ... IN-6
Bell Ditch—*canal* (2) ... ID-8
Bell Ditch—*canal* ... IN-6
Bell Ditch—*canal* ... KY-4
Bell Ditch—*canal* ... OH-6
Bell Draft—*valley* ... PA-2
Bell Drain—*canal* ... MI-6
Bell Drain—*stream* ... MI-6
*Belle* ... MP-9
**Belle**—*pop pl* ... MO-7
**Belle**—*pop pl* ... WV-2
Belle, Lake—*lake* ... FL-3
Belle, Lake—*lake* ... PA-2
Belle Acres Golf Club—*locale* ... TN-4
*Belle Air* ... NY-2
Belle Air—*hist pl* ... VA-3
Belle Air—*locale* ... IA-7
Belleair—*locale* ... VA-3
**Belleair**—*pop pl* ... FL-3
Belleair Bazaar (Shop Ctr)—*locale* ... FL-3
**Belleair Beach**—*pop pl* ... FL-3
**Belleair Bluffs**—*pop pl* ... FL-3
Belleair Bluffs Plaza (Shop Ctr)—*locale* ... FL-3
Belle Aire—*hist pl* ... VA-3
**Belle-Aire**—*pop pl* ... TN-4
**Belle Aire**—*pop pl* (2) ... TN-4
Belle Aire Canal C-1N—*canal* ... FL-3
*Belle Aire Lake* ... TN-4
Belleaire Sch—*school* ... OH-6
*Belle Air Mountain* ... NY-2
Belle Air Sch—*school* ... CA-9
Belleair Sch—*school* ... FL-3
**Belleair Shore**—*pop pl* ... FL-3
**Belleair Shores**—*pop pl* ... FL-3
**Belle Alliance**—*pop pl* ... LA-4
**Belle Amie**—*pop pl* ... LA-4
Belle and Ford Lake—*lake* ... TX-5
**Belle Arbor**—*pop pl* ... IN-6
Belleau Creek—*stream* ... MO-7
Belleau Lake—*lake* ... IL-6
Belleau Lake—*lake* ... NH-1
Belle Ayr—*locale* ... NY-2
*Belleayre* ... NY-2
**Belle Ayre Estates**—*pop pl* ... FL-3
*Belleayre Mountain* ... NY-2
Belle Ayr Mtn—*summit* ... NY-2
Belle Bayou—*stream* ... LA-4
Belle Bridge—*building* ... MS-4
**Belle Bridge**—*pop pl* ... PA-2
**Belle Brook Estate**—*pop pl* ... TN-4
**Belle Brook Estates
(subdivision)**—*pop pl* ... TN-4
Belle Campground—*locale* ... CA-9
*Belle Canton Islands* ... TN-4
*Belle Canton Shoals* ... TN-4
*Belle Carden Islands* ... TN-4
*Belle Carden Shoals* ... TN-4
*Bellecenter* ... OH-6
**Belle Center**—*pop pl* ... MO-7
**Belle Center**—*pop pl* ... OH-6
*Belle Centre* ... OH-6
Belle Ch—*church* ... LA-4
Belle Champion Mine—*mine* ... CO-8
**Belle Chaney**—*pop pl* ... LA-4
Belle Chaney Springs—*spring* ... LA-4
**Belle Chasse**—*pop pl* ... LA-4
Belle Chasse Ferry—*locale* ... LA-4
Belle Chasse State Sch—*school* ... LA-4
**Belle Chene (subdivision)**—*pop pl* ... AL-4
**Bellechester**—*pop pl* ... MN-6
Bell Echo Camp—*locale* ... CA-9
*Belle City Drainage Canal* ... LA-4
Belle Claims—*civil* ... NV-8
Belleco (site)—*locale* ... ID-8
Belle Court Apartments—*hist pl* ... OR-9
Belle Cove Bayou—*stream* ... LA-4
Belle Cove Branch—*stream* ... VA-3
*Belle Creek* ... CA-9
*Belle Creek* ... IN-6
*Belle Creek* ... MT-8
Belle Creek—*locale* ... MN-6
**Belle Creek**—*pop pl* ... MT-8
Belle Creek—*stream* ... AL-4
Belle Creek—*stream* (2) ... AK-9
Belle Creek—*stream* (2) ... ID-8
Belle Creek—*stream* (2) ... MN-6
Belle Creek—*stream* (2) ... MT-8
Belle Creek—*stream* ... TX-5
**Belle Creek (Township of)**—*pop pl* ... MN-6
*Belledeau* ... LA-4
**Belle d'Eau**—*pop pl* ... LA-4
**Belledeer Hills (subdivision)**—*pop pl* ... MS-4
*Belledu* ... FM-9
**Belle Eagle**—*pop pl* ... TN-4
Belle Eagle Ch—*church* ... TN-4
Belle Eldridge Gold Mine—*mine* ... SD-7
Belle Ellen—*locale* ... AL-4
Belle Ellen Number 1 Slope Mine
(underground)—*mine* ... AL-4
Belle Ellen Slope Mine
(underground)—*mine* ... AL-4
Bellefaire Sch—*school* ... OH-6
**Belle Farm Estates**—*pop pl* ... MD-2
**Bellefield**—*pop pl* ... PA-2
Bellefield Plantation—*locale* ... SC-3
Bellefields—*hist pl* ... MD-2
Belleflower Point—*cape* ... SC-3
**Bellefont**—*pop pl* ... KS-7
*Belle Fontaine* ... AL-4
**Bellefontaine**—*pop pl* ... AL-4
**Bellefontaine**—*pop pl* ... MS-4
**Bellefontaine**—*pop pl* (2) ... MO-7
**Bellefontaine**—*pop pl* ... OH-6
Bellefontaine Air Force Station—*military* ... OH-6
Belle Fontaine Bayu—*gut* ... MS-4
Belle Fontaine Cem—*cemetery* ... IN-6
Bellefontaine Cem—*cemetery* ... MO-7
Bellefontaine Ch—*church* ... MO-7
Bellefontaine Country Club—*other* ... OH-6
Bellefontaine Creek—*stream* ... AL-4
Bellefontaine Creek—*stream* ... MS-4
Bellefontaine Island—*island* ... OH-6
Bellefontaine Methodist Ch—*church* ... MS-4
**Bellefontaine Neighbors**—*pop pl* ... MO-7
Belle Fontaine Point—*cape* ... MS-4
Bellefontaine Post Office—*building* ... MS-4
Bellefontaine Sch—*school* ... AL-4
Bellefontaine Sch—*school* ... MO-7
Bellefontaine Sch (historical)—*school* ... MS-4
Bellefont Ch—*church* ... NC-3
*Bellefonte* ... KS-7
*Bellefonte* ... RI-1
**Bellefonte**—*pop pl* ... AL-4
**Bellefonte**—*pop pl* ... AR-4
**Bellefonte**—*pop pl* ... DE-2
**Bellefonte**—*pop pl* (2) ... KY-4
**Bellefonte**—*pop pl* ... MD-2
**Bellefonte**—*pop pl* ... PA-2
**Bellefonte**—*pop pl* ... RI-1
Bellefonte Acad—*hist pl* ... PA-2
Bellefonte Bar—*bar* ... AL-4
**Bellefonte (Bellefont)**—*pop pl* ... AL-4
Bellefonte Borough—*civil* ... PA-2
Bellefonte Cem—*cemetery* ... AL-4
Belle Fonte Ch—*church* ... VA-3
Bellefonte Country Club—*other* ... KY-4
Bellefonte Depot (historical)—*locale* ... AL-4
Bellefonte Hist Dist—*hist pl* ... PA-2
Bellefonte Island—*island* ... AL-4
Bellefonte Landing (historical)—*locale* ... AL-4
Bellefonte (Magisterial
District)—*fmr MCD* ... VA-3
Bellefonte Memeorial Cem—*cemetery* ... KY-4
Bellefonte Nuclear Plant—*building* ... AL-4
*Bellefonte Pond* ... RI-1
Bellefonte Sch—*school* ... KY-4
Bellefonte Sch (historical)—*school* ... TN-4
Bellefonte Skypark—*airport* ... PA-2
*Bellefonte Station* ... AL-4
Bellefonte Station—*locale* ... PA-2
Bellefonte (Township of)—*fmr MCD* ... AR-4
Bellefont Pond—*lake* ... RI-1
Bellefont Sch—*school* ... NC-3
**Belle Forest**—*pop pl* ... VA-3
**Belle Forest (subdivision)**—*pop pl* (2) ... TN-4
*Bellefountain* ... IN-6
*Belle Fountain* ... IA-7
Belle Fountain—*locale* ... WI-6
**Bellefountain**—*pop pl* ... IA-7
**Belle Fountain**—*pop pl* ... IA-7
**Bellefountain (Bellfountain)**—*pop pl* ... IN-6
Belle Fountain Cem—*cemetery* ... IA-7
Belle Fountain Ch—*church* ... MS-4
Belle Fountain Creek—*stream* ... WI-6
Belle Fountain Ditch—*canal* ... MO-7
*Bellefountaine* ... IN-6

*Bellefountaine* MO-7
**Bellefountaine**—*pop pl* AL-4
*Belle Fountaine Ch* MS-4
*Bellefountain Elementary School* AL-4
Belle Fountain Sch—*school* MO-7
Belle Fountain Sch—*school* WI-6
Bellefount Baptist Ch—*church* TN-4
**Belle Founte**—*pop pl* TN-4
**Bellefounte**—*pop pl* TN-4
Bellefounte Cem—*cemetery* TN-4
*Belle Founte Church* TN-4
**Belle Fourche**—*pop pl* SD-7
Belle Fourche-Cheyenne Valleys—*unorg reg* SD-7
Belle Fourche Commercial Hist Dist—*hist pl* SD-7
Belle Fourche Dam—*dam* SD-7
Belle Fourche Dam—*hist pl* SD-7
Belle Fourche Diversion Dam—*dam* SD-7
Belle Fourche Experiment Farm—*hist pl* SD-7
Belle Fourche Natl Wildlife Ref—*park* SD-7
Belle Fourche River—*stream* SD-7
Belle Fourche River—*stream* WY-8
Belle Fourche River Bridge—*hist pl* SD-7
Belle Fourche Rsvr—*reservoir* SD-7
Bellegarde Cem—*cemetery* KS-7
**Belle Glade**—*pop pl* FL-3
Belle Glade Camp (Okeechobee Farm Labor Supply Ctr.)—*CDP* FL-3
Belle Glade Elem Sch—*school* FL-3
Belle Glade-Pahokee (CCD)—*cens area* FL-3
Belle Glade Shop Ctr—*locale* FL-3
**Belleglade (subdivision)**—*pop pl* TN-4
*Belle Green* AL-4
*Belle Grove* KS-7
Belle Grove—*hist pl* VA-3
**Belle Grove**—*pop pl* MD-2
**Bellegrove**—*pop pl* MD-2
**Bellegrove**—*pop pl* PA-2
Belle Grove Ch—*church* VA-3
Belle Grove Sch—*school* AR-4
Belle Grove Sch—*school* MD-2
Belle Grove Springs—*locale* KY-4
**Bellegrove (subdivision)**—*pop pl* MS-4
Belle Hall Covered Bridge—*hist pl* OH-6
Belle Harbor—*bay* MI-6
**Belle Harbor**—*pop pl* NY-2
**Belle Haven**—*pop pl* AL-4
**Belle Haven**—*pop pl* CT-1
**Belle Haven**—*pop pl* FL-3
**Belle Haven**—*pop pl* (2) VA-3
Belle Haven—*uninc pl* CA-9
Belle Haven—*uninc pl* VA-3
Bellehaven Baptist Ch—*church* MS-4
Belle Haven Cem—*cemetery* VA-3
Belle Haven Country Club—*other* VA-3
Belle Haven Sch—*school* CA-9
Belle Haven Sch—*school* OH-6
Belle Haven Station—*locale* VA-3
Belle Hawkins Mine—*mine* TN-4
Bellehelen—*locale* NV-8
Bellehelen Canyon—*valley* NV-8
Belle Helene Plantation—*locale* LA-4
Bellehelen Lake Number One—*lake* NV-8
Bellehelen Lake Number Two—*lake* NV-8
Bellehelen Ranch—*locale* NV-8
Belle Heth Sch—*school* VA-3
Belle Hill—*summit* TN-4
Belle Hollow—*valley* NY-2
**Bellehurst (subdivision)**—*pop pl* AL-4
Belleigh Acres Hunt Club—*other* NY-2
*Belle Inlet* MA-1
*Belle Island* GA-3
Belle Island—*island* ME-1
Belle Island—*island* NH-1
Belle Island—*island* (2) NY-2
Belle Island—*island* (2) WI-6
*Belle Isle* NY-2
Belle Isle—*hist pl* MI-6
Belle Isle—*hist pl* VA-3
Belle Isle—*island* FL-3
Belle Isle—*island* GA-3
Belle Isle—*island* (3) LA-4
Belle Isle—*island* (2) MI-6
Belle Isle—*island* (2) VA-3
**Belle Isle**—*pop pl* FL-3
**Belle Isle**—*pop pl* MS-4
**Belle Isle**—*pop pl* NY-2
Belle Isle—*uninc pl* OK-5
Belle Isle Bayou—*stream* (2) LA-4
Belle Isle Campground—*locale* MI-6
*Belle Isle Canal* LA-4
Belle Isle Ch—*church* GA-3
Belle Isle Chapel—*church* SC-3
**Belle Isle Gardens**—*pop pl* SC-3
Belle Isle Gas and Oil Field—*oilfield* LA-4
Belle Isle Inlet—*stream* MA-1
Belle Isle Inlet Marshes—*swamp* MA-1
Belle Isle Lake—*lake* (2) LA-4
Belle Isle Lake—*reservoir* OK-5
Belle Isle Park—*park* MI-6
Belle Isle Point—*cape* LA-4
Belle Isle Rice Mill Chimney—*hist pl* SC-3
Belle Isle Sch—*school* OK-5
Belle Jay Slope Mine (underground)—*mine* AL-4
*Belle Lake* MT-8
*Belle Lake* WI-6
Belle Lake—*lake* AK-9
Belle Lake—*lake* (2) MN-6
Belle Lake—*lake* NE-7
Belle Lake—*lake* ND-7
Belle Lake—*lake* WI-6
Belle Lakes—*lake* MI-6
Belle Lake Sch—*school* MN-6
Belle Landing (historical)—*locale* AL-4
Belle Lateral—*canal* AK-9
Bell Elem Sch—*school* MS-4
Bellemans Ch—*church* PA-2
*Bellemead* NJ-2
**Bellemead**—*pop pl* MD-2
**Belle Mead**—*pop pl* NJ-2
**Belle Mead**—*pop pl* SC-3
*Belle Meade* NJ-2
Belle Meade—*hist pl* TN-4
Belle Meade—*locale* VA-3
**Bellemeade**—*pop pl* AL-4
**Belle Meade**—*pop pl* AR-4
**Belle Meade**—*pop pl* FL-3
**Bellemeade**—*pop pl* KY-4
**Belle Meade**—*pop pl* (3) TN-4
Bellemeade—*post sta* GA-3
Bellemeade—*uninc pl* VA-3
Belle Meade Apartments—*hist pl* TN-4
Belle Meade Branch—*stream* TN-4
Belle Meade Country Club—*other* GA-3
Belle Meade Island—*island* FL-3
Belle Meade Linden Trail—*trail* VA-3
Belle Meade Park—*park* FL-3
**Belle Meade Plantation**—*pop pl* AR-4
**Bellemeade (subdivision)**—*pop pl* (2) AL-4
**Bellemeade (subdivision)**—*pop pl* MS-4
**Bellemeade (subdivision)**—*pop pl* NC-3
**Belle Meade (subdivision)**—*pop pl* NC-3
Belle Mead General Depot—*military* NJ-2
*Belle Meadow* CA-9
Belle Meadow Pocosin—*swamp* VA-3
**Belle Meadows**—*pop pl* VA-3
**Belle Meadows Subdivision**—*pop pl* UT-8
Belle Mead Sanitarium—*hospital* NJ-2
Belle Mead Station—*locale* NJ-2
Belle Mina—*hist pl* AL-4
**Belle Mina**—*pop pl* AL-4
Belle Mina Methodist Ch—*church* AL-4
Belle Mina Post Office (historical)—*building* AL-4
*Belle Mina School* AL-4
Belle Mine—*mine* MT-8
Belle Mine—*mine* NV-8
Belle Mont—*locale* AL-4
Bellemont—*locale* OK-5
Bellemont—*locale* PA-2
**Bellemont**—*pop pl* AZ-5
**Bellemont**—*pop pl* NC-3
**Belle Monte**—*pop pl* CA-9
Bellemont Flat—*flat* AZ-5
Bellemont Mill Village Hist Dist—*hist pl* NC-3
Bellemont Post Office (historical)—*building* PA-2
Bellemont Sch—*school* PA-2
Bellemont Siding—*locale* AZ-5
*Bellemoor* DE-2
**Bellemoor**—*pop pl* DE-2
*Belle Moore* IN-6
Belle Morris Sch—*school* TN-4
Belle Mountian—*summit* PA-2
Belle Mtn—*summit* NJ-2
Bellenfant Cem—*cemetery* TN-4
Bellenita Park—*park* CA-9
Bellen Lakes—*lake* AK-9
*Belle Oak* MI-6
Belle of Arizona Mine—*mine* AZ-5
Belle of Baker Mine—*mine* OR-9
BELLE OF LOUISVILLE (steamer)—*hist pl* KY-4
Belle of the Castle Mine—*mine* MT-8
Belle of the East Mine—*mine* CO-8
Belle of the West Mine—*mine* CO-8
Belle of Tonopah—*mine* NV-8
Belle Oil Field—*oilfield* CO-8
Belle-Park Ch—*church* LA-4
Belle Pass—*channel* LA-4
Belle Passi Cem—*cemetery* OR-9
**Belle Passi (historical)**—*pop pl* OR-9
Belle Passi School (abandoned)—*locale* OR-9
**Belle Place**—*pop pl* LA-4
*Belle Plain* NJ-2
Belle Plain—*locale* TX-5
**Belle Plain**—*pop pl* CO-8
**Belleplain**—*pop pl* NJ-2
**Belle Plain**—*pop pl* TX-5
Belle Plain Cem—*cemetery* TX-5
**Belle Plaine**—*pop pl* IA-7
**Belle Plaine**—*pop pl* KS-7
**Belle Plaine**—*pop pl* MN-6
**Belle Plaine**—*pop pl* WI-6
**Belle Plaine (Town of)**—*pop pl* WI-6
*Belle Plaine Township* KS-7
**Belle Plaine Township**—*pop pl* KS-7
**Belle Plaine Township**—*pop pl* SD-7
Belle Plaine (Township of)—*civ div* MN-6
*Belle Plains* NJ-2
Belle Plains—*locale* VA-3
Belle Plain Sch—*school* MO-7
Belleplain State For—*forest* NJ-2
*Belle Point* OH-6
Belle Point—*cape* GA-3
Belle Point—*cape* MT-8
Belle Point—*locale* KY-4
**Belle Point**—*pop pl* LA-4
**Bellepoint**—*pop pl* OH-6
**Bellepoint**—*pop pl* WV-2
Bellepoint—*uninc pl* KY-4
Belle Point Creek—*stream* GA-3
Belle Point Plantation—*locale* LA-4
Belle Point Sch—*school* AR-4
*Belle Prairie* IL-6
*Belleprairie* MS-4
Belle Prairie—*flat* MT-8
Belle Prairie—*locale* MS-4
Belle Prairie—*other* IL-6
**Belle Prairie**—*pop pl* MN-6
**Belle Prairie**—*pop pl* MS-4
Belle Prairie Cem—*cemetery* KS-7
**Belle Prairie City**—*pop pl* IL-6
Belle Prairie Cut-Off—*bend* MS-4
Belle Prairie Landing—*locale* MS-4
Belle Prairie Sch—*school* NE-7
**Belle Prairie Township**—*pop pl* NE-7
**Belle Prairie Township**—*pop pl* SD-7
Belle Prairie (Township of)—*civ div* IL-6
Belle Prairie (Township of)—*civ div* MN-6
Belle Prairie Village Site—*hist pl* MN-6
Belle Pumping Station—*other* WY-8
Belle Ranch—*locale* WY-8
Belle Reve Plantation—*locale* SC-3
Beller Hollow—*valley* TN-4
Bellerica Mall—*locale* MA-1
**Belle Rive**—*pop pl* IL-6
**Bellerive**—*pop pl* MO-7
Bellerive Country Club—*other* MO-7
**Bellerive Estates**—*pop pl* MO-7
**Belle Rive Highlands (subdivision)**—*pop pl* TN-4
Bellerive Hotel—*hist pl* MO-7
Bellerive Park—*park* MO-7
**Belle River**—*pop pl* LA-4
**Belle River**—*pop pl* MI-6
**Belleriver**—*pop pl* MN-6
**Belle River**—*pop pl* MN-6
Belle River—*stream* LA-4
Belle River—*stream* MI-6
Belle River Ch—*church* LA-4
Belle River Mills—*locale* MI-6
Belle River Mills Gas Storage Area—*other* MI-6
Belle River Park—*park* MI-6
Belle River State Wildlife Mngmt Area—*park* MN-6
**Belle River (Township of)**—*pop pl* MN-6
**Belle Rive (subdivision)**—*pop pl* TN-4
Beller McCollum Ditch—*canal* IN-6
Belle Rock Light—*locale* WA-9
*Bellerose* LA-4
Bellerose—*other* LA-4
**Belle Rose**—*pop pl* LA-4
**Bellerose**—*pop pl* NY-2
**Belle Rose (Bellerose)**—*pop pl* LA-4
Belle Rose (historical)—*locale* AL-4
*Belle Rose Island* MN-6
Bellerose (P.O.)—*uninc pl* NY-2
**Bellerose Terrace**—*pop pl* NY-2
Beller Pond—*lake* MI-6
Beller Sch—*school* PA-2
Bellers Hollow—*valley* KY-4
Belle Ryan Sch—*school* NE-7
Belles Cem—*cemetery* PA-2
Belle Sch—*school* WV-2
Belle Sch (abandoned)—*school* MO-7
Belle Sch (historical)—*school* AL-4
Belles Fork—*stream* KY-4
Belle Sherman Sch—*school* NY-2
Belle Spring—*spring* AZ-5
Belle Spring Cem—*cemetery* KS-7
Belles Store (historical)—*locale* MS-4
Belle Starr Creek—*stream* OK-5
Belle Starr Mtn—*summit* OK-5
Belle's Tavern—*hist pl* KY-4
**Belle Stone School**—*pop pl* OH-6
*Belle Sumter* AL-4
*Belle Sumter Mine* AL-4
Belle Taine, Lake—*lake* MN-6
**Belle Terre**—*pop pl* (2) LA-4
**Belle Terre**—*pop pl* NY-2
Belle-Terre Airp—*airport* MS-4
Belle Terre Cem—*cemetery* NY-2
Belle Terre MS—*school* FL-3
**Belle Township**—*pop pl* NE-7
**Belle Township**—*pop pl* SD-7
**Belle Union**—*pop pl* IN-6
Belle Union Branch—*stream* IN-6
Belle Union Branch Cem—*cemetery* IN-6
Belle Union Elem Sch—*school* IN-6
**Belle Valley**—*pop pl* (2) OH-6
**Belle Valley**—*pop pl* PA-2
Belle Valley Elem Sch—*school* PA-2
Belle Valley Sch—*school* IL-6
Belle Valley Sch—*school* NE-7
Belle Valley Station (historical)—*locale* PA-2
**Belleve**—*pop pl* OH-6
*Bellevernon* PA-2
**Belle Vernon**—*pop pl* OH-6
**Belle Vernon**—*pop pl* PA-2
*Belle Vernon Boro* PA-2
Belle Vernon Borough—*civil* PA-2
Belle Vernon Cem—*cemetery* PA-2
Belle Vernon Cem—*cemetery* TN-4
Belle Vernon (sta.)—*uninc pl* PA-2
*Belleview* FL-3
*Belleview* TN-4
*Belleview* UT-8
Belleview—*hist pl* DE-2
Belleview—*hist pl* VA-3
Belleview—*locale* CA-9
Belleview—*locale* CO-8
Belleview—*locale* GA-3
Belleview—*locale* IL-6
Belleview—*locale* (2) VA-3
Belleview—*other* FL-3
Belleview—*other* VA-3
**Belleview**—*pop pl* CA-9
**Belleview**—*pop pl* FL-3
**Belleview**—*pop pl* IN-6
**Belleview**—*pop pl* LA-4
**Belleview**—*pop pl* MO-7
**Belleview**—*pop pl* NY-2
**Belleview**—*pop pl* OR-9
**Belleview**—*pop pl* (2) TN-4
**Belle View**—*pop pl* VA-3
Belleview, Bayou—*stream* (2) LA-4
Belle View, Lake—*reservoir* WI-6
*Belleview Acres* OH-6
*Belleview Baptist Church* MS-4
Belleview Beach—*beach* AK-9
**Belle View (Belleview)**—*pop pl* VA-3
Belleview-Biltmore Hotel—*hist pl* FL-3
Belleview (CCD)—*cens area* FL-3
Belleview (CCD)—*cens area* TN-4
Belleview Cem—*cemetery* AL-4
Belleview Cem—*cemetery* AR-4
Belleview Cem—*cemetery* (2) MO-7
Belleview Cem—*cemetery* NC-3
Belle View Cem—*cemetery* NC-3
Belleview Cem—*cemetery* OK-5
Belleview Cem—*cemetery* TN-4
Belleview Cem—*cemetery* WV-2
Belleview Ch—*church* AR-4
Belleview Ch—*church* GA-3
Belleview Ch—*church* NC-3
Belleview Ch—*church* SD-7
Belleview Ch—*church* TN-4
Belleview Coll—*school* CO-8
Belleview Country Club—*other* LA-4
Belleview Creek—*stream* MO-7
Belleview Division—*civil* TN-4
Belleview (Election Precinct)—*fmr MCD* IL-6
Belleview Elem Sch—*school* FL-3
Belleview Estates—*locale* TN-4
Belleview First Assembly of God—*church* FL-3
**Belleview (Grant)**—*pop pl* KY-4
**Belleview (Grant P O)**—*pop pl* KY-4
*Belleview Heights* OH-6
Belleview Heights—*locale* FL-3
**Belleview Heights**—*pop pl* (2) OH-6
**Belleview Heights**—*pop pl* PA-2
*Belleview (historical)* KS-7
Belleview (historical)—*locale* AL-4
Belleview Hollow—*valley* IL-6
Belleview Island—*island* FL-3
*Belleview Lake* CT-1
Belle View Landing—*locale* MS-4
Belleview Mtn—*summit* CO-8
Belleview Municipal Park—*park* OH-6
Belleview Park—*park* CO-8
Belleview Plantation (historical)—*locale* AL-4
*Belle View Point* OR-9
Belleview Point—*cape* NY-2
Belleview Regional Shop Ctr—*locale* FL-3
Belleview Santa Fe Union Sch—*school* CA-9
Belleview Santos HS—*school* FL-3
Belleview Sch—*school* AR-4
Belleview Sch—*school* (2) CA-9
Belleview Sch—*school* (2) CO-8
Belleview Sch—*school* KS-7
Belleview Sch—*school* MO-7
Belle View Sch—*school* VA-3
Belleview Sch (abandoned)—*school* (2) PA-2
Belleview Sch (historical)—*school* AL-4
Belleview Sch (historical)—*school* MO-7
Belleview Sch (historical)—*school* TN-4
Belleview Square (Shop Ctr)—*locale* FL-3
Belleview Township—*civil* (2) MO-7
**Belleview Township**—*pop pl* SD-7
Belleview United Methodist Ch—*church* AL-4
Belleview Valley Nursing Home—*hospital* MO-7
*Belleville* GA-3
*Belleville* PA-2
*Belleville* TN-4
Belleville—*locale* MS-4
**Belleville**—*pop pl* AL-4
**Belleville**—*pop pl* AR-4
**Belleville**—*pop pl* FL-3
**Belleville**—*pop pl* IL-6
**Belleville**—*pop pl* IN-6
**Belleville**—*pop pl* KS-7
**Belleville**—*pop pl* MI-6
**Belleville**—*pop pl* MO-7
**Belleville**—*pop pl* NJ-2
**Belleville**—*pop pl* NY-2
**Belleville**—*pop pl* OK-5
**Belleville**—*pop pl* PA-2
**Belleville**—*pop pl* RI-1
**Belleville**—*pop pl* TN-4
**Belleville**—*pop pl* VA-3
**Belleville**—*pop pl* WV-2
**Belleville**—*pop pl* WI-6
*Belleville Airport* KS-7
Belleville Annex—*post sta* NJ-2
Belleville Ave Congregational Church—*hist pl* NJ-2
Belleville Cem—*cemetery* KS-7
Belleville Cem—*cemetery* MA-1
Belleville Ch—*church* AL-4
Belleville Country Club—*other* KS-7
Belleville Creek—*stream* VA-3
Belleville Elem Sch (historical)—*school* AL-4
*Belleville Faulk Church* AL-4
Belleville Fork Ch—*church* AL-4
Belleville Gardens Playground—*park* IN-6
Belleville Heights Ch—*church* MI-6
Belleville Hist Dist—*hist pl* IL-6
Belleville (historical)—*locale* ND-7
Belleville HS—*school* KS-7
Belleville Junior Coll—*school* IL-6
Belleville Lake—*reservoir* MI-6
Belleville Lock And Dam—*dam* WV-2
Belleville Lookout Tower—*locale* AL-4
**Belleville Meadows (subdivision)**—*pop pl* VA-3
*Belleville Mill Pond* RI-1
Belleville Mine—*mine* NV-8
Belleville Municipal Airp—*airport* KS-7
**Belleville North**—*pop pl* MI-6
Belleville Park—*park* NJ-2
Belleville Pointe Park—*park* MI-6
*Belleville Pond* WI-6
Belleville Pond—*lake* RI-1
Belleville Pond—*reservoir* RI-1
Belleville Reach—*channel* NJ-2
Belleville Ridge—*ridge* AR-4
Belleville Sch—*school* LA-4
Belleville Sch—*school* MA-1
Belleville Sch—*school* NJ-2
Belleville Sch—*school* PA-2
Belleville Sch—*school* SC-3
Belleville (site)—*locale* CA-9
Belleville (Site)—*locale* NV-8
Belleville Township—*civil* KS-7
**Belleville Township**—*pop pl* KS-7
**Belleville (Township of)**—*pop pl* IL-6
**Belleville (Township of)**—*pop pl* NJ-2
Belle Vista—*hist pl* NJ-2
Belle Vista—*locale* GA-3
**Belle Vista**—*pop pl* AL-4
*Belle Vista Beach* FL-3
**Belle Vista Beach (historical)**—*pop pl* FL-3
Belle Vista Cem—*cemetery* KS-7
Bellevoir-Ormsby Village—*hist pl* KY-4
Bellevoir Sch—*school* NC-3
*Bellevue* AL-4
*Bellevue* CO-8
*Bellevue* KS-7
*Bellevue* MS-4
*Bellevue* UT-8
Bellevue—*hist pl* FL-3
Bellevue—*hist pl* GA-3
Bellevue—*hist pl* KY-4
Bellevue—*hist pl* MD-2
Bellevue—*hist pl* NC-3
Bellevue—*hist pl* OH-6
Belle Vue—*hist pl* TN-4
Bellevue—*locale* AZ-5
Bellevue—*locale* DE-2
Bellevue—*locale* GA-3
Bellevue—*locale* (2) LA-4
Bellevue—*locale* (2) PA-2
Bellevue—*locale* VA-3
Bellevue—*locale* VI-3
**Bellevue**—*pop pl* (2) AL-4
**Bellevue**—*pop pl* CA-9
**Bellevue**—*pop pl* DC-2
**Bellevue**—*pop pl* ID-8
**Bellevue**—*pop pl* IL-6
**Bellevue**—*pop pl* IA-7
**Bellevue**—*pop pl* KY-4
**Bellevue**—*pop pl* (2) LA-4
**Bellevue**—*pop pl* MD-2
**Bellevue**—*pop pl* MA-1
**Bellevue**—*pop pl* MI-6
**Bellevue**—*pop pl* NE-7
**Bellevue**—*pop pl* (2) NY-2
**Bellevue**—*pop pl* OH-6
**Bellevue**—*pop pl* OR-9
**Bellevue**—*pop pl* (2) PA-2
**Bellevue**—*pop pl* TN-4
**Bellevue**—*pop pl* TX-5
**Bellevue**—*pop pl* WA-9
**Bellevue**—*pop pl* WI-6
Bellevue—*uninc pl* GA-3
Bellevue, Lake—*lake* FL-3
Bellevue Airfield Heliport—*airport* WA-9
Bellevue Annex Sch—*school* MI-6
Bellevue Apartment Bldg—*hist pl* WI-6
Bellevue Ave Hist Dist—*hist pl* RI-1
Bellevue Avenue/Casino Hist Dist—*hist pl* RI-1
Bellevue Ave Sch—*school* CA-9
Bellevue Baptist Ch—*church* (2) AL-4
Bellevue (Bellview Heights)—*uninc pl* AL-4
Bellevue Borough—*civil* PA-2
Bellevue Canal—*canal* ID-8
Bellevue Cem—*cemetery* CA-9
Bellevue Cem—*cemetery* ID-8
Bellevue Cem—*cemetery* KY-4
Bellevue Cem—*cemetery* (3) MA-1
Bellevue Cem—*cemetery* NE-7
Bellevue Cem—*cemetery* NC-3
Bellevue Cem—*cemetery* ND-7
Bellevue Cem—*cemetery* OH-6
Bellevue Cem—*cemetery* PA-2
Bellevue Cem—*cemetery* TX-5
Bellevue Cem—*cemetery* WI-6
Bellevue Ch—*church* AL-4
Bellevue Ch—*church* KY-4
Bellevue Ch—*church* (3) LA-4
Bellevue Ch—*church* MS-4
Bellevue Ch—*church* PA-2
Bellevue Ch—*church* TX-5
Bellevue Ch—*church* VA-3
Bellevue Community Coll—*school* WA-9
Bellevue Country Club—*other* NY-2
**Bellevue Estates**—*pop pl* MD-2
**Bellevue Estates**—*pop pl* TN-4
Bellevue Flats—*flat* UT-8
**Bellevue Forest**—*pop pl* VA-3
Bellevue Heights Ch—*church* NY-2
*Bellevue Highlands* AL-4
Bellevue Hill—*summit* MA-1
Bellevue Hill—*summit* VT-1
Bellevue Hill—*summit* WI-6
Bellevue Hill Park—*park* OH-6
**Bellevue Hills (subdivision)**—*pop pl* DE-2
Bellevue Hist Dist—*hist pl* ID-8
Bellevue Hosp—*hospital* NY-2
Bellevue HS—*hist pl* KY-4
Bellevue HS—*school* TN-4
Bellevue HS—*school* WA-9
Bellevue Island—*island* (2) MI-6
Bellevue-Joy (CCD)—*cens area* TX-5
*Bellevue Junction* CO-8
Bellevue Lake—*lake* WI-6
Bellevue Lake—*reservoir* DE-2
Bellevue Lake Dam—*dam* DE-2
Bellevue Landing—*locale* MS-4
**Bellevue Manor**—*pop pl* DE-2
Bellevue Med Ctr—*hospital* NY-2
Bellevue Memorial Cem—*cemetery* FL-3
Bellevue Memorial Park—*cemetery* FL-3
Bellevue Memorial Park—*cemetery* LA-4
Bellevue Memorial Park—*park* PA-2
Bellevue Mill—*hist pl* MI-6
Bellevue Mine—*mine* CA-9
Bellevue Mtn—*summit* CO-8
Bellevue Municipal Golf Course—*other* WA-9
Bellevue No. 2—*fmr MCD* NE-7
*Bellevue Oil Field* CA-9
Bellevue Oilfield—*oilfield* LA-4
Bellevue Park—*park* CA-9
Bellevue Park—*park* TN-4
Bellevue Park—*park* TX-5
Bellevue Peak—*summit* NV-8
**Bellevue Place Subdivision**—*pop pl* UT-8
*Bellevue Plantation* MS-4
Bellevue Plantation (historical)—*locale* AL-4
*Bellevue P.O.* AL-4
Belle Vue Point—*cape* OR-9
Bellevue Point—*cape* WA-9
Bellevue Pond—*lake* MA-1
Bellevue Presbyterian Cem—*cemetery* IA-7
Bellevue Ranch—*locale* CA-9
Bellevue Range—*channel* DE-2
Bellevue Red Ch—*church* LA-4
Bellevue Rsvr—*reservoir* OH-6
Bellevue Sch—*school* CA-9
Belle Vue Sch—*school* FL-3
Bellevue Sch—*school* GA-3
Bellevue Sch—*school* IL-6
Bellevue Sch—*school* KS-7
Bellevue Sch—*school* KY-4
Bellevue Sch—*school* MI-6
Bellevue Sch—*school* NE-7
Bellevue Sch—*school* TN-4
Bellevue Sch—*school* (2) VA-3
Bellevue Sch—*school* WI-6
Bellevue Shaft—*mine* PA-2
Bellevue Slough—*stream* IA-7
Bellevue State Park—*park* DE-2
Bellevue State Park—*park* IA-7
Bellevue Stratford Hotel—*hist pl* PA-2
**Bellevue Terrace (subdivision)**—*pop pl* NC-3
**Bellevue (Town of)**—*pop pl* WI-6
*Bellevue Township* MO-7
Bellevue Township—*fmr MCD* IA-7
Bellevue (Township of)—*other* (2) OH-6
**Bellevue (Township of)**—*pop pl* MI-6
**Bellevue (Township of)**—*pop pl* MN-6
Bellevue Union Sch—*school* CA-9
**Bellevule**—*pop pl* MS-4
Bellevyria (historical)—*locale* ND-7
*Bellew Lake* MI-6
**Bellewood**—*pop pl* KY-4
**Bellewood**—*pop pl* LA-4
**Bellewood**—*pop pl* MS-4
**Bellewood**—*pop pl* NJ-2
Bellewood Cem—*cemetery* MS-4
Bellewood Ch—*church* MS-4
*Bellewood Lake* TX-5
**Bellewood (subdivision)**—*pop pl* DE-2
Bellews Ch—*church* AL-4
*Bellews Chapel* AL-4
*Bellews Creek* MO-7
Belle Yazoo Plantation (historical)—*locale* MS-4
**Bell Factory**—*pop pl* AL-4
Bell Factory Post Office (historical)—*building* AL-4
*Bell Factory Station* AL-4
Bell Farm—*locale* KY-4
Bell Farmhouse—*hist pl* DE-2
*Bellfast* PA-2
Bell Ferry (historical)—*locale* MS-4
**Bellfield**—*pop pl* PA-2
Bellfield Ch—*church* KY-4
*Bellfield Cove* VA-3
*Bellfield Creek* VA-3
Bellfield Ditch—*canal* MD-2
Bellfield Presbytyrian Ch—*church* PA-2
Bell Flat—*flat* NV-8
Bell Flat—*flat* NM-5
Bell Flats—*flat* AK-9
Bell Flats—*flat* MO-7
Bell Flat Well—*well* NV-8
**Bellflower**—*pop pl* CA-9
**Bellflower**—*pop pl* IL-6
**Bellflower**—*pop pl* MO-7
Bellflower Cem—*cemetery* IL-6
Bellflower Christian Sch—*school* CA-9
Bellflower HS—*school* CA-9
Bell Flowers Baptist Ch—*church* MS-4
Bellflower Sch—*school* CA-9
**Bellflower (Township of)**—*pop pl* IL-6
*Bellfontaine* IA-7
**Bellfontaine**—*pop pl* LA-4
*Bellfontaine Church* AL-4
*Bellfontaine Neighbors* MO-7
Bell Ford Bar—*bar* AL-4
**Bell Fork**—*pop pl* (2) NC-3
Bell Fork—*stream* KY-4
Bell Fork—*stream* MO-7
**Bell Fork Homes (subdivision)**—*pop pl* NC-3
Bell Fork Park—*park* NC-3
Bell Fork Sch—*school* NC-3
Bell Form Landing—*locale* NC-3
Bellfort East Shop Ctr—*locale* TX-5
**Bellfountain**—*pop pl* IN-6
**Bellfountain**—*pop pl* OR-9
Bellfountain Cem—*cemetery* OR-9
Bellfountain County Park—*park* OR-9
Bellfountain Junction—*locale* OR-9
Bell Fount Spring—*spring* TN-4
Bellfout Canyon—*valley* CA-9
Bell Gap—*gap* GA-3
Bell Gap—*gap* TN-4
**Bell Gardens**—*pop pl* CA-9
Bell Gardens HS—*school* CA-9
Bell Gardens JHS—*school* CA-9
Bell Gardens Sch—*school* CA-9
*Bell-Gilmore Vocational School* AL-4
Bell Gin—*locale* TX-5
Bell Ginhouse Bend—*bend* AR-4
Bellgrade (historical)—*locale* KS-7
*Bell Grove* KS-7
*Bell Grove* PA-2
Bellgrove—*locale* ID-8
Bell Grove Baptist Ch—*church* (2) MS-4
Bell Grove Cem—*cemetery* MS-4
Bell Grove Cem—*cemetery* TN-4
Bell Grove Ch—*church* (3) MS-4
Bell Grove Ch—*church* SC-3
Bell Grove Ch—*church* TN-4
Bellgrove Creek—*stream* ID-8
Bell Grove Sch—*school* WI-6
Bell Grove Sch (abandoned)—*school* MO-7
Bell Grove Sch (historical)—*school* MS-4
Bellgrove Sch II—*hist pl* ID-8
Bell Gulch—*valley* AZ-5
Bell Gulch—*valley* CA-9
Bell Gulch—*valley* (2) CO-8
Bell Gulch—*valley* ID-8
Bell Gulch Spring—*spring* AZ-5
Bell Gully—*stream* AR-4
Bellhammer Slough—*stream* AR-4
Bell Hammock—*island* FL-3
*Bell Haven* NV-8
**Bellhaven Beach**—*pop pl* MD-2
**Bell Heights**—*pop pl* WI-6
Bell Heights—*uninc pl* WI-6
**Bell Helene**—*pop pl* LA-4
Bell Hill—*summit* AL-4
Bell Hill—*summit* AR-4
Bell Hill—*summit* CA-9
Bell Hill—*summit* CT-1
Bell Hill—*summit* KY-4
Bell Hill—*summit* MA-1
Bell Hill—*summit* MO-7
Bell Hill—*summit* MT-8
Bell Hill—*summit* NH-1
Bell Hill—*summit* NM-5
Bell Hill—*summit* (2) NY-2
Bell Hill—*summit* OH-6
Bell Hill—*summit* (4) TN-4
Bell Hill—*summit* VA-3
Bell Hill—*summit* (2) WA-9
Bell Hill—*summit* WV-2
Bell Hill—*summit* WY-8
*Bell Hill Ch* MS-4
Bell Hill Ch—*church* MS-4
Bell Hill Ch—*church* NC-3
Bell Hill Meeting House—*church* ME-1
Bell Hill Mine—*mine* UT-8
Bell Hill Rsvr—*reservoir* MA-1
Bell Hill Sch—*school* KY-4
Bell Hill Sch—*school* TN-4
Bell Hill Sch (historical)—*school* PA-2
Bell (historical)—*locale* AL-4
*Bell Hollow* UT-8
Bell Hollow—*valley* (2) KY-4
Bell Hollow—*valley* (4) MO-7
Bell Hollow—*valley* NY-2
Bell Hollow—*valley* OH-6
Bell Hollow—*valley* (4) PA-2
Bell Hollow—*valley* (12) TN-4
Bell Hollow—*valley* (2) TX-5
Bell Hollow—*valley* UT-8
Bell Hollow—*valley* (3) VA-3
Bell Hollow—*valley* (3) WV-2
*Bell Hollow Run* PA-2
Bell Hosp—*hospital* VA-3
Bell House—*hist pl* AR-4
Bell House—*hist pl* OH-6

Bell House—*hist pl* VA-3
Bell HS—*school* CA-9
Bell HS—*school* FL-3
Bell HS—*school* TX-5
*Bellie McGees Creek* NC-3
Bellier Cove—*bay* ME-1
Bellile Cem—*cemetery* WI-6
Bellile Falls—*falls* WI-6
Bellilluvia Windmill—*locale* TX-5
Bellim Bay—*bay* AK-9
*Bellinda* VA-3
**Bellingar**—*pop pl* NE-7
**Bellinger**—*pop pl* SC-3
**Bellinger**—*pop pl* WI-6
Bellinger Cem—*cemetery* NY-2
Bellinger Cem—*cemetery* OR-9
Bellinger Hill—*summit* OR-9
Bellinger Hill Sch—*school* AL-4
Bellinger Landing—*locale* OR-9
*Bellinger Mountain* AL-4
Bellinger Neck—*cape* SC-3
Bellinger Ranch—*locale* NV-8
*Bellinger's Island* NY-2
**Bellingham**—*pop pl* MA-1
**Bellingham**—*pop pl* MN-6
**Bellingham**—*pop pl* WA-9
Bellingham, Mount—*summit* MA-1
Bellingham Bay—*bay* WA-9
Bellingham-Cary House—*hist pl* MA-1
Bellingham (CCD)—*cens area* WA-9
**Bellingham Center**—*pop pl* MA-1
Bellingham Center Cem—*cemetery* MA-1
Bellingham Center Sch—*school* MA-1
Bellingham Channel—*channel* WA-9
Bellingham Country Club—*other* WA-9
Bellingham Intl Airp—*airport* WA-9
Bellingham Mill Shop Ctr—*locale* WA-9
Bellingham Natl Bank Bldg—*hist pl* WA-9
Bellingham Omni Radio Range Station—*locale* WA-9
Bellingham Square Hist Dist—*hist pl* MA-1
**Bellingham (Town of)**—*pop pl* MA-1
Bellingrath Gardens—*park* AL-4
Bellingrath Gardens and Home—*hist pl* AL-4
Bellingrath JHS—*school* AL-4
Bellingrath Park—*park* AL-4
Bellingsgate Island (historical)—*island* MA-1
Bellin Hosp—*hospital* WI-6
Bell Institute (historical)—*school* AL-4
Bellin Vly—*swamp* NY-2
Bellion Creek—*stream* MT-8
Bellis Cem—*cemetery* MO-7
Bellis Dock—*locale* TN-4
Bellis Island—*island* PA-2
*Bell Island* CT-1
*Bell Island* NY-2
*Bell Island* NC-3
Bell Island—*area* NC-3
Bell Island—*island* AL-4
Bell Island—*island* (3) AK-9
Bell Island—*island* AR-4
Bell Island—*island* CT-1
Bell Island—*island* IL-6
Bell Island—*island* KY-4
Bell Island—*island* MO-7
Bell Island—*island* NC-3
Bell Island—*island* PA-2
Bell Island—*island* VT-1
Bell Island—*island* WA-9
Bell Island—*island* WI-6
Bell Island—*other* AK-9
Bell Island—*swamp* LA-4
**Bell Island Hot Springs**—*pop pl* AK-9
Bell Island Lakes—*area* AK-9
Bell Island Rec Area—*area* NC-3
Bellisle Lake—*lake* NM-5
Bell-Isle Park—*park* NY-2
Bellis Park—*park* CA-9
*Bellissima Lake* MN-6
Bellis Spring—*spring* WI-6
Bell Jellico Branch—*stream* KY-4
Bell JHS—*school* LA-4
Bell JHS—*school* OK-5
Bellknap Lake—*lake* AR-4
Bell Knob—*summit* GA-3
Bell Knob—*summit* (2) NC-3
Bell Knob Cem—*cemetery* KY-4
Bell Knob Lookout Tower—*locale* WV-2
*Bell Lake* MI-6
*Bell Lake* MN-6
Bell Lake—*lake* AL-4
Bell Lake—*lake* AK-9
Bell Lake—*lake* AR-4
Bell Lake—*lake* (2) FL-3
Bell Lake—*lake* ID-8
Bell Lake—*lake* IL-6
Bell Lake—*lake* IN-6
Bell Lake—*lake* LA-4
Bell Lake—*lake* (4) MI-6
Bell Lake—*lake* MN-6
Bell Lake—*lake* MS-4
Bell Lake—*lake* MT-8
Bell Lake—*lake* NJ-2
Bell Lake—*lake* NM-5
Bell Lake—*lake* TX-5
Bell Lake—*lake* WA-9
Bell Lake—*lake* (2) WI-6
Bell Lake—*reservoir* (2) AL-4
Bell Lake—*reservoir* FL-3
Bell Lake—*reservoir* IN-6
Bell Lake—*reservoir* MO-7
Bell Lake—*reservoir* NC-3
Bell Lake—*reservoir* VA-3
Bell Lake—*swamp* TX-5
Bell Lake Brake—*swamp* AR-4
Bell Lake Creek—*stream* ND-7
Bell Lake Dam—*dam* IN-6
Bell Lake Dam—*dam* NC-3
Bell Lake Ditch—*canal* IN-6
Bell Lake Oil Field—*other* NM-5
Bell Lake Park—*park* NJ-2
Bell Lakes—*lake* OH-6
Bell Lakes—*lake* WY-8
Bell Lakes Trail—*trail* WY-8
Bell Lake Windmill—*locale* NM-5
*Bell Landing* AL-4
Bell Landing—*locale* MI-6
Bell Lane Ch—*church* AL-4
Bell Larsen Canal—*canal* ID-8
Bell Lateral—*canal* ID-8
Bell Lateral—*canal* NM-5
Bell Lateral—*canal* TX-5
Bell Lawrence Canyon—*valley* NM-5
Bell Ledges—*summit* NH-1
Bell Lewis Hollow—*valley* WV-2
Bell Lick Run—*stream* OH-6
*Bellman Creek* NJ-2
Bellman Run—*stream* PA-2
Bellmans Creek—*stream* NJ-2
Bell Mansion—*hist pl* OH-6
Bellman's Union Church—*hist pl* PA-2
Bell Mare Creek—*stream* ID-8
Bell Mare Mining Camp (historical)—*locale* AZ-5
Bell Mare Spring—*spring* ID-8
*Bellmar HS* PA-2
Bell Marie Lake—*reservoir* MI-6
Bellmar JHS—*school* PA-2
Bell Marsh—*swamp* ME-1
Bell Marsh—*swamp* MD-2
Bell Marsh Creek—*stream* ID-8
**Bellmawr**—*pop pl* NJ-2
Bellmawr Park—*uninc pl* NJ-2
**Bellmead**—*pop pl* TX-5
**Bellmeade**—*pop pl* WV-2
Bell Meade Ch—*church* AR-4
Bell Meade Sch—*school* AR-4
**Bell Meade Subdivision**—*pop pl* TN-4
Bell Meadow—*flat* CA-9
Bell Meadow—*flat* WA-9
*Bell Meadows* CA-9
**Bell Meadows (subdivision)**—*pop pl* AL-4
Bell Memorial Ch—*church* PA-2
*Bellmena Village* TX-5
Bell Mere Lake—*reservoir* OK-5
**Bell-Merrill (subdivision)**—*pop pl* AL-4
*Bell Mill* VA-3
Bell Mill—*locale* TN-4
Bell Mills—*locale* AL-4
Bell Mine—*mine* AZ-5
Bell Mine—*mine* (3) CA-9
Bell Mine—*mine* (3) NV-8
Bell Mine—*mine* NM-5
Bell Mine—*mine* WY-8
Bellmire Ridge—*ridge* CO-8
Bellmire Rsvr—*reservoir* CO-8
Bell Mission Ch—*church* GA-3
Bell Mission (historical)—*church* MS-4
Bell Mission Sch—*school* NC-3
*Bellmont* AZ-5
*Bellmont* MS-4
**Bellmont**—*pop pl* IL-6
Bellmont Center—*locale* NY-2
Bellmont (Election Precinct)—*fmr MCD* IL-6
**Bellmont (Town of)**—*pop pl* NY-2
*Bellmore* OH-6
**Bellmore**—*pop pl* IN-6
**Bellmore**—*pop pl* NY-2
Bellmore Cem—*cemetery* AR-4
Bellmore Creek—*stream* NY-2
Bellmore Lake—*lake* WI-6
Bellmore Spring—*spring* WY-8
Bellmore (Township of)—*fmr MCD* AR-4
Bell Mound—*summit* KS-7
*Bell Mountain* GA-3
**Bell Mountain**—*pop pl* CA-9
Bell Mountain—*ridge* OR-9
Bell Mountain—*uninc pl* PA-2
Bell Mountain Brook—*stream* NY-2
Bell Mountain Canyon—*valley* ID-8
Bell Mountain Creek—*stream* ID-8
Bell Mountain Lookout Tower—*locale* MO-7
Bell Mountain Mine—*mine* NV-8
Bell Mountain Pond—*lake* NY-2
Bell Mountain Vista Picnic Area—*locale* MO-7
Bell Mountain Wash—*stream* CA-9
Bell Mountain Wilderness—*park* MO-7
Bell Mount Ch—*church* AL-4
Bell Mtn—*summit* AZ-5
Bell Mtn—*summit* AR-4
Bell Mtn—*summit* (5) CA-9
Bell Mtn—*summit* CO-8
Bell Mtn—*summit* ID-8
Bell Mtn—*summit* ME-1
Bell Mtn—*summit* MO-7
Bell Mtn—*summit* NV-8
Bell Mtn—*summit* (3) NM-5
Bell Mtn—*summit* NY-2
Bell Mtn—*summit* (4) NC-3
Bell Mtn—*summit* OR-9
Bell Mtn—*summit* PA-2
Bell Mtn—*summit* TN-4
Bell Mtn—*summit* TX-5
Bell Mtn—*summit* WY-8
Bell Neck—*cape* VA-3
Bell Neck Swamp—*swamp* VA-3
Bell No 10 Well—*well* WY-8
Bell No 11 Well—*well* WY-8
Bell No 12 Well—*well* WY-8
Bell No 14 Well—*well* WY-8
Bell No 15 Well—*well* WY-8
Bell No 16 Well—*well* WY-8
Bell No 17 Well—*well* WY-8
Bell No 24 Well—*well* WY-8
Bell No 25 Well—*well* WY-8
Bell No 5 Well—*well* WY-8
Bell No 6 Well—*well* WY-8
Bell No 8 Well—*well* WY-8
Bell Nursery Sch—*school* FL-3
**Bell Oak**—*pop pl* MI-6
**Bell Oaks Subdivision**—*pop pl* UT-8
Bell Oil Field—*oilfield* TX-5
Bello Lake—*lake* MN-6
Belloma Slough—*gut* CA-9
Bellomy Chapel—*church* WV-2
**Bellona**—*pop pl* NY-2
Bellona Arsenal—*hist pl* VA-3
Bellona Arsenal Ruins—*locale* VA-3
**Bellona Station (Gage PO)**—*pop pl* NY-2
**Bello Park Subdivision**—*pop pl* UT-8
**Bello Park Subdivision Three**—*pop pl* UT-8
Bello Spring—*spring* CA-9
Bellota—*locale* CA-9
Bellota Canyon—*valley* AZ-5
Bellota Ranch—*locale* AZ-5
Bellota Spring—*spring* (2) AZ-5
Bellota Tank—*reservoir* AZ-5
Bellot Mtn—*summit* NJ-2
Bellotosa Canyon—*valley* AZ-5
Bellotosa Tank—*reservoir* AZ-5
Bell Outing Gun Club—*other* CA-9
Bellow Branch—*stream* VA-3
Bellow Cem—*cemetery* KY-4
Bellow Corners—*locale* NY-2
Bellow Creek—*stream* MN-6
*Bellow Hill* MA-1
Bellow Island—*island* MI-6
*Bellow Lake* MI-6
Bellow Mountain Ch—*church* OK-5
Bellow Mtn—*summit* OK-5
*Bellow Park Subdivision 3* UT-8
Bellows Air Force Station (Inactive)—*military* HI-9
Bellows Bay—*bay* NC-3
Bellows Brook—*stream* CT-1
Bellows Brook—*stream* VT-1
Bellows Canyon—*valley* AZ-5
*Bellows Chapel Ch* AL-4
Bellows Creek—*stream* AK-9
Bellows Creek—*stream* CO-8
Bellows Creek—*stream* OR-9
**Bellows Falls**—*pop pl* VT-1
Bellows Falls Downtown Hist Dist—*hist pl* VT-1
Bellows Falls Village For—*forest* VT-1
Bellows Farm Mill Dam Number 1—*dam* MA-1
Bellows Field Archeol Area—*hist pl* HI-9
Bellows Free Acad—*school* (2) VT-1
*Bellows Hill* MA-1
Bellows Hill—*summit* (2) MA-1
Bellows Hollow—*valley* (2) UT-8
Bellows Lake—*lake* FL-3
Bellows Lake—*lake* (2) MI-6
Bellows Lake—*lake* NY-2
Bellows Pipe, The—*gap* MA-1
Bellows Pond—*lake* NY-2
Bellows Sch—*school* NY-2
Bellows Sch—*school* OH-6
Bellows Spring—*spring* (2) AZ-5
Bellows Spring—*spring* OR-9
Bellows Stream—*stream* ME-1
**Bellowsville**—*pop pl* PA-2
Bell Park—*park* AL-4
Bell Park—*park* AR-4
Bell Park—*park* CO-8
Bell Park—*park* GA-3
Bell Park—*park* IN-6
Bell Park—*park* NE-7
Bell Park—*park* TX-5
Bell Park Tank—*reservoir* NM-5
*Bell Pas Bayou* LA-4
Bell Pass—*gap* WA-9
*Bell Pass Bayou* LA-4
Bell Peak—*summit* MT-8
Bell Peckham Ditch—*canal* IN-6
Bell Place—*hist pl* KY-4
Bell Place-Locust Ave Hist Dist—*hist pl* NY-2
Bell Place Windmill—*locale* TX-5
Bell Plains Cem—*cemetery* TX-5
**Bell Plain (Township of)**—*pop pl* IL-6
Bell Playground—*park* IL-6
Bell Plaza Shop Ctr—*locale* AL-4
Bell Plaza Shop Ctr—*locale* AZ-5
*Bell Point* NC-3
*Bell Point* OH-6
Bell Point—*cape* CA-9
Bell Point—*cape* MT-8
Bell Point—*cape* NY-2
Bell Point—*cape* (2) NC-3
Bell Point—*cape* WA-9
Bell Point—*cliff* CA-9
Bell Point—*cliff* ID-8
Bell Point—*cliff* KS-7
**Bell Point**—*pop pl* PA-2
Bell Point—*summit* AL-4
Bell Pond—*bay* LA-4
Bell Pond—*bay* NC-3
Bell Pond—*lake* (4) FL-3
Bell Pond—*lake* IL-6
Bell Pond—*lake* (2) ME-1
Bell Pond—*lake* MI-6
Bell Pond—*lake* NY-2
Bell Pond—*reservoir* MA-1
Bell Pond—*reservoir* SC-3
Bell Pond—*swamp* (2) FL-3
Bell Pond—*swamp* IL-6
Bell Pond Ch—*church* SC-3
Bell Pond Dam—*dam* MA-1
**Bellport**—*pop pl* NY-2
Bellport Bay—*bay* NY-2
*Bellport Harbor* NY-2
Bellport HS—*school* NY-2
Bell Post Office (historical)—*building* AL-4
Bell Prairie—*flat* FL-3
Bell Prairie Township—*civil* SD-7
Bell Quarry—*mine* TN-4
Bell Quarter Hill—*summit* AL-4
Bell Ranch—*locale* AZ-5
Bell Ranch—*locale* (3) CA-9
Bell Ranch—*locale* MT-8
Bell Ranch—*locale* (2) NM-5
Bell Ranch—*locale* SD-7
Bell Ranch—*locale* (2) TX-5
Bell Ranch—*locale* (3) WY-8
Bell Ranch Canal—*canal* NM-5
Bell Ranch HQ—*hist pl* NM-5
Bell Rapids (Submerged)—*rapids* ID-8
Bell Rattle Cem—*cemetery* AL-4
Bell Ridge—*ridge* IN-6
Bell Ridge—*ridge* MT-8
Bell Ridge—*ridge* NC-3
Bell Ridge—*ridge* (2) OH-6
Bell Ridge—*ridge* OR-9
Bell Ridge—*ridge* PA-2
Bell Ridge—*ridge* (2) TN-4
Bell Ridge Ch—*church* IL-6
Bell Ridge Sch—*school* IL-6
Bell Ridge Sch—*school* TN-4
*Bell River* FL-3
Bell River—*stream* MI-6
Bell Road Ch—*church* TN-4
Bell Road Creek—*stream* OR-9
**Bell Road (historical)**—*pop pl* PA-2
Bell Rock—*pillar* CO-8
Bell Rock—*pillar* ID-8
Bell Rock—*summit* AZ-5
Bell Rock—*summit* CO-8
Bell Rock—*summit* NM-5
Bell Rock—*uninc pl* MA-1
Bell Rock Arroyo—*stream* NM-5
Bell Rock Canyon—*valley* UT-8
Bellrock Caves—*cave* PA-2
Bell Rock Cem—*cemetery* MA-1
Bell Rock Gulch—*valley* CO-8
Bell Rock Lighthouse—*locale* VA-3
Bell Rock Park—*park* MA-1
Bell Rock Ridge—*ridge* UT-8
Bell Rock Ridge—*ridge* VA-3
Bell Rock Spring—*spring* AZ-5
Bell Rock Station (historical)—*locale* MA-1
**Bell Rohr Park**—*pop pl* IN-6
**Bellrose**—*pop pl* OR-9
*Bellrose Creek* TX-5
Bellrose Slough—*gut* TX-5
Bell Rsvr—*reservoir* MT-8
*Bell Run* PA-2
**Bellrun**—*pop pl* PA-2
Bell Run—*stream* (2) IN-6
Bell Run—*stream* KY-4
Bell Run—*stream* OH-6
Bell Run—*stream* (4) PA-2
Bell Run—*stream* WV-2
Bell Run Sch (abandoned)—*school* PA-2
Bell Run Union Ch—*church* PA-2
*Bells* MS-4
*Bells* SC-3
**Bells**—*pop pl* MS-4
**Bells**—*pop pl* NC-3
**Bells**—*pop pl* PA-2
**Bells**—*pop pl* SC-3
**Bells**—*pop pl* TN-4
**Bells**—*pop pl* TX-5
Bells, Cave of The—*cave* AZ-5
Bell Saddle—*gap* ID-8
Bells Aerated Lagoon Number One Dam—*dam* TN-4
Bells Aerated Lagoon Number One Lake—*reservoir* TN-4
Bells Aerated Lagoon Number Two Dam—*dam* TN-4
Bells Aerated Lagoon Number Two Lake—*reservoir* TN-4
Bells Aerobic Lagoon Number One Dam—*dam* TN-4
Bells Aerobic Lagoon Number One Lake—*reservoir* TN-4
Bells Aerobic Lagoon Number Two Dam—*dam* TN-4
Bells Aerobic Lagoon Number Two Lake—*reservoir* TN-4
**Bells Beach**—*pop pl* WA-9
Bells Bend—*bend* (2) TN-4
Bells Branch—*stream* AL-4
Bells Branch—*stream* GA-3
Bells Branch—*stream* KY-4
Bells Branch—*stream* NC-3
Bells Branch—*stream* (2) SC-3
Bells Branch Dents Run—*stream* PA-2
Bells Bridge—*bridge* (2) NC-3
Bells Bridge—*bridge* SC-3
Bells Bridge (historical)—*bridge* TN-4
Bells Brook—*stream* ME-1
Bells Brook—*stream* NY-2
**Bellsburg**—*pop pl* TN-4
Bellsburg Sch—*school* TN-4
Bells Butte—*summit* AK-9
Bells Camp—*locale* SC-3
**Bells Camp**—*pop pl* PA-2
Bells Canyon—*valley* AZ-5
Bells Canyon—*valley* UT-8
Bells (CCD)—*cens area* TN-4
Bells Cem—*cemetery* (2) OH-6
Bells Cem—*cemetery* VA-3
Bell Scene Ch—*church* GA-3
*Bells Ch* AL-4
Bells Ch—*church* AL-4
Bells Ch—*church* SC-3
Bells Ch—*church* TN-4
Bell Sch—*school* AL-4
Bell Sch—*school* DC-2
Bell Sch—*school* GA-3
Bell Sch—*school* (6) IL-6
Bell Sch—*school* IA-7
Bell Sch—*school* (3) KS-7
Bell Sch—*school* ME-1
Bell Sch—*school* MA-1
Bell Sch—*school* (6) MI-6
Bell Sch—*school* MN-6
Bell Sch—*school* MS-4
Bell Sch—*school* MO-7
Bell Sch—*school* (2) NE-7
Bell Sch—*school* NV-8
Bell Sch—*school* NM-5
Bell Sch—*school* (3) NY-2
Bell Sch—*school* NC-3
Bell Sch—*school* (2) OH-6
Bell Sch—*school* OK-5
Bell Sch—*school* (2) SD-7
Bell Sch—*school* (2) TX-5
Bell Sch—*school* (2) WV-2
Bell Sch—*school* WI-6
Bell Sch (abandoned)—*school* FL-3
Bell Sch (abandoned)—*school* (2) MO-7
Bell Sch (abandoned)—*school* (2) PA-2
*Bells Chapel* IN-6
Bells Chapel—*church* AL-4
Bells Chapel—*church* (3) AR-4
Bells Chapel—*church* (4) KY-4
Bells Chapel—*church* MD-2
Bells Chapel—*church* MS-4
Bells Chapel—*church* TN-4
Bells Chapel—*locale* AR-4
Bells Chapel Cem—*cemetery* AR-4
Bells Chapel Cem—*cemetery* TN-4
Bells Chapel Ch—*church* AL-4
Bells Chapel Ch—*church* AR-4
Bells Chapel Ch—*church* NC-3
Bells Chapel Ch of God—*church* IN-6
Bells Chapel Sch (historical)—*school* TN-4
*Bells Chapel U H Ch of USA* NC-3
Bell Sch (historical)—*school* (3) AL-4
Bell Sch (historical)—*school* MS-4
Bell Sch (historical)—*school* PA-2
Bell Sch Number 2—*school* ND-7
Bell Sch Number 3—*school* ND-7
Bell School (historical)—*locale* MO-7
*Bell Schoolhouse* MS-4
*Bell School Number 60* IN-6
*Bells Corners* NC-3
*Bells Creek* WA-9
Bells Creek—*stream* KY-4
Bells Creek—*stream* NC-3
Bells Creek—*stream* SC-3
Bells Creek—*stream* (2) VA-3
Bells Creek—*stream* WV-2
Bells Creek Ch—*church* WV-2
Bells Crossing—*locale* NJ-2
Bells Crossroad—*locale* VA-3
**Bells Cross Road**—*pop pl* VA-3
*Bells Crossroads* NC-3
Bells Crossroads—*locale* AL-4
Bells Crossroads—*locale* (2) NC-3
Bells Crossroads—*locale* VA-3
**Bells Crossroads**—*pop pl* AL-4
**Bells Crossroads**—*pop pl* NC-3
**Bells Cross Roads**—*pop pl* NC-3
**Bells Crossroads**—*pop pl* (2) SC-3
**Bells Cross Roads**—*pop pl* VA-3
Bells Dam—*dam* AL-4
*Bells Depot Post Office* TN-4
Bells Division—*civil* TN-4
*Bells Ferry* AL-4
*Bells Ferry* TN-4
Bells Ferry (historical)—*locale* MS-4
Bells Ferry Landing—*locale* GA-3
Bells First Baptist Ch—*church* TN-4
Bell's First Home—*hist pl* OH-6
Bells Ford—*locale* TN-4
Bells Ford—*locale* WV-2
*Bells Forge* TN-4
*Bells Fork* NC-3
**Bells Fork**—*pop pl* NC-3
Bells Fork Square Shop Ctr—*locale* NC-3
Bells Gap—*gap* CO-8
Bells Gap Run—*stream* PA-2
Bells Gin (historical)—*locale* AL-4
Bells Grove Ch—*church* GA-3
Bells Grove Ch—*church* VA-3
Bells Gulley—*stream* AR-4
Bell Shaft—*mine* NV-8
Bellshead Branch—*stream* FL-3
Bell-Sherrod House—*hist pl* NC-3
*Bells Hill* PA-2
Bells Hill—*summit* MD-2
Bells Hill—*summit* NH-1
Bells Hill—*summit* PA-2
Bells Hill Sch—*school* TX-5
Bells (historical)—*locale* AL-4
**Bells (historical)**—*pop pl* MS-4
Bell Shoal—*bar* FL-3
Bell Shoals Bridge—*bridge* FL-3
Bell Shoals Ch of Christ—*church* FL-3
Bells Hollow—*valley* WV-2
Bell Shop Pond—*reservoir* CT-1
Bell Sink—*swamp* AL-4
Bell Sink Pond—*lake* AL-4
*Bell's Island* ME-1
*Bells Island* NC-3
*Bells Island* PA-2
Bells Island—*island* IL-6
Bells Island—*island* (2) NC-3
Bells Island—*island* TX-5
*Bells Lake* IN-6
*Bells Lake* WI-6
**Bells Lake**—*pop pl* NJ-2
Bells Lake—*reservoir* AL-4
Bells Lake—*reservoir* GA-3
Bells Lake—*reservoir* ID-8
Bells Lake—*reservoir* NJ-2
Bells Lake—*reservoir* NC-3
Bells Lake Dam—*dam* NJ-2
Bells Lakes—*reservoir* PA-2
Bells Landing—*locale* GA-3
Bells Landing—*locale* IL-6
Bells Landing—*locale* NC-3
Bells Landing—*locale* TN-4
**Bells Landing**—*pop pl* PA-2
Bells Landing Ch—*church* AL-4
Bells Landing Mine Station—*locale* PA-2
Bells Landing Park—*park* AL-4
**Bells Lane**—*pop pl* VA-3
Bells Leg—*stream* FL-3
Bell Slough—*gut* AR-4
Bell Slough—*gut* TN-4
*Bellsman Creek* SD-7
Bells Marsh—*swamp* ME-1
*Bells Mill* PA-2
Bells Mill—*locale* FL-3
Bells Mill—*locale* (2) MD-2
Bells Mill—*locale* TN-4
**Bells Mill**—*pop pl* VA-3
Bells Mill Access Point—*locale* GA-3
Bells Mill Bridge—*bridge* GA-3
Bells Mill (Camden Mills)—*uninc pl* VA-3
Bells Mill Creek—*stream* AL-4
Bells Mill Creek—*stream* GA-3
Bells Mill (historical)—*locale* MS-4
Bells Mill (historical)—*locale* TN-4
Bells Mill Park—*park* IA-7
Bells Mill Pond—*lake* FL-3
Bells Mill Post Office (historical)—*building* TN-4
*Bells Mills* PA-2
*Bell's Mills* VA-3
**Bells Mills**—*pop pl* PA-2
Bells Mills Covered Bridge—*hist pl* PA-2
Bells Mines Ch—*church* KY-4
Bell Smith Springs Scenic Area—*locale* IL-6
*Bells Mountain* CA-9
Bells Mtn—*summit* ME-1
Bells Mtn—*summit* WA-9
Bells Neck—*cape* MA-1
Bell's Opera House—*hist pl* OH-6
Bell Sow Bend—*bend* TX-5
Bells Oyster Gut—*bay* VA-3
*Bells Point* CA-9
Bells Point—*cape* MO-7
Bells Point—*cape* NC-3
Bells Point Landing—*locale* MO-7
Bells Pond—*reservoir* SC-3
Bells Post Office—*building* TN-4
**Bell Spring**—*pop pl* TN-4
Bell Spring—*spring* (2) AL-4
Bell Spring—*spring* (3) CA-9
Bell Spring—*spring* CO-8
Bell Spring—*spring* ID-8
Bell Spring—*spring* KY-4
Bell Spring—*spring* (2) MO-7
Bell Spring—*spring* NV-8
Bell Spring—*spring* (2) OR-9
Bell Spring—*spring* (2) TN-4
Bell Spring—*spring* (2) TX-5
Bell Spring—*spring* (2) UT-8
Bell Spring—*spring* WA-9
Bell Spring—*spring* WY-8
Bell Spring Cave—*cave* AL-4
Bell Spring Coll (historical)—*school* TN-4
Bell Spring (historical)—*locale* KS-7
Bell Spring Hollow—*valley* UT-8
*Bell Springs* CA-9
Bell Springs—*locale* (2) CA-9
**Bell Springs**—*pop pl* AL-4
Bell Springs—*spring* (2) FL-3
Bell Springs—*spring* TX-5
Bell Springs—*spring* WY-8
Bell Springs Cem—*cemetery* TX-5
Bell Springs Ch—*church* TN-4
Bell Springs Creek—*stream* CA-9
Bell Springs Mtn—*summit* CA-9
Bell Spur—*locale* (2) VA-3
Bell Square Shop Ctr—*locale* AZ-5
Bells River—*stream* FL-3
*Bells Run* PA-2
*Bells Run* WV-2
Bells Run—*locale* KY-4
Bells Run—*stream* IN-6
Bells Run—*stream* (3) OH-6
Bells Run—*stream* (2) PA-2
Bells Run—*stream* WV-2
Bells Run Cem—*cemetery* OH-6
*Bells Sch* TN-4
Bells Sch—*school* KY-4
Bells Sch—*school* MD-2
Bells Sch—*school* TN-4
Bells Sch (historical)—*school* (2) AL-4
Bells Sch (historical)—*school* PA-2
**Bells School**—*pop pl* MS-4
Bells Shute Bar—*bar* OR-9
*Bells's Peak* WY-8
Bells Spring—*spring* AZ-5
**Bells Station**—*pop pl* CA-9
Bells Store (historical)—*locale* AL-4
Bells Store (historical)—*locale* MS-4
Bells Swamp—*stream* SC-3
Bell Station—*locale* CA-9
**Bell Station**—*pop pl* AL-4
Bell Station (historical)—*locale* AL-4
Bell Station Store—*hist pl* OR-9
Bellstone—*pillar* HI-9
Bell Store—*locale* AL-4
Bells Trace Creek—*stream* KY-4
Bells Trace Sch—*school* KY-4
Bell Street Baptist Ch Number One—*church* AL-4
Bell Street Baptist Ch Number Two—*church* AL-4
Bell Street Bridge—*hist pl* MT-8
Bell Street Chapel—*hist pl* RI-1
Bell Street HS—*school* SC-3
Bell Strip Airp—*airport* NC-3
Bells Valley—*locale* VA-3
Bell Swamp—*locale* NC-3
Bell Swamp—*stream* (3) NC-3
Bell Swamp—*swamp* VA-3
Bell Swamp Branch—*stream* SC-3
Bell Swamps—*swamp* CA-9
Bell Swamp Sch—*school* NC-3
Bell Tank—*reservoir* AZ-5
Bell Tank—*reservoir* CO-8
Bell Tank—*reservoir* (3) NM-5
Bell Tank—*reservoir* TX-5
Bell Telephone Laboratories—*hist pl* NY-2
Bell Telephone of Nevada—*hist pl* NV-8
Bell Thorofare—*channel* VA-3
*Bellton* GA-3
**Bellton**—*pop pl* GA-3
**Bellton**—*pop pl* PA-2
**Bellton**—*pop pl* WV-2
Bellton Bridge—*bridge* GA-3
Bellton Ch—*church* GA-3
Bellton Creek—*stream* GA-3
Belltone Sch (historical)—*school* AL-4
Bell Top—*summit* TN-4
Bell Top Lodge—*locale* MI-6
Bell Top Mtn—*summit* NM-5
Bell Top Sch—*school* IL-6
Bell Tower—*hist pl* VA-3
**Belltower**—*pop pl* MT-8
Bell Tower—*summit* MT-8
Bell Tower, The (Shop Ctr)—*tower* FL-3
Bell Tower Bldg—*hist pl* MD-2
*Belltower Butte* MT-8
*Bell Tower Divide* MT-8
Belltower Divide—*ridge* MT-8
Bell Tower (fire tower)—*tower* FL-3
Bell Tower Sch (historical)—*school* MO-7
*Belltown* CT-1
Belltown—*locale* AL-4
Belltown—*locale* IL-6
Belltown—*locale* KY-4
Belltown—*locale* NY-2
Belltown—*locale* TN-4
**Belltown**—*pop pl* CA-9
**Belltown**—*pop pl* CT-1
**Belltown**—*pop pl* DE-2
**Belltown**—*pop pl* MD-2
**Belltown**—*pop pl* NC-3
**Belltown**—*pop pl* (2) PA-2
**Bell Town**—*pop pl* SC-3
**Belltown**—*pop pl* TN-4
**Bell Town**—*pop pl* TN-4
Belltown Cem—*cemetery* PA-2
Bell Town Cem—*cemetery* TN-4
Belltown Cem—*cemetery* TX-5
Belltown Creek—*stream* TN-4
Belltown Gap—*gap* PA-2
**Belltown Hill**—*pop pl* TN-4
Belltown Hill—*summit* CT-1
Belltown Hist Dist—*hist pl* CT-1
Belltown Mill—*locale* TN-4
**Bell (Town of)**—*pop pl* WI-6
Belltown Post Office—*locale* TN-4
Belltown Post Office (historical)—*building* TN-4
Belltown Run—*stream* DE-2
Belltown Run—*stream* PA-2
Belltown Sch—*school* IL-6
Belltown Sch (abandoned)—*school* PA-2
Belltown Sch (historical)—*school* TN-4
**Bell Township**—*pop pl* (2) KS-7
**Bell Township**—*pop pl* ND-7
Bell Township Elem Sch—*school* PA-2

Belual A Kelat—*island* PW-9
Belualasmau—*island* PW-9
Belue Branch—*stream* AL-4
Belue Cem—*cemetery* (2) MS-4
Belue Creek—*stream* SC-3
Belue Lake—*reservoir* SC-3
*Belues Landing* AL-4
Beluga Hill—*summit* AK-9
Beluga Lake—*lake* AK-9
Beluga Mtn—*summit* AK-9
Beluga Point Site—*hist pl* AK-9
Beluga River—*stream* AK-9
Beluga Shoal—*bar* AK-9
Beluga Slough—*gut* AK-9
Belus No 1 Rsvr—*reservoir* WY-8
Belus No 2 Rsvr—*reservoir* WY-8
Beluuchoar—*bar* PW-9
Beluu Lukes—*bar* PW-9
Belva—*locale* OK-5
**Belva**—*pop pl* NC-3
**Belva**—*pop pl* WV-2
Belva Cem—*cemetery* NC-3
*Belvedere* MI-6
*Belvedere* NJ-2
Belvedere—*hist pl* WV-2
Belvedere—*locale* MD-2
Belvedere—*locale* PR-3
Belvedere—*locale* VI-3
**Belvedere**—*pop pl* (2) CA-9
**Belvedere**—*pop pl* DE-2
**Belvedere**—*pop pl* ME-1
**Belvedere**—*pop pl* OH-6
**Belvedere**—*pop pl* (2) SC-3
**Belvedere**—*pop pl* (2) VA-3
**Belvedere**—*pop pl* WA-9
Belvedere—*post sta* FL-3
Belvedere—*post sta* GA-3
Belvedere—*uninc pl* VA-3
Belvedere, The—*hist pl* OK-5
Belvedere Baptist Ch—*church* FL-3
Belvedere Beach—*locale* VA-3
Belvedere Cem—*cemetery* SD-7
Belvedere Ch—*church* ME-1
Belvedere Ch of Christ—*church* MS-4
Belvedere Country Club—*other* AK-4
Belvedere Cove—*bay* CA-9
Belvedere Creek—*stream* MD-2
Belvedere Creek—*stream* SC-3
Belvedere Elem Sch—*school* FL-3
**Belvedere Estates**—*pop pl* SC-3
**Belvedere Gardens**—*pop pl* CA-9
**Belvedere Heights**—*pop pl* CA-9
**Belvedere Heights**—*pop pl* MD-2
**Belvedere Homes**—*pop pl* FL-3
Belvedere Hotel—*hist pl* MD-2
Belvedere Island—*island* AK-9
Belvedere Island—*island* CA-9
Belvedere JHS—*school* CA-9
**Belvedere Junction**—*pop pl* VT-1
Belvedere Lagoon—*lake* CA-9
Belvedere Lake—*lake* NY-2
Belvedere Memorial Cem—*cemetery* TX-5
Belvedere Park—*locale* GA-3
Belvedere Park—*park* CA-9
Belvedere Park—*park* IL-6
Belvedere Park Plaza (Shop Ctr)—*locale* FL-3
**Belvedere Plaza**—*pop pl* GA-3
Belvedere Point—*cape* GA-3
Belvedere Sch—*school* (3) CA-9
Belvedere Sch—*school* NE-7
Belvedere Sch—*school* NC-3
Belvedere Sch—*school* SC-3
Belvedere Sch—*school* VA-3
**Belvedere (subdivision)**—*pop pl* AL-4
**Belvedere (subdivision)**—*pop pl* NC-3
Belvedere-Tiburon—*uninc pl* CA-9
Belvernon Gardens—*uninc pl* CA-9
*Belvidere* DE-2
*Belvidere* IN-6
*Belvidere* MO-7
*Belvidere* WA-9
Belvidere—*hist pl* MS-4
Belvidere—*hist pl* NY-2
Belvidere—*hist pl* NC-3
Belvidere—*locale* ID-8
Belvidere—*locale* IA-7
**Belvidere**—*pop pl* IL-6
**Belvidere**—*pop pl* KS-7
**Belvidere**—*pop pl* MO-7
**Belvidere**—*pop pl* NE-7
**Belvidere**—*pop pl* NJ-2
**Belvidere**—*pop pl* NY-2
**Belvidere**—*pop pl* NC-3
**Belvidere**—*pop pl* PA-2
**Belvidere**—*pop pl* SD-7
**Belvidere**—*pop pl* TN-4
Belvidere Bay—*bay* MI-6
**Belvidere Beach**—*pop pl* VA-3
*Belvidere Brook* PA-2
Belvidere Cem—*cemetery* IL-6
Belvidere Cem—*cemetery* IA-7
Belvidere Cem—*cemetery* KS-7
Belvidere Cem—*cemetery* TN-4
**Belvidere Center**—*pop pl* VT-1
Belvidere Ch—*church* MI-6
Belvidere Ch—*church* TN-4
Belvidere Community Center—*building* TN-4
**Belvidere Corners**—*pop pl* VT-1
Belvidere Corner Sch (abandoned)—*school* PA-2
Belvidere Creek—*stream* ID-8
Belvidere Ditch—*canal* WY-8
Belvidere Ferry (historical)—*locale* PA-2
Belvidere Hist Dist—*hist pl* NJ-2
Belvidere (historical P.O.)—*locale* IA-7
Belvidere Interchange—*other* IL-6
**Belvidere Junction**—*pop pl* KS-7
**Belvidere Junction**—*pop pl* VT-1
Belvidere Medicine River Bridge—*hist pl* KS-7
Belvidere Mills—*locale* MN-6
Belvidere Mtn—*summit* VT-1
Belvidere Municipal Park—*park* IL-6
Belvidere Plantation (historical)—*locale* MS-4
Belvidere Plantation House—*hist pl* NC-3
Belvidere Post Office—*building* TN-4
Belvidere Ridge—*ridge* WI-6
Belvidere Run—*stream* PA-2
Belvidere Sch—*school* MA-1
Belvidere Sch—*school* MO-7
Belvidere Sch (historical)—*school* TN-4
Belvidere Service Area—*locale* IL-6
**Belvidere (subdivision)**—*pop pl* MA-1
Belvidere (Town name for Belvidere Center)—*other* VT-1
**Belvidere (Town of)**—*pop pl* VT-1
**Belvidere (Town of)**—*pop pl* WI-6
Belvidere Township—*civil* SD-7
Belvidere Township—*fmr MCD* IA-7
Belvidere (Township of)—*fmr MCD* NC-3
**Belvidere (Township of)**—*pop pl* IL-6
**Belvidere (Township of)**—*pop pl* MI-6
**Belvidere (Township of)**—*pop pl* MN-6
Belvidere Union Cem—*cemetery* MN-6
Belvidere United Ch of Christ—*church* TN-4
*Belview* PA-2
Belview—*locale* AR-4
**Belview**—*pop pl* MN-6
Belview Baptist Ch—*church* AL-4
Belview Cem—*cemetery* MN-6
Belview Ch—*church* MS-4
Belview Ch—*church* (3) NC-3
Belview Ch—*church* (2) TX-5
Belview Community Center—*locale* NC-3
**Belview Heights**—*pop pl* AL-4
Belview Heights Ch of Christ—*church* AL-4
Belview Heights Missionary Baptist Ch—*church* AL-4
**Belview Heights (subdivision)**—*pop pl* AL-4
*Belview Lake* CT-1
Belview Methodist Ch (historical)—*church* AL-4
Belview Mtn—*summit* NC-3
Belview Sch—*school* VA-3
Belview Sch (historical)—*school* MS-4
Belview Shelter—*locale* WA-9
Belview Shop Ctr—*locale* MS-4
*Belview Township* MO-7
*Belville* IN-6
**Belville**—*pop pl* NC-3
Belvin Ch—*church* GA-3
**Belvins**—*pop pl* TN-4
**Belvins Acres**—*pop pl* GA-3
Belvin Sch—*school* OK-5
Belvin Street Hist Dist—*hist pl* TX-5
*Belvoir* NC-3
Belvoir—*hist pl* MD-2
Belvoir—*locale* VA-3
Belvoir—*other* VA-3
**Belvoir**—*pop pl* NC-3
Bel-voir Acres Airp—*airport* MO-7
Belvoir Bluffs—*cliff* MO-7
Belvoir Ch—*church* NC-3
*Belvoir Crossroads* NC-3
*Belvoir Elementary School* NC-3
Belvoir Elem Sch—*school* KS-7
Belvoir (historical)—*locale* KS-7
Belvoir Manor—*locale* MD-2
Belvoir Ranch—*locale* WY-8
Belvoir Sch—*school* KS-7
Belvoir Sch—*school* MO-7
Belvoir Sch—*school* OH-6
**Belvoir Terrace (subdivision)**—*pop pl* TN-4
Belvoir (Township of)—*fmr MCD* (2) NC-3
*Belvue* AL-4
**Belvue**—*pop pl* KS-7
Belvue Cem—*cemetery* KS-7
Belvue Cem—*cemetery* PA-2
Belvue Ch—*church* NM-5
Belvue Ch—*church* SC-3
**Belvue Township**—*pop pl* KS-7
*Belwalasmau* PW-9
**Bel Won Enterprise Subdivision**—*pop pl* UT-8
**Belwood**—*pop pl* AL-4
**Belwood**—*pop pl* NC-3
Belwood HS—*school* NC-3
Belwood Oil Field—*oilfield* MS-4
Belwood Park—*locale* NJ-2
Belwood Sch—*school* AR-4
Belwood Sch—*school* CA-9
Belwood Sch—*school* GA-3
Belwood Swamp—*stream* VA-3
*Belyea Cove* ME-1
Belyidere Pond—*lake* VT-1
Belzar Spring—*spring* OR-9
Belz Cem—*cemetery* NE-7
*Belzer Junior High School* IN-6
Belzer MS—*school* IN-6
Belz Factory Outlet Mall—*locale* FL-3
Belz Factory Outlet Mall—*locale* MO-7
*Belzona* MS-4
Belzoni—*locale* OK-5
**Belzoni**—*pop pl* MS-4
Belzoni Cem—*cemetery* OK-5
Belzoni Lagoon Dam—*dam* MS-4
Belzoni Landing (historical)—*locale* MS-4
Belzoni Mound (22HU500)—*hist pl* MS-4
Belzoni Municipal Airp—*airport* MS-4
Belz Park—*park* TN-4
**Bem**—*pop pl* MO-7
**Beman**—*pop pl* IL-6
Beman Cem—*cemetery* KS-7
Beman (historical)—*locale* KS-7
**Bembe Beach**—*pop pl* MD-2
**Bemberg**—*pop pl* TN-4
Bemberg Shop Ctr—*locale* TN-4
Bem Branch—*stream* KY-4
**Bement**—*pop pl* IL-6
Bement Arch—*arch* UT-8
Bement Cem—*cemetery* IL-6
Bement Ch—*church* MO-7
Bement Covered Bridge—*hist pl* NH-1
*Bements Brook* CT-1
**Bement (Township of)**—*pop pl* IL-6
**Bemidji**—*pop pl* MN-6
Bemidji, Lake—*lake* MN-6
Bemidji Carnegie Library—*hist pl* MN-6
Bemidji Municipal Airp—*airport* MN-6
Bemidji State Coll—*school* MN-6
**Bemidji (Township of)**—*pop pl* MN-6
Bemis—*locale* AR-4
Bemis—*locale* LA-4
Bemis—*locale* ME-1
**Bemis**—*pop pl* SD-7
**Bemis**—*pop pl* TN-4
**Bemis**—*pop pl* WV-2
Bemis, Elbridge G., House—*hist pl* NH-1
Bemis, George, House—*hist pl* NH-1
Bemis, Judson Moss, House—*hist pl* CO-8
Bemis, Mount—*summit* NH-1
Bemis, Polly, House—*hist pl* ID-8
*Bemis Brook* MA-1
Bemis Brook—*stream* NH-1
Bemis Brook—*stream* VT-1
Bemis Cem—*cemetery* ME-1
Bemis Cem—*cemetery* OR-9
Bemis Cem—*cemetery* SD-7
Bemis Cem—*cemetery* TN-4
Bemis Cem—*cemetery* WA-9
Bemis Ch—*church* (2) SD-7
Bemis Chapel Missionary Baptist Ch—*church* TN-4
Bemis Creek—*stream* ID-8
Bemis Creek—*stream* KS-7
Bemis Ditch—*canal* CO-8
Bemis Eye Sanitarium Complex—*hist pl* NY-2
Bemis Flats—*flat* CO-8
Bemis Florist Shop—*hist pl* AR-4
Bemish Creek—*stream* MT-8
**Bemis Heights**—*pop pl* NY-2
Bemis Hill—*summit* MA-1
Bemis Hill—*summit* VT-1
Bemis Hill Campground—*locale* MN-6
Bemis Hollow—*valley* PA-2
Bemis Mill—*hist pl* MA-1
Bemis Mtn—*summit* ME-1
Bemis Omaha Bag Company Bldg—*hist pl* NE-7
Bemis Park—*park* NE-7
Bemis Plantation—*locale* AR-4
Bemis Point—*summit* ID-8
Bemis Pond—*reservoir* MA-1
Bemis Pond Lower Rsvr—*reservoir* MA-1
Bemis Pond Upper Rsvr—*reservoir* MA-1
Bemis Post Office—*building* TN-4
*Bemis Ranch* ID-8
Bemis Ridge—*ridge* NH-1
**Bemiss**—*pop pl* GA-3
Bemis Sch—*school* CA-9
Bemis Sch (historical)—*school* SD-7
Bemis-Shutts Oil Field—*oilfield* KS-7
Bemis Square Shop Ctr—*locale* TN-4
Bemiss Sch—*school* WA-9
Bemis Stream—*stream* ME-1
**Bemis (subdivision)**—*pop pl* MA-1
**Bemiston**—*pop pl* AL-4
Bemiston Baptist Ch—*church* AL-4
Bemiston United Methodist Ch—*church* AL-4
Bemis United Methodist Ch—*church* TN-4
Bemis Woods North—*woods* IL-6
Bemis Woods South—*woods* IL-6
Bemo Ledge—*rock* MA-1
*Bemon Harbor* MI-6
Bemont, Makens, House—*hist pl* CT-1
Bemrose Creek—*stream* CO-8
Bemrose Mine—*mine* CO-8
Bems Pond—*reservoir* MA-1
Bems Pond Dam—*dam* MA-1
Bemus Bay—*bay* NY-2
Bemus Creek—*stream* NY-2
*Bemus Heights* NY-2
**Bemus Point**—*pop pl* NY-2
Ben—*locale* AR-4
Ben—*locale* TX-5
Ben—*park* OR-9
Ben, Lake—*lake* MN-6
Ben, Lake—*lake* WA-9
Ben, Lake—*reservoir* AL-4
Bena—*locale* CA-9
Bena—*locale* VA-3
**Bena**—*pop pl* MN-6
Benach Lake—*lake* WI-6
*Benadad Lake* MN-6
Benada Tank—*reservoir* NM-5
Benada Windmill—*locale* TX-5
Benadito Well—*well* TX-5
Benadito Windmill—*locale* TX-5
Benado Canyon—*valley* NM-5
Benado Gap—*gap* NM-5
Benado Spring—*spring* NM-5
Benado Windmill—*locale* (2) TX-5
**Ben Air Estates (subdivision)**—*pop pl* UT-8
Benaja—*locale* NC-3
Benaja Ch—*church* NC-3
Benaja Creek—*stream* (2) NC-3
*Benakan* MH-9
Bena Lake—*lake* WI-6
Ben Ali—*locale* CA-9
Benali—*uninc pl* CA-9
Ben Ali Sch—*school* CA-9
Ben Allen Canyon—*valley* UT-8
Benally Well—*well* AZ-5
Ben Anderson Hollow—*valley* MO-7
**Benan (historical)**—*pop pl* IA-7
Ben Annis Pond—*lake* ME-1
*Benard* MS-4
Benard Cem—*cemetery* IL-6
*Benard Creek* NE-7
Benard Spring—*spring* NV-8
**Ben Arnold**—*pop pl* TX-5
Ben Arthur Trail—*trail* CA-9
Benary Hole—*cave* TN-4
Ben Ash Historical Monmt—*park* SD-7
Benathy Well—*well* NM-5
Benaur Hollow—*valley* PA-2
Benavente (Barrio)—*fmr MCD* PR-3
**Benavides**—*pop pl* TX-5
Benavides Banco Number 10—*levee* TX-5
Benavides (CCD)—*cens area* TX-5
Benavides Ranch—*locale* TX-5
Benavidez Ranch—*locale* NM-5
Benavidez Tank—*reservoir* NM-5
Benavidez Windmill—*locale* (2) NM-5
*Ben Avilla Water Hole* CA-9
*Ben Avis* MO-7
**Ben Avon**—*pop pl* (2) PA-2
**Ben Avon**—*pop pl* SC-3
Ben Avon Borough—*civil* PA-2
Ben Avon Elem Sch—*school* PA-2
**Ben Avon Heights**—*pop pl* PA-2
Ben Avon Heights Borough—*civil* PA-2
Ben Ball Bridge—*bridge* AR-4
*Ben Barrow's* ME-1
Ben Barrows Hill—*summit* ME-1
Ben Belt Mines—*mine* KY-4
Benbo Branch—*stream* NC-3
Ben Bolen Ch—*church* NC-3
Ben Bolen Creek—*stream* NC-3
Benbolt—*locale* VA-3
**Ben Bolt**—*pop pl* TX-5
Ben Bolt Oil Field—*oilfield* TX-5
Ben Bolt Ridge—*ridge* CA-9
Ben Bow—*locale* KY-4
Benbow—*locale* MO-7
Benbow—*locale* VA-3
**Benbow**—*pop pl* CA-9
**Benbow**—*pop pl* FL-3
Benbow, Charles, House—*hist pl* NC-3
Benbow, Jesse, House II—*hist pl* NC-3
Benbow Chapel—*church* NC-3
Benbow Inn—*hist pl* CA-9
Benbow Lake—*reservoir* CA-9
Benbow Lake—*reservoir* NC-3
Benbow Lake Dam—*dam* NC-3
Benbow Lakes—*lake* WA-9
Benbow Lake State Rec Area—*park* CA-9
Benbow Mine—*mine* MT-8
Benbow Number 2—*locale* FL-3
Benbow Number 3—*locale* FL-3
*Benbow Reservoir* CA-9
*Ben Branch* KY-4
Ben Branch—*stream* AL-4
Ben Branch—*stream* AR-4
Ben Branch—*stream* FL-3
Ben Branch—*stream* GA-3
Ben Branch—*stream* (2) KY-4
Ben Branch—*stream* MO-7
Ben Branch—*stream* OR-9
Ben Branch—*stream* TX-5
**Benbrook**—*pop pl* TX-5
Ben Brook—*stream* ME-1
Benbrook Dam—*dam* TX-5
Benbrook Lake—*reservoir* TX-5
*Benbrook Rsvr* TX-5
Benbrook Sch—*school* TX-5
Ben Brow Hill—*summit* CA-9
Ben Brown Canyon—*valley* NV-8
Ben Brown Spring—*spring* NV-8
Ben Brown Spring—*spring* OR-9
*Ben Burrow's* ME-1
Benbush—*locale* MO-7
**Benbush**—*pop pl* WV-2
Ben Bush Swamp—*swamp* PA-2
Ben Butler Mine—*mine* CA-9
Ben Camp—*locale* OR-9
*Ben Canyon* NM-5
Ben Canyon—*valley* WA-9
Ben Carrol Branch—*stream* KY-4
Ben Cash Memorial State Wildlife Area—*park* MO-7
Bence Mtn—*summit* AK-9
Bence Tank—*reservoir* NM-5
**Bencetown**—*pop pl* PA-2
Ben Ch—*church* AR-4
Bench—*locale* ID-8
Bench, The—*bench* MT-8
Bench, The—*bench* NV-8
Bench, The—*bench* NM-5
Bench, The—*bench* TN-4
Bench, The—*bench* (3) UT-8
Bench, The—*bench* WA-9
Bench, The—*ridge* WA-9
Bench Arch—*arch* UT-8
Ben Chase Hill—*summit* ME-1
*Bench Campground* UT-8
Bench Canal—*canal* ID-8
Bench Canal—*canal* UT-8
Bench Canal—*canal* WY-8
Bench Canyon—*valley* CA-9
Bench Canyon—*valley* OR-9
Bench Corral—*locale* WY-8
Bench Corral Rsvr No 3—*reservoir* WY-8
Bench Corral Springs—*spring* WY-8
Bench Creek—*stream* (3) AK-9
Bench Creek—*stream* AR-4
Bench Creek—*stream* (4) ID-8
Bench Creek—*stream* MT-8
Bench Creek—*stream* NV-8
Bench Creek—*stream* OR-9
Bench Creek—*stream* UT-8
Bench Creek—*stream* (4) WA-9
Bench Creek—*stream* WY-8
Bench Creek Canyon—*valley* NV-8
Bench Creek Ranch—*locale* NV-8
Bench Creek Rest Area—*locale* ID-8
Bench Creek Well—*well* NV-8
Bench Ditch—*canal* ID-8
Bench Ditch—*canal* OH-6
Bench Ditch—*canal* (2) UT-8
Bench Drain—*stream* MI-6
**Bench Drive**—*pop pl* WA-9
*Benches Pond* UT-8
*Benches Pond Dam* UT-8
*Bench Flat* CA-9
Bench Glacier—*glacier* AK-9
Bench Hollow—*valley* MO-7
Bench Lake—*lake* (2) AK-9
Bench Lake—*lake* (3) CA-9
Bench Lake—*lake* (2) CO-8
Bench Lake—*lake* (2) ID-8
Bench Lake—*lake* MN-6
Bench Lake—*lake* MT-8
Bench Lake—*lake* OK-5
Bench Lake—*lake* (3) UT-8
Bench Lake—*lake* (4) WA-9
Bench Lake—*lake* WY-8
Bench Lakes—*lake* CO-8
**Benchland**—*pop pl* MT-8
Benchland Cemetey—*cemetery* MT-8
Benchland Well—*well* NV-8
**Benchley**—*pop pl* TX-5
Benchmark—*locale* SD-7
Bench Mark Butte—*summit* OR-9
Benchmark Campground—*locale* MT-8
*Bench Mark Creek* MT-8
Benchmark Creek—*stream* MT-8
Benchmark Hill—*summit* ID-8
Benchmark Mtn—*summit* AZ-5
Benchmark Mtn—*summit* WA-9
**Benchmark Village Subdivision**—*pop pl* UT-8
Benchmark Waterhole—*lake* OR-9
Benchmark Work Center—*locale* MT-8
Bench Mtn—*summit* NC-3
Bench Mtn—*summit* (2) TN-4
Bench Mtn—*summit* TX-5
Bench Mtn—*summit* VA-3
Bench Pit—*cave* AL-4
Bench Rock—*rock* MA-1
Bench Rock Tank—*reservoir* NM-5
Bench Rsvr—*reservoir* (3) OR-9
Bench Run—*stream* IN-6
Bench Sch—*school* SD-7
Bench Slough—*gut* LA-4
Bench Spring—*spring* ID-8
Bench Spring—*spring* (2) UT-8
Bench State Wildlife Mngmt Area—*park* MN-6
Bench Tank—*reservoir* (4) AZ-5
Bench Top Waterhole—*flat* OR-9
Bench Trail—*trail* CO-8
Bench Trail—*trail* OH-6
Bench Trail Camp, The—*locale* NM-5
Bench Valley—*valley* CA-9
Bench Well—*well* AZ-5
Bench Windmill—*locale* NM-5
*Ben Clare* SD-7
Benclare—*locale* SD-7
Ben Clark Branch—*stream* KY-4
Ben Clark Cem—*cemetery* MO-7
Ben Clark Dam—*dam* SD-7
Ben Coleman Keys—*island* FL-3
Ben Courtny Creek—*stream* AK-9
Ben Cove—*valley* AR-4
Ben Cox Knob—*summit* NC-3
Ben Creek—*stream* (2) AK-9
Ben Creek—*stream* (2) GA-3
Ben Creek—*stream* MD-2
Ben Creek—*stream* MT-8
Ben Creek—*stream* NC-3
Ben Creek—*stream* TN-4
Ben Creek—*stream* WA-9
Ben Creek—*stream* WV-2
Ben Creek Mtn—*summit* WV-2
Ben Creek Sch—*school* WV-2
**Ben Creek Spur**—*pop pl* WV-2
Ben Cusenbary Ranch—*locale* TX-5
Bend—*locale* AR-4
Bend—*locale* MO-7
Bend—*locale* MT-8
Bend—*locale* SD-7
Bend—*locale* TX-5
**Bend**—*pop pl* CA-9
**Bend**—*pop pl* LA-4
**Bend**—*pop pl* OR-9
Bend, Bayou—*gut* LA-4
Bend, Lake—*bend* AL-4
Bend, Lake—*lake* TX-5
*Bend, The* AL-4
*Bend, The* IN-6
Bend, The—*bend* CA-9
Bend, The—*bend* (3) KY-4
Bend, The—*bend* NV-8
Bend,the—*bend* NY-2
Bend, The—*bend* VA-3
Bend, The—*bend* WV-2
**Bend, The**—*pop pl* OH-6
Bend About Creek—*stream* TX-5
**Bendale**—*pop pl* AL-4
**Ben Dale**—*pop pl* WV-2
**Bendale**—*pop pl* WV-2
Bendale—*uninc pl* SC-3
*Bendall* AL-4
Bendall Hollow—*valley* AL-4
Bend Amateur Atheletic Club Gymnasium—*hist pl* OR-9
*Ben Davis* IN-6
Bendavis—*locale* MO-7
**Ben Davis**—*pop pl* IN-6
Ben Davis Creek—*stream* IN-6
Ben Davis Creek Ch—*church* IN-6
Ben Davis HS—*school* IN-6
Ben Davis Independent Christian Ch—*church* IN-6
Ben Davis Island (historical)—*island* NJ-2
Ben Davis Lake—*lake* AR-4
Ben Davis Point—*cape* NJ-2
Ben Davis Point Shoal—*bar* NJ-2
**Ben Davis Station**—*pop pl* IN-6
Ben Day Gulch—*valley* WA-9
Bend Branch—*stream* KY-4
Bend Branch—*stream* TN-4
Bend Branch—*stream* (2) WV-2
Bend Bridge—*bridge* CA-9
Bend Brook—*stream* NY-2
Bend (CCD)—*cens area* OR-9
Bend Cem—*cemetery* IN-6
Bend Cem—*cemetery* OK-5
Bend Cem—*cemetery* TX-5
Bend Cemetery, The—*cemetery* KY-4
*Bend Creek* OR-9
Bend Creek—*stream* CO-8
Bend Creek—*stream* ID-8
Bend Creek—*stream* (3) OR-9
Bend Creek—*stream* SC-3
Bendder Pond—*lake* UT-8
Ben Dearman Catfish Ponds Dam—*dam* MS-4
*Ben Deer Creek* OR-9
*Ben Deer Mountain* OR-9
*Bendeir Creek* OR-9
*Bendeir Mountain* OR-9
Ben Delatour Scout Camp—*locale* CO-8
Bendeleben, Mount—*summit* AK-9
Bendeleben Mountains—*other* AK-9
Bendel Island—*island* AK-9
Bendelius—*airport* NJ-2
Bendels Pond—*lake* CT-1
**Bendemeer**—*pop pl* OR-9
**Bendemeer Valley**—*pop pl* CO-8
Bendemeer Valley—*valley* CO-8
**Bendena**—*pop pl* KS-7
Bender—*locale* OK-5
**Bender**—*pop pl* GA-3
**Bender**—*pop pl* TX-5
*Bender Canyon* WA-9
Bender Cem—*cemetery* IN-6
Bender Cem—*cemetery* IA-7
Bender Cem—*cemetery* SD-7
Bender Creek—*stream* ID-8
Bender Creek—*stream* MI-6
Bender Creek—*stream* MN-6
Bender Creek—*stream* MO-7
Bender Creek—*stream* (3) MT-8
Bender Creek—*stream* NY-2
Bender Creek—*stream* WA-9
Bender Ditch—*canal* (2) IN-6
Bender Draw—*valley* UT-8
Bender Hill—*summit* WY-8
Bender Hollow—*valley* IN-6
Bender Lake—*lake* MI-6
Bender Lake—*lake* MN-6
Bender Lake—*lake* WA-9
Bender Landing—*locale* OR-9
Bender Memorial Acad—*school* NJ-2
Bender Mine—*mine* AZ-5
Bender Mounds—*summit* KS-7
Bender Mtn—*summit* UT-8
Bender Oil Field—*oilfield* TX-5
Bender Park—*park* NM-5
*Bender Point* MI-6
Bender Point—*summit* MT-8
Bender Pup—*stream* AK-9
Bender Ridge—*ridge* IN-6
Bender Run—*stream* (2) PA-2
Bender Run—*stream* WV-2
Bender Run Ch—*church* WV-2
Benders Ch—*church* PA-2
Bender Sch—*school* IN-6
Bender Sch—*school* SD-7
Benders Ch (abandoned)—*church* PA-2
**Benders Corner**—*pop pl* NJ-2
Benders Corners—*locale* NY-2
Benders Corners—*locale* WI-6
Benders Ferry (historical)—*crossing* TN-4
Benders Ford (historical)—*crossing* TN-4
Benders Junction—*locale* PA-2
Benders Park—*park* PA-2
Bender's Restaurant-Belmont Buffet—*hist pl* OH-6
**Bendersville**—*pop pl* PA-2
Bendersville Borough—*civil* PA-2
Bendersville Station (RR name for Aspers)—*locale* PA-2
Bender Swamp—*swamp* PA-2
Bender Tank—*reservoir* AZ-5
**Bendertown**—*pop pl* PA-2
Bender Union Sch—*school* CA-9
**Benderville**—*pop pl* WI-6
Bender Wash—*stream* AZ-5
Bender Woods—*woods* WA-9
Bendetsen—*locale* TX-5
Bendewald Point—*cape* TX-5
Bend Feed Canal—*canal* OR-9
Bend Ford—*locale* AR-4
Bend Fork—*stream* OH-6
Bend Fork Ch—*church* OH-6
Bend Gate Sch—*school* KY-4
Bend Glacier—*glacier* OR-9
Bend Gulch—*valley* ID-8
Bend Gulch Creek—*stream* MT-8
Bend Gully—*valley* PA-2
Bend Gully Trail—*trail* PA-2
Bend Hill—*summit* AR-4
Bend Hill—*summit* NY-2
Bend (historical)—*locale* SD-7
Bend Hollow—*valley* AR-4
Bend Hollow—*valley* KY-4
Bendict Park—*park* CO-8
*Bendier Creek* OR-9
*Bendier Mountain* OR-9
Bendigo Airp—*airport* PA-2
Bendigo Run—*stream* PA-2
Bendigo State Park—*park* PA-2
Bendine, Lake—*reservoir* AR-4
**Bending Brook (subdivision)**—*pop pl* NC-3
Bending Chestnut—*locale* TN-4
Bending Oak Sch—*school* IL-6
Bendinsky Airp—*airport* PA-2
Bend in the Creek Spring Rsvr—*reservoir* OR-9
Bendire Canyon—*valley* CA-9
Bendire Creek—*stream* OR-9
Bendire Mtn—*summit* OR-9
Bendire Ridge—*ridge* OR-9
Bend Island—*island* TN-4
*Bendix* NJ-2
Bendix Creek—*stream* MS-4
Bendixon-Schmid House—*hist pl* MN-6
Bendix Park—*park* IN-6
Bendix Spur—*ridge* TN-4
Bendix Woods Park—*park* IN-6
Bend Lake—*lake* AL-4
Bend Lake—*lake* AR-4
Bend Lake—*lake* MN-6
Bendle Cem—*cemetery* MI-6
Bendle Drain—*canal* MI-6
Bendle East Sch—*school* MI-6
Bendle HS—*school* MI-6
Bendle South Sch—*school* MI-6
Bendle West Sch—*school* MI-6
*Bendmore Creek* CA-9
*Bendmore Valley* CA-9
Bend Mtn—*summit* (2) AK-9
Bend Municipal Airp—*airport* OR-9
Bend of Island Number Eight Revetment (historical)—*levee* MO-7
Bend of Island Number Fourteen—*bend* TN-4
Bend of Island Number Fourteen Revetment—*levee* TN-4
Bend of Island Number Sixty Three—*bend* MS-4
Bend of Island Number Thirtyfive—*bend* TN-4
Bend of Island Number Thirty-five—*bend* TN-4
Bend of Island Number Twentyfive—*bend* TN-4
Bend of Island Number Twentyfive Revetment—*levee* TN-4
**Bendon**—*pop pl* MI-6
Bendon (historical)—*locale* SD-7
Ben Doodle Branch—*stream* AR-4
Bendorf Spring—*spring* CA-9
Bend Pine Nursery—*other* OR-9
Bend Power Dam—*dam* OR-9
Ben Draw—*valley* NM-5
*Bend Ridge* ID-8
Bend Rsvr—*reservoir* ID-8
Bend Run—*stream* IN-6
Bendry Point—*cape* MI-6
Bend Sch—*school* (3) IL-6
Bend Sch—*school* SD-7
Bend Sch (abandoned)—*school* (3) MO-7
Bend School, The—*school* IL-6
Bend School, The—*school* KY-4
Bends Creek—*stream* FL-3
Bend Skyliners Lodge—*hist pl* OR-9
Bend Spur Ridge—*ridge* VA-3
Bendt, E. H. D., House—*hist pl* TX-5
Ben Duncan Mailbox Trail—*trail* CA-9
*Ben Durban* NH-1
Bendwood Park—*park* TX-5
Bendwood Sch—*school* TX-5
Bend Work Center—*locale* MT-8
Benear Sch—*school* IL-6
Ben Eberli Waterhole—*lake* CA-9

*Benecia* ... CA-9
*Benedale Green* ... IL-6
**Benedicks**—pop pl ... PA-2
*Benedict* ... MN-6
*Benedict* ... PA-2
Benedict—locale ... VA-3
**Benedict**—pop pl (2) ... GA-3
**Benedict**—pop pl ... KS-7
**Benedict**—pop pl ... MD-2
**Benedict**—pop pl ... MN-6
**Benedict**—pop pl ... NE-7
**Benedict**—pop pl ... NY-2
**Benedict**—pop pl ... ND-7
Benedict, Dr. David De Forest, House—hist pl ... OH-6
Benedict, Edwin E., House—hist pl ... OR-9
Benedict, Mount—summit ... AZ-5
Benedict, Mount—summit (2) ... MA-1
Benedict, Sarah, House—hist pl ... OH-6
**Benedicta**—pop pl ... ME-1
Benedicta (Town of)—civ div ... ME-1
**Benedict Beach**—pop pl ... NY-2
Benedict Branch—stream ... KY-4
Benedict Buttes—summit ... NE-7
Benedict Canyon—valley ... CA-9
Benedict Cem—cemetery ... KY-4
Benedict Cem—cemetery ... NY-2
Benedict Coll—school ... SC-3
Benedict College Hist Dist—hist pl ... SC-3
Benedict Creek—stream ... ID-8
Benedict Creek—stream ... KS-7
Benedict Creek—stream ... MT-8
Benedict Creek—stream ... NY-2
Benedict Gulch—valley ... MT-8
Benedict (historical)—locale ... AZ-5
Benedict Hollow—valley ... IA-7
Benedict Hollow—valley ... VT-1
Benedict House—hist pl ... NH-1
Benedictine Acad—school (2) ... NJ-2
Benedictine Coll—school ... KS-7
Benedictine College North Campus Historic Complex—hist pl ... KS-7
Benedictine Coll (South Campus)—school ... KS-7
Benedictine Convent—church ... IL-6
Benedictine HS—school ... MI-6
Benedictine HS—school ... OH-6
Benedictine Monastery—church ... NM-5
Benedict Island—island ... NY-2
Benedict Junction—locale ... KS-7
Benedict Key—island ... FL-3
*Benedict Lake* ... MI-6
Benedict Lake—lake ... ID-8
Benedict Lake—lake ... MN-6
Benedict Lake—lake (2) ... WI-6
Benedict Lateral—canal ... CA-9
Benedict Meadow—flat ... CA-9
Benedict-Miller House—hist pl ... CT-1
Benedict Outside Pond—bay ... LA-4
Benedict Park—park ... OK-5
Benedict Pond—lake ... CT-1
Benedict Pond—reservoir ... MA-1
Benedict Pond Dam—dam ... MA-1
Benedict Pond (historical)—lake ... RI-1
Benedict Ranch—locale ... CO-8
Benedict Ranch—locale (3) ... NM-5
Benedict Recreation Center—park ... CA-9
Benedicts—locale ... PA-2
Benedict Sch—school ... GA-3
Benedict Sch—school ... MD-2
Benedict Sch—school ... OH-6
Benedicts (historical)—locale ... AZ-5
*Benedicts Lake* ... MI-6
Benedicts Lake—reservoir ... TN-4
Benedicts Lake Dam—dam ... TN-4
Benedict Spring—spring ... AZ-5
Benedict Tank—reservoir ... AZ-5
**Benedict Township**—pop pl ... SD-7
Benedict (Township of)—fmr MCD ... AR-4
Benedum Airp—airport ... WV-2
Benedum Camp—locale ... TX-5
Benedum Landing—locale ... AK-9
Benedum Oil Field—oilfield ... TX-5
Benedum Theater—building ... PA-2
Bene Dunagan—locale ... NM-5
Beneficent Congregational Church—hist pl ... RI-1
Benefiel Cem—cemetery ... IN-6
**Benefiel Corner**—pop pl (2) ... IN-6
Benefiel Creek—stream ... OR-9
Benefield Cem—cemetery ... MS-4
Benefield Creek—stream ... MT-8
Benefield Creek—stream ... OR-9
Bene Field Mines—mine ... AL-4
Benefield Pond—lake ... TX-5
Benefield Spring—spring ... AL-4
Benefit—locale ... GA-3
Benefit—locale ... VA-3
Benefit Ch—church ... NC-3
**Benefit (historical)**—pop pl ... NC-3
*Beneke Creek* ... OR-9
Beneke Creek—stream ... OR-9
**Benela**—pop pl ... MS-4
Benela Cem—cemetery ... MS-4
Benela Ch—church ... MS-4
*Benela Methodist Ch* ... MS-4
Ben Elders Creek—stream ... NJ-2
Ben English Coulee—valley ... MT-8
Beneniem Ch—church ... FM-9
Beneral Sch (historical)—school ... MS-4
Benesch Ditch—canal ... CO-8
Benesh Sch—school ... MN-6
Benet, Stephen Vincent, House—hist pl ... GA-3
Benet Lake—lake ... IL-6
Benet Lake—lake ... WI-6
**Benet Lake (Religious Community)**—pop pl ... WI-6
*Benett Hill* ... NY-2
Beneva Christian Ch—church ... FL-3
Benevento Memorial Field—park ... MA-1
Beneventum Plantation—locale ... SC-3
Beneventum Plantation House—hist pl ... SC-3
Benevenue Country Club—locale ... NC-3
Benevides Ranch—locale ... NM-5
Benevides Tank—reservoir ... TX-5
Benevites Tank—reservoir ... NM-5
**Benevola**—pop pl ... AL-4
**Benevola**—pop pl ... MD-2
**Benevolence**—pop pl ... GA-3
Benevolence (CCD)—cens area ... GA-3
Benevolence Ch—church (4) ... GA-3
Benevolence Grove Ch—church ... AL-4
Benevolent Cem—cemetery ... LA-4
Benevolent Cem—cemetery ... NC-3
Benevolent Cem—cemetery (2) ... TN-4
Benevolent Grove Ch—church ... AL-4
**Benevolent Heights**—pop pl ... IL-6
Benevolent Society Cem—cemetery ... LA-4
Benevolent Society Cem—cemetery ... MS-4
*Benevolent Society Hospital* ... AL-4
Benewah—locale ... ID-8
Benewah County Courthouse—hist pl ... ID-8
Benewah Creek—stream ... ID-8
Benewah Lake—lake ... ID-8
Benewah Milk Bottle—hist pl ... WA-9
*Benezett* ... PA-2
**Benezette**—pop pl ... PA-2
Benezette (RR and Township name for Benezett)—other ... PA-2
**Benezette Township**—pop pl ... PA-2
**Benezett (RR and Township name Benezette)**—pop pl ... PA-2
Benezie Lake—lake ... MN-6
**Benfer**—pop pl ... PA-2
Ben Few Campground—locale ... AR-4
Ben F Geyer MS—school ... IN-6
Ben Ficklin Dam—dam ... TX-5
**Benfield**—pop pl ... MD-2
Ben Field Cave—cave ... AL-4
Benfield Cem—cemetery ... NC-3
Benfield Creek—stream ... NC-3
Benfield Lake—lake ... MN-6
Benfield Sch—school ... KS-7
*Benford Cem* ... AL-4
Benford Cem—cemetery ... AL-4
Benford Cem—cemetery ... MS-4
Ben Ford Ch—church ... LA-4
Benford Creek—stream ... TN-4
**Benford Heights Addition (subdivision)**—pop pl ... TN-4
Benford Tunnel—tunnel ... PA-2
Ben Fore Sch (abandoned)—school ... MO-7
*Ben Fort Creek* ... TX-5
Ben Frank Hollow—valley ... AR-4
**Ben Franklin**—pop pl ... TX-5
Ben Franklin—post sta ... AZ-5
Ben Franklin Canal—canal ... CA-9
Ben Franklin Park—park ... FL-3
Ben Franklin Sch—school ... NJ-2
Ben Franklin Sch—school ... NY-2
Ben Franklin Sch—school (2) ... PA-2
Beng, Rois—summit ... PW-9
Bengal—locale ... KY-4
Bengal—locale ... MN-6
**Bengal**—pop pl ... IN-6
**Bengal**—pop pl ... OK-5
Bengal Center Sch—school ... MI-6
Bengal Ch—church ... MI-6
Bengal Hill—summit ... MN-6
**Bengall**—pop pl ... AR-4
Bengal Lake—lake ... MN-6
Bengal Mine—mine ... MI-6
Bengal Slough—gut ... LA-4
**Bengal (Township of)**—pop pl ... MI-6
Ben Gap—gap ... GA-3
Ben Gause Bay—swamp ... SC-3
Ben-Gay—locale ... AR-4
**Ben Gay**—pop pl ... AR-4
Benge—locale ... KY-4
**Benge**—pop pl ... WA-9
Benge Branch—stream ... OK-5
Benge Cem—cemetery ... OK-5
Benge Corner—locale ... TX-5
Benge Creek—stream ... SD-7
Benge Gap—gap ... NC-3
Benge Knob—summit ... NC-3
Bengel—locale ... AR-4
*Ben George Run* ... PA-2
Benge Pond—swamp ... KY-4
Ben Geren Regional Park—park ... AR-4
Benges Branch—stream ... VA-3
Benges Creek—stream ... VA-3
Benges Gap—gap ... VA-3
**Bengies**—pop pl ... MD-2
Bengies Point—cape ... MD-2
Ben Gilbert Mine (underground)—mine ... AL-4
Ben Gile Pond—lake ... ME-1
Bengis Creek—stream (2) ... AL-4
Bengis Reservation—park ... AL-4
Ben Glazier Brook—stream ... ME-1
Ben Glenn Canyon—valley ... OR-9
Ben Glenn Ridge—ridge ... OR-9
Bengoechea Cabin—locale ... ID-8
Bengoechea Place—locale ... ID-8
Ben Good Creek—stream ... CO-8
Bengor Creek—stream ... MT-8
Bengough Hill—summit ... WY-8
Ben Graves Canyon—valley ... CA-9
Ben Gray Hollow—valley ... NY-2
Ben Green Bight—bay ... AK-9
Bengston Lake—lake ... MI-6
Bengston Lake—lake ... WA-9
Bengston Lake Dam Number Three—dam ... NC-3
Bengy Lake—lake ... AL-4
*Benhaden* ... FL-3
*Benhader* ... FL-3
Ben Haley Branch—stream ... WV-2
Ben Hall Creek—stream ... OR-9
Ben Hall Hill—summit ... SC-3
Ben Hall Spring—spring ... OR-9
*Benham* ... VA-3
**Benham**—pop pl ... IN-6
**Benham**—pop pl ... KY-4
**Benham**—pop pl ... NC-3
**Benham**—pop pl ... VA-3
Benham Branch—stream ... IN-6
Ben Ham Branch—stream ... KY-4
Benham Brook—stream ... NY-2
Benham Canal—canal ... ID-8
Benham Cem—cemetery ... IN-6
Benham Ch—church ... NC-3
Benham Creek—stream ... OR-9
Benham Creek—stream ... WA-9
Benham Drain—canal ... MI-6
Benham Falls—falls ... OR-9
Benham Falls Campground—park ... OR-9
Benham Hill—summit ... IL-6
Benham Hill—summit ... OK-5
Benham Hist Dist—hist pl ... KY-4
Benham House—hist pl ... NY-2
Benham-Hughes-Speer Cem—cemetery ... TN-4
*Benham Island* ... TN-4
Benham Mound—hist pl ... OH-6
Benham Ranch—locale ... AZ-5
**Benhams**—pop pl ... VA-3
Benham Sch—school ... KS-7
Benham Slough—gut ... OR-9
Benham Snow Play Area—park ... AZ-5
*Benhams Station* ... IN-6
*Benhams Store* ... IN-6
Benham Tank—reservoir ... AZ-5
Benhan Cem—cemetery ... NY-2
Ben Hands Thorofare—channel ... NJ-2
Ben Hanna Swamp—swamp ... PA-2
*Benhards Upper Landing* ... AL-4
Ben Harrison Gulch—valley ... UT-8
Ben Harrison Mine—mine ... OR-9
Ben Harrison Mine—mine ... UT-8
Ben Harrison Peak—summit ... OR-9
Ben Hart Creek—stream ... MT-8
Benhart Draw—valley ... WY-8
Benharts—locale ... PA-2
Benhaven HS—school ... NC-3
Ben Henry Lake—reservoir ... TN-4
Ben Henry Lake Dam—dam ... TN-4
**Ben Hill**—pop pl ... GA-3
**Benhill**—pop pl ... TN-4
Ben Hill—summit ... AR-4
**Ben Hill (County)**—pop pl ... GA-3
Ben Hill County Courthouse—hist pl ... GA-3
Ben Hill County Jail—hist pl ... GA-3
Ben Hill-Irwin Vocational Sch—school ... GA-3
Benhke Creek—stream ... MI-6
Ben Holland Hollow—valley ... TN-4
Ben Hollow—valley ... MO-7
Ben Hollow—valley ... TN-4
Ben Howard Branch—stream ... KY-4
Ben Hulse Sch—school ... CA-9
*Benhur* ... TX-5
Ben Hur—locale ... AR-4
Ben Hur—locale ... CA-9
**Ben Hur**—pop pl ... TX-5
**Ben Hur**—pop pl ... VA-3
**Ben Hur (Benhur)**—pop pl ... TX-5
Ben Hur Camp—locale ... PA-2
Ben Hur Cem—cemetery ... IN-6
Ben Hur Mine—mine ... AZ-5
Ben Hur Mine—mine ... NV-8
Ben Hur Mine (historical)—mine ... SD-7
Ben Hur Sch—school ... CA-9
*Benic* ... FM-9
**Benicia**—pop pl ... CA-9
*Benicia Arsenal* ... CA-9
Benicia Arsenal—hist pl ... CA-9
Benicia Arsenal—military ... CA-9
Benicia Capitol State Historical Monmt—park ... CA-9
Benicia Capitol State Historic Park—hist pl ... CA-9
Benicia HS—school ... CA-9
Benicia-Martinez Bridge (Toll)—bridge ... CA-9
Benicia Point—cape ... CA-9
Benicia Shoals—bar ... CA-9
*Benicke's Lake* ... WI-6
Benien Creek—stream ... OH-6
Benien Ditch—canal ... OH-6
*Benig* ... FM-9
Benight Pond—lake ... CA-9
Benign Peak—summit ... AK-9
*Benigu* ... FM-9
*Benik* ... FM-9
*Benike Lake* ... WI-6
Benilde HS—school ... MN-6
*Benington Mill* ... VA-3
*Benington Mills* ... VA-3
Benino Creek—stream ... CO-8
*Benin Water Pond* ... NY-2
Benion Bench—bench ... UT-8
*Benions Creek* ... AL-4
Ben Island—island ... ME-1
Benison, Mount—summit ... MI-6
Benitez—CDP ... PR-3
**Benitez**—pop pl ... PR-3
Benitez, Gautier, HS—hist pl ... PR-3
Benito—locale ... CA-9
Benito—locale ... KY-4
Benito Canyon—valley ... CO-8
Benito Canyon—valley ... NM-5
Benito Creek—stream ... AK-9
Benito Creek—stream ... CO-8
Benito Lake—lake ... CO-8
Benito Sch—school ... NM-5
Ben Jacobs Trail—trail ... PA-2
*Benjamen Holmes Junior Cem* ... MS-4
Ben James Ch—church ... GA-3
Benjamin—locale ... MO-7
Benjamin—locale ... PA-2
**Benjamin**—pop pl ... TX-5
**Benjamin**—pop pl ... UT-8
Benjamin—uninc pl ... PA-2
Benjamin, James, Homestead—hist pl ... NY-2
Benjamin, Lake—reservoir ... TX-5
Benjamin, Ruben M., House—hist pl ... IL-6
Benjamin Acres Sch—school ... VA-3
Benjamin Airp—airport ... PA-2
Benjamin Banneker Elem Sch—school ... DE-2
Benjamin Banneker Elem Sch—school ... IN-6
Benjamin Banneker Park—park ... DC-2
Benjamin Banneker: SW 9 Intermediate Boundary Stone—hist pl ... VA-3
Benjamin Barrow Cem—cemetery ... TX-5
Benjamin Bosse HS—school ... IN-6
Benjamin Brook—stream ... ME-1
Benjamin Canyon—valley ... CA-9
Benjamin (CCD)—cens area ... TX-5
Benjamin Cem—cemetery ... LA-4
Benjamin Cem—cemetery ... MI-6
Benjamin Cem—cemetery ... MO-7
Benjamin Cem—cemetery ... UT-8
Benjamin Ch—church ... SC-3
Benjamin Chapel Cem—cemetery ... GA-3
Benjamin Creek—stream (2) ... AK-9
Benjamin Creek—stream ... CA-9
Benjamin Creek—stream ... IA-7
Benjamin Creek—stream ... MI-6
Benjamin Flat—flat ... CA-9
Benjamin Frankin Sch—school ... TX-5
Benjamin Franklin—post sta ... DC-2
Benjamin Franklin Birthplace Site—park ... MA-1
Benjamin Franklin Bridge—bridge ... PA-2
*Benjamin Franklin Elem Sch* ... PA-2
Benjamin Franklin Elem Sch—school (4) ... IN-6
Benjamin Franklin Elem Sch—school ... PA-2
Benjamin Franklin Hotel—hist pl ... PA-2
Benjamin Franklin HS—school ... LA-4
Benjamin Franklin HS—school ... PA-2
*Benjamin Franklin JHS* ... PA-2
Benjamin Franklin JHS (abandoned)—school ... PA-2
Benjamin Franklin Lake—reservoir ... TN-4
Benjamin Franklin MS—school ... IN-6
Benjamin Franklin Sch—school ... AZ-5
Benjamin Franklin Sch—school ... CO-8
Benjamin Franklin Sch—school ... FL-3
Benjamin Franklin Sch—school (2) ... IL-6
Benjamin Franklin Sch—school ... MN-6
Benjamin Franklin Sch—school (2) ... ND-7
Benjamin Franklin Sch—school (2) ... PA-2
Benjamin Franklin Statue—park ... DC-2
Benjamin Franklin Statue—park ... MA-1
Benjamin Gulch—valley ... AZ-5
Benjamin Gulch—valley (2) ... OR-9
Benjamin Gulch—valley ... WA-9
Benjamin Harrison Elem Sch—school (3) ... IN-6
Benjamin Hill—summit ... CT-1
Benjamin Hill—summit (2) ... MA-1
Benjamin Hill—summit ... NY-2
Benjamin Hollow—valley ... PA-2
Benjamin House—hist pl ... MO-7
Benjamin Howell Cem—cemetery ... MS-4
Benjamin Island—island ... AK-9
Benjamin Island—island ... FL-3
Benjamin J Baker Elem Sch—school ... FL-3
Benjamin J Martin Elem Sch—school ... NC-3
Benjamin Lake—lake ... AR-4
Benjamin Lake—lake (3) ... MN-6
Benjamin Lake—lake ... OR-9
Benjamin Lake—lake ... WA-9
Benjamin Lake—reservoir ... NC-3
Benjamin Lake Dam—dam ... NC-3
Benjamin Marstons Mill Site—locale ... MA-1
Benjamin Mine—mine ... UT-8
Benjamin Number 10 Mine Station—locale ... PA-2
Benjamin Number 3 Mine Station—locale ... PA-2
Benjamin Number 6 Mine Station—locale ... PA-2
Benjamin Number 7 Mine Station—locale ... PA-2
Benjamin Pond—lake ... ME-1
Benjamin Pond—lake ... PA-2
Benjamin Quick Ditch—canal ... CO-8
Benjamin Ranch—locale ... MT-8
Benjamin Ranch—locale ... NM-5
Benjamin Reeves Cem—cemetery ... MS-4
Benjamin River—stream ... ME-1
Benjamin Run—stream ... MI-6
Benjamin Run—stream ... PA-2
Benjamin Rush Sch—school ... PA-2
Benjamin Sch—school ... FL-3
Benjamin Sch—school (2) ... IL-6
Benjamin Sch—school ... LA-4
Benjamin Sch—school ... MI-6
Benjamin Slough—stream ... UT-8
Benjamin Spring—spring ... AZ-5
Benjamin Spring—spring ... OR-9
Benjamin Station—locale ... UT-8
**Benjamin Switch**—pop pl ... LA-4
Benjaminville—other ... IL-6
Benjaminville Friends Meetinghouse and Burial Ground—hist pl ... IL-6
Benjamin Wall Cem—cemetery ... MS-4
**Benjestown**—pop pl ... TN-4
Benjestown Cem—cemetery ... TN-4
*Benjies* ... MD-2
*Benjies Point* ... MD-2
Benjimen Lake Dam—dam ... MS-4
**Benjoe**—pop pl ... MS-4
Ben Johnson Boy Scout Camp—locale ... MI-6
Ben Johnson Canyon—valley ... UT-8
Ben Johnson Lake—reservoir ... NC-3
Ben Johnson Lake Dam—dam ... NC-3
Ben Johnson Ridge—ridge ... AL-4
Ben Johnson Trail—trail ... CA-9
Ben Jones Spring—spring ... TX-5
Benka Lake—lake ... AK-9
Benke Drain—canal ... MI-6
**Benkelman**—pop pl ... NE-7
Benkelman Cem—cemetery ... NE-7
Benkelman No. 1—fmr MCD ... NE-7
Benkelman No. 2—fmr MCD ... NE-7
Benkelman No. 3—fmr MCD ... NE-7
Benkelman State Fish Hatchery—other ... NE-7
**Benkelman Township**—pop pl ... KS-7
Benkert Bushnell Cem—cemetery ... WI-6
Benkert Cem—cemetery ... WI-6
*Benkie Ditch* ... IN-6
*Benkleman* ... NE-7
Ben Knob—summit ... GA-3
Benko Spring—spring ... CA-9
Benlacs State Wildlife Mngmt Area—park ... MN-6
*Ben Lake* ... WI-6
Ben Lake—lake ... LA-4
Ben Lake—lake ... ME-1
Ben Lake—lake ... TX-5
Ben Lassiter Cave—cave ... MO-7
**Benld**—pop pl ... IL-6
Benleo—locale ... KY-4
Ben Lilly Campground—locale ... NM-5
Ben Lilly Pond Dam—dam ... MS-4
Ben Liner Hollow—valley ... TN-4
Ben Linn Landing—locale ... MN-6
Ben Lippen Sch—school ... NC-3
*Ben Lomand* ... TN-4
Ben Lomand Mtn—summit ... CO-8
Ben Lomond—hist pl ... VA-3
Ben Lomond—locale ... WV-2
**Ben Lomond**—pop pl ... AR-4
**Ben Lomond**—pop pl ... CA-9
Ben Lomond—summit ... CA-9
Ben Lomond—summit ... UT-8
Ben Lomond—uninc pl ... UT-8
Ben Lomond Camp—locale ... UT-8
Ben Lomond Cem—cemetery ... UT-8
**Ben Lomond Heights (subdivision)**—pop pl ... UT-8
Ben Lomond HS—school ... UT-8
Ben Lomond Landing—locale ... MS-4
Ben Lomond Mines—mine ... AZ-5
Ben Lomond Mountain Pit—cave ... TN-4
Ben Lomond Mtn—summit ... CA-9
Ben Lomond Mtn—summit ... TN-4
**Ben Lomond Park Subdivision**—pop pl ... UT-8
*Ben Lomond Peak* ... UT-8
Ben Lomond Plantation (historical)—locale (2) ... AL-4
Ben Lomond Sch—school ... CA-9
Ben Lomond Station Post Office—building ... UT-8
**Ben Lomond Suites Condominiums**—pop pl ... UT-8
Ben Lomond (Township of)—fmr MCD ... AR-4
Ben Lowe Cabin—locale ... CO-8
Ben Lowe Flats—summit ... CO-8
Ben Lowe Trail—trail ... CO-8
Ben Mann Brook—stream ... MA-1
**Benmartin**—pop pl ... OK-5
Ben May Fire Tower—locale (2) ... AL-4
Ben Milam Sch—school (2) ... TX-5
Ben Mills Flat—flat ... ID-8
*Ben Moore Creek* ... CA-9
*Ben Moore Valley* ... CA-9
**Benmore**—pop pl ... MS-4
Benmore Canyon—valley ... CA-9
*Ben More Creek* ... CA-9
Benmore Creek—stream (2) ... CA-9
Benmoreel—uninc pl ... VA-3
Benmore Experimental Pastures—flat ... UT-8
Benmore Experiment Station—locale ... UT-8
Benmore Guard Station—locale ... UT-8
Ben More Mtn—summit ... OR-9
Benmore Ridge Camp—locale ... CA-9
Benmore (Site)—locale ... UT-8
Benmore Valley—valley ... CA-9
Ben Morgan Canyon—valley ... CO-8
Ben Mtn—summit ... GA-3
*Ben Muir* ... WA-9
Benn, J. W., Bldg—hist pl ... WI-6
Bennan Lake—lake ... MI-6
*Bennay Mountain* ... CO-8
Benndale—locale ... MS-4
Benndale Fire Tower—locale ... MS-4
Benndale Post Office (historical)—building ... MS-4
Benndale Sch (historical)—school ... MS-4
Bennefield Branch—stream ... DE-2
Bennefield Cem—cemetery ... WV-2
Bennefield Prong—stream ... WV-2
Bennehoff Rsvr—reservoir ... OR-9
*Bennehoof Run* ... PA-2
Benner—locale ... VI-3
Benner Bay—bay ... VI-3
Benner Branch—stream ... MO-7
Benner Brook—stream ... ME-1
Benner Cem—cemetery (2) ... OH-6
Benner Cem—cemetery ... PA-2
Benner Corner—locale ... ME-1
*Benner Creek* ... FL-3
Benner Creek—stream (2) ... CA-9
Benner Creek—stream ... OR-9
Benner Creek Campground—locale ... CA-9
Benner Ditch—canal ... IN-6
Benner Drain—stream ... MI-6
Benner Field Airp—airport ... IN-6
Benner Gulch—valley ... SD-7
Benner Hill—ridge ... OH-6
Benner Hill—summit (2) ... ME-1
Benner Hill—summit ... PA-2
Benner Hill—summit ... VI-3
Benner Hollow—valley ... OH-6
Benner House—hist pl ... NY-2
Benner Island—island ... ME-1
Benner Lake—lake ... MO-7
Benner Run—stream ... PA-2
Benner Sch—school ... CA-9
Benner Sch—school ... IL-6
Benner Spring—spring ... CA-9
Benner Spring—spring ... PA-2
Benners Quarry—mine ... PA-2
**Benner (Township of)**—pop pl ... PA-2
*Bennerville* ... PA-2
Benne Sch—school ... CA-9
*Bennet* ... CO-8
**Bennet**—pop pl ... NE-7
Bennet, Lake—lake ... FL-3
*Bennet Bayou* ... AR-4
Bennet Bayou—stream (2) ... LA-4
*Bennet Branch* ... KY-4
*Bennet Branch* ... TN-4
*Bennet Brook* ... PA-2
*Bennet Canyon* ... CA-9
Bennet Cem—cemetery ... AR-4
Bennet Cem—cemetery ... MI-6
Bennet Ch—church ... MS-4
Bennet Cove—bay ... ME-1
*Bennet Creek* ... IL-6
Bennet Creek—stream (2) ... OR-9
Bennet Creek—stream ... PA-2
Bennet Drain—canal ... MI-6
Bennet Drain—stream ... MI-6
Bennet Farm—locale ... MS-4
Bennet Gulch—valley ... CO-8
Bennet Gulch—valley ... MT-8
Bennet Hill—park ... WY-8
Bennet Lake—reservoir ... IA-7
Bennet Lake Dam—dam ... IA-7
Bennet Peak—summit ... OR-9
Bennet Pond Ch—church ... FL-3
Bennet Ranch—locale ... TX-5
Bennet Rock Trail—trail ... WV-2
Bennet Rsvr—reservoir ... NE-7
*Bennet Run* ... PA-2
*Bennets* ... PA-2
Bennets Branch—stream ... KY-4
Bennets Branch—stream ... SC-3
Bennets Branch Sch—school ... KY-4
*Bennets Corner* ... PA-2
*Bennets Creek* ... AR-4
*Bennets Creek* ... NV-8
*Bennet's Creek* ... VA-3
*Bennets Fork* ... KY-4
*Bennets Fork* ... TN-4
*Bennets Neck* ... MA-1
Bennets Neck—cape ... MA-1
*Bennet's Point* ... MD-2
Bennets Point—summit ... OR-9
*Bennets Pond* ... MA-1
Bennets Pond—reservoir ... CT-1
*Bennet Spring Creek* ... MO-7
*Bennet Springs* ... KS-7
Bennet Springs—lake ... MI-6
Bennets Run—stream ... VA-3
Bennets Shop Ctr—locale ... VA-3
**Bennets (Stove Pipe City)**—pop pl ... NY-2
*Bennets Water Pond* ... NY-2
*Bennett* ... ID-8
*Bennett* ... IN-6
*Bennett* ... MI-6
*Bennett* ... NE-7
*Bennett* ... NC-3
Bennett—locale ... AL-4
Bennett—locale ... FL-3
Bennett—locale ... IL-6
Bennett—locale ... ME-1
Bennett—locale ... MN-6
Bennett—locale ... MO-7
Bennett—locale ... UT-8
Bennett—locale ... WV-2
**Bennett**—pop pl ... CO-8
**Bennett**—pop pl ... IA-7
**Bennett**—pop pl ... KY-4
**Bennett**—pop pl ... NJ-2
**Bennett**—pop pl ... NM-5
**Bennett**—pop pl ... NC-3
**Bennett**—pop pl ... SC-3
**Bennett**—pop pl ... TX-5
**Bennett**—pop pl ... WI-6
Bennett, George, House—hist pl ... OH-6
Bennett, Gov. Thomas, House—hist pl ... SC-3
Bennett, Henry, House—hist pl ... MI-6
Bennett, H. H., Studio—hist pl ... WI-6
Bennett, John W., House—hist pl ... NE-7
Bennett, Jonathan M., House—hist pl ... WV-2
Bennett, Lake—lake ... ND-7
Bennett, Lake—reservoir ... GA-3
Bennett, M. D., House—hist pl ... TX-5
Bennett, Nathan, House—hist pl ... GA-3
Bennett, Sue, Memorial Sch Bldg—hist pl ... KY-4
*Bennett Academy* ... MS-4
**Bennett Acres**—pop pl ... TN-4
Bennett Airp—airport ... PA-2
Bennett and Leshner Ditch—canal ... CO-8
Bennett Baseball Field—park ... GA-3
*Bennett Bay* ... GA-3
Bennett Bay—bay ... ID-8
Bennett Bay—bay ... LA-4
Bennett Bay—flat ... GA-3
Bennett Bay—swamp ... GA-3
Bennett Bay—swamp ... NC-3
**Bennett Bay Landing**—pop pl ... LA-4
*Bennett Bayou* ... AR-4
Bennett Bayou (Township of)—fmr MCD ... AR-4
Bennett Branch—stream (2) ... AL-4
Bennett Branch—stream ... AR-4
Bennett Branch—stream ... FL-3
Bennett Branch—stream (4) ... KY-4
Bennett Branch—stream (2) ... NC-3
Bennett Branch—stream ... PA-2
Bennett Branch—stream ... SC-3
Bennett Branch—stream (3) ... TN-4
Bennett Branch—stream ... TX-5
Bennett Branch—stream ... VA-3
Bennett Branch Creek—stream ... TX-5
Bennett Bridge—bridge ... ID-8
Bennett Bridge—bridge ... NC-3
Bennett Bridge—hist pl ... ME-1
**Bennett Bridge**—pop pl ... NY-2
*Bennett Brook* ... MA-1
*Bennett Brook* ... VT-1
Bennett Brook—stream ... CT-1
Bennett Brook—stream (5) ... ME-1
Bennett Brook—stream (2) ... MA-1
Bennett Brook—stream (3) ... NH-1
Bennett Brook—stream (2) ... NY-2
Bennett Brook—stream ... PA-2
Bennett Brook—stream ... VT-1
Bennett Brook Sch—school ... PA-2
Bennett Butler Tank—reservoir ... AZ-5
Bennett Butte—summit ... OR-9
Bennett Cabin—locale ... OR-9
Bennett Canal—canal ... NE-7
Bennett Canyon—valley ... CA-9
Bennett Canyon—valley ... NV-8
Bennett Canyon—valley ... OR-9
Bennett Canyon—valley ... SD-7
Bennett Causeway—bridge ... FL-3
Bennett Cave—cave ... AL-4
Bennett Cem—cemetery (6) ... AL-4
Bennett Cem—cemetery ... CA-9
Bennett Cem—cemetery ... CO-8
Bennett Cem—cemetery ... CT-1
Bennett Cem—cemetery (3) ... GA-3
Bennett Cem—cemetery ... IL-6
Bennett Cem—cemetery (3) ... IN-6
Bennett Cem—cemetery ... IA-7
Bennett Cem—cemetery (4) ... KY-4
Bennett Cem—cemetery (2) ... LA-4
Bennett Cem—cemetery ... MI-6
Bennett Cem—cemetery (2) ... MS-4
Bennett Cem—cemetery (3) ... MO-7
Bennett Cem—cemetery ... NY-2
Bennett Cem—cemetery (3) ... NC-3
Bennett Cem—cemetery (2) ... OH-6
Bennett Cem—cemetery ... OK-5
Bennett Cem—cemetery ... PA-2
Bennett Cem—cemetery (6) ... TN-4
Bennett Cem—cemetery (2) ... TX-5
Bennett Cem—cemetery ... VT-1
Bennett Cem—cemetery (3) ... VA-3
Bennett Cem—cemetery (2) ... WV-2
Bennett Cem—cemetery ... WI-6
Bennett Ch—church ... MI-6
Bennett Ch—church ... MO-7
Bennett Ch—church ... OK-5
Bennett Ch—church ... WV-2
Bennett Chapel—church ... AL-4
Bennett Chapel—church ... KY-4
Bennett Chapel—church ... MS-4
Bennett Chapel—church ... MO-7
Bennett Chapel—church ... VA-3
Bennett Chapel Sch—school ... MS-4
*Bennett Church* ... MS-4
Bennett Clarkson Hosp—hospital ... SD-7
Bennett Coal Bed Mine (underground)—mine ... AL-4
Bennett Cole Cem—cemetery ... TN-4
Bennett Coll—school ... NY-2
Bennett Coll—school ... NC-3
Bennett Corner—locale ... VA-3
Bennett Corners—locale ... PA-2
**Bennett Corners**—pop pl ... NH-1

Bennett Corral—*locale* AZ-5
Bennett Coulee—*valley* MT-8
Bennett County—*civil* SD-7
Bennett County Park—*park* IA-7
Bennett County Park—*park* OR-9
Bennett Cove—*bay* NH-1
Bennett Cove—*bay* NY-2
Bennett Cove—*cape* ME-1
Bennett Cove—*valley* AL-4
Bennett Cove—*valley* NC-3
Bennett Cove—*valley* (2) TN-4
*Bennett Creek* AR-4
*Bennett Creek* IL-6
*Bennett Creek* KY-4
*Bennett Creek* NM-5
*Bennett Creek* NY-2
*Bennett Creek* TX-5
Bennett Creek—*locale* VA-3
Bennett Creek—*stream* (3) AL-4
Bennett Creek—*stream* AK-9
Bennett Creek—*stream* (4) CA-9
Bennett Creek—*stream* (5) CO-8
Bennett Creek—*stream* (2) GA-3
Bennett Creek—*stream* (6) ID-8
Bennett Creek—*stream* IL-6
Bennett Creek—*stream* (2) IA-7
Bennett Creek—*stream* MD-2
Bennett Creek—*stream* (2) MI-6
Bennett Creek—*stream* (2) MO-7
Bennett Creek—*stream* MT-8
Bennett Creek—*stream* NJ-2
Bennett Creek—*stream* NM-5
Bennett Creek—*stream* NY-2
Bennett Creek—*stream* (2) NC-3
Bennett Creek—*stream* ND-7
Bennett Creek—*stream* OK-5
Bennett Creek—*stream* (3) OR-9
Bennett Creek—*stream* (4) TX-5
Bennett Creek—*stream* UT-8
Bennett Creek—*stream* (2) VA-3
Bennett Creek—*stream* WY-8
Bennett Creek Basin—*basin* ID-8
Bennett Creek Bridge—*bridge* ID-8
Bennett Creek Ditch—*canal* WY-8
Bennett Creek Guard Station—*locale* MT-8
Bennett Creek Light—*other* VA-3
Bennett Creek Picnic Area—*locale* CO-8
Bennett Dam—*dam* AL-4
Bennett Dam—*dam* (2) OR-9
Bennett Ditch—*canal* CA-9
Bennett Ditch—*canal* IN-6
Bennett Ditch—*canal* OH-6
Bennett Drain—*canal* (2) MI-6
Bennette Cem—*cemetery* KY-4
Bennett Elem Sch—*school* NC-3
Bennette Point—*cape* MI-6
*Bennett-Estes Lake* AL-4
Bennett Ferry (historical)—*crossing* TN-4
Bennett Field—*locale* FL-3
Bennett Field Wildlife Mngmt Area—*park* UT-8
Bennett Flat—*flat* CA-9
Bennett Flat—*flat* OR-9
Bennett Fork—*stream* KY-4
Bennett Fork—*stream* WV-2
Bennett Gap—*gap* KY-4
Bennett Gap—*gap* NC-3
Bennett Gap—*gap* WV-2
Bennett Grove Sch—*school* LA-4
Bennett Hall—*building* NC-3
**Bennett Hall**—*pop pl* MA-1
**Bennett Harbor (subdivision)**—*pop pl* VA-3
Bennett-Hemenway Sch—*school* MA-1
Bennett Hill—*summit* (3) NH-1
Bennett Hill—*summit* (5) NY-2
Bennett Hill—*summit* RI-1
Bennett Hill—*summit* WA-9
Bennett Hill—*uninc pl* WA-9
**Bennett (historical)**—*pop pl* MS-4
*Bennett Hollow* NY-2
Bennett Hollow—*valley* AR-4
Bennett Hollow—*valley* (2) MO-7
Bennett Hollow—*valley* (2) NY-2
Bennett Hollow—*valley* OH-6
Bennett Hollow—*valley* (5) TN-4
Bennett Hollow Sch—*school* NY-2
Bennett Homestead—*locale* MT-8
Bennett HS—*school* NY-2
Bennett Island—*island* NH-1
Bennett JHS—*school* CT-1
Bennett JHS—*school* OH-6
Bennett Juniper—*locale* CA-9
**Bennett (Kemper)**—*pop pl* WV-2
Bennett Knob—*summit* NC-3
*Bennett Lake* MI-6
Bennett Lake—*lake* KY-4
Bennett Lake—*lake* ME-1
Bennett Lake—*lake* (3) MI-6
Bennett Lake—*lake* MN-6
Bennett Lake—*lake* MO-7
Bennett Lake—*lake* NE-7
Bennett Lake—*lake* NY-2
Bennett Lake—*lake* OR-9
Bennett Lake—*lake* TN-4
Bennett Lake—*lake* (2) WA-9
Bennett Lake—*lake* (3) WI-6
Bennett Lake—*reservoir* AR-4
Bennett Lake—*reservoir* IN-6
Bennett Lake—*reservoir* KY-4
Bennett Lake—*reservoir* MS-4
Bennett Lake—*reservoir* TN-4
Bennett Lake—*reservoir* TX-5
Bennett Lake Dam—*dam* (2) MS-4
Bennett Lake Dam—*dam* TN-4
**Bennett (Lakota)**—*pop pl* TX-5
Bennett Landing—*locale* FL-3
Bennett Landing—*locale* IL-6
Bennett Lane Cem—*cemetery* MO-7
Bennett Lateral—*canal* (2) ID-8
Bennett Lindsay Lower Dam—*dam* UT-8
Bennett Little Field—*flat* NC-3
Bennett Lookout Tower—*locale* WI-6
Bennett Martin Dam—*dam* SD-7
Bennett-McBride House—*hist pl* MN-6
Bennett Meadow—*bench* MA-1
Bennett Meadow—*flat* (2) WA-9
Bennett Memorial Chapel—*church* WV-2
Bennett Memorial Park—*cemetery* CA-9
Bennett Mill Creek—*stream* AL-4
Bennett Mill Pond—*reservoir* (2) NC-3
Bennett Mill Pond Dam—*dam* NC-3
Bennett Mine—*mine* CO-8
Bennett Mine—*mine* MN-6
Bennett Mine—*mine* TN-4
Bennett Mine (surface)—*mine* AL-4
*Bennett Mountain* CO-8
*Bennett Mountains* WY-8
Bennett Mtn—*summit* CA-9
Bennett Mtn—*summit* CO-8
Bennett Mtn—*summit* ID-8
Bennett Mtn—*summit* NM-5
Bennett Mtn—*summit* NC-3
Bennett Mtn—*summit* TX-5
Bennett Mtn—*summit* WV-2
*Bennett Neck* MA-1
Bennett Neck—*cape* ME-1
Bennett Park—*park* MN-6
Bennett Park—*park* MO-7
Bennett Park—*park* NY-2
Bennett Park—*park* OH-6
Bennett Pass—*gap* NV-8
Bennett Pass—*gap* OR-9
Bennett Peak—*summit* (2) CA-9
Bennett Peak—*summit* CO-8
Bennett Peak—*summit* ID-8
Bennett Peak—*summit* NM-5
Bennett Peak—*summit* WY-8
Bennett Place—*locale* (2) TX-5
Bennett Place—*locale* WY-8
Bennett Place State Historic Site—*hist pl* NC-3
Bennett Plantation House and Store—*hist pl* LA-4
Bennett Point—*cape* DE-2
Bennett Point—*cape* MD-2
Bennett Point—*cape* OR-9
Bennett Point—*cape* TX-5
Bennett Point—*summit* ID-8
*Bennett Pond* NC-3
Bennett Pond—*lake* AL-4
Bennett Pond—*lake* DE-2
Bennett Pond—*lake* GA-3
Bennett Pond—*lake* ME-1
Bennett Pond—*lake* (3) MA-1
Bennett Pond—*lake* NY-2
Bennett Pond *reservoir* MA-1
Bennett Pond Dam—*dam* MA-1
Bennett Ponds—*lake* CT-1
Bennett Post Office (historical)—*building* TN-4
Bennett Ranch—*locale* AZ-5
Bennett Ranch—*locale* CO-8
Bennett Ranch—*locale* (2) ID-8
Bennett Ranch—*locale* MT-8
Bennett Ranch—*locale* (3) NM-5
Bennett Ranch—*locale* (2) TX-5
Bennett Ranch—*locale* WA-9
Bennett Ranch—*locale* (2) WY-8
*Bennett Reservoir* CO-8
Bennett Ridge—*locale* NY-2
Bennett Ridge—*ridge* ME-1
Bennett Ridge—*ridge* MS-4
Bennett Ridge—*ridge* MO-7
Bennett Ridge—*ridge* TN-4
Bennett Ridge—*ridge* WA-9
Bennett Ridge—*ridge* WI-6
*Bennett River* AR-4
Bennett Rock—*summit* OR-9
Bennett Rock Cabin—*locale* AK-9
Bennett Rockshelter—*hist pl* CT-1
Bennett Rsvr—*reservoir* CO-8
Bennett Rsvr—*reservoir* ID-8
Bennett Rsvr—*reservoir* NE-7
Bennett Rsvr—*reservoir* OR-9
Bennett Run—*stream* OH-6
Bennett Run—*stream* (3) PA-2
Bennett Run—*stream* VA-3
Bennett Run—*stream* (6) WV-2
*Bennetts* IN-6
*Bennetts* PA-2
Bennetts—*locale* (2) NY-2
Bennett's Adventure—*hist pl* MD-2
Bennett Sand Hills—*summit* TX-5
Bennetts Basin—*basin* CO-8
*Bennetts Basin Gulch* CO-8
Bennetts Bay—*bay* MT-8
Bennetts Bay—*swamp* NC-3
Bennetts Bayou—*stream* AR-4
Bennetts Bayou—*stream* MO-7
**Bennetts (Bennetts Switch)**—*pop pl* IN-6
*Bennetts Branch* PA-2
Bennetts Branch—*stream* IN-6
Bennetts Branch—*stream* KY-4
*Bennetts Branch Creek* PA-2
Bennetts Bridge—*bridge* NC-3
Bennetts Brook—*stream* MA-1
**Bennettsburg**—*pop pl* NY-2
*Bennetts Canyon* CA-9
Bennetts Canyon—*valley* UT-8
Bennetts Cem—*cemetery* TX-5
Bennett Sch—*school* (2) CA-9
Bennett Sch—*school* FL-3
Bennett Sch—*school* IL-6
Bennett Sch—*school* IN-6
Bennett Sch—*school* MA-1
Bennett Sch—*school* (4) MI-6
Bennett Sch—*school* NY-2
Bennett Sch—*school* OH-6
Bennett Sch—*school* SD-7
Bennett Sch—*school* TX-5
Bennett Sch—*school* VA-3
*Bennetts Chapel* AL-4
Bennett Sch (historical)—*school* AL-4
*Bennett School* MS-4
Bennett School (abandoned)—*locale* WI-6
Bennett Schoolhouse Road Covered Bridge—*hist pl* OH-6
Bennetts Corner—*locale* PA-2
**Bennetts Corner**—*pop pl* MA-1
Bennetts Corners—*locale* NY-2
**Bennetts Corners**—*pop pl* (3) NY-2
**Bennetts Corners**—*pop pl* OH-6
Bennetts Coulee—*valley* ND-7
*Bennetts Creek* AL-4
*Bennetts Creek* AR-4
*Bennetts Creek* CO-8
*Bennetts Creek* NJ-2
Bennetts Creek—*stream* FL-3
Bennetts Creek—*stream* NY-2
Bennetts Creek—*stream* PA-2
Bennetts Creek—*stream* (2) TN-4
Bennetts Creek—*uninc pl* VA-3
Bennetts Creek Park and Nike Site—*military* VA-3
Bennettsen Lake—*lake* WA-9
*Bennetts Ferry* TN-4
*Bennetts Fork* KY-4
Bennetts Fork—*stream* KY-4
Bennetts Fork—*stream* TN-4
Bennetts Fork Ch—*church* KY-4
Bennetts Grove—*area* ID-8
*Bennetts Harbor* VA-3
Bennetts Harbor—*uninc pl* VA-3
Bennetts Knob—*summit* MA-1
Bennetts Lake—*reservoir* AL-4
Bennetts Lake—*reservoir* NC-3
Bennetts Lake Dam—*dam* NC-3
Bennetts Lake Quarry—*mine* TN-4
Bennetts Landing—*locale* GA-3
Bennetts Landing—*locale* MS-4
Bennetts Landing (historical)—*locale* MS-4
Bennett Slough—*gut* CA-9
Bennett Slough—*gut* KY-4
Bennetts Memorial Park—*park* MS-4
Bennetts Methodist Ch (historical)—*church* TN-4
Bennetts Mill—*locale* NJ-2
Bennetts Mill—*locale* VA-3
Bennett's Mill Covered Bridge—*hist pl* KY-4
**Bennetts Mills**—*pop pl* NJ-2
Bennetts Mills Dam—*dam* NJ-2
*Bennetts Neck* MA-1
Bennetts Oil Field—*oilfield* UT-8
Bennetts Pass—*gap* ID-8
Bennetts Pier—*locale* DE-2
*Bennetts Point* FL-3
*Bennett's Point* MD-2
Bennetts Point—*cape* SC-3
Bennetts Point—*cape* VA-3
**Bennetts Point**—*pop pl* SC-3
Bennetts Point Sch—*school* SC-3
Bennetts Pond—*reservoir* NJ-2
Bennetts Pond Brook—*stream* MA-1
Bennett Spring—*spring* (2) AZ-5
Bennett Spring—*spring* CA-9
Bennett Spring—*spring* ID-8
Bennett Spring—*spring* MO-7
Bennett Spring—*spring* NV-8
Bennett Spring—*spring* NM-5
Bennett Spring—*spring* (2) OR-9
Bennett Spring—*spring* WA-9
*Bennett Spring Creek* MO-7
Bennett Spring Natural Tunnel—*tunnel* MO-7
**Bennett Springs**—*pop pl* MO-7
**Bennett Springs**—*pop pl* VA-3
Bennett Springs—*spring* NV-8
Bennett Spring State Park—*park* MO-7
Bennett Spring State Park Hatchery-Lodge Area Hist Dist—*hist pl* MO-7
Bennett Spring State Park Shelter House and Water Gauge Station—*hist pl* MO-7
Bennett Spring State Public Access Area—*area* MO-7
Bennett Springs Wash—*stream* NV-8
Bennetts Ridge—*ridge* VT-1
Bennetts River—*stream* AR-4
Bennetts River—*stream* MO-7
*Bennetts Run* PA-2
Bennetts Run—*stream* (2) PA-2
Bennetts Run—*stream* VA-3
Bennetts Spring—*spring* ID-8
*Bennetts Station* AL-4
Bennetts Store (historical)—*locale* AL-4
Bennetts Store (historical)—*locale* MS-4
**Bennetts Switch**—*pop pl* IN-6
Bennett State Wildlife Mngmt Area—*park* MN-6
**Bennettstown**—*pop pl* KY-4
Bennett Strip Airp—*airport* IN-6
**Bennett Subdivision**—*pop pl* MS-4
Bennettsville—*other* KY-4
**Bennettsville**—*pop pl* IN-6
**Bennettsville**—*pop pl* IA-7
**Bennettsville**—*pop pl* NY-2
**Bennettsville**—*pop pl* SC-3
Bennettsville Bridge (historical)—*bridge* AL-4
Bennettsville (CCD)—*cens area* SC-3
Bennettsville Creek—*stream* NY-2
Bennettsville Hist Dist—*hist pl* SC-3
Bennettsville (historical)—*locale* AL-4
Bennettsville Southwest—*CDP* SC-3
Bennett Swamp—*stream* SC-3
Bennett Swamp—*swamp* FL-3
Bennetts Well—*well* CA-9
Bennett Tank—*reservoir* (2) AZ-5
Bennett Tank—*reservoir* (2) NM-5
Bennett-Tobler-Pace-Oliver House—*hist pl* MO-7
**Bennett (Town of)**—*pop pl* WI-6
**Bennett Township**—*pop pl* KS-7
**Bennett Township**—*pop pl* NE-7
Bennett (Township of)—*fmr MCD* AR-4
Bennett Tract—*civil* CA-9
Bennett Valley—*basin* CA-9
Bennett Valley—*basin* NE-7
Bennett Valley—*valley* (2) CA-9
Bennett Valley—*valley* WI-6
Bennett Valley Grange Hall—*locale* CA-9
Bennett Valley Sch—*school* CA-9
**Bennettville**—*pop pl* MN-6
Bennettville Cem—*cemetery* MN-6
Bennett Vly—*swamp* NY-2
Bennett Wash—*stream* (2) AZ-5
Bennett Wash—*stream* CA-9
Bennett Weatherly Cem—*cemetery* NY-2
Bennett Well—*well* OR-9
Bennett Well—*well* SD-7
Bennett-Williams House—*hist pl* OR-9
Bennett York Dam—*dam* MS-4
*Bennetville* AL-4
*Bennet Water Bog* LA-4
Ben Nevis—*summit* WA-9
Ben Nevis Mtn—*summit* AZ-5
Benneys Bay—*bay* LA-4
Benneys Creek—*stream* NC-3
*Bennezette* PA-2
Bennezette Ch—*church* IA-7
Bennezette Township—*fmr MCD* IA-7
Bennie Branch—*stream* MO-7
Bennie Brook—*stream* NY-2
Bennie Creek—*stream* MT-8
Bennie Creek—*stream* UT-8
Bennie Creek Ridge—*ridge* UT-8
Bennie-Dillon Bldg—*hist pl* TN-4
Bennie Hill—*summit* MT-8
*Bennie Kill* NY-2
Bennie Peer Creek—*stream* MT-8
Bennie Peer Creek—*stream* ND-7
*Bennie Pierre Creek* MT-8
*Bennie Pierre Creek* ND-7
Bennies Branch—*stream* NC-3
Bennies Brook—*stream* NY-2
Bennie Sch—*school* MI-6
Bennie Sch (historical)—*school* MS-4
Bennies Day Care and Kindergarten—*school* FL-3
Bennies Hill Road Bridge—*hist pl* MD-2
Bennies Pass—*gut* LA-4
Bennies Pond—*bay* LA-4
*Bennie water Pond* NY-2
*Bennie Whitmore Brook* NY-2
Bennifield Cem—*cemetery* MO-7
Benning—*locale* MN-6
**Benning**—*pop pl* DC-2
Benning Bridge—*bridge* DC-2
Benning Creek—*stream* MT-8
Benninger Canyon—*valley* CA-9
Benninger Creek—*stream* (2) PA-2
Benninger Playground—*park* NY-2
*Benningers* PA-2
*Benningers Run* PA-2
Benningfield Cem—*cemetery* KY-4
Benningfield Chapel—*church* KY-4
Benningfield Creek—*stream* OK-5
**Benning Heights**—*pop pl* DC-2
**Benning Hills**—*pop pl* GA-3
Benning Hill Sch—*school* GA-3
Benninghofen House—*hist pl* OH-6
Benninghoff Ditch—*canal* IN-6
Benninghof Run—*stream* PA-2
Benning Hollow—*valley* MO-7
Benning Lake—*lake* MN-6
Benning Lookout (historical)—*locale* ID-8
Benning Mtn—*summit* ID-8
**Benning Park**—*pop pl* GA-3
Benning Ridge—*ridge* MO-7
Benning RR Yard—*locale* DC-2
*Bennings* DC-2
Benning Sch—*school* DC-2
Benningsfield Creek—*stream* SC-3
Bennington—*locale* PA-2
**Bennington**—*pop pl* ID-8
**Bennington**—*pop pl* IL-6
**Bennington**—*pop pl* IN-6
**Bennington**—*pop pl* KS-7
**Bennington**—*pop pl* MI-6
**Bennington**—*pop pl* NE-7
**Bennington**—*pop pl* NH-1
**Bennington**—*pop pl* NY-2
**Bennington**—*pop pl* OK-5
**Bennington**—*pop pl* VT-1
Bennington And Perry Drain—*canal* MI-6
Bennington Battlefield—*hist pl* NY-2
Bennington Battlefield Park—*park* NY-2
Bennington Battle Monmt—*hist pl* VT-1
Bennington Canyon—*valley* ID-8
Bennington Cem—*cemetery* MN-6
Bennington Cem—*cemetery* OH-6
Bennington Cem—*cemetery* PA-2
*Bennington Center* VT-1
Bennington Center—*other* VT-1
Bennington Ch—*church* OK-5
Bennington Chapel—*church* OH-6
Bennington Coll—*school* VT-1
*Bennington College* VT-1
**Bennington County**—*pop pl* VT-1
Bennington Drain—*canal* MI-6
Bennington Falls—*other* VT-1
Bennington Falls Covered Bridge—*hist pl* VT-1
Bennington (hitorical P.O.)—*locale* IA-7
Bennington HS—*school* KS-7
*Bennington Island* PA-2
Bennington Lake—*reservoir* IN-6
Bennington Levee—*levee* (2) IN-6
Bennington Mill—*locale* VA-3
Bennington Monument—*other* CA-9
Bennington Post Office—*hist pl* VT-1
Bennington RR Station—*hist pl* VT-1
Bennington Sch—*school* IL-6
Bennington Spring Run—*stream* PA-2
*Benningtons Spring Run* PA-2
**Bennington (Town of)**—*pop pl* NH-1
**Bennington (Town of)**—*pop pl* NY-2
**Bennington (Town of)**—*pop pl* VT-1
Bennington Township—*fmr MCD* IA-7
**Bennington Township**—*pop pl* KS-7
**Bennington (Township of)**—*pop pl* IL-6
**Bennington (Township of)**—*pop pl* MI-6
**Bennington (Township of)**—*pop pl* MN-6
**Bennington (Township of)**—*pop pl* (2) OH-6
Bennink-Douglas Cottages—*hist pl* MA-1
**Bennion**—*pop pl* UT-8
**Bennion Court Estates (subdivision)**—*pop pl* UT-8
**Bennion Cove Subdivision**—*pop pl* UT-8
Bennion Creek—*stream* (2) UT-8
**Bennion Estates (subdivision)**—*pop pl* UT-8
Bennion JHS—*school* UT-8
Bennion Lake—*lake* UT-8
Bennion Park—*flat* UT-8
**Bennion Park Subdivision**—*pop pl* UT-8
**Bennion Plaza Subdivision**—*pop pl* UT-8
Bennion Ridge—*ridge* UT-8
Bennion Sch—*school* UT-8
Bennion Spring—*spring* UT-8
Bennis Bowl—*basin* CA-9
*Bennis Brook* NY-2
Benn Knob—*summit* NC-3
Benn Memorial Park—*park* WA-9
Bennock Millpond—*reservoir* GA-3
Bennor Draw—*valley* WY-8
Bennor Rsvr—*reservoir* WY-8
Benns Branch—*stream* VA-3
**Benns Church**—*pop pl* VA-3
**Bennsville**—*pop pl* MD-2
Bennsville Siding—*locale* MD-2
Bennum—*locale* DE-2
Ben Nutt Creek—*stream* WI-6
*Bennview* TX-5
Bennview—*other* TX-5
Benny Babcock Park—*park* FL-3
*Benny Bayou* FL-3
Benny Branch—*stream* AL-4
Benny Branch—*stream* VA-3
Benny Branch—*stream* WV-2
Benny Cove—*valley* NC-3
Benny Creek—*stream* AZ-5
Benny Creek—*stream* CO-8
Benny Creek—*stream* OR-9
Benny Creek Campground—*park* AZ-5
Bennyfield Cem—*cemetery* TN-4
Benny Gray Point—*cape* MD-2
*Benny Hawk Creek* OR-9
Bennyhoof Creek—*stream* PA-2
Benny Lake—*lake* MI-6
Benny Lake—*lake* WI-6
*Benny Pierre Creek* MT-8
*Benny Pierre Creek* ND-7
Benny Ridge—*ridge* NC-3
Benny Run—*stream* WV-2
Bennys Landing—*locale* NJ-2
*Bennys Point* NJ-2
Bennys Run—*stream* (2) PA-2
*Bennys Shoal* NJ-2
*Benny Tank* AZ-5
Benny Well—*well* TX-5
Bennywood Sch (abandoned)—*school* MO-7
**Beno**—*pop pl* KY-4
**Ben Oaks**—*pop pl* MD-2
Ben Odell Rsvr—*reservoir* OR-9
Benoist, Louis Auguste, House—*hist pl* MO-7
Benoit—*locale* MN-6
Benoit—*locale* TX-5
**Benoit**—*pop pl* AL-4
**Benoit**—*pop pl* MS-4
**Benoit**—*pop pl* WI-6
Benoit, Bayou—*gut* LA-4
Benoit, Lake—*lake* LA-4
Benoit Bayou—*gut* LA-4
Benoit Bend—*bend* AL-4
Benoit Cem—*cemetery* LA-4
Benoit HS—*school* MS-4
Benoit Lake—*lake* WI-6
Benoit Post Office (historical)—*building* AL-4
Benoit Sch—*school* SD-7
Benolken Ranch—*locale* MT-8
*Benona* MI-6
Benona Sch—*school* MI-6
**Benona (Township of)**—*pop pl* MI-6
Benoni—*cape* MD-2
*Benonies Point* MD-2
Benonine—*locale* TX-5
*Benon Point* MD-2
*Benore* PA-2
Ben Ortiz Peak—*summit* NM-5
Ben Owens Creek—*stream* GA-3
Ben Parton Lookout—*summit* TN-4
Ben Phillips Cem—*cemetery* TN-4
Ben Pilot Creek—*gut* FL-3
Ben Pilot Point—*cape* FL-3
Ben Point—*summit* OR-9
Ben Pond—*swamp* SC-3
*Ben Poodle Branch* AR-4
**Ben Rancho Acres Subdivision**—*pop pl* UT-8
Ben Robins Landing—*locale* DE-2
Ben Rose Branch—*stream* KY-4
Ben Rose Cave—*cave* AL-4
Ben Ross Rsvr—*reservoir* ID-8
*Ben Routh Lake* LA-4
Benroy—*locale* WA-9
**Benroy**—*pop pl* PA-2
Ben RR Station—*building* AZ-5
Ben Run—*stream* WV-2
Bensalem—*post sta* PA-2
Ben Salem Cem—*cemetery* MS-4
Bensalem Ch—*church* NC-3
Ben Salem Ch—*church* PA-2
Bensalem Ch—*church* (2) PA-2
Bensalem Ch (historical)—*church* MS-4
Bensalem Township—*CDP* PA-2
Bensalem Township HS—*school* PA-2
**Bensalem (Township of)**—*pop pl* PA-2
Ben Saylor Branch—*stream* KY-4
Bens Bayou—*gut* LA-4
Bens Bayou—*stream* LA-4
*Bens Branch* VA-3
Bens Branch—*locale* KS-7
Bens Branch—*stream* AR-4
Bens Branch—*stream* GA-3
Bens Branch—*stream* KY-4
Bens Branch—*stream* MD-2
Bens Branch—*stream* NC-3
Bens Branch—*stream* TN-4
Bens Branch—*stream* TX-5
Bens Branch—*stream* (2) VA-3
Bens Branch Sch—*school* AR-4
Bensch Drain—*canal* MI-6
Bens Cliff—*cliff* KY-4
Benscoter Valley—*basin* NE-7
Bens Cove—*valley* NC-3
*Bens Creek* ID-8
*Bens Creek* TX-5
*Bens Creek* WV-2
**Bens Creek**—*pop pl* (3) PA-2
Bens Creek—*stream* AR-4
Bens Creek—*stream* CA-9
Bens Creek—*stream* FL-3
Bens Creek—*stream* IN-6
Bens Creek—*stream* LA-4
Bens Creek—*stream* NC-3
Bens Creek—*stream* OR-9
Bens Creek—*stream* (2) PA-2
Bens Creek—*stream* SC-3
Bens Creek Ch—*church* PA-2
Bens Dam Tank—*reservoir* AZ-5
Bensel Pond—*lake* WI-6
*Bensen* AL-4
Bensen, John N., House—*hist pl* MN-6
Bensen Cem—*cemetery* MO-7
Bensen Lake—*lake* (2) MN-6
**Bensenville**—*pop pl* IL-6
Bensenville Ditch—*canal* IL-6
Bens Flat—*flat* NE-7
Bens Flats—*flat* WV-2
Bens Fork—*stream* KY-4
Bens Fork—*stream* WV-2
Ben Shavis Park—*park* FL-3
Bens Hill—*summit* WV-2
Benshoff Hill Cem—*cemetery* PA-2
Bens Hole Branch—*stream* KY-4
Bens Hole Creek—*stream* TX-5
*Ben Silvers Lake* MI-6
Bensing Park—*park* NM-5
*Bens Island* MD-2
Bens Knob—*summit* WV-2
Bens Lake—*lake* FL-3
Bens Lake—*lake* IL-6
Bens Lake—*lake* LA-4
Bens Lake—*lake* SC-3
**Ben's Lake**—*pop pl* FL-3
Ben Slaughter Draw—*valley* NM-5
Ben Slaughter Spring—*spring* NM-5
Bensley—*CDP* VA-3
Bensley Creek—*stream* MT-8
Bensley Flat—*flat* OR-9
Bensley Park—*park* IL-6
Bensley Point—*cape* RI-1
*Bensleys Point* RI-1
**Bensley Village**—*pop pl* VA-3
Bens Lick—*stream* KY-4
Ben Slough—*gut* MS-4
Ben Smith Branch—*stream* KY-4
Ben Smith Creek—*stream* OR-9
Ben Smith Dam—*dam* MA-1
Ben Smith Hollow—*valley* OK-5
Ben Socker Hill—*summit* NY-2
*Benson* (2) AL-4
*Benson* ND-7
Benson—*fmr MCD* NE-7
Benson—*locale* IA-7
Benson—*locale* KY-4
Benson—*locale* ME-1
Benson—*locale* MI-6
Benson—*locale* MS-4
Benson—*locale* NY-2
Benson—*locale* WV-2
Benson—*locale* WI-6
**Benson**—*pop pl* AZ-5
**Benson**—*pop pl* IL-6
**Benson**—*pop pl* LA-4
**Benson**—*pop pl* MD-2
**Benson**—*pop pl* MN-6
**Benson**—*pop pl* NC-3
**Benson**—*pop pl* PA-2
**Benson**—*pop pl* UT-8
**Benson**—*pop pl* VT-1
Benson, John G., House—*hist pl* NJ-2
Benson, Judge Henry L., House—*hist pl* OR-9
Benson, Lake—*lake* MI-6
Benson, Lake—*lake* ND-7
Benson, Lake—*reservoir* NC-3
Benson, Mount—*summit* AK-9
Benson, Simon, House—*hist pl* OR-9
*Benson Acres* NE-7
Benson Airp—*airport* AZ-5
Benson Airp—*airport* PA-2
Benson Archeol Site (13WD50)—*hist pl* IA-7
Benson Bay—*bay* VT-1
Benson Bayou—*stream* TX-5
Benson Bldg—*hist pl* MD-2
Benson Block—*hist pl* IA-7
Benson Borough—*civil* PA-2
Benson Branch—*stream* AL-4
Benson Branch—*stream* GA-3
Benson Branch—*stream* MD-2
Benson Branch—*stream* NC-3
Benson Branch—*stream* TN-4
Benson Bridge—*bridge* AR-4
Benson Bridge Ch—*church* AR-4
Benson Brook—*stream* (3) ME-1
Benson Brook—*stream* MA-1
Benson Canal—*canal* LA-4
Benson Canal—*canal* UT-8
Benson Canyon—*valley* NM-5
Benson Cave—*cave* TN-4
Benson (CCD)—*cens area* AZ-5
Benson Cem—*cemetery* AZ-5
Benson Cem—*cemetery* IN-6
Benson Cem—*cemetery* IA-7
Benson Cem—*cemetery* LA-4
Benson Cem—*cemetery* (4) MS-4
Benson Cem—*cemetery* NM-5
Benson Cem—*cemetery* (2) NC-3
Benson Cem—*cemetery* SC-3
*Benson Center* NY-2
Benson Ch—*church* AL-4
Benson Ch—*church* IN-6
Benson Ch—*church* KY-4
Benson Ch—*church* NC-3
Benson Chapel—*church* IN-6
Benson City Hall—*building* AZ-5
Benson Corner—*locale* ND-7
*Benson Corners* ND-7
Benson Corners—*locale* NY-2
Benson Coulee—*valley* MT-8
Benson County—*civil* ND-7
Benson County Courthouse—*hist pl* ND-7
*Benson Creek* AR-4
Benson Creek—*stream* AL-4
Benson Creek—*stream* AK-9
Benson Creek—*stream* CO-8
Benson Creek—*stream* KY-4
Benson Creek—*stream* MI-6
Benson Creek—*stream* (2) MT-8
Benson Creek—*stream* NC-3
Benson Creek—*stream* (3) OR-9
Benson Creek—*stream* (3) UT-8
Benson Creek—*stream* (3) WA-9
Benson Creek—*stream* WI-6
Benson Creek State Wildlife Mngmt Area—*park* WI-6
Benson Dam—*dam* OR-9
Benson Dam—*dam* SD-7
Benson-Davis Ranch—*locale* CA-9
Benson Drain—*canal* ID-8
Benson Draw—*valley* MT-8
Benson Draw—*valley* UT-8
*Benson Dry Lake* CA-9
**Benson East**—*pop pl* PA-2
Benson Elem Sch—*hist pl* UT-8
Benson Elem Sch—*school* AZ-5
Benson Elem Sch—*school* NC-3
*Benson Gardens* NE-7
Benson Glacier—*glacier* OR-9
Benson Grove Ch—*church* NC-3
Benson Gulch—*valley* (2) CA-9
Benson Gulch—*valley* ID-8
Benson Gulch—*valley* (3) OR-9
**Benson Highway**—*pop pl* AZ-5
Benson Highway-Valencia Road Interchange—*crossing* AZ-5
Benson Hill—*summit* ME-1

Benwood—*locale* OH-6
**Benwood**—*pop pl* IN-6
**Benwood**—*pop pl* WV-2
Ben Wood Brook—*stream* NY-2
**Benwood Junction**—*pop pl* WV-2
Benwood Lake—*lake* AR-4
Benwood Meadow—*swamp* CA-9
Ben Wood Mtn—*summit* NY-2
Benwood Run—*stream* IN-6
**Benwood Subdivision**—*pop pl* UT-8
Benwy Canyon—*valley* WA-9
Benyan Creek—*stream* KY-4
Beny Cem—*cemetery* LA-4
Beny Hollow—*valley* PA-2
Ben Young Cave—*cave* AL-4
Ben Young Creek—*stream* OR-9
Ben Young Hill—*summit* NH-1
Benz—*locale* MT-8
Benzal—*locale* AR-4
Benzarino, Mount—*summit* WA-9
Benzeman Lake—*lake* AK-9
Benzes Draw—*valley* AZ-5
*Benzette* PA-2
Benz Hill—*summit* IN-6
*Benzi Dam* ND-7
**Benzie (County)**—*pop pl* MI-6
Benzien—*locale* MT-8
Benzie State Park—*park* MI-6
Benzinger—*locale* PA-2
**Benzinger (Township of)**—*pop pl* PA-2
Benz Lake—*lake* (2) MN-6
Benz Lake—*lake* WI-6
**Benzonia**—*pop pl* MI-6
**Benzonia (Township of)**—*pop pl* MI-6
Benz Pond—*lake* NY-2
Benz Spring—*spring* OR-9
*Beoadic Mtn* MA-1
Beoadic Mtn—*summit* MA-1
Beoshear Cem—*cemetery* MS-4
Beotia (historical)—*locale* SD-7
**Beotia Township**—*pop pl* SD-7
Beotia Township (historical)—*civil* SD-7
*Beovert Island* OR-9
**Beowawe**—*pop pl* NV 8
*Beowawe Geysers* NV-8
Beowawe Township—*inact MCD* NV-8
Bepler, August, House—*hist pl* OH-6
**Beppo (historical)**—*pop pl* MS-4
Beppo Siding—*locale* UT-8
Bequaith Cem No 1—*cemetery* IL-6
Bequaith Cem No 2—*cemetery* IL-6
Bequette Canyon—*valley* CA-9
Bequette Cem—*cemetery* MO-7
Bera Ch—*church* NC-3
Berachah Acad—*school* AL-4
Berachan Ch—*church* PA-2
*Berage Island* MP-9
Bera (historical)—*locale* AL-4
Berake—*island* MP-9
*Beran Baptist Church* AL-4
Beranek Cem—*cemetery* NE-7
*Berang* MP-9
Berangu—*island* MP-9
*Berangu Island* MP-9
Berangu Passage—*channel* MP-9
*Berangu-Suido* MP-9
*Berangu-to* MP-9
**Berard**—*pop pl* LA-4
Berard Canal, Bayou—*canal* LA-4
Berard Creek—*stream* NE-7
Bera Sch (historical)—*school* AL-4
*Berbeck* KS-7
Berbecker Park—*park* IL-6
Berby Hollow—*valley* NY-2
Bercham Cem—*cemetery* AR-4
Bercham Draw—*valley* NM-5
B'er Chayim Temple—*hist pl* MD-2
Berchfield Lake—*lake* FL-3
Berch Hole—*locale* OK-5
Berch Lake—*lake* MI-6
Berchmans Hall—*building* NH-1
Berchmans Sch—*school* IL-6
*Bercich Peak* AZ-5
Bercich Ranch—*locale* AZ-5
Berckerley Dam—*dam* ND-7
**Berclair**—*pop pl* MS-4
**Berclair**—*pop pl* TX-5
Berclair—*uninc pl* TN-4
Berclair Post Office (historical)—*building* MS-4
Berclair Sch—*school* TN-4
Berdahl-Rolvaag House—*hist pl* SD-7
**Berdan**—*pop pl* IL-6
Berdan, G. V. H., House—*hist pl* NJ-2
Berdan, Richard J., House—*hist pl* NJ-2
Berdan Bldg—*hist pl* OH-6
Berdan Heights Ch—*church* NJ-2
Berdeen Lake—*lake* WA-9
Berdeen Stream—*stream* ME-1
**Berdell Hills**—*pop pl* MO-7
*Berdick Pond* IL-6
Berdick Slough—*gut* IL-6
Berdine Bar—*bar* TN-4
**Berdines Corner**—*pop pl* NJ-2
**Berdines Corners**—*pop pl* NJ-2
Berding, A., House—*hist pl* CA-9
Berdon Plaza (Shop Ctr)—*locale* MA-1
Berdoo Canyon—*valley* CA-9
Berea—*locale* AR-4
Berea—*locale* IA-7
Berea—*locale* NY-2
Berea—*locale* ND-7
Berea—*locale* TN-4
Berea—*locale* TX-5
Berea—*locale* VA-3
**Berea**—*pop pl* KY-4
**Berea**—*pop pl* NE-7
**Berea**—*pop pl* NC-3
**Berea**—*pop pl* OH-6
**Berea**—*pop pl* SC-3
**Berea**—*pop pl* TN-4
**Berea**—*pop pl* TX-5
**Berea**—*pop pl* WV-2
*Berea Baptist Church* MS-4
Berea Baptist Church Day Sch—*school* FL-3
Berea (CCD)—*cens area* KY-4
Berea Cem—*cemetery* (2) AL-4
Berea Cem—*cemetery* KS-7
Berea Cem—*cemetery* KY-4
Berea Cem—*cemetery* MS-4
Berea Cem—*cemetery* NY-2
Berea Cem—*cemetery* (2) TN-4
Berea Cem—*cemetery* VA-3
Berea Ch—*church* (5) AL-4
Berea Ch—*church* CT-1
Berea Ch—*church* (2) FL-3
Berea Ch—*church* (2) GA-3
Berea Ch—*church* (2) IL-6
Berea Ch—*church* (4) IN-6
Berea Ch—*church* (2) IA-7
Berea Ch—*church* (6) KY-4
Berea Ch—*church* MN-6
Berea Ch—*church* (3) MS-4
Berea Ch—*church* (4) MO-7
Berea Ch—*church* NE-7
Berea Ch—*church* (11) NC-3
Berea Ch—*church* OH-6
Berea Ch—*church* PA-2
Berea Ch—*church* (6) SC-3
Berea Ch—*church* (6) TN-4
Berea Ch—*church* TX-5
Berea Ch—*church* (5) VA-3
Berea Chapel—*church* AR-4
Berea Chapel—*church* OH-6
Berea Chapel—*church* VA-3
Berea Ch (historical)—*church* TN-4
*Berea Ch of Christ* AL-4
*Berea Ch of Christ* MS-4
Berea Coll—*school* KY-4
Berea College (RR name for College)—*other* KY-4
Berea Creek—*stream* MS-4
Berea Creek—*stream* NE-7
Berea District 7 Sch—*hist pl* OH-6
Bereah—*locale* FL-3
**Berea (historical)**—*pop pl* MS-4
**Berea (historical)**—*pop pl* TN-4
Bereum Ch—*church* MS-4
Berean—*locale* MD-2
Berean Acad—*school* KS-7
Berean Acad—*school* TX-5
Berean Baptist Ch—*church* (2) AL-4
Berean Baptist Ch—*church* (2) FL-3
Berean Baptist Ch—*church* (2) UT-8
Boroan Bible Ch—*church* MS-4
Berean Cem—*cemetery* IL-6
Berean Cem—*cemetery* TX-5
*Berean Ch* AL-4
Berean Ch—*church* AL-4
Berean Ch—*church* (2) FL-3
Berean Ch—*church* GA-3
Berean Ch—*church* KY-4
Berean Ch—*church* ME-1
Berean Ch—*church* MI-6
Berean Ch—*church* (3) MN-6
Berean Ch—*church* (2) NY-2
Berean Ch—*church* PA-2
Berean Ch—*church* (4) TX-5
Berean Ch—*church* VA-3
Berean Ch—*church* WV-2
Berean Ch—*church* WI-6
Berean Christian Sch—*school* FL-3
Berean Grace Ch—*church* WI-6
Berean Mennonite Ch—*church* FL-3
Berean Mission—*church* NM-5
Berean Sch—*school* FL-3
Berean Sch—*school* IL-6
Berean Sch—*school* MO-7
Berean Sch—*school* NM-5
Berean Seventh Day Adventist Ch—*church* MS-4
Berea Sch—*school* IL-6
Berea Sch (historical)—*school* MS-4
Berea Sch (historical)—*school* (2) TN-4
*Berea (sta.)* OH-6
Berea Township (historical)—*civil* SD-7
Bereau Brook—*stream* ME-1
Berea Union Depot—*hist pl* OH-6
**Berenda**—*pop pl* CA-9
Berenda Canyon—*stream* NM-5
Berenda Creek—*stream* CA-9
Berenda Creek—*stream* NM-5
Berenda Slough—*stream* CA-9
Berenda Well—*well* TX-5
Berend Lake—*lake* MN-6
*Berendo* CA-9
Berendo JHS—*school* CA-9
*Berendo Slough* CA-9
Berendsen Lake—*lake* WI-6
Berendsen Sch (historical)—*school* TN-4
Berenice—*locale* ID-8
Berens Sch—*school* SD-7
Bererjan Island—*island* MP-9
Beresford—*locale* FL-3
**Beresford**—*pop pl* SD-7
Beresford, Lake—*lake* FL-3
Beresford Bend—*bend* FL-3
Beresford Cem—*cemetery* SD-7
Beresford Creek—*stream* SC-3
Beresford Lateral—*canal* SD-7
**Beresford Manor**—*pop pl* FL-3
Beresford Park—*park* CA-9
Beresford Park Sch—*school* CA-9
Beresford Peninsula—*cape* FL-3
Beresford Ranch—*locale* CA-9
Beresheim, August, House—*hist pl* IA-7
Berford Electric Company Lake Dam—*dam* MS-4
*Berg* WA-9
Berg—*locale* AK-9
Berg—*locale* CA-9
Berg, Henry, Bldg—*hist pl* IA-7
Berg, William H., House—*hist pl* NV-8
*Berg Adeamar* FM-9
*Berg Ademar* FM-9
Bergamot (historical)—*locale* AL-4
Bergamot Sch (historical)—*school* AL-4
Bergan Hosp—*hospital* NE-7
Bergan HS—*school* IL-6
Bergan Point—*cape* NY-2
Bergan Sch—*school* IL-6
Berg Basin—*basin* AK-9
Berg Bay—*bay* (2) AK-9
Berg Brook—*stream* IN-6
Berg Camp—*locale* WA-9
Berg Canal—*canal* LA-4
Berg Cem—*cemetery* KS-7
Berg Cem—*cemetery* MI-6
Berg Cem—*cemetery* NE-7
Berg Cem—*cemetery* SD-7
Berg Ch—*church* OH-6
Berg Coulee—*valley* ND-7
*Berg Creek* MI-6
Berg Creek—*stream* (3) AK-9
Berg Creek—*stream* ID-8
Berg Creek—*stream* MI-6
Berg Creek—*stream* (2) WA-9
Bergdahl Lake—*swamp* MN-6
Bergdahl State Wildlife Mngmt Area—*park* MN-6
*Berg Djukuielu* FM-9
*Berg Djukuram* FM-9
Bergdoll, Louis, House—*hist pl* PA-2
Bergdoll Mansion—*hist pl* PA-2
Bergdorf Township—*civil* SD-7
Berge, Lake—*lake* FL-3
Bergeau Lake—*lake* WA-9
Berge Coulee—*valley* WI-6
Berge Creek—*stream* ID-8
Bergemeyer Cove—*bay* AZ-5
Bergen—*locale* IA-7
**Bergen**—*pop pl* IL-6
**Bergen**—*pop pl* MN-6
**Bergen**—*pop pl* NJ-2
**Bergen**—*pop pl* NY-2
**Bergen**—*pop pl* ND-7
**Bergen**—*pop pl* WI-6
Bergen Basin—*bay* NY-2
**Bergen Beach**—*pop pl* (2) NY-2
**Bergen Beach**—*pop pl* WI-6
Bergen Beach Yacht Club—*other* NY-2
Bergen Branch—*stream* VA-3
*Bergen-Byron Swamp* NY-2
Bergen Cem—*cemetery* IL-6
Bergen Cem—*cemetery* IA-7
Bergen Cem—*cemetery* (2) ND-7
Bergen Ch—*church* MN-6
Bergen Ch—*church* (3) ND-7
Bergen Ch—*church* (3) SD-7
Bergen Community Coll—*school* NJ-2
**Bergen County**—*pop pl* NJ-2
Bergen County Court House Complex—*hist pl* NJ-2
Bergen Creek—*stream* CO-8
Bergen Creek—*stream* NY-2
Bergen Creek—*stream* WI-6
Bergen Dam—*dam* SD-7
Bergen Ditch—*canal* CO-8
Bergene Lake—*lake* WI-6
*Bergen Evergreen Cemetery* SD-7
**Bergenfield**—*pop pl* NJ-2
*Bergen Fields* NJ-2
Bergen (historical)—*locale* SD-7
Bergen Junction—*uninc pl* NJ-2
Bergen Lake—*lake* AR-4
Bergen Lake—*lake* MN-6
Bergen Lake—*lake* ND-7
Bergenline—*uninc pl* NJ-2
*Bergen Lutheran Church* SD-7
*Bergen Luthuran Church* SD-7
Bergen Mall—*post sta* NJ-2
Bergen Mills—*locale* NJ-2
Bergen Mtn—*summit* NC-3
Bergen Mtn—*summit* WA-9
*Bergen Neck* NJ-2
Bergen Park—*park* CO-8
Bergen Park—*park* IL-6
Bergen Park—*park* NY-2
**Bergen Park**—*pop pl* CO-8
**Bergen Park**—*pop pl* NY-2
Bergen Peak—*summit* CO-8
Bergen Pines County Hosp—*hospital* NJ-2
**Bergen Point**—*pop pl* NJ-2
Bergen Point East Reach—*channel* NJ-2
Bergen Point East Reach—*channel* NY-2
Bergen Point West Reach—*channel* NJ-2
Bergen Point West Reach—*channel* NY-2
Bergen Ranch—*locale* NE-7
Bergen Reservoirs—*reservoir* CO-8
Bergen Rock—*pillar* CO-8
Bergen Sch—*school* CO-8
Bergen Sch—*school* MN-6
Bergens (historical)—*locale* AL-4
*Bergens Mills* NJ-2
Bergen Springs—*spring* WI-6
Bergen Square Sch—*school* NJ-2
Bergen Street Sch—*school* NJ-2
**Bergen (Town of)**—*pop pl* NY-2
**Bergen (Town of)**—*pop pl* (2) WI-6
**Bergen Township**—*pop pl* ND-7
**Bergen (Township of)**—*pop pl* MN-6
Bergen Trail—*trail* CO-8
Berge Peak—*summit* ID-8
*Berger* IL-6
Berger—*locale* AR-4
Berger—*locale* ID-8
Berger—*locale* TX-5
**Berger**—*pop pl* MO-7
Berger, Jacob, House—*hist pl* AK-9
Berger Bay—*bay* AK-9
Berger Bay—*bay* CA-9
Berger Bldg—*hist pl* TN-4
*Berger Butte* AZ-5
Berger Butte—*summit* ID-8
Berger Cem—*cemetery* MO-7
Berger Cem—*cemetery* SD-7
Berger Cem—*cemetery* TX-5
*Berger Coulee* WI-6
*Berger Creek* MO-7
Berger Creek—*stream* MT-8
Berger Creek—*stream* NE-7
Berger Creek—*stream* WY-8
Berger Dam—*dam* ND-7
Berger Ditch—*canal* (3) IN-6
Bergere, Alfred M., House—*hist pl* NM-5
Berger Factory—*hist pl* MA-1
Berger-Graham House—*hist pl* AR-4
Berger Hill—*summit* IL-6
Berger Hill—*summit* NY-2
Berger Hill—*summit* WA-9
Berger Hill—*summit* WY-8
Berger Hollow—*valley* PA-2
Berger Hosp—*hospital* OH-6
Berger Island—*island* AK-9
Berger Knob—*summit* KY-4
*Berger Lake* MI-6
Berger Lake—*lake* MN-6
Berger Lake—*reservoir* OR-9
Bergeron Rapids—*rapids* WI-6
Berger Park—*park* OH-6
Berger Pond—*lake* MI-6
Berger Ranch—*locale* TX-5
Berger Ranch—*locale* (2) WY-8
Berger Road Ditch—*canal* OH-6
Berger Rsvr—*reservoir* MT-8
**Bergers**—*pop pl* PA-2
Berger Sch—*school* IL-6
Berger Sch—*school* MI-6
Berger Sch—*school* PA-2
Berger Sch—*school* (2) WI-6
Berger Sch (abandoned)—*school* PA-2
Bergers Creek—*stream* PA-2
Berger Spring—*spring* WY-8
*Bergers Run* PA-2
Bergers Station—*locale* PA-2
Berger Trail—*trail* (2) PA-2
Bergerud State Wildlife Mngmt Area—*park* MN-6
**Berge Run**—*pop pl* PA-2
Berge Run—*stream* PA-2
**Bergerville**—*pop pl* NJ-2
Bergeson Basin—*basin* NE-7
Bergeson Hill—*summit* UT-8
Bergess Lake—*lake* MI-6
**Berg Estates Subdivision**—*pop pl* UT-8
Bergey—*locale* PA-2
*Berg Falata* FM-9
*Berg Fangaden* FM-9
*Berg Fauba* FM-9
*Berg Faumuig* FM-9
Bergfeld Park—*park* TX-5
Bergfield Lake—*reservoir* TX-5
Berg-Green Gulch—*valley* ID-8
Bergguist Spring—*spring* ID-8
Bergheim—*locale* TX-5
Bergheim Cem—*cemetery* TX-5
Bergher Creek—*stream* TX-5
Berg Hill—*summit* VI-3
Bergh Lake—*lake* AK-9
**Bergholtz**—*pop pl* NY-2
Bergholtz Creek—*stream* NY-2
**Bergholz**—*pop pl* OH-6
Bergholz Cem—*cemetery* OH-6
Bergh-Stoutenburgh House—*hist pl* NY-2
Bergier Ranch—*locale* AZ-5
Bergier Tank—*reservoir* AZ-5
Bergie Springs—*spring* WA-9
Bergin Block—*hist pl* ME-1
Bergin Ditch—*canal* WI-6
Bergin Knob—*summit* KY-4
Berginville—*locale* GA-3
*Berg Irou* FM-9
Berg Island—*island* MN-6
Bergit Cem—*cemetery* MN-6
Berg Lake—*lake* AK-9
Berg Lake—*lake* (5) MN-6
Berg Lake—*lake* WI-6
Berg Lake—*reservoir* AR-4
Berg Lakes—*lake* AK-9
**Bergland**—*pop pl* MI-6
Bergland Bay—*bay* MI-6
Bergland Coulee—*valley* MT-8
*Bergland Creek* MI-6
Bergland Lake—*lake* MN-6
Bergland Lookout Tower—*locale* MI-6
**Bergland (Township of)**—*pop pl* MI-6
*Berg Leirelom* FM-9
Berglins Bay—*bay* MN-6
Berglund Gulch—*valley* OR-9
Berglund Lake—*lake* WA-9
Bergman—*other* WV-2
**Bergman**—*pop pl* AR-4
Bergman, Joseph, House—*hist pl* OR-9
Bergman Brook—*stream* MN-6
Bergman Cem—*cemetery* NE-7
Bergman Creek—*stream* AK-9
Bergman Creek—*stream* WI-6
Bergman Gulch—*valley* WA-9
Bergman Island—*island* WI-6
Bergmann Hotel—*hist pl* AK-9
Bergman Rsvr—*reservoir* WY-8
Bergman Sch—*school* AR-4
Bergman Sch—*school* WI-6
Bergman State Wildlife Mngmt Area—*park* MN-6
Bergmantown—*locale* TN-4
Berg Mine—*mine* ID-8
Berg Mtn—*summit* (2) AK-9
Berg Mtn—*summit* ID-8
*Bergner Dam* SD-7
Bergner Dam—*dam* SD-7
Bergner Dam 1—*dam* SD-7
Bergner Lake—*lake* MI-6
Bergona Lake—*lake* CA-9
**Bergoo**—*pop pl* WV-2
Bergoo Creek—*stream* WV-2
Bergquist, John, House—*hist pl* MN-6
Bergquist Sch—*school* SD-7
*Berg Ras* FM-9
Bergreen Creek—*stream* WY-8
Bergren Cave—*cave* AR-4
Bergren Ditch—*canal* IN-6
Bergs—*uninc pl* TX-5
Berg Sch—*school* IA-7
Berg Sch—*school* NE-7
Berg Sch Number 6 (historical)—*school* SD-7
*Bergs Creek* MI-6
Bergseth Field Airp—*airport* WA-9
Bergsicker Creek—*stream* MT-8
*Bergs Landing* WA-9
Berg Slough—*lake* ND-7
**Bergs Mill**—*pop pl* TX-5
Bergs Ranch—*locale* NV-8
Bergstedt Ranch—*locale* WY-8
Bergstrasse Sch—*school* PA-2
Bergstresser Covered Bridge—*hist pl* OH-6
Bergstresser Hollow—*valley* PA-2
Bergstresser Run—*stream* PA-2
Bergstrom AFB—*military* TX-5
Bergstrom Bay—*bay* MN-6
Bergstrom Canyon—*valley* CA-9
Bergstrom Gulch—*valley* AK-9
Bergstrom Hollow—*valley* PA-2
Bergstrom Park—*park* OR-9
Bergstrom Place—*locale* ID-8
Bergsvik Creek—*stream* OR-9
Bergt, Christian A., Farm—*hist pl* MO-7
Bergtal Cem—*cemetery* KS-7
Bergtal Ch—*church* KS-7
Bergtal Oil and Gas Field—*oilfield* KS-7
Bergthal Ch—*church* OK-5
Bergton—*locale* VA-3
Bergton Gospel Center—*church* VA-3
Bergton Sch—*school* VA-3
*Berg Trukianu* FM-9
*Berg Trukubei* FM-9
*Berg Trukulei* FM-9
*Berg Uitjkula* FM-9
*Berg Uitjukula* FM-9
*Berg Ulivar* FM-9
Bergum Coulee—*valley* MT-8
Bergum Coulee—*valley* WI-6
Bergundy Point—*cape* WI-6
*Berg Univar* FM-9
*Berg Ururiol* FM-9
Berg Valley—*valley* WI-6
Bergville—*locale* MN-6
Bergville Lake—*lake* MN-6
*Berg Viniboat* FM-9
*Berg Vinifei* FM-9
*Berg Viselet* FM-9
Bergy Bridge Hist Dist—*hist pl* PA-2
**Beriber**—*pop pl* PW-9
Beric Island—*island* AK-9
Bering—*locale* TX-5
Bering Creek—*stream* (2) AK-9
Bering Ditch—*canal* TX-5
Beringer—*locale* PA-2
Bering Expedition Landing Site—*hist pl* AK-9
Bering Glacier—*glacier* AK-9
Bering Lake—*lake* AK-9
Bering Land Bridge Natl Monmt—*park* AK-9
Bering Point—*cape* AK-9
Bering River—*stream* AK-9
Bering Sea—*sea* AK-9
Bering Slough—*stream* AK-9
Bering Strait—*channel* AK-9
*Beringuier* FM-9
*Beringuier Island* FM-9
**Berino**—*pop pl* NM-5
Berino Bridge—*other* NM-5
Berino Siding—*locale* NM-5
Berino Tank—*reservoir* NM-5
**Berio**—*pop pl* PR-3
Ber Juan Park—*park* MO-7
Berk, Daniel, Log House—*hist pl* PA-2
Berkalew Island—*island* NY-2
Berk Creek—*stream* WA-9
Berkebile Cem—*cemetery* OH-6
*Berkeley* KY-4
Berkeley—*hist pl* VA-3
Berkeley—*locale* VA-3
**Berkeley**—*pop pl* CA-9
**Berkeley**—*pop pl* FL-3
**Berkeley**—*pop pl* IL-6
**Berkeley**—*pop pl* MO-7
**Berkeley**—*pop pl* RI-1
**Berkeley**—*pop pl* VA-3
**Berkeley**—*pop pl* WV-2
Berkeley—*post sta* NC-3
**Berkeley, Township of**—*pop pl* NJ-2
Berkeley Apartments—*hist pl* NY-2
Berkeley Aquatic Park—*park* CA-9
Berkeley Ave Sch—*school* NJ-2
Berkeley Ball Park—*park* NC-3
Berkeley Branch—*stream* SC-3
**Berkeley (Burkley)**—*pop pl* KY-4
Berkeley (CCD)—*cens area* CA-9
**Berkeley (County)**—*pop pl* SC-3
**Berkeley (County)**—*pop pl* WV-2
Berkeley Day Nursery—*hist pl* CA-9
**Berkeley Farms**—*pop pl* DE-2
Berkeley Gardens Sch—*school* CO-8
Berkeley Hall Sch—*school* CA-9
**Berkeley Heights**—*pop pl* NJ-2
Berkeley Heights Sch—*school* NJ-2
Berkeley Heights Sch—*school* WV-2
Berkeley Heights Station—*locale* NJ-2
**Berkeley Heights (Township of)**—*pop pl* NJ-2
**Berkeley Highlands**—*pop pl* CA-9
**Berkeley Hills**—*pop pl* PA-2
**Berkeley Hills**—*pop pl* SC-3
**Berkeley Hills**—*pop pl* VA-3
Berkeley Hills—*summit* CA-9
Berkeley Hills Park—*park* CO-8
Berkeley HS—*school* CA-9
Berkeley HS—*school* VA-3
*Berkeley Island* VA-3
Berkeley Lake—*lake* CO-8
**Berkeley Lake**—*pop pl* GA-3
Berkeley Lake—*reservoir* GA-3
Berkeley Lake Park—*hist pl* CO-8
Berkeley (Magisterial District)—*fmr MCD* (2) VA-3
**Berkeley Manor Area (subdivision)**—*pop pl* NC-3
Berkeley Manor Elem Sch—*school* NC-3
Berkeley Mill Village—*hist pl* RI-1
Berkeley Muni Camp—*locale* CA-9
Berkeley Music Camp—*locale* CA-9
Berkeley Park—*flat* WA-9
Berkeley Park—*park* CA-9
Berkeley Park—*park* CO-8
Berkeley Park—*park* (2) OR-9
Berkeley Pier (abandoned)—*locale* CA-9
Berkeley Pit—*mine* MT-8
**Berkeley Place**—*pop pl* WV-2
Berkeley Preparatory Sch—*school* FL-3
Berkeley Public Library—*hist pl* CA-9
**Berkeley Ridge**—*pop pl* DE-2
Berkeley Rose Garden—*park* CA-9
Berkeley (RR name for Carlton)—*other* GA-3
Berkeley Run—*stream* WV-2
Berkeley Sch—*school* CO-8
Berkeley Sch—*school* IL-6
Berkeley Sch—*school* MO-7
Berkeley Sch—*school* NJ-2
Berkeley Sch—*school* (2) VA-3
*Berkeley Seat* RI-1
**Berkeley Shore Estates**—*pop pl* NJ-2
**Berkeley Shores**—*pop pl* NJ-2
**Berkeley Springs**—*pop pl* WV-2
*Berkeley Springs (corporate name Bath)* WV-2
Berkeley Springs State Park—*hist pl* WV-2
Berkeley Square Hist Dist—*hist pl* NJ-2
Berkeley Square Hist Dist—*hist pl* NY-2
Berkeley Street Hist Dist—*hist pl* MA-1
Berkeley Street Hist Dist (Boundary Increase)—*hist pl* MA-1
Berkeley Street Sch—*school* NJ-2
**Berkeley (subdivision)**—*pop pl* NC-3
Berkeley Tennis Club—*other* CA-9
Berkeley Terrace Sch—*school* NJ-2
*Berkeley (Township of)* NJ-2
Berkeley Training Sch—*school* SC-3
**Berkeley Village (subdivision)**—*pop pl* NC-3
Berkeley Women's City Club—*hist pl* CA-9
Berkeley Yacht Harbor—*bay* CA-9
Berkel Lake—*lake* IL-6
Berkel Mine—*mine* IL-6
Berkenshaw Creek—*stream* UT-8
*Berker Mill Creek* AL-4
Berkes Community Ch—*church* AR-4
Berkett Hollow—*valley* KY-4
**Berkey**—*pop pl* OH-6
Berkey Creek—*stream* OR-9
*Berkey Ditch* IN-6
Berkey Gulch—*valley* CO-8
Berkey Spring—*spring* CO-8
Berkhalter Cem—*cemetery* MS-4
Berkheimer Sch (abandoned)—*school* PA-2
Berkholder Rsvr—*reservoir* MT-8
Berkin Flat—*flat* MT-8
Berkin Gulch—*valley* MT-8
Berkins Bar—*bar* MT-8
Berkins Butte—*summit* MT-8
Berkland Slough—*gut* ND-7
Berkleigh Country Club—*other* PA-2
Berklet Center Inn—*locale* NC-3
*Berkley* NJ-2
*Berkley* PA-2
*Berkley* VA-3
Berkley—*locale* PA-2
**Berkley**—*pop pl* AL-4
**Berkley**—*pop pl* IA-7
**Berkley**—*pop pl* KY-4
**Berkley**—*pop pl* MD-2
**Berkley**—*pop pl* MA-1
**Berkley**—*pop pl* MI-6
**Berkley**—*pop pl* VA-3
Berkley Airp—*airport* KS-7
Berkley Bluff—*cliff* AR-4
*Berkley Branch* SC-3
Berkley Bridge—*bridge* MA-1
Berkley Bridge—*bridge* VA-3
**Berkley Bridge**—*pop pl* MA-1
Berkley Brothers Airp—*airport* KS-7
Berkley Cem—*cemetery* AR-4
Berkley Center Head Start Sch—*school* AL-4
Berkley Ch—*church* NJ-2
Berkley Ch—*church* VA-3
Berkley Creek—*stream* TX-5
Berkley Glen Sch—*school* VA-3
*Berkley Heights* NJ-2
*Berkley Heights* OH-6
**Berkley Hills**—*pop pl* AL-4
Berkley Hills Cem—*cemetery* PA-2
Berkley Hills Ch—*church* PA-2
**Berkley Hills (subdivision)**—*pop pl* AL-4
**Berkley (historical)**—*pop pl* (2) OR-9
Berkley Island—*island* VA-3
Berkley Mill Creek—*stream* AL-4
*Berkley Mills* PA-2
Berkley Mtn—*summit* NY-2
**Berkley Place (subdivision)**—*pop pl* NC-3
Berkley Post Office (historical)—*building* AL-4
Berkley Prospect—*mine* TN-4
**Berkley Run Junction**—*pop pl* WV-
Berkley Sch—*hist pl* MD-
Berkley Sch—*school* AL-
Berkley Sch—*school* MA-
Berkley Sch—*school* SD-
**Berkleys Mill**—*pop pl* PA-
Berkley Spring—*spring* OR-
*Berkley Square* CO-
*Berkley Square* IL-
**Berkley (Town of)**—*pop pl* MA-
Berkly (historical)—*locale* KS-
Berks—*locale* NE-
**Berks**—*pop pl* NE-
Berks Airp (historical)—*airport* PA-
Berks Branch—*stream* AR-
*Berks Center Penn State University* PA-
**Berks County**—*pop pl* PA-
Berks Creek—*stream* TN-
Berkshie Mill No. 1—*hist pl* MA-
**Berkshire**—*pop pl* CT-
**Berkshire**—*pop pl* MD-
**Berkshire**—*pop pl* MA-
**Berkshire**—*pop pl* (2) NY-
**Berkshire**—*pop pl* OH-
**Berkshire**—*pop pl* VT-
**Berkshire**—*pop pl* VA-
Berkshire Association—*other* NY-
**Berkshire (Berkshire Association)**—*pop pl* NY-
Berkshire Block—*hist pl* WI-
Berkshire Cem—*cemetery* CT-
Berkshire Cem—*cemetery* VT-
**Berkshire Center**—*pop pl* VT-
Berkshire Christian Coll—*school* MA-
Berkshire Common—*locale* MA-
Berkshire Community Coll—*school* MA-
Berkshire Country Club—*other* PA-
**Berkshire County**—*pop pl* MA-
Berkshire County Jail—*building* MA-
Berkshire Creek—*stream* IN-
Berkshire Creek—*stream* OR-
Berkshire Ditch—*canal* IN-
Berkshire Downs—*locale* MA-
Berkshire Elem Sch—*school* FL-
**Berkshire Estates**—*pop pl* (2) CT-
**Berkshire Estates (subdivision)**—*pop pl* AL-
Berkshire Farm For Boys—*locale* NY-
**Berkshire Forest**—*pop pl* TN-
Berkshire Gap—*gap* TN-
Berkshire Gardens Center—*park* MA-
**Berkshire Heights**—*pop pl* MA-
**Berkshire Heights (subdivision)**—*pop pl* PA-
Berkshire Hills—*range* MA-
Berkshire Hills Ch—*church* MA-
Berkshire Hills Country Club—*locale* MA-
**Berkshire Hills (subdivision)**—*pop pl* MS-
**Berkshire Hills (subdivision)**—*pop pl* PA-
Berkshire HS—*school* FL-
Berkshire Infant Care Center—*school* FL-
Berkshire JHS—*school* MI-

Berkshire Junction—pop pl ... CT-1
Berkshire Life Insurance Company Bldg—hist pl ... MA-1
Berkshire Mall—locale ... PA-2
Berkshire Mall West—locale ... PA-2
Berkshire Market Village—park ... MA-1
Berkshire Mine Ruins—locale ... WI-6
Berkshire Mountain ... MA-1
Berkshire Museum—building ... MA-1
BERKSHIRE NO. 7—hist pl ... CT-1
Berkshire Pond—lake ... MA-1
Berkshire Public Theater—building ... MA-1
Berkshire Ranch—locale ... NM-5
Berkshire Sch—school ... FL-3
Berkshire Sch—school (2) ... MD-2
Berkshire Sch—school (2) ... MA-1
Berkshire Show Basin Ski Area—locale ... MA-1
Berkshire Slough—stream ... OR-9
Berkshire Terrace—locale ... NY-2
Berkshire (Town of)—pop pl ... NY-2
Berkshire (Town of)—pop pl ... VT-1
Berkshire (Township of)—pop pl ... OH-6
Berkshire Trout Pond—reservoir ... MA-1
Berkshire Trout Pond Dam—dam ... MA-1
Berkshire Valley—pop pl ... NJ-2
Berkshire Valley Fish and Wildlife Mngmt Area—park ... NJ-2
Berkshire Village—locale ... AZ-5
Berkshire Village Hist Dist—hist pl ... NY-2
Berkshire West Subdivision—pop pl ... UT-8
Berkshire Windmill—locale ... NM-5
Berkshire Wood—pop pl ... TN-4
Berkshire Woods—uninc pl ... GA-3
Berks Slough—gut ... AR-4
Berks Station ... AZ-5
Berkswitch Run—stream ... WV-2
Berlamont—pop pl ... MI-6
Berland Homestead—locale ... MT-8
Berland Lake—lake ... MI-6
Berland Lake—lake ... NM-5
Berland Ranch—locale ... OR-9
Berland Rsvr—reservoir ... OR-9
Berl Avery Seep ... UT-8
Berle Dam—dam ... MA-1
Berlee ... PA-2
Berlein ... IN-6
Berle Lake—lake ... MN-6
Berleley Industrial Park Subdivision—locale ... UT-8
Berleman House—hist pl ... IL-6
Berle Pond—reservoir ... MA-1
Berles Creek—stream ... VA-3
Berlien—pop pl ... IN-6
Berlien Ditch—canal ... IN-6
Berlier Ranch—locale ... NM-5
Berlin ... AL-4
Berlin ... MI-6
Berlin ... NE-7
Berlin ... ND-7
Berlin ... OH-6
Berlin ... VT-1
Berlin—fmr MCD ... NE-7
Berlin—locale ... AL-4
Berlin—locale ... AR-4
Berlin—locale ... TX-5
Berlin—locale ... VA-3
Berlin—other ... MI-6
Berlin—pop pl ... AL-4
Berlin—pop pl ... CT-1
Berlin—pop pl ... GA-3
Berlin—pop pl ... IL-6
Berlin—pop pl ... IA-7
Berlin—pop pl ... KS-7
Berlin—pop pl ... KY-4
Berlin—pop pl ... MD-2
Berlin—pop pl ... MA-1
Berlin—pop pl ... MO-7
Berlin—pop pl ... NV-8
Berlin—pop pl ... NH-1
Berlin—pop pl ... NJ-2
Berlin—pop pl ... NY-2
Berlin—pop pl ... ND-7
Berlin—pop pl (2) ... OH-6
Berlin—pop pl ... OK-5
Berlin—pop pl ... OR-9
Berlin—pop pl ... PA-2
Berlin—pop pl ... SC-3
Berlin—pop pl ... TN-4
Berlin—pop pl ... VT-1
Berlin—pop pl ... WV-2
Berlin—pop pl ... WI-6
Berlin Airp—airport ... NH-1
Berlin and Ivor (Magisterial District)—fmr MCD ... VA-3
Berlin Borough—civil ... PA-2
Berlin Branch—stream ... AL-4
Berlin-Brothersvalley Joint Schools—school ... PA-2
Berlin Canyon—valley (2) ... NV-8
Berlin Cem—cemetery ... MN-6
Berlin Cem—cemetery ... MO-7
Berlin Cem—cemetery ... NJ-2
Berlin Cem—cemetery ... ND-7
Berlin Cem—cemetery ... OK-5
Berlin Cem—cemetery ... OR-9
Berlin Center—locale ... MI-6
Berlin Center—locale ... PA-2
Berlin Center—pop pl (2) ... OH-6
Berlin Center Station—locale ... OH-6
Berlin Centre ... MA-1
Berlin Centre ... NY-2
Berlin Ch—church ... GA-3
Berlin Ch—church ... IL-6
Berlin Ch—church ... OH-6
Berlin Ch—church ... PA-2
Berlin Commercial District—hist pl ... MD-2
Berlin Corners—pop pl ... VT-1
Berlin Corner Sch—school ... VT-1
Berlin Court Grand Ditch—canal ... IN-6
Berlin Cross Roads ... OH-6
Berlin Draw—valley ... WY-8
Berlin-Ellenton (CCD)—cens area ... GA-3
Berliner Lake—lake ... MN-6
Berlin Estates—pop pl ... NJ-2
Berlin Fork—stream ... PA-2
Berlin Gulch—valley ... ID-8
Berling Airp—airport ... IN-6
Berlin Heights—locale ... NJ-2
Berlin Heights—pop pl ... OH-6
Berlin Heights—uninc pl ... NJ-2
Berlin Heights (sta.)—pop pl ... OH-6
Berlin Heights Station—pop pl ... OH-6
Berlin Hill—summit ... TN-4
Berlin Hist Dist—hist pl ... NV-8
Berlin Hist Dist—hist pl ... TN-4
Berlin (historical)—locale ... AL-4
Berlin (historical)—locale ... IA-7
Berlin (historical)—locale ... ND-7
Berlin Hollow—valley ... TN-4
Berlin-Ichthyosaur State Park—park ... NV-8
Berlin-Ivor Sch—school ... VA-3
Berlin Junction—locale ... PA-2
Berlin Lake—reservoir ... OH-6
Berlin Lock Number One—dam ... WI-6
Berlin Memorial Sch—school ... MA-1
Berlin Mills ... NH-1
Berlin Mine—mine ... MT-8
Berlin Mtn—summit ... MA-1
Berlin Mtn—summit ... NY-2
Berlin Normal Sch—school ... AL-4
Berlin Oil Field—other ... MI-6
Berlin Park—park ... NJ-2
Berlin Pass—gap ... NY-2
Berlin Pond—lake ... VT-1
Berlin Post Office (historical)—building ... TN-4
Berlin Prospect—mine ... TN-4
Berlin Rsvr ... OH-6
Berlin Sch—school ... NJ-2
Berlin Sch—school ... OR-9
Berlin Sch—school ... SC-3
Berlin Sch—school ... TN-4
Berlin Sch (historical)—school ... TN-4
Berlin Sch Number 1—school ... ND-7
Berlin Sch Number 2—school ... ND-7
Berlin Sch Number 3—school ... ND-7
Berlin Sch Number 4—school ... ND-7
Berlinski Creek—stream ... MI-6
Berlin Spring—spring ... TN-4
Berlin (sta.)—pop pl ... MA-1
Berlin (sta.) (Kensington)—pop pl ... CT-1
Berlin Station—locale ... CT-1
Berlins Ville ... PA-2
Berlinsville—pop pl ... PA-2
Berlin Tank—reservoir ... NM-5
Berlin Town Hall—building ... ND-7
Berlin (Town of)—pop pl ... CT-1
Berlin (Town of)—pop pl ... MA-1
Berlin (Town of)—pop pl ... NY-2
Berlin (Town of)—pop pl ... VT-1
Berlin (Town of)—pop pl (2) ... WI-6
Berlin Township ... KS-7
Berlin Township ... ND-7
Berlin Township—pop pl (3) ... ND-7
Berlin Township (historical)—civil ... SD-7
Berlin (Township of)—pop pl ... IL-6
Berlin (Township of)—pop pl (3) ... MI-6
Berlin (Township of)—pop pl ... MN-6
Berlin (Township of)—pop pl ... NJ-2
Berlin (Township of)—pop pl (5) ... OH-6
Berlin (Township of)—pop pl ... PA-2
Berlin Union Ch—church ... OR-9
Berlin United Methodist Ch—church ... TN-4
Berlinville ... PA-2
Berlinville—pop pl ... OH-6
Berlin Well—well ... NM-5
Berl Island—island ... FL-3
Berlock Mine—mine ... NV-8
Berlson Lake—lake ... MS-4
Berly, William, House—hist pl ... SC-3
Berly, W. Q. M., House—hist pl ... SC-3
Berlyn Ave Sch—school ... CA-9
Berly Post Office (historical)—building ... AL-4
Bermadez Place—locale ... NM-5
Berman Airp (historical)—airport ... PA-2
Berman Creek ... OR-9
Bermejales (Barrio)—fmr MCD ... PR-3
Bermester ... UT-8
Bermidji ... MN-6
Bermingham Sch—school ... NY-2
Bermond ... NV-8
Bermond Sch (historical)—school ... MO-7
Bermont—locale ... ND-7
Bermont Lookout Tower—tower ... FL-3
Bermuda—locale ... GA-3
Bermuda—locale ... LA-4
Bermuda—pop pl (2) ... AL-4
Bermuda—pop pl ... GA-3
Bermuda Acad—school ... VA-3
Bermuda Bluff—cliff ... SC-3
Bermuda Cem—cemetery ... AL-4
Bermuda Cem—cemetery ... SC-3
Bermuda Ch—church ... AL-4
Bermuda Ch—church ... SC-3
Bermuda Creek—stream ... SC-3
Bermuda Dam—dam ... TX-5
Bermuda Dunes—pop pl ... CA-9
Bermuda Dunes Country Club—other ... CA-9
Bermuda Falls Spring—spring ... AZ-5
Bermuda Hill—summit ... GA-3
Bermuda Hundred—locale ... VA-3
Bermuda Hundred (sta.)—pop pl ... VA-3
Bermuda Lake—reservoir ... TX-5
Bermuda Landing (historical)—locale ... MS-4
Bermuda (Magisterial District)—fmr MCD ... VA-3
Bermuda Memorial Park—cemetery ... VA-3
Bermuda Oaks Golf Course—locale ... AL-4
Bermuda Run Golf Course—locale ... NC-3
Bermuda Run (subdivision)—pop pl ... NC-3
Bermuda Sch—school ... VA-3
Bermuda Sch (historical)—school ... AL-4
Bermudez—pop pl ... PR-3
Bermudez Bluff—summit ... AK-9
Bermudian—pop pl ... PA-2
Bermudian Ch—church ... PA-2
Bermudian Creek—stream ... PA-2
Bermudian Valley Airpark—airport ... PA-2
Bermul (historical)—locale ... AL-4
Bern ... IN-6
Bern ... NY-2
Bern—pop pl ... ID-8
Bern—pop pl ... KS-7
Bernabe M Montano—civil ... NM-5
Bernadette, Lake—lake ... FL-3
Bernadotte—pop pl ... IL-6
Bernadotte—pop pl ... MN-6
Bernadotte Bridge—hist pl ... IL-6
Bernadotte Bridge—other ... IL-6
Bernadotte (Township of)—pop pl ... IL-6
Bernadotte (Township of)—pop pl ... MN-6
Bernal—pop pl ... NM-5
Bernal—uninc pl ... CA-9
Bernal Branch—stream ... NC-3
Bernal Chavez Canyon—valley ... NM-5
Bernal Creek—stream ... NM-5
Bernaldo Creek ... TX-5
Bernal Heights—summit ... CA-9
Bernal Hollow—valley ... TN-4
Bernalillito Mesa—summit ... NM-5
Bernalillo—pop pl ... NM-5
Bernalillo Acequia—canal ... NM-5
Bernalillo (CCD)—cens area ... NM-5
Bernalillo Cem—cemetery ... NM-5
Bernalillo (County)—pop pl ... NM-5
Bernalillo East (CCD)—cens area ... NM-5
Bernalillo Interior Drain—canal ... NM-5
Bernalillo Riverside Drain—canal ... NM-5
Bernalillo West (CCD)—cens area ... NM-5
Bernal Lake—lake ... NM-5
Bernal Lateral—canal ... TX-5
Bernal Mine—mine ... CA-9
Bernal Park—park ... CA-9
Bernal Trail—trail ... NM-5
Bernander Cem—cemetery ... MS-4
Bernard—locale ... MS-4
Bernard—pop pl ... IA-7
Bernard—pop pl ... KY-4
Bernard—pop pl ... ME-1
Bernard, Bayou—gut ... LA-4
Bernard, Bayou—stream ... MS-4
Bernard, Susana Machado, House and Barn—hist pl ... CA-9
Bernard Acres (subdivision)—pop pl ... MS-4
Bernard Bayou ... MS-4
Bernard Bayou Industrial Park—locale ... MS-4
Bernard Branch ... KS-7
Bernard Branch—stream ... KS-7
Bernard Branch—stream ... TX-5
Bernard Bridge—bridge ... ID-8
Bernard Brooks Dam—dam ... AL-4
Bernard Ch—church ... KY-4
Bernard Chapel—church ... TN-4
Bernard Creek ... ID-8
Bernard Creek ... MI-6
Bernard Creek ... NC-3
Bernard Creek ... WA-9
Bernard Creek—stream ... AK-9
Bernard Creek—stream ... CO-8
Bernard Creek—stream (4) ... ID-8
Bernard Creek—stream ... MT-8
Bernard Creek—stream ... WA-9
Bernard Creek Guard Station—locale ... ID-8
Bernard Ditch—canal ... ID-8
Bernarde Mine—mine ... AZ-5
Bernard Ferry—locale ... ID-8
Bernard Frank, Lake—reservoir ... MD-2
Bernard Harbor—bay ... AK-9
Bernard Hollow—valley ... TN-4
Bernard Hollow—valley ... WY-8
Bernard-Hoover Boathouse—hist pl ... WI-6
Bernard Howell Rsvr—reservoir ... WY-8
Bernardine Convent—church ... CT-1
Bernardino—locale ... AZ-5
Bernardino Creek—stream ... CO-8
Bernard Islands—island ... VA-3
Bernard Lagoon—lake ... LA-4
Bernard Lake—lake ... ID-8
Bernard Lake—lake ... MO-7
Bernard Lakes—lake ... ID-8
Bernard Mtn—summit ... ID-8
Bernard Mtn—summit ... ME-1
Bernard Mtn—summit ... NC-3
Bernardo ... CA-9
Bernardo—locale ... NM-5
Bernardo—pop pl ... TX-5
Bernardo Arroyo—stream ... NM-5
Bernardo Mtn—summit ... CA-9
Bernardo Sch—school ... TX-5
Bernardo Segui Grant—civil ... FL-3
Bernard Park—park ... NE-7
Bernard Park—park ... OH-6
Bernard Peak—summit ... ID-8
Bernard Peak—summit ... WY-8
Bernard Place—locale ... NV-8
Bernard Point—cliff ... ID-8
Bernard Prairie—flat ... TX-5
Bernard Prairie Sch—school ... TX-5
Bernard Ridge—ridge ... KY-4
Bernards Bedground—flat ... ID-8
Bernard Sch—school ... CA-9
Bernard Sch—school (4) ... TN-4
Bernards Corrals—locale ... NV-8
Bernards Creek—stream ... VA-3
Bernard's Ferry—hist pl ... ID-8
Bernards Hill ... MA-1
Bernards Island ... MS-4
Bernard's Islands ... VA-3
Bernard Smith Pond—reservoir ... GA-3
Bernard Spit—bar ... AK-9
Bernard Stoeser Dam—dam ... SD-7
Bernardston—pop pl ... MA-1
Bernardston (Town of)—pop pl ... MA-1
Bernardston Village ... MA-1
Bernardstown—pop pl ... WV-2
Bernards (Township of)—pop pl ... NJ-2
Bernardsville ... NJ-2
Bernardsville—pop pl ... NJ-2
Bernardsville Station—hist pl ... NJ-2
Bernard Terrace—uninc pl ... LA-4
Bernard Terrace Sch—school ... LA-4
Bernard Township ... NJ-2
Bernardville ... NJ-2
Bernard Wasteway—canal ... ID-8
Bernasconi Hills—range ... CA-9
Bernasconi Pass—gap ... CA-9
Bernau Brook—stream ... NY-2
Bern Cem—cemetery ... NC-3
Bern Ch—church ... PA-2
Bernd, W. A., Bldg—hist pl ... ID-8
Bernd, William J., House—hist pl ... WI-6
Bernd Canyon—valley ... NV-8
Bernd Sch—school ... GA-3
Berndt Lake—reservoir ... MO-7
Berne—locale ... SD-7
Berne—locale ... WA-9
Berne—pop pl ... IN-6
Berne—pop pl ... IA-7
Berne—pop pl ... MI-6
Berne—pop pl ... MN-6
Berne—pop pl ... NY-2
Berne—pop pl ... PA-2
Berneathy Spring—spring ... ID-8
Berne (Carlisle)—pop pl ... OH-6
Berne Cem—cemetery ... NY-2
Bernecker—locale ... TX-5
Berne Compressor Station—locale ... OH-6
Berne Elem Sch—school ... IN-6
Berne-French Township Sch ... IN-6
Bernent Sch—school ... MA-1
Berner—locale ... GA-3
Berner—pop pl ... MN-6
Berner Creek—stream ... TN-4
Berner HS—school ... NY-2
Berner Ranch—locale ... WY-8
Berners Bay—bay ... AK-9
Berners Peaks—other ... AK-9
Berners River—stream ... AK-9
Berne Speedway—other ... PA-2
Berne Station ... WA-9
Berne (Town of)—pop pl ... NY-2
Berne (Township of)—pop pl ... OH-6
Berney Park—park ... AZ-5
Berney Points—pop pl ... AL-4
Berney Points Baptist Ch—church ... AL-4
Berney Points Ch of Christ—church ... AL-4
Berneys—locale ... AL-4
Berney Sch—school ... WA-9
Berneys Station ... AL-4
Bernhandt Sch—school ... MI-6
Bernhard, Frederick, House—hist pl ... OH-6
Bernhard Bay—bay ... NY-2
Bernhard Creek ... CO-8
Bernhard Point—cape ... NY-2
Bernhards Bay—pop pl ... NY-2
Bernhardson, Bernard, House—hist pl ... MN-6
Bernhardt, George Matthias, House—hist pl ... NC-3
Bernhardt Creek—stream ... OR-9
Bernhardt Creek—stream ... WA-9
Bernhardt Mine—mine ... WA-9
Bernhardt Mtn—summit ... NY-2
Bernhardt Ranch—locale ... WA-9
Bernhardt Trail—trail ... WA-9
Bernhart—pop pl ... IA-7
Bernhart Creek—stream ... PA-2
Bernhart Dam—dam ... PA-2
Bernhart Lake—lake ... MN-6
Bernhart Lake—swamp ... MI-6
Bernhart Rsvr—reservoir ... PA-2
Bernharts—pop pl ... PA-2
Bernheim Distillery Bottling Plant—hist pl ... KY-4
Bernheimer—locale ... MO-7
Bernheim For—woods ... KY-4
Bernheim Foundation Private Reservation ... KY-4
Bernheim House—hist pl ... OH-6
Bernheisel Ridge—ridge ... PA-2
Berni, Jacob, House—hist pl ... WI-6
Bernice ... IL-6
Bernice—locale ... KY-4
Bernice—locale ... MT-8
Bernice—locale ... OH-6
Bernice—pop pl ... AR-4
Bernice—pop pl ... IL-6
Bernice—pop pl ... LA-4
Bernice—pop pl ... OK-5
Bernice—pop pl ... PA-2
Bernice, Lake—lake ... OR-9
Bernice, Lake—reservoir ... WI-6
Bernice (Bernice Mines)—pop pl ... AR-4
Bernice Canyon—valley ... NV-8
Bernice Ch—church ... AR-4
Bernice Creek—bay ... NC-3
Bernice Creek—stream ... NV-8
Bernice (historical)—pop pl ... OR-9
BERNICE J. (skipjack)—hist pl ... MD-2
Bernice Lake ... AK-9
Bernice Lake—lake ... AK-9
Bernice Lake—lake ... CA-9
Bernice Lake—lake ... WA-9
Bernice Mines ... AR-4
Bernice Point—cape ... OK-5
Bernice Spring—spring (2) ... NV-8
Bernie—pop pl ... MO-7
Bernie—pop pl ... WV-2
Bernie Lake—lake ... GA-3
Bernie Lake—reservoir ... TX-5
Bernie Pond—lake ... NY-2
Bernier Creek—stream ... ID-8
Bernier Creek—stream ... WA-9
Bernier Point—cliff ... ID-8
Bernier Ranch—locale ... MT-8
Bernier (Trailer Park)—pop pl ... ME-1
Bernice Slough—stream ... WA-9
Bernietown—locale ... VA-3
Bernina—pop pl ... IA-7
Berning Drain—canal ... IN-6
Berning Mill—locale ... KY-4
Bern Lake—lake ... OH-6
Bern Peak—summit ... NM-5
Bern Post Office (historical)—building ... SD-7
Bern Sch—school ... PA-2
Bernstadt—pop pl ... KY-4
Bernst Creek—stream ... TX-5
Bernstein—locale ... TX-5
Bernstein Farm Pond Dam—dam ... MA-1
Bernstein JHS—school ... NY-2
Bernstein Park—park ... LA-4
Bern (Town of)—pop pl ... WI-6
Bern (Township of)—pop pl ... OH-6
Bern (Township of)—pop pl ... PA-2
Bernville—pop pl ... PA-2
Bernville Borough—civil ... PA-2
Beroun—pop pl ... MN-6
Berpen Branch ... GA-3
Berquist Lateral—canal ... NE-7
Berral Well—well ... NM-5
Berranger Creek—stream ... MI-6
Berray Creek—stream ... MT-8
Berray Mountain Trail—trail ... MT-8
Berray Mtn—summit ... MT-8
Berre Lake—lake ... ND-7
Berreman (Township of)—pop pl ... IL-6
Berrenda Creek—stream (4) ... NM-5
Berrenda Draw—valley ... TX-5
Berrenda Mtn—summit ... NM-5
Berrenda Well—well ... NM-5
Berrendo ... CA-9
Berrendo Creek—stream ... NM-5
Berrendo Recorder Well—well ... NM-5
Berrendo Sch—school ... NM-5
Berrendo Slough ... CA-9
Berrendo-Smith Recorder Well—well ... NM-5
Berrendo Windmill—locale ... NM-5
Berrendo Windmill—locale ... TX-5
Berrenth Quarry—mine ... OR-9
Berreth Lake—lake ... ND-7
Berrett—pop pl ... MD-2
Berrett Subdivision—pop pl ... UT-8
Berreyesa ... CA-9
Berrey Park—park ... TX-5
Berrian—locale ... WA-9
Berrian Mtn—summit ... CO-8
Berrian Park—flat ... CO-8
Berrian Park—park ... IL-6
Berrian Sch—school ... IL-6
Berrian School—locale ... CO-8
Berrian Spring—spring ... OR-9
Berri Creek—stream ... CO-8
Berrien Branch—stream ... GA-3
Berrien Center—pop pl ... MI-6
Berrien (County)—pop pl ... GA-3
Berrien (County)—pop pl ... MI-6
Berrien County Courthouse—hist pl ... GA-3
Berrien County Jail—hist pl ... GA-3
Berrien Springs—pop pl ... MI-6
Berrien Springs Courthouse—hist pl ... MI-6
Berrien (Township of)—pop pl ... MI-6
Berrier Island—island ... PA-2
Berrie Sch—school ... PA-2
Berrin Cem—cemetery ... MI-6
Berringer Cem—cemetery ... OH-6
Berriochoa, Ignacio, Farm—hist pl ... ID-8
Berris Landing—locale ... AL-4
Berron, Pass—channel ... AL-4
Berrong Ch—church ... MO-7
Berrong Lake—reservoir ... GA-3
Berrong Mtn ... GA-3
Berrong Mtn—summit ... GA-3
Berron Point ... AL-4
Berros—pop pl ... CA-9
Berry ... AZ-5
Berry ... MI-6
Berry—locale ... AZ-5
Berry—locale ... FL-3
Berry—locale ... MD-2
Berry—locale ... TN-4
Berry—other ... AK-9
Berry—pop pl ... AL-4
Berry—pop pl ... IL-6
Berry—pop pl ... KY-4
Berry—pop pl ... MD-2
Berry—pop pl ... MI-6
Berry, Captain James, House—hist pl ... MA-1
Berry, George O., House—hist pl ... GA-3
Berry, James E., House—hist pl ... OK-5
Berry, J. S., House—hist pl ... TX-5
Berry, Lake—lake ... FL-3
Berry, Lake—reservoir ... SD-7
Berry, Martin, House—hist pl ... NJ-2
Berry, Mount—summit ... WY-8
Berry, Thomas A., House—hist pl ... GA-3
Berry Acad—school ... GA-3
Berry Ann Lake—lake ... FL-3
Berry Baptist Ch—church ... AL-4
Berry Basin—basin ... NV-8
Berry Bay ... NC-3
Berry Bay—bay ... LA-4
Berry Bay—bay ... NH-1
Berry Bayou—stream ... LA-4
Berry Bayou—stream ... TX-5
Berry Bend—bend ... MO-7
Berry Bend Public Use Area—park ... MO-7
Berry Bluff—cliff ... MO-7
Berry Bluff State Hunting Area—locale ... MO-7
Berry Brake—swamp ... LA-4
Berry Branch—stream (3) ... AL-4
Berry Branch—stream (2) ... AR-4
Berry Branch—stream (3) ... GA-3
Berry Branch—stream ... IA-7
Berry Branch—stream ... KY-4
Berry Branch—stream ... MS-4
Berry Branch—stream (2) ... MO-7
Berry Branch—stream ... SC-3
Berry Branch—stream (4) ... TN-4
Berry Branch—stream (2) ... TX-5
Berry Branch—stream (2) ... WV-2
Berry Branch Ch—church ... WV-2
Berry Branch Lake—reservoir ... IN-6
Berry Branch Lake Dam—dam ... IN-6
Berry Branch Sch—school ... WV-2
Berry Bridge—bridge ... LA-4
Berry Bridge—other ... MI-6
Berry Brook—stream (2) ... ME-1
Berry Brook—stream (2) ... NH-1
Berry Brook—stream (2) ... NY-2
Berry Brook Flowage—lake ... ME-1
Berry-Brookshire Cem—cemetery ... AL-4
Berry Brothers Bolt Works—hist pl ... OH-6
Berryburg—pop pl ... PA-2
Berryburg—pop pl ... WV-2
Berryburg Junction—locale ... WV-2
Berryburg Mine No. 1—pop pl ... WV-2
Berry Camp—locale ... AK-9
Berry Camp—locale ... WY-8
Berry Canyon—valley (3) ... CA-9
Berry Canyon—valley ... CO-8
Berry Canyon—valley ... ID-8
Berry Canyon—valley ... NM-5
Berry Canyon—valley ... UT-8
Berry Canyon—valley ... WY-8
Berry Cave—cave ... MO-7
Berry Cave—cave ... TN-4
Berry (CCD)—cens area ... AL-4
Berry (CCD)—cens area ... KY-4
Berry Cem—cemetery (3) ... AL-4
Berry Cem—cemetery ... AR-4
Berry Cem—cemetery ... GA-3
Berry Cem—cemetery (2) ... IL-6
Berry Cem—cemetery ... ME-1
Berry Cem—cemetery ... MN-6
Berry Cem—cemetery (4) ... MS-4
Berry Cem—cemetery (7) ... MO-7
Berry Cem—cemetery ... NH-1
Berry Cem—cemetery (3) ... OH-6
Berry Cem—cemetery (6) ... TN-4
Berry Cem—cemetery (5) ... TX-5
Berry Cem—cemetery (3) ... VA-3
Berry Cem—cemetery (2) ... WV-2
Berry Ch—church ... GA-3
Berry Ch—church ... MO-7
Berry Chapel—church ... GA-3
Berry Chapel—church ... MS-4
Berry Chapel—church ... NC-3
Berry Chapel—church ... VA-3
Berry Chapel—church ... WV-2
Berry Chapel Cem—cemetery ... AL-4
Berry Ch (historical)—church ... MS-4
Berry Ch of Christ—church ... AL-4
Berry Coll—school ... GA-3
Berry Coulee—valley ... MT-8
Berry Cove—bay (2) ... ME-1
Berry Creek ... AL-4
Berry Creek ... TX-5
Berry Creek ... WA-9
Berry Creek—bay ... NC-3
Berry Creek—pop pl ... CA-9
Berry Creek—stream (2) ... AL-4
Berry Creek—stream (3) ... AK-9
Berry Creek—stream ... AR-4
Berry Creek—stream (10) ... CA-9
Berry Creek—stream (3) ... CO-8
Berry Creek—stream (2) ... GA-3
Berry Creek—stream (3) ... ID-8
Berry Creek—stream ... KY-4
Berry Creek—stream ... MI-6
Berry Creek—stream ... MN-6
Berry Creek—stream ... MS-4
Berry Creek—stream ... MO-7
Berry Creek—stream (5) ... MT-8
Berry Creek—stream (2) ... NV-8
Berry Creek—stream ... NC-3
Berry Creek—stream ... OH-6
Berry Creek—stream (10) ... OR-9
Berry Creek—stream ... SD-7
Berry Creek—stream (6) ... TX-5
Berry Creek—stream ... VA-3
Berry Creek—stream (4) ... WA-9
Berry Creek—stream ... WI-6
Berry Creek—stream ... WY-8
Berry Creek Campground—locale ... NV-8
Berry Creek Ch—church ... LA-4
Berry Creek Dam—dam ... OR-9
Berry Creek Ditch—canal ... CA-9
Berry Creek Falls—falls ... CA-9
Berry Creek Falls—falls ... OR-9
Berry Creek Forest Camp ... NV-8
Berry Creek Forest Service Recreation Site ... NV-8
Berry Creek Forest Service Station—locale ... NV-8
Berry Creek Grove—woods ... NV-8
Berry Creek Guard Station ... NV-8
Berry Creek Ind Res—pop pl ... CA-9
Berry Creek Rancheria—locale ... CA-9
Berry Creek Rsvr—reservoir ... OR-9
Berry Creek Sch—school ... CA-9
Berry Creek Trail (pack)—trail ... OR-9
Berry Creek Windmill—locale ... TX-5
Berrydale—locale ... FL-3
Berrydale—pop pl (2) ... WA-9
Berrydale Ch—church ... FL-3
Berry Dam—dam ... SD-7
Berry Ditch—canal ... CO-8
Berry Ditch—canal ... IN-6
Berry Ditch—canal ... NM-5
Berry Division—civil ... AL-4
Berry Drain—canal ... MI-6
Berry Draw—valley ... SD-7
Berry Draw—valley ... WY-8
Berry Elem Sch—school ... AL-4
Berryessa—pop pl ... CA-9
Berryessa, Lake—reservoir ... CA-9
Berryessa (CCD)—cens area ... CA-9
Berryessa Creek—stream ... CA-9
Berryessa Marina—locale ... CA-9
Berryessa Park—pop pl ... CA-9
Berryessa Peak—summit ... CA-9
Berryessa Siding—locale ... CA-9
Berry Farm Lake—reservoir ... IN-6
Berry Farm Lake Dam—dam ... IN-6
Berry Flat Ch—church ... TX-5
Berry Flats—flat ... WV-2
Berry Flat Trail—trail ... HI-9
Berry Ford (historical)—locale ... MO-7
Berry Fork—stream ... WV-2
Berry Gap—gap ... AR-4
Berry Gap—gap ... NC-3
Berry Gap—gap ... TN-4
Berry Glenn—pop pl ... CA-9
Berry Glory Hole—mine ... NV-8
Berry Grammar Sch (historical)—school ... AL-4
Berry Grove Ch—church ... GA-3
Berry Gulch—valley ... CA-9
Berry Gulch—valley (3) ... CO-8
Berry Gulch—valley ... ID-8
Berry Gulch—valley ... MT-8
Berry Gulch—valley ... NE-7
Berry Gulch—valley ... UT-8
Berry Heath—swamp ... ME-1
Berryhill ... MS-4
Berry Hill—hist pl ... KY-4
Berry Hill—hist pl (3) ... VA-3
Berry Hill—locale ... SC-3
Berry Hill—locale ... VA-3
Berry Hill—pop pl ... NC-3
Berry Hill—pop pl ... TN-4
Berry Hill—summit ... CA-9
Berry Hill—summit ... KS-7
Berry Hill—summit (3) ... ME-1
Berry Hill—summit ... MA-1
Berry Hill—summit ... MO-7
Berry Hill—summit ... NH-1
Berry Hill—summit (2) ... NY-2
Berry Hill—summit ... VA-3
Berryhill, Charles, House—hist pl ... IA-7
Berry Hill Bluff—cliff ... GA-3
Berry Hill Cave—cave ... AL-4
Berry Hill Cem—cemetery ... AL-4
Berryhill Cem—cemetery ... GA-3
Berryhill Cem—cemetery ... MS-4
Berryhill Cem—cemetery ... NC-3
Berry Hill Cem—cemetery ... VA-3
Berry Hill Ch—church ... VA-3
Berryhill Creek—stream ... OK-5
Berryhill Creek—stream ... TX-5
Berryhill Elem Sch—school ... FL-3
Berry Hill Estates—uninc pl ... CA-9
Berryhill Farms Airp—airport ... MS-4
Berryhill Gut—stream ... SC-3
Berryhill House—hist pl ... MS-4
Berryhill-Morris House—hist pl ... OH-6
Berryhill Pond—swamp ... GA-3

Berryhill Ranch—*locale* (2) NM-5
Berry Hill Sch—*school* IL-6
Berry Hill Sch—*school* NY-2
Berryhill Sch—*school* NC-3
Berryhill Sch—*school* OK-5
Berryhill Sch—*school* TX-5
**Berryhill (subdivision)**—*pop pl* NC-3
Berryhill Windmill—*locale* NM-5
**Berry (historical)**—*pop pl* OR-9
Berry Hollow—*valley* AL-4
Berry Hollow—*valley* (3) AR-4
Berry Hollow—*valley* KY-4
Berry Hollow—*valley* MO-7
Berry Hollow—*valley* (5) TN-4
Berry Hollow—*valley* (2) VA-3
Berry Hollow—*valley* (2) WV-2
Berry Hosp—*hospital* MI-6
Berry House—*hist pl* TX-5
*Berry HS* AL-4
Berry HS—*school* AL-4
Berry Hump—*summit* NY-2
Berry Island—*island* (3) AK-9
Berry Island—*island* (2) ME-1
Berry Island—*island* MN-6
Berry Island—*island* MO-7
Berry Island—*island* TN-4
Berry Island (historical)—*island* TN-4
*Berry Junction* UT-8
**Berry Junction**—*pop pl* MI-6
**Berry Junction**—*pop pl* UT-8
Berry Knob—*summit* TX-5
Berry Knob—*summit* VA-3
Berry Knoll—*summit* AK-9
Berry Knoll—*summit* AZ-5
*Berry Lake* FL-3
Berry Lake—*lake* AL-4
Berry Lake—*lake* (2) AK-9
Berry Lake—*lake* CO-8
Berry Lake—*lake* GA-3
Berry Lake—*lake* LA-4
Berry Lake—*lake* (4) MI-6
Berry Lake—*lake* (2) MT-8
Berry Lake—*lake* (2) NE-7
Berry Lake—*lake* ND-7
Berry Lake—*lake* TX-5
Berry Lake—*lake* WA-9
Berry Lake—*lake* (4) WI-6
Berry Lake—*reservoir* AL-4
Berry Lake—*reservoir* IL-6
Berry Lake—*reservoir* NM-5
Berry Lake—*reservoir* TN-4
Berry Lake—*reservoir* TX-5
Berry Lakebed—*flat* MN-6
Berry Lake Dam—*dam* AL-4
Berry Lake Dam—*dam* SD-7
Berry Lake Dam—*dam* TN-4
Berry Lakes—*lake* WA-9
Berryland—*locale* NJ-2
Berry Landing—*locale* GA-3
Berryland Playground—*park* WI-6
**Berryland (subdivision)**—*pop pl* NC-3
Berry Lateral—*canal* CO-8
Berry Ledge—*cliff* ME-1
Berry Line Sch (historical)—*school* MS-4
Berryman—*locale* WA-9
**Berryman**—*pop pl* MO-7
Berryman Branch—*stream* NJ-2
Berryman Campground—*locale* MO-7
Berryman Cem—*cemetery* GA-3
Berryman Cem—*cemetery* TN-4
Berryman Cem—*cemetery* (3) TX-5
Berryman Ch—*church* MO-7
**Berryman Corner**—*pop pl* MA-1
Berryman Creek—*stream* WA-9
Berryman Hollow—*valley* TN-4
Berryman Rsvr—*reservoir* CA-9
Berryman School (historical)—*locale* MO-7
Berrymans Corner—*locale* VA-3
Berryman Trail—*trail* MO-7
*Berryman Trail Campground* MO-7
Berryman Tunnel—*mine* NV-8
Berryman Windmill—*locale* TX-5
*Berry Meadow* MT-8
Berry Meadows—*flat* (2) MT-8
Berry Memorial Ch—*church* SC-3
Berry Methodist Ch—*church* AL-4
Berrymile Pond Trail—*trail* NY-2
Berry Mill—*locale* NC-3
Berrymill Hill—*summit* NY-2
Berrymill Pond—*lake* (2) NY-2
**Berry Mills**—*pop pl* ME-1
*Berry Mine* TN-4
Berry Mound and Village Archeol
Site—*hist pl* MS-4
Berry Mountain—*ridge* AL-4
*Berry Mtn* AL-4
*Berry Mtn* PA-2
Berry Mtn—*summit* (2) AL-4
Berry Mtn—*summit* MA-1
Berry Mtn—*summit* (3) NC-3
Berry Mtn—*summit* (2) PA-2
Berry Mtn—*summit* VA-3
Berry Mtn—*summit* WA-9
Berrynill Cem—*cemetery* OH-6
Berry Park—*park* CA-9
Berry Park—*park* CO-8
Berry Park—*park* MN-6
Berry Park—*park* OK-5
Berry Patch—*locale* WA-9
Berry Patch, The—*area* CA-9
Berry Patch Ridge—*ridge* CA-9
Berry Patch Trail—*trail* PA-2
Berry Peak—*summit* WA-9
Berry-Peters Mill—*locale* TN-4
Berry Point—*cape* AL-4
Berry Point—*cliff* CO-8
*Berry Pond* ME-1
*Berry Pond* SC-3
Berry Pond—*lake* FL-3
Berry Pond—*lake* (3) ME-1
Berry Pond—*lake* (2) MA-1
Berry Pond—*lake* (2) NH-1
Berry Pond—*lake* NY-2
Berry Pond—*lake* TN-4
Berry Pond—*lake* TX-5
Berry Pond—*reservoir* ME-1
Berry Pond Brook—*stream* NH-1
Berry Pond Brook—*stream* NY-2
Berry Pond Creek—*stream* MA-1
Berry Pond Creek—*stream* NY-2
Berryport Canyon—*valley* UT-8
Berry Ranch—*locale* ID-8
Berry Ranch—*locale* NE-7
Berry Ranch—*locale* NM-5
Berry Ranch—*locale* SD-7
Berry Ranch—*locale* TX-5
Berry Ranch—*locale* WY-8
Berry Ranch Strip—*airport* AZ-5
Berry Ridge—*ridge* CA-9
Berry Ridge—*ridge* CO-8
Berry Ridge—*ridge* IN-6
Berry Rock—*pillar* OR-9
Berry RR Station—*building* AZ-5
Berry Rsvr—*reservoir* (2) CO-8
Berry Rsvr—*reservoir* GA-3
Berry Run—*stream* IN-6
Berry Run—*stream* KY-4
Berry Run—*stream* MD-2
Berry Run—*stream* OH-6
Berry Run—*stream* PA-2
Berry Run—*stream* VA-3
Berry Run—*stream* (3) WV-2
Berrys—*locale* VA-3
Berry Sand Draw—*valley* TX-5
Berrys Bay—*bay* NC-3
Berrys Brook—*stream* NH-1
**Berrysburg**—*pop pl* PA-2
Berrysburg Borough—*civil* PA-2
Berry Sch—*school* AL-4
Berry Sch—*school* CA-9
Berry Sch—*school* CT-1
Berry Sch—*school* (4) IL-6
Berry Sch—*school* KS-7
Berry Sch—*school* KY-4
Berry Sch—*school* (2) MA-1
Berry Sch—*school* (2) MI-6
Berry Sch—*school* MO-7
Berry Sch—*school* MT-8
Berry Sch—*school* (3) TN-4
Berry Sch—*school* (2) TX-5
Berry Sch (abandoned)—*school* (2) MO-7
Berry Sch (abandoned)—*school* SD-7
Berrys Chapel—*church* AL-4
Berrys Chapel—*church* TN-4
**Berrys Chapel**—*pop pl* TN-4
Berrys Chapel Cem—*cemetery* TX-5
**Berrys Chapel Heights**—*pop pl* TN-4
*Berrys Chapel Methodist Ch* AL-4
Berry Sch (historical)—*school* AL-4
Berry Sch (historical)—*school* MS-4
Berry Sch (historical)—*school* MO-7
Berry Schools—*hist pl* GA-3
Berrys Corner—*locale* ME-1
**Berrys Corner**—*pop pl* NH-1
*Berrys Cove* ME-1
Berrys Cove—*valley* AL-4
Berrys Creek—*stream* KS-7
Berrys Creek—*stream* LA-4
Berrys Creek—*stream* NJ-2
Berrys Creek—*stream* NC-3
Berrys Creek—*stream* TX-5
Berrys Creek Canal—*canal* NJ-2
Berrys Crossroads—*locale* SC-3
Berrys Gap—*gap* NC-3
Berrys Gap—*gap* PA-2
Berrys Grove Ch—*church* NC-3
Berrys Hill—*summit* NH-1
Berrys (historical)—*locale* AL-4
*Berry Shoals* SC-3
*Berry Shoals Lake* SC-3
Berry Shoals Pond—*reservoir* SC-3
Berry Siding—*locale* WV-2
Berry-Sigler Investment
Property—*hist pl* OR-9
Berrys Island—*island* TN-4
Berrys Island Ecological Study
Area—*locale* TN-4
*Berrys Landing* GA-3
Berrys Landing—*locale* SC-3
**Berrys Lick**—*pop pl* KY-4
Berry Slough—*stream* OR-9
Berrys Millpond—*reservoir* SC-3
*Berrys Mountain* PA-2
*Berrys Pond* SC-3
Berry Spring—*spring* (2) AL-4
Berry Spring—*spring* AZ-5
Berry Spring—*spring* CA-9
Berry Spring—*spring* GA-3
Berry Spring—*spring* MO-7
Berry Spring—*spring* MT-8
Berry Spring—*spring* SD-7
Berry Spring—*spring* (2) UT-8
Berry Spring—*spring* WA-9
Berry Spring Creek—*stream* UT-8
*Berry Springs* UT-8
Berry Springs—*locale* AL-4
Berry Springs—*spring* UT-8
Berrys River—*stream* NH-1
Berrys Run—*stream* IA-7
Berrys Run—*stream* OH-6
Berrys Store—*other* KY-4
Berry Stadium—*other* TX-5
*Berry Station* AL-4
Berry Store—*locale* KY-4
Berry Street—*uninc pl* TX-5
Berry Summit—*summit* CA-9
Berry-Sutton Cem—*cemetery* MS-4
**Berrysville**—*pop pl* OH-6
Berry Swamp—*swamp* AL-4
Berry Swamp—*swamp* NY-2
*Berry-Tabernacle Church* AL-4
Berry Tank—*reservoir* (2) AZ-5
Berry Tank—*reservoir* NM-5
Berry Tank Number Two—*reservoir* AZ-5
Berry Thomas Sch (historical)—*school* MS-4
**Berryton**—*pop pl* GA-3
**Berryton**—*pop pl* KS-7
Berryton Cem—*cemetery* GA-3
Berryton United Methodist Ch—*church* KS-7
*Berry Town* DE-2
Berrytown—*locale* DE-2
Berrytown—*locale* PA-2
Berrytown—*locale* VA-3
**Berrytown**—*pop pl* KY-4
*Berrytown Branch* DE-2
**Berry (Town of)**—*pop pl* WI-6
**Berry Township**—*pop pl* ND-7
**Berry (Township of)**—*pop pl* IL-6
*Berry Trail* AZ-5
*Berryville* AL-4
Berryville—*locale* MI-6
Berryville—*other* TN-4
**Berryville**—*pop pl* AR-4
**Berryville**—*pop pl* GA-3
**Berryville**—*pop pl* (2) IL-6
**Berryville**—*pop pl* MS-4
**Berryville**—*pop pl* NY-2
**Berryville**—*pop pl* TX-5
**Berryville**—*pop pl* VA-3
**Berryville**—*pop pl* WV-2
Berryville Ch—*church* TN-4
Berryville Hist Dist—*hist pl* VA-3
Berryville Memorial Cem—*cemetery* AR-4
Berryville Rsvr—*reservoir* VA-3
Berry Water Gardens—*reservoir* NC-3
Berry Well—*locale* NM-5
Berry Well—*well* NM-5
Berry West (CCD)—*cens area* KY-4
Berry Windmill—*locale* NM-5
Berry Windmill—*locale* TX-5
Bersching Drain—*canal* MI-6
Berseth Lake—*lake* MN-6
Bersheba Sch (historical)—*school* AL-4
*Bersheba Springs Post Office* TN-4
*Bershire School* FL-3
Berskow State Wildlife Mngmt
Area—*park* MN-6
Berson Lake—*lake* TN-4
Berston Playground—*locale* MI-6
*Bersum Gardens* NH-1
**Bersum Gardens**—*pop pl* NH-1
*Bert* GA-3
Bert—*locale* WV-2
Berta Bend Conglomerate Field—*locale* TX-5
Berta Canyon—*valley* CA-9
Berta Dam JHS—*school* TX-5
Bertagnole Well—*well* UT-8
Bert Avery Seep—*spring* UT-8
Bert Bath Spring—*spring* CA-9
Bert Boroughs Pond Dam—*dam* AL-4
Bert Bros Pond—*lake* FL-3
Bert Canyon—*valley* NM-5
Bert Cook Well—*well* NM-5
Bert Creek—*stream* AR-4
Bert Creek—*stream* (2) MT-8
Bert Creek—*stream* NC-3
Bert Creek—*stream* OR-9
Bert Creek—*stream* WY-8
Bert Creek Lead—*ridge* NC-3
*Bert Dosh Lock* FL-3
**Berteleda (Douglas Park)**—*pop pl* CA-9
Berteling Bldg—*hist pl* IN-6
Bertersville (historical)—*locale* MS-4
Bert Fritz Summit—*summit* NV-8
Bert Gillaspie Ranch—*locale* WY-8
*Bertha* OH-6
Bertha—*locale* FL-3
Bertha—*locale* MD-2
Bertha—*locale* MO-7
Bertha—*locale* NE-7
Bertha—*locale* PA-2
Bertha—*locale* VA-3
**Bertha**—*pop pl* AL-4
**Bertha**—*pop pl* KY-4
**Bertha**—*pop pl* MN-6
**Bertha**—*pop pl* NC-3
**Bertha**—*pop pl* TN-4
**Bertha**—*pop pl* WV-2
Bertha, Lake—*lake* FL-3
Bertha, Lake—*lake* ND-7
Bertha, Mount—*summit* AK-9
Bertha Abess Childrens Center—*school* FL-3
Bertha Bay—*bay* AK-9
Bertha Canyon—*valley* CA-9
Bertha Canyon—*valley* WY-8
Bertha Creek—*stream* (2) AK-9
Bertha Creek—*stream* ID-8
Bertha Creek—*stream* MT-8
**Bertha (Dinsmore)**—*pop pl* PA-2
Bertha Eccles Community Art
Center—*hist pl* UT-8
Bertha Glacier—*glacier* AK-9
Bertha Gulch—*valley* CO-8
**Bertha Hill**—*pop pl* WV-2
Bertha Hill—*summit* ID-8
Bertha Hollow—*valley* KY-4
Bertha Hollow—*valley* UT-8
Bertha Lake—*lake* MI-6
Bertha Lake—*lake* MN-6
Bertha Lake—*lake* WA-9
Bertha Lake—*lake* WY-8
Bertha May Lake—*lake* WA-9
Bertha Mine—*mine* MT-8
Bertha Peak—*summit* CA-9
Bertha Ridge—*ridge* CA-9
Bertha Sch—*school* NE-7
Berthas Cupboard Cave—*cave* CA-9
**Bertha (Township of)**—*pop pl* MN-6
Berthaud Ditch—*canal* IN-6
Berthaville—*locale* VA-3
Berthelson Pond—*lake* OR-9
Berth F—*locale* GU-9
Berth H—*locale* GU-9
**Berthold**—*pop pl* ND-7
Berthold Bay—*bay* ND-7
Berthold Bay Public Use Area—*park* ND-7
Bertholdt Lake—*lake* MI-6
**Berthold Township**—*pop pl* ND-7
Berthold Updyke and Landon
Ditch—*canal* CO-8
**Berthoud**—*pop pl* CO-8
**Berthoud Falls**—*pop pl* CO-8
Berthoud Pass—*gap* CO-8
**Berthoud Pass**—*pop pl* (2) CO-8
Berthoud Pass Ditch—*canal* CO-8
Berthoud Rsvr—*reservoir* CO-8
Berthusen Memorial Park—*cemetery* WA-9
**Bertice**—*pop pl* MS-4
*Bertie* NC-3
Bertie—*locale* LA-4
Bertie—*uninc pl* NC-3
**Bertie County**—*pop pl* NC-3
Bertie County Courthouse—*hist pl* NC-3
Bertie HS—*school* NC-3
Bertie JHS—*school* NC-3
Bertie Lord Creek—*stream* MT-8
Berties Falls—*falls* NC-3
Bertie Windmill—*locale* NM-5
Bertig—*locale* AR-4
Bertino Rsvr—*reservoir* MT-8
Bert Jayne Pond—*lake* PA-2
Bert Jones Yacht Harbor—*harbor* MS-4
Bert Lake—*lake* OR-9
Bert Lee Park—*flat* AZ-5
Bert Lee Tank—*reservoir* AZ-5
Bertlesen Canyon—*valley* UT-8
Bertlesen Ditch—*canal* UT-8
Bert Lide Mine—*mine* AK-9
Bert Mertz Canyon—*valley* TX-5
Bert Mesa—*summit* UT-8
Bert Millar Cutoff—*channel* AK-9
Bert Monday Rsvr—*reservoir* ID-8
Bert Mooney Airport—*airport* MT-8
Bert Mtn—*summit* NC-3
Bertoglio-Merrill Ranch—*locale* NM-5
Bertolets Ch—*church* PA-2
Bertolini Block—*hist pl* UT-8
Bertolli Lake—*reservoir* AL-4
Bertom Lake—*lake* WI-6
Berton—*locale* VA-3
Berton Cem—*cemetery* SC-3
Berton Cem—*cemetery* SD-7
Bertoncini Island—*island* AK-9
Berton (historical)—*locale* SD-7
Bert Pierre Tank—*reservoir* AZ-5
Bert Point—*cape* AK-9
Bertram—*locale* (2) CA-9
**Bertram**—*pop pl* IA-7
**Bertram**—*pop pl* (2) TX-5
Bertram, Henry, Sr., House—*hist pl* OR-9
Bertram Branch—*stream* TX-5
Bertram (CCD)—*cens area* TX-5
*Bertram Creek* GA-3
Bertram Creek—*stream* GA-3
Bertram Ditch—*canal* WY-8
Bertram Hall at Radcliffe
College—*hist pl* MA-1
Bertram Hollow—*valley* KY-4
Bertram Lake—*lake* MN-6
Bertram Lake—*lake* WI-6
Bertram Mine—*mine* CA-9
Bertram Mtn—*summit* KY-4
*Bertram School* SD-7
Bertram Township—*fmr MCD* IA-7
*Bertramville* OH-6
Bertran Camp—*locale* IA-7
Bertrand—*locale* VA-3
**Bertrand**—*pop pl* MI-6
**Bertrand**—*pop pl* MO-7
**Bertrand**—*pop pl* NE-7
Bertrand, Bayou—*stream* LA-4
Bertrand Ave Sch—*school* CA-9
Bertrand Branch—*stream* IL-6
Bertrand Cem—*cemetery* (2) LA-4
Bertrand Cem—*cemetery* OK-5
Bertrand Creek—*stream* WA-9
Bertrand HS—*school* TN-4
Bertrand Island—*island* NJ-2
Bertrand Island—*uninc pl* NJ-2
Bertrand Ranch—*locale* NE-7
Bertrand Site—*hist pl* NE-7
**Bertrand (Township of)**—*pop pl* MI-6
**Bertrandville**—*pop pl* LA-4
Bertraud Lake—*lake* MI-6
Bertrum Mtn—*summit* KY-4
Berts Branch—*stream* KY-4
Berts Canyon—*valley* CA-9
Berts Canyon—*valley* NM-5
Bert Sch—*school* IL-6
Bertsch Cem—*cemetery* SD-7
Bertsch Creek—*stream* PA-2
*Bertsch Run* PA-2
**Bertsch Terrace**—*pop pl* CA-9
Bertschy House—*hist pl* AR-4
Berts Corner—*locale* CO-8
Bert Siddel Ditch—*canal* CO-8
*Berts Lake* MI-6
Berts Lake—*lake* CA-9
Berts Lake—*reservoir* AL-4
Berts Place Well—*well* TX-5
Berts Tank—*reservoir* (2) NM-5
Berts Well—*well* (3) NM-5
Bert Tank—*reservoir* AZ-5
Bert Tank—*reservoir* TX-5
Bert Thompson Number 1 Dam—*dam* SD-7
Bertuccini House and
Barbershop—*hist pl* MS-4
Bertwell Sch—*school* NE-7
*Bert-Wettar* KS-7
Bert Wettar—*locale* KS-7
Bert Windmill—*locale* NM-5
Bert Woods Homestead—*locale* MT-8
Berua Ch—*church* TN-4
Berube Sch—*school* ME-1
Ber Vaughn Park—*park* PA-2
Berven Bay—*bay* ID-8
**Berville**—*pop pl* MI-6
Berwet—*locale* KS-7
*Berwet Spur* KS-7
**Berwet Spur**—*pop pl* KS-7
Berwick—*locale* AL-4
Berwick—*locale* MS-4
Berwick—*locale* MO-7
**Berwick**—*pop pl* IL-6
**Berwick**—*pop pl* IA-7
**Berwick**—*pop pl* KS-7
**Berwick**—*pop pl* LA-4
**Berwick**—*pop pl* ME-1
**Berwick**—*pop pl* (2) ND-7
**Berwick**—*pop pl* OH-6
**Berwick**—*pop pl* PA-2
Berwick Acad—*hist pl* ME-1
Berwick Acad—*school* ME-1
Berwick Airp—*airport* KS-7
Berwick Airp—*airport* PA-2
Berwick Bay—*bay* LA-4
Berwick Borough—*civil* PA-2
*Berwick Branch* ME-1
Berwick Canyon—*valley* CA-9
Berwick Cem—*cemetery* IA-7
Berwick Cem—*cemetery* ND-7
Berwick Center (census name
Berwick)—*other* ME-1
Berwick Ch—*church* MO-7
Berwick Creek—*stream* WA-9
Berwick Cut—*bend* TX-5
Berwick Heights—*locale* PA-2
Berwick (historical)—*locale* KS-7
Berwick Hosp—*hospital* PA-2
Berwick Hospital Corporation
Airp—*airport* PA-2
Berwick Hotel—*hist pl* OH-6
Berwick HS—*school* LA-4
Berwick Island—*island* LA-4
Berwick Lock—*dam* LA-4
**Berwick Manor**—*pop pl* IN-6
Berwick Manor and Orchard—*hist pl* CA-9
Berwick Plaza—*locale* OH-6
*Berwick Reservoir* PA-2
Berwick Sch—*school* KS-7
Berwick Sch—*school* OH-6
**Berwick (Town of)**—*pop pl* ME-1
Berwick Township—*civil* MO-7
**Berwick Township**—*pop pl* KS-7
**Berwick Township**—*pop pl* ND-7
**Berwick (Township of)**—*pop pl* IL-6
**Berwick (Township of)**—*pop pl* PA-2
Berwick Waterworks—*locale* LA-4
Berwin—*locale* GA-3
Berwin Cem—*cemetery* GA-3
Berwin Cem—*cemetery* NY-2
**Berwind**—*pop pl* WV-2
Berwind, Lake—*reservoir* WV-2
Berwind Arroyo—*stream* CO-8
*Berwind Canyon* CO-8
Berwind Canyon—*valley* CO-8
Berwind Mines—*mine* CO-8
Berwind Ruins—*locale* CO-8
**Berwinsdale**—*pop pl* PA-2
*Berwit* KS-7
*Berwyn* OK-5
Berwyn—*locale* NY-2
Berwyn—*other* OK-5
**Berwyn**—*pop pl* IL-6
**Berwyn**—*pop pl* MD-2
**Berwyn**—*pop pl* NE-7
**Berwyn**—*pop pl* PA-2
**Berwyn Heights**—*pop pl* MD-2
Berwyn Park—*park* IL-6
Berwyn Sch—*school* MI-6
**Berwyn (subdivision)**—*pop pl* VA-3
**Berwyn Township**—*pop pl* NE-7
**Berwyn (Township of)**—*pop pl* IL-6
*Beryessa* CA-9
*Beryl* PA-2
Beryl—*locale* AR-4
Beryl—*locale* UT-8
**Beryl**—*pop pl* PA-2
**Beryl**—*pop pl* WV-2
Beryl Baptist Ch—*church* UT-8
Beryl Feldspar Mine—*mine* SD-7
Beryl Heights Sch—*school* CA-9
Beryl Hill—*summit* MA-1
Beryl Junction—*locale* UT-8
**Beryl Junction**—*pop pl* UT-8
Beryl Junction Airp—*airport* UT-8
Beryl Lake—*lake* CA-9
Beryl Lake—*lake* GA-3
Beryl Mtn—*summit* CO-8
Beryl Mtn—*summit* NH-1
Beryl-Newcastle—*cens area* UT-8
Beryl-Newcastle Division—*civil* UT-8
Beryl Spring—*spring* WY-8
Beryl Veal Dam—*dam* SD-7
Berylwood—*hist pl* CA-9
Berylwood Sch—*school* CA-9
Berzelia—*locale* GA-3
Berzelia Pond—*reservoir* GA-3
Besa Chitto Creek—*stream* MS-4
Besancon Gulch—*valley* CO-8
*Besant* SD-7
*Besant Flats* SD-7
Besant Park—*flat* SD-7
Bes Arrington Lake Dam—*dam* MS-4
Besboro Island—*island* AK-9
Besco—*locale* PA-2
**Beseck Lake**—*pop pl* CT-1
Beseck Lake—*reservoir* CT-1
Beseck Mtn—*summit* CT-1
Besela—*island* FM-9
**Beseman (Township of)**—*pop pl* MN-6
**Besemer**—*pop pl* NY-2
Besh-Ba-Gowah—*hist pl* AZ-5
Besh-Ba-Gowah Pueblo Ruins—*locale* AZ-5
Beshbito Rest Area—*locale* AZ-5
Beshbito Wash—*stream* AZ-5
Beshear, Lake—*reservoir* KY-4
Beshears Cem—*cemetery* TN-4
Beshears Point—*cape* AL-4
Beshear Spring—*spring* KY-4
**Beshel**—*pop pl* LA-4
Beshell Grade—*locale* OR-9
*Beshnalthdas Cliffs* AZ-5
*Beshnalthdas Cliffs* NM-5
Beshoar—*locale* CO-8
Besho Lake—*lake* MN-6
Beshta Bay—*bay* AK-9
Besing Cem—*cemetery* IL-6
Besk Cem—*cemetery* NE-7
Besley Cem—*cemetery* PA-2
**Besoco**—*pop pl* WV-2
Besor Ridge—*ridge* VA-3
Besosa—*locale* PR-3
**Bess**—*pop pl* TX-5
**Bess**—*pop pl* VA-3
Bess, Lake—*lake* AK-9
Bess, Lake—*lake* FL-3
Bess, Lake—*lake* MN-6
*Bessada Church* AL-4
*Bess Bend* TX-5
Bess Branch—*stream* AL-4
Bess Branch—*stream* LA-4
Bess Canyon—*valley* WY-8
Bess Cem—*cemetery* MO-7
Bess Cem—*cemetery* WV-2
Bess Chapel—*church* NC-3
Bess Creek—*stream* ID-8
Besse Bog Reservoir Dam—*dam* MA-1
Besse Bog Rsvr—*reservoir* MA-1
*Besse Creek* OR-9
*Bessee Creek* OR-9
Besse Hill—*summit* CT-1
Bess Elem Sch—*school* NC-3
*Bessember City Central Elem Sch* NC-3
*Bessember City JHS* NC-3
Bessemer—*locale* FL-3
**Bessemer**—*pop pl* AL-4
**Bessemer**—*pop pl* MI-6
**Bessemer**—*pop pl* NC-3
**Bessemer**—*pop pl* OH-6
**Bessemer**—*pop pl* (2) PA-2
**Bessemer**—*pop pl* VA-3
**Bessemer**—*pop pl* WV-2
Bessemer Airp—*airport* AL-4
Bessemer Archaeol Site (44 BO
26)—*hist pl* VA-3
Bessemer Bend—*bend* WY-8
Bessemer Borough—*civil* PA-2
**Bessemer City**—*pop pl* NC-3
Bessemer City Hall—*building* AL-4
Bessemer City HS—*school* NC-3
Bessemer City Primary Sch—*school* NC-3
Bessemer City Rsvr—*reservoir* NC-3
Bessemer Creek—*stream* MI-6
Bessemer Ditch—*canal* CO-8
Bessemer Elem Sch—*school* NC-3
**Bessemer Gardens**—*pop pl* AL-4
**Bessemer Homestead**—*pop pl* AL-4
Bessemer Junction—*locale* AL-4
Bessemer Junction—*locale* PA-2
Bessemer Mine—*mine* CA-9
Bessemer Mtn—*summit* WA-9
Bessemer Mtn—*summit* WY-8
Bessemer Municipal Golf Course—*locale* AL-4
Bessemer Narrows—*valley* WY-8
Bessemer Park—*park* CO-8
Bessemer Park—*park* IL-6
**Bessemer (RR name Walford)**—*pop pl* PA-2
Bessemer Sch—*school* CO-8
Bessemer Stadium—*other* AL-4
Bessemer State Technical Coll—*school* AL-4
Bessemer Station—*building* PA-2
Bessemer Terrace—*uninc pl* PA-2
**Bessemer (Township of)**—*pop pl* MI-6
**Bessemer (Walford Station)**—*pop pl* PA-2
*Besse Mountain* ME-1
Bessen Creek—*stream* MD-2
Bessen Landing—*locale* MD-2
Bessent—*locale* FL-3
Besse Park—*park* CA-9
Besse Park Pond—*lake* CT-1
Besser, Lake—*reservoir* MI-6
Besser JHS—*school* MI-6
Besser Natural Area—*park* MI-6
Besser Technical Sch—*school* MI-6
Bessette Creek—*stream* MT-8
Bessette Point—*cape* MN-6
Bessette Ranch—*locale* MT-8
Bessey, Anthonv W., House—*hist pl* UT-8
Bessey Creek—*stream* OR-9
Bessey Creek Point—*cape* FL-3
Bessey Lake—*lake* MI-6
Bessey Nursery—*hist pl* NE-7
Bessey Point—*cape* FL-3
Bessey Sch—*school* ME-1
*Bess Hollow* MO-7
*Bess Hollow* PA-2
*Bessie* MS-4
Bessie—*locale* (2) AL-4
Bessie—*locale* IL-6
Bessie—*locale* NC-3
**Bessie**—*pop pl* OK-5
**Bessie**—*pop pl* TN-4
Bessie, Lake—*lake* FL-3
Bessie, Lake—*lake* ND-7
Bessie Babbet Lake—*lake* WI-6
Bessie Bar (inundated)—*bar* UT-8
Bessie Beck Lake—*reservoir* AL-4
Bessie Beck Lake Dam—*dam* AL-4
Bessie Bell Mtn—*summit* VA-3
Bessie Bottom—*bend* WY-8
Bessie Branham Park—*park* GA-3
Bessie Butte—*summit* OR-9
Bessie Carmichael Sch—*school* CA-9
Bessie C Fonvielle Elem Sch—*school* AL-4
Bessie Ch—*church* OK-5
Bessie Cove—*bay* FL-3
*Bessie Creek* TX-5
Bessie Creek—*stream* (2) AK-9
Bessie Creek—*stream* OR-9
Bessie Elem Sch (historical)—*school* AL-4
Bessie Ellison Sch—*school* MO-7
Bessie Furnace—*locale* OH-6
Bessie G Mine—*mine* CO-8
Bessie Gulch—*valley* ID-8
Bessie Haynes Park—*park* TX-5
Bessie Heights—*locale* TX-5
Bessie Heights Oil And Gas Field—*oilfield* TX-5
Bessie-Helen Ranch—*locale* CO-8
Bessie Hollow—*valley* MO-7
Bessie Junction—*locale* AL-4
Bessie K—*locale* LA-4
Bessie Landing—*locale* TN-4
Bessie Mine—*mine* AK-9
Bessie Mine—*mine* CA-9
Bessie Mine—*mine* CO-8
Bessie Mines Number 3
Impoundment—*reservoir* AL-4
Bessie Mines - Number 3 Impoundment
Dam—*dam* AL-4
Bessie Mine (underground)—*mine* AL-4
Bessie Park—*flat* CO-8
Bessie Peak—*summit* AK-9
Bessie Pond—*lake* NY-2
Bessie Post Office (historical)—*building* TN-4
Bessie Rhoads Mtn—*summit* NM-5
Bessie Rock—*pillar* OR-9
Bessie Rock Trail—*trail* OR-9
Bessie Roe Branch—*stream* MS-4
Bessies Bayou—*gut* TX-5
Bessies Chapel—*church* NC-3
Bessies Creek—*stream* TX-5
Bessies Falls—*falls* CO-8
Bessie Tank—*reservoir* AZ-5
Bessie Tank—*reservoir* NM-5
Bessie Turner Mine—*mine* NV-8
Bessiola, Lake—*lake* FL-3
Bess Kaiser Hosp—*hospital* OR-9
Bess Lake—*lake* UT-8
Bess Landing—*locale* NC-3
Besslen—*locale* ID-8
Bessler Ditch—*canal* IN-6
Bessler Lakes—*lake* IL-6
Bessleys Bar—*bar* TN-4
Bessman-Kemp County Park—*park* IA-7
**Bessmay**—*pop pl* TX-5
Bessmay-Buna—*CDP* TX-5
Bess Nook—*summit* FL-3
Bess Point—*cape* SD-7

Bess Sch—school ... MO-7
Bess Slough—stream ... MO-7
Bess T Shepherd Sch—school ... TN-4
**Bessville**—pop pl ... MO-7
Bessville Sch (abandoned)—school ... MO-7
Bessy Creek—stream ... FL-3
Bessy Playground—park ... MI-6
Bessy Slough—stream ... AK-9
*Best* ... PA-2
Best—locale ... TX-5
**Best**—pop pl ... NY-2
**Best**—pop pl ... NC-3
Best—uninc pl ... PA-2
Best, Allie M., House—hist pl ... GA-3
Best, Charles, House—hist pl ... ME-1
Best Bend—bend ... TX-5
Best Bottom Cem—cemetery ... MO-7
Best Branch—stream ... TX-5
Best Brewing Company of Chicago Bldg—hist pl ... IL-6
Best Butte—summit ... CO-8
Best Canal—canal ... CA-9
Best-Cannon House—hist pl ... UT-8
Best Cem—cemetery (2) ... AR-4
Best Cem—cemetery ... KY-4
Best Cem—cemetery ... NE-7
Best Ch (abandoned)—church ... MO-7
Best Chapel—church ... GA-3
Best Chapel—church ... NC-3
Best Corner—locale ... ID-8
Best Coulee—valley ... MT-8
Best Cove—valley ... NC-3
Best Dam—dam ... AL-4
Best Ditch—canal ... IN-6
Best Drain—canal ... CA-9
Besteda Bar—bar ... AL-4
Besteda Landing (historical)—locale ... AL-4
Bester (historical)—locale ... AL-4
Bester Sch—school ... NE-7
**Bestfield**—pop pl ... DE-2
**Bestgate**—pop pl ... MD-2
Best Gulch—valley ... CO-8
Best Hill—summit ... ID-8
*Besth-kli-chee-begez* ... AZ-5
*Besth-kli-chee-begez* ... NM-5
Best Hollow—valley ... NY-2
Best HS—school ... NC-3
Best Inscription-1891—other ... UT-8
Best JHS—school ... MI-6
*Best Lake* ... MI-6
Best Lake—lake ... NJ-2
Bestland—locale ... VA-3
Best Lock Airstrip—airport ... IN-6
Best Lookout—locale ... PA-2
Best Park—park ... MI-6
Best Pit—cave ... AL-4
Bestpitch—locale ... MD-2
Bestpitch Ferry—locale ... MD-2
Best Place Rsvr—reservoir ... WY-8
Best Plaza (Shop Ctr)—locale ... FL-3
Best Pond—reservoir ... AL-4
Best Pond—reservoir ... NC-3
Best Pond Dam—dam ... NC-3
Best Ranch—locale ... WY-8
Best Rock—island ... OR-9
Bestrom Creek—stream ... WA-9
Bestrom Meadows—flat ... WA-9
*Bests* ... PA-2
**Bests**—pop pl ... NC-3
Bests Bridge—bridge ... GA-3
Bests Ch—church ... NC-3
Best Sch—school ... MI-6
Best Sch—school ... NC-3
Best's Covered Bridge—hist pl ... VT-1
*Bests Lake* ... WA-9
Best Slough—stream ... CA-9
Bests Mill (historical)—locale (2) ... TN-4
Best Spring—spring ... MT-8
Best Station—building ... PA-2
**Best Station**—pop pl ... PA-2
Best Tank—reservoir ... AZ-5
Best View—locale ... CT-1
**Bestview**—pop pl ... TN-4
**Best View Estates (subdivision)**—pop pl ... UT-8
**Best View Subdivision**—pop pl ... UT-8
Bestville—locale ... CA-9
Bestwall—locale ... KS-7
*Bestwater* ... AR-4
Bestwick Creek—stream ... MT-8
*Beşul Cape* ... PW-9
Beswick—locale ... CA-9
Beswick Cem—cemetery ... IN-6
Beswick Island—island ... FL-3
Beswick Sch—school ... CA-9
Beszivit Lake—lake ... AK-9
*Bet* ... MS-4
**Bet**—pop pl ... MS-4
Bet, Mount—summit ... NH-1
Beta—locale (2) ... CO-8
**Beta**—pop pl ... NC-3
**Beta**—pop pl ... TN-4
Beta Bell Tower—locale ... OH-6
Beta Branch—stream ... TN-4
Beta Canal—canal ... CA-9
Beta Cave—cave ... AL-4
Beta Cem—cemetery ... TN-4
Beta Ch—church ... TN-4
Beta Creek—stream ... MT-8
Beta Ditch—canal ... WY-8
Beta Key—island ... FL-3
Beta Lake—lake ... MN-6
Beta Lake—lake ... MT-8
**Betana Park**—pop pl ... VA-3
**Betances**—pop pl ... PR-3
Betania Ch—church ... ND-7
*Betany Church* ... AL-4
*Betaoto Reef* ... PW-9
*Betaot Reef* ... PW-9
Beta Pit—cave ... AL-4
Beta Post Office (historical)—building ... TN-4
Beta Rock—other ... AK-9
*Betatakin* ... AZ-5
Betatakin Canyon—valley ... AZ-5
Betatakin Overlook—locale ... AZ-5
Betatakin Ruin—locale ... AZ-5
*Betatakin Ruins* ... AZ-5
Beta Theta Pi Fraternity House, The Univ of Oklahoma—hist pl ... OK-5
Betaw Ch—church ... SC-3
Betay—summit ... AZ-5
Bet Branch—stream ... TX-5
Bet Breira Synagogue—church ... FL-3
Bet Cash Branch—stream ... KY-4
Betchler Lakes—lake ... MI-6
Betchtel Park—park ... DE-2
**Bete Grise**—pop pl ... MI-6
Bete Grise Bay—bay ... MI-6
Betel Hollow—valley ... WI-6
Betenson Flat—flat ... UT-8
Betesta Ch—church ... MN-6
*Beth* ... NY-2
Beth, Lake—lake ... AK-9
Beth, Lake—reservoir ... AL-4
Beth Aaron Cem—cemetery ... MT-8
*Bethabara* ... NC-3
Bethabara—uninc pl ... NC-3
*Bethabara Baptist Church* ... AL-4
Bethabara Cem—cemetery ... AL-4
Bethabara Ch—church (3) ... AL-4
Bethabara Ch—church ... AR-4
Bethabara Ch—church (2) ... GA-3
Bethabara Ch—church ... IN-6
Bethabara Ch—church (4) ... NC-3
Bethabara Ch—church ... SC-3
*Bethabara Creek* ... GA-3
*Bethabara Creek* ... NC-3
Bethabara Creek—stream ... NC-3
Bethabara Hist Dist—hist pl ... NC-3
Bethabara Moravian Church—hist pl ... NC-3
Bethabara Sch (historical)—school (2) ... AL-4
*Bethabera Church* ... AL-4
Bethaberry Cem—cemetery ... AL-4
Bethabra Cem—cemetery ... AL-4
Bethabra Ch—church ... GA-3
Beth Abraham Cem—cemetery ... ME-1
Beth Abraham Cem—cemetery ... NJ-2
Beth Abraham Cem—cemetery ... OH-6
Beth Abraham Home—building ... NY-2
Betha Cem—cemetery ... LA-4
Betha Ch—church ... LA-4
*Bethal* ... PA-2
Bethal Creek—stream ... MT-8
Bethal Lake—reservoir ... IN-6
Bethal Lake Dam—dam ... IN-6
Beth-Allen Park—park ... PA-2
Beth Alom Cem—cemetery ... CT-1
Bethal Ranch—locale ... CA-9
**Bethalto**—pop pl ... IL-6
Bethalto Village Hall—hist pl ... IL-6
Beth Am Cem—cemetery ... NJ-2
Beth Am Sch—school ... MA-1
Bethana Baptist Ch (historical)—church ... TN-4
Bethana Cem—cemetery ... OH-6
*Bethana Primitive Baptist Church* ... MS-4
Bethan Ch—church ... NC-3
Bethane Cem—cemetery ... ND-7
*Bethania* ... PA-2
**Bethania**—pop pl ... NC-3
Bethania Cem—cemetery ... IL-6
Bethania Cem—cemetery (3) ... MN-6
Bethania Cem—cemetery (3) ... ND-7
Bethania Cem—cemetery (6) ... SD-7
*Bethania Cemetery* ... SD-7
Bethania Ch—church (3) ... MN-6
Bethania Ch—church ... MO-7
Bethania Ch—church (2) ... ND-7
Bethania Golf Course—park ... NC-3
Bethania Hist Dist—hist pl ... NC-3
Bethania Hosp—hospital ... TX-5
Bethania Sch—school ... PW-9
**Bethania Station**—pop pl ... NC-3
Bethania (Township of)—fmr MCD ... NC-3
Bethanna—locale ... KY-4
Bethanna Ch—church ... TX-5
*Bethany* ... KS-7
*Bethany* ... NJ-2
*Bethany* ... PA-2
Bethany—locale ... AR-4
Bethany—locale ... GA-3
Bethany—locale ... NC-3
**Bethany**—pop pl ... CA-9
**Bethany**—pop pl ... CT-1
**Bethany**—pop pl ... FL-3
**Bethany**—pop pl ... GA-3
**Bethany**—pop pl ... IL-6
**Bethany**—pop pl (3) ... IN-6
**Bethany**—pop pl (2) ... KY-4
**Bethany**—pop pl ... LA-4
**Bethany**—pop pl ... MN-6
**Bethany**—pop pl ... MS-4
**Bethany**—pop pl (2) ... MO-7
**Bethany**—pop pl ... NE-7
**Bethany**—pop pl ... OH-6
**Bethany**—pop pl ... OK-5
**Bethany**—pop pl (2) ... OR-9
**Bethany**—pop pl ... PA-2
**Bethany**—pop pl ... SC-3
**Bethany**—pop pl (2) ... TN-4
**Bethany**—pop pl ... TX-5
**Bethany**—pop pl ... VA-3
**Bethany**—pop pl ... WV-2
**Bethany**—pop pl ... VI-3
Bethany, Lake—reservoir ... CT-1
Bethany Bapist Ch—church ... MS-4
*Bethany Baptist Ch* ... AL-4
*Bethany Baptist Ch* ... MS-4
Bethany Baptist Ch—church (3) ... AL-4
Bethany Baptist Ch—church (2) ... FL-3
Bethany Baptist Ch—church ... KS-7
*Bethany Baptist Church* ... NC-3
Bethany Beach—beach ... DE-2
**Bethany Beach**—pop pl ... DE-2
**Bethany Beach**—pop pl ... MI-6
Bethany Beach Canal—canal ... DE-2
**Bethany (Bethany Center)**—pop pl ... NY-2
Bethany Bible Ch—church ... FL-3
Bethany Bible Coll—school ... CA-9
Bethany Bible Sch—school ... AZ-5
Bethany Borough—civil ... PA-2
*Bethany Branch* ... GA-3
Bethany Branch—stream ... AL-4
Bethany Bridge—bridge ... GA-3
Bethany Cem—cemetery (7) ... AL-4
Bethany Cem—cemetery (2) ... AR-4
Bethany Cem—cemetery ... CA-9
Bethany Cem—cemetery (2) ... FL-3
Bethany Cem—cemetery ... GA-3
Bethany Cem—cemetery ... ID-8
Bethany Cem—cemetery (5) ... IL-6
Bethany Cem—cemetery ... IN-6
Bethany Cem—cemetery (5) ... IA-7
Bethany Cem—cemetery (5) ... KS-7
Bethany Cem—cemetery ... KY-4
Bethany Cem—cemetery ... LA-4
Bethany Cem—cemetery ... MA-1
Bethany Cem—cemetery (8) ... MN-6
Bethany Cem—cemetery (10) ... MS-4
Bethany Cem—cemetery (4) ... MO-7
Bethany Cem—cemetery (5) ... ND-7
Bethany Cem—cemetery ... OH-6
Bethany Cem—cemetery (5) ... OK-5
Bethany Cem—cemetery (2) ... PA-2
Bethany Cem—cemetery (5) ... SC-3
Bethany Cem—cemetery (6) ... SD-7
Bethany Cem—cemetery (5) ... TN-4
Bethany Cem—cemetery (6) ... TX-5
Bethany Cem—cemetery ... VA-3
Bethany Cem—cemetery ... WV-2
Bethany Cem—cemetery (3) ... WI-6
Bethany Cemetery—building ... SD-7
*Bethany Center* ... CT-1
**Bethany Center**—pop pl ... NY-2
Bethany Center Cem—cemetery ... KS-7
*Bethany Ch* ... AL-4
*Bethany Ch* ... IN-6
*Bethany Ch* ... MS-4
Bethany Ch—church (25) ... AL-4
Bethany Ch—church (5) ... AR-4
Bethany Ch—church (3) ... CT-1
Bethany Ch—church ... DE-2
Bethany Ch—church (2) ... FL-3
Bethany Ch—church (34) ... GA-3
Bethany Ch—church (15) ... IL-6
Bethany Ch—church (13) ... IN-6
Bethany Ch—church (2) ... IA-7
Bethany Ch—church (7) ... KS-7
Bethany Ch—church (15) ... KY-4
Bethany Ch—church (7) ... LA-4
Bethany Ch—church (3) ... MD-2
Bethany Ch—church (5) ... MI-6
Bethany Ch—church (14) ... MN-6
Bethany Ch—church (18) ... MS-4
Bethany Ch—church (15) ... MO-7
Bethany Ch—church ... MT-8
Bethany Ch—church (7) ... NE-7
Bethany Ch—church (2) ... NJ-2
Bethany Ch—church ... NM-5
Bethany Ch—church (3) ... NY-2
Bethany Ch—church (37) ... NC-3
Bethany Ch—church (9) ... ND-7
Bethany Ch—church (10) ... OH-6
Bethany Ch—church ... OK-5
Bethany Ch—church (12) ... PA-2
Bethany Ch—church (20) ... SC-3
Bethany Ch—church (2) ... SD-7
Bethany Ch—church (22) ... TN-4
Bethany Ch—church (8) ... TX-5
Bethany Ch—church (40) ... VA-3
Bethany Ch—church (7) ... WV-2
Bethany Ch—church (9) ... WI-6
Bethany Chapel—church ... IN-6
Bethany Chapel—church ... KS-7
Bethany Chapel—church (3) ... KY-4
Bethany Chapel—church ... MO-7
Bethany Chapel—church ... NJ-2
Bethany Chapel—church ... NY-2
Bethany Chapel—church ... NC-3
Bethany Chapel—church ... OH-6
Bethany Chapel—hist pl ... NJ-2
Bethany Ch (historical)—church ... AL-4
Bethany Ch (historical)—church (2) ... MS-4
Bethany Childrens Home Spring—spring ... PA-2
*Bethany Ch of God Prophecy* ... MS-4
Bethany Ch of Miami—church ... FL-3
Bethany Ch of the Nazarene—church ... MS-4
Bethany Christian Church-Disciples of Christ—church ... FL-3
Bethany Christian Methodist Episcopal Ch—church ... FL-3
Bethany Christian Sch—school ... FL-3
Bethany Coll—school ... KS-7
Bethany Coll—school ... MN-6
Bethany Coll—school ... OK-5
Bethany Coll—school ... WV-2
Bethany Community Kindergarten—school ... FL-3
Bethany Congregational Ch—church ... AL-4
Bethany Congregational Church—hist pl ... GA-3
Bethany Convent—church ... NY-2
Bethany Creek—stream ... VA-3
**Bethany Crossroads**—pop pl ... NC-3
**Bethany Dunes (subdivision)**—pop pl ... DE-2
Bethany East Shop Ctr—locale ... AZ-5
Bethany Evangelical Covenant Kindergarten—school ... FL-3
Bethany Free Methodist Ch—church ... NE-7
Bethany Grand Mobile Home Park—locale ... AZ-5
Bethany Hall—locale ... IA-7
*Bethany Heights* ... NE-7
**Bethany Hills**—pop pl ... TN-4
Bethany Hills Camp—locale ... TN-4
Bethany Hist Dist—hist pl ... WV-2
Bethany (historical)—locale (2) ... AL-4
Bethany (historical)—locale ... MS-4
**Bethany (historical)**—pop pl ... NC-3
Bethany Home—building ... IL-6
Bethany Hosp—hospital ... IL-6
Bethany Hosp—hospital ... KS-7
Bethany HS—school ... IN-6
Bethany Independent Christian Ch—church ... IN-6
Bethany Indian Cem—cemetery ... MI-6
Bethany Institute (historical)—school ... MS-4
Bethany Lime Ch—church ... AL-4
Bethany Longstreet Oil and Gas Field—oilfield ... LA-4
Bethany Lutheran Ch—church ... FL-3
Bethany Lutheran Ch—church ... KS-7
Bethany Lutheran Church—hist pl ... MI-6
Bethany Lutheran Kindergarten—school ... FL-3
**Bethany Manor**—pop pl ... MD-2
Bethany Memorial Airp—airport ... MO-7
Bethany Memorial Cem—cemetery ... KY-4
Bethany Memorial Chapel—hist pl ... ID-8
Bethany Methodist Cem—cemetery ... OR-9
*Bethany Methodist Ch* ... AL-4
*Bethany Missionary Baptist Ch* ... AL-4
Bethany Mission Assembly of God—church ... FL-3
Bethany Oil And Gas Field—oilfield ... TX-5
Bethany Orphan Home—building ... PA-2
Bethany Park—park ... KS-7
Bethany Park—park ... NE-7
**Bethany Park**—pop pl ... CA-9
*Bethany Pentecostal Holiness Church* ... MS-4
Bethany Pioneer Cem—cemetery ... OR-9
Bethany Place—church ... KS-7
Bethany Place Ch—church ... VA-3
*Bethany Presbyterian Ch* ... MS-4
Bethany Presbyterian Ch—church ... AL-4
Bethany Presbyterian Ch—church ... MS-4
*Bethany Primitive Baptist Ch* ... MS-4
Bethany Primitive Baptist Ch—church ... AL-4
Bethany Reformed and Lutheran Church Cemetery—hist pl ... NC-3
Bethany Ridge—ridge ... KY-4
Bethany Rsvr—reservoir ... CA-9
Bethany Rsvr—reservoir ... MO-7
Bethany Sch—school ... CA-9
Bethany Sch—school ... CT-1
Bethany Sch—school ... IL-6
Bethany Sch—school ... IN-6
Bethany Sch—school ... MI-6
Bethany Sch—school (2) ... NE-7
Bethany Sch—school ... OH-6
Bethany Sch—school ... OK-5
Bethany Sch—school (2) ... OR-9
Bethany Sch—school ... PA-2
Bethany Sch—school (3) ... VA-3
Bethany Sch (historical)—school (3) ... AL-4
Bethany Sch (historical)—school ... MO-7
Bethany Sch (historical)—school (2) ... TN-4
Bethany Seminary—school ... IL-6
Bethany Sewage Disposal—other ... OK-5
Bethany-Silver Creek Cem—cemetery ... SD-7
Bethany Springs Cem—cemetery ... MS-4
Bethany Square Shop Ctr—locale ... AZ-5
Bethany Tabernacle—church ... PA-2
**Bethany (Town of)**—pop pl ... CT-1
**Bethany (Town of)**—pop pl ... NY-2
**Bethany Township**—pop pl ... KS-7
**Bethany Township**—pop pl ... MO-7
Bethany (Township of)—fmr MCD ... NC-3
**Bethany (Township of)**—pop pl ... MI-6
Bethany United Methodist Church—hist pl ... SD-7
Bethany United Presbyterian Ch—church ... IN-6
Bethany Valley Cem—cemetery ... ND-7
Bethany Villa Adult Mobile Home Park—locale ... AZ-5
Bethany Village—locale ... PA-2
Bethany Village Nursing Home—building ... OH-6
**Bethany Village (subdivision)**—pop pl ... DE-2
Bethany West Plaza Shop Ctr—locale ... AZ-5
Bethany West Shop Ctr—locale ... AZ-5
Bethard—locale ... TX-5
*Bethavan* ... IN-6
*Bethaven* ... IN-6
Bethaven Ch—church (2) ... GA-3
Bethayres—locale ... PA-2
Bethbara Cem—cemetery ... KY-4
Bethbirei Cem—cemetery ... TN-4
Bethbirei Ch—church ... TN-4
Beth Car Ch—church ... NC-3
Bethcar Ch—church ... SC-3
Bethcar Ch—church ... TN-4
Beth David Acad—school ... CT-1
Beth-David Cem—cemetery ... NJ-2
Beth David Cem—cemetery ... NY-2
Beth David Synagogue—church ... FL-3
Bethea, Tristram, House—hist pl ... AL-4
Bethea Cem—cemetery ... MS-4
Bethea Cem—cemetery ... NC-3
Bethea Cem—cemetery ... SC-3
*Bethea Creek* ... AL-4
Bethea Creek—stream ... TX-5
Bethea Dam—dam ... AL-4
Bethea Home for the Aged—building ... SC-3
Bethea Lake—reservoir ... FL-3
Bethea Mill Creek—stream ... AL-4
Bethea Pond—reservoir ... TN-4
**Bethear**—pop pl ... SC-3
*Beth Earley Church* ... AL-4
*Betheasby Church* ... AL-4
Beth Eden—locale ... SC-3
**Betheden**—pop pl ... MS-4
Betheden Cem—cemetery ... MD-2
Betheden Cem—cemetery ... MS-4
Beth Eden Ch—church ... VA-3
Betheden Lutheran Ch—church ... MS-4
Beth Eden Sch—school ... SD-7
Bethehem Ch—church ... AR-4
Bethehen Ch—church ... KS-7
*Bethel* ... AL-4
*Bethel* ... IN-6
*Bethel* ... KS-7
*Bethel* ... MS-4
*Bethel* ... NC-3
*Bethel* ... PA-2
*Bethel* ... VA-3
Bethel—CDP ... CT-1
Bethel—fmr MCD ... NE-7
Bethel—locale ... AL-4
Bethel—locale (3) ... AR-4
Bethel—locale (2) ... DE-2
Bethel—locale ... FL-3
Bethel—locale (5) ... GA-3
Bethel—locale (5) ... MD-2
Bethel—locale ... MS-4
Bethel—locale ... NM-5
Bethel—locale (2) ... NC-3
Bethel—locale ... OH-6
Bethel—locale ... OK-5
Bethel—locale ... OR-9
Bethel—locale (2) ... PA-2
Bethel—locale (3) ... TN-4
Bethel—locale (6) ... TX-5
Bethel—locale (4) ... VA-3
**Bethel**—pop pl (11) ... AL-4
**Bethel**—pop pl ... AK-9
**Bethel**—pop pl ... AR-4
**Bethel**—pop pl ... CA-9
**Bethel**—pop pl ... CT-1
**Bethel**—pop pl ... DE-2
**Bethel**—pop pl (2) ... GA-3
**Bethel**—pop pl (3) ... IL-6
**Bethel**—pop pl (2) ... IN-6
**Bethel**—pop pl ... IA-7
**Bethel**—pop pl ... KS-7
**Bethel**—pop pl (2) ... KY-4
**Bethel**—pop pl ... LA-4
**Bethel**—pop pl ... ME-1
**Bethel**—pop pl ... MD-2
**Bethel**—pop pl ... MI-6
**Bethel**—pop pl ... MN-6
**Bethel**—pop pl (4) ... MS-4
**Bethel**—pop pl ... MO-7
**Bethel**—pop pl (2) ... NY-2
**Bethel**—pop pl (8) ... NC-3
**Bethel**—pop pl (2) ... OH-6
**Bethel**—pop pl ... OK-5
**Bethel**—pop pl (2) ... OR-9
**Bethel**—pop pl (5) ... PA-2
**Bethel**—pop pl ... RI-1
**Bethel**—pop pl ... SC-3
**Bethel**—pop pl (8) ... TN-4
**Bethel**—pop pl (2) ... TX-5
**Bethel**—pop pl ... VT-1
**Bethel**—pop pl ... VA-3
**Bethel**—pop pl ... WA-9
**Bethel**—pop pl ... WI-6
Bethel—uninc pl ... KS-7
Bethel, Lake—lake ... FL-3
**Bethel, Mount**—pop pl ... PA-2
Bethel, Mount—summit ... CO-8
Bethel Acad—school ... MS-4
Bethel Academy—other ... VA-3
Bethel Acad (historical)—school ... AL-4
Bethel Acad Site (15JS80)—hist pl ... KY-4
**Bethel Acres**—pop pl ... OK-5
Bethel African Methodist Episcopal Ch—church (3) ... DE-2
Bethel African Methodist Episcopal Ch—church (5) ... FL-3
Bethel African Methodist Episcopal Ch—church ... IN-6
Bethel African Methodist Episcopal Ch—church ... TN-4
Bethel African Methodist Episcopal Church—hist pl ... AR-4
Bethela Grove Ch—church ... TX-5
Bethel Airp—airport ... AK-9
*Bethel AME Ch* ... AL-4
Bethelame Ch—church ... AL-4
Bethel AME Ch—church ... MS-4
Bethel AME Ch (historical)—church ... AL-4
Bethel A.M.E. Church—hist pl ... IN-6
Bethel AME Church—hist pl ... IA-7
Bethel AME Church—hist pl ... KY-4
Bethel A.M.E. Church—hist pl ... PA-2
Bethel A.M.E. Church—hist pl ... SC-3
Bethel AME Church—hist pl ... WV-2
Bethel AME Church and Manse—hist pl ... NY-2
Bethel AME Zion Ch—church ... AL-4
Bethel Apostolic Temple—church ... FL-3
*Bethel Apostolic United Pentecostal Ch* ... MS-4
Bethel Assembly of God Ch—church ... AL-4
Bethel Assembly of God Ch—church ... FL-3
Bethel Assembly of God Ch—church (3) ... MS-4
Bethel Assembly of God Spanish Ch—church ... FL-3
Bethel Bank—bar ... FL-3
*Bethel Baptist Ch* ... AL-4
*Bethel Baptist Ch* ... MS-4
Bethel Baptist Ch—church (11) ... AL-4
Bethel Baptist Ch—church (6) ... FL-3
Bethel Baptist Ch—church (2) ... KS-7
Bethel Baptist Ch—church (3) ... MS-4
Bethel Baptist Ch—church (4) ... TN-4
Bethel Baptist Ch—church ... UT-8
Bethel Baptist Ch (historical)—church ... TN-4
Bethel Baptist Church—hist pl ... KY-4
Bethel Baptist Church—hist pl ... OH-6
Bethel Baptist Church—hist pl ... OR-9
Bethel Baptist Institutional Church—hist pl ... FL-3
Bethel Bayou—stream (2) ... LA-4
Bethel Beach—beach ... VA-3
Bethel Berry Ch—church ... AL-4
*Bethel Berry Ch of Christ* ... AL-4
*Bethel Berry Christian Ch* ... AL-4
**Bethel (Bethel Academy)**—pop pl ... VA-3
**Bethel (Bethelham)**—pop pl ... MD-2
Bethel Bible Camp—park ... SD-7
Bethel Bible Sch—school ... TN-4
Bethel Bible Sch (historical)—school ... TN-4
**Bethelboro**—pop pl ... PA-2
Bethel Branch—stream (4) ... AL-4
Bethel Branch—stream ... AR-4
Bethel Branch—stream ... KY-4
Bethel Branch—stream ... MS-4
Bethel Branch—stream (3) ... TN-4
Bethel Branch—stream ... VA-3
Bethel Branch Ch—church ... NC-3
Bethel Brick Ch—church ... GA-3
Bethel Bridge—bridge ... MO-7
Bethel Bridge—bridge ... TN-4
Bethel Bridge Cave—cave ... TN-4
Bethel Brook—stream ... IN-6
Bethel Camp—locale ... MN-6
Bethel Camp—park ... IN-6
Bethel Campground—locale ... SC-3
*Bethel Campground Church* ... AL-4
Bethel Canal—canal ... CA-9
Bethel Canyon—valley ... ID-8
Bethel Carr Ch—church ... OH-6
Bethel-Cass Ch—church ... TX-5
Bethel Cave—cave (2) ... AL-4
Bethel Cave—cave ... TN-4
*Bethel Cem* ... AL-4
*Bethel Cem* ... MS-4
Bethel Cem—cemetery (5) ... AL-4
Beth-El Cem—cemetery ... AL-4
Bethel Cem—cemetery (23) ... AL-4
Beth El Cem—cemetery ... AZ-5
Bethel Cem—cemetery (17) ... AR-4
Bethel Cem—cemetery ... CA-9
Bethel Cem—cemetery (2) ... CO-8
Beth-el Cem—cemetery ... CT-1
Bethel Cem—cemetery ... CT-1
Bethel Cem—cemetery ... DE-2
Bethel Cem—cemetery (3) ... FL-3
Bethel Cem—cemetery (8) ... GA-3
Bethel Cem—cemetery ... ID-8
Bethel Cem—cemetery (19) ... IL-6
Bethel Cem—cemetery (23) ... IN-6
Bethel Cem—cemetery (16) ... IA-7
Bethel Cem—cemetery (7) ... KS-7
Bethel Cem—cemetery (6) ... KY-4
Bethel Cem—cemetery (3) ... LA-4
Bethel Cem—cemetery ... MD-2
Beth El Cem—cemetery ... MA-1
Bethel Cem—cemetery (2) ... MI-6
Bethel Cem—cemetery (3) ... MN-6
Beth-el Cem—cemetery ... MN-6
Bethel Cem—cemetery (7) ... MN-6
Bethel Cem—cemetery (37) ... MS-4
Bethel Cem—cemetery (13) ... MO-7
Bethel Cem—cemetery (2) ... MT-8
Bethel Cem—cemetery (6) ... NE-7
Beth-El Cem—cemetery ... NJ-2
Bethel Cem—cemetery (2) ... NM-5
Bethel Cem—cemetery (3) ... NY-2
Beth-El Cem—cemetery ... NY-2
Bethel Cem—cemetery (7) ... NC-3
Bethel Cem—cemetery (10) ... ND-7
Bethel Cem—cemetery (21) ... OH-6
Bethel Cem—cemetery (10) ... OK-5
Bethel Cem—cemetery ... OR-9
Bethel Cem—cemetery (10) ... PA-2
Bethel Cem—cemetery (5) ... SC-3
Bethel Cem—cemetery (5) ... SD-7
Bethel Cem—cemetery (23) ... TN-4
Bethel Cem—cemetery ... TX-5
Beth El Cem—cemetery ... TX-5
Bethel Cem—cemetery (20) ... TX-5
Bethel Cem—cemetery (6) ... VA-3
Bethel Cem—cemetery (2) ... WA-9
Bethel Cem—cemetery (3) ... WV-2
Bethel Cem—cemetery (8) ... WI-6
Bethel Cem—cemetery ... WY-8
Bethel Cemetary—cemetery ... AR-4
Bethel Cemetery—church ... TN-4
**Bethel (Census Area)**—pop pl ... AK-9
Bethel Center Ch—church ... IN-6
*Bethel Ch* ... AL-4
*Bethel Ch* ... IN-6
*Bethel Ch* ... MS-4
*Bethel Ch* ... MO-7
*Bethel Ch* ... TN-4
Bethel Ch—church (107) ... AL-4
Bethel Ch—church (34) ... AR-4
Bethel Ch—church ... CA-9
Bethel Ch—church ... CT-1
Bethel Ch—church (4) ... DE-2
Bethel Ch—church (29) ... FL-3
Bethel Ch—church (107) ... GA-3
Bethel Ch—church (35) ... IL-6
Bethel Ch—church (46) ... IN-6
Bethel Ch—church (15) ... IA-7
Bethel Ch—church (10) ... KS-7
Bethel Ch—church (43) ... KY-4
Bethel Ch—church (26) ... LA-4
Bethel Ch—church ... ME-1
Bethel Ch—church (8) ... MD-2
Bethel Ch—church (18) ... MI-6
Bethel Ch—church (11) ... MN-6
Bethel Ch—church (83) ... MS-4
Bethel Ch—church (53) ... MO-7
Bethel Ch—church (9) ... NE-7
Bethel Ch—church (5) ... NJ-2
Bethel Ch—church ... NM-5
Bethel Ch—church (5) ... NY-2
Bethel Ch—church (91) ... NC-3
Bethel Ch—church (9) ... ND-7
Bethel Ch—church (48) ... OH-6
Bethel Ch—church (18) ... OK-5
Bethel Ch—church (42) ... PA-2
Bethel Ch—church (67) ... SC-3
Bethel Ch—church (4) ... SD-7
Bethel Ch—church (59) ... TN-4
Bethel Ch—church (41) ... TX-5
Bethel Ch—church (73) ... VA-3
Bethel Ch—church (3) ... WA-9
Bethel Ch—church (37) ... WV-2
Bethel Ch—church (12) ... WI-6
Bethel Ch (abandoned)—church (2) ... MO-7
Bethel Ch (abandoned)—church ... PA-2
*Bethel Chapel* ... AL-4
Bethel Chapel—church ... AR-4
Bethel Chapel—church ... GA-3
Bethel Chapel—church (2) ... IL-6
Bethel Chapel—church (2) ... IN-6
Bethel Chapel—church ... IA-7
Bethel Chapel—church (3) ... KS-7
Bethel Chapel—church (3) ... MI-6
Bethel Chapel—church (3) ... MO-7
Bethel Chapel—church ... NC-3
Bethel Chapel—church (6) ... OH-6
Bethel Chapel—church (3) ... PA-2
Bethel Chapel—church ... SC-3
Bethel Chapel—church ... TN-4
Bethel Chapel—church ... VA-3
Bethel Chapel—church (3) ... WV-2
Bethel Chapel (historical)—church ... TN-4
Bethel Chapel Pentecostal Ch of God—church ... TN-4
Bethel Ch (historical)—church (6) ... AL-4
Bethel Ch (historical)—church (10) ... MS-4
Bethel Ch (historical)—church (3) ... MO-7
Bethel Ch (historical)—church (2) ... PA-2
Bethel Ch (historical)—church (10) ... TN-4
Bethel Childrens Home—building ... KY-4
*Bethel Ch of Christ* ... AL-4
Bethel Ch of Christ—church ... TN-4
*Bethel Ch of God* ... AL-4
Bethel Ch of God—church ... AL-4
Bethel Ch of the Lord Jesus Christ—church ... MS-4
Bethel Christian Sch—school ... CA-9
Bethel Christian Sch—school ... FL-3
Bethel Church—hist pl ... IA-7
Bethel Church—hist pl ... KY-4
Bethel Church Cem—cemetery ... WV-2
Bethel City (historical)—locale ... IA-7
*Bethel CME Ch* ... AL-4
*Bethel Colbert Ch* ... AL-4
*Bethel Colbert Missionary Baptist Ch* ... AL-4
Bethel Coll—school ... IN-6
Bethel Coll—school ... KS-7
Bethel Coll—school ... KY-4
Bethel Coll—school ... MN-6
Bethel Coll—school ... TN-4
*Bethel College* ... KS-7
Bethel College Administration Bldg—hist pl ... KS-7
Bethel College Camp—locale ... TN-4
Bethel Community Baptist Ch—church ... FL-3
Bethel Community Center—building ... AL-4

Beverley—*hist pl* WV-2
Beverley, Lake—*lake* AK-9
**Beverley Beach**—*pop pl* FL-3
Beverley Cove—*bay* AK-9
**Beverley Heights (subdivision)**—*pop pl* AL-4
*Beverley Hills* CA-9
**Beverley Hills**—*pop pl* VA-3
Beverley Hist Dist—*hist pl* VA-3
*Beverley Lake* MD-2
Beverley Manor (Magisterial District)—*fmr MCD* VA-3
Beverley Mill—*hist pl* VA-3
Beverley Mill—*locale* VA-3
*Beverley Mills* VA-3
**Beverley Terrace**—*pop pl* FL-3
*Beverlies Chapel* MS-4
Beverlin Fork—*stream* WV-2
*Beverly* IA-7
*Beverly* MI-6
*Beverly* TX-5
Beverly—*hist pl* (2) MD-2
Beverly—*locale* FL-3
Beverly—*locale* GA-3
Beverly—*locale* (2) KY-4
Beverly—*locale* MO-7
Beverly—*locale* NE-7
Beverly—*locale* PA-2
**Beverly**—*pop pl* AR-4
**Beverly**—*pop pl* IL-6
**Beverly**—*pop pl* KS-7
**Beverly**—*pop pl* KY-4
**Beverly**—*pop pl* MA-1
**Beverly**—*pop pl* NJ-2
**Beverly**—*pop pl* OH-6
**Beverly**—*pop pl* SC-3
**Beverly**—*pop pl* TN-4
**Beverly**—*pop pl* TX-5
**Beverly**—*pop pl* WA-9
**Beverly**—*pop pl* WV-2
Beverly, City of—*civil* MA-1
**Beverly Acres**—*pop pl* TN-4
**Beverly Addition (subdivision)**—*pop pl* UT 8
Beverly Beach—*locale* MI-6
**Beverly Beach**—*pop pl* FL-3
**Beverly Beach**—*pop pl* MD-2
**Beverly Beach**—*pop pl* OR-9
**Beverly Beach**—*pop pl* WA-9
Beverly Beach State Park—*park* OR-9
Beverly Brook—*stream* NH-1
Beverly Cem—*cemetery* IL-6
Beverly Cem—*cemetery* KS-7
Beverly Cem—*cemetery* KY-4
Beverly Cem—*cemetery* MS-4
Beverly Cem—*cemetery* VA-3
Beverly Center Business District—*hist pl* MA-1
Beverly Ch—*church* DE-2
Beverly Channel—*channel* MA-1
Beverly Channel—*channel* NJ-2
Beverly Channel—*channel* PA-2
Beverly Chapel—*church* MS-4
Beverly Chapel—*church* TX-5
Beverly Chapel—*church* VA-3
Beverly Chapel Sch—*school* MS-4
*Beverly City* NJ-2
Beverly City Hall—*building* MA-1
Beverly Community Center—*building* MA-1
*Beverly (corporate name Beverly Hills)* TX-5
Beverly Country Club—*other* IL-6
*Beverly Cove* MA-1
Beverly Cove—*cove* MA-1
**Beverly Cove (subdivision)**—*pop pl* MA-1
*Beverly Creek* MA-1
Beverly Creek—*stream* AK-9
Beverly Creek—*stream* OR-9
Beverly Creek—*stream* SC-3
Beverly Creek—*stream* WA-9
**Beverly (Davenport Station)**—*pop pl* MS-4
**Beverly Depot**—*pop pl* IA-7
Beverlye MS—*school* AL-4
**Beverly Estates**—*pop pl* PA-2
**Beverly Farms**—*pop pl* MD-2
**Beverly Farms**—*pop pl* MA-1
**Beverly Forest**—*pop pl* VA-3
Beverly Forest Camp—*locale* WA-9
Beverly Fork—*stream* WV-2
**Beverly Gardens**—*pop pl* OH-6
**Beverly Gardens**—*pop pl* TX-5
**Beverly Glen**—*pop pl* CA-9
Beverly Grove—*locale* CO-8
Beverly Hall—*building* NC-3
Beverly Harbor—*bay* MA-1
Beverly-Harris House—*hist pl* TX-5
**Beverly Heights**—*pop pl* PA-2
**Beverly Heights**—*pop pl* VA-3
Beverly Heights—*uninc pl* GA-3
Beverly Heights Ch—*church* PA-2
Beverly Hill—*CDP* FL-3
Beverly Hill—*locale* TX-5
**Beverly Hill**—*pop pl* IN-6
*Beverly Hills* IL-6
*Beverly Hills* MI-6
*Beverly Hills* OH-6
Beverly Hills—*locale* CO-8
**Beverly Hills**—*pop pl* CA-9
**Beverly Hills**—*pop pl* (2) FL-3
**Beverly Hills**—*pop pl* GA-3
**Beverly Hills**—*pop pl* KS-7
**Beverly Hills**—*pop pl* KY-4
**Beverly Hills**—*pop pl* (2) MI-6
**Beverly Hills**—*pop pl* MO-7
**Beverly Hills**—*pop pl* NC-3
**Beverly Hills**—*pop pl* OH-6
**Beverly Hills**—*pop pl* (3) PA-2
**Beverly Hills**—*pop pl* TN-4
**Beverly Hills**—*pop pl* (2) TX-5
**Beverly Hills**—*pop pl* (2) VA-3
**Beverly Hills**—*pop pl* (2) WV-2
**Beverly Hills**—*pop pl* PR-3
Beverly Hills—*summit* PA-2
Beverly Hills—*uninc pl* TX-5
Beverly Hills Cem—*cemetery* NY-2
Beverly Hills Cem—*cemetery* WV-2
Beverly Hills Ch—*church* SC-3
Beverly Hills Ch—*church* TX-5
Beverly Hill Sch—*school* NY-2
**Beverly Hills (corporate name for Beverly)**—*pop pl* TX-5
Beverly Hills HS—*school* CA-9
Beverly Hills Memorial Gardens—*cemetery* FL-3
Beverly Hills MS—*school* PA-2
Beverly Hills Neighborhood Park—*park* NC-3
Beverly Hills Park—*park* TX-5
*Beverly Hills Sanitarium* TN-4
Beverly Hills Sch—*school* CA-9
Beverly Hills Sch—*school* NC-3
Beverly Hills Sch—*school* WV-2
Beverly Hills Shop Ctr—*locale* VA-3
**Beverly Hills (subdivision)**—*pop pl* NC-3
Beverly Hist Dist—*hist pl* WV-2
**Beverly (historical)**—*pop pl* NC-3
Beverly Hosp—*hospital* CA-9
Beverly HS—*school* MA-1
Beverly Inn Corners—*locale* NY-2
Beverly JHS—*school* KS-7
*Beverly Junction* IL-6
*Beverly Junction* MO-7
Beverly Junction—*locale* WA-9
Beverly Junction—*uninc pl* MA-1
**Beverly Knoll**—*pop pl* LA-4
Beverly Lake—*lake* AK-9
Beverly Lake—*lake* IL-6
Beverly Lake—*lake* MD-2
Beverly Lake—*lake* WI-6
Beverly Lake—*reservoir* PA-2
Beverly Lake State Wildlife Mngmt Area—*park* WI-6
Beverly Landing (historical)—*locale* MS-4
Beverly Lawn Park—*park* IL-6
Beverly (Magisterial District)—*fmr MCD* WV-2
*Beverly Manor* IL-6
**Beverly Manor**—*pop pl* IL-6
**Beverly Manor**—*pop pl* VA-3
Beverly Manor Ch—*church* VA-3
Beverly Manor Sch—*school* IL-6
Beverly Marsh—*swamp* VA-3
Beverly Marsh Creek—*stream* VA-3
Beverly Memorial JHS—*school* MA-1
*Beverly Mill* VA-3
*Beverly Mills* VA-3
Beverly Natl Cem—*cemetery* NJ-2
Bevorly Oil Field—*oilfield* MS-4
Beverly Park—*park* IL-6
Beverly Park—*park* MI-6
Beverly Park—*park* NM-5
Beverly Park—*park* WA-9
Beverly Park South—*uninc pl* WA-9
Beverly Place Plantation (historical)—*locale* MS-4
Beverly Plantation (historical)—*locale* MS-4
Beverly Plaza (Shop Ctr)—*locale* FL-3
Beverly Plaza (Shop Ctr)—*locale* MA-1
Beverly Post Office (historical)—*building* TN-4
Beverly Reservoir Dam—*dam* MA-1
Beverly Road Sch—*school* NJ-2
**Beverly Road (subdivision)**—*pop pl* MA-1
Beverly Rocks—*summit* MA-1
Beverly RR Bridge—*hist pl* WA-9
Beverly Rsvr—*reservoir* MA-1
Beverly Run—*stream* (2) VA-3
Beverly Sch—*hist pl* KY-4
Beverly Sch—*school* (3) MI-6
Beverly Sch—*school* MT-8
Beverly Sch—*school* OH-6
Beverly Sch—*school* TX-5
**Beverly Shores**—*pop pl* IN-6
Beverly Shores-Century of Progress Architectural District—*hist pl* IN-6
Beverly Shores Sch—*school* FL-3
Beverly Spring—*spring* CA-9
*Beverly Station* MO-7
**Beverly Station**—*pop pl* AL-4
Beverly Street Park—*park* NC-3
Beverly Swamp—*swamp* SC-3
**Beverly Terrace**—*pop pl* FL-3
Beverlytown—*locale* VA-3
Beverly (Township of)—*fmr MCD* AR-4
**Beverly (Township of)**—*pop pl* IL-6
Beverly Trailer Park—*locale* AZ-5
Beverlyville—*locale* VA-3
Beverly Vista Sch—*school* CA-9
Beverly Wilshire Hotel—*hist pl* CA-9
**Beverly Woods East (subdivision)**—*pop pl* NC-3
Beverly Woods Elem Sch—*school* NC-3
**Beverly Woods (subdivision)**—*pop pl* DE-2
**Beverly Woods (subdivision)**—*pop pl* NC-3
Bever Park—*park* IA-7
Bever Sch—*school* MI-6
*Bevers Lake* MI-6
**Beversville**—*pop pl* TX-5
Beverwyck Manor—*hist pl* NY-2
Bever Zoo—*locale* IA-7
Bevier—*locale* KY-4
**Bevier**—*pop pl* MO-7
Bevier, Samuel, House—*hist pl* IN-6
Bevier Ch—*church* NY-2
Bevier House—*hist pl* NY-2
Bevier Memorial Bldg—*hist pl* NY-2
Bevier Township—*civil* MO-7
Bevil Hill Cem—*cemetery* MS-4
Bevil Hill Ch—*church* MS-4
Bevil (historical)—*locale* MS-4
Bevill Airp—*airport* MO-7
*Bevill Branch* AL-4
Bevill Cem—*cemetery* TN-4
Bevill Ch—*church* AL-4
*Bevill Chapel Church* AL-4
Beville Ditch—*canal* FL-3
**Beville Heights**—*pop pl* FL-3
Beville Lake—*lake* CA-9
Beville Point—*cape* FL-3
Beville Road Ch of Christ—*church* FL-3
**Bevilles Corner**—*pop pl* FL-3
*Bevill P.O.* MS-4
*Bevills Hill Cemetery* MS-4
*Bevills Hill Methodist Church* MS-4
*Bevills Store* AL-4
**Bevil Oaks**—*pop pl* TX-5
Bevils Creek—*stream* GA-3
Bevin, Lake—*reservoir* MS-4
Bevine Fork—*stream* KY-4
**Bevington**—*pop pl* IA-7
Bevington, C. D., House and Stone Barn—*hist pl* IA-7
Bevington, C. D. and Eliza Heath, Privy—*hist pl* IA-7
Bevington Canyon—*valley* WA-9
*Bevin Lake* MI-6
**Bevins Branch**—*pop pl* KY-4
Bevins Branch—*stream* (3) KY-4
Bevins Branch—*stream* NC-3
Bevins Branch—*stream* TN-4
Bevins Cem—*cemetery* (2) VA-3
Bevins Chapel—*church* KY-4
Bevins Chapel—*church* TN-4
Bevins Creek—*stream* FL-3
Bevins Creek—*stream* KY-4
Bevins Grove Cem—*cemetery* IA-7
Bevins Lake—*lake* MI-6
Bevins Sch—*school* KY-4
**Bevinsville**—*pop pl* KY-4
**Bevis**—*pop pl* OH-6
Bevis Branch—*stream* AL-4
Bevis Ch—*church* OH-6
Bevis Corner—*locale* AR-4
Bevis Lake—*lake* WA-9
Bevis Ridge—*ridge* TN-4
Bevis Sch (historical)—*school* TN-4
Bevo Lake—*lake* MN-6
Bevos Mtn—*summit* MO-7
**Bevwood Acres Subdivision**—*pop pl* UT-8
**Bev Wood Estates Subdivision**—*pop pl* UT-8
**Bevwood Subdivision**—*pop pl* UT-8
Bewabic Park—*park* MI-6
Bewdley—*hist pl* VA-3
*Be Welcome* MS-4
Bewelcome—*locale* MS-4
Bewick Lateral—*canal* WI-6
Bewley Cem—*cemetery* TX-5
Bewley Chapel—*church* TN-4
Bewley Creek—*stream* OR-9
Bewley Island—*island* TN-4
**Bewleyville**—*pop pl* KY-4
*Bewlie* GA-3
Bewmark Lake—*lake* WY-8
Bewon Lake—*lake* MN-6
Bew Pond—*lake* MS-4
**Bew Springs**—*pop pl* MS-4
Bews Ranch—*locale* NV-8
Bexar—*locale* TX-5
**Bexar**—*pop pl* AL-4
**Bexar**—*pop pl* AR-4
**Bexar**—*pop pl* TX-5
Bexar (CCD)—*cens area* AL-4
Bexar Cem—*cemetery* AL-4
Bexar Cem—*cemetery* TX-5
Bexar Ch—*church* AL-4
**Bexar (County)**—*pop pl* TX-5
Bexar County Courthouse—*hist pl* TX-5
Bexar Division—*civil* AL-4
*Bexar United Methodist Church* AL-4
**Bexley**—*pop pl* MS-4
**Bexley**—*pop pl* OH-6
Bexley Bay—*swamp* GA-3
Bexley Cem—*cemetery* MS-4
Bexley Ch—*church* MS-4
Bexley Post Office (historical)—*building* MS-4
Bexley Sch—*school* MS-4
Bexley (Township of)—*other* OH-6
Bex Spring—*spring* ID-8
Bexten Branch—*stream* MO-7
Bexton—*locale* GA-3
Beyale Well—*well* NM-5
Beyea Pond—*reservoir* PA-2
*Beyehaven* NJ-2
**Beyer**—*pop pl* PA-2
Beyer Bay—*bay* AK-9
Beyer Cem—*cemetery* KY-4
Beyer Crossing—*locale* TX-5
Beyer Farm Airp—*airport* KS-7
Beyer Home Museum—*hist pl* WI-6
Beyerlein House—*hist pl* AR-4
Beyer Park—*park* CA-9
Beyer Park—*park* MI-6
*Beyers and Tolles Addition* UT-8
Beyers Cem—*cemetery* MO-7
Beyer Sch—*school* CA-9
Beyer Sch—*school* (2) IL-6
**Beyers Corners**—*pop pl* NY-2
Beyers Cove—*bay* WI-6
Beyer Ship Ledge—*bar* ME-1
Beyers Lake—*lake* OR-9
Beyers Lakes—*lake* CA-9
Beyers Lake Trail—*trail* CA-9
Beyers Pond—*reservoir* OR-9
**Beyersville**—*pop pl* TX-5
Beyersville Cem—*cemetery* TX-5
Beyersville Oil Field—*oilfield* TX-5
**Beyerville**—*pop pl* AZ-5
Beye Sch—*school* IL-6
**Beyles Riverside Plot Subdivision**—*pop pl* UT-8
Beymer Memorial Ch—*church* FL-3
Beynaud Ranch—*locale* WA-9
Beynroth House—*hist pl* KY-4
Beyoc—*area* GU-9
Beyota Tank—*reservoir* AZ-5
**Bezer**—*pop pl* MS-4
*Bezhick Lake* MN-6
Bezhik Creek—*stream* MN-6
Bezhik Lake—*lake* MN-6
Bezin Point—*cape* FM-9
Bezoin Cem—*cemetery* OK-5
*Bezona* KS-7
*Bezonia* KS-7
Bezue Cem—*cemetery* LA-4
Bezziel Springs Ch—*church* AL-4
Bezziel Spring Sch—*school* AL-4
Bfedwards Grant—*civil* NM-5
B.F. Good & Company Leaf Tobacco Warehouse—*hist pl* PA-2
B. F. Goodlife Airstrip—*airport* OR-9
B. F. Goodrich Company—*facility* IN-6
B. F. Goodrich Company—*facility* (2) OH-6
B. F. Goodrich Lumberton Plant—*facility* NC-3
B Flat Tank—*reservoir* AZ-5
B-Four Ranch—*locale* CA-9
B Four Ranch—*locale* WY-8
B F Overmyer Ditch—*canal* IN-6
BFP Oil Field—*oilfield* TX-5
*B F Smith Cemetery* AL-4
B F Smith Ranch—*locale* OR-9
B F Windmill—*locale* TX-5
B G Coggins Lake Dam—*dam* MS-4
B G Janous Pond Dam—*dam* MS-4
B G Powell Lake—*reservoir* AL-4
B G Powell Lake Dam—*dam* AL-4
B Greenwood Ranch*—*locale* ND-7
Bg Sandy River Drainage Ditch (historical)—*canal* TN-4
B Hanna Ranch—*locale* NE-7
B Hardy Pond Dam—*dam* MS-4
B H Cooper Lake Dam—*dam* MS-4
B Heart Spring—*spring* MT-8
*Bheeka Creek* OR-9
B Hellickson Dam—*dam* SD-7
B Hicks Ranch—*locale* MT-8
*Bhif Cold Creek Dam* SD-7
Bhif Dam—*dam* SD-7
B Hill—*summit* CA-9
B H Mine—*mine* WY-8
B Hollingsworth Catfish Pond Dam—*dam* MS-4
B Horowitz Pond Dam—*dam* MS-4
*Bi* FM-9
**Biafara**—*pop pl* (2) PR-3
Biagiotti Cem—*cemetery* TN-4
Biala Creek—*stream* TX-5
Biali Rock—*island* AK-9
Bial Point—*cape* MA-1
Bials Hill—*summit* MA-1
Bialystoker Synagogue—*hist pl* NY-2
*Bian* FM-9
**Bianchi**—*pop pl* PR-3
Bianco Road Interchange—*crossing* AZ-5
*Bianu* FM-9
*Bianu Durchfahrt* FM-9
**Biardstown**—*pop pl* TX-5
Biardstown (CCD)—*cens area* TX-5
Biardstown Cem—*cemetery* TX-5
**Bias**—*pop pl* WV-2
Bias Branch—*stream* WV-2
Bias Canyon—*valley* AZ-5
Bias Cem—*cemetery* (6) WV-2
Bias Chapel—*church* (2) WV-2
Biathalon Area—*other* NY-2
Biauswah Lake—*lake* MN-6
Biays (historical)—*locale* KS-7
*Bibalucta Creek* MS-4
Bibalucta Creek—*stream* MS-4
Biba Wila Creek—*stream* MS-4
Bibb, James H., House—*hist pl* AL-4
Bibb and Garretts Steam Mill (historical)—*locale* AL-4
Bibb Cem—*cemetery* (3) AL-4
Bibb Cem—*cemetery* MO-7
**Bibb City**—*pop pl* GA-3
**Bibb County**—*pop pl* AL-4
**Bibb (County)**—*pop pl* GA-3
Bibb County Airp—*airport* AL-4
*Bibb County Area Vocational Center* AL-4
Bibb County Courthouse—*building* AL-4
Bibb County HS—*school* AL-4
Bibb County JHS—*school* AL-4
Bibb County Lake—*reservoir* AL-4
Bibb County Vocational Sch—*school* AL-4
*Bibb Court House* AL-4
Bibbee Hollow—*valley* WV-2
Bibbee Ridge—*ridge* WV-2
Bibber Hill—*summit* ME-1
*Bibber Island* ME-1
*Bibber Ledges* ME-1
*Bibber Rocks* ME-1
*Bibbers Island* ME-1
Bibb Furnace (historical)—*locale* AL-4
*Bibb Graves High School* AL-4
Bibbins Pond—*reservoir* CT-1
Bibb Lookout Tower—*locale* AL-4
Bibb Mill—*locale* AL-4
**Bibb Mills (Ensign Mills)**—*pop pl* GA-3
Bibb Old County Hall (historical)—*locale* AL-4
*Bibbon Hill* ME-1
Bibbons Lake—*lake* MI-6
Bibb Rock—*bar* ME-1
Bibbs Cem—*cemetery* AL-4
Bibbs Chapel Cem—*cemetery* KY-4
Bibb Shoal—*bar* AK-9
Bibbs Hollow—*valley* TN-4
Bibbs Ranch—*locale* NM-5
Bibbs Sch—*school* FL-3
Bibbs Store—*locale* VA-3
Bibbs Tank—*lake* NM-5
Bibbtown Ch—*church* KY-4
Bibbville—*locale* AL-4
Bibbville Ch—*church* AL-4
Bibby Dam—*dam* OR-9
Bibby Family Cem—*cemetery* AL-4
Bibby (historical)—*locale* AL-4
Bibby Mtn—*summit* NY-2
Bibby Pond—*reservoir* OR-9
*Bibby Rsvr* OR-9
Bibbys Cem—*cemetery* WV-2
Bibbys Ferry—*locale* AL-4
Bibby Slope Mine (underground)—*mine* AL-4
*Bibi* MP-9
Bibiana Mtn—*summit* PA-2
*Bibidwayance Lake* MN-6
**Bibiroi**—*pop pl* PW-9
Bible Back Mtn—*summit* CO-8
Bible Back Mtn—*summit* ID-8
Bible Baptist Ch—*church* (3) AL-4
Bible Baptist Ch—*church* DE-2
Bible Baptist Ch—*church* (8) FL-3
Bible Baptist Ch—*church* (3) MS-4
Bible Baptist Ch—*church* TN-4
Bible Baptist Ch—*church* (2) UT-8
Bible Baptist Ch of the Redlands—*church* FL-3
Bible Baptist Church Day Care Center—*school* FL-3
Bible Baptist Seminary—*school* TX-5
Bible Baptist Temple—*church* FL-3
Bible Believers Ch—*church* AL-4
Bible Believers Fellowship Ch—*church* MS-4
Bible Branch—*stream* TN-4
Bible Camp—*locale* (2) IL-6
Bible Camp—*locale* MN-6
Bible Camp—*locale* OK-5
Bible Camp—*locale* VA-3
Bible Camp Ch—*church* MN-6
Bible Camp Park—*flat* MT-8
Bible Canyon—*valley* NM-5
Bible Cem—*cemetery* GA-3
Bible Cem—*cemetery* (2) TN-4
Bible Center Ch—*church* NC-3
*Bible Ch* PA-2
Bible Ch—*church* (2) AL-4
Bible Ch—*church* (2) AR-4
Bible Ch—*church* FL-3
Bible Ch—*church* (5) GA-3
Bible Ch—*church* (2) IL-6
Bible Ch—*church* IN-6
Bible Ch—*church* IA-7
Bible Ch—*church* (2) KY-4
Bible Ch—*church* (2) MI-6
Bible Ch—*church* MO-7
Bible Ch—*church* (2) NC-3
Bible Ch—*church* ND-7
Bible Ch—*church* (2) OK-5
Bible Ch—*church* PA-2
Bible Ch—*church* SC-3
Bible Ch—*church* SD-7
Bible Ch—*church* (2) VA-3
Bible Chapel—*church* AL-4
Bible Chapel—*church* FL-3
Bible Chapel—*church* IL-6
Bible Chapel—*church* MO-7
Bible Chapel—*church* TN-4
Bible Chapel—*church* TX-5
Bible Chapel Ch—*church* (2) AL-4
Bible Chapel Sch—*school* TN-4
Bible Ch of God—*church* AL-4
Bible Christian Ch—*church* KS-7
Bible Christian Ch—*church* MI-6
Bible Church, The—*church* GA-3
Bible Church, The—*church* PA-2
Bible Coll—*school* ID-8
Bible Coll—*school* SC-3
Bible Coll—*school* TN-4
Bible College (St. Paul Bible College)—*facility* MN-6
Bible Conference Ch—*church* PA-2
Bible Covenant Ch—*church* LA-4
Bible Creek—*stream* OR-9
Bible Creek—*stream* TN-4
Bible Deliverance Ch—*church* AL-4
Bible Faith Assembly—*church* MO-7
Bible Fellowship—*church* PA-2
Bible Fellowship Ch—*church* GA-3
Bible Fellowship Church, The—*church* KY-4
*Biblegrove* MO-7
**Bible Grove**—*pop pl* IL-6
**Biblegrove**—*pop pl* MO-7
**Bible Grove**—*pop pl* MO-7
Bible Grove Ch—*church* (2) TN-4
Bible Grove Ch (historical)—*church* MO-7
**Bible Grove (Township of)**—*pop pl* IL-6
Bible Gulf—*valley* GA-3
Bible Hill—*locale* TN-4
**Bible Hill**—*pop pl* TN-4
Bible Hill—*summit* (4) NH-1
Bible Hill—*summit* VT-1
Bible Hill Baptist Ch—*church* TN-4
Bible Hill Cem—*cemetery* TN-4
Bible Hill Ch—*church* TN-4
Bible Hill Ch (historical)—*church* TN-4
*Bible Hill Post Office* TN-4
Biblehill Post Office (historical)—*building* TN-4
Bible Institute Camp—*locale* CO-8
Bible Institute of Texas—*school* TX-5
Bible Knob—*summit* WV-2
Bible Lake—*lake* MN-6
Bible Lighthouse Church, The—*church* AL-4
Bible Memory Ch—*church* GA-3
Bible Methodist Camp—*locale* AL-4
Bible Methodist Campground—*locale* AL-4
Bible Methodist Ch—*church* (4) AL-4
Bible Mission—*church* OH-6
Bible Missionary Baptist Ch—*church* AL-4
Bible Missionary Ch—*church* (3) AL-4
Bible Missionary Ch—*church* MI-6
Bible Missionary Ch—*church* (2) NC-3
Bible Missionary Ch—*church* TN-4
Bible Missionary Church, The—*church* LA-4
Bible Mission Ch—*church* TN-4
Bible Pentecostal Ch—*church* IN-6
Bible Point—*cape* ME-1
Bible Presbyterian Ch—*church* TN-4
Bible Presbyterian Ch of Maitland—*church* FL-3
Bibler Cem—*cemetery* (2) OH-6
Bible Ridge—*ridge* VA-3
Bible Rock—*summit* CT-1
Bible Rock—*summit* WY-8
Bible Rock Brook—*stream* CT-1
Bible Rock Camp—*locale* WA-9
Bible Run—*stream* VA-3
Bible Sch—*school* LA-4
Bible Sch—*school* NY-2
Bible Sch—*school* SD-7
*Bibles Chapel Baptist Ch* TN-4
Bible School Park—*uninc pl* NY-2
Bible Shore—*beach* NC-3
Bible Spring—*spring* TN-4
Bible Spring—*spring* UT-8
Bibles State Wildlife Mngmt Area—*park* MN-6
Bible Student Cem—*cemetery* WI-6
Bible Students Cem—*cemetery* LA-4
Bible Study Chapel—*church* AR-4
Bible Tabernacle—*church* KS-7
Bible Tabernacle—*church* MS-4
Bible Tabernacle—*church* NC-3
Bible Tabernacle—*church* ND-7
Bible Tabernacle, The—*church* NC-3
Bible Top Butte—*summit* NM-5
Bible To Youth Camp—*locale* PA-2
Bible Truth Hall—*church* NY-2
Bible Union Cem—*cemetery* TN-4
Bible Union Ch—*church* TN-4
Bible Union Ch of Christ—*church* TN-4
Bible View Ch—*church* IN-6
Bibleway Baptist Ch—*church* MS-4
Bibleway Ch—*church* AL-4
Bible Way Ch—*church* MD-2
Bible Way Ch—*church* (2) MS-4
Bible Way Ch—*church* (2) NC-3
Bible Way Ch—*church* SC-3
Bible Way Ch—*church* (2) TX-5
Bible Way Ch—*church* (2) VA-3
Bibleway Chapel—*church* TX-5
Bible Way Church, The—*church* NC-3
Bibleway Pentecostal Assembly Ch—*church* KS-7
Bible Way Temple Ch of God in Christ—*church* DE-2
Biblical College Cem—*cemetery* IA-7
Biblical Garden Cem—*cemetery* MS-4
Biblioteca Carnegie—*hist pl* PR-3
Bibo—*locale* NM-5
**Bibo**—*pop pl* NM-5
Bibo Canyon—*valley* NM-5
Bibon Lake—*lake* MN-6
Bibon Lake—*lake* WI-6
Bibon Marsh—*swamp* WI-6
*Bibon Swamp* WI-6
Bibora Island—*island* AK-9
Bibo Ranch—*locale* NM-5
Bibrietz Drain—*canal* MI-6
Bibtown—*uninc pl* FL-3
Bib Town RR Station—*locale* FL-3
Bibyak—*locale* AZ-5
Biby Cabin Ridge—*ridge* NY-2
Biby Ditch—*canal* ID-8
Bice Cem—*cemetery* AL-4
Bice Creek—*stream* MI-6
Bice Creek—*stream* (2) TN-4
Bice Ditch—*canal* IN-6
Bice Hollow—*valley* KY-4
Bice Island—*island* SD-7
Bice Mtn—*summit* (2) AL-4
Bicentennial—*post sta* CA-9
Bicentennial Park—*park* AZ-5
Bicentennial Park—*park* FL-3
Bicentennial Park—*park* (2) TN-4
Bicentennial Union HS—*school* AZ-5
**Bicentennial Village**—*pop pl* DE-2
Bice Ranch—*locale* ND-7
Bichler Creek—*stream* MI-6
Bichota Canyon—*valley* CA-9
Bichota Mesa—*summit* CA-9
*Bichote Canyon* CA-9
**Bichsels Subdivision (East)**—*pop pl* UT-8
**Bichsels Subdivision (West)**—*pop pl* UT-8
Bickel—*locale* ID-8
Bickel,Emmanuel C., House—*hist pl* IN-6
Bickel Branch—*stream* IA-7
Bickel Camp—*locale* CA-9
Bickel Cem—*cemetery* WI-6
Bickel Ditch—*canal* IN-6
Bickel Ditch—*canal* WY-8
Bickel Mound Park—*park* FL-3
Bickel Mtn—*summit* ME-1
Bickel Sch—*school* ID-8
Bickel Sch—*school* NE-7
Bickels Coulee—*valley* MT-8
Bickel Spring—*spring* ID-8
Bickerdike Square Park—*park* IL-6
Bickerdyke Elem Sch—*school* KS-7
Bickers Creek—*stream* VA-3
Bickerstaff, Lake—*reservoir* AL-4
Bickerstaff Eddy—*rapids* TN-4
Bickerstaffs Pond—*reservoir* AL-4
Bickerton Drain—*canal* MI-6
**Bicker Township**—*pop pl* ND-7
Bickett Knob—*summit* WV-2
*Bickford* NH-1
Bickford Brook—*stream* ME-1
Bickford Brook Trail—*trail* ME-1
Bickford Cem—*cemetery* ME-1
Bickford Cem—*cemetery* OK-5
*Bickford Dam* MA-1
*Bickford Hill* MA-1
Bickford Hill—*summit* (2) ME-1
Bickford Hill—*summit* MA-1
Bickford Hill—*summit* NH-1
Bickford Hollow Brook—*stream* VT-1
Bickford Island—*island* ME-1
Bickford Mines (underground)—*mine* TN-4
Bickford Mountain—*ridge* NH-1
Bickford Park—*park* TN-4
Bickford Point—*cape* ME-1
Bickford Pond—*reservoir* ME-1
Bickford Pond—*reservoir* MA-1
Bickford Pond Dam—*dam* MA-1
Bickford Reservoir Dam—*dam* MA-1
Bickford Sch—*school* IL-6
Bickford Sch—*school* VT-1
Bickfords Corner—*locale* ME-1
Bickford Spring—*spring* MT-8
Bickford Trail—*trail* NH-1
Bickham—*locale* LA-4
Bickham Bayou—*stream* LA-4
Bickham Branch—*stream* LA-4
Bickham Cem—*cemetery* (3) LA-4
Bickham Cem—*cemetery* TX-5
Bickle, Jesse C., House—*hist pl* NE-7
Bickle Burke Ditch—*canal* MT-8
Bickle Cem—*cemetery* PA-2
Bickle Knob—*summit* WV-2
Bickle Run—*stream* WV-2
**Bickleton**—*pop pl* WA-9
Bickleton Ridge—*ridge* WA-9
**Bickley**—*pop pl* GA-3
Bickley Cem—*cemetery* AL-4
Bickley Cem—*cemetery* TX-5
Bickley Cem—*cemetery* (3) VA-3
Bickley Chapel—*church* GA-3
Bickley Mills—*other* VA-3
*Bickley Place* AL-4
Bickley Point—*summit* AL-4
Bickley Sch—*school* NM-5
Bickmeyer Cem—*cemetery* MO-7
**Bickmore**—*pop pl* WV-2
Bickmore Canyon—*valley* CA-9
Bickmore Ch—*church* WV-2
Bickmore Creek—*stream* OR-9
*Bickmore Neck* ME-1
Bickmore Point—*cape* ME-1
*Bicknalls Hill* RI-1
Bicknell—*locale* CA-9
**Bicknell**—*pop pl* IN-6
**Bicknell**—*pop pl* UT-8
Bicknell-Armington Lightning Splitter House—*hist pl* RI-1
Bicknell Bottoms—*flat* UT-8
*Bicknell Bottoms Waterfowl Mngmt Area* UT-8
Bicknell Branch—*stream* KY-4
Bicknell Brook—*stream* ME-1
Bicknell Brook—*stream* NH-1
Bicknell Brook—*stream* VT-1
Bicknell Cem—*cemetery* MA-1
Bicknell Cem—*cemetery* UT-8
Bicknell Cem—*cemetery* WV-2
Bicknell Country Club—*other* IN-6
*Bicknell Hill* RI-1
Bicknell House—*hist pl* KY-4
Bicknell Park—*park* CA-9
Bicknell Park Playground—*park* IN-6

Bicknell Post Office—building UT-8
Bicknell Rsvr—reservoir UT-8
Bicknell Sch—school KY-4
Bicknell Sch—school MA-1
Bicknells Hill RI-1
Bicknell's Point IL-6
Bicknell Springs—spring UT-8
Biclabito NM-5
Biclabito Spring NM-5
Bictner Cem—cemetery TX-5
Bicycle Canyon—valley TX-5
Bicycle Club Bldg—hist pl MA-1
Bicycle Creek ND-7
Bicycle Lake—flat CA-9
Bid AL-4
Bidaaii To Haali—spring AZ-5
Bidahochi—locale AZ-5
Bidahochi Butte—summit AZ-5
Bidahochi Spring—spring AZ-5
Bidahochi Trading Post—locale AZ-5
Bidahochi Wash—stream AZ-5
Bidarka Point—cape AK-9
Bidarki Creek—stream AK-9
**Bid-A-Wee—pop pl** FL-3
Biddahoochee AZ-5
Biddahoochee Wash AZ-5
**Biddeford—pop pl** ME-1
Biddeford City Hall—hist pl ME-1
Biddeford Pool ME-1
**Biddeford Pool—pop pl** ME-1
Biddeford-Saco—other ME-1
Biddehoche AZ-5
Biddehoche Wash AZ-5
Biddehochi Butte AZ-5
Bidden Creek—stream (2) CA-9
Biddick Ditch—canal WY-8
**Biddick (historical)—pop pl** IA-7
Biddick Ranch—locale WY-8
Biddie Hollow—valley KY-4
Biddie Knob—summit VT-1
Biddie Toe Creek—stream NC-3
Bidding Creek—stream OK-5
Bidding Springs—other OK-5
Biddix Cem—cemetery NC-3
Biddle OR-9
Biddle—locale KY-4
Biddle—locale MT-8
Biddle—locale OR-9
**Biddle—pop pl** AR-4
**Biddle—pop pl** PA-2
**Biddle—pop pl** SC-3
Biddleborn—locale IL-6
Biddle Branch—stream NJ-2
Biddle Bridge—bridge NC-3
Biddle Butte—summit WA-9
Biddle Canyon—valley OR-9
Biddle Cem—cemetery AL-4
Biddle Cem—cemetery IN-6
Biddle Cem—cemetery KY-4
Biddle Cem—cemetery OH-6
Biddle Cem—cemetery PA-2
Biddle Ch—church OH-6
Biddlecome Hollow—valley (2) UT-8
Biddlecome Ranch—locale UT-8
Biddlecome Ridge—ridge UT-8
Biddle Creek—stream OH-6
**Biddle Crossroads—pop pl** AL-4
Biddle Dam PA-2
Biddle Ditch—canal IN-6
Biddle Gap—gap AL-4
Biddle Hill—summit CT-1
**Biddle (historical)—pop pl** OR-9
Biddlehochi Spring AZ-5
Biddle Hollow Dam—dam PA-2
Biddle House—hist pl DE-2
Biddle Island—island IN-6
Biddle Lake—lake WA-9
Biddle Landing—locale NC-3
Biddleman Marsh—swamp MI-6
Biddleman Springs—spring NV-8
Biddle Memorial Hall, Johnson C. Smith Univ—hist pl NC-3
Biddle Oil Field—oilfield KS-7
Biddle Pass—gap OR-9
Biddle Point—cape DE-2
Biddle Point—cape MI-6
Biddle Pond—reservoir PA-2
Biddle Ridge—ridge ID-8
Biddle Sch—school MI-6
Biddles Corner—locale DE-2
Biddles Landing—locale NJ-2
Biddle Spring Branch—stream AL-4
Biddleville Sch—school NC-3
**Biddleville (subdivision)—pop pl** NC-3
Biddulph Plaza Shop Ctr—locale OH-6
Biddys Creek—stream AL-4
Bide-A-Wee Animal Cem—cemetery NY-2
Bide A Wee Flat—flat WA-9
Bideman Gully—stream LA-4
Biden Park—park DE-2
Biderman Golf Club—other DE-2
Bidleys Shoals—bar TN-4
Bidne Sch—school MN-6
Bid Post Office (historical)—building AL-4
Bidstrip Rsvr—reservoir MT-8
Biduul—cape PW-9
Bidville—locale AR-4
Bidville Cem—cemetery AR-4
Bidwell—locale IA-7
Bidwell—locale MO-7
Bidwell—locale PA-2
Bidwell—locale TN-4
**Bidwell—pop pl** OH-6
Bidwell—uninc pl NY-2
Bidwell, Mount—summit CA-9
Bidwell, Rev. Adonijah, House—hist pl MA-1
Bidwell Bar Bridge—bridge CA-9
Bidwell Bar Canyon Saddle Dam—dam CA-9
Bidwell Canyon Campground—locale CA-9
Bidwell Cem—cemetery NY-2
Bidwell Creek—stream (3) CA-9
Bidwell Creek—stream MO-7
Bidwell Creek—stream NJ-2
Bidwell Ditch NJ-2
Bidwell Ditch—canal OH-6
Bidwell Elsey Ditch—canal OH-6
Bidwell Gulch—valley MT-8
Bidwell Hill—locale PA-2
Bidwell Hill—summit CO-8
Bidwell JHS—school (2) CA-9
Bidwell Lake CA-9
Bidwell Lake—lake CO-8
Bidwell Mansion—hist pl CA-9
Bidwell Mansion State Monument—locale CA-9
Bidwell Mine—mine NV-8
Bidwell Mountain CA-9
Bidwell Mountains CA-9
Bidwell Park—park (2) CA-9
Bidwell Park—park IL-6
Bidwell Peak CA-9
Bidwell Point—cape AR-4
Bidwell Point—summit CA-9
Bidwell Pond PA-2
Bidwell-Porter Sch—school OH-6
Bidwell Post Office (historical)—building TN-4
Bidwell Ranch—locale CA-9
Bidwell River Park—park CA-9
Bidwell Sch—school (5) CA-9
Bidwell Sch—school MI-6
Bidwells Creek NJ-2
Bidwells Creek—stream NY-2
Bidwells Ditch NJ-2
Bidwell Spring—spring CA-9
Bidwell Spring—spring MT-8
Bidwell Station—locale PA-2
Biebe Island MP-9
Biebel Springs—spring CO-8
**Bieber—pop pl** CA-9
Bieber Cem—cemetery MO-7
Bieber Creek—stream PA-2
**Bieber Line Junction—pop pl** OR-9
**Bieber Station (Nubieber)—pop pl** CA-9
Bieberstedt Butte—summit OR-9
Bieberstedt Creek—stream OR-9
Bieberstedt Trail—trail OR-9
Biebertedt Butte OR-9
Biebe Spring—spring NV-8
Biebi—island MP-9
Biebi-To MP-9
Biebrach Park—park CA-9
Biedell Creek CO-8
Biedell Creek—stream CO-8
Biedeman, Mount—summit CA-9
Biedenharn Candy Company Bldg—hist pl MS-4
Biederman Bluff—cliff AK-9
Biederstaedt Grocery—hist pl WI-6
Bieger Mound—summit MO-7
**Bieglers First Addition (subdivision)—pop pl** SD-7
**Biehle—pop pl** MO-7
Biehle Sch—school TX-5
Biehn Cem—cemetery OH-6
Biehn Colony Park—park AZ-5
Biehn P O OH-6
Bieker-Wilson Village Site—hist pl IL-6
Bielowski, Mount—summit CA-9
Bielefield Sch—school CT-1
Bielenberg, Nick J., House—hist pl MT-8
Bielenberg Canyon—valley MT-8
Bielenberg Lake—lake MT-8
Bieler Bayou—gut LA-4
Bieler Ranch—locale OR-9
Bieler Run—stream OH-6
Bieler Run—stream PA-2
Bieli Rocks—area AK-9
Biel Lake—reservoir TX-5
Bieller Landing—locale MS-4
Biel Oil Field—oilfield TX-5
Bielvins Spring—spring MT-8
**Biem—pop pl** MT-8
Biemans Point—cape MD-2
Biemeret Park—park WI-6
Biene Creek—stream AR-4
Bienek Oil Field—oilfield TX-5
Bien/McNatt House—hist pl AZ-5
Bienvenue, Bayou—stream LA-4
Bienvenue Inside Pond—bay LA-4
Bienvenue Outside Pond—bay LA-4
Bienvenue Pass—channel LA-4
Bienview Sch (historical)—school AL-4
**Bienville—pop pl** LA-4
Bienville Beach—beach AL-4
Bienville Ch—church MS-4
Bienville Church AL-4
Bienville District Ranger Office—building MS-4
Bienville East Fourteen Oil Field—oilfield MS-4
Bienville Game Mngmt Area MS-4
Bienville Natl Forest—park MS-4
**Bienville Parish—pop pl** LA-4
Bienville Pines Scenic Area—park MS-4
Bienville Pumping Station—building AL-4
Bienville Rsvr—reservoir AL-4
Bienville Sch—school AL-4
Bienville Sch—school LA-4
Bienville Square—park AL-4
Bienville State Wildlife Mngmt Area—park MS-4
Bienville Work Center—building MS-4
Bieo Island MP-9
Bier—locale MD-2
Bierce Creek—stream CA-9
Bierce Creek—stream OR-9
Bierce Ditch—canal IN-6
Bierce Ridge—ridge CA-9
Bierer Creek—stream WY-8
Bierig Cem—cemetery OK-5
Bieri Lakes—lake TX-5
Bierke Sch—school SD-7
Bierly Airp—airport PA-2
Bierman Run PA-2
Bierne AR-4
Bierne Park—park AL-4
Bierney Creek—stream MT-8
Biernit Swamp—swamp WI-6
Bieroth Ranch NV-8
Bieroth Ranch—locale NV-8
Bieroth Slide—slope NV-8
Bieroth Spring—spring NV-8
Biers Cem—cemetery OH-6
Bierschwale Spring—spring TX-5
Bierschwale Windmill—locale (2) TX-5
Biers Kill NJ-2
Biers Run—stream OH-6
Bierstadt, Mount—summit CO-8
Bierstadt Lake—lake CO-8
Bierstadt Moraine—ridge CO-8
Biertuempful Park—park NJ-2
Biery Ditch—canal IN-6
Bierys Port PA-2
Biery's Port Hist Dist—hist pl PA-2
**Biesecker Gap—pop pl** PA-2
Biesecker Run—stream PA-2
Bieser Creek—stream CO-8
Biesterfeldt Site (32RM1)—hist pl ND-7
Bieto Island MP-9
Biever House—hist pl PA-2
Biffle Cove—cave TN-4
Biffle Creek—stream TN-4
Biffle Hollow—valley (2) TN-4
Biffords Branch—stream AL-4
Bifido, Arroyo—stream CA-9
Big NC-3
Big A—locale GA-3
Big Abe Fork—stream WV-2
Big Abrams Gap—gap NC-3
Big Abrams Gap—gap TN-4
Big A Cem—cemetery TX-5
Big A Ch—church VA-3
Big Acorn Hollow—valley OK-5
Big A Creek—stream CO-8
Big Adams Cem—cemetery SC-3
Big Adobe Dam—dam OR-9
Big Adobe Flat—flat NV-8
Big Adobe Rsvr—reservoir OR-9
Big African Lake—lake MI-6
Big Agingan Beach MH-9
Big Agnes Mtn—summit CO-8
Big Aguja Canyon—valley TX-5
Big Aguja Mtn—summit TX-5
Bigajele MP-9
Big Alamance Creek NC-3
Big Alamance Creek—stream NC-3
Big Alamo Tank TX-5
Big Alamo Tank—reservoir TX-5
Big Alderbed—lake NY-2
Big Alderbed Mtn—summit NY-2
Big Alder Creek—stream CO-8
Big Alder Spring—spring AZ-5
Big Alder Spring—spring OR-9
Big Alinchak Bay—bay AK-9
Big Alinchak Creek—stream AK-9
Big Alkali—flat CA-9
Big Alkali Creek—stream CO-8
Big Alkali Lake—lake CA-9
Big Alkali Lake—lake NE-7
Big Alkali Lake—reservoir CO-8
Big Alkali Spring—spring NV-8
Bigalks Creek—stream IA-7
Big Allan Mtn—summit ME-1
Big Alligator Creek—stream GA-3
Big Alligator Lake FL-3
Big Alligator Swamp—swamp NC-3
Big Alvord Creek—stream OR-9
Bigamon Pond WA-9
Big Ambejackmockamus Falls—falls ME-1
Big American Island—island MN-6
Big Amos Creek—stream KY-4
Big A Mountain Sch—school VA-3
Big A Mtn—summit AZ-5
Big A Mtn—summit VA-3
Bigan Dam—dam PA-2
Big Anderson Tank—reservoir AZ-5
Big and Little Indian Rock Petroglyphs—hist pl PA-2
Big and Little Petroglyph Canyons—hist pl CA-9
Big And Outlet Drain—canal MI-6
Big Andy Airp—airport WA-9
Big Andy Branch—stream KY-4
Big Andy Ch—church KY-4
Big Andy Ridge—ridge KY-4
Big Andy Ridge—ridge NC-3
Big Annemessex River MD-2
Big Annemessex River—stream MD-2
Big Annemessic River MD-2
Big Anne Spring—spring NE-7
Biganuo Island—island MP-9
Bigannuo-To MP-9
Bigan Pond—reservoir PA-2
Big Antelope Creek—stream NE-7
Big Antelope Creek—stream OK-5
Big Antelope Creek—stream OR-9
Big Antelope Spring—spring (2) NV-8
Big Antelope Springs—spring NV-8
Big Antelope Tank—reservoir NM-5
Big Antioch Cem—cemetery MS-4
Big Antioch Church MS-4
Big Apache Hill—summit TX-5
Big Aparejo Creek—stream ID-8
Big a Plenty Bayou—stream LA-4
Big A Plenty Landing—locale LA-4
Big Apple Sch (abandoned)—school MO-7
Big Apple Township—civil MO-7
Big Apyette Lake ID-8
Big Arbor Cem—cemetery OK-5
Big Arbor Ch—church OK-5
Big Arbor Vitae Lake—lake WI-6
Bigar Island MP-9
Big Arm—bay MT-8
Big Arm—bay OR-9
**Big Arm—pop pl** MT-8
Big Arm—ridge TN-4
Big Arm—swamp GA-3
Big Arm Branch—stream TN-4
Big Arm Creek—stream NC-3
Big Armidge Creek—stream TX-5
Big Armuchee Creek GA-3
Big Arrow Interchange—crossing AZ-5
Big Arrow Trading Post—locale AZ-5
Big Arroyo AZ-5
Big Arroyo—stream CA-9
Big Arroyo—stream CO-8
Big Arroyo Hills—range CO-8
Big Arsenic Springs Campground—locale NM-5
Big Asaph Run PA-2
Big "A" Sch—school GA-3
Big A Sch—school TN-4
Big Aso Tank—reservoir AZ-5
Big Asparos Canyon NM-5
Big Asphalt Canyon—valley UT-8
Bigateerango To MP-9
Bigaterangu-to MP-9
Bigatjelang MP-9
Big Atkinson Creek—stream CO-8
Big Atlantic Gulch—valley WY-8
Big Atoy Creek—stream TX-5
Big Attitash Mtn—summit NH-1
Bigatyeland MP-9
Bigatyeland Island MP-9
Bigatyelang Island—island MP-9
Big Austin Creek CA-9
Big Avalanche Ravine—valley CA-9
Big Averill Lake VT-1
Big Bacon Island—island DE-2
Big Badger Creek MT-8
Big Badger Creek—stream KS-7
Big Badlands SD-7
Big Bad Luck Pond—lake NY-2
Big Bahala Creek MS-4
Big Bailey Run—stream OH-6
Big Bald GA-3
Big Bald NC-3
Big Bald—summit (3) NC-3
Big Bald—summit TN-4
Big Bald Branch—stream NC-3
Big Bald Cove—basin GA-3
Big Bald Creek—stream TN-4
Big Bald Hill—summit NE-7
Big Bald Knob—summit VA-3
Big Bald Mountain NC-3
Big Bald Mtn—summit GA-3
Big Bald Mtn—summit NV-8
Big Bald of Rich NC-3
Big Bald Rock—summit CA-9
Big Baldy MT-8
Big Baldy—summit (2) CA-9
Big Baldy—summit (2) CO-8
Big Baldy—summit ID-8
Big Baldy—summit (4) OR-9
Big Baldy—summit (3) UT-8
Big Baldy Grove—woods CA-9
Big Baldy Mtn—summit CO-8
Big Baldy Mtn—summit MT-8
Big Baldy Peak—summit TX-5
Big Baldy Ridge—ridge CA-9
Big Baldy Ridge—ridge ID-8
Big Baldy Ridge Trail—trail ID-8
Big Ball—summit TN-4
Big Ballard Spring—spring UT-8
Big Ball Hill—summit TX-5
Big Ball Island—island VA-3
Big Banana Island—island WI-6
Big Baptize Lake—lake AR-4
Big Bar—bar CA-9
Big Bar—bar (2) ID-8
Big Bar—bar MS-4
Big Bar—bar NY-2
Big Bar—bar UT-8
Big Bar—locale CA-9
**Big Bar—pop pl** CA-9
Big Barbee Lake—lake IN-6
Big Bar Creek—stream AK-9
Big Bar Creek—stream CA-9
Big Bar Hill CA-9
Big Bar Mtn—summit CA-9
Big Barn Creek—stream AR-4
Big Barnes Ditch—canal CO-8
Big Baron Spire ID-8
Bigbarren TN-4
**Big Barren—pop pl** TN-4
Big Barren Cem TN-4
Big Barren Cem—cemetery TN-4
Big Barren Ch—church MO-7
Bigbarren Creek TN-4
Big Barren Creek—stream MO-7
Big Barren Creek—stream TN-4
Big Barren Creek (CCD)—cens area TN-4
Big Barren Creek Ch—church TN-4
Big Barren Creek Division—civil TN-4
Big Barren Post Office (historical)—building TN-4
Big Barren River KY-4
Big Barrett Hollow—valley TN-4
Big Bart Coulee—valley MT-8
Big Bartley Pond—lake ME-1
Big Bartons Creek TN-4
Big Basin—basin (3) CA-9
Big Basin—basin CO-8
Big Basin—basin (2) ID-8
Big Basin—basin KS-7
Big Basin—basin MS-4
Big Basin—basin NV-8
Big Basin—basin (3) OR-9
Big Basin—basin WA-9
Big Basin—basin WY-8
**Big Basin (Big Basin Redwoods State Park)—pop pl** CA-9
Big Basin Canyon—valley WY-8
Big Basin Coulee—valley MT-8
Big Basin Creek—stream CA-9
Big Basin Hollow—valley (2) PA-2
Big Basin Post Office—locale CA-9
Big Basin Redwoods State Park—park CA-9
Big Basin Rsvr—reservoir OR-9
Big Basket Spring—spring UT-8
Big Bass Bay—bay NY-2
Big Bass Lake IN-6
Big Bass Lake MI-6
Big Bass Lake MN-6
Big Bass Lake WI-6
Big Bass Lake—lake FL-3
Big Bass Lake—lake MI-6
Big Bass Lake—lake (3) MN-6
Big Bass Lake—lake PA-2
Big Bass Lake—lake (2) WI-6
Big Bass Lake—reservoir IN-6
Big Bass Lake—reservoir PA-2
Big Bass Lake Dam—dam PA-2
Big Basswood Lake—lake MN-6
Big Bateau Bay—bay AL-4
Big Bateau Lake WI-6
Big Bateau Lake—lake MI-6
**Big Battle—pop pl** WV-2
Big Battleground Creek—stream GA-3
Big Battlement Lake—reservoir CO-8
Big Battle Run—stream WV-2
Big Baxter Swamp—stream SC-3
Big Bay—basin SC-3
Big Bay—bay (4) AK-9
Big Bay—bay FL-3
Big Bay—bay ID-8
Big Bay—bay (2) LA-4
Big Bay—bay (3) MI-6
Big Bay—bay (3) MN-6
Big Bay—bay MO-7
Big Bay—bay (3) NY-2
Big Bay—bay NC-3
Big Bay—bay WI-6
**Big Bay—pop pl** IL-6
**Big Bay—pop pl** MI-6
**Big Bay—pop pl** NY-2
Big Bay—swamp (2) FL-3
Big Bay—swamp (4) GA-3
Big Bay—swamp (12) NC-3
Big Bay—swamp (6) SC-3
Big Bay, The—swamp SC-3
Big Bay Branch—stream SC-3
Big Bay (Carolina Bay)—swamp (2) NC-3
Big Bay Creek—stream NY-2
Big Bay Creek—stream SC-3
Big Bay De Noc—bay MI-6
Big Bay de Nocquet MI-6
Big Bay De Noc Shoal—bar MI-6
Big Bay De Noque MI-6
Big Bay De Noquette MI-6
Big Bay Ditch—canal AR-4
Big Bay Island—island GA-3
Big Bay John—stream AL-4
Big Bay Lagoon—lake WI-6
Big Bay Lake—lake FL-3
Big Bay Marsh—swamp MD-2
Big Bayou LA-4
Big Bayou MI-6
Big Bayou MS-4
Big Bayou TX-5
Big Bayou—bay (2) FL-3
Big Bayou—channel TX-5
Big Bayou—gut (2) FL-3
Big Bayou—gut (3) LA-4
Big Bayou—gut MO-7
Big Bayou—gut (3) TX-5
Big Bayou—lake FL-3
Big Bayou—stream AR-4
Big Bayou—stream IL-6
Big Bayou—stream IN-6
Big Bayou—stream (9) LA-4
Big Bayou—stream (2) MS-4
Big Bayou—stream TX-5
Big Bayou—uninc pl FL-3
Big Bayou Canot—stream AL-4
Big Bayou Chene—stream LA-4
Big Bayou Colyell LA-4
Big Bayou Creek IN-6
Big Bayou De Grasse—stream LA-4
Big Bayou Friejon—stream LA-4
Big Bayou Jessie—stream LA-4
Big Bayou Joe—stream LA-4
Big Bayou Jose—gut LA-4
Big Bayou Lake LA-4
Big Bayou Mallet—stream LA-4
Big Bayou Oil Field—oilfield LA-4
Big Bayou Pigeon LA-4
Big Bayou Pigeon—stream LA-4
Big Bayou Point—cape FL-3
Big Bayou Slough—gut AR-4
Big Bay Park—park WI-6
Big Bay Point—cape MD-2
Big Bay Point—cape MI-6
Big Bay Point—cape WI-6
Big Bay Point Light Station—hist pl MI-6
Big Bay Pond—lake FL-3
Big Bay Public Use Area—locale MO-7
Big Bay Ridge—ridge NC-3
Big Bay Station IL-6
Big Bay Swamp—swamp NY-2
Big Bay Swamp—swamp NC-3
Big Bay Swamp—swamp (2) SC-3
Big Beach—beach ME-1
Big Beach—beach NC-3
Big Bead Mesa—hist pl NM-5
Big Bear—CDP CA-9
Big Bear Bay—swamp FL-3
Big Bear Bayou—gut MS-4
Big Bear Beach—beach FL-3
Big Bear Branch—stream AL-4
Big Bear Branch—stream NC-3
Big Bear Camp—locale KY-4
Big Bear Camp—locale OR-9
Big Bear Campground—locale WA-9
Big Bear Canyon—valley (2) NM-5
Big Bear Canyon—valley UT-8
Big Bear Canyon—valley WY-8
Big Bear Cave TN-4
Big Bear Cave—cave AR-4
Big Bear Cave—cave MO-7
Big Bear (CCD)—cens area CA-9
**Big Bear City—pop pl** CA-9
Big Bear Cove Ridge—ridge TN-4
Big Bear Creek AL-4
Big Bear Creek AR-4
Big Bear Creek CO-8
Big Bear Creek GA-3
Big Bear Creek IA-7
Big Bear Creek MI-6
Big Bear Creek MS-4
Big Bear Creek PA-2
Big Bear Creek TX-5
Big Bear Creek—locale KY-4
Big Bear Creek—stream CA-9
Big Bear Creek—stream CO-8
Big Bear Creek—stream FL-3
Big Bear Creek—stream (4) ID-8
Big Bear Creek—stream IA-7
Big Bear Creek—stream MT-8
Big Bear Creek—stream NE-7
Big Bear Creek—stream NC-3
Big Bear Creek—stream SC-3
Big Bear Creek—stream TX-5
Big Bear Creek—stream UT-8
Big Bear Dam AZ-5
Big Bear Ditch—canal WY-8
Big Bear Flat—flat CA-9
Big Bear Flowage—reservoir WI-6
Big Bear Gulch—valley (2) CA-9
Big Bear Gulch—valley MT-8
**Big Bear Highlands—pop pl** CA-9
Big Bear Hill—summit TX-5
Big Bearhole Pond—reservoir MA-1
Big Bearhole Pond Dam—dam MA-1
Big Bear Hollow—valley UT-8
Big Bear Hollow—valley VA-3
Big Bear HS—school CA-9
Big Bear Island MN-6
Big Bear Island—island FL-3
Big Bear Lake MI-6
Big Bear Lake—lake AR-4
Big Bear Lake—lake (4) CA-9
Big Bear Lake—lake FL-3
Big Bear Lake—lake (2) MI-6
Big Bear Lake—lake MT-8
Big Bear Lake—lake WI-6
Big Bear Lake—lake WY-8
**Big Bear Lake—pop pl** CA-9
Big Bear Lake—reservoir CA-9
Big Bear Landing—locale MN-6
Big Bear Mtn—summit WA-9
Big Bear Park—flat CO-8
Big Bearpen Branch—stream NC-3
**Big Bear Pines—pop pl** CA-9
**Big Bear Pinewoods—pop pl** CA-9
Big Bear Point—cape MI-6
Big Bear Ranger Station—locale CA-9
Big Bear Ridge—ridge ID-8
Big Bear Rock Branch—stream VA-3
Big Bear Rock Gap—gap VA-3
Big Bear Shoals (historical)—bar AL-4
Big Bear Solar Observatory—building CA-9
Big Bear Swamp—swamp PA-2
Big Bear Tank—reservoir NM-5
Big Bear Tank—reservoir TX-5
Big Beartrail Ridge—ridge NC-3
Big Beartrap Branch—stream NC-3
Big Bearwallow Creek—stream NC-3
Big Bear Willow Spring—spring WA-9
Big Beavedam Creek—stream SC-3
Big Beaver MI-6
**Big Beaver—pop pl** MI-6
**Big Beaver—pop pl** PA-2
Big Beaver Basin—basin CO-8
Big Beaver Creek ID-8
Big Beaver Creek MI-6
Big Beaver Creek MO-7
Big Beaver Creek OK-5
Big Beaver Creek—gut AL-4
Big Beaver Creek—stream (2) CO-8
Big Beaver Creek—stream (2) MI-6
Big Beaver Creek—stream (2) MT-8
Big Beaver Creek—stream NE-7
Big Beaver Creek—stream (2) OH-6
Big Beaver Creek—stream PA-2
Big Beaver Creek—stream (2) SC-3
Big Beaver Creek—stream TN-4
Big Beaver Creek—stream WA-9
Big Beaver Creek—stream WV-2
Big Beaver Creek—stream WI-6
Big Beaver Creek State Public Hunting Ground—park WI-6
Big Beaver Dam—dam PA-2
Big Beaverdam Ch—church SC-3
Big Beaverdam Creek GA-3
Big Beaverdam Creek SC-3
Big Beaverdam Creek—stream NC-3
Big Beaverdam Creek—stream SC-3
Big Beaver Elem Sch—school PA-2
Big Beaver Hollow—valley OK-5
Big Beaver Island—island ME-1
Big Beaver Island Creek—stream NC-3
Big Beaver Lake—lake AK-9
Big Beaver Lake—lake IL-6
Big Beaver Oil Field—oilfield CO-8
Big Beaver Pond—lake (2) ME-1
Big Beaver Pond—reservoir PA-2
Big Beaver River PA-2
Big Beaver Rsvr—reservoir CO-8
Big Beaver Slough—stream AR-4
Big Beaver Springs—spring UT-8
Big Beaver Township—civil (2) PA-2
Big Bedground—other OR-9
Bigbee—locale AL-4
**Bigbee—pop pl** MS-4
Big Bee Branch—stream TN-4
Bigbee Branch—stream TN-4
Bigbee Cem TN-4
Bigbee Cem—cemetery (2) TN-4
Bigbee Ch—church AL-4
Bigbee Ch—church MS-4
Bigbee Chapel—church TN-4
Bigbee Chapel Cem—cemetery TN-4
Big Beech Branch—stream KY-4
Big Beech Creek—stream GA-3
Big Beechy Trail—trail WV-2
Bigbee Creek—stream OR-9
Bigbee Draw—valley NM-5
Big Beef Creek—stream WA-9
Big Beef Harbor—bay WA-9
Bigbee First Baptist Ch—church MS-4
Big Bee Mtn—summit TX-5
Bigbee Post Office (historical)—building MS-4
Bigbee Ranch—locale NM-5
Bigbee Tank—reservoir NM-5
Bigbeevale MS-4
**Bigbee Valley—pop pl** MS-4
Bigbee Valley Access Area—park AL-4
Bigbee Valley Cem—cemetery MS-4
Bigbee Valley Ch—church MS-4
Bigbee Valley Colored Methodist Ch MS-4
Bigbee Valley Post Office—building MS-4
Big Bell Estates Lake—reservoir TN-4
Big Bell Estates Lake Dam—dam TN-4
Big Bell Lake—lake AR-4
Big Belt Mountains—spring MT-8
Big Ben KS-7
Big Ben Campground—park OR-9
Big Ben Canyon—valley NV-8
Big Bench—beach ID-8
Big Bench—bench AR-4
Big Bench—bench (3) UT-8
Big Bench Hollow—valley PA-2
Big Ben Creek—stream OR-9
Big Ben Cut—canal NY-2
Big Bend AZ-5
Big Bend KS-7
Big Bend WV-2
Big Bend—area WY-8
Big Bend—bend AL-4
Big Bend—bend (2) AK-9
Big Bend—bend (2) AZ-5
Big Bend—bend (6) CA-9
Big Bend—bend GA-3
Big Bend—bend ID-8
Big Bend—bend (3) KY-4
Big Bend—bend (2) LA-4
Big Bend—bend MO-7
Big Bend—bend (4) MT-8
Big Bend—bend NC-3
Big Bend—bend OH-6
Big Bend—bend (2) OK-5
Big Bend—bend (6) OR-9
Big Bend—bend PA-2

Big Canyon Rsvr—reservoir CA-9
Big Canyon Saddle—gap ID-8
Big Canyon Spring—spring ID-8
Big Canyon Spring—spring NM-5
Big Canyon Spring—spring (2) OR-9
Big Canyon Tank—reservoir NM-5
Big Canyon Tank—reservoir TX-5
Big Canyon Tank Number One—reservoir AZ-5
Big Canyon Tank Number Two—reservoir AZ-5
Big Canyon Tyron Airp—airport CO-8
Big Capon River WV-2
Big Carencro Bayou—stream LA-4
Big Caribou Pond—lake ME-1
Big Carlos Pass—channel FL-3
Big Carlson Hollow—valley PA-2
Big Carmen Creek—stream CA-9
Big Carmen Lake—lake CA-9
Big Carnelian Lake—lake MN-6
Big Carp Lake—reservoir MO-7
Big Carrion Crow Bayou LA-4
Big Carrizo Wash AZ-5
Big Carr Lake—lake WI-6
Big Carson Creek—stream CA-9
Big Carter Pond—swamp TX-5
Big Casa Blanca Canyon—valley AZ-5
Big Cash Bayou—gut LA-4
Big Casino Creek—stream ID-8
Big Casino Gulch—valley CO-8
Big Casino Mines—mine NV-8
Big Castle Island—island AK-9
Big Castle Lake MI-6
Big Cataloochee NC-3
Big Cataloochee Knob NC-3
Big Cataloochee Mtn—summit NC-3
Big Cataluche NC-3
Big Cataluchee NC-3
Big Cat Slough—gut WI-6
Big Cat Spring—spring OR-9
Big Cattail Creek—stream VA-3
Big Cave—cave CA-9
Big Cave—cave MO-7
Big Cave—cave NV-8
Big Cave—cave TN-4
Big Cave—cave VA-3
Big Cave Lick Hollow OH-6
Big Cave Ruins—locale AZ-5
Big Cave Run—stream KY-4
Big Cave Run—stream OH-6
Big Cave Run—stream WV-2
Big Cedar—locale ID-8
**Big Cedar**—pop pl OK-5
Big Cedar Bayou—stream LA-4
Big Cedar Brake Windmill—locale TX-5
Big Cedar Branch—stream SC-3
Big Cedar Branch—stream VA-3
Big Cedar Canyon—valley (2) ID-8
Big Cedar Cem—cemetery AR-4
Big Cedar Ch—church IN-6
Big Cedar Cliffs—cliff IN-6
Big Cedar Cove—basin UT-8
Big Cedar Creek AL-4
Big Cedar Creek FL-3
Big Cedar Creek ID-8
Big Cedar Creek IA-7
Big Cedar Creek TX-5
Big Cedar Creek—stream (3) AR-4
Big Cedar Creek—stream CA-9
Big Cedar Creek—stream (3) GA-3
Big Cedar Creek—stream (2) ID-8
Big Cedar Creek—stream IN-6
Big Cedar Creek—stream KS-7
Big Cedar Creek—stream MS-4
Big Cedar Creek—stream NE-7
Big Cedar Creek—stream NV-8
Big Cedar Creek—stream NC-3
Big Cedar Creek—stream (2) OK-5
Big Cedar Creek—stream SD-7
Big Cedar Creek—stream VA-3
Big Cedar Creek Ditch—canal NV-8
Big Cedar Gulch—valley MT-8
Big Cedar Hollow—valley (2) MO-7
Big Cedar Island SD-7
Big Cedar Island—island DE-2
Big Cedar Lake MI-6
Big Cedar Lake WI-6
Big Cedar Lake—lake MI-6
Big Cedar Lake—lake WI-6
Big Cedar Lick Church TN-4
Big Cedar Mtn—summit GA-3
Big Cedar Ridge—ridge WY-8
Big Cedar River MI-6
Big Cedar Run—stream PA-2
Big Cedars County Park—park WA-9
Big Cedar Spring—spring CO-8
Big Cedar Springs—spring OR-9
Big Cedar Tank—reservoir NM-5
Big Cedar Trap—cliff AZ-5
Big Cement Tank—reservoir NM-5
Big Chain Lake WY-8
Big Chair—summit AZ-5
Big Chairs Creek FL-3
Big Chalybeate Spring AR-4
Big Chalybeate Springhouse—locale AR-4
Big Channel—channel NY-2
Big Chapman Lake—reservoir IN-6
Big Charles Bayou—gut LA-4
Big Charley Tank—reservoir TX-5
Big Charlie Lakes—lake WY-8
Big Chazy River NY-2
Big Cheif Rsvr—reservoir WY-8
Big Chemise Knob—summit CA-9
Big Chene Blanc LA-4
**Big Cherokee**—pop pl TN-4
Big Cherokee Creek TN-4
Big Cherry Canyon—valley NM-5
Big Cherry Creek—stream AZ-5
Big Cherry Creek—stream MT-8
Big Cherry Creek—stream VA-3
Big Cherry Lake—lake MT-8
Big Cherrypatch Pond—lake NY-2
Big Cherry Rsvr—reservoir VA-3
Big Chestnut Bald—summit NC-3
Big Chestnut Bald—summit TN-4
Big Chestnut Creek—stream VA-3
Big Chestnut Island—island PA-2
Big Chestnut Lick—stream KY-4
Big Chestnut Ridge—ridge VA-3
Big Chickasaw Creek LA-4
Big Chicken Hollow—valley CA-9
Big Chickies Creek PA-2
Big Chico Creek—stream CA-9
Big Chicosa Lake—lake NM-5
Big Chief UT-8
**Big Chief**—pop pl CA-9
Big Chief—summit CA-9
Big Chief, Mount—summit CO-8
Big Chief Camps—locale ME-1
Big Chief Creek—stream ID-8
Big Chief Creek Trail—trail ID-8
Big Chief Hollow—valley MO-7
Big Chief Lake—lake CA-9
Big Chief Mine—mine AZ-5
Big Chief Mine—mine (3) CA-9
Big Chief Mine—mine NV-8
Big Chief Mine—mine SD-7
Big Chief Mine—mine WA-9
Big Chief Mountain CA-9
Big Chief Mtn—summit AK-9
Big Chief Mtn—summit WA-9
Big Chief Park—flat MT-8
Big Chief Pond—lake NY-2
Big Chief Spring—spring ME-1
Big Chief Tank—reservoir AZ-5
**Big Chimney**—pop pl WV-2
Big Chimney Gulch CO-8
Big Chino Valley—valley AZ-5
Big Chino Wash—stream AZ-5
Big Chinquapin Branch NC-3
Big Chinquapin Creek—stream TX-5
Big Chippewa Lake—lake AL-4
Big Chiquesalunga Creek PA-2
Big Choctaw Bayou—stream LA-4
Big Choga Creek—stream NC-3
Big Chub Lake—lake MI-6
Big Chunky MS-4
Big Church Mtn—summit NY-2
Big Chutes—channel AK-9
Big Cienega—spring CA-9
Big Cienega—valley CA-9
Big Cienega Mtn—summit AZ-5
Big Cienega Spring—spring CA-9
Big Cimarron Campground—locale CO-8
Big Cimarron Ranch—locale CO-8
Big Cimarron River CO-8
Big Cinder Butte—summit ID-8
Big Claw—bay ME-1
Big Clear Creek ID-8
Big Clear Creek—stream WV-2
Big Clear Creek Mountain—ridge WV-2
Big Clear Lake—lake AR-4
Big Clear Lake—lake ID-8
Big Clear Pond NY-2
Big Clear Pond Mtn—summit NY-2
Big Cleveland Creek—stream TX-5
Big Cliff—cliff KY-4
Big Cliff—cliff OR-9
Big Cliff—cliff TN-4
Big Cliff Dam—dam (2) OR-9
Big Cliff Lake—reservoir OR-9
Big Cliff Mine—mine CA-9
Big Cliff Rsvr—reservoir OR-9
**Big Clifty**—pop pl KY-4
Big Clifty—summit KY-4
Big Clifty Branch—stream TN-4
Big Clifty Creek—stream AR-4
Big Clifty Creek—stream IN-6
Big Clifty Creek—stream (3) KY-4
Big Clouds Creek—stream GA-3
Big Coal Bed Branch—stream AL-4
Big Coal Gap—gap TN-4
Big Coal River—stream WV-2
Big Cobbler Mtn—summit VA-3
Big Cockroach Mound—summit FL-3
Big Cockroach Pass—channel FL-3
Big Coffeepot Spring—spring NV-8
Big Cold Brook—stream NY-2
Big Cold Creek NY-2
Big Cold Water Creek NC-3
Big Coldwater Creek—stream FL-3
Big Coldwater River FL-3
Big Colewa Bayou LA-4
Big Colewa Creek—stream LA-4
Big Collis Creek—stream GA-3
Big Colly Bay—swamp NC-3
Big Colorado Mine—mine CO-8
Big Cone Camp—locale CA-9
Bigcone Spring—spring CA-9
Big Cone Spruce Camp—locale CA-9
Big Conrad Gulch—valley CA-9
Big Constance Bayou—stream LA-4
Big Constance Lake—lake LA-4
Big Constance Lake—lake MN-6
Big Cook Island—island IA-7
Big Coolidge Mtn—summit NH-1
Big Coon Creek KS-7
Big Coon Creek—stream AL-4
Big Coon Valley—valley AL-4
Big Coppitt First Baptist Ch—church FL-3
Big Coppitt Key—CDP FL-3
Big Coppitt Key—island FL-3
Big Corazones Spring—spring TX-5
Big Cordual Branch—stream KY-4
Big Corkscrew Island—island FL-3
Big Cormorant Lake—lake MN-6
Big Cornelian Lake MN-6
Big Cornfield Tank—reservoir NM-5
Big Cornie Bayou AR-4
Big Cornie Creek AR-4
Big Cornie Creek LA-4
Big Corral—locale CO-8
Big Corral—locale MT-8
Big Corral—locale WY-8
Big Corral Ditch—canal WY-8
Big Corral Draw—valley SD-7
Big Corral Draw—valley WY-8
Big Costilla Peak—summit NM-5
Big Cotton Indian Creek—stream GA-3
Big Cotton Lake—lake AR-4
Big Cottonwood Canon UT-8
Big Cottonwood Canyon NV-8
Big Cottonwood Canyon—valley (2) NV-8
Big Cottonwood Canyon—valley (2) UT-8
Big Cottonwood Creek CO-8
Big Cottonwood Creek SD-7
Big Cottonwood Creek—stream CO-8
Big Cottonwood Creek—stream (3) ID-8
Big Cottonwood Creek—stream MT-8
Big Cottonwood Creek—stream (2) NE-7
Big Cottonwood Creek—stream NV-8
Big Cottonwood Creek—stream (2) TX-5
Big Cottonwood Creek—stream (2) UT-8
Big Cottonwood Creek—stream WY-8
Big Cottonwood Ditch—canal WY-8
Big Cottonwood Hollow—valley AR-4
Big Cottonwood Lake—lake NV-8
Big Cottonwood Mine—mine UT-8
Big Cottonwood River MN-6
Big Cottonwood Rsvr—reservoir WY-8
Big Cottonwood Windmill—locale NM-5
Big Cougar Creek—stream ID-8
Big Coulee MT-8
Big Coulee ND-7
Big Coulee—valley (19) MT-8
Big Coulee—valley (5) ND-7
Big Coulee—valley SD-7
Big Coulee—valley WI-6
Big Coulee—valley WY-8
Big Coulee Canal—canal MT-8
Big Coulee Ch—church ND-7
Big Coulee Creek MT-8
Big Coulee Creek—stream (2) MT-8
Big Coulee Creek—stream SD-7
Big Coulee Dam—dam ND-7
Big Coulee Draw—valley WY-8
Big Coulee Drop—canal MT-8
Big Cove NJ-2
Big Cove—basin (2) OR-9
Big Cove—basin (2) UT-8
Big Cove—bay CA-9
Big Cove—bay CT-1
Big Cove—bay DE-2
Big Cove—bay (2) FL-3
Big Cove—bay (2) ME-1
Big Cove—bay NJ-2
Big Cove—bay TX-5
Big Cove—bay WA-9
**Big Cove**—pop pl AL-4
Big Cove—valley AL-4
Big Cove—valley AZ-5
Big Cove—valley GA-3
Big Cove—valley ID-8
Big Cove—valley (11) NC-3
Big Cove—valley TN-4
Big Cove—valley UT-8
Big Cove Branch—stream KY-4
Big Cove Branch—stream NC-3
Big Cove Branch—stream (4) TN-4
Big Cove Branch—stream VA-3
Big Cove Campground—locale CA-9
Big Cove Canyon—valley AZ-5
Big Cove Canyon—valley WA-9
Big Cove Cem—cemetery AL-4
Big Cove Ch—church AL-4
Big Cove Ch—church NC-3
Big Cove Ch (historical)—church AL-4
Big Cove Creek—stream (2) AL-4
Big Cove Creek—stream AR-4
Big Cove Creek—stream OR-9
Big Cove Creek—stream PA-2
Big Cove Holiness Church AL-4
Big Cove Mission—church NC-3
Big Cove Presbyterian Ch—church AL-4
Big Cove Pumping Station—building AL-4
Big Cove Run—stream WV-2
Big Cove Sch—school AL-4
Big Cove Tank—reservoir AZ-5
**Big Cove Tannery**—pop pl PA-2
Big Cowan Ch—church KY-4
Big Cow Burn—area OR-9
Big Cow Canyon—valley NV-8
Big Cow Creek KS-7
Big Cow Creek OR-9
Big Cow Creek—stream TX-5
Big Cow Creek—stream WY-8
Big Cowhead Creek—stream SC-3
Big Cow Island AL-4
Big Cow Lake—lake LA-4
Big Cowpen Swamp—stream NC-3
Big Coyote Creek WA-9
Big Coyote Creek—stream TX-5
Big Coyote Point CA-9
Big Crab Island GA-3
Big Crab Key FL-3
Big Crab Orchard Site—hist pl VA-3
Big Crabtree Ch—church NC-3
Big Crabtree Creek—stream NC-3
Big Crack—other CA-9
Big Craggies—summit OR-9
Big Craggy Peak—summit WA-9
Big Cranberry Lake—lake MI-6
Big Cranberry Lake—lake MN-6
Big Crane Creek—stream CA-9
Big Crater—cliff CA-9
Big Crater Flow ID-8
Big Craters—crater ID-8
Big Craters Flow—lava ID-8
Big Crawford Creek—stream UT-8
Big Crawford Spring—spring UT-8
Big Creek AL-4
Big Creek AR-4
Big Creek CA-9
Big Creek GA-3
Big Creek ID-8
Big Creek IN-6
Big Creek KS-7
Big Creek MD-2
Big Creek MI-6
Big Creek MS-4
Big Creek NY-2
Big Creek NC-3
Big Creek OH-6
Big Creek OK-5
Big Creek OR-9
Big Creek PA-2
Big Creek SC-3
Big Creek TN-4
Big Creek TX-5
Big Creek VA-3
Big Creek WA-9
Big Creek WV-2
Big Creek—gut TX-5
Big Creek—locale (2) GA-3
Big Creek—locale NY-2
Big Creek—locale PA-2
Big Creek—locale (2) TN-4
**Big Creek**—pop pl AL-4
**Big Creek**—pop pl CA-9
**Big Creek**—pop pl ID-8
**Big Creek**—pop pl KY-4
**Big Creek**—pop pl LA-4
**Big Creek**—pop pl MS-4
**Bigcreek**—pop pl SC-3
**Big Creek**—pop pl TN-4
**Big Creek**—pop pl TX-5
**Big Creek**—pop pl WV-2
Big Creek—stream (13) AL-4
Big Creek—stream (8) AK-9
Big Creek—stream AZ-5
Big Creek—stream (28) AR-4
Big Creek—stream (20) CA-9
Big Creek—stream (2) CO-8
Big Creek—stream (4) FL-3
Big Creek—stream (22) GA-3
Big Creek—stream (17) ID-8
Big Creek—stream (12) IL-6
Big Creek—stream (9) IN-6
Big Creek—stream (5) IA-7
Big Creek—stream (5) KS-7
Big Creek—stream (6) KY-4
Big Creek—stream (12) LA-4
Big Creek—stream (10) MI-6
Big Creek—stream (20) MS-4
Big Creek—stream (14) MO-7
Big Creek—stream (7) MT-8
Big Creek—stream (2) NE-7
Big Creek—stream (4) NV-8
Big Creek—stream (2) NJ-2
Big Creek—stream NM-5
Big Creek—stream (4) NY-2
Big Creek—stream (17) NC-3
Big Creek—stream (4) OH-6
Big Creek—stream (6) OK-5
Big Creek—stream (20) OR-9
Big Creek—stream PA-2
Big Creek—stream (6) SC-3
Big Creek—stream (2) SD-7
Big Creek—stream (12) TN-4
Big Creek—stream (18) TX-5
Big Creek—stream (4) UT-8
Big Creek—stream (5) VA-3
Big Creek—stream (18) WA-9
Big Creek—stream (9) WV-2
Big Creek—stream (4) WI-6
Big Creek—stream (2) WY-8
Big Creek—swamp FL-3
Big Creek Access Point—locale GA-3
Big Creek Arm—bay OR-9
Big Creek Baldy Mtn—summit MT-8
Big Creek Baptist Ch—church (2) TN-4
Big Creek Baptist Church MS-4
Big Creek Bar—bar AL-4
Big Creek Barrier Dam—dam IA-7
Big Creek Basin—basin CA-9
Big Creek Bottoms—bend WA-9
Big Creek Bridge—bridge ID-8
Big Creek Bridge—bridge (2) NC-3
Big Creek Bridge Trail—trail CO-8
Big Creek Cabin—locale ID-8
Big Creek Cabin—locale MT-8
Big Creek Campground—locale CO-8
Big Creek Campground—locale (2) ID-8
Big Creek Campground—locale MT-8
Big Creek Campground—locale NV-8
Big Creek Campground—locale OR-9
Big Creek Campground—locale (2) WA-9
Big Creek Camp (historical)—locale ID-8
Big Creek Canyon—valley CA-9
Big Creek Canyon—valley NV-8
Big Creek Canyon—valley UT-8
Big Creek (CCD)—cens area GA-3
Big Creek (CCD)—cens area KY-4
Big Creek Cem—cemetery (2) AL-4
Big Creek Cem—cemetery IN-6
Big Creek Cem—cemetery KS-7
Big Creek Cem—cemetery (2) MS-4
Big Creek Cem—cemetery MO-7
Big Creek Cem—cemetery TN-4
Big Creek Cem—cemetery TX-5
Big Creek Cem—cemetery WI-6
Big Creek Ch AL-4
Big Creek Ch—church (4) AL-4
Big Creek Ch—church AR-4
Big Creek Ch—church (6) GA-3
Big Creek Ch—church IL-6
Big Creek Ch—church (2) KY-4
Big Creek Ch—church (3) LA-4
Big Creek Ch—church (4) MS-4
Big Creek Ch—church (4) MO-7
Big Creek Ch—church NC-3
Big Creek Ch—church SC-3
Big Creek Ch—church (3) TN-4
Big Creek Ch—church (3) WV-2
Big Creek Ch—church WI-6
Big Creek Chapel—church KS-7
Big Creek Chapel—church TN-4
Big Creek Ch (historical)—church AL-4
Big Creek Ch (historical)—church MS-4
Big Creek Community Center—locale MO-7
**Big Creek Corner**—pop pl AR-4
Big Creek Dam No. 2—dam OR-9
Big Creek Dam Number 1—dam OR-9
Big Creek Deadwater—stream MS-4
Big Creek Ditch IN-6
Big Creek Ditch—canal AR-4
Big Creek Ditch—canal (2) OR-9
Big Creek Ditch—canal WY-8
Big Creek Ditch Main Ditch—canal AR-4
Big Creek Drain—canal IL-6
Big Creek Drainage Canal—canal TN-4
Big Creek Falls—falls CO-8
Big Creek Falls—falls WY-8
Big Creek Fire Station—locale CA-9
Big Creek Forest Camp OR-9
Big Creek Forest Camp—locale OR-9
Big Creek Gap TN-4
Big Creek Gap—gap GA-3
Big Creek Gap—gap TN-4
Big Creek Gap Post Office TN-4
Big Creek Gas Field—oilfield LA-4
Big Creek Gorge—valley ID-8
Big Creek Guard Station—locale WY-8
Big Creek Hardshell Cem—cemetery GA-3
**Big Creek (historical)**—pop pl TN-4
Big Creek Hot Springs ID-8
Big Creek Knobs—ridge TN-4
Big Creek Lake LA-4
Big Creek Lake MT-8
Big Creek Lake—lake CO-8
Big Creek Lake—lake ID-8
Big Creek Lake—lake IA-7
Big Creek Lake—reservoir AL-4
Big Creek Lake—reservoir TN-4
Big Creek Lake Dam—dam AL-4
Big Creek Lakes—lake CO-8
Big Creek Lakes—lake MT-8
Big Creek Lake Site—hist pl MT-8
Big Creek Landing—locale AL-4
Big Creek Landing Rec Area—park MS-4
Big Creek Landmark Church MS-4
Big Creek Lateral No 1—canal AR-4
Big Creek Leon Drift Fence—other CO-8
Big Creek Log Pond—reservoir OR-9
Big Creek Lookout Tower—locale MS-4
Big Creek Lookout Tower (historical)—tower TN-4
Big Creek (Magisterial District)—fmr MCD WV-2
Big Creek Marsh—swamp MD-2
Big Creek Marsh—swamp VA-3
Big Creek Meadow—flat OR-9
Big Creek Meadows—flat (2) ID-8
Big Creek Methodist Church MS-4
Big Creek Missionary Baptist Ch (historical)—church AL-4
Big Creek Missionary Ch—church TX-5
Big Creek Narrows—cliff AR-4
Big Creek North WY-8
Big Creek Oil Field—oilfield TX-5
Big Creek Park—flat WY-8
Big Creek Park—park (2) IL-6
Big Creek Parkway—park OH-6
Big Creek Peak—summit ID-8
Big Creek Point—summit (3) ID-8
Big Creek Post Office TN-4
Bigcreek Post Office (historical)—building TN-4
Big Creek Pounding Area—reservoir IA-7
Big Creek Powerhouse (site)—locale CA-9
Big Creek Ranch—locale CA-9
Big Creek Ranch—locale CO-8
Big Creek Ranch—locale ID-8
Big Creek Ranch—locale (2) NV-8
Big Creek Ranch—locale WY-8
Big Creek Reservation—park OH-6
Big Creek Ridge—ridge ID-8
Big Creek Rsvr OR-9
Big Creek Rsvr—reservoir CO-8
Big Creek Rsvr No. 1—reservoir CO-8
Big Creek Rsvr No. 2—reservoir OR-9
Big Creek Sch—school AL-4
Big Creek Sch—school NC-3
Big Creek Sch—school (2) WV-2
Big Creek Sch (historical)—school AL-4
Big Creek Sch (historical)—school (2) MS-4
Big Creek Sch (historical)—school MO-7
Big Creek Sch (historical)—school (2) TN-4
Big Creek School—locale MT-8
Big Creek Shoals—bar AL-4
Big Creek Shoals—bar TN-4
Big Creek Slough—stream IN-6
Big Creek Slough—stream OR-9
Big Creek Spring—spring OR-9
Big Creek State Park—park IA-7
Big Creek State Park—park OR-9
Big Creek Station KS-7
Big Creek Station—locale MT-8
Big Creek Structure 13 Dam—dam MS-4
Big Creek Summit—summit ID-8
Big Creek Summit Trail—trail ID-8
Big Creek Terminal Dam—dam IA-7
Big Creek Township—civil (4) MO-7
Big Creek Township—fmr MCD IA-7
**Big Creek Township**—pop pl (3) KS-7
**Big Creek Township**—pop pl MO-7
Big Creek (Township of)—fmr MCD (12) AR-4
Big Creek (Township of)—fmr MCD NC-3
**Big Creek (Township of)**—pop pl IN-6
**Big Creek (Township of)**—pop pl MI-6
Big Creek Trail—trail CO-8
Big Creek Trail—trail NC-3
Big Creek Trail—trail OR-9
Big Creek Trail—trail TN-4
Big Creek Trail—trail (2) WA-9
Big Creek Utility Dam—dam TN-4
Big Creek Utility Lake—reservoir TN-4
Big Creek Valley Ch—church AR-4
Big Creek Watershed Structure 2 Dam—dam MS-4
Big Creek Watershed Structure 9 Dam—dam MS-4
Big Creek Watershed 14 Dam—dam MS-4
Big Creek Windmill—locale NM-5
Big Creek Work Center—locale MT-8
Big Crevasse Creek—stream KY-4
Big Cripple Swamp—swamp DE-2
Big Crooked Creek FL-3
Big Crooked Lake MI-6
Big Crooked Lake—lake MI-6
Big Crooked Lake—lake (2) WI-6
Big Crooked Ridge—ridge VA-3
Big Cross Bayou—stream LA-4
Big Crow Basin—basin WA-9
Big Crow Creek AL-4
Big Crow Creek TN-4
Big Crow Island—island NY-2
Big Crow Lake—lake MN-6
Big Crow Mtn—summit NY-2
Big Crownest Creek TX-5
Big Cub Ch—church WV-2
Big Cub Creek—stream VA-3
Big Cub Creek—stream WV-2
Big Cub Lake IN-6
Big Cub Lake—lake WI-6
Big Cudge Branch—stream KY-4
Big Culvert Creek—stream AL-4
Big Curltail Creek—stream SC-3
Big Current Hole—channel VI-3
Big Curve—locale NC-3
Big Curve Rsvr—reservoir OR-9
Big Curve Shop Ctr—locale AZ-5
Big Cussetah Ch—church OK-5
Big Cut AL-4
Big Cut—channel TX-5
Big Cut—gut WI-6
Big Cut—locale MI-6
Big Cut (historical)—locale AL-4
Big Cutoff—bend MO-7
Big Cutoff—gap KY-4
Big Cutoff—stream IL-6
Big Cutoff Branch—stream KY-4
Big Cut Rsvr—reservoir OR-9
Big Cut Sch—school NE-7
Big Cut Station—locale AL-4
Big Cut Station—locale VA-3
**Big Cypress**—pop pl FL-3
Big Cypress—swamp GA-3
Big Cypress—swamp IL-6
Big Cypress Baptist Ch (historical)—church AL-4
Big Cypress Bay—basin SC-3
Big Cypress Bayou—stream TX-5
Big Cypress Branch—stream FL-3
Big Cypress Bridge—bridge NC-3
Big Cypress Camp Island—island GA-3
Big Cypress Ch—church FL-3
Big Cypress Creek TX-5
Big Cypress Creek—stream (3) AR-4
Big Cypress Creek—stream FL-3
Big Cypress Creek—stream GA-3
Big Cypress Creek—stream MS-4
Big Cypress Creek—stream (2) TX-5
**Big Cypress Ind Res**—pop pl FL-3
Big Cypress Lake—lake (2) GA-3
Big Cypress Lake Dam—dam AL-4
Big Cypress Natl Preserve—park FL-3
Big Cypress Pond—swamp AL-4
Big Cypress Pond—swamp TX-5
Big Cypress Slough KY-4
Big Cypress Slough—gut TN-4
Big Cypress Swamp—stream NC-3
Big Cypress Swamp—stream SC-3
Big Cypress Swamp—swamp AR-4
Big Cypress Swamp—swamp (5) FL-3
Big Cypress Swamp—swamp GA-3
Big Cypress Tree State Natural Area TN-4
Big Cypress Tree State Park—park TN-4
Big Cypress Wildlife Mngmt Area FL-3
Big Daddys Airp—airport NC-3
Big Dailey Bayou—gut MI-6
Big Daley—valley UT-8
Big Dalton Canyon—valley CA-9
Big Dalton Rsvr—reservoir CA-9
Big Dalton Wash—stream CA-9
Big Dam—dam AZ-5
Big Dam—dam SD-7
Big Dam—dam VT-1
Big Dam—locale PA-2
Big Dam—reservoir MT-8
Big Dam Bayou—gut TX-5
Big Dam Branch—stream NC-3
Big Dam Draw—valley SD-7
Big Dam Hollow—valley PA-2
Big Dam Hollow Trail—trail (2) PA-2
Big Dam Lead—stream SC-3
Big Dam Ridge—ridge PA-2
Big Dam Rsvr—reservoir AZ-5
Big Dam Sch—school PA-2
Big Dam Swamp—stream SC-3
Big Dam Tank—reservoir AZ-5
Big Dam Tank—reservoir TX-5
Big Dam Wash—valley AZ-5
Big Dan Branch KY-4
Big Dan Branch—stream KY-4
Big Dan Creek CA-9
Big Dan Lake—reservoir NC-3
Big Dann Creek—stream CA-9
Big Darbonne Bay LA-4
Big Darbonne Bayou—stream LA-4
Big Darby Ch—church OH-6
Big Darby Creek—stream OH-6
Big Darby Peak—summit CA-9
Big Dardis Lake—lake WI-6
Big Dark Hollow—valley VA-3
Big Dark Hollow—valley WV-2
Big Dasher Island—island (2) IL-6
Big Dave Creek—stream ID-8
Big Davis Creek—stream FL-3
Big Davis Gulch—valley MT-8
Big Day Cem—cemetery MT-8
Big Deacon Creek—stream OR-9
Big Dead Creek—gut FL-3
Big Deadening Branch—stream NC-3
Big Deadening Creek—stream WV-2
Big Dead Key—island FL-3
Big Deedie Lake—lake LA-4
Big Deeper Well—well NM-5
Big Deep Lake—lake MN-6
Big Deep Marsh Island—island NC-3
Big Deer Bayou LA-4
Big Deer Branch—stream MO-7
Big Deer Canyon—valley CA-9
Big Deer Creek—stream (3) ID-8
Big Deer Creek—stream MO-7
Big Deer Lake MN-6
Big Deerlick Creek—stream NY-2
Big Deer Peak—summit WA-9
Big Deer Point—summit MT-8
Big Deer Pond—lake NY-2
Big Deer Pond Trail—trail NY-2
Big Deer Swamp—swamp PA-2
**Big Delta**—pop pl AK-9
Big Den—basin NV-8
Big Den Creek—stream NV-8
Bigden Hollow—valley KY-4
Big Den Spring—spring NV-8
Big Denver Creek—stream AK-9
Big Devil NV-8
Big Devil Bayou—lake TX-5
Big Devil Creek IA-7
Big Devil Creek—stream MI-6
Big Devil Gulch—valley OR-9
Big Devil Lake—lake WI-6
Big Devil Peak—summit WA-9
Big Devils Fork—stream AR-4
Big Devils Stairs—valley VA-3
Big Devils Stairs Trail—trail VA-3
Big Devils Table—flat NV-8
Big Devil Swamp—swamp MI-6
Big D Hollow VA-3
Big Diamond Creek AZ-5
Big Diamond Lake—lake MN-6
Big Diamond Pond—lake NY-2
Big Diamond Spring—spring WY-8
Big Diamond Springs Draw—valley WY-8
Big Dick Canyon—valley AZ-5
Big Dick Creek—stream ID-8
Big Dickey Creek AL-4
Big Dickey Lake—lake TX-5
Big Dickinson—reservoir AR-4
Big Dick Lake—lake MN-6
Big Dick Mine—mine CO-8

Biggen Hollow—valley TN-4
Big George—locale ID-8
Big George Branch—stream IL-6
Big George Branch—stream MO-7
Big George Creek VA-3
Big George Gulch—valley MT-8
Big George Tank—reservoir TX-5
Biggerann MP-9
Biggerann—island MP-9
Bigger Branch—stream WV-2
Bigger Cem—cemetery OH-6
Bigger Cem—cemetery TN-4
Bigger Creek—stream VA-3
Bigger Hollow—valley NY-2
Big German Creek—stream AL-4
Bigger Ranch—locale CO-8
Bigger Run—stream (2) PA-2
Biggers—locale TX-5
**Biggers—pop pl** AR-4
Biggers Branch—stream SC-3
Biggers Cem—cemetery GA-3
Biggers Cem—cemetery KY-4
Biggers Cem—cemetery TX-5
Biggers Ch—church SC-3
Biggers Creek—stream TX-5
Biggers Hill—summit AR-4
Biggers Hill Cave—cave AR-4
Biggers Island ME-1
Biggers Lake—reservoir GA-3
Biggers Point ME-1
Biggerstaff Bar—bar KY-4
Biggerstaff Branch—stream AL-4
Biggerstaff Branch—stream NC-3
Biggerstaff Cem—cemetery TX-5
Biggerstaff Creek—stream KY-4
Biggerstaff Mtn—summit NC-3
Biggerstown—locale PA-2
**Biggersville—pop pl** MS-4
Biggersville Ch—church MS-4
Biggersville Consolidated School MS-4
Biggersville Elem Sch—school MS-4
Biggersville First Baptist Church MS-4
Biggersville HS—school MS-4
Bigger Tank—reservoir NM-5
Biggertown PA-2
**Biggertown—pop pl** PA-2
**Bigger (Township of)—pop pl** IN-6
**Bigger Tract (subdivision)—pop pl** DE-2
Big Getaway Canyon—valley TX-5
Biggett Coulee—valley MT-8
Bigg Hurricane Creek TN-4
Big Giant Mine—mine CO-8
Big Gibson Lake—lake WI-6
Big Gimlet Creek—stream KY-4
Biggin Cem—cemetery SC-3
Biggin Church Ruins—hist pl SC-3
Biggin Corners—locale OH-6
Biggin Creek—stream SC-3
Biggins Hollow—valley TN-4
Biggins Sch—school IA-7
Biggin Swamp—swamp SC-3
Big Glacier—gut AK-9
Big Glade—flat UT-8
Big Glade Branch—stream AL-4
Big Glades—flat OR-9
Big Glades Lake FL-3
Big Glade Spring—spring OR-9
Big Glady Run—stream WV-2
Big Glass Lake FL-3
Big Goat Creek—stream WA-9
Big Goat Lake—lake AK-9
Big Goat Mtn—summit WA-9
Big Gobbler—valley TX-5
Big Goddel Bayou—stream LA-4
Big Goddet Bayou LA-4
Big Goldmine Hill—summit NY-2
Big Golf Creek OK-5
Big Gonsoulin Bayou—stream LA-4
Big Goose And Beaver Ditch—canal WY-8
Big Goose Bay WA-9
Big Goose Campground—locale WY-8
Big Goose Creek AL-4
Big Goose Creek TN-4
Big Goose Creek WY-8
Big Goose Creek—stream WY-8
Big Goose Creek Buffalo Jump—hist pl WY-8
Big Goose Lake WA-9
Big Goose Park—flat WY-8
Big Goose Pond—lake NJ-2
Big Goose Pond—lake SC-3
Big Goose Ranger Station—locale WY-8
Big Goose Sch—school WY-8
Big Gordon Gulch—valley OR-9
Big Gough Spring—spring UT-8
Big Government Mine (underground)—mine TN-4
Big Governors Creek—stream NC-3
Big Graham Creek IN-6
Big Grand Lake MI-6
Big Grand Pierre Creek—stream IL-6
Big Granite Canyon—valley UT-8
Big Granite Creek—stream AK-9
Big Granite Creek—stream CA-9
Big Granite Creek—stream OR-9
Big Granite Trail—trail CA-9
Big Granite Wash—stream AZ-5
Big Grapevine Pond—lake ME-1
Big Grass Island—island (2) FL-3
Big Grass Lake—lake AK-9
Big Grassy—flat CO-8
Big Grassy—flat ID-8
Big Grassy Bayou—stream LA-4
Big Grassy Brake—swamp AR-4
Big Grassy Butte OR-9
Big Grassy Butte—summit ID-8
Big Grassy Creek—stream NC-3
Big Grassy Island LA-4
Big Grassy Island—island (2) FL-3
Big Grassy Knob—summit GA-3
Big Grassy Mountain OR-9
Big Grassy Peak—summit MT-8
Big Grassy Pond—swamp TX-5
Big Grassy Ridge—ridge ID-8
Big Grassy Valley—valley MO-7
Big Grave Creek—other WV-2
Big Gravel Creek - in part NV-8
Big Graveling Creek—gut NJ-2
Big Gravel Slough—stream AR-4
Big Graveyard Hollow—valley KY-4
Big Graw, Bayou—stream LA-4
Big Grayling Lake—lake AK-9
Big Greasy Creek—stream MO-7
Big Greaves Creek—stream NJ-2
Big Greek Station—building TX-5
Big Green Brake—island TX-5
Big Green Brake—swamp LA-4
Big Green Break Island LA-4
Big Green Break Island TX-5
Big Greenbrier Hill—summit AR-4
Big Green Lake—lake MN-6
Big Greenland Lake—lake ME-1
Big Green Mtn—summit NC-3
Big Green Mtn—summit OR-9
Big Green River—stream WI-6
Big Green Tom Lake—lake AR-4
Big Greenwood Pond—lake ME-1
Big Greider Lake—lake WA-9
Big Grenier Pond—lake ME-1
Big Gressy Creek MO-7
Big Griffin Lake—reservoir AL-4
Big Grill Ridge—ridge NC-3
Big Grindle Cave—cave AL-4
Big Grizzly Canyon—valley CA-9
Big Grizzly Creek—stream AK-9
Big Grizzly Creek—stream (3) CA-9
Big Grizzly Flat—flat CA-9
Big Grizzly Lake—lake MT-8
Big Grizzly Mtn—summit CA-9
Big Grocery Creek—stream GA-3
Big Groundhog Branch—stream KY-4
Big Groundhog Hollow—valley KY-4
Big Grove Cem—cemetery (2) IL-6
Big Grove Cem—cemetery IA-7
Big Grove Ch—church MN-6
Big Grove (historical P.O.)—locale IA-7
Big Grove-Homer Cem—cemetery IA-7
Big Grove Townhall—building IA-7
Big Grove Township—fmr MCD (2) IA-7
**Big Grove (Township of)—pop pl** IL-6
Biggs MS-4
Biggs—locale IL-6
Biggs—locale KY-4
Biggs—locale OR-9
**Biggs—pop pl** CA-9
**Biggs—pop pl** MD-2
Biggs, Asa, House and Site—hist pl NC-3
Biggs, Gov. Benjamin T., Farm—hist pl DE-2
Biggs AFB—military TX-5
Biggs Army Air Field—uninc pl TX-5
Biggs Branch—stream KY-4
Biggs Branch—stream TN-4
Biggs (CCD)—cens area CA-9
Biggs Cem—cemetery MO-7
Biggs Cem—cemetery NE-7
Biggs Cem—cemetery OH-6
Biggs Cem—cemetery WV-2
Biggs Chapel—church AR-4
Biggs Cove OR-9
Biggs Creek—stream MT-8
Biggs Creek—stream TN-4
Biggs Creek Flat—flat MT-8
Biggs Ditch—canal IL-6
Biggs Ditch—canal OR-9
Biggs Extension—canal CA-9
Biggs Ford Bridge—bridge MD-2
Biggs Ford Site—hist pl MD-2
Biggs Gin (historical)—locale MS-4
Biggs Gridley Memorial Hosp—hospital CA-9
Biggs Gulch—valley CA-9
Biggs Hill—summit KY-4
Biggs Hollow—valley TN-4
**Biggs Junction—pop pl** OR-9
Biggs Landing—locale AR-4
Biggs Mtn—summit VA-3
Biggs Park—uninc pl NC-3
Biggs Point OR-9
Biggs Post Office (historical)—building MS-4
Biggs Ranch—locale ID-8
Biggs Ranch—locale MT-8
Biggs Ranch—locale NM-5
Biggs Run—stream VA-3
Biggs Settlement—locale MI-6
Biggs Spring—spring OR-9
Biggs Spring Branch—stream TN-4
Biggs Spring Forest Camp—locale OR-9
**Biggsville—pop pl** IL-6
Biggsville Cem—cemetery IL-6
**Biggsville (Township of)—pop pl** IL-6
Biggs Wells—well NM-5
Big Guatali River—stream GU-9
Big Guinea Creek—stream VA-3
Big Gulch—valley AK-9
Big Gulch—valley (4) CA-9
Big Gulch—valley (7) CO-8
Big Gulch—valley (5) ID-8
Big Gulch—valley MO-7
Big Gulch—valley (3) MT-8
Big Gulch—valley ND-7
Big Gulch—valley (4) OR-9
Big Gulch—valley TX-5
Big Gulch—valley (2) WA-9
Big Gulch—valley (2) WY-8
Big Gulch Creek—stream ID-8
Big Gulch Rsvr—reservoir OR-9
Big Gulf—stream NY-2
Big Gulf—valley NY-2
Big Gull Island—island NY-2
Big Gully—stream LA-4
Big Gully—stream NC-3
Big Gully—valley IA-7
Big Gully—valley LA-4
Big Gully—valley NY-2
Big Gully—valley (2) TN-4
Big Gully Creek—stream (2) FL-3
Big Gully Creek—stream MI-6
Big Gully Post Office (historical)—building TN-4
Big Gumbo Creek—stream MT-8
Big Gumbo Creek—stream ND-7
Big Gum Hollow TN-4
Big Gum Hollow—valley AR-4
Big Gum Lake—lake FL-3
Big Gum Lateral—canal AR-4
Big Gum Pond—swamp AR-4
Big Gum Pond—swamp TN-4
Big Gum Swamp—swamp FL-3
Big Gun Diggings—locale CA-9
**Big Gunpowder—pop pl** MD-2
Big Gut—bay NC-3
Big Gut—gut MD-2
Big Gut—gut NC-3
Big Gut—gut VA-3
Big Gut Branch—stream WV-2
Big Gut Slough—stream NC-3
Big Gypsum Creek—stream CO-8
Big Gypsum Ledges—cliff AZ-5
Big Gypsum Valley—valley CO-8
Big Hackberry Canyon—valley TX-5
Big Hale Creek OK-5
Big Hale Mountains ID-8
Big Half Mountain Creek—stream KY-4
Big Half Mtn—summit KY-4
Big Halfway Tank—reservoir TX-5
Bigham Branch—stream SC-3
Bigham Cem—cemetery (2) TN-4
Bigham Flat—flat WA-9
Big Ham Hole Spring—spring TX-5
Big Hamilton Run PA-2
Bigham Lake—lake ND-7
Big Hammer Creek—stream ID-8
Big Hammock FL-3
Big Hammock—island (2) FL-3
Big Hammock—lake FL-3
**Big Hammock—pop pl** FL-3
Big Hammock Ch—church LA-4
**Big Hammock (historical)—pop pl** FL-3
Big Hammock Point—bay FL-3
Big Hammock Point—cape NC-3
Bighams Lake—reservoir AZ-5
Bighams Mill (historical)—locale MS-4
Big Hand Oil Field—oilfield WY-8
Big Hand Oil Field—other MI-6
Big Haning Horn Lake MN-6
Big Hank Creek—stream ID-8
Big Hank Meadow—flat ID-8
Big Hanson Lake—lake MN-6
Big Happy Spring—spring OR-9
Big Harbor Run PA-2
Big Hard Pan—flat NV-8
Big Hardwood Island ME-1
Big Harkey Canyon—valley TX-5
Big Harper Key—island FL-3
Big Harper Lake—lake GA-3
Big Harrington Creek ID-8
Big Harris Creek—stream NC-3
Big Harrison Ditch—canal WY-8
Big Harry Island—island SC-3
Big Hart Canyon—valley CA-9
Big Hart Creek WV-2
Big Harts Creek—stream WV-2
Big Hassock—island NY-2
Big Hatch Canyon—valley UT-8
Big Hatchet Mountains—other NM-5
Big Hatchet Peak—summit NM-5
Big Hatchie MS-4
Big Hatchie River TN-4
Big Hat Creek ID-8
Big Hat Creek—stream ID-8
Big Hat Mtn—summit NV-8
Big Hawk Lake—lake MT-8
Big Hawk Mtn—summit MT-8
Big Haw Mtn—summit NC-3
Big Hayes Run PA-2
Big Hay Meadow Creek—stream WI-6
Big Haynes Creek—stream GA-3
Big Haystack Mtn—summit NY-2
Big Hazard Lake—lake ID-8
Big Hazel Creek GA-3
Big Hazy Islet—island AK-9
Big H Creek—stream ID-8
Big H Creek—stream WA-9
Big Head—cape ME-1
Big Head Branch—stream FL-3
Big Head Branch—stream NC-3
Bighead Creek—stream MT-8
Bighead Creek—stream TX-5
Big Head Mtn—summit TX-5
Bighead Rsvr—reservoir MT-8
Bigheart—locale OK-5
Big Heart Ditch—canal WY-8
Big Heart Lake—lake WA-9
Big Heath—swamp (4) ME-1
Big He Creek—stream TN-4
Big Heiser Tank—reservoir TX-5
Big Hell Canyon—valley CO-8
Big Hellgate Creek—stream VA-3
Big Hellhole Lake—lake LA-4
Big Hells Gate—gap AZ-5
Big Hen Island—island ME-1
Big Henry Branch—stream LA-4
Big Henry Hill—summit TN-4
Big Herd Spring—spring AL-4
Big Hermit Gulch—valley WY-8
Big Hickory—summit PA-2
Big Hickory Cem—cemetery AR-4
Big Hickory Creek TX-5
Big Hickory Hollow—valley VA-3
Big Hickory Island—island FL-3
Big Hickory Pass—channel FL-3
Big Hickory Pond PA-2
Big Hidatsa Village Site—hist pl ND-7
Big Hidden Lake—lake WA-9
Big Hill CA-9
Big Hill KY-4
Big Hill NH-1
Big Hill OR-9
Big Hill PA-2
Big Hill VA-3
Big Hill—cliff KS-7
Big Hill—locale AR-4
Bighill—locale KY-4
Big Hill—locale TX-5
Big Hill—locale VA-3
**Big Hill—pop pl** IN-6
**Bighill—pop pl** TX-5
Big Hill—ridge OR-9
Big Hill—ridge PA-2
Big Hill—ridge SC-3
Big Hill—summit AL-4
Big Hill—summit AK-9
Big Hill—summit AZ-5
Big Hill—summit (7) CA-9
Big Hill—summit (3) CO-8
Big Hill—summit (2) FL-3
Big Hill—summit GA-3
Big Hill—summit (5) ID-8
Big Hill—summit KY-4
Big Hill—summit (3) ME-1
Big Hill—summit MO-7
Big Hill—summit (2) MT-8
Big Hill—summit NE-7
Big Hill—summit NJ-2
Big Hill—summit (4) NY-2
Big Hill—summit NC-3
Big Hill—summit (2) OR-9
Big Hill—summit (5) PA-2
Big Hill—summit RI-1
Big Hill—summit SC-3
Big Hill—summit (7) TN-4
Big Hill—summit (11) TX-5
Big Hill—summit (6) UT-8
Big Hill—summit (5) VA-3
Big Hill—summit WA-9
Big Hill—summit WV-2
Big Hill—summit (3) WY-8
Big Hill, The CO-8
Big Hill, The VA-3
Big Hill, The—summit CA-9
Big Hill, The—summit (2) KY-4
Big Hill, The—summit MT-8
Big Hillabee Creek AL-4
Big Hill Archeol District—hist pl KS-7
Big Hill Bayou—gut TX-5
Big Hill Bayou Wildlife Mngmt Area—park TX-5
Big Hill Branch—stream IL-6
Big Hill Branch—stream TN-4
Big Hill Camp—locale HI-9
Big Hill Canyon—valley CA-9
Big Hill Cem—cemetery AL-4
Big Hill Cem—cemetery IL-6
Big Hill Cem—cemetery KY-4
Big Hill Cem—cemetery (2) TN-4
Big Hill Cem—cemetery WI-6
Big Hill Ch—church AL-4
Big Hill Ch—church MS-4
Big Hill Ch—church NC-3
Big Hill Ch—church TN-4
Big Hill Creek—stream (2) AR-4
Big Hill Creek—stream KS-7
Big Hill Creek—stream MT-8
Big Hill Dam—dam KS-7
Big Hill Gulch—valley ID-8
Big Hill Hollow—valley MO-7
Big Hill Hollow—valley WV-2
Big Hill Lake—reservoir KS-7
Big Hill Lookout Tower—locale LA-4
Big Hill Marsh—swamp SC-3
Big Hill Methodist Ch MS-4
Bighill Mtn—summit KY-4
Big Hill Oil Field—oilfield TX-5
Big Hill Park—park WI-6
Big Hill Pond—lake AL-4
Big Hill Pond—lake NY-2
Big Hill Pond—lake TN-4
Big Hill Pond Environmental Education Area—area TN-4
Big Hill Pond Lake—reservoir TN-4
Big Hill Pond Lake Dam—dam TN-4
Big Hill Post Office (historical)—building TN-4
Big Hill Rapids—rapids ID-8
Big Hill Ridge VA-3
Big Hill Ridge—ridge CA-9
Big Hill Rsvr—reservoir CO-8
Big Hill Rsvr—reservoir TX-5
Bighill Sch—school KY-4
Big Hill Sch (historical)—school TN-4
Big Hill Shaft—mine UT-8
Big Hill Shaft Headframe—hist pl UT-8
Big Hill Spring—spring OR-9
Big Hill State Game Mngmt Area KS-7
Big Hill Trail—trail CA-9
Big Hill Trail—trail PA-2
Big Hill Valley—basin NE-7
Big Hill Wildlife Area—park KS-7
Big Hit Mine—mine SD-7
Big Hob Run—stream MD-2
Big Hocter Tank—reservoir AZ-5
Big Hogan—summit AZ-5
Big Hogback, The—ridge NV-8
Big Hogback Ridge—ridge MT-8
Big Hog Bayou—gut TX-5
Big Hog Bayou—stream LA-4
Big Hog Creek IN-6
Big Hog Creek—stream TX-5
Big Hog Glade—swamp LA-4
Big Hog Ranch Creek—stream NV-8
Big Hog Slough LA-4
Big Hole HT-8
Big Hole—basin (2) UT-8
Big Hole—bay ID-8
Big Hole—bend ID-8
Big Hole—crater OR-9
Big Hole—flat NC-3
Big Hole—gut LA-4
Big Hole—lake TX-5
Big Hole—lake UT-8
Big Hole—other ID-8
Big Hole—valley CO-8
Big Hole—valley OH-6
Big Hole Basin—cens area MT-8
Bighole Butte—summit CO-8
Big Hole Butte—summit OR-9
Big Hole Canyon CO-8
Big Hole Canyon—valley CO-8
Big Hole Canyon—valley OR-9
Big Hole Creek ID-8
Big Hole Creek OK-5
Big Hole Creek—stream MT-8
Big Hole Dam—dam MT-8
Big Hole Divide—ridge MT-8
Bighole Gulch—valley CO-8
Big Hole Mtns—range ID-8
Big Hole Natl Battlefield—hist pl MT-8
Big Hole Natl Battlefield—park MT-8
Big Hole Pass—gap ID-8
Big Hole Pass—gap (2) MT-8
Big Hole Peak—summit MT-8
Big Hole Pond—lake UT-8
Big Hole Pumping Station—other MT-8
Big Hole Pumpstation—hist pl MT-8
Big Hole River—stream MT-8
Big Hole Rsvr—reservoir (2) OR-9
Big Holes—bend ID-8
Big Hole Slough—gut AL-4
Big Hole Spring—spring CO-8
Big Holes Wash UT-8
Big Hole Tank—reservoir (3) AZ-5
Big Hole Wash—valley (2) UT-8
Big Hollow ID-8
Big Hollow UT-8
Big Hollow—locale NY-2
**Big Hollow—pop pl** IL-6
Big Hollow—valley (2) AL-4
Big Hollow—valley (10) AR-4
Big Hollow—valley (2) CO-8
Big Hollow—valley FL-3
Big Hollow—valley (2) ID-8
Big Hollow—valley (13) KY-4
Big Hollow—valley (18) MO-7
Big Hollow—valley MT-8
Big Hollow—valley (2) NY-2
Big Hollow—valley OH-6
Big Hollow—valley (2) OK-5
Big Hollow—valley (8) PA-2
Big Hollow—valley (18) TN-4
Big Hollow—valley (2) TX-5
Big Hollow—valley (20) UT-8
Big Hollow—valley (7) VA-3
Big Hollow—valley (13) WV-2
Big Hollow—valley WI-6
Big Hollow—valley (3) WY-8
Big Hollow, The—basin WY-8
Big Hollow, The—locale WY-8
Big Hollow Bench—bench WY-8
Big Hollow Branch—stream (3) MO-7
Big Hollow Branch—stream NY-2
Big Hollow Branch—stream TN-4
Big Hollow Branch—stream VA-3
Big Hollow Brook—stream NY-2
Big Hollow Brook—stream VT-1
Big Hollow Cave—cave TN-4
Big Hollow Cem—cemetery WI-6
Big Hollow Creek SD-7
Big Hollow Creek—stream IL-6
Big Hollow Creek—stream NY-2
Big Hollow Creek—stream OK-5
Big Hollow Creek—stream SD-7
Big Hollow Creek—stream TX-5
Big Hollow Creek—stream WA-9
Big Hollow Creek—stream WY-8
Big Hollow Draw—valley TX-5
Big Hollow Gulch—valley CO-8
Big Hollow Gulch—valley WY-8
Big Hollow Hill—summit TN-4
Big Hollow Public Use Area—park OK-5
Big Hollow Rsvr—reservoir NY-2
Big Hollow Rsvr—reservoir UT-8
Big Hollow Rsvr—reservoir WY-8
Big Hollow Run—stream NY-2
Big Hollow Sch—school IL-6
Big Hollow Spring—spring (3) UT-8
Big Hollow Trail—trail UT-8
Big Hollow Trail—trail VA-3
Big Hollow Wash—stream AZ-5
Big Hollow Wash—valley (2) UT-8
Big Hollow Wildlife Mngmt Area—park UT-8
Big Holly Cove—bay ME-1
Big Hoodoo Mtn—summit MT-8
Big Hopkins Mtn—summit NY-2
Big Hopper Camp Branch—stream TN-4
Big Horn (2) MT-8
Bighorn WY-8
Big Horn—CDP AK-9
Big Horn—locale AK-9
Big Horn—locale AZ-5
Bighorn—locale MT-8
Big Horn—locale NM-5
**Bighorn—pop pl** CO-8
**Big Horn—pop pl** WY-8
Big Horn—valley UT-8
Bighorn Basin—basin CA-9
Bighorn Basin—basin ID-8
Bighorn Basin—basin MT-8
Big Horn Bayou—stream LA-4
Big Horn Benches—bench UT-8
Bighorn Bridge—bridge ID-8
Bighorn Butte—summit WY-8
Bighorn Campground—locale ID-8
Bighorn Campground—locale MT-8
Bighorn Campground—park OR-9
Big Horn Canal—canal MT-8
Big Horn Canal—canal WY-8
Big Horn Canyon MT-8
Big Horn Canyon WY-8
Bighorn Canyon—valley CA-9
Big Horn Canyon—valley CA-9
Bighorn Canyon—valley CA-9
Bighorn Canyon—valley ID-8
Bighorn Canyon—valley MT-8
Big Horn Canyon—valley WA-9
Bighorn Canyon—valley WY-8
Bighorn Canyon Natl Recreation Area—park MT-8
Bighorn Canyon Natl Recreation Area—park WY-8
Bighorn Cattle Company Ditch—canal CO-8
Bighorn Cave—hist pl AZ-5
Bighorn Caverns—cave MT-8
Big Horn Cem—cemetery WY-8
Big Horn Central—cens area WY-8
Bighorn Coulee—valley MT-8
Bighorn Country—area ID-8
Bighorn Cove—bay NV-8
Bighorn Crags—range ID-8
Bighorn Creek MT-8
Bighorn Creek—stream (3) CO-8
Bighorn Creek—stream (2) ID-8
Bighorn Creek—stream (2) MT-8
Bighorn Creek—stream NM-5
Bighorn Creek—stream OR-9
Big Horn Creek—stream WA-9
Bighorn Ditch Headgate—hist pl MT-8
Bighorn Draw—valley WY-8
Bighorn Enclosure—area UT-8
Bighorn Flat—flat WY-8
Bighorn Flats—flat CO-8
Bighorn Gorge—valley CA-9
Big Horn Gulch—valley CO-8
Bighorn Gulch—valley NE-7
Big Horn (historical)—locale AZ-5
Big Horn Hotel—hist pl WY-8
Bighorn Island—island NV-8
Big Horn Islands NV-8
Bighorn Lake CA-9
Big Horn Lake—lake CA-9
Bighorn Lake—lake (3) CA-9
Bighorn Lake—lake (2) CO-8
Big Horn Lake—lake MN-6
Bighorn Lake—lake MT-8
Big Horn Lake—reservoir KY-4
Bighorn Lake—reservoir MT-8
Bighorn Lake—reservoir WY-8
Big Horn Lode Mine—mine SD-7
Big Horn Low Line Canal—canal MT-8
Bighorn Mesa—summit (2) UT-8
Big Horn Mine—mine AZ-5
Big Horn Mine—mine CA-9
Bighorn Mine—mine (2) CA-9
Big Horn Mine—mine WY-8
Big Horn Mountain MT-8
Big Horn Mountains AZ-5
Big Horn Mountains—range AZ-5
Bighorn Mountains—range CA-9
Bighorn Mtn—summit AZ-5
Bighorn Mtn—summit (2) CO-8
Big Horn Mtn—summit (2) MT-8
Bighorn Mtn—summit MT-8
Bighorn Mtn—summit NE-7
Big Horn Mtn—summit UT-8
Bighorn Mtns—range WY-8
Bighorn Natl For—forest WY-8
Big Horn North—cens area WY-8
Big Horn Other Reservation Land—reserve MT-8
Bighorn Park—flat CA-9
Big Horn Pass—gap AZ-5
Bighorn Pass—gap WY-8
Bighorn Pass Trail—trail WY-8
Bighorn Peak AZ-5
Big Horn Peak—summit AZ-5
Bighorn Peak—summit CA-9
Bighorn Peak—summit MT-8
Big Horn Peak—summit MT-8
Bighorn Peak—summit NM-5
Bighorn Peak—summit WY-8
Bighorn Plateau—plain CA-9
Bighorn Point—summit ID-8
Bighorn Range CA-9
Bighorn Ranger Station—locale CO-8
Big Horn Ridge—ridge CA-9
Bighorn Ridge—ridge CO-8
Bighorn Ridge—ridge WY-8
Big Horn River MT-8
Bighorn River—stream MT-8
Bighorn River—stream WY-8
Bighorn Rsvr—reservoir WY-8
Big Hornsby Lake—lake GA-3
Big Horn Sch—school WA-9
Big Horn Sheep Canyon—valley UT-8
Big Horn South—cens area WY-8
Bighorn Tullock Ditch—canal MT-8
Bighorn Tunnel—tunnel MT-8
Big Horn Well—well AZ-5
**Big Horn Wye—pop pl** MT-8
Big Horse Basin Gap—gap ID-8
Big Horse Branch—stream TN-4
Big Horse Canyon—valley UT-8
Big Horse Canyon Creek—stream ID-8
Big Horse Cove—valley VA-3
Big Horse Creek GA-3
Big Horse Creek—stream AL-4
Big Horse Creek—stream FL-3
Big Horse Creek—stream ID-8
Big Horse Creek—stream (2) NC-3
Big Horse Creek—stream SC-3
Big Horse Creek—stream VA-3
Big Horse Creek—stream WV-2
Big Horse Creek Ch—church GA-3
Big Horse Draw—valley CO-8
Big Horse Draw Rsvr—reservoir CO-8
Big Horse Gap—gap VA-3
Big Horse Opening—flat CA-9
Big Horsepen Bay—swamp SC-3
Big Horse Run—stream WV-2
Big Horseshoe—basin UT-8
Big Horseshoe—slope UT-8
Big Horseshoe Bend—bend GA-3
Big Horseshoe Brake—lake AR-4
Big Horseshoe Lake—lake (2) AR-4
Big Horseshoe Mtn—summit OK-5
Big Horse Spring—spring ID-8
Big Horse Trails, The—trail OR-9
Big Hot Spring—spring OR-9
Big Hound Cave—cave AL-4
Big Hound Creek VA-3
Big Hounds Creek—stream VA-3
Big House—hist pl AZ-5
Big Houso, The locale AZ-5
Big House Branch—stream TX-5
Big House Canyon—valley NM-5
Big House Cem—cemetery SC-3
Big House Mtn—summit VA-3
Big Houston Lake OR-9
Big Houston Pond—lake ME-1
Big Howard Spring—spring OR-9
Big Huckleberry Butte OR-9
Big Huckleberry Butte—summit OR-9
Big Huckleberry Creek—stream TN-4
Big Huckleberry Creek—stream WA-9
Big Huckleberry Mtn—summit WA-9
Big Hudson Brook—stream ME-1
Big Hudson Creek—stream OK-5
Big Humbug Creek—stream CA-9
Big Hump—summit WA-9
Big Hungry Branch—stream TN-4
Big Hunter—summit CA-9
Big Hunting Club—locale AL-4
Big Hunting Slough—stream MO-7
Big Hurd Lake ME-1
Big Hurd Pond—lake ME-1
Big Hurrah Creek—stream AK-9
Big Hurrah Mine—mine AK-9
Big Hurricane Branch—stream KY-4
Big Hurricane Cem—cemetery AL-4
Big Hurricane Ch—church AL-4
Big Hurricane Creek AL-4
Big Hurricane Creek MO-7
Big Hurricane Creek TN-4
Big Hurricane Creek—stream AR-4
Big Hurricane Creek—stream KY-4
Big Hurricane Creek—stream NC-3
Big Hurricane Creek—stream (2) TN-4
Big Hurricane Gap—gap TN-4
Big Hurricane Hill—summit IN-6
Big Hurricane Lake—lake AR-4
Big Hurst Lake—lake WI-6
Big Huston Creek—stream AR-4
Big Huston Pond ME-1
Bigi—island MP-9

Big Ice Cave—*cave* MT-8
Big I Grade—*trail* ID-8
*Bigiian* MP-9
*Bigiiru-to* MP-9
*Bigi Island* MP-9
Big Ikie Tank—*reservoir* AZ-5
*Bigilapij Island* MP-9
Bigilapij Island—*island* MP-9
Big Inch Pipe Line—*other* IL-6
*Big Index Mtn* WA-9
Big Indian—*island* CT-1
**Big Indian**—*pop pl* NY-2
Big Indian—*summit* UT-8
*Big Indian Access* MO-7
Big Indian Branch Trail—*trail* TN-4
*Big Indian Butte* UT-8
Big Indian Camp—*locale* ID-8
Big Indian Camps—*locale* ME-1
Big Indian Canyon—*valley* TX-5
*Big Indian Creek* AR-4
*Big Indian Creek* GA-3
*Big Indian Creek* MD-2
*Big Indian Creek* MO-7
*Big Indian Creek* OR-9
*Big Indian Creek* TN-4
*Big Indian Creek* VA-3
Big Indian Creek—*stream* AL-4
Big Indian Creek—*stream* AK-9
Big Indian Creek—*stream* CA-9
Big Indian Creek—*stream* (2) GA-3
Big Indian Creek—*stream* IN-6
Big Indian Creek—*stream* IA-7
Big Indian Creek—*stream* KY-4
Big Indian Creek—*stream* MD-2
Big Indian Creek—*stream* NE-7
Big Indian Creek—*stream* NV-8
Big Indian Creek—*stream* NY-2
Big Indian Creek—*stream* NC-3
Big Indian Creek—*stream* OR-9
Big Indian Creek—*stream* TN-4
Big Indian Creek—*stream* VA-3
Big Indian Creek Public Use Area—*park* AL-4
Big Indian Farms—*hist pl* WI-6
Big Indian Hollow—*valley* NY-2
*Big Indian Lake* ME-1
Big Indian Lake—*lake* NV-8
Big Indian Mine—*mine* UT-8
Big Indian Mtn—*summit* NV-8
Big Indian Mtn—*summit* NY-2
Big Indian Pond—*lake* (2) ME-1
Big Indian Public Use Area—*locale* MO-7
Big Indian Rock—*pillar* UT-8
Big Indian Run—*stream* (2) WV-2
Big Indian Shaft—*mine* CO-8
Big Indian Swamp—*stream* NC-3
Big Indian Tank—*reservoir* AZ-5
Big Indian Valley—*valley* UT-8
Big Indian Wash—*valley* UT-8
Big Indian Waterhole Windmill—*locale* TX-5
*Bigini* MP-9
Big Injun Lake—*lake* WI-6
Big Injun Mine—*mine* CA-9
*Big Inlet* VA-3
Big Inlet—*stream* ME-1
Big Inlet—*stream* NY-2
Big Inlet—*stream* PA-2
*Big Inlet Brook* ME-1
Big Inlet Swamp—*swamp* PA-2
Biginnigar Island—*island* MP-9
*Bigin-suido* MP-9
*Bigin-To* MP-9
*Bigiramu-to* MP-9
Bigiren—*island* MP-9
*Bigiren Island* MP-9
*Bigiren-to* MP-9
Big Iron Mine—*mine* WA-9
Big Iron Ore Creek—*stream* TX-5
Big Iron River—*stream* MI-6
**Big Isaac**—*pop pl* WV-2
Big Isaac Creek—*stream* WV-2
*Big Island* ME-1
*Big Island* MD-2
*Big Island* MI-6
*Big Island* (2) MN-6
*Big Island* NY-2
*Big Island* SC-3
*Big Island* TN-4
*Big Island* WI-6
Big Island—*area* AK-9
Big Island—*bench* NV-8
Big Island—*cape* MA-1
Big Island—*flat* (2) AR-4
Big Island—*flat* MS-4
Big Island—*island* (2) AL-4
Big Island—*island* (3) AK-9
Big Island—*island* (3) AR-4
Big Island—*island* (11) FL-3
Big Island—*island* (3) GA-3
Big Island—*island* ID-8
Big Island—*island* IL-6
Big Island—*island* (2) IN-6
Big Island—*island* KY-4
Big Island—*island* (6) LA-4
Big Island—*island* (10) ME-1
Big Island—*island* (3) MD-2
Big Island—*island* (9) MN-6
Big Island—*island* (2) MS-4
Big Island—*island* MO-7
Big Island—*island* MT-8
Big Island—*island* (5) NH-1
Big Island—*island* NM-5
Big Island—*island* (12) NY-2
Big Island—*island* (11) NC-3
Big Island—*island* OH-6
Big Island—*island* (7) SC-3
Big Island—*island* (2) TN-4
Big Island—*island* (2) TX-5
Big Island—*island* UT-8
Big Island—*island* (5) VA-3
Big Island—*island* (8) WI-6
Big Island—*island* WY-8
**Big Island**—*pop pl* LA-4
**Big Island**—*pop pl* NY-2
**Big Island**—*pop pl* OH-6
**Big Island**—*pop pl* VA-3
Big Island—*summit* CO-8
Big Island—*swamp* FL-3
Big Island—*swamp* NC-3
Big Island, The—*island* MN-6
Big Island Bayou—*stream* LA-4
Big Island Branch—*stream* KY-4
Big Island Branch—*stream* MS-4
Big Island Bridge—*bridge* NC-3
Big Island Bridge—*bridge* WY-8
Big Island Camp—*locale* ME-1
Big Island CCC Tank—*reservoir* NM-5
Big Island Ch—*church* LA-4
Big Island Chute—*gut* AR-4
Big Island Chute—*stream* LA-4
Big Island Creek—*stream* NC-3
Big Island Creek—*stream* SC-3
Big Island Dam—*dam* NM-5
Big Island Gap—*channel* FL-3
Big Island (historical)—*island* (2) AL-4
Big Island (historical)—*island* TN-4
Big Island Lake—*lake* FL-3
Big Island Lake—*lake* MI-6
Big Island Lake—*lake* MN-6
Big Island Lake—*lake* WI-6
Big Island Lakes—*lake* LA-4
Big Island Oil Field—*oilfield* (2) LA-4
Big Island Pond—*lake* ME-1
Big Island Run—*stream* WV-2
Big Island Run Ch—*church* WV-2
Big Islands—*island* ME-1
Big Island Sch—*school* IL-6
Big Island Sch—*school* MO-7
Big Island Slough—*stream* TX-5
Big Island State Wildlife Area—*park* WI-6
Big Island Swamp—*swamp* (2) FL-3
**Big Island (Township of)**—*pop pl* OH-6
Big Island Wash—*valley* WY-8
Big Island Wildlife Area—*park* OH-6
*Bigitapit* MP-9
Big Ivey Hollow—*valley* TN-4
Big Ivy—*locale* TN-4
Big Ivy Cem—*cemetery* NC-3
Big Ivy Ch—*church* NC-3
*Big Ivy Creek* NC-3
Big Ivy Creek—*stream* VA-3
Big Jackass Creek—*stream* CA-9
Big Jack Creek—*stream* GA-3
Big Jack Lake—*lake* AR-4
Big Jack Lake—*lake* CA-9
Big Jack Lake—*lake* MN-6
Big Jack Ranch—*locale* NV-8
Big Jack Ridge—*ridge* VA-3
Big Jacks Creek—*stream* ID-8
Big Jackson Hollow—*valley* PA-2
Big Jackson Sch—*school* MI-6
Big Jackson Tank—*reservoir* AZ-5
Big Jacob Creek—*stream* TN-4
Big Jarrells Creek—*stream* WV-2
*Big Jarrolds Creek* WV-2
Big Jay—*summit* VT-1
Big Jensen Hollow—*valley* UT-8
Big Jensen Pass—*gap* UT-8
Big Jerry Rsvr—*reservoir* WY-8
*Big Jerusalem Baptist Church* MS-4
Big Jerusalem Ch—*church* MS-4
Big Jessie Hollow—*valley* TN-4
*Big Jessie Lake* MN-6
Big Jim Branch—*stream* LA-4
*Big Jim Creek* WA-9
Big Jim Creek—*gut* FL-3
Big Jim Creek—*stream* AK-9
Big Jim Creek—*stream* WA-9
Big Jim Draw—*valley* TX-5
Big Jim Hollow—*valley* AL-4
Big Jim Mountain Lakes—*lake* WA-9
Big Jim Mtn—*summit* WA-9
Big Jimmy Creek—*stream* (2) ID-8
Big Jimmy Gulch—*valley* CO-8
Big Jim Run—*stream* WV-2
Big Jims Branch—*stream* WV-2
Big Jim Tank—*reservoir* AZ-5
Big Joe Bald—*summit* MO-7
Big Joe Basin—*basin* CO-8
Big Joe Creek—*stream* AK-9
Big Joe Draw—*valley* CO-8
Big Joes Lake—*lake* WA-9
Big Joe Spring—*spring* KY-4
Big Joe Tank—*reservoir* NM-5
Big John Bay—*bay* AK-9
Big John Branch—*stream* (2) MS-4
Big John Brown Lake—*lake* MI-6
Big John Butte—*summit* MT-8
*Big John Church* MS-4
Big John Creek—*stream* AK-9
Big John Creek—*stream* GA-3
Big John Creek—*stream* KS-7
Big John Creek—*stream* MT-8
Big John Dick Mtn—*summit* GA-3
Big John Flat—*flat* CA-9
Big John Flat—*flat* UT-8
Big John Hackworth Hollow—*valley* KY-4
Big John Hill—*summit* AK-9
Big John Hill—*summit* CA-9
Big John Hollow—*valley* KY-4
Big John Lake—*lake* AK-9
Big John Mann Creek—*stream* TX-5
Big John Mtn—*summit* CO-8
Big Johnnie Gulch—*valley* AZ-5
Big Johnnie Shaft—*mine* AZ-5
*Big John Reservoir* UT-8
Big John Ridge—*ridge* CA-9
Big Johns Branch—*stream* KY-4
Big Johnson Creek—*stream* CO-8
Big Johnson Hollow—*valley* KY-4
Big Johnson Lake—*lake* AR-4
Big Johnson Rsvr—*reservoir* CO-8
Big John Spring—*spring* CA-9
Big Jonathan Branch—*stream* KY-4
Big Jones Creek—*stream* FL-3
Big Jones Gut—*stream* MD-2
Big Jordan Cave—*cave* TN-4
Big Jordan Lake—*lake* AR-4
Big Josephine Island—*island* LA-4
Big Joshua Creek—*stream* TX-5
Big Judson—*basin* WY-8
Big Jump Bar (historical)—*bar* AL-4
Big Junction—*locale* NC-3
Big Junction—*summit* TN-4
Big Juniper Bay—*swamp* NC-3
Big Juniper Creek—*stream* AL-4
Big Juniper Creek—*stream* CA-9
Big Juniper Creek—*stream* FL-3
Big Juniper Creek—*stream* NC-3
Big Juniper Creek—*stream* VA-3
Big Juniper Flat—*flat* OR-9
*Big Juniper Mountain* OR-9
Big Juniper Run—*stream* NC-3
Big Jureano Creek—*stream* ID-8
Big Kandiyohi Lake—*lake* MN-6
Big Kashvik Creek—*stream* AK-9
Big Kasock Mtn—*summit* NV-8
*Big Keaton Lake* AL-4
Big Kellen Hollow—*valley* KY-4
Big Keller Lake—*lake* IA-7
Big Kelley Tank—*reservoir* AZ-5
Big Kennedy Creek—*stream* NC-3
Big Kernel Tree Branch—*stream* NC-3
Big Kettle—*basin* PA-2
Big Kettle Mtn—*summit* PA-2
*Big Key* FL-3
Big Key—*island* (2) FL-3
Big Kid Hollow—*valley* TX-5
Big Kiffer Point—*cape* SC-3
*Big Kilbuck Creek* IN-6
Big Kilby Lake—*lake* MS-4
*Big Kill Buck Creek* IN-6
Big Kilsock Bay—*swamp* SC-3
Big Kimble Mine—*mine* AZ-5
Big Kimshew Creek—*stream* CA-9
*Big Kinkaid Creek* IL-6
Big Kinnakeet Coast Guard Station Abandoned—*locale* NC-3
Big Kiowa Creek—*stream* OK-5
Big Kitchens Ridge—*ridge* NC-3
Big Kitoi Lake—*lake* AK-9
Big Kitten Lake—*lake* WI-6
Big Kline Creek—*stream* CO-8
Big Knife Coulee—*valley* MT-8
Big Knife Creek—*stream* MT-8
Big Knife Lake—*lake* SC-3
Big Knife Lakes—*lake* MT-8
*Big Knife River* ND-7
*Big Knob* PA-2
*Big Knob* TN-4
Big Knob—*summit* KY-4
Big Knob—*summit* MD-2
Big Knob—*summit* (8) NC-3
Big Knob—*summit* (3) PA-2
Big Knob—*summit* SC-3
Big Knob—*summit* TN-4
Big Knob—*summit* (4) VA-3
Big Knob—*summit* (4) WV-2
Big Knob, The—*summit* WY-8
Big Knob Campground—*locale* MI-6
*Big Knob Creek* NC-3
Big Knob Grange—*locale* PA-2
Big Knob Lookout—*locale* NC-3
Big Knob Ridge—*ridge* VA-3
Big Knob Trail—*trail* PA-2
*Big Knofe Lake* MN-6
Big Knoll—*summit* IN-6
Big Knoll, The—*summit* AZ-5
Big Knot Run—*stream* WV-2
Big Koniuji Island—*island* AK-9
Big Lacassine Bayou—*gut* LA-4
Big Laddie Tank—*lake* NM-5
Big Lagoon—*bay* AK-9
Big Lagoon—*flat* KS-7
Big Lagoon—*lake* (3) CA-9
Big Lagoon—*lake* FL-3
Big Lagoon—*lake* KS-7
Big Lagoon—*lake* LA-4
**Big Lagoon**—*pop pl* CA-9
Big Lagoon County Park—*park* CA-9
**Big Lagoon Park**—*pop pl* CA-9
**Big Lagoon Rancheria (Indian Reservation)**—*pop pl* CA-9
Big Lagoon State Rec Area—*park* FL-3
*Big La Grue Bayou* AR-4
Big La Grue Cem—*cemetery* AR-4
Big La Grue Ch—*church* AR-4
Big Laguna Lake—*lake* CA-9
*Big Lake* AL-4
*Big Lake* AK-9
*Big Lake* CO-8
*Big Lake* ID-8
*Big Lake* LA-4
*Big Lake* MN-6
*Big Lake* OR-9
*Big Lake* TN-4
*Big Lake* WI-6
Big Lake—*basin* AR-4
Big Lake—*CDP* AK-9
Big Lake—*flat* AR-4
Big Lake—*flat* OR-9
Big Lake—*lake* (2) AL-4
Big Lake—*lake* (7) AK-9
Big Lake—*lake* (3) AZ-5
Big Lake—*lake* (5) AR-4
Big Lake—*lake* (6) CA-9
Big Lake—*lake* (2) CO-8
Big Lake—*lake* CT-1
Big Lake—*lake* (3) FL-3
Big Lake—*lake* (2) GA-3
Big Lake—*lake* (3) ID-8
Big Lake—*lake* (5) IL-6
Big Lake—*lake* IN-6
Big Lake—*lake* (2) IA-7
Big Lake—*lake* (8) LA-4
Big Lake—*lake* ME-1
Big Lake—*lake* (5) MI-6
Big Lake—*lake* (9) MN-6
Big Lake—*lake* (7) MS-4
Big Lake—*lake* (2) MO-7
Big Lake—*lake* (4) MT-8
Big Lake—*lake* (2) NE-7
Big Lake—*lake* NV-8
Big Lake—*lake* (4) NM-5
Big Lake—*lake* OH-6
Big Lake—*lake* OK-5
Big Lake—*lake* (3) OR-9
Big Lake—*lake* (6) SC-3
Big Lake—*lake* SD-7
Big Lake—*lake* TN-4
Big Lake—*lake* (5) TX-5
Big Lake—*lake* (6) UT-8
Big Lake—*lake* (3) WA-9
Big Lake—*lake* (9) WI-6
Big Lake—*locale* AK-9
Big Lake—*locale* AR-4
Big Lake—*locale* WA-9
**Big Lake**—*pop pl* IN-6
**Big Lake**—*pop pl* MN-6
**Big Lake**—*pop pl* MO-7
**Big Lake**—*pop pl* TX-5
Big Lake—*reservoir* AZ-5
Big Lake—*reservoir* CO-8
Big Lake—*reservoir* ID-8
Big Lake—*reservoir* MO-7
Big Lake—*reservoir* TN-4
Big Lake—*reservoir* (4) TX-5
Big Lake—*reservoir* UT-8
Big Lake—*reservoir* VA-3
Big Lake—*reservoir* WI-6
Big Lake—*swamp* MS-4
Big Lake—*swamp* MO-7
Big Lake—*swamp* SC-3
Big Lake, The—*flat* AZ-5
Big Lake Bayou—*stream* MO-7
Big Lake Campground—*locale* ME-1
Big Lake (CCD)—*cens area* TX-5
Big Lake Cem—*cemetery* ND-7
Big Lake Ch—*church* IN-6
Big Lake Ch—*church* MO-7
**Big Lake Chapel**—*pop pl* MN-6
Big Lake Creek—*stream* ID-8
Big Lake Creek—*stream* MO-7
Big Lake Creek—*stream* MT-8
Big Lake Dam—*dam* AZ-5
Big Lake Dam—*dam* TN-4
Big Lake Ditch—*canal* MO-7
Big Lake Draw—*valley* ID-8
Big Lake Draw—*valley* TX-5
Big Lake Forest Camp—*park* AZ-5
Big Lake (historical)—*lake* MS-4
**Big Lake (historical)**—*pop pl* MS-4
Big Lake Knoll—*summit* AZ-5
Big Lake Mine—*mine* WA-9
Big Lake Moreau—*lake* LA-4
Big Lake Natl Wildlife Ref—*park* AR-4
Big Lake Oil Field—*oilfield* LA-4
Big Lake Oil Field—*oilfield* TX-5
Big Lake Park—*park* IA-7
Big Lake Reservoir Dam—*dam* UT-8
Big Lake Rsvr—*reservoir* OR-9
Big Lake Run—*stream* MS-4
*Big Lakes* AZ-5
Big Lake Sch—*school* MI-6
Big Lake Tank—*reservoir* NM-5
Big Lake Tank—*reservoir* TX-5
Big Lake (Township of)—*fmr MCD* AR-4
**Big Lake (Township of)**—*pop pl* MN-6
Big Lake Twenty—*lake* MI-6
Big Lake Vienna—*lake* FL-3
Big Lake Windmill—*locale* (2) TX-5
Big Lamunyon Flats—*flat* NE-7
Bigland Gulch—*valley* CA-9
*Big Lane Brook* ME-1
Big Lane Cem—*cemetery* MS-4
Big Laramie Stage Station—*locale* WY-8
Big Larch Campground—*locale* MT-8
*Big Larto Bayou* LA-4
Big LaSalle Lake—*lake* MN-6
Big Last Chance Canyon—*valley* CA-9
Big Laurel—*locale* NC-3
**Big Laurel**—*pop pl* (2) KY-4
**Big Laurel**—*pop pl* NC-3
**Big Laurel**—*pop pl* VA-3
Big Laurel—*summit* NC-3
Big Laurel Branch—*stream* (3) KY-4
Big Laurel Branch—*stream* (2) NC-3
Big Laurel Branch—*stream* TN-4
Big Laurel Branch—*stream* VA-3
Big Laurel Cem—*cemetery* NC-3
Big Laurel Ch—*church* (3) NC-3
Big Laurel Ch—*church* WV-2
Big Laurel Creek—*stream* KY-4
Big Laurel Creek—*stream* (4) NC-3
Big Laurel Creek—*stream* (2) TN-4
Big Laurel Creek—*stream* (4) VA-3
Big Laurel Creek—*stream* (4) WV-2
Big Laurel Gap—*gap* NC-3
Big Laurel Mtn—*summit* NC-3
Big Laurel Run—*stream* MD-2
Big Laurel Run—*stream* (2) WV-2
Big Laurel Sch—*school* (2) KY-4
Big Laurel Sch—*school* WV-2
Big Laurel Thicket—*woods* WV-2
Big Lava Bed—*lava* WA-9
Big Lawler Mtn—*summit* NY-2
Big Lead Creek—*stream* MO-7
Big Lead Mine—*mine* (2) ID-8
Big Leatherwood Ch—*church* KY-4
Big Leatherwood Creek—*stream* GA-3
Big Ledge—*bar* ME-1
Big Ledge—*bench* ME-1
Big Ledge Brook—*stream* ME-1
**Bigler**—*pop pl* PA-2
Bigler Cem—*cemetery* MI-6
Bigler Mill Pond—*reservoir* VA-3
Bigler Mine—*mine* MT-8
Bigler Mtn—*summit* WA-9
*Big Leroux Spring* AZ-5
Big Leroux Spring—*spring* AZ-5
Bigler Ponds—*lake* AZ-5
Biglers Grove—*locale* IA-7
Biglers Rsvr—*reservoir* AZ-5
Bigler Tank—*reservoir* (3) AZ-5
**Bigler (Township of)**—*pop pl* PA-2
Bigler Trick Tank—*reservoir* AZ-5
**Biglerville**—*pop pl* PA-2
Biglerville Borough—*civil* PA-2
Bigler Wash—*stream* AZ-5
Big Leslie Branch—*stream* KY-4
*Big Level* VA-3
Big Level—*flat* KY-4
**Big Level**—*pop pl* MS-4
Big Level—*summit* PA-2
Big Level—*summit* TN-4
Big Level Ch—*church* MS-4
Big Level Ch—*church* NC-3
Big Level Island—*island* AK-9
Big Levels—*flat* (2) VA-3
*Big Leverentz* MI-6
Big Lewis Lake—*lake* IA-7
Bigley Cem—*cemetery* IL-6
Bigley Ridge—*ridge* OH-6
Big Lick—*locale* TN-4
**Big Lick**—*pop pl* NC-3
Big Lick—*stream* KY-4
Big Lick—*stream* OR-9
Big Lick—*stream* VA-3
Big Lick Branch—*stream* (2) KY-4
Biglick Branch—*stream* KY-4
Big Lick Branch—*stream* (4) KY-4
Biglick Branch—*stream* KY-4
Big Lick Branch—*stream* PA-2
Big Lick Branch—*stream* VA-3
Big Lick Branch—*stream* WV-2
Big Lick Cem—*cemetery* MO-7
Biglick Cem—*cemetery* OH-6
Big Lick Cem—*cemetery* TN-4
*Big Lick Creek* TN-4
Big Lick Creek—*stream* CO-8
Big Lick Creek—*stream* IN-6
Big Lick Creek—*stream* (2) VA-3
Big Lick Draft—*valley* VA-3
Big Lick Fork—*stream* KY-4
Big Lick Fork—*stream* WV-2
Big Lick Gap—*gap* KY-4
Big Lick Gap—*gap* TN-4
Big Lick Gap—*gap* VA-3
Big Lick Hill—*summit* AR-4
Big Lick (historical)—*locale* AL-4
*Big Lick Hollow* VA-3
Big Lick Hollow—*valley* (2) KY-4
Big Lick Hollow—*valley* VA-3
Big Lickinghole Creek—*stream* VA-3
Big Lick Lake—*lake* MI-6
Big Lick Mtn—*summit* PA-2
*Biglick Post Office* TN-4
Big Lick Post Office (historical)—*building* TN-4
*Biglick Run* WV-2
Biglick Run—*stream* OH-6
Big Lick Run—*stream* VA-3
Big Lick Run—*stream* (2) WV-2
Biglick Run—*stream* WV-2
Big Lick Run—*stream* WV-2
Big Lick Sch—*school* AR-4
Big Lick Sch—*school* TN-4
Big Lick Spring—*spring* CA-9
Big Lick (Township of)—*fmr MCD* NC-3
**Biglick (Township of)**—*pop pl* OH-6
Big Lige Branch—*stream* FL-3
*Big Lightning Creek* WY-8
Big Lightning Creek—*stream* MT-8
Big Lilly Lake—*lake* FL-3
Big Lily Creek—*stream* KY-4
Big Lily Lake—*lake* AK-9
*Big Limber Creek* OR-9
Big Limber Gulch—*valley* MT-8
Big Lime Mtn—*summit* NV-8
Big Limestone Creek—*stream* TN-4
Big Limestone Tank—*reservoir* AZ-5
Big Limestone Trail—*trail* KY-4
Big Lime Wash—*stream* NV-8
Biglin Bayou—*stream* MS-4
Biglins Creek—*stream* NC-3
Biglin Shaft—*mine* PA-2
Big Lizard—*glacier* WA-9
Big Lizard Creek—*stream* AL-4
*Big Loaf Mountain* MT-8
Big Loaf Mtn—*summit* MT-8
*Big Loblockee Creek* AL-4
Big Lock Pond—*lake* NY-2
Big Lodge Creek—*stream* MT-8
Big Lodge Mtn—*summit* MT-8
Big Logan—*bay* ME-1
Big Logan (Oxbow)—*bend* MN-6
Big Log Branch—*stream* VA-3
Big Log Camp—*locale* WA-9
Big Log Creek—*stream* OR-9
Big Log Gulch—*valley* MT-8
Big Log Shoals (historical)—*bar* AL-4
Big Lolly Bridge—*bridge* FL-3
*Big Lone Tree Creek* WY-8
Big Long Branch—*stream* KY-4
Big Long Creek—*stream* GA-3
*Big Long Lake* MI-6
Big Long Lake—*lake* AK-9
Big Long Lake—*lake* IN-6
Big Long Lake—*lake* MI-6
Big Lookout Lake—*lake* ID-8
Big Lookout Mtn—*summit* OR-9
*Big Loon Lake* MI-6
*Big Loop Creek* WV-2
Big Loop Hollow—*valley* NY-2
Big Lost Cove Cliffs—*cliff* NC-3
Big Lost Cove Creek—*stream* NC-3
Big Lost Cove Ridge—*ridge* NC-3
Big Lost Creek—*stream* MT-8
Big Lost Creek—*stream* (2) TN-4
*Big Lost Lake* MN-6
Big Lost Lake—*lake* ID-8
Big Lostmans Bay—*bay* FL-3
*Big Lost River* ID-8
Big Lost River—*stream* ID-8
Big Lost River Sinks—*basin* ID-8
Big Lost River Valley—*valley* ID-8
Big Louie Spring—*spring* NV-8
Big Lovely Branch—*stream* KY-4
Biglow Canyon—*valley* NM-5
Biglow Canyon—*valley* OR-9
Biglow Ch—*church* OH-6
Biglow Creek—*stream* MT-8
Big Low Gap—*gap* VA-3
*Biglow Hill* ME-1
**Biglow (historical)**—*pop pl* OR-9
Biglow Lake—*lake* PA-2
Biglows Canyon—*valley* UT-8
Biglow Street Mission—*church* TX-5
Biglow Swamp—*swamp* ME-1
*Big Loyal Sock Creek* PA-2
Big Lue Canyon—*valley* AZ-5
*Big Lue Mountain* AZ-5
Big Lue Mountains—*summit* AZ-5
Big Lue Ranch—*locale* AZ-5
Big Lue Spring—*spring* AZ-5
*Big Lumber Gulch* MT-8
Big Lute Branch—*stream* KY-4
Big Lyford Pond—*reservoir* ME-1
Big Lynn Sch—*school* WV-2
*Big M* MO-7
*Big Machias Lake* ME-1
Big Machias Lake—*lake* ME-1
Big Macks Creek—*stream* VA-3
Big Mac Lake—*lake* TX-5
Big Mac Tank—*reservoir* AZ-5
Big Maggie May—*stream* AZ-5
Big Magill Bayou—*gut* LA-4
Big Magnesia Creek—*stream* FL-3
Big Mahogany Mtn—*summit* UT-8
Big Mahogany Rsvr—*reservoir* NV-8
Big Major Mine—*mine* MT-8
*Big Malad River* ID-8
*Big Malad River* UT-8
Big Malad Spring—*spring* ID-8
Big Mallard—*lake* NV-8
Big Mallard Creek—*stream* ID-8
Big Mallard Creek Bar—*bar* ID-8
Big Mallard Rapids—*rapids* ID-8
Big Mandy Creek—*stream* KY-4
Big Mangrove Key—*island* (2) FL-3
*Big Manistee River* MI-6
Big Manitou Falls—*falls* WI-6
Big Manning Tank—*reservoir* TX-5
Big Mannington Hill—*summit* NJ-2
Big Man Panel—*other* UT-8
Big Maple Spring—*spring* UT-8
Big Mar—*lake* LA-4
*Big Marco Pass* FL-3
Big Marco Pass—*channel* FL-3
Big Marco River—*gut* FL-3
Big Margaret Lake—*lake* CA-9
Big Marine Lake—*lake* MN-6
*Big Marion Creek* MT-8
*Big Marrowbone Creek* TN-4
Big Marsh—*swamp* MD-2
Big Marsh—*swamp* (2) MI-6
Big Marsh—*swamp* MN-6
Big Marsh—*swamp* (4) NY-2
Big Marsh—*swamp* NC-3
Big Marsh—*swamp* OR-9
Big Marsh—*swamp* (3) TX-5
Big Marsh—*swamp* (2) VA-3
Big Marsh Creek—*stream* OR-9
Big Marsh Drain—*stream* MI-6
Big Marsh Gut—*stream* NC-3
Big Marsh Island—*island* GA-3
*Big Marsh Lake* MI-6
Big Marsh Lake—*lake* MI-6
Big Marsh Mtn—*summit* NY-2
*Big Marsh Point* VA-3
Big Marsh Point—*cape* DE-2
Big Marsh Point—*cape* (2) MD-2
Big Marsh Point—*cape* NC-3
Big Marsh Point—*cape* VA-3
Big Marsh Pond—*lake* ME-1
Big Marsh Pond—*lake* NY-2
Big Marsh Slough—*gut* VT-1
Big Marsh Swamp—*stream* NC-3
Big Marsh Wildlife Area—*park* IA-7
Big Marshy Lake—*lake* CA-9
*Big Marvine* CO-8
*Big Marvine Mountain* CO-8
Big Marvine Peak—*summit* CO-8
Big Marys Creek—*stream* VA-3
Big Marys Island—*island* MT-8
Big Massaug Cove—*bay* NY-2
*Big Maumelle Lake* AR-4
*Big Maumelle River* AR-4
Big Maverick Tank—*reservoir* TX-5
Big Maxson Meadow—*flat* CA-9
*Big May* LA-4
Big Mayberry Cove—*bay* ME-1
Big McAdoo Creek—*stream* TN-4
Big McCarthy Lake—*lake* MN-6
Big McCloskey Run—*stream* PA-2
Big McDonald Lake—*lake* MN-6
Big McGee Lake—*lake* CA-9
*Big McGill Pass* FL-3
Big Mc Intyre Burn—*area* CO-8
Big McNeil Slough—*reservoir* MT-8
Big Meadow—*area* UT-8
Big Meadow—*flat* (9) CA-9
Big Meadow—*flat* CO-8
Big Meadow—*flat* (2) NV-8
Big Meadow—*flat* OR-9
Big Meadow—*flat* (2) UT-8
Big Meadow—*swamp* AK-9
Big Meadow—*swamp* ND-7
*Big Meadow, The* VA-3
Big Meadow Bog—*swamp* ME-1
*Big Meadow Branch* TN-4
Big Meadow Camp—*locale* OR-9
Big Meadow Canyon—*valley* OR-9
Big Meadow Cem—*cemetery* NV-8
Big Meadow Ch—*church* KY-4
Big Meadow Ch—*church* NC-3
Big Meadow Creek—*stream* (4) CA-9
Big Meadow Creek—*stream* ID-8
Big Meadow Creek—*stream* MT-8
Big Meadow Creek—*stream* SD-7
Big Meadow Creek—*stream* WA-9
Big Meadow Ditch—*canal* CO-8
Big Meadow Ditch—*canal* WY-8
Big Meadow Drain—*canal* MI-6
Big Meadow Drain—*stream* MI-6
Big Meadow Field Firing Range—*military* TN-4
Big Meadow Forest Service Station—*locale* UT-8
Big Meadow Lake—*lake* WA-9
Big Meadow Pond—*lake* CT-1
Big Meadow Ranch—*locale* NV-8
*Big Meadow Run* PA-2
**Big Meadow Run**—*pop pl* PA-2
Big Meadow Run—*stream* PA-2
Big Meadow Run—*stream* VA-3
Big Meadow Run Station—*locale* PA-2
*Big Meadows* CA-9
*Big Meadows* CO-8
Big Meadows—*area* MT-8
Big Meadows—*flat* (4) CA-9
Big Meadows—*flat* (3) CO-8
Big Meadows—*flat* (5) ID-8
Big Meadows—*flat* NV-8
Big Meadows—*flat* (2) OR-9
Big Meadows—*flat* UT-8
Big Meadows—*flat* VA-3
Big Meadows—*flat* WA-9
Big Meadows—*flat* WY-8
Big Meadows—*locale* VA-3
**Big Meadows**—*pop pl* CA-9
Big Meadows—*swamp* NH-1
Big Meadows—*swamp* (3) OR-9
*Big Meadow School* TN-4
Big Meadows Creek—*stream* (3) CA-9
Big Meadows Guard Station—*locale* CA-9
Big Meadows Lookout Tower—*locale* MN-6
Big Meadows Rsvr—*reservoir* CA-9
Big Meadows Rsvr—*reservoir* CO-8
Big Meadows Site—*hist pl* VA-3
Big Meadows Tank Number One—*reservoir* AZ-5

Big Prairie Creek—*stream* ... AL-4
Big Prairie Creek—*stream* ... MT-8
Big Prairie Dog Creek—*stream* ... SD-7
Big Prairie-Everett Cem—*cemetery* ... MI-6
Big Prairie Ridge—*ridge* ... OK-5
Big Prairie Sch—*school* ... IL-6
Big Prairie Township—*civil* ... MO-7
**Big Prairie (Township of)**—*pop pl* ... MI-6
Big Prater Creek—*stream* ... VA-3
Big Prather Meadow—*flat* ... CA-9
*Big Proctor Creek* ... TN-4
*Big Professor* ... CO-8
Big Prospector Meadow—*flat* ... CA-9
Big Provo Cirque—*basin* ... UT-8
*Big Provo Hole* ... UT-8
Big Pryor Mtn—*summit* ... MT-8
*Big Pucketa Creek* ... PA-2
*Big Pucketta Creek* ... PA-2
Big Pug Tank—*reservoir* ... AZ-5
*Big Pumice Cone* ... OR-9
Big Pump—*hist pl* ... MO-7
Big Pup Creek—*stream* ... MI-6
Big Purcell Tank—*reservoir* ... AZ-5
**Big Q Estates**—*pop pl* ... TN-4
Big Quamino Rock—*rock* ... MA-1
Big Quilcene River—*stream* ... WA-9
Big Quinnesec Dam—*dam* ... MI-6
Big Quinnesec Dam—*dam* ... WI-6
Big Rabbit Bayou—*stream* ... AR-4
*Big Rabbit River* ... MI-6
*Big Rabbits Neck* ... MI-6
*Big Raccoon Creek* ... AL-4
Big Raccoon Creek—*stream* ... IN-6
Big Rack Club—*locale* ... AL-4
*Big Rack Heap Creek* ... OR-9
Big Rackheap Creek—*stream* ... OR-9
*Big Rafting Creek* ... SC-3
*Big Raft Swamp* ... NC-3
Big Ragland Tank—*reservoir* ... NM-5
Big Rain Barrel Lake—*lake* ... MN-6
Big Rainbow Lake—*lake* ... CO-8
Big Rainbow Lake—*lake* ... ID-8
*Big Rainy Lake* ... MN-6
Big Ramey Creek—*stream* ... ID-8
Big Ramhorn Branch—*stream* ... NC-3
Big Ram Island—*island* ... MA-1
Big Ram Lake—*lake* ... AK-9
Big Ramme Creek—*stream* ... MT-8
Big Ram Mine—*mine* ... CA-9
Big Range—*range* ... NY-2
*Big Ranier Lake* ... MN-6
**Big Rapids**—*pop pl* ... MI-6
Big Rapids—*rapids* ... ME-1
Big Rapids Park—*park* ... WI-6
**Big Rapids (Township of)**—*pop pl* ... MI-6
Big Rat Lake—*lake* ... AK-9
Big Rat Lake—*lake* ... MN-6
Big Rattlesnake Creek—*stream* ... CA-9
Big Rattlesnake Creek—*stream* ... NC-3
Big Rattlesnake Creek—*stream* ... OR-9
Big Rattlesnake Gulch—*valley* ... MT-8
Big Ravine—*valley* (3) ... CA-9
Big Ravine Creek—*stream* ... MI-6
*Big Raving Creek* ... MI-6
Big Rawhide Butte—*summit* ... WY-8
Big Rayborn Canyon—*valley* ... OR-9
**Big Ready**—*pop pl* ... KY-4
Big Rebel Mine—*mine* ... AZ-5
Big Red Butte—*summit* ... CO-8
Big Red Creek—*stream* ... MS-4
Big Red Creek—*stream* ... WY-8
Big Red Draw—*valley* ... WY-8
Big Redfish Lake—*lake* ... FL-3
Big Redfish Point—*cape* ... FL-3
Big Red Hill—*summit* ... CO-8
Big Red Hill Tank—*reservoir* ... AZ-5
Big Red Mountain Creek—*stream* ... OR-9
Big Red Mtn—*summit* ... OR-9
Big Red Park—*flat* ... CO-8
Big Red Ranch Complex—*hist pl* ... WY-8
*Big Red River* ... KS-7
Big Red Rsvr—*reservoir* ... CO-8
Big Red S Canal—*canal* ... OR-9
Big Red S Field—*flat* ... OR-9
Big Red Tank—*reservoir* ... NM-5
Big Red Tank—*reservoir* (2) ... TX-5
Big Red Windmill—*locale* ... NM-5
Big Redwood Creek—*stream* ... OR-9
Big Reedbrake Creek—*stream* ... AL-4
Big Reed Break—*stream* ... LA-4
Big Reed Creek—*stream* ... MS-4
Big Reed Island Creek—*stream* ... VA-3
Big Reed Pond—*lake* ... ME-1
Big Reed Pond—*lake* ... NY-2
Big Reedy—*locale* ... KY-4
Big Reedy Branch—*stream* ... KY-4
*Big Reedy Creek* ... AL-4
*Big Reedy Creek* ... SC-3
Big Reedy Creek—*stream* ... FL-3
Big Reedy Creek—*stream* ... KY-4
Big Reedy Creek—*stream* ... MS-4
Big Reedy Island—*island* ... DE-2
Big Reef Mill—*locale* ... AZ-5
Big Reilley Canyon—*valley* ... NV-8
Big Remington Creek—*stream* ... WY-8
Big Renox Creek—*stream* ... KY-4
*Bigrest* ... IN-6
*Big Rib Falls* ... WI-6
Big Rib River—*stream* ... WI-6
*Big Rice Lake* ... MN-6
*Big Rice Lake* ... WI-6
Big Rice Lake—*lake* (5) ... MN-6
Big Richland Creek—*stream* ... TN-4
*Big Ridge* ... AZ-5
*Big Ridge* ... PA-2
*Big Ridge* ... TN-4
Big Ridge—*locale* ... NC-3
**Big Ridge**—*pop pl* ... AL-4
**Big Ridge**—*pop pl* ... LA-4
**Big Ridge**—*pop pl* ... MO-7
Big Ridge—*ridge* (3) ... AL-4
Big Ridge—*ridge* (2) ... AZ-5
Big Ridge—*ridge* ... AR-4
Big Ridge—*ridge* (4) ... CA-9
Big Ridge—*ridge* ... CO-8
Big Ridge—*ridge* (3) ... GA-3
Big Ridge—*ridge* ... ID-8
Big Ridge—*ridge* ... IL-6
Big Ridge—*ridge* ... MD-2
Big Ridge—*ridge* ... MO-7
Big Ridge—*ridge* ... MT-8
Big Ridge—*ridge* ... NM-5
Big Ridge—*ridge* (18) ... NC-3
Big Ridge—*ridge* (2) ... OR-9
Big Ridge—*ridge* (6) ... PA-2
Big Ridge—*ridge* ... SC-3
Big Ridge—*ridge* (17) ... TN-4
Big Ridge—*ridge* (6) ... UT-8
Big Ridge—*ridge* (16) ... VA-3
Big Ridge—*ridge* (8) ... WV-2
Big Ridge—*ridge* (2) ... WY-8
*Big Ridge, The* ... TN-4
Big Ridge, The—*ridge* ... AZ-5
Big Ridge, The—*ridge* (2) ... UT-8
Big Ridge, The—*ridge* ... VT-1
*Big Ridge Baptist Church* ... MS-4
Big Ridge Branch—*stream* ... TN-4
Big Ridge Cave—*cave* ... PA-2
Big Ridge Ch—*church* ... IL-6
Big Ridge Ch—*church* ... MD-2
Big Ridge Ch—*church* ... MS-4
Big Ridge Ch—*church* ... MO-7
Big Ridge Ch—*church* ... NC-3
Big Ridge Chapel—*church* ... VA-3
Big Ridge Church (historical)—*locale* ... MO-7
*Big Ridge Dam* ... TN-4
Big Ridge Elem Sch—*school* ... TN-4
Big Ridge Lake—*lake* ... TN-4
Big Ridge Lake—*reservoir* ... TN-4
Big Ridge Lookout Tower—*locale* ... WV-2
*Big Ridge Marina* ... TN-4
Big Ridge Mine—*mine* ... NC-3
Big Ridge Mine (surface)—*mine* ... AL-4
Big Ridge Mine (underground)—*mine* ... AL-4
*Big Ridge Park* ... TN-4
**Big Ridge Park**—*pop pl* ... TN-4
*Big Ridge Park Lake* ... TN-4
Big Ridge Recreation Dam—*dam* ... TN-4
Big Ridge Rsvr—*reservoir* ... OR-9
Big Ridge Rsvr—*reservoir* ... WY-8
Big Ridges—*stream* ... MD-2
Big Ridge Sch—*school* ... MO-7
Big Ridge Sch—*school* ... TN-4
Big Ridge Sch (historical)—*school* ... AL-4
Big Ridge Slough—*gut* ... LA-4
Big Ridge State Park—*park* ... TN-4
Big Ridge Tank—*reservoir* (2) ... AZ-5
Big Ridge Trail—*trail* (2) ... PA-2
Big Rift Creek—*stream* ... PA-2
*Big Right Fork* ... WV-2
Big Righthand Fork—*stream* ... WV-2
Big Rimber Creek—*stream* ... KS-7
Big Rincon—*valley* ... NM-5
Big Rincon Tank—*reservoir* ... AZ-5
Big Riner Basin—*basin* ... OR-9
Big Ripley Island—*island* ... WI-6
*Big River* ... LA-4
**Big River**—*pop pl* ... VA-3
Big River—*post sta* ... CA-9
Big River—*stream* (5) ... AK-9
Big River—*stream* ... CA-9
Big River—*stream* ... MI-6
Big River—*stream* ... MO-7
Big River—*stream* ... NH-1
Big River—*stream* ... OR-9
Big River—*stream* ... RI-1
Big River—*stream* ... WA-9
Big River—*stream* ... WI-6
Big River Campground—*park* ... OR-9
Big River Cem—*cemetery* ... MO-7
Big River Ch—*church* ... MO-7
Big River Creek—*stream* ... MO-7
*Big River Lagoon* ... CA-9
Big River Laguna—*swamp* ... CA-9
Big River Lakes—*lake* ... AK-9
Big River Landing—*locale* ... FL-3
Big River Lobe Double Glacier—*glacier* ... AK-9
Big River Meadows—*flat* ... MT-8
Big River Mills Sch—*school* ... MO-7
Big River Roadhouse (Site)—*locale* ... AK-9
Big River Township—*civil* (2) ... MO-7
Big River Trail—*trail* ... MT-8
Big Road Sch (abandoned)—*school* ... PA-2
Big Roan Ridge—*ridge* ... NC-3
Big Roaring Bayou—*stream* ... LA-4
*Big Roaring River Lake* ... ID-8
Big Roaring River Lake—*lake* ... ID-8
Big Robar Pond—*lake* ... ME-1
Big Robe Bayou—*gut* ... AR-4
Big Robinson Ditch—*canal* ... UT-8
Big Roche a Cri Creek—*stream* ... WI-6
Big Roche a Cri Lake—*reservoir* ... WI-6
*Big Rock* ... ID-8
*Big Rock* ... PA-2
*Big Rock* ... UT-8
Big Rock—*bar* ... AK-9
Big Rock—*cliff* ... AL-4
Big Rock—*island* ... AK-9
Big Rock—*locale* ... AR-4
Big Rock—*locale* ... KY-4
Big Rock—*locale* ... MI-6
Big Rock—*locale* ... TX-5
Big Rock—*pillar* ... AL-4
Big Rock—*pillar* (5) ... CA-9
Big Rock—*pillar* ... MT-8
Big Rock—*pillar* (2) ... OR-9
Big Rock—*pillar* (3) ... TN-4
Big Rock—*pillar* (2) ... WI-6
**Big Rock**—*pop pl* ... AR-4
**Big Rock**—*pop pl* ... IL-6
**Big Rock**—*pop pl* (3) ... IA-7
**Big Rock**—*pop pl* ... OH-6
**Big Rock**—*pop pl* ... TN-4
**Big Rock**—*pop pl* ... VA-3
Big Rock—*rock* ... AL-4
Big Rock—*rock* ... MA-1
Big Rock—*summit* ... AL-4
Big Rock—*summit* (3) ... CA-9
Big Rock—*summit* ... KY-4
Big Rock—*summit* ... MO-7
Big Rock—*summit* ... MT-8
Big Rock—*summit* ... NV-8
Big Rock—*summit* ... NM-5
Big Rock—*summit* ... OH-6
Big Rock—*summit* ... OR-9
Big Rock—*summit* ... UT-8
Big Rock—*summit* (2) ... WA-9
Big Rock—*summit* ... WV-2
Big Rock Bay—*bay* ... MO-7
Big Rock Beach—*beach* ... CA-9
Big Rock Branch—*stream* ... VA-3
Big Rock Branch—*stream* ... WI-6
Big Rock Camp—*locale* ... CA-9
Big Rock Campground—*locale* ... CA-9
Big Rock Campground—*locale* ... CO-8
Big Rock Campground—*locale* ... NH-1
Big Rock Campground—*locale* ... WV-2
Big Rock Candy Mtn—*summit* ... UT-8
Big Rock Canyon—*valley* ... ID-8
Big Rock Canyon—*valley* ... NM-5
Big Rock Cave Trail—*trail* ... NH-1
Big Rock Cem—*cemetery* ... IA-7
Big Rock Cem—*cemetery* ... MS-4
Big Rock Ch—*church* ... AL-4
Big Rock Ch—*church* ... LA-4
Big Rock Ch—*church* ... MS-4
Big Rock Ch—*church* ... MO-7
Big Rock Ch—*church* (2) ... TX-5
Big Rock Corner—*locale* ... NH-1
Big Rock Coulee—*valley* ... MT-8
*Big Rock Creek* ... AL-4
*Big Rock Creek* ... IN-6
*Big Rock Creek* ... MO-7
*Big Rock Creek* ... OR-9
*Big Rock Creek* ... SC-3
Big Rock Creek—*stream* (3) ... CA-9
Big Rock Creek—*stream* ... FL-3
Big Rock Creek—*stream* ... IL-6
Big Rock Creek—*stream* ... MN-6
Big Rock Creek—*stream* ... MO-7
Big Rock Creek—*stream* ... MT-8
Big Rock Creek—*stream* ... NC-3
Big Rock Creek—*stream* (2) ... OR-9
Big Rock Creek—*stream* ... TN-4
Big Rock Creek—*stream* ... WA-9
Big Rock Creek—*stream* ... WI-6
Big Rock Creek Ch—*church* ... NC-3
Big Rock Dam—*dam* ... CA-9
Big Rock Dam—*dam* ... OR-9
Big Rock Detention—*reservoir* ... AZ-5
Big Rock Draw—*valley* ... CO-8
Big Rock Falls—*falls* ... VA-3
Big Rockfish Ch—*church* ... NC-3
Big Rockfish Presbyterian Church—*hist pl* ... NC-3
Big Rock Flat—*flat* ... OR-9
Big Rock Ford—*locale* ... TN-4
Big Rock Fork—*stream* ... CA-9
Big Rock Grange—*locale* ... CO-8
Big Rock Gulch—*valley* ... CA-9
*Big Rockheap Creek* ... OR-9
Big Rock Hill—*ridge* ... NM-5
Big Rock Hill—*summit* ... AR-4
Big Rock Hill—*summit* ... VT-1
Big Rock Hollow—*valley* ... MS-4
Big Rock Hollow—*valley* ... WV-2
*Big Rock House Branch* ... TN-4
*Big Rockhouse Creek* ... TN-4
Big Rock Island—*island* ... AL-4
Big Rock Island—*island* ... WA-9
Big Rock Island—*summit* ... TN-4
Big Rock Lake—*lake* (2) ... MN-6
Big Rock Lake—*lake* ... NY-2
Big Rock Lake—*lake* ... OR-9
Big Rock Lake—*reservoir* ... SC-3
Big Rock Lake—*reservoir* ... TX-5
Big Rock Mtn—*summit* ... AK-9
Big Rock Mtn—*summit* ... AR-4
Big Rock Mtn—*summit* ... ID-8
Big Rock Mtn—*summit* ... SC-3
Big Rock Mtn—*summit* ... TN-4
Big Rock Point—*cape* ... MI-6
Big Rock Point—*cape* ... NY-2
Big Rock Point—*cape* ... RI-1
Big Rock Point—*cliff* ... AZ-5
*Bigrock Post Office* ... TN-4
Big Rock Post Office—*building* ... TN-4
Big Rock Prospect—*mine* ... TN-4
Big Rock Ranch—*locale* (2) ... CA-9
Big Rock Ridge—*ridge* ... CA-9
**Big Rock (RR name Stric)**—*pop pl* ... VA-3
Big Rock Rsvr—*reservoir* ... MT-8
Big Rock Rsvr—*reservoir* ... OR-9
Big Rock Rsvr—*reservoir* ... WY-8
Big Rocks—*locale* ... OK-5
Big Rocks—*pillar* ... CA-9
Big Rocks—*rock* ... UT-8
Big Rocks—*summit* ... ME-1
Big Rocks—*summit* ... PA-2
Big Rocks—*summit* ... WY-8
Big Rocks Canyon—*valley* ... NM-5
Big Rock Sch—*school* (2) ... KY-4
Big Rock Sch—*school* ... TN-4
Big Rock Sch—*school* ... TX-5
Big Rock Sch (abandoned)—*school* ... PA-2
Big Rock Sink—*basin* ... FL-3
Big Rock Sink—*basin* ... GA-3
Big Rock Siphon—*canal* ... CA-9
Big Rock Spring—*spring* ... AZ-5
Big Rock Spring—*spring* ... NV-8
Big Rock Spring—*spring* ... NC-3
Big Rock Spring—*spring* ... OR-9
Big Rock Spring—*spring* ... PA-2
*Big Rock Springs* ... ID-8
Big Rock Springs—*locale* ... CA-9
Big Rock State Wildlife Mngmt Area—*park* ... MN-6
Big Rock Tank—*reservoir* ... AZ-5
Big Rock Tank—*reservoir* ... TX-5
Big Rock Top—*summit* ... TX-5
Big Rock (Township of)—*fmr MCD* ... AR-4
**Big Rock (Township of)**—*pop pl* ... IL-6
*Big Rock United Methodist Church* ... MS-4
Big Rock Vista—*locale* ... PA-2
Big Rock Vly—*swamp* ... NY-2
Big Rock Wash—*stream* ... CA-9
Big Rock Wayside Park—*park* ... WI-6
Big Rocky Branch—*stream* ... KY-4
Big Rocky Branch—*stream* ... NC-3
Big Rocky Canyon—*valley* ... ID-8
Big Rocky Canyon—*valley* ... NM-5
*Big Rocky Coulee* ... MT-8
*Big Rocky Creek* ... SC-3
Big Rocky Creek—*stream* ... ID-8
Big Rocky Creek—*stream* ... TX-5
Big Rocky Fork Bridge—*hist pl* ... IN-6
Big Rocky Mount Ch—*church* ... MS-4
Big Rocky Pond—*lake* ... MA-1
Big Rocky Row—*summit* ... VA-3
Big Rocky Run—*stream* ... VA-3
Big Rocky Tank—*reservoir* ... NM-5
Big Roger Creek—*stream* ... WA-9
Big Ronaldson Slough—*stream* ... TN-4
Big Room Cave—*cave* ... TN-4
Big Rooster Branch—*stream* ... KY-4
Big Root Run—*stream* ... WV-2
Big Rosa Canyon—*valley* ... NM-5
Big Rose Island—*island* ... AK-9
Big Rose Lake—*lake* ... MN-6
Big Rosendal Lake—*lake* ... MN-6
Big Rosy Bone Knob—*summit* ... NY-2
Big Rough Branch—*stream* ... KY-4
Big Rough Canyon—*valley* ... CA-9
Big Rough Canyon—*valley* ... UT-8
Big Rough Knob—*summit* ... NC-3
Big Round Hill—*summit* ... KY-4
*Big Round Lake* ... MN-6
*Big Round Lake* ... WI-6
Big Round Lake—*lake* ... AR-4
Big Round Lake—*lake* ... WI-6
Big Round Mtn—*summit* (2) ... KY-4
Big Round Mtn—*summit* ... OK-5
Big Round Pond—*lake* ... DE-2
Big Round Tank—*reservoir* ... AZ-5
*Big Round Top* ... PA-2
*Big Round Top* ... WA-9
Big Round Top—*summit* ... PA-2
Big Round Top Mtn—*summit* ... AR-4
Big Round Top Pond—*reservoir* ... RI-1
Big Roundtop Trail—*trail* ... PA-2
Big Round Valley—*basin* ... NV-8
Big Round Valley—*basin* ... UT-8
Big Roxanna Ch—*church* ... AL-4
Big Rsvr—*reservoir* ... AZ-5
Big Rsvr—*reservoir* (2) ... CA-9
Big Rsvr—*reservoir* (2) ... CO-8
Big Rsvr—*reservoir* ... MT-8
Big Rsvr—*reservoir* (2) ... OR-9
Big Ruddy Branch—*stream* ... SC-3
Big Ruin—*locale* ... UT-8
*Big Run* ... OH-6
*Big Run* ... PA-2
*Big Run* ... VA-3
*Big Run* ... WV-2
Big Run—*locale* ... OH-6
Big Run—*locale* (2) ... PA-2
Big Run—*locale* (4) ... WV-2
**Big Run**—*pop pl* (2) ... PA-2
**Big Run**—*pop pl* ... WV-2
Big Run—*stream* (5) ... IN-6
Big Run—*stream* (10) ... KY-4
Big Run—*stream* (2) ... MD-2
Big Run—*stream* (32) ... OH-6
Big Run—*stream* (31) ... PA-2
Big Run—*stream* ... SC-3
Big Run—*stream* (8) ... VA-3
Big Run—*stream* (67) ... WV-2
Big Run Borough—*civil* ... PA-2
Big Run Branch—*stream* ... KY-4
Big Run Branch Junction—*uninc pl* ... PA-2
Big Run Cem—*cemetery* (2) ... OH-6
Big Run Cem—*cemetery* (2) ... WV-2
Big Run Ch—*church* (2) ... IN-6
Big Run Ch—*church* ... OH-6
Big Run Ch—*church* (2) ... WV-2
Big Run Chapel—*church* ... WV-2
*Big Run Ditch* ... OH-6
Big Run Elem Sch—*school* ... PA-2
Big Run Gap—*gap* ... WV-2
Big Run Golf Club—*other* ... IL-6
**Big Run Junction**—*pop pl* ... PA-2
Big Run Knob—*summit* ... WV-2
Big Running Water Creek—*stream* ... AR-4
Big Run Overlook—*locale* ... VA-3
Big Run Park—*park* ... OH-6
Big Run Quarry Site—*hist pl* ... VA-3
Big Run Sch—*school* ... KY-4
Big Run Sch (abandoned)—*school* ... PA-2
Big Run Sch (historical)—*school* ... PA-2
*Big Run School* ... WV-2
Big Run Shelter—*locale* ... VA-3
Big Run Spur—*trail* ... PA-2
Big Run Trail—*trail* ... VA-3
Big Run Trail—*trail* (2) ... WV-2
Big Rush Lake—*lake* ... MN-6
Big Rusty Creek—*stream* ... AK-9
Big Rusty Gut—*stream* ... IN-6
Big R W Creek—*stream* ... WY-8
Big Sabine Point—*cape* ... FL-3
*Big Sable* ... MI-6
Big Sable Creek—*stream* ... FL-3
Big Sable Point—*cape* ... MI-6
Big Sable Point Light Station—*hist pl* ... MI-6
Big Sable River—*stream* ... MI-6
Big Saddle—*gap* (2) ... AZ-5
Big Saddle—*gap* (3) ... OR-9
Big Saddle Camp—*locale* ... AZ-5
Big Saddle Canyon—*valley* ... OR-9
Big Saddle Point—*cliff* ... AZ-5
Big Saddle Tank—*reservoir* ... AZ-5
Big Sag—*locale* ... MT-8
Big Sag—*valley* ... MT-8
Big Sag, The—*basin* (2) ... MT-8
Big Sag Basin—*valley* ... ME-1
Big Sag Brook—*stream* ... ME-1
Big Sag Creek—*stream* ... MT-8
Big Sage—*flat* ... UT-8
Big Sage Campground—*locale* ... CA-9
Big Sage Dam—*dam* ... CA-9
Big Sage Flats—*flat* ... OR-9
Big Sagehen Rsvr—*reservoir* ... ID-8
Big Sage Hen Spring—*spring* ... OR-9
Big Sage Rsvr—*reservoir* ... CA-9
Big Sage Rsvr—*reservoir* ... MT-8
Big Sage Rsvr—*reservoir* ... NV-8
Big Sage Rsvr—*reservoir* ... UT-8
Big Sage Valley—*valley* ... UT-8
Big Sag Lake—*lake* ... MT-8
Big Sailor Creek—*stream* ... CA-9
Big Saint Germain Lake—*lake* ... WI-6
Big Saint Martin Island—*island* ... MI-6
Big Saline Bayou—*stream* ... LA-4
Big Saline Ch—*church* ... IL-6
Big Saline Creek—*stream* ... TX-5
*Big Sallisaw Creek* ... OK-5
Big Sally Brook—*stream* ... NY-2
Big Sally Tank—*reservoir* ... TX-5
Big Salmon Creek—*stream* ... CA-9
Big Salmon Creek—*stream* ... MT-8
Big Salmon Creek—*stream* ... NY-2
Big Salmon Fork—*stream* ... AK-9
Big Salmon Lake—*lake* ... MT-8
*Big Salmon River* ... MT-8
Big Salmon River—*stream* ... AK-9
*Big Salt Creek* ... IL-6
Big Salt Creek—*stream* ... CA-9
Big Saltery Island—*island* ... AK-9
*Big Salt Fork* ... KS-7
Big Salt Lake—*lake* ... AK-9
Big Salt Marsh—*swamp* ... KS-7
Big Salt Marsh—*swamp* ... VA-3
Big Salt River—*stream* ... AK-9
Big Salt Wash—*valley* ... CO-8
Big Saluda Creek—*stream* ... IN-6
Big Sampson Swamp—*swamp* ... PA-2
Big Sampson Windmill—*locale* (2) ... TX-5
Big Sand—*flat* ... UT-8
Big Sand Bar—*bar* ... NV-8
Big Sand Bar—*rapids* ... AZ-5
Big Sand Bay—*bay* ... OH-6
Big Sand Beach—*beach* ... ME-1
Big Sand Butte—*summit* ... CA-9
Big Sand Cem—*cemetery* ... VA-3
Big Sand Coulee—*valley* ... MT-8
Big Sand Coulee—*valley* ... WY-8
*Big Sand Creek* ... AL-4
*Big Sand Creek* ... MN-6
*Big Sand Creek* ... OK-5
Big Sand Creek—*stream* ... CA-9
Big Sand Creek—*stream* (2) ... ID-8
Big Sand Creek—*stream* (2) ... MS-4
Big Sand Creek Cutoff—*channel* ... MS-4
Big Sand Creek Structure Y-32-25 Dam—*dam* ... MS-4
Big Sand Creek Structure Y-32-27 Dam—*dam* ... MS-4
Big Sand Creek Structure Y-32-31 Dam—*dam* ... MS-4
Big Sand Creek Structure Y-32-32 Dam—*dam* ... MS-4
Big Sand Creek Structure Y-32-33 Dam—*dam* ... MS-4
Big Sand Creek Structure Y-32-49 Dam—*dam* ... MS-4
Big Sand Creek Watershed Y-32-9b Dam—*dam* ... MS-4
Big Sand Draw—*valley* (2) ... WY-8
Big Sand Draw Oil And Gas Field—*oilfield* ... WY-8
Big Sand Flat—*flat* (2) ... CA-9
Big Sand Hill—*summit* ... AL-4
Big Sand Hills—*summit* ... SC-3
Big Sand Hole—*basin* ... CO-8
Big Sand Lake—*lake* ... FL-3
Big Sand Lake—*lake* ... ID-8
Big Sand Lake—*lake* (2) ... MN-6
Big Sand Lake—*lake* (2) ... WI-6
Big Sand Lake Campground—*locale* ... UT-8
Big Sand Mtn—*summit* ... CO-8
Big Sands—*bar* ... AK-9
Big Sand Spring—*spring* ... WY-8
Big Sand Springs Valley—*valley* ... NV-8
*Big Sand State Beach* ... UT-8
Big Sand State Park—*park* ... UT-8
Big Sandstone Creek—*stream* ... WY-8
Big Sand Tank—*reservoir* ... NM-5
Big Sand Wash—*stream* (2) ... AZ-5
Big Sand Wash—*valley* ... UT-8
Big Sand Wash Dam—*dam* ... UT-8
Big Sand Wash Rsvr—*reservoir* ... UT-8
Big Sand Watershed Y-32-1 Dam—*dam* ... MS-4
Big Sand Watershed Y-32-10 Dam—*dam* ... MS-4
Big Sand Watershed Y-32-11 Dam—*dam* ... MS-4
Big Sand Watershed Y-32-12 Dam—*dam* ... MS-4
Big Sand Watershed Y-32-14 Dam—*dam* ... MS-4
Big Sand Watershed Y-32-15 Dam—*dam* ... MS-4
Big Sand Watershed Y-32-16 Dam—*dam* ... MS-4
Big Sand Watershed Y-32-17 Dam—*dam* ... MS-4
Big Sand Watershed Y-32-18 Dam—*dam* ... MS-4
Big Sand Watershed Y-32-19 Dam—*dam* ... MS-4
Big Sand Watershed Y-32-2 Dam—*dam* ... MS-4
Big Sand Watershed Y-32-22 Dam—*dam* ... MS-4
Big Sand Watershed Y-32-29 Dam—*dam* ... MS-4
Big Sand Watershed Y-32-3 Dam—*dam* ... MS-4
Big Sand Watershed Y-32-4 Dam—*dam* ... MS-4
Big Sand Watershed Y-32-7 Dam—*dam* ... MS-4
Big Sand Watershed Y-32-8 Dam—*dam* ... MS-4
Big Sand Watershed Y-32-9a Dam—*dam* ... MS-4
*Big Sandy* ... MS-4
*Big Sandy* ... TN-4
Big Sandy—*locale* ... TN-4
**Big Sandy**—*pop pl* ... KY-4
**Big Sandy**—*pop pl* ... MT-8
**Big Sandy**—*pop pl* ... NE-7
**Big Sandy**—*pop pl* ... TN-4
**Big Sandy**—*pop pl* ... TX-5
**Big Sandy**—*pop pl* ... WV-2
**Big Sandy**—*pop pl* ... WY-8
Big Sandy, Bayou—*stream* ... LA-4
Big Sandy Bar—*bar* ... TN-4
Big Sandy Bayou—*stream* ... AR-4
Big Sandy Bluff—*cliff* ... CA-9
*Big Sandy Bluffs* ... CA-9
*Big Sandy Bottom Pond* ... MA-1
Big Sandy Branch—*stream* ... TN-4
Big Sandy Branch—*stream* (2) ... TX-5
Big Sandy Campground—*locale* ... CA-9
Big Sandy Campground—*locale* ... WY-8
Big Sandy (CCD)—*cens area* ... TN-4
Big Sandy (CCD)—*cens area* ... TX-5
Big Sandy Cem—*cemetery* ... AL-4
Big Sandy Cem—*cemetery* ... KS-7
Big Sandy Ch—*church* ... AL-4
Big Sandy Ch—*church* ... AR-4
Big Sandy Ch—*church* ... GA-3
*Big Sandy Creek* ... AL-4
*Big Sandy Creek* ... GA-3
*Big Sandy Creek* ... IN-6
*Big Sandy Creek* ... MS-4
*Big Sandy Creek* ... OK-5
*Big Sandy Creek* ... TX-5
*Big Sandy Creek* ... WI-6
*Big Sandy Creek* ... WY-8
Big Sandy Creek—*stream* (2) ... AL-4
Big Sandy Creek—*stream* ... AK-9
Big Sandy Creek—*stream* (2) ... CA-9
Big Sandy Creek—*stream* ... CO-8
Big Sandy Creek—*stream* (3) ... GA-3
Big Sandy Creek—*stream* (2) ... KS-7
Big Sandy Creek—*stream* ... MT-8
Big Sandy Creek—*stream* (2) ... NE-7
Big Sandy Creek—*stream* ... NC-3
Big Sandy Creek—*stream* (3) ... OK-5
Big Sandy Creek—*stream* ... PA-2
Big Sandy Creek—*stream* ... SC-3
Big Sandy Creek—*stream* (2) ... TN-4
Big Sandy Creek—*stream* (18) ... TX-5
Big Sandy Creek—*stream* (2) ... WV-2
Big Sandy Creek—*stream* ... WI-6
Big Sandy Creek Dam Number 10—*dam* ... TX-5
Big Sandy Creek Dam Number 11—*dam* ... TX-5
Big Sandy Creek Dam Number 12—*dam* ... TX-5
Big Sandy Creek Dam Number 13—*dam* ... TX-5
Big Sandy Cutoff—*bend* ... AL-4
Big Sandy Dam—*dam* ... OR-9
Big Sandy Dam—*dam* ... WY-8
Big Sandy Division—*civil* ... TN-4
Big Sandy Dock—*locale* ... TN-4
Big Sandy Dock Number Two—*locale* ... TN-4
Big Sandy Draw—*valley* ... CO-8
Big Sandy Draw—*valley* ... TX-5
Big Sandy-Duncanville (CCD)—*cens area* ... AL-4
Big Sandy-Duncanville Division—*civil* ... AL-4
Big Sandy Island—*island* ... LA-4
Big Sandy Island (historical)—*island* ... TN-4
**Big Sandy Junction**—*pop pl* ... KY-4
Big Sandy Lake—*lake* ... WY-8
Big Sandy Lake—*reservoir* ... MN-6
Big Sandy Lake—*reservoir* ... TX-5
Big Sandy Milling Company—*hist pl* ... KY-4
Big Sandy Mtn—*summit* ... AR-4
Big Sandy Mtn—*summit* ... WY-8
Big Sandy Municipal Park—*park* ... TN-4
Big Sandy Oil Field—*oilfield* ... KS-7
Big Sandy Opening—*swamp* ... WY-8
*Big Sandy Pond* ... MA-1
Big Sandy Pond—*lake* (2) ... MA-1
Big Sandy Post Office—*building* ... TN-4
Big Sandy Ridge—*ridge* ... NC-3
Big Sandy Ridge—*ridge* ... SC-3
*Big Sandy River* ... AZ-5
*Big Sandy River* ... OR-9
Big Sandy River—*stream* ... AZ-5
Big Sandy River—*stream* ... KY-4
Big Sandy River—*stream* ... TN-4
Big Sandy River—*stream* ... WV-2
Big Sandy River—*stream* ... WY-8
Big Sandy River Dewatering Area—*basin* ... TN-4
Big Sandy Rsvr—*reservoir* ... OR-9
Big Sandy Rsvr—*reservoir* ... WY-8
*Big Sandy Run* ... PA-2
*Big Sandy Run* ... SC-3
Big Sandy Run—*stream* ... NC-3
Big Sandy Run—*stream* (2) ... PA-2
Big Sandy Run—*stream* ... WV-2
Big Sandy Sch—*school* ... CO-8
Big Sandy Sch—*school* ... TN-4
Big Sandy Sch (historical)—*school* ... AL-4
Big Sandy Sch (historical)—*school* ... TN-4
Big Sandy Spring—*spring* ... AL-4
Big Sandy Spring—*spring* ... AZ-5
*Big Sandy Springs* ... AL-4
*Big Sandy Station* ... KY-4
Big Sandy Stream—*stream* ... ME-1
Big Sandy Trail—*trail* ... PA-2
Big Sandy Unit Tennessee Natl Wildlife Ref—*park* ... TN-4
Big Sandy Valley—*valley* ... CA-9
*Big Sandy Wash* ... AZ-5
Big Sandy Wash—*stream* ... CO-8
Big Sandy Wash—*stream* ... NM-5
Big Sang Kill—*stream* ... WV-2
*Big Santa Fe Lake* ... FL-3
*Big San Vicente Canon* ... TX-5
Big Sarasota Pass—*channel* ... FL-3
Big Satan Creek—*stream* ... TX-5
Big Satilla Creek—*stream* ... GA-3
Big Savage Mtn—*summit* ... MD-2
Big Savage Mtn—*summit* ... PA-2
*Big Savanna* ... NC-3
Big Savanna—*plain* (2) ... NC-3
*Big Savannah* ... NC-3
Big Savannah—*valley* ... GA-3
Big Savannah Bluff Lake—*lake* ... SC-3
Big Savannah Pond—*swamp* ... SC-3
Big Sawgrass—*swamp* ... FL-3
Big Sawgrass Swamp—*swamp* ... FL-3
Big Sawmill Basin—*basin* ... NV-8
Big Sawmill Canyon—*valley* ... NV-8
Big Sawmill Creek—*stream* ... ID-8
Big Sawmill Creek—*stream* ... NV-8
Big Sawmill Spring—*spring* ... NV-8
Bigsbie Lake—*lake* ... MI-6
Bigsby Branch—*stream* ... AR-4
Bigsby Cem—*cemetery* ... TX-5
*Bigsby Creek* ... AR-4
Bigsby Creek—*stream* ... TN-4
**Bigsby Creek Estates**—*pop pl* ... TN-4
Bigsby Hill—*summit* ... NY-2
Bigsby Lake—*lake* ... MN-6
Bigsby Pond—*lake* ... NY-2
Big Scaly—*summit* ... NC-3
*Big Scartan Creek* ... AL-4
*Big Scarum Creek* ... AL-4
Big Scary Sch—*school* ... WV-2
Big Schloss—*summit* ... VA-3
Big Schloss—*summit* ... WV-2
Big School Lot Lake—*lake* ... MI-6
Big Scirum Creek—*stream* ... AL-4
*Big Scoba Creek* ... MS-4
Big Scooba Creek—*stream* ... MS-4
*Big Scotch Bonnet* ... NJ-2
Big Scott Brook—*stream* ... ME-1
Bigs Creek—*stream* ... OR-9
Big Scrub Camp—*locale* ... FL-3
*Big Scrub Grass* ... PA-2
**Big Scrub (subdivision)**—*pop pl* ... FL-3
Big Seco Tank—*reservoir* ... NM-5
Big Seeley Spring—*spring* ... CA-9

Big Seep Rsvr—reservoir ... CO-8
Big Seep Tank—reservoir ... NM-5
Big Semoneaston Creek ... VA-3
Big Sepailnah Creek ... TN-4
Big Service Creek—stream ... OR-9
Big Seven Mine—mine ... CA-9
Big Seven Mine—mine ... MT-8
Big Seven Ridge—ridge ... CA-9
Big Sewee Creek—stream ... TN-4
Big Sewee Creek Bridge—hist pl ... TN-4
Big Sewell Ch—church ... WV-2
Big Sewickley Creek—stream ... PA-2
Big Shade Run—stream ... MD-2
Big Shade Run—stream ... PA-2
Big Shadow Lake ... AL-4
Big Shady Branch—stream ... KY-4
Big Shakey Swamp—stream ... NC-3
Big Shallow—lake ... NY-2
Big Shanon Windmill—locale ... TX-5
Big Shanty ... GA-3
**Big Shanty**—pop pl ... PA-2
Big Shanty Hill—summit ... PA-2
Big Shanty Mtn—summit ... ME-1
Big Shanty Mtn—summit ... NY-2
Big Shanty Station—locale ... PA-2
Big Shanty Village Hist Dist—hist pl ... GA-3
Big Sharpleys Creek—stream ... VA-3
Big Sharp Point—cape ... TX-5
Big Shawnee Creek—stream ... IN-6
Big Sheen Rapids—rapids ... WI-6
Big Sheep Basin—basin ... OR-9
Big Sheep Corral—locale ... AZ-5
Big Sheep Creek ... OR-9
Big Sheep Creek—stream (2) ... MT-8
Big Sheep Creek—stream ... WA-9
Big Sheepeater Creek—stream ... ID-8
Big Sheep Hammock—island ... DE-2
Big Sheep Mountains ... MT-8
Big Sheep Mtn—summit ... MT-8
Big Sheep Mtn—summit ... WY-8
Big Sheep Ridge—ridge ... OR-9
Big Sheepshead Creek—gut ... NJ-2
Big Sheep Trail Stock Driveway—trail ... OR-9
Big Shelby Branch—stream ... KY-4
Big Shell Island—island ... FL-3
Big Sherman Pond—lake ... NY-2
Big Shiloh Primitive Baptist Ch—church ... AL-4
Big Shiney Mountain—summit ... PA-2
Big Ship Island—island ... ME-1
Big Shipp Mtn—summit ... AZ-5
Big Shipp Wash—stream ... AZ-5
Big Shoal—bar ... ME-1
Big Shoal—bar ... MI-6
**Big Shoal**—pop pl ... KY-4
Big Shoal Branch—stream ... GA-3
Big Shoal Branch—stream ... NC-3
Big Shoal Cove—bay ... MI-6
Big Shoal Creek ... AL-4
Big Shoal Creek—stream ... AL-4
Big Shoal Creek—stream ... AR-4
Big Shoal Creek—stream ... KY-4
Big Shoally Creek—stream ... SC-3
Big Shoal Marsh—swamp ... NC-3
Big Shoal Park—park ... MO-7
Big Shoals—bar ... FL-3
Big Shoals—bar ... GA-3
Big Shoals—bar ... KY-4
Big Shoals—rapids ... SC-3
Big Shoals Camp—locale ... AL-4
Big Shoal Sch—school ... KY-4
Big Shoal Sch—school ... MO-7
Big Shoals Creek ... AL-4
Big Shoal Station—locale ... KY-4
**Big Shoal Village (historical)**—pop pl ... AL-4
Big Shoe Bend—bend ... MO-7
Big Shoe Heel Creek ... NC-3
Big Shoe Heel Creek ... SC-3
Big Shookum Creek—stream ... AK-9
Big Shot Mine—mine ... SD-7
Big Shuffle Branch ... VA-3
Big Shuffle Branch—stream ... VA-3
Big Shunga Park—park ... KS-7
Big Siding (historical)—locale ... TN-4
Big Sieber Lake—lake ... IA-7
Big Signal ... CA-9
Big Signal Peak—summit ... CA-9
Big Silver Creek ... LA-4
Big Silver Creek ... MS-4
Big Silver Creek—stream ... CA-9
Big Silver Creek—stream ... ID-8
Big Silver Creek—stream ... TX-5
Big Silverlead Creek—stream ... ID-8
Big Silver Mine—mine ... CA-9
Big Simmons Pond ... NY-2
Big Simoneaston Creek—stream ... VA-3
Big Simon Pond ... NY-2
Big Simons Pond ... NY-2
Big Sink—basin ... AZ-5
Big Sink—basin ... IL-6
Big Sink—basin ... KY-4
Big Sink—basin ... MO-7
Big Sink—basin ... OR-9
Big Sink—basin (5) ... TN-4
Big Sink—flat ... GA-3
Big Sink—swamp ... MI-6
Big Sink, The—basin ... TN-4
Big Sink Hole—basin ... MO-7
Big Sinkhole—reservoir ... KS-7
Big Sinking Ch—church ... KY-4
Big Sinking Creek ... MO-7
Big Sinking creek ... TN-4
Big Sinking Creek—stream (3) ... KY-4
Big Sinking Sch—school ... KY-4
Big Sinks—area ... NM-5
Big Sinks—basin ... TN-4
Big Sinks Rsvr—reservoir ... ID-8
Big Sinks Sch—school ... TN-4
Big Sink Waterhole—lake ... ID-8
Big Sioux Bend—bend ... IA-7
Big Sioux Bend—bend ... NE-7
Big Sioux Conifer Nursery—locale ... SD-7
Big Sioux County Park—park ... IA-7
Big Sioux Public Hunting Area—area ... IA-7
Big Sioux River—stream ... SD-7
**Big Sioux Township**—pop pl ... SD-7
Big Sioux Wildlife Public Hunting Area—area ... IA-7
Big Siphon Wasteway—canal ... ID-8
Big Sis Creek—stream ... TX-5
Big Siskiwit River—stream ... MI-6

Big Sister Bay—swamp ... SC-3
Big Sister Creek—stream ... IL-6
Big Sister Creek—stream ... NY-2
Big Sister Island ... FM-9
Big Sister Key—island ... FL-3
Big Sitdown Creek—stream ... AK-9
Big Six Canal—canal ... ID-8
Big Six Canal—canal ... UT-8
Big Six Ditch—canal ... CO-8
Big Six Ditch—canal ... MS-4
Big Sixmile Creek—stream ... NY-2
Big Six Mine—mine ... MT-8
Big Six Mine—mine ... NV-8
Big Six (Township of)—unorg ... ME-1
Big Six Well—well ... TX-5
Big Skeggs Hollow—valley ... VA-3
Big Skid Creek—stream ... TX-5
Big Skidder Hill—summit ... WA-9
Big Skin Bayou—stream ... OK-5
Big Skinner Creek—stream ... LA-4
Big Skirum Creek ... AL-4
Big Skookum Inlet ... WA-9
Big Skunk Creek—stream ... MT-8
**Big Sky**—pop pl (2) ... MT-8
**Big Sky Estates Subdivision**—pop pl ... UT-8
Big Sky Island—island ... MN-6
**Big Sky Meadow Village**—pop pl ... MT-8
**Big Sky Mountain Village**—pop pl ... MT-8
Big Sky Ranch Airstrip—airport ... OR-9
Big Sky RV Park—locale ... UT-8
Big Sky Shop Ctr—locale ... ND-7
Big Sky Ski Area—locale ... MT-8
Big Slash—stream (2) ... AR-4
Big Slash Mtn—summit ... NY-2
Big Sleepy Hollow—valley ... MO-7
Big Slick Ridge—ridge ... NC-3
Big Slide—cliff (2) ... MT-8
Big Slide—slope ... CA-9
Big Slide, The—cliff ... CO-8
Big Slide, The—cliff ... OR-9
Big Slide, The—summit ... MT-8
Big Slide Campground—locale ... CA-9
Big Slide Canyon—valley ... UT-8
Big Slide Creek—stream ... CA-9
Big Slide Creek—stream ... WA-9
Big Slide Hollow—valley ... PA-2
Big Slide Lake—lake ... OR-9
Big Slide Lode—mine ... OR-9
Big Slide Mtn—summit ... NY-2
Big Slide Mtn—summit ... OR-9
Big Slip—bar ... TN-4
Big Slough ... AR-4
Big Slough ... FL-3
Big Slough ... IN-6
Big Slough ... WA-9
Big Slough—channel ... IA-7
Big Slough—gut ... AL-4
Big Slough—gut (5) ... AR-4
Big Slough—gut ... FL-3
Big Slough—gut ... GA-3
Big Slough—gut ... KY-4
Big Slough—gut (3) ... LA-4
Big Slough—gut ... MN-6
Big Slough—gut ... ND-7
Big Slough—gut ... SD-7
Big Slough—gut ... TN-4
Big Slough—gut (7) ... TX-5
Big Slough—gut ... WA-9
Big Slough—lake ... MN-6
Big Slough—lake ... ND-7
Big Slough—stream (2) ... AL-4
Big Slough—stream (2) ... AR-4
Big Slough—stream ... CA-9
Big Slough—stream ... FL-3
Big Slough—stream (2) ... GA-3
Big Slough—stream (2) ... IL-6
Big Slough—stream (3) ... IN-6
Big Slough—stream (2) ... IA-7
Big Slough—stream (3) ... KS-7
Big Slough—stream (4) ... LA-4
Big Slough—stream ... MS-4
Big Slough—stream ... MO-7
Big Slough—stream (4) ... NE-7
Big Slough—stream (3) ... ND-7
Big Slough—stream ... OK-5
Big Slough—stream ... SD-7
Big Slough—stream ... TN-4
Big Slough—stream (4) ... TX-5
Big Slough—stream ... UT-8
Big Slough—stream (2) ... WI-6
Big Slough—swamp ... MN-6
Big Slough—swamp ... NC-3
Big Slough Boat Landing—locale ... GA-3
Big Slough Branch—gut ... FL-3
Big Slough Branch—swamp ... FL-3
Big Slough Canal—canal ... FL-3
Big Slough Creek ... IN-6
Big Slough Creek ... KS-7
Big Slough Creek—stream ... IA-7
Big Slough Creek—stream ... NE-7
Big Slough Ditch—canal (2) ... AR-4
Big Slough Ditch—canal ... IL-6
Big Slough Gundy Rapids—rapids ... WI-6
Big Slough (historical)—gut ... ND-7
Big Slough Lake—lake ... MN-6
Big Slough State Wildlife Mngmt Area—park ... MN-6
Big Sluice Box—area ... CA-9
Big Smith Creek—stream ... ID-8
Big Smook Lake—reservoir ... GA-3
Big Smokehouse Cove—bay ... FL-3
Big Smokehouse Key—island ... FL-3
Big Smoke Mine—mine ... SD-7
Big Smokey Creek ... ID-8
Big Smoky Campground—locale ... ID-8
Big Smoky Creek—stream ... CA-9
Big Smoky Creek—stream ... ID-8
Big Smoky Falls—falls ... WI-6
Big Smoky Guard Station—locale ... ID-8
Big Smoky Valley—valley ... NV-8
Big Snag—island ... FL-3
Big Snake Bay ... NY-2
Big Snake Creek ... GA-3
Big Snake Creek ... MT-8
Big Snapper Cut—channel ... FL-3
Big Sni-A-Bar Creek ... MO-7
Big Snow Creek ... MS-4
Big Snow Creek—stream ... MS-4
Big Snow Lake ... WI-6
Big Snow Lake—lake ... MN-6

Big Snow Lake—lake ... WA-9
Big Snow Lake Dam—dam ... MS-4
Big Snow Mtn—summit ... WA-9
Big Snowy ... MT-8
Big Snowy Mountain ... MT-8
Big Snowy Mtns—range ... MT-8
Big Snowy Peak ... MT-8
Big Snowy Rsvr—reservoir ... MT-8
Big Snyder Gulch—valley ... CA-9
Big Soap Park—flat ... CO-8
Big Soda Spring—spring ... CA-9
Big Soddy Number Seven Mine—mine ... TN-4
Big Soddy Number Three Mine—mine ... TN-4
Big Sodus Bay ... NY-2
Big Sog—swamp ... FL-3
Big Soldier Mtn—summit ... ID-8
Big Solution Hole—channel ... MO-7
**Bigson**—pop pl ... WV-2
Big Soos Creek—stream ... WA-9
Big Sound Creek—stream ... MD-2
Big Sourdough Canyon—valley ... OR-9
Big Sour Dough Creek ... WY-8
Big Sourwood Branch—stream ... KY-4
Big Sous Creek—stream ... TX-5
Big South Branch—stream ... WV-2
Big South Branch Pere Marquette River—stream ... MI-6
Big South Cache la Poudre River ... CO-8
Big South Campground—locale ... CO-8
Big South Canyon—valley ... CO-8
Big Southern Butte—summit ... ID-8
Big South Fork—stream (2) ... KY-4
Big South Fork Bottle Creek—stream ... NV-8
Big South Fork Hunter Creek—stream ... OR-9
Big South Fork Natl River and Rec. Area (Also KY)—park ... TN-4
Big South Fork Natl River & Rec. Area (Also TN)—park ... KY-4
Big South Trail—trail ... CO-8
Big South Well—well ... TX-5
Big Southwest Tank—reservoir ... NM-5
Big South Windmill—locale ... TX-5
Big Sowats Canyon—valley ... AZ-5
Big Spanish Channel—channel ... FL-3
Big Spanish Key—island ... FL-3
Big Spar Mine—mine ... AZ-5
Big Spar Number 1 Mine—mine ... SD-7
Big Spec Lake—lake ... MI-6
Big Spencer Flats—flat ... UT-8
Big Spencer Mtn—summit ... ME-1
Big Spoon Gulch—valley ... CO-8
Big Spraddle Branch—stream ... VA-3
Big Spreader Tank—reservoir ... AZ-5
Big Spread Spring—spring ... OR-9
Big Spring ... AL-4
Big Spring ... AZ-5
Big Spring ... KS-7
Big Spring ... NV-8
Big Spring ... PA-2
Big Spring ... TN-4
Bigspring ... TX-5
Big Spring—hist pl ... AL-4
Big Spring—lake ... ME-1
Big Spring—lake ... NJ-2
Big Spring—locale ... MD-2
Big Spring—locale ... MN-6
Big Spring—locale ... VA-3
**Big Spring**—pop pl ... KY-4
**Big Spring**—pop pl ... MD-2
**Bigspring**—pop pl ... MO-7
**Big Spring**—pop pl ... MO-7
**Big Spring**—pop pl ... OK-5
**Big Spring**—pop pl (3) ... PA-2
**Big Spring**—pop pl (3) ... TN-4
**Big Spring**—pop pl ... TX-5
**Big Spring**—pop pl ... WI-6
Big Spring—spring (9) ... AL-4
Big Spring—spring (12) ... AZ-5
Big Spring—spring (5) ... AR-4
Big Spring—spring (23) ... CA-9
Big Spring—spring (6) ... CO-8
Big Spring—spring ... FL-3
Big Spring—spring (2) ... GA-3
Big Spring—spring ... HI-9
Big Spring—spring (10) ... ID-8
Big Spring—spring ... IN-6
Big Spring—spring (2) ... IA-7
Big Spring—spring ... KS-7
Big Spring—spring (2) ... KY-4
Big Spring—spring ... MD-2
Big Spring—spring (2) ... MI-6
Big Spring—spring (10) ... MO-7
Big Spring—spring (6) ... MT-8
Big Spring—spring (20) ... NV-8
Big Spring—spring (3) ... NM-5
Big Spring—spring ... NC-3
Big Spring—spring ... ND-7
Big Spring—spring ... OK-5
Big Spring—spring (14) ... OR-9
Big Spring—spring (11) ... PA-2
Big Spring—spring (2) ... SD-7
Big Spring—spring (26) ... TN-4
Big Spring—spring (5) ... TX-5
Big Spring—spring (27) ... UT-8
Big Spring—spring ... VT-1
Big Spring—spring (12) ... VA-3
Big Spring—spring (2) ... WA-9
Big Spring—spring (3) ... WV-2
Big Spring—spring (3) ... WI-6
Big Spring—spring (11) ... WY-8
Big Spring—stream ... MO-7
Big Spring, The—spring (2) ... MI-6
Big Spring, The—spring ... UT-8
Big Spring Acad (historical)—school ... TN-4
Big Spring Branch ... AL-4
Big Spring Branch ... TN-4
Big Spring Branch ... VA-3
Big Spring Branch—stream ... AR-4
Big Spring Branch—stream (2) ... GA-3
Big Spring Branch—stream (4) ... KY-4
Big Spring Branch—stream (2) ... NC-3
Big Spring Branch—stream ... OR-9
Big Spring Branch—stream ... PA-2
Big Spring Branch—stream (2) ... TN-4
Big Spring Branch—stream ... TX-5
Big Spring Branch—stream (2) ... VA-3
Big Spring Branch—stream ... WA-9
Big Spring Branch—stream (2) ... WV-2
Big Spring Branch—stream ... WI-6
Big Spring Brook—stream ... ME-1

Big Spring Brook—stream ... PA-2
Big Spring Brook Trail—trail ... PA-2
Big Spring Butte—summit ... NV-8
Big Spring Campground—locale ... CA-9
Big Spring Campground—locale ... ID-8
Big Spring Campground—locale ... WA-9
Big Spring Campgrounds—park ... MO-7
Big Spring Canyon—valley (5) ... AZ-5
Big Spring Canyon—valley ... CA-9
Big Spring Canyon—valley ... NM-5
Big Spring Canyon—valley ... TX-5
Big Spring Canyon—valley (2) ... UT-8
Big Spring Canyon Overlook—locale ... UT-8
Big Spring Cave—cave ... AL-4
Big Spring Cave—cave (2) ... TN-4
Big Spring (CCD)—cens area ... TX-5
Big Spring Cem ... TN-4
Big Spring Cem—cemetery ... AR-4
Big Spring Cem—cemetery ... KY-4
Big Spring Cem—cemetery ... MN-6
Big Spring Cem—cemetery ... MS-4
Big Spring Cem—cemetery ... MO-7
Big Spring Cem—cemetery ... NE-7
Big Spring Cem—cemetery ... OH-6
Big Spring Cem—cemetery ... PA-2
Big Spring Cem—cemetery (2) ... TN-4
Big Spring Cem—cemetery ... TX-5
Big Spring Cem—cemetery ... VA-3
Big Spring Ch ... AL-4
Big Spring Ch—church (2) ... AL-4
Big Spring Ch—church ... KY-4
Big Spring Ch—church ... MS-4
Big Spring Ch—church (2) ... MO-7
Big Spring Ch—church ... NC-3
Big Spring Ch—church (4) ... TN-4
Big Spring Ch—church ... VA-3
Big Spring Ch—church ... WV-2
Big Spring Ch (historical)—church ... SD-7
Big Spring Ch (historical)—church ... TN-4
Big Spring Church—hist pl ... KY-4
Big Spring Church (historical)—locale ... MO-7
Big Spring City Wells—well ... TX-5
Big Spring Coulee—valley ... ND-7
Big Spring Country Club—other ... KY-4
Big Spring Cove—basin ... TN-4
Big Spring Cove—valley ... NC-3
Big Spring Creek ... CO-8
Big Spring Creek ... NV-8
Big Spring Creek ... OK-5
Big Spring Creek ... OR-9
Big Spring Creek ... WI-6
Big Spring Creek—stream (2) ... AL-4
Big Spring Creek—stream (3) ... CO-8
Big Spring Creek—stream (2) ... FL-3
Big Spring Creek—stream (4) ... ID-8
Big Spring Creek—stream ... IN-6
Big Spring Creek—stream ... KS-7
Big Spring Creek—stream ... MI-6
Big Spring Creek—stream ... MS-4
Big Spring Creek—stream (4) ... MT-8
Big Spring Creek—stream ... NV-8
Big Spring Creek—stream ... NC-3
Big Spring Creek—stream ... OH-6
Big Spring Creek—stream ... OR-9
Big Spring Creek—stream ... PA-2
Bigspring Creek—stream ... SC-3
Big Spring Creek—stream ... SD-7
Big Spring Creek—stream ... TN-4
Big Spring Creek—stream ... UT-8
Big Spring Creek—stream ... WA-9
Big Spring Creek—stream ... WI-6
Big Spring Creek Sch (historical)—school ... TN-4
Big Spring Creek Small Wild Area—park ... AL-4
**Big Spring Creek Subdivision (subdivision)**—pop pl ... AL-4
Big Spring Dam—dam ... PA-2
Big Spring Draft—valley ... PA-2
Big Spring Draft Trail—trail ... PA-2
Big Spring Draw—valley ... AR-4
Big Spring Draw—valley ... CO-8
Big Spring Draw—valley ... OR-9
Big Spring Draw—valley (2) ... TX-5
Big Spring-East View (CCD)—cens area ... TN-4
Big Spring-East View Division—civil ... TN-4
Big Spring Fork—stream ... UT-8
Big Spring Fork—stream (2) ... WV-2
Big Spring Gap—gap ... NC-3
Bigspring Gap—gap ... NC-3
Big Spring Gap—gap ... PA-2
Big Spring Gap—gap ... TN-4
Big Spring Gulch ... CO-8
Big Spring Gulch—valley ... CO-8
Big Spring Gulch—valley (2) ... MT-8
Big Spring High School ... PA-2
Big Spring Hill Ch—church ... TX-5
Big Spring Hist Dist—hist pl ... MO-7
Big Spring (historical)—locale ... AL-4
**Big Spring (historical)**—pop pl ... IA-7
**Big Spring (historical)**—pop pl ... TN-4
Big Spring Hollow—valley ... AR-4
Big Spring Hollow—valley (3) ... KY-4
Big Spring Hollow—valley ... MS-4
Big Spring Hollow—valley (8) ... MO-7
Big Spring Hollow—valley ... OH-6
Big Spring Hollow—valley (4) ... TN-4
Big Spring Hollow—valley (2) ... UT-8
Big Spring Island—island ... TN-4
Big Spring Junior High School ... PA-2
Big Spring Lake ... WI-6
Big Spring Lake—lake ... MT-8
Big Spring Lake—lake ... TN-4
Big Spring Lake Number Two—reservoir ... TN-4
Big Spring Lake Number Two Dam—dam ... TN-4
Big Spring Lookout Tower—locale ... MO-7
**Big Spring Mill**—pop pl ... AR-4
Big Spring Mine—mine ... NV-8
Big Spring Mtn—summit (3) ... NC-3
Bigspring Mtn—summit ... SC-3
Big Spring North (CCD)—cens area ... TX-5
Big Spring Oil Field—oilfield ... TX-5
Big Spring Park—park (2) ... AL-4
Big Spring Park—park ... MO-7
Big Spring Park—park ... TN-4
Big Spring Pasture Windmill—locale ... NM-5
Big Spring P.O. ... AL-4
Big Spring Pond—lake ... PA-2
Bigspring Post Office ... TN-4
Big Spring Post Office—building ... TN-4
Big Spring Post Office (historical)—building ... TN-4

Big Spring Ranch—locale ... CO-8
Big Spring Ranch—locale ... UT-8
Big Spring Ranger Station—locale ... MT-8
Big Spring Rec Area—locale ... UT-8
Big Spring Ridge—ridge ... GA-3
Big Spring Ridge—ridge ... NC-3
Big Spring Ridge—ridge ... VA-3
Big Spring River Access—locale ... MO-7
Big Spring Rsvr—reservoir ... NV-8
Big Spring Rsvr—reservoir ... OR-9
Big Spring Rsvr—reservoir ... PA-2
Big Spring Rsvr—reservoir ... WY-8
Big Spring Run—stream (3) ... PA-2
Big Spring Run—stream (2) ... WV-2
Big Spring R-1 Sch—school ... MO-7
Big Springs ... AL-4
Big Springs ... MS-4
Big Springs ... OR-9
Big Springs ... TX-5
Big Springs ... UT-8
Big Springs ... VA-3
Big Springs—locale ... AL-4
Big Springs—locale ... CA-9
Big Springs—locale ... MS-4
Big Springs—locale ... NJ-2
Big Springs—locale ... SD-7
Big Springs—locale ... TN-4
Big Springs—locale ... TX-5
**Big Springs**—pop pl ... AZ-5
**Big Springs**—pop pl ... AR-4
**Big Springs**—pop pl ... GA-3
**Big Springs**—pop pl ... ID-8
**Big Springs**—pop pl ... IN-6
**Big Springs**—pop pl ... KS-7
**Big Springs**—pop pl ... NE-7
**Big Springs**—pop pl ... OH-6
**Big Springs**—pop pl (4) ... TN-4
**Big Springs**—pop pl ... WV-2
Big Springs—spring ... AR-4
Big Springs—spring (9) ... CA-9
Big Springs—spring ... CO-8
Big Springs—spring (3) ... ID-8
Big Springs—spring (2) ... KS-7
Big Springs—spring ... MI-6
Big Springs—spring ... MN-6
Big Springs—spring (4) ... NV-8
Big Springs—spring (7) ... OR-9
Big Springs—spring ... PA-2
Big Springs—spring (2) ... TX-5
Big Springs—spring (5) ... UT-8
Big Springs—spring (2) ... WA-9
Big Springs—spring ... WY-8
Big Springs—springs ... IN-6
Big Springs, The—spring ... TX-5
Big Springs Access Area—park ... TN-4
Big Springs Baptist Ch—church ... TN-4
Big Springs Baptist Church ... AL-4
Big Springs Baptist Church ... MS-4
**Big Springs (Big Spring)**—pop pl ... GA-3
Big Springs Branch—stream (2) ... KY-4
Big Springs Branch—stream ... NC-3
Big Springs Branch—stream (2) ... TN-4
Big Springs Branch—stream ... VA-3
Big Springs Branch—stream ... WV-2
Big Springs Butte—summit ... ID-8
Big Springs Campground—locale ... CA-9
Big Springs Campground—locale ... CO-8
Big Springs Campground—park ... OR-9
Big Springs Canyon—valley ... AZ-5
Big Springs Canyon—valley ... CA-9
Big Springs Canyon—valley ... NV-8
Big Springs Cave—cave ... TN-4
Big Springs Cem—cemetery ... AL-4
Big Springs Cem—cemetery ... IA-7
Big Springs Cem—cemetery ... KS-7
Big Springs Cem—cemetery ... KY-4
Big Springs Cem—cemetery ... MS-4
Big Springs Cem—cemetery (4) ... TN-4
Big Springs Ch ... MS-4
Big Springs Ch ... TN-4
Big Springs Ch—church (3) ... AL-4
Big Springs Ch—church (3) ... GA-3
Big Springs Ch—church (2) ... IN-6
Big Springs Ch—church ... KY-4
Big Springs Ch—church (3) ... MS-4
Big Springs Ch—church ... NC-3
Big Springs Ch—church ... OK-5
Big Springs Ch—church (3) ... TN-4
Big Springs Ch—church ... TX-5
Big Springs Sch—school (2) ... KY-4
Big Springs Sch—school ... MS-4
Big Springs Sch—school ... ND-7
Big Springs Sch—school ... PA-2
Big Springs Sch—school ... TN-4
Big Springs Sch—school ... WI-6
Big Springs Sch (historical)—school ... MO-7
Big Springs Ch of Christ—church ... TN-4
Big Springs School (abandoned)—locale ... MO-7
Big Springs Creek—stream (2) ... CA-9
Big Springs Creek—stream ... CO-8
Big Springs Creek—stream (2) ... ID-8
Big Springs Creek—stream ... MI-6
Big Springs Creek—stream ... MN-6
Big Springs Creek—stream ... NE-7
Big Springs Creek—stream (2) ... NV-8
Big Springs Creek—stream (2) ... OR-9
Big Springs Creek—stream ... TN-4
Big Springs Cumberland Presbyterian Ch (historical)—church ... TN-4
Big Springs Draw—valley ... WY-8
Big Springs Gap—gap ... WV-2
Big Springs Guard Sch—school ... CA-9
Big Springs (historical)—locale ... AL-4
Big Springs Lookout—locale ... ID-8
Big Springs Lookout Tower—hist pl ... AZ-5
Big Springs Point—cliff ... AZ-5
Big Springs Post Office (historical)—building ... MS-4
Big Springs Presbyterian Ch—church ... TN-4
Big Springs Primitive Baptist Church ... MS-4
Big Springs Pump—other ... OR-9
Big Springs Ranch ... NV-8
Big Springs Ranch—locale ... CO-8
Big Springs Ranch—locale ... ID-8
Big Springs Ranch—locale (2) ... NV-8
Big Springs Ranger Station—locale ... AZ-5
Big Springs Rsvr—reservoir ... CA-9
Big Springs Sch—school (2) ... CA-9
Big Springs Sch—school ... KY-4
Big Springs Sch—school ... MI-6

Big Springs Sch (historical)—school (2) ... MS-4
Big Springs Sch (historical)—school (2) ... TN-4
Big Springs Shop Ctr—locale ... TN-4
Big Spring State Fish Hatchery—locale ... PA-2
Big Spring State Hosp—hospital ... TX-5
Big Spring State Park—park ... MO-7
Big Spring State Park—park ... PA-2
Big Spring State Park—park ... TX-5
**Big Springs Township**—pop pl ... SD-7
Big Springs (Township of)—fmr MCD ... AR-4
Big Springs Wash ... AZ-5
Big Springs Wash ... NV-8
Big Spring Table—summit ... NV-8
Big Spring Table—summit ... OR-9
Big Spring Township—civil ... SD-7
Big Spring (Township of)—fmr MCD ... AR-4
Big Spring (Township of)—other ... AR-4
**Big Spring (Township of)**—pop pl ... IL-6
**Big Spring (Township of)**—pop pl ... OH-6
Big Spring Union—locale ... TN-4
Big Spring Union Baptist Ch—church ... TN-4
Big Spring Union Church—hist pl ... TN-4
Big Spring Union Sch (historical)—school ... TN-4
Big Spring Valley—valley ... AL-4
Big Spring Wash—stream (2) ... AZ-5
Big Spring Wash—stream (3) ... NV-8
Big Springy Brook—stream ... ME-1
Big Spruce Cem—cemetery ... WV-2
Big Spruce Creek—stream ... AK-9
Big Spruce Creek—stream ... ID-8
Big Spruce Creek—stream ... MT-8
Big Spruce Knob—summit ... WV-2
Big Spruce Lake—lake ... CO-8
Big Spruce Mtn—summit ... ME-1
Big Spruce Mtn—summit ... VT-1
Big Spruce Pine Branch—stream ... VA-3
Big Spruce Ridge—ridge ... NC-3
Big Spruce State Wildlife Mngmt Area—park ... MN-6
Big Spunk Lake ... MN-6
Big Spur Branch—stream ... TN-4
Big Spur Mtn—summit ... NY-2
Big Spur Tank—reservoir ... AZ-5
Big Spy Mtn—summit ... VA-3
Big Square—locale ... TX-5
Big Squaw ... OR-9
Big Squaw Creek—stream ... ID-8
Big Squaw Mtn—summit ... ME-1
Big Squaw Mtn—summit ... OR-9
Big Squaw Pond—lake ... ME-1
Big Squaw (Township of)—unorg ... ME-1
Big Squaw Valley—basin ... NV-8
Big Squaw Valley—valley ... CA-9
Big Stack Gap—gap ... TN-4
Big Stack Gap Branch—stream ... TN-4
Big Stack Gap Branch Trail—trail ... TN-4
Big Stacy Park—park ... TX-5
Big Staff Branch—stream ... KY-4
Big Stake Gap—channel ... FL-3
Big Stakey Creek—stream ... SC-3
Big Stakey Mtn—summit ... SC-3
Big Stamp—gap ... GA-3
Big Stamp—gap ... NC-3
Big Stamp—summit ... NC-3
Big Stamp—summit ... TN-4
Big Stamp Gap—gap ... GA-3
Big Star Ch—church ... AR-4
Big Star Ch of God—church ... AL-4
Big Star Lake—lake ... MI-6
Big Star Lake Ch—church ... MI-6
Big Star Run—stream ... WV-2
Big Starvation Cove—bay ... FL-3
Big Station Pond—lake ... MA-1
Big Stave Hollow—valley ... KY-4
Big Steep Pond—lake ... FL-3
Big Stemilt Creek—stream ... WA-9
Big Sterling Spring—spring ... PA-2
Big Steve Mine—mine ... AZ-5
Big Stevens Creek Baptist Church—hist pl ... SC-3
Big Stevens Creek Ch—church ... SC-3
Big Stewart Canyon—valley ... OR-9
Big Stew Creek—stream ... ID-8
Big Stick ... WV-2
Big Stick—locale ... WV-2
Big Stick Creek—stream ... OR-9
Big Stick Ditch—canal ... CO-8
Big Stick Mine—mine ... AZ-5
Big Stinking Quarter Creek ... NC-3
Big Stitchihatchie Branch—stream ... GA-3
Big Stone ... SD-7
Bigstone—locale ... KY-4
Big Stone Bay—bay ... MI-6
Big Stone Beach—beach ... DE-2
Big Stone Beach—locale ... DE-2
Big Stone City ... MN-6
**Big Stone City**—pop pl ... SD-7
Big Stonecoal Branch—stream ... KY-4
**Big Stone Colony**—pop pl ... MN-6
**Big Stone (County)**—pop pl ... MN-6
Big Stone County Courthouse—hist pl ... MN-6
Big Stone Creek—stream ... MI-6
Big Stone Gap—gap ... VA-3
**Big Stone Gap**—pop pl ... VA-3
Big Stone Gap 6—gap ... KY-4
Big Stonehouse Creek ... NC-3
Big Stone House Creek—stream ... NC-3
Bigstone Lake ... SD-7
Big Stone Lake—lake (2) ... MN-6
Big Stone Lake—lake ... WI-6
Big Stone Lake—reservoir ... MN-6
Big Stone Lake—reservoir ... SD-7
Big Stone Lake State Park—park ... MN-6
Big Stone Ridge ... VA-3
Big Stone Ridge—ridge ... VA-3
Big Stone Ridge—ridge ... WV-2
**Big Stone Township**—pop pl ... ND-7
**Big Stone Township**—pop pl ... SD-7
**Big Stone (Township of)**—pop pl ... MN-6
Big Stoney Creek—stream ... WV-2
Big Stony Creek ... VA-3
Big Stony Island ... NY-2
Big Stony Lake—lake ... MN-6
Big Stony Point—cape ... IA-7
Big Stony Run ... VA-3
Big Strand—swamp ... GA-3
Big Stranger Creek ... KS-7
Big Stratton Rsvr—reservoir ... CO-8
Big Stream—stream ... NY-2
Big Stump Camp—locale ... CA-9

Big Stump Entrance Station—locale CA-9
Big Stump Grove—woods CA-9
Big Suamico River WI-6
Big Suamico (RR name for Suamico)—other WI-6
Big Sucker Brook—stream AL-4
Big Sucker Brook—stream NY-2
Big Sucker Creek—stream MI-6
Big Sucker Creek—stream MN-6
Big Sucker Lake—lake MN-6
Big Sue Branch—stream KY-4
Big Suee Creek TN-4
Big Sugar Bush Lake—lake MN-6
Big Sugar Creek IN-6
Big Sugar Creek IA-7
Big Sugar Creek KS-7
Big Sugar Creek MO-7
Big Sugar Creek NC-3
Big Sugar Creek OH-6
Big Sugar Creek SC-3
Big Sugar Creek—stream AR-4
Big Sugar Creek—stream KS-7
Big Sugar Creek—stream KY-4
Big Sugar Creek—stream MO-7
Big Sugar Hollow—valley TN-4
Big Sugar Loaf—bend NC-3
Big Sugarloaf Mtn—summit CO-8
Big Sugarloaf Peak—summit OR-9
Big Sulfur Draw—valley WY-8
Big Sulfur Spring—spring WY-8
Big Sullivan Tank—reservoir AZ-5
Big Sulphur Branch—stream KY-4
Big Sulphur Branch—stream TX-5
Big Sulphur Canyon—valley UT-8
Big Sulphur Creek TX-5
Big Sulphur Creek—stream CA-9
Big Sulphur Creek—stream ID-8
Big Sulphur Rapids—rapids ID-8
Big Sulphur Rapids—rapids OR-9
Big Summit—gap NV-8
Big Summit Prairie—flat OR-9
Big Sunday Creek—stream MT-8
Big Sunday Creek—stream TX-5
Big Sunflower River—stream MS-4
Big Sunk Cane—basin TN-4
Big Supai Tank—reservoir AZ-5
**Big Sur—pop pl** CA-9
Big Surface Workings—mine TN-4
Big Sur Guard Station—locale CA-9
Big Sur River—stream CA-9
Big Sur Trail—trail CA-9
Big Swag NC-3
Big Swag—ridge KY-4
Big Swag—summit NC-3
Big Swag Run—stream WV-2
Big Swale—flat UT-8
Big Swale—valley OH-6
Big Swale—valley UT-8
Big Swale Rsvr—reservoir OR-9
Big Swale Rsvr No 1—reservoir UT-8
Big Swale Rsvr No 2—reservoir UT-8
Big Swamp AL-4
Big Swamp—stream (4) NC-3
Big Swamp—stream VA-3
Big Swamp—swamp (3) AL-4
Big Swamp—swamp CA-9
Big Swamp—swamp FL-3
Big Swamp—swamp GA-3
Big Swamp—swamp IN-6
Big Swamp—swamp MI-6
Big Swamp—swamp (3) MS-4
Big Swamp—swamp (2) NY-2
Big Swamp—swamp NC-3
Big Swamp—swamp ND-7
Big Swamp—swamp OR-9
Big Swamp—swamp PA-2
Big Swamp—swamp (2) SC-3
Big Swamp—swamp VA-3
Big Swamp—swamp WA-9
Big Swamp—swamp WI-6
Big Swamp, The—stream VA-3
Big Swamp Annex—swamp FL-3
Big Swamp Branch—stream AL-4
Big Swamp Branch—stream SC-3
Big Swamp Canal—canal NC-3
Big Swamp Creek AL-4
Big Swamp Creek MT-8
Big Swamp Creek—stream (2) AL-4
Big Swamp Creek—stream FL-3
Big Swamp Creek—stream MN-6
Big Swamp Creek—stream MS-4
Big Swamp Creek—stream MT-8
Big Swamp Creek—stream (2) OR-9
Big Swamp Dam—dam OR-9
Big Swamp Drain—canal MI-6
Big Swamp Drain—stream MI-6
Big Swamp Fork—stream WV-2
Big Swamp Lake WI-6
Big Swamp Ridge—ridge AR-4
Big Swamp Rsvr—reservoir OR-9
Big Swamp Sch—school (2) SC-3
Big Swamp Springs—spring UT-8
Big Swamp State Public Hunting Grounds—park WI-6
Big Swan Creek—stream TN-4
Big Swan Island—island NC-3
Big Swan Lake—lake (2) MN-6
Big Swan Lake—swamp IL-6
Big Swan Lake Sch—school MN-6
Big Swan Overlook TN-4
Big Swan Pond IN-6
Big Swan Pond Slough—stream KY-4
Big Swan Pumping Station—other IL-6
Big Swan Sch—school IL-6
Big Swash—swamp NC-3
Big Swede Creek—stream AK-9
Big Swede Valley—basin NE-7
Big Sweetwater Creek—stream FL-3
Big Swift Lake MN-6
Big Sycamore—locale WV-2
Big Sycamore Canyon—valley (2) CA-9
Big Sycamore Ch—church TN-4
Big Sycamore Creek—stream TN-4
Big Table—flat NV-8
Big Table—summit OR-9
Big Table—summit UT-8
Big Tableland—flat CA-9
Big Table Mountain Spring—spring WY-8
Big Table Mtn OR-9
Big Table Mtn—summit ID-8
Big Table Mtn—summit WY-8
Big Talbot Island FL-3
Big Talk Lake—lake ID-8
Big Tallawampa Creek AL-4
Big Tallawampa Creek—stream AL-4
Big Tamarack Lake—lake MN-6
Big Tam Lake—lake MN-6
Big Tangipahoa River MS-4
Big Tank—lake TX-5
Big Tank—reservoir (19) AZ-5
Big Tank—reservoir (23) NM-5
Big Tank—reservoir OR-9
Big Tank—reservoir (19) TX-5
Big Tank Canyon—valley NM-5
Big Tank Canyon—valley (2) TX-5
Big Tank Creek—stream OR-9
Big Tank Detention Dam—dam AZ-5
Big Tank Draw—valley NM-5
Big Tank Ranch—locale TX-5
Big Tank Ridge—ridge AL-4
Big Tank Rsvr OR-9
Big Tanks—other NM-5
Big Tanks—reservoir AZ-5
Big Tanks—reservoir TX-5
Big Tank Series—reservoir AZ-5
Big Tank Well—well AZ-5
Big Tank Windmill—locale NM-5
Big Tank Windmill—locale TX-5
Big Tan Trough Branch—stream VA-3
Big Tar Canyon—valley CA-9
Big Tar Creek—stream CA-9
Big Tarkio River IA-7
Big Tarkio River MO-7
Big Tavern Creek MO-7
Big T Ch—church AR-4
Big Telico Creek—stream AR-4
Big Tenant Spring—spring CA-9
Big Tenasa Bayou—stream LA-4
Big Tenif WA-9
Big Tenmile Fork—stream WV-2
Big Ten Mine (underground)—mine AL-4
Big Ten Peak—summit NV-8
Big Ten Spring—spring NV-8
Big Ten (Township of)—unorg ME-1
Big Tepee Creek—stream MT-8
Big Tepee Creek—stream WY-8
Big Terrapin Run—stream KY-4
Big Tesuque Trail—trail NM-5
Big Texas Valley—valley GA-3
Big Therriault Lake—lake MT-8
Big Thick—swamp FL-3
Big Thick—swamp SC-3
Big Thick Branch—stream MS-4
Big Thick Creek—stream MS-4
Big Thicket—woods TX-5
Big Thicket Branch—stream KY-4
**Big Thicket Creekmore Village—pop pl** TX-5
Big Thicket (historical)—woods TX-5
**Big Thicket Loblolly—pop pl** TX-5
Big Thicket Menard Creek—stream TX-5
Big Thicket Natl Preserve—park TX-5
Big Thirteenth Lake Mtn—summit NY-2
Big Thirtynine Creek—stream MN-6
Big Thomas Mesa UT-8
Big Thompson Canyon—valley CO-8
Big Thompson Creek CO-8
Big Thompson Ditch—canal CO-8
Big Thompson Ditch No. 2—canal CO-8
Big Thompson Hollow—valley WV-2
Big Thompson Mesa UT-8
Big Thompson Power Plant—other CO-8
Big Thompson River—stream CO-8
Big Thompson Sch—school CO-8
Big Thompson Siphon—canal CO-8
Big Thomson Mesa—summit UT-8
Big Thornapple Drain MI-6
Big Thorofare—channel MD-2
Big Thorofare—channel VA-3
Big Thorofare—stream NJ-2
Big Thorofare River MD-2
Big Thorofare River West Light—locale MD-2
Big Thoroughfare MD-2
Big Thoroughfare—canal PA-2
Big Thoroughfare Bay (Carolina Bay)—swamp NC-3
Big Thoroughfare River MD-2
Big Thrasher Gut—gut VA-3
Big Three Creek Lake—reservoir OR-9
Big Three Creek Lake Dam—dam OR-9
Big Three Hollow—valley TN-4
Big Threemile Creek—stream OH-6
Big Three Mine—mine CO-8
Big Three Mine—mine ID-8
Big Thumb Creek—stream WY-8
Big Thumb Spring—spring NM-5
Big Thunder Creek—stream IN-6
Big Thunder Peak—summit MN-6
Big Tiger Wash—arroyo NV-8
Big Timber KS-7
**Big Timber—pop pl** MT-8
Big Timber Canyon—valley (2) MT-8
Big Timber Canyon—valley NM-5
Big Timber Cem—cemetery KS-7
Big Timber Creek SD-7
Big Timber Creek—stream (2) AK-9
Big Timber Creek—stream CO-8
Big Timber Creek—stream ID-8
Big Timber Creek—stream (5) KS-7
Big Timber Creek—stream MT-8
Big Timber Creek—stream NE-7
Big Timber Creek—stream NJ-2
Big Timber Creek—stream (2) TX-5
Big Timber Creek Canal—canal MT-8
Big Timber Guard Station—locale MT-8
Big Timber Gulch—valley MT-8
Big Timber Island—island WI-6
Big Timber Lakes—reservoir OK-5
Big Timber Peak—summit MT-8
Big Timbers—area CO-8
Big Timber Scout Camp—locale IL-6
Big Timber Spring—spring NV-8
Big Timber Spur—trail PA-2
**Big Timber Township—pop pl** KS-7
Big Tim Island—island NC-3
Big Tinker Creek—stream ID-8
Big Tip—summit OR-9
Big Tippecanoe Lake IN-6
Big Tizer Creek—stream MT-8
Big Tizer Wildcat Mine—mine MT-8
Big Tobin Creek—stream MT-8
Big Tobin Well—well MT-8
Big Toby Creek—stream VA-3
Big Tobyhanna NY-2
Big Toe Island—island MN-6
Big Tom—bar NY-2
Big Tom—summit NY-2
Big Tom—summit NC-3
Big Tom—summit VA-3
Big Tomahawk Creek—stream NC-3
Big Tom Brown Branch—stream KY-4
Big Tom Creek GA-3
Big Tom Creek—stream GA-3
Big Tom Folley Creek—stream OR-9
Big Tomhicken Creek PA-2
Big Tom Hill—summit SD-7
Big Tom Hollow—valley UT-8
Big Tom Mtn—summit AR-4
Big Tommy Branch—stream NC-3
Big Tom Sauk Creek MO-7
Big Toms Creek GA-3
Big To Much Lake MN-6
Big Tono—mine NV-8
Big Too Much Lake—lake MN-6
Big Tooth Rsvr—reservoir CO-8
Big Top UT-8
Big Top—summit NC-3
Big Top—summit SC-3
Big Top—summit TN-4
Big Top Mesa—summit ND-7
Big Torch Key—island FL-3
Big Torrea Tank—reservoir TX-5
Big Towaliga Creek—stream GA-3
Big Towhead Island—island FL-3
Big Town Creek—stream NC-3
Big Town Windmill—locale TX-5
Big Trace Branch—stream KY-4
Big Trade Lake—lake WI-6
Big Trail Lake—stream MS-4
Big Trail Pond—swamp FL-3
Bigtrails WY-8
Big Trails—locale WY-8
Big Trails Ch—church WY-8
Big Trails Rsvr—reservoir WY-8
Big Trail Vista—summit PA-2
Big Tramme Creek KY-4
Big Trammel Creek KY-4
Big Traverse Bay Hist Dist—hist pl MI-6
Big Traverse Run PA-2
Big Travis Spring—spring NV-8
Big Tree PA-2
Big Tree—locale OR-9
Big Tree—locale PA-2
Big Tree—other CA-9
Big Tree—other OR-9
**Big Tree—pop pl** NY-2
Big Tree—ridge ID-8
Big Tree, The—locale TX-5
Big Tree Campground—locale UT-8
Big Tree Campground—park OR-9
Big Tree Cave—cave TX-5
Big Tree Creek—stream UT-8
Big Tree Creek—stream WA-9
Big Tree Creek—stream WY-8
Bigtree Gulch—valley CA-9
Big Tree Gulch—valley CO-8
Big Tree Hollow—valley (2) PA-2
Big Tree Lake—lake TX-5
Big Tree Park—park FL-3
Big Tree Plaza (Shop Ctr)—locale FL-3
Big Tree Ranch—locale TX-5
Big Trees—locale CA-9
Big Trees—locale NV-8
**Big Trees—pop pl** CA-9
Big Trees Campsites—locale FL-3
Big Trees Creek—stream (2) CA-9
Big Trees Park CA-9
Big Trees Spring—spring OR-9
Big Tree Trail—trail CA-9
Big Trestle Draw—valley TX-5
Big Trestle Run—stream PA-2
Big Trestle Trail—trail PA-2
Big Triangle—bench UT-8
Big Triangle Pass TX-5
Big Tribble Creek—stream WV-2
Big Trickle Tube Dam SD-7
Big Trinity Lake—lake ID-8
Big Trough Creek—stream UT-8
Big Trough Spring—spring AZ-5
Big Trout Creek—stream FL-3
Big Trout Creek—stream MN-6
Big Trout Creek—stream OR-9
Big Trout Island—island MI-6
Big Trout Lake—lake (3) MI-6
Big Trout Lake—lake MN-6
Big Trudo Lake—lake LA-4
Big Trujillo Wash—valley CO-8
Big "T" Shop Ctr—locale MO-7
Big T Tank—reservoir AZ-5
Big Tub Tank—reservoir TX-5
Big Tucker Lake—lake TX-5
Big Tujunga Canyon CA-9
Big Tujunga Canyon—valley CA-9
Big Tujunga Dam—dam CA-9
Big Tujunga Station—locale CA-9
Big Tuni Creek—stream NC-3
Big Tunnel—tunnel KY-4
Big Tunnel Spring—spring CA-9
Big Turkey CO-8
Big Turkey Creek GA-3
Big Turkey Creek MO-7
Big Turkey Creek OK-5
Big Turkey Creek TX-5
Big Turkey Creek—stream MO-7
Big Turkey Creek—stream TX-5
Big Turkey Knob—summit VA-3
Big Turkey Lake—lake IN-6
Big Turkey Tail—ridge WA-9
Big Turkey Tank—reservoir AZ-5
Big Turnbull Creek TN-4
Big Turnbull Creek—stream TN-4
Big Turney Draw—valley TX-5
Big Turniptown Creek GA-3
Big Turn Run—stream VA-3
Big Turtle Creek IN-6
Big Tuttle Cove TN-4
Big Twelve Creek—stream OR-9
Big Twenty (Township of)—unorg ME-1
Big Twin Creek—stream CA-9
Big Twin Creek—stream (2) KY-4
Big Twin Creek—stream WY-8
Big Twin Lake CA-9
Big Twin Lake—lake (3) AR-4
Big Twin Lake—lake CA-9
Big Twin Lake—lake MI-6
Big Twin Lake—lake MN-6
Big Twin Lake—lake WA-9
Big Twin Lake—lake (2) WI-6
Big Twin Lakes Campground—park OR-9
Big Twist Creek—stream UT-8
Big Two Branch—stream KY-4
Big Two Hearted River MI-6
Big Twomile Creek—stream WV-2
Big Two Top Butte—summit SD-7
Big Tygart Cem—cemetery WV-2
Big Tykle Cove—bay WA-9
Big Uchee Creek AL-4
Big Ugly Creek—stream AL-4
Big Ugly Creek—stream WV-2
Big Ugly Run—stream VA-3
Big Ugly Run Trail—trail VA-3
Big Union Ch—church AL-4
Big Union Circuit—church DE-2
Big Union Creek—stream CO-8
Big Valley PA-2
Big Valley—area CA-9
Big Valley—basin UT-8
Big Valley—basin VA-3
Big Valley—bend TX-5
Big Valley—valley AZ-5
Big Valley—valley (2) CA-9
Big Valley—valley OR-9
Big Valley—valley PA-2
Big Valley—valley (2) TN-4
Big Valley—valley TX-5
Big Valley—valley WA-9
Big Valley Acad (historical)—school TN-4
Big Valley Bluff—ridge CA-9
Big Valley Bluff Lookout (Abandoned)—locale CA-9
Big Valley Brook—stream VT-1
Big Valley Canal—canal CA-9
Big Valley Canal—canal TX-5
Big Valley Canyon valley CA 9
Big Valley (CCD)—cens area CA-9
Big Valley Cem—cemetery (2) TX-5
Big Valley Cem—cemetery VA-3
Big Valley Ch—church PA-2
Big Valley Ch—church TX-5
Big Valley Community Center—locale CA-9
Big Valley Creek—stream CA-9
Big Valley Creek—stream MI-6
Big Valley Mountain CA-9
Big Valley Mountains—range CA-9
**Big Valley Rancheria—pop pl** CA-9
Big Valley Trail—trail CA-9
Big Vane VA-3
Big Vein—locale VA-3
Big Venson Bayou—stream LA-4
Big Vermilion River IL-6
Big Vermilion River IN-6
Big Vermilion River IL-6
Big Vermillion River IN-6
Big Vermillion River KS-7
Big Vicente Canon TX-5
Big V Ranch House—hist pl OK-5
Big V Rsvr—reservoir WY-8
Big Walamontage Stream ME-1
Big Waldren Fork—stream AK-9
Big Walker Mountain VA-3
Big Wall—ridge CO-8
Big Wallamatogue Stream—stream ME-1
Big Wall Creek—stream OR-9
Big Wall Lake—lake IA-7
Big Wall Lake State Public Hunting Area—park IA-7
Big Wall Oil Field—oilfield MT-8
Big Walnut Ch—church IN-6
Big Walnut Creek KS-7
Big Walnut Creek OH-6
Big Walnut Creek—stream IN-6
Big Walnut Creek—stream OH-6
Big Walnut Grove Ch—church KY-4
Big Walnut HS—school OH-6
Big Walnut Isle—island OH-6
Big Walnut Run—stream TX-5
Big Wamatogue Stream ME-1
Big Wapwallopen Creek—stream PA-2
Big War Creek—stream TN-4
Big War Creek (CCD)—cens area TN-4
Big War Creek Division—civil TN-4
Big Ward Lake—lake MI-6
Big War Gap—gap TN-4
Big Warm Cem—cemetery MT-8
Big Warm Creek—stream MT-8
Big Warm Spring—spring NV-8
Big Warm Spring Creek MT-8
Big Warren Rsvr—reservoir AZ-5
Big Warrior Creek—stream NC-3
Big Warrior Mtn—summit NC-3
Big Wash AZ-5
Big Wash CO-8
Big Wash—stream (6) AZ-5
Big Wash—stream (4) CA-9
Big Wash—stream CO-8
Big Wash—stream (3) NV-8
Big Wash—valley CA-9
Big Wash—valley (4) UT-8
Big Wash—valley WY-8
Big Wash, The NV-8
Big Wash, The—stream NV-8
Big Wash, The—valley UT-8
Big Wash Creek NV-8
Big Wash Dam—dam UT-8
Big Wash Debris Basin Dam—dam UT-8
Big Wash Debris Basin Rsvr—reservoir UT-8
Big Washout Creek—stream OR-9
Big Wash Reservoir, The—reservoir UT-8
Big Wash Rsvr—reservoir UT-8
Big Wash Spring—spring NV-8
Big Wash Well—well AZ-5
Big Watab Lake—lake MN-6
Big Watamantago brook ME-1
Big Water UT-8
Big Water—lake AZ-5
Big Water—lake UT-8
**Big Water—pop pl** UT-8
Big Water—reservoir NV-8
Big Water Arroyo—stream CO-8
Bigwater Branch—stream TX-5
Big Water Canyon UT-8
Big Water Canyon—valley CA-9
Big Water Canyon—valley UT-8
Bigwater Canyon—valley UT-8
Big Water City UT-8
Bigwater Creek—stream WA-9
Big Watered Hollow—valley TN-4
Big Wateree Creek—stream SC-3
Big Waterfall Bay—bay AK-9
Big Water Gulch—valley ID-8
Big Water Gulch—valley UT-8
Big Water Gun Club—other CA-9
Big Water Hole—bay ID-8
Big Waterhole Creek—stream OK-5
Big Waterholes—lake CA-9
Big Water Lake—lake CA-9
Big Water Lake—lake GA-3
Big Water Oak Round—bend GA-3
Big Water Pond—swamp GA-3
Big Water Prairie—swamp GA-3
Big Water Recreation Site—locale UT-8
Big Water Slide—swamp WY-8
Big Water Spring—spring CO-8
Big Water Spring—spring NM-5
Big Water Spring—spring UT-8
Big Watts Island VA-3
Big Wax Bayou—stream LA-4
Big Wea Creek IN-6
Big Weasel Springs—spring OR-9
Big Weaver Run—stream PA-2
Big Weedy Creek—stream NE-7
Big Weidmann Lake—lake AR-4
Big Weirgor Creek—stream WI-6
Big Well—well CO-8
Big Well—well (7) NM-5
Big Well—well (2) TX-5
Big Well—well WA-9
Big Well, The—well NV-8
Big Well, The—well NM-5
**Big Wells—pop pl** TX-5
Big Wells (CCD)—cens area TX-5
Big Wells Cem—cemetery TX-5
Big Wells Oil Field—oilfield TX-5
Big Well Windmill—locale TX-5
Big West Bayou—stream FL-3
Big West Branch Escanaba River MI-6
Big West Central Well—well NM-5
Big West Fork KY-4
Big West Fork TN-4
Big West Fork Creek KY-4
Big West Fork Creek TN-4
Big West Fork Plum Creek—stream TX-5
Big West Fork Red River TN-4
Big West Meadow CA-9
Big West Pond—lake MA-1
Big Westwater Ruin—hist pl UT-8
Big West Windmill—locale TX-5
Big Wet Meadow—flat CA-9
Big Wheeler Pond VT-1
Big Wheel Gap—gap TN-4
Big Wheel Gulch CA-9
Big Wheel Gulch—valley CA-9
Big Wheeling Creek WV-2
Big Wheeling Creek Sch—school WV-2
Big Whetstone Creek—stream KY-4
Big Whetstone Creek—stream OR-9
Big Whirl—lake FL-3
Big Whisenant Cave—cave AL-4
Big Whisker Well—well AZ-5
Big Whisky Creek—stream IA-7
Big White Bay—swamp NC-3
Big White Brook—stream ME-1
Big Whitefish Sch—school MI-6
Big White Gap—gap NM-5
Big White Lake—lake AR-4
Big White Oak Run—stream WV-2
Big White Pocosin NC-3
Big White Rock—island CA-9
Big White Rock Canyon—valley UT-8
Big White Sage Canyon—valley NV-8
Big White Sage Spring—spring NV-8
Big White Sand Creek MS-4
Big Whitley Gulch—valley ID-8
Big Whitney Gulch ID-8
Big Whitney Meadow—flat CA-9
Big Widger—valley PA-2
Big Widow Bayou—stream MS-4
Big Wiemer Spring—spring NV-8
Big Wildcat Spring—spring TN-4
Big Wilderness Wash—valley AZ-5
Big Wilder Pond—lake ME-1
Big Wild Horse Creek—stream MT-8
Big Wildhorse Creek—stream OK-5
Big Wild Horse Mesa—summit UT-8
Big Wilkie Mtn—summit ME-1
Big Willard Creek—stream KY-4
Big Willard Sch—school KY-4
Big Williams Lake—lake MI-6
Big Willis Creek—stream KY-4
Big Willis Gulch CO-8
Big Willow Spring—spring ID-8
Big Willow Cem—cemetery WI-6
Big Willow Creek—stream ID-8
Big Willow Creek—stream MT-8
Big Willow Creek—stream NC-3
Big Willow Creek—stream OR-9
Big Willow Creek—stream TX-5
Big Willow Creek—stream UT-8
Big Willow Creek—stream (2) WY-8
Big Willow Ditch—canal CO-8
**Big Willow Estates Subdivision—pop pl** UT-8
Big Willow Park—flat CO-8
Big Willow Spring—spring AL-4
Big Willow Spring—spring AZ-5
Big Willow Spring—spring NM-5
Big Willow Spring—spring OR-9
Big Willow Spring Canyon—valley AZ-5
Big Willow Spring Creek—stream OR-9
Big Wills Creek—stream AL-4
Big Wills Valley—valley AL-4
Big Wilson Cliffs—cliff ME-1
Big Wilson Creek VA-3
Big Wilson Creek—stream VA-3
Big Wilson Stream—stream ME-1
Big Windfall Branch—stream NC-3
Big Windmill—locale (2) AZ-5
Big Windmill—locale CO-8
Big Windmill—locale (5) NM-5
Big Windmill—locale (3) TX-5
Big Window, The UT-8
Big Windy—locale KY-4
Big Windy Creek—stream AK-9
Big Windy Creek—stream KS-7
Big Windy Creek—stream OR-9
Big Windy Peak—summit ID-8
Big Winters Creek—stream CA-9
Big Witch Creek—stream ID-8
Big Witch Creek—stream NC-3
Big Witch Gap—gap NC-3
Big Witch Overlook—locale NC-3
Big Witch Tunnel—tunnel NC-3
Big Wolf, Lake—lake MI-6
Big Wolf Arbor—swamp FL-3
Big Wolf Branch—stream NC-3
Big Wolf Creek OR-9
Big Wolf Creek—stream WA-9
Big Wolf Lake MI-6
**Big Wolf Lake—pop pl** NY-2
Bigwood Cove—bay MD-2
Big Wood Hollow—valley TX-5
Big Wood Ridge—ridge PA-2
Big Wood River ID-8
Big Wood River—stream ID-8
Big Woods—locale KY-4
Big Woods—locale MN-6
**Big Woods—pop pl** LA-4
**Bigwoods—pop pl** MD-2
Big Woods—swamp MD-2
Big Woods—woods KY-4
Big Woods—woods NC-3
Big Woods, The—woods LA-4
Big Woods Branch—stream MD-2
Big Woods Cem—cemetery MN-6
Big Woods Ch—church MN-6
Big Woods Ch—church TX-5
Big Woods Island—island LA-4
Big Woods Sch—school IL-6
**Big Woods (Township of)—pop pl** MN-6
Big Woody Creek—stream MT-8
Big Wrangel Brook NJ-2
Big W (Township of)—unorg ME-1
Big Wye Channel—channel VA-3
Big Yancopin Lake—lake AR-4
Big Yeader Tank—reservoir TX-5
Big Yellow Arroyo—valley TX-5
Big Yellow Creek AL-4
Big Yellow Creek IN-6
Big Yellow Creek KY-4
Big Yellow Creek—stream AL-4
Big Yellow Creek—stream IN-6
Big Yellow Mtn—summit NC-3
Big Yetna River—stream AK-9
Big Yoeman—summit MO-7
Big Yo-Le-Digo Creek TX-5
Big York Lake—lake AR-4
Big Younglove Hollow—valley PA-2
Big Y Plaza—locale MA-1
Big Y Shop Ctr—locale MA-1
Big Zion AME Zion Ch—church AL-4
Big Zion Ch—church AL-4
Big Zion Ch—church NC-3
Big Zion Sch—school AL-4
Big 10 Well—well NV-8
Big 4 Ch—church OH-6
Big 4 Drainage Ditch—canal IA-7
Bihalia Creek MS-4
Bihilinie Canyon—valley AZ-5
Bihmaier Gulch—valley WA-9
Bihmaier Springs—spring WA-9
Bi Ho Ba Girl Scout Camp—locale WY-8
Bihof Island—island FM-9
Bihofu To FM-9
Bihou Park CA-9
Bihy Cem—cemetery MD-2
Biijiri MP-9
Biijiri—island MP-9
Biirijiri-to MP-9
Bi Island FM-9
Bii To FM-9
Biiziri MP-9
Bijaodibae—summit AZ-5
Bijah Spring—spring WY-8
Bijia Peak—summit GU-9
Bijia Point—summit GU-9
Bijile MP-9
Bijinkur—island MP-9
Bijire—island MP-9
Bijle MP-9
Bijou CA-9
Bijou LA-4
Bijou—locale (2) CO-8
**Bijou—pop pl** CA-9
**Bijou—pop pl** LA-4
Bijou, Bayou—gut LA-4
Bijou Basin—basin CO-8
Bijou Basin Cem—cemetery CO-8
Bijou Canal—canal CO-8
Bijou Creek CO-8
Bijou Creek—stream CO-8
Bijou Dam—dam CO-8
Bijou Flats—flat CO-8
Bijou Golf Course—other CA-9
Bijou Hills SD-7
Bijou Hills—locale SD-7
Bijou Hills—range SD-7
Bijou Lake—lake MN-6
Bijou No 2 Rsvr—reservoir CO-8
**Bijou Park—pop pl** CA-9
Bijou Ridge Sch (historical)—school SD-7
Bijou (RR name for Echo)—other LA-4
Bijou Sch—school CA-9
Bijou Sch—school SD-7
Bijou Station LA-4
Bijous Trading Post (historical)—locale SD-7
Bik—island MP-9
Bikaanyanuoru-to MP-9
Bikaar MP-9
Bikadet—island MP-9
Bikadjele MP-9
Bikajaj—island MP-9
Bikajle MP-9
Bikaniyak MP-9
Bikanol—island MP-9
Bikanyanuoru MP-9
Bikanyanuoru Island—island MP-9
Bikarakku To MP-9
Bikar Atoll—island MP-9
Bikar (County-equivalent)—civil MP-9
Bikaret MP-9

Bikaridj—island MP-9
Bikarietto MP-9
Bikar Inseln MP-9
Bikar Island MP-9
Bikar Island—island MP-9
Bikar Island Passage MP-9
Bikar Island Passage—channel MP-9
Bikar Lagoon (not verified)—lake MP-9
Bikar Passage—channel MP-9
Bikat MP-9
Bikat—island MP-9
Bike MP-9
Bikechi-to MP-9
Bikeej MP-9
Bikeelang MP-9
Bikeen MP-9
Bikeendik—island MP-9
Bi Keesh Wash—valley AZ-5
Bikeichi—island MP-9
Bikeichi Island MP-9
Bike Island MP-9
Bikej MP-9
Bikej Channel MP-9
Bikej Islet MP-9
Bikelabet Island MP-9
Bikeleango MP-9
Biken MP-9
Biken—island MP-9
Bikenaj Island MP-9
Biken Channel MP-9
Bikendik—island MP-9
Bikene MP-9
Bikeneonor MP-9
Bikenerer MP-9
Bikenerjab—island MP-9
Biken Island MP-9
Bikenkar Island MP-9
Bikenkolange—island MP-9
Bikenlibw—island MP-9
Bikennel—island MP-9
Bikenrik MP-9
Biken To MP-9
Bikeol—island MP-9
Bikerappu MP-9
Bikesat MP-9
Biketokak MP-9
Biketokeak—island MP-9
Biketolon MP-9
Biketolong—island MP-9
Bikien—island MP-9
Bikien Pass—channel MP-9
Bikin MP-9
Bikinbar MP-9
Bikine—island MP-9
Bikini—island MP-9
Bikini Atoll—island MP-9
Bikini (County-equivalent)—civil MP-9
Bikini Island MP-9
Bikini Lagoon—lake MP-9
Bikinm'ao (not verified)—island MP-9
Bikinmingjairik—island MP-9
Bikirapurabu Island MP-9
Bikirapurabu Island—island MP-9
Bikirapurapu-to MP-9
Bikirin—island MP-9
Bik Island—island MP-9
Bikkenimenshaiarekku—island MP-9
Bikku Island MP-9
Bikku-to MP-9
Biklab MP-9
Biklab—island MP-9
Biklablab—island MP-9
Biklaplap MP-9
Bi Kleesh Wash AZ-5
Biko Hodo Klizg—valley AZ-5
Biko Hodo Klizg. Boo-koo-dol-klish Canyon AZ-5
Bikoj MP-9
Bikom Island MP-9
Bikommenlok Island MP-9
Bikommwan MP-9
Bikon MP-9
Bikonbwar—island MP-9
Bikoneangwod—island MP-9
Bikonele MP-9
Bikonele—island MP-9
**Bikoniing**—pop pl MP-9
Bikonmenlok MP-9
Bikonmollok MP-9
Bikonmollok (not verified)—island MP-9
Bikonwot (not verified)—other MP-9
Bikooj island MP-9
Bikoot—island MP-9
Bikootdik—island MP-9
Bikoro—island MP-9
Bikram Island MP-9
Bikren Island MP-9
Bikrik—island MP-9
Bikrik Island MP-9
Bila Hora Cem—cemetery TX-5
Bilasha—summit AZ-5
Bilawache FM-9
Bilberry Island—island NY-2
Bilberry Swamp—swamp NY-2
**Bilboa**—pop pl NC-3
Bilbo Basin—lake MS-4
Bilbo Branch—stream LA-4
Bilbo Cem—cemetery LA-4
Bilbo Creek—stream AL-4
Bilbo Dead River—lake MS-4
Bilbo Island—island AL-4
Bilbo Lake—lake AR-4
Bilbo Lake—lake LA-4
Bilbo Lake Dam—dam MS-4
Bilbo Lookout Tower—locale MS-4
Bilbos Creek AL-4
Bilbos Ferry (historical)—locale MS-4
Bilbos Island AL-4
Bilbos Landing (historical)—locale AL-4
Bilbrey—locale TN-4
Bilbrey Basin—basin NM-5
Bilbrey Cove—cave TN-4
Bilbrey Cem—cemetery TN-4
**Bilbrey Park (subdivision)**—pop pl TN-4
Bilbrey Post Office (historical)—building (2) TN-4
Bilbro Lake Dam—dam MS-4
Bilbro School (abandoned)—locale MO-7
**Bilbros Corner**—pop pl MS-4
Bildad Ch—church TN-4
Bildad Sch (historical)—school TN-4
Bildee Cem—cemetery AL-4
Bilden—island MP-9
Bilderback Creek—stream WY-8
Bile—locale GU-9
Bile Bay—bay GU-9
Bilebuoy FM-9
Bile Cem—cemetery NY-2
Biledo Meadow—flat CA-9
Biledug FM-9
Bileebugoy FM-9
Bileebuqoy—bar FM-9
Bileeduug—summit FM-9
Bileengeel—summit FM-9
Bileeroek—summit FM-9
Bileewacheg—summit FM-9
Bileewacheq FM-9
Bileeyibuw—locale FM-9
Bilegirik—bay FM-9
Bileiliy—island FM-9
Bilengel FM-9
Bile River—stream GU-9
Biler Lake—lake MS-4
Bilerok FM-9
Biles Branch—stream LA-4
Biles Cem—cemetery MO-7
Biles Cem—cemetery TN-4
Biles Corner PA-2
Biles Creek—stream PA-2
Biles Island—island PA-2
Biles Island Channel—channel NJ-2
Biles Island Channel—channel PA-2
Biles Point—cape PA-2
Biles Sch—school TN-4
Bilewache' FM-9
Bileybu' FM-9
Bileyibuw FM-9
Bileyrich—bay FM-9
Biley Spring—spring OR-9
Bilge Creek—stream AK-9
Bilger Creek—stream OR-9
Bilger Ditch—canal IN-6
Bilger Rocks—locale PA-2
Bilger Run—stream PA-2
Bilig FM-9
Bilig—summit FM-9
Bi-lingual Baptist Mission UT-8
Bilinski Airp—airport PA-2
Biliou PW-9
Bilis Coulee MT-8
Bilisky Lake MI-6
Bilk Basin—basin CO-8
Bilk Creek MT-8
Bilk Creek—stream CO-8
Bilk Creek—stream ID-8
Bilk Creek—stream NV-8
Bilk Creek Mountains—range NV-8
Bilk Creek Mountains—range OR-9
Bilk Creek Rsvr—reservoir NV-8
Bilk Gulch—valley (2) MT-8
Bilk Lake—lake ID-8
Bilk Mtn—summit ID-8
Bilk Mtn—summit MT-8
Bill—locale WY-8
**Bill**—pop pl KY-4
Bill, Gurdon, Store—hist pl CT-1
Billae—island MP-9
Bill Allen Reservoir UT-8
Billalli Mine—mine NM-5
Bill Allred Canyon—valley UT-8
Bill Allred Creek—stream UT-8
Bill Allred Ditch—canal UT-8
Bill and Fred Harral Ranch—locale TX-5
Billard Lake WI-6
Billard Municipal Airport KS-7
Billard Table, The—bench CO-8
Bill Arp—locale GA-3
**Billarp**—pop pl GA-3
Bill Arp (CCD)—cens area GA-3
Bill Arp Creek—stream AZ-5
Bill Arp Mine—mine AZ-5
Bill Arp Mine Spring—spring AZ-5
Bill Arp Spring—spring AZ-5
Bill Aseyna Tank—reservoir NM-5
Bill Autrey Branch—stream NC-3
Bill Back Butte—summit AZ-5
Bill Back Park—flat AZ-5
Bill Back Spring—spring AZ-5
Bill Baggs Cape Florida State Park—park FL-3
Bill Bar—bar CA-9
Bill Bartley Trail—trail MT-8
Bill Bay—swamp FL-3
Bill Bayou LA-4
Bill Bayou—stream LA-4
Billberg Lake—lake AK-9
Bill Berry Creek—stream CA-9
Billberry Island NY-2
Billberry Swamp—swamp CT-1
Bill Besser Lake—lake AK-9
Bill Black Peak TX-5
Bill Blacks Cave—cave AL-4
Billboard, The—cliff UT-8
Bill Book Lake—swamp LA-4
Bill Bracket Place—locale MT-8
Bill Branch NC-3
Bill Branch—stream FL-3
Bill Branch—stream GA-3
Bill Branch—stream (2) KY-4
Bill Branch—stream (2) NC-3
Bill Branch—stream (3) TN-4
Bill Branch—stream VA-3
Bill Branch—stream WV-2
Bill Brook—stream VT-1
Bill Brown Cove—valley GA-3
Bill Brown Cove—valley OR-9
Bill Brown Hollow—valley KY-4
Bill Browns Creek—stream VA-3
Bill Buress Dam—dam SD-7
Billburys Mill (historical)—locale TN-4
Bill Canal—canal LA-4
Bill Canyon—valley AZ-5
Bill Canyon—valley UT-8
Bill Cem—cemetery CT-1
Bill Chain Branch—stream KY-4
Bill Chapman Dam—dam MS-4
Bill Cloud Lake Dam—dam MS-4
Bill Cole Mtn—summit NC-3
Billcol Mtn—summit AR-4
Bill Cove—valley GA-3
Bill Cove—valley NC-3
Bill Creek AL-4
Bill Creek GA-3
Bill Creek ID-8
Bill Creek OR-9
Bill Creek UT-8
Bill Creek—stream AL-4
Bill Creek—stream CO-8
Bill Creek—stream (2) ID-8
Bill Creek—stream LA-4
Bill Creek—stream (2) MN-6
Bill Creek—stream MS-4
Bill Creek—stream (3) MT-8
Bill Creek—stream (4) OR-9
Bill Creek—stream TN-4
Bill Creek—stream WA-9
Bill Creek Trail—trail CO-8
Bill Cross Rapids—rapids WI-6
Billdad Ch—church MO-7
Billdad Sch (abandoned)—school MO-7
Bill Daniels Catfish Ponds Dam—dam MS-4
Bill Daniels Gut—gut NC-3
Bill Dardy Hollow—valley TN-4
Bill Davenport Branch—stream NC-3
**Bill Davis**—pop pl GA-3
Bill Days Reef—bar TX-5
Bill D Branch—stream KY-4
Bill Deadening Branch—stream TN-4
Bill DeAlder Draw—valley ID-8
Bill Deavors Lake Dam—dam MS-4
Bill Deavors Pond Dam—dam MS-4
Bill Deckard Hollow—valley MO-7
Bill Decker Hollow MO-7
Billdee Creek—stream AL-4
Bill Deel Branch—stream VA-3
Bill Dees Branch Sch—school KY-4
Bill Delong Well—well NV-8
Bill Dickie Draw—valley WY-8
Bill Dick Pond—lake FL-3
Bill Dick Spring—spring AZ-5
Bill Dick Tank—reservoir AZ-5
Bill Dobbs Well—well NM-5
Bill Dodd Mill Creek AL-4
Bill Earl Spring—spring AZ-5
**Billeaud**—pop pl LA-4
Billeaud, Martial, Jr., House—hist pl LA-4
Billeaud House—hist pl LA-4
Bill Ed Bayou—stream LA-4
Billee MP-9
Billee—island MP-9
Billee Island MP-9
Bill Ellis Pit—cave AL-4
Biller Ditch—canal IN-6
Billerica MA-1
**Billerica**—pop pl MA-1
**Billerica (Billerica Center)**—pop pl MA-1
Billerica Center—other MA-1
Billerica Centre MA-1
Billerica Mills Hist Dist—hist pl MA-1
Billerica Town Common District—hist pl MA-1
**Billerica (Town of)**—pop pl MA-1
Billerica Village MA-1
Billerika MA-1
Billerika River MA-1
Billers Hollow—valley VA-3
Billet IL-6
**Billet**—pop pl IL-6
Billet Bay—bay LA-4
**Billett**—pop pl IL-6
Billett Hill IL-6
Billetts Pond—lake PA-2
Bill Evans Lake—reservoir NM-5
Billey Fork—stream KY-4
Billeys Rsvr—reservoir UT-8
Bill Faris Campground—locale CA-9
Bill Fay Memorial Park—park NC-3
Bill Finds Key—island FL-3
Billfish Brook—stream ME-1
Billfish Mtn—summit ME-1
Billfish Pond—lake ME-1
Billfold Waterhole—reservoir OR-9
Bill Fruit Trail—trail CA-9
Bill Fruit Trail—trail OR-9
Bill Frye Branch—stream WV-2
Bill Gay Island—island LA-4
Bill Gays Butte—summit NV-8
Bill Gentry Hollow—valley TN-4
Bill George Spring—spring ID-8
Bill Glover Pond—lake FL-3
Bill Good Hollow—valley MO-7
Bill Gott Spring—spring OR-9
Bill Graham Ranch—locale MT-8
Bill Grey Dam—dam AL-4
Bill Gross Camp—locale AL-4
Bill Gulch ID-8
Bill Gullege Pond Dam—dam MS-4
Bill Hare Gulch—valley CO-8
Bill Harris Branch—stream KY-4
Bill Hess Creek—stream NY-2
Bill Hess Creek—stream PA-2
Bill Hill—summit AR-4
Bill Hill—summit CT-1
Bill Hill—summit (2) TX-5
Bill Hill Creek—stream MT-8
Bill Hill Hollow—valley IL-6
Bill Hill Peak—summit AR-4
Bill Hobson Pond Dam—dam MS-4
Bill Hollow—valley AL-4
Bill Hollow—valley (5) MO-7
Bill Hooker Monmt—park WY-8
Bill Howell Dam—dam OR-9
Bill Howell Rsvr—reservoir OR-9
Bill Hunter Creek CO-8
Bill Hunter Creek WY-8
Bill Hunt Mtn—summit AR-4
Billiad Church TN-4
Billiams Creek—stream TX-5
Billiard Flats—flat CA-9
Billiard Point—cape MD-2
Billiards Knob MA-1
Billiard Table—summit MT-8
Billiard Table Mountain MT-8
Billibokka Mtn—summit CA-9
Billie-Billy Hunt Trail—trail OR-9
Billick Coulee—valley MT-8
Billie, Bayou—stream MS-4
Billie Branch—stream (2) KY-4
Billie Branch—stream (2) TN-4
Billie Branch—stream TX-5
Billie Brown Canyon—valley UT-8
Billie Butte—summit MT-8
Billie Canyon—valley NV-8
Billie Creek AZ-5
Billie Creek—stream (2) OR-9
Billie Creek—stream (2) WY-8
Billie Creek Bridge—hist pl IN-6
**Billie Creek Village**—pop pl IN-6
Billie Field Cem—cemetery MS-4
Billie Flat Top—summit UT-8
Billie Gulch—valley CA-9
Billie Mtn—summit AK-9
Billie Mtn—summit CA-9
Billie Notahs Well—well NM-5
BILLIE P. HALL (log canoe)—hist pl MD-2
Billie Pond—reservoir GA-3
Billie Quarters Steen Cem—cemetery MS-4
Billies Bay—bay FL-3
Billies Branch—stream FL-3
Billies Branch—stream KY-4
Billies Creek—stream MO-7
Billies Creek—stream TN-4
Billies Draw—valley WY-8
Billie's Island MD-2
Billies Mtn—summit UT-8
Billies Run—stream PA-2
Billie Top—summit NC-3
Billigs PA-2
Billing—locale PA-2
Billinger Pond—lake SC-3
Billinghurst, Benson Dillon, House—hist pl NV-8
Billinghurst JHS—school NV-8
Billing Marsh Cove ME-1
Billings IN-6
Billings—locale MI-6
**Billings**—pop pl MO-7
**Billings**—pop pl MT-8
**Billings**—pop pl NY-2
**Billings**—pop pl OK-5
**Billings**—pop pl WV-2
Billings, Frederick, House—hist pl MA-1
Billings, Avery Brook—stream CT-1
Billings Bench—bench MT-8
Billings Bench Sch—school MT-8
Billings Bench Water Association Canal—canal MT-8
Billings Branch—stream PA-2
Billings Brook—stream CT-1
Billings Brook—stream (3) ME-1
Billings Brook—stream (2) MA-1
Billings Brook—stream VT-1
Billings Canyon—valley CO-8
Billings (CCD)—cens area OK-5
Billings Cem—cemetery GA-3
Billings Cem—cemetery MI-6
Billings Cem—cemetery TN-4
Billings Cem—cemetery (2) TX-5
Billings Cem—cemetery VT-1
Billings Chamber of Commerce Bldg—hist pl MT-8
Billings Chapel (historical)—church MS-4
Billings County KS-7
Billings County—civil ND-7
Billings County Courthouse—hist pl ND-7
Billings Cove—bay ME-1
Billings Creek—stream AK-9
Billings Creek—stream CA-9
Billings Creek—stream IN-6
Billings Creek—stream MT-8
Billings Creek—stream OR-9
Billings Creek—stream (2) PA-2
Billings Creek—stream WI-6
Billings Creek Cem—cemetery WI-6
Billings Ditch—canal CO-8
Billings Draw—valley SD-7
Billings Elem Sch—school IN-6
Billings Falls—falls ME-1
Billings Field (historical)—locale AL-4
Billings Gap—gap AZ-5
Billings Gap Tank—reservoir AZ-5
Billingsgate MA-1
Billingsgate Shoal—bar MA-1
Billings Glacier—glacier AK-9
Billings Head—cliff AK-9
**Billings Heights (subdivision)**—pop pl MT-8
Billings Hill—locale ME-1
Billings Hill—summit (2) ME-1
Billings Hill—summit VT-1
Billings Hill Brook—stream ME-1
Billings Hill Ch—church NC-3
Billings Hist Dist—hist pl MT-8
Billings-Hougaard House hist pl UT-8
Billings Island—island MO-7
Billings Junction—other OK-5
**Billings (Kyger)**—pop pl WV-2
Billings Lake—lake CO-8
Billings Lake—lake CT-1
Billings Lake—lake IL-6
Billings Lake—lake MI-6
Billings Lake—lake ND-7
Billings Lake Natl Wildlife Ref—park ND-7
Billingslea, Mount—summit OR-9
Billingslea Cem—cemetery AL-4
Billingslea Cem—cemetery GA-3
Billingslea Draw—valley TX-5
**Billingsley**—pop pl AL-4
Billingsley, Benjamin F., House—hist pl AZ-5
Billingsley (CCD)—cens area AL-4
Billingsley Cem—cemetery AL-4
Billingsley Cem—cemetery AR-4
Billingsley Cem—cemetery GA-3
Billingsley Ch—church AL-4
Billingsley Ch—church AR-4
Billingsley Ch of Christ (historical)—church TN-4
**Billingsley (corporate name for Billingsly)**—pop pl AL-4
Billingsley Creek—stream AZ-5
Billingsley Creek—stream GA-3
Billingsley Creek—stream ID-8
Billingsley Dam—dam AZ-5
Billingsley Division—civil AL-4
Billingsley Gap—gap TN-4
Billingsley-Hills House—hist pl IA-7
Billingsley HS—school AL-4
Billingsley Number Four Dam—dam AZ-5
Billingsley Number Three Dam—dam AZ-5
Billingsley Number Two Dam—dam AZ-5
Billingsley Ranch—locale MT-8
Billingsley Rsvr Number Four—reservoir AZ-5
Billingsley Rsvr Number Three—reservoir AZ-5
Billingsley Rsvr Number Two—reservoir AZ-5
Billingsley Sch (historical)—school MS-4
Billingsley Sch (historical)—school TN-4
**Billingsleys Corner**—pop pl AR-4
Billingsley Spring—spring AZ-5
Billings Logan International Airport—airport MT-8
Billingsly Cem—cemetery MO-7
Billingsly (corporate name Billingsley) AL-4
Billingsly Creek—stream UT-8
Billingsly Hill—summit SC-3
Billings Marsh—swamp VT-1
Billings Marsh Cove ME-1
Billings Mill Brook—stream PA-2
Billings Missionary Ch—church MI-6
Billings Oil Field—other MI-6
Billings Park—park WI-6
**Billings Park**—pop pl WI-6
Billings Park—uninc pl WI-6
Billings Pass—gap UT-8
Billings Point—cape AK-9
Billings Pond MA-1
Billings Pond—lake ME-1
Billings Pond—lake NH-1
Billings Pond—lake VT-1
Billings Pond—reservoir PA-2
Billings Pond Dam—dam PA-2
Billings Ponds—lake ME-1
**Billingsport**—pop pl NJ-2
Billingsport Range—channel NJ-2
Billingsport Range—channel PA-2
Billingsport Sch—school NJ-2
Billings Racetrack—other MT-8
Billings Ranch—locale (2) TX-5
Billings Rapids—rapids OR-9
Billings Sch—school KS-7
Billings Sch—school NY-2
Billings Sch—school WV-2
Billings Slough—gut MO-7
Billings Slough—stream MT-8
Billings Spring—spring CO-8
Billings Spring—spring TX-5
Billings Station—locale PA-2
**Billingstown**—pop pl OH-6
**Billings Township**—pop pl ND-7
**Billings (Township of)**—pop pl MI-6
Billings Trail—trail PA-2
Billings Union Cem—cemetery OK-5
Billings VA Hosp—hospital IN-6
Billingsville KS-7
Billingsville—locale MO-7
**Billingsville**—pop pl IN-6
Billingsville Sch—school MO-7
Billingsville Sch—school NC-3
**Billington**—pop pl TX-5
Billington Bay—bay NY-2
**Billington Bay**—pop pl NY-2
Billington Bldg—hist pl OK-5
Billington Brook—stream ME-1
Billington Cem—cemetery TX-5
Billington Ch—church TX-5
Billington Creek—stream KY-4
Billington Heights—CDP NY-2
Billington Ice Pond MA-1
Billington Lake—lake IN-6
Billington Ledge—flat MA-1
Billington Sea—reservoir MA-1
Billington Sea Dam—dam MA-1
Billion Slough—stream AK-9
Billiot, Lake—lake LA-4
Billiot Canal—canal LA-4
Billips Cem—cemetery VA-3
Billirrikey MA-1
Bill Jack Gap—gap TN-4
Bill Jack Ridge—ridge IN-6
Bill John Bayou—stream LA-4
Bill Johnston Hollow—valley TN-4
Bill Jones Ranch—locale NM-5
Bill Kamradt Ranch—locale NM-5
Bill Keen Branch—stream VA-3
Bill King Branch—stream WV-2
Bill Kinney Cove—bay ME-1
Bill Knob—summit WV-2
Bill Kutch Hollow—valley TN-4
Bill Lake—lake CA-9
Bill Lake—lake (2) MN-6
Bill Lake—lake (2) WA-9
Bill Lane Camp—locale CA-9
Bill Lee Mesa—summit NM-5
Bill Lee Spring—spring AZ-5
Bill Lewis Cienega—stream NM-5
Bill Lewis Creek—stream OR-9
Bill Lewis Tank—reservoir NM-5
Bill Lindshov Dam—dam (2) SD-7
Bill Link Pond Dam—dam (2) MS-4
Bill Little Brook—stream NH-1
Bill Long Hollow—valley KY-4
Bill Macks Creek—stream MO-7
Bill Mac Spring—spring MO-7
Bill Majors Canyon—valley NV-8
**Billman**—pop pl MO-7
Billman Canal—canal ID-8
Billman Creek—stream MT-8
Billman Ditch—canal IN-6
Billman Lake—lake SD-7
Bill Mann Branch—stream KY-4
Bill Martin Memorial Airp—airport MO-7
Bill May Lake Dam—dam MS-4
Bill McClintock Draw—valley AZ-5
Bill McLean Pond Dam—dam MS-4
Bill McNabb Gulf—valley TN-4
Bill Merill Mountain ME-1
Bill Merrill Mtn—summit ME-1
Billmeyer—locale PA-2
Billmeyer, Daniel, House—hist pl PA-2
Billmeyer, Michael, House—hist pl PA-2
Billmeyer Cem—cemetery PA-2
Billmeyer House—hist pl PA-2
Bill Miller Ridge—ridge PA-2
Bill Miller Trail—trail PA-2
Bill Moore Branch—stream KY-4
Bill Moore Canyon—valley CA-9
Bill Moore Creek—stream NC-3
Bill Moore Creek—stream OR-9
Bill Moore Lake—lake CO-8
Bill Moore Planting Company Pond Dam—dam MS-4
Bill Moore Ridge—ridge CA-9
**Bill Moores**—pop pl AK-9
Bill Moore's ANV739—reserve AK-9
**Billmore**—pop pl MO-7
Billmore Hollow—valley MO-7
Billmore Township—civil MO-7
Bill Morgan Canyon—valley ID-8
Bill Morris Pond—lake ME-1
Bill Mott Bayou—lake TX-5
Bill Mtn—summit GA-3
Bill Mtn—summit MS-4
Billmyer PA-2
**Billmyer (Billmeyer)**—pop pl PA-2
Billmyer East Cave—cave PA-2
Billmyer Station—locale PA-2
Bill Neal Island—island NC-3
Bill Neighbor Peak—summit OR-9
Bill Nye Mine—mine NV-8
Bill Nye Mine—mine OR-9
Bill Oak Branch—stream KY-4
Billo Lake—lake MN-6
Bill One Cave—cave AL-4
Billottis Slough—swamp AR-4
Billou-Stillwell-Perine House—hist pl NY-2
Billover Creek—stream SD-7
Billow Memorial Chapel—church OH-6
Billows—locale KY-4
**Billows**—pop pl KY-4
Billows Lake—lake ND-7
Billow-Thompson House—hist pl TX-5
Bill Parks Tank—reservoir NM-5
Bill Peak—summit OR-9
Bill Perry Branch—stream KY-4
Bill Pete Spring—spring OR-9
Bill Pinney Spring—spring UT-8
Bill Platt Slide UT-8
Bill Point—cape AK-9
Bill Pond NY-2
Bill Raines Mtn—summit NC-3
Bill Rice Branch—stream KY-4
Bill Ridge—ridge GA-3
Bill Ridge—ridge LA-4
Bill Ridge—ridge VA-3
Bill Riley Creek—stream AZ-5
Bill Riley Spring—spring AZ-5
Bill Rsvr—reservoir ID-8
Bill Run—stream WV-2
Bills—locale ID-8
Bills Arm—canal FL-3
Billsbach Lake—lake IL-6
Billsback IL-6
Bills Basin—basin UT-8
Bills Bay (Carolina Bay)—swamp NC-3
Bills Bayou AR-4
Bills Bayou—stream (2) AR-4
Billsboro—locale NY-2
**Billsboro Corners**—pop pl NY-2
Bills Branch—stream (4) AL-4
Bills Branch—stream AR-4
Bills Branch—stream IN-6
Bills Branch—stream (5) KY-4
Bills Branch—stream (2) LA-4
Bills Branch—stream (2) NC-3
Bills Branch—stream (2) TN-4
Bills Branch—stream VA-3
Bills Branch—stream (5) WV-2
**Billsburg**—pop pl SD-7
Bills Cabin—locale CA-9
Bills Cabin Spring—spring CA-9
Bills Canyon—valley ID-8
Bills Canyon—valley NV-8
Bills Canyon—valley UT-8
Bills Cem—cemetery AR-4
Bills Cem—cemetery IN-6
Bills Cem—cemetery MS-4
Bills Cem—cemetery (3) TN-4
Bill Sch—school MS-4
Bill Schroeder Tank—reservoir AZ-5
Bills Corner—locale OK-5
Bills Coulee—valley MT-8
Bill's Cove NY-2
Bills Creek AL-4
Bills Creek OR-9
Bills Creek TN-4
**Bills Creek**—pop pl NC-3
Bills Creek—stream CA-9
Bills Creek—stream CO-8
Bills Creek—stream ID-8
Bills Creek—stream IL-6
Bills Creek—stream IN-6
Bills Creek—stream (2) KS-7
Bills Creek—stream KY-4
Bills Creek—stream (2) LA-4
Bills Creek—stream MI-6
Bills Creek—stream (2) MO-7
Bills Creek—stream NE-7
Bills Creek—stream (3) NC-3
Bills Creek—stream (2) OK-5
Bills Creek—stream (3) OR-9
Bills Creek—stream TN-4
Bills Creek—stream TX-5
Bills Creek—stream (3) WV-2
Bills Creek—stream WI-6
Bills Creek—stream WY-8
Bills Creek Cem—cemetery TN-4
Bills Creek Landing—locale NC-3
Bills Creek Sch—school TN-4
Bills Drain—canal MI-6
Bills Draw—valley UT-8
Bills Fishpond—reservoir NV-8
Bills Fork—stream UT-8
Bills Fork—stream (2) WV-2
Bills Gulch—valley MT-8
Bills Gulch—valley OR-9
Bills Gut—gut NJ-2
Bill Shaw Canyon—valley UT-8
Bill Shaw Tank—reservoir NM-5
Bills Hill CT-1
Bills Hill—summit CA-9
Bills Hole Tank—reservoir NM-5
Bills Hollow—valley MO-7
Bill Siding—locale KY-4
Bill Simms Spring—spring AZ-5
Bills Island—island ME-1
Bills Island—island RI-1
Bills Knob—summit NC-3
Bills Lake—lake (2) ID-8
Bills Lake—lake KY-4
Bills Lake—lake MI-6
Bills Lake—lake MN-6
Bills Lake—lake UT-8
Bills Lake—lake WI-6
Bills Lakes—lake IN-6
Bills Landing—locale AL-4

Bills Lick—*stream* WV-2
Bills Marina—*locale* AL-4
Bills-McNeal Hist Dist—*hist pl* TN-4
Bill Smith Brook—*stream* ME-1
Bill Smith Creek—*stream* MT-8
Bill Smith Hollow—*valley* MO-7
Bill Smith Lake—*reservoir* TN-4
Bill Smith Lake Dam—*dam* TN-4
Bill Smith Slough—*lake* SD-7
Bill Smith Springs—*spring* NV-8
**Bill Smith Subdivision**—*pop pl* TN-4
Bills Mtn—*summit* NC-3
Bills Mtn—*summit* WY-8
Bills Park—*flat* UT-8
Bills Park—*flat* WY-8
Bills Pass—*gap* OR-9
*Bills Peak* OR-9
Bills Peak—*summit* CO-8
Bills Peak—*summit* NV-8
Bills Peak—*summit* WY-8
Bills Pier—*locale* TN-4
**Bills Place (historical)**—*pop pl* PA-2
Bills Point—*cape* NY-2
Bills Point—*cliff* IN-6
Bills Pond—*lake* GA-3
Bills Pond—*lake* LA-4
Bills Pond—*lake* (2) NY-2
Bills Pond—*lake* VA-3
Bill Spring—*spring* AZ-5
Bill Spring—*spring* NM-5
Bill Spring—*spring* OR-9
Bills Ranch Lake—*lake* CO-8
Bills Ridge—*ridge* VA-3
Bills Rohlfs Drain—*canal* MI-6
Bills Run—*stream* IL-6
Bills Sch—*school* MO-7
Bills Spring—*spring* AZ-5
Bills Spring—*spring* ID-8
Bills Spring—*spring* (2) NV-8
Bills Spring—*spring* OR-9
Bills Spring—*spring* UT-8
Bills Swamp—*stream* NC-3
Bills Tank—*lake* NM-5
Bills Tank—*reservoir* (4) AZ-5
Bill Stewart Activity Center—*school* AL-4
**Billstown**—*pop pl* AR-4
Billstown Cem—*cemetery* AR-4
Bill Strahand Lake Dam—*dam* MS-4
Bills Trail—*trail* PA-2
Bill Swamp—*swamp* FL-3
Bill Taber Cabin—*locale* OR-9
Bill Tank—*reservoir* AZ-5
Bill Tank—*reservoir* (2) NM-5
Bill Taylor Tank—*reservoir* TX-5
Bill Top—*summit* NC-3
**Billtown**—*pop pl* IN-6
Billtown Cem—*cemetery* IN-6
Bill Turner Lake Dam—*dam* MS-4
Bill Two Cave—*cave* AL-4
Bill Tyler Gulch—*valley* CO-8
Billup Creek—*stream* MT-8
Billups—*locale* MS-4
Billups Branch—*stream* IA-7
Billups Branch—*stream* MS-4
Billups Branch—*stream* MO-7
Billups Cem—*cemetery* (2) MO-7
Billup Sch—*school* MT-8
Billups Chapel—*church* MS-4
Billups Creek—*stream* MS-4
Billups Creek—*stream* VA-3
Billups Gap Cem—*cemetery* WV-2
*Billups Gate* MS-4
Billups Grove Ch—*church* GA-3
Billups Gulch—*valley* WA-9
Billups House—*hist pl* VA-3
Billups Plantation Airp—*airport* MS-4
Billups Pond—*lake* FL-3
*Billups Station* MS-4
Bill Valley—*valley* WI-6
Bill Vest Windmill—*locale* TX-5
**Billville**—*pop pl* IN-6
Bill Walker Creek—*stream* TX-5
Bill Walker Pond Dam—*dam* MS-4
Bill Wallace Ground—*bar* ME-1
Bill Wallace Lake Dam—*dam* MS-4
Bill Waller, Lake—*reservoir* MS-4
Bill Waller Lake Dam—*dam* MS-4
Bill Walters Cave—*cave* TN-4
Bill Warner Spring—*spring* PA-2
Bill Watson Lake Dam—*dam* MS-4
Bill Welch Gulch—*valley* WA-9
Bill Weller Mesa—*summit* CO-8
Bill West Draw—*valley* TX-5
Bill West Tank—*reservoir* AZ-5
Bill West Windmill—*locale* TX-5
Bill White Canyon—*valley* NE-7
Bill White Creek—*stream* NC-3
Bill White Mtn—*summit* NY-2
Bill White Run—*stream* WV-2
Bill White Spring—*spring* CO-8
Bill Wilks Swamp—*swamp* TN-4
Bill Williams Canyon—*valley* ID-8
Bill Williams Creek—*stream* CA-9
*Bill Williams Fork* AZ-5
*Bill Williams Fork River* AZ-5
Bill Williams Lake Dam—*dam* MS-4
*Bill Williams Mountains* AZ-5
Bill Williams Mountains—*range* AZ-5
Bill Williams Mtn—*summit* AZ-5
Bill Williams River—*stream* AZ-5
Bill Williams Spring—*spring* (2) AZ-5
Bill Williams Tank—*reservoir* AZ-5
Bill Wood Branch—*stream* MS-4
Billwood Creek—*stream* AL-4
Bill Woods Tank—*reservoir* AZ-5
Billy, Isaac, Homestead and Family Cemetery—*hist pl* OK-5
*Billy Ache Canyon* CA-9
Billy Alexander Pond Dam—*dam* MS-4
Billy Al Mine—*mine* KY-4
Bill Yates Rsvr—*reservoir* WY-8
Billy Back Draw—*valley* AZ-5
Billy Back Spring—*spring* AZ-5
Billy Back Tank—*reservoir* AZ-5
Billy Basin—*basin* AK-9
Billy Bayou—*stream* LA-4
Billy Bell Trail—*trail* OK-5
Billy Boy Dam—*dam* WI-6
Billy Boy Flowage—*reservoir* WI-6
*Billy Branch* AL-4
*Billy Branch* MO-7
*Billy Branch* WV-2
Billy Branch—*stream* AL-4
Billy Branch—*stream* FL-3
Billy Branch—*stream* GA-3
Billy Branch—*stream* (4) KY-4
Billy Branch—*stream* MS-4
Billy Branch—*stream* (2) NC-3
Billy Branch—*stream* SC-3
Billy Branch—*stream* TN-4
Billy Branch—*stream* (3) WV-2
Billy Branch Dam—*dam* TN-4
Billy Branch Lake—*reservoir* TN-4
Billy Branch Sch—*school* WV-2
Billy Brook—*stream* ME-1
*Billy Brown Trail* PA-2
Billy Buck Run—*stream* PA-2
Billy Burr Lake—*lake* OR-9
Billy Byrd Dam—*dam* AL-4
Billy Cabin Ridge—*ridge* NC-3
Billy Canyon—*valley* OR-9
Billy Canyon—*valley* WY-8
Billy Canyon Rsvr No 1—*reservoir* WY-8
Billy Carter Lake Dam—*dam* AL-4
Billy Cem—*cemetery* OK-5
Billy Chinook, Lake—*reservoir* OR-9
*Billy Chinook Lake* OR-9
Billy Clapp Lake—*reservoir* WA-9
Billy Coulee—*valley* MT-8
Billy Cove—*valley* AL-4
Billy Cove—*valley* (2) NC-3
Billy Cove Gap—*gap* NC-3
Billy Cove Knob—*summit* NC-3
Billy Cox Branch—*stream* KY-4
*Billy Creek* IN-6
*Billy Creek* OR-9
Billy Creek—*stream* (3) AK-9
Billy Creek—*stream* AZ-5
Billy Creek—*stream* (2) CA-9
Billy Creek—*stream* CO-8
Billy Creek—*stream* FL-3
Billy Creek—*stream* (2) GA-3
Billy Creek—*stream* (3) ID-8
Billy Creek—*stream* IN-6
Billy Creek—*stream* KY-4
Billy Creek—*stream* LA-4
Billy Creek—*stream* (2) MS-4
Billy Creek—*stream* MO-7
Billy Creek—*stream* (3) MT-8
Billy Creek—*stream* (2) OK-5
Billy Creek—*stream* (4) OR-9
Billy Creek—*stream* TX-5
Billy Creek—*stream* VA-3
Billy Creek—*stream* (2) WA-9
Billy Creek—*stream* WV-2
Billy Creek—*stream* (2) WI-6
Billy Creek—*stream* (2) WY-8
Billy Creek Sch—*school* WY-8
Billy Creek Spring—*spring* WY-8
*Billy Culp Spring* AL-4
Billy Ditch—*stream* TX-5
Billy Doe Bog—*swamp* ME-1
Billy Dotson Branch—*stream* KY-4
Billy Dowden Cem—*cemetery* LA-4
Billy Dunlop Park—*park* TN-4
Billy Ferrell Pond Dam—*dam* MS-4
Billy Fork—*stream* VA-3
Billy Fork Creek—*stream* GA-3
Billy Gap—*gap* NC-3
Billy Glen Creek—*stream* AK-9
Billy Goat Bay—*bay* LA-4
Billygoat Cave—*cave* AL-4
Billy Goat Cave—*cave* TN-4
Billy Goat Cliff—*cliff* TN-4
Billy Goat Corral—*locale* WA-9
Billy Goat Creek—*stream* (2) AK-9
Billy Goat Gulch—*valley* MT-8
Billy Goat Gulch—*valley* WA-9
**Billy Goat Hill**—*pop pl* AL-4
**Billy Goat Hill**—*pop pl* LA-4
Billy Goat Hill—*summit* AR-4
Billy Goat Hill—*summit* CO-8
Billy Goat Hill—*summit* ID-8
Billy Goat Hill—*summit* KY-4
Billygoat Hollow—*valley* WV-2
Billy Goat Island—*island* GA-3
Billy Goat Island—*island* ID-8
Billy Goat Island—*island* OR-9
Billy Goat Knolls—*summit* AZ-5
Billygoat Mtn—*summit* AK-9
Billy Goat Mtn—*summit* CA-9
Billy Goat Mtn—*summit* (2) WA-9
Billy Goat Pass—*gap* WA-9
Billy Goat Peak—*summit* CA-9
Billy Goat Peak—*summit* NV-8
Billy Goat Point—*summit* CO-8
Billy Goat Spring—*spring* AZ-5
Billy Goat Wash—*stream* AZ-5
Billy Good Lake—*lake* MI-6
Billy Gulch—*valley* CA-9
Billy Gulch—*valley* OR-9
Billy Gulch Spring—*spring* OR-9
Billy Hall Bend—*bend* OK-5
Billy Harry Pond Dam—*dam* MS-4
Billy Hawk Creek—*stream* AK-9
Billy Haws Canyon—*valley* UT-8
Billy Hill—*summit* CA-9
Billy Hill Hollow—*valley* TN-4
Billy Hill Reedy Creek—*stream* MS-4
Billy Hole—*lake* TX-5
Billy Hollow—*valley* MO-7
Billy Hollow—*valley* (2) TN-4
*Billy Island* MD-2
Billy Jack Brook—*stream* ME-1
Billy-Jack Depot—*locale* ME-1
Billy Joe Point—*cape* FL-3
Billy Johns Trail—*trail* MT-8
Billy Jones Creek—*stream* OR-9
Billy Jones Lake—*lake* OR-9
Billy June Tank—*reservoir* AZ-5
Billy King Branch—*stream* NC-3
Billy Lake—*lake* AK-9
Billy Lake—*lake* CA-9
Billy Lake—*lake* FL-3
Billy Lake—*lake* MO-7
Billy Lake—*lake* OR-9
Billy Lawrence Canyon—*valley* AZ-5
Billy Lawrence Creek—*stream* AZ-5
Billy Littles Lake—*lake* LA-4
Billy Lowe Branch—*stream* KY-4
Billy Lynch Well—*well* AZ-5
Billy Mack Canyon—*valley* CA-9
Billy Mack Flat—*flat* CA-9
Billy Mack Mine—*mine* AZ-5
Billy Mack Mtn—*summit* AZ-5
*Billy Mann Ditch* IN-6
*Billymead* VT-1
Billy Meadows—*flat* OR-9
Billy Meadows Guard Station—*locale* OR-9
Billy Methvin Creek—*stream* GA-3
*Billy Meyer Stadium* TN-4
*Billy Michel Airport* NC-3
Billy Mine—*mine* MT-8
Billy Mitchell Airp—*airport* NC-3
Billy Mitchell Air Strip—*airport* NC-3
Billy Mitchell Sch—*school* (2) CA-9
Billy Moore Creek—*stream* OR-9
Billy Moore Lake—*lake* AR-4
Billy Mtn—*summit* GA-3
Billy Mtn—*summit* NY-2
Billy Mtn—*summit* (2) OR-9
Billy Ought Hollow—*valley* TN-4
Bill Young Bayou—*stream* AR-4
Bill Young Branch—*stream* VA-3
Bill Young Creek—*stream* WY-8
Bill Young Gap—*gap* VA-3
Billy Packwood Spring—*reservoir* CA-9
Billy Pees Windmill—*locale* TX-5
Billy Pike Creek—*stream* CA-9
Billy Pike Ridge—*ridge* CA-9
Billy Place—*hist pl* GA-3
Billy Pond—*lake* MS-4
Billy Pope Spring—*spring* NV-8
Billy Quinn Grave—*cemetery* OR-9
Billy Rhodes Creek—*stream* ID-8
Billy Rice Canyon—*valley* NM-5
Billy Richardson Branch—*stream* TN-4
Billy Ridge—*ridge* AL-4
Billy Ridge—*ridge* TN-4
Billy Ridge—*ridge* WA-9
Billy Run—*stream* WV-2
Billys Bayou—*gut* LA-4
Billys Bayou Lake—*lake* LA-4
Billys Branch—*stream* (2) AL-4
Billys Branch—*stream* FL-3
Billys Branch—*stream* KY-4
Billys Branch—*stream* (2) MO-7
Billys Branch—*stream* NC-3
Billys Branch—*stream* VA-3
Billys Branch Sch—*school* KY-4
Billys Canyon—*valley* UT-8
*Billys Creek* AL-4
*Billys Creek* MO-7
Billys Creek—*stream* (2) MS-4
Billys Creek—*stream* NC-3
Billys Creek—*stream* OR-9
Billys Creek—*stream* TX-5
Billys Creek Windmill—*locale* TX-5
Billys Ditch—*canal* NC-3
Billys Ford—*locale* AL-4
Billys Gulch—*valley* CA-9
Billys Gulch—*valley* OR-9
Billy Shaw Slough—*stream* ID-8
Billy Shaw Slough—*stream* NV-8
Billys Hill—*summit* CA-9
Billys Hole—*lake* AK-9
Billys Hole Creek—*stream* ID-8
Billy Sink—*basin* AZ-5
*Billy's Island* MD-2
Billys Island—*island* GA-3
Billys Island—*island* MD-2
Billys Knob—*summit* NC-3
Billys Lake—*lake* GA-3
Billys Lake—*lake* MN-6
Billys Lake—*lake* NE-7
Billys Lake—*lake* WY-8
Billys Lake—*swamp* GA-3
Billy Slope Canyon—*valley* UT-8
Billy Small Meadow—*flat* OR-9
Billy Snipe Rsvr—*reservoir* ID-8
Billys Peak—*summit* (2) CA-9
Billys Point—*cape* FL-3
Billys Point—*cape* MD-2
Billy Spring—*spring* (2) AZ-5
Billy Spring—*spring* CA-9
Billy Spring—*spring* (2) UT-8
Billys Shore—*beach* ME-1
Billys Tank—*reservoir* AZ-5
Billy Stone Cave—*cave* TN-4
Billy Sunday Tabernacle—*church* IN-6
*Billysville* GA-3
Billys Woods—*woods* NC-3
Billy Tank—*reservoir* AZ-5
Billy The Kid Spring—*spring* NM-5
Billy Top—*summit* NC-3
Billyville—*locale* GA-3
*Billy Walters Creek* MS-4
Billy Wash—*stream* AZ-5
Billy West Canyon—*valley* UT-8
*Billy Williams Creek* CA-9
Billy Williams Creek—*stream* CA-9
Billy Williams Ridge—*ridge* CA-9
Billy Wood Spring—*spring* CO-8
Billy Young Creek—*stream* SD-7
Bilman Ridge—*ridge* PA-2
Bilodeau Brook—*stream* MA-1
Bilodeau Sch—*school* ND-7
**Bilodeau Township**—*pop pl* ND-7
Biloechaang—*locale* FM-9
**Biloxi**—*pop pl* MS-4
**Biloxi**—*pop pl* TX-5
Biloxi, Bayou—*gut* LA-4
Biloxi Bay—*bay* MS-4
Biloxi Cem—*cemetery* TX-5
Biloxi Ch—*church* TX-5
Biloxi City Hall—*building* MS-4
Biloxi Community Center—*building* MS-4
Biloxi Creek—*stream* TX-5
Biloxi Creek Ch—*church* MS-4
Biloxi District Ranger Station—*building* MS-4
Biloxi Federal Courthouse—*building* MS-4
Biloxi Garden Center—*hist pl* MS-4
Biloxi HS—*school* MS-4
Biloxi Lagoon—*lake* LA-4
Biloxi Library—*building* MS-4
Biloxi Lighthouse—*locale* MS-4
Biloxi Municipal Stadium—*park* MS-4
Biloxi Post Office—*building* MS-4
Biloxi Regional Med Ctr—*hospital* MS-4
Biloxi River—*stream* MS-4
Biloxi Sch—*school* (2) TX-5
Biloxi Seafood Industry Museum—*building* MS-4
Biloxi Small Craft Harbor—*harbor* MS-4
Biloxi State Wildlife Mngmt Area—*park* LA-4
Biloxi's Tivoli Hotel—*hist pl* MS-4
Biloxi Wash—*stream* CA-9
Biloxi Yacht Club—*locale* MS-4
Bilquist Sch—*school* OR-9
Bilsky Lake—*lake* MI-6
**Bilspur**—*pop pl* MN-6
*Biltabito* NM-5
*Biltabito Creek* NM-5
*Biltabito Spring* NM-5
*Biltmore* NC-3
**Biltmore**—*pop pl* FL-3
**Biltmore**—*pop pl* NC-3
**Biltmore**—*pop pl* TN-4
**Biltmore**—*pop pl* VA-3
Biltmore Baptist Ch—*church* TN-4
**Biltmore Beach**—*pop pl* FL-3
Biltmore (CCD)—*cens area* TN-4
Biltmore Country Club—*other* IL-6
Biltmore Division—*civil* TN-4
Biltmore Estate—*hist pl* NC-3
Biltmore Estate Office—*hist pl* NC-3
Biltmore Fashion Park Shop Ctr—*locale* AZ-5
**Biltmore Forest**—*pop pl* NC-3
Biltmore Forest Country Club—*locale* NC-3
Biltmore Forest Sch—*hist pl* NC-3
*Biltmore Gardens* OH-6
**Biltmore Gates (subdivision)**—*pop pl* (2) AZ-5
Biltmore Golf Course—*locale* FL-3
**Biltmore Greens III (subdivision)**—*pop pl* (2) AZ-5
**Biltmore Hills (subdivision)**—*pop pl* NC-3
Biltmore Hotel—*hist pl* OH-6
Biltmore Hot Springs—*locale* MT-8
Biltmore House—*building* NC-3
Biltmore Industries, Inc.—*hist pl* NC-3
Biltmore-Oteen Bank Bldg—*hist pl* NC-3
Biltmore Sch—*school* (2) FL-3
Biltmore Shoe Store—*hist pl* NC-3
Biltmore Shop Ctr—*locale* AZ-5
**Biltmore Shores**—*pop pl* NY-2
**Biltmore (subdivision)**—*pop pl* FL-3
**Biltmore (subdivision)**—*pop pl* NC-3
Biltmore Switch—*locale* AR-4
Biltmore Village Commercial Buildings—*hist pl* NC-3
Biltmore Village Cottage District—*hist pl* NC-3
Biltmore Village Cottages—*hist pl* NC-3
**Biltmore Villas (subdivision)**—*pop pl* (2) AZ-5
**Bilvia**—*pop pl* KY-4
Bilwaddy Creek—*stream* AK-9
Bilyeu Cem—*cemetery* IL-6
Bilyue Cem—*cemetery* OR-9
Bilz, Aloys, House—*hist pl* MI-6
**Bim**—*pop pl* WV-2
Bimahyook Creek—*stream* AK-9
*Bimams* MD-2
Bimba Island—*island* NH-1
Bimber Corners—*locale* PA-2
Bimber Run—*stream* PA-2
**Bimble**—*pop pl* KY-4
Bim Creek—*stream* ID-8
*Bimeleck Brook* MA-1
*Bimelick Brook* MA-1
Bimerick Creek—*stream* ID-8
Bimerick Meadows—*flat* ID-8
Bi-Metalic Gulch—*valley* MT-8
Bimetalic Mtn—*summit* WA-9
*Bi-metalic Ridge* ID-8
Bimetallic Mine—*mine* OR-9
Bimetallic Ridge—*ridge* ID-8
Bimetals Mine—*mine* AZ-5
Bimettalist Mine—*mine* CO-8
Bimini—*locale* FL-3
Bimini Basin—*lake* FL-3
Bimini Bay—*bay* FL-3
Bimiut (Site)—*locale* AK-9
Bimiut (Summer Camp)—*locale* AK-9
**Bimo**—*pop pl* MI-6
Bimson Blacksmith Shop—*hist pl* CO-8
**Bina**—*pop pl* NC-3
Binaew—*locale* FM-9
Binagami Lake—*lake* MN-6
Binajoaksmiut—*locale* AK-9
Binajoaksmiut River—*stream* AK-9
Binaksbak Bluff—*cliff* AK-9
Binakslit Bluff—*cliff* AK-9
Binalik Crater—*crater* AK-9
Binarch Creek—*stream* ID-8
Binarch Creek—*stream* WA-9
Binarch Mtn—*summit* ID-8
Binat-Ingrat Hill—*summit* AK-9
*Binau* FM-9
*Binaw* FM-9
Binckley Gulch—*valley* CO-8
Binco Place—*locale* CO-8
Binco Rsvr—*reservoir* CO-8
Binder, Lake—*park* IA-7
Binder Gulch—*valley* OR-9
Binder Lake—*lake* ID-8
Binder Lake—*lake* WI-6
Binder Lake—*reservoir* MO-7
Binder Memorial Park—*park* MO-7
Binder Slough—*stream* OR-9
Binder Spring—*spring* OR-9
Binder Spring Number Two—*spring* OR-9
Bindley Hardware Company Bldg—*hist pl* PA-2
Bindloss Brook—*stream* CT-1
Bindnagles Evangelical Lutheran Church—*hist pl* PA-2
Binegar Butte—*summit* OR-9
*Binejrak* MP-9
Binek Mine—*mine* ND-7
Bine Lake—*lake* MN-6
*Biner Lake* WA-9
**Binfield**—*pop pl* TN-4
Binfield (CCD)—*cens area* TN-4
Binfield Division—*civil* TN-4
Binfield Elem Sch—*school* TN-4
Binfield JHS (historical)—*school* TN-4
Binfield Methodist Ch—*church* TN-4
Binfield Post Office (historical)—*building* TN-4
**Binford**—*pop pl* MS-4
**Binford**—*pop pl* ND-7
**Binford**—*pop pl* WY-8
Binford, Lake—*reservoir* VA-3
Binford, Thaddeus, House—*hist pl* IA-7
Binford Cem—*cemetery* (2) AL-4
Binford Cem—*cemetery* ND-7
Binford (historical)—*locale* MS-4
*Binford Junior High School* IN-6
Binford MS—*school* IN-6
Binford Park—*locale* TX-5
Binford Park—*park* IN-6
Binford Ranch—*locale* TX-5
Binford Rsvr—*reservoir* OR-9
Binford Sch—*school* VA-3
Binford Store—*locale* VA-3
Bing—*locale* MT-8
Bingaman Canyon—*valley* OK-5
Bingaman Lake—*lake* CA-9
Bingaman Pond—*lake* WA-9
Bingamin Ranch—*locale* CA-9
**Bingamon**—*pop pl* WV-2
Bingamon Ch—*church* WV-2
Bingamon Creek—*stream* WV-2
**Bingamon Junction**—*pop pl* WV-2
Bing Branch—*stream* AL-4
Bing Canyon—*valley* WA-9
Bingell Drain—*stream* MI-6
*Bingen* (2) IN-6
*Bingen* OH-6
**Bingen**—*pop pl* AR-4
**Bingen**—*pop pl* PA-2
**Bingen**—*pop pl* WA-9
Bingen Gap—*gap* OR-9
Bingen Gap—*gap* WA-9
Bingen Range Channel—*channel* OR-9
Bingen-White Salmon (RR name for White Salmon)—*other* WA-9
**Binger**—*pop pl* OK-5
Binger Canyon—*valley* WA-9
Binger Cem—*cemetery* OK-5
Binger-Hinton (CCD)—*cens area* OK-5
**Binger (historical)**—*pop pl* OR-9
Bing Gap—*gap* WV-2
Binggeli Island—*island* MO-7
*Bingham* UT-8
Bingham—*locale* AL-4
Bingham—*locale* NM-5
Bingham—*locale* WV-2
**Bingham**—*pop pl* IL-6
**Bingham**—*pop pl* IA-7
**Bingham**—*pop pl* ME-1
**Bingham**—*pop pl* MI-6
**Bingham**—*pop pl* MN-6
**Bingham**—*pop pl* NE-7
**Bingham**—*pop pl* OH-6
**Bingham**—*pop pl* PA-2
**Bingham**—*pop pl* SC-3
**Bingham**—*pop pl* TN-4
**Bingham**—*pop pl* UT-8
Bingham, George Caleb, House—*hist pl* MO-7
Bingham, John H., House—*hist pl* TX-5
Bingham, Judge John A., House—*hist pl* WI-6
Bingham, Lake—*lake* FL-3
Bingham, Richard, House—*hist pl* AZ-5
Bingham Basin—*basin* OR-9
Bingham Bay—*bay* MI-6
Bingham-Blossom House—*hist pl* FL-3
*Bingham Branch* TX-5
Bingham Branch—*stream* (3) KY-4
Bingham Branch—*stream* (2) TN-4
Bingham-Brewer House—*hist pl* MD-2
**Bingham Bridge (historical)**—*pop pl* NC-3
Bingham Brook—*stream* VT-1
Bingham Camp—*locale* OR-9
Bingham Canyon—*locale* UT-8
Bingham Canyon—*valley* CO-8
Bingham Canyon—*valley* UT-8
Bingham Canyon Cem—*cemetery* UT-8
Bingham Canyon Open Pit Copper Mine—*hist pl* UT-8
*Bingham Cave* AL-4
Bingham Cem—*cemetery* AL-4
Bingham Cem—*cemetery* IN-6
Bingham Cem—*cemetery* (3) KY-4
Bingham Cem—*cemetery* MI-6
Bingham Cem—*cemetery* MO-7
Bingham Cem—*cemetery* OH-6
Bingham Cem—*cemetery* (3) TN-4
Bingham Cem—*cemetery* TX-5
Bingham Center—*locale* PA-2
Bingham Center (census name Bingham)—*other* ME-1
**Bingham Center (Township name Bingham)**—*pop pl* PA-2
Bingham Ch—*church* VA-3
Bingham City Cem—*cemetery* UT-8
Bingham Company Warehouse—*hist pl* OH-6
Bingham Copper Mine—*mine* UT-8
*Bingham Copper Pit Mine* UT-8
Bingham Cove—*bay* AK-9
Bingham Cove—*valley* AL-4
Bingham Cove—*valley* TN-4
*Bingham Creek* TX-5
Bingham Creek—*stream* (2) AL-4
Bingham Creek—*stream* MI-6
Bingham Creek—*stream* NE-7
Bingham Creek—*stream* (2) OR-9
Bingham Creek—*stream* TN-4
Bingham Creek—*stream* (3) TX-5
Bingham Creek—*stream* UT-8
Bingham Creek—*stream* WA-9
Bingham Creek—*stream* WI-6
Bingham Creek Dam—*dam* UT-8
Bingham Creek Reload—*locale* WA-9
Bingham Creek Rsvr—*reservoir* UT-8
Bingham Creek Trail—*trail* WA-9
Bingham Division—*civil* UT-8
Bingham Drain—*canal* MI-6
Bingham Elem Sch—*school* IN-6
**Bingham Estates (subdivision)**—*pop pl* MS-4
**Bingham Estates (subdivision)**—*pop pl* UT-8
**Bingham Estates Subdivision**—*pop pl* UT-8
Bingham Falls—*falls* VT-1
**Bingham Farms**—*pop pl* MI-6
Bingham Fire Tower—*locale* AL-4
Bingham Fort (historical)—*locale* UT-8
Bingham Free Meetinghouse—*hist pl* ME-1
Bingham Gap—*gap* KY-4
**Bingham Heights**—*pop pl* NC-3
*Bingham High School* UT-8
Bingham Hill—*summit* CO-8
Bingham Hill—*summit* NH-1
Bingham Hill—*summit* NC-3
Bingham Hill—*summit* TN-4
Bingham Hill—*summit* VT-1
Bingham-Hilliard Doll House—*hist pl* KY-4
**Bingham (historical)**—*pop pl* OR-9
Bingham Hollow—*valley* AR-4
*Bingham Hot Springs* OR-9
Bingham House—*hist pl* MI-6
Bingham HS—*school* UT-8
Bingham Island—*island* FL-3
Bingham Island (historical)—*island* TN-4
Bingham JHS—*school* MO-7
Bingham Lake—*lake* CA-9
Bingham Lake—*lake* CO-8
Bingham Lake—*lake* MI-6
Bingham Lake—*lake* MN-6
Bingham Lake—*lake* MT-8
Bingham Lake—*lake* OR-9
**Bingham Lake**—*pop pl* MN-6
Bingham Lakes—*lake* OR-9
Bingham Memorial Ch—*church* NC-3
Bingham Mills—*locale* NY-2
Bingham Mine—*mine* MN-6
Bingham MS—*school* UT-8
Bingham Mtn—*summit* AL-4
Bingham Mtn—*summit* OR-9
Bingham Mtn—*summit* VA-3
Bingham Narrows—*gap* AL-4
Bingham Park—*flat* OR-9
Bingham Park—*park* AL-4
Bingham Park—*park* IA-7
Bingham Park—*park* MI-6
*Bingham Peak* AZ-5
Bingham Peak—*summit* AK-9
Bingham Point—*cape* OR-9
Bingham Pond—*lake* CT-1
Bingham Post Office—*locale* NM-5
Bingham Post Office (historical)—*building* TN-4
Bingham Prairie—*flat* OR-9
Bingham Prairie Campground—*park* OR-9
**Binghampton**—*pop pl* IL-6
Binghampton Mine—*mine* AZ-5
**Binghampton Township**—*pop pl* ND-7
Bingham Pump Station—*locale* PA-2
Bingham Ranch—*locale* AZ-5
Bingham Ranch—*locale* MT-8
Bingham Ranch—*locale* NM-5
Bingham Ridge—*ridge* MT-8
Bingham Ridge—*ridge* OR-9
Bingham Ridge Trail—*trail* OR-9
Bingham Rsvr—*reservoir* OR-9
Bingham Run—*stream* WV-2
Binghams Bay—*bay* WI-6
Binghams Branch—*stream* AL-4
Bingham Sch—*hist pl* NC-3
Bingham Sch—*school* CT-1
Bingham Sch—*school* MA-1
Bingham Sch—*school* (2) MI-6
Bingham Sch—*school* MO-7
Bingham Sch—*school* TX-5
Binghams Chapel—*locale* GA-3
Bingham Sch (historical)—*school* MS-4
*Bingham Sch Number 84* IN-6
Bingham Spring—*spring* (3) OR-9
**Bingham Springs**—*pop pl* OR-9
Bingham Springs—*spring* OR-9
Binghams Shelter—*locale* OR-9
Bingham Station (historical)—*locale* PA-2
Bingham Street Sch—*school* MI-6
Bingham Tennis Court—*locale* NC-3
*Binghamton* ND-7
Binghamton—*locale* CA-9
**Binghamton**—*pop pl* NY-2
**Binghamton**—*pop pl* WI-6
Binghamton—*uninc pl* TN-4
Binghamton Cem—*cemetery* WI-6
Binghamton City Hall—*hist pl* NY-2
BINGHAMTON (ferryboat)—*hist pl* NJ-2
*Binghamton State Hospital* NY-2
**Binghamton (Town of)**—*pop pl* NY-2
**Binghamtown**—*pop pl* AL-4
**Binghamtown**—*pop pl* KY-4
Binghamtown Cem—*cemetery* KY-4
Bingham Town Hall—*building* ND-7
**Bingham (Town of)**—*pop pl* ME-1
Bingham Township—*fmr MCD* IA-7
**Bingham Township**—*pop pl* ND-7
Bingham (Township of)—*fmr MCD* NC-3
**Bingham (Township of)**—*pop pl* (3) MI-6
**Bingham (Township of)**—*pop pl* PA-2
Bingham Tunnel—*mine* UT-8
**Binghamville**—*pop pl* VT-1
Bingham-Waggoner House and Estate—*hist pl* MO-7
Bingham West Dip Tunnel—*mine* UT-8
Bing HS—*school* SC-3
Bing Lake—*lake* WI-6
*Bingle Creek* AR-4
Binglewood—*uninc pl* TX-5
Binglewood Park—*park* TX-5
**Bingley**—*pop pl* NY-2
Bingley Gap—*gap* WA-9
Bing Maloney Golf Course—*other* CA-9
Bingman Hollow—*valley* PA-2
Bingman Memorial Park—*park* KY-4
Bingman Ridge—*ridge* ID-8
**Bingman Station**—*pop pl* IL-6
Bingo—*locale* ME-1
Bingo, Lake—*lake* WI-6
Bingo Brook—*stream* VT-1
Bingo Cem—*cemetery* VT-1
Bingo Creek—*stream* ID-8
Bingo Creek Landing—*locale* ID-8
Bingo Hollow—*valley* WV-2
Bingo Lake—*lake* IN-6
Bingo Lake—*lake* OR-9
Bingo Mtn—*summit* AK-9
Bingo Saddle—*gap* ID-8
Bingot—*CDP* GU-9
**Bingot**—*pop pl* GU-9
Bings Branch—*stream* SC-3
Bings Ferry (historical)—*locale* MS-4
Bingshick Lake—*lake* MN-6
Bing's Hotel—*hist pl* OH-6
**Bing Spur**—*pop pl* MT-8
Bingville—*locale* WA-9
**Bingville**—*pop pl* OH-6

Bingville—*post sta* .... GA-3
Bingville Creek—*stream* .... OR-9
*Binion* .... AL-4
Binion Brake—*swamp* .... LA-4
Binion Cem—*cemetery* .... TX-5
Binion Creek—*stream* .... AL-4
Binion Creek—*stream* .... TX-5
Binion Creek Landing Park—*park* .... AL-4
**Binion Heights (subdivision)**—*pop pl* .... AL-4
Binion Hollow—*valley* .... OH-6
Binion Ranch—*locale* .... MT-8
*Binions Creek* .... AL-4
Binions Creek (historical)—*locale* .... AL-4
Binker Valley—*valley* .... PA-2
Binkey Lake—*lake* .... OR-9
Binkley—*locale* .... MO-7
**Binkley**—*pop pl* .... OK-5
Binkley Cem—*cemetery* .... MO-7
Binkley Cem—*cemetery* (3) .... TN-4
Binkley Ditch—*canal* .... OH-6
Binkley Drain—*canal* .... MI-6
Binkley Hill—*summit* .... IN-6
Binkley Ranch—*locale* .... CA-9
Binkleys Bridge Post Office (historical)—*building* .... PA-2
Binkley Sch—*school* .... TN-4
Binkleys Slough—*gut* .... AK-9
Binky Hollow—*valley* .... PA-2
*Binleb* .... MP-9
B Inlet Brook—*stream* .... ME-1
Binnacle Bay—*bay* .... AK-9
Binnacle Rock—*island* .... CA-9
Binne Etteni Canyon—*valley* .... AZ-5
Binnen Kill—*stream* .... NY-2
Binnes Lake—*lake* .... MI-6
**Binnewater**—*pop pl* .... NY-2
Binnewater Hist Dist—*hist pl* .... NY-2
Binnewater Lakes—*lake* .... NY-2
Binnewater Pond—*lake* .... NY-2
Binnewater Union Ch—*church* .... NY-2
Binney—*locale* .... IL-6
Binney Brook—*stream* .... VT-1
Binney Creek—*stream* .... ID-8
Binney Hill—*summit* .... NH-1
Binney Hill Brook—*stream* .... MA-1
Binney Hill Brook—*stream* .... NH-1
Binney Junction—*locale* .... CA-9
Binney Park—*park* .... CT-1
Binney Pond—*lake* .... NH-1
Binney Pond State Forest—*park* .... NH-1
Binning Ditch—*canal* .... WY-8
Binninger Cem—*cemetery* .... NY-2
Binning Ranch—*locale* .... WY-8
*Binnion Creek* .... AL-4
Binns Bar—*bar* .... VA-3
Binns Hall—*locale* .... VA-3
Binnsmead Sch—*school* .... OR-9
Binns Mill—*locale* .... KY-4
Binns Sch—*school* .... OH-6
*Binns Store* .... VA-3
**Binnstown**—*pop pl* .... PA-2
Binns Village—*uninc pl* .... DE-2
Binnsville—*locale* .... MS-4
Binnsville Cem—*cemetery* .... MS-4
Binnsville United Methodist Ch—*church* .... MS-4
**Bino**—*pop pl* .... PA-2
Bino Bay—*swamp* .... SC-3
Binocular Canyon—*valley* .... TX-5
Binocular Peak—*summit* .... ID-8
Binocular Prospect—*mine* .... AK-9
*Binonehouah Creek* .... MS-4
Bino Springs—*spring* .... CA-9
Binowarat—*locale* .... AK-9
Binsbacker Creek—*stream* .... MO-7
Bins Mines—*mine* .... MT-8
Binson Lake—*lake* .... MS-4
Bin Tank, The—*reservoir* .... AZ-5
Bintliff, Gen. James, House—*hist pl* .... WI-6
*Binum* .... MD-2
Binyon Well—*well* .... TX-5
Bio, Bayou—*gut* .... LA-4
Bio Ch—*church* .... GA-3
Biograph Theater Bldg—*hist pl* .... IL-6
Bio Island—*island* .... MP-9
**Biola**—*pop pl* .... CA-9
Biola Coll—*school* .... CA-9
Biola Junction—*locale* .... CA-9
**Bioleen**—*pop pl* .... MP-9
Bionaz Gulch—*valley* .... CO-8
Bion Mine—*mine* .... SD-7
Biorka—*locale* .... AK-9
Biorka Channel—*channel* .... AK-9
Biorka Island—*island* .... AK-9
Biorka Reef—*bar* .... AK-9
**Bippus**—*pop pl* .... IN-6
Bippus Ch—*church* .... TX-5
Biraga Playground—*park* .... MI-6
Birbent Canyon—*valley* (2) .... CA-9
Birch—*locale* .... MI-6
Birch—*locale* .... MN-6
Birch—*locale* .... NC-3
Birch—*locale* .... PA-2
Birch—*locale* .... TX-5
Birch—*locale* .... VA-3
Birch—*locale* .... WA-9
Birch—*locale* .... WI-6
**Birch**—*pop pl* .... KS-7
Birch, Annie, House—*hist pl* .... UT-8
Birch Acres—*other* .... PA-2
Bircham Bend—*bend* .... MA-1
Bircham Bend Ponds—*lake* .... MA-1
Bircham Creek—*stream* .... TX-5
Birchard Hill—*summit* .... PA-2
Birchard Park—*park* .... OH-6
Birchard Sch (abandoned)—*school* .... PA-2
Birchardsville Post Office (historical)—*building* .... PA-2
Birchardville—*locale* .... PA-2
Birch Basin—*basin* .... ID-8
Birch Bay—*bay* (2) .... MN-6
Birch Bay—*bay* .... WA-9
**Birch Bay**—*pop pl* .... WA-9
**Birch Bay Circle Grange**—*pop pl* .... WA-9
Birch Bay State Park—*park* .... WA-9
**Birch Beach**—*pop pl* .... MI-6
**Birch Beach**—*pop pl* .... MN-6
Birch Bed—*basin* .... IN-6
Birch Bela Oil Field—*other* .... MI-6
Birch Bluff—*summit* .... WI-6
Birch Bottom Canyon—*valley* .... UT-8
Birch Branch—*stream* (2) .... AL-4
Birch Branch—*stream* .... IL-6
Birch Branch—*stream* (2) .... KY-4
Birch Branch—*stream* .... MD-2
Birch Branch—*stream* .... MN-6
Birch Branch—*stream* (3) .... MO-7
Birch Branch—*stream* .... SC-3
Birch Branch—*stream* (4) .... TN-4
Birch Branch—*stream* .... WV-2
*Birch Brook* .... MA-1
Birch Brook—*stream* (4) .... ME-1
Birch Brook—*stream* (2) .... MA-1
Birch Brook—*stream* .... MI-6
Birch Brook—*stream* .... NH-1
Birch Brook—*stream* .... NY-2
Birch Brook Camp—*locale* .... NY-2
*Birch Campground* .... UT-8
Birch Canal—*canal* .... CA-9
Birch Canyon—*valley* .... OR-9
Birch Canyon—*valley* (9) .... UT-8
Birch Cem—*cemetery* (2) .... TX-5
Birch Cooley Cem—*cemetery* .... MN-6
Birch Cooley (Township of)—*civ div* .... MN-6
Birch Coulee—*hist pl* .... MN-6
Birch Coulee Creek—*stream* .... MN-6
Birch Coulee State Park—*park* .... MN-6
Birch Cove—*valley* .... NC-3
*Birch Creek* .... ID-8
*Birch Creek* .... MN-6
*Birch Creek* .... MT-8
*Birch Creek* .... NJ-2
*Birch Creek* .... ND-7
*Birch Creek* .... OR-9
*Birch Creek* .... PA-2
*Birch Creek* .... UT-8
*Birch Creek* .... VA-3
*Birch Creek* .... WI-6
*Birch Creek* .... WY-8
Birch Creek—*gut* .... NJ-2
Birch Creek—*locale* .... AK-9
**Birch Creek**—*pop pl* .... MI-6
Birch Creek—*stream* (4) .... AK-9
Birch Creek—*stream* .... AR-4
Birch Creek—*stream* (6) .... CA-9
Birch Creek—*stream* (2) .... CO-8
Birch Creek—*stream* (3) .... GA-3
Birch Creek—*stream* (25) .... ID-8
Birch Creek—*stream* (3) .... IL-6
Birch Creek—*stream* (2) .... IN-6
Birch Creek—*stream* (2) .... IA-7
Birch Creek—*stream* .... KS-7
Birch Creek—*stream* .... LA-4
Birch Creek—*stream* (3) .... MI-6
Birch Creek—*stream* (2) .... MN-6
Birch Creek—*stream* (2) .... MO-7
Birch Creek—*stream* (10) .... MT-8
Birch Creek—*stream* (4) .... NV-8
Birch Creek—*stream* .... NJ-2
Birch Creek—*stream* (5) .... NY-2
Birch Creek—*stream* .... NC-3
Birch Creek—*stream* (4) .... OK-5
Birch Creek—*stream* (17) .... OR-9
Birch Creek—*stream* (2) .... PA-2
Birch Creek—*stream* .... SC-3
Birch Creek—*stream* (6) .... TX-5
Birch Creek—*stream* (33) .... UT-8
Birch Creek—*stream* (2) .... VA-3
Birch Creek—*stream* (2) .... WA-9
Birch Creek—*stream* .... WI-6
Birch Creek—*stream* (5) .... WY-8
Birch Creek ANV741—*reserve* .... AK-9
Birch Creek Bridge—*bridge* .... MT-8
Birch Creek Campground—*locale* .... ID-8
Birch Creek Campground—*locale* .... UT-8
*Birch Creek Canyon* .... UT-8
Birch Creek CCC Camp—*hist pl* .... MT-8
Birch Creek Ditch—*canal* .... OR-9
Birch Creek Flats—*flat* .... MT-8
Birch Creek Hill—*summit* .... MT-8
*Birch Creek - in part* .... UT-8
Birch Creek (Magisterial District)—*fmr MCD* .... VA-3
Birch Creek Main Canal—*canal* .... MT-8
Birch Creek Meadows—*flat* .... OR-9
Birch Creek Meadows—*flat* .... UT-8
Birch Creek Mtn—*summit* .... UT-8
Birch Creek Oil Field—*oilfield* .... OK-5
Birch Creek Ranch—*locale* .... NV-8
Birch Creek Ranger Station—*locale* .... MT-8
*Birch Creek Reservoir* .... UT-8
Birch Creek Reservoirs—*reservoir* .... UT-8
Birch Creek Rock Shelters—*hist pl* .... ID-8
Birch Creek Rodeo Ground—*locale* .... MT-8
Birch Creek Rsvr—*reservoir* .... OR-9
Birch Creek Sch—*school* .... ID-8
Birch Creek Sch—*school* (2) .... MT-8
Birch Creek Sch—*school* .... SC-3
Birch Creek Sinks—*basin* .... ID-8
Birch Creek Slough—*stream* .... AK-9
Birch Creek South Oil Field—*oilfield* .... OK-5
Birch Creek Spring—*spring* .... NV-8
Birch Creek State Park—*park* .... TX-5
**Birch Creek (Town of)**—*pop pl* .... WI-6
**Birch Creek (Township of)**—*pop pl* .... MN-6
Birch Creek Valley—*valley* .... ID-8
Birchcrest Park—*park* .... MN-6
**Birchdale**—*pop pl* .... MN-6
Birchdale Cem—*cemetery* .... MN-6
Birchdale Lake—*lake* .... MN-6
Birchdale Lookout Tower—*locale* .... MN-6
Birchdale State Wildlife Mngmt Area—*park* .... MN-6
**Birchdale (Township of)**—*pop pl* .... MN-6
Birch Dam Creek—*stream* .... MD-2
*Birchen Bend* .... MA-1
*Birchen Creek* .... VA-3
Birchens Cabins—*locale* .... MI-6
*Bircher Canyon* .... NM-5
*Bircher Flats* .... NM-5
Bircher Springs—*spring* .... MT-8
*Bircher Tank* .... NM-5
Birches—*locale* .... AK-9
Birches, The—*hist pl* .... NY-2
Birches, The—*locale* (2) .... ME-1
Birches Creek—*stream* .... AK-9
Birches Creek—*stream* .... TX-5
Birches Picnic Area—*locale* .... MN-6
Birches Picnic Ground, The—*locale* .... UT-8
**Birchett Estate**—*pop pl* .... VA-3
Birchett Park—*park* .... AZ-5
Birchfield—*locale* .... NM-5
Birchfield—*locale* .... WA-9
**Birchfield**—*pop pl* .... NJ-2
Birchfield Branch—*stream* .... AR-4
Birchfield Branch—*stream* .... NC-3
Birchfield Camp Branch—*stream* .... TN-4
Birchfield Cem—*cemetery* .... TN-4
Birchfield Ch—*church* .... TN-4
Birchfield Creek—*stream* .... AR-4
Birchfield Creek—*stream* .... KY-4
Birchfield Creek—*stream* .... NC-3
Birchfield Creek—*stream* .... VA-3
Birchfield Gap—*gap* .... TN-4
Birchfield Mtn—*summit* .... AR-4
Birchfield Mtn—*summit* .... TN-4
Birchfield Ranch—*locale* .... NM-5
Birchfield Run—*stream* .... WV-2
Birchfield Sch—*school* .... MT-8
Birchfield Spring—*spring* .... CO-8
Birchfield Spring—*spring* .... TN-4
Birchfield Well—*well* .... NM-5
Birch Flat—*flat* .... ID-8
Birch Flat—*flat* .... WA-9
*Birch Fork* .... WV-2
Birch Fork—*stream* (2) .... KY-4
Birch Fork—*stream* .... NC-3
Birch Fork—*stream* (3) .... WV-2
*Birch Fork Creek* .... NC-3
Birch Gap—*gap* .... KY-4
Birch Gap—*gap* .... VA-3
Birch Glen Camp—*locale* .... VT-1
Birch Glen Picnic Ground—*locale* .... ID-8
Birch Grove Cem—*cemetery* (2) .... ME-1
Birch Grove Ch—*church* .... PA-2
Birchgrove Park—*park* .... MI-6
Birch Grove Park—*park* .... NJ-2
**Birch Groves**—*pop pl* .... CT-1
Birch Grove Sch—*school* .... MN-6
Birch Grove Sch—*school* .... MT-8
Birch Gulch—*valley* .... AK-9
Birch Gulch—*valley* .... WY-8
Birch Harbor—*bay* .... ME-1
**Birch Harbor**—*pop pl* .... ME-1
Birch Harbor Pond—*lake* .... ME-1
*Birch Hill* .... ME-1
**Birch Hill**—*pop pl* .... CA-9
**Birch Hill**—*pop pl* .... CT-1
**Birch Hill**—*pop pl* .... NH-1
Birch Hill—*ridge* .... MI-6
Birch Hill—*summit* (4) .... AK-9
Birch Hill—*summit* .... CA-9
Birch Hill—*summit* (2) .... CT-1
Birch Hill—*summit* .... ID-8
Birch Hill—*summit* (4) .... ME-1
Birch Hill—*summit* (4) .... MA-1
Birch Hill—*summit* .... MI-6
Birch Hill—*summit* (6) .... NH-1
Birch Hill—*summit* (2) .... NY-2
Birch Hill—*summit* (2) .... VT-1
Birch Hill Brook—*stream* .... MA-1
Birch Hill Camp—*locale* .... NH-1
Birch Hill Cem—*cemetery* .... AL-4
Birch Hill Cem—*cemetery* .... AK-9
Birch Hill Cem—*cemetery* (2) .... PA-2
Birch Hill Country Club—*other* .... MI-6
Birch Hill Dam—*dam* .... MA-1
Birch Hill Island—*island* .... NH-1
Birch Hill Lake—*lake* .... AK-9
Birch Hill Lookout Tower—*locale* .... MN-6
*Birch Hill Park* .... MI-6
*Birch Hills* .... MI-6
Birch Hills—*other* .... AK-9
**Birch Hills**—*pop pl* .... MI-6
**Birch Hills**—*pop pl* .... NJ-2
Birch Hills—*summit* .... WY-8
Birch (historical)—*locale* .... KS-7
*Birch Hollow* .... TX-5
Birch Hollow—*valley* .... KY-4
Birch Hollow—*valley* .... OH-6
Birch Hollow—*valley* (3) .... PA-2
Birch Hollow—*valley* .... TN-4
Birch Hollow—*valley* (2) .... UT-8
Birch Hollow—*valley* (2) .... WV-2
Birch House—*hist pl* .... VA-3
**Birchim**—*pop pl* .... IN-6
Birchim Canyon—*valley* .... CA-9
Birchim Creek—*stream* .... NV-8
Birchim Lake—*lake* .... CA-9
Birchin Creek—*stream* .... VA-3
Birchin Lake—*reservoir* .... VA-3
Birch Intervale—*basin* .... NH-1
*Birch Island* .... MN-6
*Birch Island* .... NH-1
Birch Island—*island* .... AK-9
Birch Island—*island* (22) .... ME-1
Birch Island—*island* .... MI-6
Birch Island—*island* (3) .... MN-6
Birch Island—*island* (2) .... NH-1
Birch Island—*island* (7) .... NY-2
Birch Island—*island* .... WI-6
Birch Island—*locale* .... IL-6
**Birch Island**—*pop pl* .... ME-1
Birch Island Brook—*stream* .... NH-1
Birch Island Campground—*locale* .... MI-6
Birch Island Lake—*lake* .... MN-6
Birch Island Lake—*lake* .... WI-6
Birch Island Ledge—*bar* .... ME-1
Birch Island Run—*stream* .... PA-2
Birch Islands—*island* (4) .... ME-1
Birch Isle—*island* .... MI-6
Birch Knob—*summit* .... NC-3
Birch Knob Lookout Tower—*locale* .... MN-6
**Birch Knoll**—*pop pl* .... DE-2
Birch Knoll—*summit* (2) .... ME-1
*Birch Lake* .... MI-6
*Birch Lake* .... MN-6
*Birch Lake* .... WI-6
Birch Lake—*lake* (6) .... AK-9
Birch Lake—*lake* (2) .... CA-9
Birch Lake—*lake* (5) .... MI-6
Birch Lake—*lake* (19) .... MN-6
Birch Lake—*lake* .... MT-8
Birch Lake—*lake* .... UT-8
Birch Lake—*lake* (14) .... WI-6
**Birch Lake**—*pop pl* .... AK-9
Birch Lake—*reservoir* .... PA-2
Birch Lake Campground—*locale* .... MN-6
Birch Lake Cem—*cemetery* (2) .... MN-6
Birch Lake Ch—*church* .... MI-6
Birch Lake Lookout Tower—*locale* .... MN-6
Birch Lakes—*lake* .... AK-9
Birch Lakes—*lake* .... MI-6
Birch Lake Sch—*school* (2) .... MN-6
Birch Lake Sch—*school* .... WI-6
Birch Lake State Forest—*park* .... MN-6
**Birch Lake (Township of)**—*pop pl* .... MN-6
Birch Lake (Unorganized Territory of)—*unorg* .... MN-6
Birchland Cem—*cemetery* .... ME-1
Birchland Park—*locale* .... VA-3
Birchland Park Sch—*school* .... MA-1
Birch Lane Sch—*school* .... CA-9
Birch Lane Sch—*school* .... NY-2
Birch Lateral Three—*canal* .... CA-9
Birchlawn Burial Park—*cemetery* .... VA-3
**Birchleaf**—*pop pl* .... VA-3
Birch Lick—*stream* .... WV-2
Birch Lick Branch—*stream* .... KY-4
Birchlick Branch—*stream* .... WV-2
Birch Lick Ch—*church* .... KY-4
Birch Lick Creek—*stream* .... KY-4
Birch Lick Run—*stream* .... PA-2
Birchlog Creek—*stream* .... TN-4
Birchlog Run—*stream* .... WV-2
Birchlog Trail—*trail* .... WV-2
Birch (Magisterial District)—*fmr MCD* .... WV-2
Birchmeade Canal—*canal* .... MT-8
Birch Meadow—*flat* .... MT-8
Birch Meadow Brook—*stream* (2) .... MA-1
Birch Meadow Sch—*school* .... MA-1
Birchmere Camp—*locale* .... NH-1
Birch Mesa—*summit* .... AZ-5
*Birch Mesa Airport* .... AZ-5
Birch Mesa Tanks—*reservoir* .... AZ-5
Birch Millpond—*reservoir* .... CT-1
Birch Minick Hollow—*valley* .... AR-4
**Birchmont**—*pop pl* .... MN-6
**Birchmont Subdivision**—*pop pl* .... UT-8
*Birch Mountain* .... UT-8
**Birch Mountain**—*pop pl* .... CT-1
Birch Mountain Brook—*stream* .... CT-1
*Birch Mtn* .... ME-1
Birch Mtn—*summit* .... CA-9
Birch Mtn—*summit* .... CT-1
Birch Mtn—*summit* .... ID-8
Birch Mtn—*summit* (3) .... ME-1
Birch Mtn—*summit* .... NY-2
Birch Narrows—*channel* .... MN-6
**Birch Ocean Front**—*pop pl* .... FL-3
Birch Park—*park* .... CA-9
Birch Park Ski Area—*area* .... WI-6
Birchpen Run—*stream* .... WV-2
Birch Picnic Area—*locale* .... UT-8
Birch Plain Creek—*stream* .... CT-1
Birch Point—*cape* .... CT-1
Birch Point—*cape* (25) .... ME-1
Birch Point—*cape* (5) .... MI-6
Birch Point—*cape* (3) .... MN-6
Birch Point—*cape* .... NH-1
Birch Point—*cape* (2) .... NY-2
Birch Point—*cape* .... VT-1
Birch Point—*cape* .... WA-9
Birch Point—*cape* .... WI-6
Birch Point—*summit* .... MA-1
**Birch Point Condominium**—*pop pl* .... UT-8
**Birch Pointe**—*pop pl* .... DE-2
Birch Point Ledge—*bar* .... ME-1
*Birch Pond* .... MI-6
Birch Pond—*lake* .... AR-4
Birch Pond—*lake* .... ME-1
Birch Pond—*lake* .... MN-6
Birch Pond—*lake* .... NY-2
Birch Pond—*reservoir* .... MA-1
Birch Pond Dam—*dam* .... MA-1
Birch Ranch—*locale* .... MT-8
Birch Ridge—*ridge* (2) .... ID-8
Birch Ridge—*ridge* .... NH-1
Birch Ridge—*ridge* .... NY-2
Birch Ridge—*ridge* .... NC-3
Birch Ridge Brook—*stream* .... NY-2
Birch Ridge Camp—*locale* .... NY-2
Birch Ridge Creek—*stream* .... NC-3
Birch Ridge Lookout Tower—*locale* .... ID-8
Birch Ridge Lookout Tower—*locale* .... WI-6
Birch Ridge Pond—*lake* .... NY-2
Birch Ridge Ponds—*lake* .... ME-1
**Birch River**—*pop pl* .... WV-2
Birch River—*stream* .... ME-1
Birch River—*stream* .... MN-6
Birch River—*stream* .... WV-2
Birch River Camp—*locale* .... ME-1
Birch River Narrows—*channel* .... MN-6
Birch River Union Ch—*church* .... WV-2
Birch Rock Hill—*summit* .... PA-2
Birch Rock Hollow—*valley* .... AL-4
Birchroot Run—*stream* .... WV-2
*Birch Run* .... PA-2
*Birch Run* .... WV-2
Birch Run—*locale* .... WV-2
**Birch Run**—*pop pl* .... MI-6
Birch Run—*stream* .... MI-6
Birch Run—*stream* .... NY-2
Birch Run—*stream* (9) .... PA-2
Birch Run—*stream* .... VA-3
Birch Run—*stream* (2) .... WV-2
Birch Run—*stream* .... WI-6
Birch Run Cem—*cemetery* .... MI-6
Birch Run Country Club—*other* .... NY-2
Birch Run Oil Field—*other* .... MI-6
*Birch Run Reservoir* .... PA-2
Birch Run Reservoir Dam—*dam* .... PA-2
**Birch Run (Township of)**—*pop pl* .... MI-6
*Birch Run Ville* .... PA-2
Birchrunville—*locale* .... PA-2
Birchrunville General Store—*hist pl* .... PA-2
Birchrunville Post Office—*building* .... PA-2
Birch Sch—*school* .... AK-9
Birch Sch—*school* .... IL-6
Birch Sch—*school* .... NY-2
Birch Sch (historical)—*school* .... AL-4
Birch Slough—*gut* .... MO-7
Birch Slough—*stream* .... AK-9
*Birch Spring* .... ID-8
Birch Spring—*spring* .... CA-9
Birch Spring—*spring* .... CO-8
Birch Spring—*spring* (2) .... ID-8
Birch Spring—*spring* .... ME-1
Birch Spring—*spring* .... MT-8
Birch Spring—*spring* (2) .... NV-8
Birch Spring—*spring* (2) .... OR-9
Birch Spring—*spring* (24) .... UT-8
Birchspring Branch—*stream* .... NC-3
Birch Spring Creek—*stream* .... UT-8
Birch Spring Draw—*valley* .... UT-8
Birch Spring Gap—*gap* (2) .... NC-3
*Birch Spring Gap Shelter* .... NC-3
Birch Spring Knoll—*summit* .... UT-8
Birch Spring Point—*summit* .... UT-8
Birch Springs—*spring* .... ID-8
Birch Springs—*spring* .... NM-5
Birch Springs—*spring* .... OR-9
Birch Springs—*spring* (3) .... UT-8
Birch Spring Shelter Spring—*locale* .... NC-3
Birch Springs Run—*stream* .... PA-2
Birch Still Hollow—*valley* .... PA-2
Birch Stream—*stream* (2) .... ME-1
Birch Street Sch—*school* .... GA-3
Birch Swale—*swamp* .... PA-2
Birch Swamp—*swamp* .... MA-1
*Birch Swamp Corner* .... MA-1
Birch Swamp Corner—*locale* .... RI-1
Birchton—*locale* .... WV-2
**Birchton**—*pop pl* .... NY-2
Birchtown—*locale* .... PA-2
**Birch Town**—*pop pl* .... VA-3
**Birch (Town of)**—*pop pl* .... WI-6
**Birch (Township of)**—*pop pl* .... MN-6
**Birch Tree**—*pop pl* .... MO-7
Birch Tree Cem—*cemetery* .... ME-1
Birch Tree Lake—*lake* .... AK-9
Birch Tree Point—*cape* .... MI-6
Birch Tree Township—*civil* .... MO-7
Birchum Hollow—*valley* .... TX-5
Birchum P.O. (historical)—*locale* .... AL-4
Birch Undertaker Bldg—*building* .... DC-2
**Birch Valley**—*pop pl* .... PA-2
Birch Valley Camp—*locale* .... MI-6
**Birchville**—*pop pl* .... CA-9
Birchville Mine—*mine* .... CA-9
**Birchwood**—*pop pl* .... AK-9
**Birchwood**—*pop pl* .... CT-1
**Birchwood**—*pop pl* (2) .... MI-6
**Birchwood**—*pop pl* .... MN-6
**Birchwood**—*pop pl* .... NY-2
**Birchwood**—*pop pl* .... TN-4
**Birchwood**—*pop pl* (2) .... WI-6
Birchwood—*uninc pl* .... AR-4
Birchwood Baptist Ch—*church* .... TN-4
**Birchwood Beach**—*pop pl* .... MI-6
Birchwood Ch—*church* .... TN-4
**Birchwood City**—*pop pl* .... MD-2
Birchwood City Sch—*school* .... MD-2
Birchwood Country Club—*other* .... CT-1
*Birchwood Creek* .... VA-3
**Birchwood Estates**—*pop pl* .... PA-2
**Birchwood Estates Subdivision**—*pop pl* .... UT-8
**Birchwood-Gardens**—*pop pl* .... VA-3
Birchwood Golf Course—*locale* .... PA-2
**Birchwood Hills Estates (subdivision)**—*pop pl* .... NC-3
**Birchwood Homes (subdivision)**—*pop pl* .... NC-3
Birchwood Inn—*hist pl* .... NH-1
Birchwood Lake—*lake* .... WI-6
Birchwood Lake—*reservoir* (2) .... NJ-2
Birchwood Lake Dam—*dam* (2) .... NJ-2
**Birchwood Lake Estates (subdivision)**—*pop pl* .... NC-3
**Birchwood Lakes**—*pop pl* .... NJ-2
**Birchwood Lakes**—*pop pl* .... PA-2
Birchwood Lookout Tower—*locale* .... WI-6
Birchwood Park—*park* (3) .... MN-6
Birchwood Park—*park* .... NY-2
**Birchwood Park**—*pop pl* .... DE-2
**Birchwood Park**—*pop pl* .... NJ-2
**Birchwood Park**—*pop pl* .... VA-3
**Birchwood Park (subdivision)**—*pop pl* .... NC-3
Birchwood-Pocono Airpark—*airport* .... PA-2
Birchwood Pond—*lake* .... ME-1
Birchwood Pond—*lake* .... NY-2
Birchwood Post Office—*building* .... TN-4
Birchwood Run—*stream* .... VA-3
Birchwood Sch—*school* .... MI-6
Birchwood Sch—*school* (2) .... NY-2
Birchwood Sch—*school* .... TN-4
**Birchwood Shores**—*pop pl* .... MI-6
**Birchwood (subdivision)**—*pop pl* (2) .... NC-3
**Birchwood (subdivision)**—*pop pl* .... TN-4
**Birchwood Terrace**—*pop pl* .... PA-2
**Birchwood (Town of)**—*pop pl* .... WI-6
**Birchwood Village**—*pop pl* .... MN-6
Birchy Creek—*stream* .... PA-2
Birckey Valley—*valley* .... TN-4
Birckhead Place Hist Dist—*hist pl* .... OH-6
*Bird* .... IN-6
*Bird* .... KS-7
Bird—*locale* .... AK-9
Bird—*locale* .... NY-2
**Bird**—*pop pl* .... LA-4
Bird, C. B., House—*hist pl* .... WI-6
Bird, Edward, House—*hist pl* .... UT-8
Bird, Philomen, House—*hist pl* .... KY-4
Bird, Roswell Darius, Sr., House—*hist pl* .... UT-8
Bird Bank Creek—*stream* .... SC-3
Bird Bay—*swamp* (3) .... FL-3
Bird Bay Channel—*channel* .... LA-4
Birdbill Lake—*lake* .... ID-8
Bird Bottom—*bend* .... MT-8
Bird/Boyd Farm House—*hist pl* .... MI-6
Bird Branch—*stream* .... FL-3
Bird Branch—*stream* .... GA-3
Bird Branch—*stream* .... IN-6
Bird Branch—*stream* (2) .... KY-4
Bird Branch—*stream* .... LA-4
Bird Branch—*stream* .... MS-4
Bird Branch—*stream* .... MO-7
Bird Branch—*stream* .... NC-3
Bird Branch—*stream* (6) .... TN-4
Bird Branch—*stream* .... TX-5
Bird Branch—*stream* (2) .... WV-2
Bird Branch Lookout Tower—*locale* .... KY-4
Bird Bridge—*bridge* .... TN-4
Bird Brook—*stream* .... ME-1
Bird Brook—*stream* .... NY-2
Bird Butte—*summit* .... OR-9
**Bird Cage**—*pop pl* .... NC-3
Birdcage Creek—*stream* .... MD-2
Birdcage Windmill—*locale* .... AZ-5
Bird Canyon—*valley* (2) .... AZ-5
Bird Canyon—*valley* .... CA-9
Bird Canyon—*valley* (3) .... ID-8
Bird Canyon—*valley* (2) .... UT-8
Bird Canyon—*valley* .... WY-8
Bird Cape—*cape* .... AK-9
Bird Cave—*cave* .... AL-4
Bird Cem—*cemetery* (2) .... AL-4
Bird Cem—*cemetery* .... AR-4
Bird Cem—*cemetery* (3) .... GA-3
Bird Cem—*cemetery* .... KS-7
Bird Cem—*cemetery* (3) .... MO-7
Bird Cem—*cemetery* .... NY-2
Bird Cem—*cemetery* (2) .... OH-6
Bird Cem—*cemetery* .... OK-5
Bird Cem—*cemetery* .... TN-4
Bird Cem—*cemetery* (2) .... WV-2
Bird Chapel—*church* .... LA-4
**Bird City**—*pop pl* .... KS-7
Bird City Airp—*airport* .... KS-7
Bird City Cem—*cemetery* .... KS-7
**Bird City Township**—*pop pl* .... KS-7
Bird Coulee—*valley* .... MT-8
Birdcraft Sanctuary—*hist pl* .... CT-1
*Bird Creek* .... AL-4
*Bird Creek* .... MS-4
*Bird Creek* .... TN-4
*Bird Creek* .... WI-6
*Bird Creek* .... WY-8
Bird Creek—*stream* (2) .... AL-4
Bird Creek—*stream* (4) .... AK-9
Bird Creek—*stream* .... AR-4
Bird Creek—*stream* (4) .... CA-9
Bird Creek—*stream* (2) .... CO-8
Bird Creek—*stream* (2) .... FL-3
Bird Creek—*stream* (3) .... ID-8
Bird Creek—*stream* .... KS-7
Bird Creek—*stream* .... LA-4
Bird Creek—*stream* (3) .... MI-6
Bird Creek—*stream* (3) .... MT-8
Bird Creek—*stream* .... NV-8
Bird Creek—*stream* .... NY-2
Bird Creek—*stream* (3) .... NC-3
Bird Creek—*stream* (8) .... OK-5
Bird Creek—*stream* .... PA-2
Bird Creek—*stream* (2) .... TN-4
Bird Creek—*stream* (2) .... TX-5
Bird Creek—*stream* .... VA-3
Bird Creek—*stream* (2) .... WA-9
Bird Creek—*stream* .... WI-6
Bird Creek—*stream* (2) .... WY-8
Bird Creek Camp—*locale* .... WA-9
Bird Creek Campground—*locale* .... ID-8
Bird Creek Campground—*locale* .... NV-8
Bird Creek Campground—*locale* .... WA-9
Bird Creek Cem—*cemetery* .... OK-5
Bird Creek Ch—*church* .... OK-5
*Bird Creek Forest Service Recreation Site* .... NV-8
*Bird Creek Meadow* .... WA-9
*Bird Creek Meadows* .... WA-9
Bird Creek Meadows—*flat* .... WA-9
Bird Creek Meadows Picnic Area—*locale* .... WA-9
Bird Creek Pass—*gap* .... AK-9
*Bird Creek School* .... TN-4
Bird Creek Trail—*trail* .... AK-9
**Bird Crossroads**—*pop pl* .... TN-4
Bird Drain—*canal* (2) .... MI-6
Bird Drain—*stream* .... MI-6
Bird Draw—*valley* .... WY-8
Bird Drive Park—*park* .... FL-3
Birdell—*locale* .... AR-4
Birdell—*locale* .... PA-2
**Birdella Park Subdivision**—*pop pl* .... UT-8
Birdell Ch—*church* .... AR-4
Birden Cem—*cemetery* .... AR-4
Birdeye—*locale* .... AL-4
**Birdeye**—*pop pl* .... AR-4
*Birdeye Church* .... AL-4
*Birdeye Creek* .... AL-4
Birdeye Hollow—*valley* .... KY-4
Birdeye Lake—*lake* .... FL-3
Birdeye Lake—*lake* .... NV-8
Bird Falls Branch—*stream* .... NC-3
Bird Farm Camp—*locale* .... TX-5
Bird Farm Crossing—*locale* .... TX-5
Birdfield Sch—*school* .... SC-3
Bird Flat—*flat* .... CA-9
Bird Flat—*flat* .... OK-5
Bird Flat Sch—*school* .... CA-9
Bird Fork—*stream* (2) .... TN-4
Bird-Galloway Center (Shop Ctr)—*locale* .... FL-3
Bird Gap—*gap* .... GA-3
Bird Glacier—*glacier* .... AK-9
Bird Gulch—*valley* .... ID-8
Bird Gulch—*valley* .... WY-8
Bird Hammock—*hist pl* .... FL-3
Bird Haven—*hist pl* .... WV-2
Bird Haven—*locale* .... VA-3
Birdhaven Resort—*locale* .... MI-6
Birdhead Creek—*stream* .... MT-8
**Bird Hill**—*pop pl* .... MD-2
**Bird Hill**—*pop pl* .... TN-4
Bird Hill—*summit* .... CT-1
Bird Hill—*summit* .... ME-1
Bird Hill—*summit* .... MO-7
Bird Hill—*summit* .... PA-2
Bird Hill—*summit* .... TN-4
Bird Hill—*summit* .... TX-5
Bird Hill Ch—*church* .... GA-3
Bird Hill Ch (historical)—*church* .... AL-4
Bird Hills—*summit* .... CA-9
Bird (historical)—*locale* .... AL-4
**Bird (historical)**—*pop pl* .... TN-4
Bird Hollow—*valley* .... AR-4
Bird Hollow—*valley* .... GA-3
Bird Hollow—*valley* .... IN-6
Bird Hollow—*valley* .... MO-7
Bird Hollow—*valley* .... OK-5
Bird Hollow—*valley* (4) .... TN-4
Bird Hollow—*valley* (3) .... TX-5
Bird Hollow Creek—*stream* .... IN-6
Bird Holt Gap—*gap* .... KY-4
Birdie—*locale* .... AL-4
Birdie—*locale* .... MS-4
**Birdie**—*pop pl* .... GA-3
**Birdie**—*pop pl* .... KY-4
Birdie Branch—*stream* .... MS-4
Birdie Creek—*stream* .... OR-9
Birdie Gulch—*valley* .... CO-8
Birdie Gulch—*valley* .... WY-8
Birdie Hollow—*valley* .... AR-4

**Bishop**—*pop pl* CA-9
**Bishop**—*pop pl* GA-3
**Bishop**—*pop pl* KY-4
**Bishop**—*pop pl* MD-2
**Bishop**—*pop pl* OK-5
**Bishop**—*pop pl* PA-2
**Bishop**—*pop pl* TX-5
**Bishop**—*pop pl* VA-3
**Bishop**—*pop pl* WV-2
Bishop—*uninc pl* KY-4
Bishop, A. H., House—*hist pl* WA-9
Bishop, Bernice P., Museum—*hist pl* HI-9
Bishop, James, House—*hist pl* NJ-2
Bishop, John, House—*hist pl* PA-2
Bishop, Peyton Randolph, House—*hist pl* CT-1
Bishop, Senator William, House and Office—*hist pl* WA-9
Bishop, William D., Cottage Development Hist Dist—*hist pl* CT-1
**Bishop Acres**—*pop pl* CA-9
Bishop Airp—*airport* MI-6
Bishop and Burr Rsvr—*reservoir* AZ-5
Bishop and Clerks—*bar* MA-1
Bishop Antimony Mine—*mine* CA-9
Bishop Armstrong HS—*school* CA-9
Bishop Bar—*bar* WA-9
Bishop Borgess HS—*school* MI-6
Bishop Brady HS—*school* NH-1
*Bishop Branch* TN-4
*Bishop Branch* WV-2
Bishop Branch—*stream* AL-4
Bishop Branch—*stream* AR-4
Bishop Branch—*stream* (2) FL-3
Bishop Branch—*stream* (2) KY-4
Bishop Branch—*stream* (2) MO-7
Bishop Branch—*stream* NC-3
Bishop Branch—*stream* SC-3
Bishop Branch—*stream* TX-5
Bishop Branch—*stream* (2) VA-3
Bishop Branch—*stream* WI-6
Bishop Bridge—*bridge* WI-6
Bishop Brook—*stream* ME-1
Bishop Brook—*stream* NH-1
Bishop Brook—*stream* (2) NY-2
Bishop Burn Well—*well* ID-8
Bishop Cabin—*locale* WY-8
Bishop Camp—*locale* AZ-5
Bishop Camp—*locale* TX-5
Bishop Canal—*canal* CA-9
Bishop Canyon—*valley* CO-8
Bishop Canyon—*valley* NE-7
Bishop Canyon—*valley* NV-8
Bishop Canyon—*valley* NM-5
Bishop Canyon—*valley* (4) UT-8
Bishop Canyon—*valley* WA-9
Bishop Canyon Spring—*spring* CO-8
Bishop Cap—*summit* NM-5
Bishop Carroll HS—*school* KS-7
Bishop Carroll HS—*school* PA-2
Bishop Cave—*cave* AL-4
Bishop Cave—*cave* TN-4
Bishop (CCD)—*cens area* CA-9
Bishop (CCD)—*cens area* TX-5
Bishop Cem—*cemetery* (6) AL-4
Bishop Cem—*cemetery* AR-4
Bishop Cem—*cemetery* FL-3
Bishop Cem—*cemetery* GA-3
Bishop Cem—*cemetery* (2) IL-6
Bishop Cem—*cemetery* IA-7
Bishop Cem—*cemetery* (3) KY-4
Bishop Cem—*cemetery* (2) LA-4
Bishop Cem—*cemetery* (3) MS-4
Bishop Cem—*cemetery* MO-7
Bishop Cem—*cemetery* NY-2
Bishop Cem—*cemetery* (2) OH-6
Bishop Cem—*cemetery* TX-5
Bishop Cem—*cemetery* (3) VA-3
Bishop Cem—*cemetery* WV-2
Bishop Ch—*church* GA-3
Bishop Ch—*church* TX-5
Bishop Chapel—*church* TN-4
Bishop Chapel—*church* TX-5
Bishop Chapel Cem—*cemetery* TN-4
Bishop Chatard HS—*school* IN-6
*Bishop Church* MO-7
Bishop Conaty Memorial HighSchool—*school* CA-9
*Bishop Conwell HS* PA-2
Dishop Corners—*locale* NY-2
Bishop Cottre Cem—*cemetery* MS-4
Bishop Coulee—*valley* MT-8
Bishop Cove—*bay* RI-1
Bishop Cove—*valley* AL-4
Bishop Cow Camp—*locale* WY-8
*Bishop Creek* AL-4
*Bishop Creek* MI-6
*Bishop Creek* MS-4
*Bishop Creek* NC-3
*Bishop Creek* TX-5
*Bishop Creek* UT-8
*Bishop Creek* WI-6
**Bishop Creek**—*pop pl* CA-9
Bishop Creek—*stream* AL-4
Bishop Creek—*stream* (4) AK-9
Bishop Creek—*stream* AZ-5
Bishop Creek—*stream* (2) AR-4
Bishop Creek—*stream* (3) CA-9
Bishop Creek—*stream* CO-8
Bishop Creek—*stream* FL-3
Bishop Creek—*stream* (2) GA-3
Bishop Creek—*stream* (2) ID-8
Bishop Creek—*stream* IL-6
Bishop Creek—*stream* MI-6
Bishop Creek—*stream* MS-4
Bishop Creek—*stream* (2) MT-8
Bishop Creek—*stream* NV-8
Bishop Creek—*stream* NC-3
Bishop Creek—*stream* OK-5
Bishop Creek—*stream* (4) OR-9
Bishop Creek—*stream* (3) TX-5
Bishop Creek—*stream* (3) VA-3
Bishop Creek—*stream* WY-8
Bishop Creek Canal—*canal* CA-9
*Bishop Creek Mountains* NV-8
Bishop Creek Rsvr—*reservoir* NV-8
Bishop Creek Sch—*school* IL-6
Bishop Cut—*canal* CA-9
Bishop Dale Sch—*school* IL-6
*Bishop Ditch* IN-6
Bishop Ditch—*canal* KY-4
Bishop Ditch—*canal* OR-9
Bishop Donahue HS—*school* WV-2
Bishop Drain—*canal* (2) MI-6
Bishop Dubourg HS—*school* MO-7
Bishop Duffy HS—*school* NY-2
Bishop Dwenger HS—*school* IN-6
Bishop Egan HS—*school* PA-2
Bishop Elem Sch—*school* KS-7
Bishopella Cave—*cave* AL-4
Bishop Eustace Sch—*school* NJ-2
Bishop Feehan HS—*school* MA-1
Bishop Fenwick Sch—*school* OH-6
Bishop Ferry (historical)—*locale* AL-4
Bishop Field—*park* UT-8
Bishop Flats—*flat* NV-8
Bishop Flat Spring Number Forty—*spring* NV-8
Bishop Flat Well—*well* NV-8
Bishop Foley HS—*school* MI-6
Bishop Ford HS—*school* NY-2
Bishop Fork—*stream* WV-2
Bishop Fork—*valley* UT-8
Bishop Gallagher HS—*school* MI-6
Bishop Gas And Oil Field—*oilfield* OK-5
Bishop Gibbons HS—*school* NY-2
Bishop Gorman Sch—*school* NV-8
Bishop Grove Ch—*church* MO-7
Bishop Guertain HS—*school* NH-1
Bishop Guilfoyle Sch—*school* PA-2
Bishop Gulch—*valley* CO-8
Bishop Hannan HS—*school* PA-2
Bishop Harbor—*bay* FL-3
Bishop Hare Statue—*park* SD-7
*Bishop Head* MD-2
**Bishop Heights**—*pop pl* RI-1
**Bishop Hill**—*pop pl* IL-6
Bishop Hill—*summit* ME-1
Bishop Hill—*summit* MD-2
Bishop Hill—*summit* NY-2
Bishop Hill—*summit* VT-1
Bishop Hill Ch—*church* OH-6
Bishop Hill Hist Dist—*hist pl* IL-6
Bishop (historical)—*locale* KS-7
Bishop (historical P.O.)—*locale* AL-4
Bishop Hollow—*valley* AL-4
Bishop Hollow—*valley* AR-4
Bishop Hollow—*valley* (2) MO-7
Bishop Hollow—*valley* (2) TN-4
Bishop Hollow—*valley* TX-5
Bishop Hollow—*valley* VA-3
Bishop House—*hist pl* GA-3
Bishop House—*hist pl* KY-4
Bishop Ireton HS—*school* VA-3
Bishop Island—*island* ID-8
Bishop Island—*island* IN-6
Bishop John Lamy Grant—*civil* NM-5
*Bishop Junction Island* MP-9
*Bishop Junction Islands* MP-9
Bishop Kearney HS—*school* NY-2
Bishop Kearney Sch—*school* NY-2
Bishop Knob—*summit* KY-4
Bishop Knob—*summit* WV-2
Bishop Knoll—*summit* AZ-5
Bishop Knoll Tank—*reservoir* AZ-5
*Bishop Lake* AZ-5
*Bishop Lake* CO-8
Bishop Lake—*basin* AZ-5
Bishop Lake—*lake* AK-9
Bishop Lake—*lake* CA-9
Bishop Lake—*lake* (2) MI-6
Bishop Lake—*lake* WI-6
Bishop Lake—*reservoir* GA-3
Bishop Lake—*reservoir* ID-8
Bishop Lake—*reservoir* TX-5
Bishop Lake—*swamp* FL-3
Bishop Lateral—*canal* WY-8
Bishop Laughlin HS—*school* NY-2
Bishop LeBlond HS—*school* MO-7
Bishop Luers HS—*school* IN-6
Bishop Mackay-Smith House—*hist pl* PA-2
Bishop Manogue HS—*school* CA-9
Bishop Manor Creek—*stream* AL-4
Bishop Manor Estate—*hist pl* AL-4
Bishop Marty Rectory—*hist pl* SD-7
Bishop McConnel Day Camp—*locale* NY-2
Bishop Mcdevitt HS—*school* PA-2
Bishop McGuiness Memorial HS—*school* NC-3
Bishop Merlin J. Shaw Arch—*arch* UT-8
Bishop Miege HS—*school* KS-7
Dishop Mine—*mine* WY-0
Bishop Montgomery HS—*school* CA-9
Bishop Moore HS—*school* FL-3
Bishop Mora HS—*school* CA-9
*Bishop Mountain* CO-8
*Bishop Mountain* ID-8
Bishop Mountain Brook—*stream* ME-1
Bishop Mountain Lookout—*hist pl* ID-8
Bishop Mtn—*summit* (2) AL-4
Bishop Mtn—*summit* CA-9
Bishop Mtn—*summit* ID-8
Bishop Mtn—*summit* ME-1
Bishop Mtn—*summit* NH-1
Bishop Mtn—*summit* SD-7
Bishop Mtn—*summit* WA-9
Bishop Museum—*building* HI-9
Bishop Natl Bank of Hawaii—*hist pl* HI-9
Bishop-Noble House—*hist pl* OH-6
Bishop Nose—*summit* AZ-5
Bishop Oil Field—*oilfield* TX-5
Bishop Park—*flat* CA-9
Bishop Park—*park* MI-6
Bishop Park—*park* MT-8
Bishop Park—*park* TX-5
Bishop Pass—*gap* CA-9
Bishop Peak—*summit* CA-9
Bishop Peak—*summit* CO-8
Bishop Peak—*summit* NV-8
Bishop Peak—*summit* NM-5
Bishop Peak Tank—*mine* AZ-5
Bishop Pit—*mine* NV-8
Bishop Place—*locale* AZ-5
Bishop Place—*locale* MT-8
Bishop Place (historical)—*locale* MS-4
Bishop Point—*cape* (2) AK-9
Bishop Point—*cape* FL-3
Bishop Point—*cape* HI-9
Bishop Point—*cape* RI-1
Bishop Point—*cape* WY-8
Bishop Point—*cliff* AL-4
Bishop Point—*cliff* CO-8
Bishop Pond—*lake* (2) ME-1
Bishop Pond—*lake* MI-6
Bishop Pond—*reservoir* CT-1
Bishop Pond Dam—*dam* MS-4
Bishop Pond Stream—*stream* ME-1
Bishop Post Office (historical)—*building* TN-4
Bishop Ranch—*locale* AK-9
Bishop Ranch—*locale* CO-8
Bishop Ranch—*locale* NM-5
Bishop Ranch—*locale* TX-5
**Bishop Rancheria (Indian Reservation)**—*pop pl* CA-9
Bishop Ranch Oil Field—*oilfield* WY-8
Bishop Ready HS—*school* OH-6
Bishopric, The—*summit* UT-8
Bishop Ridge—*ridge* (2) UT-8
Bishop Ridge—*ridge* WI-6
Bishop Road Sch—*school* KY-4
Bishop Road Site (48CA1612)—*hist pl* WY-8
Bishop Roberts Park—*park* IN-6
Bishop Rock—*bar* AK-9
Bishop Rock—*island* CT-1
Bishop Rock—*summit* AK-9
Bishop Rock—*summit* CO-8
Bishop Rockhouse Branch—*stream* WV-2
Bishop Rock Island—*island* AK-9
Bishop Run—*stream* IN-6
Bishop Run—*stream* NJ-2
Bishop Run—*stream* (2) OH-6
Bishop Ryan HS—*school* ND-7
Bishops—*locale* NJ-2
Bishop Saddle—*gap* ID-8
Bishops Bayou—*gut* FL-3
Bishops Bridge—*bridge* AL-4
Bishops Camps—*locale* ME-1
Bishops Canyon—*valley* UT-8
Bishops Cap—*summit* MT-8
Bishops Cave—*cave* TN-4
Bishop Sch—*hist pl* CT-1
Bishop Sch—*school* CA-9
Bishop Sch—*school* (2) CT-1
Bishop Sch—*school* FL-3
Bishop Sch—*school* (3) IL-6
Bishop Sch—*school* MA-1
Bishop Sch—*school* MN-6
Bishop Sch—*school* OK-5
Bishop Sch—*school* VA-3
Bishops Chapel—*church* VA-3
Bishop Sch (historical)—*school* AL-4
Bishop Sch (historical)—*school* TN-4
Bishops Claim—*mine* CA-9
Bishops Corner—*locale* DE-2
Bishops Corner—*locale* VA-3
**Bishop's Corner**—*pop pl* CT-1
Bishops Corners—*locale* NY-2
*Bishops Cove* RI-1
*Bishops Creek* NV-8
**Bishops Cross**—*pop pl* NC-3
**Bishops Cross (Bishops Crossing)**—*pop pl* NC-3
*Bishop's Head* MD-2
Bishops Head—*cape* MD-2
**Bishops Head**—*pop pl* MD-2
Bishops Head Marsh—*swamp* MD-2
Bishops Head Point—*cape* MD-2
Bishop's House—*hist pl* OR-9
Bishop's House/Chancery Office—*hist pl* MN-6
*Bishop's Ice Pond* CT-1
Bishop Site—*hist pl* TX-5
Bishops Lake—*lake* TN-4
Bishops Lake Dam—*dam* MS-4
Bishops Landing Airp—*airport* MO-7
Bishops Lane Retreat House—*locale* IL-6
Bishops Lodge—*locale* NM-5
*Bishop's Mill Pond* CT-1
Bishops Nose—*pillar* AZ-5
Bishop's Palace—*hist pl* TX-5
*Bishops Point* HI-9
*Bishop's Point* RI-1
Bishops Point—*cape* FL-3
Bishops Point—*cape* WA-9
Bishops Pond—*lake* (3) CT-1
Bishops Pond—*reservoir* NY-2
Bishop Spring—*spring* AL-4
Bishop Spring—*spring* (2) AZ-5
Bishop Spring—*spring* (2) ID-8
Bishop Spring—*spring* NV-8
Bishop Spring—*spring* OR-9
Bishop Spring—*spring* (3) UT-8
*Dishop Springs* UT-0
Bishop Springs—*spring* MO-7
Bishop Springs Area—*spring* UT-8
**Bishops Ridge (subdivision)**—*pop pl* NC-3
Bishops Rock—*cape* NJ-2
Bishops School, The—*school* CA-9
Bishops Summit—*summit* PA-2
Bishop Stang HS—*school* MA-1
Bishops Tank—*reservoir* AZ-5
Bishopstead—*hist pl* WI-6
Bishop Stevens Campground—*locale* CA-9
Bishop Store (historical)—*locale* MS-4
Bishop Street—*locale* NY-2
Bishop Street Sch—*school* PA-2
Bishop Swamp—*swamp* CT-1
Bishop Tank—*reservoir* (2) AZ-5
Bishopton—*hist pl* MD-2
*Bishop Toolen High School* AL-4
Bishop Top—*summit* TN-4
**Bishop (Township of)**—*pop pl* IL-6
Bishop Tract—*civil* CA-9
Bishop Verot HS—*school* FL-3
**Bishopville**—*pop pl* MD-2
**Bishopville**—*pop pl* NY-2
**Bishopville**—*pop pl* OH-6
**Bishopville**—*pop pl* SC-3
Bishopville (CCD)—*cens area* SC-3
Bishopville Cem—*cemetery* TN-4
Bishopville Ch—*church* TN-4
Bishopville Commercial Hist Dist—*hist pl* SC-3
Bishopville High School—*reservoir* SC-3
Bishopville Prong—*stream* MD-2
Bishop Walsh HS—*school* NY-2
*Bishop Waterhole* OR-9
Bishop Watterson HS—*school* OH-6
Bishop Well—*well* NM-5
Bishop Well—*well* TX-5
Bishop West Barn—*hist pl* ID-8
Bishop White House—*building* PA-2
Bishop Winston Ch of Christ—*church* AL-4
**Bishop Wood**—*pop pl* NJ-2
Bishtown—*locale* PA-2
*Bis-ii-ah Wash* AZ-5
Bis Ii Ah Wash—*stream* AZ-5
Bis Ii Ah Wash—*valley* AZ-5
*Bisinum* FM-9
*Bisinun* FM-9
*Bisivi* FM-9
Bisker—*cape* CA-9
Biskie Head—*cape* MA-1
Biskra Palms—*locale* CA-9
Biskup Rsvr—*reservoir* CO-8
Bisland Bayou—*stream* MS-4
Bisland Bayou Oil Field—*oilfield* MS-4
Bisland Cem—*cemetery* LA-4
*Bisley Canyon* CO-8
*Bismarch* WV-2
*Bismarck* AL-4
*Bismarck* KS-7
Bismarck—*locale* CA-9
Bismarck—*locale* WV-2
Bismarck—*other* PA-2
**Bismarck**—*pop pl* AR-4
**Bismarck**—*pop pl* IL-6
**Bismarck**—*pop pl* MO-7
**Bismarck**—*pop pl* ND-7
**Bismarck**—*pop pl* OH-6
Bismarck Bomb Scoring Site—*military* ND-7
*Bismarck Canyon* AZ-5
Bismarck Chapel—*church* AR-4
Bismarck Civic Auditorium—*hist pl* ND-7
Bismarck Creek—*stream* AK-9
*Bismarck Grove* KS-7
Bismarck Grove—*uninc pl* KS-7
Bismarck Junior Coll—*school* ND-7
Bismarck Lake—*lake* WI-6
Bismarck Lake—*reservoir* AZ-5
Bismarck Lookout Tower—*locale* AR-4
Bismarck Memorial Airp—*airport* MO-7
Bismarck Mesa—*summit* AZ-5
*Bismarck Mtn* AZ-5
Bismarck Mtn—*summit* WA-9
Bismarck Municipal Airp—*airport* ND-7
Bismarck Peak—*summit* WA-9
**Bismarck Township**—*pop pl* NE-7
Bismarck (Township of)—*fmr MCD* AR-4
**Bismarck (Township of)**—*pop pl* MI-6
**Bismarck (Township of)**—*pop pl* MN-6
Bismarck Trail—*trail* WA-9
Bismarck Tribune Bldg—*hist pl* ND-7
Bismarek Ch—*church* AR-4
*Bismark* IL-6
*Bismark* KS-7
*Bismark* OR-9
*Bismark* WV-2
Bismark Basin—*basin* ID-8
Bismark Canyon—*valley* AZ-5
Bismark Creek—*stream* AK-9
Bismark Creek—*stream* ID-8
Bismark Creek—*stream* MI-6
Bismark Creek—*stream* OR-9
Bismark Grove—*locale* KS-7
*Bismark Hill* UT-8
Bismark (historical P.O.)—*locale* IA-7
Bismark-Ida Florence Group Mine—*mine* SD-7
Bismark Knob—*summit* CA-9
Bismark Lake—*reservoir* SD-7
Bismark Lake Dam—*dam* SD-7
Bismark Meadows—*flat* ID-8
Bismark Mine—*mine* MT-8
Bismark Mine—*mine* SD-7
Bismark Mine—*mine* UT-8
Bismark Mtn—*summit* AK-9
Bismark Mtn—*summit* AZ-5
Bismark Mtn—*summit* (2) ID-8
Bismark Peak—*summit* NV-8
Bismark Peak—*summit* UT-8
Bismark Rsvr—*reservoir* MT-8
Bismark Sch—*school* MI-6
Bismark Station—*locale* IA-7
**Bismark Township**—*pop pl* NE-7
Bismark Trail—*trail* ID-8
Bismark Work Center—*locale* ID-8
Bismount Ch—*church* MO-7
Bismuth (historical)—*locale* SD-7
Bisnaga Alta Wash—*stream* CA-9
Bison—*locale* MT-8
Bison—*locale* WV-2
**Bison**—*pop pl* KS-7
**Bison**—*pop pl* OK-5
**Dison**—*pop pl* SD-7
Bison Basin Oil Field—*oilfield* WY-8
Bison Bone Rsvr—*reservoir* MT-8
Bison Branch—*stream* IN-6
Bison Canyon—*valley* MT-8
Bison Cem—*cemetery* OK-5
Bison Creek—*stream* CO-8
Bison Creek—*stream* (2) MT-8
Bison Creek Campground—*locale* MT-8
Bison Creek Ranch—*locale* MT-8
Bison Dam—*dam* SD-7
Bison Flats—*flat* SD-7
Bison Gulch—*valley* AK-9
Bisoni Ridge—*ridge* NV-8
*Bison Lake* MN-6
Bison Lake—*lake* CO-8
Bison Lake—*reservoir* OK-5
Bison Lake Campground—*locale* CO-8
Bison Mtn—*summit* CO-8
Bison Mtn—*summit* (2) MT-8
Bison Municipal Airp—*airport* SD-7
*Bison Peak* CO-8
Bison Peak—*summit* WY-8
Bison Post Office (historical)—*building* TN-4
Bison Range—*spring* MT-8
Bison Range HQ—*locale* MT-8
Bison Rsvr—*reservoir* CO-8
**Bison Spur**—*pop pl* ND-7
Bisonte—*locale* CO-8
**Bison Township**—*pop pl* SD-7
*Bisoue Point* MD-2
Bisphams Mill Creek—*stream* NJ-2
*Bisping* WA-9
Bisping Canyon—*valley* WA-9
Bisplinghoff Cem—*cemetery* TN-4
Bisquit Tank—*reservoir* NM-5
Biss—*locale* GA-3
**Bissaasha (historical)**—*pop pl* MS-4
Biss Cem—*cemetery* TN-4
Bissel Cove—*bay* RI-1
Bissel Creek—*stream* ID-8
Bissel Creek—*stream* MI-6
*Bissell* AL-4
Bissell—*locale* CA-9
Bissell—*locale* IL-6
Bissell—*locale* NJ-2
Bissell—*locale* OR-9
**Bissell**—*pop pl* CT-1
**Bissell**—*pop pl* MS-4
**Bissell**—*pop pl* MO-7
**Bissell**—*pop pl* PA-2
Bissell, Gen. Daniel, House—*hist pl* MO-7
*Bissel Lake* MI-6
Bissell Baptist Ch—*church* MS-4
Bissell Bluff—*cliff* KY-4
Bissell Bridge—*bridge* CT-1
Bissell Brook—*stream* CT-1
Bissell Brook—*stream* NH-1
*Bissell Canyon* ID-8
Bissell Canyon—*valley* ID-8
Bissell Cave—*cave* TN-4
Bissell Cem—*cemetery* IL-6
Bissell Covered Bridge—*bridge* MA-1
*Bissell Creek* ID-8
Bissell Creek—*stream* KS-7
Bissell Creek—*stream* KY-4
Bissell Creek—*stream* MI-6
Bissell Flat—*flat* WA-9
Bissell Grange Hall—*building* MT-8
Bissell Hill—*summit* VT-1
Bissell Hills—*range* CA-9
Bissell Hollow—*valley* TN-4
*Bissell Lake* MI-6
Bissell Lake—*lake* IL-6
Bissell Point Sch—*school* KS-7
Bissell Pond—*lake* MI-6
Bissell Pond—*lake* NY-2
*Bissell Post Office* AL-4
Bissell Sanitorium—*hospital* DE-2
Bissell Sch—*school* MT-8
Bissell Sch—*school* NJ-2
*Bissells Cove* RI-1
Bissells Lake—*lake* NE-7
Bissell Spring—*spring* ID-8
Bissell Tavern-Bissell's Stage House—*hist pl* CT-1
Bissel Park (historical)—*park* PA-2
Bissel Sch—*school* WA-9
*Bissels Cove* RI-1
*Bissels Mill* RI-1
Bissels Mounds—*summit* MN-6
Bissel Street Water Tower—*hist pl* MO-7
Bissets Ranch—*locale* CA-9
Bissette-Cooley House—*hist pl* NC-3
Bissett Mill (historical)—*locale* NC-3
Bissett Mtn—*summit* TX-5
Bissett Ranch—*locale* TX-5
Bissett Ranch Oil Field—*oilfield* TX-5
Bissett Run—*stream* PA-2
Bissett Sch—*school* MO-7
Bissig Ditch—*canal* WI-6
Bissing Cem—*cemetery* MI-6
Bissinger Cem—*cemetery* OH-6
Bissitte Bay—*bay* FL-3
Bissitt Ranch—*locale* TX-5
Bissitt Windmill—*locale* TX-5
Bissle Hill—*summit* NY-2
Bissman, B.F., House—*hist pl* OH-6
Bissman, Peter, House—*hist pl* OH-6
Bissman Block—*hist pl* OH-6
Bisson, Abraham, House—*hist pl* MN-6
Bisson, William, House—*hist pl* WA-9
Bisson Creek—*stream* MT-8
Bissonet Maned Downs Country Club—*other* LA-4
**Bissonet Plaza**—*pop pl* LA-4
Bissonet Plaza Sch—*school* LA-4
**Bissonnet**—*pop pl* LA-4
Bissonnette Pond—*reservoir* CT-1
Bi-State Development Agency Harbor—*harbor* MO-7
**Bisti**—*pop pl* NM-5
Bistineau, Lake—*reservoir* LA-4
Bistineau Ch—*church* LA-4
Bistineau Compressor Station—*other* LA-4
Bisti Oil Field—*other* NM-5
Bisti Trading Post—*locale* NM-5
Bistline Covered Bridge—*hist pl* PA-2
*Bistol* TX-5
**Bi-Stone**—*pop pl* TX-5
Di-Stone Oil Field—*oilfield* TX-5
Biswell Creek—*stream* ID-8
Biswell Hill—*summit* AR-4
*Bita Hache* AZ-5
*Bitahachee Wash* AZ-5
*Bita Hache Wash* AZ-5
*Bitahatsi Wash* AZ-5
*Bitahochee* AZ-5
*Bitahochee (Bidahochi)* AZ-5
*Bitahochee Wash* AZ-5
*Bitahotsi* AZ-5
*Bitahotsi Wash* AZ-5
*Bitang* PW-9
*Bitat-a Kin* AZ-5
Bitch Bay—*swamp* NC-3
*Bitch Creek* WY-8
Bitch Creek—*stream* (2) ID-8
Bitch Creek—*stream* WY-8
Bitch Creek Cow Camp—*locale* ID-8
Bitch Creek Narrows—*gap* WY-8
Bitch Creek Trail—*trail* WY-8
*Bitch Islands* ME-1
Bitch Lake—*lake* ID-8
Bitch Mtn—*summit* NY-2
*Biteley* MI-6
**Bitely**—*pop pl* (2) MI-6
Bitely Lake—*lake* MI-6
Biter Creek—*stream* CA-9
*Bithahotshi Wash* AZ-5
Bithers Brook—*stream* ME-1
**Bithlo**—*pop pl* FL-3
Bithynia Ch—*church* GA-3
*Bitlabito* NM-5
Bitlabito—*locale* AZ-5
Bitlabito—*locale* NM-5
*Bitlabito Sjpring* NM-5
*Bitlabito Wash* AZ-5
*Bitlabito Wash* NM-5
*Bitler* KS-7
*Bitlers Beach Cottages* NV-8
**Bitner**—*pop pl* PA-2
Bitner Butte—*summit* NV-8
Bitner Cem—*cemetery* KS-7
Bitner Cem—*cemetery* MI-6
Bitner Ranch—*locale* NV-8
Bitner Run—*stream* PA-2
Bitner Sch (abandoned)—*school* PA-2
Bitner Spring—*spring* TN-4
Bitner Spring—*spring* UT-8
Bitner Table—*flat* NV-8
**Bitney Corner**—*pop pl* CA-9
Bit O-Heather Golf Club—*other* IL-6
Bit Rock—*bar* CA-9
Bit Run—*stream* IN-6
*Bitsihuit-so* AZ-5
*Bitsihuitsoe Butte* AZ-5
*Bitsi Huitsos Butte* AZ-5
Bitsihuitsos Butte—*summit* AZ-5
*Bittabito Creek* AZ-5
*Bittahochee* AZ-5
Bittenbender Covered Bridge—*hist pl* PA-2
Bittenbender Creek—*stream* CA-9
Bittener Lake—*lake* ND-7
Bitten Lake—*lake* MI-6
Bitter Branch—*stream* AL-4
Bitter Brook—*stream* ME-1
Bitter Brook—*stream* NY-2
Bitterbrush Rsvr—*reservoir* ID-8
Bitterbush Channel—*canal* CA-9
Bitter Canyon—*valley* CA-9
Bitter Canyon—*valley* (2) NM-5
*Bitter Creek* AL-4
*Bitter Creek* CA-9
*Bittercreek* KS-7
*Bitter Creek* MT-8
*Bitter Creek* OK-5
*Bitter Creek* TX-5
*Bitter Creek* WY-8
Bitter Creek—*locale* KS-7
**Bitter Creek**—*pop pl* WY-8
Bitter Creek—*stream* AK-9
Bitter Creek—*stream* (6) AZ-5
Bitter Creek—*stream* (3) CA-9
Bitter Creek—*stream* (3) CO-8
Bitter Creek—*stream* GA-3
Bitter Creek—*stream* ID-8
Bitter Creek—*stream* IA-7
Bitter Creek—*stream* (4) KS-7
Bitter Creek—*stream* MN-6
Bitter Creek—*stream* MS-4
Bitter Creek—*stream* MO-7
Bitter Creek—*stream* (4) MT-8
Bitter Creek—*stream* (2) NM-5
Bitter Creek—*stream* (9) OK-5
Bitter Creek—*stream* OR-9
Bitter Creek—*stream* (3) SD-7
Bitter Creek—*stream* TN-4
Bitter Creek—*stream* (6) TX-5
Bitter Creek—*stream* (5) UT-8
Bitter Creek—*stream* (3) WA-9
Bitter Creek—*stream* (5) WY-8
*Bitter Creek Canyon* UT-8
Bitter Creek Canyon—*valley* CA-9
Bitter Creek Cem—*cemetery* OK-5
Bitter Creek Corral—*summit* UT-8
Bitter Creek Divide—*ridge* UT-8
Bitter Creek Gas Field—*oilfield* UT-8
Bitter Creek Mines—*mine* CO-8
Bitter Creek Oil Field—*oilfield* KS-7
Bitter Creek Ranch—*locale* TX-5
Bitter Creek Spring—*spring* (2) CA-9
Bitter Creek Tank—*reservoir* NM-5
Bitter Creek Well—*well* UT-8
Bitter End—*locale* TN-4
Bitter End Sch (historical)—*school* TN-4
Bitterfoot Mtn—*summit* WA-9
Bitter Gulch—*valley* TX-5
Bitter Head Point—*cape* MD-2
*Bitter Hot Spring* OR-9
*Bitter Lake* SD-7
Bitter Lake—*lake* NM-5
Bitter Lake—*lake* ND-7
Bitter Lake—*lake* (3) SD-7
Bitter Lake—*lake* WA-9
Bitter Lake—*reservoir* TX-5
Bitter Lake—*uninc pl* WA-9
Bitter Lake Creek—*stream* TX-5
Bitter Lake Natl Wildlife Ref—*park* NM-5
Bitter Lake State Public Shooting Area—*park* SD-7
Ditter Lick—*spring* OR-9
Bitter Lick Creek—*stream* OR-9
Bitterlick Creek—*stream* OR-9
**Bitter Lick (historical)**—*pop pl* OR-9
Bitterman Bldg—*hist pl* IN-6
*Bittermilk Canyon* CO-8
Bittern Brook—*stream* NJ-2
Bitter Ridge—*ridge* (2) NV-8
*Bitterroot* MP-9
*Bitter-root Beach* MH-9
*Bitter-root Cliffs* MH-9
Bitterroot Creek—*stream* MO-7
Bitterroot Divide—*ridge* MT-8
Bitterroot Flat Campground—*locale* MT-8
Bitterroot Irrigation District Canal—*canal* MT-8
Bitterroot Mtns—*range* ID-8
Bitterroot Mtns—*range* MT-8
Bitterroot Pass—*gap* MT-8
Bitterroot Range—*range* ID-8
Bitterroot Range—*range* MT-8
Bitterroot Range—*range* OR-9
*Bitter-Root Ravine* MH-9
*Bitterroot River* ID-8
*Bitterroot River* MT-8
*Bitter Root River* WA-9
Bitterroot River—*stream* MT-8
Bitterroot Springs—*spring* ID-8
Bitters Butte—*summit* ID-8
Bitters Creek—*stream* AK-9
Bitters Creek—*stream* ID-8
Bitter Seep—*spring* (2) UT-8
Bitter Seeps Wash—*stream* AZ-5
Bitter Seep Wash—*valley* UT-8
Bitters Peak—*summit* ID-8
*Bitter Spring* AZ-5
Bitter Spring—*spring* (6) AZ-5
Bitter Spring—*spring* CA-9
Bitter Spring—*spring* CO-8
Bitter Spring—*spring* NV-8
Bitter Spring—*spring* OR-9
Bitter Spring—*spring* TX-5
Bitter Spring—*spring* UT-8

Bitter Spring Archaeol Site (4-SBr-2659)—hist pl CA-9
Bitter Spring Canyon—valley CO-8
Bitter Spring Creek—stream UT-8
Bitter Spring Gulch—valley CO-8
Bitter Springs NV-8
**Bitter Springs**—pop pl AZ-5
Bitter Springs Sch—school WY-8
**Bitter Springs (Trading Post)**—pop pl AZ-5
Bitter Spring Valley—basin NV-8
Bitter Spring Wash NV-8
Bitter Spring Wash—valley AZ-5
**Bittersville**—pop pl PA-2
Bittersville Sch—school PA-2
Bittersweet—hist pl LA-4
Bittersweet Bridge—bridge IN-6
Bittersweet Cove—bay FL-3
Bittersweet Creek—stream KY-4
Bittersweet Creek—stream SD-7
Bittersweet Hill—summit NY-2
Bittersweet Island—island MN-6
Bittersweet Lake—lake WI-6
Bittersweet Lake—reservoir IN-6
Bittersweet Lake Dam—dam IN-6
Bitters Well AZ-5
Bitter Wash NV-8
Bitterwater—locale CA-9
Bitter Water Basin—basin AZ-5
Bitterwater Canyon—valley (2) CA-9
Bitterwater Cem—cemetery CA-9
Bitter Water Creek UT-8
Bitterwater Creek—stream (3) CA-9
Bitterwater Lake—lake CA-9
Bitterwater Pumping Station—other CA-9
Bitterwater Spring—spring CA-9
Bitter Water Springs—spring AZ-5
Bitterwater Spring (Undrinkable)—spring CA-9
Bitterwater-Tully Sch—school CA-9
Bitterwater Valley—basin CA-9
Bitterwater Valley—valley (2) CA-9
Bitter Water Wash—valley AZ-5
Bitterwater Well—well AZ-5
Bitterwater Wells—well CA-9
Bitterweed Lake—lake UT-8
Bitter Well AZ-5
Bitter Well—well (2) AZ-5
Bitter Well—well NV-8
Bitter Well—well TX-5
Bitter Well Canyon—valley TX-5
Bitter Well Mountains AZ-5
Bitter Well Mtn—summit TX-5
Bitter Wells AZ-5
Bitter Well Tank—reservoir TX-5
Bitter Well Wash—stream AZ-5
Bittick Cem—cemetery MO-7
Bittick Hollow—valley TX-5
Bittinger—locale MD-2
Bittinger—locale PA-2
Bittinger Fire Tower—locale MD-2
Bittinger Hill—summit MD-2
Bittings Mill CT-1
Bitting Spring—spring OK-5
**Bittle Heights (subdivision)**—pop pl TN-4
Bittle Ranch—locale TX-5
Bittle Sch (historical)—school PA-2
Bittner Creek—stream OR-9
Bittner Knoll—summit UT-8
Bittner Knoll Rsvr—reservoir UT-8
Bittner Lake—reservoir IN-6
Bittner Lake Dam—dam IN-6
Bittner Plaza (Shop Ctr)—locale FL-3
**Bittners Corner**—pop pl PA-2
Bittners Mill—locale PA-2
Bitton Ranch—locale ID-8
Bitton Spring—spring ID-8
Bitts Hill—summit PA-2
Bitt Shop Pond (historical)—reservoir MA-1
Bitty Branch—stream AL-4
Bitty Creek—stream SD-7
**Bitumen**—pop pl PA-2
Bitumen Mesa UT-8
Bitumul Tank—reservoir AZ-5
Bitz Drain—stream MI-6
Bitzer Sch—school PA-2
Bitzer's Mill Covered Bridge—hist pl PA-2
Bitzla River—stream AK-9
Bitzner Meadow—flat VA-3
Bitz Sch (abandoned)—school PA-2
Bitzshtini Mountains—other AK-9
Bivalve—locale CA-9
**Bivalve**—pop pl MD-2
**Bivalve**—pop pl NJ-2
Bivalve Harbor—bay MD-2
Bivalve Point—cape NC-3
Bivans Arm—lake FL-3
**Biven**—pop pl AL-4
Biven Arm Shop Ctr—locale FL-3
Biven Creek—stream OK-5
Biven Hollow—valley MO-7
**Bivens**—pop pl LA-4
**Bivens**—pop pl TN-4
Bivens Branch—stream LA-4
Bivens Branch—stream (2) TN-4
Bivens Branch—stream (2) TX-5
Bivens Cem—cemetery TN-4
Bivens Creek—stream FL-3
Bivens Creek—stream MT-8
Bivens Grove—locale IA-7
Bivens Oil Field—oilfield LA-4
**Bivins**—pop pl TX-5
Bivins Bay—swamp GA-3
Bivins Branch—stream TN-4
Bivins Camp—locale TX-5
Bivins Cem—cemetery VA-3
Bivins Channing Farm—locale TX-5
Bivins Channing Ranch—locale TX-5
Bivins Compressor Station—other TX-5
Bivins Gulch—valley MT-8
Bivins House—hist pl TX-5
Bivins Lake—reservoir TX-5
Bivins Lit Ranch—locale TX-5
Bivins-McLeod (CCD)—cens area TX-5
Bivins Ranch—locale TX-5
Bivins Sch—school TX-5
Bivins X L Ranch—locale TX-5
Bivo Island—island MN-6
Bivora Tank—reservoir TX-5
Bivouac Creek—stream ID-8
Bivouac Mountain WY-8
Bivouac Peak WY-8
Bivouac Peak—summit WY-8
Bivvins House—hist pl TN-4
**Biwabik**—pop pl MN-6
Biwabik Mine—mine MN-6
**Biwabik (Township of)**—pop pl MN-6
Biwyah MS-4
Bixby—locale MN-6
**Bixby**—pop pl IL-6
**Bixby**—pop pl KY-4
**Bixby**—pop pl MO-7
**Bixby**—pop pl NE-7
**Bixby**—pop pl NC-3
**Bixby**—pop pl OK-5
**Bixby**—pop pl SD-7
**Bixby**—pop pl TX-5
Bixby—uninc pl CA-9
Bixby, Walter E., House—hist pl MO-7
Bixby Bridge—bridge CA-9
Bixby Brook—stream MA-1
Bixby Camp—locale SD-7
Bixby Canyon—valley CA-9
Bixby Cem—cemetery OK-5
Bixby Corner—locale PA-2
Bixby Creek CA-9
Bixby Creek—stream CA-9
Bixby Creek—stream MI-6
Bixby Drain—canal MI-6
Bixby Hill—summit NY-2
Bixby Hill—summit VT-1
Bixby Hosp—hospital MI-6
Bixby Island—island VT-1
**Bixby Knolls**—pop pl CA-9
Bixby Landing—locale CA-9
Bixby Mtn—summit CA-9
Bixby Number One Well—well AZ-5
Bixby Park—park CA-9
Bixby Pond—reservoir NH-1
Bixby Post Office—building SD-7
Bixby Ranch—locale AZ-5
Bixby Ranch—locale CA-9
Bixby Ranch—locale MT-8
Bixby Res Dam—dam MA-1
Bixby Rsvr—reservoir MA-1
Bixby Sch—school (3) CA-9
Bixby Slough CA-9
Bixby Spring—spring OR-9
Bixbys Rsvr MA-1
Bixby State Park—park IA-7
Bixby Towhead—bar TN-4
Bixby Well Number Two—well AZ-5
Bixler—locale CA-9
Bixler—locale MD-2
Bixler—locale PA-2
Bixler Bridge—bridge VA-3
Bixler Cem—cemetery KS-7
Bixler Ch—church MD-2
Bixler Gap—gap PA-2
Bixler Lake—lake IN-6
Bixler Lake Ditch—canal IN-6
Bixler Mtn—summit AZ-5
Bixler Ranch—locale NM-5
Bixler Run—stream PA-2
Bixler Saddle—gap AZ-5
Bixlers Bluff—summit PA-2
Bixler Tank—reservoir AZ-5
Bixley Gulch—valley CO-8
Bixon Creek—stream OH-6
Bix Sioux Township—civil SD-7
Bixter Lake IN-6
Bixton Tunnel—tunnel PA-2
Biy—island FM-9
**Biyae**—pop pl GU-9
Biyan Gigane MH-9
Biyatabiyatto-To MP-9
Biyugoren To MP-9
Bizarreto—locale PR-3
Bizzell Brook—stream CT-1
Biz Point—cape WA-9
**Bizza Ridge (subdivision)**—pop pl NC-3
Bizzell, Asher W., House—hist pl NC-3
Bizzell Cem—cemetery AR-4
Bizzell Grove Ch—church NC-3
Bizzell Grove Memorial Gardens—cemetery NC-3
B J Blount Lake Dam—dam MS-4
B J Cave—cave AL-4
Bjerkson Flat—flat OR-9
Bjerremark—uninc pl AK-9
BJ Lake—lake WA-9
B Jones Pond Dam—dam MS-4
Bjork Canyon—valley WA-9
Bjork Lake—lake (2) MN-6
Bjorkman Hollow—valley UT-8
Bjorks Creek—stream MN-6
Bjorlie Ranch—locale MT-8
Bjorneberg Garage—hist pl MN-6
Bjornland Draw—valley SD-7
Bjornson State Wildlife Mngmt Area—park MN-6
**Bjornson Township**—pop pl ND-7
Bjorsness Cem—cemetery MN-6
B J Wye—locale NV-8
B K Corral—locale OR-9
Bkeho Bar—dam SD-7
B Kelly Ranch—locale NM-5
Bkilabad PW-9
B K Ranch—locale (2) MT-8
BK Tank—reservoir AZ-5
Bkulabekong—cape PW-9
Bkulabeluu, Elechol Ra—beach PW-9
Bkulachelid PW-9
Bkulachelid—cape PW-9
Bkuladudes—cape PW-9
Bkulaibelau—cape PW-9
Bkul a Medorm PW-9
Bkulamelmil—cape PW-9
Bkul A Ngebedangel PW-9
Bkul A Ngerimd PW-9
Bkulangriil PW-9
Bkulangrill—cape PW-9
Bkulatabriual—cape PW-9
Bkulatiull—cape PW-9
Bkulatmochegelibel—cape PW-9
Bkul Klim PW-9
Bkulklim—cape PW-9
Bkulngeblai—cape PW-9
Bkul Ngeil PW-9
Bkul-ngeiil—cape PW-9
Bkulngerbekall—cape PW-9
Bkulngetchuir—cape PW-9
Bkul Ngiil PW-9
Bkulomekerall—cape PW-9
Bkulsechuul—cape PW-9
Bkurrengel—cape PW-9
Blaamyhre Lake—lake MN-6
Blabaum Cem—cemetery WI-6
**Blabon**—pop pl ND-7
Blabon Dam—dam ND-7
Blabon Hill—summit ME-1
Blacherne—hist pl IN-6
Blachleys Hill—summit NJ-2
**Blachleyville**—pop pl OH-6
Blachleyville Cem—cemetery OH-6
**Blachly**—pop pl OR-9
Blachly Cem—cemetery IN-6
Blachly Cem—cemetery OR-9
Blachly Mountain Forest Wayside—locale OR-9
Blachman Swamp—swamp MI-6
Blach Sch—school CA-9
Black AL-4
Black MI-6
Black UT-8
Black—locale AK-9
Black—locale IL-6
Black—locale MD-2
Black—locale PA-2
Black—locale (2) TX-5
**Black**—pop pl AL-4
**Black**—pop pl ID-8
**Black**—pop pl MO-7
Black, Alfred L., House—hist pl WA-9
Black, Bayou—gut LA-4
Black, Bayou—stream (6) LA-4
Black, Benjamin Clayton, House—hist pl AR-4
Black, Dr. John A., House Complex—hist pl CO-8
Black, E. B., House—hist pl TX-5
Black, Hugo, House—hist pl AL-4
Black, John, House—hist pl UT-8
Black, John M., Cabin—hist pl TN-4
Black, Merritt, House—hist pl WI-6
Black, Philip J., House—hist pl OH-6
Black, Samuel M., House—hist pl CA-9
Black, The TN-4
Black, William, Family House—hist pl AR-4
Black, William, Homestead—hist pl PA-2
Blackaby Creek—stream MT-8
Blackaby Sch—school IL-6
Black Acres—uninc pl FL-3
Black Alder Creek—stream WI-6
Black Alder Lake—lake WI-6
Black Alder Spring—spring AZ-5
Blackamore Creek—stream KY-4
Blackamore Creek—stream TN-4
Blackamore Knob—summit OH-6
Blackamore Pond—lake RI-1
Black and Tan Creek—stream AK-9
Black and Tan Glacier—glacier AK-9
Black and White Farm Barn—hist pl NY-2
Black and White Lakes—lake WA-9
Black Angel Trail—trail NH-1
Blackankle—locale AL-4
Black Ankle—locale TX-5
Black Ankle Branch—stream AL-4
Black Ankle Creek—stream GA-3
Black Ankle Creek—stream IN-6
Black Ankle Creek—stream (2) TN-4
Black Ankle Mine (Inactive)—mine NC-3
Blackankle Sch (historical)—school TN-4
Black Ant Grasslands MH-9
Black Ant Ravine MH-9
Black Ape Mine—mine UT-8
Blackard Cem—cemetery MS-4
Blackard Hollow—valley AR-4
Blackard Hollow—valley MS-4
Black Arm Prong DE-2
Black Arm Prong—stream DE-2
Black Armuth Ditch—canal IN-6
**Black Ash**—pop pl PA-2
**Blackash**—pop pl PA-2
Black Ash Bog—swamp NY-2
Black Ash Ch—church PA-2
Black Ash Corners PA-2
Black Ash Creek—stream PA-2
Black Ash Mtn—summit (2) NY-2
Black Ash Swamp—swamp ME-1
Black Ash Swamp—swamp (7) NY-2
Black Ash Swamp—swamp (3) PA-2
Black Ash Swamp—swamp WI-6
Black Ash Swamp Natural Area—area PA-2
Black Bald—summit NC-3
Black Ball Hill—summit MA-1
Black Balsam Knob—summit NC-3
Blackband—locale OH-6
Black Bank Channel—channel MA-1
Blackbank Hassock NY-2
Black Bank Marsh—swamp NY-2
Blackbank River—channel GA-3
Black Banks NY-2
Black Banks—levee GA-3
Black Banks Creek—stream SD-7
Black Banks Hassock NY-2
Black Banks Island—island NY-2
Black Bar—bar OR-9
Black Baron—locale PA-2
Black Barren Spring—spring PA-2
Black Basin—basin CA-9
**Black Bass**—pop pl TX-5
Black Bass Bar—bar WI-6
Black Bass Bay—bay MI-6
Black Bass Lake—lake MN-6
Black Bay—bay (2) AK-9
Black Bay—bay (2) ID-8
Black Bay—bay LA-4
Black Bay—bay (2) MN-6
Black Bay—bay (2) NY-2
Black Bay—swamp FL-3
Black Bay—swamp NC-3
Black Bay—swamp SC-3
Black Bay—swamp TX-5
**Black Bay Beach**—pop pl MD-2
Black Bay (Carolina Bay)—swamp NC-3
Black Bay Lookout Tower—locale MN-6
Black Bay Narrows—channel MN-6
Black Bayou AR-4
Black Bayou LA-4
Black Bayou—gut AL-4
Black Bayou—gut AR-4
Black Bayou—gut (5) LA-4
Black Bayou—gut (5) MS-4
Black Bayou—gut (2) MO-7
**Black Bayou**—pop pl MS-4
Black Bayou—stream AR-4
Black Bayou—stream (17) LA-4
Black Bayou—stream (6) MS-4
Black Bayou—stream (2) TN-4
Black Bayou—stream (5) TX-5
Black Bayou Cem—cemetery LA-4
Black Bayou Ch (historical)—church MS-4
Black Bayou Cutoff—canal LA-4
Black Bayou Drainage Ditch—canal MS-4
Black Bayou Elementary School MS-4
Black Bayou Ferry—locale LA-4
Black Bayou Junction—locale MS-4
**Black Bayou Junction**—pop pl MS-4
Black Bayou Lagoon—lake LA-4
Black Bayou Lake—lake (2) LA-4
Black Bayou Lake—reservoir LA-4
Black Bayou Landing—locale MS-4
Black Bayou Lateral—canal AR-4
Black Bayou Oil Field—oilfield LA-4
Black Bayou Rsvr LA-4
Black Bayou Rsvr—reservoir LA-4
Black Bayou Sch—school MS-4
Black Bayou Sch (historical)—school MS-4
Black Beach MH-9
Black Beach—beach (2) MA-1
Black Beacon Point NC-3
Black Bear—locale CA-9
Black Bear—locale OK-5
**Black Bear**—pop pl ID-8
Black Bear—uninc pl PA-2
Black Bear Camp—locale CA-9
Black Bear Campground—locale MT-8
Black Bear Canyon—valley MT-8
Black Bear Cove—bay NC-3
Black Bear Creek ID-8
Black Bear Creek—stream (2) AK-9
Black Bear Creek—stream CA-9
Blackbear Creek—stream CO-8
Black Bear Creek—stream ID-8
Black Bear Creek—stream (5) MT-8
Black Bear Creek—stream (2) OK-5
Blackbeard Creek—channel GA-3
Blackbeard Island—island GA-3
Blackbeard Island Natl Wildlife Ref—park GA-3
Black Beard Pond VA-3
Blackbeard Pond—lake VA-3
Blackbeards Bluff—cliff MD-2
Blackbeards Creek—bay VA-3
Blackbeard Shoal—bar GA-3
Black Bear Forest Service Station—locale MT-8
Black Bear Guard Station—locale MT-8
Black Bear Hill—summit PA-2
Black Bear Hollow—valley AR-4
Black Bear Hump—summit MT-8
Black Bear Lake MN-6
Black Bear Lake UT-8
Black Bear Lake—lake AK-9
Black Bear Lake—lake (2) CA-9
Black Bear Lake—lake MN-6
Black Bear Mine—mine CA-9
Black Bear Mine—mine CO-8
Black Bear Mine—mine ID-8
Black Bear Mine—mine NM-5
Black Bear Mine—mine OR-9
Black Bear Mine—mine WA-9
Black Bear Mine (Inactive)—mine CA-9
Black Bear Mtn—summit MT-8
Black Bear Mtn—summit NY-2
Black Bear Mtn—summit OK-5
Black Bear Observation Post—locale AK-9
Black Bear Point—summit MT-8
Black Bear Run—stream PA-2
Black Bear Sch—school WI-6
**Black Bear Spring**—pop pl AZ-5
Black Bear Spring—spring (3) AZ-5
Black Bear Summit—gap CA-9
Black Bear Swamp—swamp OR-9
Black Bear Swamp—swamp PA-2
Black Bear Trail—trail PA-2
Black Beauty Mesa—summit NV-8
Black Beauty Mine—mine (2) AZ-5
Black Beauty Mine—mine CO-8
Black Belt—area AL-4
Black Belt—area MS-4
Black Belt Agricultural Experiment Station—locale AL-4
Black Belt Community Health Center—hospital AL-4
Black Belt Experimental Substation AL-4
Blackbelt Sch (historical)—school AL-4
Black Belt School AL-4
Blackberry—locale TX-5
**Blackberry**—pop pl MN-6
**Blackberry**—pop pl VA-3
Blackberry Branch—stream (2) KY-4
Blackberry Campground—park OR-9
Blackberry Canyon—valley OR-9
Blackberry Cem—cemetery IL-6
Blackberry Cem—cemetery MN-6
**Blackberry City**—pop pl WV-2
**Blackberry Corner**—pop pl OH-6
Blackberry Creek KY-4
Blackberry Creek—gut NJ-2
Blackberry Creek—stream (2) CA-9
Blackberry Creek—stream IL-6
Blackberry Creek—stream KY-4
Blackberry Creek—stream MO-7
Blackberry Creek—stream (2) OR-9
Blackberry Creek—stream (3) TX-5
Blackberry Creek—stream VA-3
Blackberry Creek—stream WA-9
Blackberry Fork—stream (2) KY-4
Blackberry Hay Farm Lake—reservoir MO-7
**Blackberry Heights**—pop pl IL-6
Blackberry Hill—hist pl NC-3
Blackberry Hill—ridge NH-1
Blackberry Hill—summit ME-1
Blackberry Hill—summit OK-5
Blackberry Hill—summit RI-1
Blackberry Hill—summit VT-1
Blackberry Hill—summit WI-6
**Blackberry Inn**—pop pl NC-3
Blackberry Island—island CA-9
Blackberry Island—island OH-6
Blackberry Island—island OK-5
Blackberry Island—island TX-5
Blackberry Lake—lake (2) MI-6
Blackberry Lake—lake (2) MN-6
Blackberry Lone Sch—school MO-7
Blackberry (Magisterial District)—fmr MCD VA-3
Blackberry Pond—reservoir PA-2
Blackberry River—stream CT-1
Blackberry Run—stream (3) PA-2
Blackberry Sch—school KY-4
Blackberry Sch—school PA-2
Blackberry Sch (abandoned)—school MO-7
Blackberry Spring—spring (2) AZ-5
Blackberry Spring—spring CA-9
**Blackberry (Township of)**—pop pl IL-6
**Blackberry (Township of)**—pop pl MN-6
Blackberry Trail—trail PA-2
**Blackberry Woods**—pop pl IL-6
Black Bess Point—cape MA-1
Black Bess Rocks—bar MA-1
Black Bess Shaft—mine AZ-5
Black Bess Shaft—mine UT-8
**Black Betsey**—pop pl WV-2
Black Betsey Keys FL-3
**Black Betsy**—pop pl WV-2
Black Betsy Keys—island FL-3
Black Betty Brook MA-1
Black Betty Brook—stream MA-1
Black Bill Draw—valley WY-8
Black Bill Flat AZ-5
Black Bill Park—flat AZ-5
Black Bill Peak—summit CA-9
Black Bill Ridge—ridge CA-9
Black Bill Tank—reservoir AZ-5
Black Birch Canyon—valley CA-9
Black Birch Canyon—valley UT-8
Blackbird DE-2
Blackbird—locale DE-2
Blackbird, Chief Andrew J., House—hist pl MI-6
Blackbird Bay—bay NY-2
Blackbird Bayou—gut LA-4
Black Bird Bayou Drainage Ditch MS-4
Black Bird Bend—bend IA-7
Black Bird Bend—bend NE-7
Blackbird Branch—stream KY-4
Blackbird Bridge DE-2
Blackbird Camp Ground—locale CA-9
Blackbird Ch—church NE-7
Blackbird Creek IA-7
Blackbird Creek MO-7
Blackbird Creek—stream DE-2
Blackbird Creek—stream ID-8
Blackbird Creek—stream MO-7
Blackbird Creek—stream (2) NE-7
Blackbird Creek—stream NV-8
Blackbird Creek—stream (2) OK-5
Blackbird Creek—stream WY-8
Blackbird Dam—dam CO-8
Blackbird Draw—valley WY-8
Blackbird Gulch—valley MT-8
Blackbird Gut—gut NJ-2
Blackbird Hill—hist pl NE-7
Blackbird Hill—summit NE-7
Blackbird Hill—summit NM-5
Blackbird Hundred—civil DE-2
Blackbird Island—island AK-9
Black Bird Island—island ME-1
Blackbird Island—island MI-6
Blackbird Island—island MN-6
Blackbird Island—island MO-7
Blackbird Island—island WI-6
Blackbird Knob—summit WV-2
Blackbird Knob Trail—trail WV-2
Blackbird Lake—lake CA-9
Blackbird Lake—lake MN-6
Blackbird Landing—locale DE-2
Blackbird Mine—mine AZ-5
Blackbird Mine—mine CO-8
Blackbird Mine—mine (3) ID-8
Blackbird Mine—mine SD-7
Blackbird Mine—mine UT-8
Blackbird Mine (Aban'd)—locale AK-9
Blackbird Mtn—summit ID-8
Blackbird Mtn—summit OK-5
Blackbird Point—cape WI-6
Blackbird Pond—lake LA-4
Blackbird Ranch—locale NV-8
Blackbird Reef—bar WI-6
Blackbird Rsvr—reservoir ID-8
Blackbird Sch—school MO-7
Black Birds Creek DE-2
Blackbird Slough—gut MN-6
Blackbird Spring—spring NV-8
Blackbird State Forest—forest DE-2
Blackbird State For Tybout Tract—forest DE-2
Blackbird Station DE-2
**Blackbird Township**—pop pl NE-7
Blackbird Townsite ID-8
**Blackbird Townsite**—pop pl ID-8
Blackbird Valley CA-9
Blackbird Valley—valley CA-9
Black Bluff AL-4
Black Bluff—cliff (3) AL-4
Black Bluff—cliff CO-8
Black Bluff—cliff NM-5
Black Bluff—cliff TX-5
Black Bluff—cliff UT-8
Black Bluff Ch AL-4
Black Bluff Ch—church AL-4
Black Bluff Hill—summit NH-1
Black Bluff Landing—locale AL-4
Black Bluff Landing (historical)—locale AL-4
Black Bluff Rapids—rapids MT-8
Black Bluffs—cape NM-5
Black Bluffs—cliff MT-8
Black Bluffs (historical)—cliff SD-7
Black Bob Canyon—valley CA-9
Black Bob Mine—mine CA-9
Black Bob Mine—mine NM-5
Black Bog—swamp ME-1
Black Bottom—bend IL-6
Black Bottom—bend TN-4
**Black Bottom**—pop pl AL-4
**Black Bottom**—pop pl KY-4
**Black Bottom**—pop pl WV-2
Black Bottom—valley TN-4
Black Bottom—valley TX-5
Black Bottom—valley WI-6
Black Bottom Branch—stream AL-4
Black Bottom Branch—stream LA-4
Black Bottom Crater—crater AZ-5
Black Bottom Creek—stream GA-3
Black Bottom Creek—stream TN-4
**Black Bottom (Deskins Addition)**—pop pl WV-2
Black Bottom Sch (historical)—school TN-4
Blackbourn Creek VA-3
Blackbourne Coll (historical)—school MS-4
Blackbourne Creek VA-3
Black Box—basin NV-8
Black Box—valley UT-8
Black Box, The UT-8
Blackboy Creek—stream OK-5
Black Boy Mine—mine UT-8
Blackboys—island CT-1
Black Branch FL-3
Black Branch TX-5
Black Branch VA-3
Black Branch—locale VA-3
Black Branch—stream (9) AL-4
Black Branch—stream (10) AR-4
Black Branch—stream (6) FL-3
Black Branch—stream (6) GA-3
Black Branch—stream (3) IL-6
Black Branch—stream IN-6
Black Branch—stream (5) KY-4
Black Branch—stream (8) LA-4
Black Branch—stream MD-2
Black Branch—stream (7) MS-4
Black Branch—stream (2) MO-7
Black Branch—stream (7) NC-3
Black Branch—stream SC-3
Black Branch—stream (8) TN-4
Black Branch—stream (20) TX-5
Black Branch—stream (6) VA-3
Black Branch Canal—canal FL-3
Black Branch Ch—church VA-3
Black Branch Creek TX-5
Black Branch Nulhegan River—stream VT-1
Black Branch Swamp—stream VA-3
Black Branch Swamp—swamp FL-3
Black Bridge—bridge ND-7
Black Bridge—bridge TX-5
Black Bridge—bridge UT-8
Black Bridge—hist pl CO-8
Black Bridge—locale KY-4
Blackbridge—locale NY-2
Black Bridge—other MI-6
Blackbridge Picnic Area—park AZ-5
Black Bridge Spring—spring IA-7
Black Brook MA-1
Black Brook NH-1
Black Brook NY-2
Black Brook WI-6
**Black Brook**—pop pl NY-2
Black Brook—stream (2) CT-1
Black Brook—stream IN-6
Black Brook—stream (27) ME-1
Black Brook—stream (10) MA-1
Black Brook—stream (2) MN-6
Black Brook—stream (16) NH-1
Black Brook—stream (3) NJ-2
Black Brook—stream (15) NY-2
Black Brook—stream OH-6
Black Brook—stream (3) VT-1
Black Brook—stream (5) WI-6
Black Brook County Park—park WI-6
Black Brook Cove—bay ME-1
Black Brook Creek MN-6
Black Brook Dam—dam MA-1
Black Brook Dike—dam OH-6
Black Brook Ditch—canal OH-6
Black Brook Farm—locale ME-1
Black Brook Flowage—reservoir WI-6
Black Brook Golf Course—other OH-6
Black Brook Hill—summit ME-1
Black Brook Mountains—summit ME-1
Black Brook Notch—gap ME-1
Blackbrook Park—park NJ-2
Black Brook Pond—lake (2) ME-1
Black Brook Pond—lake NY-2
Black Brook Ponds—lake ME-1
Black Brook Ponds—lake NY-2
Black Brook Rsvr—reservoir MA-1
Black Brook Sch—school WI-6
Black Brook Swamp—swamp MN-6
**Black Brook (Town of)**—pop pl NY-2
**Black Brook (Town of)**—pop pl WI-6
Black Brook Trail—trail NH-1
Black Brother Mountain NC-3
Black Brothers NC-3
Black Brothers Mountain NC-3
Black Brush Flat—flat AZ-5
Black Brush Point—cape TX-5
Black Brush Ridge—ridge TX-5
Black Buck Spring—spring UT-8
Black Bull Creek—stream OK-5
Black Bull Draw—valley SD-7
Black Bull Mine—mine MT-8
Black Bull Peak—summit NM-5
Black Bull Ranch—locale TX-5
Black Bull Saddle—gap NM-5
Blackbull Spring—spring MT-8
Black Bull Spring—spring (2) OR-9
Black Bull Spring—spring SD-7
Black Bull Springs—spring OR-9
Black Bunch—area UT-8
Blackburn KS-7
Blackburn OH-6
Blackburn—locale AK-9
Blackburn—locale AR-4
Blackburn—locale KY-4
Blackburn—locale NV-8
Blackburn—locale PA-2
Blackburn—locale WV-2
**Blackburn**—pop pl (2) AL-4
**Blackburn**—pop pl LA-4
**Blackburn**—pop pl MO-7
**Blackburn**—pop pl NC-3
**Blackburn**—pop pl OK-5
**Blackburn**—pop pl (2) PA-2
Blackburn, Ambrose, Farmstead—hist pl TN-4
Blackburn, Edward M., House—hist pl KY-4
Blackburn, Julius, House—hist pl KY-4
Blackburn, Mount—summit AK-9
Blackburn (Aban'd)—locale AK-9
Blackburn Administrative Site—locale NV-8
Blackburn Bay—bay TX-5
Blackburn Bay—gut FL-3
Blackburn Bay—swamp FL-3
Blackburn Branch—stream AL-4
Blackburn Branch—stream IL-6

Blackfoot Marsh Reservoir ID-8
Blackfoot Meadows—flat MT-8
Blackfoot Mine—mine AZ-5
Blackfoot Mine—mine IN-6
Blackfoot Mine—mine MT-8
Blackfoot Mountains ID-8
Blackfoot Mtn—summit MT-8
Blackfoot Mtns—range ID-8
Blackfoot Oil Field—oilfield TX-5
Blackfoot Peak ID-8
Blackfoot Pond—lake NY-2
Blackfoot Railway Depot—hist pl ID-8
Blackfoot Range ID-8
Blackfoot River—stream ID-8
Blackfoot River—stream MT-8
Blackfoot River Reservoir ID-8
Blackfoot Rsvr—reservoir ID-8
Blackfoot Rsvr—reservoir MT-8
Blackfoot Sch (abandoned)—school MO-7
Black For AZ-5
Black For—area CO-8
Black For—forest CO-8
Black For—woods AZ-5
Black Ford—locale NC-3
Blackford—locale VA-3
**Blackford**—pop pl KY-4
Blackford Cem—cemetery IL-6
Blackford Ch—church KY-4
**Blackford County**—pop pl IN-6
Blackford County Courthouse—hist pl IN-6
Blackford Creek—stream KY-4
Blackford HS—school CA-9
Blackford HS—school IN-6
Blackford Park—park IA-7
Blackford Sch—school CA-9
Blackford Sch—school IL-6
Blackford Sch—school WI-6
Blackford Slough—stream IL-6
Black Forest—locale NV-8
**Black Forest**—pop pl CO-8
Black Forest—uninc pl NM-5
Black Forest Baptist Assembly—other CO-8
Black Forest Ch—church CO-8
Black Forest Inn Airp—airport PA-2
Black Forest Mine—mine NV-8
Black Forest-Peyton—cens area CO-8
Black Forest Rec Area—park CO-8
Blackforest Sch—school CO-8
Black Forest Trail—trail PA-2
Black Fork OH-6
Black Fork WV-2
Black Fork WY-8
Black Fork—locale AR-4
**Blackfork**—pop pl OH-6
Black Fork—stream (3) AR-4
Black Fork—stream KY-4
Black Fork—stream NC-3
Black Fork—stream (3) OH-6
Black Fork—stream (2) OK-5
Black Fork—stream (3) WV-2
Blackfork Bayou—stream LA-4
Black Fork Cem—cemetery AR-4
Black Fork Cem—cemetery OK-5
Black Fork Ch—church AR-4
Black Fork Creek—stream TX-5
Black Fork Creek—stream UT-8
**Blackfork Junction**—pop pl OH-6
**Black Fork Junction**—pop pl OH-6
Blackfork Lake—lake LA-4
Black Fork Lateral—canal AR-4
Black Fork Lateral—trail OK-5
Black Fork (Magisterial District)—fmr MCD WV-2
Black Fork Mohican River—stream OH-6
Black Fork Mountain—ridge AR-4
Black Fork Mtn—summit OK-5
Black Fork (Township of)—fmr MCD AR-4
Black Fork Trail—trail OK-5
Black Fox—locale TN-4
**Black Fox**—pop pl TN-4
Black Fox Bluff—cliff OK-5
Black Fox Branch—stream TN-4
Black Fox Cem—cemetery OK-5
Black Fox Creek—stream TN-4
Black Foxe Military Institute—school CA-9
Black Fox Ford (historical)—crossing TN-4
Black Fox (historical)—locale SD-7
Black Fox Hollow—valley OK-5
Black Fox Hollow—valley TN-4
Black Fox Hollow—valley WV-2
Black Fox Island—island PA-2
Black Fox Lake—lake WI-6
Black Fox Methodist Ch—church TN-4
Black Fox Mine—mine TN-4
Black Fox Mtn—summit CA-9
Black Fox Post Office TN-4
Blackfox Post Office (historical)—building TN-4
Black Fox Ridge—ridge NC-3
Black Fox Rock—pillar CA-9
Black Fox Run—stream PA-2
Black Fox Sch—school TN-4
Black Fox Sch (historical)—school TN-4
Black Fox Spring—spring SD-7
Black Fox Springs TN-4
Black Fox Springs—spring OK-5
Black Fox Valley—valley (2) TN-4
Black Friday Mines—mine MT-8
Black Gap—gap AL-4
Black Gap—gap (2) AZ-5
Black Gap—gap NM-5
Black Gap—gap NC-3
Black Gap—gap (2) PA-2
Black Gap—gap SD-7
Black Gap—gap (2) TX-5
Black Gap—gap WY-8
Black Gap—locale AZ-5
**Blackgap**—pop pl PA-2
Black Gap Bridge—hist pl AZ-5
Black Gap Cave—cave AL-4
Black Gap Tank—reservoir NM-5
Black Gap Trail—trail PA-2
Black Gap Well—well AZ-5
Black Gate—gap NV-8
Black Gate Canyon—valley NV-8
Blackgate Windmill—locale TX-5
Black George Creek—stream ID-8
Black George Creek—stream MI-6
Black Giant—summit CA-9
Black Giant Peak CA-9
Black Glacier—glacier AK-9
Black Glade—stream NM-5
Black Glass Canyon—valley NV-8
Black Gnat—locale KY-4
**Black Gnat**—pop pl KY-4
Black Gold—locale KY-4
Black Gore Creek—stream CO-8
Black Gore Pass CO-8
Black Gorge—valley OR-9
Black Grama Tank—reservoir AZ-5
Black Grocery Bridge—bridge NY-2
Black Ground Bay—swamp NC-3
Black Ground Ch—church AL-4
Blackground Hollow—valley AR-4
Black Ground Mtn—summit AL-4
Black Ground Sch (historical)—school AL-4
Black Grove—basin ID-8
Black Grove—island LA-4
Black Grove—woods CA-9
Black Grove Ch—church KY-4
Black Gulch—valley (5) CA-9
Black Gulch—valley (4) CO-8
Black Gulch—valley (2) MT-8
Black Gulch—valley (2) UT-8
Black Gulch—valley (2) WY-8
Black Gulch Ditch—canal MT-8
Black Gulch Point—summit MT-8
Black Gully—valley TX-5
Black Gully Creek TX-5
**Blackgum**—pop pl OK-5
Blackgum Branch—stream NC-3
Black Gum Branch—stream (2) TN-4
Black Gum Corners (historical)—locale AL-4
Black Gum Draft—valley VA-3
Black Gum Flats—flat OK-5
Black Gum Gap—gap NC-3
Black Gum Gap—gap TN-4
Black Gum Head—valley AL-4
Black Gum Hollow—valley AL-4
Blackgum Hollow—valley TN-4
Black Gum Hollow—valley WV-2
Blackgum Landing Public Use Area—park OK-5
Blackgum Mtn—summit OK-5
Blackgun Gap—gap TN-4
Black Gut—gut PA-2
Black Gut—gut VA-3
Black Gut Creek—stream NC-3
Black Hall CT-1
**Black Hall**—pop pl CT-1
Black Hall Bay—bay NC-3
Black Hall Meadows—flat MT-8
Blackhall Mtn—summit WY-8
Blackhall Pond CT-1
Black Hall Pond—lake CT-1
Blackhall River CT-1
Black Hall River—stream CT-1
Blackham Canyon—valley UT-8
Blackham Creek—stream UT-8
Black Hammer—locale MN-6
Black Hammer Bluff—summit MN-6
Black Hammer Hill—summit ND-7
Black Hammer (Township of)—civ div MN-6
Black Hammock—island (3) FL-3
Black Hammock—island (3) GA-3
Black Hammock—island NC-3
Black Hammock Cem—cemetery FL-3
Black Hammock Island—island FL-3
Black Hammock Point—bar NC-3
Blackham Sch—school CT-1
Black Hand Narrows—gap OH-6
Black Hank Creek—stream MT-8
Black Hat Mine—mine UT-8
Blackhaw Bayou—stream MS-4
Black Haw Branch—stream MO-7
Black Haw Branch—stream VA-3
Black Haw Gulch—valley WY-8
Blackhawk (2) IN-6
Blackhawk MS-4
Black Hawk SD-7
Blackhawk—locale IL-6
Black Hawk—locale KY-4
Black Hawk—locale LA-4
Black Hawk—locale MO-7
Blackhawk—locale OH-6
**Black Hawk**—pop pl CO-8
**Blackhawk**—pop pl (2) IN-6
**Black Hawk**—pop pl IA-7
**Blackhawk**—pop pl IA-7
**Black Hawk**—pop pl MS-4
**Blackhawk**—pop pl PA-2
**Blackhawk**—pop pl SD-7
**Blackhawk**—pop pl WV-2
**Black Hawk**—pop pl WI-6
Black Hawk—summit UT-8
Black Hawk Acad (historical)—school MS-4
Black Hawk Airp—airport IN-6
Blackhawk Airp—airport MO-7
Blackhawk A Lateral—canal UT-8
Blackhawk Bar—bar CA-9
Blackhawk Bar—bar ID-8
Blackhawk Battlefield Park—park IL-6
Blackhawk Bayou—stream MS-4
**Blackhawk Beach**—pop pl IN-6
Blackhawk Bench—bench UT-8
Blackhawk B Lateral—canal UT-8
Blackhawk Bottoms Public Hunting Area—area IA-7
Blackhawk Branch—stream TX-5
Blackhawk Cabin—locale MT-8
Blackhawk Campground—locale (2) UT-8
Blackhawk Canal—canal UT-8
Blackhawk Canyon—valley (3) CA-9
Black Hawk Canyon—valley CO-8
Black Hawk Canyon—valley NM-5
Black Hawk Canyon—valley UT-8
Blackhawk Cem—cemetery SD-7
Black Hawk Ch—church MS-4
Black Hawk Coll—school IL-6
Blackhawk Coulee—valley MT-8
Blackhawk Country Club—other OH-6
Blackhawk Country Club—other WI-6
Blackhawk Country Club Mound Group (47 DA 131)—hist pl WI-6
Black Hawk County Cem—cemetery IA-7
Black Hawk County Courthouse*—building IA-7
Black Hawk County Courthouse—building IA-7
Black Hawk County Soldiers Memorial Hall—hist pl IA-7
Black Hawk Creek ND-7
Blackhawk Creek—stream CA-9
Blackhawk Creek—stream IN-6
Black Hawk Creek—stream (3) IA-7
Blackhawk Creek—stream (2) SD-7
Blackhawk Creek—stream TX-5
Blackhawk Creek—stream WI-6
Black Hawk Elementaty Sch—hist pl SD-7
**Blackhawk Forest**—pop pl IN-6
Black Hawk Gap—gap PA-2
Black Hawk Golf Course—locale PA-2
Blackhawk Gulch—valley CO-8
Blackhawk Gulch—valley NM-5
Blackhawk Heights IL-6
Blackhawk Hollow—valley TX-5
Blackhawk Hollow—valley WV-2
Blackhawk Hotel—hist pl IA-7
Blackhawk HS—school PA-2
Blackhawk Island—island IL-6
Blackhawk Island*—island IA-7
Blackhawk Island—island OH-6
Blackhawk Island—island WI-6
**Blackhawk Island**—pop pl IL-6
**Blackhawk Island**—pop pl WI-6
Blackhawk Kindergarten—school PA-2
Blackhawk Lake IA-7
Black Hawk Lake—lake CA-9
Blackhawk Lake—lake MN-6
Black Hawk Lake—reservoir IA-7
Black Hawk Lake State Game Mngmt Area—park IA-7
Black Hawk Lake State Rec Area—park IA-7
Blackhawk Lateral—canal UT-8
Black Hawk Marsh—swamp IA-7
Blackhawk Millpond MI-6
Black Hawk Mine—mine AZ-5
Blackhawk Mine—mine AZ-5
Black Hawk Mine—mine AZ-5
Blackhawk Mine—mine (2) CA-9
Blackhawk Mine—mine CO-8
Black Hawk Mine—mine (2) CO-8
Blackhawk Mine—mine ID-8
Black Hawk Mine—mine IL-6
Black Hawk Mine—mine (2) NV-8
Blackhawk Mine—mine NV-8
Blackhawk Mine—mine NM-5
Blackhawk Mine—mine UT-8
Blackhawk Mine—mine WA-9
Blackhawk Mine (Active)—mine NM-5
Blackhawk Mines—mine AZ-5
Blackhawk Mines—mine NM-5
Blackhawk Mountain CO-8
Blackhawk Mountain—ridge CA-9
Black Hawk Mtn—summit CA-9
Black Hawk Mtn—summit CO-8
Blackhawk Mtn—summit CO-8
Black Hawk Mtn—summit ID-8
Black Hawk Mtn—summit WA-9
Black Hawk Museum and Lodge—hist pl IL-6
Blackhawk Park—park IL-6
Black Hawk Park—park IA-7
Blackhawk Park—park OH-6
Blackhawk Park—park WI-6
Blackhawk Peak CO-8
Blackhawk Peak—summit CO-8
Blackhawk Pond—lake MI-6
Blackhawk Pond—lake MS-4
Blackhawk Raceway—other IL-6
Black Hawk Ranch—locale CA-9
Blackhawk Rapids—rapids ID-8
Black Hawk Ridge—ridge CA-9
Black Hawk Ridge—ridge WI-6
Blackhawk Run—stream MD-2
Blackhawk Run—stream OH-6
Blackhawk Sch—school (2) IL-6
Black Hawk Sch—school IL-6
Blackhawk Sch—school (3) IL-6
Blackhawk Sch—school IA-7
Black Hawk Sch—school (2) IA-7
Blackhawk Sch—school MD-2
Blackhawk Sch—school (2) WI-6
Black Hawk Sch—school WI-6
Blackhawk Shaft—mine CO-8
Black Hawk State Park—park IL-6
**Blackhawk (subdivision)**—pop pl NC-3
Black Hawk Tank—reservoir AZ-5
Black Hawk Township—fmr MCD (3) IA-7
Black Hawk Township Cem—cemetery IA-7
Black Hawk Township (historical)—civil SD-7
**Blackhawk (Township of)**—pop pl IL-6
Blackhawk Well—well CA-9
Black Haw Mtn—summit OK-5
Blackhaw Sch (historical)—school MS-4
Black Hay Windmill—locale NM-5
Black Head HI-9
Black Head—cape AK-9
Black Head—cliff ME-1
Black Head—summit (3) ME-1
Blackhead—summit NY-2
Blackhead Hill—summit PA-2
Blackhead Mountains—range NY-2
Blackhead Peak—summit CO-8
Black Head Rock—island CA-9
Blackheath Pond—lake VA-3
Black Henry Hollow—valley MO-7
Black Hill AZ-5
Black Hill MA-1
Black Hill WA-9
Black Hill—locale TX-5
Black Hill—ridge NH-1
Black Hill—summit (2) AK-9
Black Hill—summit (6) AZ-5
Black Hill—summit (6) CA-9
Black Hill—summit CT-1
Black Hill—summit ME-1
Black Hill—summit (2) MD-2
Black Hill—summit MA-1
Black Hill—summit NV-8
Black Hill—summit (3) NH-1
Black Hill—summit (7) NM-5
Black Hill—summit NY-2
Black Hill—summit (4) TX-5
Black Hill—summit UT-8
Black Hill—summit (2) VT-1
Black Hill—summit (2) VA-3
Black Hill—summit WA-9
Black Hill Basin—basin NE-7
Black Hill Basin Sch—school NE-7
Black Hill Branch—stream TX-5
Black Hill Cem—cemetery TX-5
Black Hill Creek UT-8
Black Hill Creek—stream NE-7
Black Hill Creek Sch—school NE-7
Black Hill Hollow—valley TX-5
Black Hill Park AZ-5
Black Hill Pond—lake ME-1
Black Hills AZ-5
Black Hills NM-5
Black Hills—other AK-9
Black Hills—other (2) CA-9
Black Hills—other NM-5
Black Hills—range AZ-5
Black Hills—range (4) CA-9
Black Hills—range CO-8
Black Hills—range NV-8
Black Hills—range SD-7
Black Hills—range (2) UT-8
Black Hills—range (2) WA-9
Black Hills—ridge AZ-5
Black Hills—ridge NM-5
Black Hills—spring MT-8
Black Hills—summit (10) AZ-5
Black Hills—summit (2) CO-8
Black Hills—summit (2) NV-8
Black Hills—summit (2) NM-5
Black Hills—summit (2) OR-9
Black Hills—summit (4) TX-5
Black Hills—summit (3) UT-8
Black Hills—summit VT-1
Black Hills—summit WY-8
Black Hills Arroyo—stream CO-8
Black Hills Cem—cemetery TX-5
Black Hill Sch—school WV-2
Black Hill Sch (historical)—school MS-4
Black Hills Community Hosp. Heliport—airport WA-9
Black Hills Corral—locale CA-9
Black Hills Country Club (historical)—locale SD-7
Black Hills Creek TX-5
Black Hills Creek—stream TX-5
Black Hills Creek—stream UT-8
Black Hills Gap—gap NV-8
Black Hills Kennel Club—locale SD-7
Black Hills Mine—mine (2) AZ-5
Black Hills Natl Cem—cemetery SD-7
Black Hills Natl Forest—park SD-7
Black Hills Ordnance Depot (abandoned)—military SD-7
Black Hills Playhouse—locale SD-7
Black Hill Spring UT-8
Black Hills RC and D Stabilization Dam—dam SD-7
Black Hills Rsvr—reservoir CA-9
Black Hills Sch (historical)—school MO-7
Black Hills Shaft—mine CO-8
Black Hills Spring—spring UT-8
Black Hills State Coll—school SD-7
Black Hills Tank—reservoir (2) AZ-5
Black Hills Tank—reservoir NM-5
Black Hills Tank—reservoir TX-5
Black Hills Trail—trail CO-8
Black Hill Stream—stream ME-1
Black Hills Tunnel—mine CO-8
Black Hills Well—well CA-9
Black Hills Well—well UT-8
Black Hills Wildlife Mngmt Area—park UT-8
Black Hill Tank—reservoir (5) AZ-5
Black Hill Tank—reservoir (2) TX-5
Black Hill Wash—stream AZ-5
**Black (historical)**—pop pl OR-9
Black Hog Gut—gut DE-2
Black Hog Hollow—valley WV-2
Black Hog Landing—locale DE-2
Black Hole—basin (2) UT-8
Black Hole—lake NY-2
Black Hole—valley CA-9
Black Hole, The—valley PA-2
Blackhole Creek PA-2
Blackhole Creek—stream MD-2
Black Hole Creek—stream PA-2
Black Hole Hollow—valley NY-2
Black Hole Hollow—valley VT-1
Black Hole Mine—mine NV-8
Blackhole Pond—lake FL-3
Black Hole Run PA-2
Blackhole Run—stream WV-2
Black Holes, The—lake FL-3
Black Hollow—locale CO-8
Black Hollow—valley (2) AL-4
Black Hollow—valley AR-4
Black Hollow—valley (2) CO-8
Black Hollow—valley IN-6
Black Hollow—valley (3) KY-4
Black Hollow—valley (5) MO-7
Black Hollow—valley OH-6
Black Hollow—valley OK-5
Black Hollow—valley PA-2
Black Hollow—valley (7) TN-4
Black Hollow—valley TX-5
Black Hollow—valley (2) UT-8
Black Hollow—valley VA-3
Black Hollow Branch—stream TN-4
**Black Hollow Junction**—pop pl CO-8
Black Hollow Oil Field—oilfield CO-8
Black Hollow Rsvr—reservoir CO-8
Blackhoof—locale MN-6
Blackhoof Creek—stream OH-6
Blackhoof Lake—lake (2) MN-6
Blackhoof River—stream MN-6
**Blackhoof (Township of)**—pop pl MN-6
Blackhoof Valley Sch—school MN-6
Blackhorn Branch—stream WV-2
Black Hornet Mine—mine ID-8
Black Horse AZ-5
Black Horse NJ-2
Blackhorse PA-2
Blackhorse—locale MD-2
Black Horse—locale NV-8
Black Horse—locale NJ-2
Black Horse—locale (2) PA-2
Black Horse—locale SD-7
**Black Horse**—pop pl MD-2
**Black Horse**—pop pl OH-6
**Blackhorse**—pop pl PA-2
**Black Horse**—pop pl (2) PA-2
Black Horse Arena—locale SD-7
Blackhorse Butte—summit OR-9
Black Horse Butte—summit SD-7
Black Horse Butte Creek—stream SD-7
Black Horse Canyon—valley CO-8
Black Horse Canyon—valley ID-8
Black Horse Canyon—valley NV-8
Black Horse Canyon—valley NM-5
Blackhorse Canyon—valley OR-9
Black Horse Canyon—valley UT-8
Black Horse Creek SD-7
Blackhorse Creek—stream AZ-5
Blackhorse Creek—stream ID-8
Blackhorse Creek—stream OR-9
Black Horse Creek—stream PA-2
Blackhorse Draw—valley OR-9
Blackhorse Forest Campground—park OR-9
Blackhorse Gap—gap VA-3
Black Horse Hotel (historical)—building PA-2
Blackhorse Island—island ME-1
Blackhorse Lake MT-8
Black Horse Lake—lake MT-8
Black Horse Lake Flat—flat MT-8
Black Horse Point—cliff UT-8
Black Horse Post Office (historical)—building PA-2
Black Horse Ridge—ridge (2) UT-8
Blackhorse Run—stream PA-2
Black Horse Sch—school PA-2
Black Horse Spring—spring ID-8
Black Horse Spring—spring UT-8
Black Horse Tavern—building PA-2
Black Horse Tavern—hist pl CT-1
Black Horse Tavern—hist pl ME-1
Black Horse Tavern—hist pl PA-2
Black Horse Tavern—locale PA-2
Blackhorse Trail DC-2
Blackhorse Wash AZ-5
Blackhorse Wash—arroyo AZ-5
Black Hosp—hospital PA-2
Black House—hist pl TN-4
Black House—locale NM-5
Black House Branch—stream TN-4
Black House Creek—stream NY-2
Black House Creek—stream TN-4
Blackhouse Creek—stream TX-5
Blackhouse Fork PA-2
Black House Mtn—summit TN-4
Blackhurst Gulch—valley CO-8
Blackie Branch—stream KY-4
Blackie Coulee—valley MT-8
Blackie Creek—stream ID-8
Blackie Lake—lake CA-9
Blackies Bay—bay MT-8
Blackies Branch—stream NC-3
Blackies Hollow—valley VA-3
Blackie Spring—spring AZ-5
Blackies Tank—reservoir AZ-5
Blackie Trap Canyon—valley AZ-5
Black Imp—summit ID-8
Blackinghouse Branch—stream KY-4
Blackington MA-1
Blackington Corners ME-1
Blackington Swamp—swamp MA-1
Black Inky Spring—spring AZ-5
Blackinton Corners ME-1
**Blackinton Corners**—pop pl ME-1
Blackinton Hist Dist—hist pl MA-1
Blackinton Houses and Park—hist pl MA-1
**Blackinton (subdivision)**—pop pl MA-1
Blackio Tank —reservoir TX-5
Black Island—island (3) AK-9
Black Island—island AR-4
Black Island—island FL-3
Black Island—island (2) GA-3
Black Island—island (13) ME-1
Black Island—island NE-7
Black Island—island NV-8
Black Island—island NH-1
Black Island—island VT-1
Black Island Cove—bay NH-1
Black Island Creek—gut GA-3
Black Island (historical) —island TN-4
Black Island Lake—lake MN-6
Black Island Ledge—bar ME-1
Blackiston—locale DE-2
Blackiston, Benjamin, House—hist pl DE-2
Blackiston Ch—church DE-2
Blackiston Cross Roads DE-2
Blackistone Island MD-2
Blackiston Heights IN-6
**Blackiston Mill**—pop pl (2) IN-6
Blackiston Run—stream IN-6
**Blackiston Village**—pop pl IN-6
Blackiston Wildlife Area—park DE-2
Blackjack MO-7
Black Jack NC-3
Black Jack TX-5
Black Jack—hist pl NC-3
Black Jack—locale KS-7
Black Jack—locale KY-4
Blackjack—locale OH-6
Blackjack—locale OK-5
Black Jack—locale TN-4
Black Jack—locale TX-5
Blackjack—locale (2) TX-5
Blackjack—mine UT-8
**Black Jack**—pop pl AR-4
**Blackjack**—pop pl GA-3
**Black Jack**—pop pl KY-4
**Blackjack**—pop pl MS-4
**Black Jack**—pop pl MS-4
**Blackjack**—pop pl MO-7
**Black Jack**—pop pl MO-7
**Black Jack**—pop pl NC-3
**Black Jack**—pop pl TN-4
**Black Jack**—pop pl TX-5
Black Jack, The TX-5
Blackjack Acad (historical)—school AL-4
Blackjack Arroyo—stream NM-5
Black Jack Branch MO-7
Blackjack Branch—stream GA-3
Black Jack Branch—stream LA-4
Blackjack Branch—stream LA-4
Black Jack Branch—stream NC-3
Blackjack Branch—stream OH-6
Black Jack Branch—stream TX-5
Black Jack Butte—summit MT-8
Blackjack Butte—summit OR-9
Blackjack Butte Rsvr—reservoir OR-9
Black Jack Cabin—locale AK-9
Black Jack Camp—locale CA-9
Black Jack Canyon—valley AZ-5
Blackjack Canyon—valley NM-5
Black Jack Cave—cave AZ-5
Blackjack Cem MS-4
Black Jack Cem—cemetery IL-6
Black Jack Cem—cemetery (4) MS-4
Blackjack Cem—cemetery OK-5
Blackjack Cem—cemetery (2) TX-5
Black Jack Cem—cemetery TX-5
Blackjack Cem—cemetery (2) TX-5
Black Jack Cem—cemetery VA-3
Blackjack Ch—church (2) AR-4
Black Jack Ch—church GA-3
Black Jack Ch—church MS-4
Blackjack Ch—church MS-4
Black Jack Ch—church (2) MS-4
Blackjack Ch—church MS-4
Blackjack Ch—church MO-7
Blackjack Ch—church (2) OK-5
Black Jack Ch—church SC-3
Black Jack Ch—church (2) TX-5
Black Jack Ch—church VA-3
Blackjack Chapel MS-4
Blackjack Chapel—church OK-5
Blackjack Corner—locale AR-4
Black Jack Creek KS-7
Black Jack Creek MO-7
Blackjack Creek—stream FL-3
Blackjack Creek—stream ID-8
Blackjack Creek—stream KS-7
Blackjack Creek—stream MI-6
Black Jack Creek—stream MO-7
Blackjack Creek—stream MO-7
Blackjack Creek—stream OK-5
Black Jack Creek—stream (2) OR-9
Blackjack Creek—stream (3) TX-5
Blackjack Creek—stream (2) WA-9
Blackjack Creek—stream WI-6
Black Jack Grove Ch—church NC-3
Blackjack Gulch—valley CO-8
Blackjack Gulch—valley UT-8
Blackjack Hill—summit TX-5
Black Jack (historical)—locale MS-4
Blackjack Hollow—valley AR-4
Blackjack Hollow—valley MO-7
Blackjack Hollow—valley (2) TX-5
Black Jack Island—island FL-3
Blackjack Island—island GA-3
Blackjack Knob—summit AR-4
Black Jack Knob—summit KY-4
Blackjack Knob—summit MO-7
Blackjack Lake—lake GA-3
Blackjack Lake—lake OH-6
Black Jack Lake—lake WY-8
**Blackjack Lodge Condominiums**—pop pl UT-8
Blackjack Lookout Tower—locale AL-4
Blackjack Marina—locale MO-7
Black Jack Methodist Church MS-4
Blackjack Mine—mine AZ-5
Black Jack Mine—mine ID-8
Black Jack Mine—mine NV-8
Blackjack Mine—mine NV-8
Blackjack Mine—mine OR-9
Black Jack Mine No 1—mine NM-5
Blackjack Missionary Baptist Ch—church MS-4
Blackjack Mountain AZ-5
Blackjack Mountains—summit AZ-5
Black Jack Mtn—summit AR-4
Black Jack Mtn—summit CA-9
Blackjack Mtn—summit (3) GA-3
Blackjack Mtn—summit NC-3
Blackjack Mtn—summit OK-5
Black Jack No 2 Mine—mine NM-5
Black Jack Peak—summit ID-8
Blackjack Peninsula TX-5
Blackjack Peninsula—cape TX-5
Black Jack Peninsula—cape TX-5
Black Jack Pocket—bay TN-4
Black Jack Point AZ-5
Black Jack Point—cape MS-4
Blackjack Point—cape TX-5
Blackjack Point—summit AZ-5
Black Jack Point Public Use Area—park MS-4
Black Jack Pond—lake GA-3
Blackjack Pond—lake TX-5
Black Jack Post Office (historical)—building TN-4
Blackjack Prairie—swamp GA-3
Blackjack Ranch—locale WY-8
Black Jack Ravine—valley CA-9
Blackjack Ridge AL-4
Black Jack Ridge—ridge AL-4
Blackjack Ridge—ridge AL-4
Black Jack Ridge—ridge AR-4
Blackjack Ridge—ridge GA-3
Black Jack Ridge—ridge MO-7
Blackjack Ridge—ridge OK-5
Black Jack Ridge—ridge TN-4
Blackjack Ridge—ridge WA-9
Blackjack Ridge Mine—mine TN-4
Blackjack Rim AZ-5
Blackjack Rsvr—reservoir NV-8
Black Jack Sch—school AR-4
Blackjack Sch—school (2) IL-6
Blackjack Sch—school MS-4
Black Jack Sch—school MS-4
Blackjack Sch—school MO-7
Black Jack Sch—school MO-7
Blackjack Sch—school MO-7
Blackjack Sch—school OK-5
Black Jack Sch (abandoned)—school MO-7
Black Jack Sch (historical)—school (2) MS-4
Blackjack Sch (historical)—school MO-7
Black Jack Sch (historical)—school MO-7
Blackjack School (historical)—locale MO-7
Black Jacks Hideout—other NM-5
Blackjack Spring—spring AZ-5
Black Jack Spring—spring (2) AZ-5
Blackjack Spring—spring AZ-5
Black Jack Spring—spring (2) AZ-5
Blackjack Spring—spring AZ-5
Black Jack Spring—spring AZ-5
Blackjack Spring—spring CA-9
Blackjack Spring—spring KS-7
Black Jack Spring—spring NV-8
Blackjack Spring—spring TX-5
Blackjack Springs—spring NV-8
Blackjack Springs—spring WI-6
Black Jack Springs Cem—cemetery TX-5
**Black Jack (subdivision)**—pop pl MS-4
Black Jack Tank—reservoir AZ-5
Blackjack Tank—reservoir AZ-5
Black Jack Tank—reservoir AZ-5
Blackjack Tank—reservoir (3) AZ-5

Blackpipe—*locale* SD-7
Black Pipe Creek—*stream* SD-7
Black Pipe Issue Station (historical)—*locale* SD-7
Black Pipe Township—*civil* SD-7
**Blackpipe Township**—*pop pl* SD-7
Black Pitch Spring—*spring* NV-8
Black Place—*locale* OR-9
**Black Plain**—*pop pl* RI-1
Black Plain Hill—*summit* RI-1
*Black Plains* NH-1
*Black Point* ME-1
*Black Point* MA-1
*Black Point* RI-1
Black Point—*bench* AZ-5
Black Point—*cape* (7) AK-9
Black Point—*cape* (6) CA-9
Black Point—*cape* CT-1
Black Point—*cape* (8) FL-3
Black Point—*cape* GA-3
Black Point—*cape* IN-6
Black Point—*cape* (10) ME-1
Black Point—*cape* MD-2
Black Point—*cape* MA-1
Black Point—*cape* (3) MI-6
Black Point—*cape* (2) MN-6
Black Point—*cape* MT-8
Black Point—*cape* NV-8
Black Point—*cape* NH-1
Black Point—*cape* NJ-2
Black Point—*cape* (4) NY-2
Black Point—*cape* (2) RI-1
Black Point—*cape* (3) TX-5
Black Point—*cape* UT-8
Black Point—*cape* (2) VA-3
Black Point—*cape* WA-9
Black Point—*cape* WI-6
Black Point—*cape* VI-3
Black Point—*cliff* AZ-5
Black Point—*cliff* (2) CO-8
Black Point—*cliff* FL-3
Black Point—*cliff* ID-8
Black Point—*cliff* OR-9
Black Point—*cliff* (3) UT-8
Black Point—*locale* FL-3
Black Point—*pillar* UT-8
**Black Point**—*pop pl* CA-9
**Black Point**—*pop pl* CT-1
**Black Point**—*pop pl* IN-6
**Black Point**—*pop pl* ME-1
Black Point—*ridge* CA-9
Black Point—*ridge* UT-8
Black Point—*summit* AZ-5
Black Point—*summit* (3) CA-9
Black Point—*summit* (4) NV-8
Black Point—*summit* NM-5
Black Point—*summit* OR-9
Black Point—*summit* TX-5
Black Point—*summit* (2) UT-8
**Black Point Beach Club**—*pop pl* CT-1
Black Point Brook—*stream* ME-1
Black Point Cem—*cemetery* ME-1
Black Point Cove—*bay* ME-1
Black Point Creek—*bay* FL-3
Black Point Creek—*channel* GA-3
Black Point Creek—*gut* NJ-2
Black Point Drain—*gut* VA-3
Black Point Draw—*valley* CO-8
Black Point (historical)—*pillar* SD-7
Black Point Landing—*locale* CA-9
Black Point Landing—*locale* VA-3
Black Point Park—*park* FL-3
Black Point Pond—*lake* MA-1
Black Point Rsvr—*reservoir* AZ-5
Black Point Rsvr—*reservoir* NV-8
Black Point Rsvr—*reservoir* (2) UT-8
Black Point Swamp—*swamp* (2) FL-3
Black Point Tank—*reservoir* AZ-5
Black Point Well—*well* NV-8
Black Point Well—*well* OR-9
Black Pole—*pillar* ID-8
*Black Pond* FL-3
*Black Pond* MA-1
*Black Pond* NY-2
Black Pond—*lake* CT-1
Black Pond—*lake* (5) FL-3
Black Pond—*lake* LA-4
Black Pond—*lake* (10) ME-1
Black Pond—*lake* (13) MA-1
Black Pond—*lake* (3) NH-1
Black Pond—*lake* (18) NY-2
Black Pond—*lake* NC-3
Black Pond—*lake* (3) TN-4
Black Pond—*lake* (2) VT-1
Black Pond—*lake* (4) VA-3
Black Pond—*locale* AL-4
Black Pond—*reservoir* (2) CT-1
Black Pond—*reservoir* GA-3
Black Pond—*reservoir* OH-6
Black Pond—*swamp* AR-4
Black Pond—*swamp* KY-4
*Black Pond Brook* NY-2
Black Pond Brook—*stream* CT-1
Black Pond Brook—*stream* NH-1
Black Pond Brook—*stream* NY-2
Black Pond Cem—*cemetery* MO-7
Black Pond Ch—*church* FL-3
Black Pond Creek—*stream* KY-4
Black Pond Creek—*stream* NY-2
Black Pond Dam—*dam* PA-2
Black Pond Hill—*summit* MA-1
Black Pond (historical)—*lake* MA-1
Black Pond Lookout Tower—*locale* AL-4
Black Pond Mine (surface)—*mine* AL-4
Black Pond Sch (historical)—*school* AL-4
Black Pond Slough—*gut* AR-4
Black Pond Slough—*gut* LA-4
Black Pond Swamp—*swamp* MA-1
Black Pond Swamp—*swamp* NY-2
Black Pond Township—*civil* MO-7
*Black Pool* ME-1
Black Pool—*lake* CO-8
Black Pool—*lake* VA-3
Black Pool Hollow—*valley* KY-4
Black Portage Lake—*lake* MN-6
Black Powder Hollow—*valley* IL-6
Black Powder Mines—*mine* WY-8
Black Prince Canyon—*valley* NM-5
Black Prince Creek—*stream* ID-8
Black Prince Island—*island* LA-4
Black Prince Mine—*mine* AZ-5
Black Prince Mine—*mine* CA-9
Black Prince Mine—*mine* NV-8
Black Prince Mine—*mine* NM-5
Black Prince Mine—*mine* (2) WA-9
Black Princess Mine—*mine* AZ-5
Black Prong—*stream* FL-3
Black Prospect—*mine* AK-9
Black Pyramid Mtn—*summit* MT-8
Black Queen Mine—*mine* (3) AZ-5
*Black Rabbit Canyon* CA-9
Black Rabbit Canyon—*valley* CA-9
Black Ranch—*locale* (3) CA-9
Black Ranch—*locale* CO-8
Black Ranch—*locale* MT-8
Black Ranch—*locale* NE-7
Black Ranch—*locale* (2) NM-5
Black Ranch—*locale* OR-9
Black Ranch—*locale* (2) TX-5
Black Ranch—*locale* UT-8
*Black Range* AZ-5
Black Range—*range* NM-5
Black Range Mine—*mine* AZ-5
*Black Ranger* AZ-5
Black Rapids—*rapids* AK-9
Black Rapids Glacier—*glacier* AK-9
Black Rapids Training Site—*other* AK-9
Black Rascal Creek—*stream* CA-9
Black Reef—*bar* AK-9
Black Reef—*ridge* MT-8
Black Reef—*spring* MT-8
Black Reef—*summit* UT-8
*Black Reservoir* CO-8
Black Rib—*summit* WY-8
*Black Ridge* LA-4
*Black Ridge* NV-8
*Black Ridge* UT-8
Blackridge—*locale* VA-3
**Black Ridge**—*pop pl* PA-2
Black Ridge—*ridge* (3) AZ-5
Black Ridge—*ridge* CA-9
Black Ridge—*ridge* (6) CO-8
Black Ridge—*ridge* ID-8
Black Ridge—*ridge* MT-8
Black Ridge—*ridge* (5) NV-8
Black Ridge—*ridge* NM-5
Black Ridge—*ridge* NC-3
Black Ridge—*ridge* TX-5
Black Ridge—*ridge* (8) UT-8
Black Ridge—*ridge* VA-3
Black Ridge—*ridge* WA-9
Blackridge Branch—*stream* AL-4
Black Ridge Cabin—*locale* NV-8
Black Ridge Caves—*cave* ID-8
Black Ridge Colliery—*building* PA-2
Black Ridge Crater—*crater* ID-8
Black Ridge Island—*island* NV-8
Black Ridge Trail—*trail* CO-8
Black Ridge Wash—*stream* NM-5
Black Ridge Well—*well* ID-8
Black Rim—*cliff* (2) OR-9
Black Rim—*cliff* WY-8
Black Rim Dam—*dam* OR-9
Black Rim Rsvr—*reservoir* OR-9
*Black River* AZ-5
*Black River* ME-1
*Black River* MA-1
*Black River* MI-6
*Black River* MS-4
*Black River* NJ-2
*Black River* NC-3
*Black River* SC-3
*Black River* TX-5
Black River—*CDP* WI-6
Black River—*locale* AZ-5
Black River—*locale* WI-6
**Black River**—*pop pl* MI-6
**Black River**—*pop pl* MN-6
**Black River**—*pop pl* NY-2
**Black River**—*pop pl* WA-9
Black River—*stream* (5) AK-9
Black River—*stream* AZ-5
Black River—*stream* AR-4
Black River—*stream* (2) GA-3
Black River—*stream* IN-6
Black River—*stream* (3) LA-4
Black River—*stream* (7) MI-6
Black River—*stream* (2) MN-6
Black River—*stream* MO-7
Black River—*stream* NM-5
Black River—*stream* (3) NY-2
Black River—*stream* (2) NC-3
Black River—*stream* OH-6
Black River—*stream* PA-2
Black River—*stream* SC-3
Black River—*stream* (2) VT-1
Black River—*stream* (2) WA-9
Black River—*stream* (4) WI-6
Black River Acad—*hist pl* VT-1
Black River Bay—*bay* NY-2
Black River Bridge—*hist pl* AZ-5
Black River Camp Picnic Area—*park* WI-6
Black River Canal—*canal* MI-6
Black River Canal—*canal* (2) NY-2
Black River Cem—*cemetery* (2) MO-7
Black River Cem—*cemetery* NY-2
Black River Ch—*church* IN-6
Black River Ch—*church* MN-6
Black River Ch—*church* MO-7
Black River Ch—*church* (2) NC-3
Black River Ch—*church* OH-6
Black River Ch—*church* (2) SC-3
Black River County Park—*park* MI-6
*Black River Creek* PA-2
Black River Crossing—*locale* AZ-5
Black River Ditch—*canal* MO-7
*Black River Drain* MI-6
Black River Drain—*stream* MI-6
Black River Extension Drain—*stream* MI-6
**Black River Falls**—*pop pl* WI-6
Black River Fish and Wildlife Mngmt Area—*park* NJ-2
Black River Grove Ch—*church* NC-3
**Black River Harbor**—*pop pl* MI-6
Black River HS—*school* OH-6
Black River HS—*school* VT-1
Black River Island—*island* GA-3
Black River Island—*island* MI-6
Black River Junction—*uninc pl* WA-9
Black River Lake—*lake* LA-4
Black River Lake—*lake* MI-6
Black River Number Two Tank—*reservoir* AZ-5
Black River Point—*cape* WI-6
Black River Pond—*lake* NJ-2
Black River Pond—*lake* NY-2
Black River Presbyterian and Ivanhoe Baptist Churches—*hist pl* NC-3
Black River Pumping Station—*locale* AZ-5
*Black River Pump Station* AZ-5
Black River Ranch Club—*other* MI-6
Black River Sch—*school* (2) MI-6
Black River Sch—*school* MN-6
Black River Sch (abandoned)—*school* PA-2
Black River Sch (historical)—*school* MO-7
Black River School—*locale* MI-6
Black River Slough—*stream* AK-9
Black River Spring—*spring* NM-5
Black River (sta.)—*uninc pl* WA-9
Black River State For—*forest* WI-6
Black River State Game Area—*park* AR-4
*Black River Swamp* SC-3
Black River Swamp—*swamp* MI-6
Black River Swamp—*swamp* (2) SC-3
Black River Tank—*reservoir* AZ-5
Black River Township—*civil* (3) MO-7
Black River (Township of)—*fmr MCD* (2) AR-4
Black River (Township of)—*fmr MCD* (2) NC-3
Black River (Township of)—*other* OH-6
**Black River (Township of)**—*pop pl* MN-6
Black River Viaduct, Baltimore And Ohio RR—*hist pl* OH-6
**Black River Village**—*pop pl* NM-5
*Black Robe* MI-6
*Black Rock* AZ-5
*Black Rock* CT-1
*Blackrock* MD-2
*Black Rock* MA-1
*Black Rock* NV-8
*Black Rock* PA-2
Black Rock—*bar* (2) ME-1
Black Rock—*bar* PA-2
Black Rock—*cape* ID-8
Black Rock—*cape* UT-8
Black Rock—*cliff* TX-5
Black Rock—*island* (2) AK-9
Black Rock—*island* (2) CA-9
Black Rock—*island* (3) CT-1
Black Rock—*island* FL-3
Black Rock—*island* (3) ME-1
Black Rock—*island* (4) OR-9
Black Rock—*island* WA-9
Black Rock—*lava* OR-9
Black Rock—*locale* AL-4
Black Rock—*locale* AZ-5
Black Rock—*locale* (2) KY-4
Black Rock—*locale* NY-2
Black Rock—*locale* OR-9
Black Rock—*locale* UT-8
Black Rock—*other* (2) AK-9
Black Rock—*pillar* (2) AZ-5
Black Rock—*pillar* (5) CA-9
Black Rock—*pillar* MT-8
Black Rock—*pillar* NV-8
Black Rock—*pillar* (4) OR-9
Black Rock—*pillar* (2) RI-1
Black Rock—*pillar* (2) UT-8
**Black Rock**—*pop pl* AR-4
**Black Rock**—*pop pl* CT-1
**Blackrock**—*pop pl* ID-8
**Black Rock**—*pop pl* IN-6
**Black Rock**—*pop pl* MA-1
**Black Rock**—*pop pl* NM-5
**Blackrock**—*pop pl* NC-3
**Blackrock**—*pop pl* PA-2
Black Rock—*rock* (6) MA-1
Black Rock—*summit* (5) AZ-5
Black Rock—*summit* (2) CA-9
Black Rock—*summit* CT-1
Black Rock—*summit* ID-8
Black Rock—*summit* (2) MD-2
Black Rock—*summit* MA-1
Black Rock—*summit* (2) MT-8
Black Rock—*summit* NV-8
Black Rock—*summit* NY-2
Black Rock—*summit* (3) OR-9
Black Rock—*summit* (3) UT-8
Blackrock—*summit* (2) VA-3
Black Rock—*summit* VA-3
Black Rock—*summit* WV-2
Black Rock—*summit* WY-8
Black Rock—*uninc pl* NY-2
Black Rock Airp—*airport* PA-2
Black Rock Bay—*bay* ID-8
Black Rock Beach—*beach* (2) MA-1
Black Rock Beach (site)—*beach* UT-8
Blackrock Branch—*stream* NC-3
Black Rock Branch—*stream* NC-3
Blackrock Branch—*stream* SC-3
Black Rock Bridge—*hist pl* PA-2
Black Rock Brook—*stream* ME-1
Black Rock Brook—*stream* RI-1
*Black Rock Butte* WY-8
Black Rock Butte—*summit* AZ-5
Black Rock Butte—*summit* OR-9
Black Rock Cairn Well—*well* AZ-5
Blackrock Camp—*locale* MD-2
Black Rock Campground—*locale* ID-8
Black Rock Canal—*channel* NY-2
*Black Rock Canyon* AZ-5
*Black Rock Canyon* UT-8
Black Rock Canyon—*valley* (4) AZ-5
Black Rock Canyon—*valley* (2) CA-9
Blackrock Canyon—*valley* ID-8
Blackrock Canyon—*valley* NV-8
Black Rock Canyon—*valley* (4) NV-8
Black Rock Canyon—*valley* NM-5
Black Rock Canyon—*valley* (2) OR-9
Black Rock Canyon—*valley* (5) UT-8
Black Rock Canyon—*valley* WA-9
Black Rock Canyon Spring—*spring* AZ-5
Black Rock Canyon Well—*well* AZ-5
*Black Rock Cape* NV-8
Black Rock Cave—*cave* UT-8
Black Rock Cem—*cemetery* OK-5
Black Rock Cem—*cemetery* PA-2
Black Rock Cem—*cemetery* WA-9
Black Rock Ch—*church* AL-4
Black Rock Ch—*church* GA-3
Blackrock Ch—*church* PA-2
Black Rock Ch—*church* SC-3
Black Rock Channel—*channel* MA-1
Black Rock Channel—*gut* MA-1
Black Rock Channel—*gut* VA-3
Black Rock Cliffs Cove—*cove* NC-3
Black Rock Coulee—*valley* WA-9
*Black Rock Creek* OR-9
Blackrock Creek—*stream* AK-9
Black Rock Creek—*stream* (6) CA-9
Black Rock Creek—*stream* FL-3
Black Rock Creek—*stream* KY-4
Black Rock Creek—*stream* MD-2
Black Rock Creek—*stream* MA-1
Blackrock Creek—*stream* MT-8
Black Rock Creek—*stream* MT-8
Blackrock Creek—*stream* NC-3
Black Rock Creek—*stream* (3) OR-9
Blackrock Creek—*stream* WY-8
Black Rock Creek—*stream* WY-8
Black Rock Creek—*swamp* MA-1
Black Rock Crossing—*locale* ID-8
Black Rock Dam—*dam* CT-1
Black Rock Dam—*dam* PA-2
Black Rock Dam Tank—*reservoir* AZ-5
*Black Rock Desert* UT-8
Black Rock Desert—*basin* NV-8
Blackrock Ditch—*canal* CA-9
Black Rock Draw—*valley* (3) WY-8
**Black Rock Estates**—*pop pl* MD-2
Black Rock Fishery—*locale* NC-3
Black Rock Flat—*flat* WY-8
Black Rock Fork—*stream* OR-9
*Black Rock Fork Umpqua River* OR-9
Blackrock Gap—*gap* VA-3
Black Rock Gap—*gap* WY-8
Black Rock Guard Station—*locale* CA-9
*Black Rock Gulch* ID-8
Black Rock Gulch—*valley* AZ-5
Blackrock Gulch—*valley* (2) ID-8
Blackrock Gulch—*valley* NV-8
Black Rock Harbor—*harbor* CT-1
Black Rock Hill—*summit* AZ-5
Blackrock Hill—*summit* VI-3
Black Rock Hill Overlook—*locale* VA-3
Black Rock Hills—*summit* UT-8
Black Rock Hist Dist—*hist pl* CT-1
Black Rock Hollow—*valley* NY-2
Black Rock Interchange—*crossing* AZ-5
Black Rock Island—*island* AK-9
Black Rock Island—*island* NY-2
Blackrock Knob—*summit* NC-3
Black Rock Knoll—*summit* NV-8
Black Rock KOA—*locale* UT-8
Black Rock Lake—*lake* CA-9
Blackrock Lake—*lake* CA-9
Black Rock Lake—*lake* CA-9
Black Rock Lake—*lake* GA-3
Black Rock Lake—*lake* WA-9
Black Rock Lake—*reservoir* CT-1
Black Rock Lake—*reservoir* PA-2
*Black Rock Landing Strip* PA-2
Black Rock Meadows—*flat* WY-8
Blackrock Mill—*locale* MD-2
Black Rock Mine—*mine* (4) AZ-5
Black Rock Mine—*mine* CA-9
Black Rock Mine—*mine* CO-8
Black Rock Mine—*mine* ID-8
Black Rock Mine—*mine* MT-8
Black Rock Mine—*mine* NV-8
Black Rock Mine—*mine* UT-8
Black Rock Mine—*mine* WA-9
*Black Rock Mines* OR-9
*Black Rock Mountain* UT-8
Black Rock Mountain State Park—*park* GA-3
Black Rock Mtn—*summit* AZ-5
Black Rock Mtn—*summit* CA-9
Blackrock Mtn—*summit* CA-9
Blackrock Mtn—*summit* GA-3
Black Rock Mtn—*summit* NV-8
Black Rock Mtn—*summit* NC-3
Blackrock Mtn—*summit* (3) NC-3
Black Rock Mtn—*summit* VA-3
Black Rock Mtn—*summit* WY-8
Black Rock Park—*park* TX-5
Black Rock Pass—*gap* CA-9
Black Rock Pass—*gap* UT-8
*Black Rock Peak* CA-9
*Black Rock Peak* NV-8
*Black Rock Peak* UT-8
Blackrock Peak—*summit* MT-8
Black Rock Pocket—*basin* ID-8
*Black Rock Point* AZ-5
Black Rock Point—*cape* MA-1
Black Rock Point—*cape* (2) MI-6
Black Rock Point—*cape* RI-1
Black Rock Point—*cliff* AZ-5
Black Rock Point—*cliff* NV-8
Black Rock Point—*ridge* UT-8
Black Rock Pond—*lake* AZ-5
Black Rock Pony Express Station Historical Marker—*park* UT-8
Black Rock Ranch—*locale* AZ-5
Black Rock Ranch—*locale* OR-9
Black Rock Range—*range* NV-8
Blackrock Ranger Station—*locale* WY-8
Black Rock Reach—*channel* VA-3
Black Rock Reservoir Dam—*dam* RI-1
*Black Rock Ridge* ID-8
Black Rock Ridge—*ridge* (2) AZ-5
Black Rock Ridge—*ridge* CA-9
Blackrock Ridge—*ridge* ID-8
Black Rock Ridge—*ridge* NM-5
Blackrock Ridge—*ridge* NC-3
*Black Rock Rsvr* CT-1
Black Rock Rsvr—*reservoir* CA-9
Black Rock Rsvr—*reservoir* (2) NV-8
Black Rock Rsvr—*reservoir* NM-5
Black Rock Rsvr—*reservoir* RI-1
Blackrock Run—*stream* MD-2
Black Rock Run—*stream* VA-3
*Black Rock Run Dam* PA-2
*Black Rocks* VA-3
Black Rocks—*bar* (2) ME-1
Black Rocks—*bar* (3) MA-1
Black Rocks—*locale* WY-8
Black Rocks—*pillar* CO-8
Black Rocks—*pillar* OR-9
Black Rocks—*summit* CA-9
Black Rocks, The—*area* AZ-5
Black Rocks, The—*bar* (2) ME-1
Black Rocks, The—*summit* AZ-5
Blackrock Sch—*school* PA-2
Blackrock Shelter—*locale* VA-3
Black Rocks Light—*locale* MA-1
Black Rock Spring—*spring* (6) AZ-5
Blackrock Spring—*spring* NV-8
Black Rock Spring—*spring* (4) NV-8
Blackrock Spring—*spring* NV-8
Black Rock Spring—*spring* NV-8
Blackrock Spring—*spring* NV-8
Black Rock Spring—*spring* (2) OR-9
Black Rock Spring—*spring* UT-8
Black Rock Spring—*spring* WA-9
Black Rock Spring—*spring* (2) WY-8
Black Rock Spring (Dry)—*spring* CA-9
Blackrock Springs—*spring* CA-9
Black Rock Springs—*spring* NV-8
Black Rock Springs—*spring* (2) WY-8
Blackrock Springs Site—*hist pl* VA-3
*Black Rocks Table* OR-9
Black Rock Standing—*pillar* AZ-5
Black Rock State Park—*park* CT-1
Black Rock Station—*locale* NY-2
Black Rock Summit—*gap* NV-8
Black Rock Tank—*reservoir* AZ-5
Black Rock (Township of)—*fmr MCD* AR-4
Black Rock Trail—*trail* AZ-5
Black Rock Trail—*trail* OR-9
Black Rock Trail Two Hundred Ninety Two—*trail* AZ-5
Black Rock Valley—*valley* UT-8
Black Rock Valley—*valley* WA-9
*Blackrock Volcano* UT-8
Black Rock Volcano—*summit* UT-8
Blackrock Wash—*stream* AZ-5
Black Rock Wash—*stream* (3) AZ-5
Blackrock Wash—*stream* NM-5
Black Rock Wash—*valley* AZ-5
Black Rock Well—*well* AZ-5
Blackrock Well—*well* CA-9
Black Rock Well—*well* NV-8
Black Rock Well—*well* UT-8
Black Rocky Point—*cliff* UT-8
Blackroot Hollow—*valley* MO-7
Black Rough Bottom—*bend* KY-4
Black Rsvr—*reservoir* CA-9
Black Rsvr—*reservoir* CO-8
Black Rsvr—*reservoir* NH-1
Black Rsvr—*reservoir* WY-8
*Black Run* PA-2
**Blackrun**—*pop pl* OH-6
**Black Run**—*pop pl* OH-6
**Black Run**—*pop pl* WV-2
Black Run—*stream* (3) IN-6
Black Run—*stream* MI-6
Black Run—*stream* NJ-2
Black Run—*stream* (5) OH-6
Black Run—*stream* (10) PA-2
Black Run—*stream* (3) VA-3
Black Run—*stream* (2) WV-2
Black Run Creek—*stream* NC-3
*Blacks* IN-6
*Blacks* PA-2
Blacks—*locale* SC-3
**Blacks**—*pop pl* IL-6
**Blacks**—*pop pl* PA-2
Black Sage Canyon—*valley* AZ-5
Black Sage Pass—*gap* CO-8
Black Salt Spring—*spring* NM-5
Black Salt Valley—*valley* NM-5
Black Sambo Mine—*mine* CA-9
Black Sand Basin—*basin* WY-8
*Black Sand Beach* HI-9
Blacksand Creek—*stream* AK-9
Black Sand Creek—*stream* AK-9
*Black Sand Geyser Basin* WY-8
Blacksand (historical)—*locale* AL-4
Black Sand Hollow—*valley* ID-8
Blacksand Island—*island* AK-9
Black Sand Island—*island* ME-1
Black Sand Mine (Site)—*mine* CA-9
Blacksand Spit—*bar* AK-9
Black Sand Spring—*spring* ID-8
Black Sand Spring—*spring* MT-8
Blacks Arm—*bay* OR-9
Black Savannah Ditch—*canal* DE-2
Black Savannah Ditch—*stream* DE-2
Blacksbear Sch—*school* TX-5
*Blacks Bluff* AL-4
Blacks Bluff—*cliff* TX-5
Blacks Bluff (historical)—*locale* AL-4
*Blacks Bluff Landing* AL-4
Blacks Branch—*stream* AL-4
Blacks Branch—*stream* (2) AR-4
Blacks Branch—*stream* GA-3
Blacks Branch—*stream* KY-4
Blacks Branch—*stream* NJ-2
Blacks Branch—*stream* SC-3
Blacks Branch Creek—*stream* TX-5
Blacksburg—*locale* (2) VA-3
**Blacksburg**—*pop pl* SC-3
**Blacksburg**—*pop pl* VA-3
Blacksburg (CCD)—*cens area* SC-3
Blacks Cabin—*locale* WY-8
Blacks Camp—*locale* CA-9
*Blacks Canyon* TX-5
Blacks Canyon—*valley* CA-9
Blacks Canyon—*valley* UT-8
Blacks Cem—*cemetery* KY-4
Blacks Cem—*cemetery* OH-6
Blacks Cem—*cemetery* (2) PA-2
*Blacks Ch* MS-4
Black Sch—*school* IL-6
Black Sch—*school* IN-6
Black Sch—*school* KS-7
Black Sch—*school* KY-4
Black Sch—*school* MI-6
Black Sch—*school* (2) MO-7
Black Sch—*school* NJ-2
Black Sch—*school* NY-2
Black Sch—*school* PA-2
Black Sch—*school* TN-4
Black Sch—*school* WI-6
Black Sch (abandoned)—*school* PA-2
Blacks Chapel—*church* AL-4
Blacks Chapel—*church* NC-3
Blacks Chapel—*church* WV-2
Blacks Chapel Baptist Ch—*church* MS-4
Black School—*locale* MI-6
Black School (abandoned)—*locale* MO-7
*Blacks Corner* ME-1
Blacks Corner—*locale* MD-2
Blacks Corner—*locale* WA-9
**Blacks Corner**—*pop pl* PA-2
Blacks Coulee—*valley* ND-7
*Blacks Creek* AL-4
*Blacks Creek* GA-3
*Black's Creek* ID-8
*Blacks Creek* MO-7
*Blacks Creek* UT-8
*Blacks Creek* WY-8
Blacks Creek—*bay* MA-1
Blacks Creek—*locale* ID-8
Blacks Creek—*stream* AL-4
Blacks Creek—*stream* CA-9
Blacks Creek—*stream* GA-3
Blacks Creek—*stream* (3) ID-8
Blacks Creek—*stream* KY-4
Blacks Creek—*stream* NJ-2
Blacks Creek—*stream* NC-3
Blacks Creek—*stream* OR-9
Blacks Creek—*stream* (3) PA-2
Blacks Creek—*stream* SC-3
Blacks Creek—*stream* TX-5
Blacks Creek—*stream* (2) VA-3
Blacks Creek Knob—*summit* GA-3
Blacks Creek Marshes—*swamp* MA-1
Blacks Creek Rsvr—*reservoir* ID-8
Blacks Creek Sch (historical)—*school* PA-2
Blacks Crossroads—*locale* AL-4
Blacks Crossroads—*locale* KY-4
Blacks Dam—*dam* MS-4
Black Sea Rsvr—*reservoir* MT-8
Black Seep—*spring* AZ-5
Black Segate Reid Drain—*canal* MI-6
*Blacks Ferry* AL-4
Blacks Ferry—*locale* KY-4
Blacks Ferry (historical)—*crossing* TN-4
Blacks Ferry (historical)—*locale* TN-4
Blacks Flat—*flat* CA-9
Blacks Ford—*locale* FL-3
Blacks Ford (historical)—*locale* TN-4
*Blacks Fork* UT-8
*Black's Fork* WY-8
Blacks Fork—*stream* UT-8
Blacks Fork—*stream* WY-8
Blacks Fork Bridge—*bridge* WY-8
Blacks Fork Canal—*canal* WY-8
*Blacks Fork Ghost Town* UT-8
Blacks Fort (historical)—*locale* TN-4
Blacks Fort (Ruins)—*locale* TX-5
Blacks Gap—*gap* VA-3
*Blacks Gulch* CO-8
Blacks Gulch—*valley* (3) CA-9
Blacks Gulch—*valley* CO-8
Black Shadow Lake—*lake* MN-6
Blackshaft Mine—*mine* TX-5
Black Shale Creek—*stream* AK-9
Blackshale Mine (underground)—*mine* AL-4
*Black Shanty Creek* PA-2
*Black Shanty Run* PA-2
Blackshare Ranch—*locale* NM-5
**Blackshear**—*pop pl* GA-3
Blackshear, Lake—*reservoir* (2) GA-3
Blackshear Branch—*stream* GA-3
Blackshear (CCD)—*cens area* GA-3
Blackshear HS—*school* (2) TX-5
**Blackshear Place**—*pop pl* GA-3
Blackshear Sch—*school* TX-5
Blackshear Staduim—*other* TX-5
Blackshear Trail Sch—*school* GA-3
Black Sheep Hollow—*valley* TN-4
Black Sheep Mine—*mine* NV-8
Black Sheep Mtn—*summit* MT-8
Blackshell Creek—*stream* AK-9
Blacksher—*locale* AL-4
Blackshere Cem—*cemetery* WV-2
Blackshere Chapel—*church* WV-2
Blacksher Lookout Tower—*locale* AL-4
Blacksher Sch—*school* AL-4
Blacks Hill—*summit* KY-4
Blacks Hill—*summit* PA-2
Blackshire Branch—*stream* MO-7
Blackshire Cem—*cemetery* GA-3
Blackshire Cem—*cemetery* TN-4
Blackshire Cem—*cemetery* WV-2
Blackshire Creek—*stream* FL-3
Blackshire Ridge—*ridge* TN-4
Blackshire Well—*well* NM-5
Black Shoals—*bar* TX-5
Black Shop Pond—*reservoir* CT-1
Black Silver Mine—*mine* AZ-5
Black Sink—*basin* MO-7
Black Sink Prairie—*swamp* FL-3
*Blacks Island* TN-4
Blacks Island—*island* (2) FL-3
Blacks Island—*island* ID-8
Blacks Island—*island* OR-9
Blacks Island Shoals—*bar* TN-4
Black Site—*hist pl* MS-4
*Blackskin Creek* ID-8
Blacks Knoll—*summit* ID-8
Blacks Lake—*lake* AL-4
Blacks Lake—*lake* CA-9
Blacks Lake—*lake* FL-3
Blacks Lake—*lake* MN-6
Blacks Lake—*lake* PA-2
Blacks Lake—*reservoir* NC-3
Blacks Lake Dam—*dam* NC-3
Blacks Lakes—*lake* WA-9
Blacks Landing—*locale* GA-3
Blacks Landing (historical)—*locale* AL-4
Black Slough—*gut* AK-9
Black Slough—*gut* (2) AR-4
Black Slough—*gut* CA-9
Black Slough—*gut* IL-6
Black Slough—*gut* (3) ND-7
Black Slough—*gut* OR-9
Black Slough—*gut* SD-7
Black Slough—*stream* ID-8
Black Slough—*stream* (2) IL-6
Black Slough—*stream* MT-8
Black Slough—*stream* TN-4
Black Slough—*stream* (3) TX-5
Black Slough—*stream* UT-8
Black Slough—*stream* WA-9
Black Slough—*stream* WI-6
Black Slough—*swamp* SD-7
*Black Slough Bayou* MS-4
Black Slough Ditch—*canal* KY-4
Blackslough Landing—*locale* CA-9

Blackwell Sch—*school* GA-3
Blackwell Sch—*school* TN-4
Blackwell Sch—*school* VA-3
**Blackwells Chapel**—*pop pl* VA-3
Blackwell Sch (historical)—*school* MS-4
Blackwells Corner—*locale* CA-9
*Blackwells Corner Oil Field* CA-9
Blackwells Creek—*stream* VA-3
Blackwells Hollow—*valley* VA-3
*Blackwell's Island* NY-2
Blackwells Landing (historical)—*locale* AL-4
Blackwells Mills—*locale* NJ-2
Blackwell Southeast Oil And Gas Field—*oilfield* OK-5
Blackwells Pond—*lake* CT-1
Blackwell Spring—*spring* NC-3
Blackwell Spring—*spring* (2) TN-4
*Blackwells Reef* NY-2
Blackwells Sch—*school* GA-3
Blackwell Stillwater—*swamp* NY-2
Blackwell Street Hist Dist—*hist pl* NJ-2
Blackwell Swamp—*swamp* AL-4
Blackwell Swamp—*swamp* PA-2
**Blackwell (Town of)**—*pop pl* WI-6
Blackwell Trail—*trail* OR-9
Blackwell-Wielandy Bldg—*hist pl* MO-7
Black Whiteman Creek—*stream* MT-8
Black Willow Canyon—*valley* UT-8
Black Willow Draw—*valley* WY-8
Black Willow Gulch—*valley* OR-9
Black Willow Siphon—*canal* OR-9
Black Willow Spring—*spring* (2) AZ-5
Black Willow Spring—*spring* CA-9
Black Willow Spring—*spring* NM-5
Black Willow Spring—*spring* (3) UT-8
Black Wills Cliff—*cliff* MA-1
Black Windmill—*locale* CO-8
Black Windmill—*locale* TX-5
*Blackwolf* KS-7
Black Wolf—*locale* WV-2
**Black Wolf**—*pop pl* KS-7
Black Wolf Creek—*stream* CO-8
Black Wolf Creek—*stream* TN-4
Black Wolf Meadows—*flat* OR-9
**Black Wolf Point**—*pop pl* WI-6
Black Wolf (reduced usage)—*locale* WI-6
Black Wolf Sch—*school* KS-7
**Black Wolf (Town of)**—*pop pl* WI-6
**Black Wolf Township**—*pop pl* KS-7
Black Wonder Mine—*mine* CA-9
Blackwood—*fmr MCD* (2) NE-7
Blackwood—*locale* GA-3
Blackwood—*locale* MT-8
Blackwood—*locale* PA-2
**Blackwood**—*pop pl* AL-4
**Blackwood**—*pop pl* NJ-2
**Blackwood**—*pop pl* NC-3
**Blackwood**—*pop pl* VA-3
Blackwood Bend—*bend* AL-4
Blackwood Cem—*cemetery* AL-4
Blackwood Cem—*cemetery* AR-4
Blackwood Cem—*cemetery* MS-4
Blackwood Cem—*cemetery* OK-5
Blackwood Cem—*cemetery* WV-2
Blackwood Ch—*church* AL-4
Blackwood Chapel—*church* NC-3
Blackwood-Cornelius Cem—*cemetery* AL-4
Blackwood Covered Bridge—*hist pl* OH-6
*Blackwood Creek* WA-9
Blackwood Creek—*stream* AL-4
Blackwood Creek—*stream* CA-9
Blackwood Creek—*stream* GA-3
Blackwood Creek—*stream* NE-7
Blackwood Creek—*stream* (2) NC-3
Blackwood Creek—*stream* WA-9
Black Wood Dam—*dam* AZ-5
Blackwood Drain—*canal* MI-6
Blackwood Golf Course—*locale* PA-2
Blackwood Grove Cem—*cemetery* MS-4
Blackwood Grove Ch—*church* MS-4
Black Wood Hill—*summit* AZ-5
Blackwood Hollow—*valley* TN-4
Blackwood Lake—*lake* MN-6
Blackwood Lake—*lake* WA-9
Blackwood Lake—*reservoir* NJ-2
Blackwood Lake Dam—*dam* NJ-2
Blackwood Lake Dam—*dam* NC-3
Blackwood Lateral Canal—*canal* NE-7
Blackwood Mtn—*summit* ME-1
Blackwood Mtn—*summit* NC-3
**Blackwood Park (subdivision)**—*pop pl* NC-3
Blackwood Ponds—*reservoir* AL-4
Blackwood Ridge—*ridge* CA-9
Black Woods—*woods* MA-1
Black Woods, The—*woods* (2) ME-1
Blackwoods Cem—*cemetery* AL-4
Blackwood Sch (historical)—*school* TN-4
*Blackwoods Creek* AL-4
Blackwoods Lake—*reservoir* NC-3
Blackwoods Sch—*school* WI-6
**Blackwood Terrace**—*pop pl* NJ-2
*Blackwoodtown* NJ-2
*Black Zion* MS-4
Blacow Sch—*school* CA-9
Blacree Slope Mine (underground)—*mine* AL-4
Bladder Canyon—*valley* AZ-5
Bladder Lake—*lake* MN-6
Bladder Lake—*lake* WI-6
Bladder Spring—*spring* AZ-5
Blad Ditch—*canal* IN-6
Blade—*locale* LA-4
Blade Ch—*church* LA-4
Blade Creek—*stream* CA-9
Blade Drain—*canal* MI-6
Blade Island—*island* AK-9
Bladeley Sch—*school* AL-4
Bladen—*locale* GA-3
Bladen—*locale* OH-6
**Bladen**—*pop pl* NE-7
**Bladenboro**—*pop pl* NC-3
Bladenboro Airp—*airport* NC-3
Bladenboro Cem—*cemetery* NC-3
Bladenboro HS—*school* NC-3
**Bladenboro North**—*pop pl* NC-3
Bladenboro Post Office—*building* NC-3
Bladenboro (Township of)—*fmr MCD* NC-3
**Bladenburg**—*pop pl* IA-7
Bladenburg Sch—*school* IL-6
**Bladen County**—*pop pl* NC-3
Bladen County Hospital Airp—*airport* NC-3
Bladen County Park—*park* NC-3
Bladen Creek—*stream* GA-3
Bladen Lakes Airp—*airport* NC-3
Bladen Lakes Sch—*school* NC-3
Bladen Lakes State For—*forest* NC-3
Bladen Memorial Gardens—*cemetery* NC-3
**Bladensburg**—*pop pl* IA-7
**Bladensburg**—*pop pl* MD-2
**Bladensburg**—*pop pl* OH-6
Bladensburg Cem—*cemetery* IA-7
Bladensburg HS—*school* MD-2
Bladensburg Sch—*school* MD-2
Bladensfield—*hist pl* VA-3
*Bladen Siding* GA-3
**Bladen Springs**—*pop pl* NC-3
*Bladen Springs Landing* AL-4
Bladens River—*stream* CT-1
Bladen Technical Institute—*school* NC-3
Bladen Union Ch—*church* NC-3
Bladenwoods—*uninc pl* MD-2
Blade Rock—*summit* AZ-5
Blades—*locale* NC-3
**Blades**—*pop pl* DE-2
**Blades, The**—*pop pl* DE-2
Blades, William, House—*hist pl* KY-4
Blades Chapel—*church* MO-7
Blades Corner—*locale* VA-3
Blades House—*hist pl* NC-3
Bladeston—*locale* KY-4
Blade Tank—*reservoir* AZ-5
Blade Well—*well* TX-5
*Bladgett Cove* ME-1
*Blad Mountian* NV-8
*Bladon Landing* AL-4
**Bladon Springs**—*pop pl* AL-4
Bladon Springs—*spring* AL-4
Bladon Springs Cem—*cemetery* AL-4
Bladon Springs Ch—*church* AL-4
Bladon Springs Landing—*locale* AL-4
Bladon Springs State Park—*park* AL-4
Bladshaw Branch—*stream* TN-4
Blaen Y Cae Cem—*cemetery* WI-6
Blaese Park—*park* WI-6
Blagg Cave—*cave* AR-4
Blagg Cem—*cemetery* AR-4
Blagg Hollow—*valley* AR-4
Blagg Ridge—*summit* AR-4
Blaggs Clove—*basin* NY-2
Blag Mtn—*summit* WA-9
Blague Lake—*swamp* LA-4
Blaha Sch—*school* SD-7
Blah Cave—*cave* AL-4
Blaides—*locale* PA-2
Blailock Creek—*stream* MS-4
*Blain* TN-4
Blain—*locale* IA-7
**Blain**—*pop pl* PA-2
Blain Borough—*civil* PA-2
Blain Cave—*cave* PA-2
Blain Cem—*cemetery* IL-6
Blain Cem—*cemetery* IA-7
Blain Cem—*cemetery* MI-6
Blain Cem—*cemetery* PA-2
Blain Cem—*cemetery* TN-4
**Blain City**—*pop pl* PA-2
Blain Dugout—*stream* TX-5
*Blaine* AL-4
*Blaine* ME-1
*Blaine* ND-7
Blaine—*fmr MCD* (3) NE-7
Blaine—*locale* GA-3
Blaine—*locale* (2) ID-8
Blaine—*locale* NE-7
Blaine—*locale* NC-3
**Blaine**—*pop pl* IL-6
**Blaine**—*pop pl* IN-6
**Blaine**—*pop pl* KS-7
**Blaine**—*pop pl* KY-4
**Blaine**—*pop pl* ME-1
**Blaine**—*pop pl* MI-6
**Blaine**—*pop pl* MN-6
**Blaine**—*pop pl* MS-4
**Blaine**—*pop pl* OH-6
**Blaine**—*pop pl* OR-9
**Blaine**—*pop pl* TN-4
**Blaine**—*pop pl* WA-9
**Blaine**—*pop pl* WV-2
**Blaine**—*pop pl* WI-6
Blaine, James G., House—*hist pl* ME-1
Blaine, Lake—*lake* MT-8
Blaine, Mount—*summit* AK-9
Blaine, Mount—*summit* (2) CO-8
Blaine Air Force Station—*military* WA-9
Blaine Baptist Ch—*church* MS-4
Blaine Basin—*basin* CO-8
Blaine Bottom—*bend* OK-5
Blaine Branch—*stream* NC-3
Blaine Bridge—*bridge* ID-8
Blaine Canal—*canal* ID-8
Blaine (CCD)—*cens area* KY-4
Blaine (CCD)—*cens area* TN-4
Blaine (CCD)—*cens area* WA-9
Blaine Cem—*cemetery* MI-6
Blaine Cem—*cemetery* OR-9
Blaine Cem—*cemetery* WA-9
Blaine Center (census name Blaine)—*other* ME-1
*Blaine Ch* MS-4
Blaine Ch—*church* MN-6
Blaine Chapel—*church* TN-4
*Blaine City* WA-9
**Blaine (County)**—*pop pl* OK-5
Blaine County Courthouse—*hist pl* ID-8
Blaine County Courthouse—*hist pl* OK-5
Blaine Creek—*stream* KY-4
Blaine Creek—*stream* MT-8
Blaine Creek—*stream* WI-6
Blaine Creek—*stream* WY-8
Blaine Division—*civil* TN-4
Blaine Drageset Dam—*dam* SD-7
Blaine Draw—*valley* CO-8
*Blaine Glacier* WA-9
**Blaine Hill**—*pop pl* PA-2
Blaine Island—*island* WV-2
Blaine JHS—*school* UT-8
Blaine JHS—*school* WA-9
Blaine Knob—*summit* NC-3
Blaine Lake—*lake* MI-6
Blaine Mansion (Rural Electrification Administration Building)—*building* DC-2
Blaine Memorial Cem—*cemetery* WV-2
Blaine Methodist Ch—*church* MS-4
Blaine Mtn—*summit* MT-8
Blaine Muni Airp—*airport* WA-9
Blaine Point—*cape* (2) AK-9
Blaine Pond—*lake* PA-2
Blaine Pond Dam—*dam* MS-4
Blaine Post Office—*building* TN-4
Blaine Post Office (historical)—*building* AL-4
Blaine Ranch—*locale* SD-7
Blaine Rock—*pillar* CO-8
Blainer Sch—*school* ME-1
Blaine Rsvr—*reservoir* WA-9
Blaine Run—*stream* IN-6
Blaine Run—*stream* KY-4
Blaines Branch—*stream* KY-4
Blaines Branch Ch—*church* KY-4
Blainesburg—*uninc pl* PA-2
Blaine Sch—*school* (2) IL-6
Blaine Sch—*school* IN-6
Blaine Sch—*school* ME-1
Blaine Sch—*school* (2) MN-6
Blaine Sch—*school* MS-4
Blaine Sch—*school* ND-7
Blaine Sch—*school* PA-2
Blaine Sch—*school* SD-7
Blaines Gap—*gap* KY-4
Blaines Lake—*reservoir* NM-5
Blaines Landing (historical)—*locale* TN-4
Blaine Spring—*spring* MT-8
Blaine Spring Creek—*stream* MT-8
Blaines Shoals—*bar* TN-4
Blaine Stadium—*other* OK-5
Blaine Stadium and Fieldhouse—*hist pl* OK-5
Blaine Store (historical)—*locale* MS-4
Blaine Street Sch—*school* IL-6
**Blaine Subdivision**—*pop pl* UT-8
Blainesville—*locale* VA-3
**Blainesville**—*pop pl* OH-6
**Blaine (Town of)**—*pop pl* ME-1
**Blaine (Town of)**—*pop pl* WI-6
*Blaine Township* KS-7
Blaine Township—*civil* (2) SD-7
Blaine Township—*fmr MCD* (2) IA-7
**Blaine Township**—*pop pl* (5) KS-7
**Blaine Township**—*pop pl* (4) NE-7
**Blaine Township**—*pop pl* ND-7
**Blaine Township**—*pop pl* (2) SD-7
**Blaine (Township of)**—*pop pl* MI-6
**Blaine (Township of)**—*pop pl* PA-2
Blaine Trace—*stream* KY-4
*Blaineville* OH-6
Blain Hollow—*valley* OH-6
Blain Hollow—*valley* PA-2
Blain Hosp—*hospital* MI-6
Blainies Dam—*dam* UT-8
Blain Island—*island* MI-6
Blain Point—*summit* AZ-5
Blain Run—*stream* PA-2
**Blainsburg**—*pop pl* PA-2
Blain Sch—*school* MI-6
Blains Creek—*stream* TX-5
*Blains Cross Roads* TN-4
Blainsport—*locale* PA-2
Blainsport Ch—*church* PA-2
Blain Thompson Hollow—*valley* TN-4
*Blainville* TN-4
**Blainville**—*pop pl* VA-3
*Blainville Post Office* TN-4
Blair—*locale* ME-1
Blair—*locale* MT-8
Blair—*locale* NV-8
Blair—*locale* NH-1
Blair—*locale* TN-4
Blair—*locale* TX-5
Blair—*locale* UT-8
**Blair**—*pop pl* (2) IL-6
**Blair**—*pop pl* KS-7
**Blair**—*pop pl* KY-4
**Blair**—*pop pl* MD-2
**Blair**—*pop pl* MS-4
**Blair**—*pop pl* NE-7
**Blair**—*pop pl* OK-5
**Blair**—*pop pl* SC-3
**Blair**—*pop pl* (2) WV-2
**Blair**—*pop pl* WI-6
Blair, Charles E., House—*hist pl* WY-8
Blair, Frank P., Sch—*hist pl* MO-7
Blair, Herbert S., House—*hist pl* OH-6
Blair, Sen. William, House—*hist pl* WI-6
Blair, William Allen, House—*hist pl* NC-3
Blair Acad—*school* NJ-2
Blair Airp—*airport* IN-6
Blair Basin—*basin* UT-8
Blair Bend—*bend* TN-4
Blair Bend Industrial Park—*locale* TN-4
Blair Bluff—*cliff* MO-7
Blair Bluff—*cliff* TN-4
Blair Branch—*stream* AR-4
Blair Branch—*stream* (6) KY-4
Blair Branch—*stream* MO-7
Blair Branch—*stream* (3) TN-4
Blair Branch—*stream* TX-5
Blair Branch—*stream* VA-3
Blair Branch Sch—*school* KY-4
Blair Bridge—*bridge* GA-3
Blair Bridge Park—*park* MO-7
*Blair Brook* MA-1
Blair Brook—*stream* MA-1
Blair Canyon—*valley* AZ-5
Blair Canyon—*valley* CA-9
Blair Canyon—*valley* NM-5
Blair Canyon—*valley* OR-9
Blair Canyon Rsvr—*reservoir* OR-9
Blair Cem—*cemetery* AL-4
Blair Cem—*cemetery* AR-4
Blair Cem—*cemetery* FL-3
Blair Cem—*cemetery* (2) IL-6
Blair Cem—*cemetery* (2) IN-6
Blair Cem—*cemetery* (3) KY-4
Blair Cem—*cemetery* MS-4
Blair Cem—*cemetery* MO-7
Blair Cem—*cemetery* NE-7
Blair Cem—*cemetery* (2) OH-6
Blair Cem—*cemetery* SD-7
Blair Cem—*cemetery* (8) TN-4
Blair Cem—*cemetery* (2) VA-3
Blair Cem—*cemetery* (2) WV-2
Blair Cemeterys—*cemetery* WV-2
Blair Ch—*church* AL-4
Blair Ch—*church* TX-5
Blair Channel—*bay* NC-3
Blair Chapel—*church* IA-7
**Blair County**—*pop pl* PA-2
Blair County Courthouse—*hist pl* PA-2
*Blair Creek* TN-4
Blair Creek—*stream* AR-4
Blair Creek—*stream* CA-9
Blair Creek—*stream* ID-8
Blair Creek—*stream* IA-7
Blair Creek—*stream* KY-4
Blair Creek—*stream* MI-6
Blair Creek—*stream* (2) MO-7
Blair Creek—*stream* NJ-2
Blair Creek—*stream* NC-3
Blair Creek—*stream* (2) OR-9
Blair Creek—*stream* PA-2
Blair Creek—*stream* TN-4
Blair Creek—*stream* (2) TX-5
Blair Creek—*stream* (2) WY-8
Blair Creek Cave—*cave* MO-7
Blair Creek Ch—*church* TN-4
*Blair Creek School* TN-4
Blair Creek State For—*forest* MO-7
Blair Crossing—*locale* MT-8
Blair Desoto Bend—*bend* NE-7
Blair District Sch—*school* CA-9
Blair Ditch—*canal* CO-8
Blair Ditch—*canal* (3) IN-6
Blair Ditch—*canal* WY-8
Blair Drain—*canal* MI-6
Blair Draw—*valley* UT-8
*Blairdstown* PA-2
Blair-Dunning House—*hist pl* IN-6
Blair (Election Precinct)—*fmr MCD* IL-6
Blair Elem Sch—*school* PA-2
Blair Flats—*hist pl* MN-6
Blair Fork—*stream* KY-4
Blair Fork—*stream* NC-3
Blair Fork—*stream* WV-2
Blairfour—*locale* PA-2
Blair Gap—*gap* PA-2
Blair Gap—*gap* TN-4
Blair Gap—*locale* TN-4
Blair Gap Branch—*stream* TN-4
Blair Gap Dam—*dam* PA-2
Blair Gap Rsvr—*reservoir* PA-2
Blair Gap Run—*stream* PA-2
Blair Grove—*woods* CA-9
Blair Gulch—*valley* CA-9
Blair Gulch—*valley* CO-8
Blair Hill—*summit* ME-1
Blair Hill—*summit* (2) PA-2
Blair Hill—*summit* TN-4
Blair Hill—*summit* VT-1
Blair Hill—*summit* WA-9
Blair Hills Park—*park* CA-9
Blair Hollow—*valley* IN-6
Blair Hollow—*valley* KY-4
Blair Hollow—*valley* MO-7
Blair Hollow—*valley* PA-2
Blair Hollow—*valley* (5) TN-4
Blair House—*building* NC-3
Blair House—*hist pl* DC-2
Blair House—*hist pl* IA-7
Blair House—*hist pl* OH-6
Blair HS—*school* CA-9
Blair HS—*school* MS-4
Blair HS—*school* VA-3
*Blair Islands* TN-4
Blair JHS—*school* VA-3
Blair Junction—*locale* NV-8
*Blair Lake* TX-5
Blair Lake—*lake* AK-9
Blair Lake—*lake* (2) CO-8
Blair Lake—*lake* MI-6
Blair Lake—*lake* (2) MN-6
Blair Lake—*lake* MT-8
Blair Lake—*lake* OR-9
Blair Lake—*lake* TN-4
Blair Lake—*lake* TX-5
Blair Lake—*reservoir* MI-6
Blair Lake—*reservoir* NJ-2
Blair Lake—*reservoir* TX-5
Blair Lake Air Force Range—*other* AK-9
Blair Lake Dam—*dam* NJ-2
Blair Lake Number 2—*reservoir* AL-4
Blair Lakes—*lake* AK-9
Blair Lake Trail—*trail* OR-9
**Blair Lane**—*pop pl* TN-4
Blair Lateral—*canal* OK-5
*Blair-Lee House* DC-2
*Blair Meadow* OR-9
Blair Meadows—*flat* OR-9
Blair Memorial Hosp—*hospital* PA-2
Blair Memorial Park—*park* PA-2
Blair Mesa—*summit* CO-8
Blair Mill Elem Sch—*school* PA-2
**Blair Mills**—*pop pl* SC-3
Blair Mill Shop Ctr—*locale* PA-2
**Blair Mill Village East**—*pop pl* PA-2
**Blair Mill Village West**—*pop pl* PA-2
Blair Mine—*mine* MT-8
Blair Mine (underground)—*mine* AL-4
**Blairmont**—*pop pl* OH-6
Blairmont Country Club—*other* PA-2
**Blairmont (subdivision)**—*pop pl* NC-3
Blairmoor Branch—*stream* WI-6
Blair Mound—*hist pl* SC-3
Blair Mtn—*summit* (2) CO-8
Blair Mtn—*summit* OK-5
Blair Mtn—*summit* TN-4
Blair Mtn—*summit* WV-2
Blair Number 1 Dam—*dam* AL-4
Blair Number 2 Dam—*dam* AL-4
Blair Oil Field—*oilfield* TX-5
Blair Park—*hist pl* KY-4
Blair Park—*park* IL-6
Blair Pass—*gap* AZ-5
Blair Point—*cape* AL-4
*Blair Pond* WI-6
Blair Pond—*lake* FL-3
Blair Pond—*lake* MA-1
Blair Pond—*reservoir* GA-3
Blair Portal—*locale* MD-2
Blair Portal—*other* DC-2
Blair Ranch—*locale* CO-8
Blair Ranch—*locale* MT-8
Blair Ravine—*valley* CA-9
Blair Ridge—*ridge* KY-4
Blair Ridge—*ridge* MO-7
Blair Road Ch—*church* NC-3
*Blair Run* OH-6
Blair Run—*stream* OH-6
Blair Run—*stream* PA-2
*Blairs* SC-3
Blairs—*locale* VA-3
**Blairs**—*pop pl* AL-4
**Blairs**—*pop pl* PA-2
**Blairs**—*pop pl* (2) VA-3
Blairs Bay—*bay* NY-2
**Blairsburg**—*pop pl* IA-7
Blairsburg Cem—*cemetery* IA-7
Blairsburg Township—*fmr MCD* IA-7
Blair Sch—*school* CA-9
Blair Sch—*school* DC-2
Blair Sch—*school* (2) IL-6
Blair Sch—*school* MO-7
Blair Sch—*school* NH-1
Blair Sch—*school* NC-3
Blair Sch—*school* SD-7
Blair Sch—*school* WA-9
Blair Sch—*school* WI-6
Blair Sch (abandoned)—*school* (2) PA-2
*Blairs Channel* NC-3
Blairs Chapel—*church* TN-4
Blair Sch (historical)—*school* PA-2
**Blairs Corners**—*pop pl* PA-2
Blairs Creek—*stream* TN-4
Blairs Creek—*stream* VA-3
Blairs Creek Sch (historical)—*school* TN-4
**Blairsden**—*pop pl* CA-9
Blairs Ferry (historical)—*locale* TN-4
Blair's Ferry Storehouse—*hist pl* TN-4
*Blairs Fork* NC-3
*Blairs Gap* PA-2
*Blairs Gap Run* PA-2
Blairs Island—*island* NC-3
*Blairs Isle* NC-3
Blairs Kiln—*locale* NY-2
Blairs (Magisterial District)—*fmr MCD* VA-3
Blairs Mills—*locale* KY-4
**Blairs Mills**—*pop pl* PA-2
Blairs Mills Ch—*church* KY-4
Blairs Pond—*reservoir* DE-2
Blairs Pond Dam—*dam* DE-2
Blair Spring—*spring* (2) AL-4
Blair Spring—*spring* CO-8
Blair Spring—*spring* KY-4
Blair Spring—*spring* UT-8
Blair Springs Branch—*stream* KY-4
Blairs Ridge—*ridge* WV-2
Blairs Ridge Ch—*church* WV-2
*Blairs Run* PA-2
Blairs Sch—*school* TN-4
Blairs Spring—*spring* AZ-5
Blairs Spring Wash—*stream* AZ-5
Blairstone Plaza (Shop Ctr)—*locale* FL-3
*Blair Store* AL-4
Blairstown—*airport* NJ-2
Blairstown—*locale* LA-4
**Blairstown**—*pop pl* IA-7
**Blairstown**—*pop pl* MO-7
**Blairstown**—*pop pl* NJ-2
Blairstown Station—*locale* NJ-2
**Blairstown (Township of)**—*pop pl* NJ-2
*Blairs Valley* PA-2
**Blairsville**—*pop pl* GA-3
**Blairsville**—*pop pl* (2) IL-6
**Blairsville**—*pop pl* IN-6
**Blairsville**—*pop pl* OH-6
**Blairsville**—*pop pl* PA-2
*Blairsville Boro* PA-2
Blairsville Borough—*civil* PA-2
Blairsville (CCD)—*cens area* GA-3
Blairsville Cem—*cemetery* PA-2
Blairsville (Election Precinct)—*fmr MCD* IL-6
*Blairsville High School* PA-2
*Blairsville Intersection* PA-2
Blairsville Intersection—*crossing* PA-2
Blairsville JHS—*school* PA-2
*Blairsville Joint HS* PA-2
Blairsville Joint HS—*school* PA-2
Blairsville Rsvr—*reservoir* PA-2
Blairsville-Trout Run Dam—*dam* PA-2
Blair Swamp—*swamp* AL-4
Blair Tank—*reservoir* NM-5
**Blairton**—*pop pl* WV-2
**Blair Town**—*pop pl* KY-4
**Blairtown**—*pop pl* PA-2
**Blairtown**—*pop pl* WY-8
**Blair (Township of)**—*pop pl* IL-6
**Blair (Township of)**—*pop pl* MI-6
**Blair (Township of)**—*pop pl* PA-2
Blair Valley—*basin* CA-9
Blair Valley—*basin* PA-2
Blair Valley—*bend* TX-5
Blair Valley—*valley* MD-2
Blair Valley Ranger Station—*locale* CA-9
**Blair Village**—*pop pl* GA-3
**Blairville**—*pop pl* NY-2
**Blairville**—*pop pl* SC-3
Blair Waterway—*channel* WA-9
Blair Windmill—*locale* NM-5
Blair Windmill—*locale* TX-5
Blaisdell—*locale* AZ-5
Blaisdell—*locale* OR-9
**Blaisdell**—*pop pl* ND-7
Blaisdell Brook—*stream* NH-1
Blaisdell Brook—*stream* VT-1
Blaisdell Canyon—*valley* CA-9
Blaisdell Cem—*cemetery* ME-1
**Blaisdell Corners**—*pop pl* ME-1
Blaisdell Creek—*stream* NY-2
Blaisdell Hill—*summit* ME-1
**Blaisdell Junction**—*pop pl* PA-2
*Blaisdell Lake* WI-6
Blaisdell Lake—*lake* NH-1
Blaisdell Lake—*lake* WI-6
Blaisdell Park—*park* CA-9
*Blaisdell Pond* NH-1
Blaisdell Pond—*lake* ME-1
Blaisdell Pond—*reservoir* ME-1
Blaisdell Sch—*school* WI-6
Blaisdell Slow Sand Filter Washing Machine—*hist pl* AZ-5
Blaise Ch—*church* NC-3
Blaise Lejuene Gully—*stream* LA-4
*Blaiseville* KS-7
Blais Hill—*summit* NY-2
*Blais Park* NH-1
Blaize Cem—*cemetery* IN-6
*Blake* UT-8
B Lake—*lake* ME-1
Blake—*locale* KS-7
Blake—*locale* KY-4
Blake—*locale* MD-2
Blake—*locale* MO-7
**Blake**—*pop pl* AL-4
**Blake**—*pop pl* FL-3
**Blake**—*pop pl* OH-6
**Blake**—*pop pl* SC-3
Blake, Amanda, Store—*hist pl* NJ-2
Blake, H. G., House—*hist pl* OH-6
Blake, James, House—*hist pl* MA-1
Blake, John, House—*hist pl* NY-2
Blake, Wallace, House—*hist pl* UT-8
Blake-Beaty-Orton House—*hist pl* TX-5
*Blake Branch* AL-4
Blake Branch—*stream* NC-3
Blake Branch—*stream* TN-4
Blake Branch—*stream* WV-2
*Blake Brook* WI-6
Blake Brook—*stream* ME-1
Blake Brook—*stream* MA-1
Blake Brook—*stream* (2) NH-1
Blake Brook—*stream* NY-2
Blake Canyon—*valley* CA-9
*Blake Cass Pond Brook* NH-1
Blake Cem—*cemetery* (2) IN-6
Blake Cem—*cemetery* KY-4
Blake Cem—*cemetery* (3) ME-1
Blake Cem—*cemetery* MA-1
Blake Cem—*cemetery* MS-4
Blake Cem—*cemetery* NC-3
Blake Cem—*cemetery* OH-6
Blake Cem—*cemetery* TN-4
Blake Cem—*cemetery* VT-1
Blake Cem—*cemetery* (2) WV-2
Blake Ch—*church* MO-7
Blake Ch—*church* SC-3
Blake Ch—*church* TX-5
Blake Channel—*channel* AK-9
Blake Channel—*channel* DE-2
Blake Channel—*channel* NJ-2
Blake Channel—*channel* PA-2
Blake Chapel—*church* WV-2
**Blake Corner**—*pop pl* ME-1
*Blake Corners* ME-1
Blake Cove—*bay* VA-3
*Blake Creek* MD-2
Blake Creek—*bay* MD-2
Blake Creek—*stream* MT-8
Blake Creek—*stream* WI-6
Blake Creek Forest Station—*locale* MT-8
**Blakedale**—*pop pl* SC-3
Blake Ditch—*canal* OH-6
Blake Ditch—*canal* UT-8
Blake Draw—*valley* TX-5
Blake Falls—*falls* VT-1
Blake Falls Rsvr—*reservoir* NY-2
Blake Ferry (historical)—*locale* AL-4
Blake Field—*airport* CO-8
Blake Flat—*flat* OR-9
Blake Ford—*locale* AL-4
Blakeford Point—*cape* MD-2
Blake Fork—*stream* KY-4
Blake Fork—*stream* WV-2
Blake Fork—*stream* WI-6
Blake Gore—*unorg* ME-1
*Blake Gulch* ID-8
Blake Gulch—*valley* ID-8
Blake Gulch—*valley* OR-9
Blake Harmon Trail—*trail* UT-8
Blake Harmony Trail—*trail* UT-8
**Blake Heights Subdivision**—*pop pl* UT-8
Blake Hill—*summit* MA-1
Blake Hill—*summit* NY-2
Blake Hill—*summit* (3) VT-1
**Blake Holley Subdivision**—*pop pl* UT-8
Blake Hollow—*valley* OH-6
Blake Hollow—*valley* UT-8
Blake Hollow—*valley* WV-2
Blake Hollow—*valley* WY-8
Blake House—*hist pl* AR-4
Blake House—*hist pl* ME-1
Blake HS—*school* FL-3
*Blake Island* MD-2
Blake Island—*island* AK-9
Blake Island—*island* (2) ME-1
Blake Island—*island* NH-1
Blake Island—*island* WA-9
*Blake Lake* WI-6
Blake Lake—*lake* ME-1
Blake Lake—*lake* MN-6
Blake Lake—*lake* SC-3
Blake Lake—*reservoir* TX-5
*Blake Lakes* WI-6
Blakeland—*locale* CO-8
*B Lake Landing* MS-4
Blakeless Creek—*stream* CA-9
Blakeley—*hist pl* AL-4
Blakeley—*hist pl* WV-2
Blakeley—*locale* AL-4
Blakeley—*locale* OR-9
**Blakeley**—*pop pl* MN-6
**Blakeley**—*pop pl* NY-2
**Blakeley**—*pop pl* WV-2
Blakeley, W. H., House—*hist pl* KY-4
Blakeley, William G., House—*hist pl* AZ-5
Blakeley Branch—*stream* AL-4
Blakeley Canal—*canal* CA-9
Blakeley Canyon—*valley* NV-8
Blakeley Cem—*cemetery* AL-4
Blakeley Cem—*cemetery* AR-4
Blakeley Cem—*cemetery* TN-4
Blakeley Island—*island* AL-4
*Blakeley Mountain Reservoir* AR-4
Blakeley Park—*park* AL-4
*Blakeley Pond* CT-1
Blakeley River—*stream* AL-4
Blakeley River Bar—*bar* AL-4
Blakeley Rsvr—*reservoir* CA-9
Blakeley Sch—*school* AL-4
Blakeley Sch—*school* NE-7
*Blakeley Township* KS-7
**Blakeley (Township of)**—*pop pl* MN-6
*Blakely* AL-4
*Blakely* MN-6
Blakely—*locale* MS-4

Blank Park—*park* IA-7
Blank Peak—*summit* CA-9
Blank Pit—*cave* AL-4
Blank Point—*cape* AK-9
Blank Point—*cape* ME-1
Blank Ridge—*ridge* IA-7
Blank Rock—*island* CA-9
Blank Rsvr—*reservoir* WY-8
**Blanks**—*pop pl* LA-4
**Blanks**—*pop pl* TX-5
Blanks Cem—*cemetery* AL-4
Blankshire Branch—*stream* MO-7
Blanks Hollow—*valley* TN-4
Blank Spring—*spring* CA-9
Blank Spring—*spring* UT-8
Blanks Sch—*school* PA-2
Blanks Tavern—*locale* VA-3
**Blankston**—*pop pl* LA-4
*Blank Tank* AZ-5
Blann Cem—*cemetery* TN-4
Blann Creek—*stream* AR-4
Blann Creek—*stream* OR-9
Blann Meadow—*locale* OR-9
Blann Meadows Rsvr—*reservoir* OR-9
Blann Meadows Rsvr Dam—*dam* OR-9
Blann Sch—*school* AR-4
Blanon Landing—*locale* NC-3
Blanquizal Islands—*area* AK-9
Blanquizal Point—*cape* AK-9
Blan Ranch—*locale* SD-7
Blan Sch—*school* MO-7
Blansett—*locale* AR-4
Blansett (Township of)—*fmr MCD* AR-4
**Blansingburg**—*pop pl* NJ-2
*Blanton* VA-3
Blanton—*locale* AR-4
Blanton—*locale* GA-3
Blanton—*locale* OK-5
Blanton—*locale* (2) TX-5
**Blanton**—*pop pl* AL-4
**Blanton**—*pop pl* FL-3
**Blanton**—*pop pl* KY-4
**Blanton**—*pop pl* MS-4
Blanton Archeol Site—*hist pl* KY-4
Blanton Branch—*stream* (3) KY-4
Blanton Branch—*stream* NC-3
Blanton Cem—*cemetery* AR-4
Blanton Cem—*cemetery* GA-3
Blanton Cem—*cemetery* (2) KY-4
Blanton Cem—*cemetery* MO-7
Blanton Cem—*cemetery* (2) SC-3
Blanton Cem—*cemetery* (2) TN-4
Blanton Cem—*cemetery* (3) TX-5
Blanton Cemeterys—*cemetery* KY-4
Blanton Chapel—*church* TN-4
Blanton Chapel—*church* TX-5
**Blanton Chapel**—*pop pl* TN-4
Blanton Chapel Cem—*cemetery* TN-4
Blanton Creek—*stream* CA-9
Blanton Creek—*stream* SC-3
Blanton Creek—*stream* (2) TX-5
Blanton Creek Cem—*cemetery* TX-5
Blanton Crossing—*locale* VA-3
Blanton-Crutcher Farm—*hist pl* KY-4
*Blanton Drain* OR-9
Blanton Drain—*canal* OR-9
Blanton Elem Sch—*school* FL-3
Blanton Flats—*locale* KY-4
Blanton Grove Ch—*church* GA-3
Blanton (historical)—*locale* KS-7
**Blanton (historical)**—*pop pl* TN-4
Blanton Hollow—*valley* AR-4
Blanton-Hooser Cem—*cemetery* TX-5
Blanton Industrial Park—*locale* NC-3
Blanton Lake—*lake* FL-3
Blanton Log House—*hist pl* NM-5
Blanton Post Office (historical)—*building* MS-4
Blanton Prairie—*flat* CA-9
Blantons—*locale* VA-3
Blanton Sch—*school* FL-3
Blanton Sch—*school* (3) TX-5
Blantons Chapel—*church* GA-3
Blanton Sch (historical)—*school* TN-4
*Blantons Gap* MS-4
Blantons Gap—*gap* MS-4
Blantons Mill—*locale* GA-3
Blantons Mill (CCD)—*cens area* GA-3
Blantons Sch (historical)—*school* TN-4
Blanton Tank—*reservoir* NM-5
**Blantyre**—*pop pl* NC-3
Blantyre Ch—*church* NC-3
**Blanville**—*pop pl* AR-4
Blan Waste—*canal* CA-9
Blaquiere Point—*cape* AK-9
Blarney Castle Spring—*spring* SD-7
Blarney Creek—*stream* AK-9
Blarney Spring—*spring* OR-9
Blasbalg Point—*cape* VI-3
Blas Canyon—*valley* NM-5
Blasde Brook—*stream* NH-1
**Blasdell**—*pop pl* NY-2
Blase—*locale* MO-7
**Blaser**—*pop pl* ID-8
**Blaser**—*pop pl* WV-2
Blaser Creek—*stream* WI-6
Blasers Airp—*airport* KS-7
Blashke Islands—*area* AK-9
**Blasina**—*pop pl* PR-3
Blasingame Branch—*stream* TX-5
Blasingame Creek—*stream* MS-4
Blasingame Creek—*stream* NV-8
Blasingame Creek—*stream* TX-5
Blasingame Fire Control Station—*other* CA-9
Blasket Point—*cape* ME-1
Blass, Gus, Department Store—*hist pl* AR-4
Blass, Lake—*reservoir* WI-6
Blas Spring—*spring* NM-5
Blas Tank—*reservoir* TX-5
Blast Metal Mine—*mine* NV-8
Blastow Cove—*bay* ME-1
Blatchford—*locale* MT-8
Blatchford—*locale* OH-6
Blatchford Creek—*stream* AK-9
Blatchley—*locale* NY-2
Blatchley Canyon—*valley* CA-9
Blatchley Hall—*hist pl* ID-8
B Lateral—*canal* CA-9
B Lateral—*canal* ID-8
Blats Hill—*summit* MI-6
Blattner Cem—*cemetery* MO-7
Blattner Creek—*stream* OR-9
Blatz, Valentin, Brewing Company Office Bldg—*hist pl* WI-6
Blatz Brewery Complex—*hist pl* WI-6
*Blatz Peak* ID-8
Blatz Pond—*reservoir* CT-1
Blau Ditch—*canal* IN-6
*Blau Fluss* AZ-5
Blauguard Island—*island* NJ-2
Blau Gully—*valley* TX-5
Blaurock Pass—*gap* WY-8
Blauser Sch—*school* PA-2
Blau's Four Mile House—*hist pl* KY-4
**Blauvelt**—*pop pl* NY-2
Blauvelt Cem—*cemetery* NE-7
Blauvelt-Demarest House—*hist pl* NJ-2
Blauvelt Hollow—*valley* PA-2
Blauvelt House—*hist pl* NJ-2
Blauvelt House—*hist pl* NY-2
Blauvelt Mtn—*summit* NY-2
Blauvelt State Park—*park* NY-2
Blavo—*locale* CA-9
**Blawenburg**—*pop pl* NJ-2
Blawn Mtn—*summit* UT-8
**Blawnox**—*pop pl* PA-2
Blawnox Borough—*civil* PA-2
Blawn Wash—*valley* UT-8
Blawn Wash Spring—*spring* UT-8
B. Lawrence Site I—*hist pl* WI-6
Blay Creek—*stream* MO-7
Blaydes House—*hist pl* KY-4
Blaylock Branch—*stream* TN-4
Blaylock Canyon—*valley* OR-9
Blaylock Canyon Spring—*spring* OR-9
Blaylock Cem—*cemetery* AL-4
Blaylock Cem—*cemetery* MS-4
Blaylock Cem—*cemetery* MO-7
*Blaylock Creek* GA-3
Blaylock Creek—*stream* AR-4
Blaylock Knob—*summit* AR-4
Blaylock Lake—*reservoir* NC-3
Blaylock Lake Dam—*dam* NC-3
Blaylock Mill—*locale* GA-3
Blaylock Mtn—*summit* (2) AR-4
Blaylock Mtn—*summit* OK-5
Blaylock Mtn—*summit* TN-4
Blaylock Pond Dam—*dam* MS-4
Blayney Meadows—*flat* CA-9
Blayney Run—*stream* WV-2
*Blays Creek* MO-7
Blaze—*locale* KY-4
*Blaze Branch* TN-4
Blaze Branch—*stream* AL-4
Blaze Branch—*stream* (2) KY-4
Blaze Branch—*stream* NC-3
Blaze Canyon—*valley* ID-8
Blaze Canyon—*valley* UT-8
Blaze Creek—*stream* MO-7
Blazed Alder Butte—*summit* OR-9
Blazed Alder Creek—*stream* OR-9
Blazed Alder Way Trail—*trail* OR-9
Blazed Creek—*stream* NC-3
*Blazed Elder Butte* OR-9
Blazed Fork—*stream* WV-2
Blazed Gap—*gap* NC-3
Blazed Pine Landing—*locale* (2) FL-3
Blazed Pine Ridge—*ridge* TN-4
Blazed Ridge—*ridge* AZ-5
Blazed Ridge—*ridge* WA-9
Blazed Tank—*reservoir* AZ-5
Blaze Fork—*stream* KS-7
Blaze Fork—*stream* (2) WV-2
*Blaze Fork Creek* KS-7
Blaze Hollow—*valley* (2) KY-4
Blazek, E. J., House—*hist pl* TX-5
Blazek Dam—*dam* SD-7
Blaze Lake—*lake* OR-9
Blaze Mtn—*summit* MT-8
Blazer Branch—*stream* TN-4
*Blazer Creek* WI-6
Blazer Gap—*gap* PA-2
Blazer Hill—*summit* WY-8
Blazer Hollow—*valley* OH-6
Blazer HS—*school* KY-4
Blazer Lake—*lake* WA-9
Blazer Lake—*reservoir* TN-4
Blazers Mill—*locale* NM-5
Blaze Valley—*valley* KY-4
Blazier Butte—*summit* MT-8
Blazo-Leavitt House—*hist pl* ME-1
Blazo Mtn—*summit* NH-1
Blazon Gap—*gap* WY-8
**Blazon Junction**—*pop pl* WY-8
Blazon Mine—*mine* WY-8
B Lazy M Ranch—*locale* CO-8
Blcomer (Township of)—*other* MN-6
Bldg at Rear, 537 W. 200 S.—*hist pl* UT-8
Bldg at 561 W. 200 S.—*hist pl* UT-8
Bldg at 592–98 W. 200 S.—*hist pl* UT-8
*Bleachery Pond* MA-1
Bleachery Pond—*lake* RI-1
Bleachery Pond—*reservoir* (2) RI-1
Bleachery Ponds—*reservoir* MA-1
*Bleachery Spring* GA-3
**Bleachery (subdivision)**—*pop pl* MA-1
Bleak—*locale* VA-3
Bleak Bay—*bay* MN-6
Bleak Butte—*summit* SD-7
Bleak Creek—*stream* ID-8
Bleak Creek Lake—*lake* ID-8
*Bleaker* AL-4
Bleak Hall Plantation Outbuildings—*hist pl* SC-3
Bleak Hill Fork—*locale* VA-3
Bleakhorn Creek—*stream* VA-3
Bleak House—*hist pl* TN-4
Bleak House Ch—*church* MS-4
**Bleakley Hill**—*pop pl* PA-2
Bleakman Spring—*spring* OR-9
Bleak Mound Sch (abandoned)—*school* MO-7
Bleak Spring—*spring* AZ-5
**Bleakwood**—*pop pl* TX-5
Bleases Crossroads—*locale* SC-3
Bleat Creek—*stream* MI-6
Bleazard Branch—*stream* MO-7
Blecha Ranch (historical)—*locale* AZ-5
**Bleckley (County)**—*pop pl* GA-3
Bleckley County Courthouse—*hist pl* GA-3
Bleckley Sch—*school* GA-3
Bledsaw Gulch—*valley* CO-8
Bledsoe—*locale* AZ-5
Bledsoe—*locale* AR-4
Bledsoe—*locale* KY-4
Bledsoe—*locale* TN-4
**Bledsoe**—*pop pl* TN-4
**Bledsoe**—*pop pl* TX-5
Bledsoe Branch—*stream* (2) AL-4
Bledsoe Branch—*stream* IN-6
Bledsoe Branch—*stream* NC-3
Bledsoe Branch—*stream* TX-5
Bledsoe Canyon—*valley* OR-9
Bledsoe Cem—*cemetery* (2) KY-4
Bledsoe Cem—*cemetery* MS-4
Bledsoe Cem—*cemetery* (3) TN-4
Bledsoe Cem—*cemetery* TX-5
Bledsoe Cem—*cemetery* (2) VA-3
Bledsoe Ch—*church* KY-4
Bledsoe Ch—*church* TN-4
Bledsoe Corner—*locale* VA-3
**Bledsoe County**—*pop pl* TN-4
Bledsoe County HS—*school* TN-4
Bledsoe Creek—*stream* KY-4
Bledsoe Creek—*stream* NC-3
Bledsoe Creek—*stream* OR-9
Bledsoe Creek—*stream* TN-4
Bledsoe Creek—*stream* TX-5
Bledsoe Creek Camping State Park—*park* TN-4
Bledsoe Creek Ch—*church* TN-4
Bledsoe Creek (historical)—*stream* TX-5
Bledsoe Ferry Public Use Area—*park* MO-7
Bledsoe Gulch—*valley* CA-9
Bledsoe (historical)—*locale* AL-4
Bledsoe Hollow—*valley* (2) TN-4
Bledsoe Lake Dam—*dam* MS-4
Bledsoe Memorial Cem—*cemetery* MO-7
Bledsoe Park—*park* MS-4
Bledsoe Place Plantation (historical)—*locale* AL-4
*Bledsoe P.O.* AL-4
Bledsoe Post Office (historical)—*building* TN-4
Bledsoe Ranch—*locale* CO-8
Bledsoe Ranch Landing Strip—*airport* SD-7
Bledsoe Sch—*school* TN-4
*Bledsoes Creek Baptist Church* TN-4
Bledsoe Stand (historical)—*locale* TN-4
Bledsoe State For—*forest* TN-4
*Bledson Branch* TX-5
**Bleecker**—*pop pl* AL-4
**Bleecker**—*pop pl* NY-2
Bleecker Cem—*cemetery* MS-4
Bleecker Center—*locale* NY-2
Bleecker Stadium—*other* NY-2
**Bleecker (Town of)**—*pop pl* NY-2
*Bleeda School* AL-4
Bleeksley Swamp—*swamp* PA-2
Blees Military Acad—*hist pl* MO-7
*Bleha Dam* SD-7
**Bleiblerville**—*pop pl* TX-5
Bleich Canyon—*valley* CA-9
Bleich Flat—*flat* CA-9
Blemhuber Lake—*lake* MI-6
**Blencoe**—*pop pl* IA-7
Blenco (historical P.O.)—*locale* IA-7
Blend—*other* TN-4
Blendale Lake—*lake* NY-2
**Blende**—*pop pl* CO-8
*Blenden Corner* OH-6
*Blendon* KS-7
*Blendon* OH-6
Blendon And Olive Drain—*canal* MI-6
Blendon Cem—*cemetery* MI-6
Blendon Cem—*cemetery* VA-3
**Blendon Corner**—*pop pl* OH-6
*Blendon Four Corners* OH-6
Blendon (Magisterial District)—*fmr MCD* VA-3
Blendon Sch—*school* SD-7
**Blendon Township**—*pop pl* SD-7
**Blendon (Township of)**—*pop pl* MI-6
**Blendon (Township of)**—*pop pl* OH-6
Blendon Woods Metropolitan Park—*park* OH-6
Blend Post Office (historical)—*building* TN-4
Blendsoe Bend—*bend* AR-4
*Blendville* MO-7
Blenheim—*hist pl* (4) VA-3
Blenheim—*locale* VA-3
**Blenheim**—*pop pl* MD-2
**Blenheim**—*pop pl* NJ-2
**Blenheim**—*pop pl* SC-3
Blenheim—*uninc pl* LA-4
Blenheim (CCD)—*cens area* SC-3
Blenheim Hill—*summit* NY-2
Blenheim Hill Cem—*cemetery* NY-2
Blenheim Lookout Tower—*locale* SC-3
Blenheim Mtn—*summit* NY-2
Blenheim Park—*park* MO-7
Blenheim Sch—*school* MO-7
Blenheim Sch—*school* SC-3
**Blenheim (Town of)**—*pop pl* NY-2
**Blenker (Sherry Station)**—*pop pl* WI-6
Blenk House—*hist pl* KY-4
Blenman Sch—*school* AZ-5
**Blennerhassett**—*pop pl* WV-2
Blennerhassett (Blennerhassett Heights)—*CDP* WV-2
Blennerhassett Heights—*other* WV-2
Blennerhassett Hotel—*hist pl* WV-2
Blennerhassett Island—*island* NC-3
Blennerhassett Island—*island* WV-2
Blennerhassett Island Hist Dist—*hist pl* WV-2
*Blennerhassetts Island* WV-2
Blennes Corner—*locale* NY-2
Blenn Run—*stream* WV-2
Blen Park—*park* OK-5
Blenz Spring—*spring* WA-9
*Bleondon Cross roads* OH-6
Blesener Creek—*stream* MN-6
Blesener Lake—*lake* MN-6
Bleshenski Drain—*canal* MI-6
*Blesner Creek* MN-6
*Blesner Lake* MN-6
Blessed Agnes Sch—*school* IL-6
Blessed Creek—*stream* MT-8
Blessed Hope Camp—*locale* MI-6
Blessed Hope Ch—*church* (2) WV-2
Blessed Hope Independent Baptist Ch—*church* IN-6
Blessed Martin Ch—*church* LA-4
Blessed Martin De Porres Sch—*school* AL-4
Blessed Redeemer Ch—*church* NE-7
Blessed Sacrament Acad—*hist pl* AL-4
Blessed Sacrament Acad—*school* NY-2
Blessed Sacrament Acad—*school* TX-5
Blessed Sacrament Cahtolic Ch—*church* TN-4
Blessed Sacrament Catholic Ch—*church* FL-3
Blessed Sacrament Cem—*cemetery* MN-6
Blessed Sacrament Cem—*cemetery* NY-2
Blessed Sacrament Ch—*church* FL-3
Blessed Sacrament Ch—*church* MT-8
Blessed Sacrament Ch—*church* NJ-2
Blessed Sacrament Ch—*church* SC-3
Blessed Sacrament Ch—*church* TX-5
Blessed Sacrament Ch—*church* VT-1
Blessed Sacrament Ch—*church* WY-8
Blessed Sacrament Novitiate—*church* MA-1
Blessed Sacrament of Fathers Sch—*school* WI-6
Blessed Sacrament Roman Catholic Ch—*church* KS-7
Blessed Sacrament Sch—*school* AL-4
Blessed Sacrament Sch—*school* (3) CA-9
Blessed Sacrament Sch—*school* (3) CT-1
Blessed Sacrament Sch—*school* FL-3
Blessed Sacrament Sch—*school* (2) IL-6
Blessed Sacrament Sch—*school* IN-6
Blessed Sacrament Sch—*school* (2) IA-7
Blessed Sacrament Sch—*school* (2) KS-7
Blessed Sacrament Sch—*school* (2) MA-1
Blessed Sacrament Sch—*school* (2) MI-6
Blessed Sacrament Sch—*school* (2) MO-7
Blessed Sacrament Sch—*school* (3) NE-7
Blessed Sacrament Sch—*school* NH-1
Blessed Sacrament Sch—*school* (2) NJ-2
Blessed Sacrament Sch—*school* (7) NY-2
Blessed Sacrament Sch—*school* NC-3
Blessed Sacrament Sch—*school* (2) OH-6
Blessed Sacrament Sch—*school* OR-9
Blessed Sacrament Sch—*school* (3) PA-2
Blessed Sacrament Sch—*school* SC-3
Blessed Sacrament Sch—*school* (3) TX-5
Blessed Sacrament Sch—*school* VA-3
Blessed Sacrament Sch—*school* WI-6
Blessed Trinity Catholic Ch—*church* (2) FL-3
Blessed Trinity Ch—*church* (2) FL-3
Blessed Trinity Ch—*church* SD-7
Blessed Trinity Mission—*church* AL-4
Blessed Trinity Roman Catholic Church Buildings—*hist pl* NY-2
Blessed Trinity Sch—*school* (2) FL-3
Blessed Trinity Sch—*school* NY-2
*Blessed Trinity Shrine Retreat* AL-4
Blessed Virgin Cem—*cemetery* PA-2
Blessed Virgin Ch—*church* PA-2
Blessed Virgin Mary Sch—*school* PA-2
Blessed Virgin Sch—*school* MI-6
Blessing—*locale* OH-6
Blessing—*locale* VA-3
Blessing—*locale* VI-3
**Blessing**—*pop pl* IA-7
**Blessing**—*pop pl* TX-5
Blessing, Carl, Outbuildings—*hist pl* ID-8
Blessing Bridge—*bridge* OH-6
Blessing Cem—*cemetery* AL-4
Blessing Cem—*cemetery* TX-5
Blessing Ch—*church* AL-4
Blessing Ch—*church* IA-7
*Blessing Ch of Christ* AL-4
Blessing Hosp—*hospital* IL-6
Blessing Mtn—*summit* PA-2
Blessing Number 1 Dam—*dam* SD-7
Blessing Plantation—*locale* SC-3
Blessing Sch—*school* TX-5
Blessing Sch (historical)—*school* AL-4
Blessington Cave—*cave* AL-4
Blessington Point—*cape* AL-4
Blessing Township—*civil* SD-7
Bless Park—*park* MO-7
Bletcher Brook—*stream* WV-2
Bletchers Creek—*stream* TN-4
Blethen, Lake—*lake* WA-9
Blethen Sch—*school* ME-1
Bletz Hollow—*valley* PA-2
Bleux Island—*island* LA-4
Blevens Cem—*cemetery* TX-5
Blevens Creek—*stream* AL-4
Blevens Hollow—*valley* AR-4
Blevens Rsvr—*reservoir* OR-9
Blevens Wash—*stream* AZ-5
Blevens Wash Well—*well* AZ-5
*Blevidere Village* MA-1
Blevin Branch—*stream* NC-3
Blevin Mill (historical)—*locale* TN-4
Blevin Ranch—*locale* WY-8
Blevins—*locale* KY-4
Blevins—*locale* TN-4
**Blevins**—*pop pl* AR-4
**Blevins**—*pop pl* TX-5
Blevins Acre—*locale* GA-3
Blevins Airp (private)—*airport* NC-3
Blevins Branch—*stream* (2) KY-4
Blevins Branch—*stream* NC-3
Blevins Branch—*stream* (5) TN-4
Blevins Branch—*stream* VA-3
*Blevins Branch Mine* TN-4
Blevins Cave—*cave* AL-4
Blevins Cem—*cemetery* AR-4
Blevins Cem—*cemetery* (2) NC-3
Blevins Cem—*cemetery* (7) TN-4
Blevins Cem—*cemetery* (3) VA-3
Blevins Cem—*cemetery* WV-2
Blevins Chapel (historical)—*church* TN-4
Blevins Corner—*locale* VA-3
*Blevins Creek* AL-4
Blevins Creek—*stream* NC-3
Blevins Creek—*stream* OR-9
Blevins Creek—*stream* VA-3
Blevins Creek Chapel—*church* NC-3
**Blevins Crossroads**—*pop pl* NC-3
Blevins Dam—*dam* OR-9
Blevins Draw—*valley* AZ-5
Blevins Forge (historical)—*locale* TN-4
Blevins Fork—*stream* KY-4
Blevins Gap—*gap* AL-4
Blevins Gap—*gap* KY-4
Blevins Hollow—*valley* AL-4
Blevins Hollow—*valley* KY-4
Blevins Hollow—*valley* (4) TN-4
Blevins Knob—*summit* NC-3
Blevins Lake—*lake* AZ-5
Blevins Mine—*mine* TN-4
Blevins Post Office (historical)—*building* TN-4
Blevins Ranch—*locale* CO-8
Blevins Ridge—*ridge* NC-3
Blevins Rsvr—*reservoir* OR-9
Blevins Sch No 2—*school* AR-4
Blevins Spring—*spring* OR-9
Blevins Spring—*spring* TN-4
Blevins Store—*locale* NC-3
Blevins Store (historical)—*locale* TN-4
**Blevinstown**—*pop pl* VA-3
Blevins Training Sch—*school* AR-4
Blevins Valley—*valley* KY-4
Blevins Valley Ch—*church* KY-4
Blewer Pond—*reservoir* LA-4
Blewett—*locale* TX-5
Blewett—*locale* WA-9
Blewett Arrastra—*hist pl* WA-9
Blewett Branch—*stream* TX-5
Blewett Cem—*cemetery* KY-4
Blewett Cem—*cemetery* TX-5
*Blewett Dam* NC-3
Blewett Falls Dam—*dam* NC-3
Blewett Falls Lake—*reservoir* NC-3
Blewett Pass—*gap* WA-9
Blewetts Point—*summit* CA-9
**Blewett (sta.)**—*pop pl* TX-5
Blewett Summit Trail—*trail* WA-9
Blewitt Falls Lake Dam—*dam* NC-3
*Blew Pond* RI-1
Blews Run—*stream* NJ-2
Blexley Run—*stream* PA-2
B L Griffin Lake Dam—*dam* MS-4
Blice Point—*cliff* IN-6
*Blichton* FL-3
**Blichton**—*pop pl* FL-3
Blickensderfer Creek—*stream* WA-9
Blickenstaff Ditch—*canal* IN-6
Blick Sch (historical)—*school* PA-2
Blieders Creek—*stream* TX-5
Bliedorn—*locale* IA-7
**Bliem Corners**—*pop pl* PA-2
**Blier**—*pop pl* ME-1
Blierdofer Ditch—*canal* OH-6
*Blig* FM-9
Bligh Field—*park* NY-2
Bligh Island—*island* AK-9
Bligh Reef—*bar* AK-9
Blights Run—*stream* VA-3
Bliler and Boswell Ditch—*canal* CO-8
Bliler And Boswell Ditch—*canal* WY-8
Blinberry Gulch—*valley* CO-8
Blinco Branch—*stream* OH-6
**Blincoe**—*pop pl* KY-4
Blind Alligator Bayou—*bay* FL-3
Blind Ash Bay—*bay* MN-6
Blind Basin—*lake* AR-4
*Blind Bay* AL-4
Blind Bay—*bay* (3) LA-4
Blind Bay—*bay* NY-2
Blind Bay—*bay* WA-9
Blind Bay—*swamp* NY-2
Blind Bayou—*bay* TX-5
Blind Bayou—*gut* (4) LA-4
Blind Bayou—*gut* (2) TX-5
Blind Bayou—*stream* (2) LA-4
Blind Beach—*beach* CA-9
Blind Biscuit Creek—*stream* MI-6
Blind Boone Park—*park* MO-7
Blind Branch—*stream* KY-4
Blind Breaker—*bay* AK-9
Blind Breed Gulch—*valley* MT-8
Blind Bridger Creek—*stream* MT-8
*Blind Brook* MA-1
Blind Brook—*stream* ME-1
Blind Brook—*stream* NY-2
Blind Brook—*stream* VT-1
Blind Brook Country Club—*other* NY-2
Blind Buck Hollow—*valley* NY-2
Blind Buck Stream—*stream* NY-2
Blind Bull Creek—*stream* WY-8
Blind Bull Lake—*lake* WY-8
Blind Bull Mine—*mine* WY-8
Blind Cabin Ridge—*ridge* OR-9
Blind Canyon—*valley* AZ-5
Blind Canyon—*valley* (6) CA-9
Blind Canyon—*valley* (4) CO-8
Blind Canyon—*valley* (6) ID-8
Blind Canyon—*valley* MT-8
Blind Canyon—*valley* NV-8
Blind Canyon—*valley* (6) NM-5
Blind Canyon—*valley* OR-9
Blind Canyon—*valley* (5) UT-8
Blind Canyon—*valley* (3) WY-8
Blind Canyon Creek—*stream* MT-8
Blind Canyon Draw—*valley* NM-5
Blind Choctaw Bayou—*stream* LA-4
Blind Corners—*locale* OH-6
Blind Coulee—*valley* MT-8
Blind Cove—*bay* AK-9
*Blind Creek* ID-8
Blind Creek—*gut* NH-1
Blind Creek—*stream* (2) AK-9
Blind Creek—*stream* (2) FL-3
Blind Creek—*stream* (7) ID-8
Blind Creek—*stream* MI-6
Blind Creek—*stream* (3) MT-8
Blind Creek—*stream* NY-2
Blind Creek—*stream* (2) OR-9
Blind Creek—*stream* SC-3
Blind Creek—*stream* SD-7
Blind Creek—*stream* (2) WY-8
Blind Creek Cove—*bay* NY-2
Blind Creek Trail—*trail* ID-8
Blind Draw—*valley* MT-8
Blind Draw—*valley* UT-8
Blind Draw Tank—*reservoir* AZ-5
*Blinde Durchfahrt* MP-9
Blinders Rocks—*island* VI-3
Blind Fish Cave—*cave* TN-4
Blind Fork—*stream* MT-8
Blind Fork—*stream* UT-8
Blind Fork Trail Creek—*stream* ID-8
Blind Gap—*gap* NM-5
Blind Girls' Home—*hist pl* MO-7
Blind Goddess Mine—*mine* AZ-5
Blind Gulch—*valley* AK-9
Blind Gulch—*valley* CO-8
Blind Gulch—*valley* ID-8
Blind Gulch—*valley* MT-8
Blind Gulch—*valley* NM-5
Blind Gulch—*valley* OR-9
Blind Gulch—*valley* SD-7
Blind Hills—*summit* CA-9
Blind Hollow—*valley* IL-6
Blind Hollow—*valley* UT-8
Blind Hollow—*valley* VA-3
Blind Horse Creek—*stream* CA-9
Blindhorse Creek—*stream* MT-8
Blind Horse Hollow—*valley* IN-6
Blind Horse Ridge—*ridge* IL-6
Blind Indian Creek—*channel* MI-6
Blind Indian Creek—*stream* AZ-5
Blind Indian Narrows—*channel* MN-6
Blind Island—*island* (2) AK-9
Blind Island—*island* TN-4
Blind Island—*island* (2) WA-9
Blind Island Campground—*locale* AK-9
Blind Johnny Hill—*summit* ND-7
Blind John Taylor Gap—*gap* KY-4
Blind Lagoon—*lake* (2) LA-4
Blind Lake—*lake* CO-8
Blind Lake—*lake* LA-4
Blind Lake—*lake* (2) MI-6
Blind Lake—*lake* (4) MN-6
Blind Lake—*lake* TX-5
Blind Lake—*lake* (3) UT-8
Blind Lake Ch—*church* MN-6
Blind Lake Creek—*stream* MN-6
Blind Lake Tank—*reservoir* AZ-5
**Blind Lake (Township of)**—*pop pl* MN-6
Blindman Butte—*summit* AZ-5
Blindman Canyon—*valley* KS-7
Blindman Hollow—*valley* TN-4
Blind Mans Gulch—*valley* CA-9
Blind Mans Vly—*lake* NY-2
Blindman Table—*summit* SD-7
Blind Mountain Spring—*spring* NV-8
Blind Mtn—*summit* NV-8
Blind Park—*flat* SD-7
Blind Pass—*channel* AK-9
Blind Pass—*channel* (3) FL-3
Blind Pass—*channel* (2) LA-4
Blind Pass—*channel* MI-6
Blind Pass—*channel* TX-5
Blind Pass—*gut* FL-3
Blind Passage—*channel* MP-9
Blind Pass Mtn—*summit* AK-9
Blind Pete Lake—*lake* MN-6
Blind Pig Channel—*channel* MN-6
Blind Pig Island—*island* MN-6
Blind Pisana Bayou—*gut* LA-4
Blind Point—*cape* (2) AK-9
Blind Point—*cape* CA-9
Blind Point—*cape* VA-3
Blind Pond—*lake* DE-2
Blind Pond—*lake* (3) NY-2
Blind Pond Outlet—*stream* NY-2
Blind Pony Wildlife Area—*park* MO-7
Blind Rigolets—*gut* LA-4
Blind River—*stream* (2) AK-9
Blind River—*stream* LA-4
Blind Rock—*rock* MA-1
Blind Sam Gulch—*valley* OR-9
*Blinds Canyon* UT-8
Blind Shady Creek—*stream* CA-9
Blinds Hammock—*island* NC-3
Blinds Hammock Bay—*bay* NC-3
Blind Sheep Creek—*stream* MT-8
Blind Shoals—*bar* AL-4
Blind Slough—*gut* (2) AK-9
Blind Slough—*gut* TX-5
Blind Slough—*gut* WA-9
Blind Slough—*stream* OR-9
Blind Slough Campground—*locale* AK-9
Blind Sodus Bay—*bay* NY-2
Blind Sodus Creek—*stream* NY-2
Blind Spring—*spring* AZ-5
Blind Spring—*spring* CA-9
Blind Spring—*spring* (2) ID-8
Blind Spring—*spring* (9) NV-8
Blind Spring—*spring* (3) UT-8
Blind Spring Basin—*basin* NV-8
Blind Spring Creek—*stream* ID-8
Blind Spring Draw—*valley* ID-8
Blind Spring Draw—*valley* UT-8
Blind Spring Hill—*ridge* (2) CA-9
Blind Spring Mtn—*summit* UT-8
Blind Springs—*spring* ID-8
Blind Springs—*spring* UT-8
Blind Springs Canyon—*valley* UT-8
Blind Spring Valley—*valley* CA-9
Blind Spruce Creek—*bay* FL-3
Blind Stream—*stream* UT-8
*Blind Stream Creek* UT-8
Blind Sucker Campground—*locale* MI-6
Blind Sucker Flooding—*lake* MI-6
Blind Sucker River—*stream* MI-6
Blind Summit—*summit* ID-8
Blind Tank—*reservoir* AZ-5
Blind Tank—*reservoir* NM-5
Blind Temperance Creek—*stream* MN-6
Blind Tensas Cut—*canal* LA-4
Blind Tiger Creek—*stream* MS-4
Blind Trail—*trail* UT-8
Blind Trail Creek—*stream* WY-8
Blind Trail Wash—*valley* UT-8
Blind Trap Tank—*reservoir* TX-5
Blind Valley—*valley* UT-8
Blind Well—*well* NM-5
B Line Canal—*canal* ID-8
Blink Bonnie—*hist pl* SC-3
Blinker Creek—*stream* MS-4
Blinker Lake—*lake* MN-6
*Blinkhorn Creek* VA-3
Blinkhorn Creek—*stream* MD-2
Blink Springs—*spring* MT-8
Blinn Ditch—*canal* IN-6
Blinn Hill—*summit* ME-1
Blinn Lake—*lake* AK-9
Blinn Sch—*school* IL-6
Blinn Spring—*spring* CA-9
Blinn Spring—*spring* OR-9
Blinsman (historical)—*locale* SD-7
**Blinsmon Township**—*pop pl* SD-7
*Blinthorn Creek* MD-2
Blisang—*bar* PW-9
Blish Cem—*cemetery* AR-4
Blish-Garret House—*hist pl* MA-1
Blish Point—*cape* MA-1
*Blishs Point* MA-1
Bliss—*locale* KY-4

Bliss—locale MI-6
Bliss—locale NV-8
**Bliss—pop pl** ID-8
**Bliss—pop pl** MO-7
**Bliss—pop pl** NY-2
Bliss, Abiah, House—hist pl MA-1
Bliss, Daniel, Homestead—hist pl MA-1
Bliss, F. T., House—hist pl ID-8
Bliss, L., House—hist pl NY-2
Bliss, Mount—summit CA-9
Bliss, Mount—summit MI-6
Bliss, Phillip Paul, House—hist pl PA-2
Blissang PW-9
Blissaol PW-9
Blissard Lake—lake TX-5
Bliss Bldg—hist pl MA-1
Bliss Bottom—bend UT-8
Bliss Branch TX-5
Bliss Brook MA-1
Bliss Brook—stream MA-1
Bliss Camp—locale ME-1
Bliss Canal—canal UT-8
Bliss Canyon—valley CA-9
Bliss Canyon—valley NV-8
Bliss Cem—cemetery IN-6
Bliss Cem—cemetery VT-1
Bliss Ch—church MI-6
Bliss Corner—locale NY-2
Bliss Corners—locale NY-2
**Bliss Corners—pop pl** RI-1
**Bliss Corner (subdivision)—pop pl** MA-1
Bliss Creek PA-2
Bliss Creek WY-8
Bliss Creek—stream MS-4
Bliss Creek—stream NV-8
Bliss Creek—stream TX-5
Bliss Creek—stream WY-8
Bliss Creek Meadows—flat WY-8
Blissdale—locale MS-4
Blissdale Sch—school MS-4
Blissdale Swamp—swamp MS-4
Bliss Ditch—canal CA-9
Bliss Drain—canal (2) MI-6
Blisset Branch—stream MS-4
Bliss Extension Robbins Ditch IN-6
**Blissfield—pop pl** MI-6
**Blissfield—pop pl** OH-6
Blissfield Cem—cemetery OH-6
**Blissfield (Township of)—pop pl** MI-6
Bliss Four Corners RI-1
Blissful Lake—lake MN-6
Bliss Hill—summit MA-1
Bliss Hill—summit OH-6
Bliss (historical)—locale (2) AL-4
**Bliss (historical)—pop pl** TN-4
Bliss Hollow—valley (2) MO-7
Bliss JHS—school MO-7
Bliss Lake—lake MI-6
Bliss Lookout Tower—locale MI-6
Bliss Mtn—summit AR-4
Bliss Park—park MI-6
Bliss Pass—gap WY-8
Bliss Point—cape ID-8
Bliss Pond MA-1
Bliss Pond—lake AZ-5
Bliss Pond—lake MA-1
Bliss Pond—lake VT-1
**Bliss Pond—pop pl** VT-1
Bliss Pond—reservoir MA-1
Bliss Pond Number Three—lake AZ-5
Bliss Pond Number Two—lake AZ-5
Bliss Post Office (historical)—building AL-4
Bliss Post Office (historical)—building TN-4
Bliss Pumping Station—locale WY-8
Bliss Ranch—locale CA-9
Bliss Ridge—ridge AR-4
Bliss Rsvr—reservoir ID-8
Bliss Run—stream OH-6
Bliss Run—stream PA-2
Bliss Sch—school CA-9
Bliss Sch—school IL-6
Bliss Sch—school MA-1
Bliss Sch (historical)—school AL-4
Bliss Sch (historical)—school MO-7
Bliss Spring—spring MO-7
Bliss Spring Campground—locale MO-7
Bliss Spring Hollow—valley AR-4
Bliss Tower—locale LA-4
Bliss Tower (fire tower)—tower FL-3
**Bliss (Township of)—pop pl** MI-6
Bliss Union Chapel—church MA-1
Blissville MI-6
**Blissville—pop pl** MA-1
**Blissville—pop pl** VT-1
Blissville (Bliss)—uninc pl NY-2
Blissville Brook—stream CT-1
Blissville Ch—church IN-6
Blissville Pond—lake CT-1
**Blissville (Township of)—pop pl** IL-6
Blister Creek—stream AK-9
Blister Creek—stream OR-9
Blistered Horn Mill—locale CO-8
Blister Run—stream WV-2
Blister Rust Creek—stream ID-8
Blister Swamp—swamp WV-2
Blitch—locale GA-3
**Blitch—pop pl** SC-3
Blitch Cem—cemetery GA-3
Blitchton—locale FL-3
**Blitchton—pop pl** GA-3
Blitchton Lookout Tower—tower FL-3
**Blitchville—pop pl** FL-3
Blithedale Ridge—ridge CA-9
Blithewold—hist pl RI-1
Blithewood Sch—school MA-1
Blitzen—locale OR-9
Blitzen, Mount—summit NV-8
Blitzen Butte—summit OR-9
Blitzen Creek—stream OR-9
Blitzen Valley—valley OR-9
Bliven Brook—stream CT-1
Bliven Cem—cemetery NY-2
Bliven Creek—stream NY-2
Bliven Hill—summit NY-2
Bliven Pond—lake NY-2
Blix—locale TX-5
Blixit Creek—stream MT-8
Blixrud Ranch—locale MT-8
Blizhni Point—cape AK-9
Blizzard Basin—basin ID-8
Blizzard Bluff—cliff NV-8
Blizzard Camp Point—cape NV-8
Blizzard Cem—cemetery IL-6
Blizzard Creek—stream AK-9
Blizzard Creek—stream WA-9
Blizzard Drain—canal MI-6
Blizzard Gap—gap OR-9
Blizzard Heights—summit WY-8
Blizzard Hill—summit MT-8
Blizzardine Peak—summit CO-8
Blizzard Lake—lake AK-9
Blizzard Lake—lake MN-6
Blizzard Lake—lake UT-8
Blizzard Mtn—summit ID-8
Blizzard Neck Gut—gut NJ-2
Blizzard Pass WA-9
Blizzard Pass—gap WA-9
Blizzard Peak—summit AK-9
Blizzard Peak—summit WA-9
Blizzard Ponds—lake KY-4
Blizzard Ponds Drainage Canal—canal KY-4
Blizzard Post Office (historical)—building TN-4
Blizzard Ridge—ridge MT-8
Blizzard Ridge—ridge (2) OR-9
Blizzard Rsvr—reservoir MT-8
Blizzard Run—stream (2) WV-2
Blizzards Creek—stream VA-3
Blizzards Crossroads—locale NC-3
Bluewing Flat NV-8
Blue Wing Flat—flat NV-8
BLM Campground UT-8
Blm Lake—lake NM-5
BLM Office-Hanksville—building UT-8
B L Moor HS—school MS-4
Bloat Gulch—valley CO-8
Bloat Lake—lake MI-6
Blochang FM-9
**Blocher—pop pl** IN-6
Blocher Cem—cemetery MD-2
Blocher Sch (historical)—school PA-2
Bloch Park—park AL-4
Bloch Sch—school MI-6
Block—locale IL-6
**Block—pop pl** KS-7
**Block—pop pl** TN-4
Block, J. S., Bldg—hist pl LA-4
Block, The—cliff WY-8
Block, The—summit (2) UT-8
Blockade, The—summit TN-4
Blockade Branch—stream NC-3
Blockade Gap—gap TN-4
Blockade Glacier—glacier AK-9
Blockade Hill—summit AR-4
Blockade Hollow—valley MO-7
Blockade Lake—lake AK-9
Blockade Shoal—bar NC-3
Block Air Village—airport MO-7
Block and Oil Field—oilfield LA-4
Block And Tackle Hill—summit WY-8
Block and Tackle Spring—spring OR-9
Block Bayou—stream TX-5
Block Bend—bend AR-4
Block Branch—stream MO-7
Block Branch—stream TX-5
Block Brook MA-1
Block Brook—stream MA-1
Block Canyon NE-7
Block Canyon—valley NM-5
Block Cem—cemetery IN-6
Block Cem—cemetery KY-4
Block Cem—cemetery LA-4
Block Cem—cemetery MO-7
Block Cem—cemetery (2) OH-6
Block Ch—church AL-4
Block Ch—church KY-4
Block Ch—church NY-2
Block Church TN-4
**Block City—pop pl** TN-4
Block Creek TX-5
Block Creek—stream AK-9
Block Creek—stream ID-8
Block Creek—stream IN-6
Block Creek—stream TX-5
Block Ditch—canal IN-6
Block Drain—canal MI-6
Blocker KS-7
**Blocker—pop pl** FL-3
**Blocker—pop pl** OK-5
**Blocker—pop pl** TX-5
Blocker Cem—cemetery AL-4
Blocker Cem—cemetery (2) MS-4
Blocker Cem—cemetery SC-3
Blocker Cem—cemetery (2) TX-5
Blocker Ch—church OK-5
Blocker Creek—stream (3) AR-4
Blocker Creek—stream GA-3
Blocker Creek—stream TX-5
Blocker Hill—summit AL-4
Blocker Hill Cem—cemetery AL-4
Blocker House—hist pl SC-3
Blocker JHS—school FL-3
Blocker Junior High School AL-4
Blocker Lake—lake FL-3
Blocker Lake—lake SC-3
Blocker Mine (underground)—mine AL-4
Blockers Chapel—church GA-3
Blocker Waterhole—lake TX-5
Block Field—park IN-6
Block Hill—summit CA-9
Block Hill—summit WA-9
Block Hole—other MO-7
Block Hollow—valley VA-3
Block Hollow—valley WV-2
Block Hollow Creek—stream CO-8
Block House PA-2
**Block House—pop pl** TN-4
**Blockhouse—pop pl** TN-4
**Blockhouse—pop pl** WA-9
Block House, The—hist pl NY-2
Blockhouse Butte—summit WA-9
Blockhouse Cem—cemetery IL-6
Blockhouse Cem—cemetery NY-2
Blockhouse Ch—church GA-3
Block House Ch—church TN-4
Blockhouse Creek—stream FL-3
Blockhouse Creek—stream KY-4
Blockhouse Creek—stream MI-6
Blockhouse Creek—stream NY-2
Blockhouse Creek—stream PA-2
Block House Creek—stream TX-5
Blockhouse Creek—stream TX-5
Blockhouse Creek—stream WA-9
Blockhouse Creek—stream WI-6
Blockhouse Hill—summit MS-4
Blockhouse Hollow—valley OH-6
Blockhouse Lake—lake WI-6
Blockhouse Mtn—summit NC-3
Blockhouse on Signal Mountain—hist pl OK-5
Block House Point ME-1
Blockhouse Point—cape ME-1
Blockhouse Point—cape MD-2
Blockhouse Point—cape VT-1
Blockhouse Pond—lake DE-2
Blockhouse Post Office (historical)—building TN-4
Block House Ranch—locale TX-5
Blockhouse Ridge—ridge NC-3
Blockhouse Run—stream (3) PA-2
Blockhouse Sch—school WI-6
Blockhouse Site—hist pl NC-3
Blockhouse Valley—valley TN-4
Block Island RI-1
Block Island—island (2) AK-9
Block Island—island IN-6
Block Island—island RI-1
Block Island Creek—stream SC-3
Block Island Harbor RI-1
Block Island North Light—hist pl RI-1
Block Island North Lighthouse—locale RI-1
Block Island Sound—bay NY-2
Block Island Sound—bay RI-1
Block Island Southeast Lighthouse—locale RI-1
Block Island State Airp—airport RI-1
Block Island State Beach—Beach RI-1
**Block Island (Town name New Shoreham)—pop pl** RI-1
Block Junior High School IN-6
Block Lake TX-5
Block Lake WI-6
Block Lake—reservoir MN-6
Blockland Mine (underground)—mine AL-4
Block Lick Run VA-3
**Blockly—pop pl** IA-7
Blockman Union Sch—school CA-9
Block Memorial Baptist Church AL-4
Blockmer Elevator ND-7
Block Mesas—summit UT-8
Block Mine—mine CO-8
Block Mtn—summit MT-8
Block Mtn—summit (2) UT-8
Block Mtn—summit WA-9
Blocknic Lake—lake MN-6
Block No 4 Gas Field—oilfield LA-4
Block Ore Ridge—ridge PA-2
Block Park—park NY-2
Block Pond—lake FL-3
Block Post Office (historical)—building TN-4
Block Ranch—locale (2) NM-5
Block Ranger Station—locale NM-5
Block Run WV-2
Block Run—stream IN-6
Block Run—stream MD-2
Block Run—stream (2) WV-2
Blocks, The—summit UT-8
Blocks Bluff—cliff MS-4
**Blocksburg—pop pl** CA-9
Blocks Canyon—valley OR-9
Block Sch—school MI-6
Block Sch—school WI-6
Block Sch (historical)—school TN-4
Block Shed Windmill—locale WY-8
Blocks Hollow—valley PA-2
Block Six of the Original Townsite—locale ND-7
Blocks Mill Creek AL-4
Blocksomes Corners VA-3
Blocksom-Rolls House—hist pl OH-6
Blocksom Sch—school DE-2
Blocks Point—cape MN-6
Block Spring—spring NM-5
Blocks Run—stream PA-2
Blockstand Creek—stream TN-4
Blockston Branch—stream MD-2
Block Thirteen Oil Field—oilfield TX-5
**Blockton—pop pl** IA-7
Blockton Junc—locale AL-4
Blockton Mine (underground)—mine AL-4
Block Tower—pillar WY-8
**Blocktown—pop pl** MD-2
Block Twenty-Four Park—park UT-8
**Blockville—pop pl** NY-2
Block Windmill—locale NM-5
Block 0-100 East Franklin Street Hist Dist—hist pl VA-3
Block 12 Oil Field—oilfield TX-5
Block 18 Oil and Gas Field—oilfield LA-4
Block 24 Oil Field—oilfield LA-4
Block 27 Oil Field—oilfield LA-4
Block 31 Oil Field—oilfield TX-5
Block 47 Oil and Gas Field—oilfield LA-4
Block 52 Oil Field—oilfield LA-4
Block 53 Oil and Gas Field—oilfield LA-4
Block 54 Oil and Gas Field—oilfield LA-4
Block 6 Oil Field—oilfield LA-4
Block 69 Oil Field—oilfield LA-4
Block 77 AZ-5
Block 83 Oil Field—oilfield LA-4
**Blocton—pop pl** AL-4
**Blocton—pop pl** WV-2
**Blocton Junction—pop pl** AL-4
Blocton Mine (underground)—mine AL-4
Blocton Number 11 Slope Mine (underground)—mine AL-4
Blodget Hill—summit NY-2
Blodgett IL-6
Blodgett—locale IL-6
Blodgett—locale KS-7
Blodgett—locale MS-4
Blodgett—locale TX-5
**Blodgett—pop pl** MO-7
**Blodgett—pop pl** OR-9
Blodgett, John W., Estate—hist pl MI-6
Blodgett, Selvy, House—hist pl WI-6
Blodgett, William, House—hist pl MA-1
Blodgett Basin—basin AZ-5
Blodgett Brook—stream (2) NH-1
Blodgett Brook—stream VT-1
Blodgett Campground—locale CO-8
Blodgett Canyon—valley CA-9
Blodgett Canyon Campground—locale MT-8
Blodgett Cem—cemetery IA-7
Blodgett Cem—cemetery MT-8
Blodgett Cem—cemetery OR-9
Blodgett Creek MT-8
Blodgett Creek NY-2
Blodgett Creek—stream CA-9
Blodgett Creek—stream CO-8
Blodgett Creek—stream KS-7
Blodgett Creek—stream MI-6
Blodgett Creek—stream MT-8
Blodgett Creek—stream (2) OR-9
Blodgett Ditch—canal OR-9
Blodgett Experimental For—forest CA-9
Blodgett Flat—flat CA-9
Blodgett Gulch—valley MT-8
Blodgett Hill NY-2
Blodgett Hill—summit NH-1
Blodgett Hollow—valley PA-2
Blodgett Island—island AK-9
Blodgett Island—island ME-1
Blodgett Lake—lake AK-9
Blodgett Lake—lake CO-8
Blodgett Lake—lake (2) MI-6
Blodgett Lake—reservoir MT-8
**Blodgett Landing—pop pl** NH-1
Blodgett Mill Brook—stream MA-1
**Blodgett Mills—pop pl** NY-2
Blodgett Mine—mine AZ-5
Blodgett Mtn—summit ID-8
Blodgett Park—park MT-8
Blodgett Pass—gap ID-8
Blodgett Pass—gap MT-8
Blodgett Peak—summit CO-8
Blodgett Peak—summit OR-9
Blodgett Rsvr—reservoir CA-9
Blodgetts Cem—cemetery IL-6
Blodgett Sch—school MI-6
Blodgett Sch—school OR-9
Blodgetts Corners—locale DE-2
Blodgetts Overflow—channel UT-8
Blodgett Tank—reservoir AZ-5
Blodgett Vly—swamp NY-2
Bloede Donovan Park—park WA-9
Bloemaerts Creek DE-2
Bloemendaal and Taylor Airfield—airport SD-7
Bloemke Lake—lake MN-6
Bloggett Lake—lake MI-6
Bloise Gulch—valley ID-8
Blom—locale MI-6
Blomberg Lake—lake WI-6
Blomberg Spring—spring SD-7
Blomberg 42 Ranch Airstrip—airport SD-7
Blom Creek—stream MI-6
Blome Ranch—locale MT-8
Blomers Lake WI-6
**Blomeyer—pop pl** MO-7
**Blomford—pop pl** MN-6
Blomgren Cemetery—cemetery NE-7
**Blomkest—pop pl** MN-6
Blomkest Cem—cemetery MN-6
Blom Lake—lake WI-6
Blommer Hill Ch—church NC-3
Blommers Creek DE-2
Blom Post Office (historical)—building SD-7
Blom Prairie Cem—cemetery SD-7
Blomquist Rsvr—reservoir MT-8
Blom Ranch—locale SD-7
Blomskog Cem—cemetery MN-6
Blomskog Ch—church MN-6
**Blom Township—pop pl** SD-7
Blonc Creek ID-8
Blonc Creek—stream ID-8
Blond—locale LA-4
Blonde Cove—bay AK-9
Blonde Creek—stream ID-8
Blonde Dam Bridge—other MI-6
Blonde Reef—bar HI-9
Blonde Spring—spring OR-9
Blondie Wash UT-8
Blondie Knoll—summit UT-8
Blond Lake WI-6
**Blondy—pop pl** TN-4
Blondy Ch—church TN-4
Blondy Hollow—valley TN-4
Blondy Pass—gap WY-8
Blondy Water—spring AZ-5
Blood, Col. James, House—hist pl KS-7
Blood, Henry, House—hist pl UT-8
Blood, Oliver, House—hist pl MT-8
Blood Bank Sch—school VT-1
Blood Brook MA-1
Blood Brook—stream (2) ME-1
Blood Brook—stream NH-1
Blood Brook—stream (2) VT-1
Blood Camp—locale OR-9
Blood Camp Branch—stream NC-3
Blood Camp Ridge—ridge (2) NC-3
Blood Canyon—valley UT-8
Blood Cem—cemetery MA-1
Blood Cem—cemetery MI-6
Blood Coulee—valley MT-8
Blood Cove—bay ME-1
Blood Creek—stream (3) KS-7
Blood Creek—stream (2) MI-6
Blood Creek—stream MT-8
Blood Creek—stream NC-3
Blood Creek—stream OR-9
Blood Creek Overlook—locale NC-3
Blood Ditch—canal IN-6
Blood Ditch—canal NJ-2
Bloodgood Brook—stream NY-2
Bloodgood Canyon—valley NM-5
Bloodgood Creek—stream WA-9
Bloodgood Place—locale NM-5
Bloodgood Sch—school NY-2
Bloodgood Sch—school SD-7
Bloodgoods Pond—reservoir NJ-2
Bloodgoods Pond Dam—dam NJ-2
Bloodgood Spring—spring WA-9
Blood Hill—summit (2) MA-1
Blood Hill—summit NH-1
Blood Hill—summit VT-1
Blood Hill Creek—stream SC-3
Bloodhound Site—hist pl LA-4
Blood Island—island PA-2
Blood Lake—lake ME-1
Blood Lake—lake (3) MI-6
**Bloodland—pop pl** MO-7
Bloodland Cem—cemetery MO-7
Blood Landing—locale FL-3
Bloodland Sch—school MO-7
Blood Lick—stream KY-4
Blood Mine Spring—spring UT-8
Blood Mountain Cove—bay GA-3
Blood Mountain Creek—stream GA-3
Blood Mtn—summit GA-3
Blood Mtn—summit ME-1
Blood Mtn—summit UT-8
Blood Mtn—summit VT-1
Blood of the Cross Ch—church NC-3
Blood Point—cape NJ-2
Blood Pond—lake ME-1
Blood Pond—lake (2) MA-1
Blood Pond—lake NH-1
Blood River KS-7
Blood River—stream KY-4
Blood River—stream LA-4
Blood River—stream NC-3
Blood River—stream TN-4
Blood River Bar—bar TN-4
Blood River Cem—cemetery KY-4
Blood River Ch—church KY-4
Blood River Ch—church (2) LA-4
Blood River Ch—church TN-4
Blood River Drainage Ditch—canal TN-4
Blood River Sch (historical)—school TN-4
Bloodroot Gap—gap VT-1
Bloodroot Mountain Trail—trail VT-1
Bloodroot Mtn—summit VT-1
Blood Run—stream IA-7
Blood Run—stream MI-6
Blood Run—stream MN-6
Blood Run—stream NC-3
Blood Run—stream OH-6
Blood Run—stream PA-2
Blood Run—stream SD-7
Blood Run—stream WV-2
Bloodrun Creek NC-3
Blood Run Site—hist pl IA-7
Blood Run Site—hist pl SD-7
Bloodsaw Hill—summit MS-4
Bloods Brook MA-1
Bloods Brook—stream NH-1
Bloods Creek—stream CA-9
Bloodsaw Lake—reservoir NM-5
Bloods Lake—reservoir UT-8
Bloods Meadow—flat CA-9
Bloods Point—cliff CA-9
Bloods Point Cem—cemetery IL-6
Bloods Pond MA-1
Bloods Pond—lake MA-1
Blood Spring—spring CO-8
Bloods Ridge—ridge CA-9
Bloods Toll Station Historical Site—locale CA-9
Bloodsucker Brook—stream ME-1
Bloodsucker Lake—lake CA-9
Bloodsucker Lake—lake NY-2
Bloodsucker Pond—lake (2) NY-2
Bloodsucker Pond—lake VT-1
Bloodsucker Wash—stream (2) AZ-5
Blood Swamp—swamp MA-1
**Bloods Wood Crossing—pop pl** IN-6
Bloodsworth Cem—cemetery AR-4
Bloodsworth Gulch—valley CO-8
Bloodsworth Island—island MD-2
Bloodsworth Point—cape MD-2
Bloodsworth Pond—lake CO-8
Bloodsworth's Island MD-2
Bloodsworth Spring—spring CO-8
Blood Tank—reservoir AZ-5
Bloodtown—locale GA-3
Bloodweed Island—island TX-5
Bloodworth Cem—cemetery GA-3
Bloodworth Cem—cemetery (3) TN-4
Bloodworth Hollow—valley TN-4
Bloodworth Island TX-5
Bloody Angles—locale MA-1
Bloody Basin—basin AZ-5
Bloody Basin Canyon—valley AZ-5
Bloody Basin Dam—dam AZ-5
Bloody Basin Interchange—crossing AZ-5
Bloody Basin Tank—reservoir AZ-5
Bloody Bayou—stream LA-4
Bloody Bluff—cliff MA-1
Bloody Bluff—cliff NC-3
**Bloody Bluff—pop pl** FL-3
Bloody Bluff Island—island FL-3
Bloody Branch—stream (2) TN-4
Bloody Branch Bay—swamp NC-3
Bloody Branch Cem—cemetery TN-4
Bloody Brook—stream CT-1
Bloody Brook—stream (2) MA-1
Bloody Brook—stream NH-1
Bloody Brook—stream RI-1
Bloody Brook—stream VT-1
Bloody Camp—locale CA-9
Bloody Canyon—valley CA-9
Bloody Canyon—valley NV-8
Bloody Canyon Mine—mine NV-8
Bloody Creek—stream KS-7
Bloody Creek—stream KY-4
Bloody Creek—stream NE-7
Bloody Dick MT-8
Bloody Dick Creek—stream MT-8
Bloody Dick Guard Station—locale MT-8
Bloody Dick Peak—summit MT-8
Bloody Fork—locale NC-3
Bloody Fork—stream NC-3
Bloody Gulch—valley CA-9
Bloody Gulch—valley NV-8
Bloody Gulch—valley SD-7
Bloody Gulch Dam—dam NV-8
Bloody Hand Pit—cave AL-4
Bloody Hands Gap—gap UT-8
Bloody Hand Site (39ST230)—hist pl SD-7
Bloody Hill—summit MO-7
Bloody Hill—summit MT-8
Bloody Hill—summit NY-2
Bloody Hollow—valley TX-5
Bloody Hollow—valley WV-2
Bloody Island—island CA-9
Bloody Island—summit CA-9
Bloody Island Massacre Historical Marker—park CA-9
Bloody Lake—lake CA-9
Bloody Lake—lake MN-6
Bloody Lake—lake WY-8
Bloody Marsh—swamp GA-3
Bloody Marsh Natl Monmt—park GA-3
Bloody Mtn—summit CA-9
Bloody Mtn—summit CT-1
Bloody Mtn—summit NY-2
Bloody Nose Creek—stream CA-9
Bloody Nose Ridge PW-9
Bloody Nose Ridge—ridge PW-9
Bloody Point—cape CA-9
Bloody Point—cape MD-2
Bloody Point—cape (3) OR-9
Bloody Point—cape (2) SC-3
Bloody Point—ridge NV-8
Bloody Point Creek—bay MD-2
Bloody Pond—lake MA-1
Bloody Pond—lake (3) NY-2
Bloody Pond—lake TN-4
Bloody Ravine—valley CA-9
Bloody Rock—summit CA-9
Bloody Run IA-7
Bloody Run—stream (2) CA-9
Bloody Run—stream (5) IA-7
Bloody Run—stream (5) KS-7
Bloody Run—stream KY-4
Bloody Run—stream NE-7
Bloody Run—stream (2) OH-6
Bloody Run—stream (8) PA-2
Bloody Run—stream SD-7
Bloody Run—stream VA-3
Bloody Run—stream WA-9
Bloody Run—stream (4) WV-2
Bloody Run—stream WI-6
Bloody Run Camp—locale PA-2
Bloody Run Canyon—valley NV-8
Bloody Run Creek WI-6
Bloody Run Creek—stream (2) CA-9
Bloody Run Creek—stream NE-7
Bloody Run Creek—stream OR-9
Bloody Run Hills—summit NV-8
Bloody Run Peak—summit NV-8
Bloody Run Ridge—ridge CA-9
Bloody Run Sch—school IA-7
Bloody Run Sch—school NE-7
Bloody Rush Creek—stream OK-5
Bloodyshin Creek—stream KY-4
Bloody Spring Branch—stream MS-4
Bloody Springs—locale MS-4
Bloody Tank—reservoir AZ-5
Bloody Tanks—reservoir AZ-5
Bloody Tanks Wash—stream AZ-5
Blooin Hollow—valley TN-4
Bloom OH-6
Bloom VA-3
Bloom—locale CO-8
Bloom—locale MD-2
Bloom—locale UT-8
**Bloom—pop pl** KS-7
**Bloom—pop pl** ND-7
Bloom, Frank G., House—hist pl CO-8
Bloom Basin—basin SD-7
Bloomberg Lake WI-6
**Bloomburg—pop pl** TX-5
**Bloomburg Village (subdivision)—pop pl** PA-2
Bloom Canyon—valley ID-8
Bloom Cem—cemetery CO-8
Bloom Cem—cemetery (2) KS-7
Bloom Cem—cemetery NY-2
**Bloom Center—pop pl (2)** OH-6
Bloom Ch—church IL-6
Bloom Ch—church OH-6
**Bloom City—pop pl** WI-6
Bloom City Cem—cemetery WI-6
Bloom Community Coll—school IL-6
Bloom Creek MT-8
Bloom Creek—stream CO-8
Bloom Creek—stream ID-8
Bloom Creek—stream (2) MO-7
Bloom Creek—stream MT-8
Bloom Creek—stream SD-7
Bloom Creek—stream WY-8
Bloom Creek Rsvr Number One—reservoir MT-8
Bloom Creek Rsvr Number Two—reservoir MT-8
Bloom Creek State For—forest MO-7
Bloom Crossing—locale VA-3
Bloom Dale MN-6
Bloomdale—locale TX-5
**Bloomdale—pop pl** OH-6
Bloomdale Cem—cemetery MI-6
Bloomdale Creek—stream CA-9
Bloomdale Sch (historical)—school MO-7
Bloom Dam—dam SD-7
Bloom Draft—valley PA-2
Bloom Draft Trail—trail PA-2
**Bloomenfield Township—pop pl** ND-7
**Bloomer—pop pl** AR-4
**Bloomer—pop pl** IN-6
**Bloomer—pop pl** OH-6
**Bloomer—pop pl** WI-6
Bloomer, Amelia, House—hist pl NY-2
Bloomer Branch—stream (2) KY-4
Bloomer Cem—cemetery MI-6
Bloomer Cem—cemetery (3) TN-4
Bloomer Cem—cemetery VA-3
Bloomer Creek—stream MS-4
Bloomer Creek—stream NY-2
Bloomer Hill—summit CA-9
Bloomer Island—island NY-2
Bloomer Lake—lake (2) CA-9
Bloomer Lake—lake MI-6
Bloomer Mill Pond WI-6
Bloomer Mine—mine CA-9
Bloomer Mtn—summit NY-2
Bloomer Oil Field—oilfield KS-7
Bloomer Peak—summit AK-9
Bloomer Ravine—valley CA-9
Bloomer Ridge—ridge AR-4
Bloomers Arch UT-8
Bloomer Sch—school AR-4
Bloomers Lake WI-6
Bloomer Spring—locale VA-3
Bloomer Swamp—swamp PA-2
**Bloomer (Town of)—pop pl** WI-6
Bloomer (Township of)—fmr MCD AR-4
**Bloomer (Township of)—pop pl** MI-6
**Bloomer (Township of)—pop pl** MN-6
**Bloomerville—pop pl** NY-2
**Bloomery—pop pl (2)** WV-2
Bloomery Bridge—bridge MD-2
Bloomery Bridge—other WV-2

Bloomery Ch—*church* MD-2
Bloomery (Magisterial District)—*fmr MCD* WV-2
Bloomery Run—*stream* WV-2
Bloomery Swamp—*stream* NC-3
*Bloomfield* IN-6
*Bloomfield* OH-6
*Bloomfield* PA-2
Bloomfield—*hist pl* DE-2
Bloomfield—*locale* AR-4
Bloomfield—*locale* (2) IL-6
Bloomfield—*locale* (2) MD-2
Bloomfield—*locale* MS-4
Bloomfield—*locale* SD-7
Bloomfield—*locale* TX-5
Bloomfield—*locale* VA-3
**Bloomfield**—*pop pl* CA-9
**Bloomfield**—*pop pl* CT-1
**Bloomfield**—*pop pl* IL-6
**Bloomfield**—*pop pl* (3) IN-6
**Bloomfield**—*pop pl* IA-7
**Bloomfield**—*pop pl* KY-4
**Bloomfield**—*pop pl* MI-6
**Bloomfield**—*pop pl* MS-4
**Bloomfield**—*pop pl* MO-7
**Bloomfield**—*pop pl* MT-8
**Bloomfield**—*pop pl* NE-7
**Bloomfield**—*pop pl* NJ-2
**Bloomfield**—*pop pl* NM-5
**Bloomfield**—*pop pl* NY-2
**Bloomfield**—*pop pl* (3) OH-6
**Bloomfield**—*pop pl* PA-2
**Bloomfield**—*pop pl* VT-1
Bloomfield Acad—*hist pl* ME-1
Bloomfield Acad—*school* OK-5
Bloomfield Acad Site—*hist pl* OK-5
Bloomfield Acres—*uninc pl* CA-9
Bloomfield Borough—*civil* PA-2
Bloomfield Branch—*stream* TX-5
Bloomfield Bridge—*bridge* PA-2
Bloomfield Burying Ground—*cemetery* PA-2
Bloomfield Campground—*locale* CA-9
Bloomfield Canyon—*valley* NM-5
Bloomfield (CCD)—*cens area* KY-4
Bloomfield (CCD)—*cens area* NM-5
Bloomfield Cem—*cemetery* AL-4
Bloomfield Cem—*cemetery* AR-4
Bloomfield Cem—*cemetery* IL-6
Bloomfield Cem—*cemetery* (3) IA-7
Bloomfield Cem—*cemetery* MI-6
Bloomfield Cem—*cemetery* (2) MN-6
Bloomfield Cem—*cemetery* MS-4
Bloomfield Cem—*cemetery* (2) MO-7
Bloomfield Cem—*cemetery* NE-7
Bloomfield Cem—*cemetery* NJ-2
Bloomfield Cem—*cemetery* NY-2
Bloomfield Cem—*cemetery* ND-7
Bloomfield Cem—*cemetery* OH-6
Bloomfield Cem—*cemetery* (2) OK-5
Bloomfield Cem—*cemetery* TX-5
Bloomfield Cem—*cemetery* VT-1
Bloomfield Cem—*cemetery* (2) WI-6
Bloomfield Central Sch—*school* NY-2
Bloomfield Ch—*church* AR-4
Bloomfield Ch—*church* GA-3
Bloomfield Ch—*church* IA-7
Bloomfield Ch—*church* MS-4
**Bloomfield (corporate name for New Bloomfield)**—*pop pl* PA-2
Bloomfield (Election Precinct)—*fmr MCD* (2) IL-6
Bloomfield Elem Sch—*school* (2) IN-6
Bloomfield Flat—*flat* NM-5
Bloomfield Gardens—*uninc pl* GA-3
Bloomfield Gardens Ch—*church* GA-3
**Bloomfield Glens**—*pop pl* MI-6
Bloomfield Green Hist Dist—*hist pl* NJ-2
**Bloomfield Highlands**—*pop pl* MI-6
**Bloomfield Hills**—*pop pl* MI-6
Bloomfield Hills Country Club—*other* MI-6
Bloomfield Hills JHS—*school* MI-6
Bloomfield (historical)—*locale* AL-4
Bloomfield (historical)—*locale* KS-7
Bloomfield HS—*school* IN-6
Bloomfield JHS—*school* CT-1
Bloomfield Junction (historical)—*locale* PA-2
Bloomfield Lake—*lake* MI-6
Bloomfield Lookout Tower—*locale* OH-6
Bloomfield Meadow—*flat* CA-9
**Bloomfield Park**—*pop pl* NY-2
Bloomfield Post Office (historical)—*building* AL-4
*Bloomfield Presbyterian Ch* MS-4
Bloomfield Ranch—*locale* CA-9
Bloomfield Rec Area—*park* NE-7
Bloomfield Ridge—*ridge* VT-1
Bloomfield Run—*stream* PA-2
Bloomfield Sch—*school* (2) CA-9
Bloomfield Sch—*school* IL-6
Bloomfield Sch—*school* (3) MI-6
Bloomfield Sch—*school* MO-7
Bloomfield Sch—*school* NY-2
Bloomfield Sch—*school* (2) PA-2
Bloomfield Sch—*school* WI-6
Bloomfield Site—*hist pl* CO-8
Bloomfield South Cem—*cemetery* IA-7
Bloomfield Square—*hist pl* IA-7
Bloomfield Station—*hist pl* NJ-2
Bloomfield Station—*locale* NJ-2
Bloomfield Street Hist Dist—*hist pl* GA-3
**Bloomfield Terrace**—*pop pl* NJ-2
Bloomfield Town Hall—*building* ND-7
**Bloomfield (Town of)**—*pop pl* CT-1
**Bloomfield (Town of)**—*pop pl* VT-1
**Bloomfield (Town of)**—*pop pl* (2) WI-6
Bloomfield Township—*fmr MCD* (3) IA-7
**Bloomfield Township**—*pop pl* (2) KS-7
**Bloomfield Township**—*pop pl* ND-7
**Bloomfield (Township of)**—*pop pl* IN-6
**Bloomfield (Township of)**—*pop pl* (3) MI-6
**Bloomfield (Township of)**—*pop pl* MN-6
**Bloomfield (Township of)**—*pop pl* NJ-2
**Bloomfield (Township of)**—*pop pl* (3) OH-6
**Bloomfield (Township of)**—*pop pl* (2) PA-2
**Bloomfield Village**—*pop pl* MI-6
Bloom Furnace Cem—*cemetery* OH-6
Bloom Furnace Creek—*stream* OH-6
Bloom Garden Cem—*cemetery* MO-7
Bloom Garden Sch (abandoned)—*school* MO-7
Bloomgren Ranch—*locale* ND-7
Bloom Hill Cem—*cemetery* SC-3
Bloom Hill Ch—*church* VA-3
Bloom Hills—*range* CO-8
Bloom Hill Windmill—*locale* CO-8
Bloom Hollow—*valley* MO-7
Bloom Hollow—*valley* WY-8
Bloom HS—*school* IL-6
Bloom HS—*school* OH-6
**Blooming**—*pop pl* OR-9
**Bloomingburg**—*pop pl* NY-2
**Bloomingburg**—*pop pl* OH-6
Bloomingburg Cem—*cemetery* MS-4
**Bloomingburg (corporate name for Bloomingburgh)**—*pop pl* NY-2
*Bloomingburgh (corporate name Bloomingburg)* NY-2
Bloomingburg Reformed Protestant Dutch Church—*hist pl* NY-2
Blooming Cem—*cemetery* OR-9
*Bloomingdale* KS-7
Bloomingdale—*hist pl* MD-2
Bloomingdale—*locale* KY-4
Bloomingdale—*locale* NC-3
Bloomingdale—*locale* PA-2
Bloomingdale—*locale* SD-7
**Bloomingdale**—*pop pl* FL-3
**Bloomingdale**—*pop pl* GA-3
**Bloomingdale**—*pop pl* IL-6
**Bloomingdale**—*pop pl* IN-6
**Bloomingdale**—*pop pl* MI-6
**Bloomingdale**—*pop pl* (2) NJ-2
**Bloomingdale**—*pop pl* NY-2
**Bloomingdale**—*pop pl* OH-6
**Bloomingdale**—*pop pl* (2) PA-2
**Bloomingdale**—*pop pl* TN-4
**Bloomingdale**—*pop pl* VA-3
**Bloomingdale**—*pop pl* WI-6
*Bloomingdale Baptist Church* SD-7
Bloomingdale Cem—*cemetery* IL-6
Bloomingdale Cem—*cemetery* IN-6
Bloomingdale Cem—*cemetery* KS-7
Bloomingdale Cem—*cemetery* NE-7
Bloomingdale Ch—*church* FL-3
Bloomingdale Ch—*church* PA-2
Bloomingdale Ch—*church* TN-4
Bloomingdale Ch—*church* WV-2
Bloomingdale Community Ch—*church* FL-3
Bloomingdale Elem Sch—*school* IN-6
Bloomingdale Firehouse—*hist pl* MA-1
Bloomingdale Grove—*park* IL-6
Bloomingdale Methodist Ch (historical)—*church* SD-7
Bloomingdale Mine—*mine* CA-9
Bloomingdale Pond—*lake* NY-2
Bloomingdale Sch—*hist pl* MA-1
Bloomingdale Sch—*school* IL-6
Bloomingdale Sch—*school* MN-6
Bloomingdale Sch—*school* NY-2
**Bloomingdale (sta.)**—*pop pl* NJ-2
**Bloomingdale (subdivision)**—*pop pl* MA-1
Bloomingdale (Township of)—*civ div* IL-6
Bloomingdale (Township of)—*civ div* MI-6
Bloomingdale Valley—*valley* PA-2
**Blooming Glen**—*pop pl* PA-2
Blooming Glen Post Office (historical)—*building* PA-2
*Blooming Grove* KS-7
Blooming Grove—*locale* NY-2
Blooming Grove—*locale* TN-4
**Blooming Grove**—*pop pl* AL-4
**Blooming Grove**—*pop pl* IN-6
**Blooming Grove**—*pop pl* OH-6
**Blooming Grove**—*pop pl* (2) PA-2
**Blooming Grove**—*pop pl* TX-5
Blooming Grove Baptist Ch—*church* TN-4
*Blooming Grove Baptist Church* AL-4
Blooming Grove (CCD)—*cens area* TX-5
Blooming Grove Cem—*cemetery* (2) AL-4
Blooming Grove Cem—*cemetery* IL-6
Blooming Grove Cem—*cemetery* KS-7
Blooming Grove Cem—*cemetery* NY-2
Blooming Grove Cem—*cemetery* (2) OH-6
Blooming Grove Cem—*cemetery* (2) TN-4
Blooming Grove Cem—*cemetery* WI-6
Blooming Grove Ch—*church* (2) AL-4
Blooming Grove Ch—*church* AR-4
Blooming Grove Ch—*church* GA-3
Blooming Grove Ch—*church* (3) IL-6
Blooming Grove Ch—*church* (2) KY-4
Blooming Grove Ch—*church* MN-6
Blooming Grove Ch—*church* (3) TN-4
Blooming Grove Creek—*stream* PA-2
Blooming Grove Creek—*stream* TN-4
Blooming Grove Meetinghouse—*church* PA-2
Blooming Grove Missionary Baptist Ch—*church* AL-4
Blooming Grove Post Office (historical)—*building* AL-4
Blooming Grove Sch—*school* KY-4
Blooming Grove Sch—*school* PA-2
Blooming Grove Sch—*school* TN-4
**Blooming Grove (Town of)**—*pop pl* NY-2
**Blooming Grove (Town of)**—*pop pl* WI-6
Blooming Grove (Township of)—*civ div* IN-6
Blooming Grove (Township of)—*civ div* MN-6
Blooming Grove (Township of)—*civ div* OH-6
**Blooming Grove (Township of)**—*pop pl* PA-2
Blooming Grove Trail—*trail* PA-2
Blooming Light Ch—*church* AL-4
Blooming Light Ch—*church* GA-3
**Bloomingport**—*pop pl* IN-6
Bloomingport Creek—*stream* IN-6
**Blooming Prairie**—*pop pl* (2) MN-6
Blooming Prairie Ch—*church* ND-7
**Blooming Prairie Township**—*pop pl* ND-7
Blooming Prairie (Township of)—*civ div* MN-6
**Blooming Rose**—*pop pl* MO-7
**Bloomingrose**—*pop pl* WV-2
Blooming Rose Camp—*locale* MO-7
Blooming Rose Ch—*church* GA-3
Blooming Rose Ch—*church* MD-2
Blooming Rose Hill—*summit* MD-2
Blooming Rose Sch—*school* KY-4
Blooming Rose Sch—*school* MO-7
**Blooming Rose Settlement**—*pop pl* MD-2
*Bloomingsport* IN-6
*Bloomington* IN-6
*Bloomington* KS-7
*Bloomington* NJ-2
Bloomington—*locale* (2) IA-7
Bloomington—*locale* KS-7
Bloomington—*locale* KY-4
Bloomington—*locale* MO-7
Bloomington—*locale* OH-6
Bloomington—*locale* OK-5
Bloomington—*locale* UT-8
**Bloomington**—*pop pl* CA-9
**Bloomington**—*pop pl* ID-8
**Bloomington**—*pop pl* IL-6
**Bloomington**—*pop pl* IN-6
**Bloomington**—*pop pl* KS-7
**Bloomington**—*pop pl* KY-4
**Bloomington**—*pop pl* MD-2
**Bloomington**—*pop pl* MN-6
**Bloomington**—*pop pl* NE-7
**Bloomington**—*pop pl* NY-2
**Bloomington**—*pop pl* NC-3
**Bloomington**—*pop pl* (2) PA-2
**Bloomington**—*pop pl* TN-4
**Bloomington**—*pop pl* TX-5
**Bloomington**—*pop pl* WI-6
Bloomington Cem—*cemetery* KS-7
Bloomington Cem—*cemetery* MN-6
Bloomington Cem—*cemetery* MO-7
Bloomington Cem—*cemetery* OH-6
Bloomington Central Business District—*hist pl* IL-6
Bloomington Ch—*church* KS-7
Bloomington Ch—*church* KY-4
Bloomington Chapel—*church* KY-4
Bloomington Ch (historical)—*church* SD-7
Bloomington City (Township of)—*civ div* IL-6
*Bloomington Creek* TN-4
*Bloomington Creek* WI-6
Bloomington Creek—*stream* ID-8
**Bloomington Ferry**—*pop pl* MN-6
Bloomington Ferry Ch—*church* MN-6
Bloomington Friend Ch—*church* IA-7
**Bloomington Heights**—*pop pl* IL-6
**Bloomington Heights**—*pop pl* TN-4
Bloomington-Hickory Bush—*CDP* NY-2
*Bloomington High School* IN-6
Bloomington Hill—*other* UT-8
**Bloomington Hills (subdivision)**—*pop pl* UT-8
Bloomington (historical)—*locale* SD-7
*Bloomington Horse Flat* ID-8
Bloomington HS—*school* CA-9
Bloomington JHS—*school* CA-9
Bloomington Lake—*lake* ID-8
Bloomington Lake—*reservoir* MD-2
Bloomington Lake—*reservoir* WV-2
Bloomington Lake Trail—*trail* ID-8
Bloomington-Normal Airp—*airport* IL-6
Bloomington Park—*park* OR-9
Bloomington Peak—*summit* ID-8
*Bloomington Post Office* TN-4
Bloomington Ridge—*ridge* KY-4
Bloomington Ridge—*ridge* OH-6
*Bloomington Rsvr* MD-2
*Bloomington Rsvr* WV-2
Bloomington Sch—*school* TN-4
Bloomington Sch—*school* UT-8
Bloomington Sch (historical)—*school* TN-4
Bloomington Sch Number 1—*school* ND-7
Bloomington Sch Number 2—*school* ND-7
Bloomington Sch Number 3—*school* ND-7
Bloomington Sch Number 4—*school* ND-7
Bloomington South HS—*school* IN-6
Bloomington Speedway—*other* IN-6
**Bloomington Springs**—*pop pl* TN-4
Bloomington Springs Post Office—*building* TN-4
Bloomington Springs Sch (historical)—*school* TN-4
Bloomington Springs Station (historical)—*locale* TN-4
**Bloomington (Town of)**—*pop pl* WI-6
Bloomington Township—*civil* MO-7
Bloomington Township—*fmr MCD* (2) IA-7
**Bloomington Township**—*pop pl* KS-7
**Bloomington Township**—*pop pl* NE-7
**Bloomington (Township of)**—*pop pl* IL-6
**Bloomington (Township of)**—*pop pl* IN-6
Bloomington Viaduct—*hist pl* MD-2
Blooming Town Hall—*building* ND-7
**Blooming Township**—*pop pl* ND-7
Blooming Turkey Farm—*locale* MD-2
**Bloomingvale**—*pop pl* SC-3
Bloomingvale Sch—*school* SC-3
**Blooming Valley**—*pop pl* PA-2
Blooming Valley—*valley* SD-7
Blooming Valley Borough—*civil* PA-2
Blooming Valley Cem—*cemetery* PA-2
Blooming Valley Sch—*school* MI-6
**Blooming Valley Township**—*pop pl* ND-7
**Blooming Valley Township**—*pop pl* SD-7
Blooming Valley (Township of)—*unorg* MN-6
**Bloomingville**—*pop pl* OH-6
Bloom Junction—*locale* OH-6
*Bloom Lake* WI-6
Bloom Lake—*lake* ID-8
Bloom Lake—*lake* MI-6
Bloom Lake—*lake* (2) MN-6
Bloom Lake—*lake* OR-9
Bloom Meadows—*flat* ID-8
*Bloomo* MS-4
Bloom Oil Field—*oilfield* KS-7
Bloom Peak—*summit* ID-8
Bloom Peak—*summit* MT-8
Bloomquist Creek—*stream* CA-9
Bloomquist Creek—*stream* WA-9
Bloomquist Ranch—*locale* WY-8
Bloom Ranch—*locale* NM-5
Bloomrose Ch—*church* OH-6
Bloom Rsvr—*reservoir* WY-8
Bloom Run Vista—*summit* PA-2
Blooms Bay—*bay* WA-9
*Bloomsburg* KS-7
*Bloomsburg* NJ-2
Bloomsburg—*locale* PA-2
**Bloomsburg**—*pop pl* PA-2
Bloomsburg Airp—*airport* PA-2
Bloomsburg Area HS—*school* PA-2
Bloomsburg Area MS—*school* PA-2
*Bloomsburgh* KS-7
Bloomsburg Hist Dist—*hist pl* PA-2
Bloomsburg Municipal Airp—*airport* PA-2
Bloomsburg Town—*civil* PA-2
**Bloomsbury**—*pop pl* MD-2
**Bloomsbury**—*pop pl* NJ-2
Bloom Sch—*school* AZ-5
Bloom Sch—*school* IL-6
Bloom Sch—*school* KY-4
Bloom Sch—*school* OH-6
Blooms Corners—*locale* NY-2
Blooms Creek—*stream* CA-9
**Bloomsdale**—*pop pl* MO-7
**Bloomsdale Gardens**—*pop pl* PA-2
Bloomsdale Sch—*school* MO-7
Blooms Ditch—*canal* WA-9
**Bloomsdorf**—*pop pl* PA-2
**Blooms Eddy (historical)**—*pop pl* IN-6
Blooms Grove Cem—*cemetery* IL-6
Bloomshade Ch—*church* LA-4
Bloom-Shearer Dam—*dam* SD-7
Bloom Site—*hist pl* SD-7
*Blooms Lake* MN-6
Blooms Mill Creek—*stream* LA-4
Bloom's Tavern, Store and House—*hist pl* WI-6
Bloomster Hollow—*valley* PA-2
Bloom Switch Cem—*cemetery* OH-6
**Bloom (Town of)**—*pop pl* WI-6
**Bloom Township**—*pop pl* (3) KS-7
**Bloom Township**—*pop pl* ND-7
Bloom Township HS—*hist pl* IL-6
**Bloom (Township of)**—*pop pl* IL-6
**Bloom (Township of)**—*pop pl* MN-6
**Bloom (Township of)**—*pop pl* (5) OH-6
**Bloom (Township of)**—*pop pl* PA-2
Bloom Trail Rsvr—*reservoir* UT-8
Bloomville—*locale* SC-3
**Bloomville**—*pop pl* NY-2
**Bloomville**—*pop pl* OH-6
**Bloomville**—*pop pl* WI-6
Bloomville Cem—*cemetery* OH-6
Bloomville Ch—*church* WI-6
Bloom Well—*well* NM-5
Bloom Windmill—*locale* NM-5
Bloomy Shade Cem—*cemetery* AR-4
Bloser Creek—*stream* PA-2
**Bloserville**—*pop pl* PA-2
Bloss—*locale* KY-4
Bloss, Frank D., and Sons Farm House—*hist pl* MI-6
Bloss Branch—*stream* KY-4
*Blossburg* AL-4
Blossburg—*locale* NM-5
**Blossburg**—*pop pl* AL-4
**Blossburg**—*pop pl* MT-8
**Blossburg**—*pop pl* PA-2
Blossburg A Mine (underground)—*mine* AL-4
Blossburg Borough—*civil* PA-2
Blossburg East Mine (underground)—*mine* (2) AL-4
Blossburg Mine (underground)—*mine* (2) AL-4
**Blosser**—*pop pl* MO-7
Blosser, Henry, House—*hist pl* MO-7
*Blosser Airport* KS-7
Blosser Arroyo—*stream* NM-5
Blosser Cem—*cemetery* OH-6
Blosser Creek—*stream* OH-6
*Blosser Field* KS-7
Blosser Gap—*gap* NM-5
**Blosser Hill**—*pop pl* PA-2
Blosser Hollow—*valley* WV-2
Blosser Mesa—*summit* NM-5
Blosser Municipal Airp—*airport* KS-7
**Blosserville**—*pop pl* PA-2
Blosseville, Point—*cape* FM-9
*Bloss Fire Tower* PA-2
Bloss Gulch—*valley* CO-8
Bloss Hollow—*valley* PA-2
Blossie Creek—*gut* NC-3
Bloss Lateral—*canal* CA-9
Bloss Lookout Tower—*locale* PA-2
Bloss Mansion—*hist pl* CA-9
Bloss Mountain Trail—*trail* PA-2
*Blossom* MP-9
Blossom—*locale* AR-4
Blossom—*locale* CA-9
Blossom—*locale* TN-4
**Blossom**—*pop pl* NY-2
**Blossom**—*pop pl* SC-3
**Blossom**—*pop pl* TX-5
Blossom, Barnabus, House—*hist pl* MA-1
Blossom, Elizabeth B., Subdivision Hist Dist—*hist pl* OH-6
Blossom Bar—*bar* OR-9
Blossom Bar Creek—*stream* OR-9
Blossom Bar Rapids—*rapids* OR-9
Blossom Brook—*stream* MA-1
Blossom Cabin (Ruin)—*locale* CA-9
Blossom Canyon—*valley* NV-8
Blossom (CCD)—*cens area* TX-5
Blossom Cem—*cemetery* NY-2
Blossom Cem—*cemetery* VT-1
Blossom Cove—*bay* NJ-2
Blossom Creek—*stream* CA-9
Blossom Creek—*stream* OR-9
Blossom Glacier—*glacier* AK-9
Blossom Gulch—*valley* OR-9
Blossom Gulch Sch—*school* OR-9
Blossom Heights Park—*park* TX-5
*Blossom Hill* IL-6
**Blossom Hill**—*pop pl* PA-2
Blossom Hill—*summit* CA-9
Blossom Hill—*summit* GA-3
Blossom Hill—*summit* MD-2
Blossom Hill—*uninc pl* CA-9
Blossom Hill Cem—*cemetery* IA-7
Blossom Hill Cem—*cemetery* NH-1
Blossom Hill Sch—*school* CA-9
Blossom Hill Sch—*school* OH-6
Blossom Hollow—*valley* IN-6
Blossom Island—*summit* AK-9
Blossom Lake—*lake* FL-3
Blossom Lake—*lake* MI-6
Blossom Lake—*lake* MT-8
Blossom Lakes—*lake* CA-9
Blossom Lakes—*lake* MT-8
Blossom Mine—*mine* NV-8
Blossom Mtn—*summit* ID-8
Blossom Park—*park* TX-5
Blossom Peak—*summit* CA-9
Blossom Point—*cape* MD-2
Blossom Post Office (historical)—*building* TN-4
Blossom Prairie—*flat* TX-5
Blossom Ranch—*locale* NV-8
Blossom River—*stream* AK-9
Blossom Rock—*bar* CA-9
Blossom Sch—*school* MI-6
Blossom Sch—*school* SC-3
Blossoms Corners—*locale* VT-1
Blossom Shoals—*bar* AK-9
Blossom Slough—*gut* TX-5
Blossom Spring—*spring* NV-8
**Blossomtown**—*pop pl* NC-3
**Blossom Valley**—*pop pl* PA-2
Blossom Valley—*uninc pl* CA-9
*Blossomville* AL-4
*Blossomwood Elementary School* AL-4
Blossomwood Sch—*school* AL-4
**Bloss (Township of)**—*pop pl* PA-2
**Blossvale**—*pop pl* NY-2
Blot Lake—*lake* MN-6
Blottner Sch (abandoned)—*school* MO-7
Blott Sch—*school* OH-6
Blotz Branch—*stream* WI-6
Bloucher—*locale* OR-9
Bloucher Ford—*locale* AL-4
Bloucher Ford Cem—*cemetery* AL-4
**Bloucher (historical)**—*pop pl* OR-9
**Blough**—*pop pl* PA-2
Blough Cem—*cemetery* OH-6
Blough Ch—*church* PA-2
Blough Sch (abandoned)—*school* PA-2
Blouin Canal—*canal* LA-4
Blount—*locale* GA-3
**Blount**—*pop pl* NC-3
**Blount**—*pop pl* WV-2
Blount, Capt. Thomas William, House—*hist pl* TX-5
Blount, William, Mansion—*hist pl* TN-4
Blount Addition Hist Dist—*hist pl* AZ-5
*Blount Bay* NC-3
Blount Bay—*bay* NC-3
**Blount Beach**—*pop pl* TN-4
Blount Cem—*cemetery* AL-4
Blount Cem—*cemetery* AR-4
Blount Cem—*cemetery* GA-3
Blount Cem—*cemetery* (2) MS-4
Blount Cem—*cemetery* MO-7
Blount Cem—*cemetery* TX-5
Blount Chapel—*church* TX-5
Blount Coll (historical)—*school* AL-4
**Blount County**—*pop pl* AL-4
**Blount County**—*pop pl* TN-4
Blount County Access Area—*park* TN-4
Blount County Courthouse—*building* TN-4
Blount County Farm (historical)—*locale* TN-4
Blount County Health Department—*hospital* TN-4
*Blount County High School* AL-4
*Blount County High School* TN-4
Blount County Industrial Park—*locale* TN-4
Blount County Library—*building* TN-4
*Blount Creek* NC-3
Blount Creek—*stream* FL-3
Blount Creek—*stream* GA-3
Blount Crossing Cem—*cemetery* GA-3
**Blount (Eight Mile)**—*pop pl* WV-2
*Blount Highland School* AL-4
Blount Highlands Sch—*school* AL-4
**Blount Hills**—*pop pl* TN-4
Blount Island—*island* FL-3
**Blount Island**—*pop pl* FL-3
Blount Island Channel—*channel* FL-3
Blount Landing—*locale* AL-4
Blount Memorial Hosp—*hospital* TN-4
Blount Mill Creek—*stream* FL-3
Blount Mountain—*ridge* AL-4
Blount MS—*school* FL-3
Blount Mtn—*summit* TX-5
Blount Occupational Education Center—*school* TN-4
Blount Park—*park* TX-5
Blount Peavy Cem—*cemetery* GA-3
Blount Pocosin—*swamp* NC-3
Blount Point—*cape* NC-3
Blount Run—*stream* OH-6
*Blounts Bay* NC-3
Blounts Bay—*bay* FL-3
Blounts Bay—*bay* NC-3
Blounts Bay—*swamp* NC-3
Blounts Branch—*stream* FL-3
Blounts Branch—*stream* NC-3
Blounts Ch—*church* TX-5
Blount Sch—*school* NC-3
Blounts Chapel—*church* (2) GA-3
Blounts Chapel Ch—*church* GA-3
Blounts Chapel Sch—*school* GA-3
**Blounts Creek**—*pop pl* NC-3
Blounts Creek—*stream* LA-4
Blounts Creek—*stream* (2) NC-3
**Blounts (historical)**—*pop pl* NC-3
*Blounts Lake* TX-5
*Blounts Landing* AL-4
**Blount Springs**—*pop pl* AL-4
Blount Springs Ch—*church* AL-4
Blount Springs Station—*locale* AL-4
**Blounts Store**—*pop pl* MS-4
*Blounts Town* NC-3
**Blountstown**—*pop pl* FL-3
Blountstown (CCD)—*cens area* FL-3
Blountstown Elem Sch—*school* FL-3
Blountstown Junior High Shcool—*school* FL-3
Blountstown Senior HS—*school* FL-3
Blountsville—*locale* GA-3
**Blountsville**—*pop pl* AL-4
**Blountsville**—*pop pl* IN-6
Blountsville Acad (historical)—*school* AL-4
Blountsville Baptist Ch—*church* AL-4
Blountsville (CCD)—*cens area* AL-4
Blountsville Division—*civil* AL-4
Blountsville Elem Sch—*school* AL-4
Blountsville HS—*school* AL-4
Blountsville United Methodist Ch—*church* AL-4
Blountsville Valley—*valley* AL-4
Blount Tank—*reservoir* TX-5
**Blount (Township of)**—*pop pl* IL-6
Blount Tunnel—*tunnel* AL-4
*Blountville* MS-4
**Blountville**—*pop pl* SC-3
**Blountville**—*pop pl* TN-4
Blountville (CCD)—*cens area* TN-4
Blountville Cem—*cemetery* TN-4
Blountville Division—*civil* TN-4
Blountville Elem Sch—*school* TN-4
Blountville Hist Dist—*hist pl* TN-4
Blountville Hist Dist—*locale* TN-4
Blountville MS—*school* TN-4
Blountville Post Office—*building* TN-4
Blountville United Methodist Ch—*church* TN-4
Blountville Water Works—*locale* TN-4
Blowback Creek—*stream* AK-9
*Blow Creek* VA-3
Blowder Creek—*stream* WA-9
Blowdown, The—*area* AZ-5
Blowdown Island—*island* AK-9
Blowdown Lake—*lake* OR-9
Blowdown Ridge—*ridge* OR-9
Blowdown Spring—*spring* UT-8
Blow Down Tank—*reservoir* AZ-5
Blowers Bluff—*cliff* WA-9
Blower Spring—*spring* AZ-5
**Blowers (Township of)**—*pop pl* MN-6
**Blowertown**—*pop pl* NC-3
*Blowey Creek* ID-8
Blowfly Campground—*locale* ID-8
Blowfly Canyon—*valley* OR-9
Blowfly Creek—*stream* ID-8
Blowfly Rsvr—*reservoir* NV-8
Blowfly Spring—*spring* OR-9
**Blow Gourd**—*pop pl* AL-4
Blowhard Hollow—*valley* UT-8
Blowhard Mtn—*summit* UT-8
Blow Hole—*cave* AL-4
Blowhole—*cave* (2) TN-4
Blowhole Cave—*cave* (2) TN-4
Blowhole Hill—*summit* UT-8
*Blowhole Lake* OR-9
Blowhorn—*locale* AL-4
Blowhorn Creek—*stream* AL-4
Blowhorn Post Office (historical)—*building* AL-4
Blowing Bat Cave—*cave* TN-4
*Blowing Cave* AL-4
*Blowing Cave* MO-7
Blowing Cave—*cave* (5) AL-4
Blowing Cave—*cave* (3) AR-4
Blowing Cave—*cave* (2) KY-4
Blowing Cave—*cave* ME-1
Blowing Cave—*cave* MO-7
Blowing Cave—*cave* (11) TN-4
Blowing Cave Creek—*stream* AR-4
Blowing Caves—*cave* TN-4
Blowing Cave Sch—*school* TN-4
Blowing Cave Spring—*spring* AL-4
Blowing Fork—*stream* VA-3
Blowing Hole Cave—*cave* AL-4
Blowing Hole Cave—*cave* TN-4
Blowing Rock—*locale* VA-3
**Blowing Rock**—*pop pl* NC-3
Blowing Rock—*summit* NC-3
Blowing Rock City Park—*park* NC-3
Blowing Rock Elem Sch—*school* NC-3
Blowing Rock Gap—*gap* KY-4
Blowing Rock Park—*park* FL-3
Blowing Rocks—*locale* FL-3
Blowing Rock (Township of)—*fmr MCD* NC-3
Blowing Slope Cave—*cave* AL-4
*Blowing Spring* AL-4
Blowing Spring—*locale* GA-3
**Blowing Spring**—*pop pl* KY-4
Blowing Spring—*spring* (9) AL-4
Blowing Spring—*spring* AR-4
Blowing Spring—*spring* (2) GA-3
Blowing Spring—*spring* MO-7
Blowing Spring—*spring* NC-3
Blowing Spring—*spring* (8) TN-4
*Blowing Spring Branch* TN-4
Blowing Spring Branch—*stream* AL-4
Blowing Spring Branch—*stream* KY-4
Blowing Spring Branch—*stream* (2) TN-4
Blowing Spring Cave—*cave* AL-4
Blowing Spring Cave—*cave* (2) TN-4
Blowing Spring Cem—*cemetery* TN-4
Blowing Spring Gap—*gap* TN-4
Blowing Spring Hollow—*valley* AL-4
Blowing Spring Hollow—*valley* (2) AR-4
Blowing Spring Hollow—*valley* (3) TN-4
*Blowing Springs* AL-4
Blowing Springs—*locale* KY-4
**Blowing Springs**—*pop pl* GA-3
**Blowing Springs**—*pop pl* TN-4
Blowing Springs—*spring* AL-4
Blowing Springs—*spring* AR-4
Blowing Springs—*spring* MO-7
Blowing Springs—*spring* (2) TN-4
Blowing Springs—*spring* VA-3
Blowing Springs Baptist Ch—*church* TN-4
*Blowing Springs Branch* TN-4
Blowing Springs Branch—*stream* TN-4
Blowing Springs Campground—*locale* VA-3
Blowing Springs Creek—*stream* TN-4
Blowing Springs Hollow—*valley* MO-7
Blowing Springs Hollow—*valley* TN-4
Blowing Springs Sch—*school* TN-4
Blowing Springs Sch (historical)—*school* TN-4
Blowing Well—*well* NM-5
Blowing Wind Cave Natl Wildlife Ref—*park* AL-4
Blow Lake—*lake* OR-9
Blow-me-down Brook—*stream* NH-1
Blow-Me-Down Covered Bridge—*hist pl* NH-1
Blow-me-down Pond—*lake* NH-1
Blown Mine (underground)—*mine* AL-4
Blowntimber Run—*stream* (3) WV-2
*Blowout* CO-8
Blowout—*basin* AZ-5
Blowout—*locale* TX-5
Blowout, The—*basin* CO-8
Blowout, The—*canal* NC-3
Blowout, The—*cliff* CO-8
Blow Out, The—*crater* ID-8
Blowout, The—*valley* CO-8
Blowout Basin—*basin* OR-9
Blowout Basin Creek—*stream* OR-9
Blowout Cave—*cave* TX-5
Blowout Cliff—*cliff* OR-9
*Blowout Creek* ID-8
Blowout Creek—*stream* AZ-5
Blowout Creek—*stream* ID-8
Blowout Creek—*stream* (2) MT-8
Blowout Creek—*stream* (3) OR-9
Blowout Creek—*stream* TX-5
Blowout Creek—*stream* WA-9

Bluefield Coll—*school* VA-3
*Bluefield Crossroads* NC-3
**Bluefield Crossroads**—*pop pl* NC-3
Bluefield Downtown Commercial Hist Dist—*hist pl* WV-2
Bluefields—*uninc pl* TN-4
Bluefield Sch—*school* KY-4
Bluefield State Teachers Coll—*school* WV-2
Blue Fin Bay—*bay* MN-6
Blue Fiord—*bay* AK-9
*Blue Fish Brook* MA-1
Bluefish Brothers—*gut* NJ-2
Bluefish Channel—*channel* FL-3
Bluefish Cove—*bay* CA-9
Blue Fish Cove—*cove* MA-1
Bluefish Creek—*gut* NJ-2
Blue Fish Harbor—*harbor* NJ-2
Bluefish Island—*island* AK-9
*Blue Fish Point* MA-1
Bluefish Point—*cape* FL-3
Bluefish Point—*cape* MA-1
*Blue Fish River* MA-1
Bluefish River—*stream* MA-1
Bluefish River Dam—*dam* MA-1
Bluefish River Marshes—*swamp* MA-1
Bluefish River Rsvr—*reservoir* MA-1
Blue Fish Rock—*rock* MA-1
Bluefish Rocks—*island* FL-3
Blue Flat—*flat* TX-5
Blue Flat Cem—*cemetery* TX-5
Blue Flat Rsvr—*reservoir* (2) UT-8
Blue Flats—*flat* (2) UT-8
*Bluefly Creek* UT-8
Blue Fly Creek—*stream* UT-8
Blue Fool Wash—*valley* UT-8
Blue For—*area* WY-8
Blueford Fork—*stream* KY-4
Blueford Hollow—*valley* KY-4
Blue Ford Landing—*locale* AL-4
*Blue Forest* AZ-5
Blue Fork—*stream* KY-4
Blue Fork Creek—*stream* UT-8
**Blue Fountain**—*pop pl* IL-6
Bluefox Bay—*bay* (2) AK-9
Blue Fox Tank—*reservoir* AZ-5
Blue Front Ranch—*locale* NM-5
Blue Front Sch—*school* IA-7
Blue Gainey Point—*cliff* TX-5
Blue Gap—*gap* AZ-5
Blue Gap—*gap* NC-3
Blue Gap—*gap* TX-5
Blue Gap—*gap* WY-8
Blue Gap—*locale* AZ-5
Blue Gap—*locale* KY-4
Blue Gap Chapter House—*building* AZ-5
Blue Gap Ditch No 19—*canal* WY-8
Blue Gap Draw—*valley* WY-8
Blue Gap (Historical Site)—*locale* TX-5
Blue Gap Knob—*summit* KY-4
Blue Gap Point—*ridge* AZ-5
*Blue Gap Run* PA-2
Blue Gap Sch—*school* AZ-5
Blue Gate—*gap* UT-8
Bluegate Creek—*stream* WY-8
Blue Gem—*locale* TN-4
Bluegem Post Office (historical)—*building* TN-4
Blue Giant Meadow Dam—*dam* PA-2
Blue Giant Meadow Lake—*reservoir* PA-2
Bluegill Canyon—*valley* MT-8
Bluegill Island—*island* CA-9
Blue Gill Island—*island* MI-6
*Blue Gill Lake* MI-6
*Blue Gill Lake* WI-6
Bluegill Lake—*lake* ID-8
Bluegill Lake—*lake* (5) MI-6
Blue Gill Lake—*lake* MI-6
Bluegill Lake—*lake* (2) MI-6
Blue Gill Lake—*lake* MS-4
Bluegill Lake—*lake* (2) WI-6
Blue Gill Lake—*lake* (2) WI-6
Bluegill Lake—*lake* (2) WI-6
Bluegill Point—*cape* KS-7
Bluegill Pond—*lake* IN-6
Bluegill Pond—*lake* MD-2
Bluegill Pond—*lake* MI-6
Bluegill Pond—*reservoir* PA-2
Blue Girth Creek—*stream* AL-4
Blue Glacier—*glacier* (2) WA-9
Blue Goat Creek—*stream* WA-9
Blue Goat Mtn—*summit* WA-9
**Blue Goose**—*pop pl* PA-2
**Blue Goose**—*pop pl* TN-4
Blue Goose Branch—*stream* MS-4
Blue Goose Creek—*stream* MS-4
Blue Goose Hill—*summit* TX-5
Blue Goose (historical)—*locale* MS-4
Blue Goose Island—*island* IL-6
Blue Goose Mine—*locale* PA-2
Blue Goose Mine—*mine* NV-8
Blue Goose Pond—*lake* LA-4
Blue Goose Pond—*lake* WV-2
Blue Goose Spring—*spring* OR-9
Blue Gouge Mine—*mine* CA-9
Blue Grade Tank—*reservoir* AZ-5
Blue Granite Lake—*lake* CA-9
*Bluegrass* IN-6
Blue Grass—*flat* UT-8
**Blue Grass**—*pop pl* IA-7
**Blue Grass**—*pop pl* MN-6
**Bluegrass**—*pop pl* ND-7
**Blue Grass**—*pop pl* PA-2
**Bluegrass**—*pop pl* TN-4
**Blue Grass**—*pop pl* VA-3
Blue Grass—*post sta* KY-4
**Blue Grass Acres Subdivision**—*pop pl* UT-8
Blue Grass Airp—*airport* KY-4
Blue Grass Airport Park—*park* KY-4
Bluegrass Branch—*stream* KY-4
Bluegrass Butte—*summit* OR-9
Blue Grass Camp—*locale* KY-4
Bluegrass Cem—*cemetery* IL-6
Blue Grass Cem—*cemetery* IL-6
Blue Grass Cem—*cemetery* IN-6
Blue Grass Cem—*cemetery* IA-7
Bluegrass Cem—*cemetery* MN-6
Bluegrass Cem—*cemetery* ND-7
Blue Grass Cem—*cemetery* VA-3
Blue Grass Ch—*church* IN-6
Blue Grass Cienega—*flat* AZ-5
Blue Grass County Club Dock—*locale* TN-4
*Blue Grass Creek* IN-6
Blue Grass Creek—*stream* IL-6
Bluegrass Creek—*stream* (2) IL-6
Bluegrass Creek—*stream* IN-6
Bluegrass Creek—*stream* IA-7
Bluegrass Creek—*stream* WY-8
Blue Grass Dock—*locale* TN-4
Blue Grass Flat—*flat* NM-5
Bluegrass Golf and Country Club—*locale* TN-4
Bluegrass Hollow—*valley* (2) MO-7
Bluegrass Hollow—*valley* TN-4
Bluegrass Hollow—*valley* VA-3
Blue Grass Island—*island* OH-6
Blue Grass Knitting, Incorporated—*facility* KY-4
Bluegrass Lake—*lake* ID-8
Blue Grass Lake—*lake* UT-8
Blue Grass (Magisterial District)—*fmr MCD* VA-3
**Bluegrass (Marshtown)**—*pop pl* IN-6
**Bluegrass Meadows (subdivision)**—*pop pl* TN-4
Blue Grass Memorial Cem—*cemetery* KY-4
Blue Grass Memorial Gardens—*cemetery* KY-4
**Blue Grass No 3**—*pop pl* KY-4
Blue Grass Ordnance Depot—*other* KY-4
Blue Grass Pond—*lake* UT-8
Blue Grass Raceway—*other* KY-4
Blue Grass Ridge—*ridge* MT-8
Bluegrass Ridge—*ridge* OH-6
Bluegrass Ridge—*ridge* OR-9
Bluegrass Ridge—*ridge* TN-4
Bluegrass Ridge—*ridge* WY-8
Bluegrass Sch—*school* IL-6
Blue Grass Sch—*school* IL-6
Blue Grass Sch—*school* NE-7
Blue Grass Sch—*school* TN-4
*Blue Grass Station* ND-7
**Bluegrass (subdivision)**—*pop pl* TN-4
Bluegrass Tank—*reservoir* AZ-5
Blue Grass Towhead—*flat* TN-4
Blue Grass Township—*fmr MCD* IA-7
Blue Grass Trail—*trail* VA-3
Bluegrass Valley—*valley* VA-3
Bluegrass Wells—*well* WY-8
Blue Gravel Creek—*stream* CO-8
Blue Grotto—*cave* FL-3
Blue Grotto Spring—*spring* MT-8
Blue Grouse Basin—*basin* WA-9
Blue Grouse Creek—*stream* (2) ID-8
Blue Grouse Mine—*mine* CA-9
Blue Grouse Mine—*mine* WA-9
Blue Grouse Mtn—*summit* WA-9
Blue Grouse Ridge—*ridge* CA-9
Blue Grouse Trail—*trail* CO-8
Blue Grove—*island* LA-4
**Bluegrove**—*pop pl* TX-5
Bluegrove Cem—*cemetery* TX-5
Bluegrove Oil Field—*oilfield* TX-5
Blue Grove Sch—*school* IL-6
Blue Grove Southwest Oil Field—*oilfield* TX-5
Blue Gulch—*valley* (3) CA-9
Blue Gulch—*valley* CO-8
Blue Gulch—*valley* (5) ID-8
Blue Gulch—*valley* (7) OR-9
Blue Gulch—*valley* WA-9
Blue Gulch—*valley* (2) WY-8
Blue Gulch Rsvr—*reservoir* WA-9
Blue Gulch Spring—*spring* ID-8
**Blue Gulf Beach**—*pop pl* FL-3
Blue Gull Hill—*summit* MD-2
Bluegum Canyon—*valley* CA-9
Bluegum Creek—*stream* CA-9
Blue Gums—*flat* CA-9
Blue Gurth Swamp—*swamp* AL-4
*Blue Gut Creek* AL-4
Bluegut Creek—*stream* AL-4
Blue Gut Creek—*stream* AL-4
Bluegut Creek—*stream* AL-4
*Blue Guttee Creek* AL-4
Blue Hammock Bayou—*stream* LA-4
Blue Haven Camp—*locale* NM-5
**Blue Haven Estates**—*pop pl* TX-5
**Blue Haven Place Subdivision**—*pop pl* UT-8
Blue Hawk Peak Ranch—*hist pl* OK-5
Blue Head—*summit* PA-2
Blue Head Branch—*stream* KY-4
Blue Head Dam—*dam* PA-2
Blue Head Rock—*summit* KY-4
Blue Head Rsvr—*reservoir* PA-2
Blue Healing Springs—*locale* VA-3
**Blue Heaven**—*pop pl* SC-3
Blue Heaven—*summit* TX-5
Blue Heaven Lake—*lake* CA-9
Blue Heights Ch—*church* GA-3
Blue Hen Farm—*hist pl* DE-2
Blue Hen Mall—*locale* DE-2
**Blue Heron**—*pop pl* KY-4
Blue Heron Bay—*bay* OR-9
Blue Heron Beach—*beach* WA-9
Blue Heron Camp—*locale* NJ-2
Blue Heron Creek—*stream* CA-9
Blue Heron Lagoon—*lake* MI-6
Blue Heron Lake—*lake* FL-3
Blue Heron Lake—*reservoir* NJ-2
Blue Heron Lake—*reservoir* NY-2
Blue Heron Lake—*reservoir* PA-2
Blue Heron Lake Dam—*dam* NJ-2
Blue Heron Rsvr—*reservoir* OR-9
*Blue Hill* ME-1
*Blue Hill* MA-1
*Blue Hill* NE-7
*Blue Hill* NC-3
Blue Hill—*gap* CO-8
Blue Hill—*locale* KS-7
Blue Hill—*locale* MS-4
Blue Hill—*locale* TN-4
Blue Hill—*locale* WY-8
Bluehill—*other* ME-1
**Blue Hill**—*pop pl* AR-4
**Blue Hill**—*pop pl* ME-1
**Blue Hill**—*pop pl* MD-2
**Blue Hill**—*pop pl* NE-7
**Blue Hill**—*pop pl* (2) PA-2
Blue Hill—*summit* AZ-5
Blue Hill—*summit* AR-4
Blue Hill—*summit* (3) CO-8
Blue Hill—*summit* CT-1
Blue Hill—*summit* FL-3
Blue Hill—*summit* ID-8
Blue Hill—*summit* ME-1
Blue Hill—*summit* MN-6
Blue Hill—*summit* (2) MS-4
Blue Hill—*summit* MT-8
Blue Hill—*summit* NH-1
Blue Hill—*summit* (2) NM-5
Blue Hill—*summit* (7) NY-2
Blue Hill—*summit* ND-7
Blue Hill—*summit* (2) PA-2
Blue Hill—*summit* UT-8
Blue Hill—*summit* (3) WY-8
*Blue Hill, The* MA-1
Blue Hill Bay—*bay* FL-3
Blue Hill Bay—*bay* ME-1
Blue Hill Bay Lighthouse—*locale* ME-1
Blue Hill Cem—*cemetery* MA-1
Blue Hill Cem—*cemetery* NE-7
Blue Hill Ch—*church* (2) MS-4
Blue Hill Country Club—*locale* MA-1
Blue Hill Country Club—*other* ME-1
Blue Hill Creek—*gut* FL-3
Blue Hill Creek—*stream* ID-8
Blue Hill Creek—*stream* SC-3
**Blue Hill Falls**—*pop pl* ME-1
Blue Hill Golf Club—*other* NY-2
Blue Hill Harbor—*bay* ME-1
Blue Hill Hist Dist—*hist pl* ME-1
Blue Hill Lateral—*canal* WY-8
Blue Hill Lookout Tower—*locale* MS-4
Blue Hill Mine—*mine* NM-5
Blue Hill Neck—*cape* ME-1
Blue Hill Pond—*lake* MI-6
Blue Hill Range—*range* MA-1
*Blue-hill River* MA-1
Blue Hill River—*stream* MA-1
Blue Hill Rsvr—*reservoir* WY-8
Blue Hills—*other* NM-5
**Blue Hills**—*pop pl* CA-9
**Blue Hills**—*pop pl* CT-1
**Blue Hills**—*pop pl* MA-1
**Blue Hills**—*pop pl* MS-4
Blue Hills—*range* (2) KS-7
Blue Hills—*ridge* UT-8
Blue Hills—*summit* AZ-5
Blue Hills—*summit* NM-5
Blue Hills—*summit* NY-2
Blue Hills—*summit* (2) TX-5
Blue Hills—*summit* WI-6
Blue Hills Cem—*cemetery* WI-6
*Blue Hill Sch* PA-2
Blue Hill Sch—*school* AR-4
Blue Hill Sch—*school* ND-7
Bluehill Sch—*school* PA-2
Blue Hills Country Club—*other* (2) MO-7
**Blue Hills Farms**—*pop pl* AZ-5
Blue Hills Golf Club—*other* VA-3
Blue Hills HQ—*hist pl* MA-1
Blue Hills Lookout Tower—*locale* WI-6
Blue Hill Southeast Oil Field—*oilfield* KS-7
*Blue Hills (P.O.)* CT-1
Blue Hill Spring—*spring* WY-8
Blue Hills Range—*summit* NH-1
Blue Hills Regional Sch—*school* MA-1
Blue Hills Reservation—*reserve* MA-1
Blue Hills Reservoir Dam—*dam* MA-1
*Blue Hills River* MA-1
Blue Hills Rsvr—*reservoir* MA-1
Blue Hills Sch—*school* CT-1
Blue Hills Upland—*plain* KS-7
**Blue Hill (Town of)**—*pop pl* ME-1
**Blue Hill Township**—*pop pl* KS-7
**Blue Hill Township**—*pop pl* ND-7
**Blue Hill (Township of)**—*pop pl* MN-6
Blue Hogan Wash—*valley* UT-8
Blue Hole—*basin* FL-3
Blue Hole—*basin* KY-4
Blue Hole—*bay* AL-4
Blue Hole—*bay* AR-4
Blue Hole—*bay* (2) FL-3
Blue Hole—*bay* GA-3
Blue Hole—*bay* MO-7
Blue Hole—*bay* (2) TN-4
Blue Hole—*bay* TX-5
Blue Hole—*bay* (2) VA-3
Blue Hole—*bay* WV-2
Blue Hole—*lake* (4) AL-4
Blue Hole—*lake* (7) AR-4
Blue Hole—*lake* CA-9
Blue Hole—*lake* FL-3
Blue Hole—*lake* IL-6
Blue Hole—*lake* (2) IN-6
Blue Hole—*lake* (3) LA-4
Blue Hole—*lake* (10) MS-4
Blue Hole—*lake* MO-7
Blue Hole—*lake* NJ-2
Blue Hole—*lake* NM-5
Blue Hole—*lake* OH-6
Blue Hole—*lake* PA-2
Blue Hole—*lake* SC-3
Blue Hole—*lake* (2) TN-4
Blue Hole—*lake* (5) TX-5
Blue Hole—*lake* WI-6
Bluehole—*locale* KY-4
Blue Hole—*locale* TX-5
Blue Hole—*locale* VA-3
Blue Hole—*other* MO-7
Blue Hole—*other* NM-5
Blue Hole—*reservoir* KS-7
Blue Hole—*reservoir* NM-5
Blue Hole—*reservoir* TX-5
Blue Hole—*spring* (2) AL-4
Blue Hole—*spring* AR-4
Blue Hole—*swamp* AR-4
Blue Hole, The—*bend* KY-4
Blue Hole, The—*lake* AL-4
Blue Hole Bayou—*gut* LA-4
Blue Hole Bluff—*cliff* TN-4
Blue Hole Branch—*stream* AL-4
Blue Hole Branch—*stream* AR-4
Blue Hole Branch—*stream* KY-4
Blue Hole Branch—*stream* MO-7
Blue Hole Branch—*stream* (2) TN-4
Blue Hole Branch—*stream* TX-5
Blue Hole Bridge—*bridge* TN-4
Blue Hole Campground—*locale* TX-5
Blue Hole Cave—*cave* AL-4
Blue Hole Creek—*gut* FL-3
Blue Hole Creek—*stream* AR-4
Blue Hole Creek—*stream* KY-4
Bluehole Creek—*stream* KY-4
Blue Hole Creek—*stream* OR-9
Blue Hole Creek—*stream* PA-2
Blue Hole Creek—*stream* (3) TX-5
Blue Hole Creek—*stream* WY-8
Bluehole Falls—*falls* TN-4
Blue Hole Hollow—*valley* (2) AR-4
Blue Hole Hollow—*valley* (2) KY-4
Blue Hole Hollow—*valley* (2) MO-7
Bluehole Hollow—*valley* TN-4
Blue Hole Hollow—*valley* TN-4
Blue Hole Lake—*lake* AR-4
Blue Hole Lake—*lake* LA-4
Blue Hole Lake—*lake* MS-4
Blue Hole on the Llano—*lake* TX-5
Blue Hole Picnic Area—*locale* AL-4
Blue Hole Point—*cape* FL-3
Blue Hole Pond—*lake* IN-6
Bluehole Pond—*lake* LA-4
Blue Hole Ridge—*ridge* KY-4
**Bluehole (RR name Rodonnel)**—*pop pl* KY-4
*Blue Hole Run* PA-2
Blue Holes—*locale* WY-8
Blue Hole Spring—*spring* (2) GA-3
Blue Hole Spring—*spring* KY-4
Blue Hole Spring—*spring* MO-7
Blue Hole Spring—*spring* NM-5
Blue Hole Spring—*spring* PA-2
Blue Hole Spring—*spring* TN-4
Blue Hole Springs—*spring* TX-5
Blue Holes Spring—*spring* AZ-5
Blue Hole Swamp—*swamp* NC-3
Blue Hollow—*valley* IL-6
Blue Hollow—*valley* (3) KY-4
Blue Hollow—*valley* (4) MO-7
Blue Hollow—*valley* OH-6
Blue Hollow—*valley* (2) TN-4
Blue Hollow—*valley* TX-5
Blue Hollow—*valley* VA-3
Blue Homestead Lake—*lake* FL-3
*Blue Homestead Pond* FL-3
Blue Hope Mine—*mine* AZ-5
Blue Horizon Mine—*mine* NV-8
Blue Hot Spring—*spring* FL-3
**Bluehouse Corners**—*pop pl* SC-3
Blue House Dam—*dam* NV-8
Blue House Ditch—*canal* NV-8
Blue House Mtn—*summit* AZ-5
Blue House Slough—*stream* NV-8
Blue House Spring—*spring* AZ-5
Bluehouse Swamp—*swamp* (2) SC-3
**Blue Inlet**—*pop pl* FL-3
Blue Island—*island* FL-3
**Blue Island**—*pop pl* IL-6
*Blue Island Junction* IL-6
Blue Islands—*island* LA-4
Blue Jacket—*other* OK-5
**Blue Jacket**—*pop pl* MI-6
**Bluejacket**—*pop pl* OK-5
**Bluejacket (Blue Jacket)**—*pop pl* OK-5
Blue Jacket Butte—*summit* CA-9
Blue Jacket Cem—*cemetery* OH-6
Bluejacket Cem—*cemetery* (2) OK-5
Bluejacket Creek—*stream* ID-8
Blue Jacket Creek—*stream* NV-8
Blue Jacket Creek—*stream* OH-6
Blue Jacket Crossing—*locale* KS-7
Bluejacket Mine—*mine* ID-8
Blue Jacket Mine—*mine* ID-8
Bluejacket Mine—*mine* ID-8
Blue Jacket Mine—*mine* NV-8
Blue Jacket Mine (underground)—*mine* AL-4
Blue Jacket Park—*park* KS-7
Blue Jacket Peak—*summit* NV-8
Blue Jacket Sch—*school* KS-7
Blue Jay—*locale* OH-6
Blue Jay—*locale* PA-2
**Blue Jay**—*pop pl* CA-9
**Blue Jay**—*pop pl* WV-2
Blue Jay Bay—*bay* CA-9
Bluejay Branch—*stream* MD-2
Blue Jay Campground—*locale* WA-9
Blue Jay Canyon—*valley* CA-9
Blue Jay Canyon—*valley* ID-8
*Blue Jay Creek* ID-8
*Blue Jay Creek* PA-2
Blue Jay Creek—*stream* (3) CA-9
Bluejay Creek—*stream* CA-9
Blue Jay Creek—*stream* (2) ID-8
Blue Jay Creek—*stream* MI-6
Blue Jay Creek—*stream* MN-6
Blue Jay Creek—*stream* NV-8
Blue Jay Creek—*stream* (3) OR-9
Bluejay Creek—*stream* OR-9
Bluejay Creek—*stream* PA-2
Bluejay Creek—*stream* WY-8
Blue Jay Farm—*locale* MO-7
Blue Jay Flat—*flat* UT-8
Bluejay Gulch—*valley* CO-8
Blue Jay Gulch—*valley* ID-8
Blue Jay Gulch—*valley* NV-8
Blue Jay Highway Maintenance Station—*locale* NV-8
Blue Jay Inn—*hist pl* CO-8
**Blue Jay Junction**—*pop pl* WV-2
Blue Jay Lake—*lake* (2) ID-8
Bluejay Lake—*lake* MI-6
Blue Jay Lake—*lake* MN-6
Blue Jay Lake—*reservoir* WV-2
Blue Jay Lakes—*lake* CA-9
Bluejay Mine—*mine* AZ-5
Bluejay Mine—*mine* CA-9
Blue Jay Mine—*mine* CA-9
Blue Jay Mine—*mine* ID-8
Blue Jay Mine—*mine* NV-8
Bluejay Mine—*mine* NV-8
Blue Jay Mine—*mine* OR-9
Blue Jay Mine—*mine* UT-8
*Bluejay Mountain* WY-8
Bluejay Mtn—*summit* CA-9
Blue Jay Mtn—*summit* WY-8
Blue Jay Peak—*summit* AZ-5
Blue Jay Point—*summit* CA-9
Blue Jay Ranch—*locale* NV-8
Blue Jay Ridge—*ridge* AZ-5
Blue Jay Ridge—*ridge* (2) CA-9
Blue Jay Ridge—*ridge* OR-9
Blue Jay Rsvr—*reservoir* OR-9
Blue Jay Sch—*school* MO-7
Blue Jay Splash—*bend* CA-9
Blue Jay Spring—*spring* MT-8
Blue Jay Spring—*spring* (2) NV-8
Blue Jay Spring—*spring* NM-5
Bluejay Spring—*spring* (2) OR-9
Blue Jay Spring—*spring* OR-9
Blue Jay Spring Rec Area—*locale* PA-2
Blue Jay Tank—*reservoir* AZ-5
**Blue Jay 6**—*pop pl* WV-2
Blue Jean Sch—*school* IL-6
Blue Jim Mine (underground)—*mine* AL-4
Blue Job Mtn—*summit* NH-1
Blue Joe Creek—*stream* ID-8
Blue Joe Lake—*lake* MI-6
Blue Joe Mtn—*summit* ID-8
Blue John—*locale* KY-4
*Blue John Canyon* UT-8
Bluejohn Canyon—*valley* UT-8
Blue John Creek—*stream* AR-4
Blue John Creek—*stream* GA-3
Blue John Hollow—*valley* KY-4
*Blue John Spring* UT-8
Bluejohn Spring—*spring* UT-8
Blue Joint—*summit* ID-8
Blue Joint Creek—*stream* MT-8
Blue Joint Drainage Ditch—*canal* IL-6
Bluejoint Lake—*reservoir* OR-9
Bluejoint Ranch—*locale* OR-9
Blue Jordan Swamp—*swamp* FL-3
*Blue Joy Creek* OR-9
Blue Juniata Camp—*locale* PA-2
Blue Kettle Ridge—*ridge* OR-9
**Blue Knob**—*pop pl* PA-2
**Blueknob**—*pop pl* PA-2
Blue Knob—*summit* GA-3
Blue Knob—*summit* IL-6
Blue Knob—*summit* MO-7
Blue Knob—*summit* (2) NC-3
Blue Knob—*summit* PA-2
Blue Knob—*summit* TN-4
Blue Knob—*summit* (2) VA-3
Blue Knob—*summit* (4) WV-2
Blue Knob Branch—*stream* GA-3
Blue Knob Branch—*stream* WV-2
Blue Knob Ch—*church* WV-2
Blue Knob Creek—*stream* WV-2
Blue Knob Fire Tower—*tower* PA-2
Blue Knob Lookout Tower—*tower* PA-2
*Blue Knob Park* PA-2
Blue Knob Rec Area(ski area)—*locale* PA-2
Blue Knob Run—*stream* PA-2
Blue Knob State Park—*park* PA-2
Blue Knob Valley Airp—*airport* PA-2
Blue Knoll—*summit* (3) UT-8
Blue Knolls—*summit* AZ-5
Blue Knoll Well—*well* UT-8
Blue Lagoon—*lake* FL-3
*Blue Lake* AL-4
*Blue Lake* CA-9
*Blue Lake* CO-8
*Blue Lake* LA-4
*Blue Lake* MI-6
*Blue Lake* MN-6
*Blue Lake* MS-4
*Blue Lake* MT-8
*Blue Lake* NV-8
*Blue Lake* SD-7
*Blue Lake* UT-8
*Blue Lake* WA-9
*Blue Lake* WI-6
Blue Lake—*flat* UT-8
Blue Lake—*gut* AR-4
Blue Lake—*lake* (2) AL-4
Blue Lake—*lake* (3) AK-9
Blue Lake—*lake* AZ-5
Blue Lake—*lake* (5) AR-4
Blue Lake—*lake* (11) CA-9
Blue Lake—*lake* (12) CO-8
Blue Lake—*lake* (14) FL-3
Blue Lake—*lake* GA-3
Blue Lake—*lake* (9) ID-8
Blue Lake—*lake* (2) IN-6
Blue Lake—*lake* (7) LA-4
Blue Lake—*lake* (13) MI-6
Blue Lake—*lake* (7) MN-6
Blue Lake—*lake* (16) MS-4
Blue Lake—*lake* (8) MT-8
Blue Lake—*lake* NE-7
Blue Lake—*lake* (2) NV-8
Blue Lake—*lake* (2) NM-5
Blue Lake—*lake* NY-2
Blue Lake—*lake* (2) ND-7
Blue Lake—*lake* OK-5
Blue Lake—*lake* (11) OR-9
Blue Lake—*lake* PA-2
Blue Lake—*lake* SC-3
Blue Lake—*lake* (10) TX-5
Blue Lake—*lake* (13) UT-8
Blue Lake—*lake* (19) WA-9
Blue Lake—*lake* (2) WI-6
Blue Lake—*lake* (2) WY-8
Blue Lake—*locale* FL-3
**Blue Lake**—*pop pl* CA-9
**Blue Lake**—*pop pl* FL-3
**Blue Lake**—*pop pl* IN-6
**Blue Lake**—*pop pl* MS-4
Blue Lake—*reservoir* AK-9
Blue Lake—*reservoir* AZ-5
Blue Lake—*reservoir* CA-9
Blue Lake—*reservoir* CO-8
Blue Lake—*reservoir* IA-7
Blue Lake—*reservoir* MS-4
Blue Lake—*reservoir* NJ-2
Blue Lake—*reservoir* (2) NM-5
Blue Lake—*reservoir* TX-5
Blue Lake—*reservoir* UT-8
Blue Lake—*swamp* LA-4
Blue Lake—*swamp* MN-6
Blue Lake Baptist Ch—*church* MS-4
*Blue Lake Basin* CO-8
Blue Lake Bayou—*swamp* MS-4
Blue Lake Brake—*swamp* MS-4
Blue Lake Cabin—*locale* NM-5
Blue Lake Camas Prairie Trail—*trail* OR-9
Blue Lake Camp—*locale* AL-4
Blue Lake Camp—*locale* OR-9
Blue Lake Campground—*park* AZ-5
Blue Lake Camp Picnic Area—*locale* WA-9
Blue Lake Canyon—*valley* CA-9
Blue Lake Cem—*cemetery* MI-6
Blue Lake Ch—*church* FL-3
Blue Lake Ch—*church* (2) TX-5
Blue Lake Chapel—*church* MS-4
Blue Lake County Park—*park* MI-6
*Blue Lake Creek* ID-8
Blue Lake Creek—*stream* (3) ID-8
Blue Lake Creek—*stream* UT-8
Blue Lake Creek—*stream* WA-9
Blue Lake Creek Campground—*locale* WA-9
Blue Lake Cut-Off—*bend* MS-4
Blue Lake Dam—*dam* AZ-5
Blue Lake Dam—*dam* UT-8
Blue Lake Drain—*canal* CA-9
Blue Lake Elem Sch—*school* FL-3
Blue Lake Field—*island* FL-3
Blue Lake Guard Station—*locale* OR-9
Blue Lake Gulch—*valley* ID-8
Blue Lake Landing—*locale* LA-4
Blue Lake Lookout Tower—*locale* LA-4
*Blue Lake Methodist Assembly* AL-4
Blue Lake Pass—*gap* CO-8
*Blue Lake Peak* OR-9
Blue Lake Public Hunting Area—*area* IA-7
Blue Lake Ranch—*locale* CA-9
Blue Lake Rec Area—*park* MS-4
*Blue Lake Reservoir* WA-9
Blue Lake Ridge—*ridge* WA-9
*Blue Lakes* UT-8
*Blue Lakes* WA-9
Blue Lakes—*lake* CA-9
Blue Lakes—*lake* (3) CO-8
Blue Lakes—*lake* MI-6
Blue Lakes—*lake* MT-8
Blue Lakes—*lake* WA-9
Blue Lakes—*lake* WY-8
Blue Lakes—*reservoir* CO-8
Blue Lakes—*reservoir* ID-8
Blue Lakes—*reservoir* UT-8
Blue Lakes Campground—*locale* CO-8
Blue Lake Sch—*school* MI-6
Blue Lakes Elem Sch—*school* FL-3
Blue Lake Slough—*stream* AR-4
Blue Lakes Park—*park* FL-3
Blue Lakes Ridge—*locale* FL-3
Blue Lakes Trail—*trail* CO-8
Blue Lake Swamp—*swamp* FL-3
Blue Lake Township (historical)—*civil* SD-7
**Blue Lake (Township of)**—*pop pl* (2) MI-6
Blue Lake Trail—*trail* (3) CO-8
Blue Lake Trail—*trail* ID-8
Blue Lake Trail—*trail* (2) OR-9
Blue Lake Wash—*stream* NM-5
Blue Lantern Farm—*hist pl* KY-4
Blue Lead Canyon—*valley* NV-8
Blue Lead Gulch—*valley* CA-9
Blue Lead Mine—*mine* CA-9
Blue Lead Mine (Abandoned)—*mine* CA-9
Bluelead Mtn—*summit* SD-7
Blue Ledge—*bench* NY-2
Blue Ledge—*cliff* VT-1
Blue Ledge Mine—*mine* CA-9
Blue Ledge Pond—*lake* NY-2
Blue Ledge Spring—*spring* AZ-5
**Blue Level**—*pop pl* KY-4
Blue Lick—*locale* KY-4
Blue Lick—*locale* MO-7
**Blue Lick**—*pop pl* IN-6
Blue Lick—*stream* IN-6
Blue Lick—*stream* WV-2
Blue Lick Branch—*stream* AL-4
Bluelick Branch—*stream* (2) WV-2
Blue Lick Cem—*cemetery* AL-4
Blue Lick Ch—*church* IN-6
Bluelick Ch—*church* KY-4
*Blue Lick Creek* KY-4
Blue Lick Creek—*stream* (2) IN-6
Blue Lick Creek—*stream* (2) KY-4
Bluelick Creek—*stream* KY-4
Blue Lick Creek—*stream* LA-4
Blue Lick Creek—*stream* OR-9
Blue Lick Creek—*stream* PA-2
Blue Lick Creek—*stream* WV-2
Blue Lick Hollow—*valley* PA-2
Bluelick Run—*stream* MD-2
Bluelick Run—*stream* OH-6
Blue Lick Run—*stream* VA-3
Bluelick Run—*stream* WV-2
Blue Lick Run—*stream* WV-2
Blue Licks Battlefield State Park—*park* KY-4
Blue Lick Sch—*school* KY-4
**Blue Lick Springs**—*pop pl* KY-4
Blue Lick Springs—*spring* MO-7
Blue Licks Spring—*locale* KY-4
Bluelight—*locale* WA-9
Bluelight Mine—*mine* NV-8
Blueline Hollow—*valley* WV-2
Blueline Trail—*trail* WV-2
Blue Link Spring—*spring* NV-8
Blue Marsh Bernville Levee—*dam* PA-2
Blue Marsh Dam—*dam* PA-2
Blue Marsh Dike A—*dam* PA-2
Blue Marsh Dike B—*dam* PA-2
Blue Marsh Dike C—*dam* PA-2
**Blue Marsh (historical)**—*pop pl* PA-2
Blue Marsh Lake—*reservoir* PA-2
*Blue Marsh Lake Detention Basin Number One* PA-2
*Blue Marsh Lake Detention Basin Number Two* PA-2
Blue Mary Spring—*spring* (2) AZ-5
Blue Mass—*basin* NV-8
Blue Mass Canyon—*valley* NV-8
Blue Mass Spring—*spring* NV-8
Blue Meadow Brook—*stream* MA-1
Blue Meadows—*flat* (2) UT-8
*Blue Meeting House* PA-2
*Blue Mesa* UT-8
Blue Mesa—*area* AZ-5
Blue Mesa—*summit* (2) CO-8
Blue Mesa—*summit* (2) NM-5
Blue Mesa—*summit* WY-8
Blue Mesa Canyon—*valley* NM-5
Blue Mesa Dam—*dam* CO-8
*Blue Mesa Reservoir* CO-8
Blue Mesa Rsvr—*reservoir* CO-8
Blue Mesa Spring—*spring* AZ-5
Blue Mesa Tank—*reservoir* NM-5
Blue Mesa Well—*well* (2) NM-5
**Blue Mill**—*pop pl* TN-4
**Blue Mills**—*pop pl* MO-7
Blue Mill Stream—*stream* NY-2
Blue Mine—*mine* CA-9
Blue Mine—*mine* KY-4

Blue Mine Brook—*stream* NJ-2
Blue Miner Lake—*lake* WY-8
*Blue Minnow Point* MD-2
Blue Monday Mine—*mine* CA-9
Blue Monday Spring—*spring* OR-9
Blue Monster Mine—*mine* CA-9
Blue Monster Spring—*spring* AZ-5
**Bluemont**—*pop pl* VA-3
Bluemont Cem—*cemetery* WV-2
Bluemont Ch—*church* VA-3
Bluemont Elem Sch—*school* KS-7
**Bluemont Hill**—*pop pl* KS-7
Bluemont Hist Dist—*hist pl* VA-3
**Bluemont Junction**—*pop pl* VA-3
**Bluemont Park**—*pop pl* VA-3
Blue Moon—*locale* KY-4
Blue Moon Bench—*bench* AZ-5
Blue Moon Creek—*stream* ID-8
Blue Moon Mine—*mine* CA-9
Blue Moon Ranch—*locale* CA-9
Blue Moon Rsvr—*reservoir* AZ-5
**Blue Mound**—*pop pl* IL-6
**Blue Mound**—*pop pl* KS-7
**Blue Mound**—*pop pl* MO-7
**Blue Mound**—*pop pl* TX-5
Blue Mound—*summit* (3) IL-6
Blue Mound—*summit* (3) KS-7
Blue Mound—*summit* (3) MO-7
Blue Mound—*summit* (3) OK-5
Blue Mound—*summit* (4) TX-5
Blue Mound Cem—*cemetery* IL-6
Blue Mound Cem—*cemetery* KS-7
Blue Mound Cem—*cemetery* MO-7
Blue Mound Cem—*cemetery* OK-5
Blue Mound Ch—*church* KS-7
Blue Mound Ch—*church* MN-6
Blue Mound Ch—*church* TX-5
*Blue Mound City Lake* KS-7
Blue Mound Country Club—*other* WI-6
Blue Mound Elem Sch—*school* KS-7
Blue Mound Rsvr—*reservoir* KS-7
*Blue Mounds* KS-7
**Blue Mounds**—*pop pl* WI-6
Blue Mounds—*summit* MN-6
Blue Mounds—*summit* WI-6
**Blue Mound (Saginaw Park)**—*pop pl* TX-5
*Blue Mounds Branch* WI-6
Blue Mound Sch—*school* IL-6
Blue Mound Sch—*school* (2) MO-7
Blue Mound Sch—*school* NE-7
Blue Mound Sch (historical)—*school* MO-7
*Blue Mounds Creek* WI-6
Blue Mounds Creek—*stream* WI-6
Blue Mounds State Park—*park* MN-6
Blue Mounds State Park—*park* WI-6
**Blue Mounds (Town of)**—*pop pl* WI-6
**Blue Mounds (Township of)**—*pop pl* MN-6
**Blue Mound Township**—*pop pl* KS-7
**Blue Mound Township**—*pop pl* (2) MO-7
**Blue Mound (Township of)**—*pop pl* (2) IL-6
Blue Mound Wayside Chapel—*church* MN-6
Blue Mount—*locale* MD-2
*Blue Mountain* AR-4
*Blue Mountain* ME-1
*Blue Mountain* NJ-2
*Blue Mountain* ND-7
Blue Mountain—*locale* MD-2
Blue Mountain—*locale* OR-9
**Blue Mountain**—*pop pl* AL-4
**Blue Mountain**—*pop pl* AR-4
**Blue Mountain**—*pop pl* CO-8
**Blue Mountain**—*pop pl* MD-2
**Blue Mountain**—*pop pl* MS-4
**Blue Mountain**—*pop pl* NY-2
**Blue Mountain**—*pop pl* VA-3
Blue Mountain—*ridge* CA-9
Blue Mountain Academy Airp—*airport* PA-2
Blue Mountain Baptist Ch—*church* AL-4
*Blue Mountain Baptist Church* MS-4
**Blue Mountain Beach**—*pop pl* FL-3
Blue Mountain Boys Ranch—*locale* WA-9
Blue Mountain Camp—*locale* MO-7
Blue Mountain Camp—*locale* OR-9
Blue Mountain Camps—*locale* PA-2
Blue Mountain Canyon—*valley* AZ-5
Blue Mountain Canyon—*valley* NV-8
Blue Mountain Cem—*cemetery* CA-9
Blue Mountain Cem—*cemetery* MS-4
Bluo Mountain Com—*comotory* MT-8
Blue Mountain Cem—*cemetery* OR-9
Blue Mountain Ch—*church* AR-4
Blue Mountain Ch—*church* (2) MS-4
Blue Mountain Childrens Home—*building* MS-4
*Blue Mountain Ch of the Lord Jesus Christ* MS-4
Blue Mountain Coll—*school* MS-4
Blue Mountain College Hist Dist—*hist pl* MS-4
Blue Mountain Community Coll—*school* OR-9
Blue Mountain Community Hall—*locale* TX-5
Blue Mountain Community Hall—*locale* WA-9
*Blue Mountain Creek* AL-4
Blue Mountain Creek—*stream* CO-8
Blue Mountain Dam—*dam* AR-4
Blue Mountain Ditch—*canal* OR-9
Blue Mountain Dude Ranch—*locale* UT-8
Blue Mountain East Elem Sch—*school* PA-2
Blue Mountain Elem Sch—*school* MS-4
**Blue Mountain Estates**—*pop pl* CO-8
*Blue Mountain Female Coll* MS-4
*Blue Mountain Female Institute* MS-4
Blue Mountain Forest Wayside—*locale* (2) OR-9
Blue Mountain Hot Springs—*spring* OR-9
Blue Mountain House Annex—*hist pl* NY-2
Blue Mountain HS—*school* MS-4
Blue Mountain HS—*school* PA-2
Blue Mountain Indian Writings—*locale* UT-8
*Blue Mountain Interchange* PA-2
Blue Mountain Lake—*lake* NY-2
Blue Mountain Lake—*lake* WI-6
**Blue Mountain Lake**—*pop pl* NY-2
Blue Mountain Lake—*reservoir* AR-4
Blue Mountain Lake—*reservoir* MO-7
Blue Mountain Lake—*reservoir* PA-2
Blue Mountain Lake Dam—*dam* PA-2
Blue Mountain Lakes—*reservoir* NJ-2
Blue Mountain Lions Park—*park* PA-2
Blue Mountain Meadows Tank—*reservoir* CA-9
Blue Mountain Memorial Garden—*cemetery* WA-9
Blue Mountain Mine—*mine* CA-9
Blue Mountain Mine—*mine* OR-9
Blue Mountain Mine (underground)—*mine* AL-4
Blue Mountain MS—*school* PA-2
Blue Mountain Pass—*gap* OR-9
**Blue Mountain Pines**—*pop pl* PA-2
Blue Mountain Ranch—*locale* CO-8
Blue Mountain Reservation—*park* NY-2
Blue Mountain Ridge—*ridge* AL-4
*Blue Mountain Rsvr* AR-4
Blue Mountain Rsvr—*reservoir* CO-8
*Blue Mountain Rsvr 4* OR-9
*Blue Mountains* AL-4
*Blue Mountains* AZ-5
*Blue Mountains* CA-9
*Blue Mountains* CO-8
*Blue Mountains* UT-8
Blue Mountains—*flat* OR-9
Blue Mountains—*range* ME-1
Blue Mountains—*range* (2) OR-9
Blue Mountains—*spring* MT-8
Blue Mountains—*summit* MI-6
Blue Mountains—*summit* WA-9
Blue Mountain Sch—*hist pl* WA-9
Blue Mountain Sch—*school* AL-4
Blue Mountain Sch—*school* CA-9
Blue Mountain Sch—*school* (2) OR-9
Blue Mountain Sch—*school* TX-5
Blue Mountain Spring—*spring* (2) AZ-5
Blue Mountain Spring—*spring* CA-9
Blue Mountain Spring—*spring* OR-9
Blue Mountain Spring No. 1—*spring* CO-8
Blue Mountain Spring No. 2—*spring* CO-8
Blue Mountain Spring No. 3—*spring* CO-8
Blue Mountain Spring No. 4—*spring* CO-8
*Blue Mountain Station* AL-4
Blue Mountain Stream—*stream* NY-2
Blue Mountain Tank—*reservoir* AZ-5
Blue Mountain (Township of)—*fmr MCD* (2) AR-4
Blue Mountain Tunnel—*tunnel* PA-2
Blue Mountain Union Sch—*school* VT-1
Blue Mountain United Methodist Ch—*church* MS-4
Blue Mountain View Golf Course—*locale* PA-2
Blue Mountain Well—*well* UT-8
Blue Mountain West Elem Sch—*school* PA-2
Blue Mountain Work Center—*building* OR-9
Blue Mount Lake—*reservoir* PA-2
Blue Mouse Cove—*bay* AK-9
Bluemouse Sch—*school* OK-5
*Blue Mtn* AL-4
*Blue Mtn* CA-9
*Blue Mtn* NY-2
*Blue Mtn* PA-2
*Blue Mtn* TX-5
Blue Mtn—*range* PA-2
Blue Mtn—*summit* (2) AL-4
Blue Mtn—*summit* AK-9
Blue Mtn—*summit* (6) AZ-5
Blue Mtn—*summit* (2) AR-4
Blue Mtn—*summit* (9) CA-9
Blue Mtn—*summit* (6) CO-8
Blue Mtn—*summit* FL-3
Blue Mtn—*summit* (2) GA-3
Blue Mtn—*summit* (3) ID-8
Blue Mtn—*summit* MI-6
Blue Mtn—*summit* MO-7
Blue Mtn—*summit* (6) MT-8
Blue Mtn—*summit* NV-8
Blue Mtn—*summit* (2) NH-1
Blue Mtn—*summit* (3) NM-5
Blue Mtn—*summit* (4) NY-2
Blue Mtn—*summit* ND-7
Blue Mtn—*summit* (6) OK-5
Blue Mtn—*summit* (3) OR-9
Blue Mtn—*summit* TN-4
Blue Mtn—*summit* (2) TX-5
Blue Mtn—*summit* (2) UT-8
Blue Mtn—*summit* (2) VT-1
Blue Mtn—*summit* VA-3
Blue Mtn—*summit* (6) WA-9
Blue Mtn—*summit* VI-3
Blue Mtn Knob—*summit* AR-4
Blue Mtn Plateau—*summit* UT-8
Blue Mtn Summit—*summit* OR-9
Blue Mud Canyon—*valley* CA-9
*Blue Mud Creek* NC-3
Bluo Mud Creek—*stream* NC-3
Blue Mud Hills—*spring* MT-8
Blue Mud Spring—*spring* AZ-5
Blue Mud Spring—*spring* CO-8
Blue Mud Spring—*spring* ID-8
Blue Mud Valley—*valley* TN-4
Blue M Well—*well* NM-5
Blue Nose—*summit* ID-8
Blue Nose—*summit* MT-8
Blue Nose Bluff—*cliff* CA-9
Blue Nose Creek—*stream* WY-8
Bluenose Mesa—*summit* CO-8
Blue Nose Mine—*mine* AZ-5
Blue Nose Mine—*mine* CA-9
Blue Nose Mtn—*summit* CA-9
Bluenose Peak—*summit* CA-9
Blue Nose Peak—*summit* NV-8
Blue Nose Ravine—*valley* CA-9
Blue Nose Ridge—*ridge* CA-9
Bluenose Ridge—*ridge* CA-9
Bluenose Rock—*summit* CA-9
Blue Notch—*gap* (2) UT-8
Blue Notch Canyon—*valley* UT-8
Blue Oak Recreation Site—*locale* CA-9
Blue Oaks—*locale* VA-3
Blue Oak Spring—*spring* CA-9
*Blue One Beach* MH-9
Blue Ouachita Mountain—*ridge* AR-4
*Blue Outtee Creek* AL-4
Blue Palm Mobile Home Park—*locale* AZ-5
Blue Paradise Lake—*lake* MT-8
*Blue Park* CO-8
Blue Park—*flat* (2) CO-8
*Blue Pass Canyon* UT-8
Blue Pasture Windmill—*locale* NM-5
Blue Peak—*summit* (2) AZ-5
Blue Peak—*summit* UT-8
Blue Peak Canyon—*valley* AZ-5
Blue Pennant—*locale* WV-2
Blue Pete Lake—*lake* FL-3
Blue Peter Lake—*lake* FL-3
Blue Pit—*cave* AL-4
Blue Pit Rsvr—*reservoir* WY-8
Blue Place Well—*well* NM-5
Blue Plains—*locale* DC-2
Blue Plateau—*plain* AZ-5
Blue Plate Mine—*mine* ID-8
*Blue Plum Station* TN-4
*Blue Plum Station Post Office* TN-4
*Blue Point* CA-9
*Blue Point* ID-8
Blue Point—*area* AR-4
Blue Point—*cape* AR-4
Blue Point—*cape* (2) LA-4
Blue Point—*cape* MD-2
Blue Point—*cape* MS-4
Blue Point—*cape* (2) NY-2
Blue Point—*cliff* (3) AZ-5
Blue Point—*cliff* WA-9
Blue Point—*cliff* WY-8
**Blue Point**—*pop pl* IL-6
**Blue Point**—*pop pl* ME-1
**Blue Point**—*pop pl* NY-2
Blue Point—*summit* AZ-5
Blue Point—*summit* (3) CA-9
Blue Point—*summit* MT-8
Blue Point—*summit* NV-8
Bluepoint Bay—*bay* NV-8
Blue Point Beach—*beach* NY-2
Blue Point Branch—*stream* MD-2
Blue Point Campground—*locale* CA-9
Blue Point Campground—*locale* ID-8
Blue Point Cem—*cemetery* IA-7
Blue Point Ch—*church* IL-6
*Blue Point Creek* ID-8
Blue Point Creek—*stream* IL-6
Blue Point Ditch—*canal* AR-4
Blue Point Farm—*locale* MS-4
Blue Point Forest Camp—*locale* AZ-5
Blue Point Hill—*summit* ME-1
Blue Point (historical P.O.)—*locale* IA-7
Blue Point Lodge—*locale* AR-4
Blue Point Mine—*mine* CA-9
Blue Point Picnic Area—*park* AZ-5
Blue Point Ranger Station—*locale* AZ-5
Blue Point Ridge—*ridge* CA-9
Blue Point Sch—*school* IL-6
*Bluepoint Spring* NV-8
Blue Point Spring—*spring* NV-8
*Blue Pond* FL-3
*Blue Pond* MO-7
Blue Pond—*lake* (6) AL-4
Blue Pond—*lake* CA-9
Blue Pond—*lake* (7) FL-3
Blue Pond—*lake* (2) GA-3
Blue Pond—*lake* KY-4
Blue Pond—*lake* LA-4
Blue Pond—*lake* ME-1
Blue Pond—*lake* (2) MD-2
Blue Pond—*lake* MA-1
Blue Pond—*lake* MO-7
Blue Pond—*lake* NH-1
Blue Pond—*lake* (4) NY-2
Blue Pond—*lake* NC-3
Blue Pond—*lake* RI-1
Blue Pond—*lake* TN-4
Blue Pond—*lake* UT-8
Blue Pond—*lake* VT-1
Blue Pond—*locale* AL-4
Blue Pond—*reservoir* AL-4
Blue Pond—*reservoir* MS-4
Blue Pond—*reservoir* (2) NC-3
Blue Pond—*reservoir* RI-1
Blue Pond—*swamp* TX-5
Blue Pond Bay—*locale* NC-3
Blue Pond Ch—*church* GA-3
Blue Pond Dam—*dam* (2) NC-3
Blue Pond Dam—*dam* RI-1
Blue Pond Ditch—*canal* IN-6
Blue Pond Fork—*stream* KY-4
Blue Pond (historical)—*lake* IN-6
Blue Pond (historical)—*lake* TN-4
Blue Pond Post Office (historical)—*building* AL-4
Blue Pond Rec Area—*park* AL-4
Blue Pond Spring—*spring* ID-8
**Blue Pond (subdivision)**—*pop pl* AL-4
Blue Pool—*lake* WA-9
Blue Pool Forest Camp—*locale* OR-9
Blue Pool Spring—*spring* TX-5
Blue Post Office—*building* AZ-5
*Blue Purden Swamp* FL-3
Blue Quartz Mine—*mine* CA-9
Blue Quartz Mine—*mine* NV-8
*Blue Range* CO-8
Blue Range—*range* AZ-5
Blue Range—*range* TX-5
Blue Ranger Station—*locale* AZ-5
**Blue Rapids**—*pop pl* KS-7
**Blue Rapids City Township**—*pop pl* KS-7
Blue Rapids Library—*hist pl* KS-7
**Blue Rapids Township**—*pop pl* KS-7
Blue Ravine—*valley* (3) CA-9
**Blue Ribbon Acres Subdivision**—*pop pl* UT-8
Blue Ribbon Airp—*airport* WA-9
Blue Ribbon Ch—*church* OK-5
Blue Ribbon Creek—*stream* CO-8
Blue Ribbon Mine—*mine* CO-8
Blue Ribbon Mine—*mine* ID-8
Blue Ribbon Mine—*mine* NV-8
Blue Ribbon Mine—*mine* OR-9
Blue Ribbon Mine—*mine* UT-8
Blue Ribbon Mtn—*summit* ID-8
Blue Ribbon Summit—*summit* UT-8
Blue Ribbon Tank—*reservoir* AZ-5
Blue Ridge—*locale* IL-6
Blue Ridge—*locale* NY-2
Blue Ridge—*locale* TX-5
**Blue Ridge**—*pop pl* GA-3
**Blue Ridge**—*pop pl* IN-6
**Blue Ridge**—*pop pl* MS-4
**Blue Ridge**—*pop pl* MO-7
**Blue Ridge**—*pop pl* (3) NC-3
**Blue Ridge**—*pop pl* PA-2
**Blue Ridge**—*pop pl* SC-3
**Blue Ridge**—*pop pl* TN-4
**Blue Ridge**—*pop pl* TX-5
**Blue Ridge**—*pop pl* VA-3
Blue Ridge—*range* NC-3
Blue Ridge—*range* TN-4
Blue Ridge—*range* VA-3
Blue Ridge—*ridge* (2) AL-4
Blue Ridge—*ridge* (3) AZ-5
Blue Ridge—*ridge* AR-4
Blue Ridge—*ridge* (17) CA-9
Blue Ridge—*ridge* (4) CO-8
Blue Ridge—*ridge* (2) GA-3
Blue Ridge—*ridge* (2) ID-8
Blue Ridge—*ridge* IL-6
Blue Ridge—*ridge* KY-4
Blue Ridge—*ridge* (2) ME-1
Blue Ridge—*ridge* MD-2
Blue Ridge—*ridge* MI-6
Blue Ridge—*ridge* (2) MT-8
Blue Ridge—*ridge* NV-8
Blue Ridge—*ridge* (2) NH-1
Blue Ridge—*ridge* (3) NY-2
Blue Ridge—*ridge* NC-3
Blue Ridge—*ridge* (2) OH-6
Blue Ridge—*ridge* (4) OR-9
Blue Ridge—*ridge* PA-2
Blue Ridge—*ridge* SC-3
Blue Ridge—*ridge* TN-4
Blue Ridge—*ridge* (2) TX-5
Blue Ridge—*ridge* (3) UT-8
Blue Ridge—*ridge* (3) WA-9
Blue Ridge—*ridge* (3) WV-2
Blue Ridge—*ridge* WI-6
Blue Ridge—*ridge* (5) WY-8
Blue Ridge Acad—*school* NC-3
Blue Ridge Academy—*other* VA-3
**Blue Ridge Acres**—*pop pl* WV-2
Blue Ridge Assembly Hist Dist—*hist pl* NC-3
Blue Ridge Baptist Ch—*church* AL-4
Blue Ridge Branch—*stream* NC-3
Blue Ridge Cabin—*locale* ID-8
Blue Ridge Camp—*locale* CA-9
Blue Ridge Campground—*park* AZ-5
Blue Ridge Catchment Dam—*dam* AZ-5
Blue Ridge (CCD)—*cens area* GA-3
Blue Ridge (CCD)—*cens area* TX-5
Blue Ridge Cem—*cemetery* AL-4
Blue Ridge Cem—*cemetery* IL-6
Blue Ridge Cem—*cemetery* IN-6
Blue Ridge Cem—*cemetery* IA-7
Blue Ridge Cem—*cemetery* (2) MO-7
Blue Ridge Cem—*cemetery* NE-7
Blue Ridge Cem—*cemetery* OH-6
Blue Ridge Cem—*cemetery* OK-5
Blue Ridge Cem—*cemetery* PA-2
Blue Ridge Cem—*cemetery* (2) TX-5
Blue Ridge Cem—*cemetery* VA-3
Blue Ridge Ch—*church* KY-4
Blue Ridge Ch—*church* LA-4
Blue Ridge Ch—*church* MS-4
Blue Ridge Ch—*church* (3) NC-3
Blue Ridge Ch—*church* (2) SC-3
Blue Ridge Ch—*church* TN-4
Blue Ridge Ch—*church* TX-5
Blue Ridge Ch—*church* (4) VA-3
Blue Ridge Chapel—*church* GA-3
Blue Ridge Chapel—*church* (2) VA-3
Blue Ridge Ch (historical)—*church* GA-3
Blue Ridge Corral Picnic Area—*area* MO-7
Blue Ridge Country Club—*other* PA-2
Blue Ridge Creek—*stream* OR-9
Blue Ridge Dam—*dam* AZ-5
Blue Ridge Dam—*dam* GA-3
Blue Ridge Depot—*hist pl* GA-3
Blue Ridge Elem Sch—*school* AZ-5
**Blue Ridge Estates**—*pop pl* AL-4
**Blue Ridge Estates**—*pop pl* TN-4
**Blue Ridge Estates (subdivision)**—*pop pl* AL-4
Blue Ridge Farm—*locale* TX-5
**Blue Ridge Farms**—*pop pl* VA-3
**Blue Ridge Forest**—*pop pl* NC-3
Blue Ridge Fork—*stream* KY-4
Blue Ridge Gap—*gap* (2) GA-3
Blue Ridge Gap—*gap* NC-3
Blue Ridge Gap—*gap* TN-4
Blue Ridge Golf Course (historical)—*locale* TN-4
*Blue Ridge Hill* ID-8
Blue Ridge Hill—*summit* KY-4
Blue Ridge Hills Lake—*reservoir* NC-3
Blue Ridge Hills Lake Dam—*dam* NC-3
Blue Ridge (historical P.O.)—*locale* IN-6
Blue Ridge HS—*school* AZ-5
Blue Ridge HS—*school* SC-3
Blue Ridge HS—*school* VA-3
Blue Ridge JHS—*school* AZ-5
Blue Ridge Lake—*reservoir* GA-3
Blue Ridge Lake Rec Area—*park* GA-3
Blue Ridge Lawn Cem—*cemetery* MO-7
Blue Ridge Lookout—*locale* CA-9
Blue Ridge Lookout Tower—*locale* CA-9
Blue Ridge Lookout Tower—*locale* PA-2
Blue Ridge (Magisterial District)—*fmr MCD* (5) VA-3
Blue Ridge Maintenance Yard—*locale* AZ-5
Blue Ridge Mall—*locale* MO-7
Blue Ridge Mall—*locale* NC-3
**Blue Ridge Manor**—*pop pl* KY-4
**Blue Ridge Manor**—*pop pl* MD-2
**Blue Ridge Manor (subdivision)**—*pop pl* PA-2
Blue Ridge Memorial Cem—*cemetery* NC-3
Blue Ridge Memorial Gardens—*cemetery* PA-2
Blue Ridge Memorial Gardens—*cemetery* WV-2
Blue Ridge Memorial Gardens Cem—*cemetery* VA-3
Blue Ridge Mill—*locale* VA-3
Blue Ridge Mine—*mine* WA-9
*Blue Ridge Mountains* AL-4
**Blue Ridge Mountains Estates**—*pop pl* VA-3
Blue Ridge MS—*school* VA-3
Blue Ridge Mtn—*summit* AZ-5
Blue Ridge Mtn—*summit* (2) NY-2
Blue Ridge Mtn—*summit* PA-2
Blue Ridge Mtn—*summit* VT-1
*Blue Ridge of the Alagany Mountains, The* NC-3
Blue Ridge Oil Field—*oilfield* TX-5
**Blue Ridge Overlook (subdivision)**—*pop pl* NC-3
Blue Ridge Park—*park* MO-7
Blue Ridge Park—*park* PA-2
Blueridge Park—*park* TX-5
Blue Ridge Parkway—*park* NC-3
Blue Ridge Parkway—*park* VA-3
Blue Ridge Parkway (Also NC)—*park* VA-3
Blue Ridge Parkway (Also VA)—*park* NC-3
*Blue Ridge Parkway Rec Area* NC-3
Blue Ridge Plaza—*locale* MO-7
Blue Ridge Ranch—*locale* CA-9
Blue Ridge Range—*ridge* NY-2
Blue Ridge Ranger Station—*locale* GA-3
Blue Ridge (RR name for Blue Ridge Summit)—*other* PA-2
Blue Ridge Rsvr—*reservoir* AZ-5
Blue Ridge Rsvr—*reservoir* WY-8
Blue Ridge Run—*stream* OH-6
Blue Ridge Sanatorium—*hospital* VA-3
Blue Ridge Sch—*school* AL-4
Blue Ridge Sch—*school* IL-6
Blue Ridge Sch—*school* KS-7
Blue Ridge Sch—*school* LA-4
Blue Ridge Sch—*school* (3) MO-7
Blue Ridge Sch—*school* NE-7
Blue Ridge Sch—*school* TX-5
Blue Ridge Sch—*school* WV-2
Blue Ridge Sch (historical)—*school* (2) GA-3
Blue Ridge Sch (historical)—*school* TN-4
Blue Ridge Sch No 130—*school* KS-7
Blue Ridge School, The—*school* VA-3
**Blue Ridge Shores**—*pop pl* VA-3
Blue Ridge Ski Lift—*other* CA-9
Blue Ridge Special Creek—*stream* IL-6
Blue Ridge Spring—*spring* OR-9
Blue Ridge Springs—*spring* CA-9
Blue Ridge State Prison Farm—*other* TX-5
Blue Ridge Station—*locale* PA-2
**Blue Ridge Summit**—*pop pl* PA-2
**Blue Ridge Summit (RR name Blue Ridge)**—*pop pl* PA-2
Blue Ridge Swag—*gap* GA-3
Blue Ridge Tabernacle—*church* (2) NC-3
Blue Ridge Tabernacle—*church* VA-3
Blue Ridge Tabernacle—*locale* VA-3
Blue Ridge Tank—*reservoir* AZ-5
Blueridge Tank—*reservoir* AZ-5
Blue Ridge Technical Coll—*school* NC-3
**Blue Ridge Township**—*pop pl* ND-7
Blue Ridge (Township of)—*fmr MCD* AR-4
Blue Ridge (Township of)—*fmr MCD* (2) NC-3
**Blue Ridge (Township of)**—*pop pl* IL-6
Blue Ridge Trail—*trail* TN-4
Blue Ridge Tunnel—*tunnel* VA-3
**Blue Ridge View**—*pop pl* MD-2
**Blue Ridge View**—*pop pl* TN-4
Blue Ridge Windmill—*locale* TX-5
Blue Ridge Y M C A Camp—*locale* NC-3
Blue Rim—*cliff* (2) WY-8
Blue Rim Drift Fence—*other* WY-8
Blue Rim Rsvr No 1—*reservoir* WY-8
Blue Rim Rsvr No 2—*reservoir* WY-8
Blue Rim Rsvr No 3—*reservoir* WY-8
Blue Rim Rsvr No 4—*reservoir* WY-8
*Blue River* AZ-5
*Blue River* CO-8
*Blue River* IN-6
*Blue River* KS-7
*Blue River* NE-7
Blue River—*locale* KY-4
**Blue River**—*pop pl* CO-8
**Blue River**—*pop pl* IN-6
**Blue River**—*pop pl* OR-9
**Blue River**—*pop pl* WI-6
Blue River—*stream* AK-9
Blue River—*stream* (2) AZ-5
Blue River—*stream* CO-8
Blue River—*stream* (2) IN-6
Blue River—*stream* KS-7
Blue River—*stream* MO-7
Blue River—*stream* NM-5
Blue River—*stream* OK-5
Blue River—*stream* OR-9
Blue River—*stream* WI-6
Blue River Arm—*bay* CO-8
Blue River Branch—*stream* KY-4
Blue River Campground—*locale* CO-8
Blue River Cave—*cave* AL-4
Blue River Cem—*cemetery* WI-6
Blue River Ch—*church* (8) IN-6
Blue River Chapel—*church* (2) IN-6
*Blue River City* NE-7
Blue River Dam—*dam* OK-5
Blue River Dam—*dam* OR-9
Blue River German Ch—*church* IN-6
Blue River Island—*island* KY-4
Blue River Lake—*reservoir* OR-9
**Blue River Lodge**—*pop pl* NE-7
Blue River Mill Sch—*school* WI-6
Blue River Mound—*summit* IN-6
Blue River One Hundred One Trail—*trail* AZ-5
Blue River Pasture—*flat* AZ-5
Blue River Ranch Lakes—*lake* CO-8
*Blue River Rsvr* OR-9
Blue River Spring—*spring* (2) AZ-5
Blue River State Rec Area—*park* NE-7
**Blue River (Township of)**—*pop pl* (4) IN-6
Blue River Valley Ch—*church* WI-6
Blue River Wildlife Area*—*park* KS-7
**Blueroan**—*pop pl* TX-5
*Blue Rock* AL-4
*Blue Rock* TN-4
Blue Rock—*bar* AL-4
Blue Rock—*bar* MS-4
Blue Rock—*cliff* PA-2
Blue Rock—*locale* WV-2
Blue Rock—*pillar* CA-9
Blue Rock—*pillar* (3) OR-9
Blue Rock—*pillar* VT-1
**Blue Rock**—*pop pl* NC-3
**Blue Rock**—*pop pl* OH-6
Blue Rock—*rock* WV-2
Blue Rock—*stream* ID-8
Blue Rock—*summit* AZ-5
Blue Rock—*summit* CA-9
Blue Rock—*summit* GA-3
Blue Rock Bluff—*cliff* AL-4
Blue Rock Branch—*stream* NC-3
Blue Rock Butte—*summit* AZ-5
Blue Rock Canyon—*valley* NV-8
Blue Rock Canyon—*valley* NM-5
Blue Rock Cem—*cemetery* OH-6
Blue Rock Ch—*church* MO-7
Blue Rock Ch—*church* OH-6
Blue Rock Ch—*church* VA-3
Blue Rock Coal Mine—*mine* WY-8
Blue Rock Creek—*stream* CA-9
Blue Rock Creek—*stream* ID-8
Blue Rock Creek—*stream* (2) OH-6
Blue Rock (historical)—*locale* AL-4
Bluerock Knob—*summit* NC-3
Blue Rock Knob—*summit* NC-3
Blue Rock Knob—*summit* WV-2
Blue Rock Lake—*lake* ID-8
Blue Rock Lake—*lake* MN-6
Blue Rock Landing (historical)—*locale* AL-4
Blue Rock Lookout Tower—*locale* OH-6
**Blue Rock Manor**—*pop pl* DE-2
Bluerock Mtn—*summit* CA-9
Blue Rock Mtn—*summit* NC-3
Bluerock Mtn—*summit* NC-3
Blue Rock Mtn—*summit* TN-4
Blue Rock Ridge—*ridge* CA-9
Blue Rocks—*summit* (2) CA-9
Blue Rocks—*summit* PA-2
*Blue Rocks Block Field* PA-2
Blue Rock Sch—*school* PA-2
Blue Rock Shoals—*bar* TN-4
Blue Rock Spring—*spring* AZ-5
Bluerock Spring—*spring* CA-9
Blue Rock Spring—*spring* CA-9
Blue Rock Spring—*spring* CO-8
Blue Rock Spring—*spring* NV-8
Bluerock Spring—*spring* UT-8
Blue Rock Springs Creek—*stream* CA-9
Blue Rock Springs Park—*park* CA-9
Blue Rock State For—*forest* OH-6
Blue Rock State Res—*park* OH-6
Blue Rock Tank—*reservoir* (3) AZ-5
Blue Rock Tank—*reservoir* NM-5
**Blue Rock (Township of)**—*pop pl* OH-6
Blue Rock Trail—*trail* OR-9
Blue Rose Mine (surface)—*mine* TN-4
Blue Rsvr—*reservoir* OR-9
Blue Rsvr—*reservoir* WY-8
Blue Run—*stream* FL-3
Blue Run—*stream* KY-4
Blue Run—*stream* (3) PA-2
Blue Run—*stream* (2) VA-3
Blue Run—*stream* WV-2
Blue Run Ch—*church* OH-6
Blue Run Sch—*school* LA-4
Blue Run Trail—*trail* PA-2
*Blues* UT-8
Blues, The—*summit* UT-8
Blue Sack Landing (historical)—*locale* MS-4
Blue Sands Canyon—*valley* OR-9
Blues Armory—*hist pl* VA-3
**Blues Beach**—*pop pl* WV-2
Blue Sch—*school* AZ-5
Blue Sch—*school* (2) IL-6
Blue Sch—*school* NH-1
Blue Sch—*school* NY-2
Blue Sch—*school* TX-5
Blue Sch—*school* WI-6
Blue Sch (abandoned)—*school* MO-7
Blue Sch (historical)—*school* MO-7
Blue Sch (historical)—*school* PA-2
Blueschist Narrows—*basin* CA-9
*Blues Creek* MS-4
Blues Creek—*stream* FL-3
Blues Creek—*stream* OH-6
Blues Creek Cem—*cemetery* OH-6
*Blues Crossing* NC-3
Blue Sea Community Bldg—*building* IN-6
Blue Sea Creek—*stream* NC-3
Blue Sea Falls—*falls* NC-3
*Blue Sea Fork* NC-3
Blue Sea Gap—*gap* WV-2
*Bluesee Creek* NC-3
Blue Seep Mtn—*summit* TX-5
Blues Gap—*gap* PA-2
Blues Gap Run—*stream* PA-2
Blues Grove Ch—*church* NC-3
Blue Shanty Canal—*canal* FL-3
Blue Shawnee Creek—*stream* MO-7
Blue Sink—*basin* (8) FL-3
Blue Sink—*lake* FL-3
Blue Sink—*lake* GA-3
Blue Sink Pond—*lake* FL-3
Blues Island—*island* GA-3
Blueskin Creek—*stream* MS-4
Blue Sky—*locale* TN-4
*Bluesky Creek* MT-8
Blue Sky Creek—*stream* MT-8
Bluesky Creek—*stream* MT-8
Blue Sky Hotel Camp—*locale* OR-9
Blue Sky Lake—*lake* MN-6
Blue Sky Mobile Estates—*locale* AZ-5
Blue Sky Park—*park* OH-6
Blues Lake—*lake* GA-3
Blue Slate Hills—*summit* UT-8
Blue Slide—*cliff* MT-8
Blue Slide—*cliff* WA-9
Blueslide—*locale* WA-9
Blue Slide—*slope* (2) CA-9
Blue Slide—*slope* NV-8
Blue Slide—*summit* CA-9
Blue Slide, The—*cliff* MT-8
Blue Slide Campground—*locale* MT-8
*Blue Slide Creek* CA-9
*Blueslide Creek* OR-9
Blue Slide Creek—*stream* (5) CA-9
Blue Slide Creek—*stream* OR-9
Blue Slide Fork—*stream* UT-8
*Blue Slide Lake* CA-9
Blue Slide Lookout Tower—*locale* WA-9
*Blue Slide Ridge* CA-9
*Blue Slides* CA-9
Blue Slides Creek—*stream* CA-9
Blue Slides Lake—*lake* CA-9
Blue Slides Ridge—*ridge* CA-9
Blue Slough—*stream* WA-9
Blues Mtn—*summit* NC-3
Blue Snow Lake—*lake* MN-6
Blue Sog—*swamp* FL-3
**Blues Old Stand**—*pop pl* AL-4
Blue Sow—*bar* MD-2
Blue Sox Sadium—*other* TX-5
Blue Sphinx Mine—*mine* NV-8
Blue Spjring—*spring* TN-4
Blues Pond—*reservoir* MO-7
*Blue Spring* AL-4
*Blue Spring* FL-3
*Blue Spring* GA-3
*Blue Spring* MO-7
*Blue Spring* NE-7

Blue Spring—*locale* KY-4
Blue Spring—*locale* PA-2
Blue Spring—*locale* TN-4
Blue Spring—*locale* WV-2
**Blue Spring**—*pop pl* TN-4
Blue Spring—*spring* (21) AL-4
Blue Spring—*spring* (6) AZ-5
Blue Spring—*spring* (3) AR-4
Blue Spring—*spring* (2) CA-9
Blue Spring—*spring* (3) CO-8
Blue Spring—*spring* (5) FL-3
Blue Spring—*spring* (5) GA-3
Blue Spring—*spring* (2) ID-8
Blue Spring—*spring* IA-7
Blue Spring—*spring* (3) KY-4
Blue Spring—*spring* (12) MO-7
Blue Spring—*spring* MT-8
Blue Spring—*spring* (3) NV-8
Blue Spring—*spring* (3) NM-5
Blue Spring—*spring* OK-5
Blue Spring—*spring* (6) OR-9
Blue Spring—*spring* (2) PA-2
Blue Spring—*spring* SC-3
Blue Spring—*spring* (26) TN-4
Blue Spring—*spring* (3) TX-5
Blue Spring—*spring* (6) UT-8
Blue Spring—*spring* (3) VA-3
Blue Spring—*spring* WY-8
Blue Spring Baptist Ch—*church* AL-4
*Blue Spring Branch* AL-4
*Blue Spring Branch* GA-3
Blue Spring Branch—*stream* (4) AL-4
Blue Spring Branch—*stream* AR-4
Blue Spring Branch—*stream* (4) GA-3
Blue Spring Branch—*stream* (7) KY-4
Blue Spring Branch—*stream* MS-4
Blue Spring Branch—*stream* MO-7
Blue Spring Branch—*stream* NC-3
Blue Spring Branch—*stream* OK-5
Blue Spring Branch—*stream* (8) TN-4
Bluespring Branch—*stream* TN-4
Blue Spring Branch—*stream* TX-5
Blue Spring Brook—*stream* AL-4
Blue Spring Campsite—*park* MO-7
Blue Spring Canyon—*valley* AZ-5
Blue Spring Canyon—*valley* NV-8
*Blue Spring Cave* AL-4
Blue Spring Cave—*cave* AL-4
Blue Spring Cave—*cave* TN-4
Blue Spring Caves—*cave* PA-2
Blue Spring Cem—*cemetery* AL-4
Blue Spring Cem—*cemetery* MO-7
Blue Spring Cem—*cemetery* (3) TN-4
Blue Spring Cem—*cemetery* TX-5
Blue Spring Ch—*church* GA-3
Blue Spring Ch—*church* (3) KY-4
Blue Spring Ch—*church* MS-4
Blue Spring Ch—*church* (2) MO-7
Bluespring Ch—*church* TN-4
Blue Spring Ch—*church* (8) TN-4
Blue Spring Ch—*church* (2) VA-3
Blue Spring Chapel—*church* AL-4
Blue Spring Cove—*valley* AL-4
Blue Spring Cove—*valley* (2) TN-4
*Blue Spring Creek* AL-4
*Blue Spring Creek* MO-7
*Blue Spring Creek* UT-8
*Blue Spring Creek* VA-3
Blue Spring Creek—*stream* AL-4
Blue Spring Creek—*stream* FL-3
Blue Spring Creek—*stream* (2) ID-8
Blue Spring Creek—*stream* (2) KY-4
Blue Spring Creek—*stream* MO-7
Blue Spring Creek—*stream* PA-2
Blue Spring Creek—*stream* (6) TN-4
Blue Spring Creek—*stream* (3) UT-8
Blue Spring Creek—*stream* (2) VA-3
Blue Spring Draw—*valley* CO-8
Blue Spring Draw—*valley* TX-5
Blue Spring Estates—*locale* KY-4
Blue Spring Fork—*stream* AL-4
Blue Spring Gap—*gap* VA-3
**Blue Spring Garden (subdivision)**—*pop pl* AL-4
Blue Spring Gulch—*valley* OR-9
Blue Spring Hill—*summit* VA-3
*Blue Spring Hills* ID-8
Blue Spring Hills—*range* UT-8
Blue Spring (historical)—*locale* AL-4
Blue Spring Hollow—*valley* AL-4
Blue Spring Hollow—*valley* (2) AR-4
Blue Spring Hollow—*valley* IL-6
Blue Spring Hollow—*valley* IN-6
Blue Spring Hollow—*valley* MO-7
Blue Spring Hollow—*valley* PA-2
Blue Spring Hollow—*valley* (3) TN-4
*Blue Spring Island* TN-4
Blue Spring Island Shoals—*bar* TN-4
Blue Spring Lake—*lake* AL-4
Blue Spring Lake—*lake* FL-3
Blue Spring Lake—*lake* WI-6
Blue Spring Mine—*mine* TN-4
Blue Spring Mtn—*summit* UT-8
Blue Spring Pond—*lake* MO-7
Blue Spring (Post Office)—*locale* AL-4
Blue Spring Ridge—*ridge* TN-4
Blue Spring River Access—*locale* MO-7
Blue Spring Run—*locale* VA-3
Blue Spring Run—*stream* VA-3
*Blue Springs* GA-3
*Blue Springs* KY-4
*Blue Springs* TN-4
Blue Springs—*locale* AL-4
Blue Springs—*locale* FL-3
Blue Springs—*locale* GA-3
Blue Springs—*locale* MO-7
Blue Springs—*locale* (2) TN-4
Blue Springs—*locale* TX-5
**Blue Springs**—*pop pl* (4) AL-4
**Blue Springs**—*pop pl* AR-4
**Blue Springs**—*pop pl* (2) FL-3
**Blue Springs**—*pop pl* GA-3
**Blue Springs**—*pop pl* MS-4
**Blue Springs**—*pop pl* MO-7
**Blue Springs**—*pop pl* NE-7
**Blue Springs**—*pop pl* TN-4
Blue Springs—*spring* AR-4
Blue Springs—*spring* (6) FL-3
Blue Springs—*spring* (3) GA-3
Blue Springs—*spring* KY-4
Blue Springs—*spring* MS-4
Blue Springs—*spring* (2) MO-7
Blue Springs—*spring* TN-4
Blue Springs—*spring* (2) UT-8
Blue Springs—*spring* (2) WI-6
Blue Springs—*spring* WY-8
Blue Springs Acad (historical)—*school* TN-4
Blue Springs Bank Mine—*mine* TN-4
*Blue Springs Baptist Ch* AL-4
Blue Springs Baptist Ch—*church* AL-4
Blue Springs Baptist Ch—*church* MS-4
Blue Springs Boy Scouts Camp—*locale* FL-3
*Blue Springs Branch* TN-4
Blue Springs Branch—*stream* AL-4
Blue Springs Branch—*stream* AR-4
Blue Springs Branch—*stream* MS-4
Blue Springs Branch—*stream* MO-7
Blue Springs Branch—*stream* (3) TN-4
Blue Springs Branch—*stream* VA-3
Blue Springs Campground—*locale* UT-8
Blue Springs Cave—*cave* PA-2
*Blue Springs Cem* AL-4
Blue Springs Cem—*cemetery* (5) AL-4
Blue Springs Cem—*cemetery* AR-4
Blue Springs Cem—*cemetery* GA-3
Blue Springs Cem—*cemetery* MS-4
Blue Springs Cem—*cemetery* (2) MO-7
Blue Springs Cem—*cemetery* NE-7
Blue Springs Cem—*cemetery* (2) TN-4
Blue Springs Ch—*church* (5) AL-4
Blue Springs Ch—*church* AR-4
Blue Springs Ch—*church* FL-3
Blue Springs Ch—*church* (3) GA-3
Blue Springs Ch—*church* MS-4
Blue Springs Ch—*church* MO-7
Blue Springs Ch—*church* (2) OK-5
Blue Springs Ch—*church* TN-4
Blue Springs Ch—*church* VA-3
Blue Spring Sch—*school* MO-7
Blue Spring Sch—*school* PA-2
Blue Spring Sch (historical)—*school* TN-4
*Blue Spring School* TN-4
*Blue Springs Creek* KY-4
*Blue Springs Creek* UT-8
Blue Springs Creek—*stream* AL-4
Blue Springs Creek—*stream* CO-8
Blue Springs Creek—*stream* GA-3
Blue Springs Creek—*stream* MO-7
Blue Springs Dock—*locale* TN-4
Blue Springs Draw—*valley* NM-5
Blue Springs Draw—*valley* WY-8
Blue Springs Elem Sch—*school* TN-4
Blue Springs Fish Camp—*locale* (2) AL-4
*Blue Springs Hills* UT-8
Blue Springs (historical)—*locale* AL-4
*Blue Spring Shoals* TN-4
Blue Springs Hollow—*valley* PA-2
Blue Springs Hollow Dock—*locale* TN-4
Blue Springs Lake—*reservoir* (2) MO-7
Blue Springs Lake Access Area—*park* TN-4
Blue Springs Landing—*locale* GA-3
**Blue Springs Landing**—*pop pl* FL-3
Blue Spring Slough—*gut* TN-4
Blue Spring Slough—*stream* MO-7
Blue Springs Normal Coll (historical)—*school* MS-4
**Blue Springs Park**—*pop pl* AL-4
Blue Springs Point—*summit* CO-8
*Blue Springs Post Office* AL-4
Blue Springs Reservoir Dam—*dam* UT-8
**Blue Springs Resort**—*pop pl* TN-4
Blue Springs Ridge—*ridge* TN-4
Blue Springs Rsvr—*reservoir* UT-8
Blue Springs Run—*bay* FL-3
*Blue Springs Sch* TN-4
Blue Springs Sch—*school* AL-4
Blue Springs Sch—*school* KY-4
Blue Springs Sch—*school* OK-5
Blue Springs Sch—*school* TN-4
Blue Springs Sch (historical)—*school* (2) AL-4
Blue Springs Sch (historical)—*school* TN-4
Blue Springs Site—*hist pl* NE-7
Blue Springs Slough—*bay* TN-4
Blue Springs State Park—*park* AL-4
*Blue Spring Station Post Office* TN-4
Bluespring Station Post Office (historical)—*building* TN-4
Blue Springs Township—*civ div* NE-7
Blue Springs (Township of)—*fmr MCD* NC-3
Blue Springs Trail—*trail* AZ-5
Blue Springs Valley—*valley* TN-4
**Bluesprings Woods (subdivision)**—*pop pl* NC-3
*Blue Spring Valley* UT-8
Blue Spring Valley—*basin* UT-8
Blue Spruce Camp—*locale* OR-9
Blue Spruce Campground—*locale* CO-8
Blue Spruce Campground—*locale* UT-8
Blue Spruce Canyon—*valley* CO-8
Blue Spruce County Park—*park* PA-2
**Blue Spruce Heights Subdivision**—*pop pl* UT-8
*Blue Spruce Rock* AK-9
**Blue Spruce Subdivision**—*pop pl* UT-8
Blues Run—*stream* OH-6
Blue Star Claim—*mine* AZ-5
Blue Star Creek—*stream* OR-9
Blue Star Hollow—*valley* WV-2
Blue Star Island—*island* OK-5
Blue Star Lower Dam—*dam* NC-3
**Blue Star Meadows Subdivision**—*pop pl* UT-8
Blue Star Mine—*mine* NV-8
Blue Star Mine—*mine* UT-8
Blue Star Mine—*mine* WA-9
Blue Star Mines—*mine* CA-9
Blue Star Mobile Home Park—*locale* AZ-5
Blue Star Ridge—*ridge* ID-8
Blue Star Safety Rest Area—*locale* OR-9
Blue Star Upper Dam—*dam* NC-3
Blue Star Upper Lake—*reservoir* NC-3
Blue Steer Branch—*stream* AR-4
*Blue Stem* KS-7
Blue Stem—*bar* UT-8
Bluestem—*locale* WA-9
Blue Stem Creek—*stream* (2) KS-7
Bluestem Creek—*stream* WA-9
Bluestem Draw—*valley* CO-8
*Blue Stem Hills* KS-7
Blue Stem (historical)—*locale* KS-7
Blue Stem Lake—*lake* NE-7
Bluestem Lake—*lake* NE-7
Bluestem Lake—*reservoir* NE-7
Bluestem Lake—*reservoir* OK-5
Bluestem Sch—*school* OK-5
Bluestem Tank—*reservoir* AZ-5
Blue Stem Wash—*valley* AZ-5
Bluestocking Branch—*stream* TN-4
Bluestocking Hollow—*valley* TN-4
Blue Stocking Sch—*school* IL-6
*Blue Stone* KS-7
Bluestone—*locale* (2) PA-2
Bluestone—*other* OH-6
**Bluestone**—*pop pl* KY-4
**Bluestone**—*pop pl* VA-3
**Bluestone**—*pop pl* WV-2
Bluestone Cem—*cemetery* PA-2
Bluestone Ch—*church* GA-3
Bluestone Ch—*church* NC-3
Bluestone Ch—*church* (2) VA-3
Bluestone Ch—*church* WV-2
Bluestone Conference Center—*locale* WV-2
Bluestone Creek—*stream* AK-9
Bluestone Creek—*stream* GA-3
Bluestone Creek—*stream* VA-3
Bluestone Creek—*stream* WV-2
Bluestone Dam—*dam* WV-2
Bluestone HS—*school* VA-3
Bluestone Lake—*reservoir* VA-3
Bluestone Lake—*reservoir* WV-2
Bluestone Landing—*locale* VA-3
Bluestone (Magisterial District)—*fmr MCD* VA-3
Bluestone Mine—*mine* NV-8
Bluestone Mtn—*summit* WV-2
Blue Stone Peak—*summit* MT-8
Bluestone Public Hunting And Fishing Area—*park* WV-2
Bluestone Quarry—*mine* PA-2
*Bluestone Reservoir* VA-3
*Bluestone Reservoir* WV-2
*Bluestone Ridge* WV-2
Bluestone Ridge—*ridge* CA-9
Bluestone River—*stream* AK-9
Bluestone River—*stream* VA-3
Bluestone River—*stream* WV-2
Bluestone River (Magisterial District)—*fmr MCD* WV-2
*Bluestone Run* WV-2
Bluestone Run—*stream* PA-2
Bluestone Sch—*school* WV-2
Bluestone State Park—*park* WV-2
Bluestone Valley Ditch—*canal* CO-8
Bluestone View Ch—*church* WV-2
**Blue Store**—*pop pl* NY-2
*Blue Stores* NY-2
**Blue Stores**—*pop pl* NY-2
Blue Streak Downs—*other* MT-8
Blue Suck—*area* TN-4
Blue Suck Branch—*stream* VA-3
Blue Suck Falls—*falls* VA-3
Blue Suck Hollow—*valley* VA-3
Blue Suck Trail—*trail* VA-3
**Blue Sulphur**—*pop pl* WV-2
Blue Sulphur Burial Park (Cemetery)—*cemetery* WV-2
Blue Sulphur (Magisterial District)—*fmr MCD* WV-2
*Blue Sulphur Springs* WV-2
Blue Sulphur Springs—*locale* WV-2
**Blue Summit**—*pop pl* MO-7
*Blue Swamp* NY-2
Blue Swamp—*swamp* CT-1
Blue Swamp—*swamp* LA-4
Blue Swamp—*swamp* NY-2
Blue Swamp—*swamp* PA-2
Blue Swamp—*swamp* WI-6
Blue Swamp Creek—*stream* NY-2
*Blue Swamp Lake* WA-9
Blue Swan Airp—*airport* PA-2
Blue Tank—*reservoir* (4) AZ-5
Blue Tank—*reservoir* NM-5
Blue Tank Canyon—*valley* (2) AZ-5
Blue Tank Canyon—*valley* TX-5
Blue Tank No 1—*reservoir* NM-5
Blue Tank No 2—*reservoir* NM-5
Blue Tank Wash—*stream* (2) AZ-5
*Bluet Creek* ID-8
Blue Tent Creek—*stream* (2) CA-9
Blue Tent Sch—*school* CA-9
Blue Tom Tunnel—*tunnel* WV-2
Blue Top—*summit* ME-1
Bluetop Sch (historical)—*school* TN-4
**Bluetown**—*pop pl* TX-5
**Blue Town (Argyle)**—*pop pl* SC-3
Blue Township—*civil* MO-7
**Blue Township**—*pop pl* KS-7
Blue Trail—*trail* ME-1
Blue Trail—*trail* UT-8
Blue Trail—*trail* WY-8
Blue Trail Canyon—*valley* UT-8
Blue Trail Creek—*stream* UT-8
Blue Trigger Gulch—*valley* OR-9
Bluett—*locale* TX-5
Bluett Creek—*stream* ID-8
*Blue Two Beach* MH-9
**Blue Valley**—*pop pl* CO-8
**Blue Valley**—*pop pl* MO-7
Blue Valley—*valley* NC-3
Blue Valley—*valley* OH-6
Blue Valley—*valley* (3) UT-8
**Blue Valley Acres**—*pop pl* CO-8
**Blue Valley Acres**—*pop pl* OH-6
Blue Valley Benches—*bench* UT-8
Blue Valley Cem—*cemetery* (3) NE-7
Blue Valley Community Hall—*building* KS-7
Blue Valley HS—*school* KS-7
Blue Valley JHS—*school* KS-7
Blue Valley Park—*park* MO-7
Blue Valley Sch—*school* (2) NE-7
Blue Valley School (Abandoned)—*locale* ID-8
**Blue Valley Township**—*pop pl* KS-7
**Blueville**—*pop pl* WV-2
Blue Violet Creek—*stream* AK-9
Blue Vista—*locale* AZ-5
*Blue Vue* MO-7
Blue-Vue Shops—*locale* MO-7
*Bluewarter Creek* AL-4
*Blue Wash* AZ-5
Blue Wash—*stream* (2) AZ-5
Blue Wash—*valley* UT-8
Blue Wash Well—*well* MT-8
Blue Water—*lake* CA-9
Blue Water—*locale* AZ-5
Bluewater—*locale* NM-5
**Bluewater**—*pop pl* NM-5
Blue Water, Lake—*lake* IN-6
Bluewater Basin—*basin* CO-8
Bluewater Battlefield Overlook Site—*locale* NE-7
**Blue Water Beach**—*pop pl* MI-6
Blue Water Beach Campground—*locale* UT-8
Bluewater Branch—*stream* NC-3
Bluewater Branch—*stream* TN-4
Bluewater Branch—*stream* WV-2
Blue Water Bridge—*other* MI-6
Blue Water Camp—*locale* MI-6
Blue Water Campground—*locale* TN-4
Bluewater Canyon—*valley* CA-9
Blue Water Canyon—*valley* CO-8
Blue Water Canyon—*valley* NM-5
Bluewater Canyon—*valley* NM-5
Bluewater Cem—*cemetery* AL-4
Bluewater Cem—*cemetery* NM-5
Blue Water Cem—*cemetery* TN-4
*Blue Water Ch* AL-4
Bluewater Ch—*church* AL-4
Bluewater Ch—*church* GA-3
Bluewater Ch—*church* TN-4
Bluewater Creek—*stream* AL-4
Blue Water Creek—*stream* AL-4
Blue Water Creek—*stream* FL-3
Bluewater Creek—*stream* GA-3
Blue Water Creek—*stream* MS-4
Bluewater Creek—*stream* MO-7
Bluewater Creek—*stream* MT-8
Bluewater Creek—*stream* (3) NM-5
Blue Water Creek—*stream* NM-5
Bluewater Creek—*stream* NM-5
Bluewater Creek—*stream* TN-4
Blue Water Estates—*locale* KY-4
Bluewater Fish Hatchery—*other* MT-8
Blue Waterhole—*lake* (2) TX-5
Blue Water Hole Spring—*spring* TX-5
Blue Waterhouse Canyon—*valley* TX-5
**Blue Water Key**—*pop pl* TX-5
Bluewater Lake—*lake* MN-6
Blue Water Lake—*lake* TN-4
Bluewater Lake—*reservoir* NM-5
Bluewater Lookout Complex—*hist pl* NM-5
Bluewater Lookout Tower—*other* NM-5
Blue Water Marina Park—*park* AZ-5
Blue Water Mesa—*summit* NM-5
Blue Water Pond—*lake* VA-3
*Bluewater Primitive Baptist Church* AL-4
*Blue Water River* AL-4
Bluewater Siding—*locale* NM-5
Bluewater Spring—*spring* MT-8
Blue Water Spring—*spring* NM-5
Bluewater Spring—*spring* NM-5
Blue Water Spring—*spring* NM-5
**Bluewater (sta.)**—*pop pl* NM-5
Bluewater State Park—*park* NM-5
Blue Water Tank—*reservoir* NM-5
Bluewater Truck Trail—*trail* CA-9
Blue Water Well—*locale* NM-5
Blue Water Well—*well* NM-5
Blue Water Windmill—*locale* NM-5
**Bluewell**—*pop pl* WV-2
Blue Well—*well* NM-5
Blue Wells Hollow—*valley* IN-6
Blue Well Windmill—*locale* TX-5
Blue West Picnic Area—*locale* TX-5
Blue Windmill—*locale* NM-5
Bluewing—*locale* TN-4
Bluewing Baptist Ch—*church* TN-4
Bluewing Ch—*church* NC-3
Bluewing Ch—*church* VA-3
**Blue Wing Church**—*pop pl* NC-3
Blue Wing Cow Camp—*locale* NV-8
*Blue Wing Creek* NC-3
*Blue Wing Creek* VA-3
Bluewing Creek—*stream* NC-3
Bluewing Creek—*stream* VA-3
*Bluewing Flat* NV-8
Blue Wing Flat—*flat* NV-8
Blue Wing Lake—*lake* MN-6
Blue Wing Lake—*reservoir* TX-5
Blue Wing Marsh—*lake* IA-7
Blue Wing Marsh State Game Mngmt Area—*park* IA-7
*Bluewing Mountains* NV-8
Blue Wing Mtns—*range* NV-8
Bluewing Pond—*bay* LA-4
Bluewing Sch (historical)—*school* TN-4
Bluewing Spring—*spring* NV-8
Blue Wing State Wildlife Mngmt Area—*park* MN-6
**Bluewood Estates (subdivision)**—*pop pl* AL-4
Blue Woods Creek—*stream* IN-6
*Bluff* AL-4
*Bluff* KS-7
Bluff—*fmr MCD* NE-7
Bluff—*locale* MS-4
Bluff—*locale* TX-5
Bluff—*mine* UT-8
**Bluff**—*pop pl* AL-4
**Bluff**—*pop pl* (2) AK-9
**Bluff**—*pop pl* NC-3
**Bluff**—*pop pl* OK-5
**Bluff**—*pop pl* PA-2
**Bluff**—*pop pl* UT-8
Bluff, Bayou—*gut* LA-4
*Bluff, The* AL-4
Bluff, The—*cliff* AK-9
Bluff, The—*cliff* CA-9
Bluff, The—*cliff* (2) ME-1
Bluff, The—*cliff* MI-6
Bluff, The—*cliff* RI-1
Bluff, The—*cliff* TX-5
Bluff, The—*locale* KY-4
Bluff, The—*locale* NC-3
Bluff Airp—*airport* UT-8
**Bluff at Hidden Valley**—*pop pl* UT-8
Bluff Ave Sch—*school* IN-6
Bluff Beach—*locale* NY-2
**Bluff Beach**—*pop pl* MI-6
Bluff Bench—*bench* UT-8
Bluff Boom—*locale* KY-4
Bluff Branch—*stream* FL-3
Bluff Branch—*stream* (2) NC-3
Bluff Branch—*stream* (2) SC-3
Bluff Branch—*stream* TX-5
Bluff Bridge—*bridge* DC-2
Bluff Cabin—*locale* AK-9
Bluff Cabin Ridge—*ridge* AK-9
Bluff Camp—*locale* CA-9
Bluff Campground—*locale* CA-9
Bluff Canal—*canal* IL-6
Bluff Canal—*canal* WY-8
Bluff Canyon—*valley* TX-5
Bluff Cave—*cave* (3) AL-4
Bluff Cave—*cave* TN-4
Bluff Cem—*cemetery* AL-4
Bluff Cem—*cemetery* AR-4
Bluff Cem—*cemetery* FL-3
Bluff Cem—*cemetery* KY-4
Bluff Cem—*cemetery* TX-5
Bluff Cem—*cemetery* UT-8
Bluff Cem—*cemetery* WI-6
Bluff Center Cem (historical)—*cemetery* SD-7
**Bluff Center (historical)**—*pop pl* SD-7
Bluff Ch—*church* MO-7
Bluff Ch—*church* NC-3
Bluff Ch—*church* OK-5
Bluff Chapel—*church* MS-4
Bluff Cienega Creek—*stream* AZ-5
Bluff City—*locale* AL-4
Bluff City—*locale* IL-6
**Bluff City**—*pop pl* AR-4
**Bluff City**—*pop pl* IL-6
**Bluff City**—*pop pl* KS-7
**Bluff City**—*pop pl* KY-4
**Bluff City**—*pop pl* TN-4
**Bluff City**—*pop pl* VA-3
Bluff City Cave—*cave* AL-4
Bluff City Cem—*cemetery* AR-4
Bluff City Cem—*cemetery* IL-6
*Bluff City Elementary School* AL-4
Bluff City Elem Sch—*school* TN-4
**Bluff City (historical)**—*pop pl* TX-5
Bluff City Landing (historical)—*locale* AL-4
Bluff City MS—*school* TN-4
Bluff City-Piney Flats (CCD)—*cens area* TN-4
Bluff City-Piney Flats Division—*civil* TN-4
Bluff City Post Office—*building* TN-4
Bluff City Post Office (historical)—*building* AL-4
Bluff City Sch—*school* AL-4
Bluff City Shell Mound (15HE160)—*hist pl* KY-4
Bluff City State Nursery—*other* AR-4
Bluff Cottage—*locale* MO-7
Bluff Cove—*bay* AK-9
Bluff Cove—*bay* CA-9
Bluff Cove—*valley* GA-3
*Bluffcreek* IN-6
*Bluff Creek* KS-7
*Bluff Creek* MS-4
*Bluff Creek* TX-5
*Bluff Creek* VA-3
Bluff Creek—*locale* TN-4
**Bluff Creek**—*pop pl* CA-9
**Bluff Creek**—*pop pl* IN-6
**Bluffcreek**—*pop pl* IN-6
**Bluff Creek**—*pop pl* IA-7
**Bluff Creek**—*pop pl* LA-4
Bluff Creek—*stream* (8) AL-4
Bluff Creek—*stream* (5) AK-9
Bluff Creek—*stream* (2) AR-4
Bluff Creek—*stream* (4) CA-9
Bluff Creek—*stream* (2) FL-3
Bluff Creek—*stream* (3) GA-3
Bluff Creek—*stream* (6) ID-8
Bluff Creek—*stream* (2) IN-6
Bluff Creek—*stream* (2) IA-7
Bluff Creek—*stream* (6) KS-7
Bluff Creek—*stream* LA-4
Bluff Creek—*stream* (2) MI-6
Bluff Creek—*stream* (3) MN-6
Bluff Creek—*stream* (7) MS-4
Bluff Creek—*stream* MO-7
Bluff Creek—*stream* (2) MT-8
Bluff Creek—*stream* NV-8
Bluff Creek—*stream* NM-5
Bluff Creek—*stream* (4) OK-5
Bluff Creek—*stream* (5) OR-9
Bluff Creek—*stream* SC-3
Bluff Creek—*stream* (4) TN-4
Bluff Creek—*stream* (25) TX-5
Bluff Creek—*stream* VA-3
Bluff Creek—*stream* WA-9
Bluff Creek—*stream* (2) WI-6
Bluff Creek—*stream* WY-8
Bluff Creek Access Area—*park* AL-4
Bluff Creek Baptist Ch of Christ (historical)—*church* AL-4
*Bluff Creek Baptist Church* MS-4
Bluff Creek Bay—*swamp* FL-3
Bluff Creek Camp—*locale* AL-4
Bluff Creek Canal—*canal* OK-5
Bluff Creek Cave—*cave* AL-4
**Bluff Creek (Cedar Point)**—*pop pl* TN-4
Bluff Creek Cem—*cemetery* GA-3
Bluff Creek Cem—*cemetery* IA-7
Bluff Creek Cem—*cemetery* (3) TX-5
Bluff Creek Ch—*church* MS-4
Bluff Creek Ch—*church* TN-4
Bluff Creek Ch—*church* TX-5
Bluff Creek Hill—*summit* AL-4
Bluff Creek Missionary Baptist Ch (historical)—*church* AL-4
*Bluffcreek Post Office* TN-4
Bluff Creek Post Office (historical)—*building* TN-4
*Bluff Creek Primitive Baptist Ch* AL-4
*Bluff Creek Reservoir* OK-5
Bluff Creek Sch—*school* IA-7
Bluff Creek Sch—*school* TN-4
Bluff Creek Sch (historical)—*school* (2) MS-4
Bluff Creek Sch (historical)—*school* TN-4
Bluff Creek State Wildlife Mngmt Area—*park* MN-6
Bluff Creek Tank—*reservoir* TX-5
Bluff Creek Township—*fmr MCD* IA-7
Bluff Creek Trail—*trail* WY-8
*Bluff Creek Water Supply* OK-5
Bluff Creek Windmill—*locale* (2) TX-5
*Bluff Dale* IL-6
**Bluff Dale**—*pop pl* TX-5
**Bluffdale**—*pop pl* UT-8
Bluffdale City Cem—*cemetery* UT-8
**Bluff Dale (RR name Bluffdale)**—*pop pl* TX-5
Bluffdale (RR name for Bluff Dale)—*other* TX-5
Bluffdale Sch—*school* (2) IL-6
Bluff Dale Suspension Bridge—*hist pl* TX-5
**Bluffdale (Township of)**—*pop pl* IL-6
Bluff Ditch—*canal* IL-6
Bluff Ditch—*canal* (3) WY-8
Bluff Divide—*ridge* ID-8
Bluff Dwellers Cave—*cave* MO-7
Bluffer Brook—*stream* ME-1
Bluffer Pond—*lake* ME-1
Bluffer Ridge—*ridge* ME-1
**Bluff Estates**—*pop pl* SC-3
Bluff Experimental Forest—*park* MS-4
Bluff Falls—*falls* CA-9
Bluff Falls Campground—*locale* CA-9
Bluff Field Mtn—*summit* AR-4
Bluff Ford (historical)—*locale* TN-4
Bluff Fork—*stream* WV-2
Bluff Gulch—*valley* AK-9
Bluff Gully—*valley* TX-5
Bluff Hall—*hist pl* AL-4
Bluff Hall—*locale* IL-6
Bluff Hall Ch—*church* IL-6
Bluff Hammock—*island* FL-3
Bluff Head—*cape* (2) ME-1
Bluff Head—*cape* NY-2
Bluff Head—*cliff* CT-1
Bluff Head—*island* ME-1
Bluff Head—*summit* ME-1
Bluff Head—*summit* RI-1
Bluffhead Branch—*stream* SC-3
Bluff Head Cem—*cemetery* CT-1
Bluff Hill—*summit* MA-1
Bluff Hill—*summit* RI-1
Bluff Hill Cem—*cemetery* MO-7
Bluff Hill Ch—*church* AR-4
Bluff Hill Cove—*bay* RI-1
Bluff (historical)—*locale* MS-4
Bluff Hollow—*valley* AL-4
Bluff Hollow—*valley* AZ-5
*Bluff Island* CT-1
Bluff Island—*island* (2) AK-9
Bluff Island—*island* CT-1
Bluff Island—*island* ME-1
Bluff Island—*island* (4) NY-2
Bluff Island—*island* NC-3
Bluff Island—*island* (2) SC-3
Bluff Islands—*island* SC-3
Bluff Junction—*locale* IL-6
*Bluff Lake* MI-6
Bluff Lake—*lake* AK-9
Bluff Lake—*lake* (3) CA-9
Bluff Lake—*lake* CO-8
Bluff Lake—*lake* (3) GA-3
Bluff Lake—*lake* (2) IL-6
Bluff Lake—*lake* MI-6
Bluff Lake—*lake* SC-3
Bluff Lake—*lake* (4) WA-9
Bluff Lake—*lake* WI-6
Bluff Lake—*reservoir* CA-9
Bluff Lake—*reservoir* MS-4
Bluff Lake—*swamp* AR-4
Bluff Lake Cem—*cemetery* WI-6
Bluff Lake Dam—*dam* MS-4
Bluff Lake Sch—*school* WI-6
Bluff Lake Trail—*trail* WA-9
Bluff Landing—*locale* (2) FL-3
Bluff Lateral—*canal* ID-8
Bluff Lick Creek—*stream* LA-4
Bluff Meadow—*flat* CA-9
Bluff Mills—*cliff* TX-5
Bluff Mine—*mine* NV-8
*Bluff Mountain* AZ-5
Bluff Mountain Creek—*stream* MT-8
Bluff Mountain Overlook—*locale* NC-3
Bluff Mountain Overlook—*locale* VA-3
Bluff Mountain Tunnel—*tunnel* VA-3
Bluff Mtn—*summit* AR-4
Bluff Mtn—*summit* ME-1
Bluff Mtn—*summit* MT-8
Bluff Mtn—*summit* NY-2
Bluff Mtn—*summit* (3) NC-3
Bluff Mtn—*summit* (3) TN-4
Bluff Mtn—*summit* VT-1
Bluff Mtn—*summit* (3) VA-3
Bluff Mtn—*summit* (2) WA-9
Bluff Mtn—*summit* WV-2
Bluff No 2—*cliff* AK-9
Bluff Park—*flat* WY-8
Bluff Park—*park* CA-9
Bluff Park—*park* IA-7
**Bluff Park**—*pop pl* AL-4
**Bluff Park**—*pop pl* IA-7
Bluff Park Creek—*stream* WY-8
*Bluff Park Elementary School* AL-4
Bluff Park Sch—*school* AL-4
Bluff Park United Methodist Ch—*church* AL-4
*Bluff Point* CT-1
*Bluff Point* TN-4
*Bluff Point* VT-1
*Bluff Point* WY-8
*Bluff Point* MH-9
Bluff Point—*cape* (5) AK-9
Bluff Point—*cape* CA-9
Bluff Point—*cape* (2) CT-1
Bluff Point—*cape* DE-2
Bluff Point—*cape* (2) ME-1
Bluff Point—*cape* (3) MD-2
Bluff Point—*cape* MA-1
Bluff Point—*cape* (9) NY-2
Bluff Point—*cape* (3) NC-3
Bluff Point—*cape* SC-3
Bluff Point—*cape* (3) VA-3
Bluff Point—*cliff* AK-9
Bluff Point—*cliff* TN-4
Bluff Point—*locale* NY-2
**Bluff Point**—*pop pl* IN-6
**Bluff Point**—*pop pl* NY-2
Bluff Point—*summit* ID-8
Bluff Point—*summit* NY-2
Bluff Point—*summit* PA-2
Bluff Point Beach—*beach* CT-1
Bluff Point Cem—*cemetery* NY-2
Bluff Point Ch—*church* VA-3
Bluff Point Hill—*summit* NY-2
**Bluffpoint (historical)**—*pop pl* TN-4

Bluff Point Neck—*cape* ... VA-3
*Bluff Point Post Office* ... TN-4
Bluffpoint Post Office (historical)—*building* ... TN-4
Bluff Pond—*lake* ... ME-1
Bluff Pool—*lake* ... MO-7
*Bluff Port* ... AL-4
Bluffport—*locale* ... AL-4
Bluffport—*locale* ... MT-8
**Bluffport**—*pop pl* ... AL-4
Bluff Port Bar—*bar* ... AL-4
Bluff Port Ferry (historical)—*locale* ... AL-4
Bluff Port Landing (historical)—*locale* ... AL-4
*Bluff Port P.O.* ... AL-4
Bluff Post Office (historical)—*building* ... MS-4
Bluff Prairie Sch—*school* ... CA-9
Bluff Ridge—*ridge* ... AL-4
Bluff Ridge—*ridge* ... NC-3
Bluff Ridge—*ridge* ... WV-2
Bluff Ridge Ch—*church* ... AL-4
**Bluff Road Subdivision**—*pop pl* ... UT-8
*Bluff Rock* ... RI-1
*Bluff Run* ... VA-3
Bluff Run—*stream* ... KS-7
Bluff Run—*stream* ... OH-6
Bluff Run—*stream* ... PA-2
Bluff Run—*stream* ... VA-3
**Bluffs**—*pop pl* ... IL-6
**Bluffs**—*pop pl* ... IN-6
*Bluffs, The* ... MA-1
*Bluffs, The* ... VT-1
Bluffs, The—*area* ... MA-1
Bluffs, The—*cliff* ... ID-8
Bluffs, The—*cliff* (2) ... IN-6
Bluffs, The—*cliff* (3) ... ME-1
Bluffs, The—*cliff* ... MI-6
Bluffs, The—*cliff* ... NV-8
Bluffs, The—*cliff* ... NY-2
Bluffs, The—*cliff* (2) ... WY-8
**Bluffs, The**—*pop pl* ... DE-2
Bluff Saddle—*gap* ... AZ-5
Bluffs Cem—*cemetery* (2) ... IL-6
Bluffs Ch—*church* ... NE-7
Bluff Sch—*school* ... MO-7
Bluff Sch—*school* ... NH-1
Bluff Sch—*school* ... TN-4
Bluff Sch—*school* ... UT-8
Bluff Sch (historical)—*school* ... AL-4
**Bluffside**—*pop pl* ... IL-6
**Bluffside**—*pop pl* ... IN-6
Bluff Side Park—*park* ... IA-7
Bluffside Park—*park* ... MN-6
**Bluff Siding**—*pop pl* ... WI-6
Bluff Slough—*gut* ... MN-6
Bluff Slough—*gut* ... WI-6
**Bluffs of Eno (subdivision)**—*pop pl* ... NC-3
*Bluff Spring* ... AL-4
*Bluff Spring* ... AZ-5
Bluff Spring—*locale* ... KY-4
**Bluff Spring**—*pop pl* ... AL-4
Bluff Spring—*spring* ... AL-4
Bluff Spring—*spring* (4) ... AZ-5
Bluff Spring—*spring* ... CA-9
Bluff Spring—*spring* ... CO-8
Bluff Spring—*spring* ... NM-5
Bluff Spring—*spring* (2) ... TN-4
Bluff Spring—*spring* ... TX-5
Bluff Spring—*spring* ... UT-8
Bluff Spring Branch—*stream* ... AL-4
Bluff Spring Branch—*stream* ... TN-4
Bluff Spring Canyon—*valley* ... AZ-5
Bluff Spring Cem—*cemetery* ... MS-4
Bluff Spring Ch—*church* ... AR-4
Bluff Spring Ch—*church* ... GA-3
Bluff Spring Ch—*church* ... LA-4
Bluff Spring Ch—*church* ... MS-4
Bluff Spring Mountain Canyon—*valley* ... AZ-5
Bluff Spring Mountain Spring—*spring* ... AZ-5
Bluff Spring Mtn—*summit* ... AZ-5
Bluff Spring P.O. (historical)—*locale* ... AL-4
Bluff Spring Post Office (historical)—*building* ... TN-4
*Bluff Springs* ... AZ-5
*Bluff Springs* ... MS-4
Bluff Springs—*locale* (2) ... AL-4
Bluff Springs—*locale* ... FL-3
Bluff Springs—*locale* ... MS-4
Bluff Springs—*locale* ... TN-4
**Bluff Springs**—*pop pl* ... IL-6
**Bluff Springs**—*pop pl* ... MS-4
**Bluff Springs**—*pop pl* (2) ... TX-5
Bluff Springs—*spring* ... CA-9
Bluff Springs—*spring* ... NM-5
Bluff Springs—*springs* ... CO-8
*Bluff Springs Baptist Church* ... AL-4
*Bluff Springs Baptist Church* ... MS-4
Bluff Springs Branch—*stream* ... GA-3
Bluff Springs Branch—*stream* ... TN-4
Bluff Springs Camp—*locale* ... MS-4
*Bluff Springs Cem* ... MS-4
Bluff Springs Cem—*cemetery* ... AL-4
Bluff Springs Cem—*cemetery* ... AR-4
Bluff Springs Cem—*cemetery* ... GA-3
Bluff Springs Cem—*cemetery* (7) ... MS-4
Bluff Springs Cem—*cemetery* ... MO-7
Bluff Springs Cem—*cemetery* ... TN-4
Bluff Springs Cem—*cemetery* ... TX-5
Bluff Springs Ch—*church* (3) ... AL-4
Bluff Springs Ch—*church* (2) ... AR-4
Bluff Springs Ch—*church* ... FL-3
Bluff Springs Ch—*church* (11) ... MS-4
Bluff Springs Ch—*church* ... MO-7
Bluff Springs Ch—*church* (2) ... TN-4
Bluff Springs Ch—*church* ... TX-5
Bluff Spring Sch—*school* ... AR-4
Bluff Spring Sch—*school* ... MO-7
Bluff Springs Ch (historical)—*church* ... AL-4
Bluff Springs Church and Sch—*hist pl* ... AR-4
Bluff Springs Coll (historical)—*school* ... TN-4
Bluff Springs (historical)—*locale* ... MS-4
**Bluff Springs (historical)**—*pop pl* ... MS-4
Bluff Springs Lake—*lake* ... FL-3
Bluff Springs Lake—*reservoir* ... MS-4
Bluff Springs Landing (historical)—*locale* ... MS-4
Bluff Springs Post Office (historical)—*building* ... MS-4
Bluff Springs Post Office (historical)—*building* ... TN-4
*Bluff Spring Spring* ... AZ-5
Bluff Springs Sch—*school* ... GA-3
Bluff Springs Sch—*school* ... IL-6
Bluff Springs Sch—*school* ... MS-4
Bluff Springs Sch—*school* ... MO-7
Bluff Springs Sch—*school* ... TX-5
Bluff Springs Sch (historical)—*school* ... AL-4
Bluff Springs Sch (historical)—*school* (7) ... MS-4
Bluff Springs Sch (historical)—*school* (2) ... TN-4
Bluff Springs (Township of)—*civ div* ... IL-6
Bluff Spur—*ridge* ... VA-3
Bluffs Recreation Site—*locale* ... UT-8
Bluff Station (historical)—*locale* ... TN-4
Bluff Street Hist Dist—*hist pl* ... WI-6
Bluff Swamp—*swamp* ... LA-4
Bluff Swamp—*swamp* ... NC-3
Bluff Tank—*reservoir* ... AZ-5
Bluff Tank—*reservoir* (2) ... NM-5
Bluff Tank—*reservoir* (2) ... TX-5
*Bluffton* ... AL-4
*Bluffton* ... MI-6
Bluffton—*locale* ... AL-4
Bluffton—*locale* ... FL-3
Bluffton—*locale* ... TN-4
Bluffton—*locale* ... TX-5
**Bluffton**—*pop pl* ... AR-4
**Bluffton**—*pop pl* ... GA-3
**Bluffton**—*pop pl* ... IN-6
**Bluffton**—*pop pl* ... IA-7
**Bluffton**—*pop pl* ... MN-6
**Bluffton**—*pop pl* ... MO-7
**Bluffton**—*pop pl* ... OH-6
**Bluffton**—*pop pl* ... SC-3
Bluffton (CCD)—*cens area* ... GA-3
Bluffton (CCD)—*cens area* ... SC-3
Bluffton Cem—*cemetery* ... AR-4
Bluffton Cem—*cemetery* ... IA-7
Bluffton Cem—*cemetery* ... SC-3
Bluffton Cem—*cemetery* ... TX-5
Bluffton Coll—*school* ... OH-6
Bluffton Fir Stand State Preserve—*park* ... IA-7
Bluffton Mtn—*summit* ... AL-4
Bluffton Number 2 Sch—*school* ... ND-7
Bluffton Number 3 Sch—*school* ... ND-7
Bluffton Post Office (historical)—*building* ... AL-4
Bluffton Post Office (historical)—*building* ... TN-4
Bluffton Sch—*school* ... MI-6
Bluffton Sch—*school* ... MO-7
Bluffton Sch—*school* ... WI-6
Bluffton Sch Number 1—*school* ... ND-7
Bluffton Sch Number 4—*school* ... ND-7
Bluffton Township—*fmr MCD* ... IA-7
Bluffton (Township of)—*fmr MCD* ... AR-4
**Bluffton (Township of)**—*pop pl* ... MN-6
**Bluff Township**—*pop pl* ... KS-7
Bluff Trail—*trail* ... GA-3
Bluff Trail—*trail* ... TN-4
Bluff Trail—*trail* ... VA-3
Bluff Trail—*trail* ... WI-6
Bluff Trail, Lake—*trail* ... TN-4
Bluffview—*locale* ... WI-6
**Bluff View**—*pop pl* ... TN-4
**Bluff View**—*pop pl* ... TX-5
Bluff View Cem—*cemetery* ... SD-7
Bluff View Park—*park* ... NE-7
*Bluff View Park (Bunkum)* ... IL-6
Bluff View Park Sch—*school* ... IL-6
Bluff View Public Use Area—*locale* ... MO-7
Bluff View Rec Area—*park* ... MO-7
Bluff View River Access—*locale* ... MO-7
Bluff View Sch—*school* ... IL-6
Bluffview Sch—*school* ... NM-5
*Bluffville* ... KS-7
Bluff Water Hole—*lake* ... TX-5
Bluff Windmill—*locale* (3) ... TX-5
Bluffwoods State For—*forest* ... MO-7
Bluffy Branch—*stream* ... AL-4
Bluffy Branch—*stream* ... TN-4
Bluffy Creek—*stream* ... GA-3
**Bluford**—*pop pl* ... IL-6
Bluford Cem—*cemetery* ... SC-3
Bluford Creek—*stream* ... CA-9
Bluford Elem Sch—*school* ... NC-3
Bluford Gulch—*valley* ... CA-9
**Bluford Heights (subdivision)**—*pop pl* ... NC-3
Bluford Oil Field—*other* ... IL-6
Bluford Sch—*school* ... IL-6
Bluford Trail—*trail* ... CA-9
*Blufton* ... GA-3
Bluhm Ditch—*canal* ... IN-6
Bluhm House Sch (historical)—*school* ... TN-4
*Bluhms* ... TN-4
Bluhm Sch—*school* ... MO-7
Bluhms Post Office (historical)—*building* ... TN-4
Bluhmtown—*locale* ... TN-4
Bluhmtown Creek—*stream* ... TN-4
Bluit—*locale* ... NM-5
Blujay Mine—*mine* ... CA-9
**Blum**—*pop pl* ... MT-8
**Blum**—*pop pl* ... TX-5
Blum, Mount—*summit* ... WA-9
Blumaer Hill—*summit* ... WA-9
*Blumauer Hill* ... WA-9
Blumbago Canyon—*valley* ... CA-9
Blumberg Camp—*locale* ... CO-8
Blumberg Canyon—*valley* ... AZ-5
Blumberg House—*hist pl* ... AZ-5
**Blumberg Spur**—*pop pl* ... TX-5
Blum (CCD)—*cens area* ... TX-5
Blum Cem—*cemetery* ... IL-6
Blum Creek—*stream* ... MT-8
Blum Creek—*stream* ... WA-9
Blume—*locale* ... LA-4
Blume Creek—*stream* ... AK-9
Blume Lake—*lake* ... FL-3
Blumel Draw—*valley* ... WY-8
**Blumengard Colony**—*pop pl* ... SD-7
Blumenschein, Ernest L., House—*hist pl* ... NM-5
Blumenthal—*locale* ... TX-5
Blumenthal Hollow—*valley* ... PA-2
Blume Sch—*school* ... OH-6
Blume Zilkey Ditch—*canal* ... OR-9
Blumfield Cem—*cemetery* ... MI-6
**Blumfield Corners**—*pop pl* ... MI-6
Blumfield Creek—*stream* ... MI-6
**Blumfield (Township of)**—*pop pl* ... MI-6
Blumhagen Spring—*spring* ... MT-8
Blum Lakes—*lake* ... WA-9
Blum Park—*park* ... NC-3
Blum Ranch—*locale* ... CA-9
*Blums Creek* ... WI-6
Blu Mtn—*summit* ... OK-5
Blun—*locale* ... GA-3
**Blundale**—*pop pl* ... GA-3
Blundale Ch—*church* ... GA-3
Blundell Creek—*stream* ... TX-5
Blundell Creek Ch—*church* ... TX-5
Blundell Hollow—*valley* ... VA-3
Blundering Point—*cape* ... VA-3
Blunder Pit—*cave* ... AL-4
Blunder Pond—*lake* ... ME-1
Blunder Rock—*pillar* ... VI-3
**Blundon**—*pop pl* ... WV-2
Blundon Corner—*locale* ... VA-3
*Blundon Run* ... KY-4
Blundon Sch—*school* ... LA-4
Blunkall Crossing—*locale* ... CA-9
Blunk Cem—*cemetery* ... IN-6
Blunk Point—*cliff* ... IN-6
Blunn Creek—*stream* ... TX-5
Blunt—*locale* (2) ... CA-9
**Blunt**—*pop pl* ... SD-7
Blunt, Ainsworth E., House—*hist pl* ... GA-3
Blunt, Point—*cape* ... CA-9
Blunt Cem—*cemetery* ... GA-3
Blunt Cem—*cemetery* ... ME-1
Blunt Cem—*cemetery* ... SD-7
Blunt Ch—*church* ... OK-5
Blunt Creek—*stream* ... TN-4
Blunt Hollow—*valley* ... TX-5
Blunt Island—*island* ... MN-6
Blunt Mtn—*summit* ... AK-9
*Blunt Point* ... CA-9
*Blunt Point* ... ME-1
Blunt Point—*cape* (2) ... AK-9
Blunt Point—*cape* ... VA-3
*Blunt Point Rock* ... CA-9
Blunt Run—*stream* ... OH-6
*Blunts* ... MS-4
Blunts Bridge—*bridge* ... VA-3
*Blunts Island* ... WA-9
Blunts Island—*island* ... NH-1
Blunts Island—*island* ... NY-2
Blunts Landing—*locale* ... TN-4
Blunts Point—*cape* ... ME-1
Blunts Point Naval Gun—*hist pl* ... AS-9
Blunts Pond—*lake* ... ME-1
Blunts Pond—*lake* ... NH-1
Blunts Reef—*bar* ... CA-9
*Blunt Store* ... MS-4
Blunt Township—*civil* ... SD-7
Bluntzer—*locale* ... TX-5
Blurock Landing—*locale* ... WA-9
Blush Ch—*church* ... MO-7
Blush Hill—*summit* ... VT-1
**Blush Hollow**—*pop pl* ... MA-1
*Blush Lake* ... MI-6
Bluster Mine—*mine* ... NV-8
Bluster Natl Forest Campground—*locale* ... NV-8
Bluster Ridge—*ridge* ... KY-4
*Blustry Point* ... WA-9
Bluzes, The—*bar* ... NY-2
**Bly**—*pop pl* ... CA-9
**Bly**—*pop pl* ... NC-3
**Bly**—*pop pl* ... OR-9
Bly, Smith, House—*hist pl* ... NY-2
Bly Bay—*bay* ... NY-2
Blyberg, O. A. E., House—*hist pl* ... MN-6
Blyburg Lake—*lake* ... NE-7
*Bly Canyon* ... CA-9
Bly Cem—*cemetery* ... TN-4
Bly Channel—*canal* ... CA-9
Bly Creek—*stream* ... MN-6
Bly Creek—*stream* ... SC-3
Blydenburg And Morgan North Ditch—*canal* ... WY-8
Blydenburg And Morgan South Ditch—*canal* ... WY-8
Blydenburg Draw—*valley* ... WY-8
Blydenburgh Park Hist Dist—*hist pl* ... NY-2
Blye Canyon—*valley* ... AZ-5
Blye Tank—*reservoir* ... AZ-5
Bly Gap—*gap* ... NC-3
Blygh Gulch—*valley* ... AK-9
Bly Hill—*summit* ... NH-1
Blyhill Cem—*cemetery* ... VT-1
Blying Sound—*bay* ... AK-9
Bly Lake—*lake* ... MI-6
Blymire Ch—*church* ... PA-2
Bly Mountain Pass—*gap* ... OR-9
Bly Mtn—*summit* ... OR-9
**Blyn**—*pop pl* ... WA-9
Blynman Canal—*channel* ... MA-1
Blynman Sch—*school* ... MA-1
Bly Point—*cape* ... NY-2
Bly Ranger Station—*hist pl* ... OR-9
Bly Ridge—*ridge* ... OR-9
Bly Sch—*school* ... MI-6
Bly Siding—*locale* ... AZ-5
Blyson Run—*stream* ... PA-2
Blystone Ditch—*canal* ... OH-6
Blystone Junction—*locale* ... PA-2
*Blystone Mill* ... PA-2
**Blystone Mill**—*pop pl* ... PA-2
Bly Tank—*reservoir* ... AZ-5
Blytha Creek—*stream* ... MS-4
Blytha Creek Ch—*church* ... MS-4
*Blythe* ... MS-4
Blythe—*locale* ... KY-4
**Blythe**—*pop pl* ... CA-9
**Blythe**—*pop pl* ... GA-3
Blythe, Benjamin, Homestead—*hist pl* ... PA-2
Blythe, Lake—*reservoir* ... KY-4
Blythe Airp—*airport* ... CA-9
Blythea Lake—*lake* ... NY-2
Blythe Ave Sch—*school* ... TN-4
Blythe Boat Club—*other* ... CA-9
Blythebourne—*uninc pl* ... NY-2
Blythe Branch—*stream* ... AR-4
Blythe Branch—*stream* (2) ... KY-4
Blythe Branch—*stream* ... NC-3
**Blytheburn**—*pop pl* ... PA-2
Blytheburn, Lake—*reservoir* ... PA-2
Blythe Cem—*cemetery* ... LA-4
*Bly the Chapel* ... MS-4
Blythe Chapel—*church* ... IN-6
**Blythe (Chappell)**—*pop pl* ... KY-4
*Blythe Creek* ... MO-7
Blythe Creek—*stream* ... NC-3
Blythe Creek—*stream* ... TX-5
Blythe Creek Cem—*cemetery* ... MS-4
**Blythe Crossing**—*pop pl* ... MS-4
**Blythedale**—*pop pl* ... MD-2
**Blythedale**—*pop pl* ... MO-7
**Blythedale**—*pop pl* ... PA-2
Blythedale Childrens Hosp—*hospital* ... NY-2
Blythe Ferry—*hist pl* ... TN-4
Blythe Ferry—*locale* ... TN-4
Blythe Ferry Cave—*cave* ... TN-4
Blythe Ferry Goose Mngmt Area—*park* ... TN-4
Blythefield Country Club—*other* ... MI-6
Blythefield Memorial Gardens—*cemetery* ... MI-6
Blythe HS—*school* ... GA-3
Blythe Intaglios—*hist pl* ... CA-9
Blythe Island—*island* ... GA-3
Blythe Island Ch—*church* ... GA-3
Blythe Island County Park—*park* ... GA-3
Blythe Island Naval Reservation—*other* ... GA-3
Blythe Lake—*lake* ... UT-8
Blythe Lake—*lake* ... WA-9
Blythe Memorial Cem—*cemetery* ... AL-4
Blythe Mill Creek—*stream* ... NC-3
Blythe Plaque—*locale* ... CA-9
Blythe (reduced usage)—*locale* ... MT-8
Blythe Ridge—*ridge* ... AR-4
Blythes Branch—*stream* ... KY-4
Blythe Sch—*school* ... IL-6
Blythe Sch—*school* ... SC-3
Blythes Chapel—*church* ... MS-4
**Blythes Chapel**—*pop pl* ... MS-4
Blythes Chapel Cem—*cemetery* ... MS-4
*Blythes Chapel Methodist Church* ... MS-4
Blythes Chapel Sch (historical)—*school* ... MS-4
Blythes Creek—*stream* ... MO-7
Blythes Ferry Post Office (historical)—*locale* ... TN-4
Blythe Shoals—*rapids* ... SC-3
*Blythe Siding* ... MT-8
Blythes Landing—*locale* ... MS-4
Blythe Slough—*lake* ... SD-7
Blythe State Public Shooting Area—*park* ... SD-7
Blythe (Township of)—*fmr MCD* (2) ... AR-4
**Blythe (Township of)**—*pop pl* ... PA-2
**Blytheville**—*pop pl* ... AR-4
Blytheville Air Force Base—*military* ... AR-4
Blytheville Greyhound Bus Station—*hist pl* ... AR-4
Blytheville Junction—*uninc pl* ... AR-4
Blythe Well—*well* ... NM-5
Blythewood—*hist pl* ... LA-4
Blythewood—*hist pl* ... TN-4
**Blythewood**—*pop pl* ... PA-2
**Blythewood**—*pop pl* ... SC-3
Blythewood (CCD)—*cens area* ... SC-3
Blythewood Island—*island* ... NY-2
Blyth Spring—*spring* ... NV-8
Blyth Spring—*spring* ... UT-8
*Blythville* ... MS-4
Blythwood—*locale* ... LA-4
Blyton—*locale* ... IL-6
**Blyvbach (historical)**—*pop pl* ... OR-9
Blyville Post Office (historical)—*building* ... TN-4
B-Main Canal—*canal* ... CA-9
B Main Drain—*canal* ... ID-8
B Main Lateral—*canal* ... AZ-5
B M Brignse Lake Dam—*dam* ... MS-4
B McKeen Ranch—*locale* ... NM-5
Bm Hill—*summit* ... ID-8
B Morris Catfish Ponds Dam—*dam* ... MS-4
*B Mountain* ... CA-9
B Mountain Lake—*lake* ... AL-4
B Mountain Lake Dam—*dam* ... AL-4
*B & M Placers* ... NV-8
BM Placers—*mine* ... NV-8
*BM Pond* ... MA-1
BM Spring—*spring* ... AZ-5
BMU Bridge over Wind River—*hist pl* ... WY-8
B'nai Abraham Cem—*cemetery* ... PA-2
B'Nai Abraham Memorial Park—*cemetery* ... NJ-2
B'nai Abraham Synagogue—*hist pl* ... MN-6
Bnai Ameth—*church* ... IA-7
B'Nai Amoona Synogogue—*hist pl* ... MO-7
Bnai Birth Cem—*cemetery* ... MA-1
B'nai B'rith Camp—*locale* ... PA-2
Bnai Brith Cem—*cemetery* ... MA-1
B'nai B'rith Cem—*cemetery* ... NY-2
Bnai Brith Home for Aged—*building* ... TN-4
B'Nai Cem—*cemetery* ... IL-6
Bnai-David Cem—*cemetery* ... MI-6
B'nai El Temple—*hist pl* ... MO-7
B'nai Israel Cem—*cemetery* ... IL-6
B'nai-Israel Cem—*cemetery* ... IN-6
Bnai Israel Cem—*cemetery* ... MD-2
B'nai Israel Cem—*cemetery* ... MS-4
B'Nai Israel Cem—*cemetery* ... MT-8
B'Nai Israel Cem—*cemetery* ... NJ-2
B'Nai Israel Cem—*cemetery* ... UT-8
B' Nai Israel Cem—*cemetery* ... WI-6
B'nai Israel Synagogue—*church* ... FL-3
B'nai Israel Temple—*hist pl* ... UT-8
B'nai Isreal—*hist pl* ... TX-5
B NAI Jacob Cem—*cemetery* ... OH-6
B'nai Jacob Cem—*cemetery* ... PA-2
B'Nai Jacob Synagogue—*hist pl* ... PA-2
B'Nai Jeshuron Cem—*cemetery* ... NJ-2
B'nail Jacob Memorial Park (Cemetery)—*cemetery* ... CT-1
B'nail Jacob Sch—*school* ... CT-1
B'nail Scholom Cem—*cemetery* ... CT-1
Bnai Moses Synagogue—*church* ... IA-7
B'nai Sholem Cem—*cemetery* ... MO-7
Bnai Sholom Cem—*cemetery* ... MI-6
B'Nai Zion Cem—*cemetery* ... TN-4
B'nal Jeshurum And Shereth Israel Cem—*cemetery* ... NY-2
Bnay Abraham Synagogue (historical)—*church* ... AL-4
B N B Lateral—*canal* ... CO-8
Bngei, Bkul A—*cape* ... PW-9
B N Junction—*locale* ... KS-7
*Boabors Point* ... VA-3
*Boads Mountain* ... VA-3
Boaga Hill—*summit* ... GU-9
Boag Creek—*stream* ... OR-9
Boags Branch—*stream* ... VA-3
Boak, Cada C., House—*hist pl* ... NV-8
Boake Run—*stream* ... PA-2
Boal—*locale* ... CA-9
Boal Gap—*gap* ... PA-2
Boal Gap Run—*stream* ... PA-2
Boal Mansion—*hist pl* ... PA-2
Boals Bridge—*bridge* ... PA-2
**Boalsburg**—*pop pl* ... PA-2
Boalsburg Elem Sch—*school* ... PA-2
Boalsburg Hist Dist—*hist pl* ... PA-2
Boal Sch (abandoned)—*school* ... PA-2
Boalt, John, House—*hist pl* ... OH-6
Bo Amalia—*post sta* ... PR-3
Boan Cem—*cemetery* ... KS-7
Boanerges Ch—*church* ... TN-4
**Boanna**—*pop pl* ... OH-6
Boar Backbone—*ridge* ... OR-9
Boar Bay—*swamp* ... SC-3
Boar Branch—*stream* ... KY-4
Boar Branch—*stream* ... TX-5
Boar Camp—*locale* ... OR-9
Boar Creek—*gut* ... NC-3
Boar Creek—*stream* ... IL-6
Boar Creek—*stream* ... OK-5
Boar Creek—*stream* ... TN-4
Boar Creek Oil Field—*oilfield* ... OK-5
**Board**—*pop pl* ... WV-2
Board-and-Batten Commercial Bldg—*hist pl* ... ID-8
Board and Batten Cottage—*hist pl* ... NV-8
Board and Batten Miners Cabin—*hist pl* ... NV-8
Board Bay—*bay* ... FL-3
*Board Branch* ... WV-2
Board Branch—*stream* ... GA-3
Board Branch—*stream* ... KY-4
Board Branch—*stream* (5) ... TX-5
Board Branch Cem—*cemetery* ... TX-5
Board Burn—*area* ... CA-9
Board Cabin Draw—*valley* ... AZ-5
Board Cabins—*locale* ... CO-8
Board Cabins Gulch—*valley* ... CO-8
Board Cabin Spring—*spring* ... CA-9
Board Cabin Spring—*spring* ... NV-8
*Board Camp* ... CA-9
**Board Camp**—*pop pl* ... AR-4
Boardcamp Branch—*stream* ... NC-3
Board Camp Branch—*stream* ... TN-4
Board Camp Branch—*stream* ... VA-3
Boardcamp Branch—*stream* ... WV-2
Board Camp Butte—*summit* ... CA-9
Board Camp Creek—*stream* ... AR-4
Board Camp Creek—*stream* ... GA-3
Board Camp Creek—*stream* ... NC-3
Board Camp Creek—*stream* ... TN-4
Board Camp Gap—*gap* ... NC-3
Board Camp Gulf—*valley* ... TN-4
Board Camp Mtn—*summit* ... CA-9
Board Camp Ridge—*ridge* ... CA-9
Boardcamp Ridge—*ridge* ... NC-3
Board Camp Spring—*spring* ... CA-9
Board Canyon—*valley* ... AZ-5
Board Canyon—*valley* ... NM-5
Board Cem—*cemetery* ... KY-4
Board Cem—*cemetery* ... VA-3
Board Cem—*cemetery* (3) ... WV-2
Board Ch—*church* ... TX-5
Board Ch—*church* ... WV-2
Board Corral Creek—*stream* ... MT-8
Board Corral Gulch—*valley* ... OR-9
Board Corral Mtn—*summit* ... OR-9
Board Corral Ranch—*locale* ... NV-8
Board Corral Rsvr—*reservoir* ... OR-9
Board Corral Spring—*spring* ... OR-9
Board Cove Branch—*stream* ... NC-3
Board Creek—*stream* ... AZ-5
Board Creek—*stream* ... CA-9
Board Creek—*stream* ... NV-8
Board Creek—*stream* (4) ... OR-9
Board Creek—*stream* (2) ... TX-5
Board Creek Spring—*spring* ... AZ-5
Board Cut Branch—*stream* ... KY-4
Boardcut Island—*island* ... KY-4
*Boarder Line Dam* ... ND-7
Board-Everett House—*hist pl* ... TX-5
Board Fork—*stream* (2) ... KY-4
Board Fork—*stream* (2) ... WV-2
Board Gap—*gap* ... NC-3
Board Gate Canyon—*valley* ... NM-5
Board Gate Dam Rsvr—*reservoir* ... NE-7
Board Gate Saddle—*gap* ... NM-5
Board Gulch—*valley* ... ID-8
Board Gulch—*valley* ... OR-9
Boardhead Branch—*stream* ... FL-3
Board Hollow—*valley* (2) ... MO-7
Board Hollow—*valley* ... OK-5
Board Hollow—*valley* ... OR-9
Board Hollow—*valley* ... VA-3
*Board Hollow Creek* ... OR-9
Board Hollow Creek—*stream* ... OK-5
Boardhouse Creek—*stream* ... TX-5
Boardhouse Spring—*spring* ... TX-5
Boarding House—*hist pl* ... ID-8
Boardinghouse Branch—*stream* (3) ... KY-4
Boardinghouse Canyon—*valley* ... AZ-5
Boardinghouse Canyon—*valley* ... UT-8
Boardinghouse Creek—*stream* ... TX-5
Boardinghouse Creek—*stream* ... WY-8
Boarding House Gulch—*valley* ... SD-7
Boarding House Hill—*summit* ... TN-4
Boarding House Hollow—*valley* ... KY-4
Boardinghouse Hollow—*valley* ... KY-4
Boardinghouse Hollow—*valley* (2) ... MO-7
Boardinghouse Hollow—*valley* ... PA-2
Boardinghouse Hollow—*valley* ... WV-2
Boardinghouse Spring—*spring* ... WY-8
*Boarding School Dam* ... SD-7
Board Lake—*lake* (2) ... MS-4
*Boardman* ... NY-2
*Boardman* ... WV-2
Boardman—*locale* ... FL-3
**Boardman**—*pop pl* ... NC-3
**Boardman**—*pop pl* ... OH-6
**Boardman**—*pop pl* ... OR-9
**Boardman**—*pop pl* ... PA-2
**Boardman**—*pop pl* ... WI-6
Boardman, Mount—*summit* ... CA-9
Boardman, The—*hist pl* ... MA-1
Boardman Airstrip—*airport* ... OR-9
Boardman Bridge—*locale* ... CT-1
Boardman Brook—*stream* ... NY-2
Boardman Camp—*locale* ... CA-9
Boardman Canal—*canal* ... CA-9
Boardman (CCD)—*cens area* ... OR-9
Boardman Cem—*cemetery* (2) ... NY-2
Boardman Cem—*cemetery* ... WI-6
Boardman Ch—*church* ... NC-3
Boardman Creek—*stream* ... CA-9
Boardman Creek—*stream* ... ID-8
Boardman Creek—*stream* ... MO-7
Boardman Creek—*stream* ... NE-7
Boardman Creek—*stream* ... NY-2
Boardman Creek—*stream* ... WA-9
Boardman Creek Camp—*locale* ... WA-9
Boardman Ditch—*canal* ... OH-6
Boardman Grove—*woods* ... CA-9
Boardman Gulch—*valley* (2) ... CA-9
Boardman Hill—*summit* ... VT-1
**Boardman (historical)**—*pop pl* ... OR-9
Boardman Hollow—*valley* ... WV-2
Boardman House—*hist pl* ... MA-1
Boardman House—*hist pl* ... NY-2
*Boardman Island* ... NJ-2
Boardman JHS—*school* ... OH-6
Boardman Junction—*locale* ... OR-9
Boardman Lake—*lake* ... WA-9
Boardman Lake—*reservoir* ... MI-6
Boardman Mtn—*summit* ... CT-1
Boardman Mtn—*summit* ... ME-1
Boardman Neighborhood Hist Dist—*hist pl* ... MI-6
Boardman Oasis Roadside Rest—*locale* ... OR-9
Boardman Park—*park* ... OR-9
Boardman Pass—*gap* ... ID-8
Boardman Plaza Shop Ctr—*locale* ... OH-6
Boardman Pond—*lake* ... CT-1
Boardman Ranch—*locale* (2) ... CA-9
Boardman Ridge—*ridge* (2) ... CA-9
Boardman Ridge—*ridge* ... PA-2
Boardman River—*stream* ... MI-6
Boardman Safety Rest Area—*locale* ... OR-9
Boardman's Bridge—*hist pl* ... CT-1
**Boardmans Bridge**—*pop pl* ... CT-1
Boardman Sch—*school* ... CT-1
Boardman Sch—*school* ... NY-2
*Boardmans Ferry* ... PA-2
Boardmans Lake—*swamp* ... LA-4
Boardmans Point—*cape* ... NH-1
Boardmans Pond—*reservoir* ... GA-3
Boardman Spring—*spring* ... UT-8
Boardman Township—*fmr MCD* ... IA-7
Boardman (Township of)—*other* ... OH-6
**Boardman (Township of)**—*pop pl* ... MI-6
**Boardman (Township of)**—*pop pl* ... OH-6
**Boardmanville**—*pop pl* ... NY-2
Boardman-Webb-Bugg House—*hist pl* ... TX-5
Boardman Windmill—*locale* ... NM-5
Board Mtn—*summit* ... OR-9
Board Mtn—*summit* ... VA-3
Board of Education Bldg—*hist pl* ... PA-2
Board of Extension of the Methodist Episcopal Church, South—*hist pl* ... KY-4
Boardpan Branch—*stream* ... NC-3
**Board Park**—*pop pl* ... IN-6
Board Pile Bay—*swamp* ... FL-3
Boardpile Branch—*stream* ... GA-3
Boardpile Branch—*stream* ... MS-4
Boardpile Brook—*stream* ... NH-1
Board Pile Ridges—*ridge* ... GA-3
Board Point—*island* ... ME-1
Board Ranch—*locale* ... UT-8
Board Ranch Windmill—*locale* ... NM-5
Board Ridge—*ridge* ... CA-9
Board Ridge—*ridge* ... WV-2
Board Rock Hollow—*valley* ... PA-2
Board Run—*stream* ... MD-2
Board Run—*stream* ... PA-2
Board Run—*stream* ... WV-2
Board Sch—*school* ... MO-7
Boards Crossing—*locale* ... CA-9
Boards Ferry—*locale* ... TX-5
Boardshack Knoll—*summit* ... AZ-5
Board Shanty Ch—*church* ... AR-4
Board Shanty Creek—*stream* ... OR-9
Board Shanty Gap—*gap* ... PA-2
Board Slough—*stream* ... TX-5
Boardson Lake—*swamp* ... MN-6
Board Spring—*spring* ... AZ-5
Board Springs—*spring* ... CA-9
Boardstand Flat—*flat* ... OK-5
Board Tank—*reservoir* ... AZ-5
Board Timber Creek—*stream* ... TX-5
*Boardtown* ... MS-4
*Boardtown Ch* ... GA-3
Boardtown Ch—*church* ... GA-3
Boardtown Creek—*stream* ... GA-3
Boardtown Sch (historical)—*school* ... GA-3
Board Tree—*locale* ... WV-2
**Board Tree**—*pop pl* ... KY-4
*Boardtree Branch* ... FL-3
Board Tree Branch—*stream* ... AL-4
Boardtree Branch—*stream* ... AR-4
Board Tree Branch—*stream* ... IL-6
Board Tree Branch—*stream* ... KY-4
Boardtree Branch—*stream* (2) ... KY-4
Boardtree Branch—*stream* (2) ... NC-3
Board Tree Branch—*stream* ... TN-4
Boardtree Branch—*stream* ... TN-4
Boardtree Branch—*stream* ... TX-5
Boardtree Branch—*stream* (2) ... WV-2
Board Tree Campground—*locale* ... CA-9
Board Tree Canyon—*valley* ... CA-9
Board Tree Canyon—*valley* ... NM-5
Boardtree Canyon—*valley* ... OR-9
*Board Tree Creek* ... KY-4
*Boardtree Creek* ... OR-9
Boardtree Creek—*stream* ... AL-4
Board Tree Creek—*stream* ... GA-3
Board Tree Creek—*stream* ... OK-5
Boardtree Creek—*stream* ... OK-5
Board Tree Creek—*stream* ... OR-9
Boardtree Creek—*stream* ... OR-9
Board Tree Creek—*stream* ... TX-5
Boardtree Creek—*stream* ... TX-5
Boardtree Fork—*stream* ... KY-4
Board Tree Gap—*gap* ... VA-3
Boardtree Gap—*gap* ... WV-2
Boardtree Gulch—*valley* ... CA-9
Boardtree Hollow—*valley* ... AR-4
Board Tree Hollow—*valley* (3) ... KY-4
Board Tree Hollow—*valley* (3) ... MO-7
Boardtree Hollow—*valley* ... TN-4
Board Tree Hollow—*valley* ... TN-4
Boardtree Hollow—*valley* ... TN-4
Board Tree Hollow—*valley* ... TX-5
Boardtree Hollow—*valley* ... WV-2
Boardtree Knob—*summit* ... NC-3
Board Tree Lake—*lake* ... LA-4

Boardtree Point—*cape* TN-4
Boardtree Ridge—*ridge* NC-3
Board Tree Run—*stream* VA-3
Boardtree Run—*stream* (4) WV-2
Board Tree Saddle—*gap* AZ-5
Board Tree Saddle Tank—*reservoir* AZ-5
Board Tree Slough—*gut* TX-5
Board Tree Spring—*spring* AZ-5
Board Tree Spring—*spring* OR-9
Board Tree Tunnel—*tunnel* WV-2
**Board Valley**—*pop pl* TN-4
Board Valley—*valley* TN-4
Board Valley Cem—*cemetery* TN-4
Board Valley Ch—*church* TN-4
Boardwalk, The (Shop Ctr)—*locale* FL-3
Boardwalk Nature Trail—*trail* MO-7
Boardway Ponds—*lake* ME-1
Boardwell Canyon—*valley* NM-5
Boardyard Sch (abandoned)—*school* PA-2
Boar Hammock—*island* (2) FL-3
Boarhog Branch—*stream* TN-4
Boar Hole—*bay* PA-2
Boar Hole—*valley* UT-8
Boar Hole Spring—*spring* UT-8
Boar Hollow—*valley* UT-8
*Boar Island* FM-9
Boar Island—*island* MD-2
Boar Knob—*summit* WV-2
*Boar Lake* WI-6
Boarman Sch (historical)—*school* MO-7
Boaro Timber Creek—*stream* TX-5
Boar Peak—*summit* CA-9
Boar Point—*cape* NC-3
Boar Ridge—*ridge* NC-3
*Boar River* AL-4
*Boar River* MS-4
Boar Run—*stream* (2) WV-2
Boars Creek—*stream* VA-3
Boars Head—*summit* NH-1
Boars Head Falls—*falls* ME-1
Boar Shoal—*bar* NC-3
Boars Nest Trail—*trail* WV-2
Boars Rapids—*rapids* WI-6
Boar Stone—*island* MS-4
Boarstone Mtn—*summit* ME-1
Boars Tusk—*ridge* UT-8
Boars Tusk—*summit* WY-8
Boar Swamp—*stream* VA-3
*Boar Swamp Creek* VA-3
**Boar Tush**—*pop pl* AL-4
Boar Tush Lookout Tower—*locale* AL-4
Boar Tusk Mtn—*summit* AR-4
Boas Cem—*cemetery* MO-7
Boas Sch (historical)—*school* PA-2
Boast Mtn—*summit* SC-3
Boas (Township of)—*fmr MCD* AR-4
Boat—*locale* KY-4
Boat Bay—*bay* NC-3
Boat Bayou—*gut* FL-3
Boat Bend Hollow—*valley* MO-7
Boat Bottom—*bend* UT-8
Boat Bottom—*bend* WY-8
Boat Branch—*stream* MO-7
Boat Branch—*stream* TN-4
Boat Canyon—*valley* CA-9
Boat Canyon—*valley* NV-8
Boat Cem—*cemetery* KY-4
*Boat Channel* PW-9
Boat Cove Creek—*stream* MA-1
*Boat Creek* MO-7
Boat Creek—*bay* NC-3
Boat Creek—*stream* AK-9
Boat Creek—*stream* AR-4
Boat Creek—*stream* CA-9
Boat Creek—*stream* FL-3
Boat Creek—*stream* NC-3
Boat Creek—*stream* OR-9
Boat Creek—*stream* WY-8
*Boat Dock* FM-9
Boat Dock Spring—*spring* OR-9
Boat Drain Ch—*church* FL-3
Boat Ford Slough—*stream* OR-9
Boat Gunnel Hollow—*valley* MO-7
Boat Gunnel Hollow—*valley* TN-4
Boat Gunwale Branch—*stream* KY-4
Boat Gunwale Creek—*stream* CA-9
Boat Gunwale Hollow—*valley* TN-4
Boat Gunwale Hollow—*valley* WV-2
Boat Gunwale Slash—*stream* AR-4
Boat Gut—*gut* DE-2
Boat Harbor—*bay* (2) AK-9
Boat Harbor—*bay* WA-9
Boat Hills—*summit* TX-5
Boat Hole—*basin* TX-5
Boathouse Campsite—*locale* ME-1
Boathouse Cove—*bay* MD-2
Boathouse Cove—*bay* NV-8
*Boathouse Creek* ID-8
Boathouse Creek—*bay* MD-2
Boathouse Creek—*gut* FL-3
Boathouse Creek—*stream* ID-8
Boathouse Creek—*stream* (2) NC-3
Boathouse Creek—*stream* VA-3
Boathouse Islands—*island* FL-3
Boathouse Lake—*lake* MI-6
Boathouse on the Lullwater of the Lake in Prospect Park—*hist pl* NY-2
Boathouse Point—*cape* FL-3
Boat House Pond—*lake* DE-2
Boathouse Pond—*lake* VA-3
Boat House Row—*hist pl* PA-2
*Boating Lake* SD-7
*Boating Lake Dam* NJ-2
Boat Island—*island* KY-4
Boat Island—*island* MD-2
Boat Island—*island* NC-3
*Boat Lake* AK-9
*Boat Lake* MI-6
Boat Lake—*lake* AK-9
Boat Lake—*lake* (4) FL-3
Boat Lake—*lake* IN-6
Boat Lake—*lake* MI-6
Boat Lake—*lake* NM-5
Boat Lake—*lake* (2) SC-3
Boat Lake—*lake* TX-5
Boat Lake—*reservoir* VA-3
**Boatland**—*pop pl* TN-4
Boatland Ch—*church* TN-4
Boat Landing Camp—*locale* ME-1
Boat Landing Island—*island* GA-3
Boat Landing Mtn—*summit* ME-1
Boatland Post Office (historical)—*building* TN-4
Boatland Sch—*school* TN-4
Boatmakers Creek—*stream* AK-9
Boatman—*locale* OK-5
Boatman-Ainsworth Hose—*hist pl* WA-9
Boatman Branch—*stream* MS-4
Boatman Brook—*stream* PA-2
Boatman Creek—*stream* GA-3
Boatman Gulch—*valley* OR-9
Boatman Island—*island* IA-7
Boatman Lake—*lake* MT-8
Boatman Mountain—*ridge* TN-4
Boatman Pass—*gap* AK-9
Boatman Point—*cape* VI-3
Boatman Sch—*school* IL-6
Boatman Sch (abandoned)—*school* MO-7
Boatman Slough—*gut* TX-5
Boatman Spring—*spring* ID-8
Boat Meadow Bog—*swamp* MA-1
Boat Meadow Brook—*stream* NH-1
Boat Meadow River—*stream* MA-1
Boat Meadow River Marshes—*swamp* MA-1
Boat Mesa—*summit* UT-8
*Boat Mountain* TN-4
*Boat Mountain* UT-8
Boat Mtn—*summit* (2) AR-4
Boat Mtn—*summit* MT-8
*Boatnam Hollow* MO-7
Boatner Brake—*swamp* LA-4
Boatner Branch—*stream* MS-4
Boatner Cem—*cemetery* MS-4
Boatner Creek—*stream* AL-4
Boatner House—*hist pl* LA-4
Boatner Sch (historical)—*school* MS-4
*Boat Pond* FL-3
*Boat Pond* MA-1
Boat Pond—*lake* (4) FL-3
Boat Pond—*swamp* FL-3
Boat Ramp—*locale* NE-7
Boat Ramp Statham Shoals—*bar* GA-3
Boat Ridge Island—*island* AR-4
Boatright Branch—*stream* MO-7
Boatright Cem—*cemetery* AL-4
Boatright Cem—*cemetery* MO-7
Boatright Cem—*cemetery* TX-5
Boatright Cem—*cemetery* (2) VA-3
Boatright Creek—*stream* AR-4
Boatright House—*hist pl* KY-4
*Boatrights Ferry* MS-4
*Boatright Slough* AL-4
Boatrigth Cem—*cemetery* AR-4
Boatroad Run—*stream* PA-2
Boat Rock—*island* OR-9
Boat Rock—*pillar* OR-9
Boat Rock Light—*locale* AK-9
Boat Rocks—*area* AK-9
**Boat Run**—*pop pl* AR-4
Boat Run—*stream* (2) OH-6
Boat Sch (historical)—*school* PA-2
Boat Slough—*gut* MS-4
*Boatsmens Hill* PA-2
Boat Spring—*spring* AZ-5
Boats Slough Landing (historical)—*locale* MS-4
Boats Tank—*reservoir* TX-5
Boatswain Creek—*stream* VA-3
Boatswain Hill—*summit* NH-1
Boatswain Pond Creek—*stream* SC-3
Boat Tank Springs—*spring* NV-8
**Boatwright**—*pop pl* KY-4
Boatwright Branch—*stream* GA-3
Boatwright Cem—*cemetery* (2) GA-3
Boatwright Cem—*cemetery* (2) MS-4
Boatwright Cem—*cemetery* TX-5
Boatwright Creek—*stream* LA-4
Boatwright Creek—*stream* SC-3
Boatwright Creek—*stream* TX-5
Boatwright Hole—*basin* KY-4
Boatwright Lakes—*lake* FL-3
Boatwright Mtn—*summit* SC-3
Boatwright Pond—*reservoir* GA-3
Boatwrights Island—*island* VA-3
Boatwright Slough—*gut* AL-4
Boatwrights Store—*locale* VA-3
Boatwright Well—*locale* NM-5
*Boatyard, The* PA-2
Boatyard Bluff—*cliff* MS-4
Boatyard Creek—*stream* TN-4
Boatyard Hist Dist—*hist pl* TN-4
Boatyard Hollow—*valley* WI-6
Boatyard Lake—*lake* AL-4
Boatyard Landing (historical)—*locale* TN-4
Boat Yard Landing (historical)—*locale* TN-4
Boatyard Run—*stream* PA-2
Boaz—*locale* NM-5
Boaz—*locale* VA-3
**Boaz**—*pop pl* AL-4
**Boaz**—*pop pl* IL-6
**Boaz**—*pop pl* KY-4
**Boaz**—*pop pl* MO-7
**Boaz**—*pop pl* WV-2
**Boaz**—*pop pl* WI-6
*Boaz Academy* AL-4
Boaz-Albertville Hosp—*hospital* AL-4
Boaz Branch—*stream* TN-4
Boaz Cem—*cemetery* (2) KY-4
Boaz Cem—*cemetery* NM-5
Boaz Cem—*cemetery* TN-4
Boaz Chapel—*church* KY-4
Boaz Ch of God—*church* AL-4
Boaz City Hall—*building* AL-4
*Boaz City School* AL-4
Boaz Corner—*locale* AL-4
Boaz Creek—*stream* TN-4
Boaz Elem Sch—*school* AL-4
Boaz First Baptist Ch—*church* AL-4
Boaz Golf and Country Club—*other* AL-4
Boaz Golf Course—*other* TX-5
Boaz Gulch—*valley* OR-9
Boaz (historical)—*locale* NV-8
Boaz HS—*school* AL-4
Boaz JHS—*school* AL-4
Boaz Lake—*lake* MI-6
*Boaz Methodist Episcopal Church* AL-4
Boaz Mine—*mine* AZ-5
Boaz Mine—*mine* MT-8
Boaz Mountains—*summit* VA-3
Boaz Mtn—*summit* OR-9
Boaz Nursing Home—*hospital* AL-4
Boaz Sch—*school* KY-4
Boaz Second Baptist Ch—*church* AL-4
*Boaz Station* KS-7
Bob, Mount—*summit* NY-2
**Bob Acres**—*pop pl* LA-4
Bob Adams Field Routt County—*airport* CO-8
Bob Allen Branch—*stream* NC-3
Bob Allen Keys—*island* FL-3
Bob Archibald Hollow—*valley* UT-8
Bob-A-Ron Lake—*lake* MI-6
*Bobasang Harbor* PW-9
Bobay Ditch—*canal* IN-6
*Bobay Hoeck* DE-2
Bobb, Barnett, House—*hist pl* PA-2
Bob Bald—*summit* NC-3
Bob Barber Hollow—*valley* TN-4
Bob Bargo Branch—*stream* KY-4
Bob Barnes Branch—*stream* AR-4
*Bob Bates Fork* AR-4
Bob Bay—*bay* MN-6
Bobb Branch—*stream* IN-6
Bobb Dixon Cem—*cemetery* NC-3
Bob Bee Tree Lake—*lake* SC-3
Bobben, Lake—*lake* GA-3
Bob Bennett Spring—*spring* OR-9
Bobb House—*hist pl* MS-4
Bobbie, Lake—*reservoir* AR-4
Bobbie Branch—*stream* KY-4
Bobbie Mine—*mine* AZ-5
Bobbies Bay—*bay* MN-6
Bobbies Branch—*stream* IL-6
Bobbies Windmill—*locale* TX-5
Bobbie Tank—*reservoir* AZ-5
Bobbin Branch—*stream* KY-4
Bobbin Mill Brook—*stream* CT-1
Bob Bishop Canyon—*valley* UT-8
Bobb Island—*island* SC-3
Bobbit Mine—*mine* OR-9
**Bobbitt**—*pop pl* NC-3
Bobbitt Bridge—*bridge* TX-5
Bobbitt Cem—*cemetery* KY-4
Bobbitt Cem—*cemetery* OH-6
Bobbitt Cem—*cemetery* TN-4
Bobbitt Cem—*cemetery* (2) TX-5
Bobbitt Creek—*stream* TX-5
Bobbitt Creek—*stream* VA-3
Bobbitt Knob—*summit* VA-3
Bobbitt Lake—*lake* TX-5
Bobbitt-Rogers House and Tobacco Manufactory District—*hist pl* NC-3
Bobbitts Branch—*stream* NC-3
**Bobbittville (historical)**—*pop pl* TX-5
Bobblers Knob—*summit* CO-8
Bobblets Gap—*gap* VA-3
Bob Branch—*stream* AL-4
Bob Branch—*stream* AR-4
Bob Branch—*stream* GA-3
Bob Branch—*stream* IL-6
Bob Branch—*stream* (3) KY-4
Bob Branch—*stream* (2) MS-4
Bob Branch—*stream* (4) NC-3
Bob Branch—*stream* (2) TN-4
Bob Branch—*stream* (2) TX-5
Bob Branch—*stream* (2) VA-3
Bob Branch—*stream* WV-2
Bob Bray Mtn—*summit* KY-4
Bob Brock Ditch—*canal* WY-8
*Bobbrook Lake* WI-6
Bob Brown Tank—*reservoir* AZ-5
Bob Brown Well—*well* AZ-5
**Bobbs**—*pop pl* KY-4
*Bobbs Creek* MO-7
Bobbs Creek—*stream* PA-2
Bob Butte—*summit* OR-9
Bobby Anderson Mine—*mine* ID-8
Bobby Anderson Ridge—*ridge* ID-8
Bobby Canyon—*valley* UT-8
Bobby Creek—*stream* ME-1
Bobby Creek—*stream* (2) OR-9
Bobby Creek—*stream* WV-2
Bobby Draw—*valley* WY-8
Bobby Duke Pass—*gap* UT-8
Bobby Duke Ridge—*ridge* UT-8
Bobby Duncan Lake Dam—*dam* MS-4
Bobbygay Lake—*lake* MI-6
Bobby Harris Pond—*reservoir* MA-1
*Bobby Island* NC-3
Bobby Island—*island* UT-8
Bobby Jones Lake—*reservoir* AL-4
Bobby Jones Lake Dam—*dam* AL-4
Bobby Lake—*lake* CA-9
Bobby Lake—*lake* MN-6
Bobby Lake—*lake* OR-9
Bobby Lake—*reservoir* NM-5
Bobby McLeod Lake—*dam* MS-4
Bobby Peters 2 Dam—*dam* SD-7
Bobby Run—*stream* (2) PA-2
**Bobbys Corners**—*pop pl* PA-2
Bobbys Hole—*basin* (2) UT-8
Bobbys Hole Canyon—*valley* UT-8
Bobby Sides Lake Dam—*dam* MS-4
Bobbys Landing—*locale* AL-4
Bobby Spring—*spring* AZ-5
Bobbys Ridge—*ridge* VA-3
Bobbys Run—*stream* NJ-2
Bobby Tank—*reservoir* AZ-5
Bobby Thompson Lake Dam—*dam* MS-4
Bobby Walker Marina—*locale* AL-4
Bob Canyon—*valley* NV-8
Bob Cat Acres Lake—*reservoir* NC-3
Bob Cat Acres Lake Dam—*dam* NC-3
Bobcat Bar—*bar* ID-8
Bobcat Basin—*basin* AZ-5
Bobcat Basin—*basin* WY-8
Bobcat Bay—*bay* MT-8
Bobcat Bluff—*cliff* TX-5
Bobcat Brook—*stream* ME-1
Bobcat Butte—*summit* AZ-5
Bobcat Butte—*summit* ID-8
Bobcat Canyon—*valley* (4) CA-9
Bobcat Canyon—*valley* (3) CO-8
Bobcat Canyon—*valley* NE-7
Bobcat Canyon—*valley* NV-8
Bobcat Canyon—*valley* (2) NM-5
Bobcat Canyon—*valley* (2) SD-7
Bobcat Canyon—*valley* TX-5
Bobcat Canyon—*valley* WY-8
Bobcat Canyon Windmill—*locale* TX-5
Bobcat Coulee—*valley* (2) MT-8
*Bobcat Creek* MT-8
Bobcat Creek—*stream* AZ-5
Bobcat Creek—*stream* CO-8
Bobcat Creek—*stream* ID-8
Bobcat Creek—*stream* MI-6
Bobcat Creek—*stream* MN-6
Bobcat Creek—*stream* (6) MT-8
Bobcat Creek—*stream* NM-5
Bobcat Creek—*stream* (3) OR-9
Bobcat Creek—*stream* (5) WY-8
Bobcat Draw—*valley* CO-8
Bobcat Draw—*valley* NM-5
Bobcat Draw—*valley* (3) WY-8
Bobcat Gulch—*valley* CO-8
Bobcat Gulch—*valley* ID-8
Bobcat Gulch—*valley* MT-8
Bobcat Gulch—*valley* OK-5
Bobcat Gulch—*valley* (2) SD-7
Bobcat Gulch—*valley* WY-8
Bobcat Hill—*summit* (2) NM-5
Bobcat Hill—*summit* WY-8
Bobcat Hills—*ridge* AZ-5
Bobcat Hills—*summit* CA-9
Bobcat Hills—*summit* TX-5
Bobcat Hollow—*valley* AL-4
*Bob Cat Lake* MI-6
Bobcat Lake—*lake* MI-6
Bobcat Lake—*lake* WI-6
Bobcat Lakes—*lake* MT-8
Bobcat Lakes Trail—*trail* MT-8
Bobcat Landing—*locale* SC-3
Bobcat Mtn—*summit* CO-8
Bobcat Mtn—*summit* MT-8
Bobcat Mtn—*summit* WA-9
Bobcat Pass—*gap* MT-8
Bobcat Pass—*gap* (2) NM-5
*Bobcat Peak* MT-8
Bobcat Point—*cape* CA-9
Bobcat Pond—*lake* FL-3
Bobcat Ridge—*ridge* OK-5
Bobcat Ridge—*ridge* WY-8
Bobcat Rsvr—*reservoir* (2) AZ-5
Bobcat Rsvr—*reservoir* CO-8
Bobcat Rsvr—*reservoir* OR-9
Bobcat Spring—*spring* CA-9
Bobcat Spring—*spring* NM-5
Bobcat Spring—*spring* OR-9
Bobcat Springs—*spring* CO-8
Bobcat Swamp—*swamp* NY-2
Bobcat Tank—*reservoir* (3) AZ-5
Bobcat Tank Number Two—*reservoir* AZ-5
Bobcat Trail Habitation Cave (50-10-30-5004)—*hist pl* HI-9
Bobcat Well—*well* NM-5
Bobcat Windmill—*locale* AZ-5
Bobcat Windmill—*locale* TX-5
Bob C Creek—*stream* MT-8
Bobcean Drain—*stream* MI-6
Bob Ch—*church* LA-4
*Bob Chitwood Branch* TN-4
*Bobcock Hole* CO-8
*Bobcock Ridge* WA-9
Bob Cooper Hollow—*valley* KY-4
Bob Coulee—*valley* MT-8
*Bob Creek* MI-6
Bob Creek—*stream* AK-9
Bob Creek—*stream* CA-9
Bob Creek—*stream* (3) CO-8
Bob Creek—*stream* ID-8
Bob Creek—*stream* IN-6
Bob Creek—*stream* MN-6
Bob Creek—*stream* NV-8
Bob Creek—*stream* NC-3
Bob Creek—*stream* OK-5
Bob Creek—*stream* (5) OR-9
Bob Creek—*stream* TN-4
Bob Creek—*stream* TX-5
Bob Creek—*stream* UT-8
Bob Creek—*stream* (3) WA-9
Bob Creek—*stream* WI-6
Bob Creek—*stream* (2) WY-8
Bob Creek Shelter—*locale* WA-9
Bob Creek Spring—*spring* CA-9
Bob Crosby Bridge—*other* NM-5
Bob Crosby Draw—*valley* NM-5
Bob Crowder Memorial Dam—*dam* AZ-5
Bob Dam Swamp—*swamp* SC-3
Bob Day Branch—*stream* KY-4
Bob Denny Hills—*range* ND-7
Bob Eaton Canyon—*valley* CO-8
Bob Elders Mine (underground)—*mine* TN-4
Bobell Hill—*summit* NY-2
Bob Everett Point—*cape* FL-3
Bob Faler Airp—*airport* KS-7
Bob Fitzpatrick Branch—*stream* KY-4
Bob Flat—*flat* OR-9
Bob Gap—*gap* KY-4
Bob Gap—*gap* VA-3
Bob George Branch—*stream* AL-4
Bob Gillforth Lake Dam—*dam* MS-4
Bob Gulch—*valley* WA-9
Bob Hall Pier—*locale* TX-5
Bob Hamilton Wash—*stream* NV-8
Bob Harris—*uninc pl* TX-5
Bob Hill Cem—*cemetery* MI-6
Bob Hill Flat—*flat* UT-8
Bob Hill Gulch—*valley* CA-9
Bob Hill Knoll—*summit* UT-8
Bob Hill Spring—*spring* UT-8
Bob Hoaglin Place—*locale* CA-9
Bob Hollow—*valley* AL-4
Bob Hollow—*valley* (2) MO-7
Bob Hollow—*valley* (2) TN-4
Bob Hollow—*valley* VA-3
Bob Hollow Branch—*stream* AL-4
Bob Hood Branch—*stream* AL-4
Bob Hughes Creek—*stream* CO-8
Bobidosh Lake—*lake* WI-6
Bobier Meadow—*flat* OR-9
Bobier Sch—*school* CA-9
Bobier Slide—*valley* OR-9
Bobilya Park—*park* IN-6
Bob Ingersoll Mine—*mine* MT-8
Bobington Branch—*stream* OR-9
Bobins Pocket Spring—*spring* CO-8
Bob Jones HS—*school* AL-4
Bob Jones Univ—*school* SC-3
*Bob Key* FL-3
Bob Keys—*island* FL-3
Bob Kiddys Hole—*basin* UT-8
Bobkies Island—*island* NE-7
Bob Knob—*summit* NC-3
Bob Kosts Pond—*reservoir* PA-2
Bob Lake—*lake* AK-9
Bob Lake—*lake* CO-8
Bob Lake—*lake* LA-4
Bob Lake—*lake* (4) MI-6
Bob Lake—*lake* MN-6
Bob Lake—*lake* SD-7
Bob Lake—*lake* WI-6
Bob Lake Creek—*stream* MI-6
Bob Lakes—*lake* WY-8
Bob Lane Cem—*cemetery* TX-5
Bob Lee Phillips Hill—*summit* KY-4
Bob Lee Spring—*spring* AZ-5
Bob Leroy Pass—*gap* UT-8
Bob Leroy Peaks—*summit* UT-8
Bob Leroy Spring—*spring* UT-8
*Boblet Lake* MI-6
Boblett Cem—*cemetery* OH-6
Boblitt Cem—*cemetery* AZ-5
Bob Locke Mission—*church* AL-4
Bob Lott Bridge—*bridge* MS-4
Bob Lowe Knob—*summit* KY-4
Bob Lyons—*uninc pl* TX-5
Bob Mac Pond—*lake* MI-6
Bob Malone Catfish Ponds Dam—*dam* MS-4
Bob Manning Canyon—*valley* TX-5
Bob McKee Mine—*mine* CA-9
Bob Meadow—*flat* OR-9
Bob Mikes Hollow—*valley* MO-7
*Bob Miller Creek* MS-4
Bob Moore Creek—*stream* ID-8
Bob Mtn—*summit* AL-4
Bob Neal Branch—*stream* AR-4
*Bobo* IN-6
Bobo—*locale* GA-3
Bobo—*locale* OH-6
**Bobo**—*pop pl* (2) AL-4
**Bobo**—*pop pl* (2) MS-4
Bobo Bayou—*stream* (2) MS-4
Bobo Branch—*stream* AL-4
Bobo Cave—*cave* TN-4
Bobo Cem—*cemetery* (2) AL-4
Bobo Cem—*cemetery* AR-4
Bobo Cem—*cemetery* GA-3
Bobo Cem—*cemetery* TN-4
Bobo Cem—*cemetery* TX-5
Bobo Ch—*church* TX-5
Bobo Creek—*stream* AL-4
Bobo Creek—*stream* AR-4
Bobo Creek—*stream* (3) TN-4
Bobo Hollow—*valley* TN-4
Bobo HS—*school* AL-4
Bobo Lake—*lake* MS-4
Bobolink Ch—*church* FL-3
Bobolink Creek—*stream* MI-6
Bob O'Link Golf Club—*other* IL-6
Bob-O-Link Golf Club—*other* MI-6
Bobo Link Lake—*lake* MN-6
Bobolink Lake—*reservoir* GA-3
Bob-O-Links Golf Course—*other* TX-5
Bobo Outlet—*stream* MS-4
Bobo Post Office (historical)—*building* AL-4
Bobo Sch (historical)—*school* MS-4
Bobo Spring—*spring* AZ-5
Bobo Spring—*spring* TN-4
Bob Owens Canyon—*valley* CA-9
Bob Pace Dam—*dam* AL-4
Bob Park Airp—*airport* KS-7
Bob Park Peak—*summit* UT-8
*Bob Pate Hollow* IN-6
Bob Payne Hollow—*valley* AL-4
Bob Peters Ditch—*canal* MT-8
Bob Peterson Bay—*swamp* NC-3
Bob Plank Spring—*spring* OR-9
Bob Post Office (historical)—*building* TN-4
Bob Prater Branch—*stream* NC-3
Bob Quarters Cem—*cemetery* MS-4
Bob Rabbit Canyon—*valley* CA-9
Bob Rabbit Place (Site)—*locale* CA-9
Bo Branch—*stream* TX-5
Bob Ray Lake Dam—*dam* MS-4
B & O Bridge—*hist pl* MD-2
Bobrof Island—*island* AK-9
Bobrovia Mtn—*summit* AK-9
Bobrovoi Point—*cape* AK-9
Bob Russ Lakes—*lake* FL-3
Bob Russ Pond, The—*lake* FL-3
*Bob Russ Ponds* FL-3
Bob Saints Cem—*cemetery* AL-4
Bob Sands Hollow—*valley* TN-4
Bobs Bay—*bay* AK-9
Bobs Bay—*swamp* OR-9
Bobs Bayou—*gut* (2) LA-4
Bobs Bayou—*stream* LA-4
Bobs Blue Hole—*lake* AR-4
Bobs Branch—*stream* (3) KY-4
Bobs Branch—*stream* MS-4
Bobs Branch—*stream* NC-3
Bobs Branch—*stream* SC-3
Bobs Branch—*stream* TN-4
Bobs Branch—*stream* (2) VA-3
Bobs Branch—*stream* WV-2
Bobs Brook—*stream* NY-2
Bobs Cabin Trail—*trail* CA-9
*Bobs Canyon* UT-8
Bobs Canyon—*valley* UT-8
Bob Scott Forest Service Recreation Site—*locale* NV-8
Bob Scotts Historical Site—*locale* NV-8
Bob Scotts Summit—*summit* NV-8
Bobs Coulee—*valley* ND-7
*Bobs Cove* ME-1
Bobs Cove—*bay* ME-1
*Bobs Creek* NC-3
**Bobs Creek**—*pop pl* KY-4
Bobs Creek—*stream* AL-4
Bobs Creek—*stream* AK-9
Bobs Creek—*stream* ID-8
Bobs Creek—*stream* IN-6
Bobs Creek—*stream* KY-4
Bobs Creek—*stream* LA-4
Bobs Creek—*stream* (2) MI-6
Bobs Creek—*stream* (2) MO-7
Bobs Creek—*stream* (3) NC-3
Bobs Creek—*stream* OR-9
Bobs Creek—*stream* PA-2
Bobs Creek—*stream* SD-7
Bobs Creek—*stream* TN-4
Bobs Creek—*stream* TX-5
Bobs Creek—*stream* VA-3
Bobs Creek—*stream* WI-6
Bobs Creek Ch—*church* NC-3
Bobs Creek Gap—*gap* PA-2
Bobs Creek Ranch—*locale* TX-5
**Bobs Cross Roads (historical)**—*pop pl* TN-4
Bobs Draw—*valley* WY-8
Bobs Farm—*locale* CA-9
Bobs Flat—*flat* AZ-5
Bobs Flat—*flat* CA-9
Bobs Flat—*flat* NV-8
Bobs Flat Trail—*trail* CA-9
Bobs Fork—*stream* KY-4
Bobs Fork—*stream* (2) WV-2
Bobs Fork Sch—*school* KY-4
Bobs Gap—*gap* CA-9
Bobs Gap—*gap* NC-3
Bobs Garden Creek—*gut* SC-3
Bobs Garden Mtn—*summit* OR-9
Bobs Garden Trail—*trail* OR-9
Bob Shannon Memorial Field (airport)—*airport* PA-2
**Bobsher**—*pop pl* TX-5
Bobs Hill—*summit* MD-2
Bobs Hole—*basin* UT-8
Bobs Hollow—*valley* KY-4
Bobs Hollow—*valley* WI-6
Bob Shrivers Tank—*reservoir* TX-5
*Bob Sikes Cut* FL-3
Bob Silkes Bridge—*bridge* FL-3
Bobs Island—*island* NC-3
Bobs Knob—*summit* MO-7
*Bobs Lake* CA-9
*Bobs Lake* LA-4
Bobs Lake—*lake* AK-9
Bobs Lake—*lake* FL-3
Bobs Lake—*lake* MI-6
Bobs Lake—*lake* MS-4
Bobs Lake—*lake* MT-8
Bobs Lake—*lake* OR-9
Bobs Lake—*lake* SC-3
Bobs Lake—*lake* UT-8
Bobs Lake—*lake* WA-9
Bobs Lake—*lake* (3) WI-6
Bobs Lake—*lake* WY-8
Bobs Lake Number One—*reservoir* TN-4
Bobs Lake Number One Dam—*dam* TN-4
Bobs Lake Number Two—*reservoir* TN-4
Bobs Lake Number Two Dam—*dam* TN-4
Bobs Lakes—*bay* LA-4
Bobs Lakes—*lake* WA-9
Bobs Landing—*locale* TN-4
Bobsled Creek—*stream* OR-9
Bobsled Hollow—*valley* PA-2
Bobsled Ridge—*ridge* OR-9
Bobsled Rips—*rapids* ME-1
Bobsled Trail—*trail* OR-9
Bob Slusher Gap—*gap* KY-4
Bob Smith Canyon—*valley* NM-5
Bob Smith Canyon—*valley* TX-5
*Bob Smith Creek* ID-8
Bob Smith Windmill—*locale* TX-5
Bobs Mtn—*summit* WA-9
Bobs Mtn—*summit* WV-2
Bobs Place—*locale* AK-9
Bobs Point—*cape* AK-9
Bobs Point—*cape* ME-1
Bobs Point—*cape* WA-9
Bobs Pond—*lake* ME-1
Bob Spring—*spring* CA-9
Bob Spring—*spring* (2) NV-8
Bob Spring—*spring* TN-4
Bob Spring—*spring* WY-8
Bobs Ridge—*ridge* NC-3
Bobs Ridge—*ridge* WV-2
*Bobs Run* PA-2
Bobs Run—*stream* OH-6
Bobs Spring—*spring* CO-8
Bobs Spur—*ridge* VA-3
Bobs String Swamp—*swamp* PA-2
Bobs Tank—*reservoir* (4) AZ-5
Bobs Tank—*reservoir* NM-5
Bobst Mtn—*summit* PA-2
Bobs Towers—*summit* WY-8
*Bobsts Manor House* PA-2
Bobs Well—*well* AZ-5
Bobs Well—*well* NM-5
Bobtail Basin—*basin* AZ-5
Bobtail Bayou—*stream* LA-4
Bobtail Canyon—*valley* NM-5
Bobtail Creek—*stream* AR-4
Bobtail Creek—*stream* CO-8
Bobtail Creek—*stream* GA-3
Bobtail Creek—*stream* (2) ID-8
Bobtail Creek—*stream* MT-8
Bobtail Creek—*stream* (2) NE-7
Bobtail Creek—*stream* OK-5
Bob Tail Dam—*dam* AZ-5
Bobtail Gulch—*valley* (2) SD-7
Bobtail Hill—*summit* CO-8
Bobtail Hill—*summit* IL-6
Bobtail Lake—*lake* AR-4
Bobtail Lake—*lake* NE-7
Bobtail Mesa—*summit* NM-5
Bobtail Mine—*mine* CO-8
Bobtail Mines—*mine* CA-9
Bobtail Peak—*summit* ID-8
Bobtail Ridge—*ridge* AZ-5
Bobtail Ridge—*ridge* MT-8
Bobtail Spring—*spring* AZ-5
Bob Tail Tank—*reservoir* AZ-5
Bobtail Tank—*reservoir* NM-5
Bobtail Tunnel—*mine* CO-8
Bob Tank—*reservoir* NM-5
Bob Taylors Pond—*bay* LA-4
Bob Thompson Dam—*dam* AL-4
Bob Thompson Lake—*reservoir* AL-4
Bob Thompson Peak—*summit* AZ-5
Bobtown—*locale* IL-6
Bobtown—*locale* (2) KY-4
Bobtown—*locale* VA-3
**Bobtown**—*pop pl* IN-6
**Bobtown**—*pop pl* PA-2
**Bobtown**—*pop pl* (2) TN-4
Bobtown Elem Sch—*school* PA-2
Bobtown Sch—*school* IL-6
Bobtown Sch—*school* KY-4
Bobtown Well—*well* NV-8
Bobville—*locale* TX-5
Bob Walden Hollow—*valley* AL-4
Bob Walker Canyon—*valley* CA-9

**Boggess Crossroad**—pop pl TN-4
Boggess Dam—dam AL-4
Boggess Hole—bay FL-3
Boggess Hollow—valley KY-4
Boggess Lake—lake FL-3
Boggess Lake—reservoir AL-4
**Boggess Meadow Estates (subdivision)**—pop pl UT-8
Boggess Point—cape FL-3
Boggess Run—stream WV-2
*Boggestow Brook* MA-1
Bogg Fork—stream WV-2
Bogg Gulch—valley MT-8
Boggie Creek—stream TX-5
*Boggie Hollow Creek* AL-4
*Boggie Hollow Creek* FL-3
Boggies, The—channel FL-3
Boggie Windmill—locale NM-5
*Boggin Branch* AR-4
Boggins Branch—stream AR-4
Boggins Cem—cemetery AR-4
*Boggister Brook* MA-1
*Boggistere Brook* MA-1
*Boggistere Pond* MA-1
Boggles Creek—stream AL-4
Bogg Mtn—summit SC-3
*Boggochoag Hills* MA-1
Bogg Pond—lake FL-3
Boggs—locale WV-2
**Boggs**—pop pl PA-2
**Boggs**—pop pl TN-4
Boggs Acad—school GA-3
Boggs Ave Elem Sch—hist pl PA-2
Boggs Bend—bend CA-9
Boggs Branch—stream GA-3
Boggs Branch—stream KY-4
Boggs Branch—stream OK-5
Boggs Cem—cemetery FL-3
Boggs Cem—cemetery (2) KY-4
Boggs Cem—cemetery LA-4
Boggs Cem—cemetery (2) OH-6
Boggs Cem—cemetery PA-2
Boggs Cem—cemetery VA-3
Boggs Cem—cemetery WV-2
Boggs Chapel—church GA-3
Boggs Chapel—church MS-4
Boggs Chapel Cem—cemetery MS-4
*Boggs Chapel Methodist Church* MS-4
*Boggs Creek* TX-5
Boggs Creek—stream AR-4
Boggs Creek—stream CA-9
Boggs Creek—stream (2) CO-8
Boggs Creek—stream GA-3
Boggs Creek—stream IN-6
Boggs Creek—stream (2) LA-4
Boggs Creek—stream MO-7
Boggs Creek—stream OH-6
Boggs Creek—stream WV-2
Boggs Creek Cem—cemetery IN-6
*Boggs Creek Reservoir* IN-6
Boggs Ditch—canal IN-6
Boggs Ditch—canal MT-8
Boggs Field—park FL-3
Boggs Flat—flat CO-8
Boggs Flat Cemeteries—cemetery KY-4
*Boggs Fork* WV-2
Boggs Fork—stream KY-4
Boggs Fork—stream OH-6
Boggs Fork—stream (3) WV-2
Boggs Fork Sch—school WV-2
Boggs Gut—gut MD-2
Boggs Gut—gut VA-3
Boggs Hightop—summit WV-2
Boggs Hollow—valley KY-4
Boggs Hollow—valley OH-6
Boggs Hollow—valley PA-2
Boggs Hollow—valley (2) VA-3
Boggs Hollow—valley WV-2
Boggs Hollow Creek—stream OK-5
Boggs Island—island MT-8
Boggs Island—island OH-6
Boggs Knob—summit (2) WV-2
Boggs Lake—lake CA-9
Boggs Lake—lake GA-3
Boggs Lake—lake OR-9
Boggs Lake—reservoir MO-7
Boggs Landing—locale AK-9
Boggs Lumber and Hardware Bldg—hist pl CO-8
Boggs Mill Sch—school ME-1
Boggs Mountain Ch—church GA-3
Boggs Mountain State For—forest CA-9
Boggs Mtn—summit CA-9
Boggs Mtn—summit (2) GA-3
Boggs Pond—lake FL-3
Boggs Pond—reservoir CT-1
Bogg Spring—spring NM-5
Boggs Ranch—locale (2) AZ-5
*Boggs Run* PA-2
Boggs Run—stream PA-2
Boggs Run—stream (4) WV-2
Boggs Run Sch—school WV-2
Boggs Sch—school IL-6
Boggs Sch—school KY-4
Boggs Sch—school VA-3
Boggs Sch (historical)—school PA-2
Boggs Slough—gut CA-9
Boggs Spring—spring OR-9
Boggs Table—summit NE-7
**Boggstown**—pop pl IN-6
**Boggstown**—pop pl PA-2
Boggstown Cem—cemetery IN-6
**Boggs (Township of)**—pop pl (3) PA-2
Boggsville—hist pl CO-8
Boggsville—locale CO-8
**Boggsville**—pop pl PA-2
Boggs Whart—locale VA-3
Boggu Bayou—stream LA-4
Bog Gut—gut VA-3
Boggy—locale AR-4
Boggy—locale GA-3
Boggy Basin—basin CO-8
Boggy Basin—basin TX-5
Boggy Bay—bay (2) FL-3
Boggy Bay—swamp (2) FL-3
Boggy Bay—swamp (2) GA-3
Boggy Bay—swamp LA-4
Boggy Bay—swamp (2) SC-3
Boggy Baygall—swamp LA-4
*Boggy Bayou* LA-4
*Boggy Bayou* TX-5
Boggy Bayou—bay (2) FL-3
Boggy Bayou—channel FL-3
Boggy Bayou—gut (2) AR-4
Boggy Bayou—gut (11) LA-4
Boggy Bayou—gut MS-4
Boggy Bayou—gut TX-5
Boggy Bayou—stream (2) AR-4
Boggy Bayou—stream (12) LA-4
Boggy Bayou—stream MS-4
Boggy Bayou—stream (4) TX-5
Boggy Bayou, Lake—lake AR-4
Boggy Bend—bend LA-4
Boggy Bend Ford—locale OK-5
Boggy Bend Sch—school OK-5
*Boggy Boyou* TX-5
*Boggy Branch* TX-5
Boggy Branch—gut (2) FL-3
Boggy Branch—gut SC-3
Boggy Branch—stream (15) AL-4
Boggy Branch—stream (15) FL-3
Boggy Branch—stream (11) GA-3
Boggy Branch—stream (9) LA-4
Boggy Branch—stream (8) MS-4
Boggy Branch—stream MO-7
Boggy Branch—stream NJ-2
Boggy Branch—stream (5) NC-3
Boggy Branch—stream (8) SC-3
Boggy Branch—stream (18) TX-5
Boggy Branch—swamp GA-3
Boggy Branch Bridge—bridge NC-3
Boggy Branch Sch—school SC-3
Boggy Brook—stream ME-1
Boggy Canyon—valley TX-5
Boggy Cem—cemetery OK-5
Boggy Cem—cemetery TX-5
*Boggy Creek* AZ-5
*Boggy Creek* AR-4
*Boggy Creek* FL-3
*Boggy Creek* GA-3
*Boggy Creek* OK-5
*Boggy Creek* TX-5
Boggy Creek—gut FL-3
Boggy Creek—stream (2) AL-4
Boggy Creek—stream (2) AZ-5
Boggy Creek—stream (3) AR-4
Boggy Creek—stream (8) FL-3
Boggy Creek—stream (2) GA-3
Boggy Creek—stream (2) LA-4
Boggy Creek—stream NE-7
Boggy Creek—stream ND-7
Boggy Creek—stream (14) OK-5
Boggy Creek—stream SC-3
Boggy Creek—stream (45) TX-5
Boggy Creek—stream WA-9
Boggy Creek—stream (3) WY-8
Boggy Creek Elem Sch—school FL-3
Boggy Creek Swamp—swamp FL-3
Boggy Cut Bayou—stream LA-4
Boggy Cutoff—channel OK-5
Boggy Cutoff—stream OK-5
Boggy Depot—locale OK-5
Boggy Depot Cem—cemetery OK-5
Boggy Depot Rec Area—park OK-5
Boggy Depot Site—hist pl OK-5
Boggy Drain—swamp GA-3
Boggy Draw—valley CO-8
Boggy Draw—valley TX-5
Boggy Draw Rsvr—reservoir CO-8
Boggy Flat—flat OK-5
Boggy Flat Bay—swamp FL-3
Boggy Gall—flat GA-3
Boggy Gall Swamp—swamp GA-3
Boggy Glade Branch—stream TX-5
Boggy Gully—gut SC-3
Boggy Gully Bay—swamp SC-3
Boggy Gully Swamp—stream SC-3
*Boggy Gut* SC-3
Boggy Gut—gut AL-4
Boggy Gut—stream GA-3
Boggy Gut—stream SC-3
*Boggy Gut Bayou* LA-4
Boggy Gut Branch—stream SC-3
Boggy Gut Creek—stream (3) GA-3
Boggy Head—valley FL-3
Boggy Head Bay—swamp GA-3
Boggy Head Bay—swamp SC-3
Boggy Hill Branch—stream NC-3
*Boggy Hollow* MS-4
Boggy Hollow—valley MS-4
Boggy Hollow—valley OK-5
Boggy Hollow Creek—stream AL-4
Boggy Hollow Creek—stream FL-3
Boggy Hollow Creek—stream OK-5
Boggy Island—island FL-3
*Boggy Jordan* FL-3
Boggy Jordan—swamp (2) FL-3
Boggy Jordan Bayou—stream FL-3
Boggy Key—island FL-3
Boggy Lake—lake AR-4
Boggy Lake—lake FL-3
Boggy Lake—lake GA-3
Boggy Lake—lake (6) LA-4
Boggy Lake—lake MN-6
Boggy Lake—lake MS-4
Boggy Lake—lake NM-5
Boggy Lake—lake OR-9
Boggy Lake—lake SC-3
Boggy Lake—lake (2) TX-5
Boggy Lake—lake WI-6
Boggy Lake—reservoir TX-5
Boggy Lakes—lake TX-5
Boggy Lake Well—well AZ-5
*Boggy Marsh* TX-5
Boggy Marsh—swamp FL-3
Boggy Meadow—flat (2) CA-9
Boggy Meadow—swamp CT-1
Boggy Meadows—flat NH-1
Boggy Meadows—flat WY-8
Boggy Meadows Lake—lake WY-8
Boggy Meadows Rim—cliff WY-8
*Boggy Point* FL-3
Boggy Point—cape FL-3
*Boggy Pond* ME-1
*Boggy Pond* WI-6
Boggy Pond—gut FL-3
Boggy Pond—lake (2) FL-3
Boggy Pond—lake GA-3
Boggy Pond—lake WI-6
Boggy Pond—swamp FL-3
Boggy Pond—swamp GA-3
Boggy Prong—stream MS-4
Boggy Rsvr—reservoir WY-8
Boggy Run—stream PA-2
Boggy Slough—gut AR-4
Boggy Slough—gut (3) TX-5
Boggy Slough—lake AR-4
Boggy Slough—stream MS-4
Boggy Slough—swamp FL-3
Boggy Slough Club—other TX-5
Boggy Spring—spring ID-8
Boggy Springs Ch—church AR-4
Boggy Springs Hollow—valley OK-5
Boggy Springs Pond—lake WY-8
Boggy Spur Drain—canal NM-5
Boggy Strand—swamp FL-3
*Boggy Swamp* FL-3
Boggy Swamp—stream (6) SC-3
Boggy Swamp—swamp NC-3
Boggy Swamp—swamp (2) SC-3
Boggy Tank—reservoir (2) AZ-5
Boggy Tank—reservoir NM-5
Boggy Tank—reservoir TX-5
Boggy Well—well TX-5
Boggy Windmill—locale TX-5
Boggy Womble Brake—swamp LA-4
*Bog Hole Spring* WY-8
Boghole Spring—spring ID-8
Boghole Spring—spring WY-8
Bog Hole Springs—spring WY-8
Bog Hole Tank—reservoir AZ-5
Bog Hollow—valley AR-4
Bog Hollow—valley PA-2
Bog Hollow Brook—stream CT-1
Bog Hollow Brook—stream NY-2
Bog Hot Ranch—locale NV-8
Bog Hot Rsvr—reservoir NV-8
Bog Hot Springs—spring NV-8
Bog Hot Valley—flat NV-8
Bog Hot Well—well (2) NV-8
**Boght Corners**—pop pl NY-2
Bogia—locale FL-3
Bogie Branch—stream KY-4
Bogie Channel—channel FL-3
Bogie Circle—hist pl KY-4
Bogie Creek—stream AK-9
Bogie Draw—valley WY-8
Bogie Hole Cave—cave AL-4
Bogie Hollow—valley OH-6
Bogie Houses and Mill Site—hist pl KY-4
Bogie Lake—lake MI-6
Bogie Rsvr—reservoir WY-8
Bogie Run—stream OH-6
Bogie Sch—school KY-4
*Bogirugumerutsu-To* MP-9
*Bogister Brook* MA-1
*Bogistow B* MA-1
Bogk, Frederick C., House—hist pl WI-6
*Bog Lake* CO-8
*Bog Lake* MN-6
*Bog Lake* WI-6
Bog Lake—lake AK-9
Bog Lake—lake (3) ME-1
Bog Lake—lake (2) MI-6
Bog Lake—lake (8) MN-6
Bog Lake—lake NY-2
Bog Lake—lake (2) TX-5
Bog Lake—lake (7) WI-6
Bog Lakes—lake WY-8
Boglebrae Farms—locale PA-2
Bogle Brook—stream MA-1
Bogle Cem—cemetery KS-7
Bogle Cem—cemetery TN-4
**Bogle Corner**—pop pl IN-6
Bogle Cove—bay MD-2
Bogle Draw—valley ID-8
Bogle Flats—flat NM-5
Bogle Hollow—valley TN-4
Bogle Knob—summit KY-4
Bogler Lake—lake WI-6
Bogles Chapel—church TN-4
Bogles Chapel Sch (historical)—school TN-4
Bogles Cotton Gin—other NM-5
*Bogles Creek* MI-6
Bogle Spring Branch—stream TN-4
Bogles Run—stream OH-6
*Bogles School* TN-4
Bogles Shoals—bar TN-4
*Bogles Store* TN-4
Bogle Street Sch—school MA-1
Bogle Tank—reservoir NM-5
**Bogle Township**—pop pl MO-7
Bogley Branch—stream MD-2
Bog Meadow—flat NY-2
Bog Meadow—swamp NY-2
Bog Meadow Brook—stream CT-1
Bog Meadow Brook—stream NY-2
Bog Meadow Pond—reservoir CT-1
Bog Meadow Pond—reservoir NY-2
Bog Meadow Rsvr—reservoir (2) CT-1
*Bog Medow Brook* NY-2
Bog Mine—mine UT-8
Bog Mound Springs—spring CA-9
Bog Mtn—summit ME-1
Bog Mtn—summit NH-1
Bog Mtn—summit NY-2
Bog Mtn—summit OK-5
Bogner Dam—dam SD-7
Bogner Field (airport)—airport SD-7
Bogokkai Island—island MP-9
*Bogokkai-to* MP-9
*Bogollep* MP-9
*Bogombogo* MP-9
Bogombogo—island MP-9
*Bogombogo Island* MP-9
*Bogon* MP-9
*Bogonarappu To* MP-9
*Bogon Island* MP-9
Bogontorinaai Island—island MP-9
*Bogontorinaai-To* MP-9
Bog Opening—swamp NC-3
*Bogoraborapu* MP-9
Bogoraborapu—island MP-9
*Bogoraborapu Island* MP-9
*Bogoraborapu-To* MP-9
Bog Ore Hollow—valley PA-2
Bog Ore Run—stream PA-2
Bogoslof Hill—summit AK-9
Bogoslof Island—island AK-9
Bogoslof Natl Wildlife Ref—park AK-9
**Bogota**—pop pl IL-6
**Bogota**—pop pl NJ-2
**Bogota**—pop pl TN-4
Bogota Baptist Ch—church TN-4
Bogota Elem Sch—school TN-4
Bogota Post Office—building TN-4
Bog Outlet, The—stream NY-2
Bog Point—cape ME-1
*Bog Pond* ME-1
*Bog Pond* MN-6
Bog Pond—lake LA-4
Bog Pond—lake (9) ME-1
Bog Pond—lake (2) MA-1
Bog Pond—lake (3) NH-1
Bog Pond—lake NY-2
Bog Pond—lake (2) VT-1
Bog Pond—reservoir (2) MA-1
Bog Pond—reservoir NH-1
Bog Pond Dam—dam MA-1
Bog Ranch—locale AZ-5
*Bog River* NY-2
Bog River—stream ME-1
Bog River—stream (2) NY-2
*Bog River Flow* NY-2
Bog Road Cem—cemetery NH-1
Bog Rsvr—reservoir MT-8
Bogs, The—stream TX-5
Bogs, The—swamp OH-6
*Bogs Branch* VA-3
Bog Scattering Pines—swamp NC-3
Bog Sch—school NH-1
Bog Sch—school WI-6
Bogs Gully—valley TX-5
Bogs Lake—reservoir AR-4
Bog Spring—spring AZ-5
Bog Spring—spring NM-5
Bog Spring—spring (3) OR-9
Bog Spring—spring TX-5
Bog Spring Branch—stream OK-5
**Bog Springs**—pop pl AR-4
Bog Springs—spring AZ-5
Bog Springs—spring WY-8
Bog Springs Campground—park AZ-5
Bog Springs Creek—stream MT-8
Bog Stream—stream (5) ME-1
Bog Stream—stream NY-2
Bog Tank—reservoir (2) AZ-5
Bog Tank Dam—dam AZ-5
Bog Tank Picnic Ground—park AZ-5
Bogucki Island—island WA-9
*Bogue* MA-1
*Bogue* MS-4
Bogue—locale CA-9
**Bogue**—pop pl KS-7
**Bogue**—pop pl NC-3
Bogue Bank Country Club—building NC-3
Bogue Banks—bar NC-3
Bogue Bay—bay MO-7
Bogue Bay—swamp SC-3
*Bogue Beach* MA-1
Bogue Branch—stream VT-1
Bogue Brook—stream CT-1
Bogue Brook Rsvr—reservoir CT-1
Bogue Cem—cemetery AR-4
Bogue Cem—cemetery CT-1
Bogue Ch—church AR-4
Bogue Ch—church MS-4
*Boguechitta Creek* AL-4
Bogue Chitta Creek—stream AL-4
*Bogue Chitto* MS-4
**Bogue Chitto**—pop pl AL-4
**Bogue Chitto**—pop pl (2) MS-4
Bogue Chitto—stream LA-4
Bogue Chitto Attendance Center—school MS-4
*Bogue Chitto Baptist Ch* MS-4
Bogue Chitto Baptist Ch—church MS-4
Bogue Chitto Cem—cemetery MS-4
Bogue Chitto Ch—church LA-4
Bogue Chitto Ch—church (2) MS-4
*Bogue Chitto Church* AL-4
*Bogue Chitto Consolidated School* MS-4
*Boguechitto Creek* AL-4
*Bogue Chitto Creek* MS-4
Bogue Chitto Creek—stream AL-4
Bogue Chitto Creek—stream MS-4
Bogue Chitto Creek Bar—bar AL-4
Bogue Chitto Indian Sch—school MS-4
Bogue Chitto Natl Wildlife Ref—park MS-4
*Bogue Chitto Park* AL-4
Bogue Chitto Public Use Area—park AL-4
*Bogue Chitto River* LA-4
*Bogue Chitto River* MS-4
*Bogue Creek* MS-4
Bogue Creek—stream AL-4
Bogue Creek—stream MI-6
Bogue Creek—stream MO-7
Bogue Creek—stream (2) OR-9
*Bogue Desha* MS-4
Bogue Elem Sch—school KS-7
*Bogue Eucaba Creek* MS-4
*Boguefala Baptist Ch* MS-4
Boguefala Cem—cemetery MS-4
Boguefala Ch—church MS-4
Boguefala Creek—stream MS-4
Bogue Falaya Cem—cemetery LA-4
Bogue Falaya Ch—church LA-4
*Bogue Falaya Creek* MS-4
Bogue Falaya Park—park LA-4
*Bogue Falaya River* LA-4
*Bogue Faliah Creek* MS-4
*Boguefelema Creek* MS-4
*Bogue Flower Creek* MS-4
*Bogue Flowers Creek* MS-4
Boguegaba Creek—stream MS-4
Bogue Gulch—valley CO-8
Bogue Gulch—valley OR-9
*Bogue Gulley* MS-4
*Bogue-hays* MS-4
*Boguehoma* MS-4
*Bogue Homa Creek* MS-4
*Bogue Home Creek* MS-4
*Bogue Homo* AL-4
*Bogue Homo* MS-4
Bogue Homo, Lake—reservoir MS-4
*Bogue Homo Creek* MS-4
Bogue Homo Sch—school MS-4
*Bogue Hooma* MS-4
Bogue Inlet—bay NC-3
*Boguelichitto Creek* AL-4
*Boguelichitto Creek* MS-4
*Bogue Loosa* AL-4
**Bogueloosa**—pop pl AL-4
*Bogueloosa Baptist Church* AL-4
Bogueloosa Ch—church AL-4
*Bogue Loosa Creek* AL-4
*Bogue Loosa Creek* MS-4
Bogueloosa Creek—stream AL-4
*Bogue Lusa* LA-4
Bogue Lusa Creek—stream LA-4
Bogue Marsh—swamp NC-3
*Bogue Mountain* CA-9
Bogue Phalia Cutoff—canal MS-4
*Bogue Phaliah* MS-4
Bogue Pilgrim Ch—church AR-4
*Bogue Pilgrim Church* MS-4
Bogue Pilgrim Sch—school AR-4
*Bogue Point* MA-1
Bogue Rsvr—reservoir CO-8
Bogues Bay—bay VA-3
Bogue Sch—school NC-3
Bogues Corner—locale ME-1
Bogue Shores—bay NC-3
*Bogues Lake* NJ-2
Bogue Sound—bay NC-3
Bogues Pond—lake NJ-2
*Bogue Statinea Creek* MS-4
Bogue Swamp—stream (2) NC-3
**Bogue Toocolo Chitto (historical)**—pop pl MS-4
Bogue (Township of)—fmr MCD NC-3
**Bogue View Shores (subdivision)**—pop pl NC-3
Bogue Watershed Y-30-104 Dam—dam MS-4
Bogue Watershed Y-30-105 Dam—dam MS-4
Bogue Watershed Y-30-106 Dam—dam MS-4
Bogue Watershed Y-30-107 Dam—dam MS-4
Bogue Watershed Y-30-108 Dam—dam MS-4
Bogue Watershed Y-30-20 Dam—dam MS-4
Bogue Watershed Y-30-31 Dam—dam MS-4
Bogue Watershed Y-30-34 Dam—dam MS-4
Bogue Watershed Y-30-43 Dam—dam MS-4
Bogue Watershed Y-30-51 Dam—dam MS-4
Bogue Watershed Y-30-52 Dam—dam MS-4
Bogue Watershed Y-30-53 Dam—dam MS-4
Bogue Watershed Y-30-54 Dam—dam MS-4
Bogue Watershed Y-30-55 Dam—dam MS-4
Bogue Watershed Y-30-57 Dam—dam MS-4
Bogue Watershed Y-30-58 Dam—dam MS-4
Bogue Watershed Y-30-66—dam MS-4
Bogue Watershed Y-30-84 Dam—dam MS-4
Bogue Watershed Y-30-85 Dam—dam MS-4
Bogue Watershed Y-30-89 Dam—dam MS-4
Bogue Watershed Y-30-90 Dam—dam MS-4
Bogue Watershed Y-30-94 Dam—dam MS-4
Bogue Watershed Y-30-95 Dam—dam MS-4
Bogue Watershed Y-30-99 Dam—dam MS-4
Bogue Watershed Y-54-38 Dam—dam MS-4
*Bogul* FM-9
B O Gunter Lake Dam—dam AL-4
Boguraburabu Island—island MP-9
*Boguraburabu-to* MP-9
*Boguriyushi Island* MP-9
Boguriyushi Island—island MP-9
*Boguryushi-To* MP-9
Bogus Basin—basin ID-8
Bogus Basin State Park—park ID-8
Bogus Bench—bench OR-9
Bogus Bench Rsvr—reservoir OR-9
Bogus Bluff—cliff (2) WI-6
Bogus Brook—stream MN-6
**Bogus Brook (Township of)**—pop pl MN-6
Bogus Canyon—valley NE-7
Bogus Chute—stream IL-6
**Bogus Corners**—pop pl PA-2
Bogus Creek—stream AK-9
Bogus Creek—stream (2) CA-9
Bogus Creek—stream (3) ID-8
Bogus Creek—stream MT-8
Bogus Creek—stream NE-7
Bogus Creek—stream (2) OR-9
Bogus Creek—stream TN-4
Bogus Creek—stream WI-6
Bogus Creek Campground—park OR-9
Bogus Creek Cave—cave OR-9
Bogus Creek Well—well OR-9
*Bogus Ditch* IN-6
Bogus Hill—summit CT-1
Bogus Hollow—valley IL-6
Bogus Hollow—valley IN-6
Bogus Hollow—valley UT-8
Bogus Island—island IL-6
Bogus Island Ditch—canal IN-6
Bogus Jim Creek—stream SD-7
Bogus Lake—lake (2) MN-6
Bogus Lake—lake OR-9
Bogus Lake—lake WI-6
Boguslavsky Triple-Deckers—hist pl MA-1
Bogus Meadow—swamp ME-1
Bogus Mountain Brook—stream CT-1
Bogus Mtn—summit CA-9
Bogus Mtn—summit CT-1
Bogus Pocket—basin UT-8
Bogus Point—cape NY-2
Bogus Point—cape NC-3
Bogus Point—summit CA-9
Bogus Point—summit ID-8
Bogus Ranch—locale OR-9
Bogus Ridge—ridge (2) AR-4
Bogus Rim—cliff OR-9
Bogus Rim Rsvr—reservoir OR-9
Bogus Run—stream IN-6
Bogus Run—stream PA-2
Bogus Sch—school CA-9
**Bogus Springs**—pop pl TX-5
Bogus Swamp—swamp WI-6
Bogus Tank—reservoir TX-5
Bogus Thunder—bend CA-9
*Boguueido To* MP-9
*Boguweido-to* MP-9
Bogville Ranch—locale WY-8
Bogweido—island MP-9
*Bogweido Island* MP-9
Bogy Branch—stream FL-3
Bogy (Township of)—fmr MCD AR-4
Bogzack Creek—stream LA-4
Bohall Lake—lake MN-6
Boham Creek—stream CO-8
Bohanan Canyon—valley NM-5
Bohanan Slouth Ditch—canal AR-4
Bohana Ridge—ridge CA-9
Bohan Cabin—locale AK-9
Bohannan Cem—cemetery AR-4
Bohannan Community Ch—church AR-4
Bohannan Hill—summit NH-1
Bohannan Mountain Ch—church AR-4
Bohannan Mtn—summit AR-4
Bohannon—locale VA-3
**Bohannon Addition**—pop pl TN-4
*Bohannon Branch* TX-5
Bohannon Bridge—bridge NH-1
Bohannon Cave—cave (2) TN-4
Bohannon Cem—cemetery OK-5
Bohannon Cem—cemetery TN-4
Bohannon Ch—church OK-5
*Bohannon Creek* MT-8
Bohannon Creek—stream ID-8
Bohannon Creek—stream MT-8
Bohannon Creek—stream OK-5
Bohannon Ford—locale AL-4
Bohannon Lake—reservoir OK-5
Bohannon Mine (underground)—mine AL-4
Bohannon Mtn—summit AR-4
Bohannon Ranch—locale OR-9
Bohannons Bar—bar (2) AL-4
Bohannon Sch—school AR-4
Bohannon Sch—school CA-9
Bohannon Sch—school TN-4
Bohannons Cutoff—bend AL-4
Bohannons Landing—locale TN-4
Bohannon Spring—spring ID-8
Bohannon (Township of)—fmr MCD AR-4
Bohanon Branch—stream TX-5
Bohanon Cem—cemetery GA-3
Bohanon Cem—cemetery MO-7
Bohanon Crossroad—locale GA-3
Bohanon Park—park MN-6
Bohart House—hist pl MT-8
Bohaynee—locale NC-3
Boheck Creek—stream SC-3
Bohee Creek—stream MT-8
Bohee Tank—reservoir AZ-5
Boheet Sch—school NE-7
Boheman Hall—locale TX-5
Bohemia—locale FL-3
**Bohemia**—pop pl LA-4
**Bohemia**—pop pl NY-2
**Bohemia**—pop pl PA-2
Bohemia, Mount—summit MI-6
Bohemia Basin—basin AK-9
Bohemia Bridge—bridge MD-2
*Bohemia Creek* DE-2
Bohemia Creek—stream AK-9
Bohemia Creek—stream (2) OR-9
Bohemia Farm—hist pl MD-2
**Bohemia (historical)**—pop pl OR-9
Bohemia Inc. Airfield—airport OR-9
Bohemia Manor—flat DE-2
Bohemia Mtn—summit OR-9
Bohemian—locale LA-4
*Bohemian Baptist Church* TN-4
Bohemian Bayou—gut LA-4
Bohemian Brethren Cem—cemetery NE-7
Bohemian Brotherhood Cem—cemetery NE-7
Bohemian Brotherhood Cem—cemetery WI-6
Bohemian Cem—cemetery (2) IL-6
Bohemian Cem—cemetery (2) IA-7
Bohemian Cem—cemetery (4) KS-7
Bohemian Cem—cemetery LA-4
Bohemian Cem—cemetery (10) MN-6
Bohemian Cem—cemetery MO-7
Bohemian Cem—cemetery (7) NE-7
Bohemian Cem—cemetery ND-7
Bohemian Cem—cemetery OK-5
Bohemian Cem—cemetery (3) SD-7
Bohemian Cem—cemetery (3) WI-6
Bohemian Ch—church KS-7
Bohemian Ch—church NE-7
*Bohemian Creek* MI-6
Bohemian Creek—stream IA-7
Bohemian Creek—stream MI-6
Bohemian Creek—stream NE-7
Bohemian Grove—woods CA-9
Bohemian Hall—building KS-7
Bohemian Hall—locale AL-4
Bohemian Home for the Aged—building IL-6
Bohemian Natl Cem—cemetery (2) IA-7
Bohemian Natl Cem—cemetery KS-7
Bohemian Natl Cem—cemetery (2) NE-7
Bohemian Natl Cem—cemetery ND-7
Bohemian Natl Cem—cemetery SD-7
*Bohemian Natl Cemetery* SD-7
Bohemian Natl Hall—hist pl OH-6
*Bohemian Presbyterian Cemetery* SD-7
Bohemian Range—range AK-9
Bohemian Ridge—ridge (2) WI-6
Bohemian Spring—spring OR-9
Bohemian State Wildlife Mngmt Area—park MN-6
Bohemian Valley—valley WI-6
Bohemia River—stream MD-2
Bohemia Saddle—gap OR-9
Bohemia Saddle Park—park OR-9
Bohemia Sch—school OR-9
Bohemias Mills—locale MD-2
*Bohemia Smith Falls* OR-9
Bohemia State Wildlife Mngmt Area—park LA-4
**Bohemia Township**—pop pl (2) NE-7
**Bohemia (Township of)**—pop pl MI-6
Bohemia Trail—trail OR-9
Bohemotash Mtn—summit CA-9
Bohen Run—stream PA-2
Bohen Trail—trail PA-2
Bohicket Creek—stream SC-3
Bohinkleman Spring—spring WA-9
Bohland Hollow—valley WI-6
Bohl Cem—cemetery MO-7
Bohle Dam—dam SD-7
Bohleen Ranch—locale MT-8
Bohlender Mine—mine CO-8
Bohler Canyon—valley CA-9
Bohler Ranch—locale MT-8
Bohler Sch—school IL-6
Bohley Cem—cemetery IN-6
**Bohleysville**—pop pl IL-6
Bohlinger Valley—valley WI-6
Bohlken Park—park OH-6
Bohls Hollow—valley TX-5
Bohlson Lateral—canal ID-8
Bohma Creek—stream CA-9

Bohman Hollow—*valley* ... UT-8
Bohme Ranch—*locale* ... AZ-5
Bohmer School (historical)—*locale* ... MO-7
Bohme Spring—*spring* ... AZ-5
Bohmier Lake—*lake* ... MI-6
Bohm Sch—*school* ... IL-6
Bohn, Joseph, House—*hist pl* ... UT-8
Bohna Creek—*stream* ... CA-9
**Bohna (historical)**—*pop pl* ... OR-9
Bohna Peak—*summit* ... CA-9
*Bohn Creek* ... CA-9
Bohn Creek—*stream* ... WI-6
Bohn Ditch—*canal* ... IN-6
Bohnemeier Cem—*cemetery* ... IL-6
*Bohner Canyon* ... AZ-5
Bohner Lake—*lake* ... WI-6
*Bohners Lake* ... WI-6
Bohners Lake—*CDP* ... WI-6
Bohnes Lake—*lake* ... WI-6
Bohnetts Canyon—*valley* ... WY-8
Bohnett Sch—*school* ... CA-9
Bohn Gulch—*valley* ... CO-8
Bohnke Ditch—*canal* ... IN-6
Bohnke Flauch Drain—*canal* ... IN-6
Bohn Lake—*lake* ... MT-8
Bohn Lake—*lake* ... WI-6
Bohn Lake—*reservoir* ... CO-8
Bohn Park—*park* ... IL-6
Bohn Ranch—*locale* ... CO-8
Bohnsack Cem—*cemetery* ... ND-7
**Bohnsack Township**—*pop pl* ... ND-7
Bohn Sch—*school* ... WI-6
Bohns Point—*cape* ... MN-6
Bohnstead Draw—*valley* ... WY-8
Bohnstein Hill—*summit* ... AR-4
Bohn Valley—*valley* ... CA-9
**Bohon**—*pop pl* ... KY-4
Bohonon Cem—*cemetery* ... VT-1
Bohoslov Cem—*cemetery* ... PA-2
Bohr, Nicholas, Barn—*hist pl* ... KS-7
Bohrer Cem—*cemetery* ... OH-6
Bohrer Park—*park* ... MO-7
**Bohri**—*pop pl* ... WI-6
Bohris Valley—*valley* ... WI-6
Bohris Valley Cem—*cemetery* ... WI-6
**Bohrmans Mill**—*pop pl* ... PA-2
Bohrnstedt, John, House—*hist pl* ... WI-6
Bohunk Hollow—*valley* (2) ... PA-2
Bohunk Trail—*trail* ... PA-2
Bohys Canyon—*valley* ... NE-7
Boian Cem—*cemetery* ... KY-4
Boice—*locale* ... MS-4
Boice Bridge—*bridge* ... OH-6
Boice Cem—*cemetery* ... MS-4
Boice Creek—*stream* ... WI-6
Boice Creek Cem—*cemetery* ... WI-6
Boice Creek Sch—*school* ... WI-6
Boice Drain—*stream* ... MI-6
Boice Fort And Village Site—*hist pl* ... OH-6
Boice Hill—*summit* ... NY-2
Boice Prairie—*flat* ... WI-6
Boice Prairie Cem—*cemetery* ... WI-6
Boice Tank—*reservoir* ... AZ-5
**Boiceville**—*pop pl* ... NY-2
**Boichott Acres**—*pop pl* ... MI-6
**Boicourt**—*pop pl* ... KS-7
Boicourt Lake—*reservoir* ... KS-7
Boicourt Mine—*mine* ... MT-8
Boicourt Spring—*spring* ... ND-7
Boidarkin Island—*island* ... AK-9
Boidore, Bayou—*stream* ... LA-4
**Boies**—*pop pl* ... IA-7
Boies Bend County Park—*park* ... IA-7
Boies Point—*cape* ... LA-4
*Boies Ranch* ... NV-8
Boies Rsvr—*reservoir* ... MT-8
Boies Rsvr—*reservoir* ... NV-8
Boike State Wildlife Mngmt Area—*park* ... MN-6
Boikin Cem—*cemetery* ... TN-4
*Boil Creek* ... ID-8
*Boil Creek* ... NV-8
Boil Creek—*stream* ... AK-9
Boiler Bay—*bay* ... OR-9
Boiler Bayou—*gut* ... TX-5
Boiler Bay State Park—*park* ... OR-9
*Boiler Bay Wayside* ... OR-9
Boiler Branch—*stream* ... AL-4
Boiler Canyon—*valley* ... CO-8
Boiler Canyon—*valley* ... UT-8
Boiler Cave Number One—*cave* ... AL-4
Boiler Cave Number Three—*cave* ... AL-4
Boiler Cave Number Two—*cave* ... AL-4
Boiler Creek—*gut* ... NJ-2
Boiler Creek—*stream* ... CO-8
Boiler Draw—*valley* ... OR-9
Boiler Draw—*valley* ... WY-8
Boiler Gap—*channel* ... FL-3
Boiler Gap—*gap* ... NM-5
Boiler Grade Creek—*stream* ... ID-8
Boiler Hill—*summit* ... CO-8
Boiler Hollow—*valley* (2) ... MO-7
Boiler Hollow—*valley* ... UT-8
Boiler Lake—*lake* ... FL-3
Boiler Lake—*lake* ... MN-6
Boiler Lake—*lake* ... MO-7
Boiler Lake—*lake* ... WI-6
Boiler Peak—*summit* ... NM-5
Boiler Point—*cape* ... AK-9
Boiler Riffle—*rapids* ... OR-9
Boiler Rock—*bar* ... ME-1
Boiler Run—*stream* ... PA-2
Boiler Run—*stream* ... VA-3
Boiler Run Trail—*trail* ... PA-2
Boilers, The—*bar* ... ME-1
Boilers, The—*locale* ... WY-8
Boiler Spring—*spring* ... AZ-5
Boiler Spring—*spring* ... CA-9
Boiler Spring—*spring* ... CO-8
Boiler Spring—*spring* ... OR-9
Boiler Spring—*spring* ... WY-8
Boiler Spring Branch—*stream* ... TX-5
Boiler Tank—*reservoir* ... AZ-5
Boiler Trail—*trail* (2) ... PA-2
Boile Run—*stream* ... PA-2
Boiling Canyon—*valley* ... NM-5
Boiling Ch—*church* ... AL-4
*Boiling Creek* ... IN-6
Boiling Creek—*stream* ... FL-3
Boiling Creek Lake—*lake* ... FL-3
*Boiling Fork* ... TN-4
Boiling Fork Creek—*stream* ... TN-4
*Boiling Fork Elk River* ... TN-4
Boiling Gulch—*valley* ... CO-8
**Boiling (historical)**—*pop pl* ... TN-4
Boiling Lake—*lake* ... WA-9
Boiling Mill Creek—*stream* ... AL-4
Boiling Mtn—*summit* ... TX-5
Boiling Over Wash—*valley* ... AZ-5
Boiling Over Well—*well* ... AZ-5
Boiling Pinnacles—*area* ... AK-9
Boiling Point—*locale* ... CA-9
**Boiling Point (historical)**—*pop pl* ... OR-9
Boiling Pond—*lake* ... TN-4
Boiling Post Office (historical)—*building* ... TN-4
Boiling Pots—*lake* ... HI-9
Boiling River—*spring* ... WY-8
*Boiling Spring* ... PA-2
Boiling Spring—*locale* ... AL-4
Boiling Spring—*locale* ... KY-4
Boiling Spring—*locale* ... VA-3
**Boiling Spring**—*pop pl* ... VA-3
Boiling Spring—*spring* (3) ... AL-4
Boiling Spring—*spring* (2) ... AZ-5
Boiling Spring—*spring* ... GA-3
Boiling Spring—*spring* (4) ... KY-4
Boiling Spring—*spring* ... MD-2
Boiling Spring—*spring* ... MI-6
Boiling Spring—*spring* (2) ... MO-7
Boiling Spring—*spring* (2) ... NE-7
Boiling Spring—*spring* ... NV-8
Boiling Spring—*spring* ... NY-2
Boiling Spring—*spring* ... OR-9
Boiling Spring—*spring* ... PA-2
Boiling Spring—*spring* (6) ... TN-4
Boiling Spring—*spring* ... TX-5
Boiling Spring—*spring* ... UT-8
Boiling Spring—*spring* ... VT-1
Boiling Spring—*spring* (3) ... VA-3
Boiling Spring Branch—*stream* (2) ... TN-4
Boiling Spring Bridge—*bridge* ... NE-7
Boiling Spring Camp—*locale* ... PA-2
Boiling Spring Cem—*cemetery* ... AL-4
Boiling Spring Ch—*church* ... AL-4
Boiling Spring Ch—*church* ... GA-3
Boiling Spring Ch—*church* ... NC-3
Boiling Spring Ch—*church* ... TN-4
Boiling Spring Creek—*stream* ... MN-6
Boiling Spring (historical)—*locale* ... AL-4
Boiling Spring Hollow—*valley* ... MO-7
Boiling Spring Hollow—*valley* ... TN-4
Boiling Spring Lake—*reservoir* ... NC-3
Boiling Spring Lake Dam—*dam* ... NC-3
**Boiling Spring Lakes**—*pop pl* ... NC-3
Boiling Spring (Magisterial District)—*fmr MCD* ... VA-3
Boiling Spring Prospect—*mine* ... TN-4
Boiling Spring Pump—*other* ... CA-9
Boiling Spring Ravine—*valley* ... CA-9
Boiling Spring Run—*stream* (2) ... PA-2
*Boiling Springs* ... NJ-2
*Boiling Springs* ... TN-4
*Boiling Springs* ... VA-3
Boiling Springs—*locale* ... AL-4
Boiling Springs—*locale* ... NC-3
**Boiling Springs**—*pop pl* ... AL-4
**Boiling Springs**—*pop pl* (2) ... NC-3
**Boiling Springs**—*pop pl* ... PA-2
**Boiling Springs**—*pop pl* (2) ... SC-3
**Boiling Springs**—*pop pl* ... TN-4
Boiling Springs—*spring* ... AL-4
Boiling Springs—*spring* ... AR-4
Boiling Springs—*spring* ... ID-8
Boiling Springs—*spring* ... KS-7
Boiling Springs—*spring* ... KY-4
Boiling Springs—*spring* ... MI-6
Boiling Springs—*spring* ... MN-6
Boiling Springs—*spring* (2) ... MO-7
Boiling Springs—*spring* ... PA-2
Boiling Springs—*spring* (2) ... TN-4
Boiling Springs—*spring* (3) ... TX-5
Boiling Springs Branch—*stream* ... NC-3
Boiling Springs Campground—*locale* ... ID-8
Boiling Springs Cave—*cave* ... AL-4
Boiling Springs (CCD)—*cens area* ... SC-3
Boiling Springs Cem—*cemetery* ... IL-6
Boiling Springs Ch—*church* ... AL-4
Boiling Springs Ch—*church* ... GA-3
Boiling Springs Ch—*church* ... KY-4
Boiling Springs Ch—*church* (2) ... NC-3
Boiling Springs Ch—*church* (2) ... OK-5
Boiling Springs Ch—*church* ... PA-2
Boiling Springs Ch—*church* (2) ... SC-3
Boiling Springs Ch—*church* (2) ... TN-4
Boiling Spring Sch—*school* ... MD-2
Boiling Spring Sch—*school* ... NE-7
Boiling Spring Sch (abandoned)—*school* ... MO-7
Boiling Springs Creek—*stream* ... MT-8
Boiling Springs Creek—*stream* ... OK-5
Boiling Springs Driveway—*trail* ... ID-8
Boiling Springs Elem Sch—*school* ... NC-3
*Boiling Springs Guard Station* ... ID-8
Boiling Springs Hist Dist—*hist pl* ... PA-2
**Boiling Springs (historical)**—*pop pl* ... TN-4
Boiling Springs Hollow—*valley* ... KY-4
Boiling Springs Hollow—*valley* ... MO-7
Boiling Springs HS—*school* ... PA-2
Boiling Springs Lake—*lake* ... CA-9
Boiling Springs Methodist Ch (historical)—*church* ... AL-4
*Boiling Springs Missionary Baptist Ch* ... AL-4
Boiling Springs Sch—*school* ... IL-6
Boiling Springs Sch—*school* ... SC-3
Boiling Springs Sch—*school* ... TN-4
Boiling Springs Work Center—*locale* ... ID-8
Boil Mtn—*summit* ... ME-1
Boilon Cem—*cemetery* ... WV-2
Boils, The—*spring* ... TN-4
Boil Spring—*spring* ... TX-5
Bois—*locale* ... WV-2
Boisaubin Manor—*hist pl* ... NJ-2
Boisberg—*locale* ... MN-6
Bois Blanc Island—*island* ... MI-6
**Bois Blanc (Township of)**—*pop pl* ... MI-6
*Bois Brule* ... MI-6
Bois Brule Bottom—*flat* ... MO-7
Bois Brule Creek—*stream* (2) ... MO-7
*Bois Brule River* ... MN-6
*Bois Brule River* ... WI-6
Bois Brule River—*stream* ... WI-6
Bois Brule Township—*civil* ... MO-7
Bois Bubert Island—*island* ... ME-1
Bois Chactas Shell Bank—*locale* ... LA-4
Bois Connie, Bayou—*stream* ... LA-4
*Boiscourt* ... KS-7
*Bois Creek* ... WI-6
*Bois-D'Arc* ... KS-7
*Bois d'Arc* ... OK-5
Bois d'Arc—*locale* ... IA-7
Bois d' Arc—*locale* ... KS-7
Bois D Arc—*locale* ... TX-5
**Bois D'Arc**—*pop pl* ... MO-7
**Bois D'Arc**—*pop pl* ... OK-5
*Bois D'Arc Bayou* ... TX-5
Bois d'arc Bayou—*gut* ... LA-4
Bois d'Arc Bayou—*stream* (2) ... AR-4
Bois D'Arc Ch—*church* ... MS-4
Bois D' Arc Ch—*church* ... TX-5
Bois D'Arc Ch—*church* ... TX-5
*Bois D'Arc Creek* ... TX-5
Bois D'Arc Creek—*stream* ... AR-4
Bois d'Arc Creek—*stream* (4) ... OK-5
Bois dArc Creek—*stream* ... OK-5
Bois d'Arc Creek—*stream* ... OK-5
Bois d'Arc Creek—*stream* (3) ... TX-5
Bois D'Arc Creek—*stream* ... TX-5
Bois d'Arc Creek—*stream* ... TX-5
Bois D'Arc Creek—*stream* (2) ... TX-5
Bois D'Arc Draw—*valley* ... TX-5
Bois d' Arc Grove Sch—*school* ... OK-5
Bois D'Arc Island—*island* ... TX-5
Bois d'Arc Lake—*lake* ... AR-4
Bois d'Arc Lake—*lake* ... TX-5
*Bois D'Arc River* ... TX-5
Bois d'Arc (Township of)—*fmr MCD* ... AR-4
**Bois D'Arc (Township of)**—*pop pl* ... IL-6
Bois D'Arc Tree (First Tree In High Plains)—*locale* ... TX-5
Bois d'Arc Windmill—*locale* ... TX-5
*Bois d'Ark Creek* ... OK-5
*Bois de Ark Creek* ... OK-5
Bois de Sioux Country Club—*locale* ... ND-7
Bois de Sioux River—*stream* ... MN-6
Bois de Sioux River—*stream* ... ND-7
Bois de Sioux River—*stream* ... SD-7
Bois Ditch—*canal* ... CA-9
*Bois-Duval* ... FM-9
Boise—*locale* ... TX-5
**Boise**—*pop pl* ... ID-8
**Boise**—*pop pl* ... WA-9
Boise, R. P., Bldg—*hist pl* ... OR-9
Boise Air Terminal—*airport* ... ID-8
Boise Bar—*bar* ... ID-8
Boise Basin—*basin* ... ID-8
Boise Basin Experiment Station—*locale* ... ID-8
Boise Capitol Area District—*hist pl* ... ID-8
Boise Cascade Camp—*locale* ... MN-6
Boise Christian Day Sch—*school* ... ID-8
**Boise City**—*pop pl* ... ID-8
**Boise City**—*pop pl* ... OK-5
Boise City Canal—*canal* ... ID-8
Boise City (CCD)—*cens area* ... OK-5
Boise City Cem—*cemetery* ... OK-5
Boise City Natl Bank—*hist pl* ... ID-8
Boise Creek—*stream* ... AK-9
Boise Creek—*stream* (2) ... CA-9
Boise Creek—*stream* ... CO-8
Boise Creek—*stream* ... ID-8
Boise Creek—*stream* ... MI-6
Boise Creek—*stream* ... WA-9
Boise Creek Campground—*locale* ... CA-9
*Boise de Sioux River* ... MN-6
*Boise de Sioux River* ... ND-7
*Boise de Sioux River* ... SD-7
*Boise Heights* ... ID-8
Boise High School Campus—*hist pl* ... ID-8
Boise Hills—*cens area* ... ID-8
**Boise Hills Village**—*pop pl* ... ID-8
*Boise Hill Village* ... ID-8
Boise Hist Dist—*hist pl* ... ID-8
Boise Junction—*locale* ... ID-8
Boise Junior College Administration Bldg—*hist pl* ... ID-8
Boise Junior High School—*hist pl* ... ID-8
Boise Lake—*lake* ... MN-6
Boise Mtns—*range* ... ID-8
Boise Natl For—*forest* ... ID-8
Boise Peak—*summit* (2) ... ID-8
*Boise Ranch* ... NV-8
Boise Ridge—*ridge* (2) ... ID-8
Boise Ridge—*ridge* ... WA-9
*Boise River* ... ID-8
Boise River—*stream* ... ID-8
Boise Sch—*school* ... OR-9
Boise Sch—*school* ... PA-2
**Boise Southern**—*pop pl* ... LA-4
Boise State Coll—*school* ... ID-8
Boise Valley—*valley* ... ID-8
Boise Valley Canal—*canal* ... ID-8
**Bois Fort**—*pop pl* ... MN-6
Bois Forte (Nett Lake) Ind Res—*reserve* ... MN-6
Boisher Cem—*cemetery* ... OH-6
Bois Piquant, Bayou—*gut* ... LA-4
Bois (RR name for Dubois)—*other* ... IL-6
Boisseau Cem—*cemetery* ... VA-3
Bois Sec, Lac—*lake* ... LA-4
**Boissevain**—*pop pl* ... VA-3
Boistfort—*locale* ... WA-9
Boistfort (CCD)—*cens area* ... WA-9
Boistfort HS—*hist pl* ... WA-9
Boistfort Peak—*summit* ... WA-9
Boistfort Prairie—*flat* ... WA-9
Boistfort Sch—*school* ... WA-9
Boisvert Camp—*locale* ... MT-8
Boisy Sch (historical)—*school* ... MS-4
Boitnott Cem—*cemetery* ... VA-3
Boji Creek—*stream* ... OK-5
Boji Windmill—*locale* ... TX-5
**B & O Junction (Baltimore Ohio)**—*pop pl* ... NY-2
*Bok* ... MP-9
Bok—*island* ... MP-9
Bok, Edward, Vocational Sch—*hist pl* ... PA-2
*Bokaanichi To* ... MP-9
*Bokadrik* ... MP-9
*Bokadrik-drik* ... MP-9
*Bokaen* ... MP-9
*Bokaidrik* ... MP-9
Bokaidrikdrik—*island* ... MP-9
*Bokairik* ... MP-9
*Bokaitoktok Island* ... MP-9
Bokak (County-equivalent)—*civil* ... MP-9
*Bokale-laj* ... MP-9
*Bokalijik-en* ... MP-9
Bokalijman—*island* ... MP-9
*Bokalikkorowa* ... MP-9
*Bokan* ... MP-9
Bokan—*island* ... MP-9
Bokanaetok—*island* ... MP-9
*Bokanaetok Island* ... MP-9
*Bokanairokku* ... MP-9
Bokanalap—*island* ... MP-9
*Bokanalap Island* ... MP-9
*Bokanarappu* ... MP-9
Bokanaujjor—*island* ... MP-9
*Bokanaujjor Island* ... MP-9
*Bokanbit* ... MP-9
Bokanbit—*island* ... MP-9
Bokanchinre Island—*island* ... MP-9
*Bokanchinre-To* ... MP-9
Bokandretok—*island* ... MP-9
*Bokanejman* ... MP-9
*Bokangeeru* ... MP-9
*Bokangeeru-To* ... MP-9
Bokanibop—*island* ... MP-9
*Bokanibop Island* ... MP-9
Bokanibwiebirok—*island* ... MP-9
*Bokanibwiebirok Island* ... MP-9
*Bokanikabwe* ... MP-9
Bokanikaiyaru Island—*island* ... MP-9
*Bokan Island* ... MP-9
*Bokaniuar* ... MP-9
Bokaniyak—*island* ... MP-9
Bokanjoio—*island* ... MP-9
Bokanjouij (not verified)—*island* ... MP-9
Bokankemej—*island* ... MP-9
*Bokankin* ... MP-9
*Bokankin Island* ... MP-9
Bokankin Island—*island* ... MP-9
Bokankiren—*island* ... MP-9
*Bokankiren Island* ... MP-9
Bokankiru—*island* ... MP-9
*Bokankiru Island* ... MP-9
*Bokankora* ... MP-9
Bokankowak—*island* ... MP-9
*Bokankowak Island* ... MP-9
Bokan Mtn—*summit* ... AK-9
*Bokanmweokan Island* ... MP-9
*Bokanpit* ... MP-9
Bokanurjen (not verified)—*bar* ... MP-9
*Bokanutekka* ... MP-9
Bokanutokku Island—*island* ... MP-9
Bokanwatman (not verified)—*island* ... MP-9
Bokanwor—*island* ... MP-9
*Bok Apissali* ... MS-4
*Bokarijiman* ... MP-9
Bokarijiman—*island* ... MP-9
*Bokarijiman Island* ... MP-9
*Bokarijiman-To* ... MP-9
*Bokarik* ... MP-9
*Bokariki* ... MP-9
Bokariki—*island* ... MP-9
*Bokariki-To* ... MP-9
*Bokariru Island* ... MP-9
Bokariru Island—*island* ... MP-9
*Bokariru-To* ... MP-9
*Bokarmij Island* ... MP-9
Bokat—*island* ... MP-9
Bokatari-nae (not verified)—*island* ... MP-9
**Bokchito**—*pop pl* ... OK-5
Bokchito Ch—*church* ... OK-5
Bokchito Creek—*stream* (3) ... OK-5
*Bokdik* ... MP-9
*Bokdjeldo* ... MP-9
*Boked* ... MP-9
**Bokeelia**—*pop pl* ... FL-3
Bokeelia Island—*island* ... FL-3
Bokelan—*island* ... MP-9
*Bokelan Island* ... MP-9
*Bokeluo* ... MP-9
*Boken* ... MP-9
Boken—*island* (3) ... MP-9
*Bokena* ... MP-9
*Bokenbako* ... MP-9
Bokenelab—*island* ... MP-9
*Bokenelap* ... MP-9
Bokengehalas Creek—*stream* ... OH-6
*Boken Island* ... MP-9
Boker—*island* ... MP-9
Bokeredj Island—*island* ... MP-9
*Boker Island* ... MP-9
Bokerok—*island* ... MP-9
*Boke's* ... OH-6
Bokes Creek—*stream* ... OH-6
Bokes Creek Cem—*cemetery* ... OH-6
**Bokes Creek (Township of)**—*pop pl* ... OH-6
**Bokhoma**—*pop pl* ... OK-5
Bokhoma Cem—*cemetery* ... OK-5
*Bok Homma* ... MS-4
Bokinwotme—*island* ... MP-9
*Bok Island* ... MP-9
Bok Kai Temple—*hist pl* ... CA-9
Bokkan Island—*island* ... MP-9
*Bokkonraito* ... MP-9
*Bokkonraito Island* ... MP-9
*Bokkonraito-to* ... MP-9
*Bokku* ... MP-9
Bokkuchechi—*bar* ... MP-9
Bokkuchechi—*island* ... MP-9
*Bokku Island* ... MP-9
Bokku Island—*island* (2) ... MP-9
Bokkukaaro—*bar* ... MP-9
Bokkumaruchi—*island* ... MP-9
*Bokkumaruchi Island* ... MP-9
*Bokkumaruchi-To* ... MP-9
Bokku (not verified)—*island* ... MP-9
*Bokku-suido* ... MP-9
*Bokku-to* ... MP-9
*Boklablab Island* ... MP-9
Boklabunlik—*island* ... MP-9
*Bokla Island* ... MP-9
Boklan—*island* ... MP-9
*Boklang Island* ... MP-9
*Boklap* ... MP-9
Boklaplap—*island* ... MP-9
Boklap (not verified)—*bar* ... MP-9
Boklelaj—*island* ... MP-9
Boklimairek—*island* ... MP-9
*Boklimairek Island* ... MP-9
Bokliplip—*island* ... MP-9
*Bokliplip Island* ... MP-9
*Boklob Island* ... MP-9
*Bok Lusa* ... MS-4
*Bokmarui Island* ... MP-9
*Bokmaruj* ... MP-9
Bok Mountain Lake Sanctuary and Singing Tower—*hist pl* ... FL-3
*Boknake* ... MP-9
Boko—*island* ... MP-9
Bokoaetokutoku—*island* ... MP-9
Bokoaetokutoku Pass—*channel* ... MP-9
*Bokoareji Island* ... MP-9
*Bokoareji-to* ... MP-9
Bokobyaadaa—*island* ... MP-9
*Bokobyaadaa Island* ... MP-9
*Bokobyaada Island* ... MP-9
*Bokoechabun Insel* ... MP-9
*Bokoechabun Island* ... MP-9
Bokoechabun Island—*island* ... MP-9
*Bokoen* ... MP-9
Bokoen—*island* ... MP-9
*Bokoen Island* ... MP-9
Bokoen Island—*island* (4) ... MP-9
*Bokoen-To* ... MP-9
*Bokoeributou* ... MP-9
Bokoeributou—*island* ... MP-9
*Bokoeributou-To* ... MP-9
*Bokoeruriito Island* ... MP-9
Bokoeruriito Island—*island* ... MP-9
*Bokoeruriito-To* ... MP-9
Bokok Creek—*stream* ... AL-4
Bokoluo—*island* ... MP-9
Bokombako—*island* ... MP-9
*Bokompoko-to* ... MP-9
*Bokon* ... MP-9
*Bokonaarappu* ... MP-9
*Bokonaarappu Island* ... MP-9
*Bokonaetok* ... MP-9
Bokonarappu—*island* ... MP-9
*Bokonarappu-to* ... MP-9
*Bokonarijowa* ... MP-9
Bokonarijowa—*island* ... MP-9
*Bokonarijowa Island* ... MP-9
*Bokonarijowa-To* ... MP-9
*Bokonarppu* ... MP-9
Bokonbitto—*island* ... MP-9
*Bokonbitto-To* ... MP-9
Bokonboten—*island* ... MP-9
*Bokoneejiromu Island* ... MP-9
Bokoneejiromu Island—*island* ... MP-9
*Bokoneejiromu-To* ... MP-9
Bokonejien—*island* ... MP-9
*Bokonenllap* ... MP-9
Bokonfuaaku—*island* ... MP-9
*Bokonfuaaku Island* ... MP-9
*Bokonfuuaku-To* ... MP-9
*Bokongoak* ... MP-9
*Bokongookku-to* ... MP-9
*Bokoniaaru* ... MP-9
*Bokoniaaru-To* ... MP-9
Bokonikaiaru Island—*island* ... MP-9
*Bokonikaiaru-To* ... MP-9
*Bokonikaiyaru Island* ... MP-9
*Bokonikaiyaru-To* ... MP-9
Bokonlabidoka (not verified)—*other* ... MP-9
*Bokonmollok* ... MP-9
*Bokonpoko To* ... MP-9
*Bokonriidokku* ... MP-9
Bokonriidokku—*island* ... MP-9
*Bokonriidokku Island* ... MP-9
*Bokonriidokku-To* ... MP-9
*Bokon-to* ... MP-9
*Bokooruo* ... MP-9
*Bokooruo To* ... MP-9
*Bokoramu* ... MP-9
Bokoramu—*island* ... MP-9
*Bokoramu Island* ... MP-9
*Bokoramu-To* ... MP-9
*Bokorappu Island* ... MP-9
Bokorappu Island—*island* ... MP-9
*Bokorappu-To* ... MP-9
*Bokorera Island* ... MP-9
Bokorera Island—*island* ... MP-9
*Bokorobioa Island* ... MP-9
Bokorobioa Island—*island* ... MP-9
Bokororyuru—*island* ... MP-9
*Bokororyuru Island* ... MP-9
Bokororyuru Pass—*channel* ... MP-9
*Bokororyuru-to* ... MP-9
Bokoru—*bar* ... MP-9
*Bokoruo-to* ... MP-9
Bokoryuren Island—*island* ... MP-9
*Bokoryuren-To* ... MP-9
**Bokoshe**—*pop pl* ... OK-5
Bokoshe Cem—*cemetery* ... OK-5
Bokoshe Ch—*church* ... OK-5
Bokoshe Lake—*reservoir* ... OK-5
Bokoshe Mtn—*summit* ... OK-5
*Bokot* ... MP-9
*Bokotana Island* ... MP-9
*Bokotona Island* ... MP-9
*Bokoto-To* ... MP-9
*Bokotrik* ... MP-9
*Bokou Island* ... MP-9
*Bokou-To* ... MP-9
*Bokoyan Island* ... MP-9
Bokoyan Island—*island* ... MP-9
*Bokoyan-To* ... MP-9
Bokoyoren—*bar* ... MP-9
*Bokoyoren-To* ... MP-9
*Bokozemon* ... MP-9
*Bokozemon-To* ... MP-9
*Bokpata* ... MP-9
*Bokrak* ... MP-9
Bokrak (not verified)—*island* ... MP-9
Bokshenya Creek—*stream* ... MS-4
*Bok Shubuta* ... MS-4
Bok Tower—*tower* ... FL-3
*Bok Tuklo* ... OK-5
*Bok Tuklo Chitto* ... MS-4
*Boktuklo Creek* ... OK-5
Boktuklo Creek—*stream* ... OK-5
Boktuklo Mountains—*range* ... OK-5
Boktuklo Trail—*trail* ... OK-5
*Boktukola Creek* ... OK-5
*Boktukola Mountains* ... OK-5
*Boku* ... MP-9
Bokujarito—*island* ... MP-9
*Bokujarito Island* ... MP-9
*Bokujarito-To* ... MP-9
Bokum Lawyer Ditch—*canal* ... MT-8
*Bokuramanunu* ... MP-9
*Bokuramanunu Island* ... MP-9
Bokuramanunu Island—*island* ... MP-9
*Bokureuetchi Island* ... MP-9
Bokureuetchi Island—*island* ... MP-9
*Bokurgrikk* ... MP-9
*Bokurigirikki* ... MP-9
Bokurigirikku—*island* ... MP-9
*Bokurigirikku-To* ... MP-9
*Bokurugeru Point* ... PW-9
Bok Vocation Sch—*school* ... PA-2
**Bolack**—*pop pl* ... ND-7
Bolack Oil Field—*oilfield* ... KS-7
Bolado Park—*park* ... CA-9
Bolair—*locale* ... WV-2
Bolam—*locale* ... CA-9
Bolam Creek—*stream* ... CA-9
Bolam Glacier—*glacier* ... CA-9
Bolam Pass—*gap* ... CO-8
**Bolan**—*pop pl* ... IA-7
Bolan, Bayou—*gut* ... MS-4
Bolan Creek—*stream* ... AR-4
Bolan Creek—*stream* ... CA-9
Bolan Creek—*stream* ... OR-9
Bolan Creek Mine—*mine* ... OR-9
*Boland* ... PA-2
Boland Airp—*airport* ... PA-2
Boland Archeol District—*hist pl* ... MO-7
Boland Canyon—*valley* ... CO-8
Boland Creek—*stream* ... NY-2
Bolander Canyon—*valley* ... NM-5
Bolander Run—*stream* ... OH-6
Boland House—*hist pl* ... KY-4
Boland Island—*island* ... AR-4
Boland Knob—*summit* ... MO-7
Boland Pond—*lake* ... MA-1
Boland Ridge—*ridge* ... SD-7
*Boland Run* ... PA-2
Boland Run—*stream* ... OH-6
Boland Spring—*spring* ... CO-8
*Bolanichi-to* ... MP-9
Bolan Lake—*lake* ... OR-9
Bolan Lake Dam—*dam* ... OR-9
Bolan Lake Trail—*trail* ... OR-9
Bolan Mine—*mine* ... OR-9
Bolan Mtn—*summit* ... OR-9
Bolanos, Mount—*summit* ... GU-9
Bolanos River—*stream* ... GU-9
Bolar—*locale* ... VA-3
Bolar Draft—*valley* ... VA-3
Bolar Gap—*gap* ... VA-3
Bolar Mtn—*summit* ... VA-3
Bolar Run—*stream* ... VA-3
Bolars Fork—*stream* ... WV-2
Bolar Spring—*spring* ... VA-3
Bolas Blancas Wash—*stream* ... AZ-5
Bola Tank—*reservoir* ... TX-5
Bolatusha—*locale* ... MS-4
Bolatusha Creek—*stream* ... MS-4
**Bolatushu**—*pop pl* ... MS-4
Bolby Sch—*school* ... NY-2
*Bolcan Mountains* ... CA-9
Bolch Hollow—*valley* ... MO-7
**Bolckow**—*pop pl* ... MO-7
**Bold**—*pop pl* ... OH-6
Bold Bluff—*summit* ... NV-8
Bold Bluff Point—*cape* ... AK-9
Bold Branch—*stream* ... NC-3
Bold Branch—*stream* ... SC-3
Bold Branch—*stream* ... TN-4
Bold Branch—*stream* (4) ... VA-3
Bold Branch Ch—*church* ... VA-3
Bold Camp Creek—*stream* ... VA-3
Bold Camp Mtn—*summit* ... VA-3
Bold Cape—*cape* ... AK-9
Bold Dick—*bar* ... ME-1
*Bold Dick Rock* ... MA-1
Bold Dick Rock—*cape* ... ME-1
**Bolden**—*pop pl* ... LA-4
Bolden Branch—*stream* ... NC-3
Bolden Branch—*stream* ... TN-4
Bolden Cem—*cemetery* ... AR-4
*Bolden Creek* ... TX-5
Bolden Draw—*valley* ... TX-5
Bolden Gulch—*valley* ... CO-8
Bolden Knight Bluff—*cliff* ... TN-4
Bolden Run—*stream* ... PA-2
Bolden Spring—*spring* (2) ... TN-4
Bolden Wash—*valley* ... UT-8
*Bolders Island* ... SC-3
Bold Face Creek—*stream* ... OH-6
Bold Face Playground—*park* ... OH-6
Bold Hill Trail—*trail* ... PA-2
**Bolding**—*pop pl* ... AR-4
Bolding Branch—*stream* ... AL-4
Boldin Hollow—*valley* ... TN-4
Boldin Mill Branch—*stream* ... AL-4
Bold Island—*island* (2) ... AK-9
Bold Island—*island* ... ME-1
**Boldman**—*pop pl* ... KY-4
*Bold Mountain* ... CO-8
Bold Mtn—*summit* ... WY-8
**Boldo**—*pop pl* ... AL-4
Boldo Cem—*cemetery* ... AL-4
Boldo Methodist Ch—*church* ... AL-4
Boldo Post Office (historical)—*building* ... AL-4
Boldo Sch—*school* ... AL-4
Bold Peak—*summit* ... AK-9
Bold Peak—*summit* ... MT-8
Bold Pilgrim Ch—*church* (2) ... MS-4
Bold Pilgrim Ch—*church* ... SC-3
Bold Point—*cape* ... RI-1
Boldrin Creek—*stream* (2) ... AK-9
Bold Rock—*island* ... CT-1
Bold Run—*stream* ... KY-4
Boldrup Plantation Archeol Site—*hist pl* ... VA-3
Bold Sluice Shoal—*bar* ... AL-4
*Bold Spring* ... GA-3
Bold Spring—*locale* ... TN-4
**Bold Spring**—*pop pl* ... GA-3
Bold Spring—*spring* ... TN-4
Bold Spring Branch—*stream* ... AR-4
Bold Spring Ch—*church* ... AL-4
Bold Spring Ch—*church* ... AR-4
Bold Spring Ch—*church* (2) ... GA-3
Bold Spring Ch—*church* ... NC-3
Bold Spring Ch—*church* ... SC-3
Bold Spring Hollow—*valley* ... TN-4
Bold Spring Post Office (historical)—*building* ... TN-4

**Bold Springs**—*pop pl* GA-3
Bold Springs Cem—*cemetery* AL-4
Bold Springs Cem—*cemetery* OK-5
Bold Springs Cem—*cemetery* TX-5
Bold Springs Ch—*church* GA-3
Bold Springs Ch—*church* OK-5
Bold Springs Ch—*church* TX-5
*Bold Springs Church* AL-4
Boldt, George C., Yacht House—*hist pl* NY-2
Boldt Bluff Public Use Area—*locale* KS-7
Boldt Castle—*other* NY-2
Boldt Gulch—*valley* CO-8
**Boldtville**—*pop pl* TX-5
Bolduc, Louis, House—*hist pl* MO-7
*Bolduc Brook* NH-1
Bold Water Point—*cape* MA-1
Bole—*locale* MT-8
Bole, Mount—*summit* MT-8
B Oleary Dam—*dam* SD-7
Bole Bench—*bench* MT-8
Bole Branch—*stream* TN-4
*Bole Creek* MT-8
*Bolees Creek* FL-3
*Bolega Swamp* AL-4
*Bolegea* AL-4
*Bolen* SC-3
Bolen—*locale* GA-3
**Bolen**—*pop pl* SC-3
Bolen, Anderson, and Jacobs Rsvr No. 2—*reservoir* CO-8
Bolen Branch—*stream* KY-4
Bolen Creek—*stream* OK-5
Bolen Creek—*stream* (2) WI-6
Bolen Creek State Public Hunting Grounds—*park* WI-6
Bolen Ditch—*canal* IN-6
Bolen Family Cem—*cemetery* MS-4
Bolen Hill—*summit* ME-1
Bolen Hollow State Public Hunting Area—*park* OK-5
Bolen Lake—*lake* MI-6
Bolen Mill Creek—*stream* SC-3
Bolen Pond—*reservoir* (2) SC-3
Bolen Post Office (historical)—*building* TN-4
Bolen Rsvr—*reservoir* CO-8
Bolens, Harry W., House—*hist pl* WI-6
Bolens Chapel—*church* TN-4
*Bolens Creek* NC-3
**Bolen Town**—*pop pl* SC-3
*Bolentown Ch* AL-4
Bolen Town Ch—*church* AL-4
Bolen Windmill—*locale* TX-5
Boler Branch—*stream* MS-4
*Boler Mountain* VA-3
*Bolern Brook* CT-1
Bolero Lookout—*locale* CA-9
*Bolers Draft* VA-3
*Boler Springs* VA-3
Bole Russell Tank—*reservoir* NM-5
Boles—*locale* CA-9
Boles—*locale* ID-8
Boles—*locale* KY-4
**Boles**—*pop pl* AR-4
**Boles**—*pop pl* MO-7
**Boles**—*pop pl* NM-5
**Boles**—*pop pl* TN-4
Boles, E., Cottage—*hist pl* OH-6
Boles Acres—*other* NM-5
Boles Branch—*stream* (2) TN-4
Boles Brook—*stream* ME-1
Boles Brook—*stream* NH-1
Boles Canyon—*valley* SD-7
Boles Cem—*cemetery* IN-6
Boles Cem—*cemetery* KS-7
Boles Cem—*cemetery* PA-2
Boles Chapel—*church* LA-4
*Boles Creek* AL-4
*Boles Creek* CA-9
*Boles Creek* MO-7
Boles Creek—*stream* AL-4
Boles Creek—*stream* (2) CA-9
Boles Creek—*stream* MT-8
Boles Creek—*stream* NC-3
*Boles Ferry* MS-4
Boles Field—*locale* TX-5
Boles Fork—*stream* KY-4
*Boles Gap* AR-4
Boles Gap—*gap* CA-9
Boles Hollow—*valley* KY-4
**Boles Home**—*pop pl* TX-5
Boles Lake—*lake* MS-4
Boles Lake—*lake* TX-5
Boles Lake—*reservoir* TX-5
Boles Meadow—*swamp* MT-8
Boles Meadows—*flat* CA-9
*Boles Mountain* AR-4
Boles Mtn—*summit* SC-3
Boles Opening—*flat* CA-9
Boles Point—*summit* MT-8
Boles Point Ch—*church* AL-4
Bole Spring—*spring* NV-8
Boles Ranch—*locale* WY-8
Boles Rector Oil Field—*oilfield* TX-5
**Boles (RR name West Vienna)**—*pop pl* IL-6
Boles Run—*stream* PA-2
Boles Sch—*school* TN-4
Boles Sch—*school* TX-5
Boles Spring—*spring* CA-9
Boles Springs—*spring* WY-8
Boles Tank—*reservoir* CA-9
Bolestown Cem—*cemetery* TN-4
Bolestown Ch—*church* TN-4
Boles Township—*civil* MO-7
Boles Trail—*trail* NH-1
Boleszpn Ch—*church* NE-7
Boletsakwa Site (FS-2, LA-136)—*hist pl* NM-5
**Boley**—*pop pl* OK-5
Boley Bldg—*hist pl* MO-7
Boley (CCD)—*cens area* OK-5
*Boley Creek* MS-4
Boley Creek—*stream* AL-4
Boley Hist Dist—*hist pl* OK-5
Boley HS—*school* LA-4
**Boleyn**—*pop pl* LA-4
Boleyn Ch—*church* LA-4
*Boleyns Brook* CT-1
Boley Sch for Boys—*school* OK-5
**Boley Springs**—*pop pl* AL-4
Boley Springs Cem—*cemetery* AL-4
Boley Springs Ch—*church* AL-4
Boley Spring Sch (historical)—*school* AL-4
Bolfing Lake—*lake* MN-6
Bolgen Creek—*stream* AK-9
Bolger Dam—*dam* WI-6
*Bolger Dam Flowage* WI-6
Bolger Flowage—*reservoir* WI-6
Bolger Hollow—*valley* KY-4
Bolian Cem—*cemetery* MS-4
Bolich Ch—*church* PA-2
Bolich JHS—*school* OH-6
Bolich Run—*stream* PA-2
Bolich Sch—*school* PA-2
Bolick Cem—*cemetery* NC-3
Bolick Spring—*spring* CO-8
*Bolif Lake* MN-6
**Boligee**—*pop pl* AL-4
Boligee Bar—*bar* AL-4
Boligee Canal—*canal* AL-4
Boligee (CCD)—*cens area* AL-4
*Boligee Creek* AL-4
Boligee Creek—*stream* AL-4
Boligee Creek Swamp—*swamp* AL-4
Boligee Division—*civil* AL-4
Boligee Hill—*hist pl* AL-4
Boligee Hill Plantation (historical)—*locale* AL-4
Boligee Lower Bar—*bar* AL-4
*Boligee Station* AL-4
*Boligee Swamp* AL-4
*Boliger* AL-4
Bolin—*locale* TX-5
**Bolinas**—*pop pl* CA-9
Bolinas Bay—*bay* CA-9
Bolinas Creek—*stream* CA-9
Bolinas Lagoon—*bay* CA-9
Bolinas Milit Reservation—*military* CA-9
Bolinas Point—*cape* CA-9
Bolinas Quail Ref—*park* CA-9
Bolinas Ridge—*ridge* CA-9
Bolinas Sch—*school* CA-9
Bolin Barn and Smokehouse—*hist pl* AR-4
Bolin Branch—*stream* AL-4
Bolin Branch—*stream* IL-6
Bolin Branch—*stream* KY-4
Bolin Branch—*stream* VA-3
Bolin Cem—*cemetery* AL-4
Bolin Cem—*cemetery* IN-6
Bolin Cem—*cemetery* OH-6
Bolin Cem—*cemetery* TN-4
Bolin Cemetary—*cemetery* AR-4
*Bolin Creek* AL-4
Bolin Creek—*stream* NC-3
Bolin Creek—*stream* WA-9
Bolinder Field-Tooele Valley Airp—*airport* UT-8
**Boling**—*pop pl* TX-5
Bolin Gap—*gap* NC-3
Boling Branch—*stream* (2) KY-4
**Bolingbroke**—*pop pl* GA-3
Bolingbroke Creek—*stream* MD-2
**Bolingbrook**—*pop pl* IL-6
Boling Cave—*cave* MO-7
Boling Cem—*cemetery* NJ-2
Boling Chapel Cem—*cemetery* KY-4
Bolingchessa Creek—*stream* MS-4
**Bolinger**—*pop pl* AL-4
**Bolinger**—*pop pl* LA-4
Bolinger Cem—*cemetery* (2) TN-4
*Bolinger Creek* CA-9
Bolinger Ditch—*canal* CO-8
Bolinger Lookout Tower—*locale* LA-4
Bolinger Oil Field—*oilfield* KS-7
Bolinger Sch—*school* IL-6
Bolinger Sch—*school* TN-4
Bolinger Sch (historical)—*school* PA-2
*Boling Green* IL-6
Boling (historical)—*locale* KS-7
Boling-Iago—*CDP* TX-5
Boling Oil Field—*oilfield* TX-5
*Boling Spring Church* AL-4
Boling Street United Methodist Ch—*church* MS-4
Bolin Hollow—*valley* IN-6
Bolin Hollow—*valley* OK-5
Bolin Knob—*summit* NC-3
Bolin Lake—*lake* MN-6
Bolin Lake—*lake* WI-6
Bolin Ridge—*ridge* KY-4
Bolin Sch—*school* (2) IL-6
Bolin Slough—*gut* AR-4
Bolins Mills—*locale* OH-6
Bolio Lake—*lake* AK-9
Bolivar—*locale* AL-4
Bolivar—*locale* GA-3
**Bolivar**—*pop pl* IN-6
**Bolivar**—*pop pl* LA-4
**Bolivar**—*pop pl* MD-2
**Bolivar**—*pop pl* MS-4
**Bolivar**—*pop pl* MO-7
**Bolivar**—*pop pl* (2) NY-2
**Bolivar**—*pop pl* OH-6
**Bolivar**—*pop pl* PA-2
**Bolivar**—*pop pl* TN-4
**Bolivar**—*pop pl* TX-5
**Bolivar**—*pop pl* WV-2
Bolivar, Lake—*lake* MS-4
Bolivar, Mount—*summit* OR-9
Bolivar Borough—*civil* PA-2
Bolivar Branch—*stream* TX-5
*Bolivar Brook* PA-2
Bolivar (CCD)—*cens area* TN-4
Bolivar Cem—*cemetery* AR-4
Bolivar Ch—*church* AR-4
Bolivar Ch—*church* TX-5
Bolivar Ch of Christ—*church* TN-4
Bolivar Chute—*gut* MS-4
Bolivar Chute—*stream* AR-4
Bolivar City Hall—*building* TN-4
Bolivar Community Hosp—*hospital* TN-4
**Bolivar County**—*pop pl* MS-4
Bolivar County Agricultural HS (historical)—*school* MS-4
Bolivar County Courthouse—*building* MS-4
Bolivar County Farm—*locale* MS-4
Bolivar County Hosp—*hospital* MS-4
Bolivar County HS—*school* MS-4
Bolivar County JHS—*school* MS-4
Bolivar Court Square Hist Dist—*hist pl* TN-4
Bolivar Creek—*stream* AL-4
Bolivar Creek—*stream* AR-4
Bolivar Creek—*stream* OR-9
Bolivar Dam—*dam* OH-6
Bolivar Division—*civil* TN-4
Bolivar Elem Sch—*school* TN-4
Bolivar First Baptist Ch—*church* TN-4
Bolivar-Hardeman County Airp—*airport* TN-4
**Bolivar (historical)**—*pop pl* MS-4
Bolivar Hollow—*valley* TX-5
Bolivar JHS—*school* TN-4
Bolivar Landing—*locale* MS-4
Bolivar Memorial Airp—*airport* MO-7
Bolivar Oil Field—*oilfield* TX-5
Bolivar Peninsula—*cape* TX-5
Bolivar Peninsula (CCD)—*cens area* TX-5
Bolivar Point—*cape* LA-4
Bolivar Pond—*reservoir* MA-1
Bolivar Pond Dam—*dam* MA-1
Bolivar Post Office—*building* TN-4
Bolivar Public Use Area—*park* MO-7
*Bolivar Reservoir* OH-6
Bolivar Roads—*channel* TX-5
Bolivar Road Sch—*school* NY-2
Bolivar Rsvr—*reservoir* PA-2
**Bolivar Run**—*pop pl* PA-2
Bolivar Run—*stream* NY-2
Bolivar Run—*stream* (2) PA-2
Bolivar Run Sch—*school* PA-2
Bolivar Spring—*spring* OR-9
Bolivar Statue—*park* DC-2
**Bolivar (Town of)**—*pop pl* NY-2
Bolivar (Township of)—*fmr MCD* (2) AR-4
**Bolivar (Township of)**—*pop pl* IN-6
*Boliver* MD-2
*Boliver Creek* AR-4
*Boliver Creek* OR-9
Bolivia—*locale* NV-8
**Bolivia**—*pop pl* IL-6
**Bolivia**—*pop pl* NC-3
Bolivia Branch—*stream* NC-3
Bolivia Lookout Tower—*locale* NC-3
Bolivian Run—*stream* OH-6
Bolivia Sch—*school* IL-6
Bolix Hollow—*basin* AZ-5
Bolkcom Cem—*cemetery* PA-2
*Bolland Creek* OR-9
Bolland District Cem—*cemetery* CT-1
*Bolland Lake* OR-9
*Bolland Mountain* OR-9
Bolland Slough—*lake* MN-6
Bollar Lake—*lake* MN-6
*Boll Creek* ID-8
*Boll Creek* NV-8
*Bollen Mill Branch* AL-4
Bollens Creek—*stream* NC-3
Bollen Wash—*stream* AZ-5
Boller House—*hist pl* MO-7
Boller Lateral—*canal* ID-8
Boller Point—*cape* NY-2
Boller Ranch—*locale* WY-8
Bollers Knob—*summit* NC-3
Bolles—*locale* WA-9
Bolles, Charles, House—*hist pl* SD-7
Bolles, Erastus, House—*hist pl* MN-6
Bolles Brook—*stream* VT-1
Bolles Canal—*canal* FL-3
Bolles Cem—*cemetery* MO-7
**Bolles Harbor**—*pop pl* MI-6
Bolles Hill—*summit* NY-2
Bolles Inlet—*bay* AK-9
Bolles Island—*island* NY-2
Bolles Ledge—*other* AK-9
Bolles Sch—*school* FL-3
Bolles Sch—*school* MI-6
Bolles Sch (abandoned)—*school* MO-7
Bolletto Ranch—*locale* OR-9
Bolley Ditch—*canal* IN-6
Boll Green Lake—*lake* FL-3
Boll Hill Ch—*church* IN-6
Bollibokka Club—*other* CA-9
Bollie Lake—*lake* UT-8
Bollie Pond—*lake* AR-4
*Bollier Butte* ND-7
*Bollinder Field-Tooele Valley Airport* UT-8
**Bolling**—*pop pl* AL-4
**Bolling**—*pop pl* NC-3
Bolling AFB (Bolling Aviation Field)—*military* DC-2
*Bolling Aviation Field (Bolling AFB)* DC-2
Bolling Branch—*stream* KY-4
Bolling Branch—*stream* TN-4
Bolling Branch—*stream* VA-3
Bolling Branch Ch (historical)—*church* TN-4
Bolling Branch Sch (historical)—*school* TN-4
Bolling Bridge—*bridge* GA-3
Bolling Cem—*cemetery* AL-4
Bolling Cem—*cemetery* VA-3
Bolling Creek—*stream* KS-7
Bollinger Branch—*stream* (2) MO-7
*Bollinger Brook* MO-7
Bollinger Canyon—*valley* (2) CA-9
Bollinger Canyon Creek—*stream* CA-9
Bollinger Cem—*cemetery* (2) MO-7
Bollinger Ch—*church* PA-2
**Bollinger County**—*pop pl* MO-7
Bollinger-Crass Memorial Airp—*airport* MO-7
*Bollinger Creek* CA-9
*Bollinger Creek* GA-3
Bollinger Creek—*stream* GA-3
Bollinger Creek—*stream* (2) MO-7
Bollinger Ditch—*canal* IN-6
Bollinger Ditch—*canal* OH-6
Bollinger Ford—*locale* MO-7
Bollinger Knob—*summit* WV-2
Bollinger Mill—*locale* MO-7
Bollinger Mill State Park—*park* MO-7
Bollinger Mtn—*summit* CA-9
Bollinger Place—*locale* CA-9
Bollinger Pond—*reservoir* NC-3
Bollinger Pond Dam—*dam* NC-3
Bollinger Ridge—*ridge* CA-9
Bollingers Chapel—*church* NC-3
Bollinger Sch (historical)—*school* MO-7
Bollinger Spring—*spring* MO-7
Bolling Grove—*woods* CA-9
Bolling Hall—*hist pl* VA-3
Bolling Island—*island* VA-3
Bolling Mill Access Point—*locale* GA-3
*Bolling Mill Creek* AL-4
Bolling Mill (historical)—*locale* AL-4
Bolling Pond—*lake* CT-1
Bolling Sch (historical)—*school* (2) AL-4
Bolling Siding—*locale* VA-3
Bolling Spring Hollow—*valley* AL-4
*Bolling Springs Hollow* MO-7
Bolling Springs State Park—*park* OK-5
**Bolling Store**—*pop pl* VA-3
Bolling Swamp—*stream* VA-3
Bollins Cem—*cemetery* VA-3
Bollin Tank—*reservoir* AZ-5
Bollman, W., and Company Bridge—*hist pl* PA-2
Bollman Cem—*cemetery* IA-7
Bollman Lake—*lake* WI-6
Bollman Suspension and Trussed Bridge—*hist pl* MD-2
Bolln Ditch—*canal* WY-8
*Bollon Creek* OR-9
*Bollon Lake* OR-9
*Bollon Mountain* OR-9
Bolls Cem—*cemetery* MS-4
Bollschweiler Tank—*reservoir* NM-5
Bolls Creek—*stream* MS-4
Boll Weevil Monmt—*hist pl* AL-4
*Bollworm Rsvr* OR-9
*Bolly Basin* UT-8
Bollybusha Creek—*stream* MS-4
**Bolly (historical)**—*pop pl* OR-9
Bolly Knob—*summit* UT-8
Bolme Lake—*lake* MN-6
*Bolocate Creek* MT-8
Bologna Airp—*airport* PA-2
Bologna Basin—*basin* OR-9
Bologna Creek—*stream* OR-9
Bologna Lake—*lake* MN-6
Bologna Spring—*spring* OR-9
*Bologne Creek* OR-9
Bologne Creek—*stream* MT-8
Bolo Lake—*lake* AK-9
*Bolong Creek* GA-3
Bolongo Bay—*bay* VI-3
Bolongo Point—*cape* VI-3
Bolon Hall Landing—*locale* SC-3
Bolon Island—*island* OR-9
Bolon Island State Park—*park* OR-9
Bolon Ridge Ch—*church* OH-6
*Bolons Island* OR-9
Bolon Spring—*spring* UT-8
Bolo Point—*cape* TX-5
**Bolo (Township of)**—*pop pl* IL-6
Bolsa—*area* CA-9
Bolsa—*uninc pl* CA-9
Bolsa Bay—*bay* CA-9
Bolsa Canyon—*valley* AZ-5
Bolsa Chica Beach State Park—*park* CA-9
Bolsa Chica Channel—*canal* CA-9
Bolsa Chica Lake—*lake* CA-9
Bolsa De Chamisal—*civil* CA-9
*Bolsa De Chemisal* CA-9
Bolsa De Las Escorpinas—*civil* CA-9
Bolsa Del Pajaro—*civil* CA-9
Bolsa Del Potrero Y Moro Cojo Or La Sagrada Familia—*civil* CA-9
Bolsa De San Cayetano—*civil* CA-9
Bolsa De San Felipe—*civil* CA-9
Bolsa Edwards Sch—*school* CA-9
Bolsa Grande HS—*school* CA-9
**Bolsa Knolls**—*pop pl* CA-9
Bolsa Nueva Y Moro Cojo—*civil* CA-9
Bolsa Point—*cape* CA-9
Bolsa Sch—*school* CA-9
Bolsa Tank—*reservoir* AZ-5
Bolsby Sch—*school* MI-6
*Bolsey Run* WV-2
Bolshers Run—*stream* VA-3
Bolshoi Island—*island* AK-9
Bolsillo Campground—*locale* CA-9
Bolsillo Creek—*stream* CA-9
Bolsinger Cem—*cemetery* IA-7
*Bolsinger Creek* MT-8
Bolstad Slough—*gut* SD-7
Bolster Bayou—*bay* FL-3
Bolster Brook—*stream* NH-1
Bolster Cem—*cemetery* VA-3
Bolster Creek—*stream* WA-9
Bolster Hill—*summit* MA-1
Bolster Hill—*summit* (2) NY-2
Bolster Hollow—*valley* OH-6
Bolster Pond—*lake* NH-1
Bolster Rsvr—*reservoir* VT-1
Bolster (Site)—*locale* WA-9
**Bolsters Mills**—*pop pl* ME-1
Bolsters Store—*locale* VA-3
Bolstridge Camp—*locale* ME-1
Bols Well—*well* NM-5
**Bolt**—*pop pl* OR-9
**Bolt**—*pop pl* WV-2
**Bolt**—*pop pl* WI-6
Bolt Brook—*stream* ME-1
Bolt Canyon—*valley* AZ-5
Bolt Cem—*cemetery* VA-3
Bolt Creek—*stream* CA-9
Bolt Creek—*stream* IL-6
Bolt Creek—*stream* WA-9
**Bolte**—*pop pl* AL-4
*Bolten Knob* KY-4
Bolten Mines (underground)—*mine* TN-4
Bolten Ranch—*locale* WY-8
Bolter Branch—*stream* AL-4
Bolter Brook—*stream* VT-1
Bolter Creek—*stream* NY-2
Bolter Island—*island* MO-7
Bolte Sch—*school* AL-4
Bolte Sch—*school* SD-7
Bolt Hill—*summit* ME-1
Bolthouse Ridge—*ridge* KY-4
Bolt Lake—*lake* MI-6
Boltman Cem—*cemetery* AR-4
Bolt Mtn—*summit* OR-9
*Boltners Bayou* LA-4
*Boltners Brake* LA-4
*Boltom Hollow* OR-9
*Bolton* PA-2
Bolton—*locale* IL-6
Bolton—*locale* KS-7
Bolton—*locale* MD-2
Bolton—*locale* MI-6
Bolton—*locale* VA-3
**Bolton**—*pop pl* CT-1
**Bolton**—*pop pl* GA-3
**Bolton**—*pop pl* IA-7
**Bolton**—*pop pl* MA-1
**Bolton**—*pop pl* MS-4
**Bolton**—*pop pl* NY-2
**Bolton**—*pop pl* NC-3
**Bolton**—*pop pl* OH-6
**Bolton**—*pop pl* OR-9
**Bolton**—*pop pl* TN-4
**Bolton**—*pop pl* VT-1
Bolton, Chester and Frances, House—*hist pl* OH-6
Bolton, Dr. W. T., House—*hist pl* CA-9
Bolton, James Wade, House—*hist pl* LA-4
Bolton Airp—*airport* NC-3
**Bolton and Company Subdivision**—*pop pl* UT-8
Bolton Attendance Center—*school* MS-4
Bolton Baptist Ch—*church* MS-4
Bolton Branch—*stream* (2) AL-4
Bolton Branch—*stream* FL-3
Bolton Branch—*stream* KY-4
Bolton Branch—*stream* MS-4
Bolton Branch—*stream* SC-3
Bolton Branch—*stream* (2) TN-4
Bolton Branch—*stream* VA-3
*Bolton Bridge* NC-3
Bolton Brook—*stream* NY-2
Bolton Brown, Mount—*summit* CA-9
Bolton Camp Hollow—*valley* IL-6
Bolton Canal—*canal* ID-8
Bolton Cedar Swamp—*swamp* MA-1
Bolton Cem—*cemetery* (2) AL-4
Bolton Cem—*cemetery* AR-4
Bolton Cem—*cemetery* IL-6
Bolton Cem—*cemetery* KY-4
Bolton Cem—*cemetery* MS-4
Bolton Cem—*cemetery* TX-5
**Bolton Center**—*pop pl* CT-1
Bolton Center Cem—*cemetery* CT-1
Bolton Ch—*church* KY-4
Bolton Ch—*church* TX-5
Bolton Chapel—*church* MS-4
Bolton Cove—*bay* ME-1
Bolton Creek—*stream* CO-8
Bolton Creek—*stream* ID-8
Bolton Creek—*stream* WY-8
Bolton Creek Oil Field—*oilfield* WY-8
Bolton Elem Sch—*school* NC-3
**Bolton Estates**—*pop pl* TN-4
Bolton Falls—*falls* VT-1
Bolton Flats Wildlife Mngmt Area—*park* MA-1
Bolton Hall—*hist pl* CA-9
Bolton Hill—*summit* ME-1
Bolton Hill Cem—*cemetery* ME-1
Bolton Hill Creek—*stream* OR-9
Bolton Hill Hist Dist—*hist pl* MD-2
*Bolton Hollow* OR-9
Bolton Hollow—*valley* KY-4
Bolton HS—*hist pl* LA-4
Bolton HS—*school* CT-1
Bolton HS—*school* LA-4
Bolton Knob—*summit* KY-4
Bolton Lake—*lake* MN-6
Bolton Lake—*lake* WI-6
Bolton Lake—*reservoir* AL-4
Bolton Lakes—*reservoir* CT-1
**Bolton Landing**—*pop pl* NY-2
Bolton Lateral—*canal* ID-8
Bolton Lodge—*locale* VT-1
Bolton Memorial Sch—*school* VT-1
Bolton Mtn—*summit* VT-1
Bolton Mtn—*summit* VA-3
Bolton Notch—*locale* CT-1
Bolton Notch—*locale* VT-1
Bolton Notch Pond—*lake* CT-1
Bolton Notch State Park—*park* CT-1
Bolton Pan Cem—*cemetery* MA-1
Bolton Park—*park* NC-3
Bolton Peninsula—*cape* WA-9
Bolton Point—*cape* MI-6
Bolton Point—*cape* TN-4
Bolton Pond Brook—*stream* CT-1
Bolton Post Office—*building* MS-4
Bolton Post Office (historical)—*building* SD-7
Bolton Priory—*hist pl* NY-2
Bolton Run—*stream* OH-6
Bolton Sch—*school* CT-1
Bolton Sch—*school* (2) OH-6
Bolton Sch (historical)—*school* MO-7
Bolton Sch Number 3 (historical)—*school* SD-7
Bolton School (Abandoned)—*locale* IA-7
*Boltons Crossroads* AL-4
*Boltons Depot* MS-4
Boltons Mill (historical)—*locale* MS-4
**Bolton Station**—*pop pl* MA-1
**Bolton (Town of)**—*pop pl* CT-1
**Bolton (Town of)**—*pop pl* MA-1
**Bolton (Town of)**—*pop pl* NY-2
**Bolton (Town of)**—*pop pl* VT-1
**Bolton Township**—*pop pl* KS-7
Bolton (Township of)—*fmr MCD* NC-3
Bolton Valley (Recreational Area)—*uninc pl* VT-1
Boltonville—*locale* IA-7
**Boltonville**—*pop pl* VT-1
**Boltonville**—*pop pl* WI-6
Boltonville Cem—*cemetery* VT-1
Bolt Park—*park* MI-6
Bolt Ranch—*locale* TX-5
Bolts Cem—*cemetery* KY-4
Bolts Corners—*locale* NY-2
Bolts Ditch—*canal* CO-8
Boltsfork—*locale* KY-4
Bolts Fork—*stream* KY-4
Bolts Lake—*reservoir* CO-8
Boltwood Park—*park* IL-6
**Boltz**—*pop pl* PA-2
Boltzer Drain—*canal* MI-6
Boltz Ridge—*ridge* OH-6
Boludo, Cerro—*summit* TX-5
Bolyard Cem—*cemetery* WV-2
Boly Bluff—*cliff* OR-9
Bolyn—*locale* KY-4
*Bolyn Brook* CT-1
Bolz Lake—*reservoir* KY-4
**Boma**—*pop pl* TN-4
Boma Coulee—*valley* WI-6
Boman Branch—*stream* TN-4
Bomante House—*hist pl* OH-6
Boman Valley—*valley* NH-1
Boma Post Office (historical)—*building* TN-4
Bomar—*locale* AL-4
**Bomar**—*pop pl* VA-3
Bomar Acad (historical)—*school* TN-4
Bomar Branch—*stream* TN-4
Bomar Cem—*cemetery* TN-4
Bomar Creek—*stream* (2) TN-4
Bomar Field-Shelbyville Municipal Airp—*airport* TN-4
Bomar Hill—*summit* NE-7
Bomar Hill—*summit* TN-4
Bomar Hill Cem—*cemetery* TN-4
Boma Ridge—*ridge* WI-6
Bomar Lake—*reservoir* TN-4
Bomar Lake Dam—*dam* TN-4
Bomar Point Cem—*cemetery* OK-5
Bomar Post Office (historical)—*building* AL-4
Bomarton—*locale* TX-5
Bomarton Cem—*cemetery* TX-5
Boma Sch (historical)—*school* TN-4
Bombard Bay—*bay* OR-9
Bombard Draw—*valley* SD-7
Bombardment Creek—*stream* AK-9
Bombay—*locale* CA-9
Bombay—*locale* MI-6
**Bombay**—*pop pl* MN-6
**Bombay**—*pop pl* NY-2
Bombay Beach—*beach* CA-9
**Bombay Beach**—*pop pl* CA-9
*Bombay Hook* DE-2
Bombay Hook Island—*island* DE-2
*Bombay Hook Migratory Waterfowl Refuge* DE-2
Bombay Hook Natl Wildlife Ref—*park* DE-2
Bombay Hook Point—*cape* DE-2
Bombay Hook Point Shoal—*bar* DE-2
*Bombay Island* DE-2
**Bombay (Town of)**—*pop pl* NY-2
Bombazee Brook—*stream* ME-1
Bombazee Rips—*rapids* ME-1
Bombazine Island—*island* ME-1
Bomber Basin—*basin* WY-8
Bomber Coulee—*valley* MT-8
Bomber Detention Diversion Dam—*dam* MT-8
Bomber Falls—*falls* WY-8
Bomberger Park—*park* OH-6
Bomberger's Distillery—*hist pl* PA-2
Bomber Lake—*lake* WY-8
Bomber Mtn—*summit* WY-8
Bomber Rsvr—*reservoir* MT-8
Bomber Windmill—*locale* TX-5
Bombing Range Rsvr—*reservoir* CO-8
Bombing Target Windmill—*locale* TX-5
Bomboy Mine—*mine* AZ-5
Bomb Point—*cape* AK-9
Bomb Range Dam—*dam* SD-7
Bombshell Creek—*stream* KY-4
Bombsight Tank—*reservoir* (3) TX-5
Bombsite Rsvr—*reservoir* WY-8
Bomb Target Tank—*reservoir* NM-5
Bomb Target Windmill—*locale* TX-5
Bomer City Park—*park* TN-4
Bomer Lake—*reservoir* TN-4
Bomford Hill—*summit* GA-3
Bomill Branch—*stream* NC-3
Bomkamp Ridge—*ridge* WI-6
Bomke Cem—*cemetery* WI-6
*Bomking Island* MA-1
*Bomkin Island* MA-1
Bommer Canyon—*valley* CA-9
Bommer Creek—*stream* KS-7
**Bommers**—*pop pl* MS-4
Bommers Ferry—*locale* MS-4
Bomont—*locale* WV-2
**Bomoseen**—*pop pl* VT-1
Bomoseen, Lake—*lake* VT-1
**Bomoseen (P.O.) (Castleton Corners)**—*pop pl* VT-1
*Bompas Creek* IL-6
*Bompties Hook* DE-2
*Bomtiens Udd* DE-2
*Bomties Hoek* DE-2
Bon—*locale* AZ-5
Bon—*locale* KY-4
Bona—*locale* TX-5
Bona—*locale* WY-8
**Bona**—*pop pl* MO-7
Bona, Mount—*summit* AK-9
**Bona Bella**—*pop pl* GA-3
*Bonabi* FM-9
Bonable Lake—*lake* FL-3
Bon Accord—*locale* IA-7
Bon Accord Placer Mine—*mine* MT-8
Bon Acre Landing—*locale* AL-4
Bon Acre Landing—*locale* GA-3
Bonadelle Ranchos-Madera Ranchos—*CDP* CA-9
*Bonadventure* FL-3
Bonafacio Gulch—*valley* CO-8
Bonafacius Branch—*stream* TN-4
Bona Fida Shelter—*locale* OR-9
Bonafide Ditch—*canal* CO-8
Bona Fide Ditch—*canal* CO-8
Bonafide Ditch No. 2—*canal* CO-8
Bonaime Field—*airport* ND-7
*Bonair* IN-6
*Bonair* TN-4
Bon Air—*hist pl* MD-2
Bonair—*locale* GA-3
Bon Air—*locale* LA-4
Bonair—*locale* PA-2
Bon Air—*locale* TN-4
**Bon Air**—*pop pl* (2) AL-4
**Bonair**—*pop pl* AR-4
**Bonair**—*pop pl* IA-7
**Bon Air**—*pop pl* KY-4
**Bon Air**—*pop pl* NJ-2
**Bon Air**—*pop pl* NC-3
**Bonair**—*pop pl* PA-2
**Bon Air**—*pop pl* (2) PA-2
**Bon Air**—*pop pl* TN-4
**Bon Air**—*pop pl* (2) VA-3
Bon-air—*uninc pl* AL-4
Bonair, Lake—*lake* CT-1
Bon Air Baptist Ch—*church* AL-4
Bonair Beach—*beach* FL-3
Bon Air Cem—*cemetery* TN-4
Bon Aire—*hist pl* VA-3
**Bonaire**—*pop pl* GA-3
**Bonaire**—*pop pl* LA-4
**Bon Aire**—*pop pl* PA-2
Bonaire Cem—*cemetery* NY-2
Bon Aire Lake—*reservoir* AL-4
*Bon Aire Lake Dam* AL-4
Bon Air Elementary and MS—*school* IN-6

Bon Air Elem Sch—school PA-2
Bonaire Park—park CA-9
Bonaire Park—park FL-3
**Bon Air Estates**—pop pl KY-4
Bon Air Golf Course—other (2) PA-2
Bon Air Hill—summit CA-9
**Bon Air Hills**—pop pl KY-4
Bon Air Hist Dist—hist pl VA-3
Bonair Lake CT-1
Bonair Methodist Ch—church IA-7
Bon Air Mines AL-4
Bon Air Oil Field—oilfield LA-4
Bon Air Park—park IN-6
Bon Air Park—park VA-3
**Bonair Place (subdivision)**—pop pl NC-3
Bonair Post Office TN-4
Bon Air Post Office (historical)—building TN-4
Bon Air Sch (historical)—school (2) TN-4
Bon Air School IN-6
Bon Air Springs Post Office TN-4
**Bon Air Terrace**—pop pl SC-3
Bonaki FM-9
Bonaldo Cem—cemetery TX-5
Bonaldo Ch—church TX-5
Bonaldo Creek—stream TX-5
Bonally Mine—mine CA-9
Bon Ami—locale FL-3
Bon Ami—locale LA-4
Bon Ami—locale TX-5
Bonami Creek—stream ID-8
Bonami No 1 Mine—mine ID-8
Bonanza NV-8
Bonanza—fmr MCD NE-7
Bonanza—locale AK-9
Bonanza—locale ID-8
Bonanza—locale KY-4
Bonanza—locale TX-5
**Bonanza**—pop pl AR-4
**Bonanza**—pop pl CO-8
**Bonanza**—pop pl MO-7
**Bonanza**—pop pl OR-9
**Bonanza**—pop pl TX-5
**Bonanza**—pop pl UT-8
Bonanza—post sta TX-5
**Bonanza Acres Subdivision**—pop pl UT-8
**Bonanza Acres #3 Subdivision**—pop pl UT-8
Bonanza Air Strip Airp—airport UT-8
Bonanza Bar—bar AK-9
Bonanza Bar—bar ID-8
Bonanza Basin—basin OR-9
Bonanza Bill Flat—flat AZ-5
Bonanza Bill Point—summit AZ-5
Bonanza Campground—locale WA-9
Bonanza Canyon—valley NV-8
Bonanza Cem—cemetery WY-8
**Bonanza City**—pop pl CO-8
Bonanza Creek MT-8
Bonanza Creek—stream (10) AK-9
Bonanza Creek—stream CO-8
Bonanza Creek—stream MT-8
Bonanza Creek—stream NM-5
Bonanza Creek—stream (2) WY-8
Bonanza Creek Experimental For—forest AK-9
Bonanza Falls—falls MI-6
Bonanza Flat—flat UT-8
Bonanza Flats—flat AK-9
**Bonanza Grove**—pop pl MN-6
Bonanza Guard Station—locale ID-8
Bonanza Gulch—valley (4) CA-9
Bonanza Gulch—valley ID-8
Bonanza Gulch—valley MT-8
Bonanza Gulch—valley NV-8
Bonanza Gulch—valley SD-7
Bonanza Hill—summit AK-9
Bonanza Hill—summit NV-8
Bonanza Hill—summit NM-5
Bonanza Hill—summit WA-9
Bonanza Hills—other AK-9
**Bonanza Hills (subdivision)**—pop pl NC-3
Bonanza Hollow—valley MO-7
Bonanza King—summit CA-9
Bonanza King Mine—mine (2) CA-9
Bonanza King Mine—mine NV-8
Bonanza King Well—well CA-9
Bonanza Lake—lake ID-8
Bonanza Lake—lake MN-6
Bonanza Lakes—lake MT-8
Bonanza Landing Strip UT-8
Bonanza Lead Mill—locale WA-9
Bonanza Memorial Park—cemetery OR-9
Bonanza Mine—mine AK-9
Bonanza Mine—mine (4) AZ-5
Bonanza Mine—mine CA-9
Bonanza Mine—mine CO-8
Bonanza Mine—mine (2) MT-8
Bonanza Mine—mine NC-3
Bonanza Mine—mine (3) OR-9
Bonanza Mine—mine TX-5
Bonanza Mine—mine UT-8
Bonanza Mine—mine WA-9
Bonanza Mines—mine KY-4
Bonanza Mtn—summit NV-8
Bonanza Oil Field—oilfield WY-8
Bonanza Peak—summit AK-9
Bonanza Peak—summit ID-8
Bonanza Peak—summit NV-8
Bonanza Peak—summit WA-9
Bonanza Plantation (historical)—locale MS-4
Bonanza Power Plant—building UT-8
Bonanza Power Plant Heliport—airport UT-8
Bonanza Pumping Station—other WY-8
Bonanza Queen Mine—mine WA-9
Bonanza Ranch—locale CA-9
Bonanza Ridge—ridge AK-9
Bonanza River—stream AK-9
Bonanza Rsvr—reservoir MT-8
Bonanza Rsvr No 1—reservoir WY-8
Bonanza Rsvr No 2—reservoir WY-8
Bonanza Rsvr No 3—reservoir WY-8
Bonanza RV and Mobile Home Campground—locale UT-8
Bonanza Sch—school NV-8
Bonanza Seeps—spring WY-8
Bonanza (Site)—locale CA-9
Bonanza Spring—spring CA-9
Bonanza Spring—spring MO-7
Bonanza Spring—spring TX-5
**Bonanza Springs**—pop pl CA-9
Bonanza State Wildlife Area—park MO-7
Bonanza Trail NV-8
Bonanza Trail—trail OR-9
Bonanza Trailhead—locale NV-8
Bonanza Tunnel—mine AZ-5
Bonanza Wash—arroyo AZ-5
Bonanza Wash—stream NV-8
Bonanzo Creek CA-9
Bonanzy Mine—mine NV-8
Bonaparte—other NY-2
**Bonaparte**—pop pl IA-7
Bonaparte, Lake—lake NY-2
Bonaparte, Mount—summit WA-9
Bonaparte City Park—park IA-7
Bonaparte Creek—gut NC-3
Bonaparte Creek—stream LA-4
Bonaparte Creek—stream NY-2
Bonaparte Creek—stream WA-9
Bonaparte Lake—lake WA-9
Bonaparte Landing—locale NJ-2
**Bonaparte Landing**—pop pl NC-3
Bonaparte Lodge—locale NC-3
Bonaparte Mine—mine ID-8
Bonaparte Mountain Cabin—hist pl WA-9
Bonaparte Township—fmr MCD IA-7
Bonaparte Trail—trail WA-9
**Bon Aqua**—pop pl TN-4
Bon Aqua Ch—church TN-4
**Bon Aqua Junction**—pop pl TN-4
Bon Aqua Lookout Tower—locale TN-4
Bonaqua Post Office TN-4
Bon Aqua Post Office—building TN-4
Bon Aqua Sch (historical)—school TN-4
Bon Aqua Springs—spring TN-4
Bonar Cem—cemetery MN-6
Bonar Creek—stream PA-2
Bonar Hall—hist pl GA-3
Bonars Island—island FL-3
Bonarva Canal—canal NC-3
Bonasa KS-7
Bonas Defeat—summit NC-3
Bonasila Dome—summit AK-9
Bonasila River—stream AK-9
Bonasila Slough—gut AK-9
Bona Spring—spring GU-9
**Bonaventure**—pop pl FL-3
Bonaventure, Lake—reservoir VA-3
Bonaventure Cem—cemetery AL-4
Bonaventure Cem—cemetery GA-3
Bon-A-Venture Cem—cemetery (2) NC-3
Bona Venture Mobile Home Park—locale AZ-5
**Bona Villa Park (subdivision)**—pop pl UT-8
**Bonaville Township**—pop pl KS-7
Bona Vista MH-9
**Bona Vista Subdivision**—pop pl UT-8
Bonavita-Weller House—hist pl KY-4
Bonayer KY-4
**Bonayer (Bon Ayr)**—pop pl KY-4
Bonayr KY-4
Bon Ayr—locale KY-4
Bon Ayre Ridge—ridge WA-9
Bon Ayre Sch—school WA-9
Bon Ayre Valley—valley WA-9
Bonbrook—locale VA-3
Bonbrook Creek—stream VA-3
Boncar WV-2
Boncarbo—locale CO-8
Boncarbo Mine—mine CO-8
Bonchefong Creek MS-4
Bonclarken, Lake—reservoir NC-3
Bonclarken Assembly Grounds—locale NC-3
Bonclarken Lake—reservoir NC-3
Bonclarken Lake Dam—dam NC-3
Boncl Sch—school MO-7
Bond KS-7
Bond MA-1
Bond—locale GA-3
Bond—locale KY-4
Bond—locale LA-4
Bond—locale MT-8
Bond—locale OK-5
Bond—locale TX-5
**Bond**—pop pl CO-8
**Bond**—pop pl FL-3
**Bond**—pop pl MD-2
**Bond**—pop pl (2) MS-4
**Bond**—pop pl TN-4
Bond, Frank, House—hist pl NM-5
Bond, J. Roy, House—hist pl KY-4
Bond, Mount—summit NH-1
Bond Academy Creek GA-3
Bondad—locale CO-8
Bondad Hill—summit CO-8
Bondad Station CO-8
Bonda Mine—mine CA-9
Bond And Palmer Drain—canal MI-6
Bond-Baker-Carter House—hist pl GA-3
Bond Baptist Church MS-4
Bond Bay—bay AK-9
Bond Bldg—hist pl DC-2
Bond Bottom—bend SD-7
Bond Branch—stream AL-4
Bond Branch—stream SC-3
Bond Branch—stream TN-4
Bond Branch—stream (2) VA-3
Bond Brook—stream (2) ME-1
Bond Brook—stream VT-1
Bondbrook Creek VA-3
Bond Butte—summit OR-9
Bond Camp—locale IL-6
Bond Canyon TX-5
Bond Canyon—valley AZ-5
Bond Canyon—valley NM-5
Bond Cem—cemetery AL-4
Bond Cem—cemetery (2) AR-4
Bond Cem—cemetery GA-3
Bond Cem—cemetery (2) IL-6
Bond Cem—cemetery IN-6
Bond Cem—cemetery (2) KY-4
Bond Cem—cemetery (2) LA-4
Bond Cem—cemetery (5) MS-4
Bond Cem—cemetery MO-7
Bond Cem—cemetery OK-5
Bond Cem—cemetery (3) TN-4
Bond Cem—cemetery VA-3
Bond Cem—cemetery WV-2
Bond Ch AL-4
Bond Ch—church (2) MS-4
Bond Chapel—church AL-4
Bond Chapel—church MD-2
Bond Chapel—church OH-6
Bondclay—locale OH-6
Bondcliff Trail—trail NH-1
**Bond (County)**—pop pl IL-6
Bond Creek OR-9
Bond Creek—stream AK-9
Bond Creek—stream AR-4
Bond Creek—stream (3) CA-9
Bond Creek—stream ID-8
Bond Creek—stream IL-6
Bond Creek—stream LA-4
Bond Creek—stream MI-6
Bond Creek—stream (2) MT-8
Bond Creek—stream NY-2
Bond Creek—stream NC-3
Bond Creek—stream (2) OR-9
Bond Creek—stream SC-3
Bond Creek—stream (2) TN-4
Bond Creek—stream WY-8
Bond Cutoff Lake—lake TN-4
Bond District—hist pl HI-9
Bond Drain—canal (2) MI-6
Bond Draw—valley NM-5
Bond Draw—valley WY-8
Bon De Croft (CCD)—cens area TN-4
Bon De Croft Division—civil TN-4
Bon De Croft Elem Sch—school TN-4
Bonde Farmhouse—hist pl MN-6
Bonde Spring—spring OR-9
Bondesson Lateral—canal AZ-5
Bondeville MA-1
Bond Falls—falls MI-6
Bond Falls Flowage—lake MI-6
Bond Gap—gap VA-3
Bond Hill MA-1
Bond Hill OH-6
**Bond Hill**—pop pl OH-6
Bond Hill—summit (3) MA-1
Bond Hill—summit NH-1
Bond Hill—summit VT-1
Bond (historical)—locale AL-4
Bondholder Meadows—flat CO-8
Bondholder Trail—trail CO-8
Bond Hollow—valley IL-6
Bond Hollow—valley MO-7
Bond Hollow—valley (2) OH-6
Bond Hollow Swamp—swamp MA-1
Bond House—hist pl MS-4
Bondi Brothers Store—hist pl AR-4
Bondie Drain—canal MI-6
Bondinesville PA-2
Bondinot Creek—stream OK-5
**Bondin (Township of)**—pop pl MN-6
Bond Island—island ME-1
Bond Island—island VT-1
Bondity Ponds Branch—stream MS-4
Bond Lake—lake ID-8
Bond Lake—lake (2) MN-6
Bond Lake—lake (2) MT-8
Bond Lake—lake NY-2
Bond Lake—lake ND-7
Bond Lake—lake (2) WI-6
Bond Lake Dam—dam (3) MS-4
Bond Lakes—reservoir GA-3
Bond Landing—locale NC-3
Bondland Lake NV-8
Bond Mill Pond—lake MI-6
**Bond Mill Woods**—pop pl MD-2
Bond Mtn—summit ME-1
Bond Number 1 Tunnel—tunnel HI-9
Bond Number 2 Tunnel—tunnel HI-9
**Bond (Onapa)**—pop pl OK-5
Bond Park—park NH-1
Bond Pass—gap CA-9
Bond Pond—lake CT-1
Bond Pond—lake MS-4
Bond Quarry—mine TN-4
Bond Quarry Cave—cave TN-4
Bond Ranch—locale MT-8
Bond Ranch—locale (2) NM-5
Bond Ranch—locale TX-5
Bond Ridge—ridge MO-7
Bond Ridge Ch—church MO-7
Bond Rsvr—reservoir CT-1
**Bonds**—pop pl GA-3
**Bonds**—pop pl IN-6
**Bonds**—pop pl MD-2
Bonds Bar Island—island NJ-2
Bonds Branch—stream FL-3
Bonds Branch—stream NC-3
Bonds Bridge—other MI-6
Bonds Cem—cemetery (2) AR-4
Bonds Cem—cemetery (2) MS-4
Bonds Cemetery AL-4
Bond Sch—school FL-3
Bond Sch—school (3) IL-6
Bond Sch—school (3) MI-6
Bond Sch—school NC-3
Bonds Ch (abandoned)—church MO-7
Bonds Chapel—church IN-6
Bonds Chapel—church MO-7
Bond Sch (historical)—school (2) TN-4
**Bonds Corner**—pop pl CA-9
**Bonds Corner**—pop pl NH-1
Bonds Corner Drain—canal CA-9
Bonds Corner Drain Five—canal CA-9
Bonds Corner Drain Four—canal CA-9
Bonds Corner Drain Six—canal CA-9
Bonds Corner Drain Three—canal CA-9
Bonds Corner Drain Two—canal CA-9
Bonds Corners—locale ME-1
Bonds Creek—stream MO-7
Bonds Creek—stream WV-2
**Bonds Crossroads**—pop pl SC-3
Bonds Ferry (historical)—locale SD-7
Bonds Flat—flat CA-9
Bonds Four Section Windmill—locale NM-5
Bonds Grove Ch—church NC-3
Bonds Hill—summit MA-1
Bonds Hollow—valley AR-4
Bonds Hollow—valley MO-7
Bonds Lake NY-2
Bonds Lake—reservoir AL-4
Bonds Lake Dam—dam AL-4
Bonds Mtn—summit MS-4
Bond Spring—spring AZ-5
Bonds Realty Company Lake Dam—dam MS-4
Bonds Run—stream WV-2
Bonds Sch—school AR-4
Bonds Sch (abandoned)—school MO-7
Bonds Trailer Park—locale AZ-5
Bond Street Sch—school NJ-2
Bonds Village MA-1
**Bondsville**—pop pl AR-4
**Bondsville**—pop pl MA-1
**Bondsville**—pop pl PA-2
Bondsville Lower Dam—dam MA-1
Bond Swamp—stream SC-3
Bond Swamp—swamp GA-3
Bonds Well—well NM-5
Bonds-Wilson HS—school SC-3
**Bondtown**—pop pl VA-3
Bondtown Cem—cemetery VA-3
**Bond (Township of)**—pop pl IL-6
**Bonduel**—pop pl WI-6
Bondurant—locale KY-4
**Bondurant**—pop pl IA-7
**Bondurant**—pop pl WY-8
Bondurant Cem—cemetery MO-7
Bondurant Cem—cemetery NC-3
Bondurant Cem—cemetery WY-8
Bondurant Chute—channel LA-4
Bondurant Creek—stream CO-8
Bondurant Creek—stream WY-8
Bondurant House—hist pl KY-4
Bondurant Landing—locale MS-4
Bondurant Mine—mine CA-9
Bondurant Oil Field—oilfield KS-7
Bondurant Sch (historical)—school MO-7
Bondurant Towhead—island LA-4
Bon Durban NH-1
Bond Valley—valley CA-9
Bond Vein—locale PA-2
Bondville—fmr MCD NE-7
**Bondville**—pop pl IL-6
**Bondville**—pop pl KY-4
**Bondville**—pop pl VT-1
Bond Windmill—locale TX-5
Bondy Ridge—ridge OH-6
Bondy Valley WI-6
Bone MP-9
Bone—locale ID-8
**Bone**—pop pl GA-3
Boneau Rsvr—reservoir MT-8
Boneawl House—locale CO-8
Bone Bank—levee IN-6
Bone Basin—basin MT-8
Bone Basin Creek—stream MT-8
Bone Basin Spring—spring MT-8
Bonebay FM-9
Bone Bend—bend TX-5
Bonebey FM-9
Bone Bluff Lake—lake FL-3
Bonebrake Cem—cemetery IN-6
Bone Branch—stream AL-4
Bone Branch—stream (4) KY-4
Bone Branch—stream MO-7
Bone Branch—stream (2) TX-5
Bone Branch—stream WV-2
Bone Brook—stream NH-1
Bone Camp AL-4
Bone Camp Cem—cemetery AL-4
Bone Camp Ch—church AL-4
Bone Camp Ch—church MO-7
Bone Camp Creek—stream NC-3
Bone Camp Creek—stream SC-3
Bone Camp Creek—stream TN-4
Bone Camp Island—area MO-7
Bone Camp Methodist Episcopal Ch AL-4
Bone Canyon—valley CA-9
Bone Canyon—valley NV-8
Bone Canyon—valley (3) OR-9
Bone Canyon—valley TX-5
Bone Cave—cave (2) AL-4
Bone Cave—cave AR-4
Bone Cave—cave MO-7
Bone Cave—cave (3) TN-4
Bone Cave—locale TN-4
Bone Cave Community Center—building TN-4
Bone Cave Hollow—valley AL-4
Bone Cave Hollow—valley AR-4
Bone Cave Mtn—summit TN-4
Bonecave Post Office TN-4
Bone Cave Post Office—building TN-4
Bone Cave Sch (historical)—school TN-4
Bone Cave State Park—park TN-4
Bone Cem—cemetery AL-4
Bone Cem—cemetery GA-3
Bone Cem—cemetery MO-7
Bone Cem—cemetery TN-4
Bone Cem—cemetery WV-2
Bone Coulee—valley MT-8
Bone Cove—bay NE-7
Bone Creek AL-4
Bone Creek MS-4
Bone Creek—stream (2) AL-4
Bone Creek—stream (2) AK-9
Bone Creek—stream (2) CA-9
Bone Creek—stream FL-3
Bone Creek—stream GA-3
Bone Creek—stream IN-6
Bone Creek—stream (2) KS-7
Bone Creek—stream MN-6
Bone Creek—stream (3) NE-7
Bone Creek—stream NY-2
Bone Creek—stream ND-7
Bone Creek—stream (2) OK-5
Bone Creek—stream (2) OR-9
Bone Creek—stream WA-9
Bone Creek—stream WV-2
Bone Creek—stream (2) WY-8
**Bone Creek Township**—pop pl NE-7
Bone Crossing—locale MT-8
Bone Dam—dam AZ-5
Bone Draw—valley (2) WY-8
Bonee Branch—stream TN-4
Bonee Gulch—valley CA-9
Bonefish Peak CO-8
Bone Flat—flat (2) CA-9
Bone Flat—flat UT-8
Bone Fork—stream KY-4
**Bone Gap**—pop pl IL-6
Bone Gap (Election Precinct)—fmr MCD IL-6
Bone Gap Oil Field—other IL-6
Bone Gulch—valley (2) CA-9
Bone Gulch—valley CO-8
Bone Gulch Creek CA-9
Bonehead Basin—basin AZ-5
Bonehead Catchment—reservoir AZ-5
Bonehead Creek—stream ID-8
Bonehead Hill—summit ID-8
Bonehead Mesa—summit AZ-5
Bonehead Spring—spring (2) AZ-5
Bonehead Tank—reservoir AZ-5
Bone Hile—cave TN-4
Bone Hill—summit AR-4
Bone Hill—summit MO-7
Bone Hill—summit TX-5
Bone Hill Creek—stream ND-7
Bone Hill Creek Diversion Dam—dam ND-7
Bone Hill Creek Lake—reservoir ND-7
Bone Hill Creek Natl Wildlife Ref—park ND-7
Bone Hill Lake—reservoir TX-5
Bone Hole Hollow—valley KY-4
Bone Hollow—valley AL-4
Bone Hollow—valley AZ-5
Bone Hollow—valley KY-4
Bone Hollow—valley (2) MO-7
Bone Hollow—valley MT-8
Bone Hollow—valley (2) OH-6
Bone Hollow—valley (3) TN-4
Bone Hollow—valley (3) TX-5
Bone Hollow—valley (4) UT-8
Bone Hollow—valley VA-3
Bone Hollow Spring—spring UT-8
Bone Hollow Tank—reservoir AZ-5
Bone Island FL-3
Bone Island OR-9
Bone Island VA-3
Boneita Springs—locale SD-7
Boneita Springs Dam—dam SD-7
Boneita Springs Sch—school SD-7
Boneita Springs Township (historical)—civil SD-7
Bone Lake MI-6
Bone Lake—lake GA-3
Bone Lake—lake MI-6
Bone Lake—lake (3) MN-6
Bone Lake—lake OR-9
Bone Lake—lake TX-5
Bone Lake—lake WA-9
Bone Lake—lake (3) WI-6
Bone Lake—reservoir AL-4
Bone Lake Dam—dam AL-4
**Bone Lake (Town of)**—pop pl WI-6
Bone Lake Trail—trail WA-9
Bone Lick—other WV-2
Bonelick Run—stream WV-2
Bonell Bay—bay AZ-5
Bonell Creek—stream IA-7
Bonell Ditch—canal CO-8
Bonell Gulch—valley CA-9
Bonelli House—hist pl AZ-5
Bonelli Landing—locale AZ-5
Bonelli Peak—summit NV-8
Bonelli Ranch—locale CA-9
Bonelli Salt Mine (historical)—mine NV-8
Bone Meadow—flat CA-9
Bone Mesa—summit CO-8
Bone Mill Brook CT-1
Bonemill Brook—stream CT-1
Bone Mocho Well—well NM-5
Bone Mound II—hist pl OH-6
Bone Mountain Pond—reservoir OR-9
Bone Mtn—summit CA-9
Bone Mtn—summit OR-9
Bone Mtn—summit VT-1
Bonen Knob MT-8
Bone of Contention Mine—mine OR-9
Bone Pile Creek—stream WY-8
Bone Pit—cave AL-4
Bone Point—cape OR-9
Bone Point (historical)—cape ND-7
Bone Pond—lake FL-3
Bone Pond—lake NY-2
Bone Pond—lake PA-2
Boner Canyon—valley AZ-5
Boner Cem—cemetery IL-6
Boner Chapel—church IL-6
Boner Flat—flat OR-9
Boner Gulch—valley OR-9
Boner Hollow—valley WV-2
Bone Ridge—ridge (2) LA-4
Bone Ridge—ridge TN-4
Bone River—stream WA-9
Boner Knob—summit MT-8
Boner Lake—lake IN-6
Boner Lake—lake WA-9
Boner Mountain VA-3
Boner Ranch—locale WY-8
Boners Hill—summit PA-2
Boner Spring—spring OR-9
Bone Run—stream IN-6
Bone Run—stream NY-2
Bones Branch—stream AL-4
Bones Branch—stream MO-7
Bones Canyon—valley AZ-5
Bones Cemetery AL-4
Bones Chapel—church TX-5
Bones Creek MS-4
Bones Creek—stream NC-3
Bones Creek—stream OR-9
Boneset Creek—stream LA-4
Boneset Sch—school IL-6
Bones Ford—crossing TN-4
Bones Ford—locale NC-3
Bones Fork—stream NC-3
Bones Fork Creek NC-3
Bones Gulch—valley CA-9
Bones Hill Cem—cemetery AL-4
Bones Hooks Park—park TX-5
Boneside Pass—gap WY-8
Bones Pond—reservoir NC-3
Bones Pond Dam—dam NC-3
Bone Spring TX-5
Bone Spring—spring AZ-5
Bone Spring—spring ID-8
Bone Spring—spring MT-8
Bone Spring—spring OR-9
Bone Spring—spring (3) TX-5
Bone Spring Campground—park OR-9
Bone Spring Canyon—valley AZ-5
Bone Spring Canyon—valley TX-5
Bone Spring Cem—cemetery TN-4
Bone Spring Draw—valley (2) TX-5
Bone Spring Hill—summit CA-9
Bone Spring Hollow—valley TN-4
Bone Spring Lookout Tower—locale OR-9
Bone Springs OR-9
Bone Spring Sch (historical)—school TN-4
Bone Springs (historical)—locale KS-7
Bone Spring Well—well AZ-5
Bones Ranch—locale MT-8
Bones Spring—spring AZ-5
Bones Tank—reservoir TX-5
**Bonesteel**—pop pl SD-7
Bonesteel Cem—cemetery NY-2
Bonesteel Creek—stream NY-2
Bone Steel Hill—summit PA-2
Bonesteel Lake—reservoir SD-7
Bonesteel Lake Dam—dam SD-7
Bonesteel Pond—lake NY-2
Bonesteel Sch—school (2) NY-2
Bonesteel Township (historical)—civil SD-7
Bone Stone Graves—hist pl OH-6
Bones Well—well NM-5
Boneta—locale UT-8
**Boneta**—pop pl OH-6
Boneta-Mountain Home Cem—cemetery UT-8
Bone Tank—reservoir AZ-5
Bone Tank—reservoir NM-5
Bone Tank Draw—valley NM-5
Bonet Lake WI-6
Bonetown Gap—gap WV-2
Bonetrail ND-7
**Bonetraill**—pop pl ND-7
**Bonetraill Township**—pop pl ND-7
Bonetta Bee Mine—mine CA-9
Bonett Cem—cemetery LA-4
Bonetti—locale CA-9
Bone Valley—locale UT-8
Bone Valley—valley TN-4
Bone Valley Cem—cemetery NC-3
Bone Valley Creek—stream NC-3
**Boneville**—pop pl (2) GA-3
Boneville Pond—reservoir GA-3
Boneville Stream—stream GA-3
Boney—locale SC-3
Boneyard—locale AZ-5
Bone Yard—summit UT-8
Boneyard Canyon—valley (2) CA-9
Bone Yard Canyon—valley NV-8
Boneyard Canyon—valley NV-8
Boneyard Canyon—valley OR-9
Boneyard Canyon—valley UT-8
Boneyard Creek—stream CA-9
Boneyard Creek—stream IL-6
Boneyard Creek—stream OR-9
Boneyard Draw—valley TX-5
Boneyard Gap—gap NC-3
Boneyard Gulch—valley CO-8
Boneyard Gulch—valley ID-8
Boneyard Gulch—valley OR-9
Boneyard (historical)—locale MS-4
Boneyard (historical), The—locale AL-4
Boneyard Hollow—valley KY-4
Bone Yard Hollow—valley PA-2
Boneyard Hollow—valley (6) TN-4
Boneyard Knob—summit KY-4
Boneyard Lake—lake GA-3
Boneyard Lake—lake (2) MS-4
Bone Yard Lake—lake MO-7
Boneyard Meadow—flat CA-9
Boneyard Park—flat CO-8
Boneyard Sch (historical)—school MS-4
Bone Yard Spring—spring NV-8
Boneyard Spring—spring NV-8
Boneyard Waterhole—lake TX-5
Boneyard Windmill—locale TX-5
Boneyback Peak—summit AZ-5
Boney Basin—basin OR-9
Boney Basin Rsvr—reservoir OR-9
Boney Branch—stream TX-5
Boney Brook—stream ME-1
Boney Canyon—valley OR-9
Boney Canyon—valley WY-8
Boney Cem—cemetery AL-4
Boney Cem—cemetery NC-3
Boney Creek LA-4
Boney Creek MS-4
Boney Creek SC-3
Boney Creek—stream AK-9
Boney Creek—stream GA-3
Boney Creek—stream SC-3
Boney Creek—stream TX-5
Boney Falls Basin—reservoir MI-6
Boney Falls Dam—dam MI-6
Boneyfiddle Commercial Disrict—hist pl OH-6
Boney Hill—summit NM-5
Boney Island—island IL-6
Boney Lake—lake AZ-5
Boney Mill Pond—reservoir NC-3
Boney Mtn—summit AR-4
Boney Mtn—summit CA-9
Boney Pond—reservoir NC-3
Boney Spring Number 1—spring OR-9
Boney Spring Number 2—spring OR-9
Boneytown VA-3
**Boneyville**—pop pl KY-4
Boney Windmill—locale TX-5
Bonfield—locale MT-8
**Bonfield**—pop pl IL-6
**Bonfils**—pop pl MO-7
Bonfils Bldg—hist pl MO-7
Bonfils Sch—school MO-7
Bonfisk Peak—summit CO-8
**Bonfouca**—pop pl LA-4
Bonfouca, Bayou—stream LA-4
**Bong**—pop pl WI-6
Bonga Lake—lake MN-6
Bonga Landing—locale MN-6
Bongarcon, Lake—lake LA-4
Bongard—locale IL-6
**Bongards**—pop pl MN-6
Bongo Lake—lake OR-9
Bonham—locale MO-7
Bonham—locale TN-4
**Bonham**—pop pl KY-4
**Bonham**—pop pl SC-3
**Bonham**—pop pl TX-5
Bonham, Isaac, House—hist pl MS-4
Bonham, James Butler, Elem Sch—hist pl TX-5
Bonham Atoll MP-9
Bonham Branch—stream WV-2
Bonham Campground—locale CO-8
Bonham (CCD)—cens area TX-5
Bonham Cem—cemetery IL-6
Bonham Cem—cemetery TN-4
Bonham Chapel—church WV-2
Bonham Creek—stream GA-3
Bonham Ditch—canal IN-6

**Bonham Heights (subdivision)**—*pop pl* NC-3
Bonham House—*hist pl* SC-3
*Bonham Inseln* MP-9
*Bonham Island* MP-9
Bonham JHS—*school* TX-5
Bonham Landing—*locale* LA-4
Bonham Post Office (historical)—*building* TN-4
**Bonhamptown**—*pop pl* NJ-2
Bonham Ranch—*locale* NV-8
Bonham Rsvr—*reservoir* CO-8
Bonham Sch—*school* NV-8
Bonham Sch—*school* OH-6
Bonham Sch—*school* (7) TX-5
Bonham Sch—*school* WV-2
Bonham Sch (abandoned)—*school* MO-7
Bonham Sch (historical)—*school* TN-4
Bonham Spring—*spring* OR-9
Bonham State Park—*park* TX-5
**Bonham Subdivision**—*pop pl* UT-8
Bonham Talc Mines—*mine* CA-9
Bonham Tank—*reservoir* NM-5
**Bonhamtown**—*pop pl* NJ-2
Bonhamtown Sch—*school* NJ-2
Bonham Well—*well* (2) NV-8
Bon Harbor Hills—*range* KY-4
Bonhardt Cem—*cemetery* MO-7
Bon Haven—*hist pl* SC-3
**Bon Haven**—*pop pl* KY-4
**Bon Haven**—*pop pl* MD-2
Bonhoff Butte—*summit* MT-8
Bon Hollow Picnic Area—*locale* KY-4
**Bonhomie**—*pop pl* MS-4
**Bon Homme**—*pop pl* MS-4
**Bon Homme**—*pop pl* MO-7
Bon Homme Cem—*cemetery* SD-7
Bonhomme Ch—*church* MO-7
Bon Homme Ch—*church* SD-7
Bon Homme Colony—*locale* SD-7
Bon Homme County—*civil* SD-7
Bon Homme County Courthouse—*hist pl* SD-7
Bonhomme Creek—*stream* MO-7
Bonhomme Creek Archeol District—*hist pl* MO-7
Bon Homme Hutterite Colony—*hist pl* SD-7
Bonhomme Island—*island* MO-7
*Bon Homme Mennonite Colony* SD-7
Bonhomme Ranch—*locale* MT-8
Bonhomme Township—*civil* MO-7
Bon Homme Township—*civil* SD-7
Bon Homme Township (historical)—*civil* SD-7
*Bon Hommie* MS-4
**Bonibrook**—*pop pl* AK-9
Bonica Run—*stream* WV-2
**Bonicord**—*pop pl* TN-4
Bonidu Creek—*stream* WA-9
Bonies Mound—*island* WI-6
Boniface Camp—*locale* MI-6
Bonifacio Hill—*summit* CA-9
Bonifant Cem—*cemetery* MD-2
Bonifas Chapel—*church* MI-6
Bonifas Creek—*stream* MI-6
*Bonifas Lake* MI-6
**Bonifay**—*pop pl* FL-3
Bonifay (CCD)—*cens area* FL-3
Bonifay Elem Sch—*school* FL-3
Bonifay Lakes—*reservoir* GA-3
Bonifels—*hist pl* PA-2
Bonifer—*locale* OR-9
Bonifield Cem—*cemetery* WV-2
Bonifield Run—*stream* WV-2
**Bonila**—*pop pl* NY-2
Bonilla—*locale* CA-9
**Bonilla**—*pop pl* SD-7
Bonilla Cem—*cemetery* SD-7
*Bonilla Island* WA-9
Bonillas Sch—*school* AZ-5
**Bonilla Township**—*pop pl* SD-7
Bonin Cem—*cemetery* TX-5
Bonin Divide—*ridge* MT-8
Bonine Canyon—*valley* NM-5
Bonine Cem—*cemetery* SD-7
Bonine Creek—*stream* MT-8
Bonine Creek—*stream* TN-4
Bonine Ditch—*canal* SD-7
Bonine Windmill—*locale* NM-5
Bonin Lake—*reservoir* PA-2
Bonin Springs—*spring* MT-8
Bonis Creek—*stream* CO-8
Bonis Gulch—*valley* CO-8
Boni Spring—*spring* ID-8
Bonis Spring—*spring* CO-8
Bonita—*locale* AL-4
Bonita—*locale* AZ-5
Bonita—*locale* CA-9
Bonita—*locale* CO-8
Bonita—*locale* KY-4
Bonita—*locale* OR-9
Bonita—*locale* WI-6
Bonita—*other* TX-5
**Bonita**—*pop pl* CA-9
**Bonita**—*pop pl* KS-7
**Bonita**—*pop pl* LA-4
**Bonita**—*pop pl* MS-4
**Bonita**—*pop pl* OR-9
**Bonita**—*pop pl* TX-5
Bonita, Lake—*lake* FL-3
Bonita, Lake—*reservoir* AZ-5
Bonita, Lake—*reservoir* NY-2
Bonita, Lake—*reservoir* ND-7
Bonita Beach—*beach* (2) FL-3
**Bonita Beach**—*pop pl* FL-3
Bonita Beach Baptist Ch—*church* FL-3
Bonita Bend—*bend* UT-8
Boni Table—*summit* ID-8
Bonita Butte—*summit* CA-9
Bonita Camp—*locale* AZ-5
Bonita Canyon—*valley* (2) AZ-5
Bonita Canyon—*valley* CO-8
Bonita Canyon—*valley* (2) NV-8
Bonita Canyon—*valley* (5) NM-5
Bonita Canyon Park—*park* CA-9
Bonita Canyon Spring—*spring* NV-8
Bonita Channel—*channel* CA-9
Bonita Community Ditch—*canal* NM-5
Bonita Cove—*bay* (2) CA-9
*Bonita Creek* AZ-5
Bonita Creek—*stream* AK-9
Bonita Creek—*stream* (3) AZ-5
Bonita Creek—*stream* (3) CA-9
Bonita Creek—*stream* CO-8
Bonita Creek—*stream* NM-5
Bonita Creek—*stream* (4) TX-5
Bonita Creek—*stream* WA-9
Bonita Creek—*stream* WI-6
Bonita Dam—*dam* AZ-5
Bonita Ditch—*canal* WY-8
Bonita Draw—*valley* NM-5
Bonita Elem Sch—*school* AZ-5
Bonita Falls—*falls* CA-9
Bonita Farms Lake—*reservoir* AL-4
Bonita Flat—*flat* CA-9
Bonita Flats—*flat* WA-9
Bonita Fork—*stream* MT-8
Bonita Golf Course—*other* CA-9
Bonita Hill—*summit* CO-8
Bonita Hollow—*valley* AR-4
Bonita HS—*school* CA-9
Bonita Junction—*locale* TX-5
Bonita-Klondyke (CCD)—*cens area* AZ-5
*Bonita Lake* FL-3
Bonita Lake—*lake* FL-3
Bonita Lake—*lake* MN-6
Bonita Lake—*reservoir* CA-9
Bonita Lake—*reservoir* KY-4
Bonita Lake—*reservoir* (2) TX-5
Bonita Meadows—*flat* CA-9
Bonita Mine—*mine* NV-8
Boni Tank—*reservoir* AZ-5
Bonita Park—*flat* AZ-5
Bonita Park—*park* CA-9
Bonita Park Sch—*school* CA-9
Bonita Peak—*summit* CO-8
Bonita Ranch—*locale* CA-9
*Bonita Ranger Station* MT-8
Bonita Ranger Station—*locale* MT-8
Bonita Ravine—*valley* CA-9
Bonita Reservoir Number 1 Dam—*dam* MS-4
Bonita Reservoir Number 2 Dam—*dam* MS-4
Bonita Reservoir Number 3 Dam—*dam* MS-4
Bonita Rsvr—*reservoir* CA-9
Bonita Rsvr—*reservoir* CO-8
Bonita Rsvr—*reservoir* MS-4
Bonita Sch—*school* (2) CA-9
*Bonita School* AZ-5
**Bonita Shores**—*pop pl* FL-3
Bonita (Site)—*locale* MT-8
Bonita Spring—*spring* (3) AZ-5
Bonita Spring—*spring* NV-8
Bonita Spring—*spring* OR-9
**Bonita Springs**—*pop pl* FL-3
Bonita Springs (CCD)—*cens area* FL-3
Bonita Springs Elem Sch—*school* FL-3
Bonita Springs Lake Dam—*dam* SD-7
Bonita Springs MS—*school* FL-3
Bonita Street Sch—*school* CA-9
Bonita Tank—*reservoir* (4) AZ-5
Bonita Tank—*reservoir* NM-5
Bonita Tank—*reservoir* (4) TX-5
Bonita Tideway—*channel* NJ-2
**Bonita Trading Post**—*pop pl* AZ-5
Bonita United Methodist Ch—*church* MS-4
Bonita Vista Ranch—*locale* CA-9
Bonita Well—*well* (2) AZ-5
Bonita Windmill—*locale* (2) TX-5
Bonita Work Center—*locale* MT-8
Bonito—*locale* NM-5
Bonito, Arroyo—*valley* TX-5
Bonito, Canon—*valley* CO-8
Bonito, Canyon—*valley* CO-8
Bonito, Cerro—*ridge* CA-9
*Bonito Campground* AZ-5
Bonito Canyon—*valley* (2) AZ-5
Bonito Canyon—*valley* CO-8
Bonito Canyon—*valley* (2) NM-5
Bonito Cienega—*flat* AZ-5
Bonito Cow Camp—*locale* NM-5
*Bonito Creek* AZ-5
*Bonito Creek* NM-5
Bonito Creek—*stream* AZ-5
Bonito Creek—*stream* (2) NM-5
Bonito Creek—*stream* TX-5
*Bonito Flat* AZ-5
Bonito Lake—*reservoir* NM-5
Bonito Lava Flow—*lava* AZ-5
Bonito Mine—*mine* AZ-5
Bonito Mtn—*summit* CO-8
Bonito Park—*flat* AZ-5
Bonito Park—*flat* NM-5
Bonito Pass—*gap* CO-8
Bonito Peak—*summit* NM-5
Bonito Prairie—*flat* AZ-5
Bonito Recreation Site—*park* AZ-5
Bonito Rock—*summit* AZ-5
Bonito Rock Cienega—*swamp* AZ-5
Bonito South Branch—*stream* TX-5
Bonito Spring—*spring* (2) AZ-5
Bonito Tank—*reservoir* NM-5
Bonito Tank, Arroyo—*reservoir* TX-5
Bonito Valle—*valley* AZ-5
*Bonito Valley* AZ-5
Bonito Valley (historical)—*valley* AZ-5
**Bonito Verde Subdivision**—*pop pl* UT-8
Bonito Windmill, Arroyo—*locale* TX-5
Bon Jellico Mtn—*summit* KY-4
Bonjetti Creek—*stream* CA-9
Bon Jon Pass—*gap* WA-9
Bonjour Ditch—*canal* IN-6
*Bonkangeeru* MP-9
Bon Lake—*lake* MN-6
**Bonlee**—*pop pl* NC-3
Bonlee Elem Sch—*school* NC-3
Bon L Lake—*reservoir* GA-3
**Bonlow**—*pop pl* WA-9
Bon Marche Shop Ctr—*locale* LA-4
*Bon Mead* PA-2
**Bon Meade**—*pop pl* PA-2
Bon Meade Elem Sch—*school* PA-2
Bonn—*locale* OH-6
Bonnabel Canal—*canal* LA-4
**Bonnabel Place**—*pop pl* LA-4
**Bonnair**—*pop pl* PA-2
*Bonnar Lake* WA-9
Bonna Vista, Bayou—*stream* LA-4
Bonne Aqua Lake—*reservoir* MO-7
**Bonneau**—*pop pl* SC-3
**Bonneau Beach**—*pop pl* SC-3
Bonneau (CCD)—*cens area* SC-3
Bonneau Ferry—*locale* SC-3
Bonneau Fire Tower—*locale* SC-3
*Bonneau Reservoir* MT-8
**Bonneauville**—*pop pl* PA-2
Bonneauville Borough—*civil* PA-2
*Bonne Branch* NC-3
Bonne Creek—*stream* WY-8
Bonne Doone Lake Dam—*dam* NC-3
Bonne Esperance—*locale* (2) VI-3
Bonne Femme Creek—*stream* (2) MO-7
Bonne Femme Township—*civil* MO-7
Bonne Fortune Key—*island* FL-3
**Bonnefoy**—*pop pl* CA-9
Bonne Idee, Bayou—*stream* LA-4
Bonnel, Mount—*summit* TX-5
*Bonnel Fork* WV-2
*Bonnel Gulch* CA-9
**Bonnell**—*pop pl* IN-6
Bonnel Lake—*lake* FL-3
Bonnell Branch—*stream* MO-7
Bonnell Cem—*cemetery* IA-7
Bonnell Cem—*cemetery* PA-2
Bonnell Creek—*stream* IA-7
*Bonnell Fork* PA-2
Bonnell Number Two Ditch—*canal* IN-6
Bonnell Ranch—*locale* NM-5
Bonnell Run—*stream* (3) PA-2
Bonnell Sch (abandoned)—*school* PA-2
**Bonnenburger**—*pop pl* IN-6
*Bonner* KS-7
*Bonner* NC-3
Bonner—*locale* NE-7
**Bonner**—*pop pl* MS-4
**Bonner**—*pop pl* MT-8
**Bonner**—*pop pl* TX-5
Bonner, George, Jr., House—*hist pl* UT-8
Bonner, George, Sr., House—*hist pl* UT-8
Bonner, William, House—*hist pl* UT-8
Bonner Arnold Coliseum—*building* MS-4
Bonner Bay—*bay* NC-3
Bonner Branch—*stream* WV-2
Bonner Branch—*stream* WI-6
Bonner Camp Well—*well* TX-5
Bonner Canal—*canal* NC-3
*Bonner Canyon* AZ-5
Bonner Canyon—*valley* NM-5
Bonner Cem—*cemetery* GA-3
Bonner Cem—*cemetery* (2) KY-4
Bonner Cem—*cemetery* LA-4
Bonner Cem—*cemetery* MS-4
Bonner Cem—*cemetery* NC-3
Bonner Cem—*cemetery* OH-6
Bonner Cem—*cemetery* TN-4
Bonner Ch—*church* TN-4
Bonner Creek—*stream* GA-3
Bonner Creek—*stream* ID-8
Bonner Creek—*stream* LA-4
Bonner Creek—*stream* (3) OR-9
Bonner Creek Ch—*church* LA-4
Bonnerdale—*locale* AR-4
Bonnerdale Ch—*church* AR-4
Bonner Dam—*dam* (2) AL-4
*Bonner Davis Pond* AL-4
Bonner Ditch—*canal* OH-6
Bonner Elem Sch—*school* FL-3
Bonner Field—*airport* KS-7
Bonner Field (airport)—*airport* AL-4
Bonner Hollow—*valley* (2) TN-4
Bonner Hollow—*valley* UT-8
Bonner Hollow Cave Number One—*cave* TN-4
Bonner Hollow Cave Number Three—*cave* TN-4
Bonner Hollow Cave Number Two—*cave* TN-4
Bonner Hollow Pit—*cave* TN-4
Bonner House—*hist pl* NC-3
Bonner Junction—*locale* MT-8
Bonner Knob—*summit* TN-4
Bonner Lake—*lake* ID-8
Bonner Lake—*lake* NM-5
Bonner Lake—*lake* NY-2
Bonner Lake—*lake* WA-9
Bonner Lake—*reservoir* (2) AL-4
Bonner Lake—*reservoir* MS-4
Bonner Landing—*locale* MI-6
Bonner Mine—*mine* CO-8
Bonner Mtn—*summit* MT-8
Bonner Mtn—*summit* (2) OR-9
Bonner Mtn—*summit* VA-3
Bonner Park—*park* MT-8
Bonner Peak—*summit* CO-8
Bonner Point—*cape* TX-5
Bonner Ridge—*ridge* MO-7
*Bonners Branch* AL-4
Bonner Sch—*school* ME-1
Bonner Sch—*school* (2) TX-5
**Bonners Ferry**—*pop pl* ID-8
Bonners Ferry Ranger Station—*locale* ID-8
Bonners Ferry Substation—*other* ID-8
Bonner-Sharp-Gunn House—*hist pl* GA-3
Bonners Hill—*summit* MA-1
Bonners Lake—*reservoir* AL-4
Bonner Slough—*gut* TX-5
Bonners Mill (historical)—*locale* AL-4
Bonners Point—*cape* NC-3
Bonner Spring—*spring* CO-8
**Bonner Springs**—*pop pl* KS-7
Bonner Springs Cem—*cemetery* KS-7
Bonner Springs Interchange—*locale* KS-7
*Bonner Station* NE-7
Bonner Store (historical)—*locale* MS-4
Bonnersville (historical)—*locale* ND-7
Bonner Tabernacle—*church* AL-4
Bonnerton—*locale* NC-3
**Bonnertown**—*pop pl* TN-4
Bonnertown Baptist Ch—*church* TN-4
Bonnertown Cem—*cemetery* TN-4
Bonnertown Methodist Ch—*church* TN-4
Bonnertown Sch (historical)—*school* TN-4
Bonnerville—*locale* TX-5
Bonner Well—*well* NM-5
Bonner-West Riverside—*CDP* MT-8
Bonnes Coulee—*valley* ND-7
Bonnet—*locale* PA-2
Bonnet, Lake—*lake* (2) FL-3
Bonnet, The—*cape* RI-1
Bonnet Bay—*swamp* GA-3
*Bonnet Branch* AL-4
*Bonnet Carre* LA-4
Bonnet Carre—*dam* LA-4
Bonnet Carre Crevasse (1874)—*basin* LA-4
Bonnet Carre Oil And Gas Field—*oilfield* LA-4
Bonnet Carre Point—*cape* LA-4
Bonnet Cem—*cemetery* TX-5
Bonnet Creek—*gut* FL-3
Bonnet Creek—*stream* AL-4
Bonnet Creek—*stream* (2) FL-3
*Bonneterre* MO-7
**Bonne Terre**—*pop pl* MO-7
Bonne Terre Depot—*hist pl* MO-7
Bonne Terre Mine—*hist pl* MO-7
Bonne Terre Municipal Airp—*airport* MO-7
Bonnet Fork—*stream* WV-2
Bonnet Gully—*stream* FL-3
Bonnet Hill—*summit* VA-3
Bonnet House—*hist pl* FL-3
Bonnet Island—*island* NJ-2
Bonnet Lake—*lake* (10) FL-3
Bonnet Lake—*lake* (2) GA-3
Bonnet Lake—*lake* MI-6
Bonnet Point—*cape* NC-3
Bonnet Point—*cape* RI-1
*Bonnet Pond* FL-3
Bonnet Pond—*lake* (9) FL-3
Bonnet Pond—*stream* FL-3
Bonnet Pond—*swamp* (2) FL-3
Bonnet Rock—*pillar* (2) CA-9
Bonnet Rock Branch—*stream* KY-4
**Bonnet Shores**—*pop pl* RI-1
Bonnet Shores Beach—*summit* RI-1
Bonnet Sink—*basin* FL-3
*Bonnets Mills* MO-7
Bonnet Spring—*spring* FL-3
Bonnet's Tavern—*hist pl* PA-2
**Bonnetsville**—*pop pl* NC-3
Bonnett Creek—*stream* CO-8
Bonnett Lake—*lake* GA-3
Bonnett Lake—*lake* MS-4
Bonnett Lake—*lake* OH-6
Bonnett Lake Landing—*locale* MS-4
Bonnett Park—*flat* CO-8
Bonnett Pond—*lake* FL-3
Bonnett Prairie Cem—*cemetery* WI-6
Bonnett Prairie Ch—*church* WI-6
Bonneval—*locale* WI-6
**Bonneville**—*pop pl* AL-4
**Bonneville**—*pop pl* OR-9
**Bonneville**—*pop pl* WY-8
Bonneville, Lake—*reservoir* OR-9
Bonneville, Mount—*summit* WY-8
**Bonneville Acres Subdivision**—*pop pl* UT-8
Bonneville Basin—*basin* WY-8
Bonneville (CCD)—*cens area* WA-9
**Bonneville Center Subdivision**—*pop pl* UT-8
Bonneville County Courthouse—*hist pl* ID-8
Bonneville Creek—*stream* WY-8
Bonneville Dam—*dam* OR-9
Bonneville Dam—*dam* WA-9
Bonneville Dam Hist Dist—*hist pl* OR-9
Bonneville Dam Hist Dist—*hist pl* WA-9
Bonneville Dam Hist Dist (Boundary Increase)—*hist pl* OR-9
Bonneville Dike—*levee* UT-8
Bonneville Elem Sch—*school* FL-3
**Bonneville Estates**—*pop pl* TN-4
**Bonneville Heights Subdivision**—*pop pl* UT-8
**Bonneville (historical)**—*pop pl* TN-4
Bonneville Hotel—*hist pl* ID-8
Bonneville Hot Springs—*spring* ID-8
Bonneville House—*hist pl* AR-4
Bonneville HS—*school* UT-8
Bonneville JHS—*school* UT-8
Bonneville Lakes—*lake* WY-8
Bonneville Monument, Lake—*pillar* UT-8
Bonneville Mtn—*summit* OR-9
Bonneville Municipal Golf Course—*other* UT-8
**Bonneville on the Hill Subdivision**—*pop pl* UT-8
Bonneville Park—*park* ID-8
Bonneville Pass—*gap* WY-8
Bonneville Peak—*summit* ID-8
Bonneville Point—*cliff* ID-8
Bonneville Power Station—*other* OR-9
Bonneville Racetrack—*other* UT-8
**Bonneville Ridge Subdivision**—*pop pl* UT-8
Bonneville Rsvr—*reservoir* WY-8
*Bonneville Salt Beds* UT-8
Bonneville Salt Flats—*flat* UT-8
*Bonneville Salt Flats Race Track* UT-8
Bonneville Salt Flats Race Track—*hist pl* UT-8
Bonneville Salt Flats State Park—*park* UT-8
Bonneville Sch—*school* ID-8
Bonneville Sch—*school* (2) UT-8
*Bonneville Speedway* UT-8
Bonneville Spur—*uninc pl* WA-9
Bonneville Supply Canal—*canal* UT-8
**Bonneville Terrace Subdivision**—*pop pl* UT-8
**Bonneville Terrace Subdivision (Number 1)**—*pop pl* UT-8
**Bonneville Terrace Subdivision (Number 2)**—*pop pl* UT-8
**Bonneville Tower Condominium**—*pop pl* UT-8
Bonney—*locale* NY-2
**Bonney**—*pop pl* TX-5
Bonney Brook—*stream* CT-1
Bonney Brook—*stream* ME-1
Bonney Brook Lake—*lake* ME-1
Bonney Butte—*summit* OR-9
Bonney Canyon—*valley* NM-5
Bonney Cem—*cemetery* OR-9
*Bonney Cemetery* SD-7
Bonney Cove—*bay* VA-3
Bonney Creek—*stream* NY-2
Bonney Creek—*stream* OR-9
Bonney Crossing—*locale* OR-9
Bonney Hill—*summit* MA-1
Bonney Hill—*summit* NY-2
Bonney Lake—*lake* WA-9
**Bonney Lake**—*pop pl* WA-9
Bonney Landing—*locale* VA-3
Bonneyman—*locale* GA-3
**Bonneymeade Farm (subdivision)**—*pop pl* PA-2
Bonney Meadows—*flat* OR-9
Bonney Meadows Campground—*park* OR-9
Bonney Meadows Trail—*trail* (2) OR-9
Bonney Oil Field—*oilfield* TX-5
Bonney Pass—*gap* WY-8
*Bonney Peak* WY-8
Bonney Point—*cape* (2) ME-1
Bonney Pond—*reservoir* MA-1
Bonney Pond Dam—*dam* MA-1
Bonney Spring Mine—*mine* NM-5
Bonney Swamp—*swamp* ME-1
*Bonneyville* WV-2
Bonneyville Cem—*cemetery* IN-6
Bonneyville Mills—*hist pl* IN-6
**Bonneyville Mills**—*pop pl* IN-6
Bonnheim Sch—*school* CA-9
**Bonni Castle**—*pop pl* NY-2
Bonnie—*locale* WV-2
**Bonnie**—*pop pl* FL-3
**Bonnie**—*pop pl* IL-6
**Bonnie**—*pop pl* KY-4
**Bonnie**—*pop pl* UT-8
Bonnie, Lake—*reservoir* AL-4
Bonnie, Loch—*lake* NY-2
**Bonnie Acres**—*pop pl* MD-2
Bonniebass Chapel—*church* NC-3
**Bonnie Bell**—*pop pl* CA-9
Bonnie Belle Lake—*lake* TX-5
Bonnie Bell Mine—*mine* AZ-5
**Bonnie Blink**—*pop pl* AZ-5
Bonnie Blue Creek—*stream* MT-8
Bonnie Blue Sch—*school* MS-4
Bonnie Brae—*hist pl* WI-6
**Bonnie Brae**—*pop pl* KS-7
**Bonnie Brae**—*pop pl* MD-2
Bonnie Brae—*uninc pl* KS-7
Bonnie Brae Farm For Boys—*locale* NJ-2
Bonnie Brae Golf Course—*locale* NC-3
Bonnie Brae Park—*park* CO-8
Bonnie Brae Ranch—*locale* AZ-5
Bonnie Brae Sch—*school* TX-5
**Bonnie Brae Subdivision**—*pop pl* UT-8
**Bonnie Brea**—*pop pl* IL-6
Bonnie Brennan Elem Sch—*school* AZ-5
Bonnie Briar Country Club—*other* NY-2
*Bonnie Brook* AL-4
**Bonnie Brook**—*pop pl* PA-2
Bonnie Brook—*stream* ME-1
Bonnie Brook—*stream* OR-9
Bonnie Brook—*stream* PA-2
Bonnie Brook—*stream* VA-3
Bonnie Brook Baptist Ch—*church* AL-4
Bonnie Brook Ch—*church* IL-6
**Bonniebrook Estates (subdivision)**—*pop pl* UT-8
Bonnie Brook Golf Course—*other* MI-6
Bonniebrook Homestead—*hist pl* MO-7
Bonnie Brook Sch—*school* IL-6
Bonnie Castle Lake—*lake* MI-6
Bonnie Chapel—*church* LA-4
Bonnie Chapel—*church* MS-4
*Bonnie Clair* NV-8
Bonnie Claire—*locale* NV-8
Bonnie Claire Flat—*flat* NV-8
Bonnie Claire Lake—*flat* NV-8
*Bonnie Clare* NV-8
*Bonnie Crags* CA-9
Bonnie Craigs—*cliff* CA-9
Bonnie Creek—*stream* AK-9
Bonnie Creek—*stream* IL-6
Bonnie Creek—*stream* IA-7
Bonnie Creek—*stream* OR-9
**Bonnie Crest**—*pop pl* NY-2
Bonnie Crest Country Club—*locale* AL-4
Bonnie Dalton Artesian Well—*well* UT-8
Bonnie Divide—*ridge* ND-7
**Bonnie Doon**—*pop pl* CA-9
**Bonnie Doone**—*pop pl* AL-4
**Bonnie Doone**—*pop pl* NC-3
Bonnie Doone Lake—*reservoir* NC-3
Bonnie Doone Mission—*church* NC-3
Bonnie Doone Number One Mine—*mine* OR-9
Bonnie Doon (historical)—*locale* KS-7
Bonnie Doon Sch—*school* CA-9
Bonnie Doon Substation—*other* CA-9
Bonnie E Cone University Center—*building* NC-3
Bonnie Falls—*falls* OR-9
Bonnie Glen—*hist pl* LA-4
**Bonnie Glen**—*pop pl* MN-6
Bonnie Hill Ch—*church* NC-3
Bonnie Jeans Cave—*cave* AL-4
Bonnie Knob—*uninc pl* MD-2
*Bonnie Lake* AL-4
*Bonnie Lake* MS-4
Bonnie Lake—*lake* AK-9
Bonnie Lake—*lake* (2) CA-9
Bonnie Lake—*lake* IA-7
Bonnie Lake—*lake* (2) MN-6
Bonnie Lake—*lake* UT-8
Bonnie Lake—*lake* (2) WA-9
*Bonnie Lake Landing* MS-4
**Bonnie Lane Condominium**—*pop pl* UT-8
**Bonnie Lane Subdivision**—*pop pl* UT-8
**Bonnie Lock**—*pop pl* FL-3
Bonnie Lure Park—*locale* OR-9
Bonnie Merrit Spring—*spring* WA-9
**Bonniemill Gardens**—*pop pl* VA-3
Bonnie Mine—*mine* FL-3
Bonnie Moor Drain—*canal* MI-6
Bonnie Oak Cem—*cemetery* TN-4
Bonnie Oaks Hist Dist—*hist pl* WI-6
Bonnie Post Office (historical)—*building* TN-4
Bonnie Public Use Area—*locale* IL-6
Bonnie Reserve—*reservoir* SC-3
**Bonnie Ridge**—*pop pl* KS-7
Bonnie Rsvr—*reservoir* WY-8
Bonnies Bay—*bay* LA-4
Bonnie's Bridge—*hist pl* NJ-2
Bonnie Shade—*hist pl* SC-3
Bonnie Spring—*spring* NM-5
Bonnie Springs—*locale* NV-8
Bonnie View—*locale* CA-9
**Bonnie View**—*pop pl* TX-5
Bonnie View Golf Course—*other* MD-2
Bonnie View Hill—*summit* MA-1
Bonnie View Oil Field—*oilfield* TX-5
Bonnieview Ranch—*locale* OR-9
**Bonnie View Subdivision**—*pop pl* UT-8
Bonnie View Trail—*trail* CA-9
**Bonnieville**—*pop pl* KY-4
Bonnieville (CCD)—*cens area* KY-4
Bonnie Webb, Lake—*reservoir* MS-4
Bonnifield Cem—*cemetery* IA-7
Bonnifield Creek—*stream* AK-9
Bonnifield Trail—*trail* AK-9
**Bonnivale**—*pop pl* WV-2
**Bonniview Estates**—*pop pl* SC-3
Bonniwell Sch—*school* WI-6
Bonniwell Spring Number One—*spring* SD-7
Bonniwell Spring Number Two—*spring* SD-7
**Bonnots Mill**—*pop pl* MO-7
*Bonnotts Mill* MO-7
Bonny—*locale* KY-4
Bonny, Lake—*lake* FL-3
Bonny Baptist Ch—*church* FL-3
Bonny Bloom Pond—*swamp* FL-3
Bonny Blue—*locale* VA-3
*Bonnybrook* PA-2
Bonny Brook—*locale* AL-4
**Bonny Brook**—*pop pl* CT-1
**Bonny Brook**—*pop pl* PA-2
Bonny Brook—*stream* (2) NY-2
Bonny Cem—*cemetery* SD-7
Bonny Ch—*church* FL-3
Bonny Chess Ledge—*bar* ME-1
Bonny Clabber Creek—*stream* SC-3
Bonnycot—*hist pl* KY-4
Bonny Creek—*stream* CO-8
Bonny Dam—*dam* CO-8
Bonny Dam Landing Strip—*airport* CO-8
*Bonny Doon* CA-9
**Bonny Doon**—*pop pl* CA-9
**Bonny Eagle**—*pop pl* ME-1
Bonny Eagle Pond—*lake* ME-1
Bonny Hill—*locale* NY-2
**Bonny Kate**—*pop pl* TN-4
Bonny Kate Sch—*school* TN-4
*Bonny Lake* MN-6
Bonny Lake—*lake* FL-3
Bonny Lake—*lake* MI-6
Bonny Lake—*lake* NY-2
Bonny Lakes—*lake* OR-9
Bonny Lodge—*locale* MS-4
**Bonnyman**—*pop pl* GA-3
**Bonnyman**—*pop pl* KY-4
**Bonnymeade**—*pop pl* PA-2
Bonny Nook—*locale* CA-9
Bonny Oaks—*hist pl* TN-4
Bonny Oaks Sch—*school* TN-4
Bonny Park—*park* CO-8
Bonny Pond—*lake* ME-1
**Bonny Rigg Corners**—*pop pl* MA-1
Bonny Rsvr—*reservoir* CO-8
**Bonny Slope**—*pop pl* OR-9
Bonny Slough—*stream* MS-4
Bonny Stairs Canyon—*valley* UT-8
Bonny State Rec Area—*park* CO-8
**Bonnyview**—*pop pl* CA-9
Bonny View Dam—*dam* OR-9
Bonnyview Sch—*school* CA-9
Bonnyview Sch—*school* UT-8
Bono—*locale* AR-4
Bono—*locale* TX-5
**Bono**—*pop pl* AR-4
**Bono**—*pop pl* (2) IN-6
**Bono**—*pop pl* OH-6
Bono Archaeol Site (12 Lr 194)—*hist pl* IN-6
Bono Cem—*cemetery* IN-6
Bono Creek—*stream* WI-6
*Bonodek* MP-9
Bonomo Ranch—*locale* WY-8
*Bono's Creek* WI-6
**Bono (Township of)**—*pop pl* IN-6
Bonpas Creek—*stream* IL-6
*Bonpass Creek* IL-6
**Bonpas (Township of)**—*pop pl* IL-6
*Bonpland Lake* CA-9
Bonsack—*locale* TN-4
**Bonsack**—*pop pl* VA-3
*Bonsacks* VA-3
**Bonsal**—*pop pl* NC-3
Bonsal Company Lake—*reservoir* NC-3
Bonsal Company Lake Dam—*dam* NC-3
Bonsall—*locale* CA-9
Bonsall Hill—*summit* CA-9
Bonsall Park—*park* DE-2
Bonsall Sch—*school* PA-2
Bonsall Union Sch—*school* CA-9
Bons Creek—*stream* MI-6
Bons Draw—*valley* WY-8
**Bon Secour**—*pop pl* AL-4
**Bon Secour**—*pop pl* LA-4
Bon Secour Bay—*bay* AL-4
Bon Secour Ch—*church* AL-4
Bon Secour River—*stream* AL-4
*Bon Secours* AL-4
*Bon Secours Bay* AL-4
Bon Secours Hosp—*hospital* FL-3
Bon Secours Hosp—*hospital* MD-2
Bon Secours Hosp—*hospital* MA-1
**Bon Secours Plantation**—*pop pl* LA-4
Bonsell Creek—*stream* WY-8
Bonser Run—*stream* OH-6
Bonser Run Ch—*church* OH-6
Bonser Run Sch—*school* OH-6
Bon Spring Hollow—*valley* TN-4
Bonspur—*locale* WA-9
**Bon Spur**—*pop pl* WA-9
Bonsted Island—*island* NY-2
Bontabile Creek—*stream* CA-9
Bonta Bridge—*bridge* NY-2
Bonta Creek—*stream* (2) CA-9
Bontadelli, Peter J., House—*hist pl* CA-9
Bonta-Owsley House—*hist pl* KY-4
Bonta Ridge—*ridge* CA-9
**Bonta Vista Estates**—*pop pl* TN-4
*Bontear* MO-7
Bon Tempe Creek—*stream* CA-9
Bon Tempe Lake—*reservoir* CA-9
Bonte Peak—*summit* CA-9
Bon Terra—*locale* FL-3
*Bontes Peak* CA-9
Bonticou Crag —*summit* NY-2
Bonto—*island* MP-9
Bon Ton Hist Dist—*hist pl* MT-8
Bon Ton House—*hist pl* OK-5
Bon Ton Mine—*mine* CO-8
Bon Ton Ravine—*valley* CA-9
Bontrager Cem—*cemetery* (3) IN-6
*Bontrager Ditch* IN-6
Bontrager Ditch—*canal* IN-6
Bontrager Park—*park* IA-7
Bontz Arroyo—*stream* NM-5
Bontz Canyon—*valley* NM-5
Bonum Creek—*stream* VA-3
Bonum Post Office (historical)—*building* TN-4
*Bonums Creek* VA-3

Bonus—locale TX-5
**Bonus**—pop pl MS-4
**Bonus**—pop pl PA-2
Bonus Ch—church TX-5
Bonus Creek CO-8
Bonus Creek WI-6
Bonus Gulch CO-8
Bonus Post Office (historical)—building MS-4
Bonus Spring CO-8
**Bonus (Township of)**—pop pl IL-6
Bon View—locale PA-2
Bon View Park—park CA-9
Bon View Sch—school CA-9
**Bonvillain**—pop pl LA-4
Bonvillain Canal—canal LA-4
Bonwell Branch—stream IL-6
Bon Well Hill—summit IN-6
Bonwell House—hist pl DE-2
**Bon Wier**—pop pl TX-5
Bon Wier Lookout Tower—locale TX-5
**Bonwood**—pop pl TN-4
Bonwood Industrial Park—locale TN-4
Bonya River—stream GU-9
Bony Bench—bench UT-8
Bony Bluff Branch—stream AL-4
Bony Branch—stream (2) GA-3
Bony Branch—stream KY-4
Bony Branch Ch—church GA-3
Bony Dog Lake—lake MN-6
Bonygutt Brook—stream NJ-2
Bony Lake WI-6
Bony Lake—lake WI-6
Bonys Run—stream VA-3
Bonys Run Ch—church VA-3
Bonzey Pond MA-1
Boob Creek—stream AK-9
Boobe Hole Creek—stream UT-8
Boobe Hole Dam—dam UT-8
Boobe Hole Mtn—summit UT-8
Boobe Hole Rsvr—reservoir UT-8
Boober Lake MN-6
Boobs Canyon—valley UT-8
Boobs creek PA-2
Booby Bar MD-2
Booby Point—cape MD-2
Booby Rock—island VI-3
Booby's Point MD-2
Boocher Cem—cemetery IN-6
Boocke Number 2 Dam—dam (2) SD-7
Boocke Rsvr—reservoir SD-7
Boock Sch—school SD-7
Booco Cem—cemetery IN-6
Booco Ryan Cem—cemetery OH-6
Boodom Creek—stream NC-3
Boody—locale VA-3
**Boody**—pop pl IL-6
Boody, Henry, House—hist pl ME-1
Boody Brook—stream (3) ME-1
Boody Cove—bay ME-1
Boody Hill—summit NY-2
Boody Lake—lake MI-6
Boody Meadow—swamp ME-1
Boody Pond—lake (2) ME-1
Boody Sch—school (2) MI-6
Booga-Boo Hollow—valley WV-2
Booge—locale SD-7
Booger Branch—stream NC-3
Booger Canyon—valley AZ-5
Booger Canyon—valley NM-5
Booger Den Hollow—valley TN-4
Booger Hill—summit TN-4
Booger Hill Cem—cemetery AL-4
Booger Hole, The—lake AL-4
Booger Hole Slough—gut MS-4
Booger Hollow—valley AR-4
Booger Hollow—valley KY-4
Booger Hollow—valley TN-4
Booger Pond—lake SC-3
Booger Red Hill—summit CO-8
Booger Spring—spring AZ-5
**Boogertown**—pop pl NC-3
Boogertown Gap—gap TN-4
Boogher Hill—summit TN-4
Boogher Hill Sch (historical)—school TN-4
Boogy Run—stream DE-2
Booher—locale WV-2
Booher Cem—cemetery AR-4
Booher Cem—cemetery TN-4
Booher Cem—cemetery VA-3
Booher Chapel—church VA-3
**Booher Corners**—pop pl PA-2
Booher Creek—stream (2) TN-4
Booher Hill—summit NY-2
Booher Knobs—ridge TN-4
Booher Lake—lake WA-9
Booher Ridge—ridge VA-3
Booher Run—stream WV-2
Booher Site (OK48)—hist pl OK-5
Boo Hollow—valley MS-4
Boohoo Ledge—rock MA-1
Boojum Rock—summit MA-1
Book—locale LA-4
**Book**—pop pl OH-6
Book Cem—cemetery PA-2
Bookcliff Country Club—other CO-8
Book Cliff Mine—mine CO-8
Book Cliffs—cliff CO-8
Book Cliffs—cliff UT-8
Book Cliffs—range UT-8
Book Cliff Sch—school UT-8
Book Cliffs Gas Field—oilfield UT-8
Book Cliffs Natural Area—area UT-8
Book Cliffs Oil and Gas Field—oilfield UT-8
Book Cliff View—locale CO-8
Bookeeper Spring—spring NV-8
Bookejabun MP-9
Booker AL-4
Booker—locale AR-4
Booker—locale KY-4
Booker—locale PA-2
Booker—locale VA-3
**Booker**—pop pl AR-4
**Booker**—pop pl TX-5
Booker, Merritt H., House—hist pl TN-4
Booker, Samuel, House—hist pl KY-4
Booker-Boyd Sch—school VA-3
Booker Branch—stream AL-4
Booker Branch—stream (3) KY-4
Booker Branch—stream LA-4
Booker Branch—stream (2) MS-4
Booker Branch—stream TN-4
Booker Branch—stream TX-5
Booker Camp—locale NM-5
Booker (CCD)—cens area TX-5
Booker Cem—cemetery AL-4
Booker Cem—cemetery IN-6
Booker Cem—cemetery LA-4
Booker Cem—cemetery MS-4
Booker Cem—cemetery OK-5
Booker Cem—cemetery TN-4
Booker Cem—cemetery TX-5
Booker Creek FL-3
Booker Creek LA-4
Booker Creek—stream CA-9
Booker Creek—stream FL-3
Booker Creek—stream KS-7
Booker Creek—stream NC-3
Booker Creek—stream (2) OR-9
Booker Fork—stream (2) KY-4
Booker Fork Sch—school KY-4
Booker-Giltner House—hist pl KY-4
**Booker Heights**—pop pl AL-4
**Booker Heights**—pop pl MD-2
Booker Hill—summit NM-5
Booker (historical)—locale AL-4
Booker Hollow—valley AR-4
Booker Hollow—valley KY-4
Booker Hollow—valley (3) TN-4
Booker Hollow—valley WV-2
Booker Independent Sch—school TX-5
Booker Island IL-6
Booker JHS—school AR-4
Booker Lake—lake UT-8
Booker Legg Spring AL-4
Booker Mtn WA-9
Booker Mtn—summit NV-8
Booker Mtn—summit WA-9
Booker Pond—reservoir MO-7
Booker Pond—swamp SC-3
Booker Ranch—locale SD-7
Booker Ridge—ridge (2) TN-4
Booker Sch—school IL-6
Booker Sch (historical)—school AL-4
Booker Sch (historical)—school MS-4
Booker Sch (historical)—school TN-4
Booker Schools—school FL-3
Bookers Creek KS-7
Booker Slough—stream MO-7
Bookers Mill—locale AL-4
Bookers Mills PA-2
Bookers Mill Stream—stream VA-3
Bookers Wharf—locale MD-2
**Booker T City**—pop pl AL-4
Booker T Memorial Park—cemetery VA-3
**Bookertown**—pop pl FL-3
Booker T Washington Cem—cemetery IL-6
Booker T Washington Cem—cemetery (2) OK-5
Booker T. Washington Community Center—building AL-4
Booker T. Washington Emancipation Proclamation Park—hist pl TX-5
Booker T Washington HS—school AR-4
Booker T Washington HS—school FL-3
Booker T Washington HS—school GA-3
Booker T Washington HS—school LA-4
Booker T Washington HS—school OK-5
Booker T Washington HS—school (3) TX-5
Booker T Washington HS—school VA-3
Booker T Washington HS (historical)—school AL-4
Booker T Washington JHS—school AL-4
Booker T. Washington JHS—school AL-4
Booker T Washington JHS—school (2) FL-3
Booker T Washington JHS—school TX-5
Booker T Washington Natl Monmt—park VA-3
Booker T Washington Park—park VA-3
Booker T Washington Public Sch (historical)—school AL-4
Booker T Washington Sch—school AL-4
Booker T Washington Sch—school AZ-5
Booker T Washington Sch—school (2) AR-4
Booker T Washington Sch—school (2) FL-3
Booker T Washington Sch—school (2) KY-4
Booker T Washington Sch—school (2) LA-4
Booker T Washington Sch—school MO-7
Booker T Washington Sch—school (3) OK-5
Booker T Washington Sch—school (2) TN-4
Booker T Washington Sch—school (3) TX-5
Booker T Washington Sch—school (3) VA-3
Booker T Washington Sch (historical)—school MS-4
Booker T Washington School—locale TX-5
Booker T Washington State Park—park TN-4
Booker T Washington State Park—park WV-2
**Booker T Washington (subdivision)**—pop pl NC-3
Booker Washington Heights—uninc pl GA-3
Booker Washington Sch—school OK-5
Bookfield Township—civil SD-7
Book Fork—stream WV-2
**Bookgreen**—pop pl SC-3
Bookhammer Landing—locale DE-2
Bookhammers Pond—lake DE-2
Book Hill—summit CT-1
Bookings Sch—school MA-1
Booklewoj MP-9
Bookman—locale SC-3
Bookman Creek—stream SC-3
Bookman Island—island SC-3
Bookman Shoals—bar SC-3
Bookmekak MP-9
Book Mine—mine MI-6
Book Mountains CO-8
Bookora MP-9
Bookout Branch—stream AL-4
Bookout Branch—stream (2) MO-7
Bookout Cem—cemetery TN-4
Bookout Creek—stream OR-9
Bookout Dam—dam NC-3
Bookout Lake—reservoir NC-3
Bookout Ranch—locale NM-5
Bookout Ranch—locale WY-8
Bookout Rsvr—reservoir TX-5
Bookout Tank—reservoir NM-5
Book Ranch—locale CO-8
Book Run—stream IN-6
Book's Covered Bridge—hist pl PA-2
Books Creek—stream ID-8
Book Siding—locale OH-6
Booksin Sch—school CA-9
Book Site (36 Jul)—hist pl PA-2
Book Spring—spring OR-9
Books Ranch—locale WA-9
Books Spring—spring ID-8
Books Woods Sch (historical)—school PA-2
Booktown—locale OH-6
Bookwalter—locale NE-7
**Bookwalter**—pop pl OH-6
Bookwalter, Francis, House—hist pl OH-6
Bookwalter Cem—cemetery PA-2
Bookwalter Church TN-4
Bookwalter Sch—school OH-6
Bookwalter United Methodist Ch—church TN-4
Bookwater Creek—stream TX-5
Boole Tree—locale CA-9
Boolsburg PA-2
Bools Island NJ-2
**Boom**—pop pl TN-4
Booman Lake OK-5
Boom Bay—bay WI-6
Boom Branch—stream TX-5
Boom Bridge—bridge CT-1
Boombridge Brook—stream ME-1
Boom Brook—stream ME-1
Boom Corners—locale PA-2
Boom Creek—stream ID-8
Boomer—locale TN-4
**Boomer**—pop pl IA-7
**Boomer**—pop pl NC-3
**Boomer**—pop pl WV-2
Boomerang, Lake—lake FL-3
Boomerang Creek—stream AK-9
Boomerang Ditch—canal CO-8
Boomerang Gulch—valley CO-8
Boomerang Gulch—valley MT-8
Boomerang Lake—lake AK-9
Boomerang Lake—lake CA-9
Boomerang Lake—lake WA-9
Boomerang Mine—summit AZ-5
Boomerang Slough—gut IL-6
Boomer Beach—beach CA-9
Boomer Branch—stream NC-3
Boomer Branch—stream TN-4
Boomer Branch—stream WV-2
Boomer Canal—canal ID-8
Boomer Canyon—valley UT-8
Boomer Cem—cemetery MO-7
Boomer Ch—church NC-3
Boomer Cove—bay NY-2
Boomer Creek—stream AK-9
Boomer Creek—stream CA-9
Boomer Creek—stream OK-5
Boomer Creek—stream (2) OR-9
Boomer Creek—stream WI-6
Boomer-Ferguson Sch—school NC-3
Boomer Flats—flat VA-3
Boomer Gulch—valley SD-7
Boomer Hill—summit OR-9
Boomer Hill—summit UT-8
Boomer Hill School (abandoned)—locale OR-9
Boomer Hollow—valley AR-4
Boomer Inn Branch—stream NC-3
Boomer Lake—reservoir OK-5
Boomer Lake Park—park OK-5
Boomer Mine—mine CA-9
Boomer Post Office (historical)—building TN-4
Boomer Road Access Area—park NC-3
Boomer Sch—school WI-6
Boomers Cove—bay AK-9
Boomers Island—island FL-3
Boomer Slough—stream ID-8
**Boomertown**—pop pl NY-2
Boomer Township—fmr MCD IA-7
Boomer (Township of)—fmr MCD NC-3
Boom Furnace—locale VA-3
Boom (historical)—locale AL-4
Boom Hole—lake KY-4
Boomhour Branch—stream VT-1
Boom House, The—locale ME-1
Boomhower Hill—summit NY-2
Booming Ground—lake ME-1
Booming Shoal Hollow—valley MO-7
Boom Island—island MN-6
Boom Island—island (2) WI-6
Boom Islands—island (2) ME-1
Boom Lake—lake MI-6
Boom Lake—lake MN-6
Boom Lake—lake WI-6
Boom Pumping Station—other PA-2
Boom Ridge—ridge KY-4
Boom Ridge—ridge TN-4
Booms Canyon—valley SD-7
Booms Drain—canal MI-6
Boomshaw Cave—cave TN-4
Boom Slough—stream WA-9
Boom Swamp—stream VA-3
Boomtien Hoeck DE-2
Boomties Hoeck DE-2
Boomtjes Hoeck DE-2
Boom Town Hist Dist—hist pl OH-6
Boomtown Hist Dist—hist pl WV-2
Boon NC-3
Boon TN-4
Boon FM-9
**Boon**—pop pl MI-6
**Boon**—pop pl MS-4
**Boon**—pop pl PA-2
Boon, John D., House—hist pl OR-9
Boon Bay—bay NY-2
Boon Brake—swamp LA-4
Boon Brick Store—hist pl OR-9
Booncamp Branch—stream TN-4
Boon Camp Hollow—valley TX-5
Boon Cem—cemetery TN-4
Boon Cem—cemetery TX-5
Boon Creek TX-5
Boon Creek—stream TN-4
Boondock Tank—reservoir AZ-5
Boone AL-4
Boone—locale AR-4
Boone—locale KY-4
Boone—locale OK-5
Boone—locale PA-2
Boone—locale TX-5
Boone—locale VA-3
**Boone**—pop pl CO-8
**Boone**—pop pl IA-7
**Boone**—pop pl MS-4
**Boone**—pop pl NE-7
**Boone**—pop pl NC-3
**Boone**—pop pl TN-4
**Boone**—pop pl WA-9
Boone, Daniel, Homestead Site and Bertolet Cabin—hist pl PA-2
Boone, Daniel, House—hist pl MO-7
Boone, Daniel, Sch—hist pl PA-2
Boone, John W., House—hist pl MO-7
Boone, Nathan, House—hist pl MO-7
Boone Ave Park—park MN-6
Boone Beach Ranch—locale NM-5
Boone Block Hollow—valley WV-2
Boone-Blowing Rock Airp—airport NC-3
Boone Bluff—cliff MO-7
Boone Branch—stream (2) AL-4
Boone Branch—stream AR-4
Boone Branch—stream IL-6
Boone Branch—stream (2) KY-4
Boone Branch—stream MO-7
Boone Branch—stream NC-3
Boone Branch—stream (2) TN-4
Boone Branch—stream TX-5
Boone Bridge—bridge NC-3
Boone Brook—stream CT-1
Boone Camp Branch—stream NC-3
Boone Canyon—valley (2) CA-9
Boone Canyon—valley NV-8
Boone Canyon—valley NM-5
Boone Canyon—valley (2) OR-9
Boone Cave—cave IN-6
Boone Cem—cemetery AL-4
Boone Cem—cemetery (2) AR-4
Boone Cem—cemetery (3) IN-6
Boone Cem—cemetery (2) KY-4
Boone Cem—cemetery MS-4
Boone Cem—cemetery NE-7
Boone Cem—cemetery (3) NC-3
Boone Cem—cemetery (2) TN-4
Boone Cem—cemetery TX-5
Boone Ch—church MS-4
Boone Channel—channel NC-3
Boone Chapel—church AL-4
Boone Country Club—other IA-7
**Boone (County)**—pop pl AR-4
**Boone (County)**—pop pl IL-6
**Boone County**—pop pl IN-6
**Boone (County)**—pop pl KY-4
**Boone County**—pop pl MO-7
**Boone (County)**—pop pl WV-2
Boone County Airp—airport AR-4
Boone County Airp—airport IN-6
Boone County Courthouse—hist pl AR-4
Boone County Courthouse—hist pl IN-6
Boone County Courthouse—hist pl IA-7
Boone County Courthouse—hist pl WV-2
Boone County Home—building IA-7
Boone County Hospital MO-7
Boone County Jail—hist pl AR-4
Boone Cove—valley TN-4
Boone Cove Gap—gap NC-3
Boone Cove Gap—gap TN-4
Boone Creek OK-5
Boone Creek—bay MD-2
Boone Creek—stream (3) AL-4
Boone Creek—stream (2) CO-8
Boone Creek—stream GA-3
Boone Creek—stream (3) ID-8
Boone Creek—stream IL-6
Boone Creek—stream (2) IN-6
Boone Creek—stream (3) KY-4
Boone Creek—stream (2) LA-4
Boone Creek—stream MD-2
Boone Creek—stream (3) MS-4
Boone Creek—stream (2) MO-7
Boone Creek—stream NV-8
Boone Creek—stream NC-3
Boone Creek—stream OK-5
Boone Creek—stream (2) OR-9
Boone Creek—stream SC-3
Boone Creek—stream TN-4
Boone Creek—stream WA-9
Boone Creek—stream WV-2
Boone Creek—stream WY-8
Boone Creek Cem—cemetery MO-7
Boone Creek Cem—cemetery TN-4
Boone Creek Ch—church GA-3
Boone Creek Ch—church MO-7
Boone Creek Mill TN-4
Boone Creek Mill (historical)—locale TN-4
Boone Creek Ranch—locale NV-8
Boone Creek Ridge—ridge WY-8
Boonecroft—hist pl PA-2
Boone Crossing (historical)—locale AL-4
Boone Dam—dam (2) TN-4
Boone Ditch—canal CO-8
Boone Ditch—canal ID-8
Boone Dome Gas Field—oilfield WY-8
Boone Draw—valley NM-5
Boone Draw—valley SD-7
Boone Falls—falls TN-4
Boone Field Landing—locale NC-3
**Boone Fork**—pop pl NC-3
Boone Fork—stream (3) KY-4
Boone Fork—stream (2) NC-3
Boone Fork Recreation Site—locale NC-3
Boone Forks Public Hunting Area—area IA-7
Boone Furnace—locale (2) KY-4
Boone Gap—gap (2) KY-4
Boone Gap—gap NC-3
**Boone (Gap)**—pop pl KY-4
**Boone Grove**—pop pl IN-6
Boone Grove Elem Sch—school IN-6
Boone Grove Junior-Senior HS—school IN-6
Boone Gulch—valley CO-8
Boone Hall Creek—stream SC-3
Boone Harrell Ferry—locale NC-3
Boone Harrell Ferry (historical)—locale NC-3
**Boone Heights**—pop pl KY-4
Boone Hill—summit CO-8
Boone Hill Ch—church SC-3
Boone Hill Hollow—valley MO-7
Boone Hollow—valley (2) AR-4
Boone Hollow—valley IN-6
Boone Hollow—valley (4) KY-4
Boone Hollow—valley MO-7
Boone Hollow—valley (2) TN-4
Boone Hollow Cave—cave TN-4
Boone Hosp Center—hospital MO-7
Boone Hospital Center Heliport—airport MO-7
Boone House—hist pl AR-4
Boone House—hist pl FL-3
Boone Howard Cem—cemetery KY-4
Boone HS—school FL-3
Boone-Hutcheson Cem—cemetery IN-6
Boone Island—island OR-9
Boone Knob—summit NC-3
Boone Lake—lake FL-3
Boone Lake—lake GA-3
Boone Lake—lake KS-7
Boone Lake—lake WY-8
Boone Lake—reservoir KY-4
Boone Lake—reservoir RI-1
Boone Lake—reservoir TN-4
Boone Lake—swamp AR-4
Boone Lake Dam—dam RI-1
Boone Lake Pond RI-1
Boone Lakes ID-8
Boone Landing—locale NC-3
Boone Lookout Tower—locale MO-7
Boone Lookout Tower—locale NC-3
Boone (Magisterial District)—fmr MCD VA-3
Boone Meadow—flat CA-9
Boone Memorial Garden—cemetery IA-7
Boone Mill VA-3
Boone Mill (corporate name Boones Mill) VA-3
Boone Moore Spring—spring AZ-5
Boone Moore Wash—stream AZ-5
Boone Moore Well—well AZ-5
Boone Mountain Fire Tower—tower PA-2
Boone Mtn—summit AR-4
Boone Mtn—summit MT-8
Boone Mtn—summit PA-2
Boone Mtn—summit TX-5
Boone-Murphy House—hist pl AR-4
Boone Neck—cape NC-3
Boone Number One Township—civil MO-7
Boone Number Two Township—civil MO-7
Boone Park—park FL-3
Boone Park—park NC-3
Boone Park Sch—school AR-4
Boone Peak—summit ID-8
Boone Prairie—flat OR-9
Boone Ranch—locale KS-7
Boone Ranch—locale NM-5
Boone Ranch—locale (2) TX-5
Booner Cem—cemetery VA-3
Boone Ridge—ridge NC-3
Boone Ridge—ridge UT-8
Boone River—stream IA-7
Boone Road Hist Dist—hist pl NC-3
Boone Road Trail—trail PA-2
Boone Rock OR-9
Booners Creek—stream OR-9
Boone Rsvr TN-4
Boone Rsvr—reservoir PA-2
Boone Run—stream (4) PA-2
Boone Run—stream VA-3
Boonesboro MD-2
**Boonesboro**—pop pl KY-4
**Boonesboro**—pop pl MO-7
Boonesboro (CCD)—cens area KY-4
Boonesboro Fork—stream KY-4
Boonesborough—locale KY-4
**Boonesborough**—pop pl WV-2
**Boonesborough (historical)**—pop pl MO-7
Boones Branch AL-4
Boones Branch—stream KY-4
Boones Branch—stream MO-7
Boones Camp MS-4
Boones Cave—cave NC-3
Boone Sch—school IL-6
Boone Sch—school IA-7
Boone Sch—school MO-7
Boone Sch—school OH-6
Boone Sch—school PA-2
Boones Chapel AL-4
Boones Chapel—church NC-3
Boones Chapel—church (2) VA-3
Boones Chapel (abandoned)—church MO-7
Boones Chapel United Methodist Church MS-4
Boones Creek KY-4
Boones Creek MS-4
**Boones Creek**—pop pl SC-3
**Boones Creek**—pop pl TN-4
Boones Creek—stream SC-3
Boones Creek—stream TN-4
Boones Creek Bible Ch—church TN-4
Boones Creek Cem—cemetery (2) TN-4
Boones Creek Ch—church (2) TN-4
Boones Creek Ch of the Brethren (historical)—church TN-4
Boones Creek Dock—locale TN-4
Boones Creek Elem Sch—school TN-4
Boones Creek Sch—school TN-4
**Boones Crossroads**—pop pl NC-3
Boones Ferry NC-3
**Boones Hill**—pop pl NC-3
Boones Hollow—valley KY-4
Boones Landing (historical)—locale IN-6
Boone Slough—stream OR-9
**Boones Mill**—pop pl VA-3
**Boones Mill (corporate name for Boone Mill)**—pop pl VA-3
Boones Millpond—lake NC-3
Boones Mill Pond Dam—dam NC-3
Boone's Mounds—hist pl AR-4
Boone Spring—spring (2) NV-8
Boone Spring—spring UT-8
Boone Spring Hills—summit NV-8
Boone Springs NV-8
Boone Springs Station—locale NV-8
Boone Square Park—park KY-4
Boone Station Sch—school OH-6
Boone's Univ Sch—hist pl CA-9
Boonesville—locale VA-3
Boonesville Ch—church IN-6
Boone Tank—reservoir AZ-5
Boone Township—civil (5) MO-7
Boone Township—fmr MCD (3) IA-7
**Boone Township**—pop pl (2) MO-7
**Boone Township**—pop pl ND-7
Boone Township Cem—cemetery IA-7
Boone (Township of)—fmr MCD (2) AR-4
Boone (Township of)—fmr MCD MO-7
Boone (Township of)—fmr MCD (2) NC-3
**Boone (Township of)**—pop pl IL-6
**Boone (Township of)**—pop pl (6) IN-6
**Boone Trail**—pop pl NC-3
Boone Trail Elem Sch—school NC-3
**Boone Trail (subdivision)**—pop pl TN-4
Boone Valley Sch—school IA-7
Boone Viaduct—hist pl IA-7
Booneville IN-6
Booneville—locale AL-4
**Booneville**—pop pl AR-4
**Booneville**—pop pl IA-7
**Booneville**—pop pl KY-4
**Booneville**—pop pl MS-4
**Booneville**—pop pl PA-2
**Booneville**—pop pl TN-4
Booneville-Baldwyn Airp—airport MS-4
Booneville Baptist Church AL-4
Booneville (CCD)—cens area KY-4
Booneville Cem—cemetery IA-7
Booneville Cem—cemetery MS-4
Booneville Ch—church AL-4
Booneville Ch—church LA-4
Booneville Channel OR-9
Booneville Channel—channel OR-9
Booneville Ch of Christ—church MS-4
Booneville Ch of God—church MS-4
Booneville Church Cem—cemetery AL-4
Booneville City Hall—building MS-4
Booneville City Park—park MS-4
Booneville Country Club—other MS-4
Booneville Creek—stream AR-4
Booneville Elementary School MS-4
Booneville Fish Lake Dam—dam MS-4
Booneville GrammarSchool MS-4
Booneville Gulch—valley ID-8
Booneville HS—school MS-4
Booneville Lake—reservoir AR-4
Booneville Lake—reservoir MS-4
Booneville MS—school MS-4
Booneville Mtn—summit AR-4
Booneville Municipal Park MS-4
Booneville Normal Sch MS-4
Booneville Post Office (historical)—building TN-4
Booneville-Prentiss County Industrial Park—locale MS-4
Booneville Presbyterian Ch—church MS-4
Booneville Sch—school MS-4
Booneville (site)—locale OR-9
Booneville Slough—stream OR-9
Boone Water Supply Dam—dam NC-3
Boone Well—locale NM-5
Boone Well—well AZ-5
Boone Windmill—locale (2) TX-5
Boone-Withers House—hist pl NC-3
Booney Hollow Trail—trail PA-2
Booney Mtn—summit PA-2
Boonford—locale NC-3
Boon Hill MA-1
Boon Hill—summit CA-9
Boon Hill Sch (historical)—school MO-7
Boon Hill (Township of)—fmr MCD NC-3
Boon (historical)—locale KS-7
Boon Island Ledge—bar ME-1
Boon Island Light Station—hist pl ME-1
Boon Lake—lake MN-6
Boon Lake—lake RI-1
**Boon Lake**—pop pl RI-1
**Boon Lake (Township of)**—pop pl MN-6
Boon Lookout Tower—locale MI-6
Boon Place—locale NM-5
Boon Pond MA-1
Boon Pond RI-1
Boon Ridge—ridge TN-4
Boonsboro AR-4
Boonsboro IN-6
Boonsboro—locale MD-2
**Boonsboro**—pop pl MD-2
**Boonsboro**—pop pl VA-3
Boonsboro Country Club—other VA-3
Boonsboro Rsvr—reservoir MD-2
Boonsborough AR-4
Boons Camp—locale KY-4
Boons Creek—stream (3) TX-5
Boons Creek Post Office (historical)—building TN-4
Boons Ford (historical)—locale NC-3
**Boonshill**—pop pl TN-4
Boons Hill—summit MA-1
Boonshill (CCD)—cens area TN-4
Boonshill Ch—church TN-4
Boonshill Division—civil TN-4
Boonshill Elem Sch—school TN-4
Boons Hill Post Office TN-4
Boonshill Post Office (historical)—building TN-4
Boonshill Sch—school TN-4
Boons Lake—lake GA-3
Boonslick State Park—hist pl MO-7
Boonslick State Park—park MO-7
Boons Lick Township—civil MO-7
Boon Slough—stream TX-5
Boons Mill VA-3
Boons Mill Pond—reservoir NC-3
Boons Pond—reservoir MA-1
Boonstra Park—park NJ-2
Boonsville IN-6
**Boonsville**—pop pl TX-5
Boonsville Gas Field—oilfield TX-5
Boonsville Oil Field—oilfield TX-5
**Boon Terrace**—pop pl PA-2
**Boonton**—pop pl NJ-2
Boonton Hist Dist—hist pl NJ-2
Boonton Public Library—hist pl NJ-2
Boonton Reservoir Dam—dam NJ-2
Boonton Rsvr NJ-2
Boonton Rsvr—reservoir NJ-2
**Boonton (Township of)**—pop pl NJ-2
Boontown Cem—cemetery TX-5
**Boon (Township of)**—pop pl IN-6
**Boon (Township of)**—pop pl MI-6
Boonville—locale TX-5
**Boonville**—pop pl CA-9
**Boonville**—pop pl IN-6
**Boonville**—pop pl MO-7
**Boonville**—pop pl NY-2
**Boonville**—pop pl NC-3
Boonville Airp—airport IN-6
Boonville Airp—airport NC-3
Boonville Cem—cemetery TX-5
Boonville Country Club—other IN-6
Boonville Elem Sch—school NC-3
Boonville Gorge State Park—park NY-2
Boonville Hist Dist—hist pl NY-2
**Boonville (historical)**—pop pl TN-4
Boonville HS—school IN-6
Boonville HS—school MO-7

Boonville JHS—school IN-6
Boonville Municipal Airp—airport MO-7
Boonville Public Square Hist Dist—hist pl IN-6
Boonville Rod and Gun Club—other NY-2
Boonville Rsvr—reservoir NY-2
**Boonville (Town of)—pop pl** NY-2
Boonville Township—civil MO-7
Boonville (Township of)—fmr MCD NC-3
Boon Well—well NM-5
Boorams Island AL-4
Boor Creek—gut SC-3
Boord Hollow—valley WV-2
Boorman, Benjamin, House—hist pl WI-6
Boorman Creek—stream MT-8
Boorman Peak—summit MT-8
Boorman Sch—school MT-8
Boos—locale IL-6
Boos Ditch—canal OH-6
Boose Hollow—valley PA-2
Booshu Camp—locale AK-9
Boos Lake—lake MN-6
Boos Lake—lake WI-6
Boos Sch—school CA-9
Booster—locale AR-4
Booster Branch—stream TN-4
Booster Park—park MN-6
Boosters Club Park—park MS-4
**Booster Station—pop pl** IL-6
Booster Windmill—locale (4) NM-5
Boot, The—ridge WA-9
Boo Tank—reservoir AZ-5
Boot Bar Sch—school SD-7
Boot Bay—bay AK-9
Boot Bay—bay NY-2
Boot Bay—bay WA-9
Boot Bay Mtn—summit NY-2
Boot Branch—stream TN-4
Boot Canyon—valley CA-9
Boot Canyon—valley NM-5
Boot Canyon—valley TX-5
Boot Cove—bay ME-1
Boot Creek—stream AR-4
Boot Creek—stream KS-7
Boot Creek—stream MN-6
Boot Creek—stream SD-7
Boot Creek—stream WI-6
Boot Creek—stream WY-8
Booten WV-2
Booten Creek—stream OR-9
Booten Creek—stream WV-2
Bootens VA-3
Bootens Gap—gap VA-3
Bootens Run—stream VA-3
Booth KS-7
Booth OH-6
Booth—locale (2) KY-4
Booth—locale MS-4
Booth—locale OH-6
Booth—locale OR-9
Booth—locale SC-3
Booth—locale TX-5
**Booth—pop pl** AL-4
**Booth—pop pl** NC-3
**Booth—pop pl** OH-6
**Booth—pop pl** WV-2
Booth, Dr. J. C., House—hist pl OR-9
Booth, Edwin Robert, House—hist pl UT-8
Booth, J. C., House—hist pl WI-6
Booth, John E., House—hist pl UT-8
Booth, O. H., Hose Company—hist pl NY-2
Booth, Oscar M., House—hist pl UT-8
Bootham Lake ID-8
Booth Arm—bay OR-9
**Boothbay—pop pl** ME-1
Boothbay Center ME-1
Boothbay Harbor—bay ME-1
**Boothbay Harbor—pop pl** ME-1
**Boothbay Harbor Center—pop pl** ME-1
Boothbay Harbor Memorial
Library—hist pl ME-1
**Boothbay Harbor (Town of)—pop pl** ME-1
Boothbay Park ME-1
**Boothbay Park—pop pl** ME-1
**Boothbay (Town of)—pop pl** ME-1
Booth Branch—stream DE-2
Booth Branch—stream KY-4
Booth Branch—stream MO-7
Booth Branch—stream SC-3
Booth Branch—stream (2) TN-4
Booth Branch—stream VA-3
Booth Branch—stream WV-2
Boothby—locale IL-6
Boothby Creek—stream AK-9
Boothby Hill ME-1
Boothby Hill—summit MD-2
Booth Canal—canal CO-8
Booth Canal—canal UT-8
Booth Canyon—valley ID-8
Booth Canyon—valley WA-9
Booth Cem—cemetery KS-7
Booth Cem—cemetery MS-4
Booth Cem—cemetery MO-7
Booth Cem—cemetery TX-5
Booth Cem—cemetery (2) VA-3
Booth Cem—cemetery (2) WV-2
Booth Cemetery AL-4
Booth Ch—church AL-4
Booth Ch—church GA-3
Booth Chapel—church MS-4
Booth Chapel—church (2) TN-4
Booth Chapel Cem—cemetery TN-4
Booth Ch Camp AL-4
Booth Cooperage—hist pl WI-6
Booth Corner PA-2
**Booth Corner—pop pl** MA-1
**Booth Corner—pop pl** PA-2
Booth Creek KS-7
Booth Creek—stream AR-4
Booth Creek—stream CO-8
Booth Creek—stream KS-7
Booth Creek—stream MT-8
Booth Creek—stream WY-8
Booth Crossing—locale CA-9
Booth Ditch—canal OH-6
Booth Drain—canal MI-6
Booth Drain—stream MI-6
Boothe—locale AR-4
Boothe—locale TX-5
Boot Head—summit ME-1
Boothe Cem—cemetery LA-4
Boothe Cem—cemetery MS-4
Boothe Cem—cemetery TN-4
Boothe Cem—cemetery TX-5
Boothe Creek—stream TX-5
Boothe Creek—stream VA-3
Boot Heel—summit WY-8
Bootheel Creek—stream FL-3
Bootheel Landing Strip—airport MO-7
Boothe Hall—building KS-7
Boothe Hill—summit NC-3
Boothe Homestead—hist pl CT-1
Boothe Lake—lake CA-9
Booth Elem Sch—school AZ-5
Booth Elem Sch—school KS-7
Boothe Memorial Park—cemetery CT-1
Boothe Run—stream PA-2
**Boothe Spur—pop pl** TX-5
**Booth Estates (subdivision)—pop pl** AL-4
**Boothetown—pop pl** AL-4
Boothe Valley—valley UT-8
Boothe Valley Hill—summit UT-8
Booth Ford—locale AL-4
Booth Fork—locale VA-3
Booth Fork—stream KY-4
Booth Gulch—valley CA-9
Booth Gulch—valley CO-8
Booth Gulch—valley OR-9
Booth Hill ID-8
Booth Hill—ridge OR-9
Booth Hill—summit (3) CT-1
Booth Hill—summit MA-1
Booth Hill—summit OH-6
Booth Hill—summit WA-9
Booth Hill Brook—stream CT-1
Booth Hills—summit AZ-5
Booth Hill Sch—school CT-1
Booth (historical)—locale ND-7
**Booth (historical)—pop pl** OR-9
Booth Hollow—valley KY-4
Booth Hollow—valley NM-5
Booth Hollow—valley TN-4
Booth Hollow—valley VA-3
Booth Homestead—hist pl OH-6
Booth Hosp—hospital IA-7
Booth Hosp—hospital KS-7
Booth Hosp—hospital (2) OH-6
Booth Hotel—hist pl KS-7
Booth House—building NC-3
Boot Hill—locale AL-4
**Boot Hill—pop pl** AL-4
Boot Hill—summit KS-7
Boot Hill—summit NM-5
Boothill Cem—cemetery AZ-5
Boot Hill Cem—cemetery ID-8
Boot Hill Cem—cemetery IA-7
Boot Hill Cem—cemetery MI-6
Boothill Cem—cemetery (3) MT-8
Boot Hill Cem—cemetery NE-7
Boot Hill Cem—cemetery NM-5
Boot Hill Cem—cemetery OR-9
Boot Hill Cem—cemetery TX-5
Boothill Cem—cemetery UT-8
Boothill Cemetery—hist pl MT-8
Boot Hill Ch—church WV-2
Boot Hill Creek—stream OR-9
Boot Hill Farm—hist pl KY-4
Booth Island—island MI-6
Booth Island—island OR-9
Booth-Kelley Lumber Company Log Pond
Dike—dam OR-9
Booth-Kelly Lumber Company Log
Pond—reservoir OR-9
Booth Knob VA-3
Booth Knoll—summit CA-9
Booth Lake—lake CO-8
Booth Lake—lake FL-3
Booth Lake—lake IN-6
Booth Lake—lake MI-6
Booth Lake—lake MN-6
Booth Lake—lake OR-9
Booth Lake—lake (2) WI-6
Booth Lake Dam—dam (2) MS-4
Booth Lake (historical)—lake MO-7
Booth Landing—locale FL-3
Booth Landing—locale OR-9
Booth Memorial Cem—cemetery IL-6
Booth Memorial Hosp—hospital CA-9
Booth Memorial Hosp—hospital CO-8
Booth Memorial Hosp—hospital IL-6
Booth Memorial Hosp—hospital NY-2
Booth Memorial Hosp—hospital (2) PA-2
Booth Memorial Park—cemetery GA-3
Booth Mill Pond PA-2
Booth Millpond—lake PA-2
Booth Mine (underground)—mine AL-4
Booth Mtn—summit CO-8
Booth Number 1 Dam—dam SD-7
Booth Park—park HI-9
Booth Park—park MI-6
Booth Park—park OR-9
Booth Park—park TN-4
Boothpoint TN-4
Booth Point—cape FL-3
Booth Point—cliff CA-9
Booth Point Dikes—levee TN-4
Booth Point Landing—locale TN-4
Booth Pond—lake GA-3
Booth Pond—reservoir RI-1
Booth Post No. 130-Grand Army of the
Republic Hall—hist pl MN-6
Booth Post Office (historical)—building MS-4
Booth Ranch—locale NM-5
Booth Ranch—locale TX-5
Booth Ridge—ridge KY-4
Booth Ridge—ridge (2) OR-9
Booth Run—stream PA-2
Booths Bay—bay VA-3
Booths Bend—bend VA-3
Booths Canyon—valley UT-8
Booth Sch—school (2) MI-6
Booth Sch—school NV-8
Booth Sch—school NY-2
Booth Sch—school PA-2
Booth Sch—school TX-5
Booth Sch (historical)—school TN-4
**Booths Corner—pop pl** PA-2
Booths Corners PA-2
Booths Creek—stream MS-4
Booths Creek—stream (2) WV-2
Booth-Setser Sch—school IN-6
Booths Hollow—valley WV-2
Booths Island TN-4
Booths Island—island FL-3
Booths Island—island NY-2
Booths Lake SC-3
Booths Lake—reservoir MS-4
Booths Point TN-4
Boothspoint—locale TN-4
Booths Point Post Office TN-4
Boothspoint Post Office
(historical)—building TN-4
Booths Pond—reservoir SC-3
Booth Spring—spring AZ-5
Booth Spring—spring HI-9
Booths Run—stream CA-9
Booths Shoals TN-4
Booth State Park OR-9
**Boothsville—pop pl** WV-2
Booth Tarkington Elem Sch—school (2) IN-6
Booth Tarkington Sch Number 92 IN-6
Booth Theater—hist pl KS-7
**Boothton—pop pl** AL-4
Boothton Cem—cemetery AL-4
Boothton Mine (underground)—mine AL-4
Boothton Station—locale AL-4
Boothtown AL-4
Booth Township—fmr MCD IA-7
**Boothville—pop pl** LA-4
Boothville Cem—cemetery LA-4
Boothville Post Office—locale LA-4
Boothville-Venice HS—school LA-4
**Boothwyn—pop pl** PA-2
Boothwyn Elem Sch—school PA-2
**Boothwyn Highlands—pop pl** PA-2
Bootis Ch (historical)—church PA-2
Boot Island—island LA-4
Boot Island—island MI-6
Boot Island—island NJ-2
Bootjack MI-6
Bootjack—locale CA-9
Bootjack—locale MD-2
**Bootjack—pop pl** MI-6
**Boot Jack—pop pl** PA-2
Bootjack Camp—locale CA-9
Boot Jack Canyon—valley NM-5
Bootjack Creek—stream CA-9
Bootjack Creek—stream (2) ID-8
Bootjack Creek—stream MT-8
Bootjack Creek—stream WI-6
Bootjack Draw—valley MT-8
Boot Jack Fire Tower—tower PA-2
Bootjack Gap—gap WY-8
Bootjack Island—island MI-6
Boot Jack Lake MN-6
Boot Jack Lake MT-8
Bootjack Lake—lake (2) MI-6
Bootjack Lake—lake (2) MT-8
Bootjack Lake—lake WI-6
Bootjack Meadow—flat MT-8
Bootjack Mine—mine (2) CA-9
Bootjack Mtn—summit TN-4
Bootjack Mtn—summit WA-9
Bootjack Pass—gap ID-8
Bootjack Prairie—flat CA-9
Bootjack Rock—pillar WA-9
Bootjack Spring—spring MD-2
Boot Junior Tank—reservoir AZ-5
Boot Key—island FL-3
Boot Key Harbor—bay FL-3
Boot Lake FL-3
Boot Lake MI-6
Boot Lake MN-6
Boot Lake—lake (2) AK-9
Boot Lake—lake AZ-5
Boot Lake—lake CO-8
Boot Lake—lake IN-6
Boot Lake—lake (8) MI-6
Boot Lake—lake (9) MN-6
Boot Lake—lake MT-8
Boot Lake—lake ND-7
Boot Lake—lake OR-9
Boot Lake—lake UT-8
Boot Lake—lake WA-9
Boot Lake—lake (9) WI-6
Boot Lake—reservoir CA-9
Boot Lake—reservoir NC-3
Boot Lake Campground—locale WI-6
Boot Lake Creek—stream CA-9
Boot Lake Dam—dam NC-3
Boot Lake Rsvr—reservoir CO-8
Boot Lakes MN-6
Boot Lake State Wildlife Area—park WI-6
Bootleg—locale TX-5
Bootleg Bend—bend AK-9
Bootleg Bottom Picnic Area—locale CO-8
Bootleg Campground—locale UT-8
Bootleg Canyon—valley AZ-5
Bootleg Canyon—valley CA-9
Bootleg Canyon—valley (3) NM-5
Bootleg Canyon—valley TX-5
Bootleg Creek—stream ID-8
Bootleg Dam—dam AZ-5
Bootlegger Canyon—valley NM-5
Bootlegger Canyon—valley TX-5
Bootlegger Canyon—valley UT-8
Bootlegger Cove AK-9
Bootlegger Crossing—locale AZ-5
Bootlegger Draw—valley MT-8
Bootlegger Gap—gap NM-5
Bootlegger Gulch—valley (2) CO-8
Bootlegger Saddle—gap AZ-5
Bootleggers Canyon—valley CA-9
Bootleggers Cave—cave (2) AL-4
Bootlegger Slough—stream AK-9
Bootleggers Point—cape NY-2
Bootlegger Spring—spring (9) AZ-5
Bootlegger Spring—spring MT-8
Bootlegger Spring—spring NV-8
Bootlegger Spring—spring (2) NM-5
Bootlegger Tank—reservoir (2) AZ-5
Bootlegger Trail—trail MT-8
Bootlegger Trap Spring—spring AZ-5
Bootlegger Wash—stream AZ-5
Bootlegger Wash—valley UT-8
Bootlegger Well—well AZ-5
Bootlegger Windmill—locale NM-5
Bootleg Lake—lake (2) MN-6
Bootleg Lake—reservoir AZ-5
Bootleg Lake Campground—park AZ-5
Bootleg Mtn—summit SC-3
Bootleg Pond—reservoir OR-9
Bootleg Ridge—ridge NM-5
Bootleg Rsvr—reservoir CA-9
Bootleg Saddle—gap AZ-5
Bootleg Spring NV-8
Bootleg Spring—spring (3) AZ-5
Bootleg Spring—spring CA-9
Bootleg Spring—spring (2) NV-8
Bootleg Spring—spring (2) OR-9
Bootleg State Wildlife Mngmt
Area—park MN-6
Bootleg Tank—reservoir AZ-5
Bootles Canyon—valley AZ-5
Bootles Canyon—valley CA-9
Bootley Wash—stream NV-8
Boot Mesa—summit AZ-5
Boot Mtn—summit CO-8
Boot Mtn—summit WA-9
Boot Neck—cape ME-1
Booton—locale WV-2
Boot Peak—summit AZ-5
Boot Point—cape (2) AK-9
Boot Pond—lake ME-1
Boot Pond—lake MA-1
Boot Ranch—locale NM-5
Boot Ranch—locale WY-8
Boot Rock—pillar TX-5
Boot Run—stream (2) IN-6
Boots Bend—bend CA-9
Boots Branch—stream KY-4
Boots Branch—stream SC-3
Boots Cem—cemetery IL-6
Boots Creek—stream IN-6
Boots Ditch—canal (2) IN-6
Boots Drain—canal MI-6
Boots Junior High School IN-6
Bootsole Creek—stream CA-9
Boots Point—cape FL-3
Boots Ranch—locale NE-7
Boots Swamp—stream NC-3
Boots Tank—reservoir NM-5
Boot Stock Tank—reservoir AZ-5
Bootstrap Mine—mine NV-8
Bootsville Gap—gap AL-4
Bootsville (historical)—locale AL-4
Boot Swamp—stream VA-3
Boot Swamp Brook—stream ME-1
Boott and Massachusetts Mill Agent House MA-1
Boot Tank—reservoir AZ-5
Boott Mill MA-1
Boott Mill Boarding House—building MA-1
Boott Mills—locale MA-1
Boot Toe Point—cape FL-3
Boottree Pond—lake NY-2
Boot Spur—trail NH-1
Boot Spur Trail—trail NH-1
Booty Branch—stream TN-4
Booty Cem—cemetery (2) LA-4
Booz TN-4
Booz Canyon—valley MT-8
Booze Cem—cemetery VA-3
Booze Creek—stream GA-3
Booze Creek—stream MD-2
Booze Creek—stream OR-9
Booze Crossing—locale AZ-5
Booze Hollow—valley AR-4
Booze Island Airp—airport MO-7
Booze Lake WI-6
Booze Lake—lake FL-3
Booze Mtn—summit GA-3
Boozer, Lemuel, House—hist pl SC-3
Boozer Cem—cemetery (2) AL-4
Boozer Cem—cemetery MS-4
Boozer Chapel—church SC-3
Boozer Dam—dam AL-4
Boozer Heights—uninc pl AL-4
Boozer (historical)—locale AL-4
Boozer Hollow—valley AR-4
Boozer Lake—reservoir AL-4
Boozer P.O. AL-4
Boozers Lake—lake (2) AL-4
Boozers Landing—locale FL-3
Boozeville—locale GA-3
Boozey Lake—lake CA-9
Booz Post Office (historical)—building TN-4
Boozy Creek—stream TN-4
Boozy Creek—stream VA-3
Bope Drain—canal MI-6
Bope Island—island OH-6
Bope Ravine—valley CA-9
Bophumpa Creek—stream MS-4
Bo Pocket—lake TN-4
Boppy Ditch—canal MT-8
Boque Mtn—summit CO-8
**Boqueron—pop pl (4)** PR-3
Boqueron, Bahia de—bay PR-3
Boqueron, Balneario Publico de—beach PR-3
Boqueron (Barrio)—fmr MCD (2) PR-3
Boque's OH-6
Boque's Creek OH-6
Boquet FM-9
**Boquet—pop pl** NY-2
**Boquet—pop pl** PA-2
Boquet Canyon Boys Camp—locale CA-9
Boquet Creek—stream ID-8
Boquet Island FM-9
Boquet Mountain NY-2
Boquet Ridge—ridge ID-8
Boquet River—stream NY-2
Boquet River Point—cape NY-2
Boquet Springs—spring ID-8
Boquillas TX-5
Boquillas—locale AZ-5
**Boquillas—pop pl** TX-5
**Boquillas—pop pl** PR-3
Boquillas Canyon—valley TX-5
Boquillas Canyon Overlook—locale TX-5
Boquillas Crossing (Ford)—locale TX-5
Boquillas Ranch—locale AZ-5
Boquillas Range TX-5
Boracho—locale TX-5
Boracho Canyon—valley TX-5
Boracho Peak—summit TX-5
Boracho Windmill—locale TX-5
Borah ID-8
**Borah—pop pl** ID-8
Bora Harbor—bay AK-9
Borah Cem—cemetery IL-6
Borah Cem—cemetery WI-6
Borah Creek—stream WI-6
Borah Lake—lake CO-8
Borah Mountain CO-8
Borah Peak—summit ID-8
Boram Lake—lake FL-3
Borams Island AL-4
Boranges Point—cape NC-3
Boran Gulch—valley CO-8
Boras Mine—mine AZ-5
Borate CA-9
Borau Swamp—swamp NY-2
Borax—locale MT-8
Borax—locale NV-8
Borax Bill Park—park CA-9
Borax Creek—stream MT-8
Borax Flat—flat CA-9
Borax Lake—lake CA-9
Borax Lake—lake OR-9
Borax Wash—stream NV-8
Borax Well—well TX-5
Borax Works (site)—locale OR-9
Borbetts Branch VA-3
Borchardt-Rosin State Wildlife Mngmt
A—park MN-6
Borcherding Cem—cemetery IA-7
Borchert Ranch—locale NV-8
Borchert Spring—spring NV-8
Borck Creek—bay VI-3
**Borculo—pop pl** MI-6
Bordache Creek SD-7
Bordas Artesian Well—well TX-5
Bordeaux—hist pl VI-3
Bordeaux—locale NE-7
Bordeaux—locale OK-5
Bordeaux—locale SC-3
Bordeaux—locale WA-9
Bordeaux—locale WY-8
**Bordeaux—pop pl** TN-4
**Bordeaux—pop pl** VA-3
**Bordeaux—pop pl** WY-8
**Bordeaux—pop pl** VI-3
Bordeaux Bay—bay VI-3
Bordeaux Canal—canal WY-8
Bordeaux Creek NE-7
Bordeaux Creek—stream NE-7
Bordeaux Ditch—canal WY-8
Bordeaux Gardens Park—cemetery TN-4
Bordeaux Hill—summit VI-3
Bordeaux Island—island MS-4
Bordeaux Mtn—summit VI-3
Bordeaux Point—cape MS-4
Bordeaux Point—cape VI-3
Bordeaux Sch—school WA-9
Bordeaux Shop Ctr—locale NC-3
**Bordeaux (subdivision)—pop pl** NC-3
Bordeaux Trading Post—hist pl NE-7
Bordeaux Windmill—locale NM-5
Borde Flats—flat WA-9
Bordell—locale PA-2
Bordelon, Alfred H., House—hist pl LA-4
Bordelon, Hypolite, House—hist pl LA-4
**Bordelonville—pop pl** LA-4
Borden—locale CA-9
Borden—locale TX-5
Borden—locale UT-8
**Borden—pop pl** IN-6
**Borden—pop pl** NY-2
**Borden—pop pl** SC-3
Borden, A.J., Bldg—hist pl MA-1
Borden, Ariadne J. and Mary A.,
House—hist pl GA-3
Borden, N. B., Sch—hist pl MA-1
Bordenax—locale LA-4
Borden Banks NC-3
Borden Basin Rsvr—reservoir UT-8
Borden Branch—stream AL-4
Borden Brook MA-1
Borden Brook—stream (2) MA-1
Borden Brook—stream RI-1
Borden Brook—stream VT-1
Borden Brook Reservoir Dam—dam MA-1
Borden Brook Rsvr—reservoir MA-1
Borden Camp—locale TX-5
Borden Cem—cemetery OH-6
Borden Cem—cemetery OK-5
Borden Cem—cemetery TX-5
Borden Cem—cemetery WV-2
Borden (corporate name New Providence) IN-6
**Borden (County)—pop pl** TX-5
Borden Creek NC-3
Borden Creek TX-5
Borden Creek—stream (2) AL-4
Borden Creek—stream MN-6
Borden Creek—stream NY-2
Borden Creek—stream VA-3
**Borden Estate—pop pl** NY-2
Borden Flats—bar MA-1
Borden Flats Light—locale MA-1
Borden Flats Light Station—hist pl MA-1
Borden Gulch—valley OR-9
**Borden Heights (subdivision)—pop pl** NC-3
**Borden Homes (subdivision)—pop pl** NC-3
Borden House—hist pl AR-4
Borden-Jennings House—building MA-1
Borden Lake—lake (2) MN-6
Borden Lake—lake MS-4
Borden Lake—lake WI-6
Borden Lake Lookout Tower—locale MN-6
Borden Marsh Run—stream VA-3
Borden Milk Co. Creamery and Ice
Factory—hist pl AZ-5
Borden Mills—uninc pl TN-4
Borden Mines Superintendent's
House—hist pl MD-2
Borden Mtn—summit MA-1
Borden Pond—lake NY-2
Borden-Pond House—hist pl MA-1
Borden Powdered Milk Plant—hist pl TN-4
Borden Rsvr—reservoir UT-8
Bordens Brook RI-1
Borden Sch—school MA-1
Bordens Creek—stream GA-3
Borden'S Flats MA-1
**Borden Shaft—pop pl** MD-2
Borden-Siding—locale TX-5
Bordens Marsh Run VA-3
Bordens Mill Branch—stream NJ-2
Bordens Mill (historical)—locale (2) AL-4
Bordens Point NC-3
**Borden Springs—pop pl** AL-4
Borden Springs—spring WA-9
Bordens Run NJ-2
Bordenstake Bay—bay VA-3
Borden Substation—other CA-9
Borden Tank—reservoir NM-5
Bordenton NJ-2
Borden Top—summit TN-4
Borden Town NJ-2
**Bordentown—pop pl** NJ-2
Bordentown Hist Dist—hist pl NJ-2
Bordentown Range—channel NJ-2
Bordentown Range—channel PA-2
Bordentown Seminary—school NJ-2
**Bordentown (Township of)—pop pl** NJ-2
Borden Tunnel—tunnel MD-2
**Borden Village—pop pl** TN-4
Bordenville—locale CO-8
Bordenville Cem—cemetery CO-8
**Borden Wheeler Springs—pop pl** AL-4
Borden-Winslow House—hist pl MA-1
**Borden Yard—pop pl** MD-2
Border—locale ID-8
Border—locale MN-6
Border—locale PA-2
**Border—pop pl** WY-8
Border—post sta AK-9
Border Canyon—valley NM-5
**Border City—pop pl** CA-9
**Border City—pop pl** NY-2
Border City—uninc pl NY-2
Border City, The MA-1
Border City Mill Number Two—building MA-1
Border City Trading Post—locale AK-9
Border City Village MA-1
Border Creek AZ-5
Border Creek NC-3
Border Creek—stream WI-6
Border Ditch—canal CO-8
Border Ditch—canal IN-6
Border Ditch—canal NM-5
Border Farm—locale NM-5
Border Farm Well—well NM-5
Border Field Naval Reservation—military CA-9
Border Hill—ridge NM-5
Border Hill—summit RI-1
Border Intercepting Drain—canal TX-5
Border International Airp—airport ND-7
Border Junction—locale WY-8
Border Lake—lake AK-9
Border Lake—lake FL-3
**Borderland—pop pl** TX-5
**Borderland—pop pl** WV-2
Borderland Bridge—bridge TX-5
Borderland Spur—canal TX-5
Borderland Spur Drain—canal TX-5
Borderland Trading Post—locale AZ-5
Borderline Cave—cave AL-4
Borderline Spring—spring OR-9
Borderline Tank—reservoir NM-5
Border Mine—mine AZ-5
Border Mtn—summit CA-9
Border Mtn—summit ID-8
Border Peak—summit MT-8
Border Plains—locale IA-7
Border Ridge—ridge WA-9
Border Rocks—area AK-9
Border Rsvr—reservoir ID-8
Border Rsvr—reservoir WY-8
Border Ruffian Flat—flat CA-9
Borders RI-1
Borders Branch—stream KY-4
Borders Cem—cemetery KY-4
Borders Cem—cemetery TX-5
Borders Chapel—church KY-4
Borders Coulee—valley MT-8
Borders Creek—stream GA-3
Borders Dam—dam AL-4
Borderside—hist pl MD-2
Borders Lake—reservoir AL-4
Borders Lake—reservoir OK-5
Border Springs Ch—church MS-4
**Border Springs (historical)—pop pl** MS-4
Border Spur Drain Number One—canal TX-5
Border Spur Drain Number Two—canal TX-5
Border Star Sch—school MO-7
Border Summit—summit ID-8
**Bordersville—pop pl** TX-5
Border Tank—reservoir (3) AZ-5
Border Tank—reservoir NM-5
**Border Town—pop pl** NV-8
**Border Township—pop pl** ND-7
Border Trail—trail MA-1
Borderview Ch—church TN-4
Border Well—well AZ-5
Border Well—well (3) NM-5
Bordgen JHS—school NC-3
Bord Gulch—valley CO-8
Bordine Drain—canal MI-6
Bord-in-hand PA-2
Bordley—locale KY-4
Bordley Ditch—canal KY-4
Bordley Point—cape MD-2
Bordner House—hist pl OH-6
Bordner Sch—school IL-6
**Bordnersville—pop pl** PA-2
Bordo Atravesado—ridge NM-5
Bordo Del Medio—ridge NM-5
Bordoli Creek—stream NV-8
Bordoli Ranch—locale NV-8
Bordon Creek TX-5
Bordo Nuevo Windmill—locale TX-5
**Bordoville—pop pl** VT-1
Bordo Well—well NM-5
Bordshaw Branch—stream AL-4
**Bordulac—pop pl** ND-7
**Bordulac Township—pop pl** ND-7
Bordwell Canyon—valley NV-8
Bordwell Creek—stream NV-8
Bordwell Park—park CA-9
Bordwell Spring—spring NV-8
Bordy Creek—stream CA-9
Borea—locale WI-6
Borea Canyon—valley CA-9
Borealis Glacier—glacier WA-9
Borealis Mine—mine NV-8
Borealis Ridge—ridge WA-9
Boreal Mtn—summit AK-9
Boreal Plateau—plain CA-9
Boreal Ridge—ridge CA-9
Boreas, Mount—summit MA-1
Boreas Ditch No 2—canal CO-8

Boreas Mtn—summit ... CO-8
Boreas Mtn—summit ... NY-2
Boreas Park—park ... LA-4
Boreas Pass—gap ... CO-8
Boreas Point—cape ... AK-9
Boreas Ponds—lake ... NY-2
Boreas River—locale ... NY-2
Boreas River—stream ... NY-2
Bore Auger Ch—church ... VA-3
Bore Auger Creek—stream ... VA-3
Bore Creek—stream ... AK-9
Bore Creek—stream ... MT-8
Bored Spring—spring ... AZ-5
Boregas Creek—stream ... TX-5
Borego ... CA-9
Borego Desert Unit ... CA-9
Borego Mountain ... CA-9
Borego Spirng ... CA-9
Borego Valley ... CA-9
Boreham, Lake—lake ... UT-8
Boreham Memorial—locale ... UT-8
Boreing—locale ... KY-4
Boreland Canyon ... TX-5
Borel Canal—canal ... CA-9
Borel Canyon—valley ... CA-9
Borel Hill—summit ... CA-9
Borelli Ditch—canal ... OK-5
Borel Powerhouse—other ... CA-9
Borel Sch—school ... CA-9
Boreman—locale ... WV-2
Boreman Sch—school ... WV-2
Bore Mill Run—stream ... PA-2
Boren, E. T., House—hist pl ... TX-5
Boren, Lake—lake ... WA-9
Boren, Lake—reservoir ... OK-5
Boren Cem—cemetery ... TX-5
Boren Creek—stream ... CO-8
Boren Creek—stream ... ID-8
Boren Creek—stream ... OR-9
Boren Ditch—canal ... UT-8
Borenfield Sch (historical)—school ... MS-4
Boren Fork—stream ... AR-4
Boren Mesa—summit ... UT-8
Borer Lake—lake ... MN-6
B & O Reservoir ... PA-2
Borestone Mountain ... ME-1
Borey Creek ... WY-8
Borgardy Run—stream ... PA-2
Borg Creek—stream ... AK-9
Borgeau Lake ... WA-9
Borgemans Ranch—locale ... WY-8
**Borger**—pop pl ... TX-5
Borger (CCD)—cens area ... TX-5
Borger Creek—stream ... PA-2
Borgerding, Christopher, House—hist pl ... MN-6
Borger Oil Field—oilfield ... TX-5
Borger Terminal—locale ... TX-5
Borge Sch—school ... SD-7
Borgess Cemetery ... MS-4
Borgess Hosp—hospital ... MI-6
Borges Spring—spring ... NV-8
Borgholm Cem—cemetery ... MN-6
**Borgholm (Township of)**—pop pl ... MN-6
Borg Lake ... MN-6
Borg Lake—lake ... MN-6
Borg Lake—lake ... ND-7
**Borgman**—pop pl ... WV-2
**Borgman (Bergman)**—pop pl ... WV-2
Borgmann Mill—hist pl ... MO-7
Borgne, Lake—lake ... LA-4
Borgne, Lake—lake ... MS-4
**Borgne Mouth**—pop pl ... LA-4
Borgne Mouth Sch—school ... LA-4
Borgstrom Creek—stream ... MI-6
Borgstrom House—hist pl ... TX-5
Borgund Ch—church ... MN-6
Borg Warner Chemical
Corporation—facility ... IL-6
Bori ... FM-9
Boriana Canyon—valley ... AZ-5
Boriana Mines—mine ... AZ-5
Boriana Well—well ... AZ-5
Boribo Lake—lake ... WI-6
Borica—locale ... NM-5
Borica Draw—valley ... NM-5
Borie—locale ... PA-2
Borie—locale ... WY-8
Borie Branch—stream ... PA-2
Boriin Creek—stream ... MN-6
Borin Cem—cemetery ... TN-4
Borin Creek—stream ... KS-7
**Boring**—pop pl ... MD-2
**Boring**—pop pl ... OR-9
**Boring**—pop pl ... TN-4
Boring Branch—stream ... TN-4
Boring Cem—cemetery ... TN-4
Boring Ch—church ... OH-6
Boring Chapel (historical)—church ... TN-4
Boring Creek—stream ... CA-9
Boring Creek—stream ... NC-3
Boring Ford (historical)—locale ... TN-4
Boring Machine Creek ... MT-8
Boring Mill Branch—stream ... NC-3
Boring Mill Ravine—valley ... CA-9
Boring Mill Run ... PA-2
Boring Pond—lake ... GA-3
Boring Post Office (historical)—building ... TN-4
Boring Ridge—ridge ... TN-4
Boring Sch—school ... OR-9
Borings Chapel ... TN-4
**Borinquen**—pop pl ... PR-3
Borinquen Air Station (Coast
Guard)—military ... PR-3
Borinquen (Barrio)—fmr MCD (2) ... PR-3
Borin Top—summit ... TN-4
Boris Lake—lake ... WI-6
Borke Drain Number Sixteen—canal ... ND-7
Borkeys Store—locale ... VA-3
Borkey Store ... VA-3
**Borkey Store**—pop pl ... VA-3
Borkholder Sch—school ... IN-6
Bork Number 1 Dam—dam ... SD-7
Bork Number 2 Dam—dam ... SD-7
Borland—locale ... MI-6
Borland—locale ... WV-2
Borland, John, House—hist pl ... NY-2
Borland Canyon ... TX-5
Borland Lateral—canal ... CA-9
**Borland Manor**—pop pl ... PA-2
Borland Manor Elem Sch—school ... PA-2
Borland Post Office (historical)—building ... PA-2
Borland Sch—school ... PA-2
Borland Sch (abandoned)—school ... PA-2
Borlands Par 3 Golf Course—locale ... PA-2
Borlandy Canyon ... TX-5
Borleske Stadium—other ... WA-9
**Bor-ley Heights**—pop pl ... TX-5
Born, Edward D., House—hist pl ... MI-6
Born, Engelbert B., House—hist pl ... MI-6
Bornabi ... FM-9
Born Again Beuevers Fellowship—church ... FL-3
Bornard Cem—cemetery ... MS-4
Born Branch—stream ... TX-5
Born Cem—cemetery ... IA-7
Borneman Cem—cemetery ... MO-7
Bornemann Lake—lake ... NE-7
Borne Mill Slough—gut ... AR-4
Borner Fork—stream ... WY-8
Borner Garden Sch—school ... WY-8
Bornes Ford—locale ... KY-4
Bornite—locale ... AK-9
Born Lake—lake ... MN-6
Born Lakes—lake ... ID-8
Bornman Sch—school ... OK-5
Born Sch—school ... MI-6
Born Sch—school ... NE-7
Borns Hollow—valley ... WI-6
Borns Lake—lake ... CO-8
Borns Lake—swamp ... WI-6
Bornt Hill—summit (2) ... NY-2
Borntraeger Airstrip—airport ... IN-6
Borntrager Ditch ... IL-6
Boro ... MP-9
Boro Brook—stream ... IN-6
Borodino ... LA-4
**Borodino**—pop pl ... LA-4
**Borodino**—pop pl ... NY-2
Borodino Cem—cemetery ... NY-2
Borodino Lake—lake ... AK-9
**Borodino Landing**—pop pl ... NY-2
Borodychuk Drain—canal ... MI-6
Borokku ... MP-9
Borom ... AL-4
**Borom**—pop pl ... AL-4
Borom Cem—cemetery ... AL-4
Borom Post Office (historical)—building ... AL-4
**Boromville**—pop pl ... AL-4
Boromville Cemetery ... AL-4
**Boron**—pop pl ... CA-9
Boron Air Force Station—military ... CA-9
Boron Air Force Station—other ... CA-9
Boronda, Jose Eusebio, Adobe—hist pl ... CA-9
Boronda Creek—stream ... CA-9
Boronda Sch—school ... CA-9
Boron Springs—spring ... CA-9
Borosa Oil Field—oilfield ... TX-5
Borosolvay—locale ... CA-9
Borough ... CT-1
Borough—other ... PA-2
**Borough, The**—pop pl ... NC-3
Borough Cem—cemetery ... ME-1
Borough Cem—cemetery ... VT-1
Borough Hall—uninc pl ... NY-2
Borough Hall of the Borough of
Waynesboro—hist pl ... PA-2
Borough House Plantation—hist pl ... SC-3
Borough-Owned Cold Stream Dam ... PA-2
Borough Park—park ... PA-2
**Borough Park**—pop pl ... NY-2
Boroughs Pond—reservoir ... AL-4
Boroughs Shopping Plaza—locale ... MA-1
Borovee Creek ... WA-9
Borracha Tank—reservoir ... TX-5
Borrachio—locale ... TX-5
Borrachito Windmill—locale ... TX-5
Borracho, Arroyo—valley ... TX-5
Borracho Arroyo ... TX-5
Borradita Windmill—locale ... TX-5
**Borras**—pop pl (2) ... PR-3
Borr Dam ... SD-7
Borree Corner—locale ... AZ-5
**Borrees Corner**—pop pl ... AZ-5
Borregas Creek—stream ... CA-9
Borrego—locale ... CA-9
Borrego Badlands—area ... CA-9
Borrego Canyon—valley ... CA-9
Borrego Canyon—valley ... CO-8
Borrego Canyon—valley (2) ... NM-5
Borrego Canyon Wash—stream ... CA-9
Borrego Cem—cemetery ... TX-5
Borrego Creek—stream (2) ... TX-5
Borrego Crossing—locale ... NM-5
Borrego Ditch—canal ... CO-8
Borrego Dome—summit ... NM-5
Borrego Draw—valley ... TX-5
Borrego Mesa—summit ... NM-5
Borrego Mountain Wash—stream ... CA-9
Borrego Mtn—summit ... CA-9
Borrego Palm Canyon—valley ... CA-9
Borrego Palms Resort—locale ... CA-9
Borrego Pass—gap ... NM-5
Borrego Pass Trading Post—locale ... NM-5
Borrego Ranger Cabin—locale ... NM-5
Borrego Sch—school ... CA-9
Borregos Chapel—church ... TX-5
Borrego Sink—basin ... CA-9
Borrego Sink Wash—stream ... CA-9
Borregos Lake—reservoir ... TX-5
Borregos Oil Field—oilfield (2) ... TX-5
Borregos Pasture—flat ... TX-5
Borrego Spring—spring ... CA-9
**Borrego Springs**—pop pl ... CA-9
Borregos Ranch—locale ... TX-5
Borregos Tank—reservoir ... TX-5
Borregos State Park ... CA-9
Borregos Windmill—locale ... TX-5
Borrego Tank ... AZ-5
Borrego Tank—reservoir ... NM-5
Borrego Tank—reservoir (2) ... TX-5
Borrego Trail—trail ... NM-5
Borrego Trick Tank—reservoir ... AZ-5
Borrego Valley—valley ... CA-9
Borrego Valley Substation—other ... CA-9
Borrego Wasteway—canal ... NM-5
**Borrego Wells**—pop pl ... CA-9
Borrego Windmill—locale ... NM-5
Borrego Windmill—locale (2) ... TX-5
Borreguero Spring—spring ... CA-9
Borregus Tank—reservoir ... TX-5
Borrel Spring—spring ... NV-8
Borreson Coulee—valley ... WI-6
Borring Cem—cemetery ... WV-2
Borris Cem—cemetery ... IN-6
Borromeo Cem—cemetery ... MO-7
Borromeo Seminary—school ... OH-6
Borroon Creek—stream ... WY-8
Borrow Creek—stream ... AL-4
Borrow Pit—mine ... MO-7
Borrow Pit Drain ... CA-9
Borrow Pit Drain—canal ... CA-9
Borrow Pit Gulch—valley ... ID-8
Borrow Pit Number One Tank—reservoir ... AZ-5
Borrow Pit Number Three Tank—reservoir ... AZ-5
Borrow Pit Number Two Tank—reservoir ... AZ-5
Borrow Pit Pond—lake ... FL-3
Borrow Pits—flat ... MO-7
Borrow Pit Tank—reservoir (3) ... AZ-5
Borrow Pit Windmill—locale ... TX-5
Borrow Rsvr—reservoir ... OR-9
Borrows Run—stream ... VA-3
Borrow Tank—reservoir (3) ... AZ-5
B & O RR Potomac River
Crossing—hist pl ... MD-2
B & O RR Potomac River
Crossing—hist pl ... WV-2
B & O RR Viaduct—hist pl ... OH-6
Borski Bayou—gut ... MI-6
Borski Creek—stream ... MI-6
Borski School—locale ... MI-6
Borst, Joseph, House—hist pl ... WA-9
Borstel Pond—reservoir ... OR-9
Borst Valley ... WI-6
Borst Valley—valley ... WI-6
Borst Valley State Public Hunting
Area—park ... WI-6
Borth—locale ... WI-6
Borthill Ferry—locale ... ID-8
Borth Lake—lake (2) ... WI-6
Bortle Drain—stream ... MI-6
Bortman Creek—stream ... MI-6
Bortner Sch (abandoned)—school ... PA-2
**Borton**—pop pl ... IL-6
Borton Coulee—valley ... MT-8
**Bortondale**—pop pl ... PA-2
Borton Landing—locale ... NJ-2
Borton Sch—school ... AZ-5
Bortsfield Cem—cemetery ... IN-6
Bortz Ch—church ... PA-2
Bortz Lake ... MI-6
Bortz-Lewis Site—hist pl ... ME-1
Boruff Cem—cemetery ... TN-4
Boruff Draw—valley ... WY-8
Borum Cem—cemetery ... TN-4
Borum Lake—lake ... WY-8
Borum Run—stream ... IN-6
Borum Spring—spring ... VA-3
**Borup**—pop pl ... MN-6
Boru Spring—spring ... MT-8
Bory ... FM-9
Bos Arnegos Mine—mine ... AZ-5
**Boscawen**—pop pl ... NH-1
Boscawen Acad and Much-I-Do-Hose
House—hist pl ... NH-1
Boscawen Public Library—hist pl ... NH-1
**Boscawen (Town of)**—pop pl ... NH-1
Bosch, John, Farmstead—hist pl ... MN-6
Bosch, Joseph, Bldg—hist pl ... MI-6
Bosch And Hulst Drain—canal ... MI-6
Bosch Canyon—valley ... CA-9
**Boschertown**—pop pl ... MO-7
**Bosco**—pop pl ... LA-4
Boscobel—hist pl ... NE-7
Boscobel—hist pl ... NY-2
Boscobel—locale ... VA-3
**Boscobel**—pop pl (2) ... WI-6
Boscobel Cottage—hist pl ... LA-4
Boscobel HS—hist pl ... WI-6
Boscobel Island—island ... NY-2
**Boscobel (Town of)**—pop pl ... WI-6
Boscoble and Double Standard
Mine—mine ... SD-7
Bosco HS—school ... WI-6
**Bosco (Hueysville Post Office)**—pop pl ... KY-4
Bosco Island—island ... LA-4
Bosco Oil Field—oilfield ... LA-4
Bosco (RR name for Hueysville)—other ... KY-4
Bosco Sch—school ... KY-4
Bosco Tank—reservoir ... AZ-5
**Boscoville**—pop pl ... LA-4
Boscow Sch—school ... OR-9
Bosebuck Camp—locale ... ME-1
Bosebuck Mtn—summit ... ME-1
Bose Cem—cemetery ... OH-6
Bose Lake—lake ... TX-5
Bose Lake—lake ... WI-6
Bosely Channel—channel ... MI-6
Bosely Lake—lake ... MN-6
Boseman Blacksmith—building ... TX-5
Boseman Cem—cemetery ... NC-3
Boseman Ch—church ... NC-3
Boseman Grist Mill (historical)—building ... TX-5
Boseman Run—stream ... OH-6
Bosenburg ... AL-4
Bosenburg Post Office ... AL-4
Bose Nukse Creek—stream ... MS-4
Boser Swamp—stream ... SC-3
Boshart Cem—cemetery ... NY-2
Boshart Creek—stream ... AL-4
Boshear Cem—cemetery ... TN-4
Boshell Branch—stream ... AL-4
Boshell Cem—cemetery ... AL-4
Boshell Hill—summit ... AL-4
Boshell's Mill—hist pl ... AL-4
Boshells Mill—locale ... AL-4
Boshell's Mill Dam—dam ... AL-4
Boshell's Mill Pond—reservoir ... AL-4
Bosher—locale ... VA-3
Bosher Dam—dam ... VA-3
Boshers Millpond—reservoir ... VA-3
Bosin Rock—pillar ... WY-8
Bosken Park—park ... OH-6
Bosket Cem—cemetery ... MS-4
Bosket Lake—lake ... NY-2
**Boskydell**—pop pl ... IL-6
**Bosky Dell**—pop pl ... MO-7
Bosky Post Office (historical)—building ... TN-4
Bos Lake—lake ... NE-7
Bos Lake—lake ... WA-9
Bosland ... KS-7
**Bosler**—pop pl ... WY-8
Bosler Cem—cemetery ... PA-2
Bosler Ditch No 3—canal (2) ... WY-8
Bosler Fireproof Garage—hist pl ... KY-4
Bosler Junction—locale ... WY-8
Bosler Ranch—locale (2) ... WY-8
Bosler Ridge—ridge ... IN-6
Bosler Rsvr—reservoir ... WY-8
Bosley ... NC-3
Bosley—other ... NC-3
Bosley Butte—summit ... OR-9
Bosley Cem—cemetery ... TX-5
Bosley Ch—church ... MD-2
Bosley Corner—locale ... NY-2
Bosley Playground—park ... IL-6
Bosley Ranch—locale ... AZ-5
Bosley Run—stream ... WV-2
Boslough Butte—summit ... MT-8
Boslough-Claycomb House—hist pl ... OR-9
Bosma Ditch—canal ... IN-6
Bosman ... MD-2
Bosman Creek—stream ... UT-8
Bosman Ditch—canal ... IN-6
Bosman Lake—lake ... TX-5
Bosman Ridge—ridge ... UT-8
Bosman Sch—school ... TX-5
Bosna (historical)—locale ... KS-7
Bosna Sch—school ... KS-7
Bosner Creek—stream ... WI-6
Boso Cem—cemetery (3) ... WV-2
Bosom Bottom Ch—church ... SC-3
Bosonberg Creek—stream ... OR-9
Bosque—locale ... AZ-5
Bosque—locale ... NM-5
Bosque—locale ... TX-5
Bosquebello Cem—cemetery ... FL-3
Bosque Canyon—valley ... NM-5
Bosque Cem—cemetery ... AZ-5
**Bosquecito**—pop pl ... NM-5
Bosquecito Ditch—canal ... NM-5
**Bosque (County)**—pop pl ... TX-5
Bosque County Courthouse—hist pl ... TX-5
Bosque County Jail—hist pl ... TX-5
Bosque Creek—stream ... TX-5
Bosque Del Apache Grant—civil ... NM-5
Bosque Drain—canal ... NM-5
Bosque Draw—valley ... NM-5
Bosque Estatal de Boqueron—forest ... PR-3
Bosque Estatal De Ceiba—forest ... PR-3
Bosque Estatal De Guajataca—forest ... PR-3
Bosque Estatal De Guanica—forest ... PR-3
Bosque Estatal De Guilarte—forest ... PR-3
Bosque Estatal De Maricao—forest ... PR-3
Bosque Estatal de Pinones—forest ... PR-3
Bosque Estatal de Rio Abajo—forest ... PR-3
Bosque Estatal De Susua—forest ... PR-3
Bosque Farm Ch—church ... NM-5
**Bosque Farms**—pop pl ... NM-5
Bosque Farms Sch—school ... NM-5
Bosque Grande Mesa—summit ... NM-5
Bosquejo—civil ... CA-9
Bosque Lateral—canal ... NM-5
Bosque Lateral No 1—canal ... NM-5
Bosque Lateral No 2—canal ... NM-5
Bosque Peak—summit ... NM-5
Bosque River ... TX-5
Bosque River—stream ... TX-5
Bosque Spring—spring ... AZ-5
Bosque Spring—spring (3) ... NM-5
**Bosqueville**—pop pl ... TX-5
Bosqueville Sch—school ... TX-5
Bosque Well—well ... AZ-5
Bosque Well—well ... NM-5
Bosrah Brook ... MA-1
Bos Ranch—locale ... NE-7
Boss—locale ... TX-5
**Boss**—pop pl ... MO-7
**Boss**—pop pl ... OK-5
Boss, A.J., House—hist pl ... GA-3
Boss Allen Lake ... WI-6
Bossard Corners ... PA-2
**Bossard Property
(subdivision)**—pop pl ... DE-2
Bossard Run—stream ... PA-2
**Bossards Corner**—pop pl ... PA-2
**Bossardsville**—pop pl ... PA-2
Bossardville ... PA-2
Boss Branch—stream ... NC-3
Boss Branch—stream ... TX-5
Bossburg—locale ... WA-9
Bossburg Cem—cemetery ... WA-9
Boss Canal—canal ... CA-9
Boss Canyon—valley ... ID-8
Bosschem Creek ... MI-6
Boss Creek ... NJ-2
Boss Creek ... WA-9
Boss Creek—stream ... AK-9
Boss Creek—stream ... MN-6
Boss Creek—stream ... OK-5
Boss Creek—stream ... WA-9
Boss Creek—stream ... WI-6
Boss Draw—valley ... WY-8
Bosse—locale ... KS-7
Bosse Field—building ... IN-6
Bosseher School—locale ... MI-6
Bosse HS ... IN-6
Bosse HS—school ... IN-6
Bosse Lake—lake ... FL-3
Bosseler Ridge—summit ... MT-8
Bossen Field—park ... MN-6
Bosserman Creek—stream ... IN-6
Bosserman Dam—dam ... ND-7
Bosserman Field—park ... TX-5
Bossert, Thomas, House—hist pl ... WI-6
**Bossert Estates**—pop pl ... NJ-2
Bossier Acad—school ... LA-4
Bossier Base—other ... LA-4
Bossier Bayou—stream ... LA-4
**Bossier City**—pop pl ... LA-4
Bossier City Rsvr—reservoir ... LA-4
**Bossier Parish**—pop pl ... LA-4
Bossier Point—cape ... LA-4
Bossier Sch—school ... LA-4
Boss Island—island ... IL-6
Boss Island Creek—stream ... AR-4
Bossis Plantation—locale ... SC-3
Bossi Woods—woods ... WA-9
Boss Jumbo Mine—mine ... NV-8
**Bossko Township**—pop pl ... SD-7
Boss Lady Rsvr—reservoir ... CO-8
Boss Lake—lake ... MI-6
Boss Lake—lake ... MN-6
Boss Lake—swamp ... MN-6
Bossler, Marcus, House—hist pl ... OH-6
Bossler Cem—cemetery ... LA-4
Bosslers Ch—church ... PA-2
Boss Mine—mine (2) ... CO-8
Boss Mine—mine ... NV-8
Bosson Ranch—locale ... NM-5
Bosson Wash—stream ... NM-5
Boss Ranch—locale (2) ... AZ-5
Boss Road—locale ... NJ-2
Boss Stogner Cem ... MS-4
Bosstown—locale ... WI-6
Boss Tweed—mine ... UT-8
Boss Tweed Mine—mine ... MT-8
Bossum Bayou ... MS-4
Bossung Ditch—canal ... IN-6
Bossung Lake—lake ... NE-7
Bossuot Lake—lake ... MN-6
Boss Wilson Pond—lake ... IL-6
Bossy Creek ... OK-5
Bossy Mtn—summit ... ME-1
Bost, Henry Connor, House—hist pl ... NC-3
Bost Cem—cemetery ... IN-6
Bost Cem—cemetery ... NC-3
Bost Cove—valley ... TN-4
Bost Creek—stream ... NC-3
Bostedt Creek ... MN-6
**Bostetter**—pop pl ... MD-2
Bostetter Campground—locale ... ID-8
Bostetter Cem—cemetery ... IN-6
Bostetter Forest Service Station—locale ... ID-8
Bostetter Pasture Spring—spring ... ID-8
Bostetter Spring—spring ... ID-8
Bost Fork—stream ... TN-4
Bost Hill Ch—church ... IL-6
Bostian Heights—locale ... NC-3
Bostian Sch—school ... NC-3
**Bostic**—pop pl ... AL-4
**Bostic**—pop pl ... NC-3
Bostica Cem—cemetery ... TN-4
Bostic Bend—bend ... TN-4
Bostic Branch—stream ... MS-4
Bostic Cem—cemetery ... MS-4
Bostic Cem—cemetery ... MT-8
Bostic Cem—cemetery ... NC-3
Bostic Cem—cemetery ... SC-3
Bostic Cem—cemetery ... VA-3
Bostic Cem—cemetery ... WV-2
Bostic Chapel—church ... TN-4
Bostic Creek ... MN-6
Bostic Elem Sch—school ... NC-3
Bostic Hill Church ... AL-4
**Bostick**—pop pl ... SC-3
**Bostick**—pop pl ... TX-5
Bostick Branch—stream ... FL-3
Bostick Cem—cemetery ... GA-3
Bostick Cem—cemetery ... IL-6
Bostick Cem—cemetery (2) ... TN-4
Bostick Creek ... KS-7
Bostick Creek—stream ... AL-4
Bostick Creek—stream ... MN-6
Bostick Creek—stream ... TN-4
Bostick Female Acad—hist pl ... TN-4
Bostick Hill Ch—church ... AL-4
Bostick Landing—locale ... SC-3
Bostick Mtn—summit ... CA-9
Bostick Sch—school ... SC-3
Bostick Spring—spring ... OR-9
Bostic Lake Rsvr—reservoir ... OR-9
Bostic Point—cape ... NC-3
Bostic Slough—stream ... TN-4
**Bostic Yard**—pop pl ... NC-3
Bostig Creek ... MN-6
Bostik Creek ... MN-6
Bost Mill Hist Dist—hist pl ... NC-3
Boston ... AL-4
Boston ... IN-6
Boston ... KS-7
Boston—locale ... AL-4
Boston—locale ... AR-4
Boston—locale ... CT-1
Boston—locale (3) ... KY-4
Boston—locale ... OH-6
Boston—locale ... TN-4
Boston—locale ... VA-3
**Boston**—pop pl ... GA-3
**Boston**—pop pl ... IN-6
**Boston**—pop pl (2) ... KY-4
**Boston**—pop pl ... LA-4
**Boston**—pop pl ... MA-1
**Boston**—pop pl ... MI-6
**Boston**—pop pl ... MO-7
**Boston**—pop pl ... NY-2
**Boston**—pop pl (3) ... OH-6
**Boston**—pop pl ... PA-2
**Boston**—pop pl ... TX-5
**Boston**—pop pl ... VA-3
Boston—uninc pl ... AL-4
Boston—uninc pl ... VA-3
Boston, City of—civil ... MA-1
Boston African American Natl Historic
Site—park ... MA-1
Boston and Lowell RR Memorial—park ... MA-1
Boston and Maine RR Depot—hist pl ... MA-1
Boston and Providence RR Bridge—hist pl ... RI-1
Boston Architectural Center—building ... MA-1
Boston Arizona Mine—mine ... AZ-5
Boston Army Base—other ... MA-1
Boston Athenaeum—hist pl ... MA-1
Boston Atoll ... MP-9
Boston Ave Methodist Church—hist pl ... OK-5
Boston Ave Sch—school ... FL-3
Boston Bar—bar ... IL-6
Boston Bar (inundated)—bar ... UT-8
Boston Basin—basin ... WA-9
Boston Bay—bay ... IL-6
Boston Bay—bay ... WI-6
Boston Bayou—stream ... LA-4
Boston Bldg—hist pl ... CO-8
Boston Block—hist pl ... IA-7
Boston Bluff—cliff ... MO-7
Boston Bluff—cliff ... OR-9
Boston Branch—stream ... GA-3
Boston Branch—stream ... MS-4
Boston Branch—stream ... MO-7
Boston Branch—stream ... NE-7
Boston Branch—stream ... SC-3
Boston Branch—stream (3) ... TN-4
Boston Branch—stream (2) ... VA-3
Boston Branch Lake—reservoir ... TN-4
Boston Branch Lake Dam—dam ... TN-4
Boston Bridge—bridge ... PA-2
Boston Brook—stream ... ID-8
Boston Brook—stream ... MA-1
Boston Brook Dam—dam ... MA-1
Boston Canal—canal ... LA-4
Boston Canyon—valley ... NE-7
Boston Canyon—valley ... OR-9
Boston (CCD)—cens area ... GA-3
Boston (CCD)—cens area ... KY-4
Boston (CCD)—cens area ... TN-4
Boston Cem—cemetery (2) ... AL-4
Boston Cem—cemetery ... CO-8
Boston Cem—cemetery ... IN-6
Boston Cem—cemetery (2) ... IA-7
Boston Cem—cemetery (2) ... KY-4
Boston Cem—cemetery ... MO-7
Boston Cem—cemetery ... PA-2
Boston Center—other ... NY-2
Boston Center Community
Building—locale ... MO-7
Boston Center Community Hall ... MO-7
Boston Ch—church ... AR-4
Boston Ch—church ... KY-4
Boston Ch—church ... NY-2
Boston Ch—church ... TN-4
Boston Chapel—church ... AR-4
Boston Chapel—church ... IL-6
Boston City Hall—building ... MA-1
Boston Coll—school ... MA-1
Boston Colliery—building ... PA-2
Boston Colliery (historical)—mine ... PA-2
Boston Common—park ... MA-1
Boston Common and Public
Garden—hist pl ... MA-1
**Boston Corner**—pop pl ... IN-6
**Boston Corner**—pop pl ... NY-2
**Boston Corners**—pop pl ... NY-2
Boston Coulee—valley ... MN-6
Boston Coulee—valley ... MT-8
Boston Coulee Sch—school ... MT-8
Boston Creek—stream (3) ... AK-9
Boston Creek—stream ... AR-4
Boston Creek—stream ... GA-3
Boston Creek—stream (2) ... IN-6
Boston Creek—stream ... MI-6
Boston Creek—stream ... VA-3
Boston Creek—stream ... WA-9
Boston Cutoff—trail ... AR-4
Boston Division—civil ... TN-4
Boston Dome—summit ... AK-9
Boston Drain—canal ... OR-9
Boston Edison Electric Illuminating
Company—hist pl ... MA-1
Boston-Edison Hist Dist—hist pl ... MI-6
Boston-Ely Shaft—mine ... NV-8
Boston Farm Lateral—canal ... CO-8
Boston Ferry Natural History
Area—other ... MO-7
Boston Flat—flat ... CA-9
Boston Flat—flat ... CO-8
Boston Flat Gulch—valley ... CA-9
Boston Flour Mill—hist pl ... OR-9
Boston Garden—building ... MA-1
Boston Glacier—glacier ... WA-9
Boston Gulch—valley (2) ... AK-9
Boston Gulch—valley ... AZ-5
Boston Gulch—valley ... ID-8
Boston Harbor ... MA-1
Boston Harbor—bay ... MA-1
Boston Harbor—bay ... NH-1
**Boston Harbor**—pop pl ... WA-9
Boston Harbor Islands Archeol
District—hist pl ... MA-1
Boston Harbor Islands State Park ... MA-1
Boston Harbor Island State Park—park ... MA-1
Boston Harbor Sch—school ... WA-9
**Boston Heights**—pop pl ... OH-6
Boston Heights (Township of)—other ... OH-6
**Boston (Hershel)**—pop pl ... KY-4
Boston Highlands ... MA-1
Boston Hill ... MA-1
Boston Hill—summit (2) ... KY-4
Boston Hill—summit (2) ... MA-1
Boston Hill—summit ... NH-1
Boston Hill—summit ... NM-5
Boston Hill—summit ... OH-6
Boston Hill—summit ... RI-1
Boston Hills—summit ... ME-1
Boston Hills Country Club—other ... OH-6
Boston Hollow ... OR-9
Boston Hollow—valley (2) ... AL-4
Boston Hollow—valley ... CT-1
Boston Hollow—valley ... PA-2
Boston Hollow—valley (2) ... TN-4
Boston Hollow Branch—stream ... TN-4
Boston Hollow Pit—cave ... AL-4
Boston Horse Camp—locale ... OR-9
Boston HS—school ... LA-4
**Bostonia**—pop pl ... CA-9
**Bostonia**—pop pl ... PA-2
Bostonian Creek—stream ... ID-8
Bostonia Sch—school ... CA-9
Boston Inner Harbor—channel ... MA-1
Boston Inseln ... MP-9
Boston Island ... MP-9
Boston Island—island ... ME-1
Boston Junior High School ... IN-6
Boston Knob—summit ... VA-3
Boston Lake—lake (2) ... MI-6
Boston Lake—lake ... MN-6
Boston Lake—reservoir ... IL-6
Boston Lateral—canal ... CO-8
Boston Latin Sch—school ... MA-1
Boston Ledge—bar ... MA-1
Boston Ledges—bench ... OH-6
Boston Lick Creek—stream ... KY-4
Boston Light—hist pl ... MA-1
Boston Light—locale ... MA-1
Boston Lighthouse—locale ... MA-1
Boston Lightship—locale ... MA-1
Boston Lookout Tower—locale ... AR-4
Boston Lot Lake—lake ... NH-1
Boston Main Channel—channel ... MA-1
Boston Manufacturing Company—hist pl ... MA-1
Boston Massacre Marker—park ... MA-1
Boston Massacre Site ... MA-1
**Boston Mill**—pop pl ... OH-6
**Boston Mills (historical)**—pop pl ... OR-9

Boston Mine—mine CO-8
Boston Mine Shaft—mine NV-8
Boston Mountain Lake—lake ID-8
Boston Mountains—range AR-4
Boston Mtn—summit ID-8
Boston Mtn—summit VA-3
Boston Natl Historic Park—park MA-1
Boston Natl Park Visitor Center—building MA-1
Boston Naval Shipyard—hist pl MA-1
Boston Neck—cape MA-1
Boston Neck—cape RI-1
Boston Neck Sch—school CT-1
Boston North Channel—channel MA-1
Boston Oil Field—oilfield OK-5
Boston Peak WA-9
Boston Peak—summit (2) CO-8
Boston Peak—summit WA-9
Boston Place Landing—locale MS-4
Boston Plantation MA-1
Boston Plantation (historical)—locale MS-4
Boston Plantation Landing MS-4
Boston Pond—lake ME-1
Boston Pool Cem—cemetery OK-5
Boston Post Office (historical)—building TN-4
Boston Post Road Hist Dist—hist pl CT-1
Boston Post Road Hist Dist—hist pl MA-1
Boston Post Road Hist Dist—hist pl NY-2
Boston Public Garden—hist pl MA-1
Boston Public Library—building MA-1
Boston Public Library—hist pl MA-1
Boston Ranch—locale CA-9
Boston Ranch—locale ME-1
**Boston Ravine**—pop pl CA-9
Boston Ridge School—locale NE-7
Boston Road Shop Ctr—locale MA-1
**Boston Run**—pop pl PA-2
Boston Run—stream (2) OH-6
Boston Run—stream PA-2
Boston Run Nature Area—area PA-2
Boston Sch—school CO-8
Boston Sch—school KY-4
Boston Sch—school MO-7
Boston Sch (abandoned)—school PA-2
Boston Sch (historical)—school AL-4
Bostons Creek PA-2
Boston Searchlight Mine—mine NV-8
Boston Searlight Mine NV-8
Boston South Channel—channel MA-1
Boston Store IN-6
Boston Store—hist pl OK-5
Boston Tank—reservoir AZ-5
Boston Tea Party Ship MA-1
Boston Tonopah—mine NV-8
Boston Town Church TN-4
**Boston (Town of)**—pop pl NY-2
Boston Township MA-1
Boston Township Number One MA-1
Boston (Township of)—fmr MCD (4) AR-4
**Boston (Township of)**—pop pl IN-6
**Boston (Township of)**—pop pl MI-6
**Boston (Township of)**—pop pl OH-6
Boston Tunnel—mine OR-9
Boston Tunnel—tunnel NV-8
Boston University—uninc pl MA-1
Boston University Sargent Camp—locale NH-1
Boston Valley—valley NE-7
Boston Valley Sch—school NE-7
Boston Valley Sch—school NY-2
Boston Water Works Reservoir MA-1
Boston Water Works Reservoirs MA-1
Boston Young Men's Christian Union—hist pl MA-1
Bost Run—stream IN-6
**Bosts Mill (historical)**—pop pl NC-3
Bostwick—hist pl MD-2
Bostwick—locale GA-3
**Bostwick**—pop pl FL-3
**Bostwick**—pop pl GA-3
**Bostwick**—pop pl NE-7
Bostwick Bay—bay NY-2
Bostwick Canyon—valley MT-8
Bostwick (CCD)—cens area GA-3
**Bostwick Corners**—pop pl NY-2
Bostwick Creek—gut NY-2
Bostwick Creek—stream AK-9
Bostwick Creek—stream MT-8
Bostwick Creek—stream NY-2
Bostwick Creek—stream WI-6
Bostwick Ditch—canal CO-8
Bostwick Inlet—bay AK-9
Bostwick Lake—lake AK-9
Bostwick Lake—lake MI-6
**Bostwick Lake**—pop pl MI-6
Bostwick Lake—reservoir NJ-2
Bostwick Park—flat CO-8
Bostwick Point—cape AK-9
Bostwick Point—cape NY-2
Bostwick Reef—bar AK-9
Bostwick's Bay NY-2
Bostwicks Pond Dam—dam NJ-2
Bostze Mine—mine IL-6
Bosuns Bluff Marsh—swamp MD-2
Boswell AL-4
Boswell—locale AR-4
**Boswell**—pop pl AR-4
**Boswell**—pop pl IN-6
**Boswell**—pop pl NC-3
**Boswell**—pop pl OK-5
**Boswell**—pop pl PA-2
Boswell, N. K., Ranch—hist pl WY-8
Boswell Bay—bay AK-9
**Boswell Bay**—pop pl AK-9
Boswell Bluff—cliff MO-7
Boswell Borough—civil PA-2
Boswell Branch—stream AL-4
Boswell Branch—stream TN-4
Boswell Camp One—locale CA-9
Boswell Cem—cemetery IN-6
Boswell Cem—cemetery IA-7
Boswell Cem—cemetery (2) MS-4
Boswell Cem—cemetery (5) TN-4
Boswell Ch—church TX-5
Boswell Chapel—church TN-4
**Boswell Corners**—pop pl NY-2
Boswell Creek—stream CO-8
Boswell Creek—stream KS-7
Boswell Creek—stream MI-6
Boswell Creek—stream OR-9
Boswell Creek—stream TX-5
Boswell Creek—stream WY-8
Boswell Diversion Ditch—canal SD-7
Boswell Elem Sch—school IN-6
Boswell Gin (historical)—locale AL-4
Boswell Golf Course—other AL-4
Boswell Gulch—valley CA-9
Boswell Gulch—valley CO-8
Boswell Hollow—valley MO-7
Boswell Hosp—hospital GA-3
Boswell JHS—school KS-7
Boswell Lake—reservoir AR-4
Boswell Landing (historical)—locale TN-4
Boswell Landing Lake Access Area—park TN-4
Boswell Levee—levee CA-9
Boswell Memorial Hosp—hospital AZ-5
Boswell Memorial Hospital Heliport—airport AZ-5
Boswell Mineral Springs—locale OR-9
Boswell Mtn—summit OR-9
Boswell (Omega) AL-4
Boswell Park—park NJ-2
Boswell Ranch—locale NM-5
Boswell Ranch—locale WY-8
Boswell Ridge—ridge CA-9
Boswell Rock—island AK-9
Boswell Rsvr—reservoir PA-2
Boswell Run—stream OH-6
Boswells Beach—locale SC-3
Boswell Sch—school MI-6
Boswell Sch (abandoned)—school MO-7
Boswell Spring—spring (2) OR-9
Boswell Spring—spring WY-8
Boswells Store—locale VA-3
Boswell's Tavern—hist pl VA-3
Boswells Tavern—locale VA-3
Boswell Tabernacle—church AL-4
Boswell Tank—reservoir (2) AZ-5
**Boswellville**—pop pl NC-3
Boswell Well—well NM-5
Boswell Windmill—locale NM-5
Boswick Creek WI-6
B Oswood Ranch—locale MT-8
Bosworth MI-6
Bosworth—locale AL-4
**Bosworth**—pop pl MO-7
Bosworth, Benjamin, House—hist pl CT-1
Bosworth, Dr. Ralph Lyman, House—hist pl OR-9
Bosworth Brook—stream CT-1
Bosworth Canyon—valley CA-9
Bosworth Cem—cemetery MA-1
Bosworth Cem—cemetery MI-6
Bosworth Creek—stream CA-9
Bosworth Falls—falls TN-4
Bosworth Homestead—locale CO-8
Bosworth Lake—lake WA-9
Bosworth Meadow—flat (2) CA-9
Bosworth Sch—school KY-4
Bota MH-9
Bota Chiquita Spring—spring AZ-5
Botah MH-9
Botaha MH-9
Botana Valley—valley WI-6
Botanical and Horticultural Laboratory—hist pl CO-8
Botanical (Botanical Gardens)—uninc pl NY-2
Botanical Gardens DC-2
Botanical Gardens—park CA-9
Botanical Gardens (Botanical) NY-2
Botany—locale IA-7
Botany Bay—bay VI-3
Botany Bay Archeol District—hist pl VI-3
Botany Bay Island—island SC-3
Botany Peak—summit AK-9
Botany Point—cape VI-3
Botchers Ferry (historical)—locale AL-4
Bot Creek TN-4
Botedore MS-4
Boteler, Lillian, House—hist pl MS-4
Boteler HS—school AL-4
Boteler Lake—dam MS-4
Boteler Peak—summit NC-3
Botella, Canada—valley CA-9
Botella Creek—stream TX-5
Botellas Windmill—locale TX-5
Botella Trap—summit TX-5
Botello Creek—stream TX-5
Botello Ranch—locale CA-9
Bote Mountain—ridge TN-4
Botens Rsvr—reservoir OR-9
Botero Ditch—canal (2) WY-8
**Botetourt (County)**—pop pl VA-3
Botetourt Sch—school VA-3
Botha—locale VA-3
Botha Creek—stream ID-8
**Bothell**—pop pl WA-9
Bothe Napa Valley State Park—park CA-9
Botheration Bayou—stream FL-3
Botheration Creek—gut FL-3
Botheration Creek—stream FL-3
Botheration Pond—lake NY-2
Bother Brook—stream ME-1
Bother Knob—summit VA-3
Bother Knob—summit WV-2
Botherment Branch—stream GA-3
Bother Ridge—ridge WV-2
Bother Ridge Trail—trail WV-2
Bothersome Creek—stream AR-4
Botherum—hist pl KY-4
Bothin Creek—stream CA-9
Bothun Sch—school SD-7
Bothwell CO-8
Bothwell—locale MS-4
**Bothwell**—pop pl UT-8
Bothwell, Dr. James J., House—hist pl AL-4
Bothwell, James, Water Tank House—hist pl ID-8
**Bothwell and McConaughy Subdivision**—pop pl UT-8
Bothwell Canal UT-8
Bothwell Cem—cemetery GA-3
Bothwell Cem—cemetery MS-4
Bothwell Cem—cemetery UT-8
Bothwell Ch—church AL-4
Bothwell Creek—stream WY-8
Bothwell Draw—valley WY-8
Bothwell Hosp—hospital MO-7
Bothwell Regional Health Center Heliport—airport MO-7
Bothwell Sch—school MO-7
Bothwell Sch—school NE-7
Bothwell Sch—school SD-7
Bothwick Creek—stream NV-8
**Botijas**—pop pl PR-3
Botijas (Barrio)—fmr MCD PR-3
Botines—locale TX-5
Botkinburg—locale AR-4
Botkin Hollow—valley VA-3
Botkin Ridge—ridge WV-2
**Botkins**—pop pl OH-6
Botkins Cem—cemetery OH-6
Botkins Elem Sch—hist pl OH-6
**Botland**—pop pl KY-4
**Botna**—pop pl IA-7
Botner Cem—cemetery MO-7
Botner Grove Cem—cemetery VA-3
Boto MH-9
Boton Artesian Well—well TX-5
Botone Cem—cemetery OK-5
Botrow MI-6
**Botsford**—pop pl CT-1
Botsford Brook—stream NY-2
Botsford Cem—cemetery GA-3
Botsford Ch—church (2) GA-3
Botsford Corners—locale NY-2
Botsford Hill—summit CT-1
Botsford Inn—hist pl MI-6
Botsford Park—park MI-6
Botsford Sch—school MI-6
Bots Sots Campground—locale MT-8
Botsugereido-To MP-9
Bott Canyon—valley UT-8
Bottchers Gap—gap CA-9
Botteen Sch—school WA-9
Bottega Favorita—hist pl AL-4
Botteiger Gap—gap PA-2
Bottenfield Sch—school IL-6
Bottenintnin Lake—lake AK-9
Bottern Ditch—canal IN-6
Bottero Park—park OR-9
Botters Cem—cemetery MS-4
Bottger, Charles A., House—hist pl NM-5
Bottger Creek—stream OR-9
Bottimore Ranch—locale CA-9
**Bottineau**—pop pl ND-7
Bottineau Country Club—locale ND-7
Bottineau County—civil ND-7
Bottineau Field—park MN-6
Bottineau Municipal Airp—airport ND-7
Botting Pond—lake ME-1
Bottivell Draw WY-8
Bottle AL-4
**Bottle, The**—pop pl AL-4
Bottle Bay—bay (2) ID-8
Bottle Bayou—gut LA-4
Bottle Bayou Pond—bay LA-4
Bottle Bay Point—cape ID-8
Bottle Branch—stream FL-3
Bottle Brook—stream ME-1
Bottle Brook—stream MA-1
Bottle Brook—stream NY-2
Bottle Butte—summit AZ-5
Bottle Camp—locale WA-9
Bottle Canyon—valley AZ-5
Bottle Cave—cave AL-4
Bottle Creek OR-9
Bottle Creek—gut AL-4
Bottle Creek—stream AL-4
Bottle Creek—stream AK-9
Bottle Creek—stream (2) CA-9
Bottle Creek—stream CO-8
Bottle Creek—stream (2) ID-8
Bottle Creek—stream MT-8
Bottle Creek—stream NE-7
Bottle Creek—stream NV-8
Bottle Creek—stream NJ-2
Bottle Creek—stream OK-5
Bottle Creek—stream (5) OR-9
Bottle Creek—stream WY-8
Bottle Creek Campground—locale WY-8
Bottle Creek Indian Mounds—hist pl AL-4
Bottle Creek Ranch—locale NV-8
Bottle Creek Slough—stream NV-8
Bottlegger Spring—spring UT-8
Bottleg Lake MN-6
Bottle Hill NJ-2
Bottle Hill—summit (2) CA-9
Bottle Hill—summit NV-8
Bottle Hill—summit NM-5
Bottle Hill Sch (abandoned)—school PA-2
Bottle Hollow—locale TN-4
Bottle Hollow—valley TN-4
Bottle Hollow—valley UT-8
Bottle Hollow Resort—locale UT-8
Bottle Hollow Rsvr—reservoir UT-8
Bottle House Block—hist pl MA-1
Bottle Island—island FL-3
Bottle Island—island ME-1
Bottle Island—island MI-6
Bottle Island Creek—gut FL-3
Bottle Key—island FL-3
Bottle Lagoon—lake LA-4
Bottle Lake WI-6
Bottle Lake—lake ID-8
Bottle Lake—lake ME-1
Bottle Lake—lake MN-6
Bottle Lake—lake WI-6
Bottle Lake Stream—stream ME-1
Bottle Mtn—summit CO-8
Bottle Mtn—summit ME-1
Bottle Mtn—summit NY-2
Bottleneck Lake—lake CA-9
Bottleneck Lake—lake (2) ID-8
Bottleneck Peak—summit ID-8
Bottleneck Peak—summit UT-8
Bottleneck Spring—spring CA-9
Bottleneck Spring—spring OR-9
Bottleneck Wash—stream (2) AZ-5
Bottleneck Wash Dam—dam AZ-5
Bottleneck Windmill—locale AZ-5
Bottle Pass—gap CO-8
Bottle Peak CA-9
Bottle Peak—summit CA-9
Bottle Peak—summit CO-8
Bottle Peak Spring—spring CA-9
Bottle Point FL-3
Bottle Point—cape SC-3
Bottle Point—summit ID-8
Bottle Point—summit MT-8
Bottle Pond—lake ME-1
Bottle Pond—lake NY-2
Bottle Prairie—flat OR-9
Bottle Prairie Trail—trail OR-9
Bottle Ridge—ridge WA-9
Bottle River—stream MN-6
Bottle Rock—pillar CO-8
Bottle Rock—pillar OR-9
Bottle Run—stream (2) PA-2
Bottle Run Point—cape NC-3
Bottle Run Sch (abandoned)—school PA-2
Bottle Spring—spring (2) AZ-5
Bottle Spring—spring CA-9
Bottle Spring—spring ID-8
Bottle Spring—spring (4) OR-9
Bottle Spring—spring WA-9
Bottle Springs—spring CA-9
Bottle Springs Creek—stream TX-5
Bottle Spring Tank—reservoir AZ-5
Bottles Sch—school MT-8
Bottle Summit—gap NV-8
Bottle Tank—reservoir (2) AZ-5
Bottley Creek—stream AK-9
Bott Memorial Ch—church VA-3
Botto—locale KY-4
Botto, Pietro, House—hist pl NJ-2
Bottoff Cem—cemetery IN-6
Bottolfsen Park—park ID-8
**Bottom**—pop pl NC-3
Bottom, H. P., House—hist pl KY-4
**Bottom Acres (subdivision)**—pop pl MS-4
Bottom Bay—swamp FL-3
Bottom Brook—stream MA-1
Bottom Cem—cemetery AL-4
Bottom Cem—cemetery KY-4
Bottom City AZ-5
Bottom Creek OR-9
**Bottom Creek**—pop pl WV-2
Bottom Creek—stream AL-4
Bottom Creek—stream CA-9
Bottom Creek—stream ID-8
Bottom Creek—stream MI-6
Bottom Creek—stream MN-6
Bottom Creek—stream (2) NV-8
Bottom Creek—stream OR-9
Bottom Creek—stream TN-4
Bottom Creek—stream VA-3
Bottom Creek—stream WV-2
Bottom Creek Ch—church VA-3
Bottom Crib Spring—spring MT-8
Bottom Dollar Creek—stream AK-9
Bottom Draw—valley CO-8
Bottom Fork—stream (2) KY-4
Bottom Fork Sch—school KY-4
Bottom Hills—locale DE-2
Bottom Hills Drain—gut DE-2
Bottom Knob—summit KY-4
Bottom Lake—lake NJ-2
Bottomless Ladder Pitch Cave—cave PA-2
Bottomless Lake—lake OR-9
Bottomless Lake—lake WA-9
Bottomless Lake—swamp MN-6
Bottomless Lakes—lake NM-5
Bottomless Lakes State Park—park NM-5
Bottomless Pit—basin AZ-5
Bottomless Pit—basin CO-8
Bottomless Pits AZ-5
Bottomless Pond—lake MA-1
Bottomly Pond MA-1
Bottom of the Inverted Kettle, The MH-9
Bottom Pasture Well—well TX-5
Bottom Run PA-2
Bottoms, The—flat UT-8
Bottoms Bridge—locale VA-3
Bottoms Brothers Airp—airport IN-6
Bottom School Park—park OR-9
Bottoms Fishery—locale FL-3
Bottoms House—hist pl AR-4
Bottoms Lake—lake GA-3
Bottoms Mill Bridge—bridge AL-4
Bottoms Neck—cape VA-3
Bottom Tank—reservoir AZ-5
Botton Cem—cemetery LA-4
Bottonwood Pond—lake FL-3
Bott Park—park CO-8
**Botts**—pop pl FL-3
**Botts**—pop pl PA-2
Botts Branch—stream KY-4
Botts Campground UT-8
Botts Cem—cemetery KY-4
Botts Cem—cemetery MS-4
Botts Cem—cemetery (3) MO-7
Botts Ch—church MS-4
Botts Creek—gut FL-3
Botts Creek—stream WY-8
Botts Dam—dam TN-4
Botts Ferry Cem—cemetery TX-5
Botts Ferry (historical)—locale AL-4
Botts Flat Picnic Ground—locale UT-8
Bottsford—locale GA-3
Botts Fork—stream KY-4
Botts Gap—gap TN-4
Botts Hollow—valley TN-4
Botts Lake—reservoir TN-4
Botts Park—park TX-5
Bott Spur—locale AR-4
Botts Ranch—locale NE-7
Botts Sch—school MS-4
Botts Sch (historical)—school MO-7
Botts Station—locale PA-2
Bottume, John, House—hist pl MA-1
Botuklo Creek OK-5
Botuon (not verified)—island MP-9
Botush Ch—church AL-4
**Botzum**—pop pl OH-6
Bouas House—hist pl MO-7
Bou Bay FM-9
Bouchard—locale TX-5
Bouchard Archeol Site, RI-1025—hist pl RI-1
Bouchard Lake—lake MT-8
Bouchard Pond—lake MA-1
Bouchea WI-6
Boucher Branch—stream KY-4
Boucher Brook—stream ME-1
Boucher Cem—cemetery IL-6
Boucher Cem—cemetery MO-7
Boucher Creek—stream AZ-5
Boucher Creek—stream MI-6
Boucher Hill—summit CA-9
Boucher Lake—reservoir AL-4
Boucher Mtn—summit CA-9
Boucher Oil Field—oilfield OK-5
Boucher Ranch—locale CO-8
Boucher Rapids—rapids AZ-5
Bouchers Camp—locale ME-1
Boucher Sch—school LA-4
Boucher Sch (historical)—school MO-7
Boucher Sch (historical)—school PA-2
Bouchers Gap CA-9
Boucher Trail—trail AZ-5
Bouchoux Brook—stream NY-2
Bouchoux Hill—summit NY-2
Bouck Drain—canal MI-6
Bouck Hollow—valley NY-2
Bouck Lake—lake WA-9
Boucks Falls—falls NY-2
Boucks Island—island NY-2
**Bouckville**—pop pl NY-2
Boudans Cem—cemetery AL-4
**Boudar**—pop pl VA-3
**Boudar Gardens**—pop pl VA-3
Bouder Lake—lake MN-6
Boudes Ferry—locale OH-6
Boudes Hill—summit WA-9
Boudinot—locale OK-5
Boudinot Ch—church OK-5
Boudinot Sch—school NJ-2
Boudish Gulch—valley CO-8
Boudreau, Bay—bay LA-4
Boudreau Bayou—stream LA-4
Boudreau Creek—stream MI-6
Boudreau Sch—school MO-7
**Boudreaux**—pop pl (2) LA-4
Boudreaux, Bayou—stream LA-4
Boudreaux, Lake—lake LA-4
Boudreaux Canal—canal LA-4
**Boudreaux Canal**—pop pl LA-4
Boudreaux Canal Sch—school LA-4
Boudreaux Lake—lake LA-4
Boudreaux Sch—school LA-4
Boue, Bayou—gut LA-4
Boue Creek MS-4
**Boueff**—pop pl AR-4
Bouffard Flat—flat ID-8
Bouffard Ridge—ridge ID-8
Boufford Lake—lake MI-6
Bougahoma Bayou MS-4
Bougainvillea Cem—cemetery FL-3
Bougainvillea Sch (historical)—school FL-3
**Bougainville (subdivision)**—pop pl NC-3
Bouge Canyon—valley MT-8
Bougemont Complex—hist pl WV-2
Bougere LA-4
**Bougere**—pop pl LA-4
Bougere Ch—church LA-4
Bougere Swamps—swamp LA-4
Bough Bend—bend AL-4
Boughcamp Branch—stream KY-4
Bough Creek AR-4
Bough Creek ID-8
Boughen NJ-2
Boughena Creek MS-4
Boughenia Creek—stream MS-4
Bougher—locale NJ-2
Bougher Hill—summit PA-2
Bougher Hill Sch (abandoned)—school PA-2
Bougher Lake IN-6
Bougher Lake MI-6
Bougher Run—stream PA-2
Bougher Run Trail—trail PA-2
Boughey Creek—stream OR-9
Boughey Ditch—canal IN-6
Boughmans Creek IA-7
Boughner Lake—lake MI-6
Bough Oil Field—other NM-5
Bough Sch (historical)—school MS-4
Bought, The (historical)—area DE-2
Boughten Cem—cemetery MI-6
Boughtman Hollow—valley OK-5
Boughton—locale PA-2
**Boughton**—pop pl (2) AR-4
Boughton Canal—canal WY-8
Boughton Cem—cemetery MI-6
Boughton Cem—cemetery OH-6
Boughton Creek—stream KS-7
Boughton Drain—canal MI-6
Boughton/Haight House—hist pl NY-2
Boughton Hill—hist pl NY-2
**Boughton Hill**—pop pl NY-2
Boughton Sch—school (2) MI-6
Boughton (Township of)—fmr MCD AR-4
**Boughtonville**—pop pl OH-6
Boug Inlet NC-3
Bougner Lake MI-6
Bouguefong Creek MS-4
Bouguet Mountain NY-2
Bouic Cem—cemetery OH-6
Bouie Cem—cemetery MS-4
Bouie Creek MS-4
Bouie River MS-4
Bouie Street Baptist Ch—church MS-4
Bouillon, Bayou—gut LA-4
Bouillon, Bayou—stream LA-4
Bouis Bridge CA-9
Boujan Swale—gut IL-6
Bouknight—locale SC-3
Bouknight, Simon, House—hist pl SC-3
Bouknight Cem—cemetery SC-3
Bouknight Pond—reservoir SC-3
Boulanger Island—island MI-6
Boulanger Landing—locale OK-5
**Boulangerville**—pop pl OK-5
Boulan Park—park MI-6
Boulaway Mine—mine MT-8
Boulde Creek OR-9
Boulden Chapel—church MD-2
Boulden Hill—summit WA-9
Boulden Ranch—locale WY-8
Boulder UT-8
Boulder—locale ID-8
Boulder—locale VA-3
**Boulder**—pop pl CO-8
**Boulder**—pop pl IL-6
**Boulder**—pop pl MT-8
**Boulder**—pop pl UT-8
**Boulder**—pop pl WY-8
Boulder Access Area—locale IL-6
Boulder and Larimer County Reservoir CO-8
Boulder and Left-hand Ditch—canal CO-8
Boulder and Weld County Ditch—canal CO-8
Boulder and Whiterock Ditch—canal CO-8
Boulder Baldy—summit MT-8
Boulder Basin—basin AZ-5
Boulder Basin—basin (3) ID-8
Boulder Basin—basin MT-8
Boulder Basin—basin (2) NV-8
Boulder Basin—basin UT-8
Boulder Basin—basin WY-8
Boulder Basin Trail—trail (2) WY-8
Boulder Bay—bay (3) AK-9
Boulder Bay—bay CA-9
Boulder Bay—bay (3) MN-6
Boulder Bay—bay NY-2
**Boulder Bay**—pop pl CA-9
Boulder Beach—beach NV-8
Boulder Beach Campground—locale NV-8
Boulder Bobs Cabin—locale AZ-5
Boulder Branch—stream NC-3
Boulder Bridge—bridge DC-2
Boulder Bridge and Ross Drive Bridge—hist pl DC-2
**Boulder Brook**—pop pl DE-2
Boulder Brook—stream CO-8
Boulder Brook—stream ME-1
Boulder Brook—stream MA-1
Boulder Brook—stream (2) NY-2
Boulder Brook Trail—trail CO-8
Boulder Butte—summit OR-9
Boulder Butte—summit WA-9
Boulder Cabin—hist pl OK-5
Boulder Camp—locale OK-5
Boulder Campground AZ-5
Boulder Camp (site)—locale OR-9
Boulder Canal ID-8
Boulder Canal—canal WY-8
Boulder Canyon AZ-5
Boulder Canyon UT-8
Boulder Canyon—valley (7) AZ-5
Boulder Canyon—valley (7) CA-9
Boulder Canyon—valley (2) ID-8
Boulder Canyon—valley (3) NV-8
Boulder Canyon—valley (2) NM-5
Boulder Canyon—valley OR-9
Boulder Canyon—valley SD-7
Boulder Canyon—valley TX-5
Boulder Canyon—valley (2) UT-8
Boulder Canyon Tank Number One—reservoir AZ-5
Boulder Canyon Tank Number Two—reservoir AZ-5
Boulder Canyon Trail—trail WY-8
Boulder Cave—cave WA-9
Boulder Cave Campground—locale WA-9
Boulder Cem—cemetery IA-7
Boulder Cem—cemetery MT-8
Boulder Cem—cemetery UT-8
Boulder Cem—cemetery WY-8
Boulder Ch—church IA-7
Boulder Chain Lakes—lake ID-8
Boulder Chain Lakes Creek—stream ID-8
Boulder Chief Mine—mine MT-8
Boulder Chief Park—flat MT-8
**Boulder City**—pop pl MO-7
**Boulder City**—pop pl NV-8
Boulder City Aqueduct—canal CO-8
Boulder City Hist Dist—hist pl NV-8
Boulder City Lateral—canal NV-8
Boulder City Municipal Airp—airport (2) NV-8
Boulder Corral—locale OR-9
Boulder Country Club—other CO-8
Boulder County Hill—summit CO-8
Boulder County Mine—mine CO-8
Boulder County Tunnel—mine CO-8
Boulder Cove—bay NH-1
Boulder Creek AZ-5
Boulder Creek CA-9
Boulder Creek CO-8
Boulder Creek ID-8
Boulder Creek OR-9
Boulder Creek UT-8
Boulder Creek WA-9
**Boulder Creek**—pop pl CA-9
Boulder Creek—stream (11) AK-9
Boulder Creek—stream (5) AZ-5
Boulder Creek—stream AR-4
Boulder Creek—stream (26) CA-9
Boulder Creek—stream (4) CO-8
Boulder Creek—stream (24) ID-8
Boulder Creek—stream IA-7
Boulder Creek—stream MI-6
Boulder Creek—stream MN-6
Boulder Creek—stream (11) MT-8
Boulder Creek—stream (6) NV-8
Boulder Creek—stream NM-5
Boulder Creek—stream (38) OR-9
Boulder Creek—stream SD-7
Boulder Creek—stream (4) UT-8
Boulder Creek—stream (24) WA-9
Boulder Creek—stream WI-6
Boulder Creek—stream (7) WY-8
Boulder Creek Campground—locale CA-9
Boulder Creek Campground—locale CO-8
Boulder Creek Campground—locale MT-8
Boulder Creek Campground—park OR-9
Boulder Creek Cem—cemetery ID-8
Boulder Creek Flats—flat AK-9
Boulder Creek Golf and Country Club—locale CA-9
Boulder Creek Lake CA-9
Boulder Creek Lakes—lake CA-9
Boulder Creek Meadows—swamp OR-9
Boulder Creek Trail—trail AZ-5
Boulder Creek Trail—trail OR-9
Boulder Creek Work Center—locale CA-9
Boulder Crescent Place Hist Dist—hist pl CO-8
Boulder Crest Sch—school GA-3
Boulder Cuesta—ridge NV-8
Boulder Dam AZ-5
Boulder Dam NV-8
Boulder Dam—dam AZ-5
Boulder Dam—dam NV-8
Boulder Dam Hotel—hist pl NV-8
Boulder Dam Natl Rec Area AZ-5
Boulder Dam Spring—spring AZ-5
Boulder Dam Tank—reservoir AZ-5
Boulder Ditch—canal CO-8
Boulder Ditch—canal ID-8
Boulder Divide—ridge ID-8
Boulder Driveway Trail—trail ID-8
Boulder East Oil Field—other IL-6
Boulder Elem Sch—hist pl UT-8

Boulder Falls—*falls* CO-8
Boulder Falls—*falls* MT-8
Boulder Falls—*falls* WA-9
Boulder Feeder Canal—*canal* CO-8
Boulder Feeder Ditch—*canal* CO-8
Boulder Field—*flat* NV-8
Boulder Field—*locale* PA-2
Boulder Field Trail—*trail* PA-2
Boulder Filtration Plant—*other* CO-8
Boulder Fish Hatchery—*locale* WY-8
*Boulder Flat* NV-8
Boulder Flat—*flat* (3) CA-9
Boulder Flat—*flat* (2) ID-8
Boulder Flat—*flat* (2) NV-8
Boulder Flat Campground—*park* OR-9
Boulder Flat Creek—*stream* CA-9
Boulder Flat (Depression)—*flat* NV-8
Boulder Flats—*other* AK-9
Boulder Ford Camp—*locale* WA-9
Boulder Fork—*stream* MO-7
Boulder Fork Cem—*cemetery* MO-7
Boulder Fortress (LA 55828)—*hist pl* NM-5
Boulder Glacier—*glacier* MT-8
Boulder Glacier—*glacier* WA-9
Boulder-Grand Pass—*gap* CO-8
Boulder Group Mine—*mine* OR-9
*Boulder Gulch* CA-9
*Boulder Gulch* WY-8
Boulder Gulch—*valley* AK-9
Boulder Gulch—*valley* (2) CA-9
Boulder Gulch—*valley* (3) CO-8
Boulder Gulch—*valley* (2) MT-8
Boulder Gulch—*valley* WY-8
Boulder Gulch Campground—*locale* CA-9
Boulder Harbor—*bay* NV-8
*Boulder Hill* WA-9
Boulder Hill—*CDP* IL-6
Boulder Hill—*summit* AK-9
Boulder Hill—*summit* CA-9
Boulder Hill—*summit* NV-8
Boulder Hill—*summit* SD-7
Boulder Hill Lookout Tower—*locale* MN-6
Boulder Hill Mine (historical)—*mine* NV-8
Boulder Hill Park—*park* CA-9
Boulder Hill Pond—*reservoir* MA-1
Boulder Hill Pond Dam—*dam* MA-1
Boulder (historical)—*locale* SD-7
Boulder Hot Springs—*locale* MT-8
Boulder Hot Springs Hotel—*hist pl* MT-8
*Boulder House* UT-8
Boulder Inn—*locale* AZ-5
Boulder Island—*island* ME-1
Boulder Island—*island* SC-3
Boulder Island—*island* WA-9
Boulder Island—*island* WY-8
*Boulder Islands* NV-8
Boulder Islands—*island* NV-8
Boulder Junction—*locale* CO-8
Boulder Junction—*locale* NV-8
**Boulder Junction**—*pop pl* WI-6
**Boulder Junction (Town of)**—*pop pl* WI-6
*Boulder Lake* MN-6
*Boulder Lake* NM-5
Boulder Lake—*lake* (2) AK-9
Boulder Lake—*lake* CA-9
Boulder Lake—*lake* (3) CO-8
Boulder Lake—*lake* CT-1
Boulder Lake—*lake* (3) ID-8
Boulder Lake—*lake* IL-6
Boulder Lake—*lake* (3) MN-6
Boulder Lake—*lake* (2) MT-8
Boulder Lake—*lake* NV-8
Boulder Lake—*lake* (2) OR-9
Boulder Lake—*lake* (4) WA-9
Boulder Lake—*lake* (2) WI-6
**Boulder Lake**—*pop pl* CT-1
Boulder Lake—*reservoir* CO-8
Boulder Lake—*reservoir* PA-2
Boulder Lake—*reservoir* WY-8
Boulder Lake Campground—*locale* WI-6
Boulder Lake Ranch—*locale* WY-8
*Boulder Lake Reservoir* NM-5
Boulder Lake Rsvr—*reservoir* CO-8
Boulder Lake Rsvr—*reservoir* MN-6
Boulder Lake Rsvr No 4—*reservoir* WY-8
Boulder Lake Rsvr No 7—*reservoir* WY-8
Boulder Lakes—*lake* ID-8
Boulder Lakes—*lake* (3) MT-8
Boulder Lake Shelter—*locale* WA-9
Boulder Lakes Trail—*trail* MT-8
Boulder Lake Trail—*trail* ID-8
Boulder Lake Trail—*trail* OR-9
Boulder Lake Trail—*trail* WA-9
Boulder Lake Way Trail—*trail* OR-9
Boulder Lookout Tower—*locale* WI-6
Boulder Mail Trail—*trail* UT-8
Boulder Meadows—*flat* ID-8
Boulder Meadows—*flat* UT-8
Boulder Meadows Rsvr—*reservoir* ID-8
Boulder Mesa—*summit* UT-8
Boulder Mine—*mine* AZ-5
Boulder Mine—*mine* (2) CA-9
Boulder Mine—*mine* (3) ID-8
*Boulder Mountain* UT-8
Boulder Mountain Park—*park* CO-8
Boulder Mountain Spring—*spring* AZ-5
*Boulder Mtn* AZ-5
Boulder Mtn—*summit* (2) AZ-5
Boulder Mtn—*summit* AR-4
Boulder Mtn—*summit* (2) CO-8
Boulder Mtn—*summit* (3) ID-8
Boulder Mtn—*summit* (3) MT-8
Boulder Mtn—*summit* NV-8
Boulder Mtn—*summit* (3) UT-8
Boulder Mtn—*summit* WA-9
Boulder Mtns—*range* ID-8
Boulder Municipal Airp—*airport* CO-8
Boulder Narrows—*gap* AZ-5
Boulder Nest Mine—*mine* CO-8
Boulder Oaks—*locale* CA-9
**Boulder Oaks**—*pop pl* CA-9
Boulder Park—*flat* (3) CO-8
Boulder Park—*flat* SD-7
Boulder Park—*flat* WA-9
Boulder Park—*park* OK-5
**Boulder Park**—*pop pl* CA-9
**Boulder Park**—*pop pl* MI-6
Boulder Park Campground—*locale* WY-8
Boulder Park Campground—*park* OR-9
Boulder Park Resort—*locale* OR-9
Boulder Park Resort Airstrip—*airport* OR-9
Boulder Park Sch—*school* SD-7
*Boulder Pass* CO-8
*Boulder Pass* ID-8
Boulder Pass—*gap* AZ-5
Boulder Pass—*gap* ID-8
Boulder Pass—*gap* (2) MT-8
Boulder Pass—*gap* OR-9
Boulder Pass—*gap* WA-9
Boulder Pass Trail—*trail* MT-8
Boulder Patch—*bar* AK-9
*Boulder Peak* CA-9
*Boulder Peak* MT-8
*Boulder Peak* TX-5
Boulder Peak—*summit* (5) CA-9
Boulder Peak—*summit* ID-8
Boulder Peak—*summit* (2) MT-8
Boulder Peak—*summit* NV-8
Boulder Peak—*summit* OR-9
Boulder Peak—*summit* WA-9
Boulder Point—*cape* (4) AK-9
Boulder Point—*cape* CA-9
Boulder Point—*cape* NV-8
Boulder Point—*cape* OR-9
Boulder Point—*cape* (2) UT-8
Boulder Point—*locale* PA-2
Boulder Point—*summit* (2) MT-8
Boulder Point—*summit* ND-7
Boulder Point—*summit* OR-9
Boulder Pond—*lake* ME-1
Boulder Pond—*lake* OR-9
**Boulder (Rangoon Post Office)**—*pop pl* WV-2
Boulder Rapids—*rapids* ID-8
Boulder Rapids—*rapids* OR-9
Boulder Recreation Site One Hundred Forty Eight—*park* AZ-5
Boulder Reef—*bar* MI-6
Boulder Reef—*bar* WA-9
Boulder Ridge—*ridge* AK-9
Boulder Ridge—*ridge* (2) CA-9
Boulder Ridge—*ridge* CO-8
Boulder Ridge—*ridge* MT-8
Boulder Ridge—*ridge* (4) OR-9
Boulder Ridge—*ridge* WA-9
Boulder Ridge—*ridge* (2) WY-8
Boulder Ridge Trail—*trail* MT-8
*Boulder River* MN-6
*Boulder River* MT-8
Boulder River—*stream* MN-6
Boulder River—*stream* (2) MT-8
Boulder River—*stream* WA-9
Boulder Rock—*pillar* OR-9
Boulder (RR name for Rangoon)—*other* WV-2
Boulder Rsvr—*reservoir* CO-8
Boulder Rsvr—*reservoir* NV-8
Boulder Rsvr—*reservoir* OR-9
Boulder Run—*stream* IN-6
Boulder Run—*stream* WV-2
Boulders, The—*summit* AZ-5
Boulders, The—*summit* MA-1
Boulder Sch—*school* NV-8
Boulder Sch—*school* UT-8
Boulders Golf Course—*other* AZ-5
Boulder Shelter—*locale* WA-9
Boulder Spring—*spring* (2) AZ-5
Boulder Spring—*spring* CA-9
Boulder Spring—*spring* ID-8
Boulder Spring—*spring* (4) NV-8
Boulder Spring—*spring* (5) OR-9
Boulder Spring—*spring* UT-8
Boulder Spring—*spring* WA-9
Boulder Spring Number 2—*spring* OR-9
*Boulder Springs* OR-9
Boulder Springs—*spring* OR-9
Boulder Station—*locale* MT-8
Boulder Summit—*summit* ID-8
Boulder Swale—*valley* UT-8
Boulder Tank—*reservoir* (11) AZ-5
Boulder Tank—*reservoir* (3) NM-5
Boulder Tank—*reservoir* (5) TX-5
Boulder Top—*summit* UT-8
Boulder Town—*locale* UT-8
**Boulder Town (Boulder Post Office)**—*pop pl* UT-8
Boulder Township—*fmr MCD* IA-7
*Boulder Trail* OR-9
Boulder Trail—*trail* AZ-5
Boulder Turnoff—*locale* OK-5
*Boulder Valley* MT-8
Boulder Valley—*valley* MT-8
Boulder Valley—*valley* NV-8
Boulder Valley Ch—*church* MT-8
Boulder Valley Grange No. 131—*hist pl* CO-8
Boulder Valley Mine—*mine* CO-8
Boulderville Ditch—*canal* UT-8
Boulder Wash—*stream* (2) NV-8
Boulder Wash—*valley* AZ-5
Boulder Waterhole—*reservoir* OR-9
Boulder Well—*well* (2) AZ-5
Boulder Windmill—*locale* NV-8
Bouldin Branch—*stream* TN-4
Bouldin Cave—*cave* AL-4
Bouldin Cem—*cemetery* AL-4
Boulding Branch—*stream* NC-3
Boulding Creek—*stream* NC-3
Bouldin-Hammond Cem—*cemetery* AL-4
Bouldin Island—*island* CA-9
Bouldin Lake—*lake* TX-5
Bouldin Memorial Ch—*church* VA-3
Bouldin Point—*cape* AL-4
*Bouler Lake* CO-8
Boulet Canon, Bayou—*stream* LA-4
Boulevard—*locale* CA-9
Boulevard—*other* VA-3
**Boulevard**—*pop pl* OH-6
Boulevard—*uninc pl* (2) FL-3
Boulevard—*uninc pl* NY-2
Boulevard—*uninc pl* NC-3
Boulevard—*uninc pl* OK-5
Boulevard—*uninc pl* PA-2
Boulevard, The—*ridge* TN-4
Boulevard Bend Shop Ctr—*locale* KS-7
Boulevard Bible Ch—*church* FL-3
Boulevard Bridge—*bridge* VA-3
Boulevard Business Center—*locale* NC-3
Boulevard Canyon—*valley* UT-8
Boulevard Cave—*cave* CA-9
Boulevard Ch—*church* (2) NC-3
Boulevard Ch—*church* OH-6
Boulevard Ch—*church* (2) PA-2
Boulevard Ch—*church* TX-5
Boulevard Chapel—*church* FL-3
Boulevard Christian Sch—*school* ID-8
Boulevard Creek—*stream* (2) AK-9
Boulevard Creek—*stream* WA-9
**Boulevard Estates**—*pop pl* VA-3
Boulevard Gardens—*uninc pl* CA-9
**Boulevard Heights**—*pop pl* MD-2
Boulevard Heights—*uninc pl* FL-3
Boulevard Heights Elem Sch—*school* FL-3
Boulevard Hist Dist—*hist pl* GA-3
Boulevard Hist Dist—*hist pl* VA-3
Boulevard Hosp—*hospital* NY-2
Boulevard Mall Shop Ctr—*locale* NY-2
*Boulevard Manor* IL-6
**Boulevard Manor**—*pop pl* PA-2
**Boulevard Manor**—*pop pl* VA-3
Boulevard Memorial Park—*cemetery* WV-2
Boulevard Park—*CDP* WA-9
Boulevard Plaza—*locale* KS-7
Boulevard Plaza (Shop Ctr)—*locale* FL-3
Boulevard Private Sch—*school* FL-3
Boulevard Prong—*stream* TN-4
Boulevard Ridge—*ridge* UT-8
Boulevard RR Station—*locale* FL-3
Boulevard Sch—*school* CO-8
Boulevard Sch—*school* FL-3
Boulevard Sch—*school* LA-4
Boulevard Sch—*school* NY-2
Boulevard Sch—*school* (2) OH-6
Boulevard Sch—*school* WI-6
Boulevard Shop Ctr—*locale* FL-3
Boulevard Shop Ctr—*other* CO-8
**Boulevard Subdivision**—*pop pl* UT-8
Boulevard Subdivision Hist Dist—*hist pl* MS-4
Boulevard Trail (pack)—*trail* OR-9
Boulger Canyon—*valley* UT-8
Boulger Rsvr—*reservoir* UT-8
Boulin Tank—*reservoir* AZ-5
Boulin Trick Tank—*locale* AZ-5
Bouller Park—*park* CO-8
Bouller Tank—*reservoir* CO-8
Boulley Brook—*stream* VT-1
**Boulogne**—*pop pl* FL-3
Boult, H. P., House—*hist pl* IL-6
Boulter—*locale* UT-8
**Boulter**—*pop pl* UT-8
Boulter Cem—*cemetery* ME-1
Boulter Creek—*stream* UT-8
Boulter JHS—*school* TX-5
Boulter Lake—*lake* WY-8
*Boulter Mountains* UT-8
Boulter Pass—*gap* UT-8
Boulter Peak—*summit* UT-8
Boulter Pond—*reservoir* ME-1
*Boulter Ridge* UT-8
Boulter Springs—*spring* UT-8
Boulter Summit—*summit* UT-8
Boulter Well—*well* NM-5
Boultinghouse Mtn—*summit* TX-5
**Boulton**—*pop pl* PA-2
Boulton Bend—*bend* TN-4
Boulton Drain—*canal* MI-6
**Boultons Beach**—*pop pl* NY-2
Boulton Sch—*school* UT-8
**Boulton Subdivision**—*pop pl* UT-8
Boulware Cave—*cave* MO-7
Boulware Cem—*cemetery* KS-7
Boulware Ford (Abandoned)—*locale* MO-7
Boulware Mound Group Archeol Site—*hist pl* MO-7
Boulware Pond—*reservoir* VA-3
Boulware Spring Waterworks—*hist pl* FL-3
Boulware Township—*civil* MO-7
Bounce—*locale* TX-5
Bounce Mine—*mine* NV-8
Bouncing Brook—*stream* MA-1
Bouncing Rock—*locale* WY-8
Boundary—*locale* AK-9
Boundary—*locale* WA-9
Boundary Bald Mtn—*summit* ME-1
Boundary Basin—*basin* CA-9
*Boundary Bay* WA-9
Boundary Bay—*bay* WA-9
Boundary Bluff—*cliff* WA-9
Boundary Bridge—*bridge* DC-2
*Boundary Brook* MA-1
Boundary Brook—*stream* ME-1
Boundary Butte—*summit* AZ-5
Boundary Butte—*summit* (2) NV-8
Boundary Butte—*summit* ND-7
Boundary Butte—*summit* (2) OR-9
Boundary Butte—*summit* (2) UT-8
Boundary Butte—*summit* (2) WA-9
Boundary Butte Mesa—*summit* UT-8
Boundary Campground—*locale* ID-8
Boundary Campground—*park* OR-9
Boundary Canal—*canal* NC-3
Boundary Canyon—*valley* (2) CA-9
Boundary Canyon—*valley* NV-8
Boundary Canyon—*valley* NM-5
Boundary Ch—*church* OH-6
*Boundary Channel* WA-9
Boundary Channel—*channel* DC-2
Boundary Channel—*channel* VA-3
**Boundary City**—*pop pl* IN-6
Boundary Cone—*summit* AZ-5
Boundary Cottage—*locale* ME-1
Boundary County Courthouse—*hist pl* ID-8
*Boundary Creek* WA-9
Boundary Creek—*stream* (4) AK-9
Boundary Creek—*stream* (3) CA-9
Boundary Creek—*stream* (8) ID-8
Boundary Creek—*stream* (2) MT-8
Boundary Creek—*stream* NJ-2
Boundary Creek—*stream* NC-3
Boundary Creek—*stream* (2) ND-7
Boundary Creek—*stream* (5) OR-9
Boundary Creek—*stream* UT-8
Boundary Creek—*stream* (6) WA-9
Boundary Creek—*stream* (2) WY-8
Boundary Creek Forest Service Station—*locale* OR-9
Boundary Creek Patrol Cabin—*locale* WY-8
Boundary Creek Trail—*trail* WY-8
Boundary Creek 3 Dam—*dam* ND-7
Boundary Dam—*dam* WA-9
Boundary Drain—*canal* CA-9
Boundary Drain—*stream* CA-9
Boundary Drain Number Five—*canal* CA-9
Boundary Drain Number Five-two—*canal* CA-9
Boundary Drain Number One—*stream* CA-9
Boundary Draw—*valley* MT-8
Boundary Draw Spring—*spring* MT-8
Boundary Glacier—*glacier* (2) AK-9
*Boundary Guard Station* OR-9
Boundary Guard Station—*locale* WA-9
Boundary Gulch—*valley* ID-8
Boundary Gulch—*valley* WY-8
Boundary Hill—*summit* AZ-5
Boundary Hill—*summit* CA-9
Boundary Hill—*summit* IN-6
Boundary Hill—*summit* NV-8
Boundary Lake—*lake* (2) AK-9
Boundary Lake—*lake* CA-9
Boundary Lake—*lake* ND-7
Boundary Lake—*lake* (2) WA-9
Boundary Lake—*lake* WI-6
Boundary Lakes—*lake* WA-9
Boundary Ledges—*bar* ME-1
Boundary Line Ch—*church* IN-6
Boundary Line Trail—*trail* PA-2
Boundary Marker No. 1—*hist pl* WA-9
Boundary Mine (historical)—*mine* AZ-5
Boundary Mound—*summit* IN-6
*Boundary Mountains* AZ-5
*Boundary Mountains* NM-5
Boundary Mountains—*ridge* MT-8
Boundary Mtn—*summit* AR-4
Boundary Mtn—*summit* MT-8
Boundary Mtn—*summit* (2) WA-9
Boundary Oak—*locale* KY-4
*Boundary Pass* OR-9
*Boundary Pass* WA-9
Boundary Pass—*channel* WA-9
*Boundary Peak* NV-8
Boundary Peak—*other* (3) AK-9
Boundary Peak—*summit* (4) AK-9
Boundary Peak—*summit* CA-9
Boundary Peak—*summit* (2) ID-8
Boundary Peak—*summit* NV-8
Boundary Peak—*summit* NM-5
Boundary Peak—*summit* NY-2
Boundary Peak—*summit* WA-9
Boundary Peak Trail—*trail* ID-8
Boundary Peak 100—*summit* AK-9
Boundary Peak 101—*summit* AK-9
Boundary Peak 102—*summit* AK-9
Boundary Peak 103—*summit* AK-9
Boundary Peak 104—*summit* AK-9
Boundary Peak 105—*summit* AK-9
Boundary Peak 106—*summit* AK-9
Boundary Peak 108—*summit* AK-9
Boundary Peak 109—*summit* AK-9
Boundary Peak 111—*summit* AK-9
Boundary Peak 144—*summit* AK-9
Boundary Peak 150—*summit* AK-9
Boundary Peak 151—*summit* AK-9
Boundary Peak 154—*summit* AK-9
Boundary Peak 155—*summit* AK-9
Boundary Peak 156—*summit* AK-9
Boundary Peak 157—*summit* AK-9
Boundary Peak 158—*summit* AK-9
Boundary Peak 159—*summit* AK-9
Boundary Peak 16—*other* AK-9
Boundary Peak 160—*summit* AK-9
Boundary Peak 161—*summit* AK-9
Boundary Peak 162—*other* AK-9
Boundary Peak 166—*summit* AK-9
Boundary Peak 167—*summit* AK-9
Boundary Peak 176—*summit* AK-9
Boundary Peak 177—*summit* AK-9
Boundary Peak 178—*summit* AK-9
Boundary Peak 179—*summit* AK-9
Boundary Peak 18—*other* AK-9
Boundary Peak 180—*summit* AK-9
Boundary Peak 181—*summit* AK-9
Boundary Peak 182—*summit* AK-9
Boundary Peak 183—*summit* AK-9
Boundary Peak 184—*summit* AK-9
Boundary Peak 185—*summit* AK-9
Boundary Peak 186—*summit* AK-9
Boundary Peak 187—*summit* AK-9
Boundary Peak 47—*other* AK-9
Boundary Peak 48—*other* AK-9
Boundary Peak 69—*other* AK-9
Boundary Peak 70—*other* AK-9
Boundary Peak 71—*other* AK-9
Boundary Peak 72—*other* AK-9
Boundary Peak 73—*other* AK-9
Boundary Peak 74—*other* AK-9
Boundary Peak 75—*other* AK-9
Boundary Peak 76—*other* AK-9
Boundary Peak 77—*other* AK-9
Boundary Peak 78—*other* AK-9
Boundary Peak 79—*other* AK-9
Boundary Peak 83—*other* AK-9
Boundary Peak 84—*other* AK-9
Boundary Peak 85—*other* AK-9
Boundary Peak 86—*other* AK-9
Boundary Peak 93—*summit* AK-9
Boundary Peak 96—*other* AK-9
Boundary Peak 98—*other* AK-9
Boundary Picnic Ground—*park* OR-9
Boundary Point—*cape* NV-8
Boundary Point—*cape* WA-9
Boundary Point—*summit* ID-8
Boundary Pond—*lake* ME-1
Boundary Pond—*lake* NH-1
Boundary Pond—*lake* NY-2
*Boundary Red Mountain* WA-9
Boundary Ridge—*ridge* AZ-5
Boundary Ridge—*ridge* CA-9
Boundary Ridge—*ridge* ID-8
Boundary Ridge—*ridge* WA-9
Boundary Roadhouse—*locale* AK-9
Boundary Rsvr—*reservoir* (2) MT-8
Boundary Rsvr—*reservoir* OR-9
Boundary Spring—*reservoir* AZ-5
Boundary Spring—*spring* (3) AZ-5
Boundary Spring—*spring* ID-8
Boundary Spring—*spring* (5) OR-9
Boundary Spring—*spring* (4) UT-8
Boundary Spring—*spring* WY-8
Boundary Springs—*spring* OR-9
Boundary Street-Newberry Cotton Mills Hist Dist—*hist pl* SC-3
Boundary Street Sch—*school* SC-3
Boundary Tank—*reservoir* (10) AZ-5
Boundary Tank—*reservoir* NM-5
Boundary Tanks—*reservoir* AZ-5
Boundary Trail—*trail* CA-9
Boundary Trail—*trail* (2) MT-8
Boundary Trail—*trail* (2) OR-9
Boundary Trail—*trail* (2) PA-2
Boundary Trail—*trail* (3) WA-9
Boundary Trail—*trail* WV-2
Boundary Trail—*trail* WY-8
*Boundbreak* NJ-2
*Bound Brook* MA-1
*Boundbrook* NJ-2
**Bound Brook**—*pop pl* (2) NJ-2
Bound Brook—*stream* (2) MA-1
Bound Brook—*stream* NJ-2
**Bound Brook Heights**—*pop pl* NJ-2
Bound Brook Island—*summit* MA-1
Bound Brook Junction—*locale* NJ-2
Bound Brook Number One—*airport* NJ-2
Bound Brook Number Two—*airport* NJ-2
Bound Brook Pond—*reservoir* MA-1
Bound Brook Pond Dam—*dam* MA-1
*Bound Brook Reservoir* NJ-2
Bound Brook Station—*hist pl* NJ-2
Bound Cem—*cemetery* IN-6
*Bound Creek* NJ-2
Bounde Creek—*stream* CA-9
Bounder Pond—*lake* MD-2
*Bound Pond* MA-1
Bound Rock—*pillar* MA-1
Bound Rock—*rock* NH-1
*Boundry* IN-6
**Boundry**—*pop pl* IN-6
Boundry Hills—*range* UT-8
Boundry Hollow—*valley* MO-7
Boundry Peak—*summit* AK-9
Bounds—*locale* MS-4
**Bounds**—*pop pl* MO-7
Bounds, Lake—*lake* MS-4
*Bounds Bay* FL-3
Bounds Bldg—*hist pl* AR-4
Bounds Branch—*stream* LA-4
Bounds Branch—*stream* MO-7
Bounds Cave—*cave* MS-4
Bounds Cem—*cemetery* MS-4
Bounds Cem—*cemetery* (2) TN-4
Bounds Ch—*church* TX-5
*Bounds Creek* ID-8
Bounds Creek—*stream* ID-8
Bounds Creek—*stream* MO-7
Bounds Creek—*stream* (2) OR-9
Bounds Crossing—*locale* FL-3
Bounds Crossroads—*locale* MS-4
Bounds Cross Roads Cem—*cemetery* MS-4
Bounds Hollow—*valley* TN-4
Bounds Lake—*lake* MS-4
Bounds Lake—*reservoir* AL-4
Bounds Lake Dam—*dam* (3) MS-4
Bounds Lott—*hist pl* MD-2
Bounds Mill (historical)—*locale* MS-4
Bounds Pond—*lake* WA-9
Bounds Pond Dam—*dam* MS-4
Bounds Post Office (historical)—*building* MS-4
Bounds Ranch—*locale* NM-5
Bounds Schoolhouse (historical)—*school* MS-4
Bound Swamp—*swamp* CT-1
Bounds Windmill—*locale* NM-5
**Bountiful**—*pop pl* CO-8
**Bountiful**—*pop pl* UT-8
**Bountiful Acres Subdivision**—*pop pl* UT-8
Bountiful Christian Ch—*church* UT-8
Bountiful Community Ch—*church* UT-8
*Bountiful Garden Apartment Homes* UT-8
**Bountiful Gardens Apartment Homes**—*pop pl* UT-8
**Bountiful Heights Subdivision**—*pop pl* UT-8
**Bountiful Hills Estates (subdivision)**—*pop pl* UT-8
Bountiful HS—*school* UT-8
Bountiful JHS—*school* UT-8
**Bountiful Lake Hills Subdivision**—*pop pl* UT-8
Bountiful Lateral—*canal* CO-8
Bountiful Memorial Park—*cemetery* UT-8
**Bountiful Park Subdivision**—*pop pl* UT-8
Bountiful Peak—*summit* UT-8
Bountiful Peak Campground—*locale* UT-8
Bountiful Peak Overlook—*locale* UT-8
Bountiful Peak Picnic Area—*locale* UT-8
Bountiful Sch—*school* UT-8
*Bountifuls Lake Hills Subdivision* UT-8
Bountiful Spring—*spring* UT-8
Bountiful Tabernacle—*hist pl* UT-8
**Bountiful Townhouses PUD (subdivision)**—*pop pl* UT-8
Bounty—*locale* ND-7
Bounty Cove—*bay* ME-1
Bounty Lake—*lake* OR-9
**Bounty Land**—*pop pl* SC-3
Bounty Sch—*school* ND-7
Bouplon Corner—*locale* VT-1
Bouque Creek—*stream* IA-7
*Bouquet* (2) NY-2
*Bouquet* PA-2
Bouquet—*other* PA-2
Bouquet, Jean, Historic/Archeol District—*hist pl* NM-5
Bouquet Campground Number Four—*locale* CA-9
Bouquet Campground Number Three—*locale* CA-9
Bouquet Canyon—*valley* CA-9
Bouquet Canyon Dam—*dam* CA-9
Bouquet Guard Station—*locale* CA-9
Bouquet Junction—*locale* CA-9
Bouquet Pipeline—*other* CA-9
Bouquet Ranch—*locale* AZ-5
*Bouquet River* NY-2
*Bouquet River Point* NY-2
Bouquet Rsvr—*reservoir* CA-9
Bouquet Table—*summit* SD-7
Bourassa Lake—*lake* MN-6
Bourassas Point—*cape* MI-6
Bourbanis Dam—*dam* ND-7
Bourbe, Bayou—*stream* LA-4
Bourbeaux, Bayou—*gut* LA-4
Bourbeaux, Bayou—*stream* (2) LA-4
*Bourbeaúx Bayou* LA-4
*Bourbeax Bayou* LA-4
*Bourbeuse River* SD-7
Bourbeuse River—*stream* MO-7
Bourbeux, Bayou—*lake* LA-4
Bourbeux, Bayou—*stream* LA-4
*Bourbeux Bayou* LA-4
Bourbois Township—*civil* MO-7
Bourbon—*locale* OR-9
**Bourbon**—*pop pl* IL-6
**Bourbon**—*pop pl* IN-6
**Bourbon**—*pop pl* KY-4
**Bourbon**—*pop pl* MS-4
**Bourbon**—*pop pl* (2) MO-7
Bourbonais Creek—*stream* KS-7
Bourbonais Creek—*stream* OK-5
Bourbon County—*civil* KS-7
**Bourbon (County)**—*pop pl* KY-4
Bourbon County Courthouse—*hist pl* KY-4
Bourbon County Dam—*dam* KS-7
Bourbon County State Lake—*reservoir* KS-7
Bourbon County State Lake Dam—*dam* KS-7
Bourbon County State Park—*park* KS-7
Bourbon Creek—*stream* AK-9
Bourbon Creek—*stream* WA-9
Bourbon Furnace (Ruins)—*locale* KY-4
Bourbon Hollow—*valley* KY-4
Bourbon Iron Works—*hist pl* KY-4
Bourbon Lake—*reservoir* UT-8
Bourbon Mist Island—*island* AK-9
**Bourbonnais**—*pop pl* IL-6
**Bourbonnais (Township of)**—*pop pl* IL-6
Bourbon Oil Field—*oilfield* MS-4
Bourbon Post Office (historical)—*building* MS-4
Bourbon Spring—*spring* OR-9
Bourbon Springs—*locale* KY-4
Bourbon State Fishing Lake And Wildlife Ref—*park* KS-7
*Bourbonton* MO-7
Bourbon Township—*civil* (3) MO-7
**Bourbon (Township of)**—*pop pl* IL-6
**Bourbon (Township of)**—*pop pl* IN-6
*Bourbony Creek* KS-7
Bourdette Draw—*valley* UT-8
Bourdeux Lake—*reservoir* LA-4
Bourdieu Valley—*valley* CA-9
Bourdon Cem—*cemetery* IL-6
Bourdon Creek—*stream* VA-3
*Bourdon Spring* OR-9
Bourdon Tank—*reservoir* AZ-5
Bourdon Windmill—*locale* AZ-5
Bouret Dam—*dam* ND-7
Bourett Cem—*cemetery* ND-7
Bourett Dam—*dam* ND-7
**Bourg**—*pop pl* LA-4
Bourgate HS—*school* AZ-5
Bourgeau Lake—*lake* WA-9
Bourgeois Canal—*canal* LA-4
Bourgeois Landing—*locale* LA-4
Bourg Gas Field—*oilfield* LA-4
Bourghs Creek—*stream* TX-5
Bourgois Lake—*lake* MI-6
Bourgowich Sch (abandoned)—*school* MO-7
**Bour (historical)**—*pop pl* OR-9
Bourke Canyon—*valley* AZ-5
Bourke Point—*cliff* AZ-5
Bourke Tank—*reservoir* AZ-5
Bourland Canyon—*valley* TX-5
Bourland Cem—*cemetery* AR-4
Bourland Cem—*cemetery* MS-4
Bourland Cem—*cemetery* OK-5
Bourland Cem—*cemetery* (2) TX-5
Bourland Creek—*stream* CA-9
Bourland Creek—*stream* MS-4
Bourland Meadow—*flat* CA-9
*Bourland Mountain* CA-9
Bourland Ranch—*locale* TX-5
Bourland Rsvr—*reservoir* OR-9
*Bourm Lake* WY-8
Bourn Ave Sch—*school* TX-5
Bourn Brook—*stream* VT-1
Bourn Cem—*cemetery* CA-9
Bourn Cem—*cemetery* WV-2
*Bourne* PA-2
Bourne—*locale* OR-9
**Bourne**—*pop pl* KY-4
**Bourne**—*pop pl* MA-1
**Bourne**—*pop pl* PA-2
Bourne-Anderson House—*hist pl* KY-4
Bourne Bridge—*bridge* MA-1
Bourne Canyon—*valley* NV-8
Bourne Cem—*cemetery* MS-4
Bourne Cem—*cemetery* TN-4
**Bourne Center**—*pop pl* MA-1
**Bourne Corners**—*pop pl* MA-1
Bourne Cove—*cove* MA-1
Bourne Cove Marshes—*swamp* MA-1
*Bourne Creek* MA-1
Bourne Creek—*stream* MI-6
Bourne Creek—*stream* MO-7
Bourne Creek—*stream* WY-8
Bourne Dairy—*hist pl* OK-5
**Bournedale**—*pop pl* MA-1
Bourne Draw—*valley* SD-7
Bourne Gulch—*valley* NV-8
*Bourne Hill* MA-1
Bourne Hill—*summit* MA-1
Bourne HS—*school* MA-1
Bourne JHS—*school* MA-1
Bourne Landing—*locale* OR-9
Bourne Mansion—*hist pl* ME-1
Bourne McGehee Dam—*dam* MS-4
**Bourne Mills**—*pop pl* PA-2
*Bourne Neck* MA-1
Bourne Point—*cape* MA-1
Bourne Pond—*lake* (2) MA-1
Bourne Ranch—*locale* SD-7
**Bournes Beach**—*pop pl* NY-2
Bournes Branch—*stream* VA-3
Bournes Branch Trail—*trail* VA-3
Bournes Brook (historical)—*stream* MA-1
Bourne Sch—*school* SD-7
*Bournes Cove* MA-1
Bournes Creek—*stream* NY-2
*Bournes Gulch* CA-9
*Bournes Hill* MA-1
*Bournes Landing* CA-9
*Bournes Landing* OR-9
Bourne Slough—*lake* SD-7
*Bournes Neck* MA-1
*Bournes Pond* MA-1
Bournes Pond—*bay* MA-1
*Bournes Rock* CA-9

**Bourne (Town of)**—pop pl ... MA-1
Bourne Trail—trail ... CA-9
Bourne Tunnel Spring—spring ... NV-8
**Bourneville**—pop pl ... OH-6
Bourne Wharf River—stream ... MA-1
Bourne Williams Ditch—canal ... IN-6
Bourn Gulch ... CA-9
Bourn-Hadley Pond—reservoir ... MA-1
Bourn - Hadley Pond Dam—dam ... MA-1
Bournham Sch (historical)—school ... MS-4
Bourn Hill—summit ... CT-1
Bourn Landing ... CA-9
Bourn Pond—lake ... NY-2
Bourn Pond—lake ... VT-1
Bourn Rock ... CA-9
Bourn-Roth Estate—hist pl ... CA-9
Bourns Gulch—valley ... CA-9
Bourn Shelter—locale ... VT-1
Bourns Landing—locale ... CA-9
Bourns Rock—island ... CA-9
Bourquim Hill—summit ... NE-7
Bourret Cem—cemetery ... MI-6
Bourret Draw—valley ... WY-8
**Bourret (Township of)**—pop pl ... MI-6
Bours Points—cliff ... IN-6
**Bouse**—pop pl ... AZ-5
Bouse Airp—airport ... AZ-5
Bouse Hills—summit ... AZ-5
Bouse Junction—locale ... OK-5
Bouser Hollow—valley ... MO-7
Bouses Run—stream ... WV-2
Bouse Wash ... AZ-5
Bouse Wash—stream ... AZ-5
Boush Creek (historical)—stream ... VA-3
Boushs Bluff—cliff ... VA-3
Boush-Tazewell House—hist pl ... VA-3
Bousic Canyon—valley ... CA-9
Bousley Ditch ... IN-6
Bouslog Branch—stream ... IN-6
Bouslog Ditch ... IN-6
Bousquet Ditch—canal ... MT-8
Bousquet Ski Area—locale ... MA-1
Boussole Bay—bay ... AK-9
Boussole Head—summit ... AK-9
Bousson Sch (historical)—school ... PA-2
Boussons Corners—locale ... PA-2
Boussuet, Birdie, Farm—hist pl ... ID-8
Boutel Cem—cemetery ... MI-6
Boutell Cem—cemetery ... ME-1
Boutell Drain—canal ... MI-6
Boutin, Frank, Jr., House—hist pl ... WI-6
**Boutin Corner**—pop pl ... NH-1
Boutlier Lake—lake ... MI-6
**Bouton**—pop pl ... IA-7
Bouton, Jay H., House—hist pl ... CO-8
Bouton Cem—cemetery ... TN-4
Bouton Hill—summit ... GA-3
Bouton Lake—lake ... CA-9
Bouton Lake—lake ... TX-5
**Boutonville**—pop pl ... NY-2
**Boutte**—pop pl ... LA-4
Boutte, Bayou—stream ... LA-4
Boutte Oil and Gas Field—oilfield ... LA-4
Boutte Sch—school ... LA-4
Boutwell Auditorium—building ... AL-4
Boutwell Branch—stream ... FL-3
Boutwell Brook—stream ... MA-1
Boutwell Brook—stream ... VT-1
Boutwell Cem—cemetery ... MN-6
Boutwell Cem—cemetery ... OH-6
Boutwell Creek—stream ... MN-6
Boutwell Hill—summit ... NY-2
Boutwell Island—island ... MA-1
Boutwell Mill Brook—stream ... NH-1
Boutwell Ranch (historical)—locale ... SD-7
Boutwell Street Sch—school ... MA-1
**Bouty**—pop pl ... KY-4
Bouvasau Bay ... MI-6
Bouve Pond—lake ... MA-1
Bouverans Plantation House—hist pl ... LA-4
Bouvey Canyon—valley ... WA-9
Bouvier Bay—bay ... MI-6
Bouvier-Lothrop House—hist pl ... CO-8
Bouwerie—hist pl ... NY-2
Bouwerie Lane Theater—hist pl ... NY-2
Bouyer Creek ... MS-4
Bouyer Creek—stream ... MO-7
Bouzier Creek—stream ... TX-5
Bova Canyon ... NE-7
Bova Creek—stream ... NY-2
Bovar ... PA-2
Bovard ... KS-7
Bovard—locale ... ID-8
**Bovard**—pop pl (2) ... PA-2
Bovard Cem—cemetery ... IN-6
Bova Ski Tow—other ... NY-2
Bovay Canyon ... NE-7
Bove Creek ... SD-7
Boveda Lake—lake ... TX-5
**Bovee**—pop pl ... SD-7
Bovee Cem—cemetery ... IL-6
Bovee Creek ... WI-6
Bovee Ditch—canal ... OH-6
Bovee Drain—stream ... MI-6
Bovee Draw—valley ... WY-8
Bovee Lake—lake (2) ... MI-6
Bovee Lateral—canal ... TX-5
Bovee Valley—basin ... NE-7
Bovell Branch—stream ... AL-4
Boven Earthwork—hist pl ... MI-6
Boven Spring Chimney Tank—reservoir ... NM-5
**Bovey**—pop pl ... MN-6
Bovido Bay ... TX-5
Bovido Creek ... TX-5
Bovie River ... MS-4
Bovier Run—stream ... PA-2
Bovier Run Trail—trail ... PA-2
**Bovill**—pop pl ... ID-8
Bovina—locale ... CO-8
Bovina—locale ... NY-2
**Bovina**—pop pl ... MS-4
**Bovina**—pop pl ... TX-5
Bovina Baptist Ch—church ... MS-4
Bovina Cem—cemetery ... WI-6
**Bovina Center**—pop pl ... NY-2
Bovina Elem Sch—school ... MS-4
Bovina (historical)—locale ... IA-7
Bovinair Airp—airport ... KS-7
Bovina Methodist Ch—church ... MS-4
Bovina Mtn—summit ... NY-2
Bovina Station ... MS-4
**Bovina (Town of)**—pop pl ... NY-2
**Bovina (Town of)**—pop pl ... WI-6
Bovine ... IN-6
Bovine ... SD-7
Bovine—locale ... AR-4
Bovine—locale ... UT-8
Bovine Mtns—range ... UT-8
Bovine Sch—school ... SD-7
Bovine Siding ... UT-8
Bovine Spring—spring ... UT-8
Bovine Township—civil ... SD-7
Bovocoap Point—cape ... VI-3
Bovoni Bay—bay ... VI-3
Bovoni Cay—island ... VI-3
Bow—locale ... KY-4
**Bow**—pop pl ... PA-2
**Bow**—pop pl ... WA-9
Bowan Cem—cemetery ... MO-7
Bowan Creek—stream ... WA-9
Bow and Arrow Creek—stream ... MT-8
Bow and Arrow Park—park ... AZ-5
Bow and Arrow Ranch—locale (2) ... MT-8
Bow And Arrow Ranch—locale ... WY-8
Bowan Mtn—summit ... WA-9
**Bowan Ridge**—pop pl ... WV-2
Bow Arrow Point—cape ... VT-1
Bowastown ... NY-2
Bowback Lake—lake ... MT-8
Bow Basin—basin ... MT-8
Bow Beach—beach ... VA-3
Bow Bell (ledge)—bar ... MA-1
**Bowbells**—pop pl ... ND-7
Bow Bells, The—bar ... MA-1
Bowbells Cem—cemetery ... ND-7
Bowbells Municipal Airp—airport ... ND-7
**Bowbells Township**—pop pl ... ND-7
**Bow Bog**—pop pl ... NH-1
Bow Bog Brook—stream ... NH-1
**Bow (Bow Mills)**—pop pl ... NH-1
Bow Branch—stream ... TX-5
Bow Bridge Creek—stream ... PA-2
Bow Brook—stream (2) ... MA-1
Bow Brook—stream ... NH-1
Bow Brook Dam—dam ... MA-1
Bow Brook Rsvr—reservoir ... MA-1
Bow Canyon ... TX-5
Bow Canyon—valley ... CA-9
Bow (CCD)—cens area ... WA-9
**Bow Center**—pop pl ... NH-1
Bow Channel—channel ... FL-3
Bow Cove—bay ... MD-2
Bow Creek—locale ... KS-7
Bow Creek—stream ... AL-4
Bow Creek—stream (3) ... AK-9
Bow Creek—stream ... CA-9
Bow Creek—stream ... GA-3
Bow Creek—stream (2) ... ID-8
Bow Creek—stream ... KS-7
Bow Creek—stream ... NE-7
Bow Creek—stream (2) ... OR-9
Bow Creek—stream (2) ... PA-2
Bow Creek—stream ... TX-5
Bow Creek Cem—cemetery (2) ... KS-7
Bow Creek Ch—church ... VA-3
Bow Creek Country Club—other ... VA-3
Bow Creek (historical)—stream ... PA-2
Bow Creek Township ... KS-7
Bowcreek Township—civ div ... KS-7
Bow Creek Township—civil (2) ... KS-7
Bowden ... AL-4
Bowden ... NC-3
Bowden—other ... NC-3
**Bowden**—pop pl ... FL-3
**Bowden**—pop pl ... OK-5
**Bowden**—pop pl ... WV-2
Bowden Branch—stream ... NC-3
Bowden Branch—stream ... TX-5
Bowden Canyon—valley ... UT-8
Bowden Cem—cemetery (2) ... AR-4
Bowden Cem—cemetery (3) ... TN-4
Bowden Ch (historical)—church ... TN-4
Bowden Creek—channel ... FL-3
Bowden Creek—stream ... GA-3
Bowden Creek—stream ... MI-6
Bowden Dam—dam ... AL-4
Bowden Draw—valley ... UT-8
Bowden Flat—flat ... CA-9
Bowden Gap—gap ... TN-4
**Bowden Grove**—pop pl ... AL-4
Bowden Grove Ch—church ... AL-4
Bowden Hall—hist pl ... NM-5
Bowdenheimer Branch ... TX-5
Bowdenheimer Creek—stream ... TX-5
Bowden Hills ... OR-9
Bowden Hills—summit ... OR-9
Bowden Hills—uninc pl ... GA-3
Bowden (historical)—locale ... ME-1
Bowden Hollow—valley ... AR-4
Bowden Hollow—valley ... TX-5
Bowden Island—island (2) ... ME-1
Bowden Island—island ... SC-3
Bowden Lake—lake ... UT-8
Bowden Lake—reservoir ... AL-4
Bowden Landing ... AL-4
Bowden Mill Creek—stream ... AL-4
Bowden Millpond—reservoir ... NC-3
Bowden Millpond Dam—dam ... NC-3
Bowden Mine (underground)—mine ... AL-4
Bowden Park—park ... CA-9
Bowden Park—park ... ID-8
Bowden Point ... MA-1
Bowden Point—cape ... ME-1
Bowden Ponds—reservoir ... WV-2
Bowden Ranch—locale ... OR-9
Bowden Ranch—locale ... TX-5
Bowden Ranch—locale ... WY-8
**Bowdens**—pop pl ... NC-3
**Bowdens (Bowden)**—pop pl ... NC-3
Bowdens Ch—church ... NC-3
Bowden Sch—school ... TN-4
Bowden Sch (historical)—school ... TN-4
Bowden Sessions Pond Dam—dam ... AL-4
Bowdens Garage—locale ... DE-2
Bowdens Landing (historical)—locale ... AL-4
Bowdens Mill (historical)—locale ... MS-4
Bowdens Pond—reservoir ... GA-3
Bowdens Store (historical)—locale ... AL-4
Bowdens Store (historical)—locale ... TN-4
Bowden Tank—reservoir ... TX-5
Bowdenville ... KS-7
Bowder Hill Ch—church ... TN-4
**Bowdertown**—pop pl ... PA-2
Bowdie Canyon—valley ... UT-8
Bowdie Point—cape ... UT-8
Bowdish Canyon—valley ... CO-8
Bowdish JHS—school ... WA-9
**Bowdish Lake**—pop pl ... RI-1
Bowdish Reservoir Dam—dam ... RI-1
Bowdish Reservoir Upper Dam ... RI-1
Bowdish Rsvr—reservoir ... RI-1
Bowdish Trail—trail ... CO-8
**Bowditch**—pop pl ... NC-3
Bowditch, Nathaniel, House—hist pl ... MA-1
Bowditch, William Ingersoll, House—hist pl ... MA-1
Bowditch Cem—cemetery ... ME-1
Bowditch Field—park ... MA-1
Bowditch Ledge—bar ... MA-1
Bowditch Point ... FL-3
Bowditch-Runnells State Forest—park ... NH-1
Bowditch's Ledge ... MA-1
**Bowdle**—pop pl ... SD-7
Bowdle Beach Rec Area—park ... SD-7
Bowdle Cem—cemetery (2) ... OH-6
Bowdle-Hosmer Dam—dam ... SD-7
Bowdle-Hosmer Lake—reservoir ... SD-7
Bowdle-Hosmer Public Shooting Area—park ... SD-7
Bowdle Municipal Airp—airport ... SD-7
**Bowdle Township**—pop pl ... SD-7
Bow-Dodge Lake—lake ... MN-6
Bowdoin—locale ... MT-8
Bowdoin, Lake—lake ... MT-8
Bowdoin, Mount—summit ... MA-1
**Bowdoin (Bowdoin Center)**—pop pl ... ME-1
Bowdoin Branch—stream ... TX-5
Bowdoin Canal—canal ... MT-8
Bowdoin Center—other ... ME-1
Bowdoin Coll—school ... ME-1
Bowdoin College Grant East—unorg ... ME-1
Bowdoin College Grant West—unorg ... ME-1
**Bowdoinham**—pop pl ... ME-1
Bowdoinham Ridge—ridge ... ME-1
**Bowdoinham (Town of)**—pop pl ... ME-1
Bowdoinham Wildlife Mngmt Area—park ... ME-1
Bowdoin Natl Wildlife Ref—park ... MT-8
Bowdoin Point—cape ... MD-2
BOWDOIN (schooner)—hist pl ... ME-1
**Bowdoin (Town of)**—pop pl ... ME-1
**Bowdon**—pop pl ... GA-3
**Bowdon**—pop pl ... ND-7
Bowdon (CCD)—cens area ... GA-3
**Bowdon Junction**—pop pl ... GA-3
Bowdon Tank—reservoir ... AZ-5
**Bowdre**—pop pl ... MS-4
Bowdre-Rees-Knox House—hist pl ... GA-3
**Bowdre (Township of)**—pop pl ... IL-6
Bowdry—locale ... MO-7
Bowdry Cemetery ... MS-4
Bowdry Lake—lake ... MO-7
Bowdy Swamp ... NC-3
Bowe Cem—cemetery ... TN-4
Bowe Ditch—canal ... MT-8
Boween River ... NC-3
Boween River ... SC-3
Bowe Gardens Shop Ctr—locale ... FL-3
Bowell Cem—cemetery ... AR-4
Bowell Cem—cemetery ... GA-3
Bowen ... MI-6
Bowen—fmr MCD ... NE-7
Bowen—locale ... AR-4
Bowen—locale ... WV-2
**Bowen**—pop pl ... IL-6
**Bowen**—pop pl ... KY-4
**Bowen**—pop pl (2) ... MO-7
**Bowen**—pop pl ... NY-2
**Bowen**—pop pl ... TN-4
Bowen, Abraham Briggs, House—hist pl ... WI-6
Bowen, Anthony, YMCA—hist pl ... DC-2
Bowen, Henry C., House—hist pl ... CT-1
Bowen, Isaac, House—hist pl ... RI-1
Bowen, James B., House—hist pl ... WI-6
Bowen, Joseph T., Country Club—hist pl ... IL-6
Bowen, Marion E., House—hist pl ... SD-7
Bowen, Mathew, Homestead—hist pl ... CT-1
Bowen, Nathan, House—hist pl ... MA-1
Bowen Anchorage—bay ... AK-9
Bowen and Brown Drain—canal ... MI-6
Bowen Branch—gut ... FL-3
Bowen Branch—stream ... AL-4
Bowen Branch—stream ... GA-3
Bowen Branch—stream (2) ... KY-4
Bowen Branch—stream ... MO-7
Bowen Branch—stream (2) ... NC-3
Bowen Branch—stream ... TN-4
Bowen Branch—stream ... TX-5
Bowen Branch—stream ... VA-3
Bowen Brook—stream (3) ... NH-1
Bowen-Campbell House—hist pl ... TN-4
Bowen Canyon—valley ... ID-8
Bowen Canyon—valley ... NV-8
Bowen Canyon—valley ... UT-8
Bowen Cave—cave (2) ... TN-4
Bowen Cem—cemetery ... GA-3
Bowen Cem—cemetery (2) ... IL-6
Bowen Cem—cemetery ... KS-7
Bowen Cem—cemetery (2) ... MO-7
Bowen Cem—cemetery ... NY-2
Bowen Cem—cemetery ... OH-6
Bowen Cem—cemetery (2) ... TN-4
Bowen Cem—cemetery (4) ... VA-3
Bowen Cem—cemetery (2) ... WV-2
Bowen Cem—cemetery ... WI-6
Bowen Ch—church ... CO-8
Bowen Ch—church ... KY-4
Bowen Chapel ... TN-4
Bowen Chapel—church ... KY-4
Bowen Chapel—church (2) ... TN-4
Bowen Chapel—church ... VA-3
Bowen Corners—locale ... OH-6
**Bowen Corners**—pop pl ... NY-2
Bowen Coulee—valley ... MT-8
Bowen Court—hist pl ... CA-9
Bowen Cove ... RI-1
Bowen Creek ... MD-2
Bowen Creek—stream ... AR-4
Bowen Creek—stream ... CO-8
Bowen Creek—stream ... KY-4
Bowen Creek—stream (2) ... MI-6
Bowen Creek—stream (2) ... MO-7
Bowen Creek—stream ... MT-8
Bowen Creek—stream ... NY-2
Bowen Creek—stream ... OR-9
Bowen Creek—stream ... TX-5
Bowen Creek—stream ... WA-9
Bowen Creek—stream ... WV-2
Bowen Creek Ch—church ... KY-4
Bowen Creek Point ... MD-2
Bowen Ditch—canal ... CO-8
Bowen Ditch—canal (2) ... IN-6
Bowen Drain—canal (2) ... CO-8
Bowen Drain—stream ... MI-6
Bowen Draw—valley ... TX-5
Bowen Field—park ... CT-1
Bowen Field—park ... VA-3
Bowen Flat—flat ... WY-8
Bowen Fork ... PA-2
Bowen Fork Run ... PA-2
Bowen Gap—gap ... VA-3
Bowen Gulch ... CA-9
Bowen Gulch—valley ... CO-8
Bowen Hill—summit ... CT-1
Bowen Hill—summit ... ME-1
Bowen Hill—summit ... NY-2
Bowen Hill—summit ... RI-1
Bowen Hill—summit ... VT-1
Bowen (historical)—locale ... AL-4
Bowen (historical)—locale ... MS-4
**Bowen (historical)**—pop pl ... OR-9
Bowen Hollow—valley ... IN-6
Bowen Hollow—valley ... KY-4
Bowen Hollow—valley ... TN-4
Bowen HS—school ... IL-6
Bowen Island—island ... SC-3
Bowen-Jordan Farm—hist pl ... NC-3
Bowen Lake ... UT-8
Bowen Lake—lake ... CO-8
Bowen Lake—lake (2) ... FL-3
Bowen Lake—lake ... GA-3
Bowen Lake—lake ... IN-6
Bowen Lake—lake ... MI-6
Bowen Lake—lake ... MT-8
Bowen Lake—lake ... SC-3
Bowen Lake—lake ... WA-9
Bowen Lake—reservoir ... IN-6
Bowen Lake—reservoir ... MN-6
Bowen Lake Dam—dam ... IN-6
Bowen Lake Dam—dam ... MS-4
Bowen Landing ... CA-9
Bowen Landing—locale ... DE-2
Bowen Mansion—hist pl ... CO-8
Bowen Mill—locale ... GA-3
Bowen Millpond—lake ... GA-3
Bowen Mine—mine ... CA-9
Bowen Mtn—summit ... CO-8
Bowen Mtn—summit ... VT-1
Bowen Mtn—summit (2) ... WA-9
Bowen Pass—gap ... CO-8
Bowen Point—cape ... CA-9
Bowen Point—cape ... NC-3
Bowen Point—other ... NC-3
Bowen Pond ... FL-3
Bowen Pond ... MA-1
Bowen Pond—reservoir (2) ... GA-3
Bowen Post Office (historical)—building ... TN-4
Bowen Ranch—locale ... CA-9
Bowen Ridge—ridge ... AR-4
Bowen Ridge—ridge ... KY-4
Bowen Ridge Ch—church ... WV-2
Bowen River ... NC-3
Bowen River ... SC-3
Bowen Rock ... CA-9
Bowen Rsvr—reservoir ... OR-9
Bowen Run—stream ... IN-6
Bowen Run—stream ... WV-2
**Bowens**—pop pl ... MD-2
Bowens Bay Creek—stream ... MS-4
Bowens Branch—stream ... MD-2
Bowens Branch—stream ... VA-3
Bowens Canyon—valley ... UT-8
Bowens Cem—cemetery ... OH-6
Bowen Sch—school ... DC-2
Bowen Sch—school (2) ... IL-6
Bowen Sch—school ... KY-4
Bowen Sch—school ... MA-1
Bowen Sch—school ... MI-6
Bowen Sch—school ... MT-8
Bowen Sch (abandoned)—school ... MO-7
Bowens Chapel ... TN-4
Bowens Chapel—church ... MD-2
Bowens Chapel—church ... NC-3
Bowen Schoolhouse Branch—stream ... AL-4
Bowens Corner—locale ... VA-3
**Bowens Corners**—pop pl ... MA-1
**Bowens Corners**—pop pl ... NY-2
Bowens Creek ... AL-4
Bowens Creek ... MI-6
Bowens Creek—stream ... MI-6
Bowens Creek—stream ... VA-3
Bowens Hill ... RI-1
Bowens Knob—summit ... VA-3
Bowens Lake—lake ... GA-3
Bowens Lake—lake ... IL-6
Bowens Lake—reservoir ... GA-3
**Bowens Mill**—pop pl ... GA-3
**Bowens Mill**—pop pl ... MI-6
**Bowens Mills**—pop pl ... MI-6
Bowens Pond ... MA-1
Bowens Pond—reservoir ... GA-3
Bowens Pond—reservoir (2) ... MA-1
Bowens Pond Dam—dam ... MA-1
Bowens Poowens Point ... NC-3
Bowens Prairie—locale ... IA-7
Bowens Prairie Cem—cemetery ... IA-7
Bowen Spring—spring ... CO-8
Bowen Spring—spring ... UT-8
Bowen Spring—spring ... WY-8
Bowens River—stream ... NC-3
Bowens River—stream ... SC-3
Bowens Run—stream ... VA-3
Bowens Store—locale ... VA-3
Bowen Station Sch—school ... MI-6
Bowensville Creek—gut ... NC-3
Bowen Swamp—stream ... VA-3
Bowentown—locale ... NJ-2
**Bowen Township**—pop pl ... ND-7
Bowen (Township of)—fmr MCD (2) ... AR-4
Bowen Trail—trail ... CO-8
Bowen Valley—valley ... OR-9
**Bowenville (subdivision)**—pop pl ... MA-1
Bowen Well—well ... ID-8
Bower ... OK-5
Bower—locale ... PA-2
Bower—locale ... WV-2
**Bower**—pop pl ... GA-3
Bower, Charles, House—hist pl ... ID-8
Bower, David S., House—hist pl ... NJ-2
Bower, The—hist pl ... WV-2
Bowe Ranch—locale ... NM-5
Bowerbank—locale ... CA-9
Bowerbank—locale ... ME-1
Bowerbank (historical)—locale ... ME-1
**Bowerbank (Town of)**—pop pl ... ME-1
Bower Branch—stream ... WV-2
Bower Brook ... MA-1
Bower Canyon—valley ... MT-8
Bower Cave—cave ... CA-9
Bower Cem—cemetery ... ID-8
Bower Cem—cemetery ... IL-6
Bower Cem—cemetery ... IN-6
Bower Cem—cemetery ... IA-7
Bower Cem—cemetery ... MS-4
Bower Cem—cemetery ... NE-7
Bower Cem—cemetery ... NY-2
Bower Cem—cemetery ... OK-5
Bower Cem—cemetery ... WV-2
Bower Chapel—church ... MO-7
Bower-Cox House—hist pl ... NC-3
Bower Creek ... IN-6
Bower Creek ... KS-7
Bower Creek—stream ... IL-6
Bower Creek—stream ... OR-9
Bower Creek—stream ... TN-4
Bower Creek—stream ... WI-6
Bower Dam—dam ... SD-7
Bower Ditch—canal ... CO-8
Bower Ditch—canal (2) ... IN-6
Bower Drain—canal ... MI-6
Bower Draw—valley ... CO-8
Bower Field—park ... TN-4
Bower Guard Station—locale ... ID-8
Bower Gulch—valley ... MT-8
**Bower Hill**—pop pl (2) ... PA-2
Bower Hill Post Office (historical)—building ... PA-2
Bower Hill Sch—school ... PA-2
Bower (historical)—locale ... KS-7
Bower Hollow—valley (2) ... TN-4
Bower Lake ... MN-6
Bower Lake—lake ... AK-9
Bower Lake—lake ... CO-8
Bower Lake—lake ... IN-6
Bower Lake—lake ... MN-6
Bower Lake—lake ... NE-7
Bowerman Airp—airport ... WA-9
Bowerman Barn—hist pl ... CA-9
Bowerman Basin—bay ... WA-9
Bowerman Brook—stream ... MN-6
Bowerman Cem—cemetery ... MI-6
Bowerman Ch—church ... PA-2
Bowerman Creek ... MA-1
Bowerman Creek—stream ... MA-1
Bowerman Drain—canal ... MI-6
Bowerman Gulch—valley ... CA-9
Bowerman Lake—lake ... OR-9
Bowerman Meadows—flat ... CA-9
Bowerman Mill ... TN-4
Bowerman Peak—summit (2) ... CA-9
Bowerman Ridge—ridge ... CA-9
Bowerman Sch—school ... MO-7
Bowermans Creek ... TN-4
Bower Memorial Baptist Ch—church ... AL-4
Bower Mills ... MO-7
Bower Mine—mine ... CA-9
Bower Mine—mine ... IL-6
Bower Park—park (2) ... IL-6
Bower Place—locale ... CO-8
Bower Ranch—locale ... MT-8
Bower Ranch—locale ... NE-7
Bower Rsvr—reservoir ... ID-8
Bower Run ... OH-6
Bower Run—stream ... WV-2
Bowers ... DE-2
Bowers—locale ... OK-5
**Bowers**—pop pl ... DE-2
**Bowers**—pop pl ... IN-6
**Bowers**—pop pl ... PA-2
**Bowers**—pop pl ... WI-6
Bowers, Dr. Wesley, House—hist pl ... NY-2
Bowers, John S. House—hist pl ... IN-6
Bowers, Jonathan, House—hist pl ... MA-1
Bowers, Joseph, House—hist pl ... MI-6
**Bowers Addition (subdivision)**—pop pl ... UT-8
Bowers Beach—beach ... DE-2
**Bowers Beach**—pop pl ... DE-2
Bowers Bluff—cliff ... FL-3
Bowers Bluff Middens Archeol District—hist pl ... FL-3
Bowers Branch ... IN-6
Bowers Branch—stream ... OR-9
Bowers Branch—stream ... TN-4
Bowers Branch Prospect—mine ... TN-4
Bowers Bridges Creek—stream ... OR-9
Bowers Brook ... MA-1
Bowers Brook—stream ... ME-1
Bowers Brook—stream ... MA-1
Bowers Brook—stream ... NH-1
Bowers Cem—cemetery ... AL-4
Bowers Cem—cemetery ... AR-4
Bowers Cem—cemetery ... GA-3
Bowers Cem—cemetery (2) ... IN-6
Bowers Cem—cemetery (2) ... MO-7
Bowers Cem—cemetery (2) ... OH-6
Bowers Cem—cemetery ... PA-2
Bowers Cem—cemetery (5) ... TN-4
Bowers Ch—church ... OK-5
Bower Sch—school ... IL-6
Bower Sch—school ... NE-7
Bower Sch—school ... NY-2
Bower Sch (abandoned)—school ... PA-2
Bowers Chapel Cem—cemetery ... TN-4
Bowers Chapel (historical)—church ... TN-4
**Bowers City**—pop pl ... TX-5
Bowers Corner—locale ... NY-2
Bowers Corner—locale ... VA-3
Bowers Coulee ... WA-9
Bowers Coulee—valley ... ND-7
Bowers Cove ... RI-1
Bowers Cove—valley ... GA-3
Bowers Covered Bridge—hist pl ... VT-1
Bowers Creek ... TX-5
Bowers Creek—stream ... CA-9
Bowers Creek—stream ... IN-6
Bowers Creek—stream ... MI-6
Bowers Creek—stream ... MT-8
Bowers Creek—stream ... NJ-2
Bowers Creek—stream ... NC-3
Bowers Creek—stream ... OR-9
Bowers Creek—stream ... PA-2
Bowers Creek—stream ... WI-6
Bowers Drain—canal ... MI-6
Bowers-Felts House—hist pl ... TX-5
Bowers Field—locale ... CA-9
Bowers Field Airp—airport ... WA-9
Bowers Field Hollow—valley ... AR-4
Bowers Fire Control Station—locale ... NV-8
Bowers Flat—flat ... UT-8
Bowers Gap—gap ... GA-3
Bowers Gap—gap ... NC-3
Bowers Gap—gap ... PA-2
Bowers Gulch—valley ... CO-8
Bowers Harbor—bay ... MI-6
Bowers Harbor Cem—cemetery ... MI-6
Bowers Hill—locale ... VA-3
**Bowers Hill**—pop pl ... WV-2
Bowers Hill (Bowers)—uninc pl ... VA-3
**Bowers (historical)**—pop pl ... OR-9
Bowers Hollow—valley (2) ... AR-4
Bowers Hollow—valley ... MO-7
Bowers Hollow—valley ... NY-2
Bowers Hollow—valley ... TN-4
Bowers House—hist pl ... WV-2
Bowers Island ... MT-8
Bowers Island—island ... CT-1
Bowers Island—island ... PA-2
Bowers Junction—locale ... OR-9
Bowers Knob—summit ... IN-6
Bowers Knoll—summit ... UT-8
Bowers Lake—lake ... FL-3
Bowers Lake—lake (2) ... WA-9
Bowers Lake—reservoir ... AL-4
Bowers Lake—reservoir ... TX-5
Bowers Lake—swamp ... WI-6
Bowers-Livingston-Osborn House—hist pl ... NJ-2
Bowers Lodge—locale ... MI-6
Bower Slough—gut ... WA-9
Bowers Mansion—hist pl ... NV-8
Bowers Mansion County Park—park ... NV-8
Bowers Mill ... PA-2
Bowers Mill—inactive ... MO-7
Bowers Mill—locale ... MO-7
Bowers Mills ... MO-7
Bowers Mine ... OR-9
Bowers Mine—mine ... TN-4
Bowers Mtn ... PA-2
Bowers Mtn—summit ... GA-3
Bowers Mtn—summit ... ME-1
Bowers Mtn—summit ... PA-2
Bowers Mtn—summit ... VA-3
Bowersock Cem—cemetery ... OH-6
Bowersocks Camp—locale ... MI-6
Bowers Oil Field—oilfield ... TX-5
Bowersox Lake—lake ... OR-9
Bowersox Sch (historical)—school ... PA-2
Bowers Park—park ... PA-2
Bowers Peak—summit ... CO-8
Bowers Peak—summit ... MT-8
Bowers Pitch—cliff ... ME-1
Bowers Pond—lake ... NY-2
Bowers Pond—reservoir ... NH-1
Bowers Post Office (historical)—building ... TN-4
Bowers Rock ... PA-2
Bowers (RR name for Bowers Hill)—other ... VA-3
Bowers Rsvr—reservoir ... MT-8
Bowers Run—stream ... PA-2
Bowers Run—stream ... WV-2
Bowers Sch—hist pl ... MA-1
Bowers Sch—hist pl ... OK-5
Bowers Sch—school ... CA-9
Bowers Sch—school ... CT-1
Bowers Sch—school ... MA-1
Bowers Sch—school ... ND-7
Bowers Sch (historical)—school ... TN-4
Bowers Slough—stream ... OR-9
Bowers Spring—spring ... AL-4
Bowers Spring—spring ... CA-9
Bowers Spring—spring ... ID-8
Bowers Spring—spring ... TN-4
Bowers Spring—spring ... UT-8
Bowers Spring—spring ... WA-9
**Bowerston**—pop pl ... OH-6
**Bowerstown**—pop pl ... IN-6
**Bowerstown**—pop pl ... NY-2
Bowersville ... DE-2
Bowersville ... IL-6
**Bowersville**—pop pl ... GA-3
**Bowersville**—pop pl ... OH-6
**Bowersville**—pop pl ... PA-2
Bowersville (CCD)—cens area ... GA-3
Bowersville Hist Dist—hist pl ... GA-3
**Bowersville (historical)**—pop pl ... OR-9
Bowers Vly—swamp ... NY-2
Bower Tank—reservoir ... AZ-5
Bowerton ... PA-2
**Bowerton**—pop pl ... MS-4
Bowertown Post Office (historical)—building ... MS-4
Bower Trout Lake—lake ... MN-6
Bower Woods—woods ... WA-9
Bowery Bay—bay ... NY-2
Bowery Campground ... UT-8
Bowery Cem—cemetery ... IN-6
Bowery Cem—cemetery ... TN-4
Bowery Creek—stream ... ID-8
Bowery Creek—stream ... IN-6
Bowery Creek—stream ... NY-2
Bowery Creek—stream (2) ... UT-8
Bowery Creek Campground—locale ... UT-8
Bowery Flat—flat ... CA-9
Bowery Flat—flat ... UT-8
Bowery Fork—valley ... UT-8
Bowery Haven—locale ... UT-8
Bowery Haven Resort—park ... UT-8
Bowery Hill—summit ... AR-4
Bowery Lake ... MI-6
Bowery Peak ... ID-8
Bowery Peak—summit ... ID-8
Bowery Peak—summit ... MT-8
Bowery Run—stream ... PA-2

Bow River Campground—*locale* WY-8
Bow River Overlook—*locale* WY-8
Bowron Lake—*lake* WI-6
Bow Run—*stream* IN-6
Bowsaw Branch—*stream* NC-3
Bow Sch—*school* KY-4
Bow Sch—*school* MI-6
Bows Corners—*locale* NY-2
*Bows Creek* OR-9
Bowser—*locale* TX-5
Bowser Cem—*cemetery* PA-2
Bowser Cem—*cemetery* TX-5
Bowser Creek—*stream* AK-9
Bowser Creek—*stream* WA-9
Bowserdale Ch—*church* PA-2
Bowser Gazebo—*hist pl* MA-1
Bowser Hollow—*valley* VA-3
Bowser Lake—*lake* MT-8
Bowser Lake—*lake* WA-9
Bowser Mine—*mine* OR-9
Bowser Pond—*lake* NH-1
Bowser Ridge—*ridge* TN-4
Bowser Sch—*school* IL-6
Bowser Sch—*school* VA-3
Bowser Spring—*spring* WA-9
**Bowsher**—*pop pl* IA-7
Bowsher Ford Bridge—*bridge* IN-6
Bowsher Ford Bridge—*hist pl* IN-6
Bowsher HS—*school* OH-6
Bowsherville Cem—*cemetery* OH-6
Bows Hollow—*valley* KY-4
Bows Lake—*lake* MI-6
Bow Spring—*spring* OR-9
Bowstead Lake—*lake* MI-6
Bow Street Hist Dist—*hist pl* MA-1
**Bowstring**—*pop pl* MN-6
Bowstring Branch—*stream* TN-4
Bowstring Hollow—*valley* TN-4
Bowstring Lake—*lake* (2) MN-6
Bowstring Lake (Unorganized Territory of)—*unorg* MN-6
*Bowstring River* MN-6
Bowstring River—*stream* MN-6
Bowstring State For—*forest* MN-6
**Bowstring (Township of)**—*pop pl* MN-6
**Bowthorpe Subdivision**—*pop pl* UT-8
*Bowtie Arch* UT-8
Bowton Ditch—*canal* IN-6
**Bow (Town of)**—*pop pl* NH-1
Bowtown (Township of)—*unorg* ME-1
**Bow Valley**—*pop pl* NE-7
Bow Valley Mills—*hist pl* NE-7
Bow Valley Mills—*locale* NE-7
Bow Willow Canyon—*valley* CA-9
Bow Willow Creek—*stream* CA-9
Bow Willow Palms—*locale* CA-9
Bow Willow Ranger Station—*locale* CA-9
**Bowyer**—*pop pl* SC-3
Bowyer Cem—*cemetery* IN-6
Bowyer Creek—*stream* WV-2
**Bowyer Creek Junction**—*pop pl* WV-2
Bowyer Flat—*flat* VA-3
Box—*locale* (2) OK-5
Box, The—*basin* (4) AZ-5
Box, The—*basin* WY-8
Box, The—*bend* AZ-5
Box, The—*bend* UT-8
Box, The—*channel* NM-5
Box, The—*summit* AZ-5
Box, The—*valley* (2) AZ-5
Box, The—*valley* CO-8
Box, The—*valley* (3) NM-5
Box, The—*valley* OR-9
Box, The—*valley* (2) UT-8
Boxam Cove—*bay* ME-1
Box Ankle—*locale* GA-3
Box Ankle Branch—*stream* MS-4
Box Arch—*arch* UT-8
Box Bailey Corral Canyon—*valley* ID-8
Box Bar Place—*locale* NM-5
Box Bar Ranch—*locale* AZ-5
Box Bay—*bay* WY-8
Boxberger West Oil Field—*oilfield* KS-7
**Boxboro**—*pop pl* MA-1
**Boxboro Station**—*pop pl* MA-1
*Boxborough* MA-1
**Boxborough (Boxboro)**—*pop pl* MA-1
**Boxborough (Town of)**—*pop pl* MA-1
Box Branch—*stream* (2) AL-4
Box Branch—*stream* FL-3
Box Branch—*stream* MS-4
Box Branch—*stream* MO-7
Box Branch—*stream* NC-3
Box Branch—*stream* SC-3
Box Branch—*stream* VA-3
Box Bridge (historical)—*bridge* MS-4
Box Butte—*fmr MCD* NE-7
Box Butte—*summit* (2) NE-7
Box Butte—*summit* OR-9
Box Butte Creek—*stream* NE-7
Box Butte Dam—*dam* NE-7
Box Butte Rsvr—*reservoir* NE-7
Box Camp—*locale* (2) CA-9
Box Camp Canyon—*valley* AZ-5
Box Camp Creek—*stream* VA-3
Box Camp Mtn—*summit* CA-9
*Box Canyon* AZ-5
*Box Canyon* CA-9
*Box Canyon* TX-5
Box Canyon—*basin* KY-4
**Box Canyon**—*pop pl* ID-8
Box Canyon—*valley* (18) AZ-5
Box Canyon—*valley* (13) CA-9
Box Canyon—*valley* (17) CO-8
Box Canyon—*valley* (14) ID-8
Box Canyon—*valley* (5) MT-8
Box Canyon—*valley* (17) NV-8
Box Canyon—*valley* (15) NM-5
Box Canyon—*valley* (17) OR-9
Box Canyon—*valley* (3) TX-5
Box Canyon—*valley* (13) UT-8
Box Canyon—*valley* (13) WA-9
Box Canyon—*valley* (6) WY-8
Box Canyon Creek—*stream* CO-8
Box Canyon Creek—*stream* ID-8
Box Canyon Creek—*stream* (3) OR-9
Box Canyon Creek—*stream* WA-9
Box Canyon Creek—*stream* WY-8
Box Canyon Dam—*dam* CO-8
Box Canyon Dam—*dam* NM-5
Box Canyon Dam—*dam* OR-9
Box Canyon Dam—*dam* WA-9
**Box Canyon Estates**—*pop pl* TX-5
Box Canyon Fire Station—*locale* CA-9
Box Canyon Guard Station—*locale* MT-8
Box Canyon Guard Station—*locale* OR-9
Box Canyon Lake—*lake* CO-8
Box Canyon Lake—*lake* WA-9
Box Canyon Number One—*valley* CA-9
Box Canyon Number Three—*valley* CA-9
Box Canyon Number Two—*valley* CA-9
Box Canyon Pass—*gap* WY-8
Box Canyon Picnic Area—*locale* WA-9
Box Canyon Placer—*mine* NV-8
Box Canyon Ranch—*locale* NM-5
Box Canyon Rsvr—*reservoir* CO-8
Box Canyon Rsvr—*reservoir* NV-8
Box Canyon Rsvr—*reservoir* (2) OR-9
Box Canyon Ruin (historical)—*locale* AZ-5
Box Canyon Spring—*spring* CO-8
Box Canyon Spring—*spring* ID-8
Box Canyon Spring—*spring* NV-8
Box Canyon Spring—*spring* UT-8
Box Canyon Spring Number Two—*spring* NV-8
Box Canyon Springs—*spring* AZ-5
Box Canyon Tank—*reservoir* (2) AZ-5
Box Canyon Tank—*reservoir* NM-5
Box Canyon Tank Number Two—*reservoir* AZ-5
Box Canyon Wash—*arroyo* AZ-5
Box Canyon Wash—*stream* AZ-5
Box Canyon Wash—*stream* CA-9
Box Canyon Wash—*valley* UT-8
Box Canyon Well—*well* AZ-5
Box Canyon Well—*well* NM-5
Box Canyon Windmill—*locale* AZ-5
Box Canyon Windmill—*locale* TX-5
Box Canyon Windmill—*summit* NM-5
Boxcar—*summit* AZ-5
Boxcar Camp—*locale* NM-5
Box Car Center—*locale* TX-5
Boxcar Creek—*stream* ID-8
Boxcar Cut—*channel* MI-6
Boxcar Flats—*flat* OR-9
Boxcar Hill—*summit* AZ-5
Boxcar Hills—*other* AK-9
Boxcar Mtn—*summit* ID-8
*Box Car Rock* NV-8
Boxcar Rock—*pillar* NV-8
*Boxcar Rocks* PA-2
Boxcar Well—*well* NM-5
Boxcar Windmill—*locale* NM-5
Boxcar Windmill—*locale* (3) TX-5
Box Cem—*cemetery* AL-4
Box Cem—*cemetery* (2) OK-5
Box Cem—*cemetery* (3) TN-4
Box Cem—*cemetery* (3) TX-5
Box Chapel—*church* MS-4
*Box Chapel Methodist Ch* MS-4
Box Church—*locale* TX-5
**Box Corner**—*pop pl* NH-1
*Box Creek* AZ-5
*Box Creek* TX-5
*Box Creek* WY-8
Box Creek—*stream* (3) AL-4
Box Creek—*stream* (3) CO-8
Box Creek—*stream* GA-3
Box Creek—*stream* (3) ID-8
Box Creek—*stream* (3) MS-4
Box Creek—*stream* MT-8
Box Creek—*stream* (2) NC-3
Box Creek—*stream* OK-5
Box Creek—*stream* (2) OR-9
Box Creek—*stream* (3) TX-5
Box Creek—*stream* UT-8
Box Creek—*stream* WA-9
Box Creek—*stream* (3) WY-8
Box Creek Divide—*ridge* WY-8
Box Creek Ranch—*locale* WY-8
Box Creek Sch—*school* TX-5
**Boxcroft (subdivision)**—*pop pl* TN-4
Box C Rsvr—*reservoir* WY-8
*Box Dam* AL-4
Box-Death Hollow Wilderness Area—*park* UT-8
Box D Gulch—*valley* CO-8
Box Ditch—*canal* (2) IN-6
Boxdorfer Sch—*school* MO-7
Box D Ranch—*locale* OR-9
Box Draw—*valley* NM-5
Box Draw—*valley* (2) WY-8
Box Draw Canyon—*valley* NM-5
*Boxeld Creek* SD-7
*Box Elder* CO-8
*Boxelder* MT-8
*Box Elder* UT-8
Box Elder—*fmr MCD* NE-7
Boxelder—*locale* WY-8
**Boxelder**—*pop pl* AR-4
**Box Elder**—*pop pl* MT-8
**Box Elder**—*pop pl* SD-7
**Box Elder**—*pop pl* TN-4
**Boxelder**—*pop pl* TX-5
Box Elder Bottom—*bend* MT-8
Boxelder Camp—*locale* SD-7
Box Elder Campground—*locale* UT-8
Box Elder Canal—*canal* UT-8
Box Elder Canyon—*valley* NE-7
Box Elder Canyon—*valley* (2) OR-9
Box Elder Canyon—*valley* (5) UT-8
Box Elder Canyon—*valley* (2) WY-8
Box Elder Cem—*cemetery* AR-4
Boxelder Cem—*cemetery* MT-8
Box Elder Cem—*cemetery* (2) NE-7
*Box Elder Coulee* MT-8
Box Elder Coulee—*valley* MT-8
Boxelder Coulee—*valley* MT-8
Box Elder Coulee—*valley* MT-8
Box Elder County—*civil* UT-8
Box Elder County Courthouse—*hist pl* UT-8
*Box Elder Creek* CO-8
*Box Elder Creek* MT-8
*Box Elder Creek* NE-7
*Box Elder Creek* SD-7
*Boxelder Creek* WY-8
Boxelder Creek—*stream* CO-8
Box Elder Creek—*stream* CO-8
Boxelder Creek—*stream* CO-8
Box Elder Creek—*stream* CO-8
Boxelder Creek—*stream* (2) KS-7
Boxelder Creek—*stream* MT-8
Box Elder Creek—*stream* (2) MT-8
Boxelder Creek—*stream* MT-8
Box Elder Creek—*stream* MT-8
Boxelder Creek—*stream* MT-8
Box Elder Creek—*stream* (3) MT-8
Boxelder Creek—*stream* MT-8
Box Elder Creek—*stream* (4) MT-8
Boxelder Creek—*stream* MT-8
Boxelder Creek—*stream* NE-7
Box Elder Creek—*stream* NE-7
Boxelder Creek—*stream* (2) NE-7
Boxelder Creek—*stream* (2) ND-7
Boxelder Creek—*stream* OK-5
Boxelder Creek—*stream* (4) SD-7
Box Elder Creek—*stream* UT-8
Boxelder Creek—*stream* WY-8
Box Elder Creek—*stream* (3) WY-8
Boxelder Creek—*stream* (2) WY-8
Box Elder Creek Bay—*bay* MT-8
Boxelder Ditch—*canal* CO-8
Box Elder Ditch—*canal* MT-8
Boxelder Ditch—*canal* WY-8
Box Elder Drain—*canal* WY-8
*Boxelder Draw* WY-8
Boxelder Draw—*valley* CO-8
Box Elder Draw—*valley* (4) WY-8
**Boxelder Estates**—*pop pl* CO-8
Box Elder Fort Site—*locale* UT-8
Box Elder Guard Station—*locale* UT-8
Boxelder Gulch—*valley* CO-8
Box Elder Gulch—*valley* CO-8
*Box Elder High School* UT-8
Box Elder Hollow—*valley* UT-8
Box Elder HS Gymnasium—*hist pl* UT-8
Box Elder JHS—*school* UT-8
*Box Elder Lake* UT-8
Boxelder Lake No. 3—*reservoir* CO-8
Box Elder Lateral—*canal* CO-8
Boxelder Line Sch—*school* WI-6
Box Elder Park—*flat* CO-8
Box Elder Pass—*gap* UT-8
Box Elder Peak—*summit* (2) UT-8
Box Elder Picnic Grounds—*locale* UT-8
Box Elder Ridge—*ridge* WY-8
Box Elder Rsvr—*reservoir* CO-8
Boxelder Rsvr No 1—*reservoir* CO-8
Box Elder Rsvr No 2—*reservoir* CO-8
Boxelder Rsvr No 2—*reservoir* CO-8
Box Elder Rsvr No 3—*reservoir* CO-8
Box Elder Rsvr No 4—*reservoir* CO-8
Box Elder Sch—*school* AR-4
Box Elder Sch—*school* CO-8
Boxelder Sch—*school* CO-8
Boxelder Sch—*school* IL-6
Box Elder Sch—*school* IA-7
Boxelder Sch—*school* IA-7
Box Elder Sch—*school* (2) MT-8
Box Elder Sch—*school* NE-7
Boxelder Sch—*school* SD-7
Box Elder Sch—*school* WY-8
Box Elder Spring—*spring* AZ-5
Boxelder Spring—*spring* CO-8
Box Elder Spring—*spring* OR-9
Boxelder Spring—*spring* WY-8
Boxelder Spring Draw—*valley* WY-8
Box Elder Stake Tabernacle—*hist pl* UT-8
Box Elder Wash—*valley* UT-8
Boxell Lake—*lake* MN-6
Boxer Bay—*bay* AK-9
Boxer Island—*island* ME-1
Boxer River—*stream* AK-9
Boxer Valley—*valley* CA-9
Boxes Cave—*cave* AL-4
*Boxes Cove* MD-2
Boxes Cove—*valley* AL-4
Boxes Cove Ch—*church* AL-4
Boxes Cove Sch (historical)—*school* AL-4
*Boxes Creek* TX-5
Boxes Creek—*stream* (2) AL-4
Boxes Creek Sch (historical)—*school* AL-4
*Boxes Ferry* AL-4
Boxes Point—*cape* MD-2
*Boxet Pond* RI-1
Box Factory—*post sta* TX-5
Box Factory Bend—*bend* AR-4
Box Factory Park—*flat* CO-8
Box Flat—*flat* ID-8
Box Flat—*flat* UT-8
**Boxford**—*pop pl* MA-1
Boxford (census name for Boxford Center)—*CDP* MA-1
Boxford Center (census name Boxford)—*other* MA-1
Boxford (historical P.O.)—*locale* MA-1
Boxford State For—*forest* MA-1
**Boxford Station**—*pop pl* MA-1
Boxford Station (historical)—*locale* MA-1
*Boxford (Town of)* MA-1
**Boxford (Town of)**—*pop pl* MA-1
Boxford Village Hist Dist—*hist pl* MA-1
Boxford Wildlife Sanctuary—*park* MA-1
Box Fork—*stream* KY-4
Box Gulch—*valley* ID-8
Box Gulch—*valley* WA-9
Box Hall Flat—*flat* CA-9
Box Hill—*summit* CT-1
Box Hill Ch (historical)—*church* AL-4
Box Hill Estate—*hist pl* NY-2
**Box (historical)**—*pop pl* OR-9
Box Hollow—*valley* (2) TN-4
Box Hollow—*valley* UT-8
**Boxholm**—*pop pl* IA-7
Box Huckleberry Natural Area—*area* PA-2
Boxiron—*locale* MD-2
Boxiron Creek—*stream* MD-2
Boxiron Landing—*locale* MD-2
Box Island—*island* AK-9
Box K Dam—*dam* AZ-5
Box K Ranch—*locale* AZ-5
Box K Tank—*reservoir* AZ-5
Box Lake—*lake* (2) CA-9
Box Lake—*lake* CO-8
Box Lake—*lake* ID-8
Box Lake—*lake* (2) NE-7
Box Lake—*lake* OR-9
Box Lake—*lake* UT-8
Box Lake—*lake* WI-6
Box Lake—*lake* WY-8
Box Lake Trail—*trail* ID-8
Boxley—*locale* AR-4
Boxley—*locale* VA-3
**Boxley**—*pop pl* IN-6
**Boxley**—*pop pl* VA-3
Boxley, Lake—*reservoir* KY-4
Boxley Bldg—*hist pl* VA-3
Boxley Cem—*cemetery* TN-4
Boxley Creek—*stream* AR-4
Boxley Creek—*stream* WA-9
**Boxley Hills**—*pop pl* (2) VA-3
Boxley Park—*park* OH-6
*Boxleytown* IN-6
*Boxley Valley* CA-9
Boxley Valley—*valley* TN-4
Boxley Valley Sch—*school* TN-4
Box Mountain Lakes—*lake* WA-9
Box M Ranch—*locale* NM-5
Box Mtn—*summit* WA-9
Box of Sevenmile, The—*locale* AZ-5
Box of Tenmile, The—*locale* AZ-5
Box O Hills—*summit* AZ-5
Box Oil Field—*oilfield* KS-7
Box Oil Field—*oilfield* TX-5
Box O Ranch—*locale* AZ-5
Box O Wash—*stream* AZ-5
Box Point—*cape* AK-9
Box Point—*cape* FL-3
Box Point—*cape* GA-3
Box Point—*cape* NC-3
Box Pond—*reservoir* MA-1
Box Pond Dam—*dam* MA-1
*Box Post Office* TN-4
Box Prairie—*locale* CO-8
Box Prairie Creek—*stream* CO-8
**Box Quarter**—*pop pl* TX-5
Box Ranch—*locale* CO-8
Box Ranch—*locale* NM-5
Box Ridge—*ridge* WA-9
Box River—*stream* AK-9
Box R Ranch—*locale* FL-3
Box Rsvr—*reservoir* UT-8
Box S Canyon—*valley* NM-5
Boxs Cem—*cemetery* MS-4
Box Sch (historical)—*school* MO-7
*Boxs Creek* MS-4
*Boxs Ferry* AL-4
Box Shack Well—*locale* NM-5
Box Shoals (historical)—*bar* AL-4
*Box Sing Creek* ID-8
Box Sing Creek—*stream* ID-8
Box Slough—*gut* TN-4
Boxs Mill (historical)—*locale* TN-4
*Box Spring* AL-4
*Box Spring* CA-9
*Box Spring* ID-8
Box Spring—*spring* (9) AZ-5
Box Spring—*spring* AR-4
Box Spring—*spring* (6) CA-9
Box Spring—*spring* (6) CO-8
Box Spring—*spring* (4) ID-8
Box Spring—*spring* MT-8
Box Spring—*spring* (6) NV-8
Box Spring—*spring* (2) NM-5
Box Spring—*spring* (10) OR-9
Box Spring—*spring* TX-5
Box Spring—*spring* (7) UT-8
Box Spring—*spring* WA-9
Box Spring—*spring* (7) WY-8
Box Spring Branch—*stream* AR-4
Box Spring Canyon—*valley* WA-9
Box Spring Creek—*stream* CO-8
Box Spring Creek—*stream* OR-9
Box Spring Creek—*stream* WY-8
Box Spring Creek Spring—*spring* NV-8
Box Spring Gulch—*valley* ID-8
Box Spring Hollow—*valley* UT-8
Box Spring Mtn—*summit* OK-5
Box Spring Ridge—*ridge* CA-9
Box Spring Rsvr—*reservoir* OR-9
Box Spring Rsvr—*reservoir* WY-8
Box Springs—*locale* AR-4
Box Springs—*locale* CA-9
**Box Springs**—*pop pl* GA-3
Box Springs—*spring* CA-9
Box Springs—*spring* (2) CO-8
Box Springs—*spring* ID-8
Box Springs—*spring* MT-8
Box Springs—*spring* NV-8
Box Springs—*spring* OR-9
Box Springs—*spring* TX-5
Box Springs—*spring* (2) WA-9
Box Springs—*spring* (2) WY-8
Box Springs Butte—*summit* OR-9
Box Springs Canyon—*valley* CA-9
Box Springs Canyon—*valley* NV-8
Box Springs Ch—*church* OK-5
Box Spring Sch—*school* GA-3
Box Springs Dam—*dam* OR-9
*Box Spring Siding* AL-4
Box Springs Lookout—*locale* CA-9
Box Springs Mountains—*range* CA-9
Box Springs Mtn—*summit* OK-5
Box Springs Rsvr No 1—*reservoir* CO-8
Box Springs Rsvr No 2—*reservoir* CO-8
Box Springs Rsvr No 3—*reservoir* CO-8
Box Springs Rsvr No 4—*reservoir* CO-8
Box Springs Rsvr No 5—*reservoir* CO-8
Box Springs (Siding)—*locale* CA-9
**Box Springs (subdivision)**—*pop pl* AL-4
Box S Springs—*spring* CA-9
Box Tank—*reservoir* (2) AZ-5
Box Tank—*reservoir* (5) NM-5
**Boxtel**—*pop pl* AL-4
Boxter Cem—*cemetery* OH-6
*Boxtown* IL-6
*Boxtown* PA-2
Boxtown—*other* IL-6
Box Township—*civil* MO-7
Box T Ranch—*locale* NE-7
Box Trap Tank—*reservoir* AZ-5
Box Tree Creek—*stream* VA-3
Box T Spring—*spring* AZ-5
Box T Tank—*reservoir* AZ-5
Boxville—*locale* KY-4
**Boxville (Township of)**—*pop pl* MN-6
Box Wash—*stream* AZ-5
Boxwell Reservation—*park* TN-4
Box Windmill—*locale* TX-5
Boxwood—*hist pl* AL-4
Boxwood—*hist pl* TN-4
Boxwood—*locale* TX-5
Boxwood—*locale* VA-3
**Boxwood**—*pop pl* DE-2
Boxwood Cem—*cemetery* NY-2
Boxwood Ch—*church* NC-3
Boxwood Gulch—*valley* CO-8
Boxwood Hall—*hist pl* NJ-2
**Boxwood Hills**—*pop pl* TN-4
Boxwoods, The—*hist pl* NC-3
**Boxwood Village**—*pop pl* MD-2
Boxwood Wildlife Sanctuary—*park* MA-1
Box X Cem—*cemetery* OK-5
Box Y Ranch—*locale* WY-8
Boyan, Mount—*summit* AK-9
Boyatt Cem—*cemetery* TN-4
Boy Bay—*bay* MN-6
Boy Brook—*stream* NH-1
*Boyce* MS-4
Boyce—*locale* KY-4
Boyce—*locale* PA-2
**Boyce**—*pop pl* LA-4
**Boyce**—*pop pl* NH-1
**Boyce**—*pop pl* TN-4
**Boyce**—*pop pl* TX-5
**Boyce**—*pop pl* VA-3
Boyce, Lake—*reservoir* NY-2
Boyce Block—*hist pl* IN-6
Boyce Branch—*stream* LA-4
Boyce Brook—*stream* MA-1
Boyce Brook—*stream* (2) NH-1
Boyce Brothers Ditch—*canal* CO-8
Boyce Canyon—*valley* NM-5
Boyce Cem—*cemetery* LA-4
Boyce Cem—*cemetery* MO-7
Boyce Cem—*cemetery* OH-6
Boyce Cem—*cemetery* (2) WV-2
Boyce Chapel—*church* WV-2
Boyce Corral—*locale* OR-9
Boyce Cove—*bay* ME-1
Boyce Creek—*stream* AR-4
Boyce Creek—*stream* ND-7
Boyce Creek—*stream* TX-5
Boyce Creek—*stream* WA-9
Boyce Drain—*canal* MI-6
Boyce Elem Sch—*school* PA-2
Boyce-Gregg House—*hist pl* TN-4
Boyce Gulch—*valley* CO-8
Boyce Hill—*summit* AR-4
Boyce Hill—*summit* MA-1
Boyce Hill—*summit* NY-2
Boyce Hill—*summit* VT-1
Boyce Hollow—*valley* TN-4
Boyce Lake—*lake* (2) MI-6
Boyce Lake—*lake* MS-4
Boyce Lake—*reservoir* AR-4
Boyce Lake—*reservoir* CO-8
Boyce Lake—*swamp* LA-4
Boy Cem—*cemetery* TN-4
Boyce Meadow Spring—*spring* MT-8
Boyce Memorial Ch—*church* NC-3
Boyce Monohan Pond Dam—*dam* MS-4
Boyce Mtn—*summit* VT-1
Boyce Oil Field—*oilfield* MS-4
Boyce Oil Field—*oilfield* TX-5
Boyce Olive Dam—*dam* NC-3
Boyce Park—*park* NY-2
Boyce Park Ski Area—*locale* PA-2
Boyce Playground—*park* IL-6
Boyce Ranch—*locale* OR-9
Boyce Ravine—*valley* CA-9
Boyce Rsvr—*reservoir* MT-8
Boyce Run—*stream* NY-2
Boyce Sch—*school* MI-6
Boyce Sch—*school* VT-1
Boyce Shelter—*locale* VT-1
Boyce Spring—*spring* AZ-5
Boyce spring—*spring* OR-9
Boyce Station—*hist pl* PA-2
Boyce Tank—*reservoir* NM-5
**Boyceville**—*pop pl* WI-6
Boyce Waterhole—*lake* OR-9
Boy Creek—*stream* KS-7
Boy Creek Campground—*park* AZ-5
Boyd—*locale* AR-4
Boyd—*locale* KS-7
Boyd—*locale* MI-6
Boyd—*locale* NV-8
Boyd—*locale* NM-5
Boyd—*locale* OK-5
Boyd—*locale* (2) PA-2
Boyd—*locale* SC-3
Boyd—*locale* TN-4
Boyd—*locale* TX-5
**Boyd**—*pop pl* AL-4
**Boyd**—*pop pl* AR-4
**Boyd**—*pop pl* (2) CA-9
**Boyd**—*pop pl* FL-3
**Boyd**—*pop pl* IL-6
**Boyd**—*pop pl* IN-6
**Boyd**—*pop pl* IA-7
**Boyd**—*pop pl* KY-4
**Boyd**—*pop pl* MN-6
**Boyd**—*pop pl* MT-8
**Boyd**—*pop pl* OR-9
**Boyd**—*pop pl* SC-3
**Boyd**—*pop pl* TX-5
**Boyd**—*pop pl* WV-2
**Boyd**—*pop pl* WI-6
Boyd, Adam, House—*hist pl* AR-4
Boyd, Charles, Homestead Group—*hist pl* OR-9
Boyd, James, House—*hist pl* NC-3
Boyd, Thomas Sloan, House—*hist pl* AR-4
Boyd, William, House—*hist pl* TN-4
**Boyd Acres (subdivision)**—*pop pl* TN-4
Boyd Basin—*basin* NV-8
Boyd Basin Spring—*spring* NV-8
Boyd Bend—*bend* KY-4
Boyd Bottoms—*basin* TN-4
*Boyd (Boyds)* MD-2
Boyd Branch—*stream* (2) AR-4
Boyd Branch—*stream* (2) GA-3
Boyd Branch—*stream* IN-6
Boyd Branch—*stream* IA-7
Boyd Branch—*stream* (3) KY-4
Boyd Branch—*stream* (2) MO-7
Boyd Branch—*stream* (2) NC-3
Boyd Branch—*stream* SC-3
Boyd Branch—*stream* (2) TN-4
Boyd Branch—*stream* (3) TX-5
Boyd Branch—*stream* (2) VA-3
Boyd Branch—*stream* (2) WV-2
Boyd Branch Knob—*summit* WV-2
Boyd Bridge—*bridge* NC-3
Boyd Bridge—*bridge* TN-4
Boyd Brook—*stream* IN-6
Boyd Brook—*stream* ME-1
Boyd Brook—*stream* RI-1
Boyd Brook—*stream* VT-1
Boyd Brothers Catfish Ponds Dam—*dam* MS-4
Boyd Brothers Lake—*reservoir* TN-4
Boyd Brothers Lake Dam—*dam* TN-4
Boyd Buchanan Sch—*school* TN-4
Boyd Callan, Lake—*lake* TX-5
Boyd Canal—*canal* SC-3
Boyd Canyon—*valley* NV-8
Boyd Canyon—*valley* TX-5
Boyd Canyon Spring—*spring* NV-8
Boyd Cave—*cave* OR-9
Boyd Cem—*cemetery* (5) AL-4
Boyd Cem—*cemetery* AR-4
Boyd Cem—*cemetery* IL-6
Boyd Cem—*cemetery* IN-6
Boyd Cem—*cemetery* IA-7
Boyd Cem—*cemetery* (4) KY-4
Boyd Cem—*cemetery* MI-6
Boyd Cem—*cemetery* (7) MS-4
Boyd Cem—*cemetery* (2) MO-7
Boyd Cem—*cemetery* NH-1
Boyd Cem—*cemetery* (3) OH-6
Boyd Cem—*cemetery* PA-2
Boyd Cem—*cemetery* SC-3
Boyd Cem—*cemetery* (12) TN-4
Boyd Cem—*cemetery* TX-5
Boyd Cem—*cemetery* (3) VA-3
Boyd Cem—*cemetery* WI-6
Boyd Cem—*cemetery* WY-8
Boyd Center Corners—*locale* PA-2
Boyd Ch—*church* (2) AR-4
Boyd Chapel—*church* MS-4
Boyd Chapel Cem—*cemetery* GA-3
Boyd Corner—*locale* ME-1
Boyd Corners Rsvr—*reservoir* NY-2
Boyd-Cothern House—*hist pl* MS-4
**Boyd (County)**—*pop pl* KY-4
Boyd County Tabernacle—*church* KY-4
*Boyd Creek* NY-2
*Boyd Creek* WY-8
Boyd Creek—*stream* AL-4
Boyd Creek—*stream* (2) AR-4
Boyd Creek—*stream* (3) CA-9
Boyd Creek—*stream* ID-8
Boyd Creek—*stream* IL-6
Boyd Creek—*stream* (2) MS-4
Boyd Creek—*stream* (3) MT-8
Boyd Creek—*stream* (2) NV-8
Boyd Creek—*stream* NC-3
Boyd Creek—*stream* OH-6
Boyd Creek—*stream* (2) OR-9
Boyd Creek—*stream* SC-3
Boyd Creek—*stream* TN-4
Boyd Creek—*stream* (2) TX-5
Boyd Creek—*stream* (2) WA-9
Boyd Creek—*stream* (2) WI-6
Boyd Creek Campground—*locale* ID-8
**Boyd Crossing**—*pop pl* AL-4
Boyd Crossroads—*locale* NC-3
Boyd Dam—*dam* AL-4
Boyd Ditch—*canal* IL-6
Boyd Ditch—*canal* (2) IN-6
*Boyd Elementary School* MS-4
**Boydell**—*pop pl* AR-4
Boydell, William C., House—*hist pl* MI-6
**Boyden**—*pop pl* IA-7
Boyden, John, House—*hist pl* UT-8
Boyden, Seth, House—*hist pl* MA-1
**Boyden Arbor**—*pop pl* SC-3
Boyden Arbor Pond—*reservoir* SC-3
Boyden Brook—*stream* NY-2
Boyden Brook—*stream* PA-2
Boyden Brook—*stream* VT-1
Boyden Cave—*cave* CA-9
Boyden Cem—*cemetery* MA-1
Boyden Cow Camp—*locale* CO-8
Boyden Creek—*stream* AK-9
*Boyden Heights* RI-1
Boyden HS—*school* NC-3
Boyden Lake—*lake* AL-4
Boyden Lake—*lake* ME-1
Boyden Lake Dam—*dam* AL-4
Boyden Rec Area—*park* IA-7
Boyden Sch—*school* NJ-2
Boyden Stream—*stream* ME-1
Boyd Ferry (historical)—*crossing* TN-4
Boyd Ferry (historical)—*locale* NC-3
Boyd Ford—*locale* IL-6
Boyd Fork—*stream* VA-3
Boyd Friendship Ch—*church* SC-3
Boyd Gap—*gap* (2) NC-3
Boyd Gap—*gap* TN-4
Boyd Gulch—*valley* CA-9
Boyd Gulch—*valley* (2) CO-8
Boyd H Anderson HS—*school* FL-3
Boyd-Harvey House—*hist pl* TN-4
Boyd Highlands—*locale* GA-3
Boyd Hill—*locale* AR-4
**Boyd Hill**—*pop pl* SC-3
Boyd Hill—*summit* CA-9
Boyd Hill—*summit* IL-6
Boyd Hill—*summit* IN-6
Boyd Hill—*summit* WA-9
Boyd Hill Cem—*cemetery* AR-4
Boyd Hill Ch—*church* KY-4
Boyd Hollow—*valley* (2) AR-4
Boyd Hollow—*valley* ID-8
Boyd Hollow—*valley* KY-4
Boyd Hollow—*valley* MO-7
Boyd Hollow—*valley* (4) TN-4
Boyd Hollow—*valley* VA-3
Boyd Hollow—*valley* WY-8
Boyd Hollow Branch—*stream* TN-4
Boyd Hollow Cave—*cave* TN-4
Boyd Hot Spring—*spring* CA-9
Boyd House—*hist pl* CA-9
Boyd HS—*school* CA-9
Boyd Island—*island* TN-4
Boyd Keller Reservoir Dam—*dam* PA-2
Boyd Knob—*summit* KY-4
Boyd Knob—*summit* TN-4
Boyd Knob Hollow—*valley* TN-4
Boyd Knoll—*summit* AZ-5
Boyd Lake—*lake* FL-3
Boyd Lake—*lake* ID-8

Boyd Lake—*lake* KY-4
Boyd Lake—*lake* ME-1
Boyd Lake—*lake* MI-6
Boyd Lake—*lake* MN-6
Boyd Lake—*lake* ND-7
Boyd Lake—*lake* TX-5
Boyd Lake—*lake* WA-9
**Boyd Lake**—*pop pl* ME-1
Boyd Lake—*reservoir* AL-4
Boyd Lake—*reservoir* CO-8
Boyd Lake—*reservoir* IN-6
Boyd Lake Branch—*stream* KY-4
Boyd Lake Dam—*dam* IN-6
Boyd Lane Baptist Ch (historical)—*church* AL-4
**Boyd Lodge**—*pop pl* TX-5
Boyd-Lynch Cem—*cemetery* TN-4
Boyd Memorial Ch—*church* NC-3
Boyd Memorial Ch—*church* TN-4
Boyd Memorial Park—*cemetery* CA-9
*Boyd Memorial Presbyterian Ch* NC-3
Boyd Mill Branch—*stream* AL-4
Boyd Mill Cem—*cemetery* MT-8
**Boyd Mill Estates (subdivision)**—*pop pl* TN-4
Boyd Millpond—*reservoir* SC-3
Boyd Mill Ruins—*hist pl* TN-4
Boyd Mine—*mine* (2) TN-4
Boyd Mountain Spring—*spring* AZ-5
Boyd Mtn—*summit* AZ-5
Boyd Mtn—*summit* (3) AR-4
Boyd Mtn—*summit* CO-8
Boyd Mtn—*summit* GA-3
Boyd Mtn—*summit* MD-2
Boyd Mtn—*summit* (2) MT-8
Boyd Mtn—*summit* VA-3
Boyd Neck—*cape* SC-3
Boyd No. 2 Rsvr—*reservoir* CO-8
Boyd Number 2 Mine (underground)—*mine* AL-4
Boyd Oil And Gas Field—*other* MI-6
Boyd Oil Field—*oilfield* KS-7
Boyd Oil Field—*oilfield* TX-5
Boyd Oil Field—*other* IL-6
Boyd Park—*park* NM-5
Boyd Park—*park* TN-4
Boyd Park—*park* WI-6
Boyd-Parker State Park—*park* NY-2
Boyd Point—*cape* AR-4
Boyd Point—*cape* MD-2
Boyd Point—*cape* NY-2
Boyd Point—*cape* NC-3
Boyd Point Cutoff—*channel* AR-4
Boyd Pond—*lake* (2) ME-1
Boyd Pond—*lake* MD-2
Boyd Pond—*lake* MO-7
Boyd Pond—*lake* NY-2
*Boyd Pony Express and Stage Station* UT-8
*Boyd Pony Express Station Ruins* UT-8
Boyd Post Office (historical)—*building* AL-4
Boyd Ranch—*locale* CA-9
Boyd Ranch—*locale* (2) NE-7
Boyd Ranch—*locale* (2) TX-5
Boyd Reid Tank—*reservoir* AZ-5
Boyd-Rhome (CCD)—*cens area* TX-5
Boyd Ridge—*ridge* TN-4
Boyd Ridge—*ridge* (2) VA-3
Boyd Ridge—*ridge* WY-8
Boyd Rsvr—*reservoir* CO-8
Boyd Rsvr—*reservoir* NV-8
Boyd Run—*stream* KY-4
Boyd Run—*stream* (2) PA-2
Boyd Run—*stream* WV-2
*Boyds* AL-4
Boyds—*locale* AL-4
Boyds—*locale* WA-9
**Boyds**—*pop pl* MD-2
**Boyds**—*pop pl* SC-3
**Boyds (Boyd)**—*pop pl* MD-2
*Boyds Branch* IN-6
Boyds Branch—*stream* KY-4
Boyds Camp (historical)—*locale* AL-4
Boyds Canyon—*valley* NM-5
Boyds Cave—*cave* NM-5
*Boyds Cem* AL-4
Boyds Cem—*cemetery* AL-4
Boyds Ch—*church* WV-2
Boyd Sch—*hist pl* OH-6
Boyd Sch—*school* AR-4
Boyd Sch—*school* CA-9
Boyd Sch—*school* CO-8
Boyd Sch—*school* KY-4
Boyd Sch—*school* (3) MI-6
Boyd Sch—*school* (2) MS-4
Boyd Sch—*school* MO-7
Boyd Sch—*school* NC-3
Boyd Sch—*school* (2) PA-2
Boyd Sch—*school* SC-3
Boyd Sch—*school* VA-3
Boyd Sch—*school* (2) WI-6
Boyd Sch (abandoned)—*school* (2) MO-7
Boyds Chapel—*locale* TX-5
Boyds Chapel Ch—*church* AL-4
Boyd Sch (historical)—*school* AL-4
Boyd Sch (historical)—*school* (2) MS-4
Boyd Sch (historical)—*school* MO-7
Boyd Sch (historical)—*school* TN-4
Boyds Corner—*locale* DE-2
Boyds Corners—*locale* (2) NY-2
Boyds Corners—*locale* OH-6
*Boyds Creek* SC-3
Boyds Creek—*locale* TN-4
Boyds Creek—*stream* AL-4
Boyds Creek—*stream* GA-3
Boyds Creek—*stream* KY-4
Boyds Creek—*stream* MO-7
Boyds Creek—*stream* NC-3
Boyds Creek—*stream* TN-4
Boyds Creek Cem—*cemetery* TN-4
Boyds Creek Ch—*church* KY-4
Boyds Creek Ch—*church* TN-4
Boyds Creek Sch—*school* TN-4
Boyds Crossing—*locale* AL-4
**Boyds Crossing**—*pop pl* KY-4
*Boyds Crossroads* VA-3
*Boyds Ferry* TN-4
Boyds Ferry (historical)—*locale* MS-4
Boyds Fork—*locale* NC-3
Boyds Gap—*gap* WV-2
Boyds Grove Ch—*church* IL-6
Boyds Hill—*summit* VT-1
*Boyd Shoals* DE-2
Boyds Hollow—*valley* IL-6
Boyds Hotel—*locale* NJ-2
Boyds Lake—*lake* FL-3
Boyds Lake—*reservoir* NC-3
Boyds Lake Dam—*dam* NC-3
Boyds Landing—*locale* AL-4
Boyds Mill—*locale* VA-3
Boyds Mill Creek—*stream* AL-4
Boyds Mills—*locale* PA-2
Boyds Mill Sch (historical)—*school* TN-4
Boyds Neck—*area* NC-3
Boydson Draw—*valley* SD-7
Boyds Pond—*lake* NY-2
Boyds Pond—*reservoir* SC-3
Boyd Spring—*spring* CA-9
Boyd Spring—*spring* MT-8
Boyd Spring—*spring* NV-8
Boyd Spring—*spring* OR-9
Boyd Spring—*spring* TN-4
Boyd Spring—*spring* WI-6
Boyd Spring Branch—*stream* AL-4
Boyd Spring Branch—*stream* TN-4
Boyd Spring Pond (historical)—*lake* TN-4
Boyd Spring Ranch—*locale* CA-9
Boyd Springs—*spring* CO-8
*Boyds Run* PA-2
Boyds Run—*stream* PA-2
Boyds Run (historical)—*stream* PA-2
Boyds Store (historical)—*locale* AL-4
*Boyds Tank* AL-4
**Boyds Tank**—*pop pl* AL-4
Boyd Station (Pony Express Station Ruins)—*locale* UT-8
*Boyd's Tavern* VA-3
Boyd's Tavern—*hist pl* VA-3
Boydston—*locale* TX-5
Boydston Cem—*cemetery* AR-4
Boydston Cem—*cemetery* TN-4
Boydston Cem—*cemetery* TX-5
Boydston Creek—*stream* AL-4
**Boydstown**—*pop pl* PA-2
Boydstown Dam—*dam* PA-2
Boydstown Rsvr—*reservoir* PA-2
Boydstun Sch—*school* TX-5
Boydstun Windmill—*locale* TX-5
Boyds Union Chapel—*church* NC-3
Boydsville—*locale* KY-4
Boydsville—*locale* MO-7
**Boydsville**—*pop pl* AR-4
**Boydsville**—*pop pl* OH-6
**Boydsville**—*pop pl* TN-4
Boydsville Cem—*cemetery* MO-7
Boydsville Cem—*cemetery* TN-4
Boydsville Ch—*church* AR-4
Boydsville Post Office (historical)—*building* TN-4
Boyd Tank—*reservoir* AZ-5
Boyd Tank—*reservoir* TX-5
Boyd Tavern—*locale* VA-3
**Boydton**—*pop pl* VA-3
Boydton (Magisterial District)—*fmr MCD* VA-3
Boydtown—*locale* KY-4
Boydtown—*locale* WI-6
**Boydtown**—*pop pl* PA-2
**Boyd Township**—*pop pl* ND-7
Boyd (Township of)—*fmr MCD* NC-3
Boyd Trail—*trail* AR-4
Boydville—*hist pl* WV-2
Boydville—*locale* (2) GA-3
Boydville Hist Dist—*hist pl* WV-2
Boyd Well—*well* TX-5
Boyd Workings—*mine* TN-4
*Boyenton Creek* AL-4
*Boyer* SC-3
Boyer—*locale* MO-7
Boyer—*locale* OR-9
**Boyer**—*pop pl* IA-7
**Boyer**—*pop pl* MS-4
**Boyer**—*pop pl* PA-2
**Boyer**—*pop pl* WV-2
Boyer, Earl, House—*hist pl* MO-7
Boyer, John F., House—*hist pl* WA-9
Boyer, Riter, House—*hist pl* PA-2
Boyer Airp—*airport* PA-2
Boyer Bend—*bend* IA-7
Boyer Bend—*bend* NE-7
Boyer Bluff—*cliff* WI-6
Boyer Branch—*stream* TN-4
Boyer Brook—*stream* PA-2
Boyer Canyon—*valley* AZ-5
Boyer Cem—*cemetery* GA-3
Boyer Cem—*cemetery* IL-6
Boyer Cem—*cemetery* (2) IA-7
Boyer Cem—*cemetery* MS-4
Boyer Cem—*cemetery* MO-7
Boyer Cem—*cemetery* PA-2
Boyer Cem—*cemetery* (2) TN-4
Boyer Cem—*cemetery* VA-3
Boyer Ch—*church* KY-4
Boyer Ch—*church* PA-2
Boyer Chapel—*church* MD-2
Boyer Chute—*stream* NE-7
*Boyer Creek* IA-7
*Boyer Creek* MS-4
Boyer Creek—*stream* (2) CA-9
Boyer Creek—*stream* ID-8
Boyer Creek—*stream* IL-6
Boyer Creek—*stream* IA-7
Boyer Creek—*stream* MS-4
Boyer Creek—*stream* MT-8
Boyer Creek—*stream* NY-2
Boyer Creek—*stream* OR-9
Boyer Creek—*stream* WA-9
Boyer Ditch—*canal* (2) IN-6
Boyer Ditch—*canal* IA-7
Boyer Gap—*gap* AZ-5
Boyer Gap—*gap* VA-3
Boyer Gulch—*valley* CO-8
Boyer Gulch—*valley* (2) ID-8
Boyer Gulch—*valley* NM-5
Boyer Island—*island* TN-4
Boyer Knob—*summit* MD-2
Boyer Lake—*lake* (2) MN-6
Boyer Lake—*lake* NY-2
Boyer Lake—*reservoir* (2) UT-8
Boyer Lake Dam—*dam* UT-8
Boyer Mine—*mine* CA-9
Boyer Mtn—*summit* WA-9
Boyer Natl Wildlife Ref—*park* ND-7
Boyer Number 1 Cave—*cave* PA-2
Boyer Number 2 Cave—*cave* PA-2
Boyer Number 3 Cave—*cave* PA-2
Boyero—*locale* CO-8
Boyero Cem—*cemetery* CO-8
Boyer Peak—*summit* AK-9
Boyer Playground—*park* MI-6
Boyer Pond—*reservoir* PA-2
Boyer Ranch—*locale* CA-9
Boyer Ranch—*locale* (2) NE-7
Boyer Ranch—*locale* NV-8
Boyer Ranch—*locale* WY-8
Boyer Ridge—*ridge* AZ-5
Boyer Ridge—*ridge* AR-4
**Boyer River**—*pop pl* IA-7
Boyer River—*stream* IA-7
Boyer Run—*stream* (2) PA-2
**Boyers**—*pop pl* PA-2
Boyers Bend—*bend* CA-9
*Boyer's Bluff* WI-6
Boyers Ch—*church* NC-3
Boyer Sch—*school* OH-6
Boyer Sch—*school* (3) PA-2
Boyer Sch (abandoned)—*school* PA-2
*Boyers Creek* MS-4
**Boyers Junction**—*pop pl* PA-2
Boyers Knob Lookout Tower—*locale* PA-2
Boyers Lake—*lake* KS-7
Boyers Landing—*locale* CA-9
Boyer Slough—*stream* ID-8
**Boyers (RR name Annandale)**—*pop pl* PA-2
Boyers Run—*stream* (2) PA-2
Boyer State Public Shooting Area—*park* SD-7
Boyer Station—*locale* PA-2
**Boyertown**—*pop pl* PA-2
Boyertown Borough—*civil* PA-2
Boyertown Reservoir Dam—*dam* PA-2
Boyertown Rsvr—*reservoir* PA-2
Boyer Township—*fmr MCD* (2) IA-7
Boyer Trail—*trail* PA-2
Boyer Trail One Hundred Fortyeight—*trail* AZ-5
Boyer Valley Township—*fmr MCD* IA-7
**Boyes**—*pop pl* MT-8
**Boyes Acres Subdivision**—*pop pl* UT-8
Boyes Creek—*stream* (2) CA-9
**Boyesen Township**—*pop pl* ND-7
**Boyes Hot Springs**—*pop pl* CA-9
Boyet Cem—*cemetery* TN-4
*Boyett* NC-3
Boyett Cem—*cemetery* LA-4
Boyett Cem—*cemetery* (2) TN-4
Boyett Cem—*cemetery* TX-5
*Boyette* NC-3
Boyette—*locale* FL-3
**Boyette**—*pop pl* MS-4
Boyette Pond—*reservoir* GA-3
Boyette Sch (historical)—*school* MS-4
*Boyettes Crossing* MS-4
Boyette Slave House—*hist pl* NC-3
Boyett Sch (historical)—*school* TN-4
Boyett Spring—*spring* TN-4
Boygan Lake—*lake* WI-6
**Boy (historical)**—*pop pl* TN-4
Boyington Brook—*stream* NY-2
Boykin—*locale* AL-4
Boykin—*locale* SC-3
**Boykin**—*pop pl* (2) AL-4
**Boykin**—*pop pl* FL-3
**Boykin**—*pop pl* GA-3
**Boykin**—*pop pl* SC-3
Boykin, Gen. Thomas, House—*hist pl* NC-3
Boykin, Maj. Francis, House—*hist pl* GA-3
**Boykin (Babcock)**—*pop pl* GA-3
*Boykin Bogue* MS-4
Boykin Branch—*stream* FL-3
Boykin Branch—*stream* GA-3
Boykin (CCD)—*cens area* SC-3
Boykin Cem—*cemetery* (2) AL-4
Boykin Cem—*cemetery* SC-3
Boykin Cem—*cemetery* (2) TX-5
Boykin Ch—*church* MS-4
Boykin Church Oil Field—*oilfield* MS-4
*Boykin Community Center* AL-4
Boykin Creek—*stream* AL-4
Boykin Creek—*stream* MS-4
Boykin Creek—*stream* OR-9
Boykin Creek—*stream* TX-5
Boykin Dam—*dam* AL-4
Boykin Elem Sch—*school* AL-4
**Boykin (Gees Bend)**—*pop pl* AL-4
Boykin (historical)—*locale* MS-4
Boykin JHS—*school* AL-4
Boykin Lake—*reservoir* AL-4
Boykin Mill Pond—*reservoir* SC-3
Boykin Park—*park* AL-4
Boykin Ponds—*lake* GA-3
Boykin RR Station—*locale* FL-3
*Boykins* MS-4
**Boykins**—*pop pl* VA-3
Boykin Sch—*school* (2) AL-4
Boykin Sch—*school* SC-3
Boykins Island—*island* VA-3
Boykins (Magisterial District)—*fmr MCD* VA-3
*Boykins Mill Pond* SC-3
Boykins Post Office (historical)—*building* MS-4
Boykin Spring—*spring* TX-5
*Boykins Sch* AL-4
Boykin State Wildlife Mngmt Area—*park* AL-4
Boykin's Tavern—*hist pl* VA-3
Boykin Truitt Cem—*cemetery* AL-4
*Boy Lake* MN-6
Boy Lake—*lake* (2) MN-6
Boy Lake—*lake* MT-8
**Boy Lake (Township of)**—*pop pl* MN-6
Boy Lake Waterhole—*reservoir* OR-9
Boylan—*uninc pl* NC-3
Boylan Cem—*cemetery* IA-7
Boylan Central HS—*school* IL-6
Boylan Ch—*church* MS-4
Boylan Chapel—*church* NC-3
Boylan Creek—*stream* IA-7
Boylan Heights—*hist pl* NC-3
Boylan Heights Sch—*school* NC-3
**Boylan Heights (subdivision)**—*pop pl* NC-3
Boylan Ranch—*locale* (2) NM-5
Boylan Sch (abandoned)—*school* PA-2
Boylans Grove (historical P.O.)—*locale* IA-7
Boyle—*locale* IL-6
Boyle—*locale* KS-7
**Boyle**—*pop pl* MS-4
**Boyle**—*pop pl* ND-7
Boyle—*uninc pl* CA-9
Boyle, John R., House—*hist pl* IA-7
Boyle, Judge John, House—*hist pl* KY-4
*Boyle Arroyo* CO-8
Boyle Bayou—*stream* LA-4
*Boyle Branch* TN-4
Boyle Branch—*stream* TX-5
Boyle Brook—*stream* NH-1
Boyle Brook—*stream* WI-6
Boyle Cabin—*locale* NV-8
Boyle Canyon—*valley* ID-8
Boyle Cem—*cemetery* KS-7
Boyle Cem—*cemetery* TX-5
Boyle Coulee—*valley* MT-8
**Boyle (County)**—*pop pl* KY-4
Boyle County Courthouse—*hist pl* KY-4
*Boyle Creek* ID-8
*Boyle Creek* WI-6
Boyle Creek—*stream* (2) ID-8
Boyle Creek—*stream* MI-6
Boyle Creek—*stream* NV-8
Boyle Creek—*stream* OR-9
Boyle Creek Rsvr—*reservoir* ID-8
Boyle Ditch—*canal* IN-6
Boyle Drain—*canal* MI-6
Boyle Gap—*gap* AL-4
Boyle Gulch—*valley* (2) MT-8
**Boyle Heights**—*pop pl* CA-9
Boyle Heights Recreation Center—*park* CA-9
Boyle/Hudspeth-Benson House—*hist pl* NJ-2
Boyle Investment Company Lake—*reservoir* TN-4
Boyle Investment Company Lake Dam—*dam* TN-4
Boyle Lake—*lake* MI-6
Boyle Lake—*lake* MT-8
Boyle Lake—*lake* WA-9
Boyle Lake—*reservoir* IN-6
Boyle Lakes—*reservoir* KS-7
Boyle Lakes (duck ponds)—*reservoir* OR-9
Boyle Mtn—*summit* ID-8
Boyle Oil Field—*oilfield* TX-5
Boyle Park—*park* AR-4
Boyle Pond—*reservoir* PA-2
Boyle Ranch—*locale* ID-8
Boyle Ravine—*valley* CA-9
Boyler Cem—*cemetery* IL-6
Boyle-Robertson-Letcher House—*hist pl* KY-4
**Boylers Mill**—*pop pl* MO-7
Boylers Mill Spring—*spring* MO-7
Boyle Rsvr—*reservoir* WY-8
*Boyle Run* PA-2
Boyles—*uninc pl* AL-4
Boyles Branch—*stream* GA-3
Boyles Branch—*stream* VA-3
Boyles Brook—*stream* WI-6
Boyles Cem—*cemetery* AL-4
Boyles Cem—*cemetery* KY-4
Boyles Cem—*cemetery* MS-4
Boyles Cem—*cemetery* OH-6
Boyle Sch—*school* PA-2
Boyles Chapel—*church* MS-4
Boyles Chapel—*church* NC-3
**Boyles Chapel**—*pop pl* NC-3
Boyles Chapel Cem—*cemetery* MS-4
*Boyles Chapel Methodist Church* MS-4
Boyles Corners—*locale* PA-2
*Boyles Creek* CA-9
*Boyles Creek* TX-5
Boyles Creek—*stream* MI-6
Boyles Ditch—*canal* IN-6
Boyles Gap—*gap* AL-4
Boyles Gap Lake—*reservoir* AL-4
Boyles Gap Lake Dam—*dam* AL-4
Boyles Gulch—*valley* ID-8
**Boyles Highlands**—*pop pl* AL-4
Boyles Hill—*summit* WY-8
Boyles Island—*island* GA-3
Boyles Lake—*lake* WA-9
Boyles Mill (historical)—*locale* MS-4
Boyles Point—*cape* ME-1
Boyles Sch—*school* KY-4
Boyles Sch—*school* OR-9
*Boyles Station* KS-7
**Boyleston**—*pop pl* IL-6
**Boyleston**—*pop pl* IN-6
Boyleston (historical P.O.)—*locale* IA-7
Boyleston Sch—*school* IL-6
*Boylestown* IL-6
*Boylestown* IN-6
Boyles 1 Drill Hole—*well* NV-8
Boyle Tunnel—*tunnel* NV-8
Boyll Lake Dam—*dam* IN-6
Boylston—*locale* WA-9
Boylston—*locale* WI-6
**Boylston**—*pop pl* AL-4
**Boylston**—*pop pl* MA-1
*Boylston, Town of* MA-1
Boylston Bldg—*hist pl* MA-1
Boylston Center—*locale* NY-2
**Boylston Center**—*pop pl* MA-1
*Boylston Centre* MA-1
*Boylston Corner* NY-2
**Boylston Creek**—*pop pl* NC-3
Boylston Creek—*stream* NC-3
Boylston Creek Ch—*church* NC-3
*Boylston District* NY-2
Boylston Junction—*locale* WI-6
Boylston Methodist Ch—*church* AL-4
Boylston Mountains—*range* WA-9
Boylston Ridge—*ridge* NC-3
Boylston Sch—*school* MA-1
Boylston Station—*locale* MA-1
**Boylston (Town of)**—*pop pl* MA-1
**Boylston (Town of)**—*pop pl* NY-2
Boy Mtn—*summit* NH-1
*Boyne* MI-6
**Boyne City**—*pop pl* MI-6
**Boyne Falls**—*pop pl* MI-6
Boyne Mtn—*summit* MI-6
Boyne River—*stream* MI-6
Boyne Valley Cem—*cemetery* MI-6
Boyne Valley (Township of)—*civ div* MI-6
*Boynton* FL-3
Boynton—*locale* IL-6
Boynton—*locale* TX-5
**Boynton**—*pop pl* AR-4
**Boynton**—*pop pl* GA-3
**Boynton**—*pop pl* MO-7
**Boynton**—*pop pl* OK-5
**Boynton**—*pop pl* PA-2
Boynton and Windsor—*hist pl* MA-1
**Boynton Beach**—*pop pl* FL-3
**Boynton Beach**—*pop pl* NJ-2
Boynton Beach-Delray Beach (CCD)—*cens area* FL-3
Boynton Beach Development Center—*school* FL-3
Boynton Beach Elem Sch—*school* FL-3
Boynton Beach Fashion Square (Shop Ctr)—*locale* FL-3
Boynton Beach Mall—*locale* FL-3
Boynton Beach Plaza (Shop Ctr)—*locale* FL-3
Boynton Brook—*stream* (3) ME-1
Boynton Canal—*canal* FL-3
Boynton Canyon—*valley* AZ-5
Boynton (CCD)—*cens area* OK-5
Boynton Cem—*cemetery* LA-4
Boynton Cem—*cemetery* MI-6
Boynton Cem—*cemetery* OH-6
Boynton Cem—*cemetery* OK-5
Boynton Cem—*cemetery* TN-4
Boynton Cem—*cemetery* TX-5
Boynton Chapel—*church* WI-6
Boynton Christian Acad—*school* FL-3
Boynton Creek—*stream* NY-2
Boynton Cutoff—*channel* FL-3
Boynton Dam—*dam* MA-1
Boynton Hill—*summit* (2) NH-1
Boynton Hill—*summit* VT-1
Boynton Hollow—*valley* VT-1
Boynton Inlet—*bay* FL-3
Boynton Inlet—*channel* FL-3
Boynton Inlet Park—*park* FL-3
*Boynton Island* MI-6
Boynton-Kent House—*hist pl* TX-5
Boynton Lake—*reservoir* AZ-5
Boynton Lake—*reservoir* OK-5
Boynton Lake Dam—*dam* AZ-5
Boynton Lakes Plaza (Shop Ctr)—*locale* FL-3
Boynton Lookout—*locale* UT-8
Boynton Park—*park* NJ-2
Boynton Park—*park* OR-9
Boynton Pass—*gap* AZ-5
Boynton Plaza (Shop Ctr)—*locale* FL-3
Boynton Pond—*lake* ME-1
Boynton Ridge—*summit* GA-3
Boynton Ridge (CCD)—*cens area* GA-3
Boynton Rsvr—*reservoir* TX-5
Boynton Sch—*school* ME-1
Boynton Sch—*school* (2) MI-6
Boynton Sch—*school* NH-1
Boyntons Hill—*summit* MA-1
Boynton Slough—*gut* CA-9
Boynton Slough—*stream* NV-8
Boynton Spring—*spring* TN-4
Boynton Street Hist Dist—*hist pl* ME-1
**Boynton (Township of)**—*pop pl* IL-6
Boynton Trail Centre (Shop Ctr)—*locale* FL-3
**Boynton Valley**—*pop pl* TN-4
**Boyntonville**—*pop pl* NY-2
Boynton West Shop Ctr—*locale* FL-3
Boynton Woman's Club—*hist pl* FL-3
Boy Post Office (historical)—*building* TN-4
**Boy River**—*pop pl* MN-6
Boy River—*stream* MN-6
Boy River Lookout Tower—*locale* MN-6
**Boy River (Township of)**—*pop pl* MN-6
Boysag Point—*cliff* AZ-5
Boysag Rim—*cliff* AZ-5
Boys and Girls Library—*hist pl* WI-6
Boys Bend—*bend* MT-8
Boys Camp—*locale* VA-3
Boy Sch (historical)—*school* (2) PA-2
Boys Club Camp—*park* IN-6
Boys Club Lake Dam—*dam* MS-4
Boys Club Park—*park* TX-5
Boy Scout—*island* AK-9
Boy Scout Bluff—*cliff* OK-5
*Boy Scout Camp* NC-3
*Boy Scout Camp* PA-2
Boy Scout Camp—*locale* (2) CA-9
Boy Scout Camp—*locale* ID-8
Boy Scout Camp—*locale* (2) MA-1
Boy Scout Camp—*locale* MO-7
Boy Scout Camp—*locale* NE-7
Boy Scout Camp—*locale* (2) OH-6
Boy Scout Camp—*park* (3) AZ-5
Boy Scout Compground—*locale* UT-8
Boy Scout Compgrounds—*park* AZ-5
Boy Scout Camp (historical)—*locale* MO-7
Boy Scout Campsite—*locale* ME-1
Boy Scout Cave—*cave* ID-8
Boy Scout Dam—*dam* AL-4
Boy Scout Hill—*summit* NE-7
Boy Scout Hollow—*valley* PA-2
Boy Scout Islands—*island* IA-7
*Boy Scout Lake* FL-3
Boy Scout Lake—*reservoir* AL-4
Boy Scout Lake—*reservoir* NJ-2
Boy Scout Lake—*reservoir* NC-3
Boy Scout Lake Dam—*dam* AL-4
Boy Scout Lake Dam—*dam* MS-4
Boy Scout Lake Dam—*dam* NC-3
Boy Scout Memorial—*other* TN-4
Boy Scout Memorial—*park* DC-2
Boy Scout Mtn—*summit* NM-5
Boy Scout Pond—*lake* IN-6
Boy Scout Pond—*reservoir* NC-3
Boy Scout Pond Dam—*dam* NC-3
Boy Scout Reservation—*locale* PA-2
Boy Scouts of America Camp—*locale* TX-5
Boy Scouts of America Camp—*locale* UT-8
Boy Scouts of America Camp (historical)—*locale* PA-2
Boy Scouts of America Dam—*dam* NC-3
Boy Scouts of America HQ—*building* UT-8
Boy Scout Spring—*spring* (2) AZ-5
Boy Scout Spring—*spring* UT-8
Boy Scouts Spring—*spring* AL-4
Boysen—*locale* WY-8
Boysen Bay—*bay* NY-2
Boysen Bay—*CDP* NY-2
Boysen Camp—*locale* WY-8
Boysen Creek—*stream* WY-8
Boysen Cut—*gap* TX-5
Boysen Dam—*dam* WY-8
Boysen Park—*park* CA-9
Boysen Peak—*summit* WY-8
Boysen Ridge—*ridge* WY-8
Boysen Rsvr—*reservoir* WY-8
Boyse Point—*cape* VA-3
Boys Estate—*locale* GA-3
Boys Farm Sch (County)—*school* IL-6
Boys Forest Ranch—*locale* OR-9
Boys Halfway River—*stream* CT-1
Boys Harbor Summer Camp—*locale* NY-2
Boys Haven—*locale* TX-5
Boys Haven—*locale* VA-3
*Boys High School* AL-4
Boys Home JHS—*school* NC-3
**Boys Home (Presbyterian Home)**—*pop pl* VA-3
Boy's HS—*hist pl* NY-2
Boys HS—*school* NY-2
Boys HS—*school* SC-3
*Boyside* RI-1
*Boys Industrial School* AL-4
*Boys Island* KY-4
*Boys Island* TN-4
Boys Island—*island* MI-6
Boys Island—*island* TN-4
*Boys Lake* MN-6
Boys Lake—*lake* MI-6
Boys Lake—*lake* MN-6
Boys Lake—*lake* MT-8
Boys Peak—*summit* TX-5
Boys Point—*cape* GA-3
Boy Spring—*spring* AZ-5
Boys Ranch—*locale* GA-3
Boys Ranch—*locale* (2) TX-5
**Boys Ranch**—*pop pl* AL-4
**Boys Ranch**—*pop pl* FL-3
**Boys Ranch**—*pop pl* MO-7
**Boys Ranch**—*pop pl* NM-5
Boy's Ranch Airp—*airport* AL-4
**Boys Ranch (Home for Boys)**—*pop pl* AZ-5
Boys Ranch Lake Dam—*dam* MS-4
Boys Ranch Post Office—*building* AZ-5
**Boys Ranch (sta.)**—*pop pl* TX-5
Boys Ranch Variety Club—*locale* TX-5
Boys Ranch West Texas—*locale* TX-5
**Boys Republic**—*pop pl* CA-9
Boys Sch—*school* NY-2
Boys School—*building* NC-3
Boys School Lake—*reservoir* NM-5
Boyston Cem—*cemetery* MS-4
**Boys Town**—*pop pl* MO-7
**Boys Town**—*pop pl* NE-7
Boystown—*post sta* NE-7
Boystown Fly-in-Ranch—*airport* RI-1
Boystown of Florida—*school* FL-3
Boys Town of Missouri—*other* MO-7
Boys Trade HS—*school* WI-6
Boys Trade Sch—*school* MA-1
Boys Village—*locale* OH-6
Boys Village Of Maryland—*locale* MD-2
Boysville of Michigan—*other* MI-6
Boysville Sch—*school* TX-5
Boys Vocational HS—*school* NY-2
Boy Tank—*reservoir* AZ-5
Boyt Church (historical)—*locale* MO-7
Boyter, Alexander, House—*hist pl* UT-8
Boyter, James, House—*hist pl* UT-8
Boyter, James, Shop—*hist pl* UT-8
Boyt Lake—*lake* TX-5
*Boyton Hill* NH-1
Boyton Hill—*summit* NY-2
Boyt Sch (abandoned)—*school* MO-7
Boyt School (historical)—*locale* MO-7
Boy with the Boot Fountain—*hist pl* OH-6
Boz—*locale* TX-5
Bozanta Tavern Bay—*bay* ID-8
Bozan Well—*well* NM-5
**Bozar**—*pop pl* TX-5
Bozard Creek—*stream* ID-8
Bozard Hill—*summit* NY-2
Bozard Pond—*reservoir* SC-3
**Bozarth**—*pop pl* OK-5
Bozarth Cem—*cemetery* AR-4
Bozarth Cem—*cemetery* IL-6
Bozarth Mesa—*summit* AZ-5
Bozarth Point—*cape* AZ-5
Bozarth Post Office (historical)—*building* TN-4
Bozarth Ranch—*locale* AZ-5
Bozarth Ranch—*locale* WY-8
Bozarth Sch—*school* MO-7
Bozarth State For—*forest* MO-7
*Bozarthtown* NJ-2
Boze Cem—*cemetery* TX-5
*Boze Creek* OR-9
Boze Creek—*stream* OR-9
Boze Lake—*lake* MN-6
*Bozeman* AL-4
**Bozeman**—*pop pl* MT-8
Bozeman Armory—*hist pl* MT-8
Bozeman Branch—*stream* LA-4
Bozeman Brewery Hist Dist—*hist pl* MT-8
Bozeman Carnegie Library—*hist pl* MT-8
Bozeman Cem—*cemetery* AL-4
Bozeman Cem—*cemetery* AR-4
Bozeman Cem—*cemetery* MS-4
Bozeman Cem—*cemetery* (3) TX-5
Bozeman Country Club—*other* MT-8
*Bozeman Creek* MT-8
Bozeman Creek—*stream* MT-8
Bozeman Fork Musselshell River—*stream* MT-8
**Bozeman Hot Springs**—*pop pl* MT-8
Bozeman Hot Springs—*spring* MT-8
Bozeman House—*hist pl* AR-4
Bozeman JHS—*school* GA-3
Bozeman Landing—*locale* AL-4
Bozeman Natl Fish Hatchery—*hist pl* MT-8
Bozeman Pass—*gap* MT-8
Bozeman Pond—*reservoir* AL-4
Bozeman Pond Dam—*dam* AL-4
Bozeman Sch—*school* TX-5
Bozeman Sheet Metal Works—*hist pl* MT-8
Bozeman Ski Lodge—*building* MT-8
Bozeman Tank—*reservoir* TX-5
Bozeman Trail—*trail* MT-8
Bozeman Trail—*trail* WY-8
Bozeman Trail Ditch—*canal* MT-8
Bozeman Trail Historical Marker—*locale* WY-8
Bozeman Trail Marker—*park* WY-8
Bozeman Trail Monmt—*park* WY-8
Bozeman Tunnel—*tunnel* MT-8
Bozeman-Waters Natl Bank—*hist pl* IN-6

**Brad Lee**—pop pl VA-3
Bradlee-McIntyre House—hist pl FL-3
Bradlee Sch—hist pl MA-1
Bradleton Lake Dam—dam AL-4
Bradley ID-8
Bradley—locale GA-3
Bradley—locale KY-4
Bradley—locale MS-4
Bradley—locale NE-7
**Bradley**—pop pl AL-4
**Bradley**—pop pl AR-4
**Bradley**—pop pl CA-9
**Bradley**—pop pl (2) IL-6
**Bradley**—pop pl IN-6
**Bradley**—pop pl ME-1
**Bradley**—pop pl MI-6
**Bradley**—pop pl MS-4
**Bradley**—pop pl MT-8
**Bradley**—pop pl NY-2
**Bradley**—pop pl OH-6
**Bradley**—pop pl OK-5
**Bradley**—pop pl SC-3
**Bradley**—pop pl SD-7
**Bradley**—pop pl (2) WV-2
**Bradley**—pop pl (2) WI-6
Bradley—uninc pl WI-6
Bradley, Dan, House—hist pl NY-2
Bradley, George M., House—hist pl RI-1
Bradley, Gov. William O., House—hist pl KY-4
Bradley, Harold C., House—hist pl WI-6
Bradley, James, House—hist pl TN-4
Bradley, John W., House—hist pl KY-4
Bradley, Mount—summit AK-9
Bradley, Mount—summit (2) CA-9
Bradley, Mount—summit (2) MT-8
Bradley, Timothy, House—hist pl CT-1
**Bradley Acres**—pop pl VA-3
Bradley Air Natl Guard Base—building CT-1
Bradley And Hubbard Reservoir CT-1
Bradley Barn Well—well TX-5
Bradley Basin—basin UT-8
Bradley Bay—bay AZ-5
Bradley Bayou—gut AR-4
**Bradley Beach**—pop pl NJ-2
Bradley Beach Station—hist pl NJ-2
Bradley Bend—bend TN-4
Bradley-Bourbonnais HS—school IL-6
Bradley Branch—stream AL-4
Bradley Branch—stream (3) AR-4
Bradley Branch—stream IL-6
Bradley Branch—stream (6) KY-4
Bradley Branch—stream MS-4
Bradley Branch—stream MO-7
Bradley Branch—stream NE-7
Bradley Branch—stream (3) NC-3
Bradley Branch—stream (2) TN-4
Bradley Branch—stream (2) TX-5
Bradley Branch—stream WV-2
Bradley Branch—stream WI-6
Bradley Bridge—bridge (2) SC-3
Bradley Bridge—bridge VA-3
Bradley Bridge—other IL-6
Bradley Brook CT-1
Bradley Brook—stream (3) CT-1
Bradley Brook—stream ME-1
Bradley Brook—stream (2) MA-1
Bradley Brook—stream (2) NH-1
Bradley Brook—stream (3) NY-2
Bradley Brook—stream VT-1
Bradley Brook Rsvr—reservoir NY-2
Bradley Brook Trail—trail NH-1
Bradley Butt—summit NC-3
Bradley Canyon—valley (3) CA-9
Bradley Canyon—valley MT-8
Bradley Canyon—valley NV-8
Bradley Canyon—valley (2) UT-8
Bradley Cem—cemetery (2) AR-4
Bradley Cem—cemetery CT-1
Bradley Cem—cemetery (3) GA-3
Bradley Cem—cemetery IL-6
Bradley Cem—cemetery (5) KY-4
Bradley Cem—cemetery (2) LA-4
Bradley Cem—cemetery ME-1
Bradley Cem—cemetery (2) MS-4
Bradley Cem—cemetery MO-7
Bradley Cem—cemetery (4) NC-3
Bradley Cem—cemetery OH-6
Bradley Cem—cemetery OK-5
Bradley Cem—cemetery (10) TN-4
Bradley Cem—cemetery VT-1
Bradley Cem—cemetery (2) VA-3
Bradley Cem—cemetery WV-2
**Bradley (census and RR name Bradley Junction)**—pop pl FL-3
Bradley Ch—church AL-4
Bradley Ch—church ME-1
Bradley Ch—church MI-6
Bradley Ch—church TX-5
Bradley Chapel—church AL-4
Bradley Chapel—church AR-4
Bradley Chapel—church MS-4
Bradley Chapel—church TN-4
**Bradley Chapel**—pop pl MS-4
Bradley Chapel Ch of Christ AL-4
Bradley Chapel United Methodist Church MS-4
Bradley Ch of God—church MS-4
Bradley Church Cem—cemetery AL-4
**Bradley Corner**—pop pl OR-9
Bradley Corners—locale PA-2
**Bradley (County)**—pop pl AR-4
**Bradley County**—pop pl TN-4
Bradley County Courthouse—building TN-4
Bradley County Courthouse and Clerk's Office—hist pl AR-4
Bradley County Health Department—hospital TN-4
Bradley County HS—school TN-4
Bradley County Nursing Home—hospital TN-4
Bradley County Park—park TN-4
Bradley County School TN-4
Bradley Covered Bridge—hist pl VT-1
Bradley Creek—stream (2) AR-4
Bradley Creek—stream CA-9
Bradley Creek—stream FL-3
Bradley Creek—stream GA-3
Bradley Creek—stream IA-7
Bradley Creek—stream (2) MI-6
Bradley Creek—stream (2) MT-8
Bradley Creek—stream NM-5
Bradley Creek—stream NY-2
Bradley Creek—stream (6) NC-3
Bradley Creek—stream (4) OR-9
Bradley Creek—stream (3) TN-4
Bradley Creek—stream TX-5
Bradley Creek—stream VA-3
Bradley Creek—stream WA-9
Bradley Creek—stream WI-6
Bradley Creek Ch—church TN-4
**Bradley Creek East Estates (subdivision)**—pop pl NC-3
Bradley Creek Elem Sch—school NC-3
Bradley Creek Mine—mine OR-9
Bradley Creek Missionary Ch—church TN-4
**Bradley Creek Point (subdivision)**—pop pl NC-3
Bradley Dam AL-4
Bradley Drain—canal MI-6
Bradley Draw—valley SD-7
Bradley East Sch—school IL-6
Bradley Elementary School MS-4
Bradley Falls—falls NC-3
**Bradley Farms**—pop pl MD-2
Bradley Flat—bar GA-3
Bradley Flat—flat OR-9
Bradley Flats—flat SD-7
Bradley Flat Spring—spring OR-9
**Bradley Forest**—pop pl VA-3
Bradley Fork—stream NC-3
Bradley Fork—stream (2) WV-2
Bradley Gap—gap AR-4
Bradley Gap—gap (3) NC-3
Bradley Gap—gap VA-3
Bradley Gap Ch—church KY-4
**Bradley Gardens**—pop pl NJ-2
Bradley Gulch—valley ID-8
Bradley Hammock—area LA-4
Bradley Hill—summit MA-1
Bradley Hill—summit NY-2
Bradley Hill—summit RI-1
Bradley Hill—summit TN-4
Bradley Hill—summit (2) VT-1
**Bradley Hills**—pop pl MD-2
**Bradley Hills Grove**—pop pl MD-2
Bradley Hollow—valley (2) AR-4
Bradley Hollow—valley KY-4
Bradley Hollow—valley (3) TN-4
Bradley House—hist pl MI-6
Bradley HS—school AR-4
Bradley-hubbard Rsvr CT-1
Bradley Hubbard Rsvr—reservoir CT-1
Bradley Industrial Park—locale TN-4
Bradley International Airp—airport CT-1
Bradley Island—island MN-6
Bradley Island Public Use Area—locale MO-7
Bradley JHS—school TN-4
Bradley Junction—locale PA-2
**Bradley Junction**—pop pl FL-3
Bradley Junction (census and RR name for Bradley)—CDP FL-3
Bradley Key—island FL-3
Bradley Lake—lake (2) AK-9
Bradley Lake—lake FL-3
Bradley Lake—lake ID-8
Bradley Lake—lake MI-6
Bradley Lake—lake (2) MN-6
Bradley Lake—lake MT-8
Bradley Lake—lake NH-1
Bradley Lake—lake (3) OR-9
Bradley Lake—lake (4) WI-6
Bradley Lake—lake WY-8
Bradley Lake—reservoir KS-7
Bradley Lake—reservoir NY-2
Bradley Lake—reservoir TN-4
Bradley Lake—swamp AR-4
Bradley Lake—swamp MN-6
Bradley Lake (historical)—lake IA-7
Bradley Lake Trail—trail WY-8
Bradley Landing—locale AL-4
Bradley Lateral—canal CA-9
Bradley-Latimer Summer House—hist pl NC-3
Bradley Memorial Camp—locale ID-8
Bradley Memorial Hosp—hospital TN-4
Bradley Mill Branch—stream SC-3
Bradley Mill Creek—stream AL-4
Bradley Mine—mine MI-6
Bradley Mine—mine UT-8
Bradley Mines—mine NM-5
Bradley MS—school TX-5
Bradley Mtn—summit CT-1
Bradley Mtn—summit ID-8
Bradley Mtn—summit MA-1
Bradley Mtn—summit (2) NY-2
Bradley Mtn—summit NC-3
Bradley Mtn—summit WY-8
Bradley Museum—building GA-3
Bradley Observatory—building GA-3
Bradleyon Butte—summit SD-7
Bradley Park—park IL-6
Bradley Park—park MS-4
Bradley Park—park (2) OR-9
Bradley Park—park WI-6
**Bradley Park**—pop pl NJ-2
**Bradley Park (subdivision)**—pop pl NC-3
Bradley Peak—summit CO-8
Bradley Peak—summit WY-8
Bradley Playground—park MI-6
Bradley Pleasure Ch—church KY-4
Bradley Point—cape CT-1
Bradley Point—cape GA-3
Bradley Point—cape NY-2
Bradley Point—cliff AZ-5
Bradley Pond OH-6
Bradley Pond—lake (3) ME-1
Bradley Pond—lake MA-1
Bradley Pond—lake MO-7
Bradley Pond—lake (2) NY-2
**Bradley Quarters**—pop pl AR-4
Bradley Ridge—ridge IN-6
Bradley Ridge—ridge OR-9
Bradley River—stream AK-9
Bradley River—stream GA-3
Bradley Rocks—pillar CT-1
Bradley Run—stream MD-2
Bradley Run—stream NJ-2
Bradley Run—stream (2) PA-2
Bradley Run—stream VA-3
Bradleys Brook—stream CT-1
Bradleys Cave—cave TN-4
Bradleys Cem—cemetery TN-4
Bradley Sch—school AL-4
Bradley Sch—school CA-9
Bradley Sch—school CO-8
Bradley Sch—school CT-1
Bradley Sch—school IL-6
Bradley Sch—school (2) KY-4
Bradley Sch—school LA-4
Bradley Sch—school MD-2
Bradley Sch—school MA-1
Bradley Sch—school MI-6
Bradley Sch—school MS-4
Bradley Sch—school NJ-2
Bradley Sch—school NM-5
Bradley Sch—school SC-3
Bradley Sch—school SD-7
Bradley Sch—school VT-1
Bradley Sch—school WV-2
Bradleys Chapel School AL-4
Bradley Sch (historical)—school TN-4
**Bradleys Corner**—pop pl ME-1
Bradley's Country Store Complex—hist pl FL-3
Bradleys Creek TN-4
Bradley Siding—locale ID-8
Bradleys Island—island NH-1
Bradley Sky Ranch—locale AK-9
Bradley Slough—gut AR-4
Bradley Slough—stream LA-4
Bradleys Mill (historical)—locale TN-4
Bradleys Mountain MA-1
Bradleys Pond—lake CT-1
Bradleys Pond—reservoir AL-4
Bradley Spring—spring MT-8
Bradley Spring—spring (3) NV-8
Bradley Springs—spring UT-8
Bradley Springs (historical)—locale KS-7
Bradley Springs Sch—school KY-4
Bradley State Public Shooting Area—park SD-7
Bradley Station NE-7
Bradley Swamp—swamp NY-2
Bradley Tank—reservoir TX-5
**Bradleyton**—pop pl AL-4
Bradleyton, Lake—reservoir AL-4
Bradleytown—locale AL-4
**Bradleytown**—pop pl PA-2
**Bradleytown**—pop pl TN-4
Bradleytown Ch—church PA-2
**Bradley (Town of)**—pop pl ME-1
**Bradley (Town of)**—pop pl WI-6
Bradley (Township of)—fmr MCD (2) AR-4
**Bradley (Township of)**—pop pl IL-6
Bradley Trail—trail OR-9
Bradley Truck Trail—trail WA-9
Bradley Univ—school IL-6
Bradleyville—locale CT-1
Bradleyville—well MI-6
**Bradleyville**—pop pl MO-7
**Bradleyville**—pop pl SC-3
Bradley Wales Picnic Area—area PA-2
Bradley Wayside OR-9
Bradley-Wayside Sch—school GA-3
Bradley Well—well TX-5
Bradley West Sch—school IL-6
Bradley-Wheeler House—hist pl CT-1
**Bradley Woods**—pop pl MD-2
Bradley Woods Reservation—park OH-6
Bradlys Island—island TN-4
Bradman—locale MT-8
**Bradman Spur**—pop pl MT-8
Bradmon Chapel—church NC-3
**Bradmoor**—pop pl MD-2
Bradmoor Island—island CA-9
**Bradmyer**—pop pl KY-4
**Bradner**—pop pl OH-6
Bradner Creek—stream NY-2
Bradner's Pharmacy—hist pl NJ-2
Bradooks Sch—school CA-9
Bradock Cem—cemetery NY-2
**Bradrick**—pop pl OH-6
Brad Rock—other AK-9
Bradsaw Branch TX-5
Brads Canyon—valley AZ-5
Brads Creek—stream OR-9
Bradsford Cem—cemetery MS-4
Bradsford Chapel—church MS-4
Bradshaw—locale KY-4
Bradshaw—locale MD-2
Bradshaw—locale TN-4
Bradshaw—locale TX-5
Bradshaw—locale VA-3
**Bradshaw**—pop pl IN-6
**Bradshaw**—pop pl KY-4
**Bradshaw**—pop pl NE-7
**Bradshaw**—pop pl (2) WV-2
Bradshaw, George, House and Joshua Salisbury/George Bradshaw Barn—hist pl UT-8
Bradshaw, George Albert, House—hist pl UT-8
Bradshaw Basin—basin ID-8
Bradshaw Bluff—cliff MO-7
Bradshaw-Booth House—hist pl MS-4
Bradshaw Brake—swamp AR-4
Bradshaw Branch TX-5
Bradshaw Branch—stream AR-4
Bradshaw Branch—stream NC-3
Bradshaw Canyon—valley WY-8
Bradshaw Cem—cemetery AR-4
Bradshaw Cem—cemetery IN-6
Bradshaw Cem—cemetery IA-7
Bradshaw Cem—cemetery KY-4
Bradshaw Cem—cemetery MO-7
Bradshaw Cem—cemetery NC-3
Bradshaw Cem—cemetery OH-6
Bradshaw Cem—cemetery (5) TN-4
Bradshaw Cem—cemetery VA-3
Bradshaw Cem—cemetery WV-2
Bradshaw-Center Point Cem—cemetery TN-4
Bradshaw Ch—church AL-4
Bradshaw Chapel—church TN-4
Bradshaw City—locale AZ-5
Bradshaw City Cem—cemetery AZ-5
Bradshaw Cove—bay AK-9
Bradshaw Creek—stream AR-4
Bradshaw Creek—stream CA-9
Bradshaw Creek—stream ID-8
Bradshaw Creek—stream IL-6
Bradshaw Creek—stream KS-7
Bradshaw Creek—stream KY-4
Bradshaw Creek—stream (2) MT-8
Bradshaw Creek—stream NV-8
Bradshaw Creek—stream OR-9
Bradshaw Creek—stream TN-4
Bradshaw Creek—stream VA-3
Bradshaw Creek—stream (2) WV-2
Bradshaw Dam—dam AL-4
Bradshaw Dam—dam OR-9
Bradshaw Drain—canal MI-6
Bradshaw Drain—stream MI-6
Bradshaw Draw—valley KS-7
Bradshaw Drop—cliff OR-9
Bradshaw Ferry (site)—locale AZ-5
Bradshaw Field—flat NV-8
Bradshaw Gas Field—oilfield KS-7
Bradshaw Gulch—valley ID-8
Bradshaw Hill—summit MI-6
Bradshaw Hill—summit WV-2
Bradshaw Hollow—valley TN-4
Bradshaw House—hist pl AL-4
Bradshaw House—hist pl KY-4
Bradshaw Lake—reservoir AL-4
Bradshaw Lake—reservoir (2) GA-3
Bradshaw Lake—swamp MN-6
Bradshaw Mill—building TN-4
Bradshaw Mountain HS—school AZ-5
Bradshaw Mountains—range AZ-5
Bradshaw Mtn—summit (2) AR-4
Bradshaw Mtn—summit UT-8
Bradshaw Mtn—summit WV-2
Bradshaw Narrows—gap AR-4
Bradshaw No. 2 Dam—dam OR-9
Bradshaw Park—park IL-6
Bradshaw Pond—reservoir VA-3
Bradshaw Pond Pit Cave—cave PA-2
Bradshaw Post Office (historical)—building TN-4
Bradshaw Ranch—locale MT-8
Bradshaw Ridge—ridge KY-4
Bradshaw Rsvr—reservoir OR-9
Bradshaw Rsvr Number Two—reservoir OR-9
Bradshaws Camp—locale KY-4
Bradshaw Sch—school KY-4
Bradshaw Sch (historical)—school AL-4
Bradshaw Sch (historical)—school MS-4
Bradshaw Sch (historical)—school MO-7
Bradshaws Corner PA-2
Bradshaws Ferry AZ-5
Bradshaw Spring—spring AZ-5
Bradshaw Spring—spring ID-8
Bradshaw Spring—spring (2) NV-8
Bradshaw Station—locale MD-2
Bradshaw Tank—reservoir AZ-5
Bradshaw Town Hall—hist pl NE-7
Bradshaw (Township of)—fmr MCD AR-4
Bradshaw (Township of)—fmr MCD NC-3
Bradshaw Trail—trail AZ-5
Bradshaw Well—well NV-8
Bradsher Sch—school NC-3
Brad Spring—spring OR-9
**Bradstreet**—pop pl MA-1
Bradstreet Cove—bay ME-1
Bradstreet Hill—summit MA-1
Bradstreet Rock—bar ME-1
Bradstreet Sch—school MA-1
Bradstreet (Township of)—unorg ME-1
Brads Water—spring AZ-5
Brad Tank—reservoir AZ-5
Bradt Cem—cemetery NY-2
Bradtmoor Island CA-9
Brad Turner Creek—stream CA-9
Bradtville WI-6
**Bradtville**—pop pl NY-2
Bradway Dam—dam MA-1
Bradway Pond—lake CT-1
Bradwell Bay—bay FL-3
Bradwell Institute HS—school GA-3
Bradwell Sch—school IL-6
**Bradwood**—pop pl OR-9
Brady PA-2
Brady WV-2
Brady—locale AK-9
Brady—locale MD-2
Brady—locale OH-6
Brady—locale OK-5
Brady—locale PA-2
Brady—other WV-2
**Brady**—pop pl KY-4
**Brady**—pop pl MT-8
**Brady**—pop pl NE-7
**Brady**—pop pl PA-2
**Brady**—pop pl TX-5
**Brady**—pop pl WA-9
Brady—post sta PA-2
Brady—uninc pl MI-6
Brady Bay—bay LA-4
Brady Bayou—stream MS-4
Brady Bend—bend TX-5
Brady Bluff—cliff TN-4
Brady-Bolibaugh House—hist pl IA-7
Brady Branch—stream AL-4
Brady Branch—stream GA-3
Brady Branch—stream KY-4
Brady Branch—stream MS-4
Brady Branch—stream (2) NC-3
Brady Branch—stream (5) TN-4
Brady Bridge—bridge PA-2
Brady Brook—stream ME-1
Brady Brook—stream NY-2
Brady Butte—summit AZ-5
Brady Butte—summit OR-9
Brady Butte Tank—reservoir AZ-5
Brady Cabin—hist pl OK-5
Brady Canal ID-8
Brady Canal—canal LA-4
Brady Canyon AZ-5
Brady Canyon—valley (4) AZ-5
Brady Canyon—valley NM-5
Brady Canyon—valley (2) SD-7
Brady (CCD)—cens area TX-5
Brady Cem—cemetery AR-4
Brady Cem—cemetery FL-3
Brady Cem—cemetery IL-6
Brady Cem—cemetery (2) MI-6
Brady Cem—cemetery MS-4
Brady Cem—cemetery NE-7
Brady Cem—cemetery OH-6
Brady Cem—cemetery (2) TN-4
Brady Center—locale MI-6
Brady Cove—bay AK-9
Brady Creek IN-6
Brady Creek MT-8
Brady Creek—stream GA-3
Brady Creek—stream ID-8
Brady Creek—stream MI-6
Brady Creek—stream (2) MS-4
Brady Creek—stream (2) MO-7
Brady Creek—stream (2) MT-8
Brady Creek—stream ND-7
Brady Creek—stream (2) OR-9
Brady Creek—stream SD-7
Brady Creek—stream (2) TX-5
Brady Creek—stream UT-8
Brady Creek—stream (2) WY-8
Brady Creek Lodge—locale TX-5
Brady Creek Reservoir TX-5
Brady Dam—dam PA-2
Brady Ditch—canal OH-6
Brady Estates OH-6
Brady Fork—stream WV-2
Brady Gap Run—stream WV-2
**Brady Gate**—pop pl WV-2
Brady Glacier—glacier AK-9
Brady Gulch—valley ID-8
Brady Heights Hist Dist—hist pl OK-5
Brady Hill—summit GA-3
Brady Hill—summit NY-2
Brady Hill—summit VA-3
Brady Hill Cem—cemetery MI-6
Brady Hills—summit MI-6
Brady Hollow—valley NY-2
Brady Hollow—valley NC-3
Brady Hollow—valley TN-4
Brady HS—school MN-6
Brady Island—island AK-9
Brady Island—island (2) FL-3
Brady Island—island MD-2
Brady Island—island NE-7
Brady Island—island TX-5
Brady Knob—summit TN-4
Brady Lake PA-2
Brady Lake—lake CO-8
Brady Lake—lake MI-6
Brady Lake—lake OH-6
**Brady Lake**—pop pl OH-6
Brady Lake—reservoir AL-4
Brady Lake—reservoir MS-4
**Brady Lake Addition**—pop pl OH-6
Brady Lake Dam PA-2
Brady Lake Dam—dam AL-4
Brady Landing—locale MS-4
Brady Memorial Chapel—hist pl ID-8
Brady Mountain Rec Area—park AR-4
Brady Mountains TN-4
Brady Mountains—range TX-5
Brady Mtn—summit AR-4
Brady Mtn—summit CA-9
Brady Mtn—summit TN-4
Brady Mtn—summit TX-5
Brady Park—flat AZ-5
Brady Park—flat MT-8
Brady Park—park NY-2
Brady Park—park TX-5
**Brady Park**—pop pl NJ-2
Brady Peak—summit AZ-5
**Brady Place Subdivision**—pop pl UT-8
Brady Point—cape MI-6
Brady Point—cliff TN-4
Brady Pond—lake (2) NY-2
Brady Ranch—locale CA-9
Brady Ranch—locale NM-5
Brady Ridge—ridge CA-9
Brady Rock Trail—trail WY-8
Brady Rsvr—reservoir NV-8
Brady Rsvr—reservoir TX-5
Brady Run—stream (2) OH-6
Brady Run—stream (3) PA-2
Brady Run Park—park PA-2
Bradys TN-4
Bradys Bend—bend PA-2
**Bradys Bend**—pop pl PA-2
Bradys Bend Cave—cave PA-2
Bradys Bend Iron Company Furnaces—hist pl PA-2
Bradys Bend Iron Furnaces Historical Site—park PA-2
**Bradys Bend (Township of)**—pop pl PA-2
Bradys Bluff—summit WI-6
Bradys Brook—stream NY-2
Bradys Camp—locale CA-9
Brady Sch—school AR-4
Brady Sch—school IL-6
Brady Sch—school (2) MI-6
Brady Sch—school (2) PA-2
Brady Sch—school SD-7
Brady Sch (historical)—school MO-7
Bradys Creek—stream IA-7
Bradys Hot Springs—locale NV-8
Bradys Island—island OH-6
Bradys Island—island WI-6
Bradys Lake—reservoir PA-2
Bradys Lake Dam—dam PA-2
Bradys Lake (PC RR name for Brady Lake)—other OH-6
Bradys Pond PA-2
Brady Spring—spring (2) AZ-5
Brady Spring—spring NV-8
Brady Spring—spring NM-5
Brady's Ranch—locale MT-8
Bradys Rock (historical)—locale TN-4
Bradys Run PA-2
Bradys Run Lake—reservoir PA-2
Bradys Switch—locale PA-2
Brady Station NE-7
Brady Station—locale PA-2
**Bradysville**—pop pl OH-6
Brady Tank—reservoir (2) AZ-5
Brady Tanks—reservoir AZ-5
Brady Township (historical)—civil SD-7
**Brady (Township of)**—pop pl (2) MI-6
**Brady (Township of)**—pop pl OH-6
**Brady (Township of)**—pop pl (5) PA-2
Brady Tunnel—tunnel PA-2
Bradyville OH-6
Bradyville—locale WV-2
**Bradyville**—pop pl OH-6
**Bradyville**—pop pl TN-4
Bradyville Ch of Christ—church TN-4
Bradyville Post Office—building TN-4
Bradyville Sch—school MI-6
Bradyville Sch (historical)—school TN-4
Brady Wash—stream AZ-5
Brady Wash—stream NV-8
**Braeburn**—pop pl ME-1
**Braeburn**—pop pl PA-2
Brae Burn Country Club—locale MA-1
Brae Burn Country Club—other TX-5
Brae-Burn Golf Club—other MI-6
Braeburn Heights—locale NJ-2
**Braeburn Park**—pop pl NJ-2
Braeburn Sch—school CT-1
Braeburn Sch—school PA-2
Braeburn Sch—school TX-5
**Braeburn (subdivision)**—pop pl PA-2
Braecher Lake—reservoir CO-8
Braehead (historical)—locale AL-4
Braehead Slope Mine (underground)—mine AL-4
**Braehead Woods**—pop pl VA-3
**Braeholm**—pop pl WV-2
Braeloch Camp—locale VT-1
Brae Loch Country Club—other IL-6
**Braemar**—pop pl TN-4
Braemar, Lake—reservoir MI-6
Braemar Country Club—other NY-2
Braemar Post Office (historical)—building TN-4
**Braemar VII (subdivision)**—pop pl (2) AZ-5
Braemer Park—park MN-6
Braen Canyon—valley CA-9
Braeside IL-6
**Braeside**—pop pl IL-6
**Braeside**—pop pl NY-2
Braeside Sch—hist pl IL-6
Braeside Sch—school IL-6
Braesmont Park—park TX-5
**Braeswood**—pop pl TX-5
Braewood Park—park AZ-5
Braezels Branch—stream WI-6
Brafees Creek—stream MN-6
**Braffetsville**—pop pl OH-6
Braffett Fork UT-8
Braffettsville OH-6
**Braffettsville**—pop pl OH-6
Braffit Fork UT-8
Braffit Ridge—ridge UT-8
Braffits Creek—stream UT-8
Braffits Fork UT-8
Braffitsville OH-6
Braffitt Fork UT-8
Braffitt Ridge UT-8
Brafford Cem—cemetery KY-4
Brafford Fork—stream KY-4
Braga Bridge—bridge MA-1
**Braganza**—pop pl GA-3
Braga Pond—lake NH-1
Bragden Ditch—canal MI-6
Bragdens Pond—reservoir SC-3
Bragdon—locale CO-8
Bragdon Brook—stream (2) ME-1
Bragdon Gulch—valley CA-9
Bragdon Island—island (2) ME-1
Bragdon Ledge—bench NH-1
Bragdon Rock—bar ME-1
Brager Lake—lake ND-7
Bragg—locale TX-5
**Bragg**—pop pl GA-3
**Bragg**—pop pl OH-6
**Bragg**—pop pl VT-1
**Bragg**—pop pl WV-2
Bragg, Caleb, Estate—hist pl NY-2
Bragg, Richard, House—hist pl AR-4
Braggadocia MO-7
**Braggadocio**—pop pl MO-7
Braggadocio Township—civil MO-7
Bragg Branch—stream MO-7
Bragg Branch—stream WV-2
Bragg Brook—stream ME-1
Bragg Brook—stream VT-1
Bragg Camp—locale ME-1
Bragg Canyon—valley NM-5
Bragg Canyon—valley WY-8
Bragg Cem—cemetery (2) AL-4
Bragg Cem—cemetery AR-4
Bragg Cem—cemetery GA-3
Bragg Cem—cemetery IA-7
Bragg Cem—cemetery ME-1
Bragg Cem—cemetery MA-1
Bragg Cem—cemetery (2) MO-7
Bragg Cem—cemetery (2) TN-4
Bragg Cem—cemetery VA-3
**Bragg City**—pop pl AR-4
**Bragg City**—pop pl MO-7
Bragg Corner WV-2
Bragg Creek—stream OR-9
Bragg Ditch—canal OH-6
Bragg Draw—valley CO-8
Bragg Fork—stream WV-2
Bragg Hill MA-1
Bragg Hill—summit NH-1
Bragg Hill Ch—church AL-4
Bragg Hill Sch—school AL-4
Bragg Hollow—valley KY-4
Bragg Hollow—valley MO-7
Bragg Hollow—valley NY-2
Bragg House—hist pl AR-4
Bragg Knob—summit WV-2
Bragg Lake—lake MI-6
Bragg Lake—reservoir AR-4
Bragg Ledge—bench NH-1
Bragg Mill Creek—stream AR-4
Bragg-Mitchell House—hist pl AL-4
Bragg Morris HS—school TX-5
Bragg Mtn—summit MS-4
Bragg Mtn—summit WY-8
Bragg No. 1 Ditch—canal CO-8
Bragg Pit Cave—cave AL-4
Bragg Pond—lake NH-1
Bragg Run—stream (2) WV-2
Braggs AR-4
**Braggs**—pop pl AL-4
**Braggs**—pop pl OK-5
Braggs Bluff—cliff AL-4
Braggs Branch—stream FL-3
Braggs Branch—stream MO-7
Braggs Canyon—valley CA-9
Braggs Cem—cemetery GA-3
Braggs Ch—church AL-4
Braggs Sch—school WI-6
Braggs Corner—locale VA-3
Braggs Corners—locale NY-2
Braggs JHS—school AL-4
Braggs Mill Creek—stream GA-3
Braggs Mill (historical)—locale TN-4

Brandon Corner—locale ... CA-9
Brandon Coulee—valley ... MT-8
Brandon Creek—stream ... ID-8
Brandon Creek—stream ... VA-3
Brandon Depot ... MS-4
Brandon Depot—locale ... MS-4
Brandon Ditch—canal ... CO-8
Brandon Ditch—canal ... IN-6
Brandon Elementary School ... MS-4
Brandon Fellowship Baptist Ch—church ... FL-3
Brandon Female Coll (historical)—school ... MS-4
Brandon Gap—gap ... VT-1
**Brandon Gardens**—pop pl ... MI-6
Brandon Grade School ... AL-4
Brandon Gulch—valley ... AK-9
Brandon Gulch—valley ... CA-9
Brandon Gut—stream ... VA-3
Brandon Hall—hist pl ... MS-4
Brandon Heights—uninc pl ... VA-3
Brandon Heights Baptist Ch—church ... FL-3
Brandon Hill—summit ... NY-2
Brandon Hill Ch—church ... MS-4
Brandon Hills—uninc pl ... SC-3
Brandon Hollow—valley ... TN-4
Brandon HS—school ... FL-3
Brandon HS—school ... MS-4
Brandon Lake—lake ... LA-4
Brandon Lake—lake ... MN-6
Brandon Lakes—lake ... ID-8
Brandon Locks—other ... IL-6
Brandon Lower Elem Sch—school ... MS-4
Brandon (Magisterial District)—fmr MCD ... VA-3
Brandon Male and Female Acad ... MS-4
Brandon Mall—locale ... FL-3
Brandon Memorial Hosp (historical)—hospital ... TN-4
Brandon Memorial Methodist Ch (historical)—church ... AL-4
Brandon Memorial Park ... MS-4
Brandon Memory Gardens—cemetery ... MS-4
Brandon MS—school ... MS-4
Brandon Oil Field—oilfield ... CO-8
Brandon Park—park ... MS-4
Brandon Park—park (2) ... PA-2
Brandon Park—uninc pl ... SD-7
**Brandon Park Subdivision**—pop pl ... UT-8
Brandon Place—uninc pl ... VA-3
Brandon Point—cape ... VA-3
Brandon Presbyterian Ch—church ... MS-4
Brandon Public Library—building ... MS-4
Brandon Sch—school (2) ... AL-4
Brandon Sch—school ... CA-9
Brandon Sch—school ... GA-3
Brandon Sch—school ... IL-6
Brandon Sch—school ... MA-1
Brandon Sch—school ... MI-6
Brandon Sch—school ... MS-4
Brandon Sch—school ... PA-2
Brandon Sch—school ... TX-5
Brandons Landing (historical)—locale ... TN-4
Brandon Spring—spring ... AL-4
Brandon Spring—spring (2) ... OR-9
Brandon Spring—spring ... TN-4
Brandon Spring Branch—stream ... TN-4
Brandon Spring Group Camp—locale ... TN-4
Brandon Springs—spring ... MS-4
Brandons Spring ... AL-4
**Brandons Store**—pop pl ... VA-3
Brandon State Sch—school ... VT-1
Brandon Station ... MS-4
**Brandon (subdivision)**—pop pl ... NC-3
Brandon Swamp—swamp ... VT-1
Brandon Tank—reservoir ... AZ-5
Brandon Terrace—uninc pl ... SD-7
**Brandontown**—pop pl ... AL-4
Brandon Town Center (Shop Ctr)—locale ... FL-3
**Brandon (Town of)**—pop pl ... NY-2
**Brandon (Town of)**—pop pl ... VT-1
Brandon Township—fmr MCD ... IA-7
**Brandon Township**—pop pl ... ND-7
**Brandon Township**—pop pl ... SD-7
**Brandon (Township of)**—pop pl ... MI-6
**Brandon (Township of)**—pop pl ... MN-6
Brandon Training Sch (historical)—school ... TN-4
Brandon Upper Elem Sch—school ... MS-4
**Brandon Village**—pop pl ... VA-3
Brandon Village Hist Dist—hist pl ... VT-1
**Brandonville**—pop pl ... PA-2
**Brandonville**—pop pl ... WV-2
Brandonville Pumping Station Dam—dam ... PA-2
Brandonville Rsvr—reservoir ... PA-2
Brandon Well—well ... OR-9
Brandow Point—cape ... NY-2
Brand Park—park (2) ... CA-9
Brand Park—park ... MI-6
Brand Park—park ... NY-2
Brand Pinnacle—summit ... NY-2
Brand Point Ditch—canal ... WY-8
B R And P Rsvr ... PA-2
**Brandreth**—pop pl ... NY-2
Brandreth Lake—lake ... NY-2
Brandreth Lake Outlet—stream ... NY-2
Brandreth Pill Factory—hist pl ... NY-2
Brandriff Beach—locale ... NJ-2
Brand Run—stream ... WV-2
Brandrup, J. R., House—hist pl ... MN-6
**Brandrup (Township of)**—pop pl ... MN-6
Brands Airfield—airport ... ND-7
Brand Sch—school ... IL-6
Brandsford Reef—bar ... MI-6
Brands Lake ... MN-6
Brands Park—park ... IL-6
Brand Spring—spring ... CA-9
Brands Ranch—locale ... CO-8
Brands Rsvr—reservoir ... CO-8
Brand Station ... TX-5
Brandstedt Slough—stream ... WA-9
Brandsville ... PA-2
**Brandsville**—pop pl ... MO-7
Brandsvold State Wildlife Mngmt Area—park ... MN-6
**Brandsvold (Township of)**—pop pl ... MN-6
Brandt ... TX-5
Brandt—locale ... OR-9
**Brandt**—pop pl ... OH-6
**Brandt**—pop pl ... PA-2
**Brandt**—pop pl ... SD-7
Brandt, Lake—reservoir ... NC-3
Brandt Bridge—bridge ... CA-9
Brandt Cem—cemetery ... MS-4
Brandt Cem—cemetery ... MO-7
Brandt Cem—cemetery ... TX-5
Brandt Lake—lake (2) ... WI-6
Brandt Oil Field—oilfield ... TX-5
Brandt Pond—reservoir ... FL-3
Brandt Ridge—ridge ... CA-9
Brandt Sch—school ... IL-6
Brandt Sch—school ... NJ-2
Brandts Creek—stream ... MI-6
Brandt-Sensenbaugh Oil Field—oilfield ... KS-7
Brandts Lake—lake ... MI-6
**Brandts Landing**—pop pl ... WA-9
**Brandtsville**—pop pl ... PA-2
**Brandt Township**—pop pl ... SD-7
**Brandt (Township of)**—pop pl ... MN-6
Brandt Well—locale ... NM-5
Brandvold Ch—church ... SD-7
Brandy- ... DE-2
Brandy ... VA-3
Brandy—stream ... PA-2
Brandy Bar—bar ... OR-9
Brandy Bay—swamp ... GA-3
Brandy Beach Pond—swamp ... FL-3
Brandy Branch ... WI-6
Brandy Branch—stream (2) ... FL-3
Brandy Branch—stream (2) ... NC-3
Brandy Branch—stream ... TX-5
Brandy Branch—stream ... VA-3
Brandy Branch Ch—church ... FL-3
Brandy Branch Mill—locale ... VA-3
Brandy Branch Swamp—swamp ... FL-3
Brandy Brook ... RI-1
Brandy Brook—locale ... NY-2
Brandy Brook—stream (2) ... CT-1
Brandy Brook—stream (8) ... ME-1
Brandy Brook—stream ... MA-1
Brandy Brook—stream (2) ... NH-1
Brandy Brook—stream (14) ... NY-2
Brandy Brook—stream (2) ... RI-1
Brandy Brook—stream ... VT-1
Brandy Brook—stream ... WI-6
Brandy Brook Flow—bay ... NY-2
Brandy Brook Sch—school ... WI-6
Brandy Brow ... MA-1
Brandybrow Hill ... MA-1
Brandy Brow Hill—summit ... MA-1
Brandy Brow Hill—summit ... NH-1
**Brandy Camp**—pop pl ... PA-2
Brandy Camp Creek—stream ... PA-2
Brandy Ch—church ... VA-3
Brandy City—locale ... CA-9
Brandy Creek ... NY-2
Brandy Creek—stream ... AK-9
Brandy Creek—stream (2) ... CA-9
Brandy Creek—stream ... FL-3
Brandy Creek—stream (2) ... MI-6
Brandy Creek—stream ... NC-3
Brandy Creek—stream (3) ... OR-9
Brandy Creek—stream ... TX-5
Brandy Creek—stream ... VA-3
Brandy Creek—stream (2) ... WI-6
**Brandy Creek Estates**—pop pl ... VA-3
Brandy Flat—flat ... CA-9
Brandy Gap—gap ... NC-3
Brandy Heath—swamp ... ME-1
**Brandy Hill**—pop pl ... CT-1
Brandy Hill—summit (2) ... CT-1
Brandy Hill—summit ... MA-1
Brandy Hollow—valley ... TN-4
Brandy Hollow—valley ... WV-2
Brandy-Hook ... PA-2
Brandy Island—island ... NE-7
**Brandy Keg**—pop pl ... KY-4
Brandy Keg Boat Dock—locale ... KY-4
Brandykeg Creek—stream ... KY-4
Brandy Keg Dike—locale ... KY-4
Brandy Lake—lake ... MN-6
Brandy Lake—lake ... NY-2
Brandy Lake—reservoir ... KS-7
Brandy Lick—stream ... KY-4
Brandy Mine—mine ... NV-8
Brandymore Castle ... VA-3
Brandymore Drain—canal ... MI-6
Brandy Peak—summit ... OR-9
Brandy Point—cape ... GA-3
Brandy Point—cape ... ME-1
Brandy Pond ... ME-1
Brandy Pond—lake (5) ... ME-1
Brandy Pond—lake ... NY-2
Brandy Ranch—locale ... CO-8
Brandy Rock Hill—summit ... NH-1
Brandy Run—canal ... MI-6
Brandy Run—stream (2) ... PA-2
Brandy Spring—spring ... CA-9
Brandy Springs Park—park ... PA-2
**Brandy Station**—pop pl ... VA-3
Brandy Stream—stream ... ME-1
Brandy Tree Tank—reservoir ... NM-5
Brandy Wine ... DE-2
Brandywine ... MS-4
Brandywine ... PA-2
Brandywine—locale ... VA-3
**Brandywine**—pop pl ... CA-9
**Brandywine**—pop pl ... DE-2
**Brandywine**—pop pl ... IL-6
**Brandywine**—pop pl ... MD-2
**Brandywine**—pop pl ... NY-2
**Brandywine**—pop pl ... OH-6
**Brandywine**—pop pl ... PA-2
**Brandywine**—pop pl ... WV-2
Brandywine Academy—building ... PA-2
Brandywine Airp—airport ... PA-2
Brandywine Ave Sch—school ... NY-2
Brandywine Battlefield—hist pl ... PA-2
Brandywine Battlefield—park ... PA-2
Brandywine Battlefield State Park—park ... PA-2
Brandywine Bldg and Loan Assoc. Rowhouses—hist pl ... PA-2
Brandywine Brook—stream ... NY-2
Brandywine (CCD)—cens area ... DE-2
Brandywine Cem—cemetery ... MS-4
Brandywine Cem—cemetery ... OH-6
Brandywine Ch—church ... IN-6
Brandywine Ch—church ... MD-2
Brandywine Ch—church ... MS-4
Brandywine Channel—channel ... VA-3
Brandywine Chute ... AR-4
Brandywine Chute ... TN-4
Brandywine Chute—gut ... TN-4
Brandywine Coll—school ... DE-2
Brandywine Community House—locale ... GA-3
Brandywine Country Club—other ... DE-2
Brandy Wine Creek ... DE-2
Brandywine Creek—stream ... DE-2
Brandywine Creek—stream ... IL-6
Brandywine Creek—stream (2) ... IN-6
Brandywine Creek—stream ... IA-7
Brandywine Creek—stream (2) ... KY-4
Brandywine Creek—stream (5) ... MI-6
Brandywine Creek—stream ... MS-4
Brandywine Creek—stream ... NY-2
Brandywine Creek—stream (4) ... OH-6
Brandywine Creek—stream (2) ... PA-2
Brandywine Creek—stream ... WI-6
Brandywine Creek Dam—dam ... DE-2
Brandywine Creek State Park—park ... DE-2
Brandywine Cross Roads ... DE-2
Brandywine Elem Sch—school ... IN-6
**Brandywine Estates**—pop pl ... DE-2
**Brandywine Estates**—pop pl ... TN-4
Brandywine Facility—building ... PA-2
**Brandywine Forge**—pop pl ... DE-2
Brandywine Fork—stream ... IN-6
Brandywine Four Corners ... DE-2
Brandywine Gulch—valley ... CO-8
**Brandywine Heights**—pop pl ... MD-2
**Brandywine Hills**—pop pl ... DE-2
**Brandywine Homes**—pop pl ... PA-2
Brandywine HS—school ... DE-2
Brandywine Hundred—civil ... DE-2
Brandywine Island—island ... AR-4
Brandywine Kill ... DE-2
Brandywine Lake—lake ... MI-6
Brandywine Lake—lake ... OH-6
Brandywine Lake—lake ... WI-6
**Brandywine Lake**—pop pl ... MI-6
Brandywine Lake—reservoir ... WV-2
Brandywine Landing—locale ... AR-4
Brandywine Manor—locale ... PA-2
**Brandywine Manor (subdivision)**—pop pl ... PA-2
Brandywine Manufacturers Sunday Sch—hist pl ... DE-2
Brandywine Methodist Church ... MS-4
Brandywine Park—hist pl ... DE-2
Brandywine Park—park ... DE-2
Brandywine Park and Kentmere Parkway (Boundary Increase)—hist pl ... DE-2
Brandywine Point—cape ... TN-4
Brandywine Powder Mills District—hist pl ... DE-2
Brandywine Raceway—other ... DE-2
Brandywine Range—channel ... NJ-2
Brandywine Rec Area—park ... WV-2
Brandywine Revetment—dam ... AR-4
Brandywine River ... PA-2
Brandywine Run—stream ... WV-2
Brandywine Sch—school ... MI-6
Brandywine Shoal—bar ... NJ-2
Brandywine Shop Ctr—locale ... DE-2
Brandywine Spring—spring ... MS-4
**Brandywine Springs**—pop pl ... DE-2
**Brandywine Springs Manor**—pop pl ... DE-2
Brandywine Springs State Park—park ... DE-2
**Brandywine (subdivision)**—pop pl (2) ... AZ-5
**Brandywine (subdivision)**—pop pl ... NC-3
**Brandywine Summit**—pop pl ... PA-2
Brandywine Summit Camp—locale ... PA-2
**Brandywine (Township of)**—pop pl (2) ... IN-6
Brandywine Township School Number 1 ... IN-6
Brandywine-Trinity United Methodist Ch—church ... DE-2
Brandywine Village ... PA-2
**Brandywine Village**—pop pl ... PA-2
Brandywine Village Hist Dist—hist pl ... DE-2
Brandywine Village Hist Dist (Boundary Increase)—hist pl ... DE-2
Brandywine Village Shop Ctr—locale ... FL-3
Brandywine Wallace Elem Sch—school ... PA-2
**Brandywine Woods**—pop pl ... MD-2
**Brandywood**—pop pl ... DE-2
Brandywood Elem Sch—school ... DE-2
Brandywood Park—park ... DE-2
Branett Sch (historical)—school ... IA-7
**Branford**—pop pl ... CT-1
**Branford**—pop pl ... FL-3
Branford (CCD)—cens area ... FL-3
Branford Center Cem—cemetery ... CT-1
Branford Center Hist Dist—hist pl ... CT-1
Branford Creek—stream ... SC-3
Branford Electric Railway Hist Dist—hist pl ... CT-1
Branford Harbor—bay ... CT-1
**Branford Hills**—pop pl ... CT-1
Branford Hills Sch—school ... CT-1
Branford-Horry House—hist pl ... SC-3
Branford House—hist pl ... CT-1
Branford HS—school ... CT-1
Branford HS—school ... FL-3
Branford Mtn—summit ... CA-9
Branford Park—park ... CA-9
Branford Point—cape ... CT-1
**Branford Point**—pop pl ... CT-1
Branford Point Hist Dist—hist pl ... CT-1
Branford Supply Ponds—lake ... CT-1
**Branford (Town of)**—pop pl ... CT-1
Branham, Richard, House—hist pl ... KY-4
Branham Branch—stream (2) ... KY-4
Branham Branch—stream ... SC-3
Branham Cem—cemetery ... KY-4
Branham Cem—cemetery ... MO-7
Branham Cem—cemetery ... OH-6
Branham Creek—stream ... KY-4
Branham Hollow—valley (2) ... TN-4
Branham House—hist pl ... KY-4
Branham Lakes—lake ... MT-8
Branham Mill Swamp—swamp ... VA-3
Branham Peaks—summit ... MT-8
Branham Rsvr—reservoir ... CA-9
Branhams Branch—stream ... KY-4
Branhams Branch Sch—school ... KY-4
Branhams Mill Swamp ... VA-3
Braniff Bldg—hist pl ... OK-5
Branigan Lake—lake ... CA-9
**Branigar Estates**—pop pl ... IL-6
Brank Cem—cemetery ... NC-3
Brank Cove—valley ... NC-3
Brank Mtn—summit ... NC-3
Bran Lake—lake ... ME-1
Branley Lake ... WI-6
Brannacks Bay ... MD-2
Brannaman ... AZ-5
Brannaman Branch—stream ... IN-6
Brannan, Sam, Cottage—hist pl ... CA-9
Brannan Cem—cemetery ... GA-3
Brannan Ch—church ... KY-4
Brannan Creek—stream ... CA-9
Brannan Gulch—valley ... OR-9
Brannan Island—island ... CA-9
Brannan JHS—school ... CA-9
Brannan Lakes—lake ... MT-8
Brannan-Montague Mine—mine ... TN-4
Brannan Mtn—summit ... CA-9
Brannan Rsvr—reservoir ... WY-8
Brannan Sch (historical)—school ... AL-4
Brannars Mills (historical)—locale ... TN-4
Brann Boardinghouse—hist pl ... NV-8
Brann Brook—stream (2) ... ME-1
**Brannen**—pop pl ... ME-1
Brannen Bay—bay ... GA-3
Brannen Cem—cemetery ... GA-3
Brannen Creek—gut ... FL-3
Brannen-Devine House—hist pl ... AZ-5
Branner Cem—cemetery ... TN-4
Branner-Hicks House—hist pl ... TN-4
Branners Knob—summit ... TN-4
Brannian Creek—stream ... WA-9
Brannigan Camp—locale ... CO-8
Brannigan Flat—flat ... AZ-5
Brannigan Flat Tank—reservoir ... AZ-5
Brannigan Park—flat ... AZ-5
Brannigan Spring—spring ... CO-8
Brannigan Tank—reservoir ... AZ-5
Brannin Creek—stream ... CA-9
Branningan Mine—mine ... CA-9
Branning Branch—stream ... FL-3
**Branning (historical)**—pop pl ... NC-3
Branning Ledge—bar ... ME-1
**Branningville**—pop pl ... PA-2
Branninsville ... PA-2
Brannock Bay—bay ... MD-2
Brannocks Bay ... MD-2
Brannom Branch—stream ... VA-3
Brannom Knob—summit ... VA-3
Brannon—locale ... AR-4
Brannon—locale ... KY-4
**Brannon**—pop pl ... LA-4
**Brannon**—pop pl ... SC-3
Brannon, S. L., House—hist pl ... TX-5
Brannon, W. A., Store-Moreland Knitting Mills—hist pl ... GA-3
Brannon Branch—stream ... VA-3
Brannon Cem—cemetery ... AL-4
Brannon Cem—cemetery ... IL-6
Brannon Cem—cemetery ... MO-7
Brannon Cem—cemetery ... SC-3
Brannon Cem—cemetery (2) ... TX-5
Brannon Cem—cemetery (2) ... WV-2
Brannon Creek—stream ... AL-4
Brannon Creek—stream ... MS-4
Brannon Creek—stream ... TN-4
Brannon Creek Dam ... TN-4
Brannon-Joyner Cem—cemetery ... MS-4
Brannon Mtn—summit ... AR-4
Brannon Park—flat ... NM-5
Brannon Park Trail (Pack)—trail ... NM-5
Brannon Pit—cave ... AL-4
Brannon Prospect—mine ... TN-4
Brannon Ranch—locale ... OK-5
Brannon Ridge—ridge ... AK-9
Brannon Run—stream (2) ... PA-2
Brannons Bridge—bridge ... GA-3
Brannon Sch—school ... WI-6
Brannons Fork—stream ... OH-6
Brannon Spring ... TN-4
Brannon Springs ... AL-4
Brannon Springs (historical)—locale ... AL-4
Brannon Springs Missionary Baptist Ch—church ... AL-4
Brannons Run—stream ... WV-2
**Brannon Stand**—pop pl ... AL-4
**Brannon Stand Heights (subdivision)**—pop pl ... AL-4
**Brannonville**—pop pl ... FL-3
Brannonville Baptist Ch—church ... FL-3
Brannon Windmill—locale ... NM-5
Brann Sch—school ... AR-4
Branns Mill Pond—lake ... ME-1
Brannthoff Lake ... MI-6
Brannum Windmill—locale ... NM-5
Branom—locale ... TX-5
**Branon**—pop pl ... NC-3
Branon Cem—cemetery ... GA-3
Branon Hollow—valley ... AL-4
Bran Point—cape ... MA-1
**Brans Chapel**—pop pl ... AL-4
Brans Chapel Congregational Methodist Ch—church ... AL-4
**Branscomb**—pop pl ... CA-9
Branscombe Cem—cemetery ... TN-4
Branscomb Hill—summit ... VA-3
Branscomb Spring ... AR-4
Branscom Cem—cemetery ... KS-7
Branscome Cem—cemetery ... MS-4
Branscum Cem—cemetery ... AR-4
Branscumb Spring ... AR-4
Branscum Spring—spring ... AR-4
Bransford—locale ... TN-4
Bransford—locale ... TX-5
Bransford Cem—cemetery ... MS-4
Bransford Cem—cemetery ... TN-4
Bransford HS—school ... TN-4
Bransford Post Office (historical)—building ... TN-4
Bransford Pumphouse—other ... KY-4
Bransford Spring—spring ... KY-4
**Branshermill (subdivision)**—pop pl ... NC-3
**Branson**—pop pl ... CO-8
**Branson**—pop pl ... MO-7
Branson Adult Community Center—building ... MO-7
Branson Airp—airport ... NC-3
Branson Bldg—hist pl ... OK-5
Branson Cave—cave ... MO-7
Branson Cem—cemetery ... GA-3
Branson Cem—cemetery ... IA-7
Branson Cem—cemetery ... KS-7
Branson Cem—cemetery (2) ... MO-7
Branson Cem—cemetery ... TN-4
Branson City Cem—cemetery ... MO-7
Branson Cove—bay ... VA-3
Branson Creek—stream ... KS-7
Branson Creek—stream ... NC-3
Branson Creek—stream ... OK-5
Branson Creek—stream (2) ... OR-9
Branson Ditch—canal ... IN-6
Branson Hill—summit ... WA-9
Branson Hills Ch—church ... MO-7
Branson JHS—school ... MO-7
Branson Lake—reservoir ... NC-3
Branson Memorial Airp—airport ... MO-7
Branson MS—school ... MO-7
Branson Post Office—building ... MO-7
Branson Public Library—building ... MO-7
Branson Ridge—ridge ... OH-6
Branson Rsvr—reservoir ... OR-9
Branson Sch—school ... MO-7
Bransons Cove ... VA-3
Branson Senior HS—school ... MO-7
Bransons Point—cape ... VA-3
Branson Spring—spring ... CO-8
Branson Spring—spring ... VA-3
Branson Township—civil ... MO-7
**Branstad**—pop pl ... WI-6
Branstad Sch—school ... WI-6
Bransteder Hollow ... MO-7
Branstetter Branch—stream ... KY-4
Branstetter Branch—stream ... TN-4
Branstetter Canyon—valley ... CA-9
Branstetter Cem—cemetery ... MO-7
Branstetter Oil Field—oilfield ... OK-5
Branstetter Park—park ... KY-4
Branstetter Ridge—ridge ... CA-9
Branstetters Cem—cemetery ... TN-4
Branstutter Cem—cemetery ... MO-7
Brant—locale ... CA-9
Brant—locale ... WI-6
**Brant**—pop pl ... MI-6
**Brant**—pop pl ... NY-2
Brant, A.A., House—hist pl ... NJ-2
Brant Bayou—channel ... LA-4
**Brant Beach**—pop pl ... NJ-2
Brant Bluff—cliff ... AK-9
Brant Brook—stream ... NY-2
Brant Cem—cemetery ... MO-7
Brant Cem—cemetery ... OH-6
Brant Cem—cemetery ... WV-2
Brant Cemeteries—cemetery ... MI-6
Brant Coulee—valley ... MT-8
Brant Creek—stream ... MI-6
Brant Creek—stream ... WI-6
Brant Ditch—canal (2) ... IN-6
Brantford—locale ... KS-7
**Brantford**—pop pl ... ND-7
Brantford Cem—cemetery ... KS-7
Brantford Cem—cemetery ... ND-7
**Brantford Township**—pop pl ... KS-7
**Brantford Township**—pop pl ... SD-7
Brantford Township (historical)—civil ... SD-7
Branther Gulch—valley ... CO-8
Brant Hill ... MA-1
Brant Hill—locale ... PA-2
Brant Hole—bay ... MD-2
Brant Hole Point—cape ... MD-2
**Brantingham**—pop pl ... NY-2
Brantingham Cem—cemetery ... NY-2
Brantingham Lake—lake ... NY-2
Brant Island ... ME-1
Brant Island—island ... AK-9
Brant Island—island ... LA-4
Brant Island—island ... MA-1
Brant Island—island ... NC-3
Brant Island—island ... TX-5
Brant Island—island ... WA-9
Brant Island Cove—cove ... MA-1
Brant Island (historical)—island ... NC-3
Brant Island Pond—lake ... NC-3
Brant Lake—lake ... FL-3
Brant Lake—lake ... MI-6
Brant Lake—lake ... MN-6
Brant Lake—lake ... NY-2
Brant Lake—lake ... SD-7
**Brant Lake**—pop pl ... NY-2
Brant Lake Drain—canal ... MI-6
Brant Lake Township (historical)—civil ... SD-7
Brant Ledges—bar ... ME-1
Brantley—locale ... GA-3
**Brantley**—pop pl (2) ... AL-4
Brantley, Dr. Hassell, House—hist pl ... NC-3
Brantley, Lake—lake ... FL-3
Brantley, Lake—reservoir ... GA-3
Brantley Assembly of God Ch—church ... AL-4
Brantley Baptist Ch—church ... AL-4
Brantley Bluff—cliff ... KY-4
Brantley Branch ... MO-7
Brantley Branch—stream ... MO-7
Brantley Branch—stream ... TX-5
Brantley (CCD)—cens area ... AL-4
Brantley Cem—cemetery ... AL-4
Brantley Cem—cemetery ... LA-4
Brantley Cem—cemetery ... MS-4
Brantley Cem—cemetery ... MO-7
Brantley Cem—cemetery ... NC-3
Brantley Cem—cemetery ... TX-5
Brantley Chapel—church ... GA-3
**Brantley (County)**—pop pl ... GA-3
Brantley Creek—stream ... GA-3
**Brantley Crossing**—pop pl ... AL-4
Brantley Dam—dam ... AL-4
Brantley Division—civil ... AL-4
Brantley Gin (historical)—locale ... AL-4
Brantley Grove Ch—church ... NC-3
Brantley Hollow—valley ... TN-4
Brantley HS—school (2) ... AL-4
Brantley Island—island ... NC-3
Brantley Lake—lake ... AL-4
Brantley Lake—lake ... FL-3
Brantley Lake—reservoir ... AL-4
Brantley Lake Dam—dam ... AL-4
Brantley Landing—locale ... LA-4
Brantley Mtn—summit ... AR-4
Brantley Pond—reservoir ... AL-4
Brantley Pond—swamp ... FL-3
Brantley Ranch Creek—stream ... AR-4
Brantleys Chapel—church ... TN-4
Brantley School ... AL-4
**Brantleys Grove**—pop pl ... NC-3
Brantleys Island ... NC-3
Brantleys Mine (underground)—mine ... AL-4
Brantleys Pond—reservoir ... NC-3
Brantleys Pond Dam—dam ... NC-3
Brantley Square (Shop Ctr)—locale ... FL-3
Brantleys Store ... TN-4
Brantleys Switch ... AL-4
Brantley Swamp—stream ... VA-3
Brantley Switch ... AL-4
Brantley Tank—reservoir ... NM-5
Brantley United Methodist Ch—church ... AL-4
**Brantleyville**—pop pl ... AL-4
Brantleyville Ch—church ... AL-4
Brantling Hill—summit ... NY-2
Brantly Cem—cemetery ... TX-5
Brantly Lake—lake ... FL-3
Brantner Ditch—canal ... CO-8
Branton ... TX-5
**Branton**—pop pl ... TX-5
Branton Bar—bar ... OR-9
Branton Manor—hist pl ... MD-2
Branton Sch—school ... GA-3
Brant Point—cape ... AK-9
Brant Point—cape ... MA-1
Brant Point—cape ... NY-2
Brant Point—cape ... WA-9
Brant Point Light—locale ... MA-1
Brant Point Light Station—hist pl ... MA-1
Brantree ... MA-1
Brantree Bay ... MA-1
**Brant Rock**—pop pl ... MA-1
Brant Rock—rock ... MA-1
Brant Rocks ... MA-1
Brant Rock Village (historical P.O.)—locale ... MA-1
Brant Sch—school ... SD-7
Brants Hill ... MA-1
Brants Hill—summit ... MI-6
Brant Shoal Channel ... NC-3
Brants Island ... MA-1
Brants Pond ... CT-1
**Brant (Town of)**—pop pl ... NY-2
**Brant (Township of)**—pop pl ... MI-6
Brant Trail—trail ... PA-2
Brantville—locale ... WV-2
**Brantwood**—pop pl ... NJ-2
**Brantwood**—pop pl ... WI-6
Brantwood Pond—reservoir ... AL-4
Brantwood Sch—school ... OH-6
Branum Cem—cemetery ... TN-4
Branum Lake—reservoir ... MT-8
Branum Well—well ... NM-5
Branville Bay—lake ... LA-4
Branville Ch—church ... TN-4
Branwood—uninc pl ... SC-3
**Branyan**—pop pl ... MS-4
Branyan Sch—school ... MS-4
Branyon Cem—cemetery ... AL-4
Branyon Cem—cemetery ... TX-5
Branyon Oil Field—oilfield ... TX-5
**Braodwells Mill**—pop pl ... AL-4
Bras—island ... FM-9
Brase Cem—cemetery ... MN-6
Brasel Branch—stream ... TN-4
Brasel Cem—cemetery ... TN-4
Brasel Creek—stream ... AR-4
Brasel Sch—school ... IL-6
**Braselton**—pop pl ... GA-3
Braseltown ... GA-3
**Brasfield**—pop pl ... AR-4
**Brasfield**—pop pl ... MS-4
Brasfield Cem—cemetery ... AL-4
Brasfield Cem—cemetery ... MO-7
Brasfield Landing—locale ... AL-4
Brasfield Landing (historical)—locale ... AL-4
Brasfield Sch (abandoned)—school ... MO-7
Brasfields Gin Landing ... AL-4
**Brashear**—pop pl ... MO-7
**Brashear**—pop pl ... TX-5
Brashear Acad (historical)—school ... MS-4
Brashear Cem—cemetery ... IN-6
Brashear Cem—cemetery ... KY-4
Brashear Cem—cemetery ... MO-7
Brashear Creek—stream ... MS-4
Brashear Creek—stream ... TN-4
Brashear Hollow—valley ... MO-7
Brashear HS—school ... PA-2
Brashear Island—island ... TN-4
Brashears ... MO-7
**Brashears**—pop pl ... AR-4
Brashears Cem—cemetery ... TX-5
Brashears Cemetery ... MO-7
Brashears Creek—stream ... KY-4
Brashears Ferry (historical)—locale ... AL-4
Brashears Run—stream ... PA-2
Brashears Shoals—bar ... TN-4
**Brashears Subdivision**—pop pl ... TN-4
Brasher ... MO-7
Brasher Bayou—stream ... MS-4
Brasher Branch—stream ... AL-4
Brasher Cove—cave ... IL-6
Brasher Cem—cemetery (4) ... AL-4
Brasher Cem—cemetery ... MO-7
Brasher Cem—cemetery ... TN-4
**Brasher Center**—pop pl ... NY-2
**Brasher Center (Brasher)**—pop pl ... NY-2
Brasher Chapel ... AL-4
Brasher Creek—stream ... AL-4
**Brasher Falls**—pop pl ... NY-2
Brasher Falls-Winthrop—CDP ... NY-2
**Brasher Iron Works**—pop pl ... NY-2
Brasher Iron Works Cem—cemetery ... NY-2
Brashers Cem—cemetery ... MO-7
Brashers Chapel Ch—church ... AL-4
Brashers Ferry ... AL-4
Brasher Spring—spring ... AL-4
Brasher Spring Camp—locale ... AL-4
Brasher Springs Camp ... AL-4
Brasher Springs Church ... AL-4
**Brasher (Town of)**—pop pl ... NY-2
Brashier Branch—stream ... TN-4
Brashier Cem—cemetery ... AL-4
Brashier Chapel ... AL-4
Brashier Chapel—church ... AL-4
Brashier Chapel Cem—cemetery ... AL-4
Brashier Chapel Sch (historical)—school ... AL-4
Brashiers Chapel Methodist Church ... AL-4
Brashiers Ferry ... AL-4
Brashy Slough ... IL-6
**Brasie Corners**—pop pl ... NY-2
Brasier Gap—gap ... AL-4
Brasier Tank—reservoir ... NM-5
Brasil Springs—spring ... AK-9
Braska House—hist pl ... IA-7

Brasket Spring—spring ... WY-8
Brassar—locale ... MI-6
Brassar Point—cape ... MI-6
Brass Cap Point—cape ... AZ-5
Brass Cap Rsvr—reservoir ... OR-9
**Brass Castle**—pop pl ... NJ-2
Brass Castle Creek—stream ... NJ-2
Brass Ch—church ... AL-4
Brass Channel—channel ... VI-3
Brass Chapel ... AL-4
Brass Creek—stream ... ID-8
Brassel Cem—cemetery ... MS-4
Brassel Cem—cemetery ... TN-4
**Brassell**—pop pl ... AL-4
**Brassell Bottom**—pop pl ... AL-4
Brassell Chapel—church ... MS-4
Brassell Ranch—locale ... NM-5
Brassel Slough—gut ... MI-6
Brasser Sch—school ... NY-2
Brassey Ranch—locale ... ID-8
Brassfield—locale ... KY-4
Brassfield—locale ... NC-3
Brassfield Baptist Church—hist pl ... NC-3
Brassfield Bend—bend ... TN-4
Brassfield Branch—stream ... TN-4
Brassfield Ch—church ... NC-3
Brassfield Sch—school ... KY-4
Brassfield (Township of)—fmr MCD ... NC-3
Brassi Brook—stream ... CT-1
Brassiere Hills—summit ... AK-9
Brass Kettle Brook—stream ... MA-1
Brass Millpond—reservoir ... MA-1
Brass Mtn—summit ... CT-1
Brass Nail Gulch—valley ... OR-9
Brasso Well—well ... TX-5
Brass Pan Creek—stream ... AK-9
Brass Ranch—locale ... NM-5
**Brasstown**—pop pl ... NC-3
**Brasstown**—pop pl ... SC-3
Brasstown Bald—summit ... GA-3
Brasstown Cem—cemetery ... NC-3
Brasstown Ch—church ... GA-3
Brasstown Ch—church ... SC-3
Brasstown Cottage—hist pl ... WI-6
Brasstown Creek—stream (2) ... GA-3
Brasstown Creek—stream ... NC-3
Brasstown Creek—stream ... SC-3
Brasstown Gap ... GA-3
Brasstown Gap—gap ... GA-3
Brasstown Knob—summit ... NC-3
Brasstown (Township of)—fmr MCD ... NC-3
Brassua—locale ... ME-1
Brassua Dam—dam ... ME-1
Brassua Lake—reservoir ... ME-1
Brassua Stream—stream ... ME-1
Brassua (Township of)—unorg ... ME-1
Brasswell Canyon—valley ... AZ-5
Brasswells Lake—reservoir ... GA-3
Brast Cem—cemetery ... TX-5
Brasures Branch—stream ... DE-2
Braswell—locale ... GA-3
Braswell—locale ... NC-3
**Braswell**—pop pl ... GA-3
Braswell Branch—stream ... AR-4
Braswell Branch—stream ... GA-3
Braswell Branch—stream ... MS-4
Braswell-Carnes House—hist pl ... GA-3
Braswell Cem—cemetery (2) ... GA-3
Braswell Cem—cemetery ... MO-7
Braswell Cem—cemetery ... NC-3
Braswell Cem—cemetery (3) ... TN-4
Braswell Ch—church ... GA-3
Braswell Creek—stream ... GA-3
Braswell Lake—reservoir ... NC-3
Braswell Lake Dam—dam (2) ... NC-3
Braswell Lookout—locale ... MO-7
Braswell Lookout Tower—tower ... MO-7
Braswell Mill ... AL-4
Braswell Sch—school ... NC-3
Braswells Crossroads—locale ... NC-3
Braswells Lake—reservoir ... NC-3
**Braswells (Pinhook)**—pop pl ... FL-3
Braswell Spring—spring ... AR-4
Braswell Well—well ... NM-5
Bratburg Butte—summit ... ND-7
**Bratcher**—pop pl ... TN-4
Bratcher, Lake—reservoir ... TX-5
Bratcher Branch—stream ... KY-4
Bratcher Branch—stream ... SC-3
Bratcher Cem—cemetery ... AR-4
Bratcher Cem—cemetery ... KY-4
Bratcher Cem—cemetery ... MO-7
Bratcher Cem—cemetery ... TX-5
Bratcher Creek—stream ... GA-3
Bratcher Gap—gap ... NC-3
Bratcher Lake—lake ... MO-7
Bratchers Crossroads—locale ... TN-4
Bratcher Slough—stream ... TX-5
**Bratenahl**—pop pl ... OH-6
Braten Ranch—locale ... WY-8
Brat Hollow—valley ... NY-2
Brat Hollow Sch—school ... NY-2
Bratle Lake ... MN-6
Bratlie, Lake—lake ... AK-9
Braton Cem—cemetery ... TN-4
Braton Creek ... MI-6
Braton Hollow—valley ... OR-9
Braton Peak ... CA-9
Braton School (Abandoned)—locale ... MN-6
**Bratsberg**—pop pl ... MN-6
Bratschi Cem—cemetery ... TN-4
**Bratt**—pop pl ... FL-3
Brattain Butte—summit ... OR-9
Brattain Canyon—valley ... OR-9
Brattain Canyon Spring—spring ... OR-9
Brattain Cem—cemetery ... OR-9
Brattain Hill—summit ... OR-9
Brattain Ranch—locale ... OR-9
Brattain Ridge—ridge ... OR-9
Brattain Sch—school ... OR-9
Brattan Spring—spring ... OR-9
Brattan Valley ... CA-9
Bratt Elem Sch—school ... FL-3
Bratten Area State Wildlife Mngmt Area—park ... SD-7
Bratten Coulee—valley ... MT-8
Bratten Creek—stream ... NE-7
Bratten Hollow—valley ... KY-4
Bratten Hollow—valley ... TN-4
Bratten Spring Creek—stream ... MO-7
Bratt Hollow—valley ... MO-7
**Brattle**—pop pl ... MA-1
Brattle, William, House—hist pl ... MA-1
Brattleboro—CDP ... VT-1
**Brattleboro**—pop pl ... VT-1
**Brattleboro Center**—pop pl ... VT-1
Brattleboro Country Club—other ... VT-1
Brattleboro Downtown Hist Dist—hist pl ... VT-1
Brattleboro Retreat—hist pl ... VT-1
Brattle Brook—stream ... MA-1
Brattle Brook Park—park ... MA-1
Brattle Hall—hist pl ... MA-1
Brattle Hill—summit ... MA-1
Brattle Lake ... MN-6
Brattle RR Station ... MA-1
Brattle Station ... MA-1
**Bratton**—pop pl ... KY-4
Bratton—uninc pl ... MS-4
Bratton Airp—airport ... PA-2
Bratton Bend—bend ... TN-4
Bratton Bluff—cliff ... TN-4
Bratton Branch—stream ... KY-4
Bratton Branch—stream ... WV-2
Bratton Cem—cemetery ... AR-4
Bratton Cem—cemetery ... KY-4
Bratton Cem—cemetery ... MO-7
Bratton Cem—cemetery ... OH-6
Bratton Cem—cemetery ... TN-4
Bratton Cem—cemetery ... TX-5
Bratton Cem—cemetery ... VA-3
Bratton Cem—cemetery ... WV-2
Bratton Creek ... VA-3
Bratton Creek—stream ... AR-4
Bratton Creek—stream ... MD-2
Bratton Ditch—canal ... OH-6
Bratton Ford—crossing ... TN-4
Bratton Ford Bridge—bridge ... TN-4
Bratton Gap—gap ... PA-2
Bratton Hollow—valley ... TN-4
Bratton Mtn—summit (2) ... VA-3
Bratton Ranch ... OR-9
Bratton Ranch—locale ... CA-9
Bratton Ridge ... OR-9
Bratton's Chapel—church ... MS-4
Brattons Creek ... VA-3
Brattons Mill (historical)—locale ... TN-4
Brattons Run—stream ... VA-3
Bratton Store—locale ... MS-4
Brattonsville Hist Dist—hist pl ... SC-3
**Brattontown**—pop pl ... TN-4
Bratton Township—civil ... PA-2
**Bratton (Township of)**—pop pl ... OH-6
**Bratton (Township of)**—pop pl ... PA-2
Bratton Union Sch—school ... NE-7
Bratton Valley—basin ... CA-9
Bratts Branch ... DE-2
Bratt Sch—school ... NY-2
Bratt-Smiley House—hist pl ... AR-4
Braucher—locale ... WV-2
Braud, Bayou—stream ... LA-4
Braud Book ... CT-1
Braud Brook ... CT-1
Braudy Branch—stream ... VA-3
Brauer Ditch—canal ... WY-8
Brauer Hill ... MI-6
Brauer Ranch—locale ... TX-5
Brauer Sch—school ... KS-7
Brauersville Sch—school ... MO-7
Braugh Stone Ditch—canal ... MT-8
Braulia Oil Field—oilfield ... TX-5
Brault Sch—school ... IL-6
**Braum**—pop pl ... OK-5
Braum Point Island ... NC-3
Braun—locale ... OR-9
Braun, Charles A., House—hist pl ... CA-9
Braun, George, House—hist pl ... TX-5
Braun, John, House—hist pl ... KY-4
Braun, Michael, House—hist pl ... NC-3
Braun Bay—bay ... NH-1
Braun Butte—summit ... ND-7
Braunch Memorial Park—cemetery ... OK-5
Braun Creek—stream ... ID-8
Braun Creek—stream ... MT-8
Braund Hill—summit ... WI-6
Braune, Gustave, House—hist pl ... AL-4
Brauner Lake—lake ... MN-6
Braunig Lake—reservoir ... TX-5
Brauns Airp—airport ... IN-6
Braun Sch—school ... PA-2
Braun Settlement Sch—school ... WI-6
Braunson Ranch—locale ... SD-7
Braunsport ... OR-9
Braunstein's Bldg—hist pl ... DE-2
Braunsweiger Lake—lake ... NE-7
Braun Windmill—locale ... NM-5
Braunworth Lake—lake ... MN-6
Brauti Creek ... OR-9
Brauti Creek—stream ... OR-9
**Brave**—pop pl ... PA-2
Brave Boat Harbor—bay ... ME-1
Brave Bull Creek—stream ... SD-7
Brave Bull Ranch Resort Airp—airport ... AZ-5
Brave Creek—stream ... ID-8
Brave Creek—stream ... IN-6
Brave Dog Mtn—summit ... MT-8
Brave (historical)—locale ... SD-7
Brave Hollow—valley ... IN-6
Brave Lake—lake ... CA-9
Bravel Slough—gut ... CA-9
Braverman HS—school ... NY-2
Brave Run—stream ... IN-6
Braves Branch ... TN-4
Brave Station—locale ... PA-2
**Bravo**—pop pl ... MI-6
Bravo Canyon—valley ... CO-8
Bravo Creek—stream ... OR-9
Bravo Creek—stream ... TX-5
Bravo Ditch—canal ... CO-8
Bravo Field Outlying—airport ... MS-4
Bravo Glacier—glacier ... AK-9
Bravo Lake—reservoir ... CA-9
Bravo Park—park ... AZ-5
Bravo Pass—gap ... AK-9
Bravo Ranch—locale ... TX-5
Bravo Ranch (historical)—locale ... OR-9
**Bravo (subdivision)**—pop pl ... AL-4
Bravo Well—well ... TX-5
Bravo Windmill—locale ... TX-5
Brawders Shoals ... TN-4
Brawl Cem—cemetery ... IL-6
Brawley—locale ... AR-4
**Brawley**—pop pl ... CA-9
Brawley, Espy Watts, House—hist pl ... NC-3
Brawley Branch—stream ... GA-3
Brawley (CCD)—cens area ... CA-9
Brawley Cem—cemetery ... GA-3
Brawley Cem—cemetery ... PA-2
Brawley Ch—church ... WV-2
Brawley Creek—stream ... MO-7
Brawley Creek—stream ... TX-5
Brawley Hollow—valley ... AR-4
Brawley Hollow—valley (6) ... MO-7
Brawley Hollow—valley ... OH-6
Brawley HS—school ... NC-3
Brawley Lake—reservoir ... TX-5
Brawley MS ... NC-3
Brawley Mtn—summit ... GA-3
Brawley Peaks—range ... CA-9
Brawley Peaks—summit ... NV-8
Brawley Pond—lake ... MO-7
Brawley Run—stream ... PA-2
Brawley Sch—school ... NC-3
Brawleys Fork—stream ... TN-4
Brawleys Fork Church ... TN-4
Brawleys Hollow—valley ... WV-2
Brawley Tank—reservoir ... NM-5
Brawley (Township of)—fmr MCD ... AR-4
Brawley Wash—stream ... AZ-5
Brawly Wash ... AZ-5
Brawner Creek—stream ... NE-7
Brawners Creek ... NE-7
Braxee Lake—lake ... MI-6
Braxon Lake—lake ... ID-8
Braxon Peak—summit ... ID-8
Braxton (2) ... IN-6
Braxton—locale ... KY-4
Braxton—locale ... WV-2
**Braxton**—pop pl ... MS-4
**Braxton**—pop pl ... TN-4
Braxton Baptist Ch—church ... MS-4
Braxton Branch ... LA-4
Braxton Branch—stream ... LA-4
Braxton Cem—cemetery ... FL-3
Braxton Cem—cemetery ... SC-3
Braxton Chapel African Methodist Episcopal Ch—church ... TN-4
Braxton Collegiate Institution (historical)—school ... MS-4
**Braxton (County)**—pop pl ... WV-2
Braxton Craven Elem Sch—school ... NC-3
Braxton Lake ... ID-8
Braxton Lakes ... ID-8
Braxton Park—park ... PA-2
Braxton Post Office (historical)—building ... TN-4
Braxtons ... IN-6
Braxton Sch—school ... NC-3
**Braxtons Siding**—pop pl ... IN-6
Bray—locale ... CA-9
Bray—locale ... TN-4
**Bray**—pop pl ... OK-5
Bray, Lake—reservoir ... MA-1
Bray, Thomas, Farm—hist pl ... MA-1
Bray-Barron House—hist pl ... AL-4
Bray Branch—stream ... AR-4
Bray Branch—stream ... GA-3
Bray Branch—stream ... KY-4
Bray Branch—stream ... TN-4
Bray Branch—stream ... TX-5
Braybrooks Sch—school ... MI-6
Bray Canyon—valley ... CA-9
Bray Cem—cemetery ... MD-2
Bray Cem—cemetery ... MI-6
Bray Cem—cemetery (2) ... MO-7
Bray Cem—cemetery (3) ... TN-4
Bray Cem—cemetery ... VA-3
Bray Cem—cemetery ... WV-2
Bray Ch—church ... GA-3
Bray Cove—bay ... TX-5
Bray Creek ... AL-4
Bray Creek—gut ... FL-3
Bray Creek—stream ... AL-4
Bray Creek—stream ... AZ-5
Bray Creek—stream ... CA-9
Bray Creek—stream ... ID-8
Bray Creek—stream ... KY-4
Bray Creek—stream ... MI-6
Bray Creek—stream ... MS-4
Brayden Creek ... MI-6
Brayden Creek—stream ... MI-6
Bray Ditch—canal ... IN-6
Bray Draw—valley ... WY-8
Braye Lakes—lake ... AK-9
Braye Pass—gap ... AK-9
Braye Sch (historical)—school ... TN-4
Bray Field Hollow—valley ... KY-4
Brayford Cem—cemetery ... IL-6
Bray Gulch—valley ... MT-8
Bray Gulch—valley ... OR-9
Bray Gully—valley ... NY-2
Bray Hill—summit ... AR-4
Bray Hill—summit ... ME-1
Bray Hill—summit ... MD-2
Bray Hill—summit ... NH-1
Bray Hill—summit ... VA-3
Bray-Hoffman House—hist pl ... NJ-2
Bray Hollow—valley (2) ... MO-7
Bray Hollow—valley ... OH-6
Bray House—hist pl ... ME-1
Brayhouse Brook—stream ... NY-2
Bray Lake—lake ... ID-8
Bray Lake—lake ... MI-6
Bray Lake—lake (2) ... MN-6
Bray Lake—reservoir ... IN-6
Bray Lake Ranch—locale ... ID-8
Bray Ledge—bar ... ME-1
Brayley Brook ... ME-1
Brayley Brook—stream ... ME-1
Brayley Pond—lake ... ME-1
Braymanville ... NY-2
Bray-Maxwell Sch—school ... OK-5
**Braymer**—pop pl ... MO-7
Braymer Cem—cemetery ... NY-2
Braymer Lake—reservoir ... MO-7
Braymer School (abandoned)—locale ... NY-2
**Braymill**—pop pl ... OR-9
Bray Mill Creek—stream ... FL-3
Bray Mine—mine ... MN-6
Bray Mine—mine ... NV-8
Bray Mine (underground)—mine ... AL-4
Bray Mtn ... OR-9
Bray Mtn—summit ... OR-9
Braynerd Bayou—gut ... FL-3
Bray Park—park ... NC-3
Bray Place—hist pl ... KY-4
Bray Point—cape (2) ... ME-1
Bray Point—cape ... OR-9
Bray Ranch—locale ... NM-5
Bray Reservoir Dam ... MA-1
Brays ... TN-4
**Brays**—pop pl ... MO-7
**Brays**—pop pl ... VA-3
Brays Bayou—stream ... TX-5
**Brays (Brays Fork)**—pop pl ... VA-3
Brays Butte—summit ... MT-8
Brays Canyon—valley ... MT-8
Brays Canyon Creek—stream ... MT-8
Brays Cem—cemetery ... KY-4
Bray Sch—school ... KY-4
Bray Sch—school ... MD-2
Bray Sch—school ... NJ-2
Brays Chapel—church ... OH-6
Bray Sch (historical)—school ... MO-7
Brays Fork—other ... VA-3
Brayshore Park—locale ... VA-3
Brays Island—island ... SC-3
Brays Knob—summit ... TN-4
Brays Lake ... PA-2
Brays Lake—reservoir ... GA-3
Brays Lake—reservoir ... MO-7
Brays Lake Dam ... PA-2
Brays Landing—locale ... VA-3
Brays Landing Cem—cemetery ... WA-9
Brays Ledge ... ME-1
**Brayson**—pop pl ... IL-6
Brays Opening—flat ... CA-9
Brays Opening Creek—stream ... CA-9
Brays Point—cape ... WI-6
Brays Post Office (historical)—building ... TN-4
Bray Spring—spring ... AR-4
**Braysville**—pop pl (2) ... IN-6
Braysville Cem—cemetery ... IN-6
Brayton ... AZ-5
Brayton—locale ... NE-7
Brayton—locale ... NY-2
Brayton—locale ... TN-4
**Brayton**—pop pl ... IA-7
Brayton Ave Sch—school ... MA-1
Brayton Ch—church ... TN-4
Brayton Drain—stream ... MI-6
Brayton Grist Mill—hist pl ... CT-1
Brayton-Hendon Community Center—locale ... TN-4
Brayton Hollow—locale ... NY-2
Brayton Hollow—valley ... NY-2
Brayton Hollow Cem—cemetery ... NY-2
Brayton Methodist Episcopal Church—hist pl ... MA-1
Brayton Point—cape ... MA-1
**Brayton Point**—pop pl ... MA-1
Brayton Point Beach—beach ... MA-1
Brayton Point Channel Range Light—locale ... MA-1
Brayton Post Office (historical)—building ... TN-4
Brayton Sch—school ... IL-6
Brayton Sch—school ... NJ-2
Brayton Sch (historical)—school ... TN-4
Brayton School—reservoir ... MA-1
Brayton Town ... RI-1
**Braytonville**—pop pl ... MA-1
**Braytown**—pop pl ... IN-6
**Braytown**—pop pl ... TN-4
**Bray (Township of)**—pop pl ... MN-6
Braywood—locale ... MI-6
Brazaletes Pueblo Site—hist pl ... AZ-5
Brazan Canal—canal ... LA-4
Brazeal Branch—stream ... AL-4
Brazeale Cem—cemetery ... AR-4
Brazeale Farm Airp—airport ... MO-7
Brazeale Homestead—hist pl ... AR-4
**Brazeau**—pop pl ... MO-7
Brazeau Cem—cemetery (2) ... WI-6
Brazeau Creek—stream ... MO-7
**Brazeau (Town of)**—pop pl ... WI-6
Brazeau Township—civil ... MO-7
Brazel Cem—cemetery ... AL-4
Brazel Hill—summit ... WA-9
**Brazelia (historical)**—pop pl ... MS-4
Brazelia Post Office (historical)—building ... MS-4
Brazell, Crawford W., House—hist pl ... GA-3
Brazell Cem—cemetery ... GA-3
Brazell Creek—stream ... WI-6
Brazell Lake—lake ... WI-6
Brazell Meadows—flat ... CA-9
Brazell Pond—reservoir ... GA-3
Brazell Pond—reservoir ... MA-1
Brazell Pond Dam—dam ... MA-1
Brazells Creek—stream ... GA-3
Brazel Park—flat ... NM-5
Brazelton, Thomas and Bettie, House—hist pl ... TX-5
Brazelton Cave—cave ... AL-4
Brazelton Cem—cemetery ... AL-4
Brazelton Cem—cemetery ... TN-4
Brazelton House—hist pl ... IA-7
Brazelton House Hotel—hist pl ... IA-7
Brazelton Sch—school ... KY-4
Brazeltons Mill (historical)—locale ... TN-4
Brazelton Spring—spring ... AL-4
**Brazen Crossroads**—pop pl ... SC-3
Brazer Canyon ... UT-8
Braziel Creek—stream ... AL-4
Braziel Creek—stream ... MT-8
Braziel Creek Cave—cave ... AL-4
Braziel Lake—lake ... MT-8
Brazie Pond ... NY-2
Brazier Canyon—valley ... UT-8
Brazier Hollow—valley ... TN-4
Braziers Church ... AL-4
Brazier Spring—spring ... UT-8
Brazil—locale ... KY-4
Brazil—locale ... MO-7
**Brazil**—pop pl ... IN-6
**Brazil**—pop pl ... IA-7
**Brazil**—pop pl ... MS-4
**Brazil**—pop pl ... TN-4
Brazil Beach—beach ... CA-9
Brazil Branch—stream ... TN-4
Brazil Cem—cemetery ... OK-5
Brazil Ch—church ... AR-4
Brazil Ch—church ... MO-7
Brazil Creek ... AL-4
Brazil Creek—stream ... KS-7
Brazil Creek—stream ... MO-7
Brazil Creek—stream ... MT-8
Brazil Creek—stream ... OK-5
Brazil Creek Campground—locale ... MO-7
Brazil Creek Trail Campground ... MO-7
Brazil-Gibson Wells (CCD)—cens area ... TN-4
Brazil-Gibson Wells Division—civil ... TN-4
Brazil Gulch—valley ... MT-8
Brazil HS—school ... IN-6
Brazil HS (historical)—school ... TN-4
Brazilian Embassy Bldg—building ... DC-2
Brazil JHS—school ... IN-6
**Brazil Junction**—pop pl ... IN-6
Brazil Lake Dam—dam ... MS-4
Brazille Flat—flat ... CA-9
Brazill Mill (historical)—locale ... AL-4
Brazil Methodist Ch—church ... TN-4
Brazil Mine (underground)—mine ... AL-4
Brazil Pack Trail—trail ... MT-8
Brazil Post Office (historical)—building ... TN-4
Brazil Ridge—ridge ... MT-8
Brazils ... AR-4
Brazil Sch Number 1—school ... ND-7
Brazil Sch Number 2—school ... ND-7
Brazil Sch Number 3—school ... ND-7
Brazil Sch Number 4—school ... ND-7
Brazils Lake—reservoir ... IN-6
Brazils Lake Dam—dam ... IN-6
**Brazil (Stover)**—pop pl ... MS-4
**Brazilton**—pop pl ... KS-7
**Brazil (Township of)**—pop pl ... IN-6
Brazil Windmill—locale ... NM-5
Brazil Windmill—locale (3) ... TX-5
Brazine Dry Creek ... KS-7
Brazito—civil ... NM-5
**Brazito**—pop pl ... MO-7
Brazito Lateral—canal ... NM-5
Brazito River Lateral—canal ... NM-5
**Brazlime**—pop pl ... TX-5
**Braznell**—pop pl ... PA-2
Brazo Canyon—valley ... NM-5
Brazo de Miraflores ... AZ-5
**Brazoria**—pop pl ... TX-5
**Brazoria (County)**—pop pl ... TX-5
Brazoria Lake ... TX-5
Brazoria Reservoir—lake ... TX-5
Brazoria-West Columbia (CCD)—cens area ... TX-5
**Brazos**—pop pl ... CA-9
**Brazos**—pop pl ... NM-5
**Brazos**—pop pl ... TX-5
Brazos Box—valley ... NM-5
Brazos Cabin—locale ... NM-5
Brazos Cliffs—cliff ... NM-5
**Brazos (County)**—pop pl ... TX-5
Brazos Cow Camp—locale ... NM-5
Brazos Creek—stream ... NM-5
Brazos Harbor—bay ... TX-5
Brazos Island—island ... TX-5
Brazos Lodge—locale ... NM-5
Brazos Meadows—flat ... NM-5
Brazos Mine—mine ... OR-9
Brazos Mountain Range ... NM-5
Brazos Peak—summit ... NM-5
**Brazos Point**—pop pl ... TX-5
Brazosport—other ... TX-5
Brazosport (CCD)—cens area ... TX-5
Brazosport HS—school ... TX-5
Brazosport Turning Basin—basin ... TX-5
Brazos River ... TX-5
Brazos River—stream ... TX-5
Brazos Santiago ... TX-5
Brazos Santiago Depot (41CF4)—hist pl ... TX-5
Brazos Santiago Pass—channel ... TX-5
Brazos Valley—basin ... TX-5
Brazos Valley Cem—cemetery ... TX-5
Brazzee Hollow ... PA-2
Brazzel Bridge—bridge ... KY-4
Brazzlemans Bridge—bridge ... SC-3
BRC Creek—stream ... ID-8
Brchan Sch—school ... SD-7
Brckenridge Ski Area—other ... CO-8
**Brea**—pop pl ... CA-9
Brea Canyon—valley (2) ... CA-9
Breach, The—gap ... UT-8
Breach, The—gap ... WA-9
Brea Chem—locale ... CA-9
**Brea Chem (Loftus)**—pop pl ... CA-9
Breach Inlet—bay ... SC-3
Breachway, The—gut ... RI-1
Brea City Hall and Park—hist pl ... CA-9
Brea Creek—stream ... CA-9
Brea Dam—dam ... CA-9
Bread and Butter Creek—gut ... SC-3
Bread And Cheese Branch—stream ... MD-2
Bread and Cheese Brook—stream ... MA-1
Bread and Cheese Creek—stream ... MD-2
Bread and Cheese Island—island ... DE-2
Bread and Cheese Run—stream ... NJ-2
Bread Creek ... MA-1
Bread Creek ... NC-3
Bread Creek—stream ... AR-4
Bread Creek Pinnacle—summit ... AR-4
Breadens Spring—spring ... TN-4
Bread Knolls—summit ... UT-8
Breadline, The—other ... AK-9
**Bread Loaf**—pop pl ... VT-1
Bread Loaf Hill—summit ... NY-2
Breadloaf Island—island ... AK-9
Bread Loaf Mtn—summit ... CT-1
Bread Loaf Mtn—summit ... VT-1
Bread Loaf Rock—summit ... ID-8
Breadpan Canyon—valley ... AZ-5
Breadpan Hill—summit ... WY-8
Breadpan Mtn—summit ... AZ-5
Bread Pan Spring ... AZ-5
Breadpan Spring—spring ... AZ-5
Breadpan Tank—reservoir ... AZ-5
Bread Spring—spring ... AZ-5
Bread Spring—spring ... NY-2
Bread Spring—spring ... OR-9
**Bread Springs**—pop pl ... NM-5
Bread Springs Wash—stream ... NM-5
Bread Springs Well—well ... NM-5
Breadsville ... PA-2
Breadtown Creek—stream ... OK-5
**Bread Tray Hill**—pop pl ... AL-4
Bread Tray Hill—summit ... TN-4
Bread Tray Hollow—valley ... AR-4
Breadtray Hollow—valley ... TN-4
Bread Tray Mtn—summit (2) ... MO-7
Bread Tray Mtn—summit (2) ... TX-5
Breadtray Ridge—ridge ... NH-1
Breadwater Point ... NC-3
Breadwinner Creek—stream ... ID-8
**Breadysville**—pop pl ... PA-2
Breadyville ... PA-2
Brea Golf Club—other ... CA-9
Brea JHS—school ... CA-9
Break, The—swamp ... TX-5
**Breakabeen**—pop pl ... NY-2
Breakabeen Hist Dist—hist pl ... NY-2
Break Creek ... MT-8
Breakdown Cave—cave ... AL-4
Breakdown Creek—stream ... OR-9
Breakdown Gulch—valley ... WA-9
Breakdown Rsvr—reservoir ... ID-8
Breakdown Saddle—gap ... AZ-5
Breakenridge Ferry (historical)—locale ... IA-7
Breaker Island—island ... NY-2
Breaker Lake—lake ... WA-9
Breaker Point—cape ... CA-9
**Breakers**—pop pl ... WA-9
Breakers, The—bar ... ME-1
Breakers, The—hist pl ... RI-1
Breakers Hotel Complex—hist pl ... FL-3
Breakers Point—cape ... AS-9
**Breakers (subdivision), The**—pop pl ... MS-4
Breakfact Branch ... MO-7
Breakfast Branch—stream ... FL-3
Breakfast Branch—stream (2) ... GA-3
Breakfast Branch—stream ... MO-7
Breakfast Branch—stream ... SC-3
Breakfast Branch—stream ... TN-4
Breakfast Canyon—valley ... AZ-5
Breakfast Canyon—valley ... CA-9
Breakfast Creek—stream ... AL-4
Breakfast Creek—stream ... GA-3
Breakfast Creek—stream (3) ... ID-8
Breakfast Creek—stream ... OK-5
**Breakfast Hill**—pop pl ... NH-1
Breakfast Hill—summit ... NH-1
Breakfast Hill Station ... NH-1
Breakfast Island—island ... MP-9
Breakfast Lake—lake ... MI-6
Breakfast Lake—lake ... WI-6
Breakfast Point—cape ... FL-3
Breakfast Rock—other ... AK-9
Breakfast Roll—summit ... MI-6
Breakfast Swamp—stream ... SC-3
Breakfield Cem—cemetery ... MS-4
Breakheart Brook—stream ... RI-1
Breakheart Hill—summit ... ME-1
Breakheart Hill—summit ... RI-1
Breakheart Pond—lake ... RI-1
Breakheart Pond—reservoir ... RI-1
Breakheart Pond Dam—dam ... RI-1
Breakheart Reservation—park ... MA-1
Break Hill Brook—stream ... CT-1
Breaking Rocks—bar ... MA-1
Break Mine—mine ... NV-8
Breakneck—locale ... CT-1
**Breakneck**—pop pl ... PA-2
Breakneck Bridge—bridge ... PA-2
Breakneck Brook—stream (2) ... ME-1
Breakneck Brook—stream (2) ... MA-1
Breakneck Brook—stream (2) ... NY-2
Breakneck Brook—stream ... VT-1
Break Neck Canyon ... CA-9
Breakneck Canyon—valley (2) ... CA-9
Breakneck Canyon—valley ... KS-7
Breakneck Cem—cemetery ... OH-6
Breakneck Creek—stream ... CA-9
Breakneck Creek—stream ... NV-8
Breakneck Creek—stream ... NY-2
Breakneck Creek—stream ... OH-6
Breakneck Creek—stream ... PA-2
Breakneck Creek—stream ... WY-8
Breakneck Dam—dam ... KS-7
Breakneck Dam—dam ... NJ-2
Breakneck Flat—flat ... WY-8
Breakneck Gulch—valley (2) ... SD-7
Break Neck Hill ... MA-1
Breakneck Hill—locale ... WY-8
Breakneck Hill—summit (2) ... CT-1
Breakneck Hill—summit ... ME-1
Breakneck Hill—summit ... MD-2
Breakneck Hill—summit (2) ... MA-1
Breakneck Hill—summit ... NH-1
Breakneck Hill—summit ... SD-7
Breakneck Hill—summit ... VT-1
Breakneck Hill—summit ... WY-8
Breakneck Island ... ME-1
Breakneck Lake—reservoir ... KS-7
Breakneck Ledge—cliff ... MA-1
Breakneck Mtn—summit ... ME-1
Breakneck Mtn—summit ... MT-8
Breakneck Mtn—summit ... NY-2
Break Neck Pass ... CO-8
Breakneck Pass—gap ... CO-8
Breakneck Point—cape ... NY-2
Breakneck Pond—lake ... CT-1
Breakneck Pond—reservoir ... NY-2
Breakneck Ponds—lake ... ME-1
Breakneck Ridge—ridge ... ME-1
Breakneck Ridge—ridge ... NY-2
Breakneck Ridge—ridge (2) ... NC-3
Breakneck Ridge—ridge ... WV-2
Breakneck Ridge Trail—trail ... NY-2
Breakneck Road Hist Dist—hist pl ... MD-2
Breakneck Run ... PA-2
Breakneck Run—stream ... PA-2
Breakneck Run—stream ... VA-3
Breakneck Run—stream ... WV-2
Break-O-Day Elem Sch—school ... IN-6
Breakover Sandbar—bar ... MS-4
Break Plantation Mine (underground)—mine ... AL-4
Break Point—cape ... MD-2
Break Reed Ford—locale ... VA-3
**Breaks**—pop pl ... VA-3
Breaks, The—cliff ... CO-8
Breaks, The—cliff ... UT-8
Breaks, The—cliff ... VA-3
Breaks, The—range ... ID-8
Breaks, The—range ... WY-8
Breaks Cem—cemetery ... IN-6
Breaks Coulee, The—valley ... MT-8
Breaks Interstate Park—park ... VA-3

Breaks Overlook, The—*locale* VA-3
Breaks Rsvr—*reservoir* OR-9
**Breakstone Village (subdivision)**—*pop pl* AL-4
Breaks Well—*well* TX-5
*Breakup Mill Spring* MO-7
Breakwater Campground—*locale* ID-8
Breakwater Creek—*stream* ID-8
Breakwater Harbor—*bay* DE-2
Breakwater Lighthouse—*locale* CT-1
Breakwater Point—*cape* RI-1
Bream—*locale* WV-2
Bream Branch—*stream* GA-3
Bream Hole Dam—*dam* TN-4
Bream Hole Lake—*reservoir* TN-4
Bream Lake—*lake* (5) FL-3
Bream Lake—*lake* MS-4
Bream Mill (historical)—*locale* PA-2
Brean Lake—*lake* AR-4
Brea Olinda HS—*school* CA-9
**Breard**—*pop pl* LA-4
Brearley Cem—*cemetery* AR-4
Breashears Cem—*cemetery* AR-4
Breasne Dam—*dam* SD-7
Breast Island—*island* AK-9
*Breast Mountain* OR-9
Breast Mtn—*summit* AK-9
*Breast Work Run* PA-2
Breastwork Run—*stream* PA-2
Breastworks Branch—*stream* FL-3
Breastworks Branch—*stream* GA-3
Breast Works Cem—*cemetery* TN-4
Breastwork Sch (abandoned)—*school* PA-2
Breastworks Creek—*stream* AL-4
Breath Bayou—*gut* MS-4
Breathed Mtn—*summit* WV-2
**Breathedsville**—*pop pl* MD-2
Breath Hill—*summit* NY-2
Breathing Spring—*spring* OR-9
**Breathitt (County)**—*pop pl* KY-4
Breathitt County Jail—*hist pl* KY-4
Breathnach Country Club—*other* OH-6
*Breaux* LA-4
**Breaux Bridge**—*pop pl* LA-4
Breaux Cem—*cemetery* LA-4
Breaux House—*hist pl* LA-4
Breaux HS—*school* LA-4
*Breawo Park* AZ-5
Breazeale Cem—*cemetery* MS-4
Breazeale Cem—*cemetery* TN-4
Breazeale Spring—*spring* ID-8
Brebeuf Preparatory Sch—*school* IN-6
*Brebeuf Sch* IN-6
Brebner Flat—*flat* ID-8
Breccia Cliffs—*cliff* WY-8
*Breccia Creek* WY-8
Breccia Knob—*summit* UT-8
Breccia Peak—*summit* WY-8
Brecheen Cem—*cemetery* TX-5
Brecheen Post Office (historical)—*building* TN-4
Brechler Cem—*cemetery* WI-6
Brechtel Park—*park* LA-4
Brechtel Sch—*school* SD-7
Brecht Sch—*school* PA-2
Breck—*locale* KY-4
Breck, Judge Daniel, House—*hist pl* KY-4
*Breck Creek* MT-8
Breckeen Creek—*stream* CA-9
*Breckenridge* KY-4
*Breckenridge* OK-5
Breckenridge—*locale* (2) IL-6
**Breckenridge**—*pop pl* CO-8
**Breckenridge**—*pop pl* IN-6
**Breckenridge**—*pop pl* MI-6
**Breckenridge**—*pop pl* MN-6
**Breckenridge**—*pop pl* MO-7
**Breckenridge**—*pop pl* TX-5
Breckenridge—*uninc pl* AR-4
Breckenridge, Justin, House—*hist pl* OH-6
Breckenridge Airp—*airport* CO-8
Breckenridge Campground—*locale* CA-9
Breckenridge Cem—*cemetery* PA-2
Breckenridge Ch—*church* WV-2
*Breckenridge County* KS-7
Breckenridge Creek—*stream* CO-8
Breckenridge Creek—*stream* WA-9
Breckenridge Creek—*stream* WV-2
Breckenridge Ditch—*canal* (2) IN-6
Breckenridge Hatter's Shop—*hist pl* TN-4
Breckenridge Hill—*summit* GA-3
**Breckenridge Hills**—*pop pl* MO-7
Breckenridge Hist Dist—*hist pl* CO-8
Breckenridge JHS—*school* VA-3
Breckenridge Lake—*lake* MN-6
Breckenridge Landing (historical)—*locale* AL-4
**Breckenridge Manor (subdivision)**—*pop pl* (2) AZ-5
Breckenridge Meadows—*flat* CA-9
Breckenridge Mtn—*summit* CA-9
Breckenridge North (CCD)—*cens area* TX-5
Breckenridge Oil Field—*oilfield* TX-5
Breckenridge Park—*park* IN-6
Breckenridge Rsvr—*reservoir* VA-3
Breckenridge Sch (historical)—*school* PA-2
Breckenridge South (CCD)—*cens area* TX-5
**Breckenridge (subdivision)**—*pop pl* MS-4
**Breckenridge (subdivision)**—*pop pl* NC-3
Breckenridge Township—*civil* MO-7
Breckenridge (Township of)—*civ div* MN-6
Breckenridge (Township of)—*fmr MCD* (2) AR-4
Breckenridge-Wahpeton Interstate Airp—*airport* ND-7
Brecke Ridge Cem—*cemetery* IA-7
Brecker Island—*island* WI-6
Breck Gulch—*valley* MT-8
*Breckinridge* MO-7
Breckinridge—*locale* KY-4
**Breckinridge**—*pop pl* OK-5
Breckinridge, C. R., House—*hist pl* AR-4
Breckinridge, Isabella, House—*hist pl* WA-9
Breckinridge, Lake—*reservoir* KY-4
Breckinridge Cem—*cemetery* IN-6
Breckinridge Cem—*cemetery* KY-4
Breckinridge Center—*CDP* KY-4
**Breckinridge (County)**—*pop pl* KY-4
Breckinridge Job Corps Center—*locale* KY-4
Breckinridge Mill—*hist pl* VA-3
Breckinridge Peak—*summit* CO-8
Breckinridge Sch—*school* KY-4
Breckinridge Southeast (CCD)—*cens area* KY-4
Breckinridge Southwest (CCD)—*cens area* KY-4
Breckner Ranch—*locale* WY-8
Brecknock—*hist pl* DE-2
Brecknock Sch—*school* PA-2
**Brecknock (Township of)**—*pop pl* (2) PA-2
Breck Sch—*school* MN-6
Brecks Knoll—*summit* UT-8
Breck's Mill Area—*hist pl* DE-2
Breck's Mill Area-Henry Clay Village Hist Dist (Boundary Increase)—*hist pl* DE-2
**Brecksville**—*pop pl* OH-6
Brecksville-Northfield High Level Bridge—*hist pl* OH-6
Brecksville Reservation—*park* OH-6
Brecksville Town Hall—*hist pl* OH-6
Breckwood Lake—*reservoir* MA-1
Breckwood Lake Dam—*dam* MA-1
Breckwood Park—*park* MA-1
*Breckwood Park Dam* MA-1
Breckwood Shop Ctr—*locale* MA-1
Brecon—*locale* OH-6
Brecon Ch—*church* AL-4
**Brecon Ridge**—*pop pl* VA-3
**Brecon (subdivision)**—*pop pl* AL-4
Brecount Lake—*lake* MS-4
Breda—*locale* MN-6
**Breda**—*pop pl* IA-7
Breda Creek—*stream* MN-6
Breda Lake—*lake* MN-6
*Bredehoff Island* MI-6
Bredehoft Place—*locale* CA-9
Bredeick-Lang House—*hist pl* OH-6
*Bredenton Post Office* TN-4
Bredeson Lake—*lake* MN-6
Bredette—*locale* MT-8
Bredfeldt Oil Field—*oilfield* KS-7
Bredinsburg—*locale* PA-2
**Bredinville**—*pop pl* PA-2
Bredlov Creek—*stream* NC-3
**Bredlow Corner**—*pop pl* AR-4
*Breds Creek* WV-2
Breece—*locale* WV-2
Breece And Wheeler Ditch—*canal* CA-9
Breece Cem—*cemetery* TN-4
Breece Creek—*stream* CO-8
Breece Ditch—*canal* IN-6
Breece Hill—*summit* CO-8
Breece Hollow—*valley* TN-4
Breece Well—*locale* NM-5
Breechbill-Davidson House—*hist pl* IN-6
Breeches Branch—*stream* NJ-2
*Breeches Pond* PA-2
Breeches Swamp—*stream* NC-3
Breeching Creek—*stream* ID-8
Breeckenridge Sch—*school* VA-3
**Breed**—*pop pl* WI-6
Breed Branch—*stream* LA-4
Breed Brook—*stream* NH-1
Breed Cem—*cemetery* GA-3
Breed Creek—*stream* (2) MT-8
Breeden—*locale* WV-2
**Breeden**—*pop pl* SC-3
Breeden Branch—*stream* (2) TN-4
Breeden Branch—*stream* (3) VA-3
Breeden Cem—*cemetery* MS-4
Breeden Cem—*cemetery* TN-4
Breeden Cem—*cemetery* VA-3
Breeden Ch—*church* MO-7
Breeden Creek—*stream* MO-7
Breeden Creek—*stream* WV-2
Breeden Gap—*gap* WV-2
Breeden Hollow—*valley* TN-4
Breeden Pond—*reservoir* TN-4
Breeden Ranch—*locale* MT-8
Breeden-Runge Wholesale Grocery Company Bldg—*hist pl* TX-5
Breeden Sch (abandoned)—*school* MO-7
Breedens Creek—*stream* KY-4
Breedens Point—*cape* MD-2
Breedens Sch (historical)—*school* TN-4
Breedenton—*locale* TN-4
*Breedenton Ferry* TN-4
Breedenton Post Office (historical)—*building* TN-4
Breed Hill—*summit* NH-1
Breed Hollow—*valley* NY-2
**Breeding**—*pop pl* KY-4
Breeding Branch—*stream* KY-4
Breeding Cem—*cemetery* AL-4
Breeding Cem—*cemetery* IA-7
Breeding Cem—*cemetery* MO-7
Breeding Cem—*cemetery* (2) TN-4
Breeding Cem—*cemetery* (2) VA-3
Breeding Chapel—*church* VA-3
Breeding Creek—*stream* KY-4
Breeding Ditch—*canal* IN-6
Breeding Industrial Park—*locale* AL-4
Breeding Mountain—*ridge* AL-4
*Breed Island* MA-1
Breed Lake—*lake* MN-6
*Breedlove* WV-2
Breedlove Branch—*stream* LA-4
Breedlove Branch—*stream* NC-3
Breedlove Branch—*stream* TN-4
Breedlove Cem—*cemetery* (2) GA-3
Breedlove Cem—*cemetery* IN-6
Breedlove Cem—*cemetery* (2) NC-3
Breedlove Ditch—*canal* IL-6
Breedlove Hollow—*valley* IN-6
Breedlove House and Water Tower—*hist pl* AR-4
Breedlove Knob—*summit* VA-3
Breedlove Lake—*lake* OK-5
Breedlove Mtn—*summit* NC-3
Breedlove Oil Field—*oilfield* TX-5
*Breed Pond* MA-1
*Breed Pond* NH-1
Breed Pond—*swamp* TX-5
Breed Ranch Airp—*airport* MO-7
**Breeds**—*pop pl* IL-6
Breed Saint Sch—*school* CA-9
Breed Sch—*school* MA-1
Breeds Cove—*cove* MA-1
*Breeds Creek* NC-3
Breeds Creek—*stream* AL-4
Breeds Flat—*flat* OR-9
*Breed's Hill* MA-1
Breeds Hill—*summit* MA-1
Breeds Hill—*summit* NY-2
Breeds Hill HS—*school* MA-1
*Breeds Island* MA-1
Breeds Lake—*lake* MI-6
Breeds Pond—*reservoir* MA-1
Breeds Pond—*reservoir* NY-2
Breeds Pond Outlet Dam—*dam* MA-1
*Breeds Pond Reservoir* MA-1
Breed Spring—*spring* AZ-5
Breed Spring—*spring* MT-8
Breed Springs—*spring* MT-8
Breeds Run—*stream* NY-2
**Breedsville**—*pop pl* MI-6
**Breed Switch**—*pop pl* IN-6
Breedtown—*locale* PA-2
**Breed (Town of)**—*pop pl* WI-6
Breeing Hollow—*valley* PA-2
Breeler Field Cem—*cemetery* SC-3
Breem Park—*park* WI-6
Breen—*locale* CO-8
*Breen Acres* MO-7
**Breen Acres**—*pop pl* MO-7
Breen Brook—*stream* NY-2
Breen Creek—*stream* MI-6
Breen Creek—*stream* MT-8
Breen Creek—*stream* NV-8
Breen Mine—*mine* CA-9
Breen Oil Field—*oilfield* WY-8
Breen Ranch—*locale* NV-8
Breen Sch—*school* MA-1
**Breen (Township of)**—*pop pl* MI-6
Breen Well—*well* NM-5
**Breese**—*pop pl* IL-6
Breese, Griffith, Farm—*hist pl* OH-6
Breese, James L., House—*hist pl* NY-2
Breese, William, Jr., House—*hist pl* NC-3
Breese, William E., Sr., House—*hist pl* NC-3
Breese Cem—*cemetery* OR-9
Breese Hollow—*valley* NY-2
Breese Hollow—*valley* PA-2
Breese Pond—*lake* VT-1
**Breese (Township of)**—*pop pl* IL-6
**Breesport**—*pop pl* NY-2
Breeze, Lake—*lake* LA-4
Breeze, Point—*cape* MA-1
Breeze, Point—*cape* NJ-2
Breeze, Point—*cape* (3) NY-2
Breeze, Point—*cape* VA-3
Breeze Basin—*basin* CO-8
Breeze Basin Coulee—*valley* MT-8
Breeze Creek—*stream* CA-9
Breezedale—*hist pl* PA-2
**Breeze Estates Subdivision**—*pop pl* UT-8
**Breeze Hill**—*pop pl* SC-3
Breeze Hill—*summit* CA-9
Breeze Hill—*summit* MA-1
Breeze Hill—*summit* NY-2
Breeze Hill—*summit* VT-1
Breeze Hill Ch—*church* IN-6
Breeze Lake—*lake* AK-9
Breeze Lake—*lake* CA-9
Breeze Lake—*lake* MN-6
Breezemont—*hist pl* WV-2
Breeze Mtn—*summit* CO-8
Breeze Park—*park* LA-4
*Breeze Point* MN-6
Breeze Point—*cape* NH-1
Breeze Point—*cape* WY-8
Breezers Branch—*stream* VA-3
Breeze Sch—*school* CO-8
Breezeswept Center (Shop Ctr)—*locale* FL-3
Breezeswept Park—*park* FL-3
**Breezeswept Park Estates**—*pop pl* FL-3
**Breezeway Bay**—*pop pl* AL-4
**Breezewood**—*pop pl* DE-2
**Breezewood**—*pop pl* IN-6
**Breezewood**—*pop pl* (2) PA-2
**Breezewood**—*pop pl* SC-3
**Breezewood Acres (subdivision)**—*pop pl* NC-3
Breezewood Elem Sch—*school* PA-2
**Breezewood Farms**—*pop pl* MD-2
**Breezewood II (subdivision)**—*pop pl* DE-2
*Breezewood Interchange* PA-2
**Breezewood Park**—*pop pl* IN-6
**Breezy Acres**—*pop pl* PA-2
Breezy Bay—*bay* AK-9
**Breezy Beach**—*pop pl* MI-6
Breezy Corner—*locale* PA-2
Breezy Creek—*stream* OR-9
Breezy Gap—*gap* WA-9
**Breezy Hill**—*pop pl* VA-3
Breezy Hill—*hist pl* VA-3
Breezy Hill—*locale* LA-4
**Breezy Hill**—*pop pl* MA-1
Breezy Hill—*summit* CT-1
Breezy Hill—*summit* KS-7
Breezy Hill—*summit* TN-4
Breezy Hill—*summit* TX-5
Breezy Hill—*summit* VT-1
Breezy Hill Sch—*school* SC-3
Breezy Hill Site (RI-957)—*hist pl* RI-1
**Breezy Hills (subdivision)**—*pop pl* TN-4
Breezy Island—*island* NH-1
Breezy Knoll—*summit* NY-2
*Breezy Lake* RI-1
Breezy Lake—*lake* AZ-5
*Breezy Lake Dam* RI-1
Breezy Meadow Camp—*locale* MA-1
Breezy Number One Tank—*reservoir* AZ-5
Breezy Number Two Tank—*reservoir* AZ-5
Breezy Point—*cape* AK-9
Breezy Point—*cape* CA-9
Breezy Point—*cape* FL-3
Breezy Point—*cape* IA-7
Breezy Point—*cape* (2) ME-1
Breezy Point—*cape* MD-2
Breezy Point—*cape* MI-6
Breezy Point—*cape* (3) NY-2
Breezy Point—*cape* OR-9
Breezy Point—*cape* VA-3
Breezy Point—*cliff* AZ-5
Breezy Point—*cliff* WA-9
Breezy Point—*lake* MN-6
Breezy Point—*locale* NH-1
Breezy Point—*locale* PA-2
**Breezy Point**—*pop pl* IN-6
**Breezy Point**—*pop pl* MD-2
**Breezy Point**—*pop pl* MN-6
**Breezy Point**—*pop pl* NY-2
Breezy Point—*summit* ID-8
*Breezy Point Beach* (2) MD-2
**Breezy Point Beach**—*pop pl* MD-2
**Breezy Point (Breezy Point Beach)**—*pop pl* MD-2
Breezy Saddle—*gap* ID-8
Breezy Tank—*reservoir* AZ-5
*Breezy Waters Valley* AZ-5
Breffel Hill—*summit* NY-2
Breford Lake—*lake* MI-6
Bregar Spring—*spring* NV-8
Bregy, F. Amedee, Sch—*hist pl* PA-2
Bregy Sch—*school* PA-2
Brehm Cem—*cemetery* OH-6
*Brehmer Creek* ID-8
Brehmer Creek—*stream* WI-6
Brehmer Ranch—*locale* TX-5
Brehm Oil and Gas Field—*oilfield* KS-7
Brehm Sch—*school* SD-7
Brehms Lane Sch—*school* MD-2
Brehnard Creek—*stream* AK-9
**Breidablick**—*pop pl* WA-9
*Breidablik* WA-9
*Breidblick* WA-9
Breidel Coulee—*valley* WI-6
Breidenbach Bldg—*hist pl* KY-4
Breidenhart—*hist pl* NJ-2
*Breidlick* WA-9
**Breien**—*pop pl* ND-7
Breier Arm—*canal* IN-6
Breier Bldg—*hist pl* ID-8
Breier Creek—*stream* IN-6
*Breier Ditch* IN-6
*Breier Ditch Arm* IN-6
Breiner Joint Ditch—*canal* IN-6
Breiner Sch—*school* PA-2
Breinig Run—*stream* PA-2
*Breinigs Run* PA-2
**Breinigsville**—*pop pl* PA-2
Breininger Gap—*gap* PA-2
*Breinizer* PA-2
**Breinizer**—*pop pl* PA-2
Breitenbach, Mount—*summit* ID-8
*Breitenbush* OR-9
**Breitenbush**—*pop pl* OR-9
*Breitenbush Butte* OR-9
Breitenbush Campground—*park* OR-9
Breitenbush Guard Station—*hist pl* OR-9
**Breitenbush Hot Springs**—*pop pl* OR-9
Breitenbush Lake—*lake* OR-9
Breitenbush Mtn—*summit* OR-9
Breitenbush River—*stream* OR-9
*Breitenbush Springs* OR-9
Breitfield Ditch—*canal* IN-6
**Breithing Park Subdivision**—*pop pl* UT-8
Breitmeyer Sch—*school* MI-6
Breitmeyer-Tobin Bldg—*hist pl* MI-6
**Breitung (Township of)**—*pop pl* MI-6
**Breitung (Township of)**—*pop pl* MN-6
Breitzman Lake—*lake* WI-6
*Breje Island* MP-9
Breke Memorial County Park—*park* IA-7
Brekhus Field—*airport* ND-7
Brekke Draw—*valley* SD-7
Brekke Lake—*lake* MN-6
Brekken, Lake—*lake* ND-7
Brekke Ranch (abandoned)—*locale* MT-8
Brekk Lake—*lake* WI-6
Brela—*locale* CA-9
**Breland**—*pop pl* MS-4
Breland Branch—*stream* MS-4
Breland Cem—*cemetery* LA-4
Breland Cem—*cemetery* (4) MS-4
Breland Eddy—*rapids* MS-4
Breland Lake—*lake* (3) MS-4
Brelsford, Lake—*reservoir* TX-5
Brelsford House—*hist pl* FL-3
Brelsford Run—*stream* OH-6
Brelsford-Seese House—*hist pl* OH-6
Breman Coal Bed Mine (underground)—*mine* AL-4
Breman Lake—*lake* NE-7
*Bremen* MO-7
Bremen—*locale* MN-6
Bremen—*locale* ND-7
**Bremen**—*pop pl* AL-4
**Bremen**—*pop pl* GA-3
**Bremen**—*pop pl* (2) IL-6
**Bremen**—*pop pl* IN-6
**Bremen**—*pop pl* KS-7
**Bremen**—*pop pl* KY-4
**Bremen**—*pop pl* ND-7
**Bremen**—*pop pl* OH-6
Bremen (CCD)—*cens area* AL-4
Bremen (CCD)—*cens area* GA-3
Bremen (CCD)—*cens area* KY-4
Bremen Cem—*cemetery* ND-7
Bremen Ch—*church* AL-4
Bremen Ch—*church* MN-6
Bremen Community Center—*building* AL-4
Bremen Creek—*stream* MN-6
Bremen Division—*civil* AL-4
Bremen (Election Precinct)—*fmr MCD* IL-6
Bremen Elementary/MS—*school* IN-6
Bremen HS—*school* IL-6
Bremenington Coulee—*valley* WI-6
Bremen Long Island—*island* ME-1
*Bremen Missionary Baptist Church* AL-4
Bremen Rsvr—*reservoir* GA-3
Bremen Sch—*school* IL-6
Bremen Sch—*school* ME-1
Bremen Sch (historical)—*school* AL-4
Bremen Senior HS—*school* IN-6
**Bremen (sta.)**—*pop pl* KY-4
**Bremen (Town of)**—*pop pl* ME-1
Bremen Township—*fmr MCD* IA-7
**Bremen Township**—*pop pl* ND-7
**Bremen (Township of)**—*pop pl* IL-6
**Bremen (Township of)**—*pop pl* MN-6
Bremer—*locale* IA-7
Bremer—*locale* WA-9
**Bremer**—*pop pl* IA-7
Bremer, Fredrika, Intermediate Sch—*hist pl* MN-6
Bremer Cem—*cemetery* OH-6
Bremer Cem—*cemetery* TX-5
Bremer County Home—*building* IA-7
Bremer Creek—*stream* CA-9
Bremer Hollow—*valley* TN-4
Bremer Mtn—*summit* WA-9
Bremer Rsvr—*reservoir* OR-9
Bremer Sch—*school* MN-6
**Bremerton**—*pop pl* WA-9
Bremerton (CCD)—*cens area* WA-9
*Bremerton East* WA-9
Bremerton Junction—*locale* WA-9
Bremerton Natl Airp—*airport* WA-9
Bremerton Naval Regional Med Ctr—*military* WA-9
Bremerton Yacht Club—*other* WA-9
Bremmer Creek—*stream* MT-8
Bremmer Longshed Camp—*locale* NM-5
Bremner—*locale* AK-9
Bremner Creek—*stream* ID-8
Bremner Glacier—*glacier* AK-9
Bremner River—*stream* AK-9
Bremner Trail—*trail* ID-8
*Bremo* VA-3
Bremo, Point—*cape* VA-3
**Bremo Bluff**—*pop pl* VA-3
**Bremo Bluff (RR name Bremo)**—*pop pl* VA-3
Bremo Creek—*stream* VA-3
Bremo Mansion—*building* VA-3
**Bremond**—*pop pl* TX-5
Bremond Block Hist Dist—*hist pl* TX-5
Bremond (CCD)—*cens area* TX-5
Bremond Cem—*cemetery* TX-5
Bremon Sch (historical)—*school* AL-4
Bremo Plantation—*hist pl* VA-3
Bremo (RR name for Bremo Bluff)—*other* VA-3
*Bremos Bluff* VA-3
Bremo Slave Chapel—*hist pl* VA-3
**Brems**—*pop pl* IN-6
Bremser Hollow—*valley* MO-7
Brenam Bayou—*stream* LA-4
*Brenan Lake* NE-7
Brenan Sch—*school* IL-6
**Brenas**—*pop pl* PR-3
Brenas, El Alto de—*summit* PR-3
Brenau Acad—*school* GA-3
Brenau Coll—*school* GA-3
Brenau College District—*hist pl* GA-3
Brenau Lake—*reservoir* GA-3
Brenda—*locale* AZ-5
**Brenda**—*pop pl* AZ-5
Brenda, Lake—*reservoir* OH-6
Brenda, Lake—*reservoir* TX-5
**Brendan Heights**—*pop pl* CT-1
*Brendan Wood* IN-6
**Brendan Wood**—*pop pl* IN-6
*Brendel* UT-8
Brendel—*locale* UT-8
Brendel, Charles, House—*hist pl* OH-6
Brendel Gulch—*valley* CO-8
Brendel Lake—*lake* MI-6
Brender Canyon—*valley* WA-9
Brender Creek—*stream* WA-9
Brendle Branch—*stream* (2) NC-3
Brendle Cem—*cemetery* AR-4
Brendle Cem—*cemetery* NC-3
Brendle Farms—*hist pl* PA-2
Brendle Mtn—*summit* NC-3
**Brendletown**—*pop pl* NC-3
*Brendonwood* IN-6
**Brendonwood**—*pop pl* IN-6
Brendvold Creek—*stream* MN-6
Breneiser Woods—*woods* PA-2
*Breneman* KS-7
Breneman Lake—*lake* WI-6
Brenford—*locale* DE-2
Brenham—*locale* KS-7
Brenham—*locale* OR-9
**Brenham**—*pop pl* TX-5
Brenham Branch—*stream* GA-3
Brenham (CCD)—*cens area* TX-5
Brenham Cem—*cemetery* TX-5
Brenham Golf Course—*other* TX-5
*Brenham Lake* MT-8
Brenham Oil Field—*oilfield* TX-5
Brenham Township—*unorg reg* KS-7
*Brenholt* OH-6
*Brenholts* OH-6
Breniman Place—*locale* WY-8
**Brenizer**—*pop pl* PA-2
Brenizer Elem Sch (abandoned)—*school* PA-2
Brenkwitz Sch—*school* CA-9
**Bren Mar Park**—*pop pl* VA-3
Bren Mar Park Sch—*school* VA-3
Brenna—*fmr MCD* NE-7
Brennaman Cem—*cemetery* CO-8
*Brennan* SD-7
Brennan—*locale* WA-9
Brennan Airp—*airport* PA-2
Brennan Airp (private)—*airport* PA-2
Brennan Basin—*basin* UT-8
Brennan Bay—*bay* AK-9
Brennan Bottom—*bend* UT-8
*Brennan Creek* NV-8
Brennan Creek—*stream* MT-8
Brennan Creek—*stream* WI-6
Brennand Ranch—*locale* NM-5
Brennan Draw—*valley* WY-8
Brennan Flat—*flat* SD-7
Brennan Hill—*summit* NH-1
Brennan Hill—*summit* SD-7
Brennan JHS—*school* MA-1
Brennan Lake—*lake* MI-6
Brennan Lake—*lake* ND-7
Brennan Park—*park* TN-4
Brennan Sch—*school* CT-1
*Brennan Spring* NV-8
Brennan Spring—*spring* NM-5
**Brennan Subdivision**—*pop pl* MS-4
Brenna Town Hall—*building* ND-7
**Brenna Township**—*pop pl* ND-7
Brennegan Creek—*stream* WA-9
Brenneis Creek—*stream* MT-8
Brenneise Cem—*cemetery* SD-7
Brenneman Cem—*cemetery* PA-2
Brenneman Hill—*summit* MD-2
Brenneman Lake—*reservoir* PA-2
Brennemann Sch—*school* IL-6
Brenneman Ranch—*locale* NE-7
Brenneman Sch (abandoned)—*school* PA-2
Brennen Creek—*stream* NV-8
Brennen Lake—*lake* MN-6
Brennen Mine—*mine* (2) NV-8
Brennen Sch—*school* SC-3
Brennen Spring—*spring* NV-8
*Brenner Canyon* OR-9
Brenner Canyon—*valley* OR-9
Brenner Cem—*cemetery* TX-5
*Brenner Coulee* WI-6
Brenner Drain—*canal* MI-6
Brenner Heights—*uninc pl* KS-7
Brenner Heights Ch—*church* KS-7
Brenner Heights Creek—*stream* KS-7
Brenner Lake—*lake* MN-6
Brenner Ranch—*locale* (2) MT-8
Brenner Sch—*school* KS-7
Brenner Sch (historical)—*school* SD-7
*Brenners Creek* MT-8
Brenners Run—*stream* OH-6
Brenner Station (historical)—*locale* KS-7
Brennersville—*locale* OH-6
**Brennyville**—*pop pl* MN-6
Brenott Drain—*stream* MI-6
Brens Corner—*locale* SD-7
Brensen Branch—*stream* AL-4
Brenson Pond—*lake* FL-3
Brent—*locale* GA-3
Brent—*locale* KY-4
Brent—*locale* SC-3
**Brent**—*pop pl* AL-4
**Brent**—*pop pl* FL-3
**Brent**—*pop pl* OK-5
**Brent**—*pop pl* PA-2
Brentano Bar—*bar* OR-9
Brentano Sch—*school* IL-6
Brent Baptist Ch—*church* AL-4
*Brent Branch* TX-5
Brent (Brentwood)—*CDP* FL-3
Brent Cem—*cemetery* AR-4
Brent Cem—*cemetery* (2) MS-4
Brent Cem—*cemetery* OK-5
Brent Cem—*cemetery* TX-5
Brent-Centreville Public Library—*building* AL-4
Brent Ch—*church* OK-5
Brent Ch of God—*church* AL-4
**Brent Creek**—*pop pl* MI-6
Brent Creek—*stream* MI-6
Brent Creek—*stream* WY-8
Brent Ditch—*canal* IN-6
Brent Elem Sch—*school* AL-4
**Brentford**—*pop pl* SD-7
Brent Gap—*gap* VA-3
**Brenthaven Park Subdivision**—*pop pl* UT-8
Brent HS—*school* MD-2
Brent Lake—*reservoir* MO-7
Brentland—*locale* MD-2
Brentlawn—*uninc pl* TN-4
Brentley Pond—*lake* GA-3
**Brentmar Circle Subdivision**—*pop pl* UT-8
Brent Marsh—*swamp* VA-3
Brentmoor—*hist pl* VA-3
Brentmoor Park, Brentmoor and Forest Ridge District—*hist pl* MO-7
Brentmoor Sch—*school* OH-6
Brentnell Sch—*school* OH-6
*Brenton* KS-7
**Brenton**—*pop pl* VA-3
**Brenton**—*pop pl* WV-2
Brenton Cabin—*locale* OR-9
Brenton Ch—*church* WV-2
Brenton Chapel—*church* IN-6
Brenton Chapel Cem—*cemetery* IN-6
Brenton Cove—*bay* RI-1
Brenton Point—*cape* RI-1
*Brentons Cove* RI-1
Brenton Slough—*gut* IA-7
*Brentons Point* RI-1
Brenton Springs—*spring* WY-8
**Brenton (Township of)**—*pop pl* IL-6
*Brenton Village* RI-1
**Brenton Village**—*pop pl* RI-1
Brent Point—*cape* VA-3
Brent Presbyterian Ch—*church* AL-4
Brent Ranch—*locale* TX-5
Brent Run—*stream* MI-6
Brents Cem—*cemetery* AR-4
Brents Cem—*cemetery* MS-4
Brent Sch—*school* (2) MD-2
Brent Sch (historical)—*school* MS-4
**Brents Cross Roads**—*pop pl* AL-4
**Brents Junction**—*pop pl* CA-9
Brents Lake—*reservoir* MS-4
Brents Landing—*locale* VA-3
Brents-Lisle House—*hist pl* KY-4
Brents Mill (historical)—*locale* MS-4
Brents Mtn—*summit* CA-9
*Brents Point* VA-3
*Brent Springs Branch* VA-3
Brentsville—*locale* VA-3
**Brentsville**—*pop pl* KY-4
Brentsville HS—*school* VA-3
Brentsville (Magisterial District)—*fmr MCD* VA-3
*Brentwood* IL-6
*Brentwood* IN-6
*Brentwood* MI-6
*Brentwood* OH-6
Brentwood—*locale* GA-3
Brentwood—*other* (2) FL-3
**Brentwood**—*pop pl* AL-4
**Brentwood**—*pop pl* AR-4
**Brentwood**—*pop pl* (2) CA-9
**Brentwood**—*pop pl* FL-3
**Brentwood**—*pop pl* GA-3
**Brentwood**—*pop pl* IN-6
**Brentwood**—*pop pl* KY-4
**Brentwood**—*pop pl* MD-2
**Brentwood**—*pop pl* MO-7
**Brentwood**—*pop pl* NH-1
**Brentwood**—*pop pl* NY-2
**Brentwood**—*pop pl* (2) OH-6
**Brentwood**—*pop pl* PA-2
**Brentwood**—*pop pl* SC-3
**Brentwood**—*pop pl* (2) TN-4
**Brentwood**—*pop pl* VA-3
Brentwood, Lake—*lake* FL-3
Brentwood Acad—*school* TN-4
**Brentwood Acres**—*pop pl* ME-1
**Brentwood Acres (subdivision)**—*pop pl* NC-3
Brentwood Assembly of God—*church* FL-3
Brentwood Borough—*civil* PA-2
Brentwood Branch—*stream* TN-4
Brentwood Business Center—*locale* TN-4
Brentwood Camp—*locale* NY-2
Brentwood (CCD)—*cens area* TN-4

Brentwood Cem—cemetery ... NH-1
Brentwood Ch—church ... OH-6
Brentwood Circle Subdivision—pop pl ... UT-8
Brentwood Corner—pop pl ... NH-1
Brentwood Corners—pop pl ... NH-1
Brentwood Country Club—locale ... TN-4
Brentwood Country Club—other ... CA-9
Brentwood Country Club—other ... CO-8
Brentwood Country Club—other ... NY-2
Brentwood Division—civil ... TN-4
Brentwood Elem Sch—school (3) ... FL-3
Brentwood Elem Sch—school (2) ... IN-6
Brentwood Elem Sch—school ... NC-3
Brentwood Estates—pop pl ... FL-3
Brentwood Estates—pop pl ... IL-6
Brentwood Estates—pop pl ... OH-6
Brentwood Estates—pop pl ... TN-4
Brentwood Estates (subdivision)—pop pl ... TN-4
Brentwood Estates Subdivision—pop pl ... UT-8
Brentwood Farm—hist pl ... MD-2
Brentwood Forest—uninc pl ... VA-3
Brentwood Forest (subdivision)—pop pl ... NC-3
Brentwood Gas Field ... CA-9
Brentwood Heights—pop pl ... CA-9
Brentwood Hills—pop pl ... AL-4
Brentwood Hills Subdivision—pop pl ... UT-8
Brentwood Hosp—hospital ... OH-6
Brentwood HS—school ... MO-7
Brentwood HS—school ... SC-3
Brentwood HS—school ... TN-4
Brentwood JHS—school ... TX-5
Brentwood Junior-Senior HS—school ... PA-2
Brentwood Lake—lake ... AK-9
Brentwood Lake—pop pl ... OH-6
Brentwood Lake—reservoir ... OH-6
Brentwood Manor—pop pl ... TX-5
Brentwood Military Acad—school ... CA-9
Brentwood Mobile Manor—locale ... AZ-5
Brentwood MS ... TN-4
Brentwood MS—school ... FL-3
Brentwood-Oak Park Sch—school ... NY-2
Brentwood Park—park ... DC-2
Brentwood Park—park (3) ... FL-3
Brentwood Park—park ... OR-9
Brentwood Park—park ... PA-2
Brentwood Park—park ... TN-4
Brentwood Park—park ... TX-5
Brentwood Park—uninc pl ... CA-9
Brentwood Park (historical)—park ... DC-2
Brentwood Park (subdivision)—pop pl ... TN-4
Brentwood Park Subdivision—pop pl ... UT-8
Brentwood-Pine Park Sch—school ... NY-2
Brentwood Place Shop Ctr—locale ... TN-4
Brentwood Plantation (historical)—locale ... AL-4
Brentwood Plaza—locale ... MO-7
Brent Woods ... IN-6
Brent Woods—pop pl ... IN-6
Brentwood Sch—school (2) ... CA-9
Brentwood Sch—school ... CO-8
Brentwood Sch—school (2) ... FL-3
Brentwood Sch—school ... IL-6
Brentwood Sch—school ... MD-2
Brentwood Sch—school (2) ... NC-3
Brentwood Sch—school ... TX-5
Brentwood Shop Ctr—locale ... FL-3
Brentwood Shop Ctr—locale ... NC-3
Brentwood Shop Ctr—other ... CO-8
Brentwood Station—pop pl ... TN-4
Brentwood (subdivision)—pop pl (3) ... AL-4
Brentwood (subdivision)—pop pl (6) ... NC-3
Brentwood (subdivision)—pop pl (4) ... TN-4
Brentwood (subdivison)—pop pl ... AL-4
Brentwood (Town of)—pop pl ... NH-1
Brentwood Utah RV Park—locale ... UT-8
Brentwood Village Playground—park ... DC-2
Brentwood Village (subdivision)—pop pl ... NC-3
Brentwood West (trailer park)—locale ... AZ-5
Brentwood West (trailer park)—pop pl ... AZ-5
Brenum Lake—lake ... MN-6
Breo Flat—flat ... OR-9
Brereton—pop pl ... IL-6
Brescia Coll—school ... KY-4
Bresee Ch—church ... IN-6
Bresee Hall—hist pl ... NY-2
Bresee Mill Brook—stream ... VT-1
Breshears Cem—cemetery ... MO-7
Bresheres Lateral—canal ... ID-8
Bresinger Sch—school ... NJ-2
Breskin Dam Number Two—dam ... PA-2
Breskin Pond—reservoir ... PA-2
Breskin Pond Dam Number One—dam ... PA-2
Breslau—pop pl ... NE-7
Breslau—pop pl ... PA-2
Breslau—pop pl ... TX-5
Breslau Cem—cemetery ... NY-2
Breslau Cem—cemetery ... TX-5
Breslau Creek—stream ... NE-7
Breslin—hist pl ... WA-9
Breslin Draw—valley ... CO-8
Breslyn Apartments—hist pl ... PA-2
Bressie Cem—cemetery ... OK-5
Bressler—pop pl ... PA-2
Bressler, Mount—summit ... AK-9
Bressler Cem—cemetery ... OH-6
Bressler Gap—gap ... PA-2
Bressler Island—island ... PA-2
Bressler Sch (historical)—school ... MO-7
Bressman Cabin—locale ... NV-8
Bressmer-Baker House—hist pl ... IL-6
Brest—pop pl ... MI-6
Brest Bay—bay ... MI-6
Brest (Lester)—pop pl ... GA-3
Breston Plantation House—hist pl ... LA-4
Brestwork Creek—stream ... AL-4
Bret Creek—stream ... CA-9
Breteche Creek—stream ... WY-8
Bret Harte Cabin—locale ... CA-9
Bret Harte HS—school ... CA-9
Bret Harte JHS—school (3) ... CA-9
Bret Harte Park—park ... CA-9
Bret Harte Sanatorium—building ... CA-9
Bret Harte Sch—school (7) ... CA-9
Brethen Ch—church ... MO-7
Bretherick Plantation (historical)—locale ... AL-4
Brethern Church ... KS-7
Bretherton, Mount—summit ... WA-9
Bret Hole—flat ... CA-9
Brethren—pop pl ... MI-6
Brethren Cem—cemetery ... KS-7
Brethren Cem—cemetery ... MI-6
Brethren Cem—cemetery ... MO-7
Brethren Cem—cemetery ... NE-7
Brethren Cem—cemetery (2) ... ND-7
Brethren Cem—cemetery ... OH-6
Brethren Cem—cemetery (3) ... OK-5
Brethren Ch—church (2) ... FL-3
Brethren Ch—church (2) ... IL-6
Brethren Ch—church (2) ... KS-7
Brethren Ch—church (6) ... MI-6
Brethren Ch—church (3) ... MN-6
Brethren Ch—church ... MO-7
Brethren Ch—church ... NE-7
Brethren Ch—church (3) ... OH-6
Brethren Ch—church (2) ... OK-5
Brethren Ch—church ... PA-2
Brethren Ch—church ... TN-4
Brethren Day Sch—school ... CA-9
Brethren HS—school ... CA-9
Brethren in Christ Cem—cemetery ... KS-7
Brethren in Christ Ch—church ... FL-3
Brethren in Christ Ch—church (2) ... MI-6
Brethren in Christ Ch—church ... OK-5
Brethren in Christ Chapel—church ... PA-2
Brethren in Christ Church—hist pl ... IN-6
Brethren in Christ Fellowship—church ... FL-3
Brethren in Christ Mission Sch—school ... NM-5
Brethren JHS—school ... CA-9
Brethren Navajo Boarding Sch—school ... NM-5
Brethren of the Woods Camp—locale ... VA-3
Brethren Run—stream ... IN-6
Brethren Summit—summit ... PA-2
Bret Kimberlin Lake—reservoir ... IN-6
Bret Kimberlin Lake Dam—dam ... IN-6
Bretland—locale ... WA-9
Breton—locale ... KY-4
Breton—locale ... LA-4
Breton—pop pl ... KS-7
Bretona Creek—stream ... CA-9
Breton Bay—bay ... MD-2
Breton Beach—pop pl ... MD-2
Breton Canal—canal ... LA-4
Breton Creek Sch—school ... MO-7
Breton Downs Sch—school ... MI-6
Breton Hills—pop pl ... PA-2
Breton Island ... LA-4
Breton Islands ... LA-4
Breton Islands—island ... LA-4
Breton Natl Wildlife Ref—park (2) ... LA-4
Bretons Bay ... MD-2
Bretons Bay—locale ... MD-2
Breton Sound—bay ... LA-4
Breton Township—civil ... MO-7
Bretonville—pop pl ... PA-2
Breton Woods—pop pl ... NJ-2
Bretschneider Cem—cemetery ... TX-5
Brett, Madam Catharyna, Homestead—hist pl ... NY-2
Brett Bay—bay ... NC-3
Brett Creek—stream ... ID-8
Brett Ditch—canal ... CO-8
Brett Hill—summit ... ME-1
Brett (historical)—locale ... KS-7
Bretthorst Cem—cemetery ... MO-7
Bretton Heights ... CT-1
Bretton Heights—pop pl ... CT-1
Bretton Hills—pop pl ... FL-3
Bretton Township—civil ... SD-7
Bretton Woods—pop pl ... NH-1
Bretton Woods Sch—school ... MI-6
Bretton Woods (subdivision)—pop pl ... MI-6
Brett Sch—school ... MA-1
Brett Sch—school ... OH-6
Brett Tank—reservoir ... AZ-5
Brettuns Mills ... ME-1
Brettuns Pond—lake ... ME-1
Brettwood—post sta ... IL-6
Bretz ... IN-6
Bretz—pop pl (2) ... WV-2
Bretz Cem—cemetery ... OH-6
Bretz Farm—hist pl ... OH-6
Bretz Mill—pop pl ... CA-9
Bretzville—pop pl ... IN-6
Bretzville Cem—cemetery ... IN-6
Breukelen—uninc pl ... NY-2
Breustedt, Andreas, House—hist pl ... TX-5
Brevard ... MS-4
Brevard—pop pl ... NC-3
Brevard—pop pl ... PA-2
Brevard, Caroline, Grammar Sch—hist pl ... FL-3
Brevard, Keziah Goodwyn Hopkins, House—hist pl ... SC-3
Brevard Airp—airport ... NC-3
Brevard Christian Sch—school ... FL-3
Brevard Coll—school ... NC-3
Brevard Coll (historical)—school ... TN-4
Brevard Community Coll—school ... FL-3
Brevard Community Coll (Cocoa Campus)—school ... FL-3
Brevard Community Coll (Melbourne)—school ... FL-3
Brevard Community Coll (Melbourne Campus)—school ... FL-3
Brevard Community Coll (Titusville Campus)—school ... FL-3
Brevard Country Club and Golf Course—locale ... NC-3
Brevard County—pop pl ... FL-3
Brevard County Game Ref—park ... FL-3
Brevard County Tutorial Systems—school ... FL-3
Brevard Creek—stream ... NC-3
Brevard Elem Sch—school ... NC-3
Brevard (historical)—pop pl ... NC-3
Brevard HS—school ... NC-3
Brevard Learning Clinic—school ... FL-3
Brevard Mall—locale ... FL-3
Brevard Memorial Park—cemetery ... FL-3
Brevard Mental Health Center and Hosp—hospital ... FL-3
Brevard MS—school ... NC-3
Brevard Music Center ... NC-3
Brevard Music Center Lake—reservoir ... NC-3
Brevard Post Office (historical)—building ... MS-4
Brevard Post Office (historical)—building ... TN-4
Brevard Sch—school ... FL-3
Brevards Ferry (historical)—crossing ... TN-4
Brevards Forge (historical)—locale ... NC-3
Brevards Landing—locale ... TN-4
Brevards Mill (historical)—locale ... TN-4
Brevard (Township of)—fmr MCD ... NC-3
Brevator—locale ... MO-7
Brevator Cem—cemetery (2) ... MN-6
Brevator (Township of)—pop pl ... MN-6
Brevelle, Bayou—stream ... LA-4
Brevet (historical)—pop pl ... MS-4
Brevick Lake—lake ... MI-6
Brevicomis Creek—stream ... WA-9
Brevier Creek—stream ... AK-9
Brevig Lagoon—lake ... AK-9
Brevig Mission—pop pl ... AK-9
Brevik—pop pl ... MN-6
Brevoart Lake ... MI-6
Brevoort ... MI-6
Brevoort—uninc pl ... NY-2
Brevoort Lake—lake ... MI-6
Brevoort Levee—levee ... IN-6
Brevoort Park—park ... OH-6
Brevoort River ... MI-6
Brevoort River—stream ... MI-6
Brevort—pop pl ... MI-6
Brevort Cem—cemetery (2) ... MI-6
Brevort Lake ... MI-6
Brevort River ... MI-6
Brevort (Township of)—pop pl ... MI-6
Brewards Islands ... FL-3
Brewbaker Dam—dam ... AL-4
Brewbaker Elem Sch—school ... AL-4
Brewbaker JHS—school ... AL-4
Brewbaker Lake—reservoir ... AL-4
Brewbaker Number Two Dam—dam ... AL-4
Brewbaker Number Two Lake—reservoir ... AL-4
Brewer—locale ... AR-4
Brewer—locale ... KS-7
Brewer—locale (2) ... MS-4
Brewer—locale ... MT-8
Brewer—pop pl ... IL-6
Brewer—pop pl ... ME-1
Brewer—pop pl ... MN-6
Brewer—pop pl ... MS-4
Brewer—pop pl ... MO-7
Brewer—pop pl ... OH-6
Brewer, A. B., Bldg—hist pl ... AR-4
Brewer, Bayou—stream ... MS-4
Brewer, C., Bldg—hist pl ... HI-9
Brewer, Capt. John, House—hist pl ... MA-1
Brewer, David J., House—hist pl ... KS-7
Brewer, Edward Hill, House—hist pl ... FL-3
Brewer, Henrietta, House—hist pl ... ME-1
Brewer, John F., House—hist pl ... AR-4
Brewer, John N.M., House—hist pl ... ME-1
Brewer, Mount—summit ... CA-9
Brewer, Selden, House—hist pl ... CT-1
Brewer Addition—pop pl ... TN-4
Brewer Baptist Ch—church ... MS-4
Brewer Basin—lake ... TN-4
Brewer Bay—stream ... MO-7
Brewer Bayou—stream ... LA-4
Brewer Bend—bend ... OK-5
Brewer Bend Public Use Area—park ... OK-5
Brewer Branch ... WV-2
Brewer Branch—stream ... AR-4
Brewer Branch—stream ... IL-6
Brewer Branch—stream ... IN-6
Brewer Branch—stream ... KY-4
Brewer Branch—stream (2) ... MO-7
Brewer Branch—stream ... NC-3
Brewer Branch—stream (2) ... TN-4
Brewer Branch—stream ... TX-5
Brewer Bridge—bridge ... NE-7
Brewer Brook—stream (3) ... MA-1
Brewer Brook Dam—dam ... MA-1
Brewer Butte—summit ... SD-7
Brewer Canyon—valley ... NV-8
Brewer Canyon—valley (2) ... UT-8
Brewer Cem—cemetery ... AL-4
Brewer Cem—cemetery ... AR-4
Brewer Cem—cemetery ... GA-3
Brewer Cem—cemetery ... IN-6
Brewer Cem—cemetery (2) ... KY-4
Brewer Cem—cemetery ... ME-1
Brewer Cem—cemetery (5) ... MS-4
Brewer Cem—cemetery ... NJ-2
Brewer Cem—cemetery ... NC-3
Brewer Cem—cemetery ... OH-6
Brewer Cem—cemetery ... OR-9
Brewer Cem—cemetery (8) ... TN-4
Brewer Cem—cemetery ... TX-5
Brewer Cem—cemetery ... VT-1
Brewer Cem—cemetery (5) ... WV-2
Brewer Cemtery—cemetery ... GA-3
Brewer Ch—church ... AR-4
Brewer Chapel—church (2) ... TN-4
Brewer Corners—locale (2) ... NY-2
Brewer Corners Cem—cemetery ... NY-2
Brewer Creek ... TN-4
Brewer Creek ... VA-3
Brewer Creek—bay ... MD-2
Brewer Creek—stream (2) ... AL-4
Brewer Creek—stream (2) ... CA-9
Brewer Creek—stream ... ID-8
Brewer Creek—stream ... MD-2
Brewer Creek—stream ... PA-2
Brewer Creek—stream (2) ... TN-4
Brewer Creek—stream ... WI-6
Brewer Dam—dam ... OR-9
Brewer Ditch—canal (2) ... IN-6
Brewer Ditch South ... IN-6
Brewer Drain—canal (2) ... MI-6
Brewer Estates (subdivision)—pop pl ... AL-4
Brewer Family Cem—cemetery ... MS-4
Brewer Flat—flat ... WY-8
Brewer Fork—stream (2) ... KY-4
Brewer Fork—stream ... PA-2
Brewer Gap—gap ... TN-4
Brewerg Bay—bay ... VI-3
Brewer Gut—gut ... VA-3
Brewer Heights ... AL-4
Brewer Heights ... OH-6
Brewer Heights—pop pl ... OH-6
Brewer Hill—pop pl ... WV-2
Brewer Hill—summit ... AR-4
Brewer Hill—summit ... IN-6
Brewer Hill—summit ... MT-8
Brewer Hill Cem—cemetery ... MD-2
Brewer Hollow—valley ... AL-4
Brewer Hollow—valley (2) ... KY-4
Brewer Hollow—valley ... MO-7
Brewer Hollow—valley ... OH-6
Brewer Hollow—valley (2) ... TN-4
Brewer Hollow—valley ... TX-5
Brewer HS—school ... SC-3
Brewer Island—island ... CA-9
Brewer Junction (RR name for Brewer)—other ... ME-1
Brewer Lake ... CO-8
Brewer Lake ... MA-1
Brewer Lake—lake ... AR-4
Brewer Lake—lake ... CA-9
Brewer Lake—lake ... FL-3
Brewer Lake—lake ... ME-1
Brewer Lake—lake ... MN-6
Brewer Lake—lake ... MO-7
Brewer Lake—lake ... NE-7
Brewer Lake—lake ... NY-2
Brewer Lake—pop pl ... ME-1
Brewer Lake—reservoir ... MS-4
Brewer Lake—reservoir (2) ... NC-3
Brewer Lake Dam ... ND-7
Brewer Lake Dam—dam ... MS-4
Brewer Lake Dam—dam (2) ... NC-3
Brewer Lake Ditch—canal ... MO-7
Brewer Log House—hist pl ... OH-6
Brewer Memorial Ch—church ... AL-4
Brewer Methodist Ch—church ... MS-4
Brewer Mtn—summit ... AL-4
Brewer Mtn—summit ... ME-1
Brewer Mtn—summit ... WA-9
Brewer Oil Field—oilfield ... TX-5
Brewer Park—park ... FL-3
Brewer Path—trail ... PA-2
Brewer Point ... NY-2
Brewer Point—cape ... AL-4
Brewer Point—cape (2) ... MD-2
Brewer Pond ... MA-1
Brewer Pond—lake ... MD-2
Brewer Pond—lake ... MA-1
Brewer-Porch Childrens Center—school ... AL-4
Brewer Ranch—locale ... MT-8
Brewer Ranch—locale ... OR-9
Brewer Ridge—ridge ... TN-4
Brewer Ridge—ridge ... UT-8
Brewer River ... GA-3
Brewer Rsvr—reservoir ... OR-9
Brewer Run ... PA-2
Brewer Run—stream (3) ... PA-2
Brewers—pop pl ... KY-4
Brewers Bar—bar ... TN-4
Brewers Bluff ... MS-4
Brewers Branch*—stream ... NE-7
Brewers Branch—stream ... VA-3
Brewers Brook—stream ... VT-1
Brewer Sch—school ... AR-4
Brewer Sch—school ... IL-6
Brewer Sch—school ... MS-4
Brewer Sch—school ... NJ-2
Brewer Sch—school ... OH-6
Brewer Sch—school ... TN-4
Brewer Sch—school (2) ... TX-5
Brewers Chapel—church ... TX-5
Brewer Sch (historical)—school ... AL-4
Brewer Sch (historical)—school ... MS-4
Brewer Sch (historical)—school ... TN-4
Brewer School ... KS-7
Brewers Corner—locale ... NY-2
Brewers Corner—locale ... VT-1
Brewers Creek—stream ... IA-7
Brewers Creek—stream ... MS-4
Brewers Creek—stream ... MO-7
Brewers Creek—stream ... VA-3
Brewers Creek Sch (abandoned)—school ... MO-7
Brewers Crossroad (historical)—locale ... AL-4
Brewers Crossroads—pop pl ... NC-3
Brewers Exchange—hist pl ... MD-2
Brewers Flat—flat ... NV-8
Brewers Landing—locale ... FL-3
Brewer Slope Mine (underground)—mine ... AL-4
Brewer's Mill—hist pl ... AR-4
Brewers Mtn ... ME-1
Brewers Neck ... GA-3
Brewers Pond ... MA-1
Brewer Spring—spring ... AL-4
Brewer Spring—spring ... AZ-5
Brewer Spring—spring ... AR-4
Brewers Spring Cave—cave ... AL-4
Brewers Store—locale ... NC-3
Brewers Store (historical)—locale ... AL-4
Brewersville—pop pl ... AL-4
Brewersville—pop pl ... IN-6
Brewersville Cem—cemetery ... AL-4
Brewert Bay—swamp ... GA-3
Brewerton—pop pl ... NY-2
Brewerton—pop pl ... SC-3
Brewerton Channel—channel ... MD-2
Brewerton Channel Eastern Extension—channel ... MD-2
Brewertown ... NJ-2
Brewer (Township of)—fmr MCD (3) ... AR-4
Brewerville ... MO-7
Brewerville (Election Precinct)—fmr MCD ... IL-6
Brewer Vly—swamp ... NY-2
Brewer-Webb Cem—cemetery ... MS-4
Brewer Well—well ... MT-8
Brewery Creek—stream ... CA-9
Brewery Creek—stream ... CO-8
Brewery Creek—stream ... KS-7
Brewery Creek—stream (2) ... MI-6
Brewery Creek—stream ... MN-6
Brewery Creek—stream ... WI-6
Brewery Creek Guard Station—locale ... CO-8
Brewery Gulch—valley ... AZ-5
Brewery Gulch Interchange—crossing ... AZ-5
Brewery Hill—cliff ... IN-6
Brewery Hill—summit ... CA-9
Brewery Hill—summit ... CO-8
Brewery Hill—summit ... NE-7
Brewery Hole—lake ... OR-9
Brewery Hollow—valley ... OH-6
Brewery Run—stream ... PA-2
Brewery Spring—spring ... CA-9
Brewery Spring—spring ... OR-9
Brew Hill—summit ... WA-9
Brewington Branch—stream ... MD-2
Brewington Cem—cemetery (2) ... MO-7
Brewington Ch—church ... SC-3
Brewington Ch—church ... TX-5
Brewington Creek—stream ... TX-5
Brewington Crossing—bridge ... SC-3
Brewington Lake—lake ... SC-3
Brewington Woods—pop pl ... IN-6
Brewis Lake—lake ... MN-6
Brew Mill—pop pl ... WA-9
Brewner Hollow—valley ... MO-7
Brewsaugh Cem—cemetery ... KY-4
Brewster—locale ... FL-3
Brewster—locale ... OR-9
Brewster—pop pl ... CO-8
Brewster—pop pl ... KS-7
Brewster—pop pl ... MA-1
Brewster—pop pl ... MN-6
Brewster—pop pl ... NE-7
Brewster—pop pl ... NY-2
Brewster—pop pl ... OH-6
Brewster—pop pl ... WA-9
Brewster—pop pl ... WV-2
Brewster, Royal, House—hist pl ... ME-1
Brewster, Walter, House—hist pl ... NY-2
Brewster Acad—school ... NH-1
Brewster Branch—stream ... KY-4
Brewster Bridge—bridge ... TN-4
Brewster Brook ... NJ-2
Brewster Brook—stream ... ME-1
Brewster Camp—locale (2) ... MT-8
Brewster Canyon—valley ... CO-8
Brewster Canyon—valley ... OR-9
Brewster Cem—cemetery (2) ... IL-6
Brewster Cem—cemetery ... KS-7
Brewster Cem—cemetery ... MA-1
Brewster Cem—cemetery ... NE-7
Brewster Cem—cemetery ... NY-2
Brewster Cem—cemetery (2) ... TN-4
Brewster Cem—cemetery (2) ... TX-5
Brewster Cem—cemetery ... WV-2
Brewster Cem—cemetery (2) ... WI-6
Brewster Chapel—church ... WV-2
Brewster Corner—locale ... ME-1
Brewster (County)—pop pl ... TX-5
Brewster County Club—locale ... MA-1
Brewster County Courthouse and Jail—hist pl ... TX-5
Brewster Creek—stream ... CO-8
Brewster Creek—stream (3) ... IL-6
Brewster Creek—stream ... KY-4
Brewster Creek—stream ... MT-8
Brewster Creek—stream (2) ... TX-5
Brewsterdale—locale ... WV-2
Brewster Ditch—canal ... IN-6
Brewster Draw—valley (2) ... WY-8
Brewster Draws—valley ... WY-8
Brewster-Dutra House—hist pl ... CA-9
Brewster Elem Sch—school ... AL-4
Brewster E Side Ditch—canal ... MT-8
Brewster Flat—flat ... WA-9
Brewster Fork ... WV-2
Brewster Gulch—valley ... MT-8
Brewster Heights—pop pl ... NY-2
Brewster Hill—summit ... NY-2
Brewster Hill (census name for Tonetta Lake Hgts.)—CDP ... NY-2
Brewster Hollow—valley ... AL-4
Brewster Hollow—valley ... PA-2
Brewster Hollow—valley ... VA-3
Brewster Hosp—hist pl ... FL-3
Brewster Hosp—hospital ... FL-3
Brewster House—hist pl ... AR-4
Brewster House—hist pl ... CA-9
Brewster HS—school ... KS-7
Brewster Island ... MA-1
Brewster Islands—island ... MA-1
Brewster Lake—lake (2) ... MI-6
Brewster Lake—lake ... WA-9
Brewster Lake—lake ... WY-8
Brewster Memorial Hall—hist pl ... NH-1
Brewster Memorial Hosp—hospital ... TX-5
Brewster Mtn—summit ... GA-3
Brewster Mtn—summit ... NY-2
Brewster Park—park ... MI-6
Brewster Park—park ... MO-7
Brewster Place Ch—church ... KS-7
Brewster Point—cape ... ME-1
Brewster Point Ledge—bar ... ME-1
Brewster Pond—lake ... CT-1
Brewster Pond—lake ... NY-2
Brewster Pond—reservoir ... PA-2
Brewster Pond Dam—dam ... PA-2
Brewster Public Access—locale ... IL-6
Brewster Ranch—locale ... MT-8
Brewster Ranch—locale ... OR-9
Brewster Ranch—locale ... TX-5
Brewster River—stream ... VT-1
Brewster Rock—pillar ... OR-9
Brewster RR YMCA/Wandle House—hist pl ... OH-6
Brewster Rsvr ... OR-9
Brewster Rsvr—reservoir ... OR-9
Brewster Rsvr—reservoir ... WY-8
Brewster Rsvr Number Two—reservoir ... OR-9
Brewsters ... MA-1
Brewsters, The ... MA-1
Brewsters Brook ... MA-1
Brewster Sch—school ... CO-8
Brewster Sch—school ... CT-1
Brewster Sch—school ... FL-3
Brewster Sch—school ... GA-3
Brewster Sch—school ... TX-5
Brewster Settling Basin—basin ... IL-6
Brewsters Islands ... MA-1
Brewster Site—hist pl ... IA-7
Brewsters Pit—cave ... AL-4
Brewsters Pond—lake ... CT-1
Brewsters Siding—locale ... GA-3
Brewster Station ... MA-1
Brewster Station (historical)—locale ... MA-1
Brewster Tank—reservoir ... NM-5
Brewstertown—pop pl ... TN-4
Brewster (Town of)—pop pl ... MA-1
Brewster Valley—valley ... OR-9
Brewster-Wakefield (CCD)—cens area ... WA-9
Brewster Well—well (2) ... AZ-5
Brewster W Side Ditch—canal ... MT-8
Brewton—locale ... SC-3
Brewton—pop pl ... AL-4
Brewton—pop pl ... GA-3
Brewton, Miles, House—hist pl ... SC-3
Brewton, Robert, House—hist pl ... SC-3
Brewton Agricultural Experiment Station—locale ... AL-4
Brewton Baptist Ch—church ... AL-4
Brewton Bridge ... AL-4
Brewton Canyon—valley ... TX-5
Brewton (CCD)—cens area ... AL-4
Brewton (CCD)—cens area ... GA-3
Brewton Cem—cemetery ... GA-3
Brewton Cem—cemetery ... IL-6
Brewton Ch—church ... AL-4
Brewton Chapel—church ... AL-4
Brewton Creek—stream (2) ... GA-3
Brewton Crossroads ... LA-4
Brewton Division—civil ... AL-4
Brewton Gap ... AL-4
Brewton Grammer Sch (historical)—school ... AL-4
Brewton Gulch—valley ... WA-9
Brewton (historical)—locale ... MS-4
Brewton Historic Commercial District—hist pl ... AL-4
Brewton HS—school ... AL-4
Brewton Institute ... AL-4
Brewton Lake—lake ... MS-4
Brewton Millpond—reservoir ... GA-3
Brewton Municipal Airp—airport ... AL-4
Brewton Parker Coll—school ... GA-3
Brewton Presbyterian Ch—church ... AL-4
Brewton Sewage Lagoon—reservoir ... AL-4
Brewton Sewage Lagoon Dam—dam ... AL-4
Brewtons Mill—gut ... LA-4
Breyfogel Ditch—canal ... IN-6
Breymann Redoubt Overlook—locale ... NY-2
B Reynolds Falls—falls ... PA-2
Brey Riddle Ditch—canal ... MT-8
Brey Valley—valley ... WI-6
Brezee Creek—stream ... WA-9
Brezina Woods—woods ... IL-6
Brezniak Ranch—locale ... OR-9
B R Gunn Pond Dam—dam ... MS-4
Brian—locale ... MO-7
Brian—pop pl ... LA-4
Brian Branch—stream ... PA-2
Brian Cem—cemetery ... IL-6
Brian Cem—cemetery ... IN-6
Brian Creek—stream ... AK-9
Brian Creek—stream ... MT-8
Brian Creek—stream ... OR-9
Brian Head—pop pl ... UT-8
Brian Head—summit ... UT-8
Brian Head Peak ... UT-8
Brian Head Ski Area—locale ... UT-8
Brianhead Ski Resort ... UT-8
Brian Point—cape ... MD-2
Brian Reservoir ... UT-8
Brian Run ... PA-2
Brian Spring—spring ... UT-8
Brian Spring Number Three—spring ... MT-8
Brian Spring Number Two—spring ... MT-8
Briant ... IN-6
Briant (Bryant) ... IN-6
Briant Park—park ... NJ-2
Briant Park Dam—dam ... NJ-2
Briant Pond—reservoir ... NJ-2
Briant Pond Dam ... NJ-2
Briants Neck—cape ... MA-1
Brian Well—well ... MT-8
Briar—locale (2) ... AR-4
Briar—pop pl ... MO-7
Briar—pop pl ... TX-5
Briar Bay—bay ... GA-3
Briar Bay Convenience Center (Shop Ctr)—locale ... FL-3
Briar Bay Golf Course—locale ... FL-3
Briar Bay Urban Park—park ... FL-3
Briar Bed—swamp ... NC-3
Briar Bluff—locale ... IL-6
Briar Branch ... TX-5
Briar Branch—stream ... AL-4
Briar Branch—stream ... AR-4
Briar Branch—stream (2) ... GA-3
Briar Branch—stream ... IL-6
Briar Branch—stream (2) ... MS-4
Briar Branch—stream ... NC-3
Briar Branch—stream (3) ... OK-5
Briar Branch—stream (2) ... SC-3
Briar Branch—stream (2) ... TN-4
Briar Branch—stream (8) ... TX-5
Briar Branch—stream ... WV-2
Briar Branch Cem—cemetery ... TX-5
Briar Branch Ch—church ... NC-3
Briar Branch Creek—stream ... OK-5
Briarbrook—pop pl ... PA-2
Briarbrook Village ... IL-6
Briar Canyon—valley ... CO-8
Briarcliff—hist pl ... GA-3
Briarcliff—pop pl ... GA-3
Briarcliff—pop pl ... NC-3
Briarcliff—pop pl ... PA-2
Briarcliff—pop pl ... TX-5
Briarcliff—uninc pl ... VA-3
Briar Cliff Coll—school ... IA-7
Briarcliff Coll—school ... NY-2
Briarcliffe ... IL-6
Briarcliffe Acres—pop pl ... SC-3
Briarcliffe Coll—school ... FL-3
Briarcliff Hotel—hist pl ... GA-3
Briarcliff Manor—pop pl ... NY-2
Briarcliff Manor (subdivision)—pop pl ... NC-3
Briarcliff Mines—mine ... CA-9
Briarcliff Park—park ... MO-7
Briarcliff Road Sch—school ... NY-2
Briarcliff Sch—school ... MO-7
Briarcliff Sch—school ... NC-3
Briarcliff (subdivision)—pop pl (2) ... AL-4
Briarcliff (subdivision)—pop pl ... MS-4
Briarcliff (subdivision)—pop pl (2) ... NC-3
Briarcliff (subdivision)—pop pl ... TN-4
Briarcliff View—pop pl ... TN-4
Briar Cove—bay ... ME-1
Briar Creek ... AR-4
Briar Creek ... GA-3
Briar Creek ... NC-3
Briar Creek ... OK-5
Briar Creek ... TX-5
Briar Creek—pop pl ... PA-2
Briar Creek—stream (3) ... AL-4
Briar Creek—stream (4) ... AR-4
Briar Creek—stream (3) ... GA-3
Briar Creek—stream ... ID-8
Briar Creek—stream (2) ... IL-6
Briar Creek—stream (2) ... MS-4
Briar Creek—stream (3) ... MO-7

Briar Creek—*stream* MT-8
Briar Creek—*stream* ND-7
Briar Creek—*stream* OK-5
Briar Creek—*stream* OR-9
Briar Creek—*stream* PA-2
Briar Creek—*stream* SC-3
Briar Creek—*stream* (3) TN-4
Briar Creek—*stream* (9) TX-5
**Briarcreek Condominium**—*pop pl* UT-8
Briar Creek Dam—*dam* PA-2
**Briarcreek Estates Subdivision**—*pop pl* UT-8
*Briar Creek Landing* GA-3
Briar Creek Park—*park* AL-4
*Briar Creek Park Lake* PA-2
Briar Creek Rsvr—*reservoir* PA-2
**Briar Creek (Township of)**—*pop pl* PA-2
Briarcrest Country Club—*other* TX-5
**Briarcrest Heights**—*pop pl* MD-2
*Briarcrest School* TN-4
**Briar Crest Woods**—*pop pl* PA-2
Briar Crest Woods Dam—*dam* PA-2
Briar Crest Woods Lake—*reservoir* PA-2
**Briardale (subdivision)**—*pop pl* TN-4
Briardam Swamp—*swamp* GA-3
Briar Ditch—*canal* CO-8
Briard Lake—*lake* WI-6
**Briarfield**—*pop pl* AL-4
Briarfield—*uninc pl* VA-3
Briarfield Acad—*school* LA-4
Briarfield Branch—*stream* KY-4
Briarfield Ridge—*ridge* KY-4
Briarfield Sch—*school* AL-4
Briarfield Sch—*school* VA-3
**Briarfield (subdivision)**—*pop pl* TN-4
*Briar Fork* AL-4
Briar Fork—*stream* (3) KY-4
Briar Fork—*stream* TN-4
Briar Fork—*stream* VA-3
Briar Fork Cem—*cemetery* AR-4
Briar Fork Ch (historical)—*church* TN-4
Briar Fork Music Camp—*locale* AL-4
Briargate Ch—*church* KY-4
**Briargate (subdivision)**—*pop pl* TN-4
**Briargate Subdivision**—*pop pl* UT-8
**Briargrove**—*pop pl* TX-5
Briargrove Park—*uninc pl* TX-5
Briargrove Sch—*school* TX-5
Briargrove Shop Ctr—*locale* TX-5
Briar Gulch—*valley* OR-9
Briar Hall Country Club—*other* NY-2
Briar Head—*swamp* FL-3
Briar Head Sch—*school* SC-3
**Briar Hill**—*pop pl* AL-4
Briar Hill—*summit* MI-6
Briar Hill—*summit* (2) NY-2
Briar Hill—*summit* (3) PA-2
Briar Hill Cem—*cemetery* MS-4
Briar Hill Cem—*cemetery* PA-2
Briar Hill Ch—*church* AL-4
Briar Hill Ch—*church* MS-4
Briar Hill Creek—*stream* MI-6
Briar Hill Lake—*reservoir* OH-6
Briar Hill Sch—*school* KY-4
Briar Hill Sch—*school* NY-2
Briar Hill Sch (historical)—*school* AL-4
Briar Hill Sch (historical)—*school* TN-4
Briar Hill Ski Jump—*other* MI-6
Briar Hill Tank—*reservoir* NM-5
Briarhill Welfare Home—*building* NJ-2
Briar Hollow—*valley* AR-4
Briar Hollow—*valley* (2) KY-4
Briar Hollow—*valley* MO-7
Briar Hollow—*valley* TN-4
**Briar Hook (subdivision)**—*pop pl* DE-2
Briarhurst—*hist pl* CO-8
Briar Island—*island* FL-3
Briar Island—*island* (3) GA-3
Briar Island (reduced usage)—*island* IL-6
Briark—*locale* AR-4
Briar Knob—*summit* TN-4
Briar Lake—*lake* AL-4
Briar Lake—*lake* (2) MN-6
Briar Lake—*lake* WI-6
Briar Lake—*reservoir* NC-3
Briar Lake Dam—*dam* NC-3
**Briar Lake Estates (subdivision)**—*pop pl* AL-4
Briar Landing—*locale* MS-4
Briar Lookout Tower—*locale* MO-7
**Briarly**—*pop pl* PA-2
Briarly Creek—*stream* OH-6
**Briar Manor**—*pop pl* NJ-2
Briar Meadow Park—*park* TX-5
Briar Mtn—*summit* MS-4
Briar Mtn—*summit* PA-2
**Briaroaks**—*pop pl* TX-5
**Briar Park**—*pop pl* DE-2
**Briar Park**—*pop pl* NY-2
Briar Patch Cem—*cemetery* LA-4
Briar Patch Lake—*lake* IL-6
Briarpatch Lake—*lake* TN-4
Briar Patch Lake—*reservoir* MS-4
*Briar Patch Mountain* VA-3
Briar Patch Pond—*swamp* TX-5
Briar Patch Road Hist Dist—*hist pl* NY-2
Briar Patch Sch—*school* MI-6
Briar Point—*cape* DE-2
Briar Point—*cape* MD-2
Briar Point—*cape* NY-2
Briar Point—*cliff* TN-4
*Briar Pond* MA-1
Briar Pond Bottom—*bend* TN-4
Briar Pond Branch—*stream* TN-4
Briar Pond (Carolina Bay)—*swamp* NC-3
Briar Ridge—*ridge* AR-4
Briar Ridge—*ridge* IN-6
Briar Ridge—*ridge* (2) TN-4
Briar Ridge Cem—*cemetery* TN-4
Briar Ridge Ch—*church* TN-4
Briar Ridge Sch (historical)—*school* TN-4
Briar Rose Mine—*mine* CO-8
Briar Run—*stream* (2) WV-2
Briars—*hist pl* MS-4
**Briars**—*pop pl* SC-3
Briar Sch—*school* OH-6
Briars Chute—*gut* MS-4
Briars Chute—*stream* LA-4
Briars Creek—*stream* SC-3
Briars Pocosin—*swamp* VA-3
*Briars Pond* MA-1
Briar Spring—*spring* ID-8
**Briars (subdivision), The**—*pop pl* MS-4
Briar Swamp—*swamp* MA-1
**Briar Thicket**—*pop pl* TN-4
*Briar Thicket Baptist Church* TN-4
Briar Thicket Ch—*church* TN-4
*Briarton* PA-2
**Briarton**—*pop pl* WI-6
**Briartown**—*pop pl* KY-4
**Briartown**—*pop pl* OK-5
Briartown Cem—*cemetery* OK-5
Briartown Creek—*stream* OK-5
Briarwood—*hist pl* WV-2
**Briarwood**—*pop pl* AR-4
**Briarwood**—*pop pl* IN-6
**Briarwood**—*pop pl* KY-4
**Briarwood**—*pop pl* MD-2
**Briarwood**—*pop pl* ND-7
**Briarwood**—*pop pl* OR-9
**Briarwood**—*pop pl* (2) TN-4
**Briarwood**—*pop pl* (2) VA-3
Briarwood—*uninc pl* GA-3
Briarwood—*uninc pl* PA-2
Briarwood, Lake—*reservoir* MO-7
Briarwood Acad—*school* GA-3
**Briarwood Acres (subdivision)**—*pop pl* NC-3
**Briarwood Acres Subdivision**—*pop pl* UT-8
**Briarwood Beach**—*pop pl* MA-1
**Briarwood Beach**—*pop pl* OH-6
Briarwood Ch—*church* AL-4
Briarwood Ch—*church* MS-4
Briarwood Ch—*church* TN-4
**Briarwood Condominium**—*pop pl* UT-8
Briarwood Country Club—*other* TX-5
Briarwood Country Club Dam—*dam* MS-4
Briarwood Drive Baptist Ch—*church* MS-4
Briarwood Elem Sch—*school* KS-7
**Briar Wood Estates**—*pop pl* GA-3
**Briarwood Estates**—*pop pl* TN-4
**Briarwood Estates**—*pop pl* WV-2
**Briarwood Estates Subdivision**—*pop pl* UT-8
Briarwood Golf Course—*other* AZ-5
**Briarwood Hills Subdivision**—*pop pl* UT-8
*Briarwood Junior High School* TN-4
Briarwood Lake—*lake* FL-3
Briarwood Lake Dam—*dam* IN-6
**Briarwood Manor**—*pop pl* KY-4
**Briarwood Manor (subdivision)**—*pop pl* DE-2
Briarwood MS—*school* TN-4
Briarwood Plaza—*locale* MA-1
Briarwood Presbyterian Ch—*church* MS-4
Briarwood Sch—*school* AL-4
Briarwood Sch—*school* CA-9
Briarwood Sch—*school* MI-6
Briarwood Sch—*school* NY-2
Briarwood Sch—*school* NC-3
Briarwood Sch (historical)—*school* TN-4
*Briarwoods Estates* IL-6
**Briarwood Springs Condo**—*pop pl* UT-8
**Briarwood Springs Townhomes**—*pop pl* UT-8
**Briarwood (subdivision)**—*pop pl* AL-4
**Briarwood (subdivision)**—*pop pl* (2) MS-4
**Briarwood (subdivision)**—*pop pl* NC-3
**Briarwood (subdivision)**—*pop pl* TN-4
**Briarwood Subdivision**—*pop pl* UT-8
**Briarwood Terrace (subdivision)**—*pop pl* NC-3
**Briarwood Trace**—*pop pl* IL-6
Briary—*locale* TX-5
Briary Bay—*swamp* (2) GA-3
Briary Bay (Carolina Bay)—*swamp* NC-3
Briary Branch—*stream* TN-4
Briary Ch—*church* KY-4
Briary Cove—*bay* MD-2
Briary Creek—*stream* KY-4
Briary Creek—*stream* TX-5
*Briary Point* MD-2
Briary Stream—*stream* NC-3
*Brice* NY-2
Brice—*locale* GA-3
Brice—*locale* MD-2
Brice—*locale* MI-6
**Brice**—*pop pl* AL-4
**Brice**—*pop pl* AR-4
**Brice**—*pop pl* IN-6
**Brice**—*pop pl* NC-3
**Brice**—*pop pl* OH-6
**Brice**—*pop pl* TX-5
Brice, Dr. Walter, House and Office—*hist pl* SC-3
Brice, Orlando, House—*hist pl* WI-6
Brice Branch—*stream* MS-4
Brice Branch—*stream* TN-4
Brice Bridge—*bridge* TN-4
Brice Brook—*stream* ME-1
**Briceburg**—*pop pl* CA-9
Brice Canyon—*valley* CO-8
Brice Cem—*cemetery* LA-4
Brice Cem—*cemetery* TN-4
Brice Creek—*stream* AL-4
Brice Creek—*stream* NC-3
Brice Creek—*stream* OR-9
Brice Creek—*stream* SC-3
Brice Creek Ch—*church* NC-3
Brice Creek Pocoson—*swamp* NC-3
Brice Creek Recreation Site—*park* NC-3
Brice Drain—*canal* MI-6
Bricefield Ch (historical)—*church* AL-4
Brice Fine Pass—*channel* FL-3
Brice Hill—*summit* SC-3
Brice Hill Country Club—*other* GA-3
Brice Hollow Run—*stream* MD-2
Brice House—*hist pl* MD-2
**Briceland**—*pop pl* CA-9
Briceland Ranch—*locale* CA-9
**Bricelyn**—*pop pl* MN-6
Bricelyn Cem—*cemetery* MN-6
Brice Point—*cape* MD-2
Brice Pond—*lake* FL-3
Brice Pond—*lake* GA-3
Brice Prairie—*flat* WI-6
Brice Prairie Cem—*cemetery* WI-6
*Brice Ridge* TN-4
Brice (RR name for Bryceland)—*other* LA-4
Brice Run—*stream* MD-2
Brice Sch (abandoned)—*school* MO-7
Brice Sch (abandoned)—*school* PA-2
Brice Sch (historical)—*school* AL-4
Brices Creek—*stream* KY-4
*Brices Cross Roads* MS-4
**Brices Crossroads**—*pop pl* NC-3
Brices Crossroads Natl Battlefield Cem—*cemetery* MS-4
Brices Cross Roads Natl Battlefield Site—*park* MS-4
Brice Spring Branch—*stream* TX-5
Brice Station—*locale* LA-4
Briceston Hollow—*valley* AL-4
**Briceton**—*pop pl* OH-6
*Briceville* GA-3
**Briceville**—*pop pl* TN-4
Briceville Elem Sch—*school* TN-4
Briceville Post Office—*building* TN-4
Brice Well—*well* NM-5
Brice Wightman Drain—*canal* MI-6
Brichetto Lateral—*canal* CA-9
Brichetto Tomb—*cemetery* CA-9
Brich Mtn—*summit* CA-9
Brichta Sch—*school* AZ-5
*Brick* AL-4
*Brick* NJ-2
**Brick**—*pop pl* AL-4
Brick—*post sta* NJ-2
Brick, Frank J., House—*hist pl* ID-8
Brick, Richard, House—*hist pl* NJ-2
Brick Acad (historical)—*school* MS-4
Brickbat Point—*cape* DE-2
Brickbat Ridge—*ridge* TN-4
Brick Block—*hist pl* MA-1
Brick Bound Swamp—*swamp* SC-3
Brick Cellar Landing—*locale* NC-3
Brick Cellar Landing (historical)—*locale* NC-3
Brick Cem—*cemetery* (3) IL-6
Brick Cem—*cemetery* MI-6
Brick Cem—*cemetery* MS-4
Brick Cem—*cemetery* MO-7
Brick Cem—*cemetery* OH-6
Brick Cem—*cemetery* WV-2
*Brick Ch* MS-4
Brick Ch—*church* (2) IL-6
Brick Ch—*church* (2) MS-4
Brick Ch—*church* NY-2
Brick Ch—*church* (2) NC-3
Brick Ch—*church* (2) OH-6
Brick Ch—*church* (2) SC-3
Brick Ch—*church* (2) TN-4
Brick Ch—*church* (4) VA-3
Brick Ch—*church* (2) WV-2
Brick Ch—*church* WI-6
Brick Chapel—*church* IA-7
Brick Chapel—*locale* NY-2
**Brick Chapel**—*pop pl* IN-6
Brick Chapel Cem—*cemetery* MI-6
Brick Ch (historical)—*church* MS-4
Brick Ch (historical)—*church* TN-4
Brick Chimney Canyon—*valley* CA-9
*Brick Church* PA-2
*Brickchurch* TN-4
Brick Church—*locale* NJ-2
Brick Church—*locale* WV-2
**Brickchurch**—*pop pl* PA-2
**Brick Church**—*pop pl* PA-2
**Brick Church**—*pop pl* TN-4
Brick Church, The—*church* VA-3
Brick Church Cem—*cemetery* IN-6
Brick Church Cem—*cemetery* MO-7
Brick Church Cem—*cemetery* NY-2
Brick Church Cem—*cemetery* (2) OH-6
Brick Church Cem—*cemetery* PA-2
Brick Church Cem—*cemetery* TN-4
Brick Church Cem—*cemetery* WI-6
Brick Church Complex—*hist pl* NY-2
Brick Church Corners—*hist pl* NY-2
Brick Church Mound and Village Site—*hist pl* TN-4
*Brick Church Post Office* TN-4
Brickchurch Post Office (historical)—*building* TN-4
Brick Church Sch—*school* NY-2
Brick Church Sch—*school* PA-2
Brick Church Sch—*school* (2) TN-4
Brick Church Sch—*school* VA-3
Brick Church Station—*hist pl* NJ-2
Brick Commercial Block—*hist pl* OH-6
Brick Creek—*stream* ID-8
Brick Creek—*stream* IN-6
Brick Creek—*stream* WA-9
Brick Creek—*stream* WI-6
**Brickdale**—*pop pl* SC-3
**Brickdale Estates (subdivision)**—*pop pl* AL-4
Brickel—*locale* TX-5
Brickel Creek—*stream* WA-9
Brickell—*post sta* FL-3
Brickell Ave Bridge—*bridge* FL-3
Brickell Christian Sch—*school* FL-3
**Brickell Hammock**—*pop pl* FL-3
Brickell Park—*park* FL-3
Brickell Plaza Mini Park—*park* FL-3
Brickell Point—*cape* FL-3
Brickell Ridge—*ridge* TN-4
Brickell Sch—*school* OH-6
*Brickenville* AL-4
**Bricker**—*pop pl* IA-7
Bricker, Lake—*lake* MI-6
Bricker Cem—*cemetery* KY-4
Bricker Cem—*cemetery* MO-7
Bricker Creek—*stream* OR-9
Bricker Crossroads—*locale* PA-2
Bricker Drain—*stream* IN-6
Bricker Lakes—*lake* NE-7
Bricker Mine—*mine* NV-8
Bricker Park—*park* TX-5
Bricker Run—*stream* PA-2
Bricker Sparrow Ditch—*canal* MT-8
**Brickersville**—*pop pl* PA-2
**Brickerville**—*pop pl* OR-9
**Brickerville**—*pop pl* PA-2
Brickerville Post Office (historical)—*building* PA-2
Brickett Falls—*falls* NH-1
Brickett Place—*hist pl* ME-1
Brickett Place—*locale* ME-1
Brickett Point—*cape* ME-1
Brickett Sch—*school* MA-1
Brickey Branch—*stream* TN-4
Brickey Cem—*cemetery* IL-6
Brickey Cem—*cemetery* TN-4
Brickey Cem—*cemetery* (2) VA-3
Brickey Hollow—*valley* AR-4
Brickeys—*locale* MO-7
**Brickeys**—*pop pl* AR-4
Brickey Sch—*school* TN-4
Brickeys Hollow—*valley* MO-7
Brickey Spring—*spring* VA-3
Brickhammer Coulee—*valley* MT-8
**Brickhaven**—*pop pl* NC-3
Brick Hill—*hist pl* MD-2
Brick Hill—*ridge* NH-1
Brickhill Bluff—*cliff* GA-3
*Brickhill Brook* RI-1
Brick Hill Creek—*stream* VA-3
Brick Hill Point—*cape* NC-3
Brickhill River—*channel* GA-3
Brick Hill Sch—*school* PA-2
Brick Hill Sch (historical)—*school* TN-4
Brick Hotel—*hist pl* DE-2
Brick House—*hist pl* NY-2
Brick House—*hist pl* VA-3
Brickhouse Bar—*bar* MD-2
Brickhouse Bend—*bend* TN-4
Brickhouse Branch—*stream* GA-3
Brickhouse Cem—*cemetery* AL-4
Brickhouse Cem—*cemetery* MS-4
**Brick House Corners**—*pop pl* NY-2
Brickhouse Cove—*bay* FL-3
Brick House Cove—*bay* NC-3
Brickhouse Crossroads—*locale* SC-3
Brickhouse Field—*airport* NC-3
Brickhouse Ford—*locale* AL-4
Brickhouse Gully—*valley* TX-5
Brickhouse Hollow—*valley* KY-4
Brick House Hollow—*valley* MO-7
Brick House Hollow—*valley* PA-2
Brickhouse Hollow—*valley* TN-4
Brick House Landing—*locale* MD-2
Brickhouse Landing—*locale* VA-3
Brickhouse Mountain Trail—*trail* MA-1
Brickhouse Neck—*cape* VA-3
Brick House on Shun Pike—*hist pl* KY-4
Brickhouse Point—*cape* NC-3
Brick House Pond—*lake* IN-6
Brick House Ruin—*hist pl* SC-3
Brickhouse Run—*stream* VA-3
Brickhouse Sch (historical)—*school* MS-4
Brick House Slough—*stream* MO-7
Brick Inn—*hist pl* KY-4
Brick Island—*island* ME-1
Brick Island—*island* MN-6
Brick Kiln Branch—*stream* NC-3
Brickkiln Branch—*stream* TX-5
Brick Kiln Branch—*stream* (2) VA-3
Brick Kiln Creek—*stream* VA-3
Brick Kiln Gulch—*valley* NM-5
Brickkiln Hollow—*valley* VA-3
Brick Lagoon—*lake* LA-4
Brick Lake—*lake* FL-3
Brick Landing—*locale* NC-3
**Brick Landing Plantation**—*pop pl* NC-3
Brickle Branch—*stream* WV-2
*Brickleg* MS-4
**Brickley**—*pop pl* SC-3
Brickley Hollow—*valley* MO-7
Brickley Place (historical)—*locale* AL-4
*Brickman Manor* IL-6
Brick Market—*hist pl* RI-1
Brick Memorial Park Cem—*cemetery* IN-6
**Brick Mill**—*pop pl* TN-4
Brick Mill Ch—*church* NC-3
Brick Mill Post Office (historical)—*building* TN-4
Brick Mill Sch (historical)—*school* TN-4
Brick Mine—*mine* AZ-5
*Brick Missionary Baptist Church* MS-4
Brick Monroe Sch—*school* MO-7
Brickpile Ranch—*locale* OR-9
Brickplant Hollow—*valley* TN-4
Brickplant Hollow Ch—*church* TN-4
Brick Row—*hist pl* CA-9
Brick Row Hist Dist—*hist pl* NY-2
Bricks—*locale* NC-3
**Bricksboro**—*pop pl* NJ-2
*Bricksburg* NJ-2
Brick Sch—*hist pl* ME-1
Brick Sch—*school* AL-4
Brick Sch—*school* CT-1
Brick Sch—*school* ID-8
Brick Sch—*school* (6) IL-6
Brick Sch—*school* KS-7
Brick Sch—*school* ME-1
Brick Sch—*school* MA-1
Brick Sch—*school* (4) MI-6
Brick Sch—*school* MO-7
Brick Sch—*school* (2) NE-7
Brick Sch—*school* PA-2
Brick Sch—*school* TN-4
Brick Sch—*school* (2) WI-6
Brick Sch (abandoned)—*school* (2) MO-7
Brick Sch (abandoned)—*school* PA-2
Brick Sch House—*hist pl* ME-1
Brick School—*locale* IL-6
Brick School (Abandoned)—*locale* MN-6
Brick School Cem—*cemetery* MA-1
**Brick School Corner**—*pop pl* NH-1
Brick Schoolhouse—*hist pl* RI-1
Brick Schoolhouse (abandoned)—*school* PA-2
**Brickson Park**—*pop pl* WI-6
Brickston—*locale* GA-3
*Brickstone* GA-3
*Brickstore* AL-4
Brick Store—*hist pl* NH-1
Brick Store—*locale* DE-2
Brick Store—*locale* GA-3
**Brick Store, The**—*pop pl* AL-4
*Brick Store Landing* DE-2
Brick Street Sch—*school* WI-6
Bricks Windmill—*locale* AZ-5
Brick Tank—*reservoir* AZ-5
Brick Tavern—*locale* NY-2
Brick Tavern—*locale* PA-2
Brickton—*locale* FL-3
Brickton—*locale* MN-6
**Brickton**—*pop pl* IL-6
**Brickton**—*pop pl* NC-3
Brickton Ch—*church* NC-3
*Bricktown* NJ-2
**Brick Town (local name Laurelton)**—*pop pl* NJ-2
Brick Township—*CDP* NJ-2
**Brick (Township of)**—*pop pl* NJ-2
Brick Union Ch—*church* KY-4
Brick Vernacular House No. 1—*hist pl* OH-6
Brick Vernacular House No. 2—*hist pl* OH-6
*Brickville* AL-4
*Brickville Church* AL-4
Brickville P.O. (historical)—*locale* AL-4
Brickwall Cem—*cemetery* KY-4
Brick Wall Landing—*locale* MD-2
Brickwood Canyon—*valley* AZ-5
Brickwoods Ranch (historical)—*locale* AZ-5
**Brickwood (subdivision)**—*pop pl* NC-3
*Brick Yard* AL-4
Brickyard—*locale* FL-3
**Brickyard**—*pop pl* AL-4
*Brickyard, The* PA-2
Brickyard Bayou—*stream* (2) MS-4
Brickyard Branch—*stream* AL-4
Brickyard Branch—*stream* (2) GA-3
Brickyard Branch—*stream* IL-6
Brickyard Branch—*stream* LA-4
Brickyard Branch—*stream* NC-3
Brickyard Branch—*stream* TN-4
Brickyard Branch—*stream* TX-5
Brickyard Branch—*stream* VA-3
*Brickyard Brook* NH-1
Brickyard Brook—*stream* (2) MA-1
Brickyard Brook—*stream* (4) NH-1
Brickyard Brook—*stream* NY-2
Brickyard Cem—*cemetery* AL-4
Brickyard Cem—*cemetery* FL-3
Brickyard Cem—*cemetery* MI-6
Brickyard Cem (Spring Hill Cemetery)—*cemetery* GA-3
Brickyard Cove—*bay* (2) ME-1
*Brick Yard Creek* SC-3
Brickyard Creek—*stream* AL-4
Brickyard Creek—*stream* AR-4
Brickyard Creek—*stream* CA-9
Brickyard Creek—*stream* FL-3
Brickyard Creek—*stream* GA-3
Brickyard Creek—*stream* MA-1
Brickyard Creek—*stream* MI-6
Brickyard Creek—*stream* MS-4
Brickyard Creek—*stream* MT-8
Brickyard Creek—*stream* NY-2
Brickyard Creek—*stream* (2) SC-3
Brickyard Creek—*stream* WA-9
Brickyard Creek—*stream* WI-6
Brickyard Cut Off—*gut* FL-3
Brickyard Falls—*falls* NY-2
Brickyard Gap—*gap* VA-3
Brickyard Hollow—*valley* TN-4
Brickyard Junction—*locale* AL-4
*Brick Yard Lake* WI-6
Brickyard Lake—*lake* AL-4
Brickyard Lake—*lake* GA-3
Brickyard Lake—*lake* LA-4
Brickyard Landing—*locale* (2) FL-3
Brickyard Mine (underground)—*mine* AL-4
Brickyard Mtn—*summit* TN-4
Brickyard Plaza (Shop Ctr)—*locale* FL-3
Brickyard Plaza Shop Ctr—*locale* UT-8
Brickyard Point—*cape* NY-2
Brickyard Point—*cape* SC-3
Brickyard Pond—*lake* CT-1
Brickyard Pond—*lake* FL-3
Brickyard Pond—*lake* NY-2
Brickyard Pond—*reservoir* RI-1
Brickyard Pond—*swamp* FL-3
Brickyard Pond—*swamp* TN-4
Brickyard Ridge—*ridge* TN-4
*Brickyard River* SC-3
Brickyard Sch—*school* AL-4
Brickyard Sch—*school* SC-3
Brickyard Sch—*school* WI-6
Brickyard Slough—*gut* FL-3
Brickyard Spring—*spring* NV-8
Brickyard Swamp—*swamp* SC-3
Bricky Branch—*stream* KY-4
Bridal Cave—*cave* MO-7
Bridal Chamber Mine—*mine* NM-5
Bridal House—*hist pl* TN-4
**Bridal Veil**—*pop pl* OR-9
Bridal Veil Basin—*basin* CO-8
Bridalveil Campground—*locale* CA-9
Bridal Veil Cove—*valley* TN-4
Bridal Veil Creek—*stream* CA-9
Bridalveil Creek—*stream* CA-9
Bridalveil Creek—*stream* CO-8
Bridal Veil Creek—*stream* CO-8
Bridal Veil Creek—*stream* OR-9
Bridal Veil Creek—*stream* TN-4
Bridal Veil Creek—*stream* (2) WA-9
Bridalveil Fall—*falls* CA-9
*Bridalveil Falls* CA-9
*Bridal Veil Falls* MT-8
Bridal Veil Falls—*falls* AK-9
Bridal Veil Falls—*falls* AR-4
Bridal Veil Falls—*falls* (3) CO-8
Bridal Veil Falls—*falls* ID-8
Bridalveil Falls—*falls* NH-1
Bridal Veil Falls—*falls* NY-2
Bridal Veil Falls—*falls* (2) NC-3
Bridal Veil Falls—*falls* OK-5
Bridal Veil Falls—*falls* OR-9
Bridal Veil Falls—*falls* SD-7
Bridal Veil Falls—*falls* TN-4
Bridal Veil Falls—*falls* UT-8
Bridal Veil Falls—*falls* (2) WA-9
Bridal Veil Falls—*falls* WY-8
Bridal Veil Falls Sky Ride—*other* UT-8
Bridal Veil Hollow—*valley* AR-4
Bridal Veil Park—*park* KS-7
Bridal Veil Spring—*spring* SD-7
Briddle Lake—*lake* MN-6
**Briddletown**—*pop pl* MD-2
**Bride**—*pop pl* TN-4
Bride Brook—*stream* CT-1
*Bridegroom Creek* MT-8
*Bridegroom Island* FM-9
Bridegroom Run—*stream* NJ-2
Bride Hill—*summit* NH-1
*Bride Island* FM-9
Bride Island—*island* ME-1
Bride Lake—*lake* CT-1
Bridenbecker Creek—*stream* NY-2
Bridenstine Ditch—*canal* OH-6
*Bride of the Mountain* AL-4
Bride Point—*cape* AK-9
Bride Post Office (historical)—*building* TN-4
*Brides* AL-4
**Bridesburg**—*pop pl* PA-2
Bridesburg Channel—*channel* PA-2
Bridesburg Sch—*school* PA-2
Bride's Hill—*hist pl* AL-4
**Brides Hill**—*pop pl* AL-4
Brides Hill Cem—*cemetery* AL-4
Brides Pocket—*valley* NM-5
Bridewell (State House of Corrections)—*building* MD-2
*Bridge* CA-9
Bridge—*bridge* NC-3
Bridge—*locale* UT-8
**Bridge**—*pop pl* ID-8
**Bridge**—*pop pl* OR-9
B Ridge—*ridge* ME-1
*Bridge, The* NJ-2
Bridge Acad—*hist pl* ME-1
Bridge Acad—*school* ME-1
Bridge Ave Ch of God—*church* AL-4
Bridge Ave Hist Dist—*hist pl* IA-7
Bridge Bay—*bay* WY-8
Bridge Bayou—*stream* (2) LA-4
Bridge Bay Resort—*locale* CA-9
Bridge between Guilford and Hamilton Townships—*hist pl* PA-2
Bridge between Madison and Mahoning Townships—*hist pl* PA-2
Bridge between Monroe and Penn Townships—*hist pl* PA-2
**Bridgeboro**—*pop pl* GA-3
**Bridgeboro**—*pop pl* NJ-2
Bridgeboro (CCD)—*cens area* GA-3
*Bridge Branch* DE-2
Bridge Branch—*stream* (6) AL-4
Bridge Branch—*stream* (2) FL-3
Bridge Branch—*stream* GA-3
Bridge Branch—*stream* (6) KY-4
Bridge Branch—*stream* LA-4
Bridge Branch—*stream* (4) MS-4
Bridge Branch—*stream* (4) NC-3
Bridge Branch—*stream* (2) TN-4
Bridge Branch—*stream* VA-3
Bridge Branch—*stream* (2) WV-2
Bridge Brook—*stream* IN-6
Bridge Brook—*stream* MA-1
Bridge Brook—*stream* NH-1
Bridge Brook—*stream* NY-2
Bridge Brook Pond—*lake* NY-2
Bridge Brook Swamp—*swamp* MA-1
**Bridgeburg**—*pop pl* PA-2
Bridgeburg Station—*locale* PA-2
Bridge Camp—*locale* CA-9
Bridge Camp—*locale* WA-9
*Bridge Campground* UT-8
Bridge Campground—*locale* CA-9
Bridge Campground—*locale* CO-8
Bridge Campground—*locale* ID-8
Bridge Campground—*locale* WY-8
*Bridge Canyon* AZ-5
*Bridge Canyon* UT-8
Bridge Canyon—*valley* AZ-5
Bridge Canyon—*valley* CA-9
Bridge Canyon—*valley* CO-8
Bridge Canyon—*valley* MT-8
Bridge Canyon—*valley* NV-8
Bridge Canyon—*valley* NM-5
Bridge Canyon—*valley* TX-5
Bridge Canyon—*valley* (5) UT-8
**Bridge Canyon Country Estates**—*pop pl* AZ-5
*Bridge Canyon Creek* UT-8
Bridge Canyon Rapids—*rapids* AZ-5
Bridge Cave—*cave* (2) AL-4
Bridge Cem—*cemetery* CT-1
Bridge Cem—*cemetery* IN-6
Bridge Cem—*cemetery* NY-2
Bridge Ch—*church* IN-6
Bridge Ch—*church* KY-4
Bridge Ch—*church* MO-7
Bridge Ch—*church* WV-2
Bridge Ch (historical)—*church* TN-4
**Bridge City**—*pop pl* LA-4
**Bridge City**—*pop pl* TX-5
Bridge City-Orangefield (CCD)—*cens area* TX-5
Bridge Corners—*locale* NY-2
Bridge Coulee—*valley* (5) MT-8
Bridge Court—*post sta* MN-6
Bridge Cove—*bay* (2) VA-3
*Bridge Creek* AL-4
*Bridge Creek* GA-3
*Bridge Creek* ID-8
*Bridge Creek* MT-8
*Bridge Creek* NC-3
*Bridge Creek* OR-9
*Bridge Creek* TN-4
*Bridge Creek* UT-8
*Bridge Creek* VA-3
*Bridge Creek* WY-8
Bridge Creek—*bay* (2) MD-2
Bridge Creek—*channel* MD-2
Bridge Creek—*stream* (5) AL-4
Bridge Creek—*stream* (3) AK-9
Bridge Creek—*stream* (7) AR-4
Bridge Creek—*stream* (9) CA-9
Bridge Creek—*stream* CO-8
Bridge Creek—*stream* (3) FL-3
Bridge Creek—*stream* (3) GA-3
Bridge Creek—*stream* (14) ID-8
Bridge Creek—*stream* (4) IN-6
Bridge Creek—*stream* IA-7
Bridge Creek—*stream* KS-7
Bridge Creek—*stream* (3) LA-4
Bridge Creek—*stream* (3) MD-2
Bridge Creek—*stream* MA-1
Bridge Creek—*stream* MN-6
Bridge Creek—*stream* (5) MS-4
Bridge Creek—*stream* (4) MO-7
Bridge Creek—*stream* (11) MT-8
Bridge Creek—*stream* NY-2
Bridge Creek—*stream* (3) NC-3
Bridge Creek—*stream* (2) OH-6
Bridge Creek—*stream* (2) OK-5
Bridge Creek—*stream* (22) OR-9
Bridge Creek—*stream* PA-2
Bridge Creek—*stream* (3) SC-3

Bridge Creek—*stream* (5) ... TN-4
Bridge Creek—*stream* (7) ... TX-5
Bridge Creek—*stream* (2) ... UT-8
Bridge Creek—*stream* (2) ... VA-3
Bridge Creek—*stream* (6) ... WA-9
Bridge Creek—*stream* (2) ... WV-2
Bridge Creek—*stream* ... WI-6
Bridge Creek—*stream* (4) ... WY-8
Bridge Creek Campground—*locale* (2) ... WA-9
Bridge Creek Canal—*canal* ... OR-9
Bridge creek Cave—*cave* ... TN-4
Bridge Creek Cem—*cemetery* ... MO-7
Bridge Creek Ch—*church* ... FL-3
Bridge Creek Ch—*church* ... GA-3
Bridge Creek Draw—*valley* ... OR-9
Bridge Creek Draw Rsvr—*reservoir* ... OR-9
Bridge Creek Fishing Club Dam—*dam* ... AL-4
Bridge Creek Flats—*flat* ... OR-9
**Bridge Creek (historical)**—*pop pl* (2) ... OR-9
Bridge Creek Lake—*reservoir* ... AL-4
Bridge Creek Meadow—*area* ... OR-9
Bridge Creek Meadow—*flat* ... OR-9
*Bridge Creek Meadows* ... OR-9
Bridge Creek Pond—*lake* ... SC-3
Bridge Creek Ranch—*locale* ... OR-9
*Bridge Creek Reservoir* ... OH-6
Bridge Creek Rsvr—*reservoir* ... MT-8
Bridge Creek Sch—*school* ... MO-7
Bridge Creek Sch—*school* ... OK-5
Bridge Creek Spring—*spring* ... MT-8
**Bridge Creek (Town of)**—*pop pl* ... WI-6
Bridge Creek Township (historical)—*civil* ... SD-7
Bridge Creek (Township of)—*fmr MCD* ... AR-4
Bridge Creek Waterhole—*reservoir* ... OR-9
Bridge Creek Well—*well* ... MT-8
**Bridgedale**—*pop pl* ... LA-4
Bridgedale Sch—*school* ... LA-4
Bridge Dam—*bridge* ... WY-8
Bridge Dam—*dam* ... AZ-5
Bridge Dam—*dam* ... TX-5
Bridge Draw—*valley* (3) ... WY-8
Bridge Flat—*flat* ... CA-9
Bridgeford Cem—*cemetery* ... OK-5
Bridgeford Ch—*church* ... GA-3
Bridge Fork—*stream* ... KY-4
Bridge Fork—*stream* ... WV-2
Bridge Fork Creek—*stream* ... SC-3
Bridgeforth Branch—*stream* ... AL-4
Bridgeforth Cem—*cemetery* ... AL-4
Bridgeforth Lake Dam—*dam* ... MS-4
Bridgeforth MS—*school* ... TN-4
Bridge Forty Creek—*stream* ... OR-9
Bridge Gap—*gap* ... GA-3
Bridge Gap—*gap* ... TX-5
Bridge Glacier—*glacier* ... AK-9
Bridge Gulch—*stream* ... OR-9
Bridge Gulch—*valley* (2) ... CA-9
Bridge Gulch—*valley* (2) ... CO-8
Bridge Gulch—*valley* (3) ... MT-8
Bridge Gulch—*valley* ... NV-8
Bridge Gulch—*valley* ... OR-9
Bridge Gut—*gut* ... VA-3
**Bridgehampton**—*pop pl* ... NY-2
Bridgehampton Ch—*church* ... MI-6
Bridgehampton Drain—*canal* ... MI-6
Bridgehampton Golf Club—*bridge* ... NY-2
*Bridgehampton River* ... MI-6
Bridgehampton (Township of)—*civ div* ... MI-6
*Bridge Haven* ... CA-9
Bridgehaven—*locale* ... CA-9
**Bridge Haven**—*pop pl* ... CA-9
Bridgehaven Lake—*reservoir* ... GA-3
Bridgehead—*locale* ... CA-9
**Bridgehead**—*pop pl* ... AL-4
Bridge Hill—*summit* ... ME-1
Bridge Hill—*summit* ... VA-3
Bridge Hill Ch—*church* ... TN-4
Bridge (historical)—*locale* ... KS-7
*Bridge Hollow* ... UT-8
Bridge Hollow—*valley* ... AR-4
Bridge Hollow—*valley* (2) ... KY-4
Bridge Hollow—*valley* ... MO-7
Bridge Hollow—*valley* ... MT-8
Bridge Hollow—*valley* ... OK-5
Bridge Hollow—*valley* (4) ... TN-4
Bridge Hollow—*valley* ... TX-5
Bridge Hollow—*valley* (3) ... UT-8
Bridge Hollow—*valley* (2) ... VA-3
Bridge House—*hist pl* ... GA-3
Bridge House—*locale* ... CA-9
Bridge in Albany Township—*hist pl* ... PA-2
Bridge in Athens Township—*hist pl* ... PA-2
Bridge in Bangor Borough—*hist pl* ... PA-2
Bridge in Brown Township—*hist pl* ... PA-2
Bridge in Buckingham Township—*hist pl* ... PA-2
Bridge in Cassandra Borough—*hist pl* ... PA-2
Bridge in Cherrytree Township—*hist pl* ... PA-2
Bridge in City of Wilkes-Barre—*hist pl* ... PA-2
Bridge in Clinton Township—*hist pl* ... PA-2
Bridge in Cumberland Township—*hist pl* ... PA-2
Bridge in Dreher Township—*hist pl* ... PA-2
Bridge in East Fallowfield Township—*hist pl* (2) ... PA-2
Bridge in Fishing Creek Township—*hist pl* ... PA-2
Bridge in Franconia Township—*hist pl* ... PA-2
Bridge in Franklin Township—*hist pl* ... PA-2
Bridge in French Creek Township—*hist pl* ... PA-2
Bridge in Gibson Borough—*hist pl* ... PA-2
Bridge in Greenwood Township—*hist pl* ... PA-2
Bridge in Hatfield Township—*hist pl* ... PA-2
Bridge in Heidelberg Township—*hist pl* ... PA-2
Bridge in Jefferson Borough—*hist pl* ... PA-2
Bridge in Jenner Township—*hist pl* ... PA-2
Bridge in Johnstown City—*hist pl* ... PA-2
Bridge in Lewis Township—*hist pl* ... PA-2
Bridge in Lykens Township No. 1—*hist pl* ... PA-2
Bridge in Lykens Township No. 2—*hist pl* ... PA-2
Bridge in Lynn Township—*hist pl* ... PA-2
Bridge in Metal Township—*hist pl* ... PA-2
Bridge in New Garden Township—*hist pl* ... PA-2
Bridge in Newport Borough—*hist pl* ... PA-2
Bridge in Nicholson Township—*hist pl* ... PA-2
Bridge in Oil Creek Township—*hist pl* ... PA-2
Bridge in Plunkett's Creek Township—*hist pl* ... PA-2
Bridge in Porter Township—*hist pl* ... PA-2
Bridge in Radnor Township No. 1—*hist pl* ... PA-2
Bridge in Radnor Township No. 2—*hist pl* ... PA-2
Bridge in Reed Township—*hist pl* ... PA-2
Bridge in Ridley Park Borough—*hist pl* ... PA-2
Bridge in Rockdale Township—*hist pl* ... PA-2
Bridge in Shaler Township—*hist pl* ... PA-2
Bridge in Snake Spring Township—*hist pl* ... PA-2
Bridge in Solebury Township—*hist pl* ... PA-2
Bridge in South Beaver Township—*hist pl* ... PA-2
Bridge in Tinicum Township—*hist pl* ... PA-2
Bridge in Tredyffrin Township—*hist pl* ... PA-2
Bridge in Upper Frederick Township—*hist pl* ... PA-2
Bridge in Upper Fredrick Township—*hist pl* ... PA-2
Bridge in Upper Merion Township—*hist pl* ... PA-2
Bridge in Washington Township—*hist pl* ... PA-2
Bridge in West Earl Township—*hist pl* ... PA-2
Bridge in West Fallowfield Township—*hist pl* ... PA-2
Bridge in West Mead Township—*hist pl* ... PA-2
Bridge in Westover Borough—*hist pl* ... PA-2
Bridge in West Wheatfield Township—*hist pl* ... PA-2
Bridge in Williams Township—*hist pl* ... PA-2
Bridge in Yardley Borough—*hist pl* ... PA-2
Bridge Island—*island* ... ID-8
Bridge Island—*island* ... IL-6
Bridge Junction—*locale* ... AR-4
Bridge Junction—*locale* ... UT-8
**Bridge Junction**—*pop pl* ... LA-4
**Bridge Junction**—*pop pl* ... WV-2
Bridge Lake—*lake* ... AK-9
Bridge Lake—*lake* ... GA-3
Bridge Lake—*lake* ... KY-4
Bridge Lake—*lake* (3) ... MI-6
Bridge Lake—*lake* ... MT-8
Bridge Lake—*lake* (2) ... WI-6
*Bridgelake Campground* ... UT-8
Bridge Lake Cem—*cemetery* ... MI-6
Bridgeland—*locale* ... UT-8
Bridge Landing (historical)—*locale* ... AL-4
**Bridgelane (Trailer Court)**—*pop pl* ... IL-6
Bridge L-158—*hist pl* ... NY-2
Bridgeman—*locale* ... MN-6
**Bridgeman**—*pop pl* ... MI-6
Bridgeman Cem—*cemetery* ... MN-6
*Bridgeman Creek* ... MT-8
Bridgeman Creek—*stream* ... VA-3
Bridgeman Ditch—*canal* ... OH-6
**Bridgeman Heights**—*pop pl* ... GA-3
Bridgeman Hill—*summit* ... VT-1
Bridgeman Hollow—*valley* ... VA-3
Bridgeman Mtn—*summit* ... KY-4
Bridgeman Pond—*lake* ... WA-9
Bridgemans Back Creek—*stream* ... VA-3
*Bridgemeadow Brook* ... MA-1
Bridge Meadow Brook—*stream* ... MA-1
Bridge Mill Farm—*hist pl* ... PA-2
Bridge Mill Power Plant—*hist pl* ... RI-1
Bridge Mtn—*summit* ... NV-8
Bridge Mtn—*summit* ... UT-8
Bridge Neck—*cape* ... VA-3
Bridge No. 1—*hist pl* ... WI-6
Bridge No. 10/Adelaide Bridge—*hist pl* ... CO-8
Bridge No. 2—*hist pl* ... WI-6
Bridge No. 3—*hist pl* ... WI-6
Bridge No. 4—*hist pl* ... WI-6
Bridge No. 4846 (1)—*hist pl* ... MN-6
Bridge No. 5—*hist pl* ... WI-6
Bridge No. 6—*hist pl* ... WI-6
Bridge of Lions—*bridge* ... FL-3
Bridge of Lions—*hist pl* ... FL-3
Bridge Of Tears—*arch* ... ID-8
Bridge of the Gods—*bridge* ... OR-9
Bridge Of The Moon—*locale* ... ID-8
Bridge over Arkansas River—*hist pl* ... CO-8
Bridge over Burro Canon—*hist pl* ... CO-8
Bridge over Fountain Creek—*hist pl* ... CO-8
Bridge Park—*park* ... AZ-5
Bridge Park—*park* ... WV-2
Bridge Pasture—*flat* ... KS-7
Bridge Plaza (Shop Ctr)—*locale* ... FL-3
*Bridge Point* ... PA-2
Bridge Point—*cape* ... AK-9
Bridge Point—*cape* ... UT-8
Bridge Point—*locale* ... PA-2
**Bridgepoint**—*pop pl* ... NJ-2
Bridge Point—*summit* ... ID-8
Bridgepoint Hist Dist—*hist pl* ... NJ-2
Bridgepoint Lake—*reservoir* ... NJ-2
Bridge Pond—*lake* ... NJ-2
*Bridgeport* ... AL-4
*Bridgeport* ... IL-6
*Bridgeport* (2) ... IN-6
*Bridgeport* ... NJ-2
*Bridgeport* ... PA-2
Bridgeport—*airport* ... NJ-2
Bridgeport—*CDP* ... MD-2
Bridgeport—*locale* ... CA-9
Bridgeport—*locale* ... CO-8
Bridgeport—*locale* ... IA-7
Bridgeport—*locale* ... MD-2
Bridgeport—*locale* ... MS-4
Bridgeport—*locale* ... OH-6
Bridgeport—*locale* (2) ... OR-9
Bridgeport—*locale* ... PA-2
Bridgeport—*locale* ... UT-8
Bridgeport—*locale* ... VA-3
**Bridgeport**—*pop pl* ... AL-4
**Bridgeport**—*pop pl* ... AZ-5
**Bridgeport**—*pop pl* (2) ... CA-9
**Bridgeport**—*pop pl* ... CT-1
**Bridgeport**—*pop pl* (2) ... FL-3
**Bridgeport**—*pop pl* ... IL-6
**Bridgeport**—*pop pl* (2) ... IN-6
**Bridgeport**—*pop pl* (2) ... IA-7
**Bridgeport**—*pop pl* ... KS-7
**Bridgeport**—*pop pl* ... KY-4
**Bridgeport**—*pop pl* ... MD-2
**Bridgeport**—*pop pl* ... MI-6
**Bridgeport**—*pop pl* ... MO-7
**Bridgeport**—*pop pl* ... NE-7
**Bridgeport**—*pop pl* ... NJ-2
**Bridgeport**—*pop pl* (2) ... NY-2
**Bridgeport**—*pop pl* (2) ... OH-6
**Bridgeport**—*pop pl* ... OK-5
**Bridgeport**—*pop pl* (6) ... PA-2
**Bridgeport**—*pop pl* ... RI-1
**Bridgeport**—*pop pl* ... TN-4
**Bridgeport**—*pop pl* ... TX-5
**Bridgeport**—*pop pl* ... WA-9
**Bridgeport**—*pop pl* ... WV-2
**Bridgeport**—*pop pl* ... WI-6
Bridgeport, Lake—*reservoir* ... TX-5
Bridgeport Baptist Ch—*church* ... AL-4
Bridgeport Baptist Ch—*church* ... IN-6
Bridgeport Bar—*bar* ... AL-4
Bridgeport Bar—*locale* ... WA-9
Bridgeport Beach—*beach* ... AL-4
Bridgeport Borough—*civil* ... PA-2
Bridgeport Canyon—*valley* ... CA-9
Bridgeport (CCD)—*cens area* ... AL-4
Bridgeport (CCD)—*cens area* ... TX-5
Bridgeport (CCD)—*cens area* ... WA-9
Bridgeport Cem—*cemetery* ... IA-7
Bridgeport Cem—*cemetery* ... OR-9
Bridgeport Cem—*cemetery* ... PA-2
Bridgeport Ch—*church* ... MO-7
Bridgeport Ch—*church* ... TN-4
Bridgeport Ch (historical)—*church* ... TN-4
Bridgeport City Hall—*hist pl* ... CT-1
**Bridgeport Colony (Indian Reservation)**—*pop pl* ... CA-9
Bridgeport Community Park—*park* ... AL-4
Bridgeport Country Club—*other* ... MI-6
Bridgeport Covered Bridge—*hist pl* ... CA-9
Bridgeport Division—*civil* ... AL-4
Bridgeport Downtown North Hist Dist—*hist pl* ... CT-1
Bridgeport Downtown South Hist Dist—*hist pl* ... CT-1
Bridgeport Elem Sch—*school* ... AL-4
Bridgeport Elem Sch—*school* ... TN-4
Bridgeport Ferry—*bridge* ... NY-2
Bridgeport Ferry—*locale* ... AL-4
Bridgeport Gas Field—*oilfield* ... TX-5
Bridgeport Grange—*locale* ... WA-9
Bridgeport Harbor—*harbor* ... CT-1
Bridgeport Hill—*uninc pl* ... WV-2
Bridgeport (historical)—*locale* ... MS-4
Bridgeport Hosp—*hospital* ... CT-1
Bridgeport HS—*school* ... AL-4
Bridgeport HS—*school* ... MI-6
*Bridgeport Island* ... AL-4
Bridgeport Landing—*locale* ... AL-4
Bridgeport Landing (Site)—*locale* ... CA-9
Bridgeport Missionary Baptist Ch—*church* ... KS-7
Bridgeport Nazarene Ch—*church* ... IN-6
Bridgeport Point—*cliff* ... WA-9
Bridgeport Post Office (historical)—*building* ... TN-4
Bridgeport Public Use Area—*park* ... AL-4
Bridgeport Ranger Station—*locale* ... CA-9
Bridgeport Rsvr—*reservoir* ... PA-2
Bridgeport Sch—*school* ... CA-9
Bridgeport Sch—*school* ... KS-7
Bridgeport Sch—*school* ... MI-6
Bridgeport Sch (historical)—*school* ... MS-4
Bridgeport State Park—*park* ... WA-9
Bridgeport State Rec Area—*park* ... NE-7
*Bridgeport-subdivision* ... PA-2
**Bridgeport (subdivision)**—*pop pl* (2) ... AZ-5
Bridgeport (Town of)—*civ div* ... CT-1
**Bridgeport (Town of)**—*pop pl* ... WI-6
Bridgeport Township—*civil* ... MO-7
**Bridgeport (Township of)**—*pop pl* ... IL-6
**Bridgeport (Township of)**—*pop pl* ... MI-6
Bridgeport United Methodist Ch—*church* ... AL-4
Bridgeport Valley—*valley* ... CA-9
Bridgeport Valley—*valley* ... OR-9
Bridge Prairie—*flat* ... OR-9
Bridger—*locale* ... WY-8
**Bridger**—*pop pl* ... MT-8
**Bridger**—*pop pl* ... SD-7
Bridger—*post sta* ... MT-8
Bridge Ranch—*locale* (2) ... NV-8
Bridger Antelope Trap—*hist pl* ... WY-8
Bridger Arms Apartments—*hist pl* ... MT-8
Bridger Basin—*basin* ... WY-8
Bridger Bay—*bay* ... UT-8
Bridger Bayou—*stream* ... LA-4
Bridger Butte—*summit* (2) ... WY-8
Bridger Butte Canal—*canal* ... WY-8
Bridger Campground—*locale* ... UT-8
Bridger Canyon—*valley* (2) ... UT-8
Bridger Cem—*cemetery* ... IL-6
Bridger Cem—*cemetery* ... MT-8
Bridger Coal Company House—*hist pl* ... MT-8
Bridger Creek—*stream* ... AR-4
Bridger Creek—*stream* ... CA-9
Bridger Creek—*stream* (3) ... MT-8
Bridger Creek—*stream* ... ND-7
Bridger Creek—*stream* ... SD-7
Bridger Creek—*stream* ... UT-8
Bridger Creek—*stream* (3) ... WY-8
Bridger Ditch—*canal* ... MT-8
Bridger Ditch—*canal* ... UT-8
Bridger Drain—*stream* ... MI-6
Bridger Flat—*flat* ... SD-7
Bridger Fork—*stream* ... WY-8
Bridger Gap—*gap* ... WY-8
Bridger Hill—*summit* ... WY-8
Bridger (historical)—*locale* ... SD-7
Bridger HS—*school* ... MO-7
Bridger Immigrant Road-Dry Creek Crossing—*hist pl* ... WY-8
Bridger Immigrant Road-Waltman Crossing—*hist pl* ... WY-8
Bridger Jack—*locale* ... UT-8
Bridger Jack Mesa—*summit* (2) ... UT-8
Bridger Jack Mesa Outstanding Natural Area—*area* ... UT-8
Bridger JHS—*school* ... NV-8
Bridger Lake—*lake* ... UT-8
Bridger Lake—*lake* ... WY-8
Bridger Lake Campground—*locale* ... UT-8
*Bridger Lake Forest Service Station* ... UT-8
Bridger Lake Guard Station—*locale* ... UT-8
Bridger Lake Oil Field—*bridge* ... UT-8
Bridger Lakes—*lake* ... WY-8
Bridgerland Shop Ctr—*locale* ... UT-8
Bridger Millpond—*reservoir* ... NC-3
Bridger Mine—*mine* ... WY-8
Bridger Mountain—*ridge* ... WV-2
Bridger Natl For—*forest* ... WY-8
Bridge Road Cem—*cemetery* ... MA-1
Bridge Rock Sch—*school* ... KY-4
Bridger Opera House—*hist pl* ... MT-8
Bridger Pass—*gap* ... WY-8
Bridger Peak—*summit* ... MT-8
Bridger Peak—*summit* ... WY-8
Bridger Range—*range* ... MT-8
Bridgers Ave Sch—*school* ... FL-3
Bridger Sch—*school* ... NC-3
Bridgers Creek—*stream* (2) ... NC-3
Bridgers Knoll—*summit* ... AZ-5
Bridger's Pass—*hist pl* ... WY-8
Bridger Spring—*spring* ... ID-8
Bridgersville—*locale* ... NC-3
Bridge Run—*stream* (3) ... WV-2
Bridger Valley—*cens area* ... WY-8
Bridges—*locale* ... FL-3
Bridges—*locale* ... VA-3
**Bridges**—*pop pl* ... MS-4
**Bridges**—*pop pl* ... OH-6
Bridges, C. A., Tobacco Warehouse—*hist pl* ... KY-4
Bridges, J.J., House—*hist pl* ... FL-3
Bridges, J. L., Home Place—*hist pl* ... GA-3
Bridges, The—*locale* ... NY-2
Bridge Saint Sch—*school* ... CA-9
Bridge Saint Sch—*school* ... ME-1
Bridges Bluff—*cliff* ... AR-4
Bridges Branch—*stream* ... LA-4
Bridges Branch—*stream* ... MS-4
Bridges Branch—*stream* ... MO-7
Bridges Branch—*stream* ... NC-3
Bridges Branch—*stream* ... TX-5
Bridges Camp Gap—*gap* ... NC-3
Bridges Cem—*cemetery* ... AL-4
Bridges Cem—*cemetery* (2) ... IL-6
Bridges Cem—*cemetery* (2) ... IN-6
Bridges Cem—*cemetery* ... KY-4
Bridges Cem—*cemetery* ... LA-4
Bridges Cem—*cemetery* ... ME-1
Bridges Cem—*cemetery* (3) ... MS-4
Bridges Cem—*cemetery* (2) ... TN-4
Bridges Cem—*cemetery* (2) ... TX-5
Bridge Sch—*school* ... IL-6
Bridge Sch—*school* ... KY-4
Bridge Sch—*school* ... MA-1
Bridge Sch—*school* ... MI-6
Bridge Sch—*school* ... MT-8
Bridge Sch—*school* ... NE-7
Bridge Sch—*school* ... NY-2
Bridge Sch—*school* ... PA-2
Bridge Sch (abandoned)—*school* ... MO-7
Bridge Sch (abandoned)—*school* ... PA-2
Bridges Chapel—*church* ... MS-4
Bridges Chapel—*church* (2) ... TN-4
Bridges Chapel—*locale* ... TX-5
Bridges Chapel Cem—*cemetery* ... TN-4
Bridge Sch (historical)—*school* ... MO-7
Bridge School, The—*locale* ... OR-9
*Bridges Creek* ... NC-3
Bridges Creek—*stream* (2) ... CA-9
Bridges Creek—*stream* ... MS-4
Bridges Creek—*stream* ... MO-7
Bridges Creek—*stream* ... OR-9
Bridges Creek—*stream* ... VA-3
Bridges Creek Access—*locale* ... MO-7
Bridges Creek Landing—*locale* ... VA-3
**Bridges Crossroad**—*pop pl* ... GA-3
Bridges Dam—*dam* ... AL-4
Bridge Set Creek—*stream* ... OK-5
Bridges Gap—*gap* ... TN-4
Bridges Grove Ch—*church* ... NC-3
Bridge Shaft—*mine* ... PA-2
Bridges Hall—*building* ... NC-3
Bridges (historical)—*locale* ... MS-4
Bridges Hollow—*valley* (2) ... MO-7
Bridges Hollow—*valley* (3) ... TN-4
Bridge Shop Ctr—*locale* ... MA-1
Bridges Island—*island* ... GA-3
Bridges Island—*island* ... MN-6
Bridges-Johnson House—*hist pl* ... TX-5
Bridges Knob—*summit* ... IL-6
*Bridges Lake* ... AL-4
*Bridges Lake* ... NC-3
*Bridges Lake* ... WA-9
Bridges Lake—*bay* ... NC-3
Bridges Lake—*lake* ... WA-9
Bridges Landing (historical)—*locale* ... MS-4
Bridge Slough—*gut* ... TN-4
Bridges- Miller Cem—*cemetery* ... TN-4
Bridges Mill (historical)—*locale* ... MS-4
Bridges Mine—*mine* ... CO-8
Bridges Mtn—*summit* ... NC-3
*Bridges Pond* ... NJ-2
Bridge Spring—*spring* ... NV-8
Bridge Spring—*spring* ... NM-5
Bridge Spring—*spring* ... OR-9
Bridge Spring—*spring* ... TX-5
Bridge Square Hist Dist—*hist pl* ... NY-2
*Bridges Run* ... PA-2
Bridges Sch (historical)—*school* ... MO-7
Bridges Spring—*spring* ... AL-4
Bridges Spring—*spring* ... GA-3
Bridges Sticks Creek—*stream* ... NJ-2
Bridges Swamp—*swamp* ... ME-1
**Bridges Switch**—*pop pl* ... CO-8
Bridges Township—*civil* ... MO-7
Bridge Street—*uninc pl* ... KY-4
Bridge Street Bridge—*bridge* ... NJ-2
Bridge Street-Broad Street Hist Dist—*hist pl* ... MI-6
Bridge Street Cem—*cemetery* (2) ... MA-1
Bridge Street Hist Dist—*hist pl* ... NM-5
Bridge Street Hist Dist—*hist pl* ... NY-2
Bridge Street Sch—*school* ... CT-1
Bridge Street Sch—*school* ... MA-1
Bridge Street Sch—*school* ... VA-3
Bridge (Suspension Bridge)—*uninc pl* ... NY-2
Bridges Well—*well* ... NV-8
Bridge Tank—*reservoir* (5) ... AZ-5
Bridget Cem—*cemetery* ... TN-4
Bridget Cove—*bay* ... AK-9
Bridget Creek—*stream* ... AK-9
Bridge Thorofare—*channel* ... MD-2
Bridge Timber Mtn—*summit* ... CO-8
*Bridgeton* ... NJ-2
Bridgeton—*locale* ... PA-2
**Bridgeton**—*pop pl* ... IN-6
**Bridgeton**—*pop pl* ... MI-6
**Bridgeton**—*pop pl* (2) ... MO-7
**Bridgeton**—*pop pl* ... NJ-2
**Bridgeton**—*pop pl* ... NC-3
**Bridgeton**—*pop pl* ... OR-9
**Bridgeton**—*pop pl* ... RI-1
Bridgeton Bridge—*hist pl* ... IN-6
Bridgeton Cem—*cemetery* ... NC-3
Bridgeton City Park—*park* ... NJ-2
Bridgeton Elementary and JHS—*school* ... IN-6
Bridgeton Hist Dist—*hist pl* ... NJ-2
Bridgeton (historical)—*locale* ... IA-7
Bridgeton Hospital—*airport* ... NJ-2
Bridgeton Junction—*locale* ... NJ-2
**Bridgeton (sta.)**—*pop pl* ... MO-7
**Bridgeton Terrace**—*pop pl* ... MO-7
Bridgeton Township Elem Sch—*school* ... PA-2
**Bridgeton (Township of)**—*pop pl* ... MI-6
**Bridgeton (Township of)**—*pop pl* ... PA-2
*Bridge Town* ... DE-2
*Bridgetown* ... NJ-2
*Bridgetown* ... PA-2
Bridgetown—*locale* ... GA-3
Bridgetown—*locale* (2) ... PA-2
Bridgetown—*locale* ... VA-3
**Bridgetown**—*pop pl* ... MD-2
**Bridgetown**—*pop pl* ... OH-6
**Bridgetown**—*pop pl* ... PA-2
**Bridgetown**—*pop pl* ... RI-1
**Bridgetown**—*pop pl* ... VA-3
Bridgetown Ch—*church* ... MD-2
Bridge Trail—*trail* ... PA-2
Bridge Valley—*locale* ... PA-2
Bridge Valley Bridge—*hist pl* ... PA-2
Bridge Valley Post Office (historical)—*building* ... PA-2
Bridge View—*locale* (2) ... UT-8
**Bridgeview**—*pop pl* ... IL-6
**Bridgeview**—*pop pl* ... OR-9
Bridge View Cem—*cemetery* ... PA-2
Bridgeview Ch—*church* ... AL-4
Bridgeview Creek—*stream* ... ID-8
Bridge View Sch—*school* ... IL-6
**Bridgeview (subdivision)**—*pop pl* ... AL-4
*Bridgeville* ... AL-4
Bridgeville—*locale* ... AL-4
Bridgeville—*locale* ... KY-4
**Bridgeville**—*pop pl* ... CA-9
**Bridgeville**—*pop pl* ... DE-2
**Bridgeville**—*pop pl* (2) ... MI-6
**Bridgeville**—*pop pl* ... NJ-2
**Bridgeville**—*pop pl* ... NY-2
**Bridgeville**—*pop pl* ... OH-6
**Bridgeville**—*pop pl* (2) ... PA-2
*Bridgeville Boro* ... PA-2
Bridgeville Borough—*civil* ... PA-2
Bridgeville Branch—*stream* ... DE-2
Bridgeville Ch—*church* ... PA-2
Bridgeville-Greenwood (CCD)—*cens area* ... DE-2
**Bridgeville Manor**—*pop pl* ... DE-2
**Bridgeville North (subdivision)**—*pop pl* ... DE-2
Bridgeville Station—*locale* ... NJ-2
Bridge Washer Tank—*reservoir* ... AZ-5
*Bridgewater* ... NJ-2
Bridgewater—*locale* ... IA-7
Bridgewater—*locale* ... OH-6
Bridgewater—*locale* ... PA-2
**Bridgewater**—*pop pl* ... CT-1
**Bridgewater**—*pop pl* ... IA-7
**Bridgewater**—*pop pl* ... ME-1
**Bridgewater**—*pop pl* ... MA-1
**Bridgewater**—*pop pl* ... MI-6
**Bridgewater**—*pop pl* ... MN-6
**Bridgewater**—*pop pl* ... NH-1
**Bridgewater**—*pop pl* ... NJ-2
**Bridgewater**—*pop pl* ... NY-2
**Bridgewater**—*pop pl* ... NC-3
**Bridgewater**—*pop pl* (2) ... PA-2
**Bridgewater**—*pop pl* ... SD-7
**Bridgewater**—*pop pl* ... VT-1
**Bridgewater**—*pop pl* ... VA-3
*Bridgewater, Town of* ... MA-1
Bridgewater Air Park—*airport* ... VA-3
Bridgewater Borough—*civil* ... PA-2
Bridgewater Cave—*cave* ... TN-4
Bridgewater Cem—*cemetery* ... KY-4
Bridgewater Cem—*cemetery* ... NY-2
Bridgewater (census name for Bridgewater Center)—*CDP* ... MA-1
**Bridgewater Center**—*pop pl* ... OH-6
**Bridgewater Center**—*pop pl* ... VT-1
Bridgewater Center Cem—*cemetery* ... MI-6
Bridgewater Center (census name Bridgewater)—*other* ... MA-1
*Bridgewater Centre* ... MA-1
Bridgewater Ch—*church* ... NC-3
Bridgewater Ch—*church* ... OH-6
Bridgewater Coll—*school* ... VA-3
**Bridgewater Corner**—*pop pl* ... ME-1
**Bridgewater Corners**—*pop pl* ... VT-1
**Bridgewater (corp and RR name for West Bridgewater)**—*pop pl* ... PA-2
Bridgewater Creek—*stream* ... OH-6
Bridgewater Dam—*dam* ... NC-3
**Bridgewater Farms**—*pop pl* ... PA-2
Bridgewater Flats—*flat* ... NY-2
Bridgewater Hist Dist—*hist pl* ... VA-3
Bridgewater (historical P.O.)—*locale* ... MA-1
Bridge Waterhold—*reservoir* ... OR-9
Bridgewater Hollow—*valley* ... IL-6
Bridgewater Hollow—*valley* ... VT-1
Bridgewater Mtn—*summit* ... NH-1
Bridgewater Post Office (historical)—*building* ... PA-2
Bridgewater Raynham Regional HS—*school* ... MA-1
*Bridgewater Reservoir* ... NC-3
Bridgewater Sch—*school* ... PA-2
Bridgewater Sch (abandoned)—*school* ... MO-7
*Bridgewaters Lake* ... AL-4
Bridgewaters Landing—*locale* ... TN-4
Bridgewater Station—*building* ... PA-2
**Bridgewater (Town of)**—*pop pl* ... CT-1
**Bridgewater (Town of)**—*pop pl* ... ME-1
**Bridgewater (Town of)**—*pop pl* ... MA-1
**Bridgewater (Town of)**—*pop pl* ... NH-1
**Bridgewater (Town of)**—*pop pl* ... NY-2
**Bridgewater (Town of)**—*pop pl* ... VT-1
Bridgewater Township—*fmr MCD* ... IA-7
**Bridgewater Township**—*pop pl* ... SD-7
**Bridgewater (Township of)**—*pop pl* ... MI-6
**Bridgewater (Township of)**—*pop pl* ... MN-6
**Bridgewater (Township of)**—*pop pl* ... NJ-2
**Bridgewater (Township of)**—*pop pl* ... OH-6
**Bridgewater (Township of)**—*pop pl* ... PA-2
Bridgewater Woolen Mill—*hist pl* ... VT-1
**Bridgeway**—*pop pl* ... WV-2
*Bridgeway Addition* ... IL-6
**Bridgeway Addition**—*pop pl* ... IL-6
Bridgeway Lake—*lake* ... MI-6
Bridge Well—*well* ... NV-8
Bridge Well—*well* ... WY-8
Bridge Windmill—*locale* ... TX-5
Bridgewood Golf Course—*bridge* ... GA-3
Bridgewood Lake—*reservoir* ... NJ-2
**Bridgewood Manor Condominium**—*pop pl* ... UT-8
Bridge 166—*bridge* ... LA-4
Bridge 184—*bridge* ... LA-4
Bridge 900—*bridge* ... WI-6
Bridgforth Cem—*cemetery* ... TN-4
Bridgham-Arch-Wilson Streets Hist Dist—*hist pl* ... RI-1
Bridgham Farm—*hist pl* ... RI-1
Bridgham Swamp—*swamp* ... ME-1
Bridghman Ranch—*locale* ... CA-9
Bridgie Bayou—*gut* ... LA-4
**Bridgman**—*pop pl* ... MI-6
Bridgman, Percy, House—*hist pl* ... MA-1
Bridgman Creek—*stream* ... MT-8
**Bridgton**—*pop pl* ... ME-1
Bridgton Compact (census name Bridgton)—*other* ... ME-1
**Bridgton (Town of)**—*pop pl* ... ME-1
*Bridie Creek* ... TN-4
**Bridle Acres Subdivision**—*pop pl* ... UT-8
Bridlebit Camp—*locale* ... TX-5
Bridle Bit Hill—*summit* ... WY-8
Bridle Bit Ranch—*locale* ... CO-8
Bridle Creek—*locale* ... VA-3
Bridle Creek—*stream* ... AZ-5
Bridle Creek—*stream* ... MT-8
Bridle Creek—*stream* ... NC-3
Bridle Creek—*stream* ... VA-3
**Bridle Creek (subdivision)**—*pop pl* ... NC-3
**Bridlemile**—*pop pl* ... OR-9
Bridlemile Sch—*school* ... OR-9
Bridle Path Acres—*locale* ... FL-3
Bridle Ridge—*ridge* ... NC-3
**Bridleshire Farms**—*pop pl* ... DE-2
**Bridle Trail**—*pop pl* ... WA-9
Bridle Trail—*trail* ... AZ-5
Bridle Trail—*trail* ... CA-9
Bridle Trail State Park—*park* ... WA-9
**Bridlewalk Subdivision**—*pop pl* ... UT-8
Bridle Well—*well* ... UT-8
**Bridlewood**—*pop pl* ... MD-2
**Bridlewood Forest Estates**—*pop pl* ... AL-4
**Bridlewood (subdivision)**—*pop pl* ... AL-4
**Bridlewood (subdivision)**—*pop pl* ... MS-4
**Bridlewood Subdivision**—*pop pl* ... UT-8
*Bridlington* ... NJ-2
*Bridlington Towne* ... NJ-2
**Bridport**—*pop pl* ... VT-1
**Bridport (Town of)**—*pop pl* ... VT-1
**Bridwell Heights**—*pop pl* ... TN-4
Bridwell Park—*park* ... TX-5
Bridwell Ranch—*locale* (3) ... TX-5
Bridy Creek—*stream* ... TN-4
Briedenbaugh Lake—*reservoir* ... IN-6
Briedenbaugh Lake Dam—*dam* ... IN-6
Briedwell—*locale* ... OR-9
Briedwell Sch—*hist pl* ... OR-9
Brief—*locale* ... WA-9
**Brief**—*pop pl* ... NC-3
Brieger, R. J., House—*hist pl* ... TX-5
Briel Ave Baptist Ch—*church* ... MS-4
**Brielle**—*pop pl* ... NJ-2
Brielmaier House—*hist pl* ... MS-4
Briem Creek—*stream* ... OR-9
Brien—*locale* ... KY-4
Brien Ranch—*locale* ... ND-7
Brien Run—*stream* ... MD-2
**Briensburg**—*pop pl* ... KY-4
**Brier**—*pop pl* ... MA-1
**Brier**—*pop pl* ... WA-9
Brier, Andrew, House—*hist pl* ... IN-6
*Brier Arm* ... IN-6
Brier Bay—*swamp* ... GA-3
Brier Bay—*swamp* ... NC-3
Brier Bend—*bend* ... TX-5
Brier Bend Cem—*cemetery* ... TX-5
*Brier Branch* ... NC-3
Brier Branch—*stream* ... AR-4
Brier Branch—*stream* (3) ... KY-4
Brier Branch—*stream* (3) ... SC-3
Brier Branch—*stream* ... TN-4
Brier Branch—*stream* (5) ... TX-5
Brier Branch—*stream* (3) ... WV-2
Brier Canyon—*valley* ... ID-8
Brier Cem—*cemetery* ... IN-6
Briercliff Sch—*school* ... WA-9
Brier Cove—*valley* ... NC-3
Brier Cove—*valley* ... VA-3
*Brier Creek* ... AR-4
*Brier Creek* ... IN-6
*Brier Creek* ... MT-8
*Brier Creek* ... OK-5
*Brier Creek* ... PA-2
*Brier Creek* ... TX-5
**Brier Creek**—*pop pl* ... KY-4
Brier Creek—*stream* ... AL-4
Brier Creek—*stream* (6) ... AR-4
Brier Creek—*stream* ... CO-8
Brier Creek—*stream* ... FL-3
Brier Creek—*stream* (3) ... GA-3
Brier Creek—*stream* ... ID-8
Brier Creek—*stream* (2) ... IL-6
Brier Creek—*stream* ... IN-6
Brier Creek—*stream* (4) ... KY-4
Brier Creek—*stream* ... NY-2
Brier Creek—*stream* (6) ... NC-3
Brier Creek—*stream* (6) ... OK-5
Brier Creek—*stream* (2) ... SC-3
Brier Creek—*stream* (3) ... TN-4
Brier Creek—*stream* (4) ... TX-5
Brier Creek—*stream* ... VA-3
Brier Creek—*stream* (2) ... WV-2
Brier Creek Bald—*summit* ... GA-3
Brier Creek Cem—*cemetery* ... TX-5
Brier Creek Ch—*church* ... NC-3
Brier Creek Ch—*church* ... TN-4
Brier Creek Country Club—*other* ... GA-3
Brier Creek Ford—*locale* ... TN-4
**Brier Creek (historical)**—*pop pl* ... NC-3
Brier Creek Landing—*locale* ... GA-3
Brier Creek Mountains—*ridge* ... AR-4
Brier Creek Sch—*school* ... KY-4
*Brier Creek School* ... TN-4

Brier Creek Tabernacle—church WV-2
**Briercrest**—pop pl WA-9
Brier Ditch IN-6
Brier Ditch—stream MD-2
Brier Ditch Arm IN-6
Brier Drain—canal MI-6
**Brierfield**—pop pl AL-4
Brierfield Branch—stream KY-4
Brierfield Branch—stream VA-3
Brierfield Cem—cemetery AL-4
Brierfield Ch—church AL-4
Brierfield Furnace—hist pl AL-4
Brierfield Gap—gap KY-4
Brierfield Gap—gap VA-3
Brierfield (historical)—locale MS-4
Brierfield Sch (historical)—school TN-4
Brier Fork—stream (2) KY-4
Brier Fork Ch—church (2) AL-4
Brier Fork Flint River—stream AL-4
Brier Fork Flint River—stream TN-4
Brier Fork Sch (historical)—school AL-4
Brier Gap—gap TN-4
**Briergate**—pop pl IL-6
Brier Hill OH-6
Brier Hill—hist pl PA-2
Brier Hill—locale TN-4
**Brier Hill**—pop pl NY-2
**Brier Hill**—pop pl OH-6
**Brier Hill**—pop pl PA-2
Brier Hill—summit MA-1
Brier Hill—summit MI-6
Brier Hill—summit NH-1
Brier Hill Cem—cemetery OH-6
Brier Hill Church MS-4
Brier Hill Creek MI-6
Brier Hill Sch—school PA-2
Brier Hill Station—locale NY-2
Brier Hollow—valley TN-4
Brier Hollow Gap—gap KY-4
Brier Knob—summit (2) NC-3
Brier Knob—summit PA-2
Brier Knob—summit TN-4
Brier Knob—summit WV-2
Brierley Park—park NY-2
Brier Lick Branch—stream AR-4
Brier Lick Branch—stream TN-4
Brier Lick Gap—gap NC-3
Brier Lick Gap—gap TN-4
Brier Lick Knob—summit NC-3
Brier Lick Knob—summit TN-4
Brierly Pond—reservoir MA-1
Brierly Pond Dam—dam MA-1
Brier Mtn—summit (2) PA-2
Brier Mtn—summit (2) VA-3
Brier Neck—cliff MA-1
Brier Neck—uninc pl MA-1
Brier Patch—flat NC-3
Brier Patch Bayou—stream LA-4
Brier Patch Ch—church GA-3
Brier Patch Island—flat LA-4
Brierpatch Lake—lake (2) GA-3
Brier Patch Mtn—summit VA-3
Brierpatch Mtn—summit WV-2
Brier Patch Sch—school CA-9
Brier Point—cape (2) MD-2
Brier Point Post Office (historical)—building TN-4
Brier Pond—reservoir OR-9
Brier Ridge—ridge (2) KY-4
Brier Ridge—ridge MD-2
Brier Ridge—ridge (2) NC-3
Brier Ridge—ridge (2) OH-6
Brier Ridge—ridge PA-2
Brier Ridge—ridge (2) TN-4
Brier Ridge—ridge VA-3
Brier Ridge Ch—church OH-6
Brier Run—stream VA-3
Brier Run—stream WV-2
Brier Sch—school CA-9
Brier Sch—school WA-9
Briers Creek MS-4
Briers Creek NC-3
Briers (historical)—locale MS-4
Briers Landing MS-4
Brier Spring—spring NV-8
Brierton Cem—cemetery TX-5
**Briertown**—pop pl NC-3
Briertown Creek NC-3
Briertown Mtn—summit NC-3
Brierwood Country Club—other IL-6
**Brierwood Hills**—pop pl IN-6
Brierwood Plaza Village (Shop Ctr)—locale FL-3
Briery—locale VA-3
Briery Bay—swamp NC-3
Briery Bay—swamp SC-3
Briery Branch—locale VA-3
Briery Branch—stream KY-4
Briery Branch—stream (2) VA-3
Briery Branch Dam—dam VA-3
Briery Branch Gap—gap VA-3
Briery Branch Gap—gap WV-2
Briery Branch Overlook—locale VA-3
Briery Ch—church VA-3
Briery Church—hist pl VA-3
Briery Country Club—other VA-3
Briery Cove MD-2
Briery Creek—stream AR-4
Briery Creek—stream KY-4
Briery Creek—stream MT-8
Briery Creek—stream (2) VA-3
Briery Creek—stream WV-2
Briery Draft—valley VA-3
Briery Fork—stream KY-4
Briery Fork Creek—stream NC-3
Briery Gap Run—stream WV-2
Briery Hall Point—cape NC-3
Briery Knob—summit (4) WV-2
Brierylick Run—stream WV-2
Briery Mountains—range WV-2
Briery Mtn—summit NC-3
Briery Point—cape MD-2
Briery Run—stream NC-3
Briery Run—stream WV-2
Briery Swamp—stream NC-3
Briery Swamp—stream VA-3
Briery Swamp Ch—church NC-3
Briese Hill—summit TX-5
Brigadier's Island ME-1
**Brigadoon**—pop pl KY-4
**Brigadoon**—pop pl NJ-2
**Brigadoon (subdivision)**—pop pl (2) NC-3
**Brigadoon (subdivision)**—pop pl PA-2
**Brigadoon Village**—pop pl MA-1
Brigance Cem—cemetery TN-4
Brigand Bay—locale NC-3
Brigand Bay—swamp NC-3
Brigand Lake—lake MN-6
Brigands Cavern—cave AL-4
**Brigantine**—pop pl NJ-2
Brigantine Bay—bay WA-9
Brigantine Beach NJ-2
Brigantine Beach—beach NJ-2
Brigantine Channel—channel NJ-2
Brigantine City NJ-2
Brigantine Inlet—bay NJ-2
Brigantine Natl Wildlife Ref—park NJ-2
Brigantine Shoal—bar NJ-2
Briggance Branch—stream TN-4
Briggance Cem—cemetery TN-4
**Brigglesville**—pop pl OH-6
Briggman, F. H. W., House—hist pl SC-3
Briggs OH-6
Briggs VT-1
Briggs—locale AZ-5
Briggs—locale OK-5
Briggs—locale VA-3
**Briggs**—pop pl AZ-5
**Briggs**—pop pl (2) CA-9
**Briggs**—pop pl IN-6
**Briggs**—pop pl NE-7
**Briggs**—pop pl NY-2
**Briggs**—pop pl OH-6
**Briggs**—pop pl TX-5
Briggs—uninc pl TX-5
Briggs, Alexander, House—hist pl IL-6
Briggs, George I., House—hist pl MA-1
Briggs, Joseph, House-Coventry Town Farm—hist pl RI-1
Briggs, Samuel and Mary Logan, House—hist pl KY-4
Briggs, William, Homestead—hist pl ME-1
Briggs Airp—airport OR-9
Briggs Airstrip—airport OR-9
Briggs and Bohn Ditch—canal CO-8
Briggs and Robertson Grant—civil FL-3
Briggs Bay—bay NY-2
Briggs Beach—locale RI-1
Briggs Branch—stream IL-6
Briggs Branch—stream KS-7
Briggs Branch—stream MO-7
Briggs Brook—stream (2) MA-1
Briggs Cabin—locale OR-9
Briggs Camp—locale UT-8
Briggs Camp Creek—stream UT-8
Briggs Canal—canal CA-9
Briggs Canyon—valley CA-9
Briggs Canyon—valley CO-8
Briggs Canyon—valley ID-8
Briggs Canyon—valley NM-5
Briggs (CCD)—cens area TX-5
Briggs Cem—cemetery AR-4
Briggs Cem—cemetery GA-3
Briggs Cem—cemetery IL-6
Briggs Cem—cemetery KS-7
Briggs Cem—cemetery LA-4
Briggs Cem—cemetery ME-1
Briggs Cem—cemetery MA-1
Briggs Cem—cemetery (3) NY-2
Briggs Cem—cemetery NC-3
Briggs Cem—cemetery TN-4
Briggs Chapel—church LA-4
Briggs Chapel—church MS-4
Briggs Chapel—church SC-3
Briggs Chapel Cem—cemetery MS-4
Briggs Chapel Hollow—valley TN-4
Briggs Cobble—summit MA-1
Briggs Colman Sch—school TX-5
Briggs Corner—locale NY-2
**Briggs Corner**—pop pl ME-1
**Briggs Corner**—pop pl MA-1
Briggs Corner—summit RI-1
Briggs Corners—locale NY-2
Briggs Coulee—valley MT-8
Briggs Cove MA-1
Briggs Creek—stream (2) CA-9
Briggs Creek—stream MN-6
Briggs Creek—stream (2) MT-8
Briggs Creek—stream NE-7
Briggs Creek—stream NY-2
Briggs Creek—stream OR-9
Briggs Creek—stream UT-8
Briggs Creek Campground—locale OR-9
**Briggsdale**—pop pl CO-8
**Briggsdale**—pop pl OH-6
Briggsdale Cem—cemetery CO-8
**Briggs Development**—pop pl DE-2
Briggs Garland Cove—valley NC-3
Briggs Gully—valley NY-2
Briggs Harbor—cove MA-1
Briggs Hardware Bldg—hist pl NC-3
Briggs Hill—summit CT-1
Briggs Hill—summit KY-4
Briggs Hill—summit ME-1
Briggs Hill—summit WA-9
Briggs Hill Cem—cemetery VT-1
Briggs (historical)—locale KS-7
**Briggs (historical)**—pop pl TN-4
Briggs Hollow—locale NY-2
Briggs Hollow—valley NY-2
Briggs Hollow—valley NC-3
Briggs Hollow—valley PA-2
Briggs Hollow—valley (2) UT-8
Briggs Island—island FL-3
Briggs Island—island TN-4
Briggs JHS—school OR-9
Briggs Lake MI-6
Briggs Lake—lake (3) MI-6
Briggs Lake—lake (2) MN-6
Briggs Lake—lake SD-7
Briggs Lake—lake WI-6
**Briggs Lake**—pop pl MN-6
Briggs Lake—reservoir KY-4
Briggs Lake—reservoir NC-3
Briggs Lake Ch—church MN-6
Briggs Lake Creek—stream MI-6
Briggs Lake Dam—dam NC-3
Briggs Lake State Public Shooting Area—park SD-7
Briggs Ledge MA-1
Briggs Marsh—swamp RI-1
Briggs Mesa—summit NM-5
Briggs Mtn—summit NY-2
**Briggs (Old Chapel)**—pop pl VA-3
**Briggson (historical)**—pop pl OR-9
Briggs Park—park MI-6
Briggs Place—locale NM-5
Briggs Point—cape RI-1
Briggs Point—cape WI-6
Briggs Pond MA-1
Briggs Pond—lake RI-1
Briggs Pond—reservoir (2) MA-1
Briggs Post Office (historical)—building TN-4
Briggs Ranch—locale CO-8
Briggs Ranch—locale MT-8
Briggs Ranch—locale OR-9
Briggs Reservoir Dam Number 1—dam MA-1
Briggs Reservoir Number 2—dam MA-1
Briggs Ridge—ridge UT-8
Briggs Rock—rock MA-1
Briggs Rsvr MA-1
Briggs Rsvr—reservoir (2) MA-1
Briggs Rsvr—reservoir OR-9
Briggs Rsvr—reservoir WY-8
Briggs Run—stream NY-2
Briggs Run—stream OH-6
Briggs Run—stream PA-2
Briggs Run—stream WV-2
Briggs Sch—school CA-9
Briggs Sch—school IL-6
Briggs Sch—school KS-7
Briggs Sch—school (2) MA-1
Briggs Sch—school MI-6
Briggs Sewage Disposal—other AZ-5
Briggs Spring—spring ID-8
Briggs Spring—spring OR-9
Briggs Spring—spring SD-7
Briggs Street Cem—cemetery NY-2
**Briggs Subdivision**—pop pl UT-8
Briggs Tavern—hist pl MA-1
**Briggs Terrace**—pop pl CA-9
Briggston—locale GA-3
Briggs Townsite—uninc pl AZ-5
Briggs Valley—valley OR-9
Briggsville MA-1
Briggsville—locale (2) PA-2
**Briggsville**—pop pl AR-4
**Briggsville**—pop pl MA-1
**Briggsville**—pop pl WI-6
Briggsville (Township of)—fmr MCD AR-4
Briggs Windmill—locale TX-5
Briggs Woods County Park—park IA-7
Briggs Woods Lake—reservoir IA-7
Briggs Woods Lake Dam—dam IA-7
Brigham UT-8
Brigham, Lake—lake WA-9
Brigham, Mount—summit UT-8
Brigham Branch—stream TN-4
Brigham Cem—cemetery MI-6
Brigham Cem—cemetery (2) TN-4
Brigham Cem—cemetery TX-5
Brigham City—hist pl AZ-5
**Brigham City**—pop pl UT-8
Brigham City Airp—airport UT-8
Brigham City Bible Ch—church UT-8
Brigham City Carnegie Library—hist pl UT-8
Brigham City Cem—cemetery UT-8
Brigham City Community Hosp—hospital UT-8
Brigham City Community Hospital Heliport—airport UT-8
Brigham City Country Club—other UT-8
Brigham City Division—civil UT-8
Brigham City Fire Station/City Hall—hist pl UT-8
Brigham City KOA—locale UT-8
Brigham City Municipal Airport UT-8
Brigham City Shop Ctr—locale UT-8
Brigham Creek—stream AK-9
Brigham Creek—stream OR-9
Brigham Face Wildlife Mngmt Area—park UT-8
Brigham Fork—valley UT-8
Brigham Hall—hist pl NY-2
Brigham Hill—summit ME-1
Brigham Hill—summit (2) MA-1
Brigham Hill—summit (2) NH-1
Brigham Hill—summit TN-4
Brigham Hill—summit VT-1
Brigham Hollow—valley (2) TN-4
Brigham Lake—lake (2) MI-6
Brigham Lake—lake WI-6
Brigham Lake Reservoir—lake ID-8
Brigham Ledge—cliff ME-1
**Brigham Madsen Subdivision**—pop pl UT-8
Brigham Park—park WI-6
Brigham Peak UT-8
Brigham Peak—summit AZ-5
Brigham Plains—flat UT-8
Brigham Point—summit (2) ID-8
Brigham Point Lake—lake ID-8
Brigham Point Trapper Cabin—locale ID-8
Brigham Pond—reservoir MA-1
Brigham Pond Dam—dam MA-1
Brigham Pond (historical)—lake MA-1
Brigham Sch—school FL-3
Brighams Cove—bay ME-1
**Brighams Cove**—pop pl ME-1
Brighams Landing—locale GA-3
Brigham's Tavern—hist pl CT-1
Brighams Tomb—summit UT-8
Brigham Tavern Brook—stream CT-1
Brigham Tea Bench—bench UT-8
**Brigham (Town of)**—pop pl WI-6
Brigham Young Branch—stream OK-5
Brigham Young Park—park UT-8
Brigham Young Springs—spring OK-5
Brigham Young Univ—school UT-8
Brigham Young Winter Home—park UT-8
Bright AL-4
Bright—locale MS-4
**Bright**—pop pl GA-3
**Bright**—pop pl IN-6
Bright—uninc pl FL-3
Bright, John, Covered Bridge—hist pl OH-6
Bright, Lake—lake FL-3
Bright and Morning Star Ch—church LA-4
Bright And Southerland Ditch—canal WY-8
Bright Angel Canyon—valley (2) AZ-5
Bright Angel Creek—stream AZ-5
Bright Angel Point AZ-5
Bright Angel Point—cliff AZ-5
Bright Angel Spring—spring AZ-5
Bright Angel Trail—trail AZ-5
Bright Angel Trail—trail UT-8
Bright Angel Wash—stream AZ-5
Bright Branch—stream KY-4
Bright Branch—stream NC-3
Bright Branch—stream TN-4
Bright Cem—cemetery (2) IL-6
Bright Cem—cemetery OH-6
Bright Cem—cemetery TN-4
Bright Cem—cemetery TX-5
Bright Corner (reduced Usage)—locale MS-4
Bright Creek—stream NC-3
Bright Dot Lake—lake CA-9
Brighten View Subdivision UT-8
Brighter Cem—cemetery AL-4
Brighter Days Mine—mine AZ-5
Bright Ferry (historical)—crossing TN-4
Bright Future Farm—locale AR-4
Bright Glade Convalescent Center—hospital TN-4
Bright Haines Ditch DE-2
Bright Haines Glade Branch—stream DE-2
Bright-Hastings Cemetery TN-4
Bright Hill—summit KY-4
Bright Hill—summit MA-1
Bright Hill Ch—church (2) TN-4
Bright Hill Sch (historical)—school TN-4
**Bright (historical)**—pop pl TN-4
Bright Hollow—valley AR-4
Bright Hollow—valley MO-7
Bright Hollow—valley TN-4
Bright Hollow—valley VA-3
Bright Hope—locale TN-4
Bright Hope Ch—church AL-4
Bright Hope Ch—church NC-3
Bright Hope Ch—church TN-4
Bright Hope Ch—church VA-3
Bright Hope Furnace (historical)—locale TN-4
Bright Hope Sch—school NC-3
Bright Hope Sch—school TN-4
Bright Horizons—school FL-3
Bright Horizons Learning Center—school MI-6
Bright Island—island ME-1
Bright Lake—lake AR-4
Bright Lake—lake FL-3
Bright Lake—lake MI-6
Bright Lake—lake (2) MN-6
Bright Lake—lake (2) WI-6
Bright-Lamkin-Easterling House—hist pl LA-4
Bright Leaf Shop Ctr—locale NC-3
Bright Light Ch—church MS-4
Bright Light Ch—church (4) NC-3
Bright Light Ch—church (2) TX-5
Brightman, Hathaway, House—hist pl MA-1
Brightman Bridge—bridge MA-1
Brightman Cem—cemetery KY-4
Brightman Cove (historical)—bay MA-1
Brightman Flat—flat CA-9
Brightman Hill—summit RI-1
Brightman House—hist pl OH-6
Brightman Pond RI-1
Brightmans Creek—stream SC-3
Brightman Swamp—stream SC-3
Brightmoor MI-6
Bright Morning Star Ch—church AL-4
Bright Morning Star Ch—church AR-4
Bright Morning Star Ch—church (3) LA-4
Bright Morning Star Ch—church MS-4
Bright Oaks IL-6
Brighton (2) OH-6
Brighton—locale CA-9
Brighton—locale KY-4
Brighton—locale NJ-2
Brighton—locale WV-2
**Brighton**—pop pl AL-4
**Brighton**—pop pl AR-4
**Brighton**—pop pl CO-8
**Brighton**—pop pl FL-3
**Brighton**—pop pl GA-3
**Brighton**—pop pl IL-6
**Brighton**—pop pl IN-6
**Brighton**—pop pl IA-7
**Brighton**—pop pl ME-1
**Brighton**—pop pl (4) MD-2
**Brighton**—pop pl MI-6
**Brighton**—pop pl MS-4
**Brighton**—pop pl MO-7
**Brighton**—pop pl (2) NY-2
**Brighton**—pop pl (2) OH-6
**Brighton**—pop pl OR-9
**Brighton**—pop pl PA-2
**Brighton**—pop pl SC-3
**Brighton**—pop pl (2) TN-4
**Brighton**—pop pl UT-8
**Brighton**—pop pl WA-9
**Brighton**—pop pl WI-6
Brighton—uninc pl NY-2
**Brighton Addition (subdivision)**—pop pl UT-8
Brighton Baptist Ch—church TN-4
Brighton Beach—beach WA-9
**Brighton Beach**—pop pl CT-1
**Brighton Beach**—pop pl NJ-2
**Brighton Beach**—pop pl NY-2
**Brighton Beach**—pop pl SC-3
**Brighton Beach**—pop pl WI-6
Brighton Branch—stream KY-4
**Brighton (Brighton Corners)**—pop pl NY-2
Brighton Brook—stream VT-1
Brighton Camp—locale MI-6
Brighton Canal—canal UT-8
Brighton Canal Extension—canal UT-8
Brighton Canyon—valley WY-8
Brighton Cave—cave WY-8
Brighton (CCD)—cens area TN-4
Brighton Cem—cemetery AL-4
Brighton Cem—cemetery IA-7
Brighton Cem—cemetery MN-6
Brighton Cem—cemetery OH-6
Brighton Cem—cemetery WI-6
Brighton Ch—church MI-6
Brighton Ch—church MN-6
Brighton City Hall—building AL-4
Brighton City Hall—building TN-4
Brighton Cliff—cliff NY-2
Brighton Community Center—building TN-4
**Brighton Corner**—pop pl ME-1
Brighton Corners—other NY-2
Brighton Creek—stream WI-6
Brighton Dam—dam MD-2
Brighton Deadwater—swamp ME-1
Brighton Ditch—canal CO-8
Brighton Division—civil TN-4
Brighton Drain—canal UT-8
Brighton Drain—stream MI-6
Brighton-Drydon Hist Dist—hist pl OH-6
Brighton Elementary School AL-4
Brighton Elem Sch—school IN-6
Brighton Elem Sch—school TN-4
Brighton Elem Sch (historical)—school AL-4
**Brighton Estates (subdivision)**—pop pl AL-4
Brighton Guard Station—locale UT-8
Brighton Heights Reformed Church—hist pl NY-2
Brighton Hill—summit ME-1
Brighton Hills Cem—cemetery MI-6
**Brighton Hills (subdivision)**—pop pl UT-8
Brighton Hollow—valley KY-4
Brighton Hosp—hospital MI-6
Brighton HS—school AL-4
Brighton HS—school MA-1
Brighton HS—school UT-8
Brighton Indian Day Sch—school FL-3
**Brighton Ind Res**—pop pl FL-3
Brighton JHS—school AL-4
Brighton Lake—lake MI-6
Brighton Lake—reservoir NJ-2
Brighton Lateral Ditch—canal CO-8
Brighton Lookout Tower—tower FL-3
Brighton Memorial Park—cemetery NY-2
Brighton Park IL-6
Brighton Park—park NY-2
**Brighton Place Condo**—pop pl UT-8
**Brighton Place (subdivision)**—pop pl (2) AZ-5
Brighton (Plantation of)—civ div ME-1
Brighton (P.O.)—uninc pl NY-2
Brighton Point—cape MN-6
**Brighton Point Subdivision**—pop pl UT-8
Brighton Post Office—building TN-4
Brighton Post Office (historical)—building TN-4
Brighton Primary School TN-4
Brighton Rec Area—locale UT-8
**Brighton Ridge Subdivision**—pop pl UT-8
Brighton Sch—hist pl CA-9
Brighton Sch—school AL-4
Brighton Sch—school CA-9
Brighton Sch—school NY-2
Brighton Sch—school VT-1
Brighton Sch—school VA-3
Brighton Sch (historical)—school TN-4
Brighton Seminole Ind Res FL-3
Brighton Ski Area—locale UT-8
Brighton Ski Area Heliport—airport UT-8
**Brighton Square**—pop pl VA-3
Brighton State Park—park VT-1
Brighton State Rec Area—park MI-6
Brighton Station (historical)—locale MA-1
**Brighton (subdivision)**—pop pl MA-1
**Brighton (Town of)**—pop pl (2) NY-2
**Brighton (Town of)**—pop pl VT-1
**Brighton (Town of)**—pop pl (2) WI-6
Brighton Township—fmr MCD (2) IA-7
**Brighton (Township of)**—pop pl IL-6
**Brighton (Township of)**—pop pl MI-6
**Brighton (Township of)**—pop pl MN-6
**Brighton (Township of)**—pop pl OH-6
**Brighton (Township of)**—pop pl PA-2
Brighton Township Sch—school PA-2
Brighton Valley—basin NE-7
**Brighton View Subdivision**—pop pl UT-8
**Brighton Village**—pop pl NY-2
Bright Park—park FL-3
Bright Penny Lake—reservoir NC-3
Bright Penny Lake Dam—dam NC-3
Bright Pond—reservoir NC-3
Bright Pond Ch—church FL-3
Bright Pond Dam—dam NC-3
Bright Post Office (historical)—building MS-4
Bright Prairie Cem—cemetery MO-7
Bright Prairie Sch—school MO-7
Bright Prospect Ch—church FL-3
Bright Prospect Ch—church MO-7
Bright Prospect Ch—church WV-2
Bright Ridge—ridge CA-9
Bright Run—stream IN-6
Bright Run—stream PA-2
Brights—locale VA-3
Brights—uninc pl NJ-2
Brights Branch DE-2
Brights Branch—stream DE-2
Brights Branch—stream MD-2
Brights Cem—cemetery OH-6
Brights Cem—cemetery PA-2
Brights Center Shop Ctr—locale MS-4
Bright Sch—school FL-3
Bright Sch—school IL-6
Bright Sch—school MA-1
Bright Sch—school NC-3
Brights Chapel—church WV-2
Bright Sch (historical)—school AL-4
Bright School, The—school TN-4
Brights Corner Sch—school IL-6
Brights Creek—stream AL-4
Brights Creek—stream NC-3
Brights Creek—stream PA-2
Brights Creek—stream VA-3
Brights Creek—stream WA-9
Brights Ditch—canal OH-6
**Brightseat**—pop pl MD-2
Brightshade—locale KY-4
Brights Hollow—valley WV-2
**Brightside**—pop pl MA-1
**Brightside**—pop pl NY-2
**Brightside**—pop pl PA-2
Brightside Apartments—hist pl MA-1
Brights Lake—lake IA-7
Brights Lake—lake NC-3
Brights Lake State Game Mngmt Area—park IA-7
Bright Spring—spring GA-3
Bright Spring—spring TN-4
Bright Spring Draw—valley WY-8
Bright Spring Knoll MO-7
Brights Ridge—ridge NC-3
Brights Run—stream WV-2
Brights Spring—spring MO-7
Brights Spring—spring OR-9
Brights Spring Knoll—summit MO-7
**Brights Station**—pop pl IN-6
Brightstar AL-4
Bright Star—locale AL-4
Brightstar—locale AR-4
Bright Star—locale TX-5
**Bright Star**—pop pl AR-4
Bright Star Canyon—valley CA-9
Bright Star Cem—cemetery AR-4
Bright Star Cem—cemetery GA-3
Bright Star Cem—cemetery TX-5
Bright Star Ch—church (3) AR-4
Bright Star Ch—church (5) GA-3
Bright Star Ch—church LA-4
Bright Star Ch—church MS-4
Bright Star Ch—church OK-5
Bright Star Ch—church SC-3
Bright Star Ch—church (2) TX-5
Bright Star Ch—church WV-2
Bright Star Ch (historical)—church MS-4
Bright Star Mine—mine (2) CA-9
**Bright Star (Sava)**—pop pl TX-5
Bright Star Sch—school LA-4
Bright Star Sch—school SD-7
Brightstone Community Ch—church MO-7
Brightstone Sch (historical)—school MO-7
**Brightsville**—pop pl FL-3
**Brightsville**—pop pl SC-3
Brights Well—well NM-5
Brightview CT-1
**Brightview**—pop pl CT-1
Brightwater—locale AR-4
Brightwater—locale ME-1
**Brightwater**—pop pl AL-4
**Brightwater**—pop pl NC-3
**Brightwater (Bestwater)**—pop pl AR-4
Brightwater Branch—stream NC-3
Bright Water Ch AL-4
Brightwater Ch—church AL-4
Brightwater Ch—church AR-4
**Brightwater East (subdivision)**—pop pl NC-3
Bright Water Lake—lake ND-7
Brightwater Methodist Ch AL-4
**Brightwaters**—pop pl NY-2
Brightwaters Canal—canal NY-2
Brightwater (Township of)—fmr MCD AR-4
Brightwell Cem—cemetery MO-7
Brightwell Mill—locale VA-3
Brightwing Cem—cemetery MT-8
Brightwood IN-6
Brightwood—hist pl MD-2
Brightwood—locale OH-6
**Brightwood**—pop pl DC-2
**Brightwood**—pop pl NC-3
**Brightwood**—pop pl OR-9
**Brightwood**—pop pl PA-2
**Brightwood**—pop pl (2) VA-3
**Brightwood Acres**—pop pl MD-2
Brightwood Beach Cottage—hist pl MN-6
Brightwood Ch—church NC-3
**Brightwood (historical)**—pop pl IN-6
Brightwood Park—park GA-3
**Brightwood Park**—pop pl DC-2
Brightwood Rec Area—park DC-2
Brightwood Saint Sch—school CA-9
Brightwood Sch—school DC-2
Brightwood Sch—school NC-3
**Brightwood (subdivision)**—pop pl MA-1
Brightwood Town Hall—building ND-7
**Brightwood Township**—pop pl ND-7
Brightwood Township (historical)—civil ND-7
Brigintine NJ-2
Brig Ledge—bench RI-1
Brig Ledge—island ME-1
Brigman Branch TN-4
Brigman Branch—stream TX-5
Brigman Cem—cemetery SC-3
Brigman Chapel—church NC-3
Brigman Coulee—valley MT-8
Brigman Coulee Sch (reduced usage)—school MT-8
Brigman Hollow—valley NC-3
Brigmon Branch TN-4
Brigmon Branch—stream TN-4
**Brignac**—pop pl LA-4
Brigner Hollow—valley OH-6
Brikles Branch—stream KY-4
Brilby Butte CO-8
Briles Rsvr—reservoir CA-9
Briles Spring—spring CA-9
Briley Brook—gut ME-1
Briley Canyon—valley OR-9
Briley Cem—cemetery AR-4
Briley Cem—cemetery MI-6
Briley Cem—cemetery TN-4
Briley Chapel—church IN-6
Briley Creek—stream AL-4
Briley Creek—stream MO-7
Briley Mtn—summit OR-9
Briley Pond—lake ME-1
Brileys Lake—lake GA-3
**Briley (Township of)**—pop pl MI-6
**Brilhart**—pop pl PA-2
Brilheart Cem—cemetery VA-3
**Brill**—pop pl WI-6
Brillante Windmill—locale NM-5
Brill Brook—stream MI-6
Brillhart—locale PA-2
Brill Hollow—valley PA-2
Brillion Mine—mine WY-8
Brilliant—locale NM-5
**Brilliant**—pop pl AL-4
**Brilliant**—pop pl OH-6
Brilliant (CCD)—cens area AL-4
Brilliant Division—civil AL-4
Brilliant Glacier—glacier AK-9
Brilliant HS—school AL-4
Brilliant Lake—reservoir AL-4
Brilliant Lake Dam—dam AL-4
Brilliant Memorial Cem—cemetery AL-4
**Brillian Township**—pop pl ND-7
Brilliant Point—cape LA-4
Brilliant Sch—school OH-6
Brilliant Shoal—bar FL-3
**Brillion**—pop pl WI-6
Brillion Ch—church WI-6
Brillion State Wildlife Area—park WI-6
**Brillion (Town of)**—pop pl WI-6

Brill Lake—lake ... MI-6
Brill Point—cape ... FL-3
Brill River—stream ... WI-6
Brill Run—stream ... OH-6
Brills—uninc pl ... NJ-2
Brills Creek—stream ... MO-7
Brills Junction—uninc pl ... NJ-2
Brills Ranch ... AZ-5
Brills Ranch—locale ... NM-5
Brills Run—stream ... PA-2
Brills Shop—locale ... VA-3
Brills Upper Ranch—locale ... NM-5
Brills Yard—locale ... NJ-2
**Brilyn Park**—pop pl ... VA-3
Brimbal Hill ... MA-1
Brimble Hill—summit ... MA-1
Brimbles—rock ... MA-1
Brimbles Rock ... MA-1
Brim Canyon—valley ... ID-8
Brim Cove—bay ... ME-1
Brim Creek—stream ... WA-9
Brim Creek School—locale ... WA-9
Brimer Brook ... NY-2
Brimer Cem—cemetery ... TN-4
Brimer Creek—stream ... TN-4
Brimer Gut ... MD-2
Brimer Heights School ... TN-4
Brimer Hill—summit ... WA-9
Brimer Town Hall—building ... ND-7
**Brimer Township**—pop pl ... ND-7
Brimestone Mine—mine ... TN-4
Brimestone Sch (historical)—school ... TN-4
Brimetone Post Office (historical)—building ... TN-4
**Brimfield**—pop pl ... IL-6
**Brimfield**—pop pl ... IN-6
**Brimfield**—pop pl ... MA-1
**Brimfield**—pop pl ... OH-6
Brimfield, Town of ... MA-1
Brimfield Centre ... MA-1
Brimfield Crossing—locale ... NJ-2
Brimfield Ditch—canal ... OH-6
Brimfield Pond ... MA-1
Brimfield State For—forest ... MA-1
Brimfield Station ... MA-1
**Brimfield Station**—pop pl ... OH-6
**Brimfield (Town of)**—pop pl ... MA-1
**Brimfield (Township of)**—pop pl ... IL-6
**Brimfield (Township of)**—pop pl ... OH-6
Brimhall, Lake—lake ... UT-8
Brimhall Bridge—arch ... UT-8
Brimhall Canyon—valley ... UT-8
**Brimhall (Coyote Canyon)**—pop pl ... NM-5
**Brimhall Estates Subdivision**—pop pl ... UT-8
Brimhall Point—cape ... UT-8
Brimhall Springs—spring ... UT-8
**Brimhall Subdivision**—pop pl ... UT-8
Brimhall Wash—stream ... NM-5
Brimhall Well—well ... AZ-5
Brim Hollow—valley ... MO-7
**Brimley**—pop pl ... MI-6
Brimley State Park—park ... MI-6
**Brimley Subdivision**—pop pl ... UT-8
Brimmage Cem—cemetery ... AR-4
Brimmer Brook—stream ... NY-2
Brimmer Creek—stream ... MI-6
Brimmer Creek—stream ... OR-9
Brimmer Divide—ridge ... WY-8
Brimmer Heights School ... TN-4
Brimmer-May Sch—school ... MA-1
Brimmer Point—cliff ... WY-8
Brimmer Sch—school ... WY-8
Brimm Hollow—valley ... TN-4
Brimminstool Ranch—locale ... NM-5
Brim Pond—lake (3) ... FL-3
**Brims Corner**—pop pl ... TN-4
Brims Grove Ch—church ... NC-3
**Brimson**—pop pl ... MN-6
**Brimson**—pop pl ... MO-7
Brimson Cem—cemetery ... MN-6
Brimstone—locale ... LA-4
**Brimstone**—pop pl ... MT-8
**Brimstone**—pop pl ... TN-4
Brimstone Basin—basin ... WY-8
Brimstone Brook—stream ... VT-1
Brimstone Ch—church ... TN-4
Brimstone Corner ... MA-1
Brimstone Corner—locale ... CO-8
Brimstone Corner—locale ... ME-1
**Brimstone Corner**—pop pl ... MA-1
**Brimstone Corner**—pop pl ... VT-1
Brimstone Corners—locale ... PA-2
Brimstone Corners—locale ... VT-1
**Brimstone Corners**—pop pl ... IN-6
Brimstone Creek—stream ... CA-9
Brimstone Creek—stream (3) ... MT-8
Brimstone Creek—stream ... NY-2
Brimstone Creek—stream ... OH-6
Brimstone Creek—stream (3) ... TN-4
Brimstone Gulch—valley ... UT-8
Brimstone Hill—summit ... ME-1
Brimstone Hill—summit (2) ... MA-1
Brimstone Hill—summit ... NY-2
Brimstone Hollow—valley ... WI-6
Brimstone Island—island (2) ... ME-1
Brimstone Island (historical)—island ... TN-4
Brimstone Mtn—summit ... ME-1
Brimstone Mtn—summit (2) ... NY-2
Brimstone Mtn—summit ... WY-8
Brimstone Neck ... NJ-2
Brimstone Pond—lake ... ME-1
Brimstone Post Office (historical)—building ... AL-4
Brimstone Ridge—ridge ... OH-6
Brimstone Ridge—ridge ... TN-4
Brimstone Rsvr—reservoir ... UT-8
Brimstone Run—stream (2) ... OH-6
Brimstone Siding—locale ... TN-4
**Brimstone (sta.)**—pop pl ... LA-4
Brimston Gulch—valley ... OR-9
Brimwood Lakes—reservoir ... AL-4
Brinan Spring—spring ... CA-9
Brin Bldg—hist pl ... WI-6
Brin Canyon—valley (2) ... CA-9
Brinckerhoff—locale ... NY-2
Brinckley ... IN-6
**Brinckley**—pop pl ... IN-6
Brinckman Gulch—valley ... AK-9
Brindle Canyon—valley ... TX-5
Brindle Corner—locale ... OH-6
Brindle Creek ... AL-4
Brindle Creek ... TX-5
Brindle Creek—stream ... NC-3
Brindle Creek—stream ... WY-8
Brindle Ditch—canal ... IN-6
Brindlee Mountain ... AL-4
Brindle Hollow—valley ... VA-3
Brindle Lake—lake ... MI-6
Brindle Lake—reservoir ... NJ-2
Brindle Lake Dam—dam ... NJ-2
Brindle Mines (historical)—locale ... NC-3
Brindle Pond—lake ... NH-1
Brindle Pond—lake (2) ... NY-2
Brindle Pup Mine—mine ... AZ-5
Brindle Ridge—ridge ... KY-4
Brindle Ridge Ch—church ... KY-4
Brindle Sch—school ... PA-2
Brindles Sch—school ... PA-2
Brindle Town ... NC-3
**Brindletown**—pop pl ... NJ-2
**Brindletown**—pop pl ... NC-3
**Brindle Town**—pop pl ... NC-3
Brindley Branch—stream ... AL-4
Brindley Branch—stream ... TN-4
Brindley Cem—cemetery (2) ... AL-4
Brindley Chapel—church ... TN-4
Brindley Creek ... AL-4
Brindley Creek—stream ... AL-4
Brindley Creek—stream ... AR-4
Brindley Farm—hist pl ... DE-2
Brindley Flat—flat ... UT-8
Brindley Hollow—valley ... AL-4
Brindley Hollow—valley ... TN-4
Brindley Hollow Spring—spring ... AL-4
Brindley Mtn—range ... AL-4
Brind Mtn—summit ... CO-8
Brindnagles Ch—church ... PA-2
Brine Creek—stream ... UT-8
**Brinegar**—pop pl ... KY-4
Brinegar Cabin—hist pl ... NC-3
Brinegar Cabin—locale ... NC-3
Brinegar Cem—cemetery ... IN-6
Brinegar Cem—cemetery ... KY-4
Brinegar Cem—cemetery ... MO-7
Brinegar District—hist pl ... NC-3
Brinegar Ranch—locale ... WY-8
Brineinger Hollow—valley ... OH-6
Brine Pond No 6—lake ... MI-6
Briner Branch—stream ... SC-3
Briner Ch—church ... SC-3
Briner Heights Sch (historical)—school ... TN-4
Brine Sch—school ... PA-2
Brine Spring—spring ... CA-9
Briney Creek—stream ... ID-8
Briney Landing Field—airport ... KS-7
Bringerhoff Coulee ... MT-8
Bringghold, Jacob, House—hist pl ... MN-6
Bringham Springs ... OR-9
Bringhurst—locale ... LA-4
**Bringhurst**—pop pl ... IN-6
Bringhurst Park—park ... LA-4
Bringhurst Woods Park—park ... DE-2
Bringier Point—cape ... LA-4
Bringle Creek—stream ... AR-4
Bringle Ferry—locale ... NC-3
Bringle Lake—reservoir ... TX-5
Bringles ... NC-3
Bringles Ferry ... NC-3
Bringleson Rsvr—reservoir ... CO-8
Bringoff Creek—stream ... MT-8
Bringoff Spring—spring ... MT-8
Bringolf Ranch—locale ... WY-8
Brin Head ... UT-8
Brining, John, House—hist pl ... WA-9
Brink—locale ... MD-2
Brink—locale ... OK-5
Brink—locale ... VA-3
**Brink**—pop pl ... VA-3
**Brink**—pop pl (2) ... WV-2
Brink, The—cliff ... UT-8
Brink Cem—cemetery ... IA-7
Brink Cem—cemetery ... ND-7
Brink Creek ... CA-9
Brinkell Sch (historical)—school ... PA-2
Brinker—locale ... TX-5
**Brinker**—pop pl ... PA-2
**Brinker and Hochstetlers Subdivision**—pop pl ... UT-8
Brinker Collegiate Institute—hist pl ... CO-8
Brinker Corners—locale ... OH-6
Brinker Creek—stream (2) ... CO-8
Brinker Creek—stream (2) ... OR-9
Brinker Drain—stream ... MI-6
Brinker Gulch—valley ... CO-8
Brinker Heights ... IN-6
Brinkerhoff—fmr MCD ... NE-7
Brinkerhoff, George M., House—hist pl ... IL-6
Brinkerhoff-Becker House—hist pl ... MI-6
Brinkerhoff-Demarest House—hist pl ... NJ-2
Brinkerhoff Hill—summit ... NY-2
Brinkerhoff House—hist pl ... NJ-2
Brinkerhoff Pond—reservoir ... UT-8
Brinkerhoff Sch—school ... IL-6
Brinkerhoff Sch—school ... OH-6
Brinkerhoff Street Hist Dist—hist pl ... NY-2
Brinkerhoff Well—well ... AZ-5
Brinker Ranch—locale ... CO-8
Brinker Run—stream ... PA-2
Brinker Run—stream ... WV-2
Brinker Sch (abandoned)—school (2) ... PA-2
Brinkerton—locale ... PA-2
**Brinkerton**—pop pl ... PA-2
Brinkerton Dam—dam ... PA-2
Brinkerton Post Office (historical)—building ... PA-2
Brinkhaus Saloon Livery Barn—hist pl ... MN-6
Brinkhaven Cem—cemetery ... OH-6
Brinkhaven (corporate name Gann;RR name Brink Haven) ... OH-6
**Brinkhaven (Gann)**—pop pl ... OH-6
Brink Haven (RR name for Brinkhaven)—other ... OH-6
Brink Hill Sch—school ... FL-3
Brinkhoff Mine—mine ... CO-8
Brink Hollow—valley ... MO-7
Brink Hollow Trail—trail ... PA-2
Brink Lake—swamp ... MN-6
**Brinkleigh**—pop pl ... MD-2
**Brinkleigh Manor**—pop pl ... MD-2
Brinkley—locale ... KY-4
**Brinkley**—pop pl ... AR-4
**Brinkley**—pop pl ... MS-4
**Brinkley**—pop pl ... NC-3
Brinkley Bayou—stream ... TN-4
Brinkley Branch—stream (3) ... TN-4
Brinkley Cem—cemetery ... AR-4
Brinkley Cem—cemetery ... NC-3
Brinkley Cem—cemetery (3) ... TN-4
Brinkley Cem—cemetery ... VA-3
Brinkley Chapel—church ... AR-4
Brinkley Chapel—church ... GA-3
Brinkley Country Club—other ... AR-4
Brinkley Creek ... TN-4
Brinkley Creek ... TX-5
Brinkley Creek—stream ... TX-5
**Brinkley Estates (subdivision)**—pop pl ... NC-3
Brinkley Farm—locale ... AR-4
Brinkley High School ... MS-4
Brinkley JHS—school ... MS-4
Brinkley Lake—lake ... UT-8
Brinkley Lake—reservoir ... AR-4
Brinkley Lake—reservoir ... NC-3
Brinkley Lake Dam—dam ... MS-4
Brinkley Lake Dam—dam ... NC-3
**Brinkley Manor**—pop pl ... MD-2
Brinkley Park—park ... TN-4
Brinkley Plantation—locale ... AR-4
Brinkley Pond—reservoir ... LA-4
Brinkley Siding—locale ... OK-5
Brinkley Slough ... TX-5
Brinkley Spring—spring ... AZ-5
Brinkleys Twin Lakes—reservoir ... NC-3
Brinkleys Twin Lakes Number One—reservoir ... NC-3
Brinkleys Twin Lakes Number One Dam—dam ... NC-3
Brinkley (Township of)—fmr MCD ... AR-4
Brinkleyville—locale ... NC-3
**Brinkleyville**—pop pl ... NC-3
Brinkleyville (Township of)—fmr MCD ... NC-3
Brinklow—locale ... MD-2
**Brinkman**—pop pl ... OK-5
Brinkman Butte—summit ... CA-9
Brinkman Cem—cemetery ... OH-6
Brinkman Creek—stream ... MO-7
Brinkman Ditch—canal ... OH-6
Brinkman Gulch—valley ... AK-9
Brinkman Lake—lake ... WI-6
Brinkmann, Otto, House—hist pl ... TX-5
Brinkman Ridge ... WI-6
Brinkman Ridge—ridge ... WI-6
Brinkman Sch—school ... IL-6
Brinkmeier Cem—cemetery ... MO-7
Brinkmeyer Ditch—canal ... IN-6
Brinkmeyer House—hist pl ... AZ-5
Brinkmeyer Point—summit ... AZ-5
Brink Ponds ... PA-2
Brink Sch—school ... NY-2
Brink Sch—school ... SD-7
Brinks Draw—valley ... CO-8
Brink Spring—spring ... UT-8
Brink Tank—reservoir ... TX-5
**Brinktown**—pop pl ... MO-7
Brink-Wagner House—hist pl ... SD-7
Brinlee Branch—stream ... TX-5
Brinlee Cem—cemetery ... TX-5
Brinley—locale ... OH-6
Brinley Ave Hist Dist—hist pl ... AZ-5
Brinley Fork ... OH-6
Brinley Fork—stream ... OH-6
Brinly Post Office (historical)—building ... TN-4
Brin Marr Ranch—locale ... CA-9
**Brinn**—pop pl ... AL-4
Brinnan Spring ... CA-9
Brinnan Springs ... CA-9
Brinnemans Headacres Airp—airport ... IN-6
Brinnen Lake ... ND-7
Brinningstool Creek—stream ... NY-2
Brinnon—locale ... WA-9
Brinnon Flats—flat ... WA-9
Brinnon Sch—school ... WA-9
Brinsfield I Site—hist pl ... MD-2
**Brinsmade**—pop pl ... ND-7
Brinsmade Cem—cemetery ... CT-1
Brinsmade Cem—cemetery ... ND-7
Brins Mesa—summit ... AZ-5
**Brinson**—pop pl ... GA-3
Brinson (CCD)—cens area ... GA-3
Brinson Cem—cemetery ... GA-3
Brinson Cem—cemetery ... MS-4
Brinson Cem—cemetery ... NC-3
Brinson Creek—stream ... NC-3
Brinson Crossing—locale ... GA-3
Brinson Family Hist Dist—hist pl ... GA-3
Brinson Memorial Sch—school ... NC-3
Brinson Millpond—reservoir ... GA-3
Brinson Point—cape ... TX-5
Brinson Ranch—locale ... TX-5
Brinson Rock Ch—church ... GA-3
Brinsons Creek—stream ... LA-4
Brintle Creek ... GA-3
Brintley Well—well ... AZ-5
Brinton—locale ... WY-8
**Brinton**—pop pl ... MI-6
**Brinton**—pop pl ... VA-3
Brinton, David B., House—hist pl ... UT-8
Brinton, Edward, House—hist pl ... PA-2
Brinton Bridge ... PA-2
Brinton Cem—cemetery ... MO-7
Brinton-Dahl House—hist pl ... UT-8
Brinton Lake—lake ... PA-2
Brinton Meadow—flat ... UT-8
Brinton Meadow Forest Service Station ... UT-8
Brinton Meadow Guard Station—locale ... UT-8
Brinton Run—stream ... PA-2
**Brintons**—pop pl ... PA-2
Brintons Bridge—locale ... PA-2
**Brintons Corners**—pop pl ... PA-2
Brinton's Mill—hist pl ... PA-2
Brintons Mill—locale ... PA-2
Brints Chapel—church ... TN-4
**Briny Breezes**—pop pl ... FL-3
Briny Bridge Creek—stream ... LA-4
Brion Creek—stream ... PA-2
Briones (CCD)—cens area ... CA-9
Briones Dam—dam ... CA-9
Briones Hills—range ... CA-9
Briones Regional Park—park ... CA-9
Briones Rsvr—reservoir ... CA-9
Briones Valley—valley (2) ... CA-9
Briones Valley Sch—school ... CA-9
Briquette—uninc pl ... PA-2
Brirton ... MI-6
Brisa Island ... RI-1
Brisbane—locale ... IL-6
**Brisbane**—pop pl ... CA-9
**Brisbane**—pop pl ... ND-7
Brisbane Lake—lake ... MN-6
Brisbane Lake—reservoir ... NJ-2
Brisbane Township—obs name ... ND-7
Brisbane Valley—valley ... CA-9
**Brisben**—pop pl ... NY-2
Brisbin—locale ... MT-8
**Brisbin**—pop pl ... PA-2
Brisbin Borough—civil ... PA-2
Brisbine Catholic Church ... SD-7
Brisbine Cemetery ... SD-7
Brisbine (historical)—locale ... SD-7
Brisbin Shaft—mine ... PA-2
Brisbois, Michael, House—hist pl ... WI-6
Brisbois Creek ... OR-9
Brisbois Creek—stream ... OR-9
Brisbois Gulch—valley ... OR-9
Brisbon—locale ... GA-3
Brisco ... TX-5
**Brisco**—pop pl ... IN-6
Brisco Butte—summit ... CA-9
Brisco Cem—cemetery ... IN-6
Briscoe ... VA-3
Briscoe—locale ... WV-2
**Briscoe**—pop pl ... AL-4
**Briscoe**—pop pl ... MO-7
**Briscoe**—pop pl ... NY-2
**Briscoe**—pop pl ... TX-5
Briscoe, Benjamin E., House—hist pl ... AZ-5
Briscoe, James, Quarters—hist pl ... KY-4
Briscoe Branch—stream ... TX-5
Briscoe Canal—canal ... TX-5
Briscoe Cem—cemetery ... AL-4
Briscoe Cem—cemetery ... MS-4
Briscoe Cem—cemetery (4) ... MO-7
Briscoe Cem—cemetery ... TX-5
Briscoe Ch—church ... WV-2
**Briscoe (County)**—pop pl ... TX-5
Briscoe Cove—bay ... NY-2
Briscoe Creek—stream ... AR-4
Briscoe Creek—stream ... CA-9
Briscoe Ditch—canal ... MT-8
Briscoe JHS—school ... MA-1
Briscoe Lake—lake ... WA-9
Briscoe Lake—reservoir ... CO-8
Briscoe Lake—reservoir ... NY-2
Briscoe Mounds—hist pl ... IL-6
Briscoe Mtn—summit ... TX-5
Briscoe Pond Dam—dam ... MS-4
Briscoe Post Office (historical)—building ... AL-4
Briscoe Ranch—locale ... NM-5
Briscoe Ranch—locale ... TX-5
Briscoe Ranch (Hdqrs)—locale ... TX-5
Briscoe Ranch Number 2—locale ... TX-5
Briscoe Rocks—summit ... CA-9
Briscoe Rsvr—reservoir ... OR-9
Briscoe Run—stream ... WV-2
Briscoe Sch—school ... IL-6
Briscoe Sch—school ... KY-4
Briscoe Sch—school ... MA-1
Briscoe Sch—school (2) ... TX-5
Briscoe's Creek ... MD-2
Briscoes Mill (historical)—locale ... MS-4
**Briscoe Springs (Perrys Corner)**—pop pl ... PA-2
Briscoe Tank—reservoir ... CO-8
Brisco Point—cape ... WA-9
Brisco Store—locale ... AL-4
Brisco Well—well ... NM-5
Brisendine Cem—cemetery ... TN-4
Brishlotte Lake—lake ... ME-1
Brish Run—stream ... PA-2
Briskey Mountain—ridge ... PA-2
Brisk & Jacobson Store—hist pl ... AL-4
Brisky Canyon—valley ... WA-9
Brislawn Sch—school ... WY-8
**Brislet (Township of)**—pop pl ... MN-6
Brison Hollow—valley ... MO-7
Brison Memorial Chapel—church ... AL-4
Brissel Ridge—ridge ... MO-7
**Brissette Beach**—pop pl ... MI-6
Brissette Sch—school ... MI-6
Brissey Branch—stream ... SC-3
Brissey Ridge—ridge ... SC-3
Briss Lake—lake ... WI-6
Brisson Bay—swamp ... NC-3
Brisson Branch—stream ... NC-3
Brisson RR Station—locale ... FL-3
Brister—locale ... AR-4
Brister—locale ... OH-6
Brister, John Willard, Library—hist pl ... TN-4
Brister Branch—stream ... MS-4
Brister Branch—stream ... TN-4
Brister Brook—stream ... NY-2
Bristerburg ... VA-3
Brister Cem—cemetery (5) ... MS-4
Brister Cem—cemetery ... TX-5
Brister Creek ... MS-4
Brister Fork—stream ... OH-6
Brister Hollow—valley ... TN-4
**Bristersburg**—pop pl ... VA-3
Brister Sch—school ... LA-4
Brister Spring—spring ... TN-4
**Bristers Store**—pop pl ... MS-4
Brister Tank—reservoir (2) ... NM-5
**Bristerville**—pop pl ... MS-4
Bristle Branch ... AR-4
Bristlecone Canyon—valley ... UT-8
Bristlecone Loop Trail—trail ... UT-8
Bristlecone Point—summit ... UT-8
Bristlecone Ridge—ridge ... UT-8
Bristlecone Trail—trail ... NV-8
**Bristle Knoll**—pop pl ... DE-2
Bristle Ridge—locale ... MO-7
Bristle Ridge—ridge (2) ... MO-7
Bristle Ridge—ridge ... NC-3
Bristleridge Cem—cemetery ... IN-6
Bristletown—locale ... KY-4
Bristo Creek—stream ... OR-9
Bristoe ... VA-3
Bristol ... MI-6
Bristol—CDP ... RI-1
Bristol—locale ... IA-7
Bristol—locale ... MD-2
Bristol—locale ... OH-6
Bristol—locale ... WA-9
**Bristol**—pop pl ... CO-8
**Bristol**—pop pl ... CT-1
**Bristol**—pop pl ... FL-3
**Bristol**—pop pl ... GA-3
**Bristol**—pop pl ... IL-6
**Bristol**—pop pl ... IN-6
**Bristol**—pop pl ... LA-4
**Bristol**—pop pl ... ME-1
**Bristol**—pop pl ... MI-6
**Bristol**—pop pl ... MN-6
**Bristol**—pop pl ... NH-1
**Bristol**—pop pl ... NY-2
**Bristol**—pop pl ... OH-6
**Bristol**—pop pl ... PA-2
**Bristol**—pop pl ... SD-7
**Bristol**—pop pl ... TN-4
**Bristol**—pop pl ... TX-5
**Bristol**—pop pl ... VT-1
**Bristol**—pop pl ... WV-2
**Bristol**—pop pl ... WI-6
Bristol—uninc pl ... CA-9
Bristol Bay ... RI-1
Bristol Bay—bay ... AK-9
Bristol Bay—bay ... UT-8
**Bristol Bay (Borough)**—pop pl ... AK-9
Bristol Bay (Census Subarea)—cens area ... AK-9
Bristol Blake State Reservoir Dam—dam ... MA-1
Bristol Blake State Rsvr—reservoir ... MA-1
Bristol Borough—civil ... PA-2
Bristol Branch—stream ... NC-3
Bristol Camp—locale ... NC-3
Bristol Carpet Mills—hist pl ... PA-2
Bristol Cave Branch—stream ... TN-4
Bristol Caverns—cave ... TN-4
Bristol (CCD)—cens area ... GA-3
Bristol (CCD)—cens area ... TN-4
Bristol Cem—cemetery (2) ... MI-6
Bristol Cem—cemetery ... MO-7
Bristol Cem—cemetery ... PA-2
Bristol Cem—cemetery ... WI-6
**Bristol Center**—pop pl ... NY-2
Bristol Ch—church ... AR-4
Bristol Ch—church ... IA-7
Bristol Ch—church ... NC-3
Bristol Ch—church ... OH-6
Bristol Ch—church ... WI-6
Bristol City Hall—building ... TN-4
Bristol Coll—school ... TN-4
Bristol Coll Johnson City Center—school ... TN-4
**Bristol Colony**—pop pl ... RI-1
Bristol Commerce Park (Shop Ctr)—locale ... PA-2
Bristol Community Coll—school ... MA-1
Bristol Community Coll East Campus—school ... MA-1
**Bristol Compact (census name Bristol)**—pop pl ... NH-1
Bristol Corners—locale ... MI-6
**Bristol County**—pop pl ... RI-1
Bristol County Agricultural HS—school ... MA-1
Bristol County Courthouse—hist pl ... RI-1
Bristol County Courthouse Complex—hist pl ... MA-1
**Bristol County (in (P)MSA 1120, 1200, 2480, 5400, 6060)**—pop pl ... MA-1
Bristol County Jail—hist pl ... RI-1
Bristol County Superior Court—hist pl ... MA-1
Bristol Cove—bay ... CT-1
Bristol Creek—stream ... ID-8
Bristol Creek—stream (2) ... NC-3
Bristol Customshouse and Post Office—hist pl ... RI-1
Bristol Division—civil ... TN-4
Bristol Downtown Hist Dist—hist pl ... VT-1
Bristol Dry Lake ... CA-9
Bristol Elem Sch—school ... IN-6
Bristol Ferry—locale ... RI-1
**Bristol Ferry**—pop pl ... RI-1
Bristol Ferry Lighthouse—hist pl ... RI-1
Bristol Flat—flat ... WA-9
Bristol Flats—flat ... VT-1
Bristol Girls' Club—hist pl ... CT-1
Bristol Golf and Country Club—locale ... TN-4
Bristol Grove Cem—cemetery ... MN-6
Bristol Gulch—stream ... ND-7
Bristol Harbor—bay ... RI-1
Bristol Head—summit ... CO-8
**Bristol Heights**—pop pl ... PA-2
**Bristol Highlands**—pop pl ... RI-1
Bristol Hill—summit ... IL-6
Bristol Hill—summit (2) ... NY-2
Bristol Hill Ch—church ... NY-2
Bristol Hist Dist—hist pl ... PA-2
**Bristol (historical)**—pop pl ... MS-4
Bristol HS—school ... PA-2
**Bristol (ind. city)**—pop pl ... VA-3
Bristol Industrial Hist Dist—hist pl ... PA-2
Bristol Industrial Park—locale ... TN-4
Bristol International Raceway ... TN-4
Bristol International Speedway—locale ... TN-4
Bristol Lake ... IN-6
Bristol Lake—lake ... CA-9
Bristol Lake—lake ... IN-6
Bristol Lake—lake ... MI-6
Bristol Lake—lake (2) ... NE-7
**Bristol Lake**—pop pl ... IL-6
Bristol Landing—locale ... MD-2
**Bristol Mansion Condominium**—pop pl ... UT-8
Bristol Memorial Hosp—hospital ... TN-4
Bristol Memorial Hosp—hospital ... VA-3
Bristol Mill Creek ... PA-2
Bristol Mills ... ME-1
Bristol Mills—other ... ME-1
Bristol Mine Run—stream ... VA-3
Bristol Mountains—range ... CA-9
Bristol Municipal Stadium—hist pl ... TN-4
Bristol Narrows—gut ... RI-1
**Bristol Narrows**—pop pl ... RI-1
Bristol Neck—cape (2) ... RI-1
Bristol Park ... AZ-5
**Bristol Park**—pop pl ... PA-2
Bristol Pass—gap ... NV-8
Bristol Peak—summit ... NH-1
Bristol Plaza—locale ... PA-2
Bristol-Plymouth Technical Sch—school ... MA-1
Bristol Point—cape ... RI-1
Bristol Pond ... VT-1
Bristol Pond—lake ... GA-3
Bristol Pond—lake ... MI-6
Bristol Post Office—building ... TN-4
Bristol Post Office (historical)—building ... PA-2
Bristol Quarry—mine ... OR-9
Bristol Range—channel ... NJ-2
Bristol Range—channel ... PA-2
Bristol Range—range ... NV-8
**Bristol Ridge**—pop pl ... IL-6
Bristol Ridge—ridge ... NC-3
Bristol Ridge—ridge (2) ... OH-6
Bristol Ridge—ridge ... WY-8
Bristol Rock—pillar ... VT-1
Bristol RR Station—hist pl ... VA-3
Bristol Rsvr—reservoir ... OR-9
Bristol Rsvr No 1—reservoir ... CT-1
Bristol Rsvr No 2—reservoir ... CT-1
Bristol Rsvr No 3—reservoir ... CT-1
Bristol Rsvr No 4—reservoir ... CT-1
Bristol Rsvr No 5—reservoir ... CT-1
Bristol Rsvr Number Six ... CT-1
Bristol Rsvr Number Three ... CT-1
Bristol Rsvr Number Two ... CT-1
Bristol Rsvr Number Two—reservoir ... NV-8
Bristol Sch—school ... CO-8
Bristol Sch—school ... MD-2
Bristol Sch—school (2) ... MO-7
Bristol Sch—school ... NV-8
Bristol Sch—school ... OH-6
Bristol Silver Mine ... NV-8
Bristol Silver Mines—mine ... NV-8
Bristols Pond—lake ... MA-1
Bristol Spring—spring ... CA-9
Bristol Spring—spring ... NV-8
**Bristol Springs**—pop pl ... NY-2
**Bristol Square (subdivision)**—pop pl (2) ... AZ-5
Bristol Station—locale ... OH-6
Bristol Station (local name for Bristol)—other ... IL-6
Bristol Store (historical)—locale ... AL-4
Bristol Terrace ... CT-1
Bristol Terrace No. 1—other ... PA-2
Bristol Terrace No. 2—other ... PA-2
**Bristol Terrace Number One**—pop pl ... PA-2
**Bristol Terrace Number Two**—pop pl ... PA-2
Bristol (Town of)—civ div ... CT-1
**Bristol (Town of)**—pop pl ... ME-1
**Bristol (Town of)**—pop pl ... NH-1
**Bristol (Town of)**—pop pl ... NY-2
**Bristol (Town of)**—pop pl ... RI-1
**Bristol (Town of)**—pop pl ... VT-1
**Bristol (Town of)**—pop pl (2) ... WI-6
Bristol Township—CDP ... PA-2
Bristol Township—civ div ... NE-7
Bristol Township—fmr MCD (2) ... IA-7
**Bristol Township**—pop pl (2) ... SD-7
Bristol Township (historical)—civil ... SD-7
Bristol (Township of)—fmr MCD ... AR-4
**Bristol (Township of)**—pop pl ... IL-6
**Bristol (Township of)**—pop pl ... MN-6
**Bristol (Township of)**—pop pl (2) ... OH-6
**Bristol (Township of)**—pop pl ... PA-2
Bristol Valley—valley ... NY-2
Bristol View Ranger Station—locale ... CO-8
Bristol Village ... OH-6
**Bristol Village**—pop pl ... OH-6
**Bristolville**—pop pl ... OH-6
**Bristolville (sta.) (Spokane)**—pop pl ... OH-6
Bristol Virginia-Tennessee Slogan Sign—hist pl ... TN-4
Bristol Virginia-Tennessee Slogan Sign—hist pl ... VA-3
Bristol Waterfront Hist Dist—hist pl ... RI-1
Bristol Waterworks—locale ... TN-4
Bristol Well—well ... NV-8
Bristol Wells Town Site—hist pl ... NV-8
Bristolwood Ch—church ... MI-6
Bristol Woods ... GA-3
Briston Cem—cemetery ... MT-8
Bristone Creek ... AL-4
Briston Fire Control HQ—locale ... FL-3
**Bristoria**—pop pl ... PA-2
Bristow—locale ... AL-4
Bristow—locale ... KY-4
Bristow—locale ... VA-3
**Bristow**—pop pl ... IN-6
**Bristow**—pop pl ... IA-7
**Bristow**—pop pl ... MS-4
**Bristow**—pop pl ... MO-7
**Bristow**—pop pl ... NE-7
**Bristow**—pop pl ... OK-5
**Bristow**—pop pl ... SC-3
**Bristow**—pop pl ... VA-3
**Bristow**—pop pl ... WI-6
**Bristow Acres (subdivision)**—pop pl ... MS-4
Bristow Bayou—stream ... LA-4
Bristow Cave—cave ... TN-4
Bristow (CCD)—cens area ... OK-5
Bristow Cem ... AL-4
Bristow Cem—cemetery ... AL-4
Bristow Cem—cemetery ... KS-7
Bristow Cem—cemetery ... NE-7
Bristow Cem—cemetery ... TN-4
Bristow Ch—church ... KY-4
Bristow Cove—valley ... AL-4
Bristow Creek—stream ... AL-4
Bristow Creek—stream ... MT-8
Bristow Creek—stream ... TX-5
Bristow (historical)—locale ... KS-7
Bristow Hollow—valley ... WI-6
Bristow Interchange—other ... OK-5
Bristow Lake—lake ... FL-3
Bristow Methodist Episcopal Ch (historical)—church ... AL-4
**Bristow Point**—pop pl ... OK-5
Bristow Post Office (historical)—building ... AL-4
Bristow Prairie—flat ... OR-9
Bristow Presbyterian Church—hist pl ... OK-5
Bristow Sch—school ... KY-4
Bristow Sch—school ... NE-7
Bristows Creek ... AL-4
Bristows Creek Watershed Dam Number 1—dam ... AL-4
Bristow Seep Spring—spring ... AZ-5
Bristow South (CCD)—cens area ... OK-5
Bristow Spring—spring ... AL-4
Bristow Spring—spring ... AZ-5
Bristow Tank—reservoir (2) ... AZ-5
**Bristow Township**—pop pl ... NE-7
Bristow (Township of)—fmr MCD ... AR-4
Bristow Trail—trail ... OR-9

**Bristow Village**—pop pl VA-3
Britain—locale VA-3
Britain Creek—stream CA-9
Britain Draw—valley WY-8
Britain Ranch—locale TX-5
Britain Ranch—locale WY-8
Britain Ridge—ridge CA-9
Britains Bay MD-2
**Britamer**—pop pl TX-5
Britania Mtn—summit WY-8
Britaniaville MA-1
Britannia MA-1
Britannia Mountain WY-8
Britanniaville MA-1
**Britanniaville**—pop pl MA-1
Britannic Mine—mine CO-8
Britans Bay MD-2
Britan Windmill—locale NM-5
Britch Creek—stream TN-4
Britches Creek—stream FL-3
Britches Leg Branch—stream KY-4
Brite Canyon—valley NM-5
Brite Cem—cemetery (3) TX-5
Brite Creek—stream CA-9
**Brite Meadows (subdivision)**—pop pl NC-3
Britenell Brook—stream ME-1
Brite Ranch—locale TX-5
Brites Creek—stream KS-7
Brite Valley—valley CA-9
Brith Sholom Cem—cemetery MI-6
Britians Corner PA-2
Britin Ranch—locale NE-7
**British Acres (subdivision)**—pop pl NC-3
British-American Canal—canal LA-4
British Canal—canal ME-1
British Cem—cemetery NC-3
British Creek—stream CO-8
British Embassy Bldg—building DC-2
Britisher Creek WY-8
**British Hollow**—pop pl WI-6
British Landing—locale MI-6
British Lane Sch—school IL-6
British Mountains—range AK-9
**British Woods (subdivision)**—pop pl (3) NC-3
Brit Lake—lake FL-3
**Britmark**—pop pl KY-4
**Britmart**—pop pl KY-4
**Britney Acres**—pop pl OH-6
Brito—locale CA-9
Brito Gun Club—other CA-9
Britons Bay MD-2
Briton Sch—school IL-6
Brito Ranch—locale NM-5
Britsch Cem—cemetery TX-5
**Britt**—pop pl IA-7
**Britt**—pop pl MN-6
Britt, Eugene W., House—hist pl CA-9
Britt, Lake—lake FL-3
Brittain OH-6
Brittain—locale AR-4
**Brittain**—pop pl OH-6
Brittain Cem—cemetery MO-7
Brittain Cem—cemetery TN-4
Brittain Cem—cemetery VA-3
Brittain Ch—church NC-3
Brittain Cove—valley NC-3
Brittain Cove Ch—church NC-3
Brittain Creek—stream NC-3
Brittain Creek—stream TX-5
Brittain Mtn—summit NC-3
Brittain School PA-2
Brittains Corner—locale PA-2
Brittains Lake—lake TX-5
Brittain Store NC-3
**Brittain Village (subdivision)**—pop pl NC-3
Brittain Well—well NM-5
Brittam School PA-2
Brittan, Patrick Henry, House—hist pl AL-4
Brittan Acres Sch—school CA-9
Brittan Creek—stream MN-6
**Brittan (historical)**—pop pl OR-9
Brittania MA-1
Brittania Station MA-1
Brittan Knoll—summit CA-9
Brittannia MA-1
Brittan Ranch—locale CA-9
Brittan Sch—school CA-9
**Brittan Square (subdivision)**—pop pl MA-1
**Brittany**—pop pl LA-4
Brittany Apartment Bldg—hist pl OH-6
Brittany Bay Park—park FL-3
**Brittany Farms**—pop pl PA-2
Brittany Lake—lake OR-9
**Brittany Ridge (subdivision)**—pop pl NC-3
**Brittany Woods (subdivision)**—pop pl MS-4
Britt Branch—stream FL-3
Britt Branch—stream SC-3
Britt Branch—stream TX-5
Britt Branch Sch—school SC-3
Britt Canyon—valley UT-8
Britt Cem MS-4
Britt Cem—cemetery MS-4
Britt Cem—cemetery (4) NC-3
Britt Creek ID-8
Britt Creek—stream (2) FL-3
Britt Creek—stream OR-9
Britt Creek—stream TN-4
Britt David Ch—church GA-3
Brittell Sch—school CA-9
Britteman Cem MS-4
Britten Creek—stream NC-3
Brittenham Tank—reservoir AZ-5
Britten Hill IL-6
Britten Mountain NC-3
Britten Ranch—locale AZ-5
Britten Sch—school IL-6
Britten Sch (historical)—school PA-2
Brittens Creek—stream GA-3
Brittenum Cem—cemetery MS-4
Britt Farm Lake Dam—dam MS-4
Britt-Fishman Lake—reservoir NC-3
Britt-Fishman Lake Dam—dam NC-3
Britt Hollow—valley TN-4
Brittian Branch—stream NC-3
Brittian Cem—cemetery TN-4
Brittian Creek—stream WA-9
**Brittian Township**—pop pl ND-7
Brittin—locale ND-7
Brittin Cem—cemetery IL-6
Brittin Cove—valley NC-3
Brittingham Branch—stream DE-2
Brittingham Park—park WI-6
Brittingham Park Boathouse—hist pl WI-6
Brittingham Ranch—locale CO-8
Britt Lake AR-4
Britt Lake—lake AR-4
Brittle, Lake—reservoir VA-3
Brittle Azra Stow Cem—cemetery VT-1
Brittle Hollow—valley MO-7
Brittle Ridge—ridge TN-4
Brittles Ferry (historical)—locale NC-3
Brittle Silver Basin—basin CO-8
Brittle Silver Mtn—summit (2) CO-8
Brittles Millpond—reservoir VA-3
Brittles Pond VA-3
Britt Mine—mine CA-9
Britt Mine—mine TN-4
Brittmount MN-6
Brittmount—locale MN-6
Britton KS-7
Britton—locale MD-2
**Britton**—pop pl MI-6
**Britton**—pop pl OK-5
**Britton**—pop pl SC-3
**Britton**—pop pl SD-7
**Britton**—pop pl TX-5
Britton, Lake—lake CA-9
Britton, Lake—lake MS-4
Britton, Lake—reservoir CA-9
Britton, Monte—summit PR-3
**Britton Acres**—pop pl TN-4
Britton Branch—stream AL-4
Britton Branch—stream IN-6
Britton Branch—stream (3) KY-4
Britton Branch—stream OK-5
Britton Branch—stream TN-4
Britton Canyon—valley TX-5
Britton Cem—cemetery AL-4
Britton Cem—cemetery AR-4
Britton Cem—cemetery IL-6
Britton Cem—cemetery IN-6
Britton Cem—cemetery OH-6
Britton Cem—cemetery SD-7
Britton Cem—cemetery TN-4
Britton Cem—cemetery TX-5
Britton Cem—cemetery WV-2
Britton Ch—church TN-4
Britton Chaffin Cem—cemetery OH-6
Britton Creek NC-3
Britton Creek—stream KY-4
Britton Creek—stream NC-3
Britton Creek—stream OR-9
Britton Creek—stream TN-4
Britton Creek—stream TX-5
Britton Creek Ch—church KY-4
**Britton Davis**—pop pl TX-5
Britton-Evans House—hist pl TX-5
Britton Ferry (historical)—locale TN-4
Britton Ford—locale TN-4
**Britton Ford**—pop pl TN-4
Britton Ford Campground—locale TN-4
Britton Gap—gap KY-4
Britton Gap—gap VA-3
Britton Hill—summit AR-4
Britton Hill—summit IN-6
Britton Hill—summit TN-4
**Britton Hills Farms**—pop pl VA-3
Britton Hollow—valley TN-4
Britton Hollow—valley VA-3
Britton Lake—lake ME-1
Britton Lake—lake MI-6
Britton Lake—lake NE-7
Britton Mtn—summit NC-3
Britton Municipal Airp—airport SD-7
Britton Neck—cape (2) SC-3
**Britton Neck**—pop pl SC-3
Britton Neck HS—school SC-3
Britton Plaza (Shop Ctr)—locale FL-3
Britton Ponds—lake GA-3
Britton Prairie—area MO-7
Britton Prospect—mine TN-4
Britton Ranch—locale NE-7
Britton Road JHS—school NY-2
Britton Run—locale PA-2
Britton Run—stream KY-4
Britton Run—stream (3) PA-2
Brittons bay MD-2
Britton Sch—school ME-1
Britton Sch—school OK-5
Brittons Creek—stream NC-3
Britton's Island NY-2
Brittons Methodist Ch (historical)—church TN-4
Brittons Neck SC-3
Brittons Neck (CCD)—cens area SC-3
Brittons Pond—lake MA-1
Britton Spring—spring CA-9
Britton Spring—spring TN-4
Britton Spring—spring WY-8
Brittons Slough—gut ND-7
Brittons Store NC-3
Britton Tank—reservoir TX-5
Brittontown—locale TN-4
Brittontown Sch—school TN-4
Britton Wharf MD-2
Britt Park—park OR-9
Britt Place—hist pl LA-4
Britt Ranch—locale TX-5
Britt Run—stream VA-3
Britt Run—stream WV-2
**Britts**—pop pl SC-3
Britt Sch—school AR-4
Britt Sch—school NJ-2
Britts Chapel Cem—cemetery TN-4
Britt School (abandoned)—locale MO-7
Britts Creek—stream MT-8
Britts Gap—gut TX-5
Britt Shoals—bar GA-3
Britts Knob—summit KY-4
Britts Landing—locale TN-4
Britts Landing Post Office (historical)—building TN-4
Britt Slough—stream WA-9
Britts Mtn—summit VA-3
Britt Spring—spring TN-4
Britts Shoal—bar ME-1
Britts Spring Hollow—valley TN-4
Britts Store—locale NC-3
Britts (Township of)—fmr MCD NC-3
Brittsville KS-7
Brittsville—locale TN-4
Brittsville Baptist Ch—church TN-4
Brittsville Post Office (historical)—building TN-4
Britt Township—fmr MCD IA-7
Britt Valley—valley WI-6
Britt Valley Sch—school WI-6
Britt Well—well TX-5
Brix, H. H., Mansion—hist pl CA-9
Brix Bay—bay WA-9
Brixey—locale MO-7
Brixey Creek—stream MO-7
Brixey Hollow—valley MO-7
Brixey Spring—spring MO-7
Brixham—locale ME-1
Brixham Grange Hall ME-1
**Brixham Lower Corners**—pop pl ME-1
**Brixham Upper Corners**—pop pl ME-1
Brixius Creek—stream NY-2
Brizendine Branch—stream TX-5
Brizendine House—hist pl TX-5
Brizendine Place—locale NM-5
Brizzee Hollow—valley PA-2
Brizzie Hollow PA-2
Brizziolari Creek—stream CA-9
Broach MS-4
Broach, H. H., House—hist pl MN-6
Broach Cem—cemetery AR-4
Broach Cem—cemetery TN-4
Broach Creek—stream GA-3
Broach Mill—locale AL-4
Broach Mine—mine TN-4
Broach Sch—school FL-3
Broachs Mill Creek—stream NC-3
Broad—locale AR-4
Broad—locale GA-3
Broadacre—locale OH-6
Broad Acres—locale DE-2
**Broad Acres**—pop pl MI-6
**Broad Acres**—pop pl NH-1
**Broadacres**—pop pl NY-2
**Broadacres**—pop pl OR-9
**Broad Acres**—pop pl PA-2
**Broad Acres**—pop pl TN-4
Broadacres—uninc pl LA-4
Broadacres—uninc pl NC-3
Broadacres Ch—church LA-4
Broadacres Hist Dist—hist pl TX-5
Broadacres Lake—reservoir NC-3
Broadacres Lake Dam—dam NC-3
Broadacres Lakes—reservoir NC-3
Broadacres Sanatorium—other NY-2
Broad Acres Sch—school MD-2
Broadacres Shop Ctr—locale MS-4
**Broad Acres (subdivision)**—pop pl (2) NC-3
Broadacres United Methodist Ch—church MS-4
**Broadalbin**—pop pl NY-2
Broadalbin Junction—locale NY-2
**Broadalbin (Town of)**—pop pl NY-2
Broad Apron Lake—lake IL-6
Broad Arch UT-8
Broad Ax Branch—stream SC-3
Broadax Draw—valley WA-9
Broadaxe PA-2
**Broad Axe**—pop pl PA-2
Broadaxe Bayou—stream LA-4
Broadaxe Creek—bay FL-3
Broadaxe Creek—stream ID-8
Broad Axe Creek—stream VA-3
Broad Axe Hill—summit TN-4
Broadaxe Ridge—ridge FL-3
Broadax Spring—spring WA-9
Broadback Island—island WV-2
Broad Bay—bay AK-9
Broad Bay—bay NH-1
Broad Bay—bay VA-3
**Broad Bay Colony**—pop pl VA-3
Broad Bayou—gut TX-5
Broad Bayou—stream MS-4
Broadbay (Township of)—fmr MCD NC-3
**Broadbent**—pop pl OR-9
Broadbent Meadow—flat UT-8
**Broadbent PUD Subdivision**—pop pl UT-8
Broadbent Swamp—swamp PA-2
Broad Bight—bay AK-9
Broad Bottom—locale KY-4
Broadbottom Branch AL-4
Broad Branch—locale FL-3
Broad Branch—stream AL-4
Broad Branch—stream DC-2
Broad Branch—stream (2) FL-3
Broad Branch—stream GA-3
Broad Branch—stream (2) KY-4
Broad Branch—stream (2) NC-3
Broad Branch—stream (2) SC-3
Broad Branch—stream TN-4
Broad Branch—stream (3) VA-3
Broad Branch—stream WV-2
Broad Branch Sch—school WV-2
**Broadbridge Station**—pop pl MI-6
Broad Brook CT-1
Broad Brook MA-1
**Broad Brook**—pop pl CT-1
Broad Brook—stream (3) CT-1
Broad Brook—stream (4) MA-1
Broad Brook—stream NH-1
Broad Brook—stream (2) NY-2
Broad Brook—stream (4) VT-1
Broad Brook Canal—canal MA-1
Broad Brook Company—hist pl CT-1
Broad Brook Elem Sch—school CT-1
Broad Brook Mill Pond CT-1
Broad Brook Millpond—lake CT-1
Broadbrook Mtn VT-1
Broad Brook Mtn—summit VT-1
Broad Brook Rsvr CT-1
Broad Brook Rsvr—reservoir (2) CT-1
Broad Brook Village Brook CT-1
Broad Canal—canal FL-3
Broad Canal—canal MA-1
Broad Canyon—valley AZ-5
Broad Canyon—valley CA-9
Broad Canyon—valley CO-8
Broad Canyon—valley ID-8
Broad Canyon—valley (3) NV-8
Broad Canyon—valley (2) NM-5
Broad Canyon—valley (10) UT-8
Broad Canyon—valley WY-8
Broad Canyon Mine—mine NV-8
Broadcast House Helistop Heliport—airport WA-9
Broadcast Park—park IA-7
Broadcast Peak—summit CA-9
Broad Channel NY-2
Broad Channel—channel (2) NY-2
**Broad Channel**—pop pl NY-2
Broad Cove ME-1
Broad Cove—bay (10) ME-1
Broad Cove—bay (2) NH-1
Broad Cove—cove (2) MA-1
Broad Cove—lake MA-1
**Broad Cove**—pop pl (2) ME-1
Broad Cove Rock—bar ME-1
Broad Creek DE-2
Broad Creek NC-3
Broad Creek WV-2
Broad Creek—bay (2) MD-2
Broad Creek—bay (2) NC-3
Broad Creek—channel FL-3
Broad Creek—channel MD-2
Broad Creek—channel NJ-2
Broad Creek—cove MA-1
Broad Creek—gut FL-3
Broad Creek—gut MA-1
Broad Creek—locale DE-2
**Broad Creek**—pop pl MD-2
**Broad Creek**—pop pl NC-3
Broad Creek—stream AK-9
Broad Creek—stream CA-9
Broad Creek—stream DE-2
Broad Creek—stream (2) FL-3
Broad Creek—stream IN-6
Broad Creek—stream (7) MD-2
Broad Creek—stream (2) MA-1
Broad Creek—stream MO-7
Broad Creek—stream NV-8
Broad Creek—stream (2) NJ-2
Broad Creek—stream (11) NC-3
Broad Creek—stream (2) SC-3
Broad Creek—stream (5) VA-3
Broad Creek—stream WY-8
Broad Creek Canal—canal NC-3
Broad Creek Ch—church MD-2
Broad Creek Ch—church NC-3
Broad Creek Ch—church VA-3
Broad Creek Channel NJ-2
Broad Creek Channel—channel NY-2
Broad Creek Chapel—church NC-3
**Broad Creek Estates (subdivision)**—pop pl DE-2
Broad Creek Gut—gut MD-2
Broad Creek (historical)—bay MA-1
Broad Creek Hundred—civil DE-2
Broad Creek Light Six—locale FL-3
Broad Creek Marsh—swamp MD-2
Broad Creek Marsh—swamp NY-2
Broad Creek Marsh—swamp NC-3
Broad Creek Memorial Scout Camp—locale MD-2
Broad Creek MS—school NC-3
Broad Creek Point—cape (4) NC-3
Broad Creek River DE-2
Broad Creek Sch (historical)—school NC-3
Broad Creek Soapstone Quarries—hist pl MD-2
**Broad Creek (subdivision)**—pop pl VA-3
Broad Creek Thorofare NJ-2
Broad Cut—channel MI-6
Broad Cut Highway—channel MI-6
Broad Door Sch—school TN-4
Broad Draft—valley VA-3
Broad Draw—valley AZ-5
Broaddus—locale VA-3
**Broaddus**—pop pl TX-5
**Broaddus**—pop pl VA-3
**Broaddus**—pop pl WV-2
Broaddus (CCD)—cens area TX-5
Broaddus Cemetery MS-4
Broaddus Creek—stream CA-9
Broaddus Mill Pond VA-3
Broaddus Pond—reservoir VA-3
Broad Dyke Canal—canal DE-2
**Broadell (subdivision)**—pop pl NC-3
Broadenaxe Gulch—valley OR-9
**Broadfield**—pop pl GA-3
**Broadfields**—pop pl KY-4
Broadfoot Hollow—valley MO-7
**Broadford**—pop pl ID-8
**Broad Ford**—pop pl KY-4
**Broad Ford**—pop pl PA-2
**Broadford**—pop pl VA-3
Broadford Bridge—bridge PA-2
Broad Ford Ch—church KY-4
Broadford Dam—dam MD-2
Broadfording—locale MD-2
**Broadford Junction**—pop pl PA-2
Broad Ford Run—stream MD-2
Broadford Sch (abandoned)—school PA-2
Broad Gap Hollow—valley KY-4
Broad Gauge Mine—mine WA-9
Broad Gulch—valley SD-7
Broad Gulch Creek—stream NV-8
Broad Gut—gut DE-2
Broadhead KY-4
Broadhead Creek PA-2
Broadhead Creek—stream (2) AL-4
Broadhead Creek—stream VA-3
Broadhead Lake—lake UT-8
Broadhead Lakes—lake UT-8
Broadhead Mtn—summit VA-3
Broadhead Pond—lake PA-2
Broadhead Run—stream KY-4
Broadhead Run—stream PA-2
Broadhead Sch—school IL-6
Broadhead Slough—stream MT-8
Broadheads Ville PA-2
Broad Hill—summit CT-1
Broad Hill—summit (2) MA-1
Broad Hill—summit RI-1
Broad Hollow UT-8
Broad Hollow—valley ID-8
Broad Hollow—valley IL-6
Broad Hollow—valley (2) KY-4
Broad Hollow—valley OH-6
Broad Hollow—valley OR-9
Broad Hollow—valley TN-4
Broad Hollow—valley (15) UT-8
Broad Hollow—valley (6) VA-3
Broad Hollow—valley (3) WV-2
Broad Hollow—valley (2) WY-8
Broad Hollow Creek—stream VA-3
Broad Hollow Run—stream PA-2
Broad Hollow Trail—trail VA-3
Broadhorn Creek—stream IA-7
**Broadhurst**—pop pl GA-3
Broadhurst Arroyo—stream NM-5
Broadhurst Canyon—valley CA-9
Broadie Lake—lake IN-6
Broadies Lake IN-6
Broad Island—island AK-9
Broad-Kenan Streets Hist Dist—hist pl NC-3
Broad Key—island FL-3
Broadkill (2) DE-2
Broadkill Beach—beach DE-2
**Broadkill Beach**—pop pl DE-2
Broadkill Creek DE-2
Broadkill Hundred—civil DE-2
Broadkill Neck—cape DE-2
Broadkill River—stream DE-2
Broadkill Sch—school DE-2
Broadkill Sound—bay DE-2
Broadkill Station—locale DE-2
Broadkiln Creek DE-2
Broadkiln Hundred DE-2
Broad Lake—lake LA-4
Broad Lake—lake (2) MS-4
Broad Lake—lake (2) SC-3
**Broadland**—pop pl SD-7
Broadland Cem—cemetery SD-7
**Broadlands**—pop pl IL-6
**Broadlands**—pop pl IN-6
**Broadland Township**—pop pl SD-7
Broad Lane—locale NJ-2
**Broadlawn Highlands**—pop pl PA-2
Broadlawn Memorial Gardens—cemetery GA-3
Broadlawns Hosp—hospital IA-7
Broadlawn Town Hall—building ND-7
**Broadlawn Township**—pop pl ND-7
Broadleaf Hollow—valley UT-8
Broadleigh Sch—school OH-6
Broadman OH-6
Broadman Ch—church OH-6
Broad Margin—hist pl SC-3
Broad Marsh—swamp MA-1
Broad Marsh River—stream MA-1
Broadmead—locale OR-9
Broad Meadow—swamp MA-1
Broad Meadow Brook—stream MA-1
Broadmeadow Brook—stream MA-1
Broad Meadow Brook—stream MA-1
Broad Meadow Creek—stream NC-3
Broad Meadows—flat MA-1
Broadmeadow Sch—school MA-1
Broadmeadow School, The—school DE-2
Broad Meadows Sch—school MA-1
Broad Meadow Swamp—swamp MA-1
Broadmeadow United Methodist Ch—church MS-4
Broad Mesa—summit WY-8
**Broadmont**—pop pl VA-3
Broadmoor IN-6
Broadmoor—CDP LA-4
Broadmoor—locale IL-6
**Broadmoor**—pop pl AK-9
**Broadmoor**—pop pl CA-9
**Broadmoor**—pop pl CO-8
**Broadmoor**—pop pl IL-6
**Broadmoor**—pop pl IN-6
**Broadmoor**—pop pl (2) LA-4
**Broadmoor**—pop pl MD-2
**Broadmoor**—pop pl TN-4
**Broadmoor**—pop pl VA-3
**Broadmoor**—pop pl WA-9
**Broadmoor**—pop pl WV-2
Broadmoor—uninc pl AL-4
Broadmoor—uninc pl LA-4
Broadmoor—uninc pl NM-5
Broadmoor—uninc pl TX-5
Broadmoor Baptist Ch MS-4
Broadmoor Baptist Ch—church MS-4
Broadmoor Ch—church MS-4
Broadmoor Ch—church TN-4
Broadmoor Country Club—other IN-6
Broadmoore Ch—church MS-4
Broadmoor Golf Club—other WA-9
Broadmoor Golf Course—other CO-8
Broadmoor Golf Course—other OR-9
Broadmoor HS—school LA-4
Broadmoor JHS—school KS-7
Broadmoor JHS—school LA-4
Broadmoor Lodge—locale CO-8
Broadmoor Mart Shop Ctr—locale MS-4
Broadmoor Park—park FL-3
Broadmoor Plaza OH-6
Broadmoor Sch—school AR-4
Broadmoor Sch—school FL-3
Broadmoor Sch—school LA-4
Broadmoor Sch—school OH-6
Broadmoor Shop Ctr—locale AR-4
Broadmoor Shop Ctr—locale NM-5
Broadmoor Shop Ctr—other NM-5
**Broadmoor (subdivision)**—pop pl AL-4
**Broadmoor Subdivision (subdivision)**—pop pl SD-7
Broadmore Ditch—canal LA-4
Broadmor Sch—school AZ-5
Broad Mountain Dam—dam PA-2
Broad Mountain Rsvr—reservoir PA-2
Broad Mountain Tower—tower PA-2
Broad Mouth Branch—stream NC-3
Broad Mouth Canyon—valley ID-8
Broadmouth Canyon—valley (4) UT-8
Broadmouth Ch—church SC-3
Broad Mouth Creek—stream SC-3
Broadmouth Hollow—valley WV-2
Broad Mtn PA-2
Broad Mtn—range PA-2
Broad Mtn—summit (3) PA-2
Broad Mtn—summit TN-4
Broad Mtn—summit TX-5
Broadnax Bar AL-4
Broadnax Landing (historical)—locale AL-4
Broadnax Woodyard Landing AL-4
Broad Neck—cape (2) MD-2
Broad Neck—cape VA-3
Broad Neck Ch—church MD-2
Broadneck Swamp—swamp NC-3
**Broad Oaks**—pop pl WV-2
**Broad Park**—pop pl IN-6
Broad Pass—gap (2) AK-9
**Broad Pass**—pop pl AK-9
Broad Point—cape (2) AK-9
Broad Point—cape ME-1
Broad Point—cape MD-2
Broad Pond—swamp IN-6
Broad Post Office (historical)—building TN-4
Broad Ranch—locale NE-7
Broad Ridge—ridge PA-2
Broad Ridge—ridge VA-3
Broad Ridge Cem—cemetery KY-4
Broadridge Ch—church NC-3
Broadridge Plaza—locale CO-8
Broad Ridge Trail—trail PA-2
Broad Ripple (2) IN-6
**Broad Ripple**—pop pl IN-6
Broad Ripple Baptist Ch—church IN-6
Broad Ripple Bridge—bridge IN-6
Broad Ripple Camp—park IN-6
Broad Ripple HS—school IN-6
Broad Ripple Nazarene Ch—church IN-6
Broad Ripple Park—park IN-6
Broad Ripple Park Carousel—hist pl IN-6
**Broad Ripple (subdivision)**—pop pl IN-6
Broad Ripple United Methodist Ch—church IN-6
Broad River GA-3
Broad River—stream FL-3
Broad River—stream GA-3
Broad River—stream NC-3
Broad River—stream (2) SC-3
Broad River Bay—bay FL-3
Broad River (CCD)—cens area (2) GA-3
Broad River Ch—church (3) GA-3
Broad River Ch—church (2) NC-3
Broad River Ch—church (2) SC-3
Broad River Dam No 1—dam GA-3
Broad River Sch—school CT-1
Broad River Sch—school SC-3
Broad River (Township of)—fmr MCD NC-3
Broad Rock—uninc pl VA-3
Broad Rock Ch—church VA-3
Broad Rock Creek—stream VA-3
Broadroom Ch—church LA-4
Broad Run—locale VA-3
**Broad Run**—pop pl MD-2
**Broad Run**—pop pl VA-3
Broad Run—stream IL-6
Broad Run—stream IN-6
Broad Run—stream (2) KY-4
Broad Run—stream (5) MD-2
Broad Run—stream NC-3
Broad Run—stream OH-6
Broad Run—stream (5) PA-2
Broad Run—stream (7) VA-3
Broad Run—stream (14) WV-2
Broad Run Bridge and Tollhouse—hist pl VA-3
Broad Run Cem—cemetery OH-6
Broad Run Cem—cemetery WV-2
Broad Run Ch—church VA-3
Broad Run Ch—church WV-2
Broad Run Dam PA-2
**Broad Run Farms**—pop pl VA-3
Broad Run HS—school VA-3
Broad Run Lake—reservoir VA-3
Broad Run (Magisterial District)—fmr MCD VA-3
Broad Run Mtn—summit VA-3
Broad Run Rsvr—reservoir PA-2
Broad Run Sch—school WV-2
Broads, The—channel NH-1
Broad Saint Ch—church NC-3
Broad Saint Sch—school NH-1
Broads Canyon—valley UT-8
Broad Sch—school GA-3
Broads Fork—stream UT-8
Broads Hill MA-1
Broad Shoal Creek—stream TN-4
Broad Shoal Hollow—valley MO-7
Broad Shoals NC-3
Broad Shoals—bar TN-4
Broad Shoals—bar VA-3
Broad Slough—bay CA-9
Broad Slough—gut CA-9
Broad Slough—gut OR-9
Broad Slough—gut (2) TN-4
Broad Sound—bay ME-1
Broad Sound—bay MA-1
Broad Sound—channel MA-1
Broad Spit—bar WA-9
Broadstone Lodge—locale NC-3
Broad Street—gut VA-3
Broad Street—post sta TN-4
Broad Street—uninc pl PA-2
Broad Street—uninc pl SC-3
Broad Street Annex—post sta NJ-2
Broad Street Apartments—hist pl OH-6
Broad Street Ave Sch—school MA-1
Broadstreet Cem—cemetery MI-6
Broad Street Christian Ch—church NC-3
Broad Street Christian Church—hist pl OH-6
Broad Street Commercial Hist Dist—hist pl GA-3
Broad Street Commercial Hist Dist—hist pl VA-3
Broad Street Elem Sch—school PA-2
Broad Street Hist Dist—hist pl CT-1
Broad Street Hist Dist—hist pl (2) GA-3
Broad Street Hist Dist—hist pl ME-1
Broad Street Hist Dist—hist pl PA-2
Broadstreet Hollow NY-2
Broadstreet Hollow—valley NY-2
Broad Street HS—school MS-4
Broad Street Lake—reservoir NJ-2
Broad Street Market—building PA-2
Broad Street Market—hist pl PA-2
Broad Street Methodist Ch—church AL-4
Broad Street Methodist Episcopal Church South—hist pl GA-3
Broad Street Presbyterian Ch—church AL-4
Broad Street Sch—hist pl CT-1
Broad Street Sch—school (2) CT-1
Broad Street Sch—school IA-7
Broad Street Sch—school MA-1
Broad Street Sch—school NJ-2
Broad Street Sch—school (4) NY-2
Broad Street Station—hist pl VA-3
Broad Street Station—locale NJ-2
Broad Street Station—locale VA-3
Broad Street United Methodist Ch—church MS-4

Broad Street United Methodist Church—*hist pl* ... OH-6
Broad Street United Methodist Church—*hist pl* ... TN-4
Broad Street-Water Street Hist Dist—*hist pl* ... NY-2
*Broad Swamp* ... MA-1
Broad Swamp—*swamp* ... VA-3
Broad Swamp Brook—*stream* ... CT-1
Broadt Airp—*airport* ... PA-2
Broad Thorofare—*channel* ... NJ-2
*Broad Timber Creek* ... TX-5
*Broadtop* ... PA-2
Broad Top—*summit* ... VA-3
**Broad Top City**—*pop pl* ... PA-2
Broad Top City Borough—*civil* ... PA-2
**Broad Top City (corporate name for Broad Top)**—*pop pl* ... PA-2
*Broad Top (corporate name Broad Top City)* ... PA-2
Broad Top Post Office (historical)—*building* ... PA-2
**Broad Top (Township of)**—*pop pl* ... PA-2
Broadtree Branch—*stream* ... KY-4
Broadtree Branch—*stream* ... TX-5
*Broadtree Creek* ... OR-9
*Broadtree Fork* ... KY-4
Broadtree Hollow—*valley* ... KY-4
Broadtree Run—*stream* (2) ... WV-2
Broaduay Channel—*channel* ... FL-3
**Broadus**—*pop pl* ... MT-8
Broadus Branch—*stream* ... KY-4
Broadus Branch—*stream* ... MO-7
Broadus Cem—*cemetery* ... IL-6
Broadus Cem—*cemetery* (2) ... MS-4
Broadus Coulee—*valley* ... MT-8
Broadus Creek—*stream* ... MT-8
Broadus Lake—*lake* ... MS-4
Broadus Lake Dam—*dam* ... MS-4
Broadus Memorial Ch—*church* ... VA-3
Broadus Mtn—*summit* ... VA-3
Broadus Wood Sch—*school* ... VA-3
*Broadview* ... IN-6
*Broadview* ... OH-6
Broadview—*locale* ... OH-6
Broadview—*locale* ... TX-5
**Broadview**—*pop pl* ... IL-6
**Broadview**—*pop pl* (2) ... IN-6
**Broadview**—*pop pl* ... MD-2
**Broadview**—*pop pl* ... MT-8
**Broadview**—*pop pl* ... NM-5
**Broadview**—*pop pl* ... NC-3
**Broadview**—*pop pl* ... PA-2
**Broadview**—*pop pl* (3) ... TN-4
Broadview—*post sta* ... GA-3
Broadview—*post sta* ... LA-4
Broadview Acad—*school* ... IL-6
**Broadview Acres**—*pop pl* ... MD-2
**Broadview Acres**—*pop pl* ... NM-5
**Broadview Acres**—*pop pl* ... NC-3
**Broadview Acres**—*pop pl* ... OH-6
Broadview Baptist Ch—*church* ... FL-3
Broadview Bench—*bench* ... MT-8
Broadview (CCD)—*cens area* ... NM-5
Broadview Ch—*church* ... TN-4
**Broadview Country Club Estates**—*pop pl* ... FL-3
Broadview Elem Sch—*school* ... TN-4
**Broadview Estates**—*pop pl* ... NC-3
Broadview Farms—*locale* ... CA-9
Broadview Guard Station—*locale* ... AK-9
**Broadview Heights**—*pop pl* ... OH-6
Broadview Heights HS—*school* ... OH-6
Broadview JHS—*school* ... NC-3
Broadview Memorial Cem—*cemetery* ... ME-1
Broadview Park—*park* ... CO-8
**Broadview Park**—*pop pl* ... ME-1
**Broadview Park (subdivision)**—*pop pl* ... FL-3
Broadview Picnic Area—*park* ... TX-5
Broadview-Pompano Park—*CDP* ... FL-3
Broadview Sanitarium—*hospital* ... CA-9
Broadview Sch—*school* ... AR-4
Broadview Sch—*school* ... FL-3
Broadview Sch—*school* (2) ... OH-6
Broadview Sch—*school* ... WA-9
Broadview Sch—*school* ... WV-2
Broad View Sch—*school* ... WI-6
**Broadview (subdivision)**—*pop pl* ... AL-4
**Broadview (subdivision)**—*pop pl* ... NC-3
**Broadview Township**—*pop pl* ... ND-7
Broadwater—*locale* ... MD-2
Broadwater—*locale* ... MO-7
Broadwater—*locale* ... VA-3
**Broadwater**—*pop pl* ... FL-3
**Broadwater**—*pop pl* ... MT-8
**Broadwater**—*pop pl* ... NE-7
Broad Water—*stream* ... SC-3
Broadwater Airp—*airport* ... MO-7
Broadwater Bay—*bay* ... MN-6
Broadwater Bay Park—*park* ... MT-8
Broadwater Branch—*stream* (2) ... SC-3
Broadwater Cem—*cemetery* ... WV-2
Broadwater Chapel—*church* ... MD-2
Broadwater Cove—*bay* ... NY-2
Broadwater Creek—*bay* ... MD-2
Broadwater Drain—*stream* ... AZ-5
**Broadwater Estates**—*pop pl* ... MD-2
Broadwater Golf Course—*locale* ... MS-4
Broadwater Hollow—*valley* ... AR-4
*Broadwater Lake* ... MT-8
Broadwater Lake—*lake* (2) ... MT-8
Broadwater Lake—*lake* ... NC-3
Broadwater Marina—*locale* ... MS-4
Broadwater Meadows—*flat* ... UT-8
Broadwater Mines—*mine* ... MT-8
Broadwater Missouri Canal—*canal* ... MT-8
Broadwater - Missouri Canal—*canal* ... MT-8
Broadwater - Missouri West Side Canal—*canal* ... MT-8
Broadwater River—*stream* ... MT-8
Broadwater Sch—*school* ... MT-8
Broadwater Sch—*school* ... SC-3
Broad Waters Muddy Creek—*other* ... MO-7
Broadwater Sun Golf Course—*locale* ... MS-4
*Broadway* ... IL-6
*Broadway* ... RI-1
*Broadway* ... TN-4
Broadway—*channel* ... MA-1
Broadway—*flat* ... VA-3
Broadway—*locale* ... KY-4
Broadway—*locale* ... NC-3
**Broadway**—*pop pl* ... MO-7
**Broadway**—*pop pl* ... NJ-2
**Broadway**—*pop pl* ... NC-3
**Broadway**—*pop pl* ... OH-6
**Broadway**—*pop pl* ... PA-2
**Broadway**—*pop pl* ... SC-3
**Broadway**—*pop pl* ... TN-4
**Broadway**—*pop pl* (3) ... TX-5
**Broadway**—*pop pl* ... VA-3
**Broadway**—*pop pl* ... WA-9
Broadway—*post sta* ... FL-3
Broadway—*post sta* ... TX-5
Broadway—*uninc pl* (2) ... CA-9
Broadway—*uninc pl* ... MA-1
Broadway—*uninc pl* ... NY-2
Broadway-Amory Hist Dist—*hist pl* ... RI-1
Broadway Ave Hist Dist—*hist pl* ... OH-6
Broadway Baptist Ch—*church* ... IN-6
Broadway Baptist Ch—*church* ... TN-4
Broadway Bldg—*hist pl* ... OH-6
Broadway Bluff Improvement—*hist pl* ... TX-5
Broadway Branch—*stream* ... MD-2
Broadway Branch—*stream* (2) ... SC-3
Broadway Bridge—*bridge* ... OR-9
Broadway Bridge—*hist pl* ... AZ-5
Broadway Bridge—*hist pl* ... CO-8
Broadway Bridge—*other* ... MO-7
Broadway Cem—*cemetery* ... IN-6
Broadway Cem—*cemetery* (2) ... NY-2
Broadway Cem—*cemetery* ... TN-4
Broadway Center—*locale* ... MO-7
**Broadway Center**—*pop pl* ... IN-6
Broadway Ch—*church* ... AL-4
Broadway Ch—*church* ... IN-6
Broadway Ch—*church* ... KY-4
Broadway Ch—*church* (2) ... MO-7
Broadway Ch—*church* ... OH-6
Broadway Ch—*church* (2) ... TN-4
Broadway Ch—*church* ... VA-3
Broadway Channel—*channel* ... TX-5
Broadway Ch of God—*church* ... FL-3
Broadway Christian Ch—*church* ... KS-7
Broadway Creek—*stream* ... SC-3
Broadway District—*hist pl* ... MO-7
Broadway Edison Sch—*school* ... WA-9
Broadway Elem Sch—*school* ... NC-3
**Broadway Estates**—*pop pl* ... CO-8
Broadway Estates Shop Ctr—*other* ... CO-8
Broadway Gap—*gap* ... NC-3
Broadway Hist Dist—*hist pl* ... ME-1
Broadway Hist Dist—*hist pl* (2) ... NY-2
Broadway Hist Dist—*hist pl* ... TN-4
Broadway Hist Dist (Boundary Increase)—*hist pl* ... NY-2
Broadway Hollow—*valley* ... KY-4
Broadway Hosp—*hospital* ... CA-9
Broadway Hotel—*hist pl* ... OK-5
Broadway Hotel—*hist pl* ... UT-8
Broadway Interchange—*crossing* ... IN-6
Broadway Junction—*locale* ... TX-5
**Broadway Junction**—*pop pl* ... NY-2
**Broadway Lake**—*pop pl* ... SC-3
Broadway Lake—*reservoir* ... SC-3
Broadway Landing—*locale* ... VA-3
Broadway Lava—*lava* ... OR-9
Broadway-Livingston Ave Hist Dist—*hist pl* ... NY-2
Broadway Manchester—*uninc pl* ... CA-9
*Broadway Manor* ... MI-6
**Broadway Manor**—*pop pl* ... PA-2
Broadway Meadows—*swamp* ... DE-2
Broadway Mine—*mine* ... WY-8
Broadway Neck—*cape* ... VA-3
Broadway Oil and Gas Field—*oilfield* ... KS-7
*Broadway Park* ... MA-1
Broadway Park—*park* ... CA-9
Broadway Park—*park* ... ME-1
Broadway Park—*park* ... OK-5
Broadway-Phelps Park Hist Dist—*hist pl* ... IA-7
Broadway Pier (Fireboat Station)—*locale* ... CA-9
Broadway Plaza Service Shop Ctr—*locale* ... AZ-5
*Broadway (RR name Broadway Junction)* ... MO-7
Broadway Rural Shop Ctr—*locale* ... AZ-5
Broadway Sch—*school* (3) ... CA-9
Broadway Sch—*school* ... CO-8
Broadway Sch—*school* ... CT-1
Broadway Sch—*school* ... KY-4
Broadway Sch—*school* ... MD-2
Broadway Sch—*school* ... MI-6
Broadway Sch—*school* ... NJ-2
Broadway Sch—*school* (3) ... NY-2
Broadway Sch—*school* ... OH-6
Broadway Sch—*school* ... OR-9
Broadway Sch—*school* (2) ... PA-2
Broadway Sch—*school* ... TX-5
Broadway Sch—*school* (2) ... WA-9
Broadway Seven Thousand Shop Ctr—*locale* ... AZ-5
Broadway Shop Ctr—*locale* ... MA-1
Broadway Shop Ctr—*other* ... ME-1
Broadway Shop Ctr, The—*locale* ... AZ-5
Broadway Speedway (historical)—*locale* ... TN-4
Broadway Spring—*spring* ... OR-9
**Broadway (sta.)**—*pop pl* ... NJ-2
Broadway Station—*locale* ... NJ-2
Broadway Station—*locale* ... NY-2
Broadway Station (historical)—*locale* ... MA-1
Broadway-Tazewell Shop Ctr—*locale* ... TN-4
Broadway Temple A.M.E. Zion Church—*hist pl* ... KY-4
Broadway Theater and Commercial District—*hist pl* ... CA-9
Broadway Tower—*hist pl* ... OK-5
Broadway Trailer Court—*locale* ... AZ-5
Broadway United Methodist Ch—*church* ... IN-6
Broadway Valentine Shop Ctr—*locale* ... MO-7
Broadway Village Shop Ctr—*locale* ... AZ-5
Broadway West Oil and Gas Field—*oilfield* ... KS-7
Broadway Wharf—*locale* ... MO-7
Broadway Yards—*locale* ... VA-3
*Broadwell* ... OH-6
Broadwell—*locale* ... CA-9
Broadwell—*locale* ... KY-4
**Broadwell**—*pop pl* ... IL-6
**Broadwell**—*pop pl* ... OH-6
Broadwell, Cyrus, House—*hist pl* ... OH-6
Broadwell Cem—*cemetery* ... NC-3
*Broadwell Dry Lake* ... CA-9
Broadwell Lake—*flat* ... CA-9
Broadwell Lake—*reservoir* ... NC-3
Broadwell Lake Dam—*dam* ... NC-3
Broadwell Mesa—*summit* ... CA-9
Broadwells Mill—*locale* ... AL-4
**Broadwell (Township of)**—*pop pl* ... IL-6
Broadwine Branch—*stream* ... VA-3
**Broadwood Manor**—*pop pl* ... MD-2
Broady Bottom—*locale* ... VA-3
Broady Cem—*cemetery* ... VA-3
Broady Creek—*stream* ... OR-9
*Broatmanville* ... NJ-2
*Brobbity Hill* ... OR-9
Brobergs Lake—*lake* ... MN-6
*Brobity Hill* ... OR-9
**Brobston**—*pop pl* ... GA-3
Brobst Sch—*school* ... OH-6
Broccy Creek—*stream* ... NY-2
Broccy Creek Rsvr—*reservoir* ... NY-2
*Broch Creek* ... IN-6
*Brocher Creek* ... OR-9
Brocher Creek—*stream* ... OR-9
Brocher Path—*trail* ... PA-2
*Brochhausen School Number 88* ... IN-6
Brocious Run—*stream* ... PA-2
*Brock* ... AL-4
Brock—*locale* ... CA-9
Brock—*locale* ... KY-4
Brock—*locale* ... MO-7
Brock—*locale* ... NC-3
Brock—*locale* ... TX-5
**Brock**—*pop pl* ... IL-6
**Brock**—*pop pl* ... NE-7
**Brock**—*pop pl* ... OH-6
**Brock**—*pop pl* ... OK-5
**Brock**—*pop pl* ... PA-2
**Brock**—*pop pl* ... SC-3
Brock, Mount—*summit* ... AK-9
Brock Adair Ditch—*canal* ... CO-8
Brockamp Creek—*stream* ... IA-7
Brockamp Duck Club—*other* ... CA-9
Brock And Pickett Cem—*cemetery* ... TN-4
Brockatonorton Bay—*bay* ... MD-2
Brockaways Branch—*stream* ... NJ-2
Brockbank Hollow—*valley* ... UT-8
Brockbank JHS—*school* ... UT-8
Brockbank Sch—*school* ... UT-8
Brock Bay—*swamp* ... FL-3
Brock Branch—*stream* ... AL-4
Brock Branch—*stream* (2) ... GA-3
Brock Branch—*stream* ... KY-4
Brock Bridge—*bridge* ... MD-2
**Brock Bridge**—*pop pl* ... MD-2
Brock Brook—*stream* ... NH-1
Brock Butte—*summit* ... CA-9
Brock Camp—*locale* ... MT-8
Brock Camp—*locale* ... WY-8
Brock Canyon—*valley* (2) ... NV-8
Brock Canyon—*valley* ... NM-5
Brock Cave—*cave* ... TN-4
Brock Cem—*cemetery* (2) ... AL-4
Brock Cem—*cemetery* ... AR-4
Brock Cem—*cemetery* (2) ... GA-3
Brock Cem—*cemetery* ... IL-6
Brock Cem—*cemetery* ... IN-6
Brock Cem—*cemetery* (2) ... KY-4
Brock Cem—*cemetery* (2) ... MS-4
Brock Cem—*cemetery* ... OH-6
Brock Cem—*cemetery* (6) ... TN-4
Brock Cem—*cemetery* ... WV-2
Brock Ch—*church* ... AL-4
Brock Chapel—*church* ... AL-4
*Brock Ch of Christ* ... AL-4
Brock Coulee—*valley* ... MT-8
Brock County Park—*park* ... MI-6
*Brock Cove* ... TN-4
Brock Cove—*bay* ... VA-3
Brock Cowcamp—*locale* ... WY-8
Brock Creek—*bay* ... FL-3
Brock Creek—*locale* ... MT-8
Brock Creek—*stream* (2) ... AR-4
Brock Creek—*stream* (2) ... CA-9
Brock Creek—*stream* ... ID-8
Brock Creek—*stream* ... IN-6
Brock Creek—*stream* ... KY-4
Brock Creek—*stream* ... MS-4
Brock Creek—*stream* ... MO-7
Brock Creek—*stream* (2) ... MT-8
Brock Creek—*stream* ... NC-3
Brock Creek—*stream* ... OK-5
Brock Creek—*stream* ... OR-9
Brock Creek—*stream* ... PA-2
Brock Creek—*stream* ... TN-4
Brock Creek—*stream* ... VA-3
Brock Creek—*stream* (2) ... WA-9
Brock Crossroad—*locale* ... FL-3
Brockdale Ch—*church* ... LA-4
Brockdell—*locale* ... TN-4
Brockdell Ch—*church* ... TN-4
Brockdell Post Office (historical)—*building* ... TN-4
Brock Ditch—*canal* (2) ... IN-6
Brock Ditch—*canal* ... OH-6
Brockel Airstrip—*airport* ... SD-7
Brockel Homestead—*locale* ... MT-8
Brockelmans Market—*building* ... MA-1
Brockels Cem—*cemetery* ... SD-7
Brockenberry Bay—*bay* ... VA-3
Brockenberry Creek—*stream* ... VA-3
Brockenbrough Airp—*airport* ... NC-3
Brockenbrough Creek—*stream* ... VA-3
*Brocker* ... WV-2
Brocker Health Center—*hospital* ... NC-3
Brockerhoff Hotel—*hist pl* ... PA-2
Brockerhoff Mill—*hist pl* ... PA-2
Brocker Place—*locale* ... CO-8
**Brocket**—*pop pl* ... ND-7
Brockett—*locale* ... AR-4
Brockett Cem—*cemetery* ... AR-4
Brockett Cem—*cemetery* (2) ... TN-4
Brockett Creek—*stream* ... IL-6
Brockett Tank—*reservoir* ... AZ-5
Brockfield (Township of)—*other* ... IL-6
Brock Flats—*flat* ... FL-3
Brock Fork—*stream* ... WY-8
Brock Gap—*gap* ... AL-4
Brock Gap—*gap* ... PA-2
Brock Gulch—*valley* (2) ... CA-9
Brock Hall—*locale* ... MD-2
Brockham Bayou—*stream* ... LA-4
Brockhausen Cem—*cemetery* ... WI-6
Brock Hill—*summit* ... VT-1
*Brock Hollow* ... TN-4
Brock Hollow—*valley* (2) ... TN-4
Brock Hollow—*valley* (2) ... TX-5
Brock House—*hist pl* ... KY-4
Brockhurst Creek—*stream* ... OR-9
**Brockie**—*pop pl* ... PA-2
Brockie Lake—*lake* ... ID-8
Brockie Lake—*reservoir* ... ID-8
Brockie Ranch—*locale* ... ID-8
Brockies Pond—*lake* ... MI-6
Brockie Spring—*spring* ... MT-8
Brockie Tank—*reservoir* ... AZ-5
**Brockington**—*pop pl* ... SC-3
Brockington Corner—*locale* ... AR-4
Brockington Creek—*stream* ... GA-3
Brockington Sch—*school* ... SC-3
Brockinton-Scott House—*hist pl* ... SC-3
Brock Island—*island* ... NC-3
Brock Junction—*locale* ... TX-5
Brock Lake—*lake* ... FL-3
Brock Lake—*lake* ... IL-6
Brock Lake—*lake* ... WI-6
Brock Lake—*reservoir* ... TX-5
**Brockland Acres**—*pop pl* ... TN-4
Brock Landing—*locale* ... IL-6
Brockland Sch—*school* ... OK-5
Brocklebank Hill—*summit* ... VT-1
Brockliss Canyon—*valley* ... CA-9
Brockliss Slough—*stream* ... NV-8
Brockman—*locale* ... CA-9
Brockman—*locale* ... NM-5
Brockman Canyon—*valley* (3) ... CA-9
Brockman Cem—*cemetery* ... AR-4
Brockman Cem—*cemetery* ... IN-6
Brockman Creek—*stream* ... ID-8
Brockman Creek—*stream* ... TX-5
Brockman Dirt Tank—*reservoir* ... NM-5
Brockman Drain—*canal* ... CA-9
Brockman Drain Two—*canal* ... CA-9
Brockman Flat Lava Beds—*lava* ... CA-9
Brockman Guard Station—*locale* ... ID-8
Brockman Gulch—*valley* ... OR-9
Brockman Hills—*other* ... NM-5
Brockman Island—*area* ... MO-7
Brockman Island—*island* ... AK-9
Brockmann Point—*cliff* ... TX-5
Brockman Pass—*channel* ... AK-9
*Brockman Point* ... MD-2
Brockman Ranch—*locale* ... NM-5
Brockman Ranch—*locale* ... OR-9
Brockman Ranch—*locale* ... TX-5
Brockman Reservoirs—*reservoir* ... CO-8
Brockman Rsvr No 1—*reservoir* ... CO-8
Brockman Rsvr No 2—*reservoir* ... CO-8
Brockman Sch—*school* (2) ... SC-3
**Brockmans Corner**—*pop pl* ... CA-9
Brockmans Horse Camp—*locale* ... CA-9
Brockman Slough—*stream* ... CA-9
Brockman Spring—*spring* ... MO-7
Brockman Tank—*reservoir* ... NM-5
Brockman Well—*well* ... NM-5
Brock Meadows—*flat* ... OR-9
Brockmeier Sch—*school* ... IL-6
*Brock Mill Branch* ... FL-3
Brock Mill Branch—*stream* ... FL-3
Brockmiller Gulch—*valley* ... ID-8
Brock Mill (historical)—*locale* ... AL-4
Brockmonte Canyon—*valley* ... AZ-5
Brock Mtn—*summit* ... AL-4
Brock Mtn—*summit* ... AR-4
Brock Mtn—*summit* ... CA-9
Brock Mtn—*summit* ... NV-8
Brock Mtn—*summit* ... NY-2
Brock Mtn—*summit* ... NC-3
Brock Mtn—*summit* ... TN-4
Brockmueller Barn—*hist pl* ... SD-7
Brock Oil Field—*oilfield* ... OK-5
Brockonbridge Gut—*gut* ... DE-2
Brockover Mesa—*summit* ... CO-8
Brockoway Tank—*reservoir* ... NM-5
Brock Page Creek—*stream* ... SC-3
Brock Park—*park* ... IL-6
Brock Park—*park* ... OK-5
Brock Park—*park* ... TX-5
Brock Point—*cliff* ... VA-3
*Brock Pond* ... FL-3
Brock Pond—*reservoir* ... NC-3
Brock Pond—*reservoir* ... WI-6
Brock Pond Dam—*dam* ... MS-4
**Brockport**—*pop pl* ... NY-2
**Brockport**—*pop pl* ... PA-2
Brockport Creek—*stream* ... NY-2
Brockport State Univ—*school* ... NY-2
Brock Post Office (historical)—*building* ... TN-4
Brock Prairie—*area* ... MO-7
Brock Ranch—*locale* ... NM-5
Brock Ridge—*ridge* ... IN-6
Brock Ridge—*ridge* ... NM-5
Brock Ridge—*ridge* ... OH-6
Brock Ridge—*ridge* ... TN-4
Brock Ridge—*ridge* ... WV-2
Brockroad—*locale* ... VA-3
Brock Run—*stream* ... VA-3
Brock Run—*stream* (2) ... WV-2
Brock Run Camping Area—*locale* ... WV-2
**Brocks**—*pop pl* ... NC-3
Brocks Bridge—*bridge* ... VA-3
**Brocksburg**—*pop pl* ... NE-7
*Brocks Cemetery* ... MS-4
Brock Sch—*school* ... NE-7
Brock Sch—*school* ... TN-4
*Brocks Chapel* ... AL-4
Brocks Chapel—*church* ... NC-3
Brocks Chapel—*locale* ... TN-4
Brocks Chapel Sch (historical)—*school* ... TN-4
Brock Sch (historical)—*school* ... AL-4
**Brocks Corner**—*pop pl* ... OH-6
Brocks Creek—*stream* ... SC-3
Brocks Gap—*gap* ... VA-3
Brocks Lake—*reservoir* ... GA-3
Brock Slough—*lake* ... ND-7
**Brocks Mill**—*pop pl* ... SC-3
Brocks Mill (historical)—*locale* ... AL-4
Brocks Pond Dam—*dam* ... MS-4
Brock Spring—*spring* ... MO-7
Brock Spring—*spring* ... TN-4
Brock Springs—*spring* ... CA-9
Brocks Spring—*spring* ... VA-3
Brockston Gully—*stream* ... LA-4
Brock Store (historical)—*locale* ... MS-4
Brock Tank—*reservoir* ... TX-5
*Brockton* ... AL-4
Brockton—*locale* ... GA-3
**Brockton**—*pop pl* ... MA-1
**Brockton**—*pop pl* ... MS-4
**Brockton**—*pop pl* ... MT-8
**Brockton**—*pop pl* ... PA-2
Brockton, City of—*civil* ... MA-1
Brockton Ave Sch—*school* ... CA-9
Brockton City Hall—*building* ... MA-1
Brockton City Hall—*hist pl* ... MA-1
Brockton East Shopping Plaza—*locale* ... MA-1
Brockton Edison Electric Illuminating Company Power Station—*hist pl* ... MA-1
Brockton Golf Club—*locale* ... MA-1
**Brockton Heights**—*pop pl* ... MA-1
Brockton (historical P.O.)—*locale* ... MA-1
Brockton HS—*school* ... MA-1
Brockton Reservoir Dam—*dam* ... MA-1
Brockton Rsvr—*reservoir* ... MA-1
Brockton Station (historical P.O.)—*locale* ... MA-1
Brocktown Cem—*cemetery* ... AR-4
*Brockville* ... AL-4
*Brockville* ... IN-6
**Brockville**—*pop pl* ... NY-2
**Brockville**—*pop pl* ... WI-6
Brockville Cem—*cemetery* ... IL-6
Brockville Rock—*island* ... NY-2
Brockville Sch—*school* ... IL-6
Brockway—*locale* ... CT-1
Brockway—*locale* ... NY-2
Brockway—*locale* ... OR-9
**Brockway**—*pop pl* ... CA-9
**Brockway**—*pop pl* ... MI-6
**Brockway**—*pop pl* ... MT-8
**Brockway**—*pop pl* ... PA-2
Brockway, Abel, House—*hist pl* ... MI-6
Brockway Borough—*civil* ... PA-2
Brockway Branch—*stream* ... TX-5
**Brockway (Brockwayville)**—*pop pl* ... PA-2
Brockway Brook—*stream* ... NY-2
Brockway Cem—*cemetery* ... IN-6
Brockway Cem—*cemetery* ... IA-7
Brockway Cem—*cemetery* ... MN-6
Brockway Ch—*church* ... MI-6
**Brockway Corner**—*pop pl* ... MA-1
Brockway Corners—*locale* ... NY-2
Brockway Coulee—*valley* (2) ... MT-8
Brockway Creek—*stream* ... AL-4
Brockway Creek—*stream* ... OR-9
Brockway Creek—*stream* ... WA-9
Brockway Golf Club—*other* ... CA-9
Brockway Guard Station—*other* ... CA-9
**Brockway (historical)**—*pop pl* ... ND-7
Brockway Island—*island* ... CT-1
Brockway Lake—*lake* ... MI-6
Brockway Lake—*lake* ... MN-6
**Brockway Landing**—*pop pl* ... CT-1
Brockway Memorial Library—*building* ... FL-3
*Brockway Mills* ... VT-1
Brockway Nose—*summit* ... MI-6
Brockway Park—*park* ... CA-9
Brockway Point—*cape* ... CA-9
Brockway Rsvr—*reservoir* (2) ... PA-2
Brockways Bar—*bar* ... AK-9
Brockway Sch—*school* ... ME-1
Brockway Sch—*school* ... NY-2
Brockway Sch No 13—*school* ... NY-2
Brockway Site (ME 90.3)—*hist pl* ... ME-1
**Brockways Mills**—*pop pl* ... VT-1
Brockway Spring—*spring* ... CA-9
Brockway Spring—*spring* ... MO-7
Brockway Spring—*spring* ... MT-8
Brockway Summit—*summit* ... CA-9
**Brockway (Town of)**—*pop pl* ... WI-6
**Brockway (Township of)**—*pop pl* ... MI-6
**Brockway (Township of)**—*pop pl* ... MN-6
*Brockwayville* ... PA-2
Brockwayville—*other* ... PA-2
**Brockwell**—*pop pl* ... AR-4
**Brockwood PUD Subdivision**—*pop pl* ... UT-8
Brocky Canyon—*valley* ... ID-8
*Brocky Lake* ... ID-8
Brocky Lake—*lake* ... MI-6
**Broco**—*pop pl* ... FL-3
*Brocton* ... GA-3
**Brocton**—*pop pl* ... IL-6
**Brocton**—*pop pl* ... NY-2
Brocton Rsvr—*reservoir* ... NY-2
Brocum Run—*stream* ... WV-2
Brodback Cem—*cemetery* ... MO-7
Brodbeck (RR name for Brodbecks)—*other* ... PA-2
Brodbecks—*locale* ... PA-2
Brodbeck Sch (abandoned)—*school* ... PA-2
**Brodbecks (RR name Brodbeck)**—*pop pl* ... PA-2
Brodbeck-Zundel Hist Dist—*hist pl* ... AL-4
Brod Creek—*stream* ... WI-6
Broddus Creek—*stream* ... GA-3
**Broddyville**—*pop pl* ... IA-7
Broderheim Ch—*church* ... MN-6
**Broderick**—*pop pl* ... CA-9
Broderick, Mount—*summit* ... CA-9
Broderick-Bryte—*CDP* ... CA-9
Broderick Cem—*cemetery* ... OH-6
Broderick Flat—*flat* ... WY-8
Broderick Sch (abandoned)—*school* ... MO-7
Broderick (Washington)—*uninc pl* ... CA-9
Broder Meadows—*flat* ... CA-9
Broders Cabin—*locale* ... CA-9
**Brodhead**—*pop pl* ... KY-4
**Brodhead**—*pop pl* ... NY-2
**Brodhead**—*pop pl* ... PA-2
**Brodhead**—*pop pl* ... WI-6
Brodhead, Mount—*summit* ... PA-2
Brodhead, Thomas, House—*hist pl* ... NY-2
Brodhead-Bell-Morton Mansion—*hist pl* ... DC-2
Brodhead Canyon—*valley* ... CO-8
Brodhead Creek—*stream* ... PA-2
Brodhead Creek SCS Dam 466—*dam* ... PA-2
Brodhead Farm—*hist pl* ... PA-2
*Brodheads Creek* ... PA-2
Brodheads Creek Dam—*dam* ... PA-2
*Brodhead Station* ... PA-2
**Brodheadsville**—*pop pl* ... PA-2
Brodie Bend Cutoff—*bend* ... AR-4
Brodie Branch—*stream* ... VA-3
Brodie Cem—*cemetery* ... IN-6
Brodie Creek—*stream* ... AR-4
Brodie Creek—*stream* ... OR-9
Brodie Draw—*valley* ... WY-8
Brodie Gulch—*valley* ... ID-8
*Brodie Lake* ... IN-6
Brodie Millpond—*reservoir* ... SC-3
*Brodie Mountain* ... WA-9
Brodie Mountain—*ridge* ... MA-1
Brodie Mountain Ski Area—*locale* ... MA-1
Brodie Sch—*school* ... NE-7
Brodie Sch—*school* ... GU-9
Brodies Ferry (historical)—*locale* ... TN-4
Brodies Landing—*locale* ... TN-4
*Brodies Landing Post Office* ... TN-4
Brodies Pond—*reservoir* ... SC-3
Brodies Post Office (historical)—*building* ... TN-4
**Brodnax**—*pop pl* ... VA-3
Brodnax, Samuel H., House—*hist pl* ... GA-3
Brodnax Bar—*bar* ... AL-4
Brodnax Cem—*cemetery* ... GA-3
Brodnax Cem—*cemetery* ... TN-4
Brodnicki Sch—*school* ... IL-6
Brodrick Branch—*stream* ... AL-4
**Brodtville**—*pop pl* ... WI-6
Brody—*locale* ... MS-4
Brody Creek—*stream* ... AZ-5
Brody Creek—*stream* ... WA-9
Brody Hills—*summit* ... AZ-5
Brody Hills Tank—*reservoir* ... AZ-5
Brody JHS—*school* ... IA-7
Brody Rsvr—*reservoir* ... WY-8
Brody Seep—*spring* ... AZ-5
Broeckling Lake—*lake* ... IL-6
**Broeck Pointe**—*pop pl* ... KY-4
**Broeker**—*pop pl* ... MN-6
*Broemmer Creek* ... WI-6
Broening Park—*park* ... MD-2
Broesche Cem—*cemetery* ... TX-5
Broetje, John F. and John H., House—*hist pl* ... OR-9
**Broe Township**—*pop pl* ... ND-7
Brogade Cem—*cemetery* ... TX-5
**Brogado**—*pop pl* ... TX-5
**Brogan**—*pop pl* ... OR-9
Brogan Branch—*stream* ... VA-3
Brogan (CCD)—*cens area* ... OR-9
Brogan Cem—*cemetery* ... OR-9
Brogan Cem—*cemetery* ... TN-4
Brogan Creek—*stream* ... AR-4
Brogan Creek—*stream* ... KS-7
Brogan Creek—*stream* ... OR-9
Brogan Ditch—*canal* ... OR-9
Brogan Hill—*summit* ... OR-9
Brogan Hill Summit—*summit* ... OR-9
**Brogan (historical)**—*pop pl* ... IA-7
Brogan Ranch—*locale* ... NE-7
Broganville—*locale* ... NE-7
Brogdan Hollow—*valley* ... MS-4
**Brogden**—*pop pl* (2) ... NC-3
Brogden Branch—*stream* ... TX-5
Brogden Cem—*cemetery* ... SC-3
Brogden Chapel—*church* ... NC-3
Brogden Hollow—*valley* ... AR-4
Brogden JHS—*school* ... NC-3
Brogden Memorial Sch—*school* ... SC-3
*Brogden River* ... AL-4
Brogden Sch—*school* ... NC-3
Brogden (Township of)—*fmr MCD* ... NC-3
**Brogdon**—*pop pl* ... SC-3
Brogdon Branch—*stream* ... SC-3
Brogdon Cem—*cemetery* ... TN-4
Brogdon Farm—*hist pl* ... TX-5
Brogdon Hill—*summit* ... GA-3
*Broggin Branch* ... AR-4
*Broggon Hill* ... GA-3
Broglan Branch—*stream* ... AL-4
Broglen Branch—*stream* ... AL-4
*Broglen Creek* ... AL-4
Broglen River—*stream* ... AL-4
Broglin Slough—*gut* ... TN-4
**Brogue**—*pop pl* ... PA-2
Brogue Branch—*stream* ... AL-4
*Brogueville* ... PA-2
Brogueville—*locale* ... PA-2
**Brogueville (Parks)**—*pop pl* ... PA-2
*Brogueville Station* ... PA-2
**Brohard**—*pop pl* ... WV-2
*Brohawn Point* ... MD-2
*Brohead Creek SCS Dam 466* ... PA-2
**Brohman**—*pop pl* (2) ... MI-6
Brohorn Creek—*stream* ... MD-2
Broiles Hollow—*valley* ... KY-4
Brokaw—*locale* ... IL-6
**Brokaw**—*pop pl* ... OH-6
**Brokaw**—*pop pl* ... WI-6
Brokaw, Norman, House—*hist pl* ... WI-6
Brokaw Creek—*stream* ... MN-6
Brokaw Hill—*summit* ... IL-6
Brokaw Hosp—*hospital* ... IL-6
Brokaw Lake—*lake* ... MN-6
Brokaw-McDougall House—*hist pl* ... FL-3
Brokaw Ranch—*locale* ... WY-8
Brokaw Site—*hist pl* ... OH-6
Brokedown Cliff—*cliff* ... KY-4
Brokehook Creek—*stream* ... GA-3
Brokeleg Branch—*stream* ... NC-3
Broke Leg Creek—*stream* ... KY-4
Brokeleg Mtn—*summit* ... TX-5
Broke Leg Windmill—*locale* ... TX-5
Broken Arch—*arch* ... UT-8
*Broken Arrow* ... AL-4
**Broken Arrow**—*pop pl* ... OK-5
**Broken Arrow Acres**—*pop pl* ... CO-8
Broken Arrow Camp—*locale* ... OR-9
Broken Arrow Ch—*church* ... AL-4
Broken Arrow Ch—*church* ... OK-5
Broken Arrow Creek—*stream* (3) ... AL-4
Broken Arrow Mine (underground)—*mine* ... AL-4
**Broken Arrow Park**—*pop pl* ... KS-7
Broken Arrow Ranch—*locale* ... AZ-5
Broken Arrow Ranch—*locale* ... NM-5
Broken Arrow Shoals—*bar* ... AL-4
Broken Arrow Slough—*gut* ... MN-6
Broken Arrow Waterworks—*other* ... OK-5
Broken Axe Trail—*trail* ... PA-2
Broken Axle Ranch—*locale* ... NE-7
Broken Axle Tank—*reservoir* ... AZ-5
Broken Back Canyon—*valley* ... UT-8
Broken Back Crater—*summit* ... NM-5
Brokenback Creek—*stream* ... WY-8
Brokenback Mtn—*summit* ... TN-4

Brookings Township Hall—*building* SD-7
Brooking Township—*civil* MO-7
Brooking Valley—*basin* NE-7
*Brookins Bay* ME-1
Brookins Cem—*cemetery* NY-2
Brookins Gulch—*valley* MT-8
*Brook Kedron* MN-6
*Brook Knoll* IN-6
Brook Knoll Sch—*school* CA-9
Brook Lake—*lake* CO-8
Brook Lake—*lake* OR-9
Brook Lake—*lake* UT-8
Brook Lake—*lake* (2) WA-9
Brook Lake—*lake* WY-8
Brook Lake (Unorganized Territory of)—*unorg* MN-6
*Brookland* AL-4
*Brookland* SC-3
*Brookland* TX-5
Brookland—*hist pl* (2) NC-3
Brookland—*locale* PA-2
**Brookland**—*pop pl* AL-4
**Brookland**—*pop pl* AR-4
**Brookland**—*pop pl* DC-2
**Brookland**—*pop pl* MD-2
Brookland-Cayce HS—*school* SC-3
Brookland-Cayce Sch Number 1—*school* SC-3
Brookland-Cayce Sch Number 2—*school* SC-3
Brookland Cem—*cemetery* PA-2
Brookland Ch—*church* NC-3
Brookland Ch—*church* VA-3
**Brookland Estates**—*pop pl* VA-3
**Brookland Gardens**—*pop pl* VA-3
Brookland HS—*school* VA-3
Brookland (Magisterial District)—*fmr MCD* VA-3
**Brookland Manor (subdivision)**—*pop pl* NC-3
Brookland Recreation Center—*locale* VA-3
**Brooklands**—*pop pl* MI-6
Brookland Sch—*school* DC-2
Brookland Sch—*school* SC-3
Brookland Sch (historical)—*school* MS-4
Brooklands Plantation—*hist pl* SC-3
Brooklands Sch—*school* MI-6
**Brookland Terrace**—*pop pl* DE-2
Brookland (Township of)—*fmr MCD* AR-4
**Brooklandville**—*pop pl* MD-2
Brooklandville House—*hist pl* MD-2
Brooklandwood—*hist pl* MD-2
Brooklane Ch—*church* AL-4
Brooklane Golf Course—*other* MI-6
Brooklane Park—*park* MN-6
**Brooklane Place**—*pop pl* AL-4
Brooklane Sch—*school* NJ-2
*Brooklawn* PA-2
**Brooklawn**—*pop pl* NJ-2
**Brooklawn**—*pop pl* PA-2
Brooklawn Cem—*cemetery* MI-6
Brooklawn Cem—*cemetery* WI-6
Brooklawn Childrens Home—*building* KY-4
Brooklawn Country Club—*other* CT-1
**Brooklawn Estates Subdivision**—*pop pl* UT-8
Brooklawn Memorial Cem—*cemetery* ME-1
Brook Lawn Memory Garden Cem—*cemetery* WI-6
Brooklawn Park—*park* MA-1
**Brooklawn Park (subdivision)**—*pop pl* NC-3
Brooklawn Sch—*school* OH-6
Brookledge Golf Course—*other* OH-6
Brookleigh Baptist Ch—*church* MS-4
**Brookleigh (subdivision)**—*pop pl* MS-4
**Brooklet**—*pop pl* GA-3
Brooklet (CCD)—*cens area* GA-3
Brookley—*uninc pl* AL-4
**Brookley Acres**—*pop pl* VA-3
Brookley AFB—*military* AL-4
Brookley Airp—*airport* AL-4
**Brooklin**—*pop pl* ME-1
**Brooklin**—*pop pl* TN-4
**Brooklin**—*pop pl* WV-2
*Brookline* MA-1
**Brookline**—*pop pl* MA-1
**Brookline**—*pop pl* NH-1
**Brookline**—*pop pl* (2) PA-2
**Brookline**—*pop pl* VT-1
**Brookline (Brookline Station P O)**—*pop pl* MO-7
Brookline Cem—*cemetery* MA-1
Brookline Cem—*cemetery* MO-7
Brookline Elem Sch—*school* PA-2
Brookline Field—*locale* MA-1
Brookline Hill HS—*school* MA-1
**Brookline Hill (subdivision)**—*pop pl* MA-1
Brookline HS—*school* MA-1
Brookline Park—*park* TX-5
Brookline Rsvr—*reservoir* MA-1
Brookline Sch—*school* NH-1
Brookline Sch—*school* PA-2
Brookline Sch—*school* TX-5
*Brookline Station* MO-7
Brookline Station (historical)—*locale* MA-1
**Brookline (subdivision)**—*pop pl* MA-1
Brookline Town Green Hist Dist—*hist pl* MA-1
**Brookline (Town of)**—*pop pl* MA-1
**Brookline (Town of)**—*pop pl* NH-1
**Brookline (Town of)**—*pop pl* VT-1
Brookline Township—*civil* MO-7
Brookline Union Sch—*school* VT-1
Brookline Village Commercial District—*hist pl* MA-1
**Brookline Village (subdivision)**—*pop pl* MA-1
Brookling Creek—*stream* OR-9
**Brooklin (Town of)**—*pop pl* ME-1
*Brook Luta* KS-7
*Brooklyn* IN-6
*Brooklyn* MN-6
*Brooklyn* NJ-2
*Brooklyn* TN-4
Brooklyn—*locale* KY-4
Brooklyn—*locale* MN-6
Brooklyn—*locale* PA-2
Brooklyn—*locale* UT-8
Brooklyn—*locale* VA-3
Brooklyn—*locale* WA-9
**Brooklyn**—*pop pl* (3) AL-4
**Brooklyn**—*pop pl* CT-1
**Brooklyn**—*pop pl* FL-3
**Brooklyn**—*pop pl* GA-3
**Brooklyn**—*pop pl* (2) IL-6
**Brooklyn**—*pop pl* IN-6
**Brooklyn**—*pop pl* IA-7
**Brooklyn**—*pop pl* (2) MD-2
**Brooklyn**—*pop pl* MI-6
**Brooklyn**—*pop pl* (2) MS-4
**Brooklyn**—*pop pl* MO-7
**Brooklyn**—*pop pl* (2) NY-2
**Brooklyn**—*pop pl* OH-6
**Brooklyn**—*pop pl* OR-9
**Brooklyn**—*pop pl* PA-2
**Brooklyn**—*pop pl* SC-3
**Brooklyn**—*pop pl* (2) WV-2
**Brooklyn**—*pop pl* WI-6
Brooklyn—*uninc pl* NC-3
Brooklyn Acad (historical)—*school* AL-4
**Brooklyn Addition (subdivision)**—*pop pl* UT-8
Brooklyn Ave Sch—*school* NY-2
Brooklyn Bank Bldg—*hist pl* OH-6
Brooklyn Basin—*harbor* CA-9
Brooklyn-Battery Tunnel—*tunnel* NY-2
Brooklyn Bay—*bay* FL-3
Brooklyn Borough Hall—*hist pl* NY-2
**Brooklyn (Borough of New York City)**—*pop pl* NY-2
Brooklyn Botanic Gardens—*park* NY-2
Brooklyn Bridge—*bridge* NY-2
Brooklyn Bridge—*hist pl* NY-2
Brooklyn Canal—*canal* UT-8
Brooklyn Cem—*cemetery* AL-4
Brooklyn Cem—*cemetery* IL-6
Brooklyn Cem—*cemetery* IN-6
Brooklyn Cem—*cemetery* KS-7
Brooklyn Cem—*cemetery* OH-6
**Brooklyn Center**—*pop pl* MN-6
Brooklyn Center HS—*school* MN-6
Brooklyn Ch—*church* (4) AL-4
Brooklyn Ch—*church* LA-4
Brooklyn Ch—*church* MN-6
Brooklyn Ch—*church* MS-4
Brooklyn Ch—*church* NC-3
Brooklyn Ch—*church* SC-3
Brooklyn Ch—*church* SD-7
Brooklyn Chapel—*church* MS-4
Brooklyn Church and Cemetery—*hist pl* LA-4
Brooklyn-Crystal Cem—*cemetery* MN-6
*Brooklyn Cumberland Presbyterian Ch* AL-4
**Brooklyn-Curtis Bay**—*pop pl* MD-2
Brooklyn Elem Sch—*school* CT-1
Brooklyn Elem Sch—*school* IN-6
Brooklyn Green Hist Dist—*hist pl* CT-1
Brooklyn Gulch—*valley* (2) CO-8
**Brooklyn Heights**—*pop pl* IN-6
**Brooklyn Heights**—*pop pl* MO-7
**Brooklyn Heights**—*pop pl* NY-2
**Brooklyn Heights**—*pop pl* OH-6
Brooklyn Heights Cem—*cemetery* OH-6
Brooklyn Heights Hist Dist—*hist pl* NY-2
Brooklyn Heights Sch—*school* TX-5
Brooklyn (historical)—*locale* KS-7
Brooklyn (historical)—*locale* MS-4
Brooklyn (historical)—*locale* SD-7
**Brooklyn (historical)**—*pop pl* MS-4
Brooklyn Hosp—*hospital* NY-2
Brooklyn Hotel—*hist pl* IA-7
Brooklyn HS—*school* MN-6
Brooklyn HS of Auto Trades—*school* NY-2
Brooklyn Junction—*uninc pl* WV-2
Brooklyn Lake—*lake* FL-3
Brooklyn Lake—*lake* WY-8
Brooklyn Lake Guard Station—*locale* WY-8
Brooklyn Landing (historical)—*locale* MS-4
**Brooklyn Manor**—*pop pl* NY-2
Brooklyn Marine Park—*park* NY-2
**Brooklyn Military Ocean Terminal**—*pop pl* NY-2
Brooklyn Mine—*mine* AZ-5
Brooklyn Mine—*mine* CA-9
Brooklyn Mine—*mine* CO-8
Brooklyn Mine—*mine* MT-8
Brooklyn Mine—*mine* OR-9
*Brooklyn Missionary Baptist Ch* AL-4
Brooklyn Museum—*hist pl* NY-2
Brooklyn Naval Support Activity—*military* NY-2
Brooklyn Park—*park* MO-7
Brooklyn Park—*park* OR-9
**Brooklyn Park**—*pop pl* MD-2
**Brooklyn Park**—*pop pl* MN-6
Brooklyn Park Ch—*church* MN-6
Brooklyn Park HS—*school* MD-2
Brooklyn Park Sch—*school* MD-2
Brooklyn Peak—*summit* AZ-5
Brooklyn Post Office (historical)—*building* MS-4
Brooklyn Preparatory Sch—*school* NY-2
Brooklyn Rest Park—*cemetery* IN-6
Brooklyn Rock—*rock* MA-1
Brooklyn Sch—*school* CA-9
Brooklyn Sch—*school* FL-3
Brooklyn Sch—*school* IL-6
Brooklyn Sch—*school* KS-7
Brooklyn Sch—*school* KY-4
Brooklyn Sch—*school* MI-6
Brooklyn Sch—*school* (2) OR-9
Brooklyn Sch—*school* SD-7
Brooklyn Sch—*school* VT-1
Brooklyn Sch—*school* WI-6
Brooklyn Shaft—*mine* NV-8
Brooklyn-South Square Hist Dist—*hist pl* NC-3
Brooklyn Spring Sch—*school* SC-3
*Brooklyn (sta.)* OH-6
Brooklyn State Hosp—*hospital* NY-2
**Brooklyn Subdivision**—*pop pl* UT-8
Brooklyn Tank—*reservoir* AZ-5
**Brooklyn (Town of)**—*pop pl* CT-1
**Brooklyn (Town of)**—*pop pl* (3) WI-6
**Brooklyn Township**—*pop pl* ND-7
**Brooklyn Township**—*pop pl* SD-7
**Brooklyn (Township of)**—*pop pl* (2) IL-6
**Brooklyn (Township of)**—*pop pl* PA-2
Brooklyn Trail—*trail* CO-8
Brooklyn-Victor Country Club—*other* IA-7
Brooklyn Well—*well* AZ-5
Brooklyn Yacht Club—*other* NY-2
*Brooklyn Zion Ch* AL-4
Brooklyn Zion Sch (historical)—*school* AL-4
Brookman—*locale* GA-3
Brookman Cem—*cemetery* KY-4
**Brookman Corners**—*pop pl* NY-2
*Brook Martin Ridge* TN-4
**Brookmead**—*pop pl* TN-4
**Brookmeade**—*pop pl* DE-2
**Brookmeade**—*pop pl* NJ-2
Brookmeade Ch—*church* (2) TN-4
Brookmeade Sch—*school* (2) TN-4
**Brookmeade (subdivision)**—*pop pl* AL-4
Brook Meadow—*flat* UT-8
*Brook Meadows* OR-9
**Brookmead (subdivision)**—*pop pl* TN-4
Brookmere Cem—*cemetery* OH-6
Brook Mine—*mine* CA-9
**Brookmont**—*pop pl* MD-2
*Brookmont Dam* MD-2
**Brookmont Farms (subdivision)**—*pop pl* DE-2
Brookmont Sch—*school* MD-2
**Brookmoor**—*pop pl* IN-6
**Brook Mount**—*pop pl* IA-7
Brook Mtn—*summit* AL-4
**Brookneal**—*pop pl* VA-3
Brookneal Rsvr—*reservoir* VA-3
Brookner, Christopher, House—*hist pl* IL-6
Brookover—*locale* KS-7
*Brook Park* MI-6
Brook Park—*park* PA-2
**Brook Park**—*pop pl* MN-6
**Brook Park**—*pop pl* OH-6
**Brook Park**—*pop pl* PA-2
Brook Park Cem—*cemetery* MN-6
Brook Park Elem Sch—*school* IN-6
Brookpark JHS—*school* OH-6
**Brook Park Junction**—*pop pl* MN-6
Brook Park Sch—*school* IL-6
**Brook Park (Township of)**—*pop pl* MN-6
Brook Plaza (Shop Ctr)—*locale* FL-3
Brook Point—*cape* ME-1
*Brook Pond* MA-1
**Brookport**—*pop pl* IL-6
Brookport Cem—*cemetery* IL-6
Brook Ranch—*locale* TX-5
Brookreson Ranch—*locale* AZ-5
Brookridge—*CDP* FL-3
**Brookridge**—*pop pl* CO-8
Brook Ridge—*ridge* TN-4
Brookridge—*uninc pl* KS-7
Brookridge Country Club—*other* KS-7
Brookridge Park—*park* CO-8
Brookridge Sch—*school* KS-7
Brookridge Sch—*school* OH-6
Brookridge Shop Ctr—*other* CO-8
**Brookridge Terrace (subdivision)**—*pop pl* NC-3
Brook Road Park—*park* NY-2
Brook Run—*stream* VA-3
Brook Run—*stream* WV-2
Brooks—*locale* AR-4
Brooks—*locale* GA-3
Brooks—*locale* KS-7
Brooks—*locale* KY-4
Brooks—*locale* TX-5
Brooks—*locale* WV-2
**Brooks**—*pop pl* AL-4
**Brooks**—*pop pl* CA-9
**Brooks**—*pop pl* (2) GA-3
**Brooks**—*pop pl* IL-6
**Brooks**—*pop pl* IN-6
**Brooks**—*pop pl* IA-7
**Brooks**—*pop pl* KY-4
**Brooks**—*pop pl* LA-4
**Brooks**—*pop pl* ME-1
**Brooks**—*pop pl* MA-1
**Brooks**—*pop pl* MI-6
**Brooks**—*pop pl* MN-6
**Brooks**—*pop pl* MS-4
**Brooks**—*pop pl* MT-8
**Brooks**—*pop pl* OR-9
**Brooks**—*pop pl* WI-6
Brooks, Charles, House—*hist pl* MA-1
Brooks, Daniel, House—*hist pl* MA-1
Brooks, Francis, House—*hist pl* MA-1
Brooks, George L., Sch—*hist pl* PA-2
Brooks, Harold C., House—*hist pl* MI-6
Brooks, Harold C., House (Boundary Increase)—*hist pl* MI-6
Brooks, James, House—*hist pl* OH-6
Brooks, Jennie, House—*hist pl* TX-5
Brooks, John, House—*hist pl* MA-1
Brooks, Jonathan, House—*hist pl* MA-1
Brooks, J. Wesley, House—*hist pl* SC-3
Brooks, Lake—*lake* AK-9
Brooks, Lake—*lake* FL-3
Brooks, Lake—*reservoir* GA-3
Brooks, Lake—*reservoir* (2) NC-3
Brooks, Luther, House—*hist pl* MA-1
Brooks, Mount—*summit* AK-9
Brooks, Paul, House—*hist pl* AZ-5
Brooks, Samuel Wallace, House—*hist pl* TX-5
Brooks, Shepherd, Estate—*hist pl* MA-1
Brooks, Solomon Neill House—*hist pl* KY-4
Brooks, Wilks, House—*hist pl* TN-4
**Brooks Acres**—*pop pl* AL-4
Brooks-Adair Sch—*school* WV-2
Brooks AFB—*military* (2) TX-5
Brooks Airp—*airport* PA-2
Brooks and Moore Bank Bldg—*hist pl* IA-7
Brooks And Walden Brook—*stream* ME-1
Brooks Arcade—*hist pl* UT-8
*Brooks Bar* MS-4
Brooks Bay—*swamp* FL-3
Brooks Bayou—*gut* AR-4
Brooks Bend—*bend* TN-4
Brooks Bluff—*cliff* ME-1
Brooks Branch—*stream* AL-4
Brooks Branch—*stream* AR-4
Brooks Branch—*stream* FL-3
Brooks Branch—*stream* KY-4
Brooks Branch—*stream* LA-4
Brooks Branch—*stream* (2) NC-3
Brooks Branch—*stream* TN-4
Brooks Branch—*stream* TX-5
Brooks Branch—*stream* WV-2
Brooks Bridge—*bridge* CO-8
Brooks Bridge—*bridge* FL-3
Brooks Bridge—*bridge* IN-6
Brooks Bridge—*bridge* TN-4
Brooks Brook—*stream* CT-1
Brooks Brook—*stream* MA-1
**Brooksburg**—*pop pl* IN-6
**Brooksburg**—*pop pl* NY-2
Brooks Cabin—*locale* OR-9
Brooks Camp—*locale* AK-9
Brooks Camp—*locale* WY-8
Brooks Canyon—*valley* CA-9
Brooks Canyon—*valley* ID-8
Brooks Canyon—*valley* NV-8
Brooks Canyon—*valley* UT-8
Brooks Cave—*cave* TN-4
Brooks (CCD)—*cens area* GA-3
Brooks Cem—*cemetery* (3) AL-4
Brooks Cem—*cemetery* (3) AR-4
Brooks Cem—*cemetery* (3) GA-3
Brooks Cem—*cemetery* (2) IL-6
Brooks Cem—*cemetery* IN-6
Brooks Cem—*cemetery* (4) IA-7
Brooks Cem—*cemetery* (4) KY-4
Brooks Cem—*cemetery* (6) MS-4
Brooks Cem—*cemetery* (4) MO-7
Brooks Cem—*cemetery* (2) NY-2
Brooks Cem—*cemetery* (4) NC-3
Brooks Cem—*cemetery* (4) OH-6
Brooks Cem—*cemetery* (2) OK-5
Brooks Cem—*cemetery* (2) PA-2
Brooks Cem—*cemetery* (16) TN-4
Brooks Cem—*cemetery* (4) TX-5
Brooks Cem—*cemetery* VT-1
Brooks Cem—*cemetery* (5) VA-3
Brooks Cem—*cemetery* WI-6
Brooks Ch—*church* GA-3
Brooks Ch—*church* (2) KY-4
Brooks Ch—*church* (2) MD-2
Brook Sch—*school* MA-1
Brook Sch—*school* MI-6
Brook Sch—*school* TX-5
*Brooks Chapel* MS-4
Brooks Chapel—*church* (3) AR-4
Brooks Chapel—*church* KY-4
Brooks Chapel—*church* (2) MS-4
Brooks Chapel—*church* NC-3
Brooks Chapel—*church* TN-4
Brooks Chapel—*church* (2) TX-5
Brooks Chapel Cem—*cemetery* LA-4
*Brooks Chapel Methodist Ch* MS-4
Brooks Chapel Sch—*school* NC-3
Brooks Corner—*locale* NY-2
Brooks Corner—*locale* SD-7
**Brooks Corner**—*pop pl* OH-6
Brooks Corners—*locale* OH-6
Brooks Coulee—*valley* MT-8
Brooks Country Club—*other* IA-7
**Brooks (County)**—*pop pl* GA-3
**Brooks (County)**—*pop pl* TX-5
Brooks County Courthouse—*hist pl* GA-3
Brooks County Jail—*hist pl* GA-3
Brooks Cove—*bay* (2) ME-1
Brooks Cove—*bay* MD-2
Brooks Cove—*valley* (4) NC-3
*Brooks Creek* TX-5
*Brooks Creek* WI-6
Brooks Creek—*bay* MD-2
Brooks Creek—*bay* (2) NC-3
Brooks Creek—*canal* NC-3
Brooks Creek—*stream* (2) AK-9
Brooks Creek—*stream* (2) AR-4
Brooks Creek—*stream* (2) CA-9
Brooks Creek—*stream* (2) GA-3
Brooks Creek—*stream* IN-6
Brooks Creek—*stream* (2) KY-4
Brooks Creek—*stream* (3) MI-6
Brooks Creek—*stream* MN-6
Brooks Creek—*stream* MO-7
Brooks Creek—*stream* (4) MT-8
Brooks Creek—*stream* NY-2
Brooks Creek—*stream* (3) NC-3
Brooks Creek—*stream* OR-9
Brooks Creek—*stream* (2) TN-4
Brooks Creek—*stream* (3) TX-5
Brooks Creek—*stream* VA-3
Brooks Creek—*stream* (2) WA-9
Brooks Creek—*stream* WV-2
Brooks Crossing—*locale* TX-5
**Brooks Crossing**—*pop pl* GA-3
Brooks Crossroads—*locale* AL-4
**Brooks Cross Roads**—*pop pl* NC-3
**Brooks Crossroads**—*pop pl* NC-3
**Brooksdale**—*pop pl* NC-3
**Brooksdale (subdivision)**—*pop pl* AL-4
Brooks Dam—*dam* AL-4
Brooks Dam—*dam* VT-1
Brooks Ditch—*canal* OR-9
Brooks Draw—*valley* OR-9
Brooks Draw—*valley* WY-8
Brooks Eddy—*lake* LA-4
Brooks Elem Sch—*school* MS-4
**Brooks Estates (subdivision)**—*pop pl* AL-4
Brooks Fall—*falls* AK-9
Brooks Falls—*falls* WV-2
Brooks Farm—*hist pl* MI-6
Brooks Farm Lake—*reservoir* AL-4
Brooks Farm Pond—*reservoir* AL-4
Brooks Farm Pond Dam—*dam* AL-4
Brooks Ferry—*locale* TN-4
**Brooks Ferry**—*pop pl* TN-4
Brooks Ferry (historical)—*crossing* TN-4
Brooks Firetower—*tower* PA-2
Brooks Ford—*locale* TN-4
Brooks Gap—*gap* AK-9
Brooks Gap—*gap* AR-4
Brooks Gap—*gap* (2) NC-3
Brooks Gap—*gap* (2) TN-4
Brooks Glacier—*glacier* AK-9
Brooks Graham Mine (surface)—*mine* TN-4
Brooks Graves—*cemetery* AL-4
**Brooks Grove**—*pop pl* NY-2
Brooks Grove Cem—*cemetery* IL-6
Brooks Gulch—*valley* CA-9
*Brooks-Henkle Family Cemetery* MS-4
Brookshier Ch—*church* TX-5
*Brooks Hill* MD-2
Brooks Hill—*locale* VI-3
Brooks Hill—*summit* AR-4
Brooks Hill—*summit* KY-4
Brooks Hill—*summit* NH-1
Brooks Hill—*summit* NY-2
Brooks Hill—*summit* PA-2
Brooks Hill—*summit* WA-9
Brooks Hill Cem—*cemetery* PA-2
Brooks Hill Cem—*cemetery* WV-2
Brooks Hill Ch—*church* PA-2
Brooks Hill Hollow—*valley* PA-2
**Brookshire**—*pop pl* TX-5
Brookshire, Houston-Yeates House—*hist pl* TX-5
Brookshire Branch—*stream* GA-3
Brookshire Campground—*locale* CA-9
Brookshire (CCD)—*cens area* TX-5
Brookshire Cem—*cemetery* AL-4
Brookshire Cem—*cemetery* KS-7
Brookshire Cem—*cemetery* MO-7
Brookshire Cem—*cemetery* TX-5
Brookshire Creek—*stream* TN-4
Brookshire Creek—*stream* TX-5
Brookshire Creek Trail—*trail* TN-4
Brookshire Elem Sch—*school* FL-3
**Brookshire Estates (subdivision)**—*pop pl* UT-8
**Brookshire Hills**—*pop pl* TN-4
Brookshire Hollow—*valley* MO-7
Brookshire Lake Dam—*dam* MS-4
*Brookshire Prospect* TN-4
Brookshire Sch (historical)—*school* MO-7
Brookshire Top—*summit* GA-3
Brooks Hollow—*valley* MO-7
Brooks Hollow—*valley* NY-2
Brooks Hollow—*valley* PA-2
Brooks Hollow—*valley* (5) TN-4
Brooks Hollow—*valley* (2) WV-2
Brook Shore Lakes—*reservoir* PA-2
Brooks Hosp—*hospital* MA-1
Brooks Hotel—*hist pl* MT-8
Brooks House—*hist pl* VT-1
Brooks HS—*school* AL-4
Brooks HS—*school* MD-2
Brooks HS—*school* NY-2
Brooks-Hughes House—*hist pl* AL-4
Brooks Hurricane Hollow—*valley* AR-4
*Brookside* IL-6
*Brookside* IA-7
*Brookside* MI-6
Brookside—*hist pl* NY-2
Brookside—*locale* AL-4
Brookside—*locale* FL-3
Brookside—*locale* MS-4
Brookside—*locale* MO-7
Brookside—*locale* (2) PA-2
Brookside—*locale* TN-4
**Brookside**—*pop pl* AL-4
**Brookside**—*pop pl* CO-8
**Brookside**—*pop pl* DE-2
**Brookside**—*pop pl* KY-4
**Brookside**—*pop pl* (2) MI-6
**Brookside**—*pop pl* NJ-2
**Brookside**—*pop pl* NC-3
**Brookside**—*pop pl* OH-6
**Brookside**—*pop pl* (6) PA-2
**Brookside**—*pop pl* (2) VT-1
**Brookside**—*pop pl* WV-2
**Brookside**—*pop pl* (2) WI-6
Brookside—*uninc pl* OK-5
Brookside Acad—*school* WA-9
Brookside (Brookside Park)—*CDP* DE-2
Brookside Campground—*locale* MN-6
Brookside Canyon—*valley* CA-9
Brookside Canyon—*valley* MT-8
Brookside (CCD)—*cens area* AL-4
Brookside Cem—*cemetery* CO-8
Brookside Cem—*cemetery* CT-1
Brookside Cem—*cemetery* (2) IN-6
Brookside Cem—*cemetery* KY-4
Brookside Cem—*cemetery* ME-1
Brookside Cem—*cemetery* (3) MA-1
Brookside Cem—*cemetery* (6) MI-6
Brookside Cem—*cemetery* NJ-2
Brookside Cem—*cemetery* (9) NY-2
Brookside Cem—*cemetery* (2) OH-6
Brookside Cem—*cemetery* OK-5
Brookside Cem—*cemetery* OR-9
Brookside Cem—*cemetery* PA-2
Brookside Cem—*cemetery* (3) VT-1
Brookside Cem—*cemetery* WI-6
Brookside Cemetery—*hist pl* MI-6
Brookside Ch—*church* AL-4
Brookside Ch—*church* NC-3
Brookside Ch—*church* TN-4
Brookside Chapel—*church* OH-6
*Brookside Church* IN-6
Brookside Col—*gap* MA-1
Brookside Country Club—*locale* PA-2
Brookside Country Club—*other* (3) OH-6
Brookside Country Club—*other* PA-2
Brookside Creek—*stream* IN-6
Brookside Creek—*stream* IA-7
Brookside Creek—*stream* OR-9
Brookside Creek—*stream* WI-6
Brookside Division—*civil* AL-4
Brookside Elem Sch—*school* AL-4
Brookside Elem Sch—*school* DE-2
Brookside Elem Sch—*school* IN-6
**Brookside Estates**—*pop pl* (2) IN-6
**Brookside Estates**—*pop pl* OH-6
**Brookside Farms**—*pop pl* PA-2
Brookside Farms Airp—*airport* PA-2
**Brookside Forest**—*pop pl* MD-2
*Brookside Golf Course* PA-2
Brookside Gulch—*valley* CO-8
**Brookside Heights**—*pop pl* NJ-2
Brookside HS—*school* AL-4
Brookside HS—*school* OH-6
Brookside JHS—*school* FL-3
Brookside JHS—*school* NY-2
Brookside Lake—*lake* TN-4
**Brookside Manor**—*pop pl* MD-2
**Brookside Manor (subdivision)**—*pop pl* NC-3
Brookside Memorial Park—*cemetery* TX-5
Brookside Methodist Ch—*church* IN-6
Brookside Mill—*locale* TN-4
Brookside Mine (underground)—*mine* AL-4
Brookside Municipal Golf Course—*locale* NV-8
*Brookside Park* DE-2
Brookside Park—*park* CA-9
Brookside Park—*park* CT-1
Brook Side Park—*park* IN-6
Brookside Park—*park* IN-6
Brookside Park—*park* IA-7
Brookside Park—*park* MN-6
Brookside Park—*park* NJ-2
Brookside Park—*park* (2) OH-6
Brookside Park—*park* PA-2
Brookside Park—*park* TX-5
**Brookside Park**—*pop pl* OH-6
Brookside Park—*uninc pl* CA-9
Brookside Park (census name for Brookside)—*CDP* DE-2
**Brookside Park Subdivision**—*pop pl* UT-8
Brookside Place Sch—*school* NJ-2
Brookside Pond—*lake* NY-2
Brookside Sch—*school* CT-1
Brookside Sch—*school* (2) IL-6
Brookside Sch—*school* KS-7
Brookside Sch—*school* MA-1
Brookside Sch—*school* (5) MI-6
Brookside Sch—*school* (2) MN-6
Brookside Sch—*school* NE-7
Brookside Sch—*school* NJ-2
Brookside Sch—*school* (6) NY-2
Brookside Sch—*school* ND-7
Brookside Sch—*school* OH-6
Brookside Sch—*school* PA-2
Brookside Sch—*school* (2) SD-7
Brookside Sch—*school* (2) TN-4
Brookside Sch—*school* UT-8
Brookside Sch—*school* (3) VT-1
Brookside Sch—*school* (3) WI-6
Brookside Sch (abandoned)—*school* MO-7
Brookside Sch (abandoned)—*school* PA-2
Brookside Sch (historical)—*school* TN-4
*Brookside School Number 54* IN-6
Brookside Shop Ctr—*locale* DE-2
Brookside Shops—*locale* MO-7
Brookside Spring—*spring* OR-9
**Brookside (sta.)**—*pop pl* WI-6
**Brookside Station**—*pop pl* MA-1
**Brookside (subdivision)**—*pop pl* AL-4
Brookside (Township of)—*other* OH-6
**Brookside (Township of)**—*pop pl* IL-6
**Brookside Village**—*pop pl* TX-5
Brooks Island—*island* CA-9
Brooks Island—*island* MN-6
Brooks Island—*island* TN-4
Brooks Island—*island* WV-2
Brooks Island (historical)—*island* TN-4
**Brooks Isle**—*pop pl* IL-6
Brooks JHS—*school* KS-7
Brooks JHS—*school* MI-6
Brooks Junction—*locale* MO-7
Brooks Knob—*summit* KY-4
Brooks Knob—*summit* NC-3
Brooks Knob—*summit* WY-8
Brooks Lake—*lake* AR-4
Brooks Lake—*lake* FL-3
Brooks Lake—*lake* ID-8
Brooks Lake—*lake* LA-4
Brooks Lake—*lake* (4) MI-6
Brooks Lake—*lake* MN-6
Brooks Lake—*lake* NM-5
Brooks Lake—*lake* (2) NY-2
Brooks Lake—*lake* (2) TX-5
Brooks Lake—*lake* UT-8
Brooks Lake—*lake* (2) WI-6
Brooks Lake—*lake* WY-8
Brooks Lake—*reservoir* AL-4
Brooks Lake—*reservoir* (2) GA-3
Brooks Lake—*reservoir* IL-6
Brooks Lake—*reservoir* NC-3
Brooks Lake—*reservoir* OK-5
Brooks Lake—*reservoir* PA-2
Brooks Lake—*reservoir* (3) TX-5
Brooks Lake—*swamp* LA-4
Brooks Lake Creek—*stream* (2) WY-8
Brooks Lake Creek Falls—*falls* WY-8
Brooks Lake Dam—*dam* (2) MS-4
Brooks Lake Dam—*dam* NC-3
Brooks Lake Lodge—*hist pl* WY-8
Brooks Lake Lodge—*locale* WY-8
Brooks Lake Number Two—*reservoir* AL-4
Brooks Landing—*locale* MS-4
Brooks Lateral—*canal* ID-8
Brooks Library—*building* MA-1
Brooks Light—*locale* MS-4
Brooks Lookout Tower—*tower* AL-4
Brooks Mansion—*hist pl* DC-2
Brooks Meadow—*flat* OR-9
Brooks Meadow Guard Station—*locale* OR-9
Brooks Memorial Art Gallery—*building* TN-4
Brooks Memorial Ch—*church* AL-4
Brooks Memorial Ch—*church* TN-4
Brooks Memorial State Park—*park* WA-9
*Brooks Mill* AL-4
Brooks Mill—*locale* CA-9
**Brooks Mill**—*pop pl* PA-2
*Brooks Mill Dam* MA-1
Brooks Mill (historical)—*locale* TN-4
*Brooks Mill Reservoir* MA-1
*Brooks Mtn* AL-4
*Brooks Mtn* AR-4
Brooks Mtn—*summit* AL-4
Brooks Mtn—*summit* AK-9
Brooks Mtn—*summit* AR-4
Brooks Mtn—*summit* GA-3
Brooks Mtn—*summit* KY-4
Brooks Mtn—*summit* MT-8
Brooks Mtn—*summit* NY-2
Brooks Mtn—*summit* TX-5
Brooks Number 2 Dam—*dam* AL-4
*Brookson* AL-4
Brooks Park—*park* IL-6
Brooks Park—*park* LA-4
Brooks Park—*park* TX-5
**Brooks Place**—*pop pl* MA-1
*Brooks Point* IL-6
Brooks Point—*cape* IL-6
Brooks Point—*cape* (2) NY-2
Brooks Point—*cape* NC-3
Brooks Point—*cape* TN-4
*Brooks Pond* MA-1
Brooks Pond—*lake* CT-1
Brooks Pond—*lake* (2) FL-3
Brooks Pond—*lake* ME-1
Brooks Pond—*lake* MO-7
Brooks Pond—*lake* TX-5
Brooks Pond—*reservoir* MA-1
Brooks Pond Dam—*dam* (2) MA-1
Brooks Post Office (historical)—*building* TN-4
Brook Spring Branch—*stream* TX-5
Brook Springs—*locale* GA-3
Brooks Ranch—*locale* CO-8
Brooks Ranch—*locale* ID-8
Brooks Ranch—*locale* (2) TX-5
Brooks Ranch—*locale* (2) WY-8

Brooks Ranch Oil Field—oilfield ... WY-8
Brooks Ridge—ridge ... CA-9
Brooks Ridge—ridge ... ME-1
Brooks Ridge—ridge ... VA-3
Brooks River—stream ... AK-9
Brooks River Archeol District—hist pl ... AK-9
Brooks Road Ch (historical)—church ... TN-4
Brooks Road Recreation Center—park ... MD-2
Brooks Road Sch—school ... MD-2
Brooks Rocks—summit ... PA-2
Brooks Round Barn—hist pl ... IA-7
Brooks Run—stream ... KY-4
Brooks Run—stream ... MD-2
Brooks Run—stream ... OH-6
Brooks Run—stream ... PA-2
Brooks Sch—school ... AL-4
Brooks Sch—school ... IL-6
Brooks Sch—school ... IA-7
Brooks Sch—school ... KY-4
Brooks Sch—school (3) ... MA-1
Brooks Sch—school (2) ... MI-6
Brooks Sch—school (2) ... MO-7
Brooks Sch—school (2) ... NC-3
Brooks Sch—school ... OR-9
Brooks Sch—school ... PA-2
Brooks Sch—school ... SD-7
Brooks Sch—school ... TN-4
Brooks Sch—school ... VA-3
Brooks Sch (abandoned)—school ... MO-7
Brooks Sch (abandoned)—school ... PA-2
Brooks Sch (historical)—school ... AL-4
Brooks Sch (historical)—school ... MS-4
Brooks Sch (historical)—school (2) ... PA-2
Brooks Sch (historical)—school ... TN-4
Brooks School, The—school ... MA-1
Brooks Shoal—rapids ... TN-4
Brooks Slough—stream ... WA-9
Brooks Spring—spring ... AL-4
Brooks Spring—spring ... TX-5
Brooks Spring Cave—cave ... AL-4
Brooks Spring Cave—cave ... PA-2
Brooks Spring (Hot)—spring ... NV-8
Brooks Spring Mtn—summit ... AL-4
Brooks Station ... KS-7
Brooks Station ... MA-1
Brooks Stephins Mtn—summit ... AR-4
**Brooks (subdivision)**—pop pl ... NC-3
Brooks Swamp—stream ... NC-3
Brooks Tank—lake ... NM-5
Brooks Tan Yard Post Office (historical)—building ... TN-4
Brooks Temple—church ... NC-3
Brookston—locale ... NC-3
**Brookston**—pop pl ... IN-6
**Brookston**—pop pl ... MN-6
**Brookston**—pop pl ... PA-2
**Brookston**—pop pl ... TX-5
Brookstone ... MN-6
**Brookstone Condo**—pop pl ... UT-8
**Brookstone (subdivision)**—pop pl ... NC-3
Brookston Mine (underground)—mine ... AL-4
Brookstown ... IN-6
**Brookstown**—pop pl ... LA-4
**Brooks (Town of)**—pop pl ... ME-1
Brookstown Sch—school ... LA-4
**Brooks (Township of)**—pop pl ... MI-6
Brookstown-Zion Ch—church ... NC-3
Brooks Trail—trail ... PA-2
Brooks Tunnel—tunnel ... PA-2
Brooks Turner Hill—summit ... ME-1
**Brooksvale**—pop pl ... CT-1
Brooksvale Recreation Park—park ... CT-1
Brooksvale Stream—stream ... CT-1
Brooks Valley—valley ... AR-4
**Brooks Village**—pop pl ... MA-1
Brooksville ... AL-4
Brooksville ... IN-6
Brooksville—locale ... GA-3
**Brooksville**—pop pl (2) ... AL-4
**Brooksville**—pop pl ... FL-3
**Brooksville**—pop pl ... KY-4
**Brooksville**—pop pl ... ME-1
**Brooksville**—pop pl ... MS-4
**Brooksville**—pop pl ... OK-5
**Brooksville**—pop pl ... SC-3
**Brooksville**—pop pl ... VT-1
Brooksville Baptist Ch—church ... MS-4
Brooksville (CCD)—cens area ... AL-4
Brooksville (CCD)—cens area ... FL-3
Brooksville (CCD)—cens area ... KY-4
Brooksville Cem—cemetery ... FL-3
Brooksville Cem—cemetery ... MS-4
Brooksville Cem—cemetery ... OK-5
Brooksville Ch—church (2) ... AL-4
Brooksville Ch—church ... WV-2
Brooksville Division—civil ... AL-4
Brooksville First Pentecostal Ch—church ... MS-4
**Brooksville (historical)**—pop pl ... TN-4
Brooksville HS—school ... MS-4
**Brooksville (local name South Brooksville)**—pop pl ... ME-1
Brooksville Missionary Baptist Church ... AL-4
Brooksville Primary Sch—school ... FL-3
Brooksville Quarry—mine ... FL-3
Brooksville Rsvr—reservoir ... KY-4
Brooksville Sch—school ... WV-2
Brooksville Sch (historical)—school ... AL-4
Brooksville Seventh-Day Adventist Sch—school ... FL-3
**Brooksville (Town of)**—pop pl ... ME-1
Brooks Well—well ... TX-5
Brooks-Wilbarger House—hist pl ... TX-5
Brooks Windmill—locale ... TX-5
Brook Tank—reservoir ... NM-5
**Brookthorpe Hills**—pop pl ... PA-2
Brookton—locale ... GA-3
**Brookton**—pop pl ... ME-1
Brookton Cem—cemetery ... ME-1
**Brookton Corners**—pop pl ... MI-6
**Brooktondale**—pop pl ... NY-2
Brookton (Township of)—unorg ... ME-1
**Brook Trails**—pop pl ... IN-6
Brooktrails Ranch—locale ... CA-9
**Brooktree Estates Subdivision**—pop pl ... UT-8
**Brooktree Park**—pop pl ... ND-7
Brooktrout Lake—lake ... NY-2
Brooktrout Point—cape ... NY-2
Brook Vale—locale ... VA-3
**Brookvale**—pop pl ... CO-8
**Brookvale**—pop pl ... NY-2
**Brookvale**—pop pl ... PA-2
Brookvale Estates—locale ... GA-3
Brook Vale HS—school ... VA-3
Brookvale Ranch—locale ... CO-8
Brook Valley—locale ... NJ-2
**Brook Valley (subdivision)**—pop pl ... NC-3
**Brook Valley Trailer Park (subdivision)**—pop pl ... NC-3
**Brookview**—pop pl ... IL-6
**Brookview**—pop pl ... MD-2
**Brookview**—pop pl ... NJ-2
**Brookview**—pop pl ... NY-2
Brookview—uninc pl ... FL-3
**Brookview Apartments**—pop pl ... DE-2
Brookview Ch—church ... FL-3
Brookview Ch—church ... TX-5
Brookview Chapel—church ... MD-2
Brookview Country Club—other ... MN-6
**Brookview Estates (subdivision)**—pop pl ... NC-3
**Brookview Manor (subdivision)**—pop pl ... AL-4
Brookview Sch—school ... CA-9
Brookview Sch—school ... FL-3
Brook View Sch—school ... IL-6
Brookview Sch—school ... MD-2
Brookview Sch—school ... NY-2
**Brookview (subdivision)**—pop pl ... DE-2
Brook Village ... MA-1
Brook Village (historical)—locale ... MA-1
Brookville ... IL-6
Brookville ... IN-6
Brookville ... KY-4
Brookville ... MD-2
Brookville ... MS-4
Brookville—locale ... IA-7
Brookville—locale ... NJ-2
**Brookville**—pop pl (2) ... IL-6
**Brookville**—pop pl ... IN-6
**Brookville**—pop pl ... KS-7
**Brookville**—pop pl ... MA-1
**Brookville**—pop pl ... MI-6
**Brookville**—pop pl ... NJ-2
**Brookville**—pop pl (2) ... NY-2
**Brookville**—pop pl ... OH-6
**Brookville**—pop pl ... PA-2
**Brookville**—pop pl (2) ... VA-3
**Brookville**—pop pl ... WI-6
Brookville Borough—civil ... PA-2
Brookville Cem—cemetery ... KS-7
Brookville Cem—cemetery ... NY-2
Brookville Cem—cemetery (2) ... WI-6
Brookville Ch—church ... MN-6
Brookville Ch—church ... VA-3
Brookville Country Club—other ... NY-2
Brookville Elem Sch—school ... IN-6
Brookville Grade Sch—hist pl ... KS-7
**Brookville Heights**—pop pl ... IN-6
Brookville Hist Dist—hist pl ... IN-6
Brookville Hist Dist—hist pl ... PA-2
Brookville Hotel—hist pl ... KS-7
Brookville HS—school ... IN-6
Brookville JHS—school ... IN-6
Brookville Junior Senior HS—school ... PA-2
**Brookville Knolls**—pop pl ... MD-2
Brookville Lake—reservoir ... IN-6
Brookville Lake Dam—dam ... IN-6
Brookville Park—park ... NY-2
**Brookville Park**—pop pl ... NY-2
Brookville Presbyterian Church and Manse—hist pl ... PA-2
Brookville Reservoir ... IN-6
Brookville Rsvr—reservoir ... PA-2
Brookville Sch—school ... AL-4
Brookville Sch—school ... NY-2
**Brookville (Township of)**—pop pl ... IL-6
**Brookville (Township of)**—pop pl ... IN-6
**Brookville (Township of)**—pop pl ... MN-6
Brookville Waterworks Dam—dam ... PA-2
Brookwalter ... OH-6
**Brookwater Park**—pop pl ... PA-2
Brook Water Sch—school ... MA-1
Brookway Baptist Ch—church ... MS-4
Brookway Ch of Christ—church ... MS-4
Brookway Park—park ... CA-9
Brookway Plaza Shop Ctr—locale ... MS-4
**Brookwild**—pop pl ... OR-9
Brookwood ... GA-3
Brookwood ... IL-6
Brookwood ... IN-6
Brookwood ... MI-6
Brookwood ... NY-2
Brookwood ... OH-6
Brookwood—locale ... GA-3
Brookwood—locale ... VA-3
Brookwood—other ... GA-3
**Brookwood**—pop pl (2) ... AL-4
**Brookwood**—pop pl ... CO-8
**Brookwood**—pop pl ... GA-3
**Brookwood**—pop pl ... IN-6
**Brookwood**—pop pl ... MD-2
**Brookwood**—pop pl ... NJ-2
**Brookwood**—pop pl ... NC-3
**Brookwood**—pop pl ... OH-6
Brookwood—uninc pl ... GA-3
Brookwood—uninc pl ... LA-4
Brookwood—uninc pl ... VA-3
Brookwood—uninc pl ... WI-6
Brookwood Apartments—uninc pl ... GA-3
Brookwood Baptist Ch—church ... AL-4
Brookwood (CCD)—cens area ... AL-4
Brookwood Cem—cemetery ... AL-4
Brookwood Ch—church ... LA-4
Brookwood Ch—church ... NC-3
Brookwood Community Hosp—hospital ... FL-3
**Brookwood Condominiums**—pop pl ... UT-8
Brookwood Country Club—locale ... MS-4
Brookwood Country Club—other ... AL-4
Brookwood Country Club—other ... IL-6
Brookwood Country Club Lake Dam—dam ... MS-4
Brookwood Covenant Ch—church ... KS-7
Brookwood Division—civil ... AL-4
Brookwood Elem Sch—school ... AL-4
Brookwood Elem Sch—school ... KS-7
Brookwood Estates ... IL-6
**Brookwood Estates (subdivision)**—pop pl ... AL-4
**Brookwood Estates (subdivision)**—pop pl ... MS-4
**Brookwood Estates Subdivision**—pop pl ... UT-8
Brookwood Farm—hist pl ... MA-1
**Brookwood Forest**—pop pl ... AL-4
Brookwood Forest Lake Dam—dam ... AL-4
Brookwood Forest Sch—school ... AL-4
**Brookwood Gardens (subdivision)**—pop pl ... NC-3
Brookwood Golf Club—locale ... NC-3
Brookwood Golf Course—other (2) ... MI-6
Brookwood Hills Hist Dist—hist pl ... GA-3
Brookwood HS—school ... AL-4
Brookwood JHS—school ... IL-6
Brookwood Med Ctr—hospital ... AL-4
Brookwood Medical Clinic—hospital ... AL-4
Brookwood Methodist Ch—church ... AL-4
Brookwood Mine (underground)—mine ... AL-4
Brookwood Park—park ... AL-4
Brookwood Park—park ... GA-3
Brookwood Park—park ... OK-5
**Brookwood Pines (subdivision)**—pop pl ... MS-4
Brookwood Point ... NY-2
Brookwood Point—cape ... NY-2
Brookwood Rsvr—reservoir ... CA-9
Brookwood Sch—school ... AR-4
Brookwood Sch—school (2) ... GA-3
Brookwood Sch—school ... IL-6
Brookwood Sch—school ... MA-1
Brookwood Sch—school ... MI-6
Brookwood Sch—school ... MO-7
Brookwood Sch—school ... NC-3
Brookwood Sch—school ... OR-9
Brookwood Sch—school ... UT-8
**Brookwood Shaft**—pop pl ... PA-2
Brookwood Shop Ctr—locale ... KS-7
Brookwood Station—locale ... GA-3
**Brookwood (subdivision)**—pop pl (2) ... AL-4
**Brookwood (subdivision)**—pop pl ... MS-4
**Brookwood Subdivision**—pop pl ... NC-3
**Brookwood (subdivision)**—pop pl (2) ... NC-3
**Brookwood Subdivision**—pop pl (2) ... UT-8
Brookwood Village Shop Ctr—locale (2) ... AL-4
Broom, Jacob, House—hist pl ... DE-2
**Broomall**—pop pl ... PA-2
Broomalls Dam—dam ... PA-2
Broomalls Lake—reservoir ... PA-2
**Broomall (Township name Marple)**—pop pl ... PA-2
Broom Bay—swamp ... FL-3
Broom Bldg—hist pl ... OH-6
Broom-Braden Stone House—hist pl ... OH-6
Broom Branch—stream (3) ... GA-3
Broom Canyon—valley ... NV-8
Broom Cem—cemetery ... AR-4
Broom Cem—cemetery ... MS-4
Broom Cem—cemetery ... NC-3
Broom Cove ... AL-4
Broom Creek—stream ... GA-3
Broom Creek—stream ... ID-8
Broom Creek—stream ... MD-2
Broom Creek—stream ... WY-8
Broom Creek Spring—spring ... WY-8
Broom Draw—valley ... WY-8
Broome—locale ... TX-5
Broome, C. A., House—hist pl ... TX-5
Broome Air Force Auxiliary Airfield (abandoned)—military ... TX-5
Broome Canyon—valley ... UT-8
Broome Cem—cemetery ... GA-3
**Broome Center**—pop pl ... NY-2
Broome Ch—church ... MS-4
Broome Community Center—building ... MS-4
**Broome (County)**—pop pl ... NY-2
Broome County Airport—other ... NY-2
Broome County Courthouse—hist pl ... NY-2
Broome County Technical Community Coll—school ... NY-2
Broome Island ... MD-2
Broome JHS—school ... MD-2
Broome Ranch—locale ... CA-9
Broome Sch—school ... MS-4
Broomes Island—island ... MD-2
**Broomes Island**—pop pl ... MD-2
Broome State For—forest ... NY-2
Broome Tank—reservoir ... NM-5
**Broome (Town of)**—pop pl ... NY-2
Broomfield ... NC-3
**Broomfield**—pop pl ... CO-8
Broomfield Center—locale ... MI-6
Broomfield Ch—church ... AR-4
Broomfield Ch—church ... SC-3
Broomfield Ch—church ... VA-3
Broomfield Ch (historical)—church ... AL-4
Broomfield Country Club—other ... CO-8
Broomfield Creek—stream ... SC-3
Broomfield Gulch—valley ... CO-8
Broomfield Gulch—valley ... MT-8
Broomfield Heights ... CO-8
Broomfield Rsvr—reservoir ... CO-8
Broomfield Sch—school ... TN-4
Broomfield Swamp Creek—stream ... NC-3
**Broomfield (Township of)**—pop pl ... MI-6
Broom Flat—flat ... CA-9
**Broom Hill**—pop pl ... IN-6
Broom Hollow ... TN-4
Broom Island—island ... ME-1
Broom Lake—lake ... AR-4
Broom Lake—lake ... MI-6
Broom Lake—lake ... ND-7
Broom Lakebed—flat ... MN-6
Broom Mine (underground)—mine ... AL-4
Broom Mtn—summit ... NM-5
Broom Mtn—summit ... UT-8
Broom Pond—reservoir ... SC-3
Broomsage Cem—cemetery ... FL-3
Broomsage Lake—lake ... IN-6
Broomsage Ranch Airp—airport ... IN-6
Broomsage Ranch Lake Dam—dam ... IN-6
Brooms Cem—cemetery ... MS-4
Brooms Island—island ... MD-2
Broom Spring—spring ... CA-9
Broomstick Cem—cemetery ... OH-6
Broomstick Ch—church ... WV-2
Broomstick Lake—lake ... NY-2
Broomstick Ledges—cliff ... CT-1
Broomstick Run—stream ... OH-6
Broomstraw Branch—stream ... AL-4
Broomstraw Branch—stream ... FL-3
Broomstraw Fork—stream ... KY-4
Broomstraw Island—island ... GA-3
Broomstraw Mtn—summit ... NC-3
Broomstraw Trail—trail ... VA-3
Broomtail Creek—stream ... ID-8
Broomtail Ridge—ridge ... MT-8
Broom Tank—reservoir ... NM-5
Broomtown ... NJ-2
**Broomtown**—pop pl ... AL-4
Broomtown Post Office (historical)—building ... AL-4
Broomtown Valley—valley ... AL-4
Broomtown Valley—valley ... GA-3
Broomy Valley—basin ... AZ-5
Broon Buttes—summit ... AK-9
Brooners Creek ... AL-4
Broons Canyon ... UT-8
**Brooten**—pop pl ... MN-6
Brooten Mountain—ridge ... OR-9
Brophy ... ND-7
Brophy, Lake—lake ... MN-6
Brophy Big Dam—dam ... SD-7
Brophy Canyon—valley ... CA-9
Brophy Creek—stream ... AK-9
Brophy Creek—stream ... IA-7
Brophy Creek—stream ... MN-6
Brophy Creek—stream ... OR-9
Brophy Field—park ... NJ-2
Brophy Hill—summit ... OR-9
Brophy Lake ... MI-6
Brophy Mine—mine ... MT-8
Brophy Pond—reservoir ... CT-1
Brophy Preparatory Sch—school ... AZ-5
Brophy Sch—school ... CA-9
Brophys Creek ... IA-7
Bropps—locale ... PA-2
Broro Neck—cape ... GA-3
Broro River—stream ... GA-3
Brorson Ch—church ... MT-8
Brorson Creek—stream ... MT-8
Brorson Oil Field—oilfield ... MT-8
Brorson Sch—school ... MT-8
Brosa Draw—valley ... WY-8
Brosay Suck—swamp ... GA-3
**Broscan**—pop pl ... FL-3
Broseco Ranch—locale ... TX-5
**Broseley**—pop pl ... MO-7
Brosewere Bay—bay ... NY-2
Broshears Cem—cemetery ... IN-6
Brosia ... WV-2
Brosius Ranch—locale (2) ... NE-7
Brosman Ditch—canal ... OR-9
Brosman Mtn—summit ... OR-9
Brosnaham Island—island ... FL-3
Bross, Mount—summit ... CO-8
Bross Cem—cemetery ... KS-7
Brosseau Mountain ... VT-1
Bross (historical)—locale ... KS-7
Brossman Sch—school ... IL-6
Brost Drain—stream ... MI-6
Brost Number 1 Dam—dam (2) ... SD-7
Brost Number 10 Dam—dam ... SD-7
Brost Number 2 Dam—dam (2) ... SD-7
Brost Number 3 Dam—dam (2) ... SD-7
Brost Number 4 Dam—dam (2) ... SD-7
Brost Number 5 Dam—dam (2) ... SD-7
Brost Number 6 Dam—dam (2) ... SD-7
Brost Number 7 Dam—dam (2) ... SD-7
Brost Number 8 Dam—dam (2) ... SD-7
Brost Number 9 Dam—dam ... SD-7
Brosville—locale ... VA-3
**Broten**—pop pl ... ID-8
Broten PO (historical)—locale ... ID-8
Brother Clarks School ... AL-4
Brotherhood Bridge—other ... AK-9
Brotherhood Cem—cemetery ... NJ-2
Brotherhood Cem—cemetery ... ND-7
Brotherhood Ch—church ... AL-4
Brotherhood Ch—church ... KY-4
Brotherhood Holiness Ch—church ... NC-3
Brotherhood of the White Temple—church ... CO-8
Brotherick Branch—stream ... AL-4
Brotherick Sch (historical)—school ... AL-4
Brotherick Spring—spring ... AL-4
Brother Island—island ... NY-2
Brother Islands—island ... AK-9
Brother Jonathan ... OR-9
Brother Knobs—summit ... AR-4
Brother of Jesus Mission—church (2) ... NM-5
Brother Ponds—lake (2) ... NY-2
Brother Rice HS—school ... IL-6
Brothers—locale ... IL-6
**Brothers**—pop pl ... OR-9
Brothers, The—area ... AK-9
Brothers, The—bar ... ME-1
Brothers, The—island (2) ... CA-9
Brothers, The—island (3) ... ME-1
Brothers, The—pillar (2) ... RI-1
Brothers, The—summit ... ME-1
Brothers, The—summit ... NY-2
Brothers, The—summit ... WA-9
Brothers And Sisters of Corinthians Hall Number One (historical)—church ... AL-4
Brothers Branch—stream ... MS-4
Brothers Brook—stream ... CT-1
Brothers Creek—stream ... NJ-2
Brothers Dam ... PA-2
**Brothersfield Township**—pop pl ... SD-7
Brothers Landing Strip—airport ... OR-9
Brothers Oasis Safety Rest Area—locale ... OR-9
Brothers of Sacred Heart Dam—dam ... MA-1
Brothers of the Holy Rosary—church ... NV-8
Brothers-O'Neil House—hist pl ... KY-4
Brothers Passage—channel ... ME-1
Brothers River—stream ... FL-3
Brothers Road Cave—cave ... TN-4
Brothers Station—other ... IL-6
**Brothersvalley (Township of)**—pop pl ... PA-2
Brothersville Cem—cemetery ... GA-3
Brothers West Canyon—valley ... NM-5
Brothers West Tank—reservoir ... NM-5
Brotherton ... NJ-2
Brotherton—locale ... TX-5
**Brotherton**—pop pl ... PA-2
**Brotherton**—pop pl (2) ... TN-4
Brotherton Baptist Ch—church ... TN-4
Brotherton Cem—cemetery ... AL-4
Brotherton Cem—cemetery (2) ... TN-4
Brotherton Creek—stream ... GA-3
Brotherton Creek—stream ... MI-6
Brotherton Farm—hist pl ... PA-2
Brotherton Field—locale ... GA-3
Brotherton House—building ... GA-3
Brotherton Post Office (historical)—building ... TN-4
Brotherton Ridge—ridge ... WV-2
Brotherton Sch (historical)—school ... TN-4
Brotherton United Methodist Ch—church ... TN-4
Brothertown—locale ... NY-2
**Brothertown**—pop pl ... WI-6
Brothertown Harbor—bay ... WI-6
**Brothertown (Town of)**—pop pl ... WI-6
Brothwell Run—stream ... PA-2
**Brotmanville**—pop pl ... NJ-2
Broton ... AL-4
Broton Hollow ... PA-2
Broton Lake—swamp ... SC-3
Brottmanville ... NJ-2
Brouchaux Gulch—valley ... OR-9
Brough—locale ... IA-7
Broughal MS—school ... PA-2
Brougham Lake—lake ... AR-4
Brough Cem—cemetery ... SC-3
Brough Dam—dam ... UT-8
Brougher Creek—stream ... MS-4
Brougher Mansion—hist pl ... NV-8
Brougher Mtn—summit ... NV-8
**Brough Estates**—pop pl ... UT-8
Brough Fork—stream ... UT-8
Broughman Cem—cemetery ... MS-4
Brough-Martinson House—hist pl ... SD-7
Brough Rsvr—reservoir (2) ... UT-8
Brough Spring—spring ... UT-8
Broughten Bridge ... AL-4
**Broughtentown**—pop pl ... KY-4
**Broughtentown (Broughtontown)**—pop pl ... KY-4
Broughton—locale ... AL-4
Broughton—locale ... CO-8
Broughton—locale ... GA-3
**Broughton**—pop pl ... IL-6
**Broughton**—pop pl ... KS-7
**Broughton**—pop pl ... OH-6
**Broughton**—pop pl ... PA-2
Broughton Beach—beach ... OR-9
Broughton Bluff—cliff ... OR-9
Broughton Branch—stream ... KY-4
Broughton Bridge ... AL-4
Broughton Brook—stream ... PA-2
Broughton Brook—stream ... VT-1
Broughton Cem—cemetery ... AL-4
Broughton Cem—cemetery ... AR-4
Broughton Cem—cemetery ... IL-6
Broughton Cem—cemetery ... KS-7
Broughton Creek—stream ... IL-6
Broughton Creek—stream ... MT-8
Broughton Dam—dam ... AL-4
Broughton Ditch—canal ... WY-8
Broughton Gap ... AL-4
Broughton Hollow—locale ... PA-2
Broughton Hollow—valley (2) ... PA-2
Broughton Homestead (abandoned)—locale ... MT-8
Broughton Hosp Hist Dist—hist pl ... NC-3
Broughton Hospital Dam—dam ... NC-3
Broughton Hospital Rsvr—reservoir ... NC-3
Broughton HS—school ... NC-3
Broughton Island—island ... GA-3
Broughton Lake—reservoir ... AL-4
Broughton Lake—reservoir ... IN-6
Broughton Lake Dam—dam ... IN-6
Broughton Ledge—bench ... NY-2
Broughton Millpond (historical)—lake ... SC-3
Broughton Park—park ... TX-5
Broughton Point—cape ... SC-3
Broughton Reach—channel ... OR-9
Broughton Reach—channel ... WA-9
Broughton Sch—school ... IL-6
Broughton Sch—school ... KY-4
Broughton Springs—spring ... AL-4
Broughton State Hosp—hospital ... NC-3
**Broughton (Township of)**—pop pl ... IL-6
Brouilets Creek ... IN-6
Brouillard Brook—stream ... VT-1
Brouillet State Wildlife Mngmt Area—park ... MN-6
**Brouillette**—pop pl ... LA-4
Brouilletts Creek—stream ... IL-6
Brouilletts Creek—stream ... IN-6
Brouilletts Creek (Township of)—civ div ... IL-6
Brouletts Creek ... IN-6
Broumbaugh Cem—cemetery ... OR-9
Brounland—locale ... WV-2
Brouse Creek—stream ... OR-9
Brouse Mine—mine ... AZ-5
Brouse Sch (abandoned)—school ... PA-2
Brouses Corners—locale ... NY-2
Brouse Spring—spring ... CO-8
Brouse Well—well ... AZ-5
**Broussard**—pop pl ... LA-4
Broussard, Amant, House—hist pl ... LA-4
Broussard, Valsin, House—hist pl ... LA-4
Broussard Bayou—stream ... LA-4
Broussard Canal—canal ... LA-4
Broussard Cem—cemetery (6) ... LA-4
Broussard Cem—cemetery (2) ... TX-5
Broussard Grove Ch—church ... LA-4
Broussard Landing—locale ... LA-4
Brousseau Mtn—summit ... VT-1
Brousseous Brook—stream ... CT-1
Brousseous Pond—lake ... CT-1
**Brousville**—pop pl ... LA-4
Brovard ... NC-3
Brow, The—cliff ... AL-4
Broward, Lake—lake ... FL-3
Broward, Napoleon Bonaparte, House—hist pl ... FL-3
Browardale—CDP ... FL-3
Broward Christian Sch—school ... FL-3
Broward Circle Park—park ... FL-3
Broward Community Chapel—church ... FL-3
Broward Community Coll (Central Campus)—school ... FL-3
Broward Community College (North Campus Library)—building ... FL-3
Broward Community Coll (North Campus)—school ... FL-3
Broward Community Coll (South Campus)—school ... FL-3
**Broward County**—pop pl ... FL-3
Broward County Law Library—building ... FL-3
Broward Creek—bay ... FL-3
Broward Estates Sch—school ... FL-3
Broward Fire Acad (Vocational/Technical-Off Campus)—school ... FL-3
**Broward Gardens**—pop pl ... FL-3
Broward General Hosp—hospital ... FL-3
Broward General Med Ctr—hospital ... FL-3
Broward Heights Sch—school ... FL-3
**Broward Highlands**—pop pl ... FL-3
Broward Islands—island ... FL-3
Broward Mall at Plantation—locale ... FL-3
Broward Point—cape ... FL-3
Broward River ... FL-3
Broward River—stream ... FL-3
Broward Sch—school ... FL-3
Broward Substation—locale ... FL-3
Brow Back Gulch ... MT-8
Brow Creek—stream ... CO-8
**Browder**—pop pl ... KY-4
**Browder**—pop pl (2) ... TN-4
**Browder**—pop pl ... TX-5
Browder Airp—airport ... TN-4
Browder Bar—bar ... TN-4
Browder Bend—bend ... TN-4
Browder Branch—stream ... MS-4
Browder Branch—stream ... TN-4
Browder Cave—cave ... AL-4
Browder Cem—cemetery ... AL-4
Browder Cem—cemetery (3) ... KY-4
Browder Cem—cemetery ... MS-4
Browder Cem—cemetery ... NC-3
Browder Cem—cemetery ... TN-4
Browder Cem—cemetery ... VA-3
Browder Ch—church ... KY-4
Browder Chapel—church ... VA-3
Browder Creek—stream ... OR-9
Browder Creek—stream ... TX-5
Browder Hollow—valley ... AR-4
Browder Hollow—valley ... TN-4
Browder Hollow—valley ... VA-3
Browder Island—island ... TN-4
Browder Memorial Ch—church ... TN-4
Browder Mtn—summit ... VA-3
Browder Ridge—ridge ... MS-4
Browder Ridge—ridge ... OR-9
Browder Ridge Trail—trail ... OR-9
Browders Branch ... TX-5
Browders Branch—stream ... NC-3
Browder Sch—school ... TN-4
Browders Chapel—church ... KY-4
Browder Schoolhouse Hollow—valley ... TN-4
Browders Creek—stream ... TX-5
Browders Ferry (historical)—locale ... TN-4
Browder Spring—spring ... AL-4
Browder Spring—spring ... TN-4
Browder Spring Branch—stream ... AL-4
Browders Shoals ... TN-4
Browder Switch Industrial Park—locale ... TN-4
Browdy Lake—lake ... IN-6
Browell Roadside Park—park ... MI-6
Browen Lake—lake ... ND-7
Brower, Abraham, House—hist pl ... NY-2
Brower, Adolph, House—hist pl ... NY-2
Brower, Adolphus W., House—hist pl ... IL-6
Brower Branch—stream ... MO-7
Brower Cem—cemetery (2) ... MS-4
Brower Cem—cemetery ... PA-2
Brower Creek—stream ... CA-9
Brower Creek—stream ... OR-9
Brower Ditch—canal ... IN-6
Brower Drain—canal ... MI-6
Brower Draw—valley ... WY-8
Brower Family Cem ... MS-4
Brower Field—airport ... NC-3
Brower Hill—summit ... NY-2
**Brower (historical)**—pop pl ... OR-9
Brower Hollow—valley ... PA-2
Brower Island—island ... MN-6
Brower Lake—lake ... MI-6
Brower Park—park ... NY-2
Brower Ridge—ridge ... AK-9
Brower Rsvr—reservoir ... WY-8
Browers Branch—stream ... MS-4
Brower's Bridge—hist pl ... PA-2
Browers Ch—church ... NC-3
Brower Sch—school ... NC-3
Brower Sch (historical)—school ... MO-7
Browers Lake—lake ... IA-7
Browers Pilgrim Ch—church ... NC-3
Brower Spring—spring ... MO-7
**Brower Subdivision**—pop pl ... UT-8
Brower Tank—reservoir ... AZ-5
Brower (Township of)—fmr MCD ... NC-3
**Browerville**—pop pl ... AK-9
**Browerville**—pop pl ... MN-6
Browe Sch—school ... IL-6
**Browfield**—pop pl ... PA-2
Browing Cem—cemetery (2) ... TN-4
Browing Home and Mather Acad—school ... SC-3
Browing Ledge—flat ... MA-1
Browington Cem—cemetery ... TN-4
Browington Ch of the Nazarene—church ... TN-4
Browlee Lake ... MI-6
Browman Creek ... KS-7
Brow Monmt—hist pl ... AZ-5
Brown ... AL-4
Brown ... OH-6
Brown ... RI-1
Brown ... VA-3
Brown—fmr MCD ... NE-7
Brown—locale ... CA-9
Brown—locale ... CO-8
Brown—locale ... LA-4
Brown—locale (2) ... MD-2
Brown—locale ... NV-8
Brown—locale ... OH-6
Brown—locale ... OK-5
Brown—locale ... TX-5
Brown—other ... OH-6
**Brown**—pop pl ... AR-4
**Brown**—pop pl ... FL-3
**Brown**—pop pl ... KY-4
**Brown**—pop pl ... MT-8
**Brown**—pop pl ... TN-4
**Brown**—pop pl (2) ... WV-2
Brown, A. D., Bldg—hist pl ... MO-7

Browning Cem—*cemetery* ... KY-4
Browning Cem—*cemetery* ... MS-4
Browning Cem—*cemetery* ... NM-5
Browning Cem—*cemetery* ... NC-3
Browning Cem—*cemetery* ... OH-6
Browning Cem—*cemetery* (2) ... TN-4
Browning Cem—*cemetery* ... TX-5
Browning Cem—*cemetery* (3) ... VA-3
Browning Cem—*cemetery* (6) ... WV-2
Browning Cement Dam Tank—*reservoir* ... AZ-5
Browning Ch—*church* (2) ... GA-3
Browning Ch—*church* ... SC-3
Browning Chapel—*church* ... GA-3
**Browning Corner**—*pop pl* ... KY-4
Browning Coulee—*valley* ... MT-8
Browning Creek—*stream* ... AR-4
Browning Creek—*stream* ... CO-8
Browning Creek—*stream* (2) ... ID-8
Browning Creek—*stream* ... KY-4
Browning Creek—*stream* ... MI-6
Browning Creek—*stream* ... MS-4
Browning Creek—*stream* ... MT-8
Browning Creek—*stream* ... OR-9
Browning Creek—*stream* ... TN-4
Browning Creek—*stream* ... TX-5
Browning Dam—*dam* ... AZ-5
Browning Dam—*dam* ... MD-2
Browning Ditch—*canal* ... CO-8
Browning Field—*park* ... IL-6
*Browning Fork* ... KY-4
Browning Fork—*stream* ... KY-4
Browning Fork—*stream* ... WV-2
Browning Fork Ch—*church* ... WV-2
Browning Heights Sch—*school* ... TX-5
Browning Hill—*summit* ... IL-6
Browning Hill—*summit* ... IN-6
Browning (historical P.O.)—*locale* ... IA-7
Browning Hollow—*valley* ... AR-4
Browning Hollow—*valley* (3) ... MO-7
Browning Hollow—*valley* ... TN-4
Browning Hosp—*hospital* ... IL-6
Browning House—*hist pl* ... TN-4
Browning Knob—*summit* ... NC-3
Browning Lake—*bay* ... WI-6
Browning Lake—*lake* ... KS-7
Browning Lake—*lake* (2) ... MI-6
Browning Lake—*lake* ... MO-7
Browning Lambert Mtn—*summit* ... WV-2
Browning Lateral—*canal* ... CA-9
Browning Manufacturing (Plant)—*facility* ... OH-6
Browning Memorial Sch—*school* ... MA-1
Browning Mill Pond—*lake* ... RI-1
Browning Mill Pond—*reservoir* ... RI-1
Browning Mill Pond Dam—*dam* ... RI-1
Browning Mine—*mine* ... UT-8
Browning Mtn—*summit* ... CO-8
Browning Oil Field—*oilfield* ... KS-7
*Browning Peak* ... NC-3
Browning Pierce Sch—*school* ... FL-3
Browning Pond—*reservoir* ... AL-4
Browning Pond—*reservoir* ... MA-1
Browning Pond Dam—*dam* ... MA-1
Browning Ranch—*locale* ... AZ-5
Browning Ranch—*locale* ... MT-8
Browning Ridge—*ridge* ... CO-8
Browning Rsvr—*reservoir* ... MT-8
Browning Run—*stream* ... OH-6
Browning Run—*stream* (2) ... WV-2
Brownings—*locale* ... NJ-2
*Brownings Beach* ... RI-1
Brownings Branch—*stream* ... AR-4
Brownings Ch—*church* ... NC-3
Browning Sch—*school* ... KY-4
Browning Sch—*school* ... LA-4
Browning Sch—*school* ... OH-6
Browning Sch—*school* ... WI-6
Browning Sch (historical)—*school* ... MS-4
Browning Sch Number 73—*school* ... IN-6
**Brownings Corner**—*pop pl* ... KY-4
Browning Shoals—*bar* ... GA-3
*Browning's Pond* ... MA-1
Browning Spring—*spring* ... CO-8
Browning Spring—*spring* ... OR-9
Browning Station—*locale* ... MT-8
**Browningsville**—*pop pl* ... MD-2
Brownington—*locale* ... KY-4
**Brownington**—*pop pl* ... MO-7
**Brownington**—*pop pl* ... TN-4
**Brownington**—*pop pl* ... VT-1
Brownington Branch—*stream* ... VT-1
Brownington Cem—*cemetery* ... MO-7
**Brownington Center**—*pop pl* ... VT-1
Brownington Pond—*lake* ... VT-1
**Brownington (Town of)**—*pop pl* ... VT-1
**Brownington Village**—*pop pl* ... VT-1
Brownington Village Hist Dist—*hist pl* ... VT-1
**Browningtown**—*pop pl* ... KY-4
**Browningtown**—*pop pl* ... TN-4
**Browning (Town of)**—*pop pl* ... WI-6
**Browning (Township of)**—*pop pl* (2) ... IL-6
Browning Trail—*trail* ... PA-2
Browning Well—*locale* ... NM-5
Brown Interior Drain—*canal* ... NM-5
*Brown Island* ... CA-9
*Brown Island* ... ME-1
*Brown Island* ... WA-9
*Brown Island* ... MP-9
Brown Island—*island* ... GA-3
Brown Island—*island* ... IN-6
Brown Island—*island* ... LA-4
Brown Island—*island* ... ME-1
Brown Island—*island* ... MA-1
Brown Island—*island* ... MI-6
Brown Island—*island* ... NY-2
Brown Island—*island* ... NC-3
Brown Island—*island* ... SC-3
Brown Island—*island* ... TN-4
Brown Island—*island* ... WA-9
Brown Island (historical)—*island* ... TN-4
*Brown Islands* ... MP-9
Brown Islands—*island* ... ME-1
Brown JHS—*school* ... KY-4
Brown JHS—*school* ... MA-1
Brown JHS—*school* ... NY-2
Brown JHS—*school* ... TX-5
**Brown Jug Corner**—*pop pl* ... IN-6
Brown Jug Draw—*valley* ... SD-7
Brown Jug Sch—*school* ... IA-7
Brown Jug Sch (historical)—*school* ... MO-7
Brown Jug Spring—*spring* ... AZ-5
Brown Jug Tank—*reservoir* ... AZ-5
Brown-Kercheval House—*hist pl* ... IN-6
*Brown Knob* ... WV-2
Brown Knob—*summit* ... KY-4
Brown Knob—*summit* ... NV-8
Brown Knoll—*summit* ... AZ-5
Brown Knoll—*summit* ... NV-8
Brown Knoll—*summit* (2) ... UT-8
Brown Knoll Rsvr—*reservoir* ... NV-8
*Brown Lake* ... MI-6
*Brown Lake* ... MN-6
*Brown Lake* ... NE-7
*Brown Lake* ... NV-8
Brown Lake—*basin* ... NM-5
Brown Lake—*lake* ... AK-9
Brown Lake—*lake* (2) ... AR-4
Brown Lake—*lake* ... CA-9
Brown Lake—*lake* ... CO-8
Brown Lake—*lake* (5) ... FL-3
Brown Lake—*lake* (2) ... GA-3
Brown Lake—*lake* ... ID-8
Brown Lake—*lake* ... IN-6
Brown Lake—*lake* (3) ... LA-4
Brown Lake—*lake* ... ME-1
Brown Lake—*lake* (10) ... MI-6
Brown Lake—*lake* (9) ... MN-6
Brown Lake—*lake* (2) ... NE-7
Brown Lake—*lake* ... NV-8
Brown Lake—*lake* ... NY-2
Brown Lake—*lake* ... OH-6
Brown Lake—*lake* (3) ... TX-5
Brown Lake—*lake* ... WA-9
Brown Lake—*lake* ... WI-6
Brown Lake—*reservoir* ... AL-4
Brown Lake—*reservoir* (2) ... IN-6
Brown Lake—*reservoir* ... MS-4
Brown Lake—*reservoir* ... MO-7
Brown Lake—*reservoir* (3) ... NC-3
Brown Lake—*reservoir* ... OK-5
Brown Lake—*reservoir* (2) ... TN-4
Brown Lake—*reservoir* ... TX-5
Brown Lake Campground—*locale* ... UT-8
Brown Lake Dam—*dam* (3) ... MS-4
Brown Lake Dam—*dam* (2) ... NC-3
Brown Lakes—*lake* ... CO-8
Brown Lakes—*lake* ... TX-5
*Brown Landing* ... OR-9
Brown Landing—*locale* ... IN-6
Brown Landing—*locale* ... MD-2
Brown Landing Strip—*airport* ... AZ-5
Brown Lateral—*canal* (2) ... NM-5
Brown Lateral—*canal* ... WA-9
Brown Lead—*ridge* ... NC-3
*Brown Leaf Hill* ... MA-1
Brownlee—*locale* ... CO-8
Brownlee—*locale* ... ID-8
Brownlee—*locale* ... PA-2
Brownlee—*locale* ... TX-5
**Brownlee**—*pop pl* ... GA-3
**Brownlee**—*pop pl* ... LA-4
**Brownlee**—*pop pl* ... NE-7
**Brownlee**—*pop pl* ... OR-9
Brownlee, Samuel, House—*hist pl* ... PA-2
Brownlee, Scott, Covered Bridge—*hist pl* ... PA-2
Brownlee Bay—*bay* ... UT-8
**Brownlee (Brownlee Dam)**—*pop pl* ... OR-9
Brownlee Cem—*cemetery* ... MS-4
Brown Lee Ch—*church* ... MS-4
Brownlee Corrals—*locale* ... WA-9
*Brownlee Creek* ... ID-8
Brownlee Creek—*stream* (2) ... ID-8
Brownlee Creek—*stream* ... MT-8
Brownlee Creek—*stream* ... TX-5
Brownlee Creek—*stream* ... WI-6
*Brown Lee Crossroads* ... SC-3
Brownlee Crossroads—*locale* ... SC-3
Brownlee Dam—*dam* ... ID-8
Brownlee Dam—*dam* ... ND-7
Brownlee Dam—*dam* ... OR-9
**Brownlee Dam**—*pop pl* ... OR-9
Brownlee Ditch—*canal* ... WY-8
Brownlee Flats—*flat* ... NE-7
Brown Lee Hill (historical)—*summit* ... TX-5
Brownlee (historical)—*locale* ... KS-7
Brownlee Hole—*lake* ... KY-4
Brownlee Lake—*lake* ... MI-6
Brownlee Lake—*reservoir* ... KS-7
**Brownlee Park**—*pop pl* ... MI-6
Brownlee Ranch—*locale* ... CO-8
Brownlee Rsvr—*reservoir* ... ID-8
Brownlee Rsvr—*reservoir* ... OR-9
Brownlee Rsvr—*reservoir* ... WY-8
Brownlee Sch—*school* ... IL-6
Brownlee Sch—*school* ... MO-7
Brownlee Sch—*school* ... OR-9
Brownlee Spur (historical)—*locale* ... MS-4
Brown Levee Ditch—*canal* ... IN-6
Brownley Lake Dam—*dam* ... MS-4
Brown Lick Branch—*stream* ... VA-3
Brownlie, Alexander, House—*hist pl* ... IA-7
Brown-Little Cem—*cemetery* ... TN-4
*Brown Loaf* ... MA-1
Brown Loaf—*summit* ... MA-1
*Brown Loaf Hill* ... MA-1
Brown Loam Branch Experiment Station—*other* ... MS-4
Brown Loennig Ditch—*canal* ... OR-9
Brown Lookout Tower—*tower* ... FL-3
**Brownlow**—*pop pl* ... WV-2
Brownlow Cem—*cemetery* ... KS-7
Brownlow Ch—*church* ... OK-5
Brownlow Creek—*stream* ... TN-4
**Brownlow (historical)**—*pop pl* ... TN-4
Brownlow Lateral—*canal* ... CO-8
Brownlow Point—*cape* ... AK-9
Brownlow Post Office (historical)—*building* ... TN-4
Brownlow Sch—*school* (2) ... TN-4
**Brownman**—*pop pl* ... MT-8
Brown-Mann House—*hist pl* ... TX-5
Brown Mare Branch—*stream* ... TN-4
Brown-Marian Slope Mine (underground)—*mine* ... AL-4
Brown Marsh—*swamp* ... NC-3
Brown Marsh Ch—*church* ... NC-3
Brown Marsh Presbyterian Church—*hist pl* ... NC-3
Brown Marsh Swamp—*stream* ... NC-3
Brown Marsh (Township of)—*fmr MCD* ... NC-3
Brown-Maynard House—*hist pl* ... MA-1
Brown Meadow—*flat* (2) ... CA-9
Brown Meadows—*flat* ... NV-8
Brown Meadows—*flat* ... OR-9
Brown Meadows—*flat* ... WY-8
Brown Meadows Creek—*stream* ... WA-9
**Brown Meadows Subdivision**—*pop pl* ... UT-8
Brown Memorial CME Ch—*church* ... AL-4
Brown Memorial Home—*building* ... KS-7
Brown Memorial Library—*hist pl* ... ME-1
Brown Memorial Park—*cemetery* ... LA-4
Brown Memorial Park—*park* ... KS-7
Brown Memorial Presbyterian Ch—*church* ... AL-4
Brown Mesa—*summit* ... CO-8
Brown Mesa—*summit* ... NM-5
Brown Military Acad—*school* ... CA-9
Brown Mill—*locale* ... GA-3
Brown Mill—*locale* ... TN-4
Brown Mill Branch—*stream* ... NC-3
Brown Mill Creek—*stream* ... GA-3
Brown Mill Park Ch—*church* ... GA-3
Brown Mill Ranch—*locale* ... CO-8
*Brown Mills* ... NJ-2
Brown Mills—*locale* ... PA-2
Brown Mine—*mine* ... CA-9
Brown Mine—*mine* ... MN-6
Brown Mine—*mine* ... NV-8
Brown Mines—*other* ... WV-2
Brown Mission Sch—*school* ... KY-4
*Brown-Mitchell Cemetery* ... TN-4
Brownmoor Sch—*school* ... AZ-5
Brown Morse Swamp—*swamp* ... NC-3
Brown Mountain—*ridge* ... TN-4
**Brown Mountain Beach**—*pop pl* ... NC-3
Brown Mountain Campground—*locale* ... WY-8
Brown Mountain Ch—*church* ... NC-3
Brown Mountain Ch—*church* ... TN-4
Brown Mountain Creek—*stream* ... VA-3
Brown Mountain Creek Shelter—*locale* ... VA-3
Brown Mountain Overlook—*locale* ... VA-3
Brown Mountain Ridge—*ridge* ... NC-3
Brown Mountain Sch—*school* ... NC-3
Brown Mountain Sch—*school* ... TN-4
Brown Mountain Trail—*trail* ... OR-9
Brown MS—*school* ... TN-4
*Brown Mtn* ... CA-9
*Brown Mtn* ... ME-1
*Brown Mtn* ... NY-2
Brown Mtn—*summit* ... AL-4
Brown Mtn—*summit* (2) ... AK-9
Brown Mtn—*summit* ... AZ-5
Brown Mtn—*summit* (2) ... AR-4
Brown Mtn—*summit* (6) ... CA-9
Brown Mtn—*summit* (2) ... CO-8
Brown Mtn—*summit* ... GA-3
Brown Mtn—*summit* ... ME-1
Brown Mtn—*summit* (2) ... MO-7
Brown Mtn—*summit* ... NH-1
Brown Mtn—*summit* (3) ... NY-2
Brown Mtn—*summit* (5) ... NC-3
Brown Mtn—*summit* (2) ... OK-5
Brown Mtn—*summit* (3) ... OR-9
Brown Mtn—*summit* ... SC-3
Brown Mtn—*summit* (4) ... TN-4
Brown Mtn—*summit* (5) ... TX-5
Brown Mtn—*summit* (3) ... VA-3
Brown Mtn—*summit* ... WA-9
Brown Mtn—*summit* ... WV-2
Brown Mtn—*summit* ... WY-8
Brown Mullin Watershed Rsvr Number Five—*reservoir* ... TX-5
Brown Mullin Watershed Rsvr Number Seven—*reservoir* ... TX-5
Brown Mullin Watershed Rsvr Number Six—*reservoir* ... TX-5
Brown Mullin Watershed Rsvr Number Two—*reservoir* ... TX-5
Brown-Neas House—*hist pl* ... TN-4
Brown & Norcott Mills—*other* ... NC-3
Brown North Well—*well* ... NM-5
*Brown Number Two Beach* ... MH-9
Brown Number 1 Slope Mine (underground)—*mine* ... AL-4
Brown Number 1 Tank—*reservoir* ... TX-5
Brown Number 10 Mine (underground)—*mine* ... AL-4
Brown Number 3 Tank—*reservoir* ... TX-5
Brown Number 5 Mine Station—*locale* ... PA-2
Brown Oaks Ch—*church* ... SC-3
Brown Oil Field—*oilfield* ... TX-5
*Brown One Beach* ... MH-9
Brown Owl Mine—*mine* ... OR-9
Brown Palace Hotel—*hist pl* ... CO-8
Brown Palace Hotel—*hist pl* ... SD-7
Brown Park—*flat* (2) ... CO-8
Brown Park—*park* ... DE-2
Brown Park—*park* ... GA-3
Brown Park—*park* ... IL-6
Brown Park—*park* ... NE-7
Brown Park—*park* ... OH-6
Brown Park—*park* ... TN-4
Brown Park—*park* (2) ... TX-5
Brown Park Sch—*school* ... NE-7
Brown Pass—*gap* (2) ... MT-8
Brown Pass Coulee—*valley* ... MT-8
Brown Peak—*summit* (2) ... AK-9
Brown Peak—*summit* (4) ... CA-9
Brown Peak—*summit* ... WA-9
Brown Pen Mtn—*summit* ... TX-5
Brown Place—*locale* (2) ... NM-5
*Brown Point* ... WA-9
Brown Point—*cape* ... CT-1
Brown Point—*cape* ... ME-1
Brown Point—*cape* ... MA-1
Brown Point—*cape* (2) ... NY-2
Brown Point—*cape* ... PA-2
Brown Point—*cape* ... RI-1
Brown Point—*cape* (2) ... WA-9
Brown Point—*summit* ... KY-4
Brown Point Cem—*cemetery* ... ME-1
*Brown Pond* ... KS-7
*Brown Pond* ... ME-1
*Brown Pond* ... MA-1
Brown Pond—*lake* (3) ... FL-3
Brown Pond—*lake* (3) ... GA-3
Brown Pond—*lake* ... KY-4
Brown Pond—*lake* (2) ... ME-1
Brown Pond—*lake* (3) ... NY-2
Brown Pond—*lake* ... PA-2
Brown Pond—*lake* ... TN-4
Brown Pond—*lake* ... VT-1
Brown Pond—*reservoir* (2) ... GA-3
Brown Pond—*reservoir* ... MA-1
Brown Pond—*reservoir* ... SC-3
Brown Pond—*swamp* ... FL-3
Brown Pond Dam—*dam* ... AL-4
Brown Pond Dam—*dam* ... MA-1
Brown Prairie—*flat* ... OR-9
Brown-Price House—*hist pl* ... MI-6
Brown-Proctor House—*hist pl* ... AL-4
Brown-Proctoria Hotel—*hist pl* ... KY-4
Brown Prospect—*mine* (2) ... TN-4
Brown Pusey House Community Center—*hist pl* ... KY-4
Brown Quarry—*mine* ... TN-4
Brown Queen Mine—*mine* ... UT-8
Brown Ranch—*locale* (2) ... AZ-5
Brown Ranch—*locale* (2) ... CA-9
Brown Ranch—*locale* ... CO-8
Brown Ranch—*locale* ... KS-7
Brown Ranch—*locale* (6) ... MT-8
Brown Ranch—*locale* ... NV-8
Brown Ranch—*locale* (3) ... ND-7
Brown Ranch—*locale* (2) ... OR-9
Brown Ranch—*locale* (6) ... TX-5
Brown Ranch—*locale* (3) ... WY-8
Brown Ranch Cem—*cemetery* ... TX-5
Brown Ranch Windmill—*locale* ... TX-5
Brown Ravine—*valley* (2) ... CA-9
*Brown Redwood Ditch Number One* ... MN-6
Brown Ridge—*ridge* ... AL-4
Brown Ridge—*ridge* ... AZ-5
Brown Ridge—*ridge* ... GA-3
Brown Ridge—*ridge* ... IN-6
Brown Ridge—*ridge* (4) ... KY-4
Brown Ridge—*ridge* ... MT-8
Brown Ridge—*ridge* (3) ... TN-4
Brown Ridge—*ridge* ... VA-3
Brown Ridge—*ridge* ... WV-2
Brown Ridge—*ridge* ... WI-6
Brown Ridge Ch—*church* (2) ... MS-4
Brown Ridge Slough—*stream* ... AL-4
Brown Riffles—*rapids* ... ME-1
Brownrigg-Harris-Kennebrew House—*hist pl* ... MS-4
Brownrigg Ranch—*locale* ... WY-8
Brown Road Cem—*cemetery* ... AL-4
Brown Rock—*island* ... AK-9
Brown Rock—*pillar* ... CA-9
Brown Rock—*summit* ... WA-9
Brown Rock Canyon—*valley* ... WY-8
Brown Rock Rsvr—*reservoir* ... WY-8
Brownrock Spring—*spring* ... AZ-5
Brown Rocky Mountain Trail—*trail* ... VA-3
**Brown Row**—*pop pl* ... PA-2
Brown Rsvr—*reservoir* ... CO-8
Brown Rsvr—*reservoir* ... MT-8
Brown Rsvr—*reservoir* ... OR-9
Brown Rsvr—*reservoir* ... WY-8
*Brown Run* ... PA-2
Brown Run—*stream* ... IL-6
Brown Run—*stream* (3) ... IN-6
Brown Run—*stream* ... NC-3
Brown Run—*stream* ... OH-6
Brown Run—*stream* ... PA-2
*Brown's* ... GA-3
*Browns* ... KS-7
*Browns* ... PA-2
*Browns* ... VA-3
*Browns* ... WV-2
Browns—*locale* ... IA-7
Browns—*locale* ... LA-4
Browns—*locale* ... MO-7
Browns—*locale* ... OH-6
Browns—*locale* ... PA-2
Browns—*locale* (2) ... TN-4
**Browns**—*pop pl* ... AL-4
**Browns**—*pop pl* ... AR-4
**Browns**—*pop pl* (2) ... GA-3
**Browns**—*pop pl* ... IL-6
**Browns**—*pop pl* ... MO-7
**Browns**—*pop pl* ... NJ-2
**Browns**—*pop pl* ... PA-2
Brown Saint Sch—*school* ... ME-1
Browns Airp—*airport* ... PA-2
Brownsand—*locale* ... GA-3
Brown Sandstone Peak—*summit* ... MT-8
Browns Arbor Ch—*church* ... NC-3
Brown's Arcade—*hist pl* ... MD-2
Browns Artesian Mill (historical)—*locale* ... AL-4
Browns Bank—*bar* ... MA-1
Browns Baptist Ch—*church* ... TN-4
Browns Bar—*bar* ... AL-4
Browns Bar—*bar* ... CA-9
Browns Bar—*bar* ... IL-6
Browns Bar Canyon—*valley* ... CA-9
Browns Basin—*basin* (2) ... ID-8
*Browns Bay* ... WA-9
Browns Bay—*bay* ... FL-3
Browns Bay—*bay* ... ID-8
Browns Bay—*bay* ... IA-7
Browns Bay—*bay* (3) ... MN-6
Browns Bay—*bay* ... VA-3
Browns Bay—*bay* ... WA-9
Browns Bay Campground—*locale* ... MN-6
Browns Bayou—*gut* (2) ... MI-6
Browns Bayou—*stream* (2) ... MS-4
Browns Bayou—*stream* ... TX-5
Browns Bench—*bench* ... ID-8
Browns Bench Ranch—*locale* ... NV-8
Browns Bend—*bend* ... AR-4
Browns Bend—*bend* ... TX-5
Browns Bluff—*cliff* ... AL-4
Browns Bluff Landing (historical)—*locale* ... AL-4
Brownsboro—*locale* ... OR-9
Brownsboro—*locale* ... TX-5
**Brownsboro**—*pop pl* ... AL-4
**Brownsboro**—*pop pl* ... KY-4
**Brownsboro**—*pop pl* ... TX-5
Brownsboro (CCD)—*cens area* ... TX-5
Brownsboro Cem—*cemetery* ... OR-9
Brownsboro Cem—*cemetery* ... TX-5
Brownsboro Ch—*church* ... KY-4
**Brownsboro Farm**—*pop pl* ... KY-4
**Brownsboro (historical)**—*pop pl* ... TN-4
Brownsboro Post Office (historical)—*building* ... AL-4
*Brownsborough* ... AL-4
*Brownsborough* ... TN-4
Brownsborough Post Office (historical)—*building* ... TN-4
**Brownsboro Village**—*pop pl* ... KY-4
Browns Bottom—*bend* ... KY-4
Browns Bottom—*bend* ... UT-8
Browns Bottom (inundated)—*bend* ... UT-8
Browns Bowl—*basin* ... NV-8
Browns Bowl Spring—*spring* ... NV-8
*Browns Branch* ... TX-5
Browns Branch—*stream* ... AL-4
Browns Branch—*stream* ... AR-4
Browns Branch—*stream* ... DE-2
Browns Branch—*stream* ... FL-3
Browns Branch—*stream* (5) ... KY-4
Browns Branch—*stream* ... MD-2
Browns Branch—*stream* ... MS-4
Browns Branch—*stream* (3) ... MO-7
Browns Branch—*stream* ... NC-3
Browns Branch—*stream* (3) ... SC-3
Browns Branch—*stream* (3) ... TN-4
Browns Branch—*stream* ... TX-5
Browns Branch—*stream* (2) ... VA-3
Browns Branch—*stream* (3) ... WV-2
Browns Bridge—*bridge* ... AL-4
Browns Bridge—*bridge* (3) ... GA-3
Browns Bridge—*bridge* ... MS-4
Browns Bridge—*bridge* ... NC-3
Browns Bridge—*bridge* ... OR-9
Browns Bridge—*bridge* ... SC-3
Browns Bridge—*bridge* ... TN-4
Browns Bridge—*locale* ... NY-2
*Brown's Brook* ... NH-1
Browns Brook—*stream* (4) ... CT-1
Browns Brook—*stream* ... ME-1
Browns Brook—*stream* (2) ... MA-1
Browns Brook—*stream* (2) ... NH-1
Browns Brook—*stream* (2) ... NY-2
Browns Brook—*stream* ... RI-1
Browns Brook—*stream* ... VT-1
Brownsburg—*locale* ... PA-2
Brownsburg—*locale* ... WV-2
**Brownsburg**—*pop pl* ... IN-6
**Brownsburg**—*pop pl* ... VA-3
Brownsburg Airp—*airport* ... IN-6
*Brownsburgh* ... IN-6
Brownsburg Hist Dist—*hist pl* ... VA-3
Brownsburg HS—*school* ... IN-6
Brownsburg Intermediate Sch—*school* ... IN-6
Brownsburg JHS—*school* ... IN-6
Brownsburg Post Office (historical)—*building* ... PA-2
Brownsburg South Elem Sch—*school* ... IN-6
Browns Cabin—*locale* ... CA-9
Browns Cabin—*locale* (2) ... CO-8
Browns Cabin—*locale* ... NV-8
Browns Cabin Spring—*spring* ... AZ-5
*Browns Camp* ... MS-4
Browns Camp—*locale* (3) ... CA-9
Browns Camp—*locale* (2) ... ID-8
Browns Camp Creek—*stream* ... ID-8
*Browns Canal* ... NE-7
*Browns Canon* ... CO-8
Browns Canon—*locale* ... CO-8
*Browns Canyon* ... CO-8
*Browns Canyon* ... ID-8
Browns Canyon—*valley* (2) ... AZ-5
Browns Canyon—*valley* (5) ... CA-9
Browns Canyon—*valley* (2) ... CO-8
Browns Canyon—*valley* (2) ... ID-8
Browns Canyon—*valley* (2) ... MT-8
Browns Canyon—*valley* ... NE-7
Browns Canyon—*valley* (2) ... NV-8
Browns Canyon—*valley* (6) ... UT-8
Browns Canyon—*valley* ... WA-9
Browns Canyon—*valley* ... WY-8
Browns Canyon Creek—*stream* ... MT-8
Browns Canyon Sch (reduced usage)—*school* ... CO-8
Browns Canyon Wash—*stream* ... AZ-5
Browns Canyon Wash—*stream* ... CA-9
Browns Cave—*cave* ... AZ-5
*Browns Cem* ... MO-7
Browns Cem—*cemetery* ... AL-4
Browns Cem—*cemetery* ... FL-3
Browns Cem—*cemetery* (2) ... GA-3
Browns Cem—*cemetery* ... IL-6
Browns Cem—*cemetery* (3) ... KY-4
Browns Cem—*cemetery* (2) ... ME-1
Browns Cem—*cemetery* ... MD-2
Browns Cem—*cemetery* (3) ... MS-4
Browns Cem—*cemetery* ... MO-7
Browns Cem—*cemetery* ... NC-3
Browns Cem—*cemetery* ... SC-3
Browns Cem—*cemetery* (2) ... TN-4
Browns Cem—*cemetery* (2) ... TX-5
Browns Cem (historical)—*cemetery* ... TN-4
*Browns Ch* ... AL-4
Browns Ch—*church* ... AL-4
Browns Ch—*church* ... AR-4
Browns Ch—*church* ... GA-3
Browns Ch—*church* ... MS-4
Browns Ch—*church* (3) ... NC-3
Browns Ch—*church* (2) ... SC-3
Browns Ch—*church* ... TN-4
Browns Ch—*church* ... VA-3
Brown Sch—*school* (2) ... AL-4
Brown Sch—*school* ... AZ-5
Brown Sch—*school* (3) ... AR-4
Brown Sch—*school* (3) ... CA-9
Brown Sch—*school* ... CO-8
Brown Sch—*school* ... FL-3
Brown Sch—*school* (12) ... IL-6
Brown Sch—*school* ... IN-6
Brown Sch—*school* (3) ... IA-7
Brown Sch—*school* ... KS-7
Brown Sch—*school* (2) ... KY-4
Brown Sch—*school* ... ME-1
Brown Sch—*school* (7) ... MA-1
Brown Sch—*school* (8) ... MI-6
Brown Sch—*school* ... MN-6
Brown Sch—*school* ... MS-4
Brown Sch—*school* (3) ... MO-7
Brown Sch—*school* (2) ... NE-7
Brown Sch—*school* (2) ... NH-1
Brown Sch—*school* (2) ... NJ-2
Brown Sch—*school* ... NM-5
Brown Sch—*school* (2) ... NY-2
Brown Sch—*school* (2) ... NC-3
Brown Sch—*school* ... ND-7
Brown Sch—*school* (3) ... OH-6
Brown Sch—*school* (3) ... PA-2
Brown Sch—*school* (4) ... SC-3
Brown Sch—*school* (8) ... TN-4
Brown Sch—*school* (6) ... TX-5
Brown Sch—*school* (2) ... VT-1
Brown Sch—*school* ... VA-3
Brown Sch—*school* ... WV-2
Brown Sch (abandoned)—*school* (2) ... MO-7
Brown Sch (abandoned)—*school* (2) ... PA-2
*Browns Chapel* ... MS-4
*Browns Chapel* ... TN-4
Browns Chapel—*church* (3) ... AL-4
Browns Chapel—*church* (2) ... AR-4
Browns Chapel—*church* (3) ... GA-3
Browns Chapel—*church* ... IL-6
Browns Chapel—*church* ... IN-6
Browns Chapel—*church* ... MS-4
Browns Chapel—*church* ... MO-7
Browns Chapel—*church* (7) ... NC-3
Browns Chapel—*church* ... OH-6
Browns Chapel—*church* (3) ... SC-3
Browns Chapel—*church* (4) ... TN-4
Browns Chapel—*church* (2) ... TX-5
Browns Chapel—*church* (3) ... WV-2
Browns Chapel—*locale* ... VA-3
**Browns Chapel**—*pop pl* ... WV-2
Browns Chapel Cem—*cemetery* ... AL-4
Browns Chapel Cem—*cemetery* ... AR-4
Browns Chapel Cem—*cemetery* ... KS-7
Browns Chapel Cem—*cemetery* ... OH-6
Browns Chapel Cem—*cemetery* ... SC-3
Browns Chapel Cem—*cemetery* ... VA-3
*Browns Chapel Cemetery* ... TN-4
Browns Chapel (historical)—*church* (2) ... AL-4
Browns Chapel Methodist Ch (historical)—*church* ... AL-4
Browns Chapel Sch—*school* ... TN-4
Brown Sch (historical)—*school* (6) ... AL-4
Brown Sch (historical)—*school* ... MS-4
Brown Sch (historical)—*school* (4) ... MO-7
Brown Sch (historical)—*school* (2) ... PA-2
Brown Sch (historical)—*school* ... TN-4
*Brown Sch Number 20* ... IN-6
Brown Sch Number 4—*school* ... ND-7
*Brown Sch Number 6* ... IN-6
Brown Sch Number 6—*school* ... IN-6
*Brown School* ... KS-7
Brown School—*locale* ... KS-7
Brown School, The—*school* ... TX-5
*Browns Corner* ... ME-1
Browns Corner—*locale* ... CA-9
Browns Corner—*locale* ... CO-8
Browns Corner—*locale* ... CT-1
Browns Corner—*locale* ... DE-2
Browns Corner—*locale* (2) ... ME-1
Browns Corner—*locale* ... MD-2
Browns Corner—*locale* (2) ... VA-3
Browns Corner—*locale* ... WV-2
Browns Corner—*other* ... ME-1
**Browns Corner**—*pop pl* ... AL-4
**Browns Corner**—*pop pl* ... IN-6
**Browns Corner**—*pop pl* ... MD-2
**Browns Corner**—*pop pl* ... MA-1
**Browns Corner**—*pop pl* ... NH-1
Browns Corner Ch—*church* ... IN-6
Browns Corners—*locale* ... MI-6
Browns Corners—*locale* ... OH-6
**Browns Corners**—*pop pl* ... NY-2
**Browns Corners**—*pop pl* ... VT-1
**Brownscott Manor Subdivision**—*pop pl* ... UT-8
Browns Coulee—*valley* ... MT-8
Browns Court Sch—*school* ... AK-9
Browns Cove—*bay* ... AZ-5
Browns Cove—*bay* (2) ... ME-1
Browns Cove—*bay* ... MD-2
Browns Cove—*bay* ... OR-9
Browns Cove—*bay* ... VA-3
Browns Cove—*locale* ... VA-3
Browns Cove—*valley* ... VA-3
Browns Cove Ch—*church* ... VA-3
*Browns Creek* ... AL-4
*Browns Creek* ... AR-4
*Browns Creek* ... GA-3
*Browns Creek* ... IN-6
*Browns Creek* ... MS-4
*Brown's Creek* ... MT-8
*Browns Creek* ... NE-7
*Browns Creek* ... NC-3
*Browns Creek* ... PA-2
*Browns Creek* ... SC-3
*Browns Creek* ... TN-4
Browns Creek—*bay* ... FL-3
Browns Creek—*stream* (3) ... AL-4
Browns Creek—*stream* (3) ... AR-4
Browns Creek—*stream* (7) ... CA-9
Browns Creek—*stream* (2) ... CO-8
Browns Creek—*stream* ... GA-3
Browns Creek—*stream* (9) ... ID-8
Browns Creek—*stream* ... KS-7
Browns Creek—*stream* (3) ... KY-4
Browns Creek—*stream* ... LA-4
Browns Creek—*stream* (2) ... MD-2
Browns Creek—*stream* ... MI-6
Browns Creek—*stream* (2) ... MN-6
Browns Creek—*stream* (4) ... MS-4
Browns Creek—*stream* ... MT-8
Browns Creek—*stream* ... NE-7
Browns Creek—*stream* ... NV-8
Browns Creek—*stream* (4) ... NY-2
Browns Creek—*stream* (2) ... NC-3
Browns Creek—*stream* (2) ... OK-5
Browns Creek—*stream* (2) ... OR-9
Browns Creek—*stream* (3) ... PA-2
Browns Creek—*stream* (2) ... SC-3
Browns Creek—*stream* (4) ... TN-4
Browns Creek—*stream* (7) ... TX-5
Browns Creek—*stream* ... UT-8
Browns Creek—*stream* (2) ... VA-3
Browns Creek—*stream* (2) ... WA-9
Browns Creek—*stream* (4) ... WV-2
Browns Creek—*stream* ... WI-6
Browns Creek—*stream* ... WY-8
Browns Creek Campground—*park* ... OR-9
Browns Creek Canal—*canal* ... NE-7
Brown's Creek CCC Camp Barracks—*hist pl* ... ID-8
Browns Creek Cem—*cemetery* ... SC-3
Browns Creek Ch—*church* ... NC-3
Browns Creek Ch—*church* ... SC-3
Browns Creek Ch—*church* (2) ... TN-4
Browns Creek Ch—*church* (2) ... WV-2

Browns Creek Channel—*canal* ... NE-7
Browns Creek Ditch—*canal* ... AR-4
Browns Creek Lake—*reservoir* ... TN-4
Browns Creek (Magisterial District)—*fmr MCD* ... WV-2
Browns Creek Sch—*school* ... TN-4
**Browns Creek Township**—*pop pl* ... KS-7
Browns Creek (Township of)—*civ div* ... MN-6
Browns Creek Trail (reduced usage)—*trail* ... CO-8
Browns Crossing—*locale* ... AZ-5
Browns Crossing—*locale* ... GA-3
Browns Crossing—*locale* ... IL-6
Browns Crossing—*locale* ... MO-7
Browns Crossing—*locale* ... NY-2
**Browns Crossing**—*pop pl* ... IN-6
**Browns Crossroad**—*pop pl* (2) ... AL-4
*Browns Crossroads* ... AL-4
Browns Crossroads—*locale* ... KY-4
Browns Crossroads—*locale* ... OH-6
Browns Crossroads—*locale* ... PA-2
Browns Crossroads—*locale* ... SC-3
**Browns Crossroads**—*pop pl* ... AL-4
**Browns Crossroads**—*pop pl* ... NC-3
Browns Dairy—*area* ... UT-8
**Brownsdale**—*pop pl* ... FL-3
**Brownsdale**—*pop pl* ... MN-6
**Brownsdale**—*pop pl* (2) ... PA-2
Brownsdale (historical)—*locale* ... SD-7
Brownsdale Station—*building* ... PA-2
Browns Dam—*dam* ... AL-4
Browns Dam—*dam* ... PA-2
Browns Dan River—*stream* ... VA-3
Browns Ditch—*canal* ... OH-6
Browns Drain—*canal* ... CA-9
Browns Draw—*valley* ... CO-8
Browns Draw—*valley* ... SD-7
Browns Draw Dam—*dam* ... UT-8
Browns Draw Rsvr—*reservoir* ... UT-8
Brownsea Trail Camp—*locale* ... NM-5
Browns (Election Precinct)—*fmr MCD* ... IL-6
**Brownsell Corner**—*pop pl* ... NY-2
Browns Fall Powerplant—*other* ... NY-2
**Browns Farm**—*pop pl* ... FL-3
Browns Farm Wildlife Mngmt Area—*park* ... FL-3
Browns Feed Canal—*canal* ... OR-9
*Browns Ferry* ... TN-4
Browns Ferry—*facility* ... AL-4
Brown's Ferry—*hist pl* ... VA-3
Browns Ferry—*locale* ... MO-7
Browns Ferry—*locale* ... SC-3
Browns Ferry—*locale* ... TN-4
Brown's Ferry Gage—*locale* ... AR-4
Brown's Ferry Gage—*other* ... MO-7
Browns Ferry (historical)—*locale* (2) ... AL-4
Browns Ferry (historical)—*locale* ... IA-7
Browns Ferry (historical)—*locale* ... MS-4
Browns Ferry Nuclear Plant—*other* ... AL-4
Brown's Ferry Tavern—*hist pl* ... TN-4
BROWN'S FERRY VESSEL—*hist pl* ... SC-3
Browns Flat—*flat* ... CA-9
Browns Flat—*flat* ... MT-8
**Browns Flat**—*pop pl* ... CA-9
*Brown's Folly* ... MA-1
*Browns Ford* ... TN-4
Browns Ford—*locale* ... MO-7
**Browns Ford**—*pop pl* ... MO-7
**Browns Ford (Boat Ramp)**—*pop pl* ... KY-4
Browns Ford Bridge—*other* ... MO-7
*Browns Fork* ... PA-2
Browns Fork—*locale* ... KY-4
Browns Fork—*stream* ... AK-9
Browns Fork—*stream* (3) ... KY-4
Browns Fork—*stream* ... TN-4
*Browns Fork Creek* ... OK-5
Browns Fork Sch—*school* ... KY-4
*Browns Gap* ... AL-4
*Browns Gap* ... TN-4
Browns Gap—*gap* ... PA-2
Browns Gap—*gap* ... TN-4
Browns Gap—*gap* ... VA-3
Browns Gap Run—*stream* ... PA-2
*Browns Grove* ... KS-7
Browns Grove—*locale* ... KY-4
**Browns Grove**—*pop pl* ... KY-4
Browns Grove Cem—*cemetery* ... KS-7
Browns Grove Ch—*church* ... AL-4
**Browns Grove Township**—*pop pl* ... KS-7
*Browns Gulch* ... CO-8
*Browns Gulch* ... MT-8
Browns Gulch—*valley* (5) ... CA-9
Browns Gulch—*valley* (2) ... CO-8
Browns Gulch—*valley* (5) ... ID-8
Browns Gulch—*valley* (12) ... MT-8
Browns Gulch—*valley* ... NV-8
Browns Gulch—*valley* (2) ... OR-9
Browns Gulch—*valley* ... WA-9
Browns Gulch Mining District—*locale* ... MT-8
Browns Gulch Spring—*spring* ... MT-8
Brown's Hall-Thompson's Opera House—*hist pl* ... NV-8
**Brown Shanty**—*pop pl* ... MO-7
*Brown's Head* ... ME-1
Browns Head—*cape* (2) ... ME-1
Browns Head Cove—*bay* ... ME-1
Browns Head Ledge—*bar* ... ME-1
Browns Head Light Station—*hist pl* ... ME-1
Brown Shed Cem—*cemetery* ... TX-5
Brown Sheep Camp—*locale* ... CO-8
**Browns Heights**—*pop pl* ... OH-6
*Browns Hill* ... CA-9
*Browns Hill* ... MA-1
*Browns Hill* ... NH-1
Browns Hill—*locale* ... SC-3
Browns Hill—*summit* ... AK-9
Browns Hill—*summit* ... CA-9
Browns Hill—*summit* ... ME-1
Browns Hill—*summit* (2) ... MA-1
Browns Hill—*summit* (2) ... NH-1
Browns Hill—*summit* ... ND-7
Browns Hill—*summit* ... PA-2
Browns Hill—*summit* ... WV-2
Browns Hill—*summit* ... WY-8
Browns Hill Mine—*mine* ... CA-9
Browns Hill Ridge—*ridge* ... CA-9
*Brown's Hills* ... CO-8
Browns Hills—*summit* ... NY-2
Browns (historical)—*locale* ... AL-4
Brown Shoal—*bar* ... DE-2
Brown Shoe Company's Homes-Take Factory—*hist pl* ... MO-7
Browns Hole—*basin* (3) ... UT-8
Browns Hole—*valley* ... UT-8
*Browns Hollow* ... PA-2
**Browns Hollow**—*pop pl* ... NY-2
Browns Hollow—*valley* ... MO-7
Browns Hollow—*valley* (2) ... NY-2
Browns Hollow—*valley* ... TN-4
Browns Hollow—*valley* ... VA-3
Browns Hollow—*valley* ... WV-2
Browns Horse Corral Waterhole—*reservoir* ... OR-9
Browns Hotel (historical)—*locale* ... ND-7
**Brown Siding**—*pop pl* ... OH-6
Browns Indian Trading Post (Ruins)—*locale* ... FL-3
Browns Inlet—*channel* ... NC-3
*Browns Island* ... AL-4
*Brown's Island* ... FL-3
*Browns Island* ... LA-4
*Brown's Island* ... ME-1
Browns Island—*island* ... CA-9
Browns Island—*island* ... FL-3
Browns Island—*island* ... IL-6
Browns Island—*island* ... LA-4
Browns Island—*island* (3) ... ME-1
Browns Island—*island* ... MA-1
Browns Island—*island* ... MN-6
Browns Island—*island* ... NH-1
Browns Island—*island* (3) ... NC-3
Browns Island—*island* ... OR-9
Browns Island—*island* ... PA-2
Browns Island—*island* ... SC-3
Browns Island—*island* ... UT-8
Browns Island—*island* ... WA-9
Browns Island—*island* ... WV-2
Brown Site (20GR21)—*hist pl* ... MI-6
Browns Knob—*summit* ... NC-3
Browns Knob—*summit* ... OH-6
Browns Knob—*summit* ... WV-2
Browns Knoll—*summit* ... UT-8
Browns Lagoon—*bay* ... AK-9
*Browns Lake* ... MI-6
*Browns Lake* ... MS-4
*Browns Lake* ... MT-8
*Browns Lake* ... TX-5
*Browns Lake* ... WA-9
*Brown's Lake* ... WI-6
Browns Lake—*lake* ... AK-9
Browns Lake—*lake* ... CA-9
Browns Lake—*lake* (2) ... CO-8
Browns Lake—*lake* ... FL-3
Browns Lake—*lake* ... GA-3
Browns Lake—*lake* ... ID-8
Browns Lake—*lake* ... IL-6
Browns Lake—*lake* ... IA-7
Browns Lake—*lake* ... LA-4
Browns Lake—*lake* (6) ... MI-6
Browns Lake—*lake* (5) ... MN-6
Browns Lake—*lake* ... MS-4
Browns Lake—*lake* ... MT-8
Browns Lake—*lake* ... NM-5
Browns Lake—*lake* ... OK-5
Browns Lake—*lake* ... TN-4
Browns Lake—*lake* (2) ... TX-5
Browns Lake—*lake* (4) ... WA-9
Browns Lake—*lake* (2) ... WI-6
Browns Lake—*reservoir* (2) ... AL-4
Browns Lake—*reservoir* ... AR-4
Browns Lake—*reservoir* ... GA-3
Browns Lake—*reservoir* ... IA-7
Browns Lake—*reservoir* ... KY-4
Browns Lake—*reservoir* ... MS-4
Browns Lake—*reservoir* (2) ... PA-2
Browns Lake—*reservoir* (2) ... SC-3
Browns Lake—*reservoir* (2) ... TN-4
Browns Lake—*reservoir* (2) ... TX-5
Browns Lake (Cedar Park)—*CDP* ... WI-6
Browns Lake Dam—*dam* (2) ... MS-4
Browns Lake Dam—*dam* (2) ... PA-2
Browns Lake Dam—*dam* ... TN-4
Browns Lakes—*lake* ... FL-3
Browns Lakes—*lake* ... GA-3
Browns Lake Well—*well* ... NM-5
Browns Landing—*locale* ... AL-4
Browns Landing—*locale* ... CA-9
Browns Landing—*locale* (3) ... FL-3
Browns Landing—*locale* ... MS-4
Browns Landing—*locale* ... NC-3
Browns Landing—*locale* ... SC-3
Browns Landing—*locale* ... WY-8
Browns Landing (historical)—*locale* ... AL-4
Browns Landing Park—*park* ... OR-9
Browns Ledge—*cliff* ... ME-1
Browns Ledges—*summit* ... VT-1
*Browns Lily Pond* ... MA-1
Brown Slope Mine (underground)—*mine* ... AL-4
Brown Slough—*bay* ... OR-9
Brown Slough—*gut* ... IL-6
Brown Slough—*gut* ... LA-4
Brown Slough—*stream* ... OR-9
Brown Slough—*stream* ... WA-9
Brown's Manor—*hist pl* ... MA-1
**Brownsmead**—*pop pl* ... OR-9
*Browns Meadow* ... CA-9
Browns Meadow—*flat* (2) ... CA-9
Browns Meadow—*flat* ... ID-8
Browns Meadow—*flat* ... MT-8
Browns Meadow Pass—*gap* ... MT-8
*Browns Methodist Episcopal Church* ... AL-4
*Browns Mill* ... GA-3
*Browns Mill* ... PA-2
*Browns Mill* ... TN-4
Brown's Mill—*hist pl* ... TN-4
Browns Mill—*locale* ... OR-9
Browns Mill—*locale* ... PA-2
Browns Mill—*locale* ... TN-4
Browns Mill—*locale* ... VT-1
Browns Mill—*locale* ... VA-3
Browns Mill—*other* ... PA-2
**Browns Mill**—*pop pl* ... IL-6
**Browns Mill**—*pop pl* ... WV-2
Browns Mill Ch (historical)—*church* ... TN-4
Browns Mill Creek—*stream* (2) ... AL-4
Browns Mill Creek—*stream* ... NC-3
Browns Mill Dam—*dam* ... TN-4
Browns Mill (historical)—*locale* ... AL-4
Browns Mill (historical)—*locale* ... TN-4
Browns Mill Hollow—*valley* (2) ... PA-2
Browns Mill Lake—*reservoir* ... TN-4
Browns Millpond—*lake* ... GA-3
Browns Mill Pond—*swamp* ... FL-3
**Browns Mills**—*pop pl* ... NJ-2
**Browns Mills**—*pop pl* ... WV-2
*Browns Mills-in-the-Pines* ... NJ-2
Browns Mill (Site)—*locale* ... CA-9
**Browns Mills Junction**—*pop pl* ... NJ-2
Browns Mill Spring—*spring* ... TN-4
Browns Mine—*mine* ... CA-9
Browns Mound—*summit* (2) ... IL-6
Browns Mountain Crossing—*locale* ... OR-9
*Brown's Mtn* ... ME-1
Browns Mtn—*summit* ... AL-4
Browns Mtn—*summit* (2) ... CA-9
Browns Mtn—*summit* ... ME-1
Browns Mtn—*summit* ... MT-8
Browns Mtn—*summit* (2) ... NY-2
Browns Mtn—*summit* ... OR-9
Browns Mtn—*summit* ... SC-3
Browns Mtn—*summit* ... VT-1
Browns Mtn—*summit* ... VA-3
Browns Mtn—*summit* ... WV-2
*Browns Mtn Creek* ... VA-3
Browns Mullin Watershed Rsvr Number Four—*reservoir* ... TX-5
Browns Old Ferry—*locale* ... NC-3
**Browns Old Ferry (historical)**—*pop pl* ... NC-3
Browns Old Mill—*locale* ... SC-3
Browns Old River—*stream* ... MS-4
**Brownson**—*pop pl* ... AL-4
**Brownson**—*pop pl* ... NE-7
Brownson Bay—*bay* ... AK-9
Brownson Cem—*cemetery* ... TX-5
*Brownson Hill* ... NY-2
Brownson House—*locale* ... PA-2
Brownson Island—*island* ... AK-9
Brownson Peak—*summit* ... AK-9
Browns Overflow—*channel* ... UT-8
Browns Park—*flat* ... AZ-5
Browns Park—*flat* (2) ... CO-8
Browns Park—*flat* ... UT-8
Browns Park Campground—*locale* ... CO-8
Browns Park Natl Wildlife Ref—*park* ... CO-8
Browns Park Natl Wildlife Refuge Dam—*dam* ... UT-8
Browns Park Natl Wildlife Refuge Rsvr—*reservoir* ... UT-8
*Browns Park Reservoir* ... UT-8
Browns Park Sch—*school* ... CO-8
*Browns Park State Waterfowl Mngmt Area* ... UT-8
**Browns Park Subdivision (Plats 1and2)**—*pop pl* ... UT-8
**Browns Park Subdivision (Plat 3)**—*pop pl* ... UT-8
Browns Park Waterfowl Mngmt Area—*park* ... UT-8
Browns Pass—*channel* ... TX-5
Browns Pass—*gap* (2) ... CO-8
Browns Pass—*gap* ... WA-9
Browns Peak—*summit* (2) ... AZ-5
Browns Peak—*summit* ... CO-8
Browns Peak—*summit* ... ID-8
Browns Peak—*summit* ... ME-1
Browns Peak—*summit* ... MT-8
Browns Peak—*summit* ... UT-8
Browns Peak—*summit* ... VA-3
Browns Peak—*summit* ... WY-8
Browns Peak Trail—*trail* ... UT-8
Brown's Pharmacy—*hist pl* ... AZ-5
*Browns Point* ... NJ-2
*Browns Point* ... NY-2
Browns Point—*cape* ... AK-9
Browns Point—*cape* ... ID-8
Browns Point—*cape* ... IN-6
Browns Point—*cape* (2) ... ME-1
Browns Point—*cape* ... MD-2
Browns Point—*cape* ... MS-4
Browns Point—*cape* ... NH-1
Browns Point—*cape* (2) ... NY-2
Browns Point—*cape* ... UT-8
Browns Point—*cape* ... VA-3
Browns Point—*cape* ... WA-9
Browns Point—*cliff* ... CO-8
**Browns Point**—*pop pl* ... MA-1
**Browns Point**—*pop pl* ... WA-9
Browns Point—*ridge* ... UT-8
Browns Point Landing—*locale* ... MS-4
Browns Point Sch—*school* ... WA-9
*Browns Pond* ... NY-2
*Browns Pond* ... PA-2
Browns Pond—*lake* (2) ... AL-4
Browns Pond—*lake* ... AR-4
Browns Pond—*lake* ... GA-3
Browns Pond—*lake* ... ID-8
Browns Pond—*lake* (2) ... IL-6
Browns Pond—*lake* ... KY-4
Browns Pond—*lake* ... ME-1
Browns Pond—*lake* ... MA-1
Browns Pond—*lake* ... MI-6
Browns Pond—*lake* ... NJ-2
Browns Pond—*lake* (2) ... NY-2
Browns Pond—*lake* (2) ... PA-2
Browns Pond—*lake* ... VT-1
Browns Pond—*lake* ... VA-3
Browns Pond—*reservoir* ... AL-4
Browns Pond—*reservoir* ... GA-3
Browns Pond—*reservoir* ... KS-7
Browns Pond—*reservoir* ... MA-1
Browns Pond—*reservoir* (3) ... NY-2
Browns Pond—*reservoir* ... NC-3
Browns Pond—*reservoir* ... SC-3
Browns Pond—*swamp* ... MI-6
*Browns Pond Dam* ... PA-2
Browns Pond Dam—*dam* ... MA-1
Browns Pond Dam—*dam* ... NC-3
Browns Pond Ditch—*canal* ... IL-6
Browns Ponds—*reservoir* ... AL-4
Browns Pond Slough—*stream* ... AR-4
Brownsport Furnace—*locale* ... TN-4
Brownsport Furnace Post Office (historical)—*building* ... TN-4
**Brownsport (historical)**—*pop pl* ... TN-4
Brownsport I Furnace (40DR85)—*hist pl* ... TN-4
Brownsport II Furnace—*hist pl* ... TN-4
Brownsport II Furnace (40DR86) (Boundary Increase)—*hist pl* ... TN-4
Brownsport Landing—*locale* ... TN-4
Brown's Post—*hist pl* ... SD-7
Browns Post Office (historical)—*building* ... TN-4
*Brown Spring* ... UT-8
Brown Spring—*spring* (2) ... AL-4
Brown Spring—*spring* (4) ... AZ-5
Brown Spring—*spring* (2) ... AR-4
Brown Spring—*spring* ... CA-9
Brown Spring—*spring* (2) ... CO-8
Brown Spring—*spring* ... KY-4
Brown Spring—*spring* (2) ... MO-7
Brown Spring—*spring* ... NV-8
Brown Spring—*spring* ... NM-5
Brown Spring—*spring* ... OR-9
Brown Spring—*spring* (5) ... TN-4
Brown Spring—*spring* ... TX-5
Brown Spring—*spring* ... WY-8
Brown Spring Branch—*stream* (2) ... TN-4
Brown Spring Ch—*church* ... SC-3
Brown Spring Ch—*church* ... TX-5
Brown Spring Draw—*valley* ... WY-8
Brown Spring Hollow—*valley* ... MO-7
*Brown Springs* ... NV-8
Brown Springs—*locale* ... AR-4
Brown Springs—*spring* ... AZ-5
Brown Springs—*spring* ... GA-3
Brown Springs—*spring* ... NV-8
Brown Springs Branch—*stream* ... AR-4
Brown Springs Ch—*church* ... TN-4
Brown Springs Creek—*stream* ... WY-8
**Brown Springs (Faber)**—*pop pl* ... AR-4
Brown Springs Ranch—*locale* ... AZ-5
Brown Springs Rec Area—*park* ... AR-4
Brown Springs (Township of)—*fmr MCD* ... AR-4
Brown Square House—*hist pl* ... MA-1
Browns Ranch—*locale* ... AZ-5
Browns Ranch—*locale* ... CA-9
Browns Ranch—*locale* ... NM-5
Browns Ranch—*locale* ... TX-5
Browns Ranch—*locale* ... WY-8
*Brownsrange* ... MP-9
*Browns Reservoir* ... PA-2
Browns Ridge—*ridge* ... ID-8
Browns Ridge—*ridge* ... LA-4
Browns Ridge—*ridge* ... NH-1
Browns Ridge—*ridge* ... PA-2
Browns Ridge—*ridge* ... UT-8
Browns Ridge—*ridge* ... VA-3
Browns Ridge—*ridge* (2) ... WV-2
Browns Riffle—*rapids* ... AZ-5
Browns Rim—*cliff* ... UT-8
Browns River—*stream* ... NH-1
Browns River—*stream* ... VT-1
Browns Road Ch—*church* ... AL-4
Browns Rock—*pillar* ... CA-9
Browns Rock—*pillar* ... ID-8
Browns Rock—*pillar* ... NY-2
Browns Rock Saddle—*gap* ... ID-8
Browns Roll Off Campground—*locale* ... UT-8
Browns Rsvr—*reservoir* ... AZ-5
Browns Rsvr—*reservoir* ... MT-8
Browns Rsvr—*reservoir* ... NY-2
Browns Rsvr—*reservoir* (4) ... OR-9
*Browns Run* ... PA-2
Browns Run—*stream* ... KY-4
Browns Run—*stream* ... NJ-2
Browns Run—*stream* ... NY-2
Browns Run—*stream* (7) ... OH-6
Browns Run—*stream* (16) ... PA-2
Browns Run—*stream* (2) ... VA-3
Browns Run—*stream* (11) ... WV-2
Browns Run Dam—*dam* ... PA-2
**Browns Run Junction**—*pop pl* ... PA-2
Browns Run Portal—*mine* ... PA-2
Browns Run Rsvr—*reservoir* (2) ... PA-2
Browns Run Trail—*trail* ... PA-2
*Browns Sch* ... TN-4
Browns Sch—*school* ... CA-9
Browns Sch—*school* ... KY-4
Browns Sch—*school* (2) ... MO-7
Browns Sch—*school* ... TN-4
Browns Sch—*school* ... VA-3
Browns Sch—*school* ... WA-9
Browns Sch (abandoned)—*school* ... MO-7
Browns Sch (historical)—*school* (2) ... AL-4
Browns Sch (historical)—*school* ... MS-4
Browns Sch (historical)—*school* (2) ... PA-2
Browns Sch (historical)—*school* ... TN-4
Browns School (abandoned)—*locale* ... MO-7
Browns School (historical)—*locale* ... MO-7
Browns Shanty Lake—*lake* ... AR-4
Browns Shoal—*bar* ... TN-4
Browns Shoals—*bar* ... TN-4
**Browns Shop**—*pop pl* ... TN-4
Browns Slough—*stream* ... AK-9
Browns Slough—*stream* ... WA-9
Browns Sound—*bay* ... NC-3
*Browns Spring* ... CO-8
**Browns Spring**—*pop pl* ... MO-7
Browns Spring—*spring* (2) ... AL-4
Browns Spring—*spring* (2) ... ID-8
Browns Spring—*spring* ... LA-4
Browns Spring—*spring* (2) ... NV-8
Browns Spring—*spring* ... PA-2
Browns Spring—*spring* ... UT-8
Browns Spring—*spring* ... WY-8
Browns Spring Creek—*stream* ... ID-8
Browns Spur—*locale* ... KS-7
*Browns Station* ... MO-7
Browns Station—*locale* ... IA-7
Browns Station—*locale* ... PA-2
Browns Station (historical)—*locale* ... MA-1
**Browns Still**—*pop pl* ... FL-3
Browns Store—*locale* ... VA-3
**Browns Store**—*pop pl* (2) ... VA-3
Browns Store and Mill (historical)—*locale* ... AL-4
Browns Store (historical)—*locale* (2) ... AL-4
Browns Store Landing—*locale* ... MS-4
Browns Store (Magisterial District)—*fmr MCD* ... VA-3
**Browns Summit**—*pop pl* ... NC-3
**Browns Summit (RR name Brown Summit)**—*pop pl* ... NC-3
Browns Summit Sch—*school* ... NC-3
Browns Swamp—*stream* (2) ... NC-3
Browns Swamp—*swamp* ... MA-1
Browns Tank—*reservoir* ... AZ-5
Brown State Fishing Lake And Wildlife Area—*park* ... KS-7
Browns Temple Ch—*church* ... TN-4
Browns Temple (historical)—*church* ... AL-4
Brownstetter House—*hist pl* ... AZ-5
Brownstone—*locale* ... KS-7
**Brownstone**—*pop pl* ... PA-2
Brownstone Basin—*basin* ... NV-8
Brownstone Canyon Archeol District—*hist pl* ... NV-8
**Brown Stone Condominium**—*pop pl* ... UT-8
Brownstone Creek—*stream* ... MT-8
Brownstone Falls—*falls* ... WI-6
Brownstone Mine—*mine* ... CA-9
Brownstone Rsvr—*reservoir* ... CA-9
Brownstown—*locale* ... AR-4
Brownstown—*locale* ... OH-6
**Brownstown**—*pop pl* ... AL-4
**Brownstown**—*pop pl* ... IL-6
**Brownstown**—*pop pl* (2) ... IN-6
**Brownstown**—*pop pl* ... MD-2
**Brownstown**—*pop pl* ... OH-6
**Brownstown**—*pop pl* (4) ... PA-2
**Brownstown**—*pop pl* ... WA-9
Brownstown Borough—*civil* ... PA-2
Brownstown Cem—*cemetery* ... AR-4
Brownstown Creek—*stream* ... IN-6
Brownstown Creek—*stream* ... MI-6
Brownstown Elem Sch—*school* ... PA-2
*Brownstown Ridge* ... TN-4
**Browns Townsite Subdivision**—*pop pl* ... UT-8
**Brownstown (Township of)**—*pop pl* ... IN-6
**Brownstown (Township of)**—*pop pl* ... MI-6
Brownstown Vocational Technical Sch—*school* ... PA-2
Browns Tract Inlet—*stream* ... NY-2
Browns Tract Pond—*lake* ... NY-2
Browns Trail—*trail* ... PA-2
Brown Street Holiness Ch—*church* ... AL-4
Brown Street Sch—*school* (2) ... WI-6
Brown Street Seventh Day Adventist Ch—*church* ... AL-4
**Brown Street (subdivision)**—*pop pl* ... DE-2
*Browns Turnout* ... NC-3
**Brown Subdivision**—*pop pl* ... UT-8
Brown Summit—*gap* ... NV-8
Brown Summit (RR name for Browns Summit)—*other* ... NC-3
Brown Summit Rsvr—*reservoir* ... NV-8
Brown Summit Truck Trail—*trail* ... NV-8
*Brown's Valley* ... MN-6
Browns Valley—*basin* ... CA-9
Browns Valley—*locale* ... KY-4
**Browns Valley**—*pop pl* ... CA-9
**Browns Valley**—*pop pl* ... IN-6
**Browns Valley**—*pop pl* ... MN-6
Browns Valley—*valley* ... AL-4
Browns Valley—*valley* (2) ... CA-9
Browns Valley—*valley* ... WI-6
Browns Valley Carnegie Public Library—*hist pl* ... MN-6
Browns Valley Ditch—*canal* ... CA-9
Browns Valley (historical)—*locale* ... AL-4
Browns Valley of Rest Cem—*cemetery* ... AR-4
Browns Valley Ridge—*ridge* ... CA-9
**Browns Valley (RR name Brown's Valley)**—*pop pl* ... KY-4
Brown's Valley (RR name for Browns Valley)—*other* ... KY-4
Browns Valley Sch—*school* (2) ... CA-9
Browns Valley Sch—*school* ... WI-6
Browns Valley (Township of)—*civ div* ... MN-6
Browns View Ch—*church* ... NC-3
Browns Village (census name Brownsville)—*other* ... FL-3
*Brownsville* ... AL-4
*Brownsville* ... CA-9
*Brownsville* ... FL-3
*Brownsville* ... IN-6
*Brownsville* ... KS-7
*Brownsville* ... MD-2
*Brownsville* ... NJ-2
*Brownsville* ... OH-6
*Brownsville* ... PA-2
Brownsville—*hist pl* ... VA-3
Brownsville—*locale* ... AL-4
Brownsville—*locale* ... AR-4
Brownsville—*locale* ... DE-2
Brownsville—*locale* ... GA-3
Brownsville—*locale* ... KY-4
Brownsville—*locale* ... NJ-2
Brownsville—*locale* ... PA-2
Brownsville—*locale* ... SD-7
Brownsville—*locale* ... WA-9
Brownsville—*other* ... PA-2
**Brownsville**—*pop pl* ... CA-9
**Brownsville**—*pop pl* ... FL-3
**Brownsville**—*pop pl* ... IL-6
**Brownsville**—*pop pl* ... IN-6
**Brownsville**—*pop pl* ... IA-7
**Brownsville**—*pop pl* ... KY-4
**Brownsville**—*pop pl* ... LA-4
**Brownsville**—*pop pl* (2) ... MD-2
**Brownsville**—*pop pl* ... MI-6
**Brownsville**—*pop pl* ... MN-6
**Brownsville**—*pop pl* ... MS-4
**Brownsville**—*pop pl* (2) ... NY-2
**Brownsville**—*pop pl* (3) ... OH-6
**Brownsville**—*pop pl* ... OR-9
**Brownsville**—*pop pl* (4) ... PA-2
**Brownsville**—*pop pl* (2) ... SC-3
**Brownsville**—*pop pl* (2) ... TN-4
**Brownsville**—*pop pl* ... TX-5
**Brownsville**—*pop pl* ... VT-1
**Brownsville**—*pop pl* ... VA-3
**Brownsville**—*pop pl* (2) ... WV-2
**Brownsville**—*pop pl* ... WI-6
Brownsville Assembly of God—*church* ... FL-3
Brownsville Baptist Ch—*church* ... FL-3
Brownsville Baptist Ch—*church* ... TN-4
Brownsville-Bawcomville—*CDP* ... LA-4
Brownsville Borough—*civil* ... PA-2
Brownsville Bridge—*hist pl* ... PA-2
Brownsville (CCD)—*cens area* ... KY-4
Brownsville (CCD)—*cens area* ... OR-9
Brownsville (CCD)—*cens area* ... TN-4
Brownsville (CCD)—*cens area* ... TX-5
Brownsville Cem—*cemetery* ... AR-4
Brownsville Cem—*cemetery* ... WV-2
Brownsville (census name for Browns Village)—*CDP* ... FL-3
Brownsville Ch—*church* (2) ... AR-4
Brownsville Ch—*church* ... MD-2
Brownsville Ch—*church* ... MS-4
Brownsville Ch—*church* ... OH-6
Brownsville Ch—*church* ... SC-3
*Brownsville Church* ... AL-4
Brownsville Country Club—*locale* ... TN-4
Brownsville Country Club—*other* ... TX-5
Brownsville Creek—*stream* ... CA-9
Brownsville Creek—*stream* ... IL-6
Brownsville Creek—*stream* ... MN-6
Brownsville Creek—*stream* ... SC-3
Brownsville Dam—*dam* ... OR-9
Brownsville Ditch—*canal* ... OR-9
Brownsville Division—*civil* ... TN-4
Brownsville Fishing Harbor—*harbor* ... TX-5
Brownsville-Haywood County Library—*building* ... TN-4
Brownsville International Airp—*airport* ... TX-5
Brownsville Island—*island* ... IL-6
Brownsville JHS—*school* ... FL-3
**Brownsville Junction**—*pop pl* ... PA-2
Brownsville Lookout Tower—*locale* ... MS-4
Brownsville MS—*school* ... FL-3
Brownsville North (CCD)—*cens area* ... KY-4
Brownsville Park—*park* ... FL-3
Brownsville Pioneer Cem—*cemetery* ... OR-9
Brownsville Post Office—*building* ... TN-4
Brownsville Road Sch—*school* ... TN-4
Brownsville Sch—*school* ... AR-4
Brownsville Sch—*school* ... IL-6
Brownsville Sch—*school* ... LA-4
Brownsville Ship Channel—*channel* ... TX-5
Brownsville Ship Harbor—*harbor* ... TX-5
Brownsville (Site)—*locale* ... CA-9
**Brownsville (Township of)**—*pop pl* ... IN-6
**Brownsville (Township of)**—*pop pl* ... MN-6
**Brownsville (Township of)**—*pop pl* ... PA-2
Browns Vista—*summit* ... PA-2
Brown Swamp—*stream* (3) ... SC-3
Brown Swamp—*swamp* ... NY-2
Brown Swamp—*swamp* ... PA-2
Brown Swamp Cem—*cemetery* ... NY-2
Brown Swamp Ch—*church* ... SC-3
Browns Wash—*stream* ... AZ-5
Browns Wash—*stream* ... CA-9
Browns Wash—*valley* ... CA-9
Browns Wash—*valley* (2) ... UT-8
Browns Well—*well* (3) ... AZ-5
Browns Well—*well* ... CA-9
Browns Well—*well* ... NV-8
Browns Well—*well* ... NM-5
**Browns Wells**—*pop pl* ... MS-4
Browns Wells—*spring* ... AL-4
Browns Well (Site)—*well* ... CA-9
Browns Wells Post Office (historical)—*building* ... MS-4
Brown Switch—*locale* ... TN-4
Browns Wonder Ch—*church* ... IN-6
*Browns Wonder Creek* ... IN-6
Browns Wonder Creek—*stream* ... IN-6
**Browns Woods**—*pop pl* ... MD-2
Brownsworth Creek—*stream* ... OR-9
*Brownsworthy Creek* ... OR-9
Brown Tank—*reservoir* (4) ... AZ-5
Brown Tank—*reservoir* (6) ... NM-5
Brown Tank—*reservoir* (5) ... TX-5
Brown Tanks—*reservoir* ... AZ-5
*Brown Tanks Spring* ... AZ-5
Brown Tavern—*hist pl* ... CT-1
Brown Taylor Cem—*cemetery* ... OH-6
Browntee Creek—*stream* ... LA-4
Brown Temple—*church* ... MS-4
Brown Temple—*church* ... SC-3
Brown Temple CME Ch—*church* ... AL-4
Brown Tobacco Warehouse—*hist pl* ... KY-4
*Brownton* ... VA-3
Brownton—*locale* ... IL-6
Brownton—*locale* ... PA-2
**Brownton**—*pop pl* ... MN-6
**Brownton**—*pop pl* ... WV-2
Brown Top—*summit* ... NM-5
*Browntown* ... MS-4
*Browntown* ... TN-4
*Brown Town* ... WV-2
Browntown—*hist pl* ... SC-3
Browntown—*locale* ... AL-4
Browntown—*locale* ... FL-3
Browntown—*locale* ... GA-3
Brown Town—*locale* ... MS-4
Browntown—*locale* ... NY-2
Brown Town—*locale* ... NC-3
Browntown—*locale* (2) ... OR-9
Browntown—*locale* ... PA-2
Browntown—*locale* (2) ... VA-3
**Browntown**—*pop pl* (2) ... AL-4
**Browntown**—*pop pl* ... IN-6
**Browntown**—*pop pl* ... MS-4
**Browntown**—*pop pl* ... NJ-2
**Brown Town**—*pop pl* ... NC-3
**Browntown**—*pop pl* ... OH-6
**Browntown**—*pop pl* (4) ... PA-2
**Browntown**—*pop pl* ... TN-4
**Browntown**—*pop pl* ... VA-3
**Brown Town**—*pop pl* ... VA-3
**Browntown**—*pop pl* ... VA-3
**Browntown**—*pop pl* ... WI-6
Browntown Cem—*cemetery* ... MI-6
Browntown Cem—*cemetery* ... TN-4
Brown Town Ch—*church* ... AL-4
Browntown Ch—*church* ... SC-3
Browntown Ch—*church* ... VA-3
**Browntown Crossroads**—*pop pl* ... NC-3
Browntown Gulch—*valley* ... OR-9
**Browntown (historical)**—*pop pl* ... TN-4
Browntown Mtn—*summit* ... PA-2
Browntown Ridge—*ridge* ... TN-4
Browntown Sch—*school* ... MI-6
Browntown Sch (historical)—*school* ... TN-4
*Brown Township* ... KS-7
Brown Township—*civil* ... MO-7
Brown Township—*civil* ... SD-7
Brown Township—*fmr MCD* ... IA-7
**Brown Township**—*pop pl* ... ND-7
Brown Township Bldg—*hist pl* ... OH-6
Brown Township Elem Sch—*school* ... PA-2
Brown Township (historical)—*civil* ... SD-7
Brown (Township of)—*fmr MCD* (2) ... AR-4
**Brown (Township of)**—*pop pl* ... IL-6
**Brown (Township of)**—*pop pl* (6) ... IN-6
**Brown (Township of)**—*pop pl* ... MI-6
**Brown (Township of)**—*pop pl* (8) ... OH-6
**Brown (Township of)**—*pop pl* (2) ... PA-2
Browntown Valley Overlook—*locale* ... VA-3
Brown Trail—*trail* (4) ... PA-2
*Brown Trout Creek* ... MI-6

*Brown Two Beach* ... MH-9
**Brown-Tye Meadows Subdivision**—pop pl ... UT-8
*Brownvale* ... KS-7
*Brown Valley* ... CA-9
*Brown Valley* ... MN-6
Brown Valley—basin ... NE-7
Brown Valley—valley ... PA-2
Brown Valley Sch—school ... CA-9
Brown Valley Sch—school ... NE-7
**Brownview**—pop pl ... LA-4
*Brownville* ... KS-7
*Brownville* ... PA-2
Brownville—locale ... IA-7
Brownville—locale ... KS-7
Brownville—locale ... NY-2
Brownville—locale ... WI-6
**Brownville**—pop pl (3) ... AL-4
**Brownville**—pop pl ... FL-3
**Brownville**—pop pl ... LA-4
**Brownville**—pop pl ... ME-1
**Brownville**—pop pl ... NE-7
**Brownville**—pop pl ... NY-2
Brownville Breaker (historical)—building ... PA-2
Brownville Ch—church (2) ... AL-4
Brownville City Hall—building ... AL-4
Brownville Hist Dist—hist pl ... NE-7
Brownville (historical)—locale ... KS-7
Brownville Hotel—hist pl ... NY-2
**Brownville Junction**—pop pl ... ME-1
Brownville Number One Sch (historical)—school ... AL-4
Brownville Number Two Sch (historical)—school ... AL-4
Brownville Sch—school ... MO-7
Brownville State Game Farm—park ... NY-2
**Brownville (subdivision)**—pop pl ... AL-4
Brownville-Summerville Hist Dist—hist pl ... AL-4
**Brownville (Town of)**—pop pl ... ME-1
**Brownville (Town of)**—pop pl ... NY-2
*Brown Wash* ... AZ-5
Brown Wash—stream (3) ... AZ-5
Brown-Washoe Sch Number 3—school ... NV-8
Brown Water Spring—spring ... NV-8
**Brownway**—pop pl ... SC-3
Brownway Branch—stream ... SC-3
Brown Well—well ... AZ-5
Brown Well—well (2) ... NV-8
Brown Well—well (5) ... NM-5
Brownwell Cem—cemetery ... KS-7
Brown Wesleyan Ch—church ... NC-3
Brown & Williamson Tobacco Corporation—facility ... GA-3
Brown-Wilson House—hist pl ... MS-4
Brown Windmill—locale (3) ... NM-5
Brown Windmill—locale (3) ... TX-5
Brown-Wing House—hist pl ... OH-6
Brown Wolf Ditch—canal ... IN-6
Brownwood—hist pl ... OH-6
Brownwood—locale ... GA-3
Brownwood—locale ... IL-6
**Brownwood**—pop pl ... MO-7
**Brownwood**—pop pl ... NC-3
**Brownwood**—pop pl (2) ... TX-5
Brownwood, Lake—reservoir ... TX-5
Brownwood Aqueduct—canal ... TX-5
Brownwood (CCD)—cens area ... TX-5
Brownwood Cem—cemetery ... GA-3
Brownwood Cem—cemetery ... MO-7
Brownwood Cem—cemetery ... OH-6
Brownwood Ch—church ... TX-5
Brownwood Dam—dam ... TX-5
Brownwood Elem Sch—school ... AL-4
Brownwood Lake—lake ... MI-6
Brownwood Lake—lake ... TX-5
**Brownwood Lake**—pop pl ... MI-6
Brownwood Lateral Watershed No 23—reservoir ... TX-5
Brownwood Lateral Watershed Number 20—reservoir ... TX-5
Brownwood Lateral Watershed Number 21—reservoir ... TX-5
Brownwood Lateral Watershed Number 22—reservoir ... TX-5
Brownwood Lateral Watershed Number 25—reservoir ... TX-5
Brownwood Lateral Watershed Number 4A—reservoir ... TX-5
Brownwood Lateral Watershed Number 4-B—reservoir ... TX-5
**Brownwood Manor**—pop pl ... KY-4
Brownwood Oil Field—oilfield ... TX-5
Brownwood Park—park ... MN-6
Brownwood Park—park ... TX-5
Brownwood Pond—lake ... NJ-2
*Brownwood Reservoir* ... TX-5
Brownwood (RR name for Lawton)—other ... WV-2
Brownwood Sch—school ... SC-3
Brownwood Senior HS—school ... TX-5
Brownwoods Kindergarden (School)—school ... TX-5
Brownwood Water Supply Canal—canal ... TX-5
Brown-Young Cem—cemetery ... NY-2
Brow Point—cape ... AK-9
*Browsdale* ... PA-2
Browse Area Guard Station—locale ... UT-8
Browse Canyon—valley ... UT-8
Browse Lake—lake ... AK-9
Browse Tank—reservoir (2) ... AZ-5
*Browse Well* ... AZ-5
Brow's Tavern—hist pl ... MA-1
*Brox Corner* ... OH-6
Brox Creek—stream ... ME-1
Brox Mcintosh Dam—dam ... AL-4
Brox Mcintosh Lake—reservoir ... AL-4
Broxon Cem—cemetery ... IN-6
Broxson—locale ... FL-3
Broxson Branch—stream ... FL-3
Broxson Creek—stream ... AL-4
Broxson Gulch—valley ... AK-9
*Broxton* ... OK-5
Broxton—locale ... OK-5
**Broxton**—pop pl ... GA-3
Broxton Bridge—bridge ... SC-3
Broxton (CCD)—cens area ... GA-3
Broxton Cem—cemetery ... FL-3
*Broxton Creek* ... GA-3
Broxton Creek—stream ... GA-3
Broyal Cem—cemetery ... TX-5
Broyer Canyon—valley ... NE-7
**Broyhill Crest**—pop pl ... VA-3
**Broyhill Forest**—pop pl ... VA-3
**Broyhill-Glen Gary Park**—pop pl ... VA-3
Broyhill Lake—reservoir ... NC-3
Broyhill Lake Dam—dam ... NC-3
**Broyhill-Langley Estates**—pop pl ... VA-3
**Broyhill-McLean Estates**—pop pl ... VA-3
Broyhill Park—park ... NC-3
**Broyhill Park**—pop pl ... VA-3
**Broyles**—pop pl ... TN-4
**Broyles**—pop pl ... TX-5
Broyles, William and Caroline, House—hist pl ... TX-5
Broyles Branch—stream ... AL-4
Broyles Branch—stream ... MO-7
Broyles Branch—stream (2) ... TN-4
Broyles Bridge—bridge ... CO-8
Broyles Cave—cave ... TN-4
Broyles Cem—cemetery ... MO-7
Broyles Cem—cemetery (3) ... TN-4
Broyles Cem—cemetery ... WV-2
Broyles Ch—church ... TX-5
Broyle Sch (abandoned)—school ... MO-7
Broyles Chapel—church (2) ... TN-4
Broyles Chapel—church ... TX-5
Broyles Creek—stream ... MS-4
Broyles Gap—gap ... VA-3
Broyles Hollow—valley ... TN-4
Broyles Island—island ... TN-4
Broyles Post Office (historical)—building ... AL-4
Broyle Spring—spring ... TN-4
Broyles Ranch—locale ... NV-8
Broyles Sch—school ... SC-3
Broylesville—locale ... TN-4
Broylesville Hist Dist—hist pl ... TN-4
Broylesville Post Office (historical)—building ... TN-4
Broyle Tank—reservoir ... NM-5
Broza Ridge—ridge ... CA-9
Broze Knoll—summit ... UT-8
**Brozville**—pop pl ... MS-4
BRR Oil Field—oilfield ... TX-5
BR Tank—reservoir ... AZ-5
**Brubaker**—pop pl ... IL-6
Brubaker Canyon—valley ... CA-9
Brubaker Cave—cave ... PA-2
Brubaker Covered Bridge—hist pl ... OH-6
Brubaker Creek—stream ... IL-6
Brubaker Creek—stream (2) ... OH-6
**Brubaker Park Subdivision**—pop pl ... UT-8
Brubaker Run—stream (5) ... PA-2
Brubaker Sch—school ... KS-7
Brubeck Spring—spring ... CA-9
*Bruce* ... MP-9
Bruce—locale ... CO-8
Bruce—locale ... IA-7
Bruce—locale ... MN-6
Bruce—locale ... NC-3
Bruce—locale ... PA-2
Bruce—locale ... VA-3
Bruce—locale ... WA-9
Bruce—locale ... WV-2
**Bruce**—pop pl ... FL-3
**Bruce**—pop pl ... IL-6
**Bruce**—pop pl ... MS-4
**Bruce**—pop pl ... OR-9
**Bruce**—pop pl ... SD-7
**Bruce**—pop pl ... WI-6
Bruce, Bayou—stream ... LA-4
Bruce, Blanche K., House—hist pl ... DC-2
Bruce, Donald, House—hist pl ... SC-3
Bruce, H. L., House—hist pl ... TN-4
Bruce, James, Round Barn—hist pl ... IL-6
Bruce, Mount—summit ... AZ-5
Bruce, William Perry, House—hist pl ... WA-9
Bruce And Armada Cem—cemetery ... MI-6
Bruce And Bar Windmill—locale ... TX-5
Bruce Bayou—stream ... MI-6
Bruce Blaum Dam—dam ... AL-4
Bruce Blaum Lake—reservoir ... AL-4
Bruce Branch—stream ... IA-7
Bruce Branch—stream ... KY-4
Bruce Branch—stream ... TX-5
Bruce Brook—stream ... CT-1
Bruce Brook—stream ... VT-1
Bruce Business Institute (historical)—school ... TN-4
Bruce Camp—locale ... OR-9
Bruce Campbell Field (airport)—airport ... MS-4
Bruce Campground—locale ... WY-8
Bruce Canyon—valley ... CA-9
Bruce Canyon—valley (2) ... ID-8
Bruce Cave—cave ... MO-7
Bruce Cem—cemetery ... CT-1
Bruce Cem—cemetery ... GA-3
Bruce Cem—cemetery (3) ... IL-6
Bruce Cem—cemetery ... IN-6
Bruce Cem—cemetery (2) ... KY-4
Bruce Cem—cemetery ... MI-6
Bruce Cem—cemetery ... MS-4
Bruce Cem—cemetery ... ND-7
Bruce Cem—cemetery ... SD-7
Bruce Cem—cemetery (4) ... TN-4
Bruce Cem—cemetery ... TX-5
Bruce Cem—cemetery (2) ... VA-3
Bruce Chapel—church ... AR-4
Bruce Chapel—church ... IL-6
Bruce Chapel—church ... KY-4
Bruce Chapel—church ... WV-2
Bruce Chapel Hollow—valley ... KY-4
Bruce Ch of Christ—church ... MS-4
Bruce Coulee—valley ... MT-8
*Bruce Creek* ... ID-8
*Bruce Creek* ... WI-6
Bruce Creek—stream ... AR-4
Bruce Creek—stream ... CO-8
Bruce Creek—stream ... FL-3
Bruce Creek—stream ... GA-3
Bruce Creek—stream ... ID-8
Bruce Creek—stream ... IL-6
Bruce Creek—stream ... IA-7
Bruce Creek—stream ... MI-6
Bruce Creek—stream ... MN-6
Bruce Creek—stream (3) ... MT-8
Bruce Creek—stream ... TN-4
Bruce Creek—stream ... WA-9
Bruce Creek—stream ... WI-6
Bruce Creek—stream ... WY-8
Bruce Creek Grange—locale ... WA-9
Bruce Creek Sch—school ... FL-3
Bruce Creek Sch—school ... WA-9
Bruce Crossing—locale ... CA-9
**Bruce Crossing**—pop pl ... MI-6
Bruce Crossing Cem—cemetery ... MI-6
Bruce Dam—dam ... SD-7
Bruce Ditch—canal ... IN-6
Bruce-Donaldson House—hist pl ... SD-7
Bruce-Dowd-Kennedy House—hist pl ... NC-3
Bruce Draw—valley (2) ... WY-8
Bruce Eddy—locale ... ID-8
Bruce Elem Sch—school ... MS-4
Bruce Field—park ... MS-4
Bruce Fork—stream ... CA-9
Bruce Gap—gap ... TN-4
Bruce Goldfish Fisheries—hist pl ... IA-7
Bruce Hagood Cem—cemetery ... SC-3
Bruce Hill—summit ... ME-1
Bruce Hill—summit ... NH-1
Bruce Hill—summit ... NY-2
Bruce Hills—summit ... AK-9
Bruce Hollow—valley (3) ... KY-4
Bruce Hollow—valley ... OR-9
Bruce Hollow—valley (4) ... TN-4
Bruce HS—school ... MS-4
Bruce HS—school ... TN-4
Bruce JHS—school ... KY-4
**Bruce Junction**—pop pl ... MS-4
Bruce Knob—summit (3) ... NC-3
Bruce Knob—summit ... TN-4
*Bruce Lake* ... IN-6
Bruce Lake—lake ... AK-9
Bruce Lake—lake ... IL-6
Bruce Lake—lake ... IN-6
Bruce Lake—lake ... PA-2
Bruce Lake—lake (2) ... WI-6
**Bruce Lake**—pop pl ... IN-6
Bruce Lake—reservoir ... GA-3
Bruce Lake—reservoir ... SC-3
Bruce Lake Cem—cemetery ... IN-6
*Bruce Lake Ditch* ... IN-6
Bruce Lake Natural Area—area ... PA-2
Bruce Lake Outlet—canal ... IN-6
**Bruce Lake Station**—pop pl ... IN-6
Bruce Lake Trail—trail ... PA-2
Bruce Lattimer Lake Dam—dam ... MS-4
Bruce Meadows—flat ... ID-8
*Bruce Mickles* ... AR-4
Bruce Mine—mine ... CO-8
Bruce Mine Headframe—hist pl ... MN-6
Bruce Mound—summit ... WI-6
Bruce Mountain—ridge ... GA-3
Bruce MS—school ... MS-4
Bruce Mtn—summit (2) ... AR-4
Bruce Mtn—summit ... MT-8
Bruce Mtn—summit ... VA-3
Bruce Mtn—summit ... WY-8
Bruce Pardue Lake Dam—dam ... AL-4
Bruce Park—park ... AL-4
Bruce Park—park ... CT-1
Bruce Park—park ... FL-3
Bruce Park—park ... NE-7
Bruce Park—park ... TX-5
Bruce Park—park ... WV-2
Bruce Place—locale ... MT-8
Bruce Place—locale ... NM-5
Bruce Place Tank—reservoir ... AZ-5
Bruce P.O. (historical)—building ... AL-4
Bruce Point—cape ... MI-6
Bruce Pond—lake ... CT-1
Bruce Pond—lake ... VT-1
Bruce Pond Number Four—reservoir ... AL-4
Bruce Pond Number One—reservoir ... AL-4
Bruce Pond Number Three—reservoir ... AL-4
Bruce Pond Number Two—reservoir ... AL-4
Bruceport—locale ... WA-9
Bruceport Park—park ... WA-9
Bruce Prospect—mine ... TN-4
Bruce Ranch—locale ... CA-9
Bruce Ranch—locale ... TX-5
Bruce Ridge—ridge ... MT-8
Bruce Ridge—ridge ... NM-5
Bruce Ridge—ridge (2) ... NC-3
Bruce Ridge—ridge ... TN-4
Bruce Rsvr—reservoir ... OR-9
Bruce Run—stream ... WV-2
Bruces Branch—stream ... GA-3
*Bruces Brook* ... CT-1
Bruce Sch—school ... DC-2
Bruce Sch—school (2) ... GA-3
Bruce Sch—school ... MA-1
Bruce Sch—school ... MO-7
Bruce Sch—school ... TN-4
Bruce Sch—school (2) ... TX-5
Bruces Chapel—church ... TN-4
Bruce Sch (historical)—school ... MS-4
Bruce's Crossing (RR name for Bruce Crossing)—other ... MI-6
Bruces Gulch—valley ... CA-9
Bruces Ice Pond—lake ... CT-1
Bruces Island—island ... MT-8
*Bruces Lake* ... IN-6
Bruces Mill Creek—stream ... AL-4
Bruces Pond—reservoir ... MA-1
Bruce Spring—spring ... AZ-5
Bruce Spring—spring ... CA-9
Bruce Spring—spring ... TN-4
Bruce Spring Branch—stream ... VA-3
Bruce Street Sch—school ... GA-3
Bruce Street Sch—school ... NJ-2
*Bruceton* ... AL-4
Bruceton—locale ... AL-4
**Bruceton**—pop pl ... PA-2
**Bruceton**—pop pl ... TN-4
Bruceton (CCD)—cens area ... TN-4
Bruceton Division—civil ... TN-4
**Bruceton Mills**—pop pl ... WV-2
Bruceton Post Office—building ... TN-4
**Brucetown**—pop pl ... VA-3
Bruce Townhall—building ... IA-7
Bruce Township—fmr MCD ... IA-7
**Bruce Township**—pop pl ... ND-7
Bruce (Township of)—fmr MCD ... NC-3
**Bruce (Township of)**—pop pl ... IL-6
**Bruce (Township of)**—pop pl (2) ... MI-6
**Bruce (Township of)**—pop pl ... MN-6
Bruce United Methodist Ch—church ... MS-4
Bruce Valley Ch—church ... WI-6
Bruce Valley Creek—stream ... WI-6
Bruceville—locale ... AL-4
Bruceville—locale ... CA-9
Bruceville—locale ... FL-3
Bruceville—locale ... VA-3
**Bruceville**—pop pl ... IN-6
**Bruceville**—pop pl (2) ... MD-2
**Bruceville**—pop pl ... NY-2
**Bruceville**—pop pl ... TN-4
**Bruceville**—pop pl ... TX-5
**Bruceville-Eddy**—pop pl ... TX-5
Bruceville P.O. (historical)—locale ... AL-4
**Brucewell**—pop pl ... IA-7
Bruce Williams Cave—cave ... AL-4
Bruce Young Spring—spring ... ID-8
Bruch Brothers Dam—dam ... SD-7
*Bruch Creek* ... IL-6
*Bruchy Fork Creek* ... IL-6
Brucite—locale ... NV-8
Brucite Mine—mine ... NV-8
Bruckarts (RR name for Silver Spring)—other ... PA-2
Bruckarts Station—locale ... PA-2
Bruck Cem—cemetery ... KS-7
Brucker Lake—lake ... MI-6
Brucker Sch—school (2) ... MI-6
Bruckert Canyon—valley ... OR-9
Bruck Herman Dam—dam ... SD-7
Brucklacher Cem—cemetery ... OH-6
Brucknell Ridge Trail—trail ... NH-1
Bruckner Island—island ... MI-6
Bruck Run—stream ... PA-2
Bruck Sch—school ... KS-7
Bruder Airp—airport ... PA-2
Bruders Lake—lake ... MI-6
**Brudickville**—pop pl ... RI-1
*Bruebeck Spring* ... CA-9
Brueckerville Sch—school ... WI-6
Brue Drain—canal ... MI-6
Bruegmann Park—park ... IA-7
*Bruellet Creek* ... IN-6
*Bruellets Creek* ... IN-6
*Bruelletts Creek* ... IN-6
Bruemmer County Park—park ... WI-6
Bruemmer Creek—stream ... WI-6
**Bruemmerville**—pop pl ... WI-6
Bruenellie Canyon—valley ... CO-8
Bruenellie Windmill—locale ... CO-8
*Bruener Meadow* ... CA-9
Brueni Ranch—locale ... ND-7
*Bruens Crossroads* ... IN-6
Brueschke Dam—dam ... SD-7
Brueyer Pond—lake ... NY-2
Bruff Cem—cemetery ... TN-4
Bruff Creek—stream ... CO-8
Bruff Draw—valley ... WY-8
Bruffey Canyon—valley ... NV-8
Bruffey Ch—church ... WV-2
Bruffey Creek—stream ... WV-2
Bruffey Homestead—locale ... MT-8
Bruffey Ranch—locale ... NV-8
Bruffman Branch—stream ... WV-2
Bruffs Island—island ... MD-2
Bruff Valley—valley ... UT-8
Bruflat Cem—cemetery ... ND-7
Bruget Sch—school ... SD-7
Bruggeman County Park—park ... IA-7
*Bruggemann* ... FM-9
Bruggerman Canyon—valley ... NM-5
Bruggman Sch—school ... IL-6
Brug-lusher Draw—valley ... WY-8
Bruhel Point—cape ... CA-9
Bruhjell Lake—lake ... MN-6
Bruhl Cem—cemetery ... LA-4
Bruhn Point—cape ... AK-9
Bruhn-Ray Mine—mine ... AK-9
Bruie Pond—reservoir ... CT-1
*Bruillett* ... IN-6
Bruin—locale ... KY-4
**Bruin**—pop pl ... PA-2
Bruin, Bayou—gut ... LA-4
Bruin, Lake—lake ... LA-4
Bruin Bay—bay ... AK-9
Bruin Borough—civil ... PA-2
Bruin Branch—stream ... TN-4
Bruin Cem—cemetery ... IN-6
Bruin Creek—stream (2) ... AK-9
Bruin Creek—stream ... CO-8
Bruin Creek—stream (4) ... ID-8
Bruin Creek—stream ... KY-4
Bruin Creek—stream (2) ... MT-8
Bruin Creek—stream ... OR-9
Bruin Creek—stream ... WY-8
Bruin Creek Campground—locale ... ID-8
Bruin Elem Sch—school ... PA-2
Bruin Flat—flat ... CA-9
**Bruing**—pop pl ... FL-3
Bruington—locale ... VA-3
Bruin Hill—summit ... ID-8
Bruin Hill—summit ... MA-1
Bruin Lake—lake ... MI-6
Bruin Lake—lake ... MN-6
Bruin Lake—lake ... MT-8
Bruin Mtn—summit ... ID-8
*Bruin Peak* ... UT-8
Bruin Peaks—summit ... MT-8
Bruin Point—cape ... AK-9
Bruin Point—locale ... UT-8
Bruin Reef—bar ... AK-9
Bruin Ridge—ridge ... ID-8
Bruin Run Campground—park ... OR-9
Bruin Run Creek—stream ... OR-9
*Bruins* ... IN-6
**Bruins**—pop pl ... AR-4
Bruinsburg—locale ... MS-4
Bruinsburg Bend—bend ... MS-4
Bruinsburg Landing—locale ... MS-4
Bruinsburg Plantation (historical)—locale ... MS-4
Bruins Chapel—church ... AR-4
Bruins Creek—stream (2) ... TX-5
*Bruins Crossroads* ... IN-6
**Bruins Landing**—pop pl ... AR-4
Bruins Sch—school ... AR-4
Bruisers Knob—summit ... VA-3
Brulay Plantation—locale ... TX-5
Brule—locale ... LA-4
**Brule**—pop pl ... LA-4
**Brule**—pop pl ... NE-7
**Brule**—pop pl ... WI-6
Brule Agency (historical)—locale ... SD-7
Bruleau Pond—lake ... ME-1
Brule Bar—island ... MT-8
Brule Bay—bay ... MN-6
Brule Bayou—gut ... LA-4
Brule Bottom State Public Hunting Area—park ... SD-7
**Brule (Brule Labadieville)**—pop pl ... LA-4
Brule Canyon—valley ... NE-7
Brule Cem—cemetery ... NE-7
Brule County—civil ... SD-7
*Brule Creek* ... WI-6
Brule Creek—stream ... SD-7
Brule Creek—stream ... WA-9
Brule Creek—stream ... WI-6
Brule Creek Ch—church ... SD-7
Brulee Creek—stream ... MT-8
Brulee Point—summit ... MI-6
*Brule Guillot* ... LA-4
**Brule Guillot**—pop pl ... LA-4
Brule (historical)—locale ... SD-7
Brule Huffman Park—park ... AZ-5
Brule Island—island ... MN-6
Brule Island Dam—dam ... MI-6
Brule Island Dam—dam ... WI-6
Brule Island (historical)—island (2) ... SD-7
**Brule Labadie**—pop pl ... LA-4
Brule Labadieville—other ... LA-4
Brule Lake—lake ... MI-6
Brule Lake—lake ... MN-6
Brule Lake Lookout Tower—locale ... MN-6
Brule Lookout Tower—locale ... MI-6
Brule Lookout Tower—locale ... WI-6
*Brule Mountain* ... CO-8
Brule Mtn—summit ... MN-6
Brule Narrows—channel ... MN-6
Brule Point—cape ... WI-6
Bruler Creek—stream ... OR-9
*brule River* ... MN-6
Brule River—stream ... MI-6
Brule River—stream ... MN-6
Brule River—stream ... WI-6
Brule River State For—forest ... WI-6
Brule River State Forest Annex—park ... WI-6
Brule Sch—school (2) ... SD-7
Brule Springs—spring ... WI-6
Brule-St. Croix Portage—hist pl ... WI-6
**Brule (Town of)**—pop pl ... WI-6
Brule Township—civil (2) ... SD-7
**Brule Township**—pop pl ... SD-7
**Brulie Maurin**—pop pl ... LA-4
Brulm Ranch—locale ... NM-5
Bruly La Croix—locale ... LA-4
Bruly McCall—locale ... LA-4
**Bruly Saint Martin**—pop pl ... LA-4
Brumagin Rapids—rapids ... NY-2
Brumalow Creek—stream ... TN-4
Brumbach Cem—cemetery ... IL-6
Brumbach Creek—stream ... IL-6
Brumbach Sch (abandoned)—school ... PA-2
Brumback Library—hist pl ... OH-6
Brumback Sch—school ... IL-6
Brumba Natl Wildlife Ref—park ... ND-7
Brumba Pool—lake ... ND-7
Brumbaugh—locale ... PA-2
Brumbaugh Cem—cemetery ... IN-6
Brumbaugh Cem—cemetery ... KS-7
Brumbaugh Cem—cemetery ... ND-7
Brumbaugh Cem—cemetery ... OH-6
Brumbaugh Cem—cemetery (2) ... PA-2
**Brumbaugh Crossing**—pop pl ... PA-2
Brumbaugh Historical House (historical)—building ... PA-2
Brumbaugh Homestead—hist pl ... PA-2
*Brumbaugh Sch* ... PA-2
Brumbley Creek—stream ... GA-3
**Brumby**—pop pl ... GA-3
Brumby, Arnoldus, House—hist pl ... GA-3
Brumfield—locale ... KY-4
Brumfield Branch—stream ... WV-2
*Brumfield Cem* ... MS-4
Brumfield Cem—cemetery (3) ... LA-4
Brumfield Cem—cemetery (4) ... MS-4
Brumfield Cem—cemetery ... OK-5
Brumfield Cem—cemetery (2) ... WV-2
Brumfield HS—school ... MS-4
Brumfieldville—other ... PA-2
Brumfield-Whittington Cem—cemetery ... MS-4
Brumit Island—island ... TN-4
Brumley—locale ... CO-8
Brumley—locale ... TX-5
**Brumley**—pop pl ... AR-4
**Brumley**—pop pl ... MO-7
Brumley Branch—stream ... AL-4
Brumley Branch—stream ... MS-4
Brumley Camp—locale ... FL-3
Brumley Cem—cemetery ... KY-4
Brumley Cem—cemetery ... MS-4
*Brumley Creek* ... TX-5
Brumley Creek—stream ... MO-7
Brumley Creek—stream (2) ... UT-8
Brumley Creek—stream ... VA-3
Brumley Creek—stream ... WY-8
Brumley Draw—valley ... CO-8
Brumley Gap—gap ... VA-3
Brumley Gap—locale ... VA-3
**Brumley Heights**—pop pl ... TN-4
Brumley Hill—summit ... NH-1
Brumley Hollow—valley ... MO-7
Brumley Lake—reservoir ... TX-5
Brumley Mtn—summit ... VA-3
Brumley Mtn—summit ... WY-8
Brumley Point—summit ... CO-8
Brumley Ridge—ridge ... UT-8
Brumley Ridge—ridge ... VA-3
Brumley Rim—ridge ... VA-3
Brumley Rsvr—reservoir ... CO-8
Brumm Ditch—canal ... IN-6
Brummel—locale ... MD-2
Brummell's Inn—hist pl ... NC-3
Brummel Ravine—valley ... CA-9
**Brummels (historical)**—pop pl ... NC-3
Brummet Island—island ... NH-1
Brummett Branch—stream ... KY-4
Brummett Cem—cemetery ... TX-5
Brummett Ch—church ... KY-4
Brummett Creek—stream ... IN-6
Brummett Creek—stream ... NC-3
Brummett Creek Ch—church ... IN-6
Brummett Creek Ch—church ... NC-3
Brummett Hollow—valley ... TN-4
Brummett Prospect—mine ... TN-4
Brummett Sch—school ... KY-4
**Brummitt**—pop pl ... AR-4
**Brummitt Acres**—pop pl ... IN-6
Brummitt Elem Sch—school ... IN-6
**Brummitts Addition (subdivision)**—pop pl ... UT-8
Brummitt Sch—school ... IL-6
Brum Spring—spring ... OR-9
Brumwell Slough—lake ... ND-7
Bruna Sch—school ... NE-7
*Bruna Valley School* ... AL-4
*Brunce's Creek* ... IL-6
Brunch Lake—lake ... MN-6
Brunckow Hill—summit ... AZ-5
**Brunco**—pop pl ... FL-3
Brunco RR Station—locale ... FL-3
Brundage—locale ... TX-5
Brundage—post sta ... CA-9
Brundage, Mount—summit ... AK-9
Brundage Bridge—bridge ... MT-8
Brundage Canyon—valley ... UT-8
Brundage Cem—cemetery ... MI-6
Brundage Cove—valley ... UT-8
Brundage Creek—stream ... ID-8
Brundage Creek—stream ... MI-6
Brundage Creek—stream (2) ... MT-8
Brundage Head—cape ... AK-9
Brundage Head—summit ... AK-9
Brundage Island—island ... OH-6
Brundage Mtn—summit ... ID-8
Brundage Rsvr—reservoir ... ID-8
Brundedge Cem—cemetery ... OH-6
**Brundidge**—pop pl ... AL-4
Brundidge (CCD)—cens area ... AL-4
*Brundidge Consolidated School* ... AL-4
Brundidge Division—civil ... AL-4
Brundidge HS (historical)—school ... AL-4
Brundidge Municipal Airp—airport ... AL-4
*Brundidge Street Chapel Baptist Church* ... AL-4
*Brundidge Street Sunday School* ... AL-4
Brundige—locale ... TN-4
Brundige Branch—stream ... TN-4
Brundige Mtn—summit ... NY-2
Brundige Sch (historical)—school ... TN-4
*Brune* ... AL-4
**Bruneau**—pop pl ... ID-8
Bruneau Canyon—valley ... ID-8
Bruneau Creek—stream ... MI-6
Bruneau Episcopal Church—hist pl ... ID-8
*Bruneau Hot Springs* ... ID-8
Bruneau Mine—mine ... NV-8
*Bruneau Peak* ... NV-8
Bruneau Ranch—locale ... NV-8
Bruneau River—stream ... ID-8
Bruneau River—stream ... NV-8
Bruneau Sch—school ... NV-8
Bruneau Spring—spring ... NV-8
**Bruneau Valley**—pop pl ... ID-8
Bruneau Valley—valley ... ID-8
Brune Cem—cemetery ... TX-5
Brune Creek—stream ... TX-5
Brune Gulch—valley ... CO-8
Brunel Trail—trail ... NH-1
**Bruner**—pop pl ... MO-7
**Bruner**—pop pl ... OK-5
**Bruner**—pop pl ... SC-3
**Bruner**—pop pl ... TX-5
Bruner Bay—swamp ... FL-3
Bruner Branch—stream ... GA-3
Bruner Branch—stream ... PA-2
Bruner Cem—cemetery ... IL-6
Bruner Cem—cemetery ... IN-6
Bruner Cem—cemetery (2) ... KY-4
Bruner Cem—cemetery (4) ... OK-5
Bruner Ch—church ... MO-7
Bruner Creek—stream (2) ... AL-4
Bruner Creek—stream ... GA-3
Bruner Creek—stream ... IN-6
Bruner Creek—stream ... OK-5
Bruner Creek—stream ... WY-8
Bruner Crossing—locale ... TN-4
Bruner Ditch—canal ... IN-6
Bruner Draw—valley ... WY-8
*Bruner Falls* ... NY-2
Bruner Falls—falls ... NY-2
**Bruner Grove**—pop pl ... TN-4
Bruner Grove United Methodist Ch—church ... TN-4
Bruner (historical)—locale ... AL-4
Bruner Hollow—valley ... PA-2
Bruner Hollow—valley (2) ... TN-4
Bruner House—hist pl ... AR-4
Bruner Lake—lake ... NE-7
Bruner Mine—mine ... CA-9
Bruner Mine—mine ... NV-8
Bruner Park—park ... CO-8
Bruner Ridge—ridge ... KY-4
Bruner Run—stream ... PA-2
**Brunersburg**—pop pl ... OH-6
Bruners Ch—church ... KY-4
Bruner Sch—school ... AL-4
Bruner Sch—school ... OH-6
Bruner Sch (abandoned)—school ... MO-7
*Bruners Creek* ... AL-4
Bruners Gin Creek—stream ... AL-4
Bruners Grove Sch (historical)—school ... TN-4
Bruners Pond—reservoir ... AL-4
Bruners Pond—reservoir ... SC-3
Bruner Spring—spring ... NM-5
Bruner Spring—spring ... OR-9
Bruner Spring Rsvr—reservoir ... OR-9
**Brunerstown**—pop pl ... IN-6
*Brunersville* ... PA-2
Brunersville Post Office (historical)—building ... PA-2
Bruner Township—civil ... MO-7
*Bruner Valley* ... AL-4
Bruner Valley Sch (historical)—school ... AL-4
Bruner Well—well ... NV-8
Brune School Section Well—well ... NM-5
Brunet—uninc pl ... WI-6
Brunet-Calaf Residence—hist pl ... PR-3
*Brunet Flowage* ... WI-6
Brunet-Fourchy House—hist pl ... MS-4
Brunet Island—island ... WI-6
Brunet Island State Park—park ... WI-6
Brunet Lookout Tower—locale ... WI-6
Brunet River—stream ... WI-6
Brunette Cove—bay ... AK-9
Brunette Point—cape ... LA-4
Brune Well—well ... NM-5

Brunfield Cem—*cemetery* MS-4
Brungart Ch (historical)—*church* PA-2
**Bruni**—*pop pl* TX-5
Bruni-Mirando (CCD)—*cens area* TX-5
**Bruning**—*pop pl* NE-7
Bruning Number 1 Dam—*dam* SD-7
**Bruningville**—*pop pl* MI-6
Bruni Ranch—*locale* TX-5
Bruni Sch—*school* TX-5
Bruni Tank—*reservoir* TX-5
Brunk, Harrison, House—*hist pl* OR-9
Brunk Cem—*cemetery* IL-6
Brunk Creek—*stream* IL-6
Brunk Ditch—*canal* IN-6
Brunker Creek—*stream* CO-8
Brunkhorst Landing—*locale* IL-6
Brunkow Sch—*school* MI-6
Brunks Corner—*locale* OR-9
Brunley Branch—*stream* TN-4
*Brunner Canyon* AZ-5
Brunner Cem—*cemetery* IN-6
Brunner Coulee—*valley* WI-6
Brunnerdale Run—*stream* PA-2
Brunnerdale Seminary—*school* OH-6
Brunner Hill—*summit* CA-9
Brunner Hill—*summit* IN-6
Brunner Hill—*summit* NY-2
Brunner Hill—*summit* WA-9
Brunner Island—*island* PA-2
Brunner Lake—*lake* MN-6
*Brunner Peak* AZ-5
Brunner Pond—*lake* FL-3
Brunner Rsvr—*reservoir* CO-8
Brunner Valley—*valley* WI-6
**Brunnerville**—*pop pl* PA-2
**Brunnet Heights**—*pop pl* AL-4
**Brunning**—*pop pl* IL-6
Brunn Point—*cape* AK-9
Bruno—*locale* MT-8
Bruno—*locale* OK-5
Bruno—*locale* VA-3
**Bruno**—*pop pl* AR-4
**Bruno**—*pop pl* MN-6
**Bruno**—*pop pl* NE-7
**Bruno**—*pop pl* OH-6
**Bruno**—*pop pl* WV-2
Bruno, Mount—*summit* OR-9
Bruno Cabin Ruins—*locale* ID-8
Bruno Canyon—*valley* AZ-5
Bruno Canyon—*valley* CO-8
Bruno Cem—*cemetery* AR-4
Bruno Cem—*cemetery* MN-6
Bruno Cem—*cemetery* OR-9
Bruno Creek—*stream* AK-9
Bruno Creek—*stream* ID-8
Bruno Creek—*stream* KS-7
Bruno Creek—*stream* MI-6
Bruno Creek—*stream* NV-8
Bruno Creek—*stream* OK-5
Bruno Creek—*stream* OR-9
Bruno Drain—*stream* MI-6
*Bruno Gulch* CO-8
Bruno Lake—*lake* WI-6
Bruno Lake Ditch—*canal* WI-6
Bruno Lakes—*lake* OR-9
Bruno Meadows—*flat* OR-9
Bruno Meadows Trail—*trail* OR-9
Bruno Peak—*summit* AZ-5
**Brunot**—*pop pl* MO-7
Bruno Tank—*reservoir* (2) AZ-5
Brunot Cem—*cemetery* IN-6
Brunot Corners—*locale* PA-2
Brunot Island—*island* PA-2
Brunot Island Station—*building* PA-2
**Bruno Township**—*pop pl* KS-7
**Bruno (Township of)**—*pop pl* MN-6
*Brunot's* PA-2
Brunots Island—*uninc pl* PA-2
Bruns—*locale* LA-4
Brunsen Creek—*stream* GA-3
Bruns Flat—*flat* WA-9
Brun Skill Number 1 Dam—*dam* SD-7
Bruns Lake—*lake* AK-9
**Brunson**—*pop pl* SC-3
Brunson, Benjamin, House—*hist pl* MN-6
Brunson Branch—*stream* (3) SC-3
Brunson (CCD)—*cens area* SC-3
Brunson Cem—*cemetery* GA-3
Brunson Ch—*church* AL-4
Brunson Ch—*church* GA-3
Brunson Chapel—*church* AL-4
Brunson-Cleora Community
Center—*locale* SC-3
Brunson Coulee—*valley* MT-8
Brunson Crossroads—*locale* SC-3
Brunson Elem Sch—*school* NC-3
Brunsoni Furnace (40SW219)—*hist pl* TN-4
Brunson Pond—*lake* FL-3
Brunson Ranch—*locale* AZ-5
Brunson Ranch—*locale* (2) TX-5
Brunson Sch—*school* SC-3
**Brunsons Crossroads**—*pop pl* SC-3
Brunson Spring—*spring* NV-8
**Brunsons Store**—*pop pl* SC-3
Brunson Swamp—*stream* SC-3
Brunson Swamp—*swamp* SC-3
Brunson Tank—*reservoir* AZ-5
**Brunson Township**—*pop pl* SD-7
Bruns Ranch—*locale* TX-5
Bruns Slough—*gut* ND-7
Brunston Swamp—*swamp* SC-3
**Brunsville**—*pop pl* IA-7
Brunsweiler River—*stream* WI-6
*Brunswick* NJ-2
Brunswick—*locale* MS-4
Brunswick—*locale* NV-8
Brunswick—*locale* TX-5
Brunswick—*locale* VA-3
**Brunswick**—*pop pl* GA-3
**Brunswick**—*pop pl* IL-6
**Brunswick**—*pop pl* (3) IN-6
**Brunswick**—*pop pl* ME-1
**Brunswick**—*pop pl* MD-2
**Brunswick**—*pop pl* MI-6
**Brunswick**—*pop pl* MN-6
**Brunswick**—*pop pl* MO-7
**Brunswick**—*pop pl* NE-7
**Brunswick**—*pop pl* NY-2
**Brunswick**—*pop pl* NC-3
**Brunswick**—*pop pl* OH-6
**Brunswick**—*pop pl* TN-4
**Brunswick**—*pop pl* TX-5
Brunswick, Lake—*lake* OH-6
**Brunswick Acres**—*pop pl* NJ-2
Brunswick-Altamaha Canal—*canal* GA-3
Brunswick Canyon—*valley* NV-8
Brunswick Canyon—*valley* OR-9
Brunswick (CCD)—*cens area* GA-3
Brunswick Cem—*cemetery* IN-6
Brunswick Cem—*cemetery* MS-4
Brunswick Cem—*cemetery* NE-7
Brunswick Center—*other* ME-1
**Brunswick Center**—*pop pl* NY-2
Brunswick Ch—*church* MN-6
Brunswick Circle Levee—*levee* MS-4
Brunswick Community Club—*other* IN-6
Brunswick Country Club—*other* GA-3
**Brunswick County**—*pop pl* NC-3
**Brunswick (County)**—*pop pl* VA-3
Brunswick County Airp—*airport* NC-3
Brunswick County Courthouse—*hist pl* NC-3
Brunswick County Courthouse
Square—*hist pl* VA-3
Brunswick County Home—*locale* NC-3
Brunswick County Sch—*school* NC-3
Brunswick Elem Sch—*school* IN-6
**Brunswick Gardens**—*pop pl* NJ-2
*Brunswick Harbor* GA-3
Brunswick Hills (Township of)—*civ div* OH-6
Brunswick Hist Dist—*hist pl* MD-2
Brunswick HS—*school* VA-3
Brunswick Junior Coll—*school* GA-3
Brunswick Landing (historical)—*locale* MS-4
Brunswick Memorial Park—*cemetery* GA-3
Brunswick Mill (Ruins)—*locale* NV-8
Brunswick Mine—*mine* CA-9
Brunswick Naval Air Station—*military* ME-1
Brunswick Nuclear Power Plant—*facility* NC-3
Brunswick Old Town—*hist pl* GA-3
Brunswick Old Town Hist Dist—*hist pl* GA-3
Brunswick Park—*park* CA-9
*Brunswick (P.O.Sta.)* IN-6
Brunswick Ridge—*ridge* CA-9
Brunswick River—*stream* GA-3
Brunswick River—*stream* NC-3
Brunswick Sch—*school* CT-1
Brunswick Sch—*school* (2) IL-6
Brunswick Sch—*school* MD-2
Brunswick Sch—*school* MI-6
**Brunswick Springs**—*pop pl* VT-1
Brunswick Station—*locale* NC-3
Brunswick Station—*other* ME-1
Brunswick Substation—*locale* NV-8
Brunswick Town Hist Dist—*hist pl* NC-3
**Brunswick (Town of)**—*pop pl* ME-1
**Brunswick (Town of)**—*pop pl* NY-2
**Brunswick (Town of)**—*pop pl* VT-1
**Brunswick (Town of)**—*pop pl* WI-6
**Brunswick Township**—*pop pl* MO-7
Brunswick (Township of)—*other* OH-6
**Brunswick (Township of)**—*pop pl* MN-6
Brunswick Town (State Historic
Site)—*park* NC-3
*Brunt Canyon* UT-8
Brunt Creek—*stream* ID-8
Brunton Pass—*gap* NV-8
Bruntwood—*hist pl* KY-4
Brunty Fork—*stream* KY-4
Brunyansky Draw—*valley* WY-8
Brunzell House—*hist pl* ID-8
Brunzell Mine—*mine* ID-8
Brunzell Slough—*stream* MT-8
Brunzell Spring—*spring* ID-8
Bruquiere Pass—*gut* LA-4
Bruriah Sch—*school* NJ-2
Brusally Tank—*reservoir* AZ-5
Bruschi Mine—*mine* CA-9
*Bruses Creek* IL-6
**Brusett**—*pop pl* MT-8
**Brush**—*pop pl* CO-8
Brush—*summit* PA-2
*Brush Arbor* TN-4
Brush Arbor—*locale* MO-7
Brush Arbor Baptist Ch—*church* FL-3
Brush Arbor Ch—*church* MO-7
Brush Arbor Christian Sch—*school* FL-3
Brush Arbor Community
Center—*building* MO-7
Brush Arbor Sch (historical)—*school* AL-4
Brushart—*locale* KY-4
Brushart Hollow—*valley* KY-4
Brusha Sch—*school* MS-4
Brush Basin—*basin* NV-8
Brush Basin—*valley* UT-8
Brush Basin Tank—*reservoir* AZ-5
Brush Bay—*bay* MT-8
Brush Bayou—*stream* LA-4
Brush Bayou—*stream* MS-4
*Brush Branch* AL-4
*Brush Branch* IA-7
Brush Branch—*stream* IL-6
Brush Branch—*stream* MS-4
Brush Branch—*stream* MO-7
Brush Brook—*stream* NH-1
Brush Brook—*stream* NY-2
Brush Brook—*stream* VT-1
*Brush Butte* CA-9
Brush Cabin Draw—*valley* WY-8
Brush Camp—*locale* CA-9
Brush Camp Fork—*stream* WV-2
Brush Camp Low Place—*locale* WV-2
*Brush Camp Run* WV-2
Brush Camp Run—*stream* WV-2
*Brush Canyon* AZ-5
*Brush Canyon* TX-5
Brush Canyon—*valley* (2) AZ-5
Brush Canyon—*valley* (4) CA-9
Brush Canyon—*valley* (4) ID-8
Brush Canyon—*valley* NE-7
Brush Canyon—*valley* NV-8
Brush Canyon—*valley* (2) NM-5
Brush Canyon—*valley* OK-5
Brush Canyon—*valley* (2) OR-9
Brush Canyon—*valley* UT-8
Brush Cem—*cemetery* OH-6
Brush Ch—*church* MS-4
Brush Coll—*school* (2) IL-6
*Brush College* IL-6
**Brush College**—*pop pl* OR-9
Brush College Creek—*stream* OR-9
Brush College No 2 School
(Abandoned)—*locale* MO-7
Brush College Park—*park* OR-9
Brush College School
(Abandoned)—*locale* MO-7
Brush Coll Sch—*school* (6) IL-6
Brush Coll Sch—*school* (2) IA-7
Brush Coll Sch—*school* (2) MO-7
Brush Coll Sch—*school* OR-9
Brush Coll Sch (abandoned)—*school* PA-2
Brush Coll Sch (historical)—*school* MO-7
Brush Corral—*locale* NV-8
Brush Corral—*locale* UT-8
Brush Corral—*locale* WA-9
Brush Corral—*locale* WY-8
Brush Corral Canyon—*valley* (2) AZ-5
*Brush Corral Creek* AZ-5
Brush Corral Rsvr—*reservoir* ID-8
Brush Corrals—*locale* AZ-5
Brush Corral Spring—*spring* AZ-5
Brush Corral Tank—*reservoir* AZ-5
Brush Coulee—*valley* MT-8
*Brush Creek* AL-4
*Brush Creek* CA-9
*Brush Creek* CO-8
*Brush Creek* IN-6
*Brush Creek* KS-7
*Brush Creek* KY-4
*Brush Creek* MS-4
*Brush Creek* MO-7
*Brush Creek* NC-3
*Brush Creek* OK-5
*Brush Creek* OR-9
*Brush Creek* PA-2
*Brush Creek* TN-4
*Brush Creek* UT-8
*Brush Creek* WY-8
Brush Creek—*fmr MCD* NE-7
Brush Creek—*locale* AR-4
Brush Creek—*locale* TN-4
Brush Creek—*other* KY-4
Brush Creek—*other* WV-2
**Brush Creek**—*pop pl* AL-4
**Brush Creek**—*pop pl* CA-9
**Brush Creek**—*pop pl* MN-6
**Brush Creek**—*pop pl* MO-7
**Brush Creek**—*pop pl* (2) TN-4
Brush Creek—*stream* (15) AL-4
Brush Creek—*stream* (2) AK-9
Brush Creek—*stream* (16) AR-4
Brush Creek—*stream* (17) CA-9
Brush Creek—*stream* (13) CO-8
Brush Creek—*stream* FL-3
Brush Creek—*stream* (4) GA-3
Brush Creek—*stream* (16) ID-8
Brush Creek—*stream* (15) IL-6
Brush Creek—*stream* (7) IN-6
Brush Creek—*stream* (12) IA-7
Brush Creek*—*stream* IA-7
Brush Creek—*stream* IA-7
Brush Creek—*stream* (14) KS-7
Brush Creek—*stream* (22) KY-4
Brush Creek—*stream* (3) LA-4
Brush Creek—*stream* (3) MI-6
Brush Creek—*stream* MN-6
Brush Creek—*stream* (9) MS-4
Brush Creek—*stream* (51) MO-7
Brush Creek—*stream* (7) MT-8
Brush Creek—*stream* (6) NE-7
Brush Creek—*stream* (4) NV-8
Brush Creek—*stream* NY-2
Brush Creek—*stream* (8) NC-3
Brush Creek—*stream* ND-7
Brush Creek—*stream* (9) OH-6
Brush Creek—*stream* (11) OK-5
Brush Creek—*stream* (19) OR-9
Brush Creek—*stream* (8) PA-2
Brush Creek—*stream* (7) SD-7
Brush Creek—*stream* (18) TN-4
Brush Creek—*stream* (4) TX-5
Brush Creek—*stream* (4) UT-8
Brush Creek—*stream* VT-1
Brush Creek—*stream* (7) VA-3
Brush Creek—*stream* (10) WA-9
Brush Creek—*stream* (6) WV-2
Brush Creek—*stream* (6) WI-6
Brush Creek—*stream* (12) WY-8
Brush Creek—*summit* ID-8
Brush Creek Access Area—*park* TN-4
Brush Creek Bank Prospect Number
One—*mine* TN-4
Brush Creek Bank Prospect Number
Two—*mine* TN-4
Brush Creek Bank Prospect Three—*mine* TN-4
Brush Creek Baptist Ch—*church* TN-4
*Brush Creek Baptist Church* AL-4
*Brush Creek Baptist Church* MS-4
Brush Creek Bar—*bar* AL-4
Brush Creek Bay—*bay* OK-5
Brush Creek Bridge—*bridge* AL-4
Brush Creek Bridge—*hist pl* (2) KS-7
**Brushcreek (Brush Creek)**—*pop pl* MO-7
Brush Creek Butte—*summit* SD-7
Brush Creek Camp—*locale* OR-9
Brush Creek Camp (historical)—*locale* AL-4
*Brush Creek Canyon* UT-8
Brush Creek Canyon Overlook—*locale* UT-8
Brush Creek Canyon State Park—*park* IA-7
Brush Creek Cave—*cave* UT-8
Brush Creek Cem—*cemetery* (3) IL-6
Brush Creek Cem—*cemetery* IN-6
Brush Creek Cem—*cemetery* (3) KS-7
Brush Creek Cem—*cemetery* (3) MO-7
Brush Creek Cem—*cemetery* OH-6
Brush Creek Cem—*cemetery* PA-2
Brush Creek Cem—*cemetery* (2) TN-4
Brush Creek Cem—*cemetery* TX-5
Brush Creek Ch—*church* AL-4
Brush Creek Ch—*church* AR-4
Brush Creek Ch—*church* (2) IL-6
Brush Creek Ch—*church* IN-6
Brush Creek Ch—*church* (3) KY-4
Brush Creek Ch—*church* (3) MO-7
Brush Creek Ch—*church* (2) NC-3
Brush Creek Ch—*church* (3) OH-6
Brush Creek Ch—*church* OK-5
Brush Creek Ch—*church* VA-3
Brush Creek Chapel—*church* NC-3
Brush Creek Ch (historical)—*church* (2) MO-7
Brush Creek Ch of Christ—*church* TN-4
*Brush Creek Church* MS-4
Brush Creek Corral—*locale* UT-8
Brush Creek Cow Camp—*locale* CO-8
Brush Creek Ditch—*canal* CO-8
Brush Creek Divide—*ridge* MT-8
Brush Creek Gap—*gap* KY-4
Brush Creek Hollow—*valley* AL-4
Brush Creek Hollow—*valley* MO-7
Brush Creek Island—*island* KY-4
Brush Creek Island (historical)—*island* AL-4
**Brush Creek Junction**—*pop pl* WV-2
Brush Creek Lakes—*lake* CO-8
Brush Creek Mine—*mine* CA-9
Brush Creek Mission—*church* VA-3
Brush Creek Mtn—*summit* TN-4
*Brush Creek Overlook* UT-8
Brush Creek Park—*park* AL-4
Brush Creek Park—*park* MO-7
*Brushcreek Post Office* TN-4
Brush Creek Post Office—*building* TN-4
Brush Creek Post Office
(historical)—*building* AL-4
Brush Creek Public Use Area—*park* MO-7
Brush Creek Ranch—*locale* WY-8
Brush Creek Ranger Station—*locale* WY-8
Brush Creek Ridge—*ridge* CA-9
Brush Creek Rsvr—*reservoir* IN-6
Brush Creek Salems Church—*hist pl* PA-2
Brush Creek Sch—*school* IL-6
Brush Creek Sch—*school* KS-7
Brush Creek Sch—*school* (2) KY-4
Brush Creek Sch—*school* (3) MO-7
Brush Creek Sch—*school* NC-3
Brush Creek Sch—*school* PA-2
Brush Creek Sch—*school* TN-4
Brush Creek Sch—*school* WI-6
Brush Creek Sch—*school* WY-8
Brush Creek Sch (abandoned)—*school* MO-7
Brush Creek Sch (abandoned)—*school* PA-2
Brush Creek Sch (historical)—*school* (2) AL-4
Brush Creek Sch (historical)—*school* MS-4
Brush Creek Sch (historical)—*school* MO-7
Brush Creek Sch (historical)—*school* (3) TN-4
Brush Creek Sewage Treatment
Plant—*building* TN-4
Brush Creek Siding—*locale* TN-4
Brush Creek Spring—*spring* UT-8
Brush Creek Springs—*spring* NV-8
Brush Creek State Fish and Wildlife
Area—*park* IN-6
*Brush Creek Station* KY-4
Brush Creek Supply Ditch—*canal* WY-8
Brush Creek Tabernacle—*church* KY-4
Brush Creek Township—*civil* (2) MO-7
Brush Creek Township—*civil* SD-7
**Brush Creek Township**—*pop pl* MO-7
Brush Creek (Township of)—*fmr MCD* AR-4
Brush Creek (Township of)—*fmr MCD* NC-3
**Brush Creek (Township of)**—*pop pl* MN-6
**Brush Creek (Township of)**—*pop pl*
(5) OH-6
**Brush Creek (Township of)**—*pop pl* PA-2
Brush Creek Trail—*trail* OR-9
Brush Creek Trail—*trail* WA-9
Brush Creek Wildlife Area—*park* OH-6
Brush Dam—*dam* UT-8
Brush Draw—*valley* CO-8
Brush Draw—*valley* OR-9
Brusher Canyon—*valley* UT-8
*Brusher Creek* MS-4
Brusher Lake—*lake* WI-6
Brushey Bayou—*stream* LA-4
**Brushey Lake**—*pop pl* AR-4
Brush Farmstead—*hist pl* NY-2
Brush Fence Ridge—*ridge* NC-3
Brush Fence Run—*stream* WV-2
*Brush Fork* IN-6
*Brush Fork* KY-4
*Brush Fork* PA-2
*Brush Fork* TN-4
**Brush Fork**—*pop pl* WV-2
Brush Fork—*stream* (2) KY-4
Brush Fork—*stream* MT-8
Brush Fork—*stream* (2) NC-3
Brush Fork—*stream* (3) OH-6
Brush Fork—*stream* (3) TN-4
Brush Fork—*stream* VA-3
Brush Fork—*stream* (3) WV-2
*Brush Fork Branch* TN-4
Brush Fork Ch—*church* KY-4
Brush Fork Ch—*church* MS-4
Brush Golf Course—*other* CO-8
Brush Grove—*locale* KY-4
Brush Gulch—*valley* CA-9
Brush Gulch—*valley* CO-8
Brush Gulch—*valley* MT-8
Brush Harbor—*locale* VA-3
Brush Harbor Ch—*church* IL-6
Brush Heap Creek—*stream* IN-6
Brushheap Knob—*summit* WV-2
Brush Heap Mtn—*summit* AR-4
*Brush Hill* MA-1
Brush Hill—*hist pl* PA-2
Brush Hill—*locale* OK-5
Brush Hill—*summit* AK-9
Brush Hill—*summit* CA-9
Brush Hill—*summit* (2) CT-1
Brush Hill—*summit* (2) ID-8
Brush Hill—*summit* (4) MA-1
Brush Hill—*summit* MN-6
Brush Hill—*summit* NH-1
Brush Hill—*summit* NY-2
Brush Hill—*summit* RI-1
Brush Hill—*summit* VT-1
Brush Hill Cem—*cemetery* MN-6
Brush Hill Ch—*church* TN-4
Brush Hills—*range* ND-7
Brush Hill Sch—*school* IL-6
Brush Hill Sch—*school* NE-7
Brush Hill Sch (abandoned)—*school* PA-2
*Brush Hole* NV-8
**Brush Hollow**—*pop pl* MA-1
Brush Hollow—*valley* KY-4
Brush Hollow—*valley* OR-9
Brush Hollow—*valley* TN-4
Brush Hollow—*valley* (2) UT-8
Brush Hollow—*valley* WI-6
Brush Hollow Canyon—*valley* UT-8
Brush Hollow Cem—*cemetery* WI-6
Brush Hollow Creek—*stream* (2) CO-8
Brush Hollow Rsvr—*reservoir* CO-8
Brush Hollow Supply Ditch—*canal* CO-8
Brush Hollow Trail—*trail* PA-2
Brush HS—*school* OH-6
Brushie Prairie—*locale* TX-5
Brushie Prairie Ch—*church* TX-5
*Brush Island* MA-1
*Brush Island* NE-7
*Brush Island* NY-2
Brush Island—*flat* AR-4
Brush Island—*island* AR-4
Brush Island—*island* (2) CT-1
Brush Island—*island* FL-3
Brush Island—*island* (2) LA-4
Brush Island—*island* (2) MA-1
Brush Island—*island* MI-6
Brush Island—*island* MN-6
Brush Island—*island* NY-2
Brush Island—*island* OR-9
**Brush Island**—*pop pl* CT-1
Brush Island Cem—*cemetery* KY-4
Brush Islands—*island* FL-3
Brushkana Campground—*locale* AK-9
Brushkana Creek—*stream* AK-9
*Brush Key* FL-3
Brush Keys—*island* FL-3
*Brush Lake* MI-6
*Brush Lake* WI-6
Brush Lake—*lake* AR-4
Brush Lake—*lake* FL-3
Brush Lake—*lake* (2) ID-8
Brush Lake—*lake* (2) IL-6
Brush Lake—*lake* LA-4
Brush Lake—*lake* (4) MI-6
Brush Lake—*lake* (2) MN-6
Brush Lake—*lake* MS-4
Brush Lake—*lake* MO-7
Brush Lake—*lake* MT-8
Brush Lake—*lake* (2) NE-7
Brush Lake—*lake* (2) ND-7
Brush Lake—*lake* OH-6
Brush Lake—*lake* SD-7
Brush Lake—*lake* TN-4
Brush Lake—*lake* TX-5
Brush Lake—*lake* WI-6
Brush Lake—*reservoir* CA-9
Brush Lake—*reservoir* OR-9
Brush Lake—*swamp* AR-4
Brush Lakebed—*flat* MN-6
Brush Lake Resort—*locale* MT-8
Brush Lateral—*canal* (2) CO-8
Brush Ledge—*bar* MA-1
*Brush Lick Run* WV-2
Brushlick Run—*stream* WV-2
Brush Lick Run—*stream* WV-2
Brushman Mtn—*summit* AK-9
Brush Marsh—*swamp* NY-2
Brush Meadow—*flat* (2) CA-9
**Brushmeadway**—*pop pl* PA-2
Brush Mountain—*ridge* AR-4
Brush Mountain Creek—*stream* MT-8
Brush Mountain Dam—*dam* PA-2
Brush Mountain Trail—*trail* TN-4
Brush Mtn—*summit* AL-4
Brush Mtn—*summit* AZ-5
Brush Mtn—*summit* AR-4
Brush Mtn—*summit* (8) CA-9
Brush Mtn—*summit* (3) CO-8
Brush Mtn—*summit* ID-8
Brush Mtn—*summit* KY-4
Brush Mtn—*summit* ME-1
Brush Mtn—*summit* MA-1
Brush Mtn—*summit* (2) MT-8
Brush Mtn—*summit* NY-2
Brush Mtn—*summit* NC-3
Brush Mtn—*summit* (2) OR-9
Brush Mtn—*summit* (2) PA-2
Brush Mtn—*summit* TN-4
Brush Mtn—*summit* (4) VA-3
Brush Mtn—*summit* (2) WA-9
Brush Narrows—*gap* OK-5
Brush Neck—*cape* NY-2
Brush Neck—*cape* RI-1
*Brush Neck Cove* RI-1
Brush Neck Cove—*bay* RI-1
Brush Oak Sch (abandoned)—*school* MO-7
Brush Park—*flat* CO-8
Brush Park—*flat* UT-8
Brush Park—*park* NY-2
Brush Pasture Tank—*reservoir* AZ-5
Brush Patch—*area* CA-9
Brush Patch Seep—*spring* UT-8
Brush Peak—*summit* AK-9
Brush Peak—*summit* CA-9
Brush Peak—*summit* NV-8
Brush Pen Hollow—*valley* TX-5
Brush Pile Pond—*lake* NV-8
*Brush Point* WA-9
Brush Point—*cape* MI-6
Brush Point Cem—*cemetery* IA-7
Brush Pond—*lake* (2) AL-4
Brush Pond—*lake* KY-4
Brush Pond—*lake* MA-1
Brush Pond—*swamp* FL-3
**Brush Prairie**—*pop pl* WA-9
Brush Prairie Cem—*cemetery* WA-9
Brush Rabbit Spring—*spring* NV-8
*Brush Reservoir* CT-1
**Brush Ridge**—*pop pl* OH-6
Brush Ridge—*ridge* AR-4
Brush Ridge—*ridge* CA-9
Brush Ridge—*ridge* (2) GA-3
Brush Ridge—*ridge* NY-2
Brush Ridge—*ridge* (2) OH-6
Brush Ridge—*ridge* (3) PA-2
Brush Ridge—*ridge* WA-9
Brush Ridge Cem—*cemetery* MI-6
Brush Ridge Lookout Tower—*locale* OH-6
Brush Ridge Sch—*school* MI-6
Brush Ridge Sch (abandoned)—*school* PA-2
Brush Ridge Trail—*trail* PA-2
Brush Rsvr—*reservoir* UT-8
Brush Rsvr—*reservoir* WY-8
*Brush Run* PA-2
Brush Run—*locale* PA-2
Brush Run—*stream* (3) KY-4
Brush Run—*stream* (11) OH-6
Brush Run—*stream* (14) PA-2
Brush Run—*stream* (18) WV-2
Brush Run Sch—*school* OH-6
Brush Run Sch—*school* PA-2
Brush Run Sch (abandoned)—*school* PA-2
Brush Run Union Ch—*church* PA-2
Brush Sch—*school* IA-7
Brush Sch—*school* MS-4
Brush Sch—*school* OH-6
Brushs Creek—*stream* NY-2
Brushshack Creek—*stream* MT-8
Brush Shanty Lake—*lake* MN-6
Brush Sink—*basin* FL-3
Brush Spray Spring—*spring* OR-9
Brush Spring—*spring* (2) AZ-5
Brush Spring—*spring* CA-9
Brush Spring—*spring* (2) NV-8
Brush Spring—*spring* (4) OR-9
Brush Spring—*spring* UT-8
Brush Spring—*well* AZ-5
Brush Spring Number Two—*spring* OR-9
Brush Tank—*reservoir* (3) AZ-5
Brush Tank—*reservoir* (2) NM-5
**Brush Tavern**—*pop pl* VA-3
**Brushton**—*pop pl* NY-2
**Brushton**—*pop pl* PA-2
Brushton (Costa Post Office)—*locale* WV-2
Brushton-Moira Sch—*school* NY-2
**Brushton (RR name for
Costa)**—*pop pl* WV-2
Brushtop Lake—*lake* SC-3
Brush Top Lake—*swamp* AR-4
Brush Top Tank—*reservoir* AZ-5
**Brushtown**—*pop pl* (2) PA-2
Brushtown Sch (abandoned)—*school* PA-2
Brush Trail—*trail* PA-2
Brush Trail Hollow—*valley* UT-8
Brush Tunnel—*tunnel* MD-2
Brushvale—*locale* MN-6
Brushvale Sch—*school* MN-6
*Brush Valley* TN-4
**Brush Valley**—*pop pl* PA-2
Brush Valley—*valley* (2) MA-1
Brush Valley—*valley* MN-6
Brush Valley—*valley* (3) PA-2
Brush Valley Cem—*cemetery* PA-2
Brush Valley Ch—*church* PA-2
Brush Valley Dam—*dam* PA-2
*Brush Valley Mountain* PA-2
Brush Valley Rsvr—*reservoir* PA-2
Brush Valley (Township of)—*civ div* PA-2
Brushville—*locale* PA-2
Brushville—*locale* WI-6
**Brushville**—*pop pl* PA-2
Brushville Lake—*reservoir* PA-2
Brushville Sch (historical)—*school* PA-2
Brush Well—*well* TX-5
Brush Wellman Plant—*facility* OH-6
Brush Windmill—*locale* TX-5
**Brushwood**—*pop pl* MA-1
Brushwood Ch—*church* IN-6
Brushwood Ch—*church* LA-4
Brushwood (historical)—*building* MO-7
Brushwood Island—*island* WI-6
Brushwood Lake—*lake* MO-7
Brushwood Pond—*reservoir* NJ-2
Brushwood Sch—*school* IL-6
Brushwood Well—*well* NM-5
*Brushy* NC-3
Brushy—*locale* OK-5
Brushy—*locale* (2) TX-5
**Brushy**—*pop pl* IA-7
Brushy Bald Mtn—*summit* OR-9
Brushy Bar—*bar* (2) OR-9
Brushy Bar Campground—*locale* OR-9
Brushy Bar Creek—*stream* OR-9
Brushy Bar Riffle—*rapids* OR-9
Brushy Basin—*basin* (8) AZ-5
Brushy Basin—*basin* UT-8
Brushy Basin Canyon—*valley* AZ-5
Brushy Basin No 3 Mine—*mine* CO-8
Brushy Basin Spring—*spring* (5) AZ-5
Brushy Basin Tank—*reservoir* (5) AZ-5
Brushy Basin Wash—*valley* UT-8
Brushy Basin Well—*well* AZ-5
*Brushy Bayou* AR-4
*Brushy Bayou* MS-4
Brushy Bayou—*gut* (3) LA-4
Brushy Bayou—*gut* MS-4
Brushy Bayou—*stream* IL-6
Brushy Bayou—*stream* (11) LA-4
Brushy Bayou—*stream* (5) MS-4
Brushy Bayou—*stream* TX-5
*Brushy Bayou - in part* MS-4
Brushy Bend—*bend* TX-5
Brushy Bend Bayou—*bay* TX-5
Brushy Bluff—*cliff* (2) TX-5
Brushy Bluff Church—*locale* TX-5
Brushy Brake—*swamp* AR-4
Brushy Brake—*swamp* LA-4
*Brushy Branch* KY-4
*Brushy Branch* TX-5
Brushy Branch—*stream* AL-4
Brushy Branch—*stream* (5) AR-4
Brushy Branch—*stream* (2) GA-3
Brushy Branch—*stream* (3) IL-6
Brushy Branch—*stream* (8) KY-4
Brushy Branch—*stream* (6) LA-4
Brushy Branch—*stream* (2) MS-4
Brushy Branch—*stream* (6) MO-7
Brushy Branch—*stream* (4) NC-3
Brushy Branch—*stream* OH-6
Brushy Branch—*stream* OK-5
Brushy Branch—*stream* (5) TN-4
Brushy Branch—*stream* (9) TX-5
Brushy Branch—*stream* (3) WV-2
Brushy Branch—*swamp* FL-3
Brushy Branch Sch—*school* IL-6
Brushy Branch Sch (historical)—*school* TN-4
Brushy Brook—*stream* RI-1
Brushy Buckeye Creek—*stream* OH-6
Brushy Butt—*summit* VA-3
Brushy Butte—*summit* (2) CA-9
Brushy Butte—*summit* OR-9
Brushy Butte—*summit* TX-5
Brushy Camp Ridge—*ridge* CA-9
Brushy Canyon—*valley* (11) AZ-5
Brushy Canyon—*valley* (8) CA-9
Brushy Canyon—*valley* ID-8
Brushy Canyon—*valley* NV-8
Brushy Canyon—*valley* (10) NM-5
Brushy Canyon—*valley* (4) TX-5
Brushy Canyon—*valley* (3) UT-8

Bryant Cem—*cemetery* MA-1
Bryant Cem—*cemetery* (4) MS-4
Bryant Cem—*cemetery* (2) MO-7
Bryant Cem—*cemetery* (3) NC-3
Bryant Cem—*cemetery* OR-9
Bryant Cem—*cemetery* (2) SC-3
Bryant Cem—*cemetery* (10) TN-4
Bryant Cem—*cemetery* TX-5
Bryant Cem—*cemetery* VA-3
Bryant Cem—*cemetery* (2) WV-2
Bryant Ch—*church* (2) AL-4
Bryant Ch—*church* GA-3
Bryant Ch—*church* IN-6
Bryant Ch—*church* OK-5
Bryant Ch—*church* PA-2
Bryant Ch—*church* VA-3
Bryant Chapel—*church* FL-3
Bryant Chapel—*church* GA-3
Bryant Chapel—*church* NC-3
Bryant Chapel—*church* SC-3
Bryant Chapel (historical)—*church* TN-4
Bryant Chapel Sch (historical)—*school* TN-4
**Bryant City (historical)**—*pop pl* OR-9
**Bryant College**—*pop pl* RI-1
Bryant Community Center—*locale* AL-4
Bryant Corkscrew Cave—*cave* AL-4
Bryant Corner—*locale* VA-3
Bryant Corners—*locale* ME-1
Bryant Cove—*valley* AR-4
Bryant Cove—*valley* GA-3
Bryant Cove—*valley* TN-4
Bryant Cove Cem—*cemetery* AR-4
*Bryant Creek* MO-7
*Bryant Creek* OR-9
Bryant Creek—*stream* AL-4
Bryant Creek—*stream* AK-9
Bryant Creek—*stream* AR-4
Bryant Creek—*stream* (2) CA-9
Bryant Creek—*stream* (5) GA-3
Bryant Creek—*stream* (3) IN-6
Bryant Creek—*stream* (2) KY-4
Bryant Creek—*stream* LA-4
Bryant Creek—*stream* MI-6
Bryant Creek—*stream* MO-7
Bryant Creek—*stream* MT-8
Bryant Creek—*stream* NV-8
Bryant Creek—*stream* OK-5
Bryant Creek—*stream* OR-9
Bryant Creek—*stream* SD-7
Bryant Creek—*stream* TN-4
Bryant Creek—*stream* VA-3
Bryant Creek—*stream* (2) WA-9
Bryant Creek Lake—*lake* IN-6
Bryant Creek Lake Dam—*dam* IN-6
Bryant Creek Mine (surface)—*mine* AL-4
Bryant Culberson Airp—*airport* AL-4
Bryant-Cushing House—*hist pl* MA-1
Bryant-Denny Stadium—*other* AL-4
Bryant Ditch—*canal* IN-6
Bryant Ditch—*canal* KY-4
Bryant Drain—*canal* CA-9
Bryant Drain—*canal* MI-6
Bryant Drain One—*canal* CA-9
*Bryant Elementary School* PA-2
Bryant Elem Sch—*school* (2) KS-7
Bryant Fork—*stream* KY-4
Bryant Fork—*stream* WV-2
**Bryant Four Corners**—*pop pl* MA-1
Bryant Gap—*gap* AL-4
Bryant Gap—*gap* GA-3
Bryant Gap—*gap* KY-4
Bryant Gap—*gap* TN-4
Bryant Gap—*gap* VA-3
Bryant Grove Ch—*church* TN-4
Bryant Gulf—*valley* AL-4
Bryant Gulley—*valley* AL-4
Bryant-Harris Cem—*cemetery* MS-4
Bryant Highway—*channel* MI-6
Bryant Hill—*range* MA-1
Bryant Hill—*summit* (2) ME-1
Bryant Hill—*summit* MA-1
Bryant Hill—*summit* (2) NY-2
Bryant Hill Creek—*stream* NY-2
Bryant Hollow—*valley* (2) AR-4
Bryant Hollow—*valley* KY-4
Bryant Hollow—*valley* (3) MO-7
Bryant Hollow—*valley* PA-2
Bryant Hollow—*valley* (6) TN-4
Bryant Hollow—*valley* WV-2
Bryant Hollow Branch—*stream* TN-4
Bryant Homestead—*locale* MA-1
Bryant House—*hist pl* KY-4
Bryant HS—*school* NY-2
Bryantine Cem—*cemetery* NM-5
Bryant Intermediate Sch—*school* UT-8
Bryant Island—*island* FL-3
Bryant Island—*island* ME-1
Bryant Island—*island* TN-4
Bryant JHS—*school* AL-4
Bryant JHS—*school* (3) MI-6
Bryant JHS—*school* MN-6
*Bryant Junior High School* UT-8
Bryant Knob—*summit* (2) MO-7
Bryant Lake—*lake* FL-3
Bryant Lake—*lake* GA-3
Bryant Lake—*lake* (2) MI-6
Bryant Lake—*lake* MN-6
Bryant Lake—*lake* OR-9
Bryant Lake—*lake* WA-9
Bryant Lake Bed—*flat* (2) OR-9
Bryant Lakes—*reservoir* VA-3
Bryant Landing—*locale* (2) AL-4
Bryant Ledge—*bench* NH-1
Bryant Leininger Ditch—*canal* IN-6
Bryant Lick—*stream* KY-4
Bryant Memorial—*park* DC-2
Bryant Memorial Cem—*cemetery* WV-2
Bryant Mill Branch—*stream* TN-4
Bryant Mill Creek—*stream* NC-3
Bryant Mill Hollow—*valley* AL-4
*Bryant Millpond* NC-3
Bryant Mound—*summit* MO-7
Bryant Mountain Dam—*dam* OR-9
Bryant Mountain Pit—*cave* AL-4
*Bryant Mountain Rsvr* OR-9
Bryant Mountain Rsvr—*reservoir* OR-9
Bryant Mtn—*summit* AL-4
Bryant Mtn—*summit* AZ-5
Bryant Mtn—*summit* ME-1
Bryant Mtn—*summit* MA-1
Bryant Mtn—*summit* NH-1
Bryant Mtn—*summit* NC-3
Bryant Mtn—*summit* OR-9
Bryant Mtn—*summit* (2) SC-3
Bryant Mtn—*summit* VT-1
Bryant Mtn—*summit* (2) VA-3
*Bryant Neck* MA-1
Bryant Oil Field—*oilfield* OK-5
Bryantown—*locale* NC-3
**Bryantown**—*pop pl* (2) MD-2
Bryantown Bridge—*bridge* MD-2
Bryan Town Hall—*building* ND-7
Bryantown Hist Dist—*hist pl* MD-2
Bryan Township—*civil* MO-7
Bryan Township—*civil* SD-7
**Bryan Township**—*pop pl* NE-7
**Bryan Township**—*pop pl* ND-7
**Bryan Township**—*pop pl* SD-7
Bryan (Township of)—*fmr MCD* (5) AR-4
Bryan (Township of)—*fmr MCD* NC-3
Bryan (Township of)—*other* OH-6
Bryant Park—*park* MI-6
Bryant Park—*park* MN-6
Bryant Park—*park* NC-3
Bryant Park—*park* OR-9
Bryant Park—*park* SD-7
Bryant Peak—*summit* (2) WA-9
Bryant Point—*cape* MA-1
Bryant Point—*summit* AZ-5
Bryant Point Light—*locale* MA-1
Bryant Pond—*lake* FL-3
Bryant Pond—*lake* (2) ME-1
Bryant Pond—*lake* MA-1
Bryant Pond—*lake* MI-6
Bryant Pond—*lake* (2) NH-1
Bryant Pond—*lake* NY-2
**Bryant Pond**—*pop pl* ME-1
Bryant Pond—*reservoir* AL-4
Bryant Pond—*reservoir* ME-1
Bryant Pond—*reservoir* MS-4
Bryant Pond—*reservoir* NJ-2
Bryant Pond—*reservoir* PA-2
Bryant Pond—*reservoir* SC-3
Bryant Pond—*reservoir* (2) VA-3
Bryant Pond Dam—*dam* PA-2
Bryant Ranch—*locale* NE-7
Bryant Ranch—*locale* (3) TX-5
Bryant Ravine—*valley* CA-9
*Bryant Reservoir* TX-5
*Bryant Ridge* TN-4
Bryant Ridge—*ridge* (2) CA-9
Bryant Ridge—*ridge* KY-4
Bryant Ridge—*ridge* (4) TN-4
Bryant Ridge—*ridge* VA-3
Bryant Ridge—*ridge* WV-2
Bryant Ridge Tank—*reservoir* AZ-5
Bryant Run—*stream* WV-2
Bryants—*locale* CA-9
*Bryants Bridge* NC-3
Bryants Bridge—*bridge* (2) NY-2
Bryants Brook—*stream* NY-2
**Bryantsburg**—*pop pl* IN-6
**Bryantsburg**—*pop pl* IA-7
*Bryants Burn Landing* AL-4
Bryants Camp—*locale* TN-4
Bryants (CCD)—*cens area* KY-4
Bryants Cem—*cemetery* GA-3
Bryants Cem—*cemetery* KY-4
*Bryants Cemetery* MS-4
Bryant Sch—*school* (5) CA-9
Bryant Sch—*school* CT-1
Bryant Sch—*school* GA-3
Bryant Sch—*school* (4) IL-6
Bryant Sch—*school* (5) IA-7
Bryant Sch—*school* KS-7
Bryant Sch—*school* KY-4
Bryant Sch—*school* MI-6
Bryant Sch—*school* (2) MN-6
Bryant Sch—*school* (3) MO-7
Bryant Sch—*school* (2) NE-7
Bryant Sch—*school* (2) NJ-2
Bryant Sch—*school* NY-2
Bryant Sch—*school* (2) OH-6
Bryant Sch—*school* OK-5
Bryant Sch—*school* OR-9
Bryant Sch—*school* PA-2
Bryant Sch—*school* TX-5
Bryant Sch—*school* (2) WA-9
Bryant Sch—*school* WI-6
Bryants Chapel—*church* NC-3
Bryants Chapel—*church* TN-4
*Bryants Chapel Cemetery* AL-4
Bryants Chapel Ch (historical)—*church* AL-4
Bryant Sch (historical)—*school* AL-4
Bryant Sch (historical)—*school* MS-4
Bryant Sch (historical)—*school* MO-7
*Bryant School* MS-4
*Bryant School* SD-7
*Bryants Corner* GA-3
*Bryants Corner* IN-6
Bryants Corner—*locale* VA-3
**Bryants Corner**—*pop pl* ME-1
*Bryants Creek* AL-4
*Bryants Creek* IN-6
Bryants Creek—*stream* AL-4
Bryants Creek—*stream* MO-7
Bryants Creek Cem—*cemetery* MO-7
Bryants Fork—*stream* UT-8
Bryants Fork Campground
(inundated)—*locale* UT-8
Bryants Fork Guard Station
(inundated)—*locale* UT-8
**Bryants Fork Summer Home
Area**—*pop pl* UT-8
Bryants Grove Ch—*church* GA-3
*Bryants Hill* MA-1
Bryants Knob—*summit* NC-3
Bryants Knob—*summit* VA-3
Bryants Landing—*locale* AL-4
Bryants Landing—*locale* FL-3
Bryant Slough—*stream* WY-8
Bryants Marsh—*swamp* TX-5
Bryants Mill—*locale* NY-2
Bryants Mill Creek—*stream* GA-3
*Bryants Neck* MA-1
Bryants Neck—*cape* MA-1
Bryants Point—*cape* NH-1
*Bryants Pond* ME-1
*Bryants Pond* MA-1
*Bryants Pond* NC-3
Bryants Pond—*other* ME-1
Bryants Pond—*reservoir* PA-2
Bryant Spring—*spring* GA-3
Bryant Spring—*spring* TN-4
Bryant Spring—*spring* WA-9
Bryant Square—*park* MN-6
**Bryant Square**—*pop pl* MD-2
Bryants Spring—*spring* CA-9
Bryants Store—*locale* KY-4
Bryants Store (historical)—*locale* (2) MS-4
Bryants Swamp—*swamp* GA-3
Bryant Stadium—*locale* FL-3
**Bryant Station**—*pop pl* TN-4
Bryant Station Bridge—*bridge* TX-5
Bryant Station Cem—*cemetery* TX-5
*Bryant Station Spring* KY-4
Bryant Street Baptist Ch—*church* AL-4
**Bryantsville**—*pop pl* IN-6
**Bryantsville**—*pop pl* KY-4
**Bryantsville Acres**—*pop pl* MA-1
Bryantsville (CCD)—*cens area* KY-4
Bryantsville Methodist Church—*hist pl* KY-4
Bryantsville Post Office and
Store—*hist pl* KY-4
Bryant Swamp—*stream* NC-3
Bryant Swamp—*stream* VA-3
Bryant Swamp—*swamp* MA-1
Bryant Swamp—*swamp* NC-3
Bryant Swamp Canal—*canal* NC-3
Bryant Swamp Ch—*church* NC-3
Bryant Tabernacle—*church* AL-4
Bryant Tabernacle—*church* NC-3
Bryant Temple Ch—*church* SC-3
Bryant Town—*locale* VA-3
Bryanttown Cem—*cemetery* TN-4
**Bryant Township**—*pop pl* KS-7
**Bryant Township**—*pop pl* NE-7
**Bryant Township**—*pop pl* ND-7
**Bryant Township**—*pop pl* (3) SD-7
Bryant (Township of)—*fmr MCD* AR-4
**Bryantville**—*pop pl* MA-1
Bryantville (historical)—*locale* MS-4
Bryantville (historical P.O.)—*locale* MA-1
Bryantville Post Office
(historical)—*building* TN-4
Bryantville Sch—*school* MA-1
Bryant-Webster Sch—*school* CO-8
Bryant Well—*well* NM-5
Bryant Wells—*well* TX-5
Bryant Windmill—*locale* NM-5
Bryant Windmill—*locale* TX-5
**Bryant Woods**—*pop pl* MD-2
Bryanville Sch (abandoned)—*school* MO-7
Bryarly—*locale* TX-5
Bryarly Ch—*church* TX-5
Bryarly Cut-off—*bend* TX-5
Bryarly Lake—*lake* OK-5
Bryarly Sch—*school* VA-3
*Bryars Dam* AL-4
*Bryars Fish Camp and Boat Landing* AL-4
Bryars Junior Lake—*reservoir* AL-4
Bryars Junior Lakes—*reservoir* AL-4
*Bryce* WV-2
Bryce—*locale* IL-6
Bryce—*other* TX-5
**Bryce**—*pop pl* AZ-5
Bryce—*post sta* UT-8
Bryce, William J., House—*hist pl* TX-5
Bryce Amphitheater—*area* UT-8
Bryce Bldg—*hist pl* TX-5
Bryce Canyon—*park* UT-8
**Bryce Canyon**—*pop pl* UT-8
Bryce Canyon—*valley* UT-8
Bryce Canyon Airp—*airport* UT-8
Bryce Canyon Airport—*hist pl* UT-8
Bryce Canyon Heliport—*airport* UT-8
Bryce Canyon Lodge—*locale* UT-8
Bryce Canyon Lodge and Deluxe
Cabins—*hist pl* UT-8
*Bryce Canyon Natl Park* UT-8
Bryce Canyon Natl Park—*park* (2) UT-8
Bryce Cem—*cemetery* AZ-5
Bryce Creek—*stream* UT-8
Bryce Drain—*stream* MI-6
Bryce (historical)—*locale* AL-4
Bryce Horse Camp Tank—*reservoir* AZ-5
Bryce Hosp—*hospital* (2) AL-4
Bryce Hospital Dam—*dam* AL-4
Bryce Hospital Lake—*reservoir* AL-4
Bryce Knoll—*summit* AZ-5
Bryce Lake—*lake* OR-9
**Bryceland**—*pop pl* LA-4
**Bryceland (RR name Brice)**—*pop pl* LA-4
*Bryce Mtn* VA-3
Bryce Mtn—*summit* AZ-5
Bryce Mtn—*summit* VA-3
Bryce Natural Bridge—*arch* UT-8
*Bryce Peak* AZ-5
Bryce Pioneer Village—*locale* UT-8
Bryce Point—*cape* UT-8
Bryce Point View Area—*locale* UT-8
Bryce Ranch—*locale* AZ-5
Bryce (RR name for Jodie)—*other* WV-2
Bryce Smith Dam—*dam* AL-4
*Bryces Mtn* VA-3
Bryce Tank—*reservoir* AZ-5
Bryce Tank—*reservoir* NM-5
*Bryce Temple* UT-8
*Bryce Valley High School* UT-8
Bryce Valley Sch—*school* UT-8
Bryceville—*locale* FL-3
Bryceville Elem Sch—*school* FL-3
*Bryce Wash* AZ-5
Bryce Woodland Estates Landing
Strip—*airport* UT-8
Bryce/Zion KOA—*locale* UT-8
Bryden—*locale* TX-5
Bryden Hill—*summit* NY-2
Bryden Hill Brook—*stream* NY-2
Bryden Ridge—*ridge* TN-4
Bryden Sch—*school* OH-6
Bryd Mine—*mine* TN-4
Brydon—*locale* WV-2
Brydon Lake—*lake* NY-2
Brye Playground—*park* MN-6
*Bryer Creek* GA-3
Bryer Point—*cape* RI-1
Bryersund—*channel* MI-6
Bry Fork Prospect—*mine* TN-4
Bryker Woods Sch—*school* TX-5
Brykill—*hist pl* NY-2
Bryland Lake—*lake* LA-4
Bryley Cem—*cemetery* IL-6
Bryman—*locale* CA-9
Bry-Man Seven Cities Plaza—*uninc pl* GA-3
**Brymar**—*pop pl* AR-4
Brymer Creek—*stream* TN-4
Brymer Mountain—*ridge* AL-4
*Brymer Mountains* AL-4
**Bryn Athyn**—*pop pl* PA-2
Bryn Athyn Acad—*school* PA-2
Bryn Athyn Borough—*civil* PA-2
Bryn Athyn-Lower Moreland
Bridge—*hist pl* PA-2
Bryner Canyon—*valley* UT-8
Bryner Cem—*cemetery* IN-6
Bryner Chapel—*church* WV-2
**Bryners**—*pop pl* PA-2
Bryner Sch (historical)—*school* PA-2
Bryners Station—*locale* PA-2
**Brynewood Park (subdivision)**—*pop pl* TN-4
Bryn Field—*airport* ND-7
**Bryn Gweled**—*pop pl* PA-2
Bryn Hyfryd Ch—*church* OH-6
Brynion, Mount—*summit* WA-9
*Bryn Mawr* IL-6
Bryn Mawr—*hist pl* OH-6
Bryn Mawr—*hist pl* PA-2
**Bryn Mawr**—*pop pl* CA-9
**Bryn Mawr**—*pop pl* (2) PA-2
**Bryn Mawr**—*pop pl* VA-3
**Bryn Mawr**—*pop pl* WA-9
Bryn Mawr Coll—*school* PA-2
Bryn Mawr College Hist Dist—*hist pl* PA-2
Bryn Mawr Country Club—*other* IL-6
Bryn Mawr Court—*locale* PA-2
Bryn Mawr Creek—*stream* AK-9
Bryn Mawr Glacier—*glacier* AK-9
Bryn Mawr Hosp—*hospital* PA-2
Bryn Mawr Hotel—*hist pl* PA-2
Bryn Mawr Meadows—*park* MN-6
**Bryn Mawr Park**—*pop pl* NY-2
Bryn Mawr Sch—*school* IL-6
Bryn Mawr Sch—*school* MD-2
Bryn Mawr Sch—*school* MA-1
Bryn Mawr Sch—*school* MN-6
Bryn Mawr-Skyway—*CDP* WA-9
Bryn Mawr Station—*locale* PA-2
Brynn Marr—*locale* NC-3
**Brynn Marr (subdivision)**—*pop pl* NC-3
Brynt Draw—*valley* WY-8
Brynteson, Mount—*summit* AK-9
**Brynwood**—*pop pl* FL-3
Brynwood Country Club—*other* WI-6
Bryn Zion Ch—*church* OH-6
Bryn Zion Ch—*church* WI-6
*Bryon* GA-3
*Bryon* MN-6
*Bryon* WA-9
Bryon Gulch—*valley* CA-9
*Bryson* NC-3
*Bryson* WV-2
Bryson—*locale* CA-9
Bryson—*locale* MO-7
Bryson—*locale* MT-8
Bryson—*locale* TN-4
**Bryson**—*pop pl* TX-5
**Bryson**—*pop pl* WV-2
Bryson, Albert Swain, House—*hist pl* NC-3
Bryson, J. R., House—*hist pl* OR-9
Bryson Apartment Hotel—*hist pl* CA-9
Bryson Archeol Site—*hist pl* OK-5
Bryson Ave Sch—*school* CA-9
Bryson Bar—*summit* AK-9
Bryson Branch—*stream* (10) NC-3
Bryson Branch—*stream* OH-6
Bryson Branch—*stream* (3) TN-4
Bryson Canyon—*valley* UT-8
Bryson Canyon Gas Field—*oilfield* UT-8
Bryson (CCD)—*cens area* TX-5
Bryson Cem—*cemetery* AR-4
Bryson Cem—*cemetery* NC-3
Bryson Cem—*cemetery* TN-4
**Bryson City**—*pop pl* NC-3
Bryson City Dam—*dam* NC-3
Bryson City Lake—*reservoir* NC-3
**Bryson City (RR name
Bryson)**—*pop pl* NC-3
Bryson City Rsvr—*reservoir* NC-3
Bryson Cove—*valley* NC-3
Bryson Cove—*valley* VA-3
Bryson Creek—*stream* (2) NC-3
Bryson Creek—*stream* OR-9
Bryson Creek—*stream* SC-3
Bryson Dam—*dam* NC-3
Bryson Gap—*gap* GA-3
Bryson Gap—*gap* NC-3
Bryson Gap—*gap* TN-4
Bryson Hill—*summit* TX-5
Bryson Hollow—*valley* MO-7
Bryson Hollow—*valley* PA-2
Bryson Hollow—*valley* (4) TN-4
Bryson Hollow—*valley* VA-3
Bryson Hollow Run—*stream* PA-2
Bryson HS—*school* SC-3
**Brysonia**—*pop pl* PA-2
Brysonia Sch—*school* PA-2
Bryson Knob—*summit* (2) NC-3
Bryson Lead—*ridge* NC-3
*Bryson Memorial Chapel* AL-4
**Bryson Mountain**—*pop pl* TN-4
Bryson Mtn—*summit* (2) NC-3
Bryson Mtn—*summit* TN-4
Bryson Oil Field—*oilfield* TX-5
*Bryson Peak* TN-4
Bryson Place—*locale* NC-3
Bryson Post Office (historical)—*building*
(2) TN-4
Bryson Ridge—*ridge* TN-4
Bryson Ridge—*ridge* UT-8
Bryson Ridge—*ridge* VA-3
Bryson (RR name for Bryson City)—*other* NC-3
Bryson Sch (abandoned)—*school* MO-7
Bryson Sch (historical)—*school* MS-4
*Brysons Cove* TN-4
Bryson Spring—*spring* (2) OR-9
Bryson Stage Coach Stop—*hist pl* TX-5
**Bryson (subdivision)**—*pop pl* TN-4
Brysonville—*locale* TN-4
Brysonville Post Office
(historical)—*building* TN-4
Bryson Wash—*valley* UT-8
Bryson Windmill—*locale* NM-5
Brytana Lakes—*reservoir* MS-4
**Bryte**—*pop pl* CA-9
Bryte Sch—*school* CA-9
Brywood Shop Ctr—*locale* MO-7
BSA Dam—*dam* SD-7
Bsaroka Ridge—*ridge* WY-8
BS Canyon—*valley* NM-5
BS Canyon Trail—*trail* NM-5
B Sch—*school* ME-1
B Schuh Dam—*dam* SD-7
BS Gap—*gap* AZ-5
B Shaft—*mine* NM-5
B Silverman Dam—*dam* SD-7
BSK Mine—*mine* AZ-5
B S Mesa—*summit* (2) NM-5
B S Ranch Airp—*airport* MO-7
B S Spring—*spring* OR-9
BS Tank—*reservoir* (2) AZ-5
B Stream—*stream* ME-1
B Street District—*hist pl* MT-8
B Street Mini Park—*park* UT-8
**Btangech Iterchobei**—*pop pl* PW-9
Btaot—*bar* PW-9
BT Butte—*summit* AZ-5
Btil—*bar* PW-9
B T Ranch—*locale* NM-5
**Btululachang Ra Rrai**—*pop pl* PW-9
B T Washington HS—*school* VA-3
*Bu* MP-9
Bubak Lake—*lake* MN-6
Bubar Island—*island* WI-6
Bub Arthurs Flat—*flat* UT-8
B.U. (Baylor University)—*uninc pl* TX-5
Bubb Canal—*canal* ID-8
Bubb Creek—*stream* AK-9
*Bubb Lake* MI-6
Bubb Lake—*lake* NY-2
Bubble Lake—*lake* CO-8
*Bubble Mountain* ME-1
Bubble Pond—*lake* ME-1
Bubbles, The—*summit* ME-1
Bubbles Lake—*reservoir* CO-8
Bubble Spring—*spring* UT-8
Bubbling Bayou—*stream* LA-4
Bubbling Branch—*stream* SC-3
Bubbling Brook—*stream* MA-1
Bubbling Lake—*lake* AK-9
Bubbling Slough—*stream* AR-4
*Bubbling Spring* NM-5
**Bubbling Spring**—*pop pl* WV-2
Bubbling Spring—*spring* AZ-5
Bubbling Spring—*spring* AR-4
Bubbling Spring—*spring* CA-9
Bubbling Spring—*spring* (2) NM-5
Bubbling Spring—*spring* OR-9
Bubbling Spring—*spring* PA-2
Bubbling Spring—*spring* TN-4
Bubbling Spring—*spring* VA-3
Bubbling Spring—*spring* WV-2
Bubbling Spring Branch—*stream* NC-3
*Bubbling Spring Camps* WV-2
Bubbling Spring Canyon—*valley* AZ-5
Bubbling Spring Hollow—*valley* AR-4
Bubbling Spring Lake—*lake* NJ-2
Bubbling Spring Rec Area—*park* VA-3
Bubbling Springs—*spring* MT-8
Bubbling Springs—*spring* NC-3
Bubbling Springs Landing Strip—*airport* MO-7
Bubbling Spring Valley—*valley* AZ-5
Bubbling Well—*well* AZ-5
Bubb Sch—*school* CA-9
Bubbs Creek—*stream* CA-9
Bubby Branch—*stream* VA-3
Bubby Branch—*stream* WV-2
*Bubby Buttes* AZ-5
Bubby Buttes—*summit* AZ-5
Bube Ditch—*canal* IN-6
Bubie, Bayou—*bay* AL-4
*Bub Lake* MI-6
Bub Lake—*lake* MI-6
Bubler Branch—*stream* AR-4
Bublitz Mine—*mine* ND-7
**Bubona (historical)**—*pop pl* IA-7
Bubs Creek—*stream* NJ-2
Bubs Creek—*stream* UT-8
Bubs Meadow—*flat* UT-8
Bubulao—*area* GU-9
Bubulao River—*stream* GU-9
Buby Gap—*gap* NC-3
B U Cabin—*locale* KY-4
**Bucana**—*pop pl* (2) PR-3
Bucana (Barrio)—*fmr MCD* PR-3
**Bucarabones**—*pop pl* PR-3
Bucarabones (Barrio)—*fmr MCD* (2) PR-3
**Bucare**—*pop pl* (2) PR-3
Bucareli Bay—*bay* AK-9
*Bucatunna* MS-4
Bucatunna—*other* MS-4
Bucatunna Ch—*church* MS-4
Buccal Gulch—*valley* ID-8
Buccaneer Creek—*stream* AK-9
**Buccaneer Estates**—*pop pl* FL-3
Buccaneer Park—*park* FL-3
Buccaneer Point—*cape* FL-3
Buccaneer Rock—*pillar* UT-8
Buccaneer State Park—*park* MS-4
Buccaneer Yacht Club—*locale* AL-4
Buccaroo Point—*cape* FL-3
Buccleuch Mansion—*hist pl* NJ-2
Buccleuch Park—*park* NJ-2
Bucell Junction—*locale* FL-3
**Bucephalia Township**—*pop pl* ND-7
Bucey Bluff—*cliff* AL-4
*Bucha'* FM-9
Buchan, A. H., Company Bldg—*hist pl* SC-3
*Buchanan* IN-6
*Buchanan* PA-2
Buchanan—*locale* CA-9
Buchanan—*locale* CO-8
Buchanan—*locale* FL-3
Buchanan—*locale* MO-7
Buchanan—*locale* NM-5
Buchanan—*locale* OR-9
**Buchanan**—*pop pl* GA-3
**Buchanan**—*pop pl* IN-6
**Buchanan**—*pop pl* IA-7
**Buchanan**—*pop pl* KY-4
**Buchanan**—*pop pl* MI-6
**Buchanan**—*pop pl* NY-2
**Buchanan**—*pop pl* ND-7
**Buchanan**—*pop pl* OH-6
**Buchanan**—*pop pl* OR-9
**Buchanan**—*pop pl* TN-4
**Buchanan**—*pop pl* VA-3
Buchanan, I. W. P., House—*hist pl* TN-4
Buchanan, James, House—*hist pl* PA-2
Buchanan, James, House—*hist pl* TN-4
Buchanan, J. C., House—*hist pl* TX-5
Buchanan, Lake—*lake* FL-3
Buchanan Airp—*airport* NC-3
Buchanan Bank—*bar* FL-3
Buchanan Baptist Ch—*church* TN-4
Buchanan Bay—*swamp* FL-3
Buchanan Bayou—*stream* LA-4
Buchanan Branch—*stream* (2) MS-4
Buchanan Branch—*stream* NC-3
Buchanan Branch—*stream* TN-4
Buchanan Branch—*stream* VA-3
Buchanan Bridge—*bridge* MA-1
Buchanan Brown Cem—*cemetery* KS-7
Buchanan Canyon—*valley* AZ-5
Buchanan Canyon—*valley* NM-5
Buchanan Cave—*cave* PA-2
Buchanan (CCD)—*cens area* GA-3
*Buchanan Cem* TN-4
Buchanan Cem—*cemetery* AL-4
Buchanan Cem—*cemetery* AR-4
Buchanan Cem—*cemetery* ID-8
Buchanan Cem—*cemetery* (2) IL-6
Buchanan Cem—*cemetery* IN-6
Buchanan Cem—*cemetery* MS-4
Buchanan Cem—*cemetery* MO-7
Buchanan Cem—*cemetery* (4) NC-3
Buchanan Cem—*cemetery* PA-2
Buchanan Cem—*cemetery* (10) TN-4
Buchanan Cem—*cemetery* (2) TX-5
Buchanan Cem—*cemetery* (6) VA-3
Buchanan Cem—*cemetery* WV-2
Buchanan Ch—*church* IL-6
Buchanan Ch—*church* NC-3
Buchanan Ch—*church* PA-2
Buchanan Ch—*church* VA-3
Buchanan Chapel—*church* KY-4
**Buchanan Corner**—*pop pl* IN-6
**Buchanan County**—*pop pl* MO-7
**Buchanan (County)**—*pop pl* VA-3
Buchanan County Courthouse—*hist pl* VA-3
Buchanan County Courthouse and
Jail—*hist pl* MO-7
Buchanan County Courthouse (Boundary
Decrease)—*hist pl* MO-7
Buchanan County Home—*building* IA-7
Buchanan Creek—*stream* AK-9
Buchanan Creek—*stream* (2) AR-4
Buchanan Creek—*stream* CO-8
Buchanan Creek—*stream* IA-7
Buchanan Creek—*stream* (3) KY-4
Buchanan Creek—*stream* MI-6
Buchanan Creek—*stream* MO-7
Buchanan Creek—*stream* NC-3
Buchanan Creek—*stream* OR-9
Buchanan Creek—*stream* (2) TN-4
Buchanan Creek—*stream* VA-3
Buchanan Crossing—*locale* TN-4
Buchanan Dam—*dam* AL-4
Buchanan Dam—*dam* TX-5
**Buchanan Dam**—*pop pl* (2) TX-5
Buchanan Ditch—*canal* OH-6
Buchanan Draw—*valley* NM-5
*Buchanan Elem Sch* PA-2
Buchanan Elem Sch—*school* PA-2
Buchanan Elem Sch—*school* TN-4
Buchanan-Elkhorn (CCD)—*cens area* TN-4
Buchanan-Elkhorn Division—*civil* TN-4
Buchanan Ferry (historical)—*locale* AL-4
Buchanan Flat—*flat* CA-9
Buchanan Ford—*locale* TN-4
Buchanan Fork—*stream* KY-4
Buchanan Hill—*summit* NY-2
Buchanan Hill Cem—*cemetery* WV-2
Buchanan (historical)—*locale* KS-7
Buchanan Hollow—*valley* AR-4
Buchanan Hollow—*valley* NC-3
Buchanan Hollow—*valley* PA-2
Buchanan Hollow—*valley* (2) TN-4
Buchanan Hollow—*valley* VA-3
*Buchanan Hollow Dam* TN-4
Buchanan House—*hist pl* TN-4
*Buchanan Island* FL-3
Buchanan JHS—*school* FL-3
Buchanan Keys—*island* FL-3
Buchanan Lake—*lake* MN-6
Buchanan Lake—*lake* TX-5
Buchanan Lake Dam—*dam* MS-4
Buchanan Landing—*locale* TN-4
Buchanan (Magisterial District)—*fmr MCD* VA-3
*Buchanan-McCollum Cemetery* TN-4
Buchanan Memorial Cem—*cemetery* GA-3
Buchanan Memorial Ch—*church* TX-5
Buchanan Mine—*mine* CA-9
Buchanan Mtn—*summit* NY-2
Buchanan Mtn—*summit* VT-1
Buchanan Mtn—*summit* VA-3
Buchanan Oil Field—*oilfield* TX-5
Buchanan Park—*park* (2) PA-2
Buchanan Pass—*gap* CO-8
Buchanan Pass Trail—*trail* CO-8
**Buchanan Peninsula**—*pop pl* AL-4
Buchanan Peninsula Cabin Area—*locale* AL-4
*Buchanan Peninsula Subdivision* AL-4
Buchanan Point—*cape* AK-9
Buchanan Post Office—*building* TN-4
Buchanan Prospects—*mine* TN-4
Buchanan Ranch—*locale* NM-5
Buchanan Read Sch—*school* PA-2
Buchanan Ridge—*ridge* AK-9
Buchanan Ridge—*ridge* VA-3
Buchanan Ridge—*ridge* WI-6
Buchanan Rsvr—*reservoir* OR-9
Buchanan Run—*stream* PA-2
Buchanan Saint Sch—*school* CA-9
Buchanans Birthplace—*locale* PA-2
Buchanan Sch—*hist pl* IA-7
Buchanan Sch—*school* DC-2
Buchanan Sch—*school* (3) IL-6
Buchanan Sch—*school* LA-4

Buchanan Sch—*school* (2) ....... MI-6
Buchanan Sch—*school* ....... NE-7
Buchanan Sch—*school* (2) ....... OH-6
Buchanan Sch—*school* ....... OK-5
Buchanan Sch—*school* (3) ....... PA-2
Buchanan Sch—*school* ....... SD-7
Buchanan Sch (abandoned)—*school* ....... PA-2
Buchanan School—*locale* ....... NE-7
Buchanans Landing (historical)—*locale* ....... TN-4
Buchanans Springs—*spring* ....... OR-9
Buchanans Resort—*locale* ....... TN-4
*Buchanans Springs* ....... IN-6
Buchanan State For—*forest* ....... PA-2
Buchanan Station—*locale* ....... PA-2
**Buchanan Subdivision**—*pop pl* ....... TN-4
Buchanan Summit—*locale* ....... PA-2
Buchanan Tank—*reservoir* ....... AZ-5
Buchanan Tank—*reservoir* ....... TX-5
**Buchanan (Town of)**—*pop pl* ....... WI-6
Buchanan Township—*civil* (2) ....... MO-7
Buchanan Township—*fmr MCD* (2) ....... IA-7
**Buchanan Township**—*pop pl* ....... MO-7
**Buchanan Township**—*pop pl* ....... ND-7
Buchanan Township (historical)—*civil* ....... ND-7
**Buchanan (Township of)**—*pop pl* ....... MI-6
Buchanan Valley—*valley* ....... MO-7
Buchanan Valley—*valley* ....... PA-2
**Buchanan Valley Township**—*pop pl* ....... ND-7
Buchanan Well—*well* ....... TX-5
Buchan Cem—*cemetery* ....... NY-2
*Buchannan* ....... KY-4
Buchannan—*locale* ....... MS-4
Buchannan Cave—*cave* ....... AL-4
Buchannan Cem—*cemetery* ....... AR-4
Buchannan Cem—*cemetery* ....... TN-4
Buchannan Creek—*stream* ....... SC-3
*Buchannan Lake* ....... AL-4
Buchannan Missionary Baptist Ch—*church* ....... MS-4
Buchannan Mtn—*summit* ....... TN-4
Buchannan Sch—*school* ....... TN-4
Buchannan Sch (historical)—*school* ....... MS-4
Buchannon Gap—*gap* ....... VA-3
Buchannon Gulch—*valley* ....... CO-8
Buchannon Lake—*lake* ....... AL-4
*Buchannon Pond* ....... NJ-2
*Buchanon School* ....... PA-2
Buchan Pond—*lake* ....... FL-3
Buchaq—*summit* ....... FM-9
Bucha Ridge—*ridge* (2) ....... CA-9
Buchau Pass—*channel* ....... FL-3
Buch Canyon—*valley* ....... UT-8
Bucheit Sch (historical)—*school* ....... PA-2
Buchel, Floyd, House—*hist pl* ....... TX-5
Buchel Community Center—*building* ....... TX-5
Buchenau Cabin—*locale* ....... CA-9
**Bucher**—*pop pl* ....... OK-5
**Bucher**—*pop pl* ....... PA-2
Bucher, Joseph, House—*hist pl* ....... PA-2
Bucher Bridge—*hist pl* ....... KS-7
Bucher Cave—*cave* ....... AL-4
Bucher Cem—*cemetery* ....... IN-6
Bucher Cem—*cemetery* ....... PA-2
Bucher Creek—*stream* ....... CA-9
*Bucher Ditch* ....... IN-6
Bucher Elem Sch—*school* ....... PA-2
Bucher Glacier—*glacier* ....... AK-9
Bucher Hollow—*valley* ....... NY-2
Bucher Hollow—*valley* ....... PA-2
Bucher Run—*stream* ....... VA-3
Bucher Sch—*school* ....... MI-6
**Buchers Mills**—*pop pl* ....... PA-2
Bucher Spring—*spring* ....... PA-2
Bucher Spring—*spring* ....... WA-9
Bucher Swamp—*swamp* ....... CA-9
Bucher Thal Hist Dist—*hist pl* ....... PA-2
Bucher Windmill—*locale* ....... NM-5
Buchhole Ranch—*locale* ....... ND-7
Buchholtz Ranch—*locale* ....... SD-7
Buchholz (historical)—*locale* ....... SD-7
Buchholz JHS—*school* ....... FL-3
*Buch Horn Branch* ....... KY-4
Buchia Creek—*stream* ....... AK-9
Buchia Ridge—*ridge* ....... AK-9
Buchite Lake—*lake* ....... MN-6
*Buchkabuchka* ....... PA-2
Buchland Sch—*school* ....... PA-2
Buchler Creek—*stream* ....... MO-7
Buchli—*locale* ....... CA-9
Buchman Bridge—*bridge* ....... AL-4
Buchman Cem—*cemetery* ....... OH-6
*Buchman Creek* ....... KY-4
Buchman Ditch—*canal* ....... OH-6
*Buchman Lake* ....... MN-6
Buchmann Cem—*cemetery* ....... ND-7
Buchman Sch—*school* ....... IA-7
Buchmiller Field—*airport* ....... ND-7
Buchmiller Park—*park* ....... PA-2
Buchner Memorial Cem—*cemetery* ....... OK-5
Buchner Park—*park* ....... WI-6
Buchner Slough—*lake* ....... SD-7
Buchner Slough State Public Shooting Area—*park* ....... SD-7
Bucholtz Park—*park* ....... WI-6
*Buc Horn Creek* ....... AL-4
Buchser HS—*school* ....... CA-9
*Buchsville* ....... PA-2
**Buchtel**—*pop pl* ....... OH-6
Buchtel Bungalow—*hist pl* ....... CO-8
Buchtel Cem—*cemetery* ....... OH-6
Buchtel HS—*school* ....... OH-6
*Buchtel Peak* ....... WY-8
*Bucht Lamoseu* ....... FM-9
*Bucht Lemadol* ....... FM-9
*Bucht Levalol* ....... FM-9
*Bucht Nevon* ....... FM-9
*Buchwalter* ....... OH-6
Buchwalter House-Appletthorpe Farm—*hist pl* ....... OH-6
*Buck* ....... DE-2
Buck—*locale* ....... PA-2
Buck—*locale* ....... VA-3
Buck—*locale* ....... WV-2
**Buck**—*pop pl* ....... NC-3
**Buck**—*pop pl* ....... TX-5
Buck, Cassius, House—*hist pl* ....... MN-6
Buck, Charles, House—*hist pl* ....... MA-1
Buck, Frank LaVerne, House—*hist pl* ....... CA-9
Buck, Jeremiah, House—*hist pl* ....... NJ-2
Buck, Jesse H., Farm House—*hist pl* ....... MI-6
Buck, John W., House—*hist pl* ....... UT-8
Buck, Pearl, House—*hist pl* ....... WV-2
*Buck, The* ....... DE-2
*Buck, The* ....... PA-2
Buck, Will H., House—*hist pl* ....... CA-9
Buck, W. J., Polygonal Barn—*hist pl* ....... IA-7
Buckabear Pond—*lake* ....... NJ-2
Buckacre Point—*cape* ....... UT-8
Buckalew Bridge—*bridge* ....... AL-4
Buckalew Cem—*cemetery* ....... AL-4
*Buckalew Fluff* ....... FL-3
Buckalew Hill—*summit* ....... AR-4
*Buckalews Bogs* ....... NJ-2
Buckaloo Branch—*stream* ....... AR-4
Buckaloo Ch—*church* ....... AL-4
Buckaloons Rec Area—*park* ....... PA-2
Buckalo Ridge—*ridge* ....... TN-4
Buckalou Creek—*stream* ....... AZ-5
Buckalou Tank—*reservoir* ....... AZ-5
Buckalue Hollow—*valley* ....... TX-5
Buck and Charley Mine—*mine* ....... NV-8
Buck and Doe Mtn—*summit* ....... VA-3
Buck And Doe Trail (bridle path)—*trail* ....... WV-2
Buck And Game Creek—*stream* ....... VA-3
Buckaroo Cabin—*locale* ....... OR-9
Buckaroo Canyon—*valley* ....... NV-8
Buckaroo Creek—*stream* ....... ID-8
Buckaroo Creek—*stream* (2) ....... OR-9
Buckaroo Dam—*dam* ....... ID-8
Buckaroo Ditch—*canal* ....... ID-8
Buckaroo Flat—*flat* ....... OR-9
Buckaroo Flat—*flat* ....... UT-8
Buckaroo Flats—*flat* ....... AZ-5
Buckaroo Gulch—*valley* ....... OR-9
Buckaroo Lake—*swamp* ....... OR-9
Buckaroo Pass—*gap* (2) ....... OR-9
Buckaroo Pass—*valley* ....... OR-9
Buckaroo Spring—*spring* (2) ....... ID-8
Buckaroo Spring—*spring* (3) ....... OR-9
Buckaroo Tank—*reservoir* ....... AZ-5
Buck Arroyo—*valley* ....... TX-5
Buck Ash Pond—*reservoir* ....... NC-3
Buck Ash Pond Dam—*dam* ....... NC-3
*Buckatabon Lake* ....... WI-6
*Buckatanna* ....... MS-4
*Buckatanne River* ....... MS-4
Buckaton Creek—*stream* ....... WI-6
*Buckatonna* ....... MS-4
**Buckatunna**—*pop pl* ....... MS-4
Buckatunna Attendance Center—*school* ....... MS-4
*Buckatunna Baptist Ch* ....... MS-4
Buckatunna Baptist Ch—*church* ....... MS-4
Buckatunna Creek—*stream* ....... MS-4
Buckatunna Lake—*lake* ....... MS-4
Buckatunna Methodist Ch—*church* ....... MS-4
Buckatunna Sch—*school* ....... MS-4
Buck Bald—*summit* ....... TN-4
Buckball Peak—*summit* ....... VT-1
Buck Bar—*bar* ....... PA-2
Buck Bar—*island* ....... NJ-2
*Buck Basin* ....... UT-8
Buck Basin—*basin* (3) ....... AZ-5
Buck Basin—*basin* (2) ....... CO-8
Buck Basin—*basin* (2) ....... OR-9
Buck Basin—*basin* ....... UT-8
Buck Basin—*lake* ....... TN-4
Buck Basin—*valley* ....... UT-8
Buck Basin Burn—*area* ....... OR-9
Buck Basin Fork—*stream* ....... OR-9
Buck Basin Rsvr—*reservoir* ....... WY-8
Buck Basin Spring—*spring* (2) ....... AZ-5
Buck Basin Tank—*reservoir* (2) ....... AZ-5
Buck Bay—*bay* ....... CA-9
Buck Bay—*bay* ....... FL-3
Buck Bay—*bay* ....... MI-6
Buck Bay—*bay* ....... NY-2
Buck Bay—*bay* ....... WA-9
Buck Bay—*swamp* (2) ....... FL-3
Buck Bay—*swamp* (3) ....... SC-3
Buck Bay Creek—*stream* ....... MI-6
Buck Bay Hollow—*valley* ....... MO-7
Buck Bayou—*gut* ....... LA-4
Buck Bayou—*gut* ....... MS-4
Buck Bayou—*stream* ....... FL-3
Buck Bayou—*stream* (2) ....... LA-4
Buck Bayou—*stream* ....... MS-4
Buckbed Number Two Tank—*reservoir* ....... AZ-5
Buckbed Spring—*spring* ....... AZ-5
Buckbed Tank Number One—*reservoir* ....... AZ-5
*Buckbed Wash* ....... AZ-5
Buckbed Wash—*stream* ....... AZ-5
Buckbee—*locale* ....... WI-6
Buckbee Hollow—*valley* ....... PA-2
Buckbee Lake—*lake* ....... MI-6
Buck Bend Lake—*lake* ....... FL-3
Buckberg Mtn—*summit* ....... NY-2
Buckberry Branch—*stream* ....... NC-3
Buckberry Branch—*stream* ....... TN-4
Buckberry Creek—*stream* ....... MT-8
Buckberry Rsvr—*reservoir* ....... MT-8
Buck Bight—*bay* ....... AK-9
Buckboard—*locale* ....... OR-9
Buckboard Camp—*locale* ....... UT-8
Buckboard Canyon—*valley* ....... ID-8
Buckboard Canyon—*valley* ....... NV-8
Buckboard Creek—*stream* ....... MN-6
Buckboard Creek—*stream* (2) ....... OR-9
Buckboard Creek—*stream* ....... UT-8
Buckboard Crossing—*locale* ....... WY-8
Buckboard Flat—*flat* ....... UT-8
Buckboard Gulch—*valley* ....... ID-8
Buckboard Lake—*lake* ....... MN-6
Buckboard Mesa—*summit* ....... NV-8
Buckboard Rsvr—*reservoir* ....... WY-8
Buckboard Spring—*spring* (2) ....... NV-8
Buckboard Spring—*spring* (2) ....... OR-9
Buckboard Spring—*spring* ....... UT-8
Buckboard Wash—*stream* ....... NV-8
Buckboard Wash—*valley* ....... WY-8
*Buck Branch* ....... MS-4
*Buck Branch* ....... SC-3
*Buck Branch* ....... TX-5
Buck Branch—*stream* (11) ....... AL-4
Buck Branch—*stream* (7) ....... AR-4
Buck Branch—*stream* (3) ....... FL-3
Buck Branch—*stream* (7) ....... GA-3
Buck Branch—*stream* (4) ....... IL-6
Buck Branch—*stream* ....... IN-6
Buck Branch—*stream* ....... IA-7
Buck Branch—*stream* (24) ....... KY-4
Buck Branch—*stream* (5) ....... LA-4
Buck Branch—*stream* (2) ....... MD-2
Buck Branch—*stream* ....... MI-6
Buck Branch—*stream* (8) ....... MS-4
Buck Branch—*stream* (10) ....... MO-7
Buck Branch—*stream* (15) ....... NC-3
Buck Branch—*stream* (5) ....... SC-3
Buck Branch—*stream* (16) ....... TN-4
Buck Branch—*stream* (10) ....... TX-5
Buck Branch—*stream* (8) ....... VA-3
Buck Branch—*stream* (6) ....... WV-2
*Buck Branch Elementary School* ....... MS-4
Buck Branch Hollow—*valley* ....... KY-4
Buck Branch Lookout Tower—*locale* ....... MS-4
Buck Branch Park—*park* ....... MD-2
Buck Branch Sch—*school* ....... IL-6
Buck Branch Sch—*school* ....... KY-4
Buck Branch Sch—*school* ....... MS-4
Buck Branch Trail—*trail* ....... KY-4
*Buck Bridge* ....... DE-2
Buck Bridge—*bridge* ....... AL-4
Buck Bridge—*bridge* ....... VA-3
*Buck Brook* ....... NY-2
Buck Brook—*stream* ....... CT-1
Buck Brook—*stream* ....... ME-1
Buck Brook—*stream* (3) ....... NY-2
Buck Brook—*stream* ....... VT-1
Buckbrush—*reservoir* ....... OR-9
Buckbrush Butte—*summit* ....... WY-8
Buckbrush Cabin—*locale* ....... NV-8
Buckbrush Canyon—*valley* ....... NV-8
Buckbrush Creek—*stream* ....... OR-9
Buckbrush Draw—*valley* ....... ID-8
Buckbrush Flats—*flat* ....... ID-8
Buckbrush Poison Butte—*summit* ....... OR-9
Buck Brush Rsvr—*reservoir* ....... ID-8
Buckbrush Slough—*gut* ....... IL-6
Buckbrush Spring—*spring* (2) ....... ID-8
Buckbrush Spring—*spring* (5) ....... NV-8
Buck Brush Spring—*spring* ....... NV-8
Buckbrush Spring—*spring* ....... NV-8
Buckbrush Spring—*spring* ....... OR-9
Buckbrush Springs—*spring* ....... NV-8
Buckbrush Well—*well* ....... NV-8
Buck Butte—*summit* ....... AZ-5
Buck Butte—*summit* ....... CA-9
Buck Butte—*summit* ....... ID-8
Buck Butte—*summit* (6) ....... OR-9
Buck Butte Dam—*dam* ....... OR-9
Buck Butte Rsvr—*reservoir* ....... OR-9
Buck Buttes—*summit* ....... CA-9
Buck Buttes—*summit* ....... WY-8
Buck Butte Tank—*reservoir* ....... AZ-5
Buck Cabin—*locale* ....... OR-9
Buck Cabin Creek—*stream* ....... OR-9
Buck Cabin Trail—*trail* ....... OR-9
Buck Camp—*locale* ....... CA-9
Buck Camp—*locale* ....... ID-8
Buck Camp—*locale* ....... NM-5
Buck Camp—*locale* ....... OR-9
Buck Camp—*locale* ....... UT-8
Buck Camp—*locale* ....... WA-9
Buck Camp—*park* ....... OR-9
Buck Camp Canyon—*valley* ....... UT-8
Buck Camp Creek—*stream* ....... WY-8
Buck Camp Ridge—*ridge* ....... CA-9
Buck Camp Spring—*spring* ....... WA-9
Buck Camp Spring—*spring* ....... WY-8
*Buck Canyon* ....... ID-8
*Buck Canyon* ....... MT-8
*Buck Canyon* ....... OR-9
*Buck Canyon* ....... UT-8
Buck Canyon—*valley* (4) ....... AZ-5
Buck Canyon—*valley* (6) ....... CA-9
Buck Canyon—*valley* (4) ....... CO-8
Buck Canyon—*valley* (4) ....... ID-8
Buck Canyon—*valley* (4) ....... NM-5
Buck Canyon—*valley* (3) ....... OR-9
Buck Canyon—*valley* ....... SD-7
Buck Canyon—*valley* ....... TX-5
Buck Canyon—*valley* (7) ....... UT-8
Buck Canyon—*valley* (4) ....... WA-9
Buck Canyon—*valley* ....... WY-8
*Buck Canyon Creek* ....... OR-9
Buck Canyon Creek—*stream* ....... TX-5
Buck Canyon Gas Field—*oilfield* ....... UT-8
Buck Canyon Overlook—*locale* ....... UT-8
Buck Canyon Spring—*spring* ....... OR-9
Buck Canyon Trail—*trail* ....... ID-8
Buck Canyon Trail—*trail* ....... OR-9
Buck Canyon Wash—*valley* ....... UT-8
Buck Cave—*cave* ....... AL-4
Buck Cem—*cemetery* ....... AR-4
Buck Cem—*cemetery* ....... IN-6
Buck Cem—*cemetery* (2) ....... MS-4
Buck Cem—*cemetery* ....... NE-7
Buck Cem—*cemetery* (2) ....... NY-2
Buck Cem—*cemetery* (4) ....... OH-6
Buck Cem—*cemetery* (5) ....... TN-4
Buck Cem—*cemetery* ....... TX-5
Buck Cem—*cemetery* ....... WV-2
Buck Corners—*locale* (2) ....... NY-2
Buck Corral Creek—*stream* ....... ID-8
Buck Coulee—*valley* ....... MT-8
Buck Cove—*swamp* ....... SC-3
Buck Cove—*valley* ....... NC-3
Buck Cove Mtn—*summit* ....... NC-3
Buck Cove Spring—*spring* ....... CA-9
*Buck Crater* ....... UT-8
*Buck Creek* ....... AL-4
*Buck Creek* ....... AZ-5
*Buck Creek* ....... CA-9
*Buck Creek* ....... ID-8
*Buck Creek* ....... IN-6
*Buck Creek* ....... KS-7
*Buckcreek* ....... NC-3
*Buck Creek* ....... OK-5
*Buck Creek* ....... OR-9
*Buck Creek* ....... TN-4
*Buck Creek* ....... TX-5
*Buck Creek* ....... WY-8
Buck Creek—*bay* ....... NC-3
Buck Creek—*gap* ....... NC-3
Buck Creek—*locale* ....... IA-7
Buck Creek—*locale* ....... KS-7
Buck Creek—*locale* ....... WI-6
**Buck Creek**—*pop pl* ....... AL-4
**Buck Creek**—*pop pl* ....... IN-6
**Buck Creek**—*pop pl* ....... IA-7
**Buck Creek**—*pop pl* ....... KY-4
**Buck Creek**—*pop pl* ....... MO-7
**Buckcreek**—*pop pl* ....... WI-6
Buck Creek—*stream* (23) ....... AL-4
Buck Creek—*stream* (3) ....... AK-9
Buck Creek—*stream* ....... AZ-5
Buck Creek—*stream* (6) ....... AR-4
Buck Creek—*stream* (13) ....... CA-9
Buck Creek—*stream* (9) ....... CO-8
Buck Creek—*stream* (5) ....... FL-3
Buck Creek—*stream* (18) ....... GA-3
Buck Creek—*stream* (20) ....... ID-8
Buck Creek—*stream* (8) ....... IL-6
Buck Creek—*stream* (18) ....... IN-6
Buck Creek—*stream* (13) ....... IA-7
Buck Creek—*stream* (4) ....... KS-7
Buck Creek—*stream* (22) ....... KY-4
Buck Creek—*stream* (5) ....... LA-4
Buck Creek—*stream* (3) ....... MI-6
Buck Creek—*stream* ....... MN-6
Buck Creek—*stream* (5) ....... MS-4
Buck Creek—*stream* (11) ....... MO-7
Buck Creek—*stream* (13) ....... MT-8
Buck Creek—*stream* ....... NE-7
Buck Creek—*stream* ....... NV-8
Buck Creek—*stream* ....... NM-5
Buck Creek—*stream* (3) ....... NY-2
Buck Creek—*stream* (8) ....... NC-3
Buck Creek—*stream* (6) ....... OH-6
Buck Creek—*stream* (13) ....... OK-5
Buck Creek—*stream* (44) ....... OR-9
Buck Creek—*stream* (3) ....... PA-2
Buck Creek—*stream* (4) ....... SC-3
Buck Creek—*stream* ....... SD-7
Buck Creek—*stream* (11) ....... TN-4
Buck Creek—*stream* (22) ....... TX-5
Buck Creek—*stream* ....... UT-8
Buck Creek—*stream* (2) ....... VA-3
Buck Creek—*stream* (11) ....... WA-9
Buck Creek—*stream* (2) ....... WI-6
Buck Creek—*stream* (17) ....... WY-8
Buck Creek Basin—*basin* ....... CO-8
Buck Creek Bridge—*bridge* ....... AL-4
Buck Creek Bridge—*bridge* ....... SC-3
Buck Creek Campground—*locale* ....... CA-9
Buck Creek Campground—*locale* ....... WA-9
Buck Creek Campground—*park* ....... OR-9
Buck Creek Cem—*cemetery* ....... OH-6
Buck Creek Cem—*cemetery* ....... OK-5
*Buck Creek Ch* ....... AL-4
Buck Creek Ch—*church* ....... AL-4
Buck Creek Ch—*church* (2) ....... GA-3
Buck Creek Ch—*church* ....... IN-6
Buck Creek Ch—*church* ....... IA-7
Buck Creek Ch—*church* ....... KY-4
Buck Creek Ch—*church* ....... MS-4
Buck Creek Ch—*church* ....... NC-3
Buck Creek Ch—*church* ....... OK-5
Buck Creek Ch—*church* (2) ....... SC-3
*Buck Creek Chapel* ....... IN-6
Buck Creek Cove—*bay* ....... MO-7
Buck Creek Cow Camp—*locale* ....... WY-8
Buck Creek Crossing—*locale* ....... OR-9
Buck Creek Ditch—*canal* ....... IN-6
Buck Creek Drift Mine (underground)—*mine* ....... AL-4
Buck Creek Ferry (historical)—*locale* ....... AL-4
Buck Creek Guard Station—*locale* ....... CA-9
Buck Creek Hills—*range* ....... WY-8
Buck Creek (historical)—*stream* ....... PA-2
Buckcreek (historical P.O.)—*locale* ....... IA-7
Buck Creek Independent Christian Chapel—*church* ....... IN-6
Buck Creek Lake—*reservoir* ....... TN-4
Buck Creek Landing (reduced usage)—*locale* ....... OK-5
Buck Creek Lodge—*park* ....... IN-6
Buck Creek Mtn—*summit* (2) ....... OK-5
Buck Creek Oil Field—*oilfield* ....... WY-8
Buck Creek Pass—*gap* ....... WA-9
Buck Creek Pond—*lake* ....... MI-6
Buck Creek Pond—*reservoir* ....... IN-6
Buck Creek Public Use Area—*park* ....... AR-4
Buck Creek Ridge—*ridge* ....... OR-9
Buck Creek Saddle—*gap* ....... ID-8
Buck Creek Sch—*hist pl* ....... KS-7
Buck Creek Sch—*school* ....... IL-6
Buck Creek Sch—*school* ....... KS-7
Buck Creek Sch—*school* (3) ....... KY-4
Buck Creek Spring—*spring* ....... AL-4
Buck Creek Spring—*spring* ....... CA-9
*Buck Creek Station* ....... KS-7
Buck Creek Tank—*reservoir* ....... AZ-5
Buck Creek Tank—*reservoir* ....... TX-5
**Buck Creek (Township of)**—*pop pl* ....... IN-6
Buck Creek Trail—*trail* ....... CA-9
Buck Creek Trail—*trail* ....... ID-8
Buck Creek Trail—*trail* ....... OR-9
Buck Creek Trail Camp—*locale* ....... NM-5
Buck Creek V S—*range* ....... WY-8
Buck Dam—*dam* ....... AZ-5
Buck Ditch—*canal* ....... IN-6
Buck Ditch—*stream* ....... AL-4
Buck Ditch—*stream* ....... TN-4
**Buck Donic**—*pop pl* ....... MO-7
*Buck Draw* ....... WY-8
Buck Draw—*valley* ....... CO-8
Buck Draw—*valley* ....... NM-5
Buck Draw—*valley* ....... OR-9
Buck Draw—*valley* (2) ....... UT-8
Buck Draw—*valley* (4) ....... WY-8
Buck Draw Rsvr—*reservoir* ....... WY-8
Buck Drive—*swamp* ....... SC-3
Buckelew Cem—*cemetery* ....... TN-4
Buckelew Creek—*stream* ....... TX-5
Buckelew Hollow—*valley* ....... WV-2
Buckelew Spring—*spring* ....... AZ-5
Buck Elk Branch—*stream* ....... MO-7
Buck Elk Creek—*stream* ....... KY-4
Buck Elk Creek—*stream* ....... MO-7
Buck Elk Sch (historical)—*school* ....... MO-7
Buckell Lake—*lake* ....... MI-6
Buckenham Hill—*summit* ....... LA-4
Bucker—*locale* ....... OK-5
Bucker Catfish Pond Dam—*dam* ....... MS-4
Bucker Catfish Ponds Dam—*dam* ....... MS-4
Bucker Creek—*stream* ....... LA-4
Bucker Creek—*stream* ....... TX-5
Bucker Ditch—*canal* ....... CO-8
Bucker Gap—*gap* ....... AR-4
Bucker Hill Cem—*cemetery* ....... IA-7
Bucker Knob—*summit* ....... IN-6
Buckeroo Spring—*spring* ....... OR-9
Bucker Pond—*lake* ....... AL-4
Bucker Pond Ditch—*canal* ....... IL-6
**Bucker Womans Town (historical)**—*pop pl* ....... FL-3
Bucket Bend—*bay* ....... LA-4
Bucket Branch—*stream* ....... FL-3
Bucket Branch—*stream* ....... KY-4
Bucket Branch—*stream* ....... TN-4
Bucket Canyon—*valley* ....... UT-8
Bucket Creek—*stream* ....... LA-4
Bucket Creek—*stream* ....... OR-9
Bucket Creek—*stream* ....... WA-9
Bucket Gut—*gut* ....... VA-3
Bucket Hollow—*valley* ....... UT-8
Bucket Hollow Rsvr—*reservoir* ....... UT-8
Bucket Lake—*lake* ....... AK-9
Bucket Lake—*lake* ....... OR-9
Bucket Mountain Tank—*reservoir* ....... AZ-5
Bucket Mtn—*summit* ....... AZ-5
Bucket Pond—*lake* ....... NY-2
Bucket Ranch Spring—*spring* ....... UT-8
Bucket Run—*stream* ....... WV-2
Bucket Spring—*spring* ....... AZ-5
Bucket Spring—*spring* ....... ID-8
Bucket Spring—*spring* ....... WA-9
Bucket Tank—*reservoir* ....... NM-5
Buckett Branch—*stream* ....... KY-4
**Buckettown**—*pop pl* ....... KY-4
*Bucketville* ....... VT-1
Buckety Creek—*stream* ....... WI-6
Buckey Cave—*cave* (2) ....... AL-4
Buckey Cem—*cemetery* ....... MS-4
Buckeye—*locale* ....... AR-4
Buckeye—*locale* ....... CA-9
Buckeye—*locale* ....... CO-8
Buckeye—*locale* ....... IA-7
Buckeye—*locale* ....... KS-7
Buckeye—*locale* ....... KY-4
Buckeye—*locale* ....... NE-7
Buckeye—*locale* ....... NV-8
Buckeye—*locale* (2) ....... OH-6
Buckeye—*locale* ....... TN-4
Buckeye—*locale* ....... VA-3
Buckeye—*locale* ....... WA-9
**Buckeye**—*pop pl* ....... AZ-5
**Buckeye**—*pop pl* ....... AR-4
**Buckeye**—*pop pl* (2) ....... CA-9
**Buckeye**—*pop pl* ....... IN-6
**Buckeye**—*pop pl* ....... IA-7
**Buckeye**—*pop pl* ....... LA-4
**Buckeye**—*pop pl* ....... NM-5
**Buckeye**—*pop pl* ....... PA-2
**Buckeye**—*pop pl* ....... TX-5
**Buckeye**—*pop pl* ....... WV-2
Buckeye, Lake—*lake* ....... FL-3
**Buckeye Addition**—*pop pl* ....... OH-6
Buckeye and Lena Mine—*mine* ....... SD-7
Buckeye Apache Mine—*mine* ....... AZ-5
*Buckeye Bald* ....... TN-4
Buckeye Bar—*bar* ....... CA-9
Buckeye Basin—*basin* ....... WA-9
Buckeye Boys Ranch—*locale* ....... OH-6
*Buckeye Branch* ....... GA-3
*Buckeye Branch* ....... PA-2
Buckeye Branch—*stream* ....... FL-3
Buckeye Branch—*stream* ....... GA-3
Buckeye Branch—*stream* ....... IL-6
Buckeye Branch—*stream* (7) ....... KY-4
Buckeye Branch—*stream* ....... LA-4
Buckeye Branch—*stream* (4) ....... NC-3
Buckeye Branch—*stream* (4) ....... TN-4
Buckeye Branch—*stream* ....... TX-5
Buckeye Branch—*stream* (3) ....... VA-3
Buckeye Branch—*stream* ....... WV-2
Buckeye Bridge—*hist pl* ....... IL-6
Buckeye Bridge—*other* ....... IL-6
Buckeye Brook—*stream* ....... RI-1
Buckeye Butte—*summit* ....... OR-9
Buckeye Camp—*locale* (2) ....... CA-9
Buckeye Canal—*canal* ....... AZ-5
Buckeye Canyon—*valley* ....... AZ-5
Buckeye Canyon—*valley* (4) ....... CA-9
Buckeye Canyon—*valley* ....... MT-8
Buckeye Canyon—*valley* ....... NM-5
Buckeye (CCD)—*cens area* ....... AZ-5
Buckeye Cem—*cemetery* ....... AR-4
Buckeye Cem—*cemetery* (2) ....... IL-6
Buckeye Cem—*cemetery* (2) ....... IA-7
Buckeye Cem—*cemetery* ....... OH-6
Buckeye Cem—*cemetery* ....... OK-5
Buckeye Cem—*cemetery* ....... TN-4
Buckeye Cem—*cemetery* ....... WV-2
Buckeye Ch—*church* (3) ....... IL-6
Buckeye Ch—*church* ....... IN-6
Buckeye Ch—*church* ....... KY-4
Buckeye Ch—*church* ....... NC-3
Buckeye Ch—*church* ....... OH-6
Buckeye Ch—*church* ....... OK-5
Buckeye Ch—*church* (2) ....... TN-4
Buckeye Ch—*church* ....... WV-2
Buckeye City Hall—*building* ....... AZ-5
Buckeye Club—*locale* ....... CA-9
Buckeye Copper Mine—*mine* ....... AZ-5
Buckeye Copper Mine Well—*well* ....... AZ-5
*Buckeye Cove* ....... GA-3
Buckeye Cove—*bay* ....... GA-3
Buckeye Cove—*valley* ....... GA-3
Buckeye Cove—*valley* (5) ....... NC-3
Buckeye Cove—*valley* (3) ....... TN-4
*Buckeye Creek* ....... CA-9
*Buckeye Creek* ....... KS-7
Buckeye Creek—*stream* ....... AL-4
Buckeye Creek—*stream* (3) ....... AK-9
Buckeye Creek—*stream* (12) ....... CA-9
Buckeye Creek—*stream* (2) ....... CO-8
Buckeye Creek—*stream* (3) ....... GA-3
Buckeye Creek—*stream* ....... IL-6
Buckeye Creek—*stream* (2) ....... IN-6
Buckeye Creek—*stream* (2) ....... IA-7
Buckeye Creek—*stream* (2) ....... KS-7
Buckeye Creek—*stream* ....... KY-4
Buckeye Creek—*stream* (2) ....... MO-7
Buckeye Creek—*stream* ....... NV-8
Buckeye Creek—*stream* (3) ....... NC-3
Buckeye Creek—*stream* (4) ....... OH-6
Buckeye Creek—*stream* (2) ....... OK-5
Buckeye Creek—*stream* (3) ....... OR-9
Buckeye Creek—*stream* (2) ....... TN-4
Buckeye Creek—*stream* ....... UT-8
Buckeye Creek—*stream* (3) ....... WA-9
Buckeye Creek—*stream* (3) ....... WV-2
Buckeye Creek—*stream* ....... WY-8
Buckeye Crossroads—*locale* ....... CO-8
Buckeye Diggings—*mine* ....... CA-9
Buckeye Ditch—*canal* ....... CA-9
Buckeye Ditch—*canal* ....... CO-8
Buckeye Ditch—*canal* ....... ID-8
Buckeye Elem Sch—*school* ....... AZ-5
Buckeye Flat—*flat* (3) ....... CA-9
Buckeye Ford—*locale* ....... NC-3
*Buckeye Fork* ....... OH-6
*Buckeye Fork* ....... WV-2
Buckeye Fork—*stream* ....... KY-4
Buckeye Fork—*stream* ....... OH-6
Buckeye Fork—*stream* (2) ....... WV-2
Buckeye FRS Dam Number One—*dam* ....... AZ-5
Buckeye FRS Dam Number Three—*dam* ....... AZ-5
Buckeye FRS Dam Number Two—*dam* ....... AZ-5
Buckeye Furnace—*hist pl* ....... OH-6
Buckeye Furnace Covered Bridge—*hist pl* ....... OH-6
Buckeye Furnace State Memorial—*park* ....... OH-6
Buckeye Gap—*gap* ....... GA-3
Buckeye Gap—*gap* (6) ....... NC-3
Buckeye Gap—*gap* (2) ....... TN-4
Buckeye Gap Prong—*stream* ....... TN-4
*Buckeye Grammar School* ....... AZ-5
Buckeye Gulch—*valley* ....... AK-9
Buckeye Gulch—*valley* (2) ....... CA-9
Buckeye Gulch—*valley* ....... CO-8
Buckeye Gulch—*valley* ....... SD-7
Buckeye Gulch—*valley* ....... WY-8
Buckeye Hill—*summit* ....... AL-4
Buckeye Hill—*summit* (2) ....... CA-9
Buckeye Hill—*summit* ....... NV-8
Buckeye Hills—*summit* ....... AZ-5
Buckeye Hills Rec Area—*park* ....... AZ-5
Buckeye (historical)—*locale* ....... AL-4
Buckeye Hollow—*valley* ....... AL-4
Buckeye Hollow—*valley* (5) ....... KY-4
Buckeye Hollow—*valley* ....... NC-3
Buckeye Hollow—*valley* ....... OH-6
Buckeye Hollow—*valley* (4) ....... TN-4
Buckeye Hollow—*valley* (3) ....... VA-3
Buckeye Hollow—*valley* (3) ....... WV-2
Buckeye Hollow Sch—*school* ....... VA-3
Buckeye Hot Spring—*spring* ....... CA-9
Buckeye HS—*school* ....... OH-6
Buckeye Island—*island* ....... TX-5
Buckeye JHS—*school* ....... OH-6
Buckeye Knob—*summit* ....... GA-3
Buckeye Knob—*summit* (3) ....... NC-3
Buckeye Knob—*summit* ....... TN-4
Buckeye Knob—*summit* ....... WV-2
Buckeye Lake—*lake* ....... CO-8
Buckeye Lake—*lake* (2) ....... MI-6
Buckeye Lake—*lake* ....... MN-6
Buckeye Lake—*lake* ....... OR-9
Buckeye Lake—*lake* ....... UT-8
**Buckeye Lake**—*pop pl* ....... OH-6
Buckeye Lake—*reservoir* (2) ....... OH-6
Buckeye Lake Campground—*park* ....... OR-9
*Buck Eyeland* ....... VA-3
Buckeye Lateral—*canal* ....... CO-8
Buckeye Lead—*ridge* ....... TN-4
Buckeye Lick Creek—*stream* ....... TN-4
Buckeye Lookout Tower—*locale* ....... WI-6
*Buckeye Military Reservation* ....... AZ-5
Buckeye Mill—*locale* ....... AZ-5
Buckeye Mine—*mine* (2) ....... AZ-5
Buckeye Mine—*mine* (3) ....... CA-9
Buckeye Mine—*mine* ....... CO-8
Buckeye Mine—*mine* ....... MN-6
Buckeye Mine—*mine* ....... MT-8
Buckeye Mine—*mine* ....... NV-8
Buckeye Mine—*mine* ....... NM-5
Buckeye Mine—*mine* (2) ....... OR-9
Buckeye Mine—*mine* ....... UT-8
Buckeye Mines—*mine* ....... CA-9
Buckeye Mine (underground)—*mine* ....... AL-4
Buckeye Mission—*church* ....... OK-5
Buckeye Mtn—*summit* ....... AZ-5
Buckeye Mtn—*summit* (2) ....... AR-4
Buckeye Mtn—*summit* (2) ....... CA-9
Buckeye Mtn—*summit* ....... CO-8
Buckeye Mtn—*summit* (3) ....... GA-3
Buckeye Mtn—*summit* ....... VA-3
Buckeye Municipal Airp—*airport* ....... AZ-5
Buckeye Natl Guard Target Range—*military* ....... AZ-5
Buckeye Park—*park* ....... TX-5
Buckeye Pass—*gap* ....... CA-9
Buckeye Peak—*summit* ....... CO-8
Buckeye Pit—*mine* ....... CA-9
Buckeye Point—*summit* ....... CA-9
Buckeye Point—*summit* ....... TX-5
Buckeye Pond—*lake* (2) ....... AL-4
Buckeye Post Office—*building* ....... AZ-5
Buckeye Post Office (historical)—*building* ....... TN-4
Buckeye Public Library—*building* ....... AZ-5
Buckeye Ranch—*locale* ....... ID-8
Buckeye Ranch—*locale* (2) ....... NM-5
Buckeye Ravine—*valley* ....... CA-9
Buckeye Reef—*bar* ....... OH-6
Buckeye Reef—*ridge* ....... UT-8
Buckeye Ridge—*ridge* (5) ....... CA-9
Buckeye Ridge—*ridge* ....... NC-3
Buckeye Ridge—*ridge* ....... PA-2
Buckeye Ridge—*ridge* (2) ....... TN-4
Buckeye Ridge—*ridge* ....... WI-6
**Buckeye Road**—*pop pl* ....... OH-6
Buckeye RR Station—*locale* ....... FL-3
Buckeye Rsvr—*reservoir* ....... CO-8
Buckeye Run—*stream* (2) ....... OH-6
Buckeye Run—*stream* ....... PA-2
Buckeye Run—*stream* ....... WV-2
Buckeye Sch—*school* (4) ....... IL-6
Buckeye Sch—*school* ....... KS-7
Buckeye Sch—*school* (3) ....... KY-4
Buckeye Sch—*school* ....... MO-7
Buckeye Sch—*school* ....... OH-6
Buckeye Sch—*school* ....... WA-9
Buckeye Sch—*school* ....... WY-8
Buckeye School—*locale* ....... MN-6
Buckeye Shaft—*mine* ....... AZ-5
Buckeye Shoal—*bar* ....... WA-9
Buckeye (Site)—*locale* ....... CA-9
Buckeye Sports Field—*park* ....... AZ-5
Buckeye Spring—*spring* (7) ....... CA-9
Buckeye Spring—*spring* ....... NC-3

Buckeye Spring—spring VA-3
Buckeye Square—locale MO-7
Buckeye State Lake Park—park OH-6
Buckeye Station—hist pl OH-6
Buckeye Station—locale KY-4
Buckeye Substation—locale AZ-5
Buckeye Swamp—swamp OH-6
Buckeye Town Park—park AZ-5
Buckeye Township—civil MO-7
Buckeye Township—civil SD-7
Buckeye Township—fmr MCD IA-7
**Buckeye Township**—pop pl (3) KS-7
**Buckeye Township**—pop pl ND-7
**Buckeye (Township of)**—pop pl IL-6
**Buckeye (Township of)**—pop pl MI-6
Buckeye Trail—trail WV-2
Buckeye Tunnel—mine CO-8
Buckeye Union HS—school AZ-5
Buckeye Valley—valley AZ-5
Buckeye Valley—valley NE-7
**Buckeyeville**—pop pl OH-6
Buckeye Wash—arroyo AZ-5
Buckeye Wash—stream AZ-5
Buckey No 1 Mine—mine NM-5
Buckey Ridge—ridge IN-6
Buckey Run—stream PA-2
Buckeys Knob NC-3
Buckeys Landing—locale TN-4
Buckeys Pond—lake NY-2
**Buckeystown**—pop pl MD-2
Buckeystown Hist Dist—hist pl MD-2
**Buckeystown Station**—pop pl MD-2
Buck Falls—falls OR-9
Buck Farm Canyon—valley AZ-5
Buck Fever Lake—lake MI-6
Buck Fever Ridge—ridge WY-8
Buck Field—flat CA-9
**Buckfield**—pop pl ME-1
Buckfield Backwater—swamp SC-3
Buckfield Cem—cemetery ME-1
Buckfield Ch—church KY-4
**Buckfield (Town of)**—pop pl ME-1
Buck Flat—flat (2) CA-9
Buck Flat—flat UT-8
Buck Flats—flat CA-9
Buckfoot Branch—stream MO-7
Buck For—area NC-3
Buck Ford—locale AL-4
Buck Ford Bend—bend AL-4
Buckford Creek—gut FL-3
Buck Ford (historical)—locale NC-3
Buck Fork—stream (3) KY-4
Buck Fork—stream OR-9
Buck Fork—stream (2) TN-4
Buck Fork—stream (6) WV-2
**Buck Fork (historical)**—pop pl OR-9
Buck Fork Pond River—stream KY-4
Buck Fork Trail—trail OR-9
Buck Fork West Branch Pond River KY-4
Buckf Windmill—locale NM-5
Buck Gap—gap KY-4
Buck Gap—gap (3) NC-3
Buck Gap—gap (2) TN-4
Buck Garden Creek—stream WV-2
Buck Grove—locale IA-7
Buck Grove—locale KY-4
**Buck Grove**—pop pl IA-7
Buck Grove Cem—cemetery IA-7
Buck Grove Ch—church KY-4
Buck Grove Sch—school (2) IL-6
Buck Gulch—stream OR-9
Buck Gulch—valley (4) CA-9
Buck Gulch—valley (6) CO-8
Buck Gulch—valley (3) ID-8
Buck Gulch—valley (3) MT-8
Buck Gulch—valley (8) OR-9
Buck Gulch Creek OR-9
Buck Gulch Mine—mine OR-9
Buck Gulch Rsvr—reservoir OR-9
Buck Gulch Spring—spring ID-8
Buck Gully—stream CA-9
Buck Gully—valley (4) TX-5
Buckhalder Pond—reservoir GA-3
Buckhall—locale VA-3
**Buck Hall**—pop pl SC-3
Buckhall Branch—stream VA-3
Buckhall Creek—stream IN-6
Buckhall Creek—stream NC-3
Buckhalter Branch—stream MS-4
Buckhalter Cemetery MS-4
Buckhalter Creek MS-4
Buckhalter Mill Creek—stream MS-4
Buckham, Thomas Scott, Memorial Library—hist pl MN-6
Buckham Gulch—valley CA-9
Buck Hammock—island (3) FL-3
Buck Hammock Field—island FL-3
Buck Hannen Mtn—summit NM-5
**Buckhannon**—pop pl WV-2
Buckhannon Branch—stream FL-3
Buckhannon Creek—stream AL-4
Buckhannon (Magisterial District)—fmr MCD WV-2
Buckhannon Memorial Cem—cemetery WV-2
Buckhannon River—stream WV-2
Buckhannon Run—stream WV-2
Buckhannon Run Ch—church WV-2
Buck Harbor—bay ME-1
Buck Harbor Camp—locale PA-2
Buck Harpsburg Ditch—canal OH-6
Buckhart—locale MO-7
**Buckhart**—pop pl IL-6
Buckhart Branch—stream MO-7
Buckhart Creek—stream IL-6
Buckhart Creek—stream IN-6
Buckhart Hollow—valley IL-6
Buckhart Hollow—valley TN-4
Buckhart Sch—school IL-6
Buckhart Spring—spring MO-7
**Buckhart (Township of)**—pop pl IL-6
Buckhatannee Creek MS-4
Buckhead—locale GA-3
**Buckhead**—pop pl (2) GA-3
**Buckhead**—pop pl NC-3
Buck Head—stream FL-3
Buck Head—valley FL-3
Buckhead Acad—school GA-3
Buck Head Bay—basin SC-3
Buckhead Branch—stream FL-3
Buck Head Branch—stream FL-3
Buckhead Branch—stream KY-4
Buckhead Branch—stream NC-3
Buckhead Branch—stream SC-3
Buckhead Canyon—valley AZ-5
Buckhead Canyon—valley NM-5
Buckhead (CCD)—cens area GA-3
Buckhead Creek—stream AR-4
Buckhead Creek—stream (2) GA-3
Buckhead Creek—stream NC-3
Buckhead Creek—stream OK-5
Buckhead Creek—stream OR-9
Buckhead Creek—stream (3) SC-3
Buckhead Creek—stream TN-4
Buckhead Draw—valley AZ-5
**Buckhead (historical)**—pop pl OR-9
Buckhead Hollow—valley MO-7
Buckhead Lake—lake MN-6
Buckhead Lake State Wildlife Mngmt Area—park MN-6
Buckhead Mesa—summit AZ-5
Buckhead Mountain Campground—park OR-9
Buckhead Mtn—summit (2) OR-9
Buckhead Point—cliff AZ-5
**Buckhead Ridge**—pop pl FL-3
Buckhead Ridge—ridge AZ-5
Buckhead Sch—school SC-3
Buckhead Slough—gut FL-3
**Buckhead (subdivision)**—pop pl AL-4
Buckhead Swamp—swamp FL-3
Buckhead Tank—reservoir (3) AZ-5
Buckhead Trail—trail OR-9
Buckheart Creek IN-6
Buckheart Creek—stream IL-6
Buckheart Creek—stream KY-4
Buckheart Hollow—valley KY-4
Buckheart Run—stream WV-2
**Buckheart (Township of)**—pop pl IL-6
Buckheaven—locale OR-9
Buckhern Swamp VA-3
Buckhill MA-1
**Buck Hill**—pop pl OH-6
Buck Hill—summit CO-8
Buck Hill—summit (3) CT-1
Buck Hill—summit (3) ME-1
Buck Hill—summit MD-2
Buck Hill—summit (5) MA-1
Buck Hill—summit MI-6
Buck Hill—summit MN-6
Buck Hill—summit NH-1
Buck Hill—summit (9) NY-2
Buck Hill—summit (2) NC-3
Buck Hill—summit ND-7
Buck Hill—summit OK-5
Buck Hill—summit (3) PA-2
Buck Hill—summit RI-1
Buck Hill—summit SC-3
Buck Hill—summit (3) TX-5
Buck Hill—summit (2) VT-1
Buck Hill—summit (6) VA-3
Buck Hill—summit WV-2
Buck Hill Bottom—bend OH-6
Buck Hill Cem—cemetery KY-4
Buck Hill Ch—church NC-3
Buck Hill Ch—church WV-2
Buck Hill Conservation Dam—dam MA-1
Buck Hill Creek—stream PA-2
Buck Hill Falls—falls PA-2
**Buck Hill Falls**—pop pl PA-2
Buck Hill Farm Covered Bridge—hist pl PA-2
Buck Hill Gap—gap NC-3
Buck Hill (historical)—locale MS-4
Buck Hill Landing—locale DE-2
Buck Hill Lookout Tower—locale MI-6
Buck Hill Mngmt Area Dam RI-1
Buckhill Pond—reservoir MA-1
Buck Hill Pond—reservoir RI-1
Buck Hill Pond Dam—dam RI-1
Buck Hills PA-2
Buck Hills—summit MI-6
Buck Hill Sch (abandoned)—school PA-2
Buck Hill School AL-4
Buck Hill Station—locale NJ-2
Buck Hill Swamp—stream GA-3
Buck (historical)—locale MS-4
Buckholder Run—stream PA-2
Buck Hole—bay GA-3
Buckhole Creek—stream NJ-2
Buck Hole Hollow—valley TN-4
Buck Holes Tank—reservoir AZ-5
Buck Hollow OR-9
Buck Hollow—locale TX-5
**Buck Hollow**—pop pl VT-1
Buck Hollow—valley (5) AR-4
Buck Hollow—valley CA-9
Buck Hollow—valley CO-8
Buck Hollow—valley IL-6
Buck Hollow—valley (2) KY-4
Buck Hollow—valley (8) MO-7
Buck Hollow—valley (2) NY-2
Buck Hollow—valley (2) OH-6
Buck Hollow—valley (6) OR-9
Buck Hollow—valley (2) PA-2
Buck Hollow—valley SC-3
Buck Hollow—valley (10) TN-4
Buck Hollow—valley (10) TX-5
Buck Hollow—valley (10) UT-8
Buck Hollow—valley VT-1
Buck Hollow—valley (2) VA-3
Buck Hollow—valley (2) WV-2
Buck Hollow—valley WY-8
Buck Hollow Branch—stream NC-3
Buck Hollow Branch—stream VA-3
Buck Hollow Cem—cemetery TN-4
Buck Hollow Creek—stream (2) OR-9
Buck Hollow Creek—stream TN-4
Buck Hollow Overlook—locale VA-3
Buck Hollow Ridge—ridge UT-8
Buck Hollow Ridge—ridge VA-3
Buck Hollow River Access—locale MO-7
Buck Hollow Sch—school VT-1
Buck Hollow Spring—spring TN-4
Buck Hollow Spring—spring UT-8
Buck Hollow Tank—reservoir TX-5
**Buckholts**—pop pl TX-5
Buckholts Branch—stream TX-5
Buckholts Bridge—bridge GA-3
Buckholts (CCD)—cens area TX-5
Buckholtz Creek—stream SC-3
Buckholz Corners—locale WI-6
Buckhorn AL-4
Buckhorn VA-3
Buckhorn—locale (2) AL-4
Buckhorn—locale AR-4
Buckhorn—locale CA-9
Buckhorn—locale FL-3
Buckhorn—locale ID-8
Buckhorn—locale IL-6
Buckhorn—locale IA-7
Buckhorn—locale MS-4
Buckhorn—locale NM-5
Buckhorn—locale OH-6
Buckhorn—locale TX-5
Buckhorn—locale WA-9
Buckhorn—locale WY-8
**Buckhorn**—pop pl AZ-5
**Buckhorn**—pop pl FL-3
**Buckhorn**—pop pl (2) KY-4
**Buckhorn**—pop pl MI-6
**Buckhorn**—pop pl (2) MO-7
**Buckhorn**—pop pl NM-5
**Buckhorn**—pop pl NC-3
**Buckhorn**—pop pl (2) PA-2
**Buckhorn**—pop pl TX-5
Buckhorn—summit OR-9
Buckhorn, Lake—lake FL-3
Buckhorn, Mount—summit CO-8
Buckhorn, The ID-8
Buckhorn Bald—summit NC-3
Buckhorn Bally—summit (2) CA-9
Buckhorn Bar—bar ID-8
Buckhorn Bar Campground—locale ID-8
Buckhorn Bar Creek—stream ID-8
Buckhorn Basin—basin (2) AZ-5
Buckhorn Basin—basin UT-8
Buckhorn Bay—swamp NC-3
Buckhorn Bayou—stream (2) LA-4
Buckhorn Bluff—island FL-3
Buckhorn Brake—swamp MS-4
Buckhorn Branch NC-3
Buckhorn Branch—stream (3) AL-4
Buckhorn Branch—stream AR-4
Buckhorn Branch—stream (2) GA-3
Buckhorn Branch—stream (4) KY-4
Buckhorn Branch—stream MD-2
Buckhorn Branch—stream (6) NC-3
Buckhorn Branch—stream (2) TX-5
Buck Horn Branch—stream TX-5
Buckhorn Branch—stream (2) VA-3
Buckhorn Bridge—bridge GA-3
Buckhorn Bridge—bridge WI-6
Buckhorn Brook RI-1
Buckhorn Brook—stream CT-1
Buckhorn Brook—stream NH-1
Buckhorn Butte—summit ND-7
Buckhorn Cabin—locale OR-9
Buckhorn Camp—locale (2) CA-9
Buck Horn Camp—locale FL-3
Buckhorn Camp—locale OR-9
Buckhorn Campground—locale ID-8
Buckhorn Camp (historical)—locale AL-4
Buckhorn Camps—locale ME-1
Buckhorn Canyon UT-8
Buckhorn Canyon—valley AZ-5
Buckhorn Canyon—valley (3) CA-9
Buckhorn Canyon—valley (2) ID-8
Buckhorn Canyon—valley (4) NM-5
Buckhorn Canyon—valley (3) OR-9
Buckhorn Canyon—valley TX-5
Buckhorn Canyon—valley (3) UT-8
Buckhorn Canyon—valley WA-9
Buckhorn Canyon—valley WY-8
Buckhorn (CCD)—cens area KY-4
Buckhorn Cem—cemetery AR-4
Buckhorn Cem—cemetery GA-3
Buckhorn Cem—cemetery OK-5
Buckhorn Cem—cemetery (2) TX-5
Buckhorn Ch—church GA-3
Buckhorn Ch—church KY-4
Buckhorn Ch—church (2) MS-4
Buckhorn Ch—church MO-7
Buckhorn Ch—church (2) NC-3
Buckhorn Ch—church OK-5
Buckhorn Ch—church (2) WV-2
Buckhorn Ch of Christ MS-4
Buckhorn Community Ch—church CO-8
Buckhorn Corner—locale OH-6
Buckhorn Corner—locale WI-6
Buckhorn Corners—locale IL-6
Buckhorn Corral—locale UT-8
Buckhorn Corrals—locale ID-8
Buckhorn Cove—bay CA-9
Buckhorn Cove—bay NC-3
Buckhorn Creek TX-5
Buckhorn Creek VA-3
Buckhorn Creek WA-9
Buckhorn Creek—stream (2) AL-4
Buckhorn Creek—stream (2) AZ-5
Buckhorn Creek—stream AR-4
Buckhorn Creek—stream (10) CA-9
Buckhorn Creek—stream (3) CO-8
Buckhorn Creek—stream (4) FL-3
Buckhorn Creek—stream (2) GA-3
Buckhorn Creek—stream (6) ID-8
Buckhorn Creek—stream IL-6
Buckhorn Creek—stream (2) IN-6
Buckhorn Creek—stream KS-7
Buckhorn Creek—stream (3) KY-4
Buck Horn Creek—stream KY-4
Buckhorn Creek—stream (2) MI-6
Buckhorn Creek—stream MS-4
Buck Horn Creek—stream MS-4
Buckhorn Creek—stream MS-4
Buckhorn Creek—stream (2) MT-8
Buckhorn Creek—stream NV-8
Buckhorn Creek—stream NJ-2
Buckhorn Creek—stream NM-5
Buckhorn Creek—stream NY-2
Buckhorn Creek—stream (7) NC-3
Buckhorn Creek—stream ND-7
Buckhorn Creek—stream (2) OH-6
Buckhorn Creek—stream (3) OK-5
Buckhorn Creek—stream (5) OR-9
Buckhorn Creek—stream (2) SC-3
Buckhorn Creek—stream (3) TN-4
Buckhorn Creek—stream (4) TX-5
Buckhorn Creek—stream (3) VA-3
Buckhorn Creek—stream WA-9
Buckhorn Creek—stream WY-8
Buckhorn Creek—swamp FL-3
**Buckhorn Crossroads**—pop pl NC-3
**Buckhorn Cross Roads**—pop pl NC-3
Buckhorn Dam—dam KY-4
Buckhorn Dam—dam NC-3
Buckhorn Dam—dam UT-8
Buckhorn Draft—valley VA-3
Buckhorn Draw—valley (2) AZ-5
Buckhorn Draw—valley CO-8
Buckhorn Draw—valley NM-5
Buckhorn Draw—valley (2) TX-5
Buckhorn Draw—valley UT-8
Buckhorn Elem Sch—school FL-3
Buckhorn Fire Control Station—locale CA-9
Buckhorn Flat—bench CA-9
Buckhorn Flat—flat CA-9
Buckhorn Flat—flat (2) UT-8
Buckhorn Fork—stream (2) KY-4
Buckhorn Fork—stream WV-2
Buckhorn Furnace—locale OH-6
Buckhorn Gap—gap KY-4
Buckhorn Gap—gap (2) NC-3
Buckhorn Gap—gap TN-4
Buckhorn Grange—locale PA-2
Buckhorn Guard Station—locale CA-9
Buckhorn Gulch—valley (2) CA-9
Buckhorn Gulch—valley CO-8
Buckhorn Gulch—valley NM-5
Buckhorn Gulch—valley OR-9
Buckhorn Highline Ditch—canal CO-8
Buckhorn Hill—summit AZ-5
Buckhorn Hill—summit WA-9
Buckhorn (historical)—locale MS-4
Buckhorn (historical P.O.)—locale IA-7
Buckhorn Hollow—valley KY-4
Buckhorn Hollow—valley (2) MO-7
Buckhorn Hollow—valley OH-6
Buckhorn Hollow—valley (2) PA-2
Buckhorn Hollow—valley TN-4
Buckhorn Hot Spring—spring ID-8
Buckhorn HS—school AL-4
Buckhorn Island—island IL-6
Buckhorn Island—island NY-2
Buckhorn Island State Park—park NY-2
Buckhorn Key—island FL-3
Buckhorn Knob—summit TN-4
Buckhorn Knob—summit (2) VA-3
Buckhorn Knob—summit WV-2
Buckhorn Knoll—summit UT-8
Buckhorn Lake—lake AK-9
Buckhorn Lake—lake (4) CA-9
Buckhorn Lake—lake ID-8
Buckhorn Lake—lake (3) MI-6
Buckhorn Lake—lake MN-6
Buckhorn Lake—lake NY-2
Buckhorn Lake—lake SC-3
Buckhorn Lake—lake TX-5
Buckhorn Lake—lake WA-9
Buckhorn Lake—reservoir GA-3
Buckhorn Lake—reservoir KY-4
Buckhorn Lake—reservoir (3) NC-3
Buckhorn Lake—reservoir TX-5
Buckhorn Lake Dam—dam (3) NC-3
Buckhorn Lakes—lake CO-8
Buckhorn Lakes Park—park CO-8
Buckhorn Lodge WA-9
Buckhorn Lodge—locale CA-9
Buckhorn Lodge—locale CO-8
Buckhorn Lodge—locale MI-6
Buckhorn Lookout—locale OR-9
Buckhorn (Magisterial District)—fmr MCD VA-3
Buckhorn Meadow—flat (2) OR-9
Buckhorn Meadow Brook CT-1
Buckhorn Meadows—flat WA-9
Buckhorn Meadows Trail—trail OR-9
Buckhorn Mesa—summit NM-5
Buckhorn Mesa—summit UT-8
Buckhorn Mine—mine (2) AZ-5
Buckhorn Mine—mine (2) CA-9
Buckhorn Mine—mine (3) ID-8
Buckhorn Mine—mine NV-8
Buckhorn Mine—mine (2) OR-9
Buckhorn Mine Airp—airport NV-8
Buckhorn Mountain ID-8
Buckhorn Mountain UT-8
Buckhorn Mountain Lake—lake ID-8
Buckhorn Mountains—summit AZ-5
Buckhorn Mtn—summit (2) AZ-5
Buckhorn Mtn—summit (2) CA-9
Buckhorn Mtn—summit CO-8
Buckhorn Mtn—summit GA-3
Buckhorn Mtn—summit (2) ID-8
Buckhorn Mtn—summit MT-8
Buckhorn Mtn—summit (2) NY-2
Buckhorn Mtn—summit NC-3
Buckhorn Mtn—summit OK-5
Buckhorn Mtn—summit (4) OR-9
Buckhorn Mtn—summit (2) PA-2
Buckhorn Mtn—summit SD-7
Buckhorn Mtn—summit TX-5
Buckhorn Mtn—summit UT-8
Buckhorn Mtn—summit VA-3
Buckhorn Mtn—summit (3) WA-9
Buckhorn Natural Area—area PA-2
Buckhorn Oil Field—oilfield LA-4
Buckhorn Pasture—summit NV-8
Buckhorn Peak—summit CA-9
Buckhorn Peak—summit NV-8
Buckhorn Pit—basin MT-8
Buckhorn P.O. MS-4
Buckhorn Point—cape VA-3
Buckhorn Point—cliff AZ-5
Buckhorn Ponds—lake NY-2
Buckhorn Post Office—building AZ-5
Buckhorn Presbyterian Church and the Greer Gymnasium—hist pl KY-4
Buckhorn (Purvis Station)—locale VA-3
Buckhorn Quarters—valley VA-3
Buckhorn Ranch—locale AZ-5
Buckhorn Ranch—locale CA-9
Buckhorn Ranch—locale ID-8
Buckhorn Ranch—locale (2) NV-8
Buckhorn Ranch—locale ND-7
Buckhorn Ranch—locale (2) OR-9
Buckhorn Ranch—locale TX-5
Buckhorn Ranger Station—locale CO-8
Buckhorn Rec Area—park CA-9
Buckhorn Reservoir KY-4
Buckhorn Ridge—ridge AZ-5
Buckhorn Ridge—ridge (5) CA-9
Buckhorn Ridge—ridge GA-3
Buckhorn Ridge—ridge ID-8
Buckhorn Ridge—ridge NV-8
Buckhorn Ridge—ridge NY-2
Buckhorn Ridge—ridge (2) NC-3
Buckhorn Ridge—ridge OR-9
Buckhorn Ridge—ridge PA-2
Buckhorn Ridge—ridge (2) VA-3
Buckhorn Ridge Fire Tower—tower PA-2
Buckhorn Roadside Rest—locale ID-8
Buckhorn Rsvr CA-9
Buckhorn Rsvr—reservoir CA-9
Buckhorn Rsvr—reservoir ID-8
Buckhorn Rsvr—reservoir NV-8
Buckhorn Rsvr—reservoir NC-3
Buckhorn Rsvr—reservoir UT-8
Buckhorn Run—stream MD-2
Buckhorn Run—stream (2) PA-2
Buckhorn Run—stream (2) WV-2
Buck Horn Saddle—gap MT-8
Buckhorn Savanna—plain NC-3
Buckhorn Sch—school FL-3
Buckhorn Sch—school (2) IL-6
Buckhorn Sch—school PA-2
Buckhorn Sch—school VA-3
Buckhorn Sch (historical)—school MS-4
Buckhorn Sch (historical)—school TN-4
Buckhorn Shop Ctr—locale AZ-5
Buckhorn Slope Tank—reservoir AZ-5
Buckhorn Slough—stream AR-4
Buckhorn Slough—stream LA-4
Buckhorn Spring—spring AL-4
Buckhorn Spring—spring (6) AZ-5
Buckhorn Spring—spring (6) CA-9
Buckhorn Spring—spring FL-3
Buckhorn Spring—spring (3) ID-8
Buckhorn Spring—spring NM-5
Buckhorn Spring—spring (7) OR-9
Buckhorn Spring—spring (4) UT-8
Buckhorn Spring—spring (2) WA-9
Buckhorn Spring—spring WI-6
Buckhorn Springs—spring CA-9
Buckhorn Springs—spring NC-3
Buckhorn Springs—spring (2) OR-9
Buckhorn Springs Ranch—locale NE-7
Buckhorn Station—locale CA-9
Buckhorn Summit—summit CA-9
Buckhorn Summit—summit ID-8
Buckhorn Swamp—stream NC-3
Buckhorn Swamp—stream (2) VA-3
Buckhorn Swamp—swamp VA-3
Buckhorn Tank—reservoir (14) AZ-5
Buckhorn Tank—reservoir (4) NM-5
Buckhorn Tank—reservoir (2) TX-5
Buckhorn Tank Number Five—reservoir AZ-5
Buckhorn Tank Number Four—reservoir AZ-5
Buckhorn Tank Number One—reservoir AZ-5
Buckhorn Tank Number Three—reservoir AZ-5
Buckhorn Tank Number Two—reservoir AZ-5
Buckhorn Tanks—reservoir AZ-5
Buckhorn Tavern—locale GA-3
Buckhorn (Township of)—fmr MCD (2) AR-4
Buckhorn (Township of)—fmr MCD (2) NC-3
**Buckhorn (Township of)**—pop pl IL-6
Buckhorn Trail—trail AZ-5
Buckhorn Trail—trail ID-8
Buckhorn Trail—trail (2) PA-2
Buckhorn Trail (Pack)—trail CA-9
Buck Horn Valley—valley AL-4
Buckhorn Wash—valley UT-8
Buckhorn Wash Rock Art Sites—hist pl UT-8
Buckhorn Waterhole—lake CA-9
Buckhorn Water Tank—reservoir AZ-5
Buckhorn Well—well NM-5
Buckhorn Well—well UT-8
Buckhorn Well No 1—well (2) WY-8
Buckhorn Well No 2—well (2) WY-8
Buckhorn Well No 4—well WY-8
Buckhorn Well No 5—well WY-8
Buckhorn Windmill—locale (2) TX-5
Buckhort Branch—stream TN-4
Buck House—hist pl MD-2
Buckhouse Bridge—bridge MT-8
Buckhouse Creek—stream ID-8
**Buckhout Corners**—pop pl NY-2
Buckhurst Oil Field—oilfield MS-4
Buckies Pond—lake MI-6
Buckindy, Mount—summit WA-9
Buckingham PA-2
Buckingham—locale FL-3
Buckingham—locale ID-8
Buckingham—locale KY-4
Buckingham—locale VA-3
**Buckingham**—pop pl (2) CO-8
**Buckingham**—pop pl CT-1
**Buckingham**—pop pl IL-6
**Buckingham**—pop pl IA-7
**Buckingham**—pop pl NJ-2
**Buckingham**—pop pl OH-6
**Buckingham**—pop pl PA-2
**Buckingham**—pop pl TX-5
**Buckingham**—pop pl (3) VA-3
Buckingham, John, House—hist pl MA-1
Buckingham, William A., House—hist pl CT-1
Buckingham Access Point—locale PA-2
Buckingham Apartments—hist pl IN-6
Buckingham Archeol Site—hist pl MD-2
Buckingham Bluffs—cliff CA-9
Buckingham Branch—stream IL-6
**Buckingham Camp**—pop pl NV-8
Buckingham Cave—cave PA-2
Buckingham Cem—cemetery FL-3
Buckingham Cem—cemetery IA-7
Buckingham Cem—cemetery MD-2
Buckingham Cem—cemetery MS-4
Buckingham Cem—cemetery GA-3
Buckingham Cem—cemetery WA-9
Buckingham Central HS—school VA-3
**Buckingham Circle**—pop pl VA-3
Buckingham Coulee—valley MT-8
**Buckingham (County)**—pop pl VA-3
**Buckingham Court House**—pop pl VA-3
Buckingham Courthouse Hist Dist—hist pl VA-3
Buckingham Creek—stream MN-6
Buckingham Draw—valley WA-9
**Buckingham Estates**—pop pl NY-2
Buckingham Exceptional Student Center—school FL-3
Buckingham Female Collegiate Institute Hist Dist—hist pl VA-3
Buckingham Flat—flat AR-4
Buckingham Flats—flat WA-9
Buckingham Ford—locale TN-4
Buckingham Fountain—other IL-6
Buckingham Grove—woods WA-9
**Buckingham Heights**—pop pl DE-2
**Buckingham Heights**—pop pl TN-4
**Buckingham (historical)**—pop pl IA-7
Buckingham (historical P.O.)—locale IA-7
Buckingham Hollow—valley TN-4
Buckingham House—hist pl CT-1
Buckingham House—hist pl TN-4
Buckingham House and Industrial Sch Complex—hist pl MD-2
Buckingham Island—island TN-4
Buckingham Lake—reservoir CO-8
Buckingham Landing—locale SC-3
Buckingham Landing Pond—reservoir SC-3
Buckingham Mine—mine NV-8
Buckingham Mountain Sch—school CA-9
Buckingham Mtn—summit CA-9
Buckingham Mtn—summit PA-2
Buckingham Park—park CO-8
Buckingham Park—park MI-6
**Buckingham Park**—pop pl CA-9
**Buckingham Park**—pop pl NJ-2
Buckingham Park Sch—school NJ-2
Buckingham Peak—summit CA-9
Buckingham Peninsula CA-9
Buckingham-Petty House—hist pl OH-6
Buckingham Plaza CO-8
Buckingham Point—cape CA-9
Buckingham Post Office (historical)—building PA-2
Buckingham Presbyterian Ch—church FL-3
Buckingham Ridge—ridge CA-9
Buckingham Ridge—ridge OH-6
Buckingham Ridge Ch—church OH-6
Buckingham Rsvr—reservoir CT-1
Buckingham Rsvr—reservoir MT-8
Buckingham Sch—school IL-6
Buckingham Sch—school (2) MD-2
Buckingham Sch—school (2) MA-1
Buckingham Sch—school MI-6
Buckingham Sch—school OR-9
Buckingham Sch—school PA-2
Buckingham Spring—spring WA-9
Buckingham Square District—hist pl CT-1
Buckingham Square Hist Dist (Boundary Increase)—hist pl CT-1
Buckinghams Shoals—bar TN-4
**Buckingham (sta.) (Buckingham Valley)**—pop pl PA-2
**Buckingham (subdivision)**—pop pl AL-4
Buckingham Tabernacle—church VA-3
**Buckingham Terrace**—pop pl MD-2
Buckingham Township—fmr MCD IA-7
**Buckingham (Township of)**—pop pl (2) PA-2
**Buckingham Valley**—pop pl PA-2
Buckingham Valley Post Office (historical)—building PA-2
**Buckingham View**—pop pl MD-2
**Buckingham Village**—pop pl NJ-2
Buckingham West—locale FL-3
Buckingham Wharf—locale MD-2
Buckinghorn Cem—cemetery IL-6
Buckinghorse Creek—stream WA-9
Bucking Mule Creek—stream WY-8
Bucking Mule Falls—falls WY-8
Buckins Creek—stream MS-4
Buck Island AR-4
Buck Island MS-4
Buck Island NY-2
Buck Island—island (3) AL-4
Buck Island—island (2) AK-9
Buck Island—island AR-4
Buck Island—island CA-9
Buck Island—island (5) FL-3
Buck Island—island (6) GA-3
Buck Island—island (2) ME-1
Buck Island—island MN-6
Buck Island—island MS-4
Buck Island—island NJ-2
Buck Island—island (4) NY-2
Buck Island—island (5) NC-3
Buck Island—island (2) OR-9
Buck Island—island SC-3
Buck Island—island UT-8
Buck Island—island WA-9
Buck Island—island (2) VI-3
Buck Island Bar—bar AL-4
Buck Island Bar—bar MS-4
Buck Island Bay—bay NC-3
Buck Island Bayou—gut (2) MS-4
Buck Island Bridge—bridge AL-4
Buck Island Channel—channel VI-3
Buck Island Chute—channel AL-4
Buck Island Creek—stream MD-2
Buck Island Creek—stream NC-3
Buck Island Creek—stream VA-3
Buck Island Drain—swamp GA-3
Buck Island (historical)—island AL-4
Buck Island Lake—lake CA-9
Buck Island Lake—lake FL-3
Buck Island No 53—flat AR-4
Buck Island Pond—lake MD-2
Buck Island Pond—lake NC-3
Buck Island Reef Natl Monmt—park VI-3
**Buck Island Subdivision (subdivision)**—pop pl AL-4
Buck Island Swamp—stream SC-3
Buck-ka-buck-ka PA-2
Buck Key—island FL-3
Buck Key Channel—channel FL-3
Buck Knob GA-3
Buck Knob—summit (2) AR-4
Buck Knob—summit CO-8
Buck Knob—summit (5) GA-3
Buck Knob—summit IL-6
Buck Knob—summit IN-6
Buck Knob—summit (4) KY-4
Buck Knob—summit (3) MO-7
Buck Knob—summit (14) NC-3
Buck Knob—summit OH-6
Buck Knob—summit SC-3
Buck Knob—summit (5) TN-4
Buck Knob—summit TX-5
Buck Knob—summit (2) VA-3
Buck Knob—summit (7) WV-2
Buck Knob Creek—stream AR-4
Buck Knob Creek—stream IN-6

**Buena Vista**—pop pl (2) ... IN-6
**Buena Vista**—pop pl ... MD-2
**Buena Vista**—pop pl ... MS-4
**Buena Vista**—pop pl ... NM-5
**Buena Vista**—pop pl (4) ... NC-3
**Buena Vista**—pop pl (3) ... OH-6
**Buena Vista**—pop pl ... OR-9
**Buena Vista**—pop pl (5) ... PA-2
**Buena Vista**—pop pl ... TN-4
**Buena Vista**—pop pl (2) ... TX-5
**Buena Vista**—pop pl ... UT-8
**Buena Vista**—pop pl ... WA-9
**Buena Vista**—pop pl ... WI-6
**Buena Vista**—pop pl (8) ... PR-3
Buena Vista—uninc pl ... WV-2
Buena Vista, Canada—stream ... CA-9
Buena Vista Baptist Church ... TN-4
Buena Vista (Barrio)—fmr MCD (4) ... PR-3
Buena Vista Branch—stream ... KY-4
Buena Vista Branch—stream ... VA-3
**Buena Vista (Buena Vista Trailer City)**—pop pl ... FL-3
Buena Vista Butte—ridge ... OR-9
Buena Vista Campground—locale ... MT-8
Buena Vista Canal—canal ... CA-9
Buena Vista Canal—canal ... OR-9
Buena Vista Canyon—valley ... CA-9
Buena Vista Cattle Camp—locale ... NM-5
Buena Vista (CCD)—cens area ... GA-3
Buena Vista Cem—cemetery ... GA-3
Buena Vista Cem—cemetery ... IL-6
Buena Vista Cem—cemetery ... LA-4
Buena Vista Cem—cemetery ... MI-6
Buena Vista Cem—cemetery ... MS-4
Buena Vista Cem—cemetery ... OK-5
Buena Vista Cem—cemetery ... OR-9
Buena Vista Cem—cemetery ... PA-2
Buena Vista Cem—cemetery ... TN-4
Buena Vista Cem—cemetery (3) ... TX-5
Buena Vista Cem—cemetery ... WI-6
Buenavista Ch—church ... IN-6
Buena Vista Ch—church ... IN-6
Buena Vista Ch—church ... MS-4
Buena Vista Ch—church (2) ... TN-4
Buena Vista Ch—church ... TX-5
Buena Vista Ch—church ... WI-6
Buena Vista Ch (historical)—church ... MS-4
Buena Vista Coll—school ... IA-7
Buenavista Community ... TX-5
Buena Vista Cotton Gin—hist pl ... MS-4
Buena Vista County Home—building ... IA-7
Buena Vista County Park—park ... IA-7
Buena Vista Creek ... WI-6
Buena Vista Creek—stream ... AZ-5
Buena Vista Creek—stream (5) ... CA-9
Buena Vista Creek—stream ... KY-4
Buena Vista Creek—stream ... NV-8
Buena Vista Creek—stream ... OR-9
Buena Vista Creek—stream ... WI-6
Buena Vista Crest—ridge ... CA-9
Buena Vista Ditch—canal ... NM-5
Buena Vista Draw ... TX-5
Buena Vista Draw—valley ... TX-5
Buena Vista Estates—locale ... KY-4
**Buena Vista Estates (subdivision)**—pop pl ... NC-3
Buena Vista Farms—hist pl ... WV-2
Buena Vista Grove—woods ... CA-9
Buena Vista Heights ... OH-6
**Buena Vista Highlands**—pop pl ... AL-4
Buena Vista Hills—other ... CA-9
Buena Vista Hills—summit ... NV-8
Buena Vista Hist Dist—hist pl ... TN-4
Buena Vista (historical)—locale ... KS-7
Buena Vista (historical)—locale ... NV-8
**Buena Vista (historical)**—pop pl ... IA-7
**Buena Vista (historical)**—pop pl ... MS-4
Buena Vista Hotel—hist pl ... AZ-5
Buena Vista Hotel—hist pl ... TX-5
Buena Vista House—hist pl ... WI-6
Buena Vista HS—school ... MI-6
Buena Vista HS (historical)—school ... MS-4
**Buena Vista (ind. city)**—pop pl ... VA-3
Buena Vista Island—island ... MS-4
Buena Vista Lagoon—lake ... CA-9
Buena Vista Lake ... CA-9
Buena Vista Lake—flat ... OR-9
Buena Vista Lake—lake ... AZ-5
Buena Vista Lake—lake ... CA-9
Buena Vista Lake—lake ... OR-9
Buena Vista Lake—reservoir ... GA-3
Buena Vista Lake Bed—flat ... CA-9
Buena Vista Lake Dam—dam ... MS-4
**Buena Vista Lakes**—pop pl ... MS-4
Buena Vista Lakes Dam—dam ... MS-4
Buena Vista Landing ... AL-4
Buena Vista Landing—locale ... MS-4
Buena Vista Landmark Baptist Ch (historical)—church ... MS-4
Buena Vista (Magisterial District)—fmr MCD ... VA-3
Buena Vista Memorial Park Cem—cemetery ... IA-7
Buena Vista Mine—mine ... CO-8
Buena Vista Mine—mine ... NV-8
Buena Vista Missionary Baptist Ch (historical)—church ... MS-4
Buena Vista Mound Cem—cemetery ... IA-7
Buena Vista Mtn—summit ... CA-9
Buena Vista Normal Coll (historical)—school ... MS-4
Buena Vista Ocean Wayside State Park—park ... OR-9
Buena Vista Overlook—locale ... VA-3
Buena Vista Park—park (2) ... CA-9
Buena Vista Park—park ... FL-3
Buena Vista Park—park ... TN-4
Buena Vista Park—park ... WI-6
Buena Vista Patrol Station—locale ... OR-9
Buena Vista Peak—summit ... AZ-5
Buena Vista Peak—summit ... CA-9
Buena Vista Peak—summit ... CO-8
Buena Vista Peaks—summit ... CA-9
Buena Vista Plantation (historical)—locale ... MS-4
Buena Vista Point—cape ... FL-3
Buenavista Post Office ... TN-4
Buena Vista Post Office—building ... TN-4
Buena Vista Presbyteran Ch (historical)—church ... MS-4
Buena Vista Pumping Plant—other ... CA-9
Buena Vista Ranch—locale ... AZ-5
Buena Vista Ranch—locale (2) ... CA-9
Buena Vista Ranch—locale ... NV-8
Buena Vista Ranch—locale ... NM-5
Buena Vista Ranch—locale (2) ... TX-5
Buena Vista Reservoir—reserve ... CA-9
Buena Vista Sch—school (6) ... CA-9
Buena Vista Sch—school ... CO-8
Buena Vista Sch—school ... FL-3
Buena Vista Sch—school ... IL-6
Buena Vista Sch—school ... IA-7
Buena Vista Sch—school ... KY-4
Buena Vista Sch—school ... MO-7
Buena Vista Sch—school ... MT-8
Buena Vista Sch—school ... NM-5
Buena Vista Sch—school ... PA-2
Buena Vista Sch—school ... TN-4
Buena Vista Sch—school ... TX-5
Buena Vista Sch—school ... WV-2
Buena Vista Sch (abandoned)—school ... PA-2
Buena Vista Sch (historical)—school (2) ... MS-4
Buena Vista Sch (historical)—school ... TN-4
Buena Vista School(Abandoned)—locale ... IA-7
**Buena Vista Shores**—pop pl ... MA-1
Buena Vista Ski Area—other ... MN-6
Buena Vista Slough ... CA-9
Buena Vista Spring—spring ... AZ-5
Buena Vista Spring—spring ... OR-9
**Buena Vista Springs**—pop pl ... PA-2
**Buena Vista (sta.)**—pop pl ... KY-4
Buena Vista State For—forest (2) ... MN-6
**Buena Vista (subdivision)**—pop pl ... AL-4
**Buena Vista (subdivision)**—pop pl ... TN-4
**Buena Vista Subdivision**—pop pl (3) ... UT-8
Buena Vista Tank—reservoir ... NM-5
Buena Vista Tank—reservoir ... TX-5
**Buena Vista (Town of)**—pop pl (2) ... WI-6
Buena Vista Township—fmr MCD (2) ... IA-7
**Buena Vista Township**—pop pl ... ND-7
Buena Vista Township (historical)—civil ... SD-7
**Buena Vista (Township of)**—pop pl ... IL-6
**Buena Vista (Township of)**—pop pl ... MI-6
**Buena Vista (Township of)**—pop pl ... NJ-2
Buena Vista Track—other ... MO-7
Buena Vista Trail—trail (2) ... CA-9
Buena Vista Trailer City—other ... FL-3
Buena Vista United Methodist Ch—church ... MS-4
Buena Vista Valley—basin ... NV-8
Buena Vista Valley—valley ... CA-9
Buena Vista Vineyards-Buena Vista Vinicultural Society—hist pl ... CA-9
Buena Vista Windmill—locale ... NV-8
Buena Vista Windmill—locale ... NM-5
Buena Vista Windmill—locale (5) ... TX-5
Buena Vista Windmills—locale ... TX-5
Buena Vista Wine Cellars—other ... CA-9
**Buen Consejo**—pop pl ... PR-3
Buenna—locale ... WA-9
Buenna Bar—bar ... WA-9
Buenna Hill—hist pl ... KY-4
Buenna Vista Landing (historical)—locale ... AL-4
Bueno Gulch ... CO-8
Bueno Lower Branch, Canal (historical)—canal ... AZ-5
Bueno Mtn—summit ... CO-8
Buenos—locale ... TX-5
Buenos Aires—locale ... AZ-5
Buenos Aires—locale ... TX-5
**Buenos Aires**—pop pl ... PR-3
Buenos Aires Artesian Well—well ... TX-5
Buenos Aires (Barrio)—fmr MCD ... PR-3
Buenos Aires Ranch—locale ... AZ-5
Buenos Aires Sch—school ... TX-5
Buenos Aires Well—well ... TX-5
Buenos Aires Windmill—locale (4) ... TX-5
Buenos Ayres ... AZ-5
Buenos Ayres Creek ... CA-9
Bueno Tank—reservoir ... AZ-5
Bueno Vista Windmill—locale ... TX-5
Buen Pastor—church ... PR-3
Buenete Creek—stream ... IN-6
Bue Passage—channel ... MP-9
Buer Branch—stream ... TX-5
Buerkle Sch—school ... AR-4
Buescher Band Instrument Company Bldg—hist pl ... IN-6
Buescher Creek—stream ... MO-7
Buescher Lake—reservoir ... TX-5
Buescher State Park—park ... TX-5
Buesch Lake—lake ... WA-9
Bue-Suido ... MP-9
Buether Dam—dam ... OR-9
Buether Rsvr—reservoir ... OR-9
Buet Island ... FM-9
Bue Township (historical)—civil ... ND-7
**Bueyeros**—pop pl ... NM-5
Bueyeros Canyon—valley ... NM-5
Bueyeros Creek—stream (2) ... NM-5
Bueyeros Windmill—locale ... NM-5
Bueyes Arroyo—valley ... TX-5
Bufalo—CDP ... PR-3
Bufa Creek ... NC-3
Buffalo ... AR-4
Buffalo ... CO-8
Buffalo ... IN-6
Buffalo ... KS-7
Buffalo ... MI-6
Buffalo ... MS-4
Buffalo ... NC-3
Buffalo ... OH-6
Buffalo ... WV-2
Buffalo ... WI-6
Buffalo—locale ... AL-4
Buffalo—locale ... KY-4
Buffalo—locale ... ME-1
Buffalo—locale ... NE-7
Buffalo—locale ... OH-6
Buffalo—locale (2) ... SC-3
Buffalo—locale (3) ... TN-4
Buffalo—locale (3) ... TX-5
Buffalo—other ... WV-2
**Buffalo**—pop pl ... AL-4
**Buffalo**—pop pl ... IL-6
**Buffalo**—pop pl (3) ... IN-6
**Buffalo**—pop pl (2) ... IA-7
**Buffalo**—pop pl ... KS-7
**Buffalo**—pop pl ... KY-4
**Buffalo**—pop pl ... MN-6
**Buffalo**—pop pl ... MO-7
**Buffalo**—pop pl ... MT-8
**Buffalo**—pop pl ... NY-2
**Buffalo**—pop pl (2) ... NC-3
**Buffalo**—pop pl ... ND-7
**Buffalo**—pop pl ... OH-6
**Buffalo**—pop pl ... OK-5
**Buffalo**—pop pl ... PA-2
**Buffalo**—pop pl ... SC-3
**Buffalo**—pop pl ... SD-7
**Buffalo**—pop pl ... TN-4
**Buffalo**—pop pl ... TX-5
**Buffalo**—pop pl ... WV-2
**Buffalo**—pop pl ... WI-6
**Buffalo**—pop pl ... WY-8
Buffalo, Lake—lake ... WY-8
Buffalo African Methodist Episcopal Ch ... MS-4
Buffalo-Alice Interchange—crossing ... ND-7
Buffalo and Erie County Historical Society—hist pl ... NY-2
Buffalo Arm No 8—canal ... AR-4
Buffalo Arroyo—stream ... CO-8
Buffalo Arroyo—valley ... TX-5
Buffalo Ave Sch—school ... FL-3
Buffalo Ave Sch—school ... NJ-2
Buffalo Basin—basin ... MT-8
Buffalo Basin—basin (3) ... WY-8
Buffalo Basin—valley ... CO-8
Buffalo Bay—bay ... MN-6
Buffalo Bay—bay ... SD-7
Buffalo Bay—bay ... UT-8
Buffalo Bay—bay ... WI-6
Buffalo Bayou ... AR-4
Buffalo Bayou—gut ... LA-4
Buffalo Bayou—gut ... MS-4
Buffalo Bayou—stream (2) ... LA-4
Buffalo Bayou—stream ... TX-5
Buffalo Bench—bench ... UT-8
**Buffalo Bend**—pop pl ... VA-3
Buffalo Bill Boyhood Home—hist pl ... WY-8
Buffalo Bill Camp—locale ... WY-8
Buffalo Bill Creek—stream ... MT-8
Buffalo Bill Dam—dam ... WY-8
Buffalo Bill Dam—hist pl ... WY-8
Buffalo Bill Homestead—locale ... IA-7
Buffalo Bill Ranch State Park—park ... NE-7
Buffalo Bill Rsvr—reservoir ... WY-8
Buffalo Bill Statue—hist pl ... WY-8
Buffalo Bluff—cliff ... TX-5
**Buffalo Bluff**—pop pl ... FL-3
Buffalo Bog—basin ... MO-7
Buffalo Boy Mine—mine ... CO-8
Buffalo Branch ... TN-4
Buffalo Branch ... VA-3
Buffalo Branch—stream ... AL-4
Buffalo Branch—stream ... IN-6
Buffalo Branch—stream (12) ... KY-4
Buffalo Branch—stream (2) ... MO-7
Buffalo Branch—stream ... NC-3
Buffalo Branch—stream (3) ... TN-4
Buffalo Branch—stream (2) ... TX-5
Buffalo Branch—stream (4) ... VA-3
Buffalo Branch—stream ... WV-2
Buffalo Breaker—building ... PA-2
Buffalo Bridge—bridge ... MT-8
Buffalo Bridge—bridge ... NC-3
Buffalo Bridge Ch—church ... TN-4
Buffalo Bridge Sch—school ... TN-4
Buffalo Brook—stream ... VT-1
Buffalo Butte—summit ... WY-8
Buffalo Buttes—range ... ND-7
Buffalo Buttes—range ... SD-7
Buffalo Calf Fork—stream ... WV-2
Buffalo Camp—locale ... CO-8
Buffalo Camp Bayou—stream ... TX-5
Buffalo Campground—locale ... ID-8
Buffalo Canal ... FL-3
Buffalo Canal—canal ... CO-8
Buffalo Canal—canal ... FL-3
Buffalo Canyon ... MT-8
Buffalo Canyon—valley ... AZ-5
Buffalo Canyon—valley ... CO-8
Buffalo Canyon—valley (2) ... MT-8
Buffalo Canyon—valley (6) ... NV-8
Buffalo Canyon—valley ... UT-8
Buffalo Canyon—valley ... WY-8
Buffalo Cave—cave ... SD-7
Buffalo Cave—cave ... TN-4
Buffalo Caves—cave ... ID-8
Buffalo Caves Flow—lava ... ID-8
Buffalo (CCD)—cens area ... KY-4
Buffalo (CCD)—cens area ... OK-5
Buffalo (CCD)—cens area ... TX-5
Buffalo Cem—cemetery ... AR-4
Buffalo Cem—cemetery ... KS-7
Buffalo Cem—cemetery ... KY-4
Buffalo Cem—cemetery ... ME-1
Buffalo Cem—cemetery (2) ... MS-4
Buffalo Cem—cemetery ... MO-7
Buffalo Cem—cemetery ... NY-2
Buffalo Cem—cemetery (2) ... OK-5
Buffalo Cem—cemetery (3) ... SD-7
Buffalo Cem—cemetery ... VA-3
Buffalo Cemetery ... TN-4
**Buffalo Center**—pop pl ... IA-7
Buffalo Ch—church (3) ... AR-4
Buffalo Ch—church ... KY-4
Buffalo Ch—church (2) ... MS-4
Buffalo Ch—church ... MO-7
Buffalo Ch—church (6) ... NC-3
Buffalo Ch—church (4) ... OK-5
Buffalo Ch—church (2) ... PA-2
Buffalo Ch—church (2) ... SC-3
Buffalo Ch—church (3) ... TN-4
Buffalo Ch—church (6) ... VA-3
Buffalo Ch—church (2) ... WV-2
Buffalo Ch—church ... WI-6
Buffalo Ch (historical)—church ... TN-4
Buffalo Ch of Christ—church ... TN-4
Buffalo City ... KS-7
**Buffalo City**—pop pl ... AR-4
**Buffalo City**—pop pl ... NC-3
**Buffalo City**—pop pl ... WI-6
**Buffalo City (Buffalo)**—pop pl ... AR-4
Buffalo City Park Pavilion—hist pl ... OK-5
Buffalo Cliff—cliff ... KY-4
Buffalo Clover Knob—summit ... VA-3
Buffalo Club—locale ... MO-7
Buffalo Coast Guard Base—military ... NY-2
Buffalo Community Ch—church ... OH-6
Buffalo Consolidated School ... PA-2
**Buffalo Corners**—pop pl ... NY-2
Buffalo Corral—locale ... AZ-5
Buffalo Coulee ... ND-7
Buffalo Coulee—stream ... ND-7
Buffalo Coulee—valley (3) ... MT-8
Buffalo Coulee—valley ... ND-7
Buffalo Country Club—other ... NY-2
Buffalo County—civil ... SD-7
**Buffalo (County)**—pop pl ... WI-6
Buffalo Cove—bay ... MO-7
Buffalo Cove—lake ... LA-4
**Buffalo Cove**—pop pl ... NC-3
Buffalo Cove—valley ... NC-3
Buffalo Cove—valley ... TN-4
Buffalo Cove Creek—stream ... TN-4
Buffalo Creek ... GA-3
Buffalo Creek ... IA-7
Buffalo Creek ... KS-7
Buffalo Creek ... KY-4
Buffalo Creek ... MN-6
Buffalo Creek ... NV-8
Buffalo Creek ... NY-2
Buffalo Creek ... NC-3
Buffalo Creek ... PA-2
Buffalo Creek ... TN-4
Buffalo Creek ... TX-5
Buffalo Creek ... VA-3
Buffalo Creek ... WY-8
Buffalo Creek—cens area ... MT-8
Buffalo Creek—other ... KY-4
**Buffalo Creek**—pop pl ... CO-8
**Buffalo Creek**—pop pl ... PA-2
**Buffalo Creek**—pop pl ... WV-2
Buffalo Creek—stream ... AL-4
Buffalo Creek—stream (2) ... AK-9
Buffalo Creek—stream (6) ... AR-4
Buffalo Creek—stream ... CA-9
Buffalo Creek—stream (8) ... CO-8
Buffalo Creek—stream (6) ... GA-3
Buffalo Creek—stream (2) ... ID-8
Buffalo Creek—stream (2) ... IL-6
Buffalo Creek—stream (3) ... IN-6
Buffalo Creek—stream (9) ... IA-7
Buffalo Creek—stream (9) ... KS-7
Buffalo Creek—stream (15) ... KY-4
Buffalo Creek—stream ... MD-2
Buffalo Creek—stream ... MI-6
Buffalo Creek—stream (4) ... MN-6
Buffalo Creek—stream (4) ... MO-7
Buffalo Creek—stream (16) ... MT-8
Buffalo Creek—stream (9) ... NE-7
Buffalo Creek—stream (5) ... NV-8
Buffalo Creek—stream ... NY-2
Buffalo Creek—stream (22) ... NC-3
Buffalo Creek—stream (5) ... ND-7
Buffalo Creek—stream (2) ... OH-6
Buffalo Creek—stream (11) ... OK-5
Buffalo Creek—stream (6) ... PA-2
Buffalo Creek—stream (8) ... SC-3
Buffalo Creek—stream (5) ... SD-7
Buffalo Creek—stream (9) ... TN-4
Buffalo Creek—stream (25) ... TX-5
Buffalo Creek—stream ... UT-8
Buffalo Creek—stream (11) ... VA-3
Buffalo Creek—stream (20) ... WV-2
Buffalo Creek—stream (12) ... WY-8
Buffalo Creek—uninc pl ... NY-2
Buffalo Creek Campground—locale ... CO-8
Buffalo Creek Campground—locale ... MO-7
Buffalo Creek Cave—cave ... PA-2
Buffalo Creek County Park—park ... IA-7
Buffalo Creek County Parkway—park ... IA-7
Buffalo Creek Dam—dam ... ND-7
Buffalo Creek Ditch—canal ... AR-4
Buffalo Creek Game Mngmt Dam—dam ... IA-7
Buffalo Creek Ranch—locale ... WY-8
Buffalo Creek Reservoir ... NC-3
Buffalo Creek Rsvr—reservoir ... WV-2
Buffalo Creek Sch—school ... KY-4
Buffalo Creek Sch—school ... NE-7
Buffalo Creek Sch—school ... SD-7
Buffalo Creek State Game Mngmt Area—park ... IA-7
Buffalo Crossing—locale ... AZ-5
Buffalo Crossing Camp—park ... AZ-5
Buffalo Cross Roads ... PA-2
**Buffalo Cross Roads**—pop pl ... PA-2
**Buffalo Crossroads**—pop pl ... PA-2
Buffalo Dam ... ND-7
Buffalo Dam—dam ... OR-9
Buffalo Ditch ... AR-4
Buffalo Ditch—canal ... WY-8
Buffalo Ditch No 1—canal ... AR-4
Buffalo Ditch No 39—canal (2) ... MO-7
Buffalo Dome—summit ... AK-9
Buffalo Draw ... TX-5
Buffalo Draw—valley ... ID-8
Buffalo Draw—valley ... NM-5
Buffalo Draw—valley (5) ... TX-5
Buffalo-Dung River ... KS-7
Buffalo Elem Sch—school ... IN-6
Buffaloe Mills (historical)—locale ... MS-4
Buffalo Falls—falls ... MT-8
Buffalo Flat—flat ... IN-6
Buffalo Flat—flat ... WY-8
Buffalo Flat Church (Abandoned)—locale ... NE-7
Buffalo Flats—flat (2) ... NE-7
Buffalo Ford ... WY-8
Buffalo Ford—locale ... VA-3
Buffalo Ford—locale ... WY-8
**Buffalo Forge**—pop pl ... VA-3
Buffalo Forge Station—locale ... VA-3
Buffalo Fork ... MT-8
Buffalo Fork ... WV-2
Buffalo Fork ... WY-8
Buffalo Fork—locale ... KY-4
Buffalo Fork—stream ... KY-4
Buffalo Fork—stream (2) ... OH-6
Buffalo Fork—stream ... VA-3
Buffalo Fork—stream (2) ... WV-2
Buffalo Fork—stream (2) ... WY-8
Buffalo Fork Dam—dam ... WV-2
Buffalo Fork Entrance Station—locale ... WY-8
Buffalo Fork (historical P.O.)—locale ... IA-7
Buffalo Fork of White River ... AR-4
Buffalo Fork Ranger Station—locale ... MT-8
Buffalo Fresh Air Mission—locale ... NY-2
Buffalo Furnace ... PA-2
Buffalo Gap—gap ... AR-4
Buffalo Gap—gap (2) ... KY-4
Buffalo Gap—gap ... OK-5
Buffalo Gap—gap ... PA-2
Buffalo Gap—gap ... SD-7
Buffalo Gap—gap ... TN-4
Buffalo Gap—gap ... TX-5
Buffalo Gap—gap ... VA-3
**Buffalo Gap**—pop pl ... SD-7
**Buffalo Gap**—pop pl (2) ... TX-5
**Buffalo Gap**—pop pl ... VA-3
Buffalo Gap Camp—locale ... WV-2
Buffalo Gap Campground—locale ... ND-7
Buffalo Gap Cem—cemetery ... SD-7
Buffalo Gap Cem—cemetery ... TX-5
Buffalo Gap Cheyenne River Bridge—hist pl ... SD-7
Buffalo Gap Post Office (historical)—building ... SD-7
Buffalo Gas Light Company Works—hist pl ... NY-2
Buffalo Golf Course—locale ... PA-2
Buffalo Grange—locale ... PA-2
Buffalo Grass Ch—church ... CO-8
Buffalo Grass Creek—stream ... NM-5
Buffalo Grounds ... IN-6
Buffalo Grove—locale ... IA-7
**Buffalo Grove**—pop pl (2) ... IL-6
Buffalo Grove Ch—church ... NE-7
Buffalo Grove Ch—church ... TN-4
Buffalo Grove (historical P.O.)—locale ... IA-7
Buffalo Grove Sch—school ... IL-6
Buffalo Gulch ... MT-8
Buffalo Gulch—valley ... AZ-5
Buffalo Gulch—valley (3) ... CO-8
Buffalo Gulch—valley ... ID-8
Buffalo Gulch—valley (2) ... MT-8
Buffalo Gulch—valley ... OR-9
Buffalo Gulch—valley (2) ... WY-8
**Buffalo Hart**—pop pl ... IL-6
Buffalo Hart Township—civil ... MO-7
Buffalo Hart (Township of)—civ div ... IL-6
Buffalo Head ... WY-8
Buffalo Head—summit ... NM-5
Buffalo Head—summit ... OK-5
Buffalo Head Gulch—valley ... MT-8
Buffalo Head Slough ... TX-5
Buffalo Head Slough—stream ... AR-4
Buffalo Head Spring—spring ... MT-8
**Buffalo Heights**—pop pl ... IA-7
Buffalo Hide Creek—stream ... TN-4
Buffalo High Point ... TN-4
**Buffalo Hill**—pop pl ... CA-9
**Buffalo Hill**—pop pl ... VA-3
Buffalo Hill—summit ... AL-4
Buffalo Hill—summit ... AZ-5
Buffalo Hill—summit (2) ... KY-4
Buffalo Hill—summit ... ME-1
Buffalo Hill—summit ... MA-1
Buffalo Hill—summit ... MS-4
Buffalo Hill—summit ... MT-8
Buffalo Hill—summit ... OK-5
Buffalo Hill—summit ... SD-7
Buffalo Hill—summit ... TN-4
Buffalo Hill Cem—cemetery ... OH-6
**Buffalo Hills**—pop pl (2) ... VA-3
Buffalo Hills—summit ... NV-8
Buffalo Hills—summit ... WV-2
Buffalo Hills Rsvr Number 10—reservoir ... NV-8
Buffalo Hills Rsvr Number 6—reservoir ... NV-8
Buffalo Hills Rsvr Number 7—reservoir ... NV-8
Buffalo Hills Rsvr Number 8—reservoir ... NV-8
Buffalo Hills Rsvr Number 9—reservoir ... NV-8
Buffalo Hill Tank—reservoir ... AZ-5
Buffalo Hole—bend ... LA-4
Buffalo Hole—lake ... MS-4
Buffalo Hollow—valley (2) ... KY-4
Buffalo Hollow—valley ... NY-2
Buffalo Hollow—valley (3) ... TN-4
Buffalo Hollow—valley (2) ... TX-5
Buffalo Hollow—valley ... UT-8
Buffalo Hollow—valley ... VA-3
Buffalo Hollow—valley ... WV-2
Buffalo Horn Branch—stream ... KY-4
Buffalo Horn Cem—cemetery ... KY-4
Buffalo Horn Creek—stream ... MT-8
Buffalo Horn Lakes—lake ... MT-8
Buffalo Horn Pass—gap ... MT-8
Buffalo Horn Ridge—ridge ... MT-8
Buffalo Horn Sch—school ... KY-4
Buffalo Horn Station—locale ... MT-8
Buffalo Hump—cliff ... AR-4
Buffalo Hump—summit ... AR-4
Buffalo Hump—summit ... ID-8
Buffalo Hump—summit (2) ... WY-8
Buffalo Hump Basin—basin ... WY-8
Buffalo Hump Lake—lake ... WY-8
Buffalo Hump Mine—mine ... NV-8
Buffalo Idaho Mine—mine ... ID-8
Buffalo Indian Village Site—hist pl ... WV-2
Buffalo Iron Works ... TN-4
Buffalo Island—area ... MO-7
Buffalo Island—island ... AL-4
Buffalo Island—island (2) ... MO-7
Buffalo Island—island ... NE-7
Buffalo Island—island ... NC-3
Buffalo Island—island ... WI-6
Buffalo Islands ... TN-4
Buffalo Jones Elem Sch—school ... KS-7
Buffalo Jump—cliff (3) ... MT-8
Buffalo Jump—summit (2) ... MT-8
Buffalo Jump Ranch—locale ... MT-8
Buffalo Jumps—cliff ... MT-8
Buffalo Junction—locale ... VA-3
Buffalo Junction—uninc pl ... NY-2
Buffalo Knob ... WV-2
Buffalo Knob—summit ... KY-4
Buffalo Knob—summit (2) ... MO-7
Buffalo Knob—summit ... NC-3
Buffalo Knob—summit ... TX-5
Buffalo Knob—summit ... VA-3
Buffalo Knob—summit ... WV-2
Buffalo Lake ... MN-6
Buffalo Lake ... TX-5
Buffalo Lake ... WI-6
Buffalo Lake—lake ... CO-8
Buffalo Lake—lake ... FL-3
Buffalo Lake—lake ... ID-8
Buffalo Lake—lake ... IL-6
Buffalo Lake—lake (7) ... MN-6
Buffalo Lake—lake ... MT-8
Buffalo Lake—lake (2) ... NM-5
Buffalo Lake—lake ... ND-7
Buffalo Lake—lake ... SD-7
Buffalo Lake—lake ... TX-5
Buffalo Lake—lake (4) ... WI-6
Buffalo Lake—lake ... WY-8
**Buffalo Lake**—pop pl ... MN-6
Buffalo Lake—reservoir ... NC-3
Buffalo Lake—reservoir (2) ... ND-7
Buffalo Lake—reservoir ... OR-9
Buffalo Lake—reservoir ... TX-5
Buffalo Lake—reservoir ... VA-3
Buffalo Lake—reservoir ... WI-6
Buffalo Lake—swamp ... LA-4
Buffalo Lake—uninc pl ... NY-2
Buffalo Lake Cem—cemetery ... MN-6
Buffalo Lake Ch—church (2) ... MN-6
Buffalo Lake Ch—church ... SD-7
Buffalo Lake Dam—dam (2) ... NC-3
Buffalo Lake Diversion Dam—dam ... ND-7
Buffalo Lake (Lake Annum)—lake ... WA-9
Buffalo Lake Natl Wildlife Ref—park ... ND-7
Buffalo Lake Natl Wildlife Ref—park ... TX-5
Buffalo Lakes ... TX-5
Buffalo Lakes—lake ... MT-8
Buffalo Lakes—lake ... SD-7
Buffalo Lakes—reservoir ... NC-3
Buffalo Lake Sch Number 2—school ... ND-7
Buffalo Lake State Wildlife Mngmt Area—park ... MN-6
Buffalo Landing—locale ... TN-4
Buffalo Launch Club—other ... NY-2
Buffalolick Branch—stream ... WV-2
Buffalo Lick Ch—church ... KY-4
Buffalo Lick Knob—summit ... KY-4
Buffalo Lick Monmt—park ... GA-3
Buffalo Lick Run—stream ... VA-3
Buffalolick Run—stream (2) ... WV-2
Buffalo Lick Sch—school ... WV-2
Buffalo Lodge—hist pl ... OK-5
Buffalo Lodge—locale ... ID-8
Buffalo Lodge Butte—summit ... ND-7
Buffalo Lodge Lake—lake ... ND-7
Buffalo Lookout Tower—locale ... AR-4
Buffalo Lookout Tower—locale ... MS-4
Buffalo (Magisterial District)—fmr MCD (2) ... VA-3
Buffalo (Magisterial District)—fmr MCD (3) ... WV-2
Buffalo Main Light—hist pl ... NY-2
Buffalo Male and Female Institute ... TN-4
Buffalo Mall (Shop Ctr)—locale ... ND-7
Buffalo Marsh Run—stream ... VA-3
Buffalo May Township—civil ... MO-7
Buffalo Meadow—flat ... WY-8
Buffalo Meadows ... WY-8
Buffalo Meadows—flat ... CO-8
Buffalo Meadows—flat (2) ... NV-8
Buffalo Meadows—flat ... WY-8
Buffalo Meadows—stream ... NC-3
Buffalo Meadows Ranch—locale ... NV-8
Buffalo Memorial Park—cemetery ... WV-2
Buffalo Mill Creek—stream ... FL-3
**Buffalo Mills**—pop pl (2) ... PA-2
Buffalo Mills Gap—gap ... PA-2
Buffalo Mine ... TN-4
Buffalo Mine—mine ... AK-9
Buffalo Mine—mine (3) ... CA-9
Buffalo Mine—mine ... OR-9
**Buffalo Mines**—pop pl ... VA-3
Buffalo Mop—locale ... TX-5
Buffalo Mound—summit ... KS-7
Buffalo Mountain Ch—church ... VA-3
Buffalo Mountain Park—park ... TN-4
Buffalo Mountain Trail—trail ... PA-2
Buffalo Mtn—summit ... AK-9
Buffalo Mtn—summit ... AR-4
Buffalo Mtn—summit (2) ... CO-8
Buffalo Mtn—summit ... MT-8
Buffalo Mtn—summit (4) ... NV-8
Buffalo Mtn—summit (3) ... OK-5
Buffalo Mtn—summit (3) ... PA-2
Buffalo Mtn—summit (3) ... TN-4
Buffalo Mtn—summit ... VA-3
Buffalo Mtn—summit (3) ... WV-2
Buffalo Municipal Airp—airport ... MO-7
Buffalo Municipal Bathing Beach—beach ... NY-2
Buffalo Natl River—park ... AR-4
Buffalo North Breakwater South End Light—hist pl ... NY-2
Buffalo Oil Field—oilfield ... SD-7
Buffalo Oil Field—oilfield ... TX-5
Buffalo Outer Harbor—bay ... NY-2
Buffalo Park ... KS-7
Buffalo Park—flat (3) ... CO-8
Buffalo Park—flat ... SD-7
Buffalo Park—flat ... WY-8
Buffalo Park—park ... AZ-5
Buffalo Park—park ... FL-3
Buffalo Park—park ... IL-6
Buffalo Park (historical)—park ... SD-7
Buffalo Park Trail—trail ... CO-8
Buffalo Pass—gap ... AZ-5
Buffalo Pass—gap (2) ... CO-8
Buffalo Pass—gap ... WA-9
Buffalo Pass Campground—locale ... CO-8
Buffalo Pass Campground—park ... AZ-5
Buffalo Pasture, The—flat ... MT-8
Buffalo Path—trail ... PA-2
Buffalo Peak ... NV-8
Buffalo Peak—summit (3) ... CO-8
Buffalo Peak—summit ... OR-9
Buffalo Peak—summit ... TX-5
Buffalo Peak—summit ... WY-8
Buffalo Plateau—area (2) ... WY-8
Buffalo Plateau—plain ... MT-8
Buffalo Plateau Trail—trail ... MT-8
Buffalo Plateau Trail—trail ... WY-8
Buffalo Point—cape ... AL-4
Buffalo Point—cape ... UT-8
Buffalo Point—cliff ... CO-8
Buffalo Point—summit ... NV-8
Buffalo Pond—lake ... GA-3
Buffalo Pond—lake ... UT-8
Buffalo Post Office (historical)—building ... TN-4
Buffalo Prairie—flat ... TX-5
**Buffalo Prairie**—pop pl ... IL-6
Buffalo Prairie Cem—cemetery ... IL-6
Buffalo Prairie Ch—church ... IL-6
Buffalo Prairie Ch—church ... MO-7

Buffalo Prairie Town Hall—*locale* IL-6
Buffalo Prairie (Township of)—*civ div* IL-6
Buffalo Presbyterian Church—*hist pl* PA-2
Buffalo Public Use Area—*park* VA-3
Buffalo Ranch—*locale* AZ-5
Buffalo Ranch—*locale* CO-8
Buffalo Ranch—*locale* (2) NV-8
Buffalo Ranch Lake—*reservoir* NC-3
Buffalo Ranch Lake Dam—*dam* NC-3
Buffalo Rapids—*rapids* ID-8
Buffalo Rapids—*rapids* WA-9
Buffalo Ridge—*locale* VA-3
Buffalo Ridge—*post sta* SD-7
Buffalo Ridge—*ridge* AZ-5
Buffalo Ridge—*ridge* CO-8
Buffalo Ridge—*ridge* ID-8
Buffalo Ridge—*ridge* IA-7
Buffalo Ridge—*ridge* MN-6
Buffalo Ridge—*ridge* MT-8
Buffalo Ridge—*ridge* OH-6
Buffalo Ridge—*ridge* PA-2
Buffalo Ridge—*ridge* (2) TN-4
Buffalo Ridge—*ridge* (2) VA-3
Buffalo Ridge—*ridge* (3) WV-2
Buffalo Ridge—*ridge* WI-6
Buffalo Ridge Cem—*cemetery* TN-4
Buffalo Ridge Ch—*church* TN-4
Buffalo Ridge Ch—*church* VA-3
**Buffalo Ridge (historical)**—*pop pl* TN-4
Buffalo Ridge Post Office (historical)—*building* TN-4
Buffalo Ridge Sch—*school* WY-8
Buffalo Ridge Trail—*trail* CO-8
*Buffalo River* VA-3
*Buffalo River* WI-6
Buffalo River—*stream* AR-4
Buffalo River—*stream* GA-3
Buffalo River—*stream* ID-8
Buffalo River—*stream* MN-6
Buffalo River—*stream* MS-4
Buffalo River—*stream* NY-2
Buffalo River—*stream* (2) TN-4
Buffalo River—*stream* VA-3
Buffalo River—*stream* WI-6
Buffalo River State Park—*hist pl* AR-4
Buffalo River State Park—*park* AR-4
Buffalo River State Park—*park* MN-6
Buffalo Road Interchange—*crossing* AZ-5
Buffalo Rock—*pillar* TN-4
Buffalo Rock—*summit* IL-6
Buffalo Rock Community Hall—*building* ND-7
Buffalo Rock Coulee—*stream* ND-7
*Buffalo Rocks Coulee* ND-7
Buffalo Rock State Park—*park* IL-6
Buffalo Rsvr—*reservoir* CO-8
Buffalo Rsvr—*reservoir* OR-9
*Buffalo Run* PA-2
**Buffalo Run**—*pop pl* MD-2
**Buffalo Run**—*pop pl* PA-2
Buffalo Run—*stream* KY-4
Buffalo Run—*stream* MD-2
Buffalo Run—*stream* (3) OH-6
Buffalo Run—*stream* (4) PA-2
Buffalo Run—*stream* (12) WV-2
Buffalo Run Ch—*church* PA-2
Buffalo Run Creek—*stream* WY-8
*Buffalo Run - in part* PA-2
Buffalo Run Sch (historical)—*school* PA-2
Buffalo Scaffold Canyon—*valley* UT-8
Buffalo Sch—*school* IL-6
Buffalo Sch—*school* IA-7
Buffalo Sch—*school* (2) KS-7
Buffalo Sch—*school* (4) KY-4
Buffalo Sch—*school* MO-7
Buffalo Sch—*school* (3) NE-7
Buffalo Sch—*school* OH-6
Buffalo Sch—*school* PA-2
Buffalo Sch—*school* SD-7
Buffalo Sch—*school* (3) TN-4
Buffalo Sch—*school* (2) WV-2
Buffalo Sch (abandoned)—*school* MO-7
Buffalo Sch (historical)—*school* MO-7
Buffalo Sch (historical)—*school* PA-2
Buffalo Sch (historical)—*school* (3) TN-4
Buffalo Scott Butte—*summit* MT-8
Buffalo Seminary—*school* NY-2
Buffalo Shoals—*bar* (2) TN-4
Buffalo Shoals Creek—*stream* NC-3
**Buffalo Shore Estates**—*pop pl* WI-6
*Buffalo Skin Creek* SD-7
Buffalo Skull Lake—*lake* ID-8
*Buffalo Slough* SD-7
Buffalo Slough—*channel* MN-6
Buffalo Slough—*channel* WI-6
Buffalo Slough—*gut* AR-4
Buffalo Slough—*gut* MN-6
Buffalo Slough—*lake* SD-7
Buffalo Slough—*stream* NV-8
Buffalo Slough—*stream* WI-6
Buffalo Slough State Game Ref—*park* SD-7
Buffalo Slu—*gut* WI-6
Buffalo Spring—*spring* KY-4
Buffalo Spring—*spring* MO-7
Buffalo Spring—*spring* (3) MT-8
Buffalo Spring—*spring* (4) NV-8
Buffalo Spring—*spring* NM-5
Buffalo Spring—*spring* (3) OK-5
Buffalo Spring—*spring* (2) TN-4
Buffalo Spring—*spring* TX-5
Buffalo Spring—*spring* (2) UT-8
Buffalo Spring—*spring* VA-3
Buffalo Spring—*spring* WA-9
Buffalo Spring—*spring* WY-8
Buffalo Spring Cem—*cemetery* KY-4
Buffalo Springs—*locale* NM-5
Buffalo Springs—*locale* ND-7
Buffalo Springs—*locale* TN-4
Buffalo Springs—*locale* TX-5
Buffalo Springs—*locale* (2) VA-3
**Buffalo Springs**—*pop pl* PA-2
**Buffalo Springs**—*pop pl* TX-5
Buffalo Springs—*spring* (3) NV-8
Buffalo Springs—*spring* (2) NM-5
Buffalo Springs—*spring* SD-7
Buffalo Springs—*spring* (2) WY-8
Buffalo Springs Cem—*cemetery* TN-4
Buffalo Springs Creek—*stream* MT-8
Buffalo Springs Creek—*stream* SD-7
Buffalo Springs Creek—*stream* WY-8
Buffalo Springs Dam—*dam* ND-7
*Buffalo Springs Fish and Game Preserve* TN-4
Buffalo Springs Game Farm—*park* TN-4
Buffalo Springs Lake—*lake* TX-5
Buffalo Springs Lake—*reservoir* ND-7
Buffalo Springs Ranch—*locale* CO-8
Buffalo Springs Reservoirs—*reservoir* CA-9
Buffalo Springs Sch—*school* CO-8
Buffalo Springs Sch—*school* NC-3
Buffalo Springs State Game Farm—*park* TN-4
Buffalo Springs State Hatchery—*locale* TN-4
Buffalo Spur—*summit* VA-3
Buffalo Square—*park* NE-7
Buffalo Stadium—*other* TX-5
Buffalo State Asylum for the Insane—*hist pl* NY-2
Buffalo State Hosp—*hist pl* NY-2
Buffalo Station—*locale* PA-2
Buffalo Station—*locale* VA-3
*Buffalo Stream* ME-1
Buffalo Stream—*stream* IN-6
Buffalo Stream—*stream* ME-1
Buffalo Summit—*summit* NV-8
*Buffalo Swamp* GA-3
Buffalo Swamp—*swamp* (3) GA-3
Buffalo Switch Hollow—*valley* PA-2
Buffalo Switch Trail—*trail* PA-2
Buffalo Tank—*reservoir* AZ-5
Buffalo Tank—*reservoir* (3) NM-5
Buffalo Tank—*reservoir* (2) TX-5
Buffalo Tanks—*reservoir* AZ-5
**Buffalo (Town of)**—*pop pl* (2) WI-6
Buffalo Township—*civ div* NE-7
Buffalo Township—*civil* (3) MO-7
Buffalo Township—*civil* (2) SD-7
Buffalo Township—*fmr MCD* (5) IA-7
**Buffalo Township**—*pop pl* (3) KS-7
**Buffalo Township**—*pop pl* MO-7
**Buffalo Township**—*pop pl* ND-7
**Buffalo Township**—*pop pl* (4) SD-7
Buffalo Township Elem Sch—*school* PA-2
Buffalo (Township of)—*fmr MCD* (2) AR-4
Buffalo (Township of)—*fmr MCD* MO-7
**Buffalo (Township of)**—*pop pl* IL-6
**Buffalo (Township of)**—*pop pl* MN-6
**Buffalo (Township of)**—*pop pl* OH-6
**Buffalo (Township of)**—*pop pl* (4) PA-2
Buffalo Trading Post—*locale* SD-7
Buffalo Trail—*trail* TN-4
Buffalo Trail Ch—*church* TN-4
Buffalo Trail Scout Camp—*locale* TX-5
Buffalo Trail Shop Ctr—*locale* TN-4
Buffalo-Trinity Cem—*cemetery* WI-6
Buffalo Tunnel—*tunnel* VA-3
Buffalo Valley—*basin* NV-8
Buffalo Valley—*locale* TN-4
**Buffalo Valley**—*pop pl* TN-4
Buffalo Valley—*valley* NM-5
Buffalo Valley—*valley* (2) PA-2
Buffalo Valley—*valley* TN-4
**Buffalo Valley (Buffalo Creek)**—*pop pl* PA-2
Buffalo Valley (CCD)—*cens area* TN-4
Buffalo Valley Ch—*church* TN-4
Buffalo Valley Ch—*church* (2) WV-2
Buffalo Valley Division—*civil* TN-4
Buffalo Valley Farm—*locale* NM-5
Buffalo Valley Hot Springs—*spring* NV-8
Buffalo Valley Mine—*mine* NV-8
Buffalo Valley Post Office—*building* TN-4
Buffalo Valley Ranch—*locale* WY-8
Buffalo Valley Rec Area—*park* TN-4
Buffalo Valley Sch—*school* OK-5
Buffalo Valley Sch (historical)—*school* (2) TN-4
**Buffalo View (subdivision)**—*pop pl* TN-4
*Buffalo Village* PA-2
**Buffaloville**—*pop pl* IN-6
Buffaloville Cem—*cemetery* IN-6
*Buffalo Wallow* AL-4
Buffalo Wallow Branch—*stream* TN-4
Buffalo Wallow Dam—*other* WY-8
Buffalo Wallow Mtn—*summit* OK-5
*Buffalo Wallows* WY-8
Buffalo Wallows—*basin* WY-8
Buffalo Wallow Sch—*school* IA-7
*Buffalo Wallows Creek* WY-8
Buffalo Well—*well* NV-8
Buffalo Well—*well* NM-5
Buffalo Well—*well* TX-5
Buffalo Windmill—*locale* CO-8
Buffalo Windmill—*locale* NM-5
Buffalo Windmill—*locale* (6) TX-5
Buffalo Woman Lake—*lake* MT-8
Buffalo Woods—*woods* IL-6
Buffalo Zoological Garden—*park* NY-2
Buffards Mtn—*summit* VA-3
Buffat, Alfred, Homestead—*hist pl* TN-4
**Buffat Heights**—*pop pl* TN-4
Buffat Heights Baptist Ch—*church* TN-4
Buff Brook—*stream* ME-1
*Buff Brown Creek* MI-6
Buff Cap Hill—*summit* CT-1
Buff Ch—*church* WI-6
*Buff Creek* CO-8
*Buff Creek* IA-7
*Buff Creek* KS-7
*Buff Creek* OK-5
Buff Creek—*stream* MI-6
Buff Creek—*stream* NC-3
Buff Creek—*stream* VA-3
Buff Creek—*stream* (2) WI-6
Buff Creek Ch—*church* NC-3
Buffehr Creek—*stream* CO-8
Buffehr Lake—*lake* CO-8
Buff Elem Sch—*school* OR-9
Buffenbarger Cem—*cemetery* OH-6
*Buffer Creek* CO-8
Bufferin Cem—*cemetery* LA-4
Buffer Run—*stream* OH-6
Buffett, Eliphas, House—*hist pl* NY-2
Buffett, Joseph, House—*hist pl* NY-2
Buffeys Branch—*stream* NC-3
Buffey Sch—*school* MI-6
Buffham Place—*locale* CO-8
*Buffington* IN-6
*Buffington* KS-7
**Buffington**—*pop pl* GA-3
**Buffington**—*pop pl* IN-6
**Buffington**—*pop pl* MO-7
**Buffington**—*pop pl* PA-2
Buffington, Calvin A., House—*hist pl* NY-2
Buffington Cem—*cemetery* AL-4
Buffington Cem—*cemetery* MO-7
Buffington Cem—*cemetery* OK-5
**Buffington Corner**—*pop pl* MA-1
Buffington Creek—*stream* IA-7
Buffington Dam—*dam* PA-2
Buffington Field—*park* AL-4
Buffington Harbor—*harbor* IN-6
Buffington Harbor Breakwater Light—*locale* IN-6
Buffington Harbor Pierhead Light—*locale* IN-6
Buffington Harbor Range Front Light—*locale* IN-6
Buffington Harbor Range Rear Light—*locale* IN-6
Buffington Hollow—*valley* MO-7
Buffington Hotel—*hist pl* OK-5
Buffington Island—*hist pl* OH-6
Buffington Island State Memorial—*park* OH-6
Buffington Memorial Ch—*church* AL-4
*Buffington Memorial Methodist* AL-4
Buffington Memorial Park—*cemetery* OR-9
Buffington Mill Creek—*stream* GA-3
*Buffington Mills* MO-7
Buffington Park—*park* IN-6
Buffington Park—*park* (2) MA-1
Buffington Pockets—*basin* NV-8
Buffington Road Ch—*church* GA-3
Buffington Run—*stream* (2) WV-2
Buffington Sch—*school* WV-2
Buffingtons Island—*island* AL-4
Buffingtons Lagoon—*bay* WA-9
**Buffington (Township of)**—*pop pl* PA-2
Buffin Meadow—*flat* CA-9
*Buffin Pond* VT-1
*Buffinton Corner* MA-1
Buffkin Cem—*cemetery* SC-3
Buffkin Pond—*reservoir* NC-3
*Buff Lake* SC-3
Buff Lake—*lake* WI-6
Buff Lake Bottoms—*bend* TX-5
Bufflehead Lake—*lake* AK-9
*Buffle Point* TX-5
**Buff Lick**—*pop pl* WV-2
Bufflick Branch—*stream* WV-2
Bufflick Fork—*stream* WV-2
Bufflick Run—*stream* WV-2
Bufflick Sch—*school* WV-2
Bufflington Island—*island* OH-6
Buffman Canyon—*valley* CO-8
Buffmeyer Draw—*valley* CO-8
Buff Mound—*summit* KS-7
Buffom Creek—*stream* CA-9
*Bufford* VA-3
Bufford Cem—*cemetery* TN-4
*Bufford Creek* TX-5
Bufford Creek—*stream* TX-5
Bufford Crossroads—*locale* VA-3
**Bufford Cross Roads**—*pop pl* VA-3
*Bufford Hill* AZ-5
Bufford Hollow—*valley* TN-4
Bufford Mtn—*summit* GA-3
Bufford Spring—*spring* TN-4
Buff Peak—*summit* NV-8
Buffs Branch—*stream* WV-2
*Buffs Canyon* UT-8
*Buff Spur* VA-3
Buffs Store (historical)—*locale* AL-4
Buff Tank—*reservoir* NM-5
*Buffton* KS-7
Buffum, Lake—*lake* FL-3
Buffum Brook—*stream* MA-1
**Buffum Hill**—*pop pl* ME-1
*Buffum Lake* VT-1
Buffum Pond—*reservoir* MA-1
Buffum Sch—*school* CA-9
**Buffumville**—*pop pl* MA-1
Buffumville Dam—*dam* MA-1
Buffumville (historical)—*locale* MA-1
Buffumville Lake—*reservoir* MA-1
*Buffumville Rsvr* MA-1
Buffville—*locale* KS-7
Bufinch Ranch—*locale* NE-7
**Bufkin**—*pop pl* IN-6
Bufkin Cem—*cemetery* MS-4
Bufkins Branch—*stream* MS-4
**Bufo (historical)**—*pop pl* OR-9
Bufo Lake—*lake* WI-6
*Buford* AL-4
*Buford* NC-3
*Buford* VA-3
Buford—*locale* AR-4
Buford—*locale* KY-4
Buford—*locale* TX-5
Buford—*locale* VA-3
**Buford**—*pop pl* CO-8
**Buford**—*pop pl* GA-3
**Buford**—*pop pl* ND-7
**Buford**—*pop pl* OH-6
**Buford**—*pop pl* SC-3
**Buford**—*pop pl* TX-5
**Buford**—*pop pl* WY-8
Buford, Spencer, House—*hist pl* TN-4
Buford Ave Sch—*school* CA-9
Buford Bay—*bay* FL-3
Buford Branch—*stream* AL-4
Buford Branch—*stream* TN-4
Buford Branch—*stream* TX-5
Buford Branch—*stream* VA-3
Buford Canyon—*valley* AZ-5
Buford Cave—*cave* AL-4
Buford Cave—*cave* MO-7
Buford (CCD)—*cens area* GA-3
Buford Cem—*cemetery* AL-4
Buford Cem—*cemetery* MS-4
Buford Cem—*cemetery* ND-7
Buford Cem—*cemetery* OH-6
Buford Cem—*cemetery* (4) TN-4
Buford Chapel—*church* MS-4
Buford Consolidated Sch (historical)—*school* MS-4
Buford County (historical)—*civil* ND-7
*Buford Creek* TX-5
Buford Creek—*stream* MS-4
Buford Creek—*stream* MT-8
Buford Creek—*stream* OR-9
Buford Creek—*stream* WA-9
Buford Dam—*dam* GA-3
Buford-Duke House—*hist pl* KY-4
Buford Grove Ch—*church* FL-3
Buford Hill—*summit* AZ-5
Buford Hill—*summit* OR-9
Buford House—*hist pl* CA-9
Buford Island—*island* VA-3
Buford JHS—*school* VA-3
*Buford Lake* GA-3
Buford Lake—*lake* MS-4
Buford Mtn—*summit* CA-9
Buford Mtn—*summit* MO-7
Buford Park—*park* GA-3
Buford Peak—*summit* CO-8
Buford Plantation—*locale* MS-4
Buford Plaza Shop Ctr—*locale* AL-4
Buford Pond—*lake* MO-7
Buford Post Office (historical)—*building* TN-4
Buford Ranger Station—*other* CO-8
Buford Rec Area—*area* OR-9
*Buford Reservoir* GA-3
Buford Ridge—*ridge* CO-8
Buford Ridge—*ridge* OR-9
Buford Ridge—*ridge* WA-9
**Bufords**—*pop pl* TN-4
*Bufords Branch* TX-5
Buford Sch—*school* SC-3
*Bufords Creek* MS-4
*Bufords Creek* TX-5
Buford Site (22TI501)—*hist pl* MS-4
*Bufords Landing* AL-4
*Bufords Station Post Office* TN-4
Bufords Store (historical)—*locale* MS-4
Bufords Store (historical)—*locale* TN-4
Buford Station—*locale* AR-4
Buford Tank—*reservoir* AZ-5
**Buford Township**—*pop pl* ND-7
Buford (Township of)—*fmr MCD* AR-4
Buford (Township of)—*fmr MCD* NC-3
Buford Trail—*trail* WY-8
Buford Waterworks—*other* GA-3
Bufram Creek—*stream* AR-4
**Bug**—*pop pl* KY-4
Bugaboo Canyon—*valley* OK-5
*Bug-a-boo Creek* NC-3
Bugaboo Creek—*stream* IL-6
Bugaboo Creek—*stream* OR-9
Bugaboo Island—*island* GA-3
Bugaboo Landing—*locale* GA-3
Bugaboo Mountain—*ridge* AL-4
Bugaboo Spring—*spring* TN-4
Bugai Site (20SA215)—*hist pl* MI-6
*Buganegan* MP-9
Buganegan—*island* MP-9
*Buganegan Island* MP-9
*Buganegar* MP-9
Bugas Draw—*valley* WY-8
Bugas Spring Creek—*stream* WY-8
Bugaw MS—*school* NC-3
**Bugbee**—*pop pl* ME-1
Bugbee Brook—*stream* ME-1
Bugbee Creek—*stream* TX-5
Bugbee Ranch—*locale* TX-5
Bug Bluff—*cliff* GA-3
Bug Branch—*stream* GA-3
Bug Branch—*stream* MS-4
Bug Branch—*stream* TN-4
Bug Brush Spring—*spring* NV-8
Bug Butte—*summit* OR-9
Bugby Creek—*stream* TX-5
Bugby Hole—*bay* OR-9
Bugby Hole—*bend* OR-9
Bugbyhole—*locale* VI-3
*Bugbys Hole* OR-9
Bug Canyon—*valley* UT-8
*Bug Creek* AZ-5
Bug Creek—*stream* (2) CA-9
Bug Creek—*stream* ID-8
Bug Creek—*stream* (2) MN-6
Bug Creek—*stream* (3) MT-8
Bug Creek—*stream* OK-5
Bug Creek—*stream* (2) OR-9
Bug Creek—*stream* (2) WY-8
Bug Creek Bay—*bay* MT-8
Bug Creek Butte—*summit* CA-9
Bug Creek Camp—*locale* OK-5
*Bugdarmagut* FM-9
Bugdarmaqut—*summit* FM-9
*Bugdarmaut* FM-9
Bugeye Pond—*lake* ME-1
Buggar Bay—*swamp* FL-3
Buggar Lick—*stream* WV-2
Bugg Cabin—*locale* CA-9
Bugg Cem—*cemetery* GA-3
Bugg Creek—*stream* KY-4
Bugge Lake—*lake* AK-9
Buggeln Hill—*summit* AZ-5
Buggeln Tank—*reservoir* AZ-5
Bugger Boo Bay—*bay* MO-7
Bugger Bottom—*basin* AL-4
Bugger Branch—*stream* LA-4
Bugger Hole—*cave* TN-4
Bugger Hole Hollow—*valley* TN-4
Bugger Hollow—*valley* TN-4
Bugger Lake—*lake* WA-9
Buggert Lake—*lake* WI-6
Bugger Well—*well* NM-5
Bugg Landing (historical)—*locale* MS-4
Bugg Lateral—*canal* NM-5
Bugg Mill Hollow—*valley* AL-4
Bugg Point—*cape* MI-6
*Bugg Pond* MA-1
Buggs Bluff—*cliff* GA-3
Buggs Branch—*stream* KY-4
Buggs Cem—*cemetery* MO-7
Bugg Sch—*school* NC-3
Buggs Chapel—*locale* AL-4
Buggs Creek—*stream* FL-3
Buggs Ferry Bridge (historical)—*bridge* MS-4
Buggs Ferry (historical)—*locale* MS-4
Buggs Island—*island* VA-3
*Buggs Island Lake* NC-3
*Buggs Island Lake* VA-3
*Buggs Island Reservoir* NC-3
Bugg Spring—*spring* FL-3
Buggs Sch (historical)—*school* MS-4
Buggtussel Ch—*church* IL-6
Bug Gulch—*valley* AK-9
Bug Gulch—*valley* CA-9
Buggy Branch—*stream* NC-3
Buggy Branch—*stream* TN-4
Buggy Branch—*stream* WV-2
Buggy Brook—*stream* (2) ME-1
Buggy Creek—*stream* MT-8
Buggy Creek—*stream* OK-5
Buggy Gulch—*valley* MT-8
Buggy Hill Cem—*cemetery* AR-4
*Buggy Hollow Creek* OK-5
**Buggy Meetinghouse**—*pop pl* ME-1
Buggy Pond—*lake* ME-1
Buggy Spring—*spring* ID-8
Buggytop Cave—*cave* TN-4
Buggytop Hill—*summit* NM-5
**Buggytown**—*pop pl* KY-4
Buggy Wheel Spring—*spring* UT-8
Buggy Wheel Tank—*reservoir* AZ-5
Buggy Whip Creek—*stream* TX-5
**Bugh**—*pop pl* MS-4
Bughall Creek—*stream* AL-4
*Bughall Creek Lake* AL-4
*Bughall Creek Lake Dam* AL-4
Bugh Ditch—*canal* IN-6
Bugher Draw—*valley* WY-8
Bughill—*locale* NC-3
**Bug Hill**—*pop pl* NC-3
Bug Hill—*summit* MA-1
Bug Hill (Township of)—*fmr MCD* NC-3
*Bughman Landing Field* KS-7
Bug Hollow—*valley* KY-4
Bug Hollow—*valley* (2) TN-4
Bughouse Lake—*lake* WI-6
Bughs Lake—*lake* WI-6
Bugies, Arroyo—*valley* TX-5
Bug Island—*island* (2) AK-9
Bug Island—*island* GA-3
Bug Island—*island* ME-1
*Bug Lake* MN-6
*Bug Lake* WI-6
Bug Lake—*lake* AK-9
Bug Lake—*lake* CA-9
Bug Lake—*lake* (4) MN-6
Bug Lake—*lake* NY-2
Bug Lake—*lake* (2) UT-8
Bug Lake—*lake* (3) WI-6
Bugle Creek—*stream* AK-9
Bugle Creek—*stream* ID-8
Bugle Creek—*stream* MT-8
Bugle Lake—*lake* CA-9
Bugle Lake—*lake* CO-8
Bugle Lake—*lake* WY-8
Bugle Lake—*reservoir* WI-6
*Bugle Mtn* MA-1
Bugle Mtn—*summit* ID-8
Bugle Mtn—*summit* MT-8
Bugle Mtn—*summit* TX-5
Bugle Point—*cape* AK-9
Bugle Ridge—*ridge* ID-8
Bugler Rsvr—*reservoir* ID-8
Bugley Spring—*spring* VA-3
Bugman Ranch—*locale* OR-9
Bug Mesa—*summit* NM-5
*Bug Mud Lake* TX-5
*Bugnall Creek* AL-4
**Bugol**—*pop pl* FM-9
Bugo Lake—*lake* MN-6
Bugomowik Pass—*stream* AK-9
Bug Park—*flat* UT-8
Bug Point—*cape* UT-8
Bug Point—*cliff* CO-8
Bug Point—*summit* CO-8
*Bug Pond* MA-1
Bug Ranch—*locale* WY-8
Bug Ridge—*ridge* WV-2
Bug Ridge Ch—*church* WV-2
Bug Run—*stream* WV-2
Bug Run Sch—*school* WV-2
**Bugscuffle**—*pop pl* TN-4
Bug Scuffle Canyon—*valley* NM-5
Bug Scuffle Ch—*church* AR-4
Bug Scuffle Hill—*summit* NM-5
*Bug Scuffle School* MS-4
Bugs Lake—*reservoir* AL-4
Bugs Lake Dam—*dam* AL-4
Bug Slope—*cliff* ID-8
Bugsmouth Hill—*summit* NH-1
Bug Spring—*spring* AZ-5
Bug Spring—*spring* (2) OR-9
Bugs Swamp—*reservoir* MA-1
Bug Suck Lake—*lake* GA-3
Bug Swamp—*stream* SC-3
Bug Table—*summit* CA-9
Bug Tank—*reservoir* AZ-5
Bug Tanks—*reservoir* AZ-5
**Bugtown**—*pop pl* IN-6
Bugtown Gulch—*valley* SD-7
Bugtown (historical)—*locale* SD-7
Bugtown Mine—*mine* CA-9
*Bugtussell* KY-4
*Bugtussell* TN-4
*Bug Tussle* AL-4
Bugtussle—*locale* KY-4
Bug Tussle—*locale* TX-5
**Bug Tussle**—*pop pl* OK-5
**Bugtussle**—*pop pl* TN-4
Bugtussle Hollow—*valley* TN-4
*Bugudramaut* FM-9
*Bugule Burey* FM-9
Buguleeburey—*summit* FM-9
Buguleek'eef—*bay* FM-9
Buguleeqaryer—*summit* FM-9
*Buguleke f* FM-9
Bug Waterhole—*reservoir* (2) OR-9
Bug Windmill—*locale* (2) TX-5
**Buhach**—*pop pl* CA-9
Buhach Grammar Sch—*hist pl* CA-9
Buhach Lateral—*canal* CA-9
Buhella Lake—*lake* MN-6
**Buhl**—*pop pl* AL-4
**Buhl**—*pop pl* ID-8
**Buhl**—*pop pl* MN-6
Buhl—*uninc pl* PA-2
Buhl, Frank H., Mansion—*hist pl* PA-2
Buhl Bldg—*hist pl* PA-2
Buhl Cem—*cemetery* ID-8
Buhl Ch—*church* AL-4
Buhl City Hall—*hist pl* ID-8
Buhl Elem Sch—*school* AL-4
Buhler—*locale* LA-4
**Buhler**—*pop pl* KS-7
Buhler, Theodore, House—*hist pl* TX-5
Buhler Elem Sch—*school* KS-7
Buhler House—*hist pl* AR-4
Buhler HS—*school* KS-7
Buhler Rsvr—*reservoir* OR-9
Buhler Sch (historical)—*school* TN-4
Buhl IOOF Bldg—*hist pl* ID-8
Buhl Lake—*lake* PA-2
Buhl Lakes—*lake* MI-6
Buhl Lookout Tower—*locale* MN-6
Buhlow, Lake—*lake* LA-4
Buhl Park—*park* MN-6
Buhl Park—*park* PA-2
Buhl Public Library—*hist pl* MN-6
Buhl Ranch—*locale* AZ-5
**Buhls**—*pop pl* PA-2
Buhl Sch—*school* ID-8
Buhl Science Center—*building* PA-2
**Buhls Station**—*pop pl* PA-2
Buhl Village Hall—*hist pl* MN-6
Buhne Point—*cape* CA-9
Buhne Spit Shoal—*bar* CA-9
Buhrer-Garrison Ditch—*canal* MT-8
Buhrer Gulch—*valley* MT-8
Buhrer Sch—*school* MT-8
Buhrig Lake—*lake* WA-9
Buhrman Field—*park* AR-4
Buhrmann Cem—*cemetery* NE-7
Buhr Park—*park* MI-6
Buhrs Run—*stream* OH-6
Buh Town Hall—*locale* MN-6
**Buh (Township of)**—*pop pl* MN-6
*Buibui* MP-9
*Buibui-to* MP-9
Buick—*locale* MO-7
**Buick**—*pop pl* CO-8
**Buick (historical)**—*pop pl* OR-9
Buick Lookout Tower—*locale* MO-7
Buick Mine—*mine* MO-7
*Buick Mine and Mill* MO-7
Buick Sch—*school* MI-6
*Buie* MS-4
**Buie**—*pop pl* AR-4
**Buie**—*pop pl* LA-4
**Buie**—*pop pl* NC-3
Buie Bldg—*hist pl* MS-4
Buie Branch—*stream* AL-4
Buie Branch—*stream* MS-4
Buie Cem—*cemetery* (2) LA-4
Buie Cem—*cemetery* (2) MS-4
Buie Cem—*cemetery* NC-3
Buie Hollow—*valley* AR-4
Buie House—*hist pl* MS-4
Buie Knob—*summit* KY-4
Buie Lake—*lake* TX-5
Buie Park—*park* TX-5
Buie Pond Big—*reservoir* NC-3
Buie Pond Dam Small—*dam* NC-3
Buie Pond Small—*reservoir* NC-3
**Buies Creek**—*pop pl* NC-3
Buies Creek—*stream* NC-3
Buies Creek Elem Sch—*school* NC-3
Buies Neck—*locale* NC-3
Bui Island—*island* MP-9
Builderback Cem—*cemetery* MO-7
Builderback Hollow—*valley* MO-7
Builders Exchange Bldg—*hist pl* CA-9
Building at High and Cannon Streets—*hist pl* DE-2
Building at Jct. of KY 395 and 1779—*hist pl* KY-4
Building at 10 Follen Street—*hist pl* MA-1
Building at 1007 Broadway—*hist pl* GA-3
Building at 1009 Broadway—*hist pl* GA-3
Building at 101 North Franklin Street—*hist pl* OH-6
Building at 10108 Northeast 1st Ave—*hist pl* FL-3
Building at 102-104 Inman Street—*hist pl* MA-1
Building at 104-106 Hancock Street—*hist pl* MA-1
Building at 105 N. Washington Street—*hist pl* AL-4
Building at 106-108 Inman St—*hist pl* MA-1
Building at 107 Northeast 96th Street—*hist pl* FL-3
Building at 108 Green Street—*hist pl* LA-4
Building at 1101-1113 Maple Ave—*hist pl* IL-6
Building at 1119-1121 W. Third Street—*hist pl* IA-7
Building at 1202 9th Street—*hist pl* NM-5
Building at 1209-1217 Maple Ave—*hist pl* IL-6
Building at 121 Northeast 100th Street—*hist pl* FL-3
Building at 1210–1214 Main Street—*hist pl* SC-3
Building at 1214 Bridge—*hist pl* NM-5
Building at 1291 Northeast 102nd Street—*hist pl* FL-3
Building at 1300 Washington Ave—*hist pl* MO-7
Building at 1301-1303 Judson Ave—*hist pl* IL-6
Building at 130–132 Biltmore Ave—*hist pl* NC-3
Building at 1305-1307 Judson Ave—*hist pl* IL-6
Building at 1316 Maple Ave—*hist pl* IL-6
Building at 133 East Commerce Street—*hist pl* MS-4
Building at 134–136 1/2 Biltmore Ave—*hist pl* NC-3
Building at 136-138 Collins Street—*hist pl* CT-1
Building at 138–142 Portland Street—*hist pl* MA-1
Building at 1389 Stuart Street—*hist pl* CO-8
Building at 1390 Stuart Street—*hist pl* CO-8
Building at 140 Biltmore Ave—*hist pl* NC-3
Building at 140 W. Main Street—*hist pl* DE-2
Building at 1400 Third Ave—*hist pl* GA-3
Building at 1401-1407 Elmwood Ave—*hist pl* IL-6
Building at 1406 Romero—*hist pl* NM-5
Building at 14–16 Pearson Street—*hist pl* IL-6
Building at 142 Collins Street—*hist pl* CT-1
Building at 1429 Second Ave—*hist pl* GA-3
Building at 1435 Stuart Street—*hist pl* CO-8
Building at 1444 Stuart Street—*hist pl* CO-8

Building at 145 Northeast 95th Street—hist pl ... FL-3
Building at 1471 Stuart Street—hist pl ... CO-8
Building at 1505-1509 Oak Ave—hist pl ... IL-6
Building at 1519 3rd Ave—hist pl ... GA-3
Building at 1520 Second Ave—hist pl ... GA-3
Building at 1524 Second Ave—hist pl ... GA-3
Building at 1531 3rd Ave—hist pl ... GA-3
Building at 1-6 Walnut Terrace—hist pl ... MA-1
Building at 1606 Third Ave—hist pl ... GA-3
Building at 1612 3rd Ave—hist pl ... GA-3
Building at 1617 Third Ave—hist pl ... GA-3
Building at 1619 Third Ave—hist pl ... GA-3
Building at 1625 Third Ave—hist pl ... GA-3
Building at 1644 Main Street—hist pl ... SC-3
Building at 1707-1709 Cambridge Street—hist pl ... MA-1
Building at 1715-1717 Cambridge Street—hist pl ... MA-1
Building at 1722-1724 Main Street—hist pl ... SC-3
Building at 1735-1737 Webster Street—hist pl ... CA-9
Building at 1813-1813B Sutter Street—hist pl ... CA-9
Building at 1840-1842 Eddy Street—hist pl ... CA-9
Building at 1921-1921 1/2 Ave D—hist pl ... TX-5
Building at 1925-1927 Market Street—hist pl ... TX-5
Building at 1929-1931 Sherman Ave—hist pl ... IL-6
Building at 200-202A High Street—hist pl ... DE-2
Building at 2005 Montezuma—hist pl ... NM-5
Building at 201 S. 3rd St.—hist pl ... ND-7
Building at 202 Park Ave—hist pl ... NM-5
Building at 202 W. Third Street—hist pl ... IA-7
Building at 205 DeMers Ave.—hist pl ... ND-7
Building at 205 East Constitution—hist pl ... TX-5
Building at 215 Ninth Street—hist pl ... GA-3
Building at 216 Bank Street—hist pl ... VA-3
Building at 218 High Street—hist pl ... DE-2
Building at 218 Spring—hist pl ... AZ-5
Building at 221 Ninth Street—hist pl ... GA-3
Building at 223 Main Street—hist pl ... IN-6
Building at 223 West High Street—hist pl ... OH-6
Building at 23-27 S. Sixth Street—hist pl ... IN-6
Building at 237-239 Main Street—hist pl ... MA-1
Building at 240 Park Ave West—hist pl ... OH-6
Building at 242 St. Charles Street—hist pl ... MS-4
Building at 247 Pleasant Ave—hist pl ... ID-8
Building at 2517 Central Street—hist pl ... IL-6
Building at 2519 Central Street—hist pl ... IL-6
Building at 252-254 Park Ave West—hist pl ... OH-6
Building at 2523 Central Street—hist pl ... IL-6
Building at 253 Northeast 99th Street—hist pl ... FL-3
Building at 257 East Delaware—hist pl ... IL-6
Building at 257 Northeast 91st Street—hist pl ... FL-3
Building at 259 Mount Auburn Street—hist pl ... MA-1
Building at 262 Northeast 96th Street—hist pl ... FL-3
Building at 27-29 Fountain Alley—hist pl ... CA-9
Building at 273 Northeast 98th Street—hist pl ... FL-3
Building at 276 Northeast 98th Street—hist pl ... FL-3
Building at 28-34 1/2 Acad Street—hist pl ... DE-2
Building at 284 Northeast 96th Street—hist pl ... FL-3
Building at 287 Northeast 96th Street—hist pl ... FL-3
Building at 303 Saluda Ave—hist pl ... SC-3
Building at 303 11th St.—hist pl ... GA-3
Building at 30-34 Station Street—hist pl ... MA-1
Building at 306 South Jackson Street—hist pl ... MS-4
Building at 308 Lamar Street—hist pl ... MS-4
Building at 309 Park Ave West—hist pl ... OH-6
Building at 310 Northeast 99th Street—hist pl ... FL-3
Building at 312 George Street—hist pl ... MS-4
Building at 312 Kittson Ave.—hist pl ... ND-7
Building at 317 S. 3rd St.—hist pl ... ND-7
Building at 33-35 Beideman Place—hist pl ... CA-9
Building at 34 Choate Street—hist pl ... DE-2
Building at 353 Northeast 91st Street—hist pl ... FL-3
Building at 357 Northeast 92nd Street—hist pl ... FL-3
Building at 361 Broadway—hist pl ... NY-2
Building at 361 Northeast 97th Street—hist pl ... FL-3
Building at 376-380 Lafayette Street—hist pl ... NY-2
Building at 384 Northeast 94th Street—hist pl ... FL-3
Building at 389 Northeast 99th Street—hist pl ... FL-3
Building at 405-407 College Ave—hist pl ... OK-5
Building at 409 College Ave—hist pl ... OK-5
Building at 415 Park Ave West—hist pl ... OH-6
Building at 417-419 Lee Street—hist pl ... IL-6
Building at 42 Edward J. Lopez Ave—hist pl ... MA-1
Building at 426 South Main Street—hist pl ... NY-2
Building at 430 Harvard Street—hist pl ... TX-5
Building at 431 Northeast 94th Street—hist pl ... FL-3
Building at 441 East Main—hist pl ... TX-5
Building at 45 East 66th Street—hist pl ... NY-2
Building at 45-57 Beideman Place—hist pl ... CA-9
Building at 477 Northeast 92nd Street—hist pl ... FL-3
Building at 500 East High Street—hist pl ... OH-6
Building at 500 Flynn Street—hist pl ... OK-5
Building at 500 White Ave—hist pl ... NM-5
Building at 500-502 East Main—hist pl ... TX-5
Building at 505 East High Street—hist pl ... OH-6
Building at 510-516 Ohio Street—hist pl ... IN-6
Building at 540 Northeast 96th Street—hist pl ... FL-3
Building at 548-606 Michigan Ave—hist pl ... IL-6
Building at 551-555 North Goodman Street—hist pl ... NY-2
Building at 553 Northeast 101st Street—hist pl ... FL-3
Building at 561 Northeast 101st Street—hist pl ... FL-3
Building at 577 Northeast 96th Street—hist pl ... FL-3
Building at 600 Main Street—hist pl ... MA-1
Building at 606 Main Street—hist pl ... MA-1
Building at 614 Main Street—hist pl ... MA-1
Building at 701 Roma NW—hist pl ... NM-5
Building at 710 South Blvd—hist pl ... MS-4
Building at 801 Chinquepin Street—hist pl ... MS-4
Building at 810 Wabash Ave—hist pl ... IN-6
Building at 813-815 Forest Ave—hist pl ... IL-6
Building at 813-815 W. Second Street—hist pl ... IA-7
Building at 8-22 Graves Ave—hist pl ... MA-1
Building at 826 North Main Street—hist pl ... AZ-5
Building at 83-85 Sigourney Street—hist pl ... CT-1
Building at 85 Leonard Street—hist pl ... NY-2
Building at 920 Ninth Ave—hist pl ... GA-3
Building at 921 Fifth Ave—hist pl ... GA-3
Building at 923-925 Michigan Ave—hist pl ... IL-6
Building at 944 Second Ave—hist pl ... GA-3
Building at 999 Michigan, 200 Lee—hist pl ... IL-6
Building No. 105, Boeing Airplane Company—hist pl ... WA-9
Building Run—stream (2) ... WV-2
Buildings at NW Corner of Commerce and Meridian Streets—hist pl ... MS-4
Buildings at 10, 12, 14, and 16 East Chase Street—hist pl ... MD-2
Buildings at 1000 Block of Seventh Street, and 649-651 New York Ave. NW—hist pl ... DC-2
Buildings at 104-128 S. Side Sq.—hist pl ... AL-4
Buildings at 110-112 Inman St.—hist pl ... MA-1
Buildings at 110-122 East Commerce Street—hist pl ... MS-4
Buildings at 1104-1110 Seward—hist pl ... IL-6
Buildings at 1200-1206 Washington Street—hist pl ... NJ-2
Buildings at 15-17 Lee St.—hist pl ... MA-1
Buildings at 1601-1830 St. Paul Street and 12-20 E. Lafayette St—hist pl ... MD-2
Buildings at 1644-1666 Park Road NW—hist pl ... DC-2
Buildings at 207-209 South Main St.—hist pl ... MO-7
Buildings at 2327-31 and 2333-35 Rutger Street—hist pl ... MO-7
Buildings at 24-30 Summer St.—hist pl ... MA-1
Buildings at 375-379 Flatbush Ave and 185-187 Sterling Place—hist pl ... NY-2
Buildings at 744, 746, 748, 750 Broadway—hist pl ... NY-2
Buildings at 80 and 88 W. Brittania St.—hist pl ... MA-1
Buildings at 815-817 Brummel and 819-821 Brummel—hist pl ... IL-6
Buildings at 860-880 Lake Shore Drive—hist pl ... IL-6
Building 309, Fort Sill Indian Sch—hist pl ... OK-5
Building 800-Austin Hall—hist pl ... AL-4
Building 836-Community College of the Air Force Bldg—hist pl ... AL-4
Bu Island ... MP-9
Bu Island—island ... MP-9
Buist—locale ... ID-8
Buist Sch—school ... SC-3
Buist Valley ... ID-8
Buist Valley ... UT-8
Bui-to ... MP-9
Buk ... MP-9
Buker Bay—bay ... WI-6
Buker Hill—summit ... VT-1
Buker Mtn—summit ... ME-1
Buker Pond—lake ... ME-1
Buker Sch—school (2) ... ME-1
Buker Sch—school ... MA-1
Bukers Prairie—area ... CA-9
Bukey Run—stream ... WV-2
Bukhti Point—cape ... AK-9
Bukolt Park—park ... WI-6
Bukonkan (not verified)—island ... MP-9
Bukon To ... MP-9
Bukowski Lakebed—flat ... MN-6
Bukrrairong—island ... PW-9
Bukti Point—cape ... AK-9
Bukubaru ... MP-9
Bukubaru—island ... MP-9
Bukubaru-To ... MP-9
Bukudotklish ... AZ-5
Bukudotklish Canyon ... AZ-5
Bukurappan ... MP-9
Bukurappon-To ... MP-9
Buky Run—stream ... WV-2
Bula—locale ... VA-3
**Bula**—pop pl ... TX-5
**Bula**—pop pl ... WV-2
Bula Church ... AL-4
**Buladean**—pop pl ... NC-3
Buladean Elem Sch—school ... NC-3
**Buladeen**—pop pl ... TN-4
Buladeen Sch (historical)—school ... TN-4
Bulah—locale ... TX-5
**Bulah**—pop pl ... MS-4
**Bulah**—pop pl ... OH-6
Bulah Baptist Church ... AL-4
Bulah Cemetery ... MS-4
Bulah Ch—church ... VA-3
Bulah Ch (historical)—church ... AL-4
Bulah Church ... AL-4
Bulah Point—cape ... NC-3
Bula HS—school ... TX-5
Bulah Springs Ch—church ... TX-5
Bu Lake—lake ... ND-7
Bulam Creek ... CA-9
Bulam Glacier ... CA-9
**Bulan**—pop pl ... KY-4
**Bulan (Duane)**—pop pl ... KY-4
Bula Sch (historical)—school ... AL-4
Bulaville—locale ... OH-6
**Bulb**—pop pl ... OR-9
Bulb Lake—lake ... MN-6
Bulcher—locale ... TX-5
Bulchitna Lake—lake ... AK-9
Bulck Canyon—valley ... OR-9
Buldir Island—island ... AK-9
Buldir Reef—bar ... AK-9
Buldir Volcano—summit ... AK-9
Bule Creek—stream ... OK-5
Bule Gulch—valley ... CA-9
Buleo, Lake—lake ... MO-7
Buleys Shoals—bar ... TN-4
Bulfinch Triangle Hist Dist—hist pl ... MA-1
Bulfrog Bayou—stream ... LA-4
Bulgarians Lake—lake ... WA-9
Bulgary Ridge—ridge ... NY-2
Bulge, The—summit ... NH-1
Bulge Hollow—valley ... UT-8
Bulge Lake—lake ... MN-6
Bulger—locale ... CO-8
Bulger—locale ... WV-2
**Bulger**—pop pl ... PA-2
Bulger Canyon—valley ... UT-8
Bulger Cem—cemetery ... WV-2
Bulger Creek ... AL-4
Bulger Creek—stream ... AL-4
Bulger Creek—stream ... IA-7
Bulger Creek—stream ... LA-4
Bulger Creek—stream ... OR-9
Bulger Creek—stream ... TX-5
Bulger Ditch—canal ... OR-9
Bulger Flat—flat ... OR-9
Bulger Head ... ME-1
Bulger Hill ... OR-9
Bulger Hill—summit ... ME-1
Bulger Hill—summit ... OR-9
Bulger Park—park ... IL-6
Bulger Ridge—ridge ... UT-8
Bulgers—locale ... AL-4
Bulgers Sch—school ... WV-2
Bulgers Hollow—locale ... IA-7
Bulgers Run—stream ... IA-7
Bulgers Run—stream ... PA-2
Bulger Windmill—locale ... CO-8
Bulging Branch—stream ... TN-4
Bulhand Sch—school ... MI-6
Bulhead Lake—lake (3) ... WI-6
Bulhead Rsvr—reservoir ... CA-9
Bulhman Schoder Ditch—canal ... IN-6
Bulito, Arroyo El—stream ... CA-9
Bulkeley Bridge—bridge ... CT-1
Bulkeley Park—park ... CT-1
Bulkeley Sch—hist pl ... CT-1
Bulkely HS—school ... CT-1
Bulkey Lake—lake ... MI-6
Bulkhead—locale ... OH-6
**Bulkhead**—pop pl ... OH-6
Bulkhead, The—channel ... GA-3
Bulkhead, The—summit ... NH-1
Bulkhead Bar Range—channel ... DE-2
Bulkhead Channel ... NC-3
Bulkhead Cove—bay ... TX-5
Bulkhead Drain—channel ... NY-2
Bulkhead Point—cape ... FL-3
Bulkhead Reef—bar ... TX-5
Bulkhead Shoal—bar ... DE-2
Bulkhead Shoal—bar ... FL-3
Bulkhead Shoal Channel—channel ... DE-2
Bulkley Brook—stream ... NY-2
Bulkley Brook—stream ... PA-2
Bulkley Creek—stream ... NY-2
Bulkley Creek—stream ... PA-2
Bulkley Mine—locale ... CO-8
Bulkley Pond—lake ... CT-1
Bulkley Ranch—locale ... CA-9
Bulkley Rsvr—reservoir ... CO-8
Bulkley Wash—stream ... CO-8
Bulk Mail Center—post sta ... PA-2
Bulks Lake—reservoir ... NJ-2
Bulky, Mount—summit ... AK-9
**Bull**—pop pl ... WV-2
Bull, Amos, House—hist pl ... CT-1
Bull, Capt. William, Tavern—hist pl ... CT-1
Bull, Henry C., House—hist pl ... MN-6
Bull, Jireh, Blockhouse Historic Site—hist pl ... RI-1
Bull, The ... ME-1
Bull, Thomas, House—hist pl ... PA-2
Bull, William, House—hist pl ... KY-4
Bull, William, III, House—hist pl ... NY-2
Bulla Cem—cemetery ... MO-7
**Bullacktown**—pop pl ... IN-6
Bullamore Forks Sch—school ... WI-6
Bull and Brown Trail—trail ... CO-8
Bullard—locale ... CA-9
Bullard—locale ... GA-3
**Bullard**—pop pl ... IA-7
**Bullard**—pop pl ... TX-5
Bullard, T. J., House—hist pl ... TX-5
Bullard Bank—bar ... FL-3
Bullard Bluff—bend ... NE-7
Bullard Bluff Campsite—locale ... MN-6
Bullard Branch—stream (2) ... AL-4
Bullard Branch—stream ... GA-3
Bullard Branch—stream ... LA-4
Bullard Branch—stream ... MS-4
Bullard Branch—stream (3) ... NC-3
Bullard Branch—stream ... TN-4
Bullard Branch—stream ... TX-5
Bullard Brook ... MA-1
Bullard Canal—canal ... CA-9
Bullard Canyon—valley ... AZ-5
Bullard Canyon—valley ... NM-5
Bullard Canyon—valley ... OR-9
Bullard (CCD)—cens area ... TX-5
Bullard Cem—cemetery ... AL-4
Bullard Cem—cemetery ... MS-4
Bullard Cem—cemetery ... NC-3
Bullard Ch—church ... FL-3
Bullard Chapel—church ... OK-5
Bullard Club ... TX-5
Bullard Creek—stream ... IN-6
Bullard Creek—stream ... KS-7
Bullard Creek—stream ... LA-4
Bullard Creek—stream ... MN-6
Bullard Creek—stream ... OR-9
Bullard Creek—stream ... PA-2
Bullard Creek—stream ... TN-4
Bullard Creek—stream (5) ... TX-5
Bullard Culb Lake ... TX-5
Bullard-Hart House—hist pl ... GA-3
Bullard-Haven Sch—school ... CT-1
Bullard Hill—summit ... MA-1
Bullard Hill—summit ... NH-1
Bullard Hill—summit ... NY-2
Bullard Hotel—hist pl ... NM-5
Bullard HS—school ... CA-9
Bullard Island ... IL-6
Bullard Knob—summit ... VA-3
Bullard Lake ... TX-5
Bullard Lake—lake ... CA-9
Bullard Lake—lake ... IL-6
Bullard Lake—reservoir ... MI-6
Bullard Landing—locale ... GA-3
Bullard Mine—mine ... AZ-5
Bullard Mtn—summit ... AK-9
Bullard Mtn—summit ... AR-4
Bullard Mtn—summit ... CA-9
Bullard Mtn—summit ... NH-1
Bullard Mtn—summit ... SC-3
Bullard Oil Field—oilfield ... TX-5
Bullard Park—park ... NY-2
Bullard Pass—gap ... AZ-5
Bullard Peak—summit (2) ... AZ-5
Bullard Peak—summit ... NM-5
Bullard Peak Canyon—valley ... NM-5
Bullard Point—cliff ... TN-4
Bullard Point Crossroads—locale ... TN-4
Bullard Pond—reservoir ... NC-3
Bullard-Ray House—hist pl ... NC-3
Bullards—locale ... OR-9
Bullards Basin—basin ... CA-9
Bullards Beach State Park—park ... OR-9
Bullards Bridge—bridge ... OR-9
Bullards Cem—cemetery ... OR-9
Bullard Sch—school ... NY-2
Bullard Sch—school ... OR-9
Bullard Sch—school ... TX-5
Bullards Chapel CME Ch—church ... MS-4
Bullard Sch (historical)—school ... MS-4
Bullard School—locale ... KS-7
Bullards Creek—stream ... GA-3
Bullards Creek Lookout Tower—locale ... GA-3
**Bullards Gap**—pop pl ... TN-4
Bullards Millpond—reservoir ... SC-3
Bullard Spring—spring ... AZ-5
Bullard Spring—spring ... OK-5
Bullard Spring—spring ... UT-8
Bullard (Township of)—fmr MCD ... AR-4
**Bullard (Township of)**—pop pl ... MN-6
**Bullardville**—pop pl ... MA-1
Bullard Wash—stream ... AZ-5
Bullard Well—well ... TX-5
Bulla Sch (abandoned)—school ... MO-7
Bullbarn Creek—stream ... AL-4
Bull Barn Flat—flat ... CA-9
Bull Barn Ranch—valley ... CA-9
Bull Basin—basin (4) ... AZ-5
Bull Basin—basin ... CO-8
Bull Basin—basin (3) ... ID-8
Bull Basin—basin (2) ... NV-8
Bull Basin—basin ... NM-5
Bull Basin—basin ... OR-9
Bull Basin Camp—locale ... ID-8
Bull Basin Canyon—valley ... AZ-5
Bull Basin Canyon—valley ... NM-5
Bull Basin Creek—stream ... ID-8
Bull Basin Mesa—summit ... AZ-5
Bull Basin Rsvr No. 1—reservoir ... CO-8
Bull Basin Rsvr No. 2—reservoir ... CO-8
Bull Basin Spring—spring ... ID-8
Bull Basin Spring—spring ... NV-8
Bull Basin Spring—spring ... NM-5
Bull Basin Tank—reservoir ... NM-5
Bull Basin Tanks—reservoir ... AZ-5
Bull Bay ... SC-3
Bull Bay—bay ... FL-3
Bull Bay—bay ... LA-4
Bull Bay—bay ... NC-3
Bull Bay—gut ... LA-4
Bull Bay—swamp ... FL-3
Bull Bay—swamp ... SC-3
Bull Bay Bayou—gut ... AL-4
Bull Bay Bend—bend ... MS-4
Bull Bay Branch—stream ... LA-4
Bull Bay Creek—stream ... TX-5
Bull Bayou ... FL-3
Bull Bayou ... LA-4
Bull Bayou—gut (2) ... LA-4
Bull Bayou—stream ... AR-4
Bull Bayou—stream (5) ... LA-4
Bull Bayou—stream ... MS-4
Bullbegger—locale ... VA-3
Bullbegger Creek—stream ... VA-3
Bull Bend—bend ... OR-9
Bullberry Coulee—valley ... MT-8
Bullberry Creek—stream (3) ... UT-8
Bullberry Flat—flat ... UT-8
Bullberry Hollow—valley ... UT-8
Bullberry Island (historical)—island ... SD-7
Bullberry Lake ... UT-8
Bullberry Lakes—lake ... UT-8
Bullberry Slough—stream ... UT-8
Bullberry Spring—spring (4) ... UT-8
Bullberry Springs ... UT-8
Bull Bluff—cliff (2) ... TN-4
Bull Bluff—cliff ... VA-3
Bull Blvd Ditch—canal ... NC-3
Bull Bottom—bend ... UT-8
Bull Bottom Bluff—cliff ... AR-4
Bull Branch ... KY-4
Bull Branch ... NJ-2
Bull Branch—stream (5) ... AL-4
Bull Branch—stream ... AR-4
Bull Branch—stream (2) ... FL-3
Bull Branch—stream (4) ... GA-3
Bull Branch—stream ... IL-6
Bull Branch—stream (5) ... KY-4
Bull Branch—stream ... LA-4
Bull Branch—stream ... ME-1
Bull Branch—stream (2) ... MS-4
Bull Branch—stream (2) ... MO-7
Bull Branch—stream (11) ... NC-3
Bull Branch—stream ... OH-6
Bull Branch—stream ... SC-3
Bull Branch—stream (5) ... TN-4
Bull Branch—stream (5) ... TX-5
Bull Branch—stream (2) ... VA-3
Bull Branch—stream (3) ... WV-2
Bull Branch—stream (2) ... WI-6
Bull Breakers—bar ... SC-3
Bull Bridge Creek—stream ... SC-3
Bull Brook ... MA-1
Bull Brook—stream (5) ... ME-1
Bull Brook—stream ... MA-1
Bull Brook—stream ... NH-1
Bull Brook—stream ... WI-6
Bull Brook Reservoir Dam—dam ... MA-1
Bull Brook Rsvr—reservoir ... MA-1
Bullbucker Creek—stream ... WA-9
Bull Butte—summit ... AZ-5
Bull Butte—summit ... MT-8
Bull Butte—summit (3) ... ND-7
**Bull Butte Township**—pop pl ... ND-7
Bull Calf Bayou—stream ... LA-4
Bull Camp—locale ... FL-3
Bull Camp—locale (2) ... NV-8
Bull Camp—locale ... NM-5
Bull Camp Butte—summit ... ID-8
Bull Camp Canyon—valley ... NM-5
Bull Camp Creek ... NV-8
Bull Camp Creek—stream (2) ... NV-8
Bull Camp Creek—stream ... WY-8
Bull Camp Hollow—valley ... MO-7
Bull Camp Park—flat ... WY-8
Bull Camp Peak—summit ... WY-8
Bull Camp Rsvr—reservoir ... ID-8
Bull Camp Spring—spring ... NV-8
Bull Camp Windmill—locale ... NM-5
Bull Canal—canal ... CO-8
Bull Canyon ... UT-8
Bull Canyon—stream ... UT-8
Bull Canyon—valley (8) ... AZ-5
Bull Canyon—valley (11) ... CA-9
Bull Canyon—valley (5) ... CO-8
Bull Canyon—valley (2) ... ID-8
Bull Canyon—valley ... NE-7
Bull Canyon—valley (2) ... NV-8
Bull Canyon—valley (7) ... NM-5
Bull Canyon—valley (7) ... OR-9
Bull Canyon—valley (4) ... TX-5
Bull Canyon—valley (12) ... UT-8
Bull Canyon—valley (3) ... WY-8
Bull Canyon Creek—stream ... NM-5
Bull Canyon Ranch—locale ... NE-7
Bull Canyon Rapids—rapids ... UT-8
Bull Canyon Rsvr—reservoir (2) ... OR-9
Bull Canyon Spring—spring ... AZ-5
Bull Canyon Well—locale ... NM-5
Bull Cap Hill ... CT-1
Bull Cove—cave ... AL-4
Bull Cove—cave ... TN-4
Bull Cem—cemetery ... AR-4
Bull Cem—cemetery (2) ... IL-6
Bull Cem—cemetery ... IN-6
Bull Cem—cemetery ... MI-6
Bull Cem—cemetery ... MS-4
Bull Cem—cemetery ... MO-7
Bull Cem—cemetery ... NY-2
Bull Cem—cemetery (2) ... TN-4
Bull Cienega—flat ... AZ-5
Bull Cienega Creek—stream ... AZ-5
Bull Cienega Spring—spring ... AZ-5
Bull Cieniga Creek ... AZ-5
Bull City ... KS-7
**Bull City**—pop pl ... AL-4
Bull Claim Hill—summit ... UT-8
Bull Clod Draw—valley ... TX-5
Bull Cod Windmill—locale ... TX-5
Bull Corral Creek—stream ... ID-8
Bull Cove—bay ... FL-3
Bull Cove—bay ... ME-1
Bull Cove—bay ... VA-3
Bull Cove—valley (2) ... NC-3
Bull Cove—valley ... TX-5
Bull Creek ... AR-4
Bull Creek ... CO-8
Bull Creek ... ID-8
Bull Creek ... IN-6
Bull Creek ... KY-4
Bull Creek ... MI-6
Bull Creek ... MT-8
Bull Creek ... SD-7
Bull Creek ... TX-5
Bull Creek ... WY-8
Bull Creek—bay ... NC-3
Bull Creek—channel ... SC-3
Bull Creek—gut ... NC-3
Bull Creek—lake ... FL-3
Bull Creek—locale ... CA-9
Bull Creek—locale ... KY-4
**Bull Creek**—pop pl ... IL-6
**Bull Creek**—pop pl ... TN-4
Bull Creek—stream (2) ... AK-9
Bull Creek—stream (4) ... AZ-5
Bull Creek—stream (3) ... AR-4
Bull Creek—stream (18) ... CA-9
Bull Creek—stream (6) ... CO-8
Bull Creek—stream (6) ... FL-3
Bull Creek—stream (8) ... GA-3
Bull Creek—stream (8) ... ID-8
Bull Creek—stream (3) ... IL-6
Bull Creek—stream (2) ... IN-6
Bull Creek—stream ... IA-7
Bull Creek—stream (7) ... KS-7
Bull Creek—stream (10) ... KY-4
Bull Creek—stream (2) ... LA-4
Bull Creek—stream ... MS-4
Bull Creek—stream (2) ... MO-7
Bull Creek—stream (12) ... MT-8
Bull Creek—stream (3) ... NE-7
Bull Creek—stream (5) ... NV-8
Bull Creek—stream ... NJ-2
Bull Creek—stream (4) ... NM-5
Bull Creek—stream (2) ... NY-2
Bull Creek—stream (5) ... NC-3
Bull Creek—stream ... ND-7
Bull Creek—stream (5) ... OH-6
Bull Creek—stream (17) ... OK-5
Bull Creek—stream (16) ... OR-9
Bull Creek—stream ... PA-2
Bull Creek—stream (4) ... SC-3
Bull Creek—stream (15) ... SD-7
Bull Creek—stream (21) ... TX-5
Bull Creek—stream (2) ... UT-8
Bull Creek—stream ... VT-1
Bull Creek—stream (2) ... VA-3
Bull Creek—stream (2) ... WA-9
Bull Creek—stream (5) ... WV-2
Bull Creek—stream ... WI-6
Bull Creek—stream (19) ... WY-8
Bull Creek Archeol District—hist pl ... UT-8
Bull Creek Baptist Ch—church ... TN-4
Bull Creek Bar—bar ... ID-8
Bull Creek Butte—summit ... SD-7
Bull Creek Campground—locale ... WY-8
Bull Creek Cem—cemetery ... CA-9
Bull Creek Cem—cemetery ... PA-2
Bull Creek Ch—church ... GA-3
Bull Creek Ch—church ... KY-4
Bull Creek Ch—church ... NC-3
Bull Creek Ch—church ... PA-2
Bull Creek Ch—church ... VA-3
Bull Creek Ch—church ... WV-2
Bull Creek Cienega—flat ... AZ-5
Bull Creek Cow Camp—locale ... CO-8
Bull Creek Crossing—locale ... ID-8
Bull Creek Dam—dam ... OR-9
Bull Creek Ditch—canal ... NV-8
Bull Creek Flats Trail—trail ... CA-9
Bull Creek Hill—summit ... AR-4
Bull Creek Hot Springs—spring ... ID-8
Bull Creek Island ... SC-3
Bull Creek Junior ... WI-6
Bull Creek Lookout—locale ... MT-8
Bull Creek Mtn—summit (2) ... OK-5
Bull Creek Oil Field—oilfield ... KS-7
Bull Creek Pass—gap ... UT-8
Bull Creek Patrol Cabin—locale ... WY-8
Bull Creek Point—summit ... ID-8
Bull Creek Polecreek Trail—trail ... MT-8
Bull Creek Pond ... FL-3
Bull Creek Pond—lake ... OR-9
Bull Creek Ranch—locale ... NV-8
Bull Creek Ridge—ridge ... ID-8
Bull Creek Rsvr—reservoir ... ID-8
Bull Creek Rsvr—reservoir ... NV-8
Bull Creek Rsvr—reservoir ... OR-9
Bull Creek Rsvr No. 1—reservoir ... CO-8
Bull Creek Rsvr No. 2—reservoir ... CO-8
Bull Creek Rsvr No. 3—reservoir ... CO-8
Bull Creek Rsvr No. 4—reservoir ... CO-8
Bull Creek Rsvr No. 5—reservoir ... CO-8
Bull Creek Sch—school ... CA-9
Bull Creek Sch—school ... KY-4
Bull Creek Sch—school ... NC-3
Bull Creek Sch—school ... SD-7
Bull Creek Sch—school ... TN-4
Bull Creek Sch—school ... WV-2
Bull Creek Sch (historical)—school ... SD-7
Bull Creek School—locale ... CO-8
Bull Creek Spring—spring ... OR-9
Bull Creek Station—locale ... TN-4
Bull Creek-Sully Township—civil ... SD-7
Bull Creek Tank—reservoir ... AZ-5
Bull Creek Tank—reservoir ... TX-5
**Bull Creek Township**—pop pl ... SD-7
Bull Creek Trail—trail ... ID-8
Bull Creek Wildlife Mngmt Area—park ... FL-3
Bull Cut—channel ... SC-3
Bulldie Creek—stream ... NC-3
Bulldie Ridge—ridge ... NC-3
Bull Ditch ... IN-6
Bull Ditch—canal (2) ... CO-8
Bull Ditch—canal ... IN-6
Bull Ditch—canal ... IA-7
Bull Ditch—canal ... NE-7
Bull Ditch—canal ... NY-2
Bull Ditch—canal ... OR-9
Bull Ditch—canal ... WA-9
Bulldog, The—bar ... ME-1
Bulldog Bench—bench ... UT-8
Bulldog Bend—bend ... AL-4
Bulldog Branch—stream ... TN-4
Bulldog Camps—locale ... ME-1
Bulldog Canyon—valley ... AZ-5
Bulldog Canyon—valley (2) ... UT-8
Bulldog Cove—bay ... AK-9
Bulldog Creek—stream ... AK-9
Bulldog Creek—stream ... CO-8
Bulldog Creek—stream ... ID-8
Bulldog Creek—stream ... MI-6
Bulldog Creek—stream ... OR-9
Bulldog Creek—stream ... TN-4
Bulldog Creek—stream ... UT-8
Bulldog Creek—stream (2) ... WA-9
Bulldog Crossing—locale ... IL-6
Bulldog Cut—bend ... NC-3
Bulldog Detention Dam—dam ... CO-8
Bulldog Gulch—valley ... SD-7
Bulldog (historical)—locale ... SD-7
Bulldog Hole—basin ... UT-8
Bulldog Hollow—valley ... KY-4
Bulldog Hollow—valley ... UT-8
Bulldog Hollow—valley ... WY-8
Bull Dog Jack Mine—mine ... NV-8
Bulldog Knolls—range ... UT-8
Bulldog Lake—lake ... MI-6
Bulldog Lake—lake ... MN-6
Bulldog Mesa—summit ... AZ-5
Bulldog Mesa—summit ... NM-5
Bulldog Mine—mine ... AZ-5
Bulldog Mountains ... AZ-5
Bulldog Mtn—summit ... CO-8
Bulldog Mtn—summit ... MT-8
Bulldog Mtn—summit ... WA-9
Bulldog Oil Field—oilfield ... OK-5
Bulldog Pass—gap ... UT-8
Bulldog Peak—summit ... UT-8
Bulldog Prairie—flat ... OR-9
Bull Dog Ranch—locale ... SD-7
Bulldog Ranch I ... SD-7
Bulldog Ridge—ridge ... ID-8
Bulldog Ridge—summit ... UT-8
Bulldog River ... MN-6

Bulldog Rock—pillar OR-9
Bulldog Run—stream MN-6
Bulldog Run—stream PA-2
*Bulldog Run River* MN-6
Bulldog Springs—spring WI-6
Bulldog Tank—reservoir NM-5
Bulldog Wash—stream AZ-5
Bull Domingo Hills—summit CO-8
*Bulldos Run River* MN-6
Bulldozer Creek—stream MT-8
Bulldozer Creek—stream OR-9
Bulldozer Mine—mine AZ-5
Bulldozer Spring—spring NM-5
Bull Draw—valley (3) CO-8
Bull Draw—valley (2) TX-5
Bull Draw—valley (2) WY-8
Bull Draw Windmill—locale TX-5
Bull Durham Tobacco Factory—hist pl NC-3
Bull Durham Resort Dock—locale TN-4
Bull Elk Canyon—valley WA-9
Bull Elk Creek—stream ID-8
Bull Elk Creek—stream UT-8
Bull Elk Creek—stream WA-9
Bull Elk Creek—stream WY-8
Bull Elk Creek Spring—spring UT-8
Bull Elk Ditch—canal CO-8
Bull Elk Draw—valley WY-8
Bull Elk Park—flat WY-8
Bull Elk Pass—gap WY-8
Bull Elk Ridge—ridge ID-8
Bullen—locale AK-9
Bullen, John, House—hist pl DE-2
Bullen Branch—stream AL-4
Bullen Cem—cemetery AL-4
Bullen Cem—cemetery MS-4
Bullen Creek—stream MS-4
Bullen Gap—gap GA-3
Bullen Hole—valley UT-8
Bullen Hollow—valley TN-4
Bullen Hollow Trail—trail TN-4
Bullen Mills—locale ME-1
Bullen Mission (historical)—church MS-4
Bullen Point—cape AK-9
Bullen Run—stream TN-4
*Bullens Bayou* MS-4
Bullen-Stratton-Cozzen House—hist pl MA-1
Bullen Valley—valley (2) TN-4
**Buller**—pop pl LA-4
Buller Bass Hatchery—other VA-3
Buller Canyon—valley NV-8
Buller Cem—cemetery NE-7
Bullerdick Hyndman Moulton Ditch—canal MT-8
Buller Lake—lake WA-9
Bullerman Branch—stream IN-6
Bullerman Cem—cemetery IN-6
Bullerman Ditch—canal IN-6
Buller Marsh—swamp LA-4
Buller Mtn—summit NV-8
Bullerton Towhead—island AR-4
Bullet Bend—bend FL-3
Bullet Branch—stream IN-6
Bullet Branch—stream MS-4
Bullet Branch—stream (3) TN-4
Bullet Canyon—valley UT-8
Bullet Canyon Spring—spring UT-8
Bullet Canyon Trailhead—locale UT-8
Bullet Chute, The—stream WI-6
Bullet Creek—locale TN-4
Bullet Creek—stream ID-8
Bullet Creek—stream OK-5
Bullet Creek—stream TN-4
Bullet Creek—stream TX-5
Bullet Creek Cem—cemetery TN-4
Bullet Creek Falls—falls TN-4
Bullet Creek Sch (historical)—school TN-4
Bullet Drain—canal MI-6
Bullet Field—island FL-3
Bullet Hill—summit CT-1
Bullet Hill—summit OK-5
Bullet Hill Brook—stream CT-1
Bullet Hill Sch—hist pl CT-1
**Bullet Hole**—pop pl NY-2
Bullet Hole—rock NY-2
Bullet Hole—valley NY-2
Bullet Hole, The—valley NY-2
Bullet Lake—lake CA-9
Bullet Lake—lake MI-6
Bullet Lake—lake MN-6
Bullet Mtn—summit TN-4
Bullet Nose Mtn—summit MT-8
Bullet Pond—lake NH-1
Bullet Pond—lake (2) NY-2
Bullet Prairie—flat OK-5
Bullet Prairie Cem—cemetery OK-5
*Bullet Run* PA-2
Bullet Run—stream WV-2
Bullets Chapel—church SC-3
*Bullets Lick* KY-4
Bullet Spring—spring ID-8
Bullette Playground—park OK-5
Bulley Creek—stream AL-4
Bull Falls—falls WI-6
Bull Falls Camping Area—locale WV-2
Bullfight Tank—reservoir AZ-5
Bullfinch Reservoirs—reservoir CO-8
Bullfinch Rsvr No. 1—reservoir CO-8
Bullfinch Rsvr No. 2—reservoir CO-8
Bull Flat—flat (5) CA-9
Bull Flat—flat OR-9
Bull Flat—flat (3) UT-8
Bull Flat Camp—locale CA-9
Bull Flat Canyon—valley AZ-5
Bull Flat Lake—lake OR-9
Bull Flats Sch—school SD-7
*Bull Foot Creek* KS-7
Bullfoot Creek—stream KS-7
Bullfoot Creek Bridge—hist pl KS-7
*Bull Fork* TN-4
Bull Fork—locale NV-8
Bull Fork—stream CO-8
Bull Fork—stream IN-6
Bull Fork—stream (3) KY-4
Bull Fork—stream (3) WV-2
Bull Fork Creek—stream KY-4
Bull Frame Canyon—valley NV-8
Bull Frame Creek—stream ID-8
Bull Frame Reservoirs—reservoir ID-8
Bullfrog—locale NV-8
Bullfrog—locale UT-8
**Bullfrog**—pop pl WA-9
Bullfrog Basin Airp—airport UT-8
Bullfrog Basin Campground—locale UT-8
Bullfrog Basin Marina—locale UT-8
Bullfrog Bay—bay UT-8
Bullfrog Branch—stream KY-4
Bullfrog Branch—stream TX-5
*Bullfrog Campground* UT-8
Bullfrog Canyon—valley AZ-5
Bullfrog Cave—cave AL-4
Bullfrog Corner—locale MS-4
Bullfrog Creek—stream AK-9
Bullfrog Creek—stream (2) FL-3
Bullfrog Creek—stream NC-3
Bullfrog Creek—stream OK-5
Bullfrog Creek—stream TX-5
Bullfrog Creek—stream UT-8
Bullfrog Creek Overlook—locale UT-8
Bullfrog Hills—summit NV-8
Bullfrog (historical)—summit AZ-5
Bullfrog Hollow—valley VT-1
Bullfrog Island—island AK-9
Bullfrog Lake—lake (2) CA-9
Bull Frog Lake—lake IL-6
Bull Frog Lake—lake MI-6
Bullfrog Lake—lake MN-6
Bull Frog Lake—lake OR-9
Bullfrog Lake—lake (2) WI-6
Bullfrog Lakes—lake CA-9
*Bullfrog Marina* UT-8
Bullfrog Meadow—flat CA-9
Bullfrog Mtn—summit NV-8
Bullfrog Mtn—summit WA-9
Bullfrog No 1 Shaft—mine NM-5
Bullfrog No 2 Shaft (Active)—mine NM-5
Bullfrog Pond—lake WA-9
Bullfrog Ravine—valley CA-9
Bullfrog Ridge—ridge AZ-5
Bullfrog Road Bridge—hist pl MD-2
Bullfrog Rsvr—reservoir CO-8
Bullfrog Rsvr—reservoir NV-8
Bull Frog Rsvr—reservoir OR-9
Bullfrog Run—stream WV-2
Bullfrog Spring—spring AZ-5
Bullfrog Spring—spring OR-9
Bullfrog Spring—spring TX-5
Bullfrog Spring—spring WA-9
*Bull Frog Springs* OR-9
*Bull Frog Town* PA-2
**Bullfrog Valley**—pop pl AR-4
Bull Gap—gap (3) GA-3
Bull Gap—gap (2) NC-3
Bull Gap—gap OR-9
Bull Gap—gap (2) VA-3
Bull Gap—gap WY-8
Bull Gap Campground—park OR-9
Bull Gap Canyon—valley NM-5
Bull Gap Spring—spring NM-5
Bull Gap Tank—reservoir NM-5
Bull Garden—flat CO-8
Bullgate Dike—levee OR-9
Bullger Creek—stream MS-4
Bullgrass Flowage—reservoir WI-6
Bullgrass Knoll—summit UT-8
Bull Grass Tank—reservoir NM-5
Bullgrouse Ridge—ridge WA-9
Bull Gulch—valley CA-9
Bull Gulch—valley (8) CO-8
Bull Gulch—valley (5) ID-8
Bull Gulch—valley OR-9
Bull Gulch—valley (2) WY-8
Bull Gulch Spring—spring OR-9
Bull Gulf—valley AL-4
Bull Gus Creek—stream WI-6
Bull Gut—gut NC-3
Bull Hall Creek—stream AL-4
Bull Hall Swamp—swamp AL-4
Bull Hammock—island FL-3
Bull Harbor—bay SC-3
Bull Head—cape AK-9
**Bullhead**—pop pl NC-3
**Bullhead**—pop pl SD-7
Bull Head—summit PA-2
Bull Head—summit TN-4
Bullhead—summit TN-4
Bullhead, Lake—lake WI-6
Bullhead Basin—basin ID-8
Bullhead Bay—basin SC-3
Bullhead Bay—bay MI-6
Bullhead Bay—bay NY-2
Bullhead Bay—swamp FL-3
Bullhead Bay—swamp SC-3
Bullhead Bayou—stream MS-4
Bullhead Bayou—stream TX-5
Bullhead Bench—bench UT-8
Bullhead Bluff—locale GA-3
Bullhead Branch—stream NC-3
Bullhead Branch—stream TN-4
Bullhead Brook—stream NY-2
Bullhead Brook—stream RI-1
Bullhead Canyon—valley CA-9
**Bullhead City**—pop pl AZ-5
Bullhead City Airp—airport AZ-5
Bullhead City Elem Sch—school AZ-5
Bullhead City Post Office—building AZ-5
Bullhead City-Riviera—CDP AZ-5
Bullhead Coulee—valley MT-8
Bullhead Creek—gut MI-6
Bullhead Creek—stream CA-9
Bullhead Creek—stream GA-3
Bullhead Creek—stream MT-8
Bullhead Creek—stream NC-3
Bullhead Creek—stream OK-5
Bullhead Creek—stream (2) TX-5
*Bullhead Dam* SD-7
Bullhead Drop—canal MT-8
Bullhead Gap—gap NC-3
Bullhead Gulch—valley CO-8
Bullhead Hollow—valley TX-5
Bullhead Island—island NY-2
*Bullhead Lake* MI-6
Bullhead Lake—lake IA-7
Bullhead Lake—lake (15) MI-6
Bullhead Lake—lake (13) MN-6
Bullhead Lake—lake MT-8
Bullhead Lake—lake NY-2
Bullhead Lake—lake (3) SD-7
Bullhead Lake—lake (14) WI-6
Bullhead Lake—swamp MN-6
Bull Headley Public Landing—locale FL-3
Bull Head Lodge and Studio—hist pl MT-8
Bullhead Mountain Overlook—locale NC-3
*Bull Head Mtn* NY-2
Bullhead Mtn—summit NY-2
Bullhead Mtn—summit (3) NC-3
Bullhead Mtn—summit (2) TX-5
Bullhead Pond—lake (12) NY-2
Bull Head Pond—lake NY-2
Bull Head Pond—lake RI-1
Bullhead Pond—lake (2) VT-1
Bullhead Pond—reservoir VA-3
Bullhead Pond—swamp MI-6
Bullhead Pond Brook—stream NY-2
Bullhead Pond Mtn—summit NY-2
*Bull Head Ranch* NV-8
Bullhead Ranch—locale NV-8
Bullhead Ridge—ridge NC-3
*Bullhead Rock* AZ-5
Bullhead Rsvr—reservoir ID-8
*Bull Head Run* SD-7
Bullhead Run—stream SC-3
Bullhead Run—stream SD-7
Bullhead Sch—school MT-8
*Bullhead Slough* CA-9
Bullhead Slough—stream CA-9
Bullhead Slu—gut WI-6
Bullhead Springs—spring MT-8
Bullhead Strand—swamp FL-3
Bullhead Swamp—swamp FL-3
Bullhead Tank—reservoir TX-5
Bull Head (Township of)—fmr MCD NC-3
Bullhead Valley—flat MT-8
Bull Head Windmill—locale TX-5
Bullhead Windmill—locale (2) TX-5
Bull Heifer Creek—stream OR-9
Bullhide Creek—stream FL-3
Bull Hide Creek—stream TX-5
Bullhide Slough—gut TX-5
**Bull Hill**—pop pl NY-2
Bull Hill—summit AZ-5
Bull Hill—summit (2) CA-9
Bull Hill—summit (4) CO-8
Bull Hill—summit (2) CT-1
Bull Hill—summit FL-3
Bull Hill—summit LA-4
Bull Hill—summit (4) ME-1
Bull Hill—summit (2) MA-1
Bull Hill—summit NV-8
Bull Hill—summit NM-5
Bull Hill—summit (8) NY-2
Bull Hill—summit OK-5
Bull Hill—summit (2) PA-2
Bull Hill—summit (3) VT-1
Bull Hill—summit VA-3
Bull Hill—summit (2) WY-8
Bull Hill Cem—cemetery CT-1
Bull Hill Cem—cemetery PA-2
Bull Hill Cem—cemetery TX-5
Bull Hill Creek—stream MI-6
Bull Hill Lookout Tower—locale VA-3
Bull Hill Mine—mine NV-8
Bullhill Run—stream VA-3
Bullhock Creek—stream CA-9
Bull Hole—bend AZ-5
Bull Hole—bend NC-3
Bull Hole—lake FL-3
Bull Hole Canal—canal LA-4
Bull Hole Landing—locale GA-3
Bull Hollow—valley AL-4
Bull Hollow—valley AZ-5
Bull Hollow—valley (2) AR-4
Bull Hollow—valley (2) IN-6
Bull Hollow—valley PA-2
Bull Hollow—valley (3) TN-4
Bull Hollow—valley (3) TX-5
Bull Hollow—valley (9) UT-8
Bull Hollow—valley (2) WV-2
Bull Hollow—valley WY-8
Bull Hollow Branch—stream KY-4
Bull Hollow Branch—stream TX-5
*Bull Hollow Canyon* AZ-5
Bull Hollow Corral—locale UT-8
Bull Hollow Gap—gap PA-2
Bull Hollow Spring—spring UT-8
Bull Hollow Trail—trail PA-2
Bull Hollow Wash—valley UT-8
Bullhook Creek—stream MT-8
Bull Hook Creek—stream ND-7
Bull Hook Creek—stream SD-7
Bullhorn Branch—stream KY-4
Bull Horn Creek—stream ID-8
Bullhorn Creek—stream NY-2
Bullhorn Wash—valley UT-8
Bulliard Basin—valley CA-9
Bullick Branch—stream KY-4
Bullick Branch—stream TX-5
Bullick Hollow—valley TX-5
*Bullier Creek* ND-7
Bullin Cem—cemetery NC-3
*Bullin Creek* NC-3
Bullinger Creek—stream TX-5
Bullinger Mtn—summit NC-3
Bullings Creek—stream NC-3
Bullings Pass—gap UT-8
*Bullington Branch* AL-4
Bullington Cem—cemetery MO-7
Bullington Creek—stream KS-7
Bullington Hill—summit TX-5
Bullington Ranch—locale NM-5
Bullington Store (historical)—locale TN-4
Bullington Warehouse—hist pl NC-3
Bullins Branch—stream KY-4
Bullins Branch—stream VA-3
Bullins Creek—stream SC-3
Bullion—locale LA-4
Bullion—locale MO-7
Bullion—locale NV-8
**Bullion**—pop pl NV-8
**Bullion**—pop pl PA-2
Bullion, Mount—summit NV-8
Bullion Basin—basin WA-9
Bullion Bend Historic Marker—park CA-9
Bullion Branch—stream TX-5
Bullion Butte—summit ND-7
Bullion Canyon—valley (3) UT-8
Bullion Cem—cemetery TX-5
Bullion Creek—stream (3) AK-9
Bullion Creek—stream (2) ID-8
Bullion Creek—stream MT-8
Bullion Creek—stream ND-7
**Bullion Falls**—pop pl UT-8
Bullion Flat—flat CA-9
Bullion Gulch—valley CA-9
Bullion Gulch—valley (2) ID-8
Bullion Hill—summit CA-9
Bullion Hollow—valley TX-5
Bullion King Lake—lake CO-8
Bullion Mine—mine AZ-5
Bullion Mine—mine (3) CA-9
Bullion Mine—mine CO-8
Bullion Mine—mine (2) ID-8
Bullion Mine—mine MT-8
Bullion Mine—mine NV-8
Bullion Mine—mine (2) SD-7
Bullion Mine—mine WA-9
Bullion Mine—mine WY-8
Bullion Mountains—range CA-9
Bullion Mtn—summit AK-9
Bullion Mtn—summit (2) LA-9
Bullion Mtn—summit CO-8
Bullion Mtn—summit NV-8
Bullion Parks—flat MT-8
Bullion Pass—gap ID-8
Bullion Pass—gap MT-8
Bullion Pasture—flat UT-8
Bullion Plaza Sch—school AZ-5
Bullion Ravine—valley NV-8
Bullion Run—stream PA-2
Bullion Shaft—mine NV-8
Bullion Spring—spring NV-8
**Bullion Subdivision**—pop pl UT-8
**Bullion Township**—pop pl ND-7
Bullion Trail—trail UT-8
Bullion Tunnel—hist pl ID-8
Bullion Tunnel—mine CO-8
Bullion View Sch—school ND-7
Bullionville—locale UT-8
Bullionville Cem—cemetery NV-8
Bullionville (Site)—locale (2) NV-8
Bullionville Spring—spring UT-8
Bullion Wash—valley CA-9
*Bullis* MS-4
Bullis, Adams H., House—hist pl MN-6
Bullis, Charles, House—hist pl NY-2
Bullis Brook—stream (2) NY-2
Bullis' Camp Site—hist pl TX-5
Bullis Canyon—valley NM-5
Bullis Cem—cemetery SD-7
*Bullis Creek* NY-2
Bullis Creek—stream (2) MT-8
Bullis Crossing—locale MI-6
Bullis Gap Range—range TX-5
Bullis Gap Tank—reservoir TX-5
Bullis Hill—summit TX-5
Bullis Hollow—valley PA-2
*Bullis Lake* MN-6
Bullis Lake—lake NM-5
Bull Island—flat DE-2
Bull Island—island (2) AK-9
Bull Island—island CA-9
Bull Island—island GA-3
Bull Island—island IL-6
Bull Island—island LA-4
Bull Island—island (2) MA-1
Bull Island—island MT-8
Bull Island—island (3) SC-3
Bull Islands—island LA-4
**Bullis Mill**—pop pl PA-2
**Bullis Mills**—pop pl PA-2
Bullis Sch—school (2) MD-2
Bullis Spring Ranch—locale NM-5
Bullis Tabernacle Ch—church NC-3
Bullit Bay—swamp SC-3
Bullit Park—park VA-3
Bullit Run—stream PA-2
Bullitsburg Ch—church KY-4
*Bullits Lick* KY-4
Bullitt Bayou—gut LA-4
**Bullitt (County)**—pop pl KY-4
Bullitt Lick Ch—church KY-4
Bullitt Lick Creek—stream KY-4
Bullitt-Longenecker House—hist pl LA-4
Bullitt Neck—cape MD-2
*Bullitts Bayou* LA-4
**Bullittsville**—pop pl KY-4
Bullivant Park—park IN-6
Bull-Jackson House—hist pl NY-2
Bull Jack Spring—spring OR-9
Bull Junior Creek—stream WI-6
Bull Key—island FL-3
Bull Kill Creek—stream MI-6
Bull Knob—summit TX-5
Bull Knoll—summit WY-8
Bull Lake—lake (2) AR-4
Bull Lake—lake (2) CA-9
Bull Lake—lake (2) CO-8
Bull Lake—lake (2) LA-4
Bull Lake—lake MN-6
Bull Lake—lake (3) MT-8
Bull Lake—lake NE-7
Bull Lake—lake (2) NM-5
Bull Lake—lake TX-5
Bull Lake—reservoir IN-6
Bull Lake—reservoir OR-9
Bull Lake—reservoir UT-8
Bull Lake—reservoir WY-8
Bull Lake Creek—stream WY-8
Bull Lake Dam—dam WY-8
Bull Lake Falls—falls WY-8
Bull Lake Glacier—glacier WY-8
*Bull Lake Glaciers* WY-8
Bull Lake Lodge—locale WY-8
Bull Lake Slough—gut AR-4
Bull Lake Slough—stream LA-4
Bull Ledge—bar ME-1
Bull Lick—stream WV-2
Bull Lot Hollow—valley MO-7
Bullman Cem—cemetery NC-3
Bullman Cem—cemetery TX-5
Bullman Creek—stream WA-9
Bull Meadow—flat (3) CA-9
Bull Meadow—flat ID-8
Bull Meadow—flat OR-9
Bull Meadow Creek—stream CA-9
Bullmill Camp—locale NM-5
**Bull Mine**—pop pl NY-2
Bull Mine Mtn—summit NY-2
Bull Minnow Point—cape MD-2
Bull Minnow Run—stream MD-2
Bullmire Branch—stream KY-4
Bull Moose Cabin—locale MT-8
Bull Moose Canal—canal LA-4
Bullmoose Creek—stream WY-8
Bull Moose Hill—summit VT-1
Bull Moose Lake—lake WI-6
Bull Moose Lode Mine—mine SD-7
**Bull Moose Township**—pop pl ND-7
**Bull Moose (Township of)**—pop pl MN-6
Bull Moose Trail—trail ID-8
Bull Moose Trail—trail MN-6
Bull Mountain—locale MT-8
Bull Mountain—locale OR-9
Bull Mountain—ridge AR-4
Bull Mountain Brook—stream CT-1
*Bull Mountain Creek* MT-8
Bull Mountain Creek—stream AL-4
Bull Mountain Creek—stream MS-4
Bull Mountain Fork—stream VA-3
Bull Mountain Game Range—park MT-8
Bull Mountain Gap—gap TN-4
*Bull Mountains* CO-8
*Bull Mountains* MT-8
Bull Mountain Tank—reservoir AZ-5
Bull Mtn—summit AL-4
Bull Mtn—summit (2) AZ-5
Bull Mtn—summit (2) AR-4
Bull Mtn—summit (3) CO-8
Bull Mtn—summit CT-1
Bull Mtn—summit GA-3
Bull Mtn—summit ME-1
Bull Mtn—summit MD-2
Bull Mtn—summit MA-1
Bull Mtn—summit MS-4
Bull Mtn—summit (2) MT-8
Bull Mtn—summit (3) NC-3
Bull Mtn—summit OK-5
Bull Mtn—summit OR-9
Bull Mtn—summit (3) UT-8
Bull Mtn—summit (2) VT-1
Bull Mtn—summit VA-3
Bull Mtn—summit WV-2
Bull Mtn—summit (2) WY-8
Bull Mtns—range MT-8
Bull Narrows—channel SC-3
Bull Neck—cape (2) VA-3
Bullneck Brake—swamp AR-4
Bullneck Creek—stream MD-2
Bull Neck Creek—stream VA-3
Bullneck Run—stream VA-3
Bull Neck Swamp—stream NC-3
Bull Nelson Creek—stream UT-8
Bull Nose Branch—stream GA-3
Bulloch Bay—swamp GA-3
Bulloch Branch—stream FL-3
Bulloch Canyon—valley UT-8
**Bulloch (County)**—pop pl GA-3
Bulloch County Courthouse—hist pl GA-3
**Bulloch Crossroads**—pop pl GA-3
Bulloch Gulch—valley UT-8
Bulloch Hall—hist pl GA-3
Bulloch Memorial Gardens—cemetery GA-3
Bulloch Spring—spring UT-8
*Bullock* IN-6
Bullock—locale AL-4
Bullock—locale TX-5
**Bullock**—pop pl NJ-2
**Bullock**—pop pl NC-3
Bullock, Benjamin Kimball, Farmhouse—hist pl UT-8
Bullock, Samuel, House—hist pl NE-7
Bullock Bend—bend CA-9
Bullock Bend—bend TX-5
Bullock Branch—stream (2) AL-4
Bullock Branch—stream AR-4
Bullock Branch—stream KY-4
Bullock Branch—stream SC-3
Bullock Bridge—bridge OR-9
Bullock Brook—stream NY-2
*Bullock Canyon* UT-8
Bullock Canyon—valley AZ-5
Bullock Canyon—valley TX-5
Bullock Cave—cave TN-4
Bullock Cem—cemetery AL-4
Bullock Cem—cemetery AR-4
Bullock Cem—cemetery IA-7
Bullock Cem—cemetery KY-4
Bullock Cem—cemetery (2) LA-4
Bullock Cem—cemetery (5) MS-4
Bullock Cem—cemetery (2) NC-3
Bullock Cem—cemetery PA-2
Bullock Cem—cemetery SC-3
Bullock Cem—cemetery (2) TN-4
Bullock Ch—church NC-3
Bullock-Clifton House—hist pl KY-4
Bullock Community Center—locale SD-7
Bullock Corners—locale NY-2
Bullock Corrals Spring—spring AZ-5
**Bullock County**—pop pl AL-4
Bullock County Courthouse—building AL-4
Bullock County Courthouse Hist Dist—hist pl AL-4
Bullock County HS—school AL-4
Bullock County Technical HS—school AL-4
Bullock Cove—bay RI-1
*Bullock Creek* VA-3
**Bullock Creek**—pop pl MI-6
**Bullock Creek**—pop pl SC-3
Bullock Creek—stream CA-9
Bullock Creek—stream LA-4
Bullock Creek—stream MD-2
Bullock Creek—stream (2) MI-6
Bullock Creek—stream MS-4
Bullock Creek—stream NY-2
Bullock Creek—stream OR-9
Bullock Creek—stream SC-3
Bullock Creek Ch—church MI-6
Bullock Creek HS—school MI-6
Bullock Creek JHS—school MI-6
Bullock-Dew House—hist pl NC-3
Bullock Ditch—canal IN-6
Bullock Drain—canal MI-6
Bullock Drain—canal OR-9
Bullock Draw—valley UT-8
Bullock Draw Dam—dam UT-8
Bullock Draw Rsvr—reservoir UT-8
*Bullock Gulch* UT-8
Bullock Gulch—valley OR-9
Bullock Hill—summit MT-8
Bullock Hill—summit NY-2
Bullock Hill Cem—cemetery AL-4
Bullock (historical)—locale MS-4
Bullock (historical)—locale SD-7
Bullock Hollow—valley MO-7
Bullock Hollow—valley (3) TN-4
Bullock Hollow Spring—spring TN-4
*Bullock Island* AL-4
Bullock Island—island MD-2
Bullock Lake—lake FL-3
Bullock Lake—lake LA-4
Bullock Lateral—canal NM-5
*Bullock Lock* IN-6
Bullock Lookout Tower—locale SD-7
Bullock Lookout Tower—tower FL-3
Bullock Neck—cape RI-1
Bullock Pen Creek—stream (2) KY-4
Bullock Pen Lake—reservoir KY-4
Bullock Point—cape AL-4
Bullock Point—cape RI-1
Bullock Pond—lake MD-2
Bullock Post Office (historical)—building MS-4
Bullock Prong—stream DE-2
Bullock Run—stream PA-2
Bullocks Cave—cave AL-4
Bullocks Ch—church TX-5
Bullock Sch—school KY-4
Bullock Sch—school MS-4
Bullock Sch—school NC-3
Bullock Sch (historical)—school AL-4
Bullocks Corner—locale VA-3
*Bullocks Cove* RI-1
*Bullocks Creek* SC-3
*Bullocks Creek Cove* RI-1
*Bullocks Crossroads* NC-3
**Bullocks Crossroads**—pop pl NC-3
*Bullocks Ferry* AL-4
Bullocks Hill—summit AL-4
*Bullock Shoals* AL-4
Bullocks Hollow—valley AL-4
Bullocks Islands—island AL-4
Bullocks Lake—reservoir GA-3
*Bullocks Neck* MD-2
Bullocks Park—park NC-3
Bullocks Park—park UT-8
*Bullocks Point* RI-1
Bullock Spring—spring CA-9
Bullocks Quarry—mine PA-2
**Bullock Subdivision**—pop pl UT-8
Bullocksville—locale NC-3
Bullock's Wilshire Bldg—hist pl CA-9
Bullock Tank—reservoir AZ-5
Bullock Tank—reservoir TX-5
**Bullocktown**—pop pl IN-6
Bull of the Woods—summit OR-9
Bull Of The Woods Gulch—valley ID-8
Bull-of-the-Woods Mtn—summit NM-5
Bull of the Woods Pass—gap MT-8
Bull-of-the-Woods Pasture—area NM-5
Bull Of The Woods Trail—trail OR-9
Bullon, Mount—summit WA-9
Bullon Lake—lake WA-9
Bullon Lakes, Mount—lake WA-9
Bull Opening—flat CA-9
Bulloughs Pond—lake MA-1
Bull Park—flat (5) CO-8
Bull Park—flat (2) UT-8
Bull Park—flat WY-8
Bull Park Rsvr—reservoir CO-8
Bull Pass—gap AZ-5
Bull Pass Canyon—valley NM-5
Bull Pass Tank—reservoir NM-5
Bull Pasture—area UT-8
Bull Pasture—flat (2) AZ-5
Bull Pasture—flat CA-9
Bull Pasture—flat OR-9
Bull Pasture—flat UT-8
Bull Pasture—hist pl AZ-5
Bull Pasture—locale ID-8
Bull Pasture—valley AZ-5
Bull Pasture, The—flat OR-9
Bullpasture Creek—stream TN-4
Bullpasture Gorge—valley VA-3
Bull Pasture Hill—summit TX-5
Bull Pasture Hills—summit TX-5
Bullpasture Landing (historical)—locale TN-4
*Bull Pasture Mountain* UT-8
*Bullpasture Mtn* VA-3
Bullpasture Mtn—summit VA-3
Bullpasture River—stream VA-3
Bullpasture River—stream WV-2
Bull Pasture Rsvr—reservoir CO-8
Bull Pasture Spring—spring (2) AZ-5
Bull Pasture Spring—spring WY-8
Bull Pasture Tank—reservoir (7) AZ-5
Bull Pasture Tank—reservoir (3) NM-5
Bull Pasture Tank—reservoir TX-5
Bull Pasture Trail—trail UT-8
Bull Pasture Well—well CO-8
Bull Pasture Well—well (3) NM-5
Bull Pasture Well—well TX-5
Bull Pasture Well—well (2) WY-8
Bull Pasture Well (Flowing)—well NM-5
Bull Pasture Windmill—locale AZ-5
Bull Pasture Windmill—locale (2) CO-8
Bull Pasture Windmill—locale (4) NM-5
Bull Pasture Windmill—locale (11) TX-5
Bull Pen—locale NV-8
Bull Pen—locale NC-3
Bull Pen—valley MT-8
Bull Pen, The—stream ID-8
Bullpen Bay, The—bay WI-6
Bull Pen Branch—stream FL-3
Bullpen Branch—stream GA-3
Bull Pen Branch—stream KY-4
Bullpen Branch—stream TN-4
Bullpen Canyon—valley CA-9
Bullpen Cove—valley NC-3
*Bullpen Creek* TN-4
Bullpen Creek—stream AL-4
Bull Pen Creek—stream AL-4
Bullpen Creek—stream AR-4
Bullpen Creek—stream MS-4
Bullpen Creek—stream OK-5
Bullpen Creek—stream TN-4
Bull Pen Creek—stream WA-9
Bullpen Creek—stream WY-8
Bullpen Fork—stream WV-2
Bullpen Hollow—valley AL-4
Bull Pen Hollow—valley AR-4
Bullpen Hollow—valley TN-4
Bullpen Lake—lake CA-9

Bullpen Lake—lake TN-4
Bull Pen Landing AL-4
Bullpen Landing—locale TN-4
Bull Pen Mtn—summit NC-3
Bullpen Mtn—summit UT-8
Bull Pen Point—cape SC-3
Bull Pen Ranch—locale AZ-5
Bull Pen Rsvr—reservoir NV-8
Bull Pen Spring—spring MT-8
Bullpen Spring—spring UT-8
Bullpen Swale—valley UT-8
Bull Pine Corners—locale DE-2
Bull Pine Gap—gap OR-9
Bull Pine Mine—mine CA-9
Bull Pine Ridge—ridge OR-9
Bull Pit—cave AL-4
Bull Pizzle Lake—lake AR-4
Bull Pocosin—swamp NC-3
Bull Point SC-3
Bull Point—cape CA-9
Bull Point—cape FL-3
Bull Point—cape ME-1
Bull Point—cape MD-2
Bull Point—cape NY-2
Bull Point—cape NC-3
Bull Point—cape RI-1
Bull Point—cape (3) SC-3
Bull Point—cape VI-3
Bull Point—cliff UT-8
Bull Point—summit AZ-5
Bull Point Island—island MD-2
Bull Point Mine—mine CA-9
Bull Points—summit UT-8
Bull Point Wash—valley AZ-5
Bull Pond—lake (2) AZ-5
Bull Pond—lake CO-8
Bull Pond—lake CT-1
Bull Pond—lake (3) FL-3
Bull Pond—lake ME-1
Bull Pond—lake SC-3
Bull Pond—reservoir NY-2
Bull Pond—reservoir SC-3
Bull Pond—swamp SC-3
Bull Pond Point—cape NC-3
Bull Ponds—swamp TX-5
Bullpout Pond—lake (2) NY-2
Bull Prairie—flat (2) OR-9
Bull Prairie Dam—dam OR-9
Bull Prairie Forest Camp OR-9
Bull Prairie Forest Camp—locale OR-9
Bull Prairie Guard Station—locale OR-9
Bull Prairie Rsvr—reservoir OR-9
Bull Prairie Spring—spring OR-9
Bull Prairie Trail—trail OR-9
Bullpup Canyon—valley UT-8
Bull Pup Creek—stream AK-9
Bull Pup Lake OR-9
Bullpup Lake—lake OR-9
Bullpush Fork—stream WV-2
Bull Ranch—locale AZ-5
Bull Ranch—locale MT-8
Bull Ranch—locale SD-7
Bull Ranch Creek—stream NV-8
Bull Rapids—rapids IN-6
Bull Rapids Bridge—bridge IN-6
Bull Ridge CA-9
Bull Ridge—ridge (2) CA-9
Bull Ridge—ridge CO-8
Bull Ridge—ridge KY-4
Bull Ridge—ridge ME-1
Bull Ridge—ridge (2) TN-4
Bull Ridge—ridge (2) UT-8
Bull Ridge—ridge WY-8
Bull Ridge Pond—lake AL-4
Bull River MT-8
Bull River—gut SC-3
Bull River—stream AK-9
Bull River—stream GA-3
Bull River—stream MT-8
Bull River—stream SC-3
Bull River—stream WV-2
Bull River Campground—locale MT-8
Bull River Ditch—canal UT-8
Bull River Guard Station—locale MT-8
Bull River Run WV-2
Bull Roaring Creek—stream MT-8
Bull Rock—bar CA-9
Bull Rock—hist pl ME-1
Bull Rock—pillar CO-8
Bull Rock pillar ME 1
Bull Rock—pillar VI-3
Bull Rock Mtn—summit NY-2
Bull Rock Point—cape NY-2
Bullrock Point—cape NY-2
Bull Rock Trail—trail AK-9
Bull Roost—summit UT-8
Bull Roost Rsvr—reservoir UT-8
Bull Rsvr—reservoir MT-8
Bull Rsvr—reservoir PA-2
Bull Run IN-6
Bull Run OH-6
Bull Run OR-9
Bullrun PA-2
Bull Run TX-5
Bull Run VA-3
Bull Run WV-2
Bull Run—basin CA-9
Bull Run—flat CA-9
Bull Run—locale LA-4
Bull Run—locale MD-2
Bull Run—locale NY-2
Bull Run—locale VA-3
**Bullrun**—pop pl OR-9
**Bull Run**—pop pl TN-4
**Bull Run**—pop pl WV-2
Bull Run—stream AL-4
Bull Run—stream CA-9
Bull Run—stream CO-8
Bull Run—stream (3) IL-6
Bull Run—stream (3) IN-6
Bull Run—stream (3) IA-7
Bull Run—stream (5) KY-4
Bull Run—stream (2) MD-2
Bull Run—stream MI-6
Bull Run—stream NJ-2
Bull Run—stream (2) NC-3
Bull Run—stream (6) OH-6
Bull Run—stream OR-9
Bull Run—stream (11) PA-2
Bull Run—stream SD-7
Bull Run—stream (3) TN-4
Bull Run—stream (2) TX-5
Bull Run—stream UT-8
Bull Run—stream VT-1
Bull Run—stream (8) VA-3
Bull Run—stream (10) WV-2
Bull Run—stream WI-6
Bull Run—uninc pl TN-4
Bull Run Basin—basin CA-9
Bull Run Basin—basin NV-8
Bull Run Bluff—cliff MO-7
Bull Run Boat Dock—locale TN-4
Bull Run Brook NY-2
Bull Run Canyon—valley NV-8
Bull Run Canyon—valley NM-5
Bull Run Canyon—valley OR-9
Bull Run Canyon—valley UT-8
Bull Run Cattle Drive—trail CA-9
Bull Run Ch—church (2) VA-3
Bull Run Corner—locale CT-1
Bull Run Cove—basin ID-8
Bull Run Creek TN-4
Bullrun Creek—stream AK-9
Bull Run Creek—stream AZ-5
Bull Run Creek—stream (4) CA-9
Bull Run Creek—stream CO-8
Bull Run Creek—stream (3) ID-8
Bull Run Creek—stream (2) KY-4
Bull Run Creek—stream MN-6
Bull Run Creek—stream (2) MT-8
Bullrun Creek—stream (2) MT-8
Bull Run Creek—stream NV-8
Bull Run Creek—stream ND-7
Bullrun Creek—stream (2) OR-9
Bull Run Creek—stream (3) OR-9
Bullrun Creek—stream OR-9
Bull Run Creek—stream (2) OR-9
Bull Run Creek—stream SC-3
Bull Run Creek—stream SD-7
Bullrun Creek—stream TN-4
Bull Run Creek—stream TX-5
Bull Run Creek—stream VA-3
Bull Run Creek—stream WY-8
Bull Run Creek Falls—falls ID-8
Bull Run Dam—dam PA-2
Bull Run Dam No. 1—dam OR-9
Bull Run Dam NO. 2—dam OR-9
**Bull Run Estates**—pop pl VA-3
Bull Run Flat—flat UT-8
Bull Run Gap—gap PA-2
Bull Run Gulch—valley MT-8
Bull Run Hollow—valley MO-7
Bull Run Knob—summit KY-4
Bull Run Knob—summit VA-3
Bull Run Knob Overlook—locale VA-3
Bull Run Lake—lake CA-9
Bull Run Lake—lake OR-9
Bull Run Lake Dam—dam OR-9
Bull Run Lake Trail—trail OR-9
Bull Run Meadow—flat CA-9
Bull Run Mine—mine NV-8
Bullrun Mine—mine OR-9
Bull Run Mine—mine UT-8
**Bull Run Mountain Estates**—pop pl VA-3
Bull Run Mountains—range VA-3
Bullrun Mtn—summit OR-9
Bull Run Mtns—range NV-8
Bull Run Park—park TN-4
Bull Run Pass—gap CA-9
Bull Run Peak—summit (2) CA-9
Bull Run Peak—summit ID-8
Bull Run Point—cape PA-2
Bull Run Post Office (historical)—building TN-4
Bull Run Rec Area—park TN-4
Bull Run Regional Park—park VA-3
Bullrun Ridge—ridge TN-4
Bull Run River NV-8
Bull Run River—stream OR-9
Bull Run Road Ch—church TN-4
Bull Run Rock—summit CA-9
Bullrun Rock—summit OR-9
Bull Run Rsvr OR-9
Bull Run Rsvr—reservoir NV-8
Bull Run Rsvr—reservoir OR-9
Bull Run Rsvr Number One—reservoir OR-9
Bull Run Rsvr Number Two—reservoir OR-9
Bull Run Sch—school OR-9
Bullrun Sch—school TN-4
Bull Run Sch—school VT-1
Bull Run Sch—school WV-2
Bull Run Sch (abandoned)—school (2) PA-2
Bull Run Shoals—bar TN-4
Bull Run Slough—stream CA-9
Bull Run Spring NV-8
Bull Run Spring—spring AZ-5
Bull Run Spring—spring NV-8
Bullrun Spring—spring OR-9
Bull Run Spring—spring OR-9
Bull Run Steam Plant—building TN-4
Bull Run Swamp—swamp LA-4
Bull Run Tank—reservoir AZ-5
Bull Run Tank—reservoir NM-5
Bull Run Trail—trail AZ-5
Bull Run Trail—trail OR-9
Bull Run Valley—flat CA-9
Bull Run Valley—valley TN-4
Bull Run Vista—locale PA-2
Bull Rush Bay—bay NY-2
Bull Rush Creek UT-8
Bullrush Creek—stream UT-8
Bull Rush Creek—stream UT-8
Bullrush Gorge—valley UT-8
Bullrush Hollow—valley UT-8
Bullrush Lake—lake AK-9
Bullrush Lake—lake MN-6
Bull Rush Peak—summit UT-8
Bull Rush Point—cape VT-1
Bullrush Spring—spring NV-8
Bull Rush Spring—spring UT-8
Bullrush Spring—spring UT-8
Bull Rush Valley UT-8
Bull Saddle—gap AZ-5
Bull Sampson Creek WI-6
Bulls Bay NC-3
Bulls Bay SC-3
Bulls Bay—bay SC-3
Bulls Bay—swamp FL-3
Bulls Bayou—gut LA-4
Bulls Bend—bend WY-8
Bulls Branch VA-3
Bulls Branch—stream KY-4
Bulls Branch—stream NJ-2
Bulls Branch—stream SC-3
Bull's Bridge—hist pl CT-1
**Bulls Bridge**—pop pl CT-1
Bulls Brook—stream ME-1
Bulls Canyon—valley UT-8
Bull Sch—school SC-3
Bull Sch (abandoned)—school PA-2
Bulls City KS-7
Bullscrape Branch—stream NC-3
Bulls Creek CT-1
Bulls Creek SC-3
Bulls Creek WV-2
Bulls Creek—stream AL-4
Bulls Creek—stream CO-8
Bulls Creek—stream SC-3
Bulls Creek—stream TN-4
Bulls Creek—stream VA-3
Bulls Creek—stream WY-8
Bulls Creek Access Area—park TN-4
Bulls Dock—locale VA-3
Bull Seal Point—cape AK-9
Bull Seep—canal CO-8
Bullseye—locale DE-2
Bullseye Bayou—gut LA-4
Bullseye Bridge—bridge ME-1
Bulls Eye Butte—summit OR-9
Bullseye Canyon—valley UT-8
Bullseye Lake—lake CA-9
Bulls-Eye Lake—lake IN-6
Bulls Eye Mine—mine CO-8
Bullseye Orchard Lake—reservoir NC-3
Bullseye Point—cape DE-2
Bulls Eye Point—summit WY-8
Bulls Eye Rock—pillar CA-9
Bullseye Spring—spring OR-9
Bulls Ford Bridge—bridge KS-7
Bulls Fork—stream ID-8
Bullsgap TN-4
Bulls Gap—gap AL-4
Bulls Gap—gap TN-4
**Bulls Gap**—pop pl TN-4
Bulls Gap (CCD)—cens area TN-4
Bulls Gap Division—civil TN-4
Bulls Gap Hist Dist—hist pl TN-4
Bulls Gap HS—school TN-4
Bullsgap Post Office TN-4
Bulls Gap Post Office—building TN-4
Bulls Gap Sch (historical)—school TN-4
Bulls Harbor SC-3
Bullshead AZ-5
Bullshead NY-2
Bulls Head—locale NY-2
**Bulls Head**—pop pl NY-2
Bulls Head—rock VT-1
Bullshead—summit CA-9
Bulls Head—summit VA-3
Bulls Head—summit WV-2
Bulls Head—uninc pl NY-2
Bulls Head Branch—stream PA-2
Bullshead Canyon—valley CA-9
Bulls Head Ch—church NY-2
Bulls Head Channel—channel CA-9
Bullshead Creek—stream TX-5
Bulls Head Point—cape CA-9
Bulls Head Rock—island AZ-5
Bulls Hill—summit SC-3
Bull Shirt Spring OR-9
**Bull Shoals**—pop pl AR-4
Bull Shoals Caverns—cave AR-4
Bull Shoals Dam—dam AR-4
Bull Shoals Lake—reservoir (2) AR-4
Bull Shoals Lake—reservoir MO-7
Bull Shoals Mtn—summit AR-4
Bull Shoals Public Use Area—park AR-4
Bull Shoals Reservoir AR-4
Bull Shoals Rsvr MO-7
Bull Shoals State Park—park AR-4
Bullshoe Mtn—summit MT-8
Bullshot Reservoir—lake ID-8
Bull Sink—lake FL-3
Bull Sink Pond FL-3
Bulls Island SC-3
Bulls Island—island IL-6
Bulls Island—island NJ-2
Bulls Island State Park—park NJ-2
Bull Skeen Windmill—locale TX-5
Bullskin Branch—stream KY-4
Bullskin Branch—stream WV-2
Bullskin Creek—stream (2) KY-4
Bullskin Creek—stream MO-7
Bullskin Creek—stream (2) OH-6
Bull Skin Creek—stream SC-3
Bullskin Creek—stream TN-4
Bullskin Creek Site—hist pl OH-6
Bullskin Elem Sch—school PA-2
Bullskin Fairgrounds—locale PA-2
Bullskin Fork—stream KY-4
Bullskin Mtn—summit MD-2
Bullskin Ridge—ridge CA-9
Bullskin Ridge—ridge TN-4
Bullskin Run—stream WV-2
**Bullskin (Township of)**—pop pl PA-2
Bull Skull Branch AL-4
Bull Skull Creek—stream AL-4
Bulls Landing—locale VA-3
Bull Slough—gut FL-3
Bull Slough—stream CA-9
Bull Sluice Lake—reservoir GA-3
Bulls Mill DE-2
Bullsnake Pond—reservoir NM-5
Bulls Narrows SC-3
Bulls Neck MA-1
Bulls Neck Island MA-1
Bulls Pass—gap UT-8
Bulls Point RI-1
Bulls Point—cape IN-6
Bulls Point—cape MD-2
Bulls Pond—lake VA-3
Bull Spring AZ-5
Bull Spring—spring (11) AZ-5
Bull Spring—spring AR-4
Bull Spring—spring (6) CA-9
Bull Spring—spring (2) CO-8
Bull Spring—spring (7) ID-8
Bull Spring—spring (3) NV-8
Bull Spring—spring (3) NM-5
Bull Spring—spring (7) OR-9
Bull Spring—spring SD-7
Bull Spring—spring (2) TX-5
Bull Spring—spring (6) UT-8
Bull Spring—spring WY-8
Bull Spring Canyon—valley AZ-5
Bull Spring Canyon—valley NM-5
Bull Spring Creek—stream OR-9
Bull Spring Creek—stream WY-8
Bull Spring Lake—lake WY-8
Bull Spring Mesa—summit AZ-5
Bull Springs—spring AZ-5
Bull Springs—spring CO-8
Bull Springs—spring ID-8
Bull Springs—spring NV-8
Bull Springs—spring NM-5
Bull Springs—spring UT-8
Bull Springs—spring (2) WY-8
Bull Springs Mine—mine AZ-5
Bull Springs Rim—cliff WY-8
Bull Springs Well—well TX-5
Bull Spring Tank—reservoir AZ-5
Bull Spring Wash—stream AZ-5
Bull Spring Wash—stream CA-9
Bull Spring Wash—valley UT-8
Bull Spring Well—well AZ-5
Bulls Run—stream MD-2
Bulls Run—stream WY-8
Bulls Shoals—rapids TN-4
Bull Stone House—hist pl NY-2
Bulls Tooth—summit WA-9
Bull Summit Waterhole—spring ID-8
Bull Swamp—stream (2) SC-3
Bull Swamp—stream VA-3
Bull Swamp—swamp OR-9
Bull Swamp Ch—church SC-3
Bull Swamp Creek—stream SC-3
Bull Swamp Sch—school SC-3
Bull Tail Creek—stream KY-4
Bulltail Creek—stream (2) NC-3
Bull Tail Valley—valley CA-9
Bull Tank—reservoir (19) AZ-5
Bull Tank—reservoir (3) NM-5
Bull Tank—reservoir (8) TX-5
Bull Tank Canyon—valley AZ-5
Bull Tank Mesa—summit AZ-5
Bull Tank Number One—reservoir AZ-5
Bull Tank Spring—spring NM-5
Bull Tavern—locale PA-2
Bull Team Gulch—valley CA-9
Bull Thistle Cave Archeol Site (44TZ92)—hist pl VA-3
Bull Thorofare—channel NJ-2
**Bullthroat**—pop pl VT-1
Bull Tongue Creek—stream TX-5
Bull Tongue Island—island SC-3
Bull Tote Road Trail—trail PA-2
Bulltown—locale AR-4
Bulltown—locale NJ-2
Bulltown—locale WV-2
Bulltown Bay—swamp SC-3
Bulltown Ditch—canal SC-3
Bulltown Schoolhouse (historical)—school PA-2
Bull Town Swamp—swamp GA-3
Bull Trail—trail CO-8
Bull Trail Mtn—summit GA-3
Bull Trap Canyon—valley NM-5
Bull Trap Tank—reservoir (3) TX-5
Bulltrap Windmill—locale NM-5
Bull Trap Windmill—locale (2) TX-5
Bull Trout Lake—lake ID-8
Bull Trout Point—cliff ID-8
Bull Tubs Tank—reservoir TX-5
Bull Tub Tank—reservoir TX-5
Bull Tub Windmill—locale TX-5
Bulluck Cem—cemetery NC-3
Bullucks Crossroads—locale NC-3
Bull Valley UT-8
Bull Valley—basin UT-8
**Bull Valley**—pop pl IL-6
Bull Valley—valley (3) UT-8
Bull Valley Branch UT-8
Bull Valley Canyon UT-8
Bull Valley Creek UT-8
Bull Valley Gorge—valley UT-8
Bull Valley Mtn—summit UT-8
Bull Valley Mtns—range UT-8
Bull Valley Spring—spring UT-8
Bull Valley Wash—stream NV-8
Bull Valley Wash—valley UT-8
**Bullville**—pop pl NY-2
Bullwacker Creek—stream OK-5
Bullwacker Creek—stream WY-8
Bullwacker Spring—spring UT-8
Bullwagga Bay NY-2
Bull Wagon Creek—stream TX-5
Bull Waterhole—lake (2) TX-5
Bull Waterhole Draw—valley TX-5
Bull Water Spring—spring AZ-5
Bull Well—well AZ-5
Bull Well—well (4) NM-5
Bull Well—well (7) TX-5
Bull Well Canyon—valley NM-5
Bullwell Windmill—locale TX-5
Bullwhacker Canyon—valley ID-8
Bullwhacker Coulee—stream MT-8
Bullwhacker Creek MT-8
Bullwhacker Creek—stream WY-8
Bullwhacker Draw—valley WY-8
Bullwhacker Mine—mine NV-8
Bullwhackers Coulee MT-8
Bullwhacker Spring—spring (2) NV-8
Bullwhacker Springs—spring NV-8
Bullwhack Spring—spring NV-8
Bullwhack Summit—locale NV-8
Bull Wheel Hollow—valley PA-2
Bullwheel Ridge—ridge CA-9
Bull Windmill—locale (3) NM-5
Bull Windmill—locale (5) TX-5
Bullwinkle Rsvr—reservoir UT-8
Bullyard Sound—bay SC-3
Bully Boy Creek—stream AK-9
Bully Branch—stream LA-4
Bully Branch—stream SC-3
Bully Camp Oil and Gas Field—oilfield LA-4
Bully Choop Mine—mine CA-9
Bully Choop Mtn—summit CA-9
Bully Creek ID-8
Bully Creek—stream ID-8
Bully Creek—stream OK-5
Bully Creek—stream (2) OR-9
Bully Creek Dam—dam OR-9
Bully Creek Ridge ID-8
Bully Creek Rsvr—reservoir OR-9
Bully Creek Sch—school OR-9
Bully Creek Siphon—other OR-9
Bull Yearling Run—stream VA-3
Bully Head Cove—cave PA-2
Bully Hill—locale CA-9
**Bully Hill**—pop pl PA-2
Bully Hill—summit CA-9
Bully Hill Sch—school PA-2
**Bully (historical)**—pop pl OR-9
Bully Hollow—valley PA-2
Bully Horselot Branch—stream FL-3
Bully Lake—lake FL-3
Bully Mtn—summit SC-3
Bullymuck Brook—stream CT-1
Bully Ridge—ridge KY-4
Bully Run—stream PA-2
Bulmer Creek—stream OR-9
Bulochang FM-9
Buloh Ch—church AL-4
Bulol FM-9
Buloochang FM-9
Bulo Point—cape OR-9
Bulow, Governor William J., House—hist pl SD-7
Bulow Campbell, Lake—reservoir GA-3
Bulow Creek—stream FL-3
Bulow Plantation Ruins—hist pl FL-3
Bulow Ruins State Monmt—park FL-3
Bulows Minde—locale VI-3
**Bulpitt**—pop pl IL-6
Bulrush Canyon—valley AZ-5
Bulrush Cove—bay NH-1
Bulrush Point—cliff AZ-5
Bulrush Wash—stream (2) AZ-5
Bulson Creek—stream WA-9
Bulsontown—locale NY-2
Bulter Cem—cemetery AR-4
Bulter Creek GA-3
Bulter Lodge—locale VT-1
Bultje Sch (historical)—school SD-7
Bulubul—island FM-9
Bulul FM-9
Bulverde—locale TX-5
Bulverde Community Center—locale TX-5
Bulverde Sch—school TX-5
Bulwagga Bay—bay NY-2
Bulwagga Mtn—summit NY-2
Bulwark Branch—stream WV-2
Bulwark Ridge—ridge CO-8
Bulwark Sch—school WV-2
Bulwark Shoal—bar ME-1
Bulwinkle Creek—stream CA-9
Bulwol—locale FM-9
Buma Hill—summit GA-3
**Buman**—pop pl OR-9
Bumback Gulch—valley CO-8
Bumback Spring—spring CO-8
Bumbay Island DE-2
Bumbee Creek—stream TN-4
Bumbers Branch—stream VA-3
Bumble Bay—bay AK-9
Bumblebee AZ-5
**Bumble Bee**—pop pl AZ-5
**Bumblebee**—pop pl CA-9
Bumblebee Canyon—valley UT-8
Bumblebee Creek AZ-5
Bumble Bee Creek—stream AZ-5
Bumblebee Creek—stream AZ-5
Bumblebee Creek—stream (2) CA-9
Bumblebee Creek—stream FL-3
Bumblebee Creek—stream ID-8
Bumble Bee Interchange—crossing AZ-5
Bumblebee Island—island (2) FL-3
Bumblebee Lake—lake UT-8
Bumblebee Meadow—flat ID-8
Bumblebee Mine—mine (2) CA-9
Bumblebee Mine—mine ID-8
Bumblebee Mtn—summit UT-8
Bumblebee Peak—summit ID-8
Bumble Bee Ridge—ridge TN-4
Bumblebee Run—stream WV-2
Bumble Bee Sch—school IL-6
Bumblebee Spring—spring OR-9
Bumblebee Spring—spring (2) UT-8
Bumblebee Springs—spring UT-8
Bumblebee Tank—reservoir AZ-5
Bumblebee Wash AZ-5
Bumbleton Courthouse—building GA-3
**Bumbletown**—pop pl MI-6
Bumbo Brook—stream MA-1
Bumbo Hill—summit NH-1
Bumbo Island DE-2
Bumboo Hill NH-1
Bumbo Pond—lake NY-2
Bumbpers Hell CA-9
Bumbrey Cem—cemetery VA-3
Bumby Canyon MT-8
Bumby Gulch—valley MT-8
Bum Canyon—valley OR-9
Bumcombe Hill—summit FL-3
Bum Creek—stream ID-8
Bum Creek—stream MN-6
Bum Creek—stream MT-8
Bum Creek—stream TN-4
Bum Drain—stream MI-6
Bum Draw—valley WY-8
Bumfagging Hill—summit NH-1
Bumfagon Brook—stream NH-1
Bum Fork—stream WV-2
Bumgard Cem—cemetery IL-6
Bumgarden Ford—locale MO-7
Bumgardiner Spring—spring TN-4
Bumgard Island—island IL-6
Bumgardner Branch—stream NC-3
Bumgardner Branch—stream VA-3
Bumgardner Cem—cemetery IL-6
Bumgardner Hollow—valley WV-2
Bumgardner Ridge—ridge NC-3
Bumgardner Sch—school KS-7
Bumgarner Branch—stream (3) NC-3
Bumgarner Cem—cemetery MO-7
Bumgarner Cem—cemetery NC-3
Bumgarner Cem—cemetery OH-6
Bumgarner Gap—gap NC-3
Bumgarner Ranch—locale CO-8
Bumgarner Sch—school IL-6
Bumgarther Mtn—summit NC-3
Bumkin Island—bar MA-1
Bumkin Island—island MA-1
Bum Lake—lake MI-6
Bum Lake—lake TX-5
**Bummer**—pop pl KY-4
Bummer Creek—stream ID-8
Bummer Creek—stream ND-7
Bummer Creek—stream (3) OR-9
Bummer Gulch—valley (2) OR-9
Bummer Lake—lake CA-9
Bummer Lake Creek—stream CA-9
Bummer Peak—summit CA-9
Bummers Flat—flat CA-9
Bummers Gulch—valley CO-8
**Bummerville**—pop pl CA-9
Bummet Brook MA-1
Bump, The—summit VA-3
Bump And Edmiston Ditch—canal CA-9
Bumpas Bottom—valley TN-4
Bumpas Cove—valley TN-4
Bumpas Creek Sch (historical)—school AL-4
Bumpas Hell CA-9
Bumpas Hot Springs CA-9
Bumpas Mountain CA-9
**Bumpass**—pop pl VA-3
Bumpass Cave Creek TN-4
Bumpass Cem—cemetery MO-7
Bumpass Cem—cemetery TN-4
Bumpass Cove TN-4
**Bumpass Cove**—pop pl TN-4
Bumpass Cove Creek TN-4
Bumpass Creek—stream AL-4
Bumpass Creek—stream MS-4
Bumpass Creek—stream MO-7
Bumpass Creek—stream TN-4
Bumpass Creek Ch—church AL-4
Bumpass Creek Freewill Baptist Ch AL-4
Bumpass Hell—flat CA-9
Bumpass Hot Springs CA-9
Bumpass Inferno CA-9
Bumpass Mtn—summit CA-9
Bumpasss Hell CA-9
Bumpass Store (historical)—locale TN-4
Bumpas-Troy House—hist pl NC-3
Bump Cem—cemetery VT-1
Bump Creek—stream (2) OR-9
Bumper, The—summit WA-9
Bumper Canyon—valley UT-8
Bumper Cem—cemetery MO-7
Bumpers Bluff—cliff TN-4
Bumpers Cem—cemetery AL-4
Bumper Tank—reservoir TX-5
Bumphead—locale GA-3
Bumphead Dam—dam OR-9
Bumphead Glade—flat CA-9
Bumphead Rsvr—reservoir OR-9
Bump Heads—summit CA-9
Bumpheads, The—other OR-9
Bump Hill—summit MA-1
Bump Hollow—valley MO-7
Bumphrey Lake—lake MI-6
Bumphs Hill Creek SC-3
Bumping Campground—locale WA-9
Bumping Crossing Campground—locale WA-9
Bumping Lake—reservoir WA-9
Bumping Lake Trail—trail WA-9
Bumping Reservoir WA-9
Bumping River—stream WA-9
Bumpin Hill—summit RI-1
Bumpity Park—flat CO-8
Bumpkin Island—island ME-1
Bump Lake—lake OR-9
Bumplanding Creek—stream NC-3
Bump Mtn—summit NY-2
Bum Point Island NC-3
Bum Point Island—island NC-3
Bum Pond—lake NY-2
Bumpous Cem—cemetery KY-4
Bump Rsvr—reservoir OR-9
Bump Run—stream PA-2
Bumps Brook—stream VT-1
Bump Sch—school VT-1
Bumps Corners—locale PA-2
Bumps Creek—gut NC-3
Bumps Creek—stream NY-2
Bumps Pond MA-1
Bumps Pond—lake MA-1
Bumps Pond—lake NY-2
Bumps River—stream MA-1
Bumpstead, John, House—hist pl NY-2
Bumpstead Archeol Site—hist pl MD-2
Bump Sullivan Ditch—canal WY-8
Bump-Sullivan Ditch—canal WY-8
Bump-Sullivan Rsvr—reservoir WY-8
Bumpus Bog—swamp MA-1
Bumpus Bog Rsvr—reservoir MA-1
Bumpus Brook—stream NH-1
Bumpus Butte—summit WY-8
Bumpus Cem—cemetery TX-5
Bumpus Corners—locale NY-2
Bumpus Cove—locale TN-4
Bumpus Cove Cem—cemetery TN-4
Bumpus Cove Creek—stream TN-4
Bumpus Creek TN-4
Bumpus Dam Number 1—dam MA-1
Bumpus Lake Dam—dam MS-4
**Bumpus Mills**—pop pl TN-4
Bumpus Mills Post Office—building TN-4
Bumpus Mills Rec Area—park TN-4
Bumpus Mills Sch—school TN-4
Bumpville—locale PA-2
Bumpville Cem—cemetery PA-2
Bumpy Bay—swamp FL-3
Bumpy Baygall—swamp TX-5
Bumpy Creek—stream FL-3
Bumpy Point—cape AK-9
Bumpy Road Well—well AZ-5
Bums Creek—stream TX-5
Bum Shot Mtn—summit MT-8
Bumskit Pond MA-1
Bum Spring—spring UT-8
Bum Springs—spring WA-9
Bums Tank—reservoir AZ-5
**Bumstead**—pop pl AZ-5
Bumstead RR Station—building AZ-5
Bumstead Spit—cape WA-9
Bum Windmill—locale TX-5
Bumyok Ridge—ridge AK-9
**Buna**—pop pl TX-5
Buna (CCD)—cens area TX-5
Buna Lookout Tower—locale TX-5

Bunatik-Hafen ... FM-9
**Bunavista**—pop pl ... TX-5
Buncan Cem—cemetery ... KY-4
Bunce Cem—cemetery ... MO-7
Bunce Creek—stream ... MI-6
Bunce Gap—gap ... AR-4
Bunce Lake ... NY-2
Bunce Lake—lake ... ND-7
Buncel Basin—basin ... ID-8
Buncel Place—locale ... ID-8
Buncel Rsvr—reservoir ... ID-8
Bunce Sch—hist pl ... CO-8
Bunce Sch—school ... CT-1
Bunce Sch—school ... MI-6
Bunce Sch (abandoned)—school ... MO-7
Bunce School—locale ... CO-8
Bunces Pass—channel ... FL-3
**Bunceton**—pop pl ... MO-7
Bunch—locale ... KY-4
Bunch—locale ... OK-5
Bunch Bar—bar ... OR-9
Bunch Beach ... FL-3
Bunch Branch—stream ... KY-4
Bunch Branch—stream ... LA-4
Bunch Brush Canyon—valley ... NV-8
Bunch Canyon—valley ... AR-4
Bunch Canyon—valley ... CA-9
Bunch Canyon—valley ... NV-8
Bunch Canyon—valley ... WA-9
Bunch Cave—cave ... MO-7
Bunch Cave—cave ... TN-4
Bunch Cem—cemetery ... AR-4
Bunch Cem—cemetery ... IA-7
Bunch Cem—cemetery ... MS-4
Bunch Cem—cemetery (2) ... MO-7
Bunch Cem—cemetery ... OH-6
Bunch Cem—cemetery (3) ... TN-4
Bunch Creek ... LA-4
Bunch Creek ... NC-3
Bunch Creek—stream (2) ... AL-4
Bunch Creek—stream ... ID-8
Bunch Creek—stream ... KY-4
Bunch Creek—stream ... OK-5
Bunch Creek—stream ... PA-2
Bunch Creek—stream ... VA-3
Bunch Ditch ... IN-6
Bunche, Ralph, House—hist pl ... NY-2
Bunche, Ralph J., House—hist pl ... CA-9
Bunche Beach—beach ... FL-3
Bunche HS—school ... GA-3
Bunche HS—school ... KY-4
Bunche HS—school ... VA-3
Bunche JHS—school ... CA-9
Bunchem Creek ... WY-8
Bunchem Creek—stream ... WY-8
Bunche Park—park ... FL-3
Bunche Park—park ... TX-5
**Bunche Park**—pop pl ... FL-3
Bunche Park Elem Sch—school ... FL-3
Bunche Park Sch—school ... FL-3
Buncher (Reusens)—uninc pl ... VA-3
**Bunches**—pop pl ... PA-2
Bunches Bald—summit ... NC-3
Bunches Bald Overlook—locale ... NC-3
Bunches Bald Tunnel—tunnel ... NC-3
Bunches Bend—bend ... MS-4
Bunches Branch ... KY-4
Bunches Branch ... TN-4
Bunches Branch—stream ... KY-4
Bunches Ch—church ... NC-3
Bunche Sch—school ... CA-9
Bunche Sch—school ... GA-3
Bunche Sch—school ... MI-6
Bunche Sch—school ... OK-5
Bunche Sch—school (3) ... TX-5
Bunches Ch (historical)—church ... TN-4
Bunches Creek ... AL-4
Bunches Creek—stream ... KY-4
Bunches Creek—stream ... NC-3
Bunches Gap—gap ... NC-3
Bunches Sch—school ... TN-4
Bunches Trace—trail (2) ... TN-4
Bunch Ford—locale ... TN-4
Bunch Gap—gap ... TN-4
Bunch Grass Basin—basin ... MT-8
Bunchgrass Butte—summit ... OR-9
Bunchgrass Campground—locale ... CA-9
Bunchgrass Creek ... OR-9
Bunchgrass Creek—stream (3) ... CA-9
Bunch Grass Creek—stream ... MT-8
Bunchgrass Creek—stream (2) ... OR-9
Bunchgrass Creek—stream ... UT-8
Bunchgrass Flat—flat ... CA-9
Bunchgrass Lake—lake ... WA-9
Bunchgrass Meadow—flat ... WA-9
Bunch Grass Meadows—flat ... OR-9
Bunchgrass Mtn—summit ... CA-9
Bunchgrass Mtn—summit ... OR-9
Bunch Grass Ridge—ridge ... CA-9
Bunchgrass Ridge—ridge (2) ... OR-9
Bunch Grass Rsvr—reservoir ... OR-9
Bunchgrass Trail—trail ... CA-9
Bunchgrass Trail—trail ... OR-9
Bunchgrass Valley—valley ... CA-9
Bunch Ground Branch Blue Creek—stream ... CO-8
Bunchground Canyon—valley ... UT-8
Bunch Ground Pond—lake ... FL-3
Bunch Gulch—valley ... MT-8
Bunch (historical P.O.)—locale ... IA-7
Bunch Hollow—valley ... MO-7
Bunch Hollow—valley (3) ... TN-4
Bunch Hollow Bridge (historical)—bridge ... TN-4
Bunch Hollow Mine—mine ... TN-4
Bunch Lake—lake ... WA-9
Bunch Landing ... MO-7
Bunch Mtn—summit ... KY-4
Bunch Mtn—summit ... OK-5
Bunch of Hair—island ... NC-3
Bunch Prong—stream ... TN-4
Bunch Reservoir Dam—dam ... AZ-5
Bunch Rsvr—reservoir ... AZ-5
Bunchs Branch—stream ... KY-4
Bunch Sch—school ... TX-5
Bunch Sch (abandoned)—school ... MO-7
Bunchs Creek ... UT-8
Bunchs Creek—stream ... ID-8
Bunchs Creek—stream ... LA-4
Bunchs Cutoff—gut ... MS-4
Bunchs Store (historical)—locale ... TN-4
Bunch Station (historical)—locale ... IA-7
Bunchtown Cem—cemetery ... TN-4
Bunchy Creek ... LA-4
Bunckley ... MS-4
Bunckley Post Office (historical)—building ... MS-4
Bunco Corners—locale ... ID-8
Bunco Creek—stream ... AK-9
Bunco Lake—lake ... AK-9
Buncom—locale ... OR-9
Buncomb ... TX-5
**Buncomb**—pop pl ... TX-5
Buncomb Branch—stream ... KY-4
Buncomb Branch—stream ... MO-7
Buncomb Branch—stream ... NC-3
Buncomb Ch—church ... MO-7
Buncomb Creek—stream ... AL-4
Buncomb Creek—stream ... KY-4
Buncombe ... IN-6
Buncombe ... TX-5
Buncombe—locale ... IA-7
**Buncombe**—pop pl ... IL-6
**Buncombe**—pop pl ... TN-4
Buncombe Branch—stream ... KY-4
Buncombe Branch—stream (2) ... SC-3
Buncombe Cemetery ... AL-4
Buncombe Ch—church ... KY-4
**Buncombe County**—pop pl ... NC-3
Buncombe County Courthouse—hist pl ... NC-3
Buncombe County Home—locale ... NC-3
Buncombe Cove—valley ... TN-4
Buncombe Creek—stream ... IA-7
Buncombe Creek—stream ... OK-5
Buncombe Creek—stream ... TX-5
Buncombe Gap—gap ... TN-4
Buncombe Hall—locale ... NC-3
Buncombe Hill—summit ... MS-4
Buncombe Hill—summit ... TN-4
Buncombe (historical)—locale ... MS-4
**Buncombe (historical)**—pop pl (2) ... LA-4
**Buncombe (historical)**—pop pl ... TN-4
Buncombe Hollow Creek—stream ... WA-9
Buncombe Horse Range Ridge—ridge ... NC-3
Buncombe Ridge—ridge ... TN-4
Buncombe Sch—school ... IA-7
Buncombe Townhall—building ... IA-7
Buncombe Township—fmr MCD ... IA-7
Buncomb Ridge—ridge ... MO-7
Buncomb Sch—school ... KY-4
Buncomb Sch (abandoned)—school ... MO-7
Buncome—locale ... TX-5
Buncum Cem—cemetery ... MS-4
Bundan Sch—school ... IL-6
Bunday Hill—summit ... MI-6
**Bunde**—pop pl ... MN-6
Bunde Drain—canal ... MI-6
Bunderson Sch—school ... UT-8
Bund Gulch—valley ... MT-8
**Bundick**—pop pl ... VA-3
Bundick, Bayou—stream ... LA-4
Bundick Cem—cemetery ... TX-5
Bundick Creek ... LA-4
Bundick Creek—stream ... LA-4
Bundick Creek—stream ... VA-3
Bundick Lake—lake ... TX-5
Bundick Lake—reservoir ... LA-4
Bundicks Branch—stream ... DE-2
Bundicks Creek ... LA-4
Bundix Branch—stream ... TX-5
Bundle Ditch ... IN-6
Bundle Hollow—valley ... PA-2
Bundle Lake—lake ... MN-6
Bundle Prairie—flat ... CA-9
Bundle Run—stream ... OH-6
Bundoora Spring—spring ... CA-9
Bund Ranch—locale ... CA-9
Bundrant Branch—stream ... TN-4
Bundren Cem—cemetery ... TN-4
Bundrick Island—island ... SC-3
Bundschu Park—park ... MO-7
Bundy—locale ... ID-8
Bundy—locale ... MT-8
Bundy—locale ... VA-3
Bundy—locale ... WI-6
Bundy, Lake—lake ... FL-3
Bundy, Mount—summit ... MI-6
Bundy Branch ... VA-3
Bundy Brook—stream ... VT-1
Bundy Canyon—valley (2) ... CA-9
Bundy Cave—cave ... VA-3
Bundy Cem—cemetery ... NY-2
Bundy Cem—cemetery (2) ... PA-2
Bundy Creek—stream ... VA-3
Bundy Creek—stream ... WI-6
Bundy Crossing—locale ... TX-5
**Bundy Crossing**—pop pl ... NY-2
Bundy Fort—military ... PR-3
**Bundy Hill**—pop pl ... CT-1
Bundy Hill—summit ... CT-1
Bundy Hollow—valley ... NY-2
Bundy Hollow—valley ... WA-9
Bundy Hollow—valley ... WI-6
Bundy Hollow Cem—cemetery ... WA-9
**Bundy (Johnsons Mill)**—pop pl ... VA-3
**Bundy Junction**—pop pl ... MO-7
Bundy Lake—lake ... CO-8
Bundy Lake—lake ... FL-3
Bundy Lake—lake ... LA-4
Bundy Mtn—summit ... NH-1
Bundy Oil Field—oilfield ... TX-5
Bundy Park—flat ... CO-8
Bundy Pond—lake ... NY-2
Bundy Ponds—lake ... AZ-5
Bundy Ranch—locale ... TX-5
Bundy-Ross Ranch—locale ... TX-5
**Bundys (Bundy Crossing)**—pop pl ... NY-2
**Bundysburg**—pop pl ... OH-6
Bundy Sch—school ... DC-2
Bundy Sch—school (2) ... IL-6
Bundy Sch—school ... NC-3
Bundy Sch—school ... VT-1
Bundy Sch—school ... WY-8
Bundys Chapel—church ... VA-3
Bundys Crossroads ... NC-3
Bundys Swamp—stream ... VA-3
Bundy Tank—reservoir ... AZ-5
Bundy Tank—reservoir ... TX-5
Bunejug Mtns—summit ... NV-8
**Bunell**—pop pl ... CO-8
Bunga Lake—lake ... MN-6
Bungalow Canal—canal ... ID-8
**Bungalow City**—pop pl ... VA-3
Bungalow Cow Camp—locale ... ID-8
Bungalow Creek—stream ... OR-9
Bungalow Creek—stream ... WA-9
Bungalow Group—locale ... MT-8
Bungalow Hill—summit ... MO-7
Bungalow Hollow—valley ... TN-4
Bungalow Inlet—gut ... VA-3
Bungalow Island—island ... MN-6
Bungalow Lookout Trail—trail ... MT-8
Bungalow Mine—mine ... WA-9
Bungalow Mtn—summit ... MT-8
**Bungalow Park**—pop pl ... PA-2
Bungalow Pass—channel ... FL-3
Bungalow Ranger Station—locale ... ID-8
Bungalow Sch—school ... IL-6
Bungalow Sch—school ... TN-4
**Bungalow Town**—pop pl ... TN-4
Bunganock Brook—stream ... ME-1
Bunganock Pond—lake ... ME-1
Bunganuc Brook ... ME-1
Bunganuc Landing—locale ... ME-1
Bunganuc Point—cape ... ME-1
Bunganuc Rock—bar ... ME-1
Bunganuc Stream—stream ... ME-1
Bunganut Pond—lake ... ME-1
Bungarmock Brook ... ME-1
Bungarmock Pond ... ME-1
Bunga Rock ... ME-1
Bungashing Creek—stream ... MN-6
**Bungay**—pop pl ... CT-1
**Bungay**—pop pl ... IL-6
Bungay Brook—stream ... MA-1
Bungay Creek—stream ... MD-2
Bungay Oil Field—other ... IL-6
Bungay Pond ... MA-1
Bungay Reservoir ... MA-1
Bungay River—stream ... MA-1
Bungay Swamp—swamp ... MA-1
Bunge, Christian, Jr., Store—hist pl ... MN-6
Bunge Creek ... MN-6
Bungee Bay ... MN-6
Bungee Brook—stream ... CT-1
Bungee Cem—cemetery ... CT-1
Bungee Hill—summit ... CT-1
Bungeon Branch—stream ... KY-4
Bunge Park—park ... TX-5
Bunger—locale ... TX-5
Bunger Cem—cemetery ... KY-4
Bunger Lake—lake ... NE-7
Bungermuck Brook ... ME-1
Bungermuck Pond ... ME-1
Bungernut Brook ... ME-1
Bungernut Pond ... ME-1
Bunger Point—summit ... AZ-5
Bunger Ranch—locale ... AZ-5
Bunger Ranch—locale (2) ... TX-5
Bungers Park—park ... IA-7
Bungey Bay—bay ... MN-6
Bunggee Creek—stream ... MN-6
Bunggee Lake—lake ... MN-6
**Bunghardts Mill (historical)**—pop pl ... OR-9
Bungie Bay ... MN-6
Bungishing Creek ... MN-6
Bungletown—locale ... VA-3
Bungo Brook ... MN-6
Bungo Creek—stream ... MN-6
Bungo Lake ... MN-6
Bungo Lake—lake ... MI-6
**Bungo (Township of)**—pop pl ... MN-6
Bungy—locale ... NH-1
Bungy Briver ... MA-1
Bungy Brook ... MA-1
Bungy Hill ... MA-1
Bungy Ledge ... ME-1
Bungy Mtn—summit ... MA-1
Bungy Rock—island ... ME-1
Buniger Canyon—valley ... CO-8
Bunion Cem—cemetery ... MS-4
Bunion Ch—church (2) ... MS-4
Bunion Creek ... AL-4
Bunion Creek—stream ... KS-7
Bunion Mtn—summit ... WY-8
Bunitlana Lake—lake ... AK-9
Bunje—locale ... IL-6
Bunjus Cem—cemetery ... TX-5
Bunk, The ... UT-8
Bunk, The—summit ... PA-2
Bunka Lake—lake ... AK-9
Bunkara River ... CO-8
Bunkava River ... CO-8
Bunk Branch—stream ... AL-4
Bunk Branch—stream ... MS-4
Bunk Clay Place—locale ... NM-5
Bunker—locale ... CA-9
Bunker—locale ... FL-3
Bunker—locale ... NY-2
Bunker—locale ... UT-8
Bunker—locale ... WA-9
**Bunker**—pop pl ... FL-3
**Bunker**—pop pl ... MO-7
Bunker, The—summit ... MD-2
Bunker Basin—basin ... CO-8
Bunker Bldg—hist pl ... MO-7
Bunker Branch—stream ... AL-4
Bunker Branch—stream (2) ... KY-4
Bunker Branch—stream ... MO-7
Bunker Brook—stream ... VT-1
**Bunker Camp (historical)**—pop pl ... MO-7
Bunker (CCD)—cens area ... WA-9
Bunker Cem—cemetery ... IN-6
Bunker Cem—cemetery ... MA-1
Bunker Cem—cemetery ... MI-6
Bunker Cem—cemetery ... MO-7
Bunker Chute—stream ... IA-7
Bunker Cove—bay ... FL-3
Bunker Cove—bay (2) ... ME-1
Bunker Creek ... UT-8
Bunker Creek—stream ... CO-8
Bunker Creek—stream ... IN-6
Bunker Creek—stream ... MT-8
Bunker Creek—stream ... NH-1
Bunker Creek—stream ... OR-9
Bunker Creek—stream ... TX-5
Bunker Creek—stream ... UT-8
Bunker Creek—stream ... WA-9
Bunker Creek—stream ... WY-8
**Bunker Donation**—pop pl ... FL-3
Bunker Draw—valley ... WY-8
Bunker Flat—flat ... NV-8
Bunker Grove Sch—school ... IL-6
Bunker Gulch—valley ... CA-9
Bunker Harbor ... ME-1
Bunker Head—cape ... ME-1
Bunker Hill ... CA-9
Bunker Hill ... CT-1
Bunkerhill ... KS-7
Bunker Hill ... MS-4
Bunker Hill ... PA-2
Bunkerhill ... TN-4
Bunker Hill ... WA-9
Bunker Hill—hist pl ... MD-2
Bunker Hill—locale ... AK-9
Bunker Hill—locale ... AR-4
Bunker Hill—locale ... CA-9
Bunker Hill—locale ... FL-3
Bunker Hill—locale ... GA-3
Bunker Hill—locale ... KY-4
Bunker Hill—locale ... MS-4
Bunker Hill—locale ... MO-7
Bunker Hill—locale (2) ... PA-2
Bunker Hill—locale ... SC-3
Bunker Hill—locale ... TN-4
Bunker Hill—locale (3) ... TX-5
Bunker Hill—locale (2) ... VA-3
Bunker Hill—locale ... WA-9
Bunker Hill—locale ... WI-6
Bunker Hill—other ... TX-5
**Bunker Hill**—pop pl ... CT-1
**Bunker Hill**—pop pl ... FL-3
**Bunker Hill**—pop pl ... IL-6
**Bunker Hill**—pop pl (5) ... IN-6
**Bunker Hill**—pop pl ... KS-7
**Bunker Hill**—pop pl ... ME-1
**Bunker Hill**—pop pl ... MI-6
**Bunker Hill**—pop pl ... MS-4
**Bunker Hill**—pop pl (2) ... MO-7
**Bunker Hill**—pop pl ... NJ-2
**Bunker Hill**—pop pl ... NC-3
**Bunker Hill**—pop pl (2) ... OH-6
**Bunkerhill**—pop pl ... OH-6
**Bunker Hill**—pop pl ... OH-6
**Bunker Hill**—pop pl ... OR-9
**Bunker Hill**—pop pl ... PA-2
**Bunker Hill**—pop pl ... SC-3
**Bunker Hill**—pop pl (2) ... TN-4
**Bunker Hill**—pop pl (2) ... WV-2
Bunker Hill—ridge ... NV-8
Bunker Hill—summit ... AK-9
Bunker Hill—summit ... AZ-5
Bunker Hill—summit (3) ... AR-4
Bunker Hill—summit (6) ... CA-9
Bunker Hill—summit (3) ... CO-8
Bunker Hill—summit (2) ... CT-1
Bunker Hill—summit (2) ... FL-3
Bunker Hill—summit (2) ... ID-8
Bunker Hill—summit (2) ... IL-6
Bunker Hill—summit (2) ... IN-6
Bunker Hill—summit ... KS-7
Bunker Hill—summit (3) ... KY-4
Bunker Hill—summit (4) ... ME-1
Bunker Hill—summit ... MD-2
Bunker Hill—summit ... MA-1
Bunker Hill—summit (2) ... MO-7
Bunker Hill—summit (2) ... MT-8
Bunker Hill—summit ... NV-8
Bunker Hill—summit (3) ... NH-1
Bunker Hill—summit (2) ... NY-2
Bunker Hill—summit ... NC-3
Bunker Hill—summit ... OH-6
Bunker Hill—summit (5) ... OR-9
Bunker Hill—summit (11) ... PA-2
Bunker Hill—summit (5) ... TN-4
Bunker Hill—summit (3) ... TX-5
Bunker Hill—summit ... VT-1
Bunker Hill—summit (2) ... VA-3
Bunker Hill—summit (3) ... WA-9
Bunker Hill—summit ... WV-2
Bunker Hill—summit (3) ... WI-6
Bunker Hill—summit (3) ... WY-8
Bunker Hill—summit ... VI-3
Bunker Hill—uninc pl ... PA-2
Bunker Hill Air Force Base ... IN-6
Bunker Hill Air Force Base—other ... IN-6
Bunker Hill Baptist Ch—church ... MS-4
Bunker Hill Branch—stream ... MD-2
Bunker Hill Branch—stream ... SC-3
Bunker Hill Branch—stream ... TN-4
Bunker Hill Brook—stream ... CT-1
Bunker Hill Campground—park ... OR-9
Bunker Hill Canal ... LA-4
Bunker Hill Canyon—valley ... CA-9
Bunker Hill Cave—cave ... MO-7
Bunker Hill Caves—cave ... TN-4
Bunker Hill Cem—cemetery ... IL-6
Bunker Hill Cem—cemetery ... IN-6
Bunker Hill Cem—cemetery (2) ... KS-7
Bunker Hill Cem—cemetery (3) ... MS-4
Bunker Hill Cem—cemetery (2) ... NH-1
Bunker Hill Cem—cemetery (2) ... NY-2
Bunker Hill Cem—cemetery (3) ... OH-6
Bunker Hill Cem—cemetery ... OR-9
Bunker Hill Cem—cemetery ... PA-2
Bunker Hill Cem—cemetery ... VT-1
Bunker Hill Center ... MI-6
Bunkerhill Ch ... MS-4
Bunker Hill Ch ... PA-2
Bunker Hill Ch—church ... FL-3
Bunker Hill Ch—church ... IN-6
Bunker Hill Ch—church ... ME-1
Bunker Hill Ch—church ... MS-4
Bunker Hill Ch—church ... MO-7
Bunker Hill Ch—church ... NJ-2
Bunker Hill Ch—church ... NC-3
Bunker Hill Ch—church ... OH-6
Bunker Hill Ch—church ... OK-5
Bunker Hill Ch—church (2) ... PA-2
Bunker Hill Community Ch—church ... PA-2
Bunker Hill Community Coll—school ... MA-1
Bunker Hill Covered Bridge—bridge ... NC-3
Bunker Hill Covered Bridge—hist pl ... NC-3
Bunker Hill Creek—stream ... AK-9
Bunker Hill Creek—stream ... CA-9
Bunker Hill Creek—stream ... MN-6
Bunker Hill Creek—stream ... MT-8
Bunker Hill Creek—stream ... VA-3
Bunker Hill Creek—stream ... WA-9
Bunker Hill Dam—dam ... NJ-2
Bunker Hill Elem Sch—school (2) ... IN-6
Bunker Hill Estates ... IL-6
Bunkerhill Ferry ... TN-4
Bunker Hill Ferry (historical)—locale ... TN-4
Bunker Hill Hist Dist—hist pl ... WV-2
Bunker Hill HS—school ... NC-3
Bunker Hill Island—island ... FL-3
Bunker Hill Lead—ridge ... TN-4
Bunker Hill Memorial Cem—cemetery ... MS-4
Bunker Hill Mill Creek—stream ... MS-4
Bunker Hill Mine—mine (2) ... AZ-5
Bunker Hill Mine—mine (6) ... CA-9
Bunker Hill Mine—mine ... ID-8
Bunker Hill Mine—mine ... NV-8
Bunker Hill Mine—mine (2) ... OR-9
Bunker Hill Mine (Site)—locale ... CA-9
Bunker Hill Monmt—hist pl ... MA-1
Bunker Hill Monmt—park ... MA-1
**Bunker Hill Park (subdivision)**—pop pl ... TN-4
Bunker Hill Pavilion—building ... MA-1
Bunker Hill Pond—reservoir ... NJ-2
Bunker Hill Post Office ... TN-4
Bunkerhill Post Office (historical)—building ... TN-4
Bunker Hill Ranch—locale ... CA-9
Bunker Hill Ranch—locale ... MO-7
Bunker Hill Resort—locale ... MI-6
Bunker Hill Ridge—ridge ... CA-9
Bunker Hill Rsvr—reservoir ... IL-6
Bunker Hills—range ... PA-2
Bunker Hills—summit ... NV-8
Bunker Hill Sch—hist pl ... MA-1
Bunker Hill Sch—school ... CO-8
Bunker Hill Sch—school ... CT-1
Bunker Hill Sch—school ... DC-2
Bunker Hill Sch—school ... GA-3
Bunker Hill Sch—school (3) ... IL-6
Bunker Hill Sch—school ... IA-7
Bunker Hill Sch—school ... KS-7
Bunker Hill Sch—school (2) ... KY-4
Bunker Hill Sch—school ... MS-4
Bunker Hill Sch—school ... MO-7
Bunker Hill Sch—school (2) ... NE-7
Bunker Hill Sch—school ... NJ-2
Bunker Hill Sch—school (2) ... OH-6
Bunker Hill Sch—school ... OR-9
Bunker Hill Sch—school ... PA-2
Bunker Hill Sch—school ... SD-7
Bunker Hill Sch—school ... TX-5
Bunker Hill Sch—school ... WV-2
Bunker Hill Sch—school ... WI-6
Bunker Hill Sch (abandoned)—school ... MO-7
Bunker Hill Sch (abandoned)—school ... PA-2
Bunker Hill Sch (historical)—school ... MS-4
Bunker Hill Sch (historical)—school ... MO-7
Bunker Hill Sch (historical)—school ... PA-2
Bunker Hill Sch (historical)—school ... TN-4
Bunker Hill Spring—spring ... AZ-5
Bunker Hill Station (reduced usage)—locale ... TX-5
**Bunker Hill (subdivision)**—pop pl ... MS-4
Bunker Hill Swamp—swamp ... NY-2
**Bunker Hill (Township of)**—pop pl ... IL-6
**Bunker Hill (Township of)**—pop pl ... MI-6
**Bunker Hill Village**—pop pl ... TX-5
Bunker (historical)—locale ... SD-7
**Bunker (historical)**—pop pl ... SD-7
Bunker Hole—bay ... ME-1
Bunker Hollow—valley ... PA-2
Bunker Hollow Sch (historical)—school ... MO-7
Bunker Homesite—park ... NC-3
Bunker Island—swamp ... FL-3
Bunker JHS—school ... MI-6
Bunker Lake—lake ... CA-9
Bunker Lake—lake (2) ... MI-6
Bunker Lake—lake (2) ... MN-6
Bunker Lake—lake ... MT-8
Bunker Lake—lake ... ND-7
Bunker Lake—lake ... WI-6
Bunker Lake State Game Mngmt Area—park ... ND-7
Bunker Ledge—bar (2) ... ME-1
Bunker Ledge Mon—bar ... ME-1
Bunker Lookout Tower—locale ... MO-7
Bunker Meadow—flat ... CA-9
Bunker Meadows—swamp ... MA-1
Bunker Mine—mine ... AZ-5
Bunker Mtn—summit ... AR-4
Bunker Mtn—summit ... CA-9
Bunker Mtn—summit ... ME-1
Bunker Neck—cape ... ME-1
Bunker Park—flat ... MT-8
Bunker Pass—gap ... NV-8
Bunker Peak—summit ... AZ-5
Bunker Peak—summit ... NV-8
Bunker Peak Wash ... NV-8
Bunker Peak Wash ... UT-8
Bunker Point—cape ... ME-1
Bunker Pond ... NJ-2
Bunker Pond—lake ... ME-1
Bunker Pond—reservoir ... NH-1
Bunker Pond—reservoir ... NJ-2
Bunker Ponds—lake ... ME-1
Bunker Prairie Lookout Tower—locale ... MN-6
Bunker Reef—bar ... ME-1
Bunker RR Station—locale ... FL-3
Bunker Run—stream ... OH-6
Bunker Run—stream ... WV-2
Bunkers ... HI-9
Bunkers Cem—cemetery ... AZ-5
Bunker Sch—school ... CA-9
Bunker Sch—school ... KS-7
Bunker Sch (abandoned)—school ... MO-7
Bunkers Cove ... ME-1
Bunkers Cove—bay ... FL-3
Bunkers Cove—bay ... ME-1
Bunkers Harbor—bay ... ME-1
**Bunkers Harbor**—pop pl ... ME-1
Bunker'S Hill ... MA-1
Bunkers Hill—summit ... KY-4
Bunkers Knob—summit ... MO-7
Bunkers Knob Picnic Area—locale ... MO-7
Bunkers Point ... ME-1
Bunkers Point—cape ... FL-3
Bunker Spring—spring ... AZ-5
Bunker Spring—spring ... NV-8
Bunker Spur—locale ... UT-8
Bunker Stream—stream ... ME-1
Bunker Tank—reservoir (2) ... AZ-5
**Bunkertown**—pop pl ... PA-2
**Bunker Township**—pop pl ... ND-7
**Bunkerville**—pop pl ... NV-8
Bunkerville Ditch—canal ... NV-8
Bunkerville Mountains ... AZ-5
Bunkerville Mountains ... NV-8
Bunkerville Ridge—ridge ... NV-8
Bunkerville Township—inact MCD ... NV-8
Bunkham Sch—school ... AR-4
Bunkham Slough—gut ... CA-9
Bunkhouse Creek ... ID-8
Bunkhouse Creek—stream (2) ... MT-8
Bunkhouse Hollow—valley ... AR-4
**Bunkie**—pop pl ... LA-4
Bunkin Hill—summit ... VA-3
Bunkle Bay—bay ... GA-3
Bunkley—locale ... MS-4
Bunkley, Dr. E. P., House and Garage—hist pl ... TX-5
Bunkley Baptist Ch—church ... MS-4
Bunkley Cem—cemetery ... MS-4
Bunkley Cem—cemetery ... TX-5
Bunkley Ch—church ... MS-4
Bunkley Woods Branch—stream ... GA-3
Bunk Robinson Peak—summit ... NM-5
Bunk Robinson Spring—spring ... NM-5
Bunks Branch—stream ... GA-3
Bunkuin ... IN-6
Bunkum ... IL-6
Bunkum ... TX-5
**Bunkum**—pop pl ... IL-6
Bunkum Cave—cave ... TN-4
Bunkum Church ... AL-4
Bunkum Creek—stream ... AL-4
Bunkum Hollow—valley ... MO-7
Bunkwater Ridge—ridge ... CO-8
Bunky Hollow—valley ... TN-4
Bunlevel ... NC-3
Bunlevel—other ... NC-3
Bunlevel Cem—cemetery ... NC-3
Bunn—locale ... ID-8
**Bunn**—pop pl ... AR-4
**Bunn**—pop pl ... NC-3
Bunn, Bennett, Plantation—hist pl ... NC-3
Bunn, John Marion, House—hist pl ... OR-9
Bunn Cem—cemetery ... GA-3
Bunn Chapel—church ... NC-3
Bunn Corners—locale ... NY-2
Bunn Coulee—valley ... MT-8
Bunn Creek—stream ... NY-2
Bunn Ditch—canal ... MD-2
Bunnel Branch ... IN-6
Bunnel Cascade—falls ... CA-9
Bunnel Creek—stream ... ID-8
Bunnel Creek—stream (2) ... OR-9
Bunnel Ditch ... IN-6
Bunn Elementary School ... NC-3
**Bunnell**—pop pl ... FL-3
Bunnell, Willard, House—hist pl ... MN-6
Bunnel Lake—lake ... MI-6
Bunnell Branch—stream ... IN-6
Bunnell Brook—stream ... CT-1
Bunnell Brook—stream ... NH-1
Bunnell Brook—stream ... VT-1
Bunnell Butte—summit ... WA-9
Bunnell Cape—cape ... AK-9
Bunnell (CCD)—cens area ... FL-3
Bunnell Cem—cemetery (2) ... IN-6
Bunnell Cem—cemetery ... PA-2
Bunnell Creek—stream ... MT-8
Bunnell Crossing—locale ... KY-4
Bunnell Elem Sch—school ... FL-3
Bunnell Hill Ch—church ... PA-2
Bunnell Hollow—valley ... PA-2
Bunnell HS—school ... CT-1
Bunnell Notch—gap ... NH-1
Bunnell Point—summit ... CA-9
Bunnell Pond ... CT-1
Bunnell Ranch—locale ... CA-9
Bunnell Ridge—ridge ... PA-2
Bunnell Ridge Trail—trail ... PA-2
Bunnell Run—stream ... PA-2
Bunnell Run—stream ... WV-2
Bunnell Sch—school ... MO-7
Bunnells Fork—stream ... UT-8
Bunnells Pond—reservoir ... CT-1
Bunnells Pond—reservoir ... PA-2
Bunnells Pond Dam—dam ... PA-2
**Bunnells Subdivision**—pop pl ... UT-8
Bunnel Point—cape ... CA-9
Bunnels Bluff—summit ... WI-6
Bunnel Spring—spring ... WA-9
Bunner Lake ... MN-6
Bunner Lake—lake ... NE-7
**Bunners Ridge**—pop pl ... WV-2
Bunners Ridge—ridge ... WV-2
Bunners Ridge Cem—cemetery ... WV-2
Bunners Ridge Ch—church ... WV-2
Bunners Run—stream ... WV-2
**Bunney**—pop pl ... AR-4
Bunney Gulch—valley ... ID-8
Bunney Ranch—locale ... WY-8
Bunn Hill—summit (2) ... NY-2
Bunn Hill Cem—cemetery ... NY-2
Bunn Hill Ch—church ... NY-2
Bunn Hill Creek—stream ... NY-2
Bunn HS—school ... NC-3
Bunnie (historical)—locale ... MS-4
Bunning Mine—mine ... WY-8
Bunning Park—park ... WY-8
Bunning Rsvr—reservoir ... WY-8
Bunningwater ... AZ-5
Bunnin Park—park ... TX-5
Bunn Lake—lake ... WA-9
Bunn Lake—reservoir ... NC-3
Bunn Lake Dam—dam ... NC-3
Bunn Level ... NC-3
**Bunnlevel**—pop pl ... NC-3
**Bunnlevel (Bunlevel)**—pop pl ... NC-3
Bunn Park—park ... IL-6
Bunns Bluff—cliff ... TX-5
Bunns Canal—canal ... TX-5
Bunn Sch—school ... IL-6
Bunn Sch—school ... OH-6
Bunn Sch (historical)—school ... TN-4
Bunns Hollow—valley ... MO-7
Bunns Lake ... NY-2
Bunns Lake—lake ... GA-3
Bunns Mtn—summit ... PA-2
Bunns Wood County Park—park ... IA-7
Bunn (Township of)—fmr MCD ... AR-4
**Bunnvale**—pop pl ... NJ-2

Bunnville—pop pl MO-7
Bunny Butte—summit OR-9
Bunny Creek MT-8
Bunny Creek—stream ID-8
Bunny Creek—stream NC-3
Bunny Dale KS-7
Bunny Flat—flat CA-9
Bunny Lake—lake AL-4
Bunny Lake—lake CA-9
Bunny Lake—lake MN-6
Bunny Run—CDP MI-6
Bunny Run Lake—lake MI-6
Bunny Tank AZ-5
Bunny Tank—reservoir AZ-5
Buno Gulch—valley CO-8
Bunola—pop pl PA-2
Bunola Run—stream PA-2
Bun Point—cape AK-9
Bun Rock—island AK-9
Buns Basin—basin CA-9
Bunselmier Spring—spring CA-9
Bunsen—pop pl TX-5
Bunsen Peak—summit WY-8
Bunsenville—pop pl IL-6
Bunshefoot Creek—stream AK-9
Bunt Brook—stream NY-2
Bunt Creek—stream NC-3
Bunte Highline Ditch—canal CO-8
Bunten Cem—cemetery NE-7
Buntin Branch—stream TN-4
Buntin Cem—cemetery IN-6
Buntin Cem—cemetery (2) MS-4
Buntin Cem—cemetery MO-7
Buntin Cem—cemetery TN-4
Buntin Ditch—canal IN-6
Bunting—locale DE-2
Bunting Branch—stream TN-4
Bunting Canyon—valley ID-8
Bunting Canyon—valley UT-8
Bunting Cem—cemetery OH-6
Bunting Lake—lake MI-6
Bunting Ranch—locale NM-5
Bunting Ranch—locale TX-5
Bunting Ranch—locale UT-8
Bunting Rsvr—reservoir ID-8
Buntings Branch—stream DE-2
Buntings Branch—stream MD-2
Bunting Sedge—island NJ-2
Buntingville—pop pl CA-9
Buntin Lake—reservoir KY-4
Bunt Lake—lake MN-6
Buntley Cemeteries—cemetery TN-4
Bunton Branch—stream TN-4
Bunton Branch—stream TX-5
Bunton Cem—cemetery TN-4
Bunton Cem—cemetery TX-5
Bunton Creek—stream NC-3
Bunton Creek—stream OR-9
Bunton Creek—stream TN-4
Bunton Drain—stream MI-6
Bunton Draw—valley TX-5
Bunton Flat—flat CA-9
Bunton Hollow Creek—stream CA-9
Bunton Overpass—locale TX-5
Bunton Ridge—ridge TN-4
Bunton Temple CME Ch—church MS-4
Buntontown—pop pl TN-4
Bunton Windmill—locale TX-5
Bunt Sisk Hills—range KY-4
Bunt Spring—spring MO-7
Bunts Run—stream PA-2
Buntyn—uninc pl TN-4
Buntyn Creek—stream MS-4
Buntyn Creek Structure Y-16A-1 Dam—dam MS-4
Buntyn Creek Structure Y-16A-2 Dam—dam MS-4
Buntyn Creek Structure Y-16A-4 Dam—dam MS-4
Buntyn Creek Structure Y-16A-6 Dam—dam MS-4
Bunuknuk—locale FM-9
Bunyan—locale CO-8
Bunyan—locale TX-5
Bunyan—locale WI-6
Bunyan—pop pl NC-3
Bunyan, Paul, and Babe the Blue Ox—hist pl MN-6
Bunyan Cem—cemetery TX-5
Bunyan Creek NC-3
Bunyan Creek—stream MT-8
Bunyan Hill Cem—cemetery AL-4
Bunyan Lake—lake MT-8
Bunyan Mtn—summit MA-1
Bunyan Peak—summit AZ-5
Bunyan Point—summit MT-8
Bunyans Hat Island—island WI-6
Bunyan Substation—locale AZ-5
Bunyard Creek—stream OR-9
Bunyard Spring—spring MO-7
Buoy Bay—bay WA-9
Buoy Creek MS-4
Buoy Creek—stream OR-9
Buoy Depot—uninc pl OR-9
Buoy Hollow—valley TN-4
Buoy Key—island FL-3
Buoy Number 1—other TX-5
Buoy Number 10—other TX-5
Buoy Number 11—other TX-5
Buoy Number 12—other TX-5
Buoy Number 13—other TX-5
Buoy Number 14—other TX-5
Buoy Number 15—other TX-5
Buoy Number 16—other TX-5
Buoy Number 17—other TX-5
Buoy Number 18—other TX-5
Buoy Number 19—other TX-5
Buoy Number 2—other TX-5
Buoy Number 20—other TX-5
Buoy Number 21—other TX-5
Buoy Number 22—other TX-5
Buoy Number 23—other TX-5
Buoy Number 24—other TX-5
Buoy Number 25—other TX-5
Buoy Number 26—other TX-5
Buoy Number 27—other TX-5
Buoy Number 28—other TX-5
Buoy Number 29—other TX-5
Buoy Number 3—other TX-5
Buoy Number 30—other TX-5
Buoy Number 31—other TX-5
Buoy Number 32—other TX-5
Buoy Number 33—other TX-5
Buoy Number 4—other TX-5
Buoy Number 5—other TX-5
Buoy Number 6—other TX-5
Buoy Number 7—other TX-5
Buoy Number 8—other TX-5
Buoy Number 9—other TX-5
Buoy Pass—channel FL-3
Buoy Pass—gut LA-4
Buoy Path Pond—lake SC-3
Buoy Point—cape AK-9
Buoy Point—cape NC-3
Buoy Pond—bay LA-4
Buoy Rocks—bar MA-1
Buoy 34—other TX-5
Buoy 35—other TX-5
Buoy 36—other TX-5
Bupps Union Ch—church PA-2
Bup Spring—spring WA-9
Bupto, Mount—summit AK-9
Bupto Creek—stream AK-9
Bura Berg FM-9
Buracker Hollow—valley VA-3
Burandt Lake—lake MN-6
Buras—locale KY-4
Buras—pop pl LA-4
Buras Bayou—gut LA-4
Buras Boat Harbor—harbor LA-4
Buras Drainage Canal—canal LA-4
Buras Pond—bay LA-4
Buras-Triumph—CDP LA-4
Burba Cem—cemetery OH-6
Burbach Block—hist pl MA-1
Burbage Crossroad NC-3
Burbage Crossroads—pop pl NC-3
Burbage Gut—gut NC-3
Burbage Hunt Club—other SC-3
Burban Fork SC-3
Burbank—locale FL-3
Burbank—locale UT-8
Burbank—pop pl AL-4
Burbank—pop pl (2) CA-9
Burbank—pop pl IL-6
Burbank—pop pl MO-7
Burbank—pop pl OH-6
Burbank—pop pl OK-5
Burbank—pop pl SD-7
Burbank—pop pl TN-4
Burbank—pop pl WA-9
Burbank, Lake—lake FL-3
Burbank, Luther, House and Garden—hist pl CA-9
Burbank Airp—airport KS-7
Burbank Blvd Sch—school CA-9
Burbank Boys Sch—school WA-9
Burbank Brook NH-1
Burbank Canyon—valley CA-9
Burbank Canyon—valley NV-8
Burbank Canyon—valley NM-5
Burbank (CCD)—cens area CA-9
Burbank (CCD)—cens area WA-9
Burbank Cem—cemetery AL-4
Burbank Cem—cemetery OH-6
Burbank Cem—cemetery OK-5
Burbank Cem—cemetery UT-8
Burbank Community Cemetery SD-7
Burbank Creek—stream ID-8
Burbank Creek—stream OR-9
Burbank Creek—stream WA-9
Burbank Creek—stream WY-8
Burbank Ditch IN-6
Burbank Ditch—canal IN-6
Burbank Draw—valley WY-8
Burbank Gardens—uninc pl TX-5
Burbank-Glendale-Pasadena Airp—airport CA-9
Burbank Gun Club—other CA-9
Burbank Heights—pop pl WA-9
Burbank Hill—summit VT-1
Burbank Hills—summit UT-8
Burbank Hollow—valley PA-2
Burbank Homestead Waterwheel—hist pl WA-9
Burbank Hosp—hospital MA-1
Burbank HS—school (2) CA-9
Burbank HS—school TX-5
Burbank JHS—school CA-9
Burbank Junction—locale CA-9
Burbank Lake—lake SD-7
Burbank-Livingston-Griggs House—hist pl MN-6
Burbank Main Post Office—building CA-9
Burbank Mtn—summit NY-2
Burbank Oil Field—oilfield OK-5
Burbank Park—park MA-1
Burbank Pass—gap UT-8
Burbank Pond—lake ME-1
Burbank Pond—lake MA-1
Burbank Pond—reservoir MA-1
Burbank Post Office (historical)—building TN-4
Burbanks Cem—cemetery KY-4
Burbank Sch—school (9) CA-9
Burbank Sch—school (4) IL-6
Burbank Sch—school MA-1
Burbank Sch—school MI-6
Burbank Sch—school (2) OK-5
Burbank Sch—school (3) WI-6
Burbank Sch (historical)—school TN-4
Burbanks Lakes—lake KY-4
Burbank Slough—gut WA-9
Burbank Spring—spring ID-8
Burbank (sta.)—pop pl OH-6
Burbank State Wildlife Mngmt Area—park MN-6
Burbank Station—locale OH-6
Burbank (Township of)—pop pl MN-6
Burbank Valley—valley WA-9
Burbank Village MA-1
Burbank Western Channel—canal CA-9
Burbank YMCA Camp—locale CA-9
Burba Oil Field—oilfield TX-5
Burbeck—locale CA-9
Burbeck Creek—stream CA-9
Burbe Cove ME-1
Burbee Brook—stream ME-1
Burbee Cove—bay ME-1
Burbee Peak—summit VT-1
Burbee Pond VT-1
Burbees Pond—reservoir VT-1
Burbick Hollow—valley MO-7
Burbon KY-4
Burbow Gulch ID-8
Burbridge Branch—stream KY-4
Burbridge Creek—stream MO-7
Burcalo Creek—stream SC-3
Burch AL-4
Burch—locale AZ-5
Burch—locale MO-7
Burch—pop pl MD-2
Burch—pop pl NC-3
Burch, Lake—reservoir SD-7
Burch, William, House—hist pl OH-6
Burch Addition (subdivision)—pop pl UT-8
Burcham Branch—stream IN-6
Burcham Cem—cemetery KY-4
Burcham Cem—cemetery TN-4
Burcham Creek ID-8
Burcham Creek NV-8
Burcham Creek—stream AL-4
Burcham Creek—stream CA-9
Burcham Creek—stream ID-8
Burcham Creek Church of Christ AL-4
Burcham Ditch—canal IA-7
Burcham Flat—flat CA-9
Burcham Hollow—valley AL-4
Burcham Hollow—valley TN-4
Burcham House—hist pl TX-5
Burcham Mills (historical)—locale AL-4
Burcham Mills P.O. AL-4
Burcham Mine—mine CA-9
Burcham Plaza Shop Ctr—locale AZ-5
Burcham Pond—lake TN-4
Burcham Rsvr OR-9
Burcham Sch—school CA-9
Burchams Creek AL-4
Burchams Creek NV-8
Burchams Sinks Creek AL-4
Burchan Creek AL-4
Burchard—pop pl MN-6
Burchard—pop pl NE-7
Burchard Branch TN-4
Burchard Branch—stream TN-4
Burchard Cem—cemetery MO-7
Burchard Cem—cemetery NE-7
Burchard Creek—stream (2) OR-9
Burchard Davison Ditch—canal IN-6
Burchard Ford—crossing TN-4
Burchard Foreman Ditch—canal IN-6
Burchard Hollow—valley MO-7
Burchard Lake—reservoir OR-9
Burchard Lake Special Use Area—park NE-7
Burchard Mine—mine TN-4
Burchard Place—locale TX-5
Burchards Creek—stream PA-2
Burchard Town Bend—bend TN-4
Burchardville PA-2
Burchars Creek AL-4
Burch Branch—stream GA-3
Burch Branch—stream MD-2
Burch Brook—stream NY-2
Burch Brothers Number 2 Dam—dam SD-7
Burch Canyon—valley UT-8
Burch Cem—cemetery AL-4
Burch Cem—cemetery AR-4
Burch Cem—cemetery (2) GA-3
Burch Cem—cemetery IN-6
Burch Cem—cemetery IA-7
Burch Cem—cemetery KY-4
Burch Cem—cemetery (2) LA-4
Burch Cem—cemetery (4) MS-4
Burch Cem—cemetery NY-2
Burch Cem—cemetery SC-3
Burch Cem—cemetery TN-4
Burch Cem—cemetery (2) TX-5
Burch Ch—church MO-7
Burch Cove Branch—stream NC-3
Burch Creek CA-9
Burch Creek TX-5
Burch Creek WY-8
Burch Creek—stream AL-4
Burch Creek—stream CA-9
Burch Creek—stream LA-4
Burch Creek—stream MI-6
Burch Creek—stream MS-4
Burch Creek—stream NY-2
Burch Creek—stream OR-9
Burch Creek—stream UT-8
Burch Creek Heights Subdivision—pop pl UT-8
Burch Creek Sch—school UT-8
Burch Creek Subdivision—pop pl UT-8
Burch Crossroads—locale SC-3
Burch Dam—dam AL-4
Burch Ditch—canal IN-6
Burchell Canal—canal LA-4
Burchenal Mound—hist pl OH-6
Burcher Canyon—valley OR-9
Burcher Sch (historical)—school PA-2
Burchers Store—pop pl VA-3
Burchett Canyon—valley ID-8
Burchett Spring—spring ID-8
Burchet Canyon—valley NM-5
Burchett Branch—stream KY-4
Burchett Branch—stream WV-2
Burchett Cem—cemetery (2) TN-4
Burchett Chapel—church NC-3
Burchette Cem—cemetery VA-3
Burchette Spring—spring AR-4
Burchett Flat Sch—school KY-4
Burchett Hollow—valley TN-4
Burchett Mtn—summit KY-4
Burchett Sch—school NC-3
Burchfiel Ch—church KS-7
Burchfield—pop pl AL-4
Burchfield—pop pl WV-2
Burchfield Branch—stream AL-4
Burchfield Cave—cave AL-4
Burchfield Cem—cemetery TN-4
Burchfield Ch—church TN-4
Burchfield Heights—pop pl TN-4
Burchfield Hollow—valley TN-4
Burchfield Lake—reservoir AL-4
Burchfield Lake—reservoir CO-8
Burchfield Sch—school TN-4
Burchfield Store—locale AL-4
Burchfield Store HS (historical)—school AL-4
Burch Hill Baptist Ch—church MS-4
Burch (historical)—locale SD-7
Burch Hollow—valley PA-2
Burch Hollow—valley UT-8
Burch Hollow—valley VA-3
Burchill Ch—church TX-5
Burchinal—pop pl IA-7
Burch Lake MI-6
Burch Lake—reservoir AL-4
Burch Lake—reservoir CO-8
Burch Lake—reservoir TN-4
Burch Lake Dam—dam TN-4
Burchman Hollow—valley AR-4
Burch Meadow—flat CA-9
Burch-Mitchell House—hist pl GA-3
Burch Mtn—summit NY-2
Burch Mtn—summit (2) WA-9
Burch Oil Field—oilfield KS-7
Burch Peak—summit AZ-5
Burch Pond—lake AL-4
Burch Pond—lake VA-3
Burch Post Office AL-4
Burchram Creek AL-4
Burch Ranch—locale MT-8
Burch Ridge—ridge WV-2
Burch Run—stream PA-2
Burch Run—stream (2) WV-2
Burch Sch (abandoned)—school MO-7
Burch Sch (historical)—school TN-4
Burch School MO-7
Burch Siding—locale GA-3
Burch Spring—spring UT-8
Burchs Run—stream OH-6
Burchsville MN-6
Burch Tank—reservoir NM-5
Burch-Taylor Mill—hist pl UT-8
Burchwell, Ray, Archeol Site—hist pl KY-4
Burchwood Cem—cemetery NC-3
Burchwood Park—park FL-3
Bur Cirque—basin AK-9
Burckhalter Rsvr No. 1—reservoir CO-8
Burckhalter Sch—school CA-9
Burckhardt, A. E., House—hist pl OH-6
Burcliff Farms—pop pl NJ-2
Bur Coulee—valley MT-8
Burdal GA-3
Burd Coleman Village—locale PA-2
Burd Coulee—valley MT-8
Burdeau Drain—stream MI-6
Burdeck Creek—stream CO-8
Burdell—locale CA-9
Burdell Branch—stream AR-4
Burdell Island—island CA-9
Burdell Mtn—summit CA-9
Burdell Sch—school CA-9
Burdell Sch—school GA-3
Burdell (Township of)—pop pl MI-6
Burdeman Branch MS-4
Burden—locale NY-2
Burden—locale NC-3
Burden—pop pl KS-7
Burden Cem—cemetery KS-7
Burden Cem—cemetery TN-4
Burden Channel—channel NC-3
Burden Creek—stream IL-6
Burden Creek—stream NC-3
Burden Dock—locale NY-2
Burden Draw—arroyo WA-9
Burden Falls—falls IL-6
Burdenfield KS-7
Burden Field—park IA-7
Burden Field-(Robbit Run) Airp—airport WA-9
Burden Ironworks Office Bldg—hist pl NY-2
Burden Iron Works Site—hist pl NY-2
Burden Lake—lake (2) MI-6
Burden Lake—lake NY-2
Burden Lake—pop pl NY-2
Burden Oil Field—oilfield KS-7
Burden Pond RI-1
Burden Pond—lake ME-1
Burden Sch—school IL-6
Burdens Creek—stream NC-3
Burdens Mill—locale NC-3
Burdens Pond RI-1
Burdens Pond—reservoir NY-2
Burdenstown NJ-2
Burden Swamp—swamp SC-3
Burdeshaw Bridge—bridge AL-4
Burdeshaw Mill Creek—stream AL-4
Burdett MS-4
Burdett SD-7
Burdett—locale CO-8
Burdett—pop pl KS-7
Burdett—pop pl MO-7
Burdett—pop pl NY-2
Burdett Cem—cemetery (2) MO-7
Burdett Ch—church TN-4
Burdett Community Airp—airport KS-7
Burdett Creek—stream CO-8
Burdette—locale IA-7
Burdette—locale PA-2
Burdette—locale SD-7
Burdette—locale VA-3
Burdette—locale WV-2
Burdette—pop pl AR-4
Burdette—pop pl MD-2
Burdette—pop pl MS-4
Burdette Cem—cemetery GA-3
Burdette Cem—cemetery SD-7
Burdette Ch—church TN-4
Burdette Chapel TN-4
Burdette Creek CO-8
Burdette Creek—stream (2) MT-8
Burdette Creek—stream WV-2
Burdette Dam—dam AZ-5
Burdette Knob—summit KY-4
Burdette Park—park IN-6
Burdette Park—park NE-7
Burdette Ridge—ridge TN-4
Burdettes MD-2
Burdette Sch—school OH-6
Burdette Springs Tabernacle—church WV-2
Burdette Township—pop pl SD-7
Burdette (Township of)—fmr MCD AR-4
Burdette-Walker Cem—cemetery WV-2
Burdett Hill—summit MA-1
Burdett (historical)—pop pl NC-3
Burdett Prairie Cem—cemetery TX-5
Burdetts MD-2
Burdetts Creek—pop pl WV-2
Burdge Sch—school WI-6
Burdgeville (historical)—locale KS-7
Burd Hill—bench MT-8
Burd Hill Lake—reservoir MT-8
Burdick—locale KY-4
Burdick—pop pl IN-6
Burdick—pop pl KS-7
Burdick, Anthony, House—hist pl IA-7
Burdick, E. E., House—hist pl NV-8
Burdick, Harold B., House—hist pl OH-6
Burdick Branch—stream IL-6
Burdick Cem—cemetery (2) NY-2
Burdick Cem—cemetery (2) PA-2
Burdick Cem—cemetery WI-6
Burdick Corners—locale PA-2
Burdick Coulee—valley MT-8
Burdick County (historical)—civil SD-7
Burdick Creek OR-9
Burdick Creek—stream PA-2
Burdick Creek—stream WA-9
Burdick Creek—stream WY-8
Burdick Crossing—locale NY-2
Burdick Hill—summit NY-2
Burdick Hills—other NM-5
Burdick Island—island NY-2
Burdick JHS—school CT-1
Burdick Lake—lake IN-6
Burdick Mine—mine CO-8
Burdick Park—park MD-2
Burdick Place—locale MT-8
Burdick Ranch—locale WY-8
Burdick Run—stream PA-2
Burdick Sch—school SD-7
Burdick Sch—school WI-6
Burdicks Crossing Cem—cemetery NY-2
Burdick Spring—spring UT-8
Burdick Township—pop pl SD-7
Burdickville—lake RI-1
Burdickville—pop pl MI-6
Burdickville—pop pl RI-1
Burdick Vocational HS—school DC-2
Burdick-West Memorial Hosp—hospital AL-4
Burdic Run—stream PA-2
Burdie Drain—canal MI-6
Burdin Corner—locale ME-1
Burdine—pop pl KY-4
Burdine Branch—stream AL-4
Burdine Cem—cemetery MS-4
Burdine Cem—cemetery (2) TN-4
Burdine Creek—stream AL-4
Burdine Creek—stream SC-3
Burdine Lake Dam—dam MS-4
Burdine Sch No 1—school KY-4
Burdine Sch No 2—school KY-4
Burdine Township—pop pl MO-7
Burdine Valley—valley KY-4
Burd Lake—lake WI-6
Burdlick Hollow—valley KY-4
Burdock—locale SD-7
Burdock Hollow—valley PA-2
Burdock Landing AL-4
Burdock Sch—school SD-7
Burdon Hill—summit WI-6
Burdon Mtn—summit WA-9
Burdon Pond MA-1
Burd-Roger Memorial Home—locale PA-2
Burd Run—stream (2) PA-2
Burdsal, Samuel, House—hist pl OH-6
Burdsall Chapel—church OH-6
Burd Sch—school NE-7
Burd Sch—school PA-2
Burds Crossing—pop pl PA-2
Bureau KS-7
Bureau—locale MD-2
Bureau—pop pl IL-6
Bureau Annex Bldg—building DC-2
Bureau Baptist Ch—church IN-6
Bureau Cem—cemetery NE-7
Bureau (corporate name Bureau Junction) IL-6
Bureau (County)—pop pl IL-6
Bureau County Ditch—canal IL-6
Bureau Creek IL-6
Bureau Junction IL-6
Bureau Junction (corporate name for Bureau)—pop pl IL-6
Bureau of Engraving and Printing Bldg—building DC-2
Bureau of Indian Affairs Coolidge Office—building AZ-5
Bureau of Indian Affairs Ranger Station—locale AZ-5
Bureau of Land Mngmt UT-8
Bureau of Land Mngmt Campground—locale UT-8
Bureau of Land Mngmt State Office—building UT-8
Bureau of Mines Oil Shale Experiment Station—locale CO-8
Bureau Of Public Roads Camp—locale WY-8
Bureau (Township of)—pop pl IL-6
Bureau Valley Country Club—other IL-6
Bureham Valley Sch (historical)—school AL-4
Burekufuasto-To MP-9
Burekufwasto-to MP-9
Burelson Ch—church AL-4
Burem—locale TN-4
Burem Bridge—bridge TN-4
Burem Island—island TN-4
Burem Lake—reservoir TN-4
Burem Lake Dam—dam TN-4
Burem Post Office (historical)—building TN-4
Burems Store TN-4
Burems Store Post Office TN-4
Burenes—pop pl PR-3
Buresahan PW-9
Buresh Archeol Site—hist pl KS-7
Buresh Cem—cemetery IA-7
Buresh Farm—hist pl IA-7
Buresh Lake—lake MN-6
Buressahan PW-9
Buresshan PW-9
Buretshian PW-9
Burfening Ranch—locale MT-8
Burfield—locale KY-4
Burfield Branch—stream AL-4
Burfield Hollow—valley KY-4
Burfield Sch—school IL-6
Burford—locale TX-5
Burford Branch—stream AL-4
Burford Branch—stream MS-4
Burford Canyon—valley OR-9
Burford Cem—cemetery AL-4
Burford Cem—cemetery MS-4
Burford Cem—cemetery MO-7
Burford Cem—cemetery (2) VA-3
Burford House—hist pl NH-1
Burford Lake—reservoir OK-5
Burford Lake Wildlife Station—locale NM-5
Burford Landing AL-4
Burford Run—stream PA-2
Burford (Site)—locale CA-9
Burfordville—pop pl MO-7
Burfordville Covered Bridge—hist pl MO-7
Burfordville Mill—hist pl MO-7
Burfor's VA-3
Burfort Cem—cemetery KY-4
Burg KY-4
Burg—locale AR-4
Burg—locale OK-5
Burg—pop pl KY-4
Burg, The—pop pl IL-6
Burgamy Millpond—reservoir GA-3
Burgan—locale SC-3
Burgan, Lake—lake MN-6
Burgan Branch—stream AL-4
Burgan Creek—stream NC-3
Burgans Lake MN-6
Burgard HS—school NY-2
Burgaw—pop pl NC-3
Burgaw Creek—stream NC-3
Burgaw Depot—hist pl NC-3
Burgaw Elem Sch—school NC-3
Burgaw JHS—school NC-3
Burgaw Savannah—swamp NC-3
Burgaw (Township of)—fmr MCD NC-3
Burg Creek MS-4
Burg Creek—stream KY-4
Burg Creek—stream MS-4
Burg Creek—stream MT-8
Burg Creek—valley KY-4
Burg Ditch—canal WY-8
Burgdorf—hist pl ID-8
Burgdorf—pop pl ID-8
Burgdorf Campground—locale ID-8
Burgdorf Creek—stream ID-8
Burgdorfer Flat—flat OR-9
Burgdorf Guard Station—locale ID-8
Burgdorf Summit—summit ID-8
Burge—pop pl NE-7
Burge Branch—stream MO-7
Burge Branch—stream TX-5
Burge Cem—cemetery (2) IL-6
Burge Cem—cemetery (2) OH-6
Burge Creek—stream KY-4
Burge Hill—summit MS-4
Burge House—hist pl TX-5
Burge Lake—reservoir AL-4
Burge Lake Dam—dam AL-4
Burge Mtn—summit NC-3
Burge Mtn—summit TN-4
Burge Mtn—summit WA-9
Burgen—locale TN-4
Burgen Branch—stream TN-4
Burgen Creek—stream OR-9
Burgener Cem—cemetery VA-3
Burgen Lake MN-6
Burgen Lake—lake MN-6
Burgen Post Office (historical)—building TN-4
Burgentine Creek—stream TX-5
Burgentine Dam—dam TX-5
Burgentine Lake—reservoir TX-5
Burge Pond MA-1
Burge Pond—lake NY-2
Burger—locale TN-4
Burger Ranch—locale NV-8
Burger Branch VA-3
Burger Branch—stream KY-4
Burger Branch—stream TN-4
Burger Butte—summit OR-9
Burger Canyon—valley CA-9
Burger Canyon—valley NE-7
Burger Cem—cemetery IN-6
Burger Cem—cemetery IA-7
Burger Cem—cemetery PA-2
Burger Cemetery AL-4
Burger Creek MT-8
Burger Creek—stream CA-9
Burger Creek—stream KS-7
Burger Creek—stream MO-7
Burger Creek—stream MT-8
Burger Creek—stream NV-8
Burger Ditch—canal MT-8
Burger Draw—valley WY-8
Burger-Gault Lateral—canal CO-8
Burger Hill—summit TX-5
Burger Hollow—valley TX-5
Burger JHS—school MI-6
Burger JHS—school NY-2
Burger Knob—summit NC-3
Burger Lake—lake CA-9
Burger Lake—lake TX-5
Burger Meadows—flat OR-9
Burger Mtn—summit NC-3
Burger Pass—gap OR-9
Burger Peak—summit UT-8
Burger Point—cape AK-9
Burger Sch—school IL-6
Burger Sch—school WV-2
Burger Town—locale NC-3
Burger Well—locale AZ-5
Burges Branch—stream KY-4
Burges Branch—stream VA-3
Burges Canyon—valley CA-9
Burges Cem—cemetery MS-4
Burges Ch—church TN-4
Burges Cove—bay RI-1
Burges Junior and Senior HS—school TX-5
Burges Lake—reservoir NC-3
Burges Lake Dam—dam NC-3
Burgeson Lake CA-9
Burgeson Ranch—locale CA-9
Burges Point RI-1
Burges Pond—lake MA-1
Burgess—locale AL-4
Burgess—locale IA-7
Burgess—locale MI-6
Burgess—locale NC-3
Burgess—locale VA-3
Burgess—pop pl IL-6
Burgess—pop pl MS-4
Burgess—pop pl MO-7
Burgess—pop pl ND-7
Burgess—pop pl SC-3
Burgess—pop pl TN-4

**Burgess**—pop pl VA-3
Burgess, Joseph Fields, House—hist pl KY-4
Burgess, Thornton W., House—hist pl MA-1
Burgess Bay—basin SC-3
Burgess Big Dam—dam SD-7
Burgess Branch—stream (2) KY-4
Burgess Branch—stream TX-5
Burgess Branch—stream VT-1
Burgess Branch—stream WV-2
Burgess Bridge—bridge AL-4
Burgess Brook—stream CT-1
Burgess Brook—stream (2) ME-1
Burgess Brook—stream PA-2
**Burgess (Burgess Store)**—pop pl VA-3
Burgess Cabin—locale CA-9
Burgess Canal—canal ID-8
Burgess Canyon—valley OR-9
Burgess Cave—cave AL-4
Burgess Cem—cemetery (3) AL-4
Burgess Cem—cemetery (2) AR-4
Burgess Cem—cemetery GA-3
Burgess Cem—cemetery KS-7
Burgess Cem—cemetery (4) KY-4
Burgess Cem—cemetery MN-6
Burgess Cem—cemetery MS-4
Burgess Cem—cemetery NY-2
Burgess Cem—cemetery (2) OK-5
Burgess Cem—cemetery SC-3
Burgess Cem—cemetery TN-4
Burgess Cem—cemetery VT-1
Burgess Cem Number One—cemetery TN-4
Burgess Cem Number Two—cemetery TN-4
Burges Sch—school TX-5
Burgess Chapel Ch—church TN-4
Burgess Chapel (historical)—church TN-4
Burgess Cove—bay ME-1
Burgess Cove—stream TN-4
*Burgess Creek* CA-9
Burgess Creek—stream CA-9
Burgess Creek—stream CO-8
Burgess Creek—stream LA-4
Burgess Creek—stream MD-2
Burgess Creek—stream (2) MS-4
Burgess Creek—stream MT-8
Burgess Creek—stream NE-7
Burgess Creek—stream OK-5
Burgess Creek—stream (3) SC-3
Burgess Creek—stream TX-5
Burgess Creek—stream (3) VA-3
Burgess Creek Ch—church MS-4
*Burgess Ditch* IN-6
Burgess Drain—stream (2) MI-6
Burgess Falls—falls TN-4
Burgess Falls Dam—dam TN-4
Burgess Falls Lake—reservoir (2) TN-4
Burgess Falls State Natural Area—park TN-4
Burgess Fork—stream KY-4
Burgess Gap—gap GA-3
Burgess Gulch—valley OR-9
Burgess Gut—gut FL-3
Burgess Hill—summit ME-1
Burgess (historical)—locale MS-4
Burgess Hollow—valley KY-4
Burgess Hollow—valley MO-7
Burgess Hollow—valley (3) TN-4
Burgess Hollow—valley WV-2
Burgess House—hist pl ME-1
*Burgess Island* MA-1
Burgess Island—island NY-2
*Burgess Junction* IL-6
Burgess Junction—locale WY-8
Burgess Junction—other IL-6
Burgess Knob—summit TN-4
Burgess Lake—lake MI-6
Burgess Lake—lake MT-8
Burgess Lake—lake OH-6
Burgess Lake Dam—dam (2) MS-4
Burgess Landing—locale FL-3
Burgess Lateral—canal CA-9
Burgess Meadow—flat WA-9
Burgess Meadows—flat CA-9
Burgess Memorial Hosp—hospital IA-7
Burgess Mica Prospect Mine—mine SD-7
Burgess Mine—mine CA-9
Burgess Mtn—summit MA-1
Burgess Mtn—summit NY-2
Burgess Museum—building MA-1
Burgess Park—park CA-9
Burgess Park—park PA-2
Burgess Peak—summit AZ-5
Burgess Picnic Area—park WY-8
Burgess Plantation (historical)—locale AL-4
Burgess Point—cape MA-1
Burgess Point—summit AL-4
*Burgess Pond* MA-1
Burgess Pond—lake AL-4
Burgess Pond—lake IL-6
Burgess Pond—lake ME-1
Burgess Pond—reservoir PA-2
Burgess Post Office (historical)—building MS-4
Burgess Ranch—locale MT-8
Burgess Ranch—locale (2) NE-7
Burgess Ranch—locale WY-8
Burgess Ranger Station—locale WY-8
**Burgess (Reed Lake)**—pop pl TX-5
Burgess Ridge—ridge CA-9
*Burgess River* VA-3
Burgess River—stream CO-8
Burgess Road Baptist Ch—church FL-3
Burgess Road Ch—church FL-3
Burgess Rsvr—reservoir MT-8
Burgess Run—stream OH-6
Burgess Run—stream WV-2
*Burgess-Salisbury Ditch* IN-6
*Burgess-Salisbury Drain* IN-6
Burgess Sch—school GA-3
Burgess Sch—school IL-6
Burgess Sch—school MA-1
Burgess Sch—school MI-6
Burgess Sch—school MS-4
Burgess Sch—school MO-7
Burgess Sch—school OR-9
Burgess Sch—school SC-3
Burgess Sch—school TN-4
Burgess Sch—school (2) TX-5
Burgess Sch (historical)—school AL-4
Burgess Sch (historical)—school TN-4
Burgess Spring Lakes—lake AL-4
Burgess Springs—spring CA-9
Burgess Springs—spring WY-8
*Burgess Store* VA-3
Burgess Store—other VA-3
**Burgesstown (historical)**—pop pl TN-4
**Burgess (Township of)**—pop pl IL-6
Burgess Wash—valley UT-8
Burgess Well—well CA-9
Burget Creek—stream NY-2
**Burge Terrace**—pop pl IN-6
*Burge Terrace Church* IN-6
Burge Terrace Independent Baptist
Ch—church IN-6
Burgetown Ch—church MS-4
Burgett Branch—stream (2) KY-4
Burgett Creek—stream OR-9
Burgett Ditch—canal IN-6
Burgette Ranch—locale NM-5
Burgett Hill—summit OR-9
Burgett House And Barn—hist pl OH-6
Burgett Lake—lake IL-6
Burgett Peak—summit WA-9
Burgett Run—stream OH-6
Burgett Sch—school KY-4
Burgetts Fork—stream PA-2
**Burgettstown**—pop pl PA-2
Burgettstown Borough—civil PA-2
Burgettstown Community Park—park PA-2
*Burgettstown Junior Senior High School* PA-2
*Burgeville* KS-7
Burggraf-Burt-Webster House—hist pl OR-9
Burggraff Ranch—locale MT-8
Burgher Branch—stream MO-7
**Burghil**—pop pl OH-6
Burghil Cem—cemetery OH-6
**Burghill**—pop pl OH-6
Burgholtshouse—hist pl PA-2
Burgholzer Creek—stream OR-9
Burghstream Point—cape FL-3
Burgh Westra—hist pl VA-3
Burgie Chapel Sch—school TN-4
*Burgies Chapel* TN-4
Burgi Hill—summit UT-8
**Burgin**—pop pl KY-4
Burgin (CCD)—cens area KY-4
Burgin Cem—cemetery KY-4
Burgin Cove—valley (2) NC-3
Burgin Lake Dam—dam (2) MS-4
Burgins Fork—stream NC-3
Burgin Slope Mine (underground)—mine AL-4
Burgis Branch—stream TN-4
Burgis Creek—stream SC-3
Burgess Knob—summit AR-4
*Burgland Creek* MI-6
*Burglar's Island* NH-1
**Burglen Hills**—pop pl IN-6
Burglund Pond—lake OR-9
Burg Mtn—summit OR-9
Burgoin Brook—stream ME-1
Burgoin Gap—gap NC-3
Burgo Lake—lake MN-6
Burgony Creek—stream AL-4
**Burgoon**—pop pl OH-6
Burgoon Church—cemetery IN-6
Burgoon Hollow—valley OH-6
Burgoon Run—stream (3) PA-2
Burgoons Gap—locale PA-2
Burgoschnich Hollow—valley MO-7
Burgoyne—locale NY-2
Burgoyne Branch—stream KY-4
Burgoyne Creek—stream CA-9
Burgoyne Pass—gap MA-1
Burgoyne Shop Ctr—locale FL-3
Burgoyne Siding—locale MT-8
*Burgreen Corner* AL-4
**Burgreen Corners**—pop pl AL-4
**Burgreen Gin**—pop pl AL-4
Burgreen Lake—reservoir AL-4
Burg Sch—school MI-6
Burg Slough—stream WA-9
Burgson Lake—lake CA-9
**Burg Township**—pop pl ND-7
Burg (Township of)—fmr MCD AR-4
Burgundy Estates—uninc pl MD-2
**Burgundy Farms**—pop pl VA-3
Burgundy Farms Sch—school VA-3
**Burgundy Hill (subdivision)**—pop pl
(2) AZ-5
Burgundy Knolls—uninc pl MD-2
**Burgundy Manor**—pop pl VA-3
**Burgundy Street Gardens**
**Subdivision**—pop pl UT-8
**Burgundy Village**—pop pl VA-3
Burgundy Village—uninc pl MD-2
Burg Wagon Works Bldg—hist pl IA-7
Burgwin Elem Sch—school PA-2
*Burgwin Sch* PA-2
Burgwins Landing (historical)—locale NC-3
Burgy Creek—stream ID-8
Burgy Creek—stream MI-6
Burham Canyon—valley CA-9
Burhams Shoals—bar TN-4
Burhans Ranch—locale CA-9
Burhans Sch—school IL-6
Burhans Wharf—locale VA-3
Burhart Chapel—church VA-3
Burheight Creek—stream NY-2
Burholme—locale PA-2
Burholme Park—park PA-2
Burial Ground For Kuamoo Battle
Warriors—cemetery HI-9
Burial Hill—summit MA-1
Burial Hill Beach—beach CT-1
Burial Island—island ME-1
*Burial Islet* ME-1
Burial Lake—lake AK-9
Burial Platform—hist pl HI-9
*Burian Lake* WA-9
Buri Buri—civil CA-9
Buri Buri Ridge—ridge CA-9
Buri Buri Sch—school CA-9
Buried City Site (41OC1)—hist pl TX-5
Buried Hills—range NV-8
Buried Mtn—summit CA-9
**Burien**—pop pl WA-9
Burien Lake—lake WA-9
Buring Point—cape ME-1
Burington Sch—school VT-1
Buris Creek—stream MO-7
Buris Hollow—valley KY-4
*Buritoma* MH-9
Buritoma—channel MH-9
Buritts Creek—stream MI-6
Burk—locale WV-2
**Burk**—pop pl IA-7
Burkalow Creek—stream MD-2
Burkard Post Office (historical)—building AL-4
Burk Branch—stream (2) KY-4
Burk Branch—stream OH-6
Burk Branch—stream TX-5
Burk Brothers and Company—hist pl PA-2
**Burkburnett**—pop pl TX-5
Burkburnett (CCD)—cens area TX-5
Burkburnett Water Supply—other TX-5
Burk Camp—locale NM-5
Burk Cave—cave (2) TN-4
Burk Cem—cemetery AL-4
Burk Cem—cemetery FL-3
Burk Cem—cemetery KY-4
Burk Cem—cemetery (2) OH-6
Burk Cem—cemetery SD-7
Burk Cem—cemetery (2) TN-4
Burk Cem—cemetery VA-3
Burk Cem—cemetery WV-2
Burk Chapel—church IA-7
Burk Creek—stream NY-2
Burk Creek—stream WV-2
**Burkdale**—pop pl VA-3
Burk Drain—stream MI-6
Burke—locale KY-4
Burke—locale LA-4
Burke—locale TN-4
**Burke**—pop pl CA-9
**Burke**—pop pl ID-8
**Burke**—pop pl NY-2
**Burke**—pop pl SD-7
**Burke**—pop pl TX-5
**Burke**—pop pl VA-3
**Burke**—pop pl WI-6
Burke, Charles H., House—hist pl NV-8
Burke, Lake—reservoir SD-7
Burke, Thomas C., House—hist pl GA-3
Burke Arroyo—stream CO-8
Burke Bay—bay WA-9
Burke Bet Island—island OK-5
Burke Bldg—hist pl PA-2
Burke Branch—stream AL-4
Burke Branch—stream KY-4
Burke Branch—stream OK-5
Burke Branch—stream TN-4
Burke Branch—stream TX-5
Burke Branch—stream WV-2
**Burke (Burke Hollow)**—pop pl VT-1
Burke Canal—canal LA-4
Burke Cem—cemetery AR-4
Burke Cem—cemetery GA-3
Burke Cem—cemetery IL-6
Burke Cem—cemetery (2) KY-4
Burke Cem—cemetery (2) MI-6
Burke Cem—cemetery NC-3
Burke Cem—cemetery (2) TN-4
Burke Cem—cemetery TX-5
Burke Cem—cemetery (3) VA-3
**Burke Center**—pop pl NY-2
Burke Center Cem—cemetery NY-2
Burke Ch—church WI-6
Burke Chapel—church AL-4
Burke Chapel—church NC-3
**Burke Chapel**—pop pl NC-3
**Burke City**—pop pl MO-7
**Burke Civil Township**—pop pl SD-7
Burke-Clark House—hist pl OR-9
*Burke County* NC-3
Burke County—civil NC-3
Burke County—civil ND-7
**Burke (County)**—pop pl GA-3
Burke County Courthouse—hist pl GA-3
Burke County Courthouse—hist pl NC-3
Burke County Courthouse—hist pl ND-7
Burke County Human Resources
Center—school NC-3
*Burke Creek* CA-9
*Burke Creek* TX-5
Burke Creek—stream AK-9
Burke Creek—stream AR-4
Burke Creek—stream (2) MI-6
Burke Creek—stream (2) MT-8
Burke Creek—stream NV-8
Burke Creek—stream NC-3
Burke Creek—stream OR-9
Burke Creek—stream SC-3
Burke Creek—stream VA-3
Burke Creek—stream WA-9
Burke Creek—stream WY-8
Burke Dam—dam SD-7
Burke Ditch—canal AR-4
Burke Ditch—canal CO-8
Burke Drain Number 15—canal ND-7
Burke Green Cem—cemetery VT-1
Burke Gulch—valley CO-8
Burke Gulch—valley MT-8
*Burkehart Station* IN-6
**Burkehaven**—pop pl NH-1
Burkehaven Hill—summit NH-1
Burkehaven Island—island NH-1
**Burke Heights**—pop pl VA-3
Burke Hill—summit CA-9
Burke Hill—summit ME-1
Burke Hill—summit MT-8
Burke Hill—summit NY-2
Burke Hill—summit (2) WA-9
**Burke Hills**—pop pl VA-3
Burke (historical P.O.)—locale IA-7
**Burke Hollow**—pop pl VT-1
Burke Hollow—valley (3) TN-4
Burke HS—school NE-7
Burke HS—school SC-3
Burke Island—island ME-1
Burke Island—island WA-9
Burke JHS—school CA-9
Burke JHS—school NM-5
Burke Knob—summit TN-4
Burke Lake—lake MI-6
Burke Lake—lake WA-9
Burke Lake—reservoir CO-8
Burke Lake—reservoir VA-3
Burke Lake—swamp OR-9
Burke Lake County Park—park VA-3
Burke Lakefront Airp—airport OH-6
Burke Landing—locale MS-4
Burke Landing Revetment—levee MS-4
Burke Lateral—canal ID-8
Burkeley Square—locale NC-3
Burke-Martin Mine—mine CO-8
Burke Memorial Cem—cemetery NC-3
Burke Memorial Hosp—hospital MA-1
Burke Memorial Park—park IA-7
Burke Mill Stream—stream VA-3
**Burkemont**—pop pl NC-3
**Burkemont (historical)**—pop pl OR-9
Burkemont Mtn—summit NC-3
**Burke Mountain**—pop pl VT-1
Burke Mtn—summit AZ-5
Burke Mtn—summit NC-3
Burke Mtn—summit VT-1
Burke Municipal Airp—airport SD-7
Burken Ch (historical)—church MS-4
Burke Park—park OH-6
Burke Park—park TN-4
**Burke Park**—pop pl NC-3
Burke Playground—park MA-1
*Burke Pond* FL-3
Burke Pond—lake FL-3
Burke Pond—lake NH-1
Burke Pond—reservoir VA-3
Burke Ponds—reservoir AL-4
Burke Post Office (historical)—building TN-4
Burke Ranch—locale AZ-5
Burke Ranch—locale NE-7
Burke Ranch—locale TX-5
Burke Ranch—locale (2) WY-8
Burke Ranch Oil Field—oilfield WY-8
Burke (reduced usage)—locale IL-6
Burke Rehabilitation Center—building NY-2
Burke Rsvr—reservoir (2) WY-8
**Burkes Addition (subdivision)**—pop pl UT-8
Burkes Bayou—stream LA-4
Burkes Branch—stream KY-4
Burkes Branch—stream TN-4
Burkes Cem—cemetery KY-4
Burkes Cem—cemetery OH-6
Burke Sch—school CO-8
Burke Sch—school GA-3
Burke Sch—school (2) IL-6
Burke Sch—school (2) MA-1
Burke Sch—school MI-6
Burke Sch—school MO-7
Burke Sch—school NE-7
Burke Sch—school NJ-2
Burke Sch—school TX-5
Burke Sch—school VA-3
Burkes Chapel—church GA-3
Burke Sch Number 1—school ND-7
Burke Sch Number 2—school ND-7
Burke Sch Number 3—school ND-7
Burke Sch Number 4—school ND-7
Burkes Corner—locale VA-3
Burkes Creek—stream KY-4
Burkes Creek—stream MS-4
Burkes Creek—stream NJ-2
Burkes Creek—stream NC-3
Burkes Garden—basin VA-3
**Burkes Garden**—pop pl VA-3
Burke's Garden Central Church And
Cemetery—hist pl VA-3
Burkes Garden Creek—stream VA-3
Burke's Garden Rural Hist Dist—hist pl VA-3
Burkes Garden Station—locale VA-3
Burke Siding—locale KY-4
*Burke's Island* WA-9
Burkes Lake Dam—dam AL-4
*Burke's Lily Pond* ME-1
Burke Slough—stream WA-9
Burke Slough—swamp SD-7
Burke Slough State Public Shooting
Area—park SD-7
*Burke Spring* NV-8
Burke Spring—spring AZ-5
Burke Spring—spring MT-8
Burke Spring—spring NM-5
Burke Spring—spring OR-9
Burke Spring Creek—stream CO-8
*Burkes Ranch* AZ-5
Burkes Ridge—ridge TX-5
Burkes Shop—locale VA-3
Burkes Spring—locale KY-4
*Burkes Station* AZ-5
Burke State Wildlife Mngmt Area—park MN-6
Burke Station Sch—school WI-6
Burke Statue—park DC-2
Burke's Tavern—hist pl VA-3
Burkes Tavern—locale VA-3
Burke Street Sch—school WV-2
Burke Substation—other WA-9
Burke Summit—summit ID-8
Burke Summit—summit MT-8
Burkesville—locale NJ-2
**Burkesville**—pop pl KY-4
Burkesville Bridge—bridge KY-4
Burkesville (CCD)—cens area KY-4
Burkesville Cem—cemetery KY-4
*Burket* PA-2
**Burket**—pop pl IN-6
Burke-Tarr Stadium—park TN-4
Burket Cem—cemetery PA-2
Burket Creek—stream GA-3
Burket Elem Sch—school IN-6
Burket Ferry Landing—locale GA-3
**Burketown**—pop pl VA-3
**Burke (Town of)**—pop pl NY-2
**Burke (Town of)**—pop pl VT-1
**Burke (Town of)**—pop pl WI-6
Burke Township—civil SD-7
**Burke Township**—pop pl ND-7
Burke (Township of)—fmr MCD AR-4
**Burke (Township of)**—pop pl MN-6
Burket Sch—school IL-6
*Burkett* MS-4
Burkett—locale KS-7
**Burkett**—pop pl NE-7
**Burkett**—pop pl TX-5
Burkett, Lake—lake FL-3
Burkett, Mount—summit AK-9
**Burkett Acres**—pop pl CA-9
Burkett Archeol Site—hist pl NE-7
Burkett Bay Swamp—swamp FL-3
Burkett Bend—bend TX-5
Burkett Cem—cemetery AR-4
Burkett Cem—cemetery IL-6
Burkett Cem—cemetery (2) IN-6
Burkett Cem—cemetery MS-4
Burkett Cem—cemetery TX-5
Burkett Ch—church GA-3
Burkett Chapel—church (2) TN-4
Burkett Chapel Cem—cemetery TN-4
*Burkett Chapel School* TN-4
*Burkett Creek* MS-4
Burkett Creek—stream LA-4
Burkett Creek—stream MI-6
Burkett Ditch—canal OH-6
**Burkett Gardens**—pop pl CA-9
Burkett Hollow—valley AL-4
Burkett Hollow—valley IL-6
Burkett Hollow Ch—church PA-2
Burkett Hollow Sch—school PA-2
Burkett Landing—locale SC-3
Burkett Mine—mine TN-4
Burkett Mine—mine WI-6
Burkett Oil Field—oilfield KS-7
Burkett Oil Field—oilfield TX-5
Burkett Park—park TX-5
Burkett Pond—reservoir PA-2
Burketts Chapel Cem—cemetery TN-4
Burketts Chapel Sch (historical)—school TN-4
Burketts Creek—stream (2) MS-4
Burketts Ranch—locale NM-5
**Burkettsville (historical)**—pop pl MS-4
Burkettsville Post Office
(historical)—building MS-4
**Burkettsville (RR name**
**Gilberts)**—pop pl OH-6
**Burkettville**—pop pl ME-1
*Burkeville* AL-4
**Burkeville**—pop pl TX-5
**Burkeville**—pop pl VA-3
*Burkeville (Burkville)* AL-4
Burkeville (CCD)—cens area TX-5
Burkeville Covered Bridge—hist pl MA-1
Burkeville Lookout Tower—locale TX-5
Burke-Yandell Cem—cemetery TX-5
Burkey Ditch—canal IN-6
Burkey Pond—lake OH-6
Burkhad Chapel (historical)—church TN-4
Burkhalter Branch—stream AL-4
Burkhalter Branch—stream SC-3
Burkhalter Cem—cemetery (2) MS-4
Burkhalter Creek—stream AL-4
Burkhalter Creek—stream MS-4
Burkhalter Ditch—canal WY-8
Burkhalter Gap—gap GA-3
Burkhalter Rsvr—reservoir OR-9
**Burkhalter Subdivision**
**(subdivision)**—pop pl AL-4
Burkham Center Park—park OH-6
*Burkhams Ferry* MS-4
Burkham Tank—reservoir NV-8
Burkhand Branch—stream TX-5
**Burkhardt**—pop pl WI-6
Burkhardt Cem—cemetery TX-5
Burkhardt Center—locale OH-6
Burkhardt Lake—lake CA-9
Burkhardt Sch—school IN-6
*Burkhardts Creek* IN-6
Burkhardt Tank—reservoir NM-5
Burkhart—locale KY-4
Burkhart—locale OH-6
Burkhart Branch—stream MO-7
Burkhart Cem—cemetery KY-4
Burkhart Ch—church MO-7
Burkhart Ch—church OH-6
Burkhart Creek—stream IN-6
Burkhart Creek—stream OK-5
Burkhart Creek—stream OR-9
Burkhart Creek—stream WI-6
Burkhart-Dibrell House—hist pl AK-9
**Burkhart Estates Subdivision**—pop pl UT-8
Burkhart Knob—summit TN-4
Burkhart Lake—lake MI-6
Burkhart Park—park OR-9
Burkhart Prairie—area MO-7
Burkhart Rapids—rapids OR-9
Burkhart Rsvr—reservoir ID-8
Burkhart Saddle—gap CA-9
Burkhart Sch—school TN-4
*Burkhart School* IN-6
Burkhartsmeyer Rsvr—reservoir MT-8
*Burkhart Station* IN-6
Burkhart Trail—trail CA-9
Burkhart Well—well NM-5
Burkhead Cem—cemetery AR-4
Burkhead Drain—canal MI-6
Burkhead Lake—reservoir MS-4
**Burkhelder**—pop pl PA-2
**Burk Hill**—pop pl NY-2
Burk (historical)—locale KS-7
*Burkholder Branch* AL-4
Burkholder Deadening—swamp KY-4
Burkholder Draw—valley UT-8
**Burk Hollow**—pop pl KY-4
Burk Hollow—valley TN-4
Burk Hollow—valley TX-5
*Burkins Branch* MS-4
**Burkinshaws Factory**—pop pl MA-1
**Burkitt**—pop pl TN-4
Burkitt-Laws Lake—reservoir IL-6
Burkitt Siding—locale TN-4
Burkittsville—hist pl MD-2
**Burkittsville**—pop pl MD-2
Burk Lake—lake MN-6
Burk Lake—lake NM-5
Burk Lake—lake OK-5
Burkland Sch—school MA-1
*Burkley* KY-4
Burkley—other KY-4
Burkley Burgess Lake Dam—dam MS-4
Burkley Coulee—valley ND-7
Burklyn Hall—hist pl VT-1
Burkman Brake—gut LA-4
Burkmere—locale SD-7
Burk Mill Branch—stream MD-2
**Burkplace**—pop pl LA-4
Burk Ranch—locale WY-8
Burk Recreation Center—park FL-3
Burks—locale MS-4
Burks Branch—stream KY-4
Burks Branch—stream TN-4
Burks Branch Ch—church KY-4
Burks Cem—cemetery WV-2
Burks Chapel—church AR-4
Burks Chapel—church TN-4
Burks Chapel Cem—cemetery IN-6
*Burks Creek* TX-5
Burks Creek—stream AL-4
Burks Creek—stream ID-8
Burks Creek—stream TX-5
Burks Creek—stream VA-3
Burks' Distillery—hist pl KY-4
Burks Fork—stream VA-3
Burks Fork Ch—church VA-3
Burks Fork (Magisterial
District)—fmr MCD VA-3
*Burk's Garden* VA-3
Burks Garden—uninc pl VA-3
**Burks Gardens**—pop pl AL-4
**Burks Garden (subdivision)**—pop pl AL-4
Burks-Guy-Hagen House—hist pl VA-3
Burks-Hart Cem—cemetery TX-5
Burkshed Sch—school AR-4
*Burks Hill* TN-4
Burks Hill—summit GA-3
Burks Hill—summit NY-2
Burks Hill—summit TN-4
Burks Hollow—valley (2) MO-7
Burks Hollow—valley OK-5
Burks House—hist pl LA-4
Burk Side Ditch—canal CA-9
Burks Lake—lake SD-7
*Burks Mill* AL-4
Burks Mtn—summit GA-3
Burks Mtn—summit VA-3
Burks Pond—lake AR-4
Burks Pond Dam—dam MS-4
Burks Precinct (historical)—locale MS-4
Burk Spring—spring AZ-5
Burks Ranch—locale NM-5
Burks Ridge—locale TX-5
Burks Run—stream VA-3
Burks Sch (historical)—school TN-4
Burks Spring—spring OR-9
Burks Springs—spring OK-5
Burk Street Sch—school AZ-5
Burks Union Ch—church VA-3
Burksville—locale MO-7
**Burksville**—pop pl (2) IL-6
Burks Well—well (2) NM-5
**Burk Township**—pop pl SD-7
Burkville—locale AL-4
**Burkville**—pop pl MA-1
**Burkville (Burkeville)**—pop pl AL-4
*Burl* AL-4
Burl—locale WV-2
**Burl**—pop pl AL-4
**Burland Ranchettes**—pop pl CO-8
Burl Branch—stream MS-4
Burl Branch—stream NC-3
Burl Cem—cemetery KS-7
Burle—island (2) MP-9
Burleele State Wildlife Mngmt
Area—park MN-6
**Burleene (Township of)**—pop pl MN-6
*Burleigh (2)* ND-7
Burleigh—hist pl MD-2
Burleigh—hist pl NC-3
Burleigh—locale TX-5
**Burleigh**—pop pl NJ-2
Burleigh, H. G., House—hist pl NY-2
Burleigh Brook—stream NH-1
Burleigh Cem—cemetery MI-6
Burleigh Ch—church NJ-2
Burleigh Corners—locale MI-6
Burleigh County—civil ND-7
Burleigh County Courthouse—hist pl ND-7
Burleigh Hamilton Sch—school MS-4
Burleigh Hill—summit ME-1
Burleigh Hill—summit NY-2
Burleigh House—hist pl LA-4
Burleigh Mine—mine CO-8
Burleigh Mtn—summit NH-1
Burleigh Ridge—ridge PA-2
Burleigh Sch—school IL-6
Burleigh Slough—channel MN-6
*Burleigh Station* ND-7
**Burleigh (Township of)**—pop pl MI-6
*Burle Island* MP-9
**Burleith**—pop pl DC-2
Burleman Branch—stream MS-4
**Burleson**—pop pl TX-5
Burleson Bald—summit NC-3
Burleson Branch—stream (2) NC-3
Burleson Branch—stream (3) TX-5
Burleson Canyon—arroyo AZ-5
Burleson Cem—cemetery (3) AL-4
Burleson Cem—cemetery LA-4
Burleson Cem—cemetery (4) NC-3
Burleson Cem—cemetery TN-4
Burleson Cem—cemetery (2) TX-5
Burleson Ch—church AL-4
Burleson Chapel—church NC-3
**Burleson (County)**—pop pl TX-5
Burleson Creek—stream TX-5
Burleson Drain—canal MI-6
Burleson Elem Sch—school AL-4
Burleson Ferry (historical)—locale AL-4
Burleson Hill—summit TX-5
Burleson Hollow—valley PA-2
Burleson-Joshua (CCD)—cens area TX-5
Burleson-Knispel House—hist pl TX-5
Burleson Lake—lake TX-5
Burleson Lake—reservoir TX-5
Burleson-Logan Family Cem—cemetery AL-4
Burleson Mtn—summit AL-4
Burleson Park—flat AZ-5
Burleson Park—park TX-5
Burleson Pond—lake VT-1
Burleson Pond—swamp NY-2
Burleson Sch—school (4) TX-5
*Burlesons Ferry* AL-4
Burlesons Ferry (historical)—locale AL-4
Burlesons Pond—reservoir AR-4
Burleson Well—locale NM-5
Burleson Well—well AZ-5
Burleston Cave—cave AL-4
Burlew Cem—cemetery LA-4
**Burley**—pop pl ID-8
**Burley**—pop pl WA-9
Burley Bluff—cliff OR-9
Burley Butte—summit ID-8
**Burley Corner**—pop pl MI-6
*Burley Corners* MI-6
*Burley Cove* MD-2
Burley Creek—stream MD-2
Burley Creek—stream MT-8

Burnt Lake Trail—*trail* OR-9
Burnt Lake Trail—*trail* WY-8
Burntland Brook—*stream* (2) ME-1
Burnt Land Brook—*stream* ME-1
Burnt Landing—*locale* ME-1
Burnt Landing—*locale* NC-3
Burnt Land Lake—*lake* ME-1
Burntland Pond—*lake* (2) ME-1
Burnt Land Pond—*lake* ME-1
Burnt Land Ridge—*ridge* ME-1
*Burnt Land Stream* ME-1
Burnt Lane Brook—*stream* MN-6
Burnt Leather Ranch—*locale* MT-8
Burnt Log Creek—*stream* ID-8
Burntlog Creek—*stream* ID-8
Burnt Log Spring—*spring* OR-9
Burnt Logs Rsvr—*reservoir* CO-8
Burnt Log Trail—*trail* ID-8
Burnt Meadow—*flat* NV-8
Burnt Meadow—*flat* WY-8
Burnt Meadow Brook—*stream* ME-1
Burnt Meadow Brook—*stream* (2) NJ-2
Burnt Meadow Brook—*stream* NY-2
Burnt Meadow Brook—*stream* VT-1
Burnt Meadow Cem—*cemetery* ME-1
Burnt Meadow Mountains—*ridge* ME-1
Burnt Meadow Pond—*lake* ME-1
Burnt Meadow Pond—*lake* MA-1
**Burnt Meadow Pond**—*pop pl* ME-1
Burnt Meadow Swamp—*swamp* MA-1
Burnt Mesa—*summit* (2) NM-5
Burnt Mesa Rsvr—*reservoir* CO-8
*Burnt Mill* NJ-2
Burnt Mill—*locale* CO-8
Burnt Mill—*locale* ME-1
*Burnt Mill Bayou* FL-3
Burnt Mill Bluff—*cliff* AR-4
*Burnt Mill Branch* MD-2
*Burnt Mill Branch* VA-3
Burnt Mill Branch—*stream* AL-4
Burnt Mill Branch—*stream* MD-2
Burnt Mill Branch—*stream* NJ-2
Burnt Mill Branch—*stream* NC-3
Burnt Mill Bridge—*bridge* AL-4
Burnt Mill Bridge—*bridge* TN-4
Burnt Mill Bridge—*bridge* VA-3
Burnt Mill Brook—*stream* NH-1
Burnt Mill Brook—*stream* NY-2
Burnt Mill Brook Trail—*trail* NH-1
Burnt Mill Canyon—*valley* CA-9
Burnt Mill Canyon—*valley* NV-8
Burnt Mill Creek—*stream* CA-9
Burnt Mill Creek—*stream* CO-8
Burnt Mill Creek—*stream* (2) FL-3
Burnt Mill Creek—*stream* MD-2
Burnt Mill Creek—*stream* NY-2
Burnt Mill Creek—*stream* (2) NC-3
Burnt Mill Creek—*stream* SC-3
Burnt Mill Creek—*stream* VA-3
Burnt Mill Hollow—*valley* TN-4
Burnt Mill Hollow Creek—*stream* TN-4
Burnt Mill Mesa—*summit* CO-8
*Burnt Mill Pond* MD-2
Burnt Millpond—*reservoir* MA-1
Burnt Millpond Dam—*dam* MA-1
Burnt Mill Ranch—*locale* AZ-5
Burnt Mill Run—*stream* VA-3
*Burnt Mills* NJ-2
Burnt Mills—*locale* NJ-2
Burnt Mills—*locale* (2) PA-2
**Burnt Mills**—*pop pl* MD-2
**Burnt Mills**—*pop pl* NC-3
Burnt Mills, Lake—*reservoir* VA-3
Burnt Mill Sch—*school* GA-3
Burnt Mill Sch (historical)—*school* MS-4
**Burnt Mills Hills**—*pop pl* MD-2
Burnt Mills (historical P.O.)—*locale* MS-4
**Burnt Mills Knolls**—*pop pl* MD-2
**Burnt Mills Manor**—*pop pl* MD-2
Burnt Mill Spring—*spring* AZ-5
Burnt Mill Spring—*spring* UT-8
Burnt Mill Spring No 2—*spring* UT-8
Burnt Mills Rsvr—*reservoir* MD-2
Burnt Mills Sch—*school* MD-2
Burnt Mills Swamp—*stream* VA-3
Burnt Mills Trail—*trail* PA-2
**Burnt Mills Village**—*pop pl* MD-2
*Burnt Mill Swamp* VA-3
Burnt Mill Valley—*valley* GA-3
Burnt Mill Vly—*swamp* NY-2
Burnt Mountain—*ridge* NV-8
Burnt Mountain—*ridge* WA-9
Burnt Mountain—*ridge* WY-8
Burnt Mountain Ch—*church* GA-3
Burnt Mountain Creek—*stream* OR-9
Burnt Mountain Meadows—*flat* OR-9
Burnt Mountain Recreation Site—*park* OR-9
Burnt Mountain Spring—*spring* OR-9
Burnt Mountain Trail (Pack)—*trail* NM-5
*Burnt Mtn* OR-9
*Burnt Mtn* TN-4
Burnt Mtn—*summit* AK-9
Burnt Mtn—*summit* (2) AZ-5
Burnt Mtn—*summit* (3) CA-9
Burnt Mtn—*summit* (4) CO-8
Burnt Mtn—*summit* GA-3
Burnt Mtn—*summit* (2) ME-1
Burnt Mtn—*summit* MI-6
Burnt Mtn—*summit* (4) MT-8
Burnt Mtn—*summit* NV-8
Burnt Mtn—*summit* (4) NY-2
Burnt Mtn—*summit* (4) NC-3
Burnt Mtn—*summit* (8) OR-9
Burnt Mtn—*summit* TN-4
Burnt Mtn—*summit* (2) UT-8
Burnt Mtn—*summit* (7) VT-1
Burnt Mtn—*summit* VA-3
Burnt Mtn—*summit* (2) WA-9
Burnt Mtn—*summit* (2) WY-8
Burnt Nubble—*summit* ME-1
*Burnt Oak Creek* TX-5
Burn Top Mtn—*summit* MT-8
*Burnt Ordinary* NC-3
**Burntout**—*pop pl* AL-4
Burnt Out Bay—*swamp* FL-3
Burntout Cem—*cemetery* AL-4
Burntout Ch—*church* AL-4
Burntout Community Center—*building* AL-4
Burntout Creek—*stream* FL-3
Burnt-Out Creek—*stream* TX-5
Burnt Out Lakebed—*flat* MN-6
Burnt Out Sch (historical)—*school* AL-4
Burnt Park—*flat* WA-9
Burnt Paw—*locale* AK-9
Burnt Peak—*summit* CA-9
Burnt Peak—*summit* MT-8
Burnt Peak—*summit* NV-8
Burnt Peak—*summit* (3) OR-9
Burnt Peak—*summit* UT-8
Burnt Peak—*summit* WA-9
Burnt Peak Canyon—*valley* CA-9
*Burnt Peak Mountains* NV-8
Burnt Peak Trail—*trail* CA-9
Burnt Peak Well (Dry)—*well* NV-8
**Burnt Pine (subdivision)**—*pop pl* AL-4
Burnt Pine Trail—*trail* MD-2
Burnt Pinon Wash —*valley* AZ-5
Burnt Place Brook—*stream* NY-2
Burnt Place Valley—*valley* AZ-5
Burnt Plain Swamp—*swamp* MA-1
Burnt Pocoson (historical)—*swamp* NC-3
*Burnt Point* OR-9
Burnt Point—*cape* AK-9
Burnt Point—*cape* FL-3
Burnt Point—*cape* ME-1
Burnt Point—*cape* NY-2
Burnt Point—*cape* OR-9
Burnt Point—*cliff* AZ-5
Burnt Point—*cliff* WY-8
Burnt Point—*summit* CA-9
Burnt Point Creek—*stream* CA-9
Burnt Point Creek—*stream* MT-8
Burnt Point Rapids—*rapids* WI-6
*Burnt Pond* ME-1
Burnt Pond—*lake* KY-4
Burnt Pond—*lake* (2) ME-1
Burnt Pond—*lake* MD-2
Burnt Pond—*lake* (3) NY-2
Burnt Pone Creek—*stream* TN-4
Burnt Poplar Fork—*stream* VA-3
Burnt Porcupine Island—*island* ME-1
Burntpot Island—*island* GA-3
**Burnt Prairie**—*pop pl* IL-6
Burnt Prairie Ch—*church* IL-6
Burnt Prairie Site (39LM207)—*hist pl* SD-7
Burnt Prairie (Township of)—*civ div* IL-6
Burnt Quarter—*hist pl* VA-3
*Burnt Quarter Creek* VA-3
Burnt Ranch—*locale* OR-9
Burnt Ranch—*locale* SD-7
**Burnt Ranch**—*pop pl* CA-9
Burnt Ranch Creek—*stream* CA-9
Burnt Ranch Ditch—*canal* WY-8
Burnt Rancheria Campground—*locale* CA-9
Burnt Ranch Falls—*falls* CA-9
Burnt Ranch Historical Monument—*locale* WY-8
Burnt Ranch Prairie—*flat* CA-9
Burnt Ranch Sch—*school* CA-9
Burnt Rapids—*rapids* OR-9
Burnt Reed Brake—*stream* MS-4
Burnt Reeds Swamp—*stream* VA-3
*Burnt Ridge* OR-9
Burnt Ridge—*ridge* (3) CA-9
Burnt Ridge—*ridge* (2) CO-8
Burnt Ridge—*ridge* GA-3
Burnt Ridge—*ridge* (2) ID-8
Burnt Ridge—*ridge* MT-8
Burnt Ridge—*ridge* NM-5
Burnt Ridge—*ridge* NY-2
Burnt Ridge—*ridge* (2) OR-9
Burnt Ridge—*ridge* PA-2
Burnt Ridge—*ridge* (4) UT-8
Burnt Ridge—*ridge* (2) VA-3
Burnt Ridge—*ridge* WA-9
Burnt Ridge—*ridge* WV-2
Burnt Ridge—*ridge* WY-8
Burnt Ridge Airstrip Airp—*airport* WA-9
Burnt Ridge Branch—*stream* NC-3
Burnt Ridge Canyon—*valley* NM-5
Burnt Ridge Cem—*cemetery* ID-8
*Burnt Ridge Creek* OR-9
Burnt Ridge Creek—*stream* CA-9
Burnt Ridge Run—*stream* WV-2
Burnt Ridges—*ridge* NY-2
Burnt Ridge Spring—*spring* UT-8
Burnt Ridge Trail—*trail* MT-8
Burnt Ridge Trail—*trail* NM-5
Burnt River—*stream* AK-9
Burnt River—*stream* OR-9
Burnt River Canyon—*valley* OR-9
Burnt River HS—*school* OR-9
*Burnt River Rsvr* OR-9
Burnt River Spring—*spring* OR-9
Burnt River Valley—*valley* OR-9
Burnt Rock—*island* OR-9
Burnt Rock—*pillar* WA-9
Burnt Rock—*summit* (3) NY-2
Burnt Rock, The (historical)—*summit* SD-7
Burnt Rock Creek—*stream* MS-4
Burnt Rock Creek—*stream* SD-7
Burnt Rock Mtn—*summit* VT-1
Burntrock Ridge—*ridge* NC-3
Burnt Rock Spring—*spring* MT-8
Burnt Rollways Dam—*dam* WI-6
Burnt Rsvr—*reservoir* NV-8
Burnt Run—*stream* OH-6
Burnt Run—*stream* WV-2
Burnt Saw Creek—*stream* WA-9
Burnt Sch (historical)—*school* (2) MS-4
Burnt School Cem—*cemetery* NC-3
Burnt Schoolhouse Branch—*stream* TX-5
Burnt School House Cem—*cemetery* AR-4
Burnt Scrub Swamp—*swamp* GA-3
Burnt Shanty Branch—*stream* NC-3
Burnt Shanty Clearing—*flat* NY-2
Burnt Shanty Creek—*stream* CA-9
Burnt Shanty Creek—*stream* WI-6
Burnt Shanty Hollow—*valley* IL-6
Burnt Shanty Lake—*lake* MN-6
Burnt Shanty Rapids—*rapids* WI-6
Burnt Shanty Run—*stream* (2) PA-2
Burnt Shed Coulee—*valley* MT-8
Burnt Ship Creek—*stream* NY-2
Burnt Shirt Branch—*stream* MO-7
Burntshirt Mtn—*summit* NC-3
Burntside—*locale* MN-6
Burntside Lake—*lake* MN-6
Burntside Lake—*locale* MN-6
Burntside Lodge Hist Dist—*hist pl* MN-6
Burntside River—*stream* MN-6
Burntside State For—*forest* MN-6
Burnt Slough—*gut* TX-5
Burnt Slough Lake—*lake* KY-4
Burnt Spot Draw—*valley* TX-5
Burnt Spot Hill—*summit* NY-2
Burnt Spot Pond—*lake* UT-8
Burnt Spring—*spring* AZ-5
Burnt Spring—*spring* CA-9
Burnt Spring—*spring* CO-8
Burnt Spring—*spring* NM-5
Burnt Spring—*spring* (3) OR-9
Burnt Spring—*spring* TX-5
Burnt Spring—*spring* (5) UT-8
*Burnt Spring Canyon* AZ-5
Burnt Spring Canyon—*valley* UT-8
Burnt Spring Gulch—*valley* ID-8
Burnt Spring Hills—*summit* TX-5
*Burnt Spring Pond* UT-8
Burnt Spring Ridge—*ridge* TN-4
Burnt Springs—*spring* CO-8
Burnt Springs—*spring* NV-8
Burnt Springs—*spring* (2) UT-8
*Burnt Springs Canyon* AZ-5
Burnt Springs Range—*range* NV-8
Burnt Spruce Ridge—*ridge* NC-3
Burnt Stand Cem—*cemetery* TN-4
Burnt Station Branch—*stream* TN-4
Burnt Stocking Branch—*stream* NC-3
Burnt Store—*locale* MD-2
Burnt Store—*locale* VA-3
Burnt Strip Mtn—*summit* ID-8
Burnt Stump Butte—*summit* OR-9
Burnt Stump Canyon—*valley* NM-5
Burnt Stump Canyon—*valley* UT-8
Burnt Stump Mesa—*summit* AZ-5
Burnt Stump Mesa Tank—*reservoir* AZ-5
Burnt Stump Rsvr—*reservoir* OR-9
Burnt Stump Spring—*spring* CO-8
Burnt Stump Spring—*spring* (2) UT-8
*Burnt Swamp* DE-2
*Burnt Swamp* MA-1
Burnt Swamp—*stream* NC-3
Burnt Swamp—*swamp* DE-2
Burnt Swamp—*swamp* ME-1
Burnt Swamp—*swamp* (2) MA-1
Burnt Swamp Brook—*stream* MA-1
Burnt Swamp Brook—*stream* RI-1
Burnt Swamp Ch—*church* NC-3
**Burnt Swamp Corner**—*pop pl* MA-1
*Burnt Swamp Meadow* MA-1
*Burnt Swamp Pond* MA-1
Burnt Swamp (Township of)—*fmr MCD* NC-3
Burnt Tank—*reservoir* (2) AZ-5
Burnt Tank—*reservoir* (2) NM-5
*Burnt Thoroughfare* ME-1
Burnt Timber Canyon—*valley* MT-8
Burnt Timber Canyon—*valley* UT-8
Burnt Timber Canyon—*valley* WY-8
Burnt Timber Creek—*stream* CO-8
Burnt Timber Creek—*stream* NV-8
Burnt Timber Gulch—*valley* CO-8
Burnt Timber Lake—*lake* WY-8
Burnt Timber Mtn—*summit* OR-9
Burnt Top—*summit* MT-8
Burnt Top—*summit* OR-9
Burnt Trail—*trail* PA-2
Burnt Trail—*trail* WY-8
**Burnt Tree**—*pop pl* VA-3
Burnt Tree Fishing Access Site—*locale* MT-8
Burnt Tree Fork—*valley* UT-8
Burnt Tree Hollow—*valley* KY-4
Burnt Tree Pond—*lake* UT-8
Burnt Tree Ridge—*ridge* CO-8
Burnt Trees Wash—*valley* AZ-5
Burnt Trough Spring—*spring* AZ-5
Burnt Valley—*valley* CA-9
Burnt Valley—*valley* WA-9
*Burnt Village Campground* AL-4
*Burnt Village Campground and Marina* AL-4
Burnt Village Park—*park* AL-4
Burnt Vly—*valley* NY-2
Burnt Wagon Basin—*basin* ID-8
Burnt Wagon Draw—*valley* WY-8
Burnt Wagon Lake—*lake* WI-6
Burnt Wagon Tank—*reservoir* AZ-5
Burnt Wash—*stream* AZ-5
Burnt Wash Number One Spring—*spring* AZ-5
Burnt Wash Spring—*spring* AZ-5
Burntwater Trading Post—*locale* AZ-5
**Burnt Water (Trading Post)**—*pop pl* AZ-5
Burntwater Wash—*valley* AZ-5
Burntwater Well—*well* AZ-5
Burnt Well—*well* AZ-5
Burnt Well—*well* NM-5
Burnt Well (historical)—*well* AZ-5
*Burnt Wells* AZ-5
Burnt Willow Canyon—*valley* ID-8
Burnt Willow Canyon—*valley* TX-5
Burnt Willow Creek—*stream* MT-8
Burnt Willow Creek—*stream* OR-9
Burnt Willow Spring—*spring* OR-9
Burnt Windmill—*locale* NM-5
*Burnt Wood* KS-7
Burntwood Branch—*stream* AL-4
Burntwood Cem—*cemetery* OH-6
*Burnt Wood Creek* KS-7
Burntwood Creek—*stream* AL-4
Burnt Wood Creek—*stream* ID-8
Burntwood Creek—*stream* KS-7
Burntwood Creek—*stream* NE-7
Burntwood Creek—*stream* OH-6
Burntwood Creek—*stream* OR-9
Burntwood (historical)—*locale* KS-7
*Burntwood Islands* VA-3
*Burnt Wood River* WI-6
Burnt Woods—*locale* TN-4
**Burnt Woods**—*pop pl* OR-9
*Burntwood Township* KS-7
**Burnugh Downs Subdivision**—*pop pl* UT-8
**Burnville**—*pop pl* AR-4
Burnville Sch—*school* AR-4
Burn Waterhole—*reservoir* OR-9
Burnwell—*locale* KY-4
**Burnwell**—*pop pl* AL-4
**Burnwell**—*pop pl* WV-2
Burnwell Mine No. 1—*mine* CO-8
Burnwell Mine No. 2—*mine* CO-8
Burnwell Mines Post Office (historical)—*building* AL-4
Burnwell Mines (underground)—*mine* AL-4
Burnwell Post Office (historical)—*building* AL-4
**Burnwell (Stringtown)**—*pop pl* KY-4
Burnwood—*locale* NY-2
Burnwood—*locale* PA-2
Bur Oak Draw—*valley* TX-5
Bur Oak Hollow—*valley* MO-7
Bur Oak Lake—*lake* IA-7
Buroak Sch—*school* AR-4
Bur Oak Spring—*spring* TX-5
Bur Oak Windmill—*locale* TX-5
Burok—*island* MP-9
Buroker—*locale* WA-9
*Burok Island* MP-9
*Burokku* MP-9
*Burokku Island* MP-9
Burokku Island—*island* MP-9
*Burokku-to* MP-9
Buron Ritakume—*bar* MP-9
Buron Roanbugi—*bar* MP-9
Buros Creek—*stream* KS-7
Burpee—*locale* OR-9
Burpee Brook—*stream* ME-1
Burpee Brook—*stream* NY-2
Burpee Farm—*hist pl* NH-1
Burpee Hill—*summit* (2) NH-1
Burpee Hill—*summit* WA-9
Burpee Mine—*mine* ID-8
Burpee Mtn—*summit* ID-8
**Burp Hollow**—*pop pl* OR-9
Burping Brook—*stream* WA-9
Burp Lake—*lake* NY-2
Bur Point—*cape* AK-9
Burquin School—*locale* IL-6
Burr—*locale* CA-9
Burr—*locale* MO-7
Burr—*locale* TX-5
Burr—*locale* WA-9
**Burr**—*pop pl* KY-4
**Burr**—*pop pl* MN-6
**Burr**—*pop pl* NE-7
Burr, Carll, Jr., House—*hist pl* NY-2
Burr, Carll S., Mansion—*hist pl* NY-2
Burr, George, House—*hist pl* OH-6
Burr, Peter, House—*hist pl* WV-2
*Burr, The* MS-4
Burr, Theodore, House—*hist pl* NY-2
Burra-Burra Creek—*stream* TN-4
Burra-Burra Mine—*mine* TN-4
Burra Burra Mine Hist Dist—*hist pl* TN-4
Burra Burra Peak—*summit* CA-9
**Burrage**—*pop pl* MA-1
**Burrage Corner**—*pop pl* MA-1
Burrage Pond—*reservoir* MA-1
Burrage Pond Dam—*dam* MA-1
Burrage Pond Dam - Upper Reservoir Flume—*dam* MA-1
Burrage Pond Lower Reservoir Dike A—*dam* MA-1
Burrage Pond Lower Reservoir Dike B—*dam* MA-1
Burrage Pond - Lower Rsvr—*reservoir* MA-1
Burrage Pond - Upper Rsvr—*reservoir* MA-1
Burrages End—*hist pl* MD-2
Burrage Upper Reservoir Dam—*dam* MA-1
*Burrageville* MA-1
Burrantown—*locale* TX-5
Burras, Cerro de los—*summit* TX-5
Burras Bend—*bend* MO-7
Burras House—*hist pl* NC-3
Burras Tank—*reservoir* TX-5
Burr-Barton Seminary—*school* VT-1
Burr Basin—*basin* OR-9
Burr Block—*hist pl* NE-7
Burr Branch—*stream* AL-4
Burr Branch—*stream* KY-4
Burr Branch—*stream* (2) TN-4
Burr Brook—*stream* CT-1
Burr Brook—*stream* MA-1
Burr Brook—*stream* NH-1
**Burr Canyon**—*pop pl* WA-9
Burr Canyon—*valley* UT-8
Burr Canyon—*valley* WA-9
Burr Cave—*hist pl* WA-9
Burr Cem—*cemetery* AR-4
Burr Cem—*cemetery* LA-4
Burr Cem—*cemetery* ME-1
Burr Creek—*bay* CT-1
Burr Creek—*stream* (2) CA-9
Burr Creek—*stream* IN-6
Burr Creek—*stream* MI-6
Burr Creek—*stream* MS-4
Burr Creek—*stream* UT-8
Burr Desert—*plain* UT-8
Burr District Cem—*cemetery* CT-1
Burrego Spring—*spring* NM-5
**Burrel**—*pop pl* CA-9
**Burrel (Burrell)**—*pop pl* CA-9
Burrel Chapel Cem—*cemetery* TX-5
*Burrel Creek* MT-8
Burrel Ditch—*canal* CA-9
Burrel Hollow—*valley* WV-2
*Burrell* CA-9
Burrell—*locale* PA-2
Burrell, Jabez and Robbins, House and Cheese Factory—*hist pl* OH-6
Burrel Lake—*reservoir* MS-4
Burrell Bay—*swamp* NC-3
Burrell Bayou—*stream* (2) MS-4
Burrell Branch—*stream* GA-3
Burrell Branch—*stream* KY-4
Burrell Branch—*stream* TN-4
*Burrell (Burrel)* CA-9
Burrell Canyon—*valley* CA-9
Burrell Cem—*cemetery* AL-4
Burrell Cem—*cemetery* AR-4
Burrell Cem—*cemetery* FL-3
Burrell Cem—*cemetery* GA-3
Burrell Cem—*cemetery* IN-6
Burrell Chapel—*church* AL-4
Burrell Chapel—*church* OH-6
*Burrell Chapel Ch* AL-4
Burrell Corners—*locale* NY-2
Burrell Cove—*bay* NC-3
*Burrell Creek* GA-3
Burrell Creek—*stream* (2) MT-8
Burrell Creek—*stream* NY-2
Burrell Creek—*stream* TN-4
Burrell Ford—*locale* GA-3
Burrell Fort—*hist pl* OH-6
Burrell Guard Station—*locale* CA-9
Burrell Gully—*valley* TX-5
Burrell Hollow—*valley* NC-3
Burrell-King House—*hist pl* OH-6
Burrell Lake—*lake* FL-3
Burrell Lake Dam—*dam* MS-4
Burrell Lakes—*lake* MI-6
Burrell Little Lake—*lake* SC-3
Burrell Memorial Hosp—*hospital* VA-3
Burrell Mtn—*summit* AR-4
Burrell Mtn—*summit* GA-3
*Burrell Normal School for Colored Students* AL-4
Burrell Orchard Site—*hist pl* OH-6
Burrell Park—*park* IL-6
Burrells Camp (historical)—*locale* ME-1
Burrell Sch—*school* IL-6
Burrell Sch—*school* MI-6
Burrell School (abandoned)—*locale* CA-9
Burrells Creek—*stream* GA-3
Burrells Ford Trail—*trail* GA-3
Burrells Mtn—*summit* SC-3
Burrell Spring—*spring* AR-4
*Burrell State Vocational Technical School* AL-4
Burrell Township—*fmr MCD* IA-7
**Burrell (Township of)**—*pop pl* (2) PA-2
Burrels Run—*stream* OH-6
*Burres Creek* OK-5
Burress—*locale* NE-7
Burress Spring—*spring* TN-4
Burretts Burrow—*cave* AL-4
Burr Ferry—*locale* LA-4
Burr Ferry Cem—*cemetery* LA-4
Burr Fork—*valley* UT-8
Burr Gulch—*valley* MT-8
Burr Gulch—*valley* WY-8
*Burr Hill* MA-1
Burr Hill—*locale* VA-3
**Burr Hill**—*pop pl* CT-1
**Burr Hill**—*pop pl* SC-3
Burr Hill—*summit* OH-6
*Burrh-Insel* MP-9
Burrh Island—*island* MP-9
Burr Hollow—*valley* AL-4
Burr Hollow—*valley* AR-4
Burr Hollow—*valley* MO-7
Burr Hollow—*valley* NY-2
Burr Hollow—*valley* OH-6
Burridge Canyon—*valley* UT-8
Burridge Sch—*school* VT-1
Burrier, John, House—*hist pl* KY-4
Burrier Ditch—*canal* IN-6
Burrier House—*hist pl* KY-4
Burright Creek—*stream* CA-9
Burrill Airfield—*airport* OR-9
*Burrill Creek* GA-3
Burrill Creek—*stream* CA-9
Burrill Hill—*summit* (3) ME-1
Burrill Hill—*summit* MA-1
Burrill Mine—*mine* NJ-2
Burrill Peak—*summit* CA-9
Burrill Sch—*school* MA-1
*Burrills Hill* MA-1
*Burrillville* RI-1
**Burrillville (Town of)**—*pop pl* RI-1
Burrington Brook—*stream* MA-1
Burrington Covered Bridge—*hist pl* VT-1
Burris—*locale* TX-5
Burris—*locale* WY-8
Burris and Nunn Ranch—*locale* NM-5
Burris Bar—*bar* TN-4
Burris Bay—*bay* NC-3
Burris Branch—*stream* AR-4
Burris Cabin—*locale* MT-8
Burris Cem—*cemetery* AR-4
Burris Cem—*cemetery* (2) IN-6
Burris Cem—*cemetery* MS-4
Burris Cem—*cemetery* OH-6
Burris Cem—*cemetery* (2) OK-5
Burris Cem—*cemetery* (3) TN-4
Burris Cem—*cemetery* TX-5
*Burris Channel* NC-3
Burris Chapel—*church* IN-6
**Burris City (historical P.O.)**—*pop pl* IA-7
Burris Creek—*stream* (2) CA-9
Burris Creek—*stream* MT-8
Burris Creek—*stream* NC-3
Burris Creek—*stream* OK-5
Burris Creek—*stream* OR-9
Burris Creek—*stream* TX-5
Burris Creek—*stream* WA-9
Burris Crossing—*locale* TX-5
Burris Crossroads—*locale* GA-3
Burris- Crowheart Sch—*school* WY-8
Burris Ditch—*canal* IN-6
Burris Draw—*valley* KS-7
Burris Draw—*valley* WY-8
Burris Elem Sch—*school* IN-6
Burris Fork—*stream* MO-7
Burris Fork Bridge—*other* MO-7
Burris Fork Township—*civil* MO-7
Burris Hall—*building* NC-3
Burris House and Potawatomi Spring—*hist pl* IN-6
Burris H W Ranch—*locale* NM-5
Burris Lake—*lake* MI-6
Burr Island—*island* CT-1
Burris Lateral—*canal* ID-8
Burris Meadow—*flat* CO-8
Burris Memorial Universalist Ch—*church* MS-4
Burris Mtn—*summit* CO-8
Burris Park—*park* AZ-5
Burris Park—*park* CA-9
Burris Pond—*lake* NY-2
Burris Ranch—*locale* CA-9
Burris Sch—*school* IN-6
Burris Sch (historical)—*school* TN-4
Burriss Creek—*gut* NC-3
Burriston Canyon—*valley* UT-8
Burriston Pass—*gap* UT-8
Burriston Ponds—*lake* UT-8
**Burristown**—*pop pl* TN-4
Burristown (CCD)—*cens area* TN-4
Burristown Division—*civil* TN-4
Burris Valley—*valley* OK-5
**Burrisville**—*pop pl* MD-2
Burrito Creek—*stream* CA-9
Burrito Tank—*reservoir* TX-5
Burritt Center Sch—*school* IL-6
Burritt Coll (historical)—*school* TN-4
Burritt Cove—*bay* CT-1
Burritt Hotel—*hist pl* CT-1
Burritt Museum—*building* AL-4
*Burritts Creek* MI-6
**Burritt (Township of)**—*pop pl* IL-6
Burr JHS—*school* CT-1
Burr Lake—*lake* LA-4
Burr Lake—*lake* (2) MN-6
Burr Lake—*lake* MO-7
Burr Lake—*lake* NE-7
Burrls Cem—*cemetery* TX-5
Burrls Flat—*flat* MT-8
**Burr Mills**—*pop pl* NY-2
Burr Mine—*mine* CA-9
Burr Mine—*mine* WY-8
Burr Mtn—*summit* CT-1
Burro, Arroyo—*stream* CA-9
Burro, Arroyo—*valley* CA-9
Burro, Arroyo—*valley* TX-5
Burro, Cuesta del—*range* TX-5
Burro, Loma del—*summit* TX-5
Burro, Mount—*summit* AZ-5
*Burr Oak* IL-6
*Burroak* KS-7
Burr Oak—*civ div* WI-6
Burr Oak—*locale* IA-7
Burr Oak—*locale* NE-7
Burr Oak—*locale* OH-6
**Burr Oak**—*pop pl* (2) IN-6
**Burr Oak**—*pop pl* IA-7
**Burr Oak**—*pop pl* KS-7
**Burr Oak**—*pop pl* MI-6
**Burr Oak**—*pop pl* WI-6
**Burr Oak Addition (subdivision)**—*pop pl* UT-8
Burr Oak Basin—*basin* MO-7
Burr Oak Bottom—*bend* KS-7
Burr Oak Branch—*stream* KS-7
*Burr Oak Canyon* NE-7
Burr Oak Canyon—*valley* NE-7
Burr Oak Cem—*cemetery* (2) IL-6
Burr Oak Cem—*cemetery* (2) IN-6
Burr Oak Cem—*cemetery* (2) IA-7
Burr Oak Cem—*cemetery* KS-7
Burr Oak Cem—*cemetery* MI-6
Burr Oak Cem—*cemetery* MN-6
Burr Oak Ch—*church* (3) IN-6
Burr Oak Ch—*church* KS-7
Burr Oak Ch—*church* MO-7
Burr Oak Ch—*church* NE-7
Burr Oak Creek—*stream* (6) IA-7
Burr Oak Creek—*stream* KS-7
Burr Oak Creek—*stream* (3) MO-7
Burr Oak Creek—*stream* NE-7
Burr Oak Creek—*stream* (4) TX-5
Burr Oak House/Masters Hotel—*hist pl* IA-7
Burr Oak HS—*school* KS-7
*Burr Oak Lake* OH-6
Burr Oak Lake—*lake* MN-6
Burr Oak Pond—*lake* IL-6
Burr Oak Rsvr—*reservoir* OH-6
**Burr Oaks**—*pop pl* IL-6
**Burr Oaks**—*pop pl* OH-6
Burr Oak Sch—*school* (4) IL-6
Burr Oak Sch—*school* KS-7
Burr Oak Sch—*school* MI-6
Burr Oak Sch—*school* MN-6
Burr Oak Sch—*school* MO-7
Burr Oak Sch—*school* NE-7
Burr Oak Sch—*school* (5) WI-6
Burr Oak Sch (abandoned)—*school* MO-7
**Burr Oaks Heights**—*pop pl* OH-6
Burr Oak Spring—*spring* TX-5
Burr Oaks Sch—*school* MN-6
Burr Oak State Park—*park* OH-6
**Burr Oak (Strouse)**—*pop pl* IN-6
Burr Oak Tavern—*hist pl* WI-6
Burr Oak Township—*civil* MO-7
Burroak Township—*civil* SD-7
Burr Oak Township—*fmr MCD* (2) IA-7
**Burr Oak Township**—*pop pl* (2) KS-7
**Burr Oak Township**—*pop pl* SD-7
**Burr Oak (Township of)**—*pop pl* MI-6
Burr Oak Woods—*woods* IL-6
Burro and Cottonwood Well—*well* AZ-5
Burro Arroyo—*stream* CO-8
Burro Bar (inundated)—*bar* UT-8
Burro Basin—*basin* (3) AZ-5
Burro Basin—*basin* NV-8
Burro Bay—*bay* NV-8
Burro Bills Creek—*stream* NV-8
Burro Bills Spring—*spring* NV-8
Burro Bridge—*bridge* (3) CO-8
Burro Bridge Campground—*locale* CO-8
*Burro Butte* AZ-5
*Burro Canyon* CA-9
Burro Canyon—*valley* (7) AZ-5
Burro Canyon—*valley* (5) CA-9
Burro Canyon—*valley* (4) CO-8
Burro Canyon—*valley* (9) NM-5
Burro Canyon—*valley* TX-5
Burro Canyon—*valley* (2) UT-8
Burro Canyon Cem—*cemetery* CO-8
Burro Canyon Wash—*stream* AZ-5
Burro Chief Mine—*mine* NM-5
Burro Cienaga—*stream* NM-5
Burro Cliffs—*cliff* AZ-5
Burro Creek—*stream* AK-9
Burro Creek—*stream* (2) AZ-5
Burro Creek—*stream* (2) CA-9
Burro Creek—*stream* (4) CO-8
Burro Creek—*stream* ID-8
Burro Creek—*stream* MT-8
Burro Creek—*stream* NV-8
Burro Creek—*stream* NM-5
Burro Creek—*stream* OR-9
Burro Creek Campground—*park* AZ-5
Burro Creek Mesa—*summit* CO-8
Burro Creek Spring—*spring* AZ-5
Burro Creek Tank—*reservoir* AZ-5
Burro Draw—*valley* NM-5
Burro Draw—*valley* TX-5
Burro Draw Tank—*reservoir* NM-5
Burro Flaco Tank—*reservoir* AZ-5
Burro Flat—*flat* WY-8
Burro Flats—*flat* AZ-5
Burro Flats—*flat* (3) CA-9
Burro Flats Painted Cave—*hist pl* CA-9
Burro Gap—*gap* (2) AZ-5
Burro Gulch—*valley* CO-8
Burro Hill—*summit* (3) NM-5
Burro Hill—*summit* WY-8
Burro John—*locale* AZ-5

Burwood Playground—*park* ... OH-6
Burwood Sch—*school* ... CA-9
Burying Ground Brook—*stream* ... CT-1
Burying Ground Hill—*summit* ... NY-2
Burying Island—*island* ... ME-1
Burying Yard Point—*cape* ... VT-1
Burys Creek—*stream* ... KS-7
Busack Dam—*dam* ... SD-7
Busane Peak—*summit* ... CA-9
Busard Ditch—*canal* ... IN-6
**Busbee**—*pop pl* ... NC-3
Busbee Cem—*cemetery* ... SC-3
Busbee Community Center—*building* ... NC-3
Busbee MS—*school* ... SC-3
Busbee Mtn—*summit* ... NC-3
Busbee Rsvr—*reservoir* ... NC-3
Busbey Sch—*school* ... IL-6
Bus Butte—*summit* ... SD-7
Busby—*locale* ... KS-7
Busby—*locale* ... TX-5
Busby—*locale* ... WA-9
**Busby**—*pop pl* ... MT-8
**Busby**—*pop pl* ... TN-4
Busby Boarding Sch—*school* ... MT-8
Busby Branch—*stream* ... AL-4
Busby Branch—*stream* ... TX-5
Busby Butte—*summit* ... MT-8
Busby Canyon—*valley* ... UT-8
Busby Cem—*cemetery* ... AL-4
Busby Cem—*cemetery* ... AR-4
Busby Cem—*cemetery* ... KS-7
Busby Cem—*cemetery* ... MS-4
Busby Cem—*cemetery* (2) ... MO-7
Busby Cem—*cemetery* ... MT-8
Busby Cem—*cemetery* ... TN-4
Busby Ch—*church* ... AL-4
Busby Ch—*church* ... IL-6
*Busby Creek* ... TN-4
Busby Creek—*stream* ... MT-8
Busby Draw—*valley* ... WY-8
Busby Drift Mine (underground)—*mine* ... AL-4
*Busby Ferry* ... AL-4
Busby Game Ref—*park* ... MS-4
Busby Hollow—*valley* ... AL-4
Busby Hollow—*valley* ... AR-4
Busby Hollow—*valley* ... KY-4
Busby Hollow—*valley* ... TX-5
Busby Island—*island* ... AK-9
Busby Mine—*mine* ... MT-8
Busby Mine (underground)—*mine* ... AL-4
Busby Office Bldg—*hist pl* ... OK-5
Busby Park—*park* ... AZ-5
Busby Sch (historical)—*school* ... MS-4
Busby Sch (historical)—*school* ... TN-4
Busbys Landing (historical)—*locale* ... MS-4
Busby Spring—*spring* ... OR-9
Busby Theatre—*hist pl* ... OK-5
Busby Trail—*trail* ... MA-1
Busbyville P.O. (historical)—*locale* ... AL-4
Bus Canyon—*valley* ... CA-9
*Buscay Bay* ... WI-6
*Busch* ... OK-5
Busch—*locale* ... MO-7
Busch—*locale* ... MT-8
**Busch**—*pop pl* ... AR-4
**Busch**—*pop pl* ... CA-9
Busch, Diedrich, House—*hist pl* ... IA-7
Buschalaugh Cove—*bay* ... CA-9
Busch Bldg—*hist pl* ... TX-5
Busch Cem—*cemetery* ... IA-7
Busch Cem—*cemetery* (2) ... MO-7
Busch Cem—*cemetery* ... PA-2
Busch Cem—*cemetery* ... TX-5
Busch Ch—*church* ... AR-4
Busch Chapel Cem—*cemetery* ... OK-5
Busch Creek—*stream* ... AK-9
Busch Creek—*stream* ... CA-9
Busch Creek—*stream* ... MO-7
Buschell Lake—*lake* ... MI-6
Busche Park—*park* ... MO-7
Buscher Cem—*cemetery* ... IN-6
Buscher Ditch—*canal* ... IN-6
Busch Gulch—*valley* ... MT-8
Busch House—*hist pl* ... MT-8
Busch Island—*island* ... MP-9
Buschmann, William, Block—*hist pl* ... IN-6
Buschmann Creek—*stream* ... AK-9
Buschmann Pass—*channel* ... AK-9
Busch Peak—*summit* ... NV-8
Busch Ranch—*locale* ... NE-7
Busch-Reisinger Museum—*building* ... MA-1
Busch Sch—*school* ... MO-7
*Buschs Creek* ... MO-7
Busch's Grove—*hist pl* ... MO-7
Buschs Lake—*lake* ... MO-7
Busch Slough—*stream* ... TX-5
Busch Spring—*spring* ... AZ-5
Busch Stadium—*other* ... MO-7
Busco—*uninc pl* ... TX-5
Buscombe Creek—*stream* ... FL-3
Buscones Peak—*summit* ... CA-9
Buscuit Knob—*summit* ... AK-9
Busenbark—*locale* ... OH-6
Busenbark Ranch—*locale* ... AZ-5
Busenburg Ditch—*canal* ... IN-6
**Busenville**—*pop pl* ... IL-6
Buser Run—*stream* ... PA-2
**Buse (Township of)**—*pop pl* ... MN-6
Busey—*locale* ... MS-4
Busey Spring—*spring* ... SD-7
Busfaloba Creek—*stream* ... MS-4
Bus Field (airport)—*airport* ... SD-7
Busfield Pond—*lake* ... NY-2
Bush—*locale* ... AL-4
Bush—*locale* ... CA-9
Bush—*locale* ... KY-4
Bush—*locale* ... MS-4
Bush—*locale* ... UT-8
**Bush**—*pop pl* ... AL-4
**Bush**—*pop pl* ... IL-6
**Bush**—*pop pl* ... LA-4
**Bush**—*pop pl* ... MD-2
**Bush**—*pop pl* ... OR-9
Bush, Asahel, House—*hist pl* ... OR-9
Bush, Capt. Robert V., House—*hist pl* ... KY-4
Bush, Cornelia, House—*hist pl* ... KY-4
Bush, John G., House—*hist pl* ... MN-6
Bush, Samuel, House—*hist pl* ... OH-6
Bush, S. S., House—*hist pl* ... KY-4
Bush, William, House—*hist pl* ... KY-4
**Bush Addition**—*pop pl* ... PA-2
Bushahatchie Landing (historical)—*locale* ... MS-4
Bush and Brey Block and Annex—*hist pl* ... OR-9
Bush And Holliday Ditch—*canal* ... WY-8
Bush and Tiller Tank—*reservoir* ... TX-5
Bush Arbor Ch—*church* ... GA-3
Bush Arbor Ch—*church* ... NC-3
*Bush Arbor Freewill Baptist Church* ... AL-4
Bushart Mtn—*summit* ... AR-4
Bush Barl—*bar* ... CA-9
Bush Bar Sch—*school* ... CA-9
Bush Bay—*basin* ... SC-3
Bush Bay—*bay* ... MI-6
Bush Bend—*bend* ... KY-4
Bush Bog—*swamp* ... ME-1
Bush Brake—*swamp* ... AR-4
*Bush Branch* ... WV-2
Bush Branch—*stream* ... AL-4
Bush Branch—*stream* ... IA-7
Bush Branch—*stream* (2) ... KY-4
Bush Branch—*stream* ... SC-3
Bush Branch—*stream* ... TX-5
Bush-Breyman Block—*hist pl* ... OR-9
Bush Brook—*stream* ... ME-1
Bush Brook—*stream* ... MA-1
Bush Brook—*stream* ... NY-2
Bush Brothers Strip Airp—*airport* ... TN-4
Bushburg—*locale* ... MO-7
Bush Butte—*summit* ... WY-8
Bushby Sch—*school* ... SD-7
Bush Cabin Run—*stream* ... MD-2
Bushcamp Run—*stream* ... WV-2
Bush Canal—*canal* ... LA-4
Bush Canyon—*valley* ... CO-8
Bush Canyon—*valley* ... WY-8
Bush (CCD)—*cens area* ... KY-4
Bush Cem—*cemetery* (4) ... AL-4
Bush Cem—*cemetery* ... AR-4
Bush Cem—*cemetery* (2) ... GA-3
Bush Cem—*cemetery* ... IN-6
Bush Cem—*cemetery* ... KY-4
Bush Cem—*cemetery* (2) ... LA-4
Bush Cem—*cemetery* ... MN-6
Bush Cem—*cemetery* (3) ... MS-4
Bush Cem—*cemetery* (3) ... MO-7
Bush Cem—*cemetery* (2) ... NY-2
Bush Cem—*cemetery* ... OH-6
Bush Cem—*cemetery* ... TN-4
Bush Cem—*cemetery* ... TX-5
Bush Cem—*cemetery* ... VT-1
Bush Cem—*cemetery* ... VA-3
Bush Cem—*cemetery* (3) ... WV-2
Bush Cem—*cemetery* ... WI-6
Bush Ch—*church* ... OH-6
Bush Chapel—*church* ... GA-3
**Bush City**—*pop pl* ... KS-7
Bush Coon Creek—*stream* ... AL-4
**Bush Corner**—*pop pl* ... NY-2
*Bush Creek* ... AL-4
*Bush Creek* ... AR-4
*Bush Creek* ... CA-9
*Bush Creek* ... IN-6
*Bush Creek* ... MI-6
*Bush Creek* ... MS-4
*Bush Creek* ... SC-3
*Bush Creek* ... SD-7
*Bush Creek* ... TX-5
*Bush Creek* ... VA-3
Bush Creek—*gut* ... NY-2
Bush Creek—*stream* ... AZ-5
Bush Creek—*stream* ... AR-4
Bush Creek—*stream* ... CA-9
Bush Creek—*stream* ... GA-3
Bush Creek—*stream* (2) ... ID-8
Bush Creek—*stream* ... IL-6
Bush Creek—*stream* ... IN-6
Bush Creek—*stream* (2) ... MD-2
Bush Creek—*stream* (4) ... MI-6
Bush Creek—*stream* ... MT-8
Bush Creek—*stream* ... NE-7
Bush Creek—*stream* (3) ... NC-3
Bush Creek—*stream* ... OH-6
Bush Creek—*stream* ... PA-2
Bush Creek—*stream* ... TN-4
Bush Creek—*stream* (2) ... TX-5
Bush Creek—*stream* (2) ... WA-9
Bush Creek—*stream* ... WI-6
Bush Creek—*stream* (3) ... WY-8
Bush Crossing—*locale* ... MS-4
Bush Dairy Lake Dam—*dam* ... MS-4
Bushdale Cem—*cemetery* ... TX-5
Bush Dam—*dam* ... AL-4
Bush-Denton Oil Field—*oilfield* ... KS-7
Bush Ditch—*canal* ... WY-8
*Bush Drain* ... MI-6
Bush Drain—*canal* ... MI-6
Bush Draw—*valley* ... CO-8
Bush-Dykes, W., House—*hist pl* ... KY-4
Bushee Creek—*stream* ... CO-8
Bushee Creek—*stream* ... NV-8
Bushelberger Mesa—*bench* ... NM-5
Bushel Branch—*stream* ... TN-4
Bushel Lake—*lake* ... MN-6
Bushel Swamp—*swamp* ... MI-6
Busher Canyon—*valley* ... TX-5
Busher Creek—*stream* ... CA-9
Busher Creek—*stream* ... NV-8
Busher Tank—*reservoir* ... TX-5
**Bushes**—*pop pl* ... LA-4
Bushes Island—*island* ... NE-7
Bushes Island—*island* ... WV-2
**Bushes Landing**—*pop pl* ... NY-2
Bush Etherington Ditch—*canal* ... MT-8
Bushey Drive Sch—*school* ... MD-2
*Bushey Hill* ... PA-2
*Bushey Hollow Brook* ... VT-1
Busheys Sch (abandoned)—*school* ... PA-2
Bush Field (Airport)—*airport* ... GA-3
Bushfield Bend—*bend* ... VA-3
Bushfield Cem—*cemetery* ... AL-4
Bushfield Creek—*stream* ... NY-2
*Bushfield Pond* ... NY-2
Bush Flat Cem—*cemetery* ... AZ-5
Bush Ford Branch—*stream* ... VA-3
*Bush Fork* ... NC-3
*Bush Grove* ... KY-4
Bush Gulch—*valley* ... CA-9
Bush Hammock Bay—*swamp* ... FL-3
*Bush Harbor* ... CT-1
Bush Head—*summit* ... AZ-5
*Bush Head Gap* ... GA-3
*Bush Head Mountain* ... GA-3
Bush Head Shoals—*bar* ... GA-3
Bush Head Tank—*reservoir* ... AZ-5
*Bushheap Mountain* ... AR-4
Bush-Herbert Bldg—*hist pl* ... TN-4
*Bush Hill* ... MA-1
*Bush Hill* ... RI-1
**Bush Hill**—*pop pl* ... VA-3
Bush Hill—*summit* ... CA-9
Bush Hill—*summit* (3) ... CT-1
Bush Hill—*summit* ... GA-3
Bush Hill—*summit* (4) ... MA-1
Bush Hill—*summit* ... NH-1
Bush Hill—*summit* (2) ... NY-2
Bush Hill—*summit* ... PA-2
Bush Hill—*summit* ... TX-5
Bush Hill Brook—*stream* ... CT-1
Bush Hill Hist Dist—*hist pl* ... CT-1
Bush Hill Sch—*school* ... VA-3
Bush Hill Sch (historical)—*school* ... PA-2
**Bush Hill Woods**—*pop pl* ... VA-3
Bush-Holley House—*hist pl* ... CT-1
Bush Hollow—*valley* ... KY-4
Bush Hollow—*valley* (3) ... PA-2
Bush Hollow—*valley* (2) ... TN-4
Bush Hollow—*valley* ... WV-2
Bush Hollow Ch—*church* ... PA-2
Bush Hosp—*hospital* ... GA-3
Bush House—*hist pl* ... AR-4
Bush House—*hist pl* ... MS-4
Bush-Hurst (RR name for Hurst)—*other* ... IL-6
**Bushing (historical)**—*pop pl* ... TN-4
Bushing Post Office (historical)—*building* ... TN-4
*Bushington* ... PA-2
Buship Hollow—*valley* ... TN-4
Bush Island—*island* (2) ... DE-2
Bush Island—*island* ... FL-3
Bush Island—*island* (2) ... GA-3
Bush Island—*island* ... KY-4
Bush Island—*island* ... ME-1
Bush Island—*island* (3) ... NC-3
Bush Island—*island* ... TN-4
Bush Island—*island* ... WY-8
Bush Island Cove—*bay* ... VA-3
Bush Islets—*area* (2) ... AK-9
*Bush Key* ... FL-3
Bush Key—*island* (2) ... FL-3
Bush Key Shoal—*bar* ... FL-3
*Bush Kill* ... NY-2
**Bushkill**—*pop pl* ... PA-2
Bush Kill—*stream* (5) ... NY-2
Bush Kill—*stream* (2) ... PA-2
Bushkill Brook—*stream* ... NJ-2
**Bushkill Center**—*pop pl* ... PA-2
Bushkill Ch—*church* ... PA-2
*Bushkill Creek* ... PA-2
Bushkill Creek—*stream* ... PA-2
Bushkill Falls—*falls* ... PA-2
*Bushkilln Creek* ... PA-2
Bushkill Park—*park* ... PA-2
Bushkill Sch (abandoned)—*school* ... PA-2
Bushkill Swamp—*swamp* ... PA-2
Bushkill Township Elem Sch—*school* ... PA-2
**Bushkill (Township of)**—*pop pl* ... PA-2
*Bushkiln Centre* ... PA-2
Bushkirk Trail—*trail* ... PA-2
Bush Knob Cem—*cemetery* ... TX-5
Bush Knob Creek—*stream* ... TX-5
Bushkos Hill—*summit* ... PA-2
*Bush Lake* ... MI-6
*Bush Lake* ... NE-7
*Bush Lake* ... WI-6
Bush Lake—*lake* ... GA-3
Bush Lake—*lake* ... LA-4
Bush Lake—*lake* (6) ... MI-6
Bush Lake—*lake* (2) ... MN-6
Bush Lake—*lake* ... MS-4
Bush Lake—*lake* ... ND-7
Bush Lake—*lake* ... TN-4
Bush Lake—*lake* ... WI-6
Bush Lake—*lake* ... WY-8
Bush Lake—*reservoir* ... MS-4
Bush Lake—*reservoir* ... TX-5
Bush Lake Ch—*church* ... MN-6
Bush Lake (historical)—*lake* ... IA-7
Bush Lake Park—*park* ... MN-6
**Bushland**—*pop pl* ... TX-5
Bush Landing—*locale* ... MN-6
Bushley Bayou—*stream* ... LA-4
Bushley Creek—*stream* ... LA-4
Bushley Ridge—*ridge* ... PA-2
Bushley Run—*stream* ... PA-2
Bushlick Branch—*stream* ... KY-4
Bush Lot Hill—*summit* ... RI-1
Bush-Lyon Homestead—*hist pl* ... NY-2
**Bushman Acres**—*pop pl* ... AZ-5
*Bushman Bayou* ... LA-4
Bushman Cem—*cemetery* ... NY-2
Bushman Creek—*stream* ... OK-5
Bushman Creek—*stream* ... TN-4
Bushman Draw—*valley* ... AZ-5
*Bushman Lake* ... WA-9
Bushman Lake—*lake* ... MN-6
**Bush Manor**—*pop pl* ... DE-2
Bushman Sch—*school* ... TX-5
Bushman Swamp—*swamp* ... MI-6
Bushmaster Park—*park* ... AZ-5
Bushmaster Peak—*summit* ... AZ-5
Bush Meadow Brook—*stream* ... CT-1
Bush Memorial Baptist Ch—*church* ... AL-4
Bushmen Lake—*lake* ... MN-6
Bush Mill—*locale* ... VA-3
Bush Mill (site)—*locale* ... OR-9
Bush Mill Stream—*stream* ... VA-3
Bushmire Well—*well* ... CO-8
Bush Mountain Stream—*stream* ... VA-3
*Bush Mtn* ... CA-9
*Bush Mtn* ... MA-1
Bush Mtn—*summit* ... AK-9
Bush Mtn—*summit* ... CA-9
Bush Mtn—*summit* ... PA-2
Bush Mtn—*summit* ... TX-5
Bush Mtn—*summit* (2) ... VA-3
Bush Neck—*cape* ... VA-3
Bushneck Bayou—*stream* ... LA-4
*Bushnell* ... MN-6
*Bushnell* ... UT-8
Bushnell—*hist pl* ... TX-5
Bushnell—*locale* ... GA-3
Bushnell—*locale* ... KS-7
**Bushnell**—*pop pl* ... FL-3
**Bushnell**—*pop pl* ... IL-6
**Bushnell**—*pop pl* ... NE-7
**Bushnell**—*pop pl* ... OH-6
**Bushnell**—*pop pl* ... SD-7
Bushnell—*uninc pl* ... UT-8
Bushnell, Elisha, House—*hist pl* ... CT-1
Bushnell, Martin, House—*hist pl* ... OH-6
Bushnell, Mount—*summit* ... CT-1
Bushnell, Mount—*summit* ... MA-1
Bushnell, Mount—*summit* ... MT-8
Bushnell Airp—*airport* ... OR-9
**Bushnell Basin**—*pop pl* ... NY-2
Bushnell Cem—*cemetery* ... NE-7
Bushnell Cem—*cemetery* (2) ... NY-2
Bushnell Cem—*cemetery* ... OH-6
Bushnell Cem—*cemetery* ... VT-1
Bushnell Ch—*church* ... OK-5
*Bushnell Creek* ... CA-9
Bushnell Creek—*stream* ... NM-5
Bushnell Creek—*stream* ... OR-9
Bushnell Creek—*stream* ... WI-6
Bushnell Creek—*stream* ... WY-8
Bushnell Ditch—*canal* ... OH-6
Bushnell Draw—*valley* ... SD-7
Bushnell Elem Sch—*school* ... FL-3
Bushnell Falls—*falls* ... NY-2
Bushnell Hill—*summit* ... MT-8
Bushnell Hollow—*valley* ... IL-6
Bushnell Lake—*lake* ... WI-6
Bushnell Lakes—*lake* ... CO-8
Bushnell Park—*hist pl* ... CT-1
Bushnell Park—*park* ... CT-1
Bushnell Peak—*summit* ... CO-8
Bushnell Pond—*reservoir* ... NY-2
Bushnell Rock—*pillar* ... OR-9
Bushnell Sch—*school* ... OH-6
Bushnell Sch—*school* ... VT-1
Bushnell Sheep Tank—*reservoir* ... AZ-5
Bushnell Summit—*gap* ... CA-9
**Bushnellsville**—*pop pl* ... NY-2
Bushnellsville Creek—*stream* ... NY-2
Bushnell Tower—*tower* ... FL-3
**Bushnell (Township of)**—*pop pl* ... IL-6
**Bushnell (Township of)**—*pop pl* ... MI-6
Bushnell Way Sch—*school* ... CA-9
Bush Notch—*gap* ... MA-1
**Bushong**—*pop pl* ... KS-7
**Bushong**—*pop pl* ... KY-4
Bushong Cem—*cemetery* ... KS-7
Bushong Lake—*lake* ... IN-6
Bushongs Forge (historical)—*locale* ... TN-4
Bush Pacific Pioneer State Park—*park* ... WA-9
Bush Park—*park* ... MI-6
Bush Park Creek—*stream* ... VA-3
Bush Pasture Park—*park* ... OR-9
**Bush Patch**—*pop pl* ... PA-2
Bush-Philips Hardware Co.—*hist pl* ... GA-3
Bush Pit—*locale* ... AZ-5
Bush Place Knob—*summit* ... WV-2
Bush Point—*cape* (2) ... AK-9
Bush Point—*cape* ... FL-3
Bush Point—*cape* (2) ... MD-2
Bush Point—*cape* ... VA-3
Bush Point—*cape* ... WA-9
**Bush Point**—*pop pl* ... WA-9
Bush Pond—*lake* ... CT-1
Bush Pond—*lake* ... FL-3
Bush Pond—*lake* ... PA-2
Bush Pond—*reservoir* ... AL-4
Bush Pond—*reservoir* ... MA-1
Bush Pond—*reservoir* ... MS-4
Bush Pond Dam—*dam* ... AL-4
Bush Pond Dam Number 2—*dam* ... MA-1
*Bush Pork Creek* ... VA-3
Bush Post Office (historical)—*building* ... MS-4
Bush Prairie—*flat* ... WA-9
Bush Prairie Sch—*school* ... WI-6
Bush (Railroad Station)—*locale* ... FL-3
Bush Ranch—*locale* ... ID-8
Bush Ranch—*locale* ... WY-8
Bush Ridge—*ridge* ... MD-2
Bush Rim—*cliff* ... WY-8
*Bush River* ... SC-3
**Bush River**—*pop pl* ... MD-2
**Bush River**—*pop pl* ... SC-3
Bush River—*stream* ... MD-2
Bush River—*stream* ... SC-3
Bush River—*stream* ... VA-3
Bush River Ch—*church* ... GA-3
Bush River Community Center—*locale* ... SC-3
Bush River Meetinghouse Cem—*cemetery* ... SC-3
Bush River Sch—*school* ... SC-3
Bush Rock—*island* (2) ... AK-9
**Bushrod**—*pop pl* ... IN-6
*Bush Rsvr* ... OR-9
*Bush Run* ... PA-2
Bush Run—*stream* ... PA-2
Bush Run—*stream* ... VA-3
Bush Sch—*school* ... AR-4
Bush Sch—*school* ... IL-6
Bush Sch—*school* (2) ... KY-4
Bush Sch—*school* ... LA-4
Bush Sch—*school* ... MI-6
Bush Sch—*school* (2) ... MO-7
Bush Sch—*school* ... OR-9
Bush Sch—*school* ... PA-2
Bushs Chapel Sch—*school* ... TN-4
Bush Sch (historical)—*school* ... MO-7
Bush Sch Number 2—*school* ... AL-4
*Bush School* ... DE-2
*Bushs Corner* ... NY-2
Bushs Corner—*locale* ... MD-2
Bushs Corners—*locale* ... NY-2
Bushs Ferry (historical)—*locale* ... MS-4
Bushs Golf Course—*locale* ... PA-2
*Bushs Harbor* ... CT-1
Bush Slough—*gut* ... CA-9
*Bush'S Notch* ... MA-1
Bushs Pond (historical)—*lake* ... MA-1
Bush Spring—*spring* ... AZ-5
Bush Spring—*spring* ... NM-5
Bushs Run—*stream* ... IN-6
Bushstake Gap—*channel* ... FL-3
Bush Still (historical)—*locale* ... AL-4
Bush Store (historical)—*locale* ... MS-4
Bush Street-Cottage Row Hist Dist—*hist pl* ... CA-9
Bush Street Hist Dist—*hist pl* ... OH-6
Bush Tank—*reservoir* ... AZ-5
Bush Terminal—*locale* ... NY-2
**Bushton**—*pop pl* ... IL-6
**Bushton**—*pop pl* ... KS-7
Bushton Cem—*cemetery* ... KS-7
Bushtop Island—*island* ... AK-9
Bush Top Island—*island* ... AK-9
Bush Tower—*locale* ... AL-4
Bushtown—*locale* (2) ... KY-4
**Bushtown**—*pop pl* ... TN-4
Bushtown Sch—*school* ... NC-3
Bushtown Sch—*school* ... PA-2
**Bush Township**—*pop pl* ... NE-7
**Bush Township**—*pop pl* ... ND-7
Bush-Usher House—*hist pl* ... GA-3
Bushville—*locale* ... IA-7
Bushville—*locale* ... LA-4
Bushville—*locale* ... NY-2
**Bushville**—*pop pl* (2) ... NY-2
Bushwack Draw—*valley* ... TX-5
Bushwacker Cave—*cave* ... MO-7
Bushwacker Hollow—*valley* ... TN-4
Bushwacker Shaft—*mine* ... CO-8
Bushwah Lake—*lake* ... MN-6
Bushwhack Creek—*stream* ... TX-5
Bushwhacker Hollow—*valley* (2) ... TN-4
**Bushwick**—*pop pl* ... NY-2
Bushwick HS—*school* ... NY-2
Bushwick Inlet—*bay* ... NY-2
**Bushwick Junction**—*pop pl* ... NY-2
Bushwick Park—*park* ... NY-2
Bushwick Yards—*locale* ... NY-2
Bush Windmill—*locale* ... TX-5
**Bushwood**—*pop pl* ... MD-2
Bushwood Cove—*bay* ... MD-2
**Bushy**—*pop pl* ... VA-3
Bushy Bay—*swamp* ... NC-3
*Bushy Beach Pond* ... MA-1
*Bushy Branch* ... KY-4
Bushy Branch—*stream* (2) ... AL-4
Bushy Branch—*stream* (2) ... SC-3
Bushy Branch Ch—*church* ... TN-4
Bushy Camp—*locale* ... CA-9
*Bushy Canyon* ... AZ-5
Bushy Canyon—*valley* ... CO-8
Bushy Ch—*church* ... TX-5
*Bushy Creek* ... AL-4
*Bushy Creek* ... TX-5
*Bushy Creek* ... WY-8
**Bushy Creek**—*pop pl* ... AL-4
Bushy Creek—*stream* (2) ... AL-4
Bushy Creek—*stream* ... AK-9
Bushy Creek—*stream* ... LA-4
Bushy Creek Cem—*cemetery* ... MO-7
Bushy Creek Ditch—*canal* ... AR-4
*Bushy Draw* ... WY-8
*Bushy Fork* ... IN-6
*Bushy Fork* ... NC-3
**Bushy Fork**—*pop pl* ... NC-3
Bushy Fork—*stream* ... NC-3
Bushy Fork—*stream* ... PA-2
Bushy Fork Creek—*stream* ... NC-3
Bushy Fork (Township of)—*fmr MCD* ... NC-3
Bushy Gap—*gap* ... TX-5
Bushy Hammock—*island* ... FL-3
Bushyhead—*locale* ... OK-5
Bushyhead Bayou—*gut* ... LA-4
Bushyhead Cem—*cemetery* ... OK-5
Bushy Head Gap—*gap* ... GA-3
Bushyhead Island—*island* ... MN-6
*Bushyhead Mountain* ... OK-5
Bushy Head Mtn—*summit* ... GA-3
Bushy Hill—*summit* (3) ... CT-1
Bushy Hill—*summit* ... PA-2
*Bushy Hill Brook* ... CT-1
Bushy Hill Cem—*cemetery* ... CT-1
Bushy Hill Pond—*reservoir* ... CT-1
*Bushy Hills* ... CT-1
Bushy Island—*island* ... AK-9
Bushy Island—*island* ... ME-1
Bushy Islands—*area* ... AK-9
Bushy Knob—*summit* ... NM-5
Bushy Knob—*summit* ... TX-5
Bushy Knoll—*summit* ... AZ-5
Bushy Knoll Tank—*reservoir* ... AZ-5
Bushy Lagoon—*swamp* ... LA-4
*Bushy Lake* ... TX-5
Bushy Lake—*lake* (3) ... AR-4
Bushy Lake—*lake* ... WI-6
Bushy Lake—*reservoir* ... TX-5
Bushy Lake—*swamp* ... NC-3
*Bushy Mountain* ... AZ-5
Bushy Mtn—*summit* ... CA-9
Bushy Oak (historical)—*locale* ... AL-4
Bushy Point—*cape* ... AK-9
Bushy Point—*cape* ... CT-1
Bushy Point Beach—*beach* ... CT-1
Bushy Point Cove—*bay* ... AK-9
Bushy Pond—*lake* ... CT-1
**Bushy Pond**—*pop pl* ... AL-4
Bushy Pond Ch—*church* ... SC-3
Bushy Prong—*stream* ... MS-4
Bushy Ridge—*ridge* ... NY-2
Bushy Ridge Trail—*trail* ... PA-2
Bushy Run—*stream* ... PA-2
Bushy Run Battlefield—*hist pl* ... PA-2
Bushy Run Battlefield State Park—*park* ... PA-2
Bushy Tank—*reservoir* ... AZ-5
Bushytop—*summit* ... VA-3
Bushy Well—*well* ... AZ-5
Busia Mtn—*summit* ... AK-9
**Busick**—*pop pl* (2) ... NC-3
Busick Ditch—*canal* ... IN-6
Busick Lake Dam—*dam* ... MS-4
Busicks Ch—*church* ... MD-2
Busick Well—*well* ... NM-5
Busiek Sch—*school* ... MO-7
Busiel-Seeburg Mill—*hist pl* ... NH-1
Business and Government Hist Dist—*hist pl* ... MD-2
**Businessburg**—*pop pl* ... OH-6
**Business Corner**—*pop pl* ... OH-6
**Business Corners**—*pop pl* ... OH-6
**Business Corners (historical)**—*pop pl* ... IA-7
*Business Creek* ... TN-4
*Business Creek* ... VA-3
Business Gulch—*valley* ... ID-8
Businger Lake—*lake* ... MN-6
Busi Ranch—*locale* ... CA-9
Buskala, Henry Ranch—*hist pl* ... SD-7
Buskala Creek—*stream* ... SD-7
Buskala Ranch—*locale* ... SD-7
Busk Creek—*stream* ... CO-8
Buske Ranch*—*locale* ... NE-7
Buskey Bay—*lake* ... WI-6
*Buskey Lake* ... WI-6
Buskin Lake—*lake* ... AK-9
Buskin River—*stream* ... AK-9
*Buskirk* ... KY-4
Buskirk—*other* ... KY-4
**Buskirk**—*pop pl* (2) ... KY-4
**Buskirk**—*pop pl* ... NY-2
Buskirk Cem—*cemetery* ... MO-7
Buskirk Covered Bridge—*hist pl* ... NY-2
Buskirk Creek—*stream* ... MI-6
Buskirk Creek—*stream* ... OH-6
Buskirk Hollow—*valley* ... PA-2
Buskirk Run—*stream* ... WV-2
Bus Kirk Sch—*school* ... WV-2
Buskirk Spring—*spring* ... OR-9
Busler Branch—*stream* ... TN-4
Busler Hollow—*valley* ... TN-4
*Busley Creek* ... TX-5
Busley Creek—*stream* ... TX-5
Bus McGall—*summit* ... CA-9
Bus Point—*cape* ... OR-9
*Bus Rsvr* ... OR-9
Bussard Cem—*cemetery* ... WV-2
Bussard Creek—*stream* ... ID-8
**Bussard (historical)**—*pop pl* ... OR-9
Bussard Lake—*lake* ... ID-8
Bussard Mtn—*summit* ... ID-8
Bussard Ranch—*locale* ... NE-7
Buss Creek—*stream* ... GA-3
Buss Creek—*stream* ... IA-7
Busse Canal—*canal* ... OR-9
Busse Coulee—*valley* ... ND-7
Busse Dam—*dam* ... OR-9
Busse House—*hist pl* ... IN-6
Bussel Creek—*stream* ... ID-8
Bussel Creek—*stream* ... MS-4
**Bussell**—*pop pl* ... TN-4
*Bussell Branch* ... AR-4
*Bussell Branch English Creek* ... AR-4
Bussell Branch English Creek—*stream* ... MO-7
Bussell Cem—*cemetery* (2) ... TN-4
Bussell Ferry—*locale* ... TN-4
Bussell Ford—*locale* ... TN-4
Bussell Island—*island* ... TN-4
*Bussell Island Shoals* ... TN-4
Bussell Island Site—*hist pl* ... TN-4
Bussell Park—*park* ... NE-7
Bussell Pond—*reservoir* ... GA-3
Bussell Sch—*school* ... TN-4
Bussell Shoals—*bar* ... TN-4
*Bussells Shoals* ... TN-4
**Busselltown**—*pop pl* ... TN-4
Busselltown Sch (historical)—*school* ... TN-4
Bussel Peak—*summit* ... ID-8
Bussel Point—*cape* ... VA-3
Bussels Bend—*bend* ... TN-4
Bussels Creek—*stream* ... NC-3
Bussels Mill (historical)—*locale* ... TN-4
**Busseltown**—*pop pl* ... TN-4
Busseltown Dewatering Area—*basin* ... TN-4
Busseltown Unit Tennessee Natl Wildlife Ref—*park* ... TN-4
**Bussen Spur**—*pop pl* ... MO-7
*Busser* ... IA-7
**Busseron**—*pop pl* ... IN-6
*Busseron Creek* ... IN-6
Busseron Creek—*stream* ... IN-6
Busseron Dam Number B-2—*dam* ... IN-6
Busseron Dam Number D-4—*dam* ... IN-6
Busseron Dam Number D-9—*dam* ... IN-6
Busseron Dam Number F-2—*dam* ... IN-6
Busseron Dam Number G-10—*dam* ... IN-6
Busseron Dam Number G-4—*dam* ... IN-6
Busseron Dam Number G-5—*dam* ... IN-6
Busseron Dam Number I-2—*dam* ... IN-6
Busseron Dam Number L-S—*dam* ... IN-6
Busseron Dam Number L-1—*dam* ... IN-6
**Busseron (Township of)**—*pop pl* ... IN-6
Busse Sch—*school* ... IL-6
Busse Sch Number 2 (historical)—*school* ... SD-7
Busse Water—*lake* ... MT-8
Busse Woods—*woods* ... IL-6
**Bussey**—*pop pl* ... AR-4
**Bussey**—*pop pl* ... IA-7
Bussey, Esek, Firehouse—*hist pl* ... NY-2
Bussey, Louis I., Sch—*hist pl* ... ME-1
Bussey Branch—*stream* ... GA-3
Bussey Cem—*cemetery* ... OH-6
*Bussey Creek* ... SC-3
**Bussey Crossroads**—*pop pl* ... GA-3
Bussey Hill—*summit* ... MA-1
Bussey Hill Chapel—*church* ... OH-6
Bussey Hollow—*valley* ... NY-2
Bussey JHS—*school* ... TX-5
Bussey Lake Dam—*dam* ... AL-4
Bussey Point—*cape* ... GA-3
Busseys Lake—*reservoir* ... AL-4
Busseyville—*locale* ... KY-4
**Busseyville**—*pop pl* ... WI-6
Busseyville Sch—*school* ... WI-6
Buss Lake—*lake* ... MN-6
Bus Spring—*spring* ... UT-8
Buss Ranch—*locale* ... AZ-5
Buss Ranch—*locale* ... CO-8
Buss Tank—*reservoir* (2) ... AZ-5
Bussy Brake—*swamp* ... LA-4
Bussy Creek—*stream* ... AK-9
Bussy Creek—*stream* ... CO-8
Bussy Creek—*stream* ... SC-3
*Bussys Lake* ... AL-4
Bustahatchee Creek—*stream* ... GA-3
**Bustamante**—*pop pl* ... TX-5
Bustard Draw—*valley* ... WY-8
Bust Buttes—*summit* ... TX-5
Busted Arm Draw—*valley* ... CO-8
Busted Boiler Draw—*valley* ... CO-8
Busted Butte—*summit* ... NV-8
Busted Mtn—*summit* ... AR-4
Busteed—*locale* ... MT-8
Busteed Hill—*summit* ... MT-8
Buster Basin—*basin* ... CO-8
Buster Basin—*basin* ... WY-8
Buster Bay—*bay* ... AK-9
Buster Boyd Bridge—*bridge* ... NC-3
Buster Boyd Bridge—*bridge* ... SC-3

Buster Branch—*stream* ... MO-7
Buster Brown Gulch—*valley* ... MT-8
Buster Brown Tank—*reservoir* ... AZ-5
Buster Butte—*summit* ... ID-8
Buster Butte—*summit* ... OR-9
Buster Camp (site)—*locale* ... OR-9
Buster Cem—*cemetery* ... KS-7
Buster Cem—*cemetery* ... MO-7
*Buster Creek* ... MN-6
*Buster Creek* ... MT-8
Buster Creek—*stream* (4) ... AK-9
Buster Creek—*stream* ... AR-4
Buster Creek—*stream* ... MO-7
Buster Creek—*stream* ... MT-8
Buster Creek—*stream* ... NM-5
Buster Creek—*stream* (3) ... OR-9
Buster Crider Pond Dam—*dam* ... MS-4
Buster Gulch—*valley* (2) ... ID-8
Buster Hill—*summit* ... KY-4
Buster Island—*island* ... FL-3
Buster Jangle Crater—*crater* ... NV-8
Buster Knob—*summit* ... WV-2
Buster Lackey Pond Dam—*dam* ... MS-4
Buster Lake—*lake* ... ID-8
Buster Lake—*lake* ... TX-5
Buster Meat Market—*hist pl* ... ID-8
Buster Mine—*mine* ... AZ-5
Buster Mine—*mine* ... ID-8
Buster Mtn—*summit* ... AZ-5
Buster Mtn—*summit* ... NV-8
Buster Mtn—*summit* ... WA-9
Buster Price Pond Dam—*dam* ... MS-4
Buster Rsvr—*reservoir* ... CO-8
Busters Bayou—*gut* ... LA-4
Busters Gin—*locale* ... TX-5
Buster Spring—*spring* ... AZ-5
Buster Spring—*spring* (2) ... NV-8
Buster Spring—*spring* (2) ... OR-9
Buster Springs—*spring* ... NV-8
Buster Spring Shelter—*locale* ... OR-9
Busters Rsvr—*reservoir* ... CA-9
**Busterville**—*pop pl* ... TX-5
Busterville Mine—*mine* ... AZ-5
Buster Wash—*stream* ... NV-8
**Busthead**—*pop pl* ... VA-3
**Busti**—*pop pl* ... NY-2
Bustic Lake—*lake* ... MN-6
Busties Lake—*lake* ... MN-6
*Bustig Creek* ... MN-6
Busti Mill—*hist pl* ... NY-2
*Bustings Island* ... ME-1
Bustins Island—*island* ... ME-1
**Bustins Island**—*pop pl* ... ME-1
*Bustins Island Ledge* ... ME-1
Bustins Ledge—*bar* ... ME-1
**Busti (Town of)**—*pop pl* ... NY-2
Bustleburg—*locale* ... VA-3
Bustle Cem—*cemetery* ... KY-4
Bustle Creek—*stream* ... WY-8
*Bustles Shoals* ... TN-4
Bustleton—*locale* ... PA-2
**Bustleton**—*pop pl* ... NJ-2
Bustleton Creek—*stream* ... NJ-2
Bustos Canyon—*valley* ... CO-8
Bustos Cem—*cemetery* ... CO-8
Bustos Flat—*flat* ... CO-8
Bustos Spring—*spring* ... CO-8
Bustos Tank—*reservoir* ... NM-5
Bustos Well—*well* (2) ... NM-5
Bustoz Sch—*school* ... AZ-5
Busty Canyon—*valley* ... WY-8
Buswell, Clara, House—*hist pl* ... MA-1
Buswell, J.E., House—*hist pl* ... MA-1
Buswell Pond—*dam* ... MA-1
Buswell Pond—*reservoir* ... MA-1
Buswell Ridges—*ridge* ... NH-1
**Busy**—*pop pl* ... KY-4
Busy Bee Preschool—*school* ... FL-3
Busy Bee Sch—*school* ... SD-7
Busy Bee School—*locale* ... CO-8
Busy Bees Day Care Center—*school* ... FL-3
Busy Bend Sch (historical)—*school* ... SD-7
Busy Corner—*locale* ... MS-4
**Busy Corner**—*pop pl* ... TN-4
**Busy Corners**—*pop pl* ... OH-6
Busy Creek—*stream* ... SD-7
Busyton (historical)—*locale* ... MS-4
Busy Wild Creek—*stream* ... WA-9
Butano—*civil* ... CA-9
Butano Creek—*stream* ... CA-9
Butano Falls—*falls* ... CA-9
**Butano Park**—*pop pl* ... CA-9
Butano Ridge—*ridge* ... CA-9
Butano State Park—*park* ... CA-9
*Butcha* ... MS-4
*Butch Canyon* ... UT-8
Butch Cassidy Campground—*locale* ... UT-8
Butch Cassidy Draw—*valley* ... UT-8
Butch Cassidy Hideout—*locale* ... UT-8
Butch Cassidy Home—*park* ... UT-8
Butch Creek—*stream* ... MI-6
Butch Creek—*stream* ... SD-7
Butch Creek—*stream* ... WA-9
Butch Drain—*canal* ... MI-6
**Butcher**—*pop pl* ... MO-7
Butcher Bar—*bar* ... ID-8
Butcher Bend—*bend* ... WV-2
Butcher Bill Creek—*stream* ... OR-9
Butcher Bill Meadow—*flat* ... OR-9
Butcher Bluff—*cliff* ... TN-4
Butcher Boy Mine—*mine* ... OR-9
Butcher Branch—*stream* ... IN-6
Butcher Branch—*stream* (2) ... KY-4
Butcher Branch—*stream* (2) ... MO-7
Butcher Branch—*stream* ... NC-3
Butcher Branch—*stream* (2) ... WV-2
Butcher Butte—*summit* ... OR-9
Butcher Camp—*locale* ... AZ-5
Butcher Canyon—*valley* ... NV-8
Butcher Cem—*cemetery* ... IN-6
Butcher Cem—*cemetery* ... MO-7
Butcher Cem—*cemetery* ... NY-2
Butcher Cem—*cemetery* (2) ... OH-6
Butcher Cem—*cemetery* (2) ... TN-4
Butcher Cem—*cemetery* (5) ... WV-2
Butcher Corner—*locale* ... NY-2
Butcher Corral—*locale* ... CA-9
Butcher Corral Point—*cliff* ... AZ-5
*Butcher Creek* ... ID-8
*Butcher Creek* ... OR-9

Butcher Creek—*stream* ... AK-9
Butcher Creek—*stream* ... AZ-5
Butcher Creek—*stream* ... CA-9
Butcher Creek—*stream* ... CO-8
Butcher Creek—*stream* (3) ... ID-8
Butcher Creek—*stream* (2) ... IA-7
Butcher Creek—*stream* ... MO-7
Butcher Creek—*stream* (3) ... MT-8
Butcher Creek—*stream* (2) ... OR-9
Butcher Creek—*stream* ... SD-7
Butcher Creek—*stream* ... TN-4
Butcher Creek—*stream* (2) ... VA-3
Butcher Creek—*stream* ... WA-9
Butcher Creek Ditch—*canal* ... MT-8
Butcher Creek Rosebud Ditch
County—*canal* ... MT-8
Butcher Dam—*dam* ... TN-4
Butcher Drain—*canal* ... NE-7
Butcher Falls—*falls* ... KS-7
Butcher Flat—*flat* ... CA-9
Butcher Flat—*flat* ... NV-8
Butcher Flat—*flat* ... OR-9
Butcher Flat—*reservoir* ... OR-9
Butcher Fork—*stream* ... VA-3
Butcher Fork—*stream* ... WV-2
Butcher Gap—*gap* ... TN-4
Butcher Greene Sch—*school* ... MO-7
Butcher Gulch—*valley* (3) ... CA-9
Butcher Gulch—*valley* (2) ... MT-8
Butcher Gulch—*valley* (2) ... OR-9
Butcher Gulch—*valley* ... SD-7
Butcher Hill—*summit* ... NY-2
Butcher Hill—*summit* ... SD-7
Butcher Hill—*summit* ... WV-2
**Butcher (historical)**—*pop pl* ... TN-4
Butcher Hollow—*valley* ... IN-6
Butcher Hollow—*valley* ... KY-4
Butcher Hollow—*valley* ... OH-6
Butcher Hollow—*valley* ... PA-2
Butcher Hollow—*valley* ... WV-2
Butcher Hollow Sch—*school* ... KY-4
Butcher JHS—*school* ... MI-6
Butcher Jones Picnic Area—*park* ... AZ-5
Butcher Knife—*summit* ... UT-8
Butcherknife, The—*ridge* ... CA-9
Butcherknife Branch—*stream* ... FL-3
Butcherknife Canyon—*valley* ... AZ-5
Butcher Knife Canyon—*valley* ... AZ-5
Butcher Knife Canyon—*valley* ... CA-9
Butcher Knife Canyon—*valley* ... MT-8
Butcherknife Canyon—*valley* ... NM-5
Butcher Knife Canyon—*valley* ... UT-8
Butcherknife Creek—*stream* ... AR-4
Butcherknife Creek—*stream* (2) ... CA-9
Butcherknife Creek—*stream* ... CO-8
Butcher Knife Creek—*stream* ... MN-6
Butcherknife Creek—*stream* ... OH-6
Butcherknife Creek—*stream* (3) ... OR-9
Butcherknife Draw—*valley* ... TX-5
Butcher Knife Draw—*valley* ... WY-8
Butcherknife Fork—*stream* ... VA-3
Butcherknife Gulch—*valley* ... CO-8
Butcherknife Gulch—*valley* (2) ... MT-8
Butcherknife Hill—*summit* ... AZ-5
Butcherknife Hill—*summit* ... PA-2
Butcherknife Hill—*summit* ... TX-5
*Butcher Knife Lake* ... MN-6
Butcherknife Mtn—*summit* ... MT-8
Butcher Knife Pocket—*valley* ... CA-9
Butcher Knife Ridge—*ridge* ... CA-9
Butcherknife Ridge—*ridge* ... ID-8
Butcher Knife Ridge—*ridge* ... OR-9
Butcherknife Spring—*spring* ... OR-9
Butcher Knife Spring—*spring* ... OR-9
Butcher Knife Spring—*spring* ... WY-8
Butcherknife Tank—*reservoir* ... AZ-5
Butcher Lake—*lake* ... ME-1
Butcher Lake—*lake* (2) ... MI-6
Butcher Lake—*reservoir* ... TN-4
Butcher Meadow—*flat* ... UT-8
Butcher Mtn—*summit* (3) ... MT-8
Butcher Mtn—*summit* ... WA-9
Butcher Peak—*summit* ... OR-9
Butcherpen Cove—*bay* ... FL-3
Butcher Pen Creek—*stream* ... FL-3
Butcher Pen Creek—*stream* ... OK-5
Butcher Pen Draw—*valley* ... TX-5
Butcher Pen Landing—*locale* ... FL-3
Butcherpen Point—*cape* ... FL-3
Butcher Point—*cape* ... OR-9
Butcher Pond—*lake* ... IL-6
Butcher Pond—*reservoir* ... PA-2
Butcher Ranch—*locale* ... CA-9
Butcher Ranch Creek—*stream* ... CA-9
Butcher Ranch Meadows—*flat* ... CA-9
Butcher Ridge—*ridge* ... TN-4
Butcher Run—*stream* ... MD-2
Butcher Run—*stream* ... PA-2
Butchers Branch—*stream* ... KY-4
Butchers Branch—*stream* ... VA-3
Butcher Sch—*school* ... IA-7
*Butcher's Creek* ... VA-3
Butchers Creek—*stream* ... TN-4
*Butchers Forge* ... NJ-2
Butchers Fork—*stream* ... WV-2
Butchers Gap—*gap* ... KY-4
Butchers Gap—*gap* ... VA-3
Butchers Hill Hist Dist—*hist pl* ... MD-2
Butchers Island—*island* ... SC-3
Butchers Knob—*summit* ... WV-2
Butcher's Mill Covered Bridge—*hist pl* ... PA-2
Butchers Pond—*lake* ... GA-3
Butchers Pond—*lake* ... NJ-2
Butcher Spring—*spring* ... CO-8
Butcher Spring—*spring* ... NV-8
Butcher Spring—*spring* ... NM-5
Butcher Spring—*spring* (2) ... UT-8
Butcher Spring Post Office
(historical)—*building* ... TN-4
Butcher Spring Trough—*locale* ... UT-8
Butchers Run—*stream* (2) ... WV-2
Butchers Spring—*spring* ... TN-4
Butchers Valley Sch (historical)—*school* ... TN-4
**Butchersville**—*pop pl* ... WV-2
*Butchers Works* ... NJ-2
Butchertown—*locale* ... KY-4
Butchertown Hist Dist—*hist pl* ... KY-4
Butcher Valley—*valley* ... TN-4
Butcher Valley Ch—*church* ... TN-4
Butcher Valley Creek—*stream* ... TN-4

*Butcher Valley School* ... TN-4
Butcher Well—*locale* ... NM-5
Butcher Windmill—*locale* ... AZ-5
Butchery Creek—*stream* ... PA-2
Butch Fork—*stream* ... WV-2
Butch Foster Saddle—*gap* ... OR-9
Butch Henry Draw—*valley* ... CO-8
Butch Hill—*summit* ... MT-8
Butch Lake—*lake* ... AK-9
Butch Lake—*lake* ... NE-7
Butch McNabb Lake—*reservoir* ... TN-4
Butch Mtn—*summit* ... AK-9
Butch Nichols Tank—*reservoir* ... AZ-5
Butch Rsvr—*reservoir* ... OR-9
Butch Spring—*spring* ... ID-8
Butch Spring—*spring* ... MT-8
Butchs Strip (Stolport)—*airport* ... MO-7
Butch Tank—*reservoir* ... AZ-5
Bute—*locale* ... MO-7
**Bute**—*pop pl* ... PA-2
Buteau, Lake—*lake* ... WI-6
Buteaux Crossing—*locale* ... MD-2
*Bute Brook* ... MA-1
*Bute Mountains* ... CA-9
Buteo Lake—*lake* ... AK-9
Butera (Siding)—*locale* ... CA-9
Buterbaugh Cave—*cave* ... TN-4
Buter Museum of Wedgwood—*building* ... PA-2
Bute Run—*stream* ... PA-2
*Butes Brooks* ... MA-1
Bute-Warner-Truax Farm—*hist pl* ... NY-2
Buthne Sch—*school* ... FL-3
Butiaur—*bar* ... PW-9
*Butler* ... KS-7
Butler—*locale* ... AR-4
Butler—*locale* ... CA-9
Butler—*locale* (2) ... IA-7
Butler—*locale* ... MN-6
Butler—*locale* ... MS-4
Butler—*locale* ... TX-5
**Butler**—*pop pl* ... AL-4
**Butler**—*pop pl* ... GA-3
**Butler**—*pop pl* ... IL-6
**Butler**—*pop pl* ... IN-6
**Butler**—*pop pl* ... KY-4
**Butler**—*pop pl* ... MD-2
**Butler**—*pop pl* ... MI-6
**Butler**—*pop pl* ... MO-7
**Butler**—*pop pl* ... NJ-2
**Butler**—*pop pl* ... OH-6
**Butler**—*pop pl* ... OK-5
**Butler**—*pop pl* ... PA-2
**Butler**—*pop pl* ... SD-7
**Butler**—*pop pl* ... TN-4
**Butler**—*pop pl* ... TX-5
**Butler**—*pop pl* ... WI-6
**Butler**—*pop pl* ... PR-3
Butler—*uninc pl* ... KY-4
Butler, A. B., House—*hist pl* ... ME-1
Butler, Bayou—*stream* ... LA-4
Butler, Charles, House—*hist pl* ... OH-6
Butler, Cyrus, House—*hist pl* ... OH-6
Butler, Decatur N., House—*hist pl* ... MS-4
Butler, Dr. John L., House—*hist pl* ... AR-4
Butler, Emmett, House—*hist pl* ... MN-6
Butler, Gen. William O., House—*hist pl* ... KY-4
Butler, James, House—*hist pl* ... CT-1
Butler, J.G., House—*hist pl* ... OH-6
Butler, Jim, Mining Company Stone Row
Houses—*hist pl* ... NV-8
Butler, Lake—*lake* (2) ... FL-3
Butler, Marion, Birthplace—*hist pl* ... NC-3
Butler, Mount—*summit* ... NV-8
Butler, Mount—*summit* ... OR-9
Butler, Pierce and Walter,
House—*hist pl* ... MN-6
Butler, Walter, Homestead—*hist pl* ... NY-2
Butler, Wesley, Archeol District—*hist pl* ... OH-6
Butler, William F., House—*hist pl* ... UT-8
Butler, Wright, House—*hist pl* ... MD-2
Butler Area Senior HS—*school* ... PA-2
Butler Ave Interchange—*crossing* ... AZ-5
Butler Ave Sch—*school* ... NJ-2
Butler Baptist Ch—*church* ... TN-4
*Butler Baptist Church* ... AL-4
Butler Bar Campground—*park* ... OR-9
Butler Basin—*basin* ... NV-8
Butler Basin—*basin* ... OR-9
Butler Bay—*bay* ... VI-3
**Butler Bay**—*pop pl* ... ID-8
**Butler Bay**—*pop pl* ... VI-3
Butler Bay—*swamp* (2) ... NC-3
Butler Bayou—*gut* ... TX-5
Butler Bayou—*stream* ... LA-4
Butler Beach—*beach* ... FL-3
Butler Beach State Park—*park* ... FL-3
Butler Beck Cabin—*locale* ... UT-8
Butler Block—*hist pl* ... MA-1
Butler Branch—*stream* (4) ... AL-4
Butler Branch—*stream* ... GA-3
Butler Branch—*stream* ... IL-6
Butler Branch—*stream* ... IN-6
Butler Branch—*stream* (7) ... KY-4
Butler Branch—*stream* ... MD-2
Butler Branch—*stream* (2) ... MS-4
Butler Branch—*stream* (2) ... NC-3
Butler Branch—*stream* ... SC-3
Butler Branch—*stream* (5) ... TN-4
Butler Branch—*stream* (4) ... TX-5
Butler Branch—*stream* (2) ... WV-2
Butler Bridge—*bridge* ... AL-4
Butler Bridge—*bridge* ... IN-6
Butler Bridge—*bridge* ... MS-4
Butler Bridge—*bridge* ... NC-3
Butler Bridge—*other* ... IL-6
Butler Brook—*stream* (2) ... ME-1
Butler Brook—*stream* ... NH-1
Butler Brook—*stream* ... NY-2
Butler Brothers Company—*hist pl* ... MN-6
Butler Brown Flats—*flat* ... WA-9
Butler Butte—*summit* ... OR-9
Butler Butte—*summit* ... WA-9
Butler Camp—*locale* ... CA-9
Butler Camp—*locale* ... TX-5
Butler Canal—*canal* ... CA-9
Butler Canyon—*valley* ... AZ-5
Butler Canyon—*valley* (2) ... CA-9
Butler Canyon—*valley* ... CO-8
Butler Canyon—*valley* ... ID-8
Butler Canyon—*valley* ... OR-9

Butler Canyon—*valley* (3) ... UT-8
*Butler Canyon - in part* ... UT-8
Butler Cave—*cave* ... MO-7
Butler (CCD)—*cens area* ... AL-4
Butler (CCD)—*cens area* ... GA-3
Butler (CCD)—*cens area* ... KY-4
Butler (CCD)—*cens area* ... OK-5
Butler (CCD)—*cens area* ... TN-4
Butler (CCD)—*cens area* ... TX-5
*Butler Cem* ... AL-4
*Butler Cem* ... TN-4
Butler Cem—*cemetery* (5) ... AL-4
Butler Cem—*cemetery* ... AR-4
Butler Cem—*cemetery* (2) ... FL-3
Butler Cem—*cemetery* (4) ... GA-3
Butler Cem—*cemetery* (3) ... IL-6
Butler Cem—*cemetery* ... IN-6
Butler Cem—*cemetery* (4) ... IA-7
Butler Cem—*cemetery* (2) ... KS-7
Butler Cem—*cemetery* (4) ... KY-4
Butler Cem—*cemetery* (6) ... LA-4
Butler Cem—*cemetery* ... MA-1
Butler Cem—*cemetery* (9) ... MS-4
Butler Cem—*cemetery* (5) ... MO-7
Butler Cem—*cemetery* ... NH-1
Butler Cem—*cemetery* (2) ... NY-2
Butler Cem—*cemetery* (4) ... NC-3
Butler Cem—*cemetery* ... OH-6
Butler Cem—*cemetery* (3) ... OK-5
Butler Cem—*cemetery* (3) ... PA-2
Butler Cem—*cemetery* (3) ... SC-3
Butler Cem—*cemetery* ... SD-7
Butler Cem—*cemetery* (13) ... TN-4
Butler Cem—*cemetery* (2) ... TX-5
Butler Cem—*cemetery* ... VT-1
Butler Cem—*cemetery* ... WI-6
Butler Center—*locale* ... IA-7
**Butler Center**—*pop pl* ... IN-6
**Butler Center**—*pop pl* ... NY-2
**Butler Center (Butler)**—*pop pl* ... NY-2
Butler Center Cem—*cemetery* ... IA-7
Butler Ch—*church* ... AL-4
Butler Ch—*church* ... MS-4
Butler Ch—*church* ... OH-6
Butler Ch—*church* ... OK-5
Butler Ch—*church* ... SC-3
Butler Ch—*church* ... TN-4
Butler Chain, Lake—*lake* ... FL-3
Butler Chapel—*church* ... AR-4
Butler Chapel—*church* ... SC-3
Butler Chapel A.M.E. Zion Church—*hist pl* ... AL-4
Butler Chapel (historical)—*church* ... MS-4
Butler-Choctaw County Airp—*airport* ... AL-4
Butler Ch of Christ—*church* ... AL-4
*Butler City* ... KS-7
Butler City—*civil* ... PA-2
Butler Coll—*school* ... TX-5
Butler Corners—*locale* ... NY-2
Butler County—*civil* ... KS-7
**Butler County**—*pop pl* ... AL-4
**Butler (County)**—*pop pl* ... KY-4
**Butler County**—*pop pl* ... MO-7
**Butler (County)**—*pop pl* ... OH-6
**Butler County**—*pop pl* ... PA-2
*Butler County Airport* ... PA-2
Butler County Area Vocational
Sch—*school* ... AL-4
Butler County Community Coll—*school* ... KS-7
Butler County Courthouse—*building* ... AL-4
Butler County Courthouse—*hist pl* ... OH-6
Butler County Courthouse—*hist pl* ... PA-2
Butler County Home—*building* ... IA-7
Butler County Jail—*hist pl* ... KY-4
Butler County Memorial
Garden—*cemetery* ... OH-6
Butler County Memorial Park
Cem—*cemetery* ... PA-2
Butler County Number 1 Dam—*dam* ... AL-4
Butler County State Lake Dam—*dam* ... KS-7
Butler County State Park—*park* ... KS-7
Butler County State Wildlife Mngmt
Area—*park* ... AL-4
Butler Cove—*bay* ... ME-1
Butler Cove—*bay* ... MD-2
Butler Cove—*bay* ... WA-9
Butler Cove—*cove* ... MA-1
Butler Cove—*valley* ... AR-4
*Butler Creeek* ... GA-3
*Butler Creek* ... AL-4
*Butler Creek* ... AR-4
*Butler Creek* ... CO-8
*Butler Creek* ... MD-2
*Butler Creek* ... NY-2
*Butler Creek* ... PA-2
*Butler Creek* ... WV-2
Butler Creek—*bay* ... VA-3
Butler Creek—*gut* ... NC-3
Butler Creek—*stream* ... AL-4
Butler Creek—*stream* (2) ... AR-4
Butler Creek—*stream* (3) ... CA-9
Butler Creek—*stream* (4) ... CO-8
Butler Creek—*stream* ... FL-3
Butler Creek—*stream* (5) ... GA-3
Butler Creek—*stream* (2) ... ID-8
Butler Creek—*stream* ... IN-6
Butler Creek—*stream* ... IA-7
Butler Creek—*stream* (4) ... KY-4
Butler Creek—*stream* (3) ... LA-4
Butler Creek—*stream* (2) ... MI-6
Butler Creek—*stream* ... MN-6
Butler Creek—*stream* (3) ... MS-4
Butler Creek—*stream* (2) ... MO-7
Butler Creek—*stream* (5) ... MT-8
Butler Creek—*stream* ... NV-8
Butler Creek—*stream* (2) ... NY-2
Butler Creek—*stream* (2) ... NC-3
Butler Creek—*stream* (2) ... OK-5
Butler Creek—*stream* (7) ... OR-9
Butler Creek—*stream* ... PA-2
Butler Creek—*stream* ... SC-3
Butler Creek—*stream* (3) ... TN-4
Butler Creek—*stream* (5) ... TX-5
Butler Creek—*stream* ... UT-8
Butler Creek—*stream* ... VA-3
Butler Creek—*stream* (5) ... WA-9
Butler Creek—*stream* ... WI-6
Butler Creek—*stream* ... WY-8
Butler Creek Ch—*church* ... AR-4
Butler Creek Ch—*church* ... OK-5
Butler Creek Rsvr—*reservoir* ... OR-9

Butler Creek Sch (historical)—*school* ... TN-4
*Butler Creek School* ... TN-4
*Butler Crossroads* ... NC-3
Butler Crossroads—*locale* ... NC-3
**Butler Crossroads**—*pop pl* ... SC-3
Butler Davidson Cem—*cemetery* ... OR-9
Butler Ditch—*canal* ... CO-8
Butler Ditch—*canal* ... IN-6
Butler Ditch—*canal* ... MT-8
Butler Ditch—*canal* ... OH-6
Butler Ditch—*canal* ... WY-8
Butler Ditch No. 4—*canal* ... CO-8
Butler Division—*civil* ... AL-4
Butler Division—*civil* ... TN-4
Butler Drain—*canal* ... MI-6
Butler Drain—*stream* ... IA-7
Butler Draw—*valley* ... NM-5
Butler Draw—*valley* (3) ... WY-8
Butler Elem Sch—*school* ... AL-4
Butler Elem Sch—*school* ... IN-6
Butler Falls—*falls* ... AL-4
Butler Falls—*falls* ... IN-6
Butler Falls Branch—*stream* ... AL-4
Butler Family Cemetery—*hist pl* ... SC-3
Butler Farm—*hist pl* ... NJ-2
*Butler Farm Show Airport* ... PA-2
Butler Farm Show Roe Airp—*airport* ... PA-2
Butler Field—*park* ... NY-2
Butler Field Airp—*airport* ... IN-6
Butler Fieldhouse—*hist pl* ... IN-6
Butler First United Methodist Ch—*church* ... AL-4
Butler Flat—*flat* ... CA-9
Butler Flat—*flat* ... UT-8
Butler Flat—*flat* (2) ... WA-9
Butler Flats—*flat* ... MA-1
Butler Flats—*flat* ... NM-5
Butler Flats Light—*locale* ... MA-1
Butler Flats Light Station—*hist pl* ... MA-1
Butler Fork—*stream* ... UT-8
Butler Gap—*gap* ... NC-3
Butler Glacier—*glacier* ... AK-9
Butler-Graham Airp—*airport* ... PA-2
Butler Grove Cem—*cemetery* ... TN-4
Butler Grove (Township of)—*civ div* ... IL-6
Butler Gulch—*valley* ... CO-8
Butler Gulch—*valley* ... MT-8
Butler Head—*cape* ... ME-1
Butler Hill—*summit* ... ME-1
Butler Hill—*summit* ... MO-7
Butler Hill—*summit* ... MT-8
Butler Hill—*summit* ... OH-6
Butler Hill—*summit* ... OK-5
Butler Hill—*summit* ... OR-9
Butler Hill—*summit* ... PA-2
Butler Hill—*summit* ... SC-3
Butler Hill—*summit* (2) ... TN-4
Butler Hill—*summit* ... TX-5
Butler Hill—*summit* ... WA-9
Butler Hill Ch—*church* ... PA-2
**Butler Hill Estates**—*pop pl* ... MO-7
Butler Hill Park—*park* ... MS-4
Butler Hill Plaza—*locale* ... MO-7
Butler Hills—*summit* ... WY-8
**Butler Hills Subdivision**—*pop pl* ... UT-8
Butler Hill Village (Shop Ctr)—*locale* ... MO-7
Butler (historical)—*locale* ... MS-4
**Butler (historical)**—*pop pl* ... FL-3
**Butler (historical)**—*pop pl* ... OR-9
Butler (historical P.O.)—*locale* ... IA-7
Butler Hole—*bay* ... FL-3
Butler Hole—*channel* ... MA-1
Butler Hollow—*valley* (2) ... AL-4
Butler Hollow—*valley* (3) ... AR-4
Butler Hollow—*valley* ... KY-4
Butler Hollow—*valley* (4) ... MO-7
Butler Hollow—*valley* (2) ... OH-6
Butler Hollow—*valley* (5) ... PA-2
Butler Hollow—*valley* (2) ... TN-4
Butler Hollow—*valley* ... UT-8
Butler Hollow Pit—*cave* ... AL-4
Butler Hosp—*hist pl* ... RI-1
Butler House—*hist pl* ... CO-8
Butler House—*hist pl* ... CT-1
Butler House—*hist pl* ... MO-7
Butler House—*hist pl* ... PA-2
Butler House—*hist pl* ... TN-4
Butler HS—*school* ... KY-4
Butler HS—*school* ... TX-5
Butler Institute Of American Art—*hist pl* ... OH-6
Butler Island—*island* ... FL-3
Butler Island—*island* ... GA-3
Butler Island—*island* ... ID-8
Butler Island—*island* ... OH-6
Butler Island—*island* ... SC-3
Butler Island—*island* ... VT-1
Butler Junction—*locale* ... PA-2
**Butler Junction**—*pop pl* ... PA-2
Butler Knob—*summit* ... NC-3
Butler Knob—*summit* ... PA-2
Butler Knobs—*summit* ... TN-4
*Butler Lake* ... WA-9
Butler Lake—*lake* (2) ... FL-3
Butler Lake—*lake* ... KY-4
Butler Lake—*lake* (3) ... MI-6
Butler Lake—*lake* ... MN-6
Butler Lake—*lake* ... MS-4
Butler Lake—*lake* ... NY-2
Butler Lake—*lake* ... ND-7
Butler Lake—*lake* ... PA-2
Butler Lake—*lake* ... TN-4
Butler Lake—*lake* ... TX-5
Butler Lake—*lake* ... WI-6
Butler Lake—*reservoir* ... IL-6
Butler Lake—*reservoir* ... MO-7
Butler Lake—*reservoir* (3) ... TX-5
Butler Lake—*swamp* ... WI-6
Butler Lake Dam—*dam* ... MS-4
Butler Lake Ditch—*canal* ... AR-4
Butler Lake Oil Field—*oilfield* ... MS-4
Butler Lakes—*reservoir* ... MO-7
Butler Landing—*gut* ... LA-4
Butler Library—*building* ... NY-2
Butler (Magisterial District)—*fmr MCD*
(2) ... WV-2
Butler Mall—*locale* ... PA-2
*Butler-Martin Cemetery* ... MS-4
Butler-Matthews Homestead—*hist pl* ... AR-4
Butler-McCook Homestead—*hist pl* ... CT-1
Butler Meadow—*flat* ... MT-8
Butler Memorial Airp—*airport* ... MO-7

Butler Memorial Bridge—*bridge* ... TN-4
Butler Memorial Ch—*church* ... AL-4
Butler Memorial Ch—*church* ... SC-3
Butler Memorial Hosp—*hospital* ... PA-2
Butler Memorial Park—*cemetery* ... PA-2
Butler Mill—*locale* ... AL-4
*Butler Mill Branch* ... DE-2
Butler Mill Branch—*stream* ... DE-2
*Butler Mill Ch* ... AL-4
Butler Mill Ch—*church* ... AL-4
Butler Mill Hollow—*valley* ... TN-4
Butler Mill Road Ch—*church* ... AL-4
Butler Mine—*mine* ... OR-9
Butler Mine—*mine* ... TN-4
Butler Mines—*mine* ... KY-4
Butler Mound and Village Site—*hist pl* ... MS-4
Butler Mountain Lookout Tower—*locale* ... AL-4
Butler Mountains—*summit* ... AZ-5
Butler MS—*school* ... UT-8
Butler Mtn—*summit* ... AL-4
Butler Mtn—*summit* ... AZ-5
Butler Mtn—*summit* (2) ... CA-9
Butler Mtn—*summit* ... ID-8
Butler Mtn—*summit* ... NV-8
Butler Mtn—*summit* (2) ... NC-3
Butler Mtn—*summit* ... OR-9
Butler Mtn—*summit* ... PA-2
Butler Mtn—*summit* ... TN-4
Butler Mtn—*summit* (2) ... VA-3
Butler Mtn—*summit* ... WV-2
Butler Neck—*cape* ... MA-1
Butler Neck Point—*cape* ... MA-1
Butler Number 1 Mine
(underground)—*mine* ... AL-4
Butler Park—*park* ... AL-4
Butler Park—*park* ... AR-4
Butler Park—*park* ... MO-7
Butler Park—*park* ... TX-5
**Butler Park**—*pop pl* ... NJ-2
Butler Pass—*gap* ... AZ-5
Butler Peak—*summit* ... AK-9
Butler Peak—*summit* ... CA-9
Butler Peak—*summit* ... NV-8
Butler Peak—*summit* ... OR-9
Butler Playfield—*park* ... MI-6
Butler Plaza II (Shop Ctr)—*locale* ... FL-3
Butler Plaza (Shop Ctr)—*locale* ... FL-3
*Butler Point* ... ME-1
Butler Point—*cape* ... GA-3
Butler Point—*cape* ... ME-1
Butler Point—*cape* ... MA-1
Butler Point—*summit* ... AZ-5
Butler Pond—*lake* ... GA-3
Butler Pond—*lake* ... LA-4
Butler Pond—*lake* (3) ... ME-1
Butler Pond—*lake* ... NJ-2
Butler Pond—*lake* ... NY-2
Butler Pond—*lake* ... PA-2
Butler Pond—*lake* ... VT-1
Butler Pond—*reservoir* (2) ... NC-3
Butler Pond Dam—*dam* ... NC-3
Butler Post Office—*building* ... TN-4
Butler Prairie—*area* ... CA-9
*Butler-Prairie Home Cemetery* ... SD-7
*Butler Ranch* ... NV-8
Butler Ranch—*locale* ... CO-8
Butler Ranch—*locale* ... MT-8
Butler Ranch—*locale* (2) ... NV-8
Butler Ranch—*locale* ... NM-5
Butler Ranch—*locale* ... OR-9
Butler Recreational Lake—*reservoir* ... MO-7
Butler Ridge—*ridge* ... OR-9
Butler River—*channel* ... GA-3
Butler Rock—*island* ... AK-9
Butler Rock—*summit* ... WI-6
*Butler-Roe Airport* ... PA-2
Butler Rsvr—*reservoir* ... CO-8
Butler Rsvr—*reservoir* (2) ... NJ-2
Butler Rsvr—*reservoir* ... OR-9
*Butler Rsvr Dam* ... NJ-2
*Butler Run* ... PA-2
Butler Run—*stream* ... OH-6
Butler Run—*stream* ... PA-2
*Butlers* ... MD-2
Butlers—*locale* ... NC-3
Butler-Savannah Cem—*cemetery* ... NY-2
Butlers Bar—*bar* ... MS-4
Butlers Bay—*swamp* ... SC-3
**Butlers Beach**—*pop pl* ... MD-2
Butlers Bluff—*cliff* ... VA-3
Butlers Branch—*stream* ... KY-4
Butlers Bridge—*bridge* ... VA-3
Butlers Camp—*locale* ... ME-1
Butler Sch—*school* ... AL-4
Butler Sch—*school* ... CO-8
Butler Sch—*school* (3) ... IL-6
Butler Sch—*school* ... IA-7
Butler Sch—*school* (2) ... LA-4
Butler Sch—*school* ... ME-1
Butler Sch—*school* (2) ... MA-1
Butler Sch—*school* (2) ... MI-6
Butler Sch—*school* (2) ... MO-7
Butler Sch—*school* ... NJ-2
Butler Sch—*school* ... OK-5
Butler Sch—*school* ... SC-3
Butler Sch—*school* ... UT-8
Butler Sch (abandoned)—*school* ... PA-2
Butlers Chapel—*church* ... TN-4
Butlers Chapel—*church* ... WV-2
Butler Sch (historical)—*school* ... MS-4
Butler Sch (historical)—*school* ... MO-7
Butler Sch (historical)—*school* (3) ... TN-4
Butler School (historical)—*locale* ... MO-7
Butlers Corner—*locale* ... ME-1
*Butlers Cove* ... MA-1
*Butlers Creek* ... NY-2
Butlers Creek—*stream* ... GA-3
Butlers Creek—*stream* ... IN-6
Butlers Creek Ch—*church* ... GA-3
**Butlers Crossroads**—*pop pl* ... NC-3
Butlers Ditch—*canal* ... AR-4
Butlers Ferry (historical)—*crossing* ... TN-4
*Butlers Ferry Post Office* ... TN-4
Butlers Fork—*locale* ... VA-3
Butlers Fork—*stream* ... KY-4
Butlers Golf Course—*other* ... PA-2
Butlers Gut—*gut* ... SC-3
Butlers Gut—*gut* ... VA-3
Butler Shaft (historical)—*mine* ... PA-2
*Butlers Hole* ... MA-1

Butler-Short Cem—cemetery MS-4
Butler Sinkhole Cave—cave AL-4
Butlers Island—island CT-1
Butlers Knob—summit AR-4
Butlers Lake—lake PA-2
Butlers Lake—reservoir PA-2
Butlers Lake Dam—dam PA-2
**Butlers Landing**—pop pl TN-4
Butlers Landing Ch of Christ—church TN-4
Butlers Landing Post Office (historical)—building TN-4
Butlers Landing Sch (historical)—school TN-4
Butler Slough—gut LA-4
Butler Slough—stream CA-9
Butlers Mill AL-4
Butlers Mill PA-2
Butlers Mill—locale OH-6
**Butlers Mill**—pop pl AL-4
Butlers Mill (historical)—locale AL-4
Butlers Mill Pond GA-3
Butlers Mountain ME-1
Butlers Park—locale NJ-2
Butlers Place—locale NJ-2
Butlers Point MA-1
Butlers Pond—reservoir GA-3
Butlers Pond—swamp AL-4
Butler Spring WA-9
Butler Spring—spring AL-4
Butler Spring—spring AZ-5
Butler Spring—spring (2) CA-9
Butler Spring—spring ID-8
Butler Spring—spring (2) OR-9
Butler Spring—spring TN-4
Butler Spring—spring UT-8
Butler Spring—spring WA-9
Butlersprings AL-4
**Butler Springs**—pop pl AL-4
Butler Springs Cem—cemetery AL-4
Butler Springs Ch—church AL-4
Butler Spring Youth Camp—locale OH-6
Butlers Public Golf Course PA-2
Butlers Ridge—ridge AR-4
Butlers Run—stream IN-6
Butlers Store—locale VA-3
Butler (sta.)—uninc pl WI-6
Butler Stadium—other TX-5
Butler Stadium—other VA-3
Butler State Fishing Lake And Wildlife Area—park KS-7
Butler State Wildlife Mngmt Area—park MN-6
Butler's Tavern MD-2
Butler's Tavern—hist pl KY-4
Butlers Toothpick MA-1
Butlers Toothpick (historical)—bar MA-1
Butler Storage Rsvr—reservoir NY-2
Butler Street Colored Methodist Episcopal Church—hist pl GA-3
Butler Street Gatehouse—hist pl PA-2
Butler Street Station—building PA-2
**Butler Subdivision**—pop pl GA-3
Butlersville—locale KY-4
Butler Switch IN-6
Butler Table—plain MT-8
Butler Tank—reservoir (2) NM-5
**Butlertown**—pop pl MD-2
**Butler (Town of)**—pop pl NY-2
**Butler (Town of)**—pop pl WI-6
Butler Township—civil (2) MO-7
Butler Township—fmr MCD (4) IA-7
**Butler Township**—pop pl MO-7
**Butler Township**—pop pl NE-7
**Butler Township**—pop pl (2) SD-7
Butler Township—unorg reg KS-7
Butler (Township of)—fmr MCD (2) AR-4
Butler (Township of)—other OH-6
**Butler (Township of)**—pop pl IL-6
**Butler (Township of)**—pop pl (3) IN-6
**Butler (Township of)**—pop pl MI-6
**Butler (Township of)**—pop pl MN-6
**Butler (Township of)**—pop pl (6) OH-6
**Butler (Township of)**—pop pl (4) PA-2
Butler Trail—trail (2) PA-2
**Butler Transfer**—pop pl PA-2
Butler Univ—school IN-6
Butler Valley—valley AZ-5
Butler Valley—valley CA-9
Butler Valley—valley UT-8
Butler Valley Dam—dam AZ-5
Butler Valley Dam—dam UT-8
Butler Valley Draw—valley UT-8
Butler Valley Interchange PA-2
Butler Valley Neck—cape UT-8
Butler Valley Ranch—locale CA-9
Butler Valley Rsvr—reservoir UT-8
Butlerville MA-1
Butlerville UT-8
Butlerville—locale IA-7
**Butlerville**—pop pl AR-4
**Butlerville**—pop pl IN-6
**Butlerville**—pop pl MA-1
**Butlerville**—pop pl NY-2
**Butlerville**—pop pl OH-6
**Butlerville**—pop pl UT-8
Butlerville Cem—cemetery IN-6
Butlerville (historical)—locale MA-1
Butler Wash—stream AZ-5
Butler Wash—stream (2) UT-8
Butler Wash—valley (2) UT-8
Butler Wash Archeol District—hist pl UT-8
Butler Wash Ruins—locale UT-8
Butler Wash Viewpoint—locale UT-8
Butler Well—well AZ-5
Butler Well—well NV-8
Butler Well—well NM-5
Butler Windmill—locale NM-5
Butlhead Cove—bay AK-9
**Butman**—pop pl MI-6
Butman Camp—locale TX-5
Butman Cem—cemetery MI-6
**Butman Corners**—pop pl WI-6
Butman Hill—summit MA-1
Butman Hill—summit NH-1
**Butman (Township of)**—pop pl MI-6
Butner—locale OK-5
**Butner**—pop pl NC-3
Butner, Lake—reservoir NC-3
Butner Cem—cemetery KS-7
Butner Cem—cemetery OK-5
Butner Ch—church OK-5
Butner Field—park OK-5
Butner Ranch—locale WY-8
Butner Sch—school MO-7
Butner-Stem Central Sch—school NC-3
Buto Lake—lake MI-6
Butputter Creek—stream MS-4
Butram Hollow—valley MO-7
Butree Run PA-2
Butrum Creek—stream VA-3
Butson Creek—stream NY-2
Butt, The—summit VA-3
Buttahatchee, Lake—lake AL-4
Buttahatchee Dam—dam AL-4
Buttahatchee Gas Field—oilfield MS-4
Buttahatchee River AL-4
Buttahatchee River—stream AL-4
Buttahatchee River—stream MS-4
Buttahatchee Sch—school AL-4
Buttahatche River AL-4
Buttahatche River MS-4
**Buttahatchie (historical)**—pop pl MS-4
Buttahatchie Post Office (historical)—building AL-4
Buttahatchie Post Office (historical)—building MS-4
Buttahatchie River AL-4
Buttahatchie River MS-4
Buttahatchy River AL-4
Buttahatchy River MS-4
Buttam Hollow—valley TN-4
Buttars Spring—spring ID-8
Butta Tank—reservoir AZ-5
Butt Branch VA-3
Butt Branch—stream KY-4
Butt Branch—stream TN-4
Butt Canyon—valley UT-8
Butt Cem—cemetery GA-3
Butt Cem—cemetery (2) TN-4
Butt Cem—cemetery WV-2
Butt Creek TN-4
Butt Creek—stream CA-9
**Butte**—pop pl MT-8
**Butte**—pop pl NE-7
**Butte**—pop pl ND-7
Butte, Anaconda and Pacific Railway Hist Dist—hist pl MT-8
Butte, Bayou la—stream LA-4
Butte, Lake—lake WA-9
Butte, Mount—summit NV-8
Butte, The CA-9
Butte, The—summit AK-9
Butte, The—summit AZ-5
Butte, The—summit ID-8
Butte, The—summit (2) OR-9
Butte, The—summit (2) WA-9
Butte, The—summit WY-8
Butte and Zenith Mine—mine MT-8
Butte Arm Canal—canal ID-8
Butte Assembly of God Ch—church MT-8
Butte Bar—bar CA-9
Butte Bar Trail (Jeep)—trail CA-9
Butte (Bodenburg Butte)—uninc pl AK-9
Butte Cabin Creek—stream MT-8
Butte Cabin Ridge Trail—trail (2) MT-8
Butte Camp—locale (3) CA-9
Butte Camp—locale WA-9
Butte Camp Dome—summit WA-9
Butte Canal—canal ID-8
Butte Canal—canal LA-4
Butte Canyon—valley CA-9
Butte Canyon—valley NV-8
Butte Cem—cemetery (2) CO-8
Butte Cem—cemetery MO-7
Butte Cem—cemetery NE-7
Butte Cem—cemetery OR-9
Butte Central HS—school MT-8
Butte Ch of God-Cleveland Tennessee Affiliates—church MT-8
Butte City AZ-5
Butte City MT-8
**Butte City**—pop pl CA-9
**Butte City**—pop pl ID-8
Butte City Cem—cemetery CA-9
Butte City (ruins)—locale CA-9
Butte-Cochran Charcoal Ovens—hist pl AZ-5
Butte Coulee—valley MT-8
Butte Country Club—other MT-8
Butte County—civil SD-7
**Butte (County)**—pop pl CA-9
Butte County Center—locale CA-9
Butte County HS—school ID-8
Butte Crater—crater ID-8
Butte Creek CO-8
Butte Creek KS-7
Butte Creek MT-8
Butte Creek NC-3
Butte Creek WA-9
Butte Creek WY-8
Butte Creek—locale MT-8
**Butte Creek**—pop pl CA-9
Butte Creek—stream (6) AK-9
Butte Creek—stream (3) AZ-5
Butte Creek—stream (9) CA-9
Butte Creek—stream (2) CO-8
Butte Creek—stream (5) ID-8
Butte Creek—stream (16) MT-8
Butte Creek—stream (2) NV-8
Butte Creek—stream ND-7
Butte Creek—stream (16) OR-9
Butte Creek—stream (3) SD-7
Butte Creek—stream TX-5
Butte Creek—stream (7) WA-9
Butte Creek—stream WY-8
Butte Creek Cabin—locale CA-9
Butte Creek Campground—locale CA-9
Butte Creek Diversion Channel—canal CA-9
Butte Creek Falls—falls OR-9
**Butte Creek (historical)**—pop pl OR-9
Butte Creek House—locale CA-9
Butte Creek Landing—locale ID-8
Butte Creek Pass—gap OR-9
Butte Creek Ranch—locale CA-9
Butte Creek Rim—cliff CA-9
Butte Creek Saddle—gap ID-8
Butte Creek Sch—school CA-9
Butte Creek Sch—school MT-8
Butte Creek Sch—school OR-9
Butte Creek Summit—summit OR-9
Butte Dam—dam OR-9
**Butte des Morts**—pop pl WI-6
Butte Des Morts, Lake—lake WI-6
Butte des Morts Sch—school WI-6
Butte Disappointment—summit OR-9
Butte Ditch—canal (2) CO-8
Butte Ditch—canal OR-9
Butte Ditch—canal WY-8
Butte Divide—ridge WY-8
Butte Dome WA-9
Butte Drain—canal OR-9
Butte Draw—valley SD-7
Butte Draw—valley (2) WY-8
Butte Falls—falls OR-9
**Butte Falls**—pop pl OR-9
Butte Falls Cem—cemetery OR-9
Butte Falls-Prospect (CCD)—cens area OR-9
Butte Falls Ranger Station—hist pl OR-9
Butte Fork CA-9
Butte Fork—stream WA-9
Butte Fork Applegate River—stream CA-9
Butte Group Mine—mine SD-7
Butte Gulch—valley ID-8
Butte Gulch—valley NV-8
Butte Gun Club—other MT-8
Butte Hill—cape WA-9
Butte Hill—summit TX-5
Butte Hist Dist—hist pl MT-8
**Butte (historical)**—pop pl OR-9
Butte HS—school MT-8
Butte Knob—summit TX-5
Butte Lake WI-6
Butte Lake—lake AK-9
Butte Lake—lake CA-9
Butte Lake—lake CO-8
Butte Lake—lake ND-7
Butte Lake—lake OR-9
Butte Lake—lake TX-5
**Butte Larose**—pop pl LA-4
**Butte La Rose**—pop pl LA-4
Butte La Rose Bay—stream LA-4
Butte La Rose Cutoff—canal LA-4
Butte Lateral—canal ID-8
Butte Lateral—canal NM-5
Butte Lateral—canal SD-7
Butte-Lawrence County Fairgrounds—hist pl SD-7
Butte Lodge Outing Club—other CA-9
Butte Market Lake Canal—canal ID-8
Butte Meadows—flat WA-9
**Butte Meadows**—pop pl CA-9
Butte Meadows Camp—locale MT-8
Butte Meadows Creek—stream WA-9
Butte Meadows Ranger Station—locale MT-8
Buttemer Ranch—locale CA-9
Butte Michaud—summit ND-7
Butte Mine—mine AZ-5
Butte Mine—mine CA-9
Butte Mine—mine NV-8
Butte Mtn—summit NC-3
Butte Mtns—range NV-8
**Buttenberry (Buttonsberry)**—pop pl KY-4
Butte of the Cross, The UT-8
Butte One Mine—mine NV-8
Butte Pacific Mine—mine MT-8
Butte Pass—gap WA-9
Butte Peak—summit AZ-5
Butte Ranch—locale ID-8
Butterass Tank—reservoir TX-5
Butterball Cove—bay WA-9
Butterball Lake—lake AK-9
Butter Ball Rock—pillar RI-1
Butterball Tank—reservoir AZ-5
Butterbean Ridge—ridge OH-6
Butterbowl—summit TX-5
Butterbowl Creek—stream MS-4
Butter Branch WV-2
Butterbread Canyon CA-9
Butterbread Peak CA-9
Butterbread Spring CA-9
Butterbread Well CA-9
Butterbredt Canyon—valley CA-9
Butterbredt Peak—summit CA-9
Butterbredt Spring—spring CA-9
Butterbredt Well—well CA-9
Butter Brook—stream MA-1
Butter Brook—stream NY-2
Butter Creek AR-4
Butter Creek MO-7
Butter Creek OR-9
Butter Creek—stream (2) AR-4
Butter Creek—stream (2) CA-9
Butter Creek—stream CO-8
Butter Creek—stream (2) ID-8
Butter Creek—stream (2) IL-6
Butter Creek—stream (2) OR-9
Butter Creek—stream (2) PA-2
Butter Creek—stream WA-9
Butter Creek Caves—cave CA-9
**Butter Creek (historical)**—pop pl OR-9
Butter Creek Junction—locale (2) OR-9
Butter Creek Meadows—flat CA-9
Buttercup MP-9
Buttercup Creek—stream ID-8
Buttercup Creek—stream TX-5
Buttercup Farms Pictograph—hist pl CA-9
Buttercup Hill—summit WA-9
Buttercup Mine—mine ID-8
Buttercup Mtn—summit ID-8
Buttercup Park—basin MT-8
Buttercup Park Trail—trail MT-8
Buttercup Rsvr—reservoir WY-8
Buttercup Spring—spring NV-8
Buttercup Spring—spring NM-5
Buttercup Spring—spring OR-9
Butterfield—locale MI-6
**Butterfield**—pop pl AR-4
**Butterfield**—pop pl IL-6
**Butterfield**—pop pl MN-6
**Butterfield**—pop pl MO-7
**Butterfield**—pop pl OR-9
Butterfield—uninc pl NY-2
Butterfield, John A., House—hist pl CA-9
Butterfield, Lake—reservoir NY-2
Butterfield Brook—stream (4) ME-1
Butterfield Canyon—valley AK-9
Butterfield Canyon—valley CA-9
Butterfield Canyon—valley TX-5
Butterfield Canyon—valley UT-8
Butterfield Cem—cemetery IN-6
Butterfield Cem—cemetery MI-6
Butterfield Cem—cemetery MN-6
Butterfield Cem—cemetery OH-6
Butterfield Cem—cemetery WI-6
Butterfield Ch—church AR-4
Butterfield Country Club—other IL-6
Butterfield Cove—bay ME-1
Butterfield Creek—stream (2) ID-8
Butterfield Creek—stream IL-6
Butterfield Creek—stream (3) MI-6
Butterfield Creek—stream (2) MN-6
Butterfield Creek—stream NV-8
Butterfield Creek—stream OR-9
Butterfield Creek—stream (2) UT-8
Butterfield Drain—canal MI-6
Butterfield Draw—valley NM-5
Butterfield Draw—valley WY-8
Butterfield Gulch—valley ID-8
Butterfield Hill—summit ME-1
Butterfield Hill—summit NH-1
Butterfield Hill—summit VT-1
Butterfield Island—island ME-1
Butterfield Island—island MI-6
Butterfield JHS—school AL-4
Butterfield Lake—lake ME-1
Butterfield Lake—lake (2) MI-6
Butterfield Lake—lake (2) MN-6
Butterfield Lake—lake NY-2
Butterfield Lake—lake OR-9
Butterfield Landing—locale ME-1
Butterfield Livestock Company House—hist pl ID-8
Butterfield Meadow—flat UT-8
Butterfield Mtn—summit VT-1
Butterfield Oil Field—other MI-6
Butterfield Overland Trail—trail KS-7
Butterfield Park—park AZ-5
Butter Field Park—park GA-3
**Butterfield Park**—pop pl NM-5
Butterfield Pass—gap AZ-5
Butterfield Peak—summit TX-5
Butterfield Peaks—summit UT-8
Butterfield Point—cape MI-6
Butterfield Pond—lake MA-1
Butterfield Pond—lake (2) NH-1
Butterfield Rapids—rapids MN-6
Butterfield Riffle—rapids OR-9
Butterfield Rock—summit NH-1
Butterfield Sch—school ME-1
Butterfield Sch—school MI-6
Butterfield Sch—school TX-5
Butterfield Shoal—bar MI-6
Butterfield Site (15McL7)—hist pl KY-4
Butterfield Spring—spring OR-9
Butterfield Springs—spring (2) NV-8
Butterfield Springs—spring OR-9
Butterfield Stage Route (historical)—trail AZ-5
Butterfield Stage Station Historical Marker—other CA-9
Butterfield Stage Station Historical Marker—park CA-9
Butterfield Tank—reservoir NM-5
Butterfield Tank—reservoir TX-5
Butterfield Township—civil MO-7
Butterfield (Township of)—fmr MCD AR-4
**Butterfield (Township of)**—pop pl MI-6
**Butterfield (Township of)**—pop pl MN-6
Butterfield Trail—trail NM-5
Butterfield Trail—trail TX-5
Butterfield Trail Campsite—park AZ-5
Butterfield Trail Sch—school AR-4
Butterfield Tunnel—mine UT-8
Butterfield Valley—valley CA-9
Butterfield Well—well NM-5
**Butterfield West**—pop pl IL-6
Butterfield-Whittemore House—hist pl MA-1
Butterfield Windmill—locale (3) NM-5
Butterfield Windmill—locale TX-5
Butterfinger Lake—lake MN-6
Butter Flat Creek—stream NE-7
Butter Flats Lighthouse—locale MA-1
Butterfly NY-2
Butterfly—fmr MCD NE-7
Butterfly—locale KY-4
Butterfly, The—summit CO-8
Butterfly Branch—stream AL-4
Butterfly Burn—area CO-8
Butterfly Butte—summit AZ-5
Butterfly Butte—summit ID-8
Butterfly Butte—summit WA-9
Butterfly Campground—locale UT-8
Butterfly Canyon—valley CA-9
Butterfly Cienega—flat AZ-5
Butterfly Cienega—swamp AZ-5
Butterfly Corners—locale NY-2
Butterfly Creek—stream AZ-5
Butterfly Creek—stream (2) CA-9
Butterfly Creek—stream CO-8
Butterfly Creek—stream ID-8
Butterfly Creek—stream (2) MT-8
Butterfly Creek—stream NE-7
Butterfly Creek—stream NY-2
Butterfly Flat—flat CA-9
Butterfly Flat—flat UT-8
Butterfly Gap—gap TN-4
Butterfly Gap Ch—church TN-4
Butterfly Glacier—glacier WA-9
**Butterfly (historical)**—pop pl TN-4
Butterfly Island—island FL-3
Butterfly Island—island OR-9
Butterfly Knob—summit KY-4
Butterfly Lake AK-9
Butterfly Lake—lake AK-9
Butterfly Lake—lake FL-3
Butterfly Lake—lake MN-6
Butterfly Lake—lake (2) UT-8
Butterfly Lake—lake WI-6
**Butterfly Lake**—pop pl MN-6
Butterfly Lake—reservoir MO-7
Butterfly Mine—mine CO-8
Butterfly Mountain CA-9
Butterfly Mtn—summit AZ-5
Butterfly Peak—summit AZ-5
Butterfly Peak—summit CA-9
Butterfly Peak Natural Area—park AZ-5
Butterfly Pond MA-1
Butterfly Pond—reservoir RI-1
Butterfly Pond Fish and Wildlife Mngmt Area—park NJ-2
Butterfly Post Office (historical)—building TN-4
Butterfly Sch—school IL-6
Butterfly Sch—school NE-7
Butterfly Seep—spring NM-5
**Butterfly (Sonia)**—pop pl KY-4
Butterfly Spring—spring AZ-5
Butterfly Spring—spring MT-8
Butterfly Spring—spring (2) NM-5
Butterfly Spring—spring (2) OR-9
Butterfly Swamp—swamp NY-2
Butterfly Valley—valley CA-9
Butterfork AL-4
Butter Fork—stream CA-9
Butterfork Creek—stream AL-4
Butter Gap—gap NC-3
Butter Gulch—valley ID-8
Butter Hill—summit CO-8
Butter Hill—summit ME-1
Butter Hill—summit MA-1
Butter Hollow—valley (2) MO-7
Butterick Sch—school MA-1
Butter Island—island ME-1
Butter Issue Station (historical)—locale SD-7
Butter Krust—uninc pl TX-5
Butter-ladle Lake—lake MI-6
Butter Lake—reservoir CO-8
Butter Landing—locale FL-3
Butterly Cem—cemetery OK-5
Buttermilk TN-4
Buttermilk WV-2
Buttermilk—locale AR-4
Buttermilk—locale KS-7
Buttermilk Bay—bay MA-1
Buttermilk Bend—bend CA-9
Buttermilk Branch—stream (2) KY-4
Buttermilk Branch—stream MS-4
Buttermilk Branch—stream (3) TN-4
Buttermilk Branch—stream VA-3
Buttermilk Brook—stream (2) ME-1
Buttermilk Brook—stream (2) NY-2
Buttermilk Butte—summit WA-9
Buttermilk Campground—locale ID-8
Buttermilk Canyon—valley CO-8
Buttermilk Canyon—valley (2) OR-9
Buttermilk Channel—channel NY-2
Buttermilk Country—area CA-9
Buttermilk Cove NJ-2
Buttermilk Cove—bay ME-1
Buttermilk Creek CO-8
Buttermilk Creek—stream (2) CA-9
Buttermilk Creek—stream (2) CO-8
Buttermilk Creek—stream IN-6
Buttermilk Creek—stream IA-7
Buttermilk Creek—stream (2) KS-7
Buttermilk Creek—stream MI-6
Buttermilk Creek—stream (2) MS-4
Buttermilk Creek—stream (2) MT-8
Buttermilk Creek—stream NE-7
Buttermilk Creek—stream NV-8
Buttermilk Creek—stream (3) NY-2
Buttermilk Creek—stream NC-3
Buttermilk Creek—stream OH-6
Buttermilk Creek—stream (3) OR-9
Buttermilk Creek—stream PA-2
Buttermilk Creek—stream (2) TX-5
Buttermilk Creek—stream (2) VA-3
Buttermilk Creek—stream (2) WA-9
Buttermilk Ditch—canal IL-6
Buttermilk Draw—valley ID-8
Butter Milk Falls VA-3
Buttermilk Falls—falls CT-1
Buttermilk Falls—falls ME-1
Buttermilk Falls—falls (12) NY-2
Buttermilk Falls—falls (3) PA-2
Buttermilk Falls—falls VT-1
**Buttermilk Falls**—pop pl PA-2
Buttermilk Falls Brook—stream (2) NY-2
Buttermilk Falls State Park—park (2) NY-2
Buttermilk Flat—flat OR-9
Buttermilk Fork Churn Creek—stream OH-6
Buttermilk Gulch—valley CO-8
Buttermilk Hill—summit (2) NY-2
Buttermilk Hill—summit OH-6
Buttermilk Hollow—valley CT-1
Buttermilk Hollow—valley (2) OH-6
Buttermilk Hollow—valley PA-2
Buttermilk Hollow—valley TN-4
Buttermilk Hollow—valley TX-5
Buttermilk Jim Gulch—valley MT-8
Buttermilk Lake—lake MI-6
Buttermilk Lake—lake OR-9
Buttermilk Lake—lake WI-6
Buttermilk Meadow—flat WA-9
Buttermilk Meadows—flat NV-8
Buttermilk Mtn—summit AL-4
Buttermilk Mtn—summit ME-1
Buttermilk Mtn—summit NC-3
Buttermilk Point—cape IN-6
Buttermilk Point—cape ME-1
**Buttermilk Point**—pop pl IN-6
Buttermilk Pond NJ-2
Buttermilk Pond—lake ME-1
Buttermilk Pond—lake NY-2
Buttermilk Ridge—ridge CO-8
Buttermilk Ridge—ridge TN-4
Buttermilk Ridge—ridge WA-9
Buttermilk Run—stream VA-3
Buttermilk Sch—school IL-6
**Buttermilk Shores**—pop pl TN-4
Buttermilk Slough—gut ID-8
Buttermilk Slough—stream FL-3
Buttermilk Slough—stream TX-5
Buttermilk Sound—bay (2) GA-3
Buttermilk Spring UT-8
Buttermilk Spring—spring CA-9
Buttermilk Springs MS-4
Buttermilk Springs—spring AR-4
Buttermilk Springs—spring NV-8
Buttermilk Summit—gap NV-8
Buttermilk Tank—reservoir TX-5
Buttermilk Trail—trail CA-9
Buttermint Lake—lake MN-6
Butternut—locale MN-6
**Butternut**—pop pl MI-6
**Butternut**—pop pl VT-1
**Butternut**—pop pl WI-6
Butternut Basin—basin MA-1
Butternut Brook—stream CT-1
Butternut Brook—stream NH-1
Butternut Brook—stream (4) NY-2
Butternut Creek MI-6
Butternut Creek NY-2
Butternut Creek—stream (2) GA-3
Butternut Creek—stream IN-6
Butternut Creek—stream (8) MI-6
Butternut Creek—stream (3) NY-2
Butternut Creek—stream OH-6
Butternut Creek—stream OR-9
Butternut Creek—stream PA-2
Butternut Creek—stream TX-5
Butternut Creek—stream (2) WI-6
Butternut Creek Drain MI-6
Butternut Drain—canal MI-6
Butternut Grove—locale PA-2
**Butternut Grove**—pop pl NY-2
Butternut Grove Run—stream PA-2
Butternut Hill—summit NY-2
Butternut Hill—summit (2) VT-1
Butternut Hollow—valley IA-7
Butternut Hollow—valley (4) PA-2
Butternut Hollow—valley WI-6
Butternut Island NY-2
Butternut Island PA-2
Butternut Island—island WI-6
Butternut Key—island FL-3
Butternut Lake—lake (2) MI-6
Butternut Lake—lake MN-6
Butternut Lake—lake (3) WI-6
Butternut Mine—mine AZ-5
Butternut Mtn—summit VT-1
Butternut Park—park WI-6
Butternut Point—cape NY-2
Butternut Pond—lake NH-1
Butternut Pond—lake NY-2
Butternut Reservoir CT-1
Butternut Ridge—ridge OH-6
Butternut Ridge—ridge VT-1
Butternut Ridge Cem—cemetery (2) OH-6
Butternut Ridge Cem—cemetery WI-6
Butternut Ridge Chapel—church OH-6
Butternut Run—stream IN-6
Butternut Run—stream NY-2
Butternut Run—stream (2) PA-2
Butternut Sch—school WI-6
Butternut Ski Area—locale MA-1
Butternut Spring UT-8
Butternut Spring—spring AZ-5
Butternut Springs—spring IN-6
**Butternuts (Town of)**—pop pl NY-2
Butternut Valley Cem—cemetery (2) NY-2
Butternut Valley (Township of)—civ div MN-6
Butte Rock—pillar CA-9
Butte Rock—pillar CO-8
Butterowe Bayou—gut TX-5
Butterpat DE-2
Butter Point—cape ME-1
Butterpoint Cem—cemetery KY-4
Butterpot DE-2
Butter Pot Point—cape MD-2
Butter Ridge—ridge IL-6
Butter Ridge Cem—cemetery IL-6
Butter Rim OR-9
Butter Run—stream VA-3
Butter Run—stream WV-2
**Butters**—pop pl NC-3
Butters, Alfred, House—hist pl CO-8
Butters Cem—cemetery LA-4
Butters Cem—cemetery OH-6
Butter Shell Hill—summit MO-7
Butter Shell Lake—lake MO-7
Butters Mtn—summit ME-1
Butterson Knob—summit TN-4
Butterstack Ridge—ridge TN-4
Buttersville—locale MI-6
Butte Rsvr OR-9
Butte Rsvr—reservoir CO-8
Butte Rsvr—reservoir OR-9
Butte Rsvr—reservoir (2) UT-8
Butte Rsvr—reservoir WY-8
Buttertly Flats—flat MT-8
Butter Valley Golf Course—locale PA-2
Butter Valley Golf Port Airp—airport PA-2
Butterview Sch—school SD-7
Butterville—locale NY-2
**Butterville**—pop pl NY-2
Butterwood Branch—stream VA-3
Butterwood Ch—church VA-3
Butterwood Creek—stream NC-3
Butterwood Creek—stream (3) VA-3
Butterwood (Township of)—fmr MCD NC-3
Butterworth—locale VA-3
Butterworth Bldg—hist pl WA-9
Butterworth Brook—stream CT-1
Butterworth Cem—cemetery TN-4
Butterworth Cem—cemetery VA-3
Butterworth Creek—stream MS-4
Butterworth Dam—dam WA-9
Butterworth Draw—valley ID-8
**Butterworth Farms**—pop pl NJ-2
Butterworth Flat—flat CO-8
**Butterworth Flat**—pop pl CO-8
Butterworth Hosp—hospital MI-6
Butterworth Island—island AK-9
Butterworth Lake—reservoir TN-4
Butterworth Lake Dam—dam TN-4
Butterworth Park—park MA-1
Butterworth Ridge—ridge MA-1
Butterworth Rsvr—reservoir WA-9
Butterworth Sch—school IL-6
Buttery Brook—stream MA-1
Buttery Brook Tributary Rsvr—reservoir MA-1
Buttery Creek—stream TX-5
Buttes CA-9
Buttes—locale CO-8
Buttes—summit WY-8
Buttes, The CA-9
Buttes, The—spring MT-8
Buttes, The—summit AZ-5
Buttes, The—summit (2) CA-9
Buttes, The—summit CO-8
Buttes, The—summit ID-8
Buttes, The—summit (2) NV-8
Buttes, The—summit ND-7
Buttes, The—summit (3) OR-9
Buttes, The—summit (2) UT-8
Buttes, The—summit WY-8
Butte Saint Junction—locale CA-9
Butte Saint Paul Historic Site—park ND-7
Buttes Area Camp—locale CA-9
Buttes Canyon—valley CA-9
Butte Sch—school CA-9
Butte Sch—school SD-7
Butte Sch—school WY-8
Butte Sch Number 2 (historical)—school ND-7

Buzzard Swamp—*swamp* DE-2
Buzzard Swamp—*swamp* PA-2
Buzzard Tank—*reservoir* (4) AZ-5
Buzzard Tank—*reservoir* NM-5
Buzzard Trail—*trail* PA-2
Buzzard Windmill—*locale* (3) TX-5
Buzzardwing Creek—*stream* TX-5
Buzzell Brook—*stream* ME-1
Buzzell Brook—*stream* NH-1
Buzzell Cove—*bay* NH-1
Buzzell Dam—*dam* VT-1
Buzzell Gap—*gap* VT-1
Buzzell Hill—*summit* (2) VT-1
*Buzzell Mtn* VT-1
Buzzell Ridge—*ridge* NH-1
Buzzell Stream—*stream* ME-1
Buzzer Branch—*stream* KY-4
Buzz Gully—*valley* IN-6
Buzz Lake—*lake* MN-6
Buzzle Ch—*church* MN-6
Buzzle Lake—*lake* MN-6
**Buzzle (Township of)**—*pop pl* MN-6
Buzz Spring—*spring* NV-8
Buzz Spring—*spring* OR-9
Buzztail Spring—*spring* CA-9
**Buzzville**—*pop pl* IL-6
Buzzy Brook—*stream* ME-1
BVD Trail—*trail* OR-9
B V Hedrick Sand and Gravel Lake—*reservoir* NC-3
B V Rsvr—*reservoir* OR-9
BW and H Mine—*mine* UT-8
*Bwar* MP-9
B W Barnes Sch—*school* OR-9
B W Cobb Lake—*reservoir* TN-4
B W Cobb Lake Dam—*dam* TN-4
B W Coleman Dam Number 1—*dam* AL-4
B W Coleman Dam Number 2—*dam* AL-4
B W Coleman Farm Dam Number 1—*dam* AL-4
B W Coleman Farm Dam Number 2—*dam* AL-4
Bwdije—*island* MP-9
*Bwerorkan Island* MP-9
*Bwibwi* MP-9
*Bwi Island* MP-9
Bwinejrak—*island* MP-9
Bwodao—*island* MP-9
Bwoj (not verified)—*locale* MP-9
*Bwokankowak* MP-9
Bwokburar—*island* MP-9
Bwoknauo—*island* MP-9
*Bwokw* MP-9
Bwokw—*island* MP-9
*Bwokwaak* MP-9
Bwokwaang—*island* MP-9
Bwokwaddel—*island* MP-9
Bwokwadebto—*island* MP-9
Bwokwadel—*island* MP-9
Bwokwajabwung—*island* MP-9
Bwokwajenmoon—*island* MP-9
Bwokwaledde—*island* MP-9
Bwokwalijakaan—*island* MP-9
Bwokwalije—*island* MP-9
Bwokwalijmwa—*island* MP-9
Bwokwalikorwa—*island* MP-9
Bwokwalojaon—*island* MP-9
Bwokwalojokdel—*island* MP-9
Bwokwalokaajlo—*island* MP-9
Bwokwalurito—*island* MP-9
*Bwokwanaeang* MP-9
Bwokwanaelok—*island* MP-9
*Bwokwanaetok* MP-9
Bwokwanaik—*island* MP-9
Bwokwanaitok—*island* MP-9
Bwokwanajbwirik—*island* MP-9
Bwokwanajdomw—*island* MP-9
Bwokwanajinwir—*island* MP-9
Bwokwanajmwaan—*island* MP-9
Bwokwanajmwaandik—*island* MP-9
Bwokwanalejwa—*island* MP-9
Bwokwanbit—*island* MP-9
Bwokwanbwutil—*island* MP-9
Bwokwanij—*island* MP-9
Bwokwanikabwe—*island* MP-9
Bwokwanjaej—*island* MP-9
Bwokwankear—*island* MP-9
Bwokwankeear—*island* MP-9
Bwokwankeer—*island* MP-9
Bwokwankin—*island* MP-9
Bwokwankomwteeang—*island* MP-9
Bwokwankora—*island* MP-9
*Bwokwankowak* MP-9
Bwokwankowak—*island* MP-9
Bwokwanlerro—*island* MP-9
Bwokwanmwiokan—*island* MP-9
Bwokwantarinae—*island* MP-9
Bwokwarmej—*island* MP-9
Bwokwarobbwon—*island* MP-9
*Bwokwato* MP-9
Bwokwdikdik—*island* MP-9
Bwokwdikdik—*range* MP-9
*Bwokwed* MP-9
Bwokwejejen—*island* MP-9
Bwokwen—*island* MP-9
Bwokwen—*locale* MP-9
Bwokwentarinae—*island* MP-9
Bwokwiur—*island* MP-9
*Bwokwkan* MP-9
Bwokwkan—*island* MP-9
Bwokwkan (not verified)—*other* MP-9
Bwokwla—*island* MP-9
*Bwokwlablab* MP-9
*Bwokwlabwunglik* MP-9
Bwokwlajulik—*island* MP-9
*Bwokwlang* MP-9
Bwokwlemjam—*island* MP-9
Bwokwlewij—*island* MP-9
Bwokwloboea—*island* MP-9
Bwokwlomwanuno—*island* MP-9
Bwokwmeej—*island* MP-9
Bwokwmokak—*island* MP-9
Bwokwodda—*island* MP-9
Bwokwonkalleb—*island* MP-9
Bwokwonmwak—*island* MP-9
Bwokworlab—*island* MP-9
Bwokwtoonal—*island* MP-9
*Bwolwilu* MP-9
Bworokulik—*island* MP-9
B W Palmer State Park—*park* MA-1
BW Ranch—*locale* ND-7
B W Robinson State Sch—*school* MO-7
Bwruon—*island* MP-9
Bwu—*island* MP-9
*Bwurwon* MP-9
Bwuwe—*island* MP-9
*Byakutai* FM-9
Byam Cem—*cemetery* PA-2
Byan Cem—*cemetery* VA-3
Byar Branch—*stream* MO-7
Byard Gap—*gap* NC-3
Byard Point—*cape* ME-1
**Byars**—*pop pl* OK-5
*Byars Branch* GA-3
Byars Cem—*cemetery* AL-4
Byars Cem—*cemetery* IL-6
Byars Cem—*cemetery* KY-4
Byars Cem—*cemetery* OK-5
Byars Cem—*cemetery* (2) VA-3
Byars Ch—*church* NC-3
Byars Creek—*stream* OR-9
Byars Creek—*stream* VA-3
Byars Gulch—*valley* OR-9
*Byars Hall High School* TN-4
Byars Lake—*reservoir* OK-5
Byars Peak—*summit* OR-9
Byars Spring—*spring* OR-9
Byas Branch—*stream* TX-5
*Byatabyatto* MP-9
*Byatabyatto-to* MP-9
Bybee—*locale* IL-6
Bybee—*locale* VA-3
**Bybee**—*pop pl* KY-4
**Bybee**—*pop pl* (2) TN-4
Bybee, Frank E., House—*hist pl* OR-9
Bybee, William, House—*hist pl* OR-9
Bybee Branch—*stream* TN-4
Bybee Branch Sch (historical)—*school* TN-4
Bybee Cem—*cemetery* IL-6
Bybee Creek—*stream* OR-9
Bybee Creek—*stream* TX-5
Bybee Creek—*stream* UT-8
Bybee Creek—*stream* WA-9
Bybee Draw—*valley* WY-8
Bybee Gulch—*valley* CA-9
Bybee Gulch—*valley* OR-9
Bybee Gulch—*valley* UT-8
Bybee Hollow—*valley* KY-4
Bybee House—*hist pl* KY-4
Bybee-Howell House—*hist pl* OR-9
Bybee Knoll—*summit* UT-8
Bybee Lake—*lake* OR-9
Bybee Ledge Channel—*channel* OR-9
Bybee Mines—*mine* WY-8
Bybee Peak—*summit* OR-9
Bybee Post Office—*building* TN-4
Bybee Road Ch—*church* VA-3
Bybee Rsvr—*reservoir* ID-8
Bybee Sch—*school* MO-7
Bybee Sch (historical)—*school* TN-4
Bybee Springs—*locale* OR-9
Bybee United Methodist Ch—*church* TN-4
**Byberry**—*pop pl* (2) PA-2
Byberry Cem—*cemetery* PA-2
Byberry Chapel—*church* PA-2
Byberry Creek—*stream* PA-2
*Bycot* PA-2
Bycot Station—*locale* PA-2
By-Day Creek—*stream* CA-9
Bye Creek—*stream* VA-3
Byecroft Farm Complex—*hist pl* PA-2
**Byeforde**—*pop pl* MD-2
*By-en-Soss Creek* WV-2
**Byer**—*pop pl* OH-6
Byer Covered Bridge—*hist pl* OH-6
Byer Lake—*lake* MN-6
Byerland Ch—*church* PA-2
Byerle—*locale* OR-9
Byerley Bend—*bend* TN-4
Byerley Chapel—*church* TN-4
**Byerley Corner**—*pop pl* OR-9
Byerley Island—*island* TN-4
Byerley Lake (historical)—*lake* TN-4
**Byerly**—*pop pl* PA-2
Byerly Cem—*cemetery* TN-4
Byerly Hosp—*hospital* SC-3
Byerly House—*hist pl* PA-2
Byers—*locale* OR-9
Byers—*locale* PA-2
**Byers**—*pop pl* CO-8
**Byers**—*pop pl* KS-7
**Byers**—*pop pl* MO-7
**Byers**—*pop pl* TX-5
Byers, Isaac W., House—*hist pl* MI-6
Byers Airp (historical)—*airport* NC-3
**Byers and Tolles Addition (subdivision)**—*pop pl* UT-8
Byers Branch—*stream* IA-7
Byers Branch—*stream* NC-3
Byers Branch—*stream* VA-3
Byers Canyon—*valley* CO-8
Byers Canyon—*valley* NV-8
Byers Canyon—*valley* WA-9
Byers Canyon Spring No 1—*spring* WA-9
Byers Canyon Spring No 3—*spring* WA-9
*Byers Cem* AL-4
Byers Cem—*cemetery* AR-4
Byers Cem—*cemetery* (2) IN-6
Byers Cem—*cemetery* IA-7
Byers Cem—*cemetery* KS-7
Byers Cem—*cemetery* LA-4
Byers Cem—*cemetery* (2) MI-6
Byers Cem—*cemetery* (2) TN-4
Byers Cem—*cemetery* VA-3
Byers Chapel—*church* TN-4
*Byer School* TN-4
**Byers Corner**—*pop pl* PA-2
Byers Creek—*stream* AK-9
Byers Creek—*stream* CO-8
Byers Creek—*stream* GA-3
Byers Creek—*stream* MI-6
Byers Creek—*stream* MS-4
Byers Creek—*stream* (3) NC-3
Byers Creek—*stream* VA-3
Byers Creek—*stream* WA-9
Byers Creek Campground—*locale* CO-8
Byers Crossroads—*locale* GA-3
**Byersdale**—*pop pl* PA-2
Byers Ditch—*canal* CO-8
*Byers Dowdy Elementary School* TN-4
Byers Drain—*canal* MI-6
Byers-Evans House—*hist pl* CO-8
Byers Hill—*summit* MA-1
Byers Island—*island* AK-9
Byers Island—*island* PA-2
Byers JHS—*school* CO-8
**Byers Junction**—*pop pl* OH-6
Byers Lake—*lake* AK-9
Byers Lake—*lake* (2) MI-6
Byers Lake—*lake* PA-2
Byers Lake—*lake* TX-5
Byers-Lyons House—*hist pl* PA-2
Byers Mine—*mine* NV-8
Byers Mtn—*summit* NC-3
*Byerson Creek* MI-6
Byers Pass—*gap* CA-9
Byers Peak—*summit* CO-8
Byers Peak Trail—*trail* CO-8
Byers-Petrolia (CCD)—*cens area* TX-5
Byer Spring—*spring* NM-5
Byers Ranch—*locale* NV-8
Byers Ranch—*locale* WY-8
Byers Ridge—*ridge* PA-2
Byers Run—*stream* NM-5
Byers Run—*stream* PA-2
Byers Sch—*school* MI-6
Byers Sch—*school* PA-2
Byers Slough—*gut* CA-9
Byers Spring—*spring* NV-8
*Byers Station* PA-2
Byers Station (historical)—*building* PA-2
*Byer Station* OR-9
**Byersville**—*pop pl* NY-2
**Byersville (historical)**—*pop pl* NC-3
Byersville Sch Number 1—*school* ND-7
Byersville Sch Number 2—*school* ND-7
Byersville Sch Number 3—*school* ND-7
Byersville Sch Number 4—*school* ND-7
**Byersville Township**—*pop pl* ND-7
Bye Rsvr—*reservoir* OR-9
Byers Well—*locale* NM-5
Byerton Sch—*school* IL-6
Bye Sch—*school* MN-6
**Byesville**—*pop pl* OH-6
**Byewood Manor (subdivision)**—*pop pl* DE-2
*Byfield* MA-1
**Byfield**—*pop pl* MA-1
Byfield Ch—*church* TX-5
Byfield Creek—*stream* TX-5
Byfield Hist Dist—*hist pl* DE-2
Byfield (historical P.O.)—*locale* MA-1
*Byfield Snuff Company Dam* MA-1
*Byfield Station* MA-1
**Byforde**—*pop pl* MD-2
Byford Sch—*school* IL-6
*Bygar* MP-9
**Bygland**—*pop pl* MN-6
Bygland Ch—*church* MN-6
**Bygland (Township of)**—*pop pl* MN-6
By Golly Creek—*stream* WI-6
By Gonney Spring—*spring* CA-9
**Byhalia**—*pop pl* MS-4
**Byhalia**—*pop pl* OH-6
Byhalia Cem—*cemetery* MS-4
Byhalia Cem—*cemetery* OH-6
Byhalia Creek—*stream* MS-4
Byhalia Creek Canal—*canal* MS-4
Byhalia Sch—*school* MS-4
Byhalia United Methodist Church—*hist pl* MS-4
Byham Sch—*school* PA-2
By-Heck, Lake—*reservoir* TX-5
Byhre Creek—*stream* WI-6
Byington—*locale* OH-6
**Byington**—*pop pl* TN-4
Byington Cem—*cemetery* GA-3
Byington Cem—*cemetery* MO-7
Byington Ch—*church* TN-4
Byington Post Office (historical)—*building* TN-4
Byington Ranch—*locale* NV-8
Byington Ranch Airp—*airport* NV-8
Byington (RR name for Karns)—*other* TN-4
By Jim Spring—*spring* CA-9
Byland Cem—*cemetery* KY-4
**Bylas**—*pop pl* AZ-5
Bylas Atheltic Field—*park* AZ-5
Bylas Day Sch—*school* AZ-5
*Byler* AL-4
Byler Bottoms—*basin* TN-4
Byler Branch—*stream* AR-4
Byler Branch—*stream* (2) MO-7
Byler Cem—*cemetery* MO-7
Byler Cem—*cemetery* TN-4
Byler Ditch—*canal* IN-6
Byler Hill—*summit* AR-4
Byler-Marchant Cem—*cemetery* TN-4
Byler Point Ch—*church* TX-5
Byler Road—*hist pl* AL-4
Byler Sch—*school* MO-7
Byler Sch (abandoned)—*school* MO-7
Byler Spring—*spring* TX-5
Byles Canyon—*valley* CA-9
Byles Johnson Camp—*locale* CA-9
Bylew Cave—*cave* KY-4
Bylew Creek—*stream* KY-4
*Bylin Dam* ND-7
Bylin Dam—*dam* ND-7
**Byllesby**—*pop pl* VA-3
Byllesby, Lake—*reservoir* MN-6
*Byllesby Rsvr* MN-6
*Byman* MD-2
Byne Crossroads—*locale* GA-3
Bynes Chapel—*church* GA-3
Bynes Grove Cem—*cemetery* GA-3
Bynes Grove Ch—*church* GA-3
**Byng**—*pop pl* OK-5
*Bynhams* MD-2
**Byno**—*pop pl* VA-3
Byno Creek—*stream* SC-3
Bynogue Branch—*stream* LA-4
Bynum—*locale* MS-4
**Bynum**—*pop pl* AL-4
**Bynum**—*pop pl* MD-2
**Bynum**—*pop pl* MS-4
**Bynum**—*pop pl* MT-8
**Bynum**—*pop pl* NC-3
**Bynum**—*pop pl* SC-3
**Bynum**—*pop pl* TX-5
Bynum Baptist Ch—*church* AL-4
Bynum Branch—*stream* GA-3
Bynum Branch—*stream* NC-3
Bynum-Brandon Cem—*cemetery* TX-5
**Bynum (Bynum Hills)**—*pop pl* MD-2
Bynum Canal—*canal* MT-8
*Bynum Cave* AL-4
Bynum Cem—*cemetery* (3) AL-4
Bynum Cem—*cemetery* GA-3
Bynum Cem—*cemetery* LA-4
Bynum Cem—*cemetery* MS-4
Bynum Cem—*cemetery* (2) TN-4
Bynum Cem—*cemetery* TX-5
Bynum Creek—*stream* (2) MS-4
Bynum Creek—*stream* MO-7
Bynum Creek—*stream* SC-3
Bynum Creek—*stream* TX-5
Bynum Creek Rec Area—*park* MS-4
Bynum Drift Mine (underground)—*mine* AL-4
Bynum Gulch—*valley* TN-4
*Bynum Hills* MD-2
Bynum (historical)—*locale* MS-4
Bynum Hollow—*valley* TN-4
Bynum Methodist Ch—*church* AL-4
Bynum Mill Branch—*stream* AL-4
Bynum Mill Creek—*stream* NC-3
Bynum Mounds—*summit* MS-4
**Bynum Park (subdivision)**—*pop pl* NC-3
Bynum Ranch—*locale* TX-5
Bynum Reservoir Ditch—*canal* MT-8
**Bynum Ridge**—*pop pl* MD-2
Bynum Ridge—*ridge* OK-5
Bynum Rsvr—*reservoir* MT-8
Bynum Run—*stream* MD-2
Bynum Run Picnic Area—*locale* MD-2
*Bynums* MD-2
Bynum Sch—*school* MS-4
Bynums Chapel—*church* MS-4
*Bynum School* AL-4
Bynums Creek (historical)—*locale* MS-4
*Bynums Mill Creek* NC-3
Bynums Mill Run—*stream* NC-3
Bynum Store—*locale* VA-3
**Bynumville**—*pop pl* MO-7
*Byobu* PW-9
*Byobu Island* PW-9
*Byobu To* PW-9
Byodo-In Temple—*church* HI-9
Byous Butte—*summit* AZ-5
Byous Spring—*spring* AZ-5
Bypass Camp—*locale* WA-9
Bypass Canal—*canal* (2) ID-8
Bypass Canal—*canal* UT-8
Bypass Tank—*reservoir* AZ-5
Bypass Trail—*trail* OR-9
**Bypro (Wheelwright) (sta.)**—*pop pl* KY-4
Byram—*locale* NJ-2
**Byram**—*pop pl* CT-1
**Byram**—*pop pl* MS-4
Byram, Lake—*lake* AL-4
Byram Baptist Ch—*church* MS-4
Byram Bay—*bay* NJ-2
Byram Bay Ch—*church* NJ-2
*Byram Branch* MS-4
Byram Bridge—*hist pl* MS-4
Byram Cem—*cemetery* MS-4
Byram Cem—*cemetery* TN-4
Byram Chapel—*church* TN-4
Byram Cove—*bay* NJ-2
**Byram Cove**—*pop pl* NJ-2
Byram Gulch—*valley* OR-9
Byram Harbor—*bay* CT-1
**Byram Heights (subdivision)**—*pop pl* AL-4
Byram Lake—*lake* MI-6
Byram Lake Rsvr—*reservoir* NY-2
Byram-Middleton House—*hist pl* IN-6
Byram Park—*park* CT-1
Byram Point—*cape* CT-1
Byram Post Office (historical)—*building* MS-4
Byram River—*stream* CT-1
Byram River—*stream* NY-2
Byram Sch—*school* CT-1
Byram Sch—*school* MS-4
Byrams Chapel Cem—*cemetery* TN-4
*Byrams Cove* NJ-2
Byrams Fork—*stream* TN-4
Byrams Fork Ch—*church* TN-4
Byrams Island—*island* AL-4
Byram Spring—*spring* UT-8
**Byram (Township of)**—*pop pl* NJ-2
Byram United Methodist Ch—*church* MS-4
Byram Well—*well* UT-8
**Byran**—*pop pl* AR-4
Byran Cem—*cemetery* TN-4
*Byran Lake* MI-6
Byrant Ridge Tank—*reservoir* AZ-5
Byrant Sch—*school* MO-7
*Byras Branch* GA-3
*Byras Creek* GA-3
Byrd—*locale* FL-3
Byrd—*locale* MS-4
Byrd—*locale* TX-5
**Byrd**—*pop pl* AL-4
**Byrd**—*pop pl* SC-3
**Byrd**—*pop pl* VA-3
**Byrd**—*pop pl* WV-2
Byrd, J. A., Mercantile Store—*hist pl* SC-3
Byrd, Lake—*lake* FL-3
Byrd Bay—*bay* TN-4
Byrd Bayou—*stream* LA-4
Byrd Bend—*bend* MS-4
Byrd Branch—*stream* IN-6
Byrd Branch—*stream* (2) MS-4
Byrd Branch—*stream* NC-3
Byrd Branch—*stream* (2) TN-4
Byrd Branch—*stream* TX-5
Byrd Bridge—*bridge* AL-4
Byrd Bridge—*bridge* MS-4
Byrd Bridge—*bridge* VA-3
Byrd Canyon—*valley* OR-9
Byrd Canyon—*valley* WA-9
Byrd Cave—*cave* AL-4
Byrd Cave—*cave* TN-4
*Byrd Cem* AL-4
*Byrd Cem* MS-4
Byrd Cem—*cemetery* (4) AL-4
Byrd Cem—*cemetery* (3) GA-3
Byrd Cem—*cemetery* KY-4
Byrd Cem—*cemetery* (9) MS-4
Byrd Cem—*cemetery* (3) MO-7
Byrd Cem—*cemetery* (5) NC-3
Byrd Cem—*cemetery* OH-6
Byrd Cem—*cemetery* SC-3
Byrd Cem—*cemetery* (8) TN-4
Byrd Cem—*cemetery* VA-3
Byrd Cemeteries—*cemetery* NC-3
Byrd Ch—*church* AL-4
Byrd Ch—*church* FL-3
Byrd Ch—*church* GA-3
Byrd Ch—*church* MO-7
Byrd Ch—*church* TN-4
Byrd Ch—*church* VA-3
Byrd Chapel—*church* NC-3
Byrd Chapel—*church* VA-3
**Byrd Chapel**—*pop pl* TN-4
**Byrdcliffe**—*pop pl* NY-2
Byrdcliffe Hist Dist—*hist pl* NY-2
Byrd-Cole Number 6 Mine (underground)—*mine* AL-4
Byrd-Cowart Cem—*cemetery* MS-4
Byrd Creek—*stream* (2) AL-4
Byrd Creek—*stream* GA-3
Byrd Creek—*stream* KY-4
Byrd Creek—*stream* MS-4
Byrd Creek—*stream* MO-7
Byrd Creek—*stream* SC-3
Byrd Creek—*stream* (3) TN-4
Byrd Creek—*stream* VA-3
Byrd Creek Dam—*dam* TN-4
Byrd Creek Lake—*reservoir* TN-4
Byrd Creek Rsvr—*reservoir* TN-4
Byrd Dam—*dam* TN-4
Byrd Draw—*valley* WY-8
*Byrd Elementary School* AL-4
Byrd Gap—*gap* NC-3
Byrd Gap—*gap* TN-4
Byrd Gap—*gap* VA-3
Byrd Grove Ch—*church* VA-3
Byrd Gully—*valley* TX-5
**Byrd Heights (subdivision)**—*pop pl* MS-4
Byrd-Helveston Cem—*cemetery* MS-4
*Byrd Hill Church* TN-4
Byrd Hills—*other* MO-7
Byrd Hollow—*valley* (2) AR-4
Byrd Hollow—*valley* (3) TN-4
Byrd Hollows—*valley* NC-3
Byrd Holt Hollow—*valley* TN-4
Byrd HS—*school* LA-4
*Byrd Island* AL-4
Byrd Island—*island* SC-3
Byrd Island Bar—*bar* AL-4
Byrd JHS—*school* CA-9
Byrd JHS—*school* OK-5
Byrd Knob—*summit* VA-3
Byrd Lake—*lake* SC-3
Byrd Lake—*lake* WI-6
Byrd Lake—*reservoir* (2) TN-4
Byrd Lake Dam—*dam* TN-4
Byrd Lakes—*reservoir* AR-4
Byrd Line Cem—*cemetery* MS-4
Byrd Line School—*locale* MS-4
Byrd (Magisterial District)—*fmr MCD* VA-3
Byrd Memorial Cem—*cemetery* AL-4
Byrd Memorial Ch—*church* NC-3
Byrd Mill—*locale* VA-3
Byrd Mill Branch—*stream* MS-4
Byrd Mill Pond—*reservoir* NC-3
Byrd Mtn—*summit* GA-3
Byrd Mtn—*summit* NC-3
Byrd Mtn—*summit* OK-5
Byrd Park—*park* MD-2
Byrd Plaza (Shop Ctr)—*locale* FL-3
Byrd Point—*cliff* VA-3
Byrd Pond—*lake* IL-6
Byrd Ranch—*locale* AZ-5
Byrd Ranch—*locale* NM-5
Byrd Reed Brake—*stream* MS-4
Byrd Ridge—*ridge* IN-6
Byrd Ridge—*ridge* KY-4
*Byrds* SC-3
Byrds—*locale* TX-5
**Byrds**—*pop pl* NC-3
Byrds African Methodist Episcopal Ch—*church* DE-2
Byrd's AME Church—*hist pl* DE-2
Byrds Branch—*stream* AL-4
Byrds Branch—*stream* NC-3
Byrds Branch—*stream* VA-3
Byrd Sch—*school* (2) AL-4
Byrd Sch—*school* (3) IL-6
Byrd Sch—*school* NJ-2
Byrd Sch—*school* (2) SC-3
Byrd Sch—*school* TN-4
Byrd Sch—*school* TX-5
Byrds Chapel—*church* GA-3
Byrds Chapel—*church* (2) MS-4
Byrds Chapel—*church* TN-4
Byrds Chapel Cem—*cemetery* MS-4
*Byrds Chapel Church of God* MS-4
*Byrd School* MS-4
**Byrds Creek**—*pop pl* WI-6
Byrds Creek—*stream* MS-4
Byrds Creek—*stream* (2) NC-3
Byrds Creek—*stream* WI-6
**Byrds Crossroads**—*pop pl* SC-3
Byrds Ferry (historical)—*locale* TN-4
*Byrds Hill Cemetery* TN-4
Byrds Island—*island* SC-3
Byrds Lake—*reservoir* GA-3
Byrds Landing—*locale* TN-4
Byrd Slough—*gut* CA-9
Byrds Marsh—*swamp* VA-3
Byrds Mill (historical)—*locale* AL-4
Byrds Millpond—*reservoir* GA-3
Byrds Millpond—*reservoir* VA-3
Byrds Mill Spring—*spring* OK-5
Byrds Mobile Park—*locale* AZ-5
Byrds Nest No 1—*summit* VA-3
Byrds Nest No 2 Shelter—*locale* VA-3
Byrds Nest No 3—*locale* VA-3
Byrds Nest No 4—*locale* VA-3
Byrds Point—*summit* OR-9
Byrds Pond—*reservoir* AL-4
Byrds Prairie Cem—*cemetery* OK-5
Byrd Spring—*spring* AL-4
Byrd Spring—*spring* TN-4
Byrd Spring Branch—*stream* AL-4
Byrd Spring Branch—*stream* TN-4
Byrd Spring Cave—*cave* AL-4
Byrd Spring Creek—*stream* VA-3
Byrd Spring Lake—*reservoir* AL-4
Byrd Spring Rod and Gun Club—*other* AL-4
*Byrd Springs Branch* TN-4
**Byrd Springs (subdivision)**—*pop pl* AL-4
Byrd Stadium—*building* MD-2
**Byrdstown**—*pop pl* TN-4
Byrdstown (CCD)—*cens area* TN-4
Byrdstown Division—*civil* TN-4
*Byrdstown Elementary School* TN-4
Byrdstown First Baptist Ch—*church* TN-4
Byrdstown Post Office—*building* TN-4
Byrds Valley—*basin* CA-9
Byrd Theatre—*hist pl* VA-3
Byrdton—*locale* VA-3
Byrdtown—*locale* TX-5
**Byrdtown**—*pop pl* MD-2
Byrd Township—*civil* MO-7
**Byrd (Township of)**—*pop pl* OH-6
Byrdview Cem—*cemetery* VA-3
Byrdville—*locale* NC-3
B Y Recreational Park Lake—*reservoir* PA-2
Byre Dam—*dam* SD-7
Byre Lake—*reservoir* SD-7
Byrge Chapel—*church* TN-4
Byrges Branch Baptist Ch—*church* TN-4
Byrges Creek—*stream* TN-4
Byrges Sch—*school* TN-4
Byrms—*cemetery* OK-5
*Byrn Athyn* PA-2
Byrne—*locale* ID-8
Byrne—*locale* MT-8
Byrne—*locale* TX-5
**Byrne**—*pop pl* WV-2
Byrne, Lake—*lake* WA-9
Byrne, Senator William T., House—*hist pl* NY-2
Byrne, Tom, House—*hist pl* ID-8
**Byrne City**—*pop pl* MS-4
Byrne Creek—*stream* (2) MT-8
Byrne Creek—*stream* WY-8
**Byrnedale**—*pop pl* PA-2
Byrne Ditch—*canal* NE-7
Byrne Ditch No 2—*canal* WY-8
Byrne House—*hist pl* CA-9
Byrne HS—*school* TN-4
Byrne Lake—*lake* MI-6
Byrne Lake—*lake* MS-4
Byrne Lake—*swamp* MN-6
Byrne No 2 Ditch—*canal* WY-8
Byrne Park—*park* MI-6
Byrne Park—*park* NY-2
Byrne Park—*park* WA-9
Byrne Post Office (historical)—*building* TN-4
Byrne Reservior—*reservoir* WY-8
Byrne Rsvr—*reservoir* WY-8
Byrne Sch—*school* AZ-5
Byrne Sch—*school* IL-6
Byrne Sch—*school* MN-6
Byrnes Corners—*locale* NY-2
Byrnes Creek—*stream* MT-8
Byrnes Creek—*stream* TX-5
Byrnes Crossing—*locale* WY-8
Byrnes Ditch—*canal* AR-4
Byrnes Ditch—*canal* MO-7
Byrnes Draw—*valley* WY-8
Byrnes HS—*school* SC-3
Byrnes Island—*island* MD-2
Byrnes & Kiefer Bldg—*hist pl* PA-2
Byrnes Lake—*lake* AL-4
Byrnes Lake—*lake* ND-7
**Byrnes Mill**—*pop pl* MO-7
Byrnes Mill (historical)—*locale* AL-4
Byrnes Park—*park* IA-7
Byrnes Run—*stream* PA-2
Byrnes Sch—*school* (2) IL-6
Byrnes Sch (historical)—*school* MS-4
Byrnes Tank—*reservoir* NM-5
**Byrnesville**—*pop pl* MO-7
**Byrnesville**—*pop pl* PA-2
Byrnesville Ch—*church* FL-3
Byrnes Windmill—*locale* TX-5
Byrneville—*locale* FL-3
**Byrneville**—*pop pl* IN-6
Byrneville Elem Sch—*school* FL-3
Byrnjulson Cem—*cemetery* ND-7
Byrns Bridge—*bridge* AR-4
Byrns Chapel—*church* VA-3
Byrns Darden Elem Sch—*school* TN-4
Byrns (historical)—*locale* MS-4
*Byrns Stratton Canal* ID-8
Byrns Stratton Canal—*canal* ID-8
**Byrnsville**—*pop pl* PA-2
*Byrnville* FL-3
**Byrnville**—*pop pl* FL-3
Byrom Cave—*cave* TN-4
*Byrom Lake* SD-7
Byromtown—*locale* PA-2
**Byromville**—*pop pl* GA-3
Byromville (CCD)—*cens area* GA-3
*Byron* SD-7
Byron—*locale* WA-9
**Byron**—*pop pl* AR-4
**Byron**—*pop pl* CA-9
**Byron**—*pop pl* GA-3
**Byron**—*pop pl* IL-6
**Byron**—*pop pl* (2) IN-6
**Byron**—*pop pl* ME-1
**Byron**—*pop pl* MI-6
**Byron**—*pop pl* MN-6
**Byron**—*pop pl* MO-7
**Byron**—*pop pl* NE-7
**Byron**—*pop pl* NY-2
**Byron**—*pop pl* OH-6
**Byron**—*pop pl* OK-5
**Byron**—*pop pl* WI-6
**Byron**—*pop pl* WY-8
Byron, Lake—*lake* MN-6
Byron, Lake—*lake* SD-7
Byron, Lewis, House—*hist pl* SD-7
Byron-Amorita Cem—*cemetery* OK-5
Byron Bay—*bay* AK-9
Byron-Bergen Swamp—*swamp* NY-2
Byron-Bethany Irrigation Canal—*canal* CA-9
Byron Camp—*locale* SD-7
Byron Carr Ford (historical)—*locale* MO-7
Byron (CCD)—*cens area* GA-3
Byron Cem—*cemetery* IA-7
Byron Cem—*cemetery* ME-1
Byron Cem—*cemetery* ND-7
Byron Cem—*cemetery* WY-8
**Byron Center**—*pop pl* MI-6
Byron Ch—*church* OH-6
Byron Ch—*church* PA-2

Byron Corners—*locale* .............................. NY-2
Byron Creek—*stream* .............................. ID-8
Byron Creek—*stream* .............................. OR-9
Byron Creek—*stream* (2) .............................. WA-9
Byron Ditch—*canal* .............................. OR-9
Byron Forge (historical)—*locale* .............................. TN-4
Byron Glacier—*glacier* .............................. AK-9
Byron Highland Park Plaza—*park* .............................. VA-3
**Byron Hills**—*pop pl* .............................. IL-6
Byron Hills Golf Course—*other* .............................. MI-6
Byron (historical)—*locale* .............................. AL-4
Byron (historical)—*locale* .............................. KS-7
Byron Historic Commercial
District—*hist pl* .............................. MI-6
Byron Hollow—*valley* .............................. MO-7
Byron Hot Springs—*spring* .............................. CA-9
Byron Hutchinson Lake Dam—*dam* .............................. MS-4
Byron Interchange—*crossing* .............................. NV-8
Byron JHS—*school* .............................. OH-6
Byron Kibler Sch—*school* .............................. WA-9
*Byron Lake* .............................. MN-6
Byron Lake—*lake* .............................. CO-8
Byron Lake—*lake* .............................. MI-6
Byron Lake—*lake* .............................. MN-6
Byron Lake—*lake* .............................. WA-9
Byron Lake Park—*park* .............................. NY-2
Byron Ledge—*bench* .............................. HI-9
Byron Millpond—*reservoir* .............................. MI-6
Byron Mtn—*summit* .............................. ME-1
Byron Notch—*gap* .............................. ME-1
Byron Oil Field—*oilfield* .............................. WY-8
Byron Peak—*summit* .............................. AK-9
Byron Ponds—*lake* .............................. WA-9
Byron Rsvr—*reservoir* .............................. OR-9
Byron Sanatorium—*hospital* .............................. IN-6
Byron Sch—*school* .............................. CA-9
Byron Sch—*school* .............................. KY-4
Byron Sch—*school* .............................. ME-1
Byron Sch—*school* .............................. OR-9
Byrons Creek—*stream* .............................. CA-9
Byron Shaft Mine (underground)—*mine* .............................. AL-4
Byron Slough—*gut* .............................. OR-9
Byron Sube Mill Pond—*lake* .............................. FL-3
**Byron (Town of)**—*pop pl* .............................. ME-1
**Byron (Town of)**—*pop pl* .............................. NY-2
**Byron (Town of)**—*pop pl* (2) .............................. WI-6
Byron Township—*civil* .............................. SD-7
Byron Township—*fmr MCD* .............................. IA-7
**Byron Township**—*pop pl* .............................. KS-7
**Byron Township**—*pop pl* .............................. ND-7
**Byron (Township of)**—*pop pl* .............................. IL-6
**Byron (Township of)**—*pop pl* .............................. MI-6
**Byron (Township of)**—*pop pl* (2) .............................. MN-6
Byron Tract—*civil* .............................. CA-9
Byron Weston Dam—*dam* .............................. MA-1
Byrum Cem—*cemetery* .............................. GA-3
Byrum Crossroads—*locale* .............................. NC-3
Bystre Lake—*lake* .............................. FL-3
Bystrom Bay—*bay* .............................. MN-6
*Byugoren-to* .............................. MP-9
B Y U-H C—*post sta* .............................. HI-9
Byus-Kirkland House—*hist pl* .............................. TX-5
Bywater Bay—*bay* .............................. WA-9
Bywater Hist Dist—*hist pl* .............................. LA-4
**Bywater Park Estates**
**(subdivision)**—*pop pl* .............................. UT-8
Bywaters—*uninc pl* .............................. LA-4
Bywatler Landing Strip—*airport* .............................. PA-2
Bywell Cow Camp—*locale* .............................. NM-5
**Bywood**—*pop pl* .............................. PA-2
Bywood Elem Sch—*school* .............................. PA-2
**Bywood Heights**—*pop pl* .............................. PA-2
*By Wy* .............................. MS-4
**Bywy**—*pop pl* .............................. MS-4
*By Wyah* .............................. MS-4
Bywy Ch—*church* .............................. MS-4
Bywy Creek—*stream* (2) .............................. MS-4
By-Wy Creek—*stream* .............................. MS-4
Bywy Overlook—*locale* .............................. MS-4
Bywy Sch (historical)—*school* .............................. MS-4
Byzandine Gulch—*valley* .............................. OR-9
Byzantine Central Sch—*school* .............................. OH-6
Byzantine Seminary—*school* .............................. PA-2
**B Z Corner**—*pop pl* .............................. WA-9
B-1 Canal—*canal* .............................. ID-8
B1 Canal—*canal* .............................. TX-5
B-1 Ditch—*canal* .............................. ID-8
B 17 Windmill—*locale* .............................. NM-5
B-29 Lake—*lake* .............................. UT-8
B 3.7 Lateral—*canal* .............................. AZ-5
B 3.8 Lateral—*canal* .............................. AZ-5
B-4 Canal—*canal* .............................. ID-8
B-52 Hill—*summit* .............................. NM-5
B 5.5 W Lateral—*canal* .............................. AZ-5
B 6.2 E Lateral—*canal* .............................. AZ-5
B 7.0 Lateral—*canal* .............................. AZ-5
B 8.0 N Lateral—*canal* .............................. AZ-5
B 8.55 Lateral—*canal* .............................. AZ-5
B-9 Structure Archeol Site—*hist pl* .............................. MO-7

# C

Caboose Spring—*spring* MT-8
Caboose Well—*well* NV-8
Caboose Windmill—*locale* TX-5
*Cabo River* AL-4
**Caborn**—*pop pl* IN-6
*Caborn Station* IN-6
*Caborn Summit* IN-6
*Caborn Summit Station* IN-6
Cabo Rojo—*cape* PR-3
**Cabo Rojo**—*pop pl* PR-3
Cabo Rojo (Municipio)—*civil* PR-3
Cabo Rojo (Pueblo)—*fmr MCD* PR-3
Cabo San Juan—*cape* PR-3
Cabo Sch (historical)—*school* TN-4
Cabot—*locale* KY-4
Cabot—*locale* WV-2
**Cabot**—*pop pl* AR-4
**Cabot**—*pop pl* LA-4
**Cabot**—*pop pl* PA-2
**Cabot**—*pop pl* VT-1
**Cabot**—*pop pl* WV-2
Cabot—*uninc pl* MA-1
Cabot, Capt. John, House—*hist pl* MA-1
Cabot, Lewis, Estate—*hist pl* MA-1
Cabot, Louis, House—*hist pl* NH-1
Cabot, Mount—*summit* (2) NH-1
Cabot, T.H., Cottage—*hist pl* NH-1
Cabot Cem—*cemetery* MI-6
*Cabot Creek* OR-9
Cabot Creek—*stream* OR-9
Cabot House—*building* MA-1
Cabot I Site—*hist pl* ME-1
Cabot Lake—*lake* OR-9
Cabot Lake Trail—*trail* OR-9
Cabot Park—*park* MA-1
Cabot Plains—*locale* VT-1
Cabot Point—*cape* WI-6
Cabot Pond—*reservoir* MA-1
**Cabot (RR name Big Mountain)**—*pop pl* WV-2
Cabot Sch—*school* MA-1
*Cabot's Pond* NH-1
**Cabot Station**—*pop pl* WV-2
Cabot Station Power Plant Dam—*dam* MA-1
Cabot Street Shop Ctr / Professional Building—*locale* MA-1
**Cabot (Town of)**—*pop pl* VT-1
*Cabotville, Town of* MA-1
Cabra Canyon—*valley* (2) NM-5
Cabra Creek—*stream* NM-5
Cabra de Tierra—*cape* PR-3
Cabra Hill—*summit* NM-5
Cabras Island—*island* GU-9
Cabras Islands—*area* AK-9
Cabra Spring—*spring* NM-5
Cabra Springs Ranch—*locale* NM-5
Cabrero Canyon—*valley* NM-5
Cabresto Canyon—*valley* NM-5
Cabresto Creek—*stream* NM-5
Cabresto Lake—*lake* NM-5
Cabresto Mesa—*summit* NM-5
Cabresto Mesa Tower Complex (LA 2138)—*hist pl* NM-5
Cabresto Park—*park* NM-5
Cabresto Peak—*summit* NM-5
Cabretta Creek—*stream* GA-3
Cabretta Inlet—*channel* GA-3
Cabretta Island—*island* GA-3
*Cabrie Island* SD-7
Cabrillo—*park* CA-9
Cabrillo—*uninc pl* CA-9
Cabrillo, Cerro—*summit* CA-9
Cabrillo Ave Sch—*school* CA-9
Cabrillo Beach Park—*beach* CA-9
Cabrillo Bridge—*bridge* CA-9
Cabrillo Coll—*school* CA-9
**Cabrillo Estates**—*pop pl* CA-9
Cabrillo Harbor—*bay* CA-9
Cabrillo Heights Park—*park* CA-9
Cabrillo Lane Sch—*school* CA-9
Cabrillo Natl Monmt—*hist pl* CA-9
Cabrillo Natl Monmt—*park* CA-9
Cabrillo Park—*park* CA-9
Cabrillo Pavillion—*building* CA-9
Cabrillo Playground—*park* CA-9
Cabrillo Sch—*school* (7) CA-9
Cabrini Canyon—*valley* CA-9
Cabrini Coll—*school* PA-2
Cabrini HS—*school* LA-4
Cabrini Sch—*school* TX-5
*Cabri River* SD-7
Cabritaberg—*locale* VI-3
Cabrita Hill—*summit* VI-3
Cabrita Point—*cape* VI-3
Cabritte Horn Point—*cape* VI-3
Cabs Creek—*gut* NC-3
*Cabt Creek* IN-6
*Cabusto* AL-4
Cabwaylingo State For—*forest* WV-2
Cacabic Lake—*lake* MN-6
C A Caines Lake—*reservoir* AL-4
C A Caines Lake Dam—*dam* AL-4
CA Camp—*locale* NM-5
C A Camp—*locale* NM-5
Cacanaugh Creek—*stream* CA-9
Cacannen Sch—*school* IN-6
**Cacao**—*pop pl* PR-3
Cacao Alto (Barrio)—*fmr MCD* PR-3
Cacao Bajo (Barrio)—*fmr MCD* PR-3
Cacao (Barrio)—*fmr MCD* (2) PR-3
Cacaos (Barrio)—*fmr MCD* PR-3
*Cacapon Bubbling Spring Camps* WV-2
Cacapon (Magisterial District)—*fmr MCD* WV-2
Cacapon Mtn—*summit* VA-3
Cacapon Mtn—*summit* (2) WV-2
Cacapon River—*stream* WV-2
*Cacapon Springs* WV-2
Cacapon State Park—*park* WV-2
*Cacawa Island* MD-2
*Cacawa Point* MD-2
Cacaway Island—*island* MD-2
Cacaway Point—*cape* MD-2
*Cacawonch Pond* RI-1
**Cacema Town (historical)**—*pop pl* FL-3
*Cachagua Creek* CA-9
Cachagua Creek—*stream* CA-9
Cachana Arroyo—*stream* NM-5
Cachana Spring—*spring* NM-5
*Cachate Creek* TX-5
Cache—*locale* AK-9
Cache—*locale* ID-8
**Cache**—*pop pl* IL-6
**Cache**—*pop pl* OK-5
Cache, The—*other* AK-9
Cache Bar—*bar* ID-8
Cache Bayou—*stream* AR-4
Cache Bottom—*flat* OK-5
Cachebox Creek—*stream* OR-9
Cachebox Meadow—*flat* OR-9
Cache Butte—*summit* UT-8
Cache Butte—*summit* WA-9
Cache Cabin—*locale* CA-9
Cache-Cache Bayou—*stream* LA-4
Cache Camp—*locale* CA-9
Cache Camp—*locale* OR-9
Cache Canyon—*valley* OR-9
Cache Cave—*cave* UT-8
Cache Cave Creek—*stream* UT-8
Cache Cave Draw—*valley* NV-8
Cache Cem—*cemetery* OK-5
Cache Chapel—*church* IL-6
Cache Cienega—*flat* AZ-5
Cache Clawson Cem—*cemetery* ID-8
Cache Col—*gap* WA-9
Cache Coulee—*valley* (2) MT-8
Cache County—*civil* UT-8
*Cache Cove Creek* UT-8
*Cache Creek* CA-9
*Cache Creek* IL-6
*Cache Creek* MT-8
*Cache Creek* OK-5
**Cache Creek**—*pop pl* CA-9
Cache Creek—*stream* (6) AK-9
Cache Creek—*stream* (3) CA-9
Cache Creek—*stream* (3) CO-8
Cache Creek—*stream* (7) ID-8
Cache Creek—*stream* (5) MT-8
Cache Creek—*stream* NE-7
Cache Creek—*stream* (2) OK-5
Cache Creek—*stream* (4) OR-9
Cache Creek—*stream* TX-5
Cache Creek—*stream* (6) WA-9
Cache Creek—*stream* (3) WY-8
Cache Creek Cabin—*locale* ID-8
Cache Creek Cem—*cemetery* OK-5
Cache Creek Cem—*cemetery* TX-5
Cache Creek Lakes—*lake* ID-8
Cache Creek Oil Field—*oilfield* OK-5
Cache Creek Patrol Cabin—*locale* WY-8
Cache Creek Ranger Station—*locale* MT-8
Cache Creek Ridge—*ridge* CA-9
Cache Creek Settling Basin—*basin* CA-9
Cache Creek Toll Station—*locale* OR-9
Cache Creek Valley Sch—*school* NE-7
Cached Lake—*lake* OR-9
Cache (Election Precinct)—*fmr MCD* (2) IL-6
Cache Fork—*stream* AR-4
Cache Hollow—*valley* IL-6
Cache Indian Mission—*church* OK-5
Cache Island—*island* AK-9
Cache Island—*island* KY-4
Cache Junction—*locale* UT-8
*Cache Lake* OR-9
Cache Lake—*lake* (2) AK-9
Cache Lake—*lake* MI-6
Cache Lake—*lake* MN-6
Cache Lake—*lake* OR-9
Cache Lake—*lake* WY-8
Cache Lake—*locale* AR-4
Cache Lake Ch—*church* AR-4
Cache Lake Trail—*trail* OR-9
Cache la Poudre Monmt—*park* CO-8
Cache la Poudre Reservoir Inlet—*canal* CO-8
*Cache lapoudre River* CO-8
Cache La Poudre River—*stream* CO-8
Cache la Poudre Sch—*school* CO-8
Cache Meadow—*flat* OR-9
Cache Meadows—*flat* ID-8
Cache Mtn—*summit* AK-9
Cache Mtn—*summit* OR-9
Cache Mtn—*summit* WY-8
*Cache Natl Forest-in part* UT-8
Cache One Lake—*lake* AK-9
Cache Peak—*summit* CA-9
Cache Peak—*summit* ID-8
Cache Peak—*summit* WY-8
Cache River—*stream* AR-4
Cache River—*stream* IL-6
Cache River—*stream* UT-8
Cache River Ditch—*canal* MO-7
Cache River Ditch No 1—*canal* AR-4
Cache Saddle—*gap* ID-8
Cache Saddle—*gap* MT-8
Cache Slough—*stream* CA-9
*Cache Slough Gas Field* CA-9
Cache (Township of)—*fmr MCD* (6) AR-4
Cache Valley—*valley* ID-8
Cache Valley—*valley* (2) UT-8
Cache Valley Bible Ch—*church* UT-8
Cache Valley Ch—*church* AR-4
Cache Valley Creek—*stream* UT-8
Cache Valley Shopping Mall—*locale* UT-8
Cache Valley Wash—*valley* UT-8
Cache Wye—*locale* OK-5
Cachil Dehe Rancheria (Indian Reservation)—*reserve* CA-9
Cachucha Windmill—*locale* TX-5
*Cachuma* CA-9
Cachuma, Lake—*reservoir* CA-9
Cachuma Bay—*bay* CA-9
**Cachuma (Cachuma Lake Recreation Area)**—*pop pl* CA-9
Cachuma Camp—*locale* CA-9
Cachuma County Park—*park* CA-9
Cachuma Creek—*stream* CA-9
Cachuma Dam—*dam* CA-9
*Cachuma Lake* CA-9
Cachuma Mtn—*summit* CA-9
Cachuma Point—*cape* CA-9
Cachuma Rec Area—*park* CA-9
*Cachuma Reservoir* CA-9
Cachuma Saddle Guard Station—*locale* CA-9
**Cachuma Village**—*pop pl* CA-9
Cackler Cem—*cemetery* OH-6
Cackler Sch—*school* IA-7
Cackley Swamp—*swamp* OH-6
Cacklin Lou Rsvr—*reservoir* WY-8
Cacona Creek—*stream* WY-8
Cacoosing—*locale* PA-2
Cacoosing Creek—*stream* PA-2
**Cacoossing**—*pop pl* PA-2
*C A Creek* AZ-5
Cactus—*locale* CA-9
Cactus—*locale* TX-5
Cactus—*locale* WA-9
**Cactus**—*pop pl* AZ-5
**Cactus**—*pop pl* TX-5
Cactus Basin—*basin* AZ-5
Cactus Bay—*bay* CA-9
Cactus Branch—*stream* TX-5
Cactus Butte—*summit* AZ-5
Cactus Butte Spring—*spring* AZ-5
*Cactus Canyon* AZ-5
Cactus Canyon—*valley* (2) AZ-5
Cactus Cem—*cemetery* TX-5
**Cactus City**—*pop pl* CA-9
**Cactus Cove**—*pop pl* TN-4
Cactus Cove Trailer Park—*locale* AZ-5
*Cactus Creek* CA-9
Cactus Creek—*stream* ID-8
Cactus Creek—*stream* KS-7
Cactus Creek—*stream* TX-5
Cactus Dam—*dam* AZ-5
Cactus Drive Sch—*school* TX-5
*Cactus Flat* SD-7
Cactus Flat—*flat* AZ-5
Cactus Flat—*flat* (2) CA-9
Cactus Flat—*flat* MT-8
Cactus Flat—*flat* NV-8
Cactus Flat—*flat* (2) NM-5
Cactus Flat—*flat* UT-8
Cactus Flat—*flat* WY-8
**Cactus Flat**—*pop pl* AZ-5
**Cactus Flat**—*pop pl* SD-7
Cactus Flat Draw—*valley* NM-5
Cactus Flat Draw—*valley* WY-8
*Cactus Flat Junction* SD-7
Cactus Flat Lake—*lake* NM-5
*Cactus Flats* MT-8
Cactus Flats—*flat* SD-7
Cactus Flats—*flat* TX-5
Cactus Flats—*flat* UT-8
Cactus Flats—*locale* SD-7
Cactus Flats Windmill—*locale* TX-5
Cactus Flat Tank—*reservoir* NM-5
Cactus Flat Tanks—*reservoir* NM-5
Cactus Flat Windmill—*locale* AZ-5
Cactus Flat Windmill—*locale* CO-8
Cactus Flat Windmill—*locale* TX-5
**Cactus Forest**—*pop pl* AZ-5
**Cactus Gale V (subdivision)**—*pop pl* (2) AZ-5
Cactus Garden—*area* CA-9
Cactus Gardens Mobile Home Park—*locale* AZ-5
**Cactus Heights (subdivision)**—*pop pl* SD-7
**Cactus Hill**—*pop pl* MD-2
Cactus Hill—*summit* OK-5
Cactus Hill Lateral—*canal* CO-8
Cactus Hill Ranch—*locale* AZ-5
Cactus Hills—*range* SD-7
Cactus Hills Country Club—*locale* SD-7
Cactus (historical)—*locale* KS-7
Cactus Inn—*hist pl* AZ-5
Cactus Islands—*island* WA-9
Cactus Lake—*lake* OH-6
Cactus Lakes—*lake* NM-5
Cactus Mine—*mine* CA-9
Cactus Mine—*mine* (2) UT-8
*Cactus Mountain* CA-9
Cactus Mtn—*summit* (2) AZ-5
Cactus Mtn—*summit* CO-8
Cactus Mtn—*summit* OR-9
Cactus Park—*flat* (2) CO-8
Cactus Park—*flat* TX-5
Cactus Park—*park* AZ-5
Cactus Park—*park* CO-8
Cactus Park—*park* UT-8
*Cactus Pass* AZ-5
Cactus Peak—*summit* (2) CA-9
Cactus Peak—*summit* NV-8
Cactus Peak—*summit* NM-5
Cactus Picnic Area—*park* AZ-5
*Cactus Plain* AZ-5
Cactus Plain—*plain* AZ-5
Cactus Plaza Shop Ctr—*locale* AZ-5
Cactus Point—*cape* AK-9
Cactus Point—*cape* CA-9
Cactus Point—*cape* FL-3
Cactus Point—*cape* NM-5
Cactus Point—*summit* CA-9
Cactus Pond—*lake* UT-8
Cactus Press-Plaza Paint Bldg—*hist pl* AZ-5
Cactus Queen Mine—*mine* AZ-5
Cactus Queen Mine—*mine* CA-9
Cactus Range—*range* NV-8
Cactus Rat Mine—*mine* UT-8
*Cactus Ridge* CA-9
Cactus Ridge—*ridge* AZ-5
Cactus Ridge—*ridge* OR-9
Cactus Rsvr—*reservoir* CO-8
Cactus Sandy Point—*cape* NC-3
Cactus Sch—*school* WY-8
Cactus Spring—*spring* (2) CA-9
Cactus Spring—*spring* (2) NV-8
Cactus Springs—*locale* NV-8
Cactus Spring Trail—*trail* CA-9
Cactus Tank—*reservoir* AZ-5
Cactus Tank—*reservoir* (2) NM-5
Cactus Tank—*reservoir* TX-5
Cactus Valley—*basin* CO-8
Cactus Valley—*valley* (2) CA-9
Cactus View School—*locale* CO-8
**Cactus Villa (subdivision)**—*pop pl* (2) AZ-5
Cactus Well—*well* AZ-5
Cactus Windmill—*locale* NM-5
Cactus Wren Mobile Park—*locale* AZ-5
Cad—*locale* GA-3
Cadams—*locale* NE-7
**Cadamy**—*pop pl* MS-4
*Cadanassa* CA-9
**Cadaretta**—*pop pl* MS-4
Cadaughrity Sch—*school* NY-2
Cadaver Gap—*gap* WA-9
Cad Bench—*bench* UT-8
Caddell—*locale* WV-2
Caddell Branch—*stream* KY-4
Caddell Island—*island* AL-4
Caddell Lake—*reservoir* AL-4
Caddell Lake Dam—*dam* AL-4
Caddell Mine—*mine* CO-8
*Caddells Bend* AL-4
Caddels Ford—*locale* AL-4
Caddenhead Prairie Branch—*stream* TX-5
Cadd Fire Trail—*trail* CA-9
Caddie Woodlawn Park—*park* WI-6
Caddin Bridge Swamp—*swamp* SC-3
*Caddington Peak* ID-8
Caddis Creek—*stream* MI-6
*Caddis Lake* AL-4
Caddis Lake Dam—*dam* AL-4
*Caddle Creek* NC-3
Caddle Creek—*stream* KY-4
Caddle Creek—*stream* NC-3
*Caddle Island* AL-4
Caddle Landing—*locale* AL-4
Caddo—*locale* KY-4
Caddo—*locale* (2) TX-5
**Caddo**—*pop pl* AL-4
**Caddo**—*pop pl* MO-7
**Caddo**—*pop pl* OK-5
Caddo—*uninc pl* LA-4
Caddoa—*locale* CO-8
**Caddoa**—*pop pl* CO-8
Caddoa Creek—*stream* CO-8
Caddo Bay—*bay* TX-5
Caddo Cake Reach—*channel* TX-5
Caddo Canyon—*valley* AZ-5
Caddo Cave—*cave* AL-4
Caddo Cem—*cemetery* OK-5
Caddo Cem—*cemetery* (2) TX-5
Caddo Ch—*church* OK-5
Caddo Community Bldg—*hist pl* OK-5
Caddo Community Chapel—*church* LA-4
Caddo Correctional Institute—*locale* LA-4
Caddo Country Club—*other* OK-5
**Caddo (County)**—*pop pl* OK-5
Caddo Creek—*stream* (2) OK-5
Caddo Creek—*stream* (5) TX-5
*Caddo Fork of Sabine River* TX-5
*Caddo Fork of the Sabine River* TX-5
Caddo Gap—*gap* AR-4
**Caddo Gap**—*pop pl* AR-4
Caddo Heights Sch—*school* LA-4
Caddo Hill—*summit* OK-5
Caddo Hills—*range* OK-5
Caddo Hills Sch—*school* AR-4
Caddo Inlet—*channel* TX-5
Caddo-Kiowa Vocational-Technical Center—*school* OK-5
Caddo Lake—*reservoir* LA-4
Caddo Lake—*reservoir* OK-5
Caddo Lake—*reservoir* (2) TX-5
Caddo Lake State Park—*park* TX-5
**Caddo Mills**—*pop pl* TX-5
Caddo Mills (CCD)—*cens area* TX-5
Caddo Mountains—*ridge* AR-4
Caddo Oil Field—*oilfield* LA-4
**Caddo Parish**—*pop pl* LA-4
Caddo Parish Penal Farm—*locale* LA-4
Caddo Peak—*summit* TX-5
Caddo Peak Cem—*cemetery* TX-5
Caddo-Pine Island Oil and Gas Field—*oilfield* LA-4
Caddo Point—*cliff* AZ-5
Caddo Point Tank—*reservoir* AZ-5
Caddo Pool Oil Field—*oilfield* OK-5
Caddo Post Office (historical)—*building* AL-4
Caddo Prairie Ch—*church* LA-4
Caddo River—*stream* AR-4
Caddo (Township of)—*fmr MCD* (2) AR-4
**Caddo Valley**—*pop pl* AR-4
Cadduggen Creek—*stream* NC-3
Caddy, Bayou—*bay* AL-4
Caddy, Bayou—*stream* MS-4
Caddy, Point—*cape* AL-4
*Caddy Brook* MA-1
Caddy Canyon—*valley* ID-8
Caddy Cemetery, Bayou—*cemetery* MS-4
Caddy Creek—*stream* UT-8
*Caddy Mountain* CA-9
**Caddy Vista**—*pop pl* WI-6
Caddy Vista Sch—*school* WI-6
Cade—*locale* OK-5
**Cade**—*pop pl* LA-4
Cade, Lake De—*lake* LA-4
Cade Archeol District—*hist pl* WI-6
Cade Bar—*bar* (2) AL-4
Cade Bend—*bend* AL-4
Cade Bend Landing (historical)—*locale* AL-4
Cade Branch—*stream* TN-4
Cade Branch—*stream* TX-5
Cade Cem—*cemetery* MS-4
Cade Chapel—*church* GA-3
Cade Chapel—*church* TX-5
Cade Chapel Missionary Baptist Ch—*church* MS-4
Cade Creek—*stream* CA-9
Cade Creek—*stream* CO-8
Cade Creek—*stream* TX-5
**Cade Hill (subdivision)**—*pop pl* NC-3
Cade Hole—*lake* TX-5
Cade Hollow—*valley* OH-6
Cade Hollow—*valley* TX-5
Cade Lake—*lake* MI-6
Cade Lake—*lake* TX-5
Cade Lakes—*reservoir* TX-5
**Cadelaria**—*pop pl* TX-5
Cadell Branch—*stream* TX-5
Cadell Creek—*stream* TX-5
Cade Mtn—*summit* CA-9
Cade Mtn—*summit* CO-8
Cadena Creek—*stream* TX-5
Cadenas Cem—*cemetery* TX-5
Cadenasso—*locale* CA-9
**Cadentown**—*pop pl* KY-4
Cadenza Creek—*stream* OR-9
Cadera Lateral—*canal* CA-9
Cade Ranch—*locale* CO-8
Cadero Ch—*church* FL-3
**Cades**—*pop pl* AR-4
**Cades**—*pop pl* SC-3
**Cades**—*pop pl* TN-4
*Cades Bar* AL-4
*Cades Branch* DE-2
Cades Branch—*stream* TN-4
Cades (CCD)—*cens area* SC-3
Cades Chapel—*church* AL-4
Cades Cove—*locale* TN-4
Cades Cove—*valley* TN-4
Cades Cove Bloomery Forge (historical)—*locale* TN-4
Cades Cove Cem—*cemetery* TN-4
Cades Cove Hist Dist—*hist pl* TN-4
Cades Cove Memorial Ch—*church* TN-4
Cades Cove Methodist Ch—*church* TN-4
Cades Cove Missionary Baptist Ch—*church* TN-4
Cades Cove Mtn—*summit* TN-4
Cades Cove Post Office (historical)—*building* TN-4
Cades Cove Primitive Baptist Ch—*church* TN-4
Cades Ferry (historical)—*crossing* TN-4
Cades Lake—*reservoir* MS-4
*Cades Pond* DE-2
Cades Post Office (historical)—*building* TN-4
Cade Spring—*spring* TX-5
**Cadet**—*pop pl* CO-8
**Cadet**—*pop pl* MO-7
**Cadet**—*pop pl* TX-5
**Cadet**—*pop pl* VA-3
Cadet, Point—*cape* MS-4
*Cadet Creek* WA-9
Cadet Creek—*stream* (2) MO-7
Cadet Creek—*stream* WA-9
Cadet Creek Cem—*cemetery* MO-7
Cadet Lake—*lake* WA-9
Cadet Peak—*summit* WA-9
*Cadet Point* MS-4
*Cadets Pond* MA-1
Cadette Creek—*stream* MT-8
Cadet Trough Spring—*spring* NV-8
Cadeville—*locale* LA-4
*Cadew Creek* KS-7
Cad Gap—*gap* GA-3
Cadick Apartments (Plaza Building)—*hist pl* IN-6
Cadillac—*locale* FL-3
Cadillac—*locale* MS-4
**Cadillac**—*pop pl* MI-6
Cadillac, Lake—*lake* MI-6
Cadillac Camp—*locale* MI-6
Cadillac Cliffs—*cliff* ME-1
Cadillac Creek—*stream* AK-9
Cadillac Drain—*canal* MI-6
**Cadillac Estates (subdivision)**—*pop pl* AL-4
Cadillac (historical)—*locale* SD-7
Cadillac Lake—*reservoir* KS-7
Cadillac Lookout Tower—*locale* MI-6
Cadillac Memorial Gardens East—*cemetery* MI-6
Cadillac Memorial Gardens West Cem—*cemetery* MI-6
Cadillac Mtn—*summit* ME-1
Cadillac Sch—*school* (2) MI-6
Cadillac Soo Camp 14—*locale* MI-6
Cadillac Square—*locale* MI-6
Cadillac Tank—*reservoir* (2) AZ-5
**Cadillac Township**—*pop pl* SD-7
Cadillac Wash—*stream* AZ-5
Cadilloso Arroyo—*stream* CO-8
Cadillo Windmill—*locale* TX-5
Cadis—*locale* PA-2
Cadiz—*locale* IL-6
Cadiz—*locale* TX-5
**Cadiz**—*pop pl* CA-9
**Cadiz**—*pop pl* IN-6
**Cadiz**—*pop pl* KY-4
**Cadiz**—*pop pl* NY-2
**Cadiz**—*pop pl* OH-6
Cadiz (CCD)—*cens area* KY-4
Cadiz Center Sch—*school* WI-6
Cadiz Country Club—*other* OH-6
Cadiz Downtown Hist Dist—*hist pl* KY-4
Cadiz Draw—*valley* WY-8
*Cadiz Dry Lake* CA-9
**Cadiz Junction**—*pop pl* OH-6
Cadiz Lake—*lake* CA-9
Cadiz Masonic Lodge No. 121 F. and A.M.—*hist pl* KY-4
Cadiz Run—*stream* IN-6
Cadiz Street Viaduct—*bridge* TX-5
Cadiz Summit—*gap* CA-9
**Cadiz (Town of)**—*pop pl* WI-6
**Cadiz (Township of)**—*pop pl* OH-6
Cadiz Valley—*valley* CA-9
Cadiz West (CCD)—*cens area* KY-4
Cadjaw Dam—*dam* PA-2
Cadjaw Pond—*reservoir* PA-2
Cad Lake—*lake* MN-6
Cadle Butte—*summit* OR-9
Cadle Creek—*bay* MD-2
Cadle Creek—*stream* MS-4
Cadle Creek—*stream* OR-9
Cadle Creek Marsh—*swamp* MD-2
Cadle Hill—*summit* OR-9
Cadle (historical)—*locale* AL-4
Cadley—*locale* GA-3
Cadman Cove—*cove* MA-1
Cadman Creek—*stream* NY-2
Cadman Creek—*stream* WA-9
Cadman Neck—*cape* MA-1
Cadman Plaza—*locale* NY-2
Cadman Sch—*school* CA-9
**Cadmus**—*pop pl* KS-7
**Cadmus**—*pop pl* MI-6
**Cadmus**—*pop pl* OH-6
Cadmus Cem—*cemetery* KS-7
Cadmus Drain—*stream* MI-6
Cadmus-Folly House—*hist pl* NJ-2
Cadmus House—*hist pl* NJ-2
Cadmus Sch—*school* KS-7
Cadney, Bayou—*gut* LA-4
Cadoceras Creek—*stream* AK-9
Cadoche, Bayou—*gut* LA-4
**Cadogan**—*pop pl* PA-2
Cadogan Point—*cape* MI-6
**Cadogan (Township of)**—*pop pl* PA-2
Cadoma—*locale* WY-8
Cadon Branch—*stream* NC-3
Cadon Gap—*gap* NC-3
**Cadosia**—*pop pl* NY-2
Cadosia Creek—*stream* NY-2
Cados Negros Windmill—*locale* TX-5
Cadot Hill—*summit* OH-6
**Cadott**—*pop pl* WI-6
*Cadotte Creek* MT-8
Cadotte Creek—*stream* MT-8
Cadotte Island (historical)—*island* SD-7
Cadotte Lake—*lake* MN-6
Cadotte Lake—*lake* (2) WI-6
Cadotte Pass—*gap* MT-8
*Cadotte's Pass* MT-8
Cadottes Point—*cape* MI-6
Cadottes Wood Yard (historical)—*locale* SD-7
*Cadott Pass* MT-8
*Cadott's Pass* MT-8
Cadron Creek—*stream* AR-4
Cadron Gap—*gap* AR-4
Cadron Ridge—*ridge* AR-4
Cadron Ridge Ch—*church* AR-4
Cadron Settlement—*hist pl* AR-4
Cadron (Township of)—*fmr MCD* (4) AR-4
Cadron Valley—*valley* AR-4
Cadron Valley Cem—*cemetery* AR-4
Cadro Pass—*gut* LA-4
Cadro Spring—*spring* NV-8
Cads Crotch—*basin* UT-8
*Cadtanmut* MA-1
*Cadue Creek* KS-7
Cadwalader Park—*park* NJ-2
Cadwalader Sch—*school* NJ-2
Cadwallader Cem—*cemetery* OH-6
*Cadwallader Park* NJ-2
Cadwallader Park—*park* CA-9
Cadwallader Sch—*school* TX-5
**Cadwell**—*pop pl* CA-9
**Cadwell**—*pop pl* GA-3
**Cadwell**—*pop pl* IL-6
*Cadwell Brook* MA-1
Cadwell Brook—*stream* MA-1
Cadwell (CCD)—*cens area* GA-3
Cadwell Cem—*cemetery* IL-6
Cadwell Creek—*stream* IL-6
Cadwell Creek—*stream* MA-1
Cadwell Creek—*stream* VA-3
Cadwell (historical)—*locale* SD-7
Cadwell Memorial For—*forest* MA-1
Cadwell Sch (historical)—*school* SD-7
Cadwells Corners—*locale* NY-2
Cadwell Slough—*stream* WY-8
Cady—*locale* VA-3
**Cady**—*pop pl* MI-6
Cady, John, House—*hist pl* CT-1
Cady, Lucinda, House—*hist pl* DC-2
*Cady Brook* MA-1
Cady Brook—*stream* CT-1
Cady Brook—*stream* (2) MA-1
Cady Brook—*stream* (2) NY-2
Cady Brook—*stream* VT-1
Cady Cem—*cemetery* IL-6
Cady Cem—*cemetery* IA-7
Cady Coulee—*valley* MT-8
*Cady Creek* OR-9
*Cady Creek* WA-9
Cady Creek—*stream* MI-6
Cady Creek—*stream* MT-8
Cady Creek—*stream* NE-7
Cady Creek—*stream* OR-9
Cady Creek—*stream* SD-7
Cady Creek—*stream* VA-3
Cady Creek—*stream* WA-9
Cady Creek—*stream* WI-6
*Cady Falls* MA-1
Cady Hill—*summit* VT-1
**Cady Hills (subdivision)**—*pop pl* MS-4
Cady Hollow—*valley* PA-2
Cady House—*hist pl* CA-9
*Cady Lake* MI-6
Cady Lake—*lake* (3) MI-6
Cady Lake—*lake* WA-9
Cady Lake—*reservoir* NC-3
Cady Lake—*reservoir* VA-3
Cady Lake—*swamp* SD-7
Cady Lake Dam—*dam* NC-3
Cady Landing—*locale* NC-3
Cady Marsh Ditch—*canal* IN-6
Cady Mountains—*range* CA-9
Cady Mtn—*summit* WA-9
Cady Pass—*gap* (2) WA-9
Cady Point—*cape* WA-9
Cady Pond—*lake* CT-1
Cady Pond—*lake* MA-1
Cady Ridge—*ridge* WA-9
*Cady River* MA-1
Cady Run—*stream* OH-6
Cady Sch—*school* MI-6
Cady Sch—*school* VT-1
**Cadys Corners**—*pop pl* MA-1
**Cadys Falls**—*pop pl* VT-1
Cady Spring—*spring* CA-9
**Cady (Town of)**—*pop pl* WI-6
**Cadyville**—*pop pl* NY-2
Cady Vly—*swamp* NY-2
Cady-Wilson Sch—*school* WI-6
*Caep Himloop* DE-2
*Caep May* NJ-2
**Caernarvon**—*pop pl* LA-4
Caernarvon Cem—*cemetery* PA-2
**Caernarvon (Township of)**—*pop pl* (2) PA-2
*Caernovan* LA-4
Caesar—*locale* TX-5
**Caesar**—*pop pl* MS-4
**Caesar**—*pop pl* TX-5
Caesar, Mount—*summit* CT-1
Caesar, Mount—*summit* NH-1
Caesar Artesian Well—*well* TX-5
Caesar Austin Branch—*stream* NC-3
Caesar Ch—*church* MS-4
*Caesar Creek* LA-4
Caesar Creek—*channel* FL-3
Caesar Creek—*stream* AL-4
Caesar Creek—*stream* CO-8
Caesar Creek—*stream* FL-3
Caesar Creek—*stream* IL-6
Caesar Creek—*stream* IN-6
Caesar Creek—*stream* LA-4
Caesar Creek—*stream* OH-6
Caesar Creek Bank—*bar* FL-3
Caesar Creek Cem—*cemetery* OH-6
Caesar Creek Ch—*church* OH-6
Caesar Creek Lake—*reservoir* OH-6
*Caesar Creek Rsvr* OH-6
Caesar Creek Sch—*school* OH-6
Caesar Creek (Township of)—*civ div* IN-6
Caesar Ditch—*canal* CA-9
Caesarea Ch—*church* KY-4
Caesarea Ch—*church* OH-6
Caesar Gap—*gap* GA-3
Caesar Grande Water Hole—*reservoir* TX-5

Calamity Creek ... TX-5
Calamity Creek—stream (2) ... AK-9
Calamity Creek—stream ... CO-8
Calamity Creek—stream (3) ... ID-8
Calamity Creek—stream (2) ... OR-9
Calamity Creek—stream ... TX-5
Calamity Creek—stream ... WA-9
Calamity Creek Wash—valley ... TX-5
Calamity Draw—valley ... CO-8
Calamity Falls—falls ... MT-8
Calamity Forest Camp—locale ... OR-9
Calamity Guard Station—locale ... ID-8
Calamity Gulch—valley ... AK-9
Calamity Gulch—valley ... MT-8
Calamity Gulch—valley ... SD-7
Calamity Gulch—valley ... WY-8
Calamity Hollow—valley (2) ... PA-2
Calamity Jane Horse Cache—bench ... MT-8
Calamity Lake—lake ... MN-6
Calamity Meadows—flat ... ID-8
Calamity Mesa—summit ... CO-8
Calamity Mesa—summit ... UT-8
Calamity Mines—mine ... CO-8
Calamity Mtn—summit ... NY-2
Calamity Pass—gap ... CO-8
Calamity Peak—summit ... SD-7
Calamity Peak—summit ... WA-9
Calamity Peak Trail—trail ... WA-9
Calamity Point ... WA-9
Calamity Point—summit ... ID-8
Calamity Pond—lake ... NY-2
Calamity Ridge—ridge ... CO-8
Calamity Wash—stream ... AZ-5
Calamo Branch—stream ... VA-3
Calamoutier—locale ... OH-6
Calams Run—stream ... MD-2
**Calamus**—pop pl ... IA-7
Calamus, Bayou—stream ... LA-4
Calamus Consolidated Sch—school ... IA-7
Calamus Creek—stream (4) ... IA-7
Calamus Creek—stream ... MN-6
Calamus Creek—stream ... WI-6
Calamus Lake—lake ... IL-6
Calamus River—stream ... NE-7
Calamus Rsvr—reservoir ... NE-7
Calamus Run—stream ... PA-2
Calamus Sch "District #50"—school ... NE-7
**Calamus (Town of)**—pop pl ... WI-6
Calamut Lake—lake ... OR-9
Calamut Way—trail ... OR-9
Calandaqua ... PA-2
**Calann Subdivision**—pop pl ... UT-8
Calapooia—locale ... OR-9
Calapooia (CCD)—cens area ... OR-9
Calapooia Creek ... OR-9
Calapooia Mountains ... OR-9
Calapooia River—stream ... OR-9
Calapooya ... OR-9
Calapooya Creek—stream ... OR-9
Calapooya Divide—ridge ... OR-9
Calapooya JHS—school ... OR-9
Calapooya Mountains—range ... OR-9
Calapooya River ... OR-9
Calapooya Trail—trail ... OR-9
Calapooya Way—trail ... OR-9
Calaroga Sch—school ... CA-9
Calatea ... CO-8
CA Lateral—canal ... TX-5
Calavale Brook—stream ... VT-1
Calavant Hill—summit ... NH-1
Calavary Cem—cemetery ... NY-2
Calavazas Windmill—locale ... TX-5
Calavera, Cerro De La—summit ... CA-9
Calavera Canyon—valley ... NV-8
Calavera Lake—reservoir ... CA-9
**Calaveras**—pop pl ... TX-5
Calaveras—uninc pl ... CA-9
Calaveras, Canada De Las—valley ... CA-9
Calaveras Bigtree Natl For—forest ... CA-9
Calaveras Big Trees State Park—park ... CA-9
Calaveras Canyon—valley ... NM-5
Calaveras Cem—cemetery ... TX-5
Calaveras Central Mine—mine ... CA-9
**Calaveras (County)**—pop pl ... CA-9
Calaveras County Bank—hist pl ... CA-9
Calaveras County Courthouse—hist pl ... CA-9
Calaveras Creek ... CA-9
Calaveras Creek—stream ... CA-9
Calaveras Creek—stream (2) ... TX-5
Calaveras Creek Dam No 3—dam ... TX-5
Calaveras Creek Dam Number 10—dam ... TX-5
Calaveras Creek Dam Number 5—dam ... TX-5
Calaveras Creek Dam Number 6—dam ... TX-5
Calaveras Creek Dam Number 7—dam ... TX-5
Calaveras Creek Dam Number 8—dam ... TX-5
Calaveras Creek Dam Number 9—dam ... TX-5
Calaveras Dome—cliff ... CA-9
Calaveras Lake—reservoir ... TX-5
Calaveras Lake Park—park ... TX-5
Calaveras Mine—mine ... CA-9
Calaveras Point—cape ... CA-9
Calaveras Public Utility Ditch—canal ... CA-9
Calaveras Ranger Station—locale ... CA-9
Calaveras River ... CA-9
Calaveras River—stream ... CA-9
Calaveras Rsvr—reservoir (2) ... CA-9
Calaveras Test Site—locale ... CA-9
Calaveras Valley—valley ... CA-9
Calaveras Well—well ... TX-5
**Calaveras Yacht and Country Club Estates**—pop pl ... CA-9
**Calaveritas**—pop pl ... CA-9
Calaveritas Creek—stream ... CA-9
**Calavo Gardens**—pop pl ... CA-9
Calawah Ridge—ridge ... WA-9
Calawah River—stream ... WA-9
Calawah Shelter—locale ... WA-9
Calaway Cem—cemetery ... AR-4
Calaway Slope Mine (underground)—mine ... AL-4
Calbaugh Cem—cemetery ... TN-4
Calbeck Mtn—summit ... GA-3
Calbero Artesian Well—well ... TX-5
Calbert Sch—school ... WV-2
Calbet Slough—swamp ... FL-3
Calbick Creek—stream ... MT-8
Calbick Creek Trail—trail ... MT-8
Cal Bluff Ch—church ... MS-4
Calbraith Mine—mine ... MN-6
Cal Branch—stream ... MS-4
Cal Branch—stream ... TN-4
Cal Branch—stream ... TX-5
Cal Canyon—valley ... NM-5
Calcasieu ... LA-4
**Calcasieu**—pop pl (2) ... LA-4
Calcasieu Ch—church ... LA-4
Calcasieu Lake—lake ... LA-4
Calcasieu Landing ... LA-4
Calcasieu Light—locale ... LA-4
Calcasieu Locks—dam ... LA-4
**Calcasieu Parish**—pop pl ... LA-4
Calcasieu Pass—channel ... LA-4
Calcasieu Point—cape ... TX-5
Calcasieu River—stream ... LA-4
Calcasieu Ship Channel—channel ... LA-4
Calcedeaver Sch—school ... AL-4
Calcedonia Baptist Church ... AL-4
Calcedonia Cem—cemetery ... AL-4
Calcedonia Ch—church (2) ... AL-4
Cal Cem—cemetery (2) ... AL-4
Calcetin Artesian Well—well ... TX-5
**Calciana**—pop pl ... NY-2
Calcie Gulch—valley ... MT-8
**Calcis**—pop pl ... AL-4
Calcite ... MI-6
Calcite—locale ... CO-8
**Calcite**—pop pl ... MI-6
Calcite, The—mine ... NV-8
Calcite (historical)—locale ... SD-7
Calcite Mine—mine ... AZ-5
Calcite Mine—mine ... CA-9
Calcite Road (Jeep Trail)—trail ... CA-9
Calcite Springs—spring ... WY-8
Calcite Wash—stream ... AZ-5
**Calcium**—pop pl ... MT-8
**Calcium**—pop pl ... NY-2
Calcium Post Office (historical)—building ... PA-2
**Calco**—pop pl ... MS-4
Calcoat Branch ... MS-4
Cal Community Sch—school ... IA-7
Cal-Cone Burn—area ... CA-9
Calcord Canyon—valley ... AZ-5
Calcord Cem—cemetery ... IL-6
Calcord Spring—spring ... AZ-5
Calcord Springs—spring ... AZ-5
Calcote Branch—stream ... MS-4
Calcote Cem—cemetery ... MS-4
Calcott Sch—school ... VA-3
Cal Cove—valley ... NC-3
**Calcutta**—pop pl ... IN-6
**Calcutta**—pop pl ... NY-2
**Calcutta**—pop pl ... OH-6
**Calcutta**—pop pl ... WV-2
Calcutta Cem—cemetery ... IN-6
Calcutta Ch—church ... OH-6
Calcutta Lake—lake ... NV-8
Calcutta Ranch—locale ... NV-8
Calcutta Run—stream ... IN-6
Calda Bank—bar ... FL-3
Calda Channel—channel ... FL-3
Calder—locale ... AK-9
**Calder**—pop pl ... ID-8
Calder, Mount—summit ... AK-9
Calder Bay—bay ... AK-9
Calder Cem—cemetery ... IL-6
Calder Cem—cemetery ... TN-4
Calder Ch—church ... TX-5
Calder Creek ... ID-8
Calder Creek—stream ... AK-9
Calder Creek—stream ... ID-8
Calder Creek—stream ... MT-8
Calder Ditch—canal ... UT-8
Calderhead—locale ... KS-7
Calder Head—stream ... FL-3
Calder Head—valley ... FL-3
**Calder Highlands**—pop pl ... TX-5
Calder Hill—summit ... NY-2
**Calder Hill Subdivision**—pop pl ... UT-8
Calder Houses—hist pl ... IA-7
Calder Mtn—summit ... ID-8
Caldero Artesian Well—well ... TX-5
Calder Point—summit ... ID-8
Calder Pond ... UT-8
Calder Race Course—park ... FL-3
Calder Ridge—ridge ... TN-4
Calder Rocks—area ... AK-9
Caldersburgh ... VT-1
Calder Sch—school ... CA-9
Calders Corner—locale ... CA-9
Calder Spring—spring ... ID-8
**Calder Terrace**—pop pl ... TX-5
Calderwood ... AZ-5
**Calderwood**—pop pl ... MI-6
**Calderwood**—pop pl ... TN-4
Calderwood Butte—summit ... AZ-5
Calderwood Creek—stream ... ID-8
Calderwood Dam—dam ... OR-9
Calderwood Dam—dam (2) ... TN-4
Calderwood Island—island ... ME-1
Calderwood Lake—reservoir ... NC-3
Calderwood Lake—reservoir (2) ... TN-4
Calderwood Neck—island ... ME-1
Calderwood Point—cape (2) ... ME-1
Calderwood Post Office (historical)—building ... TN-4
Calderwood Rock—bar ... ME-1
Calderwood Rsvr—reservoir ... OR-9
Calderwood Sch (historical)—school ... TN-4
Calderwood Spring—spring ... MT-8
Calderwood Station—locale ... AZ-5
Caldicott—hist pl ... MD-2
Caldin Hill—summit ... ME-1
Caldirola No 1 Mine—mine ... CO-8
Caldirola No 2 Mine—mine ... CO-8
Caldmont Lake—reservoir ... NC-3
Caldmont Lake Dam—dam ... NC-3
**Caldor**—pop pl ... CA-9
Caldor Mine—mine ... CA-9
Caldor Ranger Station—locale ... CA-9
**Caldors Corner (Calders Corner)**—pop pl ... CA-9
Caldor Shop Ctr—locale (2) ... MA-1
Caldron Falls Dam—dam ... WI-6
Caldron Falls Rsvr—reservoir ... WI-6
Caldron Linn—hist pl ... ID-8
Caldwell ... AL-4
Caldwell—locale ... KY-4
Caldwell—locale ... NC-3
Caldwell—locale ... TN-4
Caldwell—locale ... TX-5
Caldwell—other ... NJ-2
**Caldwell**—pop pl ... AL-4
**Caldwell**—pop pl ... AR-4
**Caldwell**—pop pl ... ID-8
**Caldwell**—pop pl (2) ... IL-6
**Caldwell**—pop pl ... KS-7
**Caldwell**—pop pl ... MT-8
**Caldwell**—pop pl ... NJ-2
**Caldwell**—pop pl ... NC-3
**Caldwell**—pop pl ... OH-6
**Caldwell**—pop pl (2) ... PA-2
**Caldwell**—pop pl ... SC-3
**Caldwell**—pop pl ... TX-5
**Caldwell**—pop pl ... WV-2
**Caldwell**—pop pl ... WI-6
Caldwell, David, Log College Site—hist pl ... NC-3
Caldwell, Luther Henry, House—hist pl ... NC-3
Caldwell, Samuel, House—hist pl ... OH-6
Caldwell, W. A., House—hist pl ... SD-7
Caldwell, William, Kitchen—hist pl ... KY-4
Caldwell, William Parker, House—hist pl ... TN-4
Caldwell Airp—airport ... MO-7
Caldwell Bar—bar ... AL-4
Caldwell Basin—basin ... WY-8
Caldwell Bayou—stream ... LA-4
Caldwell Bldg—hist pl ... AL-4
Caldwell Block—hist pl ... MA-1
Caldwell Borough (Township of)—civ div ... NJ-2
Caldwell Branch—stream ... FL-3
Caldwell Branch—stream ... GA-3
Caldwell Branch—stream ... MS-4
Caldwell Branch—stream ... MO-7
Caldwell Branch—stream ... NC-3
Caldwell Branch—stream ... TN-4
Caldwell Branch—stream ... WV-2
Caldwell Brook—stream ... ME-1
Caldwell Brook—stream ... MN-6
Caldwell Brook—stream ... NH-1
Caldwell Brook—stream ... NY-2
Caldwell Butte—summit ... CA-9
Caldwell Camp—locale ... CO-8
Caldwell Canal Feeder—canal ... ID-8
Caldwell Canyon—valley ... CA-9
Caldwell Canyon—valley ... ID-8
Caldwell Carnegie Library—hist pl ... ID-8
Caldwell Carnegie Library—hist pl ... KS-7
Caldwell Cave—cave ... TN-4
Caldwell (CCD)—cens area ... TX-5
Caldwell Cem ... GA-3
Caldwell Cem—cemetery (2) ... AL-4
Caldwell Cem—cemetery (2) ... AR-4
Caldwell Cem—cemetery ... GA-3
Caldwell Cem—cemetery ... IL-6
Caldwell Cem—cemetery ... IN-6
Caldwell Cem—cemetery ... IA-7
Caldwell Cem—cemetery (2) ... KS-7
Caldwell Cem—cemetery ... KY-4
Caldwell Cem—cemetery (2) ... LA-4
Caldwell Cem—cemetery ... ME-1
Caldwell Cem—cemetery ... MA-1
Caldwell Cem—cemetery ... MI-6
Caldwell Cem—cemetery ... MN-6
Caldwell Cem—cemetery (2) ... MO-7
Caldwell Cem—cemetery ... NE-7
Caldwell Cem—cemetery (2) ... NC-3
Caldwell Cem—cemetery (3) ... OH-6
Caldwell Cem—cemetery ... PA-2
Caldwell Cem—cemetery (8) ... TN-4
Caldwell Cem—cemetery (2) ... VA-3
Caldwell Cem—cemetery ... WV-2
Caldwell Cemetary—cemetery ... AR-4
Caldwell Ch—church ... AL-4
Caldwell Ch—church ... IL-6
Caldwell Ch—church (2) ... KY-4
Caldwell Ch—church ... LA-4
Caldwell Ch—church ... MI-6
Caldwell Ch—church ... PA-2
Caldwell Chapel—church ... KY-4
Caldwell Ch (historical)—church ... AL-4
Caldwell Ch (historical)—church ... MO-7
Caldwell-Cobb-Love House—hist pl ... NC-3
Caldwell Coll For Women—school ... NJ-2
Caldwell Community Coll—school (2) ... NC-3
Caldwell Community Park—park ... NC-3
Caldwell Corner—locale ... ME-1
Caldwell Corners ... DE-2
**Caldwell (County)**—pop pl ... KY-4
**Caldwell County**—pop pl ... MO-7
**Caldwell County**—pop pl ... NC-3
**Caldwell (County)**—pop pl ... TX-5
Caldwell County Courthouse—hist pl ... MO-7
Caldwell County Courthouse—hist pl ... NC-3
Caldwell County Courthouse Hist Dist—hist pl ... TX-5
Caldwell Creek ... IL-6
Caldwell Creek ... MA-1
Caldwell Creek ... MN-6
Caldwell Creek ... TN-4
Caldwell Creek—stream ... CA-9
Caldwell Creek—stream ... CO-8
Caldwell Creek—stream ... ID-8
Caldwell Creek—stream (2) ... KY-4
Caldwell Creek—stream ... MS-4
Caldwell Creek—stream (2) ... MO-7
Caldwell Creek—stream ... NC-3
Caldwell Creek—stream ... OR-9
Caldwell Creek—stream ... PA-2
Caldwell Creek—stream ... TN-4
Caldwell Creek—stream (2) ... WA-9
Caldwell Creek—stream ... WY-8
Caldwell Crossing—locale ... TX-5
**Caldwell Crossroad**—pop pl ... SC-3
Caldwell Ditch—canal ... MT-8
Caldwell Ditch—canal ... WY-8
Caldwell Drain—canal ... ID-8
Caldwell Draw—valley ... ID-8
Caldwell Elem Sch—school ... AL-4
Caldwell Elem Sch—school ... KS-7
Caldwell Farm—hist pl ... MO-7
Caldwell Farmstead—hist pl ... IL-6
Caldwell Ferry (historical)—locale ... AL-4
Caldwell Fork—stream ... NC-3
Caldwell Fork Trail—trail ... NC-3
Caldwell Glacier—glacier ... AK-9
Caldwell Golf Course—other ... OK-5
Caldwell Gulch—valley ... CA-9
Caldwell Gulch—valley ... CO-8
Caldwell Gulch—valley (2) ... ID-8
Caldwell Hall—hist pl ... AR-4
Caldwell Hall—hist pl ... NY-2
Caldwell-Hampton-Boylston House—hist pl ... SC-3
Caldwell High Line Canal—canal ... ID-8
Caldwell Hill ... MA-1
**Caldwell Hill**—pop pl ... OK-5
Caldwell Hist Dist—hist pl ... ID-8
**Caldwell (historical)**—pop pl ... NC-3
Caldwell Hollow—valley ... IN-6
Caldwell Homestead—locale ... MT-8
Caldwell House—hist pl (2) ... KY-4
Caldwell House—hist pl ... TX-5
Caldwell HS—school ... MS-4
Caldwell Ice Caves—cave ... CA-9
Caldwell Island—island ... ME-1
Caldwell-Johnson-Morris Cottage—hist pl ... SC-3
Caldwell Knob—summit ... TX-5
Caldwell Labor Camp—locale ... ID-8
Caldwell Lake—lake ... CA-9
Caldwell Lake—lake ... IN-6
Caldwell Lake—lake ... NM-5
Caldwell Lake—lake ... OH-6
Caldwell Lake—lake ... WA-9
Caldwell Lake—lake ... WY-8
Caldwell Lake—reservoir ... AL-4
Caldwell Lake—reservoir ... OH-6
Caldwell Lake—reservoir ... SC-3
Caldwell Lake Dam—dam ... AL-4
Caldwell Lakes—lake ... CA-9
Caldwell Landing—locale ... FL-3
Caldwell Low Line Canal—canal ... ID-8
**Caldwell Manor**—pop pl ... KY-4
Caldwell Memorial Hosp—hospital ... NC-3
Caldwell Mesa—summit ... CA-9
Caldwell-Milner Bldg—hist pl ... AL-4
Caldwell Mine—mine ... TN-4
Caldwell Minor—summit ... CA-9
Caldwell Mtn—summit ... AR-4
Caldwell Mtn—summit ... CA-9
Caldwell Mtn—summit ... VA-3
Caldwell Municipal Airp—airport ... KS-7
Caldwell Odd Fellow Home for the Aged—hist pl ... ID-8
**Caldwell Parish**—pop pl ... LA-4
Caldwell Park—park ... AL-4
Caldwell Park—park ... CA-9
Caldwell Park—park ... ID-8
Caldwell Park—park ... IA-7
Caldwell Park—park ... OH-6
Caldwell Parsonage—hist pl ... NJ-2
Caldwell Pines—locale ... CA-9
Caldwell Place—locale ... CO-8
Caldwell Playground—park ... NJ-2
**Caldwell (Pleasant Hill)**—pop pl ... AL-4
Caldwell Point—cape ... WA-9
Caldwell Pond—lake ... NH-1
Caldwell Post Office (historical)—building ... MS-4
Caldwell Prairie—flat ... WA-9
Caldwell Presbyterian Church Manse—hist pl ... NJ-2
Caldwell Ranch—locale ... CA-9
Caldwell Ranch—locale ... MT-8
Caldwell Ranch—locale ... TX-5
Caldwell Ridge—ridge (2) ... TN-4
Caldwell Run—stream ... PA-2
Caldwell Run—stream (2) ... WV-2
Caldwell Run Trail—trail ... PA-2
**Caldwells**—pop pl ... IL-6
Caldwells Bridge (historical)—bridge ... TN-4
Caldwell Sch—school ... AL-4
Caldwell Sch—school ... AR-4
Caldwell Sch—school ... FL-3
Caldwell Sch—school ... IL-6
Caldwell Sch—school ... MI-6
Caldwell Sch—school ... NE-7
Caldwell Sch—school ... NC-3
Caldwell Sch—school (2) ... PA-2
Caldwell Sch—school (2) ... TN-4
Caldwell Sch—school ... TX-5
Caldwell Sch (historical)—school ... MS-4
Caldwell Sch (historical)—school ... PA-2
Caldwell School ... IN-6
Caldwells Corners ... NY-2
Caldwells Creek—stream ... VA-3
Caldwells Field—island ... FL-3
**Caldwell Siding**—pop pl ... IA-7
Caldwell's Island ... VA-3
Caldwells Landing ... NY-2
Caldwells Point ... NY-2
Caldwell Spring—spring ... AL-4
Caldwell Spring—spring ... KY-4
Caldwell Spring—spring ... MO-7
Caldwell Spring—spring (2) ... TN-4
Caldwell Spring—spring ... UT-8
Caldwell Spring Cem—cemetery ... KY-4
Caldwell Spring Creek—stream ... KY-4
Caldwell Springs—spring ... MT-8
Caldwell Springs Ch—church ... TN-4
Caldwells Shoals—bar ... TN-4
Caldwell Station—locale ... NJ-2
Caldwell Station Creek—stream ... NC-3
Caldwell Street—post sta ... SC-3
Caldwell Street Hist Dist—hist pl ... SC-3
Caldwell Street Sch—school ... CA-9
Caldwell Swamp—swamp ... AL-4
Caldwell Tank—reservoir (2) ... TX-5
Caldwell (Town of)—other ... NY-2
Caldwell Township—civil ... MO-7
Caldwell Township—fmr MCD ... IA-7
**Caldwell Township**—pop pl ... KS-7
Caldwell (Township of)—fmr MCD ... NC-3
**Caldwell (Township of)**—pop pl ... MI-6
Caldwell Training Sch (historical)—school ... TN-4
Caldwell United Methodist Ch—church ... TN-4
Caldwell Windmill—locale (2) ... TX-5
Caldwell Zoo—other ... TX-5
**Caldwood**—pop pl ... TX-5
**Caldwood Acres**—pop pl ... TX-5
Caldwood Cutoff—canal ... TX-5
**Cale**—pop pl ... AR-4
**Cale**—pop pl ... IN-6
Caleast—locale ... KY-4
Caleb—locale ... GA-3
**Caleb**—pop pl ... FL-3
Calebasse, Lac—lake ... LA-4
Caleb Branch—stream (2) ... NC-3
Caleb Brook—stream ... NH-1
Caleb Cem—cemetery ... OR-9
Caleb Creek—stream ... IA-7
Calebee—locale ... AL-4
Calebee Church ... AL-4
Calebee Creek—stream ... AL-4
Calebee Post Office (historical)—building ... AL-4
Caleb Fork—stream ... KY-4
Caleb Hill—summit ... CT-1
**Caleb (historical)**—pop pl ... OR-9
Caleb Hollow—valley ... TN-4
Caleb Mills Elem Sch—school ... IN-6
Caleb Pond—cove ... MA-1
Caleb Pond—lake ... DE-2
Caleb Pond—lake ... MA-1
Caleb Pond Marshes—swamp ... MA-1
Caleb Pusey Historic Site—locale ... PA-2
Caleb Pusey Historic Site—park ... PA-2
Caleb Pusey House ... PA-2
Calebs Branch ... NC-3
Calebs Creek ... PA-2
Calebs Creek—stream ... NC-3
Calebs Creek—stream ... TN-4
Caleb's Discovery—hist pl ... MD-2
Calebs Hill ... MA-1
Calebs Hill—summit ... OH-6
Calebs Peak—summit ... CT-1
Calebs Pond ... MA-1
Calebs Run—stream ... PA-2
Caleb W Bucher Elementary School ... PA-2
Cale Cem—cemetery ... IN-6
Cale Creek—stream ... AK-9
Caledonia ... PA-2
Caledonia ... WA-9
Caledonia—locale ... AR-4
Caledonia—locale ... IA-7
Caledonia—locale ... KY-4
Caledonia—locale ... TX-5
**Caledonia**—pop pl ... AL-4
**Caledonia**—pop pl ... IL-6
**Caledonia**—pop pl (2) ... IN-6
**Caledonia**—pop pl ... MI-6
**Caledonia**—pop pl ... MN-6
**Caledonia**—pop pl ... MS-4
**Caledonia**—pop pl ... MO-7
**Caledonia**—pop pl ... NY-2
**Caledonia**—pop pl ... ND-7
**Caledonia**—pop pl ... OH-6
**Caledonia**—pop pl ... PA-2
**Caledonia**—pop pl ... VA-3
**Caledonia**—pop pl ... WI-6
Caledonia Adobe—hist pl ... CA-9
Caledonia Bldg—hist pl ... MA-1
Caledonia Bowstring Bridge—hist pl ... OH-6
Caledonia Campground—locale ... IL-6
Caledonia Canal—canal ... OR-9
Caledonia Cem—cemetery ... AL-4
Caledonia Cem—cemetery ... IL-6
Caledonia Cem—cemetery ... MO-7
Caledonia Cem—cemetery (2) ... WI-6
Caledonia Ch—church ... IN-6
Caledonia Ch—church ... NC-3
Caledonia Ch—church ... SC-3
Caledonia Ch—church (2) ... TN-4
Caledonia Ch—church ... WI-6
**Caledonia County**—pop pl ... VT-1
Caledonia Creek—stream ... ID-8
Caledonia Creek—stream ... MS-4
Caledonia Creek—stream ... PA-2
Caledonia Creek—stream ... SC-3
Caledonia Creek—stream ... TN-4
Caledonia Dam ... PA-2
Caledonia Dike—levee ... OR-9
Caledonia Drain—canal ... MI-6
Caledonia Elem Sch—school ... MS-4
Caledonia Gas Field—oilfield ... MS-4
Caledonia Golf Course—locale ... PA-2
Caledonia Hill—summit ... MD-2
Caledonia Hills—other ... MO-7
Caledonia Hist Dist—hist pl ... MO-7
Caledonia Hollow—valley ... VA-3
Caledonia HS—school ... MS-4
Caledonia Island ... FL-3
Caledonia Lake—reservoir ... PA-2
Caledonia Landing—locale ... IL-6
Caledonia Marsh—swamp ... OR-9
Caledonia Mine—mine ... CA-9
Caledonia Mine—mine ... CO-8
Caledonia Mine—mine ... MI-6
Caledonia Mine—mine ... NV-8
Caledonia New Shaft—mine ... NV-8
Caledonia Park—park ... IA-7
Caledonia Park—park ... NY-2
**Caledonia Park**—pop pl ... PA-2
Caledonia Run—stream ... PA-2
Caledonia Sch—school ... MI-6
Caledonia Sch—school ... OH-6
Caledonia Sch—school ... WI-6
Caledonia Sch (historical)—school ... TN-4
Caledonia Springs ... PA-2
Caledonia State Park—park ... PA-2
Caledonia State Prison Farm—locale ... NC-3
Caledonia Station ... MS-4
**Caledonia (Town of)**—pop pl ... NY-2
**Caledonia (Town of)**—pop pl (4) ... WI-6
Caledonia Township—fmr MCD ... IA-7
**Caledonia Township**—pop pl ... ND-7
Caledonia Township (historical)—civil ... ND-7
**Caledonia (Township of)**—pop pl ... IL-6
**Caledonia (Township of)**—pop pl (3) ... MI-6
**Caledonia (Township of)**—pop pl ... MN-6
Caledonia Valley—valley ... VI-3
Caledonia Water Company Dam—dam ... PA-2
Caledonia Water Company Pond—reservoir ... PA-2
Calef, Dr. John, House—hist pl ... MA-1
Calef Brook—stream ... NH-1
Calef Pond—lake ... NH-1
Cale (historical)—locale ... KS-7
Calendar—locale ... ID-8
Calendar Brook—stream ... VT-1
Calendar Canyon—valley ... ID-8
Calendar Rsvr—reservoir ... ID-8
Calendar Slough—stream ... OR-9
Calendars Run—stream ... PA-2
Calentine Well—locale ... NM-5
**Calera**—pop pl ... AL-4
**Calera**—pop pl ... OK-5
**Calera**—pop pl ... VA-3
Calera Canyon—valley ... CA-9
Calera (CCD)—cens area ... AL-4
Calera Creek—stream ... CA-9
Calera Division—civil ... AL-4
Calera Draw—valley ... AZ-5
Calera Elem Sch—school ... AL-4
Calera First United Methodist Ch—church ... AL-4
Calera HS—school ... AL-4
Calera Tank—reservoir ... AZ-5
Calera Valley—valley ... CA-9
Calera Wash—stream ... AZ-5
Caler Cove—valley ... GA-3
Caler Cove—valley ... NC-3
Caler Cove Branch—stream ... NC-3
Caler Creek Ruby Mine—mine ... NC-3
Caler Fork—stream ... NC-3
Caler Knob—summit ... NC-3
Calero, Arroyo—stream ... CA-9
Calero, Arroyo—valley ... TX-5
Calero Rsvr—reservoir ... CA-9
Cale Run—stream ... WV-2
Calesoque ... PA-2
Calestown Ch—church ... SC-3
Caleta De Cabullones—bay ... PR-3
Caleta Parguera—bay ... PR-3
Caleta Salinas—bay ... PR-3
Calet Hill—summit ... NH-1
Calevezas Creek ... CA-9
**Calexico**—pop pl ... CA-9
Calexico (CCD)—cens area ... CA-9
**Calexico Lodge**—pop pl ... CA-9
Caley Cem—cemetery ... KS-7
Caley Ch—church ... IN-6
Caley Creek—stream ... WY-8
Caley Hill—summit ... AR-4
Caley Lake ... MI-6
Caley Lake—lake ... WI-6
Caley Road Sch—school ... PA-2
Caley Spring—spring ... IL-6
Calfat, Bayou—stream ... LA-4
Calf Branch—stream ... FL-3
Calf Branch—stream ... IN-6
Calf Branch—stream ... LA-4
Calf Branch—stream ... MS-4
Calf Branch—stream ... NC-3
Calf Branch—stream ... TN-4
Calf Branch—stream ... WV-2
Calf Canyon ... UT-8
Calf Canyon—valley ... CA-9
Calf Canyon—valley (3) ... CO-8
Calf Canyon—valley ... NV-8
Calf Canyon—valley (2) ... NM-5
Calf Canyon—valley (9) ... UT-8
Calf Canyon Rapids—rapids ... UT-8
Calf Cave—cave ... AL-4
Calf Caves—cave ... TN-4
Calf Creek ... ID-8
Calf Creek ... MT-8
Calf Creek ... TX-5
Calf Creek ... UT-8
Calf Creek—fmr MCD ... NE-7
Calf Creek—locale ... KY-4
Calf Creek—locale ... TX-5
Calf Creek—stream ... AZ-5
Calf Creek—stream ... AR-4
Calf Creek—stream (4) ... CA-9
Calf Creek—stream (5) ... CO-8
Calf Creek—stream ... FL-3
Calf Creek—stream (5) ... ID-8
Calf Creek—stream (2) ... IN-6
Calf Creek—stream ... KS-7
Calf Creek—stream (2) ... KY-4
Calf Creek—stream ... MI-6
Calf Creek—stream (4) ... MT-8
Calf Creek—stream ... NE-7
Calf Creek—stream ... NY-2
Calf Creek—stream ... OK-5
Calf Creek—stream (3) ... OR-9
Calf Creek—stream ... SD-7
Calf Creek—stream (6) ... TX-5
Calf Creek—stream ... UT-8
Calf Creek—stream ... WA-9
Calf Creek—stream ... WV-2
Calf Creek—stream (4) ... WY-8
Calf Creek Campground—locale ... UT-8
Calf Creek Guard Station—locale ... MT-8
Calf Creek Hill—summit ... WY-8
Calf Creek Oil Field—oilfield ... KS-7
Calf Creek Plateau—summit ... CO-8
Calf Creek Rec Area—locale ... UT-8
Calf Creek Sch—school ... KY-4
Calf Creek Sch—school ... MT-8
Calf Creek Sch—school ... NE-7
Calf Creek Tank—reservoir ... AZ-5
Calf Creek Tank—reservoir ... TX-5
Calf Creek (Township of)—fmr MCD ... AR-4
Calf Creek Valley—basin ... NE-7
Calf Creek Waterhole—reservoir ... OR-9
Calf Draw—valley ... WY-8
Calfee Cem—cemetery ... TN-4
Calfee Cem—cemetery ... WV-2
Calfee Ch—church ... WV-2
Calfee Creek—stream ... WY-8
Calfee Creek Patrol Cabin—locale ... WY-8
Calfee Knob—summit ... VA-3
Calfee Lake—lake ... TX-5
Calfee Lake—reservoir ... AL-4
Calfee Lake Dam—dam ... AL-4
Calfee Park—park ... VA-3
Calffe Knob ... VA-3
Calf Flat—flat ... UT-8
Calf Ford Branch—stream ... NC-3
Calf Ford Branch—stream ... SC-3
Calf Gulch—valley ... CO-8
Calf Gulch—valley ... MT-8
Calf Gulch—valley ... OR-9
Calf Gully Creek—stream ... NC-3
Calfhead Pond—lake ... NY-2
Calf Hill—summit ... TX-5
Calfhill Hollow—valley ... VA-3
Calf Hollow—valley ... ID-8
Calf Hollow—valley ... KY-4
Calf Hollow—valley ... TX-5
Calf Hollow—valley (2) ... UT-8
Calf Hollow—valley ... VA-3
Calf Island ... ME-1
Calf Island—island ... FL-3
Calf Island—island (4) ... ME-1
Calf Island—island ... MA-1
Calf Island—island ... MI-6
Calf Island—island ... NY-2
Calf Island—island ... TN-4
Calf Islands—island ... CT-1
Calf Islands—island ... MA-1
Calfkiller—locale ... TN-4

Calf Killer Creek ... TN-4
Calfkiller Creek—stream ... IL-6
Calfkiller Hole—cave ... TN-4
Calf Killer Post Office (historical)—building ... TN-4
Calf-killer River ... TN-4
Calfkiller River—stream ... TN-4
Calfkiller Saltpeter Cave—cave ... TN-4
Calfkiller Sch (historical)—school ... TN-4
Calf Lake—lake ... AK-9
Calf Lake—lake ... CA-9
Calf Lake—lake ... FL-3
Calf Lake—lake ... LA-4
Calf Lake—lake ... MN-6
Calf Lake—swamp ... LA-4
Calflax—locale ... CA-9
Calflax Ranch—locale ... CA-9
Calflax Substation—other ... CA-9
Calf Lot Hollow—valley ... MO-7
Calf Lot Hollow—valley ... TN-4
Calf Mesa—summit (2) ... UT-8
Calf Mountain Overlook—locale ... VA-3
Calf Mtn—summit ... VA-3
Calf Neck—cape ... RI-1
Calfneck Bend—bend ... AR-4
Calfpasture Beach ... CT-1
Calf Pasture Beach—beach ... CT-1
Calf Pasture Cove ... MD-2
Calfpasture Cove—bay ... MD-2
Calfpasture Creek—stream ... CA-9
Calf Pasture Hollow—valley ... UT-8
Calfpasture Island ... CT-1
Calf Pasture Island—island ... CT-1
Calfpasture Point ... CT-1
Calf Pasture Point ... MA-1
Calf Pasture Point—cape ... CT-1
Calf Pasture Point—cape ... RI-1
Calf Pasture Point—cape ... UT-8
Calf Pasture River ... VA-3
Calfpasture River—stream ... VA-3
Calf Pasture Rock—pillar ... RI-1
Calf Pasture Swamp—swamp ... AL-4
Calf Pasture Tank—reservoir ... AZ-5
Calf Pasture Tank Number One—reservoir ... AZ-5
Calf Pasture Well—well ... TX-5
Calfpen Bay—bay ... VA-3
Calfpen Bay—swamp ... SC-3
Calfpen Branch—stream ... KY-4
Calf Pen Canyon—valley ... AZ-5
Calf Pen Fork—stream ... KY-4
Calfpen Gap—gap ... NC-3
Calf Pen Gulch—valley ... ID-8
Calf Pen Meadow Creek—stream ... CT-1
Calf Pen Meadow Sch—school ... CT-1
Calfpen Ridge—ridge ... NC-3
Calfpen Sch—school ... MO-7
Calfpen Swamp—swamp ... SC-3
Calf Point—cape ... ME-1
Calf Point—cliff ... CO-8
Calf Pond ... FL-3
Calf Pond—lake ... FL-3
Calf Ranch Mtn—summit ... OR-9
Calf Ranch Prairie—flat ... OR-9
Calf Ridge—ridge ... OR-9
Calf Robe Mtn—summit ... MT-8
Calf Rock—island ... VI-3
Calf Run—stream ... IN-6
Calf Run—stream ... TX-5
Calf Run—stream (2) ... WV-2
Calf Spring—spring (2) ... AZ-5
Calf Spring—spring ... CO-8
Calf Spring—spring ... UT-8
Calf Springs—spring ... UT-8
Calf Springs Creek—stream ... UT-8
Calf Stomp Gap—gap ... GA-3
Calf Stump Branch—stream ... GA-3
Calftail Cut—gap ... AR-4
Calf Tank—reservoir ... AZ-5
Calf Tank—reservoir ... TX-5
Calf Yoke Mine—mine ... TN-4
Calf Yoke Workings—mine ... TN-4
Calgary—locale ... TX-5
Calgary Cem—cemetery ... MN-6
**Calgary Woods**—pop pl ... TX-5
Calgro—locale ... CA-9
**Calhan**—pop pl ... CO-8
Calhan Rsvr—reservoir ... CO-8
Cal Hollow—valley ... PA-2
Calhoon Cabin—locale ... CA-9
Calhoon Lake—lake ... MI-6
Calhoun ... MS-4
Calhoun ... NE-7
Calhoun—locale ... AR-4
Calhoun—locale ... CO-8
Calhoun—locale ... OK-5
**Calhoun**—pop pl ... AL-4
**Calhoun**—pop pl ... AR-4
**Calhoun**—pop pl ... GA-3
**Calhoun**—pop pl ... IL-6
**Calhoun**—pop pl ... IA-7
**Calhoun**—pop pl ... KY-4
**Calhoun**—pop pl ... LA-4
**Calhoun**—pop pl (2) ... MS-4
**Calhoun**—pop pl ... MO-7
**Calhoun**—pop pl ... SC-3
**Calhoun**—pop pl (2) ... TN-4
**Calhoun**—pop pl ... WV-2
**Calhoun**—pop pl ... WI-6
Calhoun—uninc pl ... WI-6
Calhoun, George, House—hist pl ... OR-9
Calhoun, Lake—lake (2) ... MN-6
Calhoun, Patrick, Family Cemetery—hist pl ... SC-3
Calhoun, Point—summit ... AL-4
Calhoun Acad—school ... MS-4
Calhoun Bakery—hist pl ... TX-5
Calhoun Baptist Ch ... MS-4
Calhoun Baptist Ch—church ... MS-4
Calhoun Baptist Ch—church ... TN-4
Calhoun Basin—basin ... CO-8
**Calhoun Beach**—pop pl ... MN-6
Calhoun Bend—bend ... AL-4
Calhoun Bend—bend ... TN-4
Calhoun Bend Sch (historical)—school ... AL-4
Calhoun Boat Dock—locale ... TN-4
Calhoun Brake—swamp ... LA-4
Calhoun Branch ... AL-4
Calhoun Branch—stream (2) ... KY-4
Calhoun Branch—stream ... LA-4
Calhoun Branch—stream ... MS-4
Calhoun Branch—stream (3) ... NC-3
Calhoun Branch—stream ... PA-2
Calhoun Branch—stream (2) ... SC-3
Calhoun Branch—stream ... TN-4
Calhoun Bridge—bridge ... FL-3
Calhoun Bridge—bridge ... OH-6
Calhoun Butte—summit ... ID-8
Calhoun Byrd Bridge—bridge ... FL-3
Calhoun Campsite—locale ... NC-3
Calhoun (CCD)—cens area ... GA-3
Calhoun (CCD)—cens area ... KY-4
Calhoun Cem—cemetery ... CT-1
Calhoun Cem—cemetery (2) ... IL-6
Calhoun Cem—cemetery ... IA-7
Calhoun Cem—cemetery (2) ... KY-4
Calhoun Cem—cemetery ... LA-4
Calhoun Cem—cemetery ... MI-6
Calhoun Cem—cemetery (4) ... MS-4
Calhoun Cem—cemetery (2) ... MO-7
Calhoun Cem—cemetery ... NM-5
Calhoun Cem—cemetery (2) ... NC-3
Calhoun Cem—cemetery ... TN-4
Calhoun Cem—cemetery (2) ... TX-5
Calhoun Cem—cemetery (2) ... VA-3
Calhoun Cemetery ... AL-4
Calhoun Ch—church ... MS-4
Calhoun Channel—channel ... FL-3
**Calhoun City**—pop pl ... MS-4
Calhoun City Cem—cemetery ... MS-4
Calhoun City Elem Sch—school ... MS-4
Calhoun City HS—school ... MS-4
Calhoun City MS—school ... MS-4
Calhoun Coll ... AL-4
Calhoun Colored Sch ... AL-4
**Calhoun Corners**—pop pl ... CT-1
Calhoun County ... KS-7
**Calhoun County**—pop pl ... AL-4
**Calhoun (County)**—pop pl ... AR-4
**Calhoun County**—pop pl ... FL-3
**Calhoun (County)**—pop pl ... GA-3
**Calhoun (County)**—pop pl ... IL-6
**Calhoun (County)**—pop pl ... MI-6
**Calhoun County**—pop pl ... MS-4
**Calhoun (County)**—pop pl ... SC-3
**Calhoun (County)**—pop pl ... TX-5
**Calhoun (County)**—pop pl ... WV-2
Calhoun County Airp—airport ... MS-4
Calhoun County Canal—canal ... TX-5
Calhoun County Courthouse—building ... AL-4
Calhoun County Courthouse—building ... MS-4
Calhoun County Courthouse—hist pl ... AL-4
Calhoun County Courthouse—hist pl ... AR-4
Calhoun County Courthouse—hist pl ... IA-7
Calhoun County Courthouse—hist pl ... SC-3
Calhoun County Education Center—school ... FL-3
Calhoun County Home—building ... IA-7
Calhoun County Hosp—hospital ... FL-3
Calhoun County Library—hist pl ... SC-3
Calhoun County State Wildlife Mngmt Area—park ... MS-4
Calhoun County Training Sch—school ... AL-4
Calhoun County Veterans Sch (historical)—school ... AL-4
Calhoun Cow Camp—locale ... CO-8
Calhoun Creek—stream ... GA-3
Calhoun Creek—stream ... ID-8
Calhoun Creek—stream ... IA-7
Calhoun Creek—stream ... KY-4
Calhoun Creek—stream ... NY-2
Calhoun Creek—stream ... SC-3
Calhoun Creek Sch—school ... KY-4
Calhoun Cut—canal ... CA-9
Calhoun Depot—hist pl ... GA-3
Calhoun Ditch—canal ... SD-7
Calhoun Elem Sch—school ... MS-4
Calhoun Elem Sch—school ... TN-4
**Calhoun Falls**—pop pl ... SC-3
Calhoun Falls (CCD)—cens area ... SC-3
Calhoun Falls Country Club—other ... SC-3
Calhoun Falls Park—park ... SC-3
Calhoun Farmhouse—hist pl ... LA-4
Calhoun Ferry (historical)—locale ... TX-5
Calhoun Gap—gap ... GA-3
Calhoun General Hosp—hospital ... FL-3
Calhoun Gold Mine—mine ... GA-3
Calhoun Grange Coll ... AL-4
Calhoun Gulch—valley ... CO-8
Calhoun Heights Sch—school ... AR-4
Calhoun Hill—summit ... NY-2
Calhoun Hill Public Use Area—locale ... KY-4
Calhoun (historical)—locale ... KS-7
Calhoun Hollow—valley ... AL-4
Calhoun Hollow—valley ... KY-4
Calhoun Hollow—valley ... MO-7
Calhoun HS—school ... IL-6
Calhoun HS (historical)—school ... TN-4
Calhoun Industrial School ... AL-4
Calhoun Junction—locale ... AR-4
Calhoun Lake—reservoir ... IL-6
Calhoun Landing—locale ... DE-2
Calhoun Landing Strip—airport ... MO-7
Calhoun Mill—hist pl ... SC-3
Calhoun Mill—locale ... SC-3
Calhoun Mine—hist pl ... GA-3
Calhoun Mountain ... AL-4
Calhoun Normal and Industrial School ... AL-4
Calhoun Oil Field—other ... IL-6
Calhoun Park—park ... MA-1
Calhoun Point—cape ... IL-6
Calhoun Pond—reservoir ... AL-4
Calhoun Pond—reservoir ... SC-3
Calhoun Post Office—building ... TN-4
Calhoun Ranch—locale ... NE-7
Calhoun Recreation Complex—park ... FL-3
Calhoun-Riceville (CCD)—cens area ... TN-4
Calhoun-Riceville Division—civil ... TN-4
Calhoun Rsvr—reservoir ... CO-8
Calhoun Rsvr—reservoir ... OR-9
Calhoun Run—stream ... VA-3
Calhoun Sch—school ... AL-4
Calhoun Sch—school ... AR-4
Calhoun Sch—school ... FL-3
Calhoun Sch—school ... GA-3
Calhoun Sch—school (2) ... IL-6
Calhoun Sch—school ... LA-4
Calhoun Sch—school ... MN-6
Calhoun Sch Cemetery ... MS-4
Calhoun Sch (historical)—school ... MS-4
Calhoun Sch (historical)—school ... PA-2
Calhoun Sch (historical)—school ... TN-4
Calhoun Sch Principal's House—hist pl ... AL-4
Calhouns Ferry (historical)—locale ... MS-4
Calhouns Mill Pond ... SC-3
Calhoun South Oil Field—other ... IL-6
Calhoun Spring—spring ... ID-8
Calhoun State Community Coll—school ... AL-4
Calhoun Station ... MS-4
Calhoun Street Hist Dist—hist pl ... FL-3
Calhoun Township—fmr MCD (2) ... IA-7
**Calhoun Township**—pop pl ... KS-7
Calhoun (Township of)—fmr MCD ... AR-4
**Calhounville**—pop pl ... WA-9
Calhoun West (CCD)—cens area ... FL-3
Calhoun Windmill—locale ... NM-5
Calhourn River ... TN-4
Cal Hurst Branch—stream ... TN-4
Calibee Creek ... AL-4
Calibogue Creek—stream ... SC-3
Calibogue Sound ... SC-3
Calibogue Sound—bay ... SC-3
Caliche, Canal (historical)—canal ... AZ-5
Caliche, Loma—summit ... TX-5
Caliche Creek—stream ... TX-5
Caliche Lakes—lake ... WA-9
Caliche Pit (Active)—mine ... NM-5
Caliche Pits—locale ... NM-5
Caliche Pits—mine ... TX-5
Caliche Quarries—mine ... TX-5
Caliche Quarry—mine ... TX-5
Calichera Windmill—locale ... TX-5
Caliche Spring—spring ... AZ-5
Caliche Tank—reservoir ... NM-5
Caliche Tank—reservoir (7) ... TX-5
Caliche Windmill—locale (4) ... TX-5
Calichosa Well (Flowing)—well ... TX-5
Calicito Tank—reservoir ... NM-5
Calicke Park—park ... AZ-5
Calico—locale ... CA-9
Calico—locale ... NC-3
Calico—locale ... TN-4
**Calico**—pop pl ... CA-9
**Calico**—pop pl ... SC-3
Calico Basin—basin ... NV-8
Calico Bay—bay ... NV-8
Calico Bay—bay ... NC-3
Calico Bluff—cliff ... AK-9
Calico Bluff—cliff ... AR-4
Calico Branch—stream ... KY-4
Calico Branch—stream ... LA-4
Calico Branch—stream ... SC-3
Calico & Brown General Store—hist pl ... KY-4
Calico Butte—summit ... NV-8
Calico Canyon—valley ... SD-7
**Calico Colony**—pop pl ... NY-2
Calico Corner—locale ... PA-2
Calico Creek ... OR-9
Calico Creek—bay ... NC-3
Calico Creek—stream ... AK-9
Calico Creek—stream (2) ... AR-4
Calico Creek—stream ... MO-7
Calico Creek—stream ... MT-8
Calico Creek—stream ... NV-8
Calico Creek—stream ... OH-6
Calico Creek—stream (2) ... OR-9
Calico Creek Marsh—swamp ... NC-3
Calico Draw—valley ... CO-8
**Calico (Ghost Town)**—pop pl ... CA-9
Calico Gulch—valley ... OR-9
Calico Hill—summit ... FL-3
Calico Hills ... CA-9
Calico Hills—range ... NV-8
Calico Hills—summit (3) ... NV-8
Calico Island—island ... IL-6
Calico Lake—lake ... MN-6
Calico Lateral—canal ... ID-8
Calico Mountains ... NV-8
Calico Mountains—summit ... CA-9
Calico Mountains Archeol District—hist pl ... CA-9
Calico Mtn—summit ... AR-4
Calico Mtn—summit ... CO-8
Calico Mtn—summit ... TN-4
Calico Mtns—summit ... NV-8
Calico Peak ... NV-8
Calico Peak—summit ... AZ-5
Calico Peak—summit ... CA-9
Calico Peak—summit ... CO-8
Calico Peak—summit ... UT-8
Calico Peaks—summit ... CA-9
Calico Ranch—locale ... NV-8
Calico Ridge—ridge ... OH-6
Calico Rock—cliff ... VA-3
**Calico Rock**—pop pl ... AR-4
Calico Rock Hist Dist—hist pl ... AR-4
Calico Run—stream ... PA-2
Calico Sch (abandoned)—school ... MO-7
Calico Slash Ditch—canal ... IN-6
Calico Spring—spring ... CO-8
Calico Spring—spring (2) ... NV-8
Calico Spring—spring ... OR-9
Calico Valley—valley ... GA-3
Calico Wash—stream ... NV-8
Calico Workings—mine ... TN-4
**Cal-Ida**—pop pl ... CA-9
**Calida**—pop pl ... OK-5
Cal-Idaho Pit—mine ... ID-8
Cal-Ida Mine—mine ... ID-8
**Caliente**—pop pl ... CA-9
**Caliente**—pop pl ... NV-8
Caliente, Tanko—reservoir ... AZ-5
Caliente Canyon—valley ... NM-5
Caliente Creek ... CA-9
Caliente Creek—stream ... CA-9
Caliente Flight Strip Airp—airport ... NV-8
Caliente Mtn—summit ... CA-9
Caliente Ranch—locale ... CA-9
Caliente Range—range ... CA-9
Caliente RR Depot—hist pl ... NV-8
Caliente Spring—spring ... CA-9
Caliente Spring—spring ... CO-8
Caliente Township—inact MCD ... NV-8
Califa Canal—canal ... CA-9
Califa Lateral A—canal ... CA-9
Califa Lateral B—canal ... CA-9
Califa Lateral C—canal ... CA-9
Califa Lateral D—canal ... CA-9
**Califon**—pop pl ... NJ-2
Califon Hist Dist—hist pl ... NJ-2
California ... IA-7
California ... NJ-2
California ... NY-2
California ... OH-6
California ... PA-2
California—locale ... ME-1
California—locale (2) ... NC-3
California—locale ... PA-2
California—mine ... CA-9
**California**—pop pl ... KY-4
**California**—pop pl ... MD-2
**California**—pop pl ... MI-6
**California**—pop pl ... MO-7
**California**—pop pl (2) ... NC-3
**California**—pop pl ... OH-6
**California**—pop pl (2) ... PA-2
**California**—pop pl ... VA-3
California, Bay—lake ... LA-4
California Acres Ch of Christ—church ... KS-7
California Acres Shop Ctr—locale ... KS-7
California Aqueduct—canal ... CA-9
California Area Senior High School ... PA-2
California Ave Sch—school ... CA-9
California Ave Sch—school ... NY-2
California Baptist Coll—school ... CA-9
California Bar—bar ... AL-4
California Bar—bar ... AK-9
California Bar—bar ... ID-8
California Bar—locale ... OR-9
California Basin—basin ... NV-8
California Bay—bay ... AK-9
California Bay—bay ... LA-4
California Bayou—bay ... FL-3
California Bayou—gut ... LA-4
California Bend State Wildlife Ref—park ... IA-7
California Borough—civil ... PA-2
California Boulder Patch—other ... AK-9
California Brake—swamp ... AR-4
California Brake (historical)—swamp ... MS-4
California Branch—stream ... AR-4
California Branch—stream ... MO-7
California Branch—stream ... NC-3
California Branch—stream ... OH-6
California Branch—stream (2) ... SC-3
California Branch—stream ... TN-4
California Brook—stream ... ME-1
California Brook—stream ... NH-1
California Brook—stream ... PA-2
California Camp—locale ... CO-8
California Camp—locale ... MT-8
California Canal—canal ... NY-2
California Canal—gut ... LA-4
California Checking Station—other ... CA-9
California Christian Home—building ... CA-9
California City ... CA-9
**California City**—pop pl ... CA-9
California Clearing—flat ... NY-2
California Club—other ... CA-9
California Club Mall—locale ... FL-3
California Coll of Arts and Crafts—school ... CA-9
California Coll of Medicine—school ... CA-9
California Community Ch—church ... IN-6
California Concordia Coll—school ... CA-9
**California Conservation Center**—pop pl ... CA-9
California Correctional Institute—other ... CA-9
California Country Club—other ... CA-9
California County Canal—canal ... LA-4
California Creek ... FL-3
California Creek—stream (9) ... AK-9
California Creek—stream (2) ... CA-9
California Creek—stream (2) ... FL-3
California Creek—stream (3) ... ID-8
California Creek—stream ... KS-7
California Creek—stream (2) ... MT-8
California Creek—stream (2) ... NV-8
California Creek—stream ... NY-2
California Creek—stream ... NC-3
California Creek—stream ... OK-5
California Creek—stream ... PA-2
California Creek—stream ... TN-4
California Creek—stream (3) ... TX-5
California Creek—stream (2) ... WA-9
California Creek Bar Campground—locale ... ID-8
California Creek Missionary Baptist Church—hist pl ... NC-3
California Crossing Dam—dam ... TX-5
California Crossing Park—park ... TX-5
California Crossroads—locale ... VA-3
California Cutoff—channel ... IA-7
California Day Camp—locale ... OH-6
California Department of Natural Resources—building ... CA-9
California Division of Forestry—locale (4) ... CA-9
California Division of Forestry Station—locale ... CA-9
California Draw—valley ... NM-5
California Draw—valley ... UT-8
California Duck Club—other ... CA-9
California Elem Sch—school ... IN-6
California Emigrant Trail (Carson River Route)—trail ... NV-8
California Falls—falls ... CA-9
California Federation of Womens Clubs Grove—woods ... CA-9
California Flats—flat ... CA-9
California Flats Canyon—valley ... CA-9
California Fruit Store—hist pl ... WA-9
California Furnace—locale ... PA-2
California Gap—gap ... NC-3
California Golf Club—other ... CA-9
California Governor's Mansion—hist pl ... CA-9
California Gulch ... AZ-5
California Gulch—stream ... OR-9
California Gulch—valley ... AK-9
California Gulch—valley (4) ... AZ-5
California Gulch—valley (6) ... CO-8
California Gulch—valley (4) ... ID-8
California Gulch—valley (2) ... MT-8
California Gulch—valley ... NV-8
California Gulch—valley ... NM-5
California Gulch—valley (5) ... OR-9
California Gulch—valley ... SD-7
California Gulch—valley ... UT-8
California Hall—hist pl ... CA-9
California Head—cape ... AK-9
**California Heights**—pop pl ... CA-9
California Hill—hist pl ... NE-7
California Hill—summit ... NV-8
California Hill—summit ... NY-2
California Hill—summit (2) ... TX-5
California (historical)—locale ... MS-4
California Hole—bay ... TX-5
California Hollow—valley (2) ... KY-4
California Hollow—valley ... NY-2
California Hollow—valley (2) ... OH-6
California Hollow—valley (2) ... PA-2
California Hollow—valley (2) ... TN-4
California Hollow—valley (2) ... UT-8
California Hollow—valley (2) ... VA-3
California Hotel—hist pl ... CA-9
**California Hot Springs**—pop pl ... CA-9
California HS—school ... CA-9
California HS—school ... PA-2
California Institute of Technology—school (2) ... CA-9
California Institution for Men (Chino)—building ... CA-9
California Institution for Women (Frontera)—building ... CA-9
California JHS—school ... CA-9
**California Junction**—pop pl ... IA-7
California Lake—lake ... FL-3
California Lake—lake (2) ... ID-8
California Landing ... AL-4
California Lateral—canal ... NM-5
California Maritime Acad—school ... CA-9
California Medical Facility—hospital ... CA-9
California Mens Colony (los Padres Post Office)—other ... CA-9
California Mesa—summit ... CO-8
California Military Acad—school ... CA-9
California Mine—mine (3) ... AZ-5
California Mine—mine (3) ... CA-9
California Mine—mine ... CO-8
California Mine—mine ... ID-8
California Mine—mine ... NV-8
California Mine—mine ... OR-9
California Mine—mine ... UT-8
California Mine—mine ... WA-9
California Mine (abandoned)—mine ... OR-9
California Morning Star Mine—mine ... CA-9
California Mountain ... TX-5
California Mtn—summit (2) ... CO-8
California Mtn—summit ... NV-8
California Mtn—summit ... OR-9
California Natl Guard—military ... CA-9
California North Golf Course—locale ... FL-3
California Nursery Co. Guest House—hist pl ... CA-9
California Nutmeg Spring—spring ... CA-9
**California Oil Camp**—pop pl ... CO-8
California-Oregon Highway Historical Marker—other ... CA-9
California Overlook—locale ... PA-2
California Park—flat ... CO-8
California Park—flat ... NM-5
California Park—park ... IL-6
California Park Guard Station—locale ... CO-8
California Peak—summit ... CO-8
California Pines Lake ... CA-9
California Point ... CA-9
California Point—cape ... AR-4
California Point—cape ... LA-4
California Point—cape ... NY-2
California Point—cliff ... ID-8
California Pond—lake ... ME-1
California Quadrangle—hist pl ... CA-9
California Ranch—hist pl ... WA-9
California Rehabilitation Center—other ... CA-9
California Ridge—ridge ... NV-8
California Ridge—ridge ... NC-3
California Ridge—ridge ... VA-3
California Ridge—summit ... AK-9
California Ridge Trail—trail ... VA-3
California Riding And Hiking Trail—trail ... CA-9
California Riding and Hiking Trail—trail ... CA-9
California River—stream ... AK-9
California Road—locale ... ME-1
California Rock—other ... AK-9
California Rodeo Grounds—other ... CA-9
California Rsvr—reservoir ... CO-8
California Rsvr—reservoir ... WY-8
California Run—stream ... PA-2
California Sch—school (5) ... CA-9
California Sch—school (3) ... IL-6
California Sch—school ... MI-6
California Sch—school (2) ... PA-2
California Sch for Blind and Deaf—school ... CA-9
California Sch for the Deaf—school ... CA-9
California Sch (historical)—school ... PA-2
California Scrub—swamp ... FL-3
California Sea Otter State Game Refuge, The—park ... CA-9
California Sinks—basin ... FL-3
California Slough—gut ... FL-3
California Slough—stream ... MT-8
California Slough—stream ... WA-9
California Spring—spring ... AZ-5
California Spring—spring ... CO-8
California Spring—spring ... NV-8
California Spring—spring ... UT-8
California Spring Number 2—spring ... NV-8
California State Capitol—building ... CA-9
California State Capitol—hist pl ... CA-9
California State Coll At Fullerton—school ... CA-9
California State Coll At Long Beach—school ... CA-9
California State Coll At Los Angeles—school ... CA-9
California State Coll Hayward—school ... CA-9
California State Coll San Bernardino—school ... CA-9
California State Expostion—other ... CA-9
California State Polytechnic Coll (Kellogg)—school ... CA-9
California State Polytechnic Coll San Luis Obispo—school ... CA-9
California State Polytechnic Coll (Voorhees)—school ... CA-9
California State Prison—building ... CA-9
California State Sch For Boys—school ... CA-9
California State Univ Fresno—school ... CA-9
California Street Park—park ... AL-4
California Swamp—swamp (2) ... FL-3
California Tank—reservoir ... TX-5
California Township—civil ... KS-7
California (Township of)—fmr MCD (3) ... AR-4
**California (Township of)**—pop pl ... IN-6
**California (Township of)**—pop pl ... MI-6
California Trail—trail ... NY-2
California Trail—trail ... TN-4
California Trail—trail ... UT-8
California Trail (Applegate)—trail ... ID-8
California Trail (Salt Lake Alternate)—trail ... ID-8
California Trail (salt Lake Alternate)—trail ... UT-8
California Univ of Pennsylvania—school ... PA-2
**California Valley**—pop pl ... CA-9
California Valley—valley ... CA-9
California Vineyard Ditch—canal ... CA-9
California Wash ... AZ-5
California Wash—arroyo ... NV-8
California Wash—stream ... AZ-5
California Well—well ... AZ-5
California Western Univ—school ... CA-9
California Wine and Liquor Store—hist pl ... WI-6
California Youth Authority—locale ... CA-9
California Youth Authority Camp—other ... CA-9
**Caligoa**—pop pl ... MO-7
**Calimesa**—pop pl ... CA-9
Calimesa Sch—school ... CA-9
Calimus—locale ... OR-9
Calimus Butte—summit ... OR-9
Calina—locale ... TX-5
**Calio**—pop pl ... ND-7
Caliola Pumping Station—other ... CA-9
**Calion**—pop pl ... AR-4
Calion Lake—reservoir ... AR-4
**Calipatria**—pop pl ... CA-9
Calipatria Drain Number Two—canal ... CA-9
Calipatria-Westmorland (CCD)—cens area ... CA-9
Calipaya Inlet ... WA-9
Calipeen Creek—stream ... ID-8
**Calis**—pop pl ... WV-2
Calishe Tank—reservoir ... TX-5
Calispel ... MT-8
Calispel Creek ... WA-9
Calispell—locale ... WA-9
Calispel Lake ... WA-9
Calispell Basin—basin ... WA-9
Calispell Creek ... ID-8
Calispell Creek ... WA-9
Calispell Creek—stream ... WA-9
Calispell Lake—lake ... WA-9
Calispell Peak—summit ... WA-9
Calispell Peak Creek—stream ... WA-9
Calispell Ridge—ridge ... WV-2
Calispell River ... WA-9
Calispel Peak ... WA-9
Calispel River ... WA-9
Calist, Bayou—stream ... LA-4
Calista—locale ... KS-7
Calista Lake ... WI-6
**Calistia**—pop pl ... TN-4
**Calistoga**—pop pl ... CA-9
Calistoga (CCD)—cens area ... CA-9
Calistro Hole—lake ... TX-5
Calisuk ... PA-2
Calitre Mountains ... AZ-5
Calitro Mountains ... AZ-5
Caliuro Mountains ... AZ-5
Calivan Creek ... OR-9
Calizo Mountains ... AZ-5
Cal Johnson Park—park ... TN-4
Calkens Hollow—valley ... UT-8
Calkin Lake—lake ... NE-7
Calkins—locale ... OR-9
Calkins—locale ... PA-2
**Calkins**—pop pl ... MT-8
Calkins, Charles H., House—hist pl ... MI-6
Calkins, Windsor W., House—hist pl ... OR-9
Calkins Brook—stream ... MA-1
Calkins Brook—stream ... NY-2
Calkins Cem—cemetery ... OH-6
Calkins Creek—stream ... FL-3
Calkins Creek—stream ... NY-2
Calkins Creek—stream ... OR-9
Calkins Creek—stream ... PA-2
Calkins Drain—canal ... MI-6
Calkins Drain—stream ... MI-6
Calkins Equipment Company Heliport—airport ... WA-9
Calkins Hill—summit ... NY-2
Calkins JHS—school ... CO-8
Calkins Lake ... ID-8
Calkins Lake—lake ... WI-6
Calkins Lake—reservoir (2) ... CO-8
Calkins Lateral—canal ... ID-8
Calkins North Lake—lake ... WI-6
Calkins Point—cape ... WA-9
Calkins Pond ... MA-1
Calkins Pond—reservoir ... MA-1
Calkins Pond Lower Dam—dam ... MA-1
Calkins Pond Upper Dam—dam ... MA-1
Calkins Union Ch—church ... PA-2
Calk Lake ... KY-4
Calk Sch—school ... TX-5
Call—locale ... TX-5
**Call**—pop pl ... NC-3
Calla—locale ... CA-9
Calla—other ... KY-4
**Calla**—pop pl ... KY-4
**Calla**—pop pl ... OH-6
Callabee ... AL-4
Callabee Battle Ground (historical)—locale ... AL-4
Callabo (Barrio)—fmr MCD ... PR-3
**Callaboose**—pop pl ... KY-4
Calladito Lakes—reservoir ... NM-5
Calladito Tank—reservoir ... NM-5
Callagahan Branch—stream ... AR-4
Callaghan—locale ... TX-5
**Callaghan**—pop pl ... VA-3
Callaghan, Mount—summit ... NV-8
Callaghan Canyon—valley ... NV-8
Callaghan Creek—stream ... NV-8
Callaghan Creek—stream ... NC-3
Callaghan Hollow—valley ... VA-3
Callaghan Ranch—locale ... NV-8
Callaghan Ranch—locale ... TX-5
Callaghan Sch—school ... TX-5
Callaghan Tank—reservoir ... TX-5
Callaham Cem—cemetery ... VA-3
Callaham Creek ... MT-8
Callahan—locale ... OK-5
Callahan—locale ... OR-9
**Callahan**—pop pl ... CA-9
**Callahan**—pop pl ... FL-3
**Callahan**—pop pl ... KS-7
Callahan, Bayou—stream ... LA-4
Callahan, John, House—hist pl ... MD-2

Callahan, J. W., House—hist pl ... GA-3
Callahan, Matthew, Log Cabin—hist pl ... CO-8
Callahan, Mount—summit ... CO-8
Callahan, T. M., House—hist pl ... CO-8
Callahan Branch—stream (2) ... GA-3
Callahan Branch—stream ... IN-6
Callahan Branch—stream ... KY-4
Callahan Branch—stream ... LA-4
Callahan Branch—stream ... MS-4
Callahan Branch—stream ... NC-3
Callahan Branch—stream ... TN-4
Callahan Branch—stream ... VA-3
Callahan Branch—stream ... WV-2
Callahan Bridge—locale ... NV-8
Callahan Brook—stream (2) ... NY-2
Callahan Camp—locale ... CA-9
Callahan Cem—cemetery (2) ... IN-6
Callahan Cem—cemetery (4) ... KY-4
Callahan Cem—cemetery ... MS-4
Callahan Cem—cemetery ... MO-7
Callahan Cem—cemetery ... NE-7
Callahan Cem—cemetery ... OH-6
Callahan Cem—cemetery ... TN-4
Callahan Ch—church ... NE-7
**Callahan (County)**—pop pl ... TX-5
*Callahan Creek* ... NV-8
*Callahan Creek* ... TX-5
Callahan Creek—stream ... AZ-5
Callahan Creek—stream ... ID-8
Callahan Creek—stream ... MO-7
Callahan Creek—stream (2) ... MT-8
Callahan Creek—stream ... NE-7
Callahan Creek—stream (3) ... OR-9
Callahan Creek—stream ... VA-3
Callahan Ditch—canal (2) ... IN-6
Callahan Ditch—canal ... OH-6
Callahan Divide—ridge ... TX-5
Callahan Draw—valley ... TX-5
Callahan Elem Sch—school ... FL-3
Callahan Gap—gap ... AR-4
Callahan Guard Station—locale ... OR-9
Callahan Gulch—valley (2) ... CA-9
Callahan Gulch—valley ... CO-8
Callahan Hill—summit ... PA-2
Callahan-Hilliard (CCD)—cens area ... FL-3
Callahan Hollow—valley ... IN-6
Callahan Hollow—valley (2) ... MO-7
Callahan Hollow—valley ... PA-2
Callahan House—hist pl ... PA-2
Callahan JHS—school ... FL-3
Callahan JHS—school ... IA-7
Callahan Knob—summit ... AR-4
*Callahan Lake* ... MN-6
Callahan Lake—lake ... MN-6
Callahan Lake—lake ... NM-5
Callahan Lookout—locale ... OR-9
Callahan Mine—mine ... AZ-5
Callahan Mtn—summit ... AR-4
Callahan Mtn—summit ... GA-3
Callahan-Mud Lake State Wildlife Mngmt Area—park ... WI-6
Callahan Park—park ... IN-6
Callahan Playground—park ... MI-6
Callahan Pond—lake ... MA-1
*Callahan Ranch* ... NV-8
Callahan Rehabilitation Center—locale ... OR-9
Callahan Ridge—ridge ... KY-4
Callahan Road Ch—church ... TN-4
Callahan Run—stream (2) ... PA-2
**Callahans**—pop pl ... NJ-2
Callahans Beach—beach ... NY-2
Callahan Sch—school ... FL-3
Callahan Sch—school (2) ... MA-1
Callahan Sch (historical)—school ... AL-4
Callahan Sch (historical)—school ... MS-4
Callahan Sch (historical)—school ... MO-7
Callahan Sch Number 1 (historical)—school ... SD-7
Callahans Corner—locale ... VA-3
Callahans Corners—locale ... NY-2
Callahan Shelter Cabin—locale ... AK-9
Callahans Hills—locale ... VA-3
Callahan Spring—spring ... OR-9
Callahan Spring—spring ... UT-8
Callahan Spur—ridge ... VA-3
*Callahans Run* ... PA-2
Callahan Swamp—stream ... VA-3
Callahan Swamp—swamp ... MD-2
Callahan Tank—reservoir ... AZ-5
**Callahan Township**—pop pl ... ND-7
Callahan Trail—trail ... PA-2
Callalisa Creek—stream ... FL-3
*Callam* ... WA-9
Callam Creek—stream ... MI-6
Callan—locale ... TX-5
Callanan Playground—park ... MA-1
Callanans Corners—locale ... NY-2
Callan Cem—cemetery ... AR-4
Callan Creek—stream ... NY-2
Callandar Spring—spring ... AL-4
Calland Cem—cemetery ... OH-6
Callan Draw—valley ... CO-8
Callandret Sch—school ... TX-5
Callands—locale ... VA-3
Callands Ch—church ... VA-3
Callands Gretna (Magisterial District)—fmr MCD ... VA-3
Callan Lake—reservoir ... NE-7
Callan Sch—school ... VT-1
Callans Pond (historical)—lake ... TN-4
Callanwolde—hist pl ... GA-3
Callao—locale ... UT-8
**Callao**—pop pl ... MO-7
**Callao**—pop pl ... VA-3
Callao Cem—cemetery ... UT-8
Callao Landing (historical)—locale ... MS-4
Callao Sch—school ... UT-8
Callao Township—civil ... MO-7
*Callapooia River* ... OR-9
**Callapoose**—pop pl ... PA-2
*Callapooya Creek* ... OR-9
*Callapooya Mountains* ... OR-9
*Callapooya River* ... OR-9
Calla Sch—school ... CA-9
Callas Gap—gap ... SC-3
Callas Mtn—summit ... SC-3
Callas Sweet Shop—hist pl ... KY-4
**Calla (sta.)**—pop pl ... CA-9
Callaville—locale ... VA-3
Callawassie Creek—stream ... SC-3
Callawassie Island—island ... SC-3
Callaway—locale ... MD-2
**Callaway**—pop pl ... FL-3
**Callaway**—pop pl ... KY-4
**Callaway**—pop pl ... LA-4
**Callaway**—pop pl ... MN-6
**Callaway**—pop pl ... MO-7
**Callaway**—pop pl ... NE-7
**Callaway**—pop pl ... VA-3
**Callaway**—pop pl (2) ... WV-2
Callaway, Flanders, House—hist pl ... MO-7
Callaway Assembly of God Ch—church ... FL-3
Callaway Bayou—bay ... FL-3
Callaway Bluff—cliff ... MO-7
Callaway Branch—stream ... MO-7
**Callaway (Calloway)**—pop pl ... FL-3
Callaway Cem—cemetery ... AR-4
Callaway Cem—cemetery ... GA-3
Callaway Cem—cemetery ... TN-4
Callaway Center—building ... GA-3
Callaway Ch—church ... GA-3
Callaway Ch—church ... VA-3
**Callaway County**—pop pl ... MO-7
Callaway Creek—stream ... AL-4
Callaway Creek—stream ... FL-3
Callaway Fork—stream ... MO-7
Callaway Gap—gap ... KY-4
Callaway Gardens—area ... GA-3
Callaway-Gillette House—hist pl ... TX-5
Callaway Island Shoals—bar ... TN-4
Callaway Lake—reservoir ... GA-3
Callaway Memorial Gardens—cemetery ... MO-7
Callaway Memorial Tower—building ... GA-3
Callaway Mill—locale ... GA-3
Callaway Mtn—summit ... NC-3
Callaway Park—park ... IN-6
Callaway Plaza (Shop Ctr)—locale ... FL-3
Callaway Riley Spring—spring ... MO-7
Callaway Rsvr—reservoir ... MT-8
Callaway R 1 Sch—school ... MO-7
Callaway R-1 Sch—school ... MO-7
*Callaways* ... MD-2
Callaway Sch—school ... IL-6
Callaways Landing—localé ... AL-4
*Callaways Little Island* ... TN-4
Callaway Spring—spring ... TN-4
Callaway Stadium—other ... GA-3
Callaway State Wildlife Mngmt Area—park ... MN-6
Callaway-Steptoe Cem—cemetery ... VA-3
**Callaway (Township of)**—pop pl ... MN-6
Callaway Well—well ... NV-8
Callaway Well—well ... NM-5
Call-Bartlett House—hist pl ... MA-1
Call Bldg—building ... CA-9
Call Bog—swamp ... ME-1
Call-Booth House—hist pl ... CA-9
*Call Branch* ... SC-3
Call Branch—stream ... AR-4
Call Brook—stream ... NH-1
Call (CCD)—cens area ... TX-5
Call Cem—cemetery ... IL-6
Call Cem—cemetery ... ME-1
Call Cem—cemetery ... MO-7
Call Creek—stream ... NC-3
Call Creek—stream (2) ... OR-9
Call Creek—stream ... WY-8
Call Drain—canal (2) ... MI-6
**Calleaway**—pop pl ... MO-7
Callebs Creek—stream ... KY-4
Callebs Creek Cem—cemetery ... KY-4
*Calleghan Branch Fourche Creek* ... AR-4
Calle Gonzalo Marin No. 61—hist pl ... PR-3
Calleguas—civil ... CA-9
Calleguas Creek—stream ... CA-9
Calleguas Creek Site—hist pl ... CA-9
Callejones (Barrio)—fmr MCD ... PR-3
Callejon Windmill—locale (2) ... TX-5
Calle Mayor Sch—school ... CA-9
Callen, Dick, House—hist pl ... ID-8
Callender—locale ... CA-9
**Callender**—pop pl ... IA-7
Callender Cem—cemetery ... MS-4
Callender Gap Creek—stream ... PA-2
Callender House—hist pl ... TX-5
Callender Pond—reservoir ... LA-4
Callen Point—cape ... ME-1
Callen Run—stream ... PA-2
Callen Run Trail—trail ... PA-2
Callens Branch—stream ... AR-4
Callens Branch—stream ... TN-4
**Callensburg**—pop pl ... PA-2
Callensburg Borough—civil ... PA-2
Callen Sch—school ... CT-1
Callens Dock—locale ... TN-4
Callero Well—well ... AZ-5
**Callery**—pop pl ... PA-2
Callery Borough—civil ... PA-2
Calles Spring—spring ... AZ-5
*Calletano Creek* ... CA-9
Calle Vieja (Shop Ctr)—locale ... FL-3
Calleys Lake—lake ... NM-5
Call Fat Branch—stream ... VA-3
Call Field Canal—canal ... TX-5
Callham Oil Field—oilfield ... TX-5
Call Hill—summit ... ME-1
Call Hill—summit ... NY-2
Call Hill Cem—cemetery ... NY-2
Call Hollow—valley ... AR-4
Call House—hist pl ... MI-6
Callicoat Cem—cemetery ... OH-6
**Callicoon**—pop pl ... NY-2
**Callicoon Center**—pop pl ... NY-2
Callicoon Creek—stream ... NY-2
**Callicoon (Town of)**—pop pl ... NY-2
Callicott Cem—cemetery ... IL-6
Callicott Cem—cemetery ... TN-4
Callicotte Cem—cemetery ... IN-6
Callicutts Ch—church ... NC-3
Callie—locale ... TN-4
Callie Creek—stream ... AL-4
Callie Furnace—hist pl ... VA-3
Callie Furnace—locale ... VA-3
Callie Harbin Ch—church ... GA-3
Callie Lake—lake ... AR-4
Callier Branch—stream ... AL-4
Calligan Creek—stream ... WA-9
Calligan Island—island ... AK-9
Calligan Lake—lake ... WA-9
**Calliham**—pop pl ... TX-5
Calliham Mine—mine ... UT-8
Calliham Plantation House—hist pl ... LA-4
**Callihan**—pop pl ... KY-4
Callihan Cem—cemetery ... KY-4
Callihan Cem—cemetery ... NC-3
Callihan Ch—church ... KY-4
Callihan Creek—stream ... TX-5
Callihan (historical)—locale ... SD-7
Callihan Run—stream ... PA-2
**Callimont**—pop pl ... PA-2
Calling, Ernest A., House—hist pl ... NE-7
Calling All Christians Ch—church ... MS-4
Callings Hollow—valley ... UT-8
Callins Field—park ... TN-4
Calliope Mtn—summit ... AK-9
*Calliou Bay* ... LA-4
Callioud Spring—spring ... CA-9
**Callisburg**—pop pl ... TX-5
Callisburg (CCD)—cens area ... TX-5
Callisburg Cem—cemetery ... TX-5
Callisburg Oil Field—oilfield ... TX-5
Callis Creek—stream ... ID-8
Callis Creek—stream ... VA-3
Callis General Store and Post Office—hist pl ... KY-4
Callis Grove Campground—locale ... KY-4
Callis Hill—summit ... MD-2
Callis Lake Dam—dam ... MS-4
Callison—locale ... VA-3
**Callison**—pop pl ... SC-3
Callison Bluff—cliff ... MO-7
Callison Cem—cemetery ... OH-6
Callison Lateral—canal ... NM-5
**Callisons**—pop pl ... NC-3
Callis Tank—reservoir ... TX-5
Callistel Sch—school ... IL-6
**Callister Subdivision**—pop pl ... UT-8
Callisto Head—cape ... AK-9
**Calliston**—pop pl ... AL-4
Callisto Peak—summit ... AK-9
Callis Wharf—locale ... VA-3
Callis Windmill—locale ... TX-5
Call Junction—locale ... TX-5
Call Meadow—flat ... OR-9
Call Meadow Trail—trail ... OR-9
Call Mountains—other ... CA-9
Call Mtn—summit ... MT-8
Call Mtn—summit ... PA-2
*Callo De Laureles* ... TX-5
*Callo del Grullo* ... TX-5
*Callo del Infiernillo* ... TX-5
*Callo del Oso* ... TX-5
*Callo Infiernillo* ... TX-5
**Callon**—pop pl ... WI-6
Callon Hollow—valley ... IN-6
Callon Lake Dam—dam ... MS-4
Callon Tramojo—area ... GU-9
Callo Padrones—lake ... TX-5
Calloway—other ... FL-3
**Calloway**—pop pl ... IL-6
Calloway Branch—stream (2) ... KY-4
Calloway Branch—stream ... TX-5
Calloway Butte—summit ... AZ-5
Calloway Canal—canal ... CA-9
Calloway Canyon—valley ... NM-5
Calloway Cave—cave ... AL-4
Calloway Cem—cemetery (2) ... NC-3
Calloway Cem—cemetery ... WV-2
Calloway Ch—church ... KY-4
**Calloway (County)**—pop pl ... KY-4
Calloway County Courthouse—hist pl ... KY-4
Calloway Creek—stream ... GA-3
Calloway Creek—stream (3) ... KY-4
Calloway Creek—stream ... MS-4
Calloway Creek—stream (2) ... OR-9
Calloway Crossing—locale ... KY-4
Calloway Ditch—canal ... MT-8
Calloway Ford (historical)—locale ... MO-7
Calloway Gap—gap ... KY-4
Calloway Gap—gap ... NC-3
Calloway Hill—summit ... CO-8
Calloway Hill—summit ... WA-9
**Calloway (historical)**—pop pl ... OR-9
Calloway Hollow—valley ... TN-4
Calloway House—hist pl ... KY-4
Calloway HS—school ... MS-4
Calloway Island—island ... TN-4
Calloway Island (historical)—island ... TN-4
Calloway Lake—lake ... AZ-5
Calloway Landing—locale ... MD-2
Calloway Memorial Chapel—church ... GA-3
*Calloway Memorial Gardens* ... MO-7
Calloway Mines—mine ... TN-4
Calloway Peak—summit ... NC-3
Calloway Place—locale ... CO-8
Calloway Ranch—locale ... NE-7
Calloway Ridge—ridge ... TN-4
Calloway Rsvr—reservoir ... OR-9
Calloway Sch—school ... AL-4
Calloway Sch—school ... TN-4
Calloway Sinks—basin ... AL-4
Calloway Southwest (CCD)—cens area ... KY-4
Calloway Swamp—swamp ... FL-3
Calloway Tank—reservoir ... AZ-5
Calloway Weir—dam ... CA-9
Callow Cem—cemetery ... WV-2
Callow Creek—stream ... CO-8
Callow Creek—stream ... OR-9
Callows Island—island ... MT-8
*Call Peak* ... WA-9
Call Pond—lake ... ME-1
Call Ranch—locale ... CA-9
Call Ranch—locale ... WY-8
Call Road Rsvr—reservoir ... MT-8
**Calls**—pop pl ... TN-4
Calls Ch—church ... AR-4
Call Sch—school ... TX-5
Calls Creek—stream ... GA-3
Calls First Gulch—valley ... MT-8
Calls Fort—locale ... UT-8
Calls Fort Canyon—valley ... UT-8
*Calls Fort Cemetery* ... UT-8
Calls Fort Monmt—park ... UT-8
Calls Hill—summit ... NH-1
Calls Hollow—valley ... MO-7
*Calls Neck* ... NJ-2
*Calls River* ... OR-9
Calls Sch (historical)—school ... TN-4
**Call (sta.) (Call Junction)**—pop pl ... TX-5
Call Street Hist Dist—hist pl ... FL-3
**Call Subdivision**—pop pl ... UT-8
**Call Terminal**—pop pl ... IA-7
*Call Town* ... MS-4
Callum Branch—stream ... SC-3
Callum Cem—cemetery ... AR-4
*Callville Basin* ... AZ-5
*Callville Basin* ... NV-8
Callville Bay—bay ... NV-8
Callville Bay—locale ... NV-8
*Callville Islands* ... NV-8
Callville Paint—cape ... NV-8
Callville Wash—stream ... NV-8
*Callvin Lake* ... NE-7
**Calm**—pop pl ... MO-7
Calm, Lake—lake ... FL-3
Cal Maine Lake Dam—dam ... MS-4
*Calmar* ... KS-7
**Calmar**—pop pl ... IA-7
Calmar Community Cem—cemetery ... IA-7
Calmar Township—civil ... SD-7
Calmar Township—fmr MCD ... IA-7
Calmer—locale ... AR-4
Calmes, Henry W., House—hist pl ... KY-4
Calmes Neck—cape ... VA-3
*Calmet* ... SD-7
*Calmia Lake* ... CA-9
Calming Island—island ... AK-9
Calm Lake—lake ... LA-4
Calm Point—cape ... AK-9
Cal Mtn—summit ... CA-9
Calmus Creek—stream ... IA-7
Calmwood Airp—airport ... PA-2
**Caln**—pop pl ... PA-2
*Calne* ... PA-2
Caln Elem Sch—school ... PA-2
Calneva—locale ... CA-9
Calneva Lake—lake ... CA-9
**Cal-Nev-Ari**—pop pl ... NV-8
Caln Meeting House—hist pl ... PA-2
**Caln Meeting House**—pop pl ... PA-2
Calno—locale ... VA-3
**Calno**—pop pl ... NJ-2
Calno Sch—school ... NJ-2
Caln Township Airp—airport ... PA-2
**Caln (Township of)**—pop pl ... PA-2
*Calochortus Lake* ... UT-8
*Caloebee Creek* ... AL-4
Calohan Creek—stream ... TX-5
Calohan Spring—spring ... OR-9
Caloma—locale ... IA-7
Calomel Lake (reduced usage)—lake ... IL-6
Calona Station—locale ... PA-2
Calon Ranch—locale ... OR-9
Calooga Post Office (historical)—building ... MS-4
Caloosa Elementary-MS—school ... FL-3
Caloosahatchee Bridge—bridge ... FL-3
Caloosahatchee Canal—canal ... FL-3
**Caloosahatchee (historical)**—pop pl ... FL-3
Caloosahatchee River—stream ... FL-3
Caloosahatchee River State Park—park ... FL-3
Caloosahatchee Rock Mine—mine ... FL-3
Caloosa Indian Mound—summit ... FL-3
*Caloosa River* ... FL-3
*Caloosz Lake* ... FL-3
*Calophyllum Cliffs* ... MH-9
*Calophyllum Ravine* ... MH-9
Calora—locale ... NE-7
**Calor (historical)**—pop pl ... OR-9
*Caloric* ... WV-2
Calorific (historical)—locale ... KS-7
Calosa Creek—stream ... TX-5
Caloway Creek—stream ... WA-9
**Calpack**—pop pl ... CA-9
Calpak Plant No. 11—hist pl ... CA-9
Cal Peak—summit ... WA-9
**Calpella**—pop pl ... CA-9
**Calpet**—pop pl ... WY-8
Calphos—locale ... FL-3
**Calpine**—pop pl ... CA-9
Cal-Pine Mine—mine ... CA-9
**Calpine (Sierra Valley Lodge)**—pop pl ... CA-9
Cal Place—locale ... TN-4
Cals Beach—beach ... ME-1
Cals Creek—stream ... NC-3
Cals Fork Gulch—valley ... CO-8
Cals Gulch—valley ... MT-8
Cals Hammock—bay ... VA-3
Cal Ship Mesa—summit ... NM-5
Cal Smith Branch—stream ... TN-4
Cal Smith Spring—spring ... OR-9
Cal Smoak Site—hist pl ... SC-3
Calspar Quarry Pool—lake ... MI-6
Calspur—locale ... ND-7
Cal Tank—reservoir ... AZ-5
Caltech Peak—summit ... CA-9
*Calter Pond* ... UT-8
Caltharp Sch—school ... TN-4
Caltharp Sch (historical)—school ... TN-4
Calthrop Neck—cape ... VA-3
Calton Cem—cemetery ... MO-7
*Calton Creek* ... MO-7
Calton Creek—stream ... AR-4
Calton Creek—stream ... MO-7
*Calton Point* ... ME-1
**Caltor Manor**—pop pl ... MD-2
*Calumet* ... IL-6
*Calumet* ... IN-6
Calumet—locale ... AL-4
Calumet—locale ... AZ-5
Calumet—locale ... AR-4
Calumet—locale ... CO-8
Calumet—locale ... MO-7
Calumet—locale ... NV-8
**Calumet**—pop pl ... AL-4
**Calumet**—pop pl ... IA-7
**Calumet**—pop pl ... LA-4
**Calumet**—pop pl ... MI-6
**Calumet**—pop pl ... MN-6
**Calumet**—pop pl ... OK-5
**Calumet**—pop pl ... PA-2
Calumet, Lake—lake ... IL-6
Calumet Air Force Station—military ... MI-6
Calumet and Hecla Industrial District—hist pl ... MI-6
Calumet and Hecla Mine—mine ... WI-6
Calumet Ave Interchange—crossing ... IN-6
Calumet Bar—bar ... IN-6
Calumet Boating Center—locale ... IL-6
Calumet Canyon—valley ... CA-9
Calumet Cem—cemetery ... OK-5
**Calumet City**—pop pl ... IL-6
Calumet Country Club—other ... IL-6
**Calumet (County)**—pop pl ... WI-6
Calumet County Courthouse—hist pl ... WI-6
Calumet Creek—stream ... KS-7
Calumet Creek—stream ... MO-7
Calumet Creek—stream ... NE-7
Calumet Downtown Hist Dist—hist pl ... MI-6
Calumet Fire Station—hist pl ... MI-6
Calumet Gulch—valley ... AZ-5
*Calumet Harbor* ... IL-6
Calumet Harbor—harbor ... IL-6
Calumet Harbor—harbor ... IN-6
**Calumet Harbor**—pop pl ... WI-6
Calumet Harbor Breakwater South End Light—locale ... IN-6
Calumet Harbor Entrance South Side Light—locale ... IN-6
Calumet Harbor Light—locale ... IN-6
Calumet Hotel—hist pl ... MN-6
Calumet Hotel—hist pl ... OR-9
Calumet HS—school ... IL-6
Calumet Island—island ... LA-4
Calumet Island—island ... NY-2
Calumet-Kingery Interchange—other ... IL-6
*Calumet Lake* ... OR-9
Calumet Lake—lake ... MI-6
Calumet Lake—reservoir ... IN-6
Calumet Lake Dam—dam ... IN-6
Calumet Mine—mine (2) ... AZ-5
Calumet Mine—mine ... CA-9
Calumet Mine—mine ... CO-8
Calumet Mine—mine ... MI-6
Calumet Mine—mine ... NM-5
Calumet Mine—mine ... SD-7
Calumet Mine—mine ... UT-8
Calumet Mountains—range ... CA-9
Calumet-Norvelt—CDP ... PA-2
Calumet Number 2 Slope Mine (underground)—mine ... AL-4
Calumet Park—park (2) ... IL-6
**Calumet Park**—pop pl ... IL-6
Calumet Park Cem—cemetery ... IN-6
Calumet Park (sta.) (PU RR name for Calumet City)—other ... IL-6
Calumet Plant, R. R. Donnelly & Sons Company—hist pl ... IL-6
Calumet Plantation House—hist pl ... LA-4
Calumet Playground—park ... IL-6
Calumet Pond—reservoir ... MA-1
Calumet Post Office (historical)—building ... AL-4
Calumet Ranch—locale ... NM-5
Calumet Ridge—ridge ... SD-7
Calumet River—stream ... IL-6
Calumet Rsvr—reservoir ... CO-8
Calumet Run—stream ... IN-6
Calumet Sag Channel—channel ... IL-6
Calumet Sch—school ... CA-9
Calumet Sch—school ... IL-6
Calumet Sch—school ... OH-6
Calumet Sch—school ... WI-6
Calumet Sch (abandoned)—school ... MO-7
Calumet Springs—spring ... IL-6
Calumet Theatre—hist pl ... MI-6
**Calumet (Town of)**—pop pl ... WI-6
Calumet Township—civil ... MO-7
**Calumet (Township of)**—pop pl ... IL-6
**Calumet (Township of)**—pop pl ... IN-6
**Calumet (Township of)**—pop pl ... MI-6
Calumet Union Drainage Canal—canal ... IL-6
Calumet Union Drainage Ditch—canal ... IL-6
**Calumetville**—pop pl ... WI-6
Calumet Waterworks—other ... MI-6
*Calumet Western Junction* ... IL-6
Calumet Woods—woods ... IL-6
*Calumet Yard* ... IL-6
*Calumut Creek* ... MO-7
Calunchety Hollow—valley ... OK-5
*Calup Creek* ... TN-4
*Calus* ... KS-7
Calusa Club Estates Park—park ... FL-3
Calusa Country Club—locale ... FL-3
Calusa Creek—stream ... ID-8
Calusa Elem Sch—school (2) ... FL-3
Calusa Keys—island ... FL-3
**Calva**—pop pl ... AZ-5
Calva Cem—cemetery ... AR-4
Calvache (Barrio)—fmr MCD ... PR-3
Calvada Meadows Airp—airport ... NV-8
Calva Draw—valley ... AZ-5
Calvalier Cem—cemetery ... OK-5
Cal Valley—basin ... UT-8
**Calvander**—pop pl ... NC-3
Calvario Draw—valley ... NM-5
Calva RR Station—building ... AZ-5
Calvary—locale ... KY-4
Calvary—locale ... MD-2
Calvary—locale ... TX-5
Calvary—locale ... VA-3
**Calvary**—pop pl ... AL-4
**Calvary**—pop pl ... GA-3
**Calvary**—pop pl ... MS-4
**Calvary**—pop pl ... TN-4
**Calvary**—pop pl ... WI-6
Calvary Apostolic Ch—church ... AL-4
Calvary Apostolic Ch—church ... MS-4
Calvary Apostolic Pentecostal United Ch—church ... KS-7
Calvary Assembly—church ... FL-3
Calvary Assembly American Christian Sch—school ... FL-3
Calvary Assembly of God—church (3) ... FL-3
Calvary Assembly of God Ch—church (3) ... AL-4
Calvary Assembly of God Ch—church ... DE-2
Calvary Assembly of God Ch—church (2) ... FL-3
Calvary Assembly of God Ch—church ... KS-7
Calvary Assembly of God Ch—church ... MS-4
*Calvary Baptist Ch* ... AL-4
*Calvary Baptist Ch* ... MS-4
Calvary Baptist Ch—church (18) ... AL-4
Calvary Baptist Ch—church ... DE-2
Calvary Baptist Ch—church (12) ... FL-3
Calvary Baptist Ch—church ... IN-6
Calvary Baptist Ch—church ... IA-7
Calvary Baptist Ch—church (2) ... KS-7
Calvary Baptist Ch—church (22) ... MS-4
Calvary Baptist Ch—church ... SD-7
Calvary Baptist Ch—church (16) ... TN-4
Calvary Baptist Ch and Spanish Mission (Ogden)—church ... UT-8
Calvary Baptist Ch of Lake Mary—church ... FL-3
Calvary Baptist Ch (Salt Lake City)—church ... UT-8
Calvary Baptist Church—hist pl ... KS-7
Calvary Baptist Church—hist pl ... NJ-2
Calvary Baptist Church—hist pl ... OK-5
Calvary Baptist Church—hist pl ... RI-1
Calvary Baptist Church Christian Sch—school ... FL-3
Calvary Baptist Church/First Baptist Church—hist pl ... IA-7
Calvary Baptist Church Sch—school ... FL-3
Calvary Baptist Sch—school ... MS-4
Calvary Baptist Temple—church ... MS-4
Calvary Bible Ch—church ... AL-4
Calvary Bible Ch—church ... AR-4
Calvary Bible Ch—church ... FL-3
Calvary Bible Ch—church ... KS-7
Calvary Bible Ch—church ... NJ-2
Calvary Bible Ch—church ... UT-8
Calvary Bible Ch—church ... VA-3
Calvary Branch—stream ... VA-3
Calvary Cathedral Assembly of God Ch—church ... FL-3
Calvary Cem—cemetery (2) ... AL-4
Calvary Cem—cemetery (2) ... AZ-5
Calvary Cem—cemetery (7) ... AR-4
Calvary Cem—cemetery (8) ... CA-9
Calvary Cem—cemetery (2) ... CO-8
Calvary Cem—cemetery (2) ... CT-1
Calvary Cem—cemetery (23) ... IL-6
Calvary Cem—cemetery (7) ... IN-6
Calvary Cem—cemetery (29) ... IA-7
Calvary Cem—cemetery (11) ... KS-7
Calvary Cem—cemetery (4) ... KY-4
Calvary Cem—cemetery ... LA-4
Calvary Cem—cemetery (4) ... ME-1
Calvary Cem—cemetery (10) ... MA-1
Calvary Cem—cemetery (11) ... MI-6
Calvary Cem—cemetery (45) ... MN-6
Calvary Cem—cemetery (8) ... MS-4
Calvary Cem—cemetery (7) ... MO-7
Calvary Cem—cemetery (5) ... MT-8
Calvary Cem—cemetery (14) ... NE-7
Calvary Cem—cemetery (4) ... NH-1
Calvary Cem—cemetery (4) ... NJ-2
Calvary Cem—cemetery (17) ... NY-2
Calvary Cem—cemetery (13) ... ND-7
Calvary Cem—cemetery (13) ... OH-6
Calvary Cem—cemetery (5) ... OK-5
Calvary Cem—cemetery (2) ... OR-9
Calvary Cem—cemetery (19) ... PA-2
Calvary Cem—cemetery (2) ... SC-3
Calvary Cem—cemetery (6) ... SD-7
Calvary Cem—cemetery (5) ... TN-4
Calvary Cem—cemetery (8) ... TX-5
Calvary Cem—cemetery ... VT-1
Calvary Cem—cemetery ... VA-3
Calvary Cem—cemetery (4) ... WA-9
Calvary Cem—cemetery (31) ... WI-6
*Calvary Ch* ... AL-4
*Calvary Ch* ... DE-2
*Calvary Ch* ... MS-4
*Calvary Ch* ... VA-3
Calvary Ch—church (35) ... AL-4
Calvary Ch—church (12) ... AR-4
Calvary Ch—church ... CO-8
Calvary Ch—church (14) ... FL-3
Calvary Ch—church (30) ... GA-3
Calvary Ch—church (3) ... IL-6
Calvary Ch—church (8) ... IN-6
Calvary Ch—church (3) ... IA-7
Calvary Ch—church ... KS-7
Calvary Ch—church (9) ... KY-4
Calvary Ch—church (7) ... LA-4
Calvary Ch—church (4) ... MD-2
Calvary Ch—church (3) ... MA-1
Calvary Ch—church (9) ... MI-6
Calvary Ch—church (3) ... MN-6
Calvary Ch—church (28) ... MS-4
Calvary Ch—church (9) ... MO-7
Calvary Ch—church (6) ... NJ-2
Calvary Ch—church (9) ... NY-2
Calvary Ch—church (43) ... NC-3
Calvary Ch—church ... ND-7
Calvary Ch—church (10) ... OH-6
Calvary Ch—church (4) ... OK-5
Calvary Ch—church (24) ... PA-2
Calvary Ch—church (35) ... SC-3
Calvary Ch—church ... SD-7
Calvary Ch—church (16) ... TN-4
Calvary Ch—church (24) ... TX-5
Calvary Ch—church (33) ... VA-3
Calvary Ch—church (7) ... WV-2
Calvary Ch—church ... WI-6
Calvary Ch—church ... WY-8
Calvary Ch—church ... VI-3
Calvary Chapel—church ... CT-1
Calvary Chapel—church ... FL-3
Calvary Chapel—church ... IA-7
Calvary Chapel—church (4) ... OH-6
Calvary Chapel—church ... SD-7
Calvary Chapel—church ... VA-3
Calvary Chapel (American Fork)—church ... UT-8
Calvary Chapel Assembly of God Ch—church ... UT-8
Calvary Chapel (Salt Lake)—church ... UT-8
Calvary Ch of God—church ... AL-4
*Calvary Ch of the Nazarene* ... MS-4
Calvary Ch of the Nazarene—church ... FL-3
Calvary Christian Center—school ... FL-3
Calvary Christian Center (Assembly of God)—church ... UT-8
Calvary Christian Sch—school ... CA-9
Calvary Christian Sch—school (2) ... FL-3
Calvary Christian Sch—school ... TN-4
*Calvary Church* ... SD-7
**Calvary Church**—pop pl ... TX-5
Calvary Episcopal Ch (historical)—church ... MS-4
Calvary Episcopal Church—hist pl ... KY-4
Calvary Episcopal Church—hist pl ... MT-8
Calvary Episcopal Church and Churchyard—hist pl ... NC-3
Calvary Episcopal Church and Parish House—hist pl ... TN-4
Calvary Episcopal Church Sunday Sch—hist pl ... OH-6
Calvary Evangelical Ch—church ... IN-6
*Calvary Faith Center* ... MS-4
Calvary Faith Tabernacle—church ... VA-3

Calvary Faithway Missionary Ch—church MS-4
Calvary Fellowship Baptist Ch—church FL-3
Calvary Gospel Ch—church NC-3
Calvary Heights Baptist Ch—church AL-4
Calvary Hill Baptist Ch—church TN-4
Calvary Hill Cem—cemetery MN-6
Calvary Hill Cem—cemetery PA-2
Calvary Hill Cem—cemetery TX-5
Calvary Hill Ch—church AL-4
Calvary Hill Ch—church GA-3
Calvary Hill Ch—church (2) MS-4
Calvary Hill Neighborhood Center—building AL-4
Calvary Hill Park—park MN-6
Calvary Hollow—valley PA-2
Calvary Independent Baptist Ch MS-4
Calvary Independent Ch—church PA-2
Calvary Life Tabernacle CPC—church FL-3
Calvary Lutheran Ch—church KS-7
Calvary Lutheran Church & Parsonage—hist pl OR-9
Calvary Lutheran Sch—school IN-6
Calvary Memorial Ch—church GA-3
Calvary Memorial Ch—church NY-2
Calvary Memorial Gardens—cemetery GA-3
Calvary Memorial Park—cemetery VA-3
Calvary Mennonite Church AL-4
Calvary Methodist Ch—church DE-2
Calvary Methodist Church—hist pl MA-1
Calvary Mission AL-4
Calvary Missionary Baptist Ch—church FL-3
Calvary Missionary Baptist Ch—church TN-4
Calvary Missionary Baptist Church AL-4
Calvary Missionary Ch—church TN-4
Calvary Oakwood Cem—cemetery KY-4
Calvary Open Bible Ch—church FL-3
Calvary Park( Cemetery)—cemetery OH-6
Calvary Pentacostal Ch NC-3
Calvary Pentecostal Ch—church MS-4
Calvary Presbyterian Ch—church AL-4
Calvary Presbyterian Ch—church DE-2
Calvary Presbyterian Ch—church (2) FL-3
Calvary Presbyterian Ch—church TN-4
Calvary Presbyterian Church—hist pl CA-9
Calvary Presbyterian Church—hist pl WI-6
Calvary-Reno (CCD)—cens area GA-3
Calvary Revival Center—church FL-3
Calvary Ridge—ridge KY-4
Calvary Rocks—pillar VA-3
Calvary Sacket Draw—valley WY-8
Calvary Sch IN-6
Calvary Sch—school CA-9
Calvary Sch—school KY-4
Calvary Sch—school (2) MI-6
Calvary Sch—school MS-4
Calvary Sch—school MO-7
Calvary Sch—school SC-3
Calvary Sch—school TX-5
Calvary Tabernacle—church AL-4
Calvary Tabernacle—church NY-2
Calvary Tabernacle—church NC-3
Calvary Tabernacle—church TX-5
Calvary Tabernacle—church (2) VA-3
Calvary Tabernacle of the Apostolic Way—church FL-3
Calvary Temple—church AL-4
Calvary Temple—church GA-3
Calvary Temple—church (2) IN-6
Calvary Temple—church KY-4
Calvary Temple—church MO-7
Calvary Temple—church PA-2
Calvary Temple—church VA-3
Calvary Temple Assembly of God—church AL-4
Calvary Temple Assembly of God—church TN-4
Calvary Temple Assembly of God Ch—church AL-4
Calvary Temple Assembly of God Ch—church FL-3
Calvary Temple Assembly of God Ch—church MS-4
Calvary Temple Ch—church AL-4
Calvary Temple Ch—church FL-3
Calvary Temple-First Assembly of God Ch—church FL-3
Calvary Temple United Pentecostal Ch—church AL-4
Calvary United Methodist Ch—church DE-2
Calvary United Methodist Ch—church FL-3
Calvary United Methodist Ch—church MS-4
Calvary United Pentecostal Ch—church AL-4
Calvary United Pentecostal Tabernacle—church IN-6
**Cal-Vel**—pop pl NC-3
Cal-Vel Sch—school NC-3
Calven Hollow—valley OK-5
Calver Cem—cemetery TX-5
Calverdes Spring—spring NM-5
Calver Island—island PA-2
Calver Lake—lake TX-5
Calvert KY-4
Calvert—locale MT-8
Calvert—locale SC-3
Calvert—locale WI-6
**Calvert**—pop pl (2) AL-4
**Calvert**—pop pl KS-7
**Calvert**—pop pl MD-2
**Calvert**—pop pl NC-3
**Calvert**—pop pl PA-2
**Calvert**—pop pl TX-5
Calvert—post sta DC-2
Calvert—uninc pl MD-2
Calvert—uninc pl WV-2
Calvert Air Park—airport IN-6
Calvert Atoll MP-9
Calvert Bay—bay MD-2
**Calvert Beach**—pop pl MD-2
Calvert Beach Run—stream MD-2
Calvert Beauty Cem—cemetery TX-5
Calvert Branch—stream TN-4
Calvert (CCD)—cens area TX-5
Calvert Cem—cemetery (2) AL-4
Calvert Cem—cemetery (2) KY-4
Calvert Cem—cemetery LA-4
Calvert Cem—cemetery MO-7
Calvert Cem—cemetery NM-5
Calvert Cem—cemetery VA-3
Calvert Ch—church KY-4
Calvert Ch—church NC-3
**Calvert City**—pop pl KY-4
Calvert City (CCD)—cens area KY-4
**Calvert City (RR name Calvert)**—pop pl KY-4
Calvert Country Club—other TX-5
**Calvert (County)**—pop pl MD-2
Calvert Creek—bay MD-2
Calvert Creek—stream (2) MT-8
Calvert Creek—stream (2) TX-5
Calvert Field—park WV-2
Calvert Hill—summit IL-6
Calvert Hill—summit MT-8
**Calvert Hills**—pop pl MD-2
**Calvert Hills**—pop pl PA-2
Calvert Hist Dist—hist pl TX-5
**Calvert (historical)**—pop pl OR-9
Calvert HS—school OH-6
Calvert Island MP-9
Calvert Islands MP-9
Calvert Junction—locale TX-5
Calvert Lake—lake TX-5
Calvert Lakes—lake WY-8
Calvert Landing—locale AL-4
**Calvert Manor**—pop pl MD-2
Calvert Mill/Washington Mill—hist pl VA-3
Calvert Oil Field—oilfield TX-5
**Calverton**—pop pl MD-2
**Calverton**—pop pl NY-2
**Calverton**—pop pl VA-3
Calverton Ch—church VA-3
**Calverton Park**—pop pl MO-7
Calverton-Roanoke—CDP NY-2
Calverton Sch—school MD-2
Calverton Sch—school NY-2
Calvert Park—park MD-2
Calvert Peak airstrip—airport OR-9
Calvert Point—cape AL-4
Calvert Prong Little Warrior River—stream AL-4
Calvert (RR name for Calvert City)—other KY-4
Calvert Rsvr—reservoir CO-8
Calverts Bar—bar AL-4
Calvert Sch—school MD-2
Calvert Sch—school MO-7
Calvert Sch—school MT-8
Calvert Sch—school (2) NE-7
Calvert Sch—school NC-3
Calverts Chapel—church IN-6
Calvert Sch (historical)—school MO-7
Calverts Landing AL-4
Calvert Slough—stream OR-9
Calvert Spring—spring KY-4
Calverts Store (historical)—locale MS-4
Calvert (Township of)—fmr MCD AR-4
**Calvertville**—pop pl IN-6
Calvertville Cem—cemetery IN-6
Calvery Cem—cemetery OH-6
Calvery Ch AL-4
Calvery Ch—church AL-4
Calvery Ch—church AR-4
Calvery Ch—church FL-3
Calvery Ch—church GA-3
Calvery Ch—church (2) MS-4
Calvery Chapel Agape Fellowship (Layton)—church UT-8
Calvery Presbyterian Ch—church PA-2
Calvery Sch (historical)—school AL-4
Calves Island—island CT-1
Calves Islands CT-1
Calves Pasture Point—cape MA-1
Calves's Islands CT-1
Calvey Creek—stream MO-7
Calvey Township—civil MO-7
**Calville**—pop pl GA-3
Calvin KS-7
Calvin—locale AR-4
Calvin—locale GA-3
Calvin—locale VA-3
Calvin—locale WV-2
**Calvin**—pop pl IL-6
**Calvin**—pop pl KY-4
**Calvin**—pop pl LA-4
**Calvin**—pop pl MI-6
**Calvin**—pop pl (2) NC-3
**Calvin**—pop pl ND-7
**Calvin**—pop pl OK-5
**Calvin**—pop pl PA-2
**Calvin**—pop pl TX-5
Calvin Ballensky Dam—dam SD-7
Calvin Branch—stream AR-4
Calvin Branch—stream (2) TN-4
Calvin Branch—stream WV-2
Calvin Britain Sch—school MI-6
Calvin Cem—cemetery IL-6
Calvin Cem—cemetery (2) IN-6
Calvin Cem—cemetery KY-4
Calvin Cem—cemetery OK-5
**Calvin Center**—pop pl MI-6
Calvin Ch—church (2) KY-4
Calvin Ch—church MI-6
Calvin Ch—church MN-6
Calvin Ch—church NJ-2
Calvin Ch—church PA-2
Calvin Ch—church (2) WV-2
Calvin Chapel—church MS-4
Calvin Chapel—church WV-2
Calvin Chapel Ch MS-4
Calvin Chapel Sch—school MS-4
Calvin Childress Lake Dam Number 1—dam AL-4
Calvin Childress Lake Dam Number 2—dam AL-4
Calvin Childress Number One Lake—reservoir AL-4
Calvin Childress Number Two Lake—reservoir AL-4
Calvin Christian Sch—school CA-9
Calvin Clark Run—stream PA-2
Calvin Coll—school MI-6
Calvin Coolidge Birthplace—locale VT-1
Calvin Coolidge Bridge—bridge MA-1
Calvin Coolidge Sch—school IL-6
Calvin Coolidge Sch—school (2) MA-1
Calvin Coolidge State For—forest VT-1
Calvin Corners—locale PA-2
Calvin Creek OR-9
Calvin Creek—stream NC-3
Calvin Creek—stream WI-6
Calvin Creek—stream WY-8
Calvin Day Cem—cemetery WI-6
Calvin DeLoach Pond GA-3
Calvin Donaldson Elem Sch—school TN-4
Calvin Grove (historical P.O.)—locale AL-4
Calvin Hill Sch—school MI-6
Calvin Hollow—valley TN-4
Calvin Holt Cemetery TN-4
Calvin HS—school MI-6
Calvinistic Congregational Church—hist pl MA-1
Calvin Johnson Hollow TN-4
Calvin Knollcrest Coll—school MI-6
Calvin Lake NE-7
Calvin Lake—lake WY-8
Calvin Mack Cem—cemetery MS-4
Calvin Mine—mine CO-8
Calvin N Kendall Elem Sch—school IN-6
Calvin Park—park MD-2
Calvin Parsons Elem Sch—school PA-2
Calvin Point—cape NC-3
Calvin Price State For—forest WV-2
Calvin Ray Pond—reservoir NC-3
Calvin Ray Pond Dam—dam NC-3
**Calvin (RR name Page)**—pop pl KY-4
Calvin Run—stream PA-2
Calvin Sch—school (2) IL-6
Calvin Sch—school MN-6
Calvin Sch—school SD-7
Calvins Creek—stream CA-9
Calvin Smith Cem—cemetery MS-4
Calvins Pond—lake OR-9
Calvin Spring—spring AZ-5
Calvin S. Smith Sch—school UT-8
Calvin Tank—reservoir NM-5
**Calvin Township**—pop pl KS-7
**Calvin (Township of)**—pop pl MI-6
Calvits Lake—lake MS-4
Calvoria Cem—cemetery NM-5
**Calwa**—pop pl CA-9
Calwa City CA-9
Calwa Park—park CA-9
Calwell Chapel Cem—cemetery AR-4
Calwell Sch—school TX-5
**Calwood**—pop pl MO-7
Calwood Township—civil MO-7
Cal Wooten Cem—cemetery TX-5
Calx Creek—stream MT-8
Calx Mountain Trail—trail MT-8
Calx Mtn—summit MT-8
Calydon, Lake—reservoir PA-2
Calypso—locale MT-8
**Calypso**—pop pl NC-3
Calypso Cascades—falls CO-8
Calypso Elem Sch—school PA-2
Calypso Island—island FL-3
Calypso Island—island PA-2
Calypso Spring—spring MT-8
Calypso Trail—trail MT-8
Calyton Township KS-7
Calyx—locale MS-4
Calyx Post Office (historical)—building MS-4
**Calzada**—pop pl PR-3
Calzada (Barrio)—fmr MCD PR-3
Calzona—locale CA-9
Calzona Mine—mine CA-9
Cam—locale TX-5
**Cam**—pop pl MS-4
Cama Beach—locale WA-9
**Camaceyes**—pop pl PR-3
Camaceyes (Barrio)—fmr MCD PR-3
Camack Well—well NM-5
Cam-Air Airp—airport IN-6
**Camak**—pop pl GA-3
Camak (CCD)—cens area GA-3
Camak House—hist pl GA-3
Camak Mills (historical)—locale AL-4
Camak Sch—school SC-3
Camaleche Tanks—reservoir NM-5
Camal Mountain ID-8
Camal White Sch (historical)—school MS-4
**Camanche**—pop pl CA-9
**Camanche**—pop pl IA-7
Camanche Creek—stream CA-9
Camanche Dam—dam CA-9
Camanche Lake—post sta CA-9
Camanche Rsvr—reservoir CA-9
Camanche Township—fmr MCD IA-7
**Camano**—pop pl WA-9
Camano (CCD)—cens area WA-9
**Camano City**—pop pl WA-9
Camano Country Club—locale WA-9
Camano Head—cape WA-9
Camano Island—island WA-9
Camano Island Pioneer Cem—cemetery WA-9
Camano Island State Park—park WA-9
Camardelle—locale LA-4
Camarge Sch—school OH-6
Camargo—locale PA-2
**Camargo**—pop pl IL-6
**Camargo**—pop pl KY-4
**Camargo**—pop pl OK-5
**Camargo**—pop pl TN-4
Camargo Cem—cemetery OK-5
Camargo Ch—church TN-4
Camargo Country Club—other OH-6
Camargo Ferry (historical)—locale MS-4
**Camargo (historical)**—pop pl MS-4
Camargo Post Office (historical)—building MS-4
Camargo Post Office (historical)—building PA-2
Camargo Post Office (historical)—building TN-4
Camargo Sch—school TN-4
**Camargo (Township of)**—pop pl IL-6
**Camarian Estates (subdivision)**—pop pl NC-3
**Camarillo**—pop pl CA-9
Camarillo (CCD)—cens area CA-9
Camarillo Heights—CDP CA-9
Camarillo Hills—ridge CA-9
Camarillo Oak Grove County Park—park CA-9
Camarillo State Hosp—hospital CA-9
**Camark**—pop pl AR-4
Camarones—locale PR-3
Camarones (Barrio)—fmr MCD PR-3
**Camarren Cove Estates Subdivision Phases 1-6**—pop pl UT-8
**Camas**—pop pl ID-8
**Camas**—pop pl MT-8
**Camas**—pop pl WA-9
Camas A Canal—canal MT-8
Camas and Pole Creeks Archeol District—hist pl ID-8
Camas B Canal—canal MT-8
Camas Butte—summit ID-8
Camas Butte—summit OR-9
Camas Butte Well—well ID-8
Camas Canal—canal MT-8
Camas (CCD)—cens area WA-9
Camas Cow Camp—locale ID-8
Camas Creek OR-9
Camas Creek WA-9
Camas Creek—stream (5) ID-8
Camas Creek—stream (5) MT-8
Camas Creek—stream (5) OR-9
Camas Creek—stream (2) WA-9
Camas Creek Campground—park OR-9
Camas Creek Corral—locale OR-9
Camas Creek Entrance—locale MT-8
Camas Creek Overlook—locale MT-8
Camas Creek Trail—trail MT-8
Camas D Canal—canal MT-8
Camas Flats—flat ID-8
Camas Lake—lake (3) MT-8
Camas Land—flat WA-9
Camas Lookout—locale OR-9
Camas Meadows—flat (3) ID-8
Camas Mine—mine ID-8
Camas Mountain State Park—park OR-9
Camas Mtn—summit OR-9
Camas Natl Wildlife Ref—park ID-8
Camas Natl Wildlife Refuge HQ—locale ID-8
Camas Patch—flat WA-9
Camas Prairie—flat ID-8
Camas Prairie—flat MT-8
Camas Prairie—flat (3) OR-9
Camas Prairie—flat WA-9
Camas Prairie—locale MT-8
Camas Prairie—swamp (2) OR-9
Camas Prairie Basin—basin MT-8
Camas Prairie Cem—cemetery MT-8
Camas Prairie Creek ID-8
Camas Prairie Creek—stream WA-9
Camas Prairie Trail—trail OR-9
Camas Prarie UT-8
Camas Prarie WA-9
Camas Ridge—ridge (2) MT-8
Camas Slough—stream WA-9
Camas Spring—spring OR-9
Camas Substation—other MT-8
Camas Swale—valley (2) OR-9
Camas Swale Creek—stream OR-9
**Camas Valley**—pop pl OR-9
Camas Valley—valley OR-9
Camas Valley—valley WA-9
Camatta Canyon—valley CA-9
Camatta Creek—stream CA-9
Camatta Ranch—locale CA-9
Camba—locale OH-6
Cambahee Bank—bar SC-3
**Cambalache**—pop pl PR-3
Cambalache (Barrio)—fmr MCD PR-3
Cambalache Creek—stream TX-5
Cambalache Tank—reservoir TX-5
Cambell AR-4
Cambell Branch—stream TX-5
Cambell Cem—cemetery IL-6
Cambell Chapel—church AL-4
Cambell Creek—stream OR-9
Cambells Mill Cem—cemetery MS-4
Cambell Spring AZ-5
Cambellville MS-4
Cambel Ranch NV-8
Camberon Creek TX-5
Cambers Island—island GA-3
Cambest Pond—reservoir GA-3
Cambia Creek WY-8
Cambidge Common Hist Dist Amendment—hist pl MA-1
Camble Ranch—locale NV-8
Cambles Creek PA-2
Cambles Creek - in part PA-2
Camblin Ditch—canal IN-6
Camblin Ranch—locale WY-8
Cam-Boh Picnic Area—park AZ-5
Cambo Lake—lake FL-3
Cambolasse Pond—lake ME-1
Cambolasse Stream—stream ME-1
Cambon—locale IL-6
**Cambon**—pop pl FL-3
Cambon, Cape—cape AK-9
Cambon Lake—reservoir IL-6
Camborn Draw CO-8
Camborne Pond—lake MA-1
**Cambra**—pop pl PA-2
Cambrai—locale OR-9
Cam Branch—stream IN-6
Cambray—locale NM-5
Cambray Windmill—locale NM-5
Cambre House and Farm—hist pl IL-6
Cambria VA-3
Cambria—locale WY-8
**Cambria**—pop pl CA-9
**Cambria**—pop pl IL-6
**Cambria**—pop pl IN-6
**Cambria**—pop pl IA-7
**Cambria**—pop pl MD-2
**Cambria**—pop pl MI-6
**Cambria**—pop pl MN-6
**Cambria**—pop pl OK-5
**Cambria**—pop pl TN-4
**Cambria**—pop pl (2) WV-2
**Cambria**—pop pl WI-6
Cambria—uninc pl VA-3
Cambria Adult Sch—school CA-9
Cambria Air Force Station—military CA-9
Cambria Baptist Ch—church TN-4
**Cambria (Cambria Mine)**—pop pl WV-2
Cambria Casino—hist pl WY-8
Cambria Cem—cemetery CA-9
Cambria Cem—cemetery MN-6
Cambria Cem—cemetery WI-6
Cambria Cem—cemetery WY-8
**Cambria Center**—pop pl NY-2
Cambria Ch—church OK-5
**Cambria City**—pop pl PA-2
**Cambria County**—pop pl PA-2
Cambria County Courthouse—hist pl PA-2
Cambria County Jail—hist pl PA-2
Cambria Creek—stream OH-6
Cambria Creek—stream WY-8
Cambria Drain—stream MI-6
Cambria Four Mine Station—locale PA-2
Cambria Freight Station—hist pl VA-3
Cambria Furnace Creek OH-6
**Cambria Heights**—pop pl NY-2
Cambria Heights Senior HS—school PA-2
Cambria Heights 7th and 8th Wards MS—school PA-2
Cambria Hollow—valley MO-7
Cambria Hollow—valley TN-4
Cambria-Jackson Mine—mine MI-6
Cambria Millpond—reservoir MI-6
Cambria Mills Cem—cemetery PA-2
Cambria Mills (historical)—locale KS-7
Cambria Mills Sch (abandoned)—school PA-2
Cambria Mine—other WV-2
Cambrian Creek—stream TX-5
Cambria Neck—bay IL-6
Cambrian Golf Club—other CA-9
Cambrian Hills Golf—locale PA-2
**Cambrian Park**—pop pl CA-9
Cambrian Sch—school CA-9
Cambrian Village (2) CA-9
**Cambria Pines**—pop pl CA-9
**Cambria Pines Manor**—pop pl CA-9
**Cambria Pines Subdivision**—pop pl UT-8
Cambria Point—cape UT-8
Cambria Post Office (historical)—building TN-4
Cambria Public Library Bldg—hist pl PA-2
Cambria Rock—island CA-9
Cambria Sch—hist pl OK-5
Cambria Slope Mine Number Thirty-Three Dam—dam PA-2
**Cambria (sta.)**—pop pl NY-2
Cambria Station (historical)—locale TN-4
**Cambria (Town of)**—pop pl NY-2
**Cambria Township**—pop pl KS-7
**Cambria Township**—pop pl SD-7
**Cambria (Township of)**—pop pl MI-6
**Cambria (Township of)**—pop pl MN-6
**Cambria (Township of)**—pop pl PA-2
Cambric Branch—stream NC-3
Cambridge IL-6
Cambridge MA-1
Cambridge PA-2
Cambridge—locale MS-4
Cambridge—locale OK-5
Cambridge—locale SC-3
Cambridge—locale TN-4
**Cambridge**—pop pl AL-4
**Cambridge**—pop pl (3) ID-8
**Cambridge**—pop pl IL-6
**Cambridge**—pop pl (2) IA-7
**Cambridge**—pop pl KS-7
**Cambridge**—pop pl KY-4
**Cambridge**—pop pl ME-1
**Cambridge**—pop pl MD-2
**Cambridge**—pop pl MA-1
**Cambridge**—pop pl MN-6
**Cambridge**—pop pl MO-7
**Cambridge**—pop pl NE-7
**Cambridge**—pop pl (2) NJ-2
**Cambridge**—pop pl NY-2
**Cambridge**—pop pl OH-6
**Cambridge**—pop pl PA-2
**Cambridge**—pop pl TX-5
**Cambridge**—pop pl VT-1
**Cambridge**—pop pl VA-3
**Cambridge**—pop pl WI-6
Cambridge, Town of MA-1
Cambridge A—post sta MA-1
Cambridge Acad—school FL-3
Cambridge Acad—school SC-3
Cambridge B—post sta MA-1
Cambridge Baptist Ch—church MS-4
Cambridge Black Mtn—summit NH-1
Cambridgeboro PA-2
Cambridgeborough—pop pl PA-2
Cambridge C—post sta MA-1
Cambridge Canal—canal NE-7
Cambridge Cem—cemetery MA-1
Cambridge Cem—cemetery MO-7
Cambridge Cem—cemetery ND-7
Cambridge Cem—cemetery TX-5
Cambridge Center Sch—school MI-6
Cambridge Ch—church (2) AL-4
Cambridge Church Cem—cemetery AL-4
**Cambridge City**—pop pl IN-6
Cambridge City Hall—building MA-1
Cambridge City Hall Annex—building MA-1
Cambridge City Hosp—hospital MA-1
Cambridge City Infirmary—hospital MA-1
Cambridge Common—park MA-1
Cambridge Common Hist Dist—hist pl MA-1
Cambridge Common Hist Dist (Boundary Increase & Decrease—hist pl MA-1
**Cambridge Condominium**—pop pl UT-8
Cambridge Creek SC-3
Cambridge Creek—bay MD-2
Cambridge Creek—stream NY-2
Cambridge Dam NE-7
Cambridge Downs—locale PA-2
Cambridge Elem Sch—school FL-3
**Cambridge Estates (subdivision)**—pop pl AL-4
**Cambridge Estates (subdivision)**—pop pl TN-4
**Cambridge Estates (subdivision)**—pop pl UT-8
Cambridge Farms MA-1
Cambridge Flats Sch—school ME-1
**Cambridge Forest (subdivision)**—pop pl NC-3
Cambridge Harbor MD-2
**Cambridge Heights (subdivision)**—pop pl (2) AZ-5
Cambridge Hill—summit NH-1
Cambridge Hills—summit NV-8
**Cambridge Hills (subdivision)**—pop pl TN-4
Cambridge Hist Dist—hist pl NY-2
Cambridge HS—school (2) MA-1
Cambridge Industrial Park (subdivision)—locale UT-8
Cambridge JHS—school MI-6
**Cambridge Junction**—pop pl MI-6
**Cambridge Junction**—pop pl VT-1
Cambridge Junior Coll—school MA-1
Cambridge Lake—reservoir MS-4
Cambridge Meetinghouse—hist pl VT-1
Cambridge Mine—mine NV-8
Cambridge-on-the-Lake IL-6
Cambridge P.O. (historical)—locale AL-4
Cambridge Pond—lake ME-1
**Cambridgeport**—pop pl MA-1
**Cambridgeport**—pop pl VT-1
Cambridge Post Office (historical)—building PA-2
Cambridge Public Library—hist pl MA-1
Cambridge Rsvr MA-1
Cambridge Rsvr—reservoir MA-1
Cambridge Rsvr—reservoir OH-6
Cambridge Sch—school (2) CA-9
Cambridge Sch—school MI-6
Cambridge Sch—school MS-4
Cambridge Sch—school NJ-2
Cambridge Sch—school TX-5
**Cambridge Shores**—pop pl KY-4
**Cambridge Springs**—pop pl PA-2
Cambridge Springs Borough—civil PA-2
Cambridge Springs Bridge—hist pl PA-2
Cambridge Springs Elem Sch—school PA-2
Cambridge Springs Junior Senior HS—school PA-2
Cambridge State Hosp—hospital OH-6
Cambridge Street Bridge—bridge MA-1
Cambridge Street Firehouse—hist pl MA-1
Cambridge Street Sch—hist pl MA-1
**Cambridge (subdivision)**—pop pl MA-1
**Cambridge (subdivision)**—pop pl (3) NC-3
Cambridge (Town of)—civil MA-1
**Cambridge (Town of)**—pop pl ME-1
**Cambridge (Town of)**—pop pl NY-2
**Cambridge (Town of)**—pop pl VT-1
Cambridge Township—civil MO-7
Cambridge (Township of)—fmr MCD NH-1
**Cambridge (Township of)**—pop pl IL-6
**Cambridge (Township of)**—pop pl MI-6
**Cambridge (Township of)**—pop pl MN-6
**Cambridge (Township of)**—pop pl OH-6
**Cambridge (Township of)**—pop pl PA-2
Cambridge Village—other KY-4
Cambridge Village, Town of MA-1
Cambron Field (airport)—airport TN-4
Cambron Knob—summit KY-4
Cambron Lake—lake CA-9
Cambro Pond—reservoir NC-3
Cambro Pond Dam—dam NC-3
Cambry Creek SD-7
Cambus-Kenneth Estate—hist pl KY-4
**Cambute**—pop pl PR-3
Camby IN-6
Camby—locale NY-2
**Camby**—pop pl IN-6
Camby Creek—stream IN-6
Cam Creek—stream KY-4
Camden AL-4
Camden GA-3
Camden KS-7
Camden VA-3
Camden—hist pl VA-3
Camden—locale CO-8
Camden—locale WA-9
**Camden**—pop pl AL-4
**Camden**—pop pl AR-4
**Camden**—pop pl CA-9
**Camden**—pop pl DE-2
**Camden**—pop pl IL-6
**Camden**—pop pl IN-6
**Camden**—pop pl ME-1
**Camden**—pop pl MI-6
**Camden**—pop pl MS-4
**Camden**—pop pl MO-7
**Camden**—pop pl NJ-2
**Camden**—pop pl NY-2
**Camden**—pop pl NC-3
**Camden**—pop pl (2) OH-6
**Camden**—pop pl PA-2
**Camden**—pop pl SC-3
**Camden**—pop pl TN-4
**Camden**—pop pl TX-5
**Camden**—pop pl WV-2
Camden—uninc pl (2) MD-2
Camden and Petty Island Bridge—bridge NJ-2
Camden Baptist Ch—church AL-4
Camden Battlefield—hist pl SC-3
Camden Bay—bay AK-9
**Camden Bay Subdivision**—pop pl TN-4
Camden-Burlington County—airport NJ-2
Camden (CCD)—cens area AL-4
Camden (CCD)—cens area SC-3
Camden (CCD)—cens area TN-4
Camden Cem—cemetery IN-6
Camden Cem—cemetery MO-7
Camden Cem—cemetery NE-7
Camden Cem—cemetery NY-2
Camden Cem—cemetery OH-6
Camden Cem—cemetery TN-4
Camden Cem—cemetery VA-3
Camden Center (census name Camden)—other ME-1
Camden Ch—church AL-4
Camden Ch—church NC-3
Camden City Hall—building TN-4
**Camden (County)**—pop pl GA-3
**Camden County**—pop pl MO-7
**Camden County**—pop pl NJ-2
**Camden County**—pop pl NC-3
Camden County Coll—school NJ-2
Camden County Courthouse—hist pl GA-3
Camden County Courthouse—hist pl NC-3
Camden County Jail—hist pl NC-3
Camden County Park—park NJ-2
Camden Creek—stream KY-4
Camden Creek—stream NY-2
Camden Creek—stream VT-1
Camden Dewatering Area—locale TN-4
Camden Division—civil AL-4
Camden Division—civil TN-4
Camden Elem Sch—school TN-4
Camden Flats—flat WV-2
Camden Friends Meetinghouse—hist pl DE-2
Camden-Frontier Sch—school MI-6
Camden Gap—gap VA-3
Camden Heights—locale VA-3
Camden Hill—uninc pl PA-2
Camden Hill Cem—cemetery WV-2
Camden Hills State Park—park ME-1
Camden Hist Dist—hist pl DE-2
Camden Hollow—valley IL-6
Camden Hollow—valley (2) MO-7
Camden Hollow—valley WV-2
Camden Home for Children—building NJ-2

Camp Alwood—*locale* NC-3
Camp Alzafar—*locale* TX-5
Camp Amache—*locale* CO-8
Camp Amahami—*locale* NY-2
*Campamanche* CO-8
**Campamento**—*pop pl* PR-3
Campamento Banco Number 74—*levee* TX-5
Campamento Borinquen—*locale* PR-3
**Campamento Borinquen**—*pop pl* PR-3
Campamento Buena Vista—*locale* PR-3
Campamento Crozier—*locale* PR-3
Campamento de Ninos—*locale* PR-3
**Campamento de Ninos**—*pop pl* PR-3
Campamento Eliza Colberg—*locale* PR-3
Campamento Guajataca—*locale* PR-3
Campamento Guavate—*locale* PR-3
Campamento Pinones—*locale* PR-3
**Campamento Pinones**—*pop pl* PR-3
Campamento Punta Lima—*locale* PR-3
Campamento Radley—*locale* PR-3
**Campamento Real**—*pop pl* PR-3
Campamento Santana—*locale* PR-3
Campamento Susua—*locale* PR-3
**Campamento Susua**—*pop pl* PR-3
Campamento Zarzal—*locale* PR-3
Campana—*locale* CA-9
Campana—*locale* NM-5
Campana, Cerro de la—*summit* NM-5
Campana Factory—*hist pl* IL-6
Campana Factory (Boundary Decrease)—*hist pl* IL-6
Campana Oil Field—*oilfield* TX-5
Campanaya Point—*summit* GU-9
Camp Anderel—*locale* AL-4
Camp Anderson—*locale* OH-6
Camp Anderson (Site)—*locale* CA-9
Camp Andrews—*locale* AL-4
Camp Andrews—*locale* PA-2
Campanelli Sch—*school* IL-6
Campaneyan Kristo Rai—*hist pl* MH-9
*Camp Angelus* CA-9
**Camp Angelus**—*pop pl* CA-9
Campania—*locale* GA-3
Campania Farm—*locale* MI-6
Campanile, The—*pillar* AZ-5
**Campanilla**—*pop pl* PR-3
Camp Annemeekee—*locale* TN-4
Camp Anokijig—*locale* WI-6
Camp Antelope—*locale* CA-9
Camp Antioch—*locale* GA-3
Camp Antioch Sch (historical)—*school* TN-4
Campanula Creek—*stream* MT-8
Campanula Creek—*stream* WY-8
*Camp Apache* AZ-5
Camp Apex—*locale* MA-1
Camp A P Hill Military Reservation—*other* VA-3
Camp Appalachia—*locale* VA-3
**Camp Appalachia (Girls Camp)**—*pop pl* VA-3
Camp Appalachian Wilderness—*park* GA-3
Camp Aqawam—*locale* ME-1
Camp Aqua—*locale* MT-8
*Campaquas Lake* TX-5
Camp Arbolado—*locale* CA-9
Camp Arden—*locale* CT-1
Camp Area Number Five—*park* IN-6
Camp Arewa—*locale* PA-2
Camp Argyle—*locale* TX-5
Camp Armstrong—*locale* MS-4
Camp Arrah Wanna—*locale* OR-9
Camp Arrowhead—*locale* IA-7
Camp Arrowhead—*locale* MI-6
Camp Arrowhead—*locale* MO-7
Camp Arrowhead—*locale* NY-2
Camp Arrowhead—*locale* NC-3
Camp Arrowhead—*locale* OH-6
Camp Arrowhead—*locale* PA-2
Camp Arrowhead—*locale* TN-4
Camp Arrowhead—*locale* (2) TX-5
Camp Arrowhead—*locale* WV-2
Camp Arrowhead Lake—*reservoir* IA-7
Camp Arrowhead Lake Dam—*dam* IA-7
Camp Arthur—*park* IN-6
Camp Asbury—*locale* WV-2
Camp Ascension—*locale* KS-7
**Camp Ashmere**—*pop pl* MA-1
Camp Assca—*locale* AL-4
Camp Assurance—*locale* IL-6
Camp Atkins *locale* AL 4
Camp Atkinson—*locale* NC-3
Camp Attakapas—*locale* LA-4
Camp Atwater—*hist pl* MA-1
*Campau* MI-6
Campau, Joseph, House—*hist pl* MI-6
Campau Bay—*bay* MI-6
Camp Aubrey Henning—*locale* KS-7
Camp Auburn—*locale* AL-4
Campau Drain—*canal* MI-6
Camp Audubon—*locale* CO-8
Camp Augustine—*locale* NE-7
Campau Lake—*lake* (2) MI-6
Campau Park Sch—*school* MI-6
Camp Aurora—*locale* MO-7
Camp Au Sable Club—*locale* MI-6
Campau Sch—*school* (2) MI-6
Camp Austin—*locale* MN-6
Camp Austin—*locale* TN-4
Camp Aventura—*locale* CA-9
Camp Avery—*locale* MA-1
Camp Avery—*locale* MO-7
Camp Avery—*locale* OH-6
Camp Ave Sch—*school* NY-2
Camp Avoda—*park* MA-1
**Camp Avoda**—*pop pl* MA-1
Camp Awahanee—*locale* CA-9
Camp Awana—*locale* WI-6
Camp Awanee—*locale* VT-1
Camp Axton—*locale* VA-3
Camp B—*locale* FL-3
Camp Babcock Hovey—*locale* NY-2
Camp Baco—*locale* NY-2
Camp Baden Powell—*locale* IL-6
Camp Badger Sch—*school* WI-6
Camp Baird—*locale* MA-1
Camp Baiting Hollow—*locale* NY-2
Camp Baker—*locale* VA-3
Camp Baker—*locale* WA-9
Camp Baldwin—*locale* OR-9
Camp Ballou—*locale* NY-2
Camp Barakel—*locale* MI-6
Camp Barbe—*locale* WV-2
Camp Barbey—*locale* NY-2
Camp Barbour—*locale* WV-2
**Camp Barlett**—*pop pl* CA-9
Camp Barnes—*locale* DE-2
Camp Barnett—*locale* GA-3
Camp Barnhard—*locale* NC-3
Camp Barree—*locale* PA-2
Camp Barrett—*locale* MD-2
Camp Barrett—*locale* VA-3
Camp Barron—*locale* GA-3
Camp Barstow—*locale* SC-3
**Camp Bartlett**—*pop pl* CA-9
Camp Barton—*locale* MA-1
Camp Barton—*locale* NY-2
**Camp Barton**—*pop pl* MA-1
Camp Bates—*locale* OH-6
Camp Bauer—*locale* CA-9
Camp Bay—*bay* ID-8
Camp Bay—*swamp* GA-3
Camp Bay—*swamp* NC-3
Camp Bay (Carolina Bay)—*swamp* NC-3
*Camp Bayou* AR-4
*Camp Bayou* LA-4
Camp Bayou—*gut* LA-4
Camp Bayou—*stream* (2) LA-4
Camp Bayou Canal—*canal* AR-4
Camp Bayou Canal—*canal* (2) LA-4
Camp Beale Springs—*hist pl* AZ-5
Camp Bearborn—*locale* MI-6
Camp Bear Lake—*locale* UT-8
Camp Bearregard Cem—*cemetery* KY-4
Camp Beauregard—*locale* LA-4
Camp Beaver—*locale* UT-8
**Camp Becket**—*pop pl* MA-1
Camp Bedford—*locale* NY-2
*Camp Beecher* KS-7
Camp Beecher—*locale* NY-2
Camp Beechwood—*locale* NY-2
Camp Beisler—*locale* NJ-2
Camp Beisler Dam—*dam* NJ-2
*Campbell* AR-4
*Campbell* ME-1
*Campbell* ND-7
*Campbell* OH-6
*Campbell* SD-7
Camp Bell—*hist pl* TN-4
Campbell—*locale* AR-4
Campbell—*locale* IL-6
Campbell—*locale* IA-7
Campbell—*locale* LA-4
Campbell—*locale* ME-1
Campbell—*locale* MI-6
Camp Bell—*locale* MI-6
Campbell—*locale* NM-5
Campbell—*locale* NY-2
Campbell—*locale* NC-3
Campbell—*locale* OR-9
Campbell—*locale* PA-2
Campbell—*locale* VA-3
Campbell—*mine* AZ-5
**Campbell**—*pop pl* (2) AL-4
**Campbell**—*pop pl* (2) AK-9
**Campbell**—*pop pl* CA-9
**Campbell**—*pop pl* FL-3
**Campbell**—*pop pl* IL-6
**Campbell**—*pop pl* MD-2
**Campbell**—*pop pl* MN-6
**Campbell**—*pop pl* MO-7
**Campbell**—*pop pl* (2) NE-7
**Campbell**—*pop pl* NY-2
**Campbell**—*pop pl* OH-6
**Campbell**—*pop pl* SC-3
**Campbell**—*pop pl* TX-5
Campbell—*uninc pl* MS-4
Campbell, Albert, House—*hist pl* IL-6
Campbell, Alexander, Mansion—*hist pl* WV-2
Campbell, B. H., House—*hist pl* KS-7
Campbell, Col, Samuel, House—*hist pl* ME-1
Campbell, Colin, Post—*hist pl* SD-7
Campbell, Collen C., House—*hist pl* MA-1
Campbell, David C., House—*hist pl* KY-4
Campbell, David W., House—*hist pl* ME-1
Campbell, Dr. John Owen, House—*hist pl* TN-4
Campbell, Frank, House—*hist pl* ME-1
Campbell, Gen. Alexander, House—*hist pl* ME-1
Campbell, Gen. Charles T., House—*hist pl* SD-7
Campbell, Gina Smith, Bathhouse—*hist pl* SD-7
Campbell, Hamilton, House—*hist pl* OR-9
Campbell, H. E., House—*hist pl* AZ-5
Campbell, Hugh, House—*hist pl* OH-6
Campbell, James Archibald, House—*hist pl* NC-3
Campbell, John C., Folk Sch Hist Dist—*hist pl* NC-3
Campbell, John G., House—*hist pl* WI-6
Campbell, Lake—*lake* MN-6
Campbell, Lake—*lake* SD-7
Campbell, Lake—*lake* WA-9
Campbell, Lake—*reservoir* SD-7
Campbell, Mount—*summit* AK-9
Campbell, Perciphull, House—*hist pl* NC-3
Campbell, Point—*cape* CA-9
Campbell, Richard Crawford, House—*hist pl* CO-8
Campbell, Richard Posey, House—*hist pl* OR-9
Campbell, Robert E., House—*hist pl* OR-9
Campbell, Robert G., House—*hist pl* MO-7
Campbell, Sheriff Eugene P., House—*hist pl* LA-4
Campbell, T. C., Mound—*hist pl* OH-6
Campbell, Thomas D., House—*hist pl* ND-7
Campbell, William, House—*hist pl* KY-4
Campbell, William, House—*hist pl* UT-8
Campbell, William S., House—*hist pl* TN-4
Campbell Acad for the Gifted—*school* FL-3
Campbell Acad (historical)—*school* TN-4
**Campbell Acres (subdivision)**—*pop pl* TN-4
Campbell African Methodist Episcopal Zion Chapel—*church* IN-6
Campbell Air Force Base—*other* (2) KY-4
Campbell Airp—*airport* (2) PA-2
Campbell Airstrip Airp—*airport* WA-9
Campbell and Kelly Bldg—*hist pl* NV-8
Campbell Archeol Site—*hist pl* MO-7
Campbell Army Airfield (U.S. Air Force)—*other* TN-4
Campbell Ave Interchange—*crossing* AZ-5
Campbell Bay—*bay* AK-9
Campbell Bayou—*bay* TX-5
Campbell Bayou—*stream* AR-4
Campbell Bayou—*stream* LA-4
Campbell Belken Ditch—*canal* MT-8
Campbell Bend—*bend* KY-4
Campbell Bend—*bend* TN-4
Campbell Bldg—*hist pl* PA-2
Campbell Blue Creek—*stream* AZ-5
Campbell Blue Creek—*stream* NM-5
Campbell Brake—*swamp* AR-4
*Campbell Branch* ME-1
*Campbell Branch* MS-4
Campbell Branch—*stream* AL-4
Campbell Branch—*stream* AR-4
Campbell Branch—*stream* FL-3
Campbell Branch—*stream* GA-3
Campbell Branch—*stream* IL-6
Campbell Branch—*stream* IN-6
Campbell Branch—*stream* (11) KY-4
Campbell Branch—*stream* LA-4
Campbell Branch—*stream* (5) MO-7
Campbell Branch—*stream* (2) SC-3
Campbell Branch—*stream* (4) TN-4
Camp Bell Branch—*stream* TN-4
Campbell Branch—*stream* (2) TN-4
Campbell Branch—*stream* (5) TX-5
Campbell Branch—*stream* (2) VA-3
Campbell Branch—*stream* (2) WV-2
Campbell Branch Little Black River—*stream* ME-1
*Campbell Branch Little Black River South Branch Little Black River* ME-1
Campbell Branch Sch—*school* KY-4
Campbell Bridge—*bridge* IN-6
Campbell Bridge—*other* MO-7
*Campbell Brook* ME-1
Campbell Brook—*stream* (6) ME-1
Campbell Brook—*stream* (2) NY-2
Campbell Butte—*summit* ND-7
Campbell Butte—*summit* OR-9
Campbell Cabin—*locale* AK-9
Campbell Camp Number One—*locale* MT-8
Campbell Canyon—*valley* CA-9
Campbell Canyon—*valley* ID-8
Campbell Canyon—*valley* (2) OR-9
Campbell Canyon—*valley* (2) UT-8
Campbell Cave—*cave* (2) TN-4
*Campbell Cem* TN-4
Campbell Cem—*cemetery* (7) AL-4
Campbell Cem—*cemetery* (3) AR-4
Campbell Cem—*cemetery* FL-3
Campbell Cem—*cemetery* (5) IN-6
Campbell Cem—*cemetery* (3) IA-7
Campbell Cem—*cemetery* KS-7
Campbell Cem—*cemetery* (8) KY-4
Campbell Cem—*cemetery* (2) LA-4
Campbell Cem—*cemetery* MS-4
Campbell Cem—*cemetery* (10) MO-7
Campbell Cem—*cemetery* (2) NE-7
Campbell Cem—*cemetery* (2) NY-2
Campbell Cem—*cemetery* (2) NC-3
Campbell Cem—*cemetery* (6) OH-6
Campbell Cem—*cemetery* PA-2
Campbell Cem—*cemetery* (25) TN-4
Campbell Cem—*cemetery* (6) TX-5
Campbell Cem—*cemetery* (8) VA-3
Campbell Cem—*cemetery* WV-2
Campbell Cem—*cemetery* WI-6
Campbell Ch—*church* AR-4
Campbell Ch—*church* LA-4
Campbell Chapel—*church* (3) AL-4
Campbell Chapel—*church* FL-3
Campbell Chapel—*church* IN-6
Campbell Chapel—*church* (2) MS-4
Campbell Chapel—*church* OH-6
Campbell Chapel—*church* TN-4
Campbell Chapel—*church* VA-3
Campbell Chapel African Methodist Episcopal Ch—*church* TN-4
Campbell Chapel (historical)—*church* TN-4
Campbell-Christie House—*hist pl* NJ-2
Campbell Church Cem—*cemetery* AR-4
Campbell City—*other* MI-6
Campbell City Southern Baptist Ch—*church* FL-3
Campbell Coll *school* NC 3
Campbell Coll (historical)—*school* MS-4
Campbell Corner—*locale* VT-1
Campbell Corner—*locale* (2) VA-3
**Campbell Corner**—*pop pl* IN-6
**Campbell Corner**—*pop pl* MD-2
**Campbell Corner**—*pop pl* MO-7
**Campbell Corners**—*pop pl* MI-6
Campbell Corner Sch—*school* ME-1
Campbell Coulee—*valley* MT-8
Campbell Coulee—*valley* WI-6
Campbell County—*civil* SD-7
**Campbell (County)**—*pop pl* KY-4
**Campbell County**—*pop pl* TN-4
**Campbell (County)**—*pop pl* VA-3
Campbell County Airp—*airport* TN-4
Campbell County Courthouse—*hist pl* GA-3
Campbell County Courthouse—*hist pl* VA-3
Campbell County Courthouse at Newport—*hist pl* KY-4
Campbell County Memorial Gardens—*cemetery* TN-4
Campbell County Park—*park* TN-4
Campbell Cove—*bay* CA-9
Campbell Cove—*bay* ME-1
Campbell Cove—*valley* AL-4
Campbell Cove Dam—*dam* TN-4
Campbell Cove Lake—*reservoir* TN-4
Campbell Cow Camp—*locale* CA-9
Campbell Crater—*crater* AZ-5
*Campbell Creek* CA-9
*Campbell Creek* ID-8
*Campbell Creek* ME-1
*Campbell Creek* TX-5
*Campbell Creek* WA-9
*Campbell Creek* WV-2
**Campbell Creek**—*pop pl* NC-3
Campbell Creek—*stream* (3) AL-4
Campbell Creek—*stream* AK-9
Campbell Creek—*stream* AZ-5
Campbell Creek—*stream* AR-4
Campbell Creek—*stream* (10) CA-9
Campbell Creek—*stream* (5) CO-8
Campbell Creek—*stream* FL-3
Campbell Creek—*stream* GA-3
Campbell Creek—*stream* (3) ID-8
Campbell Creek—*stream* IN-6
Campbell Creek—*stream* IA-7
Campbell Creek—*stream* (2) KY-4
Campbell Creek—*stream* LA-4
Campbell Creek—*stream* ME-1
Campbell Creek—*stream* (2) MI-6
Campbell Creek—*stream* (2) MN-6
Campbell Creek—*stream* (3) MS-4
Campbell Creek—*stream* (2) MO-7
Campbell Creek—*stream* MT-8
Campbell Creek—*stream* NV-8
Campbell Creek—*stream* NY-2
Campbell Creek—*stream* (4) NC-3
Campbell Creek—*stream* (4) OK-5
Campbell Creek—*stream* (7) OR-9
Campbell Creek—*stream* PA-2
Campbell Creek—*stream* (3) SC-3
Campbell Creek—*stream* (4) SD-7
Campbell Creek—*stream* TN-4
Campbell Creek—*stream* (4) TX-5
Campbell Creek—*stream* UT-8
Campbell Creek—*stream* (5) VA-3
Campbell Creek—*stream* (5) WA-9
Campbell Creek—*stream* (4) WI-6
Campbell Creek—*stream* WY-8
Campbell Creek Camp—*locale* TX-5
Campbell Creek Campground—*locale* WY-8
Campbell Creek Canyon—*valley* AK-9
Campbell Creek Cem—*cemetery* LA-4
Campbell Creek Ch—*church* MS-4
Campbell Creek Ranch—*locale* NV-8
Campbell Creek Sch—*school* KY-4
Campbell Creek Trail—*trail* CO-8
Campbell Crossroads—*locale* SC-3
Campbell Dam—*dam* (2) OR-9
Campbell Depot Camp—*locale* ME-1
*Campbell Ditch* IN-6
Campbell Ditch—*canal* AR-4
Campbell Ditch—*canal* CA-9
Campbell Ditch—*canal* (2) CO-8
Campbell Ditch—*canal* ID-8
Campbell Ditch—*canal* (3) IN-6
Campbell Ditch—*canal* NV-8
Campbell Ditch—*canal* NM-5
Campbell Ditch—*canal* WY-8
Campbell Ditch—*stream* MD-2
*Campbell Ditch Run* MD-2
Campbell Drain—*canal* MI-6
*Campbell Draw* TX-5
Campbell Draw—*valley* KS-7
Campbell Draw—*valley* TX-5
Campbell Draw—*valley* UT-8
Campbell Draw—*valley* (2) WY-8
Campbell Draw Tank—*reservoir* AZ-5
Campbell Drive Elem Sch—*school* FL-3
Campbell Drive JHS—*school* FL-3
Campbell Drive MS—*school* FL-3
Camp Belle Aire—*locale* TN-4
Campbelle Run—*stream* PA-2
**Campbell Estates**—*pop pl* PA-2
Camp Bellewood—*locale* MS-4
Campbell Falls—*falls* MA-1
Campbell Falls—*falls* OR-9
Campbell Falls State Park—*park* CT-1
Campbell Farm Site—*hist pl* MI-6
Campbell Flat—*bar* ID-8
Campbell Flat—*flat* (2) AZ-5
Campbell Flat—*flat* (3) CA-9
Campbell Folk Sch—*school* NC-3
Campbell Ford—*crossing* TN-4
Campbell Ford—*locale* MO-7
Campbell Fork—*stream* WV-2
Campbell Francis Wash—*stream* AZ-5
Campbell Gap—*gap* AL-4
Campbell Gap—*gap* NC-3
Campbell Gap—*gap* (2) TN-4
Campbell Grade—*slope* CA-9
Campbell-Grier Cem—*cemetery* OR-9
Campbell Grove Ch—*church* MO-7
Campbell Grove Sch (historical)—*school* TN-4
*Campbell Gulch* CO-8
Campbell Gulch—*valley* CA-9
Campbell Gulch—*valley* (2) ID-8
Campbell Gulch—*valley* OR-9
Campbell Gulch *valley* SD 7
**Campbell Hall**—*pop pl* NY-2
**Campbell Hall Junction**—*pop pl* NY-2
Campbell Hall Sch—*school* CA-9
Campbell Hall Sch—*school* IL-6
**Campbell Heights Subdivision**—*pop pl* UT-8
Campbell-Hicks House—*hist pl* WV-2
*Campbell Hill* ME-1
**Campbell Hill**—*pop pl* IL-6
Campbell Hill—*summit* AL-4
Campbell Hill—*summit* AZ-5
Campbell Hill—*summit* CA-9
Campbell Hill—*summit* CT-1
Campbell Hill—*summit* GA-3
Campbell Hill—*summit* KS-7
Campbell Hill—*summit* (2) ME-1
Campbell Hill—*summit* MO-7
Campbell Hill—*summit* (2) NH-1
Campbell Hill—*summit* (3) OH-6
Campbell Hill—*summit* OR-9
Campbell Hill—*summit* TN-4
Campbell Hill—*summit* (2) WV-2
Campbell Hill—*summit* WY-8
Campbell Hill Cem—*cemetery* IL-6
Campbell Hill Ch—*church* AL-4
Campbell Hill Ch—*church* MS-4
Campbell Hill Ch—*church* SC-3
Campbell Hills—*range* CA-9
Campbell Hollow—*stream* AR-4
Campbell Hollow—*valley* AL-4
Campbell Hollow—*valley* (5) AR-4
Campbell Hollow—*valley* KY-4
Campbell Hollow—*valley* MO-7
Campbell Hollow—*valley* NY-2
Campbell Hollow—*valley* (5) PA-2
Campbell Hollow—*valley* (11) TN-4
Campbell Hollow—*valley* UT-8
Campbell Hollow—*valley* VA-3
Campbell Hollow—*valley* (4) WV-2
Campbell Hollow Branch—*stream* TN-4
Campbell Hotel—*hist pl* OR-9
**Campbell Hot Springs**—*pop pl* CA-9
Campbell House—*hist pl* AR-4
Campbell House—*hist pl* KY-4
Campbell House—*hist pl* WA-9
Campbell House Claim—*mine* AZ-5
Campbell HQ Camp—*locale* WY-8
Campbell HS—*school* GA-3
Campbell HS—*school* HI-9
Campbell HS—*school* VA-3
Campbell Inside Bayou—*gut* MS-4
Campbell Island—*island* (2) ME-1
Campbell Island—*island* MS-4
Campbell Island—*island* (2) NY-2
Campbell Island—*island* NC-3
Campbell Island—*island* TX-5
Campbell Islands—*island* TN-4
Campbellite Cem—*cemetery* AL-4
Campbellite Cem—*cemetery* (2) MS-4
Campbellite Cem—*cemetery* TN-4
Campbellite Ch (historical)—*church* MS-4
Campbell JHS—*school* FL-3
Campbell-Jordan House—*hist pl* GA-3
Campbell Junction—*locale* TN-4
Campbell Junction Post Office (historical)—*building* TN-4
Campbell Knobs—*ridge* TN-4
Campbell Lagoon—*bay* AK-9
Campbell Lagoon—*lake* MS-4
*Campbell Lake* AK-9
*Campbell Lake* IN-6
*Campbell Lake* OR-9
*Campbell Lake* WA-9
Campbell Lake—*lake* (2) AK-9
Campbell Lake—*lake* AR-4
Campbell Lake—*lake* (2) CA-9
Campbell Lake—*lake* CO-8
Campbell Lake—*lake* FL-3
Campbell Lake—*lake* GA-3
Campbell Lake—*lake* IL-6
Campbell Lake—*lake* ME-1
Campbell Lake—*lake* (4) MI-6
Campbell Lake—*lake* (5) MN-6
Campbell Lake—*lake* (2) NE-7
Campbell Lake—*lake* (2) OR-9
Campbell Lake—*lake* (4) WA-9
Campbell Lake—*lake* (3) WI-6
Campbell Lake—*lake* (2) WY-8
Campbell Lake—*reservoir* MN-6
Campbell Lake—*reservoir* PA-2
Campbell Lake—*reservoir* SC-3
Campbell Lake—*reservoir* TN-4
Campbell Lake—*reservoir* TX-5
Campbell Lake Dam—*dam* MS-4
Campbell Lake Dam—*dam* TN-4
*Campbell Lakes* CA-9
*Campbell Lakes* IL-6
Campbell Lakes—*lake* NY-2
Campbell Landing (historical)—*locale* SD-7
Campbell Lateral—*canal* CA-9
Campbell Lead—*ridge* TN-4
Campbell Ledge—*bench* PA-2
Campbell Lick—*summit* NC-3
Campbell Meadow—*flat* CA-9
Campbell Memorial Ch—*church* VA-3
Campbell Memorial Hosp—*hospital* TX-5
Campbell Memorial Park—*cemetery* OH-6
Campbell Mill—*locale* AL-4
Campbell Mill Creek—*stream* AL-4
Campbell Mine—*mine* CA-9
Campbell Mine—*mine* ID-8
Campbell Mine—*mine* NV-8
Campbell Mine—*mine* TN-4
Campbell Mine (underground)—*mine* TN-4
Campbell-Moreland Ditch—*canal* CA-9
Campbell Mound—*hist pl* OH-6
Campbell Mound—*summit* CA-9
*Campbell Mtn* NH-1
Campbell Mtn—*summit* AL-4
Campbell Mtn—*summit* (2) CA-9
Campbell Mtn—*summit* (4) CO-8
Campbell Mtn—*summit* GA-3
Campbell Mtn—*summit* ME-1
Campbell Mtn—*summit* (2) MT-8
Campbell Mtn—*summit* NH-1
Campbell Mtn—*summit* (2) NY-2
Campbell Mtn—*summit* SC-3
Campbell Mtn—*summit* (2) TN-4
Campbell Municipal Airp—*airport* MO-7
Campbell Number One Sheep Swan—*spring* NV-8
Campbell Number One Township—*civil* MO-7
Campbell Number Two Sheep Swan—*spring* NV-8
Campbell Number Two Township—*civil* MO-7
Campbell One Plaza (Shop Ctr)—*locale* FL-3
Campbell Outside Bayou—*gut* MS-4
Campbell Park—*park* FL-3
Campbell Park—*park* IL-6
Campbell Park—*park* MT-8
Campbell Park—*park* NY-2
Campbell Park Elem Sch—*school* FL-3
Campbell Park Hist Dist of Huron—*hist pl* SD-7
Campbell Peak—*summit* CO-8
Campbell Peak—*summit* UT-8
Campbell Pen Branch—*stream* TN-4
Campbell Pen Knob—*summit* TN-4
Campbell Pit—*cave* AL-4
Campbell Pit—*cave* TN-4
Campbell Place—*locale* MT-8
Campbell Playground—*park* MI-6
Campbell Plaza Shop Ctr—*locale* AZ-5
Campbell Pocket—*bay* FL-3
*Campbell Point* CA-9
Campbell Point—*cape* AR-4
Campbell Point—*cape* FL-3
Campbell Point—*cape* NY-2
Campbell Point—*summit* CO-8
Campbell Point Public Use Area—*locale* MO-7
*Campbell Pond* ME-1
Campbell Pond—*lake* FL-3
Campbell Pond—*lake* (2) ME-1
Campbell Pond—*lake* NH-1
Campbell Pond—*lake* PA-2
Campbell Pond—*lake* WA-9
Campbell Pond—*reservoir* SC-3
Campbell Ponds—*lake* ID-8
Campbell Post Office (historical)—*building* SD-7
Campbell Post Office (historical)—*building* TN-4
Campbell Ranch—*locale* CA-9
Campbell Ranch—*locale* (2) CO-8
Campbell Ranch—*locale* HI-9
Campbell Ranch—*locale* ID-8
Campbell Ranch—*locale* (3) MT-8
Campbell Ranch—*locale* NM-5
Campbell Ranch—*locale* OR-9
Campbell Ranch—*locale* TX-5
Campbell Ranch—*locale* (2) WY-8
Campbell Ranch Airp—*airport* MO-7
Campbell Ranch Ind Res—*reserve* NV-8
*Campbell Range* WY-8
Campbell Ridge—*ridge* AR-4
Campbell Ridge—*ridge* (3) CA-9
Campbell Ridge—*ridge* KY-4
Campbell Ridge—*ridge* OH-6
Campbell Ridge—*ridge* TN-4
Campbell Ridge—*ridge* (2) WI-6
Campbell Ridge—*ridge* WY-8
Campbell River—*stream* (2) AK-9
Campbell Roadside Park—*park* TX-5
Campbell Rsvr—*reservoir* (2) CO-8
Campbell Rsvr—*reservoir* (5) OR-9
Campbell-Rumsey House—*hist pl* NY-2
*Campbell Run* PA-2
Campbell Run—*stream* (2) KY-4
Campbell Run—*stream* OH-6
Campbell Run—*stream* (8) PA-2
Campbell Run—*stream* (2) VA-3
Campbell Run—*stream* (4) WV-2
Campbell Run Ch—*church* WV-2
*Campbells* ME-1
*Campbells* TN-4
Campbells—*locale* WV-2
**Campbells**—*pop pl* IN-6
*Campbells Blue Creek* AZ-5
Campbells Brake—*swamp* AR-4
Campbells Branch—*stream* MS-4
Campbells Branch—*stream* TX-5
Campbells Branch—*stream* WV-2
Campbells Bridge—*bridge* MS-4
Campbell's Bridge—*hist pl* PA-2
*Campbells Brook* NJ-2
**Campbellsburg**—*pop pl* IN-6
**Campbellsburg**—*pop pl* KY-4
Campbellsburg (CCD)—*cens area* KY-4
Campbells Burial Park—*cemetery* VA-3
Campbells Cabins—*locale* MI-6
Campbell Sch—*hist pl* OH-6
Campbell Sch—*school* AR-4
Campbell Sch—*school* CO-8
Campbell Sch—*school* FL-3
Campbell Sch—*school* IL-6
Campbell Sch—*school* KY-4
Campbell Sch—*school* ME-1
Campbell Sch—*school* (2) MA-1
Campbell Sch—*school* (4) MI-6
Campbell Sch—*school* MN-6
Campbell Sch—*school* MO-7
Campbell Sch—*school* (2) NJ-2
Campbell Sch—*school* NC-3
Campbell Sch—*school* (3) OH-6
Campbell Sch—*school* OR-9
Campbell Sch—*school* (2) TN-4
Campbell Sch—*school* TX-5
Campbell Sch—*school* WA-9
Campbell Sch—*school* WV-2
Campbell Sch (abandoned)—*school* PA-2
*Campbells Chapel* AL-4
Campbells Chapel—*church* VA-3
Campbell Sch (historical)—*school* AL-4
Campbell Sch (historical)—*school* (2) PA-2
Campbell Sch (historical)—*school* (2) TN-4
Campbell Sch Number 1—*school* ND-7
Campbell Sch Number 4—*school* ND-7
Campbells Corner—*locale* NJ-2
Campbells Corner—*locale* VA-3
**Campbells Corner**—*pop pl* MI-6
Campbells Corners—*locale* NY-2
**Campbells Corners**—*pop pl* MI-6
Campbells Corners Cem—*cemetery* MI-6
Campbells Cow Camp—*locale* ID-8
*Campbells Creek* IN-6
*Campbells Creek* MS-4
*Campbells Creek* NC-3
*Campbells Creek* PA-2
*Campbells Creek* TX-5
*Campbells Creek* VA 3
Campbells Creek—*stream* (2) TX-5
Campbells Creek—*stream* VA-3
Campbells Creek—*stream* WV-2
Campbells Crossroad—*locale* NC-3
Campbells Crossroads—*locale* (2) AL-4
Campbells Dead River—*lake* FL-3
Campbell Settlement (historical)—*locale* AL-4
*Campbells Ferry* TN-4
Campbells Ferry—*locale* ID-8
Campbells Flat—*flat* AZ-5
Campbells Flat Spring—*spring* AZ-5
*Campbells Fork* WY-8
Campbells Fork—*locale* VA-3
*Campbells Fork Lakes* WY-8
**Campbells (Fountain Creek)**—*pop pl* TN-4
Campbells Gap—*gut* TN-4
Campbell Sheep Camp—*locale* CA-9
*Campbells Hill* OH-6
Campbells Hollow—*valley* WV-2
*Campbell Shore* ME-1
Campbells Hump Ch—*church* IL-6
Campbell Siding—*locale* MS-4
Campbell Siding—*locale* MO-7
**Campbell Siding**—*pop pl* IN-6
Campbell Sink—*basin* FL-3
*Campbells Island* MS-4
*Campbell's Island* NY-2
*Campbells Island* NC-3
Campbells Island—*island* IL-6
**Campbells Island**—*pop pl* IL-6
Campbells Island State Park—*park* IL-6
Campbell's Junction—*post sta* NJ-2
*Campbells Lake* IA-7
*Campbells Lake* MN-6
*Campbells Lake* WA-9
Campbells Lake—*reservoir* AL-4
Campbells Lake—*reservoir* SC-3
*Campbells Lake Dam* AL-4
*Campbells Lakes* CA-9
Campbells Landing—*locale* AL-4

Camp Creek Springs—*spring* ... NE-7
Camp Creek Springs—*spring* ... WY-8
Camp Creek State For—*forest* ... WV-2
Camp Creek (Township of)—*fmr MCD* ... NC-3
**Camp Creek (Township of)**—*pop pl* ... OH-6
Camp Creek Trail—*trail* ... TN-4
Camp Creek West Well—*well* ... TX-5
Camp Crestview—*locale* ... PA-2
Camp Crete—*locale* ... IL-6
Camp Crile—*locale* ... MI-6
*Camp Crittenden* ... AZ-5
Camp Crockett—*locale* ... CO-8
Camp Crockett Trail—*trail* ... CO-8
**Camp Croft**—*pop pl* ... SC-3
**Camp Crook**—*pop pl* ... SD-7
*Camp Crook II* ... SD-7
Camp Crook Municipal Airp—*airport* ... SD-7
Camp Crook Township (historical)—*civil* ... SD-7
Camp Crosby—*locale* ... AL-4
Camp Crosley—*park* ... IN-6
Camp Crossed Arrows—*locale* ... AR-4
Camp Crosstie—*locale* ... TX-5
Camp Crowell—*locale* ... OH-6
Camp Crowell—*locale* ... VA-3
Camp Crucis—*locale* ... TX-5
Camp Crunch Spring—*spring* ... OR-9
Camp Cuivre—*locale* ... MO-7
Camp Cullen Summer Camp—*locale* ... AL-4
Camp Cullman—*locale* ... AL-4
Camp Cum-Ba-Ya—*locale* ... KY-4
Camp Cumorah Crest—*locale* ... CA-9
Camp Currie—*locale* ... KY-4
Camp Currier—*locale* ... MS-4
*Camp Curry* ... CA-9
Camp Curry—*locale* ... CA-9
Camp Curry Hist Dist—*hist pl* ... CA-9
Camp Curtain Early Childhood Sch—*school* ... PA-2
*Camp Curtain JHS* ... PA-2
Camp Curtin—*uninc pl* ... PA-2
Camp Curtin Fire Station—*hist pl* ... PA-2
Camp Curtis—*locale* ... WA-9
Camp Curtis Guild Natl Guard Reservation—*reserve* ... MA-1
Camp Custer—*other* ... MI-6
Camp Custer (historical)—*locale* ... SD-7
Camp Cuyamaca—*locale* ... CA-9
Camp D—*locale* ... FL-3
Camp Da-Ko-Ta—*locale* ... SD-7
**Camp Dallas**—*pop pl* ... TX-5
Camp Dallas (ROTC)—*locale* ... TX-5
Camp Dana—*locale* ... ME-1
Camp Dan Beard—*locale* ... IL-6
Camp Dan Beard—*locale* ... KY-4
**Camp Danbee**—*pop pl* ... MA-1
Camp Daniel Boone Dam—*dam* ... NC-3
Camp Daniel Boone Lake—*reservoir* ... NC-3
Camp Daniel Marshall—*locale* ... GA-3
Camp Daniel Morgan—*locale* ... GA-3
Camp Dantzler—*locale* ... MS-4
Camp Dan Valley—*locale* ... NC-3
Camp Darby—*locale* ... OK-5
Camp Dark Hollow—*locale* ... VA-3
Camp Date Creek—*locale* ... AZ-5
Camp Davella—*locale* ... OH-6
*Camp Davidson* ... KS-7
Camp Davidson—*locale* ... CA-9
Camp Davis—*locale* ... NM-5
Camp Davis—*locale* ... NC-3
Camp Davis—*locale* (2) ... PA-2
Camp Davis—*locale* ... WY-8
Camp Dawson—*locale* ... AL-4
Camp Day—*locale* ... MA-1
**Camp Day (historical)**—*pop pl* ... OR-9
Camp Dayo Creek—*stream* ... WA-9
Camp D Creek—*stream* ... WI-6
**Camp Dealy**—*pop pl* ... GU-9
Camp Dean—*locale* ... IL-6
Camp Dearborn—*locale* ... MI-6
Camp De Benneville Pines—*locale* ... CA-9
Camp Deer Creek—*locale* ... MD-2
Camp Deer Creek—*locale* ... PA-2
Camp Deerhead—*locale* ... NY-2
Camp Deer Lake—*reservoir* ... NC-3
Camp Deer Run—*locale* ... TX-5
Camp Deerwoode—*locale* ... NC-3
Camp Deerwood Forest—*locale* ... NY-2
Camp Dejacket—*locale* ... MI-6
Camp Dekanawida—*locale* ... WV-2
Camp Delaware—*locale* ... CT-1
Camp de Leon—*locale* ... TX-5
Camp Dell-O-Claire—*locale* ... WI-6
Camp Dells Campground—*locale* ... WI-6
Camp Dellwood—*park* ... IN-6
Camp Del Mar—*locale* ... CA-9
Camp Delmar—*locale* ... NY-2
Camp Delmont Dam—*dam* ... PA-2
Camp De Luz—*locale* ... CA-9
Camp Denali—*locale* ... AK-9
Campden Gap—*gap* ... WA-9
Camp Dennen—*locale* ... MA-1
**Camp Dennison**—*pop pl* (2) ... OH-6
Camp Dent—*locale* ... PA-2
Camp Derricote—*locale* ... MO-7
Camp Derry—*locale* ... VT-1
Camp De Sales—*locale* ... MI-6
**Camp Desert Rock**—*pop pl* ... NV-8
Camp De Shaw—*locale* ... IA-7
Camp De Soto—*locale* ... AL-4
Camp DeWolf—*locale* ... NY-2
**Camp Diana**—*pop pl* ... WA-9
Camp Dick Henning (Boy Scouts)—*locale* ... NC-3
Camp Dick Robinson—*locale* ... KY-4
Camp Dick Robinson HQ—*hist pl* ... KY-4
Camp Dick Runyan—*park* ... IN-6
Camp Dineen—*locale* ... NY-2
Camp Dippikill—*locale* ... NY-2
Camp Disappointment—*hist pl* ... MT-8
**Camp Discovery**—*pop pl* ... WA-9
Camp Ditch—*canal* ... CO-8
*Camp Divide* ... FL-3
*Camp Dix* ... NJ-2
Camp Dix—*locale* ... CA-9
Camp Dix—*locale* ... KY-4
Camp Dixie—*locale* ... CA-9
Camp Dixie—*locale* (2) ... GA-3
Camp Dixie—*locale* ... TN-4
Camp Dixie (historical)—*locale* ... AL-4
Camp Dixie Lake—*reservoir* ... NC-3
Camp Dixon—*locale* ... SC-3
Camp Dixon Sch—*school* ... WI-6
**Camp Dodge**—*pop pl* ... IA-7
Camp Dodge Military Reservation—*locale* ... IA-7
Camp Dodge Station (historical)—*locale* ... IA-7
Camp Dogwood—*locale* ... NC-3
Camp Dogwood—*locale* ... TN-4
Camp Dominic Savio—*locale* ... ND-7
Camp Don Bosco—*locale* ... MT-8
Camp Don Bosco—*locale* ... WA-9
**Camp Don-Lee**—*pop pl* ... NC-3
Camp Dorchester—*locale* ... MA-1
Camp Dorothy (historical)—*locale* ... ME-1
Camp Doughboy—*locale* ... AR-4
Camp Douglas—*locale* ... NV-8
**Camp Douglas**—*pop pl* ... WI-6
Camp Douglas Lake—*lake* ... WI-6
Camp Douglas Long—*locale* ... NC-3
Camp Douglass—*locale* ... MI-6
Camp Drain—*stream* (2) ... MI-6
Camp Drake—*locale* ... CA-9
Camp Drake—*locale* ... IL-6
Camp Draper—*other* ... WA-9
Camp Draw—*valley* ... NV-8
Camp Draw—*valley* ... NM-5
Camp Draw—*valley* ... UT-8
Camp Draw Trailhead—*locale* ... NV-8
Camp Drum—*post sta* ... NY-2
Camp Dry-Kye—*locale* ... ME-1
Camp Dudley—*locale* ... NY-2
Camp Dudley—*locale* ... WA-9
Camp Duesner Ditch—*canal* ... IN-6
Camp Duffield—*locale* ... NY-2
Camp Duncan—*locale* ... IL-6
Camp Dunlap Naval Reservation—*canal* ... CA-9
Camp Dunlap (Site)—*locale* ... CA-9
Camp Dunroamin—*locale* ... TN-4
Camp Durant—*locale* ... NC-3
Camp Durant Lake Number One—*reservoir* ... NC-3
Camp Durant Lake Number One Dam—*dam* ... NC-3
Camp Durant Lake Number Two—*reservoir* ... NC-3
Camp Durant Lake Number Two Dam—*dam* ... NC-3
Camp Dyer Diversion Dam—*dam* ... AZ-5
Camp E—*locale* ... FL-3
Camp Eagle—*locale* ... NE-7
Camp Earl-Anna—*locale* ... CA-9
Camp Earl Wallace—*locale* ... KY-4
**Camp Earnest**—*pop pl* ... CA-9
Camp East Creek—*stream* ... MN-6
Camp Easter Sea—*locale* ... OR-9
Camp Easterseal—*locale* ... ID-8
Camp Easter Seal—*locale* ... VA-3
Camp Eastford—*locale* ... CT-1
Camp Easton—*locale* ... CT-1
Camp Easton—*locale* ... ID-8
Camp Eastwood—*locale* ... CA-9
Camp Easy—*locale* ... FL-3
*Campeater Basin* ... UT-8
Camp Ebenezer—*locale* ... AR-4
Camp Eberhardt—*locale* ... MI-6
Camp Ecco—*locale* ... OH-6
Camp Echo—*locale* ... WV-2
Camp Echo—*park* ... MA-1
**Camp Echockotee**—*pop pl* ... FL-3
Camp Echo Dell—*locale* ... OH-6
Camp Echo Lake—*locale* ... NY-2
Camp Echo Trail—*trail* ... PA-2
Camp Eden—*locale* ... CA-9
Camp Edey—*locale* ... NY-2
*Camp Edge* ... NJ-2
Camp Edge—*locale* ... NJ-2
Camp Edith Mayo—*locale* ... MN-6
Camp Edmar—*locale* ... PA-2
Camp Edwards—*locale* ... CA-9
Camp Edwards—*locale* ... WI-6
**Camp Edwards**—*pop pl* ... MA-1
Camp Ee Da How—*locale* ... ID-8
Camp Ee-Kah-Bee—*locale* ... MN-6
Camp Egan—*locale* ... OK-5
Camp Ehawee—*locale* ... WI-6
*Camp Eight* ... HI-9
Camp Eight—*locale* (2) ... CA-9
Camp Eight Ch—*church* ... LA-4
Camp Eight Creek—*stream* ... MI-6
Camp Eight Creek—*stream* ... MN-6
Camp Eight Creek—*stream* ... WI-6
**Camp Eighteen**—*pop pl* ... CA-9
Camp Eight Flowage—*reservoir* ... WI-6
Camp Eight Lake—*lake* ... MI-6
Camp Eight Pond—*lake* ... MO-7
Camp Eight Ponds—*reservoir* ... MI-6
Camp E-Ko-Wah—*locale* ... OK-5
Camp Eldorado—*locale* ... CA-9
*Camp Elementary School* ... MS-4
Camp Eleven—*locale* ... CA-9
Camp Eleven Creek—*stream* (2) ... MI-6
Camp Eleven Creek—*stream* ... WI-6
Camp Eleven Lake—*lake* ... MI-6
Camp Eleven Lake—*lake* ... WI-6
Camp El-Har—*locale* ... TX-5
Camp Elizabeth Lupton—*locale* ... AL-4
**Camp Elkanah**—*pop pl* ... OR-9
Camp Elklore (historical)—*locale* ... TN-4
Camp Ella Fohs—*locale* ... CT-1
Camp Ellendale—*locale* ... CA-9
*Campelle Slough* ... AR-4
*Campell Hill Missionary Baptist Church* ... MS-4
Camp Elliott—*locale* ... NC-3
Camp Elliott Naval Reservation—*civil* ... CA-9
*Camp Ellis* ... ME-1
Camp Ellis—*locale* ... WA-9
**Camp Ellis**—*pop pl* ... ME-1
Camp Ellis Military Reservation—*other* ... IL-6
**Campello**—*pop pl* ... MA-1
Campello (historical P.O.)—*locale* ... MA-1
Campello Station (historical)—*locale* ... MA-1
Camp Ellowi (Campfire Girls of America)—*locale* ... TX-5
Campell Shelter—*locale* ... WA-9
Campellton-Graceville Hosp—*hospital* ... FL-3
Camp Elm—*park* ... IN-6
Camp Elmore—*military* ... VA-3
Camp Elsinore—*locale* ... NJ-2
Camp Emerson—*locale* ... CA-9
**Camp Emerson**—*pop pl* ... MA-1
Campen Creek—*stream* ... WA-9
Camp Endeavor—*locale* ... NJ-2
Camp Endicott—*hist pl* ... RI-1
Camp Endion—*locale* ... NY-2
Camp Epworth—*locale* ... IL-6
Camp Equinunk—*locale* ... PA-2
Camp Ercan—*locale* ... NM-5
Camper Cem—*cemetery* ... AL-4
Camper Cem—*cemetery* ... TN-4
Camper Creek—*stream* ... AK-9
Camp Erdman—*locale* ... HI-9
**Camperdown**—*pop pl* ... LA-4
Camper Flat—*flat* ... CA-9
Camper Hollow—*valley* ... TN-4
Camp Ernst—*locale* ... KY-4
Campers Bayou—*stream* ... LA-4
Campers Branch—*stream* ... TN-4
Campers Cove—*bay* ... AK-9
Campers Creek—*stream* ... CO-8
Campers Flat—*flat* ... OR-9
Campers Flat Forest Camp—*locale* ... OR-9
Campers Hill Campground—*locale* ... IL-6
Campers Island—*island* ... MN-6
Campers Island—*island* ... NM-5
Campers Lake—*lake* ... AK-9
Campers Lake—*lake* ... MN-6
Campers Lake—*lake* ... OR-9
Campers Point—*cape* ... AK-9
Camper Spring—*spring* ... MO-7
Campers Spring—*spring* ... UT-8
Camp Este (historical)—*locale* ... SD-7
Camp Esther Applegate—*locale* ... OR-9
Camp Eter Lake—*lake* ... MO-7
Campetine Creek—*stream* ... IA-7
Camp Eton—*locale* ... NY-2
Camp Euchee—*locale* ... FL-3
Camp Eureka—*locale* ... KS-7
Camp Evans—*locale* ... CA-9
Camp Evelyn—*locale* ... WI-6
Camp Everest—*locale* ... VT-1
Camp Everglades—*locale* (2) ... FL-3
Camp Evergreen—*locale* ... OH-6
**Camp Evers**—*pop pl* ... CA-9
Camp Ewalu—*locale* ... IA-7
Camp Exchange—*locale* ... AL-4
Camp Exton—*locale* ... NY-2
Camp Fairchance—*locale* ... WV-2
Camp Fairfield—*locale* ... PA-2
Camp Fair Haven—*locale* ... ME-1
Camp Fair Haven—*locale* ... VA-3
Camp Fairview—*locale* ... TX-5
Camp Fairwood—*locale* ... MI-6
Camp Faith Wing—*locale* ... MI-6
Camp Falcon—*locale* ... IL-6
Camp Faraway—*locale* ... OR-9
Camp Farr—*park* ... IN-6
Camp Farwell—*locale* ... MI-6
Camp Far West Ditch—*canal* ... CA-9
Camp Far West (Historic Site)—*locale* ... CA-9
Camp Far West Ranch—*locale* ... CA-9
Camp Far West Rsvr—*reservoir* ... CA-9
Camp Fatima—*locale* ... NH-1
Camp Fawcett—*locale* ... TX-5
Camp F Creek—*stream* ... WI-6
Camp Fern Brook—*locale* ... PA-2
Camp Fiddler Hollow—*valley* ... TX-5
**Campfield**—*pop pl* ... SC-3
*Campfield Branch* ... IL-6
Campfield Ch—*church* ... SC-3
Camp Field Memorial Ch—*church* ... NC-3
Camp Field Retreat Center—*locale* ... WA-9
Camp Field Rsvr—*reservoir* ... NY-2
Campfield Run—*stream* ... WV-2
Camp Field Stream—*stream* ... ME-1
Campfield Trail—*trail* ... PA-2
Camp Fife—*locale* ... WA-9
Camp Fifteen Creek—*stream* ... WI-6
Camp Fifteen (historical)—*locale* ... SD-7
Camp Fifteen Lake—*lake* ... MI-6
Camp Fifteen (site)—*locale* ... OR-9
Camp Fifteen Springs—*spring* ... WI-6
*Camp Fifty* ... KS-7
Camp Fifty—*obs name* ... KS-7
Camp Finbrook—*locale* ... MO-7
Camp Finburg—*locale* ... MA-1
Camp Findley—*locale* ... NY-2
Campfire Creek—*stream* ... IN-6
Campfire Creek—*stream* ... WY-8
Camp Firefly—*locale* ... OH-6
Camp Fire Girls, Lake—*lake* ... WA-9
Campfire Girls Camp—*locale* ... MN-6
Camp Fire Girls Camp—*locale* ... PA-2
Campfire Lake—*lake* ... AK-9
Campfire Lake—*lake* ... CA-9
Campfire Lake—*lake* ... MN-6
Campfire Lake—*lake* ... MT-8
Campfire Lake—*lake* ... NY-2
Campfire Lodge—*locale* ... MT-8
Campfire Slough—*gut* ... LA-4
Camp Firewood—*locale* ... WI-6
Camp Fitch—*locale* ... PA-2
Camp Five—*locale* (2) ... CA-9
Camp Five—*locale* (2) ... HI-9
Camp Five—*locale* ... OR-9
Camp Five Creek—*stream* ... MI-6
Camp Five Creek—*stream* ... WI-6
Camp Five Lake—*lake* ... MI-6
Camp Five Lake—*lake* ... WI-6
Camp Five Lakes—*lake* ... MN-6
Camp Five Pond—*lake* ... MO-7
Camp Five Pond—*locale* ... MO-7
Camp Five Run—*stream* ... WV-2
Camp Five Trail—*trail* ... WV-2
Camp Flambeau—*locale* ... WI-6
Camp Flat—*flat* ... OR-9
Camp Flat—*flat* ... UT-8
Camp Flather—*locale* ... VA-3
Camp Flat-Rock—*locale* ... NY-2
**Camp Flat Rock**—*pop pl* ... IN-6
Camp Flats—*flat* ... GA-3
*Camp Fletcher* ... KS-7
Camp Floodwood—*locale* ... MI-6
Camp Florence—*locale* ... AL-4
Camp Floriday (historical)—*locale* ... FL-3
Camp Flowers—*locale* ... FL-3
Camp Floyd Cem—*cemetery* ... UT-8
Camp Floyd Site—*hist pl* ... UT-8
*Camp Floyd-Stagecoach Inn State Park* ... UT-8
Camp Floyd State Historical Site—*locale* ... UT-8
Camp Flying Eagle—*locale* ... MI-6
Camp Fontanelle—*locale* ... NE-7
Camp Forestburg—*locale* ... NY-2
**Camp Forest Lake**—*pop pl* ... NH-1
Camp Forest Milit Reservation (historical)—*military* ... TN-4
Camp Forest Springs—*locale* ... WI-6
Camp Fork—*stream* ... KY-4
Camp Fork Creek—*stream* ... IN-6
Camp Forrest Cem—*cemetery* ... TN-4
Camp Forsyth—*military* ... KS-7
Camp Fort Dearborn—*locale* ... IL-6
Camp Fort Scott—*locale* ... OH-6
Camp Forty Acres—*locale* ... NY-2
Camp Forty Creek—*stream* ... ID-8
Camp Forty Creek—*stream* ... MN-6
Camp Forty Five—*locale* ... CA-9
Camp Fortyfour—*locale* ... CA-9
Camp Fortyone Lake—*lake* ... MI-6
Camp Fortythree—*locale* ... CA-9
Camp Forward—*locale* (2) ... CA-9
Camp Foss—*locale* ... NH-1
Camp Fosseen—*locale* ... WA-9
Camp Foster—*locale* ... IA-7
Camp Foster—*locale* ... NH-1
Camp Foster Creek—*stream* ... CO-8
*Camp Four* ... HI-9
Camp Four—*locale* (3) ... CA-9
Camp Four—*locale* ... GA-3
Camp Four—*locale* (2) ... HI-9
Camp Four—*locale* ... MT-8
Camp Four—*locale* ... OR-9
Camp Four—*locale* ... WA-9
Camp Four (abandoned)—*locale* ... OR-9
Camp Four Campground—*locale* ... WA-9
Camp Four Campsite—*locale* ... CA-9
Camp Four Creek—*stream* ... OR-9
Camp Four Creek—*stream* ... WI-6
Camp Four Gulch—*valley* ... MT-8
Camp Four (historical)—*locale* ... TX-5
Camp Four Lake—*lake* ... MN-6
Camp Four Lake—*lake* (3) ... WI-6
Camp Four Lakes—*lake* ... WI-6
*Camp Four School* ... TN-4
Camp Four Springs—*lake* ... WI-6
Camp Fourteen—*locale* ... CA-9
Camp Fourteen—*locale* ... OR-9
Camp Fourteen Creek—*stream* ... WI-6
Camp Frame—*locale* ... WV-2
Camp Francis—*locale* ... CT-1
Camp Francoise Barstow—*locale* ... NY-2
Camp Frank D Merrill—*military* ... GA-3
Camp Fredrickson—*locale* ... OH-6
Camp Freedman—*locale* ... CT-1
Camp Fresno—*locale* ... CA-9
Camp Friedlander—*locale* ... OH-6
Camp Friend—*locale* ... OR-9
Camp Friendship—*locale* ... MN-6
Camp Frontier—*locale* ... NC-3
Camp Fuller—*locale* ... RI-1
Camp Funston—*military* ... KS-7
Camp Gadsden Alabama State Prison (historical)—*building* ... AL-4
Camp Galahad—*locale* ... WV-2
Camp Galena (historical)—*locale* ... SD-7
Camp Galilee—*locale* ... MN-6
Camp Gap—*gap* ... NC-3
Camp Garaway Pond Dam—*dam* ... MS-4
Camp Garaywa—*locale* ... MS-4
Camp Garcia—*locale* ... TX-5
Camp Garland—*locale* ... OK-5
Camp Garrison—*locale* ... LA-4
**Campgaw**—*pop pl* ... NJ-2
Campgaw (Franklin Lakes)—*other* ... NJ-2
Campgaw Mtn—*summit* ... NJ-2
Camp Gazelle Dew—*locale* ... GA-3
Camp Geiger—*locale* ... MO-7
Camp Geiger—*military* ... NC-3
Camp Genesee—*locale* ... PA-2
Camp Geneva—*locale* ... PA-2
Camp George—*locale* ... MN-6
Camp George Creek—*stream* ... ID-8
Camp George Cullom—*park* ... IN-6
Camp George H Sharp (historical)—*locale* ... PA-2
Camp George West—*military* ... CO-8
Camp Geronimo—*locale* ... AZ-5
Camp Geronimo—*locale* ... NM-5
Camp Gibbs—*locale* ... MI-6
Camp Gideon Childrens Home—*building* ... KY-4
Camp Gilead—*locale* ... FL-3
Camp Gilead—*locale* ... WA-9
Camp Gilmont—*locale* ... TX-5
Camp Ginger Quill—*locale* ... MI-6
Camp Girard—*locale* ... PA-2
Camp Giscowhego—*locale* ... WV-2
Camp Glancy—*locale* ... TN-4
Camp Gleason—*locale* ... CA-9
Camp Glen—*locale* ... NC-3
Camp Glen—*locale* ... OH-6
Camp Glenkirk—*locale* ... VA-3
Camp Glenmere—*locale* ... MA-1
**Camp Glenmere**—*pop pl* ... MA-1
**Camp Glenn**—*pop pl* ... NC-3
Camp Glenn Elem Sch—*school* ... NC-3
Camp Glenwood—*locale* ... CA-9
Camp Glenwood—*locale* ... NJ-2
Camp Glisson—*locale* ... GA-3
Camp Glover—*locale* ... OK-5
Camp Goettge—*locale* ... VA-3
Camp Goodaire—*locale* ... OH-6
Camp Good News—*locale* ... AZ-5
Camp Good News—*locale* ... CA-9
Camp Goodwill—*locale* ... MA-1
Camp Goodwin (historical)—*locale* ... AZ-5
Camp Gordon Johnson—*military* ... FL-3
Camp Gorsuch (Boy Scouts of America)—*locale* ... AK-9
Camp Gorton—*locale* ... NY-2
Camp Grace—*locale* ... AZ-5
Camp Grace—*locale* ... WY-8
**Camp Grafton**—*pop pl* ... ND-7
Camp Graham—*locale* ... OH-6
Camp Grande—*locale* ... WA-9
Camp Grandview—*locale* ... AL-4
Camp Grandview—*locale* ... MO-7
*Camp Grant* ... AZ-5
Camp Grant—*locale* ... NY-2
Camp Grant—*locale* ... OR-9
Camp Grant—*locale* ... UT-8
Camp Grant Flat—*flat* ... CA-9
Camp Grant (Site)—*locale* ... CA-9
*Camp Grant (sta.)* ... IL-6
Camp Grant Walker—*locale* ... LA-4
Camp Grant Wash—*stream* ... AZ-5
Camp Grant Wash—*valley* ... AZ-5
Camp Grant Wash Trail—*trail* ... AZ-5
Camp Grassick—*locale* ... ND-7
**Camp Gravatt**—*pop pl* ... SC-3
Camp Gray—*locale* ... WI-6
Camp Grayback—*locale* ... OR-9
Camp Grayling—*locale* ... MI-6
Camp Grayling Milit Reservation (Michigan Natl Guard)—*military* ... MI-6
Camp Greble—*locale* ... PA-2
Camp Green Briar—*locale* ... WV-2
Camp Green Cove—*locale* ... NC-3
Camp Greene—*locale* ... OH-6
Camp Green Eyrie—*locale* ... MA-1
**Camp Green Eyrie**—*pop pl* ... MA-1
Camp Greenville—*locale* ... SC-3
Camp Greenwood—*locale* ... MN-6
Camp Gregg—*locale* ... SC-3
Camp Greilick—*locale* ... MI-6
Camp Grenada—*locale* ... FL-3
Camp Grey—*locale* ... MI-6
**Camp Greylock**—*pop pl* ... MA-1
Camp Grier—*locale* ... NC-3
Camp Grier Dam—*dam* ... NC-3
Camp Grier Lake—*reservoir* ... NC-3
Camp Grindley—*locale* ... MI-6
Camp Grist—*locale* ... AL-4
Camp Griswold—*locale* ... OH-6
Camp Grizzly—*locale* ... ID-8
Camp Gross—*locale* ... NY-2
*Camp Ground* ... TN-4
Camp Ground—*locale* (2) ... AL-4
**Camp Ground**—*pop pl* ... AL-4
**Camp Ground**—*pop pl* ... IL-6
**Camp Ground**—*pop pl* ... MS-4
**Camp Ground**—*pop pl* ... OH-6
**Camp Ground**—*pop pl* (3) ... TN-4
**Camp Ground**—*pop pl* ... WV-2
*Camp Ground Baptist Church* ... MS-4
Campground Bay—*swamp* ... FL-3
Campground Bayou—*stream* ... TX-5
*Camp Ground Branch* ... MO-7
Camp Ground Branch—*stream* ... AL-4
Campground Branch—*stream* (2) ... AL-4
Campground Branch—*stream* ... AR-4
Camp Ground Branch—*stream* ... IN-6
Campground Branch—*stream* (2) ... LA-4
Campground Branch—*stream* ... MD-2
Camp Ground Branch—*stream* ... MS-4
Campground Branch—*stream* ... NC-3
Campground Branch—*stream* ... TN-4
*Camp Ground Branch - in part* ... MS-4
Campground Bridge—*bridge* ... MD-2
Campground Cave—*cave* ... AL-4
Camp Ground (CCD)—*cens area* ... KY-4
Camp Ground (CCD)—*cens area* ... SC-3
*Camp Ground Cem* ... MS-4
Camp Ground Cem—*cemetery* ... AL-4
Campground Cem—*cemetery* ... AL-4
Camp Ground Cem—*cemetery* ... AL-4
Campground Cem—*cemetery* (3) ... AR-4
Campground Cem—*cemetery* ... FL-3
Campground Cem—*cemetery* (3) ... GA-3
Camp Ground Cem—*cemetery* ... IL-6
Campground Cem—*cemetery* (4) ... IL-6
Campground Cem—*cemetery* ... IN-6
Campground Cem—*cemetery* ... IA-7
Campground Cem—*cemetery* (3) ... KY-4
Camp Ground Cem—*cemetery* ... KY-4
Camp Ground Cem—*cemetery* ... LA-4
Campground Cem—*cemetery* ... MS-4
Camp Ground Cem—*cemetery* (2) ... MS-4
Campground Cem—*cemetery* ... MS-4
Camp Ground Cem—*cemetery* (3) ... MS-4
Campground Cem—*cemetery* ... MO-7
Camp Ground Cem—*cemetery* ... MO-7
Campground Cem—*cemetery* (4) ... MO-7
Campground Cem—*cemetery* ... SC-3
Camp Ground Cem—*cemetery* (2) ... TN-4
Campground Cem—*cemetery* (3) ... TN-4
Camp Ground Cem—*cemetery* ... TN-4
Campground Cem—*cemetery* ... TN-4
Campground Cem—*cemetery* (5) ... TX-5
*Camp Ground Ch* ... AL-4
*Campground Ch* ... AR-4
*Camp Ground Ch* ... MS-4
*Camp Ground Ch* ... TN-4
Camp Ground Ch—*church* ... AL-4
Campground Ch—*church* (7) ... AL-4
Campground Ch—*church* ... AR-4
Camp Ground Ch—*church* ... AR-4
Campground Ch—*church* (4) ... AR-4
Campground Ch—*church* ... GA-3
Campground Ch—*church* (2) ... IL-6
Camp Ground Ch—*church* ... KY-4
Campground Ch—*church* ... KY-4
Camp Ground Ch—*church* (2) ... MS-4
Campground Ch—*church* (3) ... MS-4
Camp Ground Ch—*church* ... MO-7
Campground Ch—*church* ... MO-7
Camp Ground Ch—*church* (2) ... NC-3
Campground Ch—*church* (4) ... TN-4
Camp Ground Ch—*church* (3) ... TN-4
Campground Ch—*church* ... TN-4
Camp Ground Ch—*church* ... TN-4
Campground Ch—*church* ... TN-4
Camp Ground Ch—*church* ... TN-4
Campground Ch—*church* (4) ... TX-5
Campground Ch—*church* ... VA-3
Campground Chapel—*church* ... TN-4
Camp Ground Ch (historical)—*church* ... AL-4
Camp Ground Ch (historical)—*church* ... TN-4
Camp Ground Church and Cemetary—*hist pl* ... MO-7
*Camp Ground Creek* ... AL-4
*Camp Ground Creek* ... MS-4
Campground Creek—*stream* (2) ... AR-4
Campground Creek—*stream* ... LA-4
Campground Creek—*stream* (2) ... TN-4
Camp Ground Creek—*stream* ... TN-4
Campground Creek—*stream* (3) ... TX-5
Campground Creek—*stream* ... WI-6
Campground Gap—*gap* ... NC-3
Campground Guard Station—*locale* ... CA-9
*Camp Ground Hill* ... AL-4
Campground Hill—*summit* ... CT-1
Campground Hill—*summit* ... WI-6
Camp Ground (historical)—*locale* ... MS-4
Campground (historical)—*locale* ... MS-4
Campground Hollow—*valley* (2) ... AL-4
Campground Hollow—*valley* (3) ... MO-7
Campground Hollow—*valley* (4) ... TN-4
Campground Hollow—*valley* ... VA-3
Campground Knob—*summit* ... NC-3
Campground Lake—*lake* ... FL-3
**Campground Landing**—*pop pl* ... MA-1
*Campground Methodist Church* ... MS-4
Camp Ground Methodist Church—*hist pl* ... NC-3
Campground Mtn—*summit* ... AL-4
Camp Ground Mtn—*summit* ... GA-3
Campground Mtn—*summit* ... NY-2
Campground No 1—*locale* ... IL-6
Campground Number Five—*locale* ... WI-6
Campground Number Four—*locale* ... WI-6
Campground Number One—*locale* ... WI-6
Campground Number One—*park* ... OR-9
Campground Number Three—*locale* (2) ... CA-9
Campground Number Two—*locale* ... CA-9
Campground Number Two—*locale* ... WI-6
Campground Number Two—*park* ... OR-9
Campground on the Lakeshore—*park* ... TN-4
Campground Pond—*lake* ... FL-3
Camp Ground Post Office (historical)—*building* ... TN-4
**Camp Grounds**—*pop pl* ... KY-4
**Camp Grounds**—*pop pl* ... MA-1
**Camp Grounds**—*pop pl* ... VT-1
Camp Grounds—*uninc pl* ... MS-4
Camp Grounds Cem—*cemetery* ... AR-4
Campgrounds Ch—*church* ... AR-4
Camp Ground Sch—*school* (3) ... KY-4
Camp Ground Sch—*school* ... MS-4
Campground Sch—*school* (2) ... TN-4
Camp Ground Sch (abandoned)—*school* ... MO-7
Camp Ground Sch (historical)—*school* (2) ... AL-4
Camp Ground Sch (historical)—*school* ... MS-4
Camp Ground Sch (historical)—*school* ... TN-4
Campground Sch (historical)—*school* ... TN-4
Camp Ground Sch (historical)—*school* ... TN-4
*Camp Grounds Church* ... AL-4
Camp Ground Slough—*gut* ... MS-4
Campground Spring—*spring* ... MO-7
Campground Spring—*spring* ... OK-5
Campground Spring—*spring* ... UT-8
Campground Spring Creek—*stream* ... TN-4
Campground Spring Mountain—*ridge* ... OK-5
Camp Grounds Sch (historical)—*school* ... MS-4
Campground Tabernacle—*church* ... ME-1
Campground Trail—*trail* ... NH-1
*Camp Ground United Methodist Church* ... MS-4
*Campground United Methodist Church* ... TN-4
Campground Woods—*woods* ... IL-6
*Camp Grove* ... PA-2
Camp Grove—*locale* ... PA-2
Campgrove—*other* ... IL-6
**Camp Grove**—*pop pl* ... IL-6
**Camp Grove**—*pop pl* ... PA-2
Camp Grove Ch—*church* ... GA-3
Camp Gruber (Abandoned)—*locale* ... OK-5
Camp Guernsey Rifle Range Abutment—*other* ... WY-8
Camp Guernsey State Military Reservation—*other* ... WY-8
Camp Gulch—*valley* ... AZ-5
Camp Gulch—*valley* (2) ... CA-9
Camp Gulch—*valley* (2) ... CO-8
Camp Gulch—*valley* (2) ... ID-8
Camp Gulch—*valley* (2) ... MT-8
Camp Gulch—*valley* ... NV-8
Camp Gulch—*valley* ... OR-9
Camp Gulch Spring—*spring* ... CO-8
Camp Gulick—*park* ... IN-6
**Camp Gundalow**—*pop pl* ... NH-1
Camp Gunston—*locale* ... MD-2
Camp Guyandotte—*locale* ... WV-2
Camp H—*locale* ... FL-3
Camp Habonin—*locale* ... NY-2
Camp Hacoba—*locale* ... TN-4
Camp Hadar—*locale* ... CT-1
Camp Hafer—*locale* ... WA-9
*Camp Hageman* ... OH-6
Camp Hager—*locale* ... WA-9
*Camp Hagerman* ... OH-6
Camp Haiyaka—*locale* ... TN-4
Camp Haiyaka Dam—*dam* ... TN-4
Camp Haiyaka Lake—*reservoir* ... TN-4
Camp Halburn—*locale* ... CT-1
Camp Halcyon—*locale* ... MI-6
Camp Hale—*locale* ... CO-8
Camp Ha-Lu-Sa—*locale* ... NJ-2
Camp Hamilton—*locale* ... FL-3
Camp Hamilton—*locale* ... PA-2
Camp Hammock—*island* (2) ... FL-3
Camp Hammond—*hist pl* ... ME-1
Camp Hammond—*locale* ... KS-7
Camp Hancock—*locale* ... OR-9
Camp Hancock Site—*hist pl* ... ND-7
Camp Handy—*locale* ... WA-9
Camp Hanes—*locale* ... NC-3
Camp Hanes (YMCA) Dam—*dam* ... NC-3
Camp Hanes (YMCA) Lake—*reservoir* ... NC-3
*Camp Hanna* ... ND-7
Camp Hanover—*locale* ... VA-3
Camp Hantesa—*locale* ... IA-7
Camp Happyland—*locale* ... VA-3
**Camp Hardee**—*pop pl* ... NC-3
Camp Harding—*locale* ... NE-7
**Camp Hardtner**—*pop pl* ... LA-4
Camp Hardy—*locale* ... MI-6
Camp Harley—*locale* ... NY-2
Camp Harmony—*locale* ... CO-8
Camp Harmony—*locale* ... NJ-2
Camp Harmony—*locale* ... PA-2
Camp Harmony—*locale* ... SC-3
Camp Harmony—*locale* ... WA-9
Camp Harps Shelter—*locale* ... WA-9
Camp Harrington—*locale* ... TX-5
Camp Harry H Straus—*locale* ... NC-3
Camp Harvey—*locale* ... CA-9
Camp Harvey West—*locale* ... CA-9
Camp Haswell (B S A)—*locale* ... CA-9
Camp Hat Creek—*locale* ... VA-3
Camp Hauberg—*locale* ... IL-6
Camp Haven—*locale* ... AK-9
Camp Hawthorn—*locale* ... MO-7
Camp Hawthorne—*locale* ... CA-9
Camp Hawthorne Central Area District—*hist pl* ... MO-7
Camp Hawthorne Ridge—*locale* ... PA-2

Camp Hayaston—locale MA-1
Camp Hayes—locale NY-2
Camp Hayes Lake—reservoir NE-7
Camp Hayward—locale MA-1
Camp Hazard—locale WA-9
Camp Hazen—locale CT-1
Camp H Creek—stream MI-6
Camp Healthmore—locale NY-2
Camp Heard—locale AL-4
Camp Hebron—locale MA-1
Camp Hebron—locale PA-2
**Camp Hedding**—pop pl NH-1
Camp Heermance—locale NH-1
Camp Helen—locale AL-4
Camp Helena—locale PA-2
Camphels Wharf—locale MD-2
Camp Hemenway—locale NH-1
Camp Hemlock—locale WV-2
**Camp Hemlock**—pop pl NY-2
Camp Hemlock Ridge—locale NY-2
Camp Hemohme—locale CA-9
Camp Henderson Lookout Tower—tower FL-3
Camp Henry Historic Site—locale ID-8
Camp Henry Horner—locale IL-6
**Camp Herbron**—pop pl MA-1
Camp Heritage—locale MN-6
Camp Heritage—park MA-1
Camp Herman NC-3
Camp Herman—locale NC-3
Camp Herms—locale CA-9
Camp Herrich—locale NY-2
Camp Herrick—locale OH-6
Camp Hervida—locale OH-6
Camp Heyata—locale IA-7
Camp Hiawatha—locale ME-1
Camp Hiawatha—locale MN-6
Camp Hi Boys Camp—locale OH-6
Camp Hicita—locale GA-3
Camp Hickory—locale IL-6
Camp Hickory Hill—locale NY-2
Camp Hidden Falls Dam PA-2
Camp Hidden Hollow—locale WI-6
Camp Hidden Valley—locale CA-9
Camp Hide Hollow—valley TN-4
Camp Highland—locale GA-3
Camp Highmount—locale NY-2
Camp Highroad—locale VA-3
Camp High Rock—locale VA-3
Camp High Sierra—locale (2) CA-9
Camp Hi-Hill—locale CA-9
Camp Hi Kana—locale MS-4
Camp Hilaka—locale OH-6
Camphill MS-4
Camp Hill PA-2
Camp Hill—hist pl SC-3
Camp Hill—locale MS-4
Camphill—other PA-2
**Camp Hill**—pop pl AL-4
**Camphill**—pop pl MS-4
**Camp Hill**—pop pl NY-2
**Camp Hill**—pop pl (2) PA-2
Camp Hill—summit CA-9
Camp Hill—summit CT-1
Camp Hill—summit MA-1
Camp Hill—summit MS-4
Camp Hill—summit PA-2
Camp Hill—summit SC-3
Camp Hill—summit TX-5
Camp Hill—summit VT-1
Camp Hill—summit WA-9
Camp Hill Baptist Ch—church AL-4
Camp Hill Borough—civil PA-2
Camp Hill Borough Pool—reservoir PA-2
Camp Hill (CCD)—cens area AL-4
Camp Hill Cem—cemetery MS-4
Camp Hill Cem—cemetery PA-2
Camp Hill Cem—cemetery WV-2
Camp Hill Ch—church PA-2
Camp Hillcrest—locale IL-6
Camp Hillcrest (YMCA)—locale AL-4
Camp Hill Division—civil AL-4
Camp Hill (historical)—locale AL-4
Camp Hill Junior Senior HS—school PA-2
Camp Hill Mall—locale PA-2
**Camp Hill (PC RR name Lemoyne-Camp Hill)**—pop pl PA-2
Camp Hill Post Office (historical)—building PA-2
Camp Hill Presbyterian Ch—church PA-2
Camp Hill Reservoir Dam—dam AL-4
Camp Hill Rsvr—reservoir AL-4
Camp Hill Sch—school NY-2
Camp Hill-Tallapoosa County Airp—airport AL-4
Camp Hilltop—locale NY-2
Camp Hines—locale NY-2
Camphion Gut—gut NC-3
**Camp Hironimus**—pop pl PA-2
Camp Hiwela—locale WI-6
Camp Hixson (historical)—locale TN-4
Camp Hlond Rsvr—reservoir NJ-2
Camp H.M. Smith (U.S. Marine Corps)—military HI-9
Camp Hobble Creek—locale UT-8
Camp Hoblitzelle—locale TX-5
Camp Hoffman—locale RI-1
Camp Holden—locale TX-5
Camp Holiday—locale MI-6
Camp Holiday—locale WY-8
Camp Hollar Windmill—locale TX-5
Camp Hollis—locale AL-4
Camp Hollis—locale NY-2
Camp Hollow MO-7
Camp Hollow—valley LA-4
Camp Hollow—valley MS-4
Camp Hollow—valley (3) MO-7
Camp Hollow—valley MT-8
Camp Hollow—valley OH-6
Camp Hollow—valley (2) PA-2
Camp Hollow—valley (3) TN-4
Camp Hollow—valley (2) UT-8
Camp Hollow—valley (2) VA-3
Camp Hollow—valley (3) WV-2
Camp Hollow Creek—stream MS-4
Camp Hollow Creek—stream TX-5
Camp Hollow Mine—mine TN-4
Camp Holly—locale MI-6
Camp Holly—locale VA-3
Camp Hollybrook—locale NJ-2
Camp Holly Lake—locale ID-8
Camp Holy Cross—locale MA-1
Camp Honor Bright—park IN-6
Camp Hook—locale OH-6
Camp Hoover—hist pl VA-3
Camp Hoover—locale NY-2
Camp Hoover—locale VA-3
Camp Hope—locale GA-3
Camp Hope—locale (2) NJ-2
Camp Hope—locale NC-3
Camp Hope—locale OR-9
Camp Hope Cem—cemetery GA-3
Camp Hope Run—stream PA-2
Camp Hopewell—locale MS-4
Camphora—locale CA-9
Camphor Branch—stream KY-4
Camp Horizon—locale FL-3
Camp Horn—locale MO-7
Camp Horne—locale AL-4
Camp Horne—locale PA-2
**Camp Horne**—pop pl AL-4
Camp Horne Lake AL-4
Camp Horne Lake Dam—dam AL-4
Camp Horne Lake Dam Number 1—dam AL-4
Camp Horne Lake Dam Number 2 AL-4
Camp Horne Lake Number 1—reservoir AL-4
Camp Horne Lake Number 2—reservoir AL-4
Camp Horseshoe—locale (2) PA-2
Camphose Lake—lake GA-3
Camp House—hist pl TN-4
Camphouse Dugout—stream TX-5
Camphouse Hollow—valley OH-6
Camp House Spring—spring MO-7
Camp House Windmill—locale TX-5
Camphouse Windmill—locale TX-5
Camp Housman—locale NJ-2
Camp Houston ND-7
Camp Houston—locale OK-5
Camp Howard—locale IL-6
Camp Howard—locale (2) OR-9
Camp Howard—locale TN-4
Camp Howard Cow Camp—locale ID-8
Camp Howard Ridge—ridge ID-8
Camp Howe—locale MA-1
**Camp Howe**—pop pl MA-1
Camp Huachuca AZ-5
Camp Hual-Cu-Cuish—locale CA-9
Camp Hubinger—locale CT-1
Camp Huckins—locale NH-1
Camp Hudgens—locale OK-5
Camp Hudson—locale TX-5
Camp Huffman—locale CA-9
Camp Hugh—locale AL-4
**Camp Hulen**—pop pl TX-5
Camp Hull Springs—locale VA-3
Camp Humming Hills—locale AL-4
Camp Hunt—locale AR-4
Camp Hunt—locale UT-8
Camp Huston—locale WA-9
Camp Hydaway—locale VA-3
Camp Hyde—locale KS-7
**Campia**—pop pl WI-6
Camp Icaghowan—locale WI-6
Camp Ida Spring—spring CA-9
Camp Idlewide—locale TX-5
Camp Ihduhapi—locale MN-6
Camp Illahee—locale NC-3
Camp Illana—park IN-6
Camp Immaculate—locale NY-2
**Camp Immaculate Heart**—pop pl MA-1
Camp Inawendiwin—locale NJ-2
Camp Inawendiwin Dam—dam NJ-2
Camp Inawendiwin Lake—reservoir NJ-2
Camp Independence (site)—locale TX-5
Camp Indiandale—locale PA-2
Camp Indian Head—locale FL-3
Camp Indianola—locale OH-6
Camp Indianola—locale WI-6
Camp Indian Run—locale PA-2
Camp Indian Trails—locale WI-6
Camp Indian Valley Boy Scout Camp AL-4
Camp Indi-Co-So—park IN-6
Camp Indogan—park IN-6
Campine Lake—lake WI-6
Camp Ingawanis—locale IA-7
Camping Cave Branch—stream KY-4
Camping Creek—stream NC-3
Camping Creek—stream SC-3
Camping Fork—stream NC-3
Camping Gap—gap VA-3
Camping Place Cove ME-1
Camping Ridge—ridge VA-3
Campini Mesa—summit AZ-5
Camp Inlow—locale MO-7
Camp Innabah—locale PA-2
Camp Innistree—locale MI-6
Camp Interlocken—park MA-1
**Campion**—pop pl CO-8
Campion Acad—school CO-8
Campion (Air Force) Station—military AK-9
Campion Ditch—canal AK-9
Campion HS—school WI-6
Camp Irene—locale CA-9
Camp Irondale—locale MO-7
Camp Iroquois—locale PA-2
Camp Irwin—military (2) CA-9
Camp Island—island (3) AK-9
Camp Island—island (2) FL-3
Camp Island—island GA-3
Camp Island—island (2) ME-1
Camp Island—island NH-1
Camp Island—island NY-2
Camp Island—island VA-3
Camp Island Gut—gut VA-3
Camp Island Lake—lake AK-9
Camp Islands—island NY-2
Camp Istrouma—locale LA-4
Campit Lake—reservoir LA-4
Campito Meadow—flat CA-9
Campito Mtn—summit CA-9
Camp Ivanhoe (historical)—locale SD-7
Camp Iveetok—locale AK-9
Camp Iyataka—locale SD-7
Camp Jackson—locale AL-4
Camp Jackson—locale GA-3
Camp Jackson—locale UT-8
Camp Jackson Dam—dam UT-8
Camp Jackson Rsvr—reservoir UT-8
Camp Jacobsen—locale MN-6
Camp James River—locale VA-3
Camp Jawonio—locale NY-2
Camp Jayhawk—locale KS-7
**Camp Jayson**—pop pl MA-1
Camp JCA—locale CA-9
Camp J C C—locale WI-6
Camp Jefferson Hollow—valley MO-7
Camp Jennings SD-7
Camp Jennings—locale MA-1
Camp Jeremia—locale IL-6
Camp Jewell—locale CT-1
Camp Jimmy Goodwin—locale AL-4
Camp Jo-Ann—locale PA-2
Camp Jocassee—locale SC-3
Camp Jody—locale OH-6
Camp John Knox—locale TN-4
Camp Johnson—locale PA-2
Camp Johnson—military NC-3
Camp Johnson Sch—school MN-6
Camp Jolley—locale WA-9
Camp Jolly—locale PA-2
Camp Jo-Ota—locale MO-7
**Camp Jordan**—pop pl TN-4
Camp Jordan Park—park TN-4
Camp Josepho—locale CA-9
Camp Joseph T. Robinson (Arkansas Natl Guard)—building AR-4
Camp Joseph T Robinson (national Guard Training Area)—other AR-4
Camp Joslin—locale MA-1
Camp Joubert—gap WA-9
Camp Joy—locale IL-6
Camp Joy—locale KY-4
Camp Joy—locale OH-6
Camp Joy—locale OK-5
Camp Joy—locale PA-2
Camp Joy—locale TN-4
Camp Joy—locale VA-3
Camp Joy—locale WA-9
Camp Joy—park IN-6
Camp Joy and Hope—locale NY-2
Camp Joycliff—locale GA-3
Camp Juanita Adajuan—locale CT-1
Camp Jubilee—locale CA-9
Camp Judaea—locale NC-3
Camp Judson—locale PA-2
Camp Judson (historical)—locale SD-7
Camp Juliana—locale WA-9
Camp Juliette Low—hist pl GA-3
Camp Juliette Low—locale GA-3
Camp Juniata—locale PA-2
Camp Junipero Serra—locale CA-9
Camp Kachina—locale TX-5
Camp Kaena—locale HI-9
Camp Kaetzell—locale AR-4
Camp Kahler—locale MN-6
Camp Kanata—locale NC-3
Camp Kanata Lake Number One—reservoir NC-3
Camp Kanata Lake Number One Dam—dam NC-3
Camp Kanata Lake Number Two—reservoir NC-3
Camp Kanata Lake Number Two Dam—dam NC-3
Camp Kanawha Minawha—locale NY-2
Camp Kannata—locale VA-3
Camp Kanuga—locale NC-3
Camp Kanuga (Boys)—locale NC-3
Camp Kanuga (Girls)—locale NC-3
Camp Kanza—locale KS-7
Camp Kare Free—locale AR-4
Camp Karney—locale NJ-2
Camp Karney Dam—dam NJ-2
Camp Kate Portwood—locale OK-5
Camp Katori—locale FL-3
Camp Katzenstein—locale NC-3
Camp Kaufmann—locale PA-2
Camp Kaweah—locale CA-9
**Camp Kaweah**—pop pl CA-9
Camp Keais Strand—swamp FL-3
Camp Ke-De-Ka—locale IL-6
Camp Keemosahbee—locale CT-1
Camp Keener—locale SC-3
Camp Keewana—locale MI-6
Camp Keller—locale PA-2
Camp Kemeric—locale CA-9
Camp Kenan—locale NY-2
Camp Ken-Etiwa-Pec—locale NJ-2
Camp Kenico—locale CT-1
Camp Ken-Jocket—locale OH-6
Camp Kenmont—locale CT-1
**Camp Kennedy**—pop pl KY-4
Camp Keno Taunee—locale OK-5
Camp Kent—locale CT-1
Camp Kent Wood VA-3
Camp Keown—locale MO-7
Camp Kerk State Wildlife Mngmt Area—park MN-6
Camp Kern—locale OH-6
Camp Kettle Creek—stream OR-9
Camp Kettleford—locale NH-1
Camp Kettle Gulch—valley CO-8
Camp Kettle Rsvr—reservoir OR-9
Camp Kettle Run—locale NJ-2
Camp Key FL-3
Camp Key—island (4) FL-3
Camp Keyauwee Lake—reservoir NC-3
Camp Keyauwee Lake Dam—dam NC-3
Camp Keyes—locale ME-1
Camp Keystone—locale FL-3
Camp Kici-Yapi—locale MN-6
Camp Kickapoo—locale MS-4
Camp Kickapoo—locale OK-5
Camp Kidd—locale WV-2
Camp Ki Ki Kima—locale AR-4
Camp Kikthawenund—park IN-6
Campkill Creek OR-9
Camp Killooleet—locale VT-1
Camp Kil Lo Qua—locale MI-6
Camp Killoqua—locale WA-9
Camp Killpack—locale WA-9
Camp Kilmer—locale NJ-2
Camp Kilowan—locale OR-9
Camp Kimble—locale NJ-2
Camp Kimikomuk—locale NJ-2
Camp Kingsley—locale NY-2
Camp Kingsmont—locale MA-1
**Camp Kingsmont**—pop pl MA-1
Camp Kiniya—locale VT-1
Camp Kinneywood—locale MA-1
**Camp Kinneywood**—pop pl MA-1
Camp Kinni Kinnic—locale VT-1
Camp Kinsolving—locale TX-5
Camp Kiondashawa—locale PA-2
Camp Kirby—locale MA-1
Camp Kirby—locale WA-9
Camp Kiser—locale WA-9
Camp Kitaki—locale NE-7
Camp Kitanniwa—locale MI-6
Camp Kitchi Kahniss—locale MN-6
Camp Kittamaqund—locale VA-3
Camp Kitta-Tinny—locale NJ-2
Camp Kiwanee—park MA-1
Camp Kiwania—locale AR-4
Camp Kiwanianna—locale VA-3
Camp Kiwanilong—locale OR-9
Camp Kiwanis—locale AR-4
Camp Kiwanis—locale (2) IL-6
Camp Kiwanis—locale IA-7
Camp Kiwanis—locale MI-6
Camp Kiwanis—locale MN-6
Camp Kiwanis—locale (2) NE-7
Camp Kiwanis—locale NY-2
Camp Kiwanis—locale PA-2
Camp Kiwanis—locale VA-3
**Camp Kiwanis**—pop pl (2) MA-1
Camp Kiwanis Girl Scout Camp—locale AL-4
Camp Kiwatani—locale OH-6
Camp K Lake—lake MI-6
Camp Klebit—locale TX-5
Camp Klein—locale OH-6
Camp Kline—locale PA-2
Camp Knob—summit NC-3
Camp Knoll Ridge—ridge AZ-5
Camp Knox NC-3
Camp Koch—park IN-6
Camp Koda—locale SD-7
Camp Kohahna—locale MI-6
Camp Ko-Ha-Me—locale KS-7
Camp Koholowo—locale UT-8
Camp Koinonia—locale OK-5
Camp Kole—locale CA-9
Camp Kon-O-Kwee—locale PA-2
Camp Ko-Otaga—locale WV-2
Camp K-Three—locale HI-9
Camp Kulaqua—locale FL-3
Camp Kulowiye—locale AK-9
Camp Kysoc—locale KY-4
Camp Lacupolis—locale MN-6
Camp Laghton ND-7
Camp Lagoon—locale WA-9
Camp La Guardia—locale NY-2
Complain Road Sch—school NJ-2
Camp LaJunta—locale TX-5
Camp Lake MI-6
Camp Lake MN-6
Camp Lake—lake AR-4
Camp Lake—lake CO-8
Camp Lake—lake (2) FL-3
Camp Lake—lake GA-3
Camp Lake—lake ID-8
Camp Lake—lake (6) MI-6
Camp Lake—lake (18) MN-6
Camp Lake—lake MS-4
Camp Lake—lake (2) MT-8
Camp Lake—lake NE-7
Camp Lake—lake ND-7
Camp Lake—lake OR-9
Camp Lake—lake TX-5
Camp Lake—lake (2) WA-9
Camp Lake—lake (10) WI-6
Camp Lake—lake (2) WY-8
**Camp Lake**—pop pl MI-6
**Camp Lake**—pop pl WI-6
Camp Lake Creek—stream MI-6
Camp Lake Hubert—locale MN-6
**Camp Lakeland**—pop pl NY-2
Camp Lake Number One—reservoir TN-4
Camp Lake Number One Dam—dam TN-4
Camp Lakes—lake WA-9
Camp Lakeside—locale KS-7
Camp Lakeside—locale MS-4
Camp Lake Slough—stream TX-5
Camp Lake State Game Mngmt Area—park ND-7
Camp Lake Stevens—locale MS-4
**Camp Lake (Township of)**—pop pl MN-6
Camp Lake Trail—trail CO-8
Camp Lake Trail—trail WY-8
Camp Lakeview—locale MI-6
Camp Lake Wood—park IN-6
**Camp Lakewood**—pop pl MO-7
Camp Lakodia—locale SD-7
Camp Lambec—locale PA-2
Camp Lamoille—locale NV-8
Camp Lamondi—locale UT-8
Camp Lamotte—locale MS-4
Camp Lane—locale OR-9
Camp Lane County Park—park OR-9
Camp La-No-Che—locale FL-3
Camp Lark—locale KS-7
Camp La Salle—locale NM-5
Camp Lasater—locale NC-3
Camp Lassen—locale CA-9
Camp Lassiter NC-3
Camp Latonka—locale MO-7
Camp Laurel—locale NY-2
Camp Laurel—locale VA-3
Camp Laureldell—locale AL-4
Camp Laurelwood—locale CT-1
Camp Laurie—locale IA-7
Camp LaVerne—locale CA-9
Camp Lawrence—locale WI-6
Camp Lawrie—locale MN-6
Camp Lawton—hist pl GA-3
Camp Lazarus—locale OH-6
**Camp Leach**—pop pl NC-3
Camp Lee—locale MO-7
Camp Lee—locale OR-9
Camp Legion Environmental Center—locale PA-2
Camp Lejeune—military NC-3
**Camp Lejeune Central**—pop pl NC-3
**Camp Lejeune Junction**—pop pl NC-3
Camp Lejeune Naval Regional Med Ctr—military NC-3
Camp Lejeune Sch—school NC-3
Camp Lejeune (U.S. Marine Corps)—military NC-3
Camp Lenape—locale MO-7
Camp Lenape—locale NJ-2
Camp Lenmary—park IN-6
Camp Lenni-Len-A-Pe—locale NY-2
**Camp Lenore**—pop pl MA-1
Camp Leo—locale NH-1
Camp Leonard—locale TX-5
**Camp Leonard**—pop pl WI-6
Camp Leonard Leonore—locale CT-1
**Camp Leroy Johnson**—pop pl LA-4
Camp Leroy Schuman—locale TX-5
Camp Letcher Pond—lake TX-5
Camp Letoli—locale TX-5
Camp Letts—locale MD-2
Camp Levi Levi—locale AZ-5
Camp Lewallen—locale MO-7
Camp Lewallen Cem—cemetery GA-3
Camp Lewis—locale GA-3
Camp Lewis—locale KY-4
Camp Lewtana—locale MT-8
Camp Lightfoot—locale WV-2
Camp Lilienthal—locale CA-9
Camp Liloli—locale NY-2
Camp Lincoln AZ-5
Camp Lincoln—locale IL-6
Camp Lincoln—locale MN-6
Camp Lincoln—locale NH-1
Camp Lincoln—locale TX-5
Camp Lincoln Commissary Bldg—hist pl IL-6
**Camp Lincoln Hill**—pop pl MA-1
Camp Lincoln Laurel—locale NJ-2
Camp Linden—locale TN-4
Camp Lindney PA-2
Camp Linn-Haven—locale NC-3
Camp Linwood Hayne—locale GA-3
Camp Lions—locale VA-3
Camp Little Cloud—locale IA-7
Camp Little Lemhi—locale ID-8
Camp Little Notch—locale NY-2
Camp Livingston—locale OH-6
Camp Livingston—park IN-6
Camp Livingston Lake—reservoir IN-6
Camp Livingston Lake Dam—dam IN-6
Camp Living Water—locale NC-3
Camp Loco (historical)—locale AZ-5
Camp Logan—locale IL-6
Camp Logan—locale OH-6
**Camp Logan (historical)**—pop pl OR-9
Camp Loga Vista—locale KS-7
Camp Log-N-Twig—locale PA-2
Camp Loka—locale PA-2
Camp Lokinda—locale MN-6
Camp Lo Mia—locale AZ-5
Camp Lonesome Mound—locale FL-3
**Camp Long**—pop pl SC-3
Camp Long Campground—locale NM-5
Camp Long Lake—lake WI-6
Camp Longridge—locale SC-3
Camp Lookout—locale GA-3
Camp Loucon—locale KY-4
Camp Louemma Dam NJ-2
Camp Louise—locale MD-2
Camp Louis Ernst—park IN-6
Camp Low—locale GA-3
Camp Lowell AZ-5
Camp Lowry—locale FL-3
Camp Loxley—locale AL-4
Camp Lucerne—locale WI-6
Camp Lucille—locale TX-5
Camp Ludington—locale CT-1
Camp Ludington—locale NY-2
Camp Luella May—locale OH-6
**Camp Lu Lay Lea**—pop pl MI-6
Camp Lulu Key—island FL-3
Camp Lupine—locale CA-9
Camp Lupton—locale VA-3
Camp Luther OH-6
**Camp Luther**—pop pl OH-6
Camp Lutherlyn—locale PA-2
Camp Luther Vista—locale MI-6
Camp Luthy—locale ID-8
Camp Lycogis—locale PA-2
Camp Lyndon—locale MA-1
Camp Lyon—locale NJ-2
Camp Lyon Site—hist pl ID-8
Camp Lyons (site)—locale OR-9
Camp Maacama—locale CA-9
Camp Mabry (Army Natl Guard)—building TX-5
Camp Mabry Milit Reservation (National Guard)—military TX-5
Camp Mac—locale AL-4
Camp Mac Dam Number 11 AL-4
Camp Mac Dam Number 2 AL-4
Camp Mack—locale FL-3
Camp MacKall Milit Reservation—military NC-3
Camp MacKay KS-7
Camp Mack Morris—locale TN-4
Camp Mac Lake Number 1—reservoir AL-4
Camp Mac Lake Number 2—reservoir AL-4
Camp Mac Lakes—reservoir AL-4
Camp MacLean—locale (2) WI-6
Camp Macoba—locale AL-4
Camp Macochee—locale OH-6
Camp Maddison—locale AL-4
Camp Maddox—locale TX-5
Camp Madron—locale MI-6
Camp Magruder—locale OR-9
Camp Maha—locale NE-7
Camp Ma-Hi-Ya—locale MI-6
**Camp Mah-Kee-Nac**—pop pl MA-1
Camp Mahn-Go-Tah-See—locale MI-6
Camp Mahoneqan—locale WV-2
Camp Mahoney—locale OH-6
Camp Ma-Ka-Ja-Wan—locale WI-6
Camp Makualla—locale OR-9
Camp Malakole Milit Reservation—military HI-9
Camp Mallory—park IN-6
Camp Malloy—locale NY-2
Camp Manack—locale AL-4
Camp Manakiki—locale MN-6
Camp Man Apu—locale ID-8
Camp Manatawny—locale PA-2
Camp Manatoc—locale OH-6
Camp Manistee—locale MI-6
Camp Manitou—locale NY-2
Camp Manitou—locale (2) WI-6
Camp Manitoumi—locale IL-6
Camp Mansfield—locale VT-1
Camp Manteno—locale IA-7
Camp Manzanita—locale CA-9
Camp Maplehurst—locale MI-6
Camp Maplesville—locale AL-4
Camp Maqua—locale MI-6
**Camp Maquam**—pop pl VT-1
Camp Maranatha—locale GA-3
Camp Maranatha Lake—reservoir NC-3
Camp Maranatha Lake Dam—dam NC-3
Camp Maria—locale MD-2
Camp Maria Stella—locale CA-9
Camp Marietta—locale SC-3
Camp Marimeta—locale WI-6
Camp Marion—locale CA-9
Camp Marion—locale OR-9
Camp Marion—locale WA-9
**Camp Marion White**—pop pl MA-1
Camp Maripai—locale AZ-5
Camp Marist—locale NH-1
Camp Mar-lin—locale CT-1
Camp Marshall—locale MA-1
Camp Marston—locale CA-9
Camp Martha F Madeley—locale TX-5
Camp Martha Johnston—locale GA-3
Camp Martin—locale ID-8
Camp Marudy—locale NJ-2
Camp Marudy Lake—reservoir NJ-2
**Camp Mar Vel**—pop pl MA-1
Camp Marvin Hillyard—locale MO-7
Camp Marwedel—locale CA-9
Camp Mary Day—locale MA-1
**Camp Mary Day**—pop pl MA-1
Camp Mary Louise—locale TX-5
Camp Marymount—locale TN-4
Camp Mary Orton—locale OH-6
Camp Mary White—locale NM-5
Camp Massad—locale PA-2
Camp Massanetta—locale VA-3
Camp Massapoag—locale MA-1
**Camp Massapoag**—pop pl MA-1
Camp Massasoit—locale MA-1
Camp Massasoit—locale RI-1
Camp Massawepie—locale NY-2
Camp Mataoka—locale VA-3
Camp Mather—locale OH-6
Camp Matigwa—locale TX-5
Camp Matomba—locale ME-1
Camp Mattatuck—locale CT-1
Camp Matthews—locale MI-6
Camp Mattingly—locale KS-7
Camp Mattole—locale CA-9
Camp Maumee—park IN-6
Camp Mauwehu—locale CT-1
Camp Mawain—locale FL-3
Camp Maxey—military TX-5
Camp Maxey (Station)—locale TX-5
Camp Maximiliano Luna—other NM-5
Camp Maxwell—locale AL-4
Camp May—locale NM-5
Camp Mayfair—locale NY-2
Camp Maynard—locale GA-3
Camp May Trail—trail NM-5
Camp McCain (Abandoned)—military MS-4
Camp McCain Milit Reservation—military MS-4
Camp McCallum—locale CA-9
Camp McClellan—locale CA-9
Camp McClellan—other AL-4
Camp McConnell—locale CA-9
Camp McCoy—locale WI-6
Camp McCumber—locale CA-9
Camp McDonald—hist pl GA-3
Camp McDonald—locale WA-9
Camp McDowell AZ-5
Camp McDowell—locale AL-4
Camp McFadden—locale OK-5
Camp McGarry—locale NV-8
Camp McGregor (site)—locale OR-9
Camp McKean—locale WA-9
Camp McKee AZ-5
Camp McKee—locale KY-4
Camp McKenzie Boy Scout Camp—locale GA-3
Camp McKiwanis—locale CA-9
Camp McLoughlin—locale OR-9
Camp McMillan—locale AL-4
Camp McMillan—park IN-6
Camp McQuarrie—locale FL-3
Camp Meacham—locale KY-4
Camp Mead—locale WA-9
Camp Meadowlark—locale MA-1
**Camp Meadowlark**—pop pl MA-1
Camp Meadows—swamp VT-1
Camp Medill McCormick—locale IL-6
**Camp Meeker**—pop pl CA-9
Camp Meeting Bay FL-3
Camp Meeting Ch—church FL-3
Camp Meeting Creek—stream CA-9
Camp Meeting Creek—stream (2) OR-9
Camp-meeting Creek—stream TN-4
Camp Meeting Creek—stream TX-5
Camp-meeting Creek Shoals—bar TN-4
Campmeeting Ground MS-4
Camp Meeting Ground—locale NE-7
Camp Meeting Ground—park IN-6
Camp Meeting Grounds—locale PA-2
Campmeeting Grounds—locale SC-3
Camp Meeting Grove—locale PA-2
Camp Meeting Gulch—valley CA-9
Camp Meeting Gully—stream TX-5
Campmeeting Hollow—valley MO-7
Campmeeting Point VT-1
Campmeeting Point—cape VT-1
Campmeeting Ridge—ridge CA-9
Camp Meeting Ridge—ridge CA-9
Camp Mel—locale CT-1
Camp Melakwa—locale OR-9
Camp Melvin Site—hist pl TX-5
Camp Memorial Cem—cemetery GA-3
**Camp Mendocino**—pop pl CA-9
Camp Mennoscah—locale KS-7
Camp Meriwether—locale OR-9
Camp Merrie Mill—locale NY-2
Camp Merrie Wood—locale MI-6
Camp Merriewoode—locale NH-1
Camp Merrill—locale FL-3
**Camp Merrill**—pop pl MA-1
Camp Merrimack—locale NH-1
Camp Merritt Memorial Monmt—park NJ-2
Camp Merriwood—locale MA-1
**Camp Merriwood**—pop pl MA-1
Camp Merrybrook—locale IL-6
Camp Merrydale—locale OH-6
Camp Merryelande—locale MD-2

Camp Merrywood—locale NY-2
Camp Merz—locale NY-2
Camp Metaka—locale CA-9
Camp Metamora—locale MI-6
Camp Miakonda—locale OH-6
Camp Miami—locale OH-6
Camp Michael—locale OH-6
Camp Michaux—locale PA-2
Camp Mihaska—locale MO-7
Camp Mikell—locale GA-3
Camp Mikquand—locale WI-6
Camp Miles—locale MT-8
Camp Millard—locale OR-9
Camp Milldale—locale MD-2
Camp Miller—locale PA-2
Camp Millhouse—park IN-6
Camp Millstone—locale NC-3
Camp Minco—locale WV-2
Camp Mine—mine AZ-5
Camp Minikani—locale WI-6
Camp Minis—locale PA-2
Camp Minisink—locale NJ-2
Camp Minis Kuya—locale NE-7
Camp Minnehaha—locale WV-2
Camp Minnehaha Falls—falls NC-3
Camp Minnetoska—locale MD-2
Camp Minqua—locale PA-2
Camp Miramichee—locale AR-4
Camp Misery—locale FL-3
Camp Mishannock—locale MA-1
**Camp Mishannock**—pop pl MA-1
Camp Mistake Run—stream WV-2
Camp Mi-Ta-Na—locale NH-1
Camp Mitchell—locale AR-4
Camp Mitchell—locale TX-5
Camp Mitigwa—locale IA-7
Camp Mivoden—locale ID-8
Camp Modin for Boys—locale ME-1
Camp Modin for Girls—locale ME-1
Camp Modoc—locale MI-6
Camp Mogiska—locale NJ-2
Camp Mogollon AZ-5
Camp Mohave AZ-5
Camp Mohawk—locale CT-1
Camp Mohawk—locale MA-1
Camp Mohawk—locale TX-5
**Camp Mohawk**—pop pl MA-1
Camp Mohican—locale (2) NJ-2
Camp Mohican—locale NY-2
Camp Moingona—locale IA-7
Camp Mojave AZ-5
Camp Mo-Kan—locale MO-7
Camp Monaco—locale WY-8
Camp Mondamin—locale MS-4
Camp Monocan—locale VA-3
Camp Montauga—locale AL-4
Camp Monterey—locale TN-4
**Camp Monterey Lake**—pop pl TN-4
Camp Monterey Lake—reservoir TN-4
Camp Monterey Lake Dam—dam TN-4
Camp Montgomery—locale FL-3
Camp Montgomery—locale VA-3
Camp Montvale (YMCA)—locale TN-4
Camp Moon Lake—reservoir KS-7
Camp Moon Lake Dam—dam KS-7
Camp Moonraker (Summer Camp)—locale TX-5
Camp Moore AZ-5
Camp Moore—hist pl LA-4
Camp Moore Cem—cemetery LA-4
Camp Moosehorn—locale ID-8
Camp Mooween—locale CT-1
Camp Moraine—locale MN-6
Camp Morehead—locale NC-3
Camp Moreland Spring—spring OR-9
Camp Morgan Memorial—locale MA-1
Camp Morganton—locale GA-3
Camp Moritz—locale PA-2
Camp Morrison—locale IA-7
Camp Morrison—locale OR-9
Camp Morrow—locale OR-9
Camp Moshava—locale PA-2
Camp Moss Creek—stream TN-4
Camp Mount Aetna—locale MD-2
Camp Mountaindale—locale OR-9
Camp Mountaineer—locale WV-2
Camp Mo-Val—locale MO-7
Camp Mowana—locale OH-6
Camp Mtn—summit AK-9
Camp Mtn—summit MT-8
Camp Mtn—summit NC-3
Camp Mtn—summit (2) PA-2
Camp Mtn—summit TX-5
Camp Mtn—summit VA-3
Camp Mtn Lake NC-3
Camp Mudiekewis—locale ME-1
Camp Mueller—locale OH-6
Camp Muir—locale WA-9
Camp Muir Shelter Cabin WA-9
Camp Munger—locale AL-4
Camp Munhacke—locale MI-6
Camp Munsee—locale PA-2
Camp Munsee—park IN-6
Camp Murdock—locale NC-3
Camp Muriel Flagg—locale MA-1
**Camp Muriel Flagg**—pop pl MA-1
Camp Murphy—locale FL-3
Camp Murray Natl Guard—other WA-9
Camp Muscott—locale WA-9
Camp Muskingum—locale OH-6
Camp Muskoday—locale MN-6
Camp Musquiz—locale TX-5
Camp Myler—locale PA-2
Camp Myron Kahn—locale OH-6
Camp Mystery—locale WA-9
Camp Mystic—locale PA-2
Camp Mystic—locale TX-5
Camp Nacimiento—locale CA-9
Camp Nahellu—locale MI-6
Camp Naish—locale KS-7
Camp Nakanawa—locale TN-4
Camp Nakomis—locale MI-6
Camp Namanu—locale OR-9
Camp Napowan—locale WI-6
Camp Narrin—locale MI-6
Camp Nash KS-7
Camp Nashoba—locale MA-1
**Camp Nashoba**—pop pl MA-1
Camp Naticook—locale NH-1
Camp Natoma—locale CA-9
Camp Natowa—locale TX-5
Camp Natural Bridge—locale NY-2
Camp Navajo—locale PA-2
Camp Navarro—locale CA-9
Camp Nawaka—locale AL-4
Camp Nawaka—locale MA-1
Camp Nawaka Lake—reservoir NC-3
Camp Nawaka Lake Dam Number One—dam NC-3
Camp Nawakwa—locale CA-9
Camp Na Wa Kwa—locale MI-6
Camp Nawakwa—locale PA-2
Camp Nawakwa—locale WI-6
Camp Na-Wa-Kwa—park IN-6
Camp Nazareth—locale NY-2
Camp Nehalem—locale OR-9
Camp NeKia—locale SC-3
Camp Nelson—locale CO-8
Camp Nelson—locale KY-4
**Camp Nelson**—pop pl CA-9
**Camp Nelson**—pop pl KY-4
Camp Nelson Confederate Cem—cemetery AR-4
Camp Nelson Natl Cem—cemetery KY-4
Camp Ne-O-Tez—locale MO-7
Camp Netimus Dam—dam PA-2
Camp Netimus Lake—reservoir PA-2
Camp Newatah—locale NY-2
Camp Newheart—park IN-6
Camp Newkirk Pond—reservoir NC-3
Camp Newkirk Pond Dam—dam NC-3
Camp Newman—locale NE-7
Camp Newton—locale CO-8
Camp New Wood County Park—park WI-6
Camp Ney A Ti—locale AL-4
Camp Neyati—locale MA-1
Camp Neyati—locale MI-6
**Camp Neyati**—pop pl MA-1
Camp Niagara (Site)—locale CA-9
Camp Nichols—hist pl OK-5
Camp Nick Williams—locale CA-9
Camp Nina Flat—flat CA-9
Camp Nine—locale ID-8
Camp Nine—locale MT-8
Camp Nine—locale OR-9
Camp Nine—locale WA-9
Camp Nine Lake—lake WI-6
Camp Nine Lakes—lake MI-6
Camp Nine Pond—lake MO-7
Camp Nine Springs—spring WI-6
Camp Nineteen—locale CA-9
Camp Ninty Creek—stream MN-6
Camp Ninty Seven Creek—stream MN-6
Camp Nissokone—locale MI-6
Camp Niwana—locale TX-5
Camp Nixon—locale SC-3
Camp No-Be-Bo-Sco—locale NJ-2
Camp Nockamixon—locale PA-2
Camp Nooteeming—locale NY-2
Camp Noquochoke—park MA-1
**Camp Noquochoke**—pop pl MA-1
Camp Norfleet—locale VT-1
Camp Norris—locale CA-9
Camp Norse—locale MA-1
**Camp Norse**—pop pl MA-1
Camp Norseland—locale MN-6
Camp Northfield—locale MA-1
Camp Northward—locale KY-4
Camp Norwesca—locale NE-7
Camp Norwesco—locale WI-6
Camp Norwich—locale MA-1
**Camp Notre Dame**—pop pl NH-1
Camp Noxage Spring—spring OR-9
Camp Noyo—locale CA-9
Camp No 1—locale PA-2
Camp No 11 Slough—gut MI-6
Camp No 2—locale OR-9
Camp No 2—locale PA-2
Camp No 6—locale AK-9
Camp Number Eight—locale NY-2
Camp Number Eighteen—locale HI-9
Camp Number Eighteen—locale VT-1
Camp Number Eleven—locale ME-1
Camp Number Eleven—locale NY-2
Camp Number Eleven—locale VT-1
Camp Number Fifteen—locale VT-1
Camp Number Five—locale AZ-5
Camp Number Five—locale NY-2
Camp Number Five—locale SC-3
Camp Number Five—locale (2) VT-1
Camp Number Four—locale (2) VT-1
Camp Number Fourteen—locale VT-1
Camp Number Nine—locale ME-1
Camp Number Nineteen—locale NY-2
Camp Number Nineteen—locale VT-1
Camp Number Seven—locale HI-9
Camp Number Seven (historical)—locale TN-4
Camp Number Seventeen—locale VT-1
Camp Number Six—locale HI-9
Camp Number Six—locale VT-1
Camp Number Sixteen—locale VT-1
Camp Number Ten—locale VT-1
Camp Number Thirteen—locale VT-1
Camp Number Thirty-four—locale ME-1
Camp Number Thirty-two—locale ME-1
Camp Number Three—locale HI-9
Camp Number Three—locale (2) VT-1
Camp Number Twelve—locale VT-1
Camp Number Twenty—locale VT-1
Camp Number Twentyone—locale VT-1
Camp Number Twenty-two—locale NY-2
Camp Number Two—locale HI-9
Camp Number Two—locale MN-6
Camp Number Two—locale NY-2
Camp Number Two Brook NH-1
Camp Number Two (historical)—locale ME-1
Camp Number Two Tank—reservoir AZ-5
Camp Number 12 (historical)—locale ME-1
Camp Number 17 Lake MI-6
Camp Number 2 Bridge—bridge TN-4
Camp Number 3 Mine TN-4
Camp Number 31—locale NH-1
Camp Number 32—locale NH-1
Camp Number 36—locale NH-1
Camp Number 5—locale NH-1
Camp Number 6—locale NH-1
Camp Number 7—locale NH-1
Camp Number 8—locale NH-1
Camp Number 9—locale NH-1
**Campo**—pop pl CA-9
**Campo**—pop pl CO-8
Campo—uninc pl AZ-5
Campo, Lake—lake LA-4
Camp Oak—park MA-1
**Camp Oak**—pop pl SC-3
Camp Oakarro—locale IL-6
Camp Oakes—locale CA-9
Camp Oak Grove—locale CA-9
Camp Oak Hill—locale MI-6
Camp Oak Hill—locale WI-6
Camp Oakledge—locale MO-7
Camp Oaks MS-4
**Campo Alegre**—pop pl PR-3
Campo Alegre (Barrio)—fmr MCD PR-3
**Campo Alto**—pop pl TX-5
**Campobello**—pop pl SC-3
Campobello Island—island OH-6
Campo Bonito—locale AZ-5
**Campo Bonito**—pop pl AZ-5
**Camp Ocala**—pop pl FL-3
Campo Canyon—valley NM-5
**Camp Occoneechee**—pop pl NC-3
Campo Cem—cemetery CO-8
**Camp Ocoee**—pop pl TN-4
Camp O'Connell Swimming Pool—other PA-2
Campo Creek—stream CA-9
Campo Creek—stream ID-8
Campo de Cahuenga—locale CA-9
Campo De Los Franceses—civil CA-9
Camp Odetah—locale CT-1
Camp Odum Mon—locale GA-3
Campo El Deseo—locale NM-5
Camp O'Fair Winds—locale MI-6
Campo Forest Fire Station—locale CA-9
Camp of the Cross—locale OK-5
Camp of the Woods—locale NY-2
Campo Grande Mtn—summit TX-5
Camp O'Hara Boy Scout Camp—locale GA-3
Camp Oh da ko ta—locale WI-6
Camp Ohio—locale OH-6
Camp Ohlone Regional Park—park CA-9
**Campo Ind Res**—pop pl CA-9
Camp Ojibwa—locale WI-6
Camp Okahahwis—locale VA-3
Camp Okalona—park IN-6
Camp Okitayakani—locale GA-3
Camp Oklawaha—locale FL-3
Camp Oko-Tipi—locale MO-7
Campo Lake—lake CA-9
Camp Olcott—locale MN-6
Camp Olden—park IN-6
Camp Old Indian—locale SC-3
Camp Ole Station—locale CA-9
Camp Oliver—locale AL-4
Camp Oliver—locale GA-3
Camp Oliver Shores AL-4
Camp Oljato—locale CA-9
Camp Olmsted—hist pl NY-2
Camp Olmsted—locale PA-2
Camp Olson—locale MN-6
Camp Olson—locale OR-9
Camp Olympia—locale NJ-2
Camp Olympus—locale NY-2
Campo Manana—park NM-5
Campo Mine, El—mine AZ-5
Campomocho Draw—valley AZ-5
Campo Molino—flat CO-8
Camp One—locale (2) CA-9
Camp One—locale OR-9
Camp One—locale WA-9
Camp One Creek—stream MI-6
Camp One Creek—stream WI-6
Camp One (historical)—locale SD-7
Camp One Hundred Nine—locale HI-9
Camp One Hundred Six—locale HI-9
Camp One Lake—lake (2) WI-6
Camp One (site)—locale OR-9
Camp One Spring—spring CA-9
Camp One Springs—lake WI-6
Camp One Trail—trail OR-9
Camp Onibar—locale PA-2
Camp On-Ti-Ora—locale NY-2
Camp Ontologo—locale TX-5
Campoodie Creek—stream NV-8
Campoodle Creek—stream CA-9
Camp Oo-tah-nee-noh-chee—locale TN-4
Camp Opboca—locale MO-7
Camp Orapax—locale VA-3
Camp Ord AZ-5
Camp O'Rear—locale AL-4
Camporee Spring—spring OR-9
Camp Orenda—locale PA-2
Campo Rico—CDP PR-3
**Campo Rico**—pop pl (2) PR-3
**Camporico**—pop pl VI-3
Camp Orinsekwa—locale NY-2
**Camp Orkila**—pop pl WA-9
Camp Oronoko—locale MI-6
Camp Orr—locale AR-4
Camp Ortoha—locale WA-9
Campo Santo Cem—cemetery CO-8
Campo Santo Cem—cemetery TX-5
Campo Santo del Pueblo—cemetery NM-5
Campo Santo Estrada—locale TX-5
Campo Santo Hernandez—other TX-5
Campo Santo Rodriguez—other TX-5
Camp Osborn—locale GA-3
**Camp Osborne**—pop pl NJ-2
Campos Cem—cemetery TX-5
Camp Osceola—locale CA-9
Camp Osceola—locale FL-3
Camp Osceola—locale NC-3
Campo Sch—school CA-9
**Campo Seco**—pop pl (2) CA-9
Campo Seco Ridge—ridge CA-9
Camp Osito Rancho—locale CA-9
Campo Spring—spring NM-5
Campos Ranch—locale AZ-5
Campostella Bridge—bridge VA-3
**Campostella Heights**—pop pl VA-3
Campostella JHS—school VA-3
**Campostella (subdivision)**—pop pl VA-3
Campos Verdes Junior HighSchool—school CA-9
Campos Water Spring—spring AZ-5
Camp Oswego—military NY-2
Camp Otanyao—locale TX-5
Camp O the Suwannee—locale FL-3
Camp Otis—locale MT-8
Camp Otonk—locale KY-4
Camp Otonka—locale DE-2
**Campo Tortugero**—pop pl PR-3
Camp Otsiketa—locale MI-6
Camp Otter—locale NH-1
Camp Otto Lake—reservoir IN-6
Camp Otto Lake Dam—dam IN-6
Camp Otyokwa—locale OH-6
Camp Otyokwah—locale OH-6
Camp Ouachita—locale AR-4
Camp Ousamequin—park MA-1
**Camp Ousamequin**—pop pl MA-1
Campo Valley—valley CA-9
Campo Verde Windmill—locale TX-5
Camp Overflow—locale MA-1
Camp Overton—locale TN-4
Camp Owaissa—locale NY-2
Camp Owaissa-Bauer—locale FL-3
Camp Owaisse—locale PA-2
Camp Oweki—locale MI-6
Camp Owens—locale OH-6
**Camp Owens**—pop pl CA-9
**Camp Oyo**—pop pl OH-6
Camp Ozanam—locale MI-6
Camp Ozark—locale AR-4
Camp Ozone Dam—dam TN-4
Camp Paha Sapa—locale SD-7
Camp Pahatsi—locale CA-9
Camp Pa He Tsi—locale MO-7
Camp Pahoka—park IN-6
Camp Paivika—locale CA-9
Camp Pajarito—locale CA-9
Camp Palm—locale (2) FL-3
Camp Palmer—locale CT-1
Camp Palmer—locale OH-6
Camp Palos—locale IL-6
Camp Paluxy—locale TX-5
Camp Parapet Powder Magazine—hist pl LA-4
Camp Parater—locale VA-3
**Camp Pardee**—pop pl CA-9
**Camp Park**—pop pl OH-6
Camp Parker—locale SC-3
Camp Parkman—locale AL-4
Camp Parks—locale CA-9
Camp Parks (U.S. Army)—military CA-9
Camp Parole MD-2
Camp Parsons—locale WA-9
Camp Parthenia—locale OK-5
Camp Pasquaney—locale NH-1
Camp Pass MT-8
Camp Pass—gap MT-8
Camp Pasture Windmill—locale TX-5
Camp Patmos—locale OH-6
Camp Patrick Henry Milit Reservation—military VA-3
Camp Paul Bear Bryant AL-4
Camp Paumalu—locale HI-9
Camp Pawnee—locale KS-7
Camp Paxson—locale MT-8
Camp Paxson Boy Scout Camp (24MO77)—hist pl MT-8
Camp Paxton—park IN-6
Camp Paysock—locale ME-1
Camp Pearl—locale LA-4
Camp Pearl Wheat—locale TX-5
Camp Peary Naval Reservation—military VA-3
Camp Pee Dee—locale SC-3
Camp Peet—locale OH-6
Camp Pee Wee—locale OH-6
Camp Pellissippi—locale TN-4
Camp Penacook—locale NH-1
Camp Pendleton (Marine Corps Base)—military CA-9
Camp Pendleton Naval Regional Med Ctr—military CA-9
Camp Pendleton North—CDP CA-9
Camp Pendleton South—CDP CA-9
**Camp Pendola**—pop pl CA-9
Camp Peniel—locale AR-4
Camp Peniel—locale MD-2
Camp Peniel—locale TX-5
Camp Penn—locale PA-2
Camp Pennock—locale CO-8
Camp Pequot—locale CT-1
Camp Perkins—locale ID-8
Camp Perry—locale OH-6
Camp Perry—locale PA-2
Camp Perry Air Natl Guard Station—building OH-6
Camp Perry (Boy Scouts of America)—locale TX-5
Camp Peterson—locale OR-9
Camp Peterson—locale WI-6
Camp Phillips—locale (2) WI-6
Camp Phin-Be Gota—locale WI-6
Camp Phoenix—locale ME-1
Camp Phoenix—locale MS-4
Camp Piasa—locale IL-6
Camp Pickett Milit Reservation—military VA-3
Camp Pickett (National Guard Summer Camp)—building VA-3
Camp Pierce—locale TX-5
Camp Pinal AZ-5
Camp Pinchot—locale FL-3
Camp Pinckney Ch—church GA-3
Camp Pine—locale IL-6
Camp Pine—locale NY-2
Camp Pine Acres—locale MI-6
Camp Pine Cone—locale NY-2
Camp Pine Crest—locale MS-4
Camp Pine Knot—hist pl NY-2
Camp Pinewood—locale MI-6
Camp Pinewood—locale NC-3
Camp Pine Woods—locale IL-6
Camp Pinkston—locale TX-5
Camp Pinnacle—locale NY-2
Camp Pinnacle—locale NC-3
Camp Pinnacle—locale WV-2
Camp Pin Oak—locale (2) MO-7
Camp Pin Oak Hist Dist—hist pl MO-7
Camp Piomingo—locale KY-4
Camp Pioneer—locale AR-4
Camp Pioneer—locale CT-1
Camp Pioneer—locale GA-3
Camp Pioneer—locale MS-4
Camp Pioneer—locale OR-9
Camp Pioneer—locale WV-2
**Camp Pioneer**—pop pl NY-2
Camp Pioneer Ridge—locale MO-7
Camp Pit—locale CA-9
Camp Pittenger—locale OH-6
**Camp Placid**—pop pl TN-4
Camp Playfair—locale MI-6
Camp Pleasant AZ-5
Camp Pleasant—locale WA-9
**Camp Pleasant**—pop pl KY-4
Camp Pleasant Ch—church KY-4
Camp Pleasure (historical)—locale AL-4
Camp Plymouth—locale VT-1
Camp Pocahontas—locale VA-3
Camp Pocahontas—locale WV-2
Camp Podunk—locale PA-2
Camp Point—cape (2) AK-9
Camp Point—cape NC-3
**Camp Point**—pop pl IL-6
**Camp Point (Township of)**—pop pl IL-6
Camp Pokano-Rainona—locale NJ-2
Camp Pokonokah Hills—locale WI-6
Camp Polk LA-4
Camp Polk—locale OR-9
Camp Polk Cemetery OR-9
Camp Polk Military Reservation LA-4
**Camp Polk (State Fair Grounds)**—pop pl NC-3
Camp Pollock—locale CA-9
Camp Pompeii—locale IL-6
Camp Pomponio—locale CA-9
Camp Pond PA-2
Camp Pond—lake (2) FL-3
Camp Pond—lake ME-1
Camp Pond—lake WA-9
Camp Pond—reservoir CT-1
Camp Pond—reservoir FL-3
Camp Pond—swamp TX-5
Camp Pond Bay—swamp SC-3
Camp Pond Creek KS-7
Camp Pond Creek—stream LA-4
Camp Po-Ne-Mah—locale CT-1
Camp Pope Creek—stream MN-6
Camp Portaferry—locale NY-2
Camp Post—locale TX-5
Camp Potawatomi—locale IL-6
Camp Potomac Woods—locale VA-3
Camp Powderhorn—locale KY-4
Camp Prather—locale GA-3
Camp Pratt—locale MS-4
Camp Presmont—locale OH-6
Camp Procious WV-2
Camp Prospect (historical)—locale SD-7
**Camp Providence**—pop pl TX-5
Camp Pupukea—locale HI-9
Camp Pushmataha—locale AL-4
Camp Putnam—locale MA-1
Camp Putnam—locale MO-7
Camp Pyoca—park IN-6
Camp Quaker Haven—locale KS-7
Camp Quapaw—locale AR-4
Camp Quarry—mine FL-3
Camp Quatoga—locale IL-6
Camp Quiet—locale MI-6
Camp Quinapoxet—locale NH-1
Camp Rabbit Hollow—locale NH-1
Camp Rabideau—locale MN-6
Camp Rader Run—stream VA-3
Camp Radford—locale CA-9
Camp Radziminski—hist pl OK-5
Camp Rainbow—locale NY-2
Camp Rainbow—locale PA-2
Camp Raleigh—locale NY-2
Camp Ranch—locale TX-5
Camp Ranch—locale WY-8
Camp Rancho Framasa—park IN-6
Camp Randall—hist pl WI-6
Camp Ranger—locale NJ-2
Camp Rankin—locale MI-6
Camp Rapid—locale SD-7
Camp Rapidan—locale VA-3
Camp Raven Knob—locale NC-3
Camp Rawl SC-3
**Camp Rawls**—pop pl SC-3
Camp Raynolds (historical)—locale SD-7
Camp R Creek—stream MI-6
Camp Read—locale MA-1
Camp Reagan—locale FL-3
Camp Red Buck—locale MI-6
Camp Red Bud—locale MO-7
Camp Red Canyon SD-7
Camp Red Cedar MO-7
Camp Red Cedar—locale MO-7
Camp Red Cliff—locale UT-8
Camp Red Mill—locale MD-2
Camp Red Mill Lake Dam—dam IN-6
Camp Red Rock—locale OK-5
Camp Redwing—locale PA-2
Camp Redwing—park IN-6
Camp Reed—locale GA-3
Camp Reed—locale WA-9
Camp Reese—locale GA-3
Camp Reily—locale PA-2
Camp Reinberg—locale IL-6
Camp Relax—locale TN-4
Camp Release Cem—cemetery MN-6
Camp Release State Monmt—hist pl MN-6
Camp Release (Township of)—civ div MN-6
Camp Remington—locale SD-7
Camp Reno Historical Marker—park AZ-5
Camp Rentz—locale PA-2
Camp Resolute—locale MA-1
**Camp Resolute**—pop pl MA-1
Camp Rest—locale CA-9
Camp Rest Park—park WI-6
Camp Retreat—locale NC-3
Camp Reveal—park IN-6
Camp Reynolds—locale PA-2
Camp Riamo—locale PA-2
Camp Rice Arroyo—valley TX-5
Camp Rice Rsvr Number One—reservoir TX-5
Camp Rice Tank—reservoir TX-5
Camp Rich—locale VT-1
**Camp Richardson**—pop pl CA-9
Camp Ridge—ridge CO-8
Camp Ridge—ridge MO-7
Camp Ridge—ridge NC-3
Camp Ridge—ridge VA-3
Camp Ridge (campground)—locale MO-7
Camp Ridgecrest Dam—dam NC-3
Camp Ridgecrest Lake—reservoir NC-3
Camp Ridge-Ho—locale NY-2
Camp Ridge Trail—trail VA-3
Camp Riley—park IN-6
Camp Rim Rock—locale WV-2
Camp Rio Blanco—locale TX-5
Camp Rio Roxo—locale TX-5
Camp Rio Vista—locale TX-5
Camp Ripley Junction—locale MN-6
Camp Ripley (U.S. Army)—other MN-6
Camp Rippin—locale NY-2
Camp Rips—rapids ME-1
Camp Rip Van Winkle—locale NY-2
Camp Rising Sun—locale MO-7
Camp Rising Sun—locale NY-2
Camp Ritter—locale KY-4
Camp Rivard—locale MN-6
Camp River Glen—locale CA-9
Camp Rivers (historical)—locale AZ-5
Camp Riversite—locale WI-6
Camp Ro—locale OH-6
Camp Robber Creek—stream WA-9
Camp Robber Lake—lake WA-9
Camp Robber Valley—valley WA-9
**Camp Roberts**—pop pl IN-6
Camp Robert Toombs—locale GA-3
Camp Robinson University of Kentucky Engineering Camp—locale KY-4
Camp Robinwood—locale TX-5
Camp Rock—locale CO-8
Camp Rock—pillar CA-9
Camp Rock—pillar ID-8
Camp Rock—summit VA-3
Camprock Branch—stream NC-3
Camp Rock Branch—stream NC-3
Camp Rockbrook—locale MS-4
Camp Rock Campground—locale CO-8
Camprock Creek—stream AL-4
Camp Rock Enon—locale VA-3
Camp Rock Gulch—valley CO-8
Camp Rockhaven—locale NE-7
Camp Rock Mine—mine CA-9
Camp Rockne—locale MA-1
**Camp Rockne**—pop pl MA-1
Camp Rockspar—locale PA-2
Camp Rodgers—locale CA-9
Camp Rodgers Saddle—gap CA-9
Camp Rodney—locale MD-2
Camp Roganunda—locale WA-9
Camp Roger—locale UT-8
Camp Roland—locale VA-3
Camp Roland—locale WA-9
**Camp Romaca**—pop pl MA-1
Camp Romona—park IN-6
Camp Rondaxe—locale NY-2
Camp Roosevelt—locale CA-9
Camp Roosevelt—locale MD-2
Camp Roosevelt—locale NJ-2
**Camp Roosevelt**—pop pl FL-3
**Camp Roosevelt**—pop pl OH-6
Camp Roosevelt Rec Area—park VA-3
Camp Rosalie—locale CO-8
**Camp Rose**—pop pl CA-9
Camp Rosenbaum Airstrip—airport SD-7
Camp Rosenberg (BSA)—locale CA-9
Camp Rosenita—locale CA-9
Camp Ross—locale OH-6
Camp Ross Trail—locale OH-6
Camp Rota-Kiwan—locale MI-6
Camp Rotamer—locale WI-6
Camp Rotary—locale AL-4
Camp Rotary—locale FL-3
Camp Rotary—locale IL-6
Camp Rotary—locale (2) MI-6
Camp Rotary—locale (2) MT-8
Camp Rotary—locale NC-3
Camp Rotary—park IN-6
Camp Rotary McQueen—locale IL-6
Camp Round Meadow—locale CA-9
**Camp Rowe**—pop pl MA-1
Camp Rowland—locale PA-2
**Camp Roxas**—pop pl GU-9
Camp Royaneh—locale CA-9
Camp Rsvr—reservoir (3) MT-8
Camp Rsvr—reservoir (2) OR-9
Camp Ruby—locale TX-5
Camp Rucker—other AL-4
Camp Rucker Campground—park AZ-5
Camp Rucker (historical)—locale AZ-5
Camp Run PA-2
Camp Run WV-2
Camp Run—locale WV-2
Camp Run—stream IL-6
Camp Run—stream (2) IN-6
Camp Run—stream (5) OH-6
Camp Run—stream (13) PA-2
Camp Run—stream SC-3
Camp Run—stream (21) WV-2
Camp Run Cem—cemetery (2) PA-2
Camp Run Ch (historical)—church PA-2
Camp Run Hollow OH-6
Camp Running Deer—locale TN-4
Camp Rushford—locale NY-2
Camp Russell—locale NY-2
Camp Russell—locale (2) OK-5
Camp Russell—locale WV-2
**Camp Russell**—pop pl MA-1
Camp Russell Cem—cemetery OK-5
Camp Russell (site)—locale OR-9
Camp Ruthers—locale VA-3
Camp Rutledge—locale GA-3
Camps—locale TX-5
**Camps**—pop pl FL-3
Camp Sabrina—locale CA-9
Camp Sacajawea—locale IL-6
Camp Sacajawea—locale IA-7
Camp Sacajawea—locale WI-6
Camp Sacajawea—locale WY-8
Camp Sacajqwea—locale VA-3
Camp Sacalawea—locale (2) IA-7
Camp Sachem—locale NH-1
Camp Sacramento—locale CA-9
Camp Sagamore—locale NY-2
Camp Saginaw—locale PA-2
Camp Sa -Gis -Ca—locale ME-1
Camp Sain—locale NC-3
Camp Saint Albert—locale CA-9
Camp Saint Benedict—locale NJ-2
**Camp Saint Christopher**—pop pl SC-3
Camp Saint Claret—locale IL-6
Camp Saint Edward—locale NY-2
Camp Saint George—locale GA-3
Camp Saint George—locale IL-6
Camp Saint John—locale NJ-2
Camp Saint Joseph—locale OH-6
Camp Saint Joseph—park IN-6

Canada Lake—*lake* NY-2
**Canada Lake**—*pop pl* NY-2
Canada Larga—*stream* NM-5
Canada Larga de la Cueva—*stream* NM-5
Canada Larga o Verde—*civil* CA-9
Canada las Lemitas—*stream* (2) NM-5
Canada Las Vacas—*stream* NM-5
Canada Llaves—*stream* NM-5
Canada los Frijoles—*stream* NM-5
Canada Lovato—*stream* NM-5
Canada Lucero—*stream* NM-5
*Canada Magpo* MH-9
Canada Marcelina—*stream* NM-5
**Canada Mills**—*pop pl* MA-1
Canada Milpitas—*stream* NM-5
Canada Montoso—*valley* NM-5
Canada Montuosa—*stream* NM-5
Canada Mtn—*summit* KY-4
Canada Nervio—*stream* NM-5
*Canada Ojitos* NM-5
Canada Ojitos—*valley* NM-5
*Canada Omentero* CA-9
Canada Piedra Amarilla—*stream* NM-5
Canada Pinabete—*stream* NM-5
*Canada Point* AL-4
Canada Pond—*reservoir* RI-1
Canada Popotosa—*stream* NM-5
Canada Pueblo—*stream* NM-5
Canadarago Lake—*lake* NY-2
Canada Rancho de los Chivos—*stream* NM-5
Canada Ranger Station—*locale* NM-5
Canada Ridge—*ridge* WI-6
Canada Rincon—*stream* NM-5
Canada (Ruins)—*locale* NM-5
Canada Run—*stream* OH-6
Canada Run—*stream* (2) PA-2
Canada Run—*stream* VA-3
Canada Saddle—*gap* ID-8
Canada Salada—*stream* (2) NM-5
Canada Sanchez—*stream* NM-5
Canadas Beach—*locale* DE-2
Canada Sch—*school* IL-6
Canada Sch—*school* OK-5
Canada Schmidt—*stream* NM-5
Canada School—*locale* MI-6
Canada Segura—*stream* NM-5
**Canada Shores**—*pop pl* MI-6
Canada Sierra—*stream* NM-5
Canada Simon—*valley* NM-5
Canada Spring de la Jarita—*stream* NM-5
Canada Tank—*reservoir* NM-5
Canada Tanques—*stream* NM-5
Canada Tanques—*valley* NM-5
Canada-Threadgill Cem—*cemetery* AL-4
Canada Tio Grande—*stream* NM-5
**Canada Township**—*pop pl* KS-7
Canada (Township of)—*fmr MCD* NC-3
Canada Tuloso—*stream* NM-5
Canada Tusas—*stream* NM-5
Canada Upper Pond Dam—*dam* RI-1
Canada Vaca—*stream* NM-5
*Canada Verde* CA-9
**Canada Verde**—*pop pl* TX-5
Canada Verde—*stream* NM-5
**Canada Village**—*pop pl* NM-5
Canada Village—*uninc pl* CA-9
*Canadaville* SD-7
Canadaville—*locale* TN-4
**Canadaville**—*pop pl* SD-7
Canadaville Post Office (historical)—*building* TN-4
Canadaville Sch—*school* TN-4
Canada Vivian—*stream* NM-5
Canada Viviancito—*stream* NM-5
Canada Vivorosa—*stream* NM-5
Canadaway Creek—*stream* NY-2
Canada Windmill—*locale* NM-5
*Canaday* MO-7
Canaday Cem—*cemetery* MO-7
Canaday Creek—*stream* MO-7
Canaday Sch (historical)—*school* MO-7
Canadays Ridge—*ridge* VA-3
Canaday Switch Sch (abandoned)—*school* MO-7
**Canadensis**—*pop pl* PA-2
**Canadian**—*pop pl* OK-5
**Canadian**—*pop pl* TX-5
Canadian Bar—*bar* CA-9
Canadian Bayou—*stream* LA-4
Canadian Bayou Oil and Gas Field—*oilfield* LA-4
Canadian Bench—*bench* OR-9
**Canadian City**—*pop pl* OK-5
*Canadian Coulee* MT-8
**Canadian (County)**—*pop pl* OK-5
Canadian County Jail—*hist pl* OK-5
Canadian Creek—*stream* AK-9
Canadian Creek—*stream* CA-9
Canadian Creek—*stream* MT-8
Canadian Creek—*stream* OK-5
Canadian Ditch—*canal* CO-8
Canadian Embassy—*hist pl* DC-2
**Canadian Fork**—*pop pl* OK-5
Canadian Gasoline Plant—*oilfield* TX-5
*Canadian Hill* NY-2
Canadian Hole—*bay* NC-3
Canadian Jail and Livery Stable—*hist pl* OK-5
Canadian Lakes—*lake* MI-6
Canadian Legation Bldg—*building* DC-2
Canadian Mines—*mine* AZ-5
Canadian Natl Depot—*hist pl* MN-6
Canadian North (CCD)—*cens area* TX-5
*Canadian Police Creek* MT-8
Canadian Reach—*channel* AR-4
Canadian Rec Area—*park* OK-5
*Canadian River* CO-8
Canadian River—*stream* (2) CO-8
Canadian River—*stream* NM-5
Canadian River—*stream* OK-5
Canadian River—*stream* TX-5
Canadian River Breaks (CCD)—*cens area* TX-5
Canadian River Store—*locale* TX-5
Canadian Sandy Creek—*stream* (2) OK-5
**Canadian Shores**—*pop pl* OK-5
Canadian South (CCD)—*cens area* TX-5
Canadian Top—*summit* NC-3
Canadian (Township of)—*fmr MCD* AR-4
Canadian Valley Cem—*cemetery* OK-5
Canadian Valley Vocational Sch—*school* OK-5
Canadian Windmill—*locale* NM-5
Canadice—*locale* NY-2
Canadice Hill—*summit* NY-2
Canadice Hollow Cem—*cemetery* NY-2
Canadice Lake—*lake* NY-2
Canadice Outlet—*stream* NY-2
**Canadice (Town of)**—*pop pl* NY-2
Canadochly Ch—*church* PA-2
Canadochly Creek—*stream* PA-2
Canadohta, Lake—*lake* PA-2
**Canadohta Lake**—*pop pl* PA-2
Canadohta Ski Slope—*other* PA-2
Canador Peak—*summit* NM-5
Canador Peak Windmill—*locale* NM-5
Canados Ancha—*stream* CO-8
Canady Branch—*stream* AR-4
Canady Branch—*stream* SC-3
Canady Bridge—*bridge* SC-3
Canady Cem—*cemetery* TN-4
*Canady Crossroads* SC-3
Canady Crossroads—*locale* SC-3
Canady Gulch—*valley* CA-9
Canady Hill Hollow—*valley* MO-7
Canady Landing—*locale* SC-3
Canady Point—*cape* AR-4
**Canadys**—*pop pl* SC-3
**Canadys (Cannadys)**—*pop pl* SC-3
Canady Switch—*locale* MO-7
Canah Gap—*gap* TN-4
Canah Hollow—*valley* TN-4
Cana (historical P.O.)—*locale* IN-6
Cana Island—*island* WI-6
Cana Island Lighthouse—*hist pl* WI-6
**Canajoharie**—*pop pl* NY-2
Canajoharie Creek—*stream* NY-2
Canajoharie Falls—*falls* NY-2
Canajoharie Rsvr—*reservoir* (2) NY-2
**Canajoharie (Town of)**—*pop pl* NY-2
*Canal* DE-2
*Canal* IN-6
*Canal* MD-2
*Canal* MI-6
Canal—*locale* WY-8
**Canal**—*pop pl* MD-2
Canal, A—*canal* MT-8
Canal, An—*canal* MT-8
*Canal, The* AL-4
Canal, The—*canal* AL-4
Canal, The—*canal* (3) MD-2
Canal, The—*canal* MS-4
Canal, The—*canal* NC-3
Canal, The—*gut* FL-3
Canal, The—*gut* VA-3
Canal, The—*stream* AZ-5
Canal, The—*stream* GA-3
Canal, The—*stream* MD-2
Canal, The—*stream* NC-3
Canal A—*canal* NC-3
Canal A—*canal* UT-8
Canal Aguadilla—*canal* PR-3
*Canala Island* TX-5
*Canal Ancho* AZ-5
Canalaska Mtn—*summit* AK-9
Canal B—*canal* NC-3
Canal B—*canal* UT-8
Canal Bay—*bay* MT-8
Canal Bayou—*stream* LA-4
*Canal B. Bienvenue* LA-4
Canal Blasina—*canal* PR-3
Canal Blue—*canal* LA-4
Canal Branch—*stream* (2) GA-3
Canal Branch—*stream* MO-7
Canal Branch—*stream* NC-3
Canal Branch—*stream* (4) SC-3
Canal Branch—*swamp* GA-3
*Canal Bridge* MA-1
Canal Bridge—*bridge* DE-2
Canal Bridge—*bridge* FL-3
Canal Bridge—*bridge* NC-3
Canal C—*canal* UT-8
Canal Canyon—*valley* ID-8
Canal Canyon—*valley* UT-8
Canal Caracoles—*canal* PR-3
*Canal Casas* AZ-5
*Canal Cashion* AZ-5
Canal Castanon—*canal* PR-3
**Canal Center**—*pop pl* PA-2
Canal Ch—*church* PA-2
Canal Channel—*channel* NJ-2
Canal Channel—*channel* PA-2
*Canal Colinas* AZ-5
*Canal Cottonwood* AZ-5
*Canal Creek* TX-5
Canal Creek—*stream* CA-9
Canal Creek—*stream* MD-2
Canal Creek—*stream* NC-3
Canal Creek—*stream* (3) OR-9
Canal Creek—*stream* TX-5
Canal Creek—*stream* UT-8
Canal Creek Campground—*park* OR-9
Canal Creek Oil Field—*oilfield* TX-5
Canal C-39a—*canal* FL-3
Canal C-40—*canal* FL-3
Canal C-41—*canal* FL-3
Canal C-41A—*canal* FL-3
Canal Dam—*dam* SD-7
*Canal-Daut* MH-9
Canal De Aguadilla—*canal* PR-3
*Canal de Aroo* WA-9
Canal De Cayo Norte—*channel* PR-3
Canal De Culebrita—*channel* PR-3
Canal De Florida—*canal* PR-3
Canal de Guamani Este—*canal* PR-3
Canal de Guamani Oeste—*canal* PR-3
Canal De Guanajibo—*channel* PR-3
*Canal de Haro* WA-9
Canal De Juana Diaz—*canal* PR-3
Canal Del Medio—*canal* PR-3
*Canal de Lopex de Aro* WA-9
*Canal de Lopez de Haro* WA-9
*Canal del Rio* AZ-5
Canal de Luis Pena—*channel* PR-3
Canal De Patillas—*canal* PR-3
Canal De Riego—*canal* PR-3
Canal De Tierra—*canal* PR-3
Canal Dime Savings Bank—*hist pl* SC-3
Canal Ditch, The—*canal* UT-8
Canal Doncella—*canal* PR-3
*Canal Dover* OH-6
Canale—*locale* AR-4
Canal Eighteen—*canal* CA-9
*Canal Eleven* AZ-5
*Canal Eleven Branch* AZ-5
Canal Entrance Light—*locale* WA-9
Canales Cem—*cemetery* TX-5
Canales Draw—*valley* TX-5
Canales Sch—*school* TX-5
Canales Windmill—*locale* TX-5
Canal Feeder—*canal* OH-6
*Canal Fortuna* LA-4
*Canal Fourteen* AZ-5
*Canal Fourteen Branch* AZ-5
*Canal Fourteen Lower Branch* AZ-5
**Canal Fulton**—*pop pl* OH-6
Canal Fulton Hist Dist—*hist pl* OH-6
*Canal Goal Gap* KY-4
Canal Gonzales—*canal* PR-3
Canal Gordiani—*canal* PR-3
Canal Greenbelt Park—*park* UT-8
Canal Gulch—*valley* CA-9
Canal Gulch—*valley* ID-8
Canal Gut—*stream* NC-3
Canal (historical)—*locale* AL-4
Canal House—*hist pl* IN-6
Canal Island—*island* AL-4
Canal Jobos—*canal* PR-3
Canal Juan Dolores—*canal* PR-3
**Canal Junction**—*pop pl* MA-1
Canal K—*canal* (2) MT-8
Canal L—*canal* MT-8
Canal Lake—*lake* FL-3
Canal Lake—*lake* WA-9
Canal Lake—*locale* GA-3
Canal Lake Bible Camp—*locale* GA-3
Canal Lakes—*reservoir* IN-6
Canal La Palma—*canal* PR-3
*Canal Leaut* FM-9
*Canal Lebedei* FM-9
**Canal Lewisville**—*pop pl* OH-6
Canal L 31 E—*canal* (2) FL-3
Canal Machicote—*canal* PR-3
Canal Margarita—*canal* PR-3
Canal Marine—*canal* LA-4
*Canal Mesa* AZ-5
Canal Moca—*canal* PR-3
*Canal Nine* AZ-5
Canal Norte—*channel* PR-3
Canal No 1—*canal* IL-6
Canal No 1—*canal* NE-7
Canal No 16—*canal* AR-4
Canal No 18—*canal* AR-4
Canal No 19—*canal* AR-4
Canal No 2—*canal* (2) AR-4
Canal No 2—*canal* NE-7
Canal No 20—*canal* ID-8
Canal No 3—*canal* NE-7
Canal No 3—*canal* WY-8
Canal No 4—*canal* AR-4
Canal No 4—*canal* NE-7
Canal No 43—*canal* AR-4
Canal No 45—*canal* ID-8
Canal No 66—*canal* AR-4
Canal No 67—*canal* AR-4
Canal No 81—*canal* AR-4
*Canal No. 9* AR-4
Canal Number C-110—*canal* FL-3
Canal Number Eight—*canal* (4) LA-4
Canal Number Eighteen—*canal* LA-4
Canal Number Eleven—*canal* (2) LA-4
Canal Number Fifteen—*canal* LA-4
Canal Number Five—*canal* (2) LA-4
Canal Number Four—*canal* (4) LA-4
Canal Number Fourteen—*canal* (2) LA-4
Canal Number Nine—*canal* (2) LA-4
Canal Number Nineteen—*canal* LA-4
Canal Number One—*canal* LA-4
Canal Number Seven—*canal* (3) LA-4
Canal Number Seventeen—*canal* (2) LA-4
Canal Number Six—*canal* (3) LA-4
Canal Number Sixteen—*canal* LA-4
Canal Number Ten—*canal* (2) LA-4
Canal Number Thirteen—*canal* (2) LA-4
Canal Number Three—*canal* (3) LA-4
Canal Number Twelve—*canal* (2) LA-4
Canal Number Twenty—*canal* LA-4
Canal Number Twentyfour—*canal* LA-4
Canal Number Twentyone—*canal* LA-4
Canal Number Twentythree—*canal* LA-4
Canal Number Twentytwo—*canal* LA-4
Canal Number Two—*canal* (4) LA-4
Canal O—*canal* MT-8
*Canal Oil Field* CA-9
**Canalou**—*pop pl* MO-7
Canal P—*canal* MT-8
Canal Park—*park* AZ-5
*Canal Pima* AZ-5
Canal Point—*cape* (2) AK-9
Canal Point—*cape* NC-3
**Canal Point**—*pop pl* FL-3
Canal Point Elem Sch—*school* FL-3
Canal Pond—*lake* DE-2
*Canal Primero* AZ-5
Canal Principal de Diversion—*canal* PR-3
Canal Principal De Riego Valle De Lajas—*canal* PR-3
Canal Public Use Area—*locale* KY-4
Canal Ranch—*civil* CA-9
*Canal Rio* AZ-5
*Canal Riverside* AZ-5
Canal Run—*stream* VA-3
Canal S—*canal* MT-8
Canal S (abandoned)—*canal* MT-8
Canal Saint Jean Charles—*canal* LA-4
*Canal Salado* AZ-5
Canal Sch—*school* (2) CA-9
*Canal Scottsdale* AZ-5
Canal Seventeen—*canal* CA-9
*Canal Sitio* AZ-5
Canal Station—*locale* DE-2
Canal Street—*uninc pl* NY-2
Canal Street Algiers Ferry—*locale* LA-4
Canal Street Holiness Ch—*church* AL-4
Canal Street Schoolhouse—*hist pl* VT-1
Canal Suarez—*canal* PR-3
Canal Swamp—*stream* (3) VA-3
Canal Swamp (historical)—*stream* AL-4
Canal Tank—*reservoir* NM-5
Canal Tisamond Foret—*canal* LA-4
*Canal to Coot Bay Canal* FL-3
*Canal Tolleson* AZ-5
Canal Town Creek—*stream* MI-6
Canal Town Museum—*hist pl* NY-2
Canal Township—*inact MCD* NV-8
**Canal (Township of)**—*pop pl* PA-2
Canal Tuerto—*canal* PR-3
*Canal Viejo* AZ-5
Canal Villamil—*canal* PR-3
Canal Warehouse—*hist pl* OH-6
Canal Wildlife Area—*park* DE-2
**Canal Winchester**—*pop pl* OH-6
Canal Winchester Methodist Church—*hist pl* OH-6
Canal W 20—*canal* WA-9
Canal 111—*canal* FL-3
Canal 111E—*canal* FL-3
Canamo Spring—*spring* NM-5
**Canan**—*pop pl* PA-2
*Canan Church* AL-4
**Canandaigua**—*pop pl* MI-6
**Canandaigua**—*pop pl* NY-2
Canandaigua Hist Dist—*hist pl* NY-2
Canandaigua Lake—*lake* NY-2
Canandaigua Outlet—*stream* NY-2
Canandaigua Rsvr—*reservoir* NY-2
**Canandaigua (Town of)**—*pop pl* NY-2
Canan Lake—*lake* WA-9
**Canan Station**—*pop pl* PA-2
Cana of Galilee Ch—*church* SC-3
Canapener Rapids—*rapids* ID-8
*Canapitset Channel* MA-1
*Canapitsett Channel* MA-1
Canapitsit Channel—*channel* MA-1
Canard Creek—*stream* CO-8
Canard Gris, Bayou—*gut* LA-4
*Canard Run* WV-2
*Canaresse* DE-2
*Canarical Creek* DE-2
Canario Canyon—*valley* NM-5
*Canaris Spring* CA-9
*Canarra Creek* UT-8
**Canarsie**—*pop pl* NY-2
Canarsie Beach—*beach* NY-2
Canarsie Cem—*cemetery* NY-2
Canarsie HS—*school* NY-2
Canarsie Park—*park* NY-2
Canarsie Pier—*locale* NY-2
Canarsie Pol—*island* NY-2
Canarway Gulch—*valley* MT-8
Canary—*locale* OR-9
Canary—*locale* TX-5
Canary Bird Peak—*summit* MT-8
Canary Canyon—*valley* ID-8
Canary Cottage Golf Course—*other* NJ-2
Canary Creek—*stream* DE-2
Canary Creek—*stream* ID-8
Canary Creek—*stream* OK-5
Canary Ditch—*canal* IN-6
Canary Grove Draw—*valley* WY-8
Canary-Hartnett House—*hist pl* MA-1
Canary Island—*island* MA-1
Canary Island—*island* NY-2
Canary Lake—*lake* MN-6
Canary Lake (historical)—*lake* IA-7
Canary Lake Sch—*school* IA-7
Canary Pond—*lake* NY-2
Canarys Airp—*airport* IN-6
*Canary Spring* CA-9
Canary Spring—*spring* CA-9
Canary Tank—*reservoir* AZ-5
*Canary Well* AZ-5
Canary Well—*well* AZ-5
**Canas**—*pop pl* (2) PR-3
Canas Agrias Lateral—*canal* TX-5
*Canasauga Post Office* TN-4
Canasawacta Creek—*stream* NY-2
Canas (Barrio)—*fmr MCD* PR-3
Cana Sch—*school* TX-5
**Canaseraga**—*pop pl* NY-2
Canaseraga Canal—*canal* NY-2
Canaseraga Creek—*stream* (2) NY-2
Canas Island—*island* AK-9
**Canastota**—*pop pl* NY-2
Canastota Creek—*stream* NY-2
Canastota Methodist Church—*hist pl* NY-2
Canastota Public Library—*hist pl* NY-2
Canastota Rsvr—*reservoir* NY-2
Canas Urbano (Barrio)—*fmr MCD* PR-3
Canathan Cem—*cemetery* AL-4
Canatoga Creek—*stream* NY-2
*Canaumet Neck* MA-1
*Canaun* FM-9
Canavan Bench—*bench* MT-8
Canavan Creek—*stream* IL-6
Canavan Sch—*school* OH-6
*Canavan Slough* IL-6
Canavarro, Georges de S., House—*hist pl* HI-9
Canaveral, Cape—*cape* FL-3
**Canaveral Acres (subdivision)**—*pop pl* FL-3
Canaveral Barge Canal—*canal* FL-3
**Canaveral Beach**—*pop pl* FL-3
Canaveral Bight—*bay* FL-3
**Canaveral Harbor**—*pop pl* FL-3
Canaveral Harbor Range Front Light—*locale* FL-3
Canaveral Natl Seashore—*park* FL-3
Canaveral Peninsula—*cape* FL-3
Canaveral Plaza (Shop Ctr)—*locale* FL-3
**Canaveral Port Unit**—*pop pl* FL-3
*Canaville Township* KS-7
Canawacta Creek—*stream* PA-2
*Canawai Creek* WA-9
*Canawatta Creek* PA-2
**Canawaugus**—*pop pl* NY-2
Canaway Creek—*stream* VA-3
Canaway Gulf—*valley* NY-2
Canaz Field—*area* AL-4
Canbeal—*locale* LA-4
Canboro Sch—*school* MI-6
Canby—*locale* KY-4
Canby—*locale* WA-9
**Canby**—*pop pl* CA-9
**Canby**—*pop pl* IA-7
**Canby**—*pop pl* MN-6
**Canby**—*pop pl* NC-3
**Canby**—*pop pl* OR-9
Canby Bay—*other* CA-9
Canby Bridge—*bridge* CA-9
Canby (CCD)—*cens area* OR-9
Canby Ch—*church* PA-2
Canby Commercial Hist Dist—*hist pl* MN-6
*Canby Creek* MN-6
Canby Creek—*stream* MN-6
Canby Cross—*locale* CA-9
Canby Ferry—*locale* OR-9
Canby Hill—*summit* KY-4
**Canby Hills**—*pop pl* TN-4
Canby (historical P.O.)—*locale* IA-7
Canby Mountains—*range* OR-9
Canby Mtn—*summit* CO-8
Canby Park—*park* DE-2
**Canby Park Estates**—*pop pl* DE-2
Canby Ranch—*locale* AZ-5
Canby Sch—*school* MI-6
*Canbys Ferry* PA-2
Cance, John, F., House—*hist pl* WI-6
Cance Hill—*summit* NY-2
Cancer Hill—*summit* ME-1
Cancer Spring—*spring* NV-8
*Cancharda* AL-4
*Canchardie* AL-4
*Canchatte* FL-3
**Cancienne**—*pop pl* LA-4
Cancienne Canal—*canal* LA-4
Can Creek—*stream* AK-9
Can Creek—*stream* (2) ID-8
Can Creek—*stream* MT-8
Can Creek—*stream* OK-5
Can Creek—*stream* TX-5
Cancross Creek—*stream* NY-2
*Cancy Creek* TX-5
Candado Windmill—*locale* TX-5
*Candajarago Lake* NY-2
C and A Lake—*reservoir* MO-7
Candalaria Park—*park* OR-9
Candalaria Sch—*school* OR-9
**C and C Beach**—*pop pl* IN-6
C and D Mine—*mine* MT-8
Candee Rsvr—*reservoir* CT-1
Candees Pond—*lake* CT-1
C and El Rsvr—*reservoir* IL-6
**Candelaria**—*pop pl* TX-5
**Candelaria**—*pop pl* (2) PR-3
Candelaria (Barrio)—*fmr MCD* (3) PR-3
Candelaria Cem—*cemetery* NV-8
Candelaria Hill—*summit* TX-5
Candelaria Hills—*summit* NV-8
Candelaria Junction (Site)—*locale* NV-8
Candelaria Lake—*lake* TX-5
Candelaria Mtn—*summit* NV-8
Candelaria Pipeline—*locale* NV-8
Candelaria Place—*locale* NM-5
Candelaria Pueblo—*hist pl* NM-5
Candelaria (Site)—*locale* NV-8
Candelaria Spring—*spring* AZ-5
Candelaria Waterhole—*lake* NM-5
Candelerio Peak—*summit* AZ-5
Candelero Abajo (Barrio)—*fmr MCD* PR-3
Candelero Arriba—*CDP* PR-3
Candelero Arriba (Barrio)—*fmr MCD* PR-3
**Candelglo Village**—*pop pl* IN-6
**Candero (subdivision)**—*pop pl* NC-3
C and F Ranch Dam—*dam* SD-7
**C and G Estates Subdivision**—*pop pl* UT-8
**Candia**—*pop pl* NH-1
*Candia Depot* NH-1
**Candia Four Corners**—*pop pl* NH-1
Candiana Channel—*channel* OR-9
Candiani Bar—*bar* OR-9
**Candia (Town of)**—*pop pl* NH-1
**Candia Village**—*pop pl* NH-1
Candido Tank—*reservoir* (2) NM-5
Candido Tank—*reservoir* TX-5
Candies Creek—*stream* TN-4
Candies Creek Ch—*church* TN-4
Candies Creek Company—*cemetery* TN-4
Candies Creek Ridge—*ridge* TN-4
Candies Creek Valley—*valley* TN-4
Candies Creek Wildlife Mngmt Area—*park* TN-4
Candiff Creek—*stream* NC-3
Candilia Well—*well* TX-5
Candilla Canyon—*valley* TX-5
Candilla Creek—*stream* TX-5
Candil Rantano—*basin* PR-3
C and J Holiness Ch—*church* AL-4
C and J Shaft—*mine* AZ-5
C And K Mine—*mine* CA-9
Candland Canyon—*valley* UT-8
Candland Mtn—*summit* UT-8
Candland Spring—*spring* UT-8
**Candle**—*pop pl* AK-9
**Candlebrook**—*pop pl* PA-2
Candlebrook Sch—*school* PA-2
*Candle Creek* OR-9
Candle Creek—*stream* (2) AK-9
Candle Creek—*stream* ID-8
Candle Creek—*stream* OR-9
Candle Creek Campground—*park* OR-9
Candle Ditch—*canal* AK-9
**Candleglo Village**—*pop pl* IN-6
Candle Gulch—*valley* MT-8
Candle Hill—*summit* MA-1
Candle Hills—*other* AK-9
Candle Island—*island* AK-9
Candle Landing—*locale* AK-9
Candlelight Park—*park* OR-9
Candlelight Park—*park* TX-5
**Candlelight Terrace (subdivision)**—*pop pl* AL-4
*Candle Light Village (Trailer Park)* IN-6
**Candlelite Corner Subdivision**—*pop pl* UT-8
Candle Mtn—*summit* MT-8
Candle of Hope Sch—*school* FL-3
Candle Placer—*mine* AK-9
**Candler**—*pop pl* FL-3
**Candler**—*pop pl* GA-3
**Candler**—*pop pl* NC-3
Candler Bldg—*hist pl* GA-3
Candler Bldg—*hist pl* NY-2
Candler Branch—*stream* AL-4
Candler Branch—*stream* GA-3
Candler Cem—*cemetery* OH-6
Candler Cem—*cemetery* (2) VA-3
Candler Chapel Cem—*cemetery* MS-4
Candler Cottage—*hist pl* MA-1
**Candler (County)**—*pop pl* GA-3
Candler County Courthouse—*hist pl* GA-3
Candler Creek—*stream* GA-3
**Candler Heights**—*pop pl* NC-3
Candler Hosp—*hospital* GA-3
Candle Ridge Ch—*church* KY-4
Candler Knob—*summit* NC-3
Candler Lake—*lake* AR-4
Candler Lake—*reservoir* GA-3
Candler Lookout Tower—*tower* FL-3
Candler-McAfee—*CDP* GA-3
Candler Memorial United Methodist Ch—*church* TN-4
Candler Mtn—*summit* AL-4
Candler Mtn—*summit* VA-3
Candler Park Hist Dist—*hist pl* GA-3
Candler Sch—*school* NC-3
Candlers Chapel—*church* MS-4
*Candlers Chapel Baptist Ch* MS-4
Candler Street Sch—*hist pl* GA-3
Candler Street Sch—*school* GA-3
Candler Tank—*reservoir* (2) NM-5
**Candleset Cove**—*pop pl* CT-1
Candlestand—*summit* AL-4
*Candlestand Caves* AL-4
Candlestick Cove Sch—*school* CA-9
Candlestick Creek—*stream* AR-4
Candlestick Knob—*summit* AR-4
**Candlestick Park**—*pop pl* MS-4
**Candlestick Park Subdivision**—*pop pl* UT-8
Candlestick Point—*cape* AK-9
Candlestick Point—*cape* CA-9
Candlestick Ridge—*ridge* CA-9
Candlestick Shop Ctr—*locale* MS-4
*Candlestick Spire* UT-8
Candlestick Tower—*pillar* UT-8
Candlestick Tower—*summit* UT-8
Candleview Ridge—*ridge* CT-1
**Candlewax**—*pop pl* VA-3
**Candlewicke (subdivision)**—*pop pl* DE-2
**Candlewood**—*pop pl* AR-4
**Candlewood**—*pop pl* NJ-2
Candlewood, Lake—*reservoir* CT-1
Candlewood Cove—*cave* CT-1
Candlewood Country Club—*other* CA-9
Candlewood Dam—*dam* TN-4
**Candlewood Estates (Trailer Park)**—*pop pl* IL-6
Candlewood Golf Club—*locale* MA-1
**Candlewood Hill**—*pop pl* (2) CT-1
Candlewood Hill—*summit* CT-1
Candlewood Hill—*summit* MA-1
Candlewood Hill—*summit* NH-1
Candlewood Hill—*summit* NY-2
Candlewood Hill Brook—*stream* CT-1
Candlewood Isle—*island* CT-1
**Candlewood Isle**—*pop pl* CT-1
Candlewood JHS—*school* NY-2
**Candlewood Knolls**—*pop pl* CT-1
*Candlewood Lake* CT-1
Candlewood Lake—*reservoir* TN-4
**Candlewood Lake Club**—*pop pl* CT-1
**Candlewood Lake Estates**—*pop pl* CT-1
Candlewood Ledge—*cliff* CT-1
Candlewood Lookout Tower—*locale* CT-1
Candlewood Mtn—*summit* CT-1
**Candlewood Orchards**—*pop pl* CT-1
**Candlewood Park**—*pop pl* MD-2
**Candlewood Pines**—*pop pl* CT-1
Candlewood Point—*locale* CT-1
**Candlewood Shores**—*pop pl* CT-1
Candlewood Springs—*locale* CT-1
**Candlewood (subdivision)**—*pop pl* AL-4
**Candlewood (subdivision)**—*pop pl* NC-3
Candlewood Trail—*trail* CT-1
Candlewood Trails—*locale* CT-1
**Candlewyck**—*pop pl* NJ-2
**Candlewyck (subdivision)**—*pop pl* TN-4
C And M East Farm Dam—*dam* TN-4
C And M East Farm Pond—*reservoir* TN-4
C And M Junction—*locale* PA-2
C and M Ranch—*locale* NV-8
C and M Ranch—*locale* NM-5
**Cando**—*pop pl* ND-7
Cando Cem—*cemetery* ND-7
Candock Ch—*church* MO-7
Candock Sch (abandoned)—*school* MO-7
C And O Hosp—*hospital* VA-3
Cando Municipal Airp—*airport* ND-7
Candon Ranch—*locale* CO-8
Candor—*locale* PA-2
**Candor**—*pop pl* NY-2
**Candor**—*pop pl* NC-3
Candor Cem—*cemetery* IL-6
Candor Cem—*cemetery* NC-3
Candor City Reservoir Dam—*dam* NC-3
Candor City Rsvr—*reservoir* NC-3
Candor Elem Sch—*school* NC-3
Candor Hill—*summit* NY-2
Candor Lake—*lake* MN-6
**Candor (Town of)**—*pop pl* NY-2
**Candor (Township of)**—*pop pl* MN-6
Cando Sch—*school* KY-4
**Cando Township**—*pop pl* ND-7
C and T Helistop—*airport* NJ-2
C and U Shop Ctr—*locale* FL-3
*Candutchkee Ridge* AL-4
Candy, Mount—*summit* CO-8
Candy Bayou—*gut* LA-4
Candy Branch—*stream* (2) KY-4
Candy Branch—*stream* (2) SC-3
Candy Brook—*stream* IN-6
Candy Bucket Spring—*spring* CA-9
Candy Cem—*cemetery* WV-2
Candy Corners—*locale* WI-6
*Candy Cove* AL-4
*Candy Creek* IN-6
Candy Creek—*stream* AR-4
Candy Creek—*stream* MS-4
Candy Creek—*stream* MO-7
Candy Creek—*stream* NC-3
Candy Creek—*stream* OK-5
Candy Creek—*stream* TN-4
Candy Creek—*stream* (2) WA-9
Candy Creek Dock—*locale* TN-4
Candy Creek Sch (historical)—*school* TN-4
Candy Gulch—*valley* ID-8
*Candy Hill* MS-4
Candy Hill Cem—*cemetery* MS-4
Candy Hollow—*valley* MO-7
Candy House Sch—*school* FL-3
Candy Island—*island* FL-3
Candy Island—*island* VA-3
Candy Kitchen—*locale* NM-5
Candy Lake—*lake* LA-4
Candy Lake—*lake* MN-6

**Candyland Estates**—pop pl TN-4
Candy Landing AL-4
Candy Lane Sch—school OR-9
Candy Mesa—summit NM-5
Candy Mink Creek—stream OK-5
Candy Mink Park—park OK-5
Candy Mtn—summit CA-9
Candy Mtn—summit OK-5
Candy Mtn—summit WA-9
Candy Run—stream OH-6
Candy Run Ch—church OH-6
Candy Run Tabernacle—church OH-6
Candys Chapel—church SC-3
Candys Landing—locale AL-4
**Candy Town**—pop pl OH-6
Cane NC-3
Cane—locale AZ-5
Cane—locale NC-3
Cane—locale VI-3
**Cane**—pop pl FL-3
Cane, Bayou—stream (2) LA-4
**Caneadea**—pop pl NY-2
Caneadea Creek—stream NY-2
Caneadea Dam—dam NY-2
**Caneadea (Town of)**—pop pl NY-2
Cane Bay—basin SC-3
**Canebay**—pop pl VI-3
Cane Bay—stream SC-3
Cane Bay—swamp SC-3
Cane Bayou LA-4
Cane Bayou—gut (3) LA-4
Cane Bayou—gut TX-5
Cane Bayou—stream (3) LA-4
Cane Bayou—stream (2) MS-4
Cane Bay Sch—school SC-3
Cane Beds—locale AZ-5
Cane Bend—bend LA-4
Cane Bluff—cliff MO-7
Cane Bottom—bend MO-7
Cane Bottom—bend NC-3
Cane Bottom Bluff—cliff AR-4
Cane Bottom Hollow—valley MO-7
Cane Brake LA-4
Canebrake—hist pl LA-4
Cane Brake—locale NC-3
**Canebrake**—pop pl CA-9
**Canebrake**—pop pl LA-4
**Canebrake**—pop pl WV-2
Canebrake Agricultural Experimental Station (historical)—locale AL-4
Canebrake Branch—stream NC-3
Canebrake Branch—stream SC-3
Canebrake Branch—stream TN-4
Canebrake Branch—stream WV-2
Canebrake Canyon—valley CA-9
Canebrake Creek—stream CA-9
Cane Brake Creek—stream LA-4
Canebrake Flat—flat CA-9
Canebrake Hollow—valley VA-3
Canebrake Hollow—valley WV-2
Canebrake Island—island FL-3
Canebrake Mtn—summit (2) TN-4
Canebrake Plantation—locale LA-4
Canebrake Ridge—ridge NC-3
Canebrake Ridge—ridge TN-4
Canebrake Sch—school PA-2
**Canebrake (subdivision)**—pop pl AL-4
Canebrake Wash—stream CA-9
Cane Branch VA-3
Cane Branch—gut SC-3
**Cane Branch**—pop pl NC-3
Cane Branch—stream AR-4
Cane Branch—stream GA-3
Cane Branch—stream IN-6
Cane Branch—stream IA-7
Cane Branch—stream (12) KY-4
Cane Branch—stream MS-4
Cane Branch—stream (4) NC-3
Cane Branch—stream (4) SC-3
Cane Branch—stream (5) TN-4
Cane Branch—stream (3) TX-5
Cane Branch—stream (3) VA-3
Cane Branch—stream (3) WV-2
Cane Branch Ch—church (2) SC-3
Cane Branch Ch—church TN-4
Cane Branch Ch—church WV-2
Cane Branch Hills—range AR-4
Cane Branch Sch—school AR-4
Canebreak Branch—stream NC-3
Cane Break Bridges—bridge NC-3
Canebreak Canyon AZ-5
Cane Break Canyon—valley AZ-5
Cane Break Island—island GA-3
Cane Cairn—locale AZ-5
Cane Camp Branch—stream KY-4
Cane Canyon UT-8
Cane Canyon—valley AZ-5
Cane Canyon—valley (2) CA-9
Cane Canyon—valley UT-8
Cane Cave—cave AL-4
Cane Corral—locale AZ-5
Cane Cove ME-1
Cane Creek AL-4
Cane Creek AZ-5
Cane Creek GA-3
Cane Creek MS-4
Cane Creek NV-8
Cane Creek NC-3
Cane Creek OK-5
Cane Creek TN-4
Cane Creek UT-8
Cane Creek VA-3
Cane Creek—gut SC-3
Cane Creek—locale GA-3
Cane Creek—locale KY-4
**Cane Creek**—pop pl (2) AL-4
**Cane Creek**—pop pl AR-4
**Cane Creek**—pop pl KY-4
**Cane Creek**—pop pl NC-3
**Cane Creek**—pop pl TN-4
Cane Creek—stream (26) AL-4
Cane Creek—stream AK-9
Cane Creek—stream (10) AR-4
Cane Creek—stream CA-9
Cane Creek—stream FL-3
Cane Creek—stream (7) GA-3
Cane Creek—stream ID-8
Cane Creek—stream (3) IL-6
Cane Creek—stream IN-6
Cane Creek—stream KS-7
Cane Creek—stream (13) KY-4
Cane Creek—stream (2) LA-4
Cane Creek—stream MN-6
Cane Creek—stream (13) MS-4
Cane Creek—stream (7) MO-7
Cane Creek—stream (17) NC-3
Cane Creek—stream (4) OK-5
Cane Creek—stream OR-9
Cane Creek—stream (8) SC-3
Cane Creek—stream SD-7
Cane Creek—stream (30) TN-4
Cane Creek—stream TX-5
Cane Creek—stream UT-8
Cane Creek—stream (4) VA-3
Cane Creek Baptist Ch—church TN-4
Cane Creek Baptist Church MS-4
Cane Creek Branch—stream TN-4
Cane Creek Cem—cemetery AR-4
Cane Creek Cem—cemetery GA-3
Cane Creek Cem—cemetery KY 4
Cane Creek Cem—cemetery MO-7
Cane Creek Cem—cemetery NC-3
Cane Creek Cem—cemetery SC-3
Cane Creek Cem—cemetery (2) TN-4
Cane Creek Ch AL-4
Cane Creek Ch—church (3) AL-4
Cane Creek Ch—church (2) GA-3
Cane Creek Ch—church IN-6
Cane Creek Ch—church (4) KY-4
Cane Creek Ch—church (3) MO-7
Cane Creek Ch—church (6) NC-3
Cane Creek Ch—church OK-5
Cane Creek Ch—church (6) TN-4
Cane Creek Ch—church VA-3
Cane Creek Ch (historical)—church TN-4
Cane Creek Covered Bridge (historical)—bridge AL-4
Cane Creek Cutoff—channel MS-4
Cane Creek Dam Number Fifteen—dam TN-4
Cane Creek Dam Number Nine—dam TN-4
Cane Creek Dam Number Nineteen—dam TN-4
Cane Creek Ditch—canal AR-4
Cane Creek Ditch—canal MO-7
Cane Creek Dock—locale TN-4
Cane Creek Elementary School AL-4
Cane Creek Falls—falls GA-3
Cane Creek Falls—falls TN-4
Cane Creek Gap—gap GA-3
Cane Creek Gap—gap NC-3
Cane Creek Gap Ch—church KY-4
Cane Creek (historical)—locale AL-4
**Cane Creek (historical)**—pop pl TN-4
Cane Creek Islands—island GA-3
Cane Creek Lake—reservoir NC-3
Cane Creek Lake—reservoir TN-4
Cane Creek Lake Dam—dam NC-3
Cane Creek Lake Number Fifteen—reservoir TN-4
Cane Creek Lake Number Nine—reservoir TN-4
Cane Creek Lake Number Nineteen—reservoir TN-4
Cane Creek Mtn—summit (4) NC-3
Cane Creek Mtn—summit TN-4
Cane Creek Number Five Dam—dam TN-4
Cane Creek Number Five Lake—reservoir TN-4
Cane Creek Number Three Dam—dam TN-4
Cane Creek Number Three Lake—reservoir TN-4
Cane Creek Number Twenty-two Dam—dam TN-4
Cane Creek Number Twenty-two Lake—reservoir TN-4
Cane Creek Number 2 Mine (underground)—mine AL-4
Cane Creek Park—park NC-3
Cane Creek Park—park TN-4
Cane Creek P.O. AL-4
Cane Creek Post Office (historical)—building TN-4
Cane Creek Saltpeter Cave—cave TN-4
Cane Creek Sch—school AL-4
Cane Creek Sch—school IN-6
Cane Creek Sch—school KY-4
Cane Creek Sch—school NC-3
Cane Creek Sch—school TN-4
Cane Creek Sch—school VA-3
Cane Creek Sch (historical)—school (2) MO-7
Cane Creek Sch (historical)—school TN-4
Cane Creek Township—civil MO-7
Cane Creek (Township of)—fmr MCD (2) AR-4
Cane Creek (Township of)—fmr MCD NC-3
Cane Creek Watershed Dam Fourteen A—dam TN-4
Canedy, Squire William B., House—hist pl MA-1
Canedy Gap—gap NC-3
Canedy Mtn—summit NC-3
**Canedys Corner**—pop pl MA-1
Caneel Bay—bay VI-3
Caneel Bay Plantation—locale VI-3
Caneel Harbor Boat Dock TN-4
Caneel Hill—summit VI-3
Caneer Hollow—valley TN-4
Canefield Creek AL-4
Canefield Hollow UT-8
Canefield Plantation (historical)—locale AL-4
Canefield Tunnel AL-4
Cane Ford—locale TN-4
Cane Fork IN-6
**Cane Fork**—pop pl WV-2
Cane Fork—stream (5) KY-4
Cane Fork—stream (2) WV-2
Cane Fork Creek AL-4
Cane Fork Sch—school WV-2
Cane Fork Yards—locale WV-2
Cane Gall—swamp SC-3
Cane Gap—gap GA-3
Cane Gap—gap KY-4
Cane Gap—gap TN-4
Cane Gap—gap VA-3
Cane Garden—locale VI-3
Canegarden Bay—bay VI-3
Cane Green Bottom—basin IN-6
Cane Gully Branch—stream SC-3
Cane Hammock—island FL-3
**Canehill**—pop pl AR-4
**Cane Hill**—pop pl MO-7
Cane Hill—summit AR-4
Cane Hill—summit LA-4
Canehill Cemetery—hist pl AR-4
Canehill College Bldg—hist pl AR-4
Cane Hill Sch—school IL-6
Cane Hill Sch (abandoned)—school MO-7
Cane Hill (Township of)—fmr MCD AR-4
Cane Hollow UT-8
Cane Hollow—valley AL-4
Cane Hollow—valley AR-4
Cane Hollow—valley IN-6
Cane Hollow—valley KY-4
Cane Hollow—valley (4) MO-7
Cane Hollow—valley (7) TN-4
Cane Hollow Branch—stream TN-4
Cane Island AL-4
Cane Island—flat AR-4
Cane Island—island (2) AR-4
Cane Island—island FL-3
Cane Island—island KY-4
Cane Island—island LA-4
Cane Island—island (4) SC-3
Cane Island—island (2) TN-4
Cane Island Branch—stream TX-5
Cane Island (historical)—island (2) TN-4
Cane Islands—island NC-3
Cane Island Slough—gut AR-4
Cane Island Slough Ditch—canal AR-4
Canejo Windmill—locale TX-5
Cane Junction—locale TX-5
Canel LA-4
Canela AZ-5
Canela Hills AZ-5
Canela Island TX-5
Cane Lake ND-7
Cane Lake—lake AR-4
Cane Lake—lake (3) MS-4
Cane Lake—lake NE-7
Cane Lake—lake TX-5
Cane Lake Church MS-4
Cane Lake Dam—dam MS-4
**Caneland**—pop pl LA-4
Cane Lick Branch—stream TN-4
Canello Windmill—locale TX-5
Canelo—locale AZ-5
Canelo Hills—summit AZ-5
Canelo Hills Ranch—locale AZ-5
Canelo Lake—lake TX-5
Canelo Oil Field—oilfield TX-5
Canelo Pass—gap AZ-5
Canelo Ranger Station—locale AZ-5
**Canemah**—pop pl OR-9
Canemah Hist Dist—hist pl OR-9
Canema (historical)—locale KS-7
Cane Meadow—flat CA-9
Cane Mill Branch—stream LA-4
Cane Mill Branch—stream MS-4
Cane Mill Hammock—island FL-3
Canemount—hist pl MS-4
Cane Mountain CA-9
Cane Mountains NC-3
Canemount Plantation (historical)—locale MS-4
Cane Mtn—summit NC-3
Cane Mtn—summit SC-3
Cane Mtn—summit TN-4
Cane Patch—locale FL-3
**Cane Patch**—pop pl VA-3
Canepatch Cem—cemetery VA-3
Cane Patch Ch—church VA-3
Cane Patch Creek—stream GA-3
Canepatch Creek—stream VA-3
Cane Patch Hollow—valley TN-4
Cane Patch Island—island GA-3
Cane Patch Ridge—ridge MO-7
Canepatch Ridge—ridge NC-3
Canepatch Swamp—swamp SC-3
Canepatch Swash—beach SC-3
Cane Peak—summit CA-9
Cane P. O. (historical)—locale AL-4
Cane Pond—bay LA-4
Cane Pond—lake LA-4
Cane Pond—lake TX-5
Cane Pond Branch—stream SC-3
Canerday Branch—stream AL-4
Canerday Cem—cemetery AL-4
Cane Ridge MS-4
Cane Ridge TN-4
Cane Ridge—ridge AZ-5
Cane Ridge—ridge IN-6
Cane Ridge—ridge KY-4
Cane Ridge—ridge (2) LA-4
Cane Ridge—ridge (2) MO-7
Cane Ridge—ridge OH-6
Cane Ridge—ridge TN-4
Cane Ridge—uninc pl TN-4
Cane Ridge Ch—church (2) TN-4
Cane Ridge Ch (historical)—church MS-4
Cane Ridge Ch (historical)—church TN-4
Cane Ridge Ch Number 1—church LA-4
Cane Ridge Ch Number 2—church LA-4
Cane Ridge Creek—stream KY-4
Cane Ridge Cumberland Presbyterian Church—hist pl TN-4
**Caneridge (historical)**—pop pl TN-4
Cane Ridge Meetinghouse—church KY-4
Cane Ridge Post Office TN-4
Caneridge Post Office (historical)—building TN-4
Cane Ridge Sch (historical)—school (2) TN-4
Cane Ridge Slough—gut LA-4
Cane River—stream LA-4
Cane River—stream NC-3
Cane River Bridge—bridge LA-4
Cane River Ch—church NC-3
Cane River Gap—gap NC-3
Cane River Lake—lake LA-4
**Cane River (Post Office)**—pop pl NC-3
Cane River (Township of)—fmr MCD NC-3
Caner Lakes—lake MI-6
Cane Run IN-6
Cane Run WV-2
Cane Run—stream (2) IN-6
Cane Run—stream (14) KY-4
Cane Run Camp—locale KY-4
Cane Run Ch—church (3) KY-4
Cane Run Sch—school KY-4
Cane Savannah—locale SC-3
Cane Savannah Creek—stream SC-3
Cane Savannah Raceway—other SC-3
Canes Brook NH-1
Cane Sch (historical)—school AL-4
Cane Sch (historical)—school TN-4
Canes Cove—bay ME-1
Caneseed Hollow—valley TN-4
Canes Fork—stream AR-4
Cane Slough—stream TX-5
Cane Slough—swamp FL-3
Canes Point—cliff PA-2
Cane Spring AZ-5
Cane Spring CA-9
Cane Spring OR-9
Cane Spring UT-8
Cane Spring—spring (7) AZ-5
Cane Spring—spring (2) CA-9
Cane Spring—spring (3) NV-8
Cane Spring—spring (5) UT-8
Cane Spring Canyon AZ-5
Cane Spring Canyon UT-8
Cane Spring Canyon—valley (2) AZ-5
Cane Spring Canyon—valley NM-5
Cane Spring Desert—plain UT-8
Cane Spring Gulch OR-9
Cane Spring Mountain AZ-5
Cane Spring Peak NV-8
Cane Springs UT-8
Cane Springs—spring (4) AZ-5
Cane Springs—spring (3) NV-8
Cane Springs—spring (2) UT-8
Cane Springs Canyon UT-8
Cane Springs Mountain Tank—reservoir AZ-5
Cane Springs Mtn—summit AZ-5
Cane Springs Primitive Baptist Church—hist pl KY-4
Cane Springs Wash AZ-5
Cane Springs Wash—stream AZ-5
Cane Spring Wash AZ-5
Cane Spring Wash—stream AZ-5
Cane Spring Wash—stream NV-8
Cane Spring Well—well UT-8
Cane Sprint AZ-5
Canes Run—stream KY-4
Canesto Brook—stream MA-1
Canesto Hill—summit MA-1
Cane Swamp—swamp GA-3
Cane Swamp—swamp SC-3
Cane (Township of)—fmr MCD AR-4
Canetuck AL-4
Cane Tuck Hollow—valley AL-4
Canetuck (Township of)—fmr MCD NC-3
**Canet (Weldons)**—pop pl CA-9
Cane Valley—locale VI-3
**Cane Valley**—pop pl KY-4
Cane Valley—stream AZ-5
Cane Valley—valley AZ-5
Cane Valley—valley (2) UT-8
Cane Valley (CCD)—cens area KY-4
Cane Valley Cem—cemetery KY-4
Cane Valley Ch—church KY-4
Cane Valley Ditch—canal UT-8
Cane Valley Wash—stream AZ-5
Cane Valley Wash—valley UT-8
Canevin HS—school PA-2
Cane Wash AZ-5
Cane Wash UT-8
Cane Wash—valley AZ-5
Cane Wash—valley UT-8
Cane Water Pond—lake GA-3
Cane Well—well CA-9
Canewood Plantation (historical)—locale MS-4
Caney—locale (2) AR-4
Caney—locale LA-4
Caney—locale (2) TX-5
**Caney**—pop pl AR-4
**Caney**—pop pl KS-7
**Caney**—pop pl KY-4
**Caney**—pop pl OK-5
**Caney**—pop pl TX-5
**Caney**—pop pl VA-3
Caney Airpark—airport KS-7
Caney Bay—bay TX-5
Caney Bay—swamp (2) GA-3
Caney Bayou AR-4
Caney Bayou LA-4
Caney Bayou TX-5
Caney Bayou—gut AL-4
Caney Bayou—gut (4) LA-4
Caney Bayou—stream (6) AR-4
Caney Bayou—stream (8) LA-4
Caney Bayou—stream MS-4
Caney Bayou—swamp LA-4
Caney Bayou Fork—stream AR-4
Caney Bend Public Use Area—park OK-5
Caney Boggy Creek OK-5
Caney Boggy Creek—stream OK-5
Caney Bottom Creek—stream NC-3
Caney Bottoms—flat AR-4
Caney Branch AL-4
Caney Branch LA-4
**Caney Branch**—pop pl TN-4
Caney Branch—stream (13) AL-4
Caney Branch—stream (3) AR-4
Caney Branch—stream (4) FL-3
Caney Branch—stream (8) GA-3
Caney Branch—stream (2) IL-6
Caney Branch—stream (2) IN-6
Caney Branch—stream (14) KY-4
Caney Branch—stream (12) LA-4
Caney Branch—stream (7) MS-4
Caney Branch—stream MO-7
Caney Branch—stream (2) NC-3
Caney Branch—stream (4) SC-3
Caney Branch—stream (18) TN-4
Caney Branch—stream (8) TX-5
Caney Branch—stream VA-3
Caney Branch—stream (3) WV-2
Caney Branch—swamp (2) GA-3
Caney Branch Ch—church KY-4
Caney Branch Ch—church TN-4
Caney Branch Post Office (historical)—building TN-4
Caney Branch Ridge—ridge TN-4
Caney Branch Sch—school (2) SC-3
Caney Branch Sch (historical)—school TN-4
Caney Brook—stream NY-2
Caney Canal—canal AR-4
Caney Cave—cave AR-4
Caney Cem—cemetery AR-4
Caney Cem—cemetery IL-6
Caney Cem—cemetery KY-4
Caney Cem—cemetery OK-5
Caney Ch—church (2) AR-4
Caney Ch—church MS-4
Caney Ch—church (3) TX-5
Caney Ch—church WV-2
**Caney City**—pop pl TX-5
Caney Cove—valley AL-4
Caney Cove Creek—stream AL-4
Caney Creek AL-4
Caney Creek KS-7
Caney Creek KY-4
Caney Creek NC-3
Caney Creek OK-5
Caney Creek TN-4
Caney Creek TX-5
Caney Creek—locale FL-3
Caney Creek—locale TN-4
**Caney Creek**—pop pl KY-4
**Caney Creek**—pop pl MO-7
Caney Creek—stream (9) AL-4
Caney Creek—stream (47) AR-4
Caney Creek—stream (3) FL-3
Caney Creek—stream (6) GA-3
Caney Creek—stream (4) IL-6
Caney Creek—stream (3) IN-6
Caney Creek—stream (24) KY-4
Caney Creek—stream (22) LA-4
Caney Creek—stream MD-2
Caney Creek—stream (11) MS-4
Caney Creek—stream (5) MO-7
Caney Creek—stream (13) OK-5
Caney Creek—stream (10) TN-4
Caney Creek—stream (69) TX-5
Caney Creek—stream VA-3
Caney Creek—valley AR-4
Caney Creek Campground—locale TN-4
Caney Creek Cem—cemetery LA-4
Caney Creek Cem—cemetery TN-4
Caney Creek Ch—church (3) KY-4
Caney Creek Ch—church (2) TN-4
Caney Creek Ch—church TX-5
Caney Creek Ch (historical)—church TN-4
Caney Creek Ch of Christ Holiness—church MS-4
Caney Creek Ditch—canal AR-4
Caney Creek Dock—locale TN-4
Caney Creek Drainage Ditch—canal MS-4
Caney Creek Game Mngmt Area MS-4
Caney Creek Gulch—valley TN-4
Caney Creek Island (historical)—island TN-4
Caney Creek Rsvr—reservoir TX-5
Caney Creek Sch—school OK-5
Caney Creek Sch (historical)—school (2) AL-4
Caney Creek Sch (historical)—school TN-4
Caney Creek Shoals TN-4
Caney Creek Spring—spring TN-4
Caney Creek State Wildlife Mngmt Area—park MS-4
Caney Creek Trail—trail OK-5
Caney Creek Trail—trail TN-4
Caney Dam—dam MO-7
Caney Ditch—canal AR-4
Caney Falls—falls KY-4
Caney Flat Branch—stream FL-3
Caney Flats—flat GA-3
Caney Ford Ch—church TN-4
Caney Fork KY-4
Caney Fork TN-4
**Caney Fork**—pop pl TN-4
Caney Fork—stream (3) GA-3
Caney Fork—stream IN-6
Caney Fork—stream (19) KY-4
Caney Fork—stream MO-7
Caney Fork—stream (2) NC-3
Caney Fork—stream (3) TN-4
Caney Fork—stream VA-3
Caney Fork—stream WV-2
Caney Fork Baptist Church TN-4
Caney Fork Cem—cemetery TN-4
Caney Fork Ch—church KY-4
Caney Fork Ch—church MO-7
Caney Fork Ch—church NC-3
Caney Fork Ch—church (2) TN-4
Caney Fork Ch—church VA-3
Caney Fork Ch (historical)—church TN-4
Caney Fork Creek TN-4
Caney Fork Creek—stream KY-4
Caney Fork Creek—stream SC-3
Caney Fork Creek—stream (3) TN-4
Caney Fork Furnace (historical)—locale TN-4
Caney Fork Lake TN-4
Caney Fork Missionary Baptist Ch (historical)—church TN-4
Caney Fork Post Office (historical)—building TN-4
Caney Fork Ridge—ridge KY-4
Caney Fork River TN-4
**Caney Forks**—pop pl TN-4
Caney Fork Sch—school (2) KY-4
Caney Fork Sch—school NC-3
Caney Fork Sch (historical)—school TN-4
Caney Fork (Township of)—fmr MCD NC-3
Caney Gap—gap (2) KY-4
Caney Glade Bayou—stream LA-4
Caney Hammock—swamp FL-3
Caney Head—summit TX-5
Caneyhead Branch—stream AL-4
Caney Head Ch—church GA-3
Caney Head Creek—stream MS-4
Caney Head Sch (historical)—school MS-4
Caney High Top—summit TN-4
Caney Hill Ch—church OK-5
**Caney Hollow**—pop pl TN-4
Caney Hollow—valley (3) AL-4
Caney Hollow—valley (4) AR-4
Caney Hollow—valley KY-4
Caney Hollow—valley MS-4
Caney Hollow—valley MO-7
Caney Hollow—valley (14) TN-4
Caney Hollow—valley VA-3
CAney Hollow Cave—cave TN-4
Caney Hollow Creek—stream TN-4
Caney HS—school KS-7
Caney HS—school KY-4
Caney Island—island LA-4
Caney Island—island MN-6
Caney Island—island TN-4
Caney Island—island TX-5
Caney Island Branch—stream VA-3
Caney Junior Coll—school KY-4
Caney Knob—summit KY-4
Caney Knobs—summit TN-4
Caney Lake LA-4
Caney Lake—lake MS-4
Caney Lake—lake OK-5
Caney Lakes—reservoir LA-4
Caney Lead—ridge NC-3
Caney Lookout Tower—locale MO-7
Caney Marais Bend—bend AR-4
Caney Meadow—swamp NC-3
**Caney (Morris)**—pop pl AR-4
Caney Mountain State Game Ref—park MO-7
Caney Mountain Trail—trail OK-5
Caney Mtn NC-3
Caney Mtn—summit MO-7
Caney Mtn—summit NC-3
Caney Mtn—summit (2) OK-5
Caney Picnic Area—locale MO-7
Caney Picnic Ground MO-7
Caney Point—cape AR-4
Caney Point—cape TN-4
Caney Pond—swamp FL-3
**Caney Ridge**—pop pl OK-5
Caney Ridge—ridge (2) TN-4
Caney Ridge—ridge VA-3
Caney River—stream OK-5
Caney River Mtn NC-3
Caney River Park—park OK-5
Caney Sch—school KY-4
Caney Sch—school TX-5
Caney Sch (historical)—school AL-4
Caney Shoals—bar TN-4
Caney Siding—other KY-4
Caney Sinks—basin TN-4
Caney Slash—gut AR-4
Caney Slough—canal AR-4
Caney Slough—gut AL-4
Caney Slough—gut MO-7
Caney Slough—gut (2) TX-5
Caney Slough—stream (2) AR-4
Caney Slough—stream (2) MO-7
Caneyspring TN-4
**Caney Spring**—pop pl TN-4
Caney Spring—spring TN-4
Caney Spring Post Office TN-4
Caneyspring Post Office (historical)—building TN-4
Caney Springs TN-4
Caney Springs Post Office TN-4
Caney Springs Sch (historical)—school TN-4
Caney Springs United Methodist Ch—church TN-4
Caney Swamp—stream VA-3
Caney Swamp—swamp FL-3
Caney Swamp—swamp GA-3
**Caney Township**—pop pl KS-7
Caney (Township of)—fmr MCD (4) AR-4
Caney Tunnel—tunnel VA-3
Caney Valley—basin VA-3
**Caney Valley**—pop pl AR-4
**Caney Valley**—pop pl TN-4
Caney Valley—valley MD-2
Caney Valley—valley PA-2
Caney Valley—valley (3) TN-4
Caney Valley Branch—stream TN-4
Caney Valley Ch—church (2) AR-4
Caney Valley Knobs TN-4
Caney Valley Knobs—ridge TN-4
Caney Valley Sch—school PA-2
Caney Valley Sch (historical)—school TN-4
Caneyville KS-7
**Caneyville**—pop pl KY-4
Caneyville (CCD)—cens area KY-4
Caneyville Rsvr—reservoir KY-4
Caneyville Township—civil KS-7
Canez Wash—stream AZ-5
Canfield—locale WV-2
**Canfield**—pop pl AR-4
**Canfield**—pop pl CO-8
**Canfield**—pop pl IA-7
**Canfield**—pop pl OH-6
**Canfield**—pop pl WV-2
Canfield Ave Sch—school CA-9
**Canfield Beach**—pop pl MI-6
Canfield Branch—stream KY-4
Canfield Brook—stream NH-1
Canfield Brook—stream NY-2
Canfield Casino and Congress Park—hist pl NY-2
Canfield Cem—cemetery ID-8
Canfield Cem—cemetery IA-7
Canfield Cem—cemetery MI-6
Canfield Cem—cemetery NY-2
Canfield Cem—cemetery OK-5
Canfield Cem—cemetery SC-3
Canfield Cem—cemetery TN-4
Canfield Cem—cemetery (2) WV-2
Canfield Corners NY-2
Canfield Cove—bay NH-1
Canfield Creek—stream (2) MN-6
Canfield Creek—stream OR-9
Canfield Creek—stream PA-2
Canfield Creek—stream WY-8
Canfield Grove—woods CA-9
Canfield Gulch—valley OR-9
Canfield Gulch—valley WA-9
Canfield Hill—summit OR-9
Canfield (historical)—locale ND-7
Canfield Hollow—valley AR-4
Canfield Island—island CT-1
Canfield Lake—lake (2) MI-6
Canfield Lake—lake ND-7
Canfield Mine SD-7
Canfield Oil Field—oilfield KS-7
Canfield Park—park IA-7
**Canfield (Poe Run)**—pop pl WV-2
Canfield Portage—trail MN-6
Canfield Portage Bay—bay MN-6
Canfield Ranch—locale CA-9
Canfield Ranch Oil Field CA-9
Canfield Ridge—ridge MO-7
Canfield Run—stream PA-2
Canfield Sch—school CA-9
Canfield Sch (historical)—school PA-2
Canfields Corners NY-2
Canfield Sink AL-4
Canfield Spring—spring AZ-5
Canfield Spring—spring MN-6
**Canfield Township**—pop pl ND-7
**Canfield (Township of)**—pop pl OH-6
Cangrejo Arriba (Barrio)—fmr MCD PR-3
Canham Drain—canal MI-6
Canhawa River WV-2
Caniaco (Barrio)—fmr MCD PR-3

Caniadaraga Lake ... NY-2
Caniba Brook—stream ... ME-1
Canida Peak—summit ... ID-8
Canie Canal—canal ... MS-4
Canie Creek—stream ... MS-4
Canie Creek—stream ... NC-3
Caniehead Sch—school ... FL-3
Caniff Sch—school ... MA-1
Caniilon Hill—summit ... NM-5
Canille ... AZ-5
Canille Hills ... AZ-5
Canille Mountains ... AZ-5
Canille Sch—school ... AZ-5
Canim Creek—stream ... WA-9
Canina (historical)—locale ... KS-7
Canipa Creek—stream ... NM-5
Canipa Mesa—summit ... NM-5
Canipa Spring—spring ... NM-5
Canip Creek—stream ... KY-4
Canirco, Lake—lake ... AK-9
Canisius Coll—school ... NY-2
Canisius HS—school ... NY-2
Canistear Cem—cemetery ... NJ-2
Canistear Rsvr—reservoir ... NJ-2
Canisteo—locale ... MN-6
**Canisteo**—pop pl ... NY-2
Canisteo Center—locale ... NY-2
Canisteo District General Office Bldg—hist pl ... MN-6
Canisteo Mine—mine ... MN-6
Canisteo River—stream ... NY-2
Canisteo Rsvr—reservoir ... NY-2
**Canisteo (Town of)**—pop pl ... NY-2
**Canisteo (Township of)**—pop pl ... MN-6
**Canistota**—pop pl ... SD-7
Canistota Cem—cemetery ... SD-7
**Canistota Township**—pop pl ... SD-7
**Canjilon**—pop pl ... NM-5
Canjilon Cem—cemetery ... NM-5
Canjilon Creek—stream ... NM-5
Canjilon Creek Forest Camp—locale ... NM-5
Canjilon Lakes—lake ... NM-5
Canjilon Mountain Lookout Cabin—hist pl ... NM-5
Canjilon Mtn—summit ... NM-5
Can Knoll—summit ... UT-8
**Cankton**—pop pl ... LA-4
Cankton Gas Field—oilfield ... LA-4
Canley Lake—lake ... LA-4
Can Lot—summit ... TN-4
**Canmer**—pop pl ... KY-4
Canna ... MP-9
Canna Creek—stream ... MS-4
Cannaday Cem—cemetery ... WV-2
Cannaday Ch—church ... VA-3
Cannaday Gap—locale ... VA-3
Cannady—locale ... VA-3
Cannady Cem—cemetery ... AR-4
Cannady Hill—summit ... NY-2
Cannady Hollow—valley ... MO-7
Cannadys (Canadys) ... SC-3
Cannadys (RR name for Cannadys)—other ... SC-3
Cannan Cem—cemetery ... OH-6
Cannan Ch—church ... AL-4
Cannan Ch—church ... TX-5
Cannan Grove ... TN-4
Cannan Hill Baptist Ch—church ... AL-4
Cannan Oil Field—oilfield ... TX-5
Cannan Sch—school ... NV-8
Cann Cem—cemetery ... LA-4
Cann Creek—stream ... AL-4
Cann Creek—stream ... AK-9
Canne Ch—church ... LA-4
Cann-Edi-On Camp—locale ... PA-2
Cann-edi-on YWCA Camp ... PA-2
Cannekonkan ... DE-2
**Cannelburg**—pop pl ... IN-6
**Cannel City**—pop pl ... KY-4
Cannel City (CCD)—cens area ... KY-4
Cannel Coal Gap—gap ... KY-4
Cannel Coal Hollow—valley ... KY-4
Cannel Coal Hollow—valley ... WV-2
Cannell Creek—stream ... CA-9
Cannell Meadow—flat ... CA-9
Cannell Meadow Guard Station—locale ... CA-9
Cannell Meadow Trail—trail ... CA-9
Cannell Peak—summit ... CA-9
Cannelsburg ... IN-6
Cannel Tank—reservoir ... TX-5
**Cannelton**—pop pl ... IN-6
**Cannelton**—pop pl ... PA-2
**Cannelton**—pop pl ... WV-2
Cannelton Cotton Mills—hist pl ... IN-6
Cannelton Heights (2) ... IN-6
Cannelton Hist Dist—hist pl ... IN-6
Cannelton Locks and Dam—dam ... IN-6
Cannelton Locks And Dam—dam ... KY-4
**Cannelton Mine Junction**—pop pl ... WV-2
**Cannelville**—pop pl ... OH-6
Canner Hollow—valley ... AR-4
Canners Cem—cemetery ... TN-4
Cannery ... DE-2
**Cannery**—pop pl ... AK-9
Cannery Bay—bay ... AK-9
Cannery Cove—bay (3) ... AK-9
Cannery Creek—stream (3) ... AK-9
Cannery Hill—ridge ... OR-9
Cannery Hill—summit ... OR-9
Cannery Island—island ... OR-9
Cannery Lake—lake ... WA-9
Cannery Light—locale ... OR-9
Cannery Mtn—summit ... OR-9
Cannery Point—cape (4) ... AK-9
Cannery Rock—other ... AK-9
Cannery Row—locale ... CA-9
Cannery Slough—gut ... WA-9
Cannestow River ... MA-1
Canney Brook—stream ... NH-1
Canneystone Brook ... MA-1
Cann Hill—summit ... CO-8
Cannibal Canyon—valley ... CO-8
Cannibal Draw—valley ... TX-5
Cannibal Island—island ... CA-9
Cannibal Mtn—summit ... OR-9
Cannibal Peak ... OR-9
Cannibal Plateau ... CO-8
Cannibal Plateau—summit ... CO-8
**Canning**—pop pl ... SD-7
Canning, Mount—summit ... AK-9
Canning Creek—stream ... KS-7
Canning Creek Cove Rec Area—park ... KS-7
Canning Factory Branch—stream ... TN-4
Canninghouse Cove Marsh—swamp ... MD-2
Canning Kitchen Hollow—valley ... AR-4
Canning Ranch ... TX-5
Canning Ranch—locale ... WY-8
Canning River—stream ... AK-9
Cannings Creek—stream ... WA-9
Canning Site (21NR9)—hist pl ... MN-6
Canning Township—civil ... SD-7
Cannisnia Lake—lake ... LA-4
Cannisnia Lake Basin—basin ... LA-4
Cannistear Reservoir Dam Number One—dam ... NJ-2
Cannistear Reservoir Dam Number Two—dam ... NJ-2
Cannivan Gulch—valley ... MT-8
Canniwai Creek—stream ... WA-9
Canniwai Grange Hall—locale ... WA-9
Canniwai Valley—valley ... WA-9
Cann Memorial Ch—church ... NC-3
Cannochee River ... GA-3
Cannon ... NM-5
Cannon—locale ... CA-9
Cannon—locale ... KY-4
Cannon—locale ... OH-6
**Cannon**—pop pl ... DE-2
**Cannon**—pop pl ... MO-7
**Cannon**—pop pl ... NV-8
**Cannon**—pop pl ... NM-5
**Cannon**—pop pl ... TX-5
**Cannon**—pop pl ... VA-3
Cannon, Burton, House—hist pl ... MD-2
Cannon, Dr. William Austin, House—hist pl ... AZ-5
Cannon, George M., House—hist pl ... UT-8
Cannon, Lake—lake ... FL-3
Cannon, Mount—summit ... MT-8
Cannon, Tom, Mound—hist pl ... OH-6
Cannon Air Force Base—military ... NM-5
Cannon Air Force Base Rec Area—park ... NM-5
Cannon Airp (historical)—airport ... NC-3
**Cannon Ball**—pop pl ... ND-7
Cannonball Bay—bay ... MN-6
Cannonball Beach—beach ... CA-9
Cannonball Coulee—valley ... MT-8
Cannonball Creek—stream ... AK-9
Cannon Ball Creek—stream ... CA-9
Cannonball Creek—stream ... ID-8
Cannonball Creek—stream ... MT-8
Cannonball Creek—stream ... ND-7
Cannonball Creek—stream ... WA-9
Cannonball Cut—gap ... WY-8
Cannon Ball Flat—flat ... CA-9
Cannonball Gulch—valley ... MT-8
Cannonball Hollow—valley ... VA-3
Cannonball House—hist pl ... GA-3
Cannonball House—hist pl ... MD-2
Cannonball Island ... WA-9
Cannon Ball lake ... NJ-2
Cannonball Lake—lake ... NJ-2
Cannon Ball Memorial Congregational Cem—cemetery ... ND-7
Cannon Ball Mesa—summit ... CO-8
Cannonball Mountain ... ID-8
Cannon Ball Mtn—summit ... ID-8
Cannonball Mtn—summit ... ID-8
Cannonball Ranch—locale ... WY-8
Cannon Ball River ... ND-7
Cannonball River—stream ... ND-7
Cannon Balls, The—summit ... NH-1
Cannon Ball Spring—spring ... ID-8
**Cannon Ball Township**—pop pl ... ND-7
Cannonball Trail—trail ... NJ-2
Cannon Bay—bay ... FL-3
Cannon Bayou—stream ... LA-4
Cannon Beach—beach ... OR-9
**Cannon Beach**—pop pl ... OR-9
**Cannon Beach Junction**—pop pl ... OR-9
Cannon Beach Sch—school ... OR-9
Cannon Bend—bend ... TN-4
Cannonberry ... PA-2
Cannon Bldg—hist pl ... NY-2
Cannon Bluff Sch—school ... GA-3
Cannon Branch—stream (2) ... AL-4
Cannon Branch—stream ... FL-3
Cannon Branch—stream ... GA-3
Cannon Branch—stream ... MO-7
Cannon Branch—stream (2) ... NC-3
Cannon Branch—stream (3) ... TN-4
Cannon Branch—stream (2) ... VA-3
Cannon Branch—stream ... WI-6
Cannon Branch Cem—cemetery ... VA-3
Cannon Bridge—bridge ... SC-3
Cannon Bridge—bridge ... TN-4
Cannon Brook—stream ... NH-1
Cannon Brook—stream ... NY-2
Cannonburg ... PA-2
**Cannonburg**—pop pl ... LA-4
**Cannonburg**—pop pl ... MI-6
Cannon-Calloway House—hist pl ... TN-4
Cannon Canal ... LA-4
Cannon Canyon—valley ... CA-9
Cannon Canyon—valley ... OR-9
Cannon Canyon—valley ... UT-8
Cannon Cem—cemetery ... AL-4
Cannon Cem—cemetery ... LA-4
Cannon Cem—cemetery ... MI-6
Cannon Cem—cemetery ... MS-4
Cannon Cem—cemetery (3) ... MO-7
Cannon Cem—cemetery ... NC-3
Cannon Cem—cemetery ... OH-6
Cannon Cem—cemetery ... SC-3
Cannon Cem—cemetery (3) ... TN-4
Cannon Cem—cemetery (2) ... TX-5
Cannon Ch—church ... AR-4
Cannon Ch—church ... SC-3
Cannon City ... CA-9
**Cannon City**—pop pl ... MN-6
**Cannon City (Township of)**—pop pl ... MN-6
Cannon Corners—locale ... NY-2
**Cannon Corners**—pop pl ... NY-2
Cannon Country Club—other ... MN-6
**Cannon County**—pop pl ... TN-4
Cannon County HS—school ... TN-4
Cannon Creek ... MI-6
Cannon Creek ... WI-6
Cannon Creek ... WY-8
Cannon Creek—locale ... AR-4
Cannon Creek—locale ... TN-4
Cannon Creek—stream (2) ... AR-4
Cannon Creek—stream ... FL-3
Cannon Creek—stream (2) ... ID-8
Cannon Creek—stream ... KY-4
Cannon Creek—stream ... MO-7
Cannon Creek—stream ... MT-8
Cannon Creek—stream ... NC-3
Cannon Creek—stream ... SC-3
Cannon Creek—stream (2) ... TN-4
Cannon Creek—stream (4) ... TX-5
Cannon Creek—stream ... VA-3
Cannon Creek—stream ... WY-8
Cannon Creek Diversion—canal ... MO-7
Cannon Creek Lake—reservoir ... KY-4
Cannon Creek Post Office (historical)—building ... TN-4
Cannon Creek Swamp ... MI-6
Cannon Crossing—locale ... GA-3
Cannon Crossroads—locale ... NC-3
**Cannondale**—pop pl ... CT-1
Cannon Ditch—canal (2) ... CO-8
Cannon Ditch—canal ... IN-6
Cannon Drain—stream ... MI-6
Cannon Draw ... TX-5
**Cannon Falls**—pop pl ... MN-6
Cannon Falls Sch—hist pl ... MN-6
Cannon Falls (Township of)—civ div ... MN-6
Cannon Ferry—locale ... NC-3
Cannon Field—flat ... CA-9
Cannon Gap—gap ... NC-3
**Cannon Gate**—pop pl ... GA-3
Cannon-Goyer Ditch—canal ... IN-6
Cannon Grove Ch—church ... GA-3
Cannon Gulch ... CA-9
Cannon Gulch—valley ... CA-9
Cannon Gulch—valley ... ID-8
Cannon Gulch—valley (2) ... OR-9
Cannon Gully—valley (2) ... TX-5
Cannon High School ... NC-3
Cannon Hill—ridge ... PA-2
Cannon Hill—summit ... ME-1
Cannon Hill—summit (2) ... MA-1
Cannon Hill—summit ... NH-1
Cannon Hill—summit (2) ... ND-7
Cannon Hill—summit ... PA-2
Cannon Hill—summit ... TX-5
Cannon Hill—summit ... WV-2
Cannon Hill Park—park ... WA-9
Cannon Hills—summit ... NY-2
**Cannon Hills Subdivision**—pop pl ... UT-8
Cannon (historical)—locale ... MS-4
Cannon Hole Hollow—valley ... PA-2
Cannon Hole Trail—trail ... PA-2
Cannon Hollow—valley ... AL-4
Cannon Hollow—valley ... PA-2
Cannon Hollow—valley (3) ... TN-4
Cannon Homestead Cem—cemetery ... MS-4
Cannon House—hist pl ... MS-4
Cannon House Office Bldg—building ... DC-2
Cannon International Airport—airport ... NV-8
Cannon Island—island ... AK-9
Cannon Island—island ... FL-3
Cannon JHS—school ... NC-3
Cannon Knob—summit ... KY-4
Cannon Knob—summit ... TN-4
Cannon Lake ... AL-4
Cannon Lake ... TN-4
Cannon Lake—lake ... LA-4
Cannon Lake—lake (2) ... MN-6
Cannon Lake—lake ... MT-8
Cannon Lake—lake ... SC-3
Cannon Lake—lake ... TN-4
Cannon Lake—lake ... TX-5
**Cannon Lake**—pop pl ... MN-6
Cannon Lake—reservoir ... KY-4
Cannon Lake—reservoir ... TN-4
Cannon Lake Dam—dam ... MS-4
Cannon Lake Dam—dam ... TN-4
Cannon Lake Sch—school ... MN-6
Cannon-McDaniel House—hist pl ... GA-3
Cannon Memorial Park—cemetery ... SC-3
Cannon Mill Creek—stream ... AL-4
Cannon Mine—mine ... UT-8
**Cannon Mines**—pop pl ... MO-7
Cannon Mountains—range ... TX-5
Cannon Mtn—summit ... AL-4
Cannon Mtn—summit ... CO-8
Cannon Mtn—summit ... NH-1
Cannon Mtn—summit ... SC-3
Cannon Mtn—summit ... WA-9
Cannon Park—park ... IL-6
Cannon Park—park ... KS-7
Cannon Park—park ... NC-3
Cannon Park—park ... WI-6
Cannon Place Gap—gap ... TN-4
Cannon Playground—park ... WA-9
Cannon Point—cape (2) ... NY-2
Cannon Point Landing—locale ... MS-4
Cannon Pond—lake ... CT-1
Cannon Pond—lake (2) ... FL-3
Cannon Ranch—locale ... TX-5
Cannon Ridge—ridge ... TN-4
Cannon River—stream ... MN-6
Cannon River Camp—locale ... MN-6
Cannon River Cem—cemetery ... MN-6
Cannon River Ch—church ... MN-6
Cannon Rsvr—reservoir ... CA-9
**Cannon Run**—pop pl ... PA-2
**Cannon Run West**—pop pl ... PA-2
Cannons ... DE-2
Cannonsboro ... PA-2
Cannons Branch—stream ... GA-3
Cannonsburg ... PA-2
**Cannonsburg**—pop pl ... KY-4
**Cannonsburg**—pop pl ... MI-6
**Cannonsburg**—pop pl ... MS-4
Cannonsburg (CCD)—cens area ... KY-4
Cannonsburg Cem—cemetery ... MI-6
Cannonsburg Cem—cemetery ... OH-6
Cannonsburgh ... TN-4
Cannonsburg Post Office (historical)—building ... MS-4
Cannonsburg Sch—school ... KY-4
Cannonsburg State Game Area—park ... MI-6
**Cannons Camp Ground**—pop pl ... SC-3
Cannon Sch—school ... IL-6
Cannon Sch—school ... MS-4
Cannon Sch—school ... OR-9
Cannon Sch—school ... TN-4
Cannons Chapel—church ... KY-4
Cannon School (historical)—locale ... MO-7
Cannons Creek—locale ... OH-6
Cannons Creek—stream ... OH-6
Cannons Creek—stream ... SC-3
Cannons Creek Cem—cemetery ... SC-3
Cannons Creek Prosperity Ch—church ... SC-3
Cannons Ferry ... DE-2
Cannon's Ferry—hist pl ... DE-2
Cannon Site—hist pl ... GA-3
Cannons Lake—lake ... TX-5
Cannons Mill—locale ... KY-4
**Cannons Mills**—pop pl ... OH-6
Cannonsnap Creek—stream ... TX-5
Cannons Point—cape ... GA-3
Cannons Point—locale ... KY-4
Cannon Spring—spring ... KY-4
Cannon Spring—spring ... MO-7
Cannon Spring—spring ... OR-9
Cannon Spring—spring (2) ... TN-4
Cannon Spring Public Use Area—locale ... KY-4
Cannons Sch (historical)—school ... MS-4
Cannons Store (historical)—locale ... MS-4
Cannon Street Sch—school ... GA-3
**Cannon Subdivision**—pop pl ... TN-4
**Cannon Subdivision**—pop pl ... UT-8
Cannonsville Bridge—bridge ... NY-2
Cannonsville Dam—dam ... NY-2
Cannonsville Rsvr—reservoir ... NY-2
Cannon Swamp ... NC-3
Cannon Swamp—swamp ... GA-3
Cannon Swamp—swamp ... NC-3
Cannon Tank—reservoir ... CA-9
Cannon Town—locale ... FL-3
**Cannon (Township of)**—pop pl ... MI-6
**Cannon (Township of)**—pop pl ... MN-6
Cannon Valley—valley ... WI-6
Cannon Valley Sch—school ... WI-6
**Cannonville**—pop pl ... GA-3
**Cannonville**—pop pl ... MA-1
**Cannonville**—pop pl ... UT-8
Cannonville Cem—cemetery ... MN-6
Cannonville Cem—cemetery ... UT-8
Cannonville Ch—church ... GA-3
Cannonville Ch—church ... MN-6
Cannon Windmill—locale ... NM-5
**Cannon Woods (subdivision)**—pop pl ... NC-3
Cannor Creek ... OR-9
Cannouchee River ... GA-3
Canns Lake—reservoir ... NJ-2
Cannsville ... AL-4
Cano Aguas Frias—stream ... PR-3
Canoa Interchange—crossing ... AZ-5
Canoa Ranch—locale (2) ... AZ-5
Canoa RR Station—building ... AZ-5
Canoas Creek—stream (2) ... CA-9
Canoa Spring—spring ... AZ-5
Canoas Sch—school ... CA-9
Canoa Wash—stream ... AZ-5
Canoa Well—well ... AZ-5
Cano (Barrio)—fmr MCD ... PR-3
Canobie Lake—lake ... NH-1
**Canobie Lake**—pop pl ... NH-1
Canobie Lake Park—park ... NH-1
Cano Boqueron—gut ... PR-3
Cano Boquilla—stream ... PR-3
Canob Pond—lake ... RI-1
Cano Cabo Caribe—stream ... PR-3
Cano Campanero—stream ... PR-3
Cano Canyon—valley (2) ... NM-5
Cano Carrasco—stream ... PR-3
Canochee Creek ... GA-3
Canocico—other ... NM-5
Canocito—valley ... CO-8
Cano Corazones—gut ... PR-3
Cano Cruz—gut ... PR-3
Cano De Los Nachos—gut ... PR-3
Cano De Martin Pena—stream ... PR-3
Cano de Quebrada Catalina—stream ... PR-3
Cano De San Antonio—channel ... PR-3
Cano de San Fernando—stream ... PR-3
Cano de Santiago—valley ... PR-3
Cano de Santi Ponce—valley ... PR-3
Canodys Store—locale ... VA-3
Canoe—island ... WA-9
**Canoe**—pop pl ... AL-4
**Canoe**—pop pl ... IA-7
**Canoe**—pop pl ... KY-4
Canoe, Mount—summit ... NJ-2
Canoe Bay—bay ... AK-9
Canoe Bay—bay ... MI-6
Canoe Bayou—stream ... TX-5
Canoe Bay River—stream ... AK-9
Canoe Branch ... DE-2
Canoe Branch—stream ... AL-4
Canoe Branch—stream ... NC-3
Canoe Branch—stream (2) ... TN-4
Canoe Branch—stream ... VA-3
Canoe Branch Ferry (historical)—crossing ... TN-4
Canoe Brook—stream ... CT-1
Canoe Brook—stream ... ME-1
Canoe Brook—stream ... NJ-2
Canoe Brook—stream ... VT-1
Canoe Brook Dam—dam ... NJ-2
Canoe Brook Golf Course—other ... NJ-2
Canoe Brook Lake—lake ... CT-1
Canoe Brook Rsvr Number One—reservoir ... NJ-2
Canoe Brook Rsvr Number Two—reservoir ... NJ-2
Canoe Brook Sch—school ... CT-1
Canoe Camp—locale ... ID-8
Canoe Camp—locale ... PA-2
Canoe Camp Creek—stream ... PA-2
Canoe Cave ... AL-4
Canoe Cave—cave ... TN-4
Canoe (CCD)—cens area ... KY-4
Canoe Cem—cemetery ... AL-4
Cano Echevarria—valley ... PR-3
Canoe Cove—bay ... AK-9
Canoe Creek ... AL-4
Canoe Creek ... CA-9
Canoe Creek ... ID-8
Canoe Creek ... TX-5
Canoe Creek—canal ... FL-3
**Canoe Creek**—pop pl ... PA-2
Canoe Creek—stream ... AL-4
Canoe Creek—stream (3) ... AK-9
Canoe Creek—stream ... AR-4
Canoe Creek—stream ... CA-9
Canoe Creek—stream (3) ... FL-3
Canoe Creek—stream ... ID-8
Canoe Creek—stream ... IL-6
Canoe Creek—stream ... IA-7
Canoe Creek—stream (5) ... KY-4
Canoe Creek—stream (2) ... NC-3
Canoe Creek—stream (3) ... PA-2
Canoe Creek—stream (2) ... SC-3
Canoe Creek—stream ... TX-5
Canoe Creek—stream (2) ... WA-9
Canoe Creek Dam—dam ... PA-2
Canoe Creek Lake—reservoir ... AL-4
Canoe Creek Lake—reservoir ... PA-2
Canoe Creek Lookout Tower—tower ... FL-3
Canoe Creek Marina—locale ... AL-4
Canoe Creek Mountains—ridge ... AL-4
Canoe Creek Post Office (historical)—building ... PA-2
Canoe Creek Sch—school ... KY-4
Canoe Creek State Park—park ... PA-2
**Canoe Creek (Township of)**—pop pl ... IL-6
Canoe Creek Valley—valley ... AL-4
Canoedas Point—cape ... VA-3
Canoe Fork—stream (2) ... WV-2
Canoe Furnace—locale ... PA-2
Canoe Gap Run—stream ... PA-2
Canoe Grant Sch—school ... PA-2
Canoe Gulch—valley ... MT-8
Canoe Highway—channel ... MI-6
Canoe Hill—ridge ... NV-8
Canoe Hill—summit ... CT-1
Canoe Hills—other ... AK-9
Canoe Hole Rapids—rapids ... TN-4
Canoe Hollow—valley (3) ... KY-4
Canoe Hollow—valley ... MO-7
Canoe Hollow—valley ... PA-2
Canoe Hollow—valley ... WV-2
Canoe Island—island ... MN-6
Canoe Island—island ... WA-9
Canoe Islands—island ... NY-2
Canoe Lake ... MN-6
Canoe Lake—lake (2) ... AK-9
Canoe Lake—lake (2) ... MI-6
Canoe Lake—lake (3) ... MN-6
Canoe Lake—lake ... NY-2
Canoe Lake—lake ... SC-3
Canoe Lake—lake ... TX-5
Canoe Lake—lake ... WY-8
Canoe Lake—reservoir ... AL-4
Canoe Lake Strand—swamp ... FL-3
Canoe Landing—locale ... AR-4
Canoe Landing Site—locale ... HI-9
Cano El Hato—canal ... PR-3
Canoe Meadow—flat ... NH-1
Canoe Meadows Wildlife Sanctuary—park ... MA-1
Canoe Mesa—summit ... AZ-5
Canoe Mountain—ridge ... PA-2
Canoe Mtn—summit ... AK-9
Canoe Mtn—summit ... OK-5
Canoe Neck Creek—stream ... MD-2
Canoe Pass—channel (2) ... AK-9
Canoe Pass—channel ... WA-9
Canoe Passage ... WA-9
Canoe Passage—channel (2) ... AK-9
**Canoe Place**—pop pl ... NY-2
Canoe Point—cape (2) ... AK-9
Canoe Point—cape ... ID-8
Canoe Point—cape ... ME-1
Canoe Point—cape ... MI-6
Canoe Point—cape ... NY-2
Canoe Point And Picnic Point State Park—park ... NY-2
Canoe Pond—lake ... MA-1
Canoe Pond—reservoir ... GA-3
**Canoe Ridge**—pop pl ... PA-2
Canoe Ridge—ridge ... TN-4
Canoe Ridge—ridge ... WA-9
Canoe Ripple—rapids ... PA-2
Canoe River—stream ... MA-1
Canoe Road Beach ... MH-9
Canoe Road Lagoon ... MH-9
Canoe Road Lake ... MH-9
Canoe Rock—rock ... MA-1
Canoe Rocks—bar ... MI-6
Canoe Run—locale ... PA-2
Canoe Run—stream (2) ... PA-2
Canoe Run—stream (6) ... WV-2
Canoe Run Sch (historical)—school ... PA-2
Canoe Slough—stream ... AR-4
Canoe Station ... AL-4
Canoe Swamp—swamp ... GA-3
Canoe Township—fmr MCD ... IA-7
**Canoe (Township of)**—pop pl ... PA-2
Canoe Tree Fork—stream ... WV-2
Canoe Valley—flat ... PA-2
Canoe Valley—valley ... TX-5
Canoe Village—locale ... AK-9
**Canoga**—pop pl ... NY-2
Canoga Annex—uninc pl ... CA-9
Canoga Creek—stream ... NY-2
Canoga Island—island ... NY-2
Cano Gallardo—stream ... PR-3
**Canoga Park**—pop pl ... CA-9
Cano Garcia—stream ... PR-3
Canoga Springs—locale ... NY-2
Canogas Windmill—locale ... TX-5
Canoga Windmill—locale ... TX-5
Canogita Well—well ... TX-5
Canola ... KS-7
Cano La Puente—stream ... PR-3
Cano Las Pozas—stream ... PR-3
Cano Madre Vieja—valley ... PR-3
Cano Majagual—stream ... PR-3
Cano Matos—canal ... PR-3
Cano Media Luna—valley ... PR-3
Cano Merle—stream ... PR-3
Canon ... AZ-5
Canon—locale (2) ... NM-5
**Canon**—pop pl ... CO-8
**Canon**—pop pl ... CO-8
**Canon**—pop pl ... GA-3
**Canon**—pop pl ... NM-5
Canonacut Island ... MA-1
Canon Agapito—valley ... NM-5
Canon Agua Chiquito—valley ... NM-5
Canon Agua del Corral—valley ... NM-5
Canon Agua Sarca—valley ... NM-5
Canon Alamita—valley ... NM-5
Canon Alamito—valley (2) ... NM-5
Canon Alto—valley ... NM-5
Canon Amargo—valley ... NM-5
Canon Ancho—valley (4) ... NM-5
Canon Arado—valley ... NM-5
Canon Arguella—valley ... NM-5
Canon Armenta—valley ... NM-5
Canon Atencio—valley ... NM-5
Canon Azul—valley ... NM-5
Canon Bancos—valley ... NM-5
Canon Barranco—valley ... NM-5
Canon Barranco Blanco—valley ... NM-5
Canon Bernl—valley ... NM-5
Canon Bestias—valley ... NM-5
Canon Bilbao—valley ... NM-5
Canon Biscante—valley ... NM-5
Canon Blanco—valley (4) ... NM-5
Canon Bonita—valley ... NM-5
Canon Bonito—valley (4) ... NM-5
Canon Branch ... WI-6
Canon Brethren Cem—cemetery ... NM-5
Canon Brethren Sch—school ... NM-5
Canon Brook—stream ... ME-1
Canon Burro—valley ... NM-5
Canon Calaveras—valley ... NM-5
Canon Canyon—valley ... NM-5
Canon Capulin—valley ... NM-5
Canon Carriso—valley ... NM-5
Canon Carrizaloso—valley ... NM-5
Canon Cebollita—valley ... NM-5
Canon Cedro—valley (2) ... NM-5
Canon Cencerro—stream ... NM-5
Canon Cereza ... NM-5
Canon Ch—church ... SC-3
Canon Chamisa Losa—valley ... NM-5
Canon Chamiso—valley ... NM-5
Canon Chamisolosa—valley ... NM-5
Canon Chata—valley ... NM-5
Canon Chenelle ... AZ-5
**Canonchet**—pop pl ... RI-1
Canonchet, Lake—lake ... RI-1
Canonchet Brook—stream ... RI-1
Canon Chicosa—valley ... NM-5
Canon Chief Mine—mine ... CO-8
Canon Chimayo—valley ... NM-5
Canon Chispas—valley ... NM-5
Canon Church ... AL-4
Canon Church—church ... CO-8
Canon Cibolo—valley ... NM-5
Canon Ciruela—valley ... NM-5
Canoncita—stream ... NM-5
Canoncito—locale (2) ... NM-5
**Canoncito**—pop pl (3) ... NM-5
Canoncito —valley (2) ... AZ-5
Canoncito—valley (2) ... NM-5
Canoncito Canyon—valley ... NM-5
Canoncito Cem—cemetery ... NM-5
Canoncito Colorado—stream ... NM-5
Canoncito Colorado—valley ... NM-5
Canoncito Creek—stream ... NM-5
Canoncito de La Madera—valley ... NM-5
Canoncito de las Cabras—valley ... NM-5
Canoncito de las Primallas—valley ... NM-5
Canoncito de las Yeguas ... NM-5
Canoncito de la Uva—valley ... NM-5
Canoncito del Medio—valley ... NM-5
Canoncito del Mogote—valley ... NM-5
Canoncito del Ojito—valley ... NM-5
Canoncito de los Cordovas—valley ... NM-5
Canoncito de los Ranchos—valley ... NM-5
Canoncito del Puertecito del Lemitar—valley ... NM-5
Canoncito De Milpa—valley ... NM-5
Canoncito Ind Res—969 (1980) ... NM-5
Canoncito Navajo Day Sch—school ... NM-5
Canoncito Romero—valley ... CO-8
Canoncitos—area ... NM-5
Canoncitos—valley ... NM-5
Canoncito Seco—valley (2) ... NM-5
Canoncito Siding—locale ... NM-5
Canoncito Spring—spring ... NM-5
Canoncito Tank—reservoir ... NM-5
Canoncito Tia Tona—valley ... NM-5
Canoncito Trail—trail ... NM-5
Canoncito Valley—valley ... NM-5
Canon City ... CA-9
**Canon City**—pop pl ... CO-8
Canon City Downtown Hist Dist—hist pl ... CO-8
Canon City Downtown Hist Dist (Boundary Increase)—hist pl ... CO-8
Canon City Municipal Bldg—hist pl ... CO-8
Canon Cola Larga—valley ... NM-5
Canon Colorado—valley (3) ... NM-5
Canon Commercial Hist Dist—hist pl ... GA-3
Canon Cordava—valley ... NM-5
Canon Corrales—valley ... NM-5
Canon Creek ... CA-9
Canon Creek ... MT-8
Canon Creek ... WA-9
Canon Creek ... WY-8
Canon Creek—stream ... CA-9
Canon Creek—stream ... LA-4
Canon Creek—stream ... WI-6
Canon Creek—stream ... WY-8
Canon Cuervo—valley ... NM-5
Canon Cueva—valley ... NM-5
Canon Cueva del Leon—valley ... NM-5
Canon Cuevas—valley ... NM-5
Canon Cuevitas—valley ... NM-5
Canon Dam—dam ... HI-9
Canon de Aguilar—valley ... NM-5
Canon de Alameda ... NM-5
Canon de Alamo—valley ... NM-5
Canon de Baca—valley (2) ... NM-5
Canon de Bartolo—valley ... NM-5
Canon De Califia—valley ... NM-5
Canon De Chama Grant—civil ... NM-5
Canon de Chavez—valley ... NM-5
Canon de Chilili—valley ... NM-5
Canon de Chille ... AZ-5
Canon de Cueva—valley ... NM-5
Canon de David—valley ... NM-5
Canon de Domingo Baca—valley ... NM-5
Canon de Duran—valley ... NM-5
Canon de el Challe ... AZ-5
Canon de Eugenio—valley ... NM-5
Canon de Gallegos—valley ... NM-5
Canon de Hughes—valley ... NM-5
Canon de Jaramillo—valley ... NM-5
Canon de Juei—valley ... NM-5
Canon de la Agua Blanca—valley ... NM-5
Canon De La Agua Blanca—valley ... NM-5
Canon de la Canada—valley ... NM-5

Canon de la Capilla—*valley* NM-5
Canon de la Chamizalosa—*valley* NM-5
Canon de La Cienaga—*valley* NM-5
Canon de la Cruz—*valley* NM-5
Canon de la Cueva—*valley* (2) NM-5
Canon de la Damiana—*valley* NM-5
Canon de la Fuera—*valley* NM-5
Canon de la Gallina—*valley* NM-5
Canon de la Gotera—*valley* NM-5
Canon de la Grilla—*valley* NM-5
Canon Delagua—*civil* NM-5
Canon del Agua—*valley* (6) NM-5
Canon del Agua Azul—*valley* NM-5
Canon del Agua Ranch—*locale* NM-5
Canon del Agua Spring—*spring* NM-5
Canon del Agua Springs—*spring* NM-5
Canon de la Jarita—*valley* NM-5
Canon del Alamito—*valley* (2) NM-5
Canon de la Luvina—*valley* NM-5
Canon de La Madera—*valley* NM-5
Canon de la Madera—*valley* NM-5
Canon de la Miga—*valley* NM-5
Canon de la Mina—*valley* (2) NM-5
Canon de la Mosca—*valley* NM-5
Canon de la Mula—*valley* NM-5
Canon del Angosto—*valley* NM-5
Canon del Apache—*valley* NM-5
Canon de laPaloma—*valley* NM-5
Canon de la Perra—*valley* NM-5
Canon de la Plata—*valley* NM-5
Canon de la Presta—*valley* NM-5
Canon de la Primera Agua—*valley* NM-5
Canon de Laquesta—*valley* NM-5
Canon de la Rosa—*valley* NM-5
Canon de Las Cabras—*valley* NM-5
Canon de las Canalejas—*valley* NM-5
Canon de las Cuevas—*valley* NM-5
Canon de las Mujeras—*valley* NM-5
Canon de las Palas—*valley* NM-5
Canon de las Vegitas—*valley* NM-5
Canon de las Yeguas—*valley* NM-5
Canon de la Ternera—*valley* NM-5
Canon de la Vereda—*valley* NM-5
Canon del Caloso—*valley* NM-5
Canon del Camino—*valley* (2) NM-5
Canon del Cantor—*valley* NM-5
Canon del Chato—*valley* NM-5
Canon del Cobre—*valley* NM-5
Canon del Conejo—*valley* NM-5
Canon del Coyote—*locale* NM-5
Canon del Cuervito—*valley* NM-5
Canon del Cuervo—*valley* NM-5
Canon del Desaque—*valley* NM-5
Canon del Encierro—*valley* NM-5
Canon del Horno—*valley* NM-5
Canon de Librador—*valley* NM-5
Canon del Jacinto—*valley* NM-5
Canon del Jaral—*valley* NM-5
Canon del Medio—*valley* (2) NM-5
Canon del Molino Viejo—*valley* NM-5
Canon del Muerto—*valley* (2) NM-5
Canon del Norte—*valley* (2) NM-5
Canon del Novillo—*valley* NM-5
Canon del Ojito—*valley* (2) NM-5
Canon del Ojo—*valley* NM-5
Canon del Ojo del Indio—*valley* NM-5
Canon del Ojo del Venado—*valley* NM-5
Canon del Ojo Redondo—*valley* NM-5
Canon del Ojo Sabina—*valley* NM-5
Canon de los Alamitos—*valley* NM-5
Canon de los Alamos—*valley* (2) NM-5
Canon de los Diegos—*valley* NM-5
Canon de los Frijoles—*valley* NM-5
Canon de los Maderos—*valley* NM-5
Canon de los Moyos—*valley* NM-5
Canon de los Negros—*valley* NM-5
Canon del Oso—*valley* (3) NM-5
Canon de los Ojitos—*valley* NM-5
Canon de los Pino Reales—*valley* NM-5
Canon de los Posos—*valley* NM-5
Canon de los Seis—*valley* NM-5
Canon de los Tanques—*valley* NM-5
Canon de los Trigos—*valley* NM-5
Canon del Padre—*valley* NM-5
Canon del Perry—*valley* NM-5
Canon del Pino—*valley* NM-5
Canon Del Piojo—*valley* NM-5
Canon del Puente—*valley* NM-5
Canon del Rajadero de los Negros—*valley* NM-5
Canon del Rancho Alegre—*valley* NM-5
Canon del Raphael Gallegos—*valley* NM-5
Canon Del Rio Grande—*valley* NM-5
Canon Del Santa Ana —*civil* CA-9
Canon del Tanque Hondo—*valley* NM-5
Canon del Terrero—*valley* NM-5
Canon del Trigo—*valley* NM-5
Canon del Troncon Negro—*valley* NM-5
Canon del Uta—*valley* NM-5
Canon del Venado—*valley* NM-5
Canon de Manzanita—*valley* NM-5
Canon de Montecitos—*valley* NM-5
Canon de Mucha Agua—*valley* NM-5
Canon de Pedro Padilla—*valley* NM-5
Canon de Quirino—*valley* NM-5
Canon Derecho—*valley* NM-5
Canon de Saladeta Canyon—*stream* NM-5
Canon de Salas—*valley* NM-5
Canon de Sanchez—*valley* NM-5
Canon de San Cristobal—*valley* PR-3
Canon De San Diego—*civil* NM-5
Canon De San Diego—*valley* NM-5
Canon de San Mateo—*valley* NM-5
Canon de Santa Rosa—*valley* NM-5
Canon de Savina—*valley* NM-5
Canon de Tajique—*valley* NM-5
Canon de Tijeras—*valley* NM-5
Canon de Tio Gordito—*valley* NM-5
Canon de Torreon—*valley* (3) NM-5
Canon de Turieta—*valley* NM-5
Canon de Valencia—*valley* NM-5
Canon de Valle—*valley* NM-5
*Canon Diablo* CO-8
Canon Ditch—*canal* CO-8
Canon Ditch—*canal* CO-8
Canon Ditch—*canal* WY-8
Canon dos Nieves—*valley* NM-5
Canon el Capulin—*valley* NM-5
*Canon Elementary School* AZ-5
Canon el Gachupin—*valley* NM-5
Canon el Salado—*valley* NM-5
Canon Emplazado—*valley* NM-5
Canon Encierro—*valley* NM-5
Canon Encierto—*valley* NM-5
Canoneros Camp—*locale* NM-5
Canones—*locale* NM-5
Canones—*other* NM-5
**Canones**—*pop pl* NM-5
Canones Box—*valley* NM-5
Canon Escondido—*valley* (2) NM-5
Canon Escovas—*valley* NM-5
Canones Creek—*stream* (2) NM-5
Canones Grade Sch—*school* NM-5
Canones Mesa—*summit* NM-5
Canon Florentino—*valley* NM-5
*Canon Frijoles* CO-8
Canon Gardunos—*valley* NM-5
Canon Gato—*valley* NM-5
Canon Gonzales—*valley* NM-5
Canon gordo—*valley* NM-5
**Canon Hill**—*pop pl* SC-3
Canon Hondo—*valley* (5) NM-5
*Canonicut Point* MA-1
Canon Ignacio Rico—*valley* NM-5
Canon Indio—*valley* NM-5
*Canon Inferno* CO-8
Canon Isidro—*valley* NM-5
Canonizaria Canyon—*valley* NM-5
Canon Jara Loso—*valley* NM-5
Canon Jaroso—*valley* NM-5
Canon juan Francisco—*valley* NM-5
Canon Juan Maes—*valley* NM-5
Canon Juan Maestas—*valley* NM-5
Canon Julian—*valley* NM-5
Canon la Carne Spring —*spring* AZ-5
Canon la Ciruela—*valley* NM-5
Canon La Cueva—*valley* NM-5
Canon la Madera—*valley* NM-5
Canon Landing—*locale* NM-5
Canon Largo—*valley* (7) NM-5
Canon Largo Canyon—*valley* NM-5
Canon Largo Cem—*cemetery* NM-5
Canon las Cuevas—*valley* NM-5
Canon las Cuevitas—*valley* NM-5
Canon las Palas—*valley* NM-5
Canon las Tinajas—*valley* NM-5
Canon Latigo—*valley* NM-5
Canon Lauriano—*valley* NM-5
Canon Lavirgn—*valley* NM-5
Canon Lee—*valley* NM-5
Canon Leon—*valley* NM-5
Canon Liberty Mine—*mine* CO-8
Canon los Alamos—*valley* NM-5
Canon los Joyos—*valley* NM-5
Canon los Paises—*valley* NM-5
Canon Lucero—*valley* NM-5
Canon Madera—*valley* (2) NM-5
Canon Manga—*valley* NM-5
Canon Marquez—*valley* NM-5
Canon Maximo—*valley* NM-5
Canon-McMillan HS—*school* PA-2
Canon McMillan JHS—*school* PA-2
Canon Media—*valley* NM-5
Canon Medina—*valley* NM-5
Canon Medio—*valley* NM-5
Canon Mestenito—*stream* NM-5
Canon Mesteno—*valley* (2) NM-5
Canon Mills Ditch—*canal* CO-8
Canon Monnet—*valley* NM-5
Canon Monte de Abajo—*valley* NM-5
Canon Monte del Largo—*valley* NM-5
Canon Monte Largo—*valley* NM-5
*Canon Mountain* CA-9
Canon Natl Mine—*mine* CO-8
Canon Navajo—*valley* NM-5
Canon Negro—*valley* NM-5
Canon Nuevo—*valley* NM-5
*Canon of the Colorado River* AZ-5
Canon Ojo—*valley* NM-5
Canon Ojo Sarco—*valley* NM-5
Canon Olguin—*valley* NM-5
Cano Norberto—*stream* PR-3
Canon Osha—*valley* NM-5
Canon Osito—*valley* NM-5
Canon Oso—*valley* NM-5
Canon Padilla—*valley* NM-5
Canon Pajarita—*valley* (2) NM-5
Canon Palo Blanco—*valley* NM-5
Canon Pedroso—*valley* NM-5
Canon Piedra Lumbre—*valley* NM-5
Canon Piedroso—*valley* NM-5
Canon Pinabete—*valley* NM-5
Canon Pinabetoso—*valley* NM-5
Canon Pino Real—*valley* NM-5
Canon Pintado—*hist pl* CO-8
Canon Pintado—*valley* NM-5
Canon Plaza—*locale* NM-5
**Canon Plaza**—*pop pl* NM-5
Canon Poniente—*valley* NM-5
Canon Pony Express Station Monument—*locale* UT-8
*Canon Quemado* NM-5
Canon Quemado—*valley* NM-5
Canon Ranch Archeol District—*hist pl* TX-5
Canon Ranch RR Eclipse Windmill—*hist pl* TX-5
*Canon Rincon* CO-8
Canon Rita—*valley* NM-5
Canon River—*stream* WA-9
**Canon Road Subdivision**—*pop pl* UT-8
Canon Sabinoso—*valley* NM-5
Canon Saladito—*valley* NM-5
Canon Salado—*valley* (2) NM-5
Canon Sal Si Puedes—*valley* NM-5
Canon Sanchez—*valley* NM-5
Canon Santiago—*valley* NM-5
Canon Santo Domingo—*valley* NM-5
Canon Sapato—*valley* NM-5
**Canonsburg**—*pop pl* PA-2
Canonsburg Borough—*civil* PA-2
Canonsburg Dam Number Two—*dam* PA-2
Canonsburg General Hosp—*hospital* PA-2
Canonsburg Lake—*reservoir* PA-2
Canonsburg Number Two Rsvr—*reservoir* PA-2
*Canonsburg Rsvr Number 1* PA-2
Canonsburg Town Park—*park* PA-2
Canon Sch—*hist pl* CA-9
Canon Sch —*school* CA-9
*Canon School* AZ-5
Canon Seama—*valley* NM-5
Canon Seco—*valley* (4) NM-5
Canon Seguro—*valley* NM-5
Canon Silva—*valley* NM-5
Canon Site (22-Tu-523)—*hist pl* MS-4
Canon Spring—*spring* AZ-5
*Canon Station* UT-8
Canon Tank—*reservoir* NM-5
Canon Tapia—*valley* (2) NM-5
Canon Tejon—*valley* NM-5
Canon Tio Maes—*valley* NM-5
Canon Torcido—*valley* NM-5
Canon Toro—*valley* NM-5
Canon Trigo—*valley* NM-5
Canon Turrieta—*valley* NM-5
Canon Uva—*valley* NM-5
Canon Valdez—*valley* NM-5
Canon Vegocito—*valley* NM-5
Canon Ventanas—*valley* NM-5
Canon Vercere—*valley* NM-5
Canon Vigas—*valley* NM-5
Canon Villa de Aseyna—*valley* NM-5
Canon Vivian—*valley* NM-5
*Canon Water* AZ-5
Canon Windmill—*locale* NM-5
Canon Yegua—*valley* NM-5
**Canoochee**—*pop pl* GA-3
Canoochee (CCD)—*cens area* GA-3
Canoochee Ch—*church* GA-3
*Canoochee Creek* GA-3
Canoochee Creek—*stream* (2) GA-3
Canoochee River—*stream* GA-3
Canoochee Sch—*school* GA-3
Canoose Rips—*rapids* ME-1
Cano Paludica—*stream* PR-3
*Canopaug Brook* RI-1
Canopus Ch—*church* NY-2
Canopus Creek—*stream* NY-2
Canopus Hill—*summit* NY-2
Canopus Island—*island* NY-2
Canopus Lake—*lake* NY-2
Canopus Mine—*mine* CO-8
Canopy Gap—*gap* UT-8
Canopy Spring—*spring* UT-8
Cano Rodriguez—*stream* PR-3
Cano Salado—*gut* PR-3
Cano San Isidro—*stream* PR-3
Cano San Luis—*gut* PR-3
Canosia Cem—*cemetery* MN-6
**Canosia (Township of)**—*pop pl* MN-6
Cano Square (Shop Ctr)—*locale* FL-3
Cano Tiburones—*canal* PR-3
*Canotila Wiconi Paha* SD-7
*Canouse Brook* NJ-2
Canova—*locale* VA-3
**Canova**—*pop pl* NM-5
**Canova**—*pop pl* SD-7
**Canova Beach**—*pop pl* FL-3
Canova Canyon—*valley* CO-8
Canova Cem—*cemetery* SD-7
Canova Ditch—*canal* NM-5
Canovanas—*CDP* PR-3
**Canovanas**—*pop pl* (2) PR-3
Canovanas (Barrio)—*fmr MCD* PR-3
Canovanas (Municipio)—*civil* PR-3
Canovanas (Pueblo)—*fmr MCD* PR-3
Canovanillas (Barrio)—*fmr MCD* PR-3
Canovas Canyon—*valley* (2) NM-5
Canovas Creek—*stream* AZ-5
Canovas Spring—*spring* NM-5
*Canova Station* SD-7
**Canova Township**—*pop pl* SD-7
**Cano Verde**—*pop pl* PR-3
*Canoves Creek* AZ-5
Cano Vieques—*canal* PR-3
Canovitas Spring—*spring* NM-5
Canovos Canyon—*valley* CA-9
Canoy Draw—*valley* WY-8
Canoys Cabin—*locale* WY-8
*Canoza Lake* MA-1
Cano Zequeira—*stream* PR-3
Canright Lake—*lake* MN-6
Can Rock—*island* CA-9
Cansadie Top—*summit* NC-3
*Cansas* TN-4
**Cansellers**—*pop pl* NC-3
*Canshea Creek* CA-9
*Cansler* AL-4
Cansler Cem—*cemetery* KY-4
*Cansler Post Office* AL-4
Cansler Sch (abandoned)—*school* MO-7
Canso, Gate of—*gut* MA-1
Can Spring—*spring* OR-9
*Can Spring Wash* AZ-5
Cant, James, Ranch Hist Dist—*hist pl* OR-9
**Canta Gallo**—*pop pl* PR-3
**Cantagallo**—*pop pl* PR-3
Canta Lake—*lake* MN-6
**Cantaloupe**—*pop pl* IN-6
Cantaloupe Creek—*stream* ID-8
*Cantalous* AL-4
Cantapeta Creek—*stream* ND-7
**Cantara**—*pop pl* NM-5
Cantaralo Spring—*spring* NM-5
Cantaralo Windmill—*locale* NM-5
Cantarawas Windmill—*locale* TX-5
Cantata Peak—*summit* AK-9
Cantau Creek—*stream* TX-5
Cantau Flat—*flat* TX-5
**Cantebury, Village of**—*pop pl* DE-2
**Cantebury Apartments**—*pop pl* DE-2
Cantebury Gulch—*valley* CA-9
Cantebury Heights—*uninc pl* AL-4
Canteen Canyon—*valley* NM-5
Canteen Creek—*stream* ID-8
Canteen Creek—*stream* IL-6
Canteen Creek—*stream* OR-9
Canteen Creek—*stream* WA-9
Canteen Creek—*stream* WY-8
Canteen Flats—*flat* WA-9
Canteen Lake—*lake* IL-6
Canteen Lake—*lake* NM-5
Canteen Lake—*lake* WI-6
Canteen Meadows—*flat* ID-8
Canteeno Spring—*spring* OR-9
Canteen Sch—*school* IL-6
Canteen Spring—*spring* AZ-5
Canteen Spring—*spring* OR-9
Canteen Spring—*spring* UT-8
**Canteen (Township of)**—*pop pl* IL-6
Canteen Trail—*trail* WA-9
Cantell Creek—*stream* OR-9
Cantell Spring—*spring* WY-8
**Cantelous**—*pop pl* AL-4
Cantelous Cem—*cemetery* AL-4
Cantelous Hill—*summit* AL-4
Cantelous Lookout Tower—*tower* AL-4
**Cantelous Spur**—*pop pl* AL-4
*Cantelous Station* AL-4
*Cantepeta Creek* ND-7
**Cantera**—*pop pl* PR-3
Canteras Artesian Well—*well* TX-5
Cantera Windmill—*locale* TX-5
**Canterbay Estates Subdivision**—*pop pl* UT-8
Canterberry Branch—*stream* WV-2
Canterberry Cem—*cemetery* WV-2
Canterberry House—*church* FL-3
**Canterburg**—*pop pl* VA-3
*Canterbury* OH-6
Canterbury—*locale* DE-2
**Canterbury**—*pop pl* CT-1
**Canterbury**—*pop pl* NH-1
**Canterbury**—*pop pl* PA-2
**Canterbury**—*pop pl* VA-3
**Canterbury**—*pop pl* WV-2
Canterbury Ave Sch—*school* CA-9
*Canterbury Branch* DE-2
Canterbury Brook—*stream* MA-1
**Canterbury (Canterbury Center)**—*pop pl* NH-1
Canterbury Castle—*hist pl* OR-9
Canterbury Cem—*cemetery* (2) WV-2
*Canterbury Center* NH-1
Canterbury Ch—*church* VA-3
Canterbury Ch—*church* WV-2
Canterbury Chapel Episcopal Ch—*church* AL-4
*Canterbury Creek* OR-9
Canterbury Crossroads (historical)—*locale* AL-4
**Canterbury Estates**—*pop pl* MD-2
**Canterbury Estates**—*pop pl* MA-1
Canterbury Golf Club—*other* OH-6
**Canterbury Heights (subdivision)**—*pop pl* AL-4
**Canterbury Hill**—*pop pl* NY-2
Canterbury Hill—*summit* CO-8
**Canterbury Hills**—*pop pl* DE-2
**Canterbury Hills**—*pop pl* (2) VA-3
Canterbury Hill Sch—*school* NY-2
Canterbury Hollow—*valley* WV-2
Canterbury Lake—*reservoir* TN-4
Canterbury Lake Dam—*dam* TN-4
*Canterbury Lane* IL-6
Canterbury Mtn—*summit* CA-9
Canterbury Rsvr—*reservoir* OR-9
Canterbury Sch—*school* CT-1
Canterbury Sch—*school* FL-3
Canterbury Sch—*school* IL-6
Canterbury Sch—*school* OH-6
Canterbury Shaker Village—*hist pl* NH-1
Canterbury Square—*post sta* OR-9
*Canterbury Station* DE-2
**Canterbury Station**—*pop pl* NH-1
Canterbury Street Sch—*school* MA-1
**Canterbury (subdivision)**—*pop pl* AL-4
**Canterbury (subdivision)**—*pop pl* NC-3
**Canterbury (Town of)**—*pop pl* CT-1
**Canterbury (Town of)**—*pop pl* NH-1
Canterbury United Methodist Ch—*church* AL-4
**Canterbury Woods**—*pop pl* VA-3
Canterbury Woods Sch—*school* VA-3
Canter Cem—*cemetery* AR-4
Canter Cem—*cemetery* (2) OH-6
Canterhill Swamp—*stream* SC-3
Cantero—*locale* PR-3
Canter Spring Rsvr—*reservoir* ID-8
**Cantey**—*pop pl* SC-3
Cantey, Zachariah, House—*hist pl* SC-3
Cantey Bay—*bay* SC-3
Cantey Hill—*summit* SC-3
Cantey Hill Ch—*church* SC-3
Canthook Creek—*stream* CA-9
Canthook Lake—*lake* MN-6
Canthook Lake—*lake* WI-6
Canthook Mtn—*summit* CA-9
Canthook Prairie—*area* CA-9
Cantiague Park—*park* NY-2
Cantiague Sch—*school* NY-2
Cantigny Sch—*school* MT-8
Cantigny Woods North—*woods* IL-6
Cantigny Woods South—*woods* IL-6
**Cantil**—*pop pl* CA-9
Cantilever Bridge—*bridge* DC-2
*Cantil Valley* CA-9
Cantina Rsvr—*reservoir* AZ-5
Cantinas, The—*summit* CA-9
Cantinas Canyon—*valley* NM-5
Cantinas Creek—*stream* CA-9
Cantinas Pens—*locale* TX-5
*Cantinas Rsvr* AZ-5
Cantina Wash—*stream* AZ-5
Cantine Memorial Field—*park* NY-2
Cantley Branch—*stream* AR-4
Cantley Branch—*stream* WV-2
Cantley Cem—*cemetery* WV-2
Cantley Draw—*valley* WY-8
Cantling Creek—*stream* CO-8
Cantlin Lake—*lake* MN-6
Canto—*locale* NC-3
**Canto de Sapo**—*pop pl* PR-3
*Canton* AL-4
*Canton* FL-3
*Canton* NJ-2
*Canton* ND-7
Canton—*locale* CO-8
Canton—*locale* KY-4
Canton—*locale* VA-3
Canton—*locale* WV-2
**Canton**—*pop pl* CT-1
**Canton**—*pop pl* GA-3
**Canton**—*pop pl* IL-6
**Canton**—*pop pl* IN-6
**Canton**—*pop pl* IA-7
**Canton**—*pop pl* KS-7
**Canton**—*pop pl* ME-1
**Canton**—*pop pl* MD-2
**Canton**—*pop pl* MA-1
**Canton**—*pop pl* MN-6
**Canton**—*pop pl* MS-4
**Canton**—*pop pl* MO-7
**Canton**—*pop pl* MT-8
**Canton**—*pop pl* NJ-2
**Canton**—*pop pl* NY-2
**Canton**—*pop pl* NC-3
**Canton**—*pop pl* OH-6
**Canton**—*pop pl* OK-5
**Canton**—*pop pl* PA-2
**Canton**—*pop pl* SD-7
**Canton**—*pop pl* TX-5
**Canton**—*pop pl* WI-6
Canton—*post sta* MI-6
Canton, William J., House—*hist pl* WA-9
Canton Apartments—*hist pl* GA-3
Canton Bend—*locale* AL-4
Canton Bend Sch—*school* AL-4
Canton Borough—*civil* PA-2
Canton Canyon—*valley* CA-9
Canton Canyon Devil Canyon Truck Trail—*trail* CA-9
Canton Canyon Trail—*trail* CA-9
Canton (CCD)—*cens area* GA-3
Canton (CCD)—*cens area* OK-5
Canton (CCD)—*cens area* TX-5
Canton Cem—*cemetery* LA-4
Canton Cem—*cemetery* MA-1
Canton Cem—*cemetery* OK-5
Canton Cem—*cemetery* SD-7
Canton Center—*locale* CT-1
Canton Ch—*church* NC-3
Canton Chute—*channel* IL-6
Canton Chute Public Use Area—*park* IL-6
**Canton City**—*pop pl* ND-7
Canton Commercial Hist Dist—*hist pl* GA-3
Canton Country Club—*other* GA-3
Canton Country Club—*other* IL-6
Canton Country Club Lake Dam—*dam* MS-4
Canton Country Day Sch—*school* OH-6
Canton Courthouse Square Hist Dist—*hist pl* MS-4
Canton Creek—*stream* GA-3
Canton Creek—*stream* OR-9
Canton Creek—*stream* TN-4
Canton Creek—*stream* (2) VA-3
Canton Creek Campground—*park* OR-9
Canton Creek Ch—*church* VA-3
Canton Creek Trail—*trail* OR-9
Canton Dam—*dam* OK-5
Canton Dam—*dam* SD-7
Canton Drain—*stream* NJ-2
Canton Exit—*crossing* SD-7
Canton Farm—*locale* NY-2
Canton Female Acad (historical)—*school* MS-4
Canton Ferry—*locale* IL-6
Canton Ferry—*other* MO-7
Canton Golf Course—*other* CT-1
**Canton Heights Estates**—*pop pl* KY-4
Canton Heights Sch—*school* KY-4
*Canton Hills* KY-4
Canton Hist Dist—*hist pl* MD-2
Canton Hollow—*valley* TN-4
Canton House—*hist pl* MD-2
Canton HS—*school* KS-7
Canton-Inwood Hosp—*hospital* SD-7
Canton JHS—*school* NC-3
**Canton Junction**—*pop pl* MA-1
Canton Junction—*uninc pl* MD-2
Canton Lake—*reservoir* IL-6
Canton Lake—*reservoir* OK-5
Cantonment—*hist pl* OK-5
**Cantonment**—*pop pl* FL-3
Cantonment (CCD)—*cens area* FL-3
Cantonment Ch of Christ—*church* FL-3
Cantonment Creek—*stream* CO-8
Cantonment Creek—*stream* TX-5
*Cantonment Leavenworth* KS-7
Cantonment Reno—*hist pl* WY-8
Canton Mounds—*summit* SD-7
Canton Mtn—*summit* ME-1
Canton Municipal Airp—*airport* SD-7
Canton North Oil Field—*oilfield* KS-7
Canton Plaza—*post sta* GA-3
Canton Plaza (Shop Ctr)—*locale* NC-3
Canton Point—*cape* OR-9
Canton Point—*locale* ME-1
Canton Public Library—*hist pl* OH-6
*Canton Reservoir* OK-5
Canton Ridge—*ridge* VA-3
*Canton Ridge Creek* VA-3
*Canton River* MA-1
**Canton Road**—*pop pl* OH-6
Canton Rsvr—*reservoir* NC-3
Canton Sch—*hist pl* IA-7
Canton Sch—*school* GA-3
Canton Sch—*school* MD-2
Canton Sch—*school* MT-8
Canton Sch—*school* NJ-2
Canton Sch—*school* NM-5
Canton Shelter—*locale* OR-9
*Canton Station* MA-1
Canton Townhall—*building* MA-1
**Canton (Town of)**—*pop pl* CT-1
**Canton (Town of)**—*pop pl* ME-1
**Canton (Town of)**—*pop pl* MA-1
**Canton (Town of)**—*pop pl* NY-2
**Canton (Town of)**—*pop pl* WI-6
Canton Township—*civil* MO-7
Canton Township—*civil* SD-7
Canton Township—*fmr MCD* IA-7
**Canton Township**—*pop pl* (2) KS-7
**Canton Township**—*pop pl* SD-7
Canton Township Carnegie Library—*hist pl* KS-7
**Canton (Township of)**—*pop pl* IL-6
**Canton (Township of)**—*pop pl* MI-6
**Canton (Township of)**—*pop pl* MN-6
**Canton (Township of)**—*pop pl* OH-6
**Canton (Township of)**—*pop pl* (2) PA-2
*Canton Valley Lake* MT-8
Canton Viaduct—*hist pl* MA-1
*Canton Village* ND-7
Canton Waterworks—*other* OH-6
Canton Yard—*locale* MD-2
*Cantoo-a Creek* CA-9
*Cantor Creek* NY-2
Cantor Creek—*stream* OR-9
Cantown—*locale* KY-4
Cantrail Gulch—*valley* OR-9
Cantral Bridge (historical)—*bridge* MS-4
Cantrall—*locale* IL-6
**Cantrall**—*pop pl* IL-6
Cantrall Creek—*stream* (2) CA-9
Cantrall Creek—*stream* IL-6
Cantrall Creek—*stream* OR-9
Cantrall Mill—*locale* CA-9
Cant Ranch—*locale* OR-9
Cantrel Creek—*stream* KY-4
Cantrel Hollow—*valley* MO-7
*Cantrell Branch* AL-4
Cantrell Branch—*stream* (3) AL-4
Cantrell Branch—*stream* KY-4
Cantrell Cem—*cemetery* AL-4
Cantrell Cem—*cemetery* AR-4
Cantrell Cem—*cemetery* KY-4
Cantrell Cem—*cemetery* MS-4
Cantrell Cem—*cemetery* (2) TN-4
Cantrell Cem—*cemetery* (2) VA-3
Cantrell Ch—*church* MO-7
Cantrell Chapel—*church* TN-4
Cantrell Cove—*valley* AL-4
*Cantrell Creek* OR-9
Cantrell Creek—*stream* CO-8
Cantrell Creek—*stream* KY-4
Cantrell Creek—*stream* MO-7
Cantrell Creek—*stream* (2) NC-3
Cantrell Creek—*stream* SC-3
Cantrell Creek Lodge—*locale* NC-3
Cantrelle, Bayou—*gut* LA-4
Cantrell Family Cem—*cemetery* AL-4
Cantrell Gap—*gap* KY-4
Cantrell Gap—*gap* VA-3
Cantrell Hill—*summit* OR-9
**Cantrell (historical)**—*pop pl* TN-4
Cantrell Hollow—*valley* MO-7
Cantrell Hollow—*valley* TN-4
Cantrell Hollow—*valley* VA-3
Cantrell Lake—*lake* NM-5
Cantrell Mill Creek—*stream* AL-4
Cantrell Mtn—*summit* NC-3
Cantrell Mtn—*summit* SC-3
Cantrell Mtn—*summit* TX-5
Cantrell Pond—*lake* TN-4
Cantrell Sch—*school* MO-7
Cantrells Chapel Methodist Ch (historical)—*church* TN-4
Cantrell Sch (historical)—*school* (2) MO-7
Cantrells Lake—*reservoir* TN-4
Cantrell Slough—*stream* TX-5
Cantrell Spring—*spring* AL-4
Cantrell Spring—*spring* KY-4
Cantrell Spring—*spring* OR-9
**Cantrell Subdivision**—*pop pl* TN-4
Cantrell Tank No 1—*reservoir* NM-5
Cantrell Top—*summit* NC-3
Cantrell Top—*summit* TN-4
Cantrel Ridge—*ridge* AR-4
Cantrick JHS—*school* MI-6
**Cantril**—*pop pl* IA-7
*Cantrill* IA-7
Cantrill Fork—*stream* KY-4
Cantrill House—*hist pl* KY-4
Cantrill Post Office (historical)—*building* TN-4
Cantril Ranch—*locale* CO-8
Cantu—*locale* TX-5
*Cantua Creek* CA-9
**Cantua Creek**—*pop pl* CA-9
Cantua Creek—*stream* CA-9
Cantu Artesian Well—*well* TX-5
Cantua Substation—*other* CA-9
Cantua Well—*well* CA-9
Cantu Bend—*bend* TX-5
Cantu Cem—*cemetery* (2) TX-5
*Cantuche Church* AL-4
*Cantuche Creek* AL-4
Cantu Mtn—*summit* AK-9
*Cantuna* CA-9
Cantway Slough—*gut* IL-6
*Cantwell* AL-4
*Cantwell* DE-2
*Cantwell* MO-7
Cantwell—*locale* WV-2
**Cantwell**—*pop pl* AK-9
**Cantwell**—*pop pl* MO-7
Cantwell Acad—*school* FL-3
Cantwell Airstrip—*airport* TN-4
Cantwell ANV746—*reserve* AK-9
Cantwell Branch—*stream* MS-4
Cantwell Cem—*cemetery* AR-4
Cantwell Cliffs—*cliff* OH-6
Cantwell Creek—*stream* AK-9
Cantwell Glacier—*glacier* AK-9
Cantwell HS—*school* CA-9
Cantwell Lake—*lake* NM-5
Cantwell Mill—*locale* MS-4
Cantwell Park—*park* MO-7
*Cantwells Bridge* DE-2
Cantwell Valley—*valley* TN-4
Cantwell Valley Cave—*cave* TN-4
Canty—*locale* AL-4
Canty Branch—*stream* SC-3
*Canty Cemetery* AL-4
Canty Coulee—*valley* MT-8
Canty (historical)—*locale* SD-7
Canty House—*hist pl* WV-2
Canty Meadow—*flat* CA-9
Canty Mill Creek—*stream* NC-3
Canty Sch—*school* IL-6
Cantys Lake—*reservoir* NJ-2
Cantys Lake Dam—*dam* NJ-2
Canty Trail—*trail* VT-1
Canuck Creek—*stream* ID-8
Canuck Creek—*stream* MT-8
Canuck Lake—*lake* MN-6
Canuck Pass—*gap* ID-8
Canuck Peak—*summit* MT-8
Canuon—*area* GU-9
Canupp Branch—*stream* TN-4
Canup Ridge—*ridge* NC-3
*Canuse Brook* NJ-2
**Canute**—*pop pl* OK-5
Canute Branch—*stream* NJ-2
**Canutillo**—*pop pl* TX-5
**Canvas**—*pop pl* WV-2
Canvasback Gun Club—*locale* NV-8
Canvasback Lake—*lake* AK-9
Canvasback Lake—*lake* WA-9
Canvasback Lake—*reservoir* TX-5
*Canvas Back Point* NC-3
Canvasback Point—*cape* NC-3
Canvasback Point—*cliff* OH-6
Canvasback Pond—*lake* NC-3
*Canvas Hole* AZ-5
*Canvass Back Lake* NC-3

Cape Jellison—*other* ME-1
Cape Junction—*locale* VA-3
**Cape Junction (Cape Jellison)**—*pop pl* ME-1
Cape Junken—*cape* AK-9
*Cape Kaea* HI-9
Cape Kagalus—*cape* AK-9
Cape Kagigikak—*cape* AK-9
Cape Kaguyak—*cape* AK-9
Cape Kalekta—*cape* AK-9
Cape Kanatak—*cape* AK-9
Cape Karluk—*cape* AK-9
Cape Kasiak—*cape* AK-9
Cape Kasilof—*cape* AK-9
*Cape Kawaihoa* HI-9
Cape Kayakliut—*cape* AK-9
Cape Kazakof—*cape* AK-9
Cape Kekurnoi—*cape* AK-9
*Cape Kennedy* FL-3
Cape Kiavak—*cape* AK-9
Cape Kiguga—*cape* AK-9
Cape Kigun—*cape* AK-9
Cape Kigunak—*cape* AK-9
Cape Kigushimkada—*cape* AK-9
Cape Kilokak—*cape* AK-9
Cape Kitnik—*cape* AK-9
Cape Kiugilak—*cape* AK-9
Cape Kiwanda County Park—*park* OR-9
Cape Korovin—*cape* AK-9
Cape Kostromitinof—*cape* AK-9
Cape Kovrizhka—*cape* AK-9
Cape Krenitzin—*cape* AK-9
Capek Rsvr—*reservoir* OR-9
Cape Krusenstern—*cape* AK-9
Cape Krusenstern Archeol District—*hist pl* AK-9
Cape Krusenstern Natl Monmt—*park* AK-9
Cape Kudugnak—*cape* AK-9
*Cape Kuikui* HI-9
Cape Kuliak—*cape* AK-9
Cape Kuliuk—*cape* AK-9
Cape Kumlik—*cape* AK-9
Cape Kumliun—*cape* AK-9
Cape Kunmik—*cape* AK-9
Cape Kutuzof—*cape* AK-9
*Capel* AL-4
Capel—*locale* GA-3
Cape Labelle Creek—*stream* WA-9
Cape LaCroix Creek—*stream* MO-7
Cape La Croix Creek—*stream* MO-7
Cape Lake—*lake* CA-9
Capeland Branch—*stream* AL-4
Cape Lapin—*cape* AK-9
*Cape La Warre* DE-2
Cape Lazaref—*cape* AK-9
Cape Leontovich—*cape* AK-9
Cape Lewis—*cape* AK-9
Cape Lgvak—*cape* AK-9
Cape Liakik—*cape* AK-9
Cape Lisburne—*cape* AK-9
Cape Lisburne (Air Force Station)—*military* AK-9
Cape Lises—*cape* AK-9
*Capell* AL-4
Capell—*locale* MS-4
**Capell**—*pop pl* AL-4
**Capella**—*pop pl* NC-3
Capella Bay—*bay* VI-3
*Capella Hill* PA-2
Capella Islands—*island* VI-3
Capella Mine—*mine* CO-8
*Capella Pond* CT-1
Capell Cem—*cemetery* AL-4
Capell Creek—*stream* CA-9
*Capelle* MP-9
*Capelle Creek* SD-7
Cape Llmalianuk—*cape* AK-9
Capello Pond—*lake* CT-1
Capel Lsaf Cem—*cemetery* NY-2
Capell Sch—*school* CA-9
Capell Valley—*valley* CA-9
**Cape Loch Haven**—*pop pl* MD-2
*Cape Lookoff Mtn* VT-1
Cape Lookoff Mtn—*summit* VT-1
Cape Lookout—*cape* AK-9
Cape Lookout—*cape* NC-3
**Cape Lookout**—*pop pl* NC-3
Cape Lookout Lighthouse—*locale* NC-3
Cape Lookout Light Station—*hist pl* NC-3
Cape Lookout Natl Seashore—*park* NC-3
Cape Lookout State Park—*park* OR-9
Cape Lowenstern—*cape* AK-9
Capel Point—*cape* AK-9
**Capels**—*pop pl* WV-2
**Capelsie**—*pop pl* NC-3
Capelsie Lake—*reservoir* NC-3
Capelsie Lake Dam—*dam* NC-3
Capels Mill—*locale* NC-3
**Capels (RR name Caples)**—*pop pl* WV-2
Capel Township—*fmr MCD* IA-7
Capel Ucha Ch—*church* NY-2
Cape Lutke—*cape* AK-9
Cape Lynch—*cape* AK-9
Cape Magdalena—*cape* AK-9
*Cape Malebar* MA-1
Cape Manning—*cape* AK-9
Cape Mansfield—*cape* AK-9
Cape Marie—*cape* NY-2
*Cape May* NJ-2
Cape May—*cape* GA-3
**Cape May**—*pop pl* NJ-2
*Cape May Beach* NJ-2
**Cape May Beach**—*pop pl* MD-2
Cape May Canal—*canal* NJ-2
Cape May Channel—*channel* NJ-2
Cape May County—*airport* NJ-2
**Cape May County**—*pop pl* NJ-2
Cape May County Gas—*airport* NJ-2
**Cape May Court House**—*pop pl* NJ-2
Cape May Harbor—*bay* NJ-2
Cape May Hist Dist—*hist pl* NJ-2
Cape May Inlet—*bay* NJ-2
Cape May Lighthouse—*hist pl* NJ-2
Cape May Point—*cape* NJ-2
**Cape May Point**—*pop pl* NJ-2
*Cape May Town* NJ-2
**Cape Meares**—*pop pl* OR-9
Cape Meares Lake—*lake* OR-9
Cape Meares Natl Wildlife Ref—*park* OR-9
Cape Meares State Park—*park* OR-9
*Cape Mears* OR-9
*Cape Medorom* PW-9

Cape Mendenhall—*cape* AK-9
Cape Menshikof—*cape* AK-9
Cape Miga—*cape* AK-9
Cape Misty—*cape* AK-9
Cape Moffett—*cape* AK-9
Cape Mohigan—*cape* AK-9
Cape Mordvinof—*cape* AK-9
Cape Morgan—*cape* AK-9
Cape Mtn—*summit* AK-9
Cape Mtn—*summit* OR-9
Cape Muzon—*cape* AK-9
Cape Myaughee—*cape* AK-9
Capen, Parson, House—*hist pl* MA-1
Capen-Clark Hist Dist—*hist pl* CT-1
**Cape Neddick**—*pop pl* ME-1
Cape Neddick Harbor—*bay* ME-1
Cape Neddick Lighthouse—*locale* ME-1
Cape Neddick Light Station—*hist pl* ME-1
Cape Neddick Nubble—*island* ME-1
Cape Neddick River—*stream* ME-1
Capener, William, House—*hist pl* UT-8
Cape Newenham—*cape* AK-9
Cape Newenham (Air Force Station)—*military* AK-9
Cape Newland—*cape* AK-9
Capeneys Lake—*lake* MT-8
*Cape Ngara* PW-9
*Cape Ngaramudel* PW-9
*Cape Ngariois* PW-9
*Cape Ngatpkul* PW-9
*Cape Ngatpokui* PW-9
*Cape Ngatpokul* PW-9
*Cape Ngebasangel* PW-9
Cape Ninilchik—*cape* AK-9
*Capeniur* MP-9
Cape Nome—*cape* AK-9
**Cape Nome**—*pop pl* AK-9
Cape Nome Mining District Discovery Sites—*hist pl* AK-9
Cape Nome Roadhouse—*hist pl* AK-9
Cape Northumberland—*cape* AK-9
Capen Sch—*school* MA-1
Cape Nukshak—*cape* AK-9
Cape Nuniliak—*cape* AK-9
*Cape Obiam* MH-9
Cape of Good Hope—*cliff* CO-8
Cape of Good Hope—*summit* TN-4
*Cape Orford* OR-9
*Cape Oxford* OR-9
Cape Pankof—*cape* AK-9
Cape Papatele—*cape* AS-9
Cape Paramanof—*cape* AK-9
Cape Perpetua Campground—*park* OR-9
Cape Perpetua Rec Area—*park* OR-9
*Cape Pkulamlagalp* PW-9
*Cape Pkulangelul* PW-9
*Cape Pkulatap* PW-9
*Cape Pkulataprival* PW-9
*Cape Pog* MA-1
Cape Poge Bay—*bay* MA-1
Cape Poge Bay Marshes—*swamp* MA-1
Cape Poge Elbow—*bar* MA-1
Cape Poge Flats—*flat* MA-1
Cape Poge Gut—*gut* MA-1
Cape Poge Light—*hist pl* MA-1
Cape Poge Light—*locale* MA-1
Cape Poge Lighthouse—*building* MA-1
*Cape-Poge Pond* MA-1
*Cape Pog Pond* MA-1
Cape Point—*cape* NC-3
Cape Pole—*cape* AK-9
**Cape Pole**—*pop pl* AK-9
Cape Pond—*lake* MA-1
Cape Pond—*reservoir* NY-2
**Cape Porpoise**—*pop pl* ME-1
Cape Porpoise Harbor—*bay* ME-1
Cape Potainikof—*cape* AK-9
Cape Prince of Wales—*cape* AK-9
Cape Prominence—*cape* AK-9
Cape Providence—*cape* AK-9
Cape Puget—*cape* AK-9
Cape Ranch—*locale* CA-9
Caper Chapel—*church* SC-3
*Caper Creek* SC-3
Cape Resurrection—*cape* AK-9
Cape Retreat—*cape* MS-4
Caper Hill—*summit* VT-1
Cape Ridge—*ridge* CA-9
Cape Ridge—*ridge* OR-9
Cape Riley—*cape* AK-9
*Caper Inlet* SC-3
*Caper Island* SC-3
Caper Lake—*lake* MN-6
Capernaum Cem—*cemetery* MN-6
Capernaum Cem—*cemetery* SC-3
Capernaum Ch—*church* AR-4
Capernaum Ch—*church* SC-3
**Capernium**—*pop pl* NC-3
Capernium Ch—*church* NC-3
Cape Road Plaza (Shop Ctr)—*locale* MA-1
Cape Rock—*summit* MO-7
Cape Rocks—*bar* ME-1
Cape Rodney—*cape* AK-9
Cape Romain Harbor—*bay* SC-3
Cape Romain Lighthouses—*hist pl* SC-3
*Cape Roman* FL-3
Cape Romano Island—*island* FL-3
Cape Romano Shoals—*bar* FL-3
Cape Romano-Ten Thousand Islands Aquatic Preserve—*park* FL-3
Cape Romanzof—*cape* AK-9
Cape Romanzof (Air Force Station)—*military* AK-9
Cape Rosier—*locale* ME-1
Cape Royal—*cliff* AZ-5
Cape Rozhnof—*cape* AK-9
*Cape Rozier* ME-1
Caper Peak—*summit* MT-8
Capers Cem—*cemetery* SC-3
Capers Chapel—*church* (2) SC-3
Capers C.M.E. Church—*hist pl* TN-4
*Capers Creek* SC-3
Capers Creek—*gut* SC-3
Capers Creek—*stream* SC-3
Capers Inlet—*bay* SC-3
Capers Island—*island* (3) SC-3
Capers-McKenzie House—*hist pl* LA-4
Capers Ridge—*ridge* TX-5
Caperton—*locale* WV-2
Caperton Block—*hist pl* KY-4

Caperton Canal—*canal* CA-9
Caperton Cem—*cemetery* AL-4
Caperton Cem—*cemetery* TN-4
Caperton Chapel—*church* AL-4
*Caperton Chapel Ch* AL-4
Caperton Ferry—*locale* AL-4
Caperton Hollow—*valley* TN-4
Caperton Lake—*reservoir* TN-4
Caperton Rsvr—*reservoir* CA-9
*Capertons Chapel* AL-4
*Capertons Ferry* AL-4
Capertown Mine (underground)—*mine* AL-4
Cape Ruin—*cape* AK-9
Cape Rukavitsie—*cape* AK-9
Cape Run—*stream* PA-2
Cape Sabak—*cape* AK-9
Cape Sabine—*cape* AK-9
Cape Sable (CCD)—*cens area* FL-3
Cape Sagak—*cape* AK-9
**Cape Saint Claire**—*pop pl* MD-2
*Cape Saint Cosme Rock* MO-7
Cape Saint Elias—*cape* AK-9
Cape Saint George Light—*locale* FL-3
Cape Saint George Light House—*locale* FL-3
Cape Saint George Shoal—*bar* FL-3
Cape Saint Hermogenes—*cape* AK-9
**Cape Saint John**—*pop pl* MD-2
Cape Saint Stephen—*cape* AK-9
Cape Sajaka—*cape* AK-9
Cape San Blas Light—*locale* FL-3
Cape San Blas Lighthouse—*locale* FL-3
**Cape Sandy**—*pop pl* IN-6
*Cape Sante* WA-9
Cape Sarichef—*cape* AK-9
Cape Sarichef Radio Relay Site—*other* AK-9
Cape Sasmik—*cape* AK-9
**Capes Cove (trailer park)**—*pop pl* DE-2
Cape Sebastian State Park—*park* OR-9
Cape Sedanka—*cape* AK-9
Cape Seniavin—*cape* AK-9
Cape Seppings—*cape* AK-9
Cape Shaw—*cape* AK-9
Cape Shishkin—*cape* AK-9
Cape Simpson—*cape* AK-9
Cape Sitkagi—*cape* AK-9
Capes Lake—*reservoir* GA-3
Cape Slough—*stream* AR-4
Cape Small Harbor—*bay* ME-1
*Cape Small Point* ME-1
Cape Small Pond—*lake* ME-1
Cape Spencer—*cape* AK-9
Cape Spencer Lighthouse—*hist pl* AK-9
*Cape Split Harbor* ME-1
Cape Split Harbor—*bay* ME-1
Cape Starichkof—*cape* (2) AK-9
Cape Starr—*cape* AK-9
Cape St. Claire—*CDP* MD-2
Cape St. Elias Lighthouse—*hist pl* AK-9
Cape Stephens—*cape* AK-9
Cape St. George Light—*hist pl* FL-3
**Cape St. John**—*pop pl* MD-2
**Cape Story By The Sea**—*pop pl* VA-3
Cape Stoss—*cape* AK-9
Cape Strait—*bay* AK-9
Cape Sucking—*cape* AK-9
Cape Sudak—*cape* AK-9
Cape Suwarof—*cape* AK-9
Cape Tachilni—*cape* AK-9
Cape Tadluk—*cape* AK-9
Cape Tanak—*cape* AK-9
Cape Thompson—*cape* (2) AK-9
Cape Tolstoi—*cape* AK-9
*Cape Toro* MH-9
Capetown—*locale* CA-9
Capetown Plaza (Shop Ctr)—*locale* MA-1
Capetown Shop Ctr—*locale* MA-1
Cape Trinity—*cape* AK-9
Cape Tusik—*cape* AK-9
Cape Udak—*cape* AK-9
Cape Uganik—*cape* AK-9
Cape Ugat—*cape* AK-9
Cape Ugyak—*cape* AK-9
Cape Umak—*cape* AK-9
Cape Unalishagvak—*cape* AK-9
Cape Upright—*cape* AK-9
Cape Utalug—*cape* AK-9
Cape Utes—*cape* AK-9
Cape Uyak—*cape* AK-9
Cape Vancouver—*cape* AK-9
Cape View Sch—*school* FL-3
Capeville—*locale* VA-3
Capeville Ch—*church* VA-3
Capeville (Magisterial District)—*fmr MCD* VA-3
**Cape Vincent**—*pop pl* NY-2
**Cape Vincent (Town of)**—*pop pl* NY-2
**Cape Vista**—*pop pl* FL-3
Cape Wash Island—*island* ME-1
**Cape Windsor (trailer park)**—*pop pl* DE-2
Cape Wislow—*cape* AK-9
Cape Woolley—*cape* AK-9
Cape Wrangell—*cape* AK-9
Cape Wykoff—*summit* NY-2
Cape Yakak—*cape* AK-9
Cape Yakataga—*cape* AK-9
Cape Yakataga—*locale* AK-9
Cape Yanaliuk—*cape* AK-9
Cape York—*cape* AK-9
**Cape York**—*pop pl* AK-9
Cap Fork—*stream* AR-4
*Cap Francois* FL-3
Capgage Wash—*stream* AZ-5
Cap Glacier—*glacier* AK-9
*Cap Haena* HI-9
Cap Healy Well—*well* OR-9
Cap Henry Lake—*lake* WI-6
Cap Henry Spring—*spring* NV-8
Cap Hill—*summit* VT-1
Cap Hollow—*valley* KY-4
Cap Hollow—*valley* MO-7
Cap Horn Forest Service Station—*locale* ID-8
Capidau JHS—*school* LA-4
Capidon Creek—*stream* NY-2
Capilla Bautista Betel (Midvale)—*church* UT-8
Capilla De Anones—*church* PR-3
Capilla de la Florecita—*church* PR-3
Capilla de la Milagrosa—*church* PR-3
Capilla de las Tunas—*church* PR-3
Capilla de la Virgen Inmaculada—*church* PR-3
Capilla del Carmen—*church* PR-3
Capilla del Perpetuo Socorro—*church* PR-3

Capilla del Pozo de la Virgen—*church* PR-3
Capilla del Sagrada Corazon de Jesus—*church* PR-3
Capilla del Sagrado Corazon—*church* PR-3
Capilla de Nuestra Senora de Guadalupe—*church* NM-5
Capilla de Paris—*church* PR-3
Capilla de San Alfonso—*church* PR-3
Capilla de San Antonio—*church* NM-5
Capilla de San Geraldo—*church* PR-3
Capilla de San Ignacio—*church* NM-5
Capilla de San Jose—*church* NM-5
Capilla de San Jose—*church* PR-3
Capilla de San Juan Bautista—*hist pl* CO-8
Capilla de San Miguel—*church* NM-5
Capilla de San Pedro—*church* NM-5
Capilla de San Rafael—*church* NM-5
Capilla de Santa Ana—*church* PR-3
Capilla de Santa Marta—*church* PR-3
Capilla de Santa Rita—*church* NM-5
Capilla de Santa Rosa—*church* PR-3
Capilla Fatima—*church* PR-3
Capilla La Virgen De Alta Gracia—*church* PR-3
Capilla La Virgen del Buen Conseio—*school* PR-3
Capilla La Virgen de Monserrate—*church* PR-3
Capilla Mal Paso—*church* PR-3
Capilla Peak—*summit* NM-5
Capilla Peak Observatory—*other* NM-5
Capilla San Francisco—*church* PR-3
Capilla San Jose—*church* PR-3
Capilla San Patricio—*church* PR-3
Capilla Santa Rita—*church* PR-3
Capilla Umberto Vazquez—*church* PR-3
Capinero Creek—*stream* CA-9
Capinero Saddle—*gap* CA-9
**Capioma**—*pop pl* KS-7
**Capioma Township**—*pop pl* KS-7
Capisic Pond—*reservoir* ME-1
Cap Island—*island* AK-9
**Capistrano Beach**—*pop pl* CA-9
Capistrano Bight—*bay* CA-9
**Capistrano Highlands**—*pop pl* CA-9
Capistrano Park—*park* CA-9
**Capistrano Villa Subdivision**—*pop pl* UT-8
Capistran Ranch—*locale* CA-9
Capita Canyon—*valley* CA-9
**Capital**—*pop pl* WA-9
Capital Airp—*airport* IL-6
**Capital Beltway**—*pop pl* MD-2
Capital Blvd Crossing—*hist pl* WA-9
*Capital Butte* AZ-5
Capital Camp—*locale* NV-8
*Capital Campus Penn State University* PA-2
Capital Center (Shop Ctr)—*locale* FL-3
Capital City Airp—*airport* MI-6
Capital City Airp—*airport* PA-2
Capital City Baptist Ch—*church* AL-4
Capital City Baptist Ch—*church* MS-4
Capital City Boys Club—*building* AL-4
Capital City Ch—*church* FL-3
Capital City Club—*hist pl* GA-3
Capital City Country Club—*locale* FL-3
Capital City Country Club—*other* GA-3
Capital City Mall—*locale* PA-2
Capital City Plaza—*locale* PA-2
Capital City Press Bldg—*hist pl* LA-4
Capital Club Bldg—*hist pl* NC-3
Capital District For And Game Refuge—*forest* NY-2
Capital Dome—*summit* NM-5
*Capital Dome Mountains* AZ-5
**Capital Estates**—*pop pl* MD-2
Capital Field—*park* FL-3
*Capital Heights* IA-7
Capital Heights—*uninc pl* AL-4
Capital Heights—*uninc pl* KY-4
Capital Heights—*uninc pl* LA-4
**Capital Heights (subdivision)**—*pop pl* TN-4
**Capital Hill**—*pop pl* CA-9
**Capital Hill**—*pop pl* TN-4
Capital Hotel—*hist pl* AR-4
Capital Kiwanis Club Pond Dam—*dam* NC-3
*Capital Lake* WA-9
Capital Mall (Shop Ctr)—*locale* MO-7
Capital Memorial Park (Cemetery)—*cemetery* TX-5
Capital Mtn—*summit* AK-9
Capital Park—*park* MI-6
Capital Parkway Shop Ctr—*locale* AL-4
*Capital Peak* CO-8
*Capital Peak* WA-9
Capital Plaza Shop Ctr—*locale* AL-4
Capital Plaza Shop Ctr—*locale* TX-5
Capital Prize Tunnel—*mine* CO-8
*Capital Rock* AZ-5
Capital Rock—*summit* MT-8
**Capital Township**—*pop pl* SD-7
**Capital (Township of)**—*pop pl* IL-6
**Capital Trail Farms**—*pop pl* DE-2
Capital Univ—*school* OH-6
Capital Univ Hist Dist—*hist pl* OH-6
Capital View Elem Sch—*school* KS-7
Capitan—*locale* CA-9
**Capitan**—*pop pl* LA-4
**Capitan**—*pop pl* NM-5
Capitan, Canada Del—*valley* CA-9
Capitan, Lake—*lake* MT-8
Capitan Canyon, El—*valley* AZ-5
Capitan (CCD)—*cens area* NM-5
Capitan Creek—*stream* MT-8
Capitanejo—*CDP* PR-3
**Capitanejo**—*pop pl* PR-3
Capitanejo (Barrio)—*fmr MCD* (2) PR-3
Capitan Flat, El—*flat* AZ-5
**Capitan Grande Ind Res**—*pop pl* CA-9
Capitan Hayes Tank—*reservoir* AZ-5
Capitan Hill—*locale* NM-5
Capitan Mine, El—*mine* AZ-5
Capitan Mountain, El—*summit* AZ-5
Capitan Mountains—*range* NM-5
Capitan Pass—*gap* NM-5
Capitan Peak—*summit* NM-5
Capitan Wash, El—*stream* AZ-5
Capitan Windmill—*locale* TX-5
**Capito**—*pop pl* KY-4
*Capitol* IL-6
**Capitol**—*pop pl* MT-8
Capitol—*post sta* VA-3
Capitol—*post sta* WI-6

Capitol—*uninc pl* AZ-5
Capitol—*uninc pl* LA-4
Capitol—*uninc pl* NY-2
Capitol—*uninc pl* SC-3
Capitol—*uninc pl* TX-5
Capitol—*uninc pl* WV-2
Capitol, The—*building* VA-3
Capitola—*locale* MD-2
Capitola—*locale* TX-5
**Capitola**—*pop pl* CA-9
**Capitola**—*pop pl* FL-3
Capitola Ditch—*canal* WY-8
Capitola Lake—*lake* WI-6
Capitol Annex—*building* AZ-5
Capitol Annex—*post sta* NY-2
Capitol Anthony Meldahl Lock And Dam—*dam* OH-6
Capitola Park—*park* CA-9
Capitol Area Hist Dist—*hist pl* NC-3
Capitola State Beach—*park* CA-9
**Capitola Township**—*pop pl* SD-7
Capitol Ave Sch—*school* LA-4
Capitol Baptist Ch—*church* DE-2
Capitol Bldg—*hist pl* CT-1
Capitol Bldg—*hist pl* UT-8
**Capitol Block Addition Subdivision**—*pop pl* UT-8
**Capitol Building Condominium, The**—*pop pl* UT-8
Capitol Butte—*summit* AZ-5
Capitol City—*locale* CO-8
Capitol City Ch of the Nazarene—*church* AL-4
Capitol City Junior Acad—*school* MN-6
Capitol Creek—*stream* CO-8
Capitol Creek—*stream* MT-8
Capitol Creek Guard Station—*locale* CO-8
Capitol Dome—*summit* NM-5
Capitol Dome Draw—*valley* NM-5
*Capitol Dome Mountains* AZ-5
Capitol Dome Ranch—*locale* NM-5
Capitol Extension District—*hist pl* CA-9
**Capitol Gardens Condominium**—*pop pl* UT-8
*Capitol Gorge - in part* UT-8
Capitol Green—*hist pl* MS-4
**Capitol Green**—*pop pl* DE-2
Capitol Heating Plant Bldg—*building* DC-2
**Capitol Heights**—*pop pl* IA-7
**Capitol Heights**—*pop pl* MD-2
Capitol Heights Baptist Ch—*church* AL-4
Capitol Heights Ch of Christ—*church* AL-4
**Capitol Heights Condominium**—*pop pl* UT-8
Capitol Heights JHS—*school* AL-4
Capitol Heights Methodist Ch—*church* AL-4
Capitol Heights Sch—*school* AL-4
Capitol Heights Sch—*school* MD-2
**Capitol Heights (subdivision)**—*pop pl* AL-4
**Capitol Heights Subdivision**—*pop pl* UT-8
*Capitol Hill* CO-8
Capitol Hill—*locale* TN-4
**Capitol Hill**—*pop pl* NJ-2
**Capitol Hill**—*pop pl* OR-9
**Capitol Hill**—*pop pl* WA-9
Capitol Hill—*summit* AR-4
Capitol Hill—*summit* DC-2
Capitol Hill—*summit* ID-8
Capitol Hill—*summit* ME-1
Capitol Hill—*summit* WY-8
Capitol Hill—*uninc pl* GA-3
Capitol Hill—*uninc pl* OK-5
Capitol Hill Airp—*airport* PA-2
Capitol Hill Cem—*cemetery* IN-6
Capitol Hill Ch—*church* KY-4
Capitol Hill Ch of Christ—*church* TN-4
Capitol Hill Hist Dist—*hist pl* DC-2
Capitol Hill Hist Dist—*hist pl* UT-8
Capitol Hill HS—*school* OK-5
Capitol Hill JHS—*school* OK-5
**Capitol Hills**—*pop pl* NY-2
Capitol Hills—*uninc pl* FL-3
Capitol Hill Sch—*hist pl* MI-6
Capitol Hill Sch—*school* AR-4
Capitol Hill Sch—*school* OR-9
Capitol Hill Sch—*school* TN-4
Capitol Hill Sch (historical)—*school* AL-4
Capitol Hill Sch (historical)—*school* TN-4
**Capitol Hill Subdivision**—*pop pl* UT-8
Capitol Hosp—*hospital* WI-6
Capitol HS—*school* LA-4
Capitol Island—*island* ME-1
**Capitol Island**—*pop pl* ME-1
Capitol JHS—*school* LA-4
Capitol Kiwanis Club Pond—*reservoir* NC-3
Capitol Lake—*lake* LA-4
Capitol Lake—*lake* WA-9
Capitol Lateral—*canal* ID-8
Capitol-Lincoln Terrace Hist Dist—*hist pl* OK-5
Capitol Lkae—*reservoir* CO-8
Capitol Mall Heliport—*airport* OR-9
Capitol Mesa—*summit* TX-5
Capitol Miles Standish Tree—*locale* CA-9
Capitol Mtn—*summit* MT-8
Capitol North Hist Dist—*hist pl* WY-8
**Capitol Oaks**—*pop pl* IL-6
*Capitol Park* AL-4
Capitol Park—*park* AL-4
**Capitol Park**—*pop pl* DE-2
Capitol Peak—*summit* CO-8
Capitol Peak—*summit* NV-8
Capitol Peak—*summit* NM-5
Capitol Peak—*summit* TX-5
Capitol Peak—*summit* (2) WA-9
Capitol Peak Canyon—*valley* TX-5
Capitol Peak Tank—*reservoir* NM-5
Capitol Plaza—*post sta* MD-2
Capitol Plaza (Shop Ctr)—*locale* FL-3
Capitol Reef—*ridge* UT-8
Capitol Reef Campground—*locale* UT-8
*Capitol Reef Cliffs* UT-8
Capitol Reef Natl Park—*park* (4) UT-8
Capitol Reef Natl Park Visitor Center—*locale* UT-8
Capitol Rock—*summit* CA-9
Capitol Sch—*school* AZ-5
Capitol Sch—*school* OK-5
Capitol Sch—*school* TX-5
Capitol Sch—*school* WV-2
Capitol South Metro Station—*locale* DC-2
Capitol State For—*forest* WA-9
Capitol Station Post Office—*building* AZ-5

Capitol Street United Methodist Ch—*church* MS-4
**Capitol Subdivision**—*pop pl* UT-8
Capitol Theater—*hist pl* NY-2
Capitol Theater Bldg—*hist pl* MA-1
Capitol Theatre—*hist pl* WA-9
Capitol Theatre Bldg—*hist pl* MI-6
Capitol View—*CDP* SC-3
**Capitol View**—*pop pl* DC-2
**Capitol View**—*pop pl* VA-3
Capitol View Canal—*canal* ID-8
Capitol View Cem—*cemetery* OK-5
Capitol View Ch—*church* SC-3
**Capitol View Park**—*pop pl* MD-2
Capitol View Sch—*school* GA-3
Capitol View Sch—*school* KS-7
Capitol View Sch—*school* MN-6
Capitol View Sch—*school* PA-2
**Capitol View Subdivision**—*pop pl* UT-8
Capitol Wash—*arroyo* NV-8
Capitol Wash—*valley* UT-8
*Cap Kaena* HI-9
*Cap Kalae* HI-9
Cap Knob—*summit* MO-7
*Cap Koko* HI-9
Cap-K-Ranch—*locale* CO-8
Cap Lake—*lake* MN-6
Caple Creek—*stream* AR-4
*Cap Lefanot* FM-9
**Caplen**—*pop pl* TX-5
Caplener Branch—*stream* AR-4
Caples, Richard, Bldg—*hist pl* TX-5
Caples Creek—*stream* CA-9
Caples Creek—*stream* MO-7
Caples Hollow—*valley* AR-4
Caples Lake—*lake* CA-9
Caples Landing—*locale* WA-9
Caples' Park Hist Dist—*hist pl* WI-6
Caples'-Ringlings' Estates Hist Dist—*hist pl* FL-3
Caples (RR name for Capels)—*other* WV-2
**Capleville**—*pop pl* TN-4
Capleville HS—*school* TN-4
Capleville Methodist Church—*hist pl* TN-4
Caplewood Drive Hist Dist—*hist pl* AL-4
Capley Cem—*cemetery* TN-4
*Caplin* FM-9
Caplinger Creek—*stream* OR-9
Caplinger Hollow—*valley* TN-4
**Caplinger Mills**—*pop pl* MO-7
Caplinger Pond—*swamp* IL-6
Caplinger-Smith House—*hist pl* TN-4
Capling Post Office (historical)—*building* TN-4
Capling Primitive Baptist Ch (historical)—*church* TN-4
Capling Ridge—*ridge* TN-4
Capling Sch (historical)—*school* TN-4
Caplis—*locale* LA-4
Cap Martin Mine—*mine* OR-9
Cap Mauzy Lake—*reservoir* KY-4
Cap Mountain Cem—*cemetery* TX-5
Cap Mtn—*summit* CO-8
Cap Mtn—*summit* (2) MT-8
Cap Mtn—*summit* (2) TX-5
*Capoage* MA-1
*Capoag Island* MA-1
Capo Creek—*stream* FL-3
*Capoge* MA-1
*Capoge Pond* MA-1
**Capol**—*pop pl* NC-3
Capola Mtn—*summit* VA-3
*Cap Oligabi* FM-9
Capoli Mill—*locale* IA-7
Capoli Slough—*gut* WI-6
**Capon Bridge**—*pop pl* WV-2
Capon Brook—*stream* VT-1
Capon Chapel—*church* WV-2
Capone Creek—*stream* MI-6
Caponera Peak—*summit* AZ-5
Caponera Tank—*reservoir* AZ-5
Capon Flat—*flat* OR-9
Caponia Ch—*church* SC-3
**Capon Lake**—*pop pl* WV-2
Capon (Magisterial District)—*fmr MCD* (2) WV-2
Capon Point—*cape* LA-4
*Capon River* WV-2
Capon Road—*locale* VA-3
Capon Run—*stream* VA-3
Capon Run—*stream* WV-2
Capon Sch—*school* WV-2
**Capon Springs**—*pop pl* WV-2
Capon Springs Run—*stream* WV-2
Capoolong Creek—*stream* NJ-2
Capoolong Creek Fish and Wildlife Mngmt Area—*park* NJ-2
Capoose Creek—*stream* WA-9
Caporal Tank—*reservoir* AZ-5
*Cap Oroit* FM-9
Capos Island—*island* FL-3
Capota Cem—*cemetery* TX-5
Capota Creek—*stream* TX-5
Capote Banco Number 13—*levee* TX-5
Capote Campground—*locale* CO-8
Capote Ch—*church* TX-5
Capote Creek—*stream* TX-5
*Capote Draw* TX-5
Capote Draw—*valley* TX-5
Capote Falls—*falls* TX-5
Capote Hills—*summit* TX-5
Capote Knob—*summit* TX-5
Capote Lake—*lake* MN-6
Capote Lake—*reservoir* CO-8
Capote Peak—*summit* TX-5
Capote Ranch—*locale* TX-5
Capouse Rsvr (historical)—*reservoir* PA-2
Capouse Shaft—*mine* PA-2
Capoust—*locale* PA-2
*Cap Ovoit* FM-9
Cappadocia Ch—*church* AR-4
Cappadocia Ch—*church* NC-3
*Cappahosack* VA-3
Cappallo Camp—*locale* NV-8
*Cappamet Harbor* MA-1
*Cappaqua* KS-7
Capp Branch—*stream* TN-4
Capp Cem—*cemetery* IN-6
Capp Cem—*cemetery* MS-4
Capp Cem—*cemetery* MO-7
Capp Creek—*stream* NC-3

Cap Peak—summit ... UT-8
Cappel Bayou—stream ... LA-4
Cappelen Memorial Bridge—hist pl ... MN-6
Cappelen Sch—school ... NE-7
Cappell Creek—stream ... CA-9
Cappell Flat—flat ... CA-9
Cappelli, A. F., Block—hist pl ... RI-1
**Cappeln**—pop pl ... MO-7
Cappeln Lookout (historical)—locale ... MO-7
Cappeln Sch (abandoned)—school ... MO-7
**Capperas Banks (historical)**—pop pl ... IN-6
*Capper Creek* ... VA-3
Capper Draw—valley ... KS-7
Capper JHS—school ... KS-7
Capper Ridge—ridge ... VA-3
*Cappers Ridge* ... VA-3
Cappies Rock Spring—spring ... UT-8
Capples Pond—reservoir ... NC-3
*Cappo* ... AL-4
Cappon, Isaac, House—hist pl ... MI-6
Cappo Run—stream ... WV-2
*Capps* ... TX-5
**Capps**—pop pl ... AL-4
**Capps**—pop pl ... AR-4
**Capps**—pop pl ... FL-3
**Capps**—pop pl ... MO-7
**Capps**—pop pl ... TX-5
Capps, Mount—summit ... AK-9
Capps Branch—stream ... AR-4
Capps Branch—stream ... NC-3
Capps Branch—stream (2) ... TN-4
Capps Cem—cemetery (4) ... NC-3
Capps Cem—cemetery (2) ... TN-4
Capps Cem—cemetery ... TX-5
Capps Ch—church ... AL-4
Capps City—locale ... AR-4
Capps Corner—locale ... TX-5
Capps Creek—stream ... AK-9
Capps Creek—stream (2) ... MO-7
Capps Creek—stream ... TN-4
Capps Creek—stream ... WA-9
Capps Creek Ch—church ... TN-4
Capps Creek Sch (historical)—school ... TN-4
Capps Creek Township—civil ... MO-7
Capps Crossing—locale ... CA-9
Capps Crossing (historical)—crossing ... TN-4
**Capps Ford (historical)**—pop pl ... TN-4
Capps Ford Post Office (historical)—building ... TN-4
Capps Gap—gap ... TN-4
Capps Glacier—glacier ... AK-9
Capps Hill—summit ... NC-3
*Capps Hollow* ... TN-4
Capps Hollow—valley (2) ... MO-7
Capps Hollow—valley ... NC-3
Capps Hollow—valley (5) ... TN-4
Capps Hollow Bend—bend ... TN-4
Capps Lake—lake ... NM-5
Capps Lake—reservoir ... KS-7
Capps Lake—reservoir ... NC-3
Capps Mine (underground)—mine ... AL-4
Capps Mtn—summit ... NC-3
Capps Mtn—summit ... OR-9
Capps Park—park ... TX-5
Capps Pond—reservoir ... AL-4
Capps Post Office (historical)—building ... AL-4
Capps Ranch—locale ... CO-8
Capps Sch (abandoned)—school ... MO-7
Capps Springs—spring ... CO-8
*Capps Station* ... TX-5
Capps Switch—locale ... TX-5
Capps Well—well ... NM-5
Cappy Branch—stream ... TN-4
Cappy Mtn—summit ... OR-9
Cappy Springs Branch—stream ... TN-4
Capri, Lake—lake ... NY-2
Caprice Island—island ... NY-2
Capricorn Mine (underground)—mine ... AL-4
*Caprien Bay* ... LA-4
**Capri Gardens**—pop pl ... IL-6
**Capri Islands**—pop pl ... AL-4
Capri Isle—island ... FL-3
Capri Lake—lake ... MT-8
Capri Pass—gut ... FL-3
Capri Sch—school ... CA-9
Capris Pass Approach Light—locale ... FL-3
**Caprivi**—pop pl ... PA-2
**Capri Village**—pop pl ... IL-6
Capri Village (trailer park)—locale ... AZ-5
**Capri Village (trailer park)**—pop pl ... AZ-5
Cap Rock—island ... CA-9
Cap Rock—locale ... CA-9
Caprock—locale ... NM-5
Cap Rock—locale ... TX-5
Cap Rock—pillar ... CO-8
Cap Rock—summit ... MT-8
Caprock, The—cliff ... NM-5
Cap Rock, The—cliff ... NM-5
*Caprock Butte* ... SD-7
Cap Rock Butte—summit ... MT-8
Caprock Butte—summit ... MT-8
Cap Rock Butte—summit ... TX-5
Caprock Ch—church ... NM-5
Caprock Ch—church ... TX-5
Caprock Coulee—valley ... MT-8
Caprock East Oil Field—other ... NM-5
Caprock Mtn—summit ... NM-5
Caprock Mtn—summit ... TX-5
Caprock North Oil Field—other ... NM-5
Caprock Oil Field—other (2) ... NM-5
Caprock Prong—valley ... NM-5
Caprock Ranch—locale ... NM-5
Caprock Ranch—locale ... TX-5
Cap Rock Ridge—ridge ... CO-8
Cap Rock Ridge—ridge ... MT-8
Caprock Station—locale ... TX-5
Caprock Well—well ... TX-5
Capron—locale ... IA-7
**Capron**—pop pl ... IL-6
**Capron**—pop pl ... OK-5
**Capron**—pop pl ... VA-3
Capron, Charles, House—hist pl ... MA-1
Capron, George, House—hist pl ... MA-1
Capron Cem—cemetery ... OK-5
Capron Cem—cemetery ... TX-5
Capron Cem—cemetery ... VA-3
Capron Creek—stream ... MT-8
Capron District Sch—school ... VA-3
Capron Ditch—canal ... CO-8
Capron House—hist pl ... MA-1
Capron Lookout Tower—locale ... VA-3
Capron (Magisterial District)—fmr MCD ... VA-3
Capron Mine—mine ... CO-8
Capron Park—park ... MA-1
Capron-Phillips House—hist pl ... CT-1
Capron Pond—reservoir ... RI-1
Caprons Pond—reservoir ... MA-1
Caprons Pond Dam—dam ... MA-1
Capron Spring—spring ... OR-9
Cap Run—stream ... IN-6
Cap Run—stream ... WV-2
**Caps**—pop pl ... TX-5
Caps, Ridge of the—ridge ... NH-1
*Cap Saboo* ... FM-9
*Capsante* ... WA-9
Capsante—uninc pl ... WA-9
Cap Sante Park—park ... WA-9
Caps Bay—swamp ... FL-3
*Caps Branch* ... MO-7
Caps Branch—stream ... MO-7
Caps Branch—stream ... NC-3
Caps Creek—stream ... MI-6
Caps Creek—stream ... OR-9
Caps Creek—stream ... WI-6
Capser Ranch—locale ... MT-8
Capsey Creek—stream ... AL-4
**Capshaw**—pop pl ... AL-4
Capshaw Baptist Ch—church ... AL-4
Capshaw Branch—stream ... TN-4
Capshaw Hollow—valley ... KY-4
Capshaw Hollow—valley ... TN-4
Capshaw Mill (historical)—locale ... TN-4
Capshaw Mtn—summit ... AL-4
Capshaw Post Office—building ... AL-4
Capshaw Sch—school ... TN-4
Capshaw Sch (historical)—school ... AL-4
**Capshaw Woods (subdivision)**—pop pl ... TN-4
Capsies Creek—gut ... VA-3
Capsies Creek—stream ... NC-3
Cap Smith Hill—summit ... CO-8
Cap Spring—spring (2) ... KY-4
Cap Spring Creek—stream ... KY-4
Caps Ravine—valley ... CA-9
Caps Spring—spring ... CO-8
Capstan Rock—island ... MN-6
Capstick Ranch—locale ... SD-7
**Capstone Court (subdivision)**—pop pl ... AL-4
Capstone Med Ctr—hospital ... AL-4
Capsuttle Creek—stream ... OR-9
Captain—locale ... KS-7
Captain—locale ... VA-3
Captain Adams House—hist pl ... AL-4
Captain Athony Meldahl Lock and Dam—dam ... KY-4
Captain Bangs-Hallett House—building ... MA-1
Captain Beal Gulch—valley ... CO-8
Captain Bill Creek—stream ... SC-3
Captain Bluff Camp (Abandoned)—locale ... AK-9
Captain Butte—summit ... ID-8
Captain Cem—cemetery ... OK-5
**Captain Cook**—pop pl ... HI-9
Captain Cook Point—cape ... OR-9
*Captain Cooks Monument* ... HI-9
Captain Cook State Rec Area—park ... AK-9
Captain Creek—stream ... AK-9
Captain Creek—stream ... CA-9
Captain Creek—stream ... KS-7
Captain Creek—stream ... MO-7
Captain Creek—stream ... OK-5
Captain Creek—stream ... OR-9
Captain Creek—stream ... WA-9
Captain Creek Cem—cemetery ... MO-7
Captain Creek Ch—church ... KS-7
Captain Creek Community Center—locale ... OK-5
Captain Creek Sch (abandoned)—school ... MO-7
Captain Davis Mtn—summit ... NM-5
Captain Fleming Swamp—swamp ... GA-3
Captain Freese House—hist pl ... KY-4
Captain George Cem—cemetery ... NV-8
Captain Gray Mountain—ridge ... OR-9
Captain Gray Sch—school ... WA-9
Captain Green Monmt—park ... PA-2
Captain Harbor—bay ... AK-9
Captain Harbor—bay ... CT-1
Captain Haun Creek—stream ... CA-9
*Captain Henry D Allen Park* ... AL-4
Captain Hickory Run—stream ... VA-3
*Captain Hill* ... MA-1
Captain Hollow—valley ... KY-4
Captain Jack—summit ... OR-9
Captain Jack Creek—stream ... WY-8
Captain Jack Lake—lake ... OR-9
Captain Jacks Bridge—bridge ... CA-9
Captain Jacks Cave—cave ... AL-4
Captain Jacks Dry Diggins (historical)—locale ... SD-7
Captain Jacks Ice Cave—cave ... CA-9
Captain Jack Spring—spring ... NV-8
Captain Jack's Stronghold—hist pl ... CA-9
Captain Jacobson Creek—stream ... MN-6
Captain James Booth Memorial—other ... WV-2
Captain Jims Pond—reservoir ... SC-3
Captain J Mullan Historic Monmt—park ... WA-9
Captain Joe Island—island ... FL-3
Captain John Creek—stream (2) ... ID-8
Captain John Ferry—locale ... ID-8
Captain John Gulch—valley ... CA-9
Captain John J Clark Memorial Monmt—park ... NV-8
Captain John Mtn—summit ... CA-9
Captain John Rapids—rapids ... ID-8
Captain John Rapids—rapids ... WA-9
*Captain John's Creek* ... MD-2
Captain John Smith Monmt—park ... NH-1
Captain John Snodgrass Bridge—bridge ... AL-4
Captain Keeney Pass—gap ... OR-9
Captain Key—island ... FL-3
**Captain Kidd Estates**—pop pl ... NY-2
Captain Kidd Island—island ... MI-6
Captain Kid Hollow—basin ... NY-2
Captain Kid Monument—other ... NY-2
Captain Lewis Rapids—rapids ... ID-8
Captain Lewis Rapids—rapids ... WA-9
Captain Luke Lake—lake ... MN-6
Captain Meriwether Lewis (dredge)—hist pl ... NE-7
Captain Mtn—summit ... CO-8
Captain Point—cape ... MD-2
Captain Point—cliff ... WA-9
Captain Pomin Rock—pillar ... NV-8
Captain Pond—lake ... NH-1
Captain Pond Brook—stream ... NH-1
Captain Prairie—flat ... OR-9
Captain Robert Grant Sch—school ... OR-9
*Captain Rock* ... MN-6
*Captains, The* ... AZ-5
Captain Sams Creek—stream ... SC-3
Captain Sams Inlet—gut ... SC-3
Captain Sanders Hollow—valley ... AR-4
Captains Bay—bay ... AK-9
Captains Cabin—locale ... ID-8
Captains Ch—church ... MA-1
**Captains Cove**—pop pl ... MD-2
*Captains Creek* ... KS-7
Captains Creek—stream ... SC-3
**Captains Grant (trailer park)**—pop pl ... DE-2
Captain Shelton Trail—trail ... PA-2
**Captains Hill**—pop pl ... MD-2
Captains Hill—summit ... MA-1
Captain's Houses—hist pl ... MD-2
Captain Simmons Ch—church ... MS-4
Captain's Landing—obs name ... ND-7
Captain Smiths Cem—cemetery ... AR-4
*Captain Smith's Point* ... NY-2
Captains Rock—pillar ... CO-8
Captain Taggart Sch—school ... OH-6
Captain Tom Rsvr—reservoir ... NM-5
Captain Tom Wash—stream ... NM-5
Captain Trap Spring—spring ... AZ-5
Captain Vinyard Hollow—valley ... IL-6
Captain White Hill—summit ... PA-2
*Captain William Smith House* ... MA-1
Captain York Cem—cemetery ... TX-5
Cap Tank—reservoir ... AZ-5
Capt. Harris House—hist pl ... TN-4
Captina—locale ... WV-2
**Captina**—pop pl ... OH-6
Captina Ch—church ... OH-6
Captina Creek—stream ... OH-6
Captina Island—island ... WV-2
*Captinger Creek* ... OR-9
**Captiva**—pop pl ... FL-3
Captiva Island—island ... FL-3
Captiva Pass—channel ... FL-3
Captiva Rocks—island ... FL-3
Captivas Canyon—valley ... NM-5
Captiva Shoal—bar ... FL-3
Captivas Peak—summit ... NM-5
Captive Inca Mine—mine ... CO-8
*Captive Island* ... FL-3
*Captola* ... GA-3
**Captolo**—pop pl ... GA-3
Captree Island—island ... NY-2
Captree Sch—school ... NY-2
Captree State Park—park ... NY-2
Capt St. Claire—other ... MD-2
Capt. Stone House—hist pl ... OH-6
Captured Canyon—valley ... NV-8
Capuchin Creek—stream ... KY-4
Capuchin Creek—stream ... TN-4
Capuchino HS—school ... CA-9
Capuchin Post Office (historical)—building ... TN-4
Capuchin Retreat—church ... MI-6
Capuchin Seminary—school ... IN-6
Capuein, Bayou—stream ... LA-4
*Cap Ulap* ... FM-9
**Capulin**—pop pl ... CO-8
**Capulin**—pop pl ... NM-5
Capulin Arroyo—stream ... CO-8
Capulin Cabin—locale ... NM-5
Capulin Campground—locale ... NM-5
Capulin Canyon—valley (8) ... NM-5
Capulin Canyon Trail—trail ... NM-5
Capulin Cem—cemetery ... CO-8
*Capulin Creek* ... NM-5
Capulin Creek—stream (3) ... NM-5
Capulin Ditch—canal ... CO-8
Capulin Hill—summit ... NM-5
Capulin Lake—lake ... NM-5
*Capulin Mesa* ... NM-5
Capulin Mountain Natl Monmt—park ... NM-5
Capulin Mtn—summit ... NM-5
Capulin Peak—summit (3) ... NM-5
Capulin Picnic Area—locale ... NM-5
Capulin Sch—school ... NM-5
Capulin Spring—spring ... NM-5
Capulin Trail—trail ... NM-5
*Cap Ulongong* ... FM-9
*Cap Unumou* ... FM-9
*Cap Upolu* ... HI-9
Capush Island—island ... NJ-2
**Caputa**—pop pl ... SD-7
Caputo Helistop—airport ... NJ-2
Caput Sch—school ... MO-7
Cap Wallace Gulch—valley ... MT-8
Capwell Millpond—reservoir ... RI-1
Capwells Crossroads—locale ... SC-3
Cap White Ridge—ridge ... WY-8
Cap Winn Creek—stream ... NV-8
Caquila Canyon—valley ... NM-5
Caquin Bay—lake ... LA-4
**Car A**—pop pl ... CA-9
**Cara**—pop pl ... FL-3
*Carabasset River* ... ME-1
Cara Cem—cemetery ... GA-3
Carache Canyon—valley ... NM-5
Caracita Creek—stream ... NM-5
Caracita Windmill—locale ... NM-5
Caraco Creek—stream ... WA-9
Caracol (Barrio)—fmr MCD ... PR-3
Caracol Creek—stream ... TX-5
Caracole, The—trail ... CA-9
Caracol Island—island ... AK-9
Cara Cove—bay ... MD-2
**Caradan**—pop pl ... TX-5
Cara Del Eco Ruins—locale ... UT-8
Caradine Bldg—hist pl ... WI-6
*Caraghar* ... OH-6
Caraghar—other ... OH-6
Caralampi Canyon—valley ... AZ-5
Caralampi Tank—reservoir ... AZ-5
**Caraleigh**—pop pl ... NC-3
Caralier County—civil ... ND-7
Caralita Ranch—locale ... TX-5
Caramayola Windmill—locale ... TX-5
Caramba Camp—locale ... CA-9
Carambana Windmill—locale ... TX-5
**Caramel Village**—pop pl ... TN-4
Carancahua—locale ... TX-5
Carancahua Bay—bay ... TX-5
Carancahua Bayou—stream ... TX-5
Carancahua Bend—bend ... TX-5
Carancahua Ch—church ... TX-5
Carancahua Cove—bay ... TX-5
*Carancahua Creek* ... TX-5
Carancahua Lake—lake ... TX-5
Carancahua Pass—channel ... TX-5
Carancahua Point—cape ... TX-5
Carancahua Reef—bar ... TX-5
*Carancaway Bay* ... TX-5
C A Ranch—locale ... MT-8
*Caranchahua Bay* ... TX-5
*Caranchua Bayou* ... TX-5
*Carankawa Point* ... TX-5
*Carankaway bay* ... TX-5
*Carankaway Bayou* ... TX-5
Caranti Bros Mine—mine ... NM-5
*Caraparasu To* ... PW-9
*Cara Pelau* ... FL-3
*Carapellas* ... PW-9
*Carapolis* ... PA-2
Carara—locale ... AL-4
Carasaljo, Lake—reservoir ... NJ-2
*Carasarga Mountain* ... NH-1
*Carassee Creek* ... TX-5
Caratan (Siding)—locale ... CA-9
**Caratunk**—pop pl ... ME-1
Caratunk Falls—falls ... ME-1
Caratunk Falls Archeol District—hist pl ... ME-1
Caratunk (Plantation of)—civ div ... ME-1
**Caravel Farms**—pop pl ... DE-2
**Caravelle**—pop pl ... TN-4
Caravel Park—park ... FL-3
**Caraway**—pop pl ... AR-4
*Caraway and Phifer Landing* ... FL-3
Caraway Cem—cemetery (3) ... TN-4
Caraway Cem—cemetery ... TX-5
Caraway Ch—church ... NC-3
*Caraway Creek* ... MS-4
Caraway Creek—stream ... CA-9
Caraway Creek—stream (2) ... NC-3
Caraway Dam Number One—dam ... NC-3
Caraway Dam Number Two—dam ... NC-3
Caraway Hills—summit ... TN-4
Caraway Lake—lake ... FL-3
Caraway Lake—lake ... LA-4
Caraway Lake—lake ... MN-6
Caraway Lake Number One—reservoir ... NC-3
Caraway Lake Number Two—reservoir ... NC-3
Caraway Landing—locale ... FL-3
Caraway Landing—locale ... NC-3
Caraway Mill Pond—lake ... FL-3
Caraway Mtn—summit ... NC-3
Caraway State Wildlife Mngmt Area—park ... MN-6
Cara Windmill—locale ... TX-5
Car Barn Hill—summit ... NH-1
Car Barn Pond—lake ... NH-1
Carbaugh Cem—cemetery ... IN-6
Carbaugh Drain—canal ... MI-6
Carbaugh Rsvr—reservoir ... PA-2
Carbaugh Run—stream ... PA-2
Carbaugh Run Dam—dam ... PA-2
Carbaugh Run Natural Area—area ... PA-2
Carbaugh Run Rhyolite Quarry Site (36AD30)—hist pl ... PA-2
Carbee Cem—cemetery ... NH-1
Carbella—locale ... MT-8
Carbell Swamp—stream ... VA-3
Carberry, Mount—summit ... NH-1
*Carberry Creek* ... OR-9
Carberry Creek—stream ... OR-9
Carberry Flat—flat ... CA-9
Carberry Forest Camp—locale ... OR-9
Carberry Mtn—summit ... CA-9
Carberry Rsvr—reservoir ... MT-8
Carberry Run—stream ... WV-2
Carber Sch—school ... IL-6
Carbert—locale ... MT-8
Carbide—locale ... WV-2
**Carbide**—pop pl ... FL-3
Carbide Park—park ... TN-4
Carbine Lake—lake ... MT-8
Carbinville Ch—church ... AL-4
**Carbo**—pop pl ... VA-3
**Carboco**—pop pl ... LA-4
Carbo Draw—valley ... WY-8
Carbolyn State Park—park ... KS-7
*Carbon* ... IL-6
*Carbon* ... ND-7
*Carbon* ... PA-2
*Carbon* ... WV-2
Carbon—locale ... IA-7
Carbon—locale ... OK-5
Carbon—locale ... PA-2
Carbon—locale ... WY-8
**Carbon**—pop pl ... IL-6
**Carbon**—pop pl ... IN-6
**Carbon**—pop pl ... IA-7
**Carbon**—pop pl (2) ... PA-2
**Carbon**—pop pl ... TX-5
**Carbon**—pop pl ... WV-2
Carbon, Mount—summit ... CO-8
Carbon, Mount—summit ... IL-6
*Carbona* ... KS-7
**Carbona**—pop pl ... CA-9
**Carbonado**—pop pl ... WA-9
Carbonado Cem—cemetery ... MT-8
Carbonado Ditch—canal ... MT-8
Carbonado Mine—mine ... MT-8
*Carbonale Basin* ... CO-8
Carbonate—locale ... CO-8
Carbonate Basin—basin ... CO-8
Carbonate Camp Rsvr No. 6—reservoir ... CO-8
Carbonate Camp Rsvr No. 7—reservoir ... CO-8
Carbonate Canyon—valley ... AZ-5
*Carbonate City* ... SD-7
*Carbonate Creek* ... ID-8
Carbonate Creek—stream ... CO-8
Carbonate Creek—stream ... ID-8
Carbonate Creek—stream ... NM-5
Carbonate Gulch—valley ... CA-9
Carbonate Gulch—valley ... UT-8
Carbonate Hill—summit (4) ... CO-8
Carbonate Hill—summit ... ID-8
Carbonate Hill Mine—mine ... ID-8
Carbonate Hill Mine—mine ... NM-5
Carbonate (historical)—locale ... ID-8
**Carbonate (historical)**—pop pl ... SD-7
Carbonate King Mine—mine ... CA-9
Carbonate King Mine—mine ... CO-8
Carbonate King Mine—mine ... MT-8
Carbonate Mine—mine ... MT-8
Carbonate Mine—mine (2) ... UT-8
Carbonate Mtn—summit (2) ... CO-8
Carbonate Mtn—summit ... ID-8
Carbonate Mtn—summit ... MT-8
Carbonate Peak—summit ... CA-9
Carbonate Ridge—ridge ... NV-8
Carbonate Wash—stream ... NV-8
Carbon Beach—beach ... CA-9
Carbon Butte—summit ... AZ-5
Carbon Camp—locale ... AK-9
Carbon Canal—canal ... MT-8
Carbon Canal—canal ... UT-8
**Carbon Canyon**—pop pl ... CA-9
Carbon Canyon—valley ... AZ-5
Carbon Canyon—valley (2) ... CA-9
Carbon Canyon—valley ... NM-5
Carbon Canyon Creek—stream ... CA-9
Carbon Canyon Dam—dam ... CA-9
Carbon Canyon Diversion Channel—channel ... CA-9
Carbon Cem—cemetery ... OK-5
Carbon Center—locale ... ID-8
**Carbon Center**—pop pl ... MO-7
**Carbon Center**—pop pl ... PA-2
**Carbon City**—pop pl ... AR-4
Carbon City Mine—mine ... NM-5
Carbon City Park—park ... NC-3
**Carbon Cliff**—pop pl ... IL-6
Carbon County—civil ... UT-8
**Carbon County**—pop pl ... PA-2
Carbon County Airp—airport ... PA-2
Carbon County Airp—airport ... UT-8
Carbon County Cem—cemetery ... UT-8
Carbon County Farm—locale ... PA-2
Carbon County Jail—hist pl ... PA-2
Carbon County Section of the Lehigh Canal—hist pl ... PA-2
*Carbon Creek* ... WY-8
Carbon Creek—stream (4) ... AK-9
Carbon Creek—stream ... AZ-5
Carbon Creek—stream ... CA-9
Carbon Creek—stream ... CO-8
Carbon Creek—stream ... ID-8
Carbon Creek—stream ... WY-8
Carbondale—locale ... CA-9
Carbondale—locale ... MI-6
Carbondale—locale ... TX-5
**Carbondale**—pop pl ... CO-8
**Carbondale**—pop pl ... GA-3
**Carbondale**—pop pl ... IL-6
**Carbondale**—pop pl ... IN-6
**Carbondale**—pop pl ... IA-7
**Carbondale**—pop pl ... KS-7
**Carbondale**—pop pl ... KY-4
**Carbondale**—pop pl ... OH-6
**Carbondale**—pop pl ... OK-5
**Carbondale**—pop pl ... PA-2
**Carbondale**—pop pl ... WV-2
Carbondale Cem—cemetery ... CO-8
Carbondale Cem—cemetery ... KS-7
Carbondale City—civil ... PA-2
Carbondale City Hall and Courthouse—hist pl ... PA-2
Carbondale-Clifford Airp—airport ... PA-2
Carbondale Creek—stream ... OH-6
Carbondale Number Four Dam—dam ... PA-2
Carbondale Number Four Rsvr—reservoir ... PA-2
*Carbondale Post Office* ... TN-4
Carbondale Rsvr—reservoir ... IL-6
**Carbondale Township**—pop pl ... ND-7
**Carbondale (Township of)**—pop pl ... IL-6
**Carbondale (Township of)**—pop pl ... PA-2
Carbon Dioxide Cave—cave ... AL-4
Carbon East—cens area ... MT-8
**Carbonell**—pop pl ... PR-3
Carbonera—locale ... CO-8
Carbonera Creek—stream ... CA-9
Carbonero Mine—mine ... CO-8
Carbon Fuel Mine No 2—mine ... UT-8
Carbon Fuel Mine No 3—mine ... UT-8
Carbon Glacier—glacier ... WA-9
Carbon Glow—locale ... KY-4
*Carbonhill* ... KS-7
**Carbon Hill**—pop pl ... AL-4
**Carbon Hill**—pop pl ... IL-6
**Carbon Hill**—pop pl ... OH-6
**Carbon Hill**—pop pl ... TN-4
Carbon Hill—summit ... CO-8
Carbon Hill—summit ... MT-8
Carbon Hill Breaker (historical)—building ... PA-2
Carbon Hill (CCD)—cens area ... AL-4
Carbon Hill Cem—cemetery ... OH-6
Carbon Hill Ch of Christ—church ... AL-4
Carbon Hill Division—civil ... AL-4
Carbon Hill Elem Sch—school ... AL-4
Carbon Hill Grammar Sch (historical)—school ... AL-4
Carbon Hill (historical)—locale ... KS-7
Carbon Hill HS—school ... AL-4
Carbon Hill JHS—school ... AL-4
Carbon Hill Mine (underground)—mine ... AL-4
Carbon Hill Natl Fish Hatchery—other ... AL-4
Carbon Hill Presbyterian Ch—church ... AL-4
Carbon Hill Shaft (historical)—mine ... PA-2
Carbon HS—school ... UT-8
Carbonite Mine, The—mine ... CO-8
Carbon Junction—locale ... CO-8
Carbon Junction Canyon—valley ... CO-8
Carbon Lake—lake ... AK-9
Carbon Lake—lake ... IL-6
Carbon Mtn—summit ... AK-9
Carbonneau Mansion—hist pl ... WA-9
Carbon Peak—summit ... CO-8
Carbon Ridge—ridge ... AK-9
Carbon Ridge—ridge ... NV-8
Carbon Ridge—ridge ... WA-9
Carbon River—stream ... WA-9
Carbon River Entrance—locale ... WA-9
Carbon River Ranger Station—locale ... WA-9
**Carbon (RR name South Carbon)**—pop pl ... WV-2
Carbon Run—stream (2) ... PA-2
Carbon Run Breaker Station—locale ... PA-2
Carbon Springs—spring ... NM-5
Carbon Stream—stream ... IN-6
**Carbonton**—pop pl ... NC-3
Carbonton Ch—church ... NC-3
**Carbonton Heights (subdivision)**—pop pl ... NC-3
**Carbon (Township of)**—pop pl ... PA-2
**Carbon (Trachsville)**—pop pl ... PA-2
Carbon Trail—trail ... PA-2
Carbon Trail—trail ... WA-9
**Carbonville**—pop pl ... UT-8
Carbonville Sch (historical)—school ... UT-8
Carbough Sch—school ... IL-6
**Car Branch**—pop pl ... TN-4
Car Branch—stream ... WV-2
Carbullido Sch—school ... GU-9
Carbuncle Hill—summit ... RI-1
Carbuncle Hill Archaeol District, RI-1072-1079—hist pl ... RI-1
Carbuncle Pond—lake ... MA-1
Carbuncle Pond—lake ... RI-1
Carbur—locale ... FL-3
Carbur Lookout Tower—tower ... FL-3
*Carbury* ... ND-7
**Carbury**—pop pl ... ND-7
Carbytown Cem—cemetery ... KY-4
**Carcajou**—pop pl ... WI-6
Carcajou Lake—lake ... MT-8
Carcajou Point (47 Je 2)—hist pl ... WI-6
Carcass Basin—basin ... NM-5
Carcass Branch—stream ... KY-4
Carcass Brook—stream ... NY-2
Carcass Canyon—valley ... UT-8
Carcass Coulee—valley ... MT-8
Carcass Creek—stream ... ID-8
Carcass Creek—stream ... UT-8
Carcass Gulch—valley ... CO-8
Carcassonne—locale ... KY-4
Carcass Ridge—ridge ... WY-8
Carcass Wash—valley ... UT-8
Carcel de Puerta de Tierra—hist pl ... PR-3
*Carcitas Creek* ... TX-5
Carco Air Service—building ... NM-5
Car Creek—stream ... GA-3
Car Creek—stream ... WY-8
Carcus Creek—stream ... OR-9
Card, Rupert, House—hist pl ... WA-9
Cardai Hill—cape ... WA-9
**Cardale**—pop pl ... PA-2
Cardale Elem Sch—school ... PA-2
Cardareva Bluff—cliff ... MO-7
Cardareva Mtn—summit ... MO-7
Cardareva State For—forest (2) ... MO-7
Card Bank—bar ... FL-3
Card Branch—stream ... TN-4
Card Brook—stream (2) ... ME-1
Card Campground—locale ... UT-8
Card Canyon—valley ... UT-8
*Card Canyon Forest Service Station* ... UT-8
Card Canyon Guard Station—locale ... UT-8
Card Cem—cemetery ... MI-6
Card Cem—cemetery ... NY-2
Card Cem—cemetery ... PA-2
Card Cem—cemetery (2) ... TN-4
Card Cove—bay (2) ... ME-1
Card Creek—stream ... CO-8
Card Creek—stream ... KS-7
Card Creek—stream ... KY-4
Card Creek—stream ... PA-2
Card Creek Cem—cemetery ... PA-2
Card Creek Ch—church ... KY-4
Card Creek Public Use Area—park ... KS-7
Card Creek Sch (abandoned)—school ... PA-2
Card Creek Springs—spring ... CO-8
Card Dike—dam ... WY-8
Cardell Sch (historical)—school ... MO-7
Carden—locale ... KS-7
Carden—locale ... KY-4
Carden—locale ... VI-3
Cardenas—locale ... NM-5
*Cardenas Aisle* ... AZ-5
Cardenas Butte—summit ... AZ-5
Cardenas Canyon—valley ... AZ-5
Cardenas Creek—stream ... AZ-5
Cardenas Creek—stream ... CA-9
Cardenas Mexico Museum—building ... NC-3
Cardenas Windmill—locale ... TX-5
Carden Bottom—flat ... AR-4
Carden Bottoms—locale ... AR-4
Carden Branch—stream ... AR-4
Carden Branch—stream ... GA-3
Carden Branch—stream (3) ... TN-4
*Carden Cave* ... TN-4
Carden Cave—cave ... TN-4
Carden Cem—cemetery (2) ... AL-4
Carden Cem—cemetery ... GA-3
Carden Cem—cemetery (3) ... TN-4
Carden Creek—stream ... AK-9
Carden Creek—stream ... AR-4
Carden Dagle Ditch—canal ... CO-8
Carden Gap—gap ... TN-4
Carden Hills—other ... AK-9
Carden Hollow—valley ... TN-4
Carden Lake—lake ... AK-9
Carden Point Rec Area—park ... AR-4
Carden Prospect—mine ... TN-4
Cardens Bluff—cliff ... TN-4
**Cardens Bluff (historical)**—pop pl ... TN-4
Cardens Bluff Mine—mine ... TN-4
Cardens Bluff Post Office (historical)—building ... TN-4
Cardens Bluff Sch (historical)—school ... TN-4
Carden Sch—school ... CA-9
Carden Spring—spring ... TN-4
Carde Ranch—locale ... NM-5
Carder Camp Run—stream ... WV-2
Carder Cem—cemetery ... WV-2
**Carderock**—pop pl ... MD-2
**Carderock Springs**—pop pl ... MD-2
Carder Run—stream ... WV-2
**Carders**—pop pl ... WA-9
Carder Sch—school ... CA-9
Carder Sch—school ... NY-2
Cardesa Point Campsite—locale ... ME-1
Card Gulch—valley ... CO-8
Card Hollow—valley (2) ... PA-2
Cardiac Lake—lake ... OR-9
Cardiceras Creek—stream ... AK-9
*Cardiff* ... CA-9
Cardiff—locale ... ID-8
Cardiff—locale ... IL-6
Cardiff—locale ... NJ-2
Cardiff—locale ... PA-2
Cardiff—locale ... TN-4

Cardiff—locale TX-5
**Cardiff**—pop pl AL-4
**Cardiff**—pop pl CO-8
**Cardiff**—pop pl MD-2
**Cardiff**—pop pl NY-2
**Cardiff**—pop pl PA-2
Cardiff By The Sea—uninc pl CA-9
**Cardiff-by-the-Sea (Cardiff)**—pop pl CA-9
Cardiff Cem—cemetery AL-4
Cardiff Ch—church TN-4
Cardiff Creek—stream TN-4
Cardiff Drift Mine (underground)—mine AL-4
Cardiff Hill—summit MO-7
Cardiff (historical P.O.)—locale IA-7
Cardiff Landing (historical)—locale MS-4
Cardiff Mill—locale ID-8
Cardiff Mine—mine MI-6
Cardiff Mine—mine UT-8
Cardiff Mine (underground)—mine TN-4
**Cardiff (Nettleton)**—pop pl PA-2
Cardiff Post Office (historical)—building TN-4
Cardiff Sch—school CA-9
Cardiff Sch (historical)—school TN-4
Cardiff Spur ID-8
Cardiff State Beach—park CA-9
**Cardiff (subdivision)**—pop pl DE-2
Cardigan, Mount—summit NH-1
Cardigan Junction MN-6
Cardigan Junction—locale MN-6
Cardigan Peak—summit AZ-5
**Cardigan (sta.)**—pop pl NH-1
Cardigan Station—locale NH-1
Cardill MS-4
**Cardin**—pop pl OK-5
**Cardina Forest**—pop pl VA-3
Cardinal—locale CO-8
Cardinal—locale KY-4
Cardinal—locale VA-3
**Cardinal**—pop pl MT-8
Cardinal—post sta DC-2
Cardinal—uninc pl TX-5
Cardinal, Lake—lake OH-6
Cardinal, The—summit VA-3
**Cardinal Acres**—pop pl MO-7
**Cardinal Acres (subdivision)**—pop pl TN-4
Cardinal Brook—stream VT-1
Cardinal Center (Shop Ctr)—locale NC-3
Cardinal Country Club—locale NC-3
Cardinal Country Club Dam—dam NC-3
Cardinal Country Club Lake—reservoir NC-3
Cardinal Creek—stream ID-8
Cardinal Creek—stream MI-6
Cardinal Creek—stream MT-8
Cardinal Cushing Acad—school MA-1
Cardinal Cushing Coll—school MA-1
Cardinal Cushing Hosp—hospital MA-1
Cardinal Distribution Company, Incorporated—facility IL-6
Cardinal Dougherty HS—school PA-2
**Cardinal Estates**—pop pl VA-3
Cardinal Farley Military Acad—school NY-2
**Cardinal Forest**—pop pl VA-3
Cardinal Gap—summit NM-5
Cardinal Gibbons HS—school FL-3
Cardinal Gibbour Statue—park DC-2
Cardinal Glennon Heliport—airport MO-7
**Cardinal Hill**—pop pl KY-4
Cardinal Hill Ch—church KY-4
Cardinal Hill Reservoir—hist pl KY-4
Cardinal Hill Rsvr—reservoir KY-4
**Cardinal Hills**—pop pl TN-4
Cardinal Hosp—hospital KY-4
Cardinal Hotel—hist pl WI-6
Cardinal HS—school IA-7
Cardinal Lake—lake CA-9
**Cardinal Lake**—pop pl OH-6
Cardinal Marsh State Wildlife Area—park IA-7
Cardinal McCloskey Sch—school NY-2
Cardinal Mine—mine CA-9
Cardinal Mine—mine NV-8
Cardinal Mooney HS—school NY-2
Cardinal Mooney HS—school OH-6
Cardinal Mtn—summit CA-9
Cardinal Newman HS—school FL-3
Cardinal Newman HS—school SC-3
Cardinal O'Connell Sch—school MA-1
Cardinal O'Hara HS—school PA-2
Cardinal Park Shop Ctr—locale KS-7
Cardinal Peak—summit MT-8
Cardinal Peak—summit WA-9
Cardinal Point Rec Area—park OK-5
Cardinal Ridge—ridge VA-3
Cardinal Sch—school IL-6
Cardinal Shopping Center NC-3
Cardinal Spellman HS—school NY-2
Cardinal Stritch Coll—school WI-6
Cardinal Stritch HS—school IL-6
Cardinal Stritch HS—school IA-7
**Cardinal Valley**—pop pl KY-4
Cardinal Valley Sch—school KY-4
Cardinal Village Ch—church NC-3
**Cardinal Village (subdivision)**—pop pl NC-3
Cardinal Wash—valley UT-8
Cardin Branch—stream AR-4
Cardin Bridge Swamp SC-3
Cardin Creek—stream ID-8
Carding Factory Branch—stream TX-5
Carding Machine Branch—stream VA-3
Carding Machine Hill—summit KY-4
Carding Machine Ridge—ridge NC-3
Carding Machine Spring—spring TN-4
Carding Mill Pond—lake NH-1
Carding Millpond—reservoir MA-1
Cardington—locale PA-2
**Cardington**—pop pl OH-6
**Cardington**—pop pl PA-2
**Cardington (Township of)**—pop pl OH-6
Cardiver Branch MS-4
Card Lake—lake NE-7
Card Ledge—bar ME-1
Card Machine Brook—stream MA-1
Card Machine Brook—stream RI-1
Card Machine Run—stream PA-2
Card Mill Brook ME-1
Card Mill Stream—stream ME-1
Card Mtn—summit KY-4
Cardome—hist pl KY-4
Cardome Acad—school KY-4
Cardon—locale UT-8
Cardona Residence—hist pl PR-3

Cardon Cem—cemetery AR-4
**Cardonia**—pop pl IN-6
Cardonia Run—stream IN-6
Cardovo—locale VA-3
Cardozo HS—school DC-2
Cardozo Lake—lake CA-9
Cardozo Ridge—ridge CA-9
Cardozo Sch—school CA-9
Cardozo, Mount—summit AK-9
Cardozo HS—school DC-2
Cardozo HS—school NY-2
Card Place—locale CA-9
Card Point—cape FL-3
Card Point—cape MI-6
Card Point Cut—channel FL-3
Card Pond—lake MA-1
Card Pond—lake NY-2
Card Pond Dam—dam MA-1
Card Ranch—locale NE-7
Card Rsvr—reservoir OR-9
Card Run—stream IN-6
**Cards Corners**—pop pl NY-2
Cards Grove Sch—school IL-6
Cards Hollow—valley PA-2
Cards Lake (historical)—lake IA-7
Card Sound—bay FL-3
Cards Switch (historical)—locale AL-4
Cardsville—locale MS-4
Cardsville Ch—church MS-4
Cardsville Post Office (historical)—building MS-4
**Card Switch**—pop pl AL-4
Cardtown—locale NY-2
Cardtown Sch—school MD-2
Cardville—locale ME-1
Cardville Cem—cemetery ME-1
Cardville Ch—church ME-1
Cardwell—locale FL-3
Cardwell—locale ID-8
Cardwell—locale KY-4
Cardwell—locale VA-3
**Cardwell**—pop pl MO-7
**Cardwell**—pop pl MT-8
Cardwell—uninc pl CA-9
Cardwell Branch—stream AL-4
Cardwell Branch—stream NE-7
Cardwell Branch—stream TN-4
Cardwell Branch Salt Creek NE-7
Cardwell Cem MO-7
Cardwell Cem—cemetery IL-6
Cardwell Cem—cemetery (2) KY-4
Cardwell Cem—cemetery MO-7
Cardwell Cem—cemetery OK-5
Cardwell Cem—cemetery (3) TN-4
Cardwell Ch—church TN-4
Cardwell Creek TN-4
Cardwell Creek—stream AL-4
Cardwell Creek—stream (2) OR-9
Cardwell Dam—dam AL-4
Cardwell Draw—valley CO-8
Cardwell Hollow—valley MO-7
Cardwell Island VA-3
Cardwell Lake—reservoir AL-4
Cardwell Lake—reservoir TN-4
Cardwell Mountain—hist pl TN-4
Cardwell Mtn—summit TN-4
Cardwell Park—park NM-5
Cardwell Point—cape CA-9
Cardwell Ranch—locale TX-5
Cardwell Ridge—ridge MO-7
Cardwell Ridge—ridge TN-4
Cardwell Sch—school MT-8
Cardwell Spring—spring TN-4
Cardwellton—hist pl KY-4
**Cardwell Town**—pop pl VA-3
**Cardy**—pop pl MO-7
Carea—locale MD-2
Careaga Canyon CA-9
Careaga Canyon—valley CA-9
Ca Reca, Lake—reservoir GA-3
Care Canyon UT-8
Care Creek OR-9
Careen Hill—summit VI-3
Careening Cove—bay VI-3
Career Development Center—school FL-3
**Carefree**—pop pl AZ-5
**Carefree**—pop pl IN-6
Carefree Airp—airport AZ-5
Carefree Heliport—airport AZ-5
Carefree Lake—lake MN-6
Carefree Post Office—building AZ-5
Carefree Sun Dial—park AZ-5
Careful Point—cape AK-9
Careless Creek—stream MT-8
Careless Prairie—lake FL-3
Carely Mtn—summit AR-4
**Carem**—pop pl SC-3
**Caren**—pop pl WV-2
Caren Creek IN-6
**Carencro**—pop pl LA-4
Carencro, Bayou—stream LA-4
Carencro Bay—bay LA-4
Carencro Bayou—stream LA-4
Carencro HS—school LA-4
Carencro Lake—lake LA-4
Carenero (Barrio)—fmr MCD PR-3
Carengers Mill (historical)—locale TN-4
Caress—locale WV-2
Caret—locale VA-3
Caretaker's Cabin—hist pl UT-8
Caret Bay—bay VI-3
Caret Bay Estate—locale VI-3
Caret Point—cape VI-3
**Caretta**—pop pl WV-2
**Caretta (RR name Juno)**—pop pl WV-2
Carew—locale WV-2
Carew Sch—school MA-1
Carew Street Sch—school MA-1
Carew Tower—hist pl OH-6
Carex Creek—stream AK-9
Carex Spring—spring NV-8
Carey DE-2
Carey—locale AL-4
Carey—locale GA-3
Carey—locale NJ-2
Carey—locale WY-8
**Carey**—pop pl ID-8
**Carey**—pop pl IN-6
**Carey**—pop pl LA-4
**Carey**—pop pl NE-7

**Carey**—pop pl OH-6
**Carey**—pop pl TX-5
Carey, Lake—lake PA-2
Carey, Lewis, Farmhouse—hist pl NJ-2
Carey, Mount—summit MT-8
Carey, Philip, Bldg—hist pl NC-3
Carey Airp—airport TN-4
Carey Baptist Church AL-4
Carey Basin—lake TN-4
Carey Bay—bay ID-8
Carey Bay—bay OK-5
Carey Bend—bend OR-9
Carey Branch DE-2
Carey Branch—stream KY-4
Carey Branch—stream (2) MD-2
Carey Branch—stream MO-7
Carey Brook—stream ME-1
Carey Butte—summit MT-8
Carey Camp—locale DE-2
Carey Camp Creek—stream CA-9
Carey Canyon—valley CA-9
Carey Cem—cemetery CT-1
Carey Cem—cemetery (2) DE-2
Carey Cem—cemetery IN-6
Carey Cem—cemetery KY-4
Carey Cem—cemetery OH-6
Carey Cem—cemetery TN-4
Carey Cem—cemetery TX-5
Carey Ch—church AL-4
Carey Ch—church NC-3
Carey Chapel—church MS-4
Carey Chapel Baptist Ch MS-4
Carey Chapel Cem—cemetery MS-4
Carey Chapel Church MS-4
Carey Chapel (historical)—church TN-4
**Carey Corner**—pop pl MA-1
Carey Corners—locale (2) NY-2
Carey Creek KS-7
Carey Creek MD-2
Carey Creek—stream ID-8
Carey Creek—stream (2) MN-6
Carey Creek—stream (2) OR-9
Carey Creek—stream VA-3
Carey Creek—stream WA-9
Carey Creek—stream WY-8
Carey Ditch MO-7
Carey Ditch—canal (2) MT-8
Carey Dome—summit ID-8
Carey Draw—valley WY-8
Carey Estates—uninc pl TX-5
Carey Falls—rapids ID-8
Carey Farm Site—hist pl DE-2
Carey Ford—locale TN-4
Carey Gap—gap GA-3
Carey Gulch—valley CA-9
Carey Gulch—valley MT-8
Carey Hill—summit (2) MA-1
Carey Hill—summit NY-2
Carey Hill—summit OH-6
Carey Hill—summit PA-2
Carey Hill—summit SC-3
Carey Hill Ch—church (2) SC-3
**Carey (historical)**—pop pl OR-9
Carey Hollow—valley NY-2
Carey Horse Creek Ditch No 1—canal WY-8
Carey Horse Creek Ditch No 10—canal WY-8
Carey Horse Creek Ditch No 5—canal WY-8
Carey Horse Creek Ditch No 6—canal WY-8
Carey Horse Creek Ditch No 9—canal WY-8
Carey House—hist pl KS-7
Carey HS—school NY-2
Careyhurst—locale WY-8
Careyhurst Ranch—locale WY-8
Carey JHS—school WY-8
Carey Kipuka—summit ID-8
Carey Lake MN-6
Carey Lake MS-4
Carey Lake—lake AK-9
Carey Lake—lake CO-8
Carey Lake—lake ME-1
Carey Lake—lake MI-6
Carey Lake—lake (2) MN-6
Carey Lake—lake NE-7
Carey Lake—lake OR-9
Carey Lake—lake SC-3
Carey Lake—reservoir ID-8
Carey Lateral—canal MT-8
Carey-Malone Sch—school MT-8
Carey Marina—other MD-2
Carey Marsh—lake NY-2
**Carey Mine**—pop pl KS-7
Carey Park—park KS-7
Carey Park—park OH-6
**Carey Park**—pop pl GA-3
Carey Pond NY-2
Carey Ranch—locale (2) OR-9
Carey Ridge—ridge CA-9
Carey Rock—bar ME-1
Carey Rsvr—reservoir OR-9
Carey Rsvr—reservoir WY-8
Carey Rsvr No 1—reservoir WY-8
Carey Run OH-6
Carey Run—stream MD-2
Carey Run—stream PA-2
Careys and Stallworths Mill (historical)—locale AL-4
Careys Bridge—bridge VA-3
Careys Campground DE-2
Carey's Camp Meeting Ground—hist pl DE-2
Carey Sch—school CA-9
Carey Sch—school GA-3
Carey Sch—school IL-6
Carey Sch—school IA-7
Carey Sch—school OK-5
Carey Sch—school VA-3
Carey Sch (abandoned)—school MO-7
**Careys Corners**—pop pl NY-2
**Careys Estate (trailer park)**—pop pl DE-2
Careys Lake—lake WA-9
Careys Lakes SC-3
Carey Slope Mine (underground)—mine AL-4
Carey Spring—spring OR-9
Carey Springs Baptist Church MS-4
Carey Springs Cem—cemetery MS-4
Carey Springs Ch—church MS-4
Carey Springs Sch (historical)—school MS-4
Careys Run—stream OH-6
Careys Run Cem—cemetery OH-6
Careys Run Ch—church OH-6
Carey Stearns Ranch—locale OR-9

Carey Swamp—swamp PA-2
Carey Tables—summit OR-9
Carey Tidmore Dam—dam AL-4
Carey Tidmore Lake—reservoir AL-4
Carey Towhead—island TN-4
Careytown—locale MD-2
Careytown—locale OH-6
Careytown Branch—stream MD-2
Careytown Methodist Church AL-4
**Carey (Town of)**—pop pl WI-6
Carey-Twohy Ditch—canal MT-8
Careyville MA-1
Careyville TN-4
Careyville Landing—locale AR-4
Careywood—locale ID-8
Careywood Creek—stream ID-8
Carfax—locale VA-3
Carfax Ch—church VA-3
Carfield Peak—summit CO-8
Cargal Creek AL-4
Car Gap—gap TN-4
Cargas—locale LA-4
Cargat Creek AL-4
Cargile—locale AR-4
Cargile Cem—cemetery AL-4
Cargile Spring—spring AL-4
Cargile Tank—reservoir TX-5
Cargile (Township of)—fmr MCD AR-4
Cargill, Walter Hurt—hist pl GA-3
Cargill Airp—airport PA-2
Cargill Cem—cemetery VT-1
Cargill Creek MI-6
Cargill Creek—stream MI-6
Cargill Drain—canal MI-6
Cargill Hill—summit VT-1
Cargill Pond—lake ME-1
Cargill Pond—lake MA-1
Cargill Ranch—locale CO-8
Cargill Sch—school MI-6
Cargills Creek—stream VA-3
Cargill Windmill—locale TX-5
Cargle Branch—stream NC-3
Cargle Creek—stream AL-4
Cargle Gap—gap NC-3
Cargodera Canyon—valley AZ-5
Cargodera Canyon Six Trail—trail AZ-5
Cargodera Spring—spring AZ-5
Cargo Lake—lake MN-6
Cargo Mine—mine CA-9
Cargo Muchacho Mountains—range CA-9
Cargo Slash—lake AR-4
Cargo Spring—spring WA-9
Cargray—locale TX-5
Cargyl Creek AL-4
Cargyle Creek—stream CA-9
Cargyle Meadow—flat CA-9
Carherine Lake MI-6
Car Hollow—valley MO-7
Cariant Needle CO-8
Caribau Lake MN-6
Caribbean Bureau Of Foreign Broadcast Servic—other PR-3
Caribbean Elem Sch—school FL-3
Caribbean Gardens—park FL-3
**Caribbean Key**—pop pl FL-3
Caribbean Sea—sea PR-3
Caribbean Sea—sea VI-3
Caribel—locale ID-8
Cariboo (historical)—locale KS-7
Cariboo Lake MN-6
Caribou—locale AK-9
Caribou—locale CA-9
Caribou—locale CO-8
Caribou—locale MN-6
**Caribou**—pop pl ME-1
Caribou Bar—bar OR-9
Caribou Bar—locale AK-9
Caribou Basin—basin ID-8
Caribou Basin Guard Station—locale ID-8
Caribou Bog—lake ME-1
Caribou Bog—swamp (4) ME-1
Caribou Bog—swamp MN-6
Caribou Brook—stream (3) ME-1
**Caribou Camp**—pop pl WY-8
Caribou Campground—locale MT-8
Caribou Caverns—cave AL-4
Caribou City—locale ID-8
Caribou County Courthouse—hist pl ID-8
Caribou Cove—bay ME-1
Caribou Creek ID-8
Caribou Creek MN-6
Caribou Creek—stream (9) AK-9
Caribou Creek—stream (2) CA-9
Caribou Creek—stream CO-8
Caribou Creek—stream (7) ID-8
Caribou Creek—stream (3) MI-6
Caribou Creek—stream MN-6
Caribou Creek—stream (2) MT-8
Caribou Creek—stream OR-9
Caribou Creek—stream WA-9
Caribou Creek—stream WY-8
Caribou Crossing—other AK-9
Caribou Dam—dam ME-1
Caribou Deadwater—reservoir ME-1
Caribou Falls—falls ID-8
Caribou Falls—falls MN-6
Caribou Flat—flat CO-8
Caribou Flow—stream ME-1
Caribou Gulch—valley AK-9
Caribou Gulch—valley CA-9
Caribou Hill—summit CO-8
Caribou Hill—summit ID-8
Caribou Hill—summit NV-8
Caribou Hills—other AK-9
Caribou Island—island AK-9
Caribou Island Campground—locale MI-6
Caribou Lake MI-6
Caribou Lake MN-6
Caribou Lake—lake (4) AK-9
Caribou Lake—lake CA-9
Caribou Lake—lake CO-8
Caribou Lake—lake ID-8
Caribou Lake—lake (3) ME-1
Caribou Lake—lake MI-6
Caribou Lake—lake (5) MN-6
**Caribou Lake**—pop pl MI-6
Caribou Lakes—lake ID-8
Caribou Lake Sch—school MN-6
Caribou Lookout—locale ID-8
Caribou Mine—mine ID-8

Caribou Mine—mine WY-8
Caribou Mountain MT-8
Caribou Mountains ID-8
Caribou Mtn—summit AK-9
Caribou Mtn—summit CA-9
Caribou Mtn—summit ID-8
Caribou Mtn—summit (3) ME-1
Caribou Mtn—summit MT-8
Caribou Narrows—channel (2) ME-1
Caribou Natl For—forest UT-8
Caribou Park—flat CO-8
Caribou Pass—gap (2) AK-9
Caribou Pass—gap CO-8
Caribou Pass—gap ID-8
Caribou Pass—gap NY-2
Caribou Peak—summit CA-9
Caribou Peak—summit MT-8
Caribou Peak Wild Area—locale CA-9
Caribou Point—cape (3) ME-1
Caribou Point—cape MN-6
Caribou Pond—lake (4) ME-1
Caribou Range—range ID-8
Caribou Ridge—ridge ID-8
Caribou Ridge—ridge ME-1
Caribou River—stream AK-9
Caribou River—stream MN-6
Caribou Road ME-1
Caribou Road—locale ME-1
Caribou Rock—island ME-1
Caribou Sch—school WY-8
Caribou Shaft—mine CO-8
Caribou Shelter—locale NY-2
Caribou Snare Creek—stream AK-9
Caribou Spring—spring (2) ME-1
Caribou Stream—stream (2) ME-1
**Caribou (Township of)**—pop pl MN-6
Caribou Trail—trail CO-8
Caribou Trail—trail ME-1
Caribou Trail—trail MT-8
Caribou Valley—valley ME-1
**Carico**—pop pl KY-4
**Carico**—pop pl MO-7
Carico Branch—stream VA-3
Carico Ditch—canal MT-8
Carico Hollow—valley MO-7
Carico Lake—flat NV-8
Carico Lake Ranch—locale NV-8
Carico Lake Valley—valley NV-8
Carico Ridge—ridge VA-3
Caric (Siding)—locale CA-9
Cariens Cem—cemetery IL-6
Carigo Cem—cemetery VA-3
Carillon, Mount—summit CA-9
Carillon Park—park OH-6
Carill Peak—summit ID-8
**Carimona**—pop pl MN-6
Carimona Cem—cemetery MN-6
**Carimona (Township of)**—pop pl MN-6
**Caringer (historical)**—pop pl TN-4
Caringer Post Office (historical)—building TN-4
Carington Cem—cemetery MS-4
Carino Creek—stream NJ-2
Cario Bend TN-4
Carisa—mine UT-8
Carisa Tunnel—mine UT-8
Carisbrook—locale NM-5
Caris Creek—stream OR-9
Carisco Truck Trail—trail CA-9
Carissa Draw TX-5
Carissa Mine—mine NV-8
Carissa Mine—mine WY-8
Carissa Plains CA-9
Carite (Barrio)—fmr MCD PR-3
Carithers Mill—facility GA-3
Carithers Store Bldg—hist pl IL-6
Carizales, Arroyo—valley TX-5
Carizo Creek AZ-5
Carkeek Park—park WA-9
Carkhuff, Stacy G., House—hist pl OH-6
Carklsville PA-2
Carl—locale OK-5
Carl—locale PA-2
Carl—locale TX-5
**Carl**—pop pl GA-3
**Carl**—pop pl IA-7
**Carl**—pop pl KY-4
**Carl**—pop pl WV-2
Carla—locale LA-4
Car Lake—lake MS-4
Carl Albert, Lake—reservoir OK-5
Carl Albright Dam—dam SD-7
Carl Alwin Schenck Memorial Forest—park NC-3
Carlan—locale GA-3
Carlan Creek—stream GA-3
Carlan Creek—stream IA-7
**Carland**—pop pl MI-6
Carland Beach—beach OH-6
Carl and Dowdell Hollow—valley AR-4
Carl Anderson Lake Dam—dam MS-4
Carland Wash—stream AZ-5
Carlanna—uninc pl AK-9
Carlanna Creek—stream AK-9
Carlanna Lake—lake AK-9
Carlas Corner—locale WY-8
Carl Blackwell, Lake—reservoir OK-5
Carl Branch—stream KY-4
Carl Budweg Dam—dam AL-4
Carl Canyon—valley NM-5
Carl Cem—cemetery TX-5
Carl Cowan Park—park TN-4
Carl Creek—stream AL-4
Carl Creek—stream (3) AK-9
Carl Creek—stream MT-8
Carl Creek—stream OR-9
Carl Creek—stream (2) WY-8
Carl Cronin Dam—dam SD-7
Carl Duncan Mine (surface)—mine TN-4
Carle Creek—stream OR-9
Carle Hosp—hospital IL-6
Carl Ellington—locale TX-5
Carlen Cem—cemetery TN-4
Carlen House—hist pl AL-4
Carl Ernest Airp—airport MO-7
Carle Park—park IL-6
**Carle Place**—pop pl NY-2
Carle Place Park—park NY-2
Carle Springs—locale IL-6
**Carle Terrace**—pop pl NY-2
Carl Etling, Lake—reservoir OK-5

Carleton OK-5
Carleton WA-9
Carleton—locale FL-3
**Carleton**—pop pl MI-6
**Carleton**—pop pl NE-7
**Carleton**—pop pl OK-5
Carleton, Robert, House—hist pl ME-1
Carleton Bridge—hist pl NH-1
Carleton Cem—cemetery AL-4
Carleton Coll—school MN-6
Carleton Community Ch—church MI-6
Carleton Creek—stream MI-6
Carleton Glen Golf Club—other MI-6
Carleton Island—island ME-1
Carleton Island—island NY-2
Carleton Ledges—island ME-1
Carleton Peak MN-6
Carleton Point—cape ME-1
Carleton Prize—island VT-1
Carleton Sch—school ME-1
Carleton Sch—school MI-6
Carleton Sch—school NJ-2
Carleton Sch—school WI-6
Carletons Station (historical)—locale AL-4
Carleton Stream—stream ME-1
Carletonville (Carltonville)—uninc pl MA-1
**Carley**—pop pl TX-5
Carley Brook—locale PA-2
Carley Brook—stream ME-1
Carley Brook—stream MA-1
Carley Brook—stream PA-2
Carley Cem—cemetery VT-1
Carley Ch—church IL-6
Carley Draw—valley SD-7
Carley Mills—locale NY-2
Carleys—locale AL-4
Carleys Neck MA-1
Carley State Park—park MN-6
Carley Swamp—swamp NY-2
Carley V Porter Tunnel—tunnel CA-9
Carl Feldner Coulee—valley ND-7
Carl Fisher—uninc pl FL-3
Carl Folsom Airp—airport AL-4
Carl F Well—well AZ-5
Carl G Fenner Arboretum—park MI-6
Carl G Fisher Elem Sch—school IN-6
Carl Gjemre Ditch—canal IN-6
Carl Glacier—glacier AK-9
Carl Gulch—valley ID-8
Carl Gunner Number 1 Dam—dam SD-7
Carl G. Washburne Memorial State Park—park OR-9
Carl Hamlett Lake—reservoir NC-3
Carl Hamlett Lake Dam—dam NC-3
Carl Hammond Well—well NV-8
Carl Hansen Dam—dam SD-7
Carl Hayden Hosp—hospital AZ-5
Carl Hayden Sch—school AZ-5
Carlheim—hist pl VA-3
Carl Hill—summit PA-2
Carl Hollomans Pond Dam—dam MS-4
Carl House—hist pl AR-4
Carl Humphrey Dam Number 1—dam SD-7
Carlile—locale WY-8
Carlile, James N., House—hist pl CO-8
Carlile Cem—cemetery OK-5
Carlile Junction—locale WY-8
Carlile Sch—school CO-8
Carlile Sch—school OK-5
**Carlim**—pop pl PA-2
Carlin VA-3
**Carlin**—pop pl NV-8
Carlin, Bayou—gut LA-4
Carlin, Bayou—stream (2) LA-4
Carlin, Patrick, House—hist pl OH-6
Carlin Airp—airport NV-8
Carlin Bay—bay ID-8
**Carlin Bay**—pop pl ID-8
Carlin Bottoms—bend SD-7
Carlin Branch—stream IN-6
Carlin Bridge—bridge SD-7
Carlinburg—locale KY-4
Carlin Canyon—valley CA-9
Carlin Canyon—valley NV-8
Carlin Cem—cemetery (2) MO-7
Carlin Creek—stream (3) ID-8
Carlin Creek—stream NV-8
Carlin Creek—stream NY-2
Carlin Draw—valley SD-7
Carlin Drift Fence—locale NV-8
Carline Creek—stream AK-9
Carlin (Election Precinct)—fmr MCD IL-6
Carlin Flat—flat SD-7
Carling, Benedictus, House—hist pl UT-8
Carlin-Garrett Ranch—locale SD-7
Carlin Grange—locale ID-8
Carlin Gulch—valley CO-8
Carlin (historical)—locale SD-7
Carlin Lake—lake WI-6
Carlin Mine—mine NV-8
Carlin Park—park FL-3
Carlin Peaks—summit NV-8
Carlin Pointe—cape LA-4
Carlin Pond—lake PA-2
Carlin Ranch—locale WY-8
Carlin-Rathgeber House—hist pl MO-7
Carlin Rsvr—reservoir CO-8
Carlin's VA-3
Carlin Sch—school SD-7
Carlin Spring Station VA-3
Carlin Township—inact MCD NV-8
**Carlinville**—pop pl IL-6
Carlinville, Lake—reservoir IL-6
Carlinville Chapter House—hist pl IL-6
Carlinville Country Club—other IL-6
Carlinville Hist Dist—hist pl IL-6
**Carlinville (Township of)**—pop pl IL-6
Carlinville Waterworks—other IL-6
Carl Island—island NE-7
Carl Island—island NY-2
Carlisle IL-6
Carlisle KS-7
Carlisle TX-5
Carlisle—locale LA-4
Carlisle—locale MS-4
Carlisle—locale NE-7
Carlisle—locale TX-5
Carlisle—locale VA-3
Carlisle—locale WA-9
Carlisle—other OH-6

*Caroll Branch* ... GA-3
Caroll Cem—*cemetery* ... MO-7
Caroll Sch—*school* ... TX-5
Carollwood Ch—*church* ... MD-2
Carol Number One Tank—*reservoir* ... AZ-5
Carol Number Two Tank—*reservoir* ... AZ-5
Carol Plaza (Shop Ctr)—*locale* ... FL-3
Carol Point—*cape* ... VI-3
Carol Pond—*reservoir* ... VA-3
Carols Cave—*cave* ... TN-4
Carol Spring—*spring* ... AZ-5
Carol Spring Mtn—*summit* ... AZ-5
**Carol Stream**—*pop pl* ... IL-6
Carol Tank—*reservoir* ... AZ-5
Carolton Creek—*stream* ... MA-1
Carolton Oaks Sch—*school* ... VA-3
Carol Villa Shop Ctr—*locale* ... AL-4
**Carol Villa (subdivision)**—*pop pl* ... AL-4
**Carol Villa Subdivision**—*pop pl* ... UT-8
Carol Vista Sch—*school* ... CA-9
Carolwood Ch—*church* ... AL-4
**Carolwood Estates (subdivision)**—*pop pl* ... AL-4
Carolwood Lake—*reservoir* ... AL-4
Carolwood Lake Dam—*dam* ... AL-4
*Carolwood Lakeside Subdivision* ... AL-4
**Carolwoods (subdivision)**—*pop pl* ... NC-3
**Carolwood (subdivision)**—*pop pl* ... AL-4
Carolyn—*uninc pl* ... AL-4
Carolyn, Lake—*lake* ... ME-1
Carolyn, Lake—*reservoir* ... AL-4
*Carolyn Bridge, The* ... UT-8
Carolyn Creek—*stream* ... OR-9
Carolyn Dam—*dam* ... AL-4
Carolyn Island—*island* ... AK-9
Carolyn Lake—*lake* ... UT-8
Carolyn Lake—*reservoir* ... IN-6
Carolyn Lane Shop Ctr—*locale* ... FL-3
Carolyn Park Sch—*school* ... LA-4
*Carolyn State Park* ... KS-7
Carolyn Windmill—*locale* ... TX-5
**Caromi Village**—*pop pl* ... SC-3
**Carona**—*pop pl* ... KS-7
Caron Brook—*stream* ... ME-1
*Carondelet* ... MO-7
**Carondelet**—*pop pl* ... MO-7
Carondelet HS—*school* ... CA-9
Carondelet Park—*park* ... MO-7
**Carondelet (subdivision)**—*pop pl* ... TN-4
Caronita Canyon—*valley* ... NM-5
*Caronkaway Island* ... TX-5
*Caronkaway Point* ... TX-5
*Caronkaway Reef* ... TX-5
Caron Lake—*lake* ... MN-6
Caroon Point—*cape* ... NC-3
*Caro Pelou* ... FL-3
Caro Pine Lake—*reservoir* ... TX-5
Caro Post Office (historical)—*building* ... AL-4
Caro State Hosp—*hospital* ... MI-6
Carothers Cem—*cemetery* (3) ... TN-4
Carothers Ditch—*canal* ... IN-6
Carothers Gap—*gap* ... PA-2
Carothers Gap Run—*stream* ... PA-2
Carothers Island—*island* ... TN-4
Carothers Lake—*lake* ... WY-8
Carothers Lake—*reservoir* ... NE-7
Carothers Place—*locale* ... ID-8
Carothers Tunnel—*tunnel* ... WV-2
Carousel at Glen Echo Park—*hist pl* ... MD-2
**Carousel Knoll**—*pop pl* ... DE-2
Carousel Park—*park* ... DE-2
Carousel Sch—*school* ... AR-4
Carowinds—*park* ... NC-3
Carowinds Airp—*airport* ... NC-3
Carow Park—*park* ... WI-6
*Carp* ... MI-6
**Carp**—*pop pl* ... IN-6
**Carp**—*pop pl* ... MN-6
**Carp**—*pop pl* ... NV-8
Carpas Wash—*stream* ... AZ-5
Carpathian Peak—*summit* ... AK-9
Carp Branch—*stream* ... KY-4
Carp Chapel—*church* ... MN-6
Carp Circle—*locale* ... VA-3
*Carp Creek* ... MI-6
Carp Creek—*stream* ... AK-9
Carp Creek—*stream* ... MI-6
Carpe, Bayou La—*gut* ... LA-4
Carpe, Mount—*summit* ... AK-9
Carp Elgin Interchange—*crossing* ... NV-8
Carpenders Cem—*cemetery* ... PA-2
Carpender Springs—*spring* ... WA-9
*Carpenter* ... AL-4
Carpenter—*locale* ... AL-4
Carpenter—*locale* ... CA-9
Carpenter—*locale* ... KY-4
Carpenter—*locale* ... MT-8
**Carpenter**—*pop pl* ... AL-4
**Carpenter**—*pop pl* ... DE-2
**Carpenter**—*pop pl* ... IL-6
**Carpenter**—*pop pl* ... IA-7
**Carpenter**—*pop pl* ... MS-4
**Carpenter**—*pop pl* ... NC-3
**Carpenter**—*pop pl* ... OH-6
**Carpenter**—*pop pl* ... OK-5
**Carpenter**—*pop pl* ... PA-2
**Carpenter**—*pop pl* ... SD-7
**Carpenter**—*pop pl* ... TX-5
**Carpenter**—*pop pl* ... WY-8
Carpenter, Andrew, House—*hist pl* ... NC-3
Carpenter, Christopher, House—*hist pl* ... MA-1
Carpenter, Col. Thomas, III, House—*hist pl* ... MA-1
Carpenter, David, House—*hist pl* ... MI-6
Carpenter, Elbert L., House—*hist pl* ... MN-6
Carpenter, Eugene J., House—*hist pl* ... MN-6
Carpenter, Ezra, House—*hist pl* ... MA-1
Carpenter, George, House—*hist pl* ... MA-1
Carpenter, John B., House—*hist pl* ... NY-2
Carpenter, Joseph, House—*hist pl* ... OK-5
Carpenter, Joseph, Silversmith Shop—*hist pl* ... CT-1
Carpenter, Lakeside, and Springvale Cemeteries—*hist pl* ... RI-1
Carpenter, Michael, House—*hist pl* ... WI-6
Carpenter, Wallace W., House—*hist pl* ... OH-6
Carpenter, Willard, House—*hist pl* ... IN-6
**Carpenter Addition**—*pop pl* ... TN-4
Carpenter Airp—*airport* ... MO-7
CArpenter Arm—*swamp* ... TN-4
Carpenter Ave Sch—*school* ... CA-9
Carpenter Bar—*bar* ... CA-9
Carpenter Basin—*basin* ... UT-8
*Carpenter Bayou* ... TX-5
*Carpenter Beach* ... MD-2
Carpenter Bend—*bend* ... KY-4
Carpenter Bend—*bend* ... TX-5
Carpenter Bend Cem—*cemetery* ... MO-7
**Carpenter Bottom**—*pop pl* ... NC-3
Carpenter Branch—*stream* ... AL-4
Carpenter Branch—*stream* ... FL-3
Carpenter Branch—*stream* (6) ... KY-4
Carpenter Branch—*stream* ... LA-4
Carpenter Branch—*stream* ... MI-6
Carpenter Branch—*stream* (2) ... MO-7
Carpenter Branch—*stream* (2) ... NC-3
Carpenter Branch—*stream* ... OK-5
Carpenter Branch—*stream* ... TN-4
Carpenter Branch—*stream* ... WV-2
Carpenter Bridge—*bridge* ... TN-4
Carpenter Bridge—*hist pl* ... MA-1
Carpenter Bridge (historical)—*bridge* ... AL-4
Carpenter Brook—*stream* ... CT-1
Carpenter Brook—*stream* ... MA-1
Carpenter Brook—*stream* ... NH-1
Carpenter Brook—*stream* ... VT-1
Carpenter Butte—*summit* ... OR-9
**Carpenter Campground**—*pop pl* ... TN-4
Carpenter Campground Cem—*cemetery* ... TN-4
Carpenter Canyon—*valley* ... CA-9
Carpenter Canyon—*valley* ... NV-8
Carpenter Canyon—*valley* ... NM-5
Carpenter Canyon—*valley* ... TX-5
Carpenter Cave—*cave* ... AL-4
Carpenter Cave—*cave* ... KY-4
*Carpenter Cem* ... MS-4
Carpenter Cem—*cemetery* ... AL-4
Carpenter Cem—*cemetery* (2) ... AR-4
Carpenter Cem—*cemetery* ... CT-1
Carpenter Cem—*cemetery* ... FL-3
Carpenter Cem—*cemetery* ... KS-7
Carpenter Cem—*cemetery* (3) ... KY-4
Carpenter Cem—*cemetery* ... LA-4
Carpenter Cem—*cemetery* ... MI-6
Carpenter Cem—*cemetery* (2) ... MN-6
Carpenter Cem—*cemetery* (4) ... MS-4
Carpenter Cem—*cemetery* (3) ... MO-7
Carpenter Cem—*cemetery* (2) ... NY-2
Carpenter Cem—*cemetery* ... NC-3
Carpenter Cem—*cemetery* (2) ... PA-2
Carpenter Cem—*cemetery* (4) ... TN-4
Carpenter Cem—*cemetery* ... TX-5
Carpenter Cem—*cemetery* ... VT-1
Carpenter Cem—*cemetery* ... VA-3
Carpenter Cem—*cemetery* (2) ... WV-2
Carpenter Cem—*cemetery* ... WI-6
Carpenter Center for the Visual Arts—*hist pl* ... MA-1
Carpenter Ch—*church* ... LA-4
Carpenter Ch—*church* ... PA-2
Carpenter Chapel—*church* ... KS-7
**Carpenter Corner**—*pop pl* ... PA-2
Carpenter Corners—*locale* ... KY-4
Carpenter Corners—*locale* ... PA-2
Carpenter Coulee—*valley* ... MT-8
*Carpenter Creek* ... GA-3
*Carpenter Creek* ... PA-2
*Carpenter Creek* ... TN-4
Carpenter Creek—*stream* ... AK-9
Carpenter Creek—*stream* (2) ... CA-9
Carpenter Creek—*stream* ... CO-8
Carpenter Creek—*stream* ... FL-3
Carpenter Creek—*stream* (2) ... ID-8
Carpenter Creek—*stream* ... IN-6
Carpenter Creek—*stream* ... KY-4
Carpenter Creek—*stream* (3) ... MI-6
Carpenter Creek—*stream* ... MS-4
Carpenter Creek—*stream* (5) ... MT-8
Carpenter Creek—*stream* (2) ... NM-5
Carpenter Creek—*stream* ... NY-2
Carpenter Creek—*stream* ... NC-3
Carpenter Creek—*stream* ... OH-6
Carpenter Creek—*stream* ... OK-5
Carpenter Creek—*stream* (2) ... OR-9
Carpenter Creek—*stream* ... PA-2
Carpenter Creek—*stream* ... SC-3
Carpenter Creek—*stream* ... TX-5
Carpenter Creek—*stream* (3) ... WA-9
Carpenter Creek—*stream* ... WV-2
Carpenter Creek—*stream* (3) ... WI-6
Carpenter Creek—*stream* ... WY-8
Carpenter Creek Ditch—*canal* ... MT-8
Carpenter Dam—*dam* ... AL-4
Carpenter Dam—*dam* ... AR-4
Carpenter Ditch—*canal* ... OH-6
Carpenter Ditch No. 1—*canal* ... CO-8
Carpenter Drain—*canal* ... CA-9
Carpenter Drain—*canal* ... MI-6
Carpenter Draw—*valley* (2) ... WY-8
Carpenter Falls—*falls* ... NY-2
Carpenter Flat—*flat* ... CA-9
Carpenter Flats—*summit* ... CO-8
Carpenter Fork—*stream* (2) ... KY-4
Carpenter Fork—*stream* (3) ... WV-2
Carpenter Goat Tank—*reservoir* ... TX-5
Carpenter Goat Windmill—*locale* ... TX-5
*Carpenter Gulch* ... MT-8
Carpenter Gulch—*valley* ... AZ-5
Carpenter Gulch—*valley* ... CO-8
Carpenter Gulch—*valley* ... ID-8
Carpenter Gulch—*valley* ... MT-8
Carpenter Gulch—*valley* ... OR-9
Carpenter Gulch—*valley* ... WA-9
Carpenter Hill—*summit* ... KS-7
Carpenter Hill—*summit* (2) ... MA-1
Carpenter Hill—*summit* ... NH-1
Carpenter Hill—*summit* (2) ... NY-2
Carpenter Hill—*summit* ... PA-2
Carpenter Hill—*summit* ... TX-5
Carpenter Hill—*summit* ... VT-1
Carpenter Hills—*summit* ... TX-5
Carpenter Hollow—*locale* ... PA-2
Carpenter Hollow—*valley* ... AR-4
Carpenter Hollow—*valley* (2) ... KY-4
Carpenter Hollow—*valley* ... MO-7
Carpenter Hollow—*valley* ... PA-2
Carpenter Hollow—*valley* (3) ... TN-4
Carpenter Hollow Branch—*stream* ... TN-4
*Carpenter Hollow Creek* ... OH-6
Carpenter Homestead (abandoned)—*locale* ... MT-8
Carpenter Hotel—*hist pl* ... SD-7
Carpenter House—*hist pl* ... CT-1
Carpenter House—*hist pl* ... KY-4
Carpenter House—*hist pl* ... MA-1
*Carpenteria* ... CA-9
*Carpenter Island* ... TN-4
Carpenter Island—*island* ... MD-2
Carpenter Island Park—*park* ... OR-9
*Carpenter Island Shoals* ... TN-4
Carpenter JHS—*school* ... AZ-5
Carpenter Knob—*summit* ... NC-3
*Carpenter Lake* ... KY-4
*Carpenter Lake* ... MT-8
Carpenter Lake—*lake* (6) ... MI-6
Carpenter Lake—*lake* ... MN-6
Carpenter Lake—*lake* ... MO-7
Carpenter Lake—*lake* ... MT-8
Carpenter Lake—*lake* (2) ... NE-7
Carpenter Lake—*lake* ... NM-5
Carpenter Lake—*lake* (2) ... ND-7
Carpenter Lake—*lake* (2) ... WA-9
Carpenter Lake—*lake* (2) ... WI-6
**Carpenter Lake**—*pop pl* ... MI-6
Carpenter Lake—*reservoir* ... AL-4
Carpenter Lake—*reservoir* ... MS-4
**Carpenter Landing**—*pop pl* ... MI-6
Carpenter Lateral—*canal* ... WI-6
Carpenter-Lippincott House—*hist pl* ... DE-2
Carpenter Marsh—*swamp* ... MI-6
Carpenter Memorial Methodist Ch—*church* ... AL-4
Carpenter Memorial State Wildlife Area—*park* ... MO-7
Carpenter Mesa—*summit* ... NM-5
Carpenter Mill Camp—*locale* ... WY-8
Carpenter Mill Creek—*stream* ... AL-4
Carpenter Mtn—*summit* ... ID-8
Carpenter Mtn—*summit* ... ME-1
Carpenter Mtn—*summit* ... OR-9
Carpenter Mtn—*summit* (2) ... TX-5
Carpenter Mtn—*summit* (2) ... VA-3
*Carpenter Number Two Elementary School* ... MS-4
*Carpenter Number 1 Elementary School* ... MS-4
Carpenter Park—*park* ... CO-8
Carpenter Park—*park* ... FL-3
Carpenter Park—*park* (2) ... IL-6
Carpenter Park—*park* ... MN-6
Carpenter Park—*park* ... NM-5
Carpenter Peak—*summit* ... CO-8
Carpenter Place—*locale* ... CA-9
Carpenter Point—*cape* (2) ... MD-2
Carpenter Point—*cape* ... OH-6
Carpenter Point—*cape* ... VT-1
**Carpenter Point**—*pop pl* ... MD-2
*Carpenter Pond* ... MA-1
Carpenter Pond—*lake* ... CT-1
Carpenter Pond—*lake* ... FL-3
Carpenter Pond—*lake* ... ME-1
Carpenter Pond—*lake* ... MA-1
Carpenter Pond—*lake* (2) ... NY-2
Carpenter Pond—*lake* ... OR-9
Carpenter Pond—*lake* ... PA-2
Carpenter Pond—*reservoir* ... MA-1
Carpenter Pond—*reservoir* ... NY-2
Carpenter Pond Dam—*dam* ... MA-1
Carpenter Post Office (historical)—*building* ... MS-4
Carpenter Ranch—*locale* ... AZ-5
Carpenter Ranch—*locale* (2) ... NE-7
Carpenter Ranch—*locale* ... WY-8
Carpenter Reservoir Dam—*dam* ... MA-1
Carpenter Reservoir Dike—*dam* ... MA-1
*Carpenter Ridge* ... IN-6
Carpenter Ridge—*ridge* (3) ... CA-9
Carpenter Ridge—*ridge* (2) ... CO-8
Carpenter Ridge—*ridge* (2) ... ME-1
Carpenter Ridge—*ridge* ... WV-2
Carpenter Road Ch—*church* ... TX-5
Carpenter Road Dam—*dam* ... MA-1
Carpenter Road Pond—*reservoir* ... MA-1
Carpenter Rockhouse—*cave* ... KY-4
Carpenter Rocks—*ridge* ... MA-1
Carpenter Rsvr—*reservoir* ... CO-8
Carpenter Rsvr—*reservoir* ... ID-8
Carpenter Rsvr—*reservoir* ... MA-1
Carpenter Rsvr No 1—*reservoir* ... WY-8
Carpenter Run—*stream* ... OH-6
Carpenter Run—*stream* (3) ... PA-2
Carpenter Run—*stream* (4) ... WV-2
Carpenters Bar—*bar* ... AL-4
Carpenters Bayou—*stream* ... TX-5
**Carpenters Beach**—*pop pl* ... RI-1
Carpenters Bend—*bend* ... AL-4
**Carpenters Bluff**—*pop pl* ... TX-5
Carpenters Branch—*stream* ... NC-3
Carpenters Bridge—*bridge* ... DE-2
Carpenters Bridge—*bridge* ... LA-4
*Carpenters Brook* ... MA-1
Carpenters Brook—*stream* ... NY-2
Carpenters Campground Methodist Ch—*church* ... TN-4
Carpenters Cave—*cave* ... AZ-5
Carpenter Sch—*school* ... CA-9
Carpenter Sch—*school* (3) ... IL-6
Carpenter Sch—*school* ... IN-6
Carpenter Sch—*school* ... IA-7
Carpenter Sch—*school* ... KS-7
Carpenter Sch—*school* ... KY-4
Carpenter Sch—*school* ... MA-1
Carpenter Sch—*school* (6) ... MI-6
Carpenter Sch—*school* ... MO-7
Carpenter Sch—*school* ... OH-6
Carpenter Sch—*school* ... SD-7
Carpenter Sch—*school* ... TX-5
Carpenter Sch—*school* (3) ... WI-6
Carpenters Chapel (historical)—*church* ... TN-4
Carpenter Sch (historical)—*school* ... MS-4
Carpenter Sch (historical)—*school* (3) ... TN-4
Carpenter Sch Number 1—*school* ... MS-4
*Carpenters Corner* ... RI-1
Carpenters Corner—*locale* ... DE-2
Carpenters Corner—*locale* ... MN-6
**Carpenters Corner**—*pop pl* ... RI-1
**Carpenters Corners**—*pop pl* ... NY-2
*Carpenters Creek* ... PA-2
Carpenters Creek—*stream* ... AL-4
Carpenters Creek—*stream* ... WA-9
Carpenters Grove Ch—*church* ... NC-3
Carpenters Gulch—*valley* ... ID-8
Carpenters Hall—*building* ... PA-2
Carpenters' Hall—*hist pl* ... PA-2
Carpenter Sink Creek—*stream* ... FL-3
Carpenters Island—*island* ... OR-9
Carpenters Island (historical)—*island* ... TN-4
Carpenter Site (47 Wn 246)—*hist pl* ... WI-6
Carpenters Lake—*lake* ... KY-4
Carpenters Lake—*lake* ... LA-4
Carpenters Lake—*lake* ... MS-4
Carpenters Lake—*lake* ... WA-9
Carpenters Lake—*reservoir* ... AL-4
Carpenters Lake—*reservoir* ... NC-3
Carpenters Lake Dam—*dam* ... NC-3
*Carpenters Landing* ... NJ-2
Carpenters Landing (historical)—*locale* ... MS-4
Carpenter-Smith Cem—*cemetery* ... KY-4
Carpenter-Smith House—*hist pl* ... KY-4
*Carpenters Pit* ... TN-4
Carpenters Point—*cape* ... MN-6
Carpenters Point—*cape* ... NJ-2
Carpenters Point—*cape* ... OK-5
Carpenters Pond—*reservoir* ... AL-4
Carpenters Pond—*reservoir* ... SC-3
Carpenter Spring—*spring* ... NV-8
Carpenter Spring—*spring* (3) ... TN-4
Carpenter Spring—*spring* ... TX-5
Carpenter Springs—*spring* ... NM-5
Carpenters Rapids—*rapids* ... WI-6
*Carpenters Run* ... PA-2
Carpenters Run—*stream* ... PA-2
Carpenters Shoals—*bar* ... TN-4
Carpenters Store (historical)—*locale* ... MS-4
*Carpenter Station* ... AL-4
**Carpentersville**—*pop pl* ... IL-6
**Carpentersville**—*pop pl* ... IN-6
Carpenter Swamp—*swamp* ... PA-2
Carpenter Tank—*reservoir* ... AZ-5
Carpenter Tank—*reservoir* ... NM-5
Carpenter Town—*locale* ... PA-2
**Carpentertown**—*pop pl* ... PA-2
**Carpenter Township**—*pop pl* ... ND-7
Carpenter (Township of)—*fmr MCD* ... AR-4
**Carpenter (Township of)**—*pop pl* ... IN-6
**Carpenter (Township of)**—*pop pl* ... MN-6
Carpenter Trail—*trail* ... PA-2
Carpenter Valley—*valley* ... CA-9
**Carpenterville**—*pop pl* ... NJ-2
**Carpenterville**—*pop pl* ... OR-9
Carpenterville Brookings Wayside—*locale* ... OR-9
*Carpenterville Town* ... IN-6
Carpenter Well—*well* ... AZ-5
Carpenter Wells—*well* ... TX-5
Carpenter Windmill—*locale* (2) ... NM-5
Carpenter Windmill—*locale* ... TX-5
Carpenter Woods—*park* ... PA-2
Carpentier Creek—*stream* ... IN-6
Carpentier Mission—*church* ... LA-4
Carper Branch—*stream* ... VA-3
Carper Cem—*cemetery* (2) ... WV-2
Carper Ditch—*canal* ... IN-6
Carpe Ridge—*ridge* ... AK-9
Carper Mtn—*summit* ... OK-5
Carpers Branch—*stream* ... WV-2
Carpers Creek—*stream* ... TX-5
Carpers Valley—*valley* ... VA-3
Carpers Valley Ch—*church* ... VA-3
Carpers Valley Golf Club—*other* ... VA-3
Carpers Well—*well* ... TX-5
Carper Tank—*reservoir* ... TX-5
Carper Windmill—*locale* ... NM-5
Carpet Hill Creek—*stream* ... OR-9
Carpet Peak—*summit* ... AK-9
Carpet Rock Mine (surface)—*mine* ... AL-4
Carp Hill—*summit* ... MA-1
Carpics Lake—*lake* ... MN-6
Carpie Mine—*mine* ... ID-8
Carpi Lake—*reservoir* ... NJ-2
Carpi Lake Dam—*dam* ... NJ-2
**Carpinteria**—*pop pl* ... CA-9
Carpinteria Cem—*cemetery* ... CA-9
Carpinteria Creek—*stream* ... CA-9
*Carpinteria Slough* ... CA-9
Carpinteria State Beach—*park* ... CA-9
Carpinteria Valley (CCD)—*cens area* ... CA-9
*Carpinterio Lagoon* ... CA-9
**Carpio**—*pop pl* ... ND-7
Carpio Dam—*dam* ... ND-7
Carpios Canyon—*valley* ... CO-8
Carpios Cem—*cemetery* ... CO-8
**Carpio Township**—*pop pl* ... ND-7
Carp Island—*island* ... AK-9
*Carp Lake* ... MI-6
*Carp Lake* ... MT-8
*Carp Lake* ... WA-9
Carp Lake—*lake* ... FL-3
Carp Lake—*lake* ... GA-3
Carp Lake—*lake* ... IA-7
Carp Lake—*lake* (3) ... MI-6
Carp Lake—*lake* ... NE-7
Carp Lake—*lake* (4) ... WA-9
Carp Lake—*lake* ... WI-6
**Carp Lake**—*pop pl* ... MI-6
Carp Lake—*reservoir* ... CO-8
Carp Lake Campground—*locale* ... CO-8
Carp Lake Landing—*locale* ... MI-6
Carp Lake Mine—*mine* ... MI-6
Carp Lake River—*stream* ... MI-6
Carp Lake School—*locale* ... MI-6
**Carp Lake (Township of)**—*pop pl* (2) ... MI-6
Car Point—*cape* ... RI-1
Carpond Spring—*spring* ... AL-4
**Carpow**—*pop pl* ... SC-3
Carpp Creek—*stream* ... MT-8
Carpp Lake—*lake* ... MT-8
Carpp Mine—*mine* ... MT-8
Carp Pond—*lake* ... CT-1
Carp Pond—*lake* ... IL-6
Carp Pond—*lake* (2) ... NY-2
Carp Pond—*lake* ... RI-1
Carp Post Office (historical)—*building* ... TN-4
Carpp Ridge—*ridge* ... MT-8
*Carp River* ... MI-6
Carp River—*stream* (3) ... MI-6
Carp River Campground—*locale* ... MI-6
Carp River Inlet—*stream* ... MI-6
Carp River Lake—*reservoir* ... MI-6
Carp River Point—*cape* ... MI-6
Carps Bayou—*stream* ... LA-4
Carp Sch (historical)—*school* ... TN-4
Carps Corner—*locale* ... VA-3
Carp Slough—*bay* ... TN-4
Carpsrocus Creek—*stream* ... PA-2
*Carquines Point* ... CA-9
*Carquines Strait* ... CA-9
Carquinez Bridge—*bridge* ... CA-9
Carquinez Cem—*cemetery* ... CA-9
**Carquinez Heights**—*pop pl* ... CA-9
Carquinez Strait—*channel* ... CA-9
Carquinez Strait Lighthouse—*locale* ... CA-9
*Carr* ... MO-7
Carr—*locale* ... CA-9
Carr—*locale* ... FL-3
Carr—*locale* ... MI-6
Carr—*locale* ... TX-5
**Carr**—*pop pl* ... CO-8
**Carr**—*pop pl* ... NC-3
Carr, Andrew, Sr., House—*hist pl* ... ND-7
Carr, Anna, Homestead—*hist pl* ... SD-7
Carr, Ben F., Jr., House—*hist pl* ... KY-4
Carr, Dr. George W., House—*hist pl* ... RI-1
Carr, George, Ranch House—*hist pl* ... OK-5
Carr, Jefferson Davis, House—*hist pl* ... SD-7
Carr, John Price, House—*hist pl* ... NC-3
Carr, Martin W., Sch—*hist pl* ... MA-1
Carr, Raymond, House—*hist pl* ... AZ-5
Carr, Thomas, District—*hist pl* ... GA-3
Carr, Thomas, Farmstead Site (Keeler Site RI-707)—*hist pl* ... RI-1
Carr, Titus W., House—*hist pl* ... NC-3
Carr, William V., House—*hist pl* ... IA-7
*Carrabasset* ... ME-1
Carrabassett—*locale* ... ME-1
Carrabassett River—*stream* ... ME-1
Carrabassett Stream—*stream* ... ME-1
**Carrabassett Valley**—*pop pl* ... ME-1
Carrabassett Valley (Town of)—*civ div* ... ME-1
**Carrabelle**—*pop pl* ... FL-3
**Carrabelle Beach**—*pop pl* ... FL-3
Carrabelle (CCD)—*cens area* ... FL-3
Carrabelle Harbor—*harbor* ... FL-3
Carrabelle HS—*school* ... FL-3
Carrabelle Lighthouse—*locale* ... FL-3
*Carrabelle River* ... FL-3
Carrabelle River—*stream* ... FL-3
Carracas—*locale* ... CO-8
Carracas—*locale* ... NM-5
Carracas Canyon—*valley* ... NM-5
Carracas Cem—*cemetery* ... NM-5
Carracas Mesa—*summit* (2) ... NM-5
Carracas Rim—*cliff* ... CO-8
Carracas Rim—*cliff* ... NM-5
Carr Airp—*airport* ... WA-9
**Carraizo Alto**—*pop pl* ... PR-3
Carraizo (Barrio)—*fmr MCD* ... PR-3
Carral Arroyo—*valley* ... TX-5
Carralitos Ranch—*locale* ... NM-5
Carrals Spring—*spring* ... CA-9
**Carranza (Carranza Memorial)**—*pop pl* ... NJ-2
Carranza Memorial—*park* ... NJ-2
Carranza Spring—*spring* ... CA-9
Carranza Windmill—*locale* ... TX-5
Carrara—*locale* ... NV-8
Carrara Canyon—*valley* ... NV-8
*Carratunk* ... ME-1
*Carraway* ... MS-4
Carraway—*locale* ... FL-3
Carraway Bay—*bay* ... NC-3
Carraway Cem—*cemetery* ... VA-3
Carraway Ch—*church* ... NC-3
Carraway Creek—*stream* ... NC-3
Carraway House—*hist pl* ... MS-4
Carraway Med Ctr—*hospital* ... AL-4
Carraway Rsvr—*reservoir* ... ID-8
Carraways Bluff—*cliff* ... AL-4
Carr Bailey Run—*stream* ... OH-6
**Carrboro**—*pop pl* ... NC-3
Carrboro Commercial Hist Dist—*hist pl* ... NC-3
Carrboro Elem Sch—*school* ... NC-3
Carr Brake—*swamp* ... MS-4
**Carr Branch**—*pop pl* ... TN-4
Carr Branch—*stream* ... FL-3
Carr Branch—*stream* ... GA-3
Carr Branch—*stream* ... KY-4
Carr Branch—*stream* ... MS-4
Carr Branch—*stream* (3) ... MO-7
Carr Branch—*stream* ... OK-5
Carr Branch—*stream* (5) ... TN-4
Carr Branch—*stream* ... VA-3
Carr Branch—*stream* ... WV-2
Carr Branch Ch—*church* ... TN-4
Carr Bridge—*bridge* ... FL-3
*Carr Brook* ... NY-2
*Carr Brook* ... VT-1
Carr Brook—*stream* ... CT-1
Carr Brook—*stream* (2) ... NH-1
Carr Brook—*stream* ... PA-2
Carr Brook—*stream* (2) ... VT-1
Carr Butte—*summit* ... CA-9
Carr Cabin—*locale* ... WY-8
Carr Camp—*locale* ... NH-1
Carr Canyon—*valley* ... AZ-5
Carr Canyon—*valley* ... CA-9
Carr Canyon—*valley* ... MT-8
Carr Canyon—*valley* ... NM-5
Carr Canyon—*valley* ... SD-7
Carr Canyon—*valley* ... WY-8
Carr Canyon Ranch—*locale* ... AZ-5
Carr Cem—*cemetery* (2) ... AL-4
Carr Cem—*cemetery* (2) ... AR-4
Carr Cem—*cemetery* ... FL-3
Carr Cem—*cemetery* ... IL-6
Carr Cem—*cemetery* (5) ... IN-6
Carr Cem—*cemetery* ... KS-7
Carr Cem—*cemetery* (4) ... KY-4
Carr Cem—*cemetery* (3) ... MS-4
Carr Cem—*cemetery* (2) ... MO-7
Carr Cem—*cemetery* ... NE-7
Carr Cem—*cemetery* (2) ... NY-2
Carr Cem—*cemetery* (11) ... TN-4
Carr Cem—*cemetery* ... TX-5
Carr Cem—*cemetery* ... WV-2
Carr Cemeteries—*cemetery* ... MS-4
Carr Ch—*church* ... KY-4
Carr Ch—*church* ... MS-4
Carr Ch—*church* ... MO-7
Carr Ch—*church* ... OK-5
Carr Chapel—*church* ... FL-3
Carr Chapel—*church* ... KY-4
Carr Chapel—*church* ... MS-4
Carr Chapel—*church* ... MO-7
Carr Chapel—*church* ... TN-4
Carr Corner—*locale* ... ME-1
Carr Corners—*locale* ... NY-2
*Carr Creek* ... LA-4
*Carr Creek* ... WA-9
Carr Creek—*bay* ... FL-3
Carr Creek—*bay* ... MD-2
**Carr Creek**—*pop pl* ... KY-4
Carr Creek—*stream* (2) ... AL-4
Carr Creek—*stream* (2) ... CA-9
Carr Creek—*stream* ... CO-8
Carr Creek—*stream* ... ID-8
Carr Creek—*stream* ... IL-6
Carr Creek—*stream* ... KS-7
Carr Creek—*stream* (2) ... KY-4
Carr Creek—*stream* (2) ... MI-6
Carr Creek—*stream* (2) ... MO-7
Carr Creek—*stream* ... MT-8
Carr Creek—*stream* ... NE-7
Carr Creek—*stream* ... OK-5
Carr Creek—*stream* ... OR-9
Carr Creek—*stream* ... SC-3
Carr Creek—*stream* (6) ... TN-4
Carr Creek—*stream* ... VA-3
Carr Creek—*stream* (2) ... WI-6
Carr Creek—*stream* ... WY-8
Carr Creek Ch—*church* ... MO-7
**Carr Creek Township**—*pop pl* ... KS-7
**Carrcroft**—*pop pl* ... DE-2
**Carrcroft Crest**—*pop pl* ... DE-2
Carrcroft Elem Sch—*school* ... DE-2
*Carrcroft Sch* ... DE-2
Carrcroft Station—*locale* ... DE-2
Carr-Crumley-Krouse Cem—*cemetery* ... TN-4
Carr Ditch—*canal* ... NY-2
Carr Drain—*canal* (3) ... MI-6
Carr Drain—*stream* ... MI-6
Carr Draw—*valley* ... MT-8
Carr Draw—*valley* ... WY-8
Carreker, Newton P., House—*hist pl* ... GA-3
Carrel Cem—*cemetery* ... OH-6
Carrel Chapel—*church* ... NC-3
*Carrell Branch* ... NC-3
Carrell Branch—*stream* ... TN-4
Carrell Cem—*cemetery* ... TX-5
Carr-Ellis Number 3 Mine (underground)—*mine* ... AL-4
*Carrell Knob* ... NC-3
*Carrell Lake* ... NC-3
*Carrell Mountain* ... NC-3
Carrell Sch—*school* ... TX-5
Carrel Valley—*valley* ... WI-6
Carrent Ch—*church* ... TX-5
Carrent-Deer Cem—*cemetery* ... AL-4
Carreo Spring—*spring* ... NM-5
Carreras (Barrio)—*fmr MCD* (2) ... PR-3
*Carrer Lake* ... MN-6
Carreta Creek—*stream* ... TX-5
Carretas Crossing—*locale* ... TX-5
Carretas Springs—*spring* ... NM-5
Carreta Tank—*reservoir* ... TX-5
*Carreta Windmill* ... AZ-5
Carreton Canyon—*valley* ... NM-5
*Carretts Run* ... PA-2
Carrey Busey Sch—*school* ... IL-6
Carrey Sch—*school* ... IL-6
Carr Field—*park* ... IN-6
Carr Fork—*stream* ... KY-4
Carr Fork (CCD)—*cens area* ... KY-4
Carr Fork Lake—*reservoir* ... KY-4
*Carr Fork Rsvr* ... KY-4
Carr Gap—*gap* ... GA-3
Carr Gap—*gap* ... TN-4
Carr Gulch—*valley* ... CA-9
Carr Gulch—*valley* ... CO-8
Carr Gulch—*valley* ... OR-9
Carr-Harrison Cem—*cemetery* ... IL-6
Carr Hill—*summit* ... ME-1
Carr Hill—*summit* (2) ... NY-2
Carr Hill—*summit* ... PA-2
Carr Hill—*summit* ... WA-9
Carr Hill Ch—*church* ... NC-3
Carr (historical)—*locale* ... MS-4
Carr Hollow—*valley* (2) ... AR-4
Carr Hollow—*valley* ... IN-6
Carr Hollow—*valley* ... KY-4
Carr Hollow—*valley* ... MO-7
Carr Hollow—*valley* (2) ... TN-4
Carr Hollow—*valley* ... TX-5
Carr House—*hist pl* ... CA-9
Carr House—*hist pl* ... IL-6
*Carriage Creek* ... IL-6
**Carriage Crossing Condominium**—*pop pl* ... UT-8
*Carriage Estates* ... IN-6
**Carriage Estates**—*pop pl* ... IN-6
Carriage Ford—*locale* ... VA-3
**Carriage Hill**—*pop pl* ... TN-4
**Carriage Hill**—*pop pl* (2) ... VA-3
**Carriage Hill**—*pop pl* ... WA-9
Carriage Hill—*uninc pl* ... VA-3
**Carriage Hill Estates (subdivision)**—*pop pl* ... UT-8
**Carriage Hills**—*pop pl* ... TN-4
Carriage Hills Baptist Ch—*church* ... MS-4
Carriage Hills Country Club—*other* ... MN-6
Carriage Hills Plaza Shop Ctr—*locale* ... MS-4
**Carriage Hills (subdivision)**—*pop pl* (2) ... AL-4
**Carriage Hills (subdivision)**—*pop pl* ... MS-4
**Carriage Hills (subdivision)**—*pop pl* ... NC-3
**Carriage Hill (subdivision)**—*pop pl* ... AL-4
**Carriage Lane**—*pop pl* ... DE-2
**Carriage Lane Condominium**—*pop pl* ... UT-8
**Carriage Lane (subdivision)**—*pop pl* ... AL-4
**Carriage Lane Subdivision Number Two**—*pop pl* ... UT-8
Carriage Paths, Bridges and Gatehouses—*hist pl* ... ME-1
**Carriage Place Subdivision**—*pop pl* ... UT-8
Carriage Point—*hist pl* ... OK-5
**Carriage Run (subdivision)**—*pop pl* ... DE-2
Carriage Square Shop Ctr—*locale* ... UT-8
**Carriage Square Subdivision**—*pop pl* ... UT-8
Carriage Trade Plaza (Shop Ctr)—*locale* ... FL-3
Carribbean Center for Advanced Studies—*facility* ... PR-3
Carribean Sch—*school* ... PR-3

Carribou Lake—*lake* CA-9
Carrica Ranch—*locale* CO-8
Carrice Creek—*stream* TX-5
**Carricitos**—*pop pl* TX-5
Carricitos Creek—*stream* TX-5
**Carrick**—*pop pl* PA-2
**Carrick Addition**—*pop pl* CA-9
Carrick Cove—*valley* TN-4
Carrick Creek—*stream* CA-9
Carrick Creek—*stream* SC-3
Carrick Hill—*summit* OH-6
Carrick Hollow—*valley* TN-4
Carrick HS—*school* PA-2
Carrick Knob—*summit* MD-2
Carrick Memorial Sch—*school* TN-4
Carrick Run—*stream* WV-2
Carricks Mill (historical)—*locale* AL-4
Carrick Spring—*spring* TN-4
Carrick Valley—*locale* PA-2
Carrico Caves—*cave* MO-7
Carrico Cem—*cemetery* TX-5
Carrico Cem—*cemetery* VA-3
Carrico Lake—*lake* MO-7
Carrico Lakes—*lake* NE-7
Carrico Mill—*locale* VA-3
Carrico Mine—*mine* ID-8
Carrico Spring—*spring* AZ-5
*Carricotos Creek* TX-5
Carricut Lake—*lake* CA-9
Carrie—*locale* KY-4
Carrie—*locale* VA-3
Carrie, Lake—*lake* FL-3
Carrie, Mount—*summit* WA-9
Carrie Barnett Sch—*school* CA-9
Carrie Bogan—*swamp* ME-1
Carrie Bogan Brook—*stream* ME-1
Carrie Creek—*stream* CA-9
Carrie Creek—*stream* ID-8
Carrie Creek—*stream* NC-3
Carrie Dotson Elem Sch—*school* MS-4
Carrie Downie Elem Sch—*school* DE-2
Carrie Fork—*stream* OR-9
Carrie Glacier—*glacier* WA-9
Carrie Gosch Elem Sch—*school* IN-6
**Carrie Heights Subdivision**—*pop pl* UT-8
Carrie Lake—*lake* MN-6
Carrie Lake—*lake* ND-7
Carrie Lake—*lake* WA-9
*Carrie Leonard Creek* ID-8
Carrie Leonard Mine—*mine* ID-8
Carrie Nation Creek—*stream* WY-8
**Carrier**—*pop pl* IL-6
**Carrier**—*pop pl* OK-5
**Carrier**—*pop pl* PA-2
Carrier, Lake—*lake* MS-4
Carrier, Robert M., House—*hist pl* TN-4
Carrier Bay—*bay* NY-2
Carrier Branch—*stream* TN-4
Carrier Bridge—*bridge* NC-3
Carrier Camp—*locale* NE-7
Carrier Canyon—*valley* CA-9
Carrier Cem—*cemetery* LA-4
Carrier Cem—*cemetery* OH-6
Carrier Cem—*cemetery* PA-2
Carrier Circle—*locale* NY-2
Carrier Creek—*stream* MI-6
**Carriere**—*pop pl* MS-4
*Carriere Station* MS-4
Carrier Gulch—*valley* CA-9
Carrier Hollow—*valley* TN-4
**Carrier Mills**—*pop pl* IL-6
Carrier Mills Archeol District—*hist pl* IL-6
*Carrier Mills (corporate name Carriers Mills)* IL-6
Carrier Mills Park—*park* IL-6
Carrier Recreation Center—*building* NY-2
Carrier Run—*stream* PA-2
Carrier Sch—*school* OK-5
*Carriers Lake* KY-4
**Carriers Mills (corporate name for Carrier Mills)**—*pop pl* IL-6
Carriers Mills (Township of)—*civ div* IL-6
*Carries Lake* KY-4
*Carrie Stern Elementary School* MS-4
Carrietown—*locale* ID-8
Carrigain Branch—*stream* NH-1
Carrigain Brook—*stream* NH-1
**Carrigan**—*pop pl* KY-4
Carrigan, Mount—*summit* NH-1
Carrigan Averil Ditch—*canal* CO-8
Carrigan Campground—*locale* MT-8
Carrigan Canyon—*valley* UT-8
Carrigan Cem—*cemetery* IL-6
Carrigan Drain—*canal* MI-6
Carrigan House—*hist pl* AR-4
Carrigan Lake—*lake* MN-6
Carrigan Notch—*gap* NH-1
Carrigan Notch Trail—*trail* NH-1
Carrigan Outlook—*locale* NH-1
*Carrigan Peak* AZ-5
Carrigan Pond—*lake* NH-1
Carrigan Sch—*school* TX-5
**Carrigan (Township of)**—*pop pl* IL-6
*Carrigan Well* AZ-5
*Carrigar Church* AL-4
Carrigar Sch (historical)—*school* AL-4
**Carriger**—*pop pl* AL-4
Carriger Ch—*church* AL-4
Carriger-Cowan House—*hist pl* TN-4
Carriger Creek—*stream* (2) CA-9
Carriger Post Office (historical)—*building* AL-4
Carriger Spring Branch—*stream* TN-4
Carriker Pond—*reservoir* NC-3
Carrikers Store—*locale* NC-3
Carrill Creek—*stream* ID-8
Carrillo Sch—*school* AZ-5
Carrillo Sch—*school* CA-9
Carrillo Spring—*spring* CA-9
Carrin Bayou—*bay* FL-3
Carringer Branch—*stream* TN-4
Carringer Cove—*valley* NC-3
Carringer Gap—*gap* NC-3
Carrington—*locale* OH-6
**Carrington**—*pop pl* MO-7
**Carrington**—*pop pl* ND-7
Carrington Bay—*bay* UT-8
Carrington Branch—*stream* KY-4
Carrington Branch—*stream* TN-4
Carrington Cem—*cemetery* CT-1
Carrington Cem—*cemetery* NC-3
Carrington Cem—*cemetery* ND-7
Carrington Cem—*cemetery* (2) TX-5
*Carrington Cemetery* MS-4
Carrington-Covert House—*hist pl* TX-5
*Carrington Creek* NY-2
Carrington Creek—*stream* NY-2
Carrington Creek—*stream* TX-5
Carrington Hill—*summit* CT-1
Carrington Hollow—*valley* TN-4
Carrington Island—*island* UT-8
Carrington Island—*island* WY-8
Carrington JHS—*school* NC-3
Carrington Osage Village Site—*hist pl* MO-7
Carrington Pits Picnic Area—*locale* MO-7
Carrington Point—*cape* CA-9
Carrington Pond—*lake* CT-1
Carrington Pond—*lake* TN-4
Carrington Pond—*reservoir* OH-6
Carrington Rock—*summit* KY-4
Carrington Rock Trail—*trail* KY-4
Carrington Sch—*school* MO-7
Carringtons Pond—*reservoir* CT-1
**Carrington Township**—*pop pl* ND-7
Carrington Water Works—*locale* ND-7
**Carrington Woods (subdivision)**—*pop pl* NC-3
Carr Inlet—*bay* WA-9
Carr Institute—*school* KY-4
Carrion Branch—*stream* KY-4
*Carrion Crow Bayou* LA-4
*Carrion Crow Lake* LA-4
Carrion Crow Mtn—*summit* AR-4
Carrion Run—*stream* WV-2
Carris—*locale* SC-3
Carrisa Canyon—*valley* NM-5
Carrisalito Creek—*stream* CA-9
Carrisalito Flat—*flat* CA-9
Carrisalito Spring—*spring* CA-9
Carrisalito Springs—*spring* CA-9
Carrisa Lookout Complex—*hist pl* NM-5
Carrisa Lookout Tower—*other* NM-5
Carrisa Plains Sch—*school* CA-9
Carrisa Ranch—*locale* CA-9
Carrisa Spring—*spring* NM-5
Carrisito Spring—*spring* AZ-5
Carr Island—*island* FL-3
Carr Island—*island* IL-6
Carr Island—*island* MA-1
**Carriso Gorge**—*pop pl* CA-9
*Carriso Mountains* AZ-5
*Carriso Plain* CA-9
Carriss's Feed Store—*hist pl* KY-4
Carriss's Store—*hist pl* KY-4
Carrista Creek—*stream* CA-9
Carristo Spring—*spring* AZ-5
Carrithers Chapel—*church* KY-4
*Carritunk* ME-1
Carriveau Mill—*locale* ME-1
Carrizal (Barrio)—*fmr MCD* PR-3
**Carrizales**—*pop pl* PR-3
Carrizales (Barrio)—*fmr MCD* PR-3
Carrizalillo Hills—*summit* NM-5
*Carrizelos* TX-5
Carrizitos Creek—*stream* TX-5
*Carrizo* AZ-5
Carrizo—*locale* NM-5
**Carrizo**—*pop pl* AZ-5
Carrizo, Bayou—*stream* TX-5
Carrizo, Mount—*summit* CO-8
Carrizo Aerial Gunnery Range—*other* CA-9
Carrizo Badlands—*area* CA-9
Carrizo Branch—*stream* TX-5
Carrizo Butte—*summit* AZ-5
Carrizo Camp Windmills—*locale* NM-5
*Carrizo Canyon* CA-9
Carrizo Canyon—*valley* (2) CA-9
Carrizo Canyon—*valley* (6) NM-5
Carrizo Ch—*church* NM-5
*Carrizo Creek* AZ-5
*Carrizo Creek* CA-9
*Carrizo Creek* CO-8
*Carrizo Creek* NM-5
Carrizo Creek—*stream* AZ-5
Carrizo Creek—*stream* (4) CA-9
Carrizo Creek—*stream* (8) NM-5
Carrizo Creek—*stream* (4) TX-5
*Carrizo Desert Area* CA-9
Carrizo Draw—*valley* TX-5
Carrizo Falls—*falls* CA-9
*Carrizo Gorge* CA-9
Carrizo Gorge—*locale* CA-9
Carrizo Gorge—*valley* CA-9
Carrizo Mission Sch—*school* AZ-5
*Carrizo Mountain* AZ-5
*Carrizo Mountains* NM-5
Carrizo Mountains—*range* AZ-5
Carrizo Mountains—*range* TX-5
Carrizo Mountains—*summit* TX-5
Carrizo Mtn—*summit* CA-9
Carrizo Mtn—*summit* NM-5
Carrizo Peak—*summit* (2) NM-5
Carrizo Peak—*summit* TX-5
Carrizo Peak Trail (Pack)—*trail* NM-5
Carrizo Plain—*plain* CA-9
*Carrizo Plains* CA-9
Carrizo Plain Substation—*other* CA-9
Carrizo Ranch—*locale* AZ-5
Carrizo Ridge—*ridge* AZ-5
Carrizo Spring—*spring* CA-9
Carrizo Spring—*spring* NM-5
Carrizo Springs—*locale* CO-8
**Carrizo Springs**—*pop pl* TX-5
Carrizo Springs (CCD)—*cens area* TX-5
Carrizo Springs Cem—*cemetery* CO-8
Carrizo Springs Golf Course—*other* TX-5
Carrizo Spring Windmill—*locale* TX-5
Carrizo Tank—*reservoir* AZ-5
Carrizo Tank—*reservoir* NM-5
Carrizo Valley—*valley* CA-9
*Carrizo Wash* AZ-5
*Carrizo Wash* CA-9
Carrizo Wash—*stream* (2) CA-9
Carrizo Wash—*stream* NM-5
Carrizo Wash—*valley* AZ-5
Carrizo Wash Bridge—*bridge* AZ-5
Carrizo Well—*well* AZ-5
Carrizo Well—*well* TX-5
Carrizo Windmill—*locale* (2) NM-5
Carrizo Windmill—*locale* (2) TX-5
**Carrizozo**—*pop pl* NM-5
Carrizozo Canyon—*valley* NM-5
Carrizozo (CCD)—*cens area* NM-5
*Carrizozo Creek* CO-8
*Carrizozo Creek* OK-5
Carrizozo Creek—*stream* NM-5
Carrizozo Creek—*stream* OK-5
Carrizozo Draw—*valley* NM-5
*Carrizozo Mountains* NM-5
Carrizozo Spring—*spring* NM-5
Carrizozo Well—*well* NM-5
*Carrizzo Creek* CO-8
*Carrizzo Creek* OK-5
Carr JHS—*school* MS-4
Carr JHS—*school* NC-3
Carr Lake—*lake* (2) AZ-5
Carr Lake—*lake* CA-9
Carr Lake—*lake* (2) FL-3
Carr Lake—*lake* IN-6
Carr Lake—*lake* LA-4
Carr Lake—*lake* (3) MI-6
Carr Lake—*lake* MN-6
Carr Lake—*lake* NE-7
Carr Lake—*lake* TX-5
Carr Lake—*reservoir* TX-5
Carr Lake—*reservoir* UT-8
Carr Lake Draw—*valley* AZ-5
Carr Lake Sch—*school* MN-6
Carr Lake Tank—*reservoir* AZ-5
Carr Landing—*locale* FL-3
Carr Landing Field—*airport* SD-7
**Carr Lane**—*pop pl* MO-7
Carr Lane Ch—*church* MO-7
Carr Low Gap—*gap* MO-7
Carr Memorial Cem—*cemetery* MN-6
Carr Mill—*locale* AL-4
Carr Mountain—*ridge* NH-1
Carr Mountain Trail—*trail* NH-1
Carr Mtn—*summit* AZ-5
Carr Mtn—*summit* GA-3
Carr Mtn—*summit* ME-1
Carr Mtn—*summit* NM-5
Carr Mtn—*summit* NC-3
Carr Mtn—*summit* VA-3
Carr Natl Wildlife Ref—*park* ND-7
Carr No. 60 Sch—*hist pl* SD-7
Carr Number 1 Dam—*dam* SD-7
Carr Number 2 Dam—*dam* SD-7
Carr Number 4 Dam—*dam* SD-7
Carr Number 5 Dam—*dam* SD-7
**Carro**—*pop pl* PR-3
*Carrol* TX-5
Carrol Bank Prospect—*mine* TN-4
*Carrol Butte* OR-9
Carrol Campground—*park* OR-9
*Carrol Canyon* CA-9
Carrol Canyon—*valley* CA-9
Carrol Canyon—*valley* UT-8
Carrol Chapel—*church* MD-2
Carrol Coll—*school* MT-8
**Carrol Corner**—*pop pl* AR-4
*Carrol Coulee* MT-8
*Carrol Creek* IL-6
*Carrol Creek* IN-6
*Carrol Creek* OR-9
Carrol Creek—*stream* IN-6
Carrol Creek—*stream* MT-8
Carrol Creek—*stream* OR-9
Carrol Creek—*stream* TX-5
Carrol Creek Ch—*church* LA-4
Carrol Creek Drain—*stream* MI-6
Carrol Creek (reduced usage)—*stream* CO-8
Carrol Drain—*canal* MI-6
Carrol Flats—*flat* WA-9
Carrol Gap—*gap* GA-3
*Carrol Glade* OR-9
*Carrol Glade Spring* OR-9
Carrol Gulch—*valley* ID-8
Carrol Hill—*summit* MS-4
Carrol Hollow—*valley* MO-7
Carrol HS—*school* AL-4
Carrol HS—*school* NY-2
Carrol Junction—*locale* MO-7
Carrol Knob—*summit* NC-3
*Carroll* (2) AR-4
*Carroll* NY-2
Carroll—*locale* LA-4
Carroll—*locale* ME-1
Carroll—*locale* MD-2
Carroll—*locale* MS-4
Carroll—*locale* NY-2
**Carroll**—*pop pl* FL-3
**Carroll**—*pop pl* IA-7
**Carroll**—*pop pl* NE-7
**Carroll**—*pop pl* NH-1
**Carroll**—*pop pl* NC-3
**Carroll**—*pop pl* OH-6
**Carroll**—*pop pl* PA-2
**Carroll**—*pop pl* TN-4
**Carroll**—*pop pl* TX-5
Carroll, A. R., Bldg—*hist pl* AR-4
Carroll, Chancellor James P., House—*hist pl* SC-3
Carroll, Don (Plant)—*facility* IL-6
Carroll, Dr. Clyde, House—*hist pl* KY-4
Carroll, Edward, House—*hist pl* KS-7
Carroll, J. J., House—*hist pl* TX-5
Carroll, John M., House—*hist pl* GA-3
Carroll, Lake—*lake* FL-3
Carroll, Lake—*reservoir* GA-3
Carroll, Lake—*reservoir* VA-3
Carroll, Thomas, House—*hist pl* WV-2
Carroll Acad—*school* MS-4
Carroll Acad (historical)—*school* TN-4
Carrol Lake—*lake* UT-8
Carrol Lake—*lake* WI-6
Carrol Lake—*reservoir* AL-4
Carrol Lake—*reservoir* MS-4
Carrol Lake—*reservoir* NC-3
Carrol Lake Dam—*dam* NC-3
Carrol Lake Dam—*dam* SD-7
Carrol Lakes—*reservoir* CO-8
Carroll Alsop Ditch—*canal* WY-8
Carroll Anderson Hollow—*valley* AR-4
Carrol Lane Park—*park* TX-5
Carrol Lane Sch—*school* TX-5
Carroll Avenue, 1300 Block—*hist pl* CA-9
Carroll Bell Sch—*school* TX-5
Carroll Bldg—*hist pl* CT-1
*Carroll Bluff* WA-9
*Carroll Branch* AL-4
Carroll Branch—*stream* AL-4
Carroll Branch—*stream* GA-3
Carroll Branch—*stream* (2) MD-2
Carroll Branch—*stream* MS-4
Carroll Branch—*stream* MO-7
Carroll Branch—*stream* (2) NC-3
Carroll Branch—*stream* (2) TN-4
Carroll Branch—*stream* TX-5
Carroll Branch—*stream* WV-2
Carroll Bridge—*bridge* VA-3
Carroll Brook—*stream* NY-2
Carroll Butte—*summit* OR-9
Carroll Camp—*locale* NY-2
Carroll Canal—*canal* LA-4
Carroll Canyon—*valley* AZ-5
Carroll Canyon—*valley* CA-9
Carroll Canyon—*valley* KS-7
Carroll Canyon—*valley* NE-7
Carroll Catchment Tank—*reservoir* AZ-5
Carroll Cave—*cave* TN-4
Carroll Cem—*cemetery* AL-4
Carroll Cem—*cemetery* (2) IL-6
Carroll Cem—*cemetery* KY-4
Carroll Cem—*cemetery* MA-1
Carroll Cem—*cemetery* MO-7
Carroll Cem—*cemetery* NM-5
Carroll Cem—*cemetery* NY-2
Carroll Cem—*cemetery* NC-3
Carroll Cem—*cemetery* OH-6
Carroll Cem—*cemetery* (2) PA-2
Carroll Cem—*cemetery* (7) TN-4
Carroll Cem—*cemetery* (2) TX-5
Carroll Cem—*cemetery* (2) VA-3
Carroll Ch—*church* VA-3
*Carroll Channel* WA-9
Carroll Chapel—*church* MD-2
Carroll Chapel—*church* TN-4
Carroll Chapel Cem—*cemetery* TX-5
Carroll Coll—*school* WI-6
Carroll Colony Cem—*cemetery* TX-5
*Carroll Consolidated School* IN-6
Carroll-Cook Cem—*cemetery* MS-4
*Carroll Corner* AR-4
Carroll Corners—*locale* MI-6
Carroll Corners—*locale* NY-2
Carroll Coulee—*valley* MT-8
**Carroll (County)**—*pop pl* AR-4
**Carroll (County)**—*pop pl* GA-3
**Carroll (County)**—*pop pl* IL-6
**Carroll County**—*pop pl* IN-6
**Carroll (County)**—*pop pl* KY-4
**Carroll (County)**—*pop pl* MD-2
**Carroll County**—*pop pl* MS-4
**Carroll County**—*pop pl* MO-7
**Carroll County**—*pop pl* NH-1
**Carroll (County)**—*pop pl* OH-6
**Carroll County**—*pop pl* TN-4
**Carroll (County)**—*pop pl* VA-3
Carroll County Almshouse and Farm—*hist pl* MD-2
Carroll County Courthouse—*building* TN-4
Carroll County Courthouse—*hist pl* GA-3
Carroll County Courthouse—*hist pl* IL-6
Carroll County Courthouse—*hist pl* OH-6
Carroll County Courthouse—*hist pl* VA-3
Carroll County Courthouse, Eastern District—*hist pl* AR-4
Carroll County Farm (historical)—*locale* TN-4
Carroll County Home—*building* IA-7
Carroll County Park—*park* IA-7
Carroll County Park*—*park* IA-7
Carroll County Sheriff's Quarters and Jail—*hist pl* MO-7
Carroll County Vocational Center—*school* TN-4
*Carroll Creek* TX-5
*Carroll Creek* WA-9
Carroll Creek—*stream* AL-4
Carroll Creek—*stream* AK-9
Carroll Creek—*stream* CA-9
Carroll Creek—*stream* FL-3
Carroll Creek—*stream* GA-3
Carroll Creek—*stream* IL-6
Carroll Creek—*stream* LA-4
Carroll Creek—*stream* MD-2
Carroll Creek—*stream* (2) MO-7
Carroll Creek—*stream* (2) NC-3
Carroll Creek—*stream* OR-9
Carroll Creek—*stream* SD-7
Carroll Creek—*stream* (3) TN-4
Carroll Creek—*stream* (4) TX-5
Carroll Creek—*stream* VA-3
Carroll Creek—*stream* WA-9
Carroll Creek Cem—*cemetery* TX-5
Carroll Creek Ch—*church* AL-4
Carroll Creek Spring—*spring* SD-7
Carroll Crossroads—*locale* AL-4
Carroll Ditch—*canal* (2) IN-6
Carroll Ditch—*canal* OH-6
Carroll Ditch No 1—*canal* WY-8
Carroll Ditch No 2—*canal* WY-8
Carroll Draft—*stream* VA-3
Carroll Drain—*stream* MI-6
Carrol Lentz Oil Field—*oilfield* TX-5
Carroll Gap—*gap* NC-3
Carroll Gardens Hist Dist—*hist pl* NY-2
Carroll Glacier—*glacier* AK-9
Carroll Glade—*flat* OR-9
Carroll Glade Springs—*spring* OR-9
Carroll-Harper House—*hist pl* GA-3
Carroll-Hartshorn House—*hist pl* MA-1
Carroll Heights—*uninc pl* MD-2
**Carroll Highlands**—*pop pl* MD-2
Carroll Hill—*summit* MA-1
Carroll Hill—*summit* MT-8
Carroll Hill—*summit* (2) NY-2
Carroll Hill—*summit* WV-2
Carroll Hill Sch—*school* TX-5
Carroll (historical)—*locale* SD-7
**Carroll (historical)**—*pop pl* OR-9
Carroll Hollow—*valley* NY-2
Carroll Hollow—*valley* (5) TN-4
Carroll Hollow—*valley* VA-3
Carroll Hollow Ch—*church* TN-4
Carroll HS—*school* AL-4
Carroll HS—*school* IA-7
Carroll HS—*school* LA-4
Carroll HS—*school* OH-6
Carroll HS—*school* TX-5
Carroll Inlet—*bay* AK-9
Carroll Island—*island* AK-9
Carroll Island—*island* IL-6
Carroll Island—*island* MD-2
Carroll Island—*island* WA-9
**Carroll Island**—*pop pl* MD-2
Carroll JHS—*school* MD-2
Carroll JHS—*school* NC-3
Carroll Junior-Senior HS—*school* IN-6
Carroll Knob—*summit* NC-3
**Carroll Knolls**—*pop pl* MD-2
*Carroll Lake* MN-6
Carroll Lake—*gut* LA-4
Carroll Lake—*lake* (2) MI-6
Carroll Lake—*lake* NC-3
Carroll Lake—*lake* TX-5
Carroll Lake—*lake* WI-6
Carroll Lake—*lake* WY-8
Carroll Lake—*reservoir* MS-4
Carroll Lake—*reservoir* SD-7
Carroll Lake—*reservoir* TN-4
Carroll Lake Dam—*dam* AL-4
Carroll Lake Dam—*dam* TN-4
Carroll (Magisterial District)—*fmr MCD* WV-2
**Carroll Manor**—*pop pl* (2) MD-2
Carroll Manor Sch—*school* MD-2
**Carroll Manor (subdivision)**—*pop pl* PA-2
Carroll Mansion—*hist pl* MD-2
Carroll Memory Gardens—*cemetery* GA-3
Carroll Mill Creek—*stream* NC-3
Carroll Mine—*mine* SD-7
Carroll Mine (underground)—*mine* AL-4
Carroll Mtn—*summit* NC-3
Carroll Oil Field—*oilfield* KS-7
Carroll Park—*park* MD-2
Carroll Park—*park* MI-6
Carroll Park—*park* NY-2
Carroll Park—*park* PA-2
**Carroll Park**—*pop pl* (2) PA-2
Carroll Parks—*park* CA-9
Carroll Place—*hist pl* SC-3
Carroll (Plantation of)—*civ div* ME-1
Carroll Point—*cape* AK-9
Carroll Point—*cape* MD-2
Carroll Pond—*lake* FL-3
Carroll Pond—*lake* MD-2
Carroll Post Office (historical)—*building* TN-4
Carroll Ranch—*locale* (2) MT-8
Carroll Ranch—*locale* WY-8
Carroll Reece—*uninc pl* TN-4
Carroll-Richardson Grist Mill—*hist pl* GA-3
Carroll Ridge—*ridge* AR-4
Carroll Ridge—*ridge* GA-3
Carroll Ridge—*ridge* (2) TN-4
Carroll Rim—*cliff* OR-9
Carroll Rim—*ridge* OR-9
Carroll Road Ch—*church* TX-5
Carroll RR Station—*locale* FL-3
Carroll Run—*stream* (2) OH-6
Carrolls—*locale* GA-3
**Carrolls**—*pop pl* WA-9
Carrolls Bluff—*cliff* WA-9
Carrolls Ch—*church* GA-3
Carroll Sch—*school* (2) IL-6
Carroll Sch—*school* (2) MA-1
Carroll Sch—*school* MI-6
Carroll Sch—*school* SC-3
Carroll Sch—*school* SD-7
Carroll Sch—*school* TN-4
Carroll Sch—*school* TX-5
Carrolls Channel—*channel* WA-9
Carroll Sch (historical)—*school* (2) AL-4
Carroll Sch (historical)—*school* (2) TN-4
Carroll Sch No 2—*school* KY-4
*Carrolls Corner* AR-4
**Carroll's Corner**—*pop pl* AR-4
*Carrolls Creek* AL-4
*Carrolls Creek Baptist Church* AL-4
*Carrolls Creek Ch* AL-4
Carrolls Creek Ch—*church* AL-4
Carrolls Creek Island County Park—*park* AL-4
Carroll Slough—*gut* AR-4
Carroll Slough—*stream* SC-3
Carrolls Mill (historical)—*locale* AL-4
Carrolls Pond—*lake* MA-1
Carroll Spring—*spring* AL-4
Carroll Spring—*spring* AZ-5
Carroll Spring Ch—*church* TX-5
**Carroll Springs**—*pop pl* TX-5
Carroll Stagecoach Inn—*hist pl* MO-7
Carroll State For—*forest* NH-1
Carroll Station—*locale* NH-1
**Carroll Station**—*pop pl* NV-8
Carroll Stream—*stream* NH-1
Carroll Street Cem—*cemetery* AL-4
**Carroll Subdivision**—*pop pl* MS-4
Carroll Summit—*summit* NV-8
*Carrollsville* AL-4
*Carrollton* (2) IN-6
*Carrollton* MD-2
*Carrollton* WA-9
Carrollton—*locale* MD-2
Carrollton—*locale* VA-3
Carrollton—*locale* WV-2
**Carrollton**—*pop pl* AL-4
**Carrollton**—*pop pl* AR-4
**Carrollton**—*pop pl* (2) GA-3
**Carrollton**—*pop pl* IL-6
**Carrollton**—*pop pl* (3) IN-6
**Carrollton**—*pop pl* IA-7
**Carrollton**—*pop pl* KY-4
**Carrollton**—*pop pl* MI-6
**Carrollton**—*pop pl* MS-4
**Carrollton**—*pop pl* MO-7
**Carrollton**—*pop pl* NY-2
**Carrollton**—*pop pl* OH-6
**Carrollton**—*pop pl* TX-5
Carrollton—*uninc pl* LA-4
Carrollton Baptist Ch—*church* MS-4
Carrollton Bar—*island* MI-6
Carrollton Branch—*stream* VA-3
Carrollton (CCD)—*cens area* AL-4
Carrollton (CCD)—*cens area* GA-3
Carrollton (CCD)—*cens area* KY-4
Carrollton Cem—*cemetery* AL-4
*Carrollton Channel* WA-9
Carrollton Club Pond—*lake* OH-6
Carrollton Courthouse Square Hist Dist—*hist pl* IL-6
Carrollton Dam—*dam* TX-5
Carrollton Division—*civil* AL-4
Carrollton Hist Dist—*hist pl* KY-4
Carrollton Hist Dist—*hist pl* LA-4
Carrollton Hist Dist—*hist pl* MS-4
Carrollton Hollow—*valley* AR-4
Carrollton Hollow Cem—*cemetery* AR-4
Carrollton HS—*school* AL-4
*Carrollton Location* IN-6
Carrollton Lookout Tower—*locale* MS-4
**Carrollton Manor**—*pop pl* MD-2
Carrollton Memorial Airp—*airport* MO-7
Carrollton Presbyterian Ch—*church* MS-4
Carrollton Ridge Ch—*church* IL-6
Carrollton Run—*stream* NY-2
Carrollton Sch—*school* FL-3
Carrollton Sch—*school* (2) LA-4
Carrollton Sch—*school* MD-2
Carrollton Sch of the Sacred Heart—*school* FL-3
Carrollton Shop Ctr—*locale* LA-4
**Carrollton (Town of)**—*pop pl* NY-2
**Carrollton Township**—*pop pl* MO-7
Carrollton (Township of)—*fmr MCD* (2) AR-4
**Carrollton (Township of)**—*pop pl* IL-6
**Carrollton (Township of)**—*pop pl* IN-6
**Carrollton (Township of)**—*pop pl* MI-6
Carrollton Viaduct—*hist pl* MD-2
**Carrolltown**—*pop pl* PA-2
Carrolltown Airp—*airport* PA-2
Carrolltown Borough—*civil* PA-2
Carrolltown Ch—*church* TX-5
**Carroll (Town of)**—*pop pl* NH-1
**Carroll (Town of)**—*pop pl* NY-2
**Carrolltown Road**—*pop pl* PA-2
Carrolltown Rsvr—*reservoir* PA-2
Carroll Township—*civil* (2) MO-7
Carroll Township—*fmr MCD* (2) IA-7
**Carroll Township**—*pop pl* MO-7
**Carroll Township**—*pop pl* ND-7
**Carroll Township**—*pop pl* SD-7
Carroll (Township of)—*fmr MCD* AR-4
**Carroll (Township of)**—*pop pl* IL-6
**Carroll (Township of)**—*pop pl* OH-6
**Carroll (Township of)**—*pop pl* (3) PA-2
**Carrolltown (sta.)**—*pop pl* PA-2
Carrolltown 6th Ward Elem Sch—*school* PA-2
Carroll Trail—*trail* NH-1
Carroll Tub—*well* NM-5
*Carroll Valley* PA-2
**Carroll Valley**—*pop pl* PA-2
Carroll Valley Borough—*civil* PA-2
Carroll Valley Resort Golf Course—*locale* PA-2
**Carrollville**—*pop pl* WI-6
Carrollville—*uninc pl* WI-6
Carrollville Cem—*cemetery* MS-4
Carrollville Hill—*summit* TN-4
Carrollville (historical)—*locale* MS-4
**Carrollville (historical)**—*pop pl* TN-4
Carroll Well—*well* OR-9
Carroll Windmill—*locale* NM-5
*Carrollwood* IL-6
**Carrollwood**—*pop pl* FL-3
**Carrollwood**—*pop pl* LA-4
**Carrollwood**—*pop pl* MD-2
Carrollwood Elem Sch—*school* FL-3
Carrollwood-Messiah Lutheran Ch—*church* FL-3
Carrollwood Oaks (Shop Ctr)—*locale* FL-3
Carrol Mill—*locale* VA-3
Carrol Mine—*mine* MN-6
Carrol Mtn—*summit* GA-3
Carrol Park—*park* PA-2
Carrol Rsvr—*reservoir* OR-9
Carrol Sch (historical)—*school* MO-7
Carrols Crossing—*locale* GA-3
Carrols Lake—*reservoir* AL-4
Carrol Spring—*spring* KY-4
Carrol Street Park—*park* TX-5
Carrol Tank—*reservoir* AZ-5
*Carrolton* IN-6
**Carrolton**—*pop pl* CA-9
Carrolton Cem—*cemetery* MN-6
Carrolton Covered Bridge—*hist pl* WV-2
*Carrolton Manor* MD-2
Carrolton (sta.) (RR name for North Carrollton)—*other* MS-4
**Carrolton (Township of)**—*pop pl* MN-6
*Carrol Town* DE-2
Carroltown—*locale* DE-2
*Carrol Township* SD-7
Carrol Well—*well* AZ-5
Carrol Well—*well* NM-5
Carrolwood Community Hosp—*hospital* FL-3
Carron, Bayou—*stream* LA-4
Carrona Number One, Lake—*reservoir* AL-4
Carrona Number Two, Lake—*reservoir* AL-4
Carron Cem—*cemetery* LA-4
Carron Creek—*stream* MT-8
*Carrons Pond* MA-1
Carr-Osborn House—*building* MA-1
Carros Creek—*stream* NM-5
Carrot Basin—*basin* MT-8
Carrot Bluff—*cliff* MO-7
Carrot Canyon—*valley* ID-8
*Carrot Cove* MD-2
**Carrothers**—*pop pl* OH-6
Carrot Hollow—*valley* UT-8
Carrot Island—*island* NC-3
Carrot Island Channel—*channel* NC-3
Carrot Knoll—*gap* WY-8
Carrot Lake—*lake* MN-6
Carrot Lake—*reservoir* TN-4
Carrot Men Pictograph Site—*hist pl* CO-8
Carrot Ridge—*ridge* WY-8
*Carrot Slough* NC-3
Carrot Spring—*spring* SD-7
Carrot Top Arch—*arch* UT-8
Carrousel at Palmetto (Shop Ctr)—*locale* FL-3
Carrousel Day Center—*school* FL-3
Carroway Cem—*cemetery* NC-3
*Carroway Creek* NC-3
Carroway Lake Dam—*dam* MS-4
Carroway Methodist Hosp—*hospital* AL-4
Carroway Pond Dam—*dam* MS-4
Carrow Creek—*stream* MI-6
Carrow Fork—*stream* WV-2
Carrow Hill—*summit* NY-2
Carrow Meadow—*flat* NY-2
Carr Park—*park* MI-6
Carr Park—*park* MO-7
*Carr Pass* FL-3
Carr Peak—*summit* (2) AZ-5
Carr Peak - Canyon Loop—*trail* AZ-5
Carr Peyton Branch—*stream* IN-6

Carter-Goodrich House—*hist pl* ... OR-9
**Carter Grove**—*pop pl* ... AL-4
Carter Grove Ch—*church* ... AL-4
Carter Gulch—*valley* ... CA-9
Carter Gulch—*valley* (2) ... CO-8
Carter Gully—*valley* ... NY-2
*Carter Gully Brook* ... ME-1
Carter G Woodson Elem Sch—*school* ... FL-3
Carter Hall—*hist pl* ... VA-3
Carter Hall—*locale* ... VA-3
Carter Hall Sch (abandoned)—*school* ... MO-7
Carter Heights Golf Course—*locale* ... PA-2
Carter Hill—*cape* ... WA-9
Carter Hill—*summit* ... AL-4
Carter Hill—*summit* ... CT-1
Carter Hill—*summit* ... KY-4
Carter Hill—*summit* (3) ... ME-1
Carter Hill—*summit* (2) ... MA-1
Carter Hill—*summit* (2) ... NH-1
Carter Hill—*summit* ... VT-1
Carter Hill—*uninc pl* ... MD-2
Carter Hill Ch—*church* ... GA-3
Carter Hill Ch—*church* ... MS-4
Carter Hill Ch of Christ—*church* ... AL-4
Carter Hill Sch (abandoned)—*school* ... PA-2
Carter (historical)—*locale* ... IA-7
*Carter Hollow* ... TN-4
Carter Hollow—*valley* ... AL-4
Carter Hollow—*valley* (2) ... KY-4
Carter Hollow—*valley* (2) ... MO-7
Carter Hollow—*valley* ... OH-6
Carter Hollow—*valley* (7) ... TN-4
Carter Hollow—*valley* ... WV-2
Carter Homestead—*locale* ... OR-9
Carter Horn—*cape* ... AK-9
Carter House—*hist pl* ... IA-7
Carter House—*hist pl* ... KY-4
Carter House—*hist pl* ... LA-4
Carter HS—*school* ... TN-4
Carter Island—*island* (3) ... GA-3
Carter Island—*island* ... TX-5
Carter Island—*island* ... VA-3
Carter JHS—*school* ... MA-1
Carter JHS—*school* ... TX-5
Carter-Jones House—*hist pl* ... AR-4
Carter Jones Park—*park* ... VA-3
Carter Knob—*summit* (2) ... KY-4
Carter Knob—*summit* ... TN-4
*Carter Lake* ... CO-8
*Carter Lake* ... LA-4
Carter Lake—*lake* ... AK-9
Carter Lake—*lake* (2) ... CO-8
Carter Lake—*lake* ... IA-7
Carter Lake—*lake* (3) ... MI-6
Carter Lake—*lake* ... MN-6
Carter lake—*lake* ... MN-6
Carter Lake—*lake* (2) ... MS-4
Carter Lake—*lake* ... MO-7
Carter Lake—*lake* ... MT-8
Carter Lake—*lake* ... NE-7
Carter Lake—*lake* ... OH-6
Carter Lake—*lake* ... OK-5
Carter Lake—*lake* ... OR-9
Carter Lake—*lake* ... TX-5
Carter Lake—*lake* (2) ... WA-9
**Carter Lake**—*pop pl* ... IA-7
Carter Lake—*reservoir* (2) ... AL-4
Carter Lake—*reservoir* ... CO-8
Carter Lake—*reservoir* ... GA-3
Carter Lake—*reservoir* (2) ... NC-3
Carter Lake—*reservoir* ... OK-5
Carter Lake—*reservoir* (2) ... TN-4
Carter Lake Chapel—*church* ... TX-5
Carter Lake Dam—*dam* ... AL-4
Carter Lake Dam—*dam* (2) ... NC-3
Carter Lake Dam—*dam* ... TN-4
Carter Lake Dam Number One—*dam* ... NC-3
Carter Lake Number One—*reservoir* ... NC-3
Carter Lake Rsvr—*reservoir* ... CO-8
Carter Lake Trail—*trail* ... AK-9
*Carter Landing* ... VA-3
Carter Landing—*locale* ... FL-3
Carter Landing—*locale* ... SC-3
Carter Lateral—*canal* ... AZ-5
Carter Lawrence Sch—*school* ... TN-4
Carter Ledge—*bench* ... NH-1
Carter Ledge Trail—*trail* ... NH-1
Carter Lookout Tower—*locale* ... WI-6
Carter Mansion—*hist pl* ... MA-1
Carter Meadow—*flat* (2) ... CA-9
Carter Meadows Summit—*summit* ... CA-9
Carter Meadow Trail—*trail* ... CA-9
Carter Memorial Baptist Ch—*church* ... IN-6
Carter Mesa—*summit* ... NM-5
*Carter Methodist Church* ... AL-4
Carter Mill Creek—*stream* ... AL-4
Carter Mill Creek—*stream* ... VA-3
Carter Mill (historical)—*locale* ... AL-4
Carter Mill (historical)—*locale* ... TN-4
Carter Mill Springs—*spring* ... TN-4
Carter Mine—*mine* ... CO-8
Carter Mine (surface)—*mine* ... AL-4
Carter Moriah Trail—*trail* ... NH-1
*Carter Mountain* ... MT-8
Carter Mountain Ranch—*locale* ... CO-8
Carter Mountains—*summit* ... TX-5
Carter MS—*school* ... TN-4
*Carter Mtn* ... VA-3
Carter Mtn—*summit* (2) ... AR-4
Carter Mtn—*summit* ... CO-8
Carter Mtn—*summit* ... GA-3
Carter Mtn—*summit* ... MS-4
Carter Mtn—*summit* ... MT-8
Carter Mtn—*summit* ... NC-3
Carter Mtn—*summit* ... OK-5
Carter Mtn—*summit* ... TX-5
Carter Mtn—*summit* (2) ... VA-3
Carter Mtn—*summit* ... WA-9
Carter Mtn—*summit* ... WY-8
Carter Mudhole—*swamp* ... NY-2
Carter Munsch Ch—*church* ... TX-5
**Carter Nine**—*pop pl* ... OK-5
Carter Notch—*gap* ... NH-1
Carter Notch Trail—*trail* ... NH-1
Carter Nubble—*summit* ... ME-1
Carter Oak Hollow—*valley* ... OH-6
Carter Park—*flat* ... CO-8
Carter Park—*park* ... NE-7
Carter Park—*park* ... TX-5
Carter Park—*park* ... WA-9

Carter Park—*uninc pl* ... OK-5
Carter Park Site—*park* ... TX-5
Carter-Parramore JHS—*school* ... FL-3
Carter Pass—*gap* ... AK-9
Carter Peak—*summit* ... TX-5
Carter Peak—*summit* ... UT-8
Carter P Johnson Lake—*lake* ... NE-7
Carter Plantation—*hist pl* ... LA-4
*Carter Point* ... ME-1
Carter Point—*cape* ... HI-9
Carter Point—*cape* ... ME-1
Carter Point—*cape* ... MS-4
Carter Point—*cape* ... VA-3
Carter Point—*cape* ... WA-9
Carter Point—*cliff* ... AR-4
*Carter Pond* ... MA-1
Carter Pond—*lake* ... FL-3
Carter Pond—*lake* ... GA-3
Carter Pond—*lake* ... MA-1
Carter Pond—*lake* ... NH-1
Carter Pond—*lake* (3) ... NY-2
Carter Pond—*lake* ... WA-9
Carter Pond—*reservoir* ... MA-1
Carter Pond—*reservoir* ... SC-3
Carter Pond Dam—*dam* ... MA-1
Carter Post Office (historical)—*building* ... AL-4
Carter Post Office (historical)—*building* ... TN-4
Carter-Powell Cem—*cemetery* ... MS-4
Carter Ranch—*locale* ... AZ-5
Carter Ranch—*locale* ... CA-9
Carter Ranch—*locale* ... NM-5
Carter Ranch—*locale* ... SD-7
Carter Ranch—*locale* ... WY-8
Carter Ranch (historical)—*locale* ... NV-8
Carter Ranch Pond—*swamp* ... TX-5
Carter Refinery—*other* (2) ... IL-6
*Carter Reservoir* ... CO-8
Carter-Rice Bldg—*hist pl* ... CO-8
Carter Ridge—*ridge* ... KY-4
Carter Ridge—*ridge* ... NC-3
Carter Ridge—*ridge* ... VA-3
Carter Ridge Ch—*church* ... KY-4
Carter Riverside HS—*school* ... TX-5
Carter Road Ch—*church* ... TN-4
Carter Roark Branch—*stream* ... KY-4
Carter Rsvr—*reservoir* ... MT-8
Carter Rsvr—*reservoir* ... NV-8
Carter Rsvr—*reservoir* ... OR-9
Carter Run—*stream* (2) ... OH-6
Carter Run—*stream* ... VA-3
Carter Run—*stream* ... WV-2
*Carters* ... AL-4
*Carters* ... MA-1
Carters—*locale* ... GA-3
Carters—*locale* ... MS-4
**Carters**—*pop pl* ... FL-3
Carter Saltpeter Cave—*cave* ... TN-4
Carter Sawmill Spring—*spring* ... AZ-5
*Carters Bayou* ... LA-4
Carters Bight Landing—*locale* ... GA-3
Carters Branch—*stream* ... KY-4
Carters Branch—*stream* ... SC-3
Carters Bridge—*bridge* ... VA-3
Carters Bridge—*locale* ... VA-3
Carters Brook—*stream* ... NJ-2
Carters Bulkhead—*locale* ... FL-3
**Cartersburg**—*pop pl* ... IN-6
*Carters Camp* ... AZ-5
Carters Canal—*canal* ... NC-3
Carters Cem—*cemetery* ... LA-4
*Carters Cemetery* ... AL-4
*Carter Sch* ... PA-2
Carter Sch—*school* (3) ... GA-3
Carter Sch—*school* (3) ... IL-6
Carter Sch—*school* (2) ... KY-4
Carter Sch—*school* ... LA-4
Carter Sch—*school* ... MA-1
Carter Sch—*school* ... MI-6
Carter Sch—*school* ... MN-6
Carter Sch—*school* (5) ... MO-7
Carter Sch—*school* ... MT-8
Carter Sch—*school* ... NE-7
Carter Sch—*school* ... NH-1
Carter Sch—*school* ... TN-4
Carter Sch—*school* (2) ... TX-5
Carter Sch—*school* ... VA-3
Carter Sch—*school* ... WI-6
Carter Sch (abandoned)—*school* ... MO-7
Carters Chapel—*church* (2) ... GA-3
Carters Chapel—*church* (3) ... KY-4
Carters Chapel—*church* ... NC-3
Carters Chapel—*church* ... TX-5
*Carters Chapel Church of Christ* ... MS-4
Carters Chapel Pentecostal Ch of God—*church* ... MS-4
Carter Sch (historical)—*school* ... AL-4
Carter Sch (historical)—*school* ... TN-4
Carters Chute—*gut* ... TX-5
**Carters Circle Subdivision**—*pop pl* ... UT-8
Carters Corner—*locale* ... OK-5
Carters Corner—*locale* ... VA-3
**Carters Corner**—*pop pl* ... FL-3
Carters Corners—*locale* ... PA-2
Carters Coulee—*valley* ... MT-8
*Carters Creek* ... MI-6
*Carters Creek* ... MS-4
*Carters Creek* ... NC-3
**Carters Creek**—*pop pl* ... TN-4
Carters Creek—*stream* ... AL-4
Carters Creek—*stream* ... AR-4
Carters Creek—*stream* ... GA-3
Carters Creek—*stream* ... IN-6
Carters Creek—*stream* ... KY-4
Carters Creek—*stream* (2) ... MS-4
Carters Creek—*stream* (2) ... TN-4
Carters Creek—*stream* ... TX-5
Carters Creek—*stream* ... VA-3
Carters Creek Ch—*church* ... IN-6
Carters Crossroads—*locale* (2) ... SC-3
Carters Cut—*bay* ... FL-3
Carters Dam—*dam* ... GA-3
*Carters Dam Reservoir* ... GA-3
*Carters Depot Post Office* ... TN-4
**Carter Sell (subdivision)**—*pop pl* ... TN-4
**Carter Settlement**—*pop pl* ... TX-5
**Carters Farm Subdivision**—*pop pl* ... UT-8
*Carters Fish Spring* ... TN-4
Carters Ford—*locale* ... WV-2
Carters Furnace Post Office (historical)—*building* ... TN-4

Carter's Grove—*hist pl* ... VA-3
Carters Grove—*locale* ... GA-3
Carters Grove Historical Home—*building* ... VA-3
**Carters Grove (subdivision)**—*pop pl* ... NC-3
Carter Shields Place—*locale* ... TN-4
*Carters Hill* ... MA-1
*Carters Hill* ... MS-4
Carters Hill—*locale* ... AL-4
Carters Hill—*summit* ... MA-1
Carters Hill Ch—*church* ... GA-3
Carters Hill P. O. (historical)—*locale* ... AL-4
Carters Hog Ridge—*ridge* ... OR-9
Carters Hole—*basin* ... IN-6
Carter Shop Ctr—*locale* ... FL-3
Carter Siding—*locale* ... IL-6
Carters Ironworks and Mill (historical)—*locale* ... TN-4
Carters Island—*island* ... FL-3
Carters Island—*island* ... TN-4
Carters Lake—*lake* ... MI-6
Carters Lake—*lake* (2) ... TX-5
Carters Lake—*reservoir* ... AL-4
Carters Lake—*reservoir* ... GA-3
*Carters Landing* ... VA-3
Carters Landing—*locale* ... OK-5
Carters Landing Bar—*bar* ... IN-6
Carters Landing (historical)—*locale* ... AL-4
Carters Landing Public Use Area—*park* ... OK-5
Carters Lookout—*locale* ... TX-5
Carter Slough—*bay* ... TX-5
Carter Slough—*gut* ... AR-4
Carter Slough—*gut* ... MN-6
*Carters Mill* ... MS-4
Carters Mill—*locale* ... VA-3
Carters Mill Bridge—*bridge* ... KY-4
Carters Mill Creek—*stream* ... GA-3
*Carters Mills* ... VA-3
**Carters Mills**—*pop pl* ... VA-3
Carters Mtn—*summit* ... NC-3
Carters Mtn—*summit* ... VA-3
*Carters Nubble* ... ME-1
Carter Spit—*bar* ... AK-9
Carters Pit—*cave* ... TN-4
*Carters Point* ... VA-3
Carters Point—*cape* ... TX-5
*Carters Pond* ... MA-1
Carters Pond—*lake* ... GA-3
Carters Pond—*reservoir* ... AL-4
Carters Pond Dam—*dam* ... AL-4
Carters Prairie—*swamp* ... GA-3
Carters Precinct (historical)—*locale* ... MS-4
*Carter Spring* ... NV-8
Carter Spring—*spring* ... AL-4
Carter Spring—*spring* ... CA-9
Carter Spring—*spring* ... ID-8
Carter Spring—*spring* ... ME-1
Carter Spring—*spring* ... MO-7
Carter Spring—*spring* ... NV-8
Carter Spring—*spring* ... OR-9
Carter Spring—*spring* ... TN-4
Carter Spring—*spring* (2) ... UT-8
Carter Spring—*spring* (2) ... WY-8
Carter Spring Branch—*stream* ... TN-4
Carter Spring Creek—*stream* ... WY-8
Carters Prospect—*mine* ... TN-4
Carter's Quarters—*hist pl* ... GA-3
Carters Reed Brake—*stream* ... MS-4
*Carters Reservoir* ... GA-3
Carters RR Station—*locale* ... FL-3
*Carters Run* ... OH-6
Carters Run—*stream* ... IN-6
Carters Sch (historical)—*school* ... MS-4
Carters Schoolhouse (historical)—*school* ... AL-4
Carters Shop Hollow—*valley* ... MO-7
Carters Slough—*gut* ... TX-5
Carters Springs—*spring* ... NV-8
Carters Station—*locale* ... NV-8
Carters Station Post Office (historical)—*building* ... TN-4
**Carters Store**—*pop pl* ... VA-3
Carters Store (historical)—*locale* ... MS-4
Carter Stadium—*locale* ... NC-3
Carter Station—*locale* ... NY-2
Carter's Tavern—*hist pl* ... VA-3
Carters Temple—*church* (2) ... GA-3
Carters Temple—*church* ... IL-6
Carter Store (historical)—*locale* ... AL-4
Carter Street Cem—*cemetery* ... VT-1
Carter Street Sch—*school* ... CT-1
**Carter Subdivision**—*pop pl* ... AL-4
Carter Sunset Memorial Gardens—*cemetery* ... MS-4
Carters Valley Sch—*school* ... TN-4
Carters Valley Sch (historical)—*school* (2) ... TN-4
Cartersville—*locale* ... KY-4
Cartersville—*locale* ... MT-8
Cartersville—*locale* ... OK-5
**Cartersville**—*pop pl* ... AL-4
**Cartersville**—*pop pl* ... GA-3
**Cartersville**—*pop pl* ... IA-7
**Cartersville**—*pop pl* ... NC-3
**Cartersville**—*pop pl* ... SC-3
**Cartersville**—*pop pl* (2) ... TN-4
**Cartersville**—*pop pl* ... VA-3
*Cartersville Baptist Church* ... AL-4
Cartersville Bridge—*hist pl* ... VA-3
Cartersville Canal—*canal* ... MT-8
Cartersville (CCD)—*cens area* ... GA-3
Cartersville Cem—*cemetery* ... KY-4
Cartersville Cem—*cemetery* ... VA-3
Cartersville Ch—*church* ... AL-4
Cartersville Guard Gate—*other* ... NY-2
Cartersville (historical)—*locale* ... MS-4
Cartersville Sch—*school* ... MS-4
Carter-Swain House—*hist pl* ... NC-3
Carter Swamp—*swamp* ... CT-1
Carters Wharf—*locale* ... VA-3
Carter Tank—*reservoir* (3) ... AZ-5
Carter Tank—*reservoir* (2) ... NM-5
Carter Temple African Methodist Episcopal Ch—*church* ... AL-4
Carter Temple CME Ch—*church* ... AL-4
**Carterton**—*pop pl* ... VA-3
Carter Top—*summit* ... NC-3
Cartertown—*other* ... KY-4
**Cartertown**—*pop pl* ... TN-4
Cartertown Ch—*church* ... VA-3
Carter Township—*civil* ... MO-7
**Carter Township**—*pop pl* ... ND-7
**Carter Township**—*pop pl* ... SD-7

Carter (Township of)—*fmr MCD* ... AR-4
**Carter (Township of)**—*pop pl* ... IN-6
Carter Traylor Ditch—*canal* ... IN-6
Carter Valley—*valley* (2) ... TN-4
Carter Valley—*valley* ... VA-3
*Carter Valley School* ... TN-4
*Carterville* ... MT-8
Carterville—*locale* ... CO-8
Carterville—*locale* ... LA-4
Carterville—*locale* ... NY-2
Carterville—*locale* (2) ... TX-5
**Carterville**—*pop pl* ... IL-6
**Carterville**—*pop pl* ... MA-1
**Carterville**—*pop pl* ... MS-4
**Carterville**—*pop pl* ... MO-7
Carterville Baptist Ch—*church* ... MS-4
Carterville Cem—*cemetery* ... MO-7
Carterville (Election Precinct)—*fmr MCD* ... IL-6
Carterville (historical)—*locale* ... MA-1
**Carterville (historical)**—*pop pl* ... SD-7
Carterville Oil Field—*oilfield* ... LA-4
Carterville Pond—*lake* ... NY-2
Carterville Waterworks—*other* ... IL-6
Carter Wayside—*locale* ... VA-3
Carter Well—*locale* ... NM-5
Carter Well—*well* ... NV-8
Carter Well—*well* (3) ... NM-5
Carter Windmill—*locale* ... AZ-5
Carter Windmill—*locale* ... NM-5
Carter Windmill—*locale* (2) ... TX-5
Carter Woods—*woods* ... WA-9
Carter-Worth House and Farm—*hist pl* ... PA-2
**Cartesville (historical)**—*pop pl* ... SD-7
*Carthage* ... AL-4
*Carthage* ... KS-7
*Carthage* (2) ... OH-6
Carthage—*locale* ... IL-6
Carthage—*locale* ... MS-4
Carthage—*locale* ... NM-5
Carthage—*locale* ... VA-3
**Carthage**—*pop pl* ... AR-4
**Carthage**—*pop pl* ... IL-6
**Carthage**—*pop pl* ... IN-6
**Carthage**—*pop pl* ... KY-4
**Carthage**—*pop pl* ... ME-1
**Carthage**—*pop pl* ... MS-4
**Carthage**—*pop pl* ... MO-7
**Carthage**—*pop pl* ... NM-5
**Carthage**—*pop pl* ... NY-2
**Carthage**—*pop pl* ... NC-3
**Carthage**—*pop pl* ... OH-6
**Carthage**—*pop pl* ... SD-7
**Carthage**—*pop pl* ... TN-4
**Carthage**—*pop pl* ... TX-5
Carthage, Lake—*reservoir* ... SD-7
Carthage Attendance Center—*school* ... MS-4
Carthage Bluff Landing—*locale* ... LA-4
Carthage Branch—*stream* ... AL-4
Carthage (CCD)—*cens area* ... TN-4
Carthage (CCD)—*cens area* ... TX-5
Carthage Cem—*cemetery* ... IN-6
Carthage Ch—*church* ... AL-4
Carthage Ch—*church* ... OH-6
Carthage Ch of Christ—*church* ... TN-4
Carthage Coll—*school* ... WI-6
Carthage Courthouse Square Hist Dist—*hist pl* ... IL-6
Carthage Courthouse Square Hist Dist—*hist pl* ... MO-7
*Carthage Creek* ... CA-9
Carthage Creek—*stream* ... IN-6
Carthage Cumberland Presbyterian Ch—*church* ... MS-4
Carthage Dam—*dam* ... SD-7
Carthage Division—*civil* ... TN-4
Carthage Elem Sch—*school* ... IN-6
Carthage Elem Sch—*school* ... MS-4
Carthage Elem Sch—*school* ... NC-3
Carthage Elem Sch—*school* ... TN-4
Carthage Female Acad (historical)—*school* ... MS-4
Carthage First Baptist Ch—*church* ... TN-4
Carthage Gas Field—*oilfield* (2) ... TX-5
Carthage General Hosp—*hospital* ... TN-4
Carthage (historical)—*locale* ... KS-7
**Carthage (historical)**—*pop pl* ... SD-7
Carthage Jail—*hist pl* ... IL-6
Carthage JHS—*school* ... MS-4
**Carthage Junction**—*pop pl* ... TN-4
Carthage Lake—*lake* ... IL-6
Carthage Lake—*locale* ... IL-6
Carthage Lake—*reservoir* ... IL-6
Carthage Lake Dam Number Two—*dam* ... NC-3
Carthage Lake Number Two—*reservoir* ... NC-3
Carthage Landing—*locale* ... MS-4
Carthage-Leake County Airp—*airport* ... MS-4
**Carthagena**—*pop pl* ... OH-6
Carthagena Creek—*stream* ... MD-2
Carthagena Flats—*flat* ... MD-2
*Carthagenia* ... MD-2
Carthagenia Ch—*church* ... OH-6
Carthage Point—*cape* ... MS-4
Carthage Point Oil Field—*oilfield* ... MS-4
Carthage Post Office—*building* ... TN-4
Carthage Presbyterian Ch—*church* ... MS-4
Carthage Revetment—*levee* ... MS-4
Carthage Rsvr—*reservoir* ... NY-2
Carthage Sch—*school* ... IA-7
Carthage Sewage Lagoon Dam—*dam* ... MS-4
Carthage South Hist Dist—*hist pl* ... MO-7
**Carthage (Town of)**—*pop pl* ... ME-1
**Carthage Township**—*pop pl* ... SD-7
**Carthage (Township of)**—*pop pl* ... IL-6
**Carthage (Township of)**—*pop pl* ... OH-6
Carthage-Troy Township Sch—*school* ... OH-6
Carthage United Methodist Ch—*church* ... MS-4
Carthage United Methodist Church—*hist pl* ... TN-4
Carthage Upper Bar—*bar* ... MS-4
Carthagina Island—*island* ... NH-1
*Carthaginal Island* ... NH-1
Carthay Center Sch—*school* ... CA-9
Carthens Ferry (historical)—*locale* ... AL-4
Cart Hill—*summit* ... UT-8
Cart Hollow—*valley* (2) ... ID-8
Cart Hollow—*valley* (3) ... UT-8
Cart Hollow Spring—*spring* ... UT-8
Carthon—*locale* ... OH-6
**Carthwick**—*pop pl* ... OR-9
*Carticary* ... GA-3

*Carticary River* ... GA-3
*Carticay* ... GA-3
*Carticay River* ... GA-3
Cartie Lake—*lake* ... MN-6
Cartier Field Stadium—*other* ... IN-6
Cartier Lake—*lake* ... MI-6
Cartier Park—*park* ... MI-6
Cartier Slough—*stream* ... ID-8
**Cartin**—*pop pl* ... PA-2
Carting Island—*island* ... CT-1
*Cart Island* ... NC-3
Cart Island—*island* ... GA-3
Cart Island Swamp—*swamp* ... GA-3
Cartledge Branch—*stream* ... SC-3
Cartledge Creek—*stream* ... NC-3
Cartledge Creek Ch—*church* ... NC-3
Cartledge House—*hist pl* ... SC-3
Cartledge Windmill—*locale* ... TX-5
Cartmell Gap—*gap* ... VA-3
Cartmill Cave—*cave* ... KY-4
Cartmill Cem—*cemetery* (2) ... KY-4
Cartney—*locale* ... AR-4
Cartney—*locale* ... OR-9
Carto—*locale* ... MS-4
Cartoco—*locale* ... OK-5
Carton Ranch—*locale* ... OR-9
*Cartoogaja Creek* ... NC-3
*Cartoogajay Creek* ... NC-3
*Cartoogechaye* ... NC-3
**Cartoogechaye**—*pop pl* ... NC-3
Cartoogechaye Ch—*church* ... NC-3
Cartoogechaye Creek—*stream* ... NC-3
Cartoogechaye (Township of)—*fmr MCD* ... NC-3
Car Top Butte—*summit* ... NM-5
Cartrette Cem—*cemetery* ... NC-3
Cart Ridge—*ridge* ... AZ-5
Cartridge Creek—*stream* ... CA-9
Cartridge Creek—*stream* ... WY-8
Cartridge Pass—*gap* ... CA-9
Cartridge Spring—*spring* ... CA-9
**Cartter**—*pop pl* ... IL-6
Cartter Bldg—*hist pl* ... KS-7
Cartter Pond—*reservoir* ... IL-6
Cart Trail Coulee—*valley* ... MT-8
Cartum Branch—*stream* ... SC-3
Cartwheel Bay—*swamp* ... FL-3
Cartwheel Bay—*swamp* ... SC-3
Cartwheel Branch—*stream* ... NJ-2
Cartwheel Branch—*stream* ... NC-3
Cartwheel Branch—*stream* ... SC-3
Cartwheel Landing—*locale* (2) ... SC-3
*Cartwheel Marsh* ... NY-2
Cartwheel Ridge—*ridge* ... OR-9
Cartwheel Rsvr—*reservoir* ... CO-8
Cartwhell Branch—*stream* ... NC-3
Cartwright—*locale* (2) ... TX-5
**Cartwright**—*pop pl* ... AL-4
**Cartwright**—*pop pl* ... AZ-5
**Cartwright**—*pop pl* ... KY-4
**Cartwright**—*pop pl* ... LA-4
**Cartwright**—*pop pl* ... ND-7
**Cartwright**—*pop pl* ... OK-5
**Cartwright**—*pop pl* ... PA-2
**Cartwright**—*pop pl* (2) ... TN-4
Cartwright, Matthew, House—*hist pl* (2) ... TX-5
Cartwright Branch—*stream* ... WV-2
Cartwright Canyon—*valley* ... ID-8
Cartwright Canyon—*valley* ... TX-5
Cartwright Cem—*cemetery* ... IL-6
Cartwright Cem—*cemetery* ... TX-5
Cartwright Cem—*cemetery* ... WV-2
Cartwright Ch—*church* ... IL-6
Cartwright Ch—*church* ... LA-4
Cartwright Coulee—*valley* ... MT-8
Cartwright Coulee Ditch—*canal* ... MT-8
Cartwright Creek—*stream* (2) ... ID-8
Cartwright Creek—*stream* ... KY-4
Cartwright Creek—*stream* (2) ... OR-9
Cartwright Creek—*stream* ... TN-4
*Cartwright-Crutcher Cemetery* ... AL-4
Cartwright Ditch—*canal* ... IN-6
Cartwright Ditch—*canal* ... MT-8
Cartwright Drain—*stream* ... MI-6
Cartwright Field—*park* ... HI-9
Cartwright First Baptist Ch—*church* ... TN-4
Cartwright Gap—*gap* ... TN-4
Cartwright Gulch—*valley* ... ID-8
Cartwright Gulch—*valley* ... MT-8
Cartwright Hollow—*valley* (2) ... AR-4
Cartwright Hollow—*valley* ... MO-7
Cartwright HS—*school* ... TX-5
Cartwright Island—*island* ... NY-2
Cartwright Knob—*summit* ... TN-4
Cartwright Lakes—*lake* ... MI-6
Cartwright-Moss House—*hist pl* ... TN-4
Cartwright Mtn—*summit* ... AR-4
Cartwright Plaza Shop Ctr—*locale* ... AZ-5
Cartwright Pond Dam—*dam* ... MS-4
Cartwright Post Office (historical)—*building* ... AL-4
Cartwright Post Office (historical)—*building* ... TN-4
Cartwright Ranch—*locale* ... AZ-5
Cartwright Ranch—*locale* ... NM-5
Cartwright Run—*stream* ... OH-6
Cartwright Sch—*school* ... AZ-5
Cartwright Sch—*school* (2) ... MI-6
Cartwright Sch—*school* ... MO-7
Cartwright Sch (historical)—*school* ... AL-4
Cartwright Sch (historical)—*school* ... TN-4
Cartwrights Crossing—*locale* ... PA-2
Cartwright Slough—*stream* ... OR-9
**Cartwright (Township of)**—*pop pl* ... IL-6
Carty Branch—*stream* ... KY-4
Carty Branch—*stream* (2) ... MO-7
Carty Cem—*cemetery* ... KY-4
Carty Cem—*cemetery* (2) ... MO-7
Carty Cem—*cemetery* ... VA-3
Carty Lake—*lake* ... WA-9
Carty Rsvr—*reservoir* ... OR-9
Carty West Dam—*dam* ... OR-9
Caruco Spring—*spring* ... NM-5
Caruenger Creek—*stream* ... TN-4
**Carus**—*pop pl* ... OR-9
Carus Cem—*cemetery* ... OR-9
Caruse Creek—*stream* ... AR-4
Carus Lake—*lake* ... MI-6
Caruso—*locale* ... KS-7
**Caruso**—*pop pl* ... GA-3
Caruso Sch—*school* ... ME-1

Carus Ranch—*locale* ... ND-7
Carus Sch—*school* ... OR-9
**Caruth**—*pop pl* ... MO-7
Caruth Brook—*stream* ... MA-1
Caruther Ranch—*locale* ... TX-5
**Caruthers**—*pop pl* ... CA-9
Caruthers Canyon—*valley* ... CA-9
Caruthers Hill—*summit* ... TN-4
Caruthers House—*hist pl* ... AZ-5
Caruthers Lake—*lake* ... MI-6
Caruthers Lake—*lake* ... MT-8
Caruthers Mill—*locale* ... GA-3
Caruthers-Raisin City (CCD)—*cens area* ... CA-9
Caruthers Sch—*school* ... GA-3
Caruthers Sch—*school* ... MS-4
Caruthers Substation—*other* ... CA-9
**Caruthersville**—*pop pl* ... MO-7
Caruthersville Memorial Airp—*airport* ... MO-7
Caruthersville Water Tower—*hist pl* ... MO-7
Caruth Lake—*reservoir* ... TX-5
Caruth Park—*park* ... TX-5
Carvajal Sch—*school* ... TX-5
Carvalho Park—*park* ... HI-9
Carval Rock—*island* ... VI-3
Carveacre Ranch—*locale* ... CA-9
Carve Beech Gap—*gap* ... VA-3
Carved Rock Ch—*church* ... KY-4
**Carvel**—*pop pl* ... KS-7
**Carvel Beach**—*pop pl* ... MD-2
Carvel Island—*island* ... NJ-2
*Carvel Lake Corvel Lake* ... NE-7
Carvell Cem—*cemetery* ... TN-4
Carvell Sch—*school* ... PA-2
*Carvels Islands* ... NJ-2
*Carvel Station* ... KS-7
Carver—*locale* ... AR-4
Carver—*locale* ... KY-4
**Carver**—*pop pl* ... AR-4
**Carver**—*pop pl* ... FL-3
**Carver**—*pop pl* ... MA-1
**Carver**—*pop pl* ... MN-6
**Carver**—*pop pl* ... OR-9
Carver—*uninc pl* ... FL-3
Carver—*uninc pl* ... NY-2
Carver, George Washington, Homestead Site—*hist pl* ... KS-7
Carver and Bowen Ranch—*locale* ... CA-9
Carver Bay—*bay* ... MT-8
**Carver Beach**—*pop pl* ... MN-6
Carver Bluff—*cliff* ... MS-4
Carver Bog—*swamp* ... MA-1
Carver Branch—*stream* ... MS-4
Carver Branch—*stream* ... MO-7
Carver Branch—*stream* (2) ... NC-3
Carver Branch—*stream* ... TN-4
Carver Branch—*stream* ... TX-5
Carver Branch—*stream* (2) ... VA-3
Carver Camp—*locale* ... CA-9
Carver Canyon—*valley* ... CO-8
Carver Cem—*cemetery* ... GA-3
Carver Cem—*cemetery* ... IN-6
Carver Cem—*cemetery* ... LA-4
Carver Cem—*cemetery* (2) ... MO-7
Carver Cem—*cemetery* ... NC-3
Carver Cem—*cemetery* ... SC-3
Carver Cem—*cemetery* (2) ... TN-4
Carver Cem—*cemetery* ... TX-5
Carver Cem—*cemetery* ... VA-3
*Carver Centre* ... MA-1
Carver Ch—*church* (2) ... GA-3
**Carver (County)**—*pop pl* ... MN-6
**Carver Court**—*pop pl* ... PA-2
**Carver Court**—*pop pl* ... VA-3
Carver Court—*uninc pl* ... AL-4
Carver Court Community Center—*locale* ... NC-3
Carver Court Sch—*school* ... FL-3
Carver Cove—*bay* ... ME-1
*Carver Creek* ... NE-7
Carver Creek—*stream* ... ID-8
Carver Creek—*stream* ... MN-6
Carver Creek—*stream* ... MO-7
Carver Creek—*stream* ... NC-3
Carver Creek—*stream* ... TN-4
Carver Creek School (abandoned)—*3N R3E* ... MO-7
Carverdale Sch—*school* ... TX-5
Carver Ditch—*canal* ... IN-6
Carver Drain—*stream* ... MI-6
Carver Early Childhood Center—*school* ... FL-3
*Carver Elementary School* ... AL-4
*Carver Elem Sch* ... MS-4
Carver Elem Sch—*school* ... MS-4
Carver Elem Sch—*school* (2) ... NC-3
Carver Falls Cem—*cemetery* ... VT-1
Carver Falls Dam—*dam* ... NY-2
Carver Falls Dam—*dam* ... VT-1
*Carver Family Cemetery* ... MO-7
Carver Fork—*stream* ... WV-2
Carver Gap—*gap* ... NC-3
**Carver Gardens**—*pop pl* ... VA-3
Carver Glacier—*glacier* ... OR-9
**Carver Heights**—*pop pl* ... FL-3
**Carver Heights**—*pop pl* ... MD-2
**Carver Heights**—*pop pl* ... SC-3
Carver Heights Cem—*cemetery* ... AL-4
Carver Heights Elem Sch—*school* ... NC-3
Carver Heights HS—*school* ... FL-3
**Carver Heights (subdivision)**—*pop pl* ... NC-3
*Carver High School* ... NC-3
Carver Hill—*summit* ... MA-1
Carver Hill Cem—*cemetery* ... MS-4
Carver Hist Dist—*hist pl* ... MN-6
Carver (historical P.O.)—*locale* ... MA-1
Carver Hollow—*valley* ... AL-4
Carver Hollow—*valley* ... AR-4
Carver Hollow—*valley* ... TN-4
Carver Homes Park—*park* ... FL-3
Carver Homestead—*locale* ... CO-8
*Carver HS* ... MS-4
Carver HS—*school* (4) ... AL-4
Carver HS—*school* ... AZ-5
Carver HS—*school* (4) ... FL-3
Carver HS—*school* (2) ... GA-3
Carver HS—*school* (3) ... LA-4
Carver HS—*school* ... MD-2
Carver HS—*school* ... OK-5
Carver HS—*school* (6) ... TX-5
Carver HS—*school* (3) ... VA-3
Carver HS (historical)—*school* ... MS-4
*Carver Island* ... ME-1

Carver JHS—school AL-4
Carver JHS—school CA-9
Carver JHS—school (2) FL-3
Carver JHS—school GA-3
Carver JHS—school MS-4
Carver JHS—school OK-5
Carver JHS—school TX-5
Carver Johnson Lake AL-4
Carver Johnson Lake Dam—dam AL-4
Carver Lake—lake IL-6
Carver Lake—lake (3) MN-6
Carver Lake—lake NE-7
Carver Lake—lake OR-9
Carver Lake—reservoir TX-5
**Carver Manor**—pop pl FL-3
Carver Memorial Cem—cemetery MD-2
Carver Memorial Gardens AL-4
Carver Memorial Park—cemetery NC-3
Carver Memorial Park—cemetery VA-3
Carver Memorial Park Cem—cemetery GA-3
Carver Memorial Park (Cemetery)—cemetery TX-5
Carver Mill Creek—stream AR-4
Carver MS MS-4
Carver MS—school MS-4
Carver MS—school NC-3
Carver Mtn—summit NC-3
Carver Mtn—summit OK-5
Carver Optional Elem Sch—school NC-3
Carver Park—park (2) AL-4
Carver Park—park AZ-5
Carver Park—park (2) GA-3
Carver Park—park IL-6
Carver Park—park KS-7
Carver Park—park NJ-2
Carver Park—park TN-4
Carver Park—park (2) TX-5
**Carver Park**—pop pl NV-8
Carver Park JHS—school GA-3
**Carver Park (subdivision)**—pop pl AL-4
Carver Peak—summit CA-9
Carver Point—cape AL-4
Carver Point—cape MS-4
Carver Point State Park—park MS-4
Carver Pond—lake FL-3
Carver Pond—reservoir MA-1
Carver Pond Dam—dam MA-1
Carver Price Sch—school VA-3
Carver Ranch—locale NE-7
Carver Ranch—locale SD-7
**Carver Ranches**—pop pl FL-3
Carver Ranches Center—school FL-3
**Carver Ranch Estates**—pop pl FL-3
Carver Rapids—rapids MN-6
Carver Recreation Center—building TN-4
Carver Ridge—ridge NC-3
Carver-Roehl County Park—park WI-6
Carver Run—stream IN-6
Carvers—locale NV-8
Carvers—locale NC-3
Carvers Bay MI-6
Carvers Bay—locale SC-3
Carvers Bay—swamp SC-3
Carvers Bay Creek—stream SC-3
Carvers Branch—stream TN-4
Carvers Branch—stream VA-3
Carver Sch—school (4) AL-4
Carver Sch—school AZ-5
Carver Sch—school (7) AR-4
Carver Sch—school (5) CA-9
Carver Sch—school DC-2
Carver Sch—school (2) FL-3
Carver Sch—school (4) GA-3
Carver Sch—school KY-4
Carver Sch—school (2) LA-4
Carver Sch—school MD-2
Carver Sch—school MA-1
Carver Sch—school (3) MI-6
Carver Sch—school MN-6
Carver Sch—school (3) MS-4
Carver Sch—school (2) MO-7
Carver Sch—school NM-5
Carver Sch—school (5) NC-3
Carver Sch—school OR-9
Carver Sch—school PA-2
Carver Sch—school (4) SC-3
Carver Sch—school TN-4
Carver Sch—school (19) TX-5
Carver Sch—school (5) VA-3
Carvers Chapel—church GA-3
Carver Sch (historical)—school AL-4
Carver School IN-6
Carver School Number 87 IN-6
Carvers Corner—locale ME-1
Carvers Coulee—valley MT-8
Carvers Creek—stream (2) NC-3
Carvers Creek—stream VA-3
Carvers Creek Ch—church NC-3
Carvers Creek (Township of)—fmr MCD (2) NC-3
Carvers Crossing AL-4
Carver Seam Mine (underground)—mine AL-4
Carvers Gap—gap NC-3
Carvers Gap—gap TN-4
Carvers Gap Creek—stream NC-3
Carvers Gulch—valley WA-9
Carvers Harbor—bay ME-1
Carvers Hill MA-1
Carvers Island—island ME-1
Carvers Lake—lake ND-7
Carvers Lake—reservoir MO-7
Carvers Lake—reservoir NC-3
Carvers Lake Dam—dam NC-3
Carver- Smith HS—school TN-4
Carvers Pond MA-1
Carvers Pond—lake ME-1
Carver Spring—spring CA-9
Carvers Ridge—locale PA-2
Carvers Roadside Rest Area—locale NV-8
Carvers Station NV-8
Carver State Vocational Technical Sch—school AL-4
Carver Station—locale KY-4
Carver Statue—park MO-7
**Carver Subdivision (subdivision)**—pop pl AL-4
Carversville—locale PA-2
Carversville Hist Dist—hist pl PA-2
Carversville Post Office (historical)—building PA-2
**Carverton**—pop pl PA-2
Carverton Ch—church PA-2
**Carver (Town of)**—pop pl MA-1
**Carver Village**—pop pl FL-3
**Carver Village**—pop pl GA-3
Carver Vocational Sch—school GA-3
Carville IA-7
Carville—locale MD-2
**Carville**—pop pl LA-4
Carville Basin—cove MA-1
Carville Cem—cemetery NY-2
Carville Creek—stream NV-8
Carvill Hall—hist pl MD-2
Carvin Cove Rsvr—reservoir VA-3
Carvin Creek—stream CA-9
Carvin Creek—stream VA-3
Carvin Creek Homesites—locale CA-9
Carvittville PA-2
Carvix Rsvr—reservoir OR-9
Carvosso Ch—church VA-3
Carwick OH-6
Carwile—locale OK-5
Carwile Creek—stream TX-5
Carwile Ranch—locale TX-5
Carwine Ridge—ridge MO-7
Carwin Spring—spring OR-9
**Carwood**—pop pl IN-6
Carwood, Mount—summit MI-6
Carwood Cem—cemetery KS-7
Carwood (historical)—locale KS-7
**Carwye (historical)**—pop pl SD-7
Cary NJ-2
Cary—locale FL-3
Cary—locale KY-4
**Cary**—pop pl AR-4
**Cary**—pop pl GA-3
**Cary**—pop pl IL-6
**Cary**—pop pl IN-6
**Cary**—pop pl ME-1
**Cary**—pop pl MS-4
**Cary**—pop pl NC-3
Cary, G.W., House—hist pl OH-6
Cary, Hiram W., House—hist pl OH-6
Cary, Joshua B., House—hist pl LA-4
Cary, Mary Ann Shadd, House—hist pl DC-2
Cary, Mount—summit MA-1
Cary, Otis, House—hist pl MA-1
Cary Bay VT-1
Cary Bayou—stream TX-5
Cary Bldg—hist pl MI-6
Cary Bldg—hist pl NY-2
Cary Branch—stream IL-6
Cary Branch—stream NC-3
Cary Brook—stream (2) MA-1
Cary Brook—stream VT-1
Cary Camp—park IN-6
Cary Canyon—valley CA-9
Cary Cem—cemetery KY-4
Cary Cem—cemetery OH-6
Cary Cem—cemetery SC-3
Cary Ch—church ME-1
Cary Ch—church NC-3
Cary Ch (historical)—church AL-4
Cary Country Club—other IL-6
Cary Creek AR-4
Cary Creek KS-7
Cary Creek—stream AK-9
Cary Creek—stream AR-4
Cary Creek—stream IL-6
Cary Creek—stream MS-4
Cary Creek—stream OR-9
Cary Ditch—canal CO-8
Cary Ditch—canal OH-6
Cary Elem Sch—school NC-3
Cary Flat Branch—stream NC-3
Cary Flat Cem—cemetery NC-3
Cary Gulch—valley CO-8
Cary Hill—summit ME-1
Cary Hill—summit (2) NY-2
Cary Hill Plaza (Shop Ctr)—locale MA-1
Cary Hollow—valley AL-4
Cary Home for Children—school IN-6
Cary Hunter Ditch—canal CA-9
Caryhurst—locale UT-8
Cary JHS—school TX-5
Cary Lake—lake MI-6
Cary Lake—lake NY-2
Cary Lake—lake TX-5
Caryl Brook—stream VT-1
Caryle Sch—school WV-2
Cary Library—hist pl ME-1
Caryl Lake—lake NY-2
Carylwood Sch—school OH-6
Cary Martin Springs—spring TX-5
Cary Methodist Church AL-4
Cary Mine—mine WI-6
Cary Mound—summit WI-6
Cary Mtn—summit PA-2
Cary Park—park NY-2
Cary Pasture Creek—stream CA-9
Cary Peak—summit CA-9
Cary (Plantation of)—civ div ME-1
Cary Pond—lake NY-2
Cary Post Office—building MS-4
Cary Ridge—other KY-4
Cary Rsvr—reservoir CA-9
Cary Rsvr—reservoir OR-9
Carys NJ-2
**Carys**—pop pl NJ-2
**Carysbrook**—pop pl VA-3
Carys Ch—church VA-3
Cary Sch—school MI-6
Cary Sch—school MO-7
Cary Sch—school NY-2
Cary Sch—school (2) VA-3
Cary Sch (historical)—school AL-4
Cary School—locale IA-7
Carys Corner—locale VA-3
Carys Creek MN-6
Carys Creek—stream (2) VA-3
Carys Creek Wayside—locale VA-3
Carys Ditch—canal LA-4
Cary Senior HS—school NC-3
Carysfort Lighthouse—hist pl FL-3
Carysfort Reef—bar FL-3
**Carysfort Yacht Harbor**—pop pl FL-3
Cary Site (22Sh507)—hist pl MS-4
Carys Lakes—reservoir SC-3
Carys Mill Creek AL-4
**Carys Mills**—pop pl ME-1
Carys Point—cape VA-3
Cary Spring—spring CA-9
Cary Spring—spring OR-9
Cary Stadium—other VA-3
Cary State Forest—park FL-3
Cary Station—hist pl NJ-2
**Carysville**—pop pl OH-6
Caryton - Cockburn Cemetery AL-4
Caryton (historical)—locale AL-4
Caryton P.O. AL-4
Caryton School AL-4
Carytown OH-6
**Carytown**—pop pl MO-7
Carytown Cem—cemetery AL-4
**Cary (Town of)**—pop pl WI-6
Carytown Sch—school NY-2
Cary (Township of)—fmr MCD NC-3
Cary Valley—basin NE-7
Cary Village Site—hist pl OH-6
Caryville AL-4
**Caryville**—pop pl FL-3
**Caryville**—pop pl MA-1
**Caryville**—pop pl TN-4
**Caryville**—pop pl WI-6
Caryville (CCD)—cens area FL-3
Caryville (CCD)—cens area TN-4
Caryville Dam—dam TN-4
Caryville Division—civil TN-4
Caryville Elem Sch—school TN-4
Caryville (historical P.O.)—locale MA-1
Caryville Lake—reservoir TN-4
Caryville Lake Dam—dam TN-4
Caryville Post Office—building TN-4
Caryville Station (historical)—locale MA-1
Cary Woods Sch—school AL-4
**Cary Woods (subdivision)**—pop pl AL-4
Casa—locale CO-8
**Casa**—pop pl AR-4
Casa Adobe de San Rafael—building CA-9
Casa Adobes Shopping Plaza—locale AZ-5
Casa Agostini—hist pl PR-3
Casa Alcaldia de Arecibo—hist pl PR-3
Casa Alcaldia de Ponce-City Hall—hist pl PR-3
Casa Alegre Park—park NM-5
Casa Alvarez—hist pl MO-7
Casa Banco Number 90—levee TX-5
Casa Bella Park—park TX-5
**Casa Bianco**—pop pl FL-3
Casa Blanca—locale TX-5
Casa Blanca—locale PR-3
**Casa Blanca**—pop pl AZ-5
**Casa Blanca**—pop pl CA-9
**Casa Blanca**—pop pl NM-5
**Casa Blanca**—pop pl PR-3
Casa Blanca, Lake—reservoir TX-5
Casa Blanca Canal—canal AZ-5
Casa Blanca Cem—cemetery TX-5
Casa Blanca Ch—church AZ-5
Casa Blanca Country Club—other TX-5
Casa Blanca Creek—stream TX-5
Casa Blanca Ditch—canal NM-5
Casa Blanca (historical)—locale AZ-5
Casa Blanca Historical Marker—park TX-5
Casa Blanca Interchange—crossing AZ-5
Casa Blanca Lake TX-5
Casa Blanca Mesa—summit NM-5
Casa Blanca Plaza Shop Ctr—locale AZ-5
Casa Blanca Ranch—locale (2) TX-5
Casa Blanca Sch—school CA-9
Casa Blancas Creek TX-5
Casa Blanca Spring—spring NM-5
**Casablanca (subdivision)**—pop pl NC-3
**Casablanca (subdivision)**—pop pl TN-4
Casa Blanca Tank—reservoir TX-5
Casa Blanca Windmill—locale (3) TX-5
Casa Blanco—locale FL-3
Casa Blanco Ch—church FL-3
Casabonne Peak—summit CA-9
Casa Caprona—hist pl FL-3
Casa Cautino—hist pl PR-3
Casa Chiquita Ruins—locale NM-5
Casa Coe da Sol—hist pl FL-3
Casa Colo—locale FL-3
Casa Cola Creek—stream FL-3
Casa Colina Sch—school CA-9
Casa Colorado Canal—canal NM-5
Casa Colorado Ditch—canal NM-5
Casa Colorado Drain—canal NM-5
Casa Colorado Grant—civil NM-5
Casa Colorado Sch—school NM-5
Casa Colorado—locale CO-8
Casa Colorado Rock—pillar UT-8
**Casa Conejo**—pop pl CA-9
Casa Consistorial De Mayaguez—hist pl PR-3
Casa Cordova—hist pl PR-3
Casa Correo—uninc pl CA-9
Casaday Creek—stream CO-8
Casa de Adobe—building CA-9
Casa de Cuervo—locale CA-9
Casa de Espano—hist pl PR-3
Casa de Estrella Archeol Site—hist pl NM-5
Casa de Francisco Mobile Home Park—locale AZ-5
Casa De Josefina—hist pl FL-3
Casa de la Diosa Mita—hist pl PR-3
Casa Deldra—hist pl NJ-2
Casa del Eco Mesa—summit UT-8
Casa Del Mar Light—locale FL-3
Casa del Oro—locale AZ-5
Casa de los Cerritos—building CA-9
Casa de los Ponce de Leon—hist pl PR-3
Casa del Sol Resorts Number One (trailer park)—locale AZ-5
**Casa del Sol Resorts Number One (trailer park)**—pop pl AZ-5
Casa del Sol Resorts (trailer park)—locale AZ-5
**Casa del Sol Resorts (trailer park)**—pop pl AZ-5
Casa De Muchas Flores—hist pl FL-3
**Casa de Norte Subdivision**—pop pl UT-8
**Casa de Oro**—pop pl CA-9
Casa de Oro-Mount Helix—CDP CA-9
Casa de Oro Sch—school CA-9
Casadepaga—locale AK-9
Casadepaga River—stream AK-9
Casa de Parley Johnson—hist pl CA-9
Casa de Peidras—locale TX-5
Casa de Piedra—hist pl PR-3
Casa de Piedra—locale TX-5
Casa de Tableta—hist pl CA-9
Casa Diablo—cape CA-9
Casa Diablo Hot Springs—locale CA-9
Casa Diablo Mine—mine CA-9
Casa Diablo Mtn—summit CA-9
Casad Industrial Park—facility IN-6
Casad Industrial Park Airp—airport IN-6
Casad Lateral—canal CA-9
Casador Lake—reservoir MO-7
Casados House—hist pl NM-5
Casados Ranch—locale NM-5
Casados Well—well NM-5
Casady Sch—school IA-7
Casady Sch—school OK-5
Casa Escondida—valley NM-5
Casa Fiesta Travel Trailer Resort—locale AZ-5
Casa Franceschi Antongiorgi—hist pl PR-3
Casa Fria—locale NM-5
**Casa Fria**—pop pl NM-5
Casagranda Race Track—other MI-6
Casa Grande—building AZ-5
**Casa Grande**—pop pl AZ-5
**Casa Grande**—pop pl NM-5
Casa Grande—summit NM-5
Casa Grande Canal—canal AZ-5
Casa Grande (CCD)—cens area AZ-5
Casa Grande Country Club—other AZ-5
Casa Grande Farm Labor Camp AZ-5
Casa Grande Hotel—hist pl AZ-5
Casa Grande Interchange—crossing AZ-5
Casa Grande JHS—school AZ-5
Casa Grande Military Rsvr—reservoir AZ-5
Casa Grande Mountain Park—park AZ-5
Casa Grande Mountains—ridge AZ-5
Casa Grande Municipal Airp—airport AZ-5
Casa Grande Natl Monmt AZ-5
Casa Grande Natl Monmt—hist pl AZ-5
Casa Grande Natl Monmt—park AZ-5
Casa Grande Peak—summit TX-5
Casa Grande Ranch—locale NM-5
Casa Grande RR Station—building AZ-5
Casa Grande Ruins AZ-5
Casa Grande Ruins Natl Monmt—park AZ-5
Casa Grande Spring—spring AZ-5
Casa Grande Stone Church—hist pl AZ-5
Casa Grande Turbine Station—locale AZ-5
Casa Grande Union HS and Gymnasium—hist pl AZ-5
Casa Grande Valley—valley AZ-5
Casa Grande Woman's Club Bldg—hist pl AZ-5
Casa Italino—hist pl NY-2
Casalerry Creek WA-9
Casa Linda—uninc pl TX-5
Casa Linda Ch—church TX-5
**Casa Linda Estates (subdivision)**—pop pl NC-3
Casa Linda Lake—lake FL-3
Casa Linda Sch—school TX-5
**Casa Linda (subdivision)**—pop pl (2) AZ-5
Casa Loma—locale NM-5
**Casa Loma**—pop pl CA-9
Casa Loma Canal—canal CA-9
Casa Loma Sanitarium—hospital CA-9
Casa Loma Sch—school CA-9
**Casa Loma Subdivision**—pop pl UT-8
Casa Madera Mine—mine CA-9
Casa Malpais Site—hist pl AZ-5
Casa Massa Creek—stream AR-4
Casamero Draw—valley NM-5
Casamero Lake—reservoir NM-5
Casa Mesa Diablo (LA 11100)—hist pl NM-5
Casa Montezuma AZ-5
Casa Natal de Luis Munoz Rivera—hist pl PR-3
Casa Natal Dr. Jose Celso Barbosa—hist pl PR-3
Casandro Park—park AZ-5
**Casanova**—pop pl PA-2
**Casanova**—pop pl VA-3
Casa Peralta—hist pl CA-9
Casa Piedra—locale AZ-5
Casa Piedra—locale TX-5
Casa Piedra Spring—spring AZ-5
**Casar**—pop pl NC-3
Casar Elem Sch—school NC-3
Casarez Ranch—locale (2) NM-5
**Casa Rica (subdivision)**—pop pl (2) AZ-5
Casa Rinconada Ruins—locale NM-5
Casa Roble HS—school CA-9
Casa Roig—hist pl PR-3
Casa Rosa—locale AZ-5
Casas, Canal (historical)—canal AZ-5
**Casas Adobes**—pop pl AZ-5
Casa Salazar—locale NM-5
Casa Salazar Sch—school NM-5
Casas Cem—cemetery TX-5
Casas del Campo Mobile Home Park—locale AZ-5
Casas del Medio—other NM-5
Casa Serena Mobile Home Park—locale AZ-5
Casa (Township of)—fmr MCD AR-4
Casa Ulanga—hist pl PR-3
Casaus, Jesus M., House—hist pl NM-5
Casaus Ditch—canal NM-5
Casaus Lake—lake NM-5
**Casa Verde Estates Subdivision**—pop pl UT-8
Casa Verde Windmill—locale TX-5
Casa Vieja Meadows—flat CA-9
Casa View—post sta TX-5
Casa View Sch—school TX-5
Casa Yankee Ruins—locale TX-5
Casazza Moana NV-8
Casberg Coulee—valley WI-6
Casbobas Islands MP-9
CA SBr 1008A, CA SBr 1008B, CA SBr 1008C—hist pl CA-9
Cascabel—locale AZ-5
Cascabel Ranch—locale AZ-5
Cascabel Sch—school AZ-5
Cascade SD-7
Cascade UT-8
Cascade—locale CA-9
Cascade—locale CO-8
Cascade—locale IL-6
Cascade—locale MD-2
Cascade—locale MI-6
Cascade—locale NE-7
Cascade—locale VA-3
**Cascade**—pop pl CO-8
**Cascade**—pop pl ID-8
**Cascade**—pop pl IN-6
**Cascade**—pop pl IA-7
**Cascade**—pop pl MI-6
**Cascade**—pop pl MO-7
**Cascade**—pop pl MT-8
**Cascade**—pop pl NH-1
**Cascade**—pop pl NY-2
**Cascade**—pop pl PA-2
**Cascade**—pop pl WV-2
**Cascade**—pop pl WI-6
Cascade—post sta WA-9
Cascade, Lake—reservoir CA-9
Cascade, The—basin FL-3
Cascade, The—falls MD-2
Cascade, The—falls (2) MA-1
Cascade, The—rapids MA-1
Cascade Acres—falls WY-8
Cascade Airp—airport WA-9
Cascade Airstrip—airport OR-9
Cascade Alpine Brook—stream NH-1
Cascade Bay—bay (2) AK-9
Cascade Bay—bay WA-9
Cascade Bight—bay AK-9
Cascade Boy Scout Camp—hist pl CO-8
Cascade Branch—stream GA-3
Cascade Branch—stream NC-3
Cascade Branch—stream TN-4
Cascade Brook MI-6
Cascade Brook—stream (2) ME-1
Cascade Brook—stream MA-1
Cascade Brook—stream (6) NH-1
Cascade Brook—stream (3) NY-2
Cascade Brook Trail—trail NH-1
Cascade Butte—summit MT-8
Cascade Campground—locale CO-8
Cascade Campground—locale MT-8
Cascade Canal—canal CA-9
Cascade Canal—canal MT-8
Cascade Canal—canal OR-9
Cascade Canal—canal WA-9
Cascade Canyon—valley CA-9
Cascade Canyon—valley (2) CO-8
Cascade Canyon—valley NM-5
Cascade Canyon—valley UT-8
Cascade Canyon—valley WY-8
Cascade Canyon Trail—trail WY-8
Cascade Caves—cave KY-4
Cascade (CCD)—cens area WA-9
Cascade Cem—cemetery OH-6
Cascade Ch—church FL-3
Cascade Ch—church GA-3
Cascade Chapel—church WI-6
Cascade Cirque—basin UT-8
Cascade Cliffs—cliff CA-9
Cascade Coll—school OR-9
Cascade Corner—area WY-8
Cascade Country Club—other MI-6
Cascade County Courthouse—hist pl MT-8
Cascade Creek AK-9
Cascade Creek CO-8
Cascade Creek MT-8
Cascade Creek OR-9
Cascade Creek WA-9
Cascade Creek—locale CA-9
Cascade Creek—stream (8) AK-9
Cascade Creek—stream (11) CA-9
Cascade Creek—stream (11) CO-8
Cascade Creek—stream (8) ID-8
Cascade Creek—stream (2) MI-6
Cascade Creek—stream MN-6
Cascade Creek—stream MS-4
Cascade Creek—stream (11) MT-8
Cascade Creek—stream NE-7
Cascade Creek—stream NY-2
Cascade Creek—stream (2) NC-3
Cascade Creek—stream (5) OR-9
Cascade Creek—stream (2) PA-2
Cascade Creek—stream SD-7
Cascade Creek—stream TX-5
Cascade Creek—stream (2) UT-8
Cascade Creek—stream VA-3
Cascade Creek—stream (9) WA-9
Cascade Creek—stream (6) WY-8
Cascade Creek Campground—locale MT-8
Cascade Creek (reduced usage)—stream WY-8
Cascade Creek Summer Homes—locale MT-8
Cascade Creek Trail—trail WY-8
Cascade Crest Trail—trail (2) WA-9
Cascade Dam—dam CA-9
Cascade Dam Reservoir ID-8
Cascade Divide Trail—trail OR-9
Cascade-Fairwood—CDP WA-9
Cascade Falls—falls (2) CO-8
Cascade Falls—falls GA-3
Cascade Falls—falls MI-6
Cascade Falls—falls MN-6
Cascade Falls—falls MT-8
Cascade Falls—falls NY-2
Cascade Falls—falls NC-3
Cascade Falls—falls OH-6
Cascade Falls—falls OR-9
Cascade Falls—falls SD-7
Cascade Falls—falls (2) TN-4
Cascade Falls—falls UT-8
Cascade Falls—falls WA-9
Cascade (Fort Ritchie (sta.))—uninc pl MD-2
Cascade Gap—gap AR-4
Cascade Glacier—glacier (2) AK-9
**Cascade Gorge**—pop pl OR-9
Cascade Gorge—valley OR-9
Cascade Gulch—valley CA-9
Cascade Gulch—valley (2) CO-8
Cascade Gulch—valley ID-8
Cascade Head—cape OR-9
Cascade Heights (2) IN-6
**Cascade Heights**—pop pl GA-3
Cascade Heliport—airport WA-9
Cascade-Highfield—CDP MD-2
**Cascade Hills**—pop pl GA-3
Cascade (historical)—locale KS-7
Cascade Hollow—valley TN-4
Cascade Inlet—bay AK-9
Cascade Island—island AK-9
Cascade Islands Campground—locale WA-9
Cascade JHS—school (3) OR-9
Cascade Junction—locale WA-9
Cascade Junior and Senior HS—school WA-9
Cascade Lake—lake (2) AK-9
Cascade Lake—lake (2) CA-9
Cascade Lake—lake FL-3
Cascade Lake—lake (2) MN-6
Cascade Lake—lake MT-8
Cascade Lake—lake NY-2
Cascade Lake—lake (2) WA-9
Cascade Lake—lake (2) WY-8
Cascade Lake—reservoir CO-8
Cascade Lake—reservoir MD-2
Cascade Lake—reservoir NJ-2
Cascade Lake—reservoir NY-2
Cascade Lake—reservoir NC-3
Cascade Lake—reservoir PA-2
Cascade Lake Dam—dam NJ-2
Cascade Lake Dam—dam NC-3
Cascade Lakes—lake AK-9
Cascade Lakes—lake MT-8
Cascade Lakes—reservoir CA-9
Cascade Link Trail—trail NH-1
**Cascade Locks**—pop pl OR-9
Cascade Locks (CCD)—cens area OR-9
Cascade Locks Cem—cemetery OR-9
Cascade Locks Elementary & HS—school OR-9
Cascade Locks Marine Park—hist pl OR-9
Cascade Locks-Stevenson State Airp—airport OR-9
Cascade Locks Work Center—hist pl OR-9
Cascade Lookout Tower—locale MN-6
Cascade Lookout Tower—tower MO-7
Cascadel Point—summit CA-9
Cascadel Ranch—locale CA-9
Cascade Meadows—flat WY-8
Cascade Meadows Church Camp—locale WA-9
Cascade Mill—uninc pl WA-9
Cascade Mills—locale NY-2
Cascade Mine Number One—mine CA-9
Cascade Mtn—summit AR-4
Cascade Mtn—summit (3) CO-8
Cascade Mtn—summit MT-8
Cascade Mtn—summit NH-1
Cascade Mtn—summit (2) NY-2
Cascade Mtn—summit UT-8
Cascade Mtn—summit WA-9
Cascade Mtn—summit WI-6
Cascaden Ridge—ridge AK-9
Cascade Oil Field CA-9
Cascade Overlook—locale NC-3
Cascade Park—park ID-8
Cascade Park—park IN-6
Cascade Park—park MN-6
Cascade Park—park NC-3
Cascade Park—park OH-6
Cascade Park—park PA-2
Cascade Park—park VA-3
Cascade Pass—gap WA-9
Cascade Peak—summit ID-8
Cascade Peak—summit WA-9
Cascade Picnic Area—locale CA-9
Cascade Plantation—hist pl NC-3
Cascade Plaza Shop Ctr—locale MI-6
Cascade Point—cape AK-9
Cascade Point—locale ID-8
Cascade Point Lookout Station ID-8
Cascade Pond—lake NY-2
Cascade Post Office (historical)—building SD-7
Cascade Range—range CA-9
Cascade Range—range NY-2
Cascade Range—range OR-9
Cascade Range—range WA-9
Cascade Ranger Station—locale WY-8
Cascade Rapids Channel Lower Range—channel OR-9
Cascade Ridge—ridge ID-8
Cascade River—stream MN-6
Cascade River—stream WA-9
Cascade River Campground—locale MN-6
Cascade Rsvr OR-9
Cascade Rsvr—reservoir ID-8
Cascade Rsvr—reservoir MT-8
Cascade Run—stream PA-2
Cascade Run—stream WV-2
Cascades, The—falls CA-9
Cascades, The—falls NY-2
Cascades, The—falls NC-3
Cascades, The—rapids MN-6
Cascades, The (historical)—rapids OR-9
Cascade Saddle—gap ID-8
Cascade Salmon Hatchery—other OR-9
Cascade Sanatorium—hospital CA-9
Cascades Campsite—locale NC-3
Cascade Sch—school CA-9
Cascade Sch—school GA-3
Cascade Sch—school IL-6
Cascade Sch—school IN-6
Cascade Sch—school MD-2
Cascade Sch—school NE-7
Cascade Sch—school OH-6
Cascade Sch—school UT-8
Cascade Sch—school WA-9
Cascades Creek—stream NY-2
Cascades Creek—stream VA-3
Cascades Gateway Park—park OR-9
Cascades Golf Club—other VA-3
Cascades Lake—lake NY-2
Cascades of the Firehole—falls WY-8
Cascades Park—hist pl FL-3
Cascades Park—park MA-1
Cascade Spring CA-9
Cascade Spring—spring AZ-5
Cascade Spring—spring (2) OR-9
Cascade Spring—spring TN-4
Cascade Spring—spring (2) UT-8
Cascade Springs UT-8
Cascade Springs—locale SD-7
Cascade Springs—spring CA-9
Cascade Springs—spring OR-9
Cascade Springs—spring SD-7
Cascade Spur—locale WA-9
Cascade Spur—ridge ID-8
Cascades Sch—school MI-6
Cascades Sch—school OR-9
**Cascades (subdivision)**—pop pl NC-3
**Cascades (subdivision), The**—pop pl MS-4
Cascade Station—locale VA-3
Cascade Stream—stream ME-1
Cascade Summit—locale OR-9
Cascade Swamp—swamp WI-6
Cascade Township—fmr MCD IA-7
**Cascade (Township of)**—pop pl MI-6
**Cascade (Township of)**—pop pl MN-6
**Cascade (Township of)**—pop pl PA-2

Cascade Trail—*trail* (2) CO-8
Cascade Trail—*trail* NC-3
Cascade Tunnel—*tunnel* WA-9
Cascade Union HS—*school* OR-9
Cascade Valley—*basin* WA-9
Cascade Valley—*locale* NY-2
Cascade Valley—*valley* CA-9
Cascade Valley—*valley* WI-6
Cascade Valley Cem—*cemetery* NY-2
**Cascade Vista**—*pop pl* WA-9
**Cascadia**—*pop pl* OR-9
Cascadia Ranger Station—*locale* OR-9
Cascadia Sch—*school* OR-9
Cascadia State Park—*park* OR-9
Cascadilla Creek—*stream* MT-8
Cascadilla Creek—*stream* NY-2
Cascading Glacier—*glacier* AK-9
Cascajo Hill—*summit* CA-9
Cascajo Hill—*summit* GU-9
Cascajo Tank—*reservoir* TX-5
**Cascan**—*pop pl* OR-9
Cascara Ch—*church* WV-2
Cascara Spring—*spring* CA-9
Cascara Spring—*spring* WA-9
Cascare, Bayou—*stream* LA-4
Cascavel Tank—*reservoir* TX-5
Cas Cay—*island* VI-3
CA Sch—*school* NM-5
Cascia Hall Sch—*school* OK-5
**Cascilla**—*pop pl* MS-4
*Cascilla Baptist Church* MS-4
Cascilla Ch—*church* MS-4
Cascilla Elem Sch (historical)—*school* MS-4
Cascilla Sch—*school* MS-4
Cascine—*hist pl* NC-3
Cascine (Boundary Increase)—*hist pl* NC-3
Casci Ranch—*locale* CA-9
Casco—*locale* MN-6
Casco—*locale* MO-7
Casco—*locale* VA-3
**Casco**—*pop pl* ME-1
**Casco**—*pop pl* MI-6
**Casco**—*pop pl* WI-6
Casco Bay—*bay* ID-8
Casco Bay—*bay* ME-1
Casco Bay Ferry—*trail* ME-1
Casco Ch—*church* MO-7
Casco Cove—*bay* AK-9
Casco Cove Coast Guard Station—*mil airp* AK-9
Casco Creek—*stream* WI-6
Casco Junction—*locale* WI-6
Casco Millpond—*reservoir* WI-6
Casco Passage—*channel* ME-1
Casco Peak—*summit* CO-8
Casco Point—*cape* MN-6
**Casco (Town of)**—*pop pl* ME-1
**Casco (Town of)**—*pop pl* WI-6
**Casco (Township of)**—*pop pl* (2) MI-6
*Cascowasco* NY-2
Casdorph Cem—*cemetery* WV-2
Case—*locale* AR-4
Case—*locale* MO-7
**Case**—*pop pl* NY-2
Case, Benomi, House—*hist pl* CT-1
Case, C. B., Motor Co. Bldg—*hist pl* AR-4
Case, J. I., Plow Works Bldg—*hist pl* OK-5
Case, Larnerd, House—*hist pl* IA-7
Case, Lloyd, House—*hist pl* HI-9
Case, Mount—*summit* AK-9
Case, William, Farm—*hist pl* OR-9
Casebee Lake—*lake* MN-6
Casebeer Ranch—*locale* (2) OR-9
Casebeer Road Lateral—*canal* CA-9
Casebeer Sch (historical)—*school* PA-2
Casebeer Spring—*spring* OR-9
Casebier Hill—*summit* WY-8
Case Bolt Branch—*stream* MO-7
Casebolt Cem—*cemetery* MO-7
Casebottle Heath—*swamp* ME-1
Casebow Landing (historical)—*locale* MS-4
Case Branch—*stream* (2) NC-3
Case Branch—*stream* TX-5
Case Bridge—*bridge* DC-2
Case Bridge—*bridge* NE-7
Case Bridge—*other* MI-6
Case Brook—*stream* MA-1
Case Brook—*stream* NY-2
Case Camp Ridge—*ridge* NC-3
Case Canyon—*valley* WY-8
Case Cavern—*cave* GA-3
Case Cem—*cemetery* (2) AR-4
Case Cem—*cemetery* CT-1
Case Cem—*cemetery* IN-6
Case Cem—*cemetery* (2) MI-6
Case Cem—*cemetery* MO-7
Case Cem—*cemetery* NE-7
Case Cem—*cemetery* NY-2
Case Cem—*cemetery* OH-6
Case Cem—*cemetery* PA-2
Case Cem—*cemetery* TN-4
Case Ch—*church* AR-4
Case Cove—*bay* ME-1
Case Cove—*valley* NC-3
Case Creek—*stream* AR-4
Case Creek—*stream* ID-8
Case Creek—*stream* IL-6
Case Creek—*stream* (2) OR-9
Case Creek—*stream* TX-5
Case Creek Dam Number One—*dam* OR-9
Case Creek Rsvr—*reservoir* OR-9
Case Ditch—*canal* SD-7
Case Drain—*canal* (2) MI-6
Case Farmstead—*hist pl* NJ-2
Case Flats—*flat* CO-8
Case Glen—*valley* PA-2
Case-Harmon Field—*park* WI-6
*Case Hill* ME-1
Case Hill—*summit* (2) NY-2
Case Hollow—*valley* AR-4
Case House—*hist pl* WV-2
Case HS—*school* MA-1
Case Inlet—*bay* WA-9
Case Island—*island* MI-6
Case Knife Canyon—*valley* WY-8
Case Knife Creek—*stream* OR-9
Case Knife Creek—*stream* WA-9
Case Knife Gap—*gap* NC-3
Case Knife Ridge—*ridge* OR-9
Caseknife Ridge—*ridge* VA-3
Case Knife Spring—*spring* AZ-5
Case Lake—*lake* IN-6
Case Lake—*lake* IA-7
Case Lake—*lake* MI-6
Case Lake—*lake* (2) MN-6
Case Lake—*reservoir* IN-6
Case Lateral—*canal* AZ-5
Case Library—*hist pl* KS-7
**Caselton**—*pop pl* NV-8
**Caselton Heights**—*pop pl* NV-8
Caselton Rec Area—*park* NV-8
Caselton Wash—*stream* NV-8
Case Mansion—*hist pl* OH-6
Casemate Fort, Whiting Quadrangle—*hist pl* NY-2
Case Memorial-Seymour Library—*hist pl* NY-2
Casement Cem—*cemetery* KS-7
Casement Glacier—*glacier* AK-9
Casement House—*hist pl* OH-6
Casements, The—*hist pl* FL-3
Casements Annex—*hist pl* FL-3
Case Mill (historical)—*locale* MS-4
Case Mine—*mine* AK-9
**Casemore**—*pop pl* AL-4
Casemore Sch (historical)—*school* AL-4
Case Mountain Grove (Sierra Redwoods)—*woods* CA-9
Case Mtn—*summit* CA-9
Case Mtn—*summit* TN-4
Case Municipal Golf Course—*other* CO-8
*Casenovia Branch* WI-6
Case Observatory—*building* OH-6
Case Opening—*flat* CA-9
Case Point—*cape* RI-1
Case Pond—*lake* CT-1
Case Pond—*reservoir* (2) CT-1
Case Ponds—*reservoir* PA-2
Case Ranch—*locale* CO-8
Case Ranch—*locale* TX-5
Case Ridge—*ridge* OH-6
Case Ridge—*ridge* OR-9
Case Ridge Gap—*gap* NC-3
**Caserio Dr Gandara**—*pop pl* (2) PR-3
**Caserio Dr Pila**—*pop pl* PR-3
Caserio Roig—*post sta* PR-3
Case Rock Mine (underground)—*mine* AL-4
Case Rock Number 11 Mine (underground)—*mine* AL-4
Case Rsvr No. 1—*reservoir* CO-8
Case Rsvr No. 2—*reservoir* CO-8
Case Rsvr No. 3—*reservoir* CO-8
Caserta—*hist pl* VA-3
*Cases Brook* MA-1
Case Sch—*school* CO-8
Case Sch—*school* (2) OH-6
Case Sch—*school* PA-2
Case Sch—*school* SD-7
Case Sch—*school* WI-6
Case Shoal—*bar* WA-9
Cases Point—*cape* MN-6
*Cases Pond* PA-2
Case Spring—*spring* CA-9
Case Spring—*spring* CO-8
Case Street Cem—*cemetery* VT-1
*Caseta Piedra Peak* NM-5
**Case (Township of)**—*pop pl* MI-6
Caseview Spring—*spring* OR-9
Casevill Cem—*cemetery* GA-3
**Caseville**—*pop pl* MI-6
Caseville Cem—*cemetery* GA-3
Caseville Cem—*cemetery* MI-6
**Caseville (Township of)**—*pop pl* MI-6
Case Western Reserve Univ—*school* OH-6
Case Woodland Sch—*school* OH-6
Casey—*inactive* TX-5
Casey—*locale* AR-4
Casey—*locale* KY-4
Casey—*locale* MN-6
Casey—*locale* OK-5
**Casey**—*pop pl* AL-4
**Casey**—*pop pl* IL-6
**Casey**—*pop pl* IA-7
**Casey**—*pop pl* TX-5
**Casey**—*pop pl* PR-3
Casey, Mount—*summit* ID-8
Casey, Patrick, House—*hist pl* MN-6
Casey, Silas, Farm—*hist pl* RI-1
Casey Abajo (Barrio)—*fmr MCD* PR-3
Casey Abbott Semi-Regional Park—*park* AZ-5
**Casey Acres Subdivision**—*pop pl* UT-8
Casey Arriba (Barrio)—*fmr MCD* PR-3
Casey Bay—*bay* NC-3
Casey Bayou—*stream* LA-4
Casey Bottoms—*bend* KY-4
Casey Bow Branch—*stream* NC-3
Casey Branch—*stream* (3) KY-4
Casey Branch—*stream* MO-7
Casey Branch—*stream* NC-3
Casey Branch—*stream* VA-3
Casey Bridge—*bridge* KY-4
Casey Bridge—*bridge* MA-1
Casey Brook—*stream* ME-1
Casey Brook—*stream* MA-1
Casey Brook—*stream* (2) NY-2
Casey Cabin—*locale* ID-8
Casey Canyon—*valley* CA-9
Casey Canyon—*valley* NM-5
Casey Cem—*cemetery* (3) AR-4
Casey Cem—*cemetery* (2) IL-6
Casey Cem—*cemetery* IN-6
Casey Cem—*cemetery* MS-4
Casey Cem—*cemetery* (3) MO-7
Casey Cem—*cemetery* (2) TN-4
Casey Cem—*cemetery* TX-5
Casey Cem—*cemetery* WV-2
Casey Ch—*church* SC-3
Casey Chapel—*church* NC-3
*Casey Church* AL-4
Casey City Park—*park* IA-7
Casey Copper Canyon—*valley* AZ-5
**Casey Corner**—*pop pl* CA-9
Casey Corners—*locale* NY-2
**Casey (County)**—*pop pl* KY-4
Casey County Courthouse—*hist pl* KY-4
*Casey Creek* IL-6
Casey Creek—*gut* GA-3
Casey Creek—*locale* KY-4
Casey Creek—*stream* (2) ID-8
Casey Creek—*stream* (4) KY-4
Casey Creek—*stream* MI-6
Casey Creek—*stream* MS-4
Casey Creek—*stream* (2) MT-8
Casey Creek—*stream* NY-2
Casey Creek—*stream* OR-9
Casey Creek—*stream* SC-3
Casey Creek—*stream* WA-9
Casey Creek—*stream* WV-2
Casey Creek—*stream* (3) WI-6
*Casey Creek Baptist Church* MS-4
Casey Creek (CCD)—*cens area* KY-4
Casey Creek Cem—*cemetery* MS-4
Casey Creek Ch—*church* MS-4
Casey Creek Ch—*church* SC-3
Casey Creek Sch—*school* KY-4
Casey Ditch—*canal* IL-6
Casey Drain—*canal* (2) MI-6
*Casey Draw* TX-5
Casey Draw—*valley* SD-7
Casey Draw—*valley* TX-5
*Casey Elementary School* MS-4
*Casey Flat* CA-9
Casey Flats—*flat* CA-9
Casey Ford—*locale* MO-7
**Casey Fork**—*pop pl* WV-2
Casey Fork—*stream* IL-6
Casey Fork—*stream* (2) KY-4
Casey Fork Ch—*church* KY-4
Casey Fork Sch—*school* KY-4
Casey Fork Subimpoundment Dam—*dam* IL-6
Casey Glacier—*glacier* AK-9
Casey Gulch—*valley* CA-9
Casey Gulch—*valley* ID-8
Casey Gully—*valley* TX-5
Casey Ham Cem—*cemetery* MS-4
**Casey Highlands**—*pop pl* PA-2
Casey Hill—*summit* AL-4
Casey Hill—*summit* MA-1
Casey Hill—*summit* RI-1
Casey Hollow—*valley* TN-4
Casey Hollow—*valley* VA-3
Casey Hollow Mine—*mine* TN-4
Casey House—*hist pl* AR-4
Casey House—*hist pl* TX-5
Casey Island—*island* NC-3
Casey Island—*island* WA-9
Casey JHS—*school* CO-8
Casey JHS—*school* IL-6
Casey Jones Museum—*building* TN-4
Casey Jones Wreck Site—*hist pl* MS-4
Casey Key—*island* FL-3
**Casey Key**—*pop pl* FL-3
Casey Lake—*lake* (2) MI-6
Casey Lake—*lake* (3) MN-6
Casey Lake—*lake* MT-8
Casey Lake—*lake* (3) WI-6
Casey Lake Park—*park* MN-6
Casey Lake State Wildlife Area—*park* WI-6
Casey Meadow—*flat* ID-8
Casey Meadows—*flat* MT-8
Casey Mtn—*summit* GA-3
Casey Mtn—*summit* ID-8
Casey Mtn—*summit* NY-2
Casey Mtn—*summit* TX-5
Casey Park—*park* NY-2
Casey Peak—*summit* MT-8
Casey Point—*cape* RI-1
Casey Pond—*lake* WA-9
Casey Pond—*reservoir* AL-4
Casey Pond—*swamp* TX-5
Casey Post Office (historical)—*building* SD-7
Casey Post Office (historical)—*building* TN-4
Casey-Powell Cem—*cemetery* MS-4
Casey Rapids—*rapids* ME-1
Casey Ridge—*ridge* TX-5
Casey Run—*stream* OH-6
Casey Sch—*school* CA-9
Casey Sch—*school* (2) KY-4
Casey Sch—*school* MN-6
Casey Sch—*school* MS-4
Caseys Channel—*channel* AK-9
Casey Sch (historical)—*school* AL-4
Casey Sch (historical)—*school* MS-4
Casey School—*locale* IL-6
Caseys Creek—*stream* NJ-2
*Casey's Fork* IL-6
*Caseys Island* NC-3
Caseys Island—*island* OH-6
*Caseys Key* FL-3
*Caseys Knob* PA-2
Caseys Lakes—*reservoir* GA-3
Casey Slough—*stream* OR-9
*Caseys Point* RI-1
Casey Spring—*spring* ID-8
Casey Spring—*spring* IL-6
Casey Spring—*spring* OR-9
Casey Spring Ch—*church* IL-6
Casey Springs—*spring* NV-8
Casey Springs Branch—*stream* GA-3
Casey Springs (CCD)—*cens area* GA-3
Casey Springs Ch—*church* GA-3
**Caseys Siding**—*pop pl* TN-4
Caseys Slough—*swamp* SD-7
Casey State Park—*park* OR-9
Casey Swamp—*swamp* MI-6
Casey Table—*summit* NV-8
Casey Tank—*reservoir* NM-5
**Casey (Town of)**—*pop pl* WI-6
**Casey Township**—*pop pl* ND-7
**Casey (Township of)**—*pop pl* IL-6
**Casey Tract**—*pop pl* PA-2
Casey Valley—*basin* NE-7
**Casey Village**—*pop pl* PA-2
*Caseyville* IN-6
Caseyville—*locale* GA-3
**Caseyville**—*pop pl* IL-6
**Caseyville**—*pop pl* KY-4
**Caseyville**—*pop pl* MS-4
**Caseyville**—*pop pl* MO-7
Caseyville (historical)—*locale* MS-4
*Caseyville Post Office* TN-4
Caseyville Post Office (historical)—*building* MS-4
**Caseyville (Township of)**—*pop pl* IL-6
*Cash* MD-2
Cash—*locale* KY-4
Cash—*locale* MI-6
Cash—*locale* MO-7
Cash—*locale* VA-3
**Cash**—*pop pl* AR-4
**Cash**—*pop pl* GA-3
**Cash**—*pop pl* MS-4
**Cash**—*pop pl* SC-3
**Cash**—*pop pl* TX-5
*Cashaqua Creek* NY-2
*Casha River* NC-3
Cashatt Cem—*cemetery* IN-6
Cashaw Creek—*stream* VA-3
Cashaw Creek Trail—*trail* VA-3
Cash Baptist Ch—*church* TX-5
Cashbaugh Ranch—*locale* (2) CA-9
Cash Bayou—*bay* FL-3
Cash Bayou Ch—*church* LA-4
Cash Bend—*bend* AR-4
*Cash Brake* AR-4
Cash Branch—*stream* TX-5
Cash Butte—*summit* WA-9
Cash Camp (historical)—*locale* OR-9
Cashcamp Run—*stream* WV-2
Cash Canyon—*valley* CO-8
Cash Canyon—*valley* TX-5
Cash Canyon—*valley* WY-8
Cash Cem—*cemetery* AR-4
Cash Cem—*cemetery* KY-4
Cash Cem—*cemetery* MS-4
Cash Cem—*cemetery* MO-7
Cash Cem—*cemetery* (2) TN-4
Cash Cem—*cemetery* (2) VA-3
Cash Ch—*church* MS-4
Cash City (historical)—*locale* KS-7
*Cash Corner* ME-1
Cash Corner—*locale* MD-2
Cash Corner—*locale* (2) VA-3
**Cash Corner**—*pop pl* ME-1
**Cash Corner**—*pop pl* NC-3
**Cash Corner (Hollyville)**—*pop pl* NC-3
Cash Corner No 2—*locale* NC-3
*Cash Creek* CO-8
*Cash Creek* ID-8
*Cash Creek* WA-9
Cash Creek—*stream* AK-9
Cash Creek—*stream* FL-3
Cash Creek—*stream* GA-3
Cash Creek—*stream* ID-8
Cash Creek—*stream* IL-6
Cash Creek—*stream* KY-4
Cash Creek—*stream* MT-8
Cash Creek—*stream* ND-7
Cash Creek—*stream* OR-9
Cash Creek—*stream* PA-2
Cash Creek—*stream* TN-4
Cash Creek Ch—*church* KY-4
Cash Dam—*dam* AL-4
Cash Ditch—*canal* CO-8
Cashdollar Cove—*valley* TN-4
*Cashe Creek* WA-9
**Cashel**—*pop pl* ND-7
Cash Elem Sch—*school* NC-3
**Cashel (Township of)**—*pop pl* MN-6
Cashen Coulee—*valley* MT-8
Cash Entry Mine—*mine* NM-5
Casher Cem—*cemetery* AL-4
*Cashes Creek* PA-2
Cashes Valley—*valley* GA-3
Cashes Valley Cem—*cemetery* GA-3
Cashes Valley Ch of Christ—*church* GA-3
*Cashes Valley Church* GA-3
Cashes Valley Sch (historical)—*school* GA-3
Cash-Foust Cem—*cemetery* TN-4
Cash Gulch—*valley* (2) CO-8
Cash Gulch—*valley* OR-9
Cash Hill—*summit* WY-8
Cash Hollow—*valley* (2) MO-7
Cash Hollow—*valley* OR-9
Cash Hollow—*valley* TN-4
Cash Hollow—*valley* VA-3
Cashie Branch—*stream* NC-3
Cashie Ch—*church* NC-3
*Cashier* NC-3
Cashie River—*stream* NC-3
Cashier Mine—*mine* AZ-5
Cashier Mine—*mine* CO-8
**Cashiers**—*pop pl* NC-3
Cashier's House—*hist pl* PA-2
Cashiers House and Coach House (Boundary Increase)—*hist pl* PA-2
Cashiers Lake—*reservoir* NC-3
Cashiers Lake Dam—*dam* NC-3
Cashier Spring—*spring* AZ-5
Cashiers (Township of)—*fmr MCD* NC-3
Cashiers Valley—*valley* NC-3
*Cashier Valley* NC-3
Cashin Mine—*mine* CO-8
**Cashion**—*pop pl* AZ-5
**Cashion**—*pop pl* OK-5
Cashion Archeol Site—*hist pl* AZ-5
Cashion Bend—*bend* TN-4
Cashion Community Park—*park* AZ-5
**Cashion Crossroads**—*pop pl* SC-3
Cashion Hollow—*valley* TN-4
Cashion Lake—*lake* MI-6
Cashion Post Office—*building* AZ-5
*Cashion Ranch* AZ-5
Cashion Ridge—*ridge* TN-4
Cashion Sch (abandoned)—*school* MO-7
Cashion Substation—*locale* AZ-5
Cash Island—*island* IL-6
Cashka Lake—*lake* AK-9
Cash Knob—*summit* KY-4
Cash Lake—*lake* LA-4
Cash Lake—*lake* MN-6
Cash Lake—*lake* NE-7
Cash Lake—*lake* SC-3
Cash Lake—*reservoir* GA-3
Cash Lake—*reservoir* MD-2
Cash Lake—*reservoir* NC-3
Cashlapooda Creek—*stream* CA-9
Cash Lateral—*canal* ID-8
Cashler Cem—*cemetery* NE-7
Cashman, Mount—*summit* AK-9
Cashman Cem—*cemetery* KS-7
Cashman Creek—*stream* (2) CA-9
Cashman Dam—*dam* CA-9
Cashman Field—*flat* NV-8
Cashman JHS—*school* NV-8
Cashman Park—*park* MA-1
Cashman Sch—*school* IL-6
Cashmans Lake Dam—*dam* MS-4
**Cashmere**—*pop pl* WA-9
**Cashmere**—*pop pl* WV-2
Cashmere (CCD)—*cens area* WA-9
Cashmere-dryden Airp—*airport* WA-9
Cashmere Mtn—*summit* WA-9
Cashmere Sch—*school* IL-6
*Cashmer Mtn* WA-9
Cash Mine—*mine* AK-9
Cash Mine—*mine* AZ-5
Cash Mine—*mine* CO-8
Cash Mound—*summit* FL-3
Cash Mtn—*summit* PA-2
Cashner Butte—*summit* OR-9
Cashoke Creek—*stream* NC-3
Cashoke Landing—*locale* NC-3
Cashow Flat—*flat* OR-9
Cashow Springs—*spring* OR-9
Cash Point—*cape* FL-3
Cash Point—*locale* LA-4
**Cash Point**—*pop pl* TN-4
Cash Point Baptist Ch—*church* TN-4
Cash Point-Blanche (CCD)—*cens area* TN-4
Cash Point-Blanche Division—*civil* TN-4
Cash Point Canal—*canal* LA-4
Cashpoint Plantation House—*hist pl* LA-4
Cash Point Post Office (historical)—*building* TN-4
Cash Point Sch (historical)—*school* TN-4
Cash Pond—*lake* PA-2
Cash Pond—*reservoir* GA-3
Cash Post Office (historical)—*building* AL-4
Cash Prairie—*flat* WA-9
*Cashqua Creek* NY-2
Cash Ranch—*locale* TX-5
Cash Ridge—*ridge* OH-6
Cash Ridge—*ridge* TN-4
Cash River Ch—*church* AR-4
Cash Sch—*school* MO-7
Cash Sch—*school* SD-7
Cash Sch (historical)—*school* TN-4
Cashs Corner—*locale* VA-3
Cashs Creek—*stream* TX-5
Cashs Hill—*summit* WV-2
Cashs Hill Ch—*church* WV-2
Cashs Lake—*reservoir* AL-4
Cash Spring—*spring* KY-4
Cash Spring—*spring* MO-7
Cash Spring—*spring* TN-4
Cash Spring—*spring* WY-8
Cash Swamp—*swamp* FL-3
Cash Tank—*reservoir* AZ-5
**Cashton**—*pop pl* WI-6
*Cashtown* MN-6
Cashtown—*locale* PA-2
**Cashtown**—*pop pl* MN-6
**Cashtown**—*pop pl* PA-2
**Cash Township**—*pop pl* ND-7
**Cash Township**—*pop pl* SD-7
Cash Trail—*trail* WY-8
Cashua Street-Spring Street Hist Dist—*hist pl* SC-3
*Cashumacher Creek* WA-9
*Cashumocher Creek* WA-9
Cashup—*locale* PA-2
Cashup—*locale* WA-9
Cashville—*locale* VA-3
**Cashville**—*pop pl* SC-3
Casiano Creek—*stream* TX-5
Casias Canyon—*valley* NM-5
Casias Cem—*cemetery* NM-5
Casias Creek—*stream* NM-5
Casidy Branch—*stream* TX-5
Casier Sch—*school* CA-9
**Casilla del Gobernador**—*pop pl* PR-3
Casimero Spring—*spring* AZ-5
Casimero Spring—*spring* NM-5
**Casimir**—*pop pl* WI-6
*Casimiro* AZ-5
Casimir Pulaski Elem Sch—*school* DE-2
Casimir Sch—*school* CA-9
Casin Creek—*stream* MS-4
*Casin Lake* MI-6
Casin Lake—*lake* MI-6
Casino—*locale* MN-6
Casino—*uninc pl* CA-9
Casino, Mount—*summit* KS-7
Casino Beach—*beach* IA-7
**Casino Beach**—*pop pl* IA-7
Casino-Congress Park-Circular Street Hist Dist—*hist pl* NY-2
Casino Creek—*gut* SC-3
Casino Creek—*stream* AK-9
Casino Creek—*stream* KS-7
Casino Creek—*stream* MT-8
Casino de Ponce—*hist pl* PR-3
*Casino Gulch* CO-8
Casino Hall—*hist pl* TX-5
Casino Island—*island* NY-2
*Casino Lakes* ID-8
Casino Lakes—*lake* ID-8
Casino Park—*park* TX-5
Casino Point—*cape* CA-9
Casino Ridge—*ridge* GA-3
Casino Slough—*gut* GA-3
Casis Sch—*school* TX-5
Casita de Piedra Canyon—*valley* NM-5
Casita de Piedra Peak—*summit* NM-5
*Casita Piedra Peak* NM-5
Casitas, Lake—*reservoir* CA-9
Casitas Creek—*stream* CA-9
*Casitas Reservoir* CA-9
**Casitas Springs**—*pop pl* CA-9
Casitas Valley—*valley* CA-9
Casito Spring—*spring* AZ-5
*Casitys Bayou* MS-4
*Caskaty Beach* MA-1
*Caskaty Pond* MA-1
Casket Mtn—*summit* TX-5
Casket Rock—*island* CA-9
Caskett Bayou—*gut* LA-4
**Caskey**—*pop pl* SC-3
Caskey Branch—*stream* LA-4
Caskey Cem—*cemetery* KY-4
Caskey Cem—*cemetery* SC-3
Caskey Fork—*stream* KY-4
Caskey Lake—*lake* WA-9
Caskey Sch—*school* MT-8
Caski—*locale* VA-3
**Caskie**—*pop pl* VA-3
Casky—*locale* KY-4
Caslamayomi—*civil* CA-9
Casler Cem—*cemetery* WI-6
Casley Gas and Oil Field—*oilfield* KS-7
Caslink Spring—*spring* AZ-5
Caslow Sch—*school* PA-2
Casmalia—*civil* CA-9
**Casmalia**—*pop pl* CA-9
Casmalia Canyon—*valley* CA-9
Casmalia Hills—*summit* CA-9
*Casmalia Oil Field* CA-9
Casmer Branch—*stream* MO-7
C A Smith Dam—*dam* OR-9
C A Smith L and M Company Storage Rsvr—*reservoir* OR-9
Casnau Creek—*stream* CA-9
**Casner**—*pop pl* IL-6
Casner Butte—*summit* AZ-5
Casner Cabin Draw—*valley* AZ-5
Casner Canyon—*valley* (2) AZ-5
Casner Canyon Eleven Trail—*trail* AZ-5
Casner Canyon Tank—*reservoir* AZ-5
Casner Creek—*stream* (2) ID-8
Casner Creek—*stream* KS-7
Casner Gap—*gap* TX-5
Casner Mountain Tank—*reservoir* AZ-5
Casner Mountain Trail Eight—*trail* AZ-5
Casner Mtn—*summit* AZ-5
Casner Park—*flat* (2) AZ-5
Casner Park Tank—*reservoir* AZ-5
Casner Tank—*reservoir* (3) AZ-5
**Casner (Township of)**—*pop pl* IL-6
**Casnovia**—*pop pl* MI-6
**Casnovia (Township of)**—*pop pl* MI-6
Casoade Park—*park* OH-6
Caso Artesian Well—*well* TX-5
*Casobos Island* MP-9
*Casobos Islands James* MP-9
*Cason* NC-3
Cason—*locale* FL-3
**Cason**—*pop pl* TX-5
Cason, Bayou—*stream* LA-4
Cason, La Baie a —*stream* LA-4
Casona Cesari—*hist pl* PR-3
*Cason Baptist Church* MS-4
Cason Branch—*stream* GA-3
Cason Branch—*stream* MO-7
Cason-Bynes Cem—*cemetery* GA-3
Cason Canyon—*valley* (2) OR-9
Cason Cem—*cemetery* (2) LA-4
Cason Cem—*cemetery* (3) MO-7
Cason Cem—*cemetery* TN-4
Cason Ch—*church* MS-4
Cason Cove—*bay* TX-5
Cason Creek—*stream* LA-4
Cason Dead River—*stream* GA-3
Cason Falls—*falls* TX-5
Cason Hollow—*valley* TX-5
Cason House—*hist pl* GA-3
Cason Lake—*lake* FL-3
Cason Mine—*mine* AR-4
**Cason Oil Fields**—*pop pl* NC-3
**Cason Old Field**—*pop pl* NC-3
Cason Point—*cape* NC-3
Cason Sch (historical)—*school* MS-4
Casons Knobs—*summit* TN-4
*Casons Neck* MD-2
Cason Well—*well* NM-5
Casoose Creek—*stream* CA-9
Casotte, Bayou—*stream* MS-4
Casowasco—*locale* NY-2
*Casowosco* NY-2
**Caspar**—*pop pl* CA-9
Caspar Anchorage—*bay* CA-9
Caspar Creek—*stream* CA-9
Casparis—*locale* PA-2
**Casparis (Bluestone Quarry)**—*pop pl* PA-2
*Casparis Cave* PA-2
Casparis Caves—*cave* PA-2
Caspar Orchard—*locale* CA-9
Caspar Point—*cape* CA-9
Casp-Druma—*summit* NM-5
Casp-Druma Dam—*dam* NM-5
**Casper**—*pop pl* WY-8
Casper Arm—*canal* IN-6
Casper Bank Mine—*mine* TN-4
Casper Boat Club—*other* WY-8
Casper Branch—*stream* AR-4
Casper Buffalo Trap—*hist pl* WY-8
Casper Canal—*canal* WY-8
Casper Ch—*church* IL-6
Casper Coll—*school* WY-8
Casper Coulee—*valley* MT-8
Casper Country Club—*other* WY-8
*Casper Creek* OR-9
Casper Creek—*stream* ID-8
Casper Creek—*stream* NY-2
Casper Creek—*stream* TN-4
Casper Creek—*stream* WI-6
Casper Creek—*stream* WY-8
Casper Creek Park—*park* TN-4
Casper Ditch—*canal* IN-6
Casper Gulch—*valley* SD-7
Casper Gulch Spring—*spring* SD-7
**Casper (historical)**—*pop pl* TN-4
*Casper Lake* AL-4
Casper Lake—*lake* WI-6
Casper Lake—*reservoir* TN-4
Casper Lake Dam—*dam* TN-4
Casper Lions Camp—*locale* WY-8
Casper Mountain County Park—*flat* WY-8
Casper Mtn—*summit* WY-8
Casper North—*cens area* WY-8
*Casper Range* WY-8
Casper Rsvr—*reservoir* WY-8
Casper Schumm Ditch—*canal* CO-8
Caspersen Beach—*beach* FL-3
Casper Slough—*gut* AK-9
Casperson—*locale* MN-6
Casperson, W., House—*hist pl* DE-2
Casper South—*cens area* WY-8
Casper Spring—*spring* UT-8
Casper Spring Tank—*reservoir* AZ-5
*Caspers Run* NJ-2
**Caspian**—*pop pl* MI-6
Caspiana—*locale* LA-4
Caspiana House—*hist pl* LA-4
Caspiana Lake—*lake* LA-4
Caspian Community Center—*hist pl* MI-6
Caspian Lake—*lake* VT-1
Caspian Lake—*lake* WI-6
Caspian Mine Headframe—*hist pl* MI-6
Cas Russell Creek—*stream* TX-5
*Cass* IL-6

**Castle Hills**—*pop pl* DE-2
**Castle Hills**—*pop pl* TX-5
Castle Hill Sch—*school* IA-7
Castle Hill Sch (historical)—*school* AL-4
Castle Hills Elem Sch—*school* DE-2
Castle Hill Ski Area—*locale* MT-8
*Castle Hills Sch* DE-2
**Castle Hill (Town of)**—*pop pl* ME-1
Castle Hollow—*valley* NY-2
**Castle Hot Springs**—*pop pl* AZ-5
**Castle Hot Springs (Champie)**—*pop pl* AZ-5
**Castle Hot Springs Station (Morristown)**—*pop pl* AZ-5
Castle HS—*school* HI-9
Castle HS—*school* IN-6
*Castle Island* UT-8
Castle Island—*cape* MA-1
Castle Island—*island* (2) AK-9
Castle Island—*island* (2) ME-1
Castle Island—*island* MI-6
Castle Island—*island* OH-6
Castle Island—*island* RI-1
Castle Island—*island* WA-9
Castle Islands—*area* AK-9
Castle Island Slough—*gut* AK-9
*Castle Isle* RI-1
**Castle Junction**—*pop pl* IL-6
Castle Knob—*summit* NM-5
Castle Knob—*summit* WV-2
*Castle Lake* ID-8
Castle Lake—*lake* AZ-5
Castle Lake—*lake* (2) CA-9
Castle Lake—*lake* CO-8
Castle Lake—*lake* (2) FL-3
Castle Lake—*lake* (2) ID-8
Castle Lake—*lake* MI-6
Castle Lake—*lake* (3) MT-8
Castle Lake—*lake* NE-7
Castle Lake—*lake* NV-8
Castle Lake—*lake* (3) UT-8
Castle Lake—*lake* (2) WA-9
Castle Lake—*reservoir* IN-6
Castle Lake Creek—*stream* CA-9
*Castle Lake Dam* IN-6
Castle Lakes—*lake* CO-8
Castle Lakes—*reservoir* CO-8
Castle Lake Sch—*school* CA-9
Castle Lake Trail—*trail* CA-9
Castle Mall—*locale* DE-2
Castleman—*locale* MS-4
Castleman Cem—*cemetery* KY-4
Castleman Cem—*cemetery* TX-5
*Castleman Creek* TX-5
Castleman Creek—*stream* KY-4
Castleman Creek—*stream* TX-5
Castleman Ditch—*canal* IN-6
Castleman Gulch—*valley* CO-8
**Castle Manor**—*pop pl* MD-2
Castleman Run—*stream* PA-2
Castleman Run—*stream* WV-2
Castleman Run Ch—*church* WV-2
Castlemans Ferry Bridge—*bridge* VA-3
*Castlemans Fork* TX-5
*Castlemans Spur* MS-4
**Castle Marina**—*pop pl* MD-2
Castle Meadow—*swamp* VT-1
Castle Memorial Sch—*school* KY-4
*Castlemen Creek* TX-5
Castle Mill Creek—*stream* NC-3
Castle Mill Run—*stream* VA-3
Castle Mine—*mine* CA-9
Castlemont HS—*school* CA-9
Castlemont Sch—*school* CA-9
Castle Mound—*summit* WI-6
Castle Mound Country Club—*other* WI-6
Castle Mound Rec Area—*park* WI-6
*Castle Mountain* VA-3
Castle Mountains—*other* CA-9
Castle Mountains—*summit* AZ-5
Castle Mountain Trail—*trail* WA-9
*Castle Mtn* TX-5
Castle Mtn—*summit* (4) AK-9
Castle Mtn—*summit* CA-9
Castle Mtn—*summit* (2) CO-8
Castle Mtn—*summit* (2) MT-8
Castle Mtn—*summit* (2) NV-8
Castle Mtn—*summit* NH-1
Castle Mtn—*summit* (4) TX-5
Castle Mtn—*summit* UT-8
Castle Mtn—*summit* WA-9
Castle Mtn—*summit* (2) WV-2
Castle Mtns—*range* MT-8
Castle Neck—*cape* MA-1
Castle Neck River—*stream* MA-1
Castle Neck River Marshes—*swamp* MA-1
**Castle Oaks**—*pop pl* CO-8
**Castle Oaks (subdivision)**—*pop pl* NC-3
Castle Oil Field—*oilfield* OK-5
Castle on 19th Street—*hist pl* WY-8
Castle Park—*flat* (3) CO-8
Castle Park—*park* MI-6
Castle Park—*park* PA-2
**Castle Park**—*pop pl* CA-9
**Castle Park**—*pop pl* MI-6
Castle Park—*post sta* GA-3
Castle Park HS—*school* CA-9
Castle Park JHS—*school* CA-9
Castle Park-Otay—*CDP* CA-9
Castle Park Sch—*school* CA-9
**Castle Park (subdivision)**—*pop pl* TN-4
Castle Park Well—*well* NV-8
Castle Pass—*gap* CA-9
Castle Pass—*gap* CO-8
Castle Pass—*gap* WA-9
Castle Path—*trail* NH-1
*Castle Peak* CA-9
*Castle Peak* CO-8
*Castle Peak* UT-8
*Castle Peak* WA-9
Castle Peak—*island* MA-1
Castle Peak—*pillar* ID-8
Castle Peak—*summit* AK-9
Castle Peak—*summit* (2) AZ-5
Castle Peak—*summit* (6) CA-9
Castle Peak—*summit* (3) CO-8
Castle Peak—*summit* (2) ID-8
Castle Peak—*summit* (2) NV-8
Castle Peak—*summit* SD-7
Castle Peak—*summit* (3) TX-5
Castle Peak—*summit* (2) UT-8
Castle Peak—*summit* (2) WA-9
Castle Peak Draw—*valley* UT-8
Castle Peak Mine—*mine* (2) NV-8
Castle Peak Mine—*mine* UT-8
Castle Peak Well—*well* UT-8
Castle Pinckney—*hist pl* SC-3
Castle Pinckney—*locale* SC-3
Castle Place—*locale* NV-8
*Castle Point* MI-6
Castle Point—*cape* CA-9
Castle Point—*cape* NJ-2
Castle Point—*cape* NY-2
Castle Point—*cliff* AZ-5
Castle Point—*cliff* NY-2
**Castle Point**—*pop pl* MO-7
**Castle Point**—*pop pl* NY-2
Castle Point—*summit* OR-9
Castle Point—*uninc pl* NJ-2
Castle Ranch—*locale* NE-7
Castle Reef—*bar* AZ-5
Castle Reef—*summit* MT-8
*Castle Rest Island* NY-2
Castle Ridge—*ridge* AR-4
Castle Ridge—*ridge* CA-9
Castle Ridge—*ridge* NV-8
Castle Ridge—*ridge* OR-9
Castle Ridge—*ridge* VA-3
*Castle Ridge Creek* VA-3
Castle Ridge Creek—*stream* VA-3
*Castle River* WA-9
Castle River—*stream* AK-9
*Castle Rock* CA-9
*Castle Rock* ID-8
*Castle Rock* KS-7
*Castle Rock* MO-7
*Castle Rock* MT-8
*Castle Rock* OR-9
*Castlerock* PA-2
*Castle Rock* SD-7
*Castle Rock* WA-9
*Castle Rock* WI-6
Castle Rock—*cape* ID-8
Castle Rock—*cape* MA-1
Castle Rock—*cliff* AZ-5
Castle Rock—*cliff* CO-8
Castle Rock—*cliff* ID-8
Castle Rock—*cliff* NC-3
Castle Rock—*cliff* TX-5
Castle Rock—*cliff* WY-8
Castle Rock—*fmr MCD* NE-7
Castle Rock—*hist pl* NY-2
Castle Rock—*island* AK-9
Castle Rock—*island* (4) CA-9
Castle Rock—*island* ME-1
Castle Rock—*island* MA-1
Castle Rock—*island* (2) OR-9
Castle Rock—*locale* SD-7
Castle Rock—*locale* UT-8
Castle Rock—*pillar* AK-9
Castle Rock—*pillar* (4) AZ-5
Castle Rock—*pillar* (7) CA-9
Castle Rock—*pillar* (9) CO-8
Castle Rock—*pillar* (4) ID-8
Castle Rock—*pillar* KS-7
Castle Rock—*pillar* MN-6
Castle Rock—*pillar* (2) MO-7
Castle Rock—*pillar* (3) MT-8
Castle Rock—*pillar* (2) NV-8
Castle Rock—*pillar* NM-5
Castle Rock—*pillar* NY-2
Castle Rock—*pillar* ND-7
Castle Rock—*pillar* OK-5
Castle Rock—*pillar* (5) OR-9
Castle Rock—*pillar* PA-2
Castle Rock—*pillar* (3) SD-7
Castle Rock—*pillar* (3) UT-8
Castle Rock—*pillar* (3) WA-9
Castle Rock—*pillar* WV-2
Castle Rock—*pillar* (3) WI-6
Castle Rock—*pillar* (4) WY-8
**Castle Rock**—*pop pl* CO-8
**Castle Rock**—*pop pl* MN-6
**Castle Rock**—*pop pl* MT-8
**Castle rock**—*pop pl* OR-9
**Castle Rock**—*pop pl* PA-2
**Castle Rock**—*pop pl* WA-9
**Castle Rock**—*pop pl* WI-6
Castle Rock—*summit* AK-9
Castle Rock—*summit* (4) AZ-5
Castle Rock—*summit* (8) CA-9
Castle Rock—*summit* (5) CO-8
Castle Rock—*summit* CT-1
Castle Rock—*summit* GA-3
Castle Rock—*summit* (4) ID-8
Castle Rock—*summit* MI-6
Castle Rock—*summit* (7) MT-8
Castle Rock—*summit* NE-7
Castle Rock—*summit* (2) NV-8
Castle Rock—*summit* NM-5
Castle Rock—*summit* NY-2
Castle Rock—*summit* (2) OR-9
Castle Rock—*summit* TX-5
Castle Rock—*summit* (4) UT-8
Castle Rock—*summit* VA-3
Castle Rock—*summit* (5) WA-9
Castle Rock—*summit* WV-2
Castle Rock—*summit* WI-6
Castle Rock—*summit* (7) WY-8
Castle Rock, The—*summit* WY-8
**Castle Rock Acres**—*pop pl* PA-2
Castle Rock Bay—*bay* AZ-5
Castle Rock Butte—*summit* SD-7
Castle Rock Camp—*locale* CO-8
Castle Rock Campground—*locale* UT-8
Castle Rock Campground—*park* OR-9
Castle Rock Canal—*canal* NE-7
Castle Rock Cave—*cave* PA-2
Castle Rock (CCD)—*cens area* WA-9
Castle Rock Creek—*stream* CO-8
Castle Rock Creek—*stream* ID-8
Castle Rock Creek—*stream* (2) OR-9
Castle Rock Creek—*stream* UT-8
Castle Rock Creek—*stream* WA-9
Castle Rock Creek—*stream* WY-8
Castle Rock Dam—*dam* AZ-5
Castle Rock Depot—*hist pl* CO-8
Castle Rock Ditch—*canal* WI-6
Castle Rock Ditch—*canal* WY-8
Castle Rock Elementry Sch—*hist pl* CO-8
Castle Rock Falls—*falls* CA-9
Castle Rock Fire Station—*locale* OR-9
Castle Rock Flowage—*reservoir* WI-6
Castle Rock Fork—*stream* OR-9
*Castle Rock Fork Umpqua River* OR-9
Castle Rock Glacier—*glacier* MT-8
Castle Rock Gulch—*valley* CO-8
Castle Rock Gulf—*bay* GA-3
Castle Rock Gulf—*valley* AL-4
Castle Rock Lake—*lake* WA-9
Castle Rock Lake—*reservoir* CO-8
Castlerock Lodge—*locale* OR-9
Castle Rock Mtn—*summit* MT-8
Castle Rock Park—*flat* NM-5
Castle Rock Park—*park* CA-9
Castle Rock Point—*cape* TN-4
Castle Rock Ranch—*locale* CA-9
Castle Rock Ranch—*locale* WY-8
Castle Rock Ranch Airp—*airport* KS-7
Castle Rock Ridge—*ridge* CA-9
*Castle Rock Rsvr* WI-6
Castle Rock Rsvr—*reservoir* (2) CO-8
Castle Rocks—*locale* ID-8
Castle Rocks—*locale* PA-2
Castle Rocks—*pillar* AK-9
Castle Rocks—*pillar* (2) CO-8
Castle Rocks—*pillar* MT-8
Castle Rocks—*range* ID-8
Castle Rocks—*rock* MT-8
Castle Rocks—*summit* AZ-5
Castle Rocks—*summit* (2) CA-9
Castle Rocks—*summit* OR-9
Castle Rocks—*summit* UT-8
Castle Rocks—*summit* WI-6
Castle Rocks—*summit* (2) WY-8
Castle Rock Sch—*school* CA-9
Castle Rock Sch—*school* SD-7
Castle Rock Sch—*school* WI-6
Castle Rock Sch (abandoned)—*school* MO-7
Castle Rocks (historical)—*summit* AZ-5
**Castle Rock Shores (Trailer Park)**—*pop pl* AZ-5
Castle Rocks Lake—*lake* AK-9
Castle Rock Spring—*spring* AZ-5
Castle Rock Spring—*spring* OR-9
**Castle Rock Springs**—*pop pl* CA-9
Castle Rock State Park—*park* CA-9
Castle Rock Tank—*reservoir* (2) AZ-5
Castle Rock Tank—*reservoir* NM-5
**Castle Rock Township**—*pop pl* ND-7
**Castle Rock (Township of)**—*pop pl* MN-6
Castle Rock Trail—*trail* (2) MT-8
Castle Rock Truck Trail—*trail* WA-9
Castle Rock Valley Cem—*cemetery* MN-6
Castle Rsvr—*reservoir* WY-8
Castle Run—*stream* IN-6
Castle Run—*stream* (2) VA-3
Castle Run—*stream* WV-2
Castle Run Ch—*church* VA-3
*Castles, The* SD-7
Castles, The—*pillar* CA-9
Castles, The—*pillar* (2) CO-8
Castles, The—*range* SD-7
Castle Sch—*school* CA-9
Castle Sch—*school* KY-4
Castle Sch—*school* NY-2
Castle Sch—*school* PA-2
Castles Chapel—*church* MS-4
*Castle School* IN-6
**Castle Shannon**—*pop pl* PA-2
Castle Shannon Borough—*civil* PA-2
Castle Siding—*locale* VA-3
Castle Slough—*stream* OR-9
Castle Spring—*spring* AZ-5
Castle Spring—*spring* NV-8
Castle Spring—*spring* OR-9
Castle Spring—*spring* VA-3
Castle Spring—*spring* (2) WA-9
Castle Station—*hist pl* MI-6
Castle Stevens—*locale* NJ-2
Castle Street Row—*hist pl* MA-1
**Castle Subdivision**—*pop pl* UT-8
Castle Tank—*reservoir* AZ-5
*Castle Temple* AZ-5
*Castle Terrace* OH-6
Castleton—*locale* VA-3
**Castleton**—*pop pl* IL-6
**Castleton**—*pop pl* IN-6
**Castleton**—*pop pl* KS-7
**Castleton**—*pop pl* MD-2
**Castleton**—*pop pl* VI-1
**Castleton Corners**—*pop pl* NY-2
**Castleton Corners**—*pop pl* VT-1
Castleton Ditch—*canal* CO-8
**Castleton Gardens (subdivision)**—*pop pl* NC-3
**Castleton (historical)**—*pop pl* SD-7
Castleton Medical College Bldg—*hist pl* VT-1
Castleton Mtn—*summit* VA-3
**Castleton-On-Hudson**—*pop pl* NY-2
*Castleton on Hudson (RR name Castleton-on-Hudson)* NY-2
**Castleton-on-Hudson (RR name Castleton on Hudson)**—*pop pl* NY-2
Castleton Plaza—*locale* IN-6
Castleton River—*stream* VT-1
Castleton (Site)—*locale* UT-8
Castleton Square Shop Ctr—*locale* IN-6
Castleton State Coll—*school* VT-1
**Castleton (Town of)**—*pop pl* VT-1
**Castleton Township**—*pop pl* KS-7
**Castleton (Township of)**—*pop pl* MI-6
Castleton Village Hist Dist—*hist pl* VT-1
Castle Tower—*locale* ME-1
Castle Tower Apartments—*hist pl* IL-6
Castle Town—*locale* MT-8
**Castle Township**—*pop pl* KS-7
Castle Trail—*trail* HI-9
Castlevale Sch—*school* WA-9
*Castle Valley* UT-8
Castle Valley—*locale* PA-2
**Castle Valley**—*pop pl* UT-8
Castle Valley—*valley* CA-9
Castle Valley—*valley* (4) UT-8
Castle Valley Ridge—*ridge* UT-8
Castle View Cem—*cemetery* PA-2
Castleview Hosp—*hospital* UT-8
Castleview Hospital Heliport—*airport* UT-8
Castleview Independent Baptist Ch—*church* IN-6
Castle View Ranch—*locale* CO-8
Castle View Sch—*school* CA-9
Castle View Spring—*spring* OR-9
**Castle Village**—*pop pl* LA-4
Castleville (historical)—*locale* IA-7
Castleville (historical P.O.)—*locale* IA-7
*Castle Wash* UT-8
Castle Wash—*valley* UT-8
*Castle William* MA-1
Castle William Light—*locale* NY-2
Castle Williams—*hist pl* NY-2
Castlewood—*CDP* CO-8
Castlewood—*hist pl* VA-3
**Castlewood**—*pop pl* CA-9
**Castlewood**—*pop pl* LA-4
**Castlewood**—*pop pl* MO-7
**Castlewood**—*pop pl* PA-2
**Castlewood**—*pop pl* SD-7
**Castlewood**—*pop pl* VA-3
Castlewood—*uninc pl* KY-4
Castlewood Camp—*locale* KY-4
Castlewood Country Club—*other* CA-9
Castlewood Country Club—*other* MN-6
Castlewood Grange—*locale* CO-8
Castlewood Industrial Park—*locale* DE-2
*Castlewood Island* NH-1
Castlewood (Magisterial District)—*fmr MCD* VA-3
Castlewood Park—*park* KY-4
Castlewoods Baptist Ch—*church* MS-4
Castlewood Sch—*school* NY-2
Castlewoods Country Club—*locale* MS-4
**Castlewoods (subdivision)**—*pop pl* MS-4
**Castlewood Township**—*pop pl* SD-7
Castlewood Township (historical)—*civil* SD-7
*Castleys Bayou* MS-4
*Castlman's River* PA-2
Castner, Mount—*summit* AK-9
*Castner Coulee* MT-8
Castner Coulee—*valley* MT-8
Castner Creek—*stream* AK-9
Castner Draw—*valley* NM-5
Castner Falls—*falls* MT-8
Castner Falls—*locale* MT-8
Castner Falls Cem—*cemetery* MT-8
Castner Glacier—*glacier* AK-9
Castner Range—*range* TX-5
Castner Range Archeol District—*hist pl* TX-5
Castner Sch—*school* ME-1
Castners Coulee—*valley* MT-8
Castner Tanks—*reservoir* NM-5
Cast Net Bayou—*gut* TX-5
Casto—*locale* ID-8
Casto, Santa Anna, House—*hist pl* UT-8
Casto Bluff—*cliff* UT-8
Casto Canyon—*valley* UT-8
Casto Cem—*cemetery* (3) WV-2
Casto Creek—*stream* CO-8
Casto Creek—*stream* ID-8
Casto Creek—*stream* MO-7
*Castoe Canyon* UT-8
Castoff Slough—*stream* LA-4
**Casto Gardens Subdivision**—*pop pl* UT-8
Castolon—*locale* TX-5
Castolon Hist Dist—*hist pl* TX-5
Caston—*locale* OK-5
Caston Cem—*cemetery* MS-4
Caston Creek—*stream* MS-4
Caston Creek—*stream* OK-5
Caston Elem Sch—*school* IN-6
Castonia Farm—*locale* ME-1
Caston Junior-Senior HS—*school* IN-6
**Casto Pines Condominium**—*pop pl* UT-8
Castor—*locale* MO-7
Castor—*locale* TX-5
**Castor**—*pop pl* LA-4
Castor—*uninc pl* PA-2
Castor, Bayou—*stream* (3) LA-4
Castor, Mount—*summit* MA-1
Castor Bayou—*stream* AR-4
Castor Brook—*stream* NY-2
Castor Cem—*cemetery* (2) OH-6
Castor Ch—*church* (2) LA-4
Castor Corners—*locale* NY-2
*Castor Creek* LA-4
*Castor Creek* MO-7
Castor Creek—*stream* CO-8
Castor Creek—*stream* (4) LA-4
Castor Creek—*stream* OR-9
Castor Gulch—*valley* CO-8
Castor Hill—*summit* NY-2
**Castoria**—*pop pl* NC-3
Castoria (historical P.O.)—*locale* AL-4
Castoria Post Office (historical)—*building* TN-4
Castor Lake—*lake* KY-4
Castor Lake—*lake* OK-5
Castor Lake—*lake* OR-9
Castor Lake—*lake* WA-9
Castor Lake—*reservoir* LA-4
Castor Lake—*swamp* LA-4
**Castorland**—*pop pl* NY-2
Castor Peak—*summit* WY-8
**Castor Plunge**—*pop pl* LA-4
Castor Pond—*lake* NY-2
Castor River—*stream* MO-7
Castor River Diversion Channel—*channel* MO-7
Castor River State For—*forest* MO-7
Castor Sch (historical)—*school* MO-7
Castor Spring Ch—*church* LA-4
Castor State Wildlife Mngmt Areas—*park* MN-6
Casto Rsvr—*reservoir* CO-8
Castor Temple—*summit* AZ-5
Castor Township—*civil* MO-7
**Castor Township**—*pop pl* MO-7
*Castorville* OR-9
Castor Windmill—*locale* TX-5
Casto Spring—*spring* UT-8
Casto Springs—*spring* UT-8
Casto Valley—*valley* MO-7
Casto Valley Creek—*stream* MO-7
Casto Wash—*valley* UT-8
Castro, Jose, House—*hist pl* CA-9
Castro, Jose Joaquin, Adobe—*hist pl* CA-9
*Castro Canyon* UT-8
Castro Canyon—*valley* (5) CA-9
Castro Canyon—*valley* CO-8
**Castro City**—*pop pl* CA-9
**Castro (County)**—*pop pl* TX-5
*Castro Creek* TX-5
Castro Creek—*stream* CA-9
Castro Creek—*stream* ID-8
Castro Draw—*valley* CO-8
Castro Gulch—*valley* UT-8
**Castro Heoghts Subdivision**—*pop pl* UT-8
Castro Lane Sch—*school* CA-9
Castro Memorial Gardens—*cemetery* TX-5
Castro Mine—*mine* CA-9
Castro Peak—*summit* CA-9
Castro Point—*cape* CA-9
Castro Ranch—*locale* CA-9
Castro Ranch—*locale* ID-8
Castro Ridge—*ridge* OR-9
Castro Rocks—*bar* CA-9
Castro Run—*stream* OH-6
Castro Sch—*school* (3) CA-9
Castro Spring—*spring* CA-9
Castro Spring—*spring* OR-9
Castro Table—*summit* ID-8
**Castro Valley**—*pop pl* CA-9
Castro Valley—*valley* CA-9
**Castroville**—*pop pl* CA-9
**Castroville**—*pop pl* TX-5
Castroville Air Force Auxiliary Field—*military* TX-5
Castroville (CCD)—*cens area* CA-9
Castroville Hist Dist—*hist pl* TX-5
Castroville-La Coste (CCD)—*cens area* TX-5
Castroville Moss Landing Cem—*cemetery* CA-9
Cast Steel Run—*stream* VA-3
Castteman Cave—*cave* MO-7
**Casty**—*pop pl* CA-9
Casual Branch—*stream* SC-3
Casual Swamp—*swamp* MA-1
Casualty Hosp—*hospital* DC-2
Casuela Tank—*reservoir* TX-5
Casulon Plantation—*hist pl* GA-3
Casuse Mtn—*summit* CA-9
**Casville**—*pop pl* NC-3
Caswell—*locale* AK-9
Caswell—*locale* CA-9
Caswell—*locale* NC-3
**Caswell**—*pop pl* AL-4
**Caswell**—*pop pl* TN-4
Caswell, Daniel H. and William T., Houses—*hist pl* TX-5
Caswell Air Force Station—*other* ME-1
Caswell Airpark—*airport* NC-3
Caswell Basin—*bay* NC-3
Caswell Beach—*beach* NC-3
**Caswell Beach**—*pop pl* NC-3
Caswell Branch—*stream* NC-3
Caswell Brook—*stream* MA-1
**Caswell (Caswell Center)**—*pop pl* NC-3
Caswell Cem—*cemetery* KY-4
Caswell Cem—*cemetery* MA-1
Caswell Cem—*cemetery* MI-6
Caswell Cem—*cemetery* NH-1
Caswell Coulee—*valley* MT-8
*Caswell County* TN-4
Caswell County—*civil* NC-3
Caswell County Courthouse—*hist pl* NC-3
Caswell Creek—*stream* AK-9
Caswell Game Land—*park* NC-3
Caswell (historical)—*locale* MS-4
Caswell Hollow—*valley* WI-6
Caswell House—*hist pl* MI-6
Caswell House—*hist pl* TX-5
Caswell Lake—*lake* AK-9
Caswell Lake—*lake* MS-4
Caswell Lake—*lake* NY-2
Caswell Landing—*locale* NC-3
Caswell Memorial State Park—*park* CA-9
Caswell Mtn—*summit* (2) ME-1
Caswell-Newse State Historic Site—*park* NC-3
Caswell Park—*park* TN-4
Caswell Park—*park* TX-5
Caswell Plantation—*locale* ME-1
Caswell (Plantation of)—*civ div* ME-1
Caswell Pond—*lake* (2) NH-1
Caswell Post Office (historical)—*building* MS-4
Caswell Rock—*rock* MA-1
*Caswells* TN-4
Caswell Sch—*school* CA-9
Caswell Sch—*school* MA-1
Caswell Sch—*school* MS-4
Caswell Springs—*spring* MS-4
Caswell Springs Cem—*cemetery* MS-4
Caswell Springs Ch—*church* MS-4
*Caswell Springs Methodist Ch* MS-4
Cuswells Station Post Office (historical)—*building* TN-4
**Caswell (Town of)**—*pop pl* WI-6
Caswell (Township of)—*fmr MCD* AR-4
Caswell (Township of)—*fmr MCD* NC-3
Caswell Wildlife Mgmt Area Pond One—*reservoir* NC-3
Caswell Wildlife Mgmt Area Pond Two—*reservoir* NC-3
Caswell Wildlife Mgmt Pond Dam Number Two—*dam* NC-3
Caswell Wildlife Mngmt Pond Dam Number One—*dam* NC-3
*Cataama Island* MA-1
*Catabagan Brook* MA-1
*Catacoonamuc Brook* MA-1
Catacoonamug Brook—*stream* MA-1
*Catacoonamug Pond* MA-1
Catacula—*civil* CA-9
*Catacunamuc Brook* MA-1
*Catacunemug Brook* MA-1
*Catacunnemug Brook* MA-1
**Catahoula**—*pop pl* LA-4
**Catahoula**—*pop pl* MS-4
Catahoula, Bayou—*gut* LA-4
Catahoula Bay—*bay* LA-4
Catahoula Ch—*church* LA-4
Catahoula Ch—*church* MS-4
Catahoula Coulee—*stream* LA-4
**Catahoula Cove**—*pop pl* LA-4
Catahoula Creek—*stream* MS-4
Catahoula Lake—*lake* (2) LA-4
Catahoula Lake Diversion Canal—*canal* LA-4
Catahoula Lake Oil Field—*oilfield* LA-4
Catahoula Lookout Tower—*locale* LA-4
Catahoula Natl Wildlife Ref—*park* LA-4
**Catahoula Parish**—*pop pl* LA-4
Catahoula Parish Courthouse—*hist pl* LA-4
Catahoula Post Office (historical)—*building* MS-4
Catahoula Sch (historical)—*school* MS-4
**Cataldo**—*pop pl* (2) ID-8
Cataldo Gulch—*valley* ID-8
Cataldo Mission—*church* ID-8
Cataldo Mission—*hist pl* ID-8
Cataldo Mtn—*summit* ID-8
Catale—*locale* OK-5
Catale Oil Field—*oilfield* OK-5
**Catalina**—*pop pl* AZ-5
**Catalina**—*pop pl* PR-3
Catalina—*uninc pl* CA-9
Catalina, Lake—*lake* (2) FL-3
Catalina Camp—*locale* AZ-5
*Catalina Channel* CA-9
Catalina de Jesus Hijeulas Grant—*civil* FL-3
Catalina Elem Sch—*school* FL-3
**Catalina Estates (subdivision)**—*pop pl* UT-8
**Catalina Foothills**—*pop pl* AZ-5
Catalina Foothills Sch—*school* AZ-5
**Catalina Gardens**—*pop pl* DE-2
Catalina Harbor—*bay* CA-9
Catalina Head—*summit* CA-9
Catalina HS—*school* AZ-5
*Catalina Island* CA-9
Catalina Island—*island* AK-9
Catalina Island East End Light—*locale* CA-9
Catalina Island West End Light—*locale* CA-9
Catalina JHS—*school* AZ-5
Catalina Park—*park* AZ-5
Catalina Park—*park* TX-5
Catalina Point—*cape* AL-4
Catalina Point—*cape* GU-9
Catalina Ravine—*valley* AZ-5
Catalina Sch—*school* AZ-5
**Catalina (subdivision)**—*pop pl* PA-2
Catalina Tank—*reservoir* AZ-5
Catalina Village (trailer park)—*locale* AZ-5
**Catalina Village (trailer park)**—*pop pl* AZ-5
Catalina Wash—*stream* AZ-5
Catalina Well—*well* AZ-5
Cataline Cem—*cemetery* TX-5
*Cataloochee* NC-3
*Cataloochee Bald* NC-3
Cataloochee Balsam—*summit* NC-3
*Cataloochee Creek* NC-3
Cataloochee Creek—*stream* NC-3
Cataloochee Divide—*ridge* NC-3
*Cataloochee Mountain* NC-3
Cataloochee Ranger Station—*locale* NC-3
Cataloochee (Township of)—*fmr MCD* NC-3
*Catalow Valley* OR-9
Catalpa—*hist pl* IA-7
Catalpa—*hist pl* LA-4
Catalpa—*locale* NE-7
Catalpa—*locale* TN-4
Catalpa—*locale* VA-3
**Catalpa**—*pop pl* AL-4
**Catalpa**—*pop pl* AR-4
Catalpa, Lake—*reservoir* PA-2
Catalpa Bayou—*stream* AR-4
Catalpa (Big Sandy Station)—*locale* KY-4
Catalpa Canyon—*valley* NM-5
Catalpa Cem—*cemetery* AL-4
*Catalpa Church* AL-4
Catalpa Creek—*stream* AR-4
Catalpa Creek—*stream* MS-4
Catalpa Farm—*hist pl* MD-2
Catalpa Grove Ch—*church* TN-4
*Catalpa Grove Ch of Christ* TN-4
Catalpa Lake—*lake* OR-9
Catalpa (Magisterial District)—*fmr MCD* VA-3
*Catalpa Park* OH-6
Catalpa Park—*park* CO-8
Catalpa Park—*park* OH-6
Catalpa Plantation—*locale* LA-4
*Catalpa Station* KY-4
*Catalpo* AL-4
*Cataluche Creek* NC-3
*Cataluchee Creek* NC-3
Catamint Brook—*stream* RI-1
Catamint Hill—*summit* RI-1
*Catamont Hills* MA-1
Catamount—*summit* NY-2
Catamount Brook—*stream* ME-1
Catamount Brook—*stream* (2) NH-1
Catamount Brook—*stream* VT-1
Catamount Canyon—*valley* UT-8
Catamount Cobble—*ridge* VT-1
*Catamount Creek* KS-7
Catamount Creek—*stream* CO-8
Catamount Creek—*stream* KS-7
Catamount Creek—*stream* MT-8
Catamount Creek—*stream* VA-3
*Catamount Hill* MA-1
Catamount Hill—*summit* CT-1
Catamount Hill—*summit* NH-1
Catamount Hill—*summit* (2) NY-2
Catamount Hills—*range* MA-1
Catamount Island—*island* NY-2
Catamount Knoll—*summit* NY-2
Catamount Mtn—*summit* NH-1
Catamount Mtn—*summit* (5) NY-2
Catamount Peak—*summit* NY-2
Catamount Pond—*lake* NH-1
Catamount Pond—*lake* (2) NY-2
Catamount Ridge—*ridge* NH-1
Catamount Ski Area—*locale* MA-1
Catamount State For—*forest* MA-1
Catamount Swamp—*swamp* MA-1
Catamount Trail—*trail* NH-1
*Catamout Canyon* UT-8
Cat and Kittens Rock—*island* OR-9
Catanes Tank—*reservoir* TX-5
Catanes Windmill—*locale* TX-5
Cataney Airp—*airport* PA-2
**Catan Maga**—*pop pl* GU-9
Catano—*CDP* PR-3
**Catano**—*pop pl* (2) PR-3
Catano (Barrio)—*fmr MCD* PR-3
Catano (Municipio)—*civil* PR-3
Catano (Pueblo)—*fmr MCD* PR-3
Cataouatche, Lake—*lake* LA-4
Cataract—*locale* PA-2
**Cataract**—*pop pl* IN-6
**Cataract**—*pop pl* WI-6
Cataract Basin—*basin* CO-8
Cataract Basin—*basin* (2) MT-8
Cataract Basin—*basin* UT-8
Cataract Basin—*lake* MI-6
Cataract Bight—*bay* AK-9

Cataract Branch—*stream* MS-4
Cataract Branch—*stream* TN-4
Cataract Brook—*stream* NY-2
*Cataract Canon* UT-8
*Cataract Canyon* AZ-5
Cataract Canyon—*valley* (2) AZ-5
Cataract Canyon—*valley* (3) UT-8
Cataract Cove—*bay* (2) AK-9
*Cataract Creek* AZ-5
Cataract Creek—*stream* AZ-5
Cataract Creek—*stream* AR-4
Cataract Creek—*stream* (2) CA-9
Cataract Creek—*stream* (6) CO-8
Cataract Creek—*stream* (3) ID-8
Cataract Creek—*stream* (7) MT-8
Cataract Creek—*stream* OR-9
Cataract Creek—*stream* TX-5
Cataract Creek—*stream* UT-8
Cataract Creek—*stream* (2) WA-9
Cataract Creek Trail—*trail* MT-8
Cataract Ditch—*canal* CO-8
Cataract Engine Company No. 3—*hist pl* MA-1
Cataract Falls—*falls* MT-8
Cataract Falls—*falls* WA-9
Cataract Glacier—*glacier* AK-9
Cataract Gorge—*valley* UT-8
Cataract Gulch—*valley* CA-9
Cataract Gulch—*valley* (2) CO-8
Cataract Gulch—*valley* MT-8
Cataract Hill—*summit* MO-7
Cataract Lake—*lake* AZ-5
Cataract Lake—*lake* CO-8
Cataract Lake—*lake* MN-6
Cataract Lake—*lake* MT-8
*Cataract Lake Campground* AZ-5
Cataract Lake Recreation Site—*park* AZ-5
Cataract Landing—*locale* MO-7
Cataract Lookout Tower—*locale* WI-6
Cataract Meadows—*flat* MT-8
Cataract Mtn—*summit* MT-8
Cataract Peak—*summit* ID-8
Cataract Peak—*summit* MT-8
Cataract Pumping Station—*locale* AZ-5
Cataract River—*stream* MI-6
Cataracts, The—*falls* ME-1
Cataract Sch (historical)—*school* PA-2
Cataract Spring—*spring* NV-8
Cataract Tank—*reservoir* (2) AZ-5
Cataract Wash—*stream* NV-8
Cataract Well—*well* AZ-5
Catarata Coca—*falls* PR-3
**Catarina**—*pop pl* TX-5
Catarina Creek—*stream* TX-5
Catarina Lake—*reservoir* TX-5
**Catarrh**—*pop pl* SC-3
*Catasaqua* PA-2
**Catasauqua**—*pop pl* PA-2
Catasauqua Borough—*civil* PA-2
Catasauqua Creek—*stream* PA-2
Catasauqua HS—*school* PA-2
Catasauqua Lake—*lake* PA-2
Catasauqua Residential Hist Dist—*hist pl* PA-2
**Catasauqua (sta.)**—*pop pl* PA-2
Cataska—*locale* TN-4
Cataska Mtn—*summit* TN-4
Cataska Sch (historical)—*school* TN-4
*Catasocque* PA-2
Catatoga, Lake—*reservoir* IL-6
**Catatoga Estates (subdivision)**—*pop pl* AL-4
**Catatonk**—*pop pl* NY-2
Catatonk Creek—*stream* NY-2
**Cataula**—*pop pl* GA-3
Cataula Sch—*school* GA-3
**Cataumet**—*pop pl* MA-1
Cataumet Cem—*cemetery* MA-1
*Cataumet Harbor* MA-1
*Cataumet Harbour* MA-1
Cataumet Methodist Ch—*church* MA-1
*Cataumet Neck* MA-1
Cataumet Pier—*locale* MA-1
Cataumet Rock—*rock* MA-1
**Cataumet Station**—*pop pl* MA-1
*Cataumet Village* MA-1
*Cataumut Harbor* MA-1
Catawaba Nuclear Power Plant—*facility* SC-3
*Catawba* AL-4
*Catawba* FL-3
Catawba—*locale* FL-3
Catawba—*locale* KY-4
Catawba—*locale* NJ-2
Catawba—*locale* VA-3
**Catawba**—*pop pl* MO-7
**Catawba**—*pop pl* NY-2
**Catawba**—*pop pl* NC-3
**Catawba**—*pop pl* (2) OH-6
**Catawba**—*pop pl* SC-3
**Catawba**—*pop pl* VA-3
**Catawba**—*pop pl* WV-2
**Catawba**—*pop pl* WI-6
Catawba Camp—*locale* SC-3
Catawba Cem—*cemetery* VA-3
Catawba Cem—*cemetery* WI-6
Catawba Ch—*church* NC-3
Catawba Ch—*church* (3) SC-3
Catawba Ch—*church* VA-3
Catawba Coll—*school* NC-3
**Catawba Colony (subdivision)**—*pop pl* NC-3
Catawba Country Club—*locale* NC-3
**Catawba County**—*pop pl* NC-3
Catawba County Courthouse—*hist pl* NC-3
Catawba Creek—*stream* NC-3
Catawba Creek—*stream* SC-3
Catawba Creek—*stream* (2) VA-3
*Catawba Dam* NC-3
*Catawba Dam* SC-3
**Catawba Heights**—*pop pl* NC-3
Catawba Heights Sch—*school* NC-3
**Catawba Heights (subdivision)**—*pop pl* NC-3
Catawba Hist Dist—*hist pl* NC-3
**Catawba (historical)**—*pop pl* NC-3
Catawba Ind Res—*reserve* SC-3
Catawba Island—*island* OH-6
**Catawba Island**—*pop pl* OH-6
Catawba Island Cem—*cemetery* OH-6
Catawba Island State Park—*park* OH-6
Catawba Island (Township of)—*civ div* OH-6
Catawba Island Wine Company—*hist pl* OH-6
**Catawba Junction**—*pop pl* SC-3
**Catawba Junction**—*pop pl* WV-2
*Catawba Lake* NC-3
*Catawba Lake* SC-3
Catawba Lake—*reservoir* NC-3
Catawba (Magisterial District)—*fmr MCD* VA-3
Catawba Mall—*locale* NC-3
Catawba Memorial Hosp—*hospital* NC-3
Catawba Memorial Park—*cemetery* NC-3
Catawba Mtn—*summit* VA-3
*Catawba Reservoir* NC-3
*Catawba Reservoir* SC-3
*Catawba River* NC-3
Catawba River—*stream* NC-3
Catawba River—*stream* SC-3
Catawba River Ch—*church* NC-3
Catawba River Dam—*dam* NC-3
Catawba Rosenwald Sch—*school* NC-3
Catawba Sch (abandoned)—*school* MO-7
Catawba Springs—*spring* NC-3
Catawba Springs Cem—*cemetery* AL-4
Catawba Springs Ch—*church* AL-4
Catawba Springs Ch—*church* NC-3
Catawba Springs (Township of)—*fmr MCD* NC-3
**Catawba Station**—*pop pl* OH-6
**Catawba (Town of)**—*pop pl* WI-6
Catawba (Township of)—*fmr MCD* NC-3
Catawba Valley Ch—*church* NC-3
Catawba Valley Ch—*church* VA-3
Catawba Valley Technical Institute—*school* NC-3
*Catawba View* NC-3
Catawba Village Shop Ctr—*locale* NC-3
*Catawbaw River, The* NC-3
**Catawissa**—*pop pl* MO-7
**Catawissa**—*pop pl* PA-2
Catawissa Borough—*civil* PA-2
Catawissa Creek—*stream* PA-2
Catawissa Friends Meetinghouse—*hist pl* PA-2
Catawissa Hollow—*valley* MO-7
**Catawissa Junction**—*pop pl* PA-2
Catawissa Mtn—*summit* PA-2
Catawissa Sch—*school* MO-7
**Catawissa (Township of)**—*pop pl* PA-2
*Cataymuck* MA-1
Catback Mtn—*summit* VA-3
Cat Bay—*bay* LA-4
Cat Bay—*bay* MT-8
Cat Bay—*swamp* SC-3
Cat Bayou—*gut* TX-5
Catbird—*locale* OH-6
Catbird Creek—*stream* MD-2
Catbird Creek—*stream* TN-4
*Cat Bow Brook* VT-1
Catbow Brook—*stream* VT-1
Cat Branch—*stream* AL-4
Cat Branch—*stream* AR-4
Cat Branch—*stream* (2) FL-3
Cat Branch—*stream* GA-3
Cat Branch—*stream* KY-4
Cat Branch—*stream* LA-4
Cat Branch—*stream* MS-4
Cat Branch—*stream* MO-7
Cat Branch—*stream* TN-4
Cat Branch—*stream* (3) TX-5
Cat Branch—*stream* VA-3
Cat Butte—*summit* OR-9
Catca Creek—*stream* LA-4
Cat Camp—*locale* CA-9
*Cat Canyon* NV-8
Cat Canyon—*valley* AZ-5
Cat Canyon—*valley* (5) CA-9
Cat Canyon—*valley* (3) CO-8
Cat Canyon—*valley* OK-5
Cat Canyon—*valley* (2) OR-9
Cat Canyon—*valley* TX-5
Cat Canyon—*valley* (8) UT-8
*Cat Canyon Oil Field* CA-9
Cat Canyon Rsvr—*reservoir* UT-8
Cat Canyon Spring—*spring* OR-9
Cat Cave—*cave* AL-4
Cat Cave—*cave* TN-4
**Catchall**—*pop pl* SC-3
Catchall Creek—*stream* ID-8
Catchall Creek—*stream* NC-3
Catchall Spann Sch—*school* SC-3
*Catchatu Lake* OR-9
Catch Basin—*well* AZ-5
*Catch Brook* CT-1
Catched Two Lake—*lake* OR-9
Catch-em-all, Lake—*lake* MS-4
Catchem Creek—*stream* MT-8
Catchem Creek Trail—*trail* MT-8
**Catcher**—*pop pl* AR-4
*Catching Cemetery* MS-4
Catching Creek—*stream* (3) OR-9
Catching Creek Cem—*cemetery* OR-9
Catching Rsvr—*reservoir* OR-9
Catchings—*other* MS-4
Catchings Cem—*cemetery* MS-4
Catching Slough—*stream* OR-9
*Catchings Post Office* TN-4
Catchings Post Office (historical)—*building* MS-4
**Catchpenny**—*pop pl* MD-2
*Catchpenny Corner* MD-2
Catchpole Creek—*stream* CO-8
*Catch Too Lake* OR-9
Catchup Creek—*stream* WA-9
Catclaw Canyon—*valley* NM-5
Catclaw Canyon—*valley* TX-5
Catclaw Canyon—*valley* UT-8
Catclaw Cem—*cemetery* TX-5
Catclaw Cove—*bay* NV-8
Cat Claw Creek—*stream* TX-5
Catclaw Draw—*valley* (3) NM-5
Cat Claw Draw—*valley* NM-5
Catclaw Draw—*valley* NM-5
*Cat Claw Flat* CA-9
Catclaw Flat—*flat* CA-9
Catclaw Hollow—*valley* TX-5
Catclaws Lake—*reservoir* MO-7
Cat Claw Spring—*spring* AZ-5
Catclaw Spring—*spring* TX-5
Catclaw Tank—*reservoir* AZ-5
Cat Claw Tank—*reservoir* NM-5
Catclaw Tank—*reservoir* (2) TX-5
Catclaw Wash—*stream* NV-8
Catclaw Windmill—*locale* TX-5
Cat Claw Windmill—*locale* TX-5
**Cat Corner**—*pop pl* TN-4
*Cat Corner Church* TN-4
Cat Coulee Dam—*dam* ND-7
Cat Cove—*bay* ME-1
Cat Cove—*bay* MD-2
Cat Cove—*cove* MA-1
Cat Cove—*valley* TN-4
*Cat Creek* IL-6
*Cat Creek* KS-7
*Cat Creek* MO-7
**Cat Creek**—*pop pl* MT-8
Cat Creek—*stream* (2) AL-4
Cat Creek—*stream* AK-9
Cat Creek—*stream* AZ-5
Cat Creek—*stream* (2) AR-4
Cat Creek—*stream* (2) CA-9
Cat Creek—*stream* (5) CO-8
Cat Creek—*stream* (3) FL-3
Cat Creek—*stream* (6) GA-3
Cat Creek—*stream* (10) ID-8
Cat Creek—*stream* IN-6
Cat Creek—*stream* (2) KS-7
Cat Creek—*stream* (2) KY-4
Cat Creek—*stream* MD-2
Cat Creek—*stream* MI-6
Cat Creek—*stream* (2) MN-6
Cat Creek—*stream* MO-7
Cat Creek—*stream* (9) MT-8
Cat Creek—*stream* NE-7
Cat Creek—*stream* (2) NV-8
Cat Creek—*stream* NC-3
Cat Creek—*stream* OH-6
Cat Creek—*stream* (10) OK-5
Cat Creek—*stream* (6) OR-9
Cat Creek—*stream* (3) TN-4
Cat Creek—*stream* (12) TX-5
Cat Creek—*stream* VA-3
Cat Creek—*stream* (3) WA-9
Cat Creek—*stream* WI-6
Cat Creek—*stream* WY-8
Cat Creek Campground—*locale* WA-9
Cat Creek Ch—*church* GA-3
Cat Creek Ch—*church* KY-4
Cat Creek Crossing—*locale* ID-8
Cat Creek Gap—*gap* CO-8
Cat Creek Guard Station—*locale* WA-9
Cat Creek Park—*flat* CO-8
Cat Creek Ranch—*locale* OR-9
Cat Creek Ridge—*ridge* CA-9
Cat Creek Sch—*school* MT-8
Cat Creek Sch—*school* NE-7
Cat Creek Summit—*summit* ID-8
Cat Creek Well—*well* ID-8
Cat Creek Well—*well* WY-8
*Catcunnemug Brook* MA-1
*Cat Dam* MA-1
Cat Den Bay—*swamp* NY-2
Cat Den Branch—*stream* AL-4
Cat Den Mtn—*summit* NH-1
Catden Swamp—*swamp* CT-1
Cat Draw—*valley* (3) NM-5
*Cate* AR-4
Cate, Elijah, House—*hist pl* TN-4
Cate Branch—*stream* VA-3
Cate Brook—*stream* NH-1
Cate Cem—*cemetery* (4) TN-4
Cate Cem—*cemetery* VT-1
Catechetical Center—*school* CA-9
*Catecunemaug Brook* MA-1
Catedral del Pueblo—*church* FL-3
Catedral Evangelica Reformada—*hist pl* NJ-2
**Cateechee**—*pop pl* SC-3
*Catehank Island* MA-1
Cate Hill—*summit* VT-1
Cate House—*hist pl* ME-1
Cate Island—*island* NH-1
Cat Elbow Corner—*locale* NY-2
*Catenberg Canyon* CA-9
Caten Shoals Creek—*stream* AL-4
Cater Branch—*stream* SC-3
Cater Branch—*stream* TN-4
Cater Cem—*cemetery* MO-7
*Cater Creek* GA-3
Cater Creek—*stream* GA-3
Caterpillar, The—*cliff* UT-8
*Caterpillar Arch* UT-8
Caterpillar Butte—*summit* WY-8
Caterpillar Butte Rsvr—*reservoir* OR-9
Caterpillar Draw—*valley* WY-8
Caterpillar Island—*island* WA-9
Caterpillar Lake—*reservoir* TX-5
Caterpillar Mtn—*summit* ME-1
*Caterpillar Proving Grounds* AZ-5
Caterpillar Tank—*reservoir* (2) AZ-5
Caterpillar Tractor Company—*facility* IA-7
Caterpillar Tractor Company (Aurora Plant)—*facility* IL-6
Caterpillar Tractor Company (Joliet Plant)—*facility* IL-6
Caterpillar Tractor Company (Mapleton Plant)—*facility* IL-6
Caterpillar Tractor Company (Morton Plant)—*facility* IL-6
Caterpillar Tractor Company (Mossville Plant)—*facility* IL-6
Cater Sch—*school* TX-5
*Caterskill Clove* NY-2
*Caterskill Creek* NY-2
*Caterskill Falls* NY-2
Cates—*locale* NC-3
**Cates**—*pop pl* IN-6
**Cates**—*pop pl* TN-4
Cates, John F., House—*hist pl* MS-4
Cates Airp—*airport* TN-4
Cates Bay—*basin* SC-3
Cates Bend—*bend* TN-4
Cates Branch—*stream* MO-7
Cates Branch—*stream* TN-4
Cates Bridge—*bridge* GA-3
Cates Bridge—*bridge* TN-4
Catesby—*locale* OK-5
Catesby Ch—*church* OK-5
Cates Canyon—*valley* OR-9
Cates Cem—*cemetery* GA-3
Cates Cem—*cemetery* IL-6
Cates Cem—*cemetery* IN-6
Cates Cem—*cemetery* KY-4
Cates Cem—*cemetery* ME-1
Cates Cem—*cemetery* MO-7
Cates Cem—*cemetery* TN-4
Cate Sch—*school* CA-9
Cates Creek—*stream* NC-3
Cates Creek—*stream* TN-4
Cates Draw—*valley* WY-8
Cates Hill—*summit* ME-1
Cates Hill—*summit* (2) NH-1
Cates Hill Sch—*school* NH-1
Cates (historical)—*locale* AL-4
Cates Hollow—*valley* TN-4
Cates Lake—*reservoir* GA-3
*Cates Landing* TN-4
Cates Landing—*locale* TN-4
Cates Meadows—*swamp* ME-1
*Cates Pond* NH-1
Cates Pond—*lake* MO-7
Cates Pond—*lake* TN-4
Cates Pond—*reservoir* SC-3
Cate Spring—*spring* TN-4
Cate Spring Cave—*cave* TN-4
Cates Ranch—*locale* NM-5
Cates Sch (historical)—*school* TN-4
**Cateston**—*pop pl* TN-4
Cateston Cem—*cemetery* TN-4
Cateston Post Office (historical)—*building* TN-4
*Catesville* NC-3
**Catesville**—*pop pl* AR-4
Cat Eyes Lake—*lake* MN-6
Catface Mtn—*summit* NC-3
Catface Mtn—*summit* TN-4
Catface Ridge—*ridge* TN-4
Catfarm Spring—*spring* TN-4
Catfish—*locale* NC-3
Catfish—*locale* PA-2
Catfish Bar—*bar* AL-4
Catfish Bar—*bar* WI-6
Catfish Basin—*bay* FL-3
Catfish Bay—*bay* CA-9
Catfish Bay—*bay* MT-8
Catfish Bay—*bay* NY-2
Catfish Bay—*bay* OK-5
Catfish Bay—*bay* TX-5
Catfish Bay—*bay* VT-1
Catfish Bay—*swamp* (2) SC-3
Catfish Bayou—*channel* TX-5
Catfish Bayou—*gut* LA-4
Catfish Bayou—*gut* (2) MS-4
Catfish Bayou—*stream* AL-4
Catfish Bayou—*stream* (2) LA-4
Catfish Beach—*beach* CA-9
Catfish Bend—*bend* AL-4
Catfish Bend—*bend* FL-3
Catfish Bend—*bend* IL-6
Catfish Bend—*bend* LA-4
Catfish Bend—*bend* TX-5
*Catfish Branch* DE-2
Catfish Branch—*stream* (2) FL-3
Catfish Branch—*stream* IA-7
Catfish Branch—*stream* TX-5
Catfish Bridge—*bridge* DE-2
Catfish Camp—*locale* CA-9
Catfish Canal—*canal* LA-4
Catfish Canal—*canal* SC-3
Catfish Cave—*cave* AL-4
Catfish Ch—*church* SC-3
Catfish Chute—*gut* MS-4
**Catfish Corners**—*pop pl* NY-2
Catfish Cove—*bay* KS-7
Catfish Cove—*bay* NM-5
Catfish Creek—*bay* (2) FL-3
Catfish Creek—*channel* GA-3
Catfish Creek—*stream* (4) FL-3
Catfish Creek—*stream* (2) GA-3
Catfish Creek—*stream* IL-6
Catfish Creek—*stream* IA-7
Catfish Creek—*stream* KY-4
Catfish Creek—*stream* NY-2
Catfish Creek—*stream* NC-3
Catfish Creek—*stream* OK-5
Catfish Creek—*stream* PA-2
Catfish Creek—*stream* SC-3
Catfish Creek—*stream* (2) TX-5
Catfish Creek Baptist Church—*hist pl* SC-3
Catfish Draw—*valley* TX-5
Catfish Falls—*falls* NM-5
Catfish Hatchery Ponds Dam—*dam* MS-4
Catfish Haven Dam Number One—*dam* TN-4
Catfish Haven Rsvr—*reservoir* TN-4
*Cat Fish Hole* MD-2
Catfish Hole—*bay* OR-9
Catfish Hole—*lake* TX-5
Catfish Island—*island* MO-7
Catfish Key—*island* FL-3
*Catfish Lake* WA-9
Catfish Lake—*lake* (4) CA-9
Catfish Lake—*lake* FL-3
Catfish Lake—*lake* GA-3
Catfish Lake—*lake* (2) IN-6
Catfish Lake—*lake* (3) LA-4
Catfish Lake—*lake* MS-4
Catfish Lake—*lake* NC-3
Catfish Lake—*lake* TX-5
Catfish Lake—*lake* WA-9
Catfish Lake—*lake* (2) WI-6
Catfish Lake—*reservoir* (4) AL-4
Catfish Lake—*reservoir* MS-4
Catfish Lake—*reservoir* NC-3
Catfish Lake—*reservoir* (2) TN-4
*Catfish Lake Dam* AL-4
Catfish Lake Dam—*dam* AL-4
Catfish Lake Dam—*dam* NC-3
Catfish Lake Dam—*dam* TN-4
Catfish Lake Ii—*reservoir* TN-4
Catfish Lake Ii Dam—*dam* TN-4
Catfish Lake South Wilderness—*park* NC-3
Catfish Lake Waterfowl Impoundment—*park* NC-3
Catfish Landing—*locale* LA-4
Catfish Landing—*locale* SC-3
Catfish Paradise—*locale* AZ-5
Catfish Pass—*channel* LA-4
*Catfish Point* NC-3
Catfish Point—*cape* (3) FL-3
Catfish Point—*cape* LA-4
Catfish Point—*cape* MS-4
Catfish Point—*cape* NY-2
Catfish Point—*cape* (3) NC-3
Catfish Point—*cape* OK-5
Catfish Point—*cape* WI-6
Catfish Point Landing—*locale* MS-4
Catfish Pond—*lake* CA-9
Catfish Pond—*lake* NJ-2
Catfish Pond—*lake* NY-2
Catfish Pond—*lake* NC-3
Catfish Pond—*reservoir* NJ-2
Catfish Ponds Lake Dam—*dam* MS-4
Catfish Prairie—*lake* LA-4
Catfish Ridge—*ridge* PA-2
*Catfish River* MS-4
*Catfish River* WI-6
Catfish Rock—*bar* ME-1
Catfish Rock—*pillar* NY-2
Catfish Rsvr—*reservoir* (2) CA-9
Catfish Run—*stream* (2) PA-2
Catfish Sch—*school* IL-6
Catfish Sch—*school* WI-6
Catfish Shoals—*bar* AL-4
Catfish Slough—*gut* MI-6
Catfish Slough—*gut* WI-6
Catfish Slough—*stream* FL-3
Catfish Slu—*stream* MN-6
Catfish Spring—*spring* CA-9
Catfish Swamp—*swamp* SC-3
Catfish Tank—*lake* NM-5
Catfish Tank—*reservoir* AZ-5
Catfish Tank—*reservoir* NM-5
Catfish Tank—*reservoir* (3) TX-5
Catfish Towhead—*area* MS-4
Cat Fork—*stream* (2) KY-4
Cat Gap—*gap* NC-3
Cat Gulch—*valley* (2) CO-8
Cat Gulch—*valley* ID-8
Cat Gut—*gut* NJ-2
Catgut Branch—*stream* TN-4
Cat Gut Hollow—*valley* WV-2
*Catgut Slough* WI-6
Cat Hair Creek—*stream* MS-4
Cathaline Lake—*lake* WI-6
Catham Elem Sch—*school* PA-2
Cat Hammock—*island* (2) FL-3
Cathance—*locale* ME-1
Cathance, Lake—*lake* ME-1
*Cathance River* ME-1
Cathance River—*stream* ME-1
Cathance Stream—*stream* ME-1
Cat Harbor—*bay* MI-6
Catharina Creek—*stream* CA-9
Catharinas Hope—*locale* VI-3
**Catharine**—*pop pl* IL-6
**Catharine**—*pop pl* KS-7
**Catharine**—*pop pl* NY-2
Catharine, Joseph W., Sch—*hist pl* PA-2
Catharine, Lake—*reservoir* TX-5
**Catharine (Catherine)**—*pop pl* NY-2
Catharine Creek—*stream* NY-2
Catharine Creek—*stream* NC-3
Catharine Elem Sch—*school* KS-7
**Catharine Lake**—*pop pl* NC-3
Catharine Pass—*channel* WI-6
Catharine Sch—*school* PA-2
*Catharines Crown* PA-2
Catharines Crown—*summit* PA-2
**Catharine (Town of)**—*pop pl* NY-2
Catharine Township—*civil* KS-7
**Catharine (Township of)**—*pop pl* PA-2
Catharine Valley—*valley* NY-2
Catharpin—*locale* VA-3
Catharpin Creek—*stream* VA-3
*Catharpin Run* VA-3
Catharpin Run—*stream* VA-3
*Cathay* (2) CA-9
**Cathay**—*pop pl* ND-7
Cathay Dam—*dam* ND-7
C.A. THAYER—*hist pl* CA-9
Cathay Fire Control Station—*locale* CA-9
*Cathay Mountain* CA-9
**Cathay Township**—*pop pl* ND-7
*Cathay Valley* CA-9
Cathcart—*hist pl* IN-6
Cathcart—*locale* NV-8
**Cathcart**—*pop pl* WA-9
Cathcart Cem—*cemetery* IN-6
Cathcart Cem—*cemetery* SC-3
Cathcart Creek—*stream* ID-8
Cathcart Creek—*stream* OR-9
Cathcart Flat—*flat* NV-8
Cathcart Hill—*summit* TN-4
Cathcart Hollow—*valley* MO-7
Cathcart Home—*building* PA-2
Cathcart Run—*stream* PA-2
Cathcart Springs—*spring* OR-9
Cat Head—*cape* AK-9
Cathead Bay—*bay* AK-9
Cat Head Bay—*bay* MI-6
*Cathead Creek* SD-7
Cathead Creek—*stream* GA-3
Cathead Mtn—*summit* NY-2
Cat Head Point—*cape* MI-6
Cat Head Pond—*lake* FL-3
Cat Heads—*summit* TX-5
Catheart Mtn—*summit* ME-1
Cathederal of Saint Peter and Saint Paul—*church* DC-2
*Cathedral* OR-9
Cathedral—*locale* CO-8
Cathedral—*uninc pl* MA-1
Cathedral—*uninc pl* NY-2
Cathedral, The—*church* PA-2
Cathedral, The—*summit* (2) UT-8
*Cathedral and Organ* UT-8
Cathedral Arch—*arch* UT-8
Cathedral Area Hist Dist—*hist pl* ND-7
Cathedral Baptist Ch—*church* AL-4
Cathedral Basilica of the Assumption—*hist pl* KY-4
*Cathedral Bluffs* CO-8
Cathedral Bluffs—*cliff* AK-9
Cathedral Bluffs—*cliff* CO-8
Cathedral Butte—*summit* (2) UT-8
Cathedral Camp—*park* MA-1
Cathedral Campground—*locale* CO-8
Cathedral Canyon—*valley* CA-9
Cathedral Canyon—*valley* (2) NV-8
Cathedral Canyon—*valley* UT-8
Cathedral Cave—*cave* MO-7
Cathedral Caverns—*cave* AL-4
Cathedral Caves—*cave* AZ-5
Cathedral Cem—*cemetery* DE-2
Cathedral Cem—*cemetery* MD-2
Cathedral Cem—*cemetery* PA-2
Cathedral Central HS—*school* MI-6
Cathedral Ch—*church* PA-2
Cathedral Ch—*church* TX-5
Cathedral Chapel Sch—*school* CA-9
Cathedral Ch of Saint John—*church* DE-2
Cathedral Ch of Saint Luke—*church* FL-3
Cathedral Ch of Saint Peter, The—*church* FL-3
Cathedral Church of St. Paul Complex—*hist pl* MI-6
**Cathedral City**—*pop pl* CA-9
Cathedral City-Palm Desert (CCD)—*cens area* CA-9
Cathedral Cliff—*cliff* NM-5
Cathedral Cliffs—*cliff* WY-8
Cathedral Coll—*school* NY-2
*Cathedral Cove* AZ-5
Cathedral Cove—*bay* NV-8
Cathedral Crag—*cliff* WA-9
Cathedral Creek—*stream* (5) AK-9
Cathedral Creek—*stream* (2) CA-9
Cathedral Creek—*stream* (3) CO-8
Cathedral Creek—*stream* ID-8
Cathedral Creek—*stream* MT-8
Cathedral Creek—*stream* OR-9
Cathedral Creek—*stream* WA-9
Cathedral Domes Entrance—*cave* KY-4
Cathedral Driveway—*trail* WA-9
Cathedra Ledge—*bench* NH-1
Cathedral Falls Creek—*stream* AK-9
*Cathedral Fork* CA-9
Cathedral Fork—*stream* CA-9
Cathedral Fork—*stream* WA-9
*Cathedral Fork Merced Creek* CA-9
*Cathedral Fork Merced River* CA-9
*Cathedral Fork of Merced River* CA-9
Cathedral Glen—*valley* NY-2
Cathedral Gorge—*valley* NV-8
Cathedral Gorge State Park—*park* NV-8
Cathedral Group Scenic Turnout—*locale* WY-8
Cathedral Hill Hist Dist—*hist pl* MD-2
Cathedral Hist Dist—*hist pl* IA-7
Cathedral HS—*school* CA-9
Cathedral HS—*school* CO-8
Cathedral HS—*school* IN-6
Cathedral HS—*school* MN-6
Cathedral HS—*school* MS-4
Cathedral HS—*school* NM-5
Cathedral HS—*school* TX-5
Cathedral in the Desert—*rock* UT-8
Cathedral Island—*island* AK-9
*Cathedral Lake* CA-9
*Cathedral Lake* WA-9
Cathedral Lake—*lake* (2) CA-9
Cathedral Lake—*lake* CO-8
Cathedral Lake—*lake* ID-8
Cathedral Lake—*lake* WY-8
Cathedral Lakes—*lake* CA-9
Cathedral Mother Parish Ch—*church* AL-4
Cathedral Mtn—*summit* (2) AK-9
Cathedral Mtn—*summit* (2) TX-5
Cathedral Mtn—*summit* (2) UT-8
Cathedral Nuestra Senora de Guadalupe of Ponce—*hist pl* PR-3
Cathedral Oaks Sch—*school* CA-9
Cathedral of All Saints—*hist pl* NY-2
Cathedral of Christ the King—*school* GA-3
Cathedral of Learning—*hist pl* PA-2
Cathedral of Learning—*school* PA-2
Cathedral of Our Merciful Saviour—*hist pl* MN-6
Cathedral of Our Merciful Saviour and Guild House (Boundary Increase)—*hist pl* MN-6
Cathedral of Saint Helena—*hist pl* MT-8
Cathedral of Saint John the Divine—*church* NY-2
Cathedral of Saints Peter and Paul—*hist pl* PA-2
Cathedral of Saints Peter and Paul—*hist pl* RI-1
Cathedral of St. Augustine—*hist pl* FL-3
Cathedral of St. James and Parish Hall—*hist pl* IN-6
Cathedral of St. John the Baptist—*hist pl* NJ-2
Cathedral of St. Paul—*hist pl* MA-1
Cathedral of the Assumption—*hist pl* KY-4
Cathedral of the Cross—*church* NC-3
Cathedral of the Immaculate Conception—*hist pl* CO-8
Cathedral of the Immaculate Conception—*hist pl* IN-6
Cathedral of the Immaculate Conception—*hist pl* ME-1
Cathedral of the Immaculate Conception—*hist pl* NY-2
Cathedral of the Madeleine—*church* UT-8
Cathedral of the Madeleine—*hist pl* UT-8
Cathedral of the Most Blessed Sacrament—*hist pl* MI-6
Cathedral of the Nativity of the Blessed Virgin Mary—*hist pl* NE-7
Cathedral of the Pines—*church* MS-4
Cathedral of the Pines—*locale* NH-1
Cathedral of the Sacred Heart—*church* FL-3
Cathedral of the Sacred Heart—*hist pl* NJ-2
Cathedral of the Sacred Heart—*hist pl* VA-3
Cathedral of the Scottish Rite—*church* AL-4
Cathedral Parish—*church* FL-3
*Cathedral Park* WV-2
Cathedral Park—*park* CO-8
*Cathedral Parks* CO-8
Cathedral Pass—*gap* CA-9
Cathedral Pass—*gap* WA-9
Cathedral Peak—*cliff* CA-9
Cathedral Peak—*summit* (2) AK-9
Cathedral Peak—*summit* (3) CA-9
Cathedral Peak—*summit* (2) CO-8
Cathedral Peak—*summit* ID-8
Cathedral Peak—*summit* (3) MT-8
Cathedral Peak—*summit* TX-5
Cathedral Peak—*summit* WA-9
Cathedral Peak—*summit* (3) WY-8
Cathedral Peaks—*range* NV-8
**Cathedral Pines**—*pop pl* ID-8
Cathedral Pines Assembly of God Ch—*church* FL-3
*Cathedral Point* CA-9
Cathedral Point—*cape* AK-9
Cathedral Point—*cape* MT-8
Cathedral Point—*cape* UT-8
Cathedral Preparatory HS—*school* PA-2
Cathedral Range—*ridge* CA-9

Cathedral Rapids—locale ........ AK-9
Cathedral Rapids—rapids ........ AK-9
Cathedral Rapids Creek No 1—stream ........ AK-9
Cathedral Rapids Creek No 2—stream ........ AK-9
Cathedral Ridge—ridge ........ NV-8
Cathedral Ridge—ridge ........ OR-9
Cathedral River—stream ........ AK-9
Cathedral Rock ........ AZ-5
Cathedral Rock ........ MT-8
Cathedral Rock—pillar (3) ........ AZ-5
Cathedral Rock—pillar ........ CO-8
Cathedral Rock—pillar ........ NV-8
Cathedral Rock—pillar ........ NM-5
Cathedral Rock—pillar ........ OR-9
Cathedral Rock—pillar ........ TX-5
Cathedral Rock—pillar ........ UT-8
Cathedral Rock—summit (4) ........ AZ-5
Cathedral Rock—summit ........ CO-8
Cathedral Rock—summit (2) ........ ID-8
Cathedral Rock—summit ........ WA-9
Cathedral Rock—summit ........ WY-8
Cathedral Rock Picnic Area—locale ........ NV-8
Cathedral Rocks—cliff ........ ID-8
Cathedral Rocks—island ........ AK-9
Cathedral Rocks—pillar ........ ID-8
Cathedral Rocks—summit ........ CA-9
Cathedral Rocks—summit ........ NY-2
Cathedral Rocks—summit ........ OR-9
Cathedral Rocks—summit ........ WA-9
Cathedral Rock Trail—trail ........ NV-8
Cathedral Sch—school ........ CA-9
Cathedral Sch—school ........ HI-9
Cathedral Sch—school (2) ........ IL-6
Cathedral Sch—school ........ MI-6
Cathedral Sch—school ........ MN-6
Cathedral Sch—school ........ NY-2
Cathedral Sch—school ........ ND-7
Cathedral Sch—school ........ OH-6
Cathedral Sch—school ........ OR-9
Cathedral Sch—school ........ PA-2
Cathedral Sch—school ........ TX-5
Cathedral Sch of Saint Mary—school ........ NY-2
Cathedral Spires—other ........ AK-9
Cathedral Spires—pillar ........ CA-9
Cathedral Spires—pillar ........ SD-7
Cathedral Spires—summit ........ CO-8
**Cathedral Square**—pop pl ........ IA-7
Cathedral Stairs—cliff ........ AZ-5
Cathedral State Park—park ........ WV-2
Cathedral Tank—reservoir ........ AZ-5
Cathedral Trail—trail ........ ME-1
Cathedral Tree Trail—trail ........ CA-9
Cathedral Valley ........ UT-8
Cathedral Valley—area ........ UT-8
Cathedral Valley—valley ........ AK-9
Cathedral Valley View Area—locale ........ UT-8
Cathedral Wash—arroyo ........ AZ-5
Cather, George, Farmstead—hist pl ........ NE-7
Cather, Willa, Birthplace—hist pl ........ VA-3
Cather, William, Homestead Site—hist pl ........ NE-7
Catherall Creek—stream ........ IA-7
Cather House—hist pl ........ NE-7
Catherine ........ MO-7
Catherine—locale ........ CO-8
Catherine—other ........ NY-2
**Catherine**—pop pl ........ AL-4
**Catherine**—pop pl ........ KS-7
**Catherine**—pop pl ........ KY-4
**Catherine**—pop pl ........ LA-4
**Catherine**—pop pl ........ MO-7
Catherine, Bayou—gut ........ LA-4
Catherine, Lake—lake ........ AK-9
Catherine, Lake—lake ........ CA-9
Catherine, Lake—lake (6) ........ FL-3
Catherine, Lake—lake ........ IL-6
Catherine, Lake—lake ........ MS-4
Catherine, Lake—lake ........ NC-3
Catherine, Lake—lake ........ UT-8
Catherine, Lake—reservoir ........ AR-4
Catherine, Lake—reservoir ........ MS-4
Catherine, Mount—summit ........ UT-8
Catherine, Mount—summit ........ WA-9
Catherine Acad—school ........ AL-4
Catherineberg-Jockumsdahl-Herman Farm—hist pl ........ VI-3
Catherine Branch—stream ........ TX-5
Catherine Chapel—church ........ NC-3
**Catherine Circle Subdivision**—pop pl ........ UT-8
Catherine Creek ........ OR-9
Catherine Creek—stream ........ ID-8
Catherine Creek—stream ........ IN-6
Catherine Creek—stream ........ MT-8
Catherine Creek—stream ........ NY-2
Catherine Creek—stream ........ NC-3
Catherine Creek—stream ........ OR-9
Catherine Creek—stream (3) ........ WA-9
Catherine Creek Guard Station—locale ........ OR-9
Catherine Creek Highline Canal—canal ........ OR-9
Catherine Creek Meadow—flat ........ OR-9
Catherine Creek State Park—park ........ OR-9
Catherine Furnace—hist pl ........ VA-3
Catherine Furnace—locale ........ VA-3
Catherine Island ........ MP-9
Catherine Island—island ........ AK-9
Catherine Island—island ........ FL-3
Catherine Islands ........ MP-9
Catherine Knob—summit ........ NC-3
Catherine Lake—lake ........ ID-8
Catherine Lake—lake ........ MI-6
Catherine Lake—lake (3) ........ WI-6
Catherine Lake—locale ........ NC-3
Catherine Lake—reservoir ........ TN-4
Catherine Lake Dam—dam ........ TN-4
Catherine Mine—mine ........ NV-8
Catherine Mines—mine ........ MO-7
Catherine Mtn—summit ........ ME-1
Catherine Nenny Ch—church ........ TN-4
**Catherine Place**—pop pl ........ MO-7
Catherine Sch (abandoned)—school ........ MO-7
Catherines Knob—summit ........ WV-2
Catherine Slope Mine (underground)—mine ........ AL-4
Catherine Slough—stream ........ MO-7
Catherine Spalding Coll—school ........ KY-4
**Catherine Square**—pop pl ........ NC-3
Catherine Street Fire Station—hist pl ........ FL-3
Catherine Township ........ KS-7
**Catherine Township**—pop pl ........ KS-7
Catherineville—locale ........ NY-2
Cather Lake—lake ........ WI-6
Cather Run ........ PA-2
**Cathers**—pop pl ........ OH-6
Cather Sch—school ........ IL-6
Cathers Corner—locale ........ MD-2
Cathers Draw—valley ........ WY-8
Catherson Cabin—locale ........ OR-9
Cather Springs—spring ........ CO-8
Cathers Run—stream ........ PA-2
Catherton—uninc pl ........ VA-3
Catherton Cem—cemetery ........ NE-7
Cathewood Saddle—gap ........ CA-9
Cathey Branch—stream ........ MS-4
Cathey Canyon—valley ........ NM-5
Cathey Cem—cemetery ........ MS-4
Cathey Cem—cemetery ........ NC-3
Cathey Cem—cemetery (6) ........ TN-4
Cathey Cove—valley ........ NC-3
Cathey Creek ........ AL-4
Cathey Creek—stream ........ GA-3
Cathey Creek—stream ........ MS-4
Cathey Creek—stream ........ TX-5
Cathey Gap—gap (2) ........ NC-3
Cathey Hill—summit ........ TX-5
**Cathey (historical)**—pop pl ........ NC-3
Cathey Hollow—valley ........ TN-4
Cathey Pond—lake ........ CA-9
Cathey Ridge—ridge ........ NC-3
Catheys Cem—cemetery ........ TN-4
Cathey Sch—school ........ AL-4
Cathey Sch (historical)—school ........ MS-4
Catheys Creek ........ NC-3
Catheys Creek—stream (2) ........ NC-3
Catheys Creek—stream ........ TN-4
Catheys Creek Ch—church ........ NC-3
Catheys Creek Ch—church ........ TN-4
**Catheys Creek Estates (subdivision)**—pop pl ........ NC-3
Catheys Creek Falls—falls ........ NC-3
Catheys Creek (Township of)—fmr MCD ........ NC-3
Cathey Sink—basin ........ TN-4
Catheys Mtn—summit ........ CA-9
Catheys Peak—summit ........ CA-9
Cathey Spring ........ AZ-5
**Catheys Valley**—pop pl ........ CA-9
Catheys Valley—valley ........ CA-9
**Catheys Valley (Cathay)**—pop pl ........ CA-9
Catheys Valley Cem—cemetery ........ CA-9
Catheys Valley Sch—school ........ CA-9
Cat Hill—summit ........ CA-9
Cat Hill—summit ........ DE-2
Cat Hill—summit ........ KY-4
Cat Hill—summit ........ NM-5
Cat Hill—summit (4) ........ NY-2
Cat Hill—summit ........ OR-9
Cat Hill—summit ........ RI-1
Cat Hill—summit ........ TN-4
Cat Hill—summit ........ TX-5
Cat Hill—summit ........ UT-8
Cat Hill Cem—cemetery ........ KY-4
Cat Hill Ch—church ........ KY-4
Cat Hill Marsh—swamp ........ DE-2
Cat Hills ........ DE-2
Cat Hills—summit ........ AZ-5
Cat Hills Tank—reservoir ........ AZ-5
Cat Hill Way—trail ........ OR-9
Cathis Creek—stream ........ NC-3
**Cathlamet**—pop pl ........ WA-9
Cathlamet Bay—bay ........ OR-9
Cathlamet Channel—channel ........ WA-9
Cathlamet-Elochoman (CCD)—cens area ........ WA-9
Cathland State Park—park ........ MD-2
Cathlapootle ........ WA-9
Cathledge Cem—cemetery ........ MS-4
Cathmagby Ch—church ........ AL-4
Cathmagby Sch—school ........ AL-4
Cat Hole, The—lake ........ AL-4
Cathole Branch—stream ........ WV-2
Cat Hole Creek ........ MD-2
Cathole Landing—locale ........ VA-3
Cathole Mtn—summit ........ CT-1
Cathole Spring—spring ........ MO-7
Catholic Bay—swamp ........ NC-3
Catholic Belltower—hist pl ........ FM-9
Catholic Boys HS—school ........ IL-6
Catholic Branch—stream ........ SC-3
Catholic Butte—summit ........ ID-8
Catholic Cem—cemetery ........ CA-9
Catholic Cem—cemetery ........ KS-7
Catholic Cem—cemetery (2) ........ MN-6
Catholic Cem—cemetery (2) ........ MO-7
Catholic Cem—cemetery (2) ........ NY-2
Catholic Cem—cemetery (2) ........ OR-9
Catholic Cem—cemetery (3) ........ SD-7
Catholic Cem—cemetery ........ WV-2
Catholic Cemeteries—cemetery ........ PA-2
Catholic Cemetery—hist pl ........ MS-4
Catholic Cemetery of Mobile—church ........ AL-4
Catholic Ch Blessed Trinity—church ........ FL-3
Catholic Ch Catholic Sisters Guadalupanas—church ........ FL-3
Catholic Ch Hall—church ........ FL-3
Catholic Ch of Blessed Sacrament—church ........ FL-3
Catholic Ch of the Visitation—church ........ AL-4
Catholic Ch Saint Francis Xavier—church ........ FL-3
Catholic Church and Rectory—hist pl ........ TN-4
Catholic Church of the Sacred Heart—hist pl ........ ID-8
Catholic Creek—stream ........ ID-8
Catholic Girls HS—school ........ CA-9
Catholic High School Stadium—park ........ PA-2
**Catholic Hill**—pop pl ........ SC-3
Catholic Hill—summit ........ CA-9
Catholic HS—school ........ AR-4
Catholic HS—school ........ OH-6
Catholic HS—school ........ PA-2
Catholic HS—school ........ TX-5
Catholic HS—school ........ VA-3
Catholic Knob—summit ........ KY-4
Catholic Lake—lake ........ ID-8
Catholic Mission ........ KS-7
Catholic Path—trail ........ PA-2
Catholic Peak—summit ........ AZ-5
Catholic Peak Tank—reservoir ........ AZ-5
Catholic Point—locale ........ AR-4
Catholic Point (Township of)—fmr MCD ........ AR-4
Catholic Presbyterian Church—hist pl ........ SC-3
Catholic-Protestant Chapels, Veterans Administration Center—hist pl ........ CA-9
Catholic Sisters Sch—school ........ CA-9
Catholic Univ—school ........ DC-2
Catholic University of Puerto Rico (Guayama)—facility ........ PR-3
Catholic University of Puerto Rico (Ponce)—facility ........ PR-3
Catholic-West Lawn Cemetery ........ SD-7
Cat Hollow ........ AR-4
Cat Hollow—valley (2) ........ AL-4
Cat Hollow—valley ........ KY-4
Cat Hollow—valley ........ MO-7
Cat Hollow—valley (4) ........ NY-2
Cat Hollow—valley ........ OH-6
Cat Hollow—valley (3) ........ OK-5
Cat Hollow—valley (2) ........ TN-4
Cat Hollow—valley (3) ........ TX-5
Cat Hollow—valley ........ WV-2
Cat Hollow—valley ........ WI-6
Cat House Creek—stream ........ MT-8
Cathrene Cecile Lake—lake ........ WA-9
Cathrines Rest—locale ........ VI-3
Cathrine Swamp—swamp ........ PA-2
**Cathro**—pop pl ........ MI-6
Cathy, Lake—lake ........ FL-3
Cathy Canyon ........ NM-5
Cathy Creek ........ MS-4
Cathy Draw—valley ........ WY-8
Cathy Lake—lake ........ OR-9
Cathy Ranch—locale ........ NM-5
Cathy Ridge—ridge ........ TN-4
Catilano, Bayou—gut ........ LA-4
Catino ........ IL-6
Cat Island ........ FL-3
Cat Island ........ NC-3
Cat Island ........ RI-1
Cat Island—cape ........ AR-4
Cat Island—island ........ AL-4
Cat Island—island (2) ........ AK-9
Cat Island—island ........ CT-1
Cat Island—island (2) ........ FL-3
Cat Island—island (2) ........ LA-4
Cat Island—island (2) ........ MA-1
Cat Island—island ........ MS-4
Cat Island—island (3) ........ NC-3
Cat Island—island (3) ........ SC-3
Cat Island—island ........ VA-3
Cat Island—island ........ WA-9
Cat Island—island ........ WI-6
**Cat Island**—pop pl ........ LA-4
Cat Island Arm—locale ........ AR-4
Cat Island Bend—bend ........ MS-4
Cat Island Channel—channel ........ LA-4
Cat Island Channel—channel ........ MA-1
Cat Island Channel—channel ........ MS-4
Cat Island Creek—channel ........ SC-3
Cat Island Dikes—dam ........ AR-4
Cat Island Lake—lake ........ FL-3
Cat Island Lake—lake ........ LA-4
Cat Island Lighthouse (historical)—locale ........ MS-4
Cat Island No 50—island ........ AR-4
Cat Island Pass—channel ........ LA-4
Cat Island Plantation—locale (2) ........ SC-3
Cat Island Shoal—bar ........ MS-4
Cat Island Shoal—bar ........ NY-2
Cat Island Swamp—swamp ........ FL-3
Cat Island Towhead—island ........ AR-4
Cat Key—island ........ FL-3
Cat Knob—summit ........ TX-5
Cat Knob—summit ........ VA-3
Cat Knoll—summit ........ UT-8
Cat Lake ........ MI-6
Cat Lake ........ WI-6
Cat Lake—lake ........ AK-9
Cat Lake—lake ........ FL-3
Cat Lake—lake ........ GA-3
Cat Lake—lake (2) ........ MI-6
Cat Lake—lake (2) ........ MN-6
Cat Lake—lake (3) ........ MS-4
Cat Lake—lake ........ MT-8
Cat Lake—lake ........ NE-7
Cat Lake—lake ........ NY-2
Cat Lake—lake ........ WA-9
Cat Lake—lake (2) ........ WI-6
Cat Lake—reservoir ........ NM-5
Cat Lakes—lake ........ ID-8
Cat Lakes—lake ........ OR-9
Cat Lakes—lake ........ WA-9
Cat Ledge—bar ........ ME-1
Catledge Archeol Site—hist pl ........ MS-4
Catledge Cemetery ........ MS-4
Catledge Hill Lookout Tower—locale ........ GA-3
Catledge Mounds—summit ........ MS-4
Cat Ledges—bar ........ ME-1
Catlen—locale ........ TN-4
Catlen Mills ........ TN-4
Catlens Mills ........ TN-4
Catlens Mills Post Office (historical)—building ........ TN-4
Catlet Creek ........ TX-5
Catlett—locale ........ CA-9
**Catlett**—pop pl ........ GA-3
**Catlett**—pop pl ........ VA-3
Catlett Bend—bend ........ TN-4
Catlett Cem—cemetery ........ AR-4
Catlett Creek—stream ........ TX-5
Catlett Gap—gap ........ GA-3
Catlett Gap—gap ........ VA-3
Catlett House—hist pl ........ KY-4
Catlett House—hist pl ........ VA-3
Catlett Islands—island ........ VA-3
Catlett Mountain Trail—trail ........ VA-3
Catlett Mtn—summit (2) ........ VA-3
Catlett Run—stream ........ VA-3
Catletts Branch—stream ........ VA-3
**Catlettsburg**—pop pl ........ KY-4
**Catlettsburg**—pop pl ........ TN-4
Catlettsburg (CCD)—cens area ........ KY-4
Catlettsburg Natl Bank—hist pl ........ KY-4
Catlett Sch—school ........ NC-3
Catletts Creek—stream ........ KY-4
Catlick Cem—cemetery ........ KY-4
Catlin ........ NY-2
Catlin—locale ........ GA-3
**Catlin**—pop pl ........ IL-6
**Catlin**—pop pl ........ IN-6
Catlin, Dr. Samuel, House—hist pl ........ MI-6
Catlin and Waters Drain—canal ........ MI-6
Catlin Bridge—hist pl ........ IN-6
Catlin Brook—stream (2) ........ CT-1
Catlin Brook—stream ........ PA-2
Catlin Canal—canal ........ CO-8
Catlin Canyon—valley ........ WA-9
Catlin Center Sch—school ........ NY-2
Catlin Ch—church ........ KS-7
Catlin Creek—stream ........ KS-7
Catlin Creek—stream ........ NY-2
Catlin Creek—stream ........ TX-5
Catlin Creek—stream ........ WI-6
Catlin Dam—dam ........ CO-8
Catlin Hall, Wilkes College—hist pl ........ PA-2
Catlin Hill—locale ........ NY-2
Catlin-Hillside Sch—school ........ OR-9
Catlin Hollow—valley (2) ........ PA-2
Catlin Hollow Ch—church ........ PA-2
Catlin Lake—lake ........ NY-2
Catlin Lake—lake ........ OR-9
Catlin Lot ........ MA-1
Catlin Lot Hill—summit ........ MA-1
Catlin Mill Creek—stream ........ NY-2
Catlin Mtn—summit ........ NY-2
Catlin Point ........ LA-4
Catlin Sch—school ........ WA-9
Catlin Spring—spring ........ MT-8
**Catlin (Town of)**—pop pl ........ NY-2
**Catlin Township**—pop pl ........ KS-7
**Catlin (Township of)**—pop pl ........ IL-6
Catlo Valley ........ OR-9
Catlow Mine—mine ........ NV-8
Catlow Rim—cliff ........ OR-9
Catlow (site)—locale ........ OR-9
Catlow Valley (depression)—basin ........ OR-9
Cat Mesa—bench ........ NM-5
Cat Mesa—summit (2) ........ NM-5
Cat Mountain Pond—lake ........ NY-2
Cat Mountain Ranch—locale ........ NM-5
Cat Mtn—summit ........ AL-4
Cat Mtn—summit ........ AZ-5
Cat Mtn—summit ........ CO-8
Cat Mtn—summit ........ ME-1
Cat Mtn—summit ........ NM-5
Cat Mtn—summit (4) ........ NY-2
Cat Mtn—summit (2) ........ OR-9
Cat Mtn—summit ........ TX-5
Catna Creek—stream ........ GA-3
Catnest Swamp—swamp ........ NJ-2
Catney Creek ........ TX-5
Catnip Canyon—valley ........ NV-8
Catnip Creek—stream ........ NV-8
Catnip Mtn—summit ........ NV-8
Catnip Point—cape ........ NC-3
Catnip Rsvr—reservoir ........ NV-8
Cato ........ MO-7
Cato—locale ........ KS-7
Cato—locale ........ MS-4
Cato—locale ........ OK-5
**Cato**—pop pl ........ AR-4
**Cato**—pop pl ........ IN-6
**Cato**—pop pl ........ KY-4
**Cato**—pop pl ........ MO-7
**Cato**—pop pl ........ NY-2
**Cato**—pop pl ........ TN-4
**Cato**—pop pl ........ WI-6
Cato Cave—cave ........ TN-4
Cato Cem—cemetery ........ AR-4
Cato Cem—cemetery ........ GA-3
Cato Cem—cemetery ........ MI-6
Cato Cem—cemetery ........ MS-4
Cato Cem—cemetery ........ MO-7
Cato Cem—cemetery ........ TN-4
Cato Cove—bay ........ ME-1
Cato Creek—stream ........ OK-5
Cato Creek—stream (2) ........ WA-9
Catoctin ........ MD-2
Catoctin Creek—stream ........ MD-2
Catoctin Creek—stream ........ VA-3
Catoctin Creek Bridge—hist pl ........ VA-3
**Catoctin Furnace**—pop pl ........ MD-2
Catoctin Furnace Hist Dist—hist pl ........ MD-2
**Catoctin (Lander)**—pop pl ........ MD-2
Catoctin (Magisterial District)—fmr MCD ........ VA-3
Catoctin Mountain Park—park ........ MD-2
Catoctin Mountains ........ VA-3
Catoctin Mtn—range ........ VA-3
Catoctin Mtn—summit ........ MD-2
Catoctin Recreational Demonstration Area—park ........ MD-2
Catoctin Station ........ MD-2
**Catoctin View**—pop pl ........ MD-2
Catoe Ch—church ........ SC-3
Cato Falls—falls ........ WI-6
Cato Heights Cem—cemetery ........ WI-6
Cato Hill Hist Dist—hist pl ........ RI-1
Cato Hill Hist Dist (Boundary Increase)—hist pl ........ RI-1
Catohoula Lake ........ LA-4
Cato House—hist pl ........ AL-4
Cato Lake—lake ........ FL-3
Cato Landing (historical)—locale ........ AL-4
Cato Ledge—bar ........ ME-1
Cato Levee—levee ........ MO-7
Cato Lookout Tower—locale ........ MS-4
**Catoma**—pop pl ........ AL-4
Catoma, Lake—reservoir ........ AL-4
Catoma Ch—church ........ AL-4
Catoma Creek—stream ........ AL-4
Catoma Sch—school ........ AL-4
Cato-Meridian Central Sch—school ........ NY-2
Caton ........ NC-3
Caton—locale ........ TN-4
**Caton**—pop pl ........ NY-2
Caton, Jesse H., House—hist pl ........ OR-9
Caton Bay—swamp ........ SC-3
Caton Branch—stream ........ IA-7
Caton Branch—stream ........ TN-4
Caton Cem—cemetery ........ KY-4
Caton Cem—cemetery ........ OH-6
Caton Cove—bay ........ AK-9
Caton Creek ........ IA-7
Caton Creek—stream ........ ID-8
Caton Creek—stream ........ NY-2
Caton Creek—stream ........ SC-3
Caton Creek—stream ........ WY-8
Caton Ditch ........ OH-6
**Caton Farm**—pop pl ........ IL-6
Caton Harbor—bay ........ AK-9
Caton Island—island ........ AK-9
Caton Island—island ........ ME-1
Caton Lake—lake ........ ID-8
Caton Lake Trail—trail ........ ID-8
Caton Lateral—canal ........ CA-9
Caton Meadow—flat ........ ID-8
Caton Ranch—locale ........ NV-8
Caton Sch—school ........ TN-4
**Catons Grove**—pop pl ........ TN-4
Catons Grove Methodist Ch—church ........ TN-4
Catons Grove Sch (historical)—school ........ TN-4
Caton Spring—spring ........ NV-8
Caton Springs Cem—cemetery ........ TN-4
**Catonsville**—pop pl ........ MD-2
**Catonsville Heights**—pop pl ........ MD-2
Catonsville HS—school ........ MD-2
**Catonsville Manor**—pop pl ........ MD-2
Caton Swamp—swamp ........ NY-2
**Caton (Town of)**—pop pl ........ NY-2
Catonville Cem—cemetery ........ TX-5
Cato Oil Field—other ........ NM-5
Catoosa ........ AL-4
Catoosa—locale ........ TN-4
**Catoosa**—pop pl ........ OK-5
**Catoosa Canyon**—pop pl ........ TN-4
Catoosa (CCD)—cens area ........ OK-5
**Catoosa Country**—pop pl ........ TN-4
**Catoosa (County)**—pop pl ........ GA-3
Catoosa Post Office (historical)—building ........ TN-4
Catoosa Sch—school ........ GA-3
Catoosa Sch (historical)—school ........ TN-4
Catoosa Springs—spring ........ GA-3
Catoosa Springs Branch—stream ........ GA-3
Catoosa Springs (CCD)—cens area ........ GA-3
Catoosa Tabernacle—church ........ GA-3
Catoosa Target Range—locale ........ GA-3
Catoosa Wildlife Mngmt Area—park ........ TN-4
Cato Pentecostal Ch—church ........ AR-4
Cato Point—cliff ........ AR-4
Cato Post Office (historical)—building ........ MS-4
Cato Post Office (historical)—building (2) ........ TN-4
Cato Ranch—locale ........ UT-8
**Cator Corners**—pop pl ........ NY-2
Cator Hall Lake—lake ........ SC-3
Catoroe Windmill—locale ........ TX-5
Cator Roundtop—summit ........ NY-2
Cators Cove—bay ........ MD-2
Cato Sch (historical)—school ........ MS-4
Cato Sch (historical)—school ........ TN-4
Catosh, Point—cape ........ MI-6
Cato Slough—stream ........ MO-7
Cato'S Pond ........ MA-1
Catos Pond—lake ........ MA-1
Cato Springs ........ MS-4
Cato Springs—spring ........ UT-8
Cato Springs Baptist Ch—church ........ MS-4
Cato Springs Branch—stream ........ AR-4
**Cato (Town of)**—pop pl ........ NY-2
**Cato (Town of)**—pop pl ........ WI-6
**Cato Township**—pop pl ........ ND-7
**Cato (Township of)**—pop pl ........ MI-6
Cat Passage—channel ........ AK-9
Cat Pasture—flat ........ UT-8
Cat Paw Brook ........ VT-1
Cat Peak—summit ........ UT-8
Cat Peak—summit ........ WA-9
Catpen Branch—stream ........ NC-3
Catpen Gap—gap (2) ........ NC-3
Cat Pen Hollow—valley ........ TN-4
Cat Point ........ VA-3
Cat Point—cape ........ FL-3
Cat Point—cape ........ TX-5
Cat Point Bank—bar ........ FL-3
Cat Point Creek—stream ........ VA-3
Cat Pond—lake ........ FL-3
Cat Pond—lake ........ ME-1
Cat Pond—lake ........ MD-2
Cat Pond—lake (2) ........ NY-2
Cat Pond—lake ........ UT-8
Cat Pond—swamp ........ TX-5
Cat Pond Creek—swamp ........ FL-3
Cat Ponds—reservoir ........ VA-3
Cat Ponds—swamp ........ FL-3
Catravo Windmill—locale ........ TX-5
Catrell Creek—stream ........ CA-9
Cat Ridge—ridge ........ CA-9
Cat Ridge—ridge ........ KY-4
Cat Ridge—ridge ........ NC-3
Cat River ........ VA-3
Cat River—stream ........ MN-6
Cat Rock—island ........ CA-9
Cat Rock—summit ........ MD-2
Cat Rock—summit ........ MA-1
Cat Rock—summit ........ NY-2
Cat Rock—summit ........ OR-9
Cat Rock Cove—bay ........ RI-1
Cat Rock Hill—summit ........ MA-1
Cat Rock Hollow—valley ........ WV-2
Cat Rock Mtn—summit ........ VA-3
Cat Rock Park—park ........ MA-1
Cat Rocks—pillar ........ CO-8
Cat Rocks—summit ........ CT-1
Cat Rocks—summit ........ RI-1
Catrock School—locale ........ ID-8
Cat Rock Sluice of the Roanoke Navigation—hist pl ........ VA-3
Catron—locale ........ MT-8
**Catron**—pop pl ........ AR-4
**Catron**—pop pl ........ MO-7
Catron Branch—stream ........ KY-4
Catron Branch—stream ........ TN-4
Catron Cem—cemetery ........ KY-4
Catron Cem—cemetery ........ MO-7
Catron Cem—cemetery ........ TN-4
Catron Cem—cemetery ........ VA-3
Catron Chapel—church ........ VA-3
**Catron (County)**—pop pl ........ NM-5
Catron Creek—stream ........ KY-4
Catron Creek—stream ........ TN-4
Catron Ditch—canal ........ CA-9
Catron Gap—gap ........ KY-4
Catron Hollow—valley ........ AR-4
Catron Hollow—valley ........ KY-4
Catron Irrigation Dam—dam ........ SD-7
Catron Ranch Airstrip—airport ........ SD-7
Catron School ........ TN-4
**Catron Spur**—pop pl ........ AR-4
Catron Spur—ridge ........ KY-4
Catron Wash—stream ........ NM-5
Cat Rsvr—reservoir ........ OR-9
Cat Run—gut ........ NJ-2
Cat Run—stream (2) ........ OH-6
Cat Run—stream ........ WV-2
Catsbane Brook—stream ........ NH-1
Catsbane Island—island ........ NH-1
Cat's Bay ........ VA-3
**Cats Bridge**—pop pl ........ VA-3
Cats Creek ........ PA-2
Cats Ears—other ........ AK-9
Cats Elbow Point—cape ........ NY-2
Cats Head Mtn—summit ........ CA-9
Cat Shoals—bar ........ AK-9
**Catskill**—pop pl ........ NY-2
Catskill Aqueduct—canal ........ NY-2
Catskill Ave Sch—school ........ CA-9
Catskill Cem—cemetery ........ NM-5
Catskill Charcoal Ovens—hist pl ........ NM-5
Catskill Creek—stream ........ NY-2
Catskill Mountains—range ........ NY-2
Catskill Park—park ........ NY-2
Catskill (site)—locale ........ NM-5
Catskill State Park—park (2) ........ NY-2
**Catskill (Town of)**—pop pl ........ NY-2
Catskin Brake—gut ........ LA-4
Catskin Canyon—valley ........ CA-9
Catskin Creek—stream ........ NC-3
Cat Slough—gut ........ CA-9
Cats Paw Brook ........ VT-1
Catspaw Lake—lake ........ NY-2
Catspear Hollow—valley ........ MO-7
Cats Point—cape ........ FL-3
**Cat Spring**—pop pl ........ TX-5
Cat Spring—spring ........ AZ-5
Cat Spring—spring ........ CO-8
Cat Spring—spring ........ ID-8
Cat Spring Creek—stream ........ TX-5
Cat Spur Creek—stream ........ ID-8
**Cat Square**—pop pl ........ NC-3
Cats Run—stream ........ PA-2
Cats Run Junction—locale ........ PA-2
Cats Run Junction Station (historical)—building ........ PA-2
Cats Spur Creek ........ ID-8
Catstair Branch—stream ........ NC-3
Catstair Canyon—valley ........ UT-8
Cat Stairs—cliff ........ TN-4
Catstairs, The—cliff ........ NC-3
Cat Stairs Branch—stream ........ TN-4
Catsup Creek—stream ........ CA-9
Cat Swamp—swamp (2) ........ NJ-2
Cat Swamp Pond—reservoir ........ CT-1
Cat Swamp Pond—reservoir ........ MA-1
Cattail ........ NJ-2
Cattail Bay—bay ........ ND-7
Cattail Bay—swamp ........ FL-3
Cattail Bay—swamp ........ NC-3
Cattail Branch ........ NC-3
Cattail Branch ........ VA-3
Cattail Branch—stream ........ DE-2
Cattail Branch—stream (2) ........ GA-3
Cattail Branch—stream (3) ........ MD-2
Cattail Branch—stream (3) ........ NC-3
Cattail Branch—stream ........ SC-3
Cattail Branch—stream ........ TN-4
Cattail Branch—stream ........ TX-5
Cattail Branch—stream (3) ........ VA-3
Cattail Brook ........ NJ-2
Cat Tail Brook—stream ........ NJ-2
Cattail Brook—stream ........ NJ-2
Cattail Brook—stream ........ NY-2
Cat Tail Brook Bridge—hist pl ........ NJ-2
Cattail Canyon—valley ........ TX-5
Cattail Cem—cemetery ........ NC-3
Cattail Creek—stream ........ AR-4
Cattail Creek—stream ........ IL-6
Cattail Creek—stream (2) ........ MD-2
Cattail Creek—stream (4) ........ MO-7
Cattail Creek—stream (7) ........ NC-3
Cattail Creek—stream ........ ND-7
Cattail Creek—stream ........ OH-6
Cattail Creek—stream ........ OR-9
Cattail Creek—stream (4) ........ TX-5
Cattail Creek—stream (8) ........ VA-3
Cattail Creek—stream (2) ........ WY-8
Cattail Draw—valley ........ WY-8
Cattail Falls—falls ........ TX-5
Cattail Gut—gut ........ DE-2
Cattail Hollow—valley (2) ........ TX-5
Cattail Hollow—valley ........ VA-3
Cattail Island ........ NJ-2
Cattail Island—island ........ MD-2
Cattail Lake—lake ........ FL-3
Cattail Lake—lake ........ SD-7
Cattail Lake—lake ........ TX-5
Cattail Lake—lake ........ WI-6
Cattail Lake—reservoir ........ NV-8
Cattail Lake—reservoir ........ NC-3
Cattail Lake—swamp ........ AR-4
Cattail Lakes—lake ........ FL-3
Cattail Peak—summit ........ NC-3
Cattail Pit—basin ........ WY-8
Cattail Point—cape ........ MD-2
Cattail Pond—lake ........ AL-4
Cattail Pond—lake ........ CO-8
Cattail Pond—lake ........ MD-2
Cattail Pond—lake ........ TX-5
Cattail Pond—reservoir ........ NC-3
Cattail Pond Dam—dam ........ NC-3
Cattail Ranch—locale ........ WY-8
Cattail Rec Area—park ........ ND-7
Cattail Ridge—ridge ........ WI-6
Cattail Run ........ VA-3
Cattail Run—stream (2) ........ OH-6
Cattail Run—stream (3) ........ VA-3
Cattail Run—stream (2) ........ WV-2
Cattail Rush—spring ........ AZ-5
Cattail Slough—stream ........ IL-6
Cattail Slough—stream ........ OR-9
Cattail Slough—swamp ........ IL-6
Cattail Spring—spring (2) ........ AZ-5
Cattail Swamp ........ VA-3
Cattail Swamp—stream ........ NC-3
Cattail Swamp—stream (2) ........ VA-3
Cattail Swamp—swamp ........ FL-3
Cattail Swamp—swamp (2) ........ PA-2
Cattail Swamp Drain—canal ........ MI-6
Cattail Swamp Pond—reservoir ........ VA-3
Cattail Tank—reservoir ........ UT-8
Cattail Valley—valley ........ WI-6
Cattail Valley Creek—stream ........ WI-6
Cattail Wash—valley ........ AZ-5
Cattail Well—well ........ AZ-5
Cattail Windmill—locale (2) ........ TX-5
Cattaloochee Creek ........ NC-3
Cat Tank—reservoir (4) ........ AZ-5
Cat Tank—reservoir (2) ........ TX-5
**Cattaraugus**—pop pl ........ NY-2

Cattaraugus Camp—*locale* ... NY-2
Cattaraugus Cem—*cemetery* ... WI-6
**Cattaraugus (County)**—*pop pl* ... NY-2
Cattaraugus Creek—*stream* ... NY-2
Cattaraugus Ind Res—*1855 (1980)* ... NY-2
Cattaraugus Long House Ch—*church* ... NY-2
Cattaraugus Sch—*school* ... WI-6
Catt Cem—*cemetery* ... IN-6
Catt Creek—*stream* ... WA-9
Cattell Sch—*school* ... IA-7
Cattermole Memorial Library—*hist pl* ... IA-7
Catterson Creek—*stream* ... OR-9
Catterton Cem—*cemetery* ... IL-6
Cattese—*locale* ... IA-7
Cat Thicket Branch—*stream* ... TX-5
Cattle, John, Jr., House—*hist pl* ... NE-7
Cattle Bank—*hist pl* ... IL-6
Cattle Cabin—*hist pl* ... CA-9
Cattle Camp Spring—*spring* ... NV-8
Cattle Camp Spring—*spring* ... WA-9
Cattle Camp Wash—*stream* ... NV-8
Cattle Camp Wash Well—*well* ... NV-8
Cattle Canyon—*valley* ... AZ-5
Cattle Canyon—*valley* ... CA-9
Cattle Country Mobile Home Campground—*locale* ... UT-8
Cattle Creek—*locale* ... CO-8
Cattle Creek—*stream* (2) ... CA-9
Cattle Creek—*stream* (2) ... CO-8
Cattle Creek—*stream* (2) ... ID-8
Cattle Creek—*stream* (2) ... MT-8
Cattle Creek—*stream* (4) ... OR-9
Cattle Creek—*stream* ... SC-3
Cattle Creek—*stream* ... SD-7
Cattle Creek—*stream* ... TX-5
Cattle Creek—*stream* ... UT-8
Cattle Creek—*stream* ... VA-3
Cattle Creek Campground—*hist pl* ... SC-3
Cattle Creek Ch—*church* ... SC-3
Cattle Creek Guard Station—*locale* ... CO-8
Cattle Creek Sch—*school* ... SC-3
Cattle Dock Point—*cape* (2) ... FL-3
Cattle Guard Pond—*lake* ... AZ-5
Cattle Guard Spring—*spring* ... OR-9
Cattle Guard Tank—*reservoir* ... AZ-5
Cattleguard Tank—*reservoir* ... NM-5
Cattleguard Well—*well* ... AZ-5
Cattle Guard Well—*well* ... NM-5
Cattleguard Well—*well* ... NM-5
Cattleguard Well—*well* ... TX-5
Cattleguard Windmill—*locale* ... TX-5
Cattle Gulch—*valley* ... CO-8
Cattle Gulch—*valley* ... MT-8
Cattle Gulch Lake—*lake* ... MT-8
Cattle Gulch Ridge—*ridge* ... MT-8
Cattle Hammock—*island* ... GA-3
Cattle Hill—*summit* ... CA-9
Cattle Island—*island* ... SC-3
Cattle Island—*island* ... TX-5
Cattle Knob—*summit* ... PA-2
Cattle Lot Brook—*stream* ... CT-1
Cattlemans Ditch—*canal* ... CO-8
Cattlemens Little Valley—*valley* ... UT-8
Cattle Mtn—*summit* ... CA-9
Cattle Mtn—*summit* ... CO-8
Cattle Mtn—*summit* ... NY-2
Cattle Pen Creek—*stream* ... GA-3
Cattle Pen Point—*cape* ... NC-3
Cattle Point—*cape* ... WA-9
Cattle Pond—*lake* ... MA-1
Cattle Queen Creek—*stream* ... MT-8
Cattle Rapids—*rapids* ... ID-8
Cattle Rapids—*rapids* ... OR-9
Cattle Ridge—*ridge* ... CA-9
Cattle Spring—*spring* ... NV-8
Cattle Spring—*spring* ... UT-8
Cattle Spring Mine—*mine* ... CA-9
Cattles Ranch—*locale* ... SD-7
Cattlet Creek—*stream* ... VA-3
*Cattle Wallow* ... MH-9
*Cattle Wallow Cliffs* ... MH-9
*Catton Creek* ... AR-4
Catto Sch—*school* ... NJ-2
Catto Spring—*spring* ... AR-4
Catto Tank—*reservoir* ... TX-5
Cat Town—*locale* ... CA-9
**Cattown**—*pop pl* ... NY-2
Cattrack Tank—*reservoir* ... AZ-5
Cat Track Tank—*reservoir* ... AZ-5
Cattrill Creek—*stream* ... OR-9
Cattron Cem—*cemetery* ... VA-3
Cattron Township—*civil* ... SD-7
Catt Sch—*school* ... IL-6
Catt Sch—*school* ... KS-7
Cattus Island—*island* ... NJ-2
*Cattwama* ... MA-1
Cattyman Lake—*lake* ... MN-6
Catumb Passage—*channel* ... RI-1
*Catumb Reef* ... RI-1
Catumb Rocks—*pillar* ... RI-1
Catuna—*locale* ... LA-4
Catwba Grove Sch—*school* ... WV-2
Cat Well—*well* (2) ... NM-5
Catwillow Creek—*stream* ... WI-6
Caty Creek—*stream* ... AL-4
Cauble Sch—*school* ... IL-6
*Caucas* ... FL-3
*Cauchy Creek* ... MI-6
Cauchy Creek—*stream* ... MI-6
*Caucogomoc Lake* ... ME-1
*Caucogomuc Lake* ... ME-1
Caucomgomoc Dam—*dam* ... ME-1
Caucomgomoc Lake—*lake* ... ME-1
Caucomgomoc Mtn—*summit* ... ME-1
Caucomgomoc Stream—*stream* ... ME-1
Caucus Bay—*bay* ... VA-3
Caucus Shoal—*bar* ... FL-3
Caucut Valley—*valley* ... WI-6
**Caudell (Caudill)**—*pop pl* ... KY-4
Caudill Branch—*stream* (4) ... KY-4
Caudill Branch—*stream* ... NC-3
Caudill Cabin—*locale* ... NC-3
Caudill Cem—*cemetery* (3) ... KY-4
Caudill Creek—*stream* ... KY-4
Caudill Fork—*stream* ... KY-4
Caudill Mtn—*summit* ... TX-5
Caudill Oil Field—*other* ... NM-5
Caudill Ranch—*locale* ... NM-5
Caudill Windmill—*locale* ... NM-5
Caudle Branch—*stream* ... KY-4
Caudle Branch—*stream* ... NC-3
Caudle Cem—*cemetery* ... TX-5
Caudle Ch—*church* ... MO-7
Caudle Creek—*stream* ... NV-8
Caudle Dam—*dam* ... AL-4
Caudle Family Cem—*cemetery* ... AL-4
*Caudle Mountain* ... TX-5
Caudle Ridge—*ridge* ... MO-7
Caudles Lake—*reservoir* ... AL-4
Cauerbach Canal—*canal* ... NY-2
*Cauffman Hill* ... PA-2
Caufield Gulch—*valley* ... OR-9
Caufield Marsh—*swamp* ... OR-9
Caufman Tank—*reservoir* ... AZ-5
**Caughdenoy**—*pop pl* ... NY-2
Caughdenoy Creek—*stream* ... NY-2
Caughey Sch—*school* ... IL-6
Caughlin Oil Field—*oilfield* ... TX-5
Caughman Ditch—*canal* ... CO-8
Caughmans Pond—*reservoir* (2) ... SC-3
Caughmans Road Sch—*school* ... SC-3
Caughnawaga Cem—*cemetery* ... NY-2
Caughnawaga Indian Village Site—*hist pl* ... NY-2
Caughnawaga Shelter—*locale* ... VT-1
Caughorn Prairie—*flat* ... TX-5
Caughran Spring—*spring* ... CA-9
Caughren Point—*cape* ... MN-6
Cauhape Ranch—*locale* (2) ... NM-5
Cauhape Teel Windmill—*locale* ... NM-5
Cauhaupe Ranch—*locale* ... NM-5
Cauhorn Cem—*cemetery* ... AL-4
**Cauhorn (historical)**—*pop pl* ... MS-4
*Cauley* ... AL-4
*Cauley Creek* ... OH-6
Cauley Creek—*stream* ... GA-3
Cauley Gap—*gap* ... AL-4
Cauley Lake—*lake* ... LA-4
*Cauleys Creek* ... VA-3
Cauleysville P. O. (historical)—*locale* ... AL-4
**Caulfield**—*pop pl* ... MO-7
Caulfield Plantation (historical)—*locale* ... MS-4
Caulk Branch—*stream* ... VA-3
Caulk Cove—*bay* ... MD-2
*Caulk Creek* ... MD-2
*Caulk Cut-Off* ... AR-4
Caulk Cut-off (1937)—*bend* ... AR-4
Caulk Flats—*flat* ... FL-3
Caulkins, Dr. Martin H., House and Office—*hist pl* ... IA-7
*Caulkins Creek* ... OR-9
Caulkins Lake—*lake* ... MI-6
Caulkins Park—*park* ... CT-1
Caulk Island—*island* ... AR-4
Caulk Neck—*area* ... AR-4
*Caulk Neck Cut-Off* ... AR-4
Caulk Point—*area* ... AR-4
*Caulks Creek* ... MD-2
Caulks Creek—*stream* ... MO-7
*Caulk's Point* ... AR-4
**Caulksville**—*pop pl* ... AR-4
Caulley Creek—*stream* ... OH-6
*Caulley Fork* ... OH-6
Caumsett State Park—*park* ... NY-2
*Cauquaw Run* ... OH-6
*Cauquomgomoc Lake* ... ME-1
Causar Branch—*stream* ... SC-3
Causer Well Corral—*locale* ... NV-8
Causeville Ch—*church* ... MS-4
Causeway, The—*bridge* ... NC-3
Causeway, The—*ridge* ... UT-8
Causeway, The Bridge—*bridge* ... MA-1
Causeway Bay—*swamp* ... NC-3
Causeway Brook—*stream* ... MA-1
Causeway Island—*island* ... FL-3
Causeway Island—*island* ... ME-1
Causeway Lake—*lake* ... CO-8
Causeway Landing—*locale* ... NC-3
**Causeway Manor**—*pop pl* ... OH-6
Causeway Park—*park* ... FL-3
Causeway Park—*park* ... NY-2
Causeway Plaza (Shop Ctr)—*locale* (2) ... FL-3
Causeway Square (Shop Ctr)—*locale* (2) ... FL-3
Causeway Swamp—*swamp* ... SC-3
Causey—*locale* ... KY-4
Causey—*locale* ... SC-3
**Causey**—*pop pl* ... NM-5
Causey, Israel, House—*hist pl* ... GA-3
Causey Airp—*airport* ... NC-3
Causey Branch—*stream* ... AL-4
Causey Branch—*stream* ... MS-4
Causey Cem—*cemetery* ... GA-3
Causey Cem—*cemetery* ... IN-6
Causey Cem—*cemetery* (2) ... LA-4
Causey Cem—*cemetery* (2) ... MS-4
Causey Cem—*cemetery* ... NM-5
Causey Creek—*stream* ... MS-4
Causey Dam—*dam* ... UT-8
Causey Draw—*valley* ... TX-5
**Causey Estates Subdivision**—*pop pl* ... UT-8
Causey Hollow—*valley* ... TN-4
Causey Lake—*lake* ... IN-6
Causey Lake—*lake* ... MS-4
Causey Lake—*lake* ... NC-3
Causey Lake—*reservoir* ... NC-3
Causey Lake Dam—*dam* ... NC-3
Causey Place—*locale* ... TX-5
Causey Ranch—*locale* ... TX-5
Causey Rsvr—*reservoir* ... UT-8
Causey Spring—*spring* ... UT-8
*Causeyville Baptist Church* ... MS-4
Causeyville Hist Dist—*hist pl* ... MS-4
Causey Windmill—*locale* ... TX-5
Causier Sch—*school* ... TN-4
*Causkata Pond* ... MA-1
Causland Park—*hist pl* ... WA-9
*Causons Pond* ... MA-1
Causseaux Cem—*cemetery* ... FL-3
*Causten's Bluff* ... GA-3
*Caustill Landing* ... AL-4
Caustills Landing (historical)—*locale* ... AL-4
Causton Bluff—*cliff* ... GA-3
Causy Windmill—*locale* ... NM-5
**Cauterskill**—*pop pl* ... NY-2
Cauthen, Dr. William Columbus, House—*hist pl* ... SC-3
Cauthen-Clinton Center Sch—*school* ... SC-3
Cauthen Lake Number One—*reservoir* ... AL-4
Cauthen Lake Number Two—*reservoir* ... AL-4
Cauthen Number 1 Dam—*dam* ... AL-4
Cauthen Number 2 Dam—*dam* ... AL-4
Cauthen Pond—*reservoir* ... AL-4
Cauthens Cem—*cemetery* ... AL-4
**Cauthens Crossroads**—*pop pl* ... SC-3
*Cauthorn Draw* ... TX-5
Cauthorn Draw—*valley* ... TX-5
Cauthorn Ranch—*locale* ... TX-5
Cauthorn Spring—*spring* ... OR-9
Cauthornville—*locale* ... VA-3
**Cauthron**—*pop pl* ... AR-4
Cauthron Ch—*church* ... AR-4
Cauthron (Township of)—*fmr MCD* (2) ... AR-4
*Caution* ... AL-4
Caution, Point—*cape* ... WA-9
*Caution Island* ... SD-7
Caution Island—*island* ... AK-9
Caution Pass—*channel* ... AK-9
Cautiva Tank—*reservoir* ... AZ-5
Cava Ch—*church* ... VA-3
Cavage Airp (private)—*airport* ... PA-2
**Cavalay Park**—*pop pl* ... AZ-5
**Cavalcade**—*pop pl* ... VA-3
**Cavalero Corner**—*pop pl* ... WA-9
**Cavalier**—*pop pl* ... ND-7
Cavalier, Lake—*reservoir* ... MS-4
Cavalier City Dam—*dam* ... ND-7
Cavalier Country Club—*locale* ... ND-7
Cavalier Field—*park* ... MS-4
Cavalier Lake—*lake* ... ND-7
**Cavalier Manor**—*pop pl* ... VA-3
Cavalier Manor Sch—*school* ... VA-3
Cavalier Municipal Airp—*airport* ... ND-7
Cavalier Park—*park* ... VA-3
**Cavalier Park**—*pop pl* ... VA-3
**Cavalier Park (subdivision)**—*pop pl* ... NC-3
Cavaliers Country Club—*locale* ... DE-2
**Cavaliers Country Club Apartments (subdivision)**—*pop pl* ... DE-2
Cavalier Spring—*spring* ... WA-9
**Cavalier Terrace (subdivision)**—*pop pl* ... NC-3
**Cavalier Township**—*pop pl* ... ND-7
**Cavalier Woods (subdivision)**—*pop pl* ... NC-3
Cavalier Yacht and Country Club—*other* ... VA-3
Cavallada Creek—*stream* ... CA-9
*Cavallada Gulch* ... CA-9
*Cavallado Creek* ... CA-9
Cavalliere Ranch—*locale* ... AZ-5
**Cavallo**—*pop pl* ... OH-6
Cavallo, Pass—*channel* ... TX-5
Cavallo, Point—*cape* ... CA-9
*Cavallo Pass* ... TX-5
*Cavallo Point* ... CA-9
Cavalry Bluff—*cliff* ... CA-9
Cavalry Cem—*cemetery* ... KS-7
Cavalry Corrals—*hist pl* ... AZ-5
*Cavalry Creek* ... OK-5
Cavalry Creek—*stream* (2) ... KS-7
Cavalry Creek—*stream* (2) ... OK-5
Cavalry Field—*park* ... PA-2
**Cavalry Hill**—*pop pl* ... AL-4
Cavalry Hill Sch—*school* ... AL-4
**Cavalry Park Subdivision**—*pop pl* ... UT-8
Cavalry Tank—*reservoir* ... TX-5
Cavanagh Cem—*cemetery* ... IL-6
Cavanagh Sch—*school* ... MN-6
Cavanah, C. C., House—*hist pl* ... ID-8
Cavanah Lake—*swamp* ... IL-6
Cavanal—*locale* ... OK-5
Cavanal Mtn—*summit* ... OK-5
**Cavanaugh**—*pop pl* ... AR-4
Cavanaugh, James House—*hist pl* ... UT-8
Cavanaugh, Lake—*lake* ... WA-9
Cavanaugh Bay—*bay* ... ID-8
Cavanaugh Bluff—*cliff* ... IL-6
Cavanaugh Bottom—*bend* ... IA-7
Cavanaugh Brook—*stream* ... CT-1
Cavanaugh Canyon—*valley* ... CA-9
Cavanaugh (CCD)—*cens area* ... WA-9
Cavanaugh Cem—*cemetery* ... MO-7
Cavanaugh Creek—*stream* ... AK-9
Cavanaugh Creek—*stream* ... KY-4
Cavanaugh Creek—*stream* ... OR-9
Cavanaugh Creek—*stream* ... WA-9
Cavanaugh Ditch—*canal* ... IN-6
Cavanaugh Grade—*slope* ... CA-9
Cavanaugh Gulch—*valley* ... CA-9
Cavanaugh Lake—*lake* ... MI-6
Cavanaugh Lake—*lake* ... MN-6
Cavanaugh Lake—*lake* ... ND-7
Cavanaugh-Oso Truck Trail—*trail* ... WA-9
Cavanaugh Peak—*summit* ... WY-8
Cavanaugh Pond—*lake* ... CT-1
*Cavanaughs Brook* ... CT-1
Cavanaugh Sch—*school* ... KY-4
Cavanaugh Sch—*school* ... MI-6
Cavanaugh Spring—*spring* (2) ... NV-8
Cavanaugh Wash—*stream* ... NV-8
Cavanaugh-Zetek House—*hist pl* ... IA-7
Cavaness, Garvin, House—*hist pl* ... AR-4
Cavaness Cem—*cemetery* ... MO-7
Cavanna Acad (historical)—*school* ... MS-4
Cavannah Spring—*spring* ... ID-8
Cavanough Gulch—*valley* ... CA-9
*Cavan Point* ... NJ-2
Cavasara Creek—*stream* ... TX-5
Cavasos Place—*locale* ... NM-5
Cavass Bayou—*stream* ... MS-4
*Cavasso Creek* ... TX-5
Cavasso Creek—*stream* ... TX-5
Cavasso Pens—*locale* ... TX-5
*Cavatt Creek* ... OR-9
*Cavazos* ... TX-5
Cavazos Cem—*cemetery* ... TX-5
Cavazos Windmill—*locale* ... TX-5
Cave—*locale* ... SC-3
Cave—*locale* ... TN-4
Cave—*locale* ... WV-2
Cave—*other* ... VA-3
**Cave**—*pop pl* ... KS-7
**Cave**—*pop pl* ... MO-7
*Cave, The* ... AL-4
*Cave, The* ... MH-9
Cave, The—*cave* ... AL-4
Cave, The—*cave* ... CO-8
Cave Arch—*arch* ... UT-8
*Cave Arnold Branch* ... MO-7
Cave Basin—*basin* ... CO-8
Cave Basin Creek—*stream* ... CO-8
Cave Bay—*bay* ... ID-8
Cave Bay—*bay* ... MT-8
Cave Bayou—*stream* ... MS-4
Cave Bluff—*cliff* ... MO-7
Cave Bluff—*cliff* ... TN-4
*Cave Branch* ... AR-4
*Cave Branch* ... MO-7
Cave Branch—*stream* (2) ... AL-4
Cave Branch—*stream* ... AR-4
Cave Branch—*stream* ... GA-3
Cave Branch—*stream* (15) ... KY-4
Cave Branch—*stream* ... LA-4
Cave Branch—*stream* (2) ... MO-7
Cave Branch—*stream* (10) ... TN-4
Cave Branch—*stream* ... WV-2
Cave Branch Cave—*cave* ... TN-4
Cave Branch Hollow—*valley* ... MO-7
Cave Branch Sch—*school* ... KY-4
Cave Buttes Dam—*dam* ... AZ-5
Cave Buttes Rec Area—*park* ... AZ-5
Cave Cabin Branch—*stream* ... NJ-2
Cave Campground—*locale* ... CA-9
Cave Canyon—*valley* (5) ... AZ-5
Cave Canyon—*valley* ... CO-8
Cave Canyon—*valley* (2) ... ID-8
Cave Canyon—*valley* ... MT-8
Cave Canyon—*valley* (7) ... NV-8
Cave Canyon—*valley* (7) ... NM-5
Cave Canyon—*valley* (2) ... OR-9
Cave Canyon—*valley* ... TX-5
Cave Canyon—*valley* (5) ... UT-8
Cave Canyon—*valley* ... WA-9
Cave Canyon Trail One Hundred Forty-Seven—*trail* ... AZ-5
Cave Cem—*cemetery* ... GA-3
Cave Cem—*cemetery* ... KS-7
Cave Cem—*cemetery* ... MO-7
Cave Ch—*church* ... KS-7
Cave City—*locale* ... CA-9
**Cave City**—*pop pl* ... AR-4
**Cave City**—*pop pl* ... KY-4
Cave City (CCD)—*cens area* ... KY-4
Cave City Cem—*cemetery* ... AR-4
Cave City Commercial District—*hist pl* ... KY-4
Cave Cliff—*cliff* ... UT-8
**Cave Colony**—*pop pl* ... DE-2
Cave Coulee—*valley* ... ND-7
Cave Country—*area* ... CA-9
Cave Cove—*basin* ... TN-4
Cave Cove—*bay* ... VI-3
Cave Cove—*valley* ... TN-4
Cave Cove Creek—*stream* ... TN-4
*Cavecreek* ... AZ-5
*Cave Creek* ... AR-4
*Cave Creek* ... ID-8
*Cave Creek* ... KY-4
*Cave Creek* ... OR-9
Cave Creek—*locale* ... AR-4
Cave Creek—*locale* ... TN-4
**Cave Creek**—*pop pl* ... AZ-5
**Cavecreek**—*pop pl* ... AR-4
Cave Creek—*stream* (3) ... AL-4
Cave Creek—*stream* (2) ... AK-9
Cave Creek—*stream* (7) ... AZ-5
Cave Creek—*stream* (6) ... AR-4
Cave Creek—*stream* (4) ... CA-9
Cave Creek—*stream* (4) ... CO-8
Cave Creek—*stream* (4) ... ID-8
Cave Creek—*stream* (3) ... IL-6
Cave Creek—*stream* ... KS-7
Cave Creek—*stream* (4) ... KY-4
Cave Creek—*stream* (2) ... MO-7
Cave Creek—*stream* (5) ... MT-8
Cave Creek—*stream* (3) ... NV-8
Cave Creek—*stream* (3) ... NM-5
Cave Creek—*stream* ... NC-3
Cave Creek—*stream* ... OK-5
Cave Creek—*stream* (3) ... OR-9
Cave Creek—*stream* (3) ... TN-4
Cave Creek—*stream* (4) ... TX-5
Cave Creek—*stream* ... UT-8
Cave Creek—*stream* (2) ... WA-9
Cave Creek—*stream* ... WI-6
Cave Creek—*stream* (3) ... WY-8
*Cave Creek Butte* ... WA-9
Cave Creek Camp—*locale* ... OR-9
Cave Creek Campground—*park* ... AZ-5
Cave Creek Canyon—*valley* ... AZ-5
Cave Creek Canyon—*valley* ... NV-8
Cave Creek Cave—*cave* ... TN-4
Cave Creek Cem—*cemetery* ... AZ-5
Cave Creek Cem—*cemetery* ... OK-5
Cave Creek Ch—*church* ... AR-4
Cave Creek Ch—*church* ... KY-4
Cave Creek Ch—*church* ... TN-4
Cave Creek Ch—*church* ... TX-5
Cave Creek Community Center—*building* ... TN-4
Cave Creek Dam—*dam* ... AZ-5
Cave Creek Driving Range—*other* ... AZ-5
*Cave Creek Golf Course* ... AZ-5
Cave Creek Mesa—*summit* ... NM-5
Cave Creek Park—*park* ... AZ-5
Cave Creek Post Office—*building* ... AZ-5
Cave Creek Post Office (historical)—*building* ... TN-4
Cave Creek Ranch—*locale* ... WY-8
Cave Creek Ranger Station—*locale* ... AZ-5
Cave Creek Rec Area—*park* (2) ... AZ-5
Cave Creek Rsvr—*reservoir* ... AZ-5
Cave Creek Rsvr—*reservoir* ... NV-8
Cave Creek Sch—*school* ... AZ-5
Cave Creek Sch—*school* ... NV-8
Cave Creek Sch—*school* ... TX-5
Cave Creek Sch (historical)—*school* ... TN-4
*Cave Creek Semi-regional Park* ... AZ-5
Cave Creek Spring—*spring* ... AZ-5
Cave Creek Spring—*spring* ... NV-8
**Cave Creek (subdivision)**—*pop pl* ... AZ-5
Cave Crossing—*locale* ... TX-5
Cave Draw—*valley* ... AZ-5
Cave Draw—*valley* ... ID-8
Cave Draw—*valley* ... SD-7
Cave Draw—*valley* (3) ... TX-5
Cave Draw Tank—*reservoir* ... AZ-5
Cave Falls—*falls* ... WY-8
Cave Falls Campground—*locale* ... WY-8
Cave Flat—*flat* ... UT-8
Cave Fork—*stream* ... KY-4
Cave Fork—*stream* (2) ... MO-7
Cave Fork—*stream* ... WV-2
Cave Gap Hollow—*valley* ... TN-4
Cave Gulch—*valley* (2) ... CA-9
Cave Gulch—*valley* ... CO-8
Cave Gulch—*valley* (3) ... ID-8
Cave Gulch—*valley* (4) ... MT-8
Cave Gulch—*valley* ... OR-9
Cave Gulch—*valley* ... WY-8
Cave Gulch Rsvr—*reservoir* ... WY-8
Cave Gulch Spring—*spring* ... MT-8
*Cave Hill* ... AZ-5
Cave Hill—*locale* ... KY-4
**Cavehill**—*pop pl* ... KY-4
**Cave Hill**—*pop pl* ... MO-7
Cave Hill—*summit* ... AL-4
Cave Hill—*summit* ... AR-4
Cave Hill—*summit* (2) ... CT-1
Cave Hill—*summit* ... IL-6
Cave Hill—*summit* (3) ... KY-4
Cave Hill—*summit* (2) ... ME-1
Cave Hill—*summit* (3) ... MO-7
Cave Hill—*summit* ... NV-8
Cave Hill—*summit* ... NY-2
Cave Hill—*summit* ... OH-6
Cave Hill—*summit* (2) ... PA-2
Cave Hill—*summit* ... TN-4
Cave Hill—*summit* ... TX-5
Cave Hill—*summit* (4) ... VA-3
Cave Hill Cave—*cave* ... MO-7
Cave Hill Cave—*cave* ... TN-4
Cave Hill Cem—*cemetery* ... KY-4
Cave Hill Cemetery—*hist pl* ... KY-4
Cave Hill Ch—*church* ... KY-4
Cave Hill Ch—*church* ... TN-4
Cave Hill Saltpeter Pits—*cave* ... TN-4
Cave Hills Cattle Company Ranch—*locale* ... SD-7
Cave Hills Ch—*church* ... SD-7
Cave Hills Township (historical)—*civil* ... SD-7
Cave Hollow—*valley* ... AL-4
Cave Hollow—*valley* (8) ... AR-4
Cave Hollow—*valley* ... GA-3
Cave Hollow—*valley* ... IN-6
Cave Hollow—*valley* (2) ... KY-4
Cave Hollow—*valley* (15) ... MO-7
Cave Hollow—*valley* ... OH-6
Cave Hollow—*valley* ... OR-9
Cave Hollow—*valley* ... PA-2
Cave Hollow—*valley* (10) ... TN-4
Cave Hollow—*valley* (2) ... TX-5
Cave Hollow—*valley* (3) ... UT-8
Cave Hollow—*valley* (2) ... WV-2
Cave Hollow Branch—*stream* ... KY-4
Cave Hollow Cave—*cave* ... MO-7
Cave Hollow Spring—*spring* ... OR-9
Cave Hollow Spring—*spring* ... TX-5
**Cave Hollow Subdivision**—*pop pl* ... UT-8
Cave House—*locale* ... UT-8
Cave In, The—*basin* ... IL-6
*Cave in Rock* ... IL-6
**Cave-in-Rock**—*pop pl* ... IL-6
*Cave-in-Rock (corporate name Cave-In-Rock)* ... IL-6
Cave-In-Rock (Election Precinct)—*fmr MCD* ... IL-6
Cave In Rock Ferry—*locale* ... IL-6
Cave In Rock Ferry—*locale* ... KY-4
Cave In Rock Island—*island* ... KY-4
Cave-In-Rock State Park—*park* ... IL-6
Cave Island—*island* ... KY-4
Cave Island—*island* ... VT-1
Cave Island Falls—*falls* ... OK-5
**Cave Junction**—*pop pl* ... OR-9
Cave Junction (CCD)—*cens area* ... OR-9
Cave Knob—*summit* ... WV-2
Cave Knoll—*summit* ... NY-2
Cave Knoll—*summit* ... UT-8
Ca-Vel—*uninc pl* ... NC-3
*Cave Lake* ... WI-6
Cave Lake—*cave* ... AL-4
Cave Lake—*lake* ... CA-9
Cave Lake—*lake* ... ID-8
Cave Lake—*lake* ... MN-6
Cave Lake—*lake* (2) ... MT-8
Cave Lake—*lake* ... NM-5
Cave Lake—*lake* ... WI-6
Cave Lake—*reservoir* ... MO-7
Cave Lake Forest Service Recreation Site—*locale* ... NV-8
Cave Lakes Canyon—*valley* ... UT-8
Cave Lake Sch—*hist pl* ... ID-8
*Cavelano Creek* ... CA-9
**Cavelawn**—*pop pl* ... KY-4
Cavel Creek—*stream* ... OK-5
Cavelero Beach—*locale* ... WA-9
Cave Lick Hollow—*valley* ... OH-6
Cavelick Run—*stream* ... WV-2
Cavell—*locale* ... AR-4
Cavell, Dr. William Henry, House—*hist pl* ... NV-8
Cavellero House—*hist pl* ... AL-4
Cave Lodge—*locale* ... MO-7
Cavelry Lake—*reservoir* ... CO-8
Cavel Sch—*school* ... NM-5
Caveman Lake—*lake* ... MN-6
*Cavemans Palace* ... TN-4
Cave Mesa—*summit* ... TX-5
Cave Mill—*locale* ... TN-4
Cave Mine—*mine* ... UT-8
**Cave Mountain**—*pop pl* ... VA-3
Cave Mountain Branch—*stream* ... AL-4
Cave Mountain Cave—*cave* ... AR-4
Cave Mountain Ch—*church* ... AR-4
Cave Mountain Ch—*church* ... VA-3
Cave Mountain Lake—*reservoir* ... VA-3
Cave Mountain Rec Area—*locale* ... VA-3
*Cave Mountains* ... CA-9
Cave Mountain Small Wild Area—*park* ... AL-4
Cave Mtn—*summit* (4) ... AL-4
Cave Mtn—*summit* (2) ... AZ-5
Cave Mtn—*summit* ... AR-4
Cave Mtn—*summit* (2) ... CA-9
Cave Mtn—*summit* (2) ... MT-8
Cave Mtn—*summit* ... NV-8
Cave Mtn—*summit* (2) ... NH-1
Cave Mtn—*summit* ... NY-2
Cave Mtn—*summit* ... OR-9
Cave Mtn—*summit* ... TX-5
Cave Mtn—*summit* ... VA-3
Cave Mtn—*summit* ... WA-9
Cave Mtn—*summit* ... WV-2
Cavena Cem—*cemetery* ... KY-4
Cavena Creek—*stream* ... KY-4
Caven Bend—*bend* ... KY-4
Caven Cem—*cemetery* (2) ... KY-4
Cavender Branch—*stream* (2) ... TN-4
Cavender Bridge—*bridge* ... GA-3
Cavender Cem—*cemetery* (2) ... GA-3
Cavender Cem—*cemetery* ... IN-6
Cavender Creek—*stream* (2) ... GA-3
Cavender Gap—*gap* ... GA-3
Cavender Mtn—*summit* ... GA-3
Cavender Ridge—*ridge* ... GA-3
Cavender Rsvr—*reservoir* ... WY-8
Cavender Run—*stream* ... IN-6
Cavender Sch (historical)—*school* ... TN-4
Cavenders Creek—*stream* ... GA-3
Cavenders Creek Ch—*church* ... GA-3
Cavenders Creek Sch—*school* ... GA-3
Cavender Tank—*reservoir* ... TX-5
Cavender Windmill—*locale* ... TX-5
Cavendish—*locale* ... ID-8
**Cavendish**—*pop pl* ... VT-1
**Cavendish Center**—*pop pl* ... VT-1
Cavendish Ditch—*canal* ... IN-6
Cavendish Gorge—*valley* ... VT-1
Cavendish Sch—*school* ... VT-1
**Cavendish (Town of)**—*pop pl* ... VT-1
Cavendish Universalist Church—*hist pl* ... VT-1
Cave Neck—*cape* ... DE-2
Caveness Branch—*stream* ... MS-4
Caveness Bridge—*bridge* ... MS-4
Caveness Cem—*cemetery* ... MS-4
Caveness Field—*airport* ... NC-3
Cavenger Hollow—*valley* ... VA-3
*Cavengers Mill* ... TN-4
Caven Point—*cape* ... NJ-2
Caven Point—*uninc pl* ... NJ-2
Caven Point Army Terminal—*military* ... NJ-2
Cavenpoint Post Office (historical)—*building* ... TN-4
Caven Point United States Army Reserve Center—*military* ... NJ-2
*Cavens Point* ... NJ-2
Cave Number Two—*cave* ... TN-4
Cave Number 7 Drift Mine (underground)—*mine* ... AL-4
Cave Off Cliffs—*cliff* ... AK-9
Cave of Refuge—*cave* ... HI-9
Cave of the Virgins—*cave* ... TN-4
Cave of the Winds—*cave* ... CO-8
Cave-of-the-Winds—*cave* ... IL-6
Cave Orchard Branch—*stream* ... TN-4
Cave Orchard Sch (historical)—*school* ... TN-4
Cave Peak—*summit* ... TX-5
Cave Peak—*summit* ... UT-8
Cave Peaks—*summit* ... NM-5
*Cave Place* ... FM-9
Cave Place—*hist pl* ... AL-4
Cave Place—*hist pl* ... KY-4
Cave Point—*cape* (2) ... AK-9
Cave Point—*cape* ... NY-2
Cave Point—*cape* (2) ... UT-8
Cave Point—*cape* ... WI-6
Cave Point—*summit* ... AR-4
Cave Point—*summit* ... CA-9
Cave Point—*summit* ... ID-8
Cave Pond—*lake* ... TN-4
Cave Pond—*lake* ... TX-5
Cave Post Office (historical)—*building* ... TN-4
Cave Resort—*locale* ... MO-7
**Caverhill (historical)**—*pop pl* ... OR-9
*Cave Ridge* ... KY-4
Cave Ridge—*locale* ... KY-4
Cave Ridge—*ridge* ... AZ-5
Cave Ridge—*ridge* ... MO-7
Cave Ridge—*ridge* ... MT-8
Cave Ridge—*ridge* (4) ... TN-4
Cave Ridge—*ridge* (2) ... UT-8
Cave Ridge—*ridge* (2) ... VA-3
Cave Ridge—*ridge* ... WA-9
Cave Ridge—*ridge* ... WV-2
Cave Ridge Cem—*cemetery* ... TN-4
Cave Ridge Sch—*school* ... KY-4
Caverly Hill—*summit* ... NH-1
Caverly Mtn—*summit* ... NH-1
**Caverna**—*pop pl* ... AR-4
**Caverna**—*pop pl* ... MO-7
Caverna HS—*school* ... KY-4
Caverna Memorial Hosp—*hospital* ... KY-4
Cavern Branch Sch—*school* ... SC-3
*Cavern Canyon* ... SD-7
Cavern City Air Terminal—*airport* ... NM-5
Cavern Creek—*stream* ... OR-9
Cavern Falls—*falls* ... WA-9
Cavern Gulch—*valley* ... CO-8
Cavern Lake—*lake* ... AK-9
Cavern of Sleep—*cave* ... UT-8
Cavern Passage—*locale* ... UT-8
Cavern Point—*cape* ... CA-9
Caverns, The, Hist Dist—*hist pl* ... NM-5
*Caverns of the Ridge* ... TN-4
*Cavern Spring* ... PA-2
Cavernville Sch (abandoned)—*school* ... MO-7
Cave Road Tank—*reservoir* ... AZ-5
Cave Rock—*island* ... OR-9
Cave Rock—*pillar* ... ID-8
Cave Rock—*pillar* ... NV-8
Cave Rock—*pillar* ... WI-6
Cave Rocks—*summit* ... CA-9
Cave Rock Spring (Dry)—*spring* ... NV-8
**Cavers Grove**—*pop pl* ... AL-4
Cavers Grove Ch—*church* ... AL-4
Cave Rsvr—*reservoir* (2) ... OR-9
Cavert JHS—*school* ... TN-4
Cave Ruin—*locale* ... AZ-5
Cave Run—*stream* ... IN-6
Cave Run—*stream* ... OH-6
Cave Run—*stream* (2) ... PA-2
Cave Run—*stream* ... VA-3
Cave Run—*stream* (6) ... WV-2
Cave Run Lake—*reservoir* ... KY-4
*Cave Run Rsvr* ... KY-4
Cave Run Trail—*trail* ... KY-4
Caves—*cave* ... CA-9
*Caves, The* ... CA-9
Caves, The—*basin* ... MD-2
Caves, The—*cave* ... NV-8
Caves, The—*cave* ... NC-3
Caves, The—*locale* ... CA-9
Cave Saint Sch—*school* ... AL-4
Caves Camp—*locale* ... OR-9
Cave Sch—*school* ... CA-9
Cave Sch—*school* ... KY-4
Cave Sch (historical)—*school* ... TN-4
*Caves City* ... OR-9
Caves Creek—*stream* ... WI-6

**Cecil**—*pop pl* ... OH-6
**Cecil**—*pop pl* ... PA-2
**Cecil**—*pop pl* ... VA-3
**Cecil**—*pop pl* ... WI-6
Cecil, Lake—*lake* ... NY-2
Cecil, Lake—*lake* ... TX-5
Cecil, Mount—*summit* ... AK-9
Cecil Ave Sch—*school* ... CA-9
*Cecil Bay* ... MI-6
Cecil Bay—*bay* ... MI-6
Cecil Bay—*lake* ... GA-3
Cecil Branch—*stream* (2) ... KY-4
Cecil Branch—*stream* ... VA-3
Cecil B Rigsby Sch—*school* ... TN-4
Cecil Butler Lake—*lake* ... FL-3
Cecil Cem—*cemetery* ... AR-4
Cecil Cem—*cemetery* ... KS-7
Cecil Cem—*cemetery* (2) ... KY-4
Cecil Cem—*cemetery* ... MD-2
Cecil Cem—*cemetery* ... MO-7
Cecil Cem—*cemetery* ... OH-6
Cecil Cem—*cemetery* (2) ... TN-4
Cecil Cem—*cemetery* ... VA-3
Cecil Chapel—*church* ... AR-4
Cecil Coulee—*valley* ... MT-8
**Cecil (County)**—*pop pl* ... MD-2
Cecil Creek—*stream* ... AR-4
Cecil Creek—*stream* ... CA-9
Cecil Creek—*stream* ... LA-4
Cecil Creek—*stream* ... MD-2
Cecil Creek—*stream* ... WA-9
Cecil Davis Park—*park* ... AZ-5
Cecil Dodd Tank—*reservoir* ... AZ-5
Cecil Dome—*summit* ... AK-9
Cecile—*locale* ... CA-9
**Cecile**—*pop pl* ... LA-4
Cecile, Lake—*lake* (3) ... FL-3
*Cecile Creek* ... WA-9
Cecile Lake—*lake* ... CA-9
Cecil Elem Sch—*school* ... PA-2
Cecil Field Naval Air Station—*military* ... FL-3
Cecil Fork—*stream* ... TN-4
Cecil Gas Field—*oilfield* ... AR-4
Cecil Hill—*summit* ... KY-4
Cecil (historical)—*locale* ... KS-7
Cecil Hollow—*valley* ... AR-4
Cecil Hollow—*valley* ... OH-6
Cecil Hollow—*valley* (3) ... TN-4
Cecilia—*locale* ... IA-7
**Cecilia**—*pop pl* ... KY-4
**Cecilia**—*pop pl* ... LA-4
Cecilia Canyon—*valley* ... NM-5
Cecilia (CCD)—*cens area* ... KY-4
Cecilia Creek—*stream* ... CO-8
Cecilia Lake—*lake* ... MI-6
Cecilia Memorial Christian Church—*hist pl* ... KY-4
Cecilian Acad—*school* ... PA-2
Cecilia Oil Field—*oilfield* ... LA-4
**Cecilia (RR name Cecelia)**—*pop pl* ... LA-4
Cecil JHS—*school* ... PA-2
**Cecil Junction**—*pop pl* ... MT-8
Cecil Lake—*lake* (3) ... CA-9
Cecil Lake—*lake* ... GA-3
Cecil Lake—*lake* ... OR-9
Cecil Metcalf Ditch—*canal* ... IN-6
Cecil M Harden Lake—*reservoir* ... IN-6
Cecil M Harden Lake Dam—*dam* ... IN-6
Cecil Mine—*mine* ... CO-8
Cecil Mission—*church* ... VA-3
Cecil Mtn—*summit* ... ME-1
Cecil Park—*flat* ... WY-8
Cecil Park—*park* ... CA-9
**Cecil Park**—*pop pl* ... NY-2
Cecil Point—*cape* ... CA-9
Cecil Pond—*reservoir* ... AZ-5
Cecil Post Office (historical)—*building* ... MS-4
Cecil Rhode Mtn—*summit* ... AK-9
Cecil Ridge—*ridge* (2) ... KY-4
Cecil Ridge—*ridge* ... WV-2
Cecils Canal—*canal* ... LA-4
Cecils Ch—*church* ... VA-3
Cecil Sch—*school* (2) ... NC-3
Cecil Sch Number 8—*school* ... NJ-2
Cecils Lake—*lake* ... WA-9
Cecil's Mill Hist Dist—*hist pl* ... MD-2
Cecil Tank—*reservoir* ... AZ-5
*Cecilton* ... TN-4
**Cecilton**—*pop pl* ... MD-2
Cecilton Post Office (historical)—*building* ... TN-4
**Cecil Township**—*pop pl* ... ND-7
Cecil (Township of)—*fmr MCD* ... NC-3
**Cecil (Township of)**—*pop pl* ... PA-2
Cecil Vig Dam—*dam* ... SD-7
Cecil Vig Dam Number 1—*dam* ... SD-7
Cecil Vig Dam Number 2—*dam* ... SD-7
**Cecilville**—*pop pl* ... CA-9
Cecil Well—*well* ... AZ-5
Cecil Windmill—*locale* ... NM-5
C Eckles Ranch—*locale* ... NM-5
Ceda Bluff—*cliff* ... KY-4
Cedar—*fmr MCD* ... NE-7
Cedar—*locale* ... AZ-5
Cedar—*locale* ... ID-8
Cedar—*locale* ... IA-7
Cedar—*locale* ... KS-7
Cedar—*locale* ... ME-1
Cedar—*locale* ... NV-8
Cedar—*locale* ... OK-5
Cedar—*locale* ... UT-8
Cedar—*locale* (2) ... WV-2
Cedar—*locale* ... WI-6
**Cedar**—*pop pl* ... CO-8
**Cedar**—*pop pl* ... IN-6
**Cedar**—*pop pl* ... IA-7
**Cedar**—*pop pl* ... KS-7
**Cedar**—*pop pl* ... MA-1
**Cedar**—*pop pl* ... MI-6
**Cedar**—*pop pl* ... MN-6
Cedar—*post sta* ... CA-9
Cedar, Bayou—*gut* ... LA-4
Cedar, Lake—*reservoir* ... MO-7
Cedara, Mount—*summit* ... OR-9
**Cedar Acres**—*pop pl* ... MD-2
Cedar Acres Airp (private)—*airport* ... PA-2
Cedar Acres Ch—*church* ... AL-4
*Cedar Airpark* ... KS-7
Cedar Air Park—*airport* ... KS-7
Cedar Arroyo—*valley* ... TX-5
Cedar Ave Bridge—*bridge* ... MN-6
Cedar Bank—*locale* ... MI-6
Cedar-Bank Works—*hist pl* ... OH-6
Cedar Bar Creek—*stream* ... MT-8
Cedar Basin—*basin* (9) ... AZ-5
Cedar Basin—*basin* (5) ... CA-9
Cedar Basin—*basin* ... NV-8
Cedar Basin—*basin* ... WA-9
Cedar Basin—*basin* ... WY-8
Cedar Basin Camp—*locale* ... AZ-5
Cedar Basin Camp—*locale* ... CA-9
Cedar Basin Canyon—*valley* (2) ... AZ-5
Cedar Basin Dam—*dam* ... AZ-5
Cedar Basin Ditch—*canal* (2) ... WY-8
Cedar Basin Spring—*spring* (2) ... AZ-5
Cedar Basin Tank—*reservoir* (4) ... AZ-5
*Cedar Bay* ... NY-2
*Cedar Bay* ... NC-3
Cedar Bay—*bay* ... AK-9
Cedar Bay—*bay* ... GA-3
Cedar Bay—*bay* (2) ... NC-3
Cedar Bay—*lake* ... NY-2
Cedar Bay—*locale* ... NC-3
Cedar Bay—*stream* ... MO-7
Cedar Bay—*swamp* ... NC-3
Cedar Bay—*swamp* ... SC-3
Cedar Bay Baptist Ch—*church* ... FL-3
Cedar Bay Ch—*church* ... FL-3
*Cedar Bayou* ... LA-4
Cedar Bayou—*gut* ... TX-5
Cedar Bayou—*locale* ... TX-5
Cedar Bayou—*stream* ... AR-4
Cedar Bayou—*stream* ... MS-4
Cedar Bayou—*stream* (2) ... TX-5
Cedar Bayou Archeol District—*hist pl* ... TX-5
Cedar Bayou Channel—*channel* ... TX-5
Cedar Bayou JHS—*school* ... TX-5
Cedar Bay Point—*cape* ... NC-3
*Cedar Beach* ... CT-1
Cedar Beach—*beach* (2) ... NY-2
Cedar Beach—*locale* ... DE-2
**Cedar Beach**—*pop pl* ... CT-1
**Cedar Beach**—*pop pl* ... MD-2
**Cedar Beach**—*pop pl* ... MN-6
**Cedar Beach**—*pop pl* (2) ... NJ-2
**Cedar Beach**—*pop pl* ... VT-1
Cedar Beach Bridge—*bridge* ... DE-2
Cedar Beach Creek—*bay* ... NY-2
Cedar Beach Point—*cape* ... NY-2
Cedar Bed Ground Rsvr—*reservoir* ... MT-8
Cedar Bench—*bench* (3) ... AZ-5
Cedar Bench—*bench* ... CO-8
Cedar Bench—*bench* (3) ... UT-8
Cedar Bench Tank—*reservoir* ... AZ-5
Cedar Bench Tank Number One—*reservoir* ... AZ-5
Cedar Bench Tank Number Two—*reservoir* ... AZ-5
*Cedar Bend* (2) ... AL-4
Cedar Bend—*bend* ... AL-4
Cedar Bend—*bend* ... AR-4
Cedar Bend—*bend* ... KY-4
Cedar Bend—*bend* ... TX-5
Cedar Bend—*bend* ... WI-6
**Cedar Bend**—*pop pl* ... MI-6
Cedar Bend Bridge—*bridge* ... TX-5
Cedar Bend County Park—*park* ... IA-7
Cedar Bend Park—*park* ... IA-7
Cedar Bend Plantation—*hist pl* ... LA-4
**Cedarbend (Township of)**—*pop pl* ... MN-6
Cedar Berry Bob Tank—*reservoir* ... AZ-5
Cedar-Bethel Cem—*cemetery* ... IA-7
Cedar Bight—*bay* ... AK-9
Cedar Birch Spring—*spring* ... ID-8
*Cedar Bluff* ... KS-7
*Cedarbluff* ... MS-4
Cedar Bluff—*cliff* (4) ... AR-4
Cedar Bluff—*cliff* (2) ... IL-6
Cedar Bluff—*cliff* ... IN-6
Cedar Bluff—*cliff* ... KS-7
Cedar Bluff—*cliff* ... KY-4
Cedar Bluff—*cliff* ... LA-4
Cedar Bluff—*cliff* (10) ... MO-7
Cedar Bluff—*cliff* (2) ... OK-5
Cedar Bluff—*cliff* (4) ... TN-4
Cedar Bluff—*cliff* (3) ... TX-5
Cedar Bluff—*cliff* ... VA-3
Cedar Bluff—*hist pl* ... SC-3
Cedar Bluff—*locale* ... KY-4
Cedar Bluff—*locale* ... MO-7
Cedar Bluff—*locale* ... VA-3
**Cedar Bluff**—*pop pl* ... AL-4
**Cedar Bluff**—*pop pl* ... IA-7
**Cedar Bluff**—*pop pl* ... MI-6
**Cedar Bluff**—*pop pl* ... MS-4
**Cedar Bluff**—*pop pl* (3) ... TN-4
**Cedarbluff**—*pop pl* ... TN-4
**Cedar Bluff**—*pop pl* ... VA-3
Cedar Bluff—*ridge* ... GA-3
Cedar Bluff—*summit* ... VA-3
Cedar Bluff Baptist Ch—*church* ... MS-4
Cedar Bluff Branch—*stream* ... TN-4
Cedar Bluff Camp—*locale* ... KS-7
Cedar Bluff Canal—*canal* ... KS-7
Cedar Bluff Canyon—*valley* ... TX-5
Cedar Bluff Cem—*cemetery* ... AL-4
Cedar Bluff Cem—*cemetery* ... IL-6
Cedar Bluff Cem—*cemetery* (2) ... KS-7
Cedar Bluff Cem—*cemetery* (3) ... MO-7
Cedar Bluff Ch—*church* ... AL-4
Cedar Bluff Ch—*church* ... IL-6
Cedar Bluff Ch—*church* ... KY-4
Cedar Bluff Ch—*church* (2) ... MO-7
Cedar Bluff Ch—*church* ... OK-5
Cedar Bluff Ch—*church* (2) ... TN-4
Cedar Bluff Ch—*church* (2) ... VA-3
Cedar Bluff Creek—*stream* ... MO-7
Cedar Bluff Creek—*stream* ... SD-7
Cedar Bluff Dam—*dam* ... KS-7
Cedar Bluff Draw—*valley* ... TX-5
Cedar Bluff-Gaylesville (CCD)—*cens area* ... AL-4
Cedar Bluff-Gaylesville Division—*civil* ... AL-4
Cedar Bluff (historical)—*locale* ... KS-7
Cedar Bluff HS—*school* ... AL-4
Cedar Bluff Intermediate Sch—*school* ... TN-4
Cedar Bluff Knob—*summit* ... KY-4
*Cedar Bluff Lake* ... KS-7
Cedar Bluff Landing—*locale* ... GA-3
Cedar Bluff Marina—*locale* ... AL-4
Cedar Bluff Methodist Ch—*church* ... MS-4
Cedar Bluff Mill—*locale* ... TN-4
Cedar Bluff MS—*school* ... TN-4
Cedar Bluff Natl Fish Hatchery—*park* ... KS-7
Cedar Bluff Park—*park* ... AL-4
Cedar Bluff Post Office—*building* ... AL-4
Cedarbluff Post Office (historical)—*building* ... TN-4
Cedar Bluff Primary Sch—*school* ... TN-4
Cedar Bluff Quarry—*mine* ... TN-4
Cedar Bluff Ridge—*ridge* ... MO-7
**Cedarbluff (RR name Cedar Bluff)**—*pop pl* ... MS-4
Cedar Bluff (RR name for Cedarbluff)—*other* ... MS-4
Cedar Bluff Rsvr—*reservoir* ... KS-7
Cedar Bluffs—*cliff* ... MO-7
Cedar Bluffs—*cliff* ... SD-7
**Cedar Bluffs**—*pop pl* ... KS-7
**Cedar Bluffs**—*pop pl* ... NE-7
**Cedar Bluffs**—*pop pl* ... NY-2
Cedar Bluffs Cem—*cemetery* ... KS-7
Cedar Bluff Sch—*school* (2) ... IL-6
Cedar Bluff Sch—*school* ... KS-7
Cedar Bluff Sch (abandoned)—*school* ... MO-7
Cedar Bluff School (historical)—*locale* ... MO-7
Cedar Bluff Schools—*school* ... TN-4
Cedar Bluff Shop Ctr—*locale* ... TN-4
Cedar Bluff Spring—*spring* ... AL-4
Cedar Bluff Tank—*reservoir* ... TX-5
Cedar Bluff Township—*civil* ... MO-7
Cedar Bluff Wildlife Area—*park* ... KS-7
Cedar Bluff Windmill—*locale* (2) ... TX-5
Cedar Bog Lake—*lake* ... MI-6
Cedar Bog Lake—*lake* ... MN-6
Cedar Bonnet—*swamp* ... NJ-2
**Cedar Bonnet Island**—*pop pl* ... NJ-2
Cedar Bonnet Islands—*island* ... NJ-2
Cedarbook Mall—*locale* ... PA-2
Cedar Bottom—*bend* ... AR-4
Cedar Bottom Ch—*church* ... KY-4
Cedar Bottom Ch—*church* ... MO-7
Cedar Bottom Creek—*stream* ... MO-7
Cedar Bottom Sch (abandoned)—*school* ... MO-7
Cedar Boy Creek—*stream* ... SD-7
**Cedar Brae Farm**—*pop pl* ... DE-2
Cedar Brake (Girl Scout Camp)—*locale* ... TX-5
Cedar Brake Rsvr No 1—*reservoir* ... WY-8
Cedar Brakes, The—*summit* ... TX-5
*Cedar Branch* ... AL-4
*Cedar Branch* ... ME-1
*Cedar Branch* ... NJ-2
*Cedar Branch* ... SC-3
*Cedar Branch* ... TN-4
**Cedar Branch**—*pop pl* ... VA-3
Cedar Branch—*stream* (5) ... AL-4
Cedar Branch—*stream* (9) ... AR-4
Cedar Branch—*stream* (2) ... FL-3
Cedar Branch—*stream* ... GA-3
Cedar Branch—*stream* ... KY-4
Cedar Branch—*stream* ... LA-4
Cedar Branch—*stream* ... MD-2
Cedar Branch—*stream* (3) ... MO-7
Cedar Branch—*stream* (4) ... NJ-2
Cedar Branch—*stream* (8) ... NC-3
Cedar Branch—*stream* ... OH-6
Cedar Branch—*stream* (2) ... OK-5
Cedar Branch—*stream* ... OR-9
Cedar Branch—*stream* (4) ... SC-3
Cedar Branch—*stream* (5) ... TN-4
Cedar Branch—*stream* (11) ... TX-5
Cedar Branch—*stream* (5) ... VA-3
Cedar Branch—*stream* (4) ... WV-2
Cedar Branch Cem—*cemetery* ... SC-3
Cedar Branch Ch—*church* ... AR-4
Cedar Branch Ch—*church* ... NC-3
Cedar Branch Ch—*church* ... SC-3
Cedar Branch Ch—*church* ... TX-5
Cedar Branch Hollow—*valley* ... KY-4
Cedar Branch Sch—*school* (2) ... SC-3
Cedar Branch Sch (historical)—*school* ... MO-7
Cedar Breaks—*cliff* ... NM-5
Cedar Breaks—*ridge* ... WY-8
Cedar Breaks—*summit* ... UT-8
Cedar Breaks Amphitheater—*area* ... UT-8
Cedar Breaks Archeol District—*hist pl* ... OK-5
Cedar Breaks Draw—*valley* ... WY-8
Cedar Breaks Lodge—*locale* ... UT-8
Cedar Breaks Natl Monmt—*park* ... UT-8
*Cedar Breaks Rim* ... UT-8
Cedar Breaks Visitor Center—*locale* ... UT-8
*Cedar Bridge* ... MO-7
Cedar Bridge—*bridge* ... MS-4
**Cedar Bridge**—*pop pl* ... NJ-2
*Cedar Bridge Branch* ... NJ-2
Cedar Bridge Branch—*stream* ... NJ-2
Cedar Bridge Hollow—*valley* ... VA-3
**Cedar Bridge Manor**—*pop pl* ... NJ-2
Cedar Bridge Pond—*lake* ... NY-2
*Cedarbrook* ... IL-6
*Cedar Brook* ... NJ-2
**Cedarbrook**—*pop pl* ... CA-9
**Cedar Brook**—*pop pl* ... NJ-2
**Cedarbrook**—*pop pl* ... PA-2
Cedar Brook—*stream* ... IN-6
Cedar Brook—*stream* ... KY-4
Cedar Brook—*stream* (7) ... ME-1
Cedar Brook—*stream* (3) ... MA-1
Cedar Brook—*stream* ... MN-6
Cedar Brook—*stream* (4) ... NH-1
Cedar Brook—*stream* (4) ... NJ-2
Cedar Brook—*stream* (3) ... NY-2
Cedar Brook—*stream* ... RI-1
**Cedarbrook Acres**—*pop pl* ... DE-2
Cedar Brook Camp—*park* ... IN-6
Cedarbrook Country Club—*locale* ... NC-3
Cedarbrook Country Club—*locale* ... PA-2
Cedar Brook Country Club—*other* ... NY-2
Cedarbrook Country Club—*other* ... PA-2
**Cedarbrook County Home**—*pop pl* ... PA-2
Cedarbrook Golf Course—*locale* ... PA-2
*Cedarbrook Hills* ... PA-2
**Cedarbrook Hills**—*pop pl* ... PA-2
*Cedarbrook Hills Country Club* ... PA-2
Cedar Brook Lake—*lake* ... NJ-2
Cedar Brook Lake—*reservoir* ... CO-8
Cedarbrook Lake—*reservoir* ... NC-3
Cedarbrook Lake Dam—*dam* ... NC-3
**Cedar Brook-Melrose Park**—*pop pl* ... PA-2
Cedar Brook Park—*park* ... NJ-2
Cedarbrook Plaza (Shop Ctr)—*locale* ... FL-3
*Cedar Brook Rest Home* ... PA-2
Cedar Brook Sch—*school* ... MA-1
Cedar Brook Sch—*school* ... NH-1
Cedar Brook Sch—*school* ... VA-3
**Cedar Brook (subdivision)**—*pop pl* ... AL-4
**Cedar Brook (subdivision)**—*pop pl* ... NC-3
**Cedarbrook (subdivision)**—*pop pl* (2) ... TN-4
**Cedarburg**—*pop pl* ... WI-6
Cedarburg Bog—*swamp* ... WI-6
Cedarburg Bog Wildlife Ref—*park* ... WI-6
Cedarburg Creek—*stream* ... OK-5
Cedarburg Mill—*hist pl* ... WI-6
**Cedarburg (Town of)**—*pop pl* ... WI-6
Cedarburg Woolen Co. Worsted Mill—*hist pl* ... WI-6
Cedar Burn Camp—*locale* ... OR-9
Cedar Bush Bay—*bay* ... NC-3
Cedarbush Creek—*stream* ... VA-3
**Cedar Bushes**—*pop pl* ... MA-1
Cedarbush Hole—*area* ... DE-2
Cedarbush Island—*island* ... ME-1
*Cedar Butte* ... SD-7
**Cedarbutte**—*pop pl* ... SD-7
**Cedar Butte**—*pop pl* ... SD-7
Cedar Butte—*summit* (5) ... ID-8
Cedar Butte—*summit* ... MT-8
Cedar Butte—*summit* (2) ... ND-7
Cedar Butte—*summit* (3) ... OR-9
Cedar Butte—*summit* (4) ... SD-7
Cedar Butte—*summit* ... WA-9
Cedar Butte—*summit* ... WY-8
Cedar Butte No. 4 Township—*civ div* ... SD-7
Cedar Buttes—*summit* ... OR-9
Cedar Butte Sch—*school* ... SD-7
Cedar Buttes Rsvr—*reservoir* ... WY-8
Cedarbutte Township—*civ div* ... SD-7
Cedar Butte Township—*civil* (2) ... SD-7
Cedar Butte Well—*well* ... ID-8
Cedar Cabin Mtn—*summit* ... AR-4
Cedar Cabin Spring—*spring* ... NV-8
Cedar Camp—*locale* (4) ... CA-9
Cedar Camp—*locale* ... MN-6
Cedar Camp—*locale* (3) ... OR-9
Cedar Camp—*locale* (2) ... WA-9
Cedar Camp Canyon—*valley* ... UT-8
Cedar Campground—*locale* ... MT-8
Cedar Camp Ridge—*ridge* ... UT-8
Cedar Camp Spring—*spring* ... CA-9
Cedar Camp Spring—*spring* ... UT-8
Cedar Campus Camp—*locale* ... MI-6
Cedar Canon Mine—*mine* ... CO-8
*Cedar Canyon* ... AZ-5
*Cedar Canyon* ... NV-8
Cedar Canyon—*locale* ... SD-7
**Cedar Canyon**—*pop pl* ... ID-8
Cedar Canyon—*valley* (7) ... AZ-5
Cedar Canyon—*valley* (14) ... CA-9
Cedar Canyon—*valley* ... CO-8
Cedar Canyon—*valley* ... ID-8
Cedar Canyon—*valley* ... MT-8
Cedar Canyon—*valley* (4) ... NE-7
Cedar Canyon—*valley* (4) ... NV-8
Cedar Canyon—*valley* (14) ... NM-5
Cedar Canyon—*valley* (2) ... ND-7
Cedar Canyon—*valley* (4) ... OK-5
Cedar Canyon—*valley* ... OR-9
Cedar Canyon—*valley* (3) ... SD-7
Cedar Canyon—*valley* (9) ... TX-5
Cedar Canyon—*valley* (9) ... UT-8
Cedar Canyon—*valley* ... WA-9
Cedar Canyon—*valley* (5) ... WY-8
Cedar Canyon Bridge—*hist pl* ... AZ-5
Cedar Canyon Campground—*locale* ... UT-8
Cedar Canyon Creek—*stream* ... MT-8
*Cedar Canyon Dam* ... SD-7
Cedar Canyon Mesa—*summit* ... NM-5
**Cedar Canyons**—*pop pl* ... IN-6
Cedar Canyon Ski Area—*locale* ... UT-8
Cedar Canyon Tank—*reservoir* ... AZ-5
Cedar Canyon Windmill—*locale* ... TX-5
Cedar Cave—*cave* ... AL-4
Cedar Cem—*cemetery* ... CO-8
Cedar Cem—*cemetery* (2) ... IA-7
Cedar Cem—*cemetery* ... KS-7
Cedar Cem—*cemetery* ... LA-4
Cedar Cem—*cemetery* ... MN-6
Cedar Cem—*cemetery* (2) ... MO-7
Cedar Cem—*cemetery* ... ND-7
Cedar Cem—*cemetery* (2) ... OH-6
Cedar Cem—*cemetery* ... OK-5
Cedar Cem—*cemetery* ... SD-7
Cedar Cem—*cemetery* ... TN-4
Cedar Cem—*cemetery* (2) ... TX-5
Cedar Cem—*cemetery* ... WI-6
Cedar Center Sch—*school* ... IA-7
Cedar Ch—*church* ... GA-3
Cedar Ch—*church* ... IN-6
Cedar Ch—*church* ... MN-6
Cedar Ch—*church* ... NC-3
Cedar Ch—*church* ... ND-7
Cedar Ch—*church* ... OK-5
Cedar Ch—*church* ... PA-2
Cedar Ch—*church* (2) ... SD-7
Cedar Ch—*church* ... TX-5
Cedar Ch—*church* ... VA-3
Cedar Chapel—*church* ... IN-6
Cedar Chapel—*church* ... KY-4
Cedar Chapel—*church* ... MS-4
Cedar Chapel—*church* ... OH-6
Cedar Chapel—*church* ... TN-4
**Cedar Chapel**—*pop pl* ... TN-4
Cedar Chapel Post Office (historical)—*building* ... TN-4
Cedar Chapel Sch—*school* ... MD-2
**Cedarchase**—*pop pl* ... TN-4
Cedar Circle Fish Camp—*locale* ... AL-4
**Cedar City**—*pop pl* ... IA-7
**Cedar City**—*pop pl* ... MO-7
**Cedar City**—*pop pl* ... UT-8
Cedar City Airp Heliport—*airport* ... UT-8
Cedar City Cem—*cemetery* ... MN-6
Cedar City Cem—*cemetery* ... UT-8
Cedar City Corp Storage Dam—*dam* ... UT-8
Cedar City Corp Storage Rsvr—*reservoir* ... UT-8
Cedar City Division—*civil* ... UT-8
Cedar City HS—*school* ... UT-8
Cedar City KOA—*locale* ... UT-8
Cedar City MS—*school* ... UT-8
Cedar City Municipal Airport—*airport* ... UT-8
Cedar City Post Office—*building* ... UT-8
Cedar City RR Depot—*hist pl* ... UT-8
Cedar City Sch—*school* ... MN-6
Cedar City Upland State Game Sanctuary—*park* ... UT-8
Cedar Cliff—*cliff* ... AL-4
Cedar Cliff—*cliff* ... GA-3
Cedar Cliff—*cliff* (3) ... NC-3
Cedar Cliff—*cliff* ... WI-6
Cedar Cliff—*locale* ... GA-3
Cedar Cliff—*locale* ... MD-2
Cedar Cliff—*locale* ... NY-2
**Cedar Cliff**—*pop pl* ... PA-2
Cedar Cliff—*ridge* ... NC-3
Cedar Cliff—*summit* (4) ... NC-3
Cedar Cliff, Lake—*reservoir* ... NC-3
Cedar Cliff Cem—*cemetery* ... WV-2
Cedar Cliff Ch—*church* ... KY-4
Cedar Cliff Ch—*church* (3) ... NC-3
Cedar Cliff Ch—*church* ... TN-4
Cedar Cliff Ch—*church* ... VA-3
Cedar Cliff Dam—*dam* ... NC-3
Cedarcliff Gatehouse—*hist pl* ... NY-2
Cedar Cliff Hollow—*valley* ... OH-6
Cedar Cliff HS—*school* ... PA-2
Cedar Cliff Knob—*summit* (2) ... GA-3
Cedar Cliff Knob—*summit* ... NC-3
Cedar Cliff Lake—*reservoir* ... NC-3
Cedar Cliff Mall—*locale* ... PA-2
**Cedar Cliff Manor**—*pop pl* ... PA-2
Cedar Cliff Mtn—*summit* (2) ... NC-3
Cedar Cliff Mtn—*summit* ... TN-4
*Cedar Cliff Reservoir* ... NC-3
Cedar Cliff Ridge—*ridge* (2) ... NC-3
Cedar Cliffs—*cliff* ... IN-6
Cedar Cliffs—*cliff* ... KY-4
Cedar Cliffs—*cliff* ... NC-3
Cedar Cliff Sch—*school* ... OH-6
Cedar Cliffs Park—*park* ... IN-6
Cedar Cliffs Trail—*trail* ... KY-4
Cedar Corner Ditch—*canal* ... IN-6
Cedar Corners—*locale* ... DE-2
**Cedar Corners**—*pop pl* ... OH-6
Cedar Corner Sch—*school* ... NE-7
Cedar Corral—*locale* ... AZ-5
Cedar Corral—*summit* ... UT-8
Cedar Corral Canyon—*valley* ... UT-8
*Cedar Corral Spring* ... NV-8
Cedar Corral Spring—*spring* ... NV-8
Cedar Coulee—*valley* (2) ... MT-8
Cedar Coulee—*valley* (2) ... ND-7
**Cedar County**—*pop pl* ... MO-7
Cedar County Home—*building* ... IA-7
Cedar Cove—*basin* ... AL-4
Cedar Cove—*bay* (2) ... AK-9
Cedar Cove—*bay* ... MO-7
Cedar Cove—*bay* ... TX-5
Cedar Cove—*bay* ... VA-3
Cedar Cove—*cove* ... MA-1
**Cedar Cove**—*pop pl* ... AL-4
**Cedar Cove**—*pop pl* ... CO-8
**Cedar Cove**—*pop pl* ... MS-4
Cedar Cove—*valley* ... CA-9
Cedar Cove—*valley* ... NC-3
Cedar Cove Bridge—*bridge* ... TX-5
Cedar Cove Ch—*church* ... AL-4
**Cedar Cove Estates**—*pop pl* ... AL-4
Cedar Cove Gut—*gut* ... VA-3
Cedar Cove Lake—*reservoir* ... OK-5
Cedar Cove Mine (underground)—*mine* ... AL-4
Cedar Covered Bridge—*hist pl* ... IA-7
*Cedar Creek* ... AL-4
*Cedar Creek* ... AZ-5
*Cedar Creek* ... AR-4
*Cedar Creek* ... CA-9
*Cedar Creek* ... FL-3
*Cedar Creek* ... GA-3
*Cedar Creek* ... ID-8
*Cedar Creek* ... IN-6
*Cedar Creek* ... IA-7
*Cedar Creek* ... KS-7
*Cedar Creek* ... MI-6
*Cedar Creek* ... MS-4
*Cedar Creek* ... MO-7
*Cedar Creek* ... MT-8
*Cedar Creek* ... NE-7
*Cedar Creek* ... NV-8
*Cedar Creek* ... NJ-2
*Cedar Creek* ... NC-3
*Cedar Creek* ... ND-7
*Cedar Creek* ... OK-5
*Cedar Creek* ... OR-9
*Cedar Creek* ... PA-2
*Cedar Creek* ... SD-7
*Cedar Creek* ... TN-4
*Cedar Creek* ... TX-5
*Cedar Creek* ... UT-8
*Cedar Creek* ... VA-3
*Cedar Creek* ... WI-6
*Cedar Creek* ... WY-8
Cedar Creek—*bay* ... MD-2
Cedar Creek—*bay* ... NC-3
Cedar Creek—*channel* ... FL-3
Cedar Creek—*channel* ... GA-3
Cedar Creek—*channel* ... VA-3
Cedar Creek—*gut* ... FL-3
Cedar Creek—*gut* ... NJ-2
Cedar Creek—*gut* ... NC-3
Cedar Creek—*locale* ... AR-4
Cedar Creek—*locale* ... CO-8
Cedar Creek—*locale* ... ID-8
Cedar Creek—*locale* ... PA-2
Cedar Creek—*locale* ... SC-3
Cedar Creek—*locale* ... TX-5
Cedar Creek—*locale* ... UT-8
**Cedar Creek**—*pop pl* ... AZ-5
**Cedar Creek**—*pop pl* ... AR-4
**Cedar Creek**—*pop pl* ... FL-3
**Cedar Creek**—*pop pl* ... IN-6
**Cedar Creek**—*pop pl* ... MI-6
**Cedarcreek**—*pop pl* ... MI-6
**Cedarcreek**—*pop pl* ... MO-7
**Cedar Creek**—*pop pl* ... MO-7
**Cedar Creek**—*pop pl* ... NE-7
**Cedar Creek**—*pop pl* ... NM-5
**Cedar Creek**—*pop pl* ... NC-3
**Cedar Creek**—*pop pl* ... SC-3
**Cedar Creek**—*pop pl* ... TN-4
**Cedarcreek**—*pop pl* ... TN-4
**Cedar Creek**—*pop pl* ... TX-5
**Cedar Creek**—*pop pl* ... VA-3
**Cedar Creek**—*pop pl* ... WI-6
Cedar Creek—*stream* (24) ... AL-4
Cedar Creek—*stream* (2) ... AK-9
Cedar Creek—*stream* (5) ... AZ-5
Cedar Creek—*stream* (45) ... AR-4
Cedar Creek—*stream* (35) ... CA-9
Cedar Creek—*stream* (7) ... CO-8
Cedar Creek—*stream* (2) ... DE-2
Cedar Creek—*stream* (10) ... FL-3
Cedar Creek—*stream* (23) ... GA-3
Cedar Creek—*stream* (21) ... ID-8
Cedar Creek—*stream* (13) ... IL-6
Cedar Creek—*stream* (3) ... IN-6
Cedar Creek—*stream* (10) ... IA-7
Cedar Creek—*stream* (19) ... KS-7
Cedar Creek—*stream* (13) ... KY-4
Cedar Creek—*stream* ... LA-4
Cedar Creek—*stream* (2) ... MD-2
Cedar Creek—*stream* (20) ... MI-6
Cedar Creek—*stream* (9) ... MN-6
Cedar Creek—*stream* (8) ... MS-4
Cedar Creek—*stream* (19) ... MO-7
Cedar Creek—*stream* (27) ... MT-8
Cedar Creek—*stream* (14) ... NE-7
Cedar Creek—*stream* (3) ... NV-8
Cedar Creek—*stream* (5) ... NJ-2
Cedar Creek—*stream* (3) ... NM-5
Cedar Creek—*stream* ... NY-2
Cedar Creek—*stream* (25) ... NC-3
Cedar Creek—*stream* (3) ... ND-7
Cedar Creek—*stream* (2) ... OH-6
Cedar Creek—*stream* (45) ... OK-5
Cedar Creek—*stream* (68) ... OR-9
Cedar Creek—*stream* (3) ... PA-2
Cedar Creek—*stream* (17) ... SC-3
Cedar Creek—*stream* (4) ... SD-7
Cedar Creek—*stream* (15) ... TN-4
Cedar Creek—*stream* (85) ... TX-5
Cedar Creek—*stream* (4) ... UT-8
Cedar Creek—*stream* (16) ... VA-3
Cedar Creek—*stream* (38) ... WA-9
Cedar Creek—*stream* (4) ... WV-2
Cedar Creek—*stream* (8) ... WI-6
Cedar Creek—*stream* (10) ... WY-8
Cedar Creek—*valley* ... TX-5
Cedar Creek Access Area—*park* ... TN-4
Cedar Creek Alluvial Fan—*area* ... MT-8
Cedar Creek Aqueduct—*canal* ... MT-8
Cedar Creek Baptist Ch—*church* (2) ... FL-3
Cedar Creek Bar—*bar* ... AL-4
Cedar Creek Bar—*bar* ... ID-8
**Cedar Creek Battlefield**—*pop pl* ... VA-3
Cedar Creek Battlefield and Belle Grove—*hist pl* ... VA-3
Cedar Creek Bay—*swamp* ... SC-3
Cedar Creek Bench—*bench* ... UT-8
Cedar Creek Boat Dock—*locale* ... TN-4
Cedar Creek Boat Launching Area—*locale* ... DE-2
Cedar Creek Bridge—*bridge* ... TN-4
Cedar Creek Bridge—*hist pl* ... KS-7
Cedar Creek Camp—*locale* ... OR-9
Cedar Creek Campground—*locale* ... AL-4
Cedar Creek Campground—*locale* ... CA-9
Cedar Creek Campground—*locale* ... NM-5
Cedar Creek Canal—*canal* ... DE-2
Cedar Creek Cave—*cave* ... TN-4
Cedar Creek Cem—*cemetery* (3) ... AL-4
Cedar Creek Cem—*cemetery* (2) ... AR-4
Cedar Creek Cem—*cemetery* ... FL-3
Cedar Creek Cem—*cemetery* ... GA-3
Cedar Creek Cem—*cemetery* ... IL-6
Cedar Creek Cem—*cemetery* ... IA-7
Cedar Creek Cem—*cemetery* ... KS-7
Cedar Creek Cem—*cemetery* ... KY-4
Cedar Creek Cem—*cemetery* ... MI-6
Cedar Creek Cem—*cemetery* ... MS-4
Cedar Creek Cem—*cemetery* (2) ... MO-7
Cedar Creek Cem—*cemetery* ... NC-3
Cedar Creek Cem—*cemetery* ... ND-7
Cedar Creek Cem—*cemetery* ... OK-5
Cedar Creek Cem—*cemetery* (3) ... TX-5
*Cedar Creek Ch* ... AL-4
*Cedar Creek Ch* ... MS-4
Cedar Creek Ch—*church* (9) ... AL-4
Cedar Creek Ch—*church* ... AR-4
Cedar Creek Ch—*church* ... FL-3
Cedar Creek Ch—*church* (8) ... GA-3
Cedar Creek Ch—*church* ... IL-6
Cedar Creek Ch—*church* ... IN-6
Cedar Creek Ch—*church* ... KS-7
Cedar Creek Ch—*church* (2) ... KY-4
Cedar Creek Ch—*church* ... MI-6
Cedar Creek Ch—*church* ... MS-4
Cedar Creek Ch—*church* ... MO-7
Cedar Creek Ch—*church* ... NE-7
Cedar Creek Ch—*church* (4) ... NC-3
Cedar Creek Ch—*church* (2) ... OK-5
Cedar Creek Ch—*church* (7) ... SC-3
Cedar Creek Ch—*church* (4) ... TN-4
Cedar Creek Ch—*church* (4) ... TX-5
Cedar Creek Ch—*church* (3) ... VA-3
Cedar Creek Ch—*church* ... WV-2
*Cedar Creek Channel* ... DE-2
Cedar Creek Ch (historical)—*church* ... MS-4
*Cedar Creek Ch of Christ* ... AL-4
Cedar Creek Church—*stream* ... IA-7
Cedar Creek Club Dock—*locale* ... TN-4
Cedar Creek Crossing—*locale* ... AZ-5
*Cedar Creek Cumberland Presbyterian Ch* ... AL-4
Cedar Creek Dam—*dam* ... AL-4
Cedar Creek District—*hist pl* ... OK-5
*Cedar Creek Ditch* ... IN-6
Cedar Creek Dock—*locale* ... TN-4
*Cedar Creek Drain* ... MI-6
Cedar Creek Drain—*stream* ... MI-6
Cedar Creek Falls—*falls* ... AL-4
Cedar Creek Falls—*falls* ... CA-9
Cedar Creek Falls—*falls* ... WA-9
Cedar Creek Fish Camp—*locale* ... AL-4
Cedar Creek Forest Camp—*locale* ... WA-9
*Cedar Creek Free Will Baptist Church* ... AL-4
Cedar Creek Grist Mill—*hist pl* ... WA-9
Cedar Creek Harbor—*harbor* ... CT-1
Cedar Creek Hiking Trail—*trail* ... MO-7
**Cedar Creek (historical)**—*pop pl* ... MS-4
Cedar Creek Hundred—*civil* ... DE-2
Cedar Creek Island—*island* ... TN-4
Cedar Creek Island (historical)—*island* ... SD-7
Cedar Creek Lake—*reservoir* ... NC-3
Cedar Creek Landing—*locale* ... FL-3
Cedar Creek Landing—*locale* ... SC-3

Cedar Creek Landing—locale ... TN-4
Cedar Creek Landing (historical)—locale ... AL-4
Cedar Creek Landing Post Office (historical)—building ... TN-4
Cedar Creek (Magisterial District)—fmr MCD ... VA-3
Cedar Creek Marina—locale ... AL-4
Cedar Creek Marsh—swamp ... MD-2
Cedar Creek Meadow ... WA-9
Cedar Creek Meadows—flat ... WA-9
Cedar Creek Millpond ... DE-2
Cedar Creek Millpond Dam ... DE-2
Cedar Creek Millpond (historical)—reservoir ... SC-3
Cedar Creek Mine—mine ... CO-8
Cedar Creek Mission—church ... VA-3
Cedar Creek Mtn—summit ... SC-3
Cedar Creek Natural History Area—other ... MN-6
Cedar Creek Park—park ... TX-5
**Cedar Creek Park**—pop pl ... GA-3
Cedar Creek Peak—summit ... ID-8
Cedar Creek Point—cape ... MD-2
Cedar Creek Point—cape ... NJ-2
Cedar Creek Point—cape ... NC-3
Cedar Creek Pond—reservoir ... OH-6
Cedar Creek Post Office (historical)—building ... MS-4
Cedarcreek Post Office (historical)—building ... TN-4
Cedar Creek Rec Area ... TN-4
Cedar Creek Rec Area—locale ... MO-7
Cedar Creek Rec Area—park ... SD-7
Cedar Creek-Red Rock (CCD)—cens area ... TX-5
Cedar Creek Rodeo Grounds—locale ... AZ-5
Cedar Creek Rsvr—reservoir ... AL-4
Cedar Creek Rsvr—reservoir ... ID-8
Cedar Creek Rsvr—reservoir ... OR-9
Cedar Creek Rsvr—reservoir ... SC-3
Cedar Creek Rsvr—reservoir (2) ... TX-5
Cedar Creek Sch—school ... CA-9
Cedar Creek Sch—school (2) ... IL-6
Cedar Creek Sch—school ... KY-4
Cedar Creek Sch—school ... LA-4
Cedar Creek Sch—school ... MI-6
Cedar Creek Sch—school ... MT-8
Cedar Creek Sch—school (2) ... SC-3
Cedar Creek Sch—school ... TN-4
Cedar Creek Sch—school ... TX-5
Cedar Creek Sch—school ... WA-9
Cedar Creek Sch—school ... WV-2
Cedar Creek Sch (historical)—school (2) ... AL-4
Cedar Creek Sch (historical)—school ... MS-4
Cedar Creek Sch (historical)—school ... TN-4
Cedar Creek School—locale ... WA-9
Cedar Creek Shoals—bar ... AL-4
Cedar Creek Spring—spring ... OR-9
Cedar Creek Spring—spring ... UT-8
Cedar Creek State Park—park ... AL-4
Cedar Creek State Park—park ... WV-2
Cedar Creek Station ... IN-6
Cedar Creek Stock Driveway—trail ... MT-8
**Cedar Creek (subdivision)**—pop pl (3) ... NC-3
Cedar Creek Tank—reservoir ... AZ-5
Cedar Creek Tank—reservoir ... TX-5
Cedar Creek Township—civil (2) ... MO-7
**Cedar Creek Township**—pop pl ... ND-7
Cedar Creek (Township of)—fmr MCD (2) ... AR-4
Cedar Creek (Township of)—fmr MCD ... NC-3
**Cedar Creek (Township of)**—pop pl (2) ... IN-6
**Cedar Creek (Township of)**—pop pl (2) ... MI-6
Cedar Creek Trail—trail ... WA-9
Cedar Creek Trail (Pack)—trail ... NM-5
Cedar Creek Tunnel—tunnel ... UT-8
**Cedar Creek Wayside**—pop pl ... VA-3
Cedar Crest—hist pl ... KS-7
Cedar Crest—locale ... CO-8
**Cedar Crest**—pop pl ... CA-9
**Cedarcrest**—pop pl ... KY-4
**Cedar Crest**—pop pl ... LA-4
**Cedar Crest**—pop pl ... NJ-2
**Cedar Crest**—pop pl ... NM-5
**Cedarcrest**—pop pl ... NY-2
**Cedar Crest**—pop pl ... OK-5
**Cedar Crest**—pop pl ... VA-3
Cedar Crest—ridge ... MA-1
Cedar Crest—uninc pl ... MA-1
Cedar Crest—uninc pl ... TX-5
Cedar Crest Camp Lake—reservoir ... TN-4
Cedar Crest Camp Lake Dam—dam ... TN-4
Cedar Crest Cem—cemetery ... CO-8
Cedar Crest Cem—cemetery ... IA-7
Cedar Crest Cem—cemetery ... ME-1
Cedar Crest Cem—cemetery ... TX-5
Cedar Crest Ch—church ... CA-9
Cedar Crest Ch—church ... OK-5
Cedar Crest Ch—church ... PA-2
Cedar Crest Coll—school ... PA-2
Cedar Crest Country Club—other ... TX-5
Cedar Crest Country Club—other ... VA-3
Cedar Crest Golf Course—other ... WA-9
Cedar Crest HS—school ... PA-2
Cedar Crest Lake—reservoir ... IN-6
Cedar Crest Lake—reservoir ... OK-5
**Cedar Crest Manor**—pop pl ... NJ-2
Cedarcrest Memorial Gardens—cemetery ... AR-4
Cedar Crest MS—school ... PA-2
**Cedar Crest North**—pop pl ... TN-4
Cedarcrest Ranch—locale ... CA-9
Cedar Crest Sch—school ... MI-6
Cedarcrest Sch—school ... MN-6
Cedar Crest Sch—school ... TX-5
Cedarcrest State Sanatorium—hospital ... CT-1
**Cedar Crest (subdivision)**—pop pl ... AL-4
**Cedarcrest (subdivision)**—pop pl ... NC-3
**Cedar Crest (subdivision)**—pop pl ... NC-3
Cedarcroft—hist pl ... PA-2
**Cedarcroft**—pop pl ... MD-2
**Cedar Croft**—pop pl ... NJ-2
Cedarcroft Branch—stream ... TN-4
Cedarcroft Hill—summit ... TN-4
Cedarcroft Sch—school ... NJ-2
**Cedarcroft (subdivision)**—pop pl ... TN-4
Cedar Cross Ch—church ... KY-4
Cedar Crossing ... AL-4
Cedar Crossing—locale ... CA-9
Cedar Crossing—locale ... WA-9
**Cedar Crossing**—pop pl ... GA-3
Cedar Crossing Post Office ... AL-4
Cedar Crove Cem—cemetery ... VT-1
Cedardale—locale ... OK-5
Cedardale—locale ... WA-9
**Cedardale**—pop pl ... OR-9
Cedardale Cem—cemetery ... OK-5
Cedardale Ch—church ... MI-6
Cedar Dale Ch—church ... MS-4
Cedardale Community Chapel—church ... MI-6
Cedar Dale Indian Mission—church ... OK-5
Cedar Dam—dam (2) ... AZ-5
Cedar Dam—dam ... TN-4
Cedar Dell—hist pl ... NC-3
Cedar Dell Ch—church ... TN-4
Cedar Dell Lake—lake ... MA-1
Cedar Ditch ... IN-6
Cedar Ditch—canal ... NM-5
Cedar Drain—canal ... MI-6
Cedar Drain—stream ... FL-3
Cedar Drain—stream ... MI-6
Cedar Draw ... ID-8
Cedar Draw—valley (4) ... ID-8
Cedar Draw—valley (5) ... TX-5
Cedar Draw—valley ... UT-8
Cedar Draw—valley (12) ... WY-8
Cedar Draw Creek—stream ... ID-8
Cedar Draw Lake—lake ... ID-8
Cedar Draw School—locale (2) ... ID-8
Cedar Drift Fence Tank—reservoir ... AZ-5
Cedar Dugout—channel ... TX-5
Cedar Dugout—stream ... TX-5
Cedar East Sch—school ... UT-8
**Cedaredge**—pop pl ... CO-8
Cedar Edge School—locale ... CO-8
Cedar Falls—falls ... AR-4
Cedar Falls—falls ... IL-6
Cedar Falls—falls ... MT-8
Cedar Falls—falls (2) ... OH-6
Cedar Falls—falls ... OK-5
Cedar Falls—falls ... VA-3
Cedar Falls—falls ... WA-9
**Cedar Falls**—pop pl ... IA-7
**Cedar Falls**—pop pl ... NC-3
**Cedar Falls**—pop pl ... WA-9
**Cedar Falls**—pop pl ... WI-6
Cedar Falls Branch—stream ... SC-3
Cedar Falls Cem—cemetery ... WI-6
Cedar Falls Ch—church (2) ... NC-3
Cedar Falls Ch—church (2) ... SC-3
Cedar Falls City Hall—building ... IA-7
Cedar Falls Ditch—canal ... MT-8
Cedar Falls HS—school ... IA-7
Cedar Falls Ice House—hist pl ... IA-7
Cedar Falls Junction—locale ... IA-7
Cedar Falls Sch—school ... MS-4
Cedar Falls Township—fmr MCD ... IA-7
Cedar Falls (Township of)—fmr MCD ... AR-4
**Cedar Farm**—pop pl ... VA-3
Cedar Farm Landing—locale ... IN-6
**Cedar Farms (subdivision)**—pop pl ... DE-2
Cedar Field—flat ... ID-8
Cedar Field Creek—stream ... VA-3
Cedar Flat ... NV-8
Cedar Flat—flat (4) ... AZ-5
Cedar Flat—flat (9) ... CA-9
Cedar Flat—flat ... NV-8
Cedar Flat—flat (2) ... OR-9
Cedar Flat—flat ... WA-9
Cedar Flat—locale ... KY-4
**Cedar Flat**—pop pl ... CA-9
**Cedar Flat**—pop pl ... KY-4
**Cedar Flat**—pop pl ... OR-9
Cedar Flat Cabin—locale ... CA-9
Cedar Flat Canyon—valley ... CA-9
Cedar Flat Ch—church ... TN-4
Cedar Flat Creek ... OR-9
Cedar Flat Creek—stream ... CA-9
Cedar Flat Creek—stream ... OR-9
Cedar Flats—flat ... CO-8
Cedar Flats—flat ... ID-8
Cedar Flats—flat (3) ... WA-9
Cedar Flats—locale ... KY-4
**Cedar Flats**—pop pl ... NY-2
**Cedar Flats**—pop pl ... TN-4
Cedar Flats Cem—cemetery ... KY-4
Cedar Flats Job Corps Center—locale ... ID-8
Cedar Flats Natural Area—park ... WA-9
Cedar Flat Tank—reservoir (3) ... AZ-5
Cedar Ford—locale ... MO-7
Cedar Ford Baptist Church ... TN-4
Cedar Ford Ch—church ... TN-4
Cedar Ford Post Office ... TN-4
Cedar Forest—locale ... VA-3
Cedar Forest Camp Ground—locale ... CA-9
Cedar Forest Cave—cave ... TN-4
**Cedar Forest Estates (subdivision)**—pop pl ... NC-3
Cedarfork ... TN-4
Cedar Fork—locale ... AL-4
Cedar Fork—locale ... OH-6
Cedar Fork—locale ... TN-4
Cedar Fork—locale ... VA-3
**Cedar Fork**—pop pl ... NC-3
**Cedar Fork**—pop pl ... TN-4
Cedar Fork—stream ... AL-4
Cedar Fork—stream ... IL-6
Cedar Fork—stream (2) ... MO-7
Cedar Fork—stream (2) ... NC-3
Cedar Fork—stream (2) ... OH-6
Cedar Fork—stream ... SC-3
Cedar Fork—stream ... TN-4
Cedar Fork—stream ... TX-5
Cedar Fork—stream (3) ... UT-8
Cedar Fork Baptist Ch—church ... NC-3
Cedar Fork Cem—cemetery ... AL-4
Cedar Fork Ch—church ... AL-4
Cedar Fork Ch—church ... NC-3
Cedar Fork Ch—church ... OH-6
Cedar Fork Ch—church (2) ... TN-4
Cedar Fork Creek—stream ... NC-3
Cedar Fork Creek—stream ... TN-4
Cedar Fork (historical)—locale ... KS-7
**Cedarfork (Old Cedar Fork)**—pop pl ... TN-4
Cedar Fork Post Office (historical)—building ... TN-4
Cedar Fork Sch (abandoned)—school ... MO-7
Cedar Fork (Township of)—fmr MCD ... NC-3
Cedar Fork Valley—valley ... TN-4
Cedar Fort ... SD-7
**Cedar Fort (Cedar Valley Post Office)**—pop pl ... UT-8
Cedar Fort Ditch—canal ... UT-8
Cedar Fort Station (historical)—building ... UT-8
Cedar Fourche Creek—stream ... AR-4
Cedar Fourche Landing—locale ... AR-4
Cedar Gap—gap (2) ... AL-4
Cedar Gap—gap ... CA-9
Cedar Gap—gap ... KY-4
Cedar Gap—gap (3) ... TN-4
Cedar Gap—gap (6) ... TX-5
Cedar Gap—gap ... WY-8
**Cedar Gap**—pop pl ... MO-7
Cedar Gap Baptist Church ... AL-4
Cedar Gap Branch—stream ... AR-4
Cedar Gap Cem—cemetery ... MO-7
Cedar Gap Ch—church ... AL-4
Cedar Gap Ch—church ... KY-4
Cedar Gap Lake—lake ... MO-7
Cedar Gap Mtn ... AL-4
Cedar Gap Mtn—summit ... AL-4
Cedar Gap Sch—school ... KY-4
Cedar Gap Tank—reservoir ... AZ-5
**Cedargate (subdivision)**—pop pl ... AL-4
Cedar Glade Baptist Church ... AL-4
Cedar Glade Cem—cemetery ... AZ-5
Cedar Glade Ch—church ... AL-4
Cedar Glade Ch—church ... AR-4
Cedar Glades Ch—church ... AR-4
Cedar Glade School (historical)—locale ... MO-7
Cedar Glen ... IL-6
**Cedar Glen**—pop pl ... CA-9
**Cedar Glen**—pop pl ... IL-6
**Cedar Glen**—pop pl ... LA-4
Cedar Glen Camp—locale ... CA-9
Cedar Glen Creek—stream ... IL-6
Cedar Glen Lakes—CDP ... NJ-2
**Cedar Glen West**—pop pl ... NJ-2
**Cedargold (subdivision)**—pop pl ... TN-4
Cedar Gorge—valley ... KS-7
Cedar Grade Hill—summit ... AL-4
**Cedar Green**—pop pl ... VA-3
Cedar Green Cem—cemetery ... NJ-2
Cedar Groe Seminary (historical)—school ... TN-4
Cedar Grove ... AL-4
Cedar Grove ... KS-7
Cedar Grove ... MN-6
Cedar Grove ... MS-4
Cedar Grove ... NJ-2
Cedar Grove ... RI-1
Cedar Grove ... TN-4
Cedar Grove—hist pl ... KY-4
Cedar Grove—hist pl ... MD-2
Cedar Grove—hist pl (2) ... MS-4
Cedar Grove—hist pl ... MO-7
Cedar Grove—hist pl ... NC-3
Cedar Grove—hist pl ... SC-3
Cedar Grove—hist pl ... TN-4
Cedar Grove—hist pl ... VA-3
Cedar Grove—hist pl ... WV-2
Cedar Grove—locale ... AL-4
Cedar Grove—locale ... CO-8
Cedar Grove—locale (3) ... GA-3
Cedar Grove—locale (2) ... KY-4
Cedar Grove—locale (2) ... NJ-2
Cedar Grove—locale ... NM-5
Cedar Grove—locale ... OH-6
Cedar Grove—locale ... PA-2
Cedar Grove—locale ... SC-3
Cedar Grove—locale (4) ... TN-4
Cedar Grove—locale ... TX-5
Cedar Grove—locale (3) ... VA-3
Cedar Grove—locale ... WA-9
**Cedar Grove**—pop pl (4) ... AL-4
**Cedar Grove**—pop pl (2) ... AR-4
**Cedar Grove**—pop pl (2) ... CA-9
**Cedar Grove**—pop pl ... FL-3
**Cedar Grove**—pop pl (2) ... GA-3
**Cedar Grove**—pop pl ... IN-6
**Cedar Grove**—pop pl ... KY-4
**Cedar Grove**—pop pl (5) ... LA-4
**Cedar Grove**—pop pl ... ME-1
**Cedar Grove**—pop pl (2) ... MD-2
**Cedar Grove**—pop pl ... MN-6
**Cedar Grove**—pop pl ... MS-4
**Cedargrove**—pop pl ... MO-7
**Cedar Grove**—pop pl (3) ... NJ-2
**Cedar Grove**—pop pl (3) ... NC-3
**Cedar Grove**—pop pl (2) ... PA-2
**Cedar Grove**—pop pl ... RI-1
**Cedar Grove**—pop pl (11) ... TN-4
**Cedar Grove**—pop pl (2) ... VA-3
**Cedar Grove**—pop pl (2) ... WV-2
**Cedar Grove**—pop pl ... WI-6
Cedar Grove—swamp ... NC-3
Cedar Grove—uninc pl ... TX-5
Cedar Grove—woods (3) ... UT-8
Cedar Grove Acad—school ... AL-4
Cedar Grove Access Area—park ... TN-4
**Cedar Grove Acres**—pop pl ... VA-3
Cedar Grove Airpark Airp—airport ... WA-9
Cedar Grove Baptist Ch ... MS-4
Cedar Grove Baptist Ch ... TN-4
Cedar Grove Baptist Ch—church (2) ... AL-4
Cedar Grove Baptist Ch—church (2) ... FL-3
Cedar Grove Baptist Ch—church (2) ... MS-4
Cedar Grove Baptist Ch—church (2) ... TN-4
**Cedar Grove Beach**—pop pl ... MD-2
Cedar Grove Branch—stream ... AL-4
Cedar Grove Branch—stream ... GA-3
Cedar Grove Branch—stream ... SC-3
Cedar Grove Branch—stream ... VA-3
Cedar Grove Camp—locale ... ID-8
Cedar Grove Campground—locale ... WA-9
**Cedar Grove (Campground)**—pop pl ... CA-9
Cedar Grove (CCD)—cens area ... GA-3
Cedar Grove (CCD)—cens area ... TN-4
Cedar Grove Cem—cemetery (6) ... AL-4
Cedar Grove Cem—cemetery (4) ... AR-4
Cedar Grove Cem—cemetery ... CO-8
Cedar Grove Cem—cemetery ... CT-1
Cedar Grove Cem—cemetery ... FL-3
Cedar Grove Cem—cemetery (6) ... GA-3
Cedar Grove Cem—cemetery ... IN-6
Cedar Grove Cem—cemetery ... KS-7
Cedar Grove Cem—cemetery (4) ... KY-4
Cedar Grove Cem—cemetery (2) ... LA-4
Cedar Grove Cem—cemetery ... ME-1
Cedar Grove Cem—cemetery ... MA-1
Cedar Grove Cem—cemetery (3) ... MS-4
Cedargrove Cem—cemetery ... MS-4
Cedar Grove Cem—cemetery (8) ... MS-4
Cedar Grove Cem—cemetery (2) ... MO-7
Cedar Grove Cem—cemetery ... NE-7
Cedar Grove Cem—cemetery (3) ... NJ-2
Cedar Grove Cem—cemetery (2) ... NM-5
Cedar Grove Cem—cemetery (2) ... NY-2
Cedar Grove Cem—cemetery (3) ... NC-3
Cedar Grove Cem—cemetery ... OH-6
Cedar Grove Cem—cemetery (2) ... OK-5
Cedar Grove Cem—cemetery (3) ... PA-2
Cedar Grove Cem—cemetery (2) ... SC-3
Cedar Grove Cem—cemetery (13) ... TN-4
Cedar Grove Cem—cemetery (8) ... TX-5
Cedar Grove Cem—cemetery (7) ... VA-3
Cedar Grove Cemetery—hist pl ... NC-3
Cedar Grove Ch ... AL-4
Cedar Grove Ch ... MS-4
Cedar Grove Ch ... TN-4
Cedar Grove Ch—church (26) ... AL-4
Cedar Grove Ch—church (9) ... AR-4
Cedar Grove Ch—church ... DE-2
Cedar Grove Ch—church (4) ... FL-3
Cedar Grove Ch—church (8) ... GA-3
Cedar Grove Ch—church (3) ... IL-6
Cedar Grove Ch—church ... IN-6
Cedar Grove Ch—church (13) ... KY-4
Cedar Grove Ch—church (4) ... LA-4
Cedar Grove Ch—church (2) ... MD-2
Cedar Grove Ch—church (18) ... MS-4
Cedar Grove Ch—church (8) ... MO-7
Cedar Grove Ch—church ... NJ-2
Cedar Grove Ch—church ... NM-5
Cedar Grove Ch—church (30) ... NC-3
Cedar Grove Ch—church (2) ... OH-6
Cedar Grove Ch—church (5) ... OK-5
Cedar Grove Ch—church ... OR-9
Cedar Grove Ch—church (3) ... PA-2
Cedar Grove Ch—church (16) ... SC-3
Cedar Grove Ch—church (28) ... TN-4
Cedar Grove Ch—church (10) ... TX-5
Cedar Grove Ch—church (18) ... VA-3
Cedar Grove Ch—church (3) ... WV-2
Cedar Grove Ch (historical)—church (5) ... AL-4
Cedar Grove Ch (historical)—church (2) ... MS-4
Cedar Grove Ch (historical)—church (2) ... TN-4
Cedar Grove Ch of Christ ... AL-4
Cedar Grove Ch of Christ—church ... TN-4
Cedar Grove Church—locale ... AR-4
**Cedar Grove Colony**—pop pl ... SD-7
Cedar Grove Community Center—building ... TN-4
Cedar Grove Creek—stream ... MS-4
Cedar Grove Division—civil ... TN-4
Cedar Grove Dock—locale ... TN-4
**Cedar Grove (Dogwalk)**—pop pl ... IL-6
Cedar Grove Draw—valley ... NM-5
Cedar Grove Elem Sch—school ... FL-3
Cedar Grove Elem Sch—school ... TN-4
Cedar Grove Estates—locale ... PA-2
Cedar Grove Freewill Baptist Ch ... AL-4
Cedar Grove Furnace—hist pl ... TN-4
Cedar Grove Furnace (historical)—locale ... TN-4
Cedar Grove Furnace Post Office (historical)—building ... TN-4
Cedar Grove Furnace (40PY77)(Boundary Increase)—hist pl ... TN-4
Cedar Grove Highland Cem—cemetery ... TN-4
Cedar Grove (historical)—locale ... MS-4
Cedar Grove Lake—lake ... OR-9
Cedar Grove Lookout Tower—locale ... NC-3
Cedar Grove Memorial Sch—school ... NJ-2
Cedar Grove Pentecostal Church ... MS-4
Cedar Grove Picnic Area—park ... ID-8
Cedar Grove Place—hist pl ... MS-4
**Cedar Grove Plantation**—pop pl ... LA-4
Cedar Grove P.O. (historical)—locale ... AL-4
Cedargrove Post Office ... TN-4
Cedar Grove Post Office—building ... TN-4
Cedar Grove Ranch—locale ... CA-9
Cedar Grove Ravine—valley ... CA-9
Cedar Grover Cem—cemetery ... NH-1
Cedar Grove Ridge—ridge ... ME-1
Cedar Grove River Cave—cave ... AL-4
Cedar Grove Rsvr—reservoir ... NJ-2
Cedar Groves—locale ... ME-1
Cedar Grove Sch ... AL-4
Cedar Grove Sch ... TN-4
Cedar Grove Sch—hist pl ... NJ-2
Cedar Grove Sch—school ... AL-4
Cedar Grove Sch—school ... AR-4
Cedargrove Sch—school ... CA-9
Cedar Grove Sch—school ... GA-3
Cedar Grove Sch—school ... IA-7
Cedar Grove Sch—school (4) ... KY-4
Cedar Grove Sch—school ... LA-4
Cedar Grove Sch—school (2) ... MO-7
Cedar Grove Sch—school ... NE-7
Cedar Grove Sch—school (3) ... NC-3
Cedar Grove Sch—school ... OK-5
Cedar Grove Sch—school (2) ... PA-2
Cedar Grove Sch—school (4) ... SC-3
Cedar Grove Sch—school (5) ... TN-4
Cedar Grove Sch—school ... VA-3
Cedar Grove Sch—school ... WV-2
Cedar Grove Sch (abandoned)—school ... MO-7
Cedar Grove Sch (abandoned)—school ... PA-2
Cedar Grove Sch (historical)—school (4) ... AL-4
Cedar Grove Sch (historical)—school (5) ... MS-4
Cedar Grove Sch (historical)—school (2) ... MO-7
Cedar Grove Sch (historical)—school ... NC-3
Cedar Grove Sch (historical)—school ... PA-2
Cedar Grove Sch (historical)—school (14) ... TN-4
Cedar Grove Sch No 1—school ... NC-3
Cedar Grove Sch No 2—school ... NC-3
Cedar Grove School—locale ... AR-4
Cedar Grove School (abandoned)—locale ... MO-7
Cedar Grove School (abandoned)—locale ... OR-9
Cedar Groves Park—park ... AZ-5
Cedar Grove Spring—spring ... AL-4
Cedar Grove State For—forest ... MO-7
Cedar Grove Station—locale ... NJ-2
Cedar Grove Station (historical)—locale ... MA-1
**Cedar Grove (subdivision)**—pop pl ... MA-1
Cedar Grove (Township of)—fmr MCD (2) ... NC-3
**Cedar Grove (Township of)**—pop pl ... NJ-2
Cedar Grove Trail—trail ... OH-6
Cedar Grove United Baptist Ch—church ... TN-4
Cedar Grove Well—well ... NM-5
Cedar Grove Windmill—locale ... NM-5
Cedar Guard Station—locale ... OR-9
Cedar Guard Station No. 1019—hist pl ... OR-9
Cedar Gulch ... UT-8
Cedar Gulch—valley (8) ... CA-9
Cedar Gulch—valley (4) ... CO-8
Cedar Gulch—valley (3) ... ID-8
Cedar Gulch—valley (2) ... MT-8
Cedar Gulch—valley ... NE-7
Cedar Gulch—valley (3) ... OR-9
Cedar Gulch—valley ... WA-9
Cedar Gully—valley (3) ... TX-5
Cedar Gut—gut ... DE-2
Cedar Gut—stream ... NC-3
Cedar Hall—locale ... MD-2
Cedar Hall Elementary and JHS—school ... IN-6
Cedar Hall Sch—school ... IN-6
Cedar Hammock—cape ... FL-3
Cedar Hammock—island ... CT-1
Cedar Hammock—island (5) ... FL-3
Cedar Hammock—island (3) ... GA-3
Cedar Hammock—island (4) ... NC-3
Cedar Hammock—locale ... GA-3
**Cedar Hammock**—pop pl ... FL-3
Cedar Hammock Canal—canal ... GA-3
Cedar Hammock Creek ... GA-3
Cedar Hammock Creek—stream ... FL-3
Cedar Hammock Drainage Canal—canal ... FL-3
Cedar Hammocks—island ... GA-3
Cedar Hammocks Creek—stream ... NJ-2
Cedar Haven ... MD-2
Cedarhaven—locale ... MD-2
**Cedar Haven**—pop pl ... MD-2
**Cedar Haven**—pop pl ... MI-6
Cedarhead—summit ... TX-5
Cedar Head—swamp ... FL-3
Cedar Head Branch—stream ... FL-3
Cedar Hebrew Sch—school ... TN-4
Cedar Hedge Cem—cemetery ... IN-6
Cedar Hedge Lake—lake ... MI-6
Cedar Heights ... CT-1
**Cedar Heights**—pop pl ... CT-1
**Cedar Heights**—pop pl (2) ... DE-2
**Cedar Heights**—pop pl (2) ... MD-2
**Cedar Heights**—pop pl ... NJ-2
**Cedar Heights**—pop pl ... PA-2
Cedar Heights Cem—cemetery ... NJ-2
Cedar Heights Cem—cemetery ... PA-2
Cedar Heights Ch—church ... AR-4
Cedar Heights Sch—school ... IA-7
Cedar Heights Sch—school ... OH-6
Cedar Heights Sch—school ... OK-5
Cedar Heights Shop Ctr—locale ... CA-9
Cedar Hill ... MS-4
Cedar Hill ... SC-3
Cedar Hill—cape ... TX-5
Cedar Hill—CDP ... MO-7
Cedar Hill—hist pl ... MD-2
Cedar Hill—locale ... AL-4
Cedar Hill—locale ... AR-4
Cedar Hill—locale ... CO-8
Cedarhill—locale ... ID-8
Cedar Hill—locale ... MD-2
Cedar Hill—locale (2) ... NC-3
Cedar Hill—locale ... TX-5
Cedar Hill—locale (3) ... VA-3
**Cedar Hill**—pop pl ... AL-4
**Cedar Hill**—pop pl ... MA-1
**Cedar Hill**—pop pl (2) ... MS-4
**Cedar Hill**—pop pl (2) ... NM-5
**Cedar Hill**—pop pl ... NY-2
**Cedarhill**—pop pl ... OH-6
**Cedar Hill**—pop pl ... OH-6
**Cedar Hill**—pop pl ... PA-2
**Cedar Hill**—pop pl (4) ... TN-4
**Cedar Hill**—pop pl ... TX-5
**Cedarhill**—pop pl ... VA-3
Cedar Hill—summit ... AR-4
Cedar Hill—summit ... CA-9
Cedar Hill—summit (3) ... CO-8
Cedar Hill—summit ... CT-1
Cedar Hill—summit ... DC-2
Cedar Hill—summit (2) ... ID-8
Cedar Hill—summit (2) ... KY-4
Cedar Hill—summit (3) ... MA-1
Cedar Hill—summit (2) ... MO-7
Cedar Hill—summit ... MT-8
Cedar Hill—summit ... NV-8
Cedar Hill—summit ... NH-1
Cedar Hill—summit (3) ... NM-5
Cedar Hill—summit (2) ... NY-2
Cedar Hill—summit ... OH-6
Cedar Hill—summit (2) ... PA-2
Cedar Hill—summit ... SC-3
Cedar Hill—summit (2) ... TN-4
Cedar Hill—summit (6) ... TX-5
Cedar Hill—summit (4) ... UT-8
Cedar Hill—summit ... WV-2
Cedar Hill—summit ... WI-6
Cedar Hill—summit (2) ... WY-8
Cedar Hill Baptist Ch—church ... AL-4
Cedar Hill Baptist Ch—church (3) ... TN-4
Cedar Hill Bible Camp—locale ... TX-5
Cedar Hill Boat Dock—locale ... TN-4
**Cedar Hill Camp**—pop pl ... MA-1
Cedar Hill Canyon—valley ... NV-8
Cedar Hill Cave—cave ... TN-4
Cedar Hill Cem—cemetery (3) ... AL-4
Cedar Hill Cem—cemetery ... AR-4
Cedar Hill Cem—cemetery (2) ... CO-8
Cedar Hill Cem—cemetery ... CT-1
Cedar Hill Cem—cemetery ... FL-3
Cedar Hill Cem—cemetery (2) ... GA-3
Cedar Hill Cem—cemetery ... IN-6
Cedar Hill Cem—cemetery ... IA-7
Cedar Hill Cem—cemetery (3) ... KS-7
Cedar Hill Cem—cemetery (3) ... KY-4
Cedar Hill Cem—cemetery (2) ... MD-2
Cedar Hill Cem—cemetery (3) ... MN-6
Cedar Hill Cem—cemetery (2) ... MO-7
Cedar Hill Cem—cemetery ... NE-7
Cedar Hill Cem—cemetery (5) ... NJ-2
Cedar Hill Cem—cemetery ... NM-5
Cedar Hill Cem—cemetery (2) ... NY-2
Cedar Hill Cem—cemetery (2) ... NC-3
Cedar Hill Cem—cemetery (4) ... OH-6
Cedar Hill Cem—cemetery ... OK-5
Cedar Hill Cem—cemetery (3) ... PA-2
Cedar Hill Cem—cemetery ... SD-7
Cedar Hill Cem—cemetery (5) ... TN-4
Cedar Hill Cem—cemetery (6) ... TX-5
Cedar Hill Cem—cemetery (4) ... VA-3
Cedar Hill Cem—cemetery ... WV-2
Cedar Hill Cemetery Buildings—hist pl ... OH-6
Cedar Hill Ch—church (3) ... AL-4
Cedar Hill Ch—church ... AR-4
Cedar Hill Ch—church ... GA-3
Cedar Hill Ch—church (3) ... KY-4
Cedar Hill Ch—church (2) ... MS-4
Cedar Hill Ch—church (2) ... MO-7
Cedar Hill Ch—church ... NE-7
Cedar Hill Ch—church (6) ... NC-3
Cedar Hill Ch—church (9) ... TN-4
Cedar Hill Ch—church (2) ... TX-5
Cedar Hill Ch—church (2) ... VA-3
Cedar Hill Ch (historical)—church ... AL-4
Cedar Hill Cotton Gin—locale ... TX-5
Cedar Hill Crystal Cave—cave ... TN-4
Cedar Hill Divide—gap ... TX-5
Cedar Hill Dock—locale ... TN-4
**Cedar Hill Estates**—pop pl ... AL-4
Cedar Hill Fishery—locale ... NC-3
Cedar Hill Gulch—valley ... CO-8
Cedar Hill (historical)—locale ... AL-4
**Cedar Hill (historical)**—pop pl ... MS-4
Cedar Hill IOOF Cemetery ... OR-9
Cedar Hill Island—island ... SC-3
Cedar Hill Lake—lake ... MS-4
Cedar Hill Lake—lake ... NM-5
Cedar Hill Lake—reservoir ... TN-4
Cedar Hill Lake Dam—dam ... MS-4
Cedar Hill Lake Dam—dam ... TN-4
**Cedar Hill Lakes**—pop pl ... MO-7
Cedar Hill Lakes—reservoir ... MO-7
Cedar Hill Memorial Park—cemetery ... TX-5
Cedar Hill Memorial Park (Cemetery)—cemetery ... PA-2
Cedar Hill Memory Gardens—cemetery ... FL-3
Cedar Hill Methodist Church ... AL-4
Cedar Hill Mine—mine ... NV-8
Cedar Hill Mine—mine ... TN-4
Cedar Hill Park—park ... TN-4
**Cedar Hill Park**—pop pl ... TN-4
Cedarhill Post Office ... TN-4
Cedar Hill Post Office—building ... TN-4
Cedar Hill Post Office (historical)—building ... MS-4
Cedar Hill Ranch—locale ... NM-5
Cedar Hill Ridge—ridge ... KY-4
Cedar Hills ... PA-2
Cedar Hills ... WY-8
Cedar Hills—other ... NM-5
**Cedar Hills**—pop pl ... FL-3
**Cedar Hills**—pop pl ... IA-7
**Cedar Hills**—pop pl ... OR-9
**Cedar Hills**—pop pl (2) ... TN-4
**Cedar Hills**—pop pl ... UT-8
Cedar Hills—range (2) ... ID-8
Cedar Hills—range ... UT-8
Cedar Hills—ridge ... NM-5
Cedar Hills—ridge ... ND-7
Cedar Hills—summit ... NM-5
Cedar Hills—summit ... UT-8
Cedar Hills Baptist Ch—church ... FL-3
Cedar Hills Baptist Christian Sch—school ... FL-3
Cedar Hills Cem—cemetery ... PA-2
Cedar Hill Sch—school ... GA-3
Cedar Hill Sch—school ... IL-6
Cedar Hill Sch—school ... KS-7
Cedar Hill Sch—school (2) ... KY-4
Cedar Hill Sch—school ... NE-7
Cedar Hill Sch—school ... OH-6
Cedar Hill Sch—school ... PA-2
Cedar Hill Sch—school (4) ... TN-4
Cedar Hill Sch—school ... TX-5
Cedar Hill Sch (abandoned)—school ... MO-7
Cedar Hill Sch (historical)—school ... AL-4
Cedarhill Sch (historical)—school ... AL-4
Cedar Hill Sch (historical)—school (5) ... TN-4
Cedar Hill School ... DE-2
**Cedar Hills Estates**—pop pl ... AL-4
**Cedar Hills Estates**—pop pl ... FL-3
**Cedar Hills Estates (subdivision)**—pop pl ... NC-3
Cedar Hill Sewage Disposal—other ... TX-5
Cedar Hills Golf And Country Club—locale ... TN-4
Cedar Hills Golf Course—locale ... MO-7
Cedar Hills Raceway—other ... VA-3
Cedar Hills Ranch—locale ... MT-8
Cedar Hills Sch—school ... FL-3
Cedar Hills Sch—school ... OR-9
Cedar Hills Shop Ctr—locale ... FL-3
**Cedar Hills (subdivision)**—pop pl ... MS-4
**Cedar Hill (subdivision)**—pop pl (2) ... NC-3
**Cedar Hill (subdivision)**—pop pl ... TN-4
Cedar Hill Well—well ... NM-5
Cedar (historical)—locale ... AL-4
Cedar (historical)—locale ... SD-7
Cedar Hollow—basin ... TX-5
Cedar Hollow—locale ... PA-2
**Cedar Hollow**—pop pl ... PA-2
Cedar Hollow—valley (5) ... AR-4
Cedar Hollow—valley (2) ... ID-8
Cedar Hollow—valley ... IN-6
Cedar Hollow—valley ... KS-7
Cedar Hollow—valley ... KY-4
Cedar Hollow—valley (13) ... MO-7
Cedar Hollow—valley (4) ... OK-5
Cedar Hollow—valley ... OR-9
Cedar Hollow—valley ... PA-2
Cedar Hollow—valley (3) ... TN-4
Cedar Hollow—valley (14) ... TX-5
Cedar Hollow—valley (7) ... UT-8
Cedar Hollow Cave—cave ... TN-4
Cedar Hollow Country Club—other ... NY-2
Cedar Hollow Creek—stream ... TX-5
Cedar Hollow Ditch—canal ... UT-8
Cedar Hollow Spring—spring ... ID-8
Cedar Hollow Station—locale ... PA-2
Cedarhome—locale ... WA-9
Cedar Hook Hundred ... DE-2
Cedar House Hollow—valley ... KY-4
Cedar House Hollow—valley ... MO-7
Cedarhurst ... OH-6
Cedarhurst—locale ... WA-9
**Cedarhurst**—pop pl ... CT-1
**Cedarhurst**—pop pl (2) ... MD-2
**Cedarhurst**—pop pl ... NY-2
**Cedarhurst**—pop pl ... PA-2
**Cedarhurst (Lamotte)**—pop pl ... MD-2
Cedarhurst On The Bay ... MD-2
**Cedarhurst-on-the-Bay (Cedarhurst)**—pop pl ... MD-2
**Cedarhurst Park**—pop pl ... OR-9
Cedarhurst Sch—school ... NY-2

Cedarhurst Yacht Club—*other* NY-2
Cedar Inlet—*channel* (2) NC-3
Cedar Inlet Point—*cape* NC-3
*Cedar Island* RI-1
*Cedar Island* SD-7
Cedar Island—*cape* FL-3
Cedar Island—*cape* OR-9
Cedar Island—*island* AL-4
Cedar Island—*island* (3) AK-9
Cedar Island—*island* (4) CT-1
Cedar Island—*island* FL-3
Cedar Island—*island* GA-3
Cedar Island—*island* (2) IL-6
Cedar Island—*island* IA-7
Cedar Island—*island* (4) ME-1
Cedar Island—*island* (2) MD-2
Cedar Island—*island* (3) MA-1
Cedar Island—*island* (3) MI-6
Cedar Island—*island* MN-6
Cedar Island—*island* MS-4
Cedar Island—*island* (2) MT-8
Cedar Island—*island* (3) NE-7
Cedar Island—*island* NJ-2
Cedar Island—*island* (7) NY-2
Cedar Island—*island* (6) NC-3
Cedar Island—*island* OR-9
Cedar Island—*island* RI-1
Cedar Island—*island* SC-3
Cedar Island—*island* (2) VT-1
Cedar Island—*island* (4) VA-3
Cedar Island—*island* (2) WI-6
Cedar Island—*locale* FL-3
**Cedar Island**—*pop pl* IL-6
**Cedar Island**—*pop pl* NC-3
*Cedar Island Bay* NC-3
Cedar Island Bay—*bay* (2) NC-3
Cedar Island Bay—*bay* VA-3
Cedar Island Bay Light—*tower* NC-3
Cedar Island Bayou—*bay* FL-3
Cedar Island Beach—*beach* VA-3
*Cedar Island Cove* MA-1
Cedar Island Cove—*bay* NY-2
*Cedar Island Creek* SD-7
Cedar Island Creek—*bay* MD-2
Cedar Island Creek—*channel* NY-2
Cedar Island Creek—*stream* MA-1
Cedar Island Estate—*locale* WI-6
Cedar Island (historical)—*island* (2) AL-4
*Cedar Island Lake* MI-6
Cedar Island Lake—*lake* MI-6
Cedar Island Lake—*lake* (3) MN-6
Cedar Island Lake—*swamp* MN-6
Cedar Island Ledge—*bar* ME-1
Cedar Island Light—*tower* NC-3
*Cedar Island Marsh* MD-2
Cedar Island Marsh—*island* NY-2
Cedar Island Natl Wildlife Ref—*park* NC-3
Cedar Island Natl Wildlife Refuge HQ—*locale* NC-3
Cedar Island Point—*cape* MA-1
Cedar Island Rips—*rapids* ME-1
*Cedar Islands* NY-2
Cedar Islands—*island* MD-2
Cedar Islands—*island* NY-2
Cedar Islands Archeol District—*hist pl* SD-7
Cedar Island State Park—*park* NY-2
Cedar Island Thorofare—*channel* NC-3
Cedar Island (Township of)—*fmr MCD* NC-3
*Cedar Junction* KS-7
*Cedar Key* FL-3
**Cedar Key**—*pop pl* FL-3
**Cedar Key (corporate name for Cedar Keys)**—*pop pl* FL-3
Cedar Key HS—*school* FL-3
*Cedar Keys* FL-3
Cedar Keys—*island* FL-3
*Cedar Keys (corporate name Cedar Key)* FL-3
Cedar Keys Natl Wildlife Ref—*park* FL-3
Cedar Key State Memorial and Museum—*park* FL-3
Cedar Key-Yankeetown (CCD)—*cens area* FL-3
Cedar Knob—*locale* KY-4
Cedar Knob—*pillar* KY-4
Cedar Knob—*summit* CA-9
Cedar Knob—*summit* CO-8
Cedar Knob—*summit* GA-3
Cedar Knob—*summit* ID-8
Cedar Knob—*summit* (6) KY-4
Cedar Knob—*summit* MA-1
Cedar Knob—*summit* MO-7
Cedar Knob—*summit* NM-5
Cedar Knob—*summit* (4) NC-3
Cedar Knob—*summit* (2) OK-5
Cedar Knob—*summit* (2) TN-4
Cedar Knob—*summit* (5) TX-5
Cedar Knob—*summit* (2) VA-3
Cedar Knob—*summit* (5) WV-2
Cedar Knob Ch—*church* TX-5
**Cedar Knoll**—*pop pl* PA-2
Cedar Knoll—*summit* (2) AZ-5
Cedar Knoll—*summit* CT-1
Cedar Knoll—*summit* ID-8
Cedar Knoll—*summit* OK-5
Cedar Knoll—*summit* (5) UT-8
Cedar Knoll Canyon—*valley* UT-8
*Cedar Knolles* NJ-2
**Cedar Knolls**—*pop pl* CT-1
**Cedar Knolls**—*pop pl* NJ-2
**Cedar Knolls**—*pop pl* NY-2
Cedar Knolls—*summit* (2) UT-8
Cedar Knoll Sch—*school* MD-2
**Cedar Knolls (Monroe-Cedar Knoll)**—*pop pl* NJ-2
**Cedar Knoll (subdivision)**—*pop pl* AL-4
Cedar Knoll Tank—*reservoir* AZ-5
*Cedar Lake* CT-1
*Cedar Lake* IN-6
*Cedar Lake* MA-1
*Cedar Lake* MI-6
*Cedar Lake* MN-6
*Cedar Lake* TX-5
*Cedar Lake* WA-9
Cedar Lake—*bay* TX-5
Cedar Lake—*lake* AL-4
Cedar Lake—*lake* AK-9
Cedar Lake—*lake* AZ-5
Cedar Lake—*lake* (2) CA-9
Cedar Lake—*lake* (2) CT-1
Cedar Lake—*lake* (2) FL-3
Cedar Lake—*lake* ID-8
Cedar Lake—*lake* (2) IL-6
Cedar Lake—*lake* (6) IN-6
Cedar Lake—*lake* IA-7
Cedar Lake—*lake* ME-1
Cedar Lake—*lake* MA-1
Cedar Lake—*lake* (24) MI-6
Cedar Lake—*lake* (28) MN-6
Cedar Lake—*lake* (3) MT-8
Cedar Lake—*lake* (3) NE-7
Cedar Lake—*lake* (2) NJ-2
Cedar Lake—*lake* (3) NM-5
Cedar Lake—*lake* (2) NY-2
Cedar Lake—*lake* NC-3
Cedar Lake—*lake* OH-6
Cedar Lake—*lake* (2) OR-9
Cedar Lake—*lake* (2) PA-2
Cedar Lake—*lake* (4) TX-5
Cedar Lake—*lake* VT-1
Cedar Lake—*lake* (5) WA-9
Cedar Lake—*lake* (13) WI-6
Cedar Lake—*locale* MN-6
Cedar Lake—*locale* NJ-2
Cedar Lake—*locale* TX-5
**Cedar Lake**—*pop pl* (2) AL-4
**Cedar Lake**—*pop pl* (2) IN-6
**Cedar Lake**—*pop pl* (2) MI-6
**Cedar Lake**—*pop pl* MS-4
**Cedar Lake**—*pop pl* NJ-2
**Cedar Lake**—*pop pl* NY-2
**Cedar Lake**—*pop pl* WI-6
Cedar Lake—*reservoir* AL-4
Cedar Lake—*reservoir* CA-9
Cedar Lake—*reservoir* GA-3
Cedar Lake—*reservoir* IL-6
Cedar Lake—*reservoir* IA-7
Cedar Lake—*reservoir* MN-6
Cedar Lake—*reservoir* (3) MO-7
Cedar Lake—*reservoir* (6) NJ-2
Cedar Lake—*reservoir* NC-3
Cedar Lake—*reservoir* ND-7
Cedar Lake—*reservoir* (2) OK-5
Cedar Lake—*reservoir* (2) SC-3
Cedar Lake—*reservoir* TN-4
Cedar Lake—*reservoir* TX-5
Cedar Lake—*reservoir* VA-3
Cedar Lake—*reservoir* WA-9
Cedar Lake—*swamp* IN-6
Cedar Lake—*swamp* MN-6
Cedar Lake Acad—*school* MI-6
Cedar Lake Branch—*stream* IN-6
Cedar Lake Branch—*stream* TX-5
*Cedar Lake Branch of Elder Ditch* IN-6
*Cedar Lake Brook* IN-6
Cedar Lake Camps—*locale* ME-1
Cedar Lake Cem—*cemetery* CT-1
Cedar Lake Cem—*cemetery* IN-6
Cedar Lake Cem—*cemetery* MI-6
Cedar Lake Cem—*cemetery* MN-6
Cedar Lake Cem—*cemetery* WI-6
Cedar Lake Ch—*church* IN-6
*Cedar Lake Creek* IN-6
Cedar Lake Creek—*stream* TX-5
Cedar Lake Dam—*dam* (5) NJ-2
Cedar Lake Dam—*dam* NC-3
Cedar Lake Dam—*dam* ND-7
Cedar Lake Dam Number One—*dam* TN-4
Cedar Lake Dam Number Two—*dam* TN-4
*Cedar Lake Ditch* IN-6
Cedar Lake Ditch—*canal* IN-6
Cedar Lake Draw—*valley* NM-5
Cedar Lake Golf Club—*other* IN-6
Cedar Lake Number One—*reservoir* TN-4
Cedar Lake Number Two—*reservoir* TN-4
Cedar Lake Oil Field—*oilfield* TX-5
Cedar Lake Park—*park* WI-6
*Cedar Lake Park Dam* NJ-2
Cedar Lake Post Office (historical)—*building* AL-4
*Cedar Lake Reservoir* TX-5
Cedar Lake Rsvr—*reservoir* AZ-5
*Cedar Lakes* MT-8
Cedar Lakes—*lake* KY-4
Cedar Lakes—*lake* MI-6
Cedar Lakes—*lake* NE-7
Cedar Lakes—*lake* NY-2
Cedar Lakes—*lake* OH-6
Cedar Lakes—*lake* TX-5
Cedar Lakes—*reservoir* KY-4
Cedar Lake Sch—*school* CT-1
Cedar Lake Sch—*school* (2) MI-6
Cedar Lake Sch—*school* WI-6
Cedar Lake Slough—*gut* TX-5
Cedar Lakes Sch—*school* TX-5
Cedar Lakes State Recreation Center—*park* WV-2
Cedar Lake Stream—*stream* NY-2
Cedar Lake Swamp—*swamp* MI-6
**Cedar Lake (Town of)**—*pop pl* WI-6
Cedar Lake Township—*obs name* SD-7
**Cedar Lake (Township of)**—*pop pl* MN-6
Cedar Lake Trail—*trail* ME-1
Cedar Lake United Methodist Ch—*church* MS-4
Cedar Lake Wash—*stream* AZ-5
**Cedar Land**—*pop pl* CT-1
Cedar Landing—*locale* (2) FL-3
Cedar Landing—*locale* (2) MD-2
Cedar Landing—*locale* NC-3
Cedar Landing—*locale* VA-3
Cedar Landing Ch—*church* NC-3
Cedar Lane—*hist pl* NC-3
Cedar Lane—*locale* PA-2
Cedar Lane—*locale* TX-5
Cedarlane—*other* TN-4
**Cedar Lane**—*pop pl* TN-4
Cedar Lane Ch—*church* TN-4
Cedar Lane Ch—*church* VA-3
Cedar Lane Farm—*hist pl* GA-3
Cedar Lane Post Office (historical)—*building* TN-4
Cedar Lane Sch—*school* CA-9
Cedarlane Sch—*school* CA-9
Cedar Lane Sch—*school* MI-6
Cedar Lane Sch—*school* VA-3
Cedar Lateral—*canal* CO-8
Cedar Lawn—*hist pl* WV-2
**Cedar Lawn**—*pop pl* MD-2
**Cedar Lawn**—*pop pl* VA-3
Cedar Lawn Burial Park—*cemetery* VA-3
*Cedar Lawn Cem* MS-4
Cedar Lawn Cem—*cemetery* IA-7
Cedarlawn Cem—*cemetery* MS-4
Cedar Lawn Cem—*cemetery* MS-4
Cedar Lawn Cem—*cemetery* NE-7
Cedar Lawn Cem—*cemetery* NJ-2
Cedar Lawn Cem—*cemetery* NY-2
Cedar Lawn Cem—*cemetery* PA-2
Cedar Lawn Cem—*cemetery* TN-4
Cedar Lawn Memorial Cem—*cemetery* MS-4
Cedar Lawn Plantation (historical)—*locale* AL-4
Cedar Leaf Cem—*cemetery* KY-4
Cedar Ledge—*locale* PA-2
Cedar Ledge—*summit* PA-2
Cedar Ledges—*bar* ME-1
Cedar Ledges—*island* ME-1
Cedar Lee Sch—*school* VA-3
Cedarless Flat—*flat* UT-8
**Cedar Level**—*pop pl* (2) VA-3
Cedar Lick—*stream* KY-4
Cedar Lick Branch—*stream* TX-5
*Cedar Lick Church* TN-4
Cedar Lick Creek—*stream* OH-6
Cedar Lick Hollow—*valley* TX-5
*Cedar Lodge* NC-3
Cedar Lodge—*locale* MO-7
**Cedar Lodge**—*pop pl* NC-3
Cedar Log Creek—*stream* MT-8
Cedar Log Creek—*stream* OR-9
Cedar Log Lakes—*lake* MT-8
Cedar Log Spring—*spring* AZ-5
Cedarloo Sch—*school* IA-7
**Cedar Manor**—*pop pl* NY-2
Cedar Manor Park—*park* MN-6
Cedar Manor Sch—*school* MN-6
Cedar Meadow—*flat* OR-9
Cedar Meadow Pond—*reservoir* GA-3
Cedar Meadow Pond—*reservoir* MA-1
Cedar Meadow Pond Dam—*dam* MA-1
Cedar Memorial Ch—*church* IA-7
**Cedarmere**—*pop pl* MD-2
Cedarmere-Clayton Estates—*hist pl* NY-2
*Cedar Mesa* AZ-5
Cedar Mesa—*summit* (2) AZ-5
Cedar Mesa—*summit* CO-8
Cedar Mesa—*summit* (3) UT-8
Cedar Mesa Anticline—*ridge* UT-8
Cedar Mesa Campground—*locale* UT-8
Cedar Mesa Canal—*canal* ID-8
Cedar Mesa Canyon—*valley* AZ-5
Cedar Mesa Ditch—*canal* CO-8
Cedar Mesa Ranch—*locale* UT-8
Cedar Mesa Rsvr—*reservoir* CO-8
Cedar Mesa Rsvr—*reservoir* ID-8
Cedar Mesa Tank—*reservoir* (2) AZ-5
Cedar Mesa Tanks—*reservoir* AZ-5
Cedar Mill—*locale* AZ-5
Cedar Mill—*locale* CA-9
**Cedar Mill**—*pop pl* OR-9
Cedar Mill Creek—*stream* OR-9
**Cedar Mills**—*pop pl* MN-6
**Cedar Mills**—*pop pl* OH-6
**Cedar Mills**—*pop pl* TX-5
Cedar Mills Ch—*church* OH-6
Cedar Mill Sch—*school* OR-9
**Cedar Mills (Township of)**—*pop pl* MN-6
Cedarmont—*hist pl* TN-4
Cedarmore Camp—*locale* KY-4
Cedarmore Lake—*reservoir* KY-4
Cedar Mott Draw—*valley* TX-5
Cedar Mound—*summit* (2) TX-5
Cedar Mound Cem—*cemetery* MS-4
Cedar Mound Ch—*church* MS-4
Cedar Mound Plantation (historical)—*locale* MS-4
Cedar Mound School (historical)—*locale* MO-7
*Cedar Mountain* MT-8
*Cedar Mountain* NV-8
*Cedar Mountain* WY-8
Cedar Mountain—*locale* WA-9
**Cedar Mountain**—*pop pl* NC-3
Cedar Mountain—*ridge* AL-4
Cedar Mountain—*ridge* (2) AR-4
Cedar Mountain—*ridge* ID-8
Cedar Mountain—*ridge* WY-8
Cedar Mountain Campground—*locale* UT-8
Cedar Mountain Cave—*cave* AL-4
Cedar Mountain Ch—*church* AR-4
Cedar Mountain Ch—*church* NC-3
Cedar Mountain Draw—*valley* NV-8
Cedar Mountain Gulch—*valley* CO-8
Cedar Mountain Lake—*reservoir* NC-3
Cedar Mountain (Magisterial District)—*fmr MCD* VA-3
Cedar Mountain Range—*other* NM-5
Cedar Mountain Rec Area—*park* UT-8
Cedar Mountain Ridge—*ridge* CA-9
Cedar Mountain Rsvr—*reservoir* WY-8
Cedar Mountain Rsvr No 7—*reservoir* WY-8
*Cedar Mountains* OR-9
*Cedar Mountains* UT-8
Cedar Mountains—*range* OK-5
Cedar Mountain Sch—*hist pl* ID-8
Cedar Mountain Sch—*school* ID-8
Cedar Mountain Sch (historical)—*school* AL-4
Cedar Mountain Tank—*reservoir* AZ-5
Cedar Mountain Trail—*trail* ID-8
Cedar Mountain Trick Tank—*reservoir* AZ-5
Cedar Mountain Well—*well* NV-8
Cedar Mountain Well—*well* NM-5
Cedar Mount Ch—*church* AL-4
Cedar Mount Rsvr—*reservoir* OR-9
*Cedar Mtn* AL-4
*Cedar Mtn* GA-3
Cedar Mtn—*summit* (8) AL-4
Cedar Mtn—*summit* (6) AZ-5
Cedar Mtn—*summit* (2) AR-4
Cedar Mtn—*summit* (4) CA-9
Cedar Mtn—*summit* (2) CO-8
Cedar Mtn—*summit* (2) CT-1
Cedar Mtn—*summit* (4) GA-3
Cedar Mtn—*summit* (2) ID-8
Cedar Mtn—*summit* (3) ME-1
Cedar Mtn—*summit* MA-1
Cedar Mtn—*summit* MO-7
Cedar Mtn—*summit* MT-8
Cedar Mtn—*summit* (2) NV-8
Cedar Mtn—*summit* (2) NH-1
Cedar Mtn—*summit* (4) NM-5
Cedar Mtn—*summit* (2) NY-2
Cedar Mtn—*summit* (2) NC-3
Cedar Mtn—*summit* OK-5
Cedar Mtn—*summit* (3) OR-9
Cedar Mtn—*summit* (2) PA-2
Cedar Mtn—*summit* SC-3
Cedar Mtn—*summit* (2) TN-4
Cedar Mtn—*summit* (10) TX-5
Cedar Mtn—*summit* (10) UT-8
Cedar Mtn—*summit* (2) VT-1
Cedar Mtn—*summit* (3) VA-3
Cedar Mtn—*summit* (5) WY-8
Cedar Mtn Knoll—*summit* UT-8
Cedar Mtns—*range* NV-8
Cedar Mtns—*range* (2) UT-8
Cedar Neck—*cape* (2) DE-2
Cedar Neck—*cape* MA-1
Cedar Neck—*cape* VA-3
*Cedar Neck Church* DE-2
Cedar Neck Sch—*school* DE-2
Cedar Neck United Methodist Ch—*church* DE-2
Cedar North Sch—*school* UT-8
Cedar Notch—*gap* WA-9
Cedar Oak Cem—*cemetery* AL-4
Cedar Oak Park Sch—*school* OR-9
*Cedar Oaks Cem* AL-4
Cedar Oak Sch—*school* IL-6
Cedarock Park Hist Dist—*hist pl* NC-3
Cedar Oil And Gas Field—*other* MI-6
Cedar Opening—*gap* CA-9
Cedar Overlook Beach—*beach* NY-2
Cedar Park—*flat* CO-8
Cedar Park—*flat* UT-8
Cedar Park—*hist pl* MD-2
Cedarpark—*locale* GA-3
Cedar Park—*park* TX-5
Cedar Park—*park* WI-6
**Cedar Park**—*pop pl* IL-6
**Cedar Park**—*pop pl* OH-6
**Cedar Park**—*pop pl* TX-5
**Cedar Park**—*pop pl* VA-3
**Cedar Park**—*pop pl* WI-6
Cedar Park—*uninc pl* MD-2
Cedar Park Cem—*cemetery* IL-6
Cedar Park Cem—*cemetery* NJ-2
Cedar Park Cem—*cemetery* NY-2
Cedar Park Cem—*cemetery* WI-6
Cedar Park Ditch—*canal* CO-8
Cedar Park JHS—*school* OR-9
Cedar Park Memorial Cem—*cemetery* IA-7
Cedar Pass—*channel* AK-9
Cedar Pass—*gap* CA-9
Cedar Pass—*gap* (3) NV-8
Cedar Pass—*gap* NM-5
Cedar Pass—*gap* SD-7
Cedar Pass—*gap* (3) UT-8
Cedar Pass—*gap* WY-8
Cedar Pass Campground—*locale* CA-9
Cedar Pass Rsvr—*reservoir* UT-8
Cedar Pass Wash—*valley* UT-8
Cedar Pasture Draw—*valley* TX-5
Cedar Patch Branch—*stream* SC-3
Cedar Peak—*summit* (2) MT-8
Cedar Peak—*summit* (2) NV-8
Cedar Peak—*summit* (2) UT-8
Cedar Peak Draw—*valley* UT-8
Cedar Peak Lake—*lake* UT-8
Cedar Pen Canyon—*valley* CO-8
*Cedar Pines* CA-9
**Cedar Pines**—*pop pl* PA-2
Cedar Pines Lake—*reservoir* SC-3
**Cedarpines Park**—*pop pl* CA-9
Cedar-Piney Lake—*reservoir* AR-4
Cedar Pipeline Ranch—*locale* NV-8
Cedar Plains—*locale* AL-4
Cedar Plains Ch—*church* AL-4
Cedar Plains P.O. (historical)—*locale* AL-4
Cedar Pocket Rsvr—*reservoir* AZ-5
Cedar Pockets—*range* UT-8
Cedar Pockets Wash—*valley* AZ-5
Cedar Pockets Wash—*valley* UT-8
*Cedar Point* FL-3
*Cedar Point* MD-2
*Cedar Point* MA-1
*Cedar Point* MI-6
*Cedar Point* OH-6
*Cedar Point* TX-5
Cedar Point—*cape* (2) AL-4
Cedar Point—*cape* CT-1
Cedar Point—*cape* (8) FL-3
Cedar Point—*cape* GA-3
Cedar Point—*cape* IN-6
Cedar Point—*cape* ME-1
Cedar Point—*cape* (16) MD-2
Cedar Point—*cape* MA-1
Cedar Point—*cape* MI-6
Cedar Point—*cape* (4) MN-6
Cedar Point—*cape* (4) MS-4
Cedar Point—*cape* (2) MO-7
Cedar Point—*cape* NE-7
Cedar Point—*cape* NH-1
Cedar Point—*cape* (2) NJ-2
Cedar Point—*cape* (2) NM-5
Cedar Point—*cape* (3) NY-2
Cedar Point—*cape* (11) NC-3
Cedar Point—*cape* (2) OH-6
Cedar Point—*cape* OK-5
Cedar Point—*cape* (2) OR-9
Cedar Point—*cape* RI-1
Cedar Point—*cape* (2) TN-4
Cedar Point—*cape* (4) TX-5
Cedar Point—*cape* (9) VA-3
Cedar Point—*cape* WA-9
Cedar Point—*cape* (3) WI-6
Cedar Point—*cliff* CA-9
Cedar Point—*cliff* CO-8
Cedar Point—*cliff* IN-6
Cedar Point—*cliff* (3) KY-4
Cedar Point—*cliff* MO-7
Cedar Point—*cliff* TX-5
Cedar Point—*cliff* (3) UT-8
Cedar Point—*locale* AL-4
Cedar Point—*locale* CO-8
Cedar Point—*locale* FL-3
Cedar Point—*locale* (2) KY-4
Cedar Point—*locale* OR-9
Cedar Point—*locale* VA-3
Cedar Point—*other* TN-4
**Cedar Point**—*pop pl* AL-4
**Cedar Point**—*pop pl* GA-3
**Cedar Point**—*pop pl* IL-6
**Cedar Point**—*pop pl* (2) IN-6
**Cedar Point**—*pop pl* KS-7
**Cedar Point**—*pop pl* NC-3
**Cedar Point**—*pop pl* OH-6
**Cedar Point**—*pop pl* RI-1
**Cedar Point**—*pop pl* (2) TX-5
Cedar Point—*ridge* UT-8
Cedar Point—*summit* (3) CO-8
Cedar Point—*summit* GA-3
Cedar Point—*summit* UT-8
Cedar Point Branch—*stream* KY-4
Cedar Point Camp—*locale* IL-6
Cedar Point Camp—*locale* MS-4
Cedar Point Camp—*locale* NE-7
Cedar Point Canal—*canal* ID-8
Cedar Point Canyon—*valley* TX-5
Cedar Point Causeway—*bridge* OH-6
Cedar Point Cem—*cemetery* KS-7
Cedar Point Cem—*cemetery* KY-4
Cedar Point Cem—*cemetery* OH-6
Cedar Point Cem—*cemetery* TX-5
Cedar Point Ch—*church* (2) AL-4
Cedar Point Ch—*church* AR-4
Cedar Point Ch—*church* KY-4
Cedar Point Ch—*church* MO-7
Cedar Point Ch—*church* NC-3
Cedar Point Ch—*church* TN-4
Cedar Point Ch—*church* (2) TX-5
Cedar Point Creek—*gut* FL-3
Cedar Point Creek—*stream* GA-3
Cedar Point Dikes—*levee* TN-4
Cedar Point (fishing camp)—*uninc pl* FL-3
Cedar Point Golf and Country Club—*locale* VA-3
Cedar Point Interchange—*crossing* AZ-5
Cedar Point Lake—*reservoir* KS-7
Cedar Point Landing—*locale* TN-4
Cedar Point Light—*hist pl* OH-6
Cedar Point Lighthouse—*locale* MD-2
Cedar Point Lookout—*locale* WA-9
Cedar Point Mine—*mine* TN-4
Cedar Point Natl Wildlife Ref—*park* OH-6
Cedar Point Neck—*cape* MD-2
Cedar Point Oil Field—*oilfield* TX-5
Cedar Point Oil Field—*other* NM-5
Cedar Point Public Use Area—*park* TN-4
Cedar Point Ranch—*locale* TX-5
Cedar Point Rec Area—*park* KS-7
*Cedar Point Reservoir* KS-7
Cedar Point Ridge—*ridge* KY-4
Cedarpoint Run—*stream* WV-2
Cedar Point Sch—*school* MS-4
Cedar Point Sch—*school* TX-5
Cedar Point Sch—*school* VA-3
Cedar Point Sch (historical)—*school* AL-4
Cedar Point Spring—*spring* UT-8
Cedar Point State Park—*park* NY-2
**Cedar Point (subdivision)**—*pop pl* (2) MS-4
**Cedar Point (subdivision)**—*pop pl* PA-2
**Cedar Point (subdivision)**—*pop pl* VA-3
Cedar Point Tank—*reservoir* AZ-5
Cedar Point Trading Post—*locale* AZ-5
Cedar Point Upper Bar—*bar* TN-4
Cedar Point Windmill—*locale* TX-5
Cedar Pole Cave—*cave* AL-4
Cedar Pole Hollow—*valley* MO-7
*Cedar Pond* DE-2
*Cedar Pond* MA-1
*Cedar Pond* NY-2
*Cedar Pond* TX-5
Cedar Pond—*lake* (2) AZ-5
Cedar Pond—*lake* CT-1
Cedar Pond—*lake* DE-2
Cedar Pond—*lake* FL-3
Cedar Pond—*lake* (5) ME-1
Cedar Pond—*lake* (8) MA-1
Cedar Pond—*lake* NH-1
Cedar Pond—*lake* NJ-2
Cedar Pond—*lake* (4) NY-2
Cedar Pond—*lake* SC-3
Cedar Pond—*lake* TX-5
Cedar Pond—*lake* UT-8
Cedar Pond—*reservoir* MA-1
Cedar Pond—*reservoir* NJ-2
Cedar Pond Branch—*stream* SC-3
Cedar Pond Brook—*stream* CT-1
Cedar Pond Brook—*stream* NY-2
Cedar Pond Dam—*dam* MA-1
Cedar Pond Dam—*dam* NJ-2
Cedar Ponds—*lake* MA-1
Cedar Pond Sch—*school* FL-3
Cedar Ponds Lake—*lake* WA-9
Cedar Pond Windmill—*locale* CO-8
Cedar Ranch—*locale* AZ-5
Cedar Ranch (historical)—*locale* SD-7
*Cedar Range* NV-8
Cedar Range—*range* NV-8
**Cedar Rapids**—*pop pl* IA-7
**Cedar Rapids**—*pop pl* NE-7
Cedar Rapids—*rapids* NE-7
Cedar Rapids—*rapids* (2) WI-6
Cedar Rapids Municipal Airp—*airport* IA-7
Cedar Rapids Post Office and Public Bldg—*hist pl* IA-7
**Cedar Rapids (Town of)**—*pop pl* WI-6
Cedar Ravine—*valley* (3) CA-9
Cedar Ravine—*valley* NV-8
Cedar Reef—*bar* TX-5
*Cedar Ridge* WY-8
Cedar Ridge—*locale* PA-2
**Cedar Ridge**—*pop pl* (2) CA-9
**Cedar Ridge**—*pop pl* MO-7
**Cedar Ridge**—*pop pl* OK-5
Cedar Ridge—*ridge* (5) AL-4
Cedar Ridge—*ridge* (5) AZ-5
Cedar Ridge—*ridge* (4) AR-4
Cedar Ridge—*ridge* (2) CA-9
Cedar Ridge—*ridge* (2) GA-3
Cedar Ridge—*ridge* (4) ID-8
Cedar Ridge—*ridge* KY-4
Cedar Ridge—*ridge* (2) MO-7
Cedar Ridge—*ridge* (2) MT-8
Cedar Ridge—*ridge* NV-8
Cedar Ridge—*ridge* NC-3
Cedar Ridge—*ridge* ND-7
Cedar Ridge—*ridge* (6) TN-4
Cedar Ridge—*ridge* (3) TX-5
Cedar Ridge—*ridge* (7) UT-8
Cedar Ridge—*ridge* (4) VA-3
Cedar Ridge—*ridge* WA-9
Cedar Ridge—*ridge* (5) WY-8
Cedar Ridge—*uninc pl* MD-2
Cedar Ridge Canyon—*valley* UT-8
Cedar Ridge Cave—*cave* AL-4
Cedar Ridge Cem—*cemetery* NJ-2
Cedar Ridge Ch—*church* KY-4
Cedar Ridge Ch—*church* MO-7
Cedar Ridge Ch—*church* OH-6
Cedar Ridge Ch—*church* TN-4
Cedar Ridge Country Club—*other* NJ-2
Cedar Ridge MS—*school* UT-8
Cedar Ridge Park—*park* TX-5
Cedar Ridge P O—*locale* NM-5
Cedar Ridge Rapids—*rapids* UT-8
Cedar Ridge Rsvr—*reservoir* AZ-5
Cedar Ridge Sch—*school* IL-6
Cedar Ridge Sch—*school* IA-7
Cedar Ridge Sch—*school* TX-5
Cedar Ridge Sch (historical)—*school* MS-4
Cedar Ridge Sch (historical)—*school* MO-7
Cedar Ridge Sch (historical)—*school* TN-4
Cedar Ridge Spring—*spring* UT-8
**Cedar Ridge (subdivision)**—*pop pl* (2) AZ-5
**Cedar Ridge Subdivision**—*pop pl* UT-8
**Cedar Ridge Subdivision Number Two**—*pop pl* UT-8
Cedar Ridge Tank—*reservoir* NM-5
Cedar Ridge Trading Post—*locale* AZ-5
**Cedar Ridge (Trading Post)**—*pop pl* AZ-5
Cedar Ridge Well—*well* UT-8
Cedar Riffle Branch—*stream* KY-4
*Cedar Rim* UT-8
Cedar Rim—*cliff* WY-8
Cedar Rim Draw—*valley* WY-8
Cedar Ripple (historical)—*rapids* AL-4
*Cedar River* MI-6
*Cedar River* NE-7
*Cedar River* NJ-2
*Cedar River* ND-7
**Cedar River**—*pop pl* MI-6
Cedar River—*stream* FL-3
Cedar River—*stream* IA-7
Cedar River—*stream* (3) MI-6
Cedar River—*stream* MN-6
Cedar River—*stream* NE-7
Cedar River—*stream* NY-2
Cedar River—*stream* (2) WA-9
Cedar River Access Area—*park* IA-7
Cedar River Cem—*cemetery* MI-6
Cedar River Cem—*cemetery* NY-2
Cedar River Ch—*church* OK-5
Cedar River Flow—*reservoir* NY-2
Cedar River Golf Course—*other* NY-2
Cedar River Park—*park* IA-7
*Cedar Riverside* MN-6
Cedar River Watershed—*area* WA-9
Cedar Road Sch—*school* NY-2
Cedar Road Sch—*school* PA-2
Cedar Rock—*locale* GA-3
**Cedar Rock**—*pop pl* SC-3
Cedar Rock—*summit* NM-5
Cedar Rock—*summit* NC-3
Cedar Rock Cem—*cemetery* GA-3
Cedar Rock Ch—*church* (2) GA-3
Cedar Rock Ch—*church* (5) NC-3
Cedar Rock Ch—*church* (3) SC-3
Cedar Rock Country Club—*locale* NC-3
Cedar Rock Creek—*stream* (2) NC-3
*Cedar Rock Golf Course* NC-3
Cedar Rock Lake—*reservoir* GA-3
Cedar Rock Lodge—*locale* CA-9
**Cedar Rock Lodge**—*pop pl* CA-9
Cedar Rock Mtn—*summit* (2) NC-3
Cedar Rock Mtn—*summit* (3) SC-3
**Cedarrock (Stallings)**—*pop pl* NC-3
Cedar Rock State Park—*park* IA-7
Cedar Roughs—*ridge* CA-9
Cedar Rsvr—*reservoir* NV-8
Cedar Rsvr—*reservoir* (2) OR-9
*Cedar Run* ID-8
*Cedar Run* IL-6
Cedar Run—*locale* MI-6
**Cedar Run**—*pop pl* NJ-2
**Cedar Run**—*pop pl* OH-6
**Cedar Run**—*pop pl* PA-2
Cedar Run—*stream* CO-8
Cedar Run—*stream* (3) KY-4
Cedar Run—*stream* (2) MI-6
Cedar Run—*stream* (3) NJ-2
Cedar Run—*stream* (7) OH-6
Cedar Run—*stream* (6) PA-2
Cedar Run—*stream* (6) VA-3
Cedar Run—*stream* (6) WV-2
Cedar Run Airp—*airport* PA-2
Cedar Run Canyon—*valley* ID-8
Cedar Run Cem—*cemetery* NJ-2
Cedar Run Cem—*cemetery* VA-3
Cedar Run Ch—*church* PA-2
Cedar Run Ch—*church* (2) VA-3
Cedar Run Ch—*church* WV-2
*Cedar Run Creek* MI-6
Cedar Run Creek—*stream* CA-9
Cedar Run Creek—*stream* ID-8
Cedar Run Creek—*stream* MT-8
Cedar Run Ditch—*canal* CO-8
Cedar Run (Magisterial District)—*fmr MCD* VA-3
Cedar Run Sch—*school* MI-6
Cedar Run Sch—*school* PA-2
Cedar Run Trail—*trail* VA-3
*Cedars* AL-4
Cedars—*locale* OK-5
Cedars—*locale* PA-2
**Cedars**—*pop pl* DE-2
**Cedars**—*pop pl* MS-4
**Cedars**—*pop pl* MT-8
**Cedars**—*pop pl* NY-2
Cedars, Point of—*cape* DE-2
Cedars, The—*area* CA-9
Cedars, The—*hist pl* (2) GA-3
Cedars, The—*hist pl* KY-4
Cedars, The—*hist pl* (3) MS-4
Cedars, The—*hist pl* NC-3
Cedars, The—*locale* AL-4
Cedars, The—*locale* (2) CA-9
Cedars, The—*locale* ID-8
Cedars, The—*locale* MD-2
Cedars, The—*locale* VT-1
**Cedars, The**—*pop pl* AL-4
**Cedars, The**—*pop pl* CA-9
**Cedars, The**—*pop pl* CT-1
**Cedars, The**—*pop pl* (2) DE-2

**Cedars, The**—*pop pl* .... VA-3
Cedars, The—*summit* .... CA-9
Cedars, The—*woods* .... AZ-5
Cedars, The—*woods* (3) .... NV-8
Cedars, The—*woods* .... VA-3
Cedar Salt Ground—*flat* .... AZ-5
Cedar Salt Log Creek—*stream* .... CA-9
Cedars Camp—*locale* .... MO-7
Cedars (CCD)—*cens area* .... TN-4
Cedars Cem—*cemetery* .... MS-4
Cedars Cemetery, The—*cemetery* .... NC-3
Cedar Sch—*school* (2) .... IA-7
Cedar Sch—*school* .... MA-1
Cedar Sch—*school* .... MI-6
Cedar Sch—*school* .... MN-6
Cedar Sch—*school* .... NE-7
Cedar Sch—*school* .... SD-7
Cedar Sch (historical)—*school* .... MS-4
Cedars Country Club, The—*other* .... VA-3
Cedar Scrappy—*summit* .... AR-4
Cedars Division—*civil* .... TN-4
Cedars Estate—*uninc pl* .... NC-3
*Cedar Shelter* .... CA-9
Cedars (historical), The—*locale* .... AL-4
Cedar Shoals—*bar* .... GA-3
Cedar Shoals Ch—*church* (3) .... SC-3
Cedar Shoals Creek—*stream* .... SC-3
Cedar Shoals Ford—*locale* .... TN-4
Cedars Home—*locale* .... NE-7
**Cedar Shores**—*pop pl* .... IN-6
**Cedar Shores (subdivision)**—*pop pl* .... DE-2
Cedar Sink—*basin* .... KY-4
Cedar Sinking Creek—*stream* .... KY-4
**Cedars Knoll**—*pop pl* .... DE-2
Cedars Lock—*dam* .... WI-6
**Cedar Slope**—*pop pl* .... CA-9
Cedars Med Ctr—*hospital* .... FL-3
Cedar Snag Creek—*gut* .... NC-3
Cedar Snags—*hist pl* .... ID-8
*Cedars of Lebanon Hosp* .... FL-3
Cedars of Lebanon Hosp—*hospital* .... CA-9
Cedars of Lebanon Hosp—*hospital* .... FL-3
Cedars Of Lebanon State For—*forest* .... TN-4
Cedars of Lebanon State Park—*park* .... TN-4
Cedar South Sch—*school* .... UT-8
Cedars Plantation—*hist pl* .... LA-4
Cedars Post Office (historical)—*building* .... AL-4
*Cedar Spring* .... AZ-5
*Cedar Spring* .... ID-8
*Cedar Spring* .... NV-8
*Cedar Spring* .... TN-4
Cedar Spring—*locale* .... VA-3
**Cedar Spring**—*pop pl* .... KY-4
**Cedar Spring**—*pop pl* .... SC-3
**Cedar Spring**—*pop pl* (2) .... TN-4
Cedar Spring—*spring* (2) .... AL-4
Cedar Spring—*spring* (21) .... AZ-5
Cedar Spring—*spring* (15) .... CA-9
Cedar Spring—*spring* (5) .... CO-8
Cedar Spring—*spring* (2) .... ID-8
Cedar Spring—*spring* .... MT-8
Cedar Spring—*spring* (6) .... NV-8
Cedar Spring—*spring* (3) .... NM-5
Cedar Spring—*spring* .... NY-2
Cedar Spring—*spring* (8) .... OR-9
Cedar Spring—*spring* (2) .... PA-2
Cedar Spring—*spring* .... SD-7
Cedar Spring—*spring* (2) .... TN-4
Cedar Spring—*spring* (3) .... TX-5
Cedar Spring—*spring* (9) .... UT-8
Cedar Spring—*spring* .... VA-3
Cedar Spring—*spring* .... WA-9
Cedar Spring—*spring* .... WI-6
Cedar Spring Branch—*stream* .... TX-5
Cedar Spring Canyon—*valley* .... AZ-5
Cedar Spring Canyon—*valley* .... NM-5
Cedar Spring Canyon—*valley* .... TX-5
Cedar Spring Ch—*church* .... GA-3
Cedar Spring Ch—*church* .... OK-5
Cedar Spring Ch—*church* (2) .... TN-4
*Cedar Spring Church* .... AL-4
Cedar Spring Gulch—*valley* .... CA-9
*Cedar Spring Hollow* .... KY-4
Cedar Spring Hollow—*valley* (2) .... MO-7
Cedar Spring Run—*stream* .... PA-2
Cedar Spring Run—*stream* .... VA-3
*Cedar Springs* .... NV-8
*Cedar Springs* .... UT-8
Cedar Springs—*locale* .... AZ-5
Cedar Springs—*locale* .... KY-4
Cedar Springs—*locale* .... SC-3
Cedar Springs—*locale* .... TN-4
Cedar Springs—*locale* (2) .... TX-5
**Cedar Springs**—*pop pl* (2) .... AL-4
**Cedar Springs**—*pop pl* .... CA-9
**Cedar Springs**—*pop pl* .... CT-1
**Cedar Springs**—*pop pl* .... GA-3
**Cedar Springs**—*pop pl* .... MI-6
**Cedar Springs**—*pop pl* .... MO-7
**Cedar Springs**—*pop pl* .... NJ-2
**Cedar Springs**—*pop pl* .... OH-6
**Cedar Springs**—*pop pl* .... PA-2
**Cedar Springs**—*pop pl* .... SC-3
**Cedar Springs**—*pop pl* (2) .... TN-4
**Cedar Springs**—*pop pl* .... UT-8
**Cedar Springs**—*pop pl* (2) .... VA-3
Cedar Springs—*spring* .... AZ-5
Cedar Springs—*spring* .... CA-9
Cedar Springs—*spring* .... CO-8
Cedar Springs—*spring* .... NV-8
Cedar Springs—*spring* .... NM-5
Cedar Springs—*spring* .... OR-9
Cedar Springs—*spring* (2) .... TN-4
Cedar Springs—*spring* .... WA-9
Cedar Springs Branch—*stream* .... GA-3
Cedar Springs Branch—*stream* .... TN-4
Cedar Springs Butte—*summit* .... AZ-5
Cedar Springs Campground—*locale* .... UT-8
Cedar Springs Campground—*locale* .... WA-9
Cedar Springs Camp Ground
(historical)—*locale* .... TN-4
Cedar Springs Canyon—*valley* .... NM-5
Cedar Springs Canyon—*valley* .... UT-8
Cedar Springs Cave—*cave* .... TN-4
Cedar Springs Cem—*cemetery* .... AL-4
Cedar Springs Cem—*cemetery* .... GA-3
Cedar Springs Cem—*cemetery* .... MI-6
Cedar Springs Cem—*cemetery* .... NC-3
Cedar Springs Cem—*cemetery* .... TN-4
*Cedar Springs Ch* .... SC-3
Cedar Springs Ch—*church* (3) .... AL-4
Cedar Springs Ch—*church* .... AR-4
Cedar Springs Ch—*church* (4) .... GA-3
Cedar Springs Ch—*church* (2) .... KY-4
Cedar Springs Ch—*church* .... SC-3
Cedar Springs Ch—*church* (5) .... TN-4
Cedar Springs Ch—*church* (3) .... TX-5
Cedar Spring Sch—*school* .... TN-4
Cedar Spring Sch (historical)—*school* (2) .... AL-4
Cedar Spring Sch (historical)—*school* .... PA-2
**Cedar Springs Condominium**—*pop pl* .... UT-8
Cedar Springs Creek—*stream* .... AL-4
Cedar Springs Creek—*stream* .... OR-9
Cedar Springs Creek—*stream* .... TN-4
Cedar Springs Creek—*stream* .... WI-6
Cedar Springs Draw—*valley* .... CO-8
Cedar Springs Gulch—*valley* .... CO-8
Cedar Springs Hist Dist—*hist pl* .... SC-3
Cedar Springs (historical)—*locale* .... AL-4
Cedar Springs Lookout—*locale* .... NM-5
Cedar Springs Lookout Tower—*locale* .... GA-3
*Cedar Springs Missionary Baptist Church* .... AL-4
Cedar Springs Mtn—*summit* .... CO-8
Cedar Springs Mtn—*summit* .... OR-9
Cedar Springs Park—*park* .... AL-4
Cedar Springs Post Office
(historical)—*building* .... AL-4
Cedar Springs Post Office
(historical)—*building* .... TN-4
Cedar Springs Ridge—*ridge* .... CA-9
Cedar Springs Sch—*school* .... AL-4
Cedar Springs Sch—*school* .... FL-3
Cedar Springs Shop Ctr—*locale* .... TN-4
Cedar Springs Tabernacle—*church* .... SC-3
Cedar Spring Tank—*reservoir* .... TX-5
Cedar Spring Valley—*basin* .... KY-4
Cedar Spring Wash—*valley* .... UT-8
Cedar Square Ch—*church* .... NC-3
*Cedars Sacred Heart Convent, The* .... AL-4
Cedars Sch (historical)—*school* .... MS-4
Cedar State Wildlife Mngmt Area—*park* .. MN-6
Cedar Station—*locale* .... TX-5
Cedar Straits—*channel* .... MD-2
Cedar Straits—*channel* .... VA-3
Cedar Stream—*stream* .... NH-1
Cedar Street Bridge—*other* .... IL-6
Cedar Street HS—*school* .... KY-4
Cedar Street Sch—*school* (2) .... MI-6
Cedar Street Sch—*school* .... NY-2
Cedar Street Sch—*school* .... OH-6
Cedar Summit—*gap* .... NV-8
Cedars United Methodist Ch—*church* .... DE-2
*Cedar Swamp* .... CT-1
*Cedar Swamp* .... DE-2
*Cedar Swamp* .... MA-1
*Cedar Swamp* .... OR-9
Cedar Swamp—*locale* .... NY-2
**Cedar Swamp**—*pop pl* .... SC-3
Cedar Swamp—*stream* (2) .... SC-3
Cedar Swamp—*swamp* (13) .... CT-1
Cedar Swamp—*swamp* .... DE-2
Cedar Swamp—*swamp* (2) .... FL-3
Cedar Swamp—*swamp* .... ME-1
Cedar Swamp—*swamp* (18) .... MA-1
Cedar Swamp—*swamp* (3) .... MI-6
Cedar Swamp—*swamp* (3) .... NJ-2
Cedar Swamp—*swamp* (12) .... NY-2
Cedar Swamp—*swamp* (4) .... OR-9
Cedar Swamp—*swamp* (3) .... RI-1
Cedar Swamp—*swamp* (4) .... VT-1
Cedar Swamp—*swamp* .... WA-9
Cedar Swamp Archeol District—*hist pl* .... MA-1
Cedar Swamp Bay—*swamp* .... NC-3
*Cedar Swamp Brook* .... MA-1
Cedar Swamp Brook—*stream* (6) .... CT-1
Cedar Swamp Brook—*stream* (2) .... MA-1
Cedar Swamp Brook—*stream* (2) .... RI-1
Cedar Swamp Cem—*cemetery* .... CT-1
Cedar Swamp Covered Bridge—*hist pl* .... VT-1
Cedar Swamp Creek—*stream* .... FL-3
Cedar Swamp Creek—*stream* .... NJ-2
Cedar Swamp Creek—*stream* .... NY-2
Cedar Swamp Creek—*stream* .... NC-3
Cedar Swamp Creek—*stream* (3) .... OR-9
*Cedar Swamp Mountain* .... MA-1
Cedar Swamp Mtn—*summit* .... ME-1
*Cedar Swamp Pond* .... CT-1
*Cedar Swamp Pond* .... MA-1
*Cedar Swamp Pond* .... RI-1
Cedar Swamp Pond—*lake* (2) .... CT-1
Cedar Swamp Pond—*lake* .... ME-1
Cedar Swamp Pond—*lake* (2) .... MA-1
Cedar Swamp Pond—*lake* (2) .... RI-1
Cedar Swamp Pond—*reservoir* .... MA-1
Cedar Swamp Pond—*swamp* .... NH-1
Cedar Swamp Pond Dam—*dam* .... MA-1
*Cedar Swamp Reservoir* .... CT-1
Cedar Swamp River—*stream* .... MA-1
Cedar Swamp State Memorial—*park* .... OH-6
Cedar Swamp Town For—*forest* .... MA-1
*Cedar Switch* .... AL-4
Cedar Talisman Mine—*mine* .... UT-8
*Cedar Tank* .... TX-5
Cedar Tank—*reservoir* (13) .... AZ-5
Cedar Tank—*reservoir* (6) .... NM-5
Cedar Tank—*reservoir* (8) .... TX-5
Cedar Tank Canyon—*valley* .... AZ-5
Cedar Tank (historical)—*reservoir* .... AZ-5
Cedar Tank Windmills—*locale* .... TX-5
**Cedar Terrace**—*pop pl* .... SC-3
**Cedar Terrace Subdivision**—*pop pl* .... UT-8
Cedar Through Cave—*cave* .... AL-4
Cedarton—*locale* .... LA-4
Cedar Top—*summit* .... NC-3
Cedar Top—*summit* .... WY-8
Cedar Top Butte—*summit* .... ND-7
Cedar Top Camp—*locale* .... TX-5
Cedar Top Ch—*church* .... KY-4
Cedar Top Peak—*summit* .... TX-5
Cedartop Sch—*school* .... KY-4
Cedartown—*locale* .... MD-2
**Cedartown**—*pop pl* .... GA-3
Cedartown (CCD)—*cens area* .... GA-3
Cedartown Sch—*school* .... FL-3
Cedar Township—*civil* .... KS-7
Cedar Township—*civil* (4) .... MO-7
Cedar Township—*fmr MCD* (18) .... IA-7
**Cedar Township**—*pop pl* (4) .... KS-7
**Cedar Township**—*pop pl* .... MO-7
**Cedar Township**—*pop pl* (3) .... NE-7
**Cedar Township**—*pop pl* .... ND-7
**Cedar Township**—*pop pl* .... SD-7
Cedar Township Cem—*cemetery* .... IA-7
Cedar Township Hall—*building* .... SD-7
Cedar Township (historical)—*civil* (2) .... SD-7
Cedar Township Memorial Cem—*cemetery* . IA-7
Cedar (Township of)—*fmr MCD* (3) .... AR-4
**Cedar (Township of)**—*pop pl* .... IL-6
**Cedar (Township of)**—*pop pl* .... MI-6
**Cedar (Township of)**—*pop pl* (2) .... MN-6
Cedar Trail—*trail* .... VA-3
*Cedar Tree Arch* .... UT-8
Cedar Tree Bench—*bench* .... AZ-5
Cedar Tree Cem—*cemetery* .... AL-4
Cedar Tree Ch—*church* .... TX-5
*Cedar Tree Church* .... AL-4
Cedar Tree Hills—*summit* .... AZ-5
Cedar Tree (historical)—*locale* .... AL-4
Cedar Tree Hollow—*valley* .... GA-3
Cedar Tree Landing—*locale* .... FL-3
Cedar Tree Neck—*cliff* .... MA-1
Cedar Tree Pit—*cave* .... AL-4
Cedar Tree P.O. (historical)—*locale* .... AL-4
*Cedar Tree Point* .... RI-1
Cedar Tree Point—*cape* (2) .... RI-1
Cedar Tree Spring—*spring* .... ID-8
Cedar Tree Square—*locale* .... MO-7
Cedar Tree Tower—*pillar* .... CO-8
Cedar Tree Trail Lakes—*lake* .... ID-8
Cedar Trough Camp Ground—*locale* .... CA-9
*Cedar United Church of Christ* .... SD-7
*Cedarvale* .... KS-7
Cedarvale—*hist pl* .... MT-8
Cedarvale—*locale* .... TX-5
**Cedar Vale**—*pop pl* .... KS-7
**Cedarvale**—*pop pl* .... NM-5
**Cedarvale**—*pop pl* .... NY-2
Cedarvale Canal—*canal* .... TX-5
Cedarvale Cem—*cemetery* .... IL-6
Cedarvale Cem—*cemetery* .... KS-7
Cedarvale Cem—*cemetery* .... ME-1
Cedarvale Cem—*cemetery* .... NM-5
Cedarvale Cem—*cemetery* .... NY-2
Cedar Vale Elem Sch—*school* .... KS-7
Cedarvale Sch—*school* .... KY-4
*Cedar Valley* .... UT-8
Cedar Valley—*basin* .... CA-9
Cedar Valley—*basin* .... WA-9
Cedar Valley—*locale* .... GA-3
**Cedar Valley**—*pop pl* .... IA-7
**Cedar Valley**—*pop pl* .... MO-7
**Cedar Valley**—*pop pl* .... NC-3
**Cedar Valley**—*pop pl* .... OH-6
**Cedar Valley**—*pop pl* .... OK-5
**Cedar Valley**—*pop pl* .... TX-5
**Cedar Valley**—*pop pl* .... WA-9
Cedar Valley—*valley* .... CA-9
Cedar Valley—*valley* .... NE-7
Cedar Valley—*valley* .... TN-4
Cedar Valley—*valley* (3) .... UT-8
Cedar Valley Airp—*airport* .... UT-8
Cedar Valley Cem—*cemetery* .... MI-6
Cedar Valley Cem—*cemetery* .... MN-6
Cedar Valley Cem—*cemetery* .... MO-7
Cedar Valley Cem—*cemetery* .... ND-7
Cedar Valley Cem—*cemetery* .... OK-5
Cedar Valley Cem—*cemetery* .... TN-4
Cedar Valley Ch—*church* .... GA-3
Cedar Valley Ch—*church* .... IA-7
Cedar Valley Ch—*church* .... KS-7
Cedar Valley Ch—*church* .... MN-6
Cedar Valley Ch—*church* .... MS-4
Cedar Valley Ch—*church* (2) .... MO-7
Cedar Valley Ch—*church* .... NE-7
Cedar Valley Ch—*church* .... ND-7
Cedar Valley Ch—*church* .... OK-5
Cedar Valley Ch—*church* (3) .... TN-4
Cedar Valley Ch—*church* (2) .... TX-5
Cedar Valley Chapel—*church* .... NE-7
Cedar Valley Ch (historical)—*church* .... MO-7
Cedar Valley Country Club—*other* .... GA-3
Cedar Valley (historical P.O.)—*locale* .... IA-7
Cedar Valley Lake—*lake* .... MO-7
Cedar Valley Memorial
Gardens—*cemetery* .... IA-7
Cedar Valley Mine (underground)—*mine* .... AL-4
Cedar Valley Oil Field—*oilfield* .... NE-7
Cedar Valley Park—*park* .... IA-7
Cedar Valley Sch—*school* (2) .... IA-7
Cedar Valley Sch—*school* .... MO-7
Cedar Valley Sch—*school* (3) .... NE-7
Cedar Valley Sch—*school* .... SD-7
Cedar Valley Sch—*school* .... TN-4
Cedar Valley Sch—*school* .... UT-8
Cedar Valley Seminary—*hist pl* .... IA-7
Cedar Valley Shop Ctr—*locale* .... TN-4
**Cedar Valley (subdivision)**—*pop pl* .... AL-4
**Cedar Valley (subdivision)**—*pop pl* .... TN-4
Cedar Valley (Township of)—*civ div* .... MN-6
Cedarview—*locale* .... TX-5
Cedarview—*locale* .... UT-8
Cedar View—*locale* .... VA-3
**Cedar View**—*pop pl* .... IA-7
**Cedarview**—*pop pl* .... MS-4
Cedarview—*uninc pl* .... WA-9
Cedarview Baptist Ch—*church* .... MS-4
Cedarview Canal—*canal* .... UT-8
Cedar View Cem—*cemetery* .... IA-7
Cedarview Cem—*cemetery* .... NE-7
Cedarview Cem—*cemetery* .... UT-8
Cedar View Country Club—*other* .... NE-7
Cedarview Dam—*dam* .... UT-8
Cedar View Estates—*locale* .... PA-2
Cedarview Memorial Park—*cemetery* .... PA-2
Cedar View Park—*park* .... IA-7
Cedarview Post Office
(historical)—*building* .... MS-4
Cedar View Rsvr—*reservoir* .... UT-8
Cedarview Sch—*school* .... KS-7
Cedar View School—*locale* .... CO-8
**Cedar View (subdivision)**—*pop pl* .... MS-4
Cedar View Wharf—*other* .... VA-3
**Cedar Village**—*pop pl* .... OK-5
Cedar Village Lake—*reservoir* .... NC-3
Cedar Village Lake Dam—*dam* .... NC-3
Cedar Village Shop Ctr—*locale* .... KS-7
*Cedarville* .... NJ-2
*Cedarville* .... PA-2
Cedarville—*locale* .... AL-4
Cedarville—*locale* .... MI-6
Cedarville—*locale* .... NM-5
Cedarville—*locale* .... PA-2
Cedarville—*locale* (2) .... WA-9
**Cedarville**—*pop pl* .... AR-4
**Cedarville**—*pop pl* .... CA-9
**Cedarville**—*pop pl* .... IL-6
**Cedarville**—*pop pl* .... IN-6
**Cedarville**—*pop pl* .... KY-4
**Cedarville**—*pop pl* .... MD-2
**Cedarville**—*pop pl* .... MA-1
**Cedarville**—*pop pl* .... MO-7
**Cedarville**—*pop pl* (2) .... NJ-2
**Cedarville**—*pop pl* .... NY-2
**Cedarville**—*pop pl* .... OH-6
**Cedarville**—*pop pl* .... PA-2
**Cedarville**—*pop pl* (2) .... VA-3
**Cedarville**—*pop pl* .... WV-2
**Cedarville**—*pop pl* .... WI-6
Cedarville Bay—*bay* .... MI-6
Cedarville Canyon—*valley* .... ID-8
Cedarville Cem—*cemetery* .... CA-9
Cedarville Cem—*cemetery* .... IL-6
Cedarville Cem—*cemetery* .... MA-1
Cedarville Ch—*church* .... OK-5
Cedarville Coll—*school* .... OH-6
Cedarville Community Hall—*locale* .... AL-4
Cedarville Creek—*stream* .... WI-6
**Cedarville Estates
(subdivision)**—*pop pl* .... NC-3
**Cedarville Landing**—*pop pl* .... MA-1
Cedarville Lookout Tower—*locale* .... WI-6
Cedarville Opera House—*hist pl* .... OH-6
**Cedarville Rancheria (Indian
Reservation)**—*pop pl* .... CA-9
Cedarville Rsvr—*reservoir* .... IN-6
Cedarville Sch—*school* .... MD-2
Cedarville Sch—*school* .... NE-7
Cedarville (Site)—*locale* .... CA-9
Cedarville State For—*forest* .... MD-2
**Cedarville Station**—*pop pl* .... NY-2
Cedarville (Township of)—*fmr MCD* .... AR-4
**Cedarville (Township of)**—*pop pl* .... MI-6
**Cedarville (Township of)**—*pop pl* .... OH-6
**Cedarville (trailer park)**—*pop pl* .... DE-2
**Cedar Vista**—*pop pl* .... MO-7
*Cedar Wash* .... AZ-5
*Cedar Wash* .... UT-8
Cedar Wash—*stream* (2) .... AZ-5
Cedar Wash—*stream* .... CA-9
Cedar Wash—*stream* (2) .... NV-8
Cedar Wash—*stream* .... NM-5
Cedar Wash—*valley* .... AZ-5
Cedar Wash—*valley* (2) .... UT-8
Cedar Wash Arch—*arch* .... UT-8
*Cedar Wash Reservoir* .... UT-8
Cedar Waterhole—*spring* .... TX-5
Cedar Waters—*lake* .... NH-1
Cedar Way Draw—*valley* .... TX-5
Cedar Way Sch—*school* .... WA-9
Cedar Well—*reservoir* .... ID-8
Cedar Well—*well* (2) .... AZ-5
Cedar Well—*well* .... CA-9
Cedar Well—*well* (4) .... NM-5
Cedar Well—*well* (2) .... TX-5
Cedar Wells—*well* .... NV-8
Cedar Windmill—*locale* (2) .... NM-5
Cedar Windmill—*locale* (5) .... TX-5
Cedar Windmill—*well* .... AZ-5
Cedarwood—*locale* .... CO-8
Cedarwood Canyon—*valley* .... CO-8
Cedarwood Cem—*cemetery* .... AL-4
Cedarwood Cem—*cemetery* .... NJ-2
Cedarwood Cem—*cemetery* (3) .... NC-3
Cedarwood Cem—*cemetery* .... VA-3
Cedarwood Dam—*dam* .... NC-3
Cedarwood Golf Club—*locale* .... NC-3
Cedarwood Lake—*reservoir* .... NC-3
**Cedarwood Park**—*pop pl* .... NJ-2
**Cedarwood (subdivision)**—*pop pl* .... MA-1
Cedarwood Well—*well* .... CO-8
Cedar Yard Cem—*cemetery* .... TX-5
Cedder Mtn—*summit* .... NC-3
*Cede Boy Creek* .... SD-7
Cede Lake—*lake* .... MN-6
Ceder Brook Trail—*trail* .... NH-1
*Ceder Crest* .... MA-1
Ceder Hill Camp—*locale* .... MA-1
Ceder Hollow—*valley* .... TX-5
Cederlawn Baptist Ch—*church* .... FL-3
Cederloff Hollow—*valley* .... UT-8
*Ceder Point* .... MS-4
Cederquist Park—*park* .... OH-6
*Ceder River* .... DE-2
*Ceder School* .... MS-4
Ceder Township—*civil* .... SD-7
*Cederville* .... AL-4
*Cederville* .... KS-7
*Cederville* .... NJ-2
Cedine Bible Camp—*locale* .... TN-4
CED Mental Health Center—*hospital* .... AL-4
Cedon—*locale* .... VA-3
Cedonia—*locale* .... WA-9
Cedonia Sch—*school* .... WA-9
**Cedre Pond**—*pop pl* .... NH-1
Cedric—*locale* .... MT-8
Cedrick (historical)—*locale* .... AL-4
Cedric Tank—*reservoir* .... AZ-5
Cedric Well—*well* .... AZ-5
Cedric Wright, Mount—*summit* .... CA-9
Cedrito (Barrio)—*fmr MCD* .... PR-3
**Cedro**—*pop pl* .... NM-5
Cedro Abajo (Barrio)—*fmr MCD* .... PR-3
Cedro Arriba (Barrio)—*fmr MCD* .... PR-3
Cedro (Barrio)—*fmr MCD* (3) .... PR-3
Cedro Canyon—*valley* (4) .... NM-5
Cedro Hill—*summit* .... TX-5
Cedro Hill Oil Field—*oilfield* .... TX-5
*Cedrom* .... AL-4
Cedrom Mine (underground)—*mine* .... AL-4
Cedrom Post Office (historical)—*building* .... AL-4
Cedron—*locale* (2) .... ID-8
Cedron—*locale* .... OH-6
**Cedron**—*pop pl* .... AL-4
Cedron Cem—*cemetery* .... ID-8
Cedron Cem—*cemetery* (2) .... TX-5
*Cedron Church* .... AL-4
Cedron Creek—*stream* .... TX-5
Cedron Creek Park—*locale* .... TX-5
Cedron (historical)—*locale* .... KS-7
Cedron School (Abandoned)—*locale* .... MO-7
**Cedron Township**—*pop pl* .... KS-7
Cedro Peak—*summit* .... NM-5
Cedros Windmills—*locale* .... NM-5
**Cedro Village**—*pop pl* .... NM-5
**Cedrum**—*pop pl* .... AL-4
Cedrum Ch—*church* .... AL-4
Cedrum Grove Ch—*church* .... AL-4
Cedrum Mine (surface)—*mine* .... AL-4
Cedrum Mine (underground)—*mine* .... AL-4
Cedrum Mtn—*summit* .... AL-4
Cedrum Number 1 Mine (surface)—*mine* ... AL-4
Cee Cee Ah Creek—*stream* .... WA-9
Cee Cee Ah Peak—*summit* .... WA-9
Ceejay Airp—*airport* .... PA-2
Cee Jefferson—*locale* .... MN-6
Cee Vee—*locale* .... TX-5
C E F Airp—*airport* .... MO-7
**Ceffco**—*pop pl* .... IL-6
**Ceffo**—*pop pl* .... NC-3
**Cego**—*pop pl* .... TX-5
C E Harry Dam—*dam* .... NC-3
C E Harry Lake—*reservoir* .... NC-3
**Ceiba**—*pop pl* (2) .... PR-3
Ceiba Alta (Barrio)—*fmr MCD* .... PR-3
Ceiba Baja (Barrio)—*fmr MCD* .... PR-3
Ceiba (Barrio)—*fmr MCD* (3) .... PR-3
Ceiba (Municipio)—*civil* .... PR-3
Ceiba Norte (Barrio)—*fmr MCD* .... PR-3
Ceiba (Pueblo)—*fmr MCD* .... PR-3
Ceiba Sur (Barrio)—*fmr MCD* .... PR-3
**Ceico**—*pop pl* .... OH-6
Ceja Del Raton—*valley* .... NM-5
Ceja Pelon Mesa—*summit* .... NM-5
Cejas (Barrio)—*fmr MCD* .... PR-3
Cejita—*ridge* .... NM-5
Cejita Blanca Ridge—*ridge* .... NM-5
Cejita Cem—*cemetery* .... CO-8
Cejita Cem—*cemetery* .... NM-5
Cejita De Los Comancheros—*area* .... NM-5
Cejita Windmill—*locale* .... NM-5
C E King Lake Dam—*dam* .... MS-4
**Celada**—*pop pl* .... PR-3
Celada (Barrio)—*fmr MCD* .... PR-3
Celanese Village—*other* .... GA-3
C E Lateral—*canal* .... TX-5
Celaya, Augustine, House—*hist pl* .... TX-5
Celaya-Creager House—*hist pl* .... TX-5
*Celchester Brook* .... MA-1
**Celco**—*pop pl* .... VA-3
Celco (historical)—*locale* .... MS-4
*Celco Mill* .... MS-4
Cele—*locale* .... TX-5
Celebration Baptist Ch—*church* .... FL-3
Celebration Mine—*mine* .... OR-9
Celebration Wash—*valley* .... AZ-5
Celedonio Tank—*reservoir* .... AZ-5
C E Lee Dam—*dam* .... AL-4
*Celenie Lake* .... AK-9
*Celeoth Creek* .... GA-3
Celeron Island—*island* .... MI-6
Celery Center Sch—*school* .... MI-6
Celery Creek—*stream* .... TX-5
Celery Lake—*lake* .... CA-9
Celery Lake—*lake* .... MN-6
Celery Meadow—*flat* .... WA-9
**Celeryville**—*pop pl* .... OH-6
**Celesta Vu Condominium**—*pop pl* .... UT-8
Celeste—*locale* .... GA-3
**Celeste**—*pop pl* .... AL-4
**Celeste**—*pop pl* .... TX-5
Celeste, Lake—*lake* .... NY-2
Celeste (CCD)—*cens area* .... TX-5
Celeste Cem—*cemetery* .... TX-5
**Celeste Hinkel**—*pop pl* .... NC-3
Celeste Hinkel Sch—*school* .... NC-3
**Celeste Hinkle**—*pop pl* .... NC-3
**Celeste Place Townhouses**—*pop pl* .... UT-8
Celeste Road Ch—*church* .... AL-4
Celeste Road Ch of God—*church* .... AL-4
**Celeste Subdivision**—*pop pl* .... UT-8
Celestial Lake—*lake* .... PA-2
Celestial Memorial Gardens—*cemetery* .... NC-3
Celestial Memorial Gardens—*cemetery* .... SC-3
Celestial Valley—*valley* .... CA-9
Celestin Cem—*cemetery* (2) .... LA-4
**Celestine**—*pop pl* .... IN-6
Celestine, Bayou—*stream* .... LA-4
Celestine Community Club
Lake—*reservoir* .... IN-6
Celestine Community Club Lake
Dam—*dam* .... IN-6
Celestine Elem Sch—*school* .... IN-6
Celestine HS—*school* .... LA-4
Celestine Locality—*locale* .... PA-2
Celestino Gonzalez Grant—*civil* .... FL-3
Celetom Mine—*mine* .... NV-8
*Celia* .... KS-7
**Celia**—*pop pl* .... PA-2
Celia Cem—*cemetery* .... NE-7
Celia Creek—*stream* .... NC-3
Celia Gap—*gap* .... NC-3
Celia (historical)—*locale* .... KS-7
Celia Lake—*lake* .... MN-6
Celia Pond—*lake* .... ME-1
Celia Sch—*school* .... NE-7
Celia Spring—*spring* .... OR-9
*Celia Township* .... KS-7
*Celilo* .... OR-9
**Celilo**—*pop pl* .... OR-9
Celilo, Lake—*reservoir* .... OR-9
Celilo, Lake—*reservoir* .... WA-9
Celilo Converter Station—*other* .... OR-9
*Celilo County Park* .... OR-9
Celilo Falls—*falls* (2) .... OR-9
Celilo Falls Site (historical)—*falls* .... OR-9
Celilo Indian Cem—*cemetery* .... OR-9
Celilo Light—*locale* .... OR-9
Celilo Park—*park* .... OR-9
Celilo Village—*locale* .... OR-9
Celina—*locale* .... MN-6
**Celina**—*pop pl* .... IN-6
**Celina**—*pop pl* .... OH-6
**Celina**—*pop pl* .... TN-4
**Celina**—*pop pl* .... TX-5
Celina, Lake—*reservoir* .... IN-6
Celina Bar—*bar* .... TN-4
Celina (CCD)—*cens area* .... TN-4
Celina (CCD)—*cens area* .... TX-5
Celina Division—*civil* .... TN-4
Celina Flat Mine—*mine* .... CA-9
*Celina Grand Reservoir* .... OH-6
Celina HS—*school* .... TN-4
Celina Main Street Commercial Hist
Dist—*hist pl* .... OH-6
Celina Post Office—*building* .... TN-4
Celina Ridge—*ridge* .... CA-9
Celina Sch—*school* .... OH-6
Celina Sch—*school* .... TN-4
Celina Temple—*church* .... OH-6
Celio Ranch—*locale* .... CA-9
**Cella**—*pop pl* .... CA-9
Cellar, The—*hist pl* .... NC-3
Cellar Basin—*basin* .... AZ-5
*Cellar Basin Trail* .... AZ-5
Cellar Brook—*stream* (2) .... NY-2
Cellar Canyon—*valley* .... UT-8
*Cellar Creek* .... AZ-5
Cellar Creek—*locale* .... VA-3
Cellar Creek—*stream* .... AZ-5
Cellar Creek—*stream* .... VA-3
Cellar Creek—*stream* .... WY-8
Cellar Gulch—*valley* .... MT-8
Cellar Hollow—*valley* .... VA-3
Cellar Mtn—*summit* (2) .... NY-2
Cellar Mtn—*summit* .... VA-3
Cellar Point—*cape* .... ID-8
Cellar Pond—*lake* .... NY-2
Cellar Rsvr—*reservoir* .... OR-9
Cellars Canyon—*valley* .... NM-5
*Cellars Creek* .... ID-8
*Cellar Spring* .... AZ-5
Cellar Spring—*spring* .... UT-8
*Cellar Spring Creek* .... AZ-5
Cellar Springs—*spring* .... AZ-5
*Cellar Springs Creek* .... AZ-5
Cellar Springs Creek—*stream* .... AZ-5
*Cellen Point* .... ME-1
Cellers Ranch—*locale* .... WY-8
Cellers Ranch Oil Field—*oilfield* .... WY-8
Cellesee Cove—*valley* .... NC-3
**Celo**—*pop pl* .... NC-3
Celo Knob—*summit* .... NC-3
Celora Stoddard/Lon Harmon
House—*hist pl* .... AZ-5
Celo Ridge—*ridge* .... NC-3
**Celoron**—*pop pl* .... NY-2
Celotex—*locale* .... TX-5
Celotex Corporation—*facility* .... KY-4
**Celriver**—*pop pl* .... SC-3
Celt—*locale* .... MO-7
Celt—*locale* .... VA-3
Celton (historical)—*locale* .... SD-7
Cely Ann Mine Number 2
(surface)—*mine* .... AL-4
Cely Ann Mtn—*summit* .... AL-4
**Cemar Estates**—*pop pl* .... IN-6
C E Mason Sch—*school* .... OR-9
C E McHardy Grant—*civil* .... FL-3
Cement—*locale* .... GA-3
**Cement**—*pop pl* .... OK-5
Cementario de San German—*cemetery* .... PR-3
Cementario Municipal Numero
1—*cemetery* .... PR-3
Cementario Municipal Numero
2—*cemetery* .... PR-3
Cement Banks—*levee* .... CA-9
Cement Basin—*basin* .... WA-9
Cement Bluff—*cliff* .... CA-9
Cement Cabin—*locale* .... AZ-5
Cement Canyon—*valley* .... AZ-5
Cement Canyon—*valley* (2) .... NM-5
Cement City—*locale* .... MO-7
**Cement City**—*pop pl* .... MI-6
Cement City Cem—*cemetery* .... MI-6
Cement Creek—*stream* .... AK-9
Cement Creek—*stream* (4) .... CA-9
Cement Creek—*stream* (2) .... CO-8
Cement Creek—*stream* .... MT-8
Cement Creek—*stream* .... TX-5
Cement Creek—*stream* (2) .... WA-9
Cement Dam Canyon—*valley* .... AZ-5
Cement Dam Rsvr—*reservoir* .... AZ-5
Cement Dam Tank—*reservoir* (8) .... AZ-5
Cement Dam Tank—*reservoir* .... NM-5
Cement Ditch—*canal* .... UT-8
Cementerio, Canada Del —*valley* (2) .... CA-9
Cementerio Anahuac—*cemetery* .... TX-5
Cementerio Antiguo de Ponce—*hist pl* .... PR-3
Cementerio Bautista—*cemetery* .... TX-5
Cementerio Buxeda—*cemetery* .... PR-3
Cementerio Catolico San Vicente de
Paul—*hist pl* .... PR-3
Cementerio Civi—*cemetery* .... PR-3
Cementerio de Caguas—*cemetery* .... PR-3
Cementerio de Guaynabo—*cemetery* .... PR-3
Cementerio de Isabela—*cemetery* .... PR-3
Cementerio de la Capital—*cemetery* .... PR-3
Cementerio de las Tres Marias—*cemetery* .. TX-5
Cementerio Delicias—*cemetery* .... PR-3
Cementerio del Pueblo—*cemetery* .... TX-5
Cementerio de Villa Palmeras—*cemetery* ... PR-3
Cementerio Evangelico—*cemetery* .... TX-5
Cementerio La Piedad—*cemetery* .... PR-3
Cementerio Maria Magdalena—*cemetery* ... PR-3
Cementerio Municipal de
Mayaguez—*hist pl* .... PR-3
Cementerio Porta Coeli—*cemetery* .... PR-3
Cementerio Puente Blanco—*cemetery* .... PR-3
Cementerio Puerto Rico
Memorial—*cemetery* .... PR-3
Cementerio Rural de Gurabo—*cemetery* .... PR-3
Cementerio San Antonio de
Escobares—*cemetery* .... TX-5
Cementerio San Isidro—*cemetery* .... TX-5
Cementerio San Vicente de
Paul—*cemetery* .... PR-3
Cementerio Viejo—*cemetery* .... PR-3
Cement Gap—*gap* .... OK-5
Cement Gulch—*valley* .... ID-8
Cement Gulch—*valley* .... MT-8
Cement Hill—*ridge* .... CA-9
Cement Hill—*summit* .... AK-9
Cement Hill—*summit* (3) .... CA-9
Cement Hill—*summit* .... MT-8
Cement Hills—*ridge* .... WY-8
Cement Hollow—*valley* (2) .... IL-6
Cement Junction—*locale* .... PA-2
Cement Lake—*lake* .... WA-9
Cement Lake—*reservoir* .... NM-5
Cement Mill Creek—*stream* .... TN-4

Cement Mtn—*summit* CO-8
Cement Mtn—*summit* NY-2
Cement Mtn—*summit* (2) TX-5
Cement Mtn—*summit* WA-9
Cement Mtn—*summit* WY-8
*Cementon* NJ-2
**Cementon**—*pop pl* NY-2
**Cementon**—*pop pl* PA-2
**Cementon**—*pop pl* SC-3
Cementon Rsvr—*reservoir* PA-2
Cementosa Tanks—*reservoir* AZ-5
Cementosa Wash—*stream* AZ-5
Cement Plant Pond—*lake* NY-2
Cement Pocket Well—*well* TX-5
Cement Pond—*lake* NY-2
Cement Ponds—*reservoir* UT-8
Cement Ravine—*valley* CA-9
Cement Ridge—*ridge* WY-8
Cement Rsvr—*reservoir* UT-8
Cements, The—*summit* AZ-5
Cement Sch—*school* MI-6
Cement Sch—*school* NE-7
Cement Sch—*school* WI-6
Cement Shoals—*bar* TN-4
Cement Spring—*spring* (3) AZ-5
Cement Spring—*spring* CA-9
Cement Spring—*spring* NV-8
Cement Spring—*spring* (2) OR-9
Cement Spring—*spring* UT-8
Cement Summer Home Group—*locale* CO-8
Cement Table Meadows—*flat* CA-9
Cement Tank—*reservoir* (13) AZ-5
Cement Tank—*reservoir* (3) NM-5
Cement Tank—*reservoir* (3) TX-5
Cement Tank—*spring* AZ-5
Cement Tank Spring—*spring* (2) AZ-5
Cement Tank Well—*well* NM-5
Cement Trough Canyon—*valley* AZ-5
Cement Trough Canyon Tank—*reservoir* AZ-5
Cement Trough Spring—*spring* (2) AZ-5
Cement Trough Spring—*spring* CA-9
Cement Trough Spring—*spring* NM-5
**Cementville**—*pop pl* IN-6
Cementville—*uninc pl* TX-5
Cement Well—*locale* NM-5
Cement Well—*well* NM-5
Cement Windmill—*locale* TX-5
Cemerterio de las Burras—*cemetery* TX-5
Cemetery Bayou—*stream* MS-4
Cemetery Beautiful—*cemetery* TX-5
Cemetery Bluff District—*hist pl* MS-4
Cemetery Branch—*stream* NC-3
Cemetery Branch—*stream* (3) TX-5
*Cemetery Brook* CT-1
Cemetery Brook—*stream* (4) CT-1
Cemetery Brook—*stream* (2) NH-1
Cemetery Brook—*stream* VT-1
Cemetery Butte—*summit* OR-9
Cemetery Canyon—*valley* AZ-5
Cemetery Canyon—*valley* CO-8
Cemetery Canyon—*valley* NM-5
Cemetery Cave—*cave* (2) AL-4
Cemetery Chapel—*church* KY-4
Cemetery Chapel, San Marcos
Cemetery—*hist pl* TX-5
**Cemetery Corners**—*pop pl* NH-1
Cemetery Cove—*bay* AK-9
*Cemetery Creek* VA-3
Cemetery Creek—*gut* FL-3
Cemetery Creek—*stream* IN-6
Cemetery Creek—*stream* MI-6
Cemetery Creek—*stream* OR-9
Cemetery Creek—*stream* (2) TX-5
Cemetery Creek—*stream* VA-3
Cemetery Creek—*stream* WY-8
Cemetery Ditch—*canal* WY-8
Cemetery Draw—*valley* TX-5
Cemetery Draw—*valley* WY-8
Cemetery Flats—*flat* CO-8
Cemetery Gulch—*valley* (2) CO-8
Cemetery Gulch—*valley* ID-8
Cemetery Gulch—*valley* WY-8
*Cemetery Hill* AL-4
Cemetery Hill—*cemetery* AR-4
Cemetery Hill—*cemetery* SC-3
Cemetery Hill—*cemetery* TX-5
Cemetery Hill—*summit* AL-4
Cemetery Hill—*summit* CA-9
Cemetery Hill—*summit* KY-4
Cemetery Hill—*summit* ME-1
Cemetery Hill—*summit* MT-8
Cemetery Hill—*summit* NV-8
Cemetery Hill—*summit* NH-1
Cemetery Hill—*summit* (2) OR-9
Cemetery Hill—*summit* (2) PA-2
Cemetery Hill—*summit* WI-6
Cemetery Hill Cem—*cemetery* OR-9
Cemetery Hill Ch—*church* KY-4
Cemetery Hill Ch—*church* WV-2
*Cemetery Hills* AZ-5
Cemetery Hollow—*valley* KY-4
Cemetery Hollow—*valley* PA-2
Cemetery Island—*island* IN-6
Cemetery Island—*island* MA-1
Cemetery Island—*island* MI-6
Cemetery Island—*island* (2) MN-6
Cemetery Island—*island* TN-4
*Cemetery Lake* MI-6
Cemetery Lake—*cemetery* IN-6
Cemetery Lake—*lake* AK-9
Cemetery Lake—*lake* CO-8
Cemetery Lake—*lake* (2) FL-3
Cemetery Lake—*lake* (2) MI-6
Cemetery Lake—*lake* (2) MN-6
Cemetery Lake—*lake* OR-9
Cemetery Lake—*reservoir* TX-5
Cemetery Mtn—*summit* AL-4
Cemetery Newport Elem Sch—*school* NC-3
Cemetery No 2—*cemetery* NM-5
Cemetery No 5—*cemetery* MO-7
Cemetery No 5—*cemetery* NM-5
Cemetery Number 1—*cemetery* LA-4
Cemetery Number 6—*cemetery* LA-4
Cemetery Number 7—*cemetery* LA-4
Cemetery Of The Evergreens—*cemetery* NY-2
Cemetery of the Evergreens—*cemetery* NY-2
Cemetery of the Highlands—*cemetery* NY-2
Cemetery of The Holy Cross—*cemetery* NY-2
Cemetery of the Holy
Sepulchre—*cemetery* CA-9
Cemetery of the Madonna—*cemetery* NJ-2
Cemetery of the Resurrection—*cemetery* NY-2
Cemetery of Visitation—*cemetery* NY-2
Cemetery On the Hill—*cemetery* NH-1
Cemetery On the Plains—*cemetery* NH-1
Cemetery Point—*cape* (3) AK-9
Cemetery Point—*cape* CT-1
Cemetery Point—*cape* MA-1
Cemetery Point—*cape* MI-6
Cemetery Point—*cape* TX-5
Cemetery Pond—*lake* FL-3
Cemetery Pond—*swamp* FL-3
Cemetery Pond Brook—*stream* CT-1
Cemetery Ridge—*ridge* AZ-5
Cemetery Ridge—*ridge* CA-9
Cemetery Ridge—*ridge* ID-8
Cemetery Ridge—*ridge* MS-4
Cemetery Ridge—*ridge* OR-9
Cemetery Rsvr—*reservoir* OR-9
Cemetery Run—*stream* IN-6
Cemetery Run—*stream* PA-2
Cemetery Slough—*stream* WI-6
Cemetery Spring—*spring* OR-9
Cemetery Tank—*reservoir* (5) AZ-5
Cemetery Union Ch—*church* TN-4
Cemetery Wash—*stream* AZ-5
Cemetery Wildlife Mngmt Area—*park* UT-8
*Cemitosa Tank* AZ-5
*Cemitosa Tanks* AZ-5
*Cemitosa Wash* AZ-5
Cemmons Donick—*dam* AR-4
Cemochechobee Creek—*stream* GA-3
*Cemocheechobee Creek* GA-3
*Cemocheehobbee Creek* GA-3
Cenacle, The—*church* MA-1
Cenacle, The—*church* NY-2
Cenacle Convent—*church* NJ-2
Cenacle Convent—*church* NY-2
Cenacle Retreat—*locale* TX-5
Cenacle Retreat, The—*church* MO-7
Cenacle Retreat House—*building* LA-4
*Cenaridge Creek* AL-4
*Cenchant* GA-3
Cenchat—*locale* GA-3
C E Neal Dam—*dam* AL-4
Ceneca Tank—*reservoir* AZ-5
Ceneda—*locale* CA-9
Cenetenary Ch—*church* IN-6
Cenicero Ditch—*canal* CO-8
*Cenipede Bay* FL-3
Cenizal, Loma del—*summit* TX-5
Cenizo Park Sch—*school* TX-5
Cenntial Ch—*church* AL-4
Cenotaph Island—*island* AK-9
Cenotaph Point—*cape* AK-9
Censolidated County Park—*park* WI-6
*Centa Lake* MN-6
*Centar Star* TN-4
**Centaur**—*pop pl* GA-3
**Centaur**—*pop pl* MO-7
Centaur Chute—*gut* MO-7
Centauri HS—*school* CO-8
*Cente Bonek Creek* AL-4
Centel Lake—*lake* TX-5
Centella Point—*cliff* AZ-5
**Centenary**—*pop pl* AL-4
**Centenary**—*pop pl* IN-6
**Centenary**—*pop pl* NY-2
**Centenary**—*pop pl* OH-6
**Centenary**—*pop pl* SC-3
**Centenary**—*pop pl* VA-3
Centenary—*uninc pl* LA-4
Centenary (CCD)—*cens area* SC-3
Centenary Cem—*cemetery* GA-3
Centenary Cem—*cemetery* IL-6
Centenary Cem—*cemetery* MO-7
Centenary Cem—*cemetery* NY-2
Centenary Cem—*cemetery* (4) OH-6
Centenary Cem—*cemetery* PA-2
Centenary Cem—*cemetery* (2) TN-4
Centenary Cem—*cemetery* VA-3
Centenary Ch—*church* AL-4
Centenary Ch—*church* FL-3
Centenary Ch—*church* GA-3
Centenary Ch—*church* (2) IL-6
Centenary Ch—*church* (2) IN-6
Centenary Ch—*church* MD-2
Centenary Ch—*church* (2) MO-7
Centenary Ch—*church* NY-2
Centenary Ch—*church* (4) NC-3
Centenary Ch—*church* (4) OH-6
Centenary Ch—*church* (3) SC-3
Centenary Ch—*church* (4) TN-4
Centenary Ch—*church* (8) VA-3
Centenary Ch—*church* (2) WV-2
Centenary Chapel—*church* OH-6
Centenary Ch (historical)—*church* MO-7
Centenary Church—*hist pl* VA-3
Centenary Church Camp Grounds—*locale* FL-3
Centenary Church (historical)—*locale* MO-7
Centenary Coll—*school* LA-4
Centenary Coll—*school* NJ-2
Centenary College—*hist pl* LA-4
Centenary Creek—*stream* TN-4
Centenary Female Coll
(historical)—*school* TN-4
*Centenary Holiness Ch* AL-4
Centenary Methodist Ch—*church* NC-3
Centenary Methodist Ch
(historical)—*church* TN-4
Centenary Methodist Church—*hist pl* NC-3
Centenary Ridge—*ridge* TN-4
Centenary Sch—*school* IL-6
Centenary United Methodist Ch—*church* DE-2
Centenary United Methodist Ch—*church* MS-4
Centenary United Methodist Ch—*church* TN-4
Centenary United Methodist Ch—*church* UT-8
Centennia Bridge—*bridge* IA-7
*Centennial* AZ-5
Centennial—*CDP* OR-9
Centennial—*locale* GA-3
Centennial—*locale* WV-2
**Centennial**—*pop pl* AZ-5
**Centennial**—*pop pl* IN-6
**Centennial**—*pop pl* MD-2
**Centennial**—*pop pl* MI-6
**Centennial**—*pop pl* OH-6
**Centennial**—*pop pl* (2) PA-2
**Centennial**—*pop pl* WY-8
**Centennial Acres**
**(subdivision)**—*pop pl* PA-2
**Centennial Arms**
**(subdivision)**—*pop pl* NC-3
Centennial Ave Sch—*school* NY-2
Centennial Baptist Ch—*church* MS-4
Centennial Baptist Church—*hist pl* AR-4
Centennial Bend—*bend* AR-4
Centennial Bend—*bend* TN-4
Centennial Bluff—*cliff* CA-9
Centennial Boat Yard Park—*park* TN-4
Centennial Bridge—*bridge* KS-7
Centennial Bridge—*hist pl* PA-2
Centennial Bridge (Toll)—*other* MO-7
Centennial Butte—*summit* OR-9
Centennial Canyon—*valley* CA-9
Centennial Cem—*cemetery* GA-3
Centennial Cem—*cemetery* IN-6
Centennial Cem—*cemetery* (2) IA-7
Centennial Cem—*cemetery* KS-7
Centennial Cem—*cemetery* TN-4
Centennial Cem—*cemetery* TX-5
Centennial Center—*building* AZ-5
Centennial Ch—*church* AL-4
Centennial Ch—*church* (3) GA-3
Centennial Ch—*church* IL-6
Centennial Ch—*church* IN-6
Centennial Ch—*church* KY-4
Centennial Ch—*church* (2) NC-3
Centennial Ch—*church* OH-6
Centennial Ch—*church* (3) PA-2
Centennial Ch—*church* TN-4
Centennial Ch—*church* VA-3
Centennial Ch—*church* WV-2
Centennial Chapel Cem—*cemetery* IL-6
Centennial Ch (historical)—*church* PA-2
**Centennial City (historical)**—*pop pl* SD-7
**Centennial Condominium**—*pop pl* UT-8
Centennial Cone—*summit* CO-8
Centennial Creek—*stream* CA-9
Centennial Creek—*stream* WY-8
Centennial Creek—*valley* OR-9
Centennial Cumberland Presbyterian Ch
(historical)—*church* TN-4
Centennial Cutoff—*bend* LA-4
Centennial Cutoff—*channel* MS-4
Centennial Cutoff—*gut* TN-4
Centennial Depot—*hist pl* WY-8
Centennial Ditch—*canal* CO-8
Centennial Ditch—*canal* WY-8
Centennial Divide—*ridge* MT-8
**Centennial Estates**—*pop pl* MD-2
**Centennial Estates**
**Subdivision**—*pop pl* UT-8
Centennial Eureka—*mine* UT-8
Centennial-Eureka Mine—*hist pl* UT-8
Centennial Farms—*locale* AZ-5
Centennial Field—*park* FL-3
Centennial Flat—*flat* ID-8
Centennial Flour Mill—*hist pl* WA-9
Centennial Friendship Park—*park* AZ-5
Centennial Gulch—*valley* CA-9
Centennial Gulch—*valley* (2) MT-8
Centennial Gulch—*valley* SD-7
Centennial Hall-Edward Waters
College—*hist pl* FL-3
Centennial Hall Sch (abandoned)—*school* PA-2
**Centennial Heights**—*pop pl* MI-6
**Centennial Hills**—*pop pl* PA-2
Centennial HS—*school* CA-9
Centennial HS—*school* IL-6
Centennial HS—*school* OR-9
Centennial HS—*school* TX-5
Centennial Island—*flat* TN-4
Centennial Island—*island* OR-9
Centennial JHS—*school* CO-8
Centennial JHS—*school* FL-3
Centennial JHS—*school* IL-6
Centennial JHS—*school* PA-2
Centennial Lake—*lake* LA-4
Centennial Lake—*lake* MS-4
Centennial Lake—*lake* PA-2
**Centennial Lake**—*pop pl* NJ-2
Centennial Lake—*reservoir* NJ-2
Centennial Lake Dam—*dam* NJ-2
*Centennial Mills* TN-4
Centennial Mine (Inactive)—*mine* CA-9
*Centennial Mountain* WY-8
Centennial Mtn—*summit* CA-9
Centennial Mtn—*summit* MT-8
Centennial Mtns—*range* ID-8
Centennial Mtns—*range* MT-8
Centennial Narrows Dam—*dam* AZ-5
Centennial Natl Bank—*hist pl* PA-2
Centennial Neighborhood District—*hist pl* IN-6
*Centennial Park* NY-2
Centennial Park—*park* AL-4
Centennial Park—*park* AZ-5
Centennial Park—*park* (4) IL-6
Centennial Park—*park* IN-6
Centennial Park—*park* KS-7
Centennial Park—*park* (2) MN-6
Centennial Park—*park* MO-7
Centennial Park—*park* NE-7
Centennial Park—*park* NY-2
Centennial Park—*park* OH-6
Centennial Park—*park* TN-4
Centennial Park—*summit* CO-8
*Centennial Peak* WY-8
Centennial Peak—*summit* CA-9
Centennial Post Office
(historical)—*building* TN-4
Centennial Prairie—*flat* SD-7
Centennial Racetrack—*other* CO-8
Centennial Ranch—*locale* CO-8
*Centennial Range* NV-8
Centennial Range—*range* AK-9
Centennial Ranger Station—*locale* WY-8
Centennial Ravine—*valley* CA-9
Centennial Ridge—*locale* PA-2
Centennial Ridge—*ridge* CA-9
Centennial Ridge—*ridge* WY-8
Centennial Sch—*school* AR-4
Centennial Sch—*school* (2) CA-9
Centennial Sch—*school* CO-8
Centennial Sch—*school* (7) IL-6
Centennial Sch—*school* IN-6
Centennial Sch—*school* IA-7
Centennial Sch—*school* (7) KS-7
Centennial Sch—*school* KY-4
Centennial Sch—*school* (2) MI-6
Centennial Sch—*school* (2) MN-6
Centennial Sch—*school* MO-7
Centennial Sch—*school* NE-7
Centennial Sch—*school* OH-6
Centennial Sch—*school* (2) OR-9
Centennial Sch—*school* (2) PA-2
Centennial Sch—*school* TX-5
Centennial Sch—*school* WI-6
Centennial Sch (abandoned)—*school* MO-7
Centennial Sch (abandoned)—*school* PA-2
Centennial Sch (historical)—*school* MO-7
Centennial Sch (historical)—*school* (2) PA-2
Centennial Sch (historical)—*school* TN-4
Centennial Shaft—*mine* NV-8
Centennial Shop Ctr—*locale* KS-7
Centennial Spring—*spring* SD-7
Centennial Stadium—*other* CO-8
Centennial Township—*fmr MCD* IA-7
Centennial Tunnel—*tunnel* UT-8
Centennial United Methodist Ch—*church* DE-2
*Centennial Valley* AZ-5
Centennial Valley—*valley* MT-8
Centennial Valley—*valley* WY-8
**Centennial Village**—*pop pl* DE-2
**Centennial Village**
**Subdivision**—*pop pl* UT-8
**Centennial Village Subdivision 1,**
**Two**—*pop pl* UT-8
Centennial Wash—*stream* (2) AZ-5
Centenniel Industrial Park
(subdivision)—*locale* UT-8
Centeno Park—*park* TX-5
Centeotl, Point—*cliff* AZ-5
Centeotl Point—*cliff* AZ-5
*Center* AL-4
*Center* KS-7
*Center* ME-1
*Center* MI-6
*Center* MS-4
*Center* OH-6
*Center* PA-2
Center—*fmr MCD* (2) NE-7
Center—*locale* MS-4
Center—*locale* OH-6
Center—*locale* PA-2
Center—*locale* SD-7
Center—*locale* (3) TN-4
Center—*locale* (3) TX-5
Center—*locale* UT-8
Center—*locale* WA-9
Center—*other* ME-1
**Center**—*pop pl* AL-4
**Center**—*pop pl* AR-4
**Center**—*pop pl* CO-8
**Center**—*pop pl* CT-1
**Center**—*pop pl* (3) GA-3
**Center**—*pop pl* (3) IN-6
**Center**—*pop pl* KY-4
**Center**—*pop pl* (3) MS-4
**Center**—*pop pl* MO-7
**Center**—*pop pl* NE-7
**Center**—*pop pl* (2) NC-3
**Center**—*pop pl* ND-7
**Center**—*pop pl* (2) OH-6
**Center**—*pop pl* OK-5
**Center**—*pop pl* (3) PA-2
**Center**—*pop pl* TN-4
**Center**—*pop pl* TX-5
**Center**—*pop pl* UT-8
**Center**—*pop pl* WI-6
Center—*post sta* MA-1
Center—*uninc pl* MA-1
Center—*uninc pl* NJ-2
Center, Lake—*lake* FL-3
*Center, The* IN-6
Center, The—*locale* SC-3
Center Acad—*school* FL-3
Centeral Run—*stream* IN-6
Centeral Valleys State Fish
Hatchery—*locale* CA-9
Center Annex Sch—*school* MO-7
Center at Lenox, The—*locale* MA-1
**Center Ave**—*pop pl* NY-2
Center Ave Elem Sch—*school* PA-2
Center Ave Neighborhood Residential
District—*hist pl* MI-6
*Center Ave Sch* PA-2
Center Ave Sch—*school* CA-9
Center Ave Sch—*school* NY-2
Center Baldy—*summit* NM-5
Center Baptist Ch—*church* (2) MS-4
**Center Barnstead**—*pop pl* NH-1
*Center Bartlett* NH-1
Center Basin—*basin* CA-9
Center Basin—*basin* ID-8
Center Basin Crags—*pillar* CA-9
Center Bay—*swamp* FL-3
Center Belle Ch—*church* TN-4
Center Belmont—*locale* ME-1
Center Belpre—*other* OH-6
Center Bend—*locale* OH-6
**Center Berlin**—*pop pl* NY-2
Center Berlin Cem—*cemetery* NY-2
Center Bethel Ch—*church* KS-7
Center Bldg of East Louisiana State
Hosp—*hist pl* LA-4
**Center Bluff**—*pop pl* NC-3
*Center Bluff Building* NC-3
Center Bluff Landing—*locale* NC-3
Centerboard Shoal—*bar* MA-1
*Center Branch* KY-4
*Center Branch* WI-6
Center Branch—*canal* CA-9
Center Branch—*locale* WV-2
Center Branch—*stream* MO-7
Center Branch—*stream* OH-6
Center Branch Ch—*church* LA-4
Center Branch Fox River—*stream* IA-7
Center Branch Hefty Creek—*stream* WI-6
*Center Branch Housatonic River* MA-1
*Center Branch Little Rush Creek* OH-6
Center Branch Pigeon Creek—*stream* PA-2
Center Branch Rush Creek—*stream* OH-6
Center Branch Washington Colony
Canal—*canal* CA-9
Center Branch Water Gap Wash—*valley* WY-8
*Center Bridge* NJ-2
Center Bridge—*bridge* TN-4
**Center Bridge**—*pop pl* PA-2
Center Bridge Hist Dist—*hist pl* PA-2
*Center Brook* NY-2
**Centerbrook**—*pop pl* CT-1
Center Brook—*stream* CT-1
Center Brook—*stream* ME-1
Center Brook—*stream* (2) MA-1
Center Brook—*stream* (2) NH-1
Center Brook—*stream* (2) NY-2
Center Brook—*stream* VT-1
Center Brook Ch—*church* AL-4
Centerbrook Congregational
Church—*hist pl* CT-1
*Center Brunswick* NY-2
**Center Brunswick (Brunswick)**—*pop pl* NY-2
Center Building-Minnesota Hosp for The
Insane—*hist pl* MN-6
**Centerburg**—*pop pl* OH-6
Centerburg Cem—*cemetery* OH-6
Centerbury Hill—*uninc pl* NY-2
**Center Cambridge**—*pop pl* NY-2
Center Camp—*locale* NY-2
Center Camp Ground—*locale* TN-4
Center Campground Cem—*cemetery* AR-4
Center Canal—*canal* (2) ID-8
Center Canal—*canal* (2) OR-9
Center Canyon—*valley* (3) UT-8
Center Canyon—*valley* WY-8
Center Cass Sch—*school* IL-6
Center (CCD)—*cens area* KY-4
Center (CCD)—*cens area* TX-5
Center Cem—*cemetery* (3) AL-4
Center Cem—*cemetery* AR-4
Center Cem—*cemetery* (9) CT-1
Center Cem—*cemetery* GA-3
Center Cem—*cemetery* (2) IL-6
Center Cem—*cemetery* (4) IN-6
Center Cem—*cemetery* (5) IA-7
Center Cem—*cemetery* (2) KS-7
Center Cem—*cemetery* (2) KY-4
Center Cem—*cemetery* (3) ME-1
Center Cem—*cemetery* MA-1
Center Cem—*cemetery* (5) MS-4
Center Cem—*cemetery* NE-7
Center Cem—*cemetery* (2) NH-1
Center Cem—*cemetery* ND-7
Center Cem—*cemetery* (4) OH-6
Center Cem—*cemetery* OK-5
Center Cem—*cemetery* (3) PA-2
Center Cem—*cemetery* (5) TN-4
Center Cem—*cemetery* (3) TX-5
Center Cem—*cemetery* (8) VT-1
Center Cemeteries—*cemetery* VT-1
*Center Ch* AL-4
*Center Ch* PA-2
Center Ch—*church* (9) AL-4
Center Ch—*church* (3) AR-4
Center Ch—*church* (3) GA-3
Center Ch—*church* (2) IL-6
Center Ch—*church* (9) IN-6
Center Ch—*church* (3) IA-7
Center Ch—*church* (2) KS-7
Center Ch—*church* KY-4
Center Ch—*church* LA-4
Center Ch—*church* ME-1
Center Ch—*church* (2) MO-7
Center Ch—*church* (18) NC-3
Center Ch—*church* ND-7
Center Ch—*church* (4) OH-6
Center Ch—*church* (8) PA-2
Center Ch—*church* (2) SC-3
Center Ch—*church* (4) TN-4
Center Ch—*church* (3) TX-5
Center Ch—*church* (2) VA-3
Center Chain Cem—*cemetery* MN-6
Center Chapel—*church* (2) AL-4
Center Chapel—*church* IL-6
Center Chapel—*church* (5) IN-6
Center Chapel—*church* IA-7
Center Chapel—*church* (2) KS-7
Center Chapel—*church* MO-7
Center Chapel—*church* OH-6
Center Chapel—*church* TN-4
Center Chapel—*church* WV-2
**Center Chapel**—*pop pl* AL-4
Center Chapel Cem—*cemetery* AR-4
Center Chapel Cem—*cemetery* OK-5
Center Chapel Ch—*church* IA-7
*Center Chapel School* TN-4
Center Chardon Cem—*cemetery* OH-6
Center Ch (historical)—*church* MS-4
*Center Church* MS-4
Center Church, The—*church* TN-4
**Center City**—*pop pl* FL-3
**Center City**—*pop pl* MN-6
**Center City**—*pop pl* TX-5
Center City—*post sta* OK-5
Center City—*post sta* PA-2
Center City Cem—*cemetery* TX-5
Center City Hist Dist—*hist pl* MN-6
Center City West Commercial Hist
Dist—*hist pl* PA-2
Center Clyde Sch—*school* IL-6
**Center Community**—*pop pl* AL-4
Center Community Ch—*church* IA-7
Center Consolidated Sch (historical)—*school*
(2) MS-4
**Center Conway**—*pop pl* NH-1
**Center Corner**—*pop pl* PA-2
Center Corners—*locale* OH-6
Center Country Club—*other* TX-5
**Center Court**—*pop pl* MD-2
*Center Creek* UT-8
*Center Creek* WA-9
*Center Creek* WI-6
**Center Creek**—*pop pl* UT-8
Center Creek—*stream* AK-9
Center Creek—*stream* AZ-5
Center Creek—*stream* CA-9
Center Creek—*stream* CO-8
Center Creek—*stream* (6) ID-8
Center Creek—*stream* (3) IN-6
Center Creek—*stream* KS-7
Center Creek—*stream* MI-6
Center Creek—*stream* MN-6
Center Creek—*stream* MO-7
Center Creek—*stream* MT-8
Center Creek—*stream* NE-7
Center Creek—*stream* NV-8
Center Creek—*stream* (3) OH-6
Center Creek—*stream* PA-2
Center Creek—*stream* SC-3
Center Creek—*stream* TX-5
Center Creek—*stream* (7) UT-8
Center Creek—*stream* WA-9
Center Creek—*stream* (2) WI-6
Center Creek Archeol District—*hist pl* MN-6
Center Creek Cem—*cemetery* MN-6
Center Creek Corners—*locale* OH-6
Center Creek Lakes—*lake* ID-8
Center Creek Number Five Dam—*dam* UT-8
Center Creek Number Five
Rsvr—*reservoir* UT-8
Center Creek Number One Dam—*dam* UT-8
Center Creek Number One
Rsvr—*reservoir* UT-8
Center Creek Number Three Dam—*dam* UT-8
Center Creek Number Three
Rsvr—*reservoir* UT-8
Center Creek Number Two Dam—*dam* UT-8
Center Creek Number Two Rsvr—*reservoir* UT-8
Center Creek Spring—*spring* UT-8
Center Creek (Township of)—*civ div* MN-6
Center Creek Trail—*trail* MT-8
**Centercrest**—*pop pl* AL-4
Centercrest Ch—*church* AL-4
**Center Cross**—*pop pl* VA-3
Center Cross Ch—*church* NC-3
**Center Crossroads**—*pop pl* SC-3
*Centerdale* AL-4
Centerdale—*locale* IA-7
**Center Dale**—*pop pl* AL-4
**Centerdale**—*pop pl* RI-1
Centerdale Sch (historical)—*school* AL-4
Center Dale Sch (historical)—*school* AL-4
*Center Dam* ND-7
Center Dam—*dam* NM-5
Center District Cem—*cemetery* MO-7
*Center District Drainage* WI-6
Center District One Township—*civil* KS-7
Center Ditch—*canal* CA-9
Center Ditch—*canal* (2) UT-8
Center Ditch—*canal* WY-8
Center Divide Sch—*school* NE-7
Center Drain—*canal* MI-6
Center Draw—*valley* (2) WY-8
**Centereach**—*pop pl* NY-2
Centereach Ch—*church* NY-2
Center East Sch—*school* MO-7
**Center Effingham**—*pop pl* NH-1
Center Elem Sch—*school* CT-1
Center Elem Sch—*school* (2) IN-6
Center Elem Sch—*school* PA-2
*Center-Elmore Memorial Cemetery* AL-4
*Center-Elmore Memorial Methodist Church* AL-4
Center Fait Landing—*locale* FL-3
**Center Falls**—*pop pl* NY-2
Center Farm—*locale* CO-8
Center Fayston Cem—*cemetery* VT-1
Centerfield—*locale* OH-6
**Centerfield**—*pop pl* KY-4
**Centerfield**—*pop pl* NY-2
**Centerfield**—*pop pl* UT-8
Centerfield Cem—*cemetery* UT-8
Centerfield Ch—*church* MS-4
Centerfield Coral Reef—*bar* PA-2
Centerfield Post Office—*building* UT-8
**Centerfield Subdivision**—*pop pl* UT-8
Center Filtration Plant—*other* TX-5
Centerfire Bog—*swamp* NM-5
*Centerfire Canyon* AZ-5
Centerfire Creek—*stream* (2) AZ-5
Centerfire Creek—*stream* NM-5
Center Fireline Trail—*trail* MI-6
Centerfire Tank No 1—*reservoir* NM-5
Centerfire Tank No 2—*reservoir* NM-5
Centerfit Branch—*stream* FL-3
Center Flats—*flat* CA-9
Center Ford—*locale* TN-4
Center for Education Montessori
Sch—*school* FL-3
Center Fork—*stream* KS-7
Center Fork—*stream* OH-6
Center Fork Asphalt Wash—*valley* UT-8
Center Fork Deep Creek—*stream* UT-8
Center Fork Eagle Creek—*stream* UT-8
*Center Fork East Fork Eagle Creek* UT-8
Center Fork Gilbert Creek—*stream* UT-8
Center Fork Kane Wash—*valley* UT-8
Center Fork New Wood River—*stream* WI-6
Center Fork Spring—*spring* UT-8
*Center Fork Uinta River* UT-8
Center for Practical Christianity—*church* FL-3
Center For The Arts and Technology, Pickering
Campus—*school* PA-2
Center Friends Cem—*cemetery* IA-7
Center Friends Ch—*church* IA-7
Center Furnace—*hist pl* KY-4
Center Furnace (Ruins)—*locale* KY-4
Center-Gaillard House—*hist pl* AL-4
Center Grange—*locale* PA-2
**Center Green**—*pop pl* DE-2
**Center Groton**—*pop pl* CT-1
*Center Grove* NJ-2
Center Grove—*locale* AL-4
Center Grove—*locale* TX-5
**Centergrove**—*pop pl* AL-4
**Center Grove**—*pop pl* AR-4
**Center Grove**—*pop pl* IA-7
**Center Grove**—*pop pl* MS-4
**Centergrove**—*pop pl* NC-3
**Center Grove**—*pop pl* (2) TN-4
Center Grove Baptist Ch—*church* TN-4
*Center Grove Baptist Church* MS-4
Center Grove Cem—*cemetery* (2) AL-4
Center Grove Cem—*cemetery* IL-6
Center Grove Cem—*cemetery* (2) IN-6
Center Grove Cem—*cemetery* (3) IA-7
Center Grove Cem—*cemetery* MN-6
Center Grove Cem—*cemetery* MS-4
Center Grove Cem—*cemetery* MO-7
Center Grove Cem—*cemetery* TX-5
Center Grove Ch—*church* (2) AL-4
Center Grove Ch—*church* (3) AR-4
Center Grove Ch—*church* (3) GA-3
Center Grove Ch—*church* IN-6
Center Grove Ch—*church* (2) MS-4
Center Grove Ch—*church* (2) MO-7
Center Grove Ch—*church* (8) NC-3
Center Grove Ch—*church* PA-2
Center Grove Ch—*church* (2) SC-3

Centerville Canyon Overlook—*locale* ... UT-8
Centerville (CCD)—*cens area* ... TN-4
Centerville (CCD)—*cens area* ... TX-5
Centerville Cem—*cemetery* ... AR-4
Centerville Cem—*cemetery* ... CO-8
Centerville Cem—*cemetery* ... IL-6
Centerville Cem—*cemetery* ... KS-7
Centerville Cem—*cemetery* ... LA-4
Centerville Cem—*cemetery* (4) ... MS-4
Centerville Cem—*cemetery* ... MT-8
Centerville Cem—*cemetery* ... OH-6
Centerville Cem—*cemetery* ... OK-5
Centerville Cem—*cemetery* ... PA-2
Centerville Cem—*cemetery* ... SC-3
Centerville Cem—*cemetery* ... TN-4
Centerville Cem—*cemetery* ... WA-9
Centerville Ch—*church* ... AL-4
Centerville Ch—*church* ... KS-7
Centerville Ch—*church* ... LA-4
Centerville Ch—*church* (5) ... MS-4
Centerville Ch—*church* ... NC-3
Centerville Ch—*church* ... PA-2
Centerville Ch—*church* ... SC-3
Centerville Ch—*church* (2) ... VA-3
Centerville Ch (historical)—*church* ... MS-4
Centerville Community Ch—*church* ... IN-6
Centerville Consolidated Sch (historical)—*school* ... MS-4
Centerville Corner—*locale* ... NM-5
**Centerville (Corporate Name For Thurman)**—*pop pl* ... OH-6
*Centerville Creek* ... PA-2
Centerville Creek—*stream* ... GA-3
Centerville Creek—*stream* ... PA-2
Centerville Creek—*stream* ... WI-6
**Centerville District**—*pop pl* ... CA-9
Centerville Ditch—*canal* (2) ... ID-8
Centerville Division—*civil* ... TN-4
Centerville East Oil Field—*other* ... IL-6
Centerville (Election Precinct)—*fmr MCD* ... IL-6
Centerville Elem Sch—*school* ... PA-2
Centerville Elem Sch—*school* ... TN-4
Centerville First Baptist Ch—*church* ... TN-4
Centerville Flat—*flat* ... CA-9
Centerville Golf and Country Club—*locale* . TN-4
Centerville Harbor—*bay* ... MA-1
Centerville Hist Dist—*hist pl* ... IN-6
Centerville Hist Dist—*hist pl* ... MA-1
Centerville Hist Dist—*hist pl* ... OH-6
Centerville (historical)—*locale* ... AL-4
Centerville Industrial Sch (historical)—*school* ... AL-4
Centerville JHS—*school* ... PA-2
Centerville JHS—*school* ... UT-8
Centerville Kingsburg Canal—*canal* ... CA-9
Centerville Lake—*lake* ... MN-6
Centerville Landing (historical)—*locale* ... TN-4
Centerville Memorial Park (cemetery)—*cemetery* ... UT-8
**Centerville-Mount Carmel**—*pop pl* ... CT-1
Centerville Municipal Airp—*airport* ... TN-4
Centerville Park—*park* ... AR-4
Centerville Pond Dam—*dam* ... RI-1
Centerville Post Office—*building* ... TN-4
Centerville River—*stream* ... MA-1
**Centerville (RR name Centreville)**—*pop pl* ... TN-4
Centerville (RR name for Centreville)—*other* ... MI-6
Centerville Sch—*school* ... CA-9
Centerville Sch—*school* (9) ... IL-6
Centerville Sch—*school* ... LA-4
Centerville Sch—*school* ... MA-1
Centerville Sch—*school* ... ND-7
Centerville Sch—*school* ... PA-2
Centerville Sch—*school* (2) ... SC-3
Centerville Sch—*school* (2) ... SD-7
Centerville Sch—*school* ... UT-8
Centerville Sch (historical)—*school* (3) ... MS-4
Centerville Sch (historical)—*school* ... MO-7
Centerville Sch (historical)—*school* ... PA-2
Centerville Sch (historical)—*school* (3) ... TN-4
Centerville Schoolhouse—*hist pl* ... CA-9
Centerville Sch (reduced usage)—*school* ... CO-8
Centerville Shop Ctr—*locale* ... MA-1
Centerville Slough—*gut* ... CA-9
Centerville Spring—*spring* ... UT-8
Centerville (sta.)—*uninc pl* ... CA-9
*Centerville Station* ... NY-2
Centerville Station—*building* ... VA-3
**Centerville (Town of)**—*pop pl* ... ME-1
**Centerville (Town of)**—*pop pl* ... NY-2
**Centerville (Town of)**—*pop pl* ... WI-6
**Centerville Township**—*pop pl* (2) ... KS-7
**Centerville Township**—*pop pl* (2) ... SD-7
Centerville Township Hall—*building* ... SD-7
Centerville (Township of)—*fmr MCD* ... AR-4
**Centerville (Township of)**—*pop pl* ... MI-6
Centerville Union Sch—*school* ... CA-9
Centerville Valley—*valley* ... WA-9
Center Vine—*locale* ... TX-5
Center Well—*well* ... CO-8
Center Well—*well* ... NM-5
Center Well—*well* (2) ... TX-5
**Center West**—*pop pl* ... AL-4
Center West Ch—*church* ... AL-4
Center West (Shop Ctr)—*locale* ... FL-3
Center Wheeling Market—*hist pl* ... WV-2
**Center White Creek**—*pop pl* ... NY-2
Center White Creek—*stream* ... NY-2
Center Windmill—*locale* ... NM-5
Center Windmill—*locale* (4) ... TX-5
**Centerwood Estates**—*pop pl* ... AL-4
Center "75" (Shop Ctr)—*locale* ... KS-7
Center 90—*post sta* ... WI-6
**Centex**—*pop pl* ... TX-5
Centhro Sch—*school* ... KY-4
Centinela Adobe—*hist pl* ... CA-9
Centinela Creek Channel—*canal* ... CA-9
Centinela Hosp—*hospital* ... CA-9
Centinela Mound—*summit* ... NM-5
Centinela Park—*park* ... CA-9
Centinela Sch—*school* ... CA-9
Centinela Valley Camp—*locale* ... CA-9
Centipede Bay—*bay* ... FL-3
Centipede Branch—*stream* ... TX-5
Centipede Cave—*cave* ... AL-4
Centipede Creek—*stream* ... CA-9
Centipede Creek—*stream* ... MT-8
Centipede Mesa—*summit* ... AZ-5
Centipede Mine—*mine* ... NV-8
Centipede Spring—*spring* ... AZ-5
Centipede Well—*well* ... NM-5
Centissima Reef—*bar* ... CA-9
**Centrahoma**—*pop pl* ... OK-5
*Centrailia* ... KS-7
*Central* ... CT-1
*Central* ... IA-7
*Central* (2) ... MO-7
*Central* ... OH-6
*Central* ... RI-1
Central—*locale* ... AR-4
Central—*locale* ... CA-9
Central—*locale* (2) ... MN-6
Central—*locale* (2) ... TN-4
**Central**—*pop pl* (3) ... AL-4
**Central**—*pop pl* ... AK-9
**Central**—*pop pl* ... AZ-5
**Central**—*pop pl* (3) ... AR-4
**Central**—*pop pl* ... FL-3
**Central**—*pop pl* ... ID-8
**Central**—*pop pl* ... IL-6
**Central**—*pop pl* (2) ... IN-6
**Central**—*pop pl* ... KS-7
**Central**—*pop pl* (4) ... LA-4
**Central**—*pop pl* ... MI-6
**Central**—*pop pl* ... MS-4
**Central**—*pop pl* ... MO-7
**Central**—*pop pl* ... NM-5
**Central**—*pop pl* ... NC-3
**Central**—*pop pl* (2) ... PA-2
**Central**—*pop pl* ... SC-3
**Central**—*pop pl* (2) ... TN-4
**Central**—*pop pl* (2) ... TX-5
**Central**—*pop pl* (2) ... UT-8
**Central**—*pop pl* ... VA-3
**Central**—*pop pl* ... WV-2
Central—*post sta* ... DC-2
Central—*post sta* ... WA-9
Central—*uninc pl* ... NJ-2
Central—*uninc pl* ... NY-2
Central—*uninc pl* ... OR-9
Central—*uninc pl* (2) ... PA-2
Central—*uninc pl* ... TX-5
Central—*uninc pl* ... VA-3
**Centrala**—*pop pl* ... AL-4
Central Acad—*school* ... MS-4
Central Acad—*school* ... NC-3
Central Acad—*school* ... VA-3
**Central Academy**—*pop pl* ... MS-4
Central Academy Ch—*church* ... MS-4
Central Academy Post Office (historical)—*building* ... MS-4
Central Acad HS—*school* ... FL-3
Central Acad Sch—*school* ... FL-3
Central Adams—*unorg reg* ... ND-7
Central Agency (historical)—*locale* ... MS-4
Central Aguirre—*CDP* ... PR-3
**Central Aguirre**—*pop pl* ... PR-3
Central Alabama Acad—*school* ... AL-4
Central Alabama Hosp (historical)—*hospital* ... AL-4
Central Alkali Drain—*canal* ... ID-8
Central Alkali Drain—*canal* ... OR-9
Central Annex Sch—*school* ... MA-1
**Central Area**—*pop pl* ... NC-3
Central Area HS—*school* ... WI-6
Central Area Vocational Center—*school* ... AL-4
Central Arizona Coll—*school* ... AZ-5
Central Arizona Project Aqueduct—*canal* ... AZ-5
Central Aroostook (Unorganized Territory of)—*unorg* ... ME-1
*Central Arroyo* ... TX-5
Central Assembly Ch—*church* ... MS-4
Central Assembly of God—*church* ... FL-3
Central Assembly of God Ch—*church* (3) ... AL-4
Central Assembly of God Ch—*church* ... FL-3
Central Assembly of God Ch—*church* ... TN-4
Central Assurance Company—*hist pl* ... OH-6
Central Atoka (CCD)—*cens area* ... OK-5
Central Augusta HS—*school* ... VA-3
Central Ave Baptist Ch—*church* ... FL-3
Central Ave Ch—*church* ... FL-3
Central Ave Ch of Christ—*church* ... MS-4
Central Ave Commercial Hist Dist—*hist pl* .. NJ-2
Central Ave Elem Sch—*school* ... FL-3
Central Ave Hist Dist—*hist pl* ... NY-2
Central Ave Hist Dist—*hist pl* ... OH-6
Central Ave Holiness Ch—*church* ... AL-4
Central Ave Missionary Baptist Ch—*church* ... AL-4
*Central Avenue* ... MN-6
Central Avenue—*uninc pl* ... WI-6
**Central Ave Park**—*pop pl* ... OH-6
Central Ave Sch—*school* ... CT-1
Central Ave Sch—*school* ... FL-3
Central Ave Sch—*school* ... GA-3
Central Ave Sch—*school* ... IN-6
Central Ave Sch—*school* ... IA-7
Central Ave Sch—*school* (2) ... NJ-2
Central Ave Sch—*school* ... NY-2
Central Ave Sch—*school* ... OH-6
Central Ave Sch—*school* ... WA-9
Central Ave United Methodist Ch—*church* .. IN-6
*Central Baptist Ch* ... AL-4
Central Baptist Ch—*church* (13) ... AL-4
Central Baptist Ch—*church* ... DE-2
Central Baptist Ch—*church* (8) ... FL-3
Central Baptist Ch—*church* ... IN-6
Central Baptist Ch—*church* (3) ... MS-4
Central Baptist Ch—*church* (5) ... TN-4
Central Baptist Ch (historical)—*church* ... MS-4
Central Baptist Ch of Bearden—*church* ... TN-4
Central Baptist Ch of Flagler County—*church* ... FL-3
Central Baptist Ch of Hixson—*church* ... TN-4
Central Baptist Church—*hist pl* ... OK-5
Central Baptist Church—*hist pl* ... SC-3
Central Baptist Church Child Care—*school* .. FL-3
Central Baptist Church Sch—*school* ... FL-3
Central Baptist Church Youth Camp—*locale* ... FL-3
Central Baptist College—*uninc pl* ... AR-4
**Central Barren**—*pop pl* ... IN-6
Central Barren Cem—*cemetery* ... IN-6
Central Basin—*harbor* ... CA-9
*Central Beach School* ... FL-3
Central Bethlehem Hist Dist—*hist pl* ... PA-2
Central Bethlehem Hist Dist (Boundary Increase)—*hist pl* ... PA-2
Central Bible Ch—*church* ... FL-3
Central Bible Chapel—*church* ... FL-3
Central Bible Coll—*school* ... MO-7
Central Bldg—*hist pl* ... OR-9
Central Blvd Sch—*school* ... NY-2
Central Branch—*stream* ... CO-8
Central Branch—*stream* ... TN-4
Central Branch—*stream* ... VA-3
Central Branch Kern Island Canal—*canal* ... CA-9
Central Branch Onancock Creek—*stream* ... VA-3
Central Branch Reorganized Ch of Jesus Christ of Latter Day S—*church* ... KS-7
Central Branch Tujunga Wash—*stream* ... CA-9
Central Breaker (historical)—*building* ... PA-2
Central Bridge—*bridge* ... MA-1
**Central Bridge**—*pop pl* ... NY-2
Central Bridge Cem—*cemetery* ... NY-2
Central Bridgeport Baptist Ch—*church* ... IN-6
*Central Bridgeport Southern Baptist Ch* ... IN-6
Central Building, Public Library—*hist pl* ... OR-9
Central Building, State Lunatic Asylum—*hist pl* ... GA-3
*Central Burial Ground* ... MA-1
Central Burying Ground—*cemetery* ... CT-1
Central Burying Ground—*cemetery* ... MA-1
Central Burying Grounds—*cemetery* ... CT-1
Central Business District—*hist pl* ... NH-1
Central By-Products Sewage Lagoon Dam—*dam* ... MS-4
Central Cabarrus HS—*school* ... NC-3
**Central Cambalache**—*pop pl* ... PR-3
**Central Camp**—*pop pl* ... CA-9
Central Canal—*canal* ... AZ-5
Central Canal—*canal* (2) ... CA-9
Central Canal—*canal* ... LA-4
Central Canal—*canal* ... NE-7
Central Canal—*canal* ... UT-8
Central Canovanas—*other* ... PR-3
Central Canyon—*valley* ... CA-9
Central Canyon—*valley* ... NV-8
Central Career Center—*school* ... IN-6
Central Carolina Technical Institute—*school* ... NC-3
*Central Catholic High School* ... PA-2
Central Catholic HS—*school* ... CA-9
Central Catholic HS—*school* ... FL-3
Central Catholic HS—*school* ... OK-5
Central Catholic HS—*school* ... OR-9
Central Cayey—*other* ... PR-3
Central (CCD)—*cens area* ... NM-5
Central (CCD)—*cens area* ... SC-3
Central Cem—*cemetery* ... AL-4
Central Cem—*cemetery* ... AZ-5
Central Cem—*cemetery* ... AR-4
Central Cem—*cemetery* ... CT-1
Central Cem—*cemetery* ... ID-8
Central Cem—*cemetery* (2) ... IL-6
Central Cem—*cemetery* ... IN-6
Central Cem—*cemetery* ... KS-7
Central Cem—*cemetery* ... LA-4
Central Cem—*cemetery* ... ME-1
Central Cem—*cemetery* (7) ... MA-1
Central Cem—*cemetery* ... MS-4
Central Cem—*cemetery* ... NH-1
Central Cem—*cemetery* (2) ... NY-2
Central Cem—*cemetery* ... NC-3
Central Cem—*cemetery* ... OH-6
Central Cem—*cemetery* ... OR-9
Central Cem—*cemetery* ... TX-5
Central Cem—*cemetery* ... VA-3
Central Cemetary—*cemetery* ... AR-4
Central (Census Subdistrict)—*cens area* ... VI-3
*Central Ch* ... MS-4
Central Ch—*church* (12) ... AL-4
Central Ch—*church* (6) ... AR-4
Central Ch—*church* (3) ... FL-3
Central Ch—*church* (9) ... GA-3
Central Ch—*church* (3) ... IL-6
Central Ch—*church* ... KS-7
Central Ch—*church* ... KY-4
Central Ch—*church* (4) ... LA-4
Central Ch—*church* ... MD-2
Central Ch—*church* ... MI-6
Central Ch—*church* (3) ... MN-6
Central Ch—*church* (4) ... MS-4
Central Ch—*church* (5) ... MO-7
Central Ch—*church* ... NM-5
Central Ch—*church* ... NY-2
Central Ch—*church* (10) ... NC-3
Central Ch—*church* (2) ... OH-6
Central Ch—*church* (4) ... OK-5
Central Ch—*church* (3) ... PA-2
Central Ch—*church* (5) ... SC-3
Central Ch—*church* (12) ... TN-4
Central Ch—*church* (14) ... TX-5
Central Ch—*church* (12) ... VA-3
Central Ch—*church* (2) ... WV-2
Central Channel (not verified)—*channel* ... MP-9
Central Chapel—*church* ... KS-7
Central Chapel—*church* ... MD-2
Central Chapel—*church* ... MO-7
Central Chapel Ch—*church* ... WV-2
Central Ch (historical)—*church* (2) ... AL-4
Central Ch (historical)—*church* ... TN-4
*Central Ch of Christ* ... MS-4
Central Ch of Christ—*church* (7) ... AL-4
Central Ch of Christ—*church* (2) ... FL-3
Central Ch of Christ—*church* ... KS-7
Central Ch Of Christ—*church* ... KS-7
Central Ch of Christ—*church* (2) ... MS-4
Central Ch of Christ—*church* (2) ... TN-4
Central Ch of God—*church* ... AL-4
Central Ch of God—*church* ... TN-4
Central Ch of the Nazarene—*church* (3) ... FL-3
Central Ch of the Nazarene—*church* ... MS-4
Central Ch of the Nazarene—*church* ... UT-8
Central Christian Camp—*locale* ... OK-5
Central Christian Ch—*church* ... AL-4
Central Christian Ch—*church* (2) ... FL-3
Central Christian Ch—*church* (2) ... MS-4
Central Christian Ch—*church* (4) ... TN-4
Central Christian Ch Disciples of Christ—*church* ... FL-3
Central Christian Ch (Salt Lake City)—*church* ... UT-8
Central Christian Church—*hist pl* ... KY-4
Central Christian HS—*school* (2) ... PA-2
Central Christian Sch—*school* ... DE-2
Central Christian Sch—*school* ... MI-6
Central Christian Schools—*school* ... KS-7
*Central Church* ... DE-2
Central Church, The—*church* ... KY-4
*Central City* ... KS-7
*Central City* ... OH-6
Central City—*locale* ... FL-3
**Central City**—*pop pl* ... AL-4
**Central City**—*pop pl* (2) ... AR-4
**Central City**—*pop pl* ... CO-8
**Central City**—*pop pl* (2) ... IL-6
**Central City**—*pop pl* ... IA-7
**Central City**—*pop pl* ... KY-4
**Central City**—*pop pl* ... MO-7
**Central City**—*pop pl* ... NE-7
**Central City**—*pop pl* (2) ... PA-2
**Central City**—*pop pl* ... SD-7
Central City—*post sta* ... AR-4
Central City—*post sta* ... GA-3
Central City Borough—*civil* ... PA-2
Central City (CCD)—*cens area* ... KY-4
Central City Cem—*cemetery* ... KS-7
Central City Cem—*cemetery* ... NE-7
Central City Hist Dist—*hist pl* ... CO-8
Central City Hist Dist—*hist pl* ... LA-4
Central City (historical)—*locale* ... AL-4
Central City (historical)—*locale* ... KS-7
Central City Opera House—*hist pl* ... CO-8
Central City Park Bandstand—*hist pl* ... GA-3
Central City South—*locale* ... MO-7
Central City South Shop Ctr—*locale* ... MO-7
Central City Vista—*summit* ... PA-2
Central Coal and Coke Company—*other* ... AR-4
Central Coast (CCD)—*cens area* ... CA-9
Central Coll—*school* ... AR-4
Central Coll—*school* ... KS-7
Central Coll—*school* ... MO-7
Central Coll—*school* ... OH-6
*Central College* ... IA-7
Central College Presbyterian Church—*hist pl* ... OH-6
Central Colored Sch—*hist pl* ... KY-4
Central Colusa (CCD)—*cens area* ... CA-9
Central Commercial and RR Hist Dist—*hist pl* ... MS-4
Central Community Center—*school* ... TX-5
Central Community Ch of God—*church* ... KS-7
Central Community Hall—*building* ... KS-7
Central Community Sch—*school* ... IL-6
Central Congregational Ch—*church* ... KS-7
Central Congregational Ch—*church* ... MA-1
Central Congregational Church—*hist pl* ... ME-1
Central Congregational Church—*hist pl* (2) ... MA-1
Central Congregation Jehovahs Witnesses—*church* ... KS-7
Central Constancia—*other* ... PR-3
Central Contra Costa (CCD)—*cens area* ... CA-9
Central Control—*locale* ... FL-3
Central Corson—*unorg reg* ... SD-7
Central Cortada—*other* ... PR-3
Central Costa Coll—*school* ... CA-9
Central Cove—*locale* ... ID-8
Central Covington—*uninc pl* ... KY-4
Central Creditors Association Bldg—*hist pl* ... AZ-5
Central Creek—*stream* (3) ... AK-9
Central Creek—*stream* ... IN-6
Central Creek—*stream* ... KY-4
Central Creek—*stream* ... NV-8
Central Creek—*stream* (2) ... WA-9
*Central Crossroads* ... AL-4
**Central Crossroads**—*pop pl* ... AL-4
**Central Crossroads**—*pop pl* ... SC-3
Central Cutoff Ditch—*canal* ... NE-7
Central Dauphin East HS—*school* ... PA-2
Central Dauphin East JHS—*school* ... PA-2
Central Dauphin HS—*school* ... PA-2
Central Davidson HS—*school* ... NC-3
*Central Davis Junior High School* ... UT-8
Central Delta Acad—*school* ... MS-4
Central Detention Dam—*dam* ... AZ-5
Central District—*locale* ... ME-1
Central District—*uninc pl* ... CA-9
Central District Catholic HS—*school* ... PA-2
Central Ditch—*canal* ... CO-8
Central Ditch—*canal* ... IL-6
Central Drain—*canal* (2) ... AZ-5
Central Drain—*canal* (4) ... CA-9
Central Drain—*canal* ... MI-6
Central Drain—*canal* ... NM-5
Central Drain Eight—*canal* ... CA-9
Central Drain Four—*canal* ... CA-9
Central Drain Nine—*canal* ... CA-9
Central Drain Seven—*canal* ... CA-9
Central Drain Six—*canal* ... CA-9
Central Drain Ten—*canal* ... CA-9
Central Drain Three—*canal* (2) ... CA-9
Central Drain Three A—*canal* ... CA-9
Central Drain Three C—*canal* ... CA-9
Central Drain Three E—*canal* ... CA-9
Central Drain Three F—*canal* ... CA-9
Central Drain Three H—*canal* ... CA-9
Central Drain Two—*canal* ... CA-9
Central Drain Two A—*canal* ... CA-9
Central Drain Two C—*canal* ... CA-9
Central (Election Precinct)—*fmr MCD* ... IL-6
*Central Elem Sch* ... AL-4
*Central Elem Sch* ... MS-4
*Central Elem Sch* ... NC-3
Central Elem Sch—*hist pl* ... NC-3
Central Elem Sch—*school* (2) ... AL-4
Central Elem Sch—*school* ... AZ-5
Central Elem Sch—*school* ... FL-3
Central Elem Sch—*school* (11) ... IN-6
Central Elem Sch—*school* (10) ... KS-7
Central Elem Sch—*school* ... MS-4
Central Elem Sch—*school* (4) ... NC-3
Central Elem Sch—*school* (5) ... PA-2
Central Elem Sch—*school* (4) ... TN-4
Central Elsmere Sch—*school* ... NE-7
Central Ely Sch—*school* ... NV-8
Central Emmanuel Baptist Ch—*church* ... TN-4
Central Eureka—*other* ... PR-3
Central Eureka Mine—*mine* ... CA-9
Central Fairmount Sch—*school* ... OH-6
**Central Falls**—*pop pl* ... NC-3
**Central Falls**—*pop pl* ... RI-1
Central Falls Congregational Church—*hist pl* ... RI-1
Central Falls Dam—*dam* ... RI-1
Central Falls Mill Hist Dist—*hist pl* ... RI-1
Central Falmouth Hist Dist—*hist pl* ... KY-4
*Central Female Institute* ... MS-4
Central Ferry—*locale* (2) ... WA-9
Central Ferry Canyon—*valley* ... WA-9
Central Ferry Sch—*school* ... WA-9
Central Ferry (Site)—*locale* ... CA-9
Central Fire Station—*building* ... MA-1
Central Fire Station—*building* ... TN-4
Central Fire Station—*hist pl* ... HI-9
Central Fire Station—*hist pl* ... IA-7
Central Fire Station—*hist pl* ... LA-4
Central Fire Station—*hist pl* (2) ... MA-1
Central Fire Station—*hist pl* ... MS-4
Central Fire Station—*hist pl* ... NY-2
Central Fire Station—*hist pl* ... NC-3
Central Fire Station—*hist pl* ... SD-7
*Central Fire Tower* ... AL-4
Central Florida Bible Camp—*locale* ... FL-3
Central Florida Christian Sch—*school* ... FL-3
Central Florida District Ch of the Nazarene—*church* ... FL-3
Central Florida Hosp—*hospital* ... FL-3
Central Florida Junior Coll—*school* ... FL-3
Central Florida Regional Hosp—*hospital* ... FL-3
Central Florida Regional Library—*building* .. FL-3
*Central Fork Cottonwood Creek* ... CA-9
*Central Fork Rattlesnake Creek* ... CA-9
Central Forrest Attendance Center—*school* ... MS-4
Central Forrest Sch—*school* ... MS-4
Central Foursquare Ch—*church* ... FL-3
Central Gaither Union Sch—*school* ... CA-9
Central Garage—*locale* ... VA-3
**Central Gardens**—*pop pl* ... TX-5
**Central Gardens**—*pop pl* ... VA-3
Central Gardens Hist Dist—*hist pl* ... TN-4
Central Gardens Sch—*school* ... VA-3
Central Geneva Hist Dist—*hist pl* ... IL-6
Central Gloucester Hist Dist—*hist pl* ... MA-1
Central Graded Sch—*hist pl* ... SC-3
Central Grade Sch—*school* (2) ... KS-7
Central Grammar Sch—*school* ... TN-4
Central Grammar Sch (historical)—*school* .. TN-4
Central Grammer Sch (historical)—*school* ... AL-4
Central Grant—*unorg reg* ... ND-7
**Centralgrove**—*pop pl* ... MS-4
**Central Grove**—*pop pl* ... MS-4
*Central Grove Baptist Church* ... MS-4
Central Grove Cem—*cemetery* ... TN-4
Central Grove Ch—*church* ... GA-3
Central Grove Ch—*church* (2) ... KY-4
Central Grove Ch—*church* ... MS-4
Central Grove Ch—*church* ... MO-7
Central Grove Community Center—*locale* . MO-7
Centralgrove Post Office (historical)—*building* ... MS-4
Central Grove Sch—*school* ... TX-5
Central Grove School (historical)—*locale* .. MO-7
**Central Guamani**—*pop pl* (2) ... PR-3
Central Guanica—*other* ... PR-3
Central Gulch—*valley* ... CO-8
Central Hall—*hist pl* ... IA-7
Central Hall—*hist pl* ... NY-2
Central Hall—*summit* ... MA-1
Central Hamilton Elem Sch—*school* ... FL-3
Central Hancock (Unorganized Territory of)—*unorg* ... ME-1
**Centralhatchee**—*pop pl* ... GA-3
Centralhatchee (CCD)—*cens area* ... GA-3
Centralhatchee Creek—*stream* ... GA-3
Central Heating Plant (historical)—*building* ... DC-2
*Central Heights* ... TN-4
Central Heights—*other* ... TN-4
**Central Heights**—*pop pl* ... AL-4
**Central Heights**—*pop pl* ... AZ-5
**Central Heights**—*pop pl* ... IA-7
**Central Heights**—*pop pl* (2) ... TX-5
Central Heights Baptist Ch—*church* ... AL-4
**Central Heights (Bonita)**—*pop pl* ... TX-5
Central Heights Ch of Christ—*church* ... AL-4
Central Heights-Midland City—*CDP* ... AZ-5
**Central Heights (Mill Point)**—*pop pl* ... TN-4
Central Heights Sch—*school* ... AZ-5
Central Heights Sch—*school* ... TN-4
Central Heights Sch (reduced usage)—*school* ... TX-5
Central Heights Shopping Mall—*locale* ... KS-7
**Central Heights (subdivision)**—*pop pl* .. NC-3
**Central Heights Subdivision**—*pop pl* ... UT-8
Central Heights United Methodist Ch—*church* ... AL-4
Central Hidroelectrica de Carite Numero Three—*other* ... PR-3
Central Hidroelectrica de Carite Numero 3—*building* ... PR-3
Central Hidroelectrica Numero 1—*building* ... PR-3
Central Hidroelectrica Numero 2—*building* ... PR-3
Central Hidroelectrica Numero 3—*building* ... PR-3
Central High—*locale* ... TX-5
**Central Highlands**—*pop pl* ... AL-4
**Central Highlands**—*pop pl* ... PA-2
**Central Hill**—*pop pl* ... VA-3
Central Hill—*summit* ... CA-9
Central Hill—*summit* ... CO-8
Central Hill—*summit* ... NV-8
Central Hill Ch—*church* ... WV-2
*Central Hill Church* ... AL-4
Central Hill Mine—*mine* ... CA-9
Central Hill Sch—*school* ... MO-7
Central Hill Sch—*school* ... SC-3
Central Hinds Acad—*school* ... MS-4
*Central Hinds Sch* ... MS-4
Central (historical)—*locale* ... KS-7
**Central (historical)**—*pop pl* ... OR-9
Central Holmes Acad—*school* ... MS-4
Central Holston Ch—*church* ... TN-4
*Central Honeysuckle Lake* ... MI-6
Central Hosp—*hospital* ... MO-7
Central Hotel—*hist pl* ... PA-2
Central Hotel, Hackedorn and Zimmerman Buildings—*hist pl* ... OH-6
Central House—*hist pl* ... AK-9
Central House—*hist pl* ... IN-6
Central House—*locale* ... CA-9
Central Howell Sch—*school* ... OR-9
*Central HS* ... IN-6
*Central HS* ... TX-5
Central HS—*hist pl* ... CO-8
Central HS—*hist pl* ... FL-3
Central HS—*hist pl* (2) ... OH-6
Central HS—*hist pl* ... OK-5
Central HS—*hist pl* ... PA-2
Central HS—*hist pl* ... TN-4
Central HS—*hist pl* ... PR-3
Central HS—*school* (2) ... AL-4
Central HS—*school* ... AZ-5
Central HS—*school* (4) ... AR-4
Central HS—*school* (3) ... CO-8
Central HS—*school* ... CT-1
Central HS—*school* (2) ... FL-3
Central HS—*school* (4) ... GA-3
Central HS—*school* (3) ... IL-6
Central HS—*school* (5) ... IN-6
Central HS—*school* (3) ... IA-7
Central HS—*school* ... KS-7
Central HS—*school* (2) ... KY-4
Central HS—*school* (3) ... LA-4
Central HS—*school* ... MD-2
Central HS—*school* (12) ... MI-6
Central HS—*school* (7) ... MN-6
Central HS—*school* (5) ... MS-4
Central HS—*school* (5) ... MO-7
Central HS—*school* (3) ... MT-8
Central HS—*school* (5) ... NE-7
Central HS—*school* ... NH-1
Central HS—*school* (2) ... NJ-2
Central HS—*school* ... NM-5
Central HS—*school* (20) ... NY-2
Central HS—*school* (3) ... NC-3
Central HS—*school* (2) ... ND-7
Central HS—*school* (13) ... OH-6
Central HS—*school* (6) ... OK-5
Central HS—*school* (5) ... PA-2
Central HS—*school* ... SD-7
Central HS—*school* (18) ... TN-4
Central HS—*school* (4) ... TX-5
Central HS—*school* (9) ... VA-3
Central HS—*school* ... WA-9
Central HS—*school* ... WV-2
Central HS—*school* (4) ... WI-6
Central HS—*school* ... WY-8
Central HS & Boys Vocational Sch—*hist pl* ... IN-6
Central HS East Campus—*school* ... AL-4
Central HS for Girls (historical)—*school* ... AL-4
Central HS (historical)—*school* ... NC-3
Central HS (historical)—*school* (2) ... TN-4
Central HS West Campus—*school* ... AL-4
Central Hyde—*unorg reg* ... SD-7
*Centralia* ... ND-7
Centralia—*locale* ... CA-9
Centralia—*locale* ... TX-5
**Centralia**—*pop pl* ... IL-6
**Centralia**—*pop pl* ... IA-7
**Centralia**—*pop pl* ... KS-7
**Centralia**—*pop pl* ... MO-7
**Centralia**—*pop pl* ... NY-2
**Centralia**—*pop pl* ... OK-5
**Centralia**—*pop pl* ... PA-2
**Centralia**—*pop pl* ... VA-3
**Centralia**—*pop pl* ... WA-9
**Centralia**—*pop pl* ... WV-2
Centralia, Lake—*reservoir* ... IL-6
Centralia Borough—*civil* ... PA-2
Centralia Canal—*canal* ... WA-9
Centralia Cem—*cemetery* ... KS-7
Centralia Cem—*cemetery* ... OK-5
Centralia Cem—*cemetery* ... WV-2
Centralia Ch—*church* ... IA-7
Centralia-Chehalis (CCD)—*cens area* ... WA-9
Centralia Dam—*dam* ... WA-9
*Centralia Draw* ... TX-5
Centralia Draw—*valley* ... TX-5
Centralia Elem Sch—*school* ... KS-7
Centralia Fire Tower—*locale* ... PA-2
Centralia Foundation Park—*park* ... IL-6
Centralia HS—*school* ... KS-7
Centralia Lake—*lake* ... GA-3
*Centralia Lookout Tower* ... PA-2
Centralia Mtn—*summit* ... CO-8
Centralia Oil Field—*other* ... IL-6
*Centralia Rsvr* ... IL-6
Centralia Rsvr—*reservoir* ... IL-6
Centralia Sch—*school* ... CA-9
Centralia Sch—*school* ... OH-6
Centralia Township—*civil* ... MO-7
**Centralia (Township of)**—*pop pl* ... IL-6
Centralia Union Depot—*hist pl* ... WA-9
Central Idaho Camp—*locale* ... ID-8
Central Igualdad—*other* ... PR-3
Central Illinois Public Service Company—*facility* ... IL-6
Central Industrial Park—*locale* ... MS-4
*Central Institute* ... AL-4
Central Intelligence Agency—*building* ... VA-3
*Central Irrigation Canal* ... CA-9
Central Island—*island* ... AK-9
Central Island—*island* ... FL-3
**Central Islip**—*pop pl* ... NY-2
Central Islip State Hosp—*hospital* ... NY-2
Central Jefferson—*cens area* ... CO-8
*Central Jessup District Mining Area* ... NV-8
Central JHS—*school* (2) ... AR-4
Central JHS—*school* (2) ... CA-9
Central JHS—*school* ... CT-1
Central JHS—*school* ... FL-3
Central JHS—*school* (2) ... IL-6
Central JHS—*school* (2) ... IN-6
Central JHS—*school* (4) ... IA-7
Central JHS—*school* (2) ... KS-7
Central JHS—*school* ... LA-4
Central JHS—*school* ... MA-1
Central JHS—*school* (2) ... MI-6
Central JHS—*school* (3) ... MN-6
Central JHS—*school* (2) ... MS-4
Central JHS—*school* ... MO-7
Central JHS—*school* ... MT-8
Central JHS—*school* (2) ... NM-5
Central JHS—*school* ... NY-2
Central JHS—*school* (2) ... NC-3
Central JHS—*school* (7) ... OH-6
Central JHS—*school* (4) ... OK-5
Central JHS—*school* ... SC-3
Central JHS—*school* ... TX-5
Central JHS—*school* (2) ... UT-8
Central JHS—*school* ... WV-2

Century Bogs—*swamp* MA-1
Century Campground—*locale* UT-8
*Century Canal* LA-4
Century Caverns—*cave* TX-5
Century (CCD)—*cens area* FL-3
Century Cem—*cemetery* NY-2
Century Ch—*church* LA-4
Century Ch—*church* SC-3
Century City—*locale* CA-9
**Century Condominium**—*pop pl* UT-8
Century Corners (Shop Ctr)—*locale* FL-3
Century Country Club—*other* AZ-5
Century Country Club—*other* NY-2
Century Creek—*stream* ID-8
Century Elem Sch—*school* FL-3
*Century Hill* OK-5
Century Hill—*summit* NM-5
Century Hollow—*valley* UT-8
Century House—*hist pl* SC-3
Century Inn—*building* PA-2
Century Junction—*locale* WV-2
Century Lake—*reservoir* TX-5
Century Mall—*locale* IN-6
Century Memorial Hosp—*hospital* FL-3
Century Methodist Ch—*church* AL-4
Century Mine—*mine* AZ-5
Century Mine—*mine* SD-7
Century Mine—*mine* UT-8
Century Nelson Ch—*church* GA-3
*Century No. 1* WV-2
**Century No. 2**—*pop pl* WV-2
**Century Oaks**—*pop pl* IL-6
*Century Oaks West* IL-6
Century Park—*park* OH-6
Century Park Plaza—*locale* TN-4
Century Park Sch—*school* CA-9
Century Peak—*summit* NV-8
Century Plaza Shop Ctr—*locale* AL-4
Century Plaza (Shop Ctr)—*locale* (2) FL-3
Century Ranch—*locale* CA-9
Century Sch—*school* IL-6
Century Sch—*school* IN-6
Century Senior HS—*school* FL-3
Century Shop Ctr—*locale* MA-1
Century Square Shop Ctr—*locale* TN-4
*Century Subdivision Condominium, The* UT-8
Century Village—*CDP* FL-3
**Century Village Subdivision**—*pop pl* UT-8
Century Windmill—*locale* WY-8
**Century 21 (Mobile Home Park)**—*pop pl* FL-3
Cenzo Hill Cem—*cemetery* TX-5
Cepeda Cem—*cemetery* TX-5
Ceperley Ranch—*locale* ND-7
Cephalopod Gulch—*valley* UT-8
Cephus Ch—*church* AR-4
Cephus Sch (historical)—*school* AL-4
Ceppa Field—*park* CT-1
Cepres Windmill—*locale* TX-5
**Cerain**—*pop pl* GU-9
Ceral Sch—*school* IL-6
Ceralvo—*locale* KY-4
Ceramic—*uninc pl* AL-4
**Ceramics**—*pop pl* NJ-2
Cerbat—*locale* AZ-5
Cerbat Canyon—*valley* AZ-5
Cerbat Mine—*mine* AZ-5
Cerbat Mountains—*range* AZ-5
Cerbat Peak—*summit* AZ-5
*Cerbat Range* AZ-5
Cerbat Wash—*stream* AZ-5
Cerberus, Mount—*summit* (2) AK-9
**Cercadillo**—*pop pl* PR-3
Cercadillo (Barrio)—*fmr MCD* PR-3
Cerca Oil Field—*other* NM-5
Cercey Branch—*stream* TX-5
Cerco Canyon—*valley* NM-5
Cercocapia Rsvr—*reservoir* WY-8
Cereal—*locale* IL-6
Cereal—*locale* TX-5
**Cereal**—*pop pl* PA-2
Cerebral Palsy Hosp—*hospital* MS-4
Cerebral Palsy Institute—*building* OK-5
Cerebral Palsy Sch—*school* MO-7
Cerebral Palsy Treatment Center—*hospital* TX-5
Ceredo—*locale* KY-4
**Ceredo**—*pop pl* WV-2
Ceredo (Magisterial District)—*fmr MCD* WV-2
Ceremonia Rock—*pillar* CA-9
Ceres—*locale* IA-7
Ceres—*locale* WA-9
**Ceres**—*pop pl* CA-9
**Ceres**—*pop pl* NY-2
**Ceres**—*pop pl* OK-5
**Ceres**—*pop pl* VA-3
**Ceres**—*pop pl* WV-2
Ceres Airp—*airport* PA-2
Ceres-Bethel Ch—*church* MD-2
Ceres Ch—*church* GA-3
**Ceresco**—*pop pl* MI-6
**Ceresco**—*pop pl* NE-7
Ceresco Cem—*cemetery* MI-6
Ceresco No. 4 Adit—*mine* CO-8
Ceresco Ridge—*ridge* CO-8
Ceresco Ridge Portal—*tunnel* CO-8
Ceresco Site—*hist pl* WI-6
**Ceresco (Township of)**—*pop pl* MN-6
*Cerese Creek* OR-9
*Ceres Flat* OR-9
Ceres Hill—*summit* WA-9
Ceres Main Canal—*canal* CA-9
*Ceress* WV-2
Ceres Sch—*school* CA-9
Ceres Sch—*school* IL-6
Ceres South Oil Field—*oilfield* OK-5
**Ceres (Township of)**—*pop pl* PA-2
**Ceresville**—*pop pl* MD-2
Ceres-Whitmore Park—*park* CA-9
Cereus Tank—*reservoir* AZ-5
*Cereza Canyon* NM-5
Cereza Mesa—*summit* NM-5
Cerine Creek—*stream* OR-9
Cerini Ranch (Site)—*locale* NV-8
*Cerion Key* FL-3
Cerise Gulch—*valley* CO-8
*Cerisy* FM-9
*Cerisy Island* FM-9
Cerlew Ditch—*canal* WY-8
Cermak Bldg—*hist pl* OH-6
Cermak Park—*park* IL-6
**Cerny Heights (subdivision)**—*pop pl* FL-3
Cerny Ranch—*locale* NE-7
*Cerol Isles* FL-3
Cerra de las Cabras—*summit* NM-5
**Cerrillos**—*pop pl* NM-5
**Cerrillos**—*pop pl* (2) PR-3
Cerrillos (Barrio)—*fmr MCD* PR-3
Cerrillos del Coyote—*summit* NM-5
Cerrillos Hills—*summit* NM-5
**Cerrillos (Los Cerrillos)**—*pop pl* NM-5
Cerrillos Rsvr—*reservoir* NM-5
*Cerrilo Creek* CA-9
Cerriot Negro—*summit* NM-5
Cerrita Portillo—*summit* NM-5
*Cerritas de los Linderos* AZ-5
Cerrito Amarillo—*summit* NM-5
Cerrito Arizona—*summit* NM-5
Cerrito Artesian Well—*well* TX-5
Cerrito Blanco—*ridge* NM-5
Cerrito Blanco Tank—*reservoir* TX-5
Cerrito Chato—*summit* NM-5
Cerrito Cochino—*summit* NM-5
Cerrito Colorado—*locale* NM-5
Cerrito Colorado—*summit* (2) NM-5
Cerrito Comadre—*summit* NM-5
Cerrito Creek—*stream* CA-9
Cerrito Creek—*stream* TX-5
Cerrito de la Angostura—*ridge* AZ-5
Cerrito de la Baca—*summit* NM-5
Cerrito de la Ventana—*ridge* NM-5
Cerrito del Chibato—*summit* NM-5
Cerrito del Espia—*summit* NM-5
Cerrito del Llano—*summit* NM-5
Cerrito de los Muertos—*summit* NM-5
Cerrito del Padre—*summit* NM-5
Cerrito del Relampago—*summit* NM-5
Cerrito Dormilon—*summit* NM-5
Cerrito Gato—*summit* NM-5
Cerrito Largo—*summit* NM-5
Cerrito Negro—*summit* (3) NM-5
Cerrito Ojo Frio—*summit* NM-5
Cerrito Pelado—*summit* NM-5
Cerrito Pelon—*summit* NM-5
Cerrito Picacho—*summit* NM-5
Cerrito Prieto—*summit* (2) TX-5
Cerrito Redondo—*summit* NM-5
**Cerritos**—*pop pl* NM-5
Cerritos Blancos—*summit* TX-5
Cerritos Canal—*canal* CO-8
Cerritos Channel—*channel* CA-9
Cerritos Coll—*school* CA-9
Cerritos Colorados—*summit* NM-5
**Cerritos (Dairy Valley)**—*pop pl* CA-9
Cerritos de Jaspe—*ridge* NM-5
Cerritos De Jaspe—*ridge* NM-5
Cerritos de La Jolla de Santa Rosa—*summit* NM-5
Cerritos Margaritas—*summit* NM-5
Cerritos No 2—*canal* NM-5
Cerritos Sch—*school* (2) CA-9
Cerritos Tank—*reservoir* NM-5
Cerritos Tank—*reservoir* (2) TX-5
Cerritos Windmill—*locale* (2) TX-5
Cerrito Viejo—*summit* NM-5
Cerrito Vista Park—*park* CA-9
Cerrito Yelo—*summit* NM-5
*Cerro* CO-8
Cerro—*locale* CA-9
**Cerro**—*pop pl* NM-5
Cerro Aguila—*summit* NM-5
Cerro Alesna—*summit* (2) NM-5
Cerro Alesna Tanks—*reservoir* NM-5
Cerro Algarrobo—*summit* PR-3
Cerro Algodon—*summit* PR-3
Cerro Almirante—*summit* PR-3
Cerro Alto—*summit* (2) NM-5
Cerro Alto—*summit* PR-3
Cerro Alto Campground—*locale* CA-9
Cerro Alto Mtn—*summit* TX-5
Cerro Amargura—*summit* PR-3
Cerro Americano—*summit* NM-5
Cerro Amoldadero—*summit* PR-3
Cerro Augustinillo—*summit* PR-3
Cerro Avispa—*summit* PR-3
Cerro Azui—*summit* NM-5
Cerro Balcon—*summit* PR-3
Cerro Bandero—*summit* NM-5
Cerro Bartolo—*summit* PR-3
Cerro Blanco—*summit* (4) NM-5
Cerro Blanco Trail—*trail* NM-5
Cerro Boca del Infierno—*summit* PR-3
*Cerro Boletas* NM-5
Cerro Bonanza—*summit* NM-5
Cerro Bone—*summit* PR-3
Cerro Bravo—*summit* PR-3
Cerro Brillante—*summit* NM-5
Cerro Brujos—*summit* NM-5
Cerro Buena Vista—*summit* PR-3
Cerro Camacho—*summit* PR-3
Cerro Canal—*canal* NM-5
Cerro Candelero—*summit* PR-3
Cerro Candiles—*summit* PR-3
Cerro Canta Gallo—*summit* PR-3
Cerro Cantina—*summit* NM-5
Cerro Capron—*summit* PR-3
Cerro Caracas—*summit* PR-3
Cerro Cariblanco—*summit* PR-3
Cerro Cascajillo—*summit* PR-3
*Cerro Castelon* TX-5
*Cerro Castillon* TX-5
*Cerro Castolon* TX-5
Cerro Castrado—*ridge* NM-5
Cerro Cayures—*summit* PR-3
Cerro Cedro—*summit* PR-3
Cerro Cerrote—*summit* PR-3
Cerro Chafo—*summit* NM-5
Cerro Chamisa Losa—*summit* NM-5
Cerro Charcas—*summit* PR-3
Cerro Chatito—*summit* NM-5
Cerro Chato—*summit* (3) NM-5
Cerro Chavez—*summit* NM-5
Cerro Chiflo—*summit* NM-5
Cerro Chivato—*summit* NM-5
Cerro Cibuco—*summit* PR-3
Cerro Cochino—*summit* NM-5
Cerro Collores—*summit* PR-3
Cerro Colorada—*summit* NM-5
*Cerro Colorado* NM-5
Cerro Colorado—*summit* (12) NM-5
Cerro Colorado Mine—*mine* AZ-5
*Cerro Colorado Mtn* NM-5
Cerro Colorado Tank—*reservoir* AZ-5
Cerro Colorado Tank—*reservoir* NM-5
Cerro Colorado Wash—*stream* AZ-5
Cerro Columbo—*summit* NM-5
Cerro Conde Avila—*summit* PR-3
Cerro Conejo—*summit* NM-5
**Cerro Corazon**—*pop pl* PR-3
Cerro Corazon—*summit* PR-3
Cerro Cornelia—*summit* PR-3
Cerro Corozal—*summit* PR-3
Cerro Coso Junior Coll—*school* CA-9
Cerro Cuate—*summit* (2) NM-5
Cerro Curet—*summit* PR-3
Cerro Daguey—*summit* PR-3
Cerro de Abra—*ridge* PR-3
Cerro de Arriba—*summit* NM-5
Cerro de Corazon—*summit* NM-5
Cerro de Escobas—*summit* NM-5
Cerro de Espia—*summit* NM-5
*Cerro de Fresnal* AZ-5
Cerro de Guadalupe—*summit* NM-5
Cerro De Jacobo—*summit* NM-5
*Cerro de Jaralito* AZ-5
Cerro Del, Arroyo—*stream* CA-9
Cerro de la Bandera—*summit* PR-3
Cerro del Abrevadero—*summit* NM-5
Cerro de la Candelaria—*summit* PR-3
Cerro de la Celosa—*summit* NM-5
Cerro de la Cruz—*summit* (4) NM-5
Cerro de la Garita—*summit* NM-5
Cerro Del Aire—*summit* NM-5
Cerro de la Mesa—*ridge* PR-3
Cerro Del Amole—*summit* NM-5
Cerro De La Olla—*summit* NM-5
Cerro de la Rana—*summit* NM-5
Cerro de las Avispas—*summit* PR-3
Cerro de las Cuevas—*summit* PR-3
Cerro de las Marquenas—*summit* NM-5
Cerro de Las Mulas—*summit* PR-3
Cerro de las Tijeras—*summit* NM-5
Cerro de las Velas—*summit* PR-3
Cerro de la Tabla—*summit* PR-3
Cerro del Cabro—*summit* PR-3
Cerro del Chicharo—*summit* PR-3
Cerro del Conejo—*summit* NM-5
Cerro del Diablo—*summit* PR-3
Cerro del Durazno—*summit* NM-5
Cerro del Faro—*summit* PR-3
Cerro del Grant—*summit* NM-5
Cerro del Indio—*summit* NM-5
Cerro del Indio—*summit* PR-3
Cerro Del Medio—*summit* (2) NM-5
Cerro del Miguel Antonio—*summit* NM-5
Cerro del Muerto—*summit* PR-3
Cerro del Ojo de las Yeguas—*summit* NM-5
Cerro del Ojo Frio—*summit* NM-5
Cerro del Oro—*summit* NM-5
Cerro Del Oro—*summit* NM-5
Cerro de los Arboles—*summit* NM-5
Cerro de los Bonelli—*summit* PR-3
Cerro de los Cielos—*summit* PR-3
Cerro del Oso—*summit* NM-5
Cerro de los Taoses—*summit* NM-5
Cerro del Pino—*summit* NM-5
*Cerro del Tecolote* AZ-5
*Cerro del Temporal* AZ-5
Cerro del Zopilote—*summit* CO-8
Cerro de Nuestra Madre—*summit* PR-3
Cerro de Nuestra Senora—*summit* NM-5
Cerro de Pedro Miguel—*summit* NM-5
Cerro de Punta—*summit* PR-3
Cerro de Santa Clara—*summit* NM-5
Cerro De Santa Rosa—*summit* NM-5
*Cerro de Tacca* AZ-5
Cerro de Vergara—*summit* PR-3
Cerro Ditch No 1—*canal* CO-8
Cerro Ditch No 2—*canal* CO-8
Cerro Dona Juana—*summit* PR-3
Cerro Don Quino—*summit* PR-3
Cerro Drain—*canal* NM-5
Cerro El Alto—*summit* PR-3
Cerro El Asomante—*summit* PR-3
Cerro El Bolo—*summit* PR-3
Cerro El Buey—*summit* PR-3
Cerro El Faro—*summit* PR-3
Cerro El Gato—*summit* PR-3
Cerro El Gigante—*summit* PR-3
Cerro El Indio—*summit* PR-3
Cerro El Malo—*summit* PR-3
Cerro El Peligro—*summit* PR-3
Cerro El Pico—*summit* PR-3
Cerro El Retiro—*summit* PR-3
Cerro El Sombrero—*summit* PR-3
Cerro Encierro—*summit* NM-5
Cerro Encinoso—*summit* NM-5
Cerro ermitano—*summit* NM-5
Cerro Farallon—*summit* PR-3
Cerro Flora—*summit* NM-5
Cerro Franchon—*summit* PR-3
Cerro Frio—*summit* NM-5
Cerro Garau—*summit* PR-3
Cerro Gardo Ch—*church* TN-4
Cerro Garzas—*summit* PR-3
*Cerro Gato* NM-5
Cerro Gatos—*summit* NM-5
Cerro Goden—*summit* PR-3
*Cerro Gordo* IN-6
Cerrogordo—*locale* FL-3
Cerro Gordo—*locale* MN-6
**Cerrogordo**—*pop pl* AR-4
**Cerro Gordo**—*pop pl* IL-6
**Cerro Gordo**—*pop pl* NC-3
**Cerrogordo**—*pop pl* OK-5
**Cerro Gordo**—*pop pl* TN-4
**Cerro Gordo**—*pop pl* (2) PR-3
Cerro Gordo—*post sta* PR-3
Cerro Gordo—*summit* NM-5
Cerro Gordo—*summit* PR-3
Cerro Gordo (Barrio)—*fmr MCD* (5) PR-3
Cerro Gordo County Home—*building* IA-7
Cerro Gordo Elem Sch—*school* NC-3
Cerro Gordo Landing—*locale* MS-4
Cerro Gordo Mine—*mine* CA-9
Cerro Gordo Peak—*summit* CA-9
Cerro Gordo Sch—*school* NC-3
Cerro Gordo Sch—*school* TN-4
Cerro Gordo Spring—*spring* CA-9
Cerro Gordo Tank—*reservoir* AZ-5
Cerro Gordo (Township of)—*civ div* IL-6
Cerro Gordo (Township of)—*fmr MCD* NC-3
**Cerro Gordo (Township of)**—*pop pl* IL-6
**Cerro Gordo (Township of)**—*pop pl* MN-6
Cerro Gozos—*summit* PR-3
Cerro Grande—*locale* ID-8
Cerro Grande—*summit* NM-5
Cerro Gregorio—*summit* PR-3
Cerro Gritadero—*summit* PR-3
Cerro Guaniquilla—*summit* PR-3
Cerro Guarico—*summit* PR-3
Cerro Herencia—*summit* PR-3
Cerro Honore—*summit* PR-3
Cerro Hueco—*summit* NM-5
Cerro Indio—*summit* PR-3
Cerro Jarocito—*summit* NM-5
Cerro Jobo Dulce—*summit* PR-3
Cerro La Chorrera—*summit* PR-3
Cerro La Coroza—*summit* PR-3
Cerro la Cuchilla—*summit* PR-3
Cerro La Guanica—*summit* PR-3
Cerro La Guasima—*summit* PR-3
Cerro La Jara—*summit* (2) NM-5
Cerro Lajara—*summit* PR-3
Cerro Lambedora—*summit* PR-3
Cerro La Mira—*summit* PR-3
Cerro La Monteria—*summit* PR-3
Cerro la Mula—*summit* NM-5
Cerro La Pandura—*summit* PR-3
Cerro La Parra—*summit* PR-3
Cerro La Pena—*summit* PR-3
Cerro La Quinta—*summit* PR-3
Cerro La Santa—*summit* PR-3
Cerro La Silla—*summit* PR-3
Cerro Las Pinas—*summit* PR-3
Cerro La Tiza—*summit* PR-3
Cerro La Torre—*summit* PR-3
Cerro La Torrecilla—*summit* PR-3
Cerro La Tuna—*summit* PR-3
Cerro Lazo—*summit* PR-3
Cerro Leclerc—*summit* PR-3
Cerro Legua—*cape* NM-5
Cerro Leoncilla—*summit* PR-3
Cerro Leonides—*summit* NM-5
Cerro Limones—*summit* PR-3
Cerro Lloroso—*summit* PR-3
Cerro Lobo—*summit* NM-5
Cerro Los Negrones—*summit* PR-3
Cerro Lucero—*summit* PR-3
Cerro Mabu—*summit* PR-3
Cerro Magoyo—*summit* PR-3
Cerro Magueyes—*summit* PR-3
Cerro Mala Pascua—*summit* PR-3
Cerro Malo—*summit* PR-3
Cerro Malojillo—*summit* PR-3
Cerro Maravillas—*summit* PR-3
Cerro Mariquita—*summit* PR-3
Cerro Marquesa—*summit* PR-3
Cerro Marquez—*summit* NM-5
Cerro Martineau—*summit* PR-3
Cerro Martinica—*summit* PR-3
Cerro Mata de Platano—*summit* PR-3
Cerro Matias Jalobre—*summit* PR-3
Cerro Medina—*summit* PR-3
Cerro Mercado—*summit* PR-3
Cerro Micho—*summit* NM-5
Cerro Mime—*summit* PR-3
Cerro Miraflores—*summit* PR-3
Cerro Modesto—*summit* PR-3
Cerro Mojino—*summit* NM-5
Cerro Montalva—*summit* PR-3
*Cerro Montosa* AZ-5
Cerro Montoso—*summit* (5) NM-5
Cerro Morales—*summit* PR-3
Cerro Morrillo—*summit* PR-3
Cerro Mula—*summit* PR-3
*Cerro Negro* AZ-5
Cerro Negro—*summit* CO-8
Cerro Negro—*summit* (6) NM-5
Cerro Noroeste Camp—*locale* CA-9
Cerro Novillo—*summit* PR-3
Cerro Olla—*summit* NM-5
Cerro Orqueta—*summit* NM-5
Cerro Ortiz—*summit* NM-5
Cerro Osha—*summit* NM-5
Cerro Palma—*summit* PR-3
Cerro Palo de Cafe—*summit* PR-3
Cerro Palomas—*summit* PR-3
Cerro Palo Seco—*summit* PR-3
Cerro Parido—*summit* NM-5
Cerro Pavo—*summit* NM-5
Cerro Pedernal—*summit* NM-5
Cerro Pelado—*summit* NM-5
Cerro Pelao—*summit* PR-3
Cerro Pelon—*summit* (10) NM-5
Cerro Pelota—*summit* PR-3
Cerro Petronila—*summit* PR-3
Cerro Picacho—*summit* (2) NM-5
Cerro Pichon—*summit* PR-3
Cerro Piedra Gorda—*summit* PR-3
Cerro Piedra Hueca—*summit* PR-3
Cerro Piedrita—*summit* NM-5
Cerro Pinas—*summit* PR-3
Cerro Pino—*summit* NM-5
Cerro Pinon—*summit* (3) NM-5
Cerro Pio—*summit* PR-3
Cerro Pio Juan—*summit* PR-3
Cerro Pitahaya—*summit* PR-3
Cerro Plana—*summit* PR-3
Cerro Planada—*summit* PR-3
Cerro Plan Bonito—*summit* PR-3
Cerro Playuela—*summit* PR-3
Cerro Pomo—*summit* (2) NM-5
Cerro Presidio—*summit* PR-3
Cerro Prieto—*summit* NM-5
Cerro Prieto—*summit* PR-3
Cerro Prieto Wash—*stream* AZ-5
Cerro Prieto Windmill—*locale* NM-5
Cerro Pulguillas—*summit* PR-3
Cerro Puntiagudo—*summit* NM-5
Cerro Purron—*summit* PR-3
Cerro Quemado—*summit* PR-3
Cerro Quiros—*summit* PR-3
Cerro Redondo—*summit* NM-5
Cerro Rendija—*summit* NM-5
Cerro Respaldo—*summit* PR-3
Cerro Rito—*summit* NM-5
*Cerro Romaldo* CA-9
Cerro Roman—*summit* NM-5
*Cerro Romauldo* CA-9
Cerro Roncador—*summit* PR-3
Cerro Rosa—*summit* PR-3
Cerro Rubio—*summit* (2) NM-5
Cerro Salado—*summit* NM-5
Cerro Saliente—*summit* PR-3
Cerro San Jose—*summit* PR-3
Cerro San Patricio—*ridge* NM-5
Cerro Santa Ana—*summit* PR-3
Cerro Santa Barbara—*summit* PR-3
Cerro Santa Elena—*summit* PR-3
Cerro Santa Rosa—*summit* (2) NM-5
Cerro Santo Domingo—*summit* PR-3
Cerros Colorado—*area* NM-5
Cerros Colorados—*summit* NM-5
Cerros de Amado—*summit* NM-5
Cerros De Guadalupe—*other* NM-5
Cerros de Higuillar—*other* PR-3
Cerros del Abrigo—*summit* (2) NM-5
Cerros De Las Mujeres—*other* NM-5
Cerros de Los Posos—*ridge* (2) NM-5
*Cerros de Santa Rosa* AZ-5
Cerros de Santini—*range* PR-3
Cerros de Taos Ranch—*locale* NM-5
Cerros de Trasquilar—*summit* (2) NM-5
Cerro Seguro—*summit* NM-5
Cerros Negros—*ridge* NM-5
Cerro Sonadora—*summit* PR-3
Cerros Oso—*summit* NM-5
Cerrososo Camp—*locale* NM-5
Cerrososo Canyon—*valley* NM-5
Cerrososo Creek—*stream* NM-5
Cerro Summit—*summit* CO-8
Cerro Taita—*summit* PR-3
Cerro Tank—*reservoir* AZ-5
Cerro Tank—*reservoir* NM-5
Cerrote (Barrio)—*fmr MCD* PR-3
*Cerro Tecolote* NM-5
*Cerro Tecolote Peak* NM-5
Cerrote de Penuelas—*summit* PR-3
Cerro Tejano—*summit* NM-5
Cerro Tinaja—*summit* NM-5
Cerro Tirano—*summit* PR-3
Cerro Toledo—*summit* (2) NM-5
Cerro Toro—*summit* PR-3
Cerro Trigo Tank—*reservoir* AZ-5
**Cerro Tumbado**—*pop pl* PR-3
Cerro Tumbado—*summit* PR-3
Cerro Vacio—*summit* NM-5
Cerro Vadi—*summit* PR-3
Cerro Valdez—*cliff* NM-5
Cerro Valladares—*summit* PR-3
Cerro Vaquina—*summit* PR-3
Cerro Vargas—*summit* PR-3
Cerro Venada—*summit* NM-5
Cerro Venado—*summit* NM-5
Cerro Verde—*summit* NM-5
Cerro Verdun—*summit* PR-3
Cerro Vertero—*summit* PR-3
Cerro Viento Caliente—*summit* PR-3
Cerro Vieques—*summit* PR-3
Cerro Vigia—*summit* PR-3
**Cerro Villa Heights**—*pop pl* CA-9
Cerro Vista—*summit* NM-5
Cerro Vista Alegre—*summit* PR-3
Cerro Viviana—*summit* PR-3
Cerro Well No 1—*well* NM-5
Cerro Well No 2—*well* NM-5
Cerro Yaitini—*summit* PR-3
Cerro Yaurel—*summit* PR-3
*Cerry Point* WA-9
Cerser Swamp—*swamp* FL-3
C Erstolen Ranch—*locale* ND-7
Certain Draw Point—*cape* CT-1
Certain Gap—*gap* AL-4
Certificado Tank—*reservoir* TX-5
Certificad Windmill—*locale* TX-5
Certon Creek—*stream* MI-6
**Cerulean**—*pop pl* KY-4
Cerulean (corporate name Cerulean Springs)—*inactive* KY-4
Cerulean Knob—*summit* TN-4
*Cerulean Lake* OR-9
Cerulean Lake—*lake* MT-8
Cerulean Ridge—*ridge* MT-8
*Cerulean Springs* KY-4
Cerulean Springs (CCD)—*cens area* KY-4
Cerulean Springs (corporate name for Cerulean)—*inactive* KY-4
Cerutti Well—*well* NV-8
Cervada, Canada —*valley* CA-9
*Cervantis Well* AZ-5
Cerveny JHS—*school* MI-6
Cervi Ranch—*locale* CO-8
Cervus Lake—*lake* OR-9
*Cerwercerna River* SD-7
Cesar Lake—*lake* MN-6
Cesela Park—*park* AZ-5
C E Sellers Dam—*dam* AL-4
C E Sellers Lake—*reservoir* AL-4
C E Sellers Number 2 Dam—*dam* AL-4
C E Sellers Number 3 Dam—*dam* AL-4
C E Sellers Number 4 Dam—*dam* AL-4
Cesinger Cem—*cemetery* TX-5
Cesko Slovensky Cem—*cemetery* KS-7
*Ceso* TX-5
**Cespedes**—*pop pl* (2) PR-3
Cessions Landing—*locale* MS-4
Cessions Revetment—*levee* MS-4
Cessions Towhead—*island* AR-4
Cessions Towhead Chute—*gut* AR-4
Cessna—*locale* KS-7
**Cessna**—*pop pl* PA-2
Cessna Aircraft Airp—*airport* KS-7
*Cessna Aircraft Field* KS-7
Cessna Cem—*cemetery* KY-4
Cessna Cem—*cemetery* MS-4
Cessna Cem—*cemetery* OH-6
Cessna Creek—*stream* OH-6
Cessna Ditch—*canal* IN-6
Cessna Ditch—*canal* OH-6
Cessna Elem Sch—*school* KS-7
*Cessna Landing Field* KS-7
Cessna Park—*park* KS-7
Cessna Run—*stream* PA-2
Cessna Sch (abandoned)—*school* PA-2
**Cessna (Township of)**—*pop pl* OH-6
Cessons Mill—*locale* NC-3
*Cestochowa* TX-5
*Cestohawa* TX-5
**Cestohowa**—*pop pl* TX-5
**Cestohowa (Czestochowa)**—*pop pl* TX-5
Cestos—*locale* OK-5
Cetahoma Landing—*locale* AL-4
*Ceteal Lustee Creek* AL-4
Cetenary Ch—*church* VA-3
**Cetronia**—*pop pl* PA-2
Cetronia Elem Sch—*school* PA-2
Cetti Bay—*bay* GU-9
Cetti Bay—*hist pl* GU-9
Cetti River—*stream* GU-9
*Cetuet* MA-1
*Cetuet River* MA-1
Ceva Lake—*reservoir* NJ-2
Ceva Lake Dam—*dam* NJ-2
C E Weldon Library—*building* TN-4
C E Wise Ranch—*locale* NE-7
*Ceylon* IN-6
Ceylon—*locale* GA-3
**Ceylon**—*pop pl* IN-6
**Ceylon**—*pop pl* MN-6
**Ceylon**—*pop pl* OH-6
**Ceylon**—*pop pl* PA-2
Ceylon Cem—*cemetery* GA-3
**Ceylon Junction**—*pop pl* OH-6
Ceylon Lagoon—*lake* WI-6
Ceylon State Wildlife Mngmt Areas—*park* MN-6
Ceynar Ranch—*locale* ND-7
Ceynowa Lake—*lake* MN-6
Cezar Cem—*cemetery* LA-4
*Cezaro Creek* IN-6
CF Adams HS—*school* WA-9
CF Canyon—*valley* AZ-5
CFC Mine—*mine* CO-8
C F Greene Lake Dam—*dam* MS-4
C F Green Lake—*reservoir* AL-4
C F Green Lake Dam—*dam* AL-4
CFJ Memorial Bridge—*bridge* NY-2
C F Johnson Sch—*school* NY-2
C F Ranch—*locale* NM-5
C F Smith Woods—*woods* IL-6
C F Spring—*spring* NM-5
C F Stone Estate Dam—*dam* NC-3
C F Stone Estate Lake—*reservoir* NC-3
CF Tank—*reservoir* (2) AZ-5
*C F Vigor High School* AL-4
C-G Cutoff—*canal* OR-9
C G Lateral—*canal* TX-5
C G Melgs Bridge—*bridge* FL-3
C G Thomas Lake Dam—*dam* MS-4
C G W Station—*locale* MN-6
*Chabanakongkomom Pond* MA-1
*Chabanakongkomum* MA-1
*Chab Chab* FM-9
Chabeneau Lake—*lake* MI-6
**Chable (historical)**—*pop pl* TN-4
Chable Post Office (historical)—*building* TN-4
Chablin Hill—*summit* ME-1
Chabot, Lake—*reservoir* (2) CA-9
Chabot Canal—*canal* CA-9
Chabot Coll—*school* CA-9
Chabot Observatory—*building* CA-9
Chabot Ranch—*locale* WY-8
Chabot Regional Park—*park* CA-9
Chabots Boys Ranch—*locale* CA-9
Chabot Sch—*school* (2) CA-9
**Chabot Terrace**—*pop pl* CA-9
Cha Butte—*summit* UT-8
**Chacahoula**—*pop pl* LA-4
Chacahoula Bayou—*stream* (2) LA-4
Chacahoula Oil and Gas Field—*oilfield* LA-4
Chacala Pond—*lake* FL-3
Chacaloochee Bay—*bay* AL-4
*Chacandepeco INlet* NC-3
Cha Canyon—*valley* UT-8
*Chacato* FL-3
Chace—*locale* NY-2
Chace, A. B., Rowhouses—*hist pl* MA-1
Chace Cem—*cemetery* (2) MA-1
*Chace Lake* ID-8
Chace Mills—*hist pl* MA-1
Chace Ranch—*locale* WY-8
Chaces Island—*island* MA-1
Chace Street Sch—*school* MA-1
Chace Valley—*valley* CA-9
*Chacha* MH-9
Chacha—*slope* MH-9
*Chachacust Neck* RI-1
Chachao, Mount—*summit* GU-9
Chache Creek Mission—*church* OK-5
*Chackapaucasset Neck* RI-1
*Chackawlatoher River* MS-4
**Chackbay (Chegby)**—*pop pl* LA-4
**Chaco**—*pop pl* FL-3
Chaco Canyon—*valley* NM-5
Chaco Canyon Natl Monmt—*park* NM-5
Chaco Canyon Natl Monument—*park* NM-5
Chaco Culture Natl Historical Park—*hist pl* NM-5
Chaco Culture Natl Historic Site—*park* NM-5
Chaco Lake—*lake* MN-6
Chaco Mesa—*summit* NM-5
**Chacon**—*pop pl* NM-5
Chacon Arroyo—*stream* NM-5
Chacon Camp—*locale* NM-5
Chacon Canyon—*valley* NM-5
Chacon Corral—*other* NM-5
*Chacon Creek* TX-5
Chacon Creek—*stream* (3) TX-5
Chacon Park—*flat* NM-5
Chacon Rsvr—*reservoir* TX-5
Chacon Windmill—*locale* TX-5
Chaco River—*stream* NM-5
Chaco RR Station—*locale* FL-3
Chaco Slough—*stream* TX-5
Chacowalla Water Hole—*lake* TX-5
Chaco Wash—*stream* NM-5
**Chacra**—*pop pl* CO-8
Chacra Mesa—*bench* NM-5
Cha Creek—*stream* UT-8
*Chactahatchee River* AL-4
*Chactahatchee River* MS-4
*Chactahatche River* AL-4
*Chactahatche River* MS-4
*Chactaw Hatchee* FL-3
Chactimahan, Bayou—*stream* LA-4
Chacuaco Canyon—*valley* CO-8
Chacuaco Creek—*stream* CO-8
Chad—*locale* KY-4
Chadakoin River—*stream* NY-2

Chada Lake—lake WI-6
Chadas Lake WI-6
Chadborn—locale MT-8
Chadborne Cem—cemetery ME-1
**Chadbourn**—pop pl NC-3
Chadbourn Branch—stream KY-4
Chadbourn Cem—cemetery NC-3
Chadbourne—locale CA-9
Chadbourne Cem—cemetery ME-1
Chadbourne Gulch—valley CA-9
Chadbourn Elem Sch—school NC-3
Chadbourne Ranch—locale MT-8
Chadbourne Ranch—locale WA-9
Chadbourne Sch—school (2) CA-9
Chadbourne Slough—gut CA-9
Chadbourn JHS—school NC-3
Chadbourn (Township of)—fmr MCD NC-3
Chad Branch—stream KY-4
Chadd Creek—stream CA-9
Chadderdon State Wildlife Mngmt Area—park MN-6
Chadd House—building PA-2
Chaddock, J. B., House—hist pl TX-5
Chaddock Boys Sch—school IL-6
Chadd Prairie—flat CA-9
Chaddsford CO-8
**Chadds Ford**—pop pl PA-2
Chadds Ford Hist Dist—hist pl PA-2
Chadds Ford Junction—locale PA-2
Chadds Peak Camp and Ski School (ski area)—locale PA-2
Chaddwick Lake—lake NY-2
Chad House—hist pl PA-2
Chadick Park—park OK-5
Chad Lake—lake MN-6
Chadlish KS-7
Chadman Spring—spring UT-8
Chador Mobile Home Park—locale AZ-5
Chadric Creek—stream NC-3
**Chadron**—pop pl NE-7
Chadron Creek—stream NE-7
Chadron Municipal Airp—airport NE-7
Chadron Rsvr—reservoir NE-7
Chadron State Coll—school NE-7
Chadron State Park—park NE-7
Chads Branch—stream KY-4
Chadsey HS—school MI-6
Chads Ford PA-2
Chad Spring—spring ID-8
**Chadswyck**—pop pl VA-3
Chads Wyck—uninc pl VA-3
**Chadville**—pop pl PA-2
Chadvin Bayou LA-4
Chadwell Cem—cemetery (4) TN-4
Chadwell Cem—cemetery VA-3
Chadwell Gap—gap KY-4
Chadwell Gap—gap VA-3
Chadwell Gap Trail—trail VA-3
**Chadwell (historical)**—pop pl OR-9
Chadwell Sch—school KY-4
Chadwell Sch—school OR-9
Chadwell Sch—school TN-4
Chadwick—hist pl IN-6
Chadwick—locale ND-7
**Chadwick**—pop pl IL-6
**Chadwick**—pop pl MO-7
**Chadwick**—pop pl NJ-2
**Chadwick**—pop pl NC-3
Chadwick—uninc pl NC-3
Chadwick, George, House—hist pl MS-4
Chadwick, Loren L., Cottages—hist pl MN-6
Chadwick Acres—locale NC-3
**Chadwick Acres (subdivision)**—pop pl NC-3
Chadwick Bay—bay NC-3
Chadwick Bayou—bay FL-3
**Chadwick Beach**—pop pl NJ-2
Chadwick Beach Island—island NJ-2
Chadwick-Brittan House—hist pl MA-1
Chadwick Brook—stream MA-1
Chadwick Canyon—valley OR-9
Chadwick Cem TN-4
Chadwick Cem—cemetery NC-3
Chadwick Cem—cemetery TN-4
Chadwick Ch—church NC-3
Chadwick Corners—locale MI-6
Chadwick Corners—locale OH-6
Chadwick Creek—stream AR-4
Chadwick Creek—stream (2) KY-4
Chadwick Creek—stream MI-6
Chadwick Creek—stream NC-3
Chadwick Creek—stream WA-9
Chadwick Creek Ch—church KY-4
Chadwick Ditch—canal IN-6
Chadwick Ditch No 1—canal WY-8
Chadwick Ditch No 5—canal WY-8
Chadwick Draft—valley PA-2
Chadwick Farmhouse—hist pl NY-2
Chadwick Hill—summit WA-9
Chadwick Hill Cem—cemetery ME-1
Chadwick (historical)—locale AL-4
Chadwick Hollow—valley TN-4
Chadwick Hollow—valley WI-6
Chadwick Landing (historical)—locale TN-4
**Chadwick Manor**—pop pl MD-2
Chadwick Point—cape NC-3
Chadwick Pond—reservoir MA-1
Chadwick Pond Dam—dam MA-1
Chadwick Post Office (historical)—building AL-4
Chadwick Ranch—locale TX-5
Chadwick Reservoir No 1—canal WY-8
Chadwick Reservoir No 2—canal WY-8
Chadwick Reservoir No 3—canal WY-8
Chadwicks NJ-2
**Chadwicks**—pop pl NY-2
Chadwicks Beach NJ-2
Chadwick Sch—school CA-9
Chadwick Sch—school IL-6
Chadwick Sch—school MI-6
Chadwick Sch—school SD-7
**Chadwicks Folly**—pop pl MA-1
Chadwicks Pond MA-1
**Chadwick Square (subdivision)**—pop pl MA-1
Chadwick Township—civil MO-7
Cha-ez-kia AZ-5
Cha-ez-kla Butte AZ-5
Cha-ez-kla Rock AZ-5
Chafee Sch—school CT-1
Chaffe, Bayou—stream LA-4
Chaffee—locale CA-9
Chaffee—locale PA-2
Chaffee—locale WA-9
Chaffee—locale WV-2
**Chaffee**—pop pl MO-7
**Chaffee**—pop pl NY-2
**Chaffee**—pop pl ND-7
Chaffee, Hezekiah, House—hist pl CT-1
Chaffee, Island—island CA-9
Chaffee, Lake—reservoir CT-1
Chaffee Brook—stream ME-1
Chaffee Brook—stream MA-1
Chaffee Corners—locale PA-2
Chaffee County Courthouse and Jail Buildings—hist pl CO-8
Chaffee County Poor Farm—hist pl CO-8
Chaffee Creek—stream NY-2
Chaffee Creek—stream WI-6
Chaffee Creek State Fishery Area—locale WI-6
Chaffee Field Parade Ground—locale AZ-5
Chaffee Gulch—valley CO-8
Chaffee Gulch—valley WY-8
Chaffee Hosp—hospital NY-2
Chaffee Mtn—summit VT-1
Chaffee Park—park CO-8
Chaffee Park Shop Ctr—other CO-8
Chaffee Ranch—locale SD-7
Chaffee Run—stream (3) PA-2
Chaffees PA-2
Chaffee Sch—school AL-4
Chaffee Sch—school KS-7
Chaffee Sch—school MA-1
Chaffee Sch (abandoned)—school PA-2
**Chaffee Village**—pop pl TX-5
**Chaffeeville**—pop pl CT-1
Chaffee Well—well NM-5
Chaffer Ravine—valley MN-6
Chaffer Canyon—valley OR-9
**Chaffey**—pop pl WI-6
Chaffey HS—school CA-9
Chaffey Run—stream WV-2
Chaffey Sch—school WI-6
Chaffey Trail—trail WV-2
Chaffey Union Junior Coll—school CA-9
Chaffie Creek—stream AR-4
Chaffin MA-1
**Chaffin**—pop pl MA-1
Chaffin Bar UT-8
Chaffin Bluff—cliff VA-3
Chaffin Branch—stream AR-4
Chaffin Branch—stream (2) KY-4
Chaffin Branch—stream MS-4
Chaffin Branch—stream TN-4
Chaffin Branch—stream TX-5
Chaffin Butte—summit MT-8
Chaffin Cabin (inundated)—building UT-8
Chaffin Cem—cemetery KY-4
Chaffin Cem—cemetery (3) TN-4
Chaffin Cem—cemetery TX-5
Chaffin Cem—cemetery WV-2
Chaffinch Island—island CT-1
Chaffin Creek—stream MT-8
Chaffin Creek—stream TX-5
Chaffin Crossing—locale TX-5
Chaffin Hollow—valley TN-4
Chaffin JHS—school AR-4
Chaffin Lake—lake MT-8
Chaffin Lakes MT-8
Chaffin Place—locale TX-5
Chaffin Pond—lake ME-1
Chaffin Pond—lake MA-1
Chaffin Pond Dam—dam MA-1
Chaffin Ranch—locale UT-8
Chaffin Rsvr—reservoir MA-1
Chaffins MA-1
Chaffins Brook—stream MA-1
Chaffins Pond MA-1
Chaffin Spring—spring UT-8
**Chaffinville**—pop pl MA-1
Chaff Sch—school MA-1
Chafin Branch—stream WV-2
Chafin Cem—cemetery GA-3
Chafin Cem—cemetery (2) VA-3
Chafin Cem—cemetery WV-2
Chafin Memorial Ch—church IN-6
Chafin's Bluff VA-3
Chafins Cem—cemetery KY-4
Chafin Well—well AZ-5
Chaflin Sch—school MA-1
Chagame—area GU-9
Chagame River—stream GU-9
**Chagamin Lago**—pop pl GU-9
Chager Spring—spring OK-5
Chagit Vo—lake AZ-5
Chagiy—island FM-9
Chagoopa Creek—stream CA-9
Chagoopa Falls—falls CA-9
Chagoopa Plateau—plain CA-9
**Chagrin Falls**—pop pl (2) OH-6
Chagrin Falls Park—park OH-6
Chagrin Falls Township Hall—hist pl OH-6
Chagrin Falls (Township of)—civ div OH-6
Chagrin Falls Triangle Park Commercial District—hist pl OH-6
Chagrin Falls West Side District—hist pl OH-6
Chagrin Harbor OH-6
Chagrin Point—cape AL-4
Chagrin River—stream OH-6
Chagrin (Township of)—other OH-6
Chagrin Valley Country Club—other OH-6
Chagrin Valley Parkway—park OH-6
Chaguian—area GU-9
Chagulak Island—island AK-9
Chagulak Pass—channel AK-9
Chagum Pond RI-1
Chagvan Bay—bay AK-9
Chagvan Mtn—summit AK-9
Chahalie Lake—lake AK-9
Chaha Road Interchange—locale TX-5
Chahinkapa ND-7
Chahinkapa Park—park ND-7
Chahovun Lakes—lake AK-9
Chahta-Ima HS—school LA-4
Chaichei Islands—area AK-9
Chaika Rock—island AK-9
Chaik Bay—bay AK-9
**Chaille**—pop pl TX-5
Chain—locale PA-2
Chain Bridge—bridge DC-2
Chain Bridge—hist pl PA-2
**Chain Bridge**—pop pl PA-2
Chain Bridge Battery—military DC-2
Chain Bridge (historical)—bridge PA-2
Chain Buttes—ridge MT-8
Chain Canyon—valley CO-8
Chain Canyon—valley MT-8
Chain Canyon—valley OR-9
Chain Creek—stream ID-8
Chain Creek—stream WA-9
Chain Creek—stream WY-8
Chain Dam PA-2
Chainey Mountain Creek—stream TX-5
Chainey Run—stream OH-6
Chaineys Ranch—locale NM-5
Chain Gang Gulch—valley CA-9
Chain Gang Hollow—valley GA-3
Chain Hill—locale WA-9
Chain Hollow—valley KY-4
Chain Island—island CA-9
Chain Island—island ME-1
Chain Lake IN-6
Chain Lake MN-6
Chain Lake WA-9
Chain Lake—lake (2) IL-6
Chain Lake—lake LA-4
Chain Lake—lake (2) MI-6
Chain Lake—lake (3) MN-6
Chain Lake—lake MT-8
Chain Lake—lake NE-7
Chain Lake—lake NY-2
Chain Lake—lake ND-7
Chain Lake—lake OR-9
Chain Lake—lake WA-9
Chain Lake—lake (9) WI-6
Chain Lake—reservoir MS-4
Chain Lake—reservoir WA-9
Chain Lake—swamp NE-7
Chain Lake Ch—church MI-6
Chain Lake (historical)—lake IA-7
Chain Lakes ME-1
Chain Lakes WY-8
Chain Lakes—lake AK-9
Chain Lakes—lake (3) CA-9
Chain Lakes—lake CO-8
Chain Lakes—lake ID-8
Chain Lakes—lake (2) MI-6
Chain Lakes—lake MN-6
Chain Lakes—lake MT-8
Chain Lakes—lake (2) NE-7
Chain Lakes—lake NM-5
Chain Lakes—lake TX-5
Chain Lakes—lake UT-8
Chain Lakes—lake (4) WA-9
Chain Lakes—lake (2) WI-6
Chain Lakes—lake (3) WY-8
Chain Lakes Ch—church ND-7
Chain Lake Sch—school NE-7
Chain Lakes County Park—park IA-7
Chain Lakes Flat—flat WY-8
Chain Lakes Rim—cliff WY-8
Chain Lakes State Public Shooting Area—park SD-7
**Chain Lakes Township**—pop pl ND-7
Chain Lake Stream—stream ME-1
Chain Link Mtn—summit MO-7
Chain Link Tank—reservoir AZ-5
Chainman Shaft—mine NV-8
Chain Meadows—flat ID-8
Chain Meadows—swamp ME-1
Chain Mill Creek—stream IN-6
Chain Mill Falls—falls IN-6
Chain Mountains—ridge CO-8
Chain Of Craters—crater HI-9
Chain of Lakes—lake CA-9
Chain of Lakes—lake MI-6
Chain of Lakes—lake MN-6
Chain of Lakes—lake MT-8
Chain of Lakes—lake NE-7
Chain of Lakes—lake SD-7
Chain of Lakes—lake TX-5
Chain Of Lakes—lake WA-9
Chain of Lakes—lake WI-6
Chain of Lakes—reservoir MO-7
Chain of Lakes Coulee—valley MT-8
Chain of Ponds—lake ME-1
Chain of Ponds Camp—locale ME-1
Chain of Ponds (Township of)—unorg ME-1
**Chain of Rocks**—pop pl MO-7
Chain Of Rocks Bridge—other IL-6
Chain Of Rocks Bridge—other MO-7
Chain Of Rocks Canal—canal IL-6
Chain of Rocks (historical)—bar SD-7
Chain Of Rocks Park—park MO-7
Chain O Lakes—lake FL-3
Chain O' Lakes—lake IN-6
Chain-O-Lakes—lake MI-6
Chain O' Lakes—lake MN-6
Chain O'Lakes—lake TX-5
Chain O'Lakes—lake WI-6
**Chain O Lakes**—pop pl FL-3
**Chain-O-Lakes**—pop pl IN-6
**Chain O'lakes**—pop pl IN-6
**Chain-O-Lakes**—pop pl MO-7
Chain-O-Lakes Airp—airport IN-6
Chain-O-Lakes Ditch—canal IN-6
Chain O'Lakes State Park—park IL-6
Chain O'Lakes State Park—park IN-6
Chain-O-Sloughs State Wildlife Mngmt—park MN-6
Chain Ponds ME-1
Chain Ponds—lake ME-1
Chain Ponds—lake NY-2
Chain Rock—cliff KY-4
Chainshot Island NC-3
Chain Shot Island—island NC-3
Chain Spring—spring ID-8
Chain Stream—stream ME-1
Chain Tank—reservoir AZ-5
Chaintown—locale PA-2
Chain Windmill—locale TX-5
Chairback Mtn—summit ME-1
Chairbottom Hollow—valley MO-7
Chair Branch—stream TX-5
Chair Creek—stream CA-9
Chair Creek—stream CO-8
Chair Creek—stream ID-8
Chair Creek—stream WY-8
Chair Crossing—locale AZ-5
Chair Draft—valley VA-3
**Chaires**—pop pl FL-3
Chaires Creek—stream FL-3
**Chaires Cross Roads**—pop pl FL-3
Chaires Elem Sch—school FL-3
Chair Factory Lake—lake IN-6
Chair Hill—summit NH-1
Chairmaker Branch—stream NC-3
Chair Maker Point—cape SC-3
Chairman PA-2
Chair Mountain Ranch—locale CO-8
Chair Mountain Trail—trail MT-8
Chair Mtn—summit CO-8
Chair Mtn—summit MT-8
Chair Peak—summit WA-9
Chair Peak Lake—lake WA-9
Chair Point—summit ID-8
Chair Pond—lake ME-1
Chair Pond Head—cape ME-1
Chair Riffle—rapids OR-9
Chair Rock Creek—stream NY-2
Chair Rock Flow—bay NY-2
Chair Rock Hollow—valley VA-3
Chair Rock Island—island NY-2
Chair Rock Point—cape NY-2
Chair Rock Ridge—ridge VA-3
Chair Rocks—pillar CO-8
**Chairville**—pop pl NJ-2
Chaisey Point—cape MD-2
Chaison—locale MI-6
Chaison—uninc pl TX-5
Chaison Junction—uninc pl TX-5
Chaistla Bu AZ-5
Cha istla Butte AZ-5
Chaistla Butte—summit AZ-5
Chaix Hills—other AK-9
Chaix Mtn—summit CA-9
Chaiyahi Creek—stream AZ-5
Chaiyahi Flat—flat AZ-5
Chaiyahi Rim—cliff AZ-5
Chakachamna Lake—lake AK-9
Chakachatna River—stream AK-9
**Chakaktolik**—pop pl AK-9
Chakaktolik Creek—stream AK-9
Chakaruchi-to MP-9
Chakaruuchi To MP-9
Chakchak Creek—stream AK-9
Chakchak (Site)—locale AK-9
Chakina River—stream AK-9
Chako Creek—stream OR-9
Chakok River—stream AK-9
Chakpahu—locale AZ-5
Chakwakamiut River—stream AK-9
Chakwakamiut (Summer Camp)—locale AK-9
Cha-La-Kee YMCA Camp—locale AL-4
Chalan Anite Point—summit GU-9
Chaland, Bayou—canal LA-4
Chaland, Bayou—gut LA-4
Chalan Daog—valley GU-9
Chaland Pass—channel LA-4
Chalaney Creek—stream CA-9
Chalan Kanoa Beach MH-9
Chalan Keja MH-9
Chalankesa MH-9
Chalankeza MH-9
Chalan Killa MH-9
Chalan Kiya Beach MH-9
Chalan Laulau MH-9
**Chalan Mamajanao**—pop pl GU-9
**Chalan Pago**—pop pl GU-9
Chalan Pago-Ordot (Election District)—fmr MCD GU-9
Chalan Pupulo MH-9
Chalaybeate Spring—spring AL-4
Chalberg Creek—stream MN-6
Chalcedonia Ch—church GA-3
Chalcedony Creek—stream WY-8
Chalcedony Spring—spring CO-8
Chalchihuitl, Mount—summit NM-5
**Chalco**—pop pl NE-7
Chaleco Artesian Well—well TX-5
Chalender—locale AZ-5
Chalender District Ranger Station—locale AZ-5
Chalender Underpass—crossing AZ-5
Chalet, Lake—lake MI-6
Chalet Amill—hist pl PR-3
**Chalet Subdivision**—pop pl UT-8
**Chalet Village**—pop pl TN-4
**Chalet Woods**—pop pl VA-3
**Chalfant**—pop pl CA-9
**Chalfant**—pop pl PA-2
Chalfant, Mordecai, House—hist pl KY-4
Chalfant Airp—airport NC-3
Chalfant Borough—civil PA-2
Chalfant Cem—cemetery MO-7
Chalfant Ch—church OH-6
Chalfant Church—hist pl OH-6
Chalfant Creek—stream KY-4
Chalfant Lakes—lake CA-9
Chalfant Run—stream PA-2
Chalfants—locale OH-6
Chalfant Valley—valley CA-9
**Chalfin Bridge**—pop pl IL-6
**Chalfont**—pop pl PA-2
Chalfont Borough—civil PA-2
**Chalfonte (subdivision)**—pop pl DE-2
Chalfont Post Office (historical)—building PA-2
Chalfton Chapel—church OH-6
Chalice Peak—summit MT-8
Chalifa Ditch—canal CO-8
Chaligan—area GU-9
Chaligan Creek—stream GU-9
Chalit (Site)—locale AK-9
Chalk—locale TX-5
Chalk Bank Hollow—valley MO-7
Chalkbank Hollow—valley (2) TN-4
Chalk Bank Landing—locale CA-9
Chalk Basin—basin NV-8
Chalk Basin—basin OR-9
Chalk Bluff—cliff AR-4
Chalk Bluff—cliff CA-9
Chalk Bluff—cliff IL-6
Chalk Bluff—cliff KY-4
Chalk Bluff—cliff MO-7
Chalk Bluff—cliff MT-8
Chalk Bluff—cliff (2) NV-8
Chalk Bluff—cliff NM-5
Chalk Bluff—cliff TN-4
Chalk Bluff—cliff (4) TX-5
Chalk Bluff—cliff WY-8
Chalk Bluff—hist pl AR-4
**Chalk Bluff**—pop pl TX-5
Chalk Bluff—summit CA-9
Chalk Bluff—summit (2) WY-8
Chalk Bluff Cem—cemetery OK-5
Chalk Bluff Cem—cemetery TX-5
Chalk Bluff Ch—church TX-5
Chalk Bluff Draw—valley NM-5
**Chalk Bluff (historical)**—pop pl MS-4
Chalk Bluff Ridge—ridge CA-9
Chalk Bluff Rsvr—reservoir CA-9
Chalk Bluffs—cliff CO-8
Chalk Bluffs—cliff NM-5
Chalk Bluffs—cliff WY-8
Chalk Bluff Sch (historical)—school MS-4
Chalk Bluff Spring—spring NM-5
Chalk Bluff (Township of)—fmr MCD AR-4
Chalk Branch TN-4
Chalk Branch—stream AR-4
Chalk Branch—stream KY-4
Chalk Branch—stream TN-4
Chalk Branch—stream TX-5
Chalk Branch Prospect—mine TN-4
Chalk Butte—summit (5) MT-8
Chalk Butte—summit OR-9
Chalk Butte—summit (6) WY-8
Chalk Butte Draw—valley SD-7
Chalk Butte Rsvr—reservoir MT-8
Chalk Buttes—spring MT-8
Chalk Buttes—summit CA-9
Chalk Buttes—summit NE-7
Chalk Buttes—summit (2) WY-8
Chalk Butte Spring—spring WY-8
Chalk Buttes Sch—school NE-7
Chalk Canyon—valley AZ-5
Chalk Cave—cave AL-4
Chalk Cave—cave TN-4
Chalk Cave Hollow—valley TN-4
Chalk Cem—cemetery KS-7
Chalk Cliff—cliff CA-9
Chalk Cliff and Republican River—hist pl NE-7
Chalk Cliff Fish Hatchery—park CO-8
Chalk Cliffs—cliff CO-8
Chalk Cliffs—cliff MT-8
Chalk Cliffs—cliff NV-8
Chalk Cliffs—cliff UT-8
Chalk Creek CO-8
Chalk Creek KS-7
Chalk Creek OR-9
Chalk Creek TX-5
Chalk Creek—stream AK-9
Chalk Creek—stream (2) AZ-5
Chalk Creek—stream (2) CO-8
Chalk Creek—stream ID-8
Chalk Creek—stream (2) KS-7
Chalk Creek—stream NC-3
Chalk Creek—stream (4) OR-9
Chalk Creek—stream (2) TN-4
Chalk Creek—stream (7) TX-5
Chalk Creek—stream (3) UT-8
Chalk Creek—stream (3) WY-8
Chalk Creek Basin—basin WY-8
Chalk Creek Pass—gap CO-8
Chalk Creek Sch (historical)—school TN-4
Chalk Creek Tank—reservoir AZ-5
Chalk Creek Well—well AZ-5
Chalk Cut—locale ID-8
Chalk Draw—valley (2) TX-5
Chalk Draw—valley WY-8
Chalker Beach—beach CT-1
Chalker Brook—stream CT-1
Chalker Creek—stream NY-2
Chalker Creek—stream TX-5
Chalker Drain—canal MI-6
Chalker Hill—summit CT-1
Chalker Lake—reservoir GA-3
Chalker Memorial Ch—church AL-4
Chalker Memorial United Methodist Ch AL-4
Chalker Mine—mine CA-9
**Chalkers Beach**—pop pl CT-1
Chalkers Landing MI-6
Chalkers Millpond—reservoir CT-1
Chalker United Ch AL-4
**Chalkerville**—pop pl MI-6
Chalkey Oil and Gas Field—oilfield LA-4
Chalk Flat—flat CA-9
Chalk Flat—flat ID-8
Chalk Gap—gap NM-5
Chalk Gap—gap (2) TX-5
Chalk Grade Flat—flat WA-9
Chalk Gulch OR-9
Chalk Gulch—valley ID-8
Chalk Gulch—valley OR-9
Chalkhead Ch AL-4
Chalk Head Ch—church AL-4
Chalk Hill—locale TX-5
**Chalkhill**—pop pl PA-2
Chalk Hill—ridge CA-9
Chalk Hill—summit (3) CA-9
Chalk Hill—summit (2) FL-3
Chalk Hill—summit MI-6
Chalk Hill—summit (4) TX-5
Chalk Hill—summit UT-8
Chalk Hill—summit (2) WY-8
Chalk Hill Baptist Ch AL-4
Chalk Hill Branch—stream FL-3
Chalk Hill Branch—stream GA-3
Chalk Hill Camp—locale WI-6
Chalk Hill Cem—cemetery AL-4
Chalk Hill Cem—cemetery LA-4
Chalk Hill Cem—cemetery TN-4
Chalk Hill Ch—church SC-3
Chalk Hill Ch—church TN-4
Chalk Hill Ch (historical)—church AL-4
Chalk Hill Creek—stream SC-3
Chalk Hill Dam—dam MI-6
Chalk Hill Dam—dam WI-6
Chalk Hill Hotel PA-2
Chalk Hill Millpond—reservoir SC-3
Chalk Hill Oil Field—oilfield TX-5
Chalk Hill Reservoirs—reservoir WY-8
Chalk Hills—range CA-9
Chalk Hills—range ID-8
Chalk Hills—ridge WY-8
Chalk Hills—summit ID-8
Chalk Hills—summit LA-4
Chalk Hills—summit NV-8
Chalk Hills—summit UT-8
Chalk Hills—summit WA-9
Chalk Hills—summit WY-8
Chalk Hill Sch—school WY-8
Chalk Hills Draw—valley WY-8
Chalk (historical)—locale KS-7
Chalk Hollow—valley MS-4
Chalk Hollow—valley MO-7
Chalk Hollow—valley (2) TN-4
Chalk Hollow—valley (2) TX-5
Chalk Hollow—valley (3) UT-8
Chalk Hollow Pond—lake UT-8
Chalk Knob—summit (2) TX-5
Chalk Knob Branch—stream TX-5
Chalk Knob Hollow—valley TX-5
Chalk Knolls—summit (2) UT-8
Chalk Knolls Well—well UT-8
Chalk Lake—reservoir CO-8
Chalk Level—cliff VA-3
Chalk Level—locale VA-3
**Chalk Level**—pop pl MO-7
**Chalklevel**—pop pl TN-4
**Chalk Level**—pop pl TN-4
Chalk Level Baptist Ch (historical)—church TN-4
Chalk Level Ch—church AL-4
Chalk Level Ch—church MO-7
Chalk Level Ch—church NC-3
**Chalk Level (historical)**—pop pl NC-3
Chalk Level Post Office (historical)—building TN-4
Chalk Level Sch—school MO-7
Chalk Level Sch (historical)—school TN-4
Chalk Level Township—civil MO-7
Chalkley—locale LA-4
Chalkley Sch—school VA-3
Chalkley Station—locale KY-4
Chalk Mine—mine ID-8
Chalk Mine—mine NC-3
Chalk Mine Hollow—valley MS-4
Chalk Mine Memorial Ch—church GA-3
Chalk Mine Run—stream VA-3
Chalk Mound KS-7
Chalk Mound Cem—cemetery KS-7
**Chalk Mountain**—pop pl TX-5
Chalk Mountain Ch—church TX-5
Chalk Mountain Rsvr—reservoir CO-8
Chalk Mountains—range CA-9
Chalk Mountains—range TX-5
Chalk Mountain Wash NV-8
Chalk Mtn NC-3
Chalk Mtn—summit (2) AZ-5
Chalk Mtn—summit (5) CA-9
Chalk Mtn—summit (2) CO-8
Chalk Mtn—summit (2) NV-8
Chalk Mtn—summit (2) NC-3
Chalk Mtn—summit (3) TX-5
Chalk Mtn—summit VA-3
Chalk Mtn—summit (2) WY-8
Chalk Mtns—range CO-8
Chalk Peak CO-8
Chalk Peak—summit AZ-5
Chalk Peak—summit (2) CA-9
Chalk Peak—summit TX-5
Chalk Peak Camp—locale CA-9
Chalk Pipe Gut—gut VA-3
Chalk Point—cape (2) MD-2
**Chalk Point**—pop pl MD-2
Chalk Point—summit CA-9
Chalk Point Spring—spring AZ-5
Chalk Pond—lake (3) ME-1
Chalk Pond—lake (2) NH-1
Chalk Prong—stream WY-8
Chalk Pyramids—pillar KS-7
Chalk Ridge—ridge CA-9
Chalk Ridge—ridge KY-4
Chalk Rock—pillar CA-9
Chalk Rock Hollow—valley MO-7
Chalk Rsvr—reservoir AZ-5
Chalk Rsvr—reservoir CA-9
Chalk Rsvr—reservoir NV-8
Chalk Rsvr—reservoir OR-9
Chalk Run—stream MO-7
Chalks, The—ridge CA-9
Chalk Slough—stream KY-4
Chalk Spring—spring (12) AZ-5
Chalk Spring—spring CA-9
Chalk Spring—spring (2) ID-8
Chalk Spring—spring (3) NV-8
Chalk Spring—spring (4) OR-9
Chalk Spring—spring WY-8
Chalk Spring Canyon—valley AZ-5
Chalk Spring Number Two—spring AZ-5
Chalk Springs—spring MT-8
Chalk Spur—locale ID-8
Chalkstone Creek SD-7
Chalk Tank—reservoir (6) AZ-5
Chalk Tank—reservoir TX-5
Chalk Tank Canyon—valley AZ-5
Chalkton TX-5
**Chalkville**—pop pl AL-4
Chalkville Ch—church AL-4
Chalkville Elementary School AL-4
Chalkville Sch—school AL-4
Chalk Wash—stream AZ-5
Chalk Well—locale NM-5
Chalk Wells (Site)—locale NV-8
Chalk Windmill—locale NM-5
Chalk Windmill—locale TX-5
Chalky Butte—unorg reg ND-7
Chalky Buttes—range ND-7
Chalky Butte Well—well AZ-5
**Chalkyitsik**—pop pl AK-9
Chalkyitsik ANV748—reserve AK-9
Chalkyitsik Slough—gut AK-9
Chalky Point—summit MT-8
Chalky Spring—spring AZ-5
Chalky Tank—reservoir NM-5
Challacombe—locale IL-6
Challacombe (historical)—locale KS-7
Chall Creek—stream WY-8
Challe Canyon AZ-5
**Challedon**—pop pl SC-3
Challender (historical)—locale KS-7
**Challenge**—pop pl CA-9
**Challenge**—pop pl PA-2
Challenge Cabin—locale MT-8
Challenge Canyon—valley NM-5
Challenge Creek—stream MT-8
Challenge Entrance—channel AK-9
**Challenge (Hyde Station)**—pop pl PA-2
Challenge Island—island AK-9
Challenge Mine—mine MI-6
Challenge Mine (underground)—mine AL-4
Challenger, Mount—summit WA-9

Challenge Reservation—reserve AL-4
Challenger Glacier—glacier WA-9
Challenger Lake—lake FL-3
Challenger Point—summit CO-8
Challenge Tank—reservoir TX-5
Challenge Windmill—locale NM-5
Challenge Windmill—locale TX-5
Challenor MO-7
**Challis**—pop pl ID-8
Challis Archeol Spring District—hist pl ID-8
Challis Bison Jump Site—hist pl ID-8
Challis Brewery Hist Dist—hist pl ID-8
Challis Ch—church TX-5
Challis Cold Storage—hist pl ID-8
Challis Creek—stream ID-8
Challis Creek Lakes—lake ID-8
Challis District Ranger Station—locale ID-8
Challis Hot Springs—spring ID-8
Challis HS—hist pl ID-8
Challis Lake—reservoir NC-3
Challis Lake Dam—dam NC-3
Challis Natl For—forest ID-8
Challis Pond—lake NY-2
Chall Mtn—summit CA-9
Chalman Sch—school IL-6
Chalmer Point VA-3
Chalmers TN-4
Chalmers—locale TX-5
**Chalmers**—pop pl IN-6
Chalmers Cem—cemetery IN-6
Chalmers Creek—stream VA-3
Chalmers Drain—canal MI-6
Chalmers Field—park IA-7
Chalmers Institute—hist pl MS-4
Chalmers Lake—lake MI-6
Chalmers Lake—lake TX-5
Chalmers Point—cape VA-3
**Chalmers (Township of)**—pop pl IL-6
**Chalmette**—pop pl LA-4
Chalmette Natl Cem—cemetery LA-4
Chalmette Natl Historical Park—park LA-4
Chalmette Unit of Jean Lafitte Natl Historical Park Hist Dist—hist pl LA-4
**Chalmette Vista**—pop pl LA-4
Chalon Bayou—stream LA-4
Chalone Annex Campground—locale CA-9
Chalone Creek—stream CA-9
Chalone Creek Archeol Sites—hist pl CA-9
Chalone Creek Campground—locale CA-9
Chalone Mountain CA-9
Chalone Peak Trail—trail CA-9
Chaloner Park—park NC-3
Chaloner Sch—school NC-3
Chalons MS-4
Chaloon River CA-9
Chalpin, Bayou—stream LA-4
Chalstroms Beach—beach IA-7
Chaltbeate Spring—spring PA-2
Chalth Canyon UT-8
Chalugas Bay—bay AK-9
Chaluka Site—hist pl AK-9
Chalupa Lake WY-8
Chalupnik Dam—dam ND-7
**Chalybeat**—pop pl PA-2
Chalybeate TX-5
Chalybeate—locale TN-4
**Chalybeate**—pop pl KY-4
**Chalybeate**—pop pl MS-4
**Chalybeate**—pop pl PA-2
**Chalybeate**—pop pl TX-5
Chalybeate Baptist Ch—church MS-4
Chalybeate Branch—stream KY-4
Chalybeate Cem—cemetery MS-4
**Chalybeate (Chalybeate Springs)**—pop pl NC-3
Chalybeate Creek—stream AL-4
Chalybeate Creek—stream AR-4
Chalybeate Creek—stream TX-5
Chalybeate High School MS-4
Chalybeate Hills—range KY-4
Chalybeate Institute MS-4
Chalybeate JHS (historical)—school AL-4
Chalybeate Mountain—ridge (2) AR-4
Chalybeate Mtn—summit (2) AL-4
Chalybeate Mtn—summit (2) AR-4
Chalybeate Post Office (historical)—building TN-4
Chalybeate Presbyterian Ch (historical)—church MS-4
Chalybeate Sch—school KY-4
Chalybeate Sch—school MS-4
Chalybeate Sch (historical)—school TN-4
Chalybeate Spring—spring (6) AL-4
Chalybeate Spring—spring AR-4
Chalybeate Spring—spring MS-4
Chalybeate Spring—spring (2) TN-4
Chalybeate Spring—spring VA-3
Chalybeate Spring Creek—stream AR-4
Chalybeate Spring Hollow—valley AR-4
Chalybeate Spring Mountain AL-4
Chalybeate Springs AL-4
Chalybeate Springs MS-4
Chalybeate Springs TX-5
Chalybeate Springs—locale AR-4
Chalybeate Springs—locale GA-3
**Chalybeate Springs**—pop pl AL-4
**Chalybeate Springs**—pop pl (2) AR-4
**Chalybeate Springs**—pop pl NC-3
Chalybeate Springs—spring IN-6
Chalybeate Springs Branch—stream AR-4
Chalybeate Springs Cem—cemetery AR-4
Chalybeate Springs Ch—church AL-4
Chalybeate Springs Ch—church LA-4
Chalybeate Springs Ch (historical)—church TN-4
Chalybeate Springs Hotel—hist pl PA-2
Chalybeate Springs Sch (historical)—school AL-4
Chalybeate Springs (Township of)—fmr MCD AR-4
Chalybeate Spur—ridge AR-4
Chalybeate Valley—basin AR-4
Chalybeate Valley Ch—church AR-4
Chalybeats Ridge KY-4
Chalybrite Springs Church AL-4
Chama—locale CO-8
**Chama**—pop pl CO-8
**Chama**—pop pl NM-5
**Chama**—pop pl ND-7
Chama, Rio—stream CO-8
Chama Canyon—valley NM-5
Chama Cem—cemetery (2) CO-8
Chama Cem—cemetery NM-5
Chama Lake—lake CO-8
Chama Peak—summit CO-8
Chama River CO-8
Chamascus MS-4
Chamayo Creek CO-8
Chambeam Ditch—canal OR-9
Chamber WA-9
**Chamber**—pop pl WA-9
Chamber Cem—cemetery IA-7
Chamber Creek Drainage Ditch—canal MS-4
Chamber Grove Ch—church NC-3
**Chamberino**—pop pl NM-5
Chamberino Drain—canal NM-5
Chamberino East Lateral—canal NM-5
Chamberino Main Lateral—canal NM-5
**Chamberino (Old Town)**—pop pl NM-5
Chamberino Sch—school NM-5
Chamberlain NY-2
Chamberlain TN-4
Chamberlain—locale MI-6
Chamberlain—locale MN-6
**Chamberlain**—pop pl GA-3
**Chamberlain**—pop pl ME-1
**Chamberlain**—pop pl SD-7
**Chamberlain**—pop pl TX-5
Chamberlain, Charles, House—hist pl MA-1
Chamberlain, George Earle, House—hist pl OR-9
Chamberlain, Lake—reservoir CT-1
Chamberlain, Samuel, House—hist pl MA-1
Chamberlain Basin—basin (2) ID-8
Chamberlain Bay—bay AK-9
Chamberlain Branch—stream KY-4
Chamberlain Branch—stream NJ-2
Chamberlain Branch—stream TN-4
Chamberlain Brook—stream ME-1
Chamberlain Brook—stream (2) NY-2
Chamberlain Brook—stream VT-1
Chamberlain Canyon—valley AZ-5
Chamberlain Cem—cemetery IL-6
Chamberlain Cem—cemetery IN-6
Chamberlain Cem—cemetery ME-1
Chamberlain Cem—cemetery MO-7
Chamberlain Cem—cemetery (2) NY-2
Chamberlain Cem—cemetery TN-4
Chamberlain Cem—cemetery TX-5
Chamberlain Cemetery MS-4
Chamberlain Ch—church ME-1
Chamberlain Community Center—locale TX-5
Chamberlain Corners—locale NY-2
Chamberlain Corners Cem—cemetery NY-2
Chamberlain Creek—stream AR-4
Chamberlain Creek—stream CA-9
Chamberlain Creek—stream (4) ID-8
Chamberlain Creek—stream IL-6
Chamberlain Creek—stream MI-6
Chamberlain Creek—stream (2) MT-8
Chamberlain Creek—stream NY-2
Chamberlain Creek—stream OR-9
Chamberlain Creek—stream TX-5
Chamberlain Creek Conservation Camp—locale CA-9
Chamberlain Elem Sch—school IN-6
Chamberlain Farm—locale ME-1
Chamberlain-Flagg House—hist pl MA-1
Chamberlain Glacier—glacier AK-9
Chamberlain Glen—valley VT-1
Chamberlain Gulch—valley CO-8
Chamberlain Gulch—valley (2) ID-8
Chamberlain Hill PA-2
Chamberlain Hill—summit NY-2
Chamberlain Hill—summit OR-9
Chamberlain Hill—summit (2) VT-1
Chamberlain Hollow—valley MO-7
Chamberlain Hollow—valley PA-2
Chamberlain Hollow—valley TX-5
Chamberlain House, The—building MA-1
Chamberlain-Hunt Acad—school MS-4
Chamberlain-Hunt Acad Hist Dist—hist pl MS-4
Chamberlain Island SD-7
Chamberlain-Kay House—hist pl SC-3
Chamberlain Knob—summit TN-4
Chamberlain Lake—lake AK-9
Chamberlain Lake—lake CA-9
Chamberlain Lake—lake IN-6
Chamberlain Lake—lake ME-1
Chamberlain Lake—lake (2) MI-6
Chamberlain Lake—lake OR-9
Chamberlain Lake—lake WA-9
Chamberlain Lake—lake WI-6
Chamberlain Lake—reservoir PA-2
Chamberlain Ledge—bench NH-1
Chamberlain Meadows—flat ID-8
Chamberlain Meadows—flat MT-8
Chamberlain Memorial Baptist Ch—church TN-4
Chamberlain Memorial Hosp—hospital TN-4
Chamberlain Mills—locale NY-2
Chamberlain Mountain MA-1
Chamberlain Mtn—summit ID-8
Chamberlain Mtn—summit ME-1
Chamberlain Mtn—summit MT-8
Chamberlain Municipal Airp—airport SD-7
Chamberlain Observatory—other CO-8
Chamberlain Oil Field—oilfield TX-5
Chamberlain Pass—gap SD-7
Chamberlain Pass—gap WY-8
Chamberlain-Pennell House—hist pl PA-2
Chamberlain Place—locale WY-8
Chamberlain Playground—park MI-6
Chamberlain Point VA-3
Chamberlain Pond—lake ME-1
Chamberlain Pond—lake MA-1
Chamberlain Pond—reservoir CT-1
Chamberlain Pond—reservoir PA-2
Chamberlain Pond Dam—dam PA-2
Chamberlain Post Office (historical)—building TN-4
Chamberlain Ranch—locale (2) CA-9
Chamberlain Ranch (historical)—locale SD-7
Chamberlain Rec Area—park SD-7
Chamberlain Ridge—ridge CA-9
Chamberlain Ridge—ridge ME-1
Chamberlain Run—stream PA-2
Chamberlains MI-6
**Chamberlains**—pop pl ME-1
**Chamberlains**—pop pl MI-6
Chamberlains Bed—stream VA-3
Chamberlains Bed Creek VA-3
Chamberlains Branch NJ-2
Chamberlains Camp—locale CA-9
Chamberlain Sch—school CT-1
Chamberlain Sch—school FL-3
Chamberlain Sch—school MI-6
Chamberlain Sch—school OK-5
Chamberlain Sch—school SD-7
Chamberlain Sch—school TX-5
Chamberlain Shaft—mine PA-2
Chamberlains Hill—summit PA-2
Chamberlain Slough—gut CA-9
Chamberlains Ranch—locale UT-8
**Chamberlains Subdivision**—pop pl UT-8
Chamberlain Swamp—swamp NE-7
Chamberlain Tank—reservoir AZ-5
**Chamberlain Township**—pop pl SD-7
Chamberlain Trail—trail AZ-5
Chamberlain Trail—trail ID-8
Chamberlain Valley—basin NE-7
**Chamberlain Village**—pop pl VA-3
Chamberlain Vocational HS—school DC-2
Chamberlain Ward Sch—school TX-5
Chamber Lake—lake NY-2
Chamberland Pond—lake CT-1
Chamberlayne—CDP VA-3
**Chamberlayne Farms**—pop pl VA-3
**Chamberlayne Heights**—pop pl VA-3
**Chamberlayne North**—pop pl VA-3
Chamberlayne Point—cape VA-3
Chamberlayne Sch—school VA-3
Chamberlin—locale LA-4
Chamberlin—locale TX-5
Chamberlin, Clarence D., House—hist pl IA-7
Chamberlin, Mount—summit AK-9
Chamberlin, Mount—summit CA-9
Chamberlin Branch NJ-2
Chamberlin Cem—cemetery MI-6
Chamberlin Cem—cemetery (2) MS-4
Chamberlin Creek—stream AK-9
Chamberlin Creek—stream MS-4
Chamberlin Gap—gap WV-2
Chamberlin Glacier—glacier AK-9
Chamberlin House—hist pl NH-1
Chamberlin HS—school OH-6
Chamberlin Iron Front Bldg—hist pl PA-2
Chamberlin Lake—lake MN-6
Chamberlin Lake—lake NE-7
Chamberlin Mill Covered Bridge—hist pl VT-1
Chamberlin Mtn—summit MA-1
Chamberlin Mtn—summit VT-1
Chamberlin Observatory—hist pl CO-8
Chamberlin Park—park OH-6
Chamberlin Point VA-3
Chamberlin Sch—school WV-2
Chamberlin Sch (historical)—school TN-4
Chamberlin Spring—spring OR-9
Chamberly Island—island ME-1
Chamber of Commerce—building FL-3
Chamber of Commerce—hist pl NY-2
Chamber of Commerce—locale NC-3
Chamber of Commerce Bldg—hist pl CA-9
Chamber of Commerce Bldg—hist pl IN-6
Chamber of Commerce Bldg—hist pl MD-2
Chamber of Commerce Bldg—hist pl MN-6
Chamber of Commerce Bldg—hist pl NY-2
Chamber of Commerce Bldg—hist pl SC-3
Chamber of Commerce Visitor Center—building NC-3
Chambers MS-4
Chambers PA-2
Chambers—locale AL-4
Chambers—locale AZ-5
Chambers—locale KY-4
Chambers—locale PA-2
Chambers—locale WA-9
**Chambers**—pop pl LA-4
**Chambers**—pop pl MS-4
**Chambers**—pop pl NE-7
**Chambers**—pop pl NY-2
**Chambers**—pop pl OK-5
**Chambers**—pop pl (2) TN-4
**Chambers**—pop pl WV-2
Chambers, Frank L. and Ida H., House—hist pl OR-9
Chambers, John, House—hist pl MI-6
Chambers, Lake—reservoir MD-2
Chambers, Maxwell, House—hist pl NC-3
Chambers, Robert, House—hist pl KY-4
Chambers, Whitakker, Farm—hist pl MD-2
Chambers Acad—school AL-4
Chambers Airp—airport PA-2
Chambers Attendance Center—school MS-4
Chambers Bar—bar AL-4
Chambers Bay—bay WA-9
Chambers Bay—bay WY-8
Chambers Branch—stream (2) AL-4
Chambers Branch—stream GA-3
Chambers Branch—stream KY-4
Chambers Branch—stream (2) NC-3
Chambers Branch—stream SC-3
Chambers Branch—stream (5) TN-4
Chambers Bridge—hist pl OR-9
Chambers Brook—stream NJ-2
Chambers Brook—stream NY-2
Chambersburg NJ-2
Chambersburg OH-6
Chambersburg—locale MO-7
Chambersburg—other WV-2
**Chambersburg**—pop pl IL-6
**Chambersburg**—pop pl (2) IN-6
**Chambersburg**—pop pl OH-6
**Chambersburg**—pop pl PA-2
Chambersburg—uninc pl NJ-2
Chambersburg and Bedford Turnpike Road Company Toll House—hist pl PA-2
Chambersburg Area MS—school PA-2
Chambersburg Area Senior HS—school PA-2
Chambersburg Borough—civil PA-2
Chambersburg Ch—church MO-7
Chambersburg Hist Dist—hist pl PA-2
Chambersburg Hospital Airp—airport PA-2
Chambersburg (local name Eureka)—inactive OH-6
Chambersburg Mall—locale PA-2
Chambersburg Municipal Airp—airport PA-2
Chambersburg Rsvr—reservoir (2) PA-2
Chambersburg Rsvr Dam PA-2
Chambersburg (Township of)—civ div IL-6
Chambersburg (Township of)—fmr MCD NC-3
Chambers Camp—locale PA-2
Chambers Camp—locale TX-5
Chambers Camp—locale WY-8
Chambers Canyon—valley NM-5
Chambers Cem—cemetery (3) AL-4
Chambers Cem—cemetery AR-4
Chambers Cem—cemetery (2) IN-6
Chambers Cem—cemetery (2) IA-7
Chambers Cem—cemetery (4) KY-4
Chambers Cem—cemetery LA-4
Chambers Cem—cemetery NY-2
Chambers Cem—cemetery (2) NC-3
Chambers Cem—cemetery OH-6
Chambers Cem—cemetery (3) OK-5
Chambers Cem—cemetery SC-3
Chambers Cem—cemetery (7) TN-4
Chambers Cem—cemetery TX-5
Chambers Cem—cemetery (4) WV-2
Chambers Ch—church AR-4
Chambers Chapel—church NC-3
Chambers Chapel—church TN-4
Chambers Corner MI-6
**Chambers Corner**—pop pl ME-1
**Chambers Corner**—pop pl NJ-2
Chambers Corners MI-6
Chambers Coulee—valley MT-8
**Chambers County**—pop pl AL-4
**Chambers (County)**—pop pl TX-5
Chambers County Courthouse—building AL-4
Chambers County Courthouse Square Hist Dist—hist pl AL-4
Chambers County Hosp—hospital AL-4
Chambers County HS—school AL-4
Chambers County Public Lake Dam—dam AL-4
Chambers County State Lake—reservoir AL-4
Chambers Cove—bay FL-3
Chambers Cove—bay NC-3
Chambers Cove—valley NC-3
Chambers Creek AL-4
Chambers Creek—stream AL-4
Chambers Creek—stream CA-9
Chambers Creek—stream ID-8
Chambers Creek—stream MS-4
Chambers Creek—stream MO-7
Chambers Creek—stream NY-2
Chambers Creek—stream (2) NC-3
Chambers Creek—stream TN-4
Chambers Creek—stream (7) TX-5
Chambers Creek—stream (2) WA-9
Chambers Creek—stream WI-6
Chambers Creek Gap—gap NC-3
Chambers Dam—dam AL-4
Chambers Dam—dam PA-2
Chambers Ditch—canal CO-8
Chambers Ditch—canal IN-6
Chambers Ditch—canal (2) WY-8
Chambers Drain—canal MI-6
Chambers Draw—arroyo AZ-5
Chambers Draw—arroyo TX-5
Chambersea—hist pl TX-5
Chambers Ferry NC-3
Chambers Fork—stream KY-4
Chambers Fork—stream WV-2
Chambers Gap—gap TN-4
Chambers Grove Sch—school IL-6
Chambers Gulch—valley MT-8
Chambers Gulch—valley WA-9
**Chambers Hill**—pop pl PA-2
Chambers Hill—summit TN-4
Chambers Hill Lookout—locale TX-5
Chambers Hill Sch—school PA-2
Chambers (historical)—locale AL-4
**Chambers (historical)**—pop pl NC-3
Chambers Hollow—valley (2) AR-4
Chambers Hollow—valley MO-7
Chambers Hollow—valley NY-2
Chambers Hollow—valley (6) TN-4
Chambers Hollow—valley VA-3
Chambers House—hist pl DE-2
Chambers Interchange—crossing AZ-5
Chambers Island—island FL-3
Chambers Island—island WI-6
**Chambers Island**—pop pl WI-6
Chambers Island Lighthouse—hist pl WI-6
Chambers Knob—summit WV-2
Chambers Lake IN-6
Chambers Lake—lake AR-4
Chambers Lake—lake CO-8
Chambers Lake—lake LA-4
Chambers Lake—lake (3) WA-9
Chambers Lake—reservoir AL-4
Chambers Lake—reservoir TX-5
Chambers Lake Campground—locale CO-8
Chambers Lakes—lake OR-9
Chambers Landing—locale NC-3
**Chambers Lodge**—pop pl CA-9
Chambers Memorial Hosp—hospital TX-5
**Chambers Mill**—pop pl PA-2
Chambers Mill Brook NJ-2
Chambers Mill (historical)—locale AL-4
Chambers Mine—mine MT-8
Chambers Mine—mine OR-9
Chambers Mine (underground)—mine AL-4
Chambers Mine (underground)—mine TN-4
Chambers Mtn—summit AR-4
Chambers Mtn—summit NC-3
Chambers Northeast Oil Field—oilfield KS-7
**Chambers Park Subdivision**—pop pl UT-8
Chambers Peak—summit CA-9
Chambers Point—cape FL-3
Chambers Point—cape NC-3
Chambers Pond—swamp TN-4
Chambers Pond—swamp TX-5
Chambers Post Office (historical)—building TN-4
Chambers Prairie—flat WA-9
Chamber Spring—spring OR-9
Chambers Ranch—hist pl CO-8
Chambers Ranch—locale OR-9
Chambers Ranch—locale TX-5
Chambers Ridge—ridge VA-3
Chambers Road Covered Bridge—hist pl OH-6
Chambers RR Station—building AZ-5
Chambers Rsvr—reservoir (2) CO-8
Chambers Rsvr—reservoir PA-2
Chambers Run—stream (2) OH-6
Chambers Run—stream PA-2
Chambers Sch—school IL-6
Chambers Sch—school MI-6
Chambers Sch—school NY-2
Chambers Sch—school OH-6
Chambers Sch—school SD-7
Chambers Sch—school WV-2
Chambers School—locale IL-6
Chambers Sheep Camp—locale NM-5
Chambers Spring—spring AR-4
Chambers Spring—spring NE-7
Chambers Spring—spring NM-5
Chambers Spring—spring OR-9
Chambers Spring—spring PA-2
Chambers Spring—spring TN-4
Chambers Spring—spring (2) UT-8
Chambers Spring Branch—stream TN-4
Chambers Springs—locale AL-4
Chambers Square—post sta CO-8
**Chambers Township**—pop pl NE-7
Chambers Township (historical)—civil ND-7
**Chambers Townsite Subdivision**—pop pl UT-8
Chambers Transfer & Storage Co.—hist pl AZ-5
Chambers Transfer & Storage Co.-Central Warehouse—hist pl AZ-5
Chambersville AL-4
Chambersville VA-3
Chambersville—locale AR-4
Chambersville—locale DE-2
Chambersville—locale TX-5
**Chambersville**—pop pl PA-2
**Chambersville**—pop pl VA-3
Chambersville Cem—cemetery IN-6
Chambersville Ch—church AR-4
Chambers Wash—valley UT-8
Chambers Well (Dry)—well CA-9
Chambers Windmill—locale AZ-5
Chamblee—locale LA-4
**Chamblee**—pop pl AL-4
**Chamblee**—pop pl GA-3
Chamblee Cem—cemetery MS-4
Chamblee-Doraville (CCD)—cens area GA-3
Chamblee Gap—gap GA-3
Chamblees Bridge—bridge NC-3
Chamblees Mill—locale AL-4
Chamblees Mill Creek AL-4
Chamblers Branch—stream GA-3
**Chambless**—pop pl CA-9
Chambless Hollow—valley AL-4
Chambless Mill AL-4
Chamblis Mill—locale GA-3
**Chamblis Mill**—pop pl GA-3
Chambliss—locale GA-3
Chambliss—locale TX-5
**Chambliss**—pop pl GA-3
Chamblissburg—locale VA-3
Chamblissburgh VA-3
Chambliss Cem—cemetery TN-4
Chambliss Creek—stream GA-3
Chambliss Hill—summit TN-4
Chambliss Number 1 Dam—dam SD-7
Chambliss Number 2 Dam—dam SD-7
Chambliss Number 3 Dam—dam SD-7
Chambon Lateral—canal NM-5
**Chambord**—pop pl IL-6
Chambord Apartments—hist pl CA-9
Chambre, Bayou—swamp LA-4
**Cham (Chambersburg)**—pop pl WV-2
Chaminade Coll—school HI-9
Chaminade HS—school FL-3
Chaminade HS—school NY-2
Chaminade Preparatory Sch—school NY-2
Chaminade Sch—school CA-9
Chaminade Sch—school MO-7
Chaminade Sch—school OH-6
Chamir—summit FM-9
Chamisa Canyon—valley (2) NM-5
**Chamisa Gap**—pop pl CA-9
**Chamisal**—pop pl NM-5
Chamisal Creek—stream CA-9
Chamisal Drain—canal NM-5
Chamisal Mtn—summit CA-9
Chamisa Losa Spring—spring NM-5
Chamisal Ridge—ridge CA-9
Chamisa Mesa—summit NM-5
Chamisa Rsvr—reservoir UT-8
Chamisa Tank—reservoir AZ-5
Chamisa Vega Spring Falls—falls NM-5
Chamisa Well—well NM-5
Chamise Creek—stream CA-9
Chamise Peak—summit CA-9
Chamise Tank—reservoir (2) AZ-5
Chamise Well—well NM-5
Chamiso—locale AZ-5
Chamiso RR Station—building AZ-5
Chamisoso Canyon—valley NM-5
Chamiso Well—well NM-5
Chamisso Anchorage—channel AK-9
Chamisso-Insel FM-9
Chamisso Island—island AK-9
Chamisso Natl Wildlife Ref—park AK-9
**Chamita**—pop pl NM-5
Chamita, Rio—stream CO-8
Chamita Ditch—canal NM-5
**Chamizal**—pop pl NM-5
Chamizal Creek—stream NM-5
Chamizal Ditch—canal NM-5
Chamizal Lateral—canal NM-5
Chamizal Natl Memorial—hist pl TX-5
Chamizal Natl Memorial—park TX-5
Chamizal -Ojito Tracts—civil NM-5
Chamiza Trail—trail NM-5
Chamize Mtn CA-9
Chamlee Cem—cemetery AL-4
Chamlee Ch—church GA-3
Chamlee Heights Ch—church TN-4
Chamlissburg VA-3
**Chamlissburg**—pop pl VA-3
Chamness Cem—cemetery IL-6
Chamoge MH-9
**Chamois**—pop pl MO-7
Chamokane Creek WA-9
Chamokane Creek—stream WA-9
Chamokane Falls—falls WA-9
Chamook Creek—stream ID-8
Chamook Ridge—ridge ID-8
Chamook Saddle—gap ID-8
Chamorro (Barrio)—fmr MCD PR-3
**Chamouni**—pop pl PA-2
Chamounix—hist pl PA-2
Chamoyo Creek CO-8
Champ—locale TN-4
**Champ**—pop pl MD-2
**Champ**—pop pl MO-7
**Champ**—pop pl OR-9
Champagnat Catholic Sch—school FL-3
Champagnat Catholic Sch of Hialeah—school FL-3
Champagnat Catholic Sch of Miami—school FL-3
Champagne—locale CA-9
**Champagne**—pop pl LA-4
Champagne, Lake—lake PA-2
Champagne Canyon ID-8
Champagne Creek—stream ID-8
Champagne Creek—stream OR-9
Champagne Creek Valley—valley OR-9
Champagne Ditch OR-9
Champagne Falls—falls MT-8
**Champagne Fountain**—pop pl CA-9
Champagne Gulch—valley AK-9
Champagne Island—cape NJ-2
Champagne Lake—lake WI-6
Champagne Ranch—locale MT-8
Champagne Spring—spring (2) CA-9
Champagne Spring—spring CO-8
Champagnolle—locale AR-4
Champagnolle Creek—stream AR-4
Champagnolle Landing Oil Field—oilfield AR-4
Champagnolle Oil And Gas Field—oilfield AR-4
Champagnolle (Township of)—fmr MCD AR-4
**Champaign**—pop pl IL-6
Champaign City (Township of)—civ div IL-6
**Champaign (County)**—pop pl IL-6
**Champaign (County)**—pop pl OH-6
Champaign Creek ID-8
Champaign Island NJ-2
Champaign Island—island WI-6
Champaign Point—cape WA-9
Champaign Sch (historical)—school MO-7
**Champaign (Township of)**—pop pl IL-6
Champaine Canyon ID-8
Champansville PA-2
Champayne Falls MT-8
Champbellton Sch—school NC-3
Champ Branch—stream (2) VA-3
Champ Clark Bridge—other IL-6
Champ Cooper Sch—school LA-4
Champ Creek—stream NC-3
**Champ d'Aisle**—pop pl TX-5
Champeau Sch—school WI-6
Champee Spring—spring TX-5
Champe-Fremont 1 Archeol Site—hist pl NE-7
Champe Knobs—summit WV-2
Champepadan Creek—stream MN-6
Champepadan Creek MN-6
Champepedean Creek MN-6
Champe Rocks WV-2
Champe Rocks—rock WV-2
Champers Cem—cemetery OH-6
Champey Pocket—bay TN-4
**Champie**—pop pl AZ-5
Champie Ranch—locale AZ-5
Champie Sch—school AZ-5
Champignol Lake—lake LA-4
**Champignon Subdivision**—pop pl UT-8
Champion NC-3
Champion—locale AL-4
Champion—locale MO-7
Champion—locale PA-2
Champion—locale TX-5
**Champion**—pop pl IN-6
**Champion**—pop pl MI-6
**Champion**—pop pl MT-8
**Champion**—pop pl NE-7
**Champion**—pop pl NY-2
**Champion**—pop pl NC-3
**Champion**—pop pl OH-6
**Champion**—pop pl (2) PA-2
**Champion**—pop pl WI-6
Champion, Henry, House—hist pl CT-1
Champion, Lake—lake NY-2
Champion, Mount—summit CO-8
Champion Acre Lake—reservoir IN-6
Champion Acre Lake Dam—dam IN-6
Champion Basin—basin CO-8
Champion Bend—bend TX-5
Champion Branch—stream AL-4
Champion Canal—canal NE-7
Champion Canyon CA-9
Champion Canyon—valley CA-9
Champion Canyon—valley NM-5
Champion Cem—cemetery AL-4
Champion Cem—cemetery AR-4
Champion Cem—cemetery CT-1
Champion Cem—cemetery IL-6
Champion Cem—cemetery (2) TN-4
Champion Cem—cemetery TX-5
Champion Center Cem—cemetery OH-6
Champion City—locale MO-7
Champion City Ch—church MO-7
Champion Cove—valley TN-4
Champion Creek—stream AL-4
Champion Creek—stream (3) AK-9
Champion Creek—stream AZ-5
Champion Creek—stream (3) GA-3
Champion Creek—stream (2) ID-8
Champion Creek—stream KY-4
Champion Creek—stream (2) OR-9
Champion Creek—stream PA-2
Champion Creek—stream TX-5
Champion Creek—stream WA-9
Champion Creek Rsvr—reservoir TX-5
Champion Crossroad—locale GA-3
Champion Dirt Mine—mine CO-8
Champion Drain—canal MI-6
Champion Draw—valley WY-8
Champion Gulch—valley CO-8
**Champion haty**—pop pl MO-7
Champion Heights OH-6
Champion Heights—other OH-6
Champion Heights Shop Ctr—locale NC-3
Champion Hill—locale MS-4
Champion Hill Battlefield—hist pl MS-4
Champion Hill Cem—cemetery MI-6
Champion Hill Ch—church (2) IA-7
Champion Hill Ch—church MS-4
Champion Hill Sch—school IA-7
Champion Hill Sch (historical)—school MO-7
**Champion (historical)**—pop pl OR-9
Champion Hollow—valley AL-4

Champion Huddle—locale ... NY-2
Champion Lake—lake ... TN-4
Champion Lake—lake ... TX-5
Champion Lake—reservoir ... AL-4
Champion Lake—reservoir ... TX-5
Champion Lakes—lake ... ID-8
Champion Lakes Golf Course—locale ... PA-2
Champion-McGarrah Plantation—hist pl ... GA-3
Champion Mill—hist pl ... NE-7
Champion Mill—locale ... CO-8
Champion Mine—mine ... AZ-5
Champion Mine—mine (2) ... CA-9
Champion Mine—mine (3) ... CO-8
Champion Mine—mine ... ID-8
Champion Mine—mine (2) ... MT-8
Champion Mine—mine (2) ... NV-8
Champion Mine—mine ... OR-9
Champion Mine—mine (2) ... SD-7
**Champion Mine**—pop pl ... MI-6
Champion Mine (Inactive)—mine ... NM-5
Champion Number One Mine Refuse Bank Dam—dam ... PA-2
Champion Park—park ... OR-9
Champion Pass—gap ... MT-8
Champion Point—summit ... ID-8
Champion Pond—lake (2) ... ME-1
**Champion (Roaring Run)**—pop pl ... PA-2
Champion Rod and Gun Club—other ... TX-5
Champion Run ... PA-2
Champion Run—stream ... IN-6
Champions—CDP ... TX-5
Champion Saddle—gap ... OR-9
Champion Sch—school (6) ... IL-6
Champion Sch—school ... MI-6
Champion Sch—school ... NE-7
Champion Sch—school ... OH-6
Champion Sch (historical)—school ... AL-4
Champion-Shepherdson House—hist pl ... KY-4
Champions Hill ... MS-4
**Champion Siding**—pop pl ... SD-7
Champion Slough—gut ... CA-9
Champion Spring—spring ... AL-4
Champion Spring—spring ... AZ-5
Champion Spring Branch—stream ... MO-7
Champion Springs Cove—bay ... KY-4
Champion State Rec Area—park ... NE-7
Champion Station ... OH-6
Championsville Post Office (historical)—building ... TN-4
Champion Swamp—stream ... VA-3
Champion Tank—reservoir ... AZ-5
**Champion (Town of)**—pop pl ... NY-2
Champion Township—civil ... MO-7
**Champion Township**—pop pl ... ND-7
**Champion (Township of)**—pop pl ... MI-6
**Champion (Township of)**—pop pl ... MN-6
**Champion (Township of)**—pop pl ... OH-6
Champion Valley—valley ... WI-6
Champion Valley Cem—cemetery ... WI-6
Champion Well—well ... AZ-5
Champion Windmill—locale ... NM-5
Champlain—locale ... VA-3
**Champlain**—pop pl ... NY-2
Champlain—post sta ... VT-1
Champlain, Lake—lake ... NY-2
Champlain, Lake—lake ... VT-1
Champlain Bayou—bay ... FL-3
Champlain Canal—canal ... NY-2
Champlain Canal—hist pl ... NY-2
Champlain Central HS—school ... NY-2
Champlain Corners—locale ... NY-2
Champlain Country Club—other ... VT-1
Champlain Memorial—other ... NY-2
Champlain Monument—other ... ME-1
Champlain Mtn—summit ... ME-1
**Champlain Park**—pop pl ... NY-2
Champlain Point—cape ... LA-4
Champlain River ... NY-2
Champlain Sch—hist pl ... VT-1
Champlain Sch—school ... MI-6
Champlain Speedway—other ... NY-2
**Champlain (Town of)**—pop pl ... NY-2
Champlain Valley Exposition—park ... VT-1
Champlin—locale ... IL-6
Champlin—locale ... UT-8
**Champlin**—pop pl ... MN-6
Champlin, H. D., & Son Horseshoeing and Wagonmaking—hist pl ... NY-2
Champlin, Peleg, House—hist pl ... RI-1
Champlin Cem—cemetery ... NY-2
Champlin Cem—cemetery ... PA-2
Champlin Cove—bay ... RI-1
Champlin Creek—stream ... CA-9
Champlin Creek—stream ... NY-2
Champlin Hill—summit ... RI-1
Champlin Hollow—valley (2) ... PA-2
**Champlin Meadows**—pop pl ... IN-6
Champlin Mountains ... UT-8
Champlin Neck—cape ... DE-2
Champlin Peak—summit ... UT-8
Champlin Pond—reservoir ... NH-1
Champlin Rock—pillar ... RI-1
Champlins Dock—locale ... RI-1
Champlin Slough—stream ... CA-9
Champlin (Township of)—other ... MN-6
**Champlin Village**—pop pl ... DE-2
Champman Creek ... GA-3
Champman Creek—stream ... OR-9
Champney Brook—stream ... NH-1
Champney Island—island ... GA-3
Champney River—channel ... GA-3
Champneys Slough Stream—stream ... WA-9
**Champoeg**—pop pl ... OR-9
Champoeg Cem—cemetery ... OR-9
Champoeg Creek—stream ... OR-9
Champoeg Monument—other ... OR-9
Champoeg State Park—park ... OR-9
Champoeg State Park Historic Archeol District—hist pl ... OR-9
Champ Point—cape ... MD-2
Champ Post Office (historical)—building ... TN-4
**Champ (Saint Peters Creek)**—pop pl ... MD-2
Champs Flat—flat ... CA-9
Champurrado Tank—reservoir ... AZ-5
Champurrado Wash—stream ... AZ-5
Champurrado Wash Tank—reservoir ... AZ-5
Champurrado Well—well ... AZ-5
Champwood—locale ... WV-2
**Chan**—pop pl ... OK-5
**Chana**—pop pl ... IL-6
Chanac Creek—stream ... CA-9
Chananagi (historical)—locale ... AL-4
Chanarambie Creek—stream ... MN-6
**Chanarambie (Township of)**—pop pl ... MN-6
Chanatta Peak ... TX-5
Chanatte Peak ... TX-5
Cha'n Canyon ... OR-9
Chance ... TX-5
Chance—locale ... AR-4
Chance—locale ... CO-8
Chance—locale ... KY-4
Chance—locale ... MT-8
Chance—locale ... OK-5
**Chance**—pop pl ... AL-4
**Chance**—pop pl ... MD-2
**Chance**—pop pl ... SD-7
**Chance**—pop pl ... TX-5
**Chance**—pop pl ... VA-3
Chance, Albert Bishop, House and Gardens—hist pl ... MO-7
Chance, James O., House—hist pl ... TX-5
Chance Airp—airport ... MO-7
Chance Bay—swamp ... FL-3
Chance Branch—stream ... IN-6
Chance Branch—stream ... LA-4
Chance Cem—cemetery ... KS-7
Chance Cem—cemetery ... MT-8
Chance Cove—bay ... AK-9
Chance Creek—stream ... AR-4
Chance Creek—stream ... CO-8
Chance Creek—stream ... GA-3
Chance Creek—stream ... ID-8
Chance Creek—stream ... OR-9
Chanceford ... PA-2
Chanceford Cem—cemetery ... PA-2
Chanceford Ch—church ... PA-2
Chanceford Tabernacle—church ... PA-2
**Chanceford (Township of)**—pop pl ... PA-2
Chance Gulch—valley ... CO-8
Chance Gut ... MD-2
Chance Hill Ch—church ... GA-3
Chance Hollow—valley (3) ... TN-4
Chance Hollow Hill—ridge ... MN-6
Chance Island—island ... ME-1
Chance Island—island ... MD-2
Chance Lagoon—bay ... AK-9
Chance Lateral—canal ... ID-8
Chance Lateral—canal ... OR-9
Chancellor—locale ... TX-5
**Chancellor**—pop pl ... AL-4
**Chancellor**—pop pl ... MS-4
**Chancellor**—pop pl ... SD-7
**Chancellor**—pop pl ... VA-3
Chancellor And Son Dam—dam ... TN-4
Chancellor And Son Lake—reservoir ... TN-4
Chancellor Ave Sch—school ... NJ-2
Chancellor Campground—locale ... WA-9
Chancellor Cem—cemetery ... AL-4
Chancellor Cem—cemetery ... MS-4
Chancellor Cem—cemetery (2) ... SD-7
Chancellor Cem—cemetery ... TX-5
Chancellor Ch—church ... AL-4
Chancellor Crossroads—locale ... AL-4
Chancellor Crossroads Cemetery ... AL-4
**Chancellor Green**—pop pl ... VA-3
Chancellor Hardware—hist pl ... WV-2
Chancellor (historical)—locale ... MS-4
Chancellor Lake—lake ... MI-6
Chancellor (Magisterial District)—fmr MCD ... VA-3
Chancellor Mtn—summit ... OK-5
Chancellor Mtn—summit ... VA-3
Chancellor Point—cape (2) ... MD-2
Chancellor Sch—school ... VA-3
Chancellors Ferry (historical)—locale ... AL-4
Chancellors Point ... MD-2
Chancellor Square—locale ... NY-2
Chancellors Run—stream ... WV-2
Chancellors Switch ... MS-4
Chancellor Street Sch—school ... PA-2
Chancellorsville—locale ... VA-3
Chancellorsville Battlefield—locale ... VA-3
**Chancellorville**—pop pl ... VA-3
Chance-Loeb (CCD)—cens area ... TX-5
Chance-Loeb Sch—school ... TX-5
Chance Mine—mine ... CA-9
Chance Mine—mine (2) ... NV-8
Chance Oil Field—oilfield ... KS-7
Chance Point—cape ... MD-2
Chance Pond—lake ... GA-3
Chance Pond Branch—stream ... NH-1
Chance Post Office (historical)—building ... AL-4
**Chance (Rock Creek)**—pop pl ... MD-2
Chances Branch—stream ... VA-3
Chances Cem—cemetery ... VA-3
Chance Sch—school ... MI-6
Chance Sch—school ... MO-7
Chance Sch—school ... TX-5
Chances Chapel—church ... VA-3
Chances Creek—stream ... AR-4
Chances Crossroad—locale ... AL-4
Chances Crossroad Ch—church ... AL-4
Chances Cross Roads ... AL-4
Chances Cross Roads Sch (historical)—school ... AL-4
Chances Store—locale ... TX-5
Chancetown—locale ... VA-3
Chance Township—civil ... SD-7
**Chance Township**—pop pl ... SD-7
Chanceville ... NJ-2
Chancey—locale ... FL-3
Chancey Cem—cemetery ... TN-4
Chancey Mill Creek—stream ... GA-3
Chanceytown—locale ... TN-4
Chanchelulla Creek—stream ... CA-9
Chanchelulla Gulch—valley ... CA-9
Chanchelulla Mountain ... CA-9
Chanchelulla Peak—summit ... CA-9
Chan Creek—stream ... MT-8
Chancy—locale ... MS-4
Chancy Bay—swamp ... FL-3
Chancy Bay—swamp ... NC-3
Chancy Post Office (historical)—building ... TN-4
Chanda Creek—stream ... MI-6
**Chandalar**—pop pl ... AK-9
Chandalar Creek—stream ... AK-9
Chandalar Lake—lake ... AK-9
Chandalar Mine—mine ... AK-9
Chandalar River—stream ... AK-9
Chandalar Shelf—area ... AK-9
**Chandalar South (subdivision)**—pop pl ... AL-4
Chandans Creek—stream ... CA-9
Chandeleur Islands—island ... LA-4
Chandeleur Light—hist pl ... LA-4
Chandeleur Sound—bay ... LA-4
Chandeleur Sound—bay ... MS-4
Chandelier Tree—locale ... CA-9
Chandelle Estates Airp—airport ... DE-2
Chandelower Creek—stream ... AL-4
Chander Cave—cave ... AL-4
Chander Run—stream ... PA-2
Chandler—locale ... AR-4
Chandler—locale ... MI-6
Chandler—locale ... MO-7
**Chandler**—pop pl ... AZ-5
**Chandler**—pop pl (2) ... IN-6
**Chandler**—pop pl ... MN-6
**Chandler**—pop pl ... OH-6
**Chandler**—pop pl ... OK-5
**Chandler**—pop pl (2) ... SC-3
**Chandler**—pop pl ... TN-4
**Chandler**—pop pl ... TX-5
**Chandler**—pop pl ... VA-3
Chandler, Asa, House—hist pl ... GA-3
Chandler, Capt. Ebe, House—hist pl ... DE-2
Chandler, Gen. Samuel, House—hist pl ... MA-1
Chandler, George, Sch—hist pl ... PA-2
Chandler, John, House—hist pl ... KY-4
Chandler, Joseph, House—hist pl ... DE-2
Chandler, Matthew, House—hist pl ... OH-6
Chandler, Walter S., House—hist pl ... WI-6
Chandler Acad—school ... FL-3
Chandler Airstrip—airport ... OR-9
Chandler Bay—bay ... ME-1
Chandler-Bigsby-Abbot House—hist pl ... MA-1
Chandler Bookstore—hist pl ... OK-5
Chandler Bottom—bend ... TX-5
Chandler Branch—stream ... AL-4
Chandler Branch—stream (2) ... KY-4
Chandler Branch—stream ... LA-4
Chandler Branch—stream (2) ... TX-5
Chandler Bridge—bridge ... OR-9
Chandler Bridge Creek—stream ... SC-3
Chandler Brook—stream (4) ... ME-1
Chandler Brook—stream ... MI-6
Chandler Brook—stream (2) ... NH-1
Chandler Brook—stream ... VT-1
Chandler Brook Deadwater—lake ... ME-1
Chandler Butte—summit ... WA-9
Chandler Cabin—locale ... OR-9
Chandler Camp—locale ... OK-5
Chandler Canal—canal ... WA-9
Chandler Canyon—valley (2) ... CA-9
Chandler Canyon—valley ... ID-8
Chandler Canyon—valley ... NM-5
Chandler Canyon—valley ... OR-9
Chandler Canyon—valley ... UT-8
Chandler Cave ... AL-4
Chandler Cave—cave ... TN-4
Chandler (CCD)—cens area ... AZ-5
Chandler (CCD)—cens area ... OK-5
Chandler Cem—cemetery (3) ... AL-4
Chandler Cem—cemetery ... AR-4
Chandler Cem—cemetery (4) ... GA-3
Chandler Cem—cemetery ... IL-6
Chandler Cem—cemetery (2) ... IN-6
Chandler Cem—cemetery ... IA-7
Chandler Cem—cemetery ... KY-4
Chandler Cem—cemetery (2) ... ME-1
Chandler Cem—cemetery ... MI-6
Chandler Cem—cemetery (4) ... MS-4
Chandler Cem—cemetery ... MO-7
Chandler Cem—cemetery ... OH-6
Chandler Cem—cemetery ... OK-5
Chandler Cem—cemetery ... SC-3
Chandler Cem—cemetery (2) ... TN-4
Chandler Cem—cemetery ... UT-8
Chandler Cem—cemetery ... VA-3
Chandler Cem—cemetery ... WV-2
Chandler Ch—church ... MI-6
Chandler Ch—church ... TN-4
Chandler City Park ... AZ-5
Chandler Community Hosp—hospital ... AZ-5
Chandler Cove—bay ... ME-1
Chandler Cove Landing—locale ... ME-1
Chandler Creek—stream ... AR-4
Chandler Creek—stream ... CA-9
Chandler Creek—stream ... CO-8
Chandler Creek—stream ... LA-4
Chandler Creek—stream ... NC-3
Chandler Creek—stream ... OK-5
Chandler Creek—stream (2) ... OR-9
Chandler Crossing—locale ... VA-3
Chandler Day Sch—school ... CA-9
Chandler Deadwater—lake ... ME-1
Chandler Ditch—canal ... MT-8
Chandler Ditch—canal ... NV-8
Chandler Ditch—canal ... OH-6
Chandler Ditch—stream ... TN-4
Chandler Draw—valley ... NM-5
Chandler Draw—valley ... TX-5
Chandler Elem Sch—school (2) ... IN-6
Chandler Falls—falls ... UT-8
Chandler Fire Tower—tower ... AL-4
Chandler Fork—valley ... UT-8
Chandler Gap—gap ... AL-4
Chandler Gap—gap ... NC-3
Chandler Gap—gap ... TN-4
Chandler Gardens Mobile Home Park—locale ... AZ-5
Chandler Glade—flat ... CA-9
Chandler Gray House—building ... MA-1
Chandler Grove Ch—church ... MS-4
Chandler Grove Ch—church ... NC-3
Chandler Gulch—valley ... CA-9
Chandler Hammock Slough—stream ... FL-3
**Chandler Heights**—pop pl ... AZ-5
Chandler Heights Post Office—building ... AZ-5
Chandler Heights Sch—school ... AZ-5
Chandler-Hidden House—hist pl ... MA-1
Chandler Hill—summit (2) ... CT-1
Chandler Hill—summit (4) ... ME-1
Chandler Hill—summit (3) ... MA-1
Chandler Hill—summit ... MI-6
Chandler Hill—summit (2) ... NH-1
Chandler Hill Cem—cemetery ... ME-1
Chandler Hill Cem—cemetery ... MA-1
Chandler Hill Park—park ... MA-1
Chandler Hills—summit ... MI-6
**Chandler Hill (subdivision)**—pop pl ... MA-1
Chandler (historical)—locale ... KS-7
Chandler (historical)—locale ... SD-7
**Chandler (historical)**—pop pl ... OR-9
Chandler (historical P.O.)—locale ... IA-7
Chandler Hollow—valley ... AL-4
Chandler Hollow—valley ... GA-3
Chandler Hollow—valley (2) ... MO-7
Chandler Hollow—valley ... TN-4
Chandler Hotel and Annex—hist pl ... OR-9
Chandler Hovey Park—park ... MA-1
Chandler HS—school ... AZ-5
Chandler Interchange—other ... OK-5
Chandler Island ... ME-1
Chandler Island—island ... ME-1
Chandler Isle ... MA-1
Chandler JHS—school ... AZ-5
Chandler Junction ... AZ-5
Chandler Knob—summit ... KY-4
Chandler Lake—lake ... AK-9
Chandler Lake—lake ... ME-1
Chandler Lake—lake ... MI-6
Chandler Lake—lake (2) ... MN-6
Chandler Lake—lake ... OR-9
Chandler Lake—reservoir ... GA-3
Chandler Lake—reservoir ... NC-3
Chandler Lake—reservoir ... OK-5
Chandler Lake Dam—dam ... NC-3
Chandler Lake (historical)—reservoir ... TN-4
Chandler-Linder House—hist pl ... GA-3
Chandler Maintenance Yard—locale ... AZ-5
Chandler Marsh—swamp ... MI-6
Chandler Marsh—swamp ... VA-3
Chandler Meadow—swamp ... NH-1
Chandler Meadow Brook—stream ... VT-1
Chandler Meadows—flat ... WA-9
Chandler Meadows Mobile Home Park—locale ... AZ-5
Chandler Memorial Cem—cemetery ... MN-6
Chandler Millpond—reservoir ... MA-1
Chandler Mill Stream—stream ... ME-1
Chandler Mountain ... VA-3
**Chandler Mountain**—pop pl ... AL-4
Chandler Mountain—ridge ... AL-4
Chandler Mountain Ch—church (2) ... AL-4
Chandler Mountain Community Center—building ... AL-4
Chandler Mountain Dam—dam ... AL-4
Chandler Mountain Lake—reservoir ... AL-4
Chandler Mountain Sch—school ... AL-4
Chandler Mtn—summit ... AL-4
Chandler Mtn—summit (2) ... ME-1
Chandler Mtn—summit ... NH-1
Chandler Mtn—summit (2) ... OR-9
Chandler Municipal Airp—airport ... AZ-5
Chandler Music Hall and Bethany Parish House—hist pl ... VT-1
Chandler Natural Bridge—arch ... AL-4
Chandler Normal Sch Bldg and Webster Hall—hist pl ... KY-4
Chandler Park—park ... IL-6
Chandler Park—park ... MI-6
Chandler Park—park (2) ... OK-5
Chandler Park—park ... TN-4
**Chandler Park**—pop pl ... LA-4
Chandler Parker Mtn ... ME-1
Chandler Parker Mtn—summit ... ME-1
Chandler Pass—gap ... OR-9
Chandler Pasture—flat ... UT-8
**Chandler Plan**—pop pl ... PA-2
Chandler Point—cape ... ME-1
Chandler Pond—lake ... FL-3
Chandler Pond—lake ... IL-6
Chandler Pond—lake ... ME-1
Chandler Pond—lake ... MA-1
Chandler Pond—lake ... NY-2
Chandler Pond—lake ... VT-1
Chandler Post Office—building ... AZ-5
Chandler Post Office (historical)—building ... TN-4
Chandler Power And Pumping Plant—other ... WA-9
Chandler Ranch—locale ... CA-9
Chandler Ridge—ridge ... AL-4
Chandler Ridge—ridge ... ME-1
Chandler Ridge—ridge ... NH-1
Chandler Ridge—ridge ... VT-1
Chandler River ... ME-1
Chandler River—stream ... AK-9
Chandler River—stream ... ME-1
Chandlers—locale ... SC-3
Chandler's Bay ... ME-1
Chandlers Branch—stream ... GA-3
Chandlers Branch—stream ... VA-3
Chandler Sch—school ... CA-9
Chandler Sch—school ... IL-6
Chandler Sch—school ... KS-7
Chandler Sch—school (2) ... MI-6
Chandler Sch—school ... NE-7
Chandler Sch—school ... PA-2
Chandler Sch—school ... TX-5
Chandler Sch—school ... VT-1
Chandler Sch—school (2) ... WV-2
**Chandlers Chapel**—pop pl ... KY-4
Chandler Sch (historical)—school ... SD-7
Chandlers Corner ... VA-3
Chandlers Creek—stream ... GA-3
Chandlers Ferry (historical)—locale ... AL-4
Chandlers Fork ... VA-3
Chandlers Forks—locale ... VA-3
Chandlers Hollow ... DE-2
Chandlers Island ... ME-1
Chandlers Island ... MA-1
Chandlers Island—island ... VA-3
Chandlers Lake—lake ... MI-6
Chandlers Lake—reservoir ... GA-3
Chandler Slough—gut ... FL-3
Chandlers Millpond—reservoir ... VA-3
Chandlers Mill Run—stream ... VA-3
Chandlers Mills—locale ... NH-1
Chandler Sound ... LA-4
Chandlers Peak—summit ... TX-5
Chandlers Point ... ME-1
Chandlers Pond ... MA-1
Chandlers Pond—lake ... MA-1
Chandler Spring—spring ... ID-8
Chandler Spring—spring (2) ... MT-8
Chandler Spring—spring ... TN-4
Chandler Springs—locale ... AL-4
Chandler Springs—spring ... AZ-5
Chandler Springs Ch—church ... AL-4
Chandler Springs Creek ... AL-4
Chandler Springs Sch—school ... AL-4
Chandler Spring Station (historical)—locale ... AL-4
Chandlers Purchase—civil ... NH-1
Chandlers Run—stream ... OH-6
Chandlers Sch—school ... NH-1
Chandler State Park—park ... OR-9
Chandler State Wildlife Mngmt Area—park ... MN-6
Chandler Station ... NH-1
Chandler Store—hist pl ... ME-1
Chandler Stream—stream ... ME-1
Chandler Street Sch—school (2) ... MA-1
**Chandler Subdivision**—pop pl ... UT-8
Chandler Substation—locale ... AZ-5
**Chandlers Valley**—pop pl ... PA-2
Chandlers Valley Cem—cemetery ... PA-2
**Chandlersville**—pop pl ... OH-6
Chandlersville Cem—cemetery ... OH-6
Chandler Swamp—swamp ... MA-1
Chandler Tank—reservoir ... AZ-5
Chandler Tank—reservoir ... NM-5
Chandler Temple CME Ch—church ... MS-4
**Chandler Township**—pop pl ... ND-7
**Chandler (Township of)**—pop pl (2) ... MI-6
Chandler Tunnel—mine ... CO-8
Chandlerville—locale ... KY-4
**Chandlerville**—pop pl ... IL-6
Chandlerville Sch—school ... IL-6
Chandlerville (Township of)—civ div ... IL-6
Chandler Wayside Park ... OR-9
Chandler Windmills—locale ... NM-5
Chandley Brake—swamp ... LA-4
Chandor Gardens—park ... TX-5
Chandris Cove—bay ... AK-9
Chaneandepeco Inlet (historical)—gut ... NC-3
Chanel HS—school ... OH-6
Chanels Chapel—church ... MS-4
**Chanenton Cove P R U D Subdivision**—pop pl ... UT-8
Chaney ... MS-4
Chaney—locale ... MD-2
Chaney—locale ... TX-5
**Chaney**—pop pl ... AR-4
**Chaney**—pop pl ... IA-7
Chaney, O. P., Grain Elevator—hist pl ... OH-6
Chaney Arroyo—stream ... CO-8
Chaney Arroyo—stream ... NM-5
Chaney Bluff—cliff ... AR-4
Chaney Branch ... AL-4
Chaney Branch—stream (2) ... AL-4
Chaney Branch—stream ... AR-4
Chaney Branch—stream (2) ... LA-4
Chaney Branch—stream ... MO-7
Chaney Branch—stream (2) ... TN-4
Chaney Branch—stream ... TX-5
Chaney Branch—stream ... VA-3
Chaney Cem—cemetery ... AL-4
Chaney Cem—cemetery ... AR-4
Chaney Cem—cemetery ... GA-3
Chaney Cem—cemetery (2) ... IL-6
Chaney Cem—cemetery ... IA-7
Chaney Cem—cemetery (3) ... KY-4
Chaney Cem—cemetery ... LA-4
Chaney Cem—cemetery ... MS-4
Chaney Cem—cemetery ... TN-4
Chaney Cem—cemetery ... WV-2
Chaney Ch—church ... AR-4
Chaney Chapel Cem—cemetery ... AL-4
Chaney Chapel Cem—cemetery ... MO-7
Chaney Chapel Ch—church ... AL-4
Chaney Creek ... TX-5
Chaney Creek—stream ... AL-4
Chaney Creek—stream ... IL-6
Chaney Creek—stream (3) ... MS-4
Chaney Creek—stream ... NC-3
Chaney Creek—stream ... OK-5
Chaney Creek—stream (2) ... VA-3
Chaney Ditch—canal ... IN-6
Chaney Ditch—canal ... OH-6
Chaney Fork—stream ... WV-2
Chaney Gap—gap ... TN-4
Chaney Glacier—glacier ... MT-8
Chaney Gulch—valley ... ID-8
Chaney Hill—summit ... CA-9
Chaney Hill—summit ... MA-1
Chaney Hill State For—forest ... NH-1
Chaney Hollow—valley ... AR-4
Chaney Hollow—valley ... MD-2
Chaney Hollow—valley ... TN-4
Chaney Hollow—valley ... VA-3
Chaney HS—school ... OH-6
Chaney Lake ... CO-8
Chaney Lake—lake ... AR-4
Chaney Lake—lake ... MI-6
Chaney Lake—lake ... TN-4
Chaney Lake—reservoir ... TX-5
Chaney Lakes—lake ... LA-4
Chaney Place—locale ... AZ-5
Chaney Point—cape ... MN-6
Chaney Point—summit ... TX-5
Chaney Pumping Station—other ... CA-9
Chaney Ranch—locale (2) ... CA-9
Chaney Ranch—locale ... NM-5
Chaney Ranch—locale ... UT-8
Chaney Ranch Canyon—valley ... CA-9
Chaney Rsvr—reservoir ... OR-9
Chaney Run—stream (2) ... PA-2
Chaney Run—stream ... WV-2
Chaney Rush Creek—stream ... SD-7
**Chaneys**—pop pl ... VA-3
Chaney Sch—school ... IL-6
Chaney Sch—school ... MD-2
Chaney Sch—school ... MI-6
Chaneys Landing (historical)—locale ... AL-4
Chaneys Store—locale ... VA-3
Chaney Store ... AL-4
Chaney Store (historical)—locale ... MS-4
**Chaneysville**—pop pl ... PA-2
Chaney Swamp—stream ... SC-3
Chaneyville ... IL-6
**Chaneyville**—pop pl ... MD-2
Chaneyville Run—stream ... OH-6
Chaneyville Sch—school ... LA-4
Chaney Yard—locale ... TX-5
Changad—channel ... FM-9
Change Creek—stream ... WA-9
Change Island—island ... AK-9
Change Point—cape ... MD-2
Changewater—locale ... NJ-2
Chango Lake—lake ... CA-9
Chango Tank—reservoir ... AZ-5
Chan Gurney Municipal Airp—airport ... SD-7
**Chanhassen**—pop pl ... MN-6
Chanhassen Township Hall—hist pl ... MN-6
Chaniliut—locale ... AK-9
Chaniliut Slough—stream ... AK-9
Chanin Bldg—hist pl ... NY-2
Chanis Rock—summit ... OR-9
Chanki Chitto ... MS-4
Chanki (historical)—locale ... MS-4
Chanki River ... MS-4
Chankliut Island—island ... AK-9
Chanko Pond—lake ... CT-1
Chan Lake—lake ... MT-8
Chanley Creek ... CA-9
Channahatchee ... AL-4
Channahatchee Creek—stream ... AL-4
Channahatche Hunting Club—locale ... AL-4
**Channahon**—pop pl ... IL-6
**Channahon (Township of)**—pop pl ... IL-6
**Channel**—pop pl ... MO-7
Channel, The ... FL-3
**Channel Acres (subdivision)**—pop pl ... NC-3
Channel Arm—bay ... CA-9
Channel Bay East—bay ... TX-5
Channel Bay West—bay ... TX-5
Channel Branch—stream ... GA-3
Channel Branch—stream ... MS-4
Channel Branch—stream ... TN-4
Channel Bridge—bridge ... NY-2
Channel City ... KY-4
Channel Cove—bay ... NJ-2
Channel Creek—stream ... ID-8
Channel Creek—stream ... NJ-2
Channel Creek—stream (2) ... OR-9
Channel Five—channel ... FL-3
Channel Four Airport ... UT-8
Channel Hollow—valley ... TN-4
Channel Island ... ID-8
Channel Island ... NY-2
Channel Island—island (6) ... AK-9
Channel Island—island ... AZ-5
Channel Island—island (2) ... MI-6
Channel Island—island ... MS-4
Channel Islands—area ... AK-9
Channel Islands—post sta ... CA-9
Channel Islands Harbor—harbor ... CA-9
Channel Islands Natl Monmt—park ... CA-9
Channel Islands Natl Park—park ... CA-9
Channel Key—island (2) ... FL-3
Channel Key Banks—bar ... FL-3
Channel Key Pass—channel ... FL-3
**Channell**—pop pl ... FL-3
Channel Lake ... MI-6
Channel Lake—CDP ... IL-6
Channel Lake—lake ... AK-9
Channel Lake—lake ... CA-9
Channel Lake—lake ... IL-6
Channell Cem—cemetery ... TN-4
Channell-Lee Stadium—park ... AL-4
Channel Lowery Creek ... AL-4
Channel Mtn—summit ... WY-8
Channel Park—park ... CA-9
Channel Point—cape ... AK-9
Channel Point—cape ... FL-3
Channel Point—cape ... MD-2
Channel Point—cape ... PW-9
Channel Point Gut—gut ... MD-2
Channel Pond—lake ... NY-2
Channel Reef—bar ... AZ-5
Channel Rock—bar (4) ... ME-1
Channel Rock—island (2) ... AK-9
Channel Rock—island ... CT-1
Channel Rock—island (3) ... ME-1
Channel Rock—other ... AK-9
Channel Rock—rock (2) ... MA-1
Channel Rock—summit ... ME-1
Channel Rock Hollow—valley ... VA-3
Channel Rock Island—island ... ME-1
Channel Rocks—bar ... ME-1
Channel Rocks—other ... AK-9
Channel Slough—stream ... CA-9
Channel Tank—reservoir ... AZ-5
Channel Three—harbor ... CA-9
Channel Two—channel ... FL-3
Channel Two—harbor ... CA-9
**Channolview**—pop pl ... TX-5
**Channelwood**—pop pl ... TX-5
Channey Creek—stream ... LA-4
Channey Creek—stream ... MS-4
Channey Crossing—locale ... TX-5
Channey Rsvr—reservoir ... WY-8
Channey Slough—gut ... AR-4
Channing—locale ... CO-8
**Channing**—pop pl ... MI-6
**Channing**—pop pl ... TX-5
Channing (CCD)—cens area ... TX-5
Channing Cem—cemetery ... MI-6
Channing Creek—stream ... CO-8
**Channing (historical)**—pop pl ... SD-7
Channing Meadow—flat ... CA-9
Channing Sch—school ... MA-1
Channing School—locale ... CO-8
Channings Pond—lake ... MA-1
**Channin (subdivision)**—pop pl ... DE-2
Chan Owapi Lodge (historical)—locale ... ND-7
Chanpepedan CA VAR Champepedan Creek ... MN-6
Chanpepedan Creek ... MN-6
Chanpepedean Creek ... MN-6
Chanpurado Windmill—locale ... TX-5
Chanrigerikku ... MP-9
Chan Shacha Oju Wakpa ... SD-7
Chansler Canal No 30—canal ... CO-8
Chan Southeast Oil Field—oilfield ... WY-8
Chanta Creek Ch—church ... AL-4
Chantapeta Creek ... ND-7
Chanta Peta Creek—stream (2) ... ND-7
**Chantay Acres**—pop pl ... TN-4
Chant Cem—cemetery ... AR-4
**Chanteloupe Country Estates (subdivision)**—pop pl ... NC-3
Chanters Brook ... MA-1
Chanticleer—hist pl ... PA-2
**Chanticleer**—pop pl ... AR-4
**Chanticleer**—pop pl ... FL-3
Chanticleer Gift Shop—hist pl ... LA-4
Chanticleer Point—summit ... OR-9
Chantier Creek—stream ... SD-7

Chantier Creek Rec Area—*park* SD-7
*Chantilly* IL-6
Chantilly—*hist pl* VA-3
**Chantilly**—*pop pl* NC-3
**Chantilly**—*pop pl* VA-3
Chantilly Acres—*locale* FL-3
Chantilly Branch—*stream* VA-3
Chantilly Ch—*church* LA-4
Chantilly Country Club—*other* VA-3
**Chantilly Estates**—*pop pl* VA-3
Chantilly Hill—*summit* VA-3
Chantilly Sch—*school* NC-3
Chantilly Sch (abandoned)—*school* MO-7
Chantilly Speedway—*locale* NC-3
**Chantilly Square Subdivision**—*pop pl* UT-8
**Chantilly (subdivision)**—*pop pl* NC-3
**Chantilly Subdivision**—*pop pl* UT-8
Chant Lake—*lake* MN-6
Chanto Tank—*reservoir* TX-5
Chantry Flat—*flat* CA-9
Chantry Flat Station—*locale* CA-9
*Chanty Neck* VA-3
Chanuk Creek—*stream* AK-9
Chanute—*locale* TN-4
**Chanute**—*pop pl* KS-7
Chanute AFB—*military* IL-6
Chanute Air Force Base—*other* (2) IL-6
Chanute Country Club—*other* KS-7
*Chanute Field* IL-6
*Chanute Flying Field* IL-6
Chanute HS—*school* KS-7
Chanute Martin Johnson Airp—*airport* KS-7
Chanute Post Office (historical)—*building* TN-4
Chanute Sch (historical)—*school* TN-4
Chan-Ya-Ta Site—*hist pl* IA-7
Chaol Canyon—*valley* AZ-5
Chaonia Cem—*cemetery* MO-7
Chaonia Landing Rec Area—*locale* MO-7
Chaos Canyon—*valley* CO-8
Chaos Crags—*summit* CA-9
Chaos Crags Trail—*trail* CA-9
Chaos Crater—*crater* CA-9
Chaos Creek—*stream* CO-8
Chaos Creek—*stream* NV-8
Chaos Jumbles—*area* CA-9
Chaos Knob—*summit* NV-8
*Chaos Lava Beds* CA-9
Chaos Mtn—*summit* WY-8
Chaot—*other* GU-9
*Chaotic Cliffs* WA-9
Chaot River—*stream* GU-9
*Chaouakale* AL-4
*Chap* WV-2
Chap—*locale* VA-3
*Chapace Mountain* WA-9
Chapachap—*spring* FM-9
*Chapaka Mountain* WA-9
*Chapalap River* FM-9
**Chapanoke**—*pop pl* NC-3
*Chapaquaset Pond* MA-1
*Chapaquegick* MA-1
*Chaparal* AZ-5
Chaparosa Windmill—*locale* TX-5
**Chaparral**—*pop pl* NM-5
Chaparral, Lake—*reservoir* KS-7
*Chaparral Baptist Church* MS-4
Chaparral Basin—*basin* WA-9
Chaparral Campground—*locale* (2) CA-9
Chaparral Campground—*locale* ID-8
Chaparral Canyon—*valley* UT-8
Chaparral Cem—*cemetery* MS-4
Chaparral Cem—*cemetery* OH-6
Chaparral Ch—*church* MS-4
Chaparral Country Club—*other* TX-5
Chaparral Creek—*stream* CA-9
Chaparral Creek—*stream* CO-8
Chaparral Creek—*stream* ID-8
Chaparral Creek—*stream* OR-9
Chaparral Creek—*stream* WA-9
**Chaparral Estates**
**(subdivision)**—*pop pl* UT-8
Chaparral Golf Course—*other* AZ-5
Chaparral Guard Station—*locale* CA-9
Chaparral Gulch—*valley* AZ-5
Chaparral Hill—*summit* (3) CA-9
Chaparral (historical)—*locale* AZ-5
Chaparral Hollow—*valley* ID-8
Chaparral HS—*school* AZ-5
Chaparral HS—*school* KS-7
Chaparral Lake—*lake* NM-5
Chaparral Mtn—*summit* (2) CA-9
Chaparral Oil Field—*oilfield* MS-4
Chaparral Overlook—*locale* CA-9
Chaparral Park—*park* (2) AZ-5
Chaparral Peak—*summit* CA-9
Chaparral Post Office
(historical)—*building* MS-4
Chaparral Sch—*school* AZ-5
Chaparral Sch (historical)—*school* MS-4
Chaparral Slough—*stream* FL-3
Chaparral Spring—*spring* AZ-5
Chaparral Spring—*spring* CA-9
**Chaparral (subdivision)**—*pop pl* (2) AZ-5
Chaparral Tank—*reservoir* AZ-5
Chaparral Tank—*reservoir* NM-5
**Chaparral West Subdivision**—*pop pl* UT-8
Chaparral Windmill—*locale* TX-5
Chaparra Park—*park* CA-9
Chaparra Sch—*school* CA-9
Chaparrosa Camp—*locale* TX-5
Chaparrosa Creek—*stream* TX-5
Chaparrosa Peak—*summit* CA-9
Chaparrosa Ranch—*locale* TX-5
Chaparrosa Spring—*spring* CA-9
Chaparrosa Wash—*stream* CA-9
Chapatalito—*pillar* NM-5
Chapaton Drain—*stream* MI-6
Chap Branch—*stream* KY-4
Chap Branch—*stream* SC-3
*Chap Brook* NY-2
Chap Creek—*stream* WI-6
Chapeau, Lake—*lake* LA-4
*Chapeau Islands* MI-6
Chapeau Mtn—*summit* AK-9
Chapek Draw—*valley* WY-8
Chapek Lake—*lake* MN-6
Chapek Rsvr No 1—*reservoir* WY-8
Chapek Rsvr No 2—*reservoir* WY-8
*Chapel* MD-2
*Chapel* NC-3
Chapel—*church* FL-3
Chapel—*locale* MD-2
Chapel—*locale* PA-2
Chapel—*locale* VA-3
Chapel—*other* KY-4
**Chapel**—*pop pl* MD-2
**Chapel**—*pop pl* MO-7
**Chapel**—*pop pl* WV-2
Chapel, Lake—*lake* NC-3
Chapel, The—*church* CO-8
Chapel, The—*church* CT-1
**Chapel Acres**—*pop pl* VA-3
Chapel and Lovelace Hall, Marion Military
Institute—*hist pl* AL-4
Chapel B—*church* TX-5
Chapel Baptist Ch—*church* AL-4
Chapel Bell—*church* MS-4
*Chapel Bluff* IN-6
Chapel Bluff—*cliff* MO-7
Chapel Bluff Sch (abandoned)—*school* MO-7
*Chapel Branch* DE-2
*Chapel Branch* MD-2
*Chapel Branch* SC-3
Chapel Branch—*stream* AL-4
Chapel Branch—*stream* (2) DE-2
Chapel Branch—*stream* FL-3
Chapel Branch—*stream* (2) GA-3
Chapel Branch—*stream* IN-6
Chapel Branch—*stream* KY-4
Chapel Branch—*stream* MD-2
Chapel Branch—*stream* MS-4
Chapel Branch—*stream* MO-7
Chapel Branch—*stream* (2) NC-3
Chapel Branch—*stream* OK-5
Chapel Branch—*stream* (3) SC-3
Chapel Branch—*stream* (3) TN-4
Chapel Branch Ditch—*canal* MD-2
Chapel Brook—*stream* MA-1
Chapel Brook—*stream* NH-1
Chapel by the Sea—*church* (2) FL-3
Chapel by the Sea-Captiva—*church* FL-3
Chapel Canyon—*valley* WY-8
Chapel Canyon Pit—*reservoir* WY-8
Chapel Cave—*cave* AL-4
Chapel Cem—*cemetery* AR-4
Chapel Cem—*cemetery* IL-6
Chapel Cem—*cemetery* IN-6
Chapel Cem—*cemetery* ME-1
Chapel Cem—*cemetery* MD-2
Chapel Cem—*cemetery* MI-6
Chapel Cem—*cemetery* (3) MO-7
Chapel Cem—*cemetery* NC-3
Chapel Cem—*cemetery* (8) OH-6
Chapel Cem—*cemetery* (2) PA-2
Chapel Cem—*cemetery* (2) SC-3
Chapel Cem—*cemetery* TX-5
Chapel Cem—*cemetery* VA-3
Chapel Cem—*cemetery* WV-2
*Chapel Cemetery* MS-4
*Chapel Ch* AL-4
Chapel Ch—*church* AL-4
Chapel Ch—*church* (2) GA-3
Chapel Ch—*church* IN-6
Chapel Ch—*church* KY-4
Chapel Ch—*church* OH-6
Chapel Ch—*church* VA-3
Chapel Ch (abandoned)—*church* MO-7
Chapel Ch (historical)—*church* MS-4
Chapel Church (historical)—*locale* MO-7
Chapel Corners—*locale* (2) NY-2
Chapel Cove—*bay* AK-9
Chapel Cove—*bay* MD-2
Chapel Creek—*bay* MD-2
Chapel Creek—*stream* (3) AR-4
Chapel Creek—*stream* GA-3
Chapel Creek—*stream* MI-6
Chapel Creek—*stream* MO-7
Chapel Creek—*stream* (4) NC-3
Chapel Creek—*stream* OH-6
Chapel Creek—*stream* (2) SC-3
Chapel Creek—*stream* (2) VA-3
Chapel Creek—*stream* WY-8
Chapel Creek Point—*cape* NC-3
Chapel District Sch—*school* ME-1
**Chapel Downs**—*pop pl* PA-2
Chapel Emmanuel RR Car—*hist pl* SD-7
Chapel Falls—*falls* MA-1
Chapel Falls—*falls* MI-6
Chapel Forge Sch—*school* MD-2
Chapel Gap Sch—*school* KY-4
Chapel Gardens Cem—*cemetery* MI-6
Chapel Gray Sch (historical)—*school* AL-4
*Chapel Grove Baptist Ch* MS-4
Chapel Grove Cem—*cemetery* IL-6
Chapel Grove Cem—*cemetery* MO-7
Chapel Grove Cem—*cemetery* NE-7
Chapel Grove Cem—*cemetery* TN-4
Chapel Grove Ch—*church* KY-4
Chapel Grove Ch—*church* (3) MS-4
Chapel Grove Ch—*church* (3) NC-3
Chapel Grove Ch—*church* (2) TN-4
Chapel Grove Ch—*church* (2) VA-3
*Chapel Grove Ch of the Living God* MS-4
Chapel Grove Sch—*school* NC-3
Chapel Grove Sch (historical)—*school* MS-4
*Chapel Grove West Missionary Baptist*
*Church* MS-4
Chapel Hall, Gallaudet College—*hist pl* DC-2
**Chapel Heights**—*pop pl* NJ-2
Chapel Heights Ch—*church* NJ-2
*Chapelhill* IN-6
*Chapel Hill* IN-6
*Chapel Hill* MS-4
*Chapel Hill* NY-2
*Chapelhill* TN-4
*Chapel Hill* TX-5
Chapel Hill—*hist pl* VA-3
Chapel Hill—*locale* AL-4
Chapel Hill—*locale* GA-3
Chapel Hill—*locale* IA-7
Chapel Hill—*locale* KY-4
Chapel Hill—*locale* NJ-2
Chapel Hill—*locale* NC-3
Chapel Hill—*locale* OH-6
Chapel Hill—*locale* (2) TN-4
Chapel Hill—*other* TX-5
**Chapel Hill**—*pop pl* (4) AL-4
**Chapel Hill**—*pop pl* AR-4
**Chapel Hill**—*pop pl* DE-2
**Chapel Hill**—*pop pl* FL-3
**Chapelhill**—*pop pl* IN-6
**Chapel Hill**—*pop pl* (2) IN-6
**Chapel Hill**—*pop pl* MD-2
**Chapel Hill**—*pop pl* MS-4
**Chapel Hill**—*pop pl* MO-7
**Chapel Hill**—*pop pl* NC-3
**Chapel Hill**—*pop pl* PA-2
**Chapel Hill**—*pop pl* (2) TN-4
**Chapel Hill**—*pop pl* TX-5
**Chapel Hill**—*pop pl* VA-3
Chapel Hill—*summit* AL-4
Chapel Hill—*summit* AR-4
Chapel Hill—*summit* CT-1
Chapel Hill—*summit* KY-4
Chapel Hill—*summit* MO-7
Chapel Hill—*summit* OH-6
Chapel Hill—*summit* PA-2
Chapel HIll—*summit* TN-4
Chapel Hill—*summit* TN-4
Chapel Hill—*summit* TX-5
Chapel Hill Baptist Ch—*church* FL-3
Chapel Hill Baptist Ch—*church* (3) MS-4
Chapel Hill Baptist Ch—*church* TN-4
*Chapel Hill Baptist Church* AL-4
Chapel Hill (CCD)—*cens area* TN-4
*Chapel Hill Cem* AL-4
Chapel Hill Cem—*cemetery* (3) AL-4
Chapel Hill Cem—*cemetery* AR-4
Chapel Hill Cem—*cemetery* FL-3
Chapel Hill Cem—*cemetery* (3) IL-6
Chapel Hill Cem—*cemetery* IA-7
Chapel Hill Cem—*cemetery* KS-7
Chapel Hill Cem—*cemetery* KY-4
Chapel Hill Cem—*cemetery* (6) MS-4
Chapel Hill Cem—*cemetery* NJ-2
Chapel Hill Cem—*cemetery* NY-2
Chapel Hill Cem—*cemetery* OH-6
Chapel Hill Cem—*cemetery* (5) TN-4
Chapel Hill Cem—*cemetery* TX-5
Chapel Hill Cem—*cemetery* (2) WV-2
Chapel Hill Cem—*cemetery* WI-6
*Chapel Hill Ch* IN-6
*Chapel Hill Ch* MS-4
Chapel Hill Ch—*church* (11) AL-4
Chapel Hill Ch—*church* (4) AR-4
Chapel Hill Ch—*church* (4) GA-3
Chapel Hill Ch—*church* IN-6
Chapel Hill Ch—*church* IA-7
Chapel Hill Ch—*church* (4) KY-4
Chapel Hill Ch—*church* LA-4
Chapel Hill Ch—*church* (13) MS-4
Chapel Hill Ch—*church* (4) MO-7
Chapel Hill Ch—*church* (13) NC-3
Chapel Hill Ch—*church* OH-6
Chapel Hill Ch—*church* PA-2
Chapel Hill Ch—*church* (2) SC-3
Chapel Hill Ch—*church* (9) TN-4
Chapel Hill Ch—*church* (7) TX-5
Chapel Hill Ch—*church* VA-3
Chapel Hill Ch—*church* (2) WV-2
*Chapel Hill Ch of God of Prophecy* MS-4
*Chapel Hill Creek* VA-3
Chapel Hill Cumberland Presbyterian
Church—*hist pl* TN-4
Chapel Hill Division—*civil* TN-4
**Chapel Hill Estates**—*pop pl* MA-1
**Chapel Hill Estates**—*pop pl* NY-2
Chapel Hill Gardens—*cemetery* FL-3
Chapel Hill Gardens Cem—*cemetery* IA-7
Chapel Hill Grammar Sch
(historical)—*school* MS-4
Chapel Hill Hist Dist—*hist pl* NC-3
**Chapel Hill (historical)**—*pop pl* MS-4
Chapel Hill HS—*school* NC-3
Chapel Hill Memorial—*cemetery* MI-6
Chapel Hill Memorial Cem—*cemetery* NC-3
Chapel Hill Memorial Gardens—*cemetery* CO-8
Chapel Hill Memorial Gardens—*cemetery* IN-6
Chapel Hill Memorial Gardens—*cemetery* MI-6
Chapel Hill Memorial Gardens
Cem—*cemetery* KS-7
Chapel Hill Memorial Gardens
Cem—*cemetery* OK-5
Chapel Hill Memorial Gardens
(Cemetery)—*cemetery* TX-5
Chapel Hill Memorial Park—*cemetery* FL-3
Chapel Hill Memorial Park—*cemetery* (2) TX-5
Chapel Hill Memorial Park
Cem—*cemetery* AR-4
Chapel Hill Memory Garden—*cemetery* FL-3
*Chapel Hill Methodist Ch* AL-4
Chapel Hill Methodist Ch
(historical)—*church* TN-4
*Chapel Hill Methodist Church* MS-4
*Chapel Hill Missionary Baptist Ch* AL-4
Chapel Hill Missionary Ch—*church* NC-3
Chapel Hill North Channel—*channel* NY-2
Chapel Hill Oil Field—*oilfield* TX-5
*Chapelhill Post Office* TN-4
Chapel Hill Post Office—*building* TN-4
Chapelhill Post Office
(historical)—*building* MS-4
Chapel Hill Post Office
(historical)—*building* TN-4
**Chapel Hills**—*pop pl* CO-8
Chapel Hills—*range* KY-4
*Chapel Hill Sch* MS-4
Chapel Hills Ch—*church* MN-6
Chapel Hill Sch—*school* IN-6
Chapel Hill Sch—*school* KS-7
Chapel Hill Sch—*school* MA-1
Chapel Hill Sch—*school* MI-6
Chapel Hill Sch—*school* (3) MS-4
Chapel Hill Sch—*school* MO-7
Chapel Hill Sch—*school* NY-2
Chapel Hill Sch—*school* NC-3
Chapel Hill Sch—*school* SC-3
Chapel Hill Sch—*school* TN-4
Chapel Hill Sch—*school* (2) TX-5
Chapel Hill Sch (abandoned)—*school* MO-7
Chapel Hill Sch (historical)—*school* (2) AL-4
Chapel Hill Sch (historical)—*school* (4) MS-4
Chapel Hill Sch (historical)—*school* MO-7
Chapel Hill Sch (historical)—*school* (3) TN-4
Chapel Hill School—*locale* OK-5
Chapel Hills Garden Cem—*cemetery* IL-6
Chapel Hills Gardens South
(Cemetery)—*cemetery* IL-6
Chapel Hills Golf Course—*other* OH-6
Chapel Hills Memory Gardens—*cemetery* FL-3
Chapel Hill South Channel—*channel* NJ-2
Chapel Hill South Channel—*channel* NY-2
*Chapel Hill Stream* VA-3
**Chapel Hill Subdivision**—*pop pl* UT-8
Chapel Hill (Township of)—*fmr MCD* NC-3
Chapel Hill United Methodist Ch—*church* IN-6
Chapel Hollow—*valley* TN-4
Chapel House—*hist pl* NY-2
Chapel in the Hills—*church* CO-8
Chapel in the Pines—*church* CO-8
Chapel in the Pines—*church* (2) MN-6
Chapel in the Pines—*church* NC-3
Chapel in the Pines Presbyterian
Ch—*church* AL-4
ChapelInThe Valley—*church* ID-8
Chapel in the Woods—*church* MI-6
Chapel Island—*island* AK-9
Chapel Island—*island* (2) NY-2
Chapel Lake—*lake* CA-9
Chapel Lake—*lake* MI-6
Chapel Lake—*lake* TX-5
Chapel Landing—*locale* MS-4
Chapel Lawn Cem—*cemetery* PA-2
Chapel Lawn Memorial Gardens
Cem—*cemetery* IN-6
**Chapelle**—*pop pl* NM-5
Chapelle Administration Bldg—*hist pl* SC-3
Chapelle Cem—*cemetery* SD-7
Chapelle Creek—*stream* SD-7
Chapelle Dam—*dam* SD-7
Chapel Ledge—*summit* MA-1
Chapelle (historical)—*locale* SD-7
Chapelle Lake—*reservoir* SD-7
Chapelle Sch—*school* MI-6
Chapelle Sch—*school* SD-7
Chapelle Slough—*gut* AR-4
Chapelle Township (historical)—*civil* SD-7
**Chapell Gardens (subdivision)**—*pop pl* NC-3
Chapell Hill—*summit* NY-2
*Chapell Point* ME-1
Chapells Branch—*stream* KY-4
*Chapell's Point* ME-1
Chapel (Magisterial District)—*fmr MCD* VA-3
*Chapel Manor* IN-6
**Chapel Manor**—*pop pl* IN-6
Chapel Mtn—*summit* AZ-5
Chapel Neck—*cape* VA-3
Chapel No 1—*church* WY-8
Chapel No. 1—*hist pl* CO-8
Chapel No 2—*church* OH-6
Chapel Number 2—*church* SC-3
**Chapel Oaks**—*pop pl* MD-2
**Chapel Oaks-Cedar Heights**—*pop pl* MD-2
Chapel of Boy Jesus—*church* NY-2
Chapel of Memories—*church* MS-4
Chapel of Our Lady Help of
Christians—*hist pl* NY-2
Chapel of Our Lady of the
Sierras—*church* CA-9
Chapel of Rest—*church* NC-3
Chapel of Saint Pius X—*church* WI-6
Chapel of Santa Cruz—*hist pl* NM-5
Chapel of St. Anne—*hist pl* MA-1
Chapel of St. Mary the Virgin—*hist pl* WI-6
Chapel of the Chimes—*church* IL-6
Chapel of the Cross—*hist pl* MS-4
Chapel of the Cross—*hist pl* NC-3
Chapel of the Cross Episcopal
Ch—*church* MS-4
Chapel of the Cross (historical)—*church* AL-4
Chapel of the Good Sheperd—*hist pl* MN-6
Chapel of the Good Shepherd—*church* NY-2
Chapel of the Good Shepherd—*hist pl* NY-2
Chapel of the Good Shepherd—*hist pl* NC-3
Chapel of the Holy Cross—*church* AZ-5
Chapel of the Intercession Complex and Trinity
Cemetery—*hist pl* NY-2
Chapel of the Lake—*church* NE-7
Chapel of the Lake—*church* TX-5
Chapel of the Lords New Ch—*church* PA-2
Chapel of the Ozarks—*church* MO-7
Chapel of the Pines—*church* MN-6
Chapel Of The Transfiguration—*church* WY-8
Chapel of the Transfiguration—*hist pl* WY-8
Chapel-on-the-Hill—*church* FL-3
Chapel-on-the-Hill—*church* TX-5
Chapel on the Hill United Ch of
Christ—*church* FL-3
*Chapel on the Lake* MO-7
*Chapelo Ridge* IN-6
Chapel Park—*park* NY-2
Chapel Park—*uninc pl* VA-3
Chapel Park Ch—*church* KY-4
Chapel Peak—*summit* WA-9
Chapel Point—*cape* MD-2
Chapel Pond—*lake* CT-1
Chapel Pond—*lake* NY-2
**Chapel Ridge**—*pop pl* WI-6
Chapel Ridge—*ridge* IN-6
Chapel Ridge—*ridge* KY-4
**Chapel Ridge Heights**—*pop pl* WI-6
Chapel Ridge Trail—*trail* OH-6
Chapel Rock—*pillar* MI-6
Chapel Rock Christian Ch—*church* IN-6
Chapel Rocks—*bar* MA-1
Chapel Run—*stream* IN-6
Chapel Run—*stream* PA-2
Chapel Run—*stream* VA-3
Chapel Sch—*school* IL-6
Chapel Sch—*school* IN-6
Chapel Sch—*school* MO-7
Chapel Sch—*school* (2) SC-3
Chapel Sch—*school* SD-7
Chapel Sch—*school* VT-1
Chapel Sch (historical)—*school* MS-4
Chapel Sch (historical)—*school* MO-7
Chapel Sch (historical)—*school* TN-4
Chapel Shoals—*bar* SC-3
Chapels Pond—*lake* VT-1
Chapel Spring—*spring* KY-4
Chapel Spring—*spring* OR-9
**Chapel Square**—*pop pl* VA-3
Chapel Street Hist Dist—*hist pl* CT-1
Chapel Street Sch—*school* CT-1
**Chapel Subdivision**—*pop pl* UT-8
Chapel Swamp—*stream* NC-3
Chapel Swamp—*stream* VA-3
Chapel Tank—*reservoir* AZ-5
Chapel Tanks—*reservoir* NM-5
*Chapel Town* MS-4
Chapeltown—*locale* DE-2
**Chapeltown**—*pop pl* MS-4
Chapeltown Cem—*cemetery* MS-4
Chapel Township—*civil* MO-7
Chapeluk Slough—*gut* AK-9
Chapel Union Ch—*church* KY-4
**Chapel View**—*pop pl* MD-2
**Chapel View**—*pop pl* PA-2
**Chapel Village**—*pop pl* VA-3
**Chapelville**—*pop pl* MS-4
Chapelwood Cem—*cemetery* LA-4
Chapelwood Ch—*church* GA-3
Chapelwood Ch—*church* IL-6
Chapelwood Elem Sch—*school* IN-6
Chapelwood Memorial Gardens—*cemetery* TX-5
*Chapelwood Sch Number 7* IN-6
Chapelwood Southern Baptist Ch—*church* IN-6
**Chapelwood (subdivision)**—*pop pl* AL-4
*Chapen Creek* OR-9
Chapeno Cem—*cemetery* TX-5
Chapeno Gaging Station—*other* TX-5
Chapeno Well—*well* TX-5
Chaperito—*locale* NM-5
Chaperito Ditch—*canal* NM-5
Chaperito Knob—*summit* NM-5
Chaperito Windmill—*locale* NM-5
Chaperon, Bayou—*gut* LA-4
Chapet Station (historical)—*locale* MA-1
Chapeze—*other* KY-4
Chapin—*fmr MCD* NE-7
Chapin—*locale* ID-8
Chapin—*locale* MO-7
Chapin—*locale* TX-5
Chapin—*locale* VA-3
**Chapin**—*pop pl* IL-6
**Chapin**—*pop pl* IA-7
**Chapin**—*pop pl* MI-6
**Chapin**—*pop pl* NY-2
**Chapin**—*pop pl* SC-3
Chapin, A., House—*hist pl* MA-1
Chapin, Henry A., House—*hist pl* MI-6
Chapin, Horatio, House—*hist pl* IN-6
Chapin, Lake—*lake* FL-3
Chapin, Lake—*reservoir* MI-6
Chapin, Mount—*summit* CO-8
Chapin, Mount—*summit* MA-1
Chapin, Philip, House—*hist pl* CT-1
Chapin, Thaddeus, House—*hist pl* NY-2
Chapin and Gore Bldg—*hist pl* IL-6
Chapin Bay—*bay* AK-9
Chapin Branch—*stream* MO-7
Chapin Brook—*stream* MA-1
Chapin (CCD)—*cens area* SC-3
Chapin Cem—*cemetery* KY-4
Chapin Cem—*cemetery* NY-2
Chapin Creek—*stream* CO-8
Chapin Creek—*stream* NE-7
Chapin Creek—*stream* OR-9
Chapin Creek—*stream* WA-9
Chapin Creek Trail—*trail* CO-8
Chapin Draft—*valley* VA-3
Chapin (Election Precinct)—*fmr MCD* IL-6
Chapine Res—*reserve* IN-6
Chapin Guard Station—*locale* OR-9
*Chapin Hill* NY-2
Chapin Hill—*summit* NY-2
Chapin Island—*island* AK-9
Chapin Lake—*lake* (3) MI-6
Chapin Lake—*lake* WI-6
Chapin Meadow—*flat* OR-9
Chapin Memorial Beach—*beach* MA-1
Chapin Mesa—*summit* CO-8
Chapin Mine—*reservoir* MI-6
Chapin Mine Steam Pump
Engine—*hist pl* MI-6
Chapin Natl Bank Bldg—*hist pl* MA-1
Chapin Park—*park* IL-6
Chapin Park—*park* ME-1
Chapin Park Hist Dist—*hist pl* IN-6
Chapin Pass—*gap* CO-8
Chapin Peak—*summit* AK-9
Chapin Pleasant Hill Cem—*cemetery* IL-6
*Chapin Pond* MA-1
Chapin Pond—*lake* NH-1
Chapin Pond—*lake* NY-2
Chapin Pond—*lake* SC-3
Chapin Pond—*reservoir* MA-1
Chapin Pond Dam—*dam* MA-1
*Chapin's Bluff* VA-3
Chapin Sch—*school* MA-1
Chapin Sch—*school* TX-5
Chapins Meadow Brook—*stream* CT-1
*Chapins Pond* MA-1
Chapins Pond—*lake* CT-1
Chapin Street Sch—*school* (2) MA-1
**Chapin (Township of)**—*pop pl* MI-6
*Chapinville* CT-1
**Chapinville**—*pop pl* MA-1
**Chapinville**—*pop pl* NY-2
Chapinville Cem—*cemetery* PA-2
Chapin Wash—*stream* AZ-5
*Chapita Mountain* CO-8
Chapita Wells Gas Field—*oilfield* UT-8
Chaplain, Lake—*reservoir* WA-9
Chaplain Creek—*stream* WA-9
Chaplain Point—*cape* UT-8
Chaplain Point Fisherman Access—*locale* UT-8
Chaplain's House—*hist pl* CA-9
**Chaplecroft**—*pop pl* DE-2
*Chapley Island* NH-1
**Chaplin**—*pop pl* CT-1
**Chaplin**—*pop pl* KY-4
Chaplin, Lake—*reservoir* GA-3
Chaplin Cem—*cemetery* CT-1
Chaplin Cem—*cemetery* SC-3
Chaplin-Clarke House—*hist pl* MA-1
Chaplin Creek—*stream* SC-3
Chapline, William, House—*hist pl* MD-2
Chapline Bldg—*hist pl* KY-4
Chapline Street Row Hist Dist—*hist pl* WV-2
Chaplin Fork—*stream* KY-4
Chaplin Fork Ch—*church* KY-4
Chapling Ridge—*ridge* TN-4
Chaplin Hill—*summit* MA-1
Chaplin Hist Dist—*hist pl* CT-1
Chaplin-Hood Park—*park* MO-7
Chaplin Lake—*lake* LA-4
Chaplin River—*stream* KY-4
Chaplin Sch—*school* IL-6
Chaplin Sch—*school* WY-8
Chaplins Chapel—*church* DE-2
*Chaplins Cove* RI-1
Chaplin State For—*forest* OH-6
**Chaplin (Town of)**—*pop pl* CT-1
*Chaplinville* MA-1
*Chapman* KS-7
Chapman—*locale* AL-4
Chapman—*locale* KY-4
Chapman—*locale* ME-1
Chapman—*locale* OR-9
Chapman—*locale* TX-5
Chapman—*locale* WV-2
**Chapman**—*pop pl* CA-9
**Chapman**—*pop pl* FL-3
**Chapman**—*pop pl* IL-6
**Chapman**—*pop pl* KS-7
**Chapman**—*pop pl* KY-4
**Chapman**—*pop pl* MI-6
**Chapman**—*pop pl* MT-8
**Chapman**—*pop pl* NE-7
**Chapman**—*pop pl* OH-6
**Chapman**—*pop pl* (3) PA-2
**Chapman**—*pop pl* WV-2
Chapman, A. H., House—*hist pl* CA-9
Chapman, Charles, House—*hist pl* MN-6
Chapman, J. M., House—*hist pl* NJ-2
Chapman, John, House—*hist pl* PA-2
Chapman, John, Plantation—*hist pl* GA-3
Chapman, John A., House—*hist pl* OH-6
Chapman, Lake—*lake* WI-6
Chapman, Leonard Bond, House—*hist pl* ME-1
Chapman, Mount—*summit* CO-8
Chapman, Mount—*summit* TN-4
Chapman, Oscar H., House—*hist pl* TX-5
Chapman, Taylor, House—*hist pl* CT-1
**Chapman Addition**—*pop pl* WV-2
Chapman Arm—*canal* (2) IN-6
Chapman Ave Sch—*school* CA-9
Chapman Bay—*bay* VT-1
Chapman Bay—*bay* WA-9
Chapman Bay—*swamp* LA-4
Chapman Beach—*beach* CT-1
Chapman Beach—*beach* OR-9
**Chapman Beach**—*pop pl* CT-1
Chapman Bench—*bench* WY-8
Chapman Bldg—*hist pl* CA-9
Chapman Borough—*civil* PA-2
*Chapman Branch* LA-4
Chapman Branch—*stream* CA-9
Chapman Branch—*stream* GA-3
Chapman Branch—*stream* IN-6
Chapman Branch—*stream* KY-4
Chapman Branch—*stream* MO-7
Chapman Branch—*stream* (2) TN-4
Chapman Branch—*stream* VA-3
Chapman Branch—*stream* WV-2
Chapman Branch Ch—*church* SC-3
Chapman Branch Library—*hist pl* UT-8
Chapman Bridge—*bridge* SC-3
Chapman Brook—*stream* (2) ME-1
Chapman Brook—*stream* NH-1
Chapman Brook—*stream* NY-2
Chapman Brook—*stream* PA-2
Chapman Butte—*summit* OR-9
Chapman Butte—*summit* WY-8
Chapman Campground—*locale* CO-8
Chapman Canal—*canal* UT-8
Chapman Canal—*canal* WY-8
Chapman Canyon—*valley* CO-8
Chapman Canyon—*valley* OR-9
Chapman Cave—*cave* AL-4
Chapman (CCD)—*cens area* AL-4
Chapman Cem—*cemetery* (2) AL-4
Chapman Cem—*cemetery* (5) GA-3
Chapman Cem—*cemetery* (5) IL-6
Chapman Cem—*cemetery* IA-7
Chapman Cem—*cemetery* KS-7
Chapman Cem—*cemetery* (3) KY-4
Chapman Cem—*cemetery* (2) ME-1
Chapman Cem—*cemetery* MI-6
Chapman Cem—*cemetery* MS-4
Chapman Cem—*cemetery* (2) MO-7
Chapman Cem—*cemetery* NE-7
Chapman Cem—*cemetery* NY-2
Chapman Cem—*cemetery* NC-3
Chapman Cem—*cemetery* (2) OH-6
Chapman Cem—*cemetery* (7) TN-4
Chapman Cem—*cemetery* (2) TX-5
Chapman Cem—*cemetery* VA-3
Chapman Cem—*cemetery* (4) WV-2
*Chapman Ch* MS-4
Chapman Ch—*church* MS-4
Chapman Ch—*church* NC-3
Chapman Ch—*church* PA-2
Chapman Ch—*church* WV-2
**Chapman (Chapman**
**Quarries)**—*pop pl* PA-2
*Chapman Ch of Christ* MS-4
Chapman Coll—*school* CA-9
Chapman Corner—*locale* OR-9
Chapman Corners—*locale* NY-2
Chapman Coulee—*valley* (2) MT-8
Chapman Cove—*bay* WA-9
*Chapman Creek* MT-8
*Chapman Creek* OR-9
Chapman Creek—*stream* (2) AL-4
Chapman Creek—*stream* AK-9
Chapman Creek—*stream* (2) CA-9
Chapman Creek—*stream* GA-3
Chapman Creek—*stream* (2) ID-8
Chapman Creek—*stream* IN-6
Chapman Creek—*stream* KS-7
Chapman Creek—*stream* MT-8
Chapman Creek—*stream* OH-6
Chapman Creek—*stream* (4) OR-9
Chapman Creek—*stream* PA-2
Chapman Creek—*stream* WA-9
Chapman Creek—*stream* WI-6
Chapman Dam—*dam* CO-8
Chapman Dam—*dam* OR-9
Chapman Dam—*dam* PA-2
Chapman Dam—*dam* VA-3
Chapman Dam Rsvr—*reservoir* PA-2
*Chapman Ditch* IN-6
Chapman Ditch—*canal* CO-8
Chapman Ditch—*canal* IN-6
Chapman Division—*civil* AL-4
Chapman Dovel Trail—*trail* VA-3
Chapman Drain—*canal* MI-6
Chapman Drain—*stream* MI-6

Chapman Draw—*valley* ........ NM-5
Chapman Draw—*valley* ........ SD-7
Chapman Draw—*valley* ........ TX-5
Chapman Draw—*valley* ........ WA-9
Chapman Draw—*valley* ........ WY-8
Chapman Falls—*falls* ........ CT-1
Chapman Farmhouse—*hist pl* ........ NY-2
Chapman Field—*park* ........ TX-5
Chapman Field Park—*park* ........ FL-3
Chapman Fork—*stream* ........ KY-4
Chapman Grove—*locale* ........ TN-4
Chapman Grove Ch—*church* ........ IL-6
Chapman Grove Ch—*church* ........ TN-4
Chapman Grove Ch—*church* ........ VA-3
Chapman Gulch—*valley* ........ CA-9
Chapman Gulch—*valley* (2) ........ CO-8
Chapman-Hall House—*hist pl* ........ ME-1
Chapman Hammock—*island* ........ FL-3
**Chapman Heights**—*pop pl* ........ AL-4
Chapman Highway Shop Ctr—*locale* ........ TN-4
Chapman Hill—*summit* (2) ........ CT-1
Chapman Hill—*summit* ........ OR-9
Chapman Hollow—*valley* ........ AR-4
Chapman Hollow—*valley* ........ KY-4
Chapman Hollow—*valley* ........ OR-9
Chapman Hollow—*valley* (2) ........ TN-4
Chapman Hollow Cave—*cave* ........ TN-4
Chapman Homestead—*locale* ........ WY-8
Chapman HS—*school* ........ KS-7
Chapman HS—*school* ........ SC-3
Chapman-Hutchinson House—*hist pl* ........ OH-6
Chapman Island—*island* ........ AK-9
Chapman Island—*island* ........ NH-1
Chapman JHS—*school* ........ AL-4
Chapman JHS—*school* ........ KS-7
*Chapman Lake* ........ IN-6
*Chapman Lake* ........ MI-6
Chapman Lake—*lake* (2) ........ CO-8
Chapman Lake—*lake* (3) ........ FL-3
Chapman Lake—*lake* ........ GA-3
Chapman Lake—*lake* ........ PA-2
Chapman Lake—*lake* ........ WA-9
Chapman Lake—*lake* ........ WI-6
Chapman Lake—*reservoir* ........ AL-4
Chapman Lake—*reservoir* ........ TX-5
Chapman Lake—*reservoir* ........ WI-6
Chapman Lake Dam—*dam* ........ AL-4
**Chapman Lake (subdivision)**—*pop pl* ........ PA-2
Chapman Landing—*locale* ........ MD-2
Chapman Landing—*locale* ........ OR-9
Chapman Landing—*locale* ........ VA-3
Chapman Lead—*ridge* ........ TN-4
Chapman Lookout Tower—*locale* ........ AL-4
Chapman Mill (historical)—*locale* ........ AL-4
Chapman Mine—*mine* ........ CA-9
Chapman Mine (underground)—*mine* ........ AL-4
Chapman Mtn—*summit* ........ AL-4
Chapman Mtn—*summit* ........ ME-1
Chapman Mtn—*summit* ........ SC-3
Chapman Mtn—*summit* (3) ........ VA-3
Chapman Park—*park* ........ AL-4
Chapman Park—*park* ........ CA-9
Chapman Park—*park* ........ NY-2
Chapman Park—*park* ........ TX-5
Chapman Park—*park* ........ WI-6
Chapman Peak—*summit* ........ MT-8
Chapman Pease Lake—*reservoir* ........ GA-3
Chapman Place—*locale* ........ NM-5
*Chapman Point* ........ CT-1
Chapman Point—*cape* ........ CT-1
Chapman Point—*cape* ........ MD-2
Chapman Point—*cape* (3) ........ NY-2
Chapman Point—*cape* ........ OR-9
Chapman Point—*cape* ........ TX-5
Chapman Point Sch—*school* ........ IL-6
Chapman Pond—*lake* ........ CT-1
Chapman Pond—*lake* (2) ........ ME-1
Chapman Pond—*lake* ........ MI-6
Chapman Pond—*lake* ........ NH-1
Chapman Pond—*lake* ........ RI-1
Chapman Pond—*reservoir* ........ SC-3
Chapman Ponds—*lake* ........ TX-5
Chapman Ponds—*reservoir* ........ OR-9
Chapman Prong—*stream* ........ TN-4
*Chapman Quarries* ........ PA-2
Chapman Quarries—*other* ........ PA-2
Chapman Quarters—*locale* ........ AL-4
Chapman Ranch—*locale* ........ CA-9
Chapman Ranch—*locale* (2) ........ NE-7
Chapman Ranch—*locale* ........ TX-5
Chapman Ranch Cem—*cemetery* ........ TX-5
*Chapman Reservoir* ........ UT-8
Chapman Ridge—*ridge* ........ CT-1
Chapman Ridge—*ridge* ........ ME-1
Chapman Ridge—*ridge* ........ TN-4
Chapman Rsvr—*reservoir* (2) ........ CO-8
Chapman Rsvr—*reservoir* (2) ........ OR-9
Chapman Run—*stream* ........ OH-6
Chapman Run—*stream* ........ PA-2
Chapman Run—*stream* ........ WV-2
*Chapmans* ........ PA-2
**Chapmans**—*pop pl* ........ OH-6
**Chapmans**—*pop pl* ........ TN-4
Chapmansboro—*locale* ........ TN-4
Chapmansboro Post Office—*building* ........ TN-4
**Chapmansboro (sta.)**—*pop pl* ........ TN-4
Chapmans Ch—*church* ........ NC-3
Chapman Sch—*school* ........ CA-9
Chapman Sch—*school* ........ CT-1
Chapman Sch—*school* ........ IL-6
Chapman Sch—*school* ........ MA-1
Chapman Sch—*school* (2) ........ MI-6
Chapman Sch—*school* ........ MS-4
Chapman Sch—*school* ........ OR-9
Chapmans Chapel—*church* ........ AL-4
Chapman Sch (historical)—*school* ........ AL-4
Chapman Sch (historical)—*school* ........ PA-2
*Chapmans Creek* ........ KS-7
Chapmans Crossroads—*locale* ........ SC-3
Chapmans Fork—*stream* ........ KY-4
Chapman Slough—*stream* ........ OR-9
*Chapman's Mill* ........ VA-3
Chapmans Pond—*lake* ........ CT-1
Chapmans Pond—*reservoir* ........ SC-3
Chapman Spring—*spring* ........ AR-4
Chapman Spring—*spring* ........ CO-8
Chapman Spring—*spring* ........ OR-9
Chapman Spring—*spring* ........ WA-9
*Chapmans Run* ........ PA-2
*Chapmans Station* ........ AL-4
*Chapmans Station* ........ PA-2
Chapman State Park—*park* ........ PA-2
*Chapman Station* ........ PA-2
Chapmans Upper Ranch—*locale* ........ CA-9
*Chapmansville* ........ PA-2
Chapman Swamp—*swamp* ........ TN-4
Chapman Tank—*reservoir* ........ AZ-5
**Chapmantown**—*pop pl* ........ CA-9
**Chapmantown** (census name
  **Mulberry**)—*pop pl* ........ CA-9
**Chapman (Town of)**—*pop pl* ........ ME-1
**Chapman Township**—*pop pl* (2) ........ KS-7
**Chapman Township**—*pop pl* (2) ........ NE-7
**Chapman (Township of)**—*pop pl* (2) ........ PA-2
Chapman Trail—*trail* ........ CO-8
Chapman Tunnel—*tunnel* ........ CO-8
*Chapmanville* ........ IN-6
*Chapmanville* ........ KS-7
**Chapmanville**—*pop pl* ........ PA-2
**Chapmanville**—*pop pl* ........ WV-2
Chapman Well—*well* ........ TX-5
Chapman Windmill—*locale* ........ NM-5
Chapman Windmill—*locale* ........ TX-5
**Chapman Woods**—*pop pl* ........ CA-9
Chapo Mine (Abandoned)—*mine* ........ NM-5
*Chapoquidick Island* ........ MA-1
*Chapoquoit Harbor* ........ MA-1
*Chapoquoit Point* ........ MA-1
Chapo Ranch (historical)—*locale* ........ AZ-5
Chapotal Hill—*summit* ........ TX-5
Chapotal Tank—*reservoir* ........ TX-5
Chapote Creek—*stream* ........ TX-5
Chapote Draw—*valley* ........ TX-5
Chapote Tank—*reservoir* ........ TX-5
Chapote Well (Flowing)—*well* ........ TX-5
Chapote Windmill—*locale* (4) ........ TX-5
Chapoton, Alexander, House—*hist pl* ........ MI-6
*Chapowamsic Creek* ........ VA-3
Chapo Windmill—*locale* ........ TX-5
**Chappaqua**—*pop pl* ........ NY-2
Chappaqua Brook—*stream* ........ NY-2
Chappaqua Hill—*summit* ........ NY-2
Chappaqua RR Depot and Depot
  Plaza—*hist pl* ........ NY-2
*Chappaquiddic* ........ MA-1
*Chappaquiddic Island* ........ MA-1
**Chappaquiddick**—*pop pl* ........ MA-1
Chappaquiddick Beach—*beach* ........ MA-1
Chappaquiddick Island—*island* ........ MA-1
**Chappaquiddick Island**—*pop pl* ........ MA-1
Chappaquiddick Point—*cape* ........ MA-1
*Chappaquidgick* ........ MA-1
*Chappaquidick Island* ........ MA-1
**Chappaquoit**—*pop pl* ........ MA-1
Chappaquoit Beach—*beach* ........ MA-1
Chappaquoit Point—*cape* ........ MA-1
*Chappaquonset Pond* ........ MA-1
*Chappaquonsett Pond* ........ MA-1
*Chappaquonsit Pond* ........ MA-1
Chapparal Draw—*valley* ........ WY-8
Chapparal Mobile Village—*locale* ........ AZ-5
Chapparal Park—*park* ........ AZ-5
Chapparal Tank—*reservoir* ........ AZ-5
Chapparell (historical)—*locale* ........ MS-4
Chappa Well—*well* ........ TX-5
Chappee Creek—*stream* ........ MI-6
Chappee Rapids—*rapids* ........ MI-6
Chappee Rapids—*rapids* ........ WI-6
Chappel—*locale* ........ GA-3
Chappel—*locale* ........ NM-5
Chappel—*locale* ........ TX-5
Chappel Bay—*bay* ........ PA-2
Chappel Branch—*stream* ........ SC-3
Chappel Cem—*cemetery* ........ KY-4
*Chappel Creek* ........ WI-6
Chappel Creek—*stream* ........ GA-3
Chappel Creek—*stream* ........ MT-8
Chappel Creek—*stream* ........ NC-3
Chappel Creek—*stream* ........ OH-6
Chappel Creek—*stream* ........ WY-8
Chappel Dam—*dam* ........ MI-6
Chappel Fork—*stream* ........ PA-2
Chappel Gulch—*valley* ........ OR-9
Chappel Gulch Rsvr—*reservoir* ........ OR-9
Chappel Hollow—*valley* ........ AR-4
Chappel HS—*school* ........ SC-3
*Chappell* ........ MT-8
*Chappell* ........ SC-3
Chappell—*locale* ........ KY-4
Chappell—*locale* ........ MT-8
**Chappell**—*pop pl* ........ NE-7
Chappell, Delos Allen, House—*hist pl* ........ CO-8
*Chappel Lake* ........ MI-6
Chappel Lateral—*canal* ........ CA-9
*Chappell Brook* ........ TX-5
Chappell Cem—*cemetery* ........ GA-3
Chappell Cem—*cemetery* ........ IN-6
Chappell Cem—*cemetery* ........ KY-4
Chappell Cem—*cemetery* ........ LA-4
Chappell Cem—*cemetery* ........ MS-4
Chappell Cem—*cemetery* ........ NE-7
Chappell Cem—*cemetery* (3) ........ TN-4
*Chappell (Chappells)* ........ SC-3
*Chappell Creek* ........ OR-9
Chappell Creek—*stream* ........ TX-5
Chappell Creek—*stream* ........ VA-3
Chappell Creek—*stream* ........ WY-8
Chappelle Ch—*church* ........ AL-4
*Chappelle Creek* ........ OR-9
Chappell Ledge—*bar* ........ MA-1
Chappelle (RR name for Riffle)—*other* ........ WV-2
Chappell Farmhouse—*hist pl* ........ NY-2
Chappell Grove Ch—*church* ........ NC-3
**Chappell Hill**—*pop pl* ........ AL-4
**Chappell Hill**—*pop pl* ........ TX-5
*Chappell Hill Baptist Church* ........ AL-4
**Chappell Hill (Chapel Hill)**—*pop pl* ........ TX-5
*Chappell Hill Church* ........ AL-4
Chappell Hill Circulating Library—*hist pl* ........ TX-5
Chappell Hill Methodist Episcopal
  Church—*hist pl* ........ TX-5
Chappell Hill Public Sch and Chappell Hill
  Female College Bell—*hist pl* ........ TX-5
Chappell Hollow—*valley* ........ WV-2
Chappell Hollow Branch—*stream* ........ TN-4
Chappell House—*hist pl* ........ SC-3
Chappell Lake—*lake* ........ MI-6
Chappell Lake—*lake* ........ UT-8
Chappell Methodist Ch—*church* ........ TN-4
Chappell Mine—*mine* ........ UT-8
Chappell Place (historical)—*locale* ........ MS-4
Chappell Pond—*reservoir* ........ NC-3
Chappell Pond Dam—*dam* ........ NC-3
**Chappells**—*pop pl* ........ SC-3
Chappells (CCD)—*cens area* ........ SC-3
Chappell Sch—*school* ........ FL-3
Chappell Sch—*school* ........ IL-6
Chappell Sch—*school* ........ SC-3
Chappell Sch—*school* ........ WI-6
**Chappells (Chappell)**—*pop pl* ........ SC-3
Chappells Mill—*locale* ........ GA-3
Chappells-Spade Ranch—*locale* ........ NM-5
Chappells Pond—*reservoir* ........ GA-3
Chappell Spring—*spring* ........ AL-4
Chappelow Ridge—*ridge* ........ IN-6
*Chappel Pond* ........ MI-6
Chappel Ridge—*ridge* ........ KY-4
*Chappel Rocks* ........ MA-1
Chappels—*other* ........ KY-4
Chappels Creek—*stream* ........ NC-3
Chappel Spring—*spring* ........ MT-8
Chappel Spring—*spring* ........ OR-9
Chappel-Swedenburg House—*hist pl* ........ OR-9
*Chappen Creek* ........ OR-9
Chappepeela Ch—*church* ........ LA-4
Chappepeela Creek—*stream* ........ LA-4
Chappepeela Lake—*lake* ........ LA-4
*Chappequiddick* ........ MA-1
*Chappequiddick Island* ........ MA-1
Chapperal Ridge—*ridge* ........ PA-2
Chapp Hill—*summit* ........ NY-2
Chapple Branch—*stream* ........ AL-4
Chapple Cem—*cemetery* ........ AL-4
*Chapple Creek* ........ WY-8
Chapple Creek—*stream* ........ PA-2
Chapple Creek—*stream* ........ WI-6
Chapple Drain—*canal* ........ MI-6
*Chapple Lake* ........ MI-6
Chappo—*locale* ........ CA-9
*Chappo Gulch* ........ WY-8
Chappomiss Valley—*valley* ........ MA-1
Chappo Spring—*spring* ........ AZ-5
Chappo Spring—*spring* ........ CA-9
Chapps Branch—*stream* ........ WV-2
*Chaps* ........ UT-8
Chaps Run—*stream* ........ OH-6
*Chaptanck River* ........ DE-2
*Chaptank River* ........ DE-2
Chapter House (Chinle)—*building* ........ AZ-5
Chapter House (Nazlini)—*building* ........ AZ-5
Chapter House (Pinon)—*building* ........ AZ-5
Chapter House (sawmill)—*building* ........ AZ-5
Chapter House (St Michaels)—*building* ........ AZ-5
Chapter Point—*locale* ........ MD-2
Chapter Point Marsh—*swamp* ........ MD-2
*Chapter's Point* ........ MD-2
**Chaptico**—*pop pl* ........ MD-2
Chaptico Bay—*bay* ........ MD-2
Chaptico Creek—*stream* ........ MD-2
Chaptico Point—*cape* ........ MD-2
*Chaptico Run* ........ MD-2
Chaptico Run—*stream* ........ MD-2
*Chapuchirochi* ........ MP-9
Chapultepec—*locale* ........ WI-6
*Chaquaqua Canyon* ........ CO-8
*Chaquaqua Creek* ........ CO-8
*Chaquaquo Canyon* ........ CO-8
*Chaquaquo Creek* ........ CO-8
Chaquehui Canyon—*valley* ........ NM-5
*Chara* ........ MH-9
Character Gulch—*valley* ........ ID-8
Character Peak—*summit* ........ ID-8
*Charaghar* ........ OH-6
Charaien Island—*island* ........ MP-9
*Charaien-to* ........ MP-9
Chara Lake—*lake* ........ MI-6
Charamusca Creek—*stream* ........ TX-5
Charamusca Oil Field—*oilfield* ........ TX-5
*Charamusco Creek* ........ TX-5
*Charan Danshi* ........ MH-9
*Charanjeza* ........ MH-9
*Charan Kanoa Road* ........ MH-9
*Charankanoa Swamp* ........ MH-9
*Charan Kesa* ........ MH-9
*Charan Keza* ........ MH-9
*Charan Kija* ........ MH-9
*Charan Killa* ........ MH-9
*Charan Nuebo* ........ MH-9
*Charan Tabute* ........ MH-9
*Charanusoc Creek* ........ TX-5
*Charaton River* ........ IA-7
*Charaton River* ........ MO-7
Charbon, Bayou—*gut* ........ LA-4
**Charbonneau**—*pop pl* ........ ND-7
Charbonneau,Jean Baptiste, Memorial and
  Inskip Station Ruins—*hist pl* ........ OR-9
Charbonneau Creek—*stream* ........ ND-7
Charbonneau Dam—*dam* ........ ND-7
**Charbon Township**—*pop pl* ........ ND-7
**Charbray (subdivision)**—*pop pl* ........ TN-4
**Charbulk**—*pop pl* ........ SC-3
Charcas (Barrio)—*fmr MCD* ........ PR-3
Charco—*locale* ........ AZ-5
**Charco**—*pop pl* ........ IL-6
**Charco**—*pop pl* ........ TX-5
Charcoal Bar—*bar* ........ IL-6
Charcoal Basin—*basin* ........ NV-8
Charcoal Canyon—*valley* ........ AZ-5
Charcoal Canyon—*valley* ........ NV-8
Charcoal Canyon—*valley* ........ UT-8
Charcoal Cave—*cave* ........ OR-9
Charcoal Creek—*stream* (4) ........ ID-8
Charcoal Creek—*stream* (3) ........ MT-8
Charcoal Creek—*stream* ........ VT-1
Charcoal Gulch—*valley* (2) ........ AZ-5
Charcoal Gulch—*valley* ........ CO-8
Charcoal Gulch—*valley* ........ ID-8
Charcoal Gulch—*valley* (2) ........ MT-8
Charcoal Hill—*summit* ........ CT-1
Charcoal Hill—*summit* ........ MD-2
Charcoal Island—*island* ........ AK-9
Charcoal Kilns—*hist pl* ........ ID-8
Charcoal Kilns—*hist pl* ........ UT-8
Charcoal Landing—*locale* ........ NJ-2
Charcoal Mtn—*summit* ........ MT-8
Charcoal Point—*cape* ........ AK-9
Charcoal Point—*cape* ........ OR-9
Charcoal Point—*uninc pl* ........ AK-9
Charcoal Ravine—*valley* ........ CA-9
Charcoal Ridge—*ridge* ........ CA-9
Charcoal Spring—*spring* (2) ........ AZ-5
Charcoal Spring—*spring* ........ MT-8
Charcoal Spring—*spring* ........ OR-9
Charcoal Spring—*spring* ........ WY-8
*Charcoal Tank* ........ AZ-5
Charcoal Tank—*reservoir* ........ AZ-5
*Charco de la Piedra* ........ AZ-5
Charco del Rucio Tank—*reservoir* ........ TX-5
Charco Escondido, Arroyo de—*valley* ........ TX-5
Charco Hondo—*lake* ........ TX-5
**Charco Hondo**—*pop pl* ........ PR-3
Charco Largo—*lake* ........ TX-5
Charco Largo Windmill—*locale* ........ TX-5
Charco Marrano Creek—*stream* ........ TX-5
Charcone (historical)—*locale* ........ AL-4
Charco Nine Windmill—*locale* ........ TX-5
Charco Nuevo Windmill—*locale* ........ TX-5
Charco Redondo, Arroyo—*valley* ........ TX-5
Charco Rsvr—*reservoir* ........ WY-8
Charco Southeast Gas Field—*oilfield* ........ TX-5
Charco Tank—*reservoir* (5) ........ AZ-5
Charco Tank—*reservoir* (2) ........ TX-5
Charco Three—*reservoir* ........ AZ-5
Charco Windmill—*locale* ........ TX-5
Char Creek—*stream* ........ ID-8
Chard—*locale* ........ WA-9
Chard Creek—*stream* ........ OR-9
Charden Farms Airp—*airport* ........ KS-7
Chard Gulch—*valley* ........ WA-9
Chard (historical)—*locale* ........ KS-7
Chard Lake—*lake* ........ MI-6
Chardon—*locale* ........ KS-7
Chardon—*locale* ........ PR-3
**Chardon**—*pop pl* ........ OH-6
**Chardon**—*pop pl* ........ PR-3
Chardon Cem—*cemetery* ........ KS-7
Chardon Courthouse Square
  District—*hist pl* ........ OH-6
Chardon Road Cem—*cemetery* ........ OH-6
Chardon Sch—*school* ........ KS-7
**Chardon (Township of)**—*pop pl* ........ OH-6
Chard Pond—*lake* ........ MA-1
*Chare, Cape* ........ FM-9
*Chareguam* ........ MH-9
**Charenton**—*pop pl* ........ LA-4
Charenton Drainage and Navigation
  Canal—*canal* (2) ........ LA-4
Charenton Oil and Gas Field—*oilfield* ........ LA-4
*Chareton River* ........ IA-7
*Chareton River* ........ MO-7
Charette, Bayou—*gut* ........ LA-4
Charette Gulch—*valley* ........ MT-8
Charette Lake—*lake* ........ NM-5
Charette Lake Canal—*canal* ........ NM-5
Charette Lake Diversion Canal—*canal* ........ NM-5
Charette Mesa—*summit* ........ NM-5
*Charette River* ........ IA-7
*Charette River* ........ MO-7
Char Falls—*falls* ........ ID-8
Charge Pond—*lake* ........ MA-1
Charging Creek—*stream* ........ ND-7
Charging Eagle Bay—*bay* ........ ND-7
Charging Eagle Bay Public Use
  Area—*park* ........ ND-7
Chargos Creek—*stream* ........ TX-5
Char Gulch—*valley* ........ ID-8
*Charia* ........ MH-9
Charikus Branch—*stream* ........ NC-3
**Charing**—*pop pl* ........ GA-3
Charing Cross—*locale* ........ MI-6
**Charing Cross Estates**—*pop pl* ........ MI-6
Chariot—*locale* ........ AK-9
Chariot Canyon—*valley* ........ CA-9
Chariot Gulch—*valley* ........ ID-8
Chariot Mine—*mine* ........ CA-9
Chariot Mtn—*summit* ........ CA-9
Charisma Chapel—*church* ........ FL-3
Charitable Cem—*cemetery* ........ FL-3
Chariton River Cem—*cemetery* ........ IA-7
Charit Creek—*stream* ........ TN-4
Charit Creek Campground—*locale* ........ TN-4
*Charition* ........ IA-7
Chariton—*locale* ........ MO-7
**Chariton**—*pop pl* ........ IA-7
Chariton Ch—*church* (2) ........ MO-7
Chariton City Hall—*building* ........ IA-7
**Chariton County**—*pop pl* ........ MO-7
Chariton Creek—*stream* ........ IA-7
*Charitone River* ........ IA-7
*Charitone River* ........ MO-7
Chariton Ridge Ch—*church* ........ MO-7
Chariton River—*stream* ........ IA-7
Chariton River—*stream* ........ MO-7
Chariton River Church*—*church* ........ IA-7
Chariton Sch (abandoned)—*school* ........ MO-7
Chariton Township—*civil* (4) ........ MO-7
Chariton Township—*fmr MCD* ........ IA-7
**Chariton Township**—*pop pl* ........ MO-7
Charity—*locale* ........ VA-3
**Charity**—*pop pl* ........ MO-7
**Charity**—*pop pl* ........ NC-3
**Charity**—*pop pl* ........ SC-3
**Charity**—*pop pl* ........ TN-4
Charity, Lake—*lake* ........ FL-3
Charity Branch—*stream* ........ KY-4
Charity Branch—*stream* ........ TX-5
Charity Cem—*cemetery* ........ MS-4
Charity Cem—*cemetery* (2) ........ MO-7
Charity Cem—*cemetery* ........ NC-3
Charity Cem—*cemetery* ........ SD-7
Charity Cem—*cemetery* ........ TN-4
Charity Ch—*church* ........ AL-4
Charity Ch—*church* ........ AR-4
Charity Ch—*church* ........ IL-6
Charity Ch—*church* ........ KY-4
Charity Ch—*church* ........ LA-4
Charity Ch—*church* (3) ........ NC-3
Charity Ch—*church* ........ OH-6
Charity Ch—*church* (2) ........ SC-3
Charity Ch—*church* ........ TN-4
Charity Ch—*church* (2) ........ VA-3
Charity Ch—*church* ........ WV-2
Charity Chapel—*church* ........ AL-4
Charity Chapel—*church* ........ OH-6
Charity Chapel Cem—*cemetery* ........ AL-4
Charity Chapel Ch—*church* ........ AL-4
Charity Chapel Sch (historical)—*school* ........ AL-4
Charity Christian Center—*church* ........ FL-3
*Charity Church* ........ MS-4
Charity Creek—*stream* ........ AK-9
Charity Creek—*stream* ........ TN-4
Charity Dye Elem Sch—*school* ........ IN-6
*Charity Flat* ........ ID-8
Charity Flat Sch—*school* ........ IA-7
Charity Fork—*stream* ........ WV-2
Charity Grange Hall—*locale* ........ OR-9
Charity Grove Ch—*church* ........ GA-3
Charity Gulch—*valley* ........ ID-8
Charity Gulch—*valley* ........ MT-8
Charity Hall Ch—*church* ........ TN-4
Charity Hall (historical)—*school* ........ MS-4
**Charity Hill**—*pop pl* ........ TN-4
Charity Hill—*summit* ........ MA-1
Charity Hill Ch—*church* ........ NC-3
Charity Hill Sch (historical)—*school* ........ TN-4
Charity (historical)—*locale* ........ KS-7
Charity Hosp—*hist pl* ........ GA-3
Charity Hosp—*hospital* (2) ........ LA-4
Charity Hosp—*hospital* ........ MS-4
*Charity Industrial School* ........ AL-4
Charity Island—*island* ........ FL-3
Charity Island—*island* ........ MI-6
Charity JHS—*school* ........ NC-3
*Charity Lake* ........ MN-6
Charity Lake—*lake* ........ LA-4
Charity Lake—*lake* ........ MN-6
Charity Lake—*lake* ........ MT-8
Charity Ledge—*bar* ........ ME-1
Charity Mission—*church* ........ CA-9
Charity Mission Ch—*church* ........ MS-4
Charity Neck—*cape* ........ VA-3
Charity Peak—*summit* ........ MT-8
Charity Point—*cape* ........ MD-2
Charity Post Office (historical)—*building* ........ TN-4
*Charity Rotch* ........ OH-6
**Charity Rotch**—*pop pl* ........ OH-6
Charity Sch—*school* ........ MO-7
Charity Sch—*school* ........ SC-3
Charity Sch—*school* ........ TN-4
Charity Sch (historical)—*school* ........ MO-7
Charity School (historical)—*locale* ........ MO-7
Charity's House—*hist pl* ........ KY-4
Charity Spring—*spring* ........ ID-8
Charity Spring—*spring* ........ OR-9
Charity Valley—*flat* ........ CA-9
Charity Valley Creek—*stream* ........ CA-9
Charivari Creek—*stream* ........ AR-4
Charjean Sch—*school* ........ TN-4
**Charlack**—*pop pl* ........ MO-7
Char Lake—*lake* ........ TX-5
*Charlaton River* ........ IA-7
*Charlaton River* ........ MO-7
Charlcote House—*hist pl* ........ MD-2
*Charleau Gap* ........ AZ-5
Charleaux, Bayou—*gut* ........ LA-4
Charlebois Canyon—*valley* ........ AZ-5
Charlebois Spring—*spring* ........ AZ-5
Charlebois Tanks—*reservoir* ........ AZ-5
Charlebois Trail—*trail* ........ AZ-5
**Charlefonte Manor**—*pop pl* ........ MD-2
Charlemont—*locale* ........ VA-3
**Charlemont**—*pop pl* ........ MA-1
Charlemont Creek—*stream* ........ OH-6
**Charlemont (Town of)**—*pop pl* ........ MA-1
Charlemont Village Hist Dist—*hist pl* ........ MA-1
**Charleroi**—*pop pl* ........ PA-2
Charleroi Area Junior Senior HS—*school* ........ PA-2
Charleroi Borough—*civil* ........ PA-2
Charleroi Cem—*cemetery* ........ PA-2
*Charleroi High School* ........ PA-2
Charleroi-Monessen Bridge—*hist pl* ........ PA-2
Charleroi Monessen Hosp—*hospital* ........ PA-2
Charles—*locale* ........ AL-4
**Charles**—*pop pl* (2) ........ GA-3
**Charles**—*pop pl* ........ MI-6
**Charles**—*pop pl* ........ NC-3
Charles, Cape—*cape* ........ VA-3
Charles, Lake—*lake* ........ CO-8
Charles, Lake—*lake* (4) ........ FL-3
Charles, Lake—*lake* ........ IN-6
Charles, Lake—*lake* ........ KY-4
Charles, Lake—*lake* ........ LA-4
Charles, Lake—*lake* (2) ........ MN-6
Charles, Lake—*lake* ........ WA-9
Charles, Lake—*reservoir* (2) ........ AL-4
Charles, Lake—*reservoir* ........ AR-4
Charles, Lake—*reservoir* ........ GA-3
Charles, Lake—*reservoir* ........ IL-6
Charles, Lake—*reservoir* ........ NY-2
Charles, Lake—*reservoir* (3) ........ NC-3
Charles, Lake—*reservoir* ........ VA-3
Charles, Point—*cape* ........ FL-3
Charles A Bell Sch—*school* ........ TN-4
Charles A Cannon Recreational
  Complex—*building* ........ NC-3
Charles A Lindbergh Sch—*school* ........ MN-6
Charles A Lindbergh State Park—*park* ........ MN-6
Charles and George Clarke Grant—*civil* ........ FL-3
Charles Arnold Sch—*school* ........ TX-5
Charles Asmand Claim—*civil* ........ MS-4
Charles Bagley Sch—*school* ........ TN-4
Charles Bailey Lake Dam—*dam* ........ MS-4
**Charles (Balcones Research
  Center)**—*pop pl* ........ TX-5
Charlesbank Playground—*park* ........ MA-1
*Charles Bay* ........ FL-3
Charles Bay (Carolina Bay)—*swamp* ........ NC-3
*Charles Bayou* ........ LA-4
Charles Bayou—*gut* ........ LA-4
Charles Bayou—*stream* ........ LA-4
Charles Beeler Grant—*civil* ........ FL-3
Charles Boggio Ranch—*locale* ........ MT-8
*Charles Boozers Lake* ........ AL-4
Charlesboro Ch—*church* ........ SC-3
Charles Branch—*stream* (2) ........ AL-4
Charles Branch—*stream* ........ KS-7
Charles Branch—*stream* ........ MD-2
Charles Branch—*stream* ........ MS-4
Charles Branch—*stream* ........ NC-3
Charles Branch—*stream* ........ VA-3
*Charles Brook* ........ CT-1
Charles Brook—*stream* ........ MA-1
Charles Brook—*stream* ........ NH-1
Charles Brothers Plaza—*locale* ........ PA-2
Charles Broward Grant—*civil* ........ FL-3
Charles Brown Brook—*stream* ........ VT-1
**Charlesburg**—*pop pl* ........ WI-6
Charles Butte—*summit* ........ ID-8
Charles Carroll HS—*school* ........ MD-2
Charles Cave—*cave* ........ IN-6
Charles C Bell Sch—*school* ........ NC-3
Charles C Cook State Game Mngmt
  Area—*park* ........ ND-7
Charles Cem—*cemetery* ........ IL-6
Charles Cem—*cemetery* ........ ME-1
Charles Cem—*cemetery* (2) ........ OK-5
Charles Cem—*cemetery* ........ TN-4
**Charles Chase Corner**—*pop pl* ........ ME-1
Charles Christie Bridge—*bridge* ........ MA-1
**Charles City**—*pop pl* ........ IA-7
**Charles City**—*pop pl* ........ VA-3
Charles City City Hall—*building* ........ IA-7
Charles City College Hall—*hist pl* ........ IA-7
**Charles City (County)**—*pop pl* ........ VA-3
Charles City County Courthouse—*hist pl* ........ VA-3
Charles City JHS*—*school* ........ IA-7
Charles Cole Cem—*cemetery* ........ MS-4
Charles Collins Lake Dam—*dam* ........ IN-6
Charles Collins Lake Dam—*reservoir* ........ IN-6
Charles Corner—*locale* ........ VA-3
**Charles (County)**—*pop pl* ........ MD-2
*Charles Creek* ........ GA-3
*Charles Creek* ........ ID-8
*Charles Creek* ........ MT-8
*Charles Creek* ........ NC-3
*Charles Creek* ........ TN-4
Charles Creek—*channel* ........ GA-3
Charles Creek—*stream* (2) ........ AK-9
Charles Creek—*stream* (2) ........ CA-9
Charles Creek—*stream* ........ MD-2
Charles Creek—*stream* ........ MO-7
Charles Creek—*stream* ........ MT-8
Charles Creek—*stream* ........ NJ-2
Charles Creek—*stream* (5) ........ NC-3
Charles Creek—*stream* ........ TN-4
Charles Creek—*stream* ........ TX-5
Charles Creek—*stream* ........ WV-2
Charles Creek Ch—*church* ........ TN-4
Charles Creek Park—*flat* ........ NC-3
*Charles Dam* ........ AZ-5
Charles Davis Dam—*dam* ........ AL-4
Charles De Viller Grant—*civil* ........ FL-3
Charles Ditch—*canal* ........ IN-6
Charles Ditch—*canal* ........ OH-6
Charles Draw—*valley* ........ SD-7
Charles E Bennett Elem Sch—*school* ........ FL-3
Charles Elem Sch—*school* ........ IN-6
Charles Elliott Memorial Park—*park* ........ OR-9
Charles Ellis Pond Dam—*dam* ........ MS-4
Charles E Still Hospital Heliport—*airport* ........ MO-7
Charles Evans Cem—*cemetery* ........ PA-2
Charles F Johnson Sch—*school* ........ NY-2
Charles F Lewis Natural Area—*area* ........ PA-2
Charles Fork—*stream* ........ VA-3
Charles Fork—*stream* ........ WV-2
Charles Forte—*hist pl* ........ SC-3
Charles Frazier Dam—*dam* ........ SD-7
Charles F Sibbald Grant—*civil* ........ FL-3
*Charles Fulton Canyon* ........ OR-9
Charles Gap—*gap* ........ AR-4
Charles Gibeaut Lake Dam—*dam* ........ AL-4
Charles Guin Lake Dam—*dam* ........ MS-4
*Charles Hall School* ........ TN-4
Charles Hansen Canal—*canal* ........ CO-8
Charles Hansen Feeder Canal—*canal* ........ CO-8
Charles H Boehm HS—*school* ........ PA-2
Charles H Boustead Tunnel—*tunnel* ........ CO-8
Charles Head Pond Dam—*dam* ........ AL-4
Charles Heinz Catfish Ponds Dam—*dam* ........ MS-4
Charles Heller Dam—*dam* ........ SD-7
*Charles Henderson High School* ........ AL-4
Charles Hill—*summit* ........ VT-1
Charles Hollow—*valley* ........ AR-4
Charles Hollow—*valley* ........ MO-7
Charles Hollow—*valley* ........ UT-8
Charles Howard Point—*cape* ........ ME-1
Charles Howell Scout Reservation—*locale* ........ MI-6
Charles H Russell Elem Sch—*school* ........ PA-2
Charles H Tuttle MS—*school* ........ NC-3
Charles H Wenger Airfield—*airport* ........ OR-9
Charles Hyde Dam—*dam* ........ SD-7
*Charles Island* ........ NH-1
Charles Island—*island* ........ CT-1
Charles Island—*island* ........ GA-3
Charles Island—*island* ........ NC-3
Charles Island—*island* ........ WA-9
Charles Island (historical)—*island* ........ TN-4
*Charles Island Rocks* ........ CT-1
Charles Knob—*summit* ........ WV-2
*Charles Lake* ........ WI-6
Charles Lake—*lake* ........ MI-6
Charles Lake—*lake* ........ MN-6
Charles Lake—*lake* ........ ND-7
Charles Lake—*lake* ........ OK-5
Charles Lake—*lake* ........ WI-6
*Charles Lake Creek* ........ TX-5
Charles Lathrop Pack
  Demonstration—*area* ........ WA-9
Charles Lee Tilden Regional Park—*park* ........ CA-9
Charles Long Pond Dam—*dam* ........ MS-4
Charles Ludlow Ditch—*canal* ........ IN-6
Charlesmac Run—*stream* ........ IN-6
**Charlesmac Village**—*pop pl* ........ IN-6
Charles Major Education Center—*school* ........ IN-6
**Charles Manor**—*pop pl* ........ MD-2
Charles May Ditch—*canal* ........ IN-6
Charles McEdwards Catfish Pond
  Dam—*dam* ........ MS-4
Charles Mears State Park—*park* ........ MI-6
Charles Memorial Park—*park* ........ NY-2
**Charles Mill**—*pop pl* ........ OH-6
Charles Miller Ditch—*canal* ........ MT-8
Charles Mill Lake—*reservoir* ........ OH-6
*Charles Mill Rsvr* ........ OH-6
Charles Mine—*mine* ........ AZ-5
Charles Mine—*mine* ........ NM-5
Charles Mix County—*civil* ........ SD-7
**Charlesmont**—*pop pl* ........ MD-2
Charlesmont Sch—*school* ........ MD-2
Charles Morgan Ranch—*locale* ........ NE-7
Charles Mound—*summit* ........ IL-6
Charles M. Russell—*post sta* ........ MT-8
Charles M Russell Natl Wildlife
  Ref—*park* ........ MT-8
Charles M Russell NWR Station—*locale* ........ MT-8
Charles Mtn—*summit* ........ CA-9

Charles Mtn—summit ... TN-4
Charles Nagel ... MO-7
Charles Neck ... MA-1
Charles Neck Point—cape ... MA-1
Charles Norwood Lake—reservoir ... NC-3
Charles Norwood Lake Dam—dam ... NC-3
Charles Park—uninc pl ... LA-4
Charles Phillips Mine (underground)—mine ... TN-4
Charles Pickering Catfish Ponds Dam—dam (2) ... MS-4
Charles Pickering Lake Dam—dam ... MS-4
Charles Playhouse—building ... MA-1
Charles Playhouse—hist pl ... MA-1
Charles Point ... MD-2
Charles Point—cape ... MD-2
Charles Point—cape (3) ... NY-2
Charles Point—cape ... WA-9
Charles Pond—lake (3) ... ME-1
Charles Pond State Public Hunting Grounds—park ... WI-6
Charles Price Ranch—locale ... SD-7
Charles Rayine—valley ... NH-1
Charles R. Drew Elem Sch—school ... DE-2
Charles R Drew Elem Sch—school ... FL-3
Charles R Drew Elem Sch—school ... IN-6
Charles R Drew JHS—school ... FL-3
Charles R Drew MS—school ... AL-4
Charles River ... CT-1
Charles River ... DE-2
Charles River ... MA-1
Charles River ... PA-2
Charles River ... RI-1
Charles River—stream ... ME-1
Charles River—stream ... MA-1
Charles River Basin—reservoir ... MA-1
Charles River Basin Hist Dist—hist pl ... MA-1
Charles River Country Club—locale ... MA-1
Charles River Dam—dam ... MA-1
Charles River Dam At South Natick—dam ... MA-1
**Charles River Grove**—pop pl ... MA-1
Charles River (historical P.O.)—locale ... MA-1
Charles River Plaza (Shop Ctr)—locale ... MA-1
Charles River Rsvr—reservoir (4) ... MA-1
Charles River Square—park ... MA-1
**Charles River Station**—pop pl ... MA-1
Charles River Station (historical)—locale ... MA-1
**Charles River Village**—pop pl ... MA-1
Charles Roseberry Pond Dam—dam ... MS-4
Charles Rowland Lake Dam—dam ... MS-4
Charles Run—stream ... MD-2
Charles Run—stream ... WV-2
Charles Ryan Pond ... CT-1
Charles Seton Grant—civil ... FL-3
Charles S Foos Sch—school ... PA-2
Charles Sheldon Antelope Range—park ... NV-8
Charles Shoals—bar ... TN-4
Charles Sibbold Grant—civil ... FL-3
Charles Sprayberry Regional Educational Center—school ... AL-4
Charles Spring—spring ... AZ-5
Charles Spring—spring ... FL-3
Charles Spring—spring ... NM-5
Charles Spur ... AL-4
Charles Steele Pond Dam—dam ... MS-4
Charles Street—uninc pl ... MA-1
Charles Street African Methodist Episcopal Church—hist pl ... MA-1
Charles Street Ch of God—church ... AL-4
Charles Street Elem Sch ... PA-2
Charles Street House at No. 131—hist pl ... NY-2
Charles Street Meeting House—building ... MA-1
Charles Street Sch—school ... NJ-2
Charles Street Sch—school ... NY-2
Charles S Wallace HS—school ... NC-3
Charles Tank—reservoir ... NM-5
Charles Templeton Ditch—canal ... IN-6
Charles Theriot, Bayou—gut ... LA-4
Charles T Mines—mine ... CO-8
Charleston ... AL-4
Charleston ... DE-2
Charleston ... MA-1
Charleston ... NV-8
Charleston ... NC-3
Charleston—locale ... AZ-5
Charleston—locale ... PA-2
**Charleston**—pop pl ... AR-4
**Charleston**—pop pl ... IL-6
**Charleston**—pop pl ... IA-7
**Charleston**—pop pl ... KS-7
**Charleston**—pop pl ... KY-4
**Charleston**—pop pl ... ME-1
**Charleston**—pop pl ... MI-6
**Charleston**—pop pl ... MS-4
**Charleston**—pop pl ... MO-7
**Charleston**—pop pl ... NV-8
**Charleston**—pop pl ... NJ-2
**Charleston**—pop pl (2) ... NY-2
**Charleston**—pop pl ... NC-3
**Charleston**—pop pl ... OR-9
**Charleston**—pop pl ... PA-2
**Charleston**—pop pl ... SC-3
**Charleston**—pop pl (2) ... TN-4
**Charleston**—pop pl (2) ... TX-5
**Charleston**—pop pl ... UT-8
**Charleston**—pop pl ... WA-9
**Charleston**—pop pl ... WV-2
Charleston Acad (historical)—school ... TN-4
Charleston Access Point—locale ... GA-3
Charleston AFB—military ... SC-3
Charleston Air Force Base/ Int. Airport—mil airp ... SC-3
Charleston Air Force Station—military ... ME-1
Charleston Army Depot—other ... SC-3
Charleston Baptist Ch—church ... TN-4
Charleston Beach—beach ... RI-1
Charleston Bottom Cem—cemetery ... KY-4
**Charleston Bottoms**—pop pl ... KY-4
Charleston (CCD)—cens area ... TN-4
Charleston Cem—cemetery ... IL-6
Charleston Cem—cemetery ... IA-7
Charleston Cem—cemetery (2) ... KS-7
Charleston Cem—cemetery (2) ... MI-6
Charleston Cem—cemetery ... NC-3
Charleston Cem—cemetery ... TN-4
Charleston Cem—cemetery ... UT-8
Charleston Center Sch—school ... VT-1
Charleston Ch—church ... NY-2
Charleston City Hall—building ... MS-4
Charleston City Hall—building ... TN-4
Charleston City Hall—hist pl ... WV-2
Charleston Coast Guard Base—military ... SC-3
Charleston Community Cem—cemetery ... TN-4
Charleston Consolidated Sch—school ... PA-2
Charleston Country Club—other ... IL-6
Charleston Country Club—other ... SC-3
**Charleston (County)**—pop pl ... SC-3
Charleston Creek ... ID-8
Charleston Creek ... UT-8
Charleston Creek—bay ... MD-2
Charleston Creek—stream ... NC-3
Charleston Creek—stream ... PA-2
Charleston Creek—stream ... UT-8
Charleston Crossroads—locale ... SC-3
Charleston Cumberland Presbyterian Ch—church ... TN-4
Charleston Cumberland Presbyterian Church—hist pl ... TN-4
Charleston Division—civil ... TN-4
**Charleston East**—pop pl ... NJ-2
Charleston Elem Sch—school ... MS-4
Charleston Fork ... WV-2
**Charleston Four Corners**—pop pl ... NY-2
Charleston Fuel Storage Station—facility ... SC-3
Charleston Gulch—valley ... NV-8
Charleston Harbon Ch—church ... SC-3
Charleston Harbor—bay ... SC-3
**Charleston Heights**—pop pl ... SC-3
**Charleston Heights**—pop pl ... VA-3
Charleston High School ... TN-4
Charleston Hill—summit ... NV-8
Charleston Hist Dist—hist pl ... SC-3
Charleston Hist Dist (Boundary Increase)—hist pl ... SC-3
Charleston (historical)—locale (2) ... KS-7
Charleston (historical)—locale ... NC-3
Charleston Hotel—hist pl ... LA-4
Charleston HS—school ... MS-4
Charleston Island—island ... OH-6
Charleston Lake—reservoir ... AR-4
Charleston Lead Mine—mine ... AZ-5
Charleston Lighthouse—locale ... SC-3
Charleston Mountain ... NV-8
Charleston MS—school ... MS-4
Charleston Municipal Airp—airport ... MS-4
Charleston Naval Regional Med Ctr—military ... SC-3
Charleston Naval Shipyard—military ... SC-3
Charleston Naval Station—military ... SC-3
Charleston Naval Supply Center—military ... SC-3
Charleston Naval Weapons Station—military ... SC-3
Charleston-North Charleston (CCD)—cens area ... SC-3
Charleston Old and Hist Dist (Boundary Increase)—hist pl ... SC-3
Charleston Ordinance ... IN-6
Charleston Park ... NV-8
**Charleston Park**—pop pl ... NV-8
Charleston Peak—summit ... NV-8
Charleston Peak Trail North Loop—trail ... NV-8
**Charleston (Phelan)**—pop pl ... TN-4
**Charleston Place Subdivision**—pop pl ... UT-8
Charleston Plaza—locale ... MO-7
Charleston Port Of Embarkation—facility ... SC-3
Charleston Post Office—building ... MS-4
Charleston Post Office—building ... TN-4
Charleston Rsvr—reservoir ... NV-8
Charleston Sch—school ... CA-9
Charleston Sch—school ... OH-6
Charleston Sch—school ... TN-4
Charleston's French Quarter District—hist pl ... SC-3
Charleston Shop Ctr—locale ... NC-3
Charleston (Siding)—locale ... UT-8
Charleston Slough—gut ... CA-9
Charleston Springs—locale ... NJ-2
Charleston Station ... AZ-5
Charleston Swamp—swamp ... AL-4
**Charleston (Town of)**—pop pl ... ME-1
**Charleston (Town of)**—pop pl ... NY-2
**Charleston (Town of)**—pop pl ... VT-1
Charleston Township—fmr MCD ... IA-7
**Charleston Township**—pop pl ... KS-7
Charleston (Township of)—fmr MCD ... NC-3
Charleston (Township of)—other ... OH-6
**Charleston (Township of)**—pop pl ... IL-6
**Charleston (Township of)**—pop pl ... MI-6
**Charleston (Township of)**—pop pl ... PA-2
Charleston Transportation Depot—facility ... SC-3
Charleston Upper Elem Sch—school ... MS-4
Charleston Waterworks—other ... SC-3
Charlestown ... NY-2
Charles Town ... NC-3
Charlestown ... WV-2
Charlestown—locale ... NJ-2
Charlestown—locale ... PA-2
**Charlestown**—pop pl ... IN-6
**Charlestown**—pop pl (2) ... MD-2
**Charlestown**—pop pl ... NH-1
**Charlestown**—pop pl ... OH-6
**Charlestown**—pop pl ... OR-9
**Charlestown**—pop pl (2) ... PA-2
**Charlestown**—pop pl ... RI-1
**Charles Town**—pop pl ... WV-2
Charlestown Beach ... RI-1
Charlestown Beach—locale ... RI-1
**Charlestown Beach**—pop pl ... RI-1
Charlestown Breachway—gut ... RI-1
Charlestown Cem—cemetery ... WI-6
Charlestown Ch—church ... GA-3
**Charlestown Compact (census name Charlestown)**—pop pl ... NH-1
Charles Towne ... SC-3
Charlestown Estate—uninc pl ... SC-3
**Charlestown Estates (subdivision)**—pop pl ... TN-4
Charlestowne Village, Town of ... MA-1
Charlestown Heights ... MA-1
Charlestown Hist Dist—hist pl ... MD-2
Charlestown Inlet ... RI-1
Charlestown Landing—locale ... IN-6
Charles Town (Magisterial District)—fmr MCD ... WV-2
Charlestown Main Street Hist Dist—hist pl ... NH-1
**Charlestown Manor Beach**—pop pl ... MD-2
Charlestown Ordnance Plant ... IN-6
Charlestown Pond ... RI-1
Charlestown Senior HS—school ... IN-6
**Charlestown (subdivision)**—pop pl ... MA-1
Charlestown Town Hall—hist pl ... NH-1
**Charlestown (Town of)**—pop pl ... NH-1
**Charlestown (Town of)**—pop pl ... RI-1
**Charlestown (Town of)**—pop pl ... WI-6
**Charlestown (Township of)**—pop pl ... IN-6
**Charlestown (Township of)**—pop pl ... MN-6
**Charlestown (Township of)**—pop pl ... OH-6
**Charlestown (Township of)**—pop pl ... PA-2
Charlestown Village Hist Dist—hist pl ... PA-2
Charle Sumac Estates ... IN-6
**Charle Sumac Estates**—pop pl ... IN-6
Charles Valley—valley ... CA-9
Charles Valley Creek—stream ... CA-9
Charles Vanden Bulck Bridge—bridge ... TN-4
Charles Village-Abell Hist Dist—hist pl ... MD-2
Charlesville—locale ... MD-2
Charlesville—locale ... PA-2
**Charlesville**—pop pl ... MN-6
Charlesville Station—locale ... MD-2
Charles Waters Memorial Campground—locale ... MT-8
Charles W Baker Airp—airport ... TN-4
Charles W. Bush Sch—school ... DE-2
Charles W Clarke Grant—civil ... FL-3
Charles Weiss Dam Number 1—dam ... SD-7
Charles Weiss Dam Number 2—dam ... SD-7
Charles Weiss Dam Number 3—dam ... SD-7
Charles Welch Catfish Ponds Dam—dam ... MS-4
Charles W Fairbanks Elem Sch—school ... IN-6
Charles W Green State Wildlife Area ... MO-7
Charles W Green State Wildlife Mngmt Ar—park ... MO-7
Charles W Harris Sch—school ... AZ-5
Charles Williams Spring—spring ... AZ-5
Charles W Longer Elem Sch—school ... PA-2
CHARLES W. MORGAN—hist pl ... CT-1
Charles Woodham Lake Dam—dam ... AL-4
Charles Wood Helipad—airport ... NJ-2
Charles Wood Hollow—valley ... MO-7
**Charlesworth**—pop pl ... MI-6
**Charlesworth Addition (subdivision)**—pop pl ... UT-8
**Charlesworth Corners**—pop pl ... NY-2
Charlesworth Valley—valley ... UT-8
Charles Young Cem—cemetery ... MS-4
Charleton Cem—cemetery ... MI-6
Charleton Hollow—valley ... MO-7
Charleton R ... MO-7
Charleton River ... IA-7
Charlet Ranch—locale ... KS-7
**Charlevoix**—pop pl ... MI-6
Charlevoix, Lake—lake ... MI-6
Charlevoix City Park Site—hist pl ... MI-6
**Charlevoix (County)**—pop pl ... MI-6
**Charlevoix (Township of)**—pop pl ... MI-6
Charlewan Lake—lake ... MS-4
**Charley**—pop pl ... KY-4
Charley, Lake—lake ... MN-6
Charley, Lake—reservoir ... MS-4
Charley Adams Canyon—valley ... NM-5
Charley Anderson Pond—lake ... ME-1
Charley Bald—summit ... NC-3
Charley Bell Well ... AZ-5
Charley Bob Creek ... ND-7
Charley Branch ... WV-2
Charley Branch—stream ... KY-4
Charley Branch—stream (2) ... NC-3
Charley Branch—stream ... TN-4
Charley Branch—stream ... WV-2
Charley Bridges—locale ... SC-3
Charley Brook ... MA-1
Charley Brown Park—park ... IL-6
Charley Buck Slough—gut ... LA-4
Charley Canyon—valley ... NV-8
Charley Cem—cemetery ... IN-6
Charley Cem—cemetery ... OK-5
Charley Corral—locale ... OR-9
Charley Creek ... MT-8
Charley Creek ... TN-4
Charley Creek—stream ... AK-9
Charley Creek—stream ... AR-4
Charley Creek—stream ... CA-9
Charley Creek—stream ... FL-3
Charley Creek—stream ... ID-8
Charley Creek—stream ... IN-6
Charley Creek—stream ... MT-8
Charley Creek—stream ... NV-8
Charley Creek—stream ... NJ-2
Charley Creek—stream ... NC-3
Charley Creek—stream ... OH-6
Charley Creek—stream (2) ... OK-5
Charley Creek—stream ... OR-9
Charley Creek—stream ... SD-7
Charley Creek—stream (4) ... WA-9
Charley Creek—stream ... WV-2
Charley Creek Ch—church ... WV-2
Charley Creek Rec Area—park ... SD-7
Charley Creek Sch—school ... NC-3
Charley Day Well—well ... AZ-5
Charley Earl Gulch—valley ... CO-8
Charley Flat—flat ... UT-8
Charley Gap—gap ... NC-3
Charley Glacier—glacier ... AK-9
Charley Green Creek—stream ... AK-9
Charley Gulch—valley ... MT-8
Charley Hart Tank—reservoir ... TX-5
Charley Holes—spring ... UT-8
Charley Hollow—valley ... MO-7
Charley Hollow—valley ... WA-9
Charley Hollow—valley ... WV-2
Charley Johnson Canyon—valley ... UT-8
Charley Jumper Hammock—island ... FL-3
Charley Knob—summit ... NC-3
Charley Knob—summit ... WV-2
Charley Lake—lake ... MN-6
Charley Lake—lake ... NY-2
Charleymont ... VA-3
Charley Mtn—summit ... CA-9
Charley Nichols Windmill—locale ... TX-5
Charley Pond—lake ... FL-3
Charley Pond—lake ... LA-4
Charley Pond—lake ... NY-2
Charley Pond—reservoir ... FL-3
Charley Ridge—ridge ... NC-3
Charley Ridge—ridge ... TN-4
Charley Ridge—ridge ... WV-2
Charley River—stream ... AK-9
Charley Ross Mine—mine ... NV-8
Charley Run—stream (2) ... PA-2
Charley Run—stream ... WV-2
Charley Run Creek—stream ... OH-6
**Charleys Branch**—pop pl ... TN-4
Charleys Branch—stream ... TN-4
Charleys Gulch—valley ... MT-8
Charleys Knob—summit ... NC-3
Charleys Park—flat ... UT-8
Charley Spring Branch—stream ... AL-4
Charley Springs Mtn—summit ... TX-5
Charleys Run—stream ... WV-2
Charley Tank—reservoir (2) ... AZ-5
Charley Tank—reservoir (3) ... NM-5
Charley Tank—reservoir ... TX-5
Charley Tank Draw—valley ... TX-5
Charley Thompson Springs—spring ... AZ-5
Charley Town ... DE-2
Charley Trace Fork ... WV-2
Charley Trace Fork—stream ... WV-2
Charley Valley—basin ... CA-9
Charley Well—well ... AZ-5
Charley White Draw—valley ... NM-5
Charley White Windmill—locale ... NM-5
Charley Windmill—locale ... TX-5
Charley York Hollow—valley ... TX-5
Charlia Lakes—lake ... WA-9
Charlick Lake—lake ... MI-6
Charlie—locale ... TX-5
Charlie, Lake—reservoir ... ND-7
Charlie Alley Peak—summit ... CA-9
Charlie Area—locale ... UT-8
Charlie Barns Gap—gap ... NM-5
Charlie Bell Pass—gap ... AZ-5
Charlie Bell Well—well ... AZ-5
Charlie Bent Well—well ... AZ-5
Charlie Billie Camp—locale ... FL-3
Charlie Black Butte—summit ... MT-8
Charlie Blair Branch—stream ... KY-4
**Charlie Bluff**—pop pl ... WI-6
Charlie Bob Creek—stream ... ND-7
Charlie Brackett Spring—spring ... ID-8
Charlie Branch—stream ... GA-3
Charlie Branch—stream (2) ... KY-4
Charlie Branch—stream ... MS-4
Charlie Branch—stream ... TN-4
Charlie Brooks Draw—valley ... WY-8
Charlie Brown Branch—stream ... GA-3
Charlie Brown/Fulton County Airp—airport ... GA-3
Charlie Brown Lake—lake ... WA-9
Charlie Brown's Lake ... ID-8
Charlie Brown Spring—spring ... UT-8
Charlie Brown Spring—spring ... WY-8
Charlie Buck Gulch—valley ... OR-9
Charlie Canyon—valley (2) ... CA-9
Charlie Canyon—valley ... NV-8
Charlie Creek—stream ... AL-4
Charlie Creek—stream ... AK-9
Charlie Creek—stream ... CA-9
Charlie Creek—stream ... CO-8
Charlie Creek—stream ... FL-3
Charlie Creek—stream ... GA-3
Charlie Creek—stream (2) ... ID-8
Charlie Creek—stream ... KS-7
Charlie Creek—stream (4) ... MT-8
Charlie Creek—stream ... NC-3
Charlie Creek—stream (3) ... OK-5
Charlie Creek—stream (4) ... OR-9
Charlie Creek—stream ... SD-7
Charlie Creek—stream ... TN-4
Charlie Creek—stream ... WY-8
Charlie Creek Rsvr—reservoir ... OR-9
Charlie Cypress Camp—locale ... FL-3
Charlie Died Tank—reservoir ... AZ-5
Charlie Dike—cliff ... AZ-5
Charlie Draw—valley ... WY-8
Charlie Duncan Cem—cemetery ... MS-4
Charlie Fewl Hammock—island ... FL-3
Charlie Graves Lake Dam—dam ... MS-4
Charlie Harris Canyon—valley ... NM-5
Charlie Heath State Forest and Memorial Wildlife Area—park ... MO-7
Charlie Hill—summit ... NM-5
Charlie Hill—summit ... PA-2
Charlie Hollow—valley ... AR-4
Charlie Hollow—valley ... TN-4
Charlie Hollow—valley ... WV-2
Charlie Hope—locale ... VA-3
Charlie Hope No 1 Sch—school ... VA-3
Charlie Hope No 2 Sch—school ... VA-3
Charlie Horse Cave—cave ... AL-4
Charlie House Draw—valley ... WY-8
Charlie Humphreys Catfish Ponds Dam—dam ... MS-4
Charlie Johnson Pond Dam—dam ... MS-4
Charlie Key—island ... FL-3
Charlie Knight Gulch—valley ... WA-9
Charlie Lake—lake ... AK-9
Charlie Lake—lake ... MN-6
Charlie Lakes—lake ... WA-9
Charlie Lick Branch—stream ... VA-3
Charlie Long Millpond—swamp ... NC-3
Charlie Mack Creek—stream ... OR-9
Charlie McKissack Cut—channel ... FL-3
Charlie Moore Mesa—bench ... NM-5
Charlie Moore Mtn—summit ... AZ-5
Charlie Moore Place—locale ... AZ-5
Charlie Moseley Dam Number 1—dam ... AL-4
Charlie Moseley Dam Number 2—dam ... AL-4
Charlie Moseley Lake Number One—reservoir ... AL-4
Charlie Moseley Lake Number Two—reservoir ... AL-4
Charlie Mtn—summit ... GA-3
Charlie Otto Creek—stream ... WI-6
Charlie Otto Spring—lake ... WI-6
Charlie Pond—lake ... NY-2
Charlie Pond—reservoir ... GA-3
Charlie Ray Lake Dam—dam ... MS-4
Charlie Rhea Bend—bend ... KY-4
Charlie Rhea Island—island ... KY-4
Charlie Ridge—ridge ... NC-3
Charlie Roberts Canyon ... WA-9
Charlie Rollans Mtn—summit ... AR-4
Charlie Ross Draw—valley ... TX-5
Charlie Ross Tank—reservoir ... AZ-5
Charlie Ross Tank—reservoir ... TX-5
Charlie Rsvr—reservoir ... WY-8
Charlies Bunion—summit ... NC-3
Charlies Bunion—summit ... TN-4
Charlies Butte—locale ... CA-9
Charlies Canyon—valley ... NM-5
Charlies Creek ... WA-9
Charlies Creek—stream ... AL-4
Charlies Creek—stream ... GA-3
Charlies Creek—stream ... NC-3
Charlies Creek—stream ... SC-3
Charlies Dam—dam ... AZ-5
Charlies Draw—valley ... WY-8
Charlie Secody Well—well ... AZ-5
**Charlies Grove**—pop pl ... PA-2
Charlies Hill—summit ... NY-2
Charlies Hump—cliff ... WA-9
Charlieskin Creek—stream ... AK-9
Charlieskin Village—locale ... AK-9
Charlie Smith Butte—summit ... OR-9
Charlies Pond ... LA-4
Charlie Spring—spring ... CA-9
Charlies Ridge—ridge ... NC-3
Charlies River ... WA-9
Charlies Rock—pillar ... CA-9
Charlies Rsvr—reservoir ... WY-8
Charlies Run—stream ... PA-2
Charlies Spring ... AZ-5
Charlies Tank—lake ... NM-5
Charlies Tank—reservoir ... NM-5
Charlies Waterhole—spring ... MT-8
Charlies Well—well ... AZ-5
Charlie Tank—reservoir (2) ... AZ-5
Charlie Tank—reservoir ... NM-5
Charlie Taylor Mtn—summit ... VA-3
Charlie Turner Cave—cave ... AL-4
Charlie Valley—valley ... CA-9
Charlieville ... LA-4
Charlieville—locale ... LA-4
Charlie Wash—stream ... NM-5
Charlie Waters Dam—dam ... SD-7
Charlie Well—well ... AZ-5
Charlie Well—well ... NM-5
Charlie Weston Tank—reservoir ... AZ-5
Charlie White Lake—lake ... MT-8
Charlie Windmill—locale ... TX-5
Charlie Young Canyon ... NV-8
Charlie Young Canyon—valley ... NV-8
Charlie Young Goat Corral (historical)—locale ... NV-8
Charline, Lake—lake ... OR-9
Charliton River ... IA-7
**Charlo**—pop pl ... MT-8
**Charloe**—pop pl ... OH-6
Charlo Juan Well—well ... AZ-5
Charlo Lake—lake ... LA-4
Charlos Heights—locale ... MT-8
Charlot Gluch ... ID-8
Charlotte ... VA-3
Charlotte—locale ... LA-4
Charlotte—locale ... ME-1
**Charlotte**—pop pl ... AR-4
**Charlotte**—pop pl ... IL-6
**Charlotte**—pop pl ... IA-7
**Charlotte**—pop pl ... KY-4
**Charlotte**—pop pl ... MI-6
**Charlotte**—pop pl ... NY-2
**Charlotte**—pop pl ... NC-3
**Charlotte**—pop pl ... TN-4
**Charlotte**—pop pl ... TX-5
**Charlotte**—pop pl ... VT-1
Charlotte, Lake—lake ... AK-9
Charlotte, Lake—lake ... FL-3
Charlotte, Lake—lake (4) ... MN-6
Charlotte, Lake—lake ... NY-2
Charlotte, Lake—lake ... PA-2
Charlotte, Lake—lake ... TX-5
Charlotte Amalie—11756 (1980) ... VI-3
Charlotte Amalie (Census Subdistrict)—cens area ... VI-3
Charlotte Amalie East—CDP ... VI-3
Charlotte Amalie Hist Dist—hist pl ... VI-3
Charlotte Amalie West—CDP ... VI-3
Charlotte Ave Sch—school ... NH-1
Charlotte Ave Sch—school ... NY-2
Charlotte Beach—locale ... FL-3
Charlotte Branch ... AL-4
Charlotte Branch—stream ... NC-3
Charlotteburg—locale ... NJ-2
**Charlotteburg**—pop pl ... NJ-2
Charlotteburg Dam—dam ... NJ-2
Charlotteburg Furnace ... NJ-2
Charlotteburg Rsvr—reservoir ... NJ-2
Charlotte Catholic HS—school ... NC-3
Charlotte (CCD)—cens area ... TN-4
Charlotte (CCD)—cens area ... TX-5
Charlotte Cem—cemetery ... TN-4
Charlotte Cem—cemetery ... WI-6
**Charlotte Center**—pop pl ... NY-2
**Charlotte Center (Charlotte)**—pop pl ... NY-2
Charlotte Center Hist Dist—hist pl ... VT-1
Charlotte Christian Acad—school ... FL-3
Charlotte Coliseum—locale ... NC-3
Charlotte Country Club—locale ... NC-3
Charlotte Country Sch—school ... NC-3
**Charlotte County**—pop pl ... FL-3
**Charlotte (County)**—pop pl ... VA-3
Charlotte County Courthouse—hist pl ... VA-3
Charlotte County Lookout Tower ... FL-3
Charlotte Court House ... VA-3
**Charlotte Court House**—pop pl ... VA-3
Charlotte Courthouse Square Hist Dist—hist pl ... TN-4
Charlotte Cove—valley ... NC-3
Charlotte Creek—stream ... AL-4
Charlotte Creek—stream ... CA-9
Charlotte Creek—stream ... MT-8
Charlotte Creek—stream ... NY-2
Charlotte Creek—stream (2) ... OR-9
Charlotte Division—civil ... TN-4
Charlotte/Douglas International Airport ... NC-3
Charlotte Furnace—locale ... KY-4
Charlotte Gin Branch—stream ... GA-3
Charlotte Gospel Hall—church ... NC-3
Charlotte Gulch—valley ... ID-8
**Charlotte Hall**—pop pl ... MD-2
Charlotte Hall Hist Dist—hist pl ... MD-2
Charlotte Hall Military Acad—school ... MD-2
Charlotte Hall Sch—school ... MD-2
Charlotte Harbor—bay ... FL-3
**Charlotte Harbor**—pop pl ... FL-3
Charlotte Harbor and Northern Railway Depot—hist pl ... FL-3
Charlotte Harbor Sch—school ... FL-3
Charlotte Harbour ... FL-3
**Charlotte (historical)**—pop pl ... OR-9
Charlotte HS—school ... FL-3
Charlotte HS—school ... NY-2
Charlotte Hyatt Elementary School ... MS-4
Charlotte Jane Memorial Park—cemetery ... FL-3
Charlotte Jane Memorial Park Cem—cemetery ... FL-3
Charlotte Junction—uninc pl ... NC-3
Charlotte Lake ... WI-6
Charlotte Lake—lake ... CA-9
Charlotte Lake—lake (2) ... MN-6
Charlotte Landing—locale ... MI-6
Charlotte Latin Sch—school ... NC-3
Charlotte Lookout Tower—locale ... AR-4
Charlotte Memorial Gardens ... FL-3
Charlotte Memorial Gardens—cemetery ... NC-3
Charlotte Motor Speedway—locale ... NC-3
Charlottenburg Cem—cemetery ... TX-5
Charlotte Oil Field—oilfield ... TX-5
Charlotte Park—park ... MN-6
Charlotte Park—park ... TN-4
**Charlotte Park**—pop pl ... FL-3
**Charlotte Park**—pop pl ... TN-4
Charlotte Park Sch—school ... TN-4
Charlotte Peak—summit ... MT-8
Charlotte Plastics Lake—reservoir ... NC-3
Charlotte Plastics Lake Dam—dam ... NC-3
Charlotte Plastics Lake Dam Number Two—dam ... NC-3
Charlotte Plastics Lake Number Two—reservoir ... NC-3
Charlotte Point—cliff ... NM-5
Charlotte Police and Fire Acad—school ... NC-3
Charlotte Police Dept Airp—airport ... NC-3
Charlotte Pond—lake ... FL-3
Charlotte Ridge—ridge ... AK-9
Charlotte River ... FL-3
Charlotte River ... IA-7
Charlotte River—stream ... MI-6
Charlotte Rsvr—reservoir ... NC-3
Charlottes Brook—stream ... IN-6
Charlottesburg ... NC-3
Charlottesburgh ... NC-3
Charlottes Cove—bay ... ME-1
Charlotte Shop Ctr—locale ... FL-3
Charlotte Square—post sta ... FL-3
Charlotte Square Shop Ctr—locale ... TN-4
Charlotte Street Hist Dist—hist pl ... AR-4
Charlotte Supply Company Bldg—hist pl ... NC-3
Charlottesville ... PA-2
**Charlottesville**—pop pl (2) ... IN-6
Charlottesville-Albemarle Airp—airport ... VA-3
Charlottesville and Albemarle County Courthouse Hist Dist—hist pl ... VA-3
Charlottesville Cem—cemetery ... IL-6
Charlottesville Creek—stream ... IN-6
**Charlottesville (ind. city)**—pop pl ... VA-3
Charlottesville (Magisterial District)—fmr MCD ... VA-3
Charlottesville Rsvr—reservoir (2) ... VA-3
**Charlotte (Town of)**—pop pl ... ME-1
**Charlotte (Town of)**—pop pl ... NY-2
**Charlotte (Town of)**—pop pl ... VT-1
**Charlotte Township**—pop pl ... MO-7
**Charlotte (Township of)**—pop pl ... IL-6
Charlotte Valley—valley ... NY-2
Charlotte Valley Cem—cemetery ... NY-2
Charlotteville—locale ... GA-3
**Charlotteville**—pop pl ... NY-2
Charlotte Vocational-Technical Center—school ... FL-3
Charlotte Water Works—building ... NC-3
Charlottsville ... IN-6
**Charlottsville**—pop pl ... PA-2
Charlottsville Cem—cemetery ... PA-2
**Charlson**—pop pl ... ND-7
Charlson Oil Field—oilfield ... ND-7
Charlston ... KS-7
Charlston Creek ... GA-3
Charlton ... AL-4
Charlton ... MA-1
Charlton—locale ... VA-3
**Charlton**—pop pl ... MD-2
**Charlton**—pop pl ... MA-1
**Charlton**—pop pl ... MS-4
**Charlton**—pop pl ... NY-2
**Charlton**—pop pl (2) ... PA-2
Charlton, Capt. Richard, House—hist pl ... CT-1
Charlton Bluff—cliff ... MO-7
Charlton Butte—summit ... OR-9
Charlton Canyon—valley ... WA-9
Charlton Center—other ... MA-1
Charlton Centre ... MA-1
Charlton Channel ... WA-9
**Charlton (Charlton Center)**—pop pl ... MA-1
**Charlton City**—pop pl ... MA-1
**Charlton (County)**—pop pl ... GA-3
Charlton County Courthouse—hist pl ... GA-3
Charlton Creek—stream (2) ... CA-9
Charlton Creek—stream ... OR-9
**Charlton Depot**—pop pl ... MA-1
**Charlton Depot (RR name Charlton (sta.))**—pop pl ... MA-1
Charlton Flats Picnic Grounds—locale ... CA-9
Charlton Grove Ch—church ... GA-3
**Charlton Heights**—pop pl ... WV-2
Charlton Hist Dist—hist pl ... NY-2
Charlton House—building ... NC-3
Charlton-King-Vandam Hist Dist—hist pl ... NY-2
Charlton Lake—lake ... OR-9
Charlton Lake—lake ... WA-9
Charlton Mill—hist pl ... MA-1
Charlton Park—park ... MI-6
Charlton Park—park ... TX-5
Charlton Peak—summit ... CA-9
Charlton Post Office (historical)—building ... MS-4
Charlton Rec Area—park ... AR-4
Charlton Reservoir ... MA-1
Charlton Sch—school ... PA-2
Charlton Slough—stream ... MT-8
Charlton (sta.) (RR name for Charlton Depot)—other ... MA-1
Charlton Station—locale ... CA-9
Charlton Street Sch—school ... MA-1
Charlton Street Sch—school ... NJ-2
Charlton Town Hall and Ch—church ... MI-6
**Charlton (Town of)**—pop pl ... MA-1
**Charlton (Town of)**—pop pl ... NY-2
**Charlton (Township of)**—pop pl ... MI-6

Charltonville ... MA-1
Charlyle, Lake—lake ... MI-6
Charm—pop pl ... OH-6
Charm, Lake—lake ... FL-3
Charmaine Lake—lake ... CA-9
Charman Creek—stream ... OR-9
Charman Trail—trail ... PA-2
Charmar Subdivision—pop pl ... UT-8
Charmco—pop pl ... WV-2
Charmco Ch—church ... WV-2
Charme—locale ... WI-6
Charmian—pop pl ... PA-2
Charmicles Shoals ... TN-4
Charming, Lake—reservoir ... MD-2
Charmingdale (subdivision)—pop pl ... AL-4
Charming Forge—locale ... PA-2
Charming Lake—reservoir ... MD-2
Charm Lake—lake ... MN-6
Charm Spring—spring ... CO-8
Charnac Basin—basin ... NV-8
Charnell PUD Subdivision—pop pl ... UT-8
Charnell Subdivision—pop pl ... UT-8
Charnita—pop pl ... PA-2
Charnita Dam ... PA-2
Charnita Lake—lake ... PA-2
Charnley, James, House—hist pl ... IL-6
Charnley Lake—lake ... WI-6
Charnnings Ferry—locale ... AR-4
Charnock Hill—summit (2) ... MA-1
Charnock Pass—gap ... NV-8
Charnock Ranch—locale ... NV-8
Charnock Road Sch—school ... CA-9
Charob Lake—lake ... AL-4
Charob Lake Dam—dam ... AL-4
Charold, Lake—reservoir ... AL-4
Charoleau Gap ... AZ-5
Charoley Lake ... WI-6
Charon—pop pl ... LA-4
Charons Garden Mtn—summit ... OK-5
Charo Tank—reservoir ... TX-5
Charouleau Gap—gap ... AZ-5
Charpentier Glacier—glacier ... AK-9
Charpentier Inlet—bay ... AK-9
Charquitas Creek—stream ... TX-5
Charred Creek—stream ... MT-8
Charred Hollow—valley ... OH-6
Charred Oak Estates—pop pl ... MD-2
Charrette Creek—stream ... MO-7
Charrette Township—civil ... MO-7
Charr Island—island ... FL-3
Charris Sch—school ... TX-5
Charro Windmill—locale ... TX-5
Char Tank—reservoir ... AZ-5
Chartee Creek—stream ... AL-4
Charter Branch—stream ... TN-4
Charter Brook ... CT-1
Charter Brook—stream ... CT-1
Charter Brook—stream ... NY-2
Charter Canyon Hosp—hospital ... UT-8
Charter Cem—cemetery ... CT-1
Charter Ch—church ... MO-7
Charter Creek—stream ... KY-4
Charter Glade Hosp—hospital ... FL-3
Charter Grove—pop pl ... IL-6
Charter Grove Cem—cemetery ... IL-6
Charter Hall Point—cape ... MD-2
Charterhouse Private Sch of Clay County—school ... FL-3
Charter Lake—lake ... TX-5
Charter Landing—locale ... MS-4
Charter Marsh—swamp ... NY-2
Charter Meadows (subdivision)—pop pl ... NC-3
Charteroak ... MO-7
Charteroak—locale ... PA-2
Charter Oak—locale ... WA-9
Charter Oak—pop pl ... CA-9
Charter Oak—pop pl ... IA-7
Charteroak—pop pl ... MO-7
Charter Oak—pop pl ... MO-7
Charter Oak—pop pl ... TX-5
Charter Oak Bank Bldg—hist pl ... CT-1
Charter Oak Bridge—bridge ... CT-1
Charter Oak Cem—cemetery ... AR-4
Charter Oak Cem—cemetery ... IL-6
Charter Oak Cem—cemetery ... IA-7
Charter Oak Cem—cemetery ... OH-6
Charter Oak Ch—church ... IL-6
Charter Oak Ch church ... IN 6
Charter Oak Ch—church ... LA-4
Charter Oak Ch—church ... MO-7
Charter Oak Ch—church ... PA-2
Charter Oak Creek—stream ... CA-9
Charter Oak HS—school ... CA-9
Charter Oak Mine—mine ... CO-8
Charter Oak Mines—mine ... MT-8
Charter Oak Missionary Ch—church ... LA-4
Charter Oak Park—park ... CT-1
Charter Oak Place—hist pl ... CT-1
Charter Oak Place (Boundary Increase)—hist pl ... CT-1
Charter Oaks—pop pl ... DE-2
Charter Oaks—pop pl ... PA-2
Charter Oak Sch—school ... CA-9
Charter Oak Sch—school ... CT-1
Charter Oak Sch—school ... SC-3
Charter Oak Schoolhouse—hist pl ... IL-6
Charter Oak Township—fmr MCD ... IA-7
Charters—pop pl ... KY-4
Charters Brook ... CT-1
Charters Brook—stream ... CT-1
Charters Corner—locale ... KS-7
Charters Creek ... ID-8
Charters Creek—stream ... ID-8
Charters Island—island ... VA-3
Charters Pond—reservoir ... CT-1
Charter Springs Hosp—hospital ... FL-3
Charters Saw Mill Pond ... CT-1
Charter Street Hist Dist—hist pl ... MA-1
Charter Summit Hosp—hospital ... UT-8
Charterwood—pop pl ... PA-2
Charter Wood Hosp—hospital ... AL-4
Chartier Coulee—valley ... MT-8
Chartiers—pop pl ... PA-2
Chartiers Cem—cemetery (2) ... PA-2
Chartiers Creek—stream ... PA-2
Chartiers Elem Sch—school ... PA-2
Chartiers Heights Country Club—other ... PA-2
Chartiers Hill Cem—cemetery ... PA-2
Chartiers Houston High School ... PA-2
Chartiers Houston Middle and High School ... PA-2
Chartiers Run—stream (2) ... PA-2
Chartiers School ... PA-2
Chartiers Terrace—pop pl ... PA-2
Chartiers Township HS—school ... PA-2
Chartiers (Township of)—pop pl ... PA-2
Chartier Valley HS—school ... PA-2
Chartley—pop pl ... MD-2
Chartley—pop pl ... MA-1
Chartley Brook—stream ... MA-1
Chartley Pond—reservoir ... MA-1
Chartley Pond Dam—dam ... MA-1
Chartrand HS—school ... IN-6
Chartrand Sch—school ... IL-6
Chartreuse, Lake—lake ... NY-2
Chartville Sch—school ... CA-9
Chartwood (subdivision)—pop pl ... PA-2
Chartz Spring—spring ... AZ-5
Charukuru ... MP-9
Charukuru Island ... MP-9
Charukuru Island—island ... MP-9
Charukuru-To ... MP-9
Charutonen ... MP-9
Charvers Lake Dam—dam ... MS-4
Charvez Spring—spring ... TX-5
Charvoidles Spring—spring ... AZ-5
Charwood Sch—school ... MI-6
Charybdis—summit ... CA-9
Charybdis Butte—summit ... AZ-5
Charybois ... CA-9
Chasco, Lake—lake ... FL-3
Chasco (Whitehill)—pop pl ... IL-6
Chase ... NH-1
Chase—locale ... AL-4
Chase—locale ... AK-9
Chase—locale ... CA-9
Chase—locale ... NY-2
Chase—locale ... OH-6
Chase—other ... TX-5
Chase—pop pl ... FL-3
Chase—pop pl ... IN-6
Chase—pop pl ... KS-7
Chase—pop pl ... LA-4
Chase—pop pl ... MD-2
Chase—pop pl ... MI-6
Chase—pop pl ... NE-7
Chase—pop pl ... OH-6
Chase—pop pl ... OK-5
Chase—pop pl ... PA-2
Chase—pop pl ... SD-7
Chase—pop pl ... UT-8
Chase—pop pl ... WI-6
Chase—uninc pl ... WI-6
Chase, Albon, House—hist pl ... GA-3
Chase, Capt. Josiah E., Octagon House—hist pl ... ME-1
Chase, David C., House—hist pl ... ID-8
Chase, Dr. H. H., and Henry G. Wohlhuter Bungalows—hist pl ... WI-6
Chase, Elwin, House—hist pl ... VT-1
Chase, Hezekiah, House—hist pl ... ME-1
Chase, Isaac, Mill—hist pl ... UT-8
Chase, Lake—lake ... FL-3
Chase, Lemuel B., House—hist pl ... MA-1
Chase, Mount—summit ... ME-1
Chase, Salmon P., Birthplace—hist pl ... NH-1
Chase, Squire, House—hist pl ... ME-1
Chase, William Merritt, Homestead—hist pl ... NY-2
Chase Acres Subdivision—pop pl ... UT-8
Chase Ave Sch—school ... CA-9
Chase Bayou—stream ... MS-4
Chase Bend—bend ... TN-4
Chase Bog—lake ... ME-1
Chase Bog—swamp ... ME-1
Chase Brass and Copper Company—facility ... OH-6
Chase Bridge—other ... MI-6
Chase Brook ... NH-1
Chase Brook ... WI-6
Chase Brook—stream ... CT-1
Chase Brook—stream (7) ... ME-1
Chase Brook—stream (2) ... MN-6
Chase Brook—stream (4) ... NH-1
Chase Brook—stream ... NY-2
Chase Brook—stream (6) ... VT-1
Chase Brook Cem—cemetery ... MN-6
Chase Brook Ridge—ridge ... ME-1
Chaseburg pop pl ... WI 6
Chaseburg Sch—school ... WI-6
Chase Camp—locale ... ME-1
Chase Canyon—valley (2) ... CA-9
Chase Canyon—valley ... NE-7
Chase Canyon—valley ... NM-5
Chase Carry—trail ... ME-1
Chase Cem—cemetery ... IA-7
Chase Cem—cemetery ... ME-1
Chase Cem—cemetery ... MI-6
Chase Cem—cemetery ... MN-6
Chase Cem—cemetery ... NE-7
Chase Cem—cemetery (2) ... NH-1
Chase Cem—cemetery ... NY-2
Chase Cem—cemetery ... ND-7
Chase Cem—cemetery ... OH-6
Chase Cem—cemetery ... PA-2
Chase Cem—cemetery (2) ... TN-4
Chase Cem—cemetery ... TX-5
Chase Cem—cemetery ... WV-2
Chase Ch—church ... LA-4
Chase City—pop pl ... VA-3
Chase City (Magisterial District)—fmr MCD ... VA-3
Chase Community Ch—church ... AL-4
Chase Corner—locale ... ME-1
Chase Corners—locale ... PA-2
Chase Corners—locale ... VT-1
Chase County—civil ... KS-7
Chase County Airp—airport ... KS-7
Chase County Courthouse—hist pl ... KS-7
Chase County HS—school ... KS-7
Chase County Natl Bank—hist pl ... KS-7
Chase County State Lake—reservoir ... KS-7
Chase County State Lake Dam—dam ... KS-7
Chase Cove—bay ... ME-1
Chase Cove—bay ... RI-1
Chase Creek ... MI-6
Chase Creek ... WI-6
Chase Creek—stream ... AL-4
Chase Creek—stream (2) ... AZ-5
Chase Creek—stream ... ID-8
Chase Creek—stream ... MD-2
Chase Creek—stream ... MI-6
Chase Creek—stream ... NV-8
Chase Creek—stream (4) ... NY-2
Chase Creek—stream ... ND-7
Chase Creek—stream ... UT-8
Chase Creek—stream (3) ... WI-6
Chase Creek—stream ... WY-8
Chase Crossing—pop pl ... VA-3
Chase Draw—valley ... CO-8
Chase Draw—valley ... WA-9
Chase Draw Rsvr—reservoir ... CO-8
Chase Field—park ... CA-9
Chase Field Naval Air Station—military ... TX-5
Chasefield Plantation Cem—cemetery ... FL-3
Chaseford ... NJ-2
Chase Garden Creek—stream ... MA-1
Chase-garden River ... MA-1
Chase Gardin River ... MA-1
Chase Gardner Creek ... MA-1
Chase Gorge—valley ... NY-2
Chase Gulch—valley (2) ... CA-9
Chase Gulch—valley (2) ... CO-8
Chase Hill—summit ... CO-8
Chase Hill—summit (2) ... ME-1
Chase Hill—summit ... MT-8
Chase Hill—summit (2) ... NH-1
Chase Hill—summit ... NY-2
Chase Hill—summit ... RI-1
Chase Hill—summit ... VT-1
Chase Hill—summit ... WI-6
Chase Hill Brook—stream ... ME-1
Chase (historical)—locale ... IA-7
Chase (historical)—locale ... SD-7
Chase (historical)—pop pl ... OR-9
Chase Hollow—valley ... PA-2
Chase Hotel—hist pl ... MN-6
Chase HS—school ... KS-7
Chase HS—school (2) ... NC-3
Chase-Hyde Farm—hist pl ... MA-1
Chase Island—island ... AK-9
Chase Island—island ... MD-2
Chase Island—island ... MN-6
Chase Island—island (2) ... NH-1
Chase Island Park—park ... MN-6
Chase Lake—lake ... ID-8
Chase Lake—lake ... ME-1
Chase Lake—lake (4) ... MI-6
Chase Lake—lake (4) ... MN-6
Chase Lake—lake (2) ... NY-2
Chase Lake—lake ... ND-7
Chase Lake—lake (2) ... WA-9
Chase Lake—lake ... WI-6
Chase Lake—pop pl ... NY-2
Chase Lake—reservoir ... IN-6
Chase Lake—reservoir ... ND-7
Chase Lake—unorg reg ... ND-7
Chase Lake Country Club—locale ... AL-4
Chase Lake Dam—dam ... AL-4
Chase Lake Dam—dam ... ND-7
Chase Lake Natl Wildlife Ref—park ... ND-7
Chase Lake Number One—reservoir ... TN-4
Chase Lake Number One Dam—dam ... TN-4
Chase Lake Number Three—reservoir ... TN-4
Chase Lake Number Three Dam—dam ... TN-4
Chase Lake Number Two—reservoir ... TN-4
Chase Lake Number Two Dam—dam ... TN-4
Chase Lake Outlet—stream ... NY-2
Chase Lake Sch—school ... WA-9
Chase Lake State Game Mngmt Area—lake ... ND-7
Chase Lake State Game Mngmt Area—park ... ND-7
Chase Lake Township—civil ... ND-7
Chaseland Park—park ... OH-6
Chase Lane Estates (subdivision)—pop pl ... UT-8
Chase Lane Village (subdivision)—pop pl ... UT-8
Chase Lane West Subdivision—pop pl ... UT-8
Chase Ledge—bench ... CA-9
Chaseley—pop pl ... ND-7
Chaseley Cem—cemetery ... ND-7
Chaseley Township—pop pl ... ND-7
Chase-Lloyd House—hist pl ... MD-2
Chase Meadow—flat ... ID-8
Chase Mills—locale ... ME-1
Chase Mills—pop pl ... ME-1
Chase Mills—pop pl ... NY-2
Chase Mills Inn—hist pl ... NY-2
Chase Mills Stream—stream ... ME-1
Chase Mine—mine ... MI-6
Chase Mtn—summit ... GA-3
Chase Mtn—summit ... ME-1
Chase Mtn—summit ... NH-1
Chase Mtn—summit (2) ... NY-2
Chase Mtn—summit ... OR-9
Chase Mtn—summit ... VT-1
Chase Mtn—summit ... WA-9
Chase-Newbury Cem—cemetery ... PA-2
Chase Park—park ... CT-1
Chase Park—park ... IL-6
Chase Park—park ... OK-5
Chase Park—park ... WA-9
Chase Point—cape ... ME-1
Chase Point—cape ... NH-1
Chase Point—cape ... NY-2
Chase Pond—lake ... CA-9
Chase Pond—lake (4) ... ME-1
Chase Pond—lake ... MD-2
Chase Pond—lake ... MA-1
Chase Pond—lake (2) ... NH-1
Chase Pond—lake ... NY-2
Chase Pond Mtn—summit ... ME-1
Chase Ponds—lake ... ME-1
Chase Post Office—building ... AL-4
Chase Prairie—swamp ... GA-3
Chase Ranch—locale (2) ... CA-9
Chase Ranch—locale ... CO-8
Chase Ranch—locale ... NE-7
Chase Ranch—locale ... WY-8
Chase Rapids—rapids ... ME-1
Chase Ridge—ridge ... MO-7
Chase Ripple—rapids ... IN-6
Chaser Lake—lake ... MN-6
Chase Road Dam—dam ... MA-1
Chase RR Station—locale ... FL-3
Chase Rsvr—reservoir ... AR-4
Chase Rsvr—reservoir ... CT-1
Chase Rsvr—reservoir ... OR-9
Chaserville—locale ... GA-3
Chase's, Oliver, Thread Mill—hist pl ... MA-1
Chases Brook ... MN-6
Chases Brook ... NH-1
Chases Brook—stream ... WI-6
Chase Sch—school ... CA-9
Chase Sch—school ... CT-1
Chase Sch—school (3) ... IL-6
Chase Sch—school (2) ... MD-2
Chase Sch—school ... MI-6
Chase Sch—school ... NE-7
Chase Sch—school ... NY-2
Chase Sch—school ... ND-7
Chase Sch—school ... OH-6
Chase Sch—school (2) ... SD-7
Chase Sch (historical)—school ... MS-4
Chase School ... IN-6
Chases Cove—bay ... VA-3
Chases Garden River ... MA-1
Chases Grove—pop pl ... NH-1
Chase-Silica Oil Field—oilfield ... KS-7
Chases Island—island ... NH-1
Chases Mill—locale ... NH-1
Chase's Mill—pop pl ... ME-1
Chases Mtn—summit ... VT-1
Chases Point—cape ... MI-6
Chases Point—cape ... WI-6
Chases Pond—pop pl ... ME-1
Chases Pond—reservoir ... ME-1
Chase Spring—spring ... AZ-5
Chase Spring—spring ... CO-8
Chase Spring—spring ... NV-8
Chase Spring—spring ... OR-9
Chase Springs—spring ... UT-8
Chase State Fishing Lake And Wildlife Area—park ... KS-7
Chase Station—locale ... MD-2
Chase's Theater and Riggs Bldg—hist pl ... DC-2
Chase Store (historical)—locale ... AL-4
Chase Stream—stream (3) ... ME-1
Chase Stream Mtn—summit ... ME-1
Chase Stream Pond—lake (2) ... ME-1
Chase Stream (Township of)—unorg ... ME-1
Chase Street Sch—school ... CA-9
Chase Street Sch—school ... GA-3
Chasetown—pop pl ... OH-6
Chase (Town of)—pop pl ... WI-6
Chase (Township of)—pop pl ... MI-6
Chase Tripp Hollow—valley ... TN-4
Chase Tunnel—mine ... NV-8
Chase Upper Lake—lake ... NY-2
Chase Village—pop pl ... NH-1
Chaseville—locale ... OH-6
Chaseville—locale ... TN-4
Chaseville—pop pl ... MA-1
Chaseville—pop pl ... NY-2
Chaseville Post Office (historical)—building ... TN-4
Chaseville (subdivision)—pop pl ... FL-3
Chase Vly—swamp ... NY-2
Chase Vly Creek—stream ... NY-2
Chasina Anchorage—bay ... AK-9
Chasina Island—island ... AK-9
Chasina Point—cape ... AK-9
Chaska—pop pl ... MN-6
Chaska—pop pl ... TN-4
Chaska Beach ... OH-6
Chaska Creek—stream ... MN-6
Chaska Lake—lake ... MN-6
Chaska Post Office (historical)—building ... TN-4
Chaska (Township of)—pop pl ... MN-6
Chaski Bay—bay ... OR-9
Chaslaffa Creek ... MS-4
Chasm Brook—stream ... ME-1
Chasm Creek—stream ... AZ-5
Chasm Creek—stream ... MT-8
Chasm Falls—falls ... CO-8
Chasm Falls—locale ... NY-2
Chasm Lake—lake ... CO-8
Chasm Lake—lake ... UT-8
Chasm Prong—stream ... NC-3
Chasm Tank—reservoir ... NM-5
Chas Murphy Ranch—locale ... CO-8
Chasm View—cliff (2) ... CO-8
Chason—locale ... FL-3
Chason Cem—cemetery ... GA-3
Chason Cem—cemetery ... MS-4
Chason Park—park ... GA-3
Chason Pond—lake ... FL-3
Chason Ponds—lake ... FL-3
Chasovine Cove—bay ... AK-9
Chassahowitzka—pop pl ... FL-3
Chassahowitzka Bay—bay ... FL-3
Chassahowitzka Natl Wildlife Ref—park ... FL-3
Chassahowitzka Natl Wildlife Refuge HQ—building ... FL-3
Chassahowitzka Point—cape ... FL-3
Chassahowitzka Reefs—bar ... FL-3
Chassahowitzka River—stream ... FL-3
Chassahowitzka Swamp—swamp ... FL-3
Chassant ... FM-9
Chassaquoit Point ... MA-1
Chassel Creek ... WY-8
Chassell—pop pl ... MI-6
Chassell Creek—stream ... WY-8
Chassell L—pop pl ... MI-6
Chassell (Township of)—pop pl ... MI-6
Chastain—locale ... GA-3
Chastain Branch—stream (2) ... GA-3
Chastain Cem—cemetery (2) ... AR-4
Chastain Cem—cemetery ... GA-3
Chastain Cem—cemetery ... IA-7
Chastain Cem—cemetery ... SC-3
Chastain Cem—cemetery (2) ... TN-4
Chastain Chapel—church ... AR-4
Chastain Creek—stream ... AL-4
Chastain Creek—stream ... GA-3
Chastain Memorial Park—park ... GA-3
Chastain Memorial Park Cem—cemetery ... GA-3
Chastain Ranch—locale ... WY-8
Chastains Lakes—reservoir ... GA-3
Chastain Spring—spring ... OR-9
Chastain Springs Branch—stream ... AR-4
Chastang ... AL-4
Chastang—pop pl ... AL-4
Chastang Bluff—cliff ... AL-4
Chastang Landing—locale ... AL-4
Chasteen Cem ... MS-4
Chasteen Creek—stream ... NC-3
Chasteene Cem—cemetery ... MS-4
Chasteen Meadow—flat ... OR-9
Chasteen Mtn—summit ... NC-3
Chasteen Park—park ... OK-5
Chasteen's Grove—hist pl ... CO-8
Chastian JHS—school ... MS-4
Chastine Cem—cemetery ... KY-4
Chastine Cove—flat ... AL-4
Chastine Creek—stream ... NC-3
Chasworth—pop pl ... IA-7
Chat—pop pl ... TX-5
Chataco Mine—mine ... MN-6
Chatahoochee County Jail—hist pl ... GA-3
Chatahospee Creek—stream ... AL-4
Chataignier—pop pl ... LA-4
Chataignier Ch—church ... LA-4
Chatakhospee Creek ... AL-4
Chatam Church ... MS-4
Chatanika—pop pl ... AK-9
Chatanika Gold Camp—hist pl ... AK-9
Chatanika River—stream ... AK-9
Chatanika Siphon—other ... AK-9
Chatard High School ... IN-6
Chatata ... TN-4
Chatata Acad (historical)—school ... TN-4
Chatata Creek—stream ... TN-4
Chatata Post Office ... TN-4
Chatata Valley—valley ... TN-4
Chatata Valley Sch (historical)—school ... TN-4
Chatata Valley Seminary (historical)—school ... TN-4
Chatauguay ... VT-1
Chatauqua Auditorium—hist pl ... IL-6
Chatauqua Island—island ... MD-2
Chatauqua Mine (historical)—mine ... ID-8
Chatauqua Park—park ... MN-6
Chatauque Lake ... NY-2
Chatawa—locale ... MS-4
Chatawa Creek—stream ... NE-7
Chatawa Mission—church ... MS-4
Chat Ch—church ... WI-6
Chatchee Creek ... AL-4
Chatchie Plantation House—hist pl ... LA-4
Chatcolet—pop pl ... ID-8
Chatcolet Creek ... ID-8
Chatcolet Lake—lake ... ID-8
Chat Cove—bay ... AK-9
Chat Creek—stream ... MO-7
Chateau Camp—locale ... WA-9
Chateau Ch—church ... MD-2
Chateau Charolais Lake—reservoir ... AL-4
Chateau Chevalier—hist pl ... CA-9
Chateau Creek—stream ... ID-8
Chateau Crillon Apartment House—hist pl ... PA-2
Chateau De Cypres, Bayou—gut ... LA-4
Chateau de Mores—hist pl ... ND-7
Chateau de Mores (historical site)—locale ... ND-7
Chateau Dodge Theatre—hist pl ... MN-6
Chateau Duck Club—other ... CA-9
Chateau Estates (subdivision)—pop pl ... AL-4
Chateaugay—locale ... NY-2
Chateaugay—pop pl ... NY-2
Chateaugay Chasm—valley ... NY-2
Chateaugay Narrows—channel ... NY-2
Chateaugay Park—park ... NY-2
Chateaugay River—stream ... NY-2
Chateaugay (Town of)—pop pl ... NY-2
Chateauguay—pop pl ... VT-1
Chateau Hill—summit ... NM-5
Chateau Lake—lake ... WY-8
Chateau Le Blanc (subdivision)—pop pl ... MS-4
Chateau-Park Condominium—pop pl ... UT-8
Chateau Park Subdivision—pop pl ... UT-8
Chateau Richelieu ... NH-1
Chateau Rock—pillar ... ID-8
Chateau-Sur-Mer—hist pl ... RI-1
Chateau Terrace—pop pl ... IL-6
Chateau Village Subdivision—pop pl ... UT-8
Chateau Woods—pop pl ... TX-5
Chateau Woods (subdivision)—pop pl ... NC-3
Chateen Creek—stream ... GA-3
Chateetee ... TN-4
Chateetee Creek ... TN-4
Chatelaine South ... IL-6
Chatelain Lake—lake ... AK-9
Chater Lake ... OK-5
Chatfield—locale ... OR-9
Chatfield—locale ... TX-5
Chatfield—pop pl ... AR-4
Chatfield—pop pl ... MN-6
Chatfield—pop pl ... OH-6
Chatfield and Bartholomew Ditch—canal ... CO-8
Chatfield Branch—stream ... NJ-2
Chatfield Canyon—valley ... NM-5
Chatfield Cem—cemetery ... MN-6
Chatfield Ch—church ... AR-4
Chatfield Corner—pop pl ... NY-2
Chatfield Creek—stream ... ID-8
Chatfield Estates—pop pl ... CO-8
Chatfield Golf Course—other ... CO-8
Chatfield Hollow Brook—stream ... CT-1
Chatfield Hollow State Park—park ... CT-1
Chatfield Junction—pop pl ... MN-6
Chatfield Lake—reservoir ... CO-8
Chatfield Park—park ... IA-7
Chatfield Peak—summit ... NM-5
Chatfield Pond—lake ... AZ-5
Chatfield Public Library—hist pl ... MN-6
Chatfield Reservoir ... CO-8
Chatfield Rsvr—reservoir ... CO-8
Chatfield Sch—school ... AR-4
Chatfields Pond—lake ... AL-4
Chatfields Pond Dam—dam ... AL-4
Chatfield Township—pop pl ... ND-7
Chatfield (Township of)—pop pl ... MN-6
Chatfield (Township of)—pop pl ... OH-6
Chatfield-Tupelo Community Center—locale ... TX-5
Chatgolet ... ID-8
Chatgolet Lake ... ID-8
Chatham ... IL-6
Chatham—locale ... FL-3
Chatham—locale ... KY-4
Chatham—locale ... NH-1
Chatham—pop pl ... AK-9
Chatham—pop pl ... DE-2
Chatham—pop pl ... IL-6
Chatham—pop pl ... LA-4
Chatham—pop pl ... MD-2
Chatham—pop pl ... MA-1
Chatham—pop pl ... MI-6
Chatham—pop pl ... MS-4
Chatham—pop pl ... NJ-2
Chatham—pop pl ... NY-2
Chatham—pop pl (2) ... OH-6
Chatham—pop pl ... PA-2
Chatham—pop pl ... VA-3
Chatham—pop pl ... WY-8
Chatham Aero Light—locale ... MA-1
Chatham-Arch Hist Dist—hist pl ... IN-6
Chatham Bar—bar ... MA-1
Chatham Bay ... FL-3
Chatham Bend—bend ... FL-3
Chatham Branch—stream ... AL-4
Chatham Bridge—bridge ... NJ-2
Chatham Cem—cemetery ... MS-4
Chatham Cem—cemetery ... MO-7
Chatham (census name for Chatham Center)—CDP ... MA-1
Chatham Center—pop pl ... NY-2
Chatham Centeral HS—school ... NC-3
Chatham Center (census name Chatham)—other ... MA-1
Chatham Ch—church (2) ... NC-3
Chatham Ch—church ... VA-3
Chatham Circle (subdivision)—pop pl ... NC-3
Chatham City—pop pl ... GA-3
Chatham Coll—school ... PA-2
Chatham Corners—locale ... MI-6
Chatham (County)—pop pl ... GA-3
Chatham County—pop pl ... NC-3
Chatham County Courthouse—hist pl ... NC-3
Chatham County JHS—school ... GA-3
Chatham Creek—stream ... AK-9
Chatham Hall Sch—school ... VA-3
Chatham Harbor—harbor ... MA-1
Chatham Heights—pop pl ... VA-3
Chatham Hill—pop pl ... VA-3
Chatham Hill—pop pl ... WV-2
Chatham Hill Cem—cemetery ... VA-3
Chatham Hill (Jamison Mine No.8)—pop pl ... WV-2
Chatham Hill Memorial Gardens—cemetery ... SC-3
Chatham HS—school ... MA-1
Chatham HS—school ... VA-3
Chatham Inner Harbor—harbor ... MA-1
Chatham Island—island ... AK-9
Chatham Island—island ... OR-9
Chatham Islands ... MP-9
Chatham Lake—reservoir ... LA-4
Chatham Light—locale ... MA-1
Chatham Lighthouse—locale ... MA-1
Chatham Light Station—hist pl ... MA-1
Chatham (Magisterial District)—fmr MCD ... VA-3
Chatham Memorial Park—cemetery ... NC-3
Chatham MS—school ... NC-3
Chatham Park—park ... MI-6
Chatham Park—pop pl ... PA-2
Chatham Park Elem Sch—school ... PA-2
Chatham Park Sch ... PA-2
Chatham Pond Dam—dam ... MS-4
Chathamport ... MA-1
Chatham Port—pop pl ... MA-1
Chatham River—stream ... FL-3
Chatham Roads—harbor ... MA-1
Chatham RR Depot—hist pl ... MA-1
Chatham RR Museum—building ... MA-1
Chatham Run—pop pl ... PA-2
Chatham Run—stream ... PA-2
Chatham Sch—school ... CA-9
Chatham School ... PA-2
Chatham Siding—pop pl ... NC-3
Chatham Square (Shop Ctr)—locale ... NC-3
Chatham Station—locale ... NJ-2
Chatham Station (historical)—building ... MA-1
Chatham Strait—channel ... AK-9
Chatham Street Row—hist pl ... NY-2
Chatham (Town of)—civil ... MA-1
Chatham (Town of)—pop pl ... NH-1
Chatham (Town of)—pop pl ... NY-2
Chatham (Township of)—pop pl ... IL-6
Chatham (Township of)—pop pl ... MN-6
Chatham (Township of)—pop pl ... NJ-2
Chatham (Township of)—pop pl ... OH-6
Chatham (Township of)—pop pl ... PA-2
Chatham U.S. Life Saving Station (historical)—locale ... MA-1
Chatham Village ... MA-1
Chatham Village—pop pl ... PA-2
Chatham Villas—uninc pl ... GA-3
Chatham Windmill—hist pl ... MA-1
Chatham Yacht Club—locale ... MA-1
Chathenda Creek—stream ... AK-9
Chat High Bluff—cliff ... MS-4
Chathy Creek ... NC-3
Chatiemac Brook—stream ... NY-2
Chatiemac Lake—lake ... NY-2
Chatillon-DeMenil House—hist pl ... MO-7
Chat Island—island ... AK-9
Chat Junction—pop pl ... MO-7
Chatley Sch (historical)—school ... PA-2
Chatlin Lake—lake ... LA-4
Chatlin Lake Canal—canal ... LA-4
Chatlin Well—well ... AZ-5
Chatman Bayou—stream ... LA-4
Chatman Branch—stream ... GA-3
Chatman Branch—stream ... MS-4
Chatman Branch—stream ... VA-3
Chatman Cem—cemetery ... KY-4
Chatman Cem—cemetery (2) ... MO-7
Chatman Creek—stream ... AR-4
Chatman Creek—stream ... LA-4
Chatman Creek—stream ... MI-6
Chatman Hollow—valley ... AL-4
Chatman Hollow—valley ... MO-7
Chatman Hollow—valley ... TN-4
Chatman Lake—lake ... MI-6
Chatman Ridge—ridge ... AL-4
Chatman Sch—school ... MS-4
Chatman Town—pop pl ... LA-4
Chatmar—pop pl ... FL-3
Chatmoss—locale ... VA-3
Chatmoss Country Club—other ... VA-3
Chatnicka Creek—stream ... OR-9
Chato—locale ... NM-5
Chato Flat—flat ... NM-5
Chatoksofke Creek ... AL-4
Chatol—hist pl ... MO-7

**Chatom**—*pop pl* AL-4
Chatom (CCD)—*cens area* AL-4
Chatom Division—*civil* AL-4
Chatom Elem Sch—*school* AL-4
Chatom MS—*school* AL-4
Chatom Municipal Airp—*airport* AL-4
Chatom Union Sch—*school* CA-9
*Chatooga Ridge* NC-3
*Chatooga River* NC-3
Chato School (Abandoned)—*locale* NM-5
Chatritt Lake—*lake* AK-9
Chatsey Cem—*cemetery* NY-2
**Chatsworth**—*pop pl* CA-9
**Chatsworth**—*pop pl* GA-3
**Chatsworth**—*pop pl* IL-6
**Chatsworth**—*pop pl* IA-7
**Chatsworth**—*pop pl* NJ-2
Chatsworth Apartments—*hist pl* MI-6
Chatsworth Ave Sch—*school* NY-2
Chatsworth (CCD)—*cens area* GA-3
Chatsworth Cem—*cemetery* NJ-2
Chatsworth Creek—*stream* CA-9
Chatsworth Heights Cem—*cemetery* GA-3
Chatsworth High Line—*other* CA-9
Chatsworth Hi Line—*other* CA-9
Chatsworth Hi-Line Aqueduct—*canal* CA-9
Chatsworth HS—*school* CA-9
Chatsworth Lake—*reservoir* NJ-2
Chatsworth Lake Dam—*dam* NJ-2
**Chatsworth Lake Manor**—*pop pl* (2) CA-9
Chatsworth Peak—*summit* CA-9
Chatsworth Rsvr—*reservoir* CA-9
**Chatsworth (Township of)**—*pop pl* IL-6
Chatsworth Woods—*woods* NJ-2
Chattahoocee Natl For—*forest* GA-3
**Chattahoochee**—*pop pl* FL-3
**Chattahoochee**—*pop pl* GA-3
Chattahoochee Bay—*bay* GA-3
Chattahoochee (CCD)—*cens area* FL-3
Chattahoochee Ch—*church* (2) GA-3
Chattahoochee Country Club—*other* GA-3
Chattahoochee Country Club and Golf Course—*locale* AL-4
**Chattahoochee (County)**—*pop pl* GA-3
Chattahoochee Elem Sch—*school* FL-3
Chattahoochee Gap—*gap* GA-3
Chattahoochee Golf Club—*other* GA-3
Chattahoochee HS—*school* FL-3
Chattahoochee Lookout Tower—*locale* GA-3
Chattahoochee Natl For—*forest* (2) GA-3
**Chattahoochee Plantation**—*pop pl* GA-3
**Chattahoochee River**—*pop pl* FL-3
Chattahoochee River—*stream* AL-4
Chattahoochee River—*stream* FL-3
Chattahoochee River—*stream* GA-3
Chattahoochee River Natl Rec Area—*park* GA-3
Chattahoochee Sch—*school* GA-3
Chattahoochee State Park—*park* AL-4
Chattahoochee Trail—*trail* GA-3
*Chattahospee Creek* AL-4
Chattanooga—*locale* CO-8
**Chattanooga**—*pop pl* OH-6
**Chattanooga**—*pop pl* OK-5
**Chattanooga**—*pop pl* TN-4
Chattanooga, Harrison, Georgetown & Charleston RR Tunnel—*hist pl* TN-4
*Chattanooga Arts and Sciences Sch* TN-4
Chattanooga Bank Bldg—*hist pl* TN-4
Chattanooga Car Barns—*hist pl* TN-4
Chattanooga (CCD)—*cens area* TN-4
Chattanooga Cem—*cemetery* OK-5
Chattanooga Creek—*stream* GA-3
Chattanooga Creek—*stream* TN-4
Chattanooga Division—*civil* TN-4
Chattanooga Electric Railway—*hist pl* TN-4
Chattanooga Golf and Country Club—*locale* TN-4
Chattanooga-Hamilton County Convention and Trade Center—*building* TN-4
Chattanooga-Hamilton County Public Library—*building* TN-4
Chattanooga Hill—*summit* TX-5
Chattanooga Hot Spring—*spring* ID-8
Chattanooga HS—*school* TN-4
*Chattanooga Island* TN-4
Chattanooga Memorial Park Cem—*cemetery* TN-4
Chattanooga Mtn—*summit* OR-9
Chattanooga Municipal Bldg—*building* TN-4
Chattanooga Regional History Museum—*building* TN-4
Chattanooga Rod and Gun Club (historical)—*locale* TN-4
Chattanooga Shoals—*bar* TN-4
Chattanooga State Area Vocational Technical Sch—*school* TN-4
Chattanooga State Technical Community Coll—*school* TN-4
Chattanooga Valley—*valley* GA-3
Chattanooga Valley (CCD)—*cens area* GA-3
Chattanooga Valley Ch—*church* GA-3
Chattanooga Valley HS—*school* GA-3
Chattanooga Valley Sch—*school* GA-3
Chattanooga Yacht Club—*locale* TN-4
**Chattaroy**—*pop pl* WA-9
**Chattaroy**—*pop pl* WV-2
Chattaroy Cem—*cemetery* WA-9
Chattasofka Creek—*stream* AL-4
**Chattasofkee**—*pop pl* AL-4
**Chattel Estates**—*pop pl* UT-8
**Chattel Estates Subdivision Number Four**—*pop pl* UT-8
**Chattel Number 5 Subdivision**—*pop pl* UT-8
Chattels Station Ch—*church* VA-3
Chatten- Muncy Ranch—*locale* NM-5
Chatten Spring Sch (historical)—*school* TN-4
*Chatter Creek* OR-9
Chatter Creek—*stream* WA-9
Chatter Creek Campground—*locale* WA-9
Chatter Creek Guard Station—*hist pl* WA-9
Chatterdown Creek—*stream* CA-9
Chatterly Ranch—*locale* AZ-5
Chatterton—*locale* GA-3
**Chatterton**—*pop pl* IN-6
Chatterton Ch—*church* GA-3
Chatterton Point—*cape* CT-1
Chatterton Pond—*lake* NH-1
Chatterton Spring—*spring* (2) ID-8
Chattfield Mtn—*summit* NM-5
Chattfield Mtn—*summit* TX-5
Chattin Cem—*cemetery* IN-6
Chattin Flats—*flat* ID-8
Chattin Hill—*summit* ID-8
*Chattin Spring Sch* TN-4
Chattis Branch—*stream* MS-4
Chatto Crossing—*locale* OK-5
Chatto Flats—*flat* OK-5
*Chat-toho-chee River* GA-3
*Chat-toho-che River* AL-4
*Chat-toho-che River* FL-3
Chatto Island—*island* ME-1
**Chattolanee**—*pop pl* MD-2
Chatton—*locale* IL-6
Chatton Spring Branch—*stream* TN-4
*Chattooga* GA-3
Chattooga Acad—*hist pl* GA-3
Chattooga Ch—*church* GA-3
Chattooga Cliffs—*cliff* NC-3
**Chattooga (County)**—*pop pl* GA-3
Chattooga County Courthouse—*hist pl* GA-3
*Chattooga Creek* AL-4
*Chattooga Creek* GA-3
Chattooga Creek—*stream* GA-3
Chattooga Lake—*reservoir* SC-3
Chattooga Ridge—*ridge* NC-3
Chattooga Ridge—*ridge* SC-3
Chattooga River—*stream* AL-4
Chattooga River—*stream* (2) GA-3
Chattooga River—*stream* NC-3
Chattooga River—*stream* SC-3
Chattooga Sch—*school* SC-3
*Chattoogata Mountain* GA-3
Chattoogaville—*locale* GA-3
Chatto Ridge—*ridge* OK-5
Chatto Tank—*reservoir* NM-5
Chatts Store (historical)—*locale* AL-4
*Chatuga Ridge* NC-3
*Chatuga River* NC-3
Chatuge Dam—*building* NC-3
Chatuge Dam—*dam* NC-3
Chatuge Lake—*reservoir* GA-3
Chatuge Lake—*reservoir* NC-3
*Chatuge Rsvr* GA-3
*Chatuge Rsvr* NC-3
Chatuge State Park—*park* GA-3
**Chatwood**—*pop pl* PA-2
*Chauakle* AL-4
*Chaubaqueduck* MA-1
Chaubunagungamaug, Lake—*reservoir* MA-1
*Chaubunagungamaug Pond* MA-1
*Chaubunghungamaug Lake* MA-1
*Chaucers Brook* MA-1
Chaudet Creek—*stream* KY-4
Chaudiere Casse—*locale* LA-4
Chaudoin Cem—*cemetery* KY-4
Chaudoin Cem—*cemetery* TN-4
Chaudoin Sch—*school* SD-7
**Chaudoin Township**—*pop pl* SD-7
Chaudoirs Dock County Park—*park* WI-6
Chaud Spring—*spring* OR-9
Chauekuktuli, Lake—*lake* AK-9
Chaufchivak, Mount—*summit* AK-9
Chaufty Cem—*cemetery* NY-2
Chauga Ch—*church* SC-3
*Chauga Creek* SC-3
Chauga Heights—*locale* SC-3
Chauga River—*stream* SC-3
Chaugham Lookout—*locale* CT-1
Chaughtanoonda Creek—*stream* NY-2
Chauik Mtn—*summit* AK-9
Chaumes Sch—*school* TX-5
Chaumiere des Prairies—*hist pl* KY-4
Chaumont—*locale* KY-4
**Chaumont**—*pop pl* NY-2
Chaumont Bay—*bay* NY-2
Chaumont Pond—*lake* NY-2
Chaumont River—*stream* NY-2
Chaumont Swamp—*swamp* NY-2
Chauncey—*locale* MI-6
Chauncey—*locale* NY-2
**Chauncey**—*pop pl* GA-3
**Chauncey**—*pop pl* IL-6
**Chauncey**—*pop pl* OH-6
**Chauncey**—*pop pl* PA-2
**Chauncey**—*pop pl* WV-2
Chauncey, Mount—*summit* CO-8
Chauncey Brook—*stream* MA-1
Chauncey (CCD)—*cens area* GA-3
Chauncey Cem—*cemetery* (2) GA-3
Chauncey Creek—*stream* ME-1
*Chauncey Lake* MA-1
Chauncey Peak—*summit* CT-1
*Chauncey Pond* MA-1
Chauncey Run—*stream* NY-2
Chauncey Run—*stream* PA-2
*Chauncy* MI-6
Chauncy Hayden Gulch—*valley* CO-8
Chauncy Lake—*lake* MA-1
*Chauncys Island* WA-9
Chauncy Sparks Termina—*locale* AL-4
Chauncy Sparks Trade Sch—*school* AL-4
Chaunte Canyon—*valley* NM-5
Chausse—*locale* ID-8
*Chautaugua* OH-6
Chautaugua Natl Wildlife Ref—*park* IL-6
*Chautauqua* CO-8
Chautauqua—*locale* WA-9
**Chautauqua**—*pop pl* IL-6
**Chautauqua**—*pop pl* IA-7
**Chautauqua**—*pop pl* KS-7
**Chautauqua**—*pop pl* NY-2
**Chautauqua**—*pop pl* OH-6
**Chautauqua**—*pop pl* SD-7
**Chautauqua**—*pop pl* TX-5
Chautauqua, Lake—*lake* (2) FL-3
Chautauqua, Lake—*lake* IL-6
Chautauqua, Lake—*reservoir* MS-4
Chautauqua, Point—*cape* NY-2
Chautauqua Auditorium—*hist pl* CO-8
**Chautauqua (Chautauqua Institution)**—*pop pl* NY-2
Chautauqua County—*civil* KS-7
**Chautauqua (County)**—*pop pl* NY-2
Chautauqua Creek—*stream* LA-4
Chautauqua Creek—*stream* NY-2
Chautauqua Grounds—*park* IA-7
Chautauqua Hall of Brotherhood—*hist pl* FL-3
Chautauqua Hills—*range* KS-7
Chautauqua Institution—*other* NY-2
Chautauqua Institution Hist Dist—*hist pl* NY-2
*Chautauqua Lake* PA-2
Chautauqua Lake—*lake* MN-6
Chautauqua Lake—*lake* NY-2
Chautauqua Lake—*reservoir* IL-6
Chautauqua Lake—*reservoir* MS-4
Chautauqua Lake—*reservoir* OR-9
Chautauqua Mtn—*summit* CO-8
Chautauqua Natl Migratory Waterfowl Ref—*park* IL-6
Chautauqua Park—*hist pl* IA-7
Chautauqua Park—*locale* PA-2
Chautauqua Park—*locale* SD-7
Chautauqua Park—*park* CO-8
Chautauqua Park—*park* IL-6
Chautauqua Park—*park* IA-7
Chautauqua Park—*park* KS-7
Chautauqua Park—*park* KY-4
Chautauqua Park—*park* NE-7
**Chautauqua Park**—*pop pl* (2) IL-6
Chautauqua Pavilion—*hist pl* IA-7
Chautauqua Pavilion—*hist pl* NE-7
*Chautauqua Springs* KS-7
Chautauqua Tower—*hist pl* MD-2
**Chautauqua (Town of)**—*pop pl* NY-2
*Chautauque Lake* NY-2
Chauvenet, Mount—*summit* WY-8
**Chauvin**—*pop pl* LA-4
Chauvin, Bayou—*stream* LA-4
Chauvin Bayou—*stream* LA-4
Chauvin Sch—*school* LA-4
Chauvin Swamp—*swamp* LA-4
Chaval, Mount—*summit* WA-9
Chavale HS—*school* AL-4
Chaval Lake—*lake* WA-9
Cha-Vel, Lake—*reservoir* OH-6
Chaveroo Oil Field—*other* NM-5
Chaver Pond—*lake* SC-3
Chavers Cem—*cemetery* FL-3
Chavers Creek—*stream* AL-4
Chaves, Felipe, House—*hist pl* NM-5
*Chaves Box* NM-5
Chaves Canyon—*valley* NM-5
**Chaves (County)**—*pop pl* NM-5
*Chaves Creek* NM-5
Chaves Draw—*valley* NM-5
Chaves (historical)—*locale* AZ-5
Chaves Interchange—*crossing* AZ-5
Chaves Mtn—*summit* NM-5
Chaves Place—*locale* (2) NM-5
Chavez, Juan, House—*hist pl* NM-5
Chavez, Juan de Dios, House—*hist pl* NM-5
Chavez, Rumaldo, House—*hist pl* NM-5
Chavez Arroyo—*stream* CO-8
Chavez Box—*valley* NM-5
Chavez Canyon—*valley* (9) NM-5
Chavez Cem—*cemetery* CO-8
Chavez Cem—*cemetery* TX-5
Chavez Cem—*cemetery* WY-8
Chavez City Ruins—*locale* TX-5
Chavez City Ruins (410L253)—*hist pl* TX-5
Chavez Creek—*stream* CO-8
Chavez Creek—*stream* (3) NM-5
Chavez Crossing Campground—*park* AZ-5
Chavez Draw—*valley* AZ-5
Chavez Draw—*valley* (3) NM-5
Chavez Draw Tank—*reservoir* AZ-5
Chavez Mesa—*summit* NM-5
Chavez Mtn—*summit* AZ-5
Chavez Mtn—*summit* NM-5
Chavez Pass—*gap* AZ-5
Chavez Pass Ditch—*canal* AZ-5
Chavez Ranch—*locale* AZ-5
Chavez Ranch—*locale* (7) NM-5
Chavez Ravine—*valley* CA-9
Chavez Red Tank—*reservoir* NM-5
Chavez Ruins—*locale* NM-5
Chavez Spring—*spring* (2) AZ-5
Chavez Spring—*spring* NM-5
Chavez Suburbs East and West (410L254)—*hist pl* TX-5
Chavez Tank—*reservoir* (2) AZ-5
Chavez Tank—*reservoir* (3) NM-5
Chavez Tanks—*reservoir* NM-5
Chavez Well—*well* AZ-5
Chavez Well—*well* (3) NM-5
Chavez Windmill—*locale* NM-5
**Chavies**—*pop pl* AL-4
**Chavies**—*pop pl* KY-4
Chavies Ch—*church* AL-4
Chavies Gap—*gap* AL-4
Chavies Sch—*school* KY-4
Chavis Creek—*stream* TN-4
Chavis Park—*park* NC-3
Chavis Sch (historical)—*school* TN-4
**Chavistown**—*pop pl* SC-3
Chavolda Creek—*stream* AK-9
Chavous Cem—*cemetery* GA-3
Chavous Creek—*stream* SC-3
Chavoya Canyon—*valley* CA-9
**Chawanakee**—*pop pl* CA-9
Chawanakee Flats—*flat* CA-9
Chawanakee Sch Number One—*school* CA-9
Chawanakee Sch Number Two—*school* CA-9
*Chawappa Creek* MS-4
Chawaukee, Lake—*lake* OH-6
Chawee, Bayou—*gut* LA-4
Chawee Bay—*bay* LA-4
Chawekat Mtn—*summit* AK-9
Chaweva, Lake—*reservoir* WV-2
Chazal Park—*park* FL-3
**Chazy**—*pop pl* NY-2
*Chazy Bay* NY-2
Chazy Lake—*lake* NY-2
**Chazy Lake**—*pop pl* NY-2
**Chazy Landing**—*pop pl* NY-2
*Chazy River* NY-2
**Chazy (Town of)**—*pop pl* NY-2
CH Begaye Well—*locale* NM-5
C H Block Catfish Ponds Dam—*dam* MS-4
C H Bryars Junior Dam Number 1—*dam* AL-4
C H Bryars Junior Dam Number 2—*dam* AL-4
C H Bryars Junior Dam Number 3—*dam* AL-4
CHC Hill—*summit* CO-8
C. H. Cook Memorial Church—*hist pl* AZ-5
Cheadle Cem—*cemetery* OK-5
Cheadle Falls—*falls* OK-5
Cheadle Lake—*lake* OR-9
Cheadle Sch—*school* MT-8
**Cheaha Acres (subdivision)**—*pop pl* AL-4
Cheaha Creek—*stream* AL-4
*Cheaha Creek Foundry* AL-4
Cheaha Creek Watershed Dam Number 2—*dam* AL-4
Cheaha Creek Watershed Dam Number 3—*dam* AL-4
*Cheaha Creek Watershed Dam Number 4* AL-4
*Cheaha Creek Watershed Dam Number 5* AL-4
*Cheaha Creek Watershed Dam Number 6* AL-4
*Cheaha Lake* AL-4
Cheaha Lake—*reservoir* AL-4
Cheaha Mtn—*summit* AL-4
*Cheaha Number 5Dam* AL-4
Cheaha Number 5 Dam—*dam* AL-4
*Cheaha Number 6 Lake* AL-4
Cheaha State Park—*park* AL-4
*Chea-haw-haw Church* AL-4
Cheairs, Martin, House—*hist pl* TN-4
Cheairs Cem—*cemetery* (2) TN-4
Cheairs Park—*park* CO-8
Cheama Canyon—*valley* NM-5
**Cheap Hill**—*pop pl* TN-4
*Cheaphill Post Office* TN-4
Cheap Hill Post Office (historical)—*building* TN-4
Cheap Hill Sch (historical)—*school* TN-4
Cheap John Lake—*reservoir* NM-5
*Cheapside* NJ-2
**Cheapside**—*pop pl* MA-1
**Cheapside**—*pop pl* TX-5
**Cheapside**—*pop pl* VA-3
Cheatam Creek—*stream* GA-3
Cheatam Hollow—*valley* KY-4
Cheatam Hollow—*valley* TN-4
Cheatam Lake—*lake* AR-4
Cheatbeck Basin—*basin* ID-8
Cheatbeck Canyon—*valley* ID-8
Cheat Bridge—*locale* WV-2
Cheat Creek—*stream* OR-9
Cheatem Holler Camp—*locale* OR-9
Cheatgrass Rsvr—*reservoir* ID-8
Cheatgrass Rsvr—*reservoir* OR-9
Cheat Grass Spring—*spring* NV-8
*Cheatham* AL-4
Cheatham—*locale* AR-4
Cheatham, Lake—*lake* AR-4
Cheatham Bend—*bend* TN-4
Cheatham Bldg—*hist pl* TN-4
Cheatham Branch—*stream* AL-4
Cheatham Branch—*stream* TN-4
Cheatham Cem—*cemetery* (2) AL-4
Cheatham Cem—*cemetery* AR-4
Cheatham Cem—*cemetery* IL-6
Cheatham Cem—*cemetery* MO-7
Cheatham Cem—*cemetery* (2) TN-4
Cheatham Cem—*cemetery* TX-5
Cheatham Cem—*cemetery* VA-3
Cheatham Children Cem—*cemetery* MS-4
**Cheatham County**—*pop pl* TN-4
Cheatham County Courthouse—*building* TN-4
Cheatham County Courthouse—*hist pl* TN-4
*Cheatham County HS* TN-4
Cheatham County Poor House (historical)—*building* TN-4
Cheatham Creek—*stream* AL-4
Cheatham Creek—*stream* AR-4
Cheatham Dam—*dam* (2) TN-4
Cheatham Damsite Access Area—*park* TN-4
Cheatham Damsite Tailwater Access Point—*park* TN-4
Cheatham Hill—*summit* GA-3
Cheatham Hill Community Club—*locale* GA-3
**Cheatham (historical)**—*pop pl* TN-4
Cheatham Knob—*summit* AL-4
Cheatham Lake—*reservoir* (2) TN-4
Cheatham Park—*park* LA-4
Cheatham Park Elem Sch—*school* TN-4
*Cheatham P.O.* AL-4
Cheatham Pond—*reservoir* VA-3
Cheatham Sch—*school* TX-5
Cheatham Sch (historical)—*school* AL-4
Cheatham Sch (historical)—*school* TN-4
Cheathams Ferry (historical)—*locale* AL-4
Cheatham Spring—*spring* (2) TN-4
*Cheathams Station* TN-4
Cheatham State Wildlife Mngmt Area—*park* TN-4
*Cheathamsville* NC-3
Cheat Haven—*other* PA-2
Cheat Junction—*locale* WV-2
Cheat Lake—*reservoir* WV-2
Cheat Lake JHS—*school* WV-2
Cheat Mountain—*ridge* WV-2
**Cheat Neck**—*pop pl* (2) WV-2
Cheat River—*stream* PA-2
Cheat River—*stream* WV-2
Cheat View—*summit* WV-2
Cheatwood Branch—*stream* NC-3
Cheatwood Millpond—*reservoir* VA-3
Cheaver Creek—*stream* WY-8
*Che-aw-ha Mountain* AL-4
*Chebacco* MA-1
Chebacco Lake—*lake* MA-1
*Chebacco Parish* MA-1
*Chebacco Pond* MA-1
Chebanika Creek—*stream* AK-9
**Chebanse**—*pop pl* IL-6
**Chebanse (Township of)**—*pop pl* IL-6
*Chebatowesett Island* RI-1
*Chebaulip* WA-9
*Chebeag* ME-1
*Chebeag Island* ME-1
*Chebeag Point* ME-1
**Chebeague Island**—*pop pl* ME-1
Chebeague Point—*cape* ME-1
*Chebeagu Island* ME-1
Chebomnicon Bay—*bay* WI-6
*Cheboygan* MI-6
**Cheboygan**—*pop pl* MI-6
**Cheboygan (County)**—*pop pl* MI-6
Cheboygan County Courthouse—*hist pl* MI-6
Cheboyganing Creek—*stream* MI-6
*Cheboygan Lake* MI-6
*Cheboygan Point* MI-6
Cheboygan Point—*cape* MI-6
*Cheboygan River* MI-6
Cheboygan River—*stream* MI-6
*Checagon* MI-6
Checats Cove—*bay* AK-9
Checats Creek—*stream* AK-9
Checats Point—*cape* AK-9
*Checayon* MI-6
Che-che-pin-qua Woods—*woods* IL-6
Chechero Ch—*church* GA-3
*Chechero Creek* GA-3
Chechero Creek—*stream* GA-3
Chechessee Bluff—*cliff* SC-3
Chechessee Creek—*stream* SC-3
Chechessee Point—*cape* SC-3
Chechessee River—*stream* SC-3
*Chechil Canyon* UT-8
*Chechol* PW-9
Check—*locale* VA-3
**Check**—*pop pl* TX-5
Check Cave—*cave* AL-4
Check Drain—*canal* MI-6
**Checkerberry**—*pop pl* VT-1
Checkerberry Ledge—*bench* VT-1
**Checkerberry Village**—*pop pl* VT-1
**Checkerboard**—*pop pl* MT-8
Checkerboard Creek—*stream* MT-8
Checkerboard Creek—*stream* OK-5
Checkerboard Gulch—*valley* MT-8
*Checkerboard Inn* MT-8
Checkerboard Mesa—*summit* UT-8
Checkerboard Ranger Station—*locale* MT-8
Checkered House—*locale* NY-2
Checkered House Landing (historical)—*locale* TN-4
Checkered Sch—*school* MI-6
Checkerman Creek—*stream* AK-9
**Checkero**—*pop pl* GA-3
Checker Point—*cape* MI-6
Checkers Creek—*stream* AK-9
Checker Tank—*reservoir* AZ-5
Checkerville—*locale* PA-2
*Checkley River* MA-1
Checkly Point—*cape* ME-1
Checkmaker Mine—*mine* CO-8
Checkpoint Pass—*gap* NV-8
Checkrow—*locale* IL-6
**Check Row**—*pop pl* IL-6
Checops Mine—*mine* WA-9
Checo Sch—*school* KS-7
**Checotah**—*pop pl* OK-5
Checotah Business District—*hist pl* OK-5
Checotah (CCD)—*cens area* OK-5
Chedah Dam—*dam* NC-3
Chedatna Lakes—*area* AK-9
**Cheddar**—*pop pl* SC-3
Chedic Canyon—*valley* NV-8
*Chediski Butte* AZ-5
Chediski Farms—*locale* AZ-5
*Chediski Mtn* AZ-5
Chediski Mtn—*summit* AZ-5
Chediski Peak—*summit* AZ-5
Chediski Ridge—*ridge* AZ-5
Chediski Tank—*reservoir* AZ-5
Chedister Cem—*cemetery* IA-7
Chedotlothna Glacier—*glacier* AK-9
Chedsey Creek—*stream* CO-8
Chedsey Ditch No 2—*canal* CO-8
Chedwel—*locale* NY-2
*Cheeawo Ola* AL-4
Cheechako Gulch—*valley* AK-9
Cheechee Bay—*bay* LA-4
Cheechee Creek—*stream* LA-4
Cheechilgeetho—*other* NM-5
Cheeching Mtn—*summit* AK-9
Cheeching (site)—*locale* AK-9
Chee Dodge Ranch—*locale* AZ-5
*Cheeds Creek* TN-4
*Cheehootee Creek* MS-4
Cheek—*locale* OK-5
**Cheek**—*pop pl* TX-5
Cheeka Creek—*stream* WA-9
Cheeka Peak—*summit* WA-9
Cheek Bend—*bend* (2) TN-4
Cheek Branch—*stream* NC-3
Cheek Bridge—*bridge* TN-4
*Cheek Cem* MS-4
Cheek Cem—*cemetery* AR-4
Cheek Cem—*cemetery* GA-3
Cheek Cem—*cemetery* NC-3
Cheek Cem—*cemetery* OK-5
Cheek Cem—*cemetery* SC-3
Cheek Cem—*cemetery* TN-4
Cheek Ch—*church* OK-5
Cheek Creek—*stream* MO-7
Cheek Creek—*stream* NC-3
Cheek Creek—*stream* OK-5
Cheek Creek (Township of)—*fmr MCD* NC-3
*Cheek Crossroads* TN-4
Cheek Dam—*dam* TN-4
*Cheekeleeke Creek* AL-4
Cheek Hill—*summit* WA-9
Cheek Hollow—*valley* MO-7
Cheek House—*hist pl* GA-3
Cheek Lake—*lake* AR-4
Cheek Lake—*lake* TN-4
Cheek Lake—*reservoir* NC-3
Cheek Lake—*reservoir* TN-4
Cheek Lake Dam—*dam* NC-3
Cheek Love Cem—*cemetery* OK-5
Cheek Memorial Ch—*church* GA-3
Cheek Mtn—*summit* NC-3
Cheek Reservation—*reserve* AL-4
Cheeks—*locale* NC-3
Cheek Sch (abandoned)—*school* MO-7
Cheeks Crossroads—*locale* TN-4
**Cheeks Cross Roads**—*pop pl* NC-3
Cheek Slough—*gut* IL-6
Cheeks Mill Creek—*stream* NC-3
Cheek Spring—*spring* VA-3
Cheeks Rocks—*cliff* WV-2
Cheeks Stand Cave—*cave* TN-4
Cheeks Stand (historical)—*locale* TN-4
Cheeks (Township of)—*fmr MCD* NC-3
*Cheeksville Post Office* TN-4
**Cheektowaga**—*pop pl* NY-2
Cheektowaga Central HS—*school* NY-2
**Cheektowaga Northwest**—*pop pl* NY-2
**Cheektowaga Southwest**—*pop pl* NY-2
**Cheektowaga (Town of)**—*pop pl* NY-2
**Cheektowasa (subdivision)**—*pop pl* NY-2
Chee Kung Tong Society Bldg—*hist pl* HI-9
Cheely, Bogue—*stream* MS-4
Cheely-Coleman House—*hist pl* GA-3
Cheen—*channel* FM-9
Cheeneetnuk River—*stream* AK-9
Cheeney Creek—*stream* IN-6
Cheeney Creek—*stream* OR-9
Cheeney Drain—*canal* MI-6
Cheenik Creek—*stream* AK-9
Cheenitch Creek—*stream* CA-9
*Cheeowhee* TN-4
Cheer Creek—*stream* ID-8
Cheer Creek—*stream* (2) MT-8
Cheeree Point—*cape* CT-1
Cheerful Ch Number 2—*church* AL-4
*Cheerful Church* AL-4
Cheerful Hope Ch—*church* NC-3
Cheerfull Hill Sch (abandoned)—*school* MO-7
Cheerful Sch (historical)—*school* AL-4
*Cheery Creek* CO-8
*Cheesboro Brook* MA-1
Cheesbro Brook—*stream* MA-1
Cheesbrough Ranch—*locale* WY-8
*Cheese and Bread Island* DE-2
Cheese and Raisins Hills—*range* UT-8
*Cheeseboro Brook* MA-1
Cheeseboro Canyon—*valley* CA-9
Cheeseboro Lake—*lake* IN-6
Cheesebox, The—*summit* UT-8
Cheesebox Canyon—*valley* UT-8
Cheesebrough Hill—*summit* MO-7
Cheesebrough Pond—*reservoir* PA-2
Cheese Brown Lake—*lake* MN-6
*Cheesecake Brook* MA-1
Cheese Cake Brook—*stream* MA-1
Cheesecake Cem—*cemetery* VA-3
Cheese Camp Creek—*stream* CA-9
Cheese Camp Ridge—*ridge* CA-9
Cheesecote Mtn—*summit* NY-2
Cheesecote Pond—*lake* NY-2
*Cheese Creek* NJ-2
Cheese Creek—*stream* AK-9
Cheese Creek—*stream* MO-7
Cheese Creek—*stream* NE-7
Cheese Creek—*stream* (2) VA-3
Cheese Factory Gulf—*valley* NY-2
Cheese Hill—*summit* NY-2
Cheese Hill Sch—*school* NY-2
Cheese Lake—*lake* MI-6
Cheese Lick—*stream* KY-4
Cheeseman Cem—*cemetery* MO-7
*Cheeseman Creek* VA-3
Cheeseman Island—*island* VA-3
*Cheeseman Lake* CO-8
Cheeseman Run—*stream* PA-2
*Cheesemans Creek* VA-3
Cheesemans Inlet—*gut* NC-3
Cheese Pass—*gap* WY-8
**Cheesequake**—*pop pl* NJ-2
Cheesequake Creek—*stream* NJ-2
**Cheesequake (P.O.)**—*pop pl* NJ-2
Cheesequake State Park—*park* NJ-2
Cheese Ranch—*locale* CO-8
Cheese Run—*stream* PA-2
Cheese Spring—*spring* AZ-5
**Cheesetown**—*pop pl* PA-2
Cheese-vat Factory—*hist pl* OH-6
*Cheeseville* WI-6
Cheeseville—*locale* CA-9
Chees Hollow—*valley* NM-5
Cheesman, Morton A., House—*hist pl* UT-8
Cheesman Dam—*dam* CO-8
Cheesman Lake—*reservoir* CO-8
Cheesman Mtn—*summit* CO-8
Cheesman Park—*hist pl* CO-8
Cheesman Park—*park* CO-8
Cheesman Park Duplex—*hist pl* CO-8
Cheesman Park Esplanade—*hist pl* CO-8
Cheetdeekahyu, Mount—*summit* AK-9
Cheetham Cem—*cemetery* TX-5
Cheetwood Lake—*lake* TX-5
**Cheever**—*pop pl* NH-1
Cheever, George, Farm—*hist pl* NH-1
Cheever Airp—*airport* IN-6
Cheever Creek—*stream* CO-8
Cheever Creek—*stream* MT-8
Cheever (historical)—*locale* KS-7
Cheever Lake—*lake* IA-7
Cheever Lake State Game Mgt Area—*park* IA-7
Cheever Sch—*school* CT-1
Cheever Sch—*school* NY-2
**Cheever Township**—*pop pl* KS-7
Chee Ying Society—*hist pl* HI-9
Cheff Lake—*lake* MT-8
**Chef Menteur**—*pop pl* LA-4
Chef Menteur Pass—*channel* LA-4
*Chefoncto River* LA-4
**Chefornak**—*pop pl* AK-9
Chefs Pond—*reservoir* AZ-5
*Chefuncta River* LA-4
*chefuncte river* LA-4
*Chefuncto River* LA-4
*Chegbey* LA-4
**Chegby**—*pop pl* LA-4
**Chehalem**—*pop pl* OR-9
Chehalem Center Sch—*school* OR-9
Chehalem Creek—*stream* OR-9
Chehalem Mountain (CCD)—*cens area* OR-9
Chehalem Mountains—*summit* OR-9
Chehalem Sch—*school* OR-9
Chehalem Valley—*valley* OR-9
**Chehalis**—*pop pl* WA-9
Chehalis, Point—*cape* WA-9
Chehalis-centralia Airp—*airport* WA-9
**Chehalis Ind Res**—*pop pl* WA-9
**Chehalis Junction**—*pop pl* WA-9
Chehalis River—*stream* WA-9
Chehalis Substation—*other* WA-9
Chehaski Cem—*cemetery* MO-7
**Chehaw**—*pop pl* AL-4
**Chehaw**—*pop pl* GA-3
Chehaw Ch—*church* AL-4
*Chehawhaw Creek* AL-4
*Che-haw-haw Mountain* AL-4
*Chehaw Mountain* AL-4
Chehaw Park—*park* GA-3
Chehaw Post Office (historical)—*building* AL-4
Chehaw River—*stream* SC-3
Chehaw Sch (historical)—*school* AL-4
Chehaw State Park—*park* GA-3
Chehelem Airpark—*airport* OR-9
*Chehocton Creek* PA-2
*Chehocton Pond* PA-2

Chehulpum Creek—*stream* OR-9
Chekepa Creek—*stream* SD-7
Chekhechunnjik Creek—*stream* AK-9
Chekika, Lake—*lake* FL-3
Chekika Island—*island* FL-3
Chekok—*locale* AK-9
Chekok Bay—*bay* AK-9
Chekok Creek—*stream* AK-9
Chekok Lake—*lake* AK-9
Chekok Point—*cape* AK-9
**Chekola**—*pop pl* WA-9
**Chelab**—*pop pl* PW-9
*Chelafaula Creek* AL-4
*Chelakoom* WA-9
**Chelan**—*pop pl* WA-9
Chelan, Lake—*lake* WA-9
Chelan Bank—*bar* AK-9
Chelan Butte—*summit* WA-9
Chelan (CCD)—*cens area* WA-9
**Chelan County**—*pop pl* WA-9
Chelan Creek—*stream* MT-8
**Chelan Falls**—*pop pl* WA-9
Chelan Fraternal Cem—*cemetery* WA-9
Chelan Hill—*summit* WA-9
Chelan Mountains—*range* WA-9
Chelan Muni Airp—*airport* WA-9
*Chelan Natl Forest* WA-9
Chelan River—*stream* WA-9
Chelan State Fish Hatchery—*locale* WA-9
Chelan Station—*locale* WA-9
Chelas, Bkul A—*bar* PW-9
**Chelatchie**—*pop pl* WA-9
Chelatchie Creek—*stream* WA-9
Chelatchie Prairie—*flat* WA-9
Chelatna Lake—*lake* AK-9
Chelatna Lodge—*locale* AK-9
Chelbacheb—*island* PW-9
Chelbourne Plaza—*locale* PA-2
*Chelechui* PW-9
Cheleos—*summit* PW-9
Cheleu—*island* PW-9
Cheley Camp—*locale* CO-8
**Chelford**—*pop pl* AR-4
Chelford Sch—*school* AR-4
Chelf Ridge—*ridge* KY-4
Chelf Sch—*school* KY-4
Cheli Air Force Station—*military* CA-9
*Chellis* KS-7
Chellis Bay—*bay* NY-2
Chellis Brook—*stream* ME-1
Chelly, Canyon de—*valley* AZ-5
Chellybelle Creek—*stream* NC-3
*Chelly Canyon* AZ-5
Chelly Landing—*locale* LA-4
Chelmo Cem—*cemetery* WI-6
*Chelmsford* MA-1
**Chelmsford Center**—*pop pl* MA-1
Chelmsford Center Hist Dist—*hist pl* MA-1
*Chelmsford Centre* MA-1
Chelmsford (Chelmsford Center)—*CDP* MA-1
Chelmsford Glass Works' Long
House—*hist pl* MA-1
Chelmsford HS—*school* MA-1
Chelmsford Mall—*locale* MA-1
**Chelmsford (Town of)**—*pop pl* MA-1
*Chelonia Lake* WI-6
Chelonia Lake—*lake* WI-6
Chelsea—*hist pl* DE-2
Chelsea—*hist pl* VA-3
Chelsea—*locale* GA-3
Chelsea—*locale* KS-7
Chelsea—*locale* MD-2
Chelsea—*locale* MT-8
Chelsea—*locale* PA-2
**Chelsea**—*pop pl (2)* AL-4
**Chelsea**—*pop pl* IN-6
**Chelsea**—*pop pl* IA-7
**Chelsea**—*pop pl* ME-1
**Chelsea**—*pop pl* MA-1
**Chelsea**—*pop pl* MI-6
**Chelsea**—*pop pl (2)* NY-2
**Chelsea**—*pop pl* OK-5
**Chelsea**—*pop pl* OR-9
**Chelsea**—*pop pl* SD-7
**Chelsea**—*pop pl* VT-1
**Chelsea**—*pop pl* WI-6
Chelsea—*uninc pl* NJ-2
Chelsea, City of—*civil* MA-1
*Chelsea, Town of* MA-1
*Chelsea Beach* MA-1
**Chelsea Beach**—*pop pl* MD-2
Chelsea Bridge—*bridge* MA-1
Chelsea (CCD)—*cens area* AL-4
Chelsea (CCD)—*cens area* OK-5
Chelsea Cem—*cemetery* KS-7
Chelsea Cem—*cemetery* MA-1
Chelsea Cem—*cemetery* NE-7
Chelsea Cem—*cemetery* OK-5
Chelsea Ch—*church* AL-4
Chelsea Ch—*church* KS-7
Chelsea Ch—*church* MI-6
Chelsea City Hall—*building* MA-1
*Chelsea Cove* IL-6
**Chelsea Cove Subdivision**—*pop pl* UT-8
*Chelsea Creek* MA-1
Chelsea Creek—*stream* GA-3
Chelsea Creek—*stream* MT-8
Chelsea Division—*civil* AL-4
Chelsea Elem Sch—*school* KS-7
**Chelsea Estates**—*pop pl* DE-2
**Chelsea Estates (subdivision)**—*pop pl* DE-2
Chelsea Family Hotel—*hist pl* WA-9
Chelsea Game Preserve Lake—*lake* AL-4
Chelsea Game Preserve Lake Dam—*dam* AL-4
Chelsea Grammar Sch—*hist pl* NY-2
Chelsea Gulf—*valley* GA-3
**Chelsea Heights**—*pop pl* NJ-2
Chelsea Heights Sch—*school* MN-6
**Chelsea Hill**—*pop pl* VA-3
Chelsea Hist Dist—*hist pl* NY-2
Chelsea Hist Dist (Boundary
Increase)—*hist pl* NY-2
Chelsea HS—*school* MA-1
Chelsea Island—*island* MT-8
Chelsea Lake—*lake* WI-6
Chelsea Park—*park* AL-4
Chelsea Park—*park* MO-7
Chelsea Park—*park* NY-2
Chelsea Park—*park* WA-9
Chelsea Place Hist Dist—*hist pl* AZ-5
Chelsea Plantation—*locale* SC-3
Chelsea Point—*cape* MA-1
Chelsea Pond—*reservoir* VA-3
*Chelsea River* MA-1
Chelsea River—*bay* MA-1
Chelsea Rsvr—*reservoir* OK-5
Chelsea Sch—*school* AL-4
Chelsea Sch—*school* KS-7
Chelsea Shop Ctr—*locale* KS-7
Chelsea Slough—*gut* MT-8
Chelsea Square Hist Dist—*hist pl* MA-1
Chelsea Square (Shop Ctr)—*locale* FL-3
Chelsea State Game Area—*park* MI-6
Chelsea Station (historical)—*locale* MA-1
**Chelsea (Town of)**—*pop pl* ME-1
**Chelsea (Town of)**—*pop pl* VT-1
**Chelsea (Town of)**—*pop pl* WI-6
**Chelsea Township**—*pop pl* KS-7
**Chelsea Township**—*pop pl* NE-7
Chelsea Township—*stream* KS-7
Chelsea Village Hist Dist—*hist pl* VT-1
Chelsea West Hill—*school* VT-1
Chelsea Woods—*uninc pl* MD-2
Chelsey Brook—*stream* MN-6
Chelsey Brook—*stream* NH-1
Chelsey Creek—*stream* ID-8
**Chelsey Village**—*pop pl* TN-4
Chelstrom Lake—*lake* WI-6
Cheltenham HS—*school* PA-2
Chelten Ave—*uninc pl* PA-2
*Cheltenham* PA-2
Cheltenham—*locale* MD-2
Cheltenham—*locale* PA-2
**Cheltenham Forest**—*pop pl* MD-2
Cheltenham HS—*school* PA-2
Cheltenham Mall—*locale* PA-2
Cheltenham Sch—*school (2)* PA-2
Cheltenham Station—*building* PA-2
Cheltenham Township—*CDP* PA-2
**Cheltenham (Township of)**—*pop pl* PA-2
*Cheltenham Township Senior High School* PA-2
Cheltenham United Methodist Ch—*church* PA-2
**Cheltenham Village**—*pop pl* PA-2
Cheltenham Woods Recreation
Center—*park* MD-2
*Cheltenham (79th Street)* IL-6
**Chelten Hills**—*pop pl* PA-2
Chelten Hills Cem—*cemetery* PA-2
Chelton, Lake—*lake* FL-3
Chelton Ch—*church* PA-2
*Cheltonham Elementary School* PA-2
Chelunginik River—*stream* AK-9
**Chelwood Park**—*pop pl* NM-5
**Chelyan**—*pop pl* WV-2
**Chem**—*pop pl* CO-8
Chemard Lake—*swamp* LA-4
**Chemawa**—*pop pl* OR-9
Chemawa Cem—*cemetery* OR-9
**Chemawa (Chemawa Indian
School)**—*pop pl* OR-9
Chemawa Hill—*summit* WA-9
Chemawa JHS—*school* CA-9
Chemawa Substation—*locale* OR-9
**Chemcel**—*pop pl* TX-5
Chemehuevi Indian Cem—*cemetery* CA-9
Chemehuevi Ind Res—*reserve* CA-9
*Chemehuevi Mountains* AZ-5
Chemehuevi Mountains—*range* CA-9
Chemehuevi Peak—*summit* CA-9
Chemehuevi Point—*cliff* AZ-5
*Chemehuevis Mountains* AZ-5
*Chemehuevis Mountains* CA-9
*Cheme-Huevis Valley* AZ-5
*Chemehuevitz Mountains* CA-9
Chemehuevi Valley—*basin* AZ-5
Chemehuevi Valley—*basin* CA-9
Chemehuevi Wash—*stream* AZ-5
Chemehuevi Wash—*stream* CA-9
*Chemeketa* OR-9
*Chemeketa Hills* OR-9
Chemeketa Lodge No. 1 Odd Fellows
Buildings—*hist pl* OR-9
**Chemeketa Park**—*pop pl* CA-9
Chemeketa Park-Redwood Estates—*CDP* CA-9
*Chemew Creek* MS-4
*Chemey Hill* CT-1
**Chemical**—*pop pl* FL-3
**Chemical**—*pop pl* IL-6
**Chemical**—*pop pl* PA-2
**Chemical**—*pop pl* WV-2
Chemical Bldg—*hist pl* MO-7
Chemical City—*other* WV-2
Chemical Creek—*stream* WI-6
Chemical Laboratory—*hist pl* IL-6
Chemical Station—*locale* PA-2
Chemical Turning Basin—*harbor* TX-5
Chemin-A-Haut Bayou—*stream* AR-4
Chemin-A-Haut Bayou—*stream* LA-4
Chemin-A-Haut Creek—*stream* AR-4
Chemin-A-Haut State Park—*park* LA-4
*Chemisal* CA-9
Chemisal, The—*pillar* CA-9
*Chemisal Mountain* CA-9
Chemise, Bayou—*gut* MS-4
Chemise Creek—*stream* CA-9
*Chemise Mountain* CA-9
Chemise Ridge—*ridge* CA-9
*Chemise Wash* AZ-5
*Chemiss Mountain* CA-9
Chemistry Station (historical)—*locale* MA-1
*Chemo* ME-1
Chemo Bog—*swamp* ME-1
*Chemoi* PW-9
Chemol—*island* PW-9
*Chemolite* MN-6
Chemo Pond—*lake* ME-1
*Chemo-to* MP-9
Chemoweth Airpark—*airport* OR-9
Chempholt Wharf—*locale* VA-3
*Chemquasabamtic* ME-1
*Chemquasabamtic Lake* ME-1
Chemquasabamticook Lake—*lake* ME-1
Chemquasabamticook Lake (Ross
Lake)—*lake* ME-1
Chemquasabamticook Stream—*stream* ME-1
*Chemquassabamticook* ME-1
*Chemquassabamticook Lake* ME-1
Chemstrand Pier—*locale* FL-3
**Chemult**—*pop pl* OR-9
Chemung—*locale* PA-2
**Chemung**—*pop pl* CO-8
**Chemung**—*pop pl* IL-6
**Chemung**—*pop pl* NY-2
Chemung, Lake—*lake* MI-6
*Chemunganoc Hill* RI-1
*Chemunganock Pond* RI-1
*Chemunganset Pond* RI-1
Chemung Canal Bank Bldg—*hist pl* NY-2
*Chemung Center* NY-2
**Chemung Center**—*pop pl* NY-2
**Chemung (County)**—*pop pl* NY-2
Chemung County Airp—*airport* NY-2
Chemung County Courthouse
Complex—*hist pl* NY-2
Chemung-Dunham Cem—*cemetery* IL-6
Chemung Feeder Canal—*canal* NY-2
Chemung Hill Sch—*school* MA-1
Chemung Hills Country Club—*other* MI-6
**Chemung Junction**—*pop pl* NY-2
Chemung Mine—*mine* CA-9
Chemung River—*stream* NY-2
Chemung River—*stream* PA-2
**Chemung (Town of)**—*pop pl* NY-2
**Chemung (Township of)**—*pop pl* IL-6
Chemung Valley—*valley* PA-2
*Chemung Valley Airp* PA-2
Chemung Valley Airp—*airport* PA-2
Chemung Valley Landing Strip—*airport* PA-2
Chemurgic—*locale* CA-9
Chemway—*locale* NC-3
*Chen* FM-9
Chen—*bar* FM-9
Chenab Spring—*spring* UT-8
Chena Dome—*summit* AK-9
**Chena Hot Springs**—*pop pl* AK-9
*Chenal* LA-4
**Chenal**—*pop pl* LA-4
Chenal, The—*stream* LA-4
Chenal A Bout Rond—*channel* MI-6
Chenal Cem—*cemetery* LA-4
**Chenal Crossing**—*pop pl* LA-4
*Chenal du Diable* TN-4
Chenamus Lake—*lake* WA-9
*Chenango*—*locale* LA-4
Chenango—*locale* TX-5
**Chenango Bridge**—*pop pl* NY-2
Chenango Ch—*church* NY-2
**Chenango (County)**—*pop pl* NY-2
Chenango County Courthouse
District—*hist pl* NY-2
*Chenango Creek* NY-2
**Chenango Forks**—*pop pl* NY-2
Chenango Forks Central Sch—*school* NY-2
Chenango Hosp—*hospital* NY-2
*Chenango Lake* TX-5
Chenango Lake—*lake* MI-6
Chenango Lake—*lake (2)* NY-2
Chenango Lake—*lake* TX-5
**Chenango Lake**—*pop pl* NY-2
Chenango Mtn—*summit* AK-9
Chenango Oil Field—*oilfield* TX-5
Chenango Plantation—*locale* TX-5
Chenango Pond—*lake* TX-5
Chenango River—*stream* NY-2
Chenango Sch—*school* NY-2
Chenango State For—*forest* NY-2
**Chenango (Town of)**—*pop pl* NY-2
Chenango Valley Cem—*cemetery* NY-2
Chenango Valley Central Sch—*school* NY-2
Chenango Valley State Park—*park* NY-2
Chena Pump House—*hist pl* AK-9
Chena Ridge—*ridge* AK-9
Chena River—*stream* AK-9
Chena River Campground—*locale* AK-9
Chena River Rec Area—*park* AK-9
Chena River State Rec Area—*park* AK-9
Chena Sch—*school* AK-9
Chena Slough—*stream* AK-9
**Chenauer**—*pop pl* WA-9
*Chenault* KY-4
Chenault Bridge—*bridge* KY-4
Chenault House—*hist pl* KY-4
Chenault Island—*island* AR-4
Chenault Reach—*channel* AR-4
Chenault Spring—*spring* AL-4
Chenault Spring Branch—*stream* AL-4
**Chenaults Shop**—*pop pl* VA-3
Chenaultt—*locale* KY-4
Chenaultt Sch—*school* KY-4
Chenay Bay—*bay* VI-3
Chen-Bay State Wildlife Mngmt
Area—*park* MN-6
Chenchon, I—*basin* MH-9
Chene, Alexander, House—*hist pl* MI-6
Chene, Bayou—*gut (2)* LA-4
Chene, Bayou—*stream (4)* LA-4
Cheneathda Hill—*summit* AK-9
Chene Blanc, Bayou—*stream* LA-4
*Chene Blanc Bayou* LA-4
*Chene Brook* MA-1
Chenecas Tank—*reservoir* TX-5
Chene Cut, Bayou—*canal* LA-4
**Chenega**—*pop pl* AK-9
Chenega Cove—*bay* AK-9
Chenega Glacier—*glacier* AK-9
Chenega Island—*island* AK-9
Chenega Point—*cape* AK-9
Chene Highway—*channel* MI-6
**Chenequa**—*pop pl* WI-6
**Chenequa North**—*pop pl* WI-6
Chenery Brook—*stream* ME-1
Chenes, Point Aux—*cape* MS-4
Chenes, Pointe aux—*cape* MI-6
Chenes, River aux—*gut* LA-4
Chenevert, Bayou—*stream* LA-4
Cheneworth Gap—*gap* TN-4
Cheney—*locale* IA-7
Cheney—*locale* OR-9
**Cheney**—*pop pl* KS-7
**Cheney**—*pop pl* NE-7
**Cheney**—*pop pl* WA-9
Cheney, Andrew J., House—*hist pl* GA-3
Cheney Bldg—*hist pl* CT-1
Cheneyboro—*locale* TX-5
Cheney Branch—*stream* AL-4
Cheney Branch—*stream* MO-7
*Cheney Brook* MA-1
Cheney Brook—*stream* CT-1
Cheney Brook—*stream (2)* MA-1
Cheney Brook—*stream* NH-1
Cheney Brook—*stream* VT-1
Cheney Brothers Hist Dist—*hist pl* CT-1
Cheney Canyon—*valley* CO-8
Cheney Cem—*cemetery* GA-3
Cheney Cem—*cemetery* KS-7
Cheney Cem—*cemetery* MI-6
Cheney Cem—*cemetery* NE-7
Cheney Cem—*cemetery* PA-2
Cheney Cem—*cemetery (2)* TN-4
Cheney Cem—*cemetery* VT-1
Cheney Cobble—*summit* NY-2
Cheney Cow Camp—*locale* WY-8
*Cheney Creek* OR-9
Cheney Creek—*stream* CA-9
Cheney Creek—*stream (2)* CO-8
Cheney Creek—*stream* ID-8
Cheney Creek—*stream* LA-4
Cheney Creek—*stream (2)* MI-6
Cheney Creek—*stream* MT-8
Cheney Creek—*stream* ND-7
Cheney Creek—*stream* OR-9
Cheney Creek—*stream* UT-8
*Cheney Creek Church* AL-4
Cheney Dam—*dam* KS-7
Cheney Draw—*valley* AZ-5
Cheney Elem Sch—*school* FL-3
Cheney Flat—*flat* AZ-5
Cheney Gulch—*valley* CA-9
Cheney Gun Club—*other* WA-9
Cheneyhatchee Creek—*stream* AL-4
*Cheneyhatchee Creek Park* AL-4
Cheneyhatchee Creek Rec Area—*park* AL-4
*Cheney Hill* MA-1
Cheney Hill—*summit* CT-1
Cheney Hill—*summit* MA-1
Cheney Hill—*summit* NH-1
Cheney Hill—*summit* NY-2
Cheney Hills—*summit* MI-6
Cheney Hollow—*valley* MO-7
Cheney Interurban Depot—*hist pl* WA-9
Cheney Knob—*summit* WV-2
Cheney Lake—*lake* AZ-5
Cheney Lake—*lake* WI-6
Cheney Mtn—*summit* NY-2
Cheney Park—*park* MI-6
Cheney Point—*cape* NY-2
Cheney Point—*cape* VT-1
Cheney Pond—*lake* FL-3
Cheney Pond—*lake (4)* NY-2
Cheney Pond—*reservoir* ME-1
*Cheney Ranch* CA-9
Cheney Ranch—*locale* WA-9
Cheney Ranch—*woods* UT-8
Cheney Rsvr—*reservoir* CO-8
Cheney Rsvr—*reservoir* KS-7
Cheney Run—*stream* PA-2
*Cheneys* NE-7
Cheney Sch—*school* CA-9
Cheney Sch—*school* VA-3
Cheneys Creek—*stream* VA-3
Cheney's Grove (Township of)—*civ div* IL-6
Cheney Shoal—*bar* MI-6
Cheney Slough—*stream* OR-9
Cheney Slough Irrigation Canal—*canal* CA-9
Cheneys Lower Landing
(historical)—*locale* AL-4
Cheneys Point—*cape* CA-9
**Cheneys Point**—*pop pl* NY-2
Cheney Spring—*spring* UT-8
Cheney Spring Canyon—*valley* UT-8
Cheney Springs—*spring* UT-8
Cheney Stadium—*other* GA-3
Cheney Stadium—*other* WA-9
Cheney State Park—*park* KS-7
Cheney Substation—*other* CA-9
*Cheneys Upper Landing* AL-4
*Cheneysville* PA-2
**Cheneyville**—*pop pl* IL-6
**Cheneyville**—*pop pl* LA-4
Cheneyville Oil and Gas Field—*oilfield* LA-4
Cheney Wildlife Area—*park* KS-7
Chengwatana State For—*forest* MN-6
**Chengwatana (Township of)**—*pop pl* MN-6
*Chenier Au Tigre* LA-4
**Cheniere**—*pop pl* LA-4
Cheniere, Bayou La—*stream* LA-4
Cheniere, Lake—*lake* LA-4
Cheniere au Tigre—*locale* LA-4
Cheniere Brake—*swamp* LA-4
Cheniere Caminada—*flat* LA-4
Cheniere Ch—*church* LA-4
Cheniere Creek—*stream* LA-4
Cheniere du Fond—*island* LA-4
Cheniere Lake—*reservoir* LA-4
Cheniere Pass—*gut* LA-4
*Cheniere Perdue Ridge* LA-4
Cheniere Ronquille, Bayou—*gut* LA-4
*Cheniere Transverse Bayou* LA-4
Cheniere Traverse Bayou—*gut* LA-4
Chenier Perdue Ridge—*ridge* LA-4
Chenierre Canal—*canal* LA-4
Chenik—*locale* AK-9
Chenik Head—*cape* AK-9
Chenik Lake—*lake* AK-9
Chenik Mtn—*summit* AK-9
**Cheningo**—*pop pl* NY-2
Cheningo Creek—*stream* NY-2
Chenitur—*spring* FM-9
*Chenlini Wash* AZ-5
Chennault—*locale* GA-3
Chennault Ford—*locale* TN-4
Chennault House—*hist pl* GA-3
Chennault House—*hist pl* LA-4
*Chenneby* AL-4
Chenneth Branch—*stream* KY-4
Chenney Cem—*cemetery* OH-6
Chenoa—*locale* KY-4
**Chenoa**—*pop pl (2)* IL-6
Chenoa Cem—*cemetery* KY-4
Chenoa Ch—*church* KY-4
Chenoa Lake—*reservoir* KY-4
Chenoa Sch—*school* IL-6
**Chenoa (Township of)**—*pop pl* IL-6
Chenocetah Fire Tower—*hist pl* GA-3
Chenocetah Mtn—*summit* GA-3
Chenois Creek—*locale* WA-9
Chenois Creek—*stream* WA-9
Chenois Creek Channel—*channel* WA-9
*Chenokaby Creek - in part* MS-4
**Chenot Place**—*pop pl* IL-6
Chenowee—*locale* KY-4
Chenowee Tunnel—*tunnel* KY-4
**Chenoweth**—*pop pl* OH-6
**Chenoweth**—*pop pl* OR-9
Chenoweth, Frank L., House—*hist pl* WI-6
Chenoweth, Mount—*summit* ID-8
Chenoweth Cem—*cemetery* IL-6
Chenoweth Cem—*cemetery* IN-6
*Chenoweth Creek* WV-2
Chenoweth Creek—*stream* OR-9
Chenoweth Creek—*stream* WV-2
Chenoweth Ditch—*canal (2)* OH-6
Chenoweth Elem Sch—*school* OR-9
Chenoweth Flat—*flat* OR-9
Chenoweth Fork—*stream* OH-6
Chenoweth Fort-Springhouse—*hist pl* KY-4
Chenoweth House—*hist pl* KY-4
Chenoweth Knob—*summit* WV-2
Chenoweth Lateral—*canal* CO-8
*Chenoweth Middle School* OR-9
Chenoweth Park—*park* KY-4
Chenoweth Run—*stream (2)* KY-4
Chenoweth Run Cem—*cemetery* KY-4
Chenoweth Sch—*school* KY-4
Chenoweth Sch—*school* OR-9
**Chenowith**—*pop pl* WA-9
*Chenowith Creek* OR-9
Chenoworth Cem—*cemetery* KS-7
Chenube Creek—*stream* GA-3
Chenube Indian Village Monmt—*park* GA-3
Chenuis Creek—*stream* WA-9
Chenuis Falls—*falls* WA-9
Chenuis Lakes—*lake* WA-9
Chenuis Mtn—*summit* WA-9
Chenunda Creek—*stream* NY-2
**Cheny Ridge Estates
Subdivision**—*pop pl* UT-8
*Cheoah* NC-3
**Cheoah**—*pop pl* NC-3
Cheoah Bald—*summit* NC-3
Cheoah Ch—*church* NC-3
Cheoah Dam—*building* NC-3
Cheoah Dam—*dam* NC-3
Cheoah Lake—*reservoir* NC-3
Cheoah Mountains—*ridge* NC-3
Cheoah River—*stream* NC-3
Cheoah (Township of)—*fmr MCD* NC-3
Cheoah Valley Dam—*dam* NC-3
Cheoah Valley Lake—*reservoir* NC-3
Cheohee—*locale* SC-3
Cheohee, Lake—*reservoir* SC-3
Cheohee Ch—*church* SC-3
Cheohee Creek—*stream* SC-3
*Cheops Pyramid* CO-8
Cheops Pyramid—*summit* AZ-5
Cheosa Waterhole—*lake* TX-5
*Cheowah* NC-3
*Cheowah Mountains* NC-3
*Cheowah River* NC-3
*Cheowhee* SC-3
*Cheowhee Creek* SC-3
*Cheowhee Lake* SC-3
Chepachet—*locale* NY-2
**Chepachet**—*pop pl* RI-1
*Chepachet Reservoir* RI-1
Chepachet River—*stream* RI-1
Chepachet Village Hist Dist—*hist pl* RI-1
*Chepalis Head* WA-9
**Chepanuu (historical)**—*pop pl* NC-3
*Chepatchet* RI-1
Chepat Creek—*stream* MT-8
*Chepatset* RI-1
*Chepeta Canyon* UT-8
*Chepeta Creek* UT-8
Chepeta Dam—*dam* UT-8
Chepeta Lake—*reservoir* UT-8
*Chepeta Reservoir* UT-8
*Chepita Canyon* UT-8
*Chepiwanoxet* RI-1
**Chepiwanoxet**—*pop pl* RI-1
Chepiwanoxet Island—*island* RI-1
Chepo Saddle—*gap* CA-9
Chepota Mine (underground)—*mine* AL-4
Chepps Mill (historical)—*locale* TN-4
Chepstow—*locale* KS-7
Chepstow Cem—*cemetery* KS-7
Chepultepec—*locale* AL-4
Chepultepec (Allgood)—*other* AL-4
Chequamegon Bay—*bay* WI-6
Chequamegon Point—*cape* WI-6
Chequamegon Point Light—*locale* WI-6
Chequamegon Waters Flowage—*reservoir* WI-6
*Chequaquet* MA-1
*Chequaquet Lake* MA-1
*Chequaquet Pond* MA-1
**Chequest**—*pop pl* IA-7
Chequest Creek—*stream* IA-7
Chequest Township—*fmr MCD* IA-7
Chequit Point—*cape* NY-2
*Cheraké River* MS-4
Cherami, Bayou—*stream* LA-4
Cheramie Cem—*cemetery* LA-4
**Cheraw**—*pop pl* CO-8
**Cheraw**—*pop pl* MS-4
**Cheraw**—*pop pl* SC-3
Cheraw Acad—*school* SC-3
Cheraw (CCD)—*cens area* SC-3
Cheraw Country Club—*other* SC-3
Cheraw Hist Dist—*hist pl* SC-3
Cheraw Lake—*lake* CO-8
Cheraw Natl Fish Hatchery—*other* SC-3
Cheraw State Park—*park* SC-3
Cherbourg Round Barn—*hist pl* DE-2
Cherbourg Round Barn—*park* DE-2
**Cherbourg (subdivision)**—*pop pl* NC-3
*Cherego* MH-9
*Cheregua* MH-9
Cheremoya Ave Sch—*school* CA-9
*Cherengoll* PW-9
Cherful, Lake—*reservoir* GA-3
Cheri, Bayou—*gut* LA-4
Chericke—*hist pl* VA-3
Chericoke—*locale* VA-3
*Cheriguruppu* MP-9
Cheri Lake—*lake* AK-9
**Cherill Acres Subdivision**—*pop pl* UT-8
Cherioni Wash—*stream* AZ-5
Cherisco Creek—*stream* NM-5
Cherisco Tank—*reservoir* NM-5
Cherisco Well—*well* NM-5
**Cheriton**—*pop pl* VA-3
Cherma Ch—*church* WI-6
Chermak State Wildlife Mngmt
Area—*park* MN-6
Chernabura Island—*island* AK-9
*Chernesville* WI-6
*Chernesville Hill* WI-6
Cherneyville—*locale* WI-6
Cherneyville Hill—*summit* WI-6
Cherni Island—*island* AK-9
Chernof Glacier—*glacier* AK-9
Chernof Point—*cape* AK-9
**Chernofski**—*pop pl* AK-9
Chernofski Harbor—*bay* AK-9
Chernofski Point—*cape* AK-9
*Cheroga* MH-9
*Cherokee* TX-5
Cherokee—*locale (4)* CA-9
Cherokee—*locale* GA-3
Cherokee—*locale* KY-4
Cherokee—*locale* TN-4
Cherokee—*locale* WA-9
Cherokee—*locale* WY-8
**Cherokee**—*pop pl* AL-4
**Cherokee**—*pop pl* IA-7
**Cherokee**—*pop pl* KS-7
**Cherokee**—*pop pl* ME-1
**Cherokee**—*pop pl* NC-3
**Cherokee**—*pop pl* OH-6
**Cherokee**—*pop pl* OK-5
**Cherokee**—*pop pl* SC-3
**Cherokee**—*pop pl* TN-4
**Cherokee**—*pop pl* TX-5
**Cherokee**—*pop pl (2)* WV-2
**Cherokee**—*pop pl* WI-6
Cherokee—*uninc pl* GA-3
Cherokee—*uninc pl* KY-4
Cherokee—*uninc pl* NY-2
Cherokee, Lake—*lake* FL-3
Cherokee, Lake—*reservoir* AR-4
Cherokee, Lake—*reservoir* NJ-2
Cherokee, Lake—*reservoir* NC-3
Cherokee, Lake—*reservoir* TX-5
**Cherokee Acres (subdivision)**—*pop pl* AL-4
*Cherokee Agency* TN-4
Cherokee Armory—*hist pl* OK-5
Cherokee Ave Park—*park* AZ-5
Cherokee Bar—*bar* CA-9
Cherokee Basin—*basin* WY-8
Cherokee Bay—*bay* WA-9
*Cherokee Bayou* TX-5
Cherokee Bayou—*stream* TX-5
**Cherokee Bay Park**—*pop pl* WA-9
Cherokee Beach Lake—*reservoir* AL-4
Cherokee Beach Lake Dam—*dam* AL-4
Cherokee Bend Elem Sch—*school* AL-4
Cherokee Bill Canyon—*valley* NM-5
Cherokee Bloomary Forge
(historical)—*locale* TN-4
Cherokee Bluff Cave—*cave* TN-4
Cherokee Bluffs—*cliff* TN-4
Cherokee Bluffs—*cliff* TX-5
**Cherokee Bluffs**—*pop pl* AL-4
Cherokee Boys Camp—*locale* GA-3
Cherokee Branch—*stream* AL-4
Cherokee Camp—*locale* TX-5
*Cherokee Campground* TN-4
Cherokee Canal—*canal* CA-9
Cherokee Canyon—*valley* NM-5
Cherokee Cave—*cave* AL-4
*Cherokee Caverns* TN-4
Cherokee (CCD)—*cens area* AL-4
Cherokee (CCD)—*cens area* OK-5
Cherokee Cem—*cemetery* AL-4
Cherokee Cem—*cemetery* AR-4
Cherokee Cem—*cemetery (2)* KS-7
Cherokee Cem—*cemetery* OK-5
Cherokee Cem—*cemetery (2)* TN-4
*Cherokee Ch* TN-4
Cherokee Ch—*church* NC-3
Cherokee Ch—*church* SC-3
Cherokee Ch—*church (3)* TN-4
**Cherokee (Cherokee Springs)**—*pop pl* SC-3
Cherokee Chute—*channel* OK-5
**Cherokee City**—*pop pl* AR-4
*Cherokee City Cemetery* KS-7
Cherokee City Hall—*building* IA-7
Cherokee Community Independent Freewill
Baptist Ch—*church* TN-4
Cherokee Corners Ch—*church* GA-3
Cherokee Country Club—*locale* AL-4
Cherokee Country Club—*other* GA-3
Cherokee Country Club—*other* TX-5
Cherokee County—*civil* KS-7
**Cherokee County**—*pop pl* AL-4
**Cherokee (County)**—*pop pl* GA-3
**Cherokee County**—*pop pl* NC-3
**Cherokee (County)**—*pop pl* OK-5
**Cherokee (County)**—*pop pl* SC-3
**Cherokee (County)**—*pop pl* TX-5
Cherokee County Courthouse—*building* AL-4
Cherokee County Courthouse—*hist pl* GA-3
Cherokee County Courthouse—*hist pl* NC-3
Cherokee County Fairgrounds—*locale* KS-7
Cherokee County Hosp—*hospital* AL-4
Cherokee County HS—*school* AL-4
Cherokee County Training Sch—*school* AL-4
*Cherokee County Vocational Sch* AL-4
**Cherokee Court**—*pop pl* LA-4
Cherokee Cove—*bay* GA-3
*Cherokee Creek* OH-6
*Cherokee Creek* TN-4
Cherokee Creek—*stream (2)* AR-4
Cherokee Creek—*stream (2)* CA-9
Cherokee Creek—*stream* CO-8
Cherokee Creek—*stream* GA-3
Cherokee Creek—*stream* KY-4
Cherokee Creek—*stream* MN-6
Cherokee Creek—*stream (2)* OK-5
Cherokee Creek—*stream* OR-9
Cherokee Creek—*stream (3)* SC-3
Cherokee Creek—*stream* TN-4
Cherokee Creek—*stream (2)* TX-5
Cherokee Creek—*stream (5)* WY-8
Cherokee Dam—*dam* TN-4
Cherokee Diggings—*locale* CA-9
Cherokee Ditch—*canal* WY-8
Cherokee Division—*civil* AL-4
Cherokee Dock—*locale* TN-4
Cherokee Draw—*valley* WY-8

Cherokee Elementary School ... MS-4
Cherokee Elem Sch ... NC-3
Cherokee Elem Sch—school ... AL-4
Cherokee Elem Sch—school ... AZ-5
Cherokee Elem Sch—school ... KS-7
**Cherokee Estates**—pop pl ... TN-4
**Cherokee Estates (subdivision)**—pop pl ... AL-4
**Cherokee Falls**—pop pl ... SC-3
Cherokee Female Seminary—hist pl ... OK-5
Cherokee Flat—flat (3) ... CA-9
Cherokee Flats—other ... AK-9
**Cherokee Forest**—pop pl ... AL-4
**Cherokee Forest**—pop pl ... SC-3
Cherokee Gap—gap ... KY-4
Cherokee Gap—gap ... NC-3
**Cherokee Garden**—pop pl ... KY-4
Cherokee Golf and Country Club—locale ... TN-4
Cherokee Golf Course—locale ... PA-2
**Cherokee Grdens (subdivision)**—pop pl ... TN-4
Cherokee Gulch Ditch—canal ... WY-8
Cherokee Heights—other ... IN-6
**Cherokee Heights**—pop pl (2) ... TN-4
Cherokee Heights—uninc pl ... GA-3
Cherokee Heights—uninc pl ... VA-3
Cherokee Heights Ch—church ... TN-4
Cherokee Heights District—hist pl ... GA-3
Cherokee Heights Dock—locale ... TN-4
Cherokee Heights Park—park ... MN-6
Cherokee Heights Sch—school ... WI-6
**Cherokee Heights (subdivision)**—pop pl ... MS-4
Cherokee Hill—summit ... WY-8
Cherokee Hill Cem—cemetery ... GA-3
**Cherokee Hills**—pop pl (2) ... TN-4
Cherokee Hills Baptist Ch—church ... TN-4
Cherokee Hills Camp—locale ... IL-6
Cherokee Hills Ch—church ... OK-5
Cherokee Hills Sch—school ... MI-6
Cherokee Hills Shop Ctr—locale ... KS-7
**Cherokee Hills (subdivision)**—pop pl (2) ... AL-4
**Cherokee Hills (subdivision)**—pop pl ... TN-4
Cherokee (historical)—locale ... AL-4
Cherokee (historical town)—locale ... AZ-5
Cherokee Home Mission—church ... OK-5
Cherokee HS—school ... AL-4
Cherokee HS—school ... TN-4
Cherokee Indian Land Henson Donation—civil ... NC-3
Cherokee Indian Land Tract No 2—civil ... NC-3
Cherokee Indian Land Tract No 7—civil ... NC-3
Cherokee Indian Memorial—park ... GA-3
**Cherokee Ind Res**—pop pl ... NC-3
Cherokee Industrial Park—locale ... TN-4
Cherokee IOOF Lodge No. 219—hist pl ... OK-5
Cherokee JHS—school ... FL-3
Cherokee Knob—summit ... TN-4
Cherokee Lake—lake ... CO-8
Cherokee Lake—lake ... MN-6
Cherokee Lake—lake ... OK-5
Cherokee Lake—lake ... WI-6
Cherokee Lake—reservoir ... GA-3
Cherokee Lake—reservoir (2) ... TN-4
Cherokee Lake—reservoir (2) ... TX-5
Cherokee Lake—reservoir ... VA-3
**Cherokee Lake Acres**—pop pl ... TX-5
Cherokee Lake Campground—locale ... TN-4
Cherokee Lakes—reservoir ... GA-3
Cherokee Landing—locale ... TN-4
Cherokee Landing—locale ... TX-5
Cherokee Landing State Park—park ... OK-5
Cherokee Lane Sch—school ... MD-2
Cherokee Lowlands ... KS-7
Cherokee Mans Run—stream ... OH-6
Cherokee-McCoy Cem—cemetery ... OK-5
Cherokee Memorial—park ... GA-3
Cherokee Memorial Park—park ... CA-9
Cherokee Memorial Park (Cemetery)—cemetery ... GA-3
Cherokee Memory Gardens—cemetery ... AL-4
Cherokee Mill (historical)—locale ... AL-4
Cherokee Mine—mine (2) ... CA-9
Cherokee Mine—mine (2) ... NV-8
Cherokee Mine—mine ... UT-8
Cherokee Mine No 1—mine ... WY-8
Cherokee Mine No 2—mine ... WY-8
Cherokee Mineral Springs—spring ... AL-4
Cherokee Missionary Ch—church ... TX-5
Cherokee Mobile Village—locale ... AZ-5
Cherokee Mountain Baptist Ch—church ... TN-4
Cherokee Mtn—summit ... CO-8
Cherokee Mtn—summit ... TN-4
Cherokee Natl Capitol—hist pl ... OK-5
Cherokee Natl Cemetery—hist pl ... OK-5
Cherokee Natl For—forest ... TN-4
Cherokee Natl Jail—hist pl ... OK-5
Cherokee Nuclear Power Plant—facility ... SC-3
Cherokee Orchard—woods ... TN-4
Cherokee Park—flat ... CO-8
Cherokee Park—park ... KY-4
Cherokee Park—park ... TN-4
Cherokee Park—park (2) ... WI-6
**Cherokee Park**—pop pl ... TN-4
**Cherokee Park (subdivision)**—pop pl ... TN-4
**Cherokee Pass**—pop pl ... MO-7
Cherokee Path, Sterling Land Grant—hist pl ... SC-3
Cherokee Peak—summit ... WY-8
Cherokee Pit—cave ... AL-4
Cherokee Placer Mine—mine ... CA-9
Cherokee Plains—plain ... KS-7
Cherokee Plantation—hist pl ... AL-4
Cherokee Plantation—hist pl ... LA-4
Cherokee Plantation (historical)—locale ... AL-4
Cherokee Plaza Shop Ctr—locale ... AL-4
Cherokee Point—summit ... AZ-5
Cherokee Public Library—hist pl ... IA-7
Cherokee Ranch—locale ... CO-8
Cherokee Ranch—locale ... WY-8
**Cherokee Ranch**—pop pl ... PA-2
Cherokee Rec Area—park ... AR-4
Cherokee Reservoir ... TN-4
Cherokee Ridge ... GA-3
**Cherokee Ridge**—pop pl ... TN-4
Cherokee Ridge Camp—locale ... MO-7
Cherokee Rim—cliff ... WY-8
Cherokee River ... MS-4
Cherokee Rod and Gun Club—locale ... TN-4
Cherokee Rsvr—reservoir ... MT-8
Cherokee Rsvr—reservoir ... WY-8
Cherokee Ruby and Sapphire Mine—mine ... NC-3
Cherokee Run ... OH-6
Cherokee Run—stream ... OH-6
Cherokees, Lake O'The—reservoir ... MO-7
Cherokees, Lake O' The—reservoir ... OK-5
Cherokee Sandy Creek—stream ... OK-5
Cherokee Sch—school ... AL-4
Cherokee Sch—school (2) ... FL-3
Cherokee Sch—school ... GA-3
Cherokee Sch—school ... IL-6
Cherokee Sch—school ... KS-7
Cherokee Sch—school (2) ... LA-4
Cherokee Sch—school ... MS-4
Cherokee Sch—school ... MO-7
Cherokee Sch—school ... NC-3
Cherokee Sch—school (4) ... OK-5
Cherokee Sch—school (3) ... TN-4
Cherokee Sch (Abandoned)—school ... CA-9
Cherokee Sch (abandoned)—school ... MO-7
Cherokee Sch (historical)—school ... MS-4
Cherokee Scout Reservation—reserve ... NC-3
Cherokee Sewer Site—hist pl ... IA-7
**Cherokee Shores (subdivision)**—pop pl ... AL-4
Cherokee Sink—basin ... FL-3
Cherokee South Shop Ctr—locale ... KS-7
Cherokee Speedway—other ... SC-3
Cherokee Spring—spring ... AL-4
Cherokee Spring—spring ... CA-9
Cherokee Spring—spring ... WY-8
**Cherokee Springs**—pop pl ... SC-3
Cherokee Square Shop Ctr—locale ... TN-4
Cherokee State Game Ref—park ... OK-5
Cherokee State Hosp—hospital ... IA-7
Cherokee Street Ch—church ... NC-3
Cherokee Street Hist Dist—hist pl ... GA-3
**Cherokee Strip**—pop pl ... CA-9
Cherokee Strip Bridge—bridge ... OK-5
Cherokee Strip Museum—building ... KS-7
Cherokee Strip Museum—building ... OK-5
Cherokee Supreme Court Bldg—hist pl ... OK-5
Cherokee Tank—reservoir ... AZ-5
Cherokee Tank—reservoir ... KS-7
Cherokee Tank Pond ... KS-7
**Cherokee Terrace (Cherokee Heights)**—pop pl ... IN-6
Cherokee Township—fmr MCD ... IA-7
**Cherokee Township**—pop pl (2) ... KS-7
Cherokee (Township of)—fmr MCD (2) ... AR-4
Cherokee Trail Roadside Park—park ... MO-7
Cherokee Trail Rsvr—reservoir ... WY-8
Cherokee Triangle Area Residential District—hist pl ... KY-4
Cherokee Unit Number Five—other ... KY-4
Cherokee Valley—area ... NM-5
Cherokee Valley—basin ... GA-3
Cherokee Valley Cem—cemetery ... NM-5
Cherokee Valley Ch—church ... GA-3
**Cherokee Village**—pop pl ... AL-4
**Cherokee Village**—pop pl ... AR-4
**Cherokee Village**—pop pl ... LA-4
**Cherokee Village (subdivision)**—pop pl ... TN-4
Cherokee Vocational HS—school ... AL-4
Cherokee Wash—arroyo ... AZ-5
Cherokee Wildlife Mngmt Area—park (2) ... TN-4
**Cherokee Woods**—pop pl ... DE-2
**Cherokee Woods**—pop pl ... TN-4
**Cherokee Woods (subdivision)**—pop pl ... DE-2
**Cherokee Woods (subdivision)**—pop pl ... TN-4
Cheroke Sch—school ... KY-4
Cherokita Trend Oil And Gas Field—oilfield ... OK-5
Cheroy Hill—summit ... TN-4
Cherrelyn ... CO-8
Cherrelyn Sch—school ... CO-8
Cherring ... GA-3
Cherring Creek ... GA-3
Cherrolake—lake ... TN-4
Cherry ... MS-4
Cherry ... MP-9
Cherry—locale ... AZ-5
Cherry—locale ... TX-5
Cherry—locale ... WV-2
**Cherry**—pop pl ... CO-8
**Cherry**—pop pl ... IL-6
**Cherry**—pop pl (2) ... KY-4
**Cherry**—pop pl ... MN-6
**Cherry**—pop pl ... NC-3
**Cherry**—pop pl ... TN-4
Cherry, Lake—reservoir ... AL-4
Cherry, Peter L., House—hist pl ... OR-9
**Cherry Acres**—pop pl ... VA-3
Cherry Arm—bay ... OR-9
Cherry Ave Park—park ... CA-9
Cherry Ave Sch—school ... CA-9
Cherry Ave Sch—school ... NY-2
Cherry Bayou—stream ... TN-4
**Cherry Beach**—pop pl ... MI-6
Cherry Bean Ch—church ... AR-4
**Cherry Bend**—pop pl ... MI-6
Cherry Bend Rec Area—park ... AR-4
Cherry Bluff—cliff ... AL-4
Cherry Bottom—basin ... TN-4
Cherry Bottom—valley ... MS-4
Cherry Bottom Ch—church ... TN-4
Cherry Bottom Park—park ... OH-6
Cherry Bottom Run—stream ... MD-2
**Cherry Box**—pop pl ... MO-7
Cherry Box Cem—cemetery ... MO-7
Cherry Branch ... MO-7
**Cherry Branch**—pop pl ... TN-4
Cherry Branch—stream ... AR-4
Cherry Branch—stream (2) ... FL-3
Cherry Branch—stream ... LA-4
Cherry Branch—stream ... MD-2
Cherry Branch—stream ... MO-7
Cherry Branch—stream (6) ... NC-3
Cherry Branch—stream ... SC-3
Cherry Branch—stream (5) ... TN-4
Cherry Branch—stream ... TX-5
Cherry Branch—stream ... VA-3
Cherry Branch—stream ... WI-6
Cherry Branch Creek ... WI-6
Cherry Branch - in part ... MO-7
Cherry Branch Sch—school ... WI-6
Cherrybridge Creek—stream ... MD-2
Cherry Brook—locale ... CT-1
**Cherry Brook**—pop pl ... MA-1
**Cherrybrook**—pop pl ... TN-4
Cherry Brook—stream ... CT-1
Cherry Brook—stream (2) ... MA-1
Cherry Brook—stream ... NJ-2
Cherry Brook—stream (2) ... NY-2
Cherry Brook—stream ... RI-1
Cherry Brook Sch—school ... CT-1
Cherrybush Island—island ... DE-2
Cherry Butte—summit ... ID-8
Cherry Cairn—summit ... CO-8
Cherry Camp—locale ... CA-9
Cherry Camp Creek—stream ... KY-4
Cherry Campground ... UT-8
Cherrycamp Run—stream (2) ... WV-2
Cherry Canyon ... TX-5
Cherry Canyon—valley (2) ... AZ-5
Cherry Canyon—valley (10) ... CA-9
Cherry Canyon—valley ... CO-8
Cherry Canyon—valley ... ID-8
Cherry Canyon—valley (3) ... NV-8
Cherry Canyon—valley (10) ... NM-5
Cherry Canyon—valley (2) ... TX-5
Cherry Canyon—valley (5) ... UT-8
Cherry Canyon Ranch—locale ... TX-5
Cherry Capital Airp—airport ... MI-6
Cherry Cave—cave ... TN-4
Cherry Cem—cemetery ... AL-4
Cherry Cem—cemetery (2) ... AR-4
Cherry Cem—cemetery ... IL-6
Cherry Cem—cemetery ... KY-4
Cherry Cem—cemetery ... MS-4
Cherry Cem—cemetery (6) ... TN-4
Cherry Cem—cemetery ... TX-5
Cherry Ch—church ... NC-3
Cherry Chapel—church ... MS-4
Cherry Chapel—church ... TN-4
Cherry Chapel—church ... TX-5
Cherry Chapel Cemeterys—cemetery ... TN-4
Cherry Chapel United Pentecostal Ch ... MS-4
Cherry Chase Sch—school ... CA-9
**Cherry Circle Subdivision**—pop pl ... UT-8
**Cherry City**—pop pl ... PA-2
Cherry Cooke Creek ... WA-9
Cherry Corner—locale ... PA-2
Cherry Corner—locale ... TN-4
Cherry Corner Ch—church ... KY-4
Cherry Corners—locale ... CT-1
Cherry Coulee—valley (4) ... MT-8
Cherry Cove—basin ... GA-3
Cherry Cove—bay ... CA-9
Cherry Cove—bay ... TX-5
Cherry Cove—valley (4) ... NC-3
Cherry Cove Branch—stream ... GA-3
Cherry Cove Branch—stream (2) ... NC-3
Cherry Cove Branch—stream ... SC-3
Cherry Cove Creek—stream ... MD-2
Cherry Cove Creek—stream ... NC-3
Cherry Cove Lake—lake ... WA-9
Cherry Creek ... CA-9
Cherry Creek ... CO-8
Cherry Creek ... MT-8
Cherry Creek ... NV-8
Cherry Creek ... OR-9
Cherrycreek ... TN-4
Cherry Creek ... WA-9
Cherry Creek ... WI-6
**Cherry Creek**—pop pl ... ID-8
**Cherrycreek**—pop pl ... MS-4
**Cherry Creek**—pop pl ... MS-4
**Cherry Creek**—pop pl ... NV-8
**Cherry Creek**—pop pl ... NY-2
**Cherry Creek**—pop pl ... SD-7
**Cherry Creek**—pop pl ... TN-4
Cherry Creek—stream ... AL-4
Cherry Creek—stream ... AK-9
Cherry Creek—stream (5) ... AZ-5
Cherry Creek—stream ... AR-4
Cherry Creek—stream (11) ... CA-9
Cherry Creek—stream (11) ... CO-8
Cherry Creek—stream (2) ... GA-3
Cherry Creek—stream (13) ... ID-8
Cherry Creek—stream (3) ... IA-7
Cherry Creek—stream (7) ... KS-7
Cherry Creek—stream ... LA-4
Cherry Creek—stream (2) ... MD-2
Cherry Creek—stream (5) ... MI-6
Cherry Creek—stream ... MN-6
Cherry Creek—stream (2) ... MS-4
Cherry Creek—stream (19) ... MT-8
Cherry Creek—stream (3) ... NE-7
Cherry Creek—stream (16) ... NV-8
Cherry Creek—stream (6) ... NM-5
Cherry Creek—stream (2) ... NY-2
Cherry Creek—stream (3) ... NC-3
Cherry Creek—stream ... ND-7
Cherry Creek—stream ... OH-6
Cherry Creek—stream (2) ... OK-5
Cherry Creek—stream (14) ... OR-9
Cherry Creek—stream ... PA-2
Cherry Creek—stream (2) ... SD-7
Cherry Creek—stream (2) ... TN-4
Cherry Creek—stream (11) ... TX-5
Cherry Creek—stream (7) ... UT-8
Cherry Creek—stream (2) ... VA-3
Cherry Creek—stream (4) ... WA-9
Cherry Creek—stream ... WV-2
Cherry Creek—stream (8) ... WY-8
**Cherry Creek Acres**—pop pl ... CA-9
Cherry Creek Baptist Ch—church ... MS-4
Cherry Creek Basin—basin ... MT-8
Cherry Creek Campground—locale ... CA-9
Cherry Creek Campground—locale ... CO-8
Cherry Creek Campground—locale ... ID-8
Cherry Creek Canon —valley ... NV-8
Cherry Creek Canyon—valley ... CA-9
Cherry Creek Canyon—valley ... MT-8
Cherry Creek Canyon—valley ... NM-5
Cherry Creek Canyon—valley ... WY-8
Cherry Creek Cem—cemetery ... AR-4
Cherry Creek Cem—cemetery ... TN-4
Cherry Creek Ch—church ... GA-3
Cherry Creek Ch—church ... MT-8
Cherry Creek Ch—church ... TN-4
Cherry Creek County Park ... OR-9
Cherry Creek Cove—bay ... MD-2
Cherry Creek Dam—dam ... CO-8
Cherry Creek Dam—dam ... OR-9
Cherry Creek Ditch—canal ... UT-8
Cherry Creek Drain—canal ... WY-8
Cherry Creek Forest Camp—locale ... NM-5
Cherry Creek Forest Service Facility—locale ... NV-8
Cherry Creek Forest Service Recreation Site—locale ... NV-8
Cherry Creek Hill—summit ... AZ-5
Cherry Creek Hill—summit ... WY-8
Cherry Creek HS—school ... CO-8
Cherry Creek Lake—reservoir ... CO-8
Cherry Creek Lake State Rec Area—park ... CO-8
Cherry Creek Lateral—canal ... WY-8
Cherry Creek Mine—mine ... UT-8
Cherry Creek Mining District—civil ... NV-8
Cherry Creek Missionary Baptist Ch—church ... MS-4
Cherry Creek Mound—hist pl ... TN-4
Cherry Creek Mountains ... NV-8
Cherry Creek Myrtle Preserve—reserve ... OR-9
Cherry Creek Normal Sch (historical)—school ... MS-4
Cherry Creek Park—park ... OR-9
Cherry Creek Post Office (historical)—building ... MS-4
Cherry Creek Post Office (historical)—building ... TN-4
Cherry Creek Ranch—locale (2) ... OR-9
Cherry Creek Range—range ... NV-8
Cherry Creek Ranger Station—locale ... MT-8
Cherry Creek Recreation Site—park ... OR-9
Cherry Creek Reservoir ... CO-8
Cherry Creek RR Station—building ... AZ-5
Cherry Creek Rsvr—reservoir (2) ... OR-9
Cherry Creek Rsvr—reservoir ... UT-8
Cherry Creek Sch—school (2) ... MT-8
Cherry Creek Shop Ctr—other ... CO-8
Cherry Creek Spring—spring (2) ... AZ-5
Cherry Creek Spring—spring (2) ... UT-8
Cherry Creek Station—locale ... NV-8
**Cherry Creek (subdivision)**—pop pl ... AL-4
Cherry Creek Summit—gap ... NV-8
Cherry Creek Summit—summit ... NV-8
Cherry Creek Tank—reservoir ... AZ-5
**Cherry Creek (Town of)**—pop pl ... NY-2
**Cherry Creek Township**—pop pl ... KS-7
**Cherry Creek Township**—pop pl ... NE-7
Cherry Creek Trail Two Hundred Fourteen—trail ... AZ-5
Cherry Creek Wash—valley ... UT-8
Cherry Creek Wasteway—canal ... WY-8
Cherry Creek Well—well ... AZ-5
Cherry Crest—uninc pl ... WA-9
Cherry Crossroads—locale ... NC-3
Cherry Crossroads—locale ... TN-4
Cherrydale—hist pl ... NC-3
Cherrydale—hist pl ... SC-3
**Cherrydale**—pop pl ... PA-2
**Cherry Dale**—pop pl ... PA-2
**Cherrydale**—pop pl ... VA-3
Cherrydale Sch—school ... VA-3
Cherrydale Sch (historical)—school ... MO-7
**Cherry Dale (subdivision)**—pop pl ... AL-4
**Cherrydale (subdivision)**—pop pl ... TN-4
**Cherry Downs**—pop pl ... NJ-2
Cherry Draw—valley ... CO-8
Cherry Draw—valley (2) ... TX-5
Cherry Draw—valley (3) ... WY-8
**Cherry Falls**—pop pl ... WV-2
Cherry Farm Cem—cemetery ... MS-4
**Cherry Farm Estates Subdivision**—pop pl ... UT-8
Cherry Farm Sch—school ... IL-6
Cherry Farm Sch (historical)—school ... MS-4
**Cherryfield**—pop pl ... ME-1
**Cherryfield**—pop pl ... NC-3
Cherryfield Acad—hist pl ... ME-1
Cherryfield Creek—stream ... NC-3
Cherryfield Point—cape ... MD-2
Cherryfield Pond—lake ... MD-2
**Cherryfield (Town of)**—pop pl ... ME-1
Cherry Flat—flat ... AR-4
Cherry Flat—flat (6) ... CA-9
Cherry Flat—flat ... OR-9
Cherry Flat—flat (2) ... UT-8
Cherry Flat—valley ... TN-4
Cherry Flat Rec Area—park ... AZ-5
Cherry Flat Rsvr—reservoir ... CA-9
Cherry Flats—flat ... MI-6
Cherry Flats—flat ... NC-3
Cherry Flats—locale ... PA-2
Cherry Flats Ridge—ridge ... TN-4
Cherry Ford ... WV-2
Cherry Ford—locale ... PA-2
**Cherry Fork**—pop pl ... OH-6
Cherry Fork—stream (2) ... OH-6
Cherry Fork—stream (5) ... WV-2
Cherry Fork Ch—church ... WV-2
Cherry Fork Creek—stream ... TN-4
Cherry Fork Sch—school ... TN-4
Cherry Gap—gap (2) ... CA-9
Cherry Gap—gap (6) ... NC-3
Cherry Gap—gap (2) ... TN-4
Cherry Gap Branch—stream ... NC-3
Cherry Gap Mtn—summit ... KY-4
**Cherry Gardens**—pop pl ... WA-9
Cherry Glade—flat ... OR-9
Cherry Glade Creek ... WV-2
Cherry Glade Creek—stream ... CA-9
Cherry Glade Run—stream ... MD-2
Cherry Glen—valley ... CA-9
Cherry Grove—locale ... AL-4
Cherry Grove—locale ... KY-4
Cherry Grove—locale ... NC-3
Cherry Grove—locale (3) ... PA-2
Cherry Grove—locale (2) ... VA-3
Cherry Grove—locale ... WA-9
**Cherry Grove**—pop pl ... IN-6
**Cherry Grove**—pop pl ... MN-6
**Cherry Grove**—pop pl ... NY-2
**Cherrygrove**—pop pl ... NC-3
**Cherry Grove**—pop pl ... NC-3
**Cherry Grove**—pop pl ... OH-6
**Cherry Grove**—pop pl ... OR-9
**Cherry Grove**—pop pl ... TN-4
**Cherry Grove**—pop pl ... WV-2
Cherry Grove Airp—airport ... PA-2
Cherry Grove Baptist Ch—church ... MS-4
Cherry Grove Beach—beach ... SC-3
Cherry Grove Beach—uninc pl ... SC-3
Cherry Grove Canal—canal ... ID-8
Cherry Grove Cem—cemetery (2) ... AL-4
Cherry Grove Cem—cemetery ... AR-4
Cherry Grove Cem—cemetery (2) ... IL-6
Cherry Grove Cem—cemetery (2) ... IN-6
Cherry Grove Cem—cemetery ... KY-4
Cherry Grove Cem—cemetery ... MI-6
Cherry Grove Cem—cemetery (2) ... NC-3
Cherry Grove Cem—cemetery ... OH-6
Cherry Grove Cem—cemetery ... OR-9
Cherry Grove Cem—cemetery ... PA-2
Cherry Grove Cem—cemetery ... SC-3
Cherry Grove Cem—cemetery (2) ... WV-2
Cherry Grove Ch—church ... GA-3
Cherry Grove Ch—church ... KS-7
Cherry Grove Ch—church ... KY-4
Cherry Grove Ch—church ... LA-4
Cherry Grove Ch—church ... MD-2
Cherry Grove Ch—church (3) ... MS-4
Cherry Grove Ch—church ... MO-7
Cherry Grove Ch—church (2) ... NC-3
Cherry Grove Ch—church ... OH-6
Cherry Grove Ch—church ... OK-5
Cherry Grove Ch—church (2) ... PA-2
Cherry Grove Ch—church ... SC-3
Cherry Grove Ch—church (2) ... TN-4
Cherry Grove Ch—church ... TX-5
Cherry Grove Ch (historical)—church ... AL-4
Cherry Grove Creek—stream ... VA-3
Cherry Grove Ferry—trail ... NY-2
Cherry Grove Hollow—valley ... KY-4
Cherry Grove Inlet—bay ... SC-3
Cherry Grove Park—park ... CA-9
Cherry Grove Picnic Area—locale ... NY-2
Cherry Grove Plantation—hist pl ... MS-4
Cherry Grove Post Office (historical)—building ... TN-4
Cherry Grove Sch—school ... GA-3
Cherry Grove Sch—school (2) ... IL-6
Cherry Grove Sch—school ... KY-4
Cherry Grove Sch—school ... MI-6
Cherry Grove Sch—school (2) ... MO-7
Cherry Grove Sch—school ... OK-5
Cherry Grove Sch—school (2) ... PA-2
Cherry Grove Sch—school (2) ... SC-3
Cherry Grove Sch—school ... TN-4
Cherry Grove Sch—school ... WI-6
Cherry Grove Sch (abandoned)—school ... MO-7
Cherry Grove Sch (abandoned)—school (2) ... PA-2
Cherry Grove Sch (historical)—school ... AL-4
Cherry Grove Sch (historical)—school ... MO-7
Cherry Grove-Shannon (Township of)—civ div ... IL-6
Cherry Grove Tabernacle—church ... IN-6
**Cherry Grove Tabernacle**—pop pl ... IN-6
Cherry Grove (Township of)—civ div ... MI-6
Cherry Grove (Township of)—civ div ... MN-6
**Cherry Grove (Township of)**—pop pl ... PA-2
Cherry Gulch—valley (3) ... CO-8
Cherry Gulch—valley (8) ... ID-8
Cherry Gulch—valley ... MT-8
Cherry Gulch—valley ... NV-8
Cherry Gulch—valley (2) ... OR-9
Cherry Gulch Mine—mine ... NV-8
Cherry Hall—hist pl ... KY-4
Cherry Hall—locale ... VA-3
Cherry Harbor—bay ... NY-2
**Cherry Heights**—pop pl ... OR-9
Cherry Hill ... MS-4
Cherryhill ... PA-2
Cherry Hill ... RI-1
Cherry Hill—hist pl ... NY-2
Cherry Hill—hist pl ... NC-3
Cherry Hill—hist pl ... VA-3
Cherry Hill—locale ... AR-4
Cherry Hill—locale (2) ... MD-2
Cherry Hill—locale ... NJ-2
Cherry Hill—locale ... NY-2
Cherry Hill—locale ... SC-3
Cherry Hill—locale ... VA-3
**Cherry Hill**—pop pl ... AR-4
**Cherry Hill**—pop pl ... CT-1
**Cherry Hill**—pop pl ... DE-2
**Cherry Hill**—pop pl ... IL-6
**Cherry Hill**—pop pl (3) ... MD-2
**Cherry Hill**—pop pl ... MI-6
**Cherry Hill**—pop pl ... NJ-2
**Cherry Hill**—pop pl (3) ... PA-2
**Cherry Hill**—pop pl ... SC-3
**Cherry Hill**—pop pl ... TN-4
**Cherry Hill**—pop pl ... VA-3
Cherry Hill—summit ... AL-4
Cherry Hill—summit (5) ... CA-9
Cherry Hill—summit ... CO-8
Cherry Hill—summit (4) ... CT-1
Cherry Hill—summit ... IN-6
Cherry Hill—summit ... ME-1
Cherry Hill—summit (3) ... MA-1
Cherry Hill—summit (2) ... NY-2
Cherry Hill—summit ... OH-6
Cherry Hill—summit (5) ... PA-2
Cherry Hill—summit (2) ... WA-9
Cherry Hill—summit ... WV-2
**Cherry Hill Addition (subdivision)**—pop pl ... UT-8
Cherry Hill Airp—airport ... IN-6
Cherry Hill Campground—locale ... UT-8
Cherry Hill Cem—cemetery ... AL-4
Cherry Hill Cem—cemetery ... AR-4
Cherry Hill Cem—cemetery ... CA-9
Cherry Hill Cem—cemetery ... GA-3
Cherry Hill Cem—cemetery ... MA-1
Cherry Hill Cem—cemetery ... MI-6
Cherry Hill Cem—cemetery (2) ... MS-4
Cherry Hill Cem—cemetery ... PA-2
Cherryhill Cem—cemetery ... PA-2
Cherry Hill Cem—cemetery (4) ... SC-3
Cherry Hill Cem—cemetery ... TN-4
Cherry Hill Cem—cemetery ... VT-1
Cherry Hill Ch ... AL-4
Cherry Hill Ch—church (3) ... AL-4
Cherry Hill Ch—church ... AR-4
Cherry Hill Ch—church ... GA-3
Cherry Hill Ch—church (2) ... KY-4
Cherry Hill Ch—church ... MD-2
Cherry Hill Ch—church ... NC-3
Cherryhill Ch—church ... NC-3
Cherry Hill Ch—church ... OH-6
Cherry Hill Ch—church (2) ... SC-3
Cherry Hill Ch—church (2) ... VA-3
Cherry Hill Ch (historical)—church ... MS-4
Cherry Hill Ch Number 1—church ... LA-4
Cherry Hill Ch Number 2—church ... LA-4
Cherry Hill Ch of Christ (historical)—church ... TN-4
Cherry Hill Ch of God of Prophecy—church ... FL-3
Cherry Hill Country Club—other ... IL-6
Cherry Hill Country Club—other ... MO-7
Cherry Hill Creek—stream ... AL-4
**Cherry Hill Estates**—pop pl ... NJ-2
**Cherry Hill Estates Subdivision**—pop pl ... UT-8
Cherry Hill Fire District—civil ... NC-3
Cherry Hill Freewill Baptist Ch—church ... TN-4
Cherry Hill Hosp—hospital ... NJ-2
Cherry Hill HS—school ... MI-6
Cherry Hill HS—school ... NJ-2
Cherry Hill HS West—school ... NJ-2
Cherry Hill Inn—airport ... NJ-2
Cherry Hill Knoll Island—island ... SC-3
Cherry Hill Mall—locale ... NJ-2
Cherry Hill Mine—mine ... CA-9
Cherry Hill Park—park ... IA-7
Cherry Hill Point—cape ... NY-2
Cherry Hill Pond—lake ... NY-2
Cherry Hills ... IL-6
Cherry Hill Sch—school ... MI-6
Cherry Hill Sch—school ... NJ-2
Cherry Hill Sch—school ... OH-6
Cherry Hill Sch—school ... UT-8
Cherry Hill Sch (historical)—school ... AL-4
Cherry Hill Sch (historical)—school ... TN-4
Cherry Hills Country Club—other ... CO-8
**Cherry Hills Crest**—pop pl ... CO-8
Cherry Hills Inn Golf Course—locale ... PA-2
Cherry Hills Lake—reservoir ... CO-8
**Cherry Hills Manor**—pop pl ... CO-8
Cherry Hill Spring—spring ... NV-8
Cherry Hill Spring—spring ... TN-4
Cherry Hills Sch—school ... CO-8
Cherry Hills Sch—school ... NJ-2
**Cherry Hills Subdivision**—pop pl ... UT-8
**Cherry Hill Subdivision**—pop pl ... UT-8
**Cherry Hills Village**—pop pl ... CO-8
Cherry Hill Swamp—swamp ... SC-3
Cherry Hill (Township of)—fmr MCD ... AR-4
**Cherry Hill (Township of)**—pop pl ... NJ-2
**Cherryhill (Township of)**—pop pl ... PA-2
Cherry Hill Woods—woods ... IL-6
Cherry (historical)—locale ... KS-7
**Cherryhog**—pop pl ... GA-3
Cherry Hollow—valley ... AL-4
Cherry Hollow—valley ... OH-6
Cherry Hollow—valley (3) ... PA-2
Cherry Hollow—valley ... TN-4
Cherry Hollow—valley (7) ... TX-5
Cherry Hollow—valley ... UT-8
Cherry Hollow Branch—stream ... AR-4
Cherry Hollow Trail—trail (2) ... PA-2
Cherry Hosp—hospital ... NC-3
Cherry Hotel—hist pl ... NC-3
Cherryhurst Park—park ... TX-5
**Cherrying**—pop pl ... GA-3
Cherrying Creek ... GA-3
Cherrying Sch—school ... GA-3
Cherry Island ... MA-1
Cherry Island ... NY-2
Cherry Island ... FM-9
Cherry Island—island ... DE-2
Cherry Island—island (2) ... MD-2
Cherry Island—island ... MI-6
Cherry Island—island ... MN-6
Cherry Island—island ... MT-8
Cherry Island—island (3) ... NY-2
Cherry Island—island ... PA-2
**Cherry Island**—pop pl ... MI-6
Cherry Island Bar—bar ... MA-1
Cherry Island Flats—bar ... DE-2
Cherry Island Marsh—swamp ... DE-2
Cherry Island Range—channel ... DE-2
Cherry Isle ... MI-6
Cherry King Mine—mine ... AZ-5
Cherry Knob—summit ... AR-4
Cherry Knob—summit (2) ... NC-3
Cherry Knob—summit ... WV-2
Cherry Knobs—summit ... TN-4
Cherry Knoll—summit ... VT-1
**Cherry Knolls**—pop pl ... CO-8
Cherry Lake—lake ... CA-9
Cherry Lake—lake (2) ... CO-8
Cherry Lake—lake (3) ... FL-3
Cherry Lake—lake ... IL-6
Cherry Lake—lake ... IA-7
Cherry Lake—lake ... KY-4
Cherry Lake—lake ... MI-6
Cherry Lake—lake (2) ... MN-6
Cherry Lake—lake (2) ... MT-8
Cherry Lake—lake (4) ... ND-7
Cherry Lake—lake ... SD-7
Cherry Lake—lake ... WA-9
Cherry Lake—lake ... WI-6
Cherry Lake—locale ... FL-3
**Cherry Lake**—pop pl ... FL-3
Cherry Lake—reservoir ... CA-9
Cherry Lake—reservoir ... IN-6
Cherry Lake—reservoir ... WV-2
Cherry Lake Ch—church ... FL-3
Cherry Lake Dam—dam ... IN-6
Cherry Lakes—lake ... MT-8
Cherry Lake State Public Shooting Area—park ... SD-7
**Cherry Lake Township**—pop pl ... ND-7
Cherry Lake 4 H Camp—locale ... FL-3
Cherryland—CDP ... CA-9
Cherry Landing—locale ... NC-3
Cherryland Sch—school ... CA-9
Cherry Lane ... ID-8
Cherrylane—locale ... ID-8
**Cherry Lane**—pop pl ... NC-3
**Cherry Lane**—pop pl ... PA-2
Cherry Lane Cem—cemetery ... MA-1
Cherry Lane Ch—church ... NC-3
Cherry Lane Ch—church (3) ... PA-2
**Cherry Lane Heights Subdivision**—pop pl ... UT-8
Cherry Lane Rsvr—reservoir ... CO-8
Cherry Lane Sch—school (2) ... NY-2

Chester County Area Vocational Technical Sch—school PA-2
Chester County Courthouse—building TN-4
Chester County Courthouse—hist pl PA-2
Chester County Courthouse—hist pl TN-4
Chester County/G O Carlson Airp—airport PA-2
Chester County HS—school TN-4
Chester County JHS—school TN-4
Chester County Nursing Home—building TN-4
Chester County Training Sch (historical)—school TN-4
Chester Creek—stream AK-9
Chester Creek—stream CT-1
Chester Creek—stream GA-3
Chester Creek—stream IN-6
Chester Creek—stream KY-4
Chester Creek—stream MN-6
Chester Creek—stream NY-2
Chester Creek—stream PA-2
Chester Creek—stream (2) WA-9
Chester Creek—stream WI-6
Chester Creek Hist Dist—hist pl PA-2
Chester Dam—dam SD-7
*Chester Depot* VT-1
Chester Depot—locale VT-1
Chester (Election Precinct)—fmr MCD IL-6
Chester Elem Sch—school IN-6
**Chester Estates**—pop pl VA-3
**Chester Estates (subdivision)**—pop pl TN-4
*Chesterfield* IL-6
*Chesterfield* NH-1
*Chesterfield (2)* UT-8
Chester Field—hist pl SC-3
Chesterfield—hist pl TN-4
Chesterfield—locale AL-4
Chesterfield—locale IL-6
Chesterfield—locale MD-2
Chesterfield—locale PA-2
**Chesterfield**—pop pl CT-1
**Chesterfield**—pop pl ID-8
**Chesterfield**—pop pl IL-6
**Chesterfield**—pop pl IN-6
**Chesterfield**—pop pl MA-1
**Chesterfield**—pop pl MI-6
**Chesterfield**—pop pl MO-7
**Chesterfield**—pop pl NH-1
**Chesterfield**—pop pl NJ-2
**Chesterfield**—pop pl NC-3
**Chesterfield**—pop pl SC-3
**Chesterfield**—pop pl TN-4
**Chesterfield**—pop pl VA-3
*Chesterfield, Town of* MA-1
Chesterfield Branch—stream IN-6
Chesterfield (CCD)—cens area SC-3
Chesterfield Cem—cemetery CT-1
Chesterfield Cem—cemetery NY-2
*Chesterfield Centre* MA-1
Chesterfield Ch—church AL-4
Chesterfield Ch—church MS-4
Chesterfield Ch—church SC-3
Chesterfield Ch—church VA-3
**Chesterfield (Chesterfield Court House)**—pop pl VA-3
**Chesterfield (County)**—pop pl SC-3
**Chesterfield (County)**—pop pl VA-3
Chesterfield Court House—other VA-3
*Chesterfield Ditch Number Two* OH-6
**Chesterfield Estates (subdivision)**—pop pl AL-4
Chesterfield Flats—flat NE-7
Chesterfield Heights—uninc pl VA-3
Chesterfield Heights Sch—school VA-3
**Chesterfield Heights (subdivision)**—pop pl NC-3
Chesterfield Hist Dist—hist pl ID-8
*Chesterfield Hollow* MA-1
Chesterfield Lake—reservoir NC-3
Chesterfield Lake Dam—dam NC-3
Chesterfield Mall—locale MO-7
Chesterfield Mall (Shop Ctr)—locale MO-7
Chesterfield-Marlboro Sch—school SC-3
Chesterfield Post Office (historical)—building AL-4
Chesterfield Post Office (historical)—building TN-4
Chesterfield Range—range ID-8
*Chesterfield Reservoir* ID-8
Chesterfield Rsvr—reservoir ID-8
Chesterfield Sch—school MI-6
Chesterfield Sch—school (2) MO-7
Chesterfield Sch—school NC-3
Chesterfield Sch—school (2) OH-6
Chesterfield Sch—school SC-3
Chesterfield Sch (historical)—school TN-4
**Chesterfield Shores**—pop pl MI-6
Chesterfield Smith Bridge—bridge FL-3
Chesterfield Square—park CA-9
**Chesterfield Subdivision**—pop pl UT-8
**Chesterfield (subdivision)**—pop pl VA-3
**Chesterfield (Town of)**—pop pl MA-1
**Chesterfield (Town of)**—pop pl NH-1
**Chesterfield (Town of)**—pop pl NY-2
Chesterfield (Township of)—civ div IL-6
Chesterfield (Township of)—civ div MI-6
Chesterfield (Township of)—civ div OH-6
**Chesterfield (Township of)**—pop pl NJ-2
Chesterfield Valley—valley VT-1
*Chester Frost County Park* TN-4
Chester Gap—gap VA-3
**Chester Gap**—pop pl VA-3
Chester Grove Ch—church VA-3
Chester Hall—hist pl MD-2
**Chester Harbor**—pop pl MD-2
**Chester Heights**—pop pl PA-2
Chester Heights—uninc pl NY-2
Chester Heights Borough—civil PA-2
Chester Heights Station—building PA-2
**Chesterhill**—pop pl OH-6
**Chester Hill**—pop pl PA-2
**Chester Hill**—pop pl VA-3
Chester Hill—summit ID-8
Chester Hill Borough—civil PA-2
Chester Hill Cem—cemetery IA-7
Chester Hill Country Club—other OH-6
**Chester Hill Park**—pop pl NY-2
**Chester Hill (Wigton)**—pop pl PA-2
Chester Hist Dist—hist pl SC-3
Chester Hist Dist (Boundary Increase)—hist pl SC-3
Chester (historical)—locale KS-7
Chester (historical)—locale MS-4
Chester (historical)—locale SD-7
Chester Hollow—valley (2) TN-4
Chester Hosp—hospital AR-4
Chester House Inn—hist pl NJ-2
Chester HS—school PA-2
Chester Island—island NE-7
Chester Island—island NJ-2
**Chester Junction**—pop pl NJ-2
Chester Lake—lake MN-6
Chester Lake—reservoir AK-9
**Chesterland**—pop pl OH-6
Chester Lee Lake Dam—dam MS-4
Chester Lookout Tower—locale SC-3
Chester Lyons Spring—spring NV-8
Chester Memorial Gardens—cemetery SC-3
Chester Missionary Ch—church FL-3
Chester Morse Lake—lake WA-9
Chester Morse Monmt—park WA-9
Chester Park—park MN-6
Chester Park—park PA-2
**Chester Park**—pop pl VA-3
Chester Park Sch—school MN-6
**Chester Plaza**—pop pl PA-2
Chester Ponds—reservoir UT-8
Chester Post Office—locale UT-8
Chester Presbyterian Church—hist pl VA-3
Chester Range—channel NJ-2
Chester Range—channel PA-2
*Chester River* FL-3
Chester River—stream MD-2
**Chester River Beach**—pop pl MD-2
Chester River Country Club—other MD-2
Chester Rsvr—reservoir SC-3
Chester Rsvr—reservoir VT-1
Chester Sch—school (2) CT-1
Chester Sch—school IL-6
Chester Sch—school LA-4
Chester Sch—school OH-6
Chester Shell Elem Sch—school FL-3
Chester Shoal—bar FL-3
Chester Siding (historical)—locale ME-1
Chester Spring—spring CA-9
Chester Spring—spring OR-9
**Chester Springs**—pop pl PA-2
Chester Stamp Gap—gap GA-3
Chester State Park—park SC-3
*Chester Station* MA-1
Chester-Stoddard—fmr MCD NE-7
Chester Tank—reservoir AZ-5
Chester Terrace—hist pl MN-6
**Chesterton**—pop pl CA-9
**Chesterton**—pop pl (2) IN-6
Chesterton Cem—cemetery IN-6
Chesterton Sch—school CA-9
Chesterton Senior HS—school IN-6
**Chestertown**—pop pl MD-2
**Chestertown**—pop pl NY-2
Chestertown Armory—hist pl MD-2
Chestertown Cem—cemetery MD-2
Chester Town Hall—building ND-7
Chester Town Hall—hist pl OH-6
Chestertown Hist Dist—hist pl MD-2
Chestertown Hist Dist—hist pl NY-2
Chestertown Hist Dist (Boundary Increase)—hist pl MD-2
**Chester (Town of)**—pop pl CT-1
**Chester (Town of)**—pop pl ME-1
**Chester (Town of)**—pop pl MA-1
**Chester (Town of)**—pop pl NH-1
**Chester (Town of)**—pop pl (2) NY-2
**Chester (Town of)**—pop pl VT-1
**Chester (Town of)**—pop pl WI-6
Chestertown RR Station—hist pl MD-2
Chester Township—CDP PA-2
Chester Township—fmr MCD (2) IA-7
**Chester Township**—pop pl NE-7
**Chester Township**—pop pl ND-7
**Chester Township**—pop pl (2) SD-7
Chester Township District Sch No. 2—hist pl OH-6
Chester Township (historical)—civil ND-7
Chester (Township of)—fmr MCD (3) AR-4
**Chester (Township of)**—pop pl IL-6
**Chester (Township of)**—pop pl (2) IN-6
**Chester (Township of)**—pop pl (3) MI-6
**Chester (Township of)**—pop pl (2) MN-6
**Chester (Township of)**—pop pl NJ-2
**Chester (Township of)**—pop pl (5) OH-6
**Chester (Township of)**—pop pl PA-2
Chester Township (Township of)—other PA-2
**Chestervale**—pop pl IL-6
Chester Valley—basin PA-2
Chester Valley Golf Course—other PA-2
**Chester Valley Knoll**—pop pl PA-2
Chester Valley P. O. (historical)—building PA-2
Chester View Ch—church KY-4
Chester Village Cemetery—hist pl NH-1
Chester Village Hist Dist—hist pl VT-1
Chesterville—locale NJ-2
Chesterville—locale PA-2
Chesterville—locale TX-5
**Chesterville**—pop pl IL-6
**Chesterville**—pop pl IN-6
**Chesterville**—pop pl ME-1
**Chesterville**—pop pl MD-2
**Chesterville**—pop pl MS-4
**Chesterville**—pop pl OH-6
**Chesterville**—pop pl WV-2
Chesterville Baptist Ch—church MS-4
Chesterville Brick House—hist pl MD-2
*Chesterville Calvary Ch* MS-4
Chesterville Cem—cemetery MS-4
**Chesterville Forest**—pop pl MD-2
Chesterville Hill Cem—cemetery ME-1
Chesterville Line Canal—canal TX-5
Chesterville Methodist Church—hist pl OH-6
Chesterville Oil Field—oilfield TX-5
Chesterville Plantation Site—hist pl VA-3
Chesterville Post Office (historical)—building MS-4
Chesterville Ridge—ridge IN-6
Chesterville Sch—school IL-6
Chesterville Sch—school ME-1
Chesterville Sch (historical)—school MS-4
**Chesterville (Town of)**—pop pl ME-1
Chesterville United Methodist Ch—church MS-4
Chester Well—well TX-5
Chester West (CCD)—cens area SC-3
Chester Wildlife Mngmt Area—park MA-1
Chesterwood—hist pl MA-1
Chesterwood Museum—building MA-1
*Chestimacha Lake* LA-4
**Chestina Township**—pop pl ND-7
Chest Ledge—bar MA-1
Chestline—locale IL-6
Chest Neck—cape MD-2
Chest Neck Point—cape MD-2
*Chestnee Mills* TN-4
*Chestnee Mills Post Office* TN-4
Chestney Tank—reservoir TX-5
*Chestnut* NC-3
Chestnut—locale MT-8
**Chestnut**—pop pl AL-4
**Chestnut**—pop pl IL-6
**Chestnut**—pop pl LA-4
**Chestnut**—pop pl NJ-2
Chestnut—uninc pl CA-9
Chestnut Bald—summit NC-3
Chestnut Bayou—lake IN-6
Chestnut Bend—bend TX-5
**Chestnutbloom**—pop pl TN-4
**Chestnut Bluff**—pop pl TN-4
Chestnut Bluff Bridge—bridge TN-4
*Chestnut Bluff Post Office* TN-4
Chestnutbluff Post Office (historical)—building TN-4
Chestnut Bluffs—cliff VA-3
Chestnut Bluff Sch—school TN-4
*Chestnut Bluffs Post Office* TN-4
Chestnut Bottom Ch—church WV-2
Chestnut Bottom Run—stream WV-2
*Chestnut Branch* TN-4
Chestnut Branch—stream AL-4
Chestnut Branch—stream KS-7
Chestnut Branch—stream (4) KY-4
Chestnut Branch—stream MO-7
Chestnut Branch—stream NJ-2
Chestnut Branch—stream (9) NC-3
Chestnut Branch—stream (4) TN-4
Chestnut Branch—stream (3) VA-3
Chestnut Bridge Hollow—valley PA-2
Chestnut Bridge Hollow—valley TN-4
Chestnut Brook—stream (2) CT-1
Chestnutburg—locale KY-4
Chestnut Camp Branch—stream VA-3
Chestnut Camp Branch—stream WV-2
Chestnut Camp Run—stream WV-2
Chestnut Cave—cave AL-4
Chestnut Cem—cemetery MO-7
Chestnut Cem—cemetery OH-6
Chestnut Cem—cemetery (2) SC-3
Chestnut Cem—cemetery TN-4
Chestnut Cem—cemetery VA-3
Chestnut Ch—church (2) NC-3
Chestnut Ch—church VA-3
Chestnut Chapel—church KY-4
Chestnut Cliffs—cliff KY-4
Chestnut Corners—locale PA-2
Chestnut Cove—bay AL-4
Chestnut Cove—bay NH-1
Chestnut Cove—valley (2) GA-3
Chestnut Cove—valley (5) NC-3
Chestnut Cove—valley SC-3
Chestnut Cove—valley TN-4
Chestnut Cove Branch—stream KY-4
Chestnut Cove Branch—stream (2) NC-3
Chestnut Cove Creek—stream (2) NC-3
Chestnut Cove Gap—gap GA-3
Chestnut Cove Gap—gap NC-3
*Chestnut Creek* AL-4
*Chestnut Creek* VA-3
Chestnut Creek—stream AL-4
Chestnut Creek—stream FL-3
Chestnut Creek—stream GA-3
Chestnut Creek—stream (2) KY-4
Chestnut Creek—stream (2) MS-4
Chestnut Creek—stream NY-2
Chestnut Creek—stream (3) NC-3
Chestnut Creek—stream OH-6
Chestnut Creek—stream TN-4
Chestnut Creek—stream VA-3
*Chestnut Creek Baptist Church* AL-4
Chestnut Creek Cem—cemetery AL-4
Chestnut Creek Ch—church AL-4
*Chestnut Crossroads* NC-3
Chestnut Crossroads—locale PA-2
**Chestnut Crossroads**—pop pl SC-3
Chestnut Crossroads Sch—school PA-2
**Chestnut Dale**—pop pl NC-3
**Chestnut Estates**—pop pl NJ-2
Chestnut Flat—flat AL-4
Chestnut Flat—flat (2) KY-4
Chestnut Flat—flat PA-2
Chestnut Flat—flat TN-4
Chestnut Flat—flat VA-3
Chestnut Flat—flat (4) WV-2
**Chestnutflat**—pop pl GA-3
Chestnut Flat—ridge PA-2
Chestnut Flat—summit PA-2
Chestnut Flat Branch—stream (2) NC-3
Chestnut Flat Cem—cemetery WV-2
Chestnut Flat Ch—church WV-2
Chestnut Flat Cove—valley NC-3
Chestnut Flat Mtn—summit WV-2
Chestnut Flat Ridge—ridge (2) KY-4
Chestnut Flat Ridge—ridge NC-3
Chestnut Flats—flat (2) GA-3
Chestnut Flats—flat KY-4
Chestnut Flats—flat (3) NC-3
Chestnut Flats—flat (3) TN-4
Chestnut Flats—flat (3) VA-3
Chestnut Flats—flat (3) WV-2
Chestnut Flats—ridge KY-4
Chestnut Flats—ridge VA-3
Chestnut Flats—summit (2) KY-4
Chestnut Flats—summit PA-2
Chestnut Flats Branch—stream TN-4
Chestnut Flats Branch—stream WV-2
Chestnut Flats Ch—church VA-3
Chestnut Flat Sch—school KY-4
Chestnut Flats Gap—gap TN-4
Chestnut Flats Mine—mine NC-3
Chestnut Flat Spring—spring VA-3
Chestnut Flat Trail—trail PA-2
Chestnut Fork—locale VA-3
Chestnut Fork—stream IN-6
Chestnut Fork—stream KY-4
*Chestnut Gap* GA-3
Chestnut Gap—gap (2) GA-3
Chestnut Gap—gap (2) KY-4
Chestnut Gap—gap (3) NC-3
Chestnut Gap—gap PA-2
Chestnut Gap—gap TN-4
Chestnut Gap—locale GA-3
**Chestnut Gap**—pop pl KY-4
Chestnut Gap Branch—stream (2) KY-4
Chestnut Gap Branch—stream TN-4
Chestnut Gap Cem—cemetery KY-4
Chestnut Gap Mtn—summit NC-3
**Chestnut Glade**—pop pl TN-4
Chestnut Glade-Dukedom (CCD)—cens area TN-4
Chestnut Glade-Dukedom Division—civil TN-4
Chestnut Glade Sch—school TN-4
Chestnut Grove—hist pl KY-4
Chestnut Grove—locale DE-2
Chestnut Grove—locale KY-4
Chestnut Grove—locale (2) PA-2
Chestnut Grove—locale (2) TN-4
Chestnut Grove—locale VA-3
**Chestnut Grove**—pop pl AL-4
**Chestnut Grove**—pop pl (2) MD-2
**Chestnut Grove**—pop pl NC-3
**Chestnut Grove**—pop pl PA-2
**Chestnut Grove**—pop pl (6) TN-4
**Chestnut Grove**—pop pl VA-3
Chestnut Grove—woods TN-4
Chestnut Grove Annex Cem—cemetery PA-2
Chestnut Grove Baptist Ch—church MS-4
Chestnut Grove Cem—cemetery (3) AL-4
Chestnut Grove Cem—cemetery KY-4
Chestnut Grove Cem—cemetery (2) MS-4
Chestnut Grove Cem—cemetery NJ-2
Chestnut Grove Cem—cemetery NY-2
Chestnut Grove Cem—cemetery (2) OH-6
Chestnut Grove Cem—cemetery PA-2
Chestnut Grove Cem—cemetery (5) TN-4
Chestnut Grove Cem—cemetery VA-3
Chestnut Grove Cem—cemetery WV-2
Chestnut Grove Ch—church (5) AL-4
Chestnut Grove Ch—church (3) GA-3
Chestnut Grove Ch—church IN-6
Chestnut Grove Ch—church (8) KY-4
Chestnut Grove Ch—church (3) MD-2
Chestnut Grove Ch—church MS-4
Chestnut Grove Ch—church (9) NC-3
Chestnut Grove Ch—church (3) OH-6
Chestnut Grove Ch—church (3) PA-2
Chestnut Grove Ch—church (9) TN-4
Chestnut Grove Ch—church (18) VA-3
Chestnut Grove Ch—church (9) WV-2
Chestnut Grove Ch (historical)—church (2) AL-4
Chestnut Grove JHS—school NC-3
**Chestnut Grove (Laborde)**—pop pl PA-2
Chestnut Grove Landing—locale VA-3
*Chestnut Grove Methodist Ch* AL-4
Chestnut Grove Mtn—summit AL-4
Chestnut Grove Ridge—ridge KY-4
Chestnut Grove Ridge—ridge (2) TN-4
Chestnut Grove Sch—hist pl GA-3
Chestnut Grove Sch—school AL-4
Chestnut Grove Sch—school (5) KY-4
Chestnut Grove Sch—school NY-2
Chestnut Grove Sch—school (2) PA-2
Chestnut Grove Sch—school SC-3
Chestnut Grove Sch—school (3) TN-4
Chestnut Grove Sch (abandoned)—school (3) PA-2
Chestnut Grove Sch (historical)—school MO-7
Chestnut Grove Sch (historical)—school PA-2
Chestnut Grove Sch (historical)—school (6) TN-4
Chestnut Grove School—church TN-4
Chestnut Grove United Methodist Ch—church TN-4
**Chestnut Heights (Rabbit Hill)**—pop pl WV-2
*Chestnut Hill* IN-6
*Chestnut Hill* MA-1
*Chestnuthill* PA-2
*Chestnut Hill* RI-1
Chestnut Hill—locale CT-1
Chestnut Hill—locale MD-2
Chestnut Hill—locale NC-3
Chestnut Hill—locale (3) PA-2
Chestnut Hill—locale TN-4
Chestnut Hill—locale VA-3
**Chestnut Hill**—pop pl IN-6
**Chestnut Hill**—pop pl (2) MD-2
**Chestnut Hill**—pop pl NY-2
**Chestnut Hill**—pop pl NC-3
**Chestnut Hill**—pop pl (5) PA-2
**Chestnut Hill**—pop pl (3) TN-4
**Chestnut Hill**—pop pl (2) VA-3
**Chestnut Hill**—pop pl (2) WV-2
Chestnut Hill—summit (12) CT-1
Chestnut Hill—summit DE-2
Chestnut Hill—summit KY-4
Chestnut Hill—summit (2) MD-2
Chestnut Hill—summit (12) MA-1
Chestnut Hill—summit MS-4
Chestnut Hill—summit (3) NH-1
Chestnut Hill—summit (8) PA-2
Chestnut Hill—summit VT-1
Chestnut Hill, The—hist pl MA-1
Chestnut Hill Acad—school PA-2
**Chestnut Hill (Allnutt)**—pop pl VA-3
Chestnut Hill Baptist Ch—church TN-4
Chestnut Hill Brook—stream (2) CT-1
Chestnut Hill Brook—stream MA-1
Chestnut Hill (CCD)—cens area TN-4
Chestnut Hill Cem—cemetery GA-3
Chestnut Hill Cem—cemetery IN-6
Chestnut Hill Cem—cemetery (3) MA-1
Chestnut Hill Cem—cemetery NJ-2
Chestnut Hill Cem—cemetery (4) NY-2
Chestnut Hill Cem—cemetery NC-3
Chestnut Hill Cem—cemetery OH-6
Chestnut Hill Cem—cemetery (3) PA-2
Chestnut Hill Cem—cemetery TN-4
Chestnut Hill Ch—church KY-4
Chestnut Hill Ch—church (2) NC-3
Chestnut Hill Ch—church OH-6
Chestnut Hill Ch—church (3) PA-2
Chestnut Hill Ch—church SC-3
Chestnut Hill Ch—church TN-4
Chestnut Hill Ch—church (2) VA-3
Chestnut Hill Ch—church WV-2
Chestnut Hill Ch (historical)—church AL-4
Chestnut Hill Ch (historical)—church TN-4
Chestnut Hill Coll—school PA-2
Chestnut Hill Country Club—other MD-2
Chestnut Hill Division—civil TN-4
Chestnuthill Elem Sch—school PA-2
Chestnut Hill Elem Sch—school TN-4
**Chestnut Hill Estates**—pop pl DE-2
**Chestnut Hill Estates**—pop pl MD-2
Chestnut Hill Golf Course—other OH-6
Chestnut Hill Hist Dist—hist pl AL-4
Chestnut Hill Hist Dist—hist pl NC-3
Chestnut Hill Hist Dist—hist pl PA-2
Chestnut Hill (historical)—locale AL-4
Chestnut Hill (historical P.O.)—locale IN-6
Chestnut Hill Historic Distric—hist pl MA-1
Chestnut Hill JHS—school NY-2
Chestnut Hill Landing—locale VA-3
Chestnut Hill Meeting House—building MA-1
Chestnut Hill Meetinghouse—hist pl MA-1
**Chestnut Hill Meeting House**—pop pl MA-1
Chestnut Hill Park—park CT-1
Chestnut Hill Plaza—locale MA-1
Chestnut Hill Plaza (Shop Ctr)—locale DE-2
*Chestnut Hill Post Office* TN-4
Chestnuthill Post Office (historical)—building TN-4
**Chestnut Hill Ranches (subdivision)**—pop pl FL-3
Chestnut Hill Reservoir Dam—dam MA-1
Chestnut Hill Rsvr—reservoir CT-1
Chestnut Hill Rsvr—reservoir MA-1
*Chestnut Hills* PA-2
**Chestnut Hills**—pop pl (2) MD-2
**Chestnut Hills**—pop pl SC-3
**Chestnut Hills**—pop pl TN-4
Chestnut Hills—summit MA-1
Chestnut Hill Sch—school CT-1
Chestnut Hill Sch—school MD-2
Chestnut Hill Sch—school MI-6
Chestnut Hill Sch—school PA-2
Chestnut Hill Sch—school TN-4
Chestnut Hill Sch (abandoned)—school PA-2
Chestnut Hill Sch (historical)—school TN-4
**Chestnut Hills (subdivision)**—pop pl (2) NC-3
**Chestnut Hill (subdivision)**—pop pl AL-4
**Chestnut Hill (subdivision)**—pop pl MA-1
**Chestnut Hill (subdivision)**—pop pl PA-2
Chestnut Hill (Township of)—fmr MCD NC-3
**Chestnuthill (Township of)**—pop pl PA-2
Chestnut Hollow—valley KY-4
Chestnut Hollow—valley TN-4
Chestnut Hollow—valley (2) VA-3
Chestnut Hollow Branch—stream TN-4
*Chestnut Island* PA-2
Chestnut Island—island PA-2
Chestnut Junction—uninc pl CA-9
Chestnut Knob—locale VA-3
Chestnut Knob—locale WV-2
**Chestnut Knob**—pop pl WV-2
Chestnut Knob—summit (2) AL-4
Chestnut Knob—summit (5) GA-3
Chestnut Knob—summit KY-4
Chestnut Knob—summit MD-2
Chestnut Knob—summit (11) NC-3
Chestnut Knob—summit (3) TN-4
Chestnut Knob—summit (5) VA-3
Chestnut Knob—summit (3) WV-2
Chestnut Knob Branch—stream WV-2
Chestnut Knob Cem—cemetery OH-6
Chestnut Knob Fork—stream WV-2
**Chestnut Knoll**—pop pl DE-2
Chestnut Knoll—summit NY-2
*Chestnut Lake* PA-2
Chestnut Lake—lake IN-6
Chestnut Lake—lake MI-6
Chestnut Lake—reservoir PA-2
Chestnut Lake Campground—locale PA-2
Chestnut Lakes—lake IN-6
Chestnut Landing—locale AL-4
Chestnut Lands—forest CT-1
Chestnut Lawn Cem—cemetery NY-2
Chestnut Lead—ridge GA-3
Chestnut Level—locale VA-3
**Chestnut Level**—pop pl PA-2
**Chestnut Level**—pop pl VA-3
Chestnut Level—ridge VA-3
Chestnut Level Ch—church OH-6
Chestnut Level Ch—church VA-3
Chestnut Level Post Office (historical)—building PA-2
Chestnut Level Ridge—ridge KY-4
Chestnut Levels—flat VA-3
Chestnut Level Sch—school KY-4
Chestnut Lick—stream VA-3
Chestnut Lick Branch—stream KY-4
*Chestnut Lick Hollow* VA-3
Chestnut Lick Hollow—valley VA-3
*Chestnutlick Run* WV-2
Chestnut Lick Run—stream WV-2
Chestnutlick Run—stream WV-2
Chestnutlick Run Ch—church WV-2
Chestnut Lodge—locale AL-4
Chestnut Log Branch—stream (2) KY-4
Chestnut Log Branch—stream (2) NC-3
Chestnut Log Branch—stream WV-2
*Chestnut Log Cemetery* MS-4
Chestnut Log Gap—gap KY-4
Chestnutlog Gap—gap NC-3
Chestnut Log Gap—gap NC-3
Chestnutlog Gap—gap TN-4
Chestnut Log Hollow—valley WV-2
Chestnut Memorial Cem—cemetery OH-6
Chestnut Mine—mine NV-8
**Chestnut Mound**—pop pl TN-4
Chestnut Mound Ch—church TN-4
Chestnut Mound Post Office—building TN-4
Chestnut Mound Sch (historical)—school (2) TN-4
**Chestnut Mountain**—pop pl GA-3
Chestnut Mountain—ridge GA-3
Chestnut Mountain Ch—church WV-2
*Chestnut Mountains* VA-3
Chestnut Mountain Sch—school WV-2
Chestnut Mountain Trail—trail (2) TN-4
Chestnut Mtn—summit (2) CT-1
Chestnut Mtn—summit (4) GA-3
Chestnut Mtn—summit KY-4
Chestnut Mtn—summit MA-1
Chestnut Mtn—summit MT-8
Chestnut Mtn—summit (24) NC-3
Chestnut Mtn—summit PA-2
Chestnut Mtn—summit SC-3
Chestnut Mtn—summit (8) TN-4
Chestnut Mtn—summit (6) VA-3
Chestnut Mtn—summit WV-2
Chestnut Neck—cape NJ-2
Chestnut Neck Battle Monmt—park NJ-2
Chestnut Oak Cem—cemetery KY-4
Chestnut Oak Creek—stream WV-2
Chestnut Oak Flats—flat NC-3
Chestnut Oak Knob—summit OH-6
Chestnut Oak Knob—summit VA-3
Chestnut Oak Mtn—summit KY-4
Chestnut Oak Ridge—ridge KY-4
Chestnut Oak Ridge—ridge NC-3
Chestnut Oak Ridge—ridge (2) TN-4
Chestnut Oak Ridge—ridge WV-2
**Chestnut Orchard**—pop pl TN-4
Chestnut Orchard Branch—stream (2) NC-3
*Chestnut Orchard Hollow* PA-2
Chestnut Orchard Hollow—valley TN-4
Chestnut Orchard Ridge—ridge NC-3
Chestnut Park—park CA-9
**Chestnut Park Subdivision**—pop pl UT-8
Chestnut Pit—cave AL-4
**Chestnut Place Condo**—pop pl UT-8
Chestnut P.O. (historical)—locale AL-4
Chestnut Point—cape KY-4
Chestnut Point—cape NJ-2
Chestnut Point—cape VA-3
Chestnut Point—cliff WV-2
Chestnut Point Sch—school KY-4
Chestnut Pond—lake NH-1
Chestnut Pond—reservoir NC-3
*Chestnut Ridge* GA-3
*Chestnut Ridge* PA-2
*Chestnut Ridge* TN-4
*Chestnut Ridge* VA-3
Chestnut Ridge—hist pl MD-2
Chestnutridge—locale MO-7
Chestnut Ridge—locale NJ-2
Chestnut Ridge—locale (2) TN-4
**Chestnut Ridge**—pop pl IN-6
**Chestnut Ridge**—pop pl (2) MD-2
**Chestnut Ridge**—pop pl (3) NY-2
**Chestnut Ridge**—pop pl (2) PA-2
**Chestnut Ridge**—pop pl TN-4
**Chestnutridge**—pop pl TN-4
**Chestnut Ridge**—pop pl (3) TN-4
**Chestnut Ridge**—pop pl WV-2
Chestnut Ridge—ridge (3) AL-4
Chestnut Ridge—ridge GA-3
Chestnut Ridge—ridge (2) KY-4
Chestnut Ridge—ridge MD-2
Chestnut Ridge—ridge MS-4
Chestnut Ridge—ridge MO-7
Chestnut Ridge—ridge (3) NY-2
Chestnut Ridge—ridge (16) NC-3
Chestnut Ridge—ridge (4) OH-6
Chestnut Ridge—ridge (14) PA-2
Chestnut Ridge—ridge (2) SC-3
Chestnut Ridge—ridge (27) TN-4
Chestnut Ridge—ridge (23) VA-3
Chestnut Ridge—ridge (9) WV-2
Chestnut Ridge—summit NY-2
Chestnut Ridge—summit VA-3
**Chestnut Ridge Acres**—pop pl PA-2
Chestnut Ridge Camp—locale PA-2
Chestnut Ridge Cem—cemetery AL-4
Chestnut Ridge Cem—cemetery IN-6
Chestnut Ridge Cem—cemetery MO-7
Chestnut Ridge Cem—cemetery NY-2
Chestnut Ridge Cem—cemetery (2) PA-2
Chestnut Ridge Ch—church KY-4
Chestnut Ridge Ch—church MS-4
Chestnut Ridge Ch—church (3) NC-3
Chestnut Ridge Ch—church (2) OH-6
Chestnut Ridge Ch—church (2) SC-3
Chestnut Ridge Ch—church (3) TN-4
Chestnut Ridge Ch—church VA-3
Chestnut Ridge Ch—church WV-2
Chestnut Ridge Creek—stream NC-3
*Chestnut Ridge Divide* NC-3
Chestnut Ridge Form—hist pl OH-6
Chestnut Ridge Golf Course—locale PA-2
Chestnut Ridge HS—school PA-2
Chestnut Ridge Meetinghouse—locale OH-6
Chestnut Ridge Park—park GA-3
Chestnut Ridge Park—park NY-2
Chestnut Ridge Park—park (2) OH-6
Chestnut Ridge Park—park TN-4
Chestnut Ridge Pond—lake NY-2
*Chestnut Ridge Post Office* TN-4
Chestnutridge Post Office (historical)—building TN-4
Chestnut Ridge Rsvr—reservoir CT-1
Chestnut Ridge Run—stream MD-2
Chestnut Ridge Sch—school KY-4
Chestnut Ridge Sch—school MS-4
Chestnut Ridge Sch—school MO-7
Chestnut Ridge Sch—school NY-2
Chestnut Ridge Sch—school OH-6
Chestnut Ridge Sch—school (2) PA-2
Chestnut Ridge Sch—school TN-4
Chestnut Ridge Sch—school WV-2
Chestnut Ridge Sch (abandoned)—school (3) PA-2
Chestnut Ridge Sch (historical)—school AL-4
Chestnut Ridge Sch (historical)—school MS-4
Chestnut Ridge Trail—trail VA-3
Chestnut Ridge Trail—trail WV-2
Chestnut Rsvr—reservoir CO-8
Chestnut Run—stream DE-2
Chestnut Run—stream MA-1
Chestnut Run—stream (2) NJ-2
Chestnut Run—stream (2) PA-2
Chestnut Run—stream VA-3
Chestnut Run—stream (3) WV-2
Chestnut Run Helistop—airport DE-2
Chestnut Sag—gap VA-3
Chestnut Saint Sch—school PA-2
Chestnut Sch—school IN-6
Chestnut Sch—school NC-3
Chestnut Sch—school (4) OH-6
Chestnut Sch—school PA-2
Chestnut Sch—school WI-6
Chestnut Sch (abandoned)—school PA-2
Chestnut Sch (historical)—school TN-4

Chestnut Spring—spring ... OR-9
Chestnut Spring—spring (2) ... PA-2
Chestnut Spring—spring ... TN-4
Chestnut Springs—locale ... SC-3
Chestnut Springs Sch—school ... MS-4
Chestnut Spring Trail—trail ... PA-2
Chestnut Stand Sch—school ... KY-4
Chestnut Stomp Knob—summit ... NC-3
Chestnut Street ... IL-6
Chestnut Street Adult Education Center—school ... TN-4
Chestnut Street Baptist Church—hist pl ... KY-4
Chestnut Street District—hist pl ... MA-1
Chestnut Street District (Boundary Increase)—hist pl ... MA-1
Chestnut Street Elem Sch—school ... PA-2
Chestnut Street Hist Dist—hist pl ... NY-2
Chestnut Street JHS—school ... NC-3
Chestnut Street Log House—hist pl ... PA-2
Chestnut Street Methodist Church—hist pl ... KY-4
Chestnut Street Methodist Church—hist pl ... ME-1
Chestnut Street Sch—school (2) ... NY-2
Chestnut Stump Ridge—ridge ... TN-4
**Chestnut Subdivision**—pop pl ... MS-4
Chestnut Top—summit ... GA-3
Chestnut Top—summit ... NC-3
Chestnut Top—summit ... TN-4
Chestnut Top Lead—summit ... TN-4
**Chestnut (Township of)**—pop pl ... IL-6
Chestnut Park—park ... AZ-5
Chestnut Trail—trail (2) ... PA-2
**Chestnut Trails (subdivision)**—pop pl ... NC-3
Chestnut Tree Cem—cemetery ... MA-1
Chestnut Valley—locale ... TN-4
Chestnut Valley—valley ... MT-8
Chestnut Valley—valley ... TN-4
Chestnut Valley Canal—canal ... MT-8
Chestnut Valley Cem—cemetery ... MT-8
Chestnut Valley Ironworks ... TN-4
Chestnut Valley Sch (historical)—school ... TN-4
**Chestnut View**—pop pl ... PA-2
Chestnutwold Sch—school ... PA-2
Chestnutwood Mtn—summit ... NC-3
Chestnut Woods—woods ... NY-2
Chestnut Yard—locale ... VA-3
**Chestnut Yard (Monarat)**—pop pl ... VA-3
Chestoa—locale ... TN-4
Chestoa Post Office (historical)—building ... TN-4
Chestoa Sch—school ... TN-4
Cheston, Lake—reservoir (2) ... TN-4
Cheston Creek ... MD-2
Cheston Creek—bay ... MD-2
Cheston Creek Marshes—swamp ... MD-2
Cheston Dam—dam ... TN-4
Chestonia—locale ... MI-6
Chestonia Bridge—other ... MI-6
**Chestonia (Township of)**—pop pl ... MI-6
Cheston Marsh—swamp ... MD-2
Cheston Point—cape ... MD-2
Cheston Point Marsh—swamp ... MD-2
Cheston Robbins Park—park ... PA-2
Chest Park Mini Mall—locale ... PA-2
Chestro Township ... ND-7
Chest Spring Run ... PA-2
**Chest Springs**—pop pl ... PA-2
Chest Springs Borough—civil ... PA-2
**Chest (Township of)**—pop pl (2) ... PA-2
**Chestua**—pop pl ... TN-4
Chestua Baptist Ch—church ... TN-4
Chestua Cem—cemetery ... TN-4
Chestua Mills ... TN-4
Chestuee—locale (3) ... TN-4
**Chestuee**—pop pl ... TN-4
Chestuee Baptist Church ... TN-4
Chestuee Cem—cemetery (2) ... TN-4
Chestuee Ch—church (3) ... TN-4
Chestuee Creek—stream ... TN-4
Chestuee Golf and Country Club—locale ... TN-4
Chestuee Mills (historical)—locale ... TN-4
Chestuee Mills Post Office (historical)—building ... TN-4
Chestwick ... PA-2
Che-Suido ... MP-9
**Chesuncook**—pop pl ... ME-1
Chesuncook Dam—locale ... ME-1
Chesuncook Lake—lake ... ME-1
Chesuncook Pond—lake ... ME-1
Chesuncook Stream—stream ... ME-1
Chesuncook (Township of)—unorg ... ME-1
Chesuncook Village ... ME-1
Chesuncook Village—hist pl ... ME-1
Cheswell Cem—cemetery ... NH-1
**Cheswick**—pop pl ... PA-2
Cheswick Borough—civil ... PA-2
**Cheswold**—pop pl ... DE-2
**Cheswolde**—pop pl ... MD-2
Chetac, Lake—lake ... OH-6
Chetac, Lake—lake ... WI-6
Chetaslina Glacier—glacier ... AK-9
Chetaslina River—stream ... AK-9
Chetco—locale ... OR-9
Chetco Bar—bar ... OR-9
Chetco Cove—bay ... OR-9
Chetco Divide Trail—trail ... OR-9
**Chetco (historical)**—pop pl ... OR-9
Chetco Lake—lake ... OR-9
Chetco Lookout (historical)—locale ... OR-9
Chetco Pass—gap ... OR-9
Chetco Pass Creek—stream ... OR-9
Chetco Peak ... OR-9
Chetco Peak—summit ... OR-9
Chetco Peak Trail (jeep)—trail ... OR-9
Chetco Point—cape ... OR-9
Chetco River—stream ... OR-9
**Chetco (Sanders)**—pop pl ... AZ-5
Chetco Slough—stream ... OR-9
Chet Creek—stream ... ID-8
Chetebutebu-suido ... MP-9
Chetebutebu-to ... MP-9
Chetek ... SD-7
**Chetek**—pop pl ... WI-6
Chetek, Lake—lake ... WI-6
Chetek River—stream ... WI-6
**Chetek (Town of)**—pop pl ... WI-6
Chetemacha Lake ... LA-4
Chetenham Sch—school ... CO-8
**Chethams (historical)**—pop pl ... MS-4
Chet Harritt Dam—dam ... CA-9
Chetimachas Lake ... LA-4
Chetko Point ... OR-9
Chetko River ... OR-9
Chetlechak Island—island ... AK-9
Chetlo, Lake—lake ... OR-9
Chetlo Harbor—bay ... WA-9
Che-to ... MP-9
Chetocric Swamp—stream ... VA-3
Chetolah—hist pl ... NY-2
Chetolah Creek—stream ... KS-7
Chetola Lake—reservoir ... NC-3
Chetola Lake Dam—dam ... NC-3
Chetomba Creek—stream ... MN-6
Chetonia Creek—stream ... OK-5
Chetonia Lake ... WI-6
Chetoogeta Mountain Tunnel—tunnel ... GA-3
**Chetopa**—pop pl ... AL-4
**Chetopa**—pop pl ... KS-7
Chetopa Creek ... KS-7
Chetopa Creek—stream (2) ... KS-7
Chetopa Mine - Impoundment Number 2—dam ... AL-4
Chetopa Mine - Impoundment Number 2—reservoir ... AL-4
**Chetopa Township**—pop pl (2) ... KS-7
Chetremon Golf Course—locale ... PA-2
Chet Rowe Spring—spring ... ID-8
Chetsea Cemeteries—cemetery ... WI-6
Chet Spring—spring ... AZ-5
Chet Springs—spring ... NM-5
Chet Tank—reservoir ... AZ-5
Chettle Lake—lake ... OH-6
Chettro Kettle Ruins—locale ... NM-5
Chetwood Cabin—locale ... CA-9
Chetwood Creek—stream ... CA-9
Chetwoot Lake—lake ... WA-9
Chetwot Creek—stream ... WA-9
**Chetwynd**—pop pl ... IN-6
Chetzemolka Park—park ... WA-9
Cheuetto Spring—spring ... NV-8
Cheukochatte ... FL-3
Cheur, Tooch Ra—gut ... PW-9
**Chevak**—pop pl ... AK-9
Chevalier, Xavier, House—hist pl ... NY-2
Chevalier Woods—woods ... IL-6
Cheval Island—island ... AK-9
Cheval Lake—lake ... OR-9
**Chevalle**—pop pl ... VA-3
Chevallier Cem—cemetery ... LA-4
Chevallier Ranch—locale ... MT-8
Chevally Rsvr—reservoir ... OR-9
Cheval Narrows—channel ... AK-9
Chevalons Butte ... AZ-5
Chevaux de Frise Ch—church ... WV-2
Chevaux de Frise Run—stream ... WV-2
Chevee, Bayou—gut ... LA-4
Chevelier Bay—bay ... FL-3
Chevelier Point—cape ... FL-3
Chevellons Butte ... AZ-5
**Chevelon**—pop pl ... AZ-5
Chevelon Butte—summit ... AZ-5
Chevelon Butte Sch—school ... AZ-5
Chevelon Butte Tank—reservoir ... AZ-5
Chevelon Canyon—valley ... AZ-5
Chevelon Canyon Campground—park ... AZ-5
Chevelon Canyon Dam—dam ... AZ-5
Chevelon Canyon Lake—reservoir ... AZ-5
Chevelon Creek—stream ... AZ-5
Chevelon Creek Bridge—hist pl ... AZ-5
Chevelon Crossing—locale ... AZ-5
Chevelon Lake Campground—park ... AZ-5
Chevelon Ranger Station—locale ... AZ-5
Chevelon Ridge—ridge ... AZ-5
Chevelon Ridge Truck Trail—trail ... AZ-5
Chevelon Ruin—hist pl ... AZ-5
Chevelons Butte ... AZ-5
Chevelon Tank—reservoir ... AZ-5
Chevelous Fork ... AZ-5
Chevere Sch—school ... MN-6
**Cheverly**—pop pl ... MD-2
Cheverly Community Park—park ... MD-2
Cheverly Local Park—park ... MD-2
**Cheverly Manor**—pop pl ... MD-2
Chever Park—park ... OH-6
Cheverus HS—school ... ME-1
Cheverus Sch—school ... MA-1
Cheves Creek—stream ... SC-3
Chevey Chase—locale ... LA-4
Cheviers—locale ... MI-6
Chevington Draw ... WY-8
Cheviot—locale ... WA-9
**Cheviot**—pop pl ... NY-2
**Cheviot**—pop pl ... OH-6
Cheviot Creek—stream ... OR-9
Cheviot Hills Recreation Center—park ... CA-9
Cheviot (Township of)—other ... OH-6
Chevlon Creek ... AZ-5
Chevlon Fork ... AZ-5
Chevo, Mount—summit ... WY-8
Chevra Ahavas Chesed Cem—cemetery ... MD-2
Chevra Tilum Cem—cemetery ... MA-1
Chevreau, Bayou—gut (2) ... LA-4
Chevreuil, Bayou—channel ... LA-4
Chevreuil, Bayou—gut ... LA-4
Chevreuil, Bayou—stream (2) ... LA-4
Chevreuil, Point—cape ... LA-4
Chevreuille Bayou—stream ... LA-4
**Chevrolet**—pop pl ... KY-4
Chevrolet Motor Division, General Motors Corporation—facility ... KY-4
Chevron—locale ... KS-7
Chevron Chemical Company—facility ... OH-6
Chevron Hill—summit ... AK-9
Chevron Ridge—ridge ... UT-8
Chev Spring—spring ... OR-9
Chevy Chase—CDP ... MD-2
**Chevy Chase**—pop pl ... KY-4
**Chevy Chase**—pop pl ... MD-2
Chevy Chase Circle—locale ... DC-2
Chevy Chase Circle—locale ... MD-2
Chevy Chase Country Club—other ... MD-2
**Chevy Chase Gardens**—pop pl ... MD-2
Chevy Chase Golf Club—other ... IL-6
Chevy Chase Golf Course—other ... CA-9
**Chevy Chase Heights**—pop pl ... PA-2
**Chevy Chase Lake**—pop pl ... MD-2
**Chevy Chase Manor**—pop pl ... MD-2
Chevy Chase Sch—school ... MD-2
**Chevy Chase Section Five**—pop pl ... MD-2
Chevy Chase Section Four ... MD-2
**Chevy Chase Section Three**—pop pl ... MD-2
**Chevy Chase Section 4**—pop pl ... MD-2
**Chevy Chase Subdivision**—pop pl ... UT-8
**Chevy Chase Terrace**—pop pl ... MD-2
**Chevy Chase View**—pop pl ... MD-2
**Chevy Chase Village**—pop pl ... MD-2
Chevy Hill—summit ... NH-1
Chew—locale ... WA-9
Chew, Jesse, House—hist pl ... NJ-2
Chew, Rial, Ranch Complex—hist pl ... CO-8
Chewach Creek ... WA-9
Chewack Campground—locale ... WA-9
Chewack Creek ... WA-9
Chewack Falls—falls ... WA-9
Chewack River ... WA-9
Chewacla—locale ... AL-4
Chewacla Creek—stream ... AL-4
Chewacla Lake ... AL-4
Chewacla Lime Works (historical)—mine ... AL-4
Chewacla State Park—park ... AL-4
Chewacla State Park Dam—dam ... AL-4
Chewacla State Park Lake—reservoir ... AL-4
Chewah Creek ... MS-4
Chewakala ... AL-4
**Chewalla**—pop pl ... TN-4
Chewalla Baptist Ch—church ... TN-4
Chewalla Baptist Church ... MS-4
Chewalla Cem ... MS-4
Chewalla Cem—cemetery ... MS-4
Chewalla Ch—church (2) ... MS-4
Chewalla Creek—stream ... AL-4
Chewalla Creek—stream ... MS-4
Chewalla Lake—reservoir (2) ... MS-4
Chewalla Marina—other ... AL-4
Chewalla Organization Camp—locale ... MS-4
**Chewalla Park**—pop pl ... NJ-2
Chewalla Post Office—building ... TN-4
Chewalla Primitive Baptist Church ... MS-4
Chewalla Rec Area—park ... MS-4
Chewalla Sch (historical)—school ... TN-4
**Chewalla (subdivision)**—pop pl ... AL-4
Chewallee River ... AL-4
Chewallee River ... TN-4
Chewana Post Office (historical)—building ... MS-4
**Chewaucan (historical)**—pop pl ... OR-9
Chewaucan River—stream ... OR-9
Chewawah Creek—stream ... MS-4
Chew Creek—stream ... MD-2
Chew Creek—stream ... MS-4
Chewed Nose Springs—spring ... AZ-5
Cheweka Creek—stream ... WA-9
**Chewelah**—pop pl ... WA-9
Chewelah (CCD)—cens area ... WA-9
Chewelah Creek ... WA-9
Chewelah Creek—stream ... WA-9
Chewelah Lake—lake ... WI-6
Chewelah Mtn—summit ... WA-9
Chewelah Peak ... WA-9
Chewelah Silver Mine—mine ... WA-9
Chewelah Standard Mine—mine ... WA-9
Chewey—locale ... OK-5
Chewford Creek—stream ... KY-4
Chew House—building ... PA-2
Chewiliken Creek—stream ... WA-9
Chewiliken Sch—school ... WA-9
Chewiliken Valley—valley ... WA-9
Chewing Blackbones Campground—locale ... MT-8
Chewing Gum Cove—valley ... NC-3
Chewing Gum Lake—lake ... CA-9
**Chewings Corner**—pop pl ... VA-3
Chewink Cem—cemetery ... CT-1
Chew Lake—reservoir ... IN-6
Chew Lake Dam—dam ... IN-6
Chew Mill Creek—stream ... GA-3
Chew Millpond—lake ... GA-3
Chewning Cem—cemetery ... WV-2
Chewning House—hist pl ... KY-4
Chewning JHS—school ... NC-3
Chewnings Corner—locale ... VA-3
Chewockeleehatchee Creek ... AL-4
Chewockleehatchee Creek ... AL-4
Chewonki Creek—stream ... ME-1
Chewonki Neck—cape ... ME-1
Chew Playground—park ... MA-1
Chew Pond—lake ... IN-6
Chew-Powell House—hist pl ... NJ-2
Chew Ranch—locale ... CO-8
**Chew Road**—pop pl ... NJ-2
**Chews**—pop pl ... NJ-2
Chews Lake—lake ... MD-2
Chews Landing ... NJ-2
**Chews Landing (Chews)**—pop pl ... NJ-2
Chews Landing (historical)—locale ... MS-4
Chews Memorial Ch—church ... MD-2
Chews Ridge—ridge ... CA-9
Chews Ridge Ranger Station—locale ... CA-9
Chews Sch—school ... NJ-2
**Chewsville**—pop pl (2) ... MD-2
**Chewton**—pop pl ... PA-2
Chewuch Canal—canal ... WA-9
Che-wuch Creek ... WA-9
Chewuch River—stream ... WA-9
Chewuck Creek ... WA-9
Cheyally Dam—dam ... OR-9
Cheyarha Ch—church ... OK-5
Cheyava Falls—falls ... AZ-5
Cheyene ... ND-7
Cheyenne—locale ... KS-7
**Cheyenne**—pop pl ... OK-5
**Cheyenne**—pop pl ... TX-5
**Cheyenne**—pop pl ... WY-8
Cheyenne-Black Hills Stage Route and Rawhide Buttes and Running Water Stage Stations—hist pl ... WY-8
Cheyenne Bottoms—bend ... KS-7
Cheyenne Bottoms State Waterfowl Mngmt Area ... KS-7
Cheyenne Bottoms Wildlife Area—park ... KS-7
Cheyenne Butte—summit ... OK-5
**Cheyenne Canon**—pop pl ... CO-8
Cheyenne Canyon—valley ... NE-7
Cheyenne (CCD)—cens area ... OK-5
Cheyenne Cem—cemetery ... KS-7
Cheyenne Ch—church ... KS-7
Cheyenne Country Club—other ... WY-8
Cheyenne County—civil ... KS-7
Cheyenne County Fairgrounds—locale ... KS-7
Cheyenne County Jail—hist pl ... CO-8
Cheyenne County Municipal Airp—airport ... KS-7
Cheyenne Creek ... KS-7
Cheyenne Creek ... SD-7
Cheyenne Creek—stream (2) ... AK-9
Cheyenne Creek—stream (2) ... CO-8
Cheyenne Creek—stream (4) ... KS-7
Cheyenne Creek—stream (2) ... OK-5
Cheyenne Creek—stream ... SD-7
Cheyenne Creek—stream ... TX-5
**Cheyenne Crossing**—pop pl ... SD-7
Cheyenne Ditch—canal ... MT-8
Cheyenne Draw—valley ... TX-5
Cheyenne East—cens area ... WY-8
Cheyenne Farms—locale ... TX-5
Cheyenne Feeders Landing Strip—airport ... SD-7
Cheyenne Gap—locale ... KS-7
Cheyenne Island ... SD-7
Cheyenne Lake—lake ... NE-7
Cheyenne Lake—lake ... TX-5
Cheyenne Lode Mine—mine ... SD-7
Cheyenne Lookout—summit ... CO-8
Cheyenne Memorial Gardens—cemetery ... WY-8
Cheyenne Mountain—cens area ... CO-8
Cheyenne Mountain Complex—military ... CO-8
Cheyenne Mountain HS—school ... CO-8
Cheyenne Mountain Lodge—locale ... CO-8
Cheyenne Mountain Zoo—other ... CO-8
Cheyenne Mtn—summit ... CO-8
Cheyenne Municipal Airport—airport ... WY-8
Cheyenne No. 21 Township—civ div ... SD-7
Cheyenne Oil Field—oilfield ... CO-8
Cheyenne Park—park ... IA-7
Cheyenne Pass—gap ... WY-8
Cheyenne Pit ... SD-7
Cheyenne Playground—park ... OK-5
Cheyenne Point—cape ... MI-6
Cheyenne Ridge—ridge ... WY-8
Cheyenne River—stream (2) ... SD-7
Cheyenne River—stream ... WY-8
Cheyenne River Agencies I and II (historical)—locale ... SD-7
Cheyenne River Divide—ridge ... WY-8
Cheyenne River Draw—valley ... WY-8
Cheyenne River Indian Agency (historical)—locale ... SD-7
**Cheyenne River Ind Res**—pop pl ... SD-7
Cheyenne River Post II (historical)—locale ... SD-7
Cheyenne River Sch—school (2) ... WY-8
Cheyenne Rsvr—reservoir ... MT-8
Cheyenne Sch—school ... KS-7
Cheyenne Spring—spring ... TX-5
Cheyenne Spring—spring ... WY-8
**Cheyenne Township**—pop pl (2) ... KS-7
**Cheyenne Township**—pop pl ... SD-7
Cheyenne Valley—locale ... OK-5
Cheyenne Valley—valley ... WI-6
Cheyenne Valley Cem—cemetery ... OK-5
Cheyenne Valley Ch—church ... OK-5
Cheyenne Valley Oil Field—oilfield ... OK-5
Cheyenne Valley Sch—school ... KS-7
Cheyenne View Sch—school ... KS-7
**Cheyenne Village (subdivision)**—pop pl (2) ... AZ-5
**Cheyenne Wells**—pop pl ... CO-8
Cheyenne West—cens area ... WY-8
Cheyikdilukes ... PW-9
Cheyney—locale ... PA-2
Cheyney, John, Log Tenant House and Farm—hist pl ... PA-2
Cheyney Clow's Rebellion, Scene of—hist pl ... DE-2
Cheyney Lake—lake ... AZ-5
Cheyney Shops ... PA-2
Cheyney State College ... PA-2
Cheyney Station—building ... PA-2
Cheyney Univ of Pennsylvania—school ... PA-2
Chezhin Chotah Butte—summit ... AZ-5
Chezhin dez-a Mesa ... AZ-5
Chezhindeza Mesa—summit ... AZ-5
Chgelley Canyon ... AZ-5
C H Head Lake Dam—dam ... AL-4
Chia Canyon—valley ... AZ-5
Chiachi Bay—bay ... AK-9
Chiachi Island—island ... AK-9
Chiachi Islands—island ... AK-9
Chiachi Point—cape ... AK-9
Chiaha (historical)—locale ... AL-4
Chiakan Brook ... MA-1
Chiaktuak Creek—stream ... AK-9
Chiamon Bayou—stream ... TX-5
Chiangel ... PW-9
Chianti—locale ... CA-9
**Chiapuk**—pop pl ... AZ-5
Chiaramonte Elem Sch—school ... FL-3
Chiaramonte Mine—mine ... NM-5
Chiara Ranch ... NV-8
Chiasson—locale ... LA-4
Chiatovich Creek ... NV-8
Chiatovich Creek—stream ... NV-8
Chiatovich Flats—flat ... CA-9
Chiavria Point—cliff ... AZ-5
Chiawana Park—park ... WA-9
Chiawuli Tak—locale ... AZ-5
Chibachewesa Island ... RI-1
Chibackuweset Island ... RI-1
Chibacowoda Island ... RI-1
Chibahdehl Rocks—bar ... WA-9
Chibanbehl Rocks ... WA-9
Chibujateitei—island ... MP-9
Chibujateitei Island ... MP-9
Chibujateitei-To ... MP-9
Chibukak Point—cape ... AK-9
Chiburimen ... MP-9
Chiburimen-to ... MP-9
Chiburon Island ... MP-9
Chic—locale ... TN-4
Chicachae ... MS-4
Chicachas ... AL-4
Chicacomico River ... MD-2
Chicacoan Creek ... MD-2
Chicadee Cabin—locale ... ID-8
Chicago—fmr MCD ... NE-7
Chicago—locale ... WI-6
Chicago—other ... KY-4
**Chicago**—pop pl ... IL-6
Chicago, Burlington, and Quincy RR Depot—hist pl ... IL-6
Chicago, Burlington, & Quincy Roundhouse and Locomotive Shop—hist pl ... IL-6
Chicago, Burlington and Quincy Depot—hist pl ... MO-7
Chicago, Burlington and Quincy Railroad-Creston Station—hist pl ... IA-7
Chicago, Burlington & Quincy RR Depot—hist pl ... IL-6
Chicago, Milwaukee, and St. Paul Depot—hist pl ... MN-6
Chicago, Milwaukee, and St. Paul Railroad-Grafton Station—hist pl ... IA-7
Chicago, Milwaukee, and St. Paul RR Depot—hist pl ... SD-7
Chicago, Milwaukee, St. Paul, and Pacific Depot—hist pl ... MN-6
Chicago, Milwaukee, St. Paul and Pacific Depot—hist pl (2) ... MN-6
Chicago, Milwaukee, St. Paul and Pacific Depot, Freight House and—hist pl ... MN-6
Chicago, Milwaukee, St. Paul and Pacific Depot and Lunchroom—hist pl ... MN-6
Chicago, Milwaukee, St. Paul and Pacific Freight House—hist pl ... IA-7
Chicago, Milwaukee, St. Paul and Pacific RR Company Depot—hist pl ... IA-7
Chicago, Milwaukee, St. Paul and Pacific RR Depot—hist pl ... MN-6
Chicago, Milwaukee, St. Paul and Pacific RR Depot—hist pl ... SD-7
Chicago, Milwaukee, St. Paul and Pacific RR Station—hist pl ... MI-6
Chicago, Milwaukee and Pacific Railroad-Albert City Station—hist pl ... IA-7
Chicago, Milwaukee and St. Paul Depot—hist pl ... MN-6
Chicago, Milwaukee and St. Paul Depot—hist pl ... SD-7
Chicago, Milwaukee and St. Paul Freight House—hist pl ... MN-6
Chicago, Milwaukee and St. Paul Passenger Depot—hist pl ... MT-8
Chicago, Rock Island, and Pacific RR Depot—hist pl ... AR-4
Chicago, Rock Island and Pacific Railroad-Grinnell Passenger Station—hist pl ... IA-7
Chicago,Rock Island and Pacific Railroad: Stuart Passenger Station—hist pl ... IA-7
Chicago, Rock Island and Pacific Railroad-Wilton Depot—hist pl ... IA-7
Chicago, Rock Island and Pacific RR Passenger Station—hist pl ... IA-7
**Chicago, Rock Island & Pacific Junction**—pop pl ... AR-4
Chicago, St. Paul, Minneapolis, and Omaha Depot—hist pl ... MN-6
Chicago, St. Paul, Minneapolis and Omaha RR Car Shop Hist Dist—hist pl ... WI-6
Chicago, St. Paul, Minneapolis & Omaha RR Depot—hist pl ... WI-6
Chicago and Alton Depot—hist pl ... MO-7
Chicago and Alton RR Depot at Higginsville—hist pl ... MO-7
Chicago and Eastern Illinois RR Depot—hist pl ... IL-6
Chicago and Northwestern Depot—hist pl (2) ... IL-6
Chicago and Northwestern Depot—hist pl ... SD-7
Chicago and North Western Depot—hist pl ... WI-6
Chicago and Northwestern RR Depot—hist pl ... MI-6
Chicago and North Western RR Depot—hist pl (2) ... MN-6
Chicago and Northwestern RR Depot—hist pl (2) ... SD-7
Chicago and Northwestern RR Depot—hist pl ... WY-8
Chicago and North Western Section House—hist pl ... MN-6
Chicago And Northwestern Station—locale ... IL-6
Chicago And North Western Station—locale ... WI-6
Chicago and Northwest RR Passenger Station—hist pl ... WI-6
Chicago Apartments—hist pl ... MO-7
Chicago Avenue ... IN-6
Chicago Ave Water Tower and Pumping Station—hist pl ... IL-6
Chicago Bosin—basin ... CO-8
Chicago Bay ... MN-6
Chicago Bay—bay ... MN-6
Chicago Bay—bay ... WI-6
**Chicago Bay**—pop pl ... MN-6
Chicago Beach Hotel—hist pl ... IL-6
Chicago Bee Bldg—hist pl ... IL-6
Chicago Blvd Playground—locale ... MI-6
Chicago Board of Trade Bldg—hist pl ... IL-6
Chicago Bogs—flat ... CO-8
Chicago Boy Creek—stream ... AK-9
Chicago Boys Club Camp—park ... IN-6
Chicago Branch—stream ... MS-4
Chicago Bridge and Iron Company—facility ... IL-6
Chicago Cabin—locale ... OR-9
Chicago Camp—locale ... CA-9
Chicago Camp—locale ... WA-9
Chicago Christian HS—school ... IL-6
Chicago Corner Ch—church ... IN-6
**Chicago Corners**—pop pl ... WI-6
Chicago Creek—locale ... AK-9
Chicago Creek—stream (2) ... AK-9
Chicago Creek—stream ... CA-9
Chicago Creek—stream ... CO-8
Chicago Creek—stream ... MT-8
Chicago Creek—stream ... OR-9
Chicago Creek—stream ... WI-6
Chicago Creek—stream ... WY-8
Chicago Creek Reservoir ... CO-8
Chicago Ditch—canal ... CO-8
Chicago Golden Crown Lake ... WA-9
Chicago Great Western Depot—hist pl ... MN-6
Chicago Great Western Junction ... IL-6
Chicago Gulch—valley ... AK-9
Chicago Gulch—valley ... CO-8
Chicago Gulch—valley ... MT-8
Chicago Gulch—valley ... SD-7
Chicago Harbor—bay ... AK-9
Chicago Harbor—bay ... IL-6
Chicago Harbor Lighthouse—hist pl ... IL-6
**Chicago Heights**—pop pl ... IL-6
Chicago Heights Country Club—other ... IL-6
Chicago (historical)—locale ... KS-7
Chicago Institute of Technology—school ... IL-6
Chicago Junction—locale ... WI-6
Chicago Junior Coll—school ... IL-6
Chicago Junior Coll (Bogan Branch)—school ... IL-6
Chicago Junior Coll (Fenger Branch)—school ... IL-6
Chicago Junior Coll Wright Branch—school ... IL-6
Chicago Lake ... MN-6
Chicago Lake—lake ... MI-6
Chicago Lake—lake ... MT-8
Chicago Lake—lake ... ND-7
Chicago Lakes—lake ... AK-9
Chicago Lakes—lake ... CO-8
Chicago Lakes Trail—trail ... CO-8
Chicago Lawn ... IL-6
Chicago Loop—other ... IL-6
Chicago Midway Airp—airport ... IL-6
Chicago Mill and Lumber Company Game Mngmt Area—park ... LA-4
Chicago Mine—mine ... CA-9
Chicago Mine—mine ... CO-8
Chicago Mine—mine ... WA-9
Chicago Mine—mine ... WY-8
Chicago Mine Hill—summit ... WY-8
Chicago Mine (Inactive)—mine ... MT-8
Chicago Mound Cem—cemetery ... KS-7
Chicagon—locale ... MI-6
Chicagon Lake—lake ... MI-6
**Chicagon Lake**—pop pl ... MI-6
Chicago Northwestern Depot—hist pl ... SD-7
Chicagon Slough—stream ... MI-6
Chicago O'Hare International Airport—mil airp ... IL-6
Chicago Parental Sch—school ... IL-6
Chicago Park—flat ... CO-8
Chicago Park—locale ... CA-9
Chicago Park Ditch—canal ... CA-9
Chicago Park Sch—school ... TN-4
Chicago Peak—summit ... CA-9
Chicago Peak—summit ... CO-8
Chicago Peak—summit ... MT-8
Chicago Point—cape ... AK-9
Chicago Point—cape (2) ... WI-6
Chicago Portage Natl Historic Site—park ... IL-6
Chicago Portage Natl Historic Site—hist pl ... IL-6
Chicago Portage Woods—woods ... IL-6
Chicago Public Library, Central Bldg—hist pl ... IL-6
Chicago Ravine—valley ... CA-9
**Chicago Ridge**—pop pl ... IL-6
Chicago Ridge—ridge ... CO-8
Chicago Ridge Sch—school ... IL-6
Chicago River ... IL-6
Chicago River—stream ... IL-6
Chicago Road Cem—cemetery ... IL-6
Chicago Rock—pillar ... CA-9
Chicago Rsvr—reservoir ... WY-8
Chicago Sanitarium—locale ... IL-6
Chicago Sanitary And Ship Canal—canal ... IL-6
Chicago Savings Bank Bldg—hist pl ... IL-6
Chicago Sch—school ... OH-6
Chicago Springs Trail—trail ... PA-2
Chicago Stadium—locale ... IL-6
Chicago State Hosp—hospital ... IL-6
Chicago Teachers Coll—school ... IL-6
Chicago Technical Coll—school ... IL-6
**Chicago Township**—pop pl ... ND-7
Chicago Trail—trail ... OR-9
Chicago Tunnel—mine ... CO-8
Chicago Valley—valley ... CA-9
Chicago Vocational Sch—school ... IL-6
Chicago Windmill—locale (2) ... TX-5
Chicago Yacht Club—other ... IL-6
Chicago Zoological Park—park ... IL-6
Chical—locale ... NM-5
**Chical**—pop pl ... NM-5
Chical Creek—stream ... NM-5
Chical Ditch—canal ... NM-5
Chical Indian School—locale ... NM-5
Chical Lake—reservoir ... NM-5
Chical Lateral—canal ... NM-5
Chical Mesa—summit ... NM-5
Chical Tank—reservoir ... NM-5
Chicamacomico Channel (historical)—channel ... NC-3
Chicamacomico Life Saving Station—hist pl ... NC-3
Chicamacomico River—stream ... MD-2
Chicamauga Island ... TN-4
Chicamocomico Channel ... NC-3
Chicamun Canyon—valley ... WA-9
**Chicamuxen**—pop pl ... MD-2
Chicamuxen Ch—church ... MD-2
Chicamuxen Creek—stream ... MD-2
Chicamuxen Run ... MD-2
Chicapee Country Club—locale ... MA-1
Chicapoula ... MS-4
Chicarita Creek—stream ... CA-9
Chicasanocsa Creek ... AL-4
Chicasaw Island ... AL-4
Chicaskia Ch—church ... KS-7
Chicaskia River ... KS-7
Chicaskia River ... OK-5
Chicaskia Township ... KS-7
Chiceanske Bluff ... AL-4
Chicgon ... MI-6
Chichago—uninc pl ... AK-9
Chichagof—locale ... AK-9
Chichagof, Cape—cape ... AK-9
Chichagof Bay—bay (2) ... AK-9
Chichagof Creek—stream ... AK-9
Chichagof Harbor—bay ... AK-9
Chichagof Island—island ... AK-9
Chichagof Pass—channel ... AK-9
Chichagof Peak—summit (2) ... AK-9
Chichagof Point—cape ... AK-9
Chichagof Valley—valley ... AK-9
Chichagov ... MP-9
Chichahominy Creek Dam—dam ... OR-9
Chichantna Creek—stream ... AK-9
Chichantna River—stream ... AK-9
Chichaqua Wildlife Habitat Park—park ... IA-7
Chi Charas ... LA-4
Chi Charas Bay ... LA-4
Chicharas Bay—lake ... LA-4
Chicharon Windmill—locale ... TX-5
Chichester ... PA-2
**Chichester**—pop pl ... NH-1

Chief Moses JHS—school WA-9
Chief Mountain Basin WY-8
Chief Mountain Customs—locale MT-8
Chief Mountain Lake MT-8
Chief Mountain River MT-8
Chief Mtn CA-9
Chief Mtn—summit CA-9
Chief Mtn—summit (3) CO-8
Chief Mtn—summit MT-8
Chief Mtn—summit NV-8
Chief Mtn—summit WY-8
Chief Narrows—channel WI-6
Chief Ne-Kah-Wah-She-Tun-Kah Grave and Statue—hist pl OK-5
Chief Noonday Lake—lake MI-6
Chief No 1—mine UT-8
Chief No 2—mine UT-8
Chief of the Hills Mines—mine NV-8
Chief Okemus Camp—locale MI-6
Chief One-Eye (historical)—ridge AZ-5
Chief Ouray Mine—mine CO-8
Chief Oxide—mine UT-8
Chief Peak—summit MT-8
Chief Plenty Coups Memorial—hist pl MT-8
Chief Plenty Coups Memorial State Park—park MT-8
Chief Point—cape AK-9
Chief Poseys Indian Battle Historical Marker—park UT-8
Chief Post Office (historical)—building TN-4
Chief Rancho—locale NM-5
**Chief (Rand)**—pop pl TX-5
Chief Range—range NV-8
Chief Richardville House and Miami Treaty Grounds—hist pl IN-6
Chief River State Wildlife Mngmt Area—park WI-6
Chief Run—stream IN-6
Chief Schonchin Cem—cemetery OR-9
Chief Sealth HS—school WA-9
Chief Seattle Boy Scout Reservation—locale WA-9
Chief Shabbona For Preserve—forest IL-6
Chief Shabbona Grave—cemetery IL-6
Chief Shakes Historic Site—hist pl AK-9
Chief Shakes Hot Springs—spring AK-9
Chief's Head CO-8
Chiefs Head Peak—summit CO-8
Chief's House—hist pl OK-5
Chief Sitting Bulls Grave Monmt—park SD-7
Chief Situk Grave—cemetery AK-9
Chiefs Knoll—hist pl OK-5
Chief Spokane Monmt—park WA-9
Chief Spring—spring CA-9
Chief Springs—spring TX-5
Chiefs Tank—reservoir AZ-5
Chieftain Creek—stream OR-9
Chieftain Mine—mine CA-9
Chieftain Mine—mine CO-8
Chieftain Mine—mine OR-9
Chieftains—hist pl GA-3
Chieftan Memorial—locale CO-8
Chief Tatamy Sch (abandoned)—school PA-2
Chief Theater—hist pl NM-5
Chiefton—locale WV-2
**Chiefton**—pop pl WV-2
**Chief (Township of)**—pop pl MN-6
Chief Wapello's Memorial Park—hist pl IA-7
Chief White Crane Rec Area—park SD-7
Chief Wooden Frog Campground—locale MN-6
Chief Wooden Frogs Islands—island MN-6
Chiehazhahi Wash—stream AZ-5
Chiemauni MP-9
Chiemo To MP-9
Chien, Bayou du—gut TN-4
Chien, Point au—cape LA-4
Chienmauni MP-9
Chienmauni—island MP-9
Chienmauni-To MP-9
Chien-to MP-9
Chieriko Island MP-9
Chieriko Island—island MP-9
Chieriko-To MP-9
Chierumarakku MP-9
Chierumarakku Island MP-9
Chierumarakku Island—island MP-9
Chierumarakku-To MP-9
Chie-suido MP-9
Chietebutebu MP-9
Chietebutebu Suido (2) MP-9
Chietebutebu To MP-9
Chie-to MP-9
Chiflo Campground—locale NM-5
Chiflones Canyon—valley NM-5
Chifoncte River LA-4
Chiftak (site)—locale AK-9
Chifunctee Creek LA-4
Chifunctee River LA-4
chifuncte river LA-4
Chiget, Laderon—cliff MH-9
Chiget, Puntan—cape MH-9
Chiget, Sabanetan—slope MH-9
Chiget, Unai—beach MH-9
Chigger Branch—stream TN-4
Chigger Cove—bay OK-5
Chigger Creek—stream AR-4
Chigger Creek—stream KS-7
Chigger Creek—stream TX-5
**Chigger Hill**—pop pl AL-4
Chigger Hill Church AL-4
Chigger Hollow—valley TN-4
Chigger Island (historical)—island AL-4
Chigger Point—cape TN-4
Chigger Ridge—ridge (2) GA-3
Chigger Ridge—ridge TN-4
Chigger Ridge (historical)—locale AL-4
Chigger Ridge Sch (historical)—school AL-4
Chigger Ridge Sch (historical)—school TN-4
Chiggerville Site (15OH1)—hist pl KY-4
Chiginagak, Mount—summit AK-9
Chiginagak Bay—bay AK-9
Chigley—locale OK-5
Chigley Sandy Creek—stream OK-5
Chigmit Mountains—range AK-9
Chignaki Pond—lake AK-9
**Chignik**—pop pl AK-9
Chignik Bay—bay AK-9
Chignik Flats—flat AK-9
Chignik Island—island AK-9
Chignik Lagoon—bay AK-9
Chignik Lagoon—locale AK-9
Chignik Lagoon ANV755—reserve AK-9
Chignik Lake—lake AK-9
Chignik Lake ANV756—reserve AK-9
Chignik Mtn—summit AK-9
Chignik River—stream AK-9
Chignik Spit—bar AK-9
Chigoe Branch GA-3
Chigoe Creek—stream GA-3
Chigoorhaligamiut (Summer Camp)—locale AK-9
Chiguito Creek TX-5
Chihaks Creek—stream IA-7
Chihaun ND-7
Chihohocki DE-2
**Chihuahua**—pop pl TX-5
Chihuahua Creek CA-9
Chihuahua Creek—stream CA-9
Chihuahua Creek—stream TX-5
Chihuahua Farm—locale TX-5
Chihuahua Gulch—valley CO-8
Chihuahua Gulch—valley NM-5
Chihuahua Hill—summit AZ-5
Chihuahua Hill Hist Dist—hist pl NM-5
Chihuahua Lake—reservoir NM-5
Chihuahuan Desert Research Station—other TX-5
Chihuahua Ranch—locale NM-5
Chihuahua Valley—valley CA-9
Chihuahuenos Creek—stream NM-5
Chii Point—summit GU-9
Chiiyorugan-to MP-9
Chijuk Creek—stream AK-9
Chikabi Brook MA-1
Chikabi River MA-1
Chikamin Creek—stream (3) WA-9
Chikaming Ch—church MI-6
Chikaming Country Club—other MI-6
Chikaming Sch—school MI-6
**Chikaming (Township of)**—pop pl MI-6
Chikamin Lake—lake WA-9
Chikamin Peak—summit WA-9
Chikamin Ridge—ridge (2) WA-9
Chikapanagi Mesa—summit AZ-5
Chikapanagi Point—cliff AZ-5
Chikapangi Mesa AZ-5
Chikasanoxee Creek—stream AL-4
Chikaskia Cem—cemetery KS-7
Chikaskia (historical)—locale KS-7
Chikaskia River—stream KS-7
Chikaskia River—stream OK-5
**Chikaskia Township**—pop pl (2) KS-7
Chikianese Bluff AL-4
Chikiswalungo PA-2
Chikiswalungo Ridge PA-2
Chikootna Creek—stream AK-9
Chikoot Pass—gap CA-9
Chikululnuk Creek—stream AK-9
Chikuminuk Glacier—glacier AK-9
Chikuminuk Lake—lake AK-9
Chikungamiut (Summer Camp)—locale AK-9
Chilacoom WA-9
Chiladote Tank—reservoir AZ-5
Chilanian Gulch—valley CA-9
Chilanoialna Creek CA-9
Chilanoialna Falls CA-9
Chiloo Campground—locale CA-9
Chiloo Creek—stream CA-9
Chiloo Flat—flat CA-9
Chiloo Station—locale CA-9
Chilarna Lake—reservoir VA-3
Chilatchee Creek—stream AL-4
Chilatchee Park—park AL-4
Chilbury Point—cape MD-2
Chil-Chin-Be-To AZ-5
Chilchinbeto—spring AZ-5
**Chilchinbito**—pop pl AZ-5
Chilchinbito Canyon—valley AZ-5
Chilchinbito Creek (historical)—stream AZ-5
Chilchinbito Spring—spring AZ-5
Chilchinbito Trading Post—locale AZ-5
Chilchinbito Wash—valley AZ-5
Chilchinbito Well—well AZ-5
Chilchinvito Canyon AZ-5
Chilchitna River—stream AK-9
Chil-Chi-vi-to Canyon AZ-5
Chilchukabena Lake—lake AK-9
Chilco—locale ID-8
Chilcoat Creek CA-9
Chilcoat Junction Shelter—locale OR-9
Chilcoat Run—stream PA-2
Chilco Creek—stream ID-8
Chilco Lake—lake ID-8
Chilco Mountain ID-8
Chilco Mtn—summit ID-8
**Chilcoot**—pop pl CA-9
Chilcoot Campground—locale CA-9
Chilcoot Creek—stream CA-9
Chilcoot Creek—stream OR-9
Chilcoote Canyon—valley NM-5
Chilcoot Lake—lake ID-8
Chilcoot Mountain ID-8
Chilcoot Mtn—summit OR-9
Chilcoot Pass—gap ID-8
Chilcoot Pass—gap VT-1
Chilcoot Peak—summit ID-8
Chilcoot Ridge—ridge OR-9
Chilcoot Trail—trail OR-9
Chilcoot Trail—trail WY-8
Chilcoot Tunnel—tunnel CA-9
Chilcote Cem—cemetery OH-6
Chilcote Corner—locale PA-2
Chilcotte Canal No 27—canal CO-8
Chilcutt Lake—lake WY-8
Chilcutt Cem—cemetery (2) TN-4
Chilcutt Chapel—church TN-4
Chilcutt High School TN-4
Chilcutt Sch (historical)—school TN-4
Child MD-2
Child, Francis J., House—hist pl MA-1
Child, Isaac, House—hist pl MA-1
Child, Jonathan, House & Brewster-Burke House Hist Dist—hist pl NY-2
Child, W. C., Ranch—hist pl MT-8
Child Brook MA-1
Child City—other IL-6
Child Creek—stream WY-8
Child Enrichment Center—building FL-3
Childer Creek—stream TN-4
Childers—locale AR-4
Childers—locale OK-5
Childers Airp—airport NC-3
Childers Branch—stream KY-4
Childers Branch—stream MS-4
Childers Branch—stream WV-2
**Childersburg**—pop pl AL-4
Childersburg (CCD)—cens area AL-4
Childersburg Division—civil AL-4
Childersburg Elem Sch—school AL-4
Childersburgh AL-4
Childersburg HS—school AL-4
Childersburg Shop Ctr—locale AL-4
Childersburg State Penal Camp—other AL-4
Childersburg Work Release Center AL-4
Childers Cem—cemetery (3) AL-4
Childers Cem—cemetery (3) AR-4
Childers Cem—cemetery IL-6
Childers Cem—cemetery (2) OK-5
Childers Cem—cemetery TN-4
Childers Cem—cemetery WV-2
Childers Chapel Cem—cemetery AL-4
Childers Creek—stream AL-4
Childers Creek—stream GA-3
Childers Creek—stream SC-3
Childers Creek—stream (2) TN-4
Childers Dam—dam SD-7
Childers Ditch—canal OH-6
Childers Draw—valley WA-9
Childers Family Cem—cemetery AL-4
**Childers Hill**—pop pl TN-4
Childers Hill—summit MO-7
Childers Hollow—valley AR-4
Childers Hollow—valley KY-4
Childers Hollow—valley VA-3
Childers Knob—summit WV-2
Childers Knoll AZ-5
Childers Lake OK-5
Childers Mill Branch—stream AL-4
Childers Mine (underground)—mine AL-4
Childers Park—park NC-3
Childers Peak—summit CA-9
Childers Place—locale WY-8
Childers Pond—reservoir GA-3
Childers Ridge—ridge PA-2
Childers Ridge Trail—trail PA-2
Childers Rsvr—reservoir WY-8
Childers Run—stream WV-2
Childers Sch—school WV-2
Childers Seep—spring AZ-5
Childers Slough—stream TX-5
Childers Spring—spring AL-4
Childers Spring—spring AZ-5
Childersville Post Office (historical)—building TN-4
Childers Well—well (3) AZ-5
Childhaven Children Home—building AL-4
Child Lake—lake MN-6
Childre Cem—cemetery TX-5
Children Center Sch—school GA-3
Children Ch—church PA-2
Children Garden Montessori Sch—school FL-3
Children Hospital Sch—school OR-9
Children of God House of Prayer—church FL-3
Children of Israel Cem—cemetery OH-6
Children of Israel Ch—church MA-1
Childrens Aid Society Camps—locale NY-2
Childrens Branch WV-2
Childrens Camp—locale NH-1
Childrens Cardiac Home (historical)—building FL-3
Childrens Cem—cemetery KY-4
Childrens Center—school FL-3
Childrens Center/Baptist Hospital of Miami—school FL-3
Children Sch—school FL-3
Childrens Choice Sch—school WI-6
Childrens Cottage—building PA-2
Childrens Development Center—school FL-3
**Childrens Fairyland**—pop pl CA-9
Childrens For—forest CA-9
Childrens Fresh Air Camp—locale MD-2
Childrens Home—building CA-9
Childrens Home—building MA-1
Childrens Home—building PA-2
Children's Home—hist pl MA-1
Childrens Home—locale TX-5
Childrens Home, The—building TN-4
Childrens Home Ditch—canal OH-6
Childrens Home of Lubbock—building TX-5
Childrens Hosp—hospital AL-4
Childrens Hosp—hospital AZ-5
Childrens Hosp—hospital CO-8
Childrens Hosp—hospital DC-2
Childrens Hosp—hospital IL-6
Childrens Hosp—hospital MO-7
Childrens Hosp—hospital NY-2
Childrens Hosp—hospital (2) OH-6
Childrens Hosp—hospital OK-5
Childrens Hosp—hospital PA-2
Childrens Hosp—hospital TN-4
Childrens Hosp—hospital VA-3
Childrens Hospital Sch—school MD-2
Childrens Hour Day Sch—school FL-3
Childrens House—school FL-3
Childrens Island MA-1
Childrens Museum—building MA-1
Childrens Park—park IA-7
Childrens Park—park KS-7
Childrens Personal Development Center—school FL-3
Childrens Receiving Home—building CA-9
Childrens Rehabilitation Center—hospital PA-2
Childrens Sch—school PA-2
Childrens Small World Sch—school FL-3
Childrens Village—locale NY-2
Children's Village of the Hartford Orphan Asylum—hist pl CT-1
Childrens Workshop—school (2) FL-3
Childrens World Day Care/Learning Center—school FL-3
Childrens Rsvr—reservoir MT-8
Childres Creek—stream OK-5
Childres Place—locale NM-5
Childress—locale VA-3
**Childress**—pop pl (2) AR-4
**Childress**—pop pl TN-4
**Childress**—pop pl TX-5
Childress, Lake—reservoir TX-5
Childress Bluff—cliff KY-4
Childress Branch WV-2
Childress Branch—stream (2) TN-4
Childress Branch—stream (2) VA-3
Childress (CCD)—cens area TX-5
Childress Cem—cemetery KY-4
Childress Cem—cemetery (2) MO-7
Childress Cem—cemetery (6) TN-4
Childress Cem—cemetery (2) VA-3
Childress Cem—cemetery WV-2
Childress Country Club—other TX-5
**Childress (County)**—pop pl TX-5
Childress Creek TX-5
Childress Creek—stream TX-5
Childress Creek—stream (3) VA-3
Childress Ditch—canal CA-9
Childress Ferry (historical)—locale TN-4
Childress Gap—gap TN-4
Childress Hill—summit AL-4
Childress Hollow—valley TN-4
Childress House—hist pl TN-4
Childress Lake—reservoir TN-4
Childress Lake Dam—dam TN-4
Childress Mine (underground)—mine AL-4
Childress Oil Field—oilfield TX-5
Childress Point—cape AL-4
Childress Pond—lake TX-5
Childress Post Office TN-4
Childress Ranch—locale NM-5
Childress-Ray House—hist pl TN-4
Childress Recorder Well (USGS)—well NM-5
Childress Sch—school IL-6
Childress Store—building TN-4
Childress Store (historical)—locale MS-4
Childress Tank—reservoir AZ-5
Childress Well—well NM-5
Childress Windmill—locale NM-5
Childrey Ch—church VA-3
Childrey Creek—stream VA-3
Child River MA-1
**Childry**—pop pl VA-3
Childs—locale AZ-5
Childs—locale FL-3
Childs—locale MN-6
Childs—locale MT-8
Childs—locale WV-2
**Childs**—pop pl AZ-5
**Childs**—pop pl MD-2
**Childs**—pop pl NY-2
**Childs**—pop pl (2) PA-2
Childs, Alpha Charles, House—hist pl OH-6
Childs, George W., Sch—hist pl PA-2
Childs, Robertus W., House—hist pl OH-6
Childs, Starling, Camp—hist pl CT-1
Childs Access County Park—park IA-7
**Child's Acres**—pop pl KS-7
**Childs Acres**—pop pl KS-7
**Childs Addition (subdivision)**—pop pl UT-8
Childs and Altwilkle Mine—mine AZ-5
Childs Bog—lake NH-1
Childs Branch—stream KY-4
Childs Branch—stream NC-3
Childs Bridge—bridge MA-1
Childs Brook VT-1
Childs Brook—stream ME-1
Childs Brook—stream MA-1
Childs Brook—stream NH-1
Childs Brook—stream NY-2
Childs-Brown House—hist pl RI-1
Childsburg NC-3
Childsbury—locale SC-3
Childs Canyon—valley CA-9
Childs Canyon—valley NV-8
Childs Cem—cemetery AR-4
Childs Cem—cemetery MI-6
Childs Cem—cemetery MS-4
Childs Cem—cemetery TN-4
Childs Ch—church NJ-2
Child Sch—school AR-4
Childs Chapel (historical)—church MS-4
Childs Creek MD-2
Childs Creek—stream ID-8
Childs Creek—stream OH-6
Childs Creek—stream WA-9
Childs Creek—stream WY-8
Childsdale—locale MI-6
Childs Dam NJ-2
Childs Ditch—canal CO-8
Childs Drain—canal MI-6
Childs Drain—stream MI-6
Childs Elem Sch PA-2
Child Service Center—building OR-9
**Childs (Fair Haven)**—pop pl NY-2
Childs Ferry AL-4
Childs Ferry Point—cape AL-4
Childs Glacier—glacier AK-9
Childs Hill—summit CA-9
Childs Hill—summit ME-1
Childs Hill—summit VT-1
Childs Hill Prairie—area CA-9
Childs Hollow—valley AL-4
Childs Hollow—valley MO-7
Childs Hollow—valley WI-6
Childs HS—school NY-2
Childs Island—island MA-1
Childs Lake FL-3
Childs Lake—lake MI-6
Childs Lake—reservoir MS-4
Childs Lake—swamp MN-6
Childs Lake Dam—dam MS-4
Childs Meadows—flat CA-9
**Childs Meadows**—pop pl CA-9
Childs Meadows Trail—trail CA-9
Childs Memorial Ch—church TN-4
Childs Mtn—summit AZ-5
Childs Mtn—summit VT-1
Childs Park—park MA-1
Childs Park Sch—school FL-3
Childs Place—locale GA-3
Childs Place Day Sch—school FL-3
Childs Point—cape MD-2
Childs Pond—lake GA-3
Childs Pond—lake VT-1
Childs Pond—reservoir CT-1
Childs Ponds—lake NY-2
Childs Powerplant—locale AZ-5
Childs Powerplant Tank—reservoir AZ-5
Childs Ranch—locale AZ-5
Childs Ranch—locale CA-9
Childs Residence—hist pl MD-2
Childs River—stream MA-1
Childs Sch—school MI-6
Childs Sch—school VT-1
Childs Sch—island WA-9
Childs State Forest Park PA-2
Childs State Park PA-2
Childs Station—locale FL-3
Childs Tank—reservoir NM-5
Childstown (historical)—locale SD-7
**Childstown Township**—pop pl SD-7
Childs Valley—valley AZ-5
Childs Wash AZ-5
Childwold—locale NY-2
Childwold Station—locale NY-2
Childwood NY-2
Chile IN-6
Chilean Creek CA-9
Chilean Embassy Bldg—building DC-2
Chilean Memorial Monument—locale WA-9
Chilean Mill—locale AZ-5
Chilechinbito AZ-5
Chile Gulch—valley CA-9
Chileno Camp—locale CA-9
Chileno Canyon—valley CA-9
Chileno Creek—stream (2) CA-9
Chileno Valley—valley CA-9
Chile No 5 Mine—mine CO-8
Chiles—locale KY-4
**Chiles**—pop pl CA-9
**Chiles**—pop pl KS-7
Chiles, Tarleton, House—hist pl KY-4
Chiles-Bailey House—hist pl KY-4
Chiles Branch—stream SC-3
Chiles Branch—stream TX-5
Chilesburg—locale KY-4
**Chilesburg**—pop pl VA-3
Chiles Cem—cemetery MO-7
Chiles Creek—stream CA-9
Chiles Ferry Bar—bar AL-4
Chiles Ferry (historical)—locale AL-4
Chiles Ferry Landing (historical)—locale AL-4
Chiles Ferry Point AL-4
Chiles Grist Mill—locale CA-9
Chiles Hosp—hospital KY-4
Chiles Slough—gut ND-7
Chiles Valley—area CA-9
**Chilesville**—pop pl OK-5
Chilesville Cem—cemetery OK-5
Chilhowee—locale TN-4
**Chilhowee**—pop pl MO-7
Chilhowee Airp—airport TN-4
Chilhowee Baptist Church TN-4
Chilhowee (CCD)—cens area TN-4
Chilhowee Cem—cemetery TN-4
Chilhowee Ch—church TN-4
Chilhowee Dam—dam (2) TN-4
Chilhowee Division—civil TN-4
Chilhowee Elem Sch—school TN-4
Chilhowee Forest Walk Trail—trail TN-4
Chilhowee Gap—gap TN-4
**Chilhowee Hills**—pop pl TN-4
Chilhowee Hist Dist—hist pl MO-7
Chilhowee Lake—reservoir TN-4
Chilhowee Medical Spring—spring TN-4
Chilhowee Mountain—ridge TN-4
Chilhowee Mountains TN-4
Chilhowee Mtn—summit TN-4
Chilhowee Park—park TN-4
Chilhowee Post Office (historical)—building TN-4
Chilhowee Rec Area—park TN-4
Chilhowee Shoals—bar TN-4
Chilhowee Township—civil MO-7
**Chilhowee View**—pop pl TN-4
Chilhowee View Sch—school TN-4
**Chilhowey (historical)**—pop pl TN-4
**Chilhowie**—pop pl VA-3
Chilhowie (Magisterial District)—fmr MCD VA-3
Chilhowie Mountains TN-4
**Chili**—pop pl IL-6
**Chili**—pop pl IN-6
**Chili**—pop pl NM-5
**Chili**—pop pl OH-6
**Chili**—pop pl WI-6
Chili Bar—locale CA-9
Chili Camp Gulch—valley CA-9
**Chili Center**—pop pl NY-2
Chili Center Sch—school IL-6
Chili Cortal Mountain TX-5
Chili Cortal Spring TX-5
Chili Corte Mountain TX-5
Chili Corte Spring TX-5
Chilicotal Mtn—summit TX-5
Chilicotal Spring—spring TX-5
Chilicote Canyon—valley TX-5
Chili Country Club—other NY-2
Chili Creek—stream OK-5
Chili Crossroads Ch—church OH-6
Chilies Mill (historical)—locale AL-4
Chili Gulch—valley CA-9
Chili Hill—summit CA-9
**Chili Junction**—pop pl NY-2
Chilikadrotna River—stream AK-9
**Chili (La Chuachia)**—pop pl NM-5
**Chilili**—pop pl NM-5
Chilili Ditch—canal CO-8
Chilili Grant—civil NM-5
Chili Mills Conservation Area—hist pl NY-2
Chilipatin Canyon TX-5
Chilipin Creek TX-5
Chili Pitien Windmill—locale TX-5
Chilipitin Canyon—valley TX-5
Chilipitin Creek—stream TX-5
Chilipitin Lake—reservoir TX-5
Chilipitin Tank TX-5
Chilipotin Canyon TX-5
Chili Rural Cem—cemetery NY-2
Chili Spring—spring AZ-5
**Chili (sta.)**—pop pl NY-2
Chilitipin Creek TX-5
Chilito (historical)—locale AZ-5
Chilito Mine—mine AZ-5
**Chili (Town of)**—pop pl NY-2
**Chili (Township of)**—pop pl IL-6
Chili Windmill—locale NM-5
Chili Windmill—locale TX-5
Chiliwist Butte—summit WA-9
Chiliwist Creek—stream WA-9
Chiliwist Valley—basin WA-9
Chilkat—locale (2) AK-9
Chilkat Creek—stream AK-9
Chilkat Glacier—glacier AK-9
Chilkat Inlet—bay AK-9
Chilkat Islands—island AK-9
Chilkat Lake—lake AK-9
Chilkat(native name for Klukwan) ANV757—reserve AK-9
Chilkat Oil Company Refinery Site—hist pl AK-9
Chilkat Peak—summit AK-9
Chilkat Peninsula—cape AK-9
Chilkat Range—range AK-9
Chilkat River—stream AK-9
Chilkoot—locale AK-9
Chilkoot Campground—locale CA-9
Chilkoot Coulee—valley MT-8
Chilkoot Creek—stream CA-9
Chilkoot Inlet—bay AK-9
Chilkoot Lake—lake AK-9
Chilkoot Lake—lake CA-9
Chilkoot Pass—gap AK-9
Chilkoot Pass—gap MT-8
Chilkoot Pass—gap OR-9
Chilkoot River—stream AK-9
Chilkoot Trail—hist pl AK-9
C Hill—summit NV-8
Chillasanooga Creek AL-4
Chillas Branch VA-3
Chillbury Point MD-2
Chilled Lakes—lake MT-8
Chiller Chapel—church AR-4
Chill Heal Spring—spring AZ-5
Chill-howie Mountain TN-4
Chilli—locale OK-5
**Chillicothe**—pop pl IL-6
**Chillicothe**—pop pl IA-7
**Chillicothe**—pop pl MO-7
**Chillicothe**—pop pl OH-6
**Chillicothe**—pop pl TX-5
Chillicothe Airport MO-7
Chillicothe Business District—hist pl OH-6
Chillicothe (CCD)—cens area TX-5
Chillicothe Cem—cemetery TX-5
Chillicothe Country Club—other OH-6
Chillicothe Federal Reformatory—building OH-6
Chillicothe Island—island IL-6
Chillicothe Municipal Airp—airport MO-7
Chillicothe's Old Residential District—hist pl OH-6
**Chillicothe Township**—pop pl MO-7
**Chillicothe (Township of)**—pop pl IL-6
Chillicothe Water And Power Company Pumping Station—hist pl OH-6
Chilli Creek—stream MS-4
Chillicut Spring—spring AZ-5
Chillie Point Windmill—locale NM-5
Chilligan River—stream AK-9
Chilli Lake—reservoir MS-4
Chillipin Creek TX-5
Chilli Piquin Creek TX-5
Chilli Piquin Tank TX-5
Chillipiu Creek TX-5
Chillisado Creek AL-4
**Chillisquaque**—pop pl PA-2
Chillisquaque Cem—cemetery PA-2
Chillisquaque Creek PA-2
Chillisquaque Creek—stream PA-2
Chillisquaque Dam—dam PA-2
Chillisquaque, Lake—reservoir PA-2
Chillitos Landing (historical)—locale AL-4
Chilliwack Creek WA-9
Chilliwack Pass—gap WA-9
Chilliwack River—stream WA-9
Chilliwak Creek WA-9
Chilliwhack River WA-9
Chill Lake WY-8
Chill Lakes—lake WY-8
Chillon, Arroyo—valley TX-5
Chillowist—locale WA-9
Chillson Pond—lake PA-2
Chillukweyuk River WA-9
**Chillum**—pop pl MD-2
**Chillum Gardens**—pop pl MD-2
**Chillum Heights**—pop pl MD-2
**Chillum Manor**—pop pl MD-2
Chillum Sch—school MD-2
**Chillum Station**—pop pl DC-2
Chillutes Landing AL-4
Chilly—locale ID-8
Chilly Buttes—summit ID-8
Chilly Canal—canal ID-8
Chilly Cem—cemetery ID-8
Chilly Creek—stream MT-8
Chilly Creek—stream OK-5
Chilly Creek—stream OR-9
Chilly Gulch—valley ID-8
Chilly Peak—summit UT-8
Chilly Spring Gap—gap TN-4
Chilly Spring Knob—summit TN-4
**Chilmark**—pop pl MA-1
Chilmark Cem—cemetery MA-1
Chilmark Great Pond MA-1
Chilmark Pond—lake MA-1
**Chilmark (Town of)**—pop pl MA-1
Chilnoalna Creek CA-9
Chilnoalna Falls CA-9
Chilnoialny Creek CA-9
Chilnoialny Falls CA-9
Chilnualna Creek—stream CA-9
Chilnualna Falls—falls CA-9
Chilnualna Lakes—lake CA-9
**Chilo**—pop pl OH-6
**Chilocco**—pop pl OK-5
Chilocco Creek—stream KS-7
Chilocco Creek—stream OK-5
**Chilocco (Indian Agricultural School)**—pop pl OK-5
Chilocco Indian Sch—school OK-5
Chilocco Oil Field—oilfield OK-5
Chilo Cem—cemetery OH-6
Chilogatee Branch—stream TN-4
Chilogatee Gap—gap TN-4
Chilohowee Rod And Gun Club Dam—dam TN-4
Chilohowee Rod And Gun Club Lake—reservoir TN-4
Chilon Chalet IL-6
**Chiloquin**—pop pl OR-9
Chiloquin (CCD)—cens area OR-9
Chiloquin HS—school OR-9
Chiloquin Narrows—channel OR-9
Chiloquin Rapids—rapids OR-9

Chiloquin Ridge—ridge OR-9
Chiloquin Sch—school OR-9
Chiloquin State Airport—airport OR-9
Chiloway—locale NY-2
Chilowee TN-4
Chilowee Mountain TN-4
Chiloweyuck River WA-9
Chilpotin Creek TX-5
Chilson SD-7
**Chilson—pop pl** AR-4
**Chilson—pop pl** MI-6
**Chilson—pop pl** NY-2
Chilson Brook—stream NY-2
Chilson Cabin AZ-5
Chilson Camp—locale AZ-5
Chilson Canal—canal AZ-5
Chilson Canyon—valley SD-7
Chilson Cem—cemetery MI-6
Chilson Ch—church AR-4
Chilson Chapel—church AR-4
Chilson Creek MT-8
Chilson Creek—stream MI-6
Chilson Creek—stream OR-9
Chilson Creek—stream WA-9
Chilson Impoundment—reservoir MI-6
Chilson Lake NY-2
Chilson Landing Strip—airport AZ-5
Chilson Mesa Tank—reservoir AZ-5
Chilson Mtn—summit SD-7
Chilson Pond—lake MA-1
Chilson Run—stream PA-2
Chilson Spring—spring AZ-5
Chilson Station—locale SD-7
Chilson Tank—reservoir (3) AZ-5
Chiltapin Bayou TX-5
Chiltepines Wash—stream AZ-5
Chiltipin Creek TX-5
Chiltipin Creek—stream (4) TX-5
Chiltipin Lake TX-5
Chiltipin-San Fernando Dam No 1—dam TX-5
Chiltipin-San Fernando Dam Number 6—dam TX-5
Chiltipin-San Fernando Dam Number 7—dam TX-5
Chiltipin-San Fernando Dam Number 8—dam TX-5
Chiltipin-San Fernando Dam Number 9—dam TX-5
Chiltipin Well—well TX-5
Chiltipin Windmill—locale (2) TX-5
Chiltoes Mtn—summit NC-3
Chilton—locale KY-4
**Chilton—pop pl** AL-4
**Chilton—pop pl** MO-7
**Chilton—pop pl** TX-5
**Chilton—pop pl** WI-6
Chilton, Lake—lake FL-3
Chilton, W. E. II, House—hist pl WV-2
Chilton Area Horticulture Sub-Station—locale AL-4
Chilton (CCD)—cens area TX-5
Chilton Cem—cemetery MN-6
Chilton Cem—cemetery (5) MO-7
Chilton Cem—cemetery TX-5
Chilton Ch—church AL-4
**Chilton County—pop pl** AL-4
Chilton County Courthouse—building AL-4
Chilton County Hosp and Nursing Home—hospital AL-4
Chilton County HS—school AL-4
Chilton County Industrial Sch (historical)—school AL-4
Chilton County Vocational Skills Center—school AL-4
Chilton County Vocational Technical Sch—school AL-4
Chilton Creek—stream (2) MO-7
Chilton Creek—stream ND-7
Chilton Creek Campsite—park MO-7
Chilton Creek River Access—locale MO-7
Chilton Ditch—canal IN-6
Chilton Hill—summit IN-6
Chilton (historical)—locale AL-4
Chilton Hollow—valley MO-7
Chilton House—hist pl WV-2
Chilton Lake—lake MN-6
Chilton Park—park KS-7
Chilton Park—park MN-6
Chilton Ranch—locale WY-8
**Chiltons—pop pl** VA-3
Chilton Sch—school AL-4
Chilton Sch—school MN-6
Chiltons Store (historical)—locale TN-4
Chilton Tank—reservoir NM-5
**Chilton (Town of)—pop pl** WI-6
**Chilton Township—pop pl** ND-7
**Chiltonville—pop pl** MA-1
Chiltonville (historical P.O.)—locale MA-1
Chilton Well—well WY-8
Chilton-Williams Farm Complex—hist pl MO-7
Chiltoskie Ridge—ridge NC-3
**Chimacum—pop pl** WA-9
Chimacum Creek—stream WA-9
Chimacum Post Office—hist pl WA-9
Chimacum Valley—valley WA-9
Chimal Tank—reservoir NM-5
Chimariyatori MH-9
**Chimayo—pop pl** NM-5
Chimayo (CCD)—cens area NM-5
Chimayosos Peak—summit NM-5
Chimborazo Park—park VA-3
Chimborazo Sch—school VA-3
Chim Commercial Airp—airport PA-2
Chime Bell Ch—church SC-3
Chimena Natural Area—park AZ-5
Chimenchun Creek—stream AK-9
Chimenchun Point—cape AK-9
Chimenea Canyon—valley AZ-5
Chimenea Creek—stream TX-5
Chimeneas Creek—stream TX-5
Chimenea Well—well AZ-5
Chimenticook Stream—stream ME-1
Chime Pond MA-1
Chime Run—stream IN-6
Chimes—locale AR-4
Chimes, The—locale ME-1
Chimes Chamber—cave UT-8
Chime Street Sch—school MI-6
**Chimes View Acres (subdivision)—pop pl** UT-8
Chimhuevis Mountains AZ-5
Chimicum Creek WA-9
Chimikim WA-9
Chimikim Creek WA-9
Chimiles—civil CA-9
Chimiles Farm Center—locale CA-9
Chiminea Peak—summit AZ-5
Chimineas Creek TX-5
Chimineas Ranch—locale CA-9
Chimish Lake WI-6
Chimleyville Cem—cemetery LA-4
Chimleyville Ch—church LA-4
Chimmekanee Gulch—valley CA-9
Chimney Rock—summit UT-8
Chimmey Well—locale NM-5
Chimney, The UT-8
Chimney, The—pillar AZ-5
Chimney, The—pillar NY-2
Chimney, The—pillar OR-9
Chimney, The—pillar WY-8
Chimney, The—summit KY-4
Chimney, The—summit VA-3
Chimney Bayou—stream TX-5
Chimney Bluff—cliff MO-7
Chimney Bluff—cliff NY-2
Chimney Bluff—cliff (3) TX-5
Chimney Branch—stream AL-4
Chimney Branch—stream MD-2
Chimney Branch—stream NC-3
Chimney Branch—stream (2) VA-3
Chimney Butte—pillar SD-7
Chimney Butte—summit AZ-5
Chimney Butte—summit ID-8
Chimney Butte—summit (4) MT-8
Chimney Butte—summit NE-7
Chimney Butte—summit (2) ND-7
Chimney Butte—summit SD-7
Chimney Butte—summit (2) WY-8
Chimney Butte Creek—stream ND-7
Chimney Butte Pit No 3—reservoir WY-8
Chimney Butte Rsvr—reservoir WY-8
Chimney Butte Sch—school NE-7
Chimney Butte Spring—spring AZ-5
Chimney Canyon—valley (4) AZ-5
Chimney Canyon—valley (5) CA-9
Chimney Canyon—valley (2) CO-8
Chimney Canyon—valley (2) NV-8
Chimney Canyon—valley (5) NM-5
Chimney Canyon—valley SD-7
Chimney Canyon—valley (3) UT-8
Chimney Canyons—area CO-8
Chimney Cave—cave NM-5
Chimney Corner CT-1
Chimney Corner—locale VT-1
Chimney Corner—locale WV-2
**Chimney Corner—pop pl** VA-3
**Chimney Corners—pop pl** NY-2
Chimney Corners Pond—reservoir MA-1
Chimney Corners Pond Dam—dam MA-1
Chimney Cove—bay AK-9
Chimney Cove—bay FL-3
Chimney Cove—bay TX-5
Chimney Crater—crater CA-9
Chimney Creek CO-8
Chimney Creek NV-8
Chimney Creek—stream CA-9
Chimney Creek—stream CO-8
Chimney Creek—stream GA-3
Chimney Creek—stream (8) ID-8
Chimney Creek—stream (6) MT-8
Chimney Creek—stream NE-7
Chimney Creek—stream (6) NV-8
Chimney Creek—stream NC-3
Chimney Creek—stream OK-5
Chimney Creek—stream (4) OR-9
Chimney Creek—stream (7) TX-5
Chimney Creek—stream WA-9
Chimney Creek—stream (2) WY-8
Chimney Creek Ranch—locale TX-5
Chimney Creek Reservoir NV-8
Chimney Crossing—locale MT-8
Chimney Dam—dam NV-8
Chimney Dam—dam NM-5
Chimney End Ridge—ridge NC-3
Chimney Flat—flat CA-9
Chimney Flats—flat (2) CA-9
Chimney Fork CO-8
Chimney Fork—stream AK-9
Chimney Gap—gap NC-3
Chimney Gulch—valley CA-9
Chimney Gulch—valley (2) CO-8
Chimney Gulch—valley ID-8
Chimney Gulch—valley MT-8
Chimney Gulch—valley OR-9
Chimney Gulch—valley (2) WY-8
Chimney Hill—summit MA-1
Chimney Hill—summit NM-5
Chimney Hill—summit OK-5
Chimney Hill—summit TX-5
Chimney Hill—summit UT-8
Chimney Hill—summit WY-8
Chimney Hills IN-6
**Chimney Hill (subdivision)—pop pl (2).** AZ-5
Chimney Hollow—valley CO-8
Chimney Hollow—valley KY-4
Chimney Hollow—valley NY-2
Chimney Hollow—valley (3) TN-4
Chimney Hollow—valley (3) TX-5
Chimney Hollow—valley UT-8
Chimney Hollow—valley VA-3
Chimney Hollow—valley WV-2
Chimney Hollow Spring—spring TX-5
Chimney Hollow Trail—trail (2) VA-3
Chimney Hot Spring NV-8
Chimney Island—island NY-2
Chimney Island—island SC-3
Chimney Knob—summit NC-3
Chimney Knob—summit TN-4
Chimney Lake ID-8
Chimney Lake—bay WI-6
Chimney Lake—lake (2) CA-9
Chimney Lake—lake ID-8
Chimney Lake—lake (3) NM-5
Chimney Lake—lake OR-9
Chimney Lake—reservoir TX-5
Chimney Lakes ID-8
Chimney Lakes—lake MT-8
Chimney Marine Hosp—hospital TX-5
Chimney Meadow—flat CA-9
Chimney Meadow—flat UT-8
Chimney Mountains NY-2
Chimney Mtn GA-3
Chimney Mtn NC-3
Chimney Mtn—summit AL-4
Chimney Mtn—summit (2) AK-9
Chimney Mtn—summit GA-3
Chimney Mtn—summit NY-2
Chimney Mtn—summit OK-5
Chimney Mtn—summit TN-4
Chimney Mtn—summit VA-3
Chimney Park—area UT-8
Chimney Park—flat UT-8
Chimney Park—flat WY-8
Chimney Park—park WY-8
Chimney Park Camp—locale WY-8
Chimney Pass—gap AK-9
Chimney Peak CA-9
Chimney Peak CO-8
Chimney Peak—summit AL-4
Chimney Peak—summit CA-9
Chimney Peak—summit CO-8
Chimney Peak—summit ID-8
Chimney Peak—summit ME-1
Chimney Peak—summit NV-8
Chimney Peak—summit NM-5
Chimney Peak—summit OR-9
Chimney Peak—summit WA-9
Chimney Peak Lookout Tower—locale AL-4
Chimney Peaks—summit WA-9
Chimney Peak Trail—trail OR-9
Chimney Pier Hills—range IN-6
Chimney Pier Hills Cem—cemetery IN-6
Chimney Pit Tank—reservoir NM-5
Chimney Point—cape CT-1
Chimney Point—cape NY-2
Chimney Point—locale VT-1
Chimney Point—summit NM-5
Chimney Point Tavern—hist pl VT-1
Chimney Pole Creek—stream VA-3
Chimney Pole Marsh—swamp VA-3
Chimney Pond—reservoir MA-1
Chimney Pond Campground—locale ME-1
Chimney Pond Dam—dam MA-1
Chimney Ponds (historical)—lake PA-2
Chimney Pond Trail—trail ME-1
Chimney Pot Rsvr—reservoir ID-8
Chimney Ranch—locale TX-5
Chimney Ridge—ridge CA-9
Chimney Ridge—ridge WA-9
Chimney Ridge—ridge WV-2
Chimney Ridge—ridge WY-8
Chimney Rock WI-6
Chimney Rock WY-8
Chimney Rock—bar (2) ME-1
Chimney Rock—island AK-9
Chimney Rock—island CA-9
Chimney Rock—locale MT-8
Chimney Rock—pillar AL-4
Chimney Rock—pillar (3) AZ-5
Chimney Rock—pillar (2) AR-4
Chimney Rock—pillar (13) CA-9
Chimney Rock—pillar (5) CO-8
Chimney Rock—pillar IL-6
Chimney Rock—pillar (2) KY-4
Chimney Rock—pillar MN-6
Chimney Rock—pillar (4) MT-8
Chimney Rock—pillar (2) NM-5
Chimney Rock—pillar NC-3
Chimney Rock—pillar OK-5
Chimney Rock—pillar (5) OR-9
Chimney Rock—pillar (2) TN-4
Chimney Rock—pillar TX-5
Chimney Rock—pillar (7) UT-8
Chimney Rock—pillar WV-2
Chimney Rock—pillar (2) WI-6
Chimney Rock—pillar (6) WY-8
**Chimney Rock—pop pl** CO-8
**Chimney Rock—pop pl** NJ-2
**Chimney Rock—pop pl** NC-3
**Chimney Rock—pop pl** WI-6
Chimney Rock—summit AZ-5
Chimney Rock—summit (4) CA-9
Chimney Rock—summit (3) CO-8
Chimney Rock—summit ID-8
Chimney Rock—summit KY-4
Chimney Rock—summit MD-2
Chimney Rock—summit MO-7
Chimney Rock—summit (3) MT-8
Chimney Rock—summit NE-7
Chimney Rock—summit (2) NV-8
Chimney Rock—summit (3) NM-5
Chimney Rock—summit OK-5
Chimney Rock—summit OR-9
Chimney Rock—summit PA-2
Chimney Rock—summit (2) UT-8
Chimney Rock—summit (9) VA-3
Chimney Rock—summit (2) WA-9
Chimney Rock—summit WV-2
Chimney Rock—summit (2) WI-6
Chimney Rock—summit (5) WY-8
Chimney Rock Archeol Site—hist pl CO-8
Chimney Rock Beagle Club—other PA-2
Chimney Rock Bluff—cliff AR-4
Chimney Rock Bluff—cliff KY-4
Chimney Rock Branch—stream NC-3
Chimney Rock Butte—summit OR-9
Chimney Rock Butte—summit WY-8
Chimney Rock Camp—locale KY-4
Chimney Rock Campground—park OR-9
Chimney Rock Canal—canal NE-7
Chimney Rock Canyon UT-8
Chimney Rock Canyon—valley AZ-5
Chimney Rock Canyon—valley NV-8
Chimney Rock Canyon—valley NM-5
Chimney Rock Canyon—valley (2) UT-8
Chimney Rock Cave—cave MO-7
Chimney Rock Cem—cemetery NE-7
Chimney Rock Coulee—valley MT-8
Chimney Rock Creek VA-3
Chimney Rock Creek—stream AZ-5
Chimney Rock Creek—stream CA-9
Chimney Rock Creek—stream MT-8
Chimney Rock Creek—stream WI-6
Chimney Rock Draw—valley CO-8
Chimney Rock Draw—valley UT-8
Chimney Rock Farm—hist pl VA-3
Chimney Rock Flat—summit UT-8
Chimney Rock Fork—stream VA-3
Chimney Rock Gorge—valley NJ-2
Chimney Rock Gulch—valley (2) CO-8
Chimney Rock Gulch—valley WY-8
Chimney Rock Historical Monument—other CA-9
Chimney Rock Hollow—valley OH-6
Chimney Rock Hollow—valley OK-5
Chimney Rock Indian Bluffs State Game Mgt Ar—park IA-7
Chimney Rock Lake—lake CA-9
Chimney Rock Lake—lake UT-8
Chimney Rock Mtn—summit AR-4
Chimney Rock Mtn—summit NC-3
Chimney Rock Mtn—summit VA-3
Chimney Rock Natl Historic Site—park NE-7
Chimney Rock Pass—gap UT-8
Chimney Rock Point—cliff CO-8
Chimney Rock Post Office—locale CO-8
Chimney Rock Ranch—locale (2) CA-9
Chimney Rock Ranch—locale WY-8
Chimneyrock Ridge—ridge NC-3
Chimney Rock Rsvr—reservoir WY-8
Chimney Rock Run—stream WV-2
Chimney Rocks TN-4
Chimney Rocks—cliff PA-2
Chimney Rocks—pillar CO-8
Chimney Rocks—pillar VA-3
Chimney Rocks—rock (2) AR-4
Chimney Rocks—summit KY-4
Chimney Rocks—summit OH-6
Chimney Rocks—summit (3) PA-2
Chimney Rocks—summit (3) TN-4
Chimney Rocks—summit UT-8
Chimney Rocks—summit VA-3
Chimney Rocks—summit WY-8
Chimney Rock Spring—spring NV-8
Chimney Rock State Public Hunting Grounds—park WI-6
Chimney Rock State Wetlands Area—park WI-6
Chimney Rocks Trail—trail TN-4
Chimney Rock Tank—reservoir NM-5
Chimney Rock (Township of)—fmr MCD NC-3
Chimney Rock Well—well CO-8
Chimney Rsvr—reservoir NV-8
Chimney Rsvr—reservoir (2) WY-8
Chimney Run—stream VA-3
Chimney Run Ch—church VA-3
Chimneys NC-3
Chimneys TN-4
Chimneys, The TN-4
Chimneys, The—hist pl VA-3
Chimneys, The—island CT-1
Chimneys, The—locale WY-8
Chimneys, The—pillar CO-8
Chimneys, The—pillar MT-8
Chimneys, The—pillar TN-4
Chimneys, The—pillar TX-5
Chimneys, The—summit NC-3
Chimneys, The—summit TX-5
Chimneys, The—summit WY-8
Chimneys Campground—locale TN-4
Chimney Slough—bay (2) TX-5
Chimneys of Treasure Mountain—pillar CO-8
Chimney Spring—spring (5) AZ-5
Chimney Spring—spring (3) CA-9
Chimney Spring—spring CO-8
Chimney Spring—spring ID-8
Chimney Spring—spring NV-8
Chimney Spring—spring UT-8
Chimney Spring—spring WY-8
Chimney Springs NV-8
Chimney Springs—spring MT-8
Chimney Springs—spring NV-8
Chimney Springs—spring OR-9
Chimney Springs Canyon—valley OR-9
Chimney Springs Draw—valley WY-8
Chimney Springs Hollow—valley TN-4
**Chimney Springs (subdivision)—pop pl** AL-4
Chimney Stack—pillar KY-4
Chimneystack Rock—summit PA-2
Chimneystack Run—stream PA-2
Chimneys Trail—trail TX-5
**Chimney Street Condominium—pop pl** UT-8
Chimney Sweeps Islands—island NY-2
Chimney Tank—reservoir (3) AZ-5
Chimneytop GA-3
Chimney Top NC-3
Chimney Top TN-4
Chimney Top—pillar WV-2
Chimney Top—summit GA-3
Chimneytop—summit NC-3
Chimneytop—summit SC-3
Chimneytop—summit (2) TN-4
Chimney Top Cave—cave TN-4
Chimney Top Creek—stream KY-4
Chimneytop Gap—gap SC-3
**Chimneytop (historical)—pop pl** TN-4
Chimney Top Mtn GA-3
Chimneytop Mtn—summit GA-3
Chimneytop Mtn—summit NC-3
Chimneytop Mtn—summit TN-4
Chimney Top Mtn—summit TN-4
Chimney Top Post Office (historical)—building TN-4
Chimney Top Rock—summit KY-4
Chimney Tops—summit TN-4
Chimneytop Sch (historical)—school TN-4
Chimney Town AL-4
Chimney Wash—stream AZ-5
Chimney Well—well NM-5
Chimney Well—well TX-5
Chimney Windmill—locale TX-5
Chimon Island—island CT-1
Chimon Rock—island CT-1
Chimopovy AZ-5
Chin, Bayou—stream LA-4
Chin, The—summit VT-1
China—locale NY-2
**China—pop pl** AL-4
**China—pop pl** IN-6
**China—pop pl** LA-4
**China—pop pl** ME-1
**China—pop pl** TX-5
China Bar—bar (2) CA-9
China Bar—bar OR-9
China Bar—bar (2) WA-9
China Bar Rapids—rapids (2) OR-9
China Basin—basin ID-8
China Basin—basin MT-8
China Basin—harbor CA-9
China Bayou—gut LA-4
China Belle Oil And Gas Field—other MI-6
China Bend—bend CA-9
China Bend—bend WA-9
Chinaberry—hist pl SC-3
Chinaberry Canyon—valley NM-5
Chinaberry Ch (historical)—church MS-4
Chinaberry Draw—valley NM-5
Chinaberry Draw—valley TX-5
Chinaberry Sch (historical)—school MS-4
Chinaberry Spring—spring (2) AZ-5
Chinaberry Tank—reservoir AZ-5
Chinaberry Well—well NM-5
China Bluff—cliff AL-4
China Bluff Access Area—park AL-4
China Bluff Bar—bar AL-4
China Bowl—basin CO-8
China Branch—stream TX-5
China Butte—summit ID-8
China Butte—summit WY-8
China Cabin Flat—flat CA-9
China Camp—hist pl CA-9
China Camp—locale (2) CA-9
China Camp—locale NV-8
China Camp—summit NV-8
China Camp Canyon—valley AZ-5
China Camp Canyon—valley NM-5
China Camp Spring—spring OR-9
China Canyon—valley CO-8
China Canyon—valley (3) NM-5
China Canyon—valley (2) TX-5
China Canyon Tank—reservoir TX-5
China Canyon Windmill—locale NM-5
China Cap—summit ID-8
China Cap—summit (2) OR-9
China Cap Creek—stream OR-9
China Cap Mine—mine OR-9
China Cap Mountain OR-9
China Cap Peak OR-9
China Cap Ridge—ridge OR-9
China Cem—cemetery LA-4
China Chapel—church TX-5
China Chapel Ch—church TX-5
China (Chinatown)—uninc pl CA-9
China Church MO-7
China Cove—bay AK-9
China Cove—bay (2) CA-9
China Creek ID-8
China Creek OR-9
China Creek—locale TX-5
China Creek—stream (13) CA-9
China Creek—stream CO-8
China Creek—stream (10) ID-8
China Creek—stream MT-8
China Creek—stream (4) NV-8
China Creek—stream NC-3
China Creek—stream OK-5
China Creek—stream (15) OR-9
China Creek—stream (6) TX-5
China Creek—stream (3) WA-9
China Creek Cem—cemetery TX-5
China Creek Corral Pond—lake OR-9
China Creek Ditch—canal OR-9
China Creek Placer Mine—mine CA-9
China Creek Ranch—locale ID-8
China Creek Spring—spring OR-9
China Creek Trail—trail OR-9
China Creek Windmill—locale TX-5
China Dam—dam NV-8
China Dam Tank—reservoir AZ-5
China Diggings—locale OR-9
China Diggings—mine OR-9
China Ditch—canal CA-9
China Ditch—canal (2) OR-9
China Ditch—canal WA-9
China Draw—valley AZ-5
China Draw—valley (5) NM-5
China Draw—valley (6) TX-5
China Draw Well—locale NM-5
China Flat—flat (8) CA-9
China Flat—flat ID-8
China Flat—flat OR-9
China Fork—stream (3) ID-8
China Gap—gap OR-9
China Garden—flat (4) CA-9
China Garden—locale ID-8
China Garden—locale NV-8
China Garden—locale OR-9
China Garden Creek—stream ID-8
China Garden Creek—stream NV-8
China Gardens CA-9
China Gardens—flat NV-8
China Gardens Camp (Site)—locale CA-9
China Garden Spring CA-9
China Garden Spring—spring CA-9
China Gardens Spring—spring CA-9
China Gate—gap CA-9
China Grade—slope NV-8
China Grove—hist pl LA-4
China Grove—hist pl MS-4
China Grove—hist pl NC-3
China Grove—hist pl SC-3
China Grove—locale TX-5
**China Grove—pop pl** AL-4
**China Grove—pop pl** MS-4
**China Grove—pop pl** NC-3
**China Grove—pop pl** TN-4
**China Grove—pop pl (2)** TX-5
China Grove African Methodist Episcopal Church MS-4
China Grove Airp—airport NC-3
China Grove Baptist Ch MS-4
China Grove Baptist Ch—church (2) MS-4
China Grove Baptist Ch (historical)—church MS-4
China Grove (CCD)—cens area TN-4
China Grove Cem—cemetery AL-4
China Grove Cem—cemetery (2) GA-3
China Grove Cem—cemetery LA-4
China Grove Cem—cemetery (2) MS-4
China Grove Cem—cemetery NC-3
China Grove Cem—cemetery TN-4
China Grove Cemeteries—cemetery AR-4
China Grove Ch AL-4
China Grove Ch—church AL-4
China Grove Ch—church AR-4
China Grove Ch—church (2) GA-3
China Grove Ch—church (3) LA-4
China Grove Ch—church (4) MS-4
China Grove Ch—church (4) NC-3
China Grove Ch—church (3) SC-3
China Grove Ch—church TN-4
China Grove Ch—church (2) TX-5
China Grove Cotton Mill Village—CDP NC-3
China Grove Creek—stream AL-4
China Grove Division—civil TN-4
China Grove Elem Sch—school NC-3
China Grove JHS—school NC-3
China Grove Methodist Church MS-4
China Grove Methodist Church—hist pl MS-4
China Grove Plantation—hist pl MS-4
China Grove Roller Mill—hist pl NC-3
China Grove Sch—school SC-3
China Grove Sch—school TN-4
China Grove Sch—school (2) TX-5
China Grove Sch (historical)—school TN-4
China Grove (Township of)—fmr MCD NC-3
China Grove Windmill—locale TX-5
China Gulch—valley (23) CA-9
China Gulch—valley (4) ID-8
China Gulch—valley (3) MT-8
China Gulch—valley NV-8
China Gulch—valley (9) OR-9
China Gulch—valley SD-7
China Gulch Rapids—rapids OR-9
**China Hall—pop pl** PA-2
China Harbor—bay CA-9
China Hat—locale ID-8
China Hat—summit CA-9
China Hat—summit ID-8
China Hat—summit OR-9
China Hat Creek—stream OR-9
China Hat Peak—summit OR-9
China Hat Spring—spring OR-9
China Hill MT-8
China Hill—locale GA-3
China Hill—locale ID-8
China Hill—summit ME-1
China Hill—summit OR-9
China Hill Ch—church (2) FL-3
China Hill Rsvr—reservoir OR-9
China Hole—cave TN-4
China Hollow—valley OR-9
China Hollow Creek—stream OR-9
China Hot Peak OR-9
China Island—island LA-4
China Jim Mtn—summit NV-8
China Jim Spring—spring NV-8
China Junior High School AL-4
China Knob Well—well NM-5
China Lake—flat CA-9
China Lake—lake ME-1
China Lake—lake MT-8
China Lake—lake OR-9
China Lake—lake (3) TX-5
China Lake—lake UT-8
**China Lake—pop pl** CA-9
China Lake—reservoir UT-8
China Lake Dam—dam UT-8
China Lake Golf Club—other CA-9
China Lake (Naval Weapons Center)—military CA-9
China Lee Baptist Church MS-4
Chinalee Ch—church MS-4
Chinaman Bayou—bay LA-4
Chinaman Bluff—summit WI-6
Chinaman Coulee—valley ND-7
Chinaman Cove—bay MT-8
Chinaman Diggings—mine NV-8
Chinaman Flat CA-9
Chinaman Flat—flat AZ-5
Chinaman Gulch—valley MT-8
Chinaman Hat—summit (2) OR-9
Chinaman Hat—summit TX-5
Chinaman Hill—summit MT-8
Chinaman Lagoon—bay AK-9
Chinaman Lake UT-8
Chinaman Lake—lake MN-6
Chinaman Mortar Site—hist pl CA-9
Chinamans Canyon—valley CO-8
Chinamans Cut—bay CA-9
Chinamans Hat HI-9
Chinamans Hat—summit ID-8
Chinaman Slough—stream AK-9
Chinamans Spring—spring MT-8
Chinaman Tank—reservoir AZ-5
Chinaman Trail—trail OR-9
China Meadow—flat OR-9
China Meadows—flat UT-8
China Meadows Campground—locale UT-8
China Mine (Oro Grande)—mine CA-9
China Mission Ch (historical)—church MS-4
China Mott Windmill—locale TX-5
China Mountain Spring—spring NV-8
China Mtn—summit (2) CA-9
China Mtn—summit (2) ID-8
China Mtn—summit MT-8
China Mtn—summit (2) NV-8
China Mtn—summit OR-9
China Neck—gap UT-8
China Neck Cem—cemetery ME-1
China Pass—channel LA-4
China Peak CA-9
China Peak—summit (3) AZ-5
China Peak—summit (4) CA-9
China Peak—summit (2) OR-9
China Peak Observatory—building AZ-5
China Pig Hole—cave MO-7
China Point CA-9
China Point—cape (4) CA-9
China Point—cape UT-8
China Point—cliff ID-8
China Point—cliff WA-9
China Point—summit ID-8
China Point Ridge—ridge ID-8
China Pond—lake NY-2
China Pond—reservoir NM-5
China Pond—swamp TX-5
China Poot Bay—bay AK-9
China Poot Lake—lake AK-9
China Ranch—locale CA-9
China Ranch—locale TX-5
China Rapids—rapids ID-8
China Rapids—rapids OR-9
China Ravine—valley (2) CA-9
China Ridge—ridge CA-9
China Ridge—ridge NV-8
China Road—trail NV-8
China Rock—cliff OR-9

China Row Campground—locale UT-8
China Sch—school ME-1
China Slide—slope CA-9
China Slough—gut (3) CA-9
China Slough—stream CA-9
China South Gas Field—other MI-6
**China Spring**—pop pl TX-5
China Spring—spring (2) CA-9
China Spring—spring (2) ID-8
China Spring—spring (5) NV-8
China Spring—spring OR-9
China Spring Canyon—valley NV-8
China Spring Creek—stream AZ-5
China Springs—spring CA-9
China Springs—spring NM-5
China Springs (CCD)—cens area TX-5
**China Springs (China Spring Post Office)**—pop pl TX-5
China Springs Gulch—valley CA-9
China Spring Tank—reservoir AZ-5
China Tank—reservoir (4) NM-5
China Tank—reservoir TX-5
Chinati—locale TX-5
Chinati Cem—cemetery TX-5
Chinati Mountains—range TX-5
Chinati Peak—summit TX-5
Chinatown IL-6
China Town—locale AK-9
Chinatown—locale IL-6
Chinatown—locale MT-8
Chinatown—locale NV-8
China Town—locale OR-9
**Chinatown**—pop pl CA-9
**Chinatown**—pop pl HI-9
**Chinatown**—pop pl NY-2
China Town—rock UT-8
Chinatown Cem—cemetery NV-8
Chinatown Hist Dist—hist pl HI-9
**China (Town of)**—pop pl ME-1
Chinatown Pump—other OR-9
**China (Township of)**—pop pl IL-6
**China (Township of)**—pop pl MI-6
Chinatown Spring—spring AZ-5
**Chinatown (subdivision)**—pop pl SD-7
Chinatown Wash—valley UT-8
China Union Ch—church MO-7
China Village Cem—cemetery ME-1
China Village Cem Extension—cemetery ME-1
China Village Hist Dist—hist pl ME-1
China Wall Iowa Hill Ditch (abandoned)—canal CA-9
China Wash—stream AZ-5
China Well—well NM-5
China Well (dry)—well NV-8
China Wells (Site)—locale CA-9
China Windmill—locale TX-5
Chincapin Creek MS-4
Chinchahoma Creek—stream MS-4
Chinchalo—locale OR-9
Chinchbug Well—well NM-5
Chinch Creek—stream AL-4
**Chinchilla**—pop pl PA-2
**Chinchuba**—pop pl LA-4
Chinchuba, Bayou—stream LA-4
Chinchuba Bayou MS-4
Chinchuba Cem—cemetery LA-4
Chin Chuck Camps—other HI-9
**Chin Chuck (Chin Chuck Camps)**—pop pl HI-9
Chin Chuschu Well AZ-5
Chincka Homa Creek MS-4
Chincopin Branch—stream NJ-2
**Chincoteague**—pop pl VA-3
Chincoteague Bay—bay MD-2
Chincoteague Bay—bay VA-3
Chincoteague Ch—church VA-3
Chincoteague Channel—channel VA-3
Chincoteague Creek VA-3
Chincoteague HS—school VA-3
Chincoteague Inlet—channel VA-3
Chincoteague Island VA-3
Chincoteague Island—island VA-3
Chincoteague Natl Wildlife Ref—park MD-2
Chincoteague Natl Wildlife Ref—park VA-3
Chincoteague Point—cape VA-3
Chincoteague Pumping Station—other VA-3
Chin Creek—stream NV-8
Chin Creek Ditch—canal NV-8
Chin Creek Ranch—locale NV-8
Chin Creek Rsvr—reservoir NV-8
Chin Creek Spring—spring NV-8
Chindaglekne Creek—stream AK-9
Chindagmund Lake—lake AK-9
Chindberg Oil Field—oilfield KS-7
Chinde Mesa—summit AZ-5
Chinde Point—cliff AZ-5
Chinde Wash—stream NM-5
Chine, Bayou—gut LA-4
Chinee Gulch—valley ID-8
Chineekluk Creek—stream AK-9
Chineekluk Lake—lake AK-9
Chineekluk Mtn—summit AK-9
**Chinese**—pop pl CA-9
Chinese Baptist Ch—church FL-3
Chinese Baptist Church—hist pl WA-9
Chinese Bar—bar CA-9
**Chinese Camp**—pop pl CA-9
Chinese Camp (Site)—locale NV-8
Chinese Cem—cemetery (4) CA-9
Chinese Cem—cemetery HI-9
Chinese Cem—cemetery MS-4
Chinese Corner—locale VA-3
Chinese Diggins (Placer)—mine MT-8
Chinese Garden Spring CA-9
Chinese Gulch—valley (2) CA-9
Chinese Gulch—valley (2) ID-8
Chinese Harbor—bay CA-9
Chinese Odd Fellows Bldg—hist pl ID-8
Chinese Peak—summit CA-9
Chinese Rapids—rapids CA-9
Chinese Station—locale CA-9
Chinese Tank (historical)—reservoir AZ-5
Chinese Wall—cliff CO-8
Chinese Wall—cliff ID-8
Chinese Wall—cliff PA-2
Chinese Wall—cliff UT-8
Chinese Wall—ridge MT-8
Chinese Wall—ridge WY-8
Chinese Wall (natural dike)—cliff AZ-5
Chinese Wall Trail—trail MT-8
Chine Spring Knob—summit VA-3
Chine Spring Knob—summit WV-2
Chinfiyow—summit FM-9
Chingarata Creek NJ-2
Chingarora Creek—stream NJ-2
Ching Creek—stream ID-8
Chingeeruk Point—cape AK-9
Chingekigtlik Mtn—summit AK-9
Chinguapin TX-5
Chinguapin Branch—stream (2) TX-5
Chinguapin Creek SC-3
Chinguapin Swamp NC-3
**Chingville**—pop pl MD-2
Chinhinta Park—park MN-6
Chiniak Bay—bay AK-9
Chiniak Island—island AK-9
Chiniak Lagoon—lake AK-9
Chiniak Lake—lake AK-9
Chiniak Point—cape AK-9
Chiniak River—stream AK-9
Chinibaru MP-9
Chinibaru—island MP-9
Chinibaru Island MP-9
Chinibaru-To MP-9
Chinidere Mtn—summit OR-9
Chinieero MP-9
Chinieero—island MP-9
Chinieero Island MP-9
Chinieero-To MP-9
Chinie JHS—school AZ-5
Chinierro Island MP-9
Chinigyak Cape—cape AK-9
Chiniklik, Mount—summit AK-9
Chinikluk Slough—gut AK-9
Chinimi MP-9
Chinimi—island MP-9
Chinimi Island MP-9
Chinimi-To MP-9
Chinitna, Mount—summit AK-9
Chinitna Bay—bay AK-9
Chinitna Point—cape AK-9
Chinitna River—stream AK-9
Chinit Point—cape AK-9
Chinkapin Branch—stream FL-3
Chinkapin Branch—stream NC-3
Chinkapin Bridge—bridge NC-3
Chinkapin Creek MS-4
Chinkapin Creek—stream (2) NC-3
Chinkapin Grove Ch—church TN-4
Chinkapin Knob—summit AR-4
Chinkapin Mtn—summit AR-4
Chinkapin Ridge—ridge (2) AR-4
Chink Creek—stream MD-2
Chinkelyes Creek—stream AK-9
Chinkhollow Creek—stream CA-9
Chink Ridge OR-9
Chinks Peak—summit ID-8
Chinks Point—cape MD-2
**Chinle**—pop pl AZ-5
Chinle Airp—airport AZ-5
Chinle (CCD)—cens area AZ-5
Chinle Cem—cemetery AZ-5
Chinle Community Center—building AZ-5
Chinle Creek AZ-5
Chinle Creek—stream AZ-5
Chinle Creek—stream UT-8
Chin Lee AZ-5
Chin-lee Creek AZ-5
Chin-Lee Creek UT-8
Chinle Elementary Boarding Sch—school AZ-5
Chin Lee Mesa AZ-5
Chinlee Valley AZ-5
Chinlee Wash AZ-5
Chinle Extended Care Center—hospital AZ-5
Chinle HS—school AZ-5
Chinle Post Office—building AZ-5
Chinle Public Elem Sch—school AZ-5
Chinle River AZ-5
Chinle River UT-8
Chinle Valley—basin AZ-5
Chinle Valley Store—locale AZ-5
Chin-le Wash AZ-5
Chinle Wash UT-8
Chinle Wash—stream AZ-5
Chinle Water Tank—reservoir AZ-5
Chinlini Canyon AZ-5
Chinn—locale AL-4
Chinnabar Canyon—valley CA-9
Chinnabee—locale AL-4
Chinnabee, Lake—reservoir AL-4
Chinnabee Dam—dam AL-4
Chinnabee (historical)—locale AL-4
Chinnabee P.O. (historical)—locale AL-4
Chinnabys Fort AL-4
Chinnahee AL-4
Chinn Branch—stream VA-3
Chinn Cem—cemetery AR-4
Chinn Cem—cemetery IN-6
Chinn Cem—cemetery KS-7
Chinn Cem—cemetery MO-7
Chinn Cem—cemetery TX-5
Chinn Chapel—church TX-5
Chinneby AL-4
Chinneby Camp Ground (historical)—locale AL-4
**Chinneby (Chinnabee)**—pop pl AL-4
Chinneby Creek AL-4
Chinners—locale SC-3
Chinners Swamp—stream SC-3
Chinney Creek MI-6
Chinnick Creek—stream MT-8
Chinnis Branch—stream NC-3
Chinnis Cem—cemetery NC-3
Chinn Ridge—ridge VA-3
Chinns Branch VA-3
Chinns Branch—stream KY-4
Chinn Sch—school MO-7
Chinns Chapel—church LA-4
Chinns Lake—reservoir CO-8
Chinns Pond—reservoir VA-3
Chinn Spring—spring AR-4
Chinns Run—stream VA-3
**Chino**—pop pl CA-9
Chino, Cerro—summit TX-5
Chino, Sierra de—summit TX-5
Chino Basin—basin AZ-5
Chino Bay—bay LA-4
Chino Canyon—valley AZ-5
Chino Canyon—valley CA-9
Chinock, The—gap NH-1
Chinock Dike Light—locale OR-9
Chino Community Adult Sch—school CA-9
Chino Creek AZ-5
Chino Creek NV-8
Chino Creek—stream (2) CA-9
Chino Creek—stream MT-8
Chino Creek—stream NV-8
Chino Downs—other CA-9
Chino Draw—valley AZ-5
Chino Dry Lake—lake NM-5
Chino Flat—flat (3) CA-9
Chino Hills—range CA-9
Chino HS—school CA-9
Chinois Creek WA-9
Chino Island—island FL-3
Chinois Pass—channel LA-4
Chino Junior Fairgrounds—locale CA-9
Chino Mesa—summit NM-5
Chinom Point—cape WA-9
**Chinook**—pop pl IN-6
**Chinook**—pop pl MT-8
**Chinook**—pop pl WA-9
Chinook Bay Campground—locale ID-8
Chinook Bend—bend OR-9
Chinook Campground—locale ID-8
Chinook Cem—cemetery MT-8
Chinook Creek—stream AK-9
Chinook Creek—stream (2) WA-9
Chinook Jetty—locale WA-9
Chinook JHS—school WA-9
Chinook Lake—lake MT-8
Chinook Mtn—summit ID-8
Chinook Park—park OR-9
Chinook Pass—gap WA-9
Chinook Point—cape WA-9
Chinook Point—hist pl WA-9
Chinook River—stream WA-9
Chino Peak—summit NM-5
Chino Point—cliff (2) AZ-5
Chino Ridge—ridge CA-9
Chinos, Arroyo De Los—stream CA-9
Chino Spring—spring (3) AZ-5
Chino Spring Stockman Station—locale AZ-5
Chino Spring Tank AZ-5
Chino Station—locale AZ-5
Chino Tank—reservoir (4) AZ-5
Chino Valley AZ-5
**Chino Valley**—pop pl AZ-5
Chino Valley—valley AZ-5
Chino Valley Cem—cemetery AZ-5
Chino Valley Irrigation Ditch—canal AZ-5
Chino Valley Post Office—building AZ-5
Chino Valley Sch—school AZ-5
Chino Wash AZ-5
Chino Wash—stream AZ-5
Chino Well—well AZ-5
**Chinowths Corner**—pop pl CA-9
Chin Point—cape AK-9
Chinqua-Penn Camp—locale NC-3
Chinqua Penn Plantation (Historical Landmar—park NC-3
Chinquapin AR-4
Chinquapin—area NC-3
Chinquapin—locale (2) TX-5
**Chinquapin**—pop pl MS-4
**Chinquapin**—pop pl NC-3
Chinquapin, Lake—reservoir SC-3
Chinquapin Basin—basin CA-9
Chinquapin Bay—swamp NC-3
Chinquapin Bay—swamp SC-3
Chinquapin Bayou—gut TX-5
Chinquapin Brake—swamp MS-4
Chinquapin Branch—stream AR-4
Chinquapin Branch—stream GA-3
Chinquapin Branch—stream MS-4
Chinquapin Branch—stream (2) NC-3
Chinquapin Branch—stream (2) TX-5
Chinquapin Branch—stream VA-3
Chinquapin Butte—summit CA-9
Chinquapin Butte—summit OR-9
Chinquapin Canal—canal LA-4
Chinquapin Cem—cemetery TX-5
Chinquapin Ch—church AR-4
Chinquapin Ch—church NC-3
Chinquapin Ch—church SC-3
Chinquapin Ch—church (2) TN-4
Chinquapin Chapel—church NC-3
Chinquapin Creek AL-4
Chinquapin Creek TX-5
Chinquapin Creek—stream AL-4
Chinquapin Creek—stream (4) AR-4
Chinquapin Creek—stream CA-9
Chinquapin Creek—stream LA-4
Chinquapin Creek—stream (3) MS-4
Chinquapin Creek—stream (2) NC-3
Chinquapin Creek—stream (2) SC-3
Chinquapin Creek—stream (5) TX-5
Chinquapin Elem Sch—school NC-3
Chinquapin Falls—falls CA-9
**Chinquapin Falls**—pop pl SC-3
Chinquapin Falls Creek CA-9
Chinquapin Gap—gap NC-3
Chinquapin Grove—locale TN-4
Chinquapin Gulch—valley CA-9
Chinquapin Hill—summit PA-2
Chinquapin Hill—summit TN-4
Chinquapin Hill—summit TX-5
Chinquapin II Elem Sch—school NC-3
Chinquapin Knob—summit (2) AR-4
Chinquapin Knob—summit TN-4
Chinquapin Lake—lake CA-9
Chinquapin Lake Dam—dam MS-4
Chinquapin Lakes—lake CA-9
Chinquapin Landing—locale TX-5
Chinquapin Mtn—summit AR-4
Chinquapin Mtn—summit NC-3
Chinquapin Mtn—summit OK-5
Chinquapin Mtn—summit OR-9
Chinquapin Mtn—summit TN-4
Chinquapin Park—park MD-2
Chinquapin Point—cape (2) OR-9
Chinquapin Pond—lake GA-3
Chinquapin Post Office (historical)—building MS-4
Chinquapin Ranger Station—locale CA-9
Chinquapin Ridge AL-4
Chinquapin Ridge—ridge AL-4
Chinquapin Ridge—ridge AR-4
Chinquapin Ridge—ridge (2) GA-3
Chinquapin Ridge—ridge MS-4
Chinquapin Ridge—ridge NC-3
Chinquapin Ridge—ridge (3) TN-4
Chinquapin Ridge—ridge TX-5
Chinquapin Run—stream MD-2
Chinquapin Sch—school AR-4
Chinquapin Sch—school IA-7
Chinquapin Sch—school TN-4
Chinquapin Spring—spring AR-4
Chinquapin Spring Ridge—ridge AR-4
Chinquapin Swamp—stream VA-3
**Chinquapin Village**—pop pl VA-3
Chinquapir Ridge—ridge AL-4
Chinquapir Ridge—ridge NC-3
Chinsegut Hill—summit FL-3
Chinsegut Natl Wildlife Ref (historical)—park FL-3
**Chins Springs (historical)**—pop pl MS-4
Chintimini OR-9
Chintimini Creek—stream OR-9
Chinty Lake—lake WI-6
**Chinubee**—pop pl TN-4
Chinubee Cem—cemetery TN-4
Chin Whisker Hill—summit MI-6
Chiowith's Fork OH-6
**Chip**—pop pl (2) NC-3
Chipco Creek—stream AL-4
Chipco Lake—lake FL-3
Chip Coulee—stream MT-8
Chip Cove—bay AK-9
Chip Creek—stream ID-8
Chip Creek—stream MT-8
Chip Creek—stream WY-8
Chipeta—locale CO-8
Chipeta Canyon—valley UT-8
Chipeta Mtn—summit CO-8
Chipeta State Park—park CO-8
Chipilly Woods—woods IL-6
**Chipita Park**—pop pl CO-8
Chip Lake MI-6
Chip Lake—lake MI-6
Chip Lake—lake MN-6
Chip Lake—lake WI-6
Chipley GA-3
Chipley—locale TX-5
Chipley—other GA-3
**Chipley**—pop pl FL-3
Chipley, Lake—lake FL-3
Chipley (CCD)—cens area FL-3
Chipley Creek—stream FL-3
Chipley HS—school FL-3
Chipley Lake Dam—dam MS-4
Chipley-Pine Mountain Town Hall—hist pl GA-3
Chipley Sch—school GA-3
Chipman—locale NY-2
Chipman—locale TN-4
Chipman Canyon—valley NV-8
Chipman Canyon—valley UT-8
Chipman Cem—cemetery MO-7
Chipman Cem—cemetery OH-6
**Chipman Corners**—pop pl NY-2
Chipman Creek UT-8
Chipman Creek—stream UT-8
Chipman Gulch—valley OR-9
Chipman Hill—summit MA-1
Chipman Hill—summit VT-1
Chipman House—hist pl KY-4
Chipman Lake—lake VT-1
**Chipman Lake**—pop pl VT-1
Chipman Meadow—flat NV-8
Chipman Peak—summit UT-8
Chipman Point—cape CT-1
Chipman Point—cape VT-1
Chipman Pond—reservoir DE-2
Chipman Pond Dam—dam DE-2
Chipman Post Office (historical)—building TN-4
Chipman Ridge—ridge KY-4
Chipman Sch—school CA-9
Chipman Sch (historical)—school TN-4
Chipman Seep—spring UT-8
Chipman's Mill—hist pl DE-2
Chipmans Point VT-1
**Chipmans Point**—pop pl VT-1
Chipmonk NY-2
**Chipmonk**—pop pl NY-2
Chipmonk Creek NY-2
Chipmonk Spring AZ-5
Chipmunck NY-2
Chipmunck Creek NY-2
Chipmunck Hollow PA-2
**Chipmunk**—pop pl NY-2
Chipmunk Bay—bay NY-2
Chipmunk Bluff—summit CA-9
Chipmunk Canyon—valley NM-5
Chipmunk Coulee WI-6
Chipmunk Coulee—valley WI-6
Chipmunk Coulee Cem—cemetery WI-6
Chipmunk Creek—stream (2) CA-9
Chipmunk Creek—stream (2) MI-6
Chipmunk Creek—stream MT-8
Chipmunk Creek—stream NY-2
Chipmunk Creek—stream (2) WA-9
Chipmunk Creek—stream WY-8
Chipmunk Falls—falls (2) MI-6
Chipmunk Falls—falls MN-6
Chipmunk Flat—flat CA-9
Chipmunk Gulch—valley CO-8
Chipmunk Gulch—valley MT-8
Chipmunk Hill—ridge NV-8
Chipmunk Hollow—valley NY-2
Chipmunk Hollow—valley PA-2
Chipmunk Lake—lake CA-9
Chipmunk Lake—lake CO-8
Chipmunk Lake—lake MN-6
Chipmunk Meadow—flat (2) CA-9
Chipmunk Meadow—flat ID-8
Chipmunk Mine—mine CA-9
Chipmunk Peak—summit MT-8
Chipmunk Rapids—rapids ID-8
Chipmunk Rapids—rapids (3) WI-6
Chipmunk Rapids Campground—locale WI-6
Chipmunk Ridge—ridge CA-9
Chipmunk Ridge—ridge OR-9
Chipmunk Ridge—ridge WI-6
Chipmunk Rsvr—reservoir (2) CO-8
Chipmunk Spring—spring AZ-5
Chipmunk Spring—spring (2) CA-9
Chipmunk Spring—spring ID-8
Chipmunk Spring—spring (2) NV-8
Chipmunk Spring—spring NM-5
Chipmunk Spring—spring (2) OR-9
Chipmunk Spring—spring UT-8
Chipmunk Tank—reservoir AZ-5
Chipmunk Trail—trail CA-9
Chipmunk Trail—trail PA-2
Chipoaks Bay VA-3
Chip Off Mountain AR-4
Chi Point—cape AK-9
Chipola—locale FL-3
**Chipola**—pop pl FL-3
**Chipola**—pop pl LA-4
Chipola Cem—cemetery FL-3
Chipola Creek—stream (2) AL-4
Chipola Cutoff—bend FL-3
Chipola Junior Coll—school FL-3
Chipola Park—locale FL-3
Chipola River—stream (2) FL-3
**Chipola Terrace**—pop pl FL-3
Chippacurset Island RI-1
Chippanazie Creek—stream WI-6
Chippanazie Lake—lake WI-6
Chippanogset Island RI-1
Chippawa Channel Niagara River—stream NY-2
Chipp-A-Water Park—park MI-6
Chippean Canyon—valley UT-8
Chippean Ridge—ridge UT-8
Chippean Rocks—summit UT-8
Chippekokee Park—park IN-6
Chippendale IL-6
Chippendale Sch—school MI-6
**Chippenhaven Square (subdivision)**—pop pl NC-3
Chippen Hill—summit CT-1
**Chippenhook**—pop pl VT-1
Chippens Hill CT-1
Chippeny Creek—stream MI-6
Chipperfield, Mount—summit MT-8
Chipper Swamp—swamp SC-3
Chippeua Natl For—forest MN-6
Chippewa DE-2
Chippewa IN-6
Chippewa—locale PA-2
**Chippewa**—pop pl IL-6
Chippewa, Lake—reservoir TN-4
Chippewa, Lake—reservoir WI-6
Chippewa Agency Hist Dist—hist pl MN-6
Chippewa Bank—bar MI-6
Chippewa Bay—bay NY-2
**Chippewa Bay**—pop pl NY-2
**Chippewa Beach**—pop pl MI-6
Chippewa Bottoms—bend WI-6
Chippewa Campground—locale MN-6
Chippewa Campground—locale WI-6
Chippewa Cem—cemetery MI-6
Chippewa Cem—cemetery MN-6
Chippewa Ch—church MI-6
Chippewa Ch—church OH-6
**Chippewa City**—pop pl MN-6
**Chippewa (County)**—pop pl MI-6
**Chippewa (County)**—pop pl MN-6
**Chippewa (County)**—pop pl WI-6
Chippewa County Bank—hist pl MN-6
Chippewa County Courthouse—hist pl MI-6
Chippewa County International Airp—airport MI-6
Chippewa Creek MI-6
Chippewa Creek—stream IA-7
Chippewa Creek—stream (2) MI-6
Chippewa Creek—stream (2) MT-8
Chippewa Creek—stream NY-2
Chippewa Creek—stream (2) OH-6
Chippewa Creek—stream OK-5
Chippewa Creek—stream WY-8
Chippewa Ditch OH-6
Chippewa Elementary School PA-2
Chippewa Falls—falls MI-6
**Chippewa Falls**—pop pl WI-6
Chippewa Falls (Township of)—civ div MN-6
Chippewa Golf Course—locale PA-2
Chippewa Harbor—bay MI-6
Chippewa Harbor Campground—locale MI-6
Chippewa Harbour MI-6
Chippewa Hill MI-6
Chippewa Hills—range KS-7
Chippewa Hills Cem—cemetery KS-7
Chippewa HS—school OH-6
Chippewa Hunt Post—other MI-6
Chippewa Island—island OH-6
Chippewa Island—island WI-6
Chippewa JHS—school IL-6
Chippewa JHS—school (2) MI-6
Chippewa Lake—lake MI-6
Chippewa Lake—lake (3) MN-6
Chippewa Lake—lake WI-6
**Chippewa Lake**—pop pl MI-6
Chippewa Lake—reservoir MN-6
Chippewa Lake—reservoir OH-6
Chippewa Lake—reservoir PA-2
Chippewa Lake—reservoir WV-2
Chippewa Lake Cem—cemetery MI-6
Chippewa Lake (corporate name Chippewa-on-the-Lake)—5other OH-6
**Chippewa Lake Park**—pop pl OH-6
Chippewa Mall—locale PA-2
Chippewanuck Creek—stream IN-6
Chippewanuck Ditch IN-6
**Chippewa-on-the-Lake**—pop pl OH-6
Chippewa Park—park IL-6
Chippewa Park—park PA-2
Chippewa Playground—park OH-6
Chippewa Point—cape (2) MI-6
Chippewa Point—cape NY-2
Chippewa Point (historical)—cape ND-7
Chippewa Ranch Airp—airport KS-7
Chippewa Ridge IL-6
Chippewa River MN-6
Chippewa River—stream MI-6
Chippewa River—stream MN-6
Chippewa River—stream WI-6
Chippewa River State For—forest MI-6
Chippewa Sch—school IN-6
Chippewa Sch—school KS-7
Chippewa Sch—school MI-6
Chippewa Sch—school OH-6
Chippewassee Sch—school MI-6
Chippewa State Wildlife Mngmt Area—park MN-6
Chippewa Station Ch—church NY-2
**Chippewa Terrace**—pop pl GA-3
**Chippewa (Town of)**—pop pl WI-6
**Chippewa (Township of)**—pop pl (3) MI-6
**Chippewa (Township of)**—pop pl OH-6
**Chippewa (Township of)**—pop pl PA-2
Chippewa Trail—trail NH-1
Chippewa United Ch—church MI-6
Chippewa Valley Ch—church WI-6
Chippewa Valley HS—school MI-6
**Chippewa Vista**—pop pl MI-6
**Chippeway Park**—pop pl NM-5
Chippey Chapel Ch—church DE-2
Chippiannock Cem—cemetery IL-6
Chippie Creek—stream ID-8
Chip Pile Lake MI-6
Chipping Creek—stream MI-6
Chippoak Creek VA-3
Chippoak Point VA-3
Chippoaks Bay VA-3
Chippokes—locale VA-3
Chippokes Bay VA-3
Chippokes Plantation—hist pl VA-3
Chippokes Point—cape VA-3
Chipp Peak—summit AK-9
Chipp River—stream AK-9
Chipps—locale CA-9
Chipps—locale IL-6
Chipps Creek—stream (2) ID-8
Chipps Island—island CA-9
Chipps Mine—mine CA-9
Chipps Spring—spring OR-9
Chipp Trail—trail PA-2
Chippy Creek—stream ID-8
Chippy Creek—stream (3) MT-8
Chippy Spur—locale CA-9
Chips Cabin—locale AK-9
Chips Cave—cave AL-4
Chips Creek—stream CA-9
Chips Flat—locale CA-9
Chips Island—island AK-9
Chips Lake—lake CA-9
Chips Slough—stream AK-9
Chiputneticook Lakes—lake ME-1
Chipuxet River—stream RI-1
**Chipwood**—pop pl MS-4
Chiquapin Creek—stream OR-9
Chiquaqua Canyon CO-8
Chiquaqua Creek CO-8
Chiquasatunga Creek PA-2
Chiques PA-2
Chiquesatonga Creek PA-2
Chiquesatunga Creek PA-2
Chiques Church PA-2
Chiques Creek PA-2
Chiques Ridge PA-2
**Chiquita**—pop pl CA-9
Chiquita, Cabeza—cape PR-3
Chiquita, Canada —valley CA-9
Chiquita, Canon —valley TX-5
Chiquita, Mount—summit CO-8
Chiquita Canyon—valley CA-9
Chiquita Creek—stream CO-8
Chiquita Creek—stream OK-5
Chiquita Creek—stream TX-5
Chiquita Lake—lake CO-8
Chiquita Lake—lake MT-8
Chiquita Lake—reservoir CA-9
Chiquita Mine—mine NV-8
Chiquita Pass CA-9
Chiquitas, Las Piedras—ridge PR-3
Chiquito AZ-5
Chiquito FL-3
Chiquito Creek OK-5
Chiquito Creek—stream (2) CA-9
Chiquito Lake—lake CA-9
Chiquito Lake—lake OR-9
Chiquito Pass—gap CA-9
Chiquito Peak—summit CA-9
Chiquito Peak—summit CO-8
Chiquito Ridge—ridge CA-9
Chiquito Spring—spring CA-9
Chiquone Creek MD-2
Chiran—island MP-9
Chiran Island MP-9
Chiran-to MP-9
**Chireno**—pop pl TX-5
Chireno-Martinsville (CCD)—cens area TX-5
Chireno Sch—school TX-5
**Chiriaco Summit**—pop pl CA-9
Chiribon MP-9
Chiricahua—locale AZ-5
Chiricahua Butte—summit AZ-5
Chiricahua Ind Res (historical)—reserve AZ-5
Chi-ri-ca-hua Mountain AZ-5
Chiricahua Mountains—range AZ-5
Chiricahua Natl Monmt—park AZ-5
Chiricahua Peak—summit AZ-5
Chiricahua Siding Tank—reservoir AZ-5
Chiricahua Tank—reservoir AZ-5
Chiricahua Wilderness—park AZ-5
Chirichua Butte AZ-5
Chirikof, Cape—summit AK-9
Chirikof Island—island AK-9
Chirikof Point—cape AK-9
Chirochi-to MP-9
Chiroskey River—stream AK-9
Chirpchatter Mtn—summit CA-9
Chirreones Arroyo—valley AZ-5
Chirreon Wash—stream AZ-5
Chirubon—island MP-9
Chirubon-to MP-9
Chirutaken—island MP-9
**Chisago City**—pop pl MN-6
**Chisago (County)**—pop pl MN-6
Chisago County Courthouse—hist pl MN-6
Chisago Lake—lake MN-6
Chisago Lake Cem—cemetery MN-6
Chisago Lakes Golf Club—other MN-6
Chisago Lakes Sch—school MN-6
Chisago Lake (Township of)—civ div MN-6
Chisak Bay—bay AK-9
Chisak Island—island AK-9
Chisam Cem—cemetery TN-4
Chisana—locale AK-9
Chisana Creek—stream OR-9
Chisana Glacier—glacier AK-9
Chisana Hist Dist—hist pl AK-9
Chisana Mtn—summit AK-9
Chisana Pass—gap AK-9
Chisana River—stream AK-9
**Chisca**—pop pl AL-4
Chisca Depot Settlement AL-4

Chisca (historical)—locale AL-4
Chisca Mine (underground)—mine AL-4
Chise—locale NM-5
Chisel Branch—stream MD-2
Chiselfinger Ridge—ridge WV-2
Chisel Knob—summit VA-3
Chisel Lake—lake IL-6
Chisel Run—stream VA-3
Chisel Springs—spring WI-6
Chisels Run VA-3
**Chiselville**—pop pl VT-1
Chisem Post Office (historical)—building TN-4
Chisenhall Bar—bar AL-4
Chisenhall Branch—stream AL-4
Chisenhall Cem—cemetery (2) AL-4
Chisenhall Spring—spring AL-4
Chisenhall Spring Cave—cave AL-4
**Chisenhall Subdivision**—pop pl AL-4
Chisford—locale VA-3
Chishoktak Ch—church OK-5
Chisholm SC-3
**Chisholm**—pop pl AL-4
**Chisholm**—pop pl KY-4
**Chisholm**—pop pl ME-1
**Chisholm**—pop pl MN-6
**Chisholm**—pop pl TX-5
Chisholm—uninc pl KS-7
Chisholm, Jesse, Grave Site—hist pl OK-5
Chisholm, Mount—summit MT-8
Chisholm Baptist Ch—church AL-4
Chisholm Branch—stream AL-4
Chisholm Branch—stream MS-4
Chisholm Brook—stream ME-1
Chisholm Cabin—locale MT-8
Chisholm Campground—locale MT-8
Chisholm Canyon—valley OR-9
Chisholm Cem—cemetery AL-4
Chisholm Cem—cemetery KY-4
Chisholm Cem—cemetery MS-4
Chisholm Cem—cemetery OK-5
Chisholm Cem—cemetery SC-3
Chisholm Cem—cemetery TX-5
Chisholm Ch—church OK-5
Chisholm Ch of Christ—church AL-4
Chisholm Creek AL-4
Chisholm Creek—stream AL-4
Chisholm Creek—stream KS-7
Chisholm Creek—stream OK-5
Chisholm Creek—stream (2) TN-4
Chisholm Creek—stream VA-3
Chisholm Elem Sch—school AL-4
Chisholm Elem Sch—school KS-7
Chisholm Field—park FL-3
Chisholm Heights Ch—church AL-4
Chisholm-Hibbing Airp—airport MN-6
Chisholm Hills Country Club—other MI-6
**Chisholm Hills (subdivision)**—pop pl AL-4
Chisholm Hollow—valley AR-4
Chisholm Islands SC-3
**Chisholm Junction**—pop pl MN-6
Chisholm Lake—lake AK-9
Chisholm Lake—lake TN-4
Chisholm Methodist Ch—church AL-4
Chisholm Mine—mine NV-8
Chisholm Mission—church MS-4
Chisholm MS—school KS-7
Chisholm Mtn—summit MT-8
Chisholm Number 1 Dam—dam SD-7
Chisholm-Nydegger Cem—cemetery MD-2
Chisholm Park—park AL-4
Chisholm Point—cape MN-6
Chisholm Pond—lake ME-1
Chisholm Pond—lake NY-2
Chisholm Ranch—locale MT-8
Chisholm Ranch—locale SD-7
Chisholm Ranch Landing Field—airport SD-7
Chisholm Run—stream MD-2
Chisholm Sch—school ME-1
Chisholm Sch—school NJ-2
Chisholm Sch (historical)—school AL-4
Chisholm School AL-4
Chisholm's Creek VA-3
Chisholms Islands—island SC-3
Chisholm Swamp—swamp GA-3
Chisholm Trail Elem Sch—school KS-7
Chisholm Trail Lake OK-5
Chisholm Trail Park—park TX-5
Chisholm Valley—valley MN-6
Chishom Point—cape NY-2
Chisik Island—island AK-9
Chiska Creek—stream NC-3
Chisler Cem—cemetery WV-2
Chisler Knob—summit WV-2
Chisley Fork WV-2
Chisley Run VA-3
Chisleys Run VA-3
Chislhom Creek VA-3
Chism—locale OK-5
**Chism**—pop pl AL-4
Chismahoo Creek—stream CA-9
Chismahoo Mtn—summit CA-9
**Chisman**—pop pl NC-3
Chisman Cem—cemetery IA-7
Chisman Creek—stream VA-3
Chismans Creek VA-3
Chism Bluff—cliff TX-5
Chism Cem—cemetery KY-4
Chism Creek AL-4
Chism Creek—stream KY-4
Chism Creek—stream OK-5
Chism Ditch—canal CA-9
Chism Gulch—valley SD-7
Chism (historical)—locale MS-4
Chism Lake—reservoir GA-3
Chism Lake Dam—dam MS-4
Chismore Butte—summit OR-9
Chism Ridge—ridge KY-4
**Chism Subdivision**—pop pl MS-4
Chismville—locale AR-4
Chisna—locale AK-9
Chisna Creek—stream AK-9
Chisna Pass—gap AK-9
Chisna River—stream AK-9
Chisney—other OK-5
**Chisolm**—pop pl SC-3
Chisolm Cem—cemetery NC-3
Chisolm Cem—cemetery SC-3
Chisolm Creek MT-8
Chisolm Creek OK-5
Chisolm HS—school FL-3
Chisolm Island SC-3
Chisolm Pit—mine MS-4
Chisolms island SC-3
Chisos Basin TX-5
Chisos Mountain Lodge—locale TX-5
Chisos Mountains—range TX-5
Chispa—locale TX-5
Chispa Creek TX-5
Chispa Hills—summit NV-8
Chispa Mtn—summit TX-5
Chiss-chetan River ND-7
Chissolms Ford—locale TN-4
Chissovun Lake—lake AK-9
Chistiakof Island—island AK-9
Chistmas Crossing MS-4
**Chistochina**—pop pl AK-9
Chistochina ANV758—reserve AK-9
Chistochina Glacier—glacier AK-9
Chistochina River—stream AK-9
Chisum—locale NM-5
Chisum Canyon—valley TX-5
Chisum House—hist pl AR-4
Chisum Spring—spring TX-5
Chiswell Island—island AK-9
Chiswell Islands—island AK-9
Chiswell's Inheritance—hist pl MD-2
Chita—locale TX-5
**Chita (historical)**—pop pl MS-4
Chitanana River—stream AK-9
Chitanatala Mountains—other AK-9
Chita Post Office (historical)—building MS-4
Chitick Cem—cemetery IN-6
Chiticote Ranch—locale TX-5
Chitigue, Bayou—gut LA-4
**Chitimacha Ind Res**—pop pl LA-4
Chitimacha Lake LA-4
**Chitina**—pop pl AK-9
Chitina ANV759—reserve AK-9
Chitina Glacier—glacier AK-9
Chitina River—stream AK-9
Chitina Tin Shop—hist pl AK-9
Chitiok, Mount—summit AK-9
Chitistone Falls—falls AK-9
Chitistone Glacier—glacier AK-9
Chitistone Gorge—valley AK-9
Chitistone Mtn—summit AK-9
Chitistone Pass—gap AK-9
Chitistone River—stream AK-9
Chititu Camp—locale AK-9
Chititu Creek—stream AK-9
Chitka Cove—bay AK-9
Chitka Point—cape AK-9
Chitlam Creek—stream OR-9
Chitman Point—cape ME-1
Chitna Creek—stream AK-9
Chitna Pass—gap AK-9
Chito Beach—beach WA-9
Chito Branch—stream FL-3
Chito Creek—stream MT-8
Chitolah River KS-7
Chitopeni (historical)—locale AL-4
Chitothibi (historical)—locale AL-4
Chitsey Spring—spring OR-9
Chitsia Creek—stream AK-9
Chitsia Mtn—summit AK-9
Chitta Creek AL-4
Chittakain—locale MP-9
Chittakinmatoroen Island MP-9
Chittakinmatoroen (not verified)—island MP-9
Chittakinmatoroen-To MP-9
Chittakow Draw—valley AZ-5
Chittaloosa River MS-4
Chittam Creek—stream ID-8
Chittamo—locale WI-6
Chittam Rapids—rapids ID-8
Chittam Sch—school VA-3
Chittel Sch—school MI-6
**Chittenango**—pop pl NY-2
Chittenango Creek—stream NY-2
Chittenango Falls—falls NY-2
**Chittenango Falls**—pop pl NY-2
Chittenango Falls State Park—park NY-2
Chittenango Springs NY-2
**Chittenango Springs**—pop pl NY-2
Chittenango (sta.) NY-2
Chittenango Station Sch—school NY-2
Chittenden IL-6
**Chittenden**—pop pl (2) CA-9
**Chittenden**—pop pl VT-1
Chittenden, Martin, House—hist pl VT-1
Chittenden, Mount—summit WY-8
Chittenden, Russell Henry, House—hist pl CT-1
Chittenden Bridge—bridge WY-8
Chittenden Brook—stream VT-1
Chittenden Brook Campground—locale VT-1
Chittenden Brook Trail—trail VT-1
**Chittenden County**—pop pl VT-1
Chittenden County Courthouse—hist pl VT-1
Chittenden Dam—dam VT-1
Chittenden Lake—lake CA-9
Chittenden Lake—lake MI-6
Chittenden Locks—other WA-9
Chittenden Locks and Lake Washington Ship Canal—hist pl WA-9
Chittenden Mtn—summit CO-8
Chittenden Park—park FL-3
Chittenden Pass—gap CA-9
Chittenden Peak—summit CA-9
Chittenden Pond—lake ME-1
Chittenden Rock—rock MA-1
Chittenden Rsvr—reservoir VT-1
Chittenden Shaft (historical)—mine PA-2
**Chittenden (Town of)**—pop pl VT-1
Chitterden Ridge—ridge CA-9
Chitterling Creek—stream AL-4
Chittick Spring—spring MT-8
Chittim Gas Field—oilfield TX-5
Chittim Gulch—valley WY-8
Chittim Ranch—locale TX-5
Chittimwood Cave—cave AL-4
Chitto, Bogue—stream (2) AL-4
Chitto, Bogue—stream (4) MS-4
Chittobochiah Creek—stream MS-4
Chittoin—locale MP-9
**Chittum**—pop pl TN-4
Chittum Chapel—church TN-4
Chitty Bridge—bridge AL-4
Chitty Canyon—valley AZ-5
Chitty Canyon Trail Thirty Four—trail AZ-5
Chitty Cem—cemetery IL-6
Chitty Cove TN-4
Chitty Cove—valley TN-4
Chittys Store—locale NC-3
**Chittyville**—pop pl IL-6
Chitwood MO-7
Chitwood—locale OR-9
**Chitwood**—pop pl MO-7
**Chitwood**—pop pl OK-5
Chitwood Branch—stream TN-4
Chitwood Branch South Apache Creek—stream CO-8
Chitwood Bridge—hist pl OR-9
Chitwood Cave—cave TN-4
Chitwood Cem—cemetery AL-4
Chitwood Cem—cemetery GA-3
Chitwood Cem—cemetery KY-4
Chitwood Cem—cemetery (3) MO-7
Chitwood Cem—cemetery OK-5
Chitwood Cem—cemetery OR-9
Chitwood Cem—cemetery TN-4
Chitwood Cem—cemetery VA-3
Chitwood Creek AL-4
Chitwood Creek—stream AL-4
Chitwood Creek—stream (2) OR-9
Chitwood Dam—dam AL-4
Chitwood Falls—falls OR-9
Chitwood Gap—gap AL-4
Chitwood Hollow MO-7
Chitwood Hollow—valley AL-4
Chitwood Hollow—valley (2) KY-4
Chitwood Hollow—valley MO-7
Chitwood Hollow—valley TN-4
Chitwood Hollow—valley WI-6
Chitwood Lake—lake WA-9
Chitwood Mine—mine ID-8
Chitwood Mtn—summit TN-4
Chitwood Oil Field—oilfield KS-7
Chitwood Park—park OK-5
Chitwood Sch—school OK-5
Chitwoods Lake—reservoir AL-4
Chitwood Trail—trail OR-9
Chiu-chius-chiu AZ-5
Chiu Chiuschu AZ-5
Chiu Chuischa AZ-5
Chiu Chuischui AZ-5
Chiugai', I—slope MH-9
Chiukak—locale AK-9
Chiukapin Bridge—bridge NC-3
Chiuki River—stream AK-9
Chiuli AZ-5
Chiuli Kam AZ-5
Chiulikam—locale AZ-5
Chiuli Shaik—locale AZ-5
Chiulos Canyon—valley UT-8
Chiulos Spring—spring UT-8
Chivas Tank—reservoir AZ-5
Chivas Wash, Las—stream AZ-5
Chivata Canyon—valley NM-5
Chiva Tank—reservoir AZ-5
Chivatos Canyon—valley NM-5
Chivatos Canyon Tank—reservoir NM-5
Chivericks Cove—bay ME-1
Chiver Ledge—bar ME-1
Chivers, Bill, House—hist pl ID-8
Chivers, Thomas, Cellar—hist pl ID-8
Chivers, Thomas, House—hist pl ID-8
Chivers Memorial Church—hist pl MT-8
Chivers Spring—spring UT-8
Chivery Dam—dam LA-4
**Chivington**—pop pl CO-8
Chivington Draw WY-8
Chivington Draw—valley WY-8
Chivington Hill—summit CO-8
Chivington Rsvr No 4—reservoir CO-8
Chivler Creek—stream IL-6
Chivo Canyon—valley CA-9
Chivo Canyon—valley NM-5
Chivo Falls—falls AZ-5
Chivos Lake—reservoir TX-5
Chivos Windmill—locale TX-5
Chivo Tank—reservoir TX-5
Chivo Well—well NM-5
Chivo Windmill—locale (3) TX-5
Chiwak Creek WA-9
**Chiwapa**—pop pl MS-4
Chiwapa Creek—stream MS-4
Chiwapa Creek Structure 1 Dam—dam MS-4
Chiwapa Structure 13 Dam—dam MS-4
Chiwapa Structure 2 Dam—dam MS-4
Chiwapa Structure 24 Dam—dam MS-4
Chiwapa Structure 29 Dam—dam MS-4
Chiwapa Structure 3 Dam—dam MS-4
Chiwapa Structure 49 Dam—dam MS-4
Chiwapa Structure 6 Dam—dam MS-4
Chiwapa Structure 65 Dam—dam MS-4
Chiwapa Structure 7 Dam—dam MS-4
Chiwappa MS-4
Chiwappa Creek MS-4
Chiwappa Post Office (historical)—building MS-4
Chiwap Park—park AZ-5
Chiwappa Sch (historical)—school MS-4
**Chiwaukee**—pop pl WI-6
Chiwaukum—locale WA-9
Chiwaukum Creek—stream WA-9
Chiwaukum Lake—lake WA-9
Chiwaukum Mountains—range WA-9
Chiwawa Mtn—summit WA-9
Chiwawa Ridge—ridge (2) WA-9
Chiwawa River—stream WA-9
Chiweton Hill—summit AZ-5
Chiyorugan MP-9
Chiyorugan Passage MP-9
Chiyorugan Passage—channel MP-9
Chiyou PW-9
Chiyuru FM-9
Chizuk Amuno Synagogue—hist pl MD-2
Chizum Ditch—canal IN-6
Chlarsons Canyon AZ-5
C H Lateral—canal TX-5
Chleca Lakes—lake AK-9
C H Lewis Ranch—locale NM-5
Chloe—locale MO-7
**Chloe**—pop pl KY-4
**Chloe**—pop pl LA-4
**Chloe**—pop pl NM-5
**Chloe**—pop pl WV-2
Chloe, Lake—lake FL-3
Chloe, Lake—lake NY-2
Chloe Creek Ch—church KY-4
Chloe Gap—gap KY-4
Chloe Lake—lake KY-4
Chloe Sch—school NE-7
Chloeta—locale OK-5
Chlora Point—cape MD-2
Chloras Point MD-2
Chlore Mtn—summit MO-7
Chloride—locale MO-7
**Chloride**—pop pl AZ-5
**Chloride**—pop pl NM-5
Chloride Canyon—valley UT-8
Chloride City—locale CA-9
Chloride Cliff—summit CA-9
Chloride Community Park—park AZ-5
Chloride Creek—stream NM-5
Chloride Elem Sch—school AZ-5
Chloride Flat—flat NM-5
Chloride Gulch—valley (2) CO-8
Chloride Gulch—valley ID-8
Chloride Mine—mine CO-8
Chloride Mine—mine OR-9
Chloride Point Mine—mine UT-8
Chloride Post Office—building AZ-5
Chloride Queen Mine—mine WA-9
Chloride Ridge—ridge OR-9
Chlota AL-4
Chloupek Lake—lake MN-6
Chloya Lake—lake AK-9
Chmela Dam SD-7
Chmela Dam—dam SD-7
Chmela Dam 1—dam SD-7
Chnle River AZ-5
Choases Canyon—valley NM-5
Choases Tank—reservoir NM-5
Choat—locale IL-6
Choate—locale DE-2
Choate—locale WI-6
**Choate**—pop pl MI-6
**Choate**—pop pl TX-5
Choate, Rufus, House—hist pl MA-1
Choate Bend—bend TN-4
Choate Bldg—hist pl MN-6
Choate Branch—stream TN-4
Choate Bridge—hist pl MA-1
Choate Brook—stream CT-1
Choate Brook—stream ME-1
Choate Brook—stream NH-1
Choate Cabin—hist pl OK-5
Choate Cem—cemetery AL-4
Choate Cem—cemetery IL-6
Choate Cem—cemetery NY-2
Choate Cem—cemetery (5) TN-4
Choate Cem—cemetery TX-5
Choate Creek—stream MI-6
Choate Creek—stream MS-4
Choate Creek—stream (2) TN-4
Choate Creek Ch—church TN-4
Choate George Branch—stream AR-4
Choate Hill—summit ME-1
Choate Hill—summit MA-1
Choate Hill—summit NH-1
Choate Hollow—valley (2) TN-4
Choate Island MA-1
Choate Memorial Hosp—hospital MA-1
Choate Mtn—summit TX-5
Choate Pond—lake NY-2
Choate Pond—lake VT-1
Choate Prairie—flat OK-5
Choate Prairie Cem—cemetery OK-5
Choate Prairie Ch—church OK-5
Choate Sch—school CT-1
Choates Creek—stream TX-5
Choates Creek Cem—cemetery TN-4
Choateville Ch—church KY-4
**Choatville**—pop pl KY-4
Chobchob—bay FM-9
Chobie Dock—locale FL-3
Chobota MS-4
Choca Creek—stream AK-9
Chocalata Bay AL-4
Chocalog Pond MA-1
Chocchuma Ferry (historical)—locale MS-4
Chocchuma (historical)—locale MS-4
**Choccolocco**—pop pl AL-4
Choccolocco Bridge AL-4
Choccolocco (CCD)—cens area AL-4
Choccolocco Creek—stream AL-4
Choccolocco Creek Lake Number 24 AL-4
Choccolocco Creek Lake Number 7—reservoir AL-4
Choccolocco Creek Sewage Treatment Plant—building AL-4
Choccolocco Division—civil AL-4
Choccolocco Elem Sch—school AL-4
**Choccolocco Estates (subdivision)**—pop pl AL-4
Choccolocco Lake—reservoir AL-4
Choccolocco Mills (historical)—locale AL-4
Choccolocco Mountain—ridge AL-4
Choccolocco Number 11 Lake—reservoir AL-4
Choccolocco Number 2 Dam—dam AL-4
Choccolocco Number 6 Lake AL-4
Choccolocco Primitive Baptist Ch—church AL-4
Choccolocco Ranger Station—locale AL-4
Choccolocco Shoal AL-4
Choccolocco Shoals (historical)—bar AL-4
Choccolocco Wildlife Mngmt Area—park AL-4
Chocco Springs AL-4
Chocetopa Creek CO-8
Chocetopa Hills CO-8
Chocetopa Pass CO-8
Chocetopa River NH-1
Chochechiwick Pond MA-1
Chochechiwick River MA-1
Chochichawicke River MA-1
Chochichawick Pond MA-1
Chochogo—area GU-9
Chockalang River RI-1
Chockalaug Brook RI-1
Chockalaug River MA-1
Chockaloc Pond MA-1
Chockalog Pond—lake MA-1
Chockalog River—stream MA-1
Chockalog River—stream RI-1
Chock Creek—stream NC-3
Chockfoot Creek OR-9
Chockie—locale OK-5
Chock Island—island AK-9
Chockley Cem—cemetery IL-6
Chockolocko Creek AL-4
Chockolog Pond MA-1
Chockowinity NC-3
Chockowinity Bay NC-3
Chockowinity Creek NC-3
Chockoyotte Ch—church NC-3
Chockoyotte Creek—stream NC-3
Chocktaw Sch—school IL-6
Chocktoot Creek—stream OR-9
Chocktoot Spring—spring OR-9
Choclafola Creek AL-4
Chocle Windmill—locale NM-5
Chocolata Bay AL-4
Chocolate Bay—bay (2) TX-5
Chocolate Bayou—locale TX-5
Chocolate Bayou—stream (2) TX-5
Chocolate Bayou Oil Field—oilfield TX-5
Chocolate Bayou Rice Canal—canal TX-5
Chocolate Butte—summit NV-8
Chocolate Butte—summit ND-7
Chocolate Canyon—valley CA-9
Chocolate Creek NC-3
Chocolate Creek TX-5
Chocolate Creek—stream AK-9
Chocolate Creek—stream MO-7
Chocolate Creek—stream NC-3
Chocolate Creek—stream WA-9
Chocolate Drop—summit CA-9
Chocolate Drop—summit NV-8
Chocolate Drop—summit UT-8
Chocolate Drop Dam—dam ND-7
Chocolate Drop Hill—summit MD-2
Chocolate Drops—pillar UT-8
Chocolate Drops—range UT-8
Chocolate Glacier—glacier WA-9
Chocolate Hill OK-5
Chocolate Hole—bay VI-3
Chocolate Hollow—valley TX-5
Chocolate Lakes—lake CA-9
Chocolate Mountain AZ-5
Chocolate Mountains—range CA-9
Chocolate Mountains—summit AZ-5
Chocolate Mtn—summit (2) NV-8
Chocolate Peak—summit (2) CA-9
Chocolate Peak—summit NV-8
Chocolate Peak—summit NM-5
Chocolate Peak—summit UT-8
Chocolate Pots—spring WY-8
Chocolate Rsvr—reservoir WY-8
Chocolate Run—stream OH-6
Chocolate Springs—locale TX-5
Chocolate Swale—stream TX-5
Chocolate Windmill—locale TX-5
Chocolay River—stream MI-6
**Chocolay (Township of)**—pop pl MI-6
Choc-o-loc Shoal AL-4
Chocomount—summit NY-2
Chocomount Beach—beach NY-2
Chocomount Cove—bay NY-2
Chocomuxen Creek MD-2
**Choconickla (historical)**—pop pl FL-3
**Choconut**—pop pl PA-2
**Choconut Center**—pop pl NY-2
Choconut Chapel—church PA-2
Choconut Creek—stream NY-2
Choconut Creek—stream PA-2
Choconut Lake PA-2
Choconut Lake—reservoir PA-2
**Choconut (Township of)**—pop pl PA-2
Chocoolocco Creek AL-4
**Chocorua**—pop pl NH-1
Chocorua, Mount—summit NH-1
Chocorua Brook Trail—trail NH-1
Chocorua Island—island NH-1
Chocorua Lake—lake NH-1
Chocorua River—stream NH-1
**Chocowinity**—pop pl NC-3
Chocowinity Bay—bay NC-3
Chocowinity Creek—stream NC-3
Chocowinity HS—school NC-3
Chocowinity (Township of)—fmr MCD NC-3
Choctafaula Creek—stream AL-4
Choctahatchee Creek—stream AL-4
Choctahatchee Creek—stream GA-3
Choctaw (2) AL-4
Choctaw—locale FL-3
Choctaw—locale IL-6
Choctaw—locale (2) MS-4
**Choctaw**—pop pl AR-4
**Choctaw**—pop pl (3) LA-4
**Choctaw**—pop pl MS-4
**Choctaw**—pop pl OK-5
Choctaw—uninc pl MS-4
Choctaw, Bayou—stream LA-4
Choctaw Agency MS-4
Choctaw Agency—hist pl OK-5
Choctaw Agency (historical)—locale MS-4
Choctawatchee AL-4
Choctaw Baptist Church MS-4
Choctaw Bar—bar AL-4
Choctaw Bar Island—island AR-4
Choctaw Basin—bay TN-4
Choctaw Basin Drainage Canal—canal LA-4
**Choctaw Bay Estates (subdivision)**—pop pl FL-3
Choctaw Bayou LA-4
Choctaw Bayou TX-5
Choctaw Bayou—gut (2) AR-4
Choctaw Bayou—gut (2) LA-4
Choctaw Bayou—stream (4) LA-4
Choctaw Bayou—stream MS-4
**Choctaw Beach**—pop pl (2) FL-3
Choctaw Bend—bend (2) AL-4
Choctaw Bend—bend MS-4
Choctaw Bluff AL-4
Choctaw Bluff—cliff (2) AL-4
Choctaw Bluff—locale AL-4
Choctaw Bluff Landing (historical)—locale AL-4
Choctaw Bluffs AL-4
Choctaw Branch—stream AL-4
Choctaw Branch—stream LA-4
Choctaw Cem—cemetery AR-4
Choctaw Cem—cemetery (2) MS-4
Choctaw Cem—cemetery OK-5
Choctaw Central HS—school MS-4
Choctaw Ch—church LA-4
Choctaw Ch—church (2) MS-4
Choctaw Ch—church OK-5
Choctaw Chapel—church LA-4
Choctaw Ch (historical)—church MS-4
**Choctaw City**—pop pl AL-4
**Choctaw City (Choctaw)**—pop pl AL-4
**Choctaw Corner**—pop pl AL-4
Choctaw Corner Cem—cemetery AL-4
Choctaw Council House MS-4
Choctaw Country Club—other AL-4
Choctaw Country Club—other OK-5
**Choctaw County**—pop pl AL-4
**Choctaw County**—pop pl MS-4
**Choctaw (County)**—pop pl OK-5
Choctaw County Hosp—hospital MS-4
Choctaw County HS—school AL-4
Choctaw County Saddle Club—locale AL-4
Choctaw County School Lake—reservoir AL-4
Choctaw County School Lake Dam—dam AL-4
Choctaw County Vocational Technical Sch—school MS-4
Choctaw Creek AL-4
Choctaw Creek—stream AL-4
Choctaw Creek—stream (2) AR-4
Choctaw Creek—stream (4) LA-4
Choctaw Creek—stream (4) MS-4
Choctaw Creek—stream (2) OK-5
Choctaw Creek—stream TX-5
Choctaw District Sch (historical)—school MS-4
Choctaw Game Mngmt Area MS-4
Choctaw Hammock—island FL-3
Choctawhatchee, Lake—lake AL-4
Choctawhatchee Bay—bay FL-3
Choctawhatchee HS—school FL-3
Choctawhatchee Number 1 Dam—dam AL-4
Choctawhatchee Number 2 Dam—dam AL-4
Choctawhatchee River AL-4
Choctawhatchee River—stream AL-4
Choctawhatchee River—stream FL-3
Choctawhatchee Wells—well AL-4
Choctawhatchie Bay FL-3
Choctawhatchie River AL-4
Choctawhatchie River FL-3
**Choctaw (historical)**—pop pl MS-4
Choctaw Indian Acad—hist pl KY-4
Choctaw Ind Res—2756 (1980) MS-4
Choctaw Ind Res (MS Part)—other MS-4
Choctaw Island—island TN-4
Choctaw Island No 78—island AR-4
Choctaw Lake—lake AL-4
Choctaw Lake—lake AR-4
Choctaw Lake—reservoir MS-4
Choctaw Lake—reservoir OH-6
Choctaw Lake Dam—dam (2) MS-4
Choctaw Lake Rec Area—park MS-4
Choctaw Landing—locale MS-4
Choctaw Landing (historical)—locale MS-4
Choctaw Lookout Tower—locale MS-4
Choctaw Mine—mine AZ-5
Choctaw Mine—mine OK-5
Choctaw Natl Wildlife Ref—park AL-4
Choctaw Pass—channel AL-4
Choctaw Point—cape AL-4
Choctaw Public Use Area—park MS-4
Choctaw Rec Area—park AR-4
Choctaw Revetment—levee MS-4
Choctaw Ridge MS-4
Choctaw Ridge—ridge MS-4
Choctaw Ridge Oil Field—oilfield AL-4
Choctaw River AL-4
Choctaw River FL-3
Choctaw Route Station—hist pl AR-4
Choctaw Sch—school (2) LA-4
Choctaw Sch—school MO-7
Choctaw Sch—school TN-4
Choctaw Slough—gut TX-5
Choctaw State Wildlife Mngmt Area—park MS-4
Choctaw (Township of)—fmr MCD (2) AR-4
**Choctaw Village (subdivision)**—pop pl MS-4
Choctawville (historical)—locale MS-4
Choctaw Work Center—building MS-4
Choctaw Youth Center—building MS-4
Chocton River NY-2
Choctoo Creek OR-9
Choctoot Creek OR-9
Choctow Corner—uninc pl AL-4
Chocwich Campground—locale WA-9
Chocwich Creek—stream WA-9
Chodikee Lake—lake NY-2
Choeffenington NC-3
Choehee Creek SC-3
Choehee Lake SC-3
Choestoe—locale GA-3
Choestoea Creek—stream SC-3
Choffo Tank—reservoir AZ-5
Choga Butt Knob—summit NC-3
Choggam Brook—stream CT-1
Chogol FM-9
Chohalaboohulka FL-3
Choice—locale MN-6
Choice—locale TX-5
Choice Cem—cemetery MN-6
Choice Cem—cemetery TX-5
Choice Valley—valley CA-9
Choice Valley Sch—school CA-9
Choimer PW-9
Choiskai Mountains AZ-5
Choiskai Mountains NM-5
Chokatalbi Creek AL-4
Choke-A-Man Draw—valley NV-8
Chokeberry Branch—stream NC-3
Chokeberry Canyon—valley NV-8
Chokeberry Creek NV-8
Chokeberry Island NY-2
Chokeberry Spring—spring (3) NV-8
Chokebore Creek—stream ID-8
Chokecherry Campground—locale UT-8
Chokecherry Canyon—valley CA-9
Chokecherry Canyon—valley CO-8
Chokecherry Canyon—valley ID-8
Chokecherry Canyon—valley (3) NV-8
Chokecherry Canyon—valley NM-5
Chokecherry Canyon—valley (7) UT-8
Chokecherry Creek ID-8
Chokecherry Creek MT-8
Chokecherry Creek—stream ID-8
Chokecherry Creek—stream (2) NV-8
Choke Cherry Creek—stream OR-9
Chokecherry Creek—stream (7) UT-8
Chokecherry Creek—stream (2) WY-8
Chokecherry Dam—other WY-8
Choke Cherry Draw—valley CO-8
Chokecherry Draw—valley UT-8

Christian Camp—locale WA-9
Christian Camp Branch—stream VA-3
Christian Camp Home Mission—church GA-3
Christian Campus House—church FL-3
Christian Canyon—valley CO-8
Christian Cave—cave TN-4
Christian Cem—cemetery IL-6
Christian Cem—cemetery IN-6
Christian Cem—cemetery KS-7
Christian Cem—cemetery KY-4
Christian Cem—cemetery (2) MD-2
Christian Cem—cemetery MS-4
Christian Cem—cemetery (3) MO-7
Christian Cem—cemetery (2) NY-2
Christian Cem—cemetery OH-6
Christian Cem—cemetery (3) TN-4
Christian Cem—cemetery TX-5
Christian Cem—cemetery VA-3
Christian Cem—cemetery WV-2
Christian Cemetery GA-3
**Christian Center**—pop pl MO-7
Christian Center Acad—school FL-3
Christian Ch AL-4
Christian Ch MS-4
Christian Ch—church (2) AL-4
Christian Ch—church AR-4
Christian Ch—church DE-2
Christian Ch—church IL-6
Christian Ch—church MI-6
Christian Ch—church ND-7
Christian Ch—church OH-6
Christian Ch—church WV-2
Christian Chapel—church (2) AL-4
Christian Chapel—church AR-4
Christian Chapel—church (2) IL-6
Christian Chapel—church (2) IN-6
Christian Chapel—church KY-4
Christian Chapel—church (2) MS-4
Christian Chapel—church (2) NC-3
Christian Chapel—church OH-6
Christian Chapel—church (5) TN-4
**Christian Chapel**—pop pl TN-4
Christian Chapel Cem—cemetery MO-7
Christian Chapel Cem—cemetery TX-5
Christian Chapel Ch of Christ AL-4
Christian Chapel Ch of Christ MS-4
Christian Chapel Sch—school KY-4
Christian Chapel Sch (historical)—school TN-4
Christian Ch (historical)—church AL-4
Christian Ch (historical)—church (2) MS-4
Christian Ch (historical)—church MO-7
Christian Ch (historical), The—church AL-4
Christian Ch in Florida-Disciples of Christ—church FL-3
Christian Ch in Kansas—church KS-7
Christian Ch of Mobile—church AL-4
Christian Ch of Panama City—church FL-3
Christian Ch of the Ozarks—church MO-7
**Christian (Christians)**—pop pl VA-3
Christian Church PA-2
Christian Church—hist pl ID-8
Christian Church and Parsonage—hist pl AL-4
Christian Church-Capital City—church FL-3
Christian Church of Gilroy—hist pl CA-9
Christian Church-University Disciples of Christ—church FL-3
Christian Clemens Sch—school MI-6
Christian Coll—school NE-7
Christian Community of Wichita—church KS-7
Christian Corner—locale PA-2
Christian Corners—locale NY-2
**Christian (County)**—pop pl IL-6
**Christian (County)**—pop pl KY-4
**Christian County**—pop pl MO-7
Christian Covenant Community Acad—school FL-3
Christian Creek DE-2
Christian Creek IN-6
Christian Creek MI-6
Christian Creek VA-3
Christian Creek—stream (2) AK-9
Christian Creek—stream AR-4
Christian Creek—stream MO-7
Christian Creek—stream NC-3
Christian Creek—stream OH-6
Christian Creek—stream WY-8
Christian Creek Ch—church NC-3
Christian Creek Sewage Disposal Plant—building AL-4
Christiancy Sch—school MI-6
Christiancy Street Sch—school MI-6
Christian Day Care Center—school FL-3
Christian Day Sch—school (4) CA-9
Christian Day Sch—school FL-3
Christian Dells Bible Camp—locale AL-4
Christian-Ellis House—hist pl MI-6
Christian Faith Ch—church UT-8
Christian Family Life Sch—school FL-3
Christian Fellowship Center—church AL-4
Christian Fellowship Ch—church AL-4
Christian Fellowship Ch—church ND-7
Christian Fellowship Evangelistic Tabernacle—church VA-3
Christian Fellowship Full Gospel Ch—church AL-4
Christian-Floyd Prospect—mine TN-4
Christian Fork WV-2
Christian Fork—stream WV-2
Christian Fork Lake—reservoir WV-2
Christian Friendship Center—church MI-6
Christian Golden Rule Ch—church AR-4
Christian Grove Ch—church AL-4
Christian Grove Ch—church (3) MS-4
Christian Grove Ch—church OK-5
Christian Grove Sch—school IL-6
Christian Gulch—valley CA-9
Christian Gulch—valley (2) ID-8
Christian Harbor Youth Camp—locale WI-6
Christian Heights Ch—church KY-4
Christian Heritage Acad—school FL-3
Christian Heritage Ch—church FL-3
Christian Heritage Pentecostal Holiness Ch—church FL-3
Christian Hill—locale NY-2
**Christian Hill**—pop pl NY-2
**Christian Hill**—pop pl PA-2
Christian Hill—summit (2) ME-1
Christian Hill—summit (6) MA-1
Christian Hill—summit NH-1
Christian Hill—summit NY-2
Christian Hill—summit VT-1
Christian Hill Baptist Ch—church MS-4
Christian Hill Cem—cemetery OK-5
Christian Hill Cem—cemetery PA-2
Christian Hill Ch—church AL-4
Christian Hill Ch—church GA-3
Christian Hill Ch—church MS-4
Christian Hill Hist Dist—hist pl IL-6
Christian Hills Camp—locale KS-7
Christian Hill Sch—school MI-6
**Christian Hollow**—pop pl NH-1
Christian Hollow—valley (2) MO-7
Christian Hollow—valley (4) NY-2
Christian Hollow—valley (5) TN-4
Christian Hollow Cem—cemetery IL-6
Christian Hollow Cem—cemetery NY-2
Christian Home and Bible Sch—school FL-3
Christian Home Cem—cemetery VA-3
Christian Home Ch AL-4
Christian Home Ch—church (5) AL-4
Christian Home Ch—church FL-3
Christian Home Ch—church (2) GA-3
Christian Home Ch—church (2) IL-6
Christian Home Ch—church KY-4
Christian Home Ch—church (3) MS-4
Christian Home Ch—church MO-7
Christian Home Ch—church NC-3
Christian Home Ch of Christ AL-4
Christian Home (historical)—locale AL-4
Christian Home Orphanage—building TN-4
Christian Hope Cem—cemetery TX-5
Christian Hope Ch—church (2) AL-4
Christian Hope Ch—church (2) GA-3
Christian Hope Ch—church (2) NC-3
Christian Hope Ch—church SC-3
Christian Hosp—hospital (2) MO-7
Christian HS—school CO-8
Christian HS—school (2) MI-6
Christian HS—school NC-3
Christian HS—school VA-3
Christian HS—school WA-9
Christiania Ch—church ND-7
**Christiania Township**—pop pl ND-7
**Christiania (Township of)**—pop pl MN-6
Christian Indian Sch—school AZ-5
Christian Industrial Sch (historical)—school AL-4
Christian Island—island VA-3
Christian Islands—island TN-4
Christian JHS—school (2) MI-6
Christian Knob—summit WV-2
Christian Lake MI-6
Christian Lake—lake NY-2
Christian Lake—lake WI-6
Christian Lake Mtn—summit NY-2
Christian Lane Cem—cemetery CT-1
Christian Life Assembly of God Ch—church MS-4
Christian Life Cem—cemetery MS-4
Christian Life Center—church (2) FL-3
Christian Life Fellowship—church FL-3
Christian Life Tabernacle—church MS-4
Christian Light Baptist Ch—church MS-4
Christian Light Ch AL-4
Christian Light Ch—church (2) AL-4
Christian Light Ch—church NC-3
Christian Love Ch—church MS-4
Christian Love Spiritual Ch—church AL-4
Christian Memorial Estates—cemetery MI-6
Christian Mennonite Sch—school OH-6
Christian Military Acad—school FL-3
Christian Mill Creek—stream VA-3
Christian Mine—mine CA-9
Christian Mission—church VA-3
Christian Missionary Alliance Ch—church PA-2
Christian Mission Ch—church AL-4
Christian Mission Ch—church IN-6
Christian Mission Church, The—church AL-4
Christian Mtn—summit AL-4
Christianna Creek DE-2
Christianna Lake MI-6
Christiann Creek IN-6
Christiann Creek MI-6
Christian Neck Sch—school IL-6
Christiann Lake MI-6
Christian Opportunity Center—school IA-7
Christian Order Church TN-4
Christian Park—park IN-6
Christian Park—park MN-6
Christian Park Acad—school GA-3
Christian Park Elem Sch—school IN-6
Christian Park Kingdom Hall—church IN-6
Christian Park School Number 82 IN-6
Christian Petersen Courtyard Sculptures, and Dairy Industry Bldg—hist pl IA-7
Christian Plain Ch—church NC-3
Christian Plains Cem—cemetery MI-6
Christian Point—cape AL-4
Christian Point—cape FL-3
Christian Point Trail—trail FL-3
Christianpol Marsh—swamp NY-2
Christian Pond—lake WY-8
Christian Privilege Cem—cemetery KY-4
Christian Prospect Number Four—mine TN-4
Christian Prospect Number One—mine TN-4
Christian Prospect Number Three—mine TN-4
Christian Prospect Number Two—mine TN-4
Christian Ranch—locale NE-7
Christian Record Bldg—hist pl NE-7
Christian Reformed Ch—church MN-6
Christian Reformed Ch—church WI-6
Christian Reformed Ch (Brigham City)—church UT-8
Christian Reformed Ch (Ogden)—church UT-8
Christian Reformed Church, The—church IN-6
Christian Rest Ch—church MS-4
Christian Retreat Campground—locale FL-3
Christian Ridge—ridge AR-4
Christian Ridge—ridge WV-2
Christian Ridge Ch—church WV-2
Christian River—stream AK-9
Christian Rsvr—reservoir MT-8
Christian Run—stream VA-3
Christian Run Sch—school IL-6
Christian Run Trail—trail VA-3
Christians PA-2
Christian Sachau Saloon—hist pl MO-7
Christians Bend Sch (historical)—school TN-4
**Christiansburg**—pop pl IN-6
**Christiansburg**—pop pl OH-6
**Christiansburg**—pop pl VA-3
Christiansburg Institute—school MS-4
Christiansburg-Jackson HS—school OH-6
Christiansburg Post Office (historical)—building TN-4
Christiansburg Presbyterian Church—hist pl VA-3
Christian Sch—school AL-4
Christian Sch—school AZ-5
Christian Sch—school (6) CA-9
Christian Sch—school CO-8
Christian Sch—school (5) FL-3
Christian Sch—school (2) IL-6
Christian Sch—school IN-6
Christian Sch—school (4) IA-7
Christian Sch—school ME-1
Christian Sch—school (2) MA-1
Christian Sch—school (7) MI-6
Christian Sch—school MN-6
Christian Sch—school MO-7
Christian Sch—school PA-2
Christian Sch—school (2) WI-6
Christian Sch No 1—school GA-3
Christian Sch No 2—school GA-3
Christian Sch of Fine Arts—school FL-3
Christian Sch of York—school PA-2
Christian Science Ch—church (3) FL-3
Christian Science Ch (historical)—church AL-4
Christian Science Complex—building MA-1
Christian Science Society—church FL-3
Christian Science Society Ch—church AL-4
Christian Science Society of Ocean Springs Ch—church MS-4
Christians Cre DE-2
Christians Creek—stream VA-3
Christian Seminary—school IN-6
Christiansen Canyon—valley UT-8
Christiansen Creek OR-9
Christiansen Lake—lake AK-9
Christiansen Mound—summit MO-7
Christiansen Ranch—locale AZ-5
Christiansen Wash—valley UT-8
Christiansen Well—well NV-8
Christian Service Camp—locale VA-3
Christians Ford—locale TN-4
Christian Shore NH-1
**Christian Shore**—pop pl NH-1
Christians Island—island TN-4
Christianson Cem—cemetery ND-7
Christianson Cove WA-9
Christianson House and Store—hist pl MN-6
Christianson Lagoon—lake AK-9
Christianson Lake—lake MN-6
Christianson Meadows—flat ID-8
Christianson Ranch—locale MT-8
Christianson Spring—spring SD-7
Christian Sound—bay AK-9
Christian Spring PA-2
Christian Spring—spring ME-1
Christian Spring—spring MO-7
Christian Spring—spring NV-8
Christian Spring—spring TN-4
Christian Springs NV-8
**Christian Springs**—pop pl PA-2
Christian Springs Baptist Ch—church AL-4
Christian Springs Ch—church GA-3
Christians Sch—school IL-6
Christians Shoals—bar TN-4
Christiansted—2856 (1980) VI-3
Christiansted (Census Subdistrict)—cens area VI-3
Christiansted Harbor—bay VI-3
Christiansted Hist Dist—hist pl VI-3
Christiansted Natl Historic Site—hist pl VI-3
Christiansted Natl Historic Site—park VI-3
Christian Street Cem—cemetery VT-1
Christian Tabernacle—church DE-2
Christian Tabernacle—church (2) IN-6
Christian Tabernacle—church NC-3
Christian Tabernacle—church VA-3
Christian Tabernacle Acad—school DE-2
Christian Tank—reservoir NM-5
Christian Temple—church IL-6
Christian Temple—church OH-6
Christiantown Memorial Cem—cemetery MA-1
Christian (Township of) AR-4
Christian Union Baptist Ch—church AL-4
Christian Union Baptist Ch—church MS-4
Christian Union Cem—cemetery AL-4
Christian Union Cem—cemetery MN-6
Christian Union Ch—church (2) AL-4
Christian Union Ch—church IN-6
Christian Union Ch—church MI-6
Christian Union Ch—church (4) MS-4
Christian Union Ch—church (2) MO-7
Christian Union Ch (historical)—church MS-4
Christian Union Primitive Baptist Ch—church AL-4
Christian Union Sch—school TX-5
Christian Union Society Meetinghouse—hist pl VT-1
Christian Valley—valley CA-9
Christian Valley Baptist Ch—church AL-4
Christian Valley Ch—church (3) AL-4
Christian Valley Ch—church MS-4
Christian Valley Ch (historical)—church (3) AL-4
Christian Valley Sch—school (2) AL-4
Christian View Ch—church NC-3
Christian View Ch—church VA-3
Christian Way Baptist Ch—church AL-4
Christie KS-7
Christie—locale CA-9
Christie—locale OK-5
Christie—locale OR-9
Christie—locale VA-3
**Christie**—pop pl WI-6
Christie, Christopher Columbus, House—hist pl KY-4
Christie, Mount—summit MI-6
Christie, Mount—summit WA-9
Christie Brook—stream WI-6
Christie Canyon—valley NM-5
Christie Cem—cemetery NY-2
Christie Ch—church OK-5
Christie Chapel—church KY-4
Christie Chapel Cem—cemetery KY-4
Christie Creek—stream CO-8
Christie Creek—stream ID-8
Christie Creek—stream IA-7
Christie Creek—stream KY-4
Christie Creek—stream NY-2
Christie-Eismann House—hist pl OR-9
Christie Ford NC-3
Christie Gulch—valley CA-9
Christie Heights Park—park NE-7
Christie Hill TN-4
**Christie Hill**—pop pl TN-4
Christie Hill—summit CA-9
Christie Hill Sch—school TN-4
**Christie (historical)**—pop pl OR-9
**Christie (historical)**—pop pl TN-4
Christie Hollow—valley PA-2
Christie Lake—lake GA-3
Christie Lake—lake MI-6
Christie Lake—lake WI-6
**Christie Lake**—pop pl MI-6
Christie Lookout Tower—tower FL-3
Christie Mound—summit WI-6
Christian Bridge DE-2
Christiense Spring UT-8
Christie-Parsels House—hist pl NJ-2
Christie Point—cape AK-9
Christie Pond—bay LA-4
Christie Pond—lake NY-2
Christie Prairie—swamp GA-3
Christiersen Spring—spring UT-8
Christie Rsvr—reservoir NY-2
Christie Run—stream PA-2
Christies Branch—stream AR-4
Christie Sch—school MI-6
Christie Sch—school OR-9
Christies Chapel—church AR-4
Christie's Creek ID-8
Christie Spur—other LA-4
**Christie Spur**—pop pl CA-9
Christie Tank—reservoir AZ-5
Christie Tank—reservoir NM-5
Christie Township KS-7
Christi HS—school MI-6
**Christilla Heights**—pop pl WI-6
Christilla Heights—uninc pl WI-6
**Christina**—pop pl FL-3
**Christina**—pop pl MT-8
Christina, Lake—lake MN-6
Christina, Lake—lake WY-8
Christina Cem—cemetery MN-6
Christina Draw—valley AZ-5
Christina Draw Tank—reservoir AZ-5
Christinahamn DE-2
Christina Lake—lake FL-3
Christina Lake—reservoir WY-8
Christina Lake Ch—church MN-6
Christina Lake Trail—trail (2) WY-8
**Christina Manor**—pop pl DE-2
Christina Park—park DE-2
Christina Pass—gap WY-8
Christina Peak—summit NV-8
Christina Plantation (historical)—locale MS-4
Christina River—stream DE-2
Christina River—stream MD-2
Christina River—stream PA-2
Christine—locale KY-4
**Christine**—pop pl ND-7
**Christine**—pop pl TX-5
Christine, Lake—lake VA-3
Christine, Lake—lake WA-9
Christine, Lake—reservoir IL-6
Christine Cem—cemetery ND-7
Christine Creek—stream TX-5
Christine Dam—dam ND-7
Christine Falls—falls NY-2
Christine Falls—falls WA-9
Christine Lake WY-8
Christine Lake—lake AK-9
Christine Lake—lake MN-6
Christine Lake—lake NH-1
Christine Lake—lake WY-8
Christine Manor—uninc pl DE-2
Christines Hill—summit PA-2
Christine State Wildlife Mngmt Area—park MN-6
Christine Tank—reservoir NM-5
Christine Windmill—locale NM-5
Christins Hollow—valley MO-7
Christiorsson Canyon—valley NV-8
Christi Ranch—locale CA-9
Christ Irvington Lutheran Ch—church IN-6
Christisen Creek—stream MT-8
Christison Ranch—locale MT-8
Christ Johns Cem—cemetery NY-2
Christ King Sch—school MA-1
Christ King Sch—school (2) OK-5
Christ Lake—lake AK-9
Christ Lake—lake NE-7
Christley Run—stream MD-2
Christleys Branch VA-3
Christleys Mills—locale PA-2
Christleys Run—stream VA-3
Christ Lutheran Cem—cemetery OK-5
Christ Lutheran Ch—church (2) AL-4
Christ Lutheran Ch—church CO-8
Christ Lutheran Ch—church FL-3
Christ Lutheran Ch—church (2) KS-7
Christ Lutheran Ch—church MS-4
Christ Lutheran Ch—church UT-8
Christ Lutheran School—church MS-4
Christman, Daniel, Homestead—hist pl OH-6
Christman, Nicholas, House—hist pl OH-6
Christman, Philip, House—hist pl PA-2
Christman Bird and Wildlife Sanctuary—hist pl NY-2
Christman Cem—cemetery NY-2
Christman Cem—cemetery TN-4
Christman Covered Bridge—hist pl OH-6
Christman Dam—dam PA-2
Christman Detention Dam—dam AZ-5
Christman Fire Tower (historical)—tower PA-2
Christman Harbor MP-9
Christman Landing Field—airport CO-8
Christman Park—park IL-6
Christman Pond—reservoir AZ-5
**Christmans**—pop pl PA-2
Christman Sch—school IA-7
Christmans Corners—locale NY-2
Christmans Sch (historical)—school PA-2
Christmansville—locale PA-2
Christ-Mar Sch—school FL-3
Christmas—locale MS-4
Christmas—locale TN-4
**Christmas**—pop pl AZ-5
**Christmas**—pop pl FL-3
**Christmas**—pop pl MI-6
Christmas Airp—airport MS-4
Christmas Bay—bay TX-5
Christmas Bay—swamp FL-3
Christmas Bay—swamp GA-3
Christmas Branch GA-3
Christmas Branch—stream GA-3
Christmas Branch—stream MS-4
Christmas Camp Lake—lake LA-4
Christmas Canyon—valley CA-9
Christmas Canyon—valley (2) WA-9
Christmas Canyon Dome UT-8
Christmas Cave—cave AL-4
Christmas Cem—cemetery FL-3
Christmas Cem—cemetery SC-3
Christmas Circle—locale CA-9
Christmas City—locale UT-8
Christmas Coulee—valley MT-8
Christmas Cove—bay (3) ME-1
**Christmas Cove**—pop pl ME-1
Christmas Creek—bay GA-3
Christmas Creek—stream AK-9
Christmas Creek—stream FL-3
Christmas Creek—stream ID-8
Christmas Creek—stream OR-9
Christmas Creek—stream TN-4
Christmas Creek—stream TX-5
Christmas Creek—stream WA-9
Christmas Creek—stream WI-6
Christmas Creek Camp—locale OR-9
Christmas Gas Pool—oilfield MS-4
Christmas Gift Mine—mine (2) AZ-5
Christmas Harbor—harbor MP-9
Christmas Hill—summit CA-9
Christmas Hill Diggings—mine CA-9
Christmas Hollow—valley TX-5
Christmas Island WA-9
Christmas Island—island AK-9
Christmas Island—island FL-3
Christmas Knob—summit AR-4
Christmas Knob—summit NY-2
Christmas Lake—lake FL-3
Christmas Lake—lake GA-3
Christmas Lake—lake (3) MN-6
Christmas Lake—lake OR-9
Christmas Lake—lake WY-8
Christmas Lake—reservoir IN-6
Christmas Lake Branch—stream MS-4
Christmas Lake Dam—dam IN-6
Christmas Lake Valley—basin OR-9
Christmas Lake Village—post sta IN-6
Christmas Landing—locale AL-4
Christmas Meadows—flat UT-8
Christmas Meadows Campground—locale UT-8
**Christmas Meadow Summer Home Area**—pop pl UT-8
Christmas Mesa UT-8
Christmas Mill and Mine—mine AZ-5
Christmas Mill Lake—reservoir SC-3
Christmas Mine—mine CA-9
Christmas Mine—mine NV-8
Christmas Mountain TX-5
Christmas Mountains—summit TX-5
Christmas Mtn—summit AK-9
Christmas Mtn—summit ID-8
Christmas Oil Field—oilfield TX-5
Christmas Park (county park)—park FL-3
Christmas Pass—channel FL-3
Christmas Pass—gap AZ-5
Christmas Plantation (historical)—locale MS-4
Christmas Point—cape FL-3
Christmas Point—cape TX-5
Christmas Point Reef—bar TX-5
Christmas Prairie—area CA-9
Christmas Ranch—locale NM-5
Christmas Ridge—ridge UT-8
Christmas River OR-9
Christmas Rock—island CA-9
Christmas Rocks—summit OH-6
Christmas Run Park—park OH-6
Christmas Spring AZ-5
Christmas Spring—spring TX-5
Christmas Tailings Dam Number Five—dam AZ-5
Christmas Tailings Dam Number One—dam AZ-5
Christmas Tailings Dam Number Seven—dam AZ-5
Christmas Tailings Dam Number Six—dam AZ-5
Christmas Tailings Dam Number Three—dam AZ-5
Christmas Tailings Dam Number Two—dam AZ-5
Christmas Tree Camp—locale MN-6
Christmas Tree Canyon—valley (2) NV-8
Christmas Tree Coulee—valley MT-8
Christmas Tree Creek—stream UT-8
Christmas Tree Dam—dam AZ-5
Christmas Tree Gulch—valley ID-8
Christmas Tree Lake—reservoir AZ-5
Christmas Tree Pass—gap NV-8
Christmas Tree Plaza (Shop Ctr)—locale MA-1
Christmas Tree Point—cape AK-9
Christmas Tree Ruin (LA 11097)—hist pl NM-5
Christmas Tree Tank—reservoir AZ-5
Christmas Valley—locale OR-9
Christmas Valley Airstrip—airport OR-9
Christmasville—locale TN-4
**Christmasville**—pop pl TN-4
Christmasville Post Office (historical)—building TN-4
Christmas Well—well MT-8
Christmas Well—well NM-5
Christmas Wells Tank—reservoir TX-5
Christ Memorial Baptist Ch—church DE-2
Christ Memorial Baptist Ch—church FL-3
Christ Memorial Ch—church MO-7
Christ Memorial Sch—school WI-6
Christ Memorial Temple—church IN-6
Christ Methodist Ch—church MS-4
Christ Methodist Episcopal Church—hist pl CO-8
Christ Missionary Ch—church GA-3
Christ Mtn—summit CO-8
Christner Cem—cemetery OK-5
Christner Hill—summit PA-2
Christner Lake—lake WI-6
Christner Run—stream PA-2
Christo Ch—church VA-3
Christodelphian Ch—church KY-4
Christodora House—hist pl NY-2
Christoferson Lake MN-6
Christofferson Dam—valley WY-8
Christoff Trail—trail WA-9
Christ of King Ch—church IN-6
Christ of the Lakes Ch—church MI-6
Christ of the Ozarks—other AR-4
Christ Olson Lake—lake MN-6
Christon Ranch—locale WA-9
Christophel Ditch—canal IN-6
Christopher—locale GA-3
Christopher—locale MO-7
Christopher—locale WA-9
**Christopher**—pop pl IL-6
**Christopher**—pop pl KY-4
Christopher, Lake—reservoir CA-9
Christopher, Mount—summit ME-1
Christopher Branch AL-4
Christopher Cem—cemetery AL-4
Christopher Cem—cemetery AR-4
Christopher Cem—cemetery KY-4
Christopher Cem—cemetery OH-6
Christopher Cem—cemetery (2) TN-4
Christopher Center (Shop Ctr)—locale FL-3
Christopher Ch—church GA-3
Christopher Chapel Cem—cemetery AL-4
Christopher Chapel Ch—church AL-4
Christopher Chapel United Methodist Ch AL-4
Christopher City University of Arizona—locale AZ-5
Christopher Columbus Elem Sch—school PA-2
Christopher Columbus HS—school (2) FL-3
Christopher Columbus HS—school NY-2
Christopher Columbus JHS—school CA-9
Christopher Columbus Memorial Fountain—park DC-2
Christopher Creek OR-9
**Christopher Creek**—pop pl AZ-5
Christopher Creek—stream AZ-5
Christopher Creek—stream (2) FL-3
Christopher Creek—stream MT-8
Christopher Creek—stream VA-3
Christopher Creek Campground—park AZ-5
Christopher Fork—locale VA-3
Christopher Gist Cave—cave PA-2
**Christopher Hills (subdivision)**—pop pl MS-4
Christopher Lake—lake MT-8
Christopher Lake—reservoir IL-6
Christopher Lake—reservoir KS-7
Christopher Mills—locale NJ-2
Christopher Minchen Grant—civil FL-3
Christopher Mountain—ridge AZ-5
Christopher Mtn—summit AR-4
Christopher Park—park AL-4
Christopher Place—locale NM-5
Christopher Point—cape FL-3
Christopher Ranch—locale CO-8
Christopher Rsvr—reservoir IL-6
Christopher Run—stream WV-2
Christopher Sch—school CA-9
Christopher Sch—school IL-6
Christopher Sch (abandoned)—school PA-2
Christopherson Bay—bay MN-6
Christopherson Creek—stream WY-8
Christopherson Lake—lake (2) MN-6
Christopherson Slough—gut IA-7
Christopherson State Public Shooting Area—park (2) SD-7
Christopherson State Wildlife Mngmt Are—park MN-6
Christophers Sch—school NY-2
Christopher Tank—reservoir AZ-5
Christopher Young Cemetery MS-4
Christopher Rsvr—reservoir TX-5
Christ Orwick Dam—dam (2) SD-7
Christ Our King Ch—church DE-2
Christ Our King Sch—school DE-2
Christ Our King Sch—school OH-6
Christ Our Redeemer Lutheran Sch—school FL-3
Christ Our Redeemer Lutheran Sch—school OR-9
**Christoval**—pop pl TX-5
Chris-Town Golf Course—other AZ-5
Chris-Town Mall—locale AZ-5
Christown Plaza—locale AZ-5
Chris-Town Travel Trailer and Mobile Home Park—locale AZ-5
Christ Presbyterian Ch—church FL-3
Christ Run PA-2
Christ Sanctified Holy Ch—church MS-4
Christ Sanctified Holy Ch—church VA-3
Christs Anglican Ch—church KS-7
Christs Butte CO-8
Christs Ch—church MO-7
Christs Ch—church OK-5
Christ Sch—school CA-9
Christ Sch—school (4) IL-6
Christ Sch—school MI-6
Christ Sch—school NC-3
Christ Sch—school WI-6
Christs Forty Acres Camp—locale OK-5
Christs Manger Sch—school WI-6
Christs Mission Camp—locale OH-6
**Christs Rock**—pop pl MD-2
Christs Sanctified Holy Ch—church NC-3
Christ Tabernacle MS-4
Christ Temple—church MS-4
Christ Temple—church TN-4
Christ Temple African Methodist Episcopal Zion Ch—church TN-4
Christ Temple Apostolic Ch—church AL-4
Christ Temple Apostolic Faith Ch—church MS-4
Christ Temple Baptist Ch—church MS-4
Christ Temple Ch—church (2) AL-4
Christ Temple Ch—church KY-4
Christ Temple Ch—church MS-4
Christ Temple Ch of Christ Holiness—church (2) MS-4
Christ Temple Ch of God in Christ—church MS-4
Christ the King—church FL-3
Christ the King Catholic Ch—church (2) FL-3
Christ the King Catholic Ch—church (2) MS-4
Christ the King Catholic Ch—church UT-8
Christ the King Catholic Sch—school FL-3

Church Creek—*stream* (2) OR-9
Church Creek—*stream* (2) SC-3
Church Creek—*stream* SD-7
Church Creek—*stream* (3) TX-5
Church Creek—*stream* VA-3
Church Creek—*stream* (2) WA-9
Church Creek—*stream* WV-2
Church Creek Ch—*church* SD-7
Church Creek Divide—*gap* CA-9
*Church Creek Point* FL-3
Church Creek Shelter—*locale* WA-9
Church Creek Trail—*trail* CA-9
**Church Crossroads**—*pop pl* NC-3
Church Ditch—*canal* (2) CO-8
Church Ditch—*canal* MT-8
Church Ditch—*canal* WY-8
Church Dome—*summit* CA-9
Church Drain—*stream* MI-6
Church Dulce Nombre de Jesus of Humacao—*hist pl* PR-3
Churches—*obs name* CO-8
*Churches Cove* RI-1
*Churches Hill* NY-2
*Churches Point* RI-1
Churches Post Office (historical)—*building* TN-4
Church Farm—*hist pl* CT-1
Church Farm Sch—*school* PA-2
Church Farm Sch Hist Dist—*hist pl* PA-2
Church Flat—*flat* WA-9
Church Flats—*flat* SC-3
Church Flats—*flat* UT-8
Church Fork—*stream* KY-4
Church Fork—*stream* UT-8
Church Fork—*stream* WV-2
Church Fork Elk Creek—*stream* CO-8
*Church Fork Recreation Site* UT-8
Church Furniture Store—*hist pl* GA-3
Church Green—*hist pl* MA-1
Church Green—*park* MA-1
*Church Grove* TN-4
Church Grove Cem—*cemetery* MS-4
Church Grove Cem—*cemetery* MO-7
Church Grove Cem—*cemetery* TN-4
Church Grove Ch—*church* KY-4
Church Grove Ch—*church* TN-4
*Church Grove Church* MS-4
Church Grove Post Office (historical)—*building* TN-4
Church Grove Rec Area—*park* NE-7
Church Grove Sch (historical)—*school* MS-4
Church Gulch—*valley* CA-9
*Church Harbor* RI-1
**Church Heights Subdivision**—*pop pl* UT-8
*Church Hill* AL-4
*Church Hill* NH-1
Church Hill—*church* TX-5
Church Hill—*hist pl* VA-3
Church Hill—*locale* GA-3
Church Hill—*locale* KY-4
Church Hill—*locale* (2) MD-2
Church Hill—*locale* MS-4
Church Hill—*locale* NC-3
Church Hill—*locale* (2) PA-2
**Church Hill**—*pop pl* DE-2
**Church Hill**—*pop pl* MD-2
**Church Hill**—*pop pl* MT-8
**Church Hill**—*pop pl* (4) PA-2
**Church Hill**—*pop pl* TN-4
**Church Hill**—*pop pl* TX-5
**Church Hill**—*pop pl* VA-3
Church Hill—*summit* CA-9
Church Hill—*summit* (4) CT-1
Church Hill—*summit* ME-1
Church Hill—*summit* (2) MA-1
Church Hill—*summit* MS-4
Church Hill—*summit* MT-8
Church Hill—*summit* (3) NY-2
Church Hill—*summit* ND-7
Church Hill—*summit* (5) PA-2
Church Hill—*summit* TN-4
Church Hill—*summit* VT-1
Church Hill—*summit* (2) VA-3
Church Hill Airp (historical)—*airport* PA-2
Church Hill (CCD)—*cens area* TN-4
Church Hill Cem—*cemetery* AL-4
Church Hill Cem—*cemetery* CT-1
Church Hill Cem—*cemetery* ME-1
Church Hill Cem—*cemetery* PA-2
Church Hill Cem—*cemetery* SC-3
Church Hill Cem—*cemetery* VA-3
Church Hill Cem—*cemetery* WI-6
Church Hill Ch—*church* AR-4
Church Hill Ch—*church* (2) MS-4
Church Hill Ch—*church* OH-6
Church Hill Ch—*church* PA-2
Church Hill Ch—*church* TN-4
Church Hill Division—*civil* TN-4
Church Hill Elem Sch—*school* TN-4
**Church Hill Estates Subdivision**—*pop pl* UT-8
Church Hill Farm—*hist pl* PA-2
Church Hill Grange Hall—*hist pl* KY-4
Church Hill (historical)—*locale* AL-4
Church Hill Industrial District—*hist pl* RI-1
Church Hill Lookout Tower—*locale* MS-4
*Church Hill Manor* PA-2
**Church Hill Manor**—*pop pl* PA-2
Church Hill MS—*school* TN-4
Church Hill Post Office—*building* MS-4
Church Hill Post Office—*building* TN-4
Church Hill Road Covered Bridge—*hist pl* OH-6
Church Hill Sch—*school* (2) TX-5
Church Hill Sch (abandoned)—*school* PA-2
*Church Hill School* TN-4
Church Hill Shop Ctr—*locale* TN-4
**Church Hills Subdivision**—*pop pl* UT-8
Church Hill Village—*locale* DE-2
Church Hollow—*valley* AL-4
Church Hollow—*valley* AR-4
Church Hollow—*valley* CO-8
Church Hollow—*valley* ID-8
Church Hollow—*valley* MO-7
Church Hollow—*valley* NY-2
Church Hollow—*valley* PA-2
Church Hollow—*valley* VA-3
Church Hollow—*valley* (2) WV-2
Church Hollow Cem—*cemetery* NY-2
Church Home Hosp—*hospital* MD-2
Church House—*hist pl* TN-4
Churchhouse Branch—*stream* FL-3
Church House Branch—*stream* GA-3
Church House Branch—*stream* MS-4
Church House Creek—*stream* TX-5
Church House Gully—*valley* TX-5
Church House Hill—*summit* TN-4
Church House Hollow—*valley* (2) MO-7
Church House Hollow—*valley* TN-4
Churchhouse Hollow—*valley* TN-4
Churchhouse Hollow—*valley* WY-8
Churchhouse Lake—*lake* OK-5
Churchhouse Pond—*lake* TX-5
*Church House Rock* AZ-5
*Churchill* IL-6
*Churchill* KS-7
*Churchill* MI-6
Churchill—*locale* IL-6
Churchill—*locale* MN-6
Churchill—*locale* NV-8
**Churchill**—*pop pl* MD-2
**Churchill**—*pop pl* MN-6
**Churchill**—*pop pl* NC-3
**Churchill**—*pop pl* OH-6
**Churchill**—*pop pl* PA-2
**Churchill**—*pop pl* VA-3
Churchill, Mount—*summit* AK-9
Churchill, O. A., Store—*hist pl* MN-6
Churchill, Richard, House—*hist pl* IL-6
Churchill Acad—*school* FL-3
Churchill Airp—*airport* KS-7
Churchill Bayou—*channel* TX-5
Churchill Bayou—*stream* FL-3
Churchill Bend—*bend* MT-8
Churchill Borough—*civil* PA-2
**Churchill Bridge**—*pop pl* TX-5
Churchill Brook—*stream* (2) ME-1
Churchill Brook—*stream* MA-1
Churchill Brook—*stream* NH-1
Churchill Butte—*summit* MT-8
Churchill Butte—*summit* NV-8
Churchill Camp—*locale* ME-1
Churchill Camp (historical)—*stream* ME-1
Churchill Canyon—*valley* NV-8
Churchill Canyon—*valley* OR-9
Churchill Canyon Well—*well* NV-8
Churchill Cem—*cemetery* IN-6
Churchill Cem—*cemetery* ME-1
Churchill Cem—*cemetery* MA-1
Churchill Cem—*cemetery* PA-2
Churchill Cem—*cemetery* VA-3
Churchill Ch—*church* MI-6
Churchill County—*civil* NV-8
Churchill Creek—*stream* ID-8
Churchill Dam—*dam* ME-1
Churchill Dam Campsite—*locale* ME-1
Churchill Depot—*locale* ME-1
Churchill Downs—*hist pl* KY-4
**Churchill Downs (subdivision)**—*pop pl* AL-4
**Churchill Downs (subdivision)**—*pop pl* NC-3
Churchill Draw—*valley* WA-9
Churchill Farms—*locale* LA-4
Churchill Hill—*summit* CT-1
Churchill Hill—*summit* ME-1
Churchill Hollow—*valley* MO-7
Churchill HS—*school* OR-9
Churchill HS—*school* PA-2
Churchill JHS—*school* UT-8
*Churchill Lake* FL-3
*Churchill Lake* MI-6
Churchill Lake—*lake* (2) ME-1
Churchill Lake—*lake* (2) MI-6
Churchill Lake—*lake* (2) MN-6
Churchill Lake—*lake* PA-2
**Churchill Landing**—*pop pl* MA-1
Churchill Manor—*hist pl* CA-9
Churchill Memorial Ch—*church* NY-2
Churchill Mine—*mine* WA-9
Churchill Mtn—*summit* ID-8
Churchill Mtn—*summit* NY-2
Churchill Mtn—*summit* WA-9
Churchill Narrows—*gap* NV-8
Churchill Oil Field—*oilfield* KS-7
Churchill Park—*park* CT-1
Churchill Park—*park* IL-6
Churchill Park—*park* KY-4
Churchill Park—*park* OH-6
Churchill Park Hist Dist—*hist pl* NY-2
Churchill Peaks—*other* AK-9
Churchill Point—*cape* MI-6
*Churchill Pond* MI-6
*Churchill Pond* PA-2
Churchill-Porter Sch—*school* MI-6
Churchill Rapids—*rapids* OR-9
Churchill Ridge—*ridge* AR-4
Churchill Ridge—*ridge* ME-1
Churchill Ridge—*ridge* WA-9
Churchill Road Sch—*school* VA-3
Churchill Sch—*school* CA-9
Churchill Sch—*school* IL-6
Churchill Sch—*school* (2) MI-6
Churchill Sch—*school* MN-6
Churchill Sch—*school* OR-9
**Churchill Shores**—*pop pl* MA-1
Churchill (Siding)—*locale* ID-8
Churchill (Site)—*locale* ID-8
Churchill Stream—*stream* ME-1
Churchill Swamp—*swamp* GA-3
**Churchill (Township of)**—*pop pl* MI-6
Churchill Valley—*basin* NV-8
**Churchill Valley**—*pop pl* PA-2
Churchill Valley—*valley* NV-8
Churchill Valley Country Club—*other* PA-2
Churchill Woods—*woods* IL-6
Church Inmaculada Conception of Vega Alta—*hist pl* PR-3
Church in the Pines—*church* AL-4
Church In The Valley—*church* TX-5
Church In The Wilderness—*church* PA-2
Church in the Wildwood—*church* ME-1
Church in the Wildwood—*church* NY-2
Church in the Wildwood—*church* OR-9
*Church Island* UT-8
Church Island—*island* NC-3
Church Island—*island* SC-3
Church Island Channel—*channel* NC-3
Church Lake—*lake* (4) FL-3
Church Lake—*lake* (3) MI-6
Church Lake—*lake* (5) MN-6
Church Lake—*lake* NE-7
Church Lake—*lake* NM-5
Church Lake—*lake* WA-9
Church Lake—*reservoir* (2) AL-4
Church Lake—*reservoir* CO-8
Church Lake—*reservoir* TN-4
Church Lake—*swamp* MI-6
Church Lake Dam—*dam* MS-4
Church Lake Dam—*dam* TN-4
Church Lake Prairie—*swamp* FL-3
Church Lakes—*lakes* CO-8
**Churchland**—*pop pl* NC-3
**Churchland**—*pop pl* VA-3
Churchland Bridge—*bridge* VA-3
Churchland HS—*school* VA-3
Church Landing—*locale* NJ-2
Church Landing—*locale* NC-3
Churchland JHS—*school* VA-3
Churchland Sch—*school* NC-3
Churchland Sch—*school* VA-3
Church Lateral—*canal* AZ-5
Church Lateral—*canal* ID-8
*Church Ledge* MA-1
Church (Magisterial District)—*fmr MCD* WV-2
Churchman, John, House—*hist pl* MD-2
Churchman Coll—*school* PA-2
Churchman Creek—*stream* CA-9
Churchman Creek—*stream* IN-6
Churchman Ditch—*canal* IN-6
Church Manufacturing Company Dam—*dam* MA-1
Church Meadows—*flat* CA-9
Church Mesa—*summit* UT-8
Church Mills Branch—*stream* VA-3
Church Mine—*mine* CA-9
Church Missions House—*hist pl* NY-2
*Church Mountain* AL-4
*Church Mtn* TX-5
Church Mtn—*summit* MO-7
Church Mtn—*summit* NM-5
Church Mtn—*summit* NY-2
Church Mtn—*summit* TX-5
Church Mtn—*summit* VA-3
Church Mtn—*summit* WA-9
Church Mtns—*range* UT-8
Church Neck—*cape* VA-3
Church Neck Point—*cape* MD-2
Church No 10—*church* AR-4
Church Nuestra Senora de la Asuncion of Cayey—*hist pl* PR-3
Church Nuestra Senora de la Candelaria y San Matias of Manati—*hist pl* PR-3
Church Nuestra Senora de la Concepcion y San Fernando of Toa Alta—*hist pl* PR-3
Church Nuestra Senora del Carmen of Hatillo—*hist pl* PR-3
Church Nuestra Senora del Rosario of Naguabo—*hist pl* PR-3
Church of Abundant Life—*church* FL-3
Church of All Nations—*church* VA-3
Church of Christ—*church* (47) AL-4
Church of Christ—*church* (3) AR-4
Church of Christ—*church* (4) DE-2
Church of Christ—*church* (19) FL-3
Church Of Christ—*church* GA-3
Church of Christ—*church* (2) IL-6
Church of Christ—*church* (4) KS-7
Church of Christ—*church* MI-6
Church of Christ—*church* (8) MS-4
Church Of Christ—*church* MS-4
Church of Christ—*church* (30) MS-4
Church Of Christ—*church* MS-4
Church of Christ—*church* (5) MS-4
Church of Christ—*church* (10) MO-7
Church of Christ—*church* (3) MT-8
Church of Christ—*church* NE-7
Church of Christ—*church* NM-5
Church of Christ—*church* (2) NC-3
Church of Christ—*church* (2) OH-6
Church Of Christ—*church* OH-6
Church of Christ—*church* OK-5
Church of Christ—*church* (2) PA-2
Church of Christ—*church* (6) TN-4
Church of Christ—*church* TX-5
Church of Christ—*church* UT-8
Church of Christ—*church* WI-6
Church of Christ—*hist pl* MA-1
Church of Christ Andrews Ave—*church* FL-3
Church of Christ at Flomich Ave—*church* FL-3
Church of Christ at Lake Ellen—*church* FL-3
Church of Christ at Lincoln—*church* AL-4
Church of Christ (Brigham City)—*church* UT-8
Church of Christ-Call Street—*church* FL-3
Church of Christ (Cedar City)—*church* UT-8
Church of Christ Cem—*cemetery* GA-3
Church of Christ Cem—*cemetery* WI-6
Church of Christ Clearwater—*church* FL-3
Church of Christ Dunedin—*church* FL-3
Church of Christ-East Bradenton—*church* FL-3
Church of Christ-Goulds—*church* FL-3
Church of Christ Hialeah—*church* FL-3
Church of Christ (historical)—*church* (3) AL-4
Church of Christ (historical)—*church* MS-4
Church of Christ Holiness—*church* MS-4
Church of Christ Holiness Unto the Lord—*church* FL-3
Church of Christ in God—*church* AL-4
Church of Christ in LaRoche Township—*hist pl* SD-7
Church of Christ in Margate—*church* FL-3
Church of Christ (Kaysville)—*church* UT-8
Church of Christ Largo—*church* FL-3
Church of Christ Myrtle Grove—*church* FL-3
Church of Christ Northeast—*church* FL-3
Church of Christ Northwest—*church* FL-3
Church Of Christ No 1—*church* IA-7
Church Of Christ No 2—*church* IA-7
Church of Christ of Columbus—*church* MS-4
Church of Christ of Jacksonville Beach—*church* FL-3
*Church of Christ of Rocky Creek* MS-4
Church of Christ of South Madison—*church* MS-4
Church of Christ (Ogden)—*church* UT-8
Church of Christ Palm Harbor—*church* FL-3
Church of Christ (Salt Lake City)—*church* UT-8
Church of Christ-Sebastian—*church* FL-3
Church of Christ-Seminole—*church* FL-3
Church of Christ Sixth Street—*church* FL-3
Church of Christ Skyview—*church* FL-3
Church of Christ Southwest—*church* FL-3
Church of Christ-Timberlane—*church* FL-3
Church of Christ (Tooele)—*church* UT-8
Church of Christ-University—*church* FL-3
Church of Christ University City—*church* FL-3
Church of Christ (Vernal)—*church* UT-8
Church of Christ-Vero Beach—*church* FL-3
Church of Christ Westside—*church* (2) FL-3
Church of Christ Written in Heaven—*church* FL-3
Church of Christ Written in Heaven Number 2—*church* FL-3
Church of Christ 43rd Street—*church* FL-3
Church of Crucifixion—*church* FL-3
Church of Faith—*church* FL-3
Church of First Born—*church* OK-5
*Church of God* AL-4
*Church of God* MS-4
Church of God—*church* (48) AL-4
Church of God—*church* AR-4
Church of God—*church* (13) FL-3
Church of God—*church* (2) IL-6
Church of God—*church* (2) KS-7
Church Of God—*church* KY-4
Church of God—*church* (3) MI-6
Church of God—*church* (25) MS-4
Church Of God—*church* MS-4
Church of God—*church* (2) MS-4
Church Of God—*church* MS-4
Church of God—*church* (11) MS-4
Church Of God—*church* MS-4
Church of God—*church* (7) MS-4
Church of God—*church* (7) MO-7
Church Of God—*church* MO-7
Church of God—*church* (6) MO-7
Church of God—*church* NM-5
Church Of God—*church* OH-6
Church of God—*church* OH-6
Church Of God—*church* OH-6
Church of God—*church* (2) OH-6
Church of God—*church* OK-5
Church of God—*church* (3) TN-4
Church of God—*church* TX-5
Church of God—*church* (3) WI-6
Church of God, The—*church* AR-4
Church of God and Christ—*church* AL-4
Church of God and Christ—*church* GA-3
Church of God and Christ—*church* MS-4
Church of God and Christ—*church* TX-5
Church of God-Apopka—*church* FL-3
Church of God at Taft—*church* FL-3
Church of God by Faith—*church* (4) FL-3
Church of God Calvary Temple—*church* FL-3
Church of God Camp—*locale* MI-6
Church of God Cem—*cemetery* KS-7
Church of God Cem—*cemetery* (4) MS-4
Church of God Cem—*cemetery* ND-7
Church of God Cem—*cemetery* OH-6
Church of God Chapel—*church* MO-7
*Church of God Church* MS-4
**Church of God Colony**—*pop pl* CA-9
Church of God Cypress Pathway—*church* FL-3
Church of God Deliverance Center—*church* FL-3
Church of God Eastland Temple—*church* FL-3
Church of God Ferndale—*church* FL-3
Church of God Haverhill Road—*church* FL-3
Church of God Hawthorne—*church* FL-3
Church of God-Highlands Chapel—*church* FL-3
Church of God (historical)—*church* MS-4
Church of God Holiness—*church* MS-4
Church of God House of Deliverance—*church* AL-4
Church of God in Christ—*church* (8) AL-4
Church of God in Christ—*church* (3) AR-4
Church of God in Christ—*church* FL-3
Church of God in Christ—*church* IN-6
Church of God in Christ—*church* (3) KS-7
Church of God in Christ—*church* LA-4
Church of God in Christ—*church* MI-6
Church of God in Christ—*church* (8) MS-4
Church of God in Christ—*church* UT-8
Church of God in Christ Antioch Temple—*church* FL-3
Church of God in Christ Holiness—*church* AL-4
Church of God in Christ House of Prayer—*church* IN-6
Church of God in Christ of Eatonville—*church* FL-3
Church of God in Christ Revival Center—*church* KS-7
Church of God Independent Holiness—*church* KS-7
Church of God in Naples—*church* FL-3
Church of God-Largo—*church* FL-3
Church of God Latin-American Mission—*church* FL-3
Church of God-Longwood—*church* FL-3
Church of God New Testament Judaism—*church* FL-3
Church of God North Jacksonville—*church* FL-3
Church of God-North Lane Ave—*church* FL-3
Church of God of Deliverance—*church* AL-4
Church of God of Jacksonville Beach—*church* FL-3
Church of God of Ocoee—*church* FL-3
Church of God of Prophecy—*church* (16) AL-4
Church of God of Prophecy—*church* (5) FL-3
Church of God of Prophecy—*church* GA-3
Church of God of Prophecy—*church* IN-6
Church of God of Prophecy—*church* KS-7
Church of God of Prophecy—*church* (8) MS-4
Church of God of Prophecy—*church* (3) TN-4
Church of God of Prophecy (Moab)—*church* UT-8
Church of God of Prophecy-Ocoee—*church* FL-3
Church of God of Prophecy (Ogden)—*church* UT-8
Church of God of Prophecy (Salt Lake City)—*church* UT-8
Church of God of the United Assembly—*church* AL-4
Church of God on Orange Ave—*church* FL-3
Church of God Orphanage—*building* TN-4
*Church of God Pentecostal* AL-4
Church of God Pentecostal—*church* (3) AL-4
Church of God-Plymouth—*church* FL-3
Church of God Pompano Beach—*church* FL-3
Church of God-Praise Cathedral—*church* FL-3
Church of God Prophecy—*church* (2) FL-3
Church of God Prophecy-Apopka—*church* FL-3
Church of God Riviera Beach—*church* FL-3
Church of God Springfield—*church* FL-3
Church of God-West Jacksonville—*church* FL-3
Church of God-Winter Park—*church* FL-3
Church of Good Shepherd—*church* FL-3
Church of Good Shepherd—*church* TX-5
Church of Jesus—*church* MO-7
Church of Jesus Christ—*church* AL-4
Church of Jesus Christ—*church* AR-4
Church of Jesus Christ—*church* IL-6
Church of Jesus Christ—*church* (3) MI-6
Church of Jesus Christ—*church* (2) MS-4
Church of Jesus Christ—*church* MO-7
Church Of Jesus Christ—*church* OH-6
Church of Jesus Christ, The—*church* VA-3
Church of Jesus Christ Latter-Day Saints—*church* FL-3
Church of Jesus Christ Latter Day Saints—*church* FL-3
Church of Jesus Christ Latter Day Saints—*church* MS-4
Church of Jesus Christ Latter Day Saints—*church* TN-4
Church of Jesus Christ of Latter-Day Saints—*building* FL-3
Church of Jesus Christ of Latter Day Saints—*church* AL-4
Church Of Jesus Christ Of Latter-Day Saints—*church* AL-4
Church of Jesus Christ of Latter Day Saints—*church* AL-4
Church of Jesus Christ of Latter Day Saints—*church* DE-2
Church of Jesus Christ of Latter Day Saints—*church* FL-3
Church of Jesus Christ of Latter-Day Saints—*church* FL-3
Church of Jesus Christ of Latter Day Saints—*church* (4) FL-3
Church of Jesus Christ of Latter-Day Saints—*church* FL-3
Church of Jesus Christ of Latter Day Saints—*church* FL-3
Church of Jesus Christ of Latter-Day Saints—*church* FL-3
Church of Jesus Christ of Latter Day Saints—*church* FL-3
Church of Jesus Christ of Latter-Day Saints—*church* (2) FL-3
Church of Jesus Christ of Latter Day Saints—*church* (3) FL-3
Church of Jesus Christ of Latter-Day Saints—*church* (2) FL-3
Church of Jesus Christ of Latter Day Saints—*church* (3) KS-7
Church of Jesus Christ of Latter Day Saints—*church* (5) MS-4
Church of Jesus Christ of Latter-Day Saints—*church* MO-7
Church of Jesus Christ of Latter Day Saints—*church* TN-4
Church of Jesus Christ of Latter Day Saints, The—*church* FL-3
Church of Jesus Christ of Latter Day Saints, The—*church* MO-7
Church of Jesus Christ of Latter-Day Saints, The—*church* MT-8
Church of Jesus Christ of Latter Day Saints-Crawfordville—*church* FL-3
Church of Jesus Christ of the Latter Day Saints—*church* KS-7
Church of Jesus Christ Pentacostal—*church* TN-4
Church of Jesus Name—*church* MS-4
Church of Latter Day Saints—*church* AL-4
Church of Latter Day Saints—*church* SD-7
Church of Leonard Street—*church* FL-3
Church of Light and Truth—*church* FL-3
Church of Little Flower—*church* FL-3
Church of Living God—*church* DE-2
Church of Living God—*church* FL-3
Church of Mercy—*church* PA-2
Church of Montgomery—*church* AL-4
Church of Nazarene—*church* MI-6
Church of New Birth Sch—*school* FL-3
Church of Notre Dame and Rectory—*hist pl* NY-2
Church of Nuestra Senora de la Candelaria y Guadalupe—*hist pl* TX-5
Church of Our Lady, The—*church* TN-4
Church of Our Lady of Fatima—*church* NY-2
Church of Our Lady of Lourdes—*church* WA-9
Church of Our Lord—*church* AL-4
Church of Our Lord—*church* IN-6
Church of our Lord—*church* MS-4
Church of Our Merciful Saviour—*hist pl* KY-4
Church of Our Redeemer—*church* MS-4
Church of Our Savio-Episcopal—*hist pl* MN-6
Church of Our Savior—*church* MI-6
Church of Our Savior—*church* NJ-2
Church of Our Savior—*church* PA-2
Church Of Our Savior—*hist pl* OH-6
Church of Our Savior-Episcopal—*church* FL-3
Church of Our Saviour, Friend of Children—*hist pl* MI-6
Church of Peace—*church* AL-4
Church of Peace Cem—*cemetery* MN-6
Church of Peace (historical)—*church* AL-4
Church of Prayer—*church* AL-4
Church of Prayer For All People—*church* FL-3
Church of Resurrection—*church* FL-3
Church of Saint Bernard de Clairvoux—*church* FL-3
Church of Saint Gabriel—*church* NJ-2
Church of Saint George—*church* WI-6
Church of Saint George-Eastern Orthodox—*church* FL-3
Church of Saint John of the Mountain—*church* NJ-2
Church of Saint Martin, The—*church* VA-3
Church of Saint Mary the Virgin and Greeley Grove—*hist pl* NY-2
Church of Saint Michael and All Angels—*church* AL-4
Church of San Fernando of Carolina—*hist pl* PR-3
Church of San Isidro Labrador and Santa Maria de la Cabeza of Sabana Grande—*hist pl* PR-3
Church of San Mateo de Cangrejos of Santurce—*hist pl* PR-3
Church of Saratoga (historical)—*church* MS-4
Church of Scientology Mission of Fort Lauderdale—*church* FL-3
Church of Scientology Mission of Indianapolis—*church* IN-6
Church of Scientology of Orlando—*church* FL-3
Church of St. Adrian-Catholic—*hist pl* MN-6
Church of St. Agnes-Catholic—*hist pl* MN-6
Church of St. Bernard-Catholic—*hist pl* MN-6
Church of St. Bridget-Catholic—*hist pl* MN-6
Church of St. Casimir-Catholic—*hist pl* MN-6
Church of St. Francis Xavier-Catholic—*hist pl* (2) MN-6
Church of St. Hubertus-Catholic—*hist pl* MN-6
Church of St. Ignatius Loyola Complex—*hist pl* NY-2
Church of St. James the Less—*hist pl* PA-2
Church of St. John the Baptist—*hist pl* IA-7
Church of St. John the Evangelist—*hist pl* NY-2
Church of St. Joseph-Catholic—*hist pl* (2) MN-6
Church of St. Lawrence—*hist pl* NC-3
Church of St. Mary Help of Christians-Catholic—*hist pl* MN-6
Church of St Mary's-Catholic—*hist pl* MN-6
Church of St. Michael-Catholic—*hist pl* MN-6
Church of St. Patrick-Catholic—*hist pl* MN-6
Church of St. Peter-Catholic—*hist pl* MN-6
Church of St. Philip-in-the-Field and Bear Canon Cemetery—*hist pl* CO-8
Church of Sts. Joseph and Mary-Catholic—*hist pl* MN-6
Church of Sts. Peter and Paul-Catholic—*hist pl* MN-6
Church of St. Stanislaus-Catholic—*hist pl* MN-6
Church of St. Stephen-Catholic—*hist pl* MN-6
Church of St. Thomas the Apostle—*hist pl* WI-6
Church of St. Wenceslaus-Catholic—*hist pl* MN-6
Church of the—*church* FL-3
Church of the Advent—*church* AL-4
Church of the Advent—*hist pl* MN-6
Church of the Advent, Episcopal—*hist pl* KY-4
Church of the Annunciation—*church* FL-3
Church of the Annunciation—*church* MN-6
Church of the Annunciation—*hist pl* KY-4
Church of the Annunciation-Catholic—*hist pl* MN-6
Church of The Apostle Faith—*church* AL-4
Church of the Ascension—*church* AL-4
Church of the Ascension—*church* DE-2
Church of the Ascension—*church* (2) FL-3
Church of the Ascension—*church* MA-1
Church of The Ascension—*church* NY-2
Church of the Ascension—*church* SC-3
Church of the Ascension—*church* TN-4
Church of the Ascension—*hist pl* DC-2
Church of the Ascension—*hist pl* KY-4
Church of the Ascension—*hist pl* MA-1
Church of the Ascension—*hist pl* NJ-2
Church of the Ascension-Episcopal—*church* FL-3
Church of the Ascension (Protestant Episcopal)—*hist pl* NY-2
Church Of The Assumption—*church* PA-2
Church of the Assumption—*hist pl* ID-8
Church of the Assumption—*hist pl* TN-4
Church of the Assumption-Catholic—*hist pl* MN-6
Church of the Assumption of the Blessed Virgin Mary—*hist pl* LA-4
Church of the Assumption of the Virgin Mary—*hist pl* AK-9
Church of the Atonement—*hist pl* WI-6
Church of the Bible—*church* NC-3
Church Of The Bible Covenant—*church* IA-7
Church of the Bible Covenant—*church* KS-7
Church of the Bible Covenant—*church* MI-6
Church of the Blessed Sacrament, Priory, and School—*hist pl* WA-9
Church of the Blessed Sacrement—*church* AL-4
Church Of The Blessed Trinity, The—*church* VA-3
Church of the Blessed Virgin Mary, the Queen of Peace—*hist pl* TX-5
Church of the Brethren—*church* AL-4
Church of the Brethren—*church* CO-8
Church of the Brethren—*church* FL-3
Church of the Brethren—*church* IL-6
Church of the Brethren—*church* KS-7
Church of the Brethren—*church* MI-6
Church of The Brethren—*church* MN-6
Church of the Brethren—*church* MO-7
Church of the Brethren—*church* (2) PA-2
Church of the Brethren—*hist pl* CO-8
Church of the Christian Brotherhood—*church* PA-2
Church of the Confession—*church* MN-6
Church of the Covenant—*church* DC-2
Church of the Covenant—*church* MA-1
Church Of The Covenant—*church* PA-2
Church of the Cross—*church* FL-3
Church of the Cross—*church* MN-6
Church of the Cross—*hist pl* SC-3
Church of the Epiphany—*church* NY-2
Church of the Epiphany—*hist pl* DC-2
Church of the Epiphany, The—*church* FL-3
Church of the Escarpment—*church* NY-2
Church of the First Born—*church* AR-4
Church of the First Born—*church* (2) CO-8
Church of the First Born—*church* (3) OK-5
Church of the Firstborn—*church* OK-5
Church of the First Born—*church* TX-5
Church of the First Born House of Prayer—*church* MS-4
Church of the Forest—*church* AL-4
*Church of the Good Samaritan* TN-4
Church Of The Good Samaritan—*church* (2) PA-2
Church of the Good Shepherd—*church* (3) AL-4
Church of the Good Shepherd—*church* (2) FL-3
Church of the Good Shepherd—*church* NJ-2
Church Of The Good Shepherd—*church* OH-6
Church of the Good Shepherd—*church* OH-6
Church of the Good Shepherd—*church* PA-2
Church of the Good Shepherd—*church* TN-4
Church of the Good Shepherd—*church* TX-5

Church of the Good Shepherd—*church* (2) VA-3
Church of the Good Shepherd—*hist pl* GA-3
Church of the Good Shepherd—*hist pl* MN-6
Church of the Good Shepherd—*hist pl* NC-3
Church of the Good Shepherd and Parish House—*hist pl* CT-1
Church of the Good Shepherd-Episcopal—*hist pl* CA-9
Church of the Good Shepherd-Episcopal—*hist pl* MN-6
Church of the Guardian Angel—*hist pl* TX-5
Church of the Heights—*church* NJ-2
Church of the Hill—*church* NY-2
Church of the Holy Angels—*church* PA-2
Church of the Holy Apostles—*church* FL-3
Church of the Holy Apostles—*hist pl* NY-2
Church of the Holy Apostles, Episcopal—*hist pl* SC-3
Church of the Holy Apostles Rectory—*hist pl* SC-3
Church of the Holy Ascension—*hist pl* AK-9
Church of the Holy Bible—*church* AL-4
Church of the Holy City—*church* DC-2
Church of the Holy Comforter—*hist pl* NY-2
Church of the Holy Comforter-Episcopal—*hist pl* MN-6
Church of the Holy Communion—*church* FL-3
Church of The Holy Communion—*church* NY-2
Church of the Holy Communion—*hist pl* NJ-2
Church of the Holy Communion and Buildings—*hist pl* NY-2
Church of the Holy Communion-Episcopal—*hist pl* MN-6
Church of the Holy Cross—*church* AL-4
Church of the Holy Cross—*church* MI-6
Church of the Holy Cross—*church* SC-3
Church of the Holy Cross—*hist pl* NY-2
Church of the Holy Cross-Episcopal—*hist pl* MN-6
Church of the Holy Family—*hist pl* GA-3
Church of the Holy Family—*hist pl* IL-6
Church of the Holy Family (Catholic)—*hist pl* MN-6
Church of the Holy God—*church* GA-3
Church of the Holy Innocents—*hist pl* NJ-2
Church of the Holy Innocents—*hist pl* NY-2
Church of the Holy Innocents and Rectory—*hist pl* NY-2
Church Of The Holy Martyr—*church* PA-2
Church of the Holy Maternity—*church* NJ-2
Church of the Holy Name—*hist pl* CT-1
Church of the Holy Spirit—*church* NY-2
Church of the Holy Spirit Episcopal—*church* FL-3
Church of the Holy Trinity—*church* NC-3
Church of the Holy Trinity—*hist pl* MS-4
Church of the Holy Trinity—*hist pl* PA-2
Church of the Holy Trinity—*hist pl* SC-3
Church of the Holy Trinity and Rectory—*hist pl* CT-1
Church of the Holy Trinity-Catholic—*hist pl* MN-6
Church of the Immaculate Conception—*church* AL-4
Church of the Immaculate Conception—*church* MS-4
Church of the Immaculate Conception—*hist pl* SD-7
Church of the Immaculate Conception and Clergy Houses—*hist pl* NY-2
Church of the Immaculate Conception-Catholic—*hist pl* MN-6
Church of the Immaculate Conception of Blessed Virgin Mary—*hist pl* TX-5
Church of the Incarnation—*church* (2) FL-3
Church of the Incarnation—*church* NJ-2
Church of the Incarnation—*church* NY-2
Church of the Incarnation and Parish House—*hist pl* NY-2
Church of the Intercession Episcopal—*church* FL-3
Church of the Kingdom of God—*church* FL-3
Church Of The Lakes—*church* OH-6
Church of the Little Flower—*church* AL-4
Church Of The Little Flower—*church* IN-6
Church of the Living God—*church* (2) AL-4
Church of the Living God—*church* FL-3
Church Of The Living God—*church* GA-3
Church of the Living God—*church* IN-6
Church of the Living God—*church* (5) MS-4
Church of the Living God—*church* NC-3
Church of the Living God—*church* (2) OK-5
Church of The Living God—*church* TX-5
Church of the Lord—*church* MS-4
Church of the Lord Jesus—*church* FL-3
Church of the Lord Jesus—*church* LA-4
Church of the Lord Jesus—*church* VA-3
Church of the Lord Jesus, The—*church* AL-4
Church Of The Lord Jesus Christ—*church* GA-3
Church of the Lord Jesus Christ—*church* (3) MS-4
Church of the Lord Jesus Christ of the Apostolic Faith—*church* FL-3
Church of the Lord Jesus Christ of the Apostolic Faith—*church* (2) MS-4
Church of the Lutheran Hour—*church* AL-4
Church of the Madonna—*hist pl* NJ-2
Church of the Magdalen—*church* KS-7
Church of the Manger—*church* PA-2
Church of the Master—*church* CO-8
Church of the Master—*church* IN-6
Church of the Master—*church* MI-6
Church of the Mediator—*church* (2) FL-3
Church of the Mediator—*church* MI-6
Church of the Mediator—*church* MS-4
Church of the Messiah—*hist pl* KY-4
Church of the Messiah—*hist pl* TN-4
Church of the Messiah-Episcopal—*church* FL-3
Church of the Messiah Episcopal Ch—*church* TN-4
*Church of the Nativity* IN-6
Church of the Nativity—*church* AL-4
Church of the Nativity—*church* DE-2
Church of the Nativity—*church* (2) FL-3
Church of the Nativity—*church* MS-4
Church of the Nativity—*church* NJ-2
Church of the Nativity—*church* OH-6
Church of the Nativity—*church* PA-2
Church of the Nativity—*hist pl* CA-9
Church of the Nativity—*hist pl* LA-4
*Church of the Nazarene* MS-4
Church of the Nazarene—*church* (2) AL-4
Church of the Nazarene—*church* (3) DE-2
Church of the Nazarene—*church* (6) FL-3
Church of the Nazarene—*church* IL-6
Church of the Nazarene—*church* KS-7
Church of the Nazarene—*church* (2) MI-6
Church of the Nazarene—*church* (2) MS-4
Church of the Nazarene—*church* MO-7
Church of the Nazarene—*church* NC-3
Church of the Nazarene—*church* TN-4
Church of The Nazarene—*church* TX-5
Church of the Nazarene—*church* WI-6
Church of the Nazarene—*hist pl* NY-2
Church of the Nazarene, The—*church* AL-4
Church of the Nazarene Bayshore—*church* FL-3
Church of the Nazarene-Bradenton—*church* FL-3
Church of the Nazarene Camp—*locale* IL-6
Church of the Nazarene North—*church* FL-3
Church of the Nazarene of Lake Park—*church* FL-3
Church of the Nazarene of Lake Worth—*church* FL-3
Church of the Nazarene of West Palm Beach—*church* FL-3
Church of the Nazarene (Provo)—*church* UT-8
Church of the Nazarene (Vernal)—*church* UT-8
Church of the Nazareth—*church* AL-4
Church of the New Covenant—*church* FL-3
Church of the New Jerusalem—*church* MI-6
Church of the New Jerusalem—*hist pl* ME-1
Church of the New Jerusalem—*hist pl* MA-1
Church of the Open Bible—*church* NJ-2
Church of the Open Door—*church* (2) AL-4
Church of the Open Door—*church* MS-4
Church of the Open Door—*church* OH-6
Church Of The Open Door—*church* PA-2
Church of the Palms—*church* FL-3
Church of the Presidents—*hist pl* NJ-2
Church of the Pure in Heart—*church* AL-4
Church of the Redeemer—*church* (2) FL-3
Church of The Redeemer—*church* MN-6
Church of the Redeemer—*church* MS-4
Church of the Redeemer—*church* PA-2
Church of the Redeemer—*church* TN-4
Church of the Redeemer—*hist pl* GA-3
Church of the Redeemer—*hist pl* MS-4
Church of the Redeemer—*hist pl* NC-3
Church of the Redeemer-Episcopal—*hist pl* MN-6
Church of the Redeemer Episcopal Ch—*church* MS-4
Church of the Regeneration—*church* NY-2
Church of the Resurrection—*church* KS-7
Church of the Resurrection—*church* MI-6
Church of the Sacred Heart-Catholic—*hist pl* MN-6
Church of the Sacred Heart of Jesus—*hist pl* GA-3
*Church of the Saint Andrew* AL-4
Church of the Shepherd—*church* NJ-2
Church of the St. Sava Serbian Orthodox Monastery—*hist pl* IL-6
Church Of The Transfiguration—*church* OH-6
Church of the Transfiguration—*hist pl* (2) NY-2
Church of the Transfiguration—*hist pl* NC-3
Church of the Transfiguration and Rectory—*hist pl* NY-2
Church of the United Brethren in Christ—*church* FL-3
Church of the Valley—*church* MT-8
Church of the Valley, The—*church* AL-4
Church of the Visitation—*hist pl* AL-4
Church of the Visitation of the Blessed Virgin Mary—*hist pl* NE-7
Church Of Truth—*church* VA-3
Church of Truth, The—*church* VA-3
Church on the Hill—*hist pl* MA-1
Church on the Rock—*church* FL-3
Church on 94, The—*church* OH-6
Churchouse Hollow—*valley* KY-4
Church Park—*flat* CO-8
Church Park Hist Dist—*hist pl* NY-2
Church Park Picnic Ground—*locale* UT-8
Church Pasture Windmill—*locale* NM-5
Church Peak—*summit* AK-9
Church Peak—*summit* NV-8
Church Peak—*summit* (2) TX-5
Church Pine Lake—*lake* WI-6
Church Point—*cape* AK-9
Church Point—*cape* (2) MD-2
Church Point—*cape* RI-1
Church Point—*cape* (4) VA-3
Church Point—*cape* WA-9
Church Point—*locale* VA-3
**Church Point**—*pop pl* LA-4
Church Point Gas Field—*oilfield* LA-4
*Church Pond* PA-2
Church Pond—*lake* ME-1
Church Pond—*lake* MO-7
Church Pond—*lake* (2) NY-2
Church Pond—*swamp* FL-3
Church Ponds—*lake* NH-1
Church Pond Trail—*trail* NH-1
*Church Prong* VA-3
Church Prong—*stream* VA-3
Church Ranch—*locale* CA-9
Church Ridge—*ridge* PA-2
Church Ridge—*ridge* TN-4
Church Road—*locale* VA-3
*Church Rock* CO-8
Church Rock—*island* CA-9
Church Rock—*other* AK-9
Church Rock—*pillar* AZ-5
Church Rock—*pillar* CA-9
Church Rock—*pillar* UT-8
**Church Rock**—*pop pl* NM-5
Church Rock—*rock* (2) MA-1
Church Rock—*summit* MA-1
Church Rock—*summit* VA-3
Church Rock Branch—*stream* VA-3
Church Rock Mine—*mine* NM-5
Church Rocks—*other* NM-5
Church Rock Valley—*valley* AZ-5
*Church Run* VA-3
Church Run—*stream* IN-6
Church Run—*stream* MD-2
Church Run—*stream* NJ-2
Church Run—*stream* (3) PA-2
Church Run—*stream* (2) VA-3
Church Run Oil Field—*oilfield* PA-2
Church Saddle—*gap* WA-9
Church Saint Sch—*school* NC-3
Church San Blas de Illescas of Coamo—*hist pl* PR-3
Church San Carlos Borromeo of Aguadilla—*hist pl* PR-3
Church San German Auxerre of San German—*hist pl* PR-3
Church San Jose of Aibonito—*hist pl* PR-3
Church San Jose of Gurabo—*hist pl* PR-3
Church San Juan Bautista of Maricao—*hist pl* PR-3
Church San Juan Bautista y San Ramon Nonato of Juana Diaz—*hist pl* PR-3
Church San Miguel Arcangel of Utuado—*hist pl* PR-3
Church San Sebastian Martir of San Sebastian—*hist pl* PR-3
Church Santa Cruz of Bayamon—*hist pl* PR-3
Church Santa Maria del Rosario of Vega Baja—*hist pl* PR-3
Church Santiago Apostol of Fajardo—*hist pl* PR-3
Churchs Camp—*locale* CA-9
Church Sch—*school* (2) IL-6
Church Sch—*school* MI-6
Church Sch—*school* (2) PA-2
Churchs Corners—*locale* MI-6
**Churchs Ferry**—*pop pl* ND-7
*Churchs Hill* NY-2
Church Slough—*gut* MT-8
Church Slough—*stream* AK-9
Church-Smith-Harris Street Hist Dist—*hist pl* GA-3
*Churchs Point* RI-1
Church Spring—*spring* MT-8
Church Spring—*spring* UT-8
Church Spring Branch—*stream* VA-3
Church Spring Ditch—*canal* UT-8
Church Spring Wash—*valley* UT-8
**Church Spur**—*pop pl* LA-4
Church Square—*hist pl* GA-3
Church Square—*locale* AL-4
Churchs Spring—*spring* CA-9
Church State Wildlife Mngmt Area—*park* MN-6
Church Station—*locale* PA-2
Church St Cem—*cemetery* VT-1
*Church Street* MI-6
Church Street—*uninc pl* NY-2
Church Street-Caddy Hill Hist Dist (Boundary Increase)—*hist pl* MA-1
Church Street Cem—*cemetery* AL-4
Church Street Cem—*cemetery* MA-1
Church Street-Cherokee Street Hist Dist—*hist pl* GA-3
Church Street Ch of Christ—*church* TN-4
Church Street Commercial District—*hist pl* MO-7
Church Street East Hist Dist—*hist pl* AL-4
*Church Street Elementary School* MS-4
Church Street Hist Dist—*hist pl* DE-2
Church Street Hist Dist—*hist pl* ME-1
Church Street Hist Dist—*hist pl* (2) MA-1
Church Street Hist Dist—*hist pl* NY-2
Church Street Hist Dist—*hist pl* SC-3
Church Street Hist Dist—*hist pl* TX-5
Church Street Hist Dist (Boundary Increase)—*hist pl* AL-4
*Church Street Methodist Episcopal Church* AL-4
Church Street Plaza Shop Ctr—*locale* AL-4
Church Street Row—*hist pl* NY-2
Church Street Sch—*school* CT-1
Church Street Sch—*school* GA-3
Church Street Sch—*school* MD-2
Church Street Sch—*school* MS-4
Church Street Sch—*school* (2) NY-2
Church Street Sch—*school* PA-2
**Church Street Subdivision**—*pop pl* UT-8
Church Street United Methodist Ch—*church* AL-4
Church Street United Methodist Ch—*church* TN-4
Church Swamp—*stream* VA-3
Church Swamp—*swamp* MD-2
Church Swamp—*swamp* VA-3
Church Tabernacle—*church* DE-2
Church Tank—*reservoir* AZ-5
**Churchton**—*pop pl* MD-2
**Churchton**—*pop pl* TN-4
Churchton Rec Area—*park* MD-2
Church-Tory House—*building* MA-1
Church Tower—*pillar* CA-9
*Churchtown* TN-4
**Churchtown**—*pop pl* NJ-2
**Churchtown**—*pop pl* NY-2
**Churchtown**—*pop pl* OH-6
**Churchtown**—*pop pl* (2) PA-2
Churchtown Post Office (historical)—*building* PA-2
Churchtown Rsvr—*reservoir* NY-2
Church Valley—*valley* (2) WI-6
Church Valley Cem—*cemetery* WI-6
Church Valley Sch—*school* NE-7
**Church View**—*pop pl* VA-3
**Church View Circle Subdivision**—*pop pl* UT-8
*Churchville* PA-2
Churchville—*locale* PA-2
**Churchville**—*pop pl* IL-6
**Churchville**—*pop pl* IA-7
**Churchville**—*pop pl* MD-2
**Churchville**—*pop pl* (2) NY-2
**Churchville**—*pop pl* (4) PA-2
**Churchville**—*pop pl* VA-3
**Churchville**—*pop pl* WV-2
Churchville-Chili HS—*school* NY-2
Churchville Elem Sch—*school* PA-2
Churchville Greene—*uninc pl* NY-2
*Churchville Lake* PA-2
Churchville Park—*park* NY-2
Churchville Point—*cape* MI-6
Churchville Post Office (historical)—*building* PA-2
Churchville Presbyterian Church—*hist pl* MD-2
Churchville Sch—*school* IL-6
Church-Waddel-Brumby House—*hist pl* GA-3
Churchwalla Well—*well* CA-9
Church Well—*well* WY-8
Churchwell Bend—*bend* TN-4
Churchwell Cem—*cemetery* MS-4
Churchwell Cem—*cemetery* TN-4
Churchwell Ford—*locale* TN-4
Churchwell High Bluff—*cliff* MS-4
Churchwell Landing—*locale* TN-4
Churchwell Prospects—*mine* TN-4
Churchwell Spring—*spring* TN-4
Churchwell Spring Branch—*stream* TN-4
Church Windmill—*locale* NM-5
**Churchwood**—*pop pl* CT-1
*Churck Creek* VA-3
**Churdan**—*pop pl* IA-7
*Churdantown* IA-7
*Churea Island* MP-9
*Churea-to* MP-9
Churehill Sch—*school* WY-8
Churhc of the Savior—*church* TN-4
*Churigurappu Island* MP-9
*Churigurappu-to* MP-9
*Churin Island* MP-9
Churin Island—*island* MP-9
*Churiqurappa-to* MP-9
Chur-Lee Educational Day Care Center—*school* FL-3
Churn Creek—*stream* CA-9
Churn Creek—*stream* MD-2
Churn Creek—*stream* (2) MT-8
Churn Creek—*stream* (2) OH-6
Churn Creek Bottom—*bend* CA-9
Churn Creek Ch—*church* OH-6
Churn Creek Farm—*locale* MD-2
Churn Creek Rsvr—*reservoir* OH-6
Churn Hollow—*valley* TN-4
Churn Lake—*lake* MN-6
Churn Ranch—*locale* NE-7
Churntop Branch—*stream* KY-4
**Churntown**—*pop pl* AL-4
**Churubusco**—*pop pl* IN-6
**Churubusco**—*pop pl* NY-2
Churubusco Branch—*stream* IN-6
Chusa Windmill—*locale* TX-5
*Chusca Mountains* AZ-5
*Chusca Mountains* NM-5
*Chusetown* CT-1
*Chushgai Mountains* AZ-5
*Chushgai Mountains* NM-5
Chuska Lake—*reservoir* NM-5
Chuska Mountains—*range* AZ-5
Chuska Mountains—*range* NM-5
Chuska Peak—*summit* NM-5
Chuska Plateau—*area* AZ-5
Chuska Sch—*school* NM-5
Chuska Wash—*stream* NM-5
*Chustanaluyi* AL-4
Chute, La—*stream* NY-2
Chute, River De—*stream* ME-1
Chute, The—*bay* LA-4
Chute, The—*lake* TN-4
Chute, The—*stream* AR-4
Chute, The—*stream* IN-6
Chute, The—*stream* LA-4
Chute, The—*stream* NE-7
Chute, The—*valley* UT-8
Chute Branch—*stream* NC-3
Chute Branch—*stream* TN-4
Chute Canyon—*valley* MT-8
Chute Canyon—*valley* UT-8
Chute Canyon Spring Number One—*spring* MT-8
Chute Canyon Spring Number Two—*spring* MT-8
Chute Cem—*cemetery* AR-4
Chute Creek—*stream* AK-9
Chute Creek—*stream* (6) ID-8
Chute Creek—*stream* MT-8
Chute Creek—*stream* OR-9
Chute Creek—*stream* (3) WA-9
Chute Grand Tank—*reservoir* NM-5
Chute Gulch—*valley* CO-8
Chute Gulch—*valley* MT-8
Chute Gulch—*valley* OR-9
Chute Island—*island* ME-1
*Chute Island 73* AR-4
Chute Lake—*lake* MS-4
Chute Mesa—*ridge* NM-5
Chute Mtn—*summit* MT-8
Chute of Island—*gut* AR-4
Chute of Island No 14—*channel* MO-7
Chute Of Island No 35—*channel* TN-4
Chute of Island No 7—*lake* MO-7
Chute of Island No 73—*island* AR-4
Chute Of Island No 8—*stream* KY-4
Chute of Island Number Thirty-five Revetment—*levee* TN-4
Chute of Island Number Thirtyfive Revetment—*levee* TN-4
Chute of Island Thirty-nine—*channel* TN-4
Chute of Island 68—*gut* AR-4
Chute of Island 69—*gut* AR-4
Chute Park—*flat* CO-8
Chute Pond—*reservoir* WI-6
Chute Ravine—*valley* CA-9
Chute Ridge—*ridge* MO-7
Chutes—*locale* OR-9
*Chutes, The* OR-9
Chutes Cem—*cemetery* WV-2
Chute Sch (historical)—*school* (2) MO-7
Chute Spring—*spring* CA-9
Chute Square—*park* MN-6
*Chutes River* OR-9
Chute 38—*stream* AR-4
Chutla Peak—*summit* WA-9
Chuttoh Bluffs—*cliff* AK-9
Chutum Vaya—*locale* AZ-5
Chutum Vaya Pass—*gap* AZ-5
Chutum Vaya Wash—*stream* AZ-5
*Chuwallee River* AL-4
*Chuwallee River* TN-4
*Chuwanten Creek* WA-9
*Chuwho* FM-9
**Chuwut Murk**—*pop pl* AZ-5
Chuwut Murk Well—*well* AZ-5
C H Warner Dam—*dam* AL-4
*Chyachya* MH-9
*Chyelan* WV-2
*Chyle Dam* ND-7
Chynes Creek—*stream* MI-6
Chynoweth Canyon—*valley* UT-8
Chyphers, John T., House—*hist pl* MN-6
Chypit Sch—*school* MA-1
*Chyrchya* MH-9
**Ciales**—*pop pl* PR-3
Ciales (Municipio)—*civil* PR-3
Ciales (Pueblo)—*fmr MCD* PR-3
Cialitos (Barrio)—*fmr MCD* PR-3
Ciana Run—*stream* PA-2
*Cianell Cabin* CA-9
Ciatana Creek—*stream* CA-9
Ciba-Geigy—*airport* NJ-2
Ciba Geigy McIntosh Plant Pond 1—*reservoir* AL-4
Ciba Geigy McIntosh Plant Pond 2—*reservoir* AL-4
Cibao (Barrio)—*fmr MCD* (2) PR-3
Cibbets Flat—*flat* CA-9
**Cibecue**—*pop pl* AZ-5
Cibecue Canyon—*valley* AZ-5
Cibecue Canyon Tank—*reservoir* AZ-5
Cibecue Chapter House—*building* AZ-5
Cibecue Creek—*locale* AZ-5
Cibecue Creek—*stream* AZ-5
Cibecue Day Sch—*school* AZ-5
Cibecue Peak—*summit* AZ-5
Cibecue Ridge—*ridge* AZ-5
Cibecue Ridge Tank—*reservoir* AZ-5
Cibecue Rim Tank—*reservoir* AZ-5
Cibecue Trading Post—*building* AZ-5
*Cibicu* AZ-5
Cibilo Cem—*cemetery* TX-5
*Ciblo Draw* NM-5
Cibola—*locale* AZ-5
**Cibola**—*pop pl* AZ-5
Cibola Bridge—*bridge* AZ-5
Cibola Camp—*locale* AZ-5
Cibola Canyon—*valley* NM-5
**Cibola (County)**—*pop pl* NM-5
Cibola Lake—*reservoir* AZ-5
Cibola Natl Wildlife Ref—*park* AZ-5
Cibola Natl Wildlife Ref—*park* CA-9
*Cibola Park* NV-8
Cibola Spring—*spring* NM-5
Cibola Valley—*valley* AZ-5
*Cibolo* TX-5
**Cibolo**—*pop pl* TX-5
Cibolo Canyon—*valley* NM-5
Cibolo Creek—*stream* NM-5
Cibolo Creek—*stream* (4) TX-5
*Cibolo Draw* NM-5
Cibolo Ranch—*locale* (2) TX-5
*Cibolo River* TX-5
Cibolo Spring—*spring* NM-5
Cibolo Tank—*reservoir* TX-5
Cibolo Windmill—*locale* TX-5
Cibo Peak—*summit* CA-9
**Cibro**—*pop pl* NY-2
Cibuco (Barrio)—*fmr MCD* (2) PR-3
**Cicalla**—*pop pl* AR-4
*Cicco Brook* NJ-2
Cicely, Lake—*lake* AK-9
Cicero—*locale* KS-7
Cicero—*locale* WA-9
**Cicero**—*pop pl* IL-6
**Cicero**—*pop pl* IN-6
**Cicero**—*pop pl* NY-2
**Cicero**—*pop pl* WI-6
Cicero Cem—*cemetery* IN-6
**Cicero Center**—*pop pl* NY-2
Cicero Center Cem—*cemetery* NY-2
Cicero Creek—*stream* IN-6
Cicero Creek—*stream* MO-7
**Cicero Heights**—*pop pl* IN-6
Cicero (historical)—*locale* AL-4
Cicero Interchange—*other* NY-2
Cicero Loudermilk Cove—*valley* GA-3
Cicerone—*locale* WV-2
Cicero Peak—*summit* SD-7
Cicero Sch—*school* IL-6
Cicero State Game Mngmt Area—*park* NY-2
Cicero Swamp—*swamp* NY-2
Cicero Tank—*reservoir* TX-5
**Cicero (Town of)**—*pop pl* NY-2
**Cicero (Town of)**—*pop pl* WI-6
Cicero (Township of)—*civ div* IL-6
**Cicero (Township of)**—*pop pl* IN-6
*Cichicwaukie Pond* ME-1
*Cico* AL-4
Cicott, Lake—*lake* IN-6
**Cid**—*pop pl* NC-3
Cider Brook Cem—*cemetery* CT-1
Cider Fork—*stream* IN-6
**Cider Hill**—*pop pl* ME-1
Cider Hill—*summit* CT-1
Cider Hill Creek—*stream* ME-1
Cider Mill Brook—*stream* CT-1
*Cider Mill Pond* ME-1
Cider Mill Pond—*lake* CT-1
Cider Mill Pond—*lake* ME-1
Cider Millpond—*lake* MA-1
Cider Mill Pond—*lake* NH-1
Cider Millpond—*reservoir* MA-1
Cider Path—*trail* PA-2
Cider Press Hollow—*valley* TN-4
Cider Run—*stream* (3) PA-2
Cider Run—*stream* WV-2
Cid Field—*park* IL-6
Cid Gitus Windmill—*locale* TX-5
**Cidra**—*pop pl* PR-3
Cidra (Barrio)—*fmr MCD* PR-3
Cidral (Barrio)—*fmr MCD* PR-3
Cidra (Municipio)—*civil* PR-3
Cidra (Pueblo)—*fmr MCD* PR-3
Cidwell Branch—*stream* TX-5
Ciela Grande Mobile Home Park—*locale* AZ-5
Cielito Park—*park* AZ-5
**Cielo Vista**—*pop pl* TX-5
Cielo Vista Sch—*school* CA-9
Cienaga Alta (Barrio)—*fmr MCD* PR-3
Cienaga Baja (Barrio)—*fmr MCD* PR-3
Cienaga (Barrio)—*fmr MCD* PR-3
Cienaga Campground—*locale* CA-9
Cienaga Canyon—*valley* (2) CA-9
Cienaga de Cuevas—*swamp* PR-3
Cienaga de las Cucharillas—*swamp* PR-3
Cienaga de San Pedro—*swamp* PR-3
Cienaga El Guayabal—*swamp* PR-3
Cienaga Flats—*flat* CA-9
Cienaga Grande—*swamp* CA-9
Cienaga Isabel—*swamp* PR-3
Cienaga La Picua—*swamp* PR-3
*Cienaga Larga* CA-9
Cienaga Pozo Hondo—*swamp* PR-3
Cienaga Prieta—*swamp* PR-3
*Cienaga Redonda* CA-9
Cienaga Redonda—*area* NM-5
*Cienaga Rincon* CA-9
Cienagas (Barrio)—*fmr MCD* PR-3
Cienaga Seca—*plain* CA-9
Cienaga Seca Creek—*stream* CA-9
Cienaga Spring—*spring* CA-9
Cienaga Spring—*spring* NM-5
Cienagita Spring—*spring* AZ-5
Cienega—*locale* CA-9
Cienega, Arroyo—*valley* TX-5
Cienega, La—*area* AZ-5
Cienega, The—*swamp* AZ-5
Cienega Amarilla—*stream* NM-5
Cienega Basin—*basin* TX-5
Cienega Bridge—*hist pl* AZ-5
Cienega Camp—*locale* (2) CA-9
*Cienega Canyon* AZ-5
Cienega Canyon—*valley* AZ-5
Cienega Canyon—*valley* (4) NM-5
Cienega Cem—*cemetery* NM-5
*Cienega Creek* TX-5
Cienega Creek—*stream* (10) AZ-5
Cienega Creek—*stream* (2) CA-9
Cienega Creek—*stream* NM-5
Cienega Creek—*stream* (3) TX-5
Cienega Del Gabilan—*civil* CA-9
Cienega del Oso—*swamp* NM-5
Cienega De Los Paicines—*civil* CA-9
Cienega Draw—*valley* (3) AZ-5
Cienega Draw—*valley* NM-5
Cienega Larga—*swamp* CA-9
Cienega Mirth—*locale* CA-9
Cienega Mountains—*summit* TX-5
Cienega Mtn—*summit* TX-5
Cienega O Paso De La Tijera—*civil* CA-9
Cienega Picnic Area—*locale* NM-5
Cienega Ranch—*locale* (2) AZ-5
Cienega Ranch—*locale* (2) NM-5
Cienega Redonda—*area* CA-9
Cienega Redonda—*swamp* NM-5
Cienega Redondo Camp—*locale* AZ-5
Cienega Sch—*school* (3) CA-9
Cienega Sch—*school* (2) NM-5
Cienegas Creek—*stream* TX-5
*Cienegas de las Pimas* AZ-5
*Cienegas de los Pinos* AZ-5
Cienega Spring—*spring* (5) AZ-5
Cienega Spring—*spring* CA-9
Cienega Spring—*spring* (3) NM-5
Cienega Springs—*locale* AZ-5
**Cienega Springs**—*pop pl* AZ-5
Cienega Springs—*spring* (2) NM-5
Cienega Tank—*reservoir* (4) AZ-5
Cienega Tank—*reservoir* NM-5
Cienega Tank, La—*reservoir* AZ-5
Cienega Trap Tank—*reservoir* AZ-5
Cienega Valley—*valley* (2) CA-9
*Cienega Wash* AZ-5
Cienega Wash—*stream* AZ-5
Cienega Well—*well* AZ-5
*Cienegita Canyon* AZ-5
Cienegita Canyon—*valley* NM-5
*Cienegita Spring* NM-5
Cienegita Spring—*spring* AZ-5
Cienegueta (Barrio)—*fmr MCD* PR-3
Cieneguilla Ch—*church* NM-5
Cieneguilla Creek—*stream* (2) NM-5
Cieneguilla Grant—*civil* NM-5
Cieneguilla Mtn—*summit* NM-5
Cieneguita Canyon—*valley* AZ-5
Cieneguitas Creek—*stream* CA-9
Cieneguita Windmill—*well* AZ-5
Ciengaga Tiburones—*swamp* PR-3
Ciengita Spring—*spring* NM-5
Cierbo, Canada Del —*valley* CA-9
Ciervo, Arroyo—*stream* CA-9
Ciervo Hills—*other* CA-9
Ciervo Mountain—*ridge* CA-9
Cifax—*locale* VA-3
Cigar Creek Canyon—*valley* UT-8
Cigarette Creek—*stream* MT-8
Cigarette Creek Trail—*trail* MT-8
Cigarette Hills—*summit* CA-9
Cigarette Hollow—*valley* UT-8
Cigarette Hollow—*valley* VA-3
Cigarette Landing—*locale* AR-4
Cigarette Rock—*summit* MT-8
Cigarette Spring—*spring* CA-9
Cigarette Spring—*spring* UT-8
Cigarette Spring Cave—*cave* UT-8
Cigarette Tank—*reservoir* AZ-5
Cigar Factory—*hist pl* SC-3
Cigar Lake—*lake* OR-9
Cigar Mtn—*summit* TX-5
Cigar Spring—*spring* TX-5
Cihak Farmstead—*hist pl* SD-7
Cile Ch—*church* LA-4
Cilek Creek—*stream* NE-7
Cille Lake—*lake* WI-6
Cilley, Mount—*summit* NH-1
Cilley Brook—*stream* (2) NH-1
Cilley Covered Bridge—*hist pl* VT-1
Cilley Hill—*summit* (2) NH-1
**Cilley (historical)**—*pop pl* NC-3
Cilleys Cave—*cave* NH-1
**Cilleyville**—*pop pl* NH-1
Cilly Creek—*stream* MT-8
*Cilmeton* VA-3
*Ciltipin Creek* TX-5
Cima—*locale* CA-9
Cima—*locale* TX-5
Cima Hill—*summit* CA-9
Cima Park—*gap* AZ-5
Cima Ranger Station—*locale* AZ-5
*Cimarona Peak* CO-8
Cimaron Tank—*reservoir* NM-5
Cimarron—*locale* CA-9
**Cimarron**—*pop pl* CO-8
**Cimarron**—*pop pl* KS-7
**Cimarron**—*pop pl* NM-5
Cimarron—*uninc pl* OK-5
**Cimarrona**—*pop pl* PR-3
Cimarrona Campground—*locale* CO-8
Cimarrona Creek—*stream* CO-8
*Cimarron Airport* KS-7

Cimarrona Peak—summit CO-8
Cimarron Ave Sch—school CA-9
Cimarron Breaks KS-7
Cimarron Canyon—valley NM-5
Cimarron Canyon (historical)—valley AZ-5
Cimarron Canyon Wildlife Area—park NM-5
Cimarron (CCD)—cens area NM-5
Cimarroncita (Girls Camp)—locale NM-5
Cimarroncito Base Camp—locale NM-5
Cimarroncito Creek—stream NM-5
Cimarroncito Peak—summit NM-5
Cimarroncito Rsvr—reservoir NM-5
**Cimarron City**—pop pl OK-5
**Cimarron (County)**—pop pl OK-5
Cimarron County Courthouse—hist pl OK-5
Cimarron Creek CO-8
Cimarron Creek OK-5
Cimarron Creek—stream AZ-5
Cimarron Creek—stream CO-8
Cimarron Crossing Park—park KS-7
Cimarron Ditch—canal CO-8
Cimarron Feeder Garnet Ditch—canal CO-8
Cimarron Hills—CDP CO-8
Cimarron Hills—summit AZ-5
Cimarron Hotel—hist pl KS-7
Cimarron Lake—reservoir AZ-5
Cimarron Mesa—summit NM-5
Cimarron Mountains AZ-5
Cimarron Mountains—range NM-5
Cimarron Mountains—summit AZ-5
Cimarron Municipal Airp—airport KS-7
Cimarron Natl Grassland—forest KS-7
Cimarron Peak—summit AZ-5
Cimarron Point—cliff CO-8
Cimarron Range—range NM-5
Cimarron Redoubt—hist pl KS-7
Cimarron Ridge—ridge CO-8
Cimarron River OK-5
Cimarron River—stream (2) CO-8
Cimarron River—stream KS-7
Cimarron River—stream NM-5
Cimarron River—stream OK-5
Cimarron River Campground—locale KS-7
Cimarron River Picnic Ground—park KS-7
Cimarron Saddle—gap AZ-5
Cimarron Sch—school TX-5
Cimarron Spring—spring AZ-5
**Cimarron (subdivision)**—pop pl (2) AZ-5
**Cimarron Subdivision**—pop pl UT-8
Cimarron Tank—reservoir AZ-5
Cimarron Township—civil KS-7
**Cimarron Township**—pop pl (2) KS-7
Cimarron Valley Cem—cemetery OK-5
Cimarron Valley Ch—church OK-5
Cima Saddle—gap AZ-5
Cimeron Mtn—summit AZ-5
Cimeron Spring—spring AZ-5
Cimic—locale IL-6
Cimino Cove—cave PA-2
Cimmaron Hist Dist—hist pl NM-5
Cimmaron Mine—mine CO-8
Cimmarron River KS-7
Cimmerian Lake—lake MT-8
Cimney Park—flat WY-8
Cimota City—locale KY-4
Cinabar Creek WA-9
Cinca de Mayo Windmill—locale TX-5
Cincades Creek MS-4
Cincas Creek CA-9
Cincha Lake—lake OR-9
Cinch Creek—stream CA-9
Cinch Creek—stream (2) ID-8
Cinch Creek—stream WA-9
Cinch Hook Butte—summit AZ-5
Cinch Mine—mine NV-8
Cincinati MS-4
Cincinnati—locale MO-7
**Cincinnati**—pop pl AR-4
**Cincinnati**—pop pl (2) IN-6
**Cincinnati**—pop pl IA-7
**Cincinnati**—pop pl OH-6
Cincinnati Belle Mine—mine CA-9
Cincinnati Bible Seminary—church OH-6
Cincinnati Bluff—cliff TX-5
Cincinnati Branch—stream (2) KY-4
Cincinnati Cem—cemetery IL-6
Cincinnati Cem—cemetery NE-7
Cincinnati Cem—cemetery TX-5
Cincinnati City Hall—hist pl OH-6
Cincinnati Country Club—other OH-6
Cincinnati Country Day Sch—school OH-6
Cincinnati Creek—stream AR-4
Cincinnati Creek—stream NY-2
Cincinnati Enquirer Bldg—hist pl OH-6
Cincinnati Gardens—park OH-6
Cincinnati Gas & Electric
Company—facility KY-4
Cincinnati Gymnasium and Athletic
Club—hist pl OH-6
Cincinnati Hollow—valley KY-4
Cincinnati Landing—locale IL-6
Cincinnati Music Hall—hist pl OH-6
Cincinnati Observatory Bldg—hist pl OH-6
Cincinnati Street Gas Lamps—hist pl OH-6
Cincinnati Tennis Club—hist pl OH-6
Cincinnati Township—fmr MCD IA-7
**Cincinnati (Township of)**—pop pl (2) IL-6
Cincinnati Union Terminal—hist pl OH-6
Cincinnati Waterworks—other OH-6
Cincinnati Work House and Hosp—hist pl OH-6
Cincinnati Zoo Historic
Structures—hist pl OH-6
**Cincinnatus**—pop pl NY-2
Cincinnatus Branch WV-2
Cincinnatus Hist Dist—hist pl NY-2
Cincinnatus Lake—lake NY-2
**Cincinnatus (Town of)**—pop pl NY-2
**Cinclare**—pop pl LA-4
Cinclare Landing—locale LA-4
Cinco—locale CA-9
**Cinco**—pop pl WV-2
Cinco Bayou—bay FL-3
**Cinco Bayou**—pop pl FL-3
Cinco Canoas Canyon—valley CA-9
Cinco Canyon—valley AZ-5
Cinco de Mayo, Canon —valley TX-5
Cinco de Mayo Crossing—locale TX-5
Cinco de Mayo Ranch—locale TX-5
Cinco de Mayo Well—well AZ-5
Cinco de Mayo Windmill—locale (2) TX-5
Cincoe Lake—lake WI-6
Cinco Poses Spring—spring CA-9
Cinco Poses Trail—trail CA-9
**Cinco Soles (subdivision)**—pop pl (2) AZ-5
Cincotta—locale CA-9
Cinco Well—well NM-5
Cinco Windmill—well AZ-5
CINCPAC HQ—hist pl HI-9
Cincue Lateral—canal TX-5
Cinda—locale KY-4
Cindas Creek—stream KY-4
Cindell Spur SD-7
Cinder Basin—basin AZ-5
Cinder Bluffs—cliff CO-8
Cinder Branch—stream SC-3
Cinder Butte—summit (3) CA-9
Cinder Butte—summit CO-8
Cinder Butte—summit (2) ID-8
Cinder Butte—summit NM-5
Cinder Butte—summit OR-9
Cinder Butte Well—well OR-9
Cinder Cone WA-9
Cinder Cone—summit (4) CA-9
Cinder Cone—summit HI-9
Cinder Cone—summit (2) OR-9
Cinder Cone Butte—summit ID-8
Cinder Crater—crater UT-8
Cinder Creek—channel NY-2
Cinder Creek—stream SC-3
**Cinderella**—pop pl WV-2
Cinderella Day Nursery—school FL-3
**Cinderella Hills**—pop pl GA-3
Cinderella Mine (historical)—mine OR-9
Cinderella Rsvr—reservoir UT-8
Cinderella Sch—school FL-3
Cinderella South Mine—mine CO-8
Cinderella Spring—spring OR-9
Cinder Flat—flat AZ-5
Cinder Ford—locale TN-4
Cinder Gulch—valley CO-8
Cinder Gulch—valley NM-5
Cinder Hill CA-9
Cinder Hill—summit AZ-5
Cinder Hill—summit CA-9
Cinder Hill—summit OR-9
Cinder Hill—summit TN-4
Cinder Hill—summit UT-8
Cinder Hills—summit AZ-5
Cinder Hills—summit HI-9
Cinder Island—island NY-2
Cinder Knob—summit KY-4
Cinder Knoll—summit AZ-5
Cinder Knoll Pond—reservoir AZ-5
Cinder Lake WA-9
Cinder Lake—flat AZ-5
Cinder Mtn—summit (2) AZ-5
Cinder Mtn—summit NV-8
Cinder Mtn—summit NM-5
Cinder Pile Spring—spring PA-2
Cinder Pit—crater ID-8
Cinder Pit Tank—reservoir AZ-5
Cinder Point—cape AK-9
Cinder Point—cape SC-3
Cinder Point Mtn—summit AZ-5
Cinder Point Tank—reservoir AZ-5
Cinder Prairie Lookout—locale OR-9
Cinder Prairie Way—trail OR-9
Cinder River—stream AK-9
Cinders, The—lava UT-8
Cinders Bond Ch (historical)—church MS-4
Cinder Spring—spring CA-9
Cinder Tank AZ-5
Cinder Tank—reservoir (4) AZ-5
Cindy, Lake—reservoir GA-3
Cindy, Lake—reservoir TX-5
Cindy, Mount—summit CO-8
Cindy Branch—stream (3) NC-3
Cindy Cliff—cliff KY-4
Cindy Cove—basin GA-3
Cindy Cove—valley TN-4
Cindy Creek—stream OK-5
Cindy Creek—stream OR-9
Cindy Creek—stream TN-4
Cindy Edwards Branch—stream NC-3
Cindy Fork—stream VA-3
Cindy Hole FL-3
Cindy Hole Mine—mine TN-4
Cindy Lake—lake FL-3
Cindy Lake—lake WI-6
Cindy Linda Lake—reservoir NY-2
**Cindy Park**—pop pl LA-4
Cindy Windmill—locale TX-5
Cinebar—locale WA-9
Cinebar Creek WA-9
Cinebar Mountain ID-8
Cinega Canyon AZ-5
Cinema Park Village Shop Ctr—locale AZ-5
Cinemas East Plaza—locale KS-7
Cine Mtn—summit NV-8
Cinesa Tank—reservoir AZ-5
Cinger Creek—stream OR-9
Cinigita Canyon AZ-5
Cinigita Tank—reservoir AZ-5
**Ciniza**—pop pl NM-5
Ciniza Refinery—other NM-5
Cinkers Mine—mine MT-8
Cinko Lake—lake CA-9
Cinnabar AZ-5
Cinnabar Basin—basin MT-8
Cinnabar Camp—locale CA-9
Cinnabar Canyon—valley CA-9
Cinnabar Canyon—valley NV-8
Cinnabar City Mine—mine NV-8
Cinnabar Creek—stream AK-9
Cinnabar Creek—stream (4) ID-8
Cinnabar Creek—stream (2) MT-8
Cinnabar Creek—stream OR-9
Cinnabar Creek—stream (2) WA-9
Cinnabar Gap—gap OR-9
Cinnabar Gulch—valley CA-9
Cinnabar Gulch—valley OR-9
Cinnabar Hill—summit NV-8
Cinnabar Mine—mine (2) AZ-5
Cinnabar Mine—mine (3) CA-9
Cinnabar Mine—mine OR-9
Cinnabar Mtn OR-9
Cinnabar Mtn—summit ID-8
Cinnabar Mtn—summit MT-8
Cinnabar Mtn—summit (3) OR-9
Cinnabar Park—locale WY-8
Cinnabar Peak—summit ID-8
Cinnabar Point—summit MT-8
Cinnabar Ridge—ridge NV-8
Cinnabar Rsvr—reservoir ID-8
Cinnabar Saddle—gap MT-8
Cinnabar Sch—school (2) CA-9
Cinnabar Sch—school MT-8
Cinnabar Spring—spring NV-8
Cinnabar Springs—spring CA-9
Cinnabar Wash AZ-5
Cinnabar Wash—valley AZ-5
**Cinnaminson**—pop pl NJ-2
Cinnaminson HS—school NJ-2
**Cinnaminson (Township of)**—pop pl NJ-2
Cinnamon Bay—bay VI-3
Cinnamon Bay—locale VI-3
Cinnamon Bay Plantation—hist pl VI-3
Cinnamon Bear Creek—stream (2) MT-8
Cinnamon Bear Point—summit MT-8
Cinnamon Bear Saddle—gap MT-8
Cinnamon Butte—summit OR-9
Cinnamon Canyon—valley OK-5
Cinnamon Cay—island VI-3
Cinnamon Creek IL-6
Cinnamon Creek—stream CA-9
Cinnamon Creek—stream (2) CO-8
Cinnamon Creek—stream (2) ID-8
Cinnamon Creek—stream (2) MT-8
Cinnamon Creek—stream ND-7
Cinnamon Creek—stream UT-8
Cinnamon Creek—stream WA-9
Cinnamon Gap—gap CA-9
Cinnamon Gulch—valley CO-8
**Cinnamon Hills**—pop pl PA-2
Cinnamon Lake—lake NY-2
Cinnamon Mtn—summit (2) CO-8
Cinnamon Mtn—summit MT-8
**Cinnamon Park Subdivision**—pop pl UT-8
Cinnamon Pass—gap CO-8
Cinnamon Peak—summit MT-8
Cinnamon Peak—summit OR-9
Cinnamon Peak—summit WA-9
**Cinnamon Ridge (subdivision)**—pop pl NC-3
**Cinnamon Ridge Subdivision**—pop pl UT-8
Cinnamon Spring—spring MT-8
Cinnamon Station—locale MT-8
**Cinnimon Woods**
**(subdivision)**—pop pl NC-3
Cinque Hommes Creek—stream MO-7
Cinque Hommes Township—civil MO-7
Cin State Wildlife Mngmt Area—park MN-6
Cintra—hist pl PA-2
Cintrona (Barrio)—fmr MCD PR-3
**Cintrona Primera**—pop pl PR-3
**Cintrona Segunda**—pop pl PR-3
Cintura Hill—summit AZ-5
**Cinuecue Park**—pop pl TX-5
Cinyon Otah—summit AZ-5
Ciochetto Canyon—valley UT-8
Ci-pau-lo-vi AZ-5
Ciperts and Chapson Ditch—canal CO-8
Cipole—locale OR-9
Cipole Sch—school OR-9
**Cipper Mills**—pop pl OH-6
Cipra Branch—stream IA-7
Cipres—locale TX-5
Cipriani Sch—school CA-9
**Cipriano**—pop pl PR-3
Cipriano Hills—summit AZ-5
Cipriano Pass—gap (2) AZ-5
Cipriano Well—well AZ-5
**Cipsco Park**—pop pl IL-6
Cirac Mountain NV-8
Cirac Valley—valley NV-8
Cirby Creek CA-9
Cirby Creek—stream (2) CA-9
Cirby Meadow—flat CA-9
Cirby Sch—school CA-9
Circe Flat—flat AZ-5
Circleville (Township of)—other OH-6
Circle—locale (2) TX-5
**Circle**—pop pl AK-9
**Circle**—pop pl MT-8
**Circle**—pop pl NJ-2
Circle—valley WY-8
Circle, The—flat UT-8
Circle, The—other CA-9
Circle ANV762—reserve AK-9
Circle A Ranch—locale NM-5
Circle A Ranch Dam—dam AL-4
Circle A Ranch Lake—reservoir AL-4
Circle Back—locale TX-5
Circle Baptist Ch—church FL-3
Circle Bar—locale OR-9
Circle Bar Basin—flat CO-8
Circle Bar Coulee—valley MT-8
Circle Bar Draw—valley AZ-5
Circle Bar Draw—valley MT-8
Circle Bar Golf Club—other OR-9
Circle Bar J Boys Ranch—locale WA-9
Circle Bar Lake—lake (2) WY-8
Circle Bar Number 1 Spring—spring NV-8
Circle Bar Number 2 Spring—spring NV-8
Circle Bar Number 3 Spring—spring NV-8
Circle Bar Ranch—locale CO-8
Circle Bar Ranch—locale NM-5
Circle Bar Ranch—locale (2) OR-9
Circle Bar Ranch—locale (2) TX-5
Circle Bar Ranch—locale WY-8
Circle Bar Sheep Camp—locale WY-8
Circle Bar Spring—spring MT-8
Circle Bar Spring—spring OR-9
Circle Bar Well—well WY-8
Circle Bay—bay AK-9
Circle Beach—beach CT-1
**Circle Beach**—pop pl CT-1
Circle Bluff—cliff TX-5
Circle B Ranch—locale (2) CA-9
Circle Branch—stream MO-7
Circle Bridge—bridge MT-8
Circle Butte—summit NM-5
Circle Butte—summit OR-9
Circle Buttes—range ND-7
Circle Cave—cave AL-4
Circle Cem—cemetery (2) IN-6
Circle Cem—cemetery LA-4
**Circle City**—pop pl AZ-5
**Circle City**—pop pl MO-7
Circle City Community Hall—building AZ-5
Circle Cliffs—cliff UT-8
Circle C Number 1 Dam—dam SD-7
Circle C Number 2 Dam—dam SD-7
Circle Court Ch—church NC-3
**Circle Court Subdivision**—pop pl UT-8
Circle C Ranch—locale (2) ID-8
Circle Creek—stream AK-9
Circle Creek—stream CO-8
Circle Creek—stream ID-8
Circle Creek—stream (3) MT-8
Circle Creek—stream NV-8
Circle Creek—stream OR-9
Circle Creek—stream WA-9
Circle Creek—stream WY-8
Circle Creek Rsvr—reservoir NV-8
Circle Creek Well—well NV-8
Circle Cross Ranch—locale NM-5
Circle Cross Ranch HQ—hist pl NM-5
Circle Cross Rsvr—reservoir NV-8
Circle C Sch—school TN-4
Circle Dart Lake—reservoir KY-4
Circle Diamond Lake—lake NM-5
Circle Diamond Sch—school MT-8
Circle Ditch—canal IN-6
Circle Ditch—canal MO-7
Circle Ditch—canal WY-8
Circle Dot Gulch—valley CO-8
Circle Dot Ranch—locale (2) TX-5
Circle D Ranch—locale TX-5
Circle Eagle Dam—dam SD-7
Circle End Creek—stream ID-8
Circle E Ranch—locale (2) CA-9
Circle Flat—flat UT-8
Circle F Ranch—locale NM-5
Circle F Ranch Lake Dam—dam MS-4
**Circle Green**—pop pl OH-6
Circle Grove Cem—cemetery IA-7
Circle Grove Elem Sch—school KS-7
Circle Grove Sch (historical)—school SD-7
Circle Gulch—valley MT-8
**Circle Haven (trailer park)**—pop pl DE-2
**Circle Hill**—pop pl (2) OH-6
Circle Hill—summit MS-4
Circle Hill—summit WI-6
Circle Hill Cem—cemetery IN-6
Circle Hill Cem—cemetery MI-6
Circle Hill Cem—cemetery PA-2
Circle Hill Ch—church FL-3
Circle Hill Plantation (historical)—locale AL-4
Circle Hill Sch—school NY-2
**Circle Hot Springs (Circle Springs Post**
**Off)**—pop pl AK-9
Circle H Ranch—locale WY-8
Circle H Ranch Lake—reservoir TN-4
Circle H Spring—spring AL-4
Circle I Hills—range AZ-5
Circle Island—island (2) AK-9
Circle Island—island CA-9
Circle Island—island LA-4
Circle Island—island OH-6
Circle Island Drain—canal CA-9
Circle I Waters Spring—spring CO-8
Circle J Ranch—locale CA-9
Circle J Ranch—locale WY-8
Circle K Ranch—locale CO-8
Circle K Resort—locale SD-7
Circle Lake—lake AK-9
Circle Lake—lake KS-7
Circle Lake—lake MI-6
Circle Lake—lake (5) MN-6
Circle Lake—lake MT-8
Circle Lake—lake OR-9
Circle Lake—lake (2) TX-5
Circle Lake—lake UT-8
Circle Lake—lake WA-9
Circle Lily Lake—lake WI-6
Circle L Moblie Home Park—locale UT-8
Circle L Ranch—locale (3) NV-8
Circle L Ranch Airp—airport NV-8
**Circle M**—pop pl TN-4
Circle Meadow—flat CA-9
Circle Mesa—summit NM-5
Circle Mound Cem—cemetery NE-7
Circle Mountain ID-8
Circle Mountain WY-8
Circle M Ranch—locale CA-9
Circle M Ranch—locale OR-9
Circle M Spring—spring AZ-5
Circle Mtn—summit MT-8
Circle Oil Field—oilfield TX-5
Circle One Airstrip—airport MS-4
Circle Park—flat WY-8
Circle Park—park CA-9
Circle Park—park (2) FL-3
Circle Park—park (2) IN-6
Circle Park—park KS-7
Circle Park—park MS-4
**Circle Park**—pop pl IN-6
Circle Park Creek—stream WY-8
Circle Park Sch—school TX-5
Circle Peak—summit WA-9
Circle P Flats—flat SD-7
**Circle Pine Center**—pop pl MI-6
**Circle Pines**—pop pl MN-6
Circle Point—cape AK-9
Circle Point—cape CA-9
Circle Pond—lake (2) IL-6
Circle Post Office (historical)—building TN-4
Circle P Springs—spring SD-7
Circle R—airport NJ-2
Circle Ranch—hist pl WY-8
Circle Ranch—locale AZ-5
Circle Ranch—locale NV-8
Circle Ranch—locale NM-5
Circle Ranch—locale TX-5
Circle R Camp—locale NE-7
Circle Resort—locale OH-6
Circle Ridge—ridge CO-8
Circle Ridge—ridge WY-8
Circle Ridge Oil Field—oilfield WY-8
Circle R Industrial Park
Subdivision—locale UT-8
Circle R Ranch—locale CA-9
Circle R Sky Ranch—locale TX-5
Circle Rsvr—reservoir WY-8
Circle Run—stream IN-6
Circle Sch (abandoned)—school PA-2
Circle Seven Creek—stream NM-5
Circle Seven Ranch—locale AZ-5
Circle Seven Well—well NM-5
Circle Shop Ctr—locale AZ-5
Circle Six Ranch—locale CA-9
Circle Slough—gut AK-9
Circle S Mesa—summit NM-5
Circle Spring—spring (2) UT-8
Circle Springs—spring WY-8
Circle Springs Draw—valley WY-8
Circle Square Ranch—locale FL-3
Circle S Ranch—locale (3) CA-9
Circle-S Ranch—locale MT-8
Circle S Ranch—locale WY-8
Circle S Wash—stream AZ-5
Circle Tank—reservoir (3) AZ-5
Circle Tanks—reservoir AZ-5
Circle Theater—hist pl IN-6
Circle Three Lakes—reservoir AL-4
Circle T Lake—reservoir NC-3
Circle Trail—trail CO-8
Circle Trail—trail MA-1
**Circle Tree Subdivision**—pop pl UT-8
Circle Valley—valley (2) UT-8
Circle V Bar Eightmile Ranch—locale CO-8
Circle V Bar Line Camp—locale CO-8
Circle V Bar Ranch—locale CO-8
**Circle View**—pop pl WV-2
Circle View Cem—cemetery GA-3
**Circle View Heights**
**Subdivision**—pop pl UT-8
Circle View Sch—school CA-9
**Circle View Subdivision**—pop pl UT-8
Circleville IN-6
Circleville—locale TX-5
**Circleville**—pop pl IN-6
**Circleville**—pop pl KS-7
**Circleville**—pop pl NY-2
**Circleville**—pop pl OH-6
**Circleville**—pop pl PA-2
**Circle Ville**—pop pl PA-2
**Circleville**—pop pl UT-8
**Circleville**—pop pl WV-2
Circleville Canyon—valley UT-8
Circleville Cem—cemetery KS-7
Circleville Cem—cemetery UT-8
Circleville District Ranger Station—locale UT-8
Circleville Division—civil UT-8
Circleville Hist Dist—hist pl OH-6
Circleville (Magisterial
District)—fmr MCD WV-2
Circleville Mtn—summit UT-8
Circleville Post Office—building UT-8
Circleville Sch—school IL-6
Circleville Sch—school UT-8
**Circleville (Township of)**—pop pl OH-6
Circle V Ranch—locale TX-5
Circle Wash—stream NV-8
Circle Wash Rsvr—reservoir NV-8
Circle Wash Spring—spring NV-8
Circle West Shop Ctr—locale AL-4
Circlewood Baptist Ch—church AL-4
**Circlewood (subdivision)**—pop pl AL-4
Circle W Ranch-Condon Airstrip—airport OR-9
Circle Y Tank—reservoir NM-5
Circle Z Ranch—locale AZ-5
Circle 3 E Ranch—locale NM-5
Circle 6 Gun Club—other NM-5
Circ Twins Mine—mine ID-8
Circular Butte—summit ID-8
Circular Congregational Church and Parish
House—hist pl SC-3
Circular Tank—reservoir AZ-5
Circular White Ridge—ridge AZ-5
Circulo Cubano de Tampa—hist pl FL-3
Circus Creek—stream MT-8
Circus Heliport—airport NV-8
Circus Hollow Wildlife Mngmt Area—park UT-8
Circus Peak—summit MT-8
Cirek, Bayou—gut LA-4
Cirhuelas Canyon—valley NM-5
Cirildo Tank—reservoir TX-5
Cirilli Lake WI-6
Cirque Creek—stream (2) AK-9
Cirque Creek—stream CA-9
Cirque Crest—ridge CA-9
Cirque Lake—lake (2) CA-9
Cirque Lake—lake CO-8
Cirque Lake—lake ID-8
Cirque Lake—lake (2) MT-8
Cirque Lake—lake UT-8
Cirque Lake—lake WA-9
Cirque Lake—lake (2) WY-8
Cirque Mtn—summit CA-9
Cirque Mtn—summit CO-8
Cirque Of The Towers—summit WY-8
Cirque Peak—summit CA-9
Cirque Rsvr—reservoir ID-8
Cirrus, Mount—summit CO-8
Cirtsville—locale WV-2
Cirtsville Sch—school WV-2
Ciruela—locale NM-5
Ciruela Canyon—valley CO-8
Ciruela Creek—stream NM-5
Ciruela Mesa—summit NM-5
Ciruelas Canyon—valley NM-5
Ciruelas Spring—spring NM-5
Cisca Lake—lake AK-9
Cisco—locale AR-4
Cisco—locale GA-3
Cisco—locale KY-4
Cisco—locale UT-8
Cisco—locale WV-2
**Cisco**—pop pl CA-9
**Cisco**—pop pl IL-6
**Cisco**—pop pl MA-1
**Cisco**—pop pl NC-3
**Cisco**—pop pl OK-5
**Cisco**—pop pl TX-5
Cisco, Lake—reservoir TX-5
Cisco Beach—beach MA-1
Cisco Beach—beach UT-8
Cisco Branch MI-6
Cisco Branch—stream TN-4
Cisco Branch Ontonagon River—stream MI-6
Cisco Brook—stream NY-2
Cisco Butte—summit CA-9
Cisco Canyon (historical)—valley AZ-5
Cisco (CCD)—cens area GA-3
Cisco (CCD)—cens area TX-5
**Cisco (Cisco Grove)**—pop pl CA-9
Cisco Cove—valley NC-3
Cisco Creek CO-8
**Cisco Grove**—pop pl CA-9
Cisco Hist Dist—hist pl TX-5
Cisco Hollow—valley MO-7
Cisco Hollow—valley TN-4
Cisco Junior Coll—school TX-5
Cisco Lake—lake MI-6
Cisco Lake—lake WI-6
**Cisco Lake**—pop pl MI-6
Cisco Landing—locale UT-8
Cisco Mesa—summit UT-8
Cisco Mine—mine AZ-5
Cisco Mtn—summit NC-3
Cisco Sch—school OK-5
Cisco Sch (abandoned)—school MO-7
Cisco Spring—spring TN-4
Cisco Springs—spring UT-8
Cisco Springs Gas and Oil Field—oilfield UT-8
Cisco Springs North Gas Field—oilfield UT-8
Cisco Wash—valley UT-8
Cisko WV-2
**Cisky Park**—pop pl FL-3
Cisler Terrace—hist pl OH-6
**Cismont**—pop pl VA-3
Cisna Creek—stream WI-6
Cisna Run—locale PA-2
Cisna Run—stream PA-2
Cisna Sch (abandoned)—school PA-2
Cisne KS-7
**Cisne**—pop pl IL-6
Cisne Cem—cemetery (2) IL-6
Cisneros Canyon—valley NM-5
Cisneros Cem—cemetery CO-8
Cisneros Creek CO-8
Cisneros Creek—stream CO-8
Cisneros Park—area NM-5
Cisneros Spring—spring NM-5
Cisneros Trail—trail CO-8
Cispus—locale WA-9
Cispus Job Corps Conservation
Center—building WA-9
Cispus Pass—gap WA-9
Cispus River—stream (2) WA-9
**Cissel Farms**—pop pl MD-2
Cissell Lake—lake NM-5
Cissels Creek—stream KY-4
Cisselville—locale KY-4
Cissillini Canyon—valley NV-8
**Cissna Junction**—pop pl IL-6
**Cissna Park**—pop pl IL-6
Cissom Creek—stream SC-3
Ciss Stream—stream ME-1
Cisten Tank AZ-5
Cistercian Monastery—church NJ-2
Cistercian Monastery of
Gerowval—church MS-4
Cisterian Monastery—church TX-5
Cistern MH-9
**Cistern**—pop pl TX-5
Cisterna Alta Windmill—locale TX-5
Cistern Canyon—valley AZ-5
Cistern Canyon—valley (2) NM-5
Cistern Canyon—valley TX-5
Cistern Canyon—valley UT-8
Cistern Cliffs MH-9
Cistern Hill Baptist Ch MS-4
Cistern Hill Cem—cemetery MS-4
Cistern Hill Ch—church (2) MS-4
Cistern Hill Sch—school MS-4
Cistern Hollow—valley TX-5
Cistern Lakes—lake MI-6
Cistern Point MH-9
Cistern Spring—spring TX-5
Cistern Tank—reservoir AZ-5
Cistern Tank—reservoir (2) NM-5
Cistern Tanks—reservoir UT-8
Cistern Windmill—locale CO-8
Cita Canyon Methodist Camp—locale TX-5
Cita Creek—stream TX-5
**Citadel**—pop pl VA-3
Citadel—uninc pl SC-3
Citadel, The—school SC-3
Citadel, The—summit AK-9
Citadel, The—summit CA-9
Citadel, The (LA 55828)—hist pl NM-5
Citadel Mtn—summit MT-8
Citadel Mtn—summit NV-8
Citadel Mtn—summit WY-8
Citadel Peaks—ridge MT-8
Citadel Plateau—summit CO-8
Citadel Post Office (historical)—building TN-4
Citadel Rock—hist pl MT-8
Citadel Rock—pillar MT-8
Citadel Rock—pillar SD-7
Citadel Ruin—locale AZ-5
Citadel Sch (historical)—school TN-4
Citadel Sink—basin AZ-5
**Citadel (subdivision), The**—pop pl (2) AZ-5
Citadel Wash—stream AZ-5
Cita Glen Christian Camp—locale TX-5
Citamon, Bayou—stream LA-4
**Citation Lake Estates**—pop pl IL-6
Citellus Lake—lake AK-9
Citica AL-4
Citico—locale AL-4
Citico Bar—bar TN-4
Citico Beach—locale TN-4
Citico Bridge—bridge TN-4
Citico Cem—cemetery TN-4
Citico Ch—church TN-4
Citico Creek—stream (2) TN-4
**Citico (historical)**—pop pl (2) TN-4
Citico Mtn—summit TN-4
Citico Post Office (historical)—building TN-4
Citico Rec Area—park TN-4
Citico Site—hist pl TN-4
Citico Warden Station—locale TN-4
Citico Yards TN-4
Cities of Rocks ID-8
Cities Service Company (Pigments
Division)—facility MO-7
Cities Service Lake—reservoir KS-7
Cities Services Company—facility WV-2
Cities Services Dam—dam TN-4
Cities Services Oil Company—facility WI-6
Citing Rock—pillar RI-1
Citizen Canyon—valley AZ-5
Citizen Canyon—valley NM-5
Citizen Cem—cemetery TN-4
Citizen's and Southern Bank
Bldg—hist pl GA-3

Citizens and Southern Natl Bank of South Carolina—*hist pl* ... SC-3
Citizens Animas Ditch—*canal* ... CO-8
Citizens Bank—*hist pl* ... IN-6
Citizens Bank—*hist pl* ... WI-6
Citizens Bank Bldg—*hist pl* ... OK-5
Citizens Banking Company—*hist pl* ... GA-3
Citizen's Banking & Trust Co. Bldg—*hist pl* ... OR-9
Citizens Bank of Lafourche—*hist pl* ... LA-4
Citizens Bldg—*hist pl* ... AR-4
Citizens Cem—*cemetery* ... CA-9
Citizens Cem—*cemetery* ... GA-3
Citizens Cem—*cemetery* ... IN-6
Citizens Cem—*cemetery* ... SC-3
Citizens Cem—*cemetery* (2) ... TN-4
Citizens Cem—*cemetery* ... TX-5
Citizens Cem—*cemetery* ... VA-3
Citizens Ditch—*canal* ... NM-5
Citizen's Dock—*hist pl* ... WA-9
Citizens Dock—*locale* ... CA-9
Citizens Hall—*hist pl* ... MA-1
Citizenship Ch—*church* ... AR-4
Citizens Hosp—*hospital* ... AL-4
Citizens Hosp—*hospital* ... OH-6
Citizens Natl Bank—*hist pl* ... IN-6
Citizens' Natl Bank—*hist pl* ... MN-6
Citizens Natl Bank—*hist pl* ... WV-2
Citizens Natl Life Insurance Bldg—*hist pl* .. KY-4
Citizen Spring—*spring* ... NM-5
Citizens Publishing Company Bldg—*hist pl* ... CA-9
*Citizens Spur* ... KS-7
Citizens State Bank—*hist pl* ... ID-8
Citizen's State Bank—*hist pl* ... OK-5
Citizens State Bank—*hist pl* ... OK-5
Citizens' Trust Company Bldg—*hist pl* ... IN-6
Citizens Water Company Dam—*dam* ... PA-2
Citizen Tank—*reservoir* ... AZ-5
**Cito**—*pop pl* ... PA-2
Citra—*locale* ... OK-5
**Citra**—*pop pl* ... FL-3
Citra Cem—*cemetery* ... OK-5
Citriana Sch—*school* ... TX-5
Citro—*locale* ... CA-9
**Citro Junction**—*pop pl* ... CA-9
**Citrona**—*pop pl* ... CA-9
Citron Creek—*stream* ... WI-6
Citronelle—*locale* ... FL-3
**Citronelle**—*pop pl* ... AL-4
Citronelle Branch—*stream* ... AL-4
Citronelle (CCD)—*cens area* ... AL-4
Citronelle Coll (historical)—*school* ... AL-4
Citronelle Division—*civil* ... AL-4
Citronelle HS—*school* ... AL-4
Citronelle Lake—*reservoir* ... AL-4
*Citronelle Municipal Park Lake* ... AL-4
Citronelle Municipal Park Lake Dam—*dam* ... AL-4
Citron Hill—*summit* ... ME-1
Citron Valley—*valley* ... WI-6
Citrus—*CDP* ... CA-9
Citrus—*locale* ... CA-9
Citrus—*post sta* ... FL-3
Citrus, Lake—*lake* ... FL-3
Citrus Ave Sch—*school* ... CA-9
Citrus Canal—*canal* ... LA-4
Citrus Center—*locale* ... FL-3
Citrus Christian Acad—*school* ... FL-3
Citrus City—*locale* ... TX-5
**Citrus County**—*pop pl* ... FL-3
Citrus County Adult Community Program—*school* ... FL-3
Citrus Cove—*basin* ... CA-9
Citrus Ditch—*canal* ... AZ-5
Citrus Elem Sch—*school* ... FL-3
Citrus Gardens (trailer park)—*locale* ... AZ-5
**Citrus Gardens (Trailer Park)**—*pop pl* ... AZ-5
Citrus Grove JHS—*school* ... FL-3
Citrus Grove Occupational Training Center—*school* ... FL-3
Citrus Grove Sch—*school* ... FL-3
Citrus Grove School (Abandoned)—*locale* ... TX-5
Citrus Grove Trailer Court—*locale* ... AZ-5
Citrus Grove Trailer Park—*locale* ... AZ-5
**Citrus Heights**—*pop pl* ... CA-9
Citrus Heights Sch—*school* ... CA-9
**Citrus Hills (subdivision)**—*pop pl* (2) ... AZ-5
Citrus HS—*school* ... FL-3
Citrus Junior Coll—*school* ... CA-9
Citrus Laboratory Sch—*school* ... CA-9
Citrus Memorial Hosp—*hospital* ... FL-3
**Citrus Park**—*pop pl* ... AZ-5
**Citrus Park**—*pop pl* ... FL-3
Citrus Park Assembly of God Ch—*church* ... FL-3
Citrus Park Elem Sch—*school* ... FL-3
Citrus Park-Fern Lake (CCD)—*cens area* ... FL-3
Citrus Park (Siding)—*locale* ... AZ-5
Citrus Plaza (Shop Ctr)—*locale* (2) ... FL-3
Citrus Sch—*school* (2) ... CA-9
Citrus-South Tule Sch—*school* ... CA-9
**Citrus Springs**—*pop pl* ... FL-3
Citrus Tower—*uninc pl* ... FL-3
*Citrus Tree Island* ... FM-9
Citrus Valley—*valley* ... AZ-5
Citrus Valley Interchange—*crossing* ... AZ-5
Citrus Wildlife Mngmt Area—*park* ... FL-3
*Cittico* ... TN-4
*Cittico Creek* ... TN-4
*City* ... MN-6
City—*fmr MCD* ... NE-7
**City, Arroyo**—*pop pl* ... TX-5
City and County Bldg—*hist pl* ... WY-8
City and Suburban Homes Company's First Ave Estate Historic Dist—*hist pl* ... NY-2
City Bank Bldg—*hist pl* ... MO-7
City Bay—*bay* ... VT-1
City Beach Park—*park* ... FL-3
City Blacksmith Shop—*hist pl* ... MN-6
City Bldg—*hist pl* ... IL-6
City Block—*uninc pl* ... MD-2
City Bridge—*bridge* ... MS-4
City Brook—*stream* ... IN-6
City Brook—*stream* ... MA-1
City Brook—*stream* (2) ... NY-2
**City-by-the Sea**—*pop pl* ... TX-5
City Cabin—*locale* ... WA-9
City Camp Landing—*locale* ... ME-1
City Canal—*canal* ... ID-8
City Canal—*canal* ... UT-8
City Canyon—*valley* ... UT-8
City Cem—*cemetery* (2) ... FL-3
City Cem—*cemetery* (2) ... IL-6
City Cem—*cemetery* ... IA-7
City Cem—*cemetery* ... KS-7
City Cem—*cemetery* ... NY-2
City Cem—*cemetery* ... OH-6
City Cem—*cemetery* (3) ... TX-5
City Cem—*cemetery* ... WI-6
*City Cemetery* ... SD-7
City Cemetery—*hist pl* ... GA-3
City Cemetery—*hist pl* ... TX-5
City Center—*post sta* ... WA-9
City Center Square—*locale* ... MO-7
*City Channel* ... NJ-2
City Coll—*school* (2) ... CA-9
City Coll of San Francisco—*school* ... CA-9
City-County Airp—*airport* ... OR-9
City County Park—*park* ... IL-6
City Cove—*bay* ... ME-1
City Creek—*stream* ... AZ-5
City Creek—*stream* ... CA-9
City Creek—*stream* ... CO-8
City Creek—*stream* (2) ... ID-8
City Creek—*stream* (2) ... OR-9
City Creek—*stream* ... SD-7
City Creek—*stream* (7) ... UT-8
City Creek—*stream* ... WI-6
City Creek Campground—*locale* ... UT-8
City Creek Canyon—*valley* ... UT-8
City Creek Canyon Hist Dist—*hist pl* ... UT-8
City Creek Meadows—*flat* ... UT-8
City Creek Park—*park* ... UT-8
City Creek Peak—*summit* ... UT-8
City Creek Shelter—*locale* ... OR-9
City Creek Station—*locale* ... CA-9
City Creek Truck Trail—*trail* ... CA-9
City Creek Well—*well* ... AZ-5
**City Crest Condominium**—*pop pl* ... UT-8
City Dam—*dam* ... AZ-5
City Ditch—*canal* ... CA-9
City Ditch—*canal* ... CO-8
City Ditch—*canal* ... IN-6
City Ditch—*canal* (4) ... UT-8
City Ditch—*canal* (2) ... WY-8
City Drain—*canal* ... UT-8
City Drain—*stream* ... IN-6
City Drainage Canal—*canal* ... GA-3
City Farm—*locale* ... OR-9
**City Farm**—*pop pl* ... VA-3
City Farm Pond—*reservoir* ... MA-1
City Federal—*airport* ... NJ-2
City Fire Department—*hist pl* ... GA-3
City Gomingo—*locale* ... VA-3
City Gulch—*valley* ... CA-9
City Gulch—*valley* (3) ... OR-9
City Hall—*building* ... NC-3
City Hall—*hist pl* ... AR-4
City Hall—*hist pl* ... CA-9
City Hall—*hist pl* ... DC-2
City Hall—*hist pl* ... IN-6
City Hall—*hist pl* ... KY-4
City Hall—*hist pl* ... MD-2
City Hall—*hist pl* (2) ... MA-1
City Hall—*hist pl* ... MI-6
City Hall—*hist pl* ... MS-4
City Hall—*hist pl* ... MO-7
City Hall—*hist pl* ... MT-8
City Hall—*hist pl* ... NE-7
City Hall—*hist pl* (2) ... NY-2
City Hall—*hist pl* ... OH-6
City Hall—*hist pl* ... OK-5
City Hall—*hist pl* ... PA-2
City Hall—*hist pl* ... TX-5
City Hall—*hist pl* ... VA-3
City Hall—*hist pl* ... WA-9
City Hall—*hist pl* ... WI-6
City Hall—*hist pl* ... WY-8
City Hall—*uninc pl* ... CA-9
City Hall and Auditorium—*hist pl* ... NE-7
City Hall and Jail—*hist pl* ... AZ-5
City Hall Annex—*hist pl* ... OH-6
City Hall Complex Heliport—*airport* ... NV-8
City Hall Hist Dist—*hist pl* ... MA-1
City Hall Hist Dist—*hist pl* ... NY-2
City Hall Hist Dist (Boundary Increase)—*hist pl* ... MA-1
City Hall Mall—*locale* ... CA-9
City Hall-Monument District—*hist pl* ... CT-1
City Hall of Colorado City—*hist pl* ... CO-8
City Hall Park—*park* ... UT-8
City Hall Park Hist Dist—*hist pl* ... VT-1
City Hall/Thalian Hall—*hist pl* ... NC-3
City Hill—*summit* ... AZ-5
City Hill—*summit* ... CT-1
City Hill Cem—*cemetery* ... NY-2
City Hose Company No. 9—*hist pl* ... MO-7
City Hosp—*hist pl* ... NY-2
City Hosp (historical)—*hospital* ... AL-4
City Hotel—*hist pl* ... CA-9
City Hotel—*hist pl* ... WI-6
City Infirmary (historical)—*hospital* ... AL-4
*City Island* ... TN-4
City Island—*island* ... FL-3
City Island—*island* ... PA-2
**City Island**—*pop pl* ... NY-2
City Island—*stream* ... PA-2
City Island Bridge—*bridge* ... NY-2
City Island Harbor—*harbor* ... NY-2
City Island (historical)—*cape* ... IA-7
*City Lake* ... IL-6
*City Lake* ... IN-6
*City Lake* ... TX-5
City Lake—*lake* ... IN-6
City Lake—*lake* (2) ... NC-3
City Lake—*lake* ... OK-5
City Lake—*lake* ... TX-5
City Lake—*lake* ... WA-9
City Lake—*reservoir* (3) ... AL-4
City Lake—*reservoir* ... GA-3
City Lake—*reservoir* ... KS-7
City Lake—*reservoir* (2) ... KY-4
City Lake—*reservoir* (5) ... MO-7
City Lake—*reservoir* ... NC-3
City Lake—*reservoir* ... OK-5
City Lake—*reservoir* ... TN-4
City Lake—*reservoir* (10) ... TX-5
City Lake, Bay—*lake* ... MI-6
City Lake Number One—*lake* ... IN-6
City Lake Number One—*reservoir* ... TX-5
City Lake Number Two—*lake* ... IN-6
City Lake Number Two—*reservoir* ... TX-5
City Lake Park—*park* ... AL-4
City Lake Park—*park* ... MO-7
City Lakes—*reservoir* ... MO-7
City Lakes—*reservoir* ... TX-5
City Lands of Los Angeles—*civil* ... CA-9
City Lands of Monterey—*civil* (2) ... CA-9
City Line Ave Bridge—*hist pl* ... PA-2
City Line Shop Ctr—*locale* ... PA-2
City Market—*hist pl* ... IN-6
City Market—*hist pl* ... IA-7
City Market—*hist pl* ... VA-3
City Market—*hist pl* ... WI-6
City Marsh—*swamp* ... WI-6
City Memorial Hosp—*hospital* ... NC-3
**City Mills**—*pop pl* ... MA-1
City Mills Bldg—*hist pl* ... OH-6
City Mills Dam—*dam* ... GA-3
City Mills Pond—*reservoir* ... MA-1
City Mills Pond Dam—*dam* ... MA-1
City Mills Ponds—*lake* ... CT-1
City Mound (22Hi672)—*hist pl* ... MS-4
City Mtn—*summit* ... CO-8
City Natl Bank—*hist pl* ... AL-4
City Natl Bank—*hist pl* ... TX-5
City Natl Bank Bldg—*hist pl* ... IA-7
City Natl Bank Bldg—*hist pl* ... OH-6
City Natl Bank Bldg and Creighton Orpheum Theater—*hist pl* ... NE-7
City of Adair Waterworks—*other* ... OK-5
*City of Aurora* ... IN-6
City of Birmingham - Roebuck Plaza Lake—*reservoir* ... AL-4
City of Brest Park—*park* ... CO-8
City Of Butler Sewage Lagoon—*reservoir* ... AL-4
City Of Butler Sewage Lagoon Dam—*dam* ... AL-4
City of Camden Hist Dist—*hist pl* ... SC-3
City of Children Sch—*school* ... NY-2
City Of Colorado Springs Municipal Airport—*airport* ... CO-8
*City of Commerce* ... CA-9
City of Detroit Recreation Camp—*locale* ... MI-6
*City of Devils Lake* ... ND-7
City Of East Point Rsvr—*reservoir* ... GA-3
City Of Elyria Cem—*cemetery* ... OH-6
*City Of Erie* ... PA-2
City of Fairfax Hist Dist—*hist pl* ... VA-3
*City of Flowing Wells* ... AL-4
City of Fresno Sewage Treatment Plant—*other* ... CA-9
*City of High Forest* ... TN-4
City of Hope Natl Med Ctr—*hospital* ... CA-9
*City of Industry (Industry)* ... CA-9
City Of Jackson Sewage Lagoon—*reservoir* ... AL-4
City Of Jackson Sewage Lagoon Dam—*dam* ... AL-4
City of Los Angeles—*locale* ... CA-9
**City of Los Angeles**—*pop pl* (4) ... CA-9
City Of Lubbock Industrial Area—*locale* ... TX-5
City of Madisonville Dam—*dam* ... TN-4
City of Miami Administration Bldg—*building* ... FL-3
City of Monterey Lake—*reservoir* ... TN-4
City of Monterey Water Supply Dam—*dam* ... TN-4
City of Murdo Number 2 Dam—*dam* ... SD-7
City of New York Delaware Water Supply—*other* ... NY-2
*City of Oneida Dam* ... TN-4
City of Orange (Township of)—*civ div* ... NJ-2
City of Paris Bldg—*hist pl* ... CA-9
City of Patterson Sewage Disposal—*other* ... CA-9
*City Of Pawhuska Lake* ... OK-5
City of Port Isabel Rsvr—*reservoir* ... TX-5
City of Portland No. 1 Dam—*dam* ... OR-9
City of Portland No. 3 Dam—*dam* ... OR-9
City of Portland No. 4 Dam—*dam* ... OR-9
City of Portland No. 5 Dam—*dam* ... OR-9
City of Portland No. 6 Dam—*dam* ... OR-9
City of Portland Rsvr No. 1—*reservoir* ... OR-9
City of Portland Rsvr No. 3—*reservoir* ... OR-9
City of Portland Rsvr No. 4—*reservoir* ... OR-9
City of Portland Rsvr No. 5—*reservoir* ... OR-9
City of Portland Rsvr No. 6—*reservoir* ... OR-9
City Of Ref Natl Historical Park—*park* ... HI-9
*City of Refuge (National Historical Park)* ... HI-9
City of Refuge (Sanitorium)—*hospital* ... GA-3
City Of Rexburg Ditch—*canal* ... ID-8
City of Rocks—*hist pl* ... ID-8
City Of Rocks—*pillar* (2) ... ID-8
City of Rocks State Park—*park* ... NM-5
City of Rome Dark Swamp—*swamp* ... PA-2
City of Rome Rsvr—*reservoir* ... NY-2
City of Rome Swamp—*swamp* ... PA-2
*City of Saint Louis* ... MO-7
City Of Saint Louis Bellefontaine Farm—*locale* ... MO-7
City of San Antonio Municipal Auditorium—*hist pl* ... TX-5
City Of Seattle Rock—*bar* ... WA-9
City of Six Mine—*mine* ... CA-9
City of Six Ridge—*ridge* ... CA-9
City of Sunrise (Br. P.980. name for Sunrise)—*other* ... FL-3
*City of the Dalles* ... OR-9
**City of the Dalles**—*pop pl* ... OR-9
City of Topeka Rock—*other* ... AK-9
City of Tulsa Water Intake—*other* ... OK-5
City of Victoria Pumping Plant-Waterworks—*hist pl* ... TX-5
City of Vinita Water Intake—*other* ... OK-5
City of Wyoming Waterworks—*other* ... MI-6
City Opera House—*hist pl* ... MI-6
*City Park* ... IL-6
City Park—*hist pl* ... CO-8
City Park—*park* ... AL-4
City Park—*park* (3) ... AZ-5
City Park—*park* ... NE-7
City Park—*park* (4) ... TX-5
**City Park Addition (subdivision)**—*pop pl* ... UT-8
City Park Brewery—*hist pl* ... PA-2
City Park Carousel—*hist pl* ... CO-8
City Park Esplanade—*hist pl* ... CO-8
City Park Golf—*hist pl* ... CO-8
City Park Lake—*lake* ... LA-4
City Park Sch—*school* ... GA-3
City Park Sch—*school* ... TN-4
City Park Sch—*school* ... TX-5
**City Park Subdivision**—*pop pl* ... UT-8
City Pharmacy—*hist pl* ... NE-7
City Pier A—*hist pl* ... NY-2
City Plaza—*locale* ... SD-7
City Plaza—*park* ... CA-9
*City Point* ... CT-1
City Point—*cape* ... CT-1
City Point—*cape* ... ME-1
City Point—*cape* ... MA-1
City Point—*cape* ... VA-3
City Point—*locale* ... FL-3
**City Point**—*pop pl* ... CT-1
**City Point**—*pop pl* ... ME-1
**City Point**—*pop pl* ... WI-6
City Point Cem—*cemetery* ... WI-6
City Point Hist Dist—*hist pl* ... VA-3
City Point (historical)—*locale* ... MS-4
**City Point (subdivision)**—*pop pl* ... MA-1
**City Point (Town of)**—*pop pl* ... WI-6
City Pond—*lake* ... ME-1
City Pond—*lake* ... MA-1
City Pond—*reservoir* ... MA-1
City Pond—*reservoir* ... NC-3
City Pond Dam—*dam* ... NC-3
*City Price* ... LA-4
*City Pump Pond* ... AL-4
City Ranch—*locale* ... CA-9
City Reef—*bar* ... VT-1
City Rock—*pillar* ... CA-9
City Rock—*pillar* ... WI-6
City Rock Bluff—*cliff* ... AR-4
City Rsvr—*reservoir* ... AZ-5
City Rsvr—*reservoir* (2) ... CO-8
City Rsvr—*reservoir* ... IL-6
City Rsvr—*reservoir* ... MO-7
City Rsvr—*reservoir* (2) ... NM-5
City Rsvr—*reservoir* ... OH-6
City Rsvr—*reservoir* ... PA-2
City Rsvr—*reservoir* ... VA-3
City Rsvr—*reservoir* ... WV-2
City Rsvr—*reservoir* ... WY-8
City Run—*stream* (2) ... IN-6
City Sch (historical)—*school* ... PA-2
City Servant Kingdom Hall—*church* ... IN-6
City Services Diversion Dam—*dam* ... TN-4
City Services Diversion Lake—*reservoir* ... TN-4
City Services Rention Pond—*reservoir* ... TN-4
City Services Retention Dam—*dam* ... TN-4
City Service Well—*well* ... NM-5
City Spring—*spring* ... AL-4
City Spring—*spring* ... ID-8
City Spring—*spring* ... TN-4
City Spring—*spring* ... UT-8
City Springs—*spring* ... WY-8
City Square—*park* ... MA-1
City Square (Shop Ctr)—*locale* ... FL-3
City Stream—*stream* ... VT-1
City Tavern—*building* ... PA-2
**City Terrace**—*pop pl* ... CA-9
City Terrace Park—*park* ... CA-9
City Terrace Sch—*school* ... CA-9
**City Township**—*pop pl* ... MO-7
**City Trailer Park**—*pop pl* ... FL-3
City Tubercular Hosp—*hospital* ... TX-5
City Union Mission Camp—*locale* ... MO-7
City Univ Of New York Brooklyn Coll—*school* ... NY-2
City Univ of New York Comm Coll—*school* ... NY-2
City Univ Of New York Hunter Coll—*school* (2) ... NY-2
City Univ Of New York Queens Coll—*school* ... NY-2
City Univ Of New York The City Coll—*school* ... NY-2
*City View* ... NC-3
City View—*locale* ... OK-5
**City View**—*pop pl* ... FL-3
**Cityview**—*pop pl* ... NC-3
**City View**—*pop pl* ... SC-3
City View—*uninc pl* ... NC-3
**City View Addition (subdivision)**—*pop pl* (2) ... UT-8
City View Baptist Ch—*church* ... TN-4
City View Cem—*cemetery* ... OR-9
City View Cem—*cemetery* ... WA-9
**City View Heights**—*pop pl* ... OH-6
City View Heights Sch—*school* ... IA-7
City View Hosp—*hospital* ... CA-9
City View Park—*park* ... NV-8
City View Park—*park* ... TX-5
City View Rsvr—*reservoir* ... OR-9
City View Sch—*school* ... MO-7
Cityview Sch—*school* ... NC-3
City View Sch—*school* ... TX-5
**City Village**—*pop pl* ... GA-3
City Waterway—*bay* ... WA-9
City Waterway Bridge—*hist pl* ... WA-9
City Waterworks—*hist pl* ... FL-3
City Water Works—*hist pl* ... TX-5
City Water Works Lake—*reservoir* ... NC-3
City 1—*island* ... PA-2
Citzens Cem—*cemetery* ... IL-6
Ciudad, Canal (historical)—*canal* ... AZ-5
Ciutan Park—*park* ... OH-6
Civa Airp—*airport* ... NV-8
C Iverson Dam—*dam* ... SD-7
Civet Cat Canyon—*valley* ... NV-8
Civet Cat Cave—*cave* ... NV-8
Civet Creek—*stream* ... MN-6
Civic Arena—*building* ... PA-2
Civic Art Gallery—*hist pl* ... CA-9
Civic Center—*building* ... NC-3
Civic Center—*post sta* (3) ... CA-9
Civic Center—*post sta* ... GA-3
Civic Center—*post sta* ... KS-7
Civic Center—*post sta* ... MN-6
Civic Center—*post sta* ... MO-7
Civic Center—*post sta* ... TX-5
Civic Center—*post sta* ... VA-3
Civic Center Annex—*post sta* ... CA-9
Civic Center Financial District—*hist pl* ... CA-9
Civic Center Hist Dist—*hist pl* ... CO-8
Civic Center Hist Dist—*hist pl* ... IA-7
Civic Center (Marin County Civic Center)—*post sta* ... CA-9
Civic Center Park—*park* ... CA-9
Civic Center Park—*park* ... MI-6
Civic Center Park—*park* ... MN-6
Civic Center Park—*park* ... UT-8
Civic Club—*hist pl* ... NY-2
Civic Field Parking Area Heliport—*airport* ... WA-9
Civic League Park—*park* ... TX-5
Civic Park—*park* ... OH-6
Civic Park—*park* ... TX-5
Civic Park Hist Dist—*hist pl* ... MI-6
Civic Park Sch—*school* ... MI-6
Civie Memorial HS—*school* ... IL-6
Civil Bend—*bend* ... OR-9
Civil Bend—*locale* ... MO-7
Civil Bend Cem—*cemetery* ... MO-7
Civil Bend Cem—*cemetery* ... OR-9
Civil Bend Cem—*cemetery* ... SD-7
Civil Bend Center Sch (historical)—*school* ... MO-7
Civil Bend Christian Cem—*cemetery* ... MO-7
**Civil Bend (historical)**—*pop pl* ... OR-9
Civil Bend Sch—*school* ... SD-7
**Civil Bend Township**—*pop pl* ... SD-7
Civil Cem—*cemetery* ... SD-7
Civilian Conservatino Corps Camp TVA Number 33 (historical)—*locale* ... TN-4
Civilian Conservation Camp Number 27 (historical)—*locale* ... TN-4
Civilian Conservation Corps Camp F1456 (historical)—*locale* ... TN-4
Civilian Conservation Corps Camp Number F3 (historical)—*locale* ... AL-4
Civilian Conservation Corps Camp Number F9 (historical)—*locale* ... AL-4
Civilian Conservation Corps Camp Number (historical)—*locale* ... TN-4
*Civilian Conservation Corps Camp Number S-79* ... TN-4
Civilian Conservation Corps Camp Number 1451 (historical)—*locale* ... TN-4
Civilian Conservation Corps Camp Number 1452 (historical)—*locale* ... TN-4
Civilian Conservation Corps Camp Number 1455 (historical)—*locale* ... TN-4
Civilian Conservation Corps Camp Number 1463 (historical)—*locale* ... TN-4
Civilian Conservation Corps Camp Number 1466 (historical)—*locale* ... TN-4
Civilian Conservation Corps Camp Number 1467 (historical)—*locale* ... TN-4
Civilian Conservation Corps Camp Number 1468 (historical)—*locale* ... TN-4
Civilian Conservation Corps Camp Number 1472 (historical)—*locale* ... TN-4
Civilian Conservation Corps Camp Number 19 (historical)—*locale* ... TN-4
Civilian Conservation Corps Camp Number 2427—*locale* ... TN-4
Civilian Conservation Corps Camp Number 26 (historical)—*locale* ... TN-4
Civilian Conservation Corps Camp Number 423 (historical)—*locale* ... TN-4
Civilian Conservation Corps Camp Number 4493 (historical)—*locale* ... TN-4
Civilian Conservation Corps Camp Number 4495 (historical)—*locale* ... TN-4
Civilian Conservation Corps Camp Number 495 (historical)—*locale* ... TN-4
Civilian Conservation Corps Camp Number 497 (historical)—*locale* ... TN-4
Civilian Conservation Corps Camp Number 8 (historical)—*locale* ... TN-4
Civilian Conservation Corps Camp Shelby (historical)—*locale* ... TN-4
Civilian Conservation Corps Camp TVA Number 13 (historical)—*locale* ... TN-4
Civilian Conservation Corps Camp 3459 (historical)—*locale* ... TN-4
Civilian Conservation Corps Camp 3467 (historical)—*locale* ... TN-4
Civil Ridge Ch—*church* ... MS-4
Civil Run—*stream* ... IN-6
*Civil Service Commission Bldg* ... DC-2
Civil War Cave—*cave* ... AR-4
Civil War Cem—*cemetery* (2) ... MO-7
Civil War Drill Hall and Armory—*hist pl* ... NJ-2
Civil War Earthworks at Tallahatchie Crossing—*hist pl* ... MS-4
Civil War Fortification—*hist pl* ... TN-4
Civil War Fort Sites—*hist pl* ... DC-2
Civil War Fort Sites (Boundary Increase)—*hist pl* ... DC-2
Civil War Fort Sites (Boundary Increase)—*hist pl* ... MD-2
Civil War Fort Sites (Boundary Increase)—*hist pl* ... VA-3
Civil War Memorial—*hist pl* ... MI-6
Civil War Monuments in Washington, DC—*hist pl* ... DC-2
Civil War Trail—*trail* ... WV-2
**Civit**—*pop pl* ... OK-5
Civitan Camp—*locale* ... SC-3
Civitan Cem—*cemetery* ... AL-4
Civitan Park—*park* ... NC-3
Civitan Park—*park* ... OK-5
Civitan Park—*park* ... TN-4
Civitan Park—*park* ... TX-5
Civitan Park—*park* ... VA-3
Civitan Park—*park* ... WY-8
Civitan Sch—*school* ... AR-4
Civit Cem—*cemetery* ... OK-5
*Ciyatciya* ... MH-9
CJ Harris Community Hosp—*hospital* ... NC-3
C J Holy Ch—*church* ... AL-4
C J Jorgenson Sch—*school* ... AZ-5
C J K Airp—*airport* ... PA-2
C J King, Junior Pond—*lake* ... FL-3
C J Larson Number 1 Dam—*dam* ... SD-7
C J Mtn—*summit* ... TX-5
C Jordan Dam—*dam* ... SD-7
C J Perry Catfish Ponds Dam—*dam* ... MS-4
C J Strike Rsvr—*reservoir* (2) ... ID-8
C K Canyon—*valley* ... AZ-5
C K Creek—*stream* ... MT-8
C Keim Ranch—*locale* ... NE-7
C Klein Dam—*dam* ... SD-7
*Ckotol* ... PW-9
CKP Ditch—*canal* ... CO-8
C K Ridge—*ridge* ... MT-8
C K Tank—*reservoir* ... AZ-5
CKW Bridge over Powder River—*hist pl* ... WY-8
C K Well—*well* ... AZ-5
Clabaugh Draw—*valley* ... WY-8
Clabber Branch—*stream* (2) ... NC-3
Clabber Creek—*stream* (2) ... AR-4
Clabber Creek—*stream* ... MS-4
Clabber Creek—*stream* (2) ... MO-7
Clabber Creek—*stream* ... MT-8
Clabber Creek—*stream* ... OR-9
Clabber Creek—*stream* ... TX-5
Clabber Creek—*swamp* ... FL-3
Clabber Flats Cem—*cemetery* ... OK-5
Clabber Hill Ranch—*locale* ... NM-5
Clabber Hill Ranch—*locale* ... TX-5
Clabber Landing—*locale* ... GA-3
Clabber Peak—*summit* ... NY-2
Clabber Point—*cape* ... NC-3
Clabber Point—*cape* ... TX-5
Clabber Top Hill—*summit* ... NM-5
Clabber Town Cem—*cemetery* ... TX-5
Clabboard Cem—*cemetery* ... OH-6
Clabby Sch—*school* ... IL-6
Clabo Ridge—*ridge* ... TN-4
Claborn Sch (historical)—*school* ... AL-4
*Claburn* ... IL-6
**Clack**—*pop pl* ... MS-4
Clack, H. Earl, House—*hist pl* ... MT-8
**Clackamas**—*pop pl* ... OR-9
Clackamas Cem—*cemetery* ... OR-9
**Clackamas County**—*pop pl* ... OR-9
**Clackamas Heights**—*pop pl* ... OR-9
Clackamas Heights Airstrip—*airport* ... OR-9
Clackamas HS—*school* ... OR-9
Clackamas Lake—*lake* ... OR-9
Clackamas Lake Forest Camp—*locale* ... OR-9
Clackamas Lake Ranger Station Hist Dist—*hist pl* ... OR-9
Clackamas Rapids—*rapids* ... OR-9
Clackamas River—*stream* ... OR-9
Clackamas Sch—*school* ... OR-9
Clackamette Island—*island* ... OR-9
Clackamette Lake—*lake* ... OR-9
*Clackamus Lake* ... OR-9
Clack Branch—*locale* ... TN-4
Clack Branch—*stream* ... TN-4
Clack Branch Cem—*cemetery* ... TN-4
Clack Bridge—*bridge* ... GA-3
Clack Canyon—*valley* ... AZ-5
*Clack Cem* ... TN-4
Clack Cem—*cemetery* ... IL-6
Clack Creek—*stream* ... MT-8
Clack Creek—*stream* ... WI-6
Clack Lake—*lake* ... MI-6
Clackmas Mtn—*summit* ... WA-9
Clack Mtn—*summit* ... KY-4
Clack Mtn—*summit* ... MT-8
*Clackomas Lake* ... OR-9
Clacks Gap—*gap* ... TN-4
Clacks Gap—*locale* ... TN-4
Clacks Gap Sch—*school* ... TN-4
*Clacks Mill* ... TN-4
Clack Spring—*spring* ... TN-4
Clackville—*locale* ... AL-4
*Clade Creek* ... OR-9
Cladonia Creek—*stream* ... AK-9
Claer Well—*locale* ... NM-5
Claeys Sch—*school* ... SD-7
**Claflin**—*pop pl* ... KS-7
Claflin, Adams, House—*hist pl* ... MA-1
Claflin College Hist Dist—*hist pl* ... SC-3
*Claflin Drain* ... MI-6
Claflin HS—*school* ... KS-7
Claflin-Richards House—*hist pl* ... MA-1
Claflin Sch—*hist pl* ... MA-1
Clagett Butte—*summit* ... WY-8
Clagett Cem—*cemetery* ... WV-2
Clagett Ch—*church* ... KY-4
Clagett Hollow—*valley* ... TN-4
Clagett Island—*island* ... MD-2
*Clagetts* ... MI-6
Clagget Hill—*summit* ... MT-8
*Clagget Lake* ... OR-9
Claggett Cem—*cemetery* ... OR-9
Claggett Creek—*stream* ... OR-9
Claggett Creek Park—*park* ... OR-9
Claggett Lake—*lake* ... OR-9
**Claggettsville**—*pop pl* ... MD-2
Claghorn—*locale* ... PA-2
Claghorn Sch—*school* ... PA-2
Clago Creek—*stream* ... IN-6
Clagstone—*locale* ... ID-8
Clague House—*hist pl* ... OH-6
Clague Park—*park* ... OH-6
Clague Sch—*school* ... MI-6
Clagus, Lake—*lake* ... NE-7
Claibert Lake—*lake* ... LA-4
*Claiborne* ... MS-4
Claiborne—*locale* ... VA-3
**Claiborne**—*pop pl* ... AL-4
**Claiborne**—*pop pl* (2) ... LA-4
**Claiborne**—*pop pl* ... MD-2
**Claiborne**—*pop pl* ... MS-4
**Claiborne**—*pop pl* ... OH-6
Claiborne, Lake—*reservoir* ... LA-4
Claiborne, Lake—*reservoir* ... MS-4
Claiborne Bluff—*cliff* ... AL-4
*Claiborne Box* ... MS-4
Claiborne Cem—*cemetery* ... AL-4
Claiborne Cem—*cemetery* ... MO-7
Claiborne Cem—*cemetery* ... OH-6
Claiborne Ch—*church* ... IN-6
*Claiborne Chapel* ... MS-4
Claiborne Chapel—*church* ... AR-4
Claiborne-Cotton Mine—*mine* ... TN-4
**Claiborne County**—*pop pl* ... MS-4
**Claiborne County**—*pop pl* ... TN-4
Claiborne County Courthouse—*building* ... MS-4
Claiborne County Hosp—*hospital* ... MS-4
Claiborne County Hosp—*hospital* ... TN-4
Claiborne County HS—*school* ... TN-4
Claiborne County Vocational Center—*school* ... TN-4
Claiborne Creek—*stream* ... CA-9
Claiborne Ferry (historical)—*locale* ... AL-4
**Claiborne Hill**—*pop pl* ... LA-4
**Claiborne (historical)**—*pop pl* ... MS-4
Claiborne Island—*island* ... LA-4
Claiborne Lake—*reservoir* ... AL-4
Claiborne Landing—*locale* ... AL-4
Claiborne Lock And Dam—*dam* ... AL-4

Claiborne-Murphy Bridge—*bridge* AL-4
**Claiborne Parish**—*pop pl* LA-4
Claiborne Parish Courthouse—*hist pl* LA-4
Claiborne Peak—*summit* CA-9
Claiborne Run—*stream* VA-3
Claiborne Sch—*school* (2) LA-4
*Claibornes Island* LA-4
Claiborne Site (22Ha501)—*hist pl* MS-4
Claiborne State Dock—*locale* AL-4
Claibornes View—*summit* TN-4
**Claibornesville (historical)**—*pop pl* MS-4
Claiborne (Township of)—*fmr MCD* AR-4
Claiborne Wells Dam—*dam* TN-4
Claiborne Wells Lake—*reservoir* TN-4
Claibourne Branch—*stream* LA-4
Claibourne Cem—*cemetery* LA-4
Claibourne Chapel—*church* LA-4
**Claibourne Gardens**—*pop pl* LA-4
**Claibourne (Township of)**—*pop pl* OH-6
Claim Canyon—*valley* NV-8
Claim Creek—*stream* CA-9
Claim (historical)—*locale* KS-7
Claim Point—*cape* AK-9
Clair—*locale* MO-7
Clair, Bayou—*stream* LA-4
Clair, Lac—*lake* LA-4
**Clair Black Subdivision**—*pop pl* UT-8
*Clairborne* AL-4
Clairbourn Sch—*school* CA-9
*Clair Branch Creek* GA-3
Clairbrone Ch—*church* MS-4
Clair Brook—*stream* IN-6
Clair Camp—*locale* CA-9
Clair Carpenter Ranch—*locale* NE-7
Clair Creek—*stream* CO-8
Claire, Lake—*lake* (2) FL-3
Claire, Lake—*lake* ND-7
Claire Branch—*stream* LA-4
**Claire City**—*pop pl* SD-7
*Claire Engle Lake* CA-9
Claire Lake—*lake* WI-6
**Clairemont**—*pop pl* CA-9
**Clairemont**—*pop pl* TX-5
Clairemont Cem—*cemetery* TX-5
Clairemont East Oil Field—*oilfield* TX-5
**Clairemont Farms**—*pop pl* NY-2
Clairemont HS—*school* CA-9
Clairemont North Oil Field—*oilfield* TX-5
Clairemont Oil Field—*oilfield* TX-5
Clair Engle Lake—*reservoir* CA-9
**Clairette**—*pop pl* TX-5
Clairette Cem—*cemetery* TX-5
Claireville Flat—*flat* CA-9
**Clairfield**—*pop pl* TN-4
Clairfield (CCD)—*cens area* TN-4
Clairfield Division—*civil* TN-4
Clairfield Elem Sch—*school* TN-4
Clairfield Missionary Baptist Ch—*church* TN-4
Clairfield Post Office—*building* TN-4
Clairfield Rsvr—*reservoir* CO-8
*Clair Haven* MI-6
Clair Haven—*other* MI-6
**Clair Haven West**—*pop pl* MI-6
Clair Lake—*lake* IN-6
Clair Lake—*lake* MI-6
Clair Lake—*lake* WI-6
Clair Mel (alternate name for Clair-Mel City)—*uninc pl* FL-3
**Clair-Mel City (alternate name Clair Mel)**—*pop pl* FL-3
**Clair-Mel City (subdivision)**—*pop pl* FL-3
Clair-Mel Elem Sch—*school* FL-3
Clair Milton Ranch—*locale* WY-8
*Clairmont* TX-5
Clairmont—*locale* VI-3
**Clairmont**—*pop pl* NC-3
Clairmont Cem—*cemetery* CO-8
Clairmont Ch—*church* GA-3
Clairmont Gap—*gap* AL-4
Clairmont Sch—*school* GA-3
**Clairmont Springs**—*pop pl* AL-4
**Clairmont (subdivision)**—*pop pl* NC-3
Clair Pond—*lake* (2) FL-3
Clair Rose Gulch—*valley* ID-8
**Clairton**—*pop pl* PA-2
Clairton City—*civil* PA-2
Clairton HS—*school* PA-2
Clairton Intermediate Elem Sch—*school* PA-2
Clairton Junction—*uninc pl* PA-2
Clairton Lake—*reservoir* PA-2
Clairville Sch—*school* WI-6
**Clairway (subdivision)**—*pop pl* NC-3
*Claiton Graveyard* MS-4
Clakamas County Redsoils Airstrip—*airport* OR-9
C Lake—*lake* AZ-5
*Clakre Ledges* ME-1
*Clallam* WA-9
Clallam Bay—*bay* WA-9
**Clallam Bay**—*pop pl* WA-9
Clallam Bay-Neah Bay (CCD)—*cens area* WA-9
**Clallam County**—*pop pl* WA-9
Clallam County Courthouse—*hist pl* WA-9
Clallam Honor Camp—*locale* WA-9
*Clallam Point* WA-9
Clallam River—*stream* WA-9
*Clam* MI-6
**Clam**—*pop pl* VA-3
Clambank—*locale* SC-3
Clambank Creek—*gut* SC-3
Clambar Bay—*bay* FL-3
Clambar Bayou—*bay* FL-3
Clam Bay—*bay* AK-9
Clam Bay—*bay* WA-9
Clam Bay—*gut* LA-4
Clam Bayou—*bay* FL-3
Clam Bayou—*lake* FL-3
Clam Beach—*beach* CA-9
**Clam Beach**—*pop pl* CA-9
Clam Beach County Park—*park* CA-9
*Clam Brook* MA-1
Clam Cove—*bay* (3) AK-9
Clam Cove—*bay* (2) ME-1
*Clam Creek* FL-3
*Clam Creek* NJ-2
Clam Creek—*bay* NY-2
Clam Creek—*gut* NC-3
Clam Creek—*stream* AK-9
Clam Creek—*stream* GA-3
Clam Creek—*stream* MT-8
Clam Creek—*stream* NJ-2
*Clamet River* OR-9
Clam Factory Shoal—*bar* FL-3
**Clam Falls**—*pop pl* WI-6
Clam Falls Flowage—*reservoir* WI-6
**Clam Falls (Town of)**—*pop pl* WI-6
**Clam Gulch**—*pop pl* AK-9
Clam Gulch—*valley* AK-9
Clam Harbor Tumps—*bar* MD-2
Clam Island—*island* (4) AK-9
Clam Island—*island* CT-1
Clam Island—*island* (2) ME-1
Clam Island—*island* NJ-2
Clam Island—*island* NY-2
*Clam Key* FL-3
Clam Key—*island* FL-3
Clam Lagoon—*lake* AK-9
*Clam Lake* MN-6
Clam Lake—*lake* (2) AK-9
Clam Lake—*lake* CO-8
Clam Lake—*lake* (3) MI-6
Clam Lake—*lake* (3) MN-6
Clam Lake—*lake* TX-5
Clam Lake—*lake* WA-9
Clam Lake—*lake* WI-6
**Clam Lake**—*pop pl* WI-6
Clam Lake Cem—*cemetery* MI-6
Clam Lake Cem—*cemetery* WI-6
Clam Lake Dam—*dam* MA-1
Clam Lake Lookout Tower—*locale* WI-6
Clam Lake Oil Field—*oilfield* TX-5
Clam Lake Rsvr—*reservoir* MA-1
Clam Lake Sch—*school* MI-6
Clam Lake School—*locale* MI-6
**Clam Lake (Township of)**—*pop pl* MI-6
Clam Ledge—*bar* ME-1
Clam Ledges—*bar* ME-1
Clammer Branch—*stream* MO-7
Clammer Creek—*stream* OR-9
Clamming Creek—*stream* NJ-2
*Clammitte* CA-9
*Clammitte River* OR-9
Clam Mtn—*summit* WA-9
Clam Pass—*channel* FL-3
Clamp Creek—*stream* ID-8
Clamper Flat—*flat* CA-9
Clampet Cem—*cemetery* IL-6
Clampit Hollow—*valley* TN-4
Clampit Island—*island* NH-1
*Clam Point* MD-2
Clam Point—*cape* AK-9
Clam Point—*cape* CT-1
Clam Point—*cape* FL-3
Clam Point—*cape* ME-1
Clam Pond—*bay* NY-2
Clam Pools—*lake* MA-1
Clam Pudding Pond—*lake* MA-1
**Clam River**—*pop pl* MI-6
Clam River—*stream* MA-1
Clam River—*stream* MI-6
Clam River—*stream* WI-6
Clam River Cem—*cemetery* WI-6
Clam River Flowage—*reservoir* WI-6
Clam River Watershed Dam—*dam* MA-1
Clam River Watershed Rsvr—*reservoir* MA-1
Clam Shell, The—*locale* CT-1
Clamshell Canyon—*valley* CA-9
Clamshell Cove—*bay* ME-1
Clamshell Lake—*lake* MN-6
Clamshell Peak—*summit* CA-9
*Clam Shell Pond* MA-1
Clamshell Pond—*lake* MA-1
Clamshell Pond—*lake* NY-2
Clam Shoal—*bar* NC-3
Clam Thorofare—*channel* NJ-2
*Clamtown* NJ-2
*Clamtown* PA-2
**Clamtown**—*pop pl* PA-2
Clam Union Cem—*cemetery* MI-6
**Clam Union (Township of)**—*pop pl* MI-6
Clam Valley—*valley* MT-8
Clan Alpine—*locale* NV-8
Clan Alpine Mtns—*range* NV-8
Clan Alpine Ranch—*locale* NV-8
*Clan Alpine Range* NV-8
*Clancey* (2) MT-8
*Clancey Creek* MT-8
*Clanceytown* TN-4
Clancie—*locale* VA-3
Clan Cove—*bay* AK-9
**Clancy**—*pop pl* MT-8
Clancy, Cornelius Lawrence, House—*hist pl* TN-4
Clancy Creek—*stream* MT-8
Clancy Island—*island* NJ-2
Clancy Lake—*lake* MI-6
Clancy Lake—*lake* MN-6
Clancy Mine—*mine* MT-8
Clancy Sch—*school* LA-4
Clancy Sch—*school* MN-6
Claney Cem—*cemetery* KS-7
C Lange Ranch—*locale* ND-7
Clan House 1—*locale* AZ-5
Clank—*locale* IL-6
Clank Hollow—*valley* CA-9
Clanpit Cove—*valley* NC-3
**Clanricarde**—*pop pl* IN-6
Clanson Memorial Park—*cemetery* AR-4
Clansy Branch—*stream* AL-4
**Clanton**—*pop pl* AL-4
Clanton Baptist Ch—*church* AL-4
Clanton Branch—*stream* AL-4
Clanton (CCD)—*cens area* AL-4
Clanton Cem—*cemetery* (2) AL-4
Clanton Cem—*cemetery* GA-3
Clanton City Hall—*building* AL-4
Clanton Coulee—*valley* MT-8
*Clanton Creek* SD-7
Clanton Creek—*stream* IA-7
Clanton Creek—*stream* KY-4
Clanton Division—*civil* AL-4
Clanton Draw—*valley* NM-5
Clanton Elem Sch—*school* AL-4
*Clanton Ford* AL-4
Clanton Golf and Country Club—*locale* AL-4
*Clanton Grammar School* AL-4
Clanton Hill—*summit* AZ-5
*Clanton Hills* AZ-5
Clanton Hills—*summit* AZ-5
Clanton (historical)—*locale* IA-7
Clanton Lake Dam—*dam* MS-4
Clanton Landing (historical)—*locale* AL-4
Clanton Number 1 Dam—*dam* SD-7
Clanton Plains Ch—*church* SC-3
Clanton-Price Family Cem—*cemetery* MS-4
Clanton Pumping Station—*other* AL-4
Clantons Bar—*bar* AL-4
Clanton Sch (historical)—*school* MO-7
Clantons Landing (historical)—*locale* (2) AL-4
Clanton Spreader Dam—*dam* SD-7
*Clantons Well* AZ-5
**Clantonville**—*pop pl* AR-4
Clanton Wash—*stream* AZ-5
Clanton Well—*well* AZ-5
Clapboard Branch—*stream* SC-3
Clapboard Canyon—*valley* CA-9
Clapboard Canyon—*valley* KS-7
*Clapboard Corner* IN-6
Clapboard Creek—*stream* FL-3
Clapboard Gulch—*valley* (2) CA-9
Clapboard Gulch—*valley* OR-9
Clapboard Hill—*summit* (3) CT-1
Clapboard Island—*island* ME-1
**Clapboard Island**—*pop pl* ME-1
Clapboard Lookout Tower—*tower* FL-3
Clapboard Oak Brook—*stream* CT-1
Clapboard Run—*stream* PA-2
Clapboard Run—*stream* WV-2
Clapboard Swamp—*swamp* FL-3
**Clapham**—*pop pl* NM-5
Claphand Creek—*stream* TX-5
Clapp, Charles Q., Block—*hist pl* ME-1
Clapp, Charles Q., House—*hist pl* ME-1
Clapp, L. W., House—*hist pl* KS-7
Clapp, Silas, House—*hist pl* RI-1
Clapp Brook—*stream* MA-1
Clapp Cem—*cemetery* IL-6
Clapp Cem—*cemetery* TN-4
Clapp Cem—*cemetery* TX-5
*Clapp Creek* LA-4
*Clapp Creek* MS-4
Clapp Creek—*stream* KY-4
Clapp Creek—*stream* NE-7
Clapp-Cunningham Bldg—*hist pl* OK-5
Clapper—*locale* MO-7
Clapper Cem—*cemetery* NY-2
Clapper Cem—*cemetery* OH-6
Clapper Cem—*cemetery* PA-2
Clapper Creek—*stream* NV-8
Clapper Creek—*stream* OR-9
Clapper Creek—*stream* VA-3
Clapper Hill—*summit* NY-2
Clapper Hollow—*valley* NY-2
Clapper Hollow Sch—*school* NY-2
Clapper Lake—*lake* NE-7
Clapper Lake—*lake* NY-2
Clapper Lake—*reservoir* MO-7
Clapper Marsh—*swamp* NE-7
Clappers—*locale* MN-6
Clappers Flat—*flat* MT-8
Clappers Hollow—*valley* UT-8
**Clappertown**—*pop pl* PA-2
**Clapp Farm**—*pop pl* PA-2
Clapp Gulch—*valley* CA-9
Clapp Hill—*summit* NY-2
Clapp Hollow—*valley* TN-4
Clapp Houses—*hist pl* MA-1
**Clapp Lease**—*pop pl* PA-2
Clapp Meadow—*flat* OR-9
Clapp Memorial Park—*park* KS-7
Clap Pond—*lake* NY-2
Clapp Park—*park* MA-1
Clapp Park—*park* TX-5
Clapp Point—*cape* PA-2
*Clapp Pond* MA-1
Clapp Pond—*lake* (2) MA-1
Clapp Pond—*lake* NH-1
Clapp Pond—*reservoir* NC-3
Clapp Pond Dam—*dam* NC-3
Clapp Ranch—*locale* WY-8
Clapps Bar—*bar* MN-6
Clapp Sch—*school* MA-1
Clapp Sch—*school* (2) MI-6
Clapp Sch—*school* MO-7
Clapps Chapel—*church* NC-3
Clapps Chapel—*church* TN-4
**Clapps Corner**—*pop pl* MA-1
Clapps Creek—*stream* TX-5
Clapps Island—*island* MA-1
Clapps Pond—*lake* MA-1
Clapp Spring—*spring* (2) CA-9
Clapp Spring—*spring* MO-7
Clapp Spring—*spring* WY-8
Clapps Round Pond—*lake* MA-1
Clapp Swamp—*stream* SC-3
*Clappville* MA-1
**Clappville**—*pop pl* PA-2
*Clappville Pond* MA-1
Claquato—*locale* WA-9
Claquato Cem—*cemetery* WA-9
Claquato Church—*hist pl* WA-9
*Clara* ID-8
*Clara* MP-9
Clara—*locale* FL-3
Clara—*locale* PA-2
**Clara**—*pop pl* IA-7
**Clara**—*pop pl* MD-2
**Clara**—*pop pl* MS-4
**Clara**—*pop pl* MO-7
**Clara**—*pop pl* TX-5
Clara, Lake—*lake* FL-3
Clara, Lake—*lake* MN-6
Clara, Lake—*lake* (2) WI-6
Clara, Lake—*reservoir* GA-3
Clara Attendance Center—*school* MS-4
**Clara Barton**—*pop pl* NJ-2
Clara Barton Elem Sch—*school* (2) PA-2
*Clara Barton Home* MA-1
Clara Barton HS—*school* NY-2
Clara Barton Natl Historic Site—*hist pl* MD-2
Clara Barton Natl Historic Site—*park* MD-2
*Clara Barton Sch* PA-2
Clara Barton Sch—*school* (2) CA-9
Clara Barton Sch—*school* MD-2
Clara Barton Sch—*school* MA-1
Clara Barton Sch—*school* (2) NJ-2
Clara Barton Sch—*school* PA-2
**Clara Belle Camp (historical)**—*pop pl* SD-7
Clara Belle Mine—*mine* SD-7
Clara Burton Mine—*mine* MT-8
Clara Cem—*cemetery* ID-8
Clara Cem—*cemetery* MN-6
Clara Cem—*cemetery* SD-7
Clara Cem—*cemetery* TX-5
Clara Ch—*church* (2) MN-6
Clara Ch—*church* MS-4
Clara Ch—*church* MO-7
Clara Ch—*church* SD-7
Clara Ch—*church* TX-5
Clara Chapel—*church* IA-7
*Clara Ch of God* MS-4
**Clara City**—*pop pl* MN-6
Clara Couch Oil Field—*oilfield* TX-5
Clara Creek—*stream* (3) AK-9
Clara Creek—*stream* PA-2
Claradean, Lake—*lake* MO-7
Clara Driscoll Oil Field—*oilfield* TX-5
Clarady Bluff—*cliff* MO-7
Clara Elem Sch—*school* MS-4
*Clara Hearne Elementary School* NC-3
Clara Hill—*summit* PA-2
Clara H Mine—*mine* CA-9
*Clara Lake* MI-6
Clara Lake—*lake* VT-1
Clara Lake—*lake* WA-9
Clara Lake—*lake* WI-6
Clara Lakes, La—*lake* KY-4
Clara Mine—*mine* MT-8
Clara Oil Field—*oilfield* TX-5
Clara Park—*park* MT-8
Clara Peak—*locale* NM-5
Clara Peak—*summit* AZ-5
Clara Post Office (historical)—*building* TN-4
Clara Sch (abandoned)—*school* PA-2
Clara Smith Glacier—*glacier* AK-9
Clara Spring—*spring* OR-9
Clara Town Hall—*building* ND-7
**Clara Township**—*pop pl* ND-7
**Clara (Township of)**—*pop pl* PA-2
Clara Tunnel—*tunnel* CA-9
Clara United Methodist Ch—*church* MS-4
Claraville—*locale* CA-9
**Claraville**—*pop pl* VA-3
Claraville Flat—*locale* CA-9
*Clara Well* AZ-5
**Clarcona**—*pop pl* FL-3
*Clarconal* FL-3
Clardie Creek—*stream* VA-3
Clardy—*locale* TX-5
Clardy, U. P., House—*hist pl* TX-5
Clardy Cem—*cemetery* (2) AL-4
Clardy Lakes—*lake* FL-3
Clardy-Lee House—*hist pl* AR-4
Clardy Sch—*school* MO-7
Clardy Sch—*school* TX-5
Clardy Sch (historical)—*school* MO-7
Clardy Tank—*reservoir* NM-5
Clare—*locale* KS-7
Clare—*locale* KY-4
Clare—*locale* LA-4
Clare—*locale* NY-2
Clare—*locale* OH-6
**Clare**—*pop pl* IL-6
**Clare**—*pop pl* IN-6
**Clare**—*pop pl* IA-7
**Clare**—*pop pl* MI-6
Clare, J. H., House—*hist pl* TX-5
Clare Cem—*cemetery* SD-7
Clare Ch—*church* SD-7
**Clare (County)**—*pop pl* MI-6
*Clare Creek* MO-7
Clare Creek—*stream* AL-4
Clare Creek—*stream* NY-2
Clare Creek—*stream* TX-5
Clare Creek School (Abandoned)—*locale* TX-5
Clare Island—*island* AK-9
Clare Island—*island* WI-6
Clareknoll Novitiate—*church* IL-6
Clare Lake—*lake* IN-6
Clare Mill—*locale* CA-9
*Claremont* MI-6
Claremont—*hist pl* CO-8
Claremont—*hist pl* MS-4
Claremont—*locale* SC-3
Claremont—*locale* WV-2
**Claremont**—*pop pl* CA-9
**Claremont**—*pop pl* IL-6
**Claremont**—*pop pl* MN-6
**Claremont**—*pop pl* MS-4
**Claremont**—*pop pl* NH-1
**Claremont**—*pop pl* NC-3
**Claremont**—*pop pl* SD-7
**Claremont**—*pop pl* (2) VA-3
Claremont—*summit* (2) CA-9
Claremont—*uninc pl* MD-2
Claremont—*uninc pl* NJ-2
Claremont—*uninc pl* WA-9
Claremont Cem—*cemetery* WV-2
*Claremont Center* NH-1
Claremont City Hall—*hist pl* NH-1
Claremont Country Club—*other* CA-9
Claremont Creek—*stream* (2) CA-9
Claremont Creek—*stream* MT-8
Claremont Elem Sch—*school* NC-3
Claremont Glacier—*glacier* AK-9
Claremont Golf Course—*other* CA-9
Claremont Graduate Sch—*school* CA-9
Claremont Hotel—*hist pl* ME-1
Claremont HS—*school* CA-9
Claremont HS Hist Dist—*hist pl* NC-3
Claremont JHS—*school* CA-9
*Claremont Junction* NH-1
**Claremont Junction**—*pop pl* NH-1
Claremont Manor—*locale* VA-3
Claremont Mens Coll—*school* CA-9
Claremont Park—*park* NY-2
Claremont Park—*park* TX-5
**Claremont Place (subdivision)**—*pop pl* (2) AZ-5
Claremont Plantation (historical)—*locale* MS-4
Claremont Sch—*school* NY-2
Claremont Sch—*school* (2) VA-3
Claremont School, The—*school* DE-2
Claremont Stables—*hist pl* NY-2
Claremont Street Cem—*cemetery* MN-6
**Claremont (subdivision)**—*pop pl* NC-3
**Claremont (subdivision)**—*pop pl* TN-4
Claremont Terminal—*locale* NJ-2
Claremont Terminal Channel—*channel* NJ-2
**Claremont Township**—*pop pl* SD-7
**Claremont (Township of)**—*pop pl* IL-6
**Claremont (Township of)**—*pop pl* MN-6
Claremont Trail—*trail* CA-9
Claremont Tunnel—*tunnel* CA-9
Claremont Warehouse No. 34—*hist pl* NH-1
Claremont Water Tunnel—*tunnel* CA-9
Claremont Yards—*locale* NJ-2
**Claremore**—*pop pl* OK-5
Claremore, Lake—*reservoir* OK-5
Claremore (CCD)—*cens area* OK-5
Claremore Creek—*stream* OK-5
Claremore Interchange—*other* OK-5
Claremore Mound—*summit* OK-5
*Claren* WV-2
Clarenback Point—*cliff* CA-9
*Clarence* KS-7
Clarence—*locale* KY-4
Clarence—*locale* WV-2
**Clarence**—*pop pl* AL-4
**Clarence**—*pop pl* IL-6
**Clarence**—*pop pl* IA-7
**Clarence**—*pop pl* LA-4
**Clarence**—*pop pl* MO-7
**Clarence**—*pop pl* NY-2
**Clarence**—*pop pl* PA-2
Clarence A Boswell Elem Sch—*school* FL-3
Clarence Baker Ditch—*canal* IN-6
Clarence Cannon Dam—*dam* MO-7
Clarence Cannon Memorial Airp—*airport* MO-7
Clarence Cannon Natl Wildlife Ref—*park* MO-7
Clarence (CCD)—*cens area* AL-4
Clarence Cem—*cemetery* IA-7
Clarence Cem—*cemetery* WI-6
**Clarence (census name for Clarence Compact)**—*pop pl* NY-2
Clarence Center—*locale* MI-6
**Clarence Center**—*pop pl* NY-2
Clarence Center Cem—*cemetery* NY-2
Clarence Center Ch—*church* NY-2
Clarence Central HS—*school* NY-2
Clarence Ch—*church* WV-2
Clarence Compact (census name Clarence)—*other* NY-2
Clarence Coulee—*valley* MT-8
Clarence Creek—*stream* MT-8
Clarence Creek—*stream* OR-9
Clarence Creek—*stream* UT-8
Clarence Creek Spring—*spring* UT-8
CLARENCE CROCKETT—*hist pl* MD-2
Clarence Division—*civil* AL-4
Clarence Fahnestock Memorial State Park—*park* NY-2
Clarence Fillmore Cem—*cemetery* NY-2
Clarence Goff Dam—*dam* SD-7
Clarence H Eades Fire Station—*building* TN-4
Clarence (historical)—*locale* KS-7
Clarence King, Mount—*summit* CA-9
Clarence King Lake—*lake* CA-9
*Clarence King Mountain* CO-8
Clarence Kopp Lake—*reservoir* IN-6
Clarence Kopp Lake Dam—*dam* IN-6
Clarence Kramer Peak—*summit* AK-9
Clarence Lake—*lake* AK-9
Clarence Lake—*lake* FL-3
Clarence Lake—*lake* MI-6
Clarence Lake—*lake* MN-6
Clarence L Farrington JHS—*school* IN-6
Clarence M Gockley Elem Sch—*school* PA-2
Clarence River—*stream* AK-9
**Clarence (RR name Snow Shoe (sta.))**—*pop pl* PA-2
Clarence Smith Dam—*dam* SD-7
Clarence Strait—*channel* AK-9
Clarence (Susan Moore)—*other* AL-4
**Clarence (Town of)**—*pop pl* NY-2
**Clarence Township**—*pop pl* KS-7
**Clarence (Township of)**—*pop pl* MI-6
*Clarenceville* MI-6
**Clarenceville**—*pop pl* MI-6
Clarenceville Cem—*cemetery* MI-6
Clarenceville HS—*school* MI-6
Clarenceville JHS—*school* MI-6
Clarence Vinson Bridge—*bridge* DE-2
Clarence Well—*well* NM-5
*Clarenden Hills* MA-1
Clarendon—*locale* NC-3
**Clarendon**—*pop pl* AR-4
**Clarendon**—*pop pl* MI-6
**Clarendon**—*pop pl* NY-2
**Clarendon**—*pop pl* NC-3
**Clarendon**—*pop pl* PA-2
**Clarendon**—*pop pl* TX-5
**Clarendon**—*pop pl* VT-1
**Clarendon**—*pop pl* VA-3
Clarendon and Eckford Drain Number Three—*canal* MI-6
Clarendon Borough—*civil* PA-2
Clarendon (CCD)—*cens area* TX-5
Clarendon Cem—*cemetery* MI-6
Clarendon Ch—*church* NC-3
Clarendon Congregational Church—*hist pl* VT-1
Clarendon Country Club—*other* TX-5
**Clarendon (County)**—*pop pl* SC-3
Clarendon Creek—*stream* MS-4
*Clarendon Drain* MI-6
Clarendon Gorge—*valley* VT-1
Clarendon Hall Sch—*school* SC-3
**Clarendon Heights**—*pop pl* PA-2
*Clarendon Hill* MA-1
Clarendon Hill—*summit* MA-1
**Clarendon Hills**—*pop pl* IL-6
Clarendon Hills Cem—*cemetery* IL-6
**Clarendon Hills (subdivision)**—*pop pl* MA-1
**Clarendon Hill (subdivision)**—*pop pl* MA-1
Clarendon Hot Springs—*locale* ID-8
Clarendon House—*hist pl* VT-1
Clarendon Lake—*reservoir* TX-5
Clarendon Methodist-Episcopal Church South—*hist pl* AR-4
Clarendon MS—*school* AL-4
Clarendon Park—*park* IL-6
Clarendon Plantation House—*hist pl* LA-4
Clarendon River—*stream* VT-1
Clarendon Sch—*school* AZ-5
Clarendon Sch—*school* OH-6
**Clarendon Springs**—*pop pl* VT-1
**Clarendon (Town of)**—*pop pl* NY-2
**Clarendon (Town of)**—*pop pl* VT-1
**Clarendon (Township of)**—*pop pl* MI-6
**Clarenford**—*pop pl* VA-3
Clareno, Arroyo —*valley* TX-5
Clarenoon Sch—*school* OR-9
Claren (RR name for Hensley)—*other* WV-2
*Claren Station* WV-2
Claresville—*locale* VA-3
Claresville Ch—*church* VA-3
**Clare Switch**—*pop pl* OH-6
Claret Branch—*stream* AR-4
Clareton—*locale* WY-8
Clareton Oil Field—*oilfield* WY-8
**Clare (Town of)**—*pop pl* NY-2
**Clare Township**—*pop pl* SD-7
Clare Township Hall—*building* SD-7
Clareville—*locale* TX-5
**Clareville**—*pop pl* TN-4
Clarey Branch—*stream* TN-4
Clarey Lake—*lake* WI-6
Clarey Ranch—*locale* AZ-5
Clareys Pond—*lake* ME-1
Clarfield Sch—*school* OH-6
*Clargeons Creek* NC-3
Claribel—*locale* CA-9
Claribel Lateral—*canal* CA-9
Clarice, Lake—*lake* WA-9
Clarice Lake—*lake* CA-9
**Claridge**—*pop pl* PA-2
**Claridge**—*pop pl* TN-4
**Claridge Court (subdivision)**—*pop pl* DE-2
Claridge Manor Apartments—*hist pl* AL-4
**Claridon**—*pop pl* (2) OH-6
Claridon Cem—*cemetery* OH-6
Claridon Congregational Church—*hist pl* OH-6
Claridon Revival Center—*church* OH-6
Claridon Sch—*school* OH-6
**Claridon (Township of)**—*pop pl* (2) OH-6
Claridy Creek—*stream* OK-5
**Clarinda**—*pop pl* IA-7
Clarinda Cem—*cemetery* IA-7
Clarinda HS—*school* IA-7
**Clarinda Junction (historical)**—*pop pl* IA-7
Clarinda Mental Health Institute—*hospital* IA-7
**Clarinda Subdivision**—*pop pl* UT-8
**Clarington**—*pop pl* OH-6
**Clarington**—*pop pl* PA-2
**Clarington**—*pop pl* WV-2
Clarington Cem—*cemetery* OH-6
Clarington Station—*locale* WV-2
Clarion—*locale* IL-6
Clarion—*locale* OH-6
**Clarion**—*pop pl* IA-7
**Clarion**—*pop pl* MI-6
**Clarion**—*pop pl* PA-2
Clarion Borough—*civil* PA-2
Clarion Branch—*stream* TN-4
Clarion Ch—*church* IL-6
**Clarion County**—*pop pl* PA-2
Clarion County Airp—*airport* PA-2
Clarion County Courthouse and Jail—*hist pl* PA-2
Clarion Heliport—*airport* MO-7
Clarion (historical)—*locale* KS-7
Clarion Island—*island* PA-2
**Clarion Junction**—*pop pl* (2) PA-2
Clarion Junction Station—*locale* PA-2
Clarion-Limestone HS—*school* PA-2
Clarion River—*stream* PA-2
Clarion (RR name for Lynch Station)—*other* VA-3
*Clarion State College* PA-2
*Clarion State College - Venango Campus* PA-2
Clarion Summit—*summit* PA-2
**Clarion (Township of)**—*pop pl* IL-6
**Clarion (Township of)**—*pop pl* PA-2
Clarion Univ of Pennsylvania—*school* PA-2
**Clarissa**—*pop pl* MN-6
**Clarita**—*pop pl* OK-5
Clarita Oil And Gas Field—*oilfield* OK-5
*Clark* IN-6
*Clark* KS-7
*Clark* MS-4
Clark—*locale* (2) CO-8
Clark—*locale* IL-6
Clark—*locale* IA-7
Clark—*locale* MS-4
Clark—*locale* NJ-2
Clark—*locale* NC-3
Clark—*locale* TX-5
Clark—*locale* WI-6
Clark—*locale* WY-8
**Clark**—*pop pl* AL-4
**Clark**—*pop pl* FL-3
**Clark**—*pop pl* KY-4
**Clark**—*pop pl* MS-4
**Clark**—*pop pl* MO-7
**Clark**—*pop pl* NV-8
**Clark**—*pop pl* NY-2
**Clark**—*pop pl* NC-3
**Clark**—*pop pl* OH-6
**Clark**—*pop pl* PA-2
**Clark**—*pop pl* SD-7
Clark—*uninc pl* WV-2
Clark, Alexander, House—*hist pl* IA-7
Clark, Andrew, House—*hist pl* CT-1
Clark, Ansel, House—*hist pl* OH-6
Clark, Benjamin, House—*hist pl* NJ-2
Clark, Capt. John, House—*hist pl* CT-1
Clark, Charles W., Mansion—*hist pl* MT-8
Clark, Dr., House—*hist pl* OH-6
Clark, Dr. George C., House—*hist pl* CA-9
Clark, Ezra, House—*hist pl* NY-2
Clark, Frank Chamberlain, House—*hist pl* OR-9
Clark, Gerome, House—*hist pl* IA-7
Clark, Gov. James A., Mansion—*hist pl* KY-4
Clark, Henry A., House—*hist pl* TN-4
Clark, Isaac Newton, House—*hist pl* NE-7
Clark, James Beauchamp, House—*hist pl* MO-7
Clark, Jared, House—*hist pl* OH-6
Clark, J. M., House—*hist pl* AZ-5
Clark, John, House—*hist pl* KY-4
Clark, John Hector, House—*hist pl* NC-3
Clark, Jonathan, House—*hist pl* WI-6
Clark, Lake—*lake* AK-9
Clark, Lake—*lake* TX-5
Clark, Lake—*reservoir* AL-4
Clark, Mollie, House—*hist pl* MS-4
Clark, Mount—*summit* CA-9
Clark, Mount—*summit* VT-1
Clark, Mount—*summit* WA-9
Clark, Orin, House—*hist pl* IN-6

Clark, Peter, House—hist pl UT-8
Clark, Reuben, House—hist pl VA-3
Clark, Robert, House—hist pl TX-5
Clark, Silas M., House—hist pl PA-2
Clark, W. A., Mansion—hist pl MT-8
Clark, Whitney, House—hist pl OH-6
Clark, William, House—hist pl NJ-2
Clark, William, House—hist pl WI-6
Clark, William S., House—hist pl CA-9
Clark Acad—school MS-4
**Clark Addition**—pop pl TN-4
*Clark Airfield* PA-2
*Clark Airp* MO-7
Clark Airp—airport IN-6
Clark Airp—airport MO-7
Clark Airp—airport UT-8
Clark and Brown Canyon—valley NM-5
*Clark And Kinneys Spring* AZ-5
Clark and McCormack Quarry and House—hist pl MN-6
Clark Bank—mine MO-7
Clark Banks—levee NC-3
Clark Bay—bay (2) AK-9
Clark Bay—bay MN-6
Clark Bay—bay VA-3
Clark Bay—swamp FL-3
Clark Bayou—gut (2) LA-4
Clark Bayou—stream AR-4
Clark Bayou—stream (3) MS-4
Clark Bayou Ch—church MS-4
**Clark Bayshore**—pop pl MI-6
Clark Bench—bench UT-8
Clark Bend—bend TX-5
Clark-Blackwell House—hist pl IA-7
Clark Bluff—cliff AL-4
Clark Bluff Cave—cave AL-4
Clark Bluff Cem—cemetery GA-3
Clark Borough—civil PA-2
Clark Bottom—bend TX-5
Clark Brake—swamp AR-4
*Clark Branch* MO-7
Clark Branch—stream (3) AL-4
Clark Branch—stream AR-4
Clark Branch—stream (2) FL-3
Clark Branch—stream (2) IL-6
Clark Branch—stream (6) KY-4
Clark Branch—stream (2) LA-4
Clark Branch—stream MS-4
Clark Branch—stream (3) MO-7
Clark Branch—stream (2) NJ-2
Clark Branch—stream (6) NC-3
Clark Branch—stream OR-9
Clark Branch—stream (6) TN-4
Clark Branch—stream (5) TX-5
Clark Branch—stream VA-3
Clark Branch—stream (2) WV-2
Clark Branch Creek—stream TN-4
Clark Branch Sch—school KY-4
*Clark Bridge* GA-3
Clark Bridge—bridge GA-3
Clark Bridge—bridge KY-4
Clark Bridge—bridge ME-1
Clark Bridge—other IL-6
Clark Bridge—other MO-7
Clark Bridge Access Point—bridge GA-3
Clark Brook—stream (2) CT-1
Clark Brook—stream (9) ME-1
Clark Brook—stream (2) MA-1
Clark Brook—stream (5) NH-1
Clark Brook—stream (3) NY-2
Clark Brook—stream OR-9
Clark Brook—stream (4) VT-1
Clark Brook Trail—trail VT-1
Clark Brothers Factory No. 1—hist pl CT-1
Clark Brothers Factory No. 2—hist pl CT-1
Clark Brothers Ranch—locale (2) TX-5
Clark Brothers Ranch (abandoned)—locale MT-8
Clark-Brown House—hist pl WI-6
**Clarkburg**—pop pl MS-4
Clark Butte—summit ND-7
Clark Butte—summit OR-9
Clark Butte—summit TX-5
Clark Butte—summit WY-8
Clark Cabin Campground—locale CO-8
Clark Cabin Spring—spring CO-8
*Clark Canyon* OR-9
Clark Canyon—valley AZ-5
Clark Canyon—valley (8) CA-9
Clark Canyon—valley CO-8
Clark Canyon—valley ID-8
Clark Canyon—valley MT-8
Clark Canyon—valley NV-8
Clark Canyon—valley NM-5
Clark Canyon—valley (2) OR-9
Clark Canyon—valley (2) UT-8
Clark Canyon—valley WA-9
Clark Canyon Dam—dam MT-8
Clark Canyon-Horse Prairie—cens area MT-8
Clark Canyon Reservoir Rec Area—park MT-8
Clark Canyon Rsvr—reservoir MT-8
Clark Canyon Rsvr—reservoir OR-9
Clark Canyon Rsvr Number Two—reservoir OR-9
Clark-Cardwell House—hist pl MT-8
Clark Cem—cemetery (7) AL-4
Clark Cem—cemetery (5) AR-4
Clark Cem—cemetery (5) GA-3
Clark Cem—cemetery (9) IL-6
Clark Cem—cemetery (6) IN-6
Clark Cem—cemetery (2) IA-7
Clark Cem—cemetery (8) KY-4
Clark Cem—cemetery LA-4
Clark Cem—cemetery (2) ME-1
Clark Cem—cemetery (2) MA-1
Clark Cem—cemetery (2) MI-6
Clark Cem—cemetery (9) MS-4
Clark Cem—cemetery (9) MO-7
Clark Cem—cemetery NM-5
Clark Cem—cemetery (7) NY-2
Clark Cem—cemetery (6) NC-3
Clark Cem—cemetery (10) OH-6
Clark Cem—cemetery (2) OK-5
Clark Cem—cemetery (3) PA-2
Clark Cem—cemetery (3) SC-3
Clark Cem—cemetery (24) TN-4
Clark Cem—cemetery (6) TX-5
Clark Cem—cemetery VT-1
Clark Cem—cemetery (6) VA-3
Clark Cem—cemetery (4) WV-2
Clark Cem—cemetery WY-8
*Clark Center* SD-7
**Clark Center**—pop pl IL-6
Clark Center Ch—church SD-7
Clark Ch—church KY-4
Clark Ch—church MS-4
Clark Ch—church TX-5
Clark Ch—church VA-3
Clark-Chalker House—hist pl FL-3
Clark Chapel—church IL-6
Clark Chapel—church MD-2
Clark Chapel—church (2) NC-3
Clark Chapel—church OH-6
Clark Chapel Cem—cemetery IN-6
Clark Chapel Cem—cemetery MS-4
Clark Chapel Cem—cemetery TX-5
Clark Chapel Sch—school IL-6
Clark Chapel Sch—school NC-3
Clark-Chapman Ditch—canal IN-6
**Clark City**—pop pl MO-7
Clark City Cem—cemetery MO-7
Clark City (historical)—locale ND-7
Clark Coll—school GA-3
Clark Coll—school WA-9
**Clark Colony**—pop pl SD-7
Clark Community Club—other KS-7
Clark Corner Cutoff—bend AR-4
*Clark Corners* OH-6
Clark Corners—locale MD-2
Clark Corners—locale NY-2
Clark Corners—locale OH-6
**Clark Corners**—pop pl MI-6
**Clark Corners**—pop pl (2) NY-2
**Clark Corners**—pop pl OH-6
Clarkco State Park—park MS-4
Clark Cotton Gin—building TX-5
Clark Coulee—valley MT-8
Clark County—civil KS-7
Clark County—civil NV-8
Clark County—civil SD-7
**Clark (County)**—pop pl AR-4
**Clark (County)**—pop pl IL-6
**Clark County**—pop pl IN-6
**Clark (County)**—pop pl KY-4
**Clark County**—pop pl MO-7
**Clark (County)**—pop pl OH-6
**Clark County**—pop pl WA-9
**Clark (County)**—pop pl WI-6
Clark County Airp—airport SD-7
Clark County Airp—airport WA-9
Clark County Courthouse—hist pl AR-4
Clark County Courthouse—hist pl KY-4
Clark County Courthouse—hist pl MO-7
Clark County Fairgrounds—locale KS-7
Clark County Industrial Plant Area—locale NV-8
Clark County Jail—hist pl WI-6
Clark County Library—hist pl AR-4
*Clark County State Forest* IN-6
Clark County State Lake—reservoir KS-7
Clark County State Lake Dam—dam KS-7
Clark County Youth Camp—locale NV-8
*Clark Cove* ME-1
*Clark Cove* MA-1
Clark Cove—bay CT-1
Clark Cove—bay (5) ME-1
Clark Cove—cove MA-1
Clark Cove—valley NC-3
*Clark Creek* AL-4
*Clark Creek* FL-3
*Clark Creek* ID-8
*Clark Creek* KS-7
*Clark Creek* NC-3
*Clark Creek* ND-7
*Clark Creek* OR-9
*Clark Creek* TX-5
*Clark Creek* WA-9
Clark Creek—gut SC-3
Clark Creek—stream (2) AL-4
Clark Creek—stream (2) AK-9
Clark Creek—stream (4) AR-4
Clark Creek—stream (5) CA-9
Clark Creek—stream CO-8
Clark Creek—stream CT-1
Clark Creek—stream (2) FL-3
Clark Creek—stream (2) GA-3
Clark Creek—stream (5) ID-8
Clark Creek—stream IN-6
Clark Creek—stream IA-7
Clark Creek—stream KS-7
Clark Creek—stream LA-4
Clark Creek—stream MI-6
Clark Creek—stream (4) MS-4
Clark Creek—stream (2) MO-7
Clark Creek—stream (6) MT-8
Clark Creek—stream (2) NE-7
Clark Creek—stream (3) NY-2
Clark Creek—stream (5) NC-3
Clark Creek—stream (9) OR-9
Clark Creek—stream PA-2
Clark Creek—stream (2) SC-3
Clark Creek—stream TN-4
Clark Creek—stream (2) TX-5
Clark Creek—stream VA-3
Clark Creek—stream (6) WA-9
Clark Creek—stream WI-6
Clark Creek—stream (2) WY-8
Clark Creek Ch—church NC-3
Clark Creek Furnace (historical)—locale TN-4
Clark Creek Guard Station—locale OR-9
Clark Creek Trail—trail TN-4
*Clark Crossing* OH-6
Clark Crossroads—locale AL-4
*Clarkdale* AR-4
**Clarkdale**—pop pl AL-4
**Clarkdale**—pop pl AZ-5
**Clarkdale**—pop pl GA-3
**Clarkdale**—pop pl IA-7
*Clarkdale (Clarkedale)* AR-4
Clarkdale Elem Sch—school AZ-5
Clarkdale Elem Sch—school MS-4
Clarkdale Hist Dist—hist pl GA-3
*Clarkdale HS* MS-4
*Clarkdale-Jerome Elem Sch* AZ-5
Clarkdale JHS—school AZ-5
Clarkdale Mine—mine NV-8
Clarkdale Park—park AZ-5
Clarkdale Post Office—building AZ-5
Clarkdale RR Station—building AZ-5
Clarkdale Sch—school MS-4
Clark Dam No. 1—dam OR-9
Clark Dam No. 2—dam OR-9
Clark Ditch—canal (2) CA-9
Clark Ditch—canal (3) IN-6
Clark Ditch—canal KY-4
Clark Ditch—canal MT-8
Clark Ditch—canal NM-5
Clark Ditch—canal WY-8
Clark Drain—canal (3) MI-6
Clark Drain—stream (2) MI-6
Clark Draw—valley (2) MT-8
Clark Draw—valley (2) NM-5
Clark Draw—valley (3) WY-8
*Clarke (2)* IN-6
*Clarke* TX-5
Clarke—locale OR-9
**Clarke**—pop pl AL-4
Clarke, Boscom B., House—hist pl WI-6
Clarke, Henry B., House—hist pl IL-6
Clarke, James F., House—hist pl IA-7
Clarke, Lake—lake FL-3
Clarke, Lake—reservoir PA-2
Clarke, Luther, House—hist pl NY-2
Clarke, Nehemiah P., House—hist pl MN-6
Clarke, Pitt, House—hist pl MA-1
Clark-Eames House—hist pl MA-1
Clarke and Atkinson Grant—civil FL-3
Clarke And Bunker Drain—canal MI-6
Clarke and Lake Company Archeol Site—hist pl ME-1
Clarke Bayou—stream LA-4
Clarke Brook—stream RI-1
Clarke Canyon—valley CA-9
Clarke Cem—cemetery IN-6
Clarke Cem—cemetery IA-7
Clarke Cem—cemetery NY-2
Clarke Cem—cemetery TN-4
*Clarke City* MO-7
Clarke City—locale IL-6
Clarke Coll—school IA-7
**Clarke County**—pop pl AL-4
**Clarke (County)**—pop pl GA-3
**Clarke County**—pop pl MS-4
**Clarke (County)**—pop pl VA-3
Clarke County Airp—airport MS-4
Clarke County Baptist Center—church MS-4
Clarke County Courthouse (Old)—hist pl VA-3
Clarke County Farm (historical)—locale AL-4
Clarke County HS—school AL-4
Clarke County Jail—hist pl GA-3
Clarke County State Park Lake Dam—dam MS-4
*Clarke Creek* KS-7
Clarke Creek—stream ID-8
Clarke Creek—stream NC-3
Clarke Creek—stream TN-4
*Clarke Creek - in part* TN-4
**Clarke Dale**—pop pl GA-3
**Clarkedale (Clarkdale)**—pop pl AR-4
Clarke Edwards Canal—canal ID-8
Clarkeen Cem—cemetery AR-4
Clarke Falls—falls PA-2
Clarke Farm Site—hist pl OH-6
*Clarke Fork* ID-8
*Clarke Fork* MT-8
*Clarke Fork* WA-9
**Clarke Gardens (subdivision)**—pop pl AL-4
Clarke Gulch—valley MT-8
Clarke Hotel—hist pl NE-7
Clarke HS—school NY-2
Clarke JHS—school VA-3
*Clarke Junction* IN-6
**Clarke Junction**—pop pl IN-6
*Clarke Lake* MN-6
*Clarke Lake* NE-7
*Clarke Lake* PA-2
Clarke Lake—lake MI-6
Clarke Lake—lake (2) MN-6
Clarke Lake—lake WI-6
Clarke Lake Dam—dam MS-4
*Clarke Elementary School* AL-4
Clarke Elem Sch—school KS-7
*Clarke Memorial Baptist Junior College* MS-4
Clarke Mtn—summit AL-4
Clarke Mtn—summit ID-8
Clarke Mtn—summit TN-4
Clarke Park—park WI-6
*Clarke Point* DE-2
*Clarke Point* ME-1
Clarke Point—cape NY-2
Clarke Point Shoal—bar IL-6
Clarke Pond—reservoir NY-2
Clarke Ranch—locale (2) CA-9
*Clarke Range* MT-8
*Clarke Ridge* ME-1
Clarke Run—stream PA-2
**Clarkes**—pop pl OR-9
Clarkes Cem—cemetery OR-9
Clarke Sch—school AL-4
Clarke Sch—school IN-6
Clarke Sch—school MI-6
Clarke Sch—school TX-5
Clarke Sch—school VA-3
Clarke Sch (historical)—school MS-4
*Clarkes Creek* NC-3
Clarkes Creek—stream FL-3
*Clarkes Ferry* TN-4
Clarkes Gap—gap AL-4
Clarkes Gap—locale VA-3
Clarkes Hill—summit MA-1
Clarkes Lake—lake SC-3
*Clarkes Mills* RI-1
*Clarkes Point* DE-2
*Clarke's Point* ME-1
*Clarkes Pond* CT-1
Clarkes Springs—spring OR-9
Clarke Springs Park—park VA-3
*Clarkes Ridge* ME-1
Clarkes Sch—school OR-9
Clarkes Store (historical)—locale MS-4
Clarke Street Meeting House—hist pl RI-1
Clarke Street Sch—school WI-6
*Clarkesville* AL-4
*Clarkesville* NJ-2
*Clarkesville* PA-2
**Clarkesville**—pop pl GA-3
Clarkesville (CCD)—cens area GA-3
**Clarkesville (corporate name for Clarksville)**—pop pl GA-3
Clarkesville Ferry (historical)—locale AL-4
Clarkesville Garage—hist pl GA-3
*Clarketown* PA-2
Clarketown—locale TN-4
Clarketown Sch (historical)—school TN-4
Clarke Watkins Lake Dam—dam MS-4
Clark Farm—locale UT-8
Clark Farm Lake—reservoir TN-4
Clark Farm Lake Dam—dam TN-4
Clark Farm Trail—trail PA-2
*Clark Ferry* TN-4
Clark Field—park CA-9
Clark Field—park IN-6
**Clarkfield**—pop pl MN-6
Clarkfield Cem—cemetery MN-6
Clark Field House—locale IA-7
Clarkfield Ranch—locale NV-8
Clark Flat—flat CA-9
Clark Ford—locale MO-7
*Clark Fork* MT-8
*Clark Fork* WA-9
**Clark Fork**—pop pl ID-8
Clark Fork—stream (2) CA-9
Clark Fork—stream ID-8
Clark Fork—stream (2) KY-4
Clark Fork—stream (2) MO-7
Clark Fork—stream MT-8
Clark Fork—stream NC-3
Clark Fork—stream SC-3
Clark Fork Campground—locale CA-9
*Clark Fork Columbia River* MT-8
Clark Fork Meadow—flat CA-9
Clark Fork Muddy Creek—stream MT-8
*Clark Fork of the Columbia River* MT-8
*Clark Fork of the Yellowstone River* MT-8
*Clark Fork Ranger Station* ID-8
Clark Fork Ranger Station (historical)—locale ID-8
*Clark Fork River* ID-8
*Clark Fork River* MT-8
Clark Fork Township—civil MO-7
*Clark Fork Yellowstone River* MT-8
*Clark Fork Yellowstone River* WY-8
*Clark Furnace* TN-4
Clark Furnace (historical)—locale TN-4
Clark Furnace Mines—mine TN-4
Clark Furnace (40SW212)—hist pl TN-4
*Clark Gap* VA-3
Clark Gap—gap NC-3
Clark Gap—gap TN-4
Clark Gap—gap WV-2
Clark Gap Ch—church WV-2
Clark Glacier—glacier AK-9
Clark Glacier—glacier OR-9
Clark Glacier—glacier WA-9
Clark Griffith Park—park NC-3
Clark Grove—woods CA-9
Clark Grove Ch—church GA-3
Clark Grove Ch—church TN-4
*Clark Gulch* CO-8
*Clark Gulch* MT-8
Clark Gulch—valley CA-9
Clark Gulch—valley (2) ID-8
Clark Gulch—valley (2) MT-8
Clark Gully—valley NY-2
Clark Hardware Company Bldg—hist pl KY-4
Clark Hatch Brook—stream VT-1
**Clark Heights**—pop pl NY-2
*Clarkhill* IN-6
*Clark Hill* SC-3
**Clark Hill**—pop pl KY-4
**Clark Hill**—pop pl NH-1
Clark Hill—summit (2) AR-4
Clark Hill—summit CA-9
Clark Hill—summit CO-8
Clark Hill—summit (4) CT-1
Clark Hill—summit IN-6
Clark Hill—summit MA-1
Clark Hill—summit (2) NH-1
Clark Hill—summit (5) NY-2
Clark Hill—summit OH-6
Clark Hill—summit PA-2
Clark Hill—summit (3) VT-1
Clark Hill Cem—cemetery AR-4
*Clark Hill (Clarks Hill)* SC-3
*Clark Hill Dam* GA-3
Clark Hill Dam—dam SC-3
*Clark Hill Lake* GA-3
*Clark Hill Lake* SC-3
Clark Hill Marina—locale SC-3
*Clark Hill Reservoir* GA-3
*Clark Hill Reservoir* SC-3
**Clark Hills (subdivision)**—pop pl NC-3
Clark-Hinkle Cem—cemetery KY-4
Clark (historical)—locale AL-4
*Clark Hollow* TN-4
*Clark Hollow* UT-8
Clark Hollow—valley AL-4
Clark Hollow—valley (4) AR-4
Clark Hollow—valley (3) KY-4
Clark Hollow—valley LA-4
Clark Hollow—valley (2) MO-7
Clark Hollow—valley (4) NY-2
Clark Hollow—valley OH-6
Clark Hollow—valley (2) PA-2
Clark Hollow—valley (6) TN-4
Clark Hollow—valley TX-5
Clark Hollow—valley (2) UT-8
Clark Hollow—valley (2) VT-1
Clark Hollow Bay—bay NY-2
Clark Hollow Brook—stream VT-1
Clark Hollow Mine (underground)—mine AL-4
Clark Hollow Trail—trail PA-2
Clark Homestead—hist pl CT-1
Clark Homestead—locale CO-8
Clark Homestead—locale MT-8
Clark Hosp—hospital WI-6
Clark Hotel—hist pl TX-5
Clark House—hist pl AZ-5
Clark House—hist pl AR-4
Clark House—hist pl ID-8
Clark House—hist pl MA-1
Clark House—hist pl (2) NY-2
Clark House—hist pl TX-5
Clark House, The—locale ID-8
Clark Houses—hist pl MA-1
Clark HS—school (2) LA-4
Clark HS—school NV-8
Clark HS—school PA-2
Clark HS—school TX-5
**Clarkia**—pop pl ID-8
Clarkia Peak—summit ID-8
Clarking—locale GA-3
*Clark Island* MA-1
*Clark Island* MN-6
Clark Island—island AK-9
Clark Island—island FL-3
Clark Island—island (2) IL-6
Clark Island—island ME-1
Clark Island—island MA-1
Clark Island—island (2) MI-6
Clark Island—island MN-6
Clark Island—island NE-7
Clark Island—island NH-1
Clark Island—island OH-6
Clark Island—island PA-2
Clark Island—island (2) TX-5
Clark Island—island WA-9
Clark Island—island WI-6
**Clark Island**—pop pl ME-1
Clark Island Ledge—bar ME-1
Clark Island Shoal—bar NY-2
Clark Island State Park—park WA-9
Clark JHS—school CA-9
Clark JHS—school KY-4
Clark JHS—school LA-4
Clark JHS—school OH-6
Clark Joubert Sch—school SD-7
*Clark Junior High School* IN-6
Clark-King House—hist pl AR-4
Clark Knob—summit WV-2
*Clark Lake* MI-6
*Clark Lake* WA-9
Clark Lake—flat CA-9
Clark Lake—lake AR-4
Clark Lake—lake (2) FL-3
Clark Lake—lake ID-8
Clark Lake—lake IL-6
Clark Lake—lake (8) MI-6
Clark Lake—lake (4) MN-6
Clark Lake—lake (2) MS-4
Clark Lake—lake (3) NE-7
Clark Lake—lake OH-6
Clark Lake—lake OK-5
Clark Lake—lake (2) OR-9
Clark Lake—lake SD-7
Clark Lake—lake UT-8
Clark Lake—lake (2) WA-9
Clark Lake—lake (4) WI-6
Clark Lake—lake WY-8
**Clarklake**—pop pl MI-6
Clark Lake—reservoir AL-4
Clark Lake—reservoir CO-8
Clark Lake—reservoir NC-3
Clark Lake—reservoir OH-6
Clark Lake—reservoir TX-5
Clark Lakebed—flat MN-6
Clark Lake Dam—dam AL-4
Clark Lake Dam—dam MS-4
Clark Lake Dam—dam NC-3
Clark Lake Dam—dam OR-9
Clark Lake (historical)—lake TN-4
Clark Lakes—lake CA-9
Clarklake Sch—school MI-6
Clark Lake Wildlife Area—park OH-6
Clarkland Farms—hist pl GA-3
Clark Landing—locale KY-4
**Clark Landing**—pop pl NH-1
Clark Lane Sch—school CT-1
Clark Lateral—canal CA-9
Clark Lateral—canal ID-8
Clark Lateral—canal NM-5
**Clark Learning Office Center (subdivision)**—pop pl UT-8
*Clark Ledge* ME-1
Clark Ledge—bar (2) ME-1
*Clark Ledges* ME-1
Clark Logan (Oxbow)—bend MN-6
**Clark Manor**—pop pl PA-2
**Clark Manor (subdivision)**—pop pl TN-4
Clark Mansion—hist pl WA-9
Clark Meadow—flat OR-9
Clark Meadow Brook—stream ME-1
Clark Memorial Bridge—bridge KY-4
Clark Memorial Campground—locale MT-8
Clark Memorial Clubhouse—hist pl AZ-5
Clark Memorial Coll—school MS-4
Clark Memorial Garden—cemetery NY-2
Clark Memorial Hall—hist pl MI-6
Clark Memorial Home—building MI-6
Clark Memorial Park—cemetery CA-9
Clark Memorial Park—park LA-4
Clark Memorial Park—park NJ-2
Clark Mill Branch—stream SC-3
*Clark Mill Creek* AL-4
*Clark Mill Creek* FL-3
Clark Mill Creek—stream NC-3
Clark Millpond—lake NC-3
Clark Millpond—reservoir VA-3
*Clark Mills* WI-6
**Clark Mills**—pop pl NY-2
**Clark Mills (Clarks Mills)**—pop pl WI-6
Clark Mills House (historical)—building DC-2
Clark Mine—mine AZ-5
Clark Mine—mine CA-9
Clark Mine—mine CO-8
Clark Mine—mine ID-8
Clark Mine—mine WY-8
Clark Mine (underground)—mine (2) AL-4
Clark Monmt Number 4—park TX-5
Clark Monmt Number 7—park TX-5
Clark Monmt 10—park TX-5
Clark Monmt 9—park TX-5
Clark Morey Drain—stream MI-6
Clark Mountain Station—locale CA-9
Clark Mountain Trail—trail VA-3
*Clark Mtn* CA-9
*Clark Mtn* VA-3
Clark Mtn—summit (3) CA-9
Clark Mtn—summit GA-3
Clark Mtn—summit (3) ME-1
Clark Mtn—summit MA-1
Clark Mtn—summit MO-7
Clark Mtn—summit (2) MT-8
Clark Mtn—summit NV-8
Clark Mtn—summit (2) NY-2
Clark Mtn—summit NC-3
Clark Mtn—summit OR-9
Clark Mtn—summit SD-7
Clark Mtn—summit (2) TN-4
Clark Mtn—summit VT-1
Clark Mtn—summit (3) VA-3
Clark Mtn—summit WA-9
Clark Mtn Range—range CA-9
*Clark Natl Forest* MO-7
Clark-Northrup House—hist pl MA-1
Clark-Norton House—hist pl OR-9
Clark Oil Field—oilfield TX-5
Clark Opening—flat CA-9
Clark Park—flat SD-7
Clark Park—locale WY-8
Clark Park—park AZ-5
Clark Park—park (2) IL-6
Clark Park—park KY-4
Clark Park—park MI-6
Clark Park—park PA-2
Clark Park—park WA-9
Clark Park Cem—cemetery PA-2
Clark Park Trail Three hundred one—trail AZ-5
*Clark Pass* MT-8
Clark Peak—summit AK-9
Clark Peak—summit AZ-5
Clark Peak—summit CA-9
Clark Peak—summit (2) CO-8
Clark Peak—summit NM-5
Clark Peak—summit WA-9
Clark Peak Ranger Station—locale AZ-5
Clark Place Draw—valley TX-5
**Clark Place (subdivision)**—pop pl MS-4
Clark Place Well—well WY-8
Clark Playfield—park WA-9
Clark Playground—locale MA-1
Clark Pleasant JHS—school IN-6
*Clark Point* MA-1
Clark Point—cape CT-1
Clark Point—cape DE-2
Clark Point—cape ID-8
Clark Point—cape (5) ME-1
Clark Point—cape MD-2
Clark Point—cape NH-1
Clark Point—cape (2) NY-2
Clark Point—cape (2) NC-3
Clark Point—cape SC-3
Clark Point—cape VT-1
Clark Point—cape VA-3
Clark Point—cape WA-9
Clark Point—cliff CO-8
**Clark Point**—pop pl NY-2
*Clark Pond* MA-1
*Clark Pond* VT-1
Clark Pond—lake (3) CT-1
Clark Pond—lake IL-6
Clark Pond—lake (3) ME-1
Clark Pond—lake (4) MA-1
Clark Pond—lake (5) NH-1
Clark Pond—lake (2) NJ-2
Clark Pond—lake (3) NY-2
Clark Pond—lake PA-2
Clark Pond—lake WA-9
Clark Pond—reservoir AL-4
Clark Pond—reservoir RI-1
Clark Pond—reservoir SC-3
Clark Pond—swamp TX-5
Clark Pond Brook—stream (2) NH-1
Clark Pond Dam—dam (3) MS-4
Clark Pond Loop—trail NH-1
*Clark Post Office* AL-4
Clark Prairie—flat FL-3
Clark-Pratt House—hist pl DE-2
Clark Ranch—locale (4) AZ-5
Clark Ranch—locale (3) CA-9
Clark Ranch—locale (3) CO-8
Clark Ranch—locale (2) ID-8
Clark Ranch—locale (5) MT-8
Clark Ranch—locale (4) NM-5
Clark Ranch—locale ND-7
Clark Ranch—locale OR-9
Clark Ranch—locale SD-7
Clark Ranch—locale TX-5
Clark Ranch—locale (3) UT-8
Clark Ranch—locale (2) WY-8
**Clarkrange**—pop pl TN-4
Clark Range—summit CA-9
Clarkrange Baptist Ch—church TN-4
Clarkrange (CCD)—cens area TN-4
Clarkrange Cem—cemetery TN-4
Clarkrange Ch—church TN-4
Clarkrange Division—civil TN-4
Clarkrange Elem Sch—school TN-4
Clarkrange HS—school TN-4
Clarkrange Post Office—building TN-4
Clarkrange United Methodist Ch—church TN-4
Clark Reservation State Park—park NY-2
Clark Reservoir Dam—dam MA-1
Clarkridge—locale AR-4
Clark Ridge—ridge CA-9
Clark Ridge—ridge CO-8
Clark Ridge—ridge ME-1
Clark Ridge—ridge VA-3
Clark Ridge—ridge WA-9
Clark Ridge—ridge WV-2
Clark Ridge Cem—cemetery TX-5
Clark Ridge Trail—trail WA-9
Clark River—stream AK-9
*Clark Road* IN-6
Clark Round Barn—hist pl IA-7
Clark Row House—hist pl WI-6
Clark Rsvr—reservoir (2) CA-9
Clark Rsvr—reservoir (3) CO-8
Clark Rsvr—reservoir MA-1
Clark Rsvr—reservoir MT-8
Clark Rsvr—reservoir OR-9
Clark Rsvr No 1—reservoir CO-8
Clark Run—stream IL-6
Clark Run—stream (2) IN-6
Clark Run—stream (2) MD-2
Clark Run—stream (3) OH-6
Clark Run—stream (3) PA-2
*Clarks* IN-6
*Clarks* LA-4
*Clark's* OH-6
*Clarks* PA-2
**Clarks**—pop pl CO-8
**Clarks**—pop pl IN-6
**Clarks**—pop pl LA-4
**Clarks**—pop pl NE-7
**Clarks**—pop pl TX-5
Clarks Saint Sch—school NC-3
Clarks Basin—basin CA-9
Clarks Basin—basin UT-8
Clarks Basin Creek—stream UT-8

Clarks Basin Spring—*spring* UT-8
*Clarks Bay* MN-6
Clarks Bay—*bay* NC-3
Clarks Bay—*swamp* FL-3
Clarks Bayou—*gut* LA-4
Clarks Bayou—*stream* LA-4
Clarks Bench—*bench* CO-8
Clarks Bluff—*cliff* GA-3
Clarks Bluff—*locale* GA-3
Clarksboro—*locale* GA-3
Clarksboro—*locale* NY-2
**Clarksboro**—*pop pl* NJ-2
*Clarks Branch* MO-7
*Clarks Branch* NJ-2
Clarks Branch—*stream* IA-7
Clarks Branch—*stream* KY-4
Clarks Branch—*stream* (2) MO-7
Clarks Branch—*stream* (2) NC-3
Clarks Branch—*stream* (3) TX-5
Clarks Bridge—*bridge* ME-1
*Clarks Brook* MA-1
Clarks Brook—*stream* (2) CT-1
Clarks Brook—*stream* ME-1
*Clarksburg* CA-9
*Clarksburg* IN-6
*Clarksburg* MS-4
**Clarksburg**—*pop pl* CA-9
**Clarksburg**—*pop pl* IL-6
**Clarksburg**—*pop pl* IN-6
**Clarksburg**—*pop pl* KY-4
**Clarksburg**—*pop pl* MD-2
**Clarksburg**—*pop pl* MI-6
**Clarksburg**—*pop pl* MS-4
**Clarksburg**—*pop pl* MO-7
**Clarksburg**—*pop pl* NJ-2
**Clarksburg**—*pop pl* NY-2
**Clarksburg**—*pop pl* (2) OH-6
**Clarksburg**—*pop pl* PA-2
**Clarksburg**—*pop pl* TN-4
**Clarksburg**—*pop pl* WV-2
Clarksburg Branch—*stream* KY-4
Clarksburg (CCD)—*cens area* CA-9
Clarksburg (CCD)—*cens area* TN-4
Clarksburg Cem—*cemetery* KS-7
Clarksburg Cem—*cemetery* MA-1
Clarksburg Cem—*cemetery* MO-7
Clarksburg Ch—*church* PA-2
Clarksburg Ch—*church* (2) VA-3
Clarksburg Country Club—*other* WV-2
Clarksburg Division—*civil* TN-4
Clarksburg Downtown Hist Dist—*hist pl* WV-2
*Clarksburgh* IN-6
Clarksburg (historical)—*locale* KS-7
*Clarksburgh Post Office* TN-4
Clarksburg HS—*school* TN-4
*Clarksburg Mountain* MA-1
Clarksburg Post Office—*building* TN-4
Clarksburg Post Office (historical)—*building* MS-4
*Clarksburg Reservoir* MA-1
Clarksburg Sch—*hist pl* MD-2
Clarksburg Sch—*school* KS-7
Clarksburg Sch—*school* MD-2
Clarksburg Sch—*school* MA-1
*Clarksburg School* TN-4
Clarksburg State For—*forest* MA-1
Clarksburg State Park—*park* MA-1
**Clarksburg (Town of)**—*pop pl* MA-1
**Clarksburg (Township of)**—*pop pl* IL-6
Clarksburg Valley Chapel—*church* KS-7
Clarksbury Ch—*church* (2) NC-3
Clarksbury Ch—*church* VA-3
*Clarks Butte* ND-7
Clarks Butte—*summit* CA-9
Clarks Butte—*summit* OR-9
Clarks Camp (inundated)—*locale* UT-8
*Clarks Canyon* OR-9
Clarks Canyon—*valley* (2) CA-9
Clarks Canyon—*valley* (2) MT-8
Clarks Canyon—*valley* OR-9
Clarks Canyon—*valley* UT-8
Clarks Cem—*cemetery* AR-4
Clarks Cem—*cemetery* IL-6
Clarks Cem—*cemetery* LA-4
Clarks Cem—*cemetery* MA-1
Clarks Cem—*cemetery* MO-7
Clarks Cem—*cemetery* NE-7
Clarks Cem—*cemetery* TX-5
*Clark Sch* AL-4
*Clark Sch* IN-6
*Clark Sch* MS-4
*Clark Sch* PA-2
Clarks Ch—*church* AR-4
Clarks Ch—*church* VA-3
Clark Sch—*school* AL-4
Clark Sch—*school* AZ-5
Clark Sch—*school* CA-9
Clark Sch—*school* ID-8
Clark Sch—*school* (7) IL-6
Clark Sch—*school* IN-6
Clark Sch—*school* (2) IA-7
Clark Sch—*school* (3) KY-4
Clark Sch—*school* LA-4
Clark Sch—*school* (2) ME-1
Clark Sch—*school* (2) MA-1
Clark Sch—*school* (5) MI-6
Clark Sch—*school* MS-4
Clark Sch—*school* (3) MO-7
Clark Sch—*school* MT-8
Clark Sch—*school* NH-1
Clark Sch—*school* NJ-2
Clark Sch—*school* (2) OH-6
Clark Sch—*school* OR-9
Clark Sch—*school* (2) PA-2
Clark Sch—*school* SC-3
Clark Sch—*school* (2) SD-7
Clark Sch—*school* (2) TX-5
Clark Sch—*school* VA-3
Clark Sch—*school* WA-9
Clark Sch—*school* WI-6
Clark Sch—*school* WY-8
Clark Sch (abandoned)—*school* MO-7
Clark Sch (abandoned)—*school* (2) PA-2
Clarks Chapel—*church* AL-4
Clarks Chapel—*church* (2) AR-4
Clarks Chapel—*church* GA-3
Clarks Chapel—*church* (4) MS-4
Clarks Chapel—*church* MO-7
Clarks Chapel—*church* (2) NC-3
Clarks Chapel—*church* (2) OH-6
Clarks Chapel—*church* TX-5
Clarks Chapel—*church* VA-3
*Clarks Chapel Baptist Ch* MS-4
Clarks Chapel Cem—*cemetery* NY-2
*Clarks Chapel Ch* AL-4
Clarks Chapel Ch—*church* GA-3
Clark Sch for the Deaf—*school* MA-1
Clark Sch (historical)—*school* (3) MS-4
Clark Sch (historical)—*school* (2) MO-7
Clark Sch (historical)—*school* (2) PA-2
Clark Sch (historical)—*school* SD-7
Clark Sch (historical)—*school* (4) TN-4
Clark School—*locale* MI-6
*Clarks Church* MS-4
Clark's Conveniency—*hist pl* MD-2
*Clarks Corner* DE-2
Clarks Corner—*locale* KY-4
Clarks Corner—*locale* (2) ME-1
Clarks Corner—*locale* VA-3
**Clarks Corner**—*pop pl* AR-4
**Clarks Corner**—*pop pl* CT-1
**Clarks Corner**—*pop pl* NY-2
Clarks Corner Drain—*canal* MI-6
Clarks Corners—*locale* NY-2
Clarks Corners—*locale* PA-2
**Clarks Corners**—*pop pl* NY-2
Clarks Corner Sch—*school* MI-6
*Clarks Cove* ME-1
Clarks Cove—*bay* MA-1
*Clarks Creek* CA-9
*Clarks Creek* DE-2
*Clarks Creek* FL-3
*Clarks Creek* NY-2
*Clarks Creek* NC-3
*Clarks Creek* OR-9
*Clarks Creek* PA-2
*Clarks Creek* SC-3
Clarks Creek—*stream* (2) CA-9
Clarks Creek—*stream* (4) GA-3
Clarks Creek—*stream* ID-8
Clarks Creek—*stream* IN-6
Clarks Creek—*stream* KS-7
Clarks Creek—*stream* KY-4
Clarks Creek—*stream* MI-6
Clarks Creek—*stream* (2) MS-4
Clarks Creek—*stream* MO-7
Clarks Creek—*stream* MT-8
Clarks Creek—*stream* (2) NC-3
Clarks Creek—*stream* ND-7
Clarks Creek—*stream* (3) OR-9
Clarks Creek—*stream* PA-2
Clarks Creek—*stream* SC-3
Clarks Creek—*stream* (2) TN-4
Clarks Creek—*stream* (2) TX-5
Clarks Creek—*stream* VA-3
Clarks Creek—*stream* WA-9
Clarks Creek Cem—*cemetery* KS-7
Clarks Creek Cem—*cemetery* TN-4
Clarks Creek Ch—*church* GA-3
Clarks Creek Ch—*church* KY-4
Clarks Creek Ch—*church* MS-4
Clarks Creek Ch—*church* TN-4
Clarks Creek Ch—*church* VA-3
Clarks Creek Ditch—*canal* OR-9
Clarks Creek Public Use Area—*park* ND-7
Clarks Creek Sch (historical)—*school* MS-4
Clarks Creek Sch (historical)—*school* TN-4
Clarks Creek Shoals—*bar* TN-4
*Clarks Creek Township* KS-7
Clarks Crossing—*locale* CA-9
Clarks Crossing—*locale* VA-3
*Clarks Crossroads* AL-4
*Clarks Cross Roads* IN-6
Clarks Crossroads—*locale* NC-3
Clarks Crossroads—*locale* SC-3
Clarks Cut—*gap* ID-8
*Clarksdale* GA-3
Clarksdale—*locale* IL-6
**Clarksdale**—*pop pl* IN-6
**Clarksdale**—*pop pl* MS-4
**Clarksdale**—*pop pl* MO-7
Clarksdale Baptist Ch—*church* MS-4
*Clarksdale Baptist Church* AL-4
Clarksdale Cem—*cemetery* MO-7
Clarksdale City Hall—*building* MS-4
Clarksdale Country Club—*locale* MS-4
Clarksdale HS—*school* MS-4
Clarksdale JHS—*school* MS-4
Clarksdale Post Office—*building* MS-4
Clarksdale Seventh Day Adventist Ch—*church* MS-4
Clarksdale Shop Ctr—*locale* MS-4
Clarks Desert Spring—*spring* MT-8
Clarks Ditch—*canal* CA-9
Clarks Ditch—*canal* MI-6
Clarks Ditch (historical)—*gut* DE-2
*Clarks Draw* WY-8
Clarksean State Public Shooting Area—*park* SD-7
Clark Sennett Ditch—*canal* MT-8
**Clarks Falls**—*pop pl* CT-1
Clarks Farm—*locale* AR-4
*Clarks Ferry* TN-4
Clarks Ferry—*locale* TX-5
Clarks Ferry Bridge—*bridge* PA-2
Clarks Ferry (historical)—*crossing* TN-4
**Clarksfield**—*pop pl* OH-6
**Clarksfield (Township of)**—*pop pl* OH-6
Clarks Flat—*flat* CA-9
Clarks Ford—*crossing* TN-4
*Clarks Fork* ID-8
*Clarks Fork* MT-8
*Clark's Fork* WA-9
Clarks Fork—*locale* MO-7
Clarks Fork—*stream* GA-3
Clarks Fork—*stream* ID-8
Clarks Fork—*stream* MT-8
Clarks Fork and Silver Tip Ditch—*canal* MT-8
Clarks Fork Canyon—*valley* WY-8
Clarks Fork Canyon Creek—*stream* MT-8
Clarks Fork Creek—*stream* NM-5
Clarks Fork Creek—*stream* OR-9
Clarks Fork Creek—*stream* SD-7
Clarks Fork Ditch—*canal* MT-8
Clarks Fork Kings River—*stream* CA-9
Clarks Fork Morrisy Coulee—*valley* MT-8
*Clark's Fork of the Columbia Riv* MT-8
*Clark's Fork of the Yellowstone River* MT-8
Clarks Fork Trail Camp—*locale* NM-5
Clarks Fork Yellowstone River—*stream* MT-8
Clarks Fork Yellowstone River—*stream* WY-8
Clarks Gap—*gap* VA-3
Clarks Gin (historical)—*locale* MS-4
Clarks Grant Park—*park* IN-6
**Clarks Green**—*pop pl* PA-2
Clarks Green Borough—*civil* PA-2
**Clarks Grove**—*pop pl* MN-6
Clarks Grove Cem—*cemetery* MN-6
Clarks Grove Cem—*cemetery* TN-4
Clarks Grove Ch—*church* GA-3
Clarks Grove Ch—*church* NC-3
Clarks Grove Ch—*church* PA-2
Clarks Grove Cooperative Creamery—*hist pl* MN-6
Clarks Gulch—*valley* (2) CA-9
Clarks Gulch—*valley* MT-8
Clarks Gulch—*valley* WY-8
**Clarks Heights**—*pop pl* OK-5
**Clarks Hill**—*pop pl* IN-6
**Clarks Hill**—*pop pl* SC-3
Clarks Hill—*summit* CT-1
Clarks Hill—*summit* MA-1
Clarks Hill Airp—*airport* PA-2
**Clarks Hill (Clark Hill)**—*pop pl* SC-3
Clarks Hill Dam—*dam* GA-3
Clarks Hill Elem Sch—*school* IN-6
Clarks Hill Lake—*lake* SC-3
Clarks Hill Lake—*reservoir* GA-3
**Clark Siding**—*pop pl* IN-6
Clarks Island—*island* GA-3
Clarks Island—*island* ID-8
Clarks Island—*island* IL-6
Clarks Island—*island* ME-1
Clarks Island—*island* MA-1
Clarks Island—*island* NY-2
Clarks Island—*island* NC-3
Clarks Island—*island* PA-2
Clarks Knob—*summit* PA-2
*Clarks Lake* MI-6
*Clarks Lake* MN-6
Clarks Lake—*lake* (3) MI-6
Clarks Lake—*lake* MS-4
Clarks Lake—*reservoir* (2) AL-4
Clarks Lake—*reservoir* IA-7
Clarks Lake—*reservoir* MS-4
Clarks Lake—*reservoir* (2) NC-3
Clarks Lake Dam—*dam* MS-4
Clarks Lake Dam—*dam* (2) NC-3
Clarks Lake (historical)—*reservoir* AL-4
Clarks Landing—*locale* GA-3
Clarks Landing—*locale* IN-6
Clarks Landing—*locale* MD-2
Clarks Landing—*locale* (2) NJ-2
Clarks Landing—*locale* NC-3
Clarks Landing—*locale* VA-3
**Clarks Landing**—*pop pl* LA-4
**Clarks Landing**—*pop pl* NH-1
Clarks Landing (historical)—*locale* TN-4
Clark Slough—*gut* CA-9
Clark Slough—*gut* FL-3
Clark Slough—*gut* OR-9
Clark Slough—*stream* AK-9
Clarks Memorial Ch—*church* NC-3
*Clarks Mill* ME-1
Clarks Mill—*locale* GA-3
Clarks Mill—*locale* (2) NJ-2
**Clarks Mill**—*pop pl* ME-1
**Clarks Mill**—*pop pl* NY-2
*Clarks Mill Branch* MS-4
Clarks Mill Burying Ground—*cemetery* NJ-2
Clarks Mill Ch—*church* VA-3
*Clarks Mill Creek* AL-4
*Clarks Mill Creek* FL-3
Clarks Mill Creek—*stream* SC-3
Clarks Mill (historical)—*locale* MS-4
Clarks Mill (historical)—*locale* (3) TN-4
Clarks Mill Pond—*lake* GA-3
Clarks Millpond—*reservoir* SC-3
Clarks Mills—*locale* NJ-2
**Clarks Mills**—*pop pl* ME-1
**Clarks Mills**—*pop pl* PA-2
**Clarks Mills**—*pop pl* WI-6
Clarks Mill Stream—*stream* NJ-2
Clarks Monmt—*park* TX-5
Clarks Monument—*other* NM-5
Clarks Mound—*summit* IL-6
Clarks Mountain Cem—*cemetery* VA-3
*Clarkson* AL-4
*Clarkson* KS-7
Clarkson—*locale* ID-8
Clarkson—*locale* TX-5
**Clarkson**—*pop pl* KY-4
**Clarkson**—*pop pl* MS-4
**Clarkson**—*pop pl* NE-7
**Clarkson**—*pop pl* NY-2
**Clarkson**—*pop pl* (2) OH-6
**Clarksona**—*pop pl* CA-9
**Clarkson Addition (subdivision)**—*pop pl* SD-7
Clarkson Baptist Ch—*church* MS-4
Clarkson Bridge—*hist pl* AL-4
Clarkson (CCD)—*cens area* KY-4
Clarkson Cem—*cemetery* KY-4
Clarkson Cem—*cemetery* MS-4
Clarkson Cem—*cemetery* OK-5
Clarkson Cem—*cemetery* TN-4
Clarkson Ch—*church* TX-5
Clarkson Chapel—*hist pl* NY-2
Clarkson Coll—*school* NY-2
*Clarkson Creek* UT-8
Clarkson Ditch—*canal* IN-6
Clarkson Drain—*canal* MI-6
Clarkson Farm Complex—*hist pl* SC-3
Clarkson Fork—*stream* WV-2
Clarkson Hill—*summit* WY-8
**Clarkson (historical)**—*pop pl* IA-7
**Clarkson (historical)**—*pop pl* TN-4
Clarkson Hollow—*valley* KY-4
Clarkson Hollow—*valley* OH-6
Clarkson Home—*building* NY-2
Clarkson Hosp—*hospital* NE-7
Clarkson House—*hist pl* KY-4
Clarkson Methodist Ch—*church* MS-4
Clarkson Mission Ch—*church* SC-3
*Clarkson Mountain* UT-8
Clarkson Plaza—*locale* MO-7
Clarkson Pond—*lake* ME-1
Clarkson Pond—*reservoir* SC-3
Clarkson Post Office (historical)—*building* AL-4
Clarkson Post Office (historical)—*building* MS-4
Clarkson Ranch—*locale* TX-5
Clarkson Ranch—*locale* WY-8
Clarkson Sch—*school* IA-7
Clarkson Sch—*school* NE-7
Clarkson Sch—*school* NY-2
Clarkson Sch (historical)—*school* MS-4
Clarksons Crossroads—*locale* DE-2
Clarkson Spring—*spring* MO-7
Clarkson Tank—*reservoir* NM-5
**Clarkson (Town of)**—*pop pl* NY-2
**Clarkson Valley**—*pop pl* MO-7
Clarkson-Watson House—*hist pl* PA-2
Clark Southeast (CCD)—*cens area* KY-4
Clarks Park—*park* MN-6
Clarks Park—*park* MT-8
Clarks Park—*park* NC-3
Clarks Pass—*gap* CA-9
*Clarks Peak* CA-9
Clarks Peak—*summit* (2) CA-9
Clark Spit—*bar* AK-9
*Clarks Point* AK-9
*Clarks Point* ME-1
Clarks Point—*cape* (2) MA-1
Clarks Point—*cape* MN-6
Clarks Point—*cape* RI-1
Clarks Point—*cape* WI-6
**Clark's Point**—*pop pl* AK-9
**Clarks Point**—*pop pl* AK-9
**Clarks Point**—*pop pl* WI-6
*Clarks Point of View* OR-9
*Clarks Pond* AL-4
Clarks Pond—*lake* AK-9
Clarks Pond—*lake* CT-1
Clarks Pond—*lake* NJ-2
Clarks Pond—*lake* (2) NY-2
Clarks Pond—*lake* OR-9
Clarks Pond—*lake* VT-1
Clarks Pond—*reservoir* CT-1
Clarks Pond—*reservoir* MA-1
Clarks Pond—*reservoir* NJ-2
Clarks Pond—*reservoir* NC-3
Clarks Pond Dam—*dam* NJ-2
Clarks Pond Dam—*dam* NC-3
Clarks Pond Fish and Wildlife Mngmt Area—*park* NJ-2
Clark Spring—*spring* AL-4
Clark Spring—*spring* (3) AZ-5
Clark Spring—*spring* CO-8
Clark Spring—*spring* ID-8
Clark Spring—*spring* (3) NV-8
Clark Spring—*spring* NM-5
Clark Spring—*spring* (3) OR-9
Clark Spring—*spring* (2) UT-8
Clark Spring Branch—*stream* AL-4
Clark Spring Canyon—*valley* NM-5
Clark Spring Fish Hatchery—*locale* AL-4
Clark Spring No 1—*spring* CO-8
Clark Spring No 2—*spring* CO-8
Clark Springs—*spring* OR-9
Clark Springs Ch—*church* LA-4
Clark Springs Ch (historical)—*church* TN-4
Clark Springs Group—*locale* MT-8
Clark Square Park—*park* IL-6
Clarks Ravine—*valley* CA-9
Clarks Ridge—*ridge* ID-8
*Clarksriff* HI-9
*Clarks River* NC-3
*Clarks River* OR-9
Clarks River—*stream* KY-4
Clarks River Ch—*church* KY-4
*Clarks Rsvr* MA-1
Clarks Rsvr—*reservoir* CA-9
Clarks Run—*stream* (2) KY-4
Clarks Run—*stream* NJ-2
Clarks Run—*stream* (3) PA-2
Clarks Run—*stream* VA-3
Clarks Sch (abandoned)—*school* PA-2
*Clarks Schoolhouse Graveyard* MS-4
Clarks Shoals—*bar* TN-4
Clarks Site—*hist pl* NE-7
Clarks Spring—*spring* NV-8
Clarks Spring—*spring* UT-8
*Clarks Station* IN-6
*Clarks Station* NV-8
Clarks Store—*locale* NC-3
Clarks Store (historical)—*locale* AL-4
Clarks Store (historical)—*locale* MS-4
Clarks Store (historical)—*locale* NC-3
Clarks Summit—*gap* CA-9
**Clarks Summit**—*pop pl* PA-2
Clarks Summit Borough—*civil* PA-2
Clarks Summit State Hosp—*hospital* PA-2
Clark State Fish Hatchery—*other* KY-4
Clark State Fishing Lake And Wildlife Area—*park* KS-7
Clark State For—*forest* IN-6
Clark Station—*locale* NV-8
Clark Station Ch—*church* GA-3
Clark Station Homesites—*locale* CA-9
*Clarkston* UT-8
Clarkston—*locale* MT-8
**Clarkston**—*pop pl* GA-3
**Clarkston**—*pop pl* MI-6
**Clarkston**—*pop pl* UT-8
**Clarkston**—*pop pl* WA-9
Clarkston (CCD)—*cens area* WA-9
Clarkston Cem—*cemetery* FL-3
Clarkston Cem—*cemetery* VA-3
Clarkston City Cem—*cemetery* UT-8
*Clarkston Creek* UT-8
Clarkston Creek—*stream* UT-8
Clarkston Golf and Country Club—*other* WA-9
**Clarkston Heights**—*pop pl* WA-9
*Clarkston Mountain* UT-8
Clarkston Mtn—*summit* UT-8
Clarkston Public Library—*hist pl* WA-9
Clarkston Sch—*school* TX-5
**Clarkston (sta.)**—*pop pl* MI-6
Clarkston (station)—*locale* MI-6
Clarkston Tithing Granary—*hist pl* UT-8
Clarkston Village Hist Dist—*hist pl* MI-6
Clark Store (historical)—*locale* MS-4
Clarkstown—*locale* NJ-2
**Clarkstown**—*pop pl* PA-2
Clarkstown Cem—*cemetery* IN-6
Clarkstown HS—*school* NY-2
Clarkstown JHS—*school* NY-2
*Clarkstown Post Office* TN-4
Clarkstown Post Office (historical)—*building* TN-4
**Clarkstown (Town of)**—*pop pl* NY-2
Clark Street Baptist Ch—*church* TN-4
Clark Street Ch of Christ—*church* KS-7
Clark Street Ch of God—*church* AL-4
Clark Street MS—*school* MS-4
Clark Street Sch—*school* AZ-5
Clark Street Sch—*school* (2) MA-1
Clark-Stringham Site—*hist pl* MI-6
Clark Summit—*summit* NH-1
*Clarks Valley* AZ-5
Clarks Valley—*basin* CA-9
Clarks Valley—*valley* (2) CA-9
Clarks Valley Ranch—*locale* CA-9
**Clarks View**—*pop pl* PA-2
**Clarks Village**—*pop pl* CT-1
**Clarks Village**—*pop pl* RI-1
*Clarksville* GA-3
*Clarksville* IN-6
*Clarksville* MS-4
*Clarksville* NH-1
*Clarksville* NY-2
*Clarksville* PA-2
Clarksville—*locale* AL-4
Clarksville—*locale* DE-2
Clarksville—*locale* IL-6
Clarksville—*locale* NJ-2
Clarksville—*locale* OR-9
Clarksville—*other* PA-2
**Clarksville**—*pop pl* AR-4
**Clarksville**—*pop pl* CA-9
**Clarksville**—*pop pl* (2) FL-3
**Clarksville**—*pop pl* ID-8
**Clarksville**—*pop pl* IL-6
**Clarksville**—*pop pl* (2) IN-6
**Clarksville**—*pop pl* IA-7
**Clarksville**—*pop pl* MD-2
**Clarksville**—*pop pl* MI-6
**Clarksville**—*pop pl* MO-7
**Clarksville**—*pop pl* NJ-2
**Clarksville**—*pop pl* NY-2
**Clarksville**—*pop pl* (2) OH-6
**Clarksville**—*pop pl* OK-5
**Clarksville**—*pop pl* (2) PA-2
**Clarksville**—*pop pl* TN-4
**Clarksville**—*pop pl* TX-5
**Clarksville**—*pop pl* (2) VA-3
Clarksville Acad—*school* TN-4
Clarksville Architectural District—*hist pl* TN-4
Clarksville Baptist Coll—*school* TN-4
Clarksville Base Physical Fitness Center—*building* TN-4
Clarksville Base (U.S. Navy)—*other* TN-4
Clarksville Boat Club—*locale* TN-4
Clarksville Borough—*civil* PA-2
Clarksville Branch—*stream* DE-2
Clarksville Bridge—*bridge* OH-6
Clarksville (CCD)—*cens area* TN-4
Clarksville (CCD)—*cens area* TX-5
Clarksville Cem—*cemetery* MI-6
Clarksville Cem—*cemetery* MS-4
Clarksville Cem—*cemetery* OH-6
Clarksville Cem—*cemetery* OK-5
Clarksville Ch—*church* NC-3
Clarksville Ch—*church* VA-3
Clarksville Ch (historical)—*church* AL-4
*Clarksville Church* AL-4
*Clarksville City* MO-7
**Clarksville City**—*pop pl* TX-5
Clarksville City Hall—*building* TN-4
*Clarksville (corporate name Clarkesville)* GA-3
Clarksville Country Club—*locale* TN-4
Clarksville Division—*civil* TN-4
Clarksville Federal Bldg—*hist pl* TN-4
Clarksville Foundry—*locale* TN-4
Clarksville Foundry and Machine Works—*hist pl* TN-4
**Clarksville Hill**—*pop pl* PA-2
Clarksville Hist Dist—*hist pl* TX-5
Clarksville HS—*hist pl* TN-4
Clarksville HS—*school* TN-4
Clarksville Industrial District—*hist pl* TN-4
Clarksville Iron Furnace—*hist pl* TN-4
Clarksville Island—*island* IL-6
*Clarksville Lake* TN-4
*Clarksville Lake Dam* TN-4
Clarksville Landing—*locale* AL-4
Clarksville (Magisterial District)—*fmr MCD* VA-3
*Clarksville Memorial Hosp* TN-4
Clarksville Methodist Church—*hist pl* TN-4
Clarksville-Montgomery County Corporate Business Park—*locale* TN-4
Clarksville-Montgomery County Historical Museum—*building* TN-4
Clarksville MS—*school* IN-6
Clarksville Mtn—*summit* AL-4
Clarksville Notch—*gap* NY-2
Clarksville Plaza—*locale* IN-6
Clarksville Pond—*lake* NH-1
Clarksville Pond Sch—*school* NH-1
Clarksville Post Office—*building* TN-4
**Clarksville Ridge**—*pop pl* MD-2
*Clarksville River* VT-1
Clarksville Sch—*school* TX-5
Clarksville Senior HS—*school* IN-6
Clarksville Square Shop Ctr—*locale* TN-4
Clarksville State Game Ref—*park* MO-7
Clarksville Town Hall—*locale* NH-1
**Clarksville (Town of)**—*pop pl* NH-1
**Clarksville (Town of)**—*pop pl* NY-2
**Clarksville Township**—*pop pl* NE-7
Clarksville (Township of)—*fmr MCD* NC-3
Clark Swamp—*stream* VA-3
Clarks Well—*well* AZ-5
Clarks Well—*well* NV-8
Clarks Woods Park—*park* IA-7
Clark Tank—*reservoir* (3) AZ-5
Clark Tank—*reservoir* (3) NM-5
Clark Tanks—*reservoir* NM-5
Clark-Taylor House—*hist pl* UT-8
Clark Thread Company Hist Dist—*hist pl* NJ-2
Clarkton—*locale* VA-3
**Clarkton**—*pop pl* MO-7
**Clarkton**—*pop pl* NC-3
Clarkton Creek—*stream* AL-4
Clarkton Depot—*hist pl* NC-3
Clarkton HS—*school* NC-3
Clarkton United Ch—*church* NC-3
Clark Towhead—*area* MS-4
Clarktown—*locale* TN-4
Clarktown—*locale* TX-5
**Clarktown**—*pop pl* OH-6
**Clarktown (Clarkstown)**—*pop pl* NJ-2
Clarktown Pond—*lake* CT-1
Clark Township—*civil* (3) MO-7
Clark Township—*fmr MCD* IA-7
**Clark Township**—*pop pl* KS-7
**Clark Township**—*pop pl* (2) MO-7
**Clark Township**—*pop pl* NE-7
**Clark Township**—*pop pl* ND-7
**Clark Township**—*pop pl* (3) SD-7
Clark (Township of)—*fmr MCD* (6) AR-4
**Clark (Township of)**—*pop pl* (3) IN-6
**Clark (Township of)**—*pop pl* MI-6
**Clark (Township of)**—*pop pl* (2) MN-6
**Clark (Township of)**—*pop pl* NJ-2
**Clark (Township of)**—*pop pl* (4) OH-6
Clark Trail—*trail* (2) CA-9
Clark Trail—*trail* NH-1
Clark Trail—*trail* (2) PA-2
Clark Tree—*locale* ID-8
Clark Tunnel—*mine* CO-8
Clark Tunnel—*tunnel* CA-9
Clark Tunnel—*tunnel* HI-9
Clark Tunnel—*tunnel* PA-2
Clark Univ—*hist pl* MA-1
Clark Univ—*school* GA-3
Clark Univ—*school* MA-1
*Clark Valley* AZ-5
*Clark Valley* CA-9
Clark Valley—*basin* CA-9
Clark Valley—*basin* ID-8
Clark Valley—*basin* UT-8
Clark Valley—*valley* (4) CA-9
Clark Valley—*valley* MN-6
*Clark Valley Reservoir* UT-8
**Clark Village Gardens Subdivision**—*pop pl* UT-8
*Clarkville* ID-8
*Clarkville* IN-6
Clarkville—*locale* CO-8
Clarkville—*locale* NY-2
Clarkville—*locale* RI-1
Clarkville Cem—*cemetery* AL-4
Clarkville Pond—*reservoir* RI-1
Clarkville Pond Dam—*dam* RI-1
Clark Ward Ch—*church* ID-8
Clark Wash—*stream* AZ-5
Clark Wash—*stream* CO-8
Clark Waterhole—*lake* TX-5
Clark Well—*locale* AZ-5
Clark Well—*well* AZ-5
Clark Well—*well* CA-9
Clark Well—*well* ID-8
Clark Well—*well* (2) NM-5
Clark Well—*well* (2) TX-5
Clark-Whitton House—*hist pl* TX-5
Clarkwild—*locale* FL-3
*Clarkwilde* FL-3
Clark Windmill—*locale* NM-5
**Clarkwood**—*pop pl* TX-5
Clarmar, Lake—*reservoir* AL-4
Clarmar Sch—*school* NE-7
**Clarmatan**—*pop pl* WV-2
**Clarmin**—*pop pl* IL-6
**Clarmont**—*pop pl* MS-4
Clarmont Memorial Gardens—*cemetery* KY-4
Clarmount Park—*park* OR-9
**Clarnie**—*pop pl* OR-9
**Clarno**—*pop pl* OR-9
**Clarno**—*pop pl* WI-6
Clarno Cem—*cemetery* OR-9
Clarno Cove—*bay* AK-9
Clarno (historical)—*locale* SD-7
Clarno Lake—*lake* MN-6
Clarno Rapids—*stream* OR-9
**Clarno (Town of)**—*pop pl* WI-6
**Clarno Township**—*pop pl* SD-7
Claron, Mount—*summit* UT-8
Claronaton Post Office (historical)—*building* TN-4
Clar-Re, Lake—*lake* WI-6
Clarrissa—*locale* NC-3
Clarrmont Central Sch—*school* NC-3
Clarr Tunnel—*tunnel* ID-8
Clarry Hill—*summit* ME-1
Clarsona—*locale* CA-9
Clary—*locale* VA-3
Clary Branch—*stream* KY-4
Clary Cem—*cemetery* FL-3
Clary Cem—*cemetery* (2) MO-7
Clary Cem—*cemetery* (2) VA-3
Clary Coulee—*valley* MT-8
Clary Creek—*stream* IL-6
Clary Creek—*stream* SC-3
Clary Ditch—*canal* IN-6
Clary JHS—*school* NY-2
Clary Lake—*lake* ME-1
Clary Spring—*spring* IL-6
Clarysville—*locale* MS-4
**Clarysville**—*pop pl* MD-2
Clarysville Post Office (historical)—*building* MS-4
Clary Tank—*reservoir* TX-5
**Claryville**—*pop pl* KY-4
**Claryville**—*pop pl* MO-7
**Claryville**—*pop pl* NY-2
Clashman Cem—*cemetery* IN-6
*Clasoil* MT-8
Clasoil—*locale* MT-8
*Clason* NY-2
Clason Point—*cape* NY-2
**Clason Point**—*pop pl* NY-2
Clason Prairie Sch—*school* WI-6
Clason Sch—*school* NY-2
*Clason's Point* NY-2
*Class Creek* PA-2
Classen, Lake—*lake* MN-6
Classen Cem—*cemetery* TX-5
Classen Falls—*falls* OK-5
Classen Hill—*summit* TX-5
Classen HS—*school* OK-5
Classen Rsvr—*reservoir* OR-9
Classen Sch—*school* IL-6
Classen Sch—*school* KS-7
Classet Creek—*stream* WA-9
*Class Eye Canyon* UT-8
Classical HS—*school* MA-1

Claypit Tanks—reservoir NM-5
Claypit Well—well NE-7
Clay Plaza (Shop Ctr)—locale FL-3
Clay Point MD-2
Clay Point—cape AK-9
Clay Point—cape FL-3
Clay Point—cape MD-2
Clay Point—cape MS-4
Clay Point—cape NH-1
Clay Point—cape NY-2
Clay Point—cape OR-9
Clay Point—cape UT-8
Clay Point—cape VT-1
Clay Point—cape VA-3
Clay Point—cliff ID-8
**Clay Point**—pop pl SD-7
Clay Point—summit CA-9
Clay Point Cem—cemetery SD-7
Clay Point Ch—church WV-2
Clay Point Park—park MS-4
Claypole Branch—stream NC-3
Claypole Cem—cemetery IA-7
Claypole Hills IN-6
Claypole Mtn—summit NC-3
Claypole Pond—lake IN-6
Claypole Run OH-6
Clay Pond—lake (2) MA-1
Clay Pond—lake NH-1
Clay Pond—lake NY-2
Claypool—locale WV-2
**Claypool**—pop pl AZ-5
**Claypool**—pop pl IL-6
**Claypool**—pop pl IN-6
**Claypool**—pop pl KY-4
**Claypool**—pop pl WV-2
Claypool Branch—stream VA-3
Claypool Branch—stream WV-2
Claypool Bridge—bridge OH-6
Claypool Butte—summit OR-9
Claypool Cem—cemetery OH-6
Claypool Cem—cemetery OR-9
Claypool Cem—cemetery VA-3
Claypool Ch—church OK-5
Claypool Clinic—hospital AZ-5
Claypool Ditch—canal IL-6
Claypoole Butte OR-9
**Claypoole Heights**—pop pl PA-2
Claypool Elem Sch—school (2) IN-6
**Claypool Hill**—pop pl VA-3
Claypool Hill—summit VA-3
Claypool Hollow—valley WV-2
Claypool Knob—summit OH-6
Claypool Pond IN-6
Claypool Post Office—building AZ-5
Claypool Rsvr—reservoir AR-4
Claypool Run—stream OH-6
Claypool Spring—spring OR-9
Clay Post Office (historical)—building MS-4
Clay Pot Bend—island FL-3
Clay Prairie—flat IN-6
Clay Prairie Ch—church IN-6
Clay Ranch—locale CO-8
Clay Ranch—locale MT-8
Clay Ranch—locale NM-5
**Clay Ridge**—pop pl PA-2
Clay Ridge Sch—school NE-7
Clay Ridge Sch—school PA-2
Clay Ridge School (abandoned)—locale WI-6
Clay Rock Ch—church TX-5
Clay Roost Bayou MO-7
Clayroot—locale NC-3
**Clayroot**—pop pl NC-3
Clay Root Bayou—stream MO-7
Clayroot Swamp—stream NC-3
Clay Rsvr—reservoir MT-8
Clay Run—stream IN-6
Clay Run—stream PA-2
Clay Run—stream (2) WV-2
Clay Run Sch—school PA-2
Clay Run Trail—trail WV-2
Clays Bar—bar AL-4
Clays Bluff—cliff AL-4
Clays Branch—stream WV-2
Claysburg IN-6
**Claysburg**—pop pl PA-2
Claysburg Kimmel HS—school PA-2
Clay Sch—school (2) CA-9
Clay Sch—school (3) IL-6
Clay Sch—school KS-7
Clay Sch—school KY-4
Clay Sch—school (3) MO-7
Clay Sch—school OH-6
Clay Sch—school VA-3
Clay Sch—school WV-2
Clay Sch—school WI-6
Clay Sch (abandoned)—school PA-2
Clay Sch (historical)—school AL-4
Clay School, The—hist pl MI-6
Clays Corner—locale TX-5
Clays Corner—locale VA-3
Clays Creek—stream MA-1
Clays Creek—stream TX-5
Clay Seep—spring (3) UT-8
Clay Seep Spring—spring AZ-5
Clays Ferry—locale KY-4
Clays Fork—stream MO-7
Clay's Hope—hist pl MD-2
**Clay Siding**—pop pl IA-7
Clay Sink—locale FL-3
Clays Jack Fork—stream KY-4
**Clays Landing**—pop pl MI-6
Clays Landing (historical)—locale AL-4
Clay Slough—stream UT-8
Clay Slough—swamp FL-3
Clays Mill—locale VA-3
**Clays Mills**—pop pl VA-3
Clays Mill Sch—school KY-4
Clay Smith Peak—summit TX-5
Clayson, George, House—hist pl IL-6
Clays Park—park OH-6
Clays Pond—lake ME-1
Clays Prairie—locale IL-6
Clay Spring—spring (6) AZ-5
Clay Spring—spring NV-8
Clay Spring—spring NM-5
Clay Spring—spring OR-9
Clay Spring—spring (4) UT-8
**Clay Springs**—pop pl AZ-5
Clay Springs—spring AZ-5
Clay Springs Post Office—building AZ-5
Clay Springs Sch—school AZ-5
Clay Springs Tank—reservoir AZ-5
Clay Spring Wash—valley UT-8
Clay Spur—locale WY-8
**Clays Ranchettes Subdivision**—pop pl UT-8
Clays Run—stream PA-2
Clays Station AL-4
Clays Store (historical)—locale MS-4
Claystone Park—park GA-3
Clay Street Baptist Ch—church AL-4
Clay Street Cem—cemetery AK-9
Clay Street Cemetery (AHRS Site No. FAI-164)—hist pl AK-9
Clay Street Elementary School NC-3
Clay Street Park—park IA-7
Clay Street Sch—school IL-6
Clay Street Sch (abandond)—school PA-2
Claysville IN-6
Claysville MS-4
Claysville—locale AL-4
Claysville—locale MD-2
Claysville—locale MO-7
Claysville—locale TN-4
**Claysville**—pop pl IL-6
**Claysville**—pop pl IN-6
**Claysville**—pop pl KY-4
**Claysville**—pop pl OH-6
**Claysville**—pop pl PA-2
**Claysville**—pop pl WV-2
Claysville Borough—civil PA-2
Claysville Cem—cemetery TN-4
Claysville Ch—church AL-4
Claysville Ch—church WV-2
Claysville JHS—school AL-4
Claysville Methodist Ch—church TN-4
Claysville Number One Dam—dam PA-2
Claysville Number One Rsvr—reservoir PA-2
Claysville Post Office (historical)—building TN-4
Claysville Sch—hist pl OH-6
Claysville Sch (abandoned)—school MO-7
Claysville Sch (historical)—school TN-4
Claysvill Number One Rsvr PA-2
Clays Well Canyon—valley AZ-5
Clay Tank—reservoir (9) AZ-5
Clay Tank—reservoir NM-5
Clay Tank—reservoir (8) TX-5
Clay Tank Canyon—valley AZ-5
Clay Tank Canyon—valley NM-5
Clay Tank Windmill—locale TX-5
Clayton WI-6
Clayton—locale CA-9
Clayton—locale PA-2
Clayton—locale SC-3
Clayton—locale TX-5
Clayton—locale WV-2
Clayton—locale WY-8
**Clayton**—pop pl AL-4
**Clayton**—pop pl CA-9
**Clayton**—pop pl DE-2
**Clayton**—pop pl GA-3
**Clayton**—pop pl ID-8
**Clayton**—pop pl IL-6
**Clayton**—pop pl IN-6
**Clayton**—pop pl IA-7
**Clayton**—pop pl KS-7
**Clayton**—pop pl LA-4
**Clayton**—pop pl MD-2
**Clayton**—pop pl MA-1
**Clayton**—pop pl MI-6
**Clayton**—pop pl MS-4
**Clayton**—pop pl MO-7
**Clayton**—pop pl NJ-2
**Clayton**—pop pl NM-5
**Clayton**—pop pl (2) NY-2
**Clayton**—pop pl NC-3
**Clayton**—pop pl (3) OH-6
**Clayton**—pop pl OK-5
**Clayton**—pop pl SD-7
**Clayton**—pop pl TN-4
**Clayton**—pop pl TX-5
**Clayton**—pop pl WA-9
**Clayton**—pop pl (2) WI-6
Clayton, Henry D., House—hist pl AL-4
Clayton, Lake—lake MN-6
Clayton, Mount—summit NM-5
Clayton, Russell, Bungalow—hist pl ID-8
Clayton, W. H. H., House—hist pl AR-4
Clayton, William L., Summer House—hist pl TX-5
Clayton Airpark—airport NC-3
Clayton Baptist Ch—church AL-4
Clayton Basin—basin NM-5
Clayton Bay—swamp (2) NC-3
Clayton Bayou—gut TX-5
Clayton Bldg—hist pl UT-8
Clayton Branch—stream AL-4
Clayton Branch—stream AR-4
Clayton Branch—stream KY-4
Clayton Branch—stream NC-3
Clayton Branch—stream (3) TN-4
Clayton Brook—stream (2) ME-1
Clayton Brownlee Elem Sch—school IN-6
Clayton Camp—locale NM-5
Clayton Camp Branch—stream TN-4
Clayton Canal—canal CA-9
Clayton (CCD)—cens area AL-4
Clayton (CCD)—cens area GA-3
Clayton Cem TN-4
Clayton Cem—cemetery AL-4
Clayton Cem—cemetery CA-9
Clayton Cem—cemetery (2) IL-6
Clayton Cem—cemetery (3) IN-6
Clayton Cem—cemetery (2) IA-7
Clayton Cem—cemetery KS-7
Clayton Cem—cemetery MI-6
Clayton Cem—cemetery MN-6
Clayton Cem—cemetery (4) MS-4
Clayton Cem—cemetery MO-7
Clayton Cem—cemetery NM-5
Clayton Cem—cemetery (2) NC-3
Clayton Cem—cemetery ND-7
Clayton Cem—cemetery OK-5
Clayton Cem—cemetery SC-3
Clayton Cem—cemetery SD-7
Clayton Cem—cemetery TN-4
Clayton Cem—cemetery WI-6
Clayton Cemeteries—cemetery IN-6
Clayton Center—locale NY-2
**Clayton Center**—pop pl IA-7
Clayton Ch—church (2) AL-4
Clayton Ch—church TX-5
Clayton Chapel—church AR-4
Clayton Coll for Boys—school CO-8
Clayton Cone—summit CO-8
Clayton Corral—locale NM-5
Clayton Coulee—valley MT-8
**Clayton (County)**—pop pl GA-3
Clayton County Courthouse—hist pl IA-7
Clayton County Fairgrounds—locale IA-7
Clayton County Farm—building IA-7
Clayton County Park PA-2
Clayton County Rsvr—reservoir GA-3
Clayton County Waterworks—other GA-3
Clayton Cove—valley (2) AL-4
Clayton Creek—gut NC-3
Clayton Creek—stream AR-4
Clayton Creek—stream CA-9
Clayton Creek—stream ID-8
Clayton Creek—stream KY-4
Clayton Creek—stream MO-7
Clayton Creek—stream MT-8
Clayton Creek—stream NM-5
Clayton Creek—stream NC-3
Clayton Creek—stream (4) OR-9
Clayton Creek—stream TX-5
Clayton Dam—dam AL-4
Clayton ditch IN-6
Clayton Ditch—canal CO-8
Clayton Ditch—canal MT-8
Clayton Division—civil AL-4
Clayton Draw—valley (2) SD-7
Clayton Draw—valley TX-5
Clayton Draw—valley WY-8
Clayton Elem Sch—school DE-2
Clayton Elem Sch—school KS-7
Clayton Elem Sch—school (2) NC-3
Clayton Elem Sch—school PA-2
Clayton Field—park NC-3
Clayton Fish Pond—reservoir AL-4
Clayton Ford Bridge—bridge AL-4
Clayton Gulch—valley WA-9
Clayton Hill—summit WA-9
Clayton Hist Dist—hist pl NY-2
Clayton Hollow—valley IL-6
Clayton Hollow—valley (2) MO-7
Clayton Hollow—valley (3) TN-4
Clayton House—hist pl TX-5
Clayton Howard Pond—lake FL-3
Clayton HS—school NC-3
Clayton HS-Auditorium—hist pl OK-5
Claytonia NE-7
Claytonia—locale ID-8
**Claytonia**—pop pl PA-2
Claytonia Creek NE-7
Clayton Intermediate Sch—school UT-8
Clayton JHS—school NV-8
Clayton Junction—uninc pl LA-4
Clayton Junior High School UT-8
Clayton Knob—summit TN-4
Clayton Lake MI-6
Clayton Lake—lake CO-8
Clayton Lake—lake LA-4
Clayton Lake—lake (2) ME-1
Clayton Lake—lake MN-6
Clayton Lake—lake MT-8
Clayton Lake—lake TX-5
Clayton Lake—locale ME-1
**Clayton Lake**—pop pl OK-5
Clayton Lake—reservoir AL-4
Clayton Lake—reservoir IL-6
Clayton Lake—reservoir NM-5
Clayton Lake—reservoir OK-5
Clayton Lake State Park—park NM-5
Clayton Lake State Rec Area—park OK-5
**Clayton Manor**—pop pl MD-2
Clayton Marina—locale MD-2
Clayton Memorial Ch—church SC-3
Clayton Mesa—summit NM-5
Clayton Mesa Trail (Pack)—trail NM-5
Clayton Methodist Ch—church AL-4
Clayton Mill Creek—stream VA-3
Clayton Mine—mine ID-8
Clayton Mtn—summit TX-5
Clayton Mtn—summit WY-8
Clayton Municipal Airp—airport AL-4
Clayton North (CCD)—cens area NM-5
Clayton Number 1 Cem—cemetery OH-6
Clayton Number 2 Cem—cemetery OH-6
Clayton Oil And Gas Field—other MI-6
Clayton Oil Field—oilfield LA-4
Clayton Oil Field—oilfield (2) TX-5
Clayton Park—flat CO-8
Clayton Park—park AL-4
Clayton Park—park CO-8
Clayton Park—park DE-2
Clayton Park—park MO-7
Clayton Park—park PA-2
**Clayton Park (subdivision)**—pop pl NC-3
Clayton Peak—summit UT-8
Clayton Plaza (Shop Ctr)—locale FL-3
Clayton Point—cape OR-9
Clayton Pond—lake ME-1
Clayton Post Office (historical)—building MS-4
Clayton Post Office (historical)—building TN-4
Clayton Presbyterian Ch—church AL-4
Clayton Primary Sch—school NC-3
Clayton Ranch—locale MT-8
Clayton Ranch—locale (2) NM-5
Clayton Ranch—locale (4) TX-5
Clayton Ranger Station—locale ID-8
Clayton Ridge—ridge MO-7
Clayton Ridge—ridge NV-8
Clayton RR Station—hist pl DE-2
Clayton Rsvr IL-6
Clayton Rsvr—reservoir CO-8
Clayton Rsvr—reservoir OR-9
Clayton Sch—hist pl IA-7
Clayton Sch—school CO-8
Clayton Sch—school IL-6
Clayton Sch—school MI-6
Clayton Sch—school MS-4
Clayton Sch—school ND-7
Clayton Sch—school OH-6
Clayton Sch—school PA-2
Clayton Sch—school SD-7
Clayton Sch—school TX-5
Clayton Sch—school WI-6
Claytons Chapel—church OK-5
Clayton Sch (historical)—school MS-4
Claytons Corner—locale NJ-2
Clayton Slope Mine (underground)—mine AL-4
Clayton's Mill Creek VA-3
Clayton South (CCD)—cens area NM-5
Claytons Pond—reservoir (2) AL-4
Clayton Spring—spring CO-8
Clayton Spring—spring NM-5
Clayton Spring—spring OR-9
Clayton Spring—spring TX-5
Clayton Spring—spring UT-8
Clayton Station—locale MD-2
Clayton Store (historical)—locale MS-4
Clayton Stream—stream ME-1
Clayton Street HS (historical)—school AL-4
Clayton Street Methodist Episcopal Ch—church AL-4
Clayton Street Sch—school CO-8
**Clayton Subdivision**—pop pl UT-8
Clayton Tank—reservoir TX-5
**Clayton (Town of)**—pop pl (3) WI-6
Clayton Township—civil MO-7
Clayton Township—fmr MCD (2) IA-7
**Clayton Township**—pop pl ND-7
**Clayton Township**—pop pl SD-7
Clayton (Township of)—fmr MCD (2) AR-4
Clayton (Township of)—fmr MCD NC-3
**Clayton (Township of)**—pop pl (2) IL-6
**Clayton (Township of)**—pop pl (2) MI-6
**Clayton (Township of)**—pop pl MN-6
**Clayton (Township of)**—pop pl OH-6
Clayton Trail—trail OK-5
Clayton Valley—basin NV-8
Clayton Valley—valley CA-9
Clayton Valley HS—school CA-9
Clayton Valley Sch—school CA-9
Clayton Village—locale MO-7
**Clayton Village**—pop pl MS-4
Clayton Village (Shop Ctr)—locale MO-7
Clayton Village Shop Ctr—locale NC-3
**Clayton Villa Subdivision**—pop pl UT-8
Claytonville—locale TX-5
Claytonville—locale VA-3
**Claytonville**—pop pl IL-6
**Claytonville**—pop pl TX-5
Claytonville Cem—cemetery KS-7
Clayton Ville (historical)—locale KS-7
Claytonville Oil Field—oilfield TX-5
Clayton Vineyards-DeMartini Winery—hist pl CA-9
Clayton Well—well NM-5
Clayton Wells—well NM-5
Claytor Dam—dam VA-3
Claytor Lake—reservoir VA-3
Claytor Lake State Park—park VA-3
Claytor Ranch—locale (2) WY-8
Claytor Sch—school WY-8
**Claytown**—pop pl MS-4
**Clay (Town of)**—pop pl NY-2
Clay Township—civ div NE-7
Clay Township—civil (13) MO-7
Clay Township—fmr MCD (11) IA-7
**Clay Township**—pop pl (2) KS-7
**Clay Township**—pop pl (4) MO-7
**Clay Township**—pop pl ND-7
Clay Township Cem—cemetery IA-7
Clay (Township of)—fmr MCD (3) AR-4
Clay (Township of)—fmr MCD NC-3
**Clay (Township of)**—pop pl (17) IN-6
**Clay (Township of)**—pop pl MI-6
**Clay (Township of)**—pop pl (9) OH-6
**Clay (Township of)**—pop pl (3) PA-2
Clay (Unorganized Territory of)—unorg MN-6
Clay Valley—valley UT-8
Clay Valley Sch—school SD-7
Clayview Country Club—other MO-7
**Clay Village**—pop pl KY-4
Clayville PA-2
Clayville—locale CT-1
Clayville—locale IL-6
Clayville—locale NJ-2
**Clayville**—pop pl NY-2
**Clayville**—pop pl RI-1
**Clayville**—pop pl VA-3
Clayville Hist Dist—hist pl RI-1
Clayville Pond—lake CT-1
Clayville Sch—school NJ-2
Clayville Tavern—hist pl IL-6
Clay Waterhole—lake TX-5
Claywell—locale KY-4
Clay Well—well AZ-5
Clay Well—well NM-5
Claywell Creek—stream KS-7
Claywell Elem Sch—school FL-3
Clay Well (historical)—locale NM-5
Claywell Sch—school IL-6
Clay West Oil Field—oilfield TX-5
Claywill Ch—church KY-4
Clay Windmill—locale NM-5
**Claywood**—pop pl WI-6
Claywood, Mount—summit WA-9
Claywood Cem—cemetery FL-3
Claywood Ch—church FL-3
Claywood Lake—lake WA-9
**Clayworks**—pop pl IA-7
Clay-Yankton Ditch SD-7
C Lazy U Ranch—locale CO-8
C L Creek—stream MT-8
Cleage, Samuel, House—hist pl TN-4
Cleages Chapel African Methodist Episcopal Zion Ch—church TN-4
Cleale, Joseph, House—hist pl MA-1
Clealum WA-9
Clealum Lake WA-9
Clealum River WA-9
Clean Claw Mtn—summit AL-4
Clean Creek—stream WA-9
Clean Fork WV-2
Clean Fork—stream OH-6
Clean Shore—beach MA-1
Clean-Washed MH-9
Clean-Washed Beach MH-9
Clear—post sta AK-9
Clear, Bayou—stream LA-4
Clear, Lake—lake NY-2
Clear, Lake—lake SC-3
**Clear, Lake**—pop pl NY-2
Clear, Lake—reservoir TX-5
Clear, Point—cape MS-4
Clear Basin—lake FL-3
Clear Bay—bay CA-9
Clear Bayou—stream (2) LA-4
Clear Boggy Creek—stream OK-5
Clear Bonnet—island NJ-2
Clear Bottom Lake—lake MI-6
Clear Bottom Pond—lake MA-1
Clear Branch MS-4
Clear Branch NC-3
Clear Branch TX-5
**Clear Branch**—pop pl MS-4
**Clearbranch**—pop pl TN-4
Clear Branch—stream (6) AL-4
Clear Branch—stream AR-4
Clear Branch—stream FL-3
Clear Branch—stream (3) IN-6
Clear Branch—stream (3) KY-4
Clear Branch—stream (11) LA-4
Clear Branch—stream (5) MS-4
Clear Branch—stream (5) MO-7
Clear Branch—stream (6) NC-3
Clear Branch—stream OR-9
Clear Branch—stream SC-3
Clear Branch—stream (9) TN-4
Clear Branch—stream (10) TX-5
Clear Branch Baptist Ch—church TN-4
Clear Branch Cem—cemetery MS-4
Clear Branch Ch—church (3) MS-4
Clear Branch Ch—church NC-3
Clear Branch Ch—church (2) TN-4
Clear Branch Ch—church VA-3
Clear Branch Gap—gap AL-4
Clear Branch Post Office TN-4
Clearbranch Post Office (historical)—building TN-4
Clear Branch Sch—school NC-3
Clear Brook ME-1
Clear Brook NY-2
Clearbrook—locale WA-9
**Clearbrook**—pop pl MN-6
**Clearbrook**—pop pl PA-2
**Clear Brook**—pop pl VA-3
**Clearbrook**—pop pl VA-3
Clear Brook—stream CT-1
Clear Brook—stream DE-2
Clear Brook—stream IN-6
Clear Brook—stream MA-1
Clear Brook—stream (2) NH-1
Clear Brook—stream (2) NY-2
Clearbrook Ch—church VA-3
Clearbrook Lake—lake MN-6
Clearbrook Run—stream VA-3
Clearbrook Sch—school VA-3
**Clearbrook Village**—pop pl PA-2
Clear Canyon—valley OK-5
Clear Cem—cemetery TN-4
Clearco—locale WV-2
Clear Cortright Creek WA-9
Clear Creek AL-4
Clear Creek AZ-5
Clear Creek AR-4
Clear Creek CO-8
Clear Creek ID-8
Clear Creek IN-6
Clear Creek IA-7
Clear Creek KS-7
Clear Creek KY-4
Clear Creek MI-6
Clear Creek MS-4
Clear Creek MO-7
Clear Creek OR-9
Clear Creek TN-4
Clear Creek TX-5
Clearcreek UT-8
Clear Creek WA-9
Clear Creek—fmr MCD NE-7
Clear Creek—locale CA-9
Clear Creek—locale TX-5
Clear Creek—locale UT-8
Clear Creek—other KY-4
**Clear Creek**—pop pl AZ-5
**Clear Creek**—pop pl CA-9
**Clear Creek**—pop pl CO-8
**Clear Creek**—pop pl IN-6
**Clear Creek**—pop pl KY-4
**Clear Creek**—pop pl MO-7
**Clear Creek**—pop pl NY-2
**Clearcreek**—pop pl NC-3
**Clear Creek**—pop pl OR-9
**Clear Creek**—pop pl UT-8
**Clear Creek**—pop pl WV-2
Clear Creek—post sta TX-5
Clear Creek—stream (19) AL-4
Clear Creek—stream (11) AK-9
Clear Creek—stream (3) AZ-5
Clear Creek—stream (22) AR-4
Clear Creek—stream (29) CA-9
Clear Creek—stream (14) CO-8
Clear Creek—stream (4) FL-3
Clear Creek—stream (13) GA-3
Clear Creek—stream (18) ID-8
Clear Creek—stream (13) IL-6
Clear Creek—stream (10) IN-6
Clear Creek—stream (2) IA-7
Clear Creek*—stream IA-7
Clear Creek—stream (6) IA-7
Clear Creek—stream (10) KS-7
Clear Creek—stream (18) KY-4
Clear Creek—stream (11) LA-4
Clear Creek—stream (12) MI-6
Clear Creek—stream (6) MN-6
Clear Creek—stream (24) MS-4
Clear Creek—stream (23) MO-7
Clear Creek—stream (18) MT-8
Clear Creek—stream (6) NE-7
Clear Creek—stream (8) NV-8
Clear Creek—stream (4) NM-5
Clear Creek—stream (4) NY-2
Clear Creek—stream (9) NC-3
Clear Creek—stream (2) ND-7
Clear Creek—stream (11) OH-6
Clear Creek—stream (22) OK-5
Clear Creek—stream (32) OR-9
Clear Creek—stream (3) PA-2
Clear Creek—stream SC-3
Clear Creek—stream SD-7
Clear Creek—stream (19) TN-4
Clear Creek—stream (35) TX-5
Clear Creek—stream (11) UT-8
Clear Creek—stream (3) VA-3
Clear Creek—stream (10) WA-9
Clear Creek—stream WV-2
Clear Creek—stream (7) WI-6
Clear Creek—stream (15) WY-8
Clear Creek Acad (historical)—school TN-4
Clear Creek Baptist Ch (historical)—church AL-4
Clear Creek Baptist Church AL-4
Clear Creek Baptist Church MS-4
Clear Creek Bridge—bridge AZ-5
Clear Creek Butte—summit AK-9
Clear Creek Camp—locale OR-9
Clear Creek Camp—park OR-9
Clear Creek Camp Ground—locale CA-9
Clear Creek Campground—locale NM-5
Clear Creek Campground—locale (2) UT-8
Clear Creek Campground—park AZ-5
Clear Creek Campground—park OR-9
Clear Creek Canal—canal TN-4
Clear Creek Canyon AZ-5
Clear Creek Canyon—valley CO-8
Clear Creek Canyon—valley UT-8
Clear Creek Cem—cemetery AL-4
Clear Creek Cem—cemetery AZ-5
Clear Creek Cem—cemetery AR-4
Clear Creek Cem—cemetery CA-9
Clear Creek Cem—cemetery IN-6
Clear Creek Cem—cemetery (2) KS-7
Clear Creek Cem—cemetery KY-4
Clear Creek Cem—cemetery (4) MS-4
Clear Creek Cem—cemetery MO-7
Clear Creek Cem—cemetery MT-8
Clear Creek Cem—cemetery NE-7
Clear Creek Cem—cemetery (2) OK-5
Clear Creek Cem—cemetery (2) TN-4
Clear Creek Cem—cemetery (3) TX-5
Clear Creek Cem—cemetery UT-8
Clear Creek Ch AL-4
Clear Creek Ch—church (3) AL-4
Clear Creek Ch—church AR-4
Clear Creek Ch—church (3) GA-3
Clear Creek Ch—church (3) IN-6
Clear Creek Ch—church (2) KY-4
Clear Creek Ch—church LA-4
Clear Creek Ch—church (11) MS-4
Clear Creek Ch—church (3) MO-7
Clear Creek Ch—church (4) NC-3
Clear Creek Ch—church ND-7
Clear Creek Ch—church OH-6
Clear Creek Ch—church (2) OK-5
Clear Creek Ch—church PA-2
Clear Creek Ch—church (5) TN-4
Clear Creek Ch—church (3) TX-5
Clear Creek Channel—channel TX-5
Clear Creek Ch (historical)—church (2) AL-4
Clear Creek Ch (historical)—church TN-4
Clear Creek Church—hist pl AZ-5
Clear Creek Dam—dam OR-9
Clear Creek Dam Number One—dam AZ-5
Clear Creek Ditch—canal CO-8
Clear Creek Ditch—canal IL-6
Clear Creek Ditch—canal MT-8
Clear Creek Ditch—canal OR-9
**Clear Creek Estates**—pop pl AL-4
Clear Creek Falls—falls WY-8
Clear Creek Flats—flat UT-8
Clear Creek Forest Camp—locale OR-9
Clear Creek Furnace—locale KY-4
Clear Creek Gold Discovery Historical Marker—other CA-9
Clear Creek Guard Station—locale ID-8
Clear Creek Guard Station—locale UT-8
Clear Creek Gulf—valley TN-4
Clear Creek Harbor—locale AL-4
Clear Creek (historical)—locale KS-7
**Clear Creek (historical)**—pop pl NC-3
Clear Creek (historical P.O.)—locale IA-7
Clear Creek Hunting Club—locale AL-4
Clear Creek Junction KY-4
Clear Creek Junction—locale CA-9
Clear Creek Junction—locale TN-4
**Clear Creek Junction**—pop pl CA-9
**Clear Creek Junction**—pop pl KY-4
Clear Creek Lake—lake WY-8
Clear Creek Lake—reservoir AZ-5
Clear Creek Lake—reservoir KS-7
Clear Creek Lake—reservoir OK-5
Clear Creek Lake—reservoir TN-4
Clear Creek Lake—reservoir TX-5
Clear Creek Lake—reservoir VA-3
Clear Creek Lake Dam—dam TN-4
Clear Creek Landing Public Use Area—park MS-4
Clear Creek Lateral—canal CA-9
Clear Creek (locale)—locale PA-2
Clear Creek Marina—locale AL-4
Clear Creek Meadow—flat NV-8
Clear Creek Methodist Ch—church AL-4
Clear Creek Mill—locale (2) TN-4
Clear Creek Mine—mine (2) CA-9
Clear Creek Mines No 3—mine UT-8
Clear Creek Mines No 4—mine UT-8
Clear Creek Mountains UT-8
Clear Creek Mtn—summit NM-5
Clear Creek Mtn—summit UT-8
Clear Creek Natural Bridge—arch WY-8
Clear Creek Number Four Spring—spring AZ-5
Clear Creek Number One Spring—spring AZ-5
Clear Creek Number Three ID-8
Clear Creek Number Three Spring—spring AZ-5
Clear Creek Number Two Dam—dam AZ-5
Clear Creek Number Two Spring—spring AZ-5
Clear Creek Oil and Gas Field—oilfield ND-7
Clear Creek Oil Field—oilfield LA-4
Clear Creek Oil Field—oilfield TX-5
Clear Creek Park—park IN-6
Clear Creek Park—park MO-7
**Clear Creek Park**—pop pl AK-9
Clear Creek P. O. AL-4
Clear Creek Pond—reservoir GA-3
Clear Creek Post Office (historical)—building TN-4
Clear Creek Primitive Baptist Ch AL-4
Clear Creek Public Use Area—park AR-4
Clear Creek Pueblo and Caves—hist pl AZ-5
Clear Creek Ranch—locale (3) NV-8
Clear Creek Ranch—other MS-4
Clear Creek Range WY-8
Clear Creek Rec Area—park TN-4
Clear Creek Recreation Site UT-8
Clear Creek Reservoir WA-9
Clear Creek Ridge—ridge NC-3

Clear Creek Ridge—*ridge* UT-8
Clear Creek Ridge Tank—*reservoir* AZ-5
Clear Creek Rsvr—*reservoir* AZ-5
Clear Creek Rsvr—*reservoir* CO-8
Clear Creek Rsvr—*reservoir* OR-9
Clear Creek Sch—*school* AR-4
Clear Creek Sch—*school* (3) CA-9
Clear Creek Sch—*school* IL-6
Clear Creek Sch—*school* IA-7
Clear Creek Sch—*school* KS-7
Clear Creek Sch—*school* (2) KY-4
Clear Creek Sch—*school* MT-8
Clear Creek Sch—*school* (3) NE-7
Clear Creek Sch—*school* (2) NC-3
Clear Creek Sch (abandoned)—*school* MO-7
Clear Creek Sch (historical)—*school* (4) MS-4
Clear Creek Sch (historical)—*school* NC-3
Clear Creek Sch (historical)—*school* TN-4
Clear Creek School Camp—*locale* CA-9
Clear Creek Sinks (historical)—*basin* AL-4
Clear Creek Spring—*spring* MO-7
Clear Creek Spring—*spring* TN-4
**Clear Creek Springs**—*pop pl* KY-4
Clear Creek Springs—*spring* NE-7
Clear Creek Springs—*spring* TN-4
Clear Creek State Park—*park* PA-2
Clear Creek State Park Day Use District—*hist pl* PA-2
Clear Creek State Park Family Cabin District—*hist pl* PA-2
Clear Creek State Waterfowl Mngmt Area—*park* NE-7
Clear Creek Station—*locale* CA-9
Clear Creek Store—*locale* NM-5
**Clear Creek (subdivision)**—*pop pl* NC-3
Clear Creek Summit—*summit* (3) ID-8
**Clear Creek (Town of)**—*pop pl* WI-6
Clear Creek Township—*civil* MO-7
Clear Creek Township—*fmr MCD* (3) IA-7
**Clear Creek Township**—*pop pl* (5) KS-7
**Clear Creek Township**—*pop pl* MO-7
**Clear Creek Township**—*pop pl* NE-7
Clear Creek (Township of)—*fmr MCD* (3) AR-4
Clear Creek (Township of)—*fmr MCD* NC-3
**Clear Creek (Township of)**—*pop pl* (2) IN-6
**Clear Creek (Township of)**—*pop pl* (3) OH-6
Clear Creek Trail—*trail* AZ-5
Clear Creek Trail—*trail* CA-9
Clear Creek Trail—*trail* ID-8
Clear Creek Trail—*trail* NM-5
Clear Creek Trail—*trail* OK-5
Clear Creek Trail—*trail* TN-4
Clear Creek Trail—*trail* WY-8
Clear Creek Trail Camp—*locale* NM-5
Clear Creek Trout Pond—*lake* MI-6
Clear Creek Tunnel—*tunnel* CA-9
Clear Creek (Unorganized Territory of)—*unorg* MN-6
Clear Creek Valley—*valley* WA-9
Clear Creek Way Trail—*trail* OR-9
Clear Creek Youth Center—*building* NV-8
Clearcrest Country Club—*other* IN-6
*Clear Crooked Lake* WI-6
Clear Cut Cem—*cemetery* KS-7
*Cleardale* KS-7
Clear Dale (historical)—*locale* KS-7
Clear Drain—*stream* WV-2
Clear Falls Pond—*reservoir* MA-1
Clearfield—*locale* KS-7
Clearfield—*locale* SD-7
**Clearfield**—*pop pl* IA-7
**Clearfield**—*pop pl* KY-4
**Clearfield**—*pop pl* MD-2
**Clearfield**—*pop pl* NY-2
**Clearfield**—*pop pl* (2) PA-2
**Clearfield**—*pop pl* UT-8
**Clearfield**—*pop pl* VA-3
**Clearfield**—*pop pl* WV-2
Clearfield And Curwensville Country Club—*other* PA-2
Clearfield Area HS—*school* PA-2
Clearfield Area MS—*school* PA-2
Clearfield Borough—*civil* PA-2
*Clearfield Bridge* PA-2
Clearfield Ch—*church* PA-2
Clearfield City Cem—*cemetery* UT-8
Clearfield Community Ch—*church* UT-8
**Clearfield County**—*pop pl* PA-2
Clearfield County Courthouse—*hist pl* PA-2
Clearfield Creek—*stream* PA-2
**Clearfield Estates Subdivision**—*pop pl* UT-8
Clearfield Farm—*hist pl* DE-2
**Clearfield Heights Subdivision**—*pop pl* UT-8
Clearfield HS—*school* UT-8
Clearfield JHS (abandoned)—*school* PA-2
Clearfield Junction—*locale* PA-2
Clearfield-Lawrence Airp—*airport* PA-2
**Clearfield & Mahoning Junction**—*pop pl* PA-2
*Clearfield Nursery* PA-2
Clearfield Rsvr—*reservoir* PA-2
Clearfield Sch—*school* PA-2
Clearfield Shop Ctr—*locale* UT-8
Clearfield State Tree Nursery—*forest* PA-2
**Clearfield (subdivision)**—*pop pl* DE-2
**Clearfield Terrace Subdivision**—*pop pl* UT-8
Clearfield Town Hall—*building* ND-7
**Clearfield (Town of)**—*pop pl* WI-6
**Clearfield Township**—*pop pl* ND-7
**Clearfield (Township of)**—*pop pl* (2) PA-2
**Clearfield Villa Subdivision**—*pop pl* UT-8
*Clear Fork* AZ-5
*Clear Fork* TN-4
*Clear Fork* TX-5
Clear Fork—*locale* VA-3
**Clearfork**—*pop pl* VA-3
**Clear Fork**—*pop pl* WV-2
Clear Fork—*stream* AL-4
Clear Fork—*stream* AK-9
Clear Fork—*stream* (2) AR-4
Clear Fork—*stream* (2) CO-8
Clear Fork—*stream* (2) IN-6
Clear Fork—*stream* KS-7
Clear Fork—*stream* (6) KY-4
Clear Fork—*stream* LA-4
Clear Fork—*stream* MI-6
Clear Fork—*stream* (4) MO-7
Clear Fork—*stream* (6) OH-6
Clear Fork—*stream* OR-9
Clear Fork—*stream* (5) TN-4
Clear Fork—*stream* (2) TX-5
Clear Fork—*stream* (2) VA-3
Clear Fork—*stream* (5) WV-2
*Clear Fork Big Nance Creek* AL-4
Clear Fork Blackwater River—*stream* MO-7
Clear Fork Branch—*stream* (2) KY-4
Clear Fork Branch—*stream* VA-3
Clear Fork Branch—*stream* WV-2
Clear Fork Butte—*summit* OR-9
Clear Fork Cem—*cemetery* (2) KY-4
Clearfork Cem—*cemetery* MO-7
Clear Fork Cem—*cemetery* OH-6
Clear Fork Ch—*church* IN-6
Clear Fork Ch—*church* (6) KY-4
Clear Fork Ch—*church* (2) OH-6
Clear Fork Ch—*church* OK-5
Clear Fork Ch—*church* TN-4
Clear Fork Ch—*church* (2) TX-5
Clear Fork Ch—*church* VA-3
Clear Fork Cowlitz River—*stream* WA-9
*Clear Fork Creek* CO-8
*Clear Fork Creek* TN-4
Clear Fork Creek—*stream* KY-4
Clear Fork Creek—*stream* TN-4
Clear Fork Creek—*stream* (3) TX-5
*Clear Fork Denton Creek* TX-5
*Clear Fork Ditch* IN-6
Clear Fork Ditch—*canal* CO-8
*Clearfork Gap* WV-2
Clear Fork Gap—*gap* WV-2
**Clear Fork Junction**—*pop pl* WV-2
Clear Fork Lake—*reservoir* MO-7
Clear Fork Licking River—*stream* OH-6
Clear Fork Little Muskingum River—*stream* OH-6
Clear Fork (Magisterial District)—*fmr MCD* VA-3
Clear Fork (Magisterial District)—*fmr MCD* WV-2
Clear Fork Mohican River—*stream* OH-6
Clear Fork Muddy Creek—*stream* WY-8
*Clear Fork of Brazos River* TX-5
Clear Fork Park—*flat* CO-8
Clear Fork Plum Creek—*stream* TX-5
Clear Fork Ridge—*ridge* KY-4
*Clear Fork River* TN-4
Clear Fork Rsvr—*reservoir* OH-6
*Clear Fork Sandies Creek* TX-5
Clearfork Sch—*school* MO-7
Clear Fork Ski Haven—*other* TX-5
**Clear Fork Township**—*pop pl* KS-7
Clear Fork Trail—*trail* WA-9
Clear Fork Trinity River—*stream* TX-5
Clear Fork Valley Ch—*church* WV-2
Clear Glacier—*glacier* AK-9
Clear Gulch—*valley* CA-9
Clear Hill—*summit* MA-1
*Clearing* IL-6
**Clearing**—*pop pl* IL-6
Clearing, The—*flat* CA-9
Clearing, The—*hist pl* WI-6
Clearing Creek—*stream* OR-9
**Clearing House**—*pop pl* CA-9
Clearing Point—*cape* AK-9
Clearing Ridge—*ridge* TN-4
*Clearing (sta.)* IL-6
*Clear Lake* AR-4
*Clear Lake* CA-9
*Clear Lake* IL-6
*Clear Lake* IN-6
*Clear Lake* LA-4
*Clear Lake* MI-6
*Clear Lake* MN-6
*Clear Lake* ND-7
*Clear Lake* SD-7
*Clear Lake* WA-9
*Clear Lake* WI-6
Clear Lake—*bay* LA-4
Clear Lake—*lake* AL-4
Clear Lake—*lake* (2) AK-9
Clear Lake—*lake* AZ-5
Clear Lake—*lake* (12) AR-4
Clear Lake—*lake* (6) CA-9
Clear Lake—*lake* (3) CO-8
Clear Lake—*lake* CT-1
Clear Lake—*lake* (13) FL-3
Clear Lake—*lake* (2) GA-3
Clear Lake—*lake* (8) IL-6
Clear Lake—*lake* (4) IN-6
Clear Lake—*lake* (2) IA-7
Clear Lake—*lake* KS-7
Clear Lake—*lake* KY-4
Clear Lake—*lake* (10) LA-4
Clear Lake—*lake* ME-1
Clear Lake—*lake* (33) MI-6
Clear Lake—*lake* (36) MN-6
Clear Lake—*lake* (8) MS-4
Clear Lake—*lake* (3) MO-7
Clear Lake—*lake* (3) MT-8
Clear Lake—*lake* (7) NE-7
Clear Lake—*lake* NV-8
Clear Lake—*lake* (7) NY-2
Clear Lake—*lake* (5) ND-7
Clear Lake—*lake* (5) OK-5
Clear Lake—*lake* (10) OR-9
Clear Lake—*lake* (5) SD-7
Clear Lake—*lake* TN-4
Clear Lake—*lake* (16) TX-5
Clear Lake—*lake* UT-8
Clear Lake—*lake* (13) WA-9
Clear Lake—*lake* (22) WI-6
Clear Lake—*lake* (3) WY-8
Clear Lake—*locale* AR-4
Clear Lake—*locale* OK-5
Clear Lake—*locale* TX-5
Clear Lake—*locale* UT-8
**Clearlake**—*pop pl* CA-9
**Clear Lake**—*pop pl* FL-3
**Clear Lake**—*pop pl* (2) IL-6
**Clear Lake**—*pop pl* IN-6
**Clear Lake**—*pop pl* (2) MI-6
**Clear Lake**—*pop pl* MN-6
**Clear Lake**—*pop pl* OR-9
**Clear Lake**—*pop pl* SD-7
**Clear Lake**—*pop pl* WA-9
**Clear Lake**—*pop pl* WI-6
Clear Lake—*reservoir* AR-4
Clear Lake—*reservoir* CO-8
Clear Lake—*reservoir* FL-3
Clear Lake—*reservoir* (2) GA-3
Clear Lake—*reservoir* ID-8
Clear Lake—*reservoir* IL-6
Clear Lake—*reservoir* (2) LA-4
Clear Lake—*reservoir* MN-6
Clear Lake—*reservoir* MO-7
Clear Lake—*reservoir* NY-2
Clear Lake—*reservoir* OR-9
Clear Lake—*reservoir* PA-2
Clear Lake—*reservoir* TX-5
Clear Lake—*reservoir* WA-9
Clear Lake—*swamp* IL-6
Clear Lake—*swamp* (2) LA-4
Clear Lake—*swamp* MN-6
Clear Lake Ave Interchange—*other* IL-6
Clear Lakebed—*flat* (2) MN-6
Clear Lake Butte—*summit* OR-9
Clear Lake Camp—*locale* MI-6
Clear Lake Campground—*locale* CO-8
Clear Lake Campground—*locale* FL-3
Clear Lake (CCD)—*cens area* WA-9
Clear Lake Cem—*cemetery* MI-6
Clear Lake Cem—*cemetery* MS-4
Clear Lake Cem—*cemetery* MT-8
Clear Lake Cem—*cemetery* OK-5
Clear Lake Cem—*cemetery* SD-7
Clear Lake Cem—*cemetery* (2) TX-5
Clear Lake Ch—*church* (2) AR-4
Clear Lake Ch—*church* IN-6
Clear Lake Ch—*church* (2) LA-4
Clear Lake Ch—*church* (2) MN-6
Clear Lake Ch—*church* MS-4
**Clear Lake City**—*pop pl* TX-5
Clear Lake City Square—*park* IA-7
**Clear Lake (Clear Lake City)**—*pop pl* IA-7
Clear Lake Dam—*dam* OR-9
Clear Lake Dam—*dam* PA-2
Clear Lake Drain—*canal* TN-4
Clear Lake Golf Course—*other* OR-9
**Clearlake Highlands**—*pop pl* CA-9
Clearlake Highlands-Clearlake Park—*CDP* CA-9
Clear Lake Hills—*summit* CA-9
Clear Lake (historical)—*lake* MS-4
Clear Lake (historical)—*lake* (2) TN-4
Clear Lake JHS—*school* CO-8
Clear Lake Junction—*locale* AR-4
**Clear Lake Junction**—*pop pl* IA-7
Clearlake MS—*school* FL-3
Clear Lake Mtn—*summit* ME-1
Clear Lake Municipal Airp—*airport* SD-7
Clear Lake Natl Wildlife Ref—*park* CA-9
**Clearlake Oaks**—*pop pl* CA-9
Clearlake Oaks (Stubbs)—*CDP* CA-9
Clear Lake Oil Field—*oilfield* TX-5
Clear Lake One—*reservoir* LA-4
Clear Lake Outing Club—*other* IL-6
Clear Lake Parish House—*church* MN-6
*Clear Lake Park* CA-9
Clear Lake Park—*park* MI-6
Clear Lake Park—*park* TX-5
**Clearlake Park**—*pop pl* CA-9
Clear Lake Post Office (historical)—*building* SD-7
Clear Lake Recreation Site—*park* OR-9
**Clear Lake Resort**—*pop pl* OR-9
**Clearlake (RR name Clear Lake)**—*pop pl* WA-9
Clear Lake (RR name for Clearlake)—*other* WA-9
Clear Lake Rsvr—*reservoir* CA-9
Clear Lake Rsvr—*reservoir* ID-8
Clear Lakes—*lake* AK-9
Clear Lakes—*lake* ID-8
Clear Lakes—*lake* TX-5
Clear Lake Sch—*school* (2) MI-6
Clear Lake Sch—*school* MN-6
Clear Lake Sch—*school* OR-9
Clear Lake Sch—*school* TX-5
Clear Lakes Golf Course—*other* ID-8
**Clear Lake Shores**—*pop pl* TX-5
Clear Lake Site—*hist pl* IL-6
Clear Lake State Game Mngmt Area—*park* IA-7
Clear Lake State Park—*park* CA-9
Clear Lake Tank—*reservoir* AZ-5
**Clear Lake (Town of)**—*pop pl* WI-6
Clear Lake Township—*fmr MCD* (2) IA-7
**Clear Lake Township**—*pop pl* (2) ND-7
**Clear Lake Township**—*pop pl* (3) SD-7
Clear Lake (Township of)—*fmr MCD* AR-4
**Clear Lake (Township of)**—*pop pl* IL-6
**Clear Lake (Township of)**—*pop pl* IN-6
**Clear Lake (Township of)**—*pop pl* MN-6
Clear Lake Village Park—*park* WI-6
Clear Lake Waterfowl Mngmt Area—*park* UT-8
Clear Lick Hollow—*valley* IN-6
Clear Lost Trail—*trail* WA-9
**Clearman**—*pop pl* MS-4
Clearman Camp—*locale* MI-6
Clearman Post Office (historical)—*building* MS-4
Clear Marais—*lake* LA-4
*Clear Meadow Branch* TN-4
Clear Mews—*other* AK-9
Clear Missile Early Warning Station—*military* AK-9
Clearmont—*locale* TN-4
**Clearmont**—*pop pl* MO-7
**Clearmont**—*pop pl* SC-3
**Clearmont**—*pop pl* WY-8
Clearmont Cem—*cemetery* NC-3
Clearmont Ch—*church* NC-3
Clearmont Jail—*hist pl* WY-8
Clearmont Post Office (historical)—*building* TN-4
Clearmont Sch—*school* IL-6
Clearmont Sch—*school* NC-3
Clearmount Sch—*school* OH-6
Clear Peak—*summit* MT-8
Clear Point—*cape* (2) AK-9
Clear Point—*locale* AR-4
Clear Point—*summit* OR-9
Clearpoint Creek—*stream* AR-4
Clear Pointe Plaza Shop Ctr—*locale* MS-4
*Clear Pond* MA-1
*Clear Pond* NY-2
Clear Pond—*lake* AR-4
Clear Pond—*lake* (4) FL-3
Clear Pond—*lake* (2) IL-6
Clear Pond—*lake* IN-6
Clear Pond—*lake* (3) KY-4
Clear Pond—*lake* (2) ME-1
Clear Pond—*lake* (3) MA-1
Clear Pond—*lake* MO-7
Clear Pond—*lake* (16) NY-2
Clear Pond—*lake* NC-3
Clear Pond—*lake* (2) SC-3
Clear Pond—*lake* TX-5
Clear Pond—*lake* VT-1
Clear Pond—*locale* SC-3
Clear Pond—*reservoir* KS-7
Clear Pond—*reservoir* MA-1
Clear Pond Dam—*dam* MA-1
*Clear Pond Ditch* IN-6
Clear Pond Ditch—*canal* IL-6
Clear Pond Ditch—*canal* IN-6
Clear Pond Inlet—*stream* NY-2
Clear Pond Mtn—*summit* ME-1
Clear Pond Mtn—*summit* NY-2
Clear Pond Sch—*school* SC-3
Clear Pond Trail—*trail* NY-2
Clear Pond West Dike—*dam* MA-1
Clear Pool—*lake* NY-2
Clear Pool Camp—*locale* NY-2
Clearport—*locale* OH-6
Clear Prong—*stream* AL-4
Clear Prong—*stream* KY-4
Clear Prong—*stream* LA-4
Clear Prong—*stream* MS-4
Clear Prong—*stream* TN-4
Clear Prong—*stream* TX-5
**Clear Ridge**—*pop pl* MD-2
**Clear Ridge**—*pop pl* (2) PA-2
Clear Ridge—*ridge* CA-9
Clear Ridge—*ridge* (2) PA-2
Clear Ridge Ch—*church* PA-2
*Clear River* MN-6
Clear River—*stream* (2) AK-9
Clear River—*stream* RI-1
*Clear Run* MA-1
Clear Run—*hist pl* NC-3
Clear Run—*locale* NC-3
**Clear Run**—*pop pl* KY-4
**Clear Run**—*pop pl* PA-2
Clear Run—*stream* IN-6
Clear Run—*stream* (3) KY-4
Clear Run—*stream* LA-4
Clear Run—*stream* MS-4
Clear Run—*stream* NJ-2
Clear Run—*stream* NC-3
Clear Run—*stream* (7) PA-2
Clear Run Brook—*stream* MA-1
Clear Run Cem—*cemetery* IN-6
Clear Run Ch—*church* KY-4
Clear Run MS—*school* NC-3
Clear Runner—*stream* LA-4
Clear Runner Branch—*stream* LA-4
Clear Running Branch—*stream* AL-4
Clear Run Sch (historical)—*school* PA-2
*Clear Run Swamp* NC-3
Clear Shade Creek—*stream* PA-2
Clear Shade Wild Area—*area* PA-2
Clear Site (Clear Missile Early Warning Station)—*other* AK-9
Clear Slough—*gut* MI-6
Clear Spot Flat—*flat* UT-8
*Clear Spot Reservoir* UT-8
Clear Spot Reservoirs—*reservoir* UT-8
*Clearspring* PA-2
*Clear Spring* TN-4
Clear Spring—*locale* AR-4
Clear Spring—*locale* MO-7
Clear Spring—*locale* PA-2
**Clear Spring**—*pop pl* IN-6
**Clear Spring**—*pop pl* MD-2
**Clear Spring**—*pop pl* PA-2
**Clearspring**—*pop pl* SC-3
**Clear Spring**—*pop pl* TX-5
Clear Spring—*spring* AL-4
Clear Spring—*spring* AR-4
Clear Spring—*spring* CA-9
Clear Spring—*spring* NV-8
Clear Spring—*spring* (2) OR-9
Clear Spring—*spring* (4) TN-4
Clear Spring—*spring* UT-8
Clear Spring—*stream* IN-6
Clear Spring Branch—*stream* MS-4
Clear Spring Branch—*stream* NC-3
Clear Spring Branch—*stream* TN-4
Clear Spring Branch—*stream* (2) VA-3
Clear Spring Camp—*locale* AR-4
Clear Spring Cem—*cemetery* OK-5
Clear Spring Cem—*cemetery* TN-4
Clear Spring Cem—*cemetery* TX-5
Clear Spring Ch—*church* AR-4
Clear Spring Ch—*church* IN-6
Clear Spring Ch—*church* (2) KY-4
Clear Spring Ch—*church* SC-3
Clear Spring Ch—*church* TX-5
Clear Spring Creek—*stream* GA-3
Clear Spring Creek—*stream* IN-6
Clear Spring (historical)—*locale* MS-4
Clear Spring Pond—*reservoir* PA-2
Clear Spring Post Office (historical)—*building* TN-4
Clear Spring Ridge—*ridge* KY-4
*Clear Springs* AL-4
*Clear Springs* TN-4
Clear Springs—*locale* AL-4
Clear Springs—*locale* (2) FL-3
Clear Springs—*locale* KY-4
Clear Springs—*locale* MS-4
Clear Springs—*locale* MO-7
Clear Springs—*locale* TN-4
Clear Springs—*locale* TX-5
**Clear Springs**—*pop pl* AL-4
**Clear Springs**—*pop pl* FL-3
**Clear Springs**—*pop pl* PA-2
**Clear Springs**—*pop pl* (2) TN-4
Clear Springs—*spring* MS-4
Clear Springs—*spring* NV-8
Clear Springs—*spring* (2) TN-4
*Clear Springs Baptist Church* MS-4
Clear Springs Branch—*stream* TN-4
Clear Springs Cem—*cemetery* AL-4
Clear Springs Cem—*cemetery* (5) MS-4
Clear Springs Cem—*cemetery* TN-4
Clear Springs Ch—*church* (4) AL-4
Clear Springs Ch—*church* FL-3
Clear Springs Ch—*church* GA-3
Clear Springs Ch—*church* IL-6
Clear Springs Ch—*church* LA-4
Clear Springs Ch—*church* (6) MS-4
Clear Springs Ch—*church* MO-7
Clear Springs Ch—*church* (3) TN-4
Clear Spring Sch—*school* MO-7
Clearspring Sch (abandoned)—*school* PA-2
Clear Spring Sch (historical)—*school* TN-4
Clear Springs Creek—*stream* MS-4
Clear Springs Dam—*dam* MS-4
Clear Spring Shaft (historical)—*mine* PA-2
Clear Springs (historical)—*locale* AL-4
**Clear Springs (historical)**—*pop pl* TN-4
**Clear Springs (Jockey)**—*pop pl* TN-4
Clear Springs Lake—*reservoir* MS-4
Clear Springs Marina—*locale* AL-4
*Clear Springs Methodist Church* AL-4
Clear Springs Mine—*mine* FL-3
Clear Springs Oil Field—*oilfield* MS-4
Clear Springs Plantation—*hist pl* NC-3
*Clear Springs Primitive Baptist Church* MS-4
Clear Springs Rec Area—*park* MS-4
Clear Springs RR Station—*locale* FL-3
Clear Springs Sch—*school* IL-6
Clear Springs Sch—*school* MN-6
Clear Springs Sch—*school* TN-4
Clear Springs Sch (abandoned)—*school* MO-7
Clear Springs Sch (historical)—*school* AL-4
Clear Springs Sch (historical)—*school* MS-4
**Clearspring (Township of)**—*pop pl* IN-6
Clear Stream—*stream* AK-9
Clear Stream—*stream* CA-9
Clear Stream—*stream* NH-1
Clearstream Ave Sch—*school* NY-2
Clear Tank—*reservoir* AZ-5
Clear Tank—*reservoir* (4) TX-5
Clear Township—*civil* SD-7
*Clearview* OH-6
Clearview—*hist pl* VA-3
Clearview—*locale* AL-4
Clearview—*locale* GA-3
Clear View—*locale* MO-7
**Clearview**—*pop pl* AL-4
**Clearview**—*pop pl* GA-3
**Clearview**—*pop pl* MD-2
**Clearview**—*pop pl* (3) OH-6
**Clearview**—*pop pl* OK-5
**Clear View**—*pop pl* PA-2
**Clearview**—*pop pl* PA-2
**Clearview**—*pop pl* TX-5
**Clearview**—*pop pl* WA-9
**Clearview**—*pop pl* WV-2
Clearview—*uninc pl* FL-3
**Clearview Acres (subdivision)**—*pop pl* NC-3
Clearview Ave Sch—*school* FL-3
Clearview Baptist Ch—*church* FL-3
Clear View Camp—*locale* PA-2
Clearview Cem—*cemetery* AR-4
Clearview Cem—*cemetery* IN-6
Clearview Cem—*cemetery* (2) OK-5
Clearview Cem—*cemetery* WI-6
Clearview Ch—*church* GA-3
Clearview Ch—*church* IA-7
Clearview Ch—*church* KY-4
Clearview Ch—*church* (2) NC-3
Clear View Ch—*church* NC-3
Clearview Ch—*church* NC-3
**Clearview City**—*pop pl* KS-7
Clear View Country Club—*locale* MA-1
Clearview Elem Sch—*school* PA-2
Clearview Estates—*locale* PA-2
**Clearview Estates**—*pop pl* PA-2
**Clearview Heights**—*pop pl* AZ-5
**Clearview Heights**—*pop pl* CT-1
**Clearview Heights**—*pop pl* PA-2
**Clearview Heights (subdivision)**—*pop pl* TN-4
**Clearview Hills (subdivision)**—*pop pl* AL-4
**Clearview Hills (subdivision)**—*pop pl* (2) AZ-5
**Clearview Homes Subdivision**—*pop pl* UT-8
Clearview Lake—*lake* FL-3
Clearview Lake—*reservoir* NJ-2
Clearview Lake Dam—*dam* NJ-2
**Clearview Manor**—*pop pl* DE-2
**Clearview Manor**—*pop pl* VA-3
**Clearview Manor (subdivision)**—*pop pl* PA-2
Clearview Mission Ch—*church* AL-4
Clearview Oil Field—*oilfield* OK-5
Clearview Park—*park* OH-6
Clearview Park—*park* PA-2
Clearview Park—*park* TN-4
Clearview Plaza Shop Ctr—*locale* TN-4
Clearview Regional HS—*school* NJ-2
Clearview Rsvr—*reservoir* PA-2
*Clearview Sch* PA-2
Clearview Sch—*school* IL-6
CLEARVIEW Sch—*school* MN-6
Clearview Sch—*school* NE-7
Clearview Sch—*school* OH-6
Clearview Sch—*school* PA-2
Clear View Sch—*school* SC-3
Clearview Sch—*school* TN-4
Clearview Sch—*school* VA-3
Clearview Sch—*school* WI-6
Clear View Sch (historical)—*school* MO-7
Clearview Sch (historical)—*school* MO-7
**Clearview (subdivision)**—*pop pl* TN-4
**Clearview Village**—*pop pl* MD-2
**Clearville**—*pop pl* PA-2
Clear Vue Farm—*locale* TX-5
Clearwater—*fmr MCD* (2) NE-7
Clearwater—*locale* MT-8
Clearwater—*locale* OR-9
Clearwater—*locale* TX-5
Clearwater—*locale* WA-9
**Clearwater**—*pop pl* AR-4
**Clearwater**—*pop pl* FL-3
**Clearwater**—*pop pl* ID-8
**Clearwater**—*pop pl* KS-7
**Clearwater**—*pop pl* LA-4
**Clearwater**—*pop pl* MN-6
**Clearwater**—*pop pl* (2) MO-7
**Clearwater**—*pop pl* NE-7
**Clearwater**—*pop pl* NJ-2
**Clearwater**—*pop pl* SC-3
**Clearwater**—*pop pl* TN-4
Clearwater, Lake—*lake* FL-3
**Clearwater Acres**—*pop pl* TN-4
*Clearwater Assembly of God Ch* AL-4
*Clearwater Baptist Ch* AL-4
Clearwater Baptist Ch—*church* TN-4
Clearwater Battlefield Site—*locale* ID-8
*Clearwater Bay* FL-3
Clearwater Bay—*bay* FL-3
Clearwater Bayou—*gut* LA-4
*Clearwater Beach* FL-3
**Clearwater Beach**—*pop pl* FL-3
**Clear Water Beach**—*pop pl* MD-2
**Clearwater Beach**—*pop pl* MD-2
Clearwater Beach Island—*island* FL-3
Clearwater Branch—*stream* (2) FL-3
Clearwater Branch—*stream* (3) SC-3
Clearwater Branch—*stream* TN-4
Clearwater Branch Ch—*church* SC-3
Clearwater Brook—*stream* (2) ME-1
Clearwater Camp—*locale* AK-9
Clearwater Canyon—*valley* CA-9
Clearwater Canyon—*valley* NV-8
Clearwater Canyon—*valley* UT-8
Clearwater (CCD)—*cens area* FL-3
Clearwater Cem—*cemetery* ID-8
Clearwater Cem—*cemetery* (3) MN-6
Clearwater Cem—*cemetery* NE-7
Clearwater Cem—*cemetery* TX-5
Clearwater Ch—*church* AL-4
Clearwater Ch—*church* AR-4
Clearwater Ch—*church* FL-3
Clear Water Ch—*church* LA-4
Clearwater Ch—*church* MN-6
Clearwater Chapel—*church* MI-6
Clearwater Christian Church—*school* FL-3
Clearwater Community Hosp—*hospital* FL-3
Clearwater Comp MS—*school* FL-3
**Clearwater (County)**—*pop pl* MN-6
**Clearwater Cove**—*pop pl* TX-5
*Clear Water Creek* AL-4
*Clear Water Creek* KS-7
*Clearwater Creek* MS-4
*Clear Water Creek* NE-7
*Clearwater Creek* OR-9
Clearwater Creek—*stream* AL-4
Clearwater Creek—*stream* (4) AK-9
Clearwater Creek—*stream* (3) CA-9
Clearwater Creek—*stream* (2) FL-3
Clearwater Creek—*stream* (2) KS-7
Clearwater Creek—*stream* LA-4
Clearwater Creek—*stream* (2) MN-6
Clearwater Creek—*stream* NE-7
Clear Water Creek—*stream* SC-3
Clearwater Creek—*stream* UT-8
Clearwater Creek—*stream* (5) WA-9
Clearwater Creek—*stream* WI-6
Clearwater Creek—*stream* WY-8
Clear Water Crossing Ranger Station—*locale* MT-8
Clearwater Dam—*dam* MO-7
Clear Water Ditch—*canal* OR-9
Clearwater Drain—*canal* AZ-5
Clearwater East—*post sta* FL-3
**Clearwater Estates (subdivision)**—*pop pl* AL-4
Clearwater Falls—*falls* OR-9
Clearwater Falls—*falls* SC-3
**Clearwater Forest (subdivision)**—*pop pl* NC-3
Clearwater Fork—*stream* AK-9
Clearwater Guard Station—*locale* WA-9
Clearwater Gulch—*valley* CA-9
Clearwater Gulch—*valley* ID-8
*Clearwater Harbor* FL-3
Clearwater Harbor—*bay* FL-3
**Clearwater Hills**—*pop pl* AZ-5
Clear Waterhole—*reservoir* OR-9
Clearwater Hollow—*valley* OK-5
Clearwater HS—*school* KS-7
*Clearwater Inlet* ME-1
*Clearwater Lake* MN-6
*Clearwater Lake* VA-3
Clearwater Lake—*lake* AL-4
Clearwater Lake—*lake* AK-9
Clearwater Lake—*lake* (7) FL-3
Clear Water Lake—*lake* FL-3
Clearwater Lake—*lake* FL-3
Clearwater Lake—*lake* MI-6
Clearwater Lake—*lake* (8) MN-6
Clearwater Lake—*lake* MT-8
Clearwater Lake—*lake* ND-7
Clearwater Lake—*lake* PA-2
Clearwater Lake—*lake* SC-3
Clearwater Lake—*lake* (2) WI-6
**Clearwater Lake**—*pop pl* WI-6
Clearwater Lake—*reservoir* AR-4
Clearwater Lake—*reservoir* GA-3
Clearwater Lake—*reservoir* MN-6
Clearwater Lake—*reservoir* MO-7
Clearwater Lake—*reservoir* NJ-2
Clearwater Lake—*reservoir* NC-3
Clearwater Lake Dam—*dam* NC-3
Clearwater Lakes—*reservoir* OH-6
Clearwater Lake State Wildlife Mngmt Area—*park* MO-7
Clearwater Lodge—*hist pl* MN-6
Clearwater Mall—*locale* FL-3
Clearwater Masonic Lodge-Grand Army of the Republic Hall—*hist pl* MN-6
Clearwater Mine—*mine* (2) ID-8
Clearwater Mountains—*range* AK-9
Clearwater MS—*school* KS-7
Clearwater Mtns—*range* ID-8
Clearwater Natl For—*forest* ID-8
Clearwater Number One Diversion Dam—*dam* OR-9
Clearwater Number One Forebay—*reservoir* OR-9
Clearwater Number One Forebay Dam—*dam* OR-9
Clearwater Number Two Forebay—*reservoir* OR-9
Clearwater Number Two Forebay Dam—*dam* OR-9
Clearwater Number 2 Forebay—*reservoir* OR-9
Clearwater Oil Field—*oilfield* KS-7
Clearwater Park—*park* FL-3
Clear Water Park—*park* IN-6
**Clearwater Park**—*pop pl* VA-3
Clearwater Pass—*channel* FL-3
Clearwater Picnic Area—*park* WY-8
Clearwater Point—*cape* FL-3

Clear Water Point—cliff ... AZ-5
Clearwater Pond—lake (3) ... FL-3
Clearwater Pond—lake (3) ... ME-1
Clearwater Pond—lake ... TN-4
Clearwater Post Office (historical)—building ... SD-7
Clearwater Post Office (historical)—building ... TN-4
Clearwater Ranch—locale ... AK-9
Clearwater Rec Area—park ... FL-3
Clearwater Reservoir ... MO-7
Clear Water River ... AL-4
Clearwater River ... WI-6
Clearwater River—stream ... ID-8
Clearwater River—stream (2) ... MN-6
Clearwater River—stream ... MT-8
Clearwater River—stream ... OR-9
Clearwater River—stream (2) ... WA-9
Clearwater River Memorial Bridge—bridge ... ID-8
Clear Water Rsvr—reservoir ... MT-8
Clear Water Run ... PA-2
Clearwater Sch (historical)—school ... MS-4
Clearwater Sch (historical)—school ... TN-4
Clearwater Senior HS—school ... FL-3
Clearwater Slough—stream ... AK-9
Clear Water Spring—spring ... AZ-5
Clearwater Spring—spring ... AZ-5
Clearwater Spring—spring ... TN-4
**Clearwater Springs**—pop pl ... GA-3
Clearwater Springs—spring ... WY-8
Clearwater State For—forest ... MT-8
Clearwater State Wildlife Mngmt Area—park ... MN-6
Clearwater Tank—reservoir ... TX-5
Clearwater Timber Protective Assoc Headqtrs—locale ... ID-8
**Clearwater Township**—pop pl ... NE-7
**Clearwater Township**—pop pl ... ND-7
**Clearwater Township**—pop pl ... SD-7
**Clearwater (Township of)**—pop pl ... MI-6
**Clearwater (Township of)**—pop pl ... MN-6
Clearwater Trail—trail ... WA-9
Clearwater Valley HS—school ... ID-8
Clear West Peak—summit ... WA-9
**Cleary**—pop pl ... MS-4
Cleary (Abandoned)—locale ... AK-9
Cleary Baptist Ch—church ... MS-4
Cleary Cem—cemetery ... MS-4
Cleary Creek—stream (2) ... AK-9
Cleary Ditch—canal (2) ... OR-9
**Cleary Heights (subdivision)**—pop pl ... MS-4
Cleary Hill—summit ... MI-6
Cleary Hill Mine—mine ... AK-9
**Cleary (historical)**—pop pl ... MS-4
Cleary Lake—lake ... MN-6
Cleary Lake—reservoir ... MS-4
Cleary Lake Dam—dam ... MS-4
Cleary Post Office (historical)—building ... MS-4
Cleary Sch—school (2) ... IL-6
Cleary Sch—school ... NJ-2
Cleary Sch—school ... NY-2
Cleary Spring—spring ... OR-9
Cleary Summit—locale ... AK-9
Cleary Summit Lodge—locale ... AK-9
**Cleary Township**—pop pl ... ND-7
**Cleaton**—pop pl ... GA-3
**Cleaton**—pop pl ... KY-4
**Cleator**—pop pl ... AZ-5
Cleator Bend Picnic Area—park ... OR-9
Cleave Creek—stream ... AK-9
Cleave Creek Glacier—glacier ... AK-9
**Cleaveland**—pop pl ... AZ-5
Cleaveland Elem Sch—school ... KS-7
Cleavelands Pond ... MA-1
Cleaver—locale ... NY-2
Cleaver, The—ridge ... CA-9
Cleaver, The—summit ... CO-8
Cleaver Cem—cemetery ... AR-4
Cleaver Creek—stream ... TN-4
Cleaver Creek—stream ... WI-6
Cleaver Female Institute (historical)—school ... MS-4
Cleaver House—hist pl ... DE-2
Cleaver Lake—lake ... MN-6
Cleaver Mine—mine ... CA-9
Cleaver Peak—summit ... NV-8
Cleaver Peak—summit ... WY-8
Cleaves, Benjamin, House—hist pl ... ME-1
Cleaves Brook—stream ... ME-1
Cleaves Cove—bay ... ME-1
Cleaves Fork—locale ... MD-2
Cleaves Landing—locale ... ME-1
Cleaves' Point ... NY-2
Cleaves Point—cape ... NY-2
**Cleavesville**—pop pl ... MO-7
Cleavesville Sch (abandoned)—school ... MO-7
**Cleavet Springs (historical)**—pop pl ... TN-4
Cleavland Athletic Field—park ... NE-7
Cleawok Lake ... OR-9
Cleawox Lake—lake ... OR-9
**Clebit**—pop pl ... OK-5
Clebit Ridge—ridge ... OK-5
Clebitt Branch—stream ... KY-4
Clebitt Hill—summit ... KY-4
Cleburne—locale ... AL-4
**Cleburne**—pop pl ... IL-6
**Cleburne**—pop pl ... TX-5
Cleburne, Lake—reservoir ... AL-4
Cleburne Carnegie Library—hist pl ... TX-5
Cleburne (CCD)—cens area ... TX-5
**Cleburne County**—pop pl ... AL-4
**Cleburne (County)**—pop pl ... AR-4
Cleburne County Courthouse—building ... AL-4
Cleburne County Courthouse—hist pl ... AL-4
Cleburne County Courthouse—hist pl ... AR-4
Cleburne County HS—school ... AL-4
Cleburne County Vocational Sch—school ... AL-4
Cleburne (historical)—locale ... KS-7
Cleburne Memorial Garden—cemetery ... AL-4
Cleburne Memorial Park—cemetery ... TX-5
Cleburne State Park—park ... TX-5
Cleburne (Township of)—fmr MCD (2) ... AR-4
C L Edwards Memorial Park—park ... TN-4
Cleeces Ferry—locale ... TN-4
Clee Creek—stream ... ID-8
Clee Drain—stream ... MI-6
Cleek Branch—stream ... TN-4
Cleek Cem—cemetery ... VA-3
**Cleek (historical)**—pop pl ... OR-9
Cleek Spring—spring ... TN-4
**Cle Elum**—pop pl ... WA-9
Cle Elum (CCD)—cens area ... WA-9
Cle Elum Lake—reservoir ... WA-9
Cle Elum Muni Airp—airport ... WA-9
Cle Elum Point—summit ... WA-9
Cle Elum Reservoir ... WA-9
Cle Elum Ridge—ridge ... WA-9
Cle Elum River—stream ... WA-9
Cle Elum-Roslyn Beneficial Association Hospital—hist pl ... WA-9
**Cleeos Acres Subdivision**—pop pl ... UT-8
Cleetwood Cove—bay ... OR-9
Clef, Mount—summit ... CA-9
Cleft—locale ... ID-8
Cleft, The—cliff ... ME-1
Cleft Arch—arch ... UT-8
Cleft Creek—stream ... MT-8
Cleft Creek—stream ... OR-9
Cleft Falls—falls ... WY-8
Cleft Island—island ... AK-9
Cleft Lake—lake ... MN-6
Cleft Mountain Canon ... UT-8
Cleft Rock—pillar ... MT-8
Cleft Rock—rock ... MA-1
Cleft Rock Mtn—summit ... MT-8
Clefty Mine (underground)—mine ... AL-4
Clegern Sch—school ... OK-5
Clegg—locale ... TX-5
**Clegg**—pop pl (2) ... NC-3
Clegg, John H., House—hist pl ... TX-5
Clegg, L. B., House—hist pl ... TX-5
Clegg, Luther, House—hist pl ... NC-3
**Clegg Addition (subdivision)**—pop pl ... UT-8
Clegg and Pearson Dam—dam ... AL-4
Clegg And Pearson Lake—reservoir ... AL-4
Clegg Canyon—valley ... UT-8
Clegg Cem—cemetery ... TX-5
Clegg Creek—stream ... AR-4
Clegg Creek—stream ... IN-6
Clegg Lake—lake ... UT-8
Clegg Ranch—locale ... TX-5
Cleggs Ch—church ... NC-3
Clegg Sch—school ... IN-6
Cleggs Mill (historical)—locale ... MS-4
Clegg Windmill—locale ... TX-5
Cleghern Cem—cemetery ... TN-4
**Cleghorn**—pop pl ... IA-7
**Cleghorn**—pop pl ... WI-6
Cleghorn—uninc pl ... MA-1
Cleghorn Bar—bar ... CA-9
Cleghorn Bar Campground—locale ... CA-9
Cleghorn Bar Trail (Jeep)—trail ... CA-9
Cleghorn Canyon—valley ... CA-9
Cleghorn Canyon—valley ... SD-7
Cleghorn Cem—cemetery ... OK-5
Cleghorn Creek—stream ... CA-9
Cleghorn Creek—stream ... NC-3
Cleghorn Creek—stream ... OR-9
Cleghorn Creek—stream ... TN-4
Cleghorn Flat—flat ... CA-9
Cleghorn Hollow—valley ... TN-4
Cleghorn Lakes—flat ... CA-9
Cleghorn Meadow ... CA-9
Cleghorn Meadows—flat ... CA-9
Cleghorn Mtn—summit ... CA-9
Cleghorn Pass—gap (2) ... CA-9
Cleghorn Ravine—valley ... CA-9
Cleghorn Ridge—ridge ... CA-9
Cleghorn Rsvr—reservoir ... CA-9
Cleghorn Sch—school ... SD-7
Cleghorn Spring—spring ... GA-3
Cleghorn Valley—valley ... VA-3
Cleghorn Valley Ch—church ... VA-3
Cleghorn Valley Creek—stream ... VA-3
Cleghorn Valley Sch—school ... VA-3
Cleighton Creek—stream ... OR-9
Cleiman Mound and Village Site—hist pl ... IL-6
Cleitts Dam—dam ... AL-4
Cleitts Lake—reservoir ... AL-4
Cleiv—locale ... MT-8
Cleiv Spring—spring ... MT-8
Cleland Bay—bay ... ID-8
Cleland Cem—cemetery ... LA-4
Cleland Crossroads—locale ... SC-3
**Cleland Heights**—pop pl ... DE-2
Cleland Mtn—summit ... CA-9
Cleland Sch (abandoned)—school ... PA-2
Cleland Spring—spring ... OR-9
Clell—locale ... VA-3
Clelland House—hist pl ... WV-2
Clem—locale ... GA-3
Clem—locale ... MS-4
Clem—locale ... OR-9
Clem—locale ... WV-2
Clem Akina Park—park ... HI-9
Cleman Mtn—summit ... WA-9
Clemans Elem Sch—school ... FL-3
Clemans Mountains ... WA-9
Clemans Run—stream ... PA-2
Clemans Smith Ditch—canal ... IN-6
Clemans Tank—reservoir ... AZ-5
Clemansville Sch—school ... WI-6
Clemantha Mine—mine ... MT-8
Clemar Creek—stream ... LA-4
Clematis Brook ... MA-1
Clematis Brook—stream ... MA-1
Clematis Brook—uninc pl ... MA-1
**Clematis Brook Station**—pop pl ... MA-1
Clematis Creek—stream ... MT-8
Clematis Creek—stream ... WY-8
Clematis Rsvr—reservoir ... WY-8
Clem Branch—stream ... KY-4
Clem Cem—cemetery ... IL-6
Clem Cem—cemetery ... IN-6
Clem Creek—stream ... OK-5
Clem Creek—stream ... TN-4
Clemenceau—locale ... AZ-5
Clemenceau-Cottonwood Airport ... AZ-5
Clemenceau Public Sch—hist pl ... AZ-5
Clemenceau Public Sch—school ... AZ-5
Clemence-Irons House—hist pl ... RI-1
Clemen Creek Sch (historical)—school ... MS-4
Clemeng Creek ... WI-6
Clemens ... TX-5
**Clemens**—pop pl ... KS-7
Clemens, Michael, House—hist pl ... OR-9
Clemens, Orion, House—hist pl ... NV-8
Clemens Bend—bend ... AL-4
Clemens Bluff—cliff ... MO-7
Clemens Brake—swamp ... AR-4
Clemens Branch—stream ... TX-5
Clemens Brook ... WI-6
Clemens Cave—cave ... AL-4
Clemens Cem—cemetery ... GA-3
Clemens Cem—cemetery ... IL-6
Clemens Cem—cemetery ... OH-6
Clemens Creek ... OR-9
Clemens Creek—stream ... MO-7
Clemens Creek—stream ... TX-5
Clemens Creek—stream ... WI-6
Clemens Dam—dam ... OR-9
Clemens Ditch—canal ... OH-6
Clemens Field—park ... MO-7
Clemens Hollow—valley ... MO-7
Clemens Hollow—valley ... TX-5
Clemens House—hist pl ... AL-4
Clemens House—hist pl ... MS-4
Clemens House-Columbia Brewery District—hist pl ... MO-7
Clemens House-Columbia Brewery District (Boundary Increase)—hist pl ... MO-7
Clemens Log Pond—reservoir ... OR-9
Clemens Log Pond Dam—dam ... OR-9
Clemens Ranch—locale ... OR-9
Clemens Ranchhouse—hist pl ... NM-5
Clemens Rsvr—reservoir ... OR-9
Clemens Sch—school ... CA-9
Clemens Sch—school ... TX-5
Clemens Sch—school ... WI-6
Clemens Shop Ctr—locale ... PA-2
Clemens Well—well ... OR-9
Clemens Well (Dry)—well ... CA-9
Clement ... KS-7
Clement—locale ... MO-7
Clement—locale ... ND-7
**Clement**—pop pl ... NC-3
**Clement**—pop pl ... OH-6
Clement, C. C., House—hist pl ... MN-6
Clement, George S., House—hist pl ... OH-6
Clement, Jesse, House—hist pl ... NC-3
Clement Ave Sch—school ... WI-6
Clement Bend—bend ... AL-4
Clement Brook—stream ... NH-1
Clement Canyon—valley ... NM-5
Clement Cem—cemetery ... AR-4
Clement Cem—cemetery ... MI-6
Clement Cem—cemetery ... MS-4
Clement Cem—cemetery ... TN-4
Clement Cem—cemetery ... VT-1
Clement Ch—church (2) ... NC-3
Clement Cove—bay ... MD-2
Clement Creek ... LA-4
Clement Creek—stream ... KY-4
Clement Ditch—canal ... OR-9
Clement Drain—canal ... MI-6
Clemente Well—well ... NM-5
Clemente Well—well ... TX-5
Clemente Windmill—locale ... AZ-5
Clement Hill—summit ... ME-1
Clement Hill—summit (3) ... NH-1
Clement Hollow—valley (2) ... UT-8
**Clementine**—pop pl ... MO-7
Clementine Mine—mine ... NV-8
Clement Island—island ... TX-5
Clement JHS—school ... CA-9
Clement Junction—locale ... CA-9
Clement Lake—lake ... NJ-2
Clement Lake—reservoir ... TN-4
Clement Lake—reservoir ... UT-8
Clement Lake Dam—dam ... UT-8
**Clement Lake Estates (subdivision)**—pop pl ... TN-4
Clement Mine—mine ... KY-4
Clement-Nagel House—hist pl ... TX-5
**Clementon**—pop pl ... NJ-2
Clementon Heights—other ... NJ-2
Clementon Lake—reservoir ... NJ-2
Clementon Lake Dam—dam ... NJ-2
Clementown Mills—locale ... VA-3
Clement Point—cape ... ME-1
Clement Pond—lake ... NH-1
Clement Powell Butte—summit ... AZ-5
Clement Ranch—locale ... OR-9
Clement Run—stream ... PA-2
**Clements**—pop pl ... CA-9
**Clements**—pop pl ... IL-6
**Clements**—pop pl ... KS-7
**Clements**—pop pl ... MD-2
**Clements**—pop pl ... MN-6
**Clements**—pop pl ... WV-2
Clements, James, Airport Administration Bldg—hist pl ... MI-6
Clements, Le Vega, House—hist pl ... KY-4
Clements Bend ... AL-4
Clements Bend—bend ... AL-4
Clements Bottom—bend ... KY-4
Clements Branch—stream ... GA-3
Clements Branch—stream ... KY-4
Clements Branch Ch—church ... GA-3
**Clements Bridge**—pop pl ... NJ-2
Clements Brook—stream (2) ... ME-1
Clements Cem—cemetery (2) ... AL-4
Clements Cem—cemetery ... GA-3
Clements Cem—cemetery ... IL-6
Clements Ch—church ... NC-3
Clement Sch—school ... AL-4
Clement Sch—school ... GA-3
Clement Sch—school ... MI-6
Clement Sch—school ... NC-3
Clements Chapel—church ... GA-3
Clements Circle Park—park ... MI-6
Clements Corners—locale ... PA-2
Clements Creek—stream ... GA-3
Clements Creek—stream ... MD-2
Clements Creek—stream ... UT-8
Clements Curve—locale ... NC-3
Clements Depot ... AL-4
Clements Draw—valley ... TX-5
Clements Glen View Cem—cemetery ... CA-9
Clements Hall—hist pl ... TX-5
Clements (historical)—locale ... AL-4
Clements Hollow—valley ... MO-7
Clements HS ... AL-4
Clements Island—island ... NC-3
Clements Lake—lake ... NM-5
Clements Lake—lake ... UT-8
Clements Landing—locale ... AL-4
Clements Mill ... AL-4
Clements Mill (historical)—locale ... AL-4
Clements Mine (surface)—mine ... AL-4
Clements Mine (underground)—mine ... AL-4
Clements Mtn—summit ... GA-3
Clements Mtn—summit ... MT-8
Clements Mtn—summit ... NY-2
**Clementson**—pop pl ... MN-6
Clementson Cem—cemetery ... MN-6
Clements Point—cape ... NH-1
Clements Pond—lake ... AL-4
Clements Pond—lake ... NY-2
Clements Pond—reservoir ... GA-3
Clements Ranch—locale ... CA-9
Clements Ranch—locale ... ID-8
Clements Ranch—locale ... NM-5
Clements Reef—bar ... WA-9
Clements Ridge—ridge ... CA-9
Clements Rowhouse—hist pl ... CO-8
Clements Sch—school ... KS-7
Clements Sch—school ... KY-4
Clements Sch—school ... WI-6
Clements Spori Ditch—canal ... ID-8
Clements Spring ... AL-4
Clements State Bank Bldg—hist pl ... MN-6
Clements State Tree Nursery—other ... WV-2
Clements Station (historical)—locale ... AL-4
Clements Stone Arch Bridge—hist pl ... KS-7
Clement Station—locale ... PA-2
Clementsville ... NC-3
Clementsville—locale ... TN-4
**Clementsville**—pop pl ... ID-8
**Clementsville**—pop pl ... KY-4
**Clementsville**—pop pl ... ND-7
Clementsville (CCD)—cens area ... KY-4
Clementsville Ch of Christ—church ... TN-4
Clementsville Mill (historical)—locale ... TN-4
Clementsville Post Office (historical)—building ... TN-4
Clements Well—well ... NM-5
Clement Town Hall—building ... ND-7
**Clement Township**—pop pl ... ND-7
**Clement (Township of)**—pop pl ... IL-6
**Clement (Township of)**—pop pl ... MI-6
Clementville (historical)—locale ... KS-7
Clementwood—hist pl ... VT-1
Clem Hollow—valley ... UT-8
Cleminson Sch—school ... CA-9
**Clem Jones Heights (subdivision)**—pop pl ... TN-4
Clem Lookout Tower—locale ... MS-4
Clemments Mill (historical)—locale ... AL-4
Clemments Mtn—summit ... AL-4
Clemmer Campsite—park ... TN-4
Clemmer Cem—cemetery ... TN-4
Clemmer Cove—valley ... TN-4
Clemmer Hill—summit ... MS-4
Clemmers-Fishers Cem—cemetery ... IN-6
Clemmer Theater—hist pl ... WA-9
Clemmer Trail—trail ... TN-4
Clemmitt Branch—valley ... TN-4
**Clemmons**—pop pl ... NC-3
Clemmons, W.C., Mound—hist pl ... OH-6
Clemmons Bay—swamp ... FL-3
Clemmons Bottom—valley ... TN-4
Clemmons Cem—cemetery ... NE-7
Clemmons Cem—cemetery ... NY-2
Clemmons Cem—cemetery ... TN-4
Clemmons Center—locale ... NC-3
Clemmons City ... AL-4
Clemmons Creek—stream ... TN-4
Clemmons Creek School ... MS-4
Clemmons Elem Sch—school ... NC-3
Clemmons Gin Branch—stream ... AL-4
Clemmons Gully—valley ... TX-5
Clemmons Hollow—valley ... AR-4
Clemmons Memorial Park—cemetery ... NC-3
Clemmons Point—cape ... AL-4
Clemmons Point—cape ... TN-4
**Clemmons Station**—pop pl ... NC-3
Clemmons Village Shop Ctr—locale ... NC-3
Clemmonsville (Township of)—fmr MCD ... NC-3
**Clemmons West (subdivision)**—pop pl ... NC-3
Clem Mtn—summit ... AK-9
**Clemo**—pop pl ... PA-2
Clemo Lake ... PA-2
Clemon ... TX-5
Clemones Cem—cemetery ... GA-3
Clemons—locale ... KY-4
Clemons—locale ... TX-5
**Clemons**—pop pl ... IA-7
**Clemons**—pop pl ... NY-2
Clemons, Alexander, House—hist pl ... OH-6
Clemons Branch—stream ... AL-4
Clemons Branch—stream ... MS-4
Clemons Branch—stream ... SC-3
Clemons Cave—cave ... TN-4
Clemons Cem—cemetery ... AR-4
Clemons Cem—cemetery ... KY-4
Clemons Cem—cemetery ... ME-1
Clemons Cem—cemetery ... TX-5
Clemons Cem—cemetery ... VA-3
Clemons Cemetery ... AL-4
Clemons Ch—church ... KY-4
Clemons Chapel—church ... GA-3
**Clemons Clemons Grove Station**—pop pl ... IA-7
Clemons Coulee—valley ... MT-8
Clemons Creek ... MS-4
Clemons Creek—stream ... IA-7
Clemons Creek—stream ... MI-6
Clemons Creek—stream ... MT-8
Clemons Creek—stream ... TX-5
Clemons Crossroad—locale ... AL-4
Clemons Fork—stream ... KY-4
Clemons Grove ... IA-7
Clemons Grove Chapel—church ... NC-3
Clemons HS—school ... NC-3
Clemons HS—school ... TX-5
Clemons Lake—lake ... MI-6
Clemons Mtn—summit ... MO-7
Clemons Place ... OR-9
Clemons Pond—lake ... ME-1
Clemons Sch—school ... TN-4
Clemons Sch—school ... TX-5
**Clemont**—pop pl ... NC-3
Clemont Cem—cemetery ... MS-4
Clemonts Cem—cemetery ... MS-4
Clemo Pond—reservoir ... PA-2
Clemow Cow Camp—locale ... MT-8
Clem Point—cape ... MD-2
Clem Post Office (historical)—building ... MS-4
Clempson Island ... PA-2
Clems Branch—stream ... NC-3
Clems Branch—stream ... SC-3
Clems Branch—stream ... VA-3
Clem Sch—school ... OH-6
Clem Sch (historical)—school ... MS-4
Clem Sch (historical)—school ... OR-9
**Clemscot**—pop pl ... OK-5
**Clemscott**—pop pl ... OK-5
Clems Flat—flat ... CA-9
**Clemson**—pop pl ... SC-3
Clemson Agricultural Coll—school ... SC-3
Clemson Branch—stream ... MD-2
Clemson (CCD)—cens area ... SC-3
Clemson College ... SC-3
Clemson College Coastal Experiment Station—other ... SC-3
Clemson College Experiment Farm—locale ... SC-3
Clemson Island—island ... PA-2
Clemson Island Prehistoric District—hist pl ... PA-2
Clemson Lookout Tower—locale ... SC-3
Clemson (P.O.) ... SC-3
Clemson Shoal—bar ... IL-6
**Clemson University**—pop pl ... SC-3
Clemson University Sandhill Experiment Station—other ... SC-3
Clemsonville—locale ... MD-2
Clem's Opera House—hist pl ... NE-7
Clem Spring—spring ... OR-9
Clems Run—stream ... NJ-2
Clem Thorofare—channel ... NJ-2
Clemtown—locale ... WV-2
**Clemville**—pop pl ... TX-5
Clemville Oil Field—oilfield ... TX-5
Clendaniel Pond—reservoir ... DE-2
Clendaniel Pond Dam—dam ... DE-2
Clendenen-Carleton House—hist pl ... TX-5
Clendenen Cem—cemetery ... VA-3
Clendenen Creek—stream ... WA-9
**Clendenenville**—pop pl ... WV-2
**Clendenin**—pop pl ... WV-2
Clendenin Branch—stream ... PA-2
Clendenin Cem—cemetery ... WV-2
Clendenin Creek—stream ... TN-4
Clendenin Creek—stream ... WV-2
Clendening Corners—locale ... PA-2
Clendening Creek—stream ... TX-5
Clendening Dam—dam ... OH-6
Clendening Lake—reservoir ... OH-6
Clendening Rsvr ... OH-6
Clendening Rsvr—reservoir ... OH-6
Clendenin (Magisterial District)—fmr MCD ... WV-2
Clendenin Mtn—summit ... MT-8
**Clendenin (RR name Clendennin)**—pop pl ... WV-2
Clendenin Rsvr ... OH-6
Clendenin Well—well ... NM-5
Clendennin ... WV-2
Clendennin Creek—stream ... VA-3
Clendenning Creek ... CA-9
Clendenning Lake—lake ... WY-8
Clendenning Sch (historical)—school ... PA-2
Clendenning Well—locale ... NM-5
Clendennin (RR name for Clendenin)—other ... WV-2
Clendenon Branch—stream ... TN-4
Clendenon Cem—cemetery ... IL-6
Clendining Creek—stream ... TX-5
Clendon Brook—stream ... NY-2
Clenega Windmill—locale ... TX-5
Clenmoore Sch—school ... PA-2
Clenny ... TN-4
Clenny Branch—stream ... AR-4
Clenny Post Office (historical)—building ... TN-4
Cleo ... OK-5
Cleo ... TN-4
Cleo—locale ... OR-9
Cleo—locale ... TX-5
**Cleo**—pop pl ... MS-4
Cleo (corporate name Cleo Springs) ... OK-5
Cleo Creek—stream ... AK-9
Cleo Creek—stream ... WY-8
Cleodis, Lake—lake ... LA-4
Cleofas Canyon—valley ... NM-5
Cleofas Well—locale ... NM-5
Cleo Florence Ditch—canal ... OH-6
Cleo (historical)—locale ... KS-7
Cleola—other ... GA-3
Cleo Lake—lake ... OR-9
Cleona ... IN-6
**Cleona**—pop pl ... PA-2
Cleona Borough—civil ... PA-2
Cleona Elem Sch—school ... PA-2
Cleona Township—fmr MCD ... IA-7
Cleone—locale ... IL-6
**Cleone**—pop pl ... CA-9
Cleone, Lake—lake ... CA-9
Cleones Tank—reservoir ... NM-5
**Cleon (Township of)**—pop pl ... MI-6
Cleopatra—locale ... KY-4
Cleopatra—locale ... MO-7
Cleopatra Cove—bay ... NV-8
Cleopatra Lookout (historical)—locale ... OR-9
Cleopatra Mine—mine ... AZ-5
Cleopatra Mine—mine ... CA-9
Cleopatra Mine—mine ... SD-7
Cleopatra Mine—mine ... WA-9
Cleopatra Rsvr—reservoir ... WY-8
Cleopatras Chair—summit ... UT-8
Cleopatras Charr ... UT-8
Cleopatras Couch—summit ... CO-8
Cleopatras Needle—pillar ... NM-5
Cleopatra Wash—stream ... NV-8
Cleo Post Office (historical)—building ... TN-4
Cleopus—locale ... VA-3
Cleora—locale ... CO-8
Cleora—locale ... OK-5
Cleora—locale ... SC-3
Cleora Brake—swamp ... LA-4
Cleora Cem—cemetery ... CO-8
Cleora Sch—school ... OK-5
**Cleo Springs**—pop pl ... OK-5
Cleo Springs Cem—cemetery ... OK-5
**Cleo Springs (corporate name for Cleo)**—pop pl ... OK-5
Cleo Tank—reservoir ... TX-5
Clequa Tank—reservoir ... NM-5
Clercy Branch—stream ... NC-3
Cleremont Crags ... PA-2
Clerenger Cem—cemetery ... OH-6
Clerk Hill Cem—cemetery ... ME-1
Clerkins Ranch—locale ... CA-9
Clerk's Office—hist pl ... VA-3
Clermont—hist pl ... NY-2
**Clermont**—pop pl ... FL-3
**Clermont**—pop pl ... GA-3
**Clermont**—pop pl ... IN-6
**Clermont**—pop pl ... IA-7
**Clermont**—pop pl ... KY-4
**Clermont**—pop pl ... MT-8
**Clermont**—pop pl (2) ... NJ-2
**Clermont**—pop pl ... NY-2
**Clermont**—pop pl ... PA-2
Clermont Acad—hist pl ... NY-2
Clermont Airp—airport ... IN-6
Clermont (CCD)—cens area ... FL-3
Clermont (CCD)—cens area ... GA-3
Clermont Cem—cemetery ... PA-2
Clermont Ch—church ... MS-4
Clermont Ch (historical)—church ... MS-4
**Clermont (County)**—pop pl ... OH-6
Clermont Crag—cliff ... PA-2
Clermont Creek—stream ... IN-6
Clermont Elem Sch—school ... FL-3
Clermont Estates Hist Dist—hist pl ... NY-2
**Clermont Harbor**—pop pl ... MS-4
Clermont Harbor Sch—school ... MS-4
**Clermont Heights**—pop pl ... IN-6
Clermont Hill ... CA-9
Clermont HS—school ... FL-3
Clermont JHS—school ... FL-3
**Clermont Junction**—pop pl ... PA-2
Clermont Northeastern HS—school ... OH-6
Clermont Post Office ... TN-4
Clermont Residential Hist Dist—hist pl ... GA-3
Clermont Sch—school ... MO-7
Clermont Sch Number 4—school ... IN-6
Clermont Shop Ctr—locale ... FL-3
Clermont State Park—park ... NY-2
Clermont Street Parkway—hist pl ... CO-8
**Clermont (subdivision)**—pop pl ... DE-2
**Clermont (Town of)**—pop pl ... NY-2
Clermont Township—fmr MCD ... IA-7
**Clermont Township**—pop pl ... ND-7
Clermont Township Dam ... ND-7
**Clermontville**—pop pl ... OH-6
**Clermont Woods**—pop pl ... VA-3
Clertoma ... OH-6
**Clertoma**—pop pl ... OH-6
Cles Ranch—locale ... WY-8
Clesson Brook—stream ... MA-1
Clessons Brook ... MA-1
Clessons River ... MA-1
Clester, Joseph, House—hist pl ... OH-6
Cleta—locale ... TX-5
Cleto Lake—lake ... NM-5
Cletomus Creek ... MT-8
**Cletonia**—pop pl ... MS-4
Cleto Well—well ... NV-8
Cleur Creek ... NC-3
Cleva Bay—bay ... AK-9
**Cleve**—pop pl ... WV-2
Cleve Creek—stream ... NV-8
Cleve Creek—stream ... WA-9
Cleve Creek Administrative Site—locale ... NV-8
Cleve Creek Baldy—summit ... NV-8
Cleve Creek Campground—locale ... NV-8
Cleve Creek Forest Service Recreation Site ... NV-8
Clevedale—locale ... SC-3
Cleve Hinton Creek—stream ... FL-3
Cleveland ... AL-4
Cleveland—fmr MCD (3) ... NE-7
Cleveland—locale ... AL-4
Cleveland—locale ... ME-1
Cleveland—locale ... OR-9
Cleveland—locale ... TX-5
Cleveland—locale ... WA-9
Cleveland—mine ... UT-8
**Cleveland**—pop pl ... AL-4
**Cleveland**—pop pl ... AR-4
**Cleveland**—pop pl ... FL-3
**Cleveland**—pop pl ... GA-3
**Cleveland**—pop pl ... ID-8
**Cleveland**—pop pl ... IL-6
**Cleveland**—pop pl ... IN-6
**Cleveland**—pop pl ... KS-7
**Cleveland**—pop pl ... KY-4
**Cleveland**—pop pl ... MN-6
**Cleveland**—pop pl (2) ... MS-4
**Cleveland**—pop pl ... MO-7
**Cleveland**—pop pl ... MT-8
**Cleveland**—pop pl ... NM-5
**Cleveland**—pop pl ... NY-2
**Cleveland**—pop pl ... NC-3
**Cleveland**—pop pl ... ND-7
**Cleveland**—pop pl ... OH-6
**Cleveland**—pop pl ... OK-5
**Cleveland**—pop pl ... SC-3
**Cleveland**—pop pl ... TN-4
**Cleveland**—pop pl ... TX-5
**Cleveland**—pop pl ... UT-8
**Cleveland**—pop pl ... VA-3
**Cleveland**—pop pl ... WV-2
**Cleveland**—pop pl ... WI-6
Cleveland, A. S., House—hist pl ... TX-5
Cleveland, Cincinnati, Chicago and St. Louis RR Station—hist pl ... IL-6
Cleveland, Edward L., House—hist pl ... ME-1
Cleveland, Grover, Home—hist pl ... NJ-2
Cleveland, Lake—reservoir ... ID-8
Cleveland, Mount—summit (2) ... AK-9
Cleveland, Mount—summit ... MT-8
Cleveland, Mount—summit ... VT-1
Cleveland, Robert, Log House—hist pl ... NC-3
Cleveland Airp—airport ... MO-7
Cleveland Airp—airport ... NC-3
Cleveland And Pittsburgh RR Bridge—hist pl ... OH-6
Cleveland Arcade—hist pl ... OH-6
Cleveland Army Tank Automotive Plant—other ... OH-6
Cleveland Ave Ch of Christ—church ... AL-4
Cleveland Ave Sch—school ... AR-4
Cleveland Ave Sch—school ... GA-3
Cleveland Ave Sch—school (2) ... NY-2
Cleveland Bayou—gut ... TX-5
Cleveland Boys Sch—school ... OH-6

Cleveland-Bradley County Industrial Park—*locale* TN-4
Cleveland Branch—*stream* AL-4
Cleveland Branch—*stream* MS-4
Cleveland Branch—*stream* (3) TX-5
Cleveland Brook—*stream* MA-1
Cleveland Brook—*stream* VT-1
Cleveland Brook Reservoir Dam—*dam* MA-1
Cleveland Brook Rsvr—*reservoir* MA-1
Cleveland Canal—*canal* UT-8
Cleveland (CCD)—*cens area* AL-4
Cleveland (CCD)—*cens area* GA-3
Cleveland (CCD)—*cens area* OK-5
Cleveland (CCD)—*cens area* TN-4
Cleveland (CCD)—*cens area* TX-5
Cleveland Cem—*cemetery* (2) AL-4
Cleveland Cem—*cemetery* (2) AR-4
Cleveland Cem—*cemetery* FL-3
Cleveland Cem—*cemetery* (2) GA-3
Cleveland Cem—*cemetery* ID-8
Cleveland Cem—*cemetery* IL-6
Cleveland Cem—*cemetery* IN-6
Cleveland Cem—*cemetery* (2) KS-7
Cleveland Cem—*cemetery* LA-4
Cleveland Cem—*cemetery* MI-6
Cleveland Cem—*cemetery* MN-6
Cleveland Cem—*cemetery* MO-7
Cleveland Cem—*cemetery* NE-7
Cleveland Cem—*cemetery* NY-2
Cleveland Cem—*cemetery* OR-9
Cleveland Cem—*cemetery* (2) TN-4
Cleveland Cem—*cemetery* TX-5
Cleveland Cem—*cemetery* UT-8
Cleveland Cem—*cemetery* (2) WI-6
*Cleveland Cemetery* MS-4
Cleveland Center Ditch—*canal* UT-8
Cleveland Ch—*church* (2) AL-4
Cleveland Ch—*church* (2) GA-3
Cleveland Ch—*church* IN-6
Cleveland Ch—*church* NE-7
Cleveland Ch—*church* NC-3
Cleveland Ch—*church* TX-5
Cleveland Chapel—*church* GA-3
*Cleveland Ch of Christ* AL-4
Cleveland Circle—*locale* MA-1
Cleveland City Hall—*building* TN-4
Cleveland Cliff—*cliff* SC-3
Cleveland Cliffs Basin—*reservoir* MI-6
Cleveland Cliffs Lake—*lake* MI-6
*Cleveland Clift Lake* MI-6
Cleveland Coll (historical)—*school* MS-4
Cleveland Colored Consolidated Sch (historical)—*school* MS-4
Cleveland Community Hosp—*hospital* TN-4
**Cleveland Corner**—*pop pl* VT-1
**Cleveland Corners**—*pop pl* VT-1
Cleveland Country Club—*locale* NC-3
**Cleveland (County)**—*pop pl* AR-4
**Cleveland County**—*pop pl* NC-3
**Cleveland (County)**—*pop pl* OK-5
Cleveland County Clerk's Bldg—*hist pl* AR-4
Cleveland County Courthouse—*hist pl* AR-4
Cleveland County Courthouse—*hist pl* NC-3
Cleveland County Fairgrounds—*locale* NC-3
Cleveland County Historical Museum—*building* NC-3
Cleveland County Technical Institute—*locale* NC-3
Cleveland Court Sch—*school* FL-3
*Cleveland Creek* MT-8
*Cleveland Creek* TX-5
Cleveland Creek—*stream* AL-4
Cleveland Creek—*stream* AK-9
Cleveland Creek—*stream* ID-8
Cleveland Creek—*stream* (3) MI-6
Cleveland Creek—*stream* (2) MT-8
Cleveland Creek—*stream* OR-9
Cleveland Creek—*stream* SC-3
Cleveland Creek—*stream* WI-6
Cleveland Crossing—*locale* MS-4
Cleveland Crossroads—*locale* AL-4
**Cleveland Crossroads (Elias)**—*pop pl* AL-4
Cleveland Dam—*dam* UT-8
Cleveland Dam—*reservoir* SD-7
Cleveland Day Sch—*school* TN-4
Cleveland Ditch—*canal* CO-8
Cleveland Division—*civil* AL-4
Cleveland Division—*civil* TN-4
Cleveland Drain—*canal* CA-9
Cleveland Draw—*valley* TX-5
Cleveland Draw—*valley* WY-8
Cleveland East Ledge—*rock* MA-1
Cleveland Elem Sch—*school* NC-3
Cleveland Elem Sch—*school* PA-2
Cleveland Fairgounds—*locale* TN-4
Cleveland Ferry (historical)—*locale* AL-4
Cleveland Filtration Plant—*building* TN-4
Cleveland Fisheries Dam—*dam* MS-4
Cleveland Golf and Country Club—*locale* TN-4
Cleveland Grays Armory—*hist pl* OH-6
Cleveland Grove Ch—*church* GA-3
Cleveland Gulch—*valley* (2) CO-8
Cleveland Gulch—*valley* (2) ID-8
Cleveland Gulch—*valley* NM-5
Cleveland Hall—*hist pl* TN-4
Cleveland Harbor Station, U.S. Coast Guard—*hist pl* OH-6
**Cleveland Heights**—*pop pl* OH-6
Cleveland Heights—*ridge* NC-3
Cleveland Heights—*ridge* SC-3
Cleveland Heights Ch—*church* FL-3
Cleveland Heights Cottage Sch—*school* CO-8
Cleveland Heights Country Club—*locale* FL-3
**Cleveland Hill**—*pop pl* NY-2
Cleveland Hill—*ridge* CA-9
Cleveland Hill—*summit* GA-3
Cleveland Hill—*summit* ID-8
Cleveland Hill—*summit* NH-1
Cleveland Hill—*summit* (2) NY-2
Cleveland Hill—*summit* OR-9
Cleveland Hill—*summit* (2) VT-1
Cleveland Hill Sch—*school* NY-2
Cleveland Hill South Sch—*school* NY-2
Cleveland (historical)—*locale* AL-4
**Cleveland (historical)**—*pop pl* OR-9
Cleveland Hollow—*valley* PA-2
Cleveland Home For Aged Colored People—*hist pl* OH-6
Cleveland-Hopkins International Airp—*airport* OH-6
Cleveland House Of Correction—*building* OH-6
Cleveland HS—*school* AL-4
Cleveland HS—*school* CA-9
Cleveland HS—*school* MS-4
Cleveland HS—*school* MO-7
Cleveland HS—*school* NY-2
Cleveland HS—*school* OR-9
Cleveland HS—*school* TN-4
Cleveland HS—*school* WA-9
Cleveland Industrial Park—*locale* MS-4
Cleveland Irrigation Canal—*canal* ID-8
Cleveland Island—*island* MA-1
Cleveland Island—*island* VA-3
Cleveland JHS—*school* NJ-2
Cleveland JHS—*school* OH-6
Cleveland JHS—*school* OK-5
Cleveland JHS—*school* SC-3
Cleveland JHS—*school* TN-4
Cleveland Knob—*summit* AR-4
Cleveland Lake—*lake* CO-8
Cleveland Lake—*lake* (2) MI-6
Cleveland Lake—*lake* NY-2
Cleveland Lake—*lake* TX-5
Cleveland Lake—*lake* (2) UT-8
Cleveland Lake—*lake* WA-9
Cleveland Lake—*lake* WI-6
Cleveland Lake—*swamp* MI-6
Cleveland Lakes—*lake* AK-9
Cleveland Law Range—*hist pl* SC-3
Cleveland Ledge—*rock* MA-1
Cleveland Ledge Channel Range Light—*locale* MA-1
Cleveland Ledge Light—*locale* MA-1
Cleveland Ledge Lighthouse—*locale* MA-1
Cleveland Ledge Light Station—*hist pl* MA-1
Cleveland Lloyd Dinosaur Quarry—*locale* UT-8
Cleveland-Lloyd Dinosaur Quarry Campground—*locale* UT-8
Cleveland Lookout Tower—*locale* SC-3
Cleveland Mall—*hist pl* OH-6
Cleveland Mall—*locale* NC-3
Cleveland Mall Shop Ctr—*locale* TN-4
Cleveland Meadow—*flat* CA-9
**Cleveland Meadows (subdivision)**—*pop pl* AL-4
Cleveland Memorial Hosp—*hospital* NC-3
Cleveland Memorial Park—*cemetery* NC-3
Cleveland Methodist Ch—*church* AL-4
Cleveland Mills—*locale* AL-4
Cleveland Mills Ch—*church* AL-4
**Cleveland Mills (historical)**—*pop pl* NC-3
Cleveland Mine—*mine* (2) CA-9
Cleveland Mine—*mine* CO-8
Cleveland Mine—*mine* MT-8
Cleveland Mine—*mine* NV-8
Cleveland Mine—*mine* OR-9
Cleveland Mine—*mine* WA-9
Cleveland Mines—*mine* CA-9
Cleveland Mtn—*summit* CO-8
Cleveland Mtn—*summit* MA-1
Cleveland Mtn—*summit* MT-8
Cleveland Mtn—*summit* NH-1
Cleveland Mtn—*summit* WA-9
Cleveland Mtn—*summit* WV-2
Cleveland Municipal Airp—*airport* MS-4
Cleveland Municipal Airp—*airport* TX-5
Cleveland Municipal Stadium—*hist pl* OH-6
Cleveland Naval Finance Center—*military* OH-6
Cleveland Notch—*gap* NH-1
Cleveland Oil Field—*oilfield* OK-5
Cleveland Ordinance Plant (U.S. Military Reservation)—*other* OH-6
Cleveland Ordnance Plant—*military* OH-6
Cleveland Packard Bldg—*hist pl* OH-6
Cleveland Park—*flat* ND-7
Cleveland Park—*park* IN-6
Cleveland Park—*park* IA-7
Cleveland Park—*park* NY-2
Cleveland Park—*park* OH-6
Cleveland Park—*park* (2) SC-3
Cleveland Park—*park* TN-4
Cleveland Park—*park* TX-5
**Cleveland Park**—*pop pl* DC-2
Cleveland Park Hist Dist—*hist pl* DC-2
Cleveland-Partlow House—*hist pl* TX-5
Cleveland Pass—*gap* UT-8
Cleveland Passage—*channel* AK-9
Cleveland Peak—*summit* CO-8
Cleveland Peak—*summit* TX-5
Cleveland Peak—*summit* UT-8
Cleveland Peninsula—*cape* AK-9
Cleveland Plaza (Shop Ctr)—*locale* FL-3
Cleveland Pond—*lake* ME-1
Cleveland Pond—*lake* NY-2
Cleveland Pond—*reservoir* IN-6
Cleveland Pond—*reservoir* MA-1
Cleveland Pond Dam—*dam* IN-6
Cleveland Pond Dam—*dam* MA-1
Cleveland Post Office—*building* MS-4
Cleveland Post Office—*building* TN-4
Cleveland Post Office—*building* UT-8
Cleveland Public Library—*building* TN-4
Cleveland Public Square—*hist pl* OH-6
Cleveland Ranch—*locale* CA-9
Cleveland Ranch—*locale* NM-5
Cleveland Ranch—*locale* OR-9
Cleveland Rapids—*rapids* OR-9
Cleveland Ridge—*ridge* OR-9
Cleveland Road Ch of God—*church* AL-4
Cleveland Rock—*summit* CA-9
Cleveland-Rogers House—*hist pl* KY-4
Cleveland Rsvr—*reservoir* ID-8
Cleveland Rsvr—*reservoir* NY-2
Cleveland Rsvr—*reservoir* OK-5
Cleveland Rsvr—*reservoir* UT-8
Cleveland Run—*stream* KS-7
**Cleveland Run Township**—*pop pl* KS-7
Cleveland Sch—*school* (7) CA-9
Cleveland Sch—*school* DC-2
Cleveland Sch—*school* FL-3
Cleveland Sch—*school* (4) IL-6
Cleveland Sch—*school* IA-7
Cleveland Sch—*school* (2) KS-7
Cleveland Sch—*school* ME-1
Cleveland Sch—*school* MA-1
Cleveland Sch—*school* (6) MI-6
Cleveland Sch—*school* (3) MN-6
Cleveland Sch—*school* MO-7
Cleveland Sch—*school* NE-7
Cleveland Sch—*school* NH-1
Cleveland Sch—*school* (5) NJ-2
Cleveland Sch—*school* (2) NY-2
Cleveland Sch—*school* NC-3
Cleveland Sch—*school* (2) ND-7
Cleveland Sch—*school* (5) OH-6
Cleveland Sch—*school* (4) OK-5
Cleveland Sch—*school* PA-2
Cleveland Sch—*school* SC-3
Cleveland Sch—*school* (2) SD-7
Cleveland Sch—*school* TX-5
Cleveland Sch—*school* UT-8
Cleveland Sch—*school* WA-9
Cleveland Sch—*school* WV-2
Cleveland Sch—*school* (3) WI-6
Cleveland Sch (abandoned)—*school* MO-7
Cleveland Sch (historical)—*school* MO-7
Cleveland Sch Monument—*school* SC-3
*Cleveland School* AL-4
Cleveland Sewage Lagoon Dam—*dam* MS-4
Clevelands Ferry (historical)—*locale* AL-4
Cleveland Shoals—*bar* AL-4
Cleveland Siding—*locale* ME-1
Cleveland Slough—*stream* IL-6
Cleveland South (census name South Cleveland)—*uninc pl* TN-4
*Clevelands Pond* MA-1
Cleveland Spring—*spring* AZ-5
Cleveland Spring Ch—*church* KY-4
**Cleveland Spring (historical)**—*pop pl* NC-3
**Cleveland Springs (Cleveland Springs Estates)**—*pop pl* NC-3
*Clevelands Store* AL-4
Cleveland State Community Coll—*school* TN-4
**Cleveland Station**—*pop pl* GA-3
Cleveland Store (historical)—*locale* AL-4
Cleveland Street—*uninc pl* FL-3
Cleveland Street Cem—*cemetery* OH-6
Cleveland Street District—*hist pl* NC-3
Cleveland Street Post Office—*hist pl* FL-3
Cleveland Street Presbyterian Ch—*church* MS-4
Cleveland Street Sch—*school* NJ-2
Cleveland Street Station—*locale* NJ-2
Cleveland Temple—*church* TN-4
*Clevelandtown* MD-2
**Cleveland (Town of)**—*pop pl* (4) WI-6
Cleveland Township—*civil* MO-7
Cleveland Township—*civil* (2) SD-7
Cleveland Township—*fmr MCD* (2) IA-7
**Cleveland Township**—*pop pl* (4) KS-7
**Cleveland Township**—*pop pl* (3) NE-7
**Cleveland Township**—*pop pl* ND-7
**Cleveland Township**—*pop pl* (3) SD-7
Cleveland (Township of)—*fmr MCD* (8) AR-4
Cleveland (Township of)—*fmr MCD* (2) NC-3
**Cleveland (Township of)**—*pop pl* (2) IN-6
**Cleveland (Township of)**—*pop pl* MI-6
**Cleveland (Township of)**—*pop pl* MN-6
**Cleveland (Township of)**—*pop pl* PA-2
**Clevelandtown (subdivision)**—*pop pl* MA-1
Cleveland Trail (Jeep)—*trail* NV-8
Cleveland Trust Company—*hist pl* OH-6
**Clevelandville**—*pop pl* MD-2
Cleveland Warehouse District—*hist pl* OH-6
Cleveland West Pierhead Light—*hist pl* OH-6
Cleveland Worsted Mills Company—*hist pl* OH-6
Cleveland Worsted Mills Redfern Mill—*hist pl* OH-6
Cleveland Zoological Park—*park* OH-6
*Clevelon Fork* AZ-5
Cleve Marsh—*swamp* VA-3
Cleve Mine—*mine* MT-8
Cleve Mtn—*summit* MT-8
**Clevenger**—*pop pl* TN-4
Clevenger, Lowery, House—*hist pl* NM-5
Clevenger Butte—*summit* OR-9
Clevenger Canyon—*valley* CA-9
Clevenger Cem—*cemetery* MO-7
Clevenger Cem—*cemetery* OH-6
Clevenger Cem—*cemetery* TN-4
Clevenger Creek—*stream* OR-9
Clevenger Hollow—*valley* WV-2
Clevenger Park—*park* MI-6
Clevenger Sch—*school* (2) MO-7
*Clevengers Cross Roads* TN-4
Clevengers Marina—*locale* AL-4
Clevenger Spring—*spring* MT-8
Cleve Park—*flat* MT-8
**Clever**—*pop pl* MO-7
**Clever Creek**—*pop pl* TX-5
Clever Creek—*stream* KS-7
Clever Creek—*stream* MO-7
Clever Creek Cem—*cemetery* MO-7
**Cleverdale**—*pop pl* NY-2
**Cleversburg**—*pop pl* PA-2
Cleversburg Den Cave Four—*cave* PA-2
Cleversburg Den Cave One—*cave* PA-2
Cleversburg Den Cave Three—*cave* PA-2
Cleversburg Den Cave Two—*cave* PA-2
Cleversburg Junction—*locale* PA-2
Cleversburg Sink—*basin* PA-2
Clevers Oak Ch—*church* VA-3
**Cleves**—*pop pl* IA-7
**Cleves**—*pop pl* OH-6
Cleves Cove—*bay* OR-9
*Cleves Point* NY-2
Clevet Springs Ch—*church* AR-4
**Clevewood (subdivision)**—*pop pl* NC-3
Clevidence Draw—*valley* WY-8
Clevinger Branch—*stream* MO-7
Clevinger Knob Lookout Tower—*locale* KY-4
Clevingers Branch—*stream* KY-4
Clevise Lake—*lake* MN-6
*Clevit School* AL-4
*Clevlon Creek* AZ-5
*Clevlons Fork* AZ-5
*Clewalee Creek* AL-4
*Clewalla Creek* AL-4
Clewis Cem—*cemetery* TX-5
Clewis Corner—*locale* NC-3
Clewis Island—*island* GA-3
Clewis Ridge—*ridge* NC-3
Clewis Swamp—*swamp* FL-3
**Clewiston**—*pop pl* FL-3
Clewiston (CCD)—*cens area* FL-3
Clewiston Community Sch—*school* FL-3
Clewiston HS—*school* FL-3
Clewiston Intermediate Sch—*school* FL-3
Clewiston MS—*school* FL-3
Clewiston Primary Sch—*school* FL-3
Clewleyville Corners—*locale* ME-1
*Clew Pond* MA-1
*Clews Harbor Island* GA-3
Clews Ridge—*ridge* CA-9
*Clewwallee Creek* AL-4
Cleydael—*hist pl* VA-3
Cleyeland—*locale* IA-7
C L Hardaman Lake Dam—*dam* MS-4
C L Huff Lake Dam—*dam* MS-4
Cliatt Branch—*stream* AL-4
Cliatt Creek—*stream* GA-3
*Cliatts P.O.* AL-4
Cliburn Branch—*stream* MS-4
Cliburn Cem—*cemetery* MS-4
Cliburn Cem—*cemetery* TN-4
Cliche Creek—*stream* MI-6
Click—*locale* TX-5
*Click Branch* MO-7
*Click Branch* TX-5
Click Branch—*stream* (2) TN-4
Click Cem—*cemetery* AL-4
Click Cem—*cemetery* KS-7
Click Cem—*cemetery* MO-7
Click Cem—*cemetery* NC-3
Click Cem—*cemetery* (3) TN-4
Click Cem—*cemetery* (2) VA-3
*Click Creek* TN-4
Click Creek—*stream* TX-5
Click Creek Cave—*cave* TN-4
Click Gap—*gap* TX-5
Click Hollow—*valley* AL-4
Click Hollow—*valley* (2) MO-7
Click Mill—*locale* TN-4
Click Ridge—*ridge* TN-4
Clicks—*locale* ID-8
Clicks Creek—*stream* CA-9
Clicks Forge (historical)—*locale* TN-4
Clicks Mill (historical)—*locale* AL-4
Click Southeast Oil Field—*oilfield* KS-7
Click Tank—*reservoir* AZ-5
Click Tank—*reservoir* NM-5
Click Tank—*reservoir* TX-5
Click Tank No 2—*reservoir* NM-5
Click Tank No 7—*reservoir* NM-5
Click Tunnel—*tunnel* TN-4
**Clicquot (subdivision)**—*pop pl* MA-1
Clide Creek—*stream* WA-9
Cliett Cem—*cemetery* GA-3
Cliett Cem—*cemetery* TX-5
Clietts Post Office (historical)—*building* AL-4
Cliett Windmills—*locale* TX-5
**Clifdale**—*pop pl* NC-3
**Clifdale**—*pop pl* VA-3
*Cliff* (2) CO-8
*Cliff* MA-1
*Cliff* MN-6
Cliff—*locale* CA-9
Cliff—*locale* ID-8
Cliff—*locale* MO-7
Cliff—*locale* TX-5
**Cliff**—*pop pl* KY-4
**Cliff**—*pop pl* NM-5
**Cliff**—*pop pl* UT-8
*Cliff, The* MA-1
Cliff, The—*cliff* NY-2
Cliff, The—*cliff* OR-9
Cliff, The—*cliff* PA-2
Cliff, The—*cliff* WV-2
Cliff, Walter, Ranch District—*hist pl* NV-8
Cliff Arch—*arch* UT-8
Cliff Bay—*bay* (2) AK-9
Cliff Beach—*beach* MA-1
Cliff Branch—*stream* AL-4
Cliff Branch—*stream* (2) KY-4
Cliff Branch—*stream* NC-3
Cliff Branch—*stream* (2) TN-4
Cliff Bridge—*bridge* FL-3
Cliff Bridge—*locale* CA-9
Cliff Bromide Springs—*spring* OK-5
Cliff Camp—*locale* CA-9
Cliff Camp—*locale* WA-9
Cliff Canyon—*valley* (3) CA-9
Cliff Canyon—*valley* CO-8
Cliff Canyon—*valley* (3) ID-8
Cliff Canyon—*valley* NV-8
Cliff Canyon—*valley* NM-5
Cliff Canyon—*valley* (2) UT-8
Cliff Canyon Spring—*spring* CA-9
**Cliff Cave**—*pop pl* MO-7
Cliff Cem—*cemetery* IN-6
Cliff Cem—*cemetery* OK-5
Cliff Cem—*cemetery* TN-4
Cliff Ch—*church* KY-4
Cliff Ch—*church* NE-7
Cliff Ch—*church* PA-2
*Cliff City Point* MD-2
*Cliff Creek* CO-8
*Cliff Creek* OR-9
Cliff Creek—*stream* AK-9
Cliff Creek—*stream* CA-9
Cliff Creek—*stream* (6) CO-8
Cliff Creek—*stream* (2) GA-3
Cliff Creek—*stream* (12) ID-8
Cliff Creek—*stream* MN-6
Cliff Creek—*stream* (7) MT-8
Cliff Creek—*stream* OH-6
Cliff Creek—*stream* (4) OR-9
Cliff Creek—*stream* TN-4
Cliff Creek—*stream* TX-5
Cliff Creek—*stream* (2) UT-8
Cliff Creek—*stream* VA-3
Cliff Creek—*stream* WA-9
Cliff Creek—*stream* (3) WY-8
Cliff Creek Ch—*church* TN-4
Cliff Creek Falls—*falls* WY-8
Cliff Creek Pass—*gap* WY-8
Cliff Creek Trail—*trail* ID-8
*Cliffdale* NV-8
Cliffdale—*locale* CO-8
Cliffdale—*locale* IL-6
**Cliffdale**—*pop pl* NC-3
Cliffdale Ch—*church* TX-5
Cliff Dale Ch—*church* VA-3
Cliffdale Elem Sch—*school* NC-3
Cliffdale Hollow—*valley* MO-7
Cliffdale Park—*locale* NJ-2
Cliffdale Pond—*reservoir* NY-2
Cliffdell—*locale* WA-9
Cliff Dweller Canyon—*valley* NM-5
Cliff Dweller Canyon—*valley* UT-8
Cliff Dweller Flat—*flat* UT-8
Cliffdweller Mine—*mine* CO-8
Cliffdweller Mines—*mine* CO-8
Cliff Dweller Ridge—*ridge* UT-8
Cliff Dwellers Canyon—*valley* NE-7
Cliff Dwellers Canyon—*valley* NM-5
Cliff Dwellers Lodge—*other* AZ-5
Cliff Dwellers Lodge Airp—*airport* AZ-5
Cliff Dweller Spring—*spring* AZ-5
Cliff Dwelling—*locale* AZ-5
*Cliff Dwelling Airport* AZ-5
Cliff Dwelling Canyon—*valley* NM-5
*Cliff Dwelling Mountain* UT-8
Cliff Dwelling Tank—*reservoir* AZ-5
Cliff Fees Dam—*dam* SD-7
*Cliff Flag Peak* UT-8
Cliff Graham Rsvr No 3—*reservoir* WY-8
Cliff Gulch—*valley* OR-9
*Cliff Hamblin Natural Arch* UT-8
Cliffhanger Cave—*cave* AL-4
*Cliff Hare Stadium* AL-4
**Cliff Haven**—*pop pl* AL-4
**Cliff Haven**—*pop pl* CA-9
**Cliff Haven**—*pop pl* NY-2
**Cliff Heights Subdivision**—*pop pl* UT-8
Cliff Hill—*summit* KY-4
Cliff Hill—*summit* NC-3
Cliff Hill Ch—*church* KY-4
Cliff (historical)—*locale* MS-4
Cliff Hollow—*valley* AR-4
Cliff Hollow—*valley* ID-8
Cliff House—*building* CA-9
Cliff House—*hist pl* CO-8
Cliff House—*locale* NM-5
**Cliffield**—*pop pl* VA-3
Cliffield Mtn—*summit* NC-3
*Cliff Island* ME-1
Cliff Island—*island* AK-9
Cliff Island—*island* ME-1
Cliff Island—*island* WA-9
**Cliff Island**—*pop pl* ME-1
Cliff Island Landing—*locale* ME-1
Cliff JHS—*school* AL-4
Cliff Kill Site—*hist pl* VA-3
*Cliff Lake* MN-6
*Cliff Lake* UT-8
*Cliff Lake* WA-9
Cliff Lake—*lake* AK-9
Cliff Lake—*lake* (5) CA-9
Cliff Lake—*lake* (3) CO-8
Cliff Lake—*lake* FL-3
Cliff Lake—*lake* (3) ID-8
Cliff Lake—*lake* ME-1
Cliff Lake—*lake* (3) MN-6
Cliff Lake—*lake* (8) MT-8
Cliff Lake—*lake* (3) OR-9
Cliff Lake—*lake* UT-8
Cliff Lake—*lake* (3) WA-9
Cliff Lake—*lake* (6) WY-8
Cliff Lake—*locale* MT-8
Cliff Lake—*reservoir* NY-2
Cliff Lake—*reservoir* (2) UT-8
Cliff Lake Bench—*bench* MT-8
Cliff Lake Campground—*park* (2) OR-9
Cliff Lake Camp Grounds—*locale* MT-8
Cliff Lake Dam—*dam* (2) UT-8
Cliff Lake Rsvr—*reservoir* CO-8
Cliff Lakes—*lake* CO-8
Cliff Lake Shelter—*locale* OR-9
Cliff Lake Trail—*trail* WY-8
Cliffland—*locale* IA-7
Cliffland (historical P.O.)—*locale* IA-7
**Cliff Lodge Subdivision, The**—*pop pl* UT-8
Cliff Lookout Tower—*locale* MI-6
Cliff Meadow—*flat* CA-9
Cliff Mills—*locale* VA-3
Cliff Mine—*locale* AK-9
Cliff Mine—*locale* PA-2
Cliff Mine—*mine* OR-9
Cliff Mine—*mine* WY-8
*Cliff Mountain* MT-8
Cliff Mtn—*summit* GA-3
Cliff Mtn—*summit* ID-8
Cliff Mtn—*summit* (2) MT-8
Cliff Mtn—*summit* NY-2
Cliff Mtn—*summit* (2) VA-3
Cliff Nature Trail—*trail* OR-9
Cliff Oil Field—*oilfield* CO-8
*Clifford* VA-3
Clifford—*locale* CO-8
Clifford—*locale* IL-6
Clifford—*locale* KY-4
Clifford—*locale* MD-2
Clifford—*locale* NV-8
Clifford—*locale* WI-6
**Clifford**—*pop pl* IN-6
**Clifford**—*pop pl* MA-1
**Clifford**—*pop pl* MI-6
**Clifford**—*pop pl* MS-4
**Clifford**—*pop pl* NY-2
**Clifford**—*pop pl* ND-7
**Clifford**—*pop pl* OH-6
**Clifford**—*pop pl* (2) PA-2
**Clifford**—*pop pl* VA-3
**Clifford**—*pop pl* WI-6
Clifford, George B., House—*hist pl* ND-7
Clifford, John D., House—*hist pl* ME-1
Clifford, Mount—*summit* AK-9
*Clifford and Holcombs Brook* MA-1
Clifford Annex—*hist pl* ND-7
Clifford Bay—*bay* ME-1
Clifford Branch—*stream* TN-4
Clifford Bridge—*bridge* NE-7
*Clifford Brook* ME-1
Clifford Brook—*stream* NH-1
Clifford Brook—*stream* NY-2
Clifford (CCD)—*cens area* KY-4
Clifford Cem—*cemetery* KS-7
Clifford Cem—*cemetery* LA-4
Clifford Cem—*cemetery* ND-7
Clifford Cem—*cemetery* PA-2
Clifford Ch—*church* VA-3
Clifford Chapel—*church* MA-1
*Clifford Corners* PA-2
Clifford Creek—*stream* (2) AK-9
Clifford Creek—*stream* IN-6
Clifford Creek—*stream* (2) MT-8
Clifford Creek—*stream* NE-7
Clifford Creek—*stream* SD-7
Clifford Falls—*falls* NY-2
Clifford Hill—*ridge* NH-1
Clifford (historical)—*locale* KS-7
Clifford Hollow—*valley* MD-2
Clifford Hollow—*valley* WV-2
Clifford House—*hist pl* FL-3
Clifford House—*hist pl* NV-8
Clifford Island—*island* AK-9
Clifford Island—*island* IL-6
Clifford Island—*island* NY-2
*Clifford Lake* MA-1
Clifford Lake—*lake* ME-1
Clifford Lake—*lake* (3) MI-6
Clifford Lake—*lake* MN-6
Clifford M Dible Elementary—*school* PA-2
Clifford Mine—*mine* MT-8
Clifford Mine—*mine* NV-8
Clifford Mine (underground)—*mine* AL-4
Clifford Oil Field—*oilfield* MS-4
Clifford Park—*park* ME-1
Clifford Park—*park* MI-6
Clifford Park—*park* PA-2
**Clifford Park**—*pop pl* IN-6
Clifford Point—*cape* AK-9
Clifford Point—*summit* MT-8
Clifford Pond—*lake* ME-1
Clifford Post Office (historical)—*building* MS-4
Clifford Road Dam—*dam* MA-1
Clifford Road Pond—*reservoir* MA-1
Clifford Sch—*school* CA-9
Clifford Sch—*school* MA-1
Clifford Sch—*school* MI-6
Cliffords Grove Ch—*church* GA-3
Clifford Shaft—*mine* NM-5
Clifford Shaft—*mine* PA-2
Clifford (site)—*locale* OR-9
Cliffords Landing (historical)—*locale* MS-4
Clifford Spring—*spring* NV-8
Clifford Station—*locale* PA-2
Clifford Stream—*stream* (2) ME-1
Clifford Street Sch—*school* CA-9
**Clifford Township**—*pop pl* KS-7
**Clifford (Township of)**—*pop pl* PA-2
Clifford-Warren House—*hist pl* MA-1
Clifford Wash—*stream* AZ-5
Clifford Well—*well* AZ-5
Clifford-Wyrick House—*hist pl* MO-7
Cliff Palace—*locale* CO-8
Cliff Palace View Point—*locale* CO-8
Cliff Park—*park* WA-9
Cliff Park—*post sta* NJ-2
Cliff Park Brook—*stream* NY-2
Cliff Park Inn Golf Course—*locale* PA-2
Cliff Peak—*summit* CA-9
Cliff Point—*cape* (3) AK-9
Cliff Point—*cape* (2) WA-9
Cliff Point—*summit* MT-8
Cliff Pond—*lake* MA-1
Cliff Pond—*lake* NY-2
Cliff Pond—*lake* SD-7
Cliff Post Office (historical)—*building* MS-4
Cliff Post Office (historical)—*building* TN-4
Cliff Ranch—*locale* AZ-5
Cliff Ranch—*locale* (2) OR-9
Cliff Range—*ridge* MI-6
Cliff Ridge—*ridge* CA-9
Cliff Ridge—*ridge* GA-3
Cliff Ridge—*ridge* ME-1
Cliff Ridge—*ridge* NC-3
Cliff Ridge—*ridge* TN-4
Cliff Ridge—*ridge* UT-8
Cliff Ridge—*ridge* WA-9
Cliffridge Park—*park* CA-9
Cliff River—*stream* MI-6
Cliff Rose Hill—*summit* AZ-5
Cliff Rose Hill Wash—*valley* AZ-5
Cliff Rose Tank—*reservoir* AZ-5
Cliffrose Tank—*reservoir* AZ-5
Cliff Roy Mine—*mine* NM-5
Cliff Rsvr—*reservoir* NV-8
Cliff Rsvr—*reservoir* UT-8
Cliff Run—*stream* (2) WV-2
Cliffs—*locale* AZ-5
Cliffs—*locale* ID-8
Cliffs—*locale* WA-9
*Cliffs, The* AL-4
*Cliffs, The* WY-8
Cliffs, The—*cliff* AR-4
Cliffs, The—*cliff* CA-9
Cliffs, The—*cliff* MA-1
Cliffs, The—*cliff* NV-8
Cliffs, The—*cliff* TN-4
Cliffs, The—*hist pl* PA-2
Cliffs, The—*summit* NV-8
Cliffs, The—*summit* NH-1
*Cliffs Bay* GA-3
Cliffs Bight—*bay* MD-2
Cliffs Camp—*locale* OR-9
Cliff Sch—*school* KS-7
Cliff Sch (historical)—*school* PA-2
Cliff Sch (historical)—*school* TN-4
**Cliffs City**—*pop pl* MD-2
Cliff Scott Airp—*airport* MO-7
Cliffs Creek—*stream* OR-9
Cliffs Fishing Camp—*locale* AL-4
**Cliffs (historical)**—*pop pl* PA-2
*Cliffside* NV-8
Cliffside—*hist pl* VA-3
**Cliffside**—*pop pl* CA-9
**Cliffside**—*pop pl* KY-4
**Cliffside**—*pop pl* NY-2
**Cliffside**—*pop pl* NC-3
**Cliffside**—*pop pl* TN-4
**Cliffside**—*pop pl* TX-5
Cliffside Dam—*dam* NC-3
Cliffside Elem Sch—*school* NC-3
Cliffside Gas Field Camp—*locale* TX-5
Cliffside Hose Company No. 4—*hist pl* NJ-2
**Cliffside Junction**—*pop pl* NC-3
Cliffside Lake—*reservoir* NC-3
Cliffside Mine—*mine* NM-5
**Cliffside Park**—*pop pl* NJ-2
Cliffside State For—*forest* NY-2
Cliffside Trail—*trail* OK-5
Cliffside Well—*well* NV-8
Cliff Siding—*locale* MS-4
*Cliffs Landing* TN-4
Cliffs Mill (historical)—*locale* TN-4
Cliffs Mines—*mine* MI-6

Cliffs Of ... ME-1
Cliffs Of The Neuse State Park—park ... NC-3
Cliffs of the Seven Double Pillars—cliff ... IN-6
Cliffs Picnic Area—area ... PA-2
Cliffs Plantation—hist pl ... MS-4
Cliffs Plateau—plain ... ND-7
Cliff's Point ... MD-2
Cliffs Point—cape ... MD-2
Cliff Spring—spring ... AK-9
Cliff Spring—spring (6) ... AZ-5
Cliff Spring—spring ... ID-8
Cliff Spring—spring ... MO-7
Cliff Spring—spring ... MT-8
Cliff Spring—spring (5) ... NV-8
Cliff Spring—spring (2) ... NM-5
Cliff Spring—spring (2) ... OR-9
Cliff Spring—spring ... UT-8
Cliff Spring—spring ... WY-8
Cliff Spring Canyon—valley ... AZ-5
Cliff Spring Rsvr—reservoir ... OR-9
**Cliff Springs**—pop pl ... TN-4
Cliff Springs—spring ... AZ-5
Cliff Springs—spring ... NV-8
Cliff Springs Ch—church ... AL-4
Cliffsprings Post Office (historical)—building ... TN-4
Cliff Spring Valley—valley ... AZ-5
Cliffs Station—locale ... DE-2
Cliffstone ... ME-1
Cliffs Wharf—locale ... MD-2
Cliff Tank—reservoir (2) ... AZ-5
Cliff Tank—reservoir ... TX-5
Clifft Cemetery—cemetery ... TN-4
Cliff Temple Baptist Church ... MS-4
Cliff Temple Ch—church ... MS-4
**Clifftop**—pop pl (2) ... WV-2
Cliff Top—summit ... TN-4
Cliff Top—summit ... TX-5
**Clifftops**—pop pl ... TN-4
Clifftops Lake—reservoir ... TN-4
Clifftops Lake Dam—dam ... TN-4
**Cliff Township**—pop pl ... NE-7
Cliffty Branch—stream ... MO-7
Cliff Valley—valley ... CA-9
Cliff Valley Golf Course—other ... AZ-5
Cliffview—locale ... VA-3
Cliffview Ch—church ... VA-3
**Cliff Village**—pop pl ... MO-7
Cliff Walker Pond Dam—dam ... MS-4
Cliff White Rsvr—reservoir ... WY-8
**Cliffwilliams**—pop pl ... MS-4
**Cliff Williams**—pop pl ... MS-4
**Cliffwood**—pop pl ... NJ-2
Cliffwood Beach—beach ... NJ-2
**Cliffwood Beach**—pop pl ... NJ-2
Cliffwood Bluff—cliff ... WI-6
Cliffwood Ch—church ... NJ-2
**Cliffwood Lake**—pop pl ... NJ-2
Cliffwood Lake—reservoir ... NJ-2
**Cliffwood Park Subdivision**—pop pl ... UT-8
Cliffwood Station—locale ... NJ-2
**Cliffwood (subdivision)**—pop pl ... NC-3
Clifside—locale ... NV-8
**Clift Acres**—pop pl ... AL-4
Clift Arch—arch ... UT-8
Clift Bldg—hist pl ... UT-8
Clift Cem—cemetery ... AL-4
Clift Cem—cemetery ... TN-4
Clift Coulee—valley ... MT-8
Clift Creek—stream ... AR-4
Clift Creek—stream ... ID-8
Clift Creek—stream ... TN-4
Clift Ditch—canal ... IN-6
Clift Drain—canal ... MI-6
Clift Mines (underground)—mine ... AL-4
Clifton ... AL-4
Clifton ... MS-4
Clifton ... MO-7
Clifton ... OH-6
Clifton ... PA-2
Clifton ... TN-4
Clifton—hist pl ... IA-7
Clifton—hist pl ... MD-2
Clifton—hist pl ... VA-3
Clifton—locale ... AK-9
Clifton—locale ... ID-8
Clifton—locale ... IA-7
Clifton—locale ... KY-4
Clifton—locale ... LA-4
Clifton—locale ... OH-6
Clifton—locale ... OK-5
Clifton—locale ... PA-2
Clifton—locale ... UT-8
Clifton—locale (2) ... VA-3
Clifton—locale ... WY-8
**Clifton**—pop pl ... AZ-5
**Clifton**—pop pl ... CA-9
**Clifton**—pop pl ... CO-8
**Clifton**—pop pl ... CT-1
**Clifton**—pop pl ... ID-8
**Clifton**—pop pl ... IL-6
**Clifton**—pop pl (2) ... IN-6
**Clifton**—pop pl ... KS-7
**Clifton**—pop pl (2) ... KY-4
**Clifton**—pop pl ... LA-4
**Clifton**—pop pl ... ME-1
**Clifton**—pop pl (2) ... MD-2
**Clifton**—pop pl ... MN-6
**Clifton**—pop pl (2) ... MS-4
**Clifton**—pop pl ... NJ-2
**Clifton**—pop pl (2) ... NY-2
**Clifton**—pop pl ... NC-3
**Clifton**—pop pl ... ND-7
**Clifton**—pop pl (2) ... OH-6
**Clifton**—pop pl (2) ... OR-9
**Clifton**—pop pl (2) ... PA-2
**Clifton**—pop pl ... SC-3
**Clifton**—pop pl ... TN-4
**Clifton**—pop pl (2) ... TX-5
**Clifton**—pop pl ... VA-3
**Clifton**—pop pl ... WV-2
**Clifton**—pop pl ... WI-6
Clifton—uninc pl ... FL-3
Clifton—uninc pl ... KY-4
Clifton—uninc pl ... MD-2
Clifton, Lake—lake ... FL-3
Clifton Ave Hist Dist—hist pl ... OH-6
Clifton Ave Sch—school ... NJ-2
Clifton Baptist Ch—church ... MS-4
Clifton Basin—basin ... ID-8
Clifton Bayou—stream ... LA-4
Clifton Beach—beach ... MD-2
**Clifton Beach**—pop pl ... TX-5
Clifton Bend—bend (2) ... TN-4
Clifton Bluff—cliff ... GA-3
Clifton Boat Harbor ... TN-4
Clifton Branch—stream ... AL-4
Clifton Branch—stream ... NC-3
Clifton Branch—stream ... TX-5
Clifton Branch—stream ... VA-3
Clifton Canyon—valley ... WY-8
Clifton Casa Grande Bldg—hist pl ... AZ-5
Clifton Catholic Cem—cemetery ... AZ-5
Clifton (CCD)—cens area ... AZ-5
Clifton (CCD)—cens area ... TX-5
Clifton Cem—cemetery ... AZ-5
Clifton Cem—cemetery (3) ... GA-3
Clifton Cem—cemetery ... MS-4
Clifton Cem—cemetery (2) ... MO-7
Clifton Cem—cemetery ... NE-7
Clifton Cem—cemetery ... ND-7
Clifton Cem—cemetery ... PA-2
Clifton Cem—cemetery ... SD-7
Clifton Cem—cemetery (4) ... TN-4
Clifton Cem—cemetery (4) ... TX-5
Clifton Cem—cemetery ... VA-3
Clifton Cem—cemetery (2) ... WV-2
Clifton Cem—cemetery ... WI-6
Clifton Ch—church ... GA-3
Clifton Ch—church (2) ... KY-4
Clifton Ch—church ... MS-4
Clifton Ch—church ... SC-3
Clifton Ch—church ... TN-4
Clifton Channel—channel ... OR-9
Clifton Channel—channel ... TX-5
Clifton Chapel—church ... VA-3
**Clifton City**—pop pl ... MO-7
Clifton City (corporate name Clifton)) ... TN-4
Clifton City Hall—building ... AZ-5
Clifton City Park—park ... TN-4
Clifton-Clyde HS—school ... KS-7
Clifton Community Center and Church—hist pl ... CO-8
Clifton Corners—locale ... ME-1
Clifton Corners Sch—school ... WI-6
**Clifton (corporate name for Clifton City)**—pop pl ... TN-4
Clifton Court Forebay—reservoir ... CA-9
Clifton Creek—stream (2) ... ID-8
Clifton Creek—stream ... IN-6
Clifton Creek—stream ... MD-2
Clifton Creek—stream ... MI-6
Clifton Creek—stream ... MO-7
Clifton Creek—stream ... TN-4
Clifton Crossing—locale ... LA-4
**Cliftondale**—pop pl ... MA-1
**Cliftondale (Cliftondale Park)**—pop pl ... VA-3
**Cliftondale Park**—pop pl ... VA-3
Cliftondale Station—locale ... MA-1
**Cliftondale (Tell)**—pop pl ... GA-3
Clifton Ditch—canal ... CO-8
Clifton Ditch—canal ... IN-6
Clifton-East End—post sta ... MD-2
Clifton Elem Sch—school ... KS-7
Clifton Falls—falls ... NY-2
Clifton Farms ... OH-6
Clifton Ferry—locale ... TN-4
Clifton Ferry (historical)—locale ... AL-4
Clifton Ferry Public Use Area—park ... AL-4
Clifton Flat—flat ... UT-8
Clifton F McClintic State Wildlife Station—park ... WV-2
Clifton Ford—locale ... WV-2
Clifton Forge HS—school ... VA-3
**Clifton Forge (ind. city)**—pop pl ... VA-3
**Clifton Forge (subdivision)**—pop pl ... NC-3
Clifton Fork—stream ... VA-3
Clifton Furnace—hist pl ... VA-3
Clifton Furnace Ruins—locale ... NY-2
**Clifton Gardens**—pop pl ... NY-2
Clifton Gorge—valley ... OH-6
**Clifton Heights**—pop pl ... MA-1
**Clifton Heights**—pop pl ... MO-7
**Clifton Heights**—pop pl ... NY-2
**Clifton Heights**—pop pl ... PA-2
Clifton Heights Borough—civil ... PA-2
Clifton Heights Ch—church ... KY-4
Clifton Heights Historic Distruct—hist pl ... MS-4
**Clifton Heights (RR name Clifton)**—pop pl ... PA-2
Clifton Highlands Golf Course—other ... WI-6
Clifton Hill ... ID-8
**Clifton Hill**—pop pl ... MO-7
**Clifton Hill**—pop pl ... VI-3
Clifton Hill—summit ... VA-3
Clifton Hill Baptist Ch—church ... TN-4
**Clifton Hills**—pop pl ... TN-4
Clifton Hills—summit ... NM-5
Clifton Hills—summit ... UT-8
Clifton Hill Sch—school ... NE-7
Clifton Hills Sch—school ... TN-4
Clifton Hist Dist—hist pl ... KY-4
Clifton Hist Dist—hist pl ... VA-3
Clifton (historical)—locale (2) ... AL-4
Clifton (historical)—locale ... SD-7
**Clifton (historical)**—pop pl ... OR-9
Clifton (historical P.O.)—locale ... MA-1
Clifton Hollow—valley ... WI-6
Clifton Hollow—valley ... WY-8
Clifton Hollow Golf Club—other ... WI-6
Clifton Hot Springs—spring ... AZ-5
Clifton House—locale ... NM-5
Clifton House and Mill Site—hist pl ... NC-3
Clifton House Hotel—hist pl ... TX-5
Clifton HS—school ... AZ-5
Clifton Island—island ... NC-3
Clifton Junction—locale ... TN-4
Clifton Knob—summit ... WV-2
Clifton Knolls—CDP ... NY-2
**Clifton Knolls**—pop pl ... NY-2
Clifton Lake—reservoir ... MI-6
Clifton Lake—reservoir ... TX-5
Clifton Maddox Dam—dam ... AL-4
Clifton (Magisterial District)—fmr MCD ... VA-3
Clifton Marina—locale ... TN-4
Clifton McLeod Lake—dam ... MS-4
Clifton-Metropolitan Hotel—hist pl ... IA-7
Clifton Mill—locale ... MI-6
Clifton Mills ... MD-2
Clifton Mills—locale ... KY-4
Clifton Mills—locale ... PA-2
**Clifton Mills**—pop pl ... WV-2
Clifton Mine (underground)—mine ... AL-4
Clifton Mountain—ridge ... AR-4
Clifton-Natural Bridge (CCD)—cens area ... TN-4
Clifton-Natural Bridge Division—civil ... TN-4
Clifton Park—park ... DE-2
Clifton Park—park ... KS-7
Clifton Park—park ... MO-7
Clifton Park—park ... NY-2
**Clifton Park**—pop pl ... MD-2
Clifton Park And Golf Course—park ... MD-2
**Clifton Park Center**—pop pl ... NY-2
Clifton Park JHS—school ... MD-2
Clifton Park Lakefront District—hist pl ... OH-6
**Clifton Park Manor**—pop pl ... DE-2
**Clifton Park (Town of)**—pop pl ... NY-2
Clifton Park Valve House—hist pl ... MD-2
**Clifton Park Village**—pop pl ... MD-2
Clifton Peak—summit ... AZ-5
Clifton Place—hist pl (2) ... TN-4
Clifton Plantation (historical)—locale ... AL-4
Clifton Plantation House—hist pl ... MS-4
Clifton Point—cape ... MD-2
Clifton Point—cape ... NY-2
Clifton Point—cape ... VA-3
Clifton Pond—reservoir ... NC-3
Clifton Pond Dam—dam ... NC-3
Clifton Post Office—building ... AZ-5
Clifton Post Office—building ... TN-4
Clifton Post Office (historical)—building ... AL-4
Clifton Public School ... AZ-5
Clifton Ridge—ridge ... CA-9
Clifton Ridge—ridge ... VA-3
Clifton Ridge—ridge ... WI-6
**Clifton Ridge (subdivision)**—pop pl ... NC-3
Clifton Road Lake—lake ... KY-4
Clifton (RR name for Clifton Heights)—other ... PA-2
Clifton RR Station—building ... AZ-5
Clifton Run—stream ... WV-2
**Cliftons**—pop pl ... KY-4
Clifton Sch—hist pl ... MD-2
Clifton Sch—school (3) ... CA-9
Clifton Sch—school ... IL-6
Clifton Sch—school (2) ... KY-4
Clifton Sch—school ... ND-7
Clifton Sch—school ... OH-6
Clifton Sch—school (3) ... SD-7
Clifton Sch—school ... TX-5
Clifton Sch (abandoned)—school ... MO-7
Clifton Sch (historical)—school ... MO-7
Clifton School—locale ... WY-8
Clifton School (Abandoned)—locale ... IL-6
Clifton School Hollow—valley ... MO-7
Clifton (Site)—locale ... NV-8
Clifton Spring—spring ... ID-8
**Clifton Springs**—pop pl ... NY-2
Clifton Springs—spring ... FL-3
Clifton Springs Rsvr—reservoir ... NY-2
Clifton Springs Sanitarium—hist pl ... NY-2
Clifton Square—locale ... KS-7
Clifton Station ... MA-1
Clifton Station ... VA-3
Clifton Station—building ... PA-2
Clifton Station—locale ... NJ-2
Clifton Station—locale ... PA-2
**Clifton Station**—pop pl ... SC-3
Clifton Station (historical)—locale ... MA-1
**Clifton (subdivision)**—pop pl ... MA-1
Clifton Summit Cem—cemetery ... TN-4
Clifton Tank—reservoir (2) ... TX-5
**Clifton Terrace**—pop pl ... IL-6
Clifton Town Hall—building ... ND-7
**Clifton (Town of)**—pop pl ... ME-1
**Clifton (Town of)**—pop pl ... NY-2
**Clifton (Town of)**—pop pl (3) ... WI-6
Clifton Township—civil ... MO-7
Clifton Township—civil ... SD-7
**Clifton Township**—pop pl (2) ... KS-7
**Clifton Township**—pop pl ... ND-7
**Clifton Township**—pop pl (2) ... SD-7
Clifton (Township of)—fmr MCD ... AR-4
Clifton (Township of)—fmr MCD ... NC-3
**Clifton (Township of)**—pop pl (2) ... MN-6
**Clifton (Township of)**—pop pl ... PA-2
Clifton View Ch—church ... TN-4
Cliftonville—locale ... FL-3
**Cliftonville**—pop pl ... MS-4
**Cliftonville**—pop pl ... NC-3
Cliftonville Post Office (historical)—building ... MS-4
Clift Ridge ... CA-9
Clift Ridge ... GA-3
Clifts Landing—locale ... TN-4
Clifty ... AL-4
Clifty (2) ... IN-6
Clifty—locale ... TN-4
Clifty—locale ... WV-2
**Clifty**—pop pl ... AL-4
**Clifty**—pop pl ... AR-4
**Clifty**—pop pl ... KY-4
Clifty, Mount—summit ... WA-9
Clifty Baptist Ch (historical)—church ... TN-4
Clifty Branch—stream ... AL-4
Clifty Branch—stream (2) ... IN-6
Clifty Branch—stream (2) ... KY-4
Clifty Canyon—valley ... AR-4
Clifty Cem—cemetery ... MO-7
Clifty Cem—cemetery ... TN-4
Clifty Ch—church ... KY-4
Clifty Ch—church ... WV-2
Clifty Chapel—church ... IN-6
Clifty Coal Bed Mine (underground)—mine ... AL-4
Clifty Creek ... IN-6
Clifty Creek—stream (6) ... AL-4
Clifty Creek—stream (3) ... AR-4
Clifty Creek—stream ... ID-8
Clifty Creek—stream (3) ... IL-6
Clifty Creek—stream (2) ... IN-6
Clifty Creek—stream (10) ... KY-4
Clifty Creek—stream (2) ... MO-7
Clifty Creek—stream ... OK-5
Clifty Creek—stream (5) ... TN-4
Clifty Creek—stream ... TX-5
Clifty Creek Ditch—canal ... IL-6
Clifty Creek Elem Sch—school ... IN-6
Clifty Creek Park—park ... IN-6
Clifty Creek Power Plant—other ... IN-6
Clifty Falls—falls ... IN-6
Clifty Falls State Park—park ... IN-6
Clifty Fork ... AL-4
Clifty Fork—stream ... MO-7
Clifty Grove Ch—church ... KY-4
**Clifty Heights**—pop pl ... IL-6
Clifty Hill—summit ... KY-4
Clifty Hollow—valley (2) ... AR-4
Clifty Hollow—valley (2) ... KY-4
Clifty Hollow—valley ... MO-7
Clifty Hollow—valley ... TN-4
Clifty Mine—mine ... KY-4
Clifty Mtn—summit ... ID-8
Clifty Number One Mine (underground)—mine ... TN-4
Clifty Number Three Mine (underground)—mine ... TN-4
Clifty Post Office (historical)—building ... AL-4
Clifty Post Office (historical)—building ... TN-4
Clifty Sch—school ... KY-4
Clifty Sch (abandoned)—school ... MO-7
Clifty Sch (historical)—school (2) ... TN-4
Clifty School ... IN-6
Clifty Spring—spring ... MO-7
Clifty (Township of)—fmr MCD ... AR-4
**Clifty (Township of)**—pop pl ... IN-6
**Clifty Village**—pop pl ... IN-6
Clikapudi Creek—stream ... CA-9
Clima—locale ... CA-9
Clima Mesa—summit ... CA-9
Climax—locale ... AL-4
Climax—locale ... IA-7
Climax—locale ... KY-4
Climax—locale ... OR-9
Climax—locale ... SC-3
Climax—locale (2) ... TX-5
Climax—locale ... WA-9
**Climax**—pop pl ... CO-8
**Climax**—pop pl ... GA-3
**Climax**—pop pl ... KS-7
**Climax**—pop pl ... MI-6
**Climax**—pop pl ... MN-6
**Climax**—pop pl ... NM-5
**Climax**—pop pl ... NY-2
**Climax**—pop pl ... NC-3
**Climax**—pop pl ... OH-6
**Climax**—pop pl (2) ... PA-2
**Climax**—pop pl ... VA-3
Climax Camp—locale ... CO-8
Climax Canyon Park—park ... NM-5
Climax (CCD)—cens area ... GA-3
Climax Ch—church ... KY-4
Climax Creek—stream ... CO-8
Climax Creek—stream ... NC-3
Climax Gulch—valley ... MT-8
Climax Hollow—valley ... PA-2
Climax Lake—lake ... MN-6
Climax Mica Mine—mine ... SD-7
Climax Mine—mine (4) ... AZ-5
Climax Mine—mine ... CO-8
Climax Mine—mine ... ID-8
Climax Mine—mine ... NV-8
Climax Mine (underground)—mine ... AL-4
Climax Sch—school ... AR-4
Climax Sch—school (2) ... IL-6
Climax Sch—school ... MO-7
Climax Sch—school ... NE-7
Climax Sch—school ... VA-3
Climax Sch—school ... WI-6
Climax Sch (historical)—school ... MO-7
Climax Sch Number 3—school ... ND-7
Climax Shaft—mine ... NV-8
**Climax Springs**—pop pl ... MO-7
Climax Springs Cem—cemetery ... MO-7
Climax Springs Lookout Tower—locale ... MO-7
**Climax (sta.)**—pop pl ... PA-2
**Climax Township**—pop pl ... ND-7
Climax Township (historical)—civil ... ND-7
**Climax (Township of)**—pop pl ... MI-6
Climb Creek ... ID-8
Climb Creek—stream ... ID-8
Climbdown Cave—cave ... AL-4
Climber Lake—lake ... MN-6
Climbers Run—stream ... PA-2
Climbing Arrow Ranch—locale ... MT-8
**Climbing Hill**—pop pl ... IA-7
Climbing Hill Sch—school ... SD-7
Climbing Spring—spring ... CA-9
**Climer**—pop pl ... TN-4
Climer Branch—stream ... TN-4
Climer Cem—cemetery ... IN-6
Climer Post Office (historical)—building ... TN-4
Climer Ridge ... TN-4
Clinard Coulee—valley ... MT-8
Clinard Lake—lake ... CO-8
Clinard Lake—reservoir ... NC-3
Clinch—locale ... VA-3
**Clinch**—pop pl ... FL-3
**Clinch**—pop pl ... IL-6
Clinch, Lake—lake ... FL-3
Clinch Ave Park—park ... TN-4
**Clinchburg**—pop pl ... VA-3
**Clinchco**—pop pl ... VA-3
**Clinch (County)**—pop pl ... GA-3
Clinch County Courthouse—hist pl ... GA-3
Clinch County Jail—hist pl ... GA-3
**Clinchcross**—pop pl ... NC-3
Clinchdale Sch (historical)—school ... TN-4
Clinchfield—locale ... VA-3
**Clinchfield**—pop pl ... GA-3
**Clinchfield**—pop pl ... NC-3
Clinchfield Ch—church ... NC-3
Clinchfield Moss Mines—mine ... VA-3
Clinchfield Overlook—locale ... VA-3
Clinchfield RR Station—hist pl ... TN-4
**Clinchfield (Siemp)**—pop pl ... VA-3
Clinch Knob—summit ... KY-4
Clinch Lookout Tower—locale ... TN-4
Clinch Memorial Hosp—hospital ... GA-3
**Clinchmore**—pop pl ... TN-4
Clinchmore (CCD)—cens area ... TN-4
Clinchmore Division—civil ... TN-4
Clinchmore Mine (surface)—mine ... TN-4
Clinch Mountains ... TN-4
Clinch Mountains ... VA-3
Clinch Mountain Sch—school ... TN-4
Clinch Mountain State Wildlife Mngmt Area—park ... VA-3
Clinch Mtn—range ... TN-4
Clinch Mtn—range ... VA-3
Clinch Mtn Spur—range ... VA-3
Clinch Park Zoo—other ... MI-6
**Clinchport**—pop pl ... VA-3
Clinchport Tunnel—tunnel ... VA-3
Clinch Post Office (historical)—building ... TN-4
Clinch River—locale ... TN-4
Clinch River—stream ... TN-4
Clinch River—stream ... VA-3
Clinch River Bridge Dock—locale ... TN-4
Clinch River Ch—church ... TN-4
**Clinch River (historical)**—pop pl (2) ... TN-4
Clinch River Industrial Park—locale ... TN-4
Clinch River Post Office (historical)—building ... TN-4
Clinch River Sch—school ... TN-4
Clinch River Steam Plant—other ... VA-3
Clinch Sch—school ... TN-4
Clinchs Chapel—church ... GA-3
Clinch Valley—valley ... TN-4
Clinch Valley—valley ... VA-3
Clinch Valley Coll (University Of Virginia)—school ... VA-3
Clinch Valley Memorial Cem—cemetery ... VA-3
Clinch Valley Roller Mills—hist pl ... VA-3
**Clinch View**—pop pl ... TN-4
Clinch View Ch—church ... TN-4
Clinchview Ch—church ... VA-3
**Clinchview Heights**—pop pl ... TN-4
Clinch View Sch (historical)—school ... TN-4
Clinchview Sch (historical)—school ... TN-4
Cline ... GA-3
Cline—locale ... MT-8
Cline—locale ... OH-6
Cline—locale ... TX-5
Cline—locale ... WA-9
**Cline**—pop pl ... VA-3
Cline Ave Interchange—crossing ... IN-6
Cline-Bass House—hist pl ... TX-5
Cline Branch—stream ... IA-7
Cline Branch—stream ... LA-4
Cline Branch—stream ... TN-4
Cline Branch—stream ... WV-2
Cline Brook—stream ... IN-6
Cline Buttes—summit ... OR-9
Cline Cabin—locale ... AZ-5
C-Line Canal—canal ... ID-8
C Line Canal—canal ... ID-8
C-Line Canal East—canal ... ID-8
C-Line Canal West—canal ... ID-8
Cline Cave—cave ... TN-4
Cline Cem—cemetery ... IN-6
Cline Cem—cemetery ... KY-4
Cline Cem—cemetery ... MN-6
Cline Cem—cemetery ... OH-6
Cline Cem—cemetery ... OK-5
Cline Cem—cemetery (3) ... TN-4
Cline Cem—cemetery ... VA-3
Cline Cem—cemetery (4) ... WV-2
Cline Chapel—church ... OH-6
Cline-Clark Campground—park ... OR-9
Cline Creek ... AZ-5
Cline Creek—stream ... AZ-5
Cline Creek—stream ... CA-9
Cline Creek—stream ... IN-6
Cline Creek—stream ... IA-7
Cline Creek—stream ... MT-8
Cline Creek—stream (2) ... NC-3
Cline Creek—stream ... OR-9
Cline Creek—stream ... WA-9
Cline Crossroad ... GA-3
Cline Ditch—canal ... IN-6
Cline Drain—canal ... MI-6
Cline Draw—arroyo ... OR-9
Cline Falls—falls ... OR-9
Cline Falls Air Park—airport ... OR-9
Cline Falls State Park—flat ... OR-9
Cline Flat ... OR-9
Cline Gulch—valley ... CA-9
Cline Gulch—valley ... MT-8
Cline Hill—summit ... OR-9
Cline Hill Sch—school ... MO-7
Cline Knob—summit ... OH-6
Cline Knob—summit (2) ... TN-4
Cline Lake ... MI-6
Cline Lake—lake ... IN-6
Cline Mesa—summit (2) ... AZ-5
Cline Microwave Relay Station—other ... CA-9
Cline Mtn—summit ... ID-8
Cline Mtn—summit ... TX-5
Cline Pasture Tank—reservoir ... AZ-5
Cline Point—cape ... TX-5
Cline Point—summit ... AZ-5
Cline Pond—lake ... PA-2
Cline Prairie Cem—cemetery ... TX-5
Cline Ranch—locale ... AZ-5
Cline Ranch—locale ... NE-7
Cline Ranch—locale ... NM-5
Cline Ridge—ridge (2) ... TN-4
Cline Ridge Cabin Sites—locale ... TN-4
Cline Rsvr—reservoir (2) ... CO-8
Cline Run—stream ... PA-2
Cline Run—stream ... WV-2
Clines Branch—stream ... MO-7
Cline Sch—school ... NE-7
Cline Sch—school ... NC-3
Cline Sch—school (2) ... TN-4
Cline Sch—school ... WV-2
**Clines Corners**—pop pl ... NM-5
Clines Hacking—locale ... VA-3
Clines Island—island ... MO-7
**Clines Island**—pop pl ... MO-7
Clines Lake ... MI-6
Clinesmith Ranch Airp—airport ... WA-9
Clines Point—cape ... NY-2
Clines Pond—lake ... NY-2
Clines Ponds ... NY-2
Clines Sch—school ... TN-4
Clines (Township of)—fmr MCD ... NC-3
Cline Tank—reservoir ... AZ-5
Clinetop Cow Camp—locale ... CO-8
Clinetop Mesa—summit ... CO-8
Cline Well—well (2) ... AZ-5
Cline Well—well ... NM-5
Cliney Flat—flat ... OR-9
Clingan Ditch—canal ... OH-6
Clingan Ridge Ch—church ... TN-4
Clingan Sch—school ... KS-7
Clingans Junction—locale ... CA-9
Clingback Mtn—summit ... MT-8
Cling Branch—stream ... NC-3
Cling Creek ... OR-9
Clinger Branch Boston Farm Lateral—canal ... CO-8
Clinger Campground—park ... OR-9
Clinger Mine—mine ... UT-8
Clinger-Moses Mill Complex—hist pl ... PA-2
Clinger Spring—spring ... OR-9
Clingham Creek ... OK-5
Clingham Memorial Cem—cemetery ... SC-3
Clinging Cem—cemetery ... OK-5
Clinging Creek—stream ... OK-5
**Clingman**—pop pl ... NC-3
Clingman Mine Branch—stream ... NC-3
Clingmans Creek—stream ... NC-3
Clingmans Dome—summit ... NC-3
Clingmans Dome—summit ... TN-4
Clingmans Peak—summit ... NC-3
Clinical Laboratories Airp—airport ... TN-4
Clinkenbeard, William, House—hist pl ... KY-4
Clinker Knob—summit ... CO-8
Clinker Lake—lake ... MN-6
Clinkingbeard Creek—stream ... MO-7
Clink Trail—trail ... WA-9
Clinkum Hollow—valley ... VA-3
Clink Webster Mtn—summit ... NC-3
Clino Tank—reservoir ... AZ-5
Clint—locale ... CA-9
**Clint**—pop pl ... TX-5
Clint Canyon—valley ... WA-9
Clint Creek—stream ... WY-8
Clinter—uninc pl ... CA-9
Clint Hill Cem—cemetery ... TN-4
Clint Hill Sch (historical)—school ... TN-4
Clint Hollow—valley ... AR-4
Clint Hollow—valley ... WV-2
Clint Lateral—canal ... TX-5
Clint Millpond—lake ... NJ-2
Clinto—locale ... PA-2
Clinton ... PA-2
Clinton—CDP ... CT-1
Clinton—locale ... CA-9
Clinton—locale ... MO-7
Clinton—locale ... NJ-2
Clinton—locale ... PA-2
Clinton—locale ... UT-8
Clinton—locale ... VA-3
Clinton—locale ... WV-2
**Clinton**—pop pl ... AL-4
**Clinton**—pop pl ... AR-4
**Clinton**—pop pl ... CT-1
**Clinton**—pop pl ... GA-3
**Clinton**—pop pl (2) ... IL-6
**Clinton**—pop pl (2) ... IN-6
**Clinton**—pop pl ... IA-7
**Clinton**—pop pl ... KS-7
**Clinton**—pop pl ... KY-4
**Clinton**—pop pl ... LA-4
**Clinton**—pop pl ... ME-1
**Clinton**—pop pl ... MD-2
**Clinton**—pop pl ... MA-1
**Clinton**—pop pl ... MI-6
**Clinton**—pop pl ... MN-6
**Clinton**—pop pl ... MS-4
**Clinton**—pop pl ... MO-7
**Clinton**—pop pl ... MT-8
**Clinton**—pop pl ... NE-7
**Clinton**—pop pl ... NH-1
**Clinton**—pop pl (2) ... NJ-2
**Clinton**—pop pl ... NY-2
**Clinton**—pop pl ... NC-3
**Clinton**—pop pl (3) ... OH-6
**Clinton**—pop pl ... OK-5
**Clinton**—pop pl (4) ... PA-2
**Clinton**—pop pl ... SC-3
**Clinton**—pop pl ... TN-4
**Clinton**—pop pl (2) ... TX-5
**Clinton**—pop pl ... UT-8
**Clinton**—pop pl ... WA-9
**Clinton**—pop pl ... WV-2
**Clinton**—pop pl ... WI-6
Clinton, Charles, Stone Row House—hist pl ... NV-8
Clinton, Lake—reservoir ... IL-6
Clinton Acad ... MS-4
Clinton Acad—school ... MS-4
**Clinton Acres**—pop pl ... MD-2
Clinton Airp—airport ... IN-6
Clinton Airp—airport ... MS-4
Clinton Amphitheatre—basin ... CO-8
Clinton And Ionia Drain—canal ... MI-6
Clinton Ave Hist Dist—hist pl (2) ... NY-2
Clinton Ave Sch—school ... CT-1
Clinton Basin—harbor ... CA-9
Clinton Beach—beach ... CT-1
**Clinton Beach**—pop pl ... CT-1
Clinton Blvd Ch of Christ—church ... MS-4
Clinton Blvd Shop Ctr—locale ... MS-4
Clinton Branch—stream ... AL-4
Clinton Branch—stream ... LA-4
Clinton Branch—stream ... SC-3
Clinton Breaker—building ... PA-2
Clinton Brick Ch—church ... IN-6
Clinton Brook ... NH-1
Clinton Brook—stream ... NJ-2
Clinton Brook—stream ... NY-2
Clinton Brook Valley—valley ... NJ-2
Clinton (CCD)—cens area ... KY-4
Clinton (CCD)—cens area ... OK-5
Clinton (CCD)—cens area ... SC-3
Clinton (CCD)—cens area ... TN-4
Clinton Cem—cemetery ... KS-7
Clinton Cem—cemetery (2) ... MS-4
Clinton Cem—cemetery (2) ... NJ-2
Clinton Cem—cemetery ... OK-5
Clinton Cem—cemetery (2) ... PA-2
Clinton Cem—cemetery ... UT-8
Clinton Cem—cemetery (2) ... WI-6
**Clinton Center**—pop pl ... CT-1
**Clinton Center**—pop pl ... IA-7
Clinton Center (census name Clinton)—other ... ME-1
Clinton Central Elem Sch—school ... IN-6
Clinton Central HS—school ... IN-6
Clinton Ch—church ... AL-4
Clinton Ch—church ... IN-6
Clinton Ch—church ... MD-2
Clinton Ch—church ... NJ-2
Clinton Ch—church (2) ... PA-2
Clinton Ch—church (2) ... SC-3
Clinton Ch—church ... WV-2

Clinton Chapel—*church* AR-4
*Clinton Chapel AME Church* AL-4
Clinton Chapel AME Zion Ch—*church* (2) AL-4
Clinton Chapel Cem—*cemetery* IN-6
Clinton Ch (historical)—*church* AL-4
Clinton Ch of Christ—*church* MS-4
Clinton Ch of Christ—*church* TN-4
Clinton Christian Day Sch—*school* IN-6
*Clinton City Cemetery* UT-8
Clinton City Hall—*building* MS-4
Clinton City Hall—*building* NC-3
Clinton City Park—*park* TN-4
Clinton Coll (historical)—*school* TN-4
Clinton Commercial Hist Dist—*hist pl* SC-3
Clinton Community Sch—*school* IN-6
**Clinton Corners**—*pop pl* NY-2
Clinton Corners Cem—*cemetery* WI-6
Clinton Country Club—*other* IL-6
Clinton Country Club—*other* IA-7
**Clinton (County)**—*pop pl* IL-6
**Clinton County**—*pop pl* IN-6
**Clinton (County)**—*pop pl* KY-4
**Clinton (County)**—*pop pl* MI-6
**Clinton County**—*pop pl* MO-7
**Clinton (County)**—*pop pl* NY-2
**Clinton (County)**—*pop pl* OH-6
**Clinton County**—*pop pl* PA-2
Clinton County Airp—*airport* NY-2
Clinton County Courthouse—*hist pl* IN-6
Clinton County Courthouse—*hist pl* IA-7
Clinton County Courthouse Complex—*hist pl* NY-2
Clinton County Farm Cem—*cemetery* IA-7
Clinton County Home—*building* IA-7
Clinton Creek—*stream* (2) AK-9
Clinton Creek—*stream* CO-8
Clinton Creek—*stream* ID-8
Clinton Creek—*stream* MI-6
Clinton Creek—*stream* WA-9
Clinton Creek Ditch—*canal* CO-8
Clintondale—*locale* PA-2
**Clintondale**—*pop pl* NY-2
Clintondale HS—*school* MI-6
**Clintondale Station**—*pop pl* NY-2
Clinton Dam—*dam* KS-7
Clinton Depot—*hist pl* NC-3
Clinton District Courthouse—*building* MA-1
Clinton Ditch—*canal* TX-5
Clinton Division—*civil* TN-4
**Clinton Downs Subdivision**—*pop pl* UT-8
Clinton Elem Sch—*school* PA-2
Clinton Elem Sch—*school* TN-4
**Clinton Estates**—*pop pl* MD-2
*Clinton Falls* IN-6
**Clinton Falls**—*pop pl* IN-6
**Clinton Falls**—*pop pl* MN-6
Clinton Falls Mill and Dam—*hist pl* MN-6
Clinton Falls (Township of)—*civ div* MN-6
Clinton Field—*park* MN-6
Clinton First Baptist Ch—*church* TN-4
Clinton Fish and Wildlife Mngmt Area—*park* NJ-2
Clinton Forest Nursery (historical)—*locale* TN-4
Clinton Frame Ch—*church* IN-6
Clinton Furnace—*hist pl* NJ-2
Clinton Furnace—*locale* WV-2
**Clinton Gardens**—*pop pl* MD-2
**Clinton Grove**—*pop pl* NH-1
Clinton Grove Acad (historical)—*school* TN-4
Clinton Grove Cem—*cemetery* MI-6
Clinton Grove Sch—*school* MD-2
Clinton Gulch—*valley* MT-8
Clinton Gun Club—*other* IN-6
Clinton Hall—*hist pl* NY-2
Clinton Hamilton Branch—*stream* KY-4
Clinton Harbor—*bay* CT-1
Clinton-Hardy House—*hist pl* OK-5
**Clinton Heights**—*pop pl* FL-3
**Clinton Heights**—*pop pl* MD-2
**Clinton Heights**—*pop pl* NY-2
Clinton Hill—*summit* CT-1
Clinton Hill—*summit* MO-7
Clinton Hill—*uninc pl* NJ-2
Clinton Hill Hist Dist—*hist pl* NY-2
Clinton Hill South Hist Dist—*hist pl* NY-2
**Clinton Hills (subdivision)**—*pop pl* NC-3
**Clinton (historical)**—*pop pl* OR-9
**Clinton Hollow**—*pop pl* NY-2
Clinton Hollow—*valley* AR-4
Clinton Hosp—*hospital* MA-1
Clinton House—*hist pl* MO-7
Clinton House—*hist pl* (2) NY-2
Clinton HS—*school* IA-7
Clinton HS—*school* MS-4
Clinton HS—*school* NC-3
Clinton HS—*school* SC-3
Clinton HS—*school* TN-4
**Clintonia (Township of)**—*pop pl* IL-6
Clinton Illinois Bridge—*other* IL-6
Clinton Industrial Park—*locale* MS-4
Clinton Irrigation District Canal—*canal* MT-8
Clinton Island—*island* NY-2
Clinton Island—*island* TN-4
Clinton Island Shoals—*bar* TN-4
Clinton JHS—*school* MI-6
Clinton JHS—*school* MS-4
Clinton JHS—*school* NY-2
Clinton JHS—*school* OH-6
Clinton JHS—*school* OK-5
Clinton JHS—*school* TN-4
**Clinton Junction**—*pop pl* MA-1
Clinton Junction—*uninc pl* OK-5
**Clinton Junction (RR name for Clinton)**—*pop pl* WI-6
Clinton Junior-Senior HS—*school* MA-1
Clinton-Kalamazoo Canal—*hist pl* MI-6
Clinton Knob—*summit* WA-9
Clinton Lake—*lake* MI-6
Clinton Lake—*lake* TX-5
Clinton Lake—*reservoir* KS-7
Clinton Lake—*reservoir* OK-5
Clinton Landing Field (historical)—*airport* TN-4
*Clinton Locks* IN-6
Clinton Lookout Tower—*locale* LA-4
Clinton Lookout Tower—*locale* NC-3
Clinton Male and Female Acad (historical)—*school* AL-4
Clinton Mall Shop Ctr—*locale* MS-4
Clinton Marina—*locale* TN-4
Clinton Memorial Airp—*airport* MO-7
Clinton Memorial Cem—*cemetery* IA-7
Clinton Memorial Cem—*cemetery* SC-3
*Clinton Mill Pond* MA-1
Clinton Mills—*locale* NY-2
Clinton Mills—*locale* PA-2
Clinton Mills Dam—*dam* NJ-2
Clinton Mine (historical)—*mine* SD-7
Clinton Mountain—*ridge* AR-4
Clinton MS—*school* MA-1
Clinton Mtn—*summit* AR-4
Clinton Municipal Airp—*airport* IA-7
Clinton Nuclear Power Plant—*facility* IL-6
Clinton Park—*park* CT-1
Clinton Park—*park* KS-7
Clinton Park—*park* MS-4
Clinton Park—*park* NY-2
Clinton Park—*park* OH-6
Clinton Park—*park* OK-5
Clinton Park—*park* OR-9
**Clinton Park**—*pop pl* (2) NY-2
**Clinton Park**—*pop pl* TX-5
**Clinton Park**—*pop pl* WA-9
Clinton Park Elem Sch—*school* MS-4
Clinton Peak—*summit* CA-9
Clinton Peak—*summit* CO-8
Clinton Place JHS—*school* NJ-2
Clinton Plaza—*uninc pl* MS-4
Clinton Plaza Shop Ctr—*locale* MS-4
Clinton Plaza Shop Ctr—*locale* TN-4
*Clinton Point* WI-6
Clinton Point—*cape* NY-2
Clinton Post Office—*building* MS-4
Clinton Post Office—*building* TN-4
Clinton Prairie Junior-Senior HS—*school* IN-6
*Clinton Public Library* MS-4
Clinton Public Library—*hist pl* IA-7
Clinton Ranch—*locale* AZ-5
Clinton-Raymond Road Baptist Ch—*church* MS-4
Clinton Realty Company Pond Dam—*dam* MS-4
Clinton Reservoir Dam—*dam* NJ-2
Clinton Ridge—*ridge* WI-6
Clinton River—*stream* MI-6
*Clinton River Meadows* MI-6
Clinton River Spillway—*canal* MI-6
Clinton-Rosekrans Law Bldg—*hist pl* NY-2
Clinton Rsvr—*reservoir* NJ-2
Clinton Rsvr—*reservoir* NY-2
Clinton Rsvr—*reservoir* TN-4
Clinton Sch—*school* CA-9
Clinton Sch—*school* (2) IL-6
Clinton Sch—*school* IA-7
Clinton Sch—*school* (2) MI-6
Clinton Sch—*school* MN-6
Clinton Sch—*school* MO-7
Clinton Sch—*school* (2) NE-7
Clinton Sch—*school* NJ-2
Clinton Sch—*school* (3) NY-2
Clinton Sch—*school* OH-6
Clinton Sch—*school* OK-5
Clinton Sch—*school* (2) SC-3
Clinton Sch—*school* TX-5
Clinton Sch—*school* UT-8
Clinton Sch (abandoned)—*school* PA-2
*Clinton School* PA-2
Clintons Chute—*gut* TX-5
Clintons Ditch—*canal* NY-2
Clinton Seminary (historical)—*school* TN-4
Clinton Sewage Lagoon Dam—*dam* MS-4
Clinton-Sherman Air Force Base—*military* OK-5
Clinton (site)—*locale* CA-9
*Clinton Slough* WI-6
Clinton South (CCD)—*cens area* TN-4
Clinton South Division—*civil* TN-4
Clintons Pond—*lake* CT-1
Clintons Pool—*reservoir* AZ-5
Clinton Spring—*spring* CA-9
Clinton Spring—*spring* MO-7
Clinton State For—*forest* NY-2
Clinton State For Number Eight—*forest* NY-2
Clinton State Park—*park* KS-7
Clinton State Prison—*other* NY-2
**Clinton Stock Yards**—*pop pl* IA-7
Clinton Street Hist Dist—*hist pl* PA-2
Clinton (Surrattsville)—*CDP* MD-2
**Clinton (Town of)**—*pop pl* ME-1
**Clinton (Town of)**—*pop pl* MA-1
**Clinton (Town of)**—*pop pl* (2) NY-2
**Clinton (Town of)**—*pop pl* (3) WI-6
*Clinton Township* KS-7
Clinton Township—*civil* (2) MO-7
Clinton Township—*fmr MCD* (4) IA-7
**Clinton Township**—*pop pl* KS-7
**Clinton Township**—*pop pl* (2) MO-7
**Clinton Township**—*pop pl* ND-7
**Clinton Township**—*pop pl* SD-7
Clinton Township (historical)—*civil* SD-7
Clinton (Township of)—*other* OH-6
**Clinton (Township of)**—*pop pl* IL-6
**Clinton (Township of)**—*pop pl* (7) IN-6
**Clinton (Township of)**—*pop pl* (3) MI-6
**Clinton (Township of)**—*pop pl* (2) MN-6
**Clinton (Township of)**—*pop pl* NJ-2
**Clinton (Township of)**—*pop pl* (7) OH-6
**Clinton (Township of)**—*pop pl* (5) PA-2
Clinton Trail—*trail* PA-2
Clinton Union Cem—*cemetery* IN-6
*Clinton United Methodist Church* MS-4
Clinton Valley Sch—*school* MI-6
*Clinton Village* MA-1
**Clinton Village**—*pop pl* MI-6
**Clinton Village**—*pop pl* NH-1
Clinton Village Hall—*hist pl* WI-6
Clinton Village Hist Dist—*hist pl* NY-2
Clintonville—*locale* NY-2
**Clintonville**—*pop pl* AL-4
**Clintonville**—*pop pl* CT-1
**Clintonville**—*pop pl* (2) KY-4
**Clintonville**—*pop pl* MI-6
**Clintonville**—*pop pl* (2) NY-2
**Clintonville**—*pop pl* PA-2
**Clintonville**—*pop pl* WV-2
**Clintonville**—*pop pl* WI-6
Clintonville—*post sta* OH-6
Clintonville Borough—*civil* PA-2
Clintonville Cem—*cemetery* MO-7
Clintonville Ch—*church* AL-4
Clintonville Ch—*church* MI-6
Clintonville Sch—*school* MO-7
**Clinton Vista**—*pop pl* MD-2
Clinton Vocational Center—*school* MS-4
Clinton Water Tower—*hist pl* WI-6
Clinton Waterworks—*other* AR-4
Clinton Wildlife Area—*park* KS-7
Clinton Young Elem Sch—*school* IN-6
Clints Cabin—*locale* WA-9
*Clints Canyon* UT-8
Clints Canyon—*valley* UT-8
Clints Coves—*slope* UT-8
Clints Run—*stream* WV-2
Clints Spring—*spring* UT-8
Clints Tank—*reservoir* AZ-5
**Clints Well**—*pop pl* AZ-5
*Clints Well Campground* AZ-5
**Clint Village Subdivision**—*pop pl* UT-8
Clint Wells Campground—*park* AZ-5
Clint Williams Spring—*spring* MO-7
**Clintwood**—*pop pl* VA-3
Clintwood Bible Ch—*church* VA-3
Clintwood (Magisterial District)—*fmr MCD* VA-3
Clio—*locale* FL-3
Clio—*locale* KY-4
**Clio**—*pop pl* AL-4
**Clio**—*pop pl* CA-9
**Clio**—*pop pl* IA-7
**Clio**—*pop pl* LA-4
**Clio**—*pop pl* MI-6
**Clio**—*pop pl* SC-3
**Clio**—*pop pl* WV-2
Clio Baptist Ch—*church* AL-4
Clio (CCD)—*cens area* AL-4
Clio (CCD)—*cens area* SC-3
Clio Cem—*cemetery* MO-7
Clio Ch—*church* NC-3
Clio Depot—*hist pl* MI-6
Clio Division—*civil* AL-4
Clio Golf Course—*other* MI-6
Clio Hist Dist—*hist pl* SC-3
Clio HS—*school* AL-4
Clio Methodist Ch—*church* AL-4
Clio Mine—*mine* CA-9
Clione Sch—*school* MO-7
Clio Sch—*school* SC-3
Clio School (historical)—*locale* MO-7
*Clip* AZ-5
*Clip Creek* KY-4
Clip Hill—*summit* NY-2
*Clip Mill Site* AZ-5
Clip Mill (site)—*locale* AZ-5
Clip Mine—*mine* AZ-5
Clippard Cem—*cemetery* MO-7
*Clippenger Run* PA-2
Clipper—*locale* AR-4
Clipper—*locale* IA-7
Clipper—*locale* WA-9
Clipper Bullion Mine—*mine* ID-8
Clipper Canal—*canal* UT-8
Clipper Cem—*cemetery* AR-4
Clipper Creek—*stream* (2) CA-9
**Clipper Gap**—*pop pl* CA-9
Clipper Gap—*summit* NV-8
Clipper Gap Canyon—*valley* NV-8
**Clippergap (Clipper Gap)**—*pop pl* CA-9
Clipper Gap Spring—*spring* NV-8
Clipper Gulch—*valley* CA-9
Clipper Gulch—*valley* MT-8
Clipper (historical)—*locale* AL-4
Clipper (historical P.O.)—*locale* IA-7
Clipper Mill Bridge—*bridge* CA-9
**Clipper Mills**—*pop pl* CA-9
**Clipper Mills**—*pop pl* OH-6
Clipper Mills Sch—*school* CA-9
Clipper Mine—*mine* CA-9
Clipper Mine—*mine* MT-8
Clipper Mine—*mine* NV-8
Clipper Mine—*mine* WA-9
Clipper Mine (underground)—*mine* AL-4
Clipper Mountains—*range* CA-9
Clipper Peak—*summit* UT-8
Clipper Ridge—*ridge* UT-8
Clipper Sch—*school* MI-6
Clippership Mine—*mine* CA-9
Clipper Valley—*valley* CA-9
Clipper Wash—*stream* AZ-5
Clipper Wash—*stream* CA-9
Clipper Well—*well* AZ-5
Clipper Western Canal—*canal* UT-8
Clippingers Run—*stream* PA-2
*Clipp Lake* MT-8
Clip Ranch—*locale* TX-5
Clips Mill—*locale* WV-2
Clip Wash—*stream* AZ-5
**Cliquot**—*pop pl* MO-7
Cliquot Township—*civil* MO-7
Clirliah Creek—*stream* CA-9
Clisby (historical)—*locale* MS-4
**Clisby Park (subdivision)**—*pop pl* AL-4
Clisby Sch—*school* GA-3
Clise, James W., House—*hist pl* WA-9
Clise Drain—*canal* MI-6
Clish Pond—*lake* ME-1
Clissold HS—*school* IL-6
*Clistowacka* PA-2
Clistowackin—*locale* PA-2
**Clitherall**—*pop pl* MN-6
Clitherall Lake—*lake* MN-6
**Clitherall (Township of)**—*pop pl* MN-6
Clitheral (RR name for Clitherall)—*other* MN-6
Clito—*locale* GA-3
**Clito**—*pop pl* VA-3
Clito Ch—*church* GA-3
Clito Mill—*locale* VA-3
Clitonia Cem—*cemetery* MS-4
C Little Wounded Dam—*dam* SD-7
*Clitts Post Office* AL-4
Clitty Lake—*lake* MN-6
Clive—*locale* UT-8
**Clive**—*pop pl* IA-7
Cliveden—*hist pl* PA-2
**Cliveden**—*pop pl* VA-3
Cliveden Park—*park* PA-2
Clive Key—*island* FL-3
Clive Sch—*school* IA-7
**Clives Subdivision**—*pop pl* UT-8
Clizer Cem—*cemetery* MO-7
C L Mullins Dam—*dam* AL-4
Cloak Island—*island* VT-1
Cloak Lake—*lake* CA-9
Cloar—*locale* AR-4
Cloar Cem—*cemetery* AR-4
Cloat Run—*stream* WV-2
Clochacohua Lake—*lake* AK-9
Clock Branch Sch—*school* SC-3
Clock Cem—*cemetery* NY-2
Clock Creek—*stream* IN-6
Clock Creek—*stream* TN-4
Clock Creek—*stream* WA-9
Clock Farm—*hist pl* ME-1
Clock Farm Corner—*locale* ME-1
Clock Lake—*lake* CO-8
Clockmaker Sch—*school* WI-6
Clockmill Corners—*locale* NY-2
Clockmill Pond—*lake* NY-2
**Clocks Corner**—*pop pl* VA-3
*Clocks Creek* NY-2
Clock Spring—*spring* NV-8
Clocktower Creek—*stream* WY-8
**Clockville**—*pop pl* NY-2
Clockville Creek—*stream* NY-2
Cloddy Field Branch—*stream* KY-4
Clodfelter Cem—*cemetery* IN-6
Clodfelter Lake—*reservoir* NC-3
Clodfelter Lake Dam—*dam* NC-3
Clodine—*locale* TX-5
Clod Ridge—*ridge* MO-7
**Cloe**—*pop pl* PA-2
Cloe Dam—*dam* PA-2
Cloe Lake—*reservoir* PA-2
Cloer Branch—*stream* NC-3
Cloers Mill (historical)—*locale* TN-4
*Cloesterman Bayou* FL-3
*Cloesterman Point* FL-3
**Cloester Valley**—*pop pl* AL-4
Clog Gulch—*valley* SD-7
Clogston Ranch Airp—*airport* KS-7
Clogston Ranch Landing Strip—*airport* KS-7
Clogston Sch—*school* VT-1
Clohesy Lake—*lake* CO-8
*Cloice Branch* TX-5
Cloice Creek—*stream* TX-5
Cloie Branch—*stream* IA-7
Cloister Arch—*arch* UT-8
Cloisters, The—*church* NY-2
Cloisters, The—*hist pl* MD-2
**Cloisters (subdivision), The**—*pop pl* NC-3
**Clokey**—*pop pl* PA-2
Clokey Bridge—*bridge* PA-2
**Clokeyville**—*pop pl* PA-2
Clonch Canyon—*valley* NV-8
Clonch Creek—*stream* AL-4
Cloney Gulch—*valley* CA-9
Cloninger Creek—*stream* TX-5
Clonmel—*locale* KS-7
Clonmell—*locale* PA-2
Clonmell Creek—*stream* NJ-2
**Clontarf**—*pop pl* MN-6
**Clontarf (Township of)**—*pop pl* MN-6
Clonts Cem—*cemetery* NC-3
Clonts Ranch—*locale* TX-5
Clontz Branch—*stream* NC-3
Cloochman Creek—*stream* ID-8
Cloochman Saddle—*gap* ID-8
Cloonan JHS—*school* CT-1
Clooney Island—*island* LA-4
Cloos Cem—*cemetery* PA-2
C Loper Catfish Pond Dam—*dam* MS-4
Clopine—*locale* GA-3
Clopine, Lake—*lake* GA-3
Clopper—*locale* MD-2
*Cloppers Point* TX-5
Clopp Hollow—*valley* MO-7
Cloptins Crossing—*locale* TX-5
Clopton—*locale* VA-3
**Clopton**—*pop pl* AL-4
**Clopton**—*pop pl* TN-4
**Clopton**—*pop pl* VA-3
Clopton, Lake—*reservoir* TX-5
Clopton Cem—*cemetery* FL-3
Clopton Cem—*cemetery* MO-7
Clopton Cem—*cemetery* TN-4
Clopton Ch—*church* (2) AL-4
Clopton Ch—*church* TN-4
*Clopton Community Ch* AL-4
Clopton Ranch—*locale* AZ-5
Clopton Road Ch—*church* TX-5
Clopton Sch—*school* MO-7
Clopton Swamp—*stream* VA-3
Cloquallum Creek—*stream* WA-9
Cloquallum Grange—*locale* WA-9
Cloquallum Truck Trail—*trail* WA-9
**Cloquet**—*pop pl* AR-4
**Cloquet**—*pop pl* MN-6
Cloquet City Hall—*hist pl* MN-6
Cloquet Forest Experiment Station—*other* MN-6
Cloquet Golf Club—*other* MN-6
Cloquet Island—*island* MN-6
Cloquet Lake—*lake* MN-6
Cloquet Lookout Tower—*locale* MN-6
Cloquet-Northern Office Bldg—*hist pl* MN-6
Cloquet River—*stream* MN-6
Cloquet Valley Lookout Tower—*locale* MN-6
Cloquet Valley Ranger Station—*locale* MN-6
Cloquet Valley State For—*forest* MN-6
Cloquet Waterworks—*other* MN-6
Clora Creek—*stream* MN-6
Clora Creek—*stream* NY-2
*Cloras Point* MD-2
Clore, Albert E., House—*hist pl* KY-4
Clore, James, House—*hist pl* KY-4
Clorinda Creek—*stream* MT-8
Close, Bayou—*stream* LA-4
Close, M. T., and Company Flaxseed Warehouse—*hist pl* IA-7
Close Bay—*bay* AK-9
Close Brothers Land Company Tenant House—*hist pl* MN-6
Close Butte—*summit* CA-9
Close Call Ditch—*canal* WY-8
Close Cem—*cemetery* CT-1
**Close City**—*pop pl* TX-5
**Close City (Ragtown)**—*pop pl* TX-5
Close Creek—*stream* NJ-2
Closed Canyon—*valley* TX-5
Closed Chapel Sch—*school* OK-5
Closed Creek—*stream* WY-8
Close House—*hist pl* IA-7
Close Lake—*lake* AK-9
Close Lake—*lake* LA-4
Close Mtn—*summit* WV-2
Close Park—*park* OH-6
Close Pond—*lake* NY-2
Close Post Office (historical)—*building* TN-4
Close Ranch—*locale* SD-7
Close Ranch—*locale* TX-5
Closer Walk Ch—*church* NC-3
Close Sch—*school* IL-6
Close Sch—*school* MI-6
Close Sch (historical)—*school* TN-4
Closes Creek—*stream* PA-2
Close Slu—*gut* WI-6
Closes Pond—*lake* CT-1
**Closplint**—*pop pl* KY-4
Closs—*locale* NC-3
Clossman Hardware Store—*hist pl* OH-6
Closson Cove—*bay* ME-1
Closson Island—*island* ME-1
Closson Point—*cape* (2) ME-1
Closson Well—*well* NM-5
*Closter* NJ-2
Closter—*locale* NE-7
**Closter**—*pop pl* NJ-2
Closter Park—*park* CA-9
Closton Hill—*summit* NH-1
Clotfelter Cave—*cave* AL-4
Clotfelter Cem—*cemetery* TN-4
Clothespole Bay—*bay* GA-3
Clothier—*locale* OK-5
**Clothier**—*pop pl* WV-2
Clothier Field—*park* PA-2
Clothier Hollow—*valley* NY-2
Clothier Landing Field—*airport* KS-7
Clothier Oil Field—*oilfield* OK-5
Clotho—*locale* MN-6
**Clotho**—*pop pl* CA-9
*Clothopas Temple* AZ-5
*Clothos Temple* AZ-5
**Clotilda**—*pop pl* LA-4
Clots Lake—*lake* NJ-2
*Cloud* KS-7
**Cloud**—*pop pl* IA-7
Cloud, Aaron G., House—*hist pl* IL-6
Cloud, Mount—*summit* AK-9
Cloud Bayou—*stream* TX-5
Cloud Branch—*stream* (2) KY-4
Cloud Branch—*stream* TN-4
Cloud Brook—*stream* VT-1
Cloudburst Canyon—*valley* AZ-5
Cloudburst Canyon—*valley* (5) CA-9
Cloudburst Creek—*stream* (2) CA-9
Cloudburst Creek—*stream* MT-8
Cloudburst Creek—*stream* WY-8
Cloudburst Rsvr—*reservoir* MT-8
Cloudburst Spring—*spring* AZ-5
Cloudburst Summit—*gap* CA-9
Cloud Canyon—*valley* (2) CA-9
Cloud Canyon—*valley* NM-5
Cloudcap—*summit* OR-9
Cloudcap Bay—*bay* OR-9
Cloud Cap Inn—*hist pl* OR-9
Cloud Cap Inn—*locale* OR-9
*Cloud Cap Peak* WA-9
Cloud Cap Saddle Campground—*park* OR-9
Cloud Cap-Tilly Jane Rec Area Hist Dist—*hist pl* OR-9
Cloud Cathedral—*church* VA-3
Cloud Cem—*cemetery* (2) AL-4
Cloud Cem—*cemetery* GA-3
Cloud Cem—*cemetery* IL-6
Cloud Cem—*cemetery* MO-7
Cloud Cem—*cemetery* TN-4
**Cloud Chief**—*pop pl* OK-5
Cloud Chief Cem—*cemetery* OK-5
**Cloud Country Estates**—*pop pl* NM-5
Cloud County—*civil* KS-7
Cloud Cove—*valley* AL-4
Cloud Cove Ch—*church* AL-4
Cloud Creek—*locale* TN-4
Cloud Creek—*stream* AK-9
Cloud Creek—*stream* (2) OK-5
Cloud Creek—*stream* TN-4
Cloud Creek—*stream* WY-8
Cloud Creek Cem—*cemetery* OK-5
Cloud Creek Ch—*church* (2) OK-5
*Cloud Creek School* TN-4
**Cloud Crest Hills**—*pop pl* IN-6
**Cloudcroft**—*pop pl* NM-5
Cloudcroft Peaks—*summit* MT-8
Cloud Crossing—*locale* KY-4
Cloud Elem Sch—*school* KS-7
Clouder Gulch—*valley* ID-8
*Cloud Ferry* TN-4
Cloud Ford—*locale* TN-4
Cloud Ford (historical)—*crossing* TN-4
Cloud Gulch—*valley* CO-8
Cloud Hollow—*valley* TX-5
Cloud Home—*hist pl* PA-2
Cloud House—*hist pl* KY-4
Cloudis Cem—*cemetery* MO-7
Cloud Lake—*lake* AK-9
Cloud Lake—*lake* AR-4
Cloud Lake—*lake* WI-6
**Cloud Lake**—*pop pl* FL-3
Cloud Lake Group—*lake* OR-9
**Cloudland**—*pop pl* GA-3
Cloudland Brook—*stream* VT-1
Cloudland Canyon State Park—*park* (2) GA-3
Cloudland Ch—*church* NC-3
Cloudland HS—*school* TN-4
Cloudland Mtn—*summit* TN-4
Cloudland Park Cave—*cave* AL-4
Cloudland Pit—*cave* AL-4
Cloudland Post Office (historical)—*building* TN-4
Cloudland Sch—*school* GA-3
Cloudland Sch—*school* TN-4
Cloudland Spring—*spring* TN-4
Cloudman Bay—*bay* AK-9
Cloudmont Airpark—*airport* AL-4
Cloudmont Park—*park* AL-4
Cloudmont Resort—*locale* AL-4
Cloud Mtn—*summit* AL-4
Cloud Mtn—*summit* TX-5
Cloud Park—*park* TN-4
Cloud Peak—*summit* (2) AK-9
Cloud Peak—*summit* MI-6
Cloud Peak—*summit* WY-8
*Cloud Peak Lake* WY-8
Cloud Peak Rsvr—*reservoir* WY-8
Cloud Point—*cape* TX-5
Cloud Point—*cliff* TX-5
Cloud Pond—*lake* ME-1
Cloud Pond Brook—*stream* ME-1
Cloudrest Peak—*summit* MT-8
Cloud Ridge—*ridge* TN-4
Cloud Ridge—*ridge* VA-3
Cloud Ridge Terrace—*uninc pl* AZ-5
Cloud Rim Girl Scout Camp—*locale* UT-8
Cloud Rim Girl Scout Lodge—*hist pl* UT-8
Cloud Rsvr—*reservoir* WY-8
**Clouds**—*pop pl* TN-4
Clouds, Lake—*lake* (2) CO-8
Clouds, Lake of the—*lake* MI-6
Clouds, Lake Of The—*lake* MN-6
Clouds, Lake of the—*lake* MT-8
Clouds, Lake of the—*lake* VT-1
Clouds, Lake of the—*reservoir* IN-6
Clouds, Lakes of the—*lake* NH-1
Clouds Bend—*bend* TN-4
Clouds Bend Ch—*church* TN-4
Clouds Branch—*stream* OK-5
*Clouds Brook* CT-1
Cloud Sch—*school* CA-9
Cloud Sch (historical)—*school* AL-4
Clouds Creek—*stream* GA-3
Clouds Creek—*stream* SC-3
Clouds Creek Cem—*cemetery* GA-3
Clouds Creek Ch—*church* GA-3
Clouds Creek Sch (historical)—*school* TN-4
*Clouds Ferry* TN-4
Cloud Shoals—*bar* TN-4
Clouds Home Peak—*summit* WY-8
Clouds Lake—*lake* ND-7
Clouds Memorial Baptist Ch—*church* TN-4
Cloud Splitter—*arch* KY-4
Cloud Splitter—*summit* CA-9
Clouds Post Office (historical)—*building* TN-4
Cloud Spring—*spring* AL-4
*Cloud Spring Creek* OR-9
Clouds Rest—*summit* CA-9
Clouds Rest Island—*island* NY-2
Clouds Rest Trail—*trail* CA-9
Clouds Sch (historical)—*school* TN-4
Clouds Shoals—*bar* TN-4
Cloud-Stark House—*hist pl* TX-5
Cloud State Bank—*hist pl* IL-6
*Clouds Town* AL-4
Cloudt Draw—*valley* TX-5
Cloudt Waterhole—*lake* TX-5
Cloudveil Dome—*summit* WY-8
**Cloudy**—*pop pl* OK-5
Cloudy—*uninc pl* TX-5
Cloudy Bend—*bend* CA-9
*Cloudy Canyon* CA-9
Cloudy Cape—*cape* AK-9
Cloudy Cem—*cemetery* OK-5
Cloudy Ch—*church* OK-5
Cloudy Creek—*stream* OK-5
Cloudy Lake—*lake* AK-9
Cloudy Lake—*lake* WA-9
Cloudy Lookout Tower—*locale* OK-5
Cloudy Mtn—*summit* (2) AK-9
Cloudy Nashoba Trail—*trail* OK-5
Cloudy Pass—*gap* CO-8
Cloudy Pass—*gap* WA-9
*Cloudy Pass Peak* WA-9
Cloudy Peak—*summit* WA-9
Cloudy Spring—*spring* CO-8
Cloudy Spring Creek—*stream* MN-6
*Clouge Canyon* WA-9
*Clough* AL-4
**Clough**—*pop pl* AL-4
**Clough**—*pop pl* SD-7
Clough, Lake—*lake* FL-3
Clough, Mount—*summit* NH-1
*Clough and Corbin Creek* MI-6
Clough Branch—*stream* NH-1
Clough Brook—*stream* (2) CT-1
Clough Brook—*stream* NH-1
Clough Brook—*stream* VT-1
Clough Canyon—*valley* CA-9
Clough Cave—*cave* CA-9
Clough Cem—*cemetery* ME-1
Clough Cem—*cemetery* MN-6
Clough Ch—*church* OH-6
Clough Corners—*locale* (2) NY-2
Clough Creek—*stream* CA-9
Clough Creek—*stream* OH-6
Clough Creek and Sand Ridge Archeol District—*hist pl* OH-6
Clough Ditch—*canal* CA-9
Clough Ditch—*canal* OH-6
Clough Gulch—*valley* CA-9
Clough Gulch—*valley* (2) OR-9
**Clough Heights**—*pop pl* OH-6
Clough Hill—*summit* ME-1
Clough Hill—*summit* (2) NH-1
Clough Hill Cem—*cemetery* MI-6
Clough (historical)—*locale* SD-7
Clough Hollow—*valley* MO-7
Clough Island—*island* WI-6
Clough Lake—*lake* MN-6
Clough Lake—*lake* (2) NE-7
Clough Point—*cape* ME-1
Clough Point—*cape* NY-2
Clough Pond—*lake* (2) NH-1
Clough Post Office (historical)—*building* (2) AL-4
*Cloughs* AL-4
Cloughs Bay—*swamp* GA-3
*Cloughs Brook* CT-1
Clough Sch—*school* ME-1
Clough Sch—*school* MA-1
Clough Springs—*spring* MT-8
*Cloughs Store Post Office* AL-4
Clough State For—*forest* NH-1
Clough State Park—*park* NH-1
Clough Township Hall—*hist pl* MN-6
Clough Township (historical)—*civil* SD-7
**Clough (Township of)**—*pop pl* MN-6
Clough Valley—*valley* KS-7
Clough Valley Ch—*church* KS-7
*Cloulda* LA-4
Clounch Well—*well* AZ-5
Clouse Branch—*stream* TN-4
Clouse Cave—*cave* TN-4
Clouse Cem—*cemetery* KY-4
Clouse Cem—*cemetery* NY-2
Clouse Cem—*cemetery* TN-4

**Clouse Hill**—*pop pl* TN-4
Clouse Hill—*summit* TN-4
Clouse Hill Cem—*cemetery* TN-4
Clouse Hill Mines—*mine* TN-4
Clouse Hill Post Office (historical)—*building* TN-4
Clouse Hill Sch—*school* TN-4
Clouse Hollow—*valley* TN-4
Clouse Lake—*reservoir* OH-6
Clouse Lake Wildlife Area—*park* OH-6
Clouse Ranch—*locale* ND-7
Clouser Cem—*cemetery* IN-6
*Clousers Mills* IN-6
Clous Ledge—*bar* ME-1
Clousley Hill—*summit* TX-5
**Clouston**—*pop pl* WV-2
Clouter Creek—*stream* SC-3
Cloutier, Alexis, House—*hist pl* LA-4
**Cloutierville**—*pop pl* LA-4
Cloutler Creek—*stream* NY-2
Cloutman Point—*cape* MA-1
Cloutman Pond—*lake* ME-1
Cloutman Ridge—*ridge* ME-1
**Cloutman Spur**—*pop pl* KS-7
Clove—*locale* NY-2
**Clove**—*pop pl* NY-2
Clove, The—*valley* NY-2
Clove Acres Lake—*lake* NJ-2
Clove Brook—*stream* (2) NJ-2
Clove Brook—*stream* (2) NY-2
Clove Cem—*cemetery* NJ-2
Clove Cem—*cemetery* NY-2
Clove Ch—*church* NC-3
Clove Chapel—*church* NY-2
*Clove Creek* NJ-2
Clove Creek—*stream* NY-2
**Clove Hill**—*pop pl* MS-4
Clove Lake—*lake* MN-6
Clove Lake—*lake* NY-2
Clove Lakes Park—*park* NY-2
*Clovelly* NH-1
Clovelly Farms—*locale* LA-4
Clovelly Garden Apartments—*hist pl* OR-9
Clovelly Oil and Gas Field—*oilfield* LA-4
Clove Mtn—*summit* NY-2
Cloven Cliffs—*cliff* NC-3
*Clove Point* MD-2
*Clover* KY-4
*Clover* MP-9
Clover—*locale* GA-3
Clover—*locale* ID-8
Clover—*locale* KY-4
Clover—*locale* OH-6
Clover—*locale* UT-8
Clover—*locale* WV-2
**Clover**—*pop pl* PA-2
**Clover**—*pop pl* SC-3
**Clover**—*pop pl* (2) VA-3
**Clover**—*pop pl* WV-2
**Clover**—*pop pl* WI-6
Clover Ave Sch—*school* CA-9
**Clover Bank**—*pop pl* NY-2
Clover Basin—*basin* (2) MT-8
Clover Basin Camp—*locale* CA-9
Clover Basin Ditch—*canal* CO-8
Clover Basin Rsvr—*reservoir* CO-8
Clover Bay—*bay* AK-9
Clover Belt Sch—*school* WI-6
Clover Bend—*bend* AR-4
**Clover Bend**—*pop pl* AR-4
Clover Bend Cem—*cemetery* AR-4
Clover Bend HS—*hist pl* AR-4
*Clover Bottom* TN-4
Clover Bottom—*bend* TN-4
Clover Bottom—*locale* KY-4
**Clover Bottom**—*pop pl* MO-7
Clover Bottom Ch—*church* (2) KY-4
Clover Bottom Ch—*church* VA-3
Clover Bottom Creek—*stream* KY-4
**Cloverbottom (historical)**—*pop pl* TN-4
Clover Bottom Mansion—*hist pl* TN-4
Clover Bottom Post Office (historical)—*building* TN-4
Clover Bottom Sch—*school* TN-4
Clover Branch—*stream* AR-4
Clover Branch—*stream* KY-4
Clover Branch—*stream* NC-3
Clover Branch—*stream* TN-4
Clover Butte—*ridge* OR-9
Clover Butte—*summit* CA-9
Clover Butte—*summit* (2) OR-9
Clover Camp—*locale* AZ-5
Clover Camp—*locale* OR-9
Clover Canyon—*valley* (2) AZ-5
Clover Canyon—*valley* UT-8
Clover (CCD)—*cens area* SC-3
Clover Cem—*cemetery* CO-8
Clover Cem—*cemetery* IL-6
Clover Cem—*cemetery* (2) MN-6
Clover Cem—*cemetery* OH-6
Clover Cem—*cemetery* UT-8
Clover Cem—*cemetery* VA-3
Clover Cem—*cemetery* WA-9
Clover Cem—*cemetery* WV-2
Clover Ch—*church* MN-6
Clover Ch—*church* TX-5
Clover Chapel Cem—*cemetery* SC-3
Clover Chapel Ch—*church* IL-6
Clover Cliff Ranch House—*hist pl* KS-7
*Clover Creek* AR-4
*Clover Creek* CA-9
*Clover Creek* MN-6
*Clover Creek* OR-9
*Clover Creek* TN-4
*Clovercreek* VA-3
Clover Creek—*locale* PA-2
Clover Creek—*locale* VA-3
Clovercreek—*other* PA-2
Clover Creek—*stream* AK-9
Clover Creek—*stream* (3) AZ-5
Clover Creek—*stream* (8) CA-9
Clover Creek—*stream* CO-8
Clover Creek—*stream* (4) ID-8
Clover Creek—*stream* (2) KY-4
Clover Creek—*stream* (2) MT-8
Clover Creek—*stream* (7) NV-8
Clover Creek—*stream* (13) OR-9
Clover Creek—*stream* PA-2
Clover Creek—*stream* (2) TN-4
Clover Creek—*stream* (2) UT-8
Clover Creek—*stream* (2) VA-3
Clover Creek—*stream* WA-9
Clover Creek—*stream* WV-2
Clover Creek—*stream* WI-6
Clover Creek—*stream* WY-8
Clover Creek Bridge—*bridge* UT-8
Clover Creek Cem—*cemetery* TN-4
Clover Creek Ch—*church* TN-4
*Clover Creek Post Office* TN-4
Clover Creek Ranch—*locale* OR-9
Clover Creek Springs—*spring* CA-9
Clover Creek Valley—*valley* OR-9
**Clover Crest Subdivision - Number 2**—*pop pl* UT-8
**Clover Crest Subdivision - Number 3**—*pop pl* UT-8
Clovercroft—*locale* TN-4
Clovercroft Lake—*reservoir* TN-4
Clovercroft Lake Dam—*dam* TN-4
*Cloverdale* IL-6
*Clover Dale* IN-6
*Cloverdale* VA-3
Cloverdale—*locale* GA-3
Cloverdale—*locale* KS-7
Cloverdale—*locale* LA-4
Cloverdale—*locale* OH-6
Cloverdale—*locale* (2) OR-9
Cloverdale—*locale* VA-3
Cloverdale—*locale* WI-6
**Cloverdale**—*pop pl* (5) AL-4
**Cloverdale**—*pop pl* AR-4
**Cloverdale**—*pop pl* (2) CA-9
**Cloverdale**—*pop pl* ID-8
**Cloverdale**—*pop pl* (2) IL-6
**Cloverdale**—*pop pl* IN-6
**Cloverdale**—*pop pl* IA-7
**Cloverdale**—*pop pl* KS-7
**Cloverdale**—*pop pl* MI-6
**Cloverdale**—*pop pl* MN-6
**Cloverdale**—*pop pl* MS-4
**Cloverdale**—*pop pl* MO-7
**Cloverdale**—*pop pl* NM-5
**Cloverdale**—*pop pl* (2) NC-3
**Cloverdale**—*pop pl* OH-6
**Cloverdale**—*pop pl* OR-9
**Cloverdale**—*pop pl* (2) TN-4
**Cloverdale**—*pop pl* VT-1
**Cloverdale**—*pop pl* (2) VA-3
**Cloverdale**—*pop pl* WA-9
**Cloverdale**—*pop pl* WV-2
Cloverdale—*uninc pl* KS-7
Cloverdale—*uninc pl* KY-4
Cloverdale—*uninc pl* (2) NJ-2
Cloverdale Baptist Ch—*church* (2) AL-4
Cloverdale Baptist Ch—*church* MS-4
*Cloverdale Basin* WY-8
Cloverdale Basin—*basin* CO-8
Cloverdale (CCD)—*cens area* AL-4
*Cloverdale Cem* OR-9
Cloverdale Cem—*cemetery* CA-9
Cloverdale Cem—*cemetery* LA-4
Clover Dale Cem—*cemetery* MO-7
Cloverdale Cem—*cemetery* OR-9
Cloverdale Cem—*cemetery* TN-4
Cloverdale Ch—*church* AL-4
Cloverdale Ch—*church* AR-4
Cloverdale Ch—*church* GA-3
Cloverdale Ch—*church* (2) IN-6
Cloverdale Ch—*church* MO-7
Cloverdale Ch—*church* (2) TN-4
Cloverdale Ch—*church* VA-3
Cloverdale Ch—*church* WV-2
Cloverdale Ch of Christ—*church* AL-4
Cloverdale Christian Ch—*church* AL-4
Cloverdale Corners—*locale* PA-2
Cloverdale Creek—*stream* CA-9
Cloverdale Creek—*stream* NV-8
Cloverdale Creek—*stream* NM-5
Cloverdale Creek—*stream* TN-4
Cloverdale Creek—*stream* VA-3
*Cloverdale Crossroads* DE-2
Cloverdale Ditch—*canal* OR-9
Cloverdale Division—*civil* AL-4
*Cloverdale Elementary School* AL-4
Cloverdale Elem Sch—*school* IN-6
**Cloverdale Estates (subdivision)**—*pop pl* AL-4
**Cloverdale Estates (subdivision)**—*pop pl* TN-4
Cloverdale-Geyserville (CCD)—*cens area* CA-9
**Cloverdale Heights**—*pop pl* AL-4
Cloverdale Hist Dist—*hist pl* AL-4
Cloverdale Junior/Senior HS—*school* IN-6
*Clover Dale Lake* AL-4
Cloverdale Lake—*lake* MI-6
Cloverdale Lake—*lake* OH-6
Cloverdale Lake Dam—*dam* AL-4
Cloverdale Memorial Park—*cemetery* ID-8
Cloverdale Methodist Ch—*church* AL-4
Cloverdale Mine—*mine* CO-8
Cloverdale Mine HQ—*mine* CA-9
Cloverdale Oil Field—*oilfield* MS-4
Cloverdale Park—*park* PA-2
**Cloverdale Park**—*pop pl* PA-2
Cloverdale Peak—*summit* CA-9
Cloverdale Plaza (Shop Ctr)—*locale* NC-3
Cloverdale Ranch—*locale* CA-9
Cloverdale Ranch—*locale* NV-8
**Cloverdale Rancheria**—*pop pl* CA-9
Cloverdale Ridge—*ridge* AR-4
Cloverdale RR Station—*hist pl* CA-9
Cloverdale Sch—*school* (3) AL-4
Cloverdale Sch—*school* (2) IL-6
Cloverdale Sch—*school* MI-6
Cloverdale Sch—*school* (3) MN-6
Cloverdale Sch—*school* (2) NE-7
Cloverdale Sch—*school* NY-2
Cloverdale Sch—*school* NC-3
Cloverdale Sch—*school* OK-5
Cloverdale Sch—*school* (2) OR-9
Cloverdale Sch—*school* TN-4
Cloverdale Sch—*school* WA-9
Cloverdale Sch—*school* WV-2
Cloverdale Sch—*school* WI-6
Cloverdale Sch (abandoned)—*school* MO-7
Cloverdale Sch (historical)—*school* MS-4
*Cloverdale Shopping Center* NC-3
**Cloverdale (subdivision)**—*pop pl* (2) AL-4
**Cloverdale (subdivision)**—*pop pl* NC-3
Cloverdale Summit—*gap* NV-8
**Cloverdale (Township of)**—*pop pl* IN-6
Cloverdale Valley—*valley* WI-6
Clover Dam—*dam* PA-2
**Clover-Darby**—*pop pl* KY-4
Cloverden—*hist pl* MA-1
Clover Ditch—*canal* CO-8
Clover Divide—*ridge* MT-8
**Clover Estates Subdivision**—*pop pl* UT-8
Clover Field—*flat* VA-3
Clover Field—*park* CT-1
Clover Field Branch—*stream* KY-4
Cloverfield Branch—*stream* TN-4
Cloverfield Hollow—*valley* TN-4
Cloverfield Hollow—*valley* WV-2
Cloverfields—*hist pl* WA-9
**Cloverfields**—*pop pl* MD-2
*Clover Flat* UT-8
Clover Flat—*flat* CA-9
Clover Flat—*flat* OR-9
Clover Flat—*flat* UT-8
Clover Flat—*locale* CA-9
Clover Flat Pit—*locale* CA-9
Clover Flats—*flat* WA-9
Clover Flat Sch—*school* CA-9
Clover Flat Tank—*reservoir* AZ-5
Clover Flat Tank No.2—*reservoir* AZ-5
*Clover Fork* KY-4
Clover Fork—*stream* KY-4
Clover Fork—*stream* WV-2
Clover Fork Ch—*church* WV-2
Clover Fork Cumberland River—*stream* KY-4
*Clover Fork Tributary Cumberland River* KY-4
Clover Gap Branch—*stream* KY-4
**Clover Garden**—*pop pl* NC-3
Clover Garden Ch—*church* NC-3
Clover Garden Ch—*church* TN-4
Clover Garden Sch—*school* TN-4
Clover Groff Ditch—*canal* OH-6
Clover Gulch—*valley* (3) CA-9
Clover Gulch—*valley* CO-8
Clover Haven Ch—*church* TX-5
Clover Heights Park—*park* PA-2
*Clover Hill* MS-4
*Clover Hill* NJ-2
*Clover Hill* PA-2
Clover Hill—*CDP* MD-2
Clover Hill—*CDP* NJ-2
Clover Hill—*hist pl* KY-4
Clover Hill—*hist pl* MD-2
Clover Hill—*hist pl* NC-3
Clover Hill—*locale* AL-4
Clover Hill—*locale* MS-4
Clover Hill—*locale* (2) OH-6
Clover Hill—*locale* VA-3
**Cloverhill**—*pop pl* NJ-2
**Cloverhill**—*pop pl* OH-6
**Clover Hill**—*pop pl* OH-6
**Clover Hill**—*pop pl* PA-2
**Cloverhill**—*pop pl* TN-4
**Clover Hill**—*pop pl* TN-4
Clover Hill—*summit* (2) NY-2
Clover Hill—*summit* (2) PA-2
Clover Hill—*summit* TN-4
Clover Hill—*summit* WA-9
Clover Hill Cem—*cemetery* AL-4
Clover Hill Cem—*cemetery* IN-6
Clover Hill Cem—*cemetery* TN-4
Clover Hill Cem—*cemetery* TX-5
Clover Hill Ch—*church* AL-4
Clover Hill Ch—*church* (2) KY-4
Clover Hill Ch—*church* (2) MS-4
Clover Hill Ch—*church* MO-7
Clover Hill Ch—*church* NC-3
Clover Hill Ch—*church* TN-4
Cloverhill Ch—*church* TX-5
Clover Hill Creek—*stream* PA-2
**Clover Hill Estates**—*pop pl* TN-4
Clover Hill Hist Dist—*hist pl* NJ-2
Clover Hill Hosp—*hospital* MA-1
Clover Hill (Magisterial District)—*fmr MCD* (2) VA-3
Clover Hill Mill (historical)—*locale* TN-4
Clover Hill Park Cem—*cemetery* MI-6
Clover Hill Pond—*lake* MN-6
*Cloverhill Post Office* TN-4
Cloverhill Post Office (historical)—*building* MS-4
Clover Hill Post Office (historical)—*building* TN-4
Clover Hill Ridge—*ridge* TN-4
*Clover Hills* IA-7
Clover Hill Sch—*school* IA-7
Clover Hill Sch—*school* KS-7
Clover Hill Sch—*school* MN-6
Cloverhill Sch—*school* MO-7
Clover Hill Sch (abandoned)—*school* MO-7
Clover Hill Sch (abandoned)—*school* PA-2
**Clover Hills Subdivision**—*pop pl* UT-8
**Clover (historical)**—*pop pl* OR-9
Clover Hollow—*flat* ID-8
**Clover Hollow**—*pop pl* UT-8
Clover Hollow—*valley* KY-4
Clover Hollow—*valley* TN-4
Clover Hollow—*valley* VA-3
Clover Hollow—*valley* WV-2
Clover Hollow Cem—*cemetery* VA-3
Clover Hollow Ch—*church* VA-3
**Clover Hollow Condo**—*pop pl* UT-8
Clover Hollow Mtn—*summit* VA-3
Clover Hotel—*hist pl* OK-5
Clover Island—*island* AK-9
Clover Island—*island* WA-9
*Clove River* NJ-2
Clove River Dam—*dam* NJ-2
Clover Knoll—*summit* ID-8
Clover Knoll Ditch—*canal* CO-8
*Clover Lake* MI-6
*Clover Lake* MN-6
Clover Lake—*lake* AK-9
Clover Lake—*lake* (2) MN-6
Clover Lake—*lake* OR-9
Clover Lake—*lake* WA-9
Clover Lake—*lake* WI-6
Clover Lake—*reservoir* GA-3
Clover Lakes—*lake* TN-4
Cloverland—*locale* WA-9
Cloverland—*locale* WI-6
**Cloverland**—*pop pl* IN-6
**Cloverland**—*pop pl* VA-3
Cloverland Cem—*cemetery* WA-9
**Cloverland Estates Subdivision**—*pop pl* UT-8
Cloverland Garage—*hist pl* WA-9
Cloverland Hotel—*hist pl* MI-6
Cloverland Park—*park* TX-5
Cloverlands—*building* TN-4
Cloverlands—*hist pl* TN-4
Cloverland Sch—*school* CA-9
Cloverland Shop Ctr—*locale* AL-4
Cloverland (subdivision)—*post sta* AL-4
**Cloverland (Town of)**—*pop pl* (2) WI-6
Clover Lawn—*hist pl* IL-6
Clover Lea—*hist pl* VA-3
**Cloverlea**—*pop pl* MD-2
**Cloverleaf**—*pop pl* (2) IL-6
**Clover Leaf**—*pop pl* KY-4
**Cloverleaf**—*pop pl* TX-5
Cloverleaf Baptist Ch—*church* AL-4
Cloverleaf Branch—*stream* KY-4
Cloverleaf Camp—*locale* AL-4
Cloverleaf Campground—*locale* ID-8
Cloverleaf Cem—*cemetery* MN-6
Cloverleaf Cem—*cemetery* NJ-2
Cloverleaf Cem—*cemetery* WV-2
Cloverleaf Ch—*church* GA-3
Clover Leaf Ch—*church* IN-6
Cloverleaf Ch—*church* KY-4
Cloverleaf Ch—*church* TN-4
**Cloverleaf Colony**—*pop pl* SD-7
Cloverleaf Creek—*stream* ID-8
**Cloverleaf Farm Estates**—*pop pl* VA-3
Cloverleaf Golf Course—*locale* PA-2
Cloverleaf Golf Course—*other* IL-6
Cloverleaf Grange—*locale* ID-8
Cloverleaf HS—*school* OH-6
Cloverleaf Island—*island* AK-9
Cloverleaf Lake—*lake* CA-9
Cloverleaf Lake—*lake* (2) MI-6
Cloverleaf Lake—*lake* MN-6
Clover Leaf Lake—*lake* MN-6
Clover Leaf Lake—*lake* PA-2
Cloverleaf Lake—*lake* WI-6
Cloverleaf Lake—*lake* WY-8
Cloverleaf Lakes—*lake* MT-8
**Clover Leaf Lakes**—*pop pl* NJ-2
Cloverleaf Mall Shop Ctr—*locale* MS-4
Clover Leaf Mine—*mine* SD-7
Cloverleaf Plaza Shop Ctr—*locale* AL-4
Cloverleaf Ranch—*locale* AZ-5
Cloverleaf Rest Cem—*cemetery* TX-5
Cloverleaf Sch—*school* GA-3
Cloverleaf Sch—*school* IL-6
Cloverleaf Sch—*school* (2) KS-7
Cloverleaf Shop Ctr—*locale* NC-3
Cloverleaf Speedway—*other* OH-6
Cloverleaf Spring Number Two—*spring* OR-9
**Cloverleaf (subdivision)**—*pop pl* (2) AL-4
**Cloverleaf (subdivision)**—*pop pl* (2) AZ-5
**Clover Leaf (Township of)**—*pop pl* MN-6
Cloverleaf Valley—*valley* CO-8
Cloverleaf Yard—*locale* OH-6
*Cloverlick* WV-2
**Clover Lick**—*pop pl* WV-2
Cloverlick Branch—*stream* (2) WV-2
*Cloverlick Creek* WV-2
Clover Lick Creek—*stream* IN-6
Clover Lick Creek—*stream* KY-4
Cloverlick Creek—*stream* KY-4
Cloverlick Creek—*stream* OH-6
Clover Lick Hollow—*valley* (2) VA-3
**Cloverlick Junction**—*pop pl* KY-4
Clover Lick Knob—*summit* VA-3
Cloverlick Mtn—*summit* WV-2
Clover Lick Ridge—*ridge* VA-3
Cloverlot Hollow—*valley* PA-2
Cloverly—*locale* CO-8
**Cloverly**—*pop pl* MD-2
**Cloverly Acres**—*pop pl* PA-2
**Cloverly Heights**—*pop pl* PA-2
Cloverly Park—*park* PA-2
Cloverly Sch—*school* CA-9
Cloverly Sch—*school* MD-2
Clover (Magisterial District)—*fmr MCD* WV-2
Clover Meadow—*flat* (3) CA-9
Clover Meadow—*flat* OR-9
Clover Meadow Ditch—*canal* CO-8
Clover Meadow Ranger Station—*locale* CA-9
Clover Meadows—*flat* MT-8
Clover Meadows Campground—*locale* MT-8
Clover Meadow Sch—*school* CO-8
Clover Mill Creek—*stream* NY-2
Clover Mount—*hist pl* VA-3
Clover Mountain—*cliff* MA-1
Clover Mtn—*summit* AK-9
Clover Mtn—*summit* CA-9
Clover Mtn—*summit* CO-8
Clover Mtn—*summit* ID-8
Clover Mtn—*summit* NV-8
Clover Mtns—*range* NV-8
Clover Mtns—*range* (2) UT-8
Clovernook—*hist pl* OH-6
Clovernook Country Club—*other* OH-6
Clovernook Home—*building* OH-6
Clovernook Playground—*park* WI-6
Clovernook Sch—*school* OH-6
**Clover Park**—*pop pl* PA-2
**Clover Park**—*pop pl* WA-9
Clover Park Vocational Technical School Airp—*airport* WA-9
Clover Pass—*CDP* AK-9
Clover Passage—*channel* AK-9
Clover Pass Ch—*church* AK-9
Clover Patch—*flat* CA-9
Clover Patch Branch—*stream* NC-3
Cloverpatch Butte—*summit* OR-9
Cloverpatch Creek—*stream* OR-9
Cloverpatch Trail—*trail* OR-9
Clover Point—*cape* AK-9
Clover Point Tank—*reservoir* AZ-5
Clover Port—*other* TN-4
**Cloverport**—*pop pl* KY-4
**Cloverport**—*pop pl* TN-4
Cloverport Baptist Ch—*church* TN-4
Cloverport (CCD)—*cens area* KY-4
Cloverport Chapel—*church* TN-4
Cloverport Chapel Cem—*cemetery* TN-4
**Cloverport (Clover Port)**—*pop pl* TN-4
Cloverport Hist Dist—*hist pl* KY-4
Clover Ridge—*ridge* (2) OH-6
Clover Ridge—*ridge* (2) OR-9
Clover Ridge—*ridge* WV-2
Clover Ridge Cem—*cemetery* MS-4
Clover Ridge Oil Field—*other* WV-2
Clover Ridge Sch—*school* OR-9
**Clover Ridge Subdivision**—*pop pl* UT-8
Clover Rock—*island* AK-9
*Clover Run* PA-2
Clover Run—*locale* PA-2
Clover Run—*stream* OH-6
Clover Run—*stream* PA-2
Clover Run—*stream* (2) WV-2
Clover Sch—*school* CA-9
Clover Sch—*school* CO-8
Clover Sch—*school* IL-6
Clover Sch—*school* MI-6
Clover Sch—*school* MN-6
Clover Sch—*school* SD-7
Clover Sch—*school* TX-5
Clover School—*locale* CA-9
*Clover Slough* NV-8
Clover Spring—*spring* (5) AZ-5
Clover Spring—*spring* ID-8
Clover Spring—*spring* (2) NV-8
Clover Spring—*spring* (2) WA-9
Clover Springs Picnic Ground—*locale* UT-8
Clover Spring Tank—*reservoir* AZ-5
Clover Station—*locale* UT-8
**Clover Station (historical)**—*pop pl* OR-9
Clover Street Sch—*school* CT-1
Clover Swale—*basin* OR-9
Clover Swale—*valley* CA-9
Clover Swale—*valley* OR-9
Clover Swale Creek—*stream* CA-9
Clover Tank—*reservoir* (3) AZ-5
**Cloverton**—*pop pl* MN-6
Cloverton Cem—*cemetery* NE-7
Cloverton Sch—*hist pl* MN-6
**Clovertown**—*pop pl* KY-4
**Clover (Town of)**—*pop pl* WI-6
**Clover (Township of)**—*pop pl* IL-6
**Clover (Township of)**—*pop pl* (4) MN-6
**Clover (Township of)**—*pop pl* PA-2
*Clover Valley* CA-9
Clover Valley—*basin* CA-9
Clover Valley—*basin* NV-8
Clover Valley—*fmr MCD* NE-7
Clover Valley—*valley* (4) CA-9
Clover Valley—*valley* IN-6
Clover Valley—*valley* NV-8
Clover Valley—*valley* (2) WA-9
Clover Valley Ch—*church* MS-4
Clover Valley Creek—*stream* CA-9
*Clover Valley Mountains* NV-8
*Clover Valley Mountains* UT-8
Clover Valley Pond—*lake* AL-4
Clover Valley Ranch—*locale* (2) CA-9
Clover Valley Rsvr—*reservoir* CA-9
Clover Valley Sch—*school* MN-6
Clover Valley Sch—*school* NV-8
Clover Valley Sch—*school* WA-9
Clover Valley Wildlife Rsvr—*reservoir* NV-8
**Clover Village**—*pop pl* IN-6
**Cloverville**—*pop pl* MI-6
Cloverville Ch—*church* MI-6
Clover Wash—*stream* AZ-5
Clover Well—*well* AZ-5
**Cloverwood Subdivision**—*pop pl* UT-8
Clove Sch—*school* NY-2
Clove Spring—*spring* NY-2
**Clove Valley**—*pop pl* NY-2
Clove Valley—*valley* NY-2
Clovin Bay—*swamp* FL-3
*Clovino Bay* FL-3
**Clovis**—*pop pl* CA-9
**Clovis**—*pop pl* NM-5
Clovis, Lake—*lake* OR-9
Clovis Baptist Hosp—*hist pl* NM-5
Clovis Canyon—*valley* TX-5
Clovis (CCD)—*cens area* NM-5
Clovis Cem—*cemetery* CA-9
Clovis Central Fire Station—*hist pl* NM-5
Clovis Ditch—*canal* CA-9
Clovis Gulch—*valley* MT-8
Clovis Municipal Airp—*airport* NM-5
Clovis Park—*park* WI-6
Clovista S D A Sch—*school* CA-9
**Clow**—*pop pl* AR-4
Clow Canyon—*valley* CA-9
Clow Cem—*cemetery* TX-5
**Clow Corner**—*pop pl* OR-9
Clow Corporation (Plant)—*facility* IL-6
Clower—*locale* TX-5
Clower Knob—*summit* VA-3
Clower RR Station (historical)—*locale* FL-3
Clowers Cem—*cemetery* GA-3
Clowers Ch—*church* GA-3
Clowers Crossroads—*locale* AL-4
Clowers Shop Ctr—*locale* AL-4
*Clowes* DE-2
Clow Mtn—*summit* CA-9
Clow Ridge—*ridge* CA-9
Clowry—*locale* MI-6
*Clows* DE-2
Clowser Gap—*gap* VA-3
Clows Hill—*summit* NH-1
Clow State For—*forest* MO-7
**Clow (Township of)**—*pop pl* MN-6
Cloyd, John, House—*hist pl* TN-4
Cloyd Branch—*stream* KY-4
Cloyd Cem—*cemetery* IN-6
Cloyd Ch—*church* TN-4
Cloyd Creek—*stream* KY-4
Cloyd Creek—*stream* TN-4
Cloyd Creek Ch—*church* TN-4
**Cloyd Creek (historical)**—*pop pl* TN-4
Cloyd Hotel—*hist pl* TN-4
Cloyd Lateral—*canal* AZ-5
Cloyd (Magisterial District)—*fmr MCD* VA-3
Cloyd Ridge—*ridge* KY-4
*Cloyds Creek* TN-4
Cloyds Creek Cem—*cemetery* TN-4
Cloyds Creek Post Office (historical)—*building* TN-4
Cloyds Landing—*locale* KY-4
Cloyds Landing Island—*island* KY-4
Cloyds Mtn—*summit* VA-3
Cloyds Pond—*lake* UT-8
Cloyd Valley Cem—*cemetery* SD-7
**Cloyd Valley Township**—*pop pl* SD-7
Cloyed Carpenter Ranch—*locale* NE-7
Cloyes Hill—*summit* VT-1
*Cloyses Lake* CO-8
*Clrkes Fork* WA-9
*C L Salter Elementary School* AL-4
C L Salter Sch—*school* AL-4
C L Scarborough JHS—*school* AL-4
**Clubb**—*pop pl* MO-7
Club Bay—*swamp* NC-3
Clubb Cem—*cemetery* (3) MO-7
Clubb Creek—*stream* MO-7
Clubb Creek Ch—*church* MO-7
Clubb Hill—*summit* AR-4
Clubbing Rocks, The—*island* AK-9
Club Blvd Sch—*school* NC-3
Club Bridge Creek—*stream* SC-3
Clubbs Creek—*channel* GA-3
Clubbs MS—*school* FL-3
*Clubb Springs* TN-4
Clubb Springs Post Office (historical)—*building* TN-4
*Clubb Store* MO-7
Club Canal—*canal* LA-4
Club Canal—*canal* NM-5
Club Canyon—*valley* ID-8
**Club Court**—*pop pl* VA-3
Club Cove—*bay* MD-2
Club Cow Camp—*locale* CO-8
*Club Creek* TN-4
Club Creek—*stream* ID-8
Club Creek—*stream* MO-7
Club Creek—*stream* MT-8
Club Creek Hill—*summit* KY-4
Club Creek State For—*forest* MO-7
Club Draw—*valley* NM-5
**Club Estates (subdivision)**—*pop pl* PA-2
*Clubfoot Canal* NC-3
Clubfoot Creek—*stream* MT-8
Clubfoot Creek—*stream* NC-3
Clubfoot Hollow—*valley* OR-9
Club Gap—*gap* NC-3
Club Gulch—*valley* CO-8
Club Gulch—*valley* MT-8
Club Gulch Rsvr—*reservoir* CO-8
Club Harbor—*hist pl* WI-6
Club Haven Shop Ctr—*locale* NC-3
Club Head Creek—*stream* MA-1
Club Heights Sch—*school* UT-8
**Club Hill**—*pop pl* MD-2
Club Hill—*summit* PA-2
Clubhouse Branch—*stream* SC-3
*Club House Creek* NJ-2
*Clubhouse Creek* NC-3
Clubhouse Creek—*gut* (2) SC-3
Clubhouse Creek—*stream* MO-7
Clubhouse Creek—*stream* NJ-2
**Clubhouse Crossroads**—*pop pl* (2) SC-3
Clubhouse Extension Mines—*mine* AR-4
Clubhouse Farm—*locale* TX-5
Clubhouse Gut—*gut* VA-3
Club House Heights—*uninc pl* KY-4
Club House Hill—*summit* PA-2
Clubhouse Island—*island* WI-6
*Clubhouse Lake* WI-6
Clubhouse Lake—*lake* FL-3
Clubhouse Lake—*lake* MN-6
Clubhouse Lake—*lake* NE-7
Clubhouse Lake—*lake* SD-7
Clubhouse Lake—*lake* WI-6
Club House Landing—*locale* DE-2
**Clubhouse Landing**—*pop pl* LA-4
Clubhouse Marsh—*swamp* VA-3
Clubhouse Mine—*mine* AR-4
Clubhouse Municipal Park—*park* AZ-5
*Clubhouse Point* PA-2
Clubhouse Point—*cape* SC-3
Club House Point—*summit* PA-2
Clubhouse Pond—*lake* CT-1
Clubhouse Ridge—*ridge* GA-3
Clubhouse Run—*stream* WV-2
Clubhouse Slough—*lake* SD-7
Clubhouse Spring—*spring* AR-4
Clubhouse Spring Branch—*stream* AR-4
Clubhouse Springpond—*lake* WI-6
Clubhouse Springpond State Fishery Area—*park* WI-6
Clubine Ranch—*locale* CO-8
Club Island—*island* CT-1
Club Island—*island* MI-6
Club Island—*island* NY-2
Club Key—*island* FL-3
*Club Lake* IL-6
*Club Lake* TX-5
Club Lake—*lake* FL-3
Club Lake—*lake* (2) MI-6
Club Lake—*lake* (2) MN-6
Club Lake—*lake* (2) OK-5
Club Lake—*lake* (2) TX-5
Club Lake—*lake* WI-6
Club Lake—*reservoir* (2) GA-3
Club Lake—*reservoir* (2) MS-4
Club Lake—*reservoir* MO-7
Club Lake—*reservoir* NC-3
Club Lake—*reservoir* (2) OK-5
Club Lake—*reservoir* PA-2
Club Lake—*reservoir* (5) TX-5
Club Lake Bay—*bay* TX-5
Club Lake Branch—*stream* TX-5
Club Lake Cove—*bay* TX-5
Club Lake Dam—*dam* MS-4
**Club Lake Estates**—*pop pl* TX-5
Club Meadows—*flat* ID-8
Club Mines—*mine* CO-8
Club Moderne—*hist pl* MT-8
Club Mtn—*summit* AK-9
Club No 7 Mine—*mine* CO-8
Club of Christ Hosp—*hospital* TX-5
**Club Pines (subdivision)**—*pop pl* NC-3
Club Point—*cape* AK-9
Club Point—*summit* ID-8
*Club Pond* NC-3
Club Pond—*bay* LA-4
Club Pond—*lake* NH-1
Club Pond—*lake* NY-2
Club Pond—*lake* NC-3
Club Pond—*reservoir* AL-4
Club Pond—*reservoir* MA-1
Club Pond Dam—*dam* MA-1
Club Ranch—*locale* AZ-5
Club Ranch—*locale* CO-8
Club Ranch Trail—*trail* AZ-5

Coal Draw—*valley* CO-8
Coal Draw—*valley* MT-8
Coal Draw—*valley* UT-8
Coal Draw—*valley* (11) WY-8
Coal Dump Canyon—*valley* NM-5
Coal Dump Spring—*spring* NM-5
Coaledo—*locale* OR-9
Coalen Ground Branch—*stream* TN-4
Coalen Ground Ridge—*ridge* TN-4
Coaler—*locale* IL-6
**Coaler (historical)**—*pop pl* MS-4
Coales Branch—*stream* AL-4
Coalfield—*locale* WA-9
Coalfield—*locale* WV-2
**Coalfield**—*pop pl* TN-4
Coalfield Camp Number 1 (historical)—*locale* TN-4
Coalfield Camp Number 2 (historical)—*locale* TN-4
Coalfield (CCD)—*cens area* TN-4
Coalfield Division—*civil* TN-4
*Coalfield High School* TN-4
Coalfield (historical P.O.)—*locale* IA-7
Coalfield Hollow—*valley* KY-4
Coalfield Post Office—*building* TN-4
Coalfield Sch—*school* TN-4
**Coalfield Township**—*pop pl* ND-7
Coal Field Windmill—*locale* AZ-5
**Coal Fire**—*pop pl* AL-4
Coal Fire Ch—*church* AL-4
Coal Fire Creek—*stream* AL-4
Coal Fire Creek Bar—*bar* AL-4
Coalfire Cut Off—*channel* AL-4
*Coal Fork* UT-8
*Coal Fork* WV-2
**Coal Fork**—*pop pl* WV-2
Coal Fork—*stream* UT-8
Coal Fork—*stream* (3) WV-2
Coal Gap—*gap* TN-4
Coal Gap—*gap* VA-3
Coal Gap Post Office (historical)—*building* TN-4
Coal Gap Sch—*school* AR-4
Coalgate—*locale* OH-6
**Coalgate**—*pop pl* OK-5
Coalgate Cem—*cemetery* OK-5
Coalgate Sch Gymnasium-Auditorium—*hist pl* OK-5
Coal Glacier—*glacier* AK-9
**Coalglen**—*pop pl* NC-3
**Coal Glen**—*pop pl* PA-2
Coal Glen—*school* IA-7
Coal Glen Sch—*school* IA-7
**Coalgood (RR name Merna)**—*pop pl* KY-4
**Coal Grove**—*pop pl* OH-6
*Coal Gulch* CO-8
*Coal Gulch* ID-8
Coal Gulch—*valley* CA-9
Coal Gulch—*valley* (5) CO-8
Coal Gulch—*valley* (3) MT-8
Coal Gulch—*valley* (5) WY-8
*Coal Harbor* ND-7
*Coal Harbor* VA-3
Coal Harbor—*bay* AK-9
Coal Harbor—*locale* AK-9
*Coal Harbor Creek* VA-3
Coal Hearth Cem—*cemetery* NH-1
*Coal Hill* PA-2
Coal Hill—*locale* MO-7
Coal Hill—*locale* OH-6
Coal Hill—*locale* (2) TN-4
**Coal Hill**—*pop pl* AR-4
**Coal Hill**—*pop pl* PA-2
Coal Hill—*summit* CO-8
Coal Hill—*summit* MT-8
Coal Hill—*summit* ND-7
Coal Hill—*summit* OK-5
Coal Hill—*summit* (2) PA-2
Coal Hill—*summit* UT-8
Coal Hill—*summit* WY-8
Coal Hill—*valley* PA-2
*Coal Hill Baptist Church* TN-4
Coal Hill Cem—*cemetery* NY-2
Coal Hill Ch—*church* AR-4
Coal Hill Ch—*church* TN-4
Coal Hill Mtn—*summit* TN-4
Coal Hill Ridge—*ridge* UT-8
Coal Hill Sch (historical)—*school* PA-2
Coal (historical)—*locale* AL-4
*Coal Hollow* OH-6
Coal Hollow—*locale* IL-6
**Coal Hollow**—*pop pl* (2) PA-2
Coal Hollow—*valley* AR-4
Coal Hollow—*valley* (2) IL-6
Coal Hollow—*valley* (2) IN-6
Coal Hollow—*valley* (5) KY-4
Coal Hollow—*valley* MO-7
Coal Hollow—*valley* NM-5
Coal Hollow—*valley* (2) OH-6
Coal Hollow—*valley* PA-2
Coal Hollow—*valley* (10) UT-8
Coal Hollow—*valley* (12) WV-2
Coal Hollow—*valley* WY-8
Coal Hollow Spring—*spring* MT-8
Coal Hollow Spring—*spring* UT-8
**Coal Hollow (Toby Mines)**—*pop pl* PA-2
Coal House—*hist pl* WV-2
Coaling—*locale* TN-4
**Coaling**—*pop pl* AL-4
**Coalinga**—*pop pl* CA-9
Coalinga (CCD)—*cens area* CA-9
Coalinga Mineral Springs—*spring* CA-9
Coalinga Nose—*summit* CA-9
Coalinga Number 2 Substation—*other* CA-9
*Coalinga Oil Field* CA-9
Coalinga Polk Street Sch—*hist pl* CA-9
Coalinga Pumping Station—*other* CA-9
Coaling Baptist Ch—*church* AL-4
Coaling Cem—*cemetery* AL-4
Coaling Grounds Ridge—*ridge* TN-4
Coaling Hollow—*valley* MO-7
Coaling Hollow—*valley* (3) TN-4
Coalings, The—*summit* TN-4
Coaling Sch—*school* TN-4
Coaling United Methodist Ch—*church* AL-4
Coaling-Vance (CCD)—*cens area* AL-4
Coaling-Vance Division—*civil* AL-4
Coal Iron Creek—*stream* TX-5
Coalit Creek—*stream* AK-9
Coal Junction—*locale* PA-2
*Coal Junction Station* PA-2
Coal Kiln—*locale* VA-3
Coal Kiln Canyon—*valley* ID-8
Coal Kiln Creek—*stream* LA-4
Coalkiln Creek—*stream* TX-5
Coal Kiln Crossing—*locale* VA-3
Coal Kiln Draw—*valley* TX-5
Coal Kiln Hill—*summit* TX-5
Coal Kiln Spring—*spring* ID-8
Coal King Mine—*mine* CO-8
Coal Knob—*summit* PA-2
Coal Knob—*summit* WV-2
Coal Knob Lookout Tower—*tower* PA-2
Coal Knobs—*summit* IN-6
Coal Lake—*lake* AK-9
Coal Lake—*lake* MN-6
Coal Lake—*lake* ND-7
Coal Lake—*lake* WA-9
Coal Lake Coulee—*stream* ND-7
Coal Lake Coulee—*valley* ND-7
Coal Landing—*locale* VA-3
Coal Landing (historical)—*locale* AL-4
Coal Land Ridge—*ridge* WY-8
Coal Lick Ch—*church* PA-2
Coal Lick Run—*stream* (2) PA-2
Coal Lick Run—*stream* WV-2
Coallick Run—*stream* WV-2
Coal Lick Run—*stream* WV-2
Coalman Glacier—*glacier* OR-9
Coalman Mine (underground)—*mine* AL-4
Coalmans Branch—*stream* WV-2
Coal Marsh Ch—*church* WV-2
Coal Mine—*mine* ID-8
**Coal Mine**—*pop pl* TX-5
**Coal Mine**—*pop pl* VA-3
Coal Mine Basin—*basin* ID-8
Coal Mine Basin—*basin* NV-8
Coal Mine Basin—*basin* UT-8
Coal Mine Basin Creek—*stream* ID-8
Coal Mine Basin Creek—*stream* OR-9
Coal Mine Brook—*stream* MA-1
Coal Mine Campground—*locale* UT-8
*Coalmine Canyon* AZ-5
Coal Mine Canyon—*valley* (2) AZ-5
Coalmine Canyon—*valley* CA-9
Coal Mine Canyon—*valley* CO-8
Coalmine Canyon—*valley* ID-8
Coal Mine Canyon—*valley* NV-8
Coal Mine Canyon—*valley* (2) NM-5
Coal Mine Canyon—*valley* WY-8
Coalmine Canyon Campground—*park* AZ-5
Coal Mine Coulee—*stream* (2) MT-8
Coalmine Coulee—*valley* MT-8
Coal Mine Coulee—*valley* (7) MT-8
*Coal Mine Creek* AK-9
*Coal Mine Creek* MT-8
Coal Mine Creek—*stream* (2) AK-9
Coal Mine Creek—*stream* MN-6
Coal Mine Creek—*stream* NV-8
Coal Mine Creek—*stream* NM-5
Coal Mine Creek—*stream* ND-7
Coal Mine Creek—*stream* OR-9
Coalmine Creek—*stream* OR-9
Coal Mine Creek—*stream* OR-9
Coal Mine Creek—*stream* UT-8
Coal Mine Creek—*stream* WY-8
Coal Mine Drain—*canal* MI-6
Coal Mine Draw—*valley* CO-8
Coal Mine Draw—*valley* UT-8
Coal Mine Draw—*valley* (6) WY-8
Coalmine Draw—*valley* WY-8
Coal Mine Draw—*valley* (6) WY-8
Coalmine Fork—*stream* ID-8
Coal Mine Gulch—*valley* ID-8
Coal Mine Gulch—*valley* (2) WY-8
Coal Mine Gulch Spring—*spring* ID-8
Coal Mine Hill—*ridge* NM-5
Coal Mine Hill—*summit* MO-7
Coal Mine Hill—*summit* MT-8
Coalmine Hill—*summit* OR-9
Coal Mine Hill—*summit* UT-8
Coal Mine Hill—*summit* WY-8
**Coal Mine (historical)**—*pop pl* TN-4
Coalmine Hollow—*valley* KY-4
Coal Mine Hollow—*valley* PA-2
Coal Mine Hollow—*valley* TX-5
Coal Mine Hollow—*valley* UT-8
Coal Mine Lake—*reservoir* ND-7
Coal Mine Landing—*locale* NC-3
Coalmine Lick—*spring* OR-9
**Coal Mine Mesa**—*pop pl* AZ-5
Coal Mine Mesa—*summit* AZ-5
Coal Mine Mesa Sch—*school* AZ-5
Coal Mine Mtn—*summit* TX-5
Coal Mine Mtn—*summit* WY-8
Coal Mine Park—*flat* CO-8
Coal Mine Pass—*gap* NV-8
Coal Mine Project Well—*well* MT-8
Coal Mine Ranch—*locale* TX-5
Coal Mine Ridge—*ridge* CA-9
Coal Mine Ridge—*ridge* IN-6
Coal Mine Ridge—*ridge* WY-8
Coal Mine Rim—*ridge* MT-8
Coal Mine Rodeo Grounds—*locale* AZ-5
Coal Miners Chapel—*church* WV-2
Coal Mine Rsvr—*reservoir* WY-8
Coal Mine Sch—*school* WY-8
Coal Mine Spring—*spring* AZ-5
Coal Mine Spring—*spring* MT-8
Coal Mine Spring—*spring* (2) NM-5
Coal Mine Spring—*spring* UT-8
Coal Mine Spring—*spring* WY-8
Coal Mine Trail—*trail* CA-9
Coal Mine Tunnels—*tunnel* CA-9
Coal Mine Wash—*arroyo* UT-8
Coal Mine Wash—*stream* NM-5
Coal Mine Wash—*valley* (2) AZ-5
Coal Mine Wash—*valley* UT-8
Coal Mine Well—*well* AZ-5
Coalmont—*locale* CO-8
**Coalmont**—*pop pl* AL-4
**Coalmont**—*pop pl* IN-6
**Coalmont**—*pop pl* PA-2
**Coalmont**—*pop pl* TN-4
Coalmont Borough—*civil* PA-2
Coalmont Cem—*cemetery* TN-4
Coalmont Hollow—*valley* OH-6
Coalmont Mine A—*mine* TN-4
Coalmont Mine B—*mine* TN-4
Coalmont Mine C—*mine* TN-4
Coalmont Mine D—*mine* TN-4
Coalmont Mine E—*mine* TN-4
Coalmont Mine F—*mine* TN-4
Coalmont Mine G—*mine* TN-4
Coalmont Mine (underground)—*mine* AL-4
Coalmont Number 4 Mine (underground)—*mine* AL-4
Coalmont Post Office—*building* TN-4
Coalmont Sch—*school* TN-4
Coalmont United Methodist Ch—*church* TN-4
**Coalmount**—*pop pl* PA-2
**Coal Mountain**—*pop pl* GA-3
**Coal Mountain**—*pop pl* WV-2
Coal Mountain Sch—*school* WV-2
*Coal Mtn* PA-2
Coal Mtn—*summit* AL-4
Coal Mtn—*summit* AK-9
Coal Mtn—*summit* (3) CO-8
Coal Mtn—*summit* PA-2
Coal Mtn—*summit* TX-5
Coal Mtn—*summit* WA-9
Coal Mtn—*summit* WV-2
Coal Mtn—*summit* WY-8
Coalney Branch—*stream* NC-3
Coal Oil Basin—*basin* CO-8
Coal Oil Canyon—*valley* CA-9
Coal Oil Corner—*locale* MS-4
Coal Oil Creek—*stream* AK-9
Coal Oil Ditch—*canal* MO-7
Coal Oil Gulch—*valley* CO-8
Coal Oil Johnnie Tank—*reservoir* NM-5
Coal Oil Johnny Ditch—*canal* MO-7
Coal Oil Point—*cape* CA-9
Coal Oil Rim—*cliff* CO-8
*Coal Oil Works* OH-6
Coalora—*locale* NM-5
Coal Pass—*gap* AK-9
Coal Pass—*gap* WA-9
Coal Pit Archeol Site—*hist pl* MO-7
Coalpit Branch—*stream* VA-3
Coal Pit Butte—*summit* ID-8
Coalpit Canyon—*valley* CA-9
Coal Pit Canyon—*valley* UT-8
*Coal Pit Creek* MT-8
Coalpit Creek—*stream* ID-8
Coal Pit Creek—*stream* ID-8
Coalpit Creek—*stream* (2) MT-8
Coal Pit Creek—*stream* NV-8
Coal Pit Creek—*stream* OR-9
Coal Pit Creek—*stream* UT-8
Coal Pit Gulch—*valley* (2) CA-9
Coalpit Gulch—*valley* ID-8
Coalpit Gulch—*valley* UT-8
Coalpit Hill—*summit* CA-9
Coal Pit Hollow—*valley* AR-4
Coalpit Hollow—*valley* IN-6
Coalpit Hollow—*valley* KY-4
Coalpit Hollow—*valley* MO-7
Coal Pit Hollow—*valley* MO-7
Coalpit Hollow—*valley* (2) MO-7
Coalpit Hollow—*valley* TN-4
Coal Pit Knob—*summit* KY-4
Coalpit Knob—*summit* VA-3
Coal Pit Mtn—*summit* NC-3
Coal Pit Mtn—*summit* OR-9
Coal Pit Peak—*summit* NV-8
Coalpit Ridge—*ridge* VA-3
Coalpit Run—*stream* (2) PA-2
Coalpit Run—*stream* VA-3
Coalpit Slough—*gut* WI-6
Coal Pit Spring—*spring* ID-8
Coal Pit Spring—*spring* NV-8
Coal Pit Spring—*spring* OR-9
Coal Pit Spring—*spring* UT-8
Coalpit Springs—*spring* OR-9
Coal Pit Springs—*spring* UT-8
Coalpits Wash—*valley* UT-8
Coal Pit Tank—*reservoir* (2) AZ-5
Coal Pit Wash—*valley* UT-8
Coal Point—*cape* (3) AK-9
Coal Point—*cape* NY-2
Coal Point—*cape* OR-9
Coal Point—*cliff* AZ-5
**Coalpoint**—*pop pl* KY-4
Coalpont Lake—*reservoir* OK-5
*Coalport* OH-6
Coal Port—*locale* IA-7
**Coalport**—*pop pl* OH-6
**Coalport**—*pop pl* (2) PA-2
*Coalport Borough* PA-2
Coalport Borough—*civil* PA-2
Coal Post Office (historical)—*building* AL-4
*Coal Ridge* WV-2
Coalridge—*locale* WV-2
**Coalridge**—*pop pl* MT-8
**Coal Ridge**—*pop pl* OH-6
**Coalridge**—*pop pl* OH-6
Coal Ridge—*ridge* AR-4
Coal Ridge—*ridge* (3) CO-8
Coal Ridge—*ridge* (2) MT-8
Coal Ridge—*summit* AR-4
Coal Ridge Church Cem—*cemetery* IA-7
Coal Ridge Dam—*dam* CO-8
Coal Ridge Ditch—*canal* CO-8
Coal Ridge Lookout Tower—*locale* MT-8
Coal Ridge Sch—*school* IA-7
Coal Ridge Sch—*school* KS-7
Coal Ridge Trail—*trail* MT-8
Coal Riffle—*rapids* OR-9
*Coal River* WV-2
Coal River—*stream* AK-9
Coal River—*stream* WV-2
*Coal River Mtn* WV-2
Coal River Mtn—*summit* WV-2
*Coal Road Draw* MT-8
*Coal Run* PA-2
**Coal Run**—*pop pl* OH-6
**Coal Run**—*pop pl* (4) PA-2
Coal Run—*stream* IN-6
Coal Run—*stream* KY-4
Coal Run—*stream* (8) OH-6
Coal Run—*stream* (16) PA-2
Coal Run—*stream* VA-3
Coal Run—*stream* (9) WV-2
Coal Run June—*locale* PA-2
Coal Run (Post Office)—*locale* KY-4
**Coal Run (RR name Coalrun)**—*pop pl* KY-4
Coalrun (RR name for Coal Run)—*other* KY-4
Coalsburg (historical)—*locale* KS-7
*Coals Creek* IN-6
Coal Shaft Bridge—*other* IL-6
Coal Siding—*locale* WV-2
**Coal Siding (historical)**—*pop pl* IA-7
Coal Siding Run—*stream* WV-2
Coal Slack Coulee—*valley* MT-8
*Coalsmouth* WV-2
Coalson Canyon—*valley* AZ-5
Coalson Cem—*cemetery* TX-5
Coalson Draw—*valley* TX-5
Coalson Mesa—*bench* AZ-5
Coalson Peak—*summit* AZ-5
Coalson Ranch—*locale* AZ-5
Coalson Ranch—*locale* NM-5
Coalson Spring—*spring* AZ-5
Coalson Tank—*reservoir* AZ-5
Coalson Windmill—*locale* TX-5
*Coal Spring* PA-2
Coal Spring—*spring* AL-4
Coal Spring—*spring* (2) AZ-5
Coal Spring—*spring* CO-8
Coal Spring—*spring* ID-8
Coal Spring—*spring* (2) NV-8
Coal Spring—*spring* NM-5
Coal Spring Canyon—*valley* AZ-5
*Coal Spring Fork* WV-2
*Coal Spring Furnace* PA-2
Coal Spring Lake—*lake* FL-3
Coal Spring Rsvr—*reservoir* CO-8
**Coal Springs**—*pop pl* SD-7
Coal Springs—*spring* TX-5
Coal Springs Canyon—*valley* OK-5
Coal Springs Ch—*church* AL-4
Coal Spring Sch—*school* SD-7
Coal Springs Dam—*dam* SD-7
Coal Springs Draw—*valley* WY-8
Coal Springs (historical)—*locale* AL-4
Coal Stone Branch—*stream* KY-4
Coalstone Branch—*stream* (2) KY-4
Coalstone Run—*stream* WV-2
Coalstone Sch—*school* KY-4
Coal Tar Bay—*bay* LA-4
Coal Tar Run—*stream* PA-2
Coalton—*locale* IL-6
**Coalton**—*pop pl* IL-6
**Coalton**—*pop pl* KY-4
**Coalton**—*pop pl* OH-6
**Coalton**—*pop pl* OK-5
**Coalton**—*pop pl* WV-2
*Coalton Brook* NH-1
Coalton Cem—*cemetery* OH-6
*Coalton (corp* WV-2
Coalton (historical)—*locale* AL-4
Coalton (historical P.O.)—*locale* IA-7
Coalton Post Office (historical)—*building* AL-4
*Coaltown* AL-4
**Coaltown**—*pop pl* (2) PA-2
Coal Town Cem—*cemetery* MS-4
**Coal Township**—*pop pl* MO-7
Coal (Township of)—*fmr MCD* AR-4
**Coal (Township of)**—*pop pl* (2) OH-6
**Coal (Township of)**—*pop pl* PA-2
Coaltown Slough—*gut* IL-6
**Coalvale**—*pop pl* KS-7
Coal Valley—*basin* NV-8
Coal Valley—*locale* IA-7
**Coal Valley**—*pop pl* AL-4
**Coal Valley**—*pop pl* IL-6
**Coal Valley**—*pop pl* PA-2
**Coal Valley**—*pop pl* WV-2
Coal Valley—*valley* AK-9
Coal Valley—*valley* WV-2
Coal Valley Cem—*cemetery* IL-6
Coal Valley Creek—*stream* IA-7
Coal Valley Drift Mine (underground)—*mine* AL-4
Coal Valley Mine (Abandoned)—*mine* IL-6
Coal Valley Mine (surface)—*mine* TN-4
Coal Valley Number 1 Mine (underground)—*mine* AL-4
Coal Valley Number 10 Mine (underground)—*mine* AL-4
Coal Valley Number 11 Mine (underground)—*mine* AL-4
Coal Valley Post Office (historical)—*building* AL-4
Coal Valley Rsvr—*reservoir* NV-8
Coal Valley Sch—*school* MO-7
Coal Valley Sch (abandoned)—*school* PA-2
Coal Valley Sch Number 3—*school* ND-7
**Coal Valley (Township of)**—*pop pl* IL-6
Coal View—*locale* CO-8
Coal View Gulch—*valley* CO-8
Coal Village Site—*hist pl* AK-9
*Coalville* KS-7
Coalville—*locale* NC-3
Coalville—*locale* TX-5
**Coalville**—*pop pl* IA-7
**Coalville**—*pop pl* MS-4
**Coalville**—*pop pl* UT-8
Coalville Cem—*cemetery* UT-8
Coalville Ch—*church* MS-4
Coalville Division—*civil* UT-8
Coalville (historical)—*locale* AL-4
Coalville Post Office—*building* UT-8
Coalville Sch—*school* IL-6
*Coalville United Methodist Ch* MS-4
Coal Wash—*valley* (2) UT-8
Coal Well—*well* NM-5
Coal Well Canyon—*valley* NM-5
Coalwood—*locale* MI-6
Coalwood—*locale* MT-8
**Coalwood**—*pop pl* WV-2
Coalwood Lookout Tower—*locale* WV-2
Coaly Hollow—*valley* OH-6
Coaly Wash—*valley* UT-8
**Coamo**—*pop pl* PR-3
Coamo Arriba (Barrio)—*fmr MCD* PR-3
Coamo (Municipio)—*civil* PR-3
Coamo (Pueblo)—*fmr MCD* PR-3
Coan—*locale* VA-3
Coan Ch—*church* VA-3
Coan Corners—*locale* NY-2
*Coan Creek* NE-7
Coane—*locale* NM-5
Coan House—*hist pl* MN-6
*Coanini Plateau* AZ-5
*Coanjock* NC-3
Coan Millpond—*lake* MI-6
Coan Mill Stream—*stream* VA-3
COA No 1 Windmill—*locale* NM-5
Coan Pond—*lake* CT-1
Coan Pond—*lake* NY-2
Coan River—*stream* VA-3
Coan Stage—*locale* VA-3
Coantag Creek—*stream* WY-8
*Coar Creek* PA-2
Coards Branch—*stream* VA-3
Coards Marshes—*swamp* VA-3
Coarra Ranch—*locale* AZ-5
Coarsegold—*locale* CA-9
Coarse Gold Canyon—*valley* CA-9
Coarse Gold Creek—*stream* (2) AK-9
Coarse Gold Creek—*stream* (2) CA-9
Coarse Gold Creek—*stream* OR-9
Coarse Gold Fire Station—*locale* CA-9
Coarse Money Creek—*stream* AK-9
**Coars Springs (historical)**—*pop pl* MS-4
*Coarsville* MS-4
*Coassati* AL-4
Coastal—*post sta* SC-3
Coastal Bend Youth City—*locale* TX-5
Coastal Carolina Community Coll—*school* NC-3
Coastal (CCD)—*cens area* CA-9
Coastal Empire Christian Camp—*locale* GA-3
Coastal Hunting Club—*other* LA-4
Coastal Industrial Water Authority Canal—*canal* TX-5
Coastal Middle and Senior HS—*school* FL-3
Coastal Plain Experimental Station—*locale* NC-3
Coastal Prairie Trail—*trail* FL-3
Coastal Shop Ctr—*locale* FL-3
**Coastal Shores (subdivision)**—*pop pl* NC-3
Coast Blvd Park—*park* CA-9
Coast Campground—*locale* CA-9
Coast Creek—*stream* CA-9
Coast Creek—*stream* OR-9
Coast Creek Park—*park* OR-9
*Coasters Harbor* RI-1
Coasters Harbor—*bay* RI-1
Coasters Harbor Island—*island* RI-1
*Coasters Island* RI-1
**Coast Fork (historical)**—*pop pl* OR-9
Coast Fork Willamette River—*stream* OR-9
Coast Guard Alameda Base—*military* CA-9
Coast Guard Island—*island* CA-9
Coast Guard Mast—*military* CA-9
Coast Guard Station—*building* MA-1
Coast Guard Station—*locale* TX-5
Coast Guard Station Number 105—*locale* FL-3
Coast Guard Training Center—*military* NJ-2
Coast Lake—*lake* AK-9
Coast Mountains—*range* AK-9
Coast Range—*range* AK-9
Coast Range—*range* OR-9
Coast Range (CCD)—*cens area* OR-9
Coast Trail—*trail* CA-9
Coast Union HS—*school* CA-9
*Coat* MS-4
*Coataway Creek* MO-7
Coat Baptist Ch—*church* MS-4
Coatcook Brook—*stream* VT-1
Coat Creek—*stream* GA-3
Coates—*locale* AL-4
**Coates**—*pop pl* MN-6
Coates, Moses, Jr., Farm—*hist pl* PA-2
**Coates and Corums Lake Breeze Subdivision**—*pop pl* UT-8
**Coates and Corums South Gale Subdivision**—*pop pl* UT-8
**Coates and Corums Subdivision**—*pop pl* UT-8
Coates Bay—*swamp* FL-3
Coates Branch—*stream* FL-3
Coates Branch—*stream* KY-4
Coates Branch—*stream* MO-7
Coates Canyon—*valley* OR-9
Coates Cem—*cemetery* NC-3
Coates Cem—*cemetery* (2) TN-4
Coates Creek—*stream* CO-8
Coates Creek—*stream* IL-6
Coates Creek—*stream* NE-7
Coates Creek—*stream* UT-8
Coates Creek—*stream* WA-9
Coates Creek Sch—*school* CO-8
Coates Drain—*canal* ID-8
Coates Drain—*canal* OR-9
Coates Drain—*stream* MI-6
Coates Drainage System—*canal* CO-8
**Coates Estates (subdivision)**—*pop pl* UT-8
Coates Hill—*summit* FL-3
Coates Hollow—*valley* UT-8
Coates House—*hist pl* MN-6
Coates House Hotel—*hist pl* MO-7
Coates Island—*island* VT-1
Coates Mtn—*summit* VA-3
Coates Point—*cape* NJ-2
Coates Point—*cape* NY-2
Coates Pond—*lake* MT-8
Coates Ranch—*locale* TX-5
Coates Rsvr—*reservoir* UT-8
Coates Run—*stream* OH-6
Coates Sch—*school* IL-6
Coates Sch—*school* MI-6
Coates Sch—*school* NC-3
Coates Sch—*school* VA-3
Coates Sch (historical)—*school* MO-7
Coates Spring—*spring* OR-9
Coatesville—*locale* VA-3
**Coatesville**—*pop pl* IN-6
**Coatesville**—*pop pl* PA-2
Coatesville Area Senior HS—*school* PA-2
Coatesville Cem—*cemetery* MO-7
Coatesville City—*civil* PA-2
Coatesville Country Club—*other* PA-2
Coatesville Hist Dist—*hist pl* PA-2
Coatesville Rsvr—*reservoir* PA-2
*Coatesville Veterans Hosp* PA-2
Coatesville Veterans Hosp—*hospital* PA-2
Coates Windmill—*locale* TX-5
Coateswood—*hist pl* SC-3
Coaticook River—*stream* VT-1
Coatigan Run—*stream* MD-2
Coati Point—*cape* CA-9
Coat Mine Rsvr—*reservoir* WY-8
Coatner Spring Branch—*stream* AR-4
Coatney Branch—*stream* MO-7
Coatney Hill—*summit* CT-1
Coatney Hollow—*valley* MO-7
Coatney Hollow—*valley* TN-4
Coatney Ridge—*ridge* KY-4
Coato Bend (historical)—*locale* AL-4
**Coatopa**—*pop pl* AL-4
Coatopa Ch—*church* AL-4
Coatopa Creek—*stream* AL-4
**Coatraw (historical)**—*pop pl* MS-4
Coats—*locale* MS-4
Coats—*locale* OH-6
**Coats**—*pop pl* KS-7
**Coats**—*pop pl* NC-3
Coats Bend—*bend* AL-4
Coats Bend Sch (historical)—*school* AL-4
Coats Branch—*stream* TN-4
**Coatsburg**—*pop pl* IL-6
Coats Cem—*cemetery* AR-4
Coats Cem—*cemetery* KS-7
Coats Cem—*cemetery* MS-4
Coats Cem—*cemetery* NC-3
Coats Cem—*cemetery* OH-6
*Coats Chapel* MS-4
Coats Creek—*stream* CA-9
Coats Creek—*stream* MS-4
*Coats Crossroad* NC-3
**Coats Crossroad**—*pop pl* SC-3
**Coats Cross Roads**—*pop pl* NC-3
**Coats Crossroads**—*pop pl* NC-3
Coats Dike Mine—*mine* SD-7
Coats Drain—*stream* MI-6
Coats Elem Sch—*school* NC-3
**Coats Estates Subdivision - Number 7**—*pop pl* UT-8
**Coats Grove**—*pop pl* MI-6
Coats Hill—*summit* KY-4
Coats House—*hist pl* NC-3
Coats Lake—*lake* NM-5
*Coats Landing* VA-3
Coats Meadow—*flat* CA-9
Coats Oil Field—*oilfield* TX-5
Coats Point—*cape* MI-6
Coats Post Office (historical)—*building* TN-4
Coat Spring—*spring* AZ-5
Coats Run—*stream* WV-2
Coats Sch—*hist pl* AR-4
Coats Sch (historical)—*school* TN-4
**Coats Spring**—*pop pl* IN-6
Coats Spring—*spring* CA-9
Coats Tank—*reservoir* TX-5
*Coatstown Post Office* TN-4
*Coatsville* IN-6
*Coatsville* VA-3
**Coatsville**—*pop pl* MO-7
**Coatsville (RR name Coatesville)**—*pop pl* MO-7
Coats Windmill—*locale* NM-5
Coattail Lake—*lake* MI-6
Coatue—*bar* MA-1
Coatue Beach—*beach* MA-1
*Coatue Neck* MA-1
*Coatue Point* MA-1
Coatue Point—*cape* MA-1
*Coatuit* MA-1
*Coatuit Harbor* MA-1
Coax Ch—*church* LA-4
*Cobabi* AZ-5
*Cobabi Mountain* AZ-5
*Cobabi Mountains* AZ-5
*Cobabi Well* AZ-5
Cobal Canyon—*valley* CA-9
*Cobalt* ID-8
Cobalt—*locale* CT-1
**Cobalt**—*pop pl* ID-8
Cobalt Canyon—*valley* NV-8
**Cobalt City**—*pop pl* MO-7
Cobalt Creek—*stream* AK-9
Cobalt Creek—*stream* MN-6
*Cobalt Forest Service Station* ID-8
Cobalt Hollow—*valley* MO-7
Cobalt Junction—*locale* OK-5
Cobalt Lake—*lake* MT-8
Cobalt Lake—*lake* NY-2
Cobalt Landing—*locale* CT-1
Cobalt Mine (Inactive)—*locale* ID-8
Cobalt Ranger Station—*locale* ID-8
**Cobalt Ridge**—*pop pl* PA-2
**Cobalt Village**—*pop pl* MO-7
Cobamong Pond—*lake* NY-2
Coba Mtn—*summit* NV-8
CO Bar Tank—*reservoir* AZ-5
Cobas Hollow—*valley* NY-2
Cobas Well—*well* TX-5
Cobas Windmill—*locale* TX-5
*Cobats Pond* NH-1
*Cobb* AL-4
*Cobb* CA-9
*Cobb* KS-7
Cobb—*locale* (2) MO-7
Cobb—*locale* MT-8
Cobb—*locale* OR-9
Cobb—*locale* TX-5
Cobb—*locale* WV-2
**Cobb**—*pop pl* CA-9
**Cobb**—*pop pl* GA-3
**Cobb**—*pop pl* ID-8
**Cobb**—*pop pl* IN-6
**Cobb**—*pop pl* KY-4
**Cobb**—*pop pl* LA-4
**Cobb**—*pop pl* NE-7
**Cobb**—*pop pl* NY-2
**Cobb**—*pop pl* OK-5
**Cobb**—*pop pl* WI-6
Cobb, Cyrus B., House—*hist pl* MN-6
Cobb, George, House—*hist pl* MA-1
Cobb, George N., House—*hist pl* WI-6
Cobb, John Franklin, House—*hist pl* NC-3
Cobb, Mount—*summit* PA-2
Cobb, Mount—*summit* VT-1
Cobb, T. R. R., House—*hist pl* GA-3
Cobban—*locale* WI-6
*Cobbats Pond* NH-1
Cobb Ave Sch—*school* AL-4
Cobb Bay—*bay* VA-3
Cobb Bay—*swamp* FL-3
Cobb Bay Pond—*lake* FL-3
Cobb Bethel Ch—*church* GA-3
Cobb Bldg—*hist pl* OK-5
Cobb Bldg—*hist pl* WA-9
Cobb Bluff—*cliff* MO-7
Cobb Bluff—*cliff* NC-3
Cobb Branch—*stream* (2) AL-4
Cobb Branch—*stream* (2) FL-3

Cochran Cem—*cemetery* ... NC-3
Cochran Cem—*cemetery* ... OH-6
Cochran Cem—*cemetery* (2) ... PA-2
Cochran Cem—*cemetery* ... SC-3
Cochran Cem—*cemetery* (5) ... TN-4
Cochran Cem—*cemetery* (3) ... TX-5
Cochran Cem—*cemetery* ... VA-3
Cochran Ch—*church* ... NC-3
Cochran Ch—*church* ... VA-3
Cochran Channel—*channel* ... NJ-2
Cochran Channel—*channel* ... PA-2
Cochran Chapel—*church* ... MS-4
Cochran Chapel—*church* ... TX-5
Cochran Community Center—*locale* ... TN-4
**Cochran (County)**—*pop pl* ... TX-5
Cochran Cove—*bay* (2) ... FL-3
Cochran Cove—*valley* ... NC-3
*Cochran Creek* ... GA-3
*Cochran Creek* ... OK-5
Cochran Creek—*stream* (2) ... GA-3
Cochran Creek—*stream* ... ID-8
Cochran Creek—*stream* ... LA-4
Cochran Creek—*stream* ... MT-8
Cochran Creek—*stream* (2) ... NC-3
Cochran Creek—*stream* ... OK-5
Cochran Creek—*stream* (3) ... OR-9
Cochran Creek—*stream* (2) ... TN-4
Cochran Creek—*stream* ... WV-2
Cochran Creek Ch—*church* ... WV-2
Cochrandale Cem—*cemetery* ... MS-4
Cochran Dead River—*gut* ... MS-4
Cochran Drain—*canal* ... MI-6
Cochran Draw—*valley* ... ID-8
Cochrane—*locale* ... CA-9
Cochrane—*locale* ... KS-7
**Cochrane**—*pop pl* ... AL-4
**Cochrane**—*pop pl* ... WI-6
Cochrane, Lake—*lake* ... SD-7
Cochrane Bay—*bay* ... AK-9
Cochrane Branch—*stream* ... MS-4
Cochrane Bridge—*bridge* ... AL-4
Cochrane Bridge—*bridge* ... CA-9
Cochrane Canyon—*valley* ... NM-5
Cochrane Cem—*cemetery* ... AL-4
*Cochrane Creek* ... GA-3
*Cochrane Creek Falls* ... GA-3
Cochrane Dam—*dam* ... MA-1
Cochrane Dam—*dam* ... MT-8
Cochrane Ditch—*canal* ... CO-8
Cochrane Ferry (historical)—*locale* ... AL-4
Cochrane-Fountain City Community Sch—*school* ... WI-6
Cochrane Hill—*summit* ... AZ-5
**Cochrane (historical)**—*pop pl* ... OR-9
Cochrane Hollow—*valley* ... PA-2
Cochrane Lake—*lake* ... ME-1
Cochrane Rec Area—*park* ... AL-4
Cochrane Sch—*school* ... KY-4
Cochrane Springs Ch—*church* ... AL-4
*Cochrane Springs Missionary Baptist Ch* ... AL-4
Cochrane Springs Sch (historical)—*school* ... AL-4
*Cochran Falls* ... GA-3
Cochran Family Cem—*cemetery* ... AL-4
Cochran Farm—*hist pl* ... OH-6
Cochran Field—*other* ... GA-3
Cochran Field Acad—*school* ... GA-3
Cochran Grange—*hist pl* ... DE-2
Cochran Grove Ch—*church* ... GA-3
Cochran Grove Sch (historical)—*school* ... TN-4
Cochran Gulch—*valley* ... MT-8
Cochran Gulch—*valley* (2) ... OR-9
Cochran-Helton-Lindley House—*hist pl* ... IN-6
Cochran Hill—*summit* ... CA-9
Cochran Hill—*summit* ... KY-4
Cochran Hill—*summit* ... NH-1
Cochran Hill—*summit* ... PA-2
Cochran Hollow—*valley* ... IL-6
Cochran Hollow—*valley* ... TN-4
Cochran Island—*island* ... FL-3
Cochran Islands—*island* ... OR-9
Cochran JHS—*school* ... NC-3
Cochran JHS—*school* ... PA-2
Cochran Knob—*summit* ... WV-2
Cochran Lake—*flat* ... NM-5
Cochran Lake—*lake* ... FL-3
Cochran Lake—*lake* ... MI-6
Cochran Lake—*lake* ... NE-7
Cochran Lake—*lake* ... WI-6
Cochran Lake—*reservoir* ... AL-4
Cochran Lake Dam—*dam* ... AL-4
Cochran Landing—*locale* ... AL-4
Cochran Landing—*locale* ... FL-3
Cochran-Lime Sink—*basin* ... GA-3
Cochran Mountains—*summit* ... TX-5
Cochran Mtn—*summit* ... PA-2
Cochran Park—*park* ... GA-3
Cochran Park—*park* ... IA-7
Cochran Park—*park* ... NY-2
Cochran Pond—*lake* ... MA-1
Cochran Pond—*reservoir* ... GA-3
Cochran Pond—*reservoir* ... OR-9
*Cochran Post Office* ... MS-4
Cochran Post Office (historical)—*building* ... TN-4
Cochran Ranch—*locale* ... NE-7
Cochran Ranch—*locale* ... WY-8
Cochran Rapids—*rapids* ... OR-9
Cochran Ridge Ch—*church* ... GA-3
Cochran RR Station—*building* ... AZ-5
Cochran Rsvr—*reservoir* ... CO-8
Cochran Run—*stream* ... OH-6
Cochran Saint Ch—*church* ... NC-3
Cochran Sch—*school* ... GA-3
Cochran Sch—*school* ... KY-4
Cochran Sch—*school* ... MI-6
Cochran Sch—*school* ... PA-2
Cochran Sch—*school* ... TX-5
Cochran Sch (abandoned)—*school* ... PA-2
*Cochrans Creek* ... GA-3
Cochrans Creek—*stream* ... GA-3
*Cochrans Creek Falls* ... GA-3
Cochrans Falls—*falls* ... GA-3
Cochrans Lake—*reservoir* ... AL-4
*Cochrans Lake Dam* ... AL-4
**Cochrans Mill**—*pop pl* ... PA-2
Cochrans Mills—*locale* ... PA-2
Cochrans Mills Ch—*church* ... PA-2
Cochrans Opening—*swamp* ... MO-7
Cochrans Pass—*channel* ... FL-3
Cochrans Pond—*lake* ... MD-2
Cochran Spring—*spring* ... CA-9
Cochran Spring—*spring* ... OR-9
Cochran Spring—*spring* ... UT-8
Cochran Springs—*spring* ... AL-4
Cochran Springs (historical)—*locale* ... AL-4
Cochran Store—*hist pl* ... AR-4
Cochran Store (historical)—*locale* ... TN-4
Cochran Tank—*reservoir* (2) ... AZ-5
**Cochranton**—*pop pl* ... PA-2
*Cochranton Area Elementary School* ... PA-2
Cochranton Area Junior Senior HS—*school* ... PA-2
Cochranton Area Sch—*school* ... PA-2
Cochranton Borough—*civil* ... PA-2
**Cochrantown**—*pop pl* ... SC-3
Cochran Valley—*basin* ... NE-7
**Cochranville**—*pop pl* ... PA-2
Cochran Windmill—*locale* ... CO-8
*Cochrons Mills* ... PA-2
Cochrun Ranch—*locale* ... WY-8
Cocio Wash—*stream* ... AZ-5
Cock, Lake—*lake* ... LA-4
Cockalorum Spring—*spring* ... NV-8
Cockalorum Wash—*stream* ... NV-8
*Cockampoag Pond* ... RI-1
Cockaponset State For—*forest* ... CT-1
**Cockatoo Grove**—*pop pl* ... CA-9
*Cockburn* ... NY-2
Cockburn Lake—*lake* ... MN-6
*Cockburns Post Office* ... NC-3
*Cocke* ... LA-4
**Cocke**—*pop pl* ... LA-4
Cocke, William, House—*hist pl* ... TN-4
*Cock East Pond* ... MA-1
Cockeast Pond—*lake* ... MA-1
Cocke Cem—*cemetery* ... IL-6
**Cocke County**—*pop pl* ... TN-4
Cocke County Baptist Hosp—*hospital* ... TN-4
Cocke County Courthouse—*building* ... TN-4
Cocke County Farm (historical)—*locale* ... TN-4
Cocke County HS—*school* ... TN-4
Cocke County Vocational Sch—*school* ... TN-4
Cocke Creek—*stream* ... VA-3
Cocked Hat—*locale* ... DE-2
Cockedhat Mtn—*summit* ... AK-9
*Cocked Hat Pond* ... NJ-2
Cocke Fish Hatchery—*other* ... GA-3
Cockenoe Harbor—*bay* ... CT-1
Cockenoe Island—*island* ... CT-1
*Cockenoe Island Harbor* ... CT-1
Cockenoe Reef—*bar* ... CT-1
Cockenoe Shoal—*bar* ... CT-1
*Cockenoe's Island* ... CT-1
Cockerel Branch—*stream* ... IL-6
*Cockerel Creek* ... TX-5
*Cockerel Creek* ... VA-3
Cockerel Creek—*stream* ... LA-4
Cockerel Creek—*stream* ... MO-7
Cockerell Branch—*stream* ... AL-4
Cockerell Canyon—*valley* ... CA-9
*Cockerell Creek* ... TX-5
*Cockerell Fork* ... KY-4
Cockerell Fork Cem—*cemetery* ... KY-4
Cockerell Fork Sch—*school* ... KY-4
Cockerell Trace Branch—*stream* ... KY-4
Cockerel Spring—*spring* ... MT-8
Cockerene Ferry Site (historical)—*locale* ... NC-3
Cockerham Cem—*cemetery* (3) ... MS-4
*Cockerham Chapel* ... MS-4
Cockerham Creek—*stream* ... OR-9
Cockerham Lake—*lake* ... TX-5
Cockerham Lake—*reservoir* ... MS-4
**Cockerill**—*pop pl* ... KS-7
Cockerill House—*hist pl* ... OH-6
**Cockerills Addition (subdivision)**—*pop pl* ... UT-8
*Cockerill School* ... KS-7
Cocker Lick Branch—*stream* ... KY-4
Cockermouth River—*stream* ... NH-1
Cockers Branch—*stream* ... KS-7
*Cockers Creek* ... KS-7
Cocker Spring—*spring* ... TN-4
Cocke Tank—*reservoir* ... NM-5
Cocke Well—*well* ... NM-5
Cockey Creek—*stream* ... MD-2
Cockeye Creek—*stream* ... WA-9
Cockeyed Ridge—*ridge* ... NV-8
Cockey Hollow—*valley* ... UT-8
**Cockeysville**—*pop pl* ... MD-2
Cockfield Bay—*basin* ... SC-3
Cock Hat Hill—*summit* ... NH-1
Cock Hill—*summit* ... NH-1
Cock House—*hist pl* ... TX-5
*Cock Lake* ... MN-6
*Cockle Bay* ... AK-9
Cockleberry Tank—*reservoir* ... NM-5
*Cocklebur* ... AZ-5
Cocklebur Bayou—*gut* ... LA-4
Cocklebur Bayou—*stream* ... LA-4
Cocklebur Beach—*beach* ... CA-9
Cocklebur Bend—*bend* ... TX-5
Cocklebur Ch—*church* ... AR-4
Cocklebur Creek—*stream* ... CO-8
Cocklebur Creek—*stream* (2) ... KS-7
Cocklebur Creek—*stream* ... TX-5
Cocklebur Draw—*valley* ... CO-8
Cocklebur Draw—*valley* ... NM-5
Cocklebur Draw—*valley* ... TX-5
Cocklebur Flat—*locale* ... OK-5
Cocklebur Island—*island* ... LA-4
Cocklebur Lake—*lake* ... AR-4
Cocklebur Lake—*lake* ... NM-5
Cocklebur Lake—*swamp* ... LA-4
Cocklebur Lakes—*lake* ... AR-4
Cocklebur Lakes—*lake* ... NM-5
*Cockleburr* ... AZ-5
Cockleburr Bay—*bay* ... LA-4
Cockleburr Canyon—*valley* ... CA-9
Cockleburr Creek—*stream* ... OR-9
Cockle Burr Lake—*lake* ... NM-5
Cockleburr Lake—*lake* ... TN-4
Cockleburr Lake—*lake* ... UT-8
Cockleburr Lake—*lake* ... WA-9
*Cockleburr Slough* ... AR-4
Cockle Burr Slough Ditch—*canal* ... AR-4
Cockleburr Spring—*spring* ... AZ-5
Cockleburr Springs—*spring* ... CO-8
Cockleburr Tank—*reservoir* ... TX-5
Cockleburr Wash Petroglyphs—*hist pl* ... UT-8
Cocklebur Slough—*gut* ... IL-6
Cocklebur Slough—*stream* ... AR-4
Cocklebur Slough—*stream* ... TX-5
Cocklebur Spring—*spring* ... NV-8
Cocklebur Tank—*reservoir* ... AZ-5
Cocklebur Tank—*reservoir* (2) ... NM-5
Cocklebur Windmill—*locale* ... NE-7
Cocklebur Windmill—*locale* ... TX-5
Cockle Cove—*cove* ... MA-1
Cockle Cove Creek—*stream* ... MA-1
*Cockle Creek* ... VA-3
Cockle Creek—*stream* (2) ... VA-3
Cockle Hill—*summit* ... CT-1
Cockle Hill—*summit* ... ME-1
Cockle Marsh Island—*island* ... NC-3
Cockle Point—*cape* ... NC-3
Cockle Point—*cape* ... VA-3
Cockle Point Creek—*channel* ... VA-3
Cockler Bay—*bay* ... LA-4
Cockle Run—*stream* ... WV-2
*Cockles Harbor* ... NY-2
Cockle Shoal Light—*tower* ... NC-3
Cockllbur Spring—*spring* ... CO-8
Cock Pen Branch—*stream* ... VA-3
Cockpit Cave—*cave* ... AL-4
Cockpit Point—*cape* ... VA-3
Cockram Millpond—*reservoir* ... VA-3
Cockran Cem—*cemetery* ... OK-5
Cockran Ch—*church* ... SC-3
Cockran Creek—*stream* ... AR-4
Cockran Hollow—*valley* ... AR-4
*Cockran Landing* ... FL-3
*Cockran Pond* ... NY-2
**Cockrans**—*pop pl* ... TX-5
Cockran Sch—*school* ... NE-7
Cockran Sch—*school* ... SC-3
Cockran Spring—*spring* ... VA-3
Cockrel Creek—*channel* ... NC-3
Cockrel Creek Island—*island* ... NC-3
**Cockrell**—*pop pl* ... MO-7
Cockrell, Samuel W., House—*hist pl* ... AL-4
**Cockrell Beach**—*pop pl* ... NC-3
Cockrell Bridge—*bridge* ... NC-3
Cockrell Canyon—*valley* ... NV-8
Cockrell Cem—*cemetery* ... AL-4
Cockrell Cem—*cemetery* ... MO-7
Cockrell Cem—*cemetery* ... TX-5
Cockrell-Cofield Cem—*cemetery* ... AL-4
Cockrell Creek—*stream* ... AR-4
Cockrell Creek—*stream* ... LA-4
Cockrell Creek—*stream* ... VA-3
Cockrell Ditch—*canal* ... MT-8
Cockrell Fork—*stream* ... KY-4
**Cockrell Hill**—*pop pl* ... TX-5
Cockrell Lake Dam—*dam* ... MS-4
Cockrell Mtn—*summit* ... AL-4
Cockrell Neck—*cape* ... VA-3
Cockrell Plantation (historical)—*locale* ... MS-4
Cockrell Point—*cape* (2) ... VA-3
Cockrell Ranch—*locale* ... NV-8
**Cockrell Run**—*pop pl* ... OH-6
Cockrell Run—*stream* ... OH-6
Cockrells Chapel—*church* ... NC-3
*Cockrells Creek* ... VA-3
Cockrells Crossroads—*locale* ... NC-3
Cockrells Ferry (historical)—*locale* ... MS-4
**Cockrell Township**—*pop pl* ... MO-7
Cockrell Trough—*spring* ... NV-8
Cockrell-West Cem—*cemetery* ... AL-4
*Cockrel Run* ... OH-6
Cockrene Pond—*lake* ... NY-2
Cockrill Bend—*bend* ... TN-4
Cockrill Fork—*stream* ... KY-4
Cockrill Sch—*school* ... TN-4
Cockrin Trail—*trail* ... CA-9
Cockroach Bay—*bay* ... FL-3
Cockroach Bay Aquatic Preserve—*park* ... FL-3
Cockroach Channel—*channel* ... FL-3
Cockroach Creek—*stream* ... FL-3
Cockroach Island—*island* ... VI-3
Cockroach Key—*hist pl* ... FL-3
Cockroach Mound—*cape* ... FL-3
Cock Robin Island—*island* ... CA-9
Cock Robin Point—*summit* ... CA-9
**Cockrum**—*pop pl* ... MS-4
Cockrum, William M., House—*hist pl* ... IN-6
Cockrum Airp—*airport* ... KS-7
Cockrum Cem—*cemetery* ... MO-7
Cockrum Post Office (historical)—*building* ... MS-4
Cockrum Sch—*school* ... MS-4
*Cockrums Cross Roads* ... MS-4
Cockrun Hollow—*valley* ... OK-5
Cocks Branch—*stream* ... AL-4
Cockscomb—*ridge* ... CA-9
Cocks Comb—*ridge* ... UT-8
Cockscomb—*ridge* ... WA-9
Cocks Comb—*summit* (2) ... UT-8
Cockscomb, The—*pillar* ... AK-9
Cockscomb, The—*ridge* (2) ... AZ-5
Cockscomb, The—*ridge* (2) ... UT-8
Cockscomb, The—*summit* ... AZ-5
Cockscomb, The—*summit* ... OR-9
Cockscomb Butte—*summit* ... AZ-5
Cockscomb Creek—*stream* ... AK-9
*Cockscomb Crest* ... CA-9
*Cockscomb Gap* ... AL-4
Cockscomb Hill—*summit* ... WY-8
Cockscomb Lakes—*lake* ... CA-9
Cockscomb Mtn—*summit* ... WA-9
*Cockscomb Peak* ... CA-9
Cockscomb Point—*cape* ... AS-9
Cockscomb Ridge—*ridge* ... NV-8
Cockscomb Ridge—*ridge* ... UT-8
Cocks Combs—*ridge* ... AZ-5
*Cocks Combs, The* ... AZ-5
Cocks Landing—*locale* ... NC-3
Cockspur Branch—*stream* ... TN-4
Cockspur Island—*island* ... GA-3
Cockspur Knob—*summit* ... TN-4
Cockspur Lake—*lake* ... LA-4
Cockspur Lead—*ridge* ... TN-4
Cock Spurs—*ridge* ... AR-4
Cocktown Creek—*stream* ... MD-2
Cockwood Coulee—*valley* ... MN-6
Coco—*locale* ... WV-2
**Coco**—*pop pl* ... PR-3
Coco, Bayou—*stream* ... MS-4
**Cocoa**—*pop pl* ... FL-3
**Cocoa Beach**—*pop pl* ... FL-3
Cocoa Beach-Cape Canaveral (CCD)—*cens area* ... FL-3
Cocoa Beach HS—*school* ... FL-3
Cocoa Beach Public Library—*building* ... FL-3
Cocoa HS—*school* ... FL-3
Cocoa Mtn—*summit* ... ME-1
*Cocoanut Grove* ... FL-3
Cocoanut Hammock—*island* ... FL-3
*Cocoanut Island* ... HI-9
Cocoanut Key—*island* ... FL-3
*Cocoanut Point* ... HI-9
Cocoanut Sch (historical)—*school* ... TN-4
Cocoa Plum Beach—*beach* ... FL-3
Cocoa Public Library—*building* ... FL-3
Cocoa-Rockledge (CCD)—*cens area* ... FL-3
Cocoa-Rockledge (RR name for Cocoa)—*other* ... FL-3
**Cocoa (RR name Cocoa-Rockledge)**—*pop pl* ... FL-3
Cocoa West—*CDP* ... FL-3
Cocoa Yacht Basin—*harbor* ... FL-3
Coco Canal—*canal* ... LA-4
Coco Creek—*stream* ... AK-9
**Cocodrie**—*pop pl* ... LA-4
Cocodrie, Bayou—*gut* ... LA-4
Cocodrie, Bayou—*stream* (6) ... LA-4
Cocodrie, Lake—*lake* ... LA-4
Cocodrie, Lake—*swamp* ... LA-4
Cocodrie Bayou—*stream* ... LA-4
Cocodrie Ch—*church* ... LA-4
*Cocodrie Creek* ... LA-4
Cocodrie Lake—*lake* (2) ... LA-4
Coco Harbor—*bay* ... AK-9
Cocohatchee River—*stream* ... FL-3
Coco Lake—*lake* ... LA-4
**Cocolalla**—*pop pl* ... ID-8
Cocolalla Creek—*stream* ... ID-8
Cocolalla Lake—*lake* ... ID-8
Cocolalla Siding—*locale* ... ID-8
**Cocolamus**—*pop pl* ... PA-2
**Cocolamus (Browns Mill)**—*pop pl* ... PA-2
Cocolamus Creek—*stream* ... PA-2
Cocomongo Mine—*mine* ... CO-8
Cocomongo Mtn—*summit* ... NV-8
Coco Mtn—*summit* ... WA-9
Cocomunga Canyon—*valley* ... AZ-5
*Coconino* ... AZ-5
Coconino—*locale* ... AZ-5
*Coconino Caverns* ... AZ-5
Coconino (CCD)—*cens area* ... AZ-5
Coconino Country Club—*other* ... AZ-5
**Coconino County**—*pop pl* ... AZ-5
*Coconino County Fairgrounds and Park* ... AZ-5
Coconino County Highway Department—*building* ... AZ-5
Coconino County Hosp Complex—*hist pl* ... AZ-5
Coconino County Recreation Site—*park* ... AZ-5
Coconino Dam—*dam* ... AZ-5
Coconino HS—*school* ... AZ-5
Coconino Lake—*reservoir* ... AZ-5
Coconino Natl For—*forest* ... AZ-5
*Coconino Plateau* ... AZ-5
Coconino Plateau—*plain* ... AZ-5
Coconino Point—*cliff* ... AZ-5
Coconino Rim—*cliff* ... AZ-5
Coconino RR Station—*building* ... AZ-5
Coconino Siding—*locale* ... AZ-5
Coconino Substation—*locale* ... AZ-5
Coconino Wash—*stream* ... AZ-5
Coconino Wash Tank—*reservoir* ... AZ-5
Coconut—*locale* ... FL-3
Coconut Bayou—*bay* ... FL-3
Coconut Bluff—*cliff* ... FL-3
**Coconut Creek**—*pop pl* ... FL-3
Coconut Creek Elem Sch—*school* ... FL-3
Coconut Creek HS—*school* ... FL-3
**Coconut Creek Park**—*pop pl* ... FL-3
Coconut Creek Plaza (Shop Ctr)—*locale* ... FL-3
Coconut Grove—*locale* ... ID-8
**Coconut Grove**—*pop pl* ... FL-3
**Coconut Grove**—*pop pl* ... HI-9
Coconut Grove Bay Front Park—*park* ... FL-3
Coconut Grove Christian Sch—*school* ... FL-3
Coconut Grove Creek—*stream* ... ID-8
Coconut Grove Exhibition Center—*building* ... FL-3
Coconut Grove Mini Park—*park* ... FL-3
Coconut Grove Sch—*school* ... FL-3
Coconut Grove Station RR Station—*locale* ... FL-3
*Coconut Island* ... HI-9
Coconut Island—*island* ... FL-3
Coconut Island—*island* ... HI-9
Coconut Point—*cape* (3) ... FL-3
Coconut Point—*cape* ... HI-9
Coconut Point—*cape* ... AS-9
Cocoon Mtns—*range* ... NV-8
Cocopah Canal—*canal* ... CA-9
*Cocopah Damsite Number Three* ... AZ-5
Cocopah Drain—*canal* ... AZ-5
Cocopah Elem Sch—*school* ... AZ-5
**Cocopah Ind Res**—*pop pl* ... AZ-5
*Cocopah Point* ... AZ-5
Cocopa Point—*cliff* ... AZ-5
*Cocopa Reservoir* ... AZ-5
Cocoplum Plaza—*locale* ... FL-3
Cocoplum Waterway—*canal* ... FL-3
*Cocoran Creek* ... OK-5
*Cocoraqu Butte* ... AZ-5
Cocoraque Butte—*summit* ... AZ-5
Cocoraque Butte Archeol District—*hist pl* ... AZ-5
Cocoraque Ranch—*locale* ... AZ-5
*Cocoraqui Butte* ... AZ-5
Cocoris Park—*park* ... FL-3
Cocos (Barrio)—*fmr MCD* ... PR-3
Cocos Island—*island* ... GU-9
Cocos Lagoon—*bay* ... GU-9
**Cocoville**—*pop pl* ... LA-4
CoCo Windmill—*locale* ... TX-5
*Cocran Creek* ... OK-5
Coculus Point—*cape* ... VI-3
Coculus Rock—*island* ... VI-3
*Cocumcusset* ... RI-1
Cocumcussoc—*summit* ... RI-1
Cocumcussoc Brook—*stream* ... RI-1
*Cocumcussoc Harbor* ... RI-1
*Cocumscussoc* ... RI-1
Cod, Cape—*cape* ... FL-3
Cod, Cape—*cape* ... MA-1
Cod, Cape—*cape* ... WA-9
Cod Cove—*bay* ... ME-1
Cod Creek—*stream* ... DE-2
Cod Creek—*stream* ... MD-2
Cod Creek—*stream* ... OR-9
Cod Creek—*stream* (2) ... VA-3
**Coddes Beach**—*pop pl* ... MI-6
Codding—*locale* ... PA-2
Codding Brook—*stream* ... MA-1
Codding Brook—*stream* ... VT-1
Codding Cem—*cemetery* ... NY-2
Codding Ranch—*locale* ... OK-5
Coddington—*locale* ... WI-6
Coddington Cove—*bay* ... RI-1
Coddington Creek—*stream* ... ID-8
Coddington Lake—*lake* ... MN-6
Coddington Peak—*summit* ... ID-8
*Coddington Point* ... RI-1
Coddington Point—*cape* ... RI-1
Coddington Ranch—*locale* ... NM-5
Coddington Ranch (historical)—*locale* ... UT-8
Coddington Sch—*school* ... WI-6
Coddingtown—*post sta* ... CA-9
**Coddingville**—*pop pl* ... OH-6
Coddingville Cem—*cemetery* ... OH-6
Coddle Creek—*stream* ... NC-3
Coddle Creek Associate Reformed Presbyterian Ch, Session House—*hist pl* ... NC-3
Coddle Creek Ch—*church* ... NC-3
**Coddle Creek (historical)**—*pop pl* ... NC-3
Coddle Creek (Township of)—*fmr MCD* ... NC-3
Coddon Hill—*summit* ... MA-1
*Coddons Hill* ... MA-1
Codds Creek—*gut* ... NC-3
*Coddude* ... MA-1
Code Cem—*cemetery* ... LA-4
Code Creek—*stream* ... OR-9
**Codell**—*pop pl* ... KS-7
Codell Lake—*lake* ... KY-4
**Coden**—*pop pl* ... AL-4
Coden, Bayou—*stream* ... AL-4
Coder—*locale* ... PA-2
*Coder Creek* ... DE-2
Coder Run—*stream* ... PA-2
Code Sch—*school* ... MI-6
Codes Point—*cape* ... MD-2
Codfish Cem—*cemetery* ... IA-7
Codfish Cove—*bay* ... AK-9
Codfish Creek—*stream* ... CA-9
Codfish Falls—*falls* ... CA-9
Codfish Hill—*locale* ... CT-1
Codfish Hill Mine—*mine* ... CA-9
**Codfish Park**—*pop pl* ... MA-1
Codfish Point—*cape* ... LA-4
Codfish Point—*ridge* ... CA-9
Codfish Ridge—*ridge* ... ME-1
**Cod Fish Village**—*pop pl* ... HI-9
Cod Harbor—*bay* ... VA-3
Codhead Ledge—*bar* ... ME-1
Codington County—*civil* ... SD-7
Codington County Courthouse—*hist pl* ... SD-7
Codington County State Public Shooting Area—*park* ... SD-7
Codington Creek—*stream* ... NE-7
*Codjaw Pond* ... PA-2
Codjus Cove—*bay* ... MD-2
Cod Lake—*lake* ... AK-9
Cod Ledges—*bar* ... ME-1
Codman—*locale* (2) ... TX-5
Codman, Col. Charles, Estate—*hist pl* ... MA-1
Codman Bldg—*hist pl* ... MA-1
Codman-Davis House—*hist pl* ... DC-2
Codman Hill—*summit* ... NH-1
Codman House Museum—*building* ... MA-1
Codman Point—*cape* ... MA-1
Codman Square District—*hist pl* ... MA-1
C O D Mine—*mine* (2) ... AZ-5
Codo—*locale* ... CO-8
Codora—*locale* ... CA-9
Codora Four Corners—*locale* ... CA-9
Codora Sch—*school* ... CA-9
Codornices Creek—*stream* ... CA-9
Codornices Park—*park* ... CA-9
**Codorniz**—*pop pl* ... CA-9
Codorniz Canyon—*valley* ... TX-5
Codorus Cem—*cemetery* ... PA-2
Codorus Ch—*church* ... PA-2
*Codorus (corporate name Jefferson)* ... PA-2
Codorus Creek—*stream* (2) ... PA-2
Codorus Creek Dam—*dam* ... PA-2
Codorus Furnace—*locale* ... PA-2
Codorus Mills—*uninc pl* ... PA-2
Codorus Mills Station—*locale* ... PA-2
Codorus Rsvr—*reservoir* ... PA-2
Codorus State Park—*park* ... PA-2
**Codorus (Township of)**—*pop pl* ... PA-2
Cod Point—*cape* ... AK-9
Cod Point—*cape* ... VA-3
Cod Pond—*lake* ... NY-2
C O D Ranch—*locale* ... AZ-5
*Codrie Creek* ... LA-4
Cod Rocks, The—*cape* ... ME-1
Cods Hammocks (historical)—*island* ... DE-2
C O D Spring—*spring* ... AZ-5
Codwater Campground—*park* ... OR-9
*Cody* ... MI-6
Cody—*locale* ... AL-4
Cody—*locale* ... FL-3
Cody—*locale* (2) ... OK-5
Cody—*locale* ... VA-3
**Cody**—*pop pl* ... AR-4
**Cody**—*pop pl* ... KY-4
**Cody**—*pop pl* ... MO-7
**Cody**—*pop pl* ... NE-7
**Cody**—*pop pl* ... WY-8
Cody Bar—*bar* ... CA-9
Cody Branch—*stream* ... AL-4
Cody Branch—*stream* (4) ... NC-3
Cody Branch—*stream* ... TN-4
Cody Brook—*stream* ... NY-2
Cody Butte—*summit* ... WA-9
Cody Canal—*canal* ... WY-8
Cody Cem—*cemetery* (2) ... OH-6
Cody Ch—*church* ... AL-4
Cody Ch—*church* ... VA-3
*Cody Creek* ... CA-9
Cody Creek—*stream* ... AK-9
Cody Creek—*stream* (3) ... CA-9
Cody Creek—*stream* ... MS-4
Cody Creek—*stream* (2) ... MT-8
Cody Creek—*stream* (2) ... NC-3
Cody Creek—*stream* ... WI-6
Cody Ditch—*canal* ... CA-9
Cody Field Branch—*stream* ... TN-4
Cody Gap—*gap* ... NC-3
Cody Grove Ch—*church* ... GA-3
Cody Gulch—*valley* ... CO-8
Cody Gulch Spring—*spring* ... CO-8
**Cody (historical)**—*pop pl* ... MO-7
Cody Hollow—*valley* ... MO-7
Cody Hollow—*valley* ... PA-2
Cody Hollow—*valley* ... TN-4
Cody Homestead—*hist pl* ... IA-7
Cody HS—*school* ... MI-6
*Cody Lake* ... MI-6
Cody Lake—*lake* ... CA-9
Cody Lake—*lake* ... MN-6
Cody Lake—*lake* ... MT-8
Cody Lake—*lake* (3) ... NE-7
Cody Lake—*lake* ... SD-7
Cody Lake—*lake* ... WA-9
Cody Lake Sch—*school* ... NE-7
Cody Landing—*locale* ... GA-3
Cody Lateral Ditch—*canal* ... WY-8
Cody Meadow—*flat* ... CA-9
Cody Municipal Airport—*obs name* ... WY-8
Cody Park—*flat* ... CO-8
Cody Park—*park* ... NE-7
Cody Park—*park* ... NC-3
**Cody Park**—*pop pl* ... CO-8
Cody Peak—*summit* ... WY-8
Cody Pond—*lake* ... FL-3
Cody Pond—*lake* ... NY-2
Cody Ponds—*lake* ... OR-9
Cody Post Office (historical)—*building* ... AL-4
Cody Road Hist Dist—*hist pl* ... IA-7
Codys Camp—*locale* ... OR-9
Cody Sch—*school* ... MI-6
Cody Sch—*school* ... NE-7
Codys Corner—*locale* ... FL-3
Cody Spring—*spring* ... CO-8
**Cody Township**—*pop pl* ... SD-7
Codyville—*locale* ... ME-1
**Codyville**—*pop pl* ... KY-4
Codyville (Plantation of)—*civ div* ... ME-1
Cody-Yellowhand Battlefield—*park* ... NE-7
Coe—*locale* ... KY-4
Coe—*locale* ... WV-2
**Coe**—*pop pl* ... IN-6
**Coe**—*pop pl* ... MI-6
Coe, Amos B., House—*hist pl* ... MN-6
Coe, Lake—*lake* ... ND-7
Coe, Mount—*summit* ... ME-1
Coebourn Sch—*school* ... PA-2
*Coe Branch* ... TX-5
Coe Branch—*stream* ... OR-9
**Coeburn**—*pop pl* ... VA-3
Coe Canyon—*valley* ... NM-5
*Coeccles Harbor* ... NY-2
Coe Cem—*cemetery* ... MI-6
Coe Cem—*cemetery* ... MO-7
Coe Cem—*cemetery* ... NM-5
Coe Cem—*cemetery* ... NY-2
*Coeckle's Harbor* ... NY-2
*Coecl* ... NY-2
*Coecle Harbor Inlet* ... NY-2
*Coecles* ... NY-2
Coecles Harbor—*bay* ... NY-2
*Coecle's Harbor Inlet* ... NY-2
*Coecles Inlet* ... NY-2
Coe Coll—*school* ... IA-7
Coe Creek—*stream* ... AR-4
Coe Creek—*stream* ... ID-8
Coe Creek—*stream* ... IA-7
Coe Creek—*stream* ... KY-4
Coe Creek—*stream* ... MI-6
Coe Ditch No. 1—*canal* ... CO-8
Coe Ditch No. 2—*canal* ... CO-8
Coe Drain—*canal* ... MI-6
Coee Cem—*cemetery* ... AL-4
*Coees Creek* ... IN-6
Coefield Branch—*stream* ... NC-3
Coefield Cem—*cemetery* ... NC-3
Coefield Creek—*stream* ... KY-4
Coefield Creek—*stream* ... NC-3
Coe Glacier—*glacier* ... OR-9
Coe Gulch—*valley* ... CA-9
Coe Hill—*summit* ... CT-1
Coe Hill—*summit* ... NY-2
Coe Hill Sch—*school* ... NY-2
*Coehn Dry Lake* ... CA-9
Coe Hollow—*valley* ... KY-4
Coe Hollow—*valley* ... OH-6
Coe Hollow—*valley* ... WI-6
*Coe Lake* ... MI-6
Coe Lake—*lake* ... MN-6
Coe Lateral—*canal* ... ID-8
Coelleda Hollow—*valley* ... MO-7
*Coello (corporate name North City)* ... IL-6
**Coello (North City)**—*pop pl* ... IL-6
Coe Lodge—*locale* ... WY-8
Coe Mound—*hist pl* ... OH-6
Coen Cem—*cemetery* ... WV-2
Coen Ch—*church* ... OH-6
*Coenjock* ... NC-3
Coen Pasture—*flat* ... KS-7
Coen Tunnel—*tunnel* ... OH-6
Coe Park—*park* ... ME-1
Coe Point—*cape* ... ME-1
Coe Ranch—*locale* ... CA-9
Coe Ranch—*locale* (2) ... NM-5
Coe Ranch—*locale* ... SD-7
Coe Ridge Cem—*cemetery* ... OH-6
Coe Rsvr—*reservoir* ... WY-8
Coe Sch—*school* ... AZ-5
Coe Sch—*school* ... KY-4
Coe Sch—*school* ... OH-6
Coe Sch—*school* ... WA-9
Coe Sch (historical)—*school* ... AL-4
Coes Corners—*locale* ... NY-2
Coesfield—*locale* ... TX-5
Coes Landing—*locale* ... FL-3
Coes Neck Park—*park* ... NY-2
Coes Place Sch—*school* ... NJ-2
Coes Pond—*reservoir* ... MA-1
Coes Reservoir Dam—*dam* ... MA-1
Coes Rsvr—*reservoir* ... MA-1
**Coesse**—*pop pl* ... IN-6
Coesse Ch—*church* ... IN-6
**Coesse Corners**—*pop pl* ... IN-6
Coessens Park—*park* ... NY-2
Coetas Creek—*stream* ... TX-5
**Coe (Township of)**—*pop pl* ... IL-6
**Coe (Township of)**—*pop pl* ... MI-6

**Coeur Dalane Estates (subdivision)**—pop pl UT-8
**Coeur d'Alene**—pop pl ID-8
Coeur d'Alene, Mount—summit ID-8
Coeur d'Alene City Hall—hist pl ID-8
Coeur d'Alene Country Club—other ID-8
Coeur d'Alene Creek—stream AK-9
Coeur d'Alene Federal Bldg—hist pl ID-8
**Coeur d'Alene Ind Res**—pop pl ID-8
Coeur d'Alene Junction—locale ID-8
Coeur d'Alene Lake—reservoir ID-8
Coeur d'Alene Masonic Temple—hist pl ID-8
Coeur d'Alene Mine—mine ID-8
Coeur d'Alene Mission of the Sacred Heart—hist pl ID-8
Coeur d'Alene Mtns—range ID-8
Coeur D'Alene Mtns—range MT-8
Coeur D'Alene Natl For—forest ID-8
Coeur D'Alene Natl For—forest ID-8
Coeur D'Alene Park—park WA-9
Coeur d'Alene River—stream ID-8
Coeur d'Alene Saint Joe Divide—ridge ID-8
Coey—locale WA-9
Coey Creek—stream NY-2
Coey Hill—summit NY-2
Coey Hollow—valley OH-6
**Coeymans**—pop pl NY-2
Coeymans, Ariaanje, House—hist pl NY-2
*Coeyman's Creek* NY-2
Coeymans Creek—stream NY-2
**Coeymans Hollow**—pop pl NY-2
Coeymans Hollow Cem—cemetery NY-2
Coeymans Sch—hist pl NY-2
**Coeymans (Town of)**—pop pl NY-2
*Cofachique* KS-7
Cofelt Ranch—locale OR-9
Cofer—locale KY-4
Cofer and Tedder Jellico Mine (surface)—mine TN-4
Cofer Cem—cemetery MO-7
Cofer Cem—cemetery TN-4
Cofer Dam—dam AZ-5
Cofer (historical)—locale MS-4
Cofer Hot Spring—spring AZ-5
Cofer Pond—reservoir SC-3
Cofers Ch—church TN-4
Cofer Sch—school IL-6
Cofer Spring—spring TN-4
Coffadeliah Creek—stream MS-4
Coffadeliah (historical)—locale MS-4
*Coffalos* ME-1
*Coffalos Lake* ME-1
Coff Cem—cemetery IL-6
*Coff Creek* AL-4
*Coff Ditch* IN-6
Coffe Branch—stream MS-4
Coffe Creek—stream AK-9
*Coffedelia* MS-4
Coffee—locale GA-3
Coffee—locale VA-3
**Coffee**—pop pl CA-9
Coffee And Tea Creek—stream OH-6
Coffee Bar—bar OR-9
Coffee Bay—lake LA-4
Coffee Bayou—gut AR-4
Coffee Bayou—gut IN-6
Coffee Bayou—gut LA-4
Coffee Bayou—stream AL-4
Coffee Bayou—stream IN-6
Coffee Bayou—stream LA-4
Coffee Bay Rest Shelter—locale GA-3
Coffeebean Creek—stream KS-7
Coffee Bean Creek—stream OK-5
Coffee Bean Slough—lake TX-5
Coffee Bend Bar—bar AL-4
Coffee Bluff—cliff AL-4
Coffee Bluff—cliff GA-3
Coffee Bluff—locale GA-3
Coffee Bogue—stream MS-4
*Coffee Bogue Creek* MS-4
Coffee Bottom—bend TN-4
Coffee Branch—channel FL-3
Coffee Branch—stream AL-4
Coffee Branch—stream (2) GA-3
Coffee Branch—stream (2) KY-4
Coffee Branch—stream NC-3
Coffee Branch—stream TN-4
Coffee Branch—stream TX-5
Coffee Branch—swamp FL-3
Coffee Break Lake—lake MN-6
Coffee Brook—stream PA-2
Coffee Butte—summit (2) OR-9
Coffee Butte—summit SD-7
Coffee Camp Rsvr—reservoir CO-8
Coffee Can Creek—stream CA-9
*Coffee Can Island* OR-9
Coffee Can Lake—lake AK-9
Coffee Can Saddle—gap ID-8
Coffee Canyon—valley AZ-5
Coffee Canyon—valley (2) CA-9
Coffee Cave—cave (2) AL-4
Coffee Cem—cemetery (3) AL-4
Coffee Cem—cemetery (2) IL-6
Coffee Cem—cemetery (3) TN-4
Coffee Cem—cemetery (3) TX-5
Coffee Cem—cemetery VA-3
Coffee Cem—cemetery WV-2
Coffee Ch—church MO-7
Coffee Chute—channel OR-9
Coffee City—locale TX-5
**Coffee City**—pop pl TX-5
Coffee Corner P.O. (historical)—locale AL-4
Coffee Corners—locale OH-6
*Coffee County* KS-7
**Coffee County**—pop pl AL-4
**Coffee (County)**—pop pl GA-3
**Coffee County**—pop pl TN-4
Coffee County Central HS—school TN-4
Coffee County Court House—building TN-4
Coffee County Courthouse—hist pl AL-4
Coffee County Courthouse—hist pl TN-4
Coffee County Health Department—hospital TN-4
Coffee County HS—school TN-4
Coffee County Med Ctr—hospital TN-4
*Coffee County Memorial Hosp* AL-4
*Coffee County Public Lake* AL-4
Coffee County Public Lake Dam—dam AL-4
Coffee County Rec Area—park TN-4
*Coffee Cove* GA-3
Coffee Cove—bay AK-9
*Coffee Creek* AL-4
*Coffee Creek* IN-6
*Coffee Creek* MT-8
*Coffee Creek* SC-3
*Coffee Creek* TX-5
*Coffee Creek* VA-3
*Coffee Creek* WA-9
Coffee Creek—locale AK-9
**Coffee Creek**—pop pl MT-8
Coffee Creek—stream (3) AL-4
Coffee Creek—stream (5) AK-9
Coffee Creek—stream AZ-5
Coffee Creek—stream (5) AR-4
Coffee Creek—stream (3) CA-9
Coffee Creek—stream CO-8
Coffee Creek—stream (2) ID-8
Coffee Creek—stream (2) IL-6
Coffee Creek—stream (2) IN-6
Coffee Creek—stream IA-7
Coffee Creek—stream KS-7
Coffee Creek—stream KY-4
Coffee Creek—stream MI-6
Coffee Creek—stream MN-6
Coffee Creek—stream MO-7
Coffee Creek—stream MT-8
Coffee Creek—stream NE-7
Coffee Creek—stream (2) NC-3
Coffee Creek—stream (4) OH-6
Coffee Creek—stream (3) OK-5
Coffee Creek—stream (8) OR-9
Coffee Creek—stream PA-2
Coffee Creek—stream (4) SD-7
Coffee Creek—stream TN-4
Coffee Creek—stream TX-5
Coffee Creek—stream WA-9
Coffee Creek—stream (3) WI-6
Coffee Creek—stream WY-8
Coffee Creek—swamp FL-3
Coffee Creek Ch—church IN-6
Coffee Creek Channel—channel AK-9
Coffee Creek Conservation Club—other IN-6
Coffee Creek Cow Camp—locale TX-5
Coffee Creek Guard Station—locale CA-9
Coffee Creek Ranch—locale CA-9
Coffee Creek Sch—school AR-4
Coffee Creek Sch—school CA-9
Coffee Creek Slope Mine (underground)—mine AL-4
Coffee Creek Swamp—swamp SC-3
Coffee Cup Lake—lake ID-8
Coffee Ditch—canal CA-9
Coffee Dome—summit (2) AK-9
Coffee (Election Precinct)—fmr MCD IL-6
*Coffee Ferry* AL-4
Coffee Flat—flat AZ-5
Coffee Flat—flat SD-7
Coffee Flat—flat TX-5
Coffee Flat Canyon—valley AZ-5
Coffee Flat Mtn—summit AZ-5
Coffee Flats—flat SD-7
Coffee Flat Sch—school SD-7
Coffee Flat Trail—trail AZ-5
Coffee Gap—gap GA-3
Coffee Gap—gap OR-9
Coffee Ground Cove—bay LA-4
Coffee Gulch—valley ID-8
Coffee Gulch—valley MT-8
Coffee Gulch—valley NM-5
*Coffeehigui* KS-7
Coffee Hill—locale MD-2
Coffee Hill Run—stream MD-2
Coffee Hill Sch—school PA-2
Coffee (historical P.O.)—locale IN-6
Coffee Hollow—valley MD-2
Coffee Hollow—valley MO-7
Coffee Hollow—valley OH-6
Coffee Hollow—valley TX-5
Coffee House—hist pl NJ-2
Coffee House Stream—stream ME-1
Coffee HS—hist pl AL-4
Coffee HS—school AL-4
Coffee Island—island IN-6
Coffee Island—island OR-9
Coffee Knob—summit OH-6
Coffee Lake—lake AZ-5
Coffee Lake—lake AR-4
Coffee Lake—lake GA-3
Coffee Lake—lake MI-6
Coffee Lake—lake (4) MN-6
Coffee Lake—lake NE-7
Coffee Lake—lake OR-9
Coffee Lake—lake TN-4
Coffee Lake—lake TX-5
Coffee Lake—lake WA-9
Coffee Lake—lake (3) WI-6
Coffee Landing—locale TN-4
*Coffeeles Pond* ME-1
*Coffeelos Lake* ME-1
Coffeelos Pond—lake ME-1
Coffee Mill Butte—summit NE-7
Coffee Mill Country Club—other MN-6
Coffee Mill Creek—stream TX-5
Coffee Mill Flat—flat CA-9
Coffee Mill Gulch—valley CA-9
Coffee Mill Hammock—island FL-3
Coffee Mill Lake—reservoir TX-5
Coffee Mill Meadow—flat CA-9
*Coffeemill Rsvr* TX-5
Coffee Mill Spring—spring CA-9
Coffee Mtn—summit NY-2
**Coffeen**—pop pl IL-6
Coffeen, Goldsmith, House—hist pl OH-6
Coffeen Creek—stream WY-8
Coffeen Lake—reservoir IL-6
Coffeen Park—park WY-8
Coffeen Sch—school WY-8
Coffee Peak—summit UT-8
Coffee Pit—cave AL-4
*Coffee Point* WY-8
Coffee Point—cape (3) AK-9
Coffee Point—cape LA-4
Coffee Point—locale ID-8
Coffee Point Rsvr—reservoir ID-8
Coffee Pond—lake FL-3
Coffee Pond—lake ME-1
Coffee Pond—lake NY-2
Coffeepot—locale AZ-5
Coffee Pot—summit CA-9
Coffeepot Bayou—bay FL-3
Coffeepot Butte—summit WA-9
Coffeepot Canyon—valley AZ-5
Coffeepot Canyon—valley CA-9
Coffee Pot Canyon—valley NM-5
Coffee Pot Canyon—valley TX-5
Coffeepot Cove—cove FL-3
Coffeepot Crater—crater OR-9
*Coffee Pot Creek* UT-8
Coffeepot Creek—stream CO-8
Coffee Pot Creek—stream ID-8
Coffee Pot Creek—stream MT-8
Coffeepot Creek—stream NV-8
Coffeepot Creek—stream OK-5
Coffeepot Creek—stream (4) OR-9
Coffeepot Creek—stream UT-8
Coffee Pot Dam—dam AZ-5
Coffeepot Flat—flat OR-9
Coffee Pot Hill—summit CO-8
Coffee Pot Hollow—valley AR-4
Coffee Pot Hot Springs—spring WY-8
Coffee Pot Island—island OR-9
*Coffee Pot Lake* WA-9
Coffeepot Lake—lake WA-9
Coffee Pot Landing—locale MN-6
Coffeepot Mtn—summit AZ-5
Coffee Pot Mtn—summit NC-3
Coffeepot Park—flat CO-8
*Coffee Pot Pass* CO-8
Coffeepot Pass—gap CO-8
Coffee Pot Rapids—rapids ID-8
Coffeepot Ridge—ridge UT-8
Coffeepot Rock—summit AZ-5
Coffee Pot Rock—summit UT-8
Coffee Pot Rsvr—reservoir OR-9
Coffeepot Rsvr—reservoir OR-9
Coffee Pot Ruins—locale UT-8
*Coffee Pot Spring* UT-8
Coffeepot Spring—spring CO-8
Coffee Pot Spring—spring OK-5
Coffee Pot Spring—spring OR-9
Coffeepot Spring—spring (3) OR-9
Coffeepot Spring—spring UT-8
Coffeepot Spring—spring (2) WA-9
Coffee Pot Spring Campground—locale CO-8
Coffeepot Tank—reservoir AZ-5
Coffee Pot Tank—reservoir NM-5
Coffee Pot Trail—trail OR-9
Coffeepot Trail—trail OR-9
Coffee Pot Well—well AZ-5
Coffeepot Well—well AZ-5
Coffee Prairie—flat AR-4
Coffee Ridge—locale TN-4
Coffee Ridge—ridge MO-7
Coffee Ridge—ridge NC-3
Coffee Ridge—ridge TN-4
Coffee Ridge Baptist Ch—church TN-4
Coffee Ridge Creek—stream TN-4
Coffee Ridge Sch (historical)—school TN-4
Coffee River—stream AK-9
Coffee Rosenwald Sch (historical)—school AL-4
*Coffee Run* PA-2
**Coffee Run**—pop pl DE-2
Coffee Run—stream (2) OH-6
Coffee Run—stream (3) PA-2
Coffee Run Mission Site—hist pl DE-2
Coffee Run Overlook—locale PA-2
Coffee Run Spring—spring PA-2
Coffee Run Spring Cave—cave PA-2
Coffee Sch—school KY-4
Coffee Sch (abandoned)—school MO-7
*Coffee Settlement* AL-4
Coffee Sink—basin FL-3
*Coffees Island* AL-4
*Coffees Landing* TN-4
Coffee Slough—stream AL-4
Coffee Spring—spring NV-8
Coffee Spring—spring UT-8
**Coffee Springs**—pop pl AL-4
Coffee Springs—spring AL-4
*Coffee Springs Baptist Church* AL-4
Coffee Springs Cem—cemetery AL-4
Coffee Springs Ch of Christ—church AL-4
Coffee Springs Cumberland Presbyterian Ch (historical)—church AL-4
Coffee Springs Elem Sch—school AL-4
Coffee Springs HS—school AL-4
Coffee Springs Methodist Ch—church AL-4
Coffee Swamp—swamp WI-6
Coffee Tank—reservoir (2) AZ-5
Coffee Tank—reservoir NM-5
Coffee Tank—reservoir TX-5
Coffeetown—locale PA-2
**Coffeetown**—pop pl (2) PA-2
Coffeetown Grist Mill—hist pl PA-2
Coffee Valley—valley VA-3
*Coffeeville* AL-4
**Coffeeville**—pop pl AL-4
**Coffeeville**—pop pl AR-4
**Coffeeville**—pop pl MS-4
**Coffeeville**—pop pl TX-5
Coffeeville Acad (historical)—school MS-4
Coffeeville (CCD)—cens area AL-4
Coffeeville Cem—cemetery TX-5
Coffeeville Ch—church AL-4
Coffeeville Ch—church IL-6
Coffeeville Ch—church TN-4
Coffeeville Division—civil AL-4
Coffeeville Elem Sch—school AL-4
Coffeeville Elem Sch—school MS-4
Coffeeville Ferry (historical)—locale AL-4
Coffeeville First Baptist Ch—church MS-4
Coffeeville Hotel—hist pl MS-4
Coffeeville HS—school MS-4
Coffeeville Lake—reservoir AL-4
Coffeeville Lake Public Use Area—park AL-4
Coffeeville Landing—locale AL-4
Coffeeville Lock And Dam—dam AL-4
Coffeeville Lookout Tower—tower MS-4
Coffeeville Male and Female Acad (historical)—school MS-4
*Coffeeville Trade School* AL-4
Coffee Well—well NM-5
Coffee Windmill—locale NM-5
*Coffelest Lake* ME-1
Coffelt Cem—cemetery AR-4
Coffelt Draw—valley NM-5
Coffelt Lamoreaux Park—park AZ-5
*Coffelt Park* AZ-5
Coffelt Sch—school OK-5
Coffelt Tank—reservoir NM-5
Coffenbury Lake—lake OR-9
Coffer Creek—stream NC-3
Coffer Creek—stream SC-3
Coffer Run—stream OH-6
Cofferville—locale TX-5
Coffey Cem—cemetery MI-6
**Coffey**—pop pl MO-7
Coffey, Col. J. K., House—hist pl MS-4
Coffey Branch—stream KS-7
Coffey Branch—stream KY-4
Coffey Branch—stream NC-3
Coffey Branch—stream TN-4
Coffey Brook—stream CT-1
Coffey Cave—cave AL-4
Coffey Cem—cemetery (3) AL-4
Coffey Cem—cemetery IN-6
Coffey Cem—cemetery (5) KY-4
Coffey Cem—cemetery (3) TN-4
Coffey Cem—cemetery TX-5
Coffey Chapel—church TN-4
Coffey Corner—locale VA-3
Coffey County—civil KS-7
Coffey Cove—bay GA-3
Coffey Cove—valley NC-3
Coffey Creek—stream (2) NC-3
Coffey Gap—gap NC-3
Coffey Grove Sch—school KY-4
Coffey Hill—summit ME-1
Coffey Hollow—valley (2) KY-4
Coffey Hollow—valley MO-7
Coffey Hollow—valley TN-4
Coffey Lake—reservoir GA-3
Coffey Mill Gulch—valley CA-9
Coffey Mountain—ridge GA-3
Coffey Mtn—summit KY-4
Coffey Narrows—gap AL-4
Coffey Run—stream PA-2
Coffeys—locale NC-3
Coffey Sch—school KY-4
Coffey Sch—school MI-6
Coffey Sch (historical)—school MS-4
Coffey Sch (historical)—school MO-7
Coffeys Crossing—locale PA-2
Coffeys Ferry—locale AL-4
Coffey Site—hist pl KS-7
Coffey Slough—gut FL-3
Coffeys Point—cape MS-4
*Coffeys Store* AL-4
**Coffey Subdivision**—pop pl IN-6
Coffeyton—locale MO-7
*Coffeytown* PA-2
Coffey (Township of)—fmr MCD AR-4
Coffey Trout Lake—reservoir NC-3
Coffey Valley Ch—church OK-5
**Coffeyville**—pop pl KS-7
Coffeyville Carnegie Public Library Bldg—hist pl KS-7
*Coffeyville College* KS-7
Coffeyville Community Coll—school KS-7
Coffeyville Country Club—other KS-7
*Coffeyville Dam* AL-4
Coffeyville Memorial Hospital Airp—airport KS-7
Coffeyville Municipal Airp—airport KS-7
Coffield Cem—cemetery AR-4
Coffield House—building NC-3
Coffield Lake—lake MI-6
Coffield Ridge—ridge WV-2
Coffield Run—stream WV-2
Coffield Sch—school IL-6
Coffin, Henry, House—hist pl ID-8
Coffin, Jethro, House—hist pl MA-1
Coffin, Levi, House—hist pl IN-6
Coffin, Lorenzo S., Burial Plot—hist pl IA-7
Coffin, Mount—summit WY-8
Coffin, Stephen, House—hist pl ME-1
Coffinberry Sch—school OH-6
Coffin Bog—swamp ME-1
Coffin Branch—stream NC-3
Coffin Brook—stream (6) ME-1
Coffin Brook—stream NH-1
*Coffin Butte* ND-7
Coffin Butte—summit (2) MT-8
Coffin Butte—summit (2) OR-9
Coffin Butte—summit WY-8
Coffin Butte Lookout—locale OR-9
Coffin Buttes—range ND-7
Coffin Canyon—valley CA-9
Coffin Canyon—valley OR-9
Coffin Cem—cemetery IN-6
Coffin Creek—stream AK-9
Coffin Creek—stream ID-8
Coffin Creek—stream MT-8
Coffin Creek—stream NV-8
Coffin Creek—stream OK-5
Coffin Creek—stream OR-9
Coffin Creek—stream SC-3
**Coffing**—pop pl CA-9
Coffing Brothers Dam—dam IN-6
Coffing Brothers Lake—reservoir IN-6
Coffinger Park—park AZ-5
Coffin Hill—summit (2) NH-1
Coffin Hill—summit NJ-2
Coffin Hollow—valley AL-4
Coffin Hollow—valley CA-9
Coffin House Museum—building MA-1
*Coffin Island* UT-8
Coffin Lake—lake CO-8
Coffin Lake—lake MN-6
Coffin Lake—lake MT-8
Coffin Lake—lake UT-8
Coffin Lake—lake WA-9
Coffin Lateral—canal TX-5
Coffin Mountain Trail—trail OR-9
Coffin Mtn—summit CO-8
Coffin Mtn—summit MT-8
Coffin Mtn—summit NV-8
Coffin Mtn—summit OR-9
Coffin Mtn—summit TX-5
Coffin Park—park GA-3
Coffin Peak—summit CA-9
Coffin Point—cape FL-3
Coffin Point—cape ME-1
Coffin Point—cape MD-2
Coffin Point—cape MA-1
Coffin Point—cape NY-2
Coffin Point—cape SC-3
Coffin Point—cape VA-3
Coffin Point Cem—cemetery SC-3
Coffin Point Plantation—hist pl SC-3
Coffin Pond—lake ME-1
Coffin Pond—lake (2) NH-1
Coffin Ranch—locale NM-5
Coffin Ranch—locale WA-9
*Coffin Road* RI-1
Coffin Rock—pillar OR-9
Coffin Rock—rock MA-1
Coffin Rock—summit OR-9
Coffin Rock Ch—church PA-2
Coffin Rock Fire Tower—tower PA-2
Coffin Rocks—bar WA-9
Coffin Rocks Tower (historical)—tower PA-2
Coffins Beach—beach MA-1
Coffin Sch—school ME-1
Coffin Sch—school MA-1
**Coffins Corner**—pop pl NJ-2
*Coffins Creek* IA-7
Coffins Creek—stream IA-7
Coffins Grove Cem—cemetery IA-7
Coffin's Grove Stagecoach House—hist pl IA-7
Coffins Grove Township—fmr MCD IA-7
Coffin Shop—hist pl AL-4
Coffin Site—hist pl NY-2
**Coffins Mill**—pop pl NH-1
**Coffins Mills**—pop pl NY-2
Coffins Neck—cape ME-1
Coffins Patch—bar FL-3
*Coffins Patches* FL-3
Coffins Patch Light 20—locale FL-3
Coffins Point—cape (2) ME-1
Coffins Point—cape MD-2
Coffin Spring—spring (2) CA-9
Coffin Spring—spring TN-4
Coffin Spring—spring TX-5
Coffin Spring—spring WA-9
Coffin Springs Canyon—valley TX-5
*Coffins Station* IN-6
Coffin State For—forest MO-7
Coffin Tank—reservoir NM-5
Coffinton—locale GA-3
Coffintop Gulch—valley CO-8
Coffintop Mtn—summit CO-8
Coffman—locale AR-4
Coffman—locale KY-4
Coffman—locale PA-2
**Coffman**—pop pl AR-4
**Coffman**—pop pl MO-7
Coffman, Fletcher, House—hist pl OH-6
Coffman Bend—bend MO-7
Coffman Bluff—summit IL-6
Coffman Branch—stream AL-4
Coffman Branch—stream KY-4
Coffman Branch—stream MO-7
Coffman Bridge—bridge KY-4
Coffman Butte—summit WY-8
Coffman Camp—locale PA-2
Coffman Camp—locale TN-4
Coffman Camp Trail—trail OR-9
Coffman Cem—cemetery (3) AR-4
Coffman Cem—cemetery (2) IN-6
Coffman Cem—cemetery KY-4
Coffman Cem—cemetery (2) MO-7
Coffman Cem—cemetery OH-6
Coffman Cem—cemetery (3) TN-4
Coffman Cem—cemetery TX-5
Coffman Cem—cemetery WV-2
Coffman Ch—church VA-3
Coffman Ch—church WV-2
Coffman Cove—bay AK-9
Coffman Cove—bay AR-4
Coffman Cove—CDP AK-9
Coffman Creek—stream AK-9
Coffman Creek—stream LA-4
Coffman Drain—canal MI-6
Coffman Hill—cliff WV-2
Coffman Hill—summit PA-2
Coffman Hill Chapel—church WV-2
Coffman Hollow—valley MO-7
Coffman Hollow—valley TN-4
Coffman Island—island AK-9
Coffman Knob—summit OH-6
Coffman Lake—lake IL-6
Coffman Lookout Tower—tower MO-7
*Coffman Marsh* MD-2
Coffman Mtn—summit AR-4
Coffman Orr Cem—cemetery OH-6
Coffman Run—stream OH-6
Coffman Sch—school MO-7
Coffmans Lake—lake KY-4
Coffmans Lake—reservoir NC-3
Coffmans Lake Dam—dam NC-3
Coffman Spring—spring GA-3
Coffmans Store (historical)—locale TN-4
Coffman Tower Site State Public Hunting Area—locale MO-7
*Coffolos Lake* ME-1
Coffren, John W., House and Store—hist pl MD-2
**Cofield**—pop pl NC-3
Cofield Bend—bend AL-4
**Cofield Corner**—pop pl IN-6
Cofield Lake—lake GA-3
Cofinan Run—stream PA-2
*Cofoco* WV-2
**Cofoco**—pop pl WV-2
Cofo Lake Dam—dam MS-4
*Cogaminck River* NY-2
Cogan, Bernard, House—hist pl MA-1
Cogan, James, House—hist pl MA-1
Cogan House—locale PA-2
Cogan House Covered Bridge—hist pl PA-2
Cogan House Sch—school PA-2
**Cogan House (Township of)**—pop pl PA-2
Cogan Pond—reservoir MA-1
Cogan Station—locale PA-2
Cogan Station P. O. (historical)—building PA-2
*Cogan Valley* PA-2
*Cogan Valley Station* PA-2
Cogar—locale OK-5
Cogar Ch—church OK-5
Cogbill Cem—cemetery AR-4
Cogburn Cem—cemetery TX-5
Cogburn Creek—stream GA-3
Cogburn Windmill—locale NM-5
**Cogdell**—pop pl GA-3
Cogdell Branch—stream SC-3
Cogdell Cem—cemetery NC-3
Cogdell Oil Field—oilfield TX-5
Cogdells Pond—reservoir NC-3
Cogdels Creek—stream NC-3
Cogden Branch—stream TX-5
Cogden Lake—lake GA-3
Cogdill Center—locale AZ-5
Cogdill Chapel—church TN-4
Cogdill Sch (abandoned)—school MO-7
Coger Hill Ch—church AL-4
Coger House—hist pl AR-4
Coger (RR name for Gem)—other WV-2
Cogers Pond—lake CT-1
*Cogeshalls Cove* RI-1
Coggans Hill—summit ME-1
Cogger Lake—lake MI-6
**Coggeshall**—pop pl RI-1
Coggeshall Cove—bay RI-1
Coggeshall Ledge—bench RI-1
*Coggeshall Point* RI-1
*Coggeshalls Beach* RI-1
*Coggeshalls Ledge* RI-1
Coggeshell Point—cape RI-1
Coggin, Gilman, House—hist pl MA-1
Coggin Cem—cemetery GA-3
Coggin Cem—cemetery TN-4
Coggin Creek—stream SC-3
Coggin Elem Sch—school TX-5
Coggin House Sch (historical)—school TN-4
Coggin Lake—reservoir TX-5
Coggin Memorial Sch—school TX-5
Coggins, J. R., House—hist pl TX-5
Coggins Bend—bend NC-3
Coggins Branch—stream NC-3
Coggins Camp—locale NM-5
Coggins Corner—locale PA-2
Coggins Creek—stream NC-3
Coggins Drain—canal MI-6
Coggins-Greer Cem—cemetery TN-4
Coggins Head—summit ME-1
Coggins Hill—summit NC-3
Coggins Knob—summit WV-2
Coggins Mine—locale NC-3
Coggins Park—park CA-9
Coggins Point—cape VA-3
Coggins Saddle—gap OR-9
**Coggin Subdivision**—pop pl MS-4
Coggman Bridge—bridge VT-1
Coggman Creek—stream VT-1
Coggman Pond—lake VT-1
**Coggon**—pop pl IA-7
Coggon Cem—cemetery IA-7
**Cog Hill**—pop pl TN-4
Cog Hill—summit TN-4
Coghill Cem—cemetery (2) IL-6
Cog Hill Cem—cemetery KY-4
Cog Hill Ch—church TN-4
Cog Hill Country Club—other IL-6
Coghill Hollow—valley MO-7
Coghill Lake—lake AK-9
Coghill Point—cape AK-9
*Cog Hill Post Office* TN-4
Coghill Post Office (historical)—building TN-4
Coghill Ridge—ridge VA-3
Coghill River—stream AK-9
Coghill Sch—school LA-4
**Coghill (subdivision)**—pop pl NC-3
Coghlan Island—island AK-9
Coginchaug River—stream CT-1
Coglan Buttes—summit OR-9
Coglan Canyon—valley OR-9
*Coglans Mill Creek* MS-4
*Coglar Buttes* OR-9
Cogley Island—island PA-2
Cogley Run—stream PA-2
*Coglin Creek* NC-3
**Cognac**—pop pl NC-3
Cognac, Bayou—gut LA-4
Cognevich Pass—gut LA-4
Cogo Windmill—locale NM-5
Cograge Windmill—locale TX-5
Cogsdell Brook—stream PA-2
Cogsdill Sch—school MI-6
Cogshell Lake—lake TN-4
Cogswell—locale KY-4
**Cogswell**—pop pl ND-7
Cogswell Ave Industrial Park—locale AL-4
Cogswell Butte—summit AZ-5
Cogswell Cem—cemetery OH-6
Cogswell Corners—locale NY-2
*Cogswell Creek* OR-9
Cogswell Creek—stream (2) OR-9
Cogswell Dam—dam CA-9
Cogswell Hill—summit NH-1
Cogswell Mtn—summit NH-1
Cogswell Point—cape UT-8
Cogswell Polytechnical Coll—school CA-9
Cogswell Ravine—valley CA-9
Cogswell Rsvr—reservoir CA-9
Cogswell Sch—school CA-9
Cogswell Sch—school (2) MA-1
Cogswell Spring—spring WY-8
Cogur Fork—stream KY-4
*Cohabadia Creek* AL-4
Cohab Canyon—valley UT-8
Cohabie Creek—stream AL-4
Cohabie Mtn—summit AL-4
Cohackett Brook—stream MA-1
**Cohagen**—pop pl MT-8
Cohagen Cem—cemetery MT-8
**Cohala**—pop pl CA-9
Cohannet Sch—school MA-1
*Cohannett, Town of* MA-1
Cohan Park—park OH-6
*Cohansey* NJ-2
**Cohansey**—pop pl NJ-2
*Cohansey Bridge* NJ-2
Cohansey Country Club—other NJ-2
Cohansey Cove—bay NJ-2
*Cohansey Creek* NJ-2
Cohansey Inner Light—locale NJ-2
Cohansey Outer Light—locale NJ-2
Cohansey Point—cape NJ-2
Cohansey River—stream NJ-2
*Cohanzey Creek* NJ-2
Cohanzie Sch—school CT-1
*Cohanzy* NJ-2
*Cohanzy Creek* NJ-2
*Cohanzy River* NJ-2
Coharie Country Club—locale NC-3
Cohas Brook—stream NH-1
Cohasse Brook—stream CT-1
Cohasse Brook—stream MA-1
Cohasse Brook Rsvr—reservoir MA-1

*Coldwater River* NC-3
Coldwater River—*stream* (3) MI-6
Coldwater River—*stream* MS-4
Coldwater River County Park—*park* MI-6
Cold Water Run—*stream* NJ-2
Coldwater Sch—*school* AL-4
Coldwater Sch—*school* IL-6
Coldwater Sch—*school* (2) MO-7
Coldwater Sch—*school* SC-3
Coldwater Sch—*school* (2) TN-4
Coldwater Sch (abandoned)—*school* MO-7
Coldwater Sch (historical)—*school* MS-4
Coldwater Sch (historical)—*school* TN-4
Cold Water Seep—*spring* AZ-5
Cold Water Slough—*stream* AR-4
*Cold Water Spring* AL-4
Coldwater Spring—*spring* AL-4
Cold Water Spring—*spring* (3) AZ-5
Coldwater Spring—*spring* (2) AZ-5
Coldwater Spring—*spring* (2) AR-4
Coldwater Spring—*spring* (2) CA-9
Coldwater Spring—*spring* ID-8
Coldwater Spring—*spring* MO-7
Coldwater Spring—*spring* NV-8
Coldwater Spring—*spring* OR-9
Coldwater Spring—*spring* TN-4
Cold Water Spring—*spring* UT-8
Coldwater Spring—*spring* (3) UT-8
Coldwater Spring Branch—*stream* AL-4
*Coldwater Springs* AL-4
Cold Water Springs—*spring* UT-8
Cold Water Springs State Wildlife Area—*area* IA-7
Coldwater State For—*forest* MO-7
Coldwater State Home and Training Sch—*school* MI-6
Coldwater Station—*locale* AL-4
Cold Water Tank—*reservoir* AZ-5
Coldwater Tank Number One—*reservoir* AZ-5
Coldwater Tank Number Two—*reservoir* AZ-5
Coldwater Tavern (historical)—*locale* ME-1
Coldwater Township—*civil* MO-7
Coldwater Township—*fmr MCD* IA-7
**Coldwater Township**—*pop pl* KS-7
Coldwater (Township of)—*fmr MCD* AR-4
**Coldwater (Township of)**—*pop pl* (2) MI-6
Cold Water Trail—*trail* AZ-5
Coldwater Trail—*trail* CA-9
Coldwater Trail—*trail* WA-9
Cold Water Trail Number Twenty Seven—*trail* AZ-5
Coldwater United Methodist Ch—*church* AL-4
Coldwater United Methodist Ch—*church* MS-4
Cold Water Wash—*arroyo* AZ-5
Cold Water Well—*well* NM-5
Coldweather Creek—*stream* KY-4
Cold Weather Rsvr—*reservoir* NV-8
Cold Well Cem—*cemetery* SC-3
*Coldwell Corner* DE-2
Coldwell Corners—*locale* DE-2
Coldwell Post Office (historical)—*building* TN-4
Coldwell Sch—*school* TX-5
Coldwell (Township of)—*fmr MCD* AR-4
*Cole* AZ-5
Cole—*locale* AR-4
Cole—*locale* CA-9
Cole—*locale* LA-4
Cole—*locale* MT-8
Cole—*locale* OH-6
Cole—*mine* AZ-5
**Cole**—*pop pl* IN-6
**Cole**—*pop pl* OK-5
**Cole**—*pop pl* TX-5
Cole—*uninc pl* CA-9
Cole, Alex, Cabin—*hist pl* TN-4
Cole, Anna Russell, Auditorium—*hist pl* TN-4
Cole, David, House—*hist pl* OR-9
Cole, Frank W., House—*hist pl* MI-6
Cole, James Omar, House—*hist pl* IN-6
Cole, John, Farm—*hist pl* RI-1
Cole, Thomas, House—*hist pl* NY-2
Cole, Warren Z., House—*hist pl* PA-2
Cole Airp—*airport* PA-2
Cole-Allaire House—*hist pl* NJ-2
Cole and Forrester Dam—*dam* OR-9
Coleanor—*locale* AL-4
Coleanor Number 1 Mine (underground)—*mine* AL-4
Coleanor Slope Mine (underground)—*mine* AL-4
Cole Ave Sch—*school* CA-9
Coleback Lake—*lake* ME-1
Colebank—*locale* WV-2
Cole Bay—*bay* NY-2
Cole Bend—*bend* (2) TN-4
Cole Black Creek—*stream* CO-8
Colebough Drain—*canal* MI-6
Cole Branch—*stream* (2) AL-4
Cole Branch—*stream* AR-4
Cole Branch—*stream* IL-6
Cole Branch—*stream* IN-6
Cole Branch—*stream* (2) KY-4
Cole Branch—*stream* MS-4
Cole Branch—*stream* (2) MO-7
Cole Branch—*stream* NC-3
Cole Branch—*stream* SC-3
Cole Branch—*stream* TN-4
Cole Bridge Ch (historical)—*church* AL-4
*Cole Brook* NY-2
**Colebrook**—*pop pl* CT-1
**Colebrook**—*pop pl* NH-1
**Colebrook**—*pop pl* OH-6
**Colebrook**—*pop pl* PA-2
Cole Brook—*stream* (4) ME-1
Cole Brook—*stream* (3) NH-1
Cole Brook—*stream* (3) NY-2
Cole Brook—*stream* VT-1
Colebrook Brook—*stream* CT-1
Colebrook Butte—*summit* OR-9
Colebrook Cem—*cemetery* MA-1
Colebrook Ch—*church* PA-2
**Colebrook Compact (census name Colebrook)**—*pop pl* NH-1
*Colebrookdale* PA-2
Colebrookdale—*locale* PA-2
Colebrookdale Station (historical)—*locale* PA-2
**Colebrookdale (Township of)**—*pop pl* PA-2
Colebrook Dam—*dam* PA-2
**Colebrooke**—*pop pl* MD-2
*Colebrooke Butte* OR-9
Colebrook Manor—*hist pl* PA-2
Colebrook River Burying Ground—*cemetery* CT-1
Colebrook River Lake—*reservoir* CT-1
Colebrook River Lake—*reservoir* MA-1
*Colebrook River Rsvr* CT-1
*Colebrook River Rsvr* MA-1
Colebrook Sch—*school* NY-2
Colebrook Store—*hist pl* CT-1
Colebrook Swamp—*swamp* MA-1
**Colebrook (Town of)**—*pop pl* CT-1
**Colebrook (Town of)**—*pop pl* NH-1
**Colebrook (Township of)**—*pop pl* OH-6
**Colebrook (Township of)**—*pop pl* PA-2
Cole Butte—*summit* WA-9
**Cole Camp**—*pop pl* MO-7
Cole Campbell Tank—*reservoir* AZ-5
Cole Camp Cave—*cave* MO-7
Cole Camp Cem—*cemetery* MO-7
Cole Camp Creek—*stream* MO-7
Cole Camp Creek Arm—*bay* MO-7
**Cole Camp Junction**—*pop pl* MO-7
Cole Camp Memorial Cem—*cemetery* MO-7
Cole Camp Station—*locale* MO-7
Cole Canyon—*valley* CA-9
Cole Canyon—*valley* (2) ID-8
Cole Canyon—*valley* (4) NV-8
Cole Canyon—*valley* (2) OR-9
Cole Canyon—*valley* UT-8
Cole Canyon—*valley* WY-8
Cole Cave—*cave* MO-7
Cole Cem—*cemetery* (3) AL-4
Cole Cem—*cemetery* AR-4
Cole Cem—*cemetery* (3) GA-3
Cole Cem—*cemetery* IL-6
Cole Cem—*cemetery* IN-6
Cole Cem—*cemetery* KS-7
Cole Cem—*cemetery* KY-4
Cole Cem—*cemetery* (3) LA-4
Cole Cem—*cemetery* (2) ME-1
Cole Cem—*cemetery* MI-6
Cole Cem—*cemetery* (3) MS-4
Cole Cem—*cemetery* (4) MO-7
Cole Cem—*cemetery* (2) NY-2
Cole Cem—*cemetery* (4) OH-6
Cole Cem—*cemetery* (3) PA-2
Cole Cem—*cemetery* (11) TN-4
Cole Cem—*cemetery* (3) VA-3
Cole Cem—*cemetery* WI-6
Cole Cemeteries—*cemetery* ME-1
*Cole Center* LA-4
**Cole Central**—*pop pl* LA-4
Cole Ch—*church* AL-4
Cole Ch—*church* MI-6
Cole Ch—*church* MS-4
Cole Ch—*church* OK-5
Cole Ch—*church* TX-5
Cole Ch—*church* VA-3
Cole Chapel—*church* VA-3
Cole Chapel Cem—*cemetery* OK-5
Cole Chapel Sch—*hist pl* OK-5
Colechester, Lake—*reservoir* IA-7
*Colechester, Town of* MA-1
Cole Chuck Meadow—*flat* OR-9
Cole City—*locale* GA-3
Cole City Creek—*stream* GA-3
Cole City Creek—*stream* TN-4
*Cole Corner* WA-9
Cole Corner—*locale* ME-1
**Cole Corner**—*pop pl* MA-1
Cole Corner HS—*school* MA-1
Cole Corners—*locale* NY-2
**Cole County**—*pop pl* MO-7
Cole County Courthouse and Jail-Sheriff's House—*hist pl* MO-7
Cole County Historical Society Bldg—*hist pl* MO-7
*Cole Creek* AR-4
*Cole Creek* CA-9
*Cole Creek* KS-7
*Cole Creek* OK-5
*Cole Creek* TN-4
*Cole Creek* WA-9
Cole Creek—*stream* AR-4
Cole Creek—*stream* (4) CA-9
Cole Creek—*stream* CO-8
Cole Creek—*stream* GA-3
Cole Creek—*stream* (3) ID-8
Cole Creek—*stream* (2) IL-6
Cole Creek—*stream* IA-7
Cole Creek—*stream* (4) KS-7
Cole Creek—*stream* KY-4
Cole Creek—*stream* LA-4
Cole Creek—*stream* ME-1
Cole Creek—*stream* MD-2
Cole Creek—*stream* (9) MI-6
Cole Creek—*stream* MS-4
Cole Creek—*stream* (5) MO-7
Cole Creek—*stream* (7) MT-8
Cole Creek—*stream* NE-7
Cole Creek*—*stream* NE-7
Cole Creek—*stream* NE-7
Cole Creek—*stream* (2) NV-8
Cole Creek—*stream* NY-2
Cole Creek—*stream* NC-3
Cole Creek—*stream* ND-7
Cole Creek—*stream* OH-6
Cole Creek—*stream* (2) OK-5
Cole Creek—*stream* (6) OR-9
Cole Creek—*stream* PA-2
Cole Creek—*stream* (2) SC-3
Cole Creek—*stream* SD-7
Cole Creek—*stream* (3) TN-4
Cole Creek—*stream* (5) TX-5
Cole Creek—*stream* VA-3
Cole Creek—*stream* (3) WA-9
Cole Creek—*stream* (2) WI-6
Cole Creek—*stream* (2) WY-8
Cole Creek Cabin—*locale* CA-9
Cole Creek (historical)—*locale* MS-4
Cole Creek Lakes—*lake* CA-9
Cole Creek Manor—*uninc pl* TX-5
Cole Creek Oil Field—*oilfield* WY-8
Cole Creek Picnic Area—*locale* WA-9
Cole Creek Sch—*school* KS-7
Cole Dam—*dam* SD-7
Cole Ditch—*canal* CA-9
Cole Ditch—*canal* CO-8
Cole Ditch—*canal* (2) IN-6
Cole Ditch—*canal* MI-6
Cole Ditch—*canal* MO-7
Cole Ditch—*canal* MT-8
Cole Ditch—*canal* OH-6
Cole Ditch—*canal* OR-9
Coledon—*locale* AZ-5
Cole Draft—*valley* PA-2
Cole Drain—*canal* CA-9
Cole Drain—*canal* MI-6
Cole Drain—*stream* (3) MI-6
Cole Draw—*valley* SD-7
Cole Draw—*valley* WY-8
Colee—*uninc pl* FL-3
Cole Eddy—*bay* GA-3
Coleen Lake—*lake* MN-6
Coleen Mtn—*summit* AK-9
Coleen River—*stream* AK-9
Cole Field—*park* MA-1
Colefield Post Office (historical)—*building* AL-4
Cole Flat—*flat* CA-9
Cole Ford—*locale* ND-7
Cole Ford (historical)—*locale* MO-7
Cole Fork—*stream* AR-4
Cole Fork—*stream* (2) KY-4
*Cole Fork Creek* AR-4
Cole Gap—*gap* (2) NC-3
Colegio Adventista—*school* PR-3
Colegio Bautista de Carolina—*school* PR-3
Colegio Cayey U P R—*school* PR-3
Colegio Central—*school* PR-3
Colegio de las Madres del Sagrado Corazon—*hist pl* PR-3
Colegio del Carmen—*school* PR-3
Colegio del Perpetuo Socorro—*school* PR-3
Colegio del Sagrado Corazon—*school* PR-3
Colegio Maria Auxiliadora—*school* PR-3
Colegio Nuestra Senora del Pilar—*school* PR-3
Colegio Nuestra Senora del Rosario—*school* PR-3
Colegio Nuestra Senora La Merced—*school* PR-3
Colegio Padres Dominicos—*school* PR-3
Colegio Ponceno de Varones—*school* PR-3
Colegio Regional—*post sta* PR-3
Colegio Sagrado Corazon—*school* PR-3
Colegio San Antonio Abad—*school* PR-3
Colegio San Benito—*school* PR-3
Colegio San Carlos Sch—*school* PR-3
Colegio San Ignacio de Loyola—*school* PR-3
Colegio San Jose—*school* PR-3
Colegio San Miguel—*school* PR-3
Colegio Santa Clara—*school* PR-3
Colegio Santa Maria de Los Angeles—*school* PR-3
Colegio Santos Angeles Custodios—*school* PR-3
Colegio San Vicente de Paul—*school* PR-3
Colegio San Vincente Ferrer—*school* PR-3
Colegio Senora de La Providencia—*school* PR-3
Colegio Universitario—*post sta* PR-3
Colegio Vedruna—*school* PR-3
*Colegove Butte* OR-9
Colegrave—*locale* NY-2
Colegrove—*locale* PA-2
Cole Grove Branch—*stream* KY-4
Colegrove Brook—*stream* PA-2
Colegrove Butte—*summit* OR-9
Colegrove Cem—*cemetery* OH-6
*Cole Grove Corner* RI-1
Colegrove Gas And Oil Field—*oilfield* PA-2
Colegrove Hill—*summit* CT-1
Colegrove Sch (abandoned)—*school* PA-2
Cole Gulch—*valley* (2) CO-8
Cole Gulch—*valley* WY-8
Cole Gully—*stream* LA-4
**Coleharbor**—*pop pl* ND-7
Coleharbor Cem—*cemetery* ND-7
*Cole Harbor Cove* RI-1
Coleharbor Water Supply Dam—*dam* ND-7
Cole-Hatcher-Hampton Wholesale Grocers—*hist pl* GA-3
Cole Hill—*locale* (2) PA-2
Cole Hill—*ridge* NH-1
Cole Hill—*summit* CA-9
Cole Hill—*summit* NH-1
Cole Hill—*summit* (4) NY-2
Cole Hill—*summit* (3) PA-2
Cole Hill—*summit* (2) VT-1
Cole Hill Cem—*cemetery* ME-1
Cole Hill Cem—*cemetery* (2) NY-2
Cole Hills—*range* TX-5
Cole Hill Sch—*school* NY-2
Cole Hill Sch (historical)—*school* PA-2
Cole-Hipp House—*hist pl* TX-5
Cole Hist Dist—*hist pl* WI-6
**Cole (historical)**—*pop pl* TN-4
Cole Hole Hollow—*valley* MO-7
Cole Hollow—*valley* AR-4
Cole Hollow—*valley* (2) MO-7
Cole Hollow—*valley* (3) NY-2
Cole Hollow—*valley* (2) TN-4
Cole Hollow—*valley* (2) VA-3
Cole Homestead—*locale* MT-8
Cole Hosp—*hospital* IL-6
Cole Hotel—*hist pl* ND-7
*Colehour* IL-6
Cole House—*hist pl* ID-8
Cole House—*hist pl* TN-4
Cole HS—*school* TX-5
*Cole Island* ME-1
*Cole Island* SC-3
Cole Island—*island* AK-9
Cole Island—*island* NY-2
Cole Island—*island* (2) OR-9
Cole Island—*island* (2) SC-3
Cole JHS—*school* CO-8
Cole Junction—*locale* MO-7
Cole Knob—*summit* TN-4
*Cole Lake* NE-7
*Cole Lake* WA-9
Cole Lake—*lake* (3) MI-6
Cole Lake—*lake* (2) MN-6
Cole Lake—*lake* TX-5
Cole Lake—*lake* WI-6
Cole Lake—*reservoir* AL-4
Cole Lake—*reservoir* (2) GA-3
Cole Lake—*reservoir* MS-4
Cole Lake—*reservoir* MO-7
Cole Lake—*reservoir* TN-4
Cole Lake Dam—*dam* AL-4
Cole Lake Dam—*dam* MS-4
Cole Lake Dam—*dam* TN-4
Cole Landing Strip—*airport* MO-7
Cole Lateral—*canal* ID-8
*Cole Lick Creek* NC-3
*Coleman* MS-4
Coleman—*fmr MCD* NE-7
Coleman—*locale* AL-4
Coleman—*locale* AR-4
Coleman—*locale* ID-8
Coleman—*locale* KS-7
Coleman—*locale* LA-4
Coleman—*locale* MO-7
Coleman—*locale* NC-3
Coleman—*locale* OH-6
Coleman—*locale* PA-2
**Coleman**—*pop pl* FL-3
**Coleman**—*pop pl* GA-3
**Coleman**—*pop pl* IL-6
**Coleman**—*pop pl* KY-4
**Coleman**—*pop pl* MD-2
**Coleman**—*pop pl* MI-6
**Coleman**—*pop pl* OK-5
**Coleman**—*pop pl* (3) PA-2
**Coleman**—*pop pl* TX-5
**Coleman**—*pop pl* WV-2
**Coleman**—*pop pl* WI-6
Coleman, George L., Sr., House—*hist pl* OK-5
Coleman, House—*hist pl* KY-4
Coleman, James W., House—*hist pl* GA-3
Coleman, John, House—*hist pl* AL-4
Coleman, Lake—*reservoir* (2) TX-5
Coleman, William, House—*hist pl* UT-8
Coleman, William E., House—*hist pl* MT-8
Coleman, William L., House—*hist pl* KY-4
Coleman Arm—*bay* OR-9
Coleman-Banks House—*hist pl* AL-4
Coleman Basin—*basin* UT-8
Coleman Bay—*bay* AK-9
Coleman Bayou—*stream* LA-4
Coleman Beach—*beach* CA-9
Coleman Bench—*bench* MT-8
*Coleman Branch* AL-4
Coleman Branch—*stream* AL-4
Coleman Branch—*stream* GA-3
Coleman Branch—*stream* (3) KY-4
Coleman Branch—*stream* (2) LA-4
Coleman Branch—*stream* NC-3
Coleman Branch—*stream* OH-6
Coleman Branch—*stream* SC-3
Coleman Branch—*stream* (5) TN-4
Coleman Branch—*stream* (2) TX-5
Coleman Branch—*stream* VA-3
Coleman Branch—*stream* (3) WV-2
Coleman Branch Mine (surface)—*mine* TN-4
Coleman Bridge—*bridge* AL-4
Coleman Brook—*stream* VT-1
Coleman Butte—*summit* WA-9
Coleman Butte—*summit* WY-8
Coleman Canal—*canal* CA-9
Coleman Canyon—*valley* (2) CA-9
Coleman Canyon—*valley* CO-8
Coleman Canyon—*valley* ID-8
Coleman Canyon—*valley* (2) NV-8
Coleman Canyon—*valley* OR-9
Coleman Canyon—*valley* (2) WA-9
Coleman Catfish Ponds Dam—*dam* (2) MS-4
Coleman Cave—*cave* (2) TN-4
Coleman (CCD)—*cens area* TX-5
Coleman Cem—*cemetery* (2) AL-4
Coleman Cem—*cemetery* FL-3
Coleman Cem—*cemetery* (3) GA-3
Coleman Cem—*cemetery* IN-6
Coleman Cem—*cemetery* (4) KY-4
Coleman Cem—*cemetery* (2) LA-4
Coleman Cem—*cemetery* (5) MS-4
Coleman Cem—*cemetery* (7) MO-7
Coleman Cem—*cemetery* (2) NY-2
Coleman Cem—*cemetery* NC-3
Coleman Cem—*cemetery* OH-6
Coleman Cem—*cemetery* (2) OK-5
Coleman Cem—*cemetery* (9) TN-4
Coleman Cem—*cemetery* (4) TX-5
Coleman Cem—*cemetery* (3) VA-3
Coleman Cem—*cemetery* WV-2
Coleman Ch—*church* AL-4
Coleman Ch—*church* MS-4
Coleman Ch—*church* VA-3
Coleman Chapel—*church* AR-4
Coleman Chapel—*church* OK-5
Coleman Chapel—*church* PA-2
*Coleman Chapel AME Zion Church* MS-4
Coleman Clerk Ch—*church* GA-3
Coleman-Cole House—*hist pl* TX-5
**Coleman Corner**—*pop pl* VT-1
Coleman Coulee—*valley* MT-8
**Coleman (County)**—*pop pl* TX-5
Coleman Cove—*bay* ME-1
*Coleman Creek* AL-4
*Coleman Creek* TX-5
*Coleman Creek* WA-9
Coleman Creek—*stream* AL-4
Coleman Creek—*stream* AK-9
Coleman Creek—*stream* AZ-5
Coleman Creek—*stream* (2) AR-4
Coleman Creek—*stream* (3) CA-9
Coleman Creek—*stream* (2) CO-8
Coleman Creek—*stream* (2) GA-3
Coleman Creek—*stream* KS-7
Coleman Creek—*stream* LA-4
Coleman Creek—*stream* (4) MS-4
Coleman Creek—*stream* NE-7
Coleman Creek—*stream* (2) NV-8
Coleman Creek—*stream* NC-3
Coleman Creek—*stream* (5) OR-9
Coleman Creek—*stream* PA-2
Coleman Creek—*stream* (2) TX-5
Coleman Creek—*stream* (3) VA-3
Coleman Creek—*stream* (2) WA-9
Coleman Creek—*stream* WV-2
Coleman Cutoff Trail—*trail* CO-8
Coleman Dam—*dam* AL-4
Coleman Dam—*dam* NY-2
Coleman Dam—*dam* PA-2
Coleman Ditch—*canal* NY-2
Coleman Diversion Dam—*dam* NV-8
Coleman Drain—*canal* MI-6
Coleman Draw—*valley* MT-8
Coleman Draw—*valley* WY-8
*Coleman Elementary School* TN-4
**Coleman Falls**—*pop pl* VA-3
Coleman Family Cem—*cemetery* MS-4
Coleman Farm Ponds—*reservoir* AL-4
Coleman Ferry (historical)—*locale* AL-4
Coleman Field—*flat* CA-9
Coleman Filtration Plant—*other* TX-5
Coleman Fish Hatchery—*locale* CA-9
Coleman Flat—*flat* (2) CA-9
Coleman Flat—*flat* UT-8
Coleman Ford—*locale* AL-4
Coleman Forebay—*lake* CA-9
*Coleman Fork* AL-4
Coleman Fork—*stream* TN-4
Coleman Fork—*stream* WV-2
Coleman-Furlong House—*hist pl* WA-9
Coleman Gap—*gap* (3) NC-3
Coleman Gap—*gap* TN-4
Coleman Glacier—*glacier* WA-9
Coleman Gulch—*valley* CO-8
Coleman Gully—*stream* LA-4
Coleman Hall—*hist pl* MO-7
Coleman Hammock—*island* FL-3
*Coleman Heights* MA-1
**Coleman Heights**—*pop pl* TN-4
*Coleman Hill* MA-1
Coleman Hill—*range* WA-9
Coleman Hill—*summit* CA-9
Coleman Hill—*summit* PA-2
Coleman Hill—*summit* TN-4
Coleman Hill Creek—*stream* MA-1
Coleman Hills—*summit* MA-1
**Coleman (historical)**—*pop pl* OR-9
Coleman Hollow—*locale* NJ-2
Coleman Hollow—*valley* (5) MO-7
Coleman Hollow—*valley* (2) OK-5
Coleman Hollow—*valley* PA-2
Coleman Hollow—*valley* (3) TN-4
Coleman Hollow Prospect—*mine* TN-4
Coleman Hollow Wash—*valley* UT-8
Coleman House—*hist pl* DE-2
Coleman HS—*school* AR-4
Coleman HS—*school* MS-4
Coleman Industrial Subdivision—*locale* UT-8
Coleman Island—*island* IL-6
Coleman Island—*island* MN-6
Coleman Island—*island* SC-3
Coleman Island—*island* VA-3
Coleman Islands—*island* WI-6
*Coleman JHS* MS-4
*Coleman Junction* TX-5
Coleman Junction North Oil Field—*oilfield* TX-5
Coleman Knob—*summit* AR-4
Coleman Knob—*summit* KY-4
Coleman Knoll—*summit* AZ-5
Coleman Lake—*bay* SC-3
Coleman Lake—*lake* IL-6
Coleman Lake—*lake* MI-6
Coleman Lake—*lake* (2) MN-6
Coleman Lake—*lake* (2) NE-7
Coleman Lake—*lake* OR-9
Coleman Lake—*lake* SC-3
Coleman Lake—*lake* TX-5
Coleman Lake—*lake* WI-6
Coleman Lake—*reservoir* AL-4
Coleman Lake—*reservoir* TN-4
Coleman Lake—*swamp* AZ-5
Coleman Lake Campground and Picnic Area—*park* AL-4
Coleman Lake Dam—*dam* (3) MS-4
*Coleman Lake Number 3* AL-4
Coleman Lakes—*reservoir* (2) AL-4
Coleman Lakes Number 1 Dam—*dam* AL-4
*Coleman Lakes Number 7* AL-4
Coleman Landing—*locale* FL-3
Coleman Memorial Bridge—*bridge* VA-3
Coleman Memorial United Methodist Ch—*church* TN-4
**Coleman Mill**—*pop pl* VA-3
Coleman Mill Branch—*stream* NC-3
Coleman Mill (historical)—*locale* AL-4
*Coleman Mtn* VA-3
Coleman Mtn—*summit* OR-9
Coleman Mtn—*summit* VA-3
Cole Manor Sch—*school* PA-2
Coleman Park—*park* TN-4
Coleman Park—*park* TX-5
Coleman Peak—*summit* AK-9
Coleman Peak—*summit* WA-9
Coleman Pinnacle—*pillar* WA-9
**Coleman Place**—*pop pl* VA-3
Coleman Point—*cape* NH-1
Coleman Point—*cape* WA-9
Coleman Point—*cliff* OR-9
Coleman Point—*summit* OR-9
*Coleman Pond* PA-2
Coleman Pond—*lake* AL-4
Coleman Pond—*lake* FL-3
Coleman Pond—*lake* GA-3
Coleman Pond—*lake* ME-1
Coleman Pond—*lake* MA-1
Coleman Pond—*lake* NE-7
Coleman Pond—*lake* SC-3
Coleman Pond—*reservoir* AL-4
Coleman Pond—*reservoir* MA-1
Coleman Pond—*reservoir* VA-3
Coleman Ponds Dam—*dam* MS-4
Coleman Powerhouse—*other* CA-9
Coleman Ranch—*locale* AZ-5
Coleman Ranch—*locale* CO-8
Coleman Ranch—*locale* NV-8
Coleman Ranch—*locale* OR-9
Coleman Ranch—*locale* (2) TX-5
Coleman-Raymon Cem—*cemetery* TN-4
Coleman Recreational Center—*park* NC-3
Coleman Reef—*bar* AK-9
Coleman Ridge—*ridge* KY-4
Coleman Ridge—*ridge* OH-6
Coleman Ridge—*ridge* OK-5
Coleman Ridge—*ridge* OR-9
Coleman Ridge—*ridge* TN-4
Coleman Ridge—*ridge* VA-3
Coleman Ridge—*ridge* WA-9
Coleman Ridge Ch—*church* SC-3
Coleman Rim—*cliff* (2) OR-9
Coleman River—*stream* GA-3
Coleman River—*stream* NC-3
Coleman River Wildlife Mngmt Area—*park* GA-3
Coleman Rsvr—*reservoir* CO-8
Coleman Rsvr—*reservoir* MT-8
Coleman Rsvr—*reservoir* (2) UT-8
Coleman Run—*stream* KY-4
Coleman Run—*stream* PA-2
Coleman Run—*stream* SC-3
Coleman Run—*stream* WV-2
*Colemans* AR-4
*Colemans* NY-2
Colemans—*other* NY-2
**Colemans**—*pop pl* OH-6
Colemans Cem—*cemetery* GA-3
*Coleman Sch* TN-4
Colemans Ch—*church* PA-2
Coleman Sch—*school* CA-9
Coleman Sch—*school* (2) FL-3
Coleman Sch—*school* IL-6
Coleman Sch—*school* IA-7
Coleman Sch—*school* (3) MS-4
Coleman Sch—*school* MO-7
Coleman Sch—*school* NJ-2
Coleman Sch—*school* PA-2
Coleman Sch—*school* (2) SD-7
Coleman Sch—*school* TN-4
Coleman Sch—*school* TX-5
Coleman Sch—*school* VA-3
Coleman Sch—*school* WI-6
Coleman Sch (abondoned)—*school* PA-2
Colemans Chapel—*church* AL-4
Colemans Chapel—*church* GA-3
Colemans Chapel (historical)—*church* AL-4
Coleman Sch (historical)—*school* AL-4
Coleman Sch (historical)—*school* PA-2
Coleman Sch (historical)—*school* TN-4
Coleman Sch Number 2 (historical)—*school* SD-7
Coleman School (historical)—*locale* MO-7
Coleman-Scott House—*hist pl* OR-9
Colemans Creek—*stream* GA-3
Colemans Creek—*stream* NC-3
Colemans Creek—*stream* VA-3
Colemans Crossroads—*locale* SC-3
Colemans Exxon & RV Park—*locale* UT-8
Colemans Failure Chute—*channel* MO-7
*Colemans Falls* VA-3
Colemans Ferry (historical)—*locale* MS-4
*Colemans Hills* MA-1
**Colemans (historical)**—*pop pl* NC-3
Coleman Siding—*locale* PA-2
Colemans Lake—*lake* GA-3
**Colemans Lake**—*pop pl* GA-3
Colemans Lake—*reservoir* VA-3
Colemans Lake Dam—*dam* MS-4
Colemans Landing (historical)—*locale* (2) AL-4
*Coleman Slough* WI-6
Coleman Slough—*stream* IL-6
Coleman Slough—*swamp* MN-6
Colemans Mill—*locale* VA-3
Colemans Mill Crossing—*locale* VA-3
Colemans Mill (historical)—*locale* MS-4
Colemans Millpond—*reservoir* VA-3
**Colemans Mills**—*pop pl* NY-2
**Colemans Mills (Colemans)**—*pop pl* NY-2
Colemans Mills Post Office (historical)—*building* TN-4
*Colemans Point* MA-1
Coleman Spring—*spring* AZ-5
Coleman Spring—*spring* CA-9
Coleman Spring—*spring* CO-8
Coleman Spring—*spring* NV-8
Coleman Spring—*spring* (3) OR-9
Coleman Spring—*spring* TX-5
Coleman Spring Branch—*stream* AL-4
Coleman Spring Branch—*stream* TN-4
Coleman Spring Draw—*valley* TX-5
Colemans Shoals—*bar* AL-4
Colemans Store—*locale* VA-3
Coleman State Wildlife Mngmt Area—*park* MN-6
*Coleman Station* MS-4
Coleman Station—*building* PA-2
**Coleman Station**—*pop pl* NY-2
Colemans Tunnel—*tunnel* VA-3
**Coleman Subdivision**—*pop pl* TN-4
**Colemansville**—*pop pl* KY-4
Coleman Swamp—*swamp* VA-3
Coleman Thankful Ch—*church* SC-3
Coleman Theatre—*hist pl* OK-5
Colemantown—*locale* NJ-2
**Coleman Town**—*pop pl* LA-4
**Coleman Township**—*pop pl* KS-7
**Coleman Township**—*pop pl* NE-7
Coleman Valley—*valley* CA-9
Coleman Valley—*valley* NV-8
Coleman Valley—*valley* OR-9
Coleman Valley Creek—*stream* CA-9
**Colemanville**—*pop pl* PA-2
Colemanville Ch—*church* PA-2
Colemanville Covered Bridge—*hist pl* PA-2
Colemanville Post Office (historical)—*building* PA-2
Coleman Wash—*valley* UT-8
Coleman Weedpatch—*area* WA-9
Coleman-White House—*hist pl* NC-3
Coleman Wildlife Park—*park* MT-8
Coleman Windmill—*locale* (2) TX-5
Coleman-Winston Memorial Bridge—*bridge* TN-4
Cole Meadow—*flat* MA-1
Cole Memorial Park—*cemetery* IL-6
**Cole Mill**—*pop pl* MA-1
Cole Mill Branch—*stream* AL-4
*Cole Mill Creek* MS-4
Cole Mill Pond—*reservoir* MA-1
Cole Mill Pond Dam—*dam* MA-1
Cole Mine (underground)—*mine* AL-4
Cole Mission—*church* AR-4
Cole Motor Car Company—*hist pl* IN-6
Cole Mtn—*summit* (2) AR-4
Cole Mtn—*summit* MA-1
Cole Mtn—*summit* (2) NC-3
Cole Mtn—*summit* OR-9
Cole Mtn—*summit* VA-3
Colen Branch—*stream* KY-4
Colen Sch—*school* MO-7
Cole Number Three—*mine* AZ-5
Colen Williams Bay—*swamp* NC-3
Coleoatchee Creek—*stream* GA-3
Cole Oil Field—*oilfield* TX-5
Cole Park—*park* AZ-5
Cole Park—*park* CO-8
Cole Park—*park* IL-6
Cole Park—*park* NJ-2

Cole Park—park (2) ... TX-5
Cole Park—park ... WI-6
Cole Park Golf Course—locale ... TN-4
Cole Peak—summit ... CA-9
Cole Place—locale ... NM-5
Cole Plain—flat ... NH-1
Cole Point ... VA-3
Cole Point—cape ... FL-3
Cole Point—cape ... ME-1
Cole Point—cape ... MI-6
Cole Point—cape ... WA-9
Cole Point—ridge ... CA-9
Cole Pond ... ME-1
Cole Pond ... MA-1
Cole Pond—lake ... ME-1
Cole Pond—lake ... NH-1
Cole Pond—lake ... VT-1
Cole Post Office (historical)—building ... AL-4
Cole Post Office (historical)—building ... TN-4
Cole Prospect—mine ... TN-4
Coler—locale ... AR-4
Colerain ... PA-2
Colerain—locale ... GA-3
Colerain—other ... PA-2
**Colerain**—pop pl ... NC-3
**Colerain**—pop pl ... OH-6
**Colerain**—pop pl ... PA-2
Colerain, Town of ... MA-1
**Colerain Beach**—pop pl ... NC-3
Colerain Central School ... PA-2
Colerain Ch—church ... OH-6
Colerain Ch—church ... PA-2
Coleraine ... MA-1
Coleraine ... NC-3
**Coleraine**—pop pl ... MN-6
Coleraine, Town of ... MA-1
Coleraine Carnegie Library—hist pl ... MN-6
Coleraine Junction—locale ... MN-6
Coleraine Methodist Episcopal Church—hist pl ... MN-6
Colerain Forge ... PA-2
**Colerain Forge**—pop pl ... PA-2
**Colerain Heights**—pop pl ... OH-6
Colerain Landing—locale ... NC-3
Colerain Park ... PA-2
Colerain Picnic Area—area ... PA-2
Colerain Post Office (historical)—building ... PA-2
Colerain Sch—school ... MI-6
Colerain Sch—school (2) ... OH-6
Colerain (Township of)—fmr MCD ... NC-3
**Colerain (Township of)**—pop pl (3) ... OH-6
**Colerain (Township of)**—pop pl (2) ... PA-2
Colerain Trail—trail ... PA-2
Colerain Works Archeol District—hist pl ... OH-6
Cole Ranch—locale ... CA-9
Cole Ranch—locale ... CO-8
Cole Ranch—locale (2) ... MT-8
Cole Ranch—locale ... NE-7
Cole Ranch—locale ... NV-8
Cole Ranch—locale (2) ... TX-5
Cole Ranch—locale (2) ... WY-8
Colerian Landing—locale ... NC-3
Cole Ridge—bar ... MA-1
Cole Ridge—locale ... AR-4
**Coleridge**—pop pl ... NE-7
**Coleridge**—pop pl ... NC-3
Cole Ridge—ridge ... KY-4
Cole Ridge Ch—church ... AL-4
Coleridge Elem Sch—school ... NC-3
Coleridge Hist Dist—hist pl ... NC-3
Cole Ridge (historical)—locale ... AL-4
Coleridge (Site)—locale ... CA-9
Coleridge (Township of)—fmr MCD ... NC-3
Cole River—stream ... MA-1
Cole River Pond—reservoir ... MA-1
Cole River Pond Dam—dam ... MA-1
Coler Memorial Hosp And Home—hospital ... NY-2
Colers Ordinary ... NC-3
Cole Rsvr—reservoir ... CO-8
Cole Rsvr No. 1—reservoir ... CO-8
Cole Rsvr No. 2—reservoir ... CO-8
Cole Rsvr No. 4—reservoir ... CO-8
Cole Rsvr No. 5—reservoir ... CO-8
Cole Run ... WV-2
Cole Run—stream (4) ... PA-2
Cole Run—stream (3) ... WV-2
Cole Run Falls—falls ... PA-2
Coles ... RI-1
Coles—locale ... ME-1
**Coles**—pop pl ... IL-6
**Coles**—pop pl ... MS-4
**Coles**—pop pl ... PA-2
**Coles**—pop pl ... RI-1
Coles, Samuel, House—hist pl ... NJ-2
Colesaine ... PA-2
Coles Bar—bar ... AL-4
Coles Bay—bay ... MI-6
Coles Bayou—stream ... LA-4
Coles Bayou—stream ... MS-4
Coles Bend Bar (historical)—bar ... AL-4
**Coles Bend (Berrys Store)**—pop pl ... KY-4
Coles Brake—swamp ... AR-4
Coles Branch ... MA-1
Coles Branch—stream ... KY-4
Coles Branch—stream ... LA-4
Coles Branch—stream ... NC-3
Coles Branch—stream ... TN-4
Coles Branch—stream ... TX-5
Coles Bridge—bridge (2) ... AL-4
Coles Bridge—bridge ... OR-9
Cole'S Brook ... MA-1
Coles Brook—stream (2) ... MA-1
Coles Brook—stream ... NJ-2
**Colesburg**—pop pl ... GA-3
**Colesburg**—pop pl ... IA-7
**Colesburg**—pop pl ... KY-4
**Colesburg**—pop pl ... PA-2
**Colesburg**—pop pl ... TN-4
Coles Camp—locale ... NM-5
Coles Campground Ch—church ... KY-4
Coles Canyon—valley ... WY-8
Coles Cem—cemetery (2) ... MO-7
Coles Cem—cemetery ... NC-3
Coles Cem—cemetery ... PA-2
Coles Cem—cemetery ... VA-3
Coles Cem—cemetery ... WI-6
Coles Ch ... AL-4
Cole Sch—school (2) ... CA-9
Cole Sch—school ... ID-8
Cole Sch—school ... KS-7
Cole Sch—school ... ME-1
Cole Sch—school (4) ... MA-1
Cole Sch—school (2) ... MI-6
Cole Sch—school ... MT-8
Cole Sch—school ... OK-5
Cole Sch—school ... TN-4
Cole Sch—school ... VT-1
Cole Sch—school ... WY-8
Cole Sch and Gymnasium—hist pl ... ID-8
Coles Chapel—church (2) ... AL-4
Coles Chapel—church ... AR-4
Coles Chapel—church ... IL-6
Coles Chapel—church ... KY-4
Coles Chapel Ch ... AL-4
Coles Chapel Sch—school ... TN-4
Cole Sch (historical)—school ... MO-7
Cole Sch (historical)—school (2) ... SD-7
Coles Clove—valley ... NY-2
Coles Corner ... IN-6
Coles Corner—cape ... ME-1
Coles Corner—locale ... VT-1
Coles Corner—locale ... WA-9
**Coles Corner**—pop pl ... ME-1
**Coles Corner**—pop pl ... MD-2
**Cole's Corner**—pop pl ... WA-9
Coles Corners ... IN-6
Coles Corners—locale ... NY-2
Coles Corner Sch—school ... WI-6
**Coles (County)**—pop pl ... IL-6
Coles County Courthouse—hist pl ... IL-6
Coles County Memorial Airp—airport ... IL-6
Coles Cove—valley ... NC-3
Coles Cove Ch—church ... NC-3
Coles Creek ... MS-4
Coles Creek—locale ... PA-2
Coles Creek—locale ... VA-3
**Coles Creek**—pop pl ... MS-4
Coles Creek—stream ... IL-6
Coles Creek—stream ... IN-6
Coles Creek—stream (2) ... MD-2
Coles Creek—stream (2) ... MI-6
Coles Creek—stream (3) ... MS-4
Coles Creek—stream ... NY-2
Coles Creek—stream (2) ... PA-2
Coles Creek—stream ... SC-3
Coles Creek—stream ... TX-5
Coles Creek—stream (2) ... VA-3
Coles Creek Access Area—locale ... IL-6
Coles Creek Camping Area—park ... NY-2
Coles Creek Ch—church ... MS-4
Coles Creek Ch—church ... VA-3
Coles Creek Oil Field—oilfield ... MS-4
Coles Creek Sch—school ... MS-4
Coles Crossing—locale ... GA-3
**Coles Crossing**—pop pl ... SC-3
Coles Ferry Access Area—park ... TN-4
Coles Ferry (historical)—crossing ... TN-4
Coles Ferry Post Office (historical)—building ... TN-4
Cole's Five Cypress Farm—hist pl ... CA-9
Coles Flat—flat ... CA-9
Coles Ford Lake—lake ... MS-4
Coles Fork—stream (3) ... KY-4
Coles Gulch—valley ... MT-8
Coles Gully ... LA-4
Cole's Hill—hist pl ... MA-1
Coles Hill—locale ... VA-3
Coles Hill—summit ... ME-1
Coles Hill—summit ... MA-1
Coles Hill—summit ... NY-2
Coles Hill—summit ... VA-3
Coles Hill Cem—cemetery ... NY-2
Coles Hollow—valley ... VA-3
Coles Island ... MS-4
Coles Island ... SC-3
Coles Island—cape ... MA-1
Coles Island—island ... LA-4
Coles Island Number 113 ... MS-4
Coles JHS—school ... TX-5
Coles Knob—summit (2) ... VA-3
Cole's Lake ... MI-6
Coles Lake—lake ... MI-6
Coles Lake—lake ... MN-6
Coles Lake—reservoir ... GA-3
Coles Landing—locale ... MO-7
Coles Ledge—bar ... ME-1
Cole Slough—gut ... OR-9
Cole Slough—gut ... TX-5
Cole Slough—stream ... CA-9
Cole Slough Canal—canal (2) ... CA-9
Coles (Magisterial District)—fmr MCD ... VA-3
Coles Mill—locale ... PA-2
Coles Mill (historical)—locale ... TN-4
Coles Mill Road Dam ... NJ-2
Coles Mountain Fire Trail—trail ... VA-3
Coles Mountain Trail—trail ... WV-2
Coles Mtn—summit ... VA-3
Coles Mtn—summit ... WV-2
Coles Neck ... NJ-2
Coles Neck—cape ... VA-3
Coleson Bayou—gut ... MS-4
Coles Park—park ... NE-7
**Coles Park**—pop pl ... OH-6
Coles Peak—summit ... WI-6
Coles Point—cape ... ME-1
Coles Point—cape ... MS-4
Coles Point—cape ... NY-2
Coles Point—cape ... VA-3
Coles Point—locale ... VA-3
Coles Point Ch—church ... VA-3
Coles Point Neck ... VA-3
Coles Point Public Use Area—park ... MS-4
Coles Pond ... MA-1
Coles Pond—lake ... MA-1
Coles Pond—lake ... NJ-2
Coles Pond—lake ... VT-1
Cole Spring ... AZ-5
Cole Spring ... WY-8
**Cole Spring**—pop pl ... AL-4
Cole Spring—spring (2) ... AL-4
Cole Spring—spring ... AZ-5
Cole Spring—spring (2) ... CA-9
Cole Spring—spring ... GA-3
Cole Spring—spring ... IL-6
Cole Spring—spring ... MO-7
Cole Spring—spring (3) ... NV-8
Cole Spring—spring (2) ... NM-5
Cole Spring—spring (2) ... OR-9
Cole Spring—spring ... UT-8
Cole Spring—spring (2) ... WY-8
Cole Spring Branch—stream ... AL-4
Cole Spring Campground—locale ... CA-9
Cole Spring Ch—church ... KY-4
Cole Spring Ch—church ... MO-7
Cole Spring Creek—stream ... WY-8
Cole Spring Hollow—valley ... MO-7
Cole Spring Run ... PA-2
Cole Springs Cem—cemetery ... TX-5
Cole Spring Wash—stream ... NV-8
**Cole Spur**—pop pl ... AR-4
Cole Spur—ridge ... KY-4
Cole Spur Cem—cemetery ... OK-5
Coles Quarter—cape ... VA-3
Coles Ranch—locale ... WY-8
Coles River ... MA-1
Coles Run ... VA-3
Coles Run—stream (2) ... VA-3
Coles Run—stream (2) ... WV-2
Coles Sch—school ... IL-6
Coles Sch—school ... NY-2
Coles Sch—school ... WI-6
Coles School (historical)—church ... MO-7
Coles Spring—spring ... CA-9
Coles Spring Church ... MS-4
Coles Station ... MA-1
Coles Station—locale ... CA-9
**Coles Store**—pop pl ... TN-4
Coles Store (historical)—locale ... AL-4
Coles Store (historical)—locale ... MS-4
**Coles Subdivision**—pop pl ... MS-4
Coles Summit—summit ... PA-2
Cole Station Sch—school ... AL-4
Colestein ... OR-9
Colestin—locale ... OR-9
Colestine ... OR-9
**Colestine**—pop pl ... OR-9
Colestown ... NJ-2
**Colestown**—pop pl ... NJ-2
Colestown Cem—cemetery ... NJ-2
**Coles Valley**—pop pl ... OR-9
Coles Valley—valley ... OR-9
Coles Valley—valley ... PA-2
Coles Valley—valley ... WI-6
Coles Valley Ch (historical)—church ... PA-2
Coles Valley Creek—stream ... OR-9
Coles Valley Sch—school ... WI-6
Colesville—CDP ... MD-2
**Colesville**—pop pl ... MD-2
**Colesville**—pop pl ... NJ-2
**Colesville**—pop pl ... PA-2
Colesville Gardens ... MD-2
**Colesville Manor**—pop pl ... MD-2
**Colesville Park**—pop pl ... MD-2
Colesville Post Office (historical)—building ... TN-4
Colesville Sch—school ... MD-2
**Colesville (Town of)**—pop pl ... NY-2
Coles Wash—stream ... AZ-5
**Coleta**—pop pl ... AL-4
**Coleta**—pop pl ... IL-6
Cole Tank—reservoir ... NM-5
Cole Temple Ch—church ... AL-4
Coleto Creek ... TX-5
Coleto Creek—stream ... TX-5
Coleto Creek Oil Field—oilfield ... TX-5
Coletoville—locale ... TX-5
**Coletown**—pop pl ... KY-4
**Coletown**—pop pl ... OH-6
**Coletown**—pop pl ... TN-4
Coletown Cemetery ... MS-4
Cole Town District—hist pl ... GA-3
Coletown Missionary Ch—church ... GA-3
Coletown Missionary Ch—church ... TN-4
Cole Township—civil ... MO-7
Cole (Township of)—fmr MCD ... AR-4
Cole Trip Camp—locale ... VA-3
Coletta Mine—mine ... SD-7
Colette Creek ... MN-6
Cole Village—post sta ... ID-8
Coleville ... KS-7
Coleville ... NJ-2
**Coleville**—pop pl ... CA-9
**Coleville**—pop pl ... NC-3
**Coleville**—pop pl (2) ... PA-2
Coleville Cem—cemetery ... MS-4
Coleville Community Hall—building ... MO-7
**Coleville (historical)**—pop pl ... MS-4
Coleville Post Office (historical)—building ... MS-4
Coleville Sch (historical)—school ... MS-4
Colewa Bayou—stream ... LA-4
Colewa Ch—church ... LA-4
Colewa Creek ... LA-4
Cole Watch Tower—hist pl ... WI-6
Cole Well—well (2) ... AZ-5
Cole Well Draw—valley ... TX-5
**Colewood Acres**—pop pl ... NC-3
**Colewood Acres (subdivision)**—pop pl ... NC-3
Coley—locale ... GA-3
Coley Bldg—hist pl ... AL-4
Coley Branch—stream ... KY-4
Coley Branch—stream ... NC-3
Coley Branch—stream ... TN-4
Coley Cem—cemetery ... AL-4
Coley Cem—cemetery ... NC-3
Coley Cem—cemetery ... TN-4
Coley Chapel—church ... AL-4
Coley Creek—stream ... AL-4
Coley Creek—stream (2) ... GA-3
Coley Creek—stream (2) ... NC-3
Coley Creek—stream ... SC-3
Coley Creek—stream ... TN-4
Coley Creek—stream ... TX-5
Coley Creek Cem—cemetery ... TX-5
Coley Creek Sewage Disposal Plant—building ... AL-4
Coley Dam—dam ... AL-4
**Coley Forest (subdivision)**—pop pl ... NC-3
Coley Gap—gap ... NC-3
Coley Island—island ... MS-4
Coley Knob—summit ... AR-4
Coley Lake ... MI-6
Coley Lake—reservoir ... AL-4
**Coley Lakes (subdivision)**—pop pl ... NC-3
Coley Pond—reservoir ... NC-3
Coley Pond Dam—dam ... NC-3
Coleys Chapel—church ... AR-4
Coley Sch (historical)—school ... AL-4
Coleys Crossroads ... NC-3
Coleys Lake—reservoir ... AL-4
Coley Springs Ch—church ... NC-3
Coleysville ... TX-5
Coleytown Cem—cemetery ... CT-1
Coleytown Run—stream ... VA-3
Coleytown Sch—school ... CT-1
Coleyville—locale ... TX-5
Colfax ... KS-7
Colfax ... MS-4
Colfax—fmr MCD ... NE-7
Colfax—locale ... KY-4
Colfax—locale ... MI-6
Colfax—locale ... NM-5
Colfax—locale ... PA-2
Colfax—locale ... TX-5
**Colfax**—pop pl ... AR-4
**Colfax**—pop pl ... CA-9
**Colfax**—pop pl ... FL-3
**Colfax**—pop pl ... GA-3
**Colfax**—pop pl ... IL-6
**Colfax**—pop pl ... IN-6
**Colfax**—pop pl ... IA-7
**Colfax**—pop pl ... LA-4
**Colfax**—pop pl ... NC-3
**Colfax**—pop pl ... ND-7
**Colfax**—pop pl ... OH-6
**Colfax**—pop pl ... WA-9
**Colfax**—pop pl ... WV-2
**Colfax**—pop pl ... WI-6
Colfax, Mount—summit ... NY-2
Colfax Ave Sch—school ... CA-9
Colfax Cem—cemetery ... IA-7
Colfax Cem—cemetery ... MI-6
Colfax Cem—cemetery ... WA-9
Colfax Center Cem—cemetery ... IA-7
Colfax Center Ch—church ... IA-7
Colfax Ch—church ... KS-7
Colfax Ch—church ... MI-6
Colfax Corner—locale ... SD-7
Colfax County ... MS-4
**Colfax (County)**—pop pl ... NM-5
Colfax County Courthouse—hist pl ... NE-7
Colfax County Courthouse—hist pl ... NM-5
Colfax County Courthouse in Springer—hist pl ... NM-5
Colfax Creek—stream ... IL-6
Colfax Drain—canal ... MI-6
Colfax Elem Sch—hist pl ... PA-2
Colfax Elem Sch—school ... NC-3
Colfax Elem Sch—school (2) ... PA-2
Colfax Gulch—valley ... MT-8
Colfax Hill—summit ... CA-9
Colfax Lookout Tower—locale ... LA-4
Colfax Mine—mine ... CO-8
Colfax-Palouse (CCD)—cens area ... WA-9
Colfax Peak—summit ... WA-9
Colfax Public Hunting Area—area ... IA-7
Colfax Road Park—park ... NJ-2
Colfax Sch ... PA-2
Colfax Sch—school ... CO-8
Colfax Sch—school ... IN-6
Colfax Sch—school ... MI-6
Colfax Sch (historical)—school ... MS-4
Colfax Spring—locale ... CA-9
Colfax-Summit (CCD)—cens area ... CA-9
Colfax Theater—hist pl ... IN-6
Colfax Townhall—building ... IA-7
**Colfax (Town of)**—pop pl ... WI-6
Colfax Township—civil ... MO-7
Colfax Township—fmr MCD (6) ... IA-7
**Colfax Township**—pop pl (3) ... KS-7
**Colfax Township**—pop pl (3) ... MO-7
**Colfax Township**—pop pl ... ND-7
Colfax Township Hall—locale (2) ... IA-7
Colfax (Township of)—fmr MCD ... NC-3
**Colfax (Township of)**—pop pl ... IL-6
**Colfax (Township of)**—pop pl ... IN-6
**Colfax (Township of)**—pop pl (5) ... MI-6
**Colfax (Township of)**—pop pl ... MN-6
Colfelt Branch—stream ... MO-7
Colfer Sloughs—gut ... CO-8
Colfred—locale ... AZ-5
Colfred Airp—airport ... AZ-5
Colfred Floodway—channel ... AZ-5
Colf Sch—school ... MI-6
**Colgan**—pop pl ... ND-7
Colgan Creek Flood Control Channel—canal ... CA-9
Colgan Sch—school ... IL-6
Colgan Sch Number 10—school ... IN-6
Colgate—locale ... MT-8
**Colgate**—pop pl ... ND-7
**Colgate**—pop pl ... WI-6
Colgate—uninc pl ... MD-2
Colgate—uninc pl ... NY-2
Colgate, Robert, House—hist pl ... NY-2
**Colgate Creek**—pop pl ... MD-2
Colgate Creek—stream ... ID-8
Colgate Creek—stream ... MD-2
Colgate-Jersey City—airport ... NJ-2
Colgate Lake—reservoir ... NY-2
Colgate Park—park ... IN-6
Colgate-Piscataway—airport ... NJ-2
Colgate Powerhouse—locale ... CA-9
Colgate Rochester Divinity Sch—school ... NY-2
Colgate Sch—school ... IN-6
Colgate Sch (historical)—school ... PA-2
**Colgate Township**—pop pl ... ND-7
Colgate Tunnel—tunnel ... CA-9
Colgate Univ—school ... NY-2
Colgate Warm Springs—spring ... ID-8
Colgin Hill—hist pl ... AL-4
Colgins Island (historical)—island ... AL-4
**Colgrade**—pop pl ... LA-4
Colgrade Lookout Tower—locale ... LA-4
Colgrove Branch—stream ... CA-9
Colgrove Sch Number 1—school ... ND-7
Colgrove Sch Number 2—school ... ND-7
Colic Bayou—gut ... WI-6
Colic Mtn—summit ... WV-2
Colicum Reservior ... MA-1
Colicum Reservoir ... MA-1
Colie Flat—flat ... UT-8
**Colier**—pop pl ... VA-3
Colier Hardy Quarters (historical)—locale ... MS-4
Colier Spring—spring ... CA-9
Colie Wash ... UT-8
Colils Hill Ch of Christ Holiness—church ... MS-4
Colima—locale ... GA-3
**Colima**—pop pl ... CA-9
**Colina**—pop pl ... AL-4
Colina del Sol Park—park ... CA-9
Colinas de la Parguera—locale ... PR-3
Colin Creek—stream ... AK-9
Coline, Bayou—gut ... LA-4
Coline Oil Field—oilfield ... TX-5
Colin Field—park ... PA-2
**Coling**—pop pl ... VA-3
Coling Bible Chapel—church ... VA-3
Colington—locale ... NC-3
Colington Bay ... NC-3
Colington Creek—gut ... NC-3
Colington Cut—gut ... NC-3
Colington Cut Ditch ... NC-3
Colington Ditch ... NC-3
Colington Island—island ... NC-3
Colington Island Shoal—bar ... NC-3
Colin Kelly JHS—school ... OR-9
Colins Chapel Cem—cemetery ... OH-6
Coliseum—hist pl ... OH-6
Coliseum—pillar ... UT-8
Coliseum Shop Ctr—locale ... NC-3
Coliseum Street Sch—school ... CA-9
Coliseum Theater—hist pl ... WA-9
Coliseum Theatre—hist pl ... MS-4
Colita—locale ... TX-5
Colita Ch—church ... TX-5
Colitown Junction—locale ... KY-4
Colkins Neck—cape ... NC-3
Colk-Kail Creek ... VA-3
Collabar—locale ... NY-2
Collabergh Pond ... NY-2
Collaberg Lake ... NY-2
Collaberg Mtn—summit ... NY-2
Collaberg Pond ... NY-2
Colladay Bay—bay ... WI-6
Colladay Point—cape ... WI-6
Collado—locale (2) ... TX-5
Collage Hill Ch—church ... MS-4
Collage Shelter Site—hist pl ... CO-8
Collaliekishi Creek ... MS-4
Collamar Ch (historical)—church ... SD-7
**Collamer**—pop pl ... IN-6
**Collamer**—pop pl (2) ... NY-2
Collamer P. O. (historical)—building ... PA-2
Collamore Ledge—bar ... MA-1
Collamores Ledge ... MA-1
Collano—locale ... KS-7
Collapsed Barn Cave—cave ... TN-4
Collar and Elbow Basin—basin ... NV-8
Collar and Elbow Spring—spring (2) ... NV-8
Collar Back ... NY-2
Collarbone Branch—stream ... NC-3
Collarbone Creek ... IN-6
Collar Brook—stream ... ME-1
Collar Brook—stream ... MA-1
Collar Creek—stream ... MI-6
Collard Creek ... TX-5
Collard Creek—stream ... MI-6
Collard Creek—stream ... OR-9
Collard Creek—stream ... TX-5
Collard Lake—lake ... OR-9
Collard Lake—lake ... TX-5
Collard Pond—lake ... AL-4
Collard Ranch—locale ... CO-8
Collar Draw—valley ... ND-7
Collard Valley Ch—church ... GA-3
Collard Woods—woods ... WA-9
Collar Gulch—valley ... MT-8
Collar Hollow—valley ... WV-2
Collar Peak—summit ... MT-8
Collary Cove—valley ... NC-3
Collawash Mtn—summit ... OR-9
Collawash River—stream ... OR-9
Collayomi—civil ... CA-9
Collayomi Valley—valley ... CA-9
Coll Bay ... NY-2
Collbran—locale ... AL-4
**Collbran**—pop pl ... CO-8
Collbran Gap—gap (2) ... AL-4
Colleague Pond—lake ... NH-1
Colle Branch—stream ... VA-3
Colle Canyon—valley ... NM-5
Collector Ledge—bar ... ME-1
Col Ledyard Cem—cemetery ... CT-1
**Colleen**—pop pl ... VA-3
College ... UT-8
**College**—pop pl ... AK-9
**College**—pop pl ... CO-8
**College**—pop pl ... MO-7
**College**—pop pl ... PA-2
**College**—pop pl ... TN-4
**College**—pop pl ... UT-8
College—post sta ... PR-3
College—uninc pl ... AZ-5
College—uninc pl ... KS-7
College—uninc pl ... MS-4
College—uninc pl ... NY-2
College—uninc pl ... NC-3
College—uninc pl ... PA-2
College—uninc pl ... TN-4
College—uninc pl ... VA-3
College A—post sta ... PA-2
**College Acres**—pop pl ... SC-3
**College Acres (subdivision)**—pop pl ... NC-3
**College Ave**—pop pl ... IL-6
College Ave Baptist Ch—church ... IN-6
College Ave First Baptist Ch—church ... AL-4
College Ave Hist Dist—hist pl (2) ... WI-6
College Ave Sch—school ... AL-4
College Ave Sch—school ... GA-3
College Block Bldg—hist pl ... IA-7
College Block-Lisbon Block—hist pl ... ME-1
**Collegeboro**—pop pl ... GA-3
College Branch—stream ... MS-4
College Branch—stream ... NC-3
College Bridge—bridge ... NJ-2
College Brook—stream ... NH-1
College Camp—locale ... CA-9
College Campus—uninc pl ... KY-4
College Cave—cave ... TN-4
College Cem—cemetery ... IA-7
College Cem—cemetery ... MA-1
College Cem—cemetery ... TN-4
**College Center**—pop pl ... CA-9
College Center Plaza (Shop Ctr)—locale ... FL-3
College Church—hist pl ... MS-4
**College City**—pop pl ... AR-4
**College City**—pop pl ... CA-9
College Club House and Gymnasium—hist pl ... MI-6
**College Corner**—pop pl (4) ... IN-6
**College Corner**—pop pl ... OH-6
College Corner Branch—stream ... IN-6
College Corner Cem—cemetery ... IN-6
College Corner Elem Sch—school ... IN-6
College Corners—locale ... IL-6
College Corner Sch—school (3) ... IL-6
College Corner (sta.) ... IN-6
College Corner Station ... IN-6
**College Court (subdivision)**—pop pl ... NC-3
College Cove—bay ... CA-9
College Creek ... TX-5
College Creek—stream (2) ... AK-9
College Creek—stream ... GA-3
College Creek—stream ... IA-7
College Creek—stream ... KS-7
College Creek—stream ... MD-2
College Creek—stream ... MO-7
College Creek—stream ... OH-6
College Creek—stream ... OR-9
College Creek—stream ... TN-4
College Creek—stream ... TX-5
College Creek—stream ... VA-3
College Creek Ranger Station—locale ... OR-9
**College Crest**—pop pl ... IN-6
**College Crest**—pop pl ... OR-9
**Collegedale**—pop pl ... TN-4
Collegedale Gap—gap ... TN-4
Collegedale Memorial Park—cemetery ... TN-4
Collegedale Municipal Airp—airport ... TN-4
Collegedale Post Office—building ... TN-4
**College Downs (subdivision)**—pop pl ... NC-3
College Estates—unincpl ... MD-2
College Farm—locale ... NH-1
College Farm—other ... KY-4
College Field—park ... PA-2
College Fiord—bay ... AK-9
College (Fort Valley State Coll)—school ... GA-3
**College Gardens**—pop pl ... CA-9
College Gardens—unincpl ... MD-2
College Glacier—glacier ... AK-9
College Green—locale ... MD-2
College Green Park—park ... IA-7
College Green Pasture—flat ... KS-7
**College Grove**—pop pl (2) ... TN-4
College Grove Center—post sta ... CA-9
College Grove Ch (historical)—church ... AL-4
College Grove Church ... TN-4
College Grove Elem Sch—school ... TN-4
College Grove Methodist Church—hist pl ... TN-4
Collegegrove Post Office ... TN-4
College Grove Post Office—building ... TN-4
College Grove Sch—school ... IL-6
**College Grove (subdivision)**—pop pl ... AL-4
College Hall—hist pl ... IA-7
College Hall—hist pl ... OH-6
College Hall—hist pl ... VT-1
College Hall, Univ Of Pennsylvania—hist pl ... PA-2
College Hall, Wilmington College—hist pl ... OH-6
College Head—valley ... FL-3
College Heights ... CO-8
College Heights ... SC-3
**College Heights**—pop pl ... AR-4
**College Heights**—pop pl (3) ... CA-9
**College Heights**—pop pl ... GA-3
**College Heights**—pop pl ... IL-6
**College Heights**—pop pl ... MD-2
**College Heights**—pop pl ... PA-2
College Heights—unincpl ... CA-9
College Heights—unincpl ... GA-3
College Heights—unincpl ... KY-4
College Heights—unincpl ... TN-4
College Heights Baptist Ch—church ... TN-4
College Heights Cem—cemetery ... TN-4
College Heights Ch—church ... FL-3
College Heights Ch—church ... KY-4
College Heights Ch—church (2) ... TX-5
College Heights Ch (historical)—church ... TN-4
**College Heights Estates**—pop pl ... MD-2
College Heights Park—park ... OR-9
College Heights Sch—school ... CA-9
College Heights Sch—school ... PA-2
College Heights Sch—school (2) ... TX-5
**College Heights (subdivision)**—pop pl ... TN-4
**College Heights Subdivision**—pop pl ... UT-8
College Hill ... IN-6
Collegehill ... MS-4
College Hill ... OH-6
College Hill ... PA-2
College Hill—hist pl ... GA-3
College Hill—locale ... AR-4
College Hill—locale ... KY-4
College Hill—locale ... OH-6
College Hill—locale ... TX-5
**College Hill**—pop pl ... MS-4
**College Hill**—pop pl (2) ... OH-6
**College Hill**—pop pl ... OR-9
**College Hill**—pop pl ... PA-2
**College Hill**—pop pl ... TN-4
College Hill—summit ... AL-4
College Hill—summit ... CT-1
College Hill—summit ... IN-6
College Hill—summit ... MA-1
College Hill—summit ... MS-4
College Hill—summit ... MO-7
College Hill—summit ... NY-2
College Hill—summit ... TN-4
College Hill—summit ... TX-5
College Hill—summit ... VT-1
College Hill—summit (2) ... WV-2
College Hill Cem—cemetery ... AR-4
College Hill Cem—cemetery ... IL-6
College Hill Cem—cemetery ... IN-6
College Hill Cem—cemetery ... KS-7
College Hill Cem—cemetery (2) ... MS-4
College Hill Cem—cemetery ... MO-7
College Hill Ch—church ... AL-4
College Hill Ch—church ... IN-6
College Hill Ch—church ... MS-4
College Hill Ch—church ... MO-7
College Hill Ch—church ... OH-6
College Hill Ch—church ... TN-4
College Hill Ch—church ... WV-2
College Hill Ch (historical)—church ... MS-4
College Hill Christian Methodist Episcopal Church ... MS-4
**Collegehill (College Hill)**—pop pl ... AR-4
College Hill Community Center—building ... TN-4
College Hill District—hist pl ... KY-4

College Hill Elementary School ... TN-4
College Hill Elem Sch—school ... KS-7
**College Hill Heights (subdivision)**—pop pl ... MS-4
College Hill Hist Dist—hist pl ... AL-4
College Hill Hist Dist—hist pl ... NE-7
College Hill Hist Dist—hist pl ... RI-1
College Hill Hist Dist—hist pl ... TN-4
College Hill Hosp—hospital ... OH-6
College Hill Junction ... OH-6
College Hill Park—park ... KS-7
College Hill Park—park ... NY-2
College Hill Park—park ... TX-5
College Hill Presbyterian Ch—church ... MS-4
**College Hills**—pop pl ... LA-4
**College Hills**—pop pl ... OH-6
College Hill Sch—school ... AR-4
College Hill Sch—school ... FL-3
College Hill Sch—school ... IL-6
College Hill Sch—school ... KS-7
College Hill Sch—school (2) ... NE-7
College Hill Sch—school ... OH-6
College Hill Sch—school (3) ... TN-4
College Hill Sch—school ... TX-5
College Hill Sch (historical)—school ... MS-4
College Hill Sch (historical)—school ... MO-7
College Hill Sch (historical)—school (3) ... TN-4
**College Hills (subdivision)**—pop pl ... AL-4
**College Hills (subdivision)**—pop pl ... TN-4
College Hill Station—locale ... MS-4
**College Hill (subdivision)**—pop pl ... MA-1
College Hill Town Hall—hist pl ... OH-6
College Home/Smith Hall—hist pl ... GA-3
College HS—school ... OK-5
College Inn Bar—hist pl ... WY-8
College Island—island ... ME-1
College Knob Sch—school ... NE-7
College Lake—lake ... AL-4
College Lake—lake ... CA-9
College Lake—lake ... LA-4
College Lake—reservoir ... AL-4
College Lake—reservoir ... CO-8
College Lake—reservoir ... NC-3
College Lake—reservoir ... TX-5
College Lake—reservoir ... VA-3
College Lake Dam—dam ... AL-4
College Lake Dam—dam ... NC-3
College Lake (dry)—lake ... CA-9
College Lakes Elem Sch—school ... NC-3
**College Lakes (subdivision)**—pop pl ... NC-3
College Landing—hist pl ... VA-3
College Landing—other ... MI-6
College (Magisterial District)—fmr MCD ... VA-3
College Mall Shop Ctr—locale ... IN-6
College Manor Chapel—church ... FL-3
**College Meadows**—pop pl ... IN-6
College Memorial Park Cem—cemetery ... TX-5
**College Misericordia**—pop pl ... PA-2
College Mound—locale ... TX-5
**College Mound**—pop pl ... MO-7
College Mound Sch—school ... MO-7
College Mtn—summit ... MD-2
College Oaks Sch—school ... LA-4
College Observatory—building ... AZ-5
College of Boca Raton—school ... FL-3
College of Charleston—hist pl ... SC-3
College Of Charleston—school ... SC-3
College of Eastern Utah—school ... UT-8
College of Emporia ... KS-7
College of Ganado—school ... AZ-5
College of Great Falls—school ... MT-8
College of Guam—school ... GU-9
College of Human Services—school ... FL-3
College of Idaho—school ... ID-8
College Of Mount Saint Joseph—school ... OH-6
College of Mount Saint Vincent—school ... NY-2
College Of New Rochelle—school ... NY-2
College of Notre Dame—school ... CA-9
College of Saint Albert—school ... CA-9
College of Saint Catherine—school ... MN-6
College of Saint Elizabeth—school ... NJ-2
College of Saint Francis—school ... IL-6
College Of Saint Rose—school ... NY-2
College of Saint Teresa—school ... MN-6
College of Saint Teresa—school ... MO-7
College of Santa Fe—school ... NM-5
College of Southern Utah—school ... UT-8
College of Steubenville, The—school ... OH-6
College of the Albermarle—school ... NC-3
College of the City of New York—hist pl ... NY-2
College Of The Desert—school ... CA-9
College of the Ozarks—school ... AR-4
College of the Palm Beaches—school ... FL-3
College of The Redwoods—school ... CA-9
College of the Sequoias—school ... CA-9
College of The Southwest—school ... NM-5
College of the Virgin Islands—school ... VI-3
College Of William And Mary—school ... VA-3
College of Wooster—hist pl ... OH-6
College Of Wooster—school ... OH-6
College (Oklahoma State University)—uninc pl ... OK-5
College Park ... IL-6
College Park ... MI-6
College Park—locale ... FL-3
College Park—park ... CA-9
College Park—park ... MN-6
College Park—park ... MS-4
College Park—park ... SD-7
**College Park**—pop pl ... CA-9
**College Park**—pop pl ... DE-2
**College Park**—pop pl (3) ... FL-3
**College Park**—pop pl ... GA-3
**College Park**—pop pl ... MD-2
**College Park**—pop pl ... NY-2
**College Park**—pop pl (2) ... PA-2
**College Park**—pop pl ... TN-4
**College Park**—pop pl (3) ... VA-3
**College Park**—pop pl ... PR-3
College Park—uninc pl ... CA-9
College Park—uninc pl ... FL-3
College Park—uninc pl ... NC-3
College Park—uninc pl ... VA-3
College Park Airport—hist pl ... MD-2
College Park Baptist Ch—church ... FL-3
College Park (CCD)—cens area (2) ... GA-3
College Park Cem—cemetery ... GA-3
College Park Ch—church ... FL-3
College Park Ch—church ... IN-6
College Park Ch—church (2) ... NC-3
College Park Ch of God—church ... FL-3
College Park Elem Sch—school ... MS-4
College Park Elem Sch—school ... NC-3
**College Park Estates**—pop pl ... TN-4
College Park HS—school ... CA-9
College Park JHS—school ... NC-3
College Park Mall Shop Ctr—locale ... MS-4
**College Park North (subdivision)**—pop pl ... NC-3
College Park Sch—school (2) ... CA-9
College Park Sch—school ... FL-3
College Park Sch—school ... MD-2
College Park Shop Ctr—locale (2) ... AZ-5
College Park Shop Ctr—locale (2) ... FL-3
**College Park South (subdivision)**—pop pl ... NC-3
**College Park (subdivision)**—pop pl (2) ... AZ-5
**College Park (subdivision)**—pop pl (2) ... NC-3
College Park United Methodist Ch—church ... FL-3
College Park View Cem—cemetery ... GA-3
**College Park Woods**—pop pl ... MD-2
College Peaks—summit ... AZ-5
**College Place**—pop pl ... WA-9
College Place Sch—school ... MT-8
College Plaza—post sta ... CA-9
College Plaza (Shop Ctr)—locale (2) ... FL-3
College Plaza Shop Ctr—locale (2) ... NC-3
College Plaza (Shop Ctr)—post sta ... FL-3
College Plaze Shop Ctr—locale ... TN-4
College Point—cape ... AK-9
College Point—cape ... FL-3
College Point—cape ... LA-4
College Point—cape ... NY-2
**College Point**—pop pl ... FL-3
**College Point**—pop pl ... NY-2
College Point Reef—bar ... NY-2
College Point Shore Front Park—park ... NY-2
College Pond—lake ... MA-1
Collegeport—locale ... TX-5
Collegeport Cem—cemetery ... TX-5
College Post Office (historical)—building ... TN-4
College Road Baptist Ch—church ... FL-3
College Rock—summit ... MA-1
College (RR name Berea College)—uninc pl ... KY-4
College Run—stream ... VA-3
College Sch—school ... IL-6
College School ... UT-8
Colleges of The Seneca—locale ... NY-2
College (Southeastern)—uninc pl ... LA-4
College Spring—spring ... AL-4
**College Springs**—pop pl ... IA-7
**College Springs**—pop pl ... OH-6
College Spur—uninc pl ... SC-3
College Square Elem Sch—school ... PA-2
College Square Hist Dist—hist pl ... IA-7
College Square Mall (Shop Ctr)—locale ... IA-7
College Square Shop Ctr—locale ... CA-9
College Square Shop Ctr—locale ... TN-4
College Station ... AR-4
College Station—locale ... FL-3
College Station—locale ... PA-2
College Station—locale ... TN-4
**College Station**—pop pl ... AR-4
**College Station**—pop pl ... TX-5
College Station Cem—cemetery ... TX-5
College Station (Genevia) ... AR-4
College Station Sch—school ... AR-4
College Street Baptist Ch—church ... TN-4
College Street Bridge—hist pl ... KY-4
College Street Ch—church ... OH-6
College Street Ch of Christ—church ... TN-4
College Street Hist Dist—hist pl ... AL-4
College Street Hist Dist—hist pl (2) ... KY-4
College Street Hist Dist—hist pl ... NC-3
College Street Hist Dist—hist pl ... SC-3
College Street Presbyterian Church—hist pl ... KY-4
College Street Sch—school (3) ... GA-3
College Street Sch—school ... KY-4
College Street Sch—school ... SC-3
College Street Sch—school ... TN-4
**College (subdivision)**—pop pl ... PA-2
College Swamp—swamp ... ME-1
College Swamp Brook—stream ... ME-1
**Collegetown**—pop pl ... LA-4
**College Town**—pop pl ... MI-6
College Town—uninc pl ... LA-4
College Township—fmr MCD ... IA-7
**College (Township of)**—pop pl ... OH-6
**College (Township of)**—pop pl ... PA-2
College Town Shop Ctr—locale ... NJ-2
Collegetown Shop Ctr—locale ... NC-3
Collegeview—obs name ... NE-7
**College View**—pop pl ... CO-8
**College View**—pop pl ... IL-6
**College View**—pop pl ... MD-2
**College View**—pop pl ... NE-7
**College View**—pop pl ... TN-4
College View—uninc pl ... NC-3
College View Acad—school ... NE-7
College View Cem—cemetery ... NE-7
College View Ch of Christ—church ... AL-4
College View Park—park ... NE-7
College View Public Library—hist pl ... NE-7
College View Sch—school ... CA-9
College View Sch—school ... CO-8
**College View (subdivision)**—pop pl ... MS-4
**College View (subdivision)**—pop pl ... NC-3
College Village Shop Ctr—locale ... NC-3
**College Village (subdivision)**—pop pl ... NC-3
Collegeville ... PA-2
**Collegeville**—pop pl ... AR-4
**Collegeville**—pop pl ... CA-9
**Collegeville**—pop pl ... IN-6
**Collegeville**—pop pl ... MN-6
**Collegeville**—pop pl ... PA-2
Collegeville Borough—civil ... PA-2
Collegeville Shop Ctr—locale ... PA-2
Collegeville (Township of)—civ div ... MN-6
Collegeville-Trappe HS—school ... PA-2
Collegeville-Trappe Sch—school ... PA-2
**College Vista (subdivision)**—pop pl ... MS-4
**College Ward**—pop pl ... UT-8
College (Washington State University)—school ... WA-9
College (Western Maryland College)—uninc pl ... MD-2
College Women's Club—hist pl ... CA-9
College Wood Elem Sch—school ... IN-6
Collegewood Sch—school ... CA-9
**College Woods (subdivision)**—pop pl ... AL-4
Collegiate HS—school ... VA-3
Collegiate Peaks Campground—locale ... CO-8
Collegiate Sch—school (2) ... VA-3
Collen Brook—stream ... PA-2
Collen Brook Farm—hist pl ... PA-2
Collens Landing—locale ... MI-6
Collen's Pond ... GA-3
Coller, Julius A., House—hist pl ... MN-6
Coller Cem—cemetery ... MA-1
Collet Lake ... MN-6
**Colleton**—pop pl ... SC-3
**Colleton (County)**—pop pl ... SC-3
Colleton County Courthouse—hist pl ... SC-3
Colleton Neck—cape ... SC-3
Colleton River—stream ... SC-3
Collets Canyon ... UT-8
Colletsville ... NC-3
Collett—locale ... IA-7
**Collett**—pop pl ... IN-6
Collett Camp Branch—stream ... NC-3
Collett Cem—cemetery ... IN-6
Collett Cem—cemetery ... KY-4
Collett Cem—cemetery ... MO-7
Collett Cem—cemetery ... OK-5
Collett Cem—cemetery ... WV-2
Collett Creek ... WY-8
Collett Creek—stream ... KS-7
Collett Creek—stream ... MN-6
Collett Creek—stream ... NC-3
Collett Creek—stream ... WY-8
Collett Drain ... WY-8
**Collettes Grove**—pop pl ... NH-1
Collett Flat—flat ... WY-8
Collett Gap—gap ... WV-2
Collett Gap Run—stream ... WV-2
Collett Lake—lake ... MN-6
Collet Top—summit ... UT-8
Collett Orphanage—school ... IN-6
Collett Park ... IN-6
Collett Park—hist pl ... IN-6
Collett Park—park ... IN-6
Collett Park Sch—school ... NM-5
Collett Pond—lake ... IN-6
Collett Ridge—ridge ... NC-3
Collett Sch—school ... CA-9
Collett Sch—school ... IL-6
Collett Sch—school ... IN-6
Colletts Hill—summit ... KY-4
Collett Springs—spring ... TX-5
Collett Street Recreation Center—park ... NC-3
**Collettsville**—pop pl ... NC-3
Collettsville Sch—school ... NC-3
Collett Wash ... UT-8
Collet Wash ... UT-8
Colley—locale ... VA-3
**Colley**—pop pl ... LA-4
**Colley**—pop pl ... PA-2
Colley, Peter, Tavern and Barn—hist pl ... PA-2
Colley Branch—stream ... AR-4
Colley Cem—cemetery ... GA-3
Colley Cem—cemetery ... OK-5
Colley Cem—cemetery ... TN-4
Colley Cem—cemetery ... VA-3
Colley Creek ... KY-4
Colley Creek—stream ... MT-8
Colley Creek—stream ... TX-5
Colley Elem Sch—school ... AL-4
Colley Fork—stream ... KY-4
Colley Gulch—valley ... CA-9
Colley Hill—summit ... VT-1
Colley Hollow—valley ... MO-7
Colley Lake—lake ... MI-6
Colley Lake—lake ... MT-8
Colley Lake—reservoir ... AL-4
Colley Lake—reservoir ... GA-3
Colley Pond ... AL-4
Colley Pond Dam—dam ... AL-4
Colleys Brook ... NJ-2
Colley Swamp—stream ... VA-3
**Colley (Township of)**—pop pl ... PA-2
**Colleyville**—pop pl ... TX-5
Colley Wright Brook—stream ... ME-1
Collicon Lake—lake ... LA-4
Collicum Pond ... MA-1
Collicut Brook—stream ... ME-1
Collidge, Mount—summit ... SD-7
Collidge Sch—school ... MI-6
Collie Branch—stream ... LA-4
Collie Cem—cemetery (2) ... KY-4
Collie Cem—cemetery ... VA-3
Collie Creek—stream ... ID-8
Collie Flat—flat ... CA-9
Collie Hollow—valley ... MO-7
Collie Hollow Cem—cemetery ... MO-7
Collie Lake—lake ... ID-8
Collier ... MS-4
Collier ... SC-3
Collier—locale ... GA-3
Collier—locale ... PA-2
Collier—locale ... TX-5
Collier—locale ... VA-3
**Collier**—pop pl ... CA-9
**Collier**—pop pl ... PA-2
**Collier**—pop pl ... VA-3
Collier—uninc pl ... CA-9
Collier Bar—bar ... OR-9
Collier Bay—bay ... FL-3
Collier Bend—bend ... TN-4
Collier Bluff—cliff ... MO-7
Collier Branch ... TN-4
Collier Branch—stream (3) ... AL-4
Collier Branch—stream (2) ... MO-7
Collier Branch—stream (2) ... TN-4
Collier Branch—stream ... VA-3
Collier Bridge—bridge ... AL-4
Collier Bridge—locale ... NY-2
Collier Brook—stream ... CT-1
Collier Butte—summit ... OR-9
Collier Canyon—valley ... CA-9
Collier Cave ... AL-4
Collier Cave—cave ... AL-4
Collier Cave—cave ... TN-4
Collier Cem ... TN-4
Collier Cem—cemetery (6) ... AL-4
Collier Cem—cemetery ... AR-4
Collier Cem—cemetery (2) ... GA-3
Collier Cem—cemetery (2) ... IL-6
Collier Cem—cemetery (2) ... IN-6
Collier Cem—cemetery ... KY-4
Collier Cem—cemetery ... ME-1
Collier Cem—cemetery ... MI-6
Collier Cem—cemetery (2) ... MS-4
Collier Cem—cemetery (2) ... MO-7
Collier Cem—cemetery (10) ... TN-4
Collier Cem—cemetery ... TX-5
Collier Cem—cemetery ... VA-3
Collier Cemeteries—cemetery ... TN-4
Collier Ch—church ... GA-3
Collier City—CDP ... FL-3
Collier City—other ... FL-3
Collier City North ... FL-3
Collier Cone—summit ... OR-9
Collier Coulee—valley ... WA-9
**Collier County**—pop pl ... FL-3
Collier County Free Public Library—building ... FL-3
Collier County Tower—tower ... FL-3
Collier County Vocational-Technical Center—school ... FL-3
Collier Cove—basin ... CA-9
Collier Creek ... TX-5
Collier Creek ... VA-3
Collier Creek—stream (2) ... AL-4
Collier Creek—stream ... AR-4
Collier Creek—stream ... CO-8
Collier Creek—stream ... IL-6
Collier Creek—stream ... MD-2
Collier Creek—stream ... MI-6
Collier Creek—stream (2) ... MO-7
Collier Creek—stream ... OR-9
Collier Creek—stream ... TX-5
Collier Creek Ch—church ... KY-4
Collier-Crichlow House—hist pl ... TN-4
Collier Ditch—canal ... CO-8
Collier Ditch—canal (2) ... IN-6
Collier Draw—valley ... NM-5
Collier Draw—valley ... TX-5
Collier Draw—valley ... UT-8
**Collier Estates (subdivision)**—pop pl ... FL-3
Collier Glacier—glacier ... OR-9
Collier Glacier View—locale ... OR-9
Collier Hill—ridge ... NM-5
Collier Hill—summit ... AL-4
Collier Hill—summit ... TN-4
Collier Hole—bend ... UT-8
Collier Hollow—valley ... MD-2
Collier Hollow—valley ... PA-2
Collier Hollow—valley (2) ... TN-4
Collier Hollow—valley ... TX-5
Collier Hollow—valley ... UT-8
Collier House—hist pl ... AR-4
Collie Ridge—ridge ... KY-4
Collier Island—island ... NY-2
Collier JHS—school ... CA-9
Collier-Jones Cem—cemetery ... TN-4
Collier Lake—lake ... AL-4
Collier Lake—lake ... MN-6
Collier Lake—lake ... NE-7
Collier Lake—reservoir ... TN-4
Collier Lake Dam—dam ... MS-4
Collier Landing—locale ... TN-4
Collier Landing (historical)—locale ... AL-4
Collier-Lane-Crichlow House—hist pl ... TN-4
Collier Ledge—bar ... MA-1
Collier Manor-Cresthaven—CDP ... FL-3
**Collier Manor (subdivision)**—pop pl ... FL-3
Collier Memorial Garden—cemetery ... KY-4
Collier Mesa—summit ... TX-5
Collier Mill—locale ... VA-3
Collier Mtn—summit ... AR-4
Collier Mtn—summit ... CO-8
Collier Mtn—summit ... MD-2
Collier Oil Field—oilfield ... TX-5
Collier-Overby House—hist pl ... AL-4
Collier Park—park (2) ... CA-9
Collier Park—park ... TX-5
**Collier Park**—pop pl ... FL-3
Collier Pass—gap ... UT-8
Collier Peak—summit ... ID-8
Collier Place—locale ... ID-8
Collier Ranch—locale (2) ... NE-7
Collier Ranch—locale ... NM-5
Collier Ridge—ridge ... IN-6
Collier Road Ch—church ... MI-6
Collier Rocks—summit ... KY-4
Collier (RR name for Colliers)—other ... WV-2
Collier Run ... PA-2
Collier Run—stream ... MD-2
Colliers ... GA-3
Colliers—locale ... SC-3
**Colliers**—pop pl ... GA-3
**Colliers**—pop pl ... WV-2
Colliers Bar ... OR-9
Colliers Cemetery ... AL-4
Colliers Ch—church ... NC-3
Collier Sch—school ... AZ-5
Collier Sch—school ... FL-3
Collier Sch—school ... KY-4
Collier Sch—school ... SC-3
Collier Sch—school ... TX-5
Colliers Chapel—church ... NC-3
Colliers Chapel—church ... TX-5
Colliers Chapel Cem—cemetery ... TX-5
Colliers Chapel Ch—church ... AL-4
Collier Sch (historical)—school ... MS-4
**Colliers Corner**—pop pl ... TN-4
Colliers Cove—valley ... VA-3
Colliers Creek—stream ... KY-4
Colliers Creek—stream ... TX-5
Colliers Creek—stream ... VA-3
Colliers Creek Sch—school ... KY-4
Collier-Seminole State Park—park ... FL-3
Colliers Ferry—locale ... TX-5
Colliers Hill—summit ... OH-6
Colliers Island—island ... IN-6
Colliers Lake—reservoir ... NJ-2
Colliers Lake Park—park ... NC-3
Colliers Ledge ... MA-1
**Colliers Mills**—pop pl ... NJ-2
Colliers Mills Dam—dam ... NJ-2
Colliers Mills Fish and Wildlife Mngmt Area—park ... NJ-2
Colliers Pond—lake ... AL-4
Colliers Pond—reservoir ... NJ-2
Collier Spring—spring ... AR-4
Collier Spring Ch—church ... KY-4
**Collier Spur**—pop pl ... TX-5
**Colliers (RR name Collier)**—pop pl ... WV-2
Colliers (RR name for Colliersville)—other ... NY-2
Colliers Run—stream ... OH-6
Colliers Slick Bone Cave—cave ... AL-4
Colliers Spring—spring ... AL-4
Colliers Store ... AL-4
Colliers Tanyard (historical)—locale ... MS-4
Collier State Park—park ... OR-9
Collier Station ... GA-3
**Collierstown**—pop pl ... VA-3
**Colliersville**—pop pl ... NY-2
**Colliersville (RR name Colliers)**—pop pl ... NY-2
Collier Tank—reservoir ... NM-5
Collier Tank Draw—valley ... NM-5
Collier (Township of)—fmr MCD ... AR-4
**Collier (Township of)**—pop pl ... PA-2
Collier Trail—trail ... PA-2
**Collierville**—pop pl ... CA-9
**Collierville**—pop pl ... TN-4
Collierville (CCD)—cens area ... TN-4
Collierville Division—civil ... TN-4
Collierville Sch—school ... TN-4
Collier Well—locale ... NM-5
Collier Windmill—locale ... TX-5
Collier Yard—locale ... VA-3
Collie Swamp ... NC-3
Collie Swamp—stream ... NC-3
Collietown—locale ... AR-4
Collie Wash—valley ... UT-8
Collie Well—well ... AZ-5
Colligan Hill—summit ... NY-2
Colligan Point—cape ... NY-2
Collin—locale ... TX-5
Collina—hist pl ... MS-4
Collina Plantation (historical)—locale ... MS-4
Collin Cem—cemetery ... KY-4
Collin Chapel—church ... FL-3
**Collin (County)**—pop pl ... TX-5
Collin County Mill and Elevator Company—hist pl ... TX-5
Collin Cove ... MA-1
Colling—locale ... MI-6
**Collingdale**—pop pl ... PA-2
Collingdale Borough—civil ... PA-2
Collinge Spring—spring ... MT-8
Collin Grove Ch—church ... MS-4
Collings, James, Jr., House—hist pl ... ID-8
Collings Gulch ... OR-9
Collings Gulch—valley ... OR-9
Collings Hill—summit ... NY-2
Collings-Knight Homestead—hist pl ... NJ-2
**Collings Lakes**—pop pl ... NJ-2
Collings Mtn—summit ... OR-9
**Collingswood**—pop pl ... NJ-2
Collingswood HS—school ... NJ-2
Collingswood Theatre—hist pl ... NJ-2
Collingsworth Ch—church ... GA-3
**Collingsworth (County)**—pop pl ... TX-5
Collington ... NC-3
**Collington**—pop pl ... MD-2
Collington Branch—stream ... MD-2
Collington Branch Park—park ... MD-2
**Collington (Colington)**—pop pl ... NC-3
Collington Creek ... NC-3
Collington Island ... NC-3
Collington Square—park ... MD-2
Collingwood—locale ... VA-3
**Collingwood**—pop pl ... NY-2
Collingwood Cem—cemetery ... OH-6
Collingwood Creek*—stream ... NE-7
**Collingwood Estates**—pop pl ... NY-2
**Collingwood Estates (subdivision)**—pop pl ... NC-3
Collingwood HS—school ... TN-4
Collingwood Opera House and Office Bldg—hist pl ... NY-2
**Collingwood Park**—pop pl ... NJ-2
**Collingwood (subdivision)**—pop pl ... AL-4
**Collingwood (subdivision)**—pop pl ... TN-4
Collin Lake—lake ... SC-3
Collin Lake Dam—dam ... MS-4
Collin Peak ... ID-8
Collins ... KS-7
Collins ... MS-4
Collins—dam ... AL-4
Collins—locale ... AL-4
Collins—locale ... CA-9
Collins—locale ... ID-8
Collins—locale ... IL-6
Collins—locale ... PA-2
Collins—locale ... TX-5
**Collins**—pop pl ... AR-4
**Collins**—pop pl ... GA-3
**Collins**—pop pl (2) ... IL-6
**Collins**—pop pl ... IN-6
**Collins**—pop pl ... IA-7
**Collins**—pop pl ... KY-4
**Collins**—pop pl ... ME-1
**Collins**—pop pl ... MI-6
**Collins**—pop pl ... MS-4
**Collins**—pop pl ... MO-7
**Collins**—pop pl ... MT-8
**Collins**—pop pl ... NY-2
**Collins**—pop pl ... OH-6
**Collins**—pop pl ... SC-3
**Collins**—pop pl ... TN-4
**Collins**—pop pl ... VA-3
**Collins**—pop pl ... WV-2
**Collins**—pop pl ... WI-6
**Collins**—pop pl ... WY-8
Collins—uninc pl ... TN-4
Collins, Frederick, House—hist pl ... MA-1
Collins, James E., House—hist pl ... TN-4
Collins, John, House—hist pl ... WI-6
Collins, Jonathan C., House and Cemetery—hist pl ... NY-2
Collins, Lake—lake ... GA-3
Collins, Lake—reservoir ... GA-3
Collins, Mount—summit ... TN-4
Collins, Nathaniel Bishop, House—hist pl ... NY-2
Collins, Timothy Edwards, Mansion—hist pl ... MT-8
Collins, William, House—hist pl ... MA-1
Collins, William, House—hist pl ... WI-6
Collins and Culver Ditch—canal ... DE-2
Collins and Pancoast Hall—hist pl ... NJ-2
**Collins and Russell Development**—pop pl ... DE-2
Collins and Townley Streets District—hist pl ... CT-1
Collins Archeol District—hist pl ... IL-6
Collins Bar Creek—stream ... CA-9
Collins Bay—swamp ... FL-3
Collins Bay—swamp ... GA-3
Collins Bayou ... AL-4
Collins Bayou ... MS-4
Collins Bayou—stream ... AR-4
Collins Bayou Landing (historical)—locale ... MS-4
Collins Beach—locale ... DE-2
Collins Bend—bend ... AL-4
Collins Block-Aspen Lumber and Supply—hist pl ... CO-8
Collins Branch—bay ... ME-1
Collins Branch—stream ... AL-4
Collins Branch—stream ... AR-4
Collins Branch—stream (5) ... GA-3
Collins Branch—stream (9) ... KY-4
Collins Branch—stream ... LA-4
Collins Branch—stream ... NC-3
Collins Branch—stream (2) ... SC-3
Collins Branch—stream (10) ... TN-4
Collins Branch—stream ... TX-5
Collins Branch—stream ... WV-2
Collins Bridge—bridge ... KY-4
Collins Bridge—bridge ... NC-3
Collins Brook ... CT-1
Collins Brook—stream ... ME-1
Collins Brook—stream ... MA-1
Collins Brook—stream ... NH-1
Collins Brook—stream (3) ... NY-2
Collins Brook—stream ... PA-2
Collinsburg—locale ... LA-4
**Collinsburg**—pop pl ... PA-2
Collinsburg Cem—cemetery ... LA-4
Collinsburg Creek—stream (2) ... LA-4
Collinsburg Sch—school ... PA-2
Collins Butte—summit ... OR-9
Collins Cabin—locale ... OR-9
Collins Camp—locale ... NM-5
Collins Camp—locale ... OR-9
Collins Canal—canal (3) ... CA-9
Collins Canal—canal ... FL-3
Collins Canyon—valley ... AZ-5
Collins Canyon—valley ... NM-5
Collins Canyon—valley ... UT-8
Collins Canyon—valley ... WA-9
Collins (CCD)—cens area ... GA-3
Collins Cem—cemetery (4) ... AL-4
Collins Cem—cemetery (2) ... AR-4
Collins Cem—cemetery ... CT-1
Collins Cem—cemetery (3) ... GA-3
Collins Cem—cemetery (3) ... IL-6
Collins Cem—cemetery ... IN-6
Collins Cem—cemetery ... IA-7
Collins Cem—cemetery (10) ... KY-4
Collins Cem—cemetery ... LA-4
Collins Cem—cemetery ... ME-1
Collins Cem—cemetery (6) ... MS-4
Collins Cem—cemetery (8) ... MO-7
Collins Cem—cemetery (3) ... NY-2
Collins Cem—cemetery ... NC-3
Collins Cem—cemetery (2) ... OH-6
Collins Cem—cemetery ... OK-5
Collins Cem—cemetery (2) ... SC-3
Collins Cem—cemetery ... SD-7
Collins Cem—cemetery (9) ... TN-4
Collins Cem—cemetery ... TX-5
Collins Cem—cemetery (3) ... VT-1
Collins Cem—cemetery ... VA-3
Collins Cem—cemetery (3) ... WV-2
Collins Cem—cemetery ... WY-8
**Collins Center**—pop pl ... NY-2
Collins Ch—church (2) ... GA-3
Collins Channel—canal ... CA-9
Collins Chapel—church ... AL-4
Collins Chapel—church ... IN-6
Collins Chapel—church ... NC-3
Collins Chapel—church ... TN-4
**Collins Chapel**—pop pl ... AL-4
Collins Chapel Church ... AL-4
Collins Chapel Sch (historical)—school ... AL-4
Collins City Hall—building ... MS-4
Collins Conduit—cave ... TN-4
Collins Corner—locale ... MI-6
**Collins Corner**—pop pl ... MA-1
Collins Corners Sch—school ... NY-2
Collins Cove—bay ... ME-1
Collins Cove—bay ... NJ-2
Collins Cove—bay ... VA-3
Collins Cove—cove ... MA-1
Collins Cove—valley (2) ... TN-4
Collins Covered Bridge—bridge ... IN-6
Collins Creek ... MD-2
Collins Creek ... MT-8
**Collins Creek**—pop pl ... SC-3
Collins Creek—stream (3) ... AL-4
Collins Creek—stream ... AK-9
Collins Creek—stream (2) ... AR-4
Collins Creek—stream (3) ... CA-9
Collins Creek—stream ... CO-8
Collins Creek—stream ... DE-2
Collins Creek—stream ... ID-8
Collins Creek—stream ... KY-4
Collins Creek—stream (2) ... LA-4
Collins Creek—stream (2) ... MI-6
Collins Creek—stream (6) ... MS-4
Collins Creek—stream ... MT-8
Collins Creek—stream ... NY-2
Collins Creek—stream (3) ... NC-3
Collins Creek—stream ... OH-6
Collins Creek—stream (6) ... OR-9
Collins Creek—stream ... PA-2
Collins Creek—stream (3) ... SC-3
Collins Creek—stream (2) ... TN-4
Collins Creek—stream (4) ... TX-5
Collins Creek—stream ... UT-8
Collins Creek—stream (2) ... WA-9
Collins Creek—stream (2) ... WY-8
Collins Creek Bald ... NC-3
Collins Creek Baldy Lookout—locale ... CA-9
Collins Creek Cabin—locale ... ID-8
Collins Creek Ch—church ... SC-3
**Collins Creek Estates**—pop pl ... DE-2
Collins Crossing—locale ... MS-4
Collins Crossing—locale ... VA-3
Collins Cross Roads ... DE-2
Collins Cutoff Creek—stream ... WY-8
**Collinsdale**—pop pl ... WV-2

**Colonial Place**—*pop pl* VA-3
Colonial Place—*uninc pl* VA-3
Colonial Place Ch—*church* VA-3
Colonial Playground—*park* CA-9
Colonial Plaza—*locale* OH-6
Colonial Plaza—*locale* PA-2
**Colonial Plaza Condominium**—*pop pl* UT-8
Colonial Plaza Mall—*locale* FL-3
Colonial Point—*cape* MI-6
Colonial Pond—*lake* IN-6
**Colonial Port Trailer Park**—*pop pl* VA-3
Colonial Reality Dam—*dam* IN-6
**Colonial Ridge**—*pop pl* IL-6
Colonial Rsvr—*reservoir* PA-2
Colonial Sch—*school* NY-2
Colonial Sch—*school* NC-3
Colonial Sch—*school* OH-6
Colonial Sch—*school* PA-2
Colonial Sch—*school* TN-4
Colonial Sch—*school* TX-5
Colonial Sch—*school* VA-3
Colonial Shop Ctr—*locale* (2) FL-3
Colonial Shop Ctr—*locale* (4) MA-1
Colonial Shop Ctr, The—*locale* PA-2
**Colonial Shores (subdivision)**—*pop pl* TN-4
**Colonial Springs**—*pop pl* NY-2
Colonial Square (Shop Ctr)—*locale* FL-3
Colonial Square (Shop Ctr)—*locale* UT-8
**Colonial Square Subdivision**—*pop pl* UT-8
**Colonial Subdivision**—*pop pl* UT-8
**Colonial Terrace**—*pop pl* KY-4
**Colonial Terrace**—*pop pl* NJ-2
Colonial Terrace Golf Club—*other* NJ-2
Colonial Terrace Shop Ctr—*locale* FL-3
**Colonial Terrace (subdivision)**—*pop pl* PA-2
Colonial Theatre—*building* MA-1
Colonial Theatre—*hist pl* MD-2
Colonial Theatre—*hist pl* PA-2
Colonialtown—*uninc pl* FL-3
**Colonia Lujan**—*pop pl* (2) PR-3
*Colonial Village* IL-6
*Colonial Village* IA-7
Colonial Village—*hist pl* VA-3
**Colonial Village**—*pop pl* DC-2
**Colonial Village**—*pop pl* IL-6
**Colonial Village**—*pop pl* IN-6
**Colonial Village**—*pop pl* (2) MD-2
**Colonial Village**—*pop pl* NY-2
**Colonial Village**—*pop pl* (2) PA-2
**Colonial Village**—*pop pl* TN-4
**Colonial Village**—*pop pl* VA-3
**Colonial Village Apartments**—*pop pl* DE-2
Colonial Village (Shop Ctr)—*locale* (2) FL-3
**Colonial Village (subdivision)**—*pop pl* TN-4
Colonial White HS—*school* OH-6
Colonial Williamsburg—*post sta* VA-3
**Colonial Woods South (subdivision)**—*pop pl* PA-2
**Colonial Woods (subdivision)**—*pop pl* DE-2
**Colonial Woods (subdivision)**—*pop pl* NC-3
**Colonial Woods (subdivision)**—*pop pl* PA-2
**Colonial Wood (subdivision)**—*pop pl* PA-2
**Colonia Manzanillo**—*pop pl* CA-9
**Colonia Puerto Real**—*pop pl* PR-3
Colonias—*locale* NM-5
Colonias Camp—*locale* NM-5
Colonias Cem—*cemetery* NM-5
Colonias de San Jose Hist Dist—*hist pl* NM-5
Colonia Station—*locale* NJ-2
Colonia Verde Shop Ctr—*locale* AZ-5
**Colonie**—*pop pl* NY-2
Colonie Central HS—*school* NY-2
Colonie Country Club—*other* NY-2
Colonie Rsvr—*reservoir* NY-2
**Colonies, The (subdivision)**—*pop pl* TN-4
**Colonie-Schenectady (sta.)**—*pop pl* NY-2
Colonies North—*uninc pl* TX-5
Colonies North Sch—*school* TX-5
**Colonies of East Pointe Subdivision**—*pop pl* UT-8
**Colonies of East Pointe Subdivision Phase Five**—*pop pl* UT-8
**Colonie (Town of)**—*pop pl* NY-2
**Colonie-Watervliet (sta.)**—*pop pl* NY-2
Colonite Creek—*stream* MT-8
Colon Mtn—*summit* AR-4
Colon Mtn—*summit* MI-6
Colonnade—*building* MS-4
Colonnade—*cliff* WA-9
Colonnade, The—*summit* AZ-5
Colonnade Court—*hist pl* IL-6
Colonnade Falls—*falls* WY-8
Colonnade Shop Ctr, The—*locale* AZ-5
Colonnade (Shop Ctr), The—*locale* NC-3
Colonsay Plantation—*hist pl* GA-3
**Colon (Township of)**—*pop pl* MI-6
Colon Trail—*trail* PA-2
Colonville—*locale* MI-6
*Colony* FM-9
Colony—*locale* TX-5
Colony—*locale* WY-8
**Colony**—*pop pl* (2) AL-4
**Colony**—*pop pl* KS-7
**Colony**—*pop pl* KY-4
**Colony**—*pop pl* MO-7
**Colony**—*pop pl* OK-5
**Colony**—*pop pl* VA-3
**Colony**—*pop pl* WY-8
Colony—*uninc pl* AL-4
Colony, The—*locale* AL-4
**Colony, The**—*pop pl* TX-5
Colony, The—*uninc pl* KY-4
**Colony Acres**—*pop pl* VA-3
**Colony Acres (subdivision)**—*pop pl* NC-3
**Colony Arms**—*pop pl* PA-2
Colony Baldy—*summit* CO-8
**Colony Biltmore IV (subdivision)**—*pop pl* (2) AZ-5
Colony Branch Nubmer Three Canal—*canal* CA-9
Colony Branch Number Five—*canal* CA-9
Colony Branch Number Four—*canal* CA-9
Colony Branch Number Two Canal—*canal* CA-9
Colony (CCD)—*cens area* KY-4
Colony (CCD)—*cens area* TX-5
Colony Cem—*cemetery* KS-7
Colony Cem—*cemetery* (2) TX-5
Colony Ch—*church* AR-4
Colony Ch—*church* SC-3
Colony Ch—*church* (2) TX-5
Colony Community Ch—*church* AR-4
Colony Cove Yacht Club—*locale* AL-4
Colony Creek—*stream* IN-6
Colony Creek—*stream* TX-5
Colony Creek—*stream* WA-9
Colony Ditch—*canal* CA-9
Colony Ditch—*canal* NV-8
Colony East Ditch—*canal* CA-9
**Colony East Estates Subdivision**—*pop pl* UT-8
**Colony East Subdivision**—*pop pl* UT-8
**Colony Estates (subdivision)**—*pop pl* NC-3
**Colony Estates (subdivision)**—*pop pl* TN-4
**Colony Estates (subdivision)**—*pop pl* UT-8
Colony Farm—*locale* CA-9
Colony Farm Correctional Institue—*building* GA-3
Colony Glacier—*glacier* AK-9
**Colony Hills**—*pop pl* DE-2
**Colony Hills (subdivision)**—*pop pl* AL-4
Colony House—*hist pl* CA-9
*Colony Koronia* FM-9
Colony Lake—*lake* NC-3
**Colony (Lynchburg Training School and Hospital)**—*pop pl* VA-3
Colony Main Canal—*canal* (2) CA-9
Colony Meadow—*flat* CA-9
Colony Mill Ranger Station—*locale* CA-9
Colony Mine (Site)—*locale* CA-9
Colony Mtn—*summit* AR-4
**Colony North Subdivision**—*pop pl* UT-8
Colony of Mercy Home for the Aged—*building* SD-7
*Colony Park* IL-6
Colony Park—*park* CA-9
Colony Park—*park* PA-2
**Colony Park**—*pop pl* NC-3
Colony Park—*uninc pl* LA-4
Colony Park Airp—*airport* TN-4
Colony Park Pavilion—*hist pl* OK-5
**Colony Park (subdivision)**—*pop pl* NC-3
**Colony Park (subdivision)**—*pop pl* TN-4
Colony Peak—*summit* CA-9
Colony Plaza—*locale* PA-2
*Colony Point* IL-6
Colony Point—*cape* AK-9
Colony Pond—*lake* CT-1
Colony's Block—*hist pl* NH-1
Colony Sch—*school* AL-4
Colony Sch—*school* CA-9
Colony Sch—*school* IA-7
Colony Sch—*school* KY-4
Colony Sch—*school* MI-6
Colony Sch (historical)—*school* SD-7
Colony Shop Ctr—*locale* AL-4
Colony Shop Ctr—*locale* FL-3
Colony Shoppes—*locale* FL-3
**Colony South (subdivision)**—*pop pl* (2) AZ-5
**Colony South Subdivision**—*pop pl* UT-8
*Colony Station* KS-7
Colony Street-West Main Street Hist Dist—*hist pl* CT-1
**Colony Subdivision, The**—*pop pl* UT-8
Colony Substation—*other* CA-9
*Colony Town* FM-9
Colony Town—*locale* MS-4
Colony Township—*civil* KS-7
Colony Township—*civil* MO-7
Colony Township—*fmr MCD* (2) IA-7
Colony Wash—*arroyo* AZ-5
**Colony West Estates Subdivision**—*pop pl* UT-8
**Colony West Subdivision**—*pop pl* UT-8
**Colony West Subdivision - Numbers 13, 14 and 15**—*pop pl* UT-8
**Colony Woods (subdivision)**—*pop pl* NC-3
Colony-Woods Substation—*other* CA-9
*Coloose* VA-3
**Colora**—*pop pl* MD-2
Colorada, Laguna—*lake* NM-5
Colorada Tank—*reservoir* TX-5
Colorade Gulch—*valley* ID-8
Coloraditas Windmill—*locale* TX-5
Coloradium Mine—*mine* CO-8
*Colorado* AZ-5
*Colorado* KS-7
*Colorado* TX-5
Colorado—*locale* PA-2
**Colorado**—*pop pl* AK-9
**Colorado**—*pop pl* CA-9
**Colorado**—*pop pl* TX-5
Colorado, Arroyo—*stream* TX-5
Colorado, Arroyo—*valley* CA-9
Colorado, Canyon—*valley* TX-5
Colorado, Cerro—*summit* AZ-5
Colorado, Cerro—*summit* CA-9
Colorado, Rito—*stream* CO-8
Colorado Acad—*school* CO-8
Colorado Agricultural Canal—*canal* CO-8
Colorado Alpine Coll—*school* CO-8
Colorado and Southern Railway Depot—*hist pl* CO-8
Colorado Belle Mine—*mine* CO-8
Colorado Camp—*locale* (2) CA-9
Colorado Canal—*canal* CO-8
*Colorado Canyon* CO-8
Colorado Canyon—*valley* CO-8
Colorado Canyon—*valley* (2) NM-5
Colorado Cem—*cemetery* (2) TX-5
Colorado Chautauqua—*hist pl* CO-8
Colorado Chief—*mine* UT-8
*Colorado Chiquita* AZ-5
*Colorado Chiquito* AZ-5
Colorado Christian Home—*other* CO-8
*Colorado City* AZ-5
*Colorado City* CO-8
**Colorado City**—*pop pl* AZ-5
**Colorado City**—*pop pl* CO-8
**Colorado City**—*pop pl* TX-5
Colorado City, Lake—*reservoir* TX-5
Colorado City (CCD)—*cens area* TX-5
Colorado City Elem Sch—*school* AZ-5
Colorado City Municipal Airp—*airport* AZ-5
Colorado City Post Office—*building* AZ-5
Colorado City-Rye—*cens area* CO-8
**Colorado City (Short Creek)**—*pop pl* AZ-5
Colorado Clark Mine—*mine* AZ-5
Colorado Coll—*school* CO-8
Colorado Colony Ditch—*canal* WY-8
**Colorado (County)**—*pop pl* TX-5
Colorado County Courthouse—*hist pl* TX-5
Colorado County Courthouse Hist Dist—*hist pl* TX-5
*Colorado Creek* MT-8
Colorado Creek—*stream* (8) AK-9
Colorado Creek—*stream* CA-9
Colorado Creek—*stream* (3) CO-8
Colorado Creek—*stream* ID-8
Colorado Creek—*stream* MT-8
Colorado Creek Mine—*mine* AK-9
*Colorado Crossing* AZ-5
Colorado Cutoff, Arroyo—*channel* TX-5
Colorado Drain—*canal* NM-5
Colorado Feldspar Company Mine—*mine* CO-8
Colorado Flats Draw—*valley* WY-8
Colorado Flat Tank—*reservoir* TX-5
Colorado Game and Fish Res—*park* (2) CO-8
Colorado Gap—*gap* TN-4
Colorado General Hosp—*hospital* CO-8
Colorado Goodwill Hill Grand Valley Oil Field—*oilfield* PA-2
Colorado Governor's Mansion—*hist pl* CO-8
**Colorado Gulch**—*pop pl* MT-8
Colorado Gulch—*valley* AK-9
Colorado Gulch—*valley* (2) AZ-5
Colorado Gulch—*valley* CO-8
Colorado Gulch—*valley* MT-8
Colorado Gulch—*valley* NV-8
*Colorado Heights* KS-7
Colorado Hill—*summit* CA-9
Colorado Hollow—*valley* TN-4
Colorado Island—*island* TX-5
Colorado Lagoon—*lake* CA-9
Colorado Lake—*lake* OR-9
Colorado Memorial Shrine—*other* CO-8
Colorado Millennial Site—*hist pl* CO-8
Colorado Mine—*mine* AK-9
Colorado Mine—*mine* AZ-5
Colorado Mine—*mine* (2) CA-9
Colorado Mine—*mine* OR-9
Colorado Mine (historical)—*mine* UT-8
Colorado Mines Peak—*summit* CO-8
Colorado Mountain Coll—*school* CO-8
**Colorado Mountain Estates**—*pop pl* CO-8
Colorado Mountains, Cerro—*summit* AZ-5
Colorado Mtn—*summit* CO-8
Colorado Mtn—*summit* MT-8
Colorado Natl Guard Armory—*hist pl* CO-8
Colorado Natl Monument—*park* CO-8
Colorado Natl Monument HQ—*locale* CO-8
Colorado No 1—*mine* UT-8
Colorado No 2—*mine* UT-8
Colorado Oil Field—*oilfield* TX-5
Colorado Outward Bound Sch—*school* CO-8
Colorado Peak—*summit* NM-5
**Colorado Place Addition (subdivision)**—*pop pl* UT-8
Colorado Placer Mine—*mine* NV-8
*Colorado Plateau* AZ-5
Colorado Ranch—*locale* CO-8
Colorado Reef—*bar* AK-9
Colorado River—*stream* AZ-5
Colorado River—*stream* CA-9
Colorado River—*stream* CO-8
Colorado River—*stream* NV-8
Colorado River—*stream* TX-5
Colorado River—*stream* UT-8
Colorado River Aqueduct—*canal* CA-9
Colorado River Day Sch—*school* AZ-5
Colorado River Divide Great Basin—*basin* WY-8
Colorado River Gorge Outlook—*locale* AZ-5
Colorado River Indian Agency HQ—*building* AZ-5
Colorado River Indian Tribes Administration—*other* AZ-5
**Colorado River Ind Res**—*pop pl* AZ-5
Colorado River Ind Res (Also AZ)—*reserve* CA-9
Colorado River Ind Res (Also CA)—*reserve* AZ-5
Colorado River Overlook—*locale* UT-8
Colorado River Trail—*trail* CO-8
Colorado River Tunnel—*tunnel* CA-9
Colorado River Water Pollution Control Center—*building* AZ-5
Colorado Sch—*school* CA-9
Colorado Sch—*school* IA-7
Colorado Sch—*school* TX-5
Colorado Sch (historical)—*school* PA-2
Colorado Sch of Mines—*school* CO-8
Colorado School of Mines Experimental Mine—*mine* CO-8
Colorado School of Mines Summer Camp—*locale* CO-8
Colorado School of Mines Tunnel—*mine* CO-8
Colorado Southern RR Depot—*hist pl* LA-4
Colorado Spring—*spring* (2) AZ-5
**Colorado Springs**—*pop pl* CO-8
Colorado Springs Country Club—*other* CO-8
Colorado Springs Fine Arts Center—*hist pl* CO-8
Colorado Springs Hosp—*hospital* CO-8
Colorado Springs Ranch—*locale* CO-8
Colorado Standard School—*locale* CO-8
Colorado State For—*forest* CO-8
Colorado State Hosp Superintendent's House—*hist pl* CO-8
Colorado State Univ—*school* CO-8
Colorado State University San Juan Basin Branch Agricultural Experimental Station—*locale* CO-8
*Colorado State Veterans Center* CO-8
Colorado Street Bridge—*hist pl* CA-9
**Colorado Subdivision**—*pop pl* UT-8
Colorado Tank—*reservoir* AZ-5
Colorado Tank—*reservoir* NM-5
Colorado Tank—*reservoir* (3) TX-5
**Colorado Township**—*pop pl* KS-7
Colorado Township Elem Sch—*school* KS-7
Colorado Ute Power Plant—*hist pl* CO-8
*Colorado Valley* AZ-5
Colorado Vista Sch—*school* CA-9
Colorado Wash—*stream* (2) AZ-5
Colorado Well Number One—*well* TX-5
Colorado Well Number Three—*well* TX-5
Colorado Well Number Two—*well* TX-5
Colorado Windmill—*locale* (3) TX-5
Colora Meetinghouse—*hist pl* MD-2
Color Back Mine—*mine* NV-8
Color Creek—*stream* (2) ID-8
Color Creek—*stream* MN-6
Colored Cemetery—*hist pl* GA-3
**Colored Hill**—*pop pl* WV-2
*Colored Methodist Episcopal High School* TN-4
Colored Pass—*gap* UT-8
Colored Windmill—*locale* NM-5
Colores—*locale* WY-8
Colorful Creek—*stream* CA-9
Colorinda Creek—*gut* FL-3
Colorita Windmill—*locale* TX-5
Colorock Quarry—*mine* NV-8
Colorow Canyon—*valley* CO-8
Colorow Canyon—*valley* NM-5
Colorow Creek—*stream* TX-5
Colorow Gulch—*valley* CO-8
Colorow Hill—*summit* CO-8
*Colorow Lake* UT-8
Colorow Mountain Park—*park* CO-8
Colorow Mtn—*summit* CO-8
Colorow Sch—*school* CO-8
Colo Sch—*school* KY-4
**Coloso**—*pop pl* PR-3
Colo Spring—*spring* OR-9
Colo Springs Dam—*dam* SD-7
Colossal Cave—*cave* AZ-5
Colossal Cave—*cave* KY-4
Colossal Cave Park—*park* AZ-5
Colossal Mine—*mine* NM-5
**Colosse**—*pop pl* NY-2
**Colosse**—*pop pl* VA-3
Colosse Ch—*church* VA-3
Colosseum, The—*cape* NE-7
Colosseum Gorge—*valley* CA-9
Colosseum Mine—*mine* CA-9
Colosseum Mtn—*summit* CA-9
Colos Valley Cem—*cemetery* OR-9
Colo-Tex Refinery—*other* TX-5
**Colp**—*pop pl* IL-6
Colpien Ranch—*locale* CA-9
Colpitt Sch—*school* IL-6
*Colpitts Mountain* OR-9
Colpitts Spring—*spring* OR-9
Colp Lake—*lake* AK-9
Colp Lake Trail—*trail* AK-9
*Colquhoun Mountain* WA-9
Colquhoun Peak—*summit* WA-9
**Colquhoun Township**—*pop pl* ND-7
*Colquit* LA-4
*Colquitt* AL-4
Colquitt—*locale* TX-5
**Colquitt**—*pop pl* GA-3
**Colquitt**—*pop pl* LA-4
Colquitt (CCD)—*cens area* GA-3
Colquitt Ch—*church* GA-3
Colquitt Ch—*church* LA-4
**Colquitt (County)**—*pop pl* GA-3
Colquitt County Courthouse—*hist pl* GA-3
Colquitt County Jail—*hist pl* GA-3
*Colquitt Draw* TX-5
Colquitt Draw—*valley* TX-5
Colquitt-Tigner Mine—*mine* TX-5
Colquitt Town Square Hist Dist—*hist pl* GA-3
**Colrain**—*pop pl* MA-1
Colrain Central Sch—*school* MA-1
*Colrain Centre* MA-1
Colrain Mtn—*summit* MA-1
**Colrain (Town of)**—*pop pl* MA-1
Colrio Mine—*mine* AZ-5
Col Seth Warner Camp—*locale* VT-1
Colson—*locale* KY-4
Colson Basin—*basin* ID-8
Colson Branch—*stream* ME-1
Colson Branch—*stream* MS-4
Colson Canyon—*valley* CA-9
Colson Canyon—*valley* ID-8
Colson Canyon Campgrounds—*locale* CA-9
Colson (CCD)—*cens area* KY-4
Colson Cem—*cemetery* VA-3
Colson Creek—*stream* ID-8
Colson Creek—*stream* KY-4
Colson Creek—*stream* TN-4
Colson Gulch—*valley* CA-9
**Colson (historical)**—*pop pl* OR-9
Colson Hollow Overlook—*locale* KY-4
Colson Pond—*reservoir* NV-8
Colson Sch—*school* KY-4
Colson Store—*locale* GA-3
Colson Stream—*stream* ME-1
Colston Branch—*stream* SC-3
Colston Creek—*stream* LA-4
Colston Draw—*valley* TX-5
Colston-Gohmert House—*hist pl* TX-5
Colston Mtn—*summit* GA-3
Colston Sch—*school* SC-3
Colston Sch—*school* TX-5
**Colstrip**—*pop pl* MT-8
Colsub (Amory Junction)—*uninc pl* MS-4
**Colt**—*pop pl* AR-4
**Colt**—*pop pl* LA-4
Colt, James B., House—*hist pl* CT-1
**Colta**—*pop pl* AL-4
Colta Mine (underground)—*mine* AL-4
*Coltan* ND-7
Colt Branch—*stream* WV-2
Colt Canyon—*valley* OR-9
Colt Creek—*stream* (4) ID-8
Colt Creek—*stream* MT-8
Colt Creek—*stream* NC-3
Colt Creek—*stream* OR-9
Colt Creek—*swamp* FL-3
Colt Creek Cabin—*locale* ID-8
Colt Creek Campground—*locale* ID-8
Colt Dam—*dam* ND-7
Colt Ditch—*canal* CO-8
Coltens Cliff—*cliff* TN-4
Colter—*locale* WY-8
Colter Bay—*bay* WY-8
**Colter Bay**—*pop pl* WY-8
**Colter Bay Village**—*pop pl* WY-8
Colter Butte—*summit* AZ-5
Colter Canyon—*valley* KS-7
Colter Canyon—*valley* NE-7
Colter Canyon—*valley* WY-8
Colter Cem—*cemetery* MO-7
*Colter Creek* WY-8
Colter Creek—*stream* AZ-5
Colter Creek—*stream* MT-8
Colter Draw—*valley* (2) WY-8
Colter Gulch—*valley* MT-8
Colter Pass—*gap* MT-8
Colter Peak—*summit* WY-8
Colter Ranch—*locale* CO-8
Colter Ranch—*locale* NM-5
Colter Reservoir—*lake* AZ-5
Colter Sch (abandoned)—*school* PA-2
Colters Creek—*stream* MS-4
Colters Ferry (historical)—*locale* AL-4
Colter's Hell—*hist pl* WY-8
Colter Spring—*spring* AZ-5
Colter Spring—*spring* CA-9
**Coltexo**—*pop pl* TX-5
Coltharp Cem—*cemetery* TN-4
Colt Head Island—*island* ME-1
**Colthorp**—*pop pl* TX-5
Colthorp Historical Marker—*park* TX-5
Colthorp Post Office (historical)—*building* TX-5
Colthorp Presbyterian Ch (historical)—*church* TX-5
Colthorp Sch (historical)—*school* TX-5
Colthurst—*locale* VA-3
Colt Industrial District—*hist pl* CT-1
Coltins Cem—*cemetery* MS-4
Colt Island—*island* AK-9
Colt Killed Creek—*stream* ID-8
Colt Lake—*lake* CA-9
Colt Lake—*lake* ID-8
Colt Lake—*lake* MT-8
Colt Lake—*lake* OR-9
Colt Ledge—*bar* (2) ME-1
**Coltman**—*pop pl* ID-8
Coltman Ward Ch—*church* ID-8
Colt Mesa—*summit* UT-8
Colt Mtn—*summit* ID-8
Colt Mtn—*summit* TX-5
*Colton* MD-2
Colton—*locale* TX-5
Colton—*locale* UT-8
**Colton**—*pop pl* CA-9
**Colton**—*pop pl* KY-4
**Colton**—*pop pl* NE-7
**Colton**—*pop pl* NY-2
**Colton**—*pop pl* OH-6
**Colton**—*pop pl* OR-9
**Colton**—*pop pl* SD-7
**Colton**—*pop pl* WA-9
Colton, Albert and Freeman, H. H., House—*hist pl* AZ-5
Colton, Benjamin, House—*hist pl* CT-1
Colton Bay—*bay* MI-6
Colton Brook—*stream* ME-1
Colton (CCD)—*cens area* OR-9
Colton Crater—*crater* AZ-5
Colton Creek—*stream* LA-4
Colton Creek—*stream* NY-2
Colton Creek—*stream* SD-7
Colton Crossing—*locale* AR-4
Colton Dam—*dam* OR-9
Colton Elem Sch—*school* OR-9
Colton Flowage—*channel* WI-6
Colton Hill—*summit* ME-1
Colton Hill—*summit* (2) NY-2
Colton Hill—*summit* VT-1
Colton Hills—*summit* CA-9
**Colton Hollow**—*pop pl* MA-1
Colton Hollow—*valley* UT-8
Colton HS—*school* NY-2
Colton HS—*school* OR-9
Colton JHS—*school* LA-4
Colton JHS—*school* OR-9
Colton Lutheran Cem—*cemetery* OR-9
Colton Plunge Park—*park* CA-9
*Colton Point* MD-2
Colton Point—*cliff* PA-2
Colton Point Park—*park* PA-2
*Colton Point State Park* PA-2
Colton Point State Park—*hist pl* PA-2
Colton Pond—*lake* AL-4
Colton Pond—*lake* VT-1
Colton Ranger Station—*locale* UT-8
Colton Recreation Lake—*lake* CA-9
*Coltons* MD-2
Colton's Block—*hist pl* MA-1
Colton Sheep Camp—*locale* CO-8
Coltons Mill—*locale* VA-3
Coltons Point—*cape* MD-2
**Coltons Point**—*pop pl* MD-2
Colton Spring—*spring* OR-9
Colton Spring—*spring* UT-8
**Colton (Town of)**—*pop pl* NY-2
Colton Wash—*stream* CA-9
Colton Well—*well* CA-9
Colt Park—*park* CT-1
Coltranes Mill—*locale* NC-3
Coltrane-Webb Sch—*school* NC-3
Coltrell Flat—*flat* CA-9
Colt Ridge—*ridge* VA-3
Colt Ridge—*ridge* (2) WV-2
Coltrin Cem—*cemetery* IN-6
Coltrins Camp—*locale* TX-5
Colt Rsvr—*reservoir* CO-8
Colt Run—*stream* WV-2
Colts—*locale* KY-4
Colt Sch—*school* IL-6
Colt Sch—*school* MI-6
Colts Creek—*stream* MT-8
*Colts Foot Mtn* CT-1
Coltsfoot Mtn—*summit* CT-1
Colts Fork—*stream* KY-4
*Coltsneck* NJ-2
Colts Neck—*airport* NJ-2
**Colts Neck**—*pop pl* NJ-2
**Colts Neck (Township of)**—*pop pl* NJ-2
*Colts Pond* MA-1
Colts Pond—*lake* CT-1
Colt Spring—*spring* OR-9
Colt Spring—*spring* (2) UT-8
Colt Spring Campground—*locale* CO-8
Colts Ridge—*ridge* NC-3
Colts Station—*locale* PA-2
*Colt Station* PA-2
**Coltsville**—*pop pl* MA-1
Colt Ware Ditch—*canal* OR-9
Colum-Bel Cut—*canal* LA-4
Columbe Mtn—*summit* NY-2
Columbet Creek—*stream* ID-8
Columbet Creek—*stream* NV-8
*Columbia* AL-4
*Columbia* IN-6
*Columbia* KS-7
*Columbia* NJ-2
*Columbia* (2) OH-6
Columbia—*hist pl* MI-6
Columbia—*hist pl* VA-3
Columbia—*locale* AZ-5
Columbia—*locale* DE-2
Columbia—*locale* LA-4
Columbia—*locale* ME-1
Columbia—*locale* OH-6
Columbia—*locale* WA-9
**Columbia**—*pop pl* AL-4
**Columbia**—*pop pl* CA-9
**Columbia**—*pop pl* CT-1
**Columbia**—*pop pl* FL-3
**Columbia**—*pop pl* IL-6
**Columbia**—*pop pl* IN-6
**Columbia**—*pop pl* IA-7
**Columbia**—*pop pl* KY-4
**Columbia**—*pop pl* LA-4
**Columbia**—*pop pl* MD-2
**Columbia**—*pop pl* MS-4
**Columbia**—*pop pl* MO-7
**Columbia**—*pop pl* NH-1
**Columbia**—*pop pl* NJ-2
**Columbia**—*pop pl* NC-3
**Columbia**—*pop pl* (3) OH-6
**Columbia**—*pop pl* PA-2
**Columbia**—*pop pl* SC-3
**Columbia**—*pop pl* SD-7
**Columbia**—*pop pl* TN-4
**Columbia**—*pop pl* UT-8
**Columbia**—*pop pl* VA-3
**Columbia**—*pop pl* WA-9
**Columbia**—*pop pl* WV-2
**Columbia**—*pop pl* WI-6
**Columbia**—*pop pl* PR-3
Columbia, Lake—*lake* MI-6
Columbia, Lake—*reservoir* MS-4
Columbia, Mount—*summit* CO-8
Columbia Acad—*school* (2) MS-4
Columbia Acad—*school* WA-9
Columbia Ag Airp—*airport* WA-9
Columbia Ag 2 Airp—*airport* WA-9
Columbia Arsenal—*hist pl* TN-4
Columbia Ave Ch—*church* GA-3
Columbia Ave Hist Dist—*hist pl* IA-7
Columbia Ave Presbyterian Ch—*church* AL-4
Columbia Baptist Cemetery—*hist pl* OH-6
Columbia Baptist Ch—*church* AL-4
Columbia Baptist Church—*hist pl* OH-6
Columbia Basin—*basin* NV-8
Columbia Basin Coll—*school* WA-9
Columbia Basin Hospital Heliport—*airport* WA-9
Columbia Bay—*bay* AK-9
Columbia Bay—*bay* IL-6
Columbia Beach—*locale* OR-9
**Columbia Beach**—*pop pl* MD-2
**Columbia Beach**—*pop pl* WA-9
Columbia Bible Coll—*school* SC-3
Columbia Bldg—*hist pl* OH-6
Columbia Bogs—*swamp* MA-1
Columbia Borough—*civil* PA-2
*Columbia Bottom* MO-7
Columbia Bottom—*bend* MO-7
*Columbia Bottoms* MO-7
Columbia Bridge—*bridge* NH-1
Columbia Bridge—*bridge* PA-2
Columbia Bridge—*locale* NJ-2
Columbia Brook—*stream* NH-1
Columbia Camp—*locale* CA-9
Columbia Camp—*locale* SC-3
Columbia Canal—*canal* CA-9
Columbia Canal—*canal* SC-3
Columbia Canal—*canal* WA-9
Columbia Canal—*hist pl* SC-3
Columbia Canal No 1—*canal* WA-9
Columbia Canal No 2—*canal* WA-9
Columbia Canal No 3—*canal* WA-9
Columbia (CCD)—*cens area* AL-4
Columbia (CCD)—*cens area* KY-4
Columbia (CCD)—*cens area* SC-3
Columbia (CCD)—*cens area* TN-4
Columbia (CCD)—*cens area* WA-9
Columbia Cem—*cemetery* AR-4
Columbia Cem—*cemetery* CO-8
Columbia Cem—*cemetery* CT-1
Columbia Cem—*cemetery* IN-6
Columbia Cem—*cemetery* IA-7
Columbia Cem—*cemetery* MI-6
Columbia Cem—*cemetery* MO-7
Columbia Cem—*cemetery* NE-7
Columbia Cem—*cemetery* OH-6
Columbia Cem—*cemetery* OR-9
Columbia Cem—*cemetery* PA-2
Columbia Cem—*cemetery* WI-6
*Columbia Center* CT-1
Columbia Center—*locale* WA-9
**Columbia Center**—*pop pl* NY-2
**Columbia Center**—*pop pl* (2) OH-6
**Columbia Center (Columbia)**—*pop pl* NY-2
Columbia Central HS—*hist pl* TN-4
Columbia Central HS—*school* MI-6
Columbia Ch—*church* GA-3
Columbia Ch—*church* IN-6
Columbia Ch—*church* IA-7
Columbia Ch—*church* MD-2
Columbia Ch—*church* NY-2
Columbia Ch—*church* SC-3
Columbia Chapel—*church* CO-8
Columbia Chapel—*church* (2) OH-6
Columbia Christian Coll—*school* OR-9
Columbia Church Camp—*locale* AL-4
*Columbia City* FL-3
*Columbia City* WA-9
**Columbia City**—*pop pl* IN-6
**Columbia City**—*pop pl* OR-9
Columbia City Cem—*cemetery* MS-4
Columbia City Hall—*building* MS-4
Columbia City Hall—*hist pl* SC-3
Columbia City Hist Dist—*hist pl* IN-6
Columbia City Hist Dist—*hist pl* WA-9
Columbia City Joint HS—*school* IN-6
Columbia City Range—*channel* OR-9
Columbia City Range—*channel* WA-9
Columbia City Sch—*school* OR-9
Columbia Clinic Hosp (historical)—*hospital* MS-4
Columbia Club—*hist pl* IN-6

Colvin Run—*stream* VA-3
**Colvin Run (Leighs Corner)**—*pop pl* VA-3
Colvin Run Mill—*hist pl* VA-3
Colvin Run Mill—*post sta* VA-3
Colvin Run Mill Park—*park* VA-3
Colvins Bay (carolina bay)—*swamp* NC-3
*Colvins Brook* RI-1
Colvin Sch (historical)—*school* MO-7
Colvin School (historical)—*locale* MO-7
Colvins Cove—*bay* NC-3
Colvins Creek—*stream* NC-3
*Colvins Gap* AL-4
**Colvins Gap**—*pop pl* AL-4
Colvins Island—*island* AL-4
Colvin Street Ch of Christ—*church* AL-4
Colvin Timbers—*woods* OR-9
Colvintown—*locale* RI-1
**Colvin Township**—*pop pl* ND-7
**Colvin (Township of)**—*pop pl* MN-6
Colvos—*locale* WA-9
Colvos Passage—*channel* WA-9
Colvos Rocks—*bar* WA-9
Colwash Cem—*cemetery* WA-9
Colwell—*locale* GA-3
**Colwell**—*pop pl* AL-4
**Colwell**—*pop pl* IA-7
**Colwell**—*pop pl* PA-2
Colwell, David B., House—*hist pl* MI-6
Colwell Bar—*bar* TN-4
Colwell Branch—*stream* MS-4
Colwell Cem—*cemetery* GA-3
Colwell Cem—*cemetery* OH-6
Colwell Cem—*cemetery* WI-6
Colwell Ch—*church* GA-3
Colwell County Park—*park* IA-7
Colwell Creek—*stream* AL-4
Colwell Creek—*stream* TX-5
Colwell Cut Viaduct—*hist pl* PA-2
Colwell Fork—*stream* KY-4
Colwell Hill—*summit* MA-1
Colwell Hill—*summit* NY-2
Colwell Lake—*lake* MI-6
*Colwells* PA-2
Colwell Sch—*school* CO-8
Colwell Spring—*spring* AZ-5
Colwell Station—*locale* PA-2
**Colwich**—*pop pl* KS-7
**Colwick**—*pop pl* NJ-2
Colwick, John and Mary, Farm—*hist pl* TX-5
Colwick Branch—*stream* TN-4
**Colwick (historical)**—*pop pl* TN-4
Colwood—*locale* MI-6
Colwood Ch—*church* MI-6
Colwood Golf Course—*other* OR-9
Col Wright Elem Sch—*school* OR-9
Colwyck Elem Sch—*school* DE-2
*Colwyck JHS* DE-2
*Colwyck Sch* DE-2
**Colwyn**—*pop pl* PA-2
Colwyn Borough—*civil* PA-2
Colwyne Elem Sch—*school* PA-2
Colyear Springs—*spring* CA-9
Colyell, Bayou—*gut* LA-4
Colyell Bay—*bay* LA-4
Colyell Ch—*church* LA-4
Colyell Creek—*stream* LA-4
Colyer—*locale* PA-2
Colyer Canyon—*valley* NM-5
Colyer Cem—*cemetery* KS-7
Colyer Hill—*summit* GA-3
Colyer Lake—*lake* PA-2
Colyer Lake—*reservoir* PA-2
Colyer Lake Dam—*dam* PA-2
Colyer Sch—*school* KS-7
*Colyer Springs* CA-9
Colyn State Wildlife Area—*park* IA-7
Colyotte Hollow—*valley* MO-7
**Colza**—*pop pl* PA-2
Colza Creek—*stream* WA-9
Coma, Lake—*reservoir* NC-3
*Coma-a Spring* AZ-5
*Co-Mac* NY-2
*Comache Peak* CO-8
*Comache Reservoir* CO-8
*Comach Peak* CO-8
*Comack* NY-2
Coma Creek—*stream* (2) TX-5
Comal—*locale* AR-4
**Comal**—*pop pl* TX-5
Coma Lake—*lake* FL-3
Comal Artesian Well—*well* TX-5
Comal Cem—*cemetery* TX-5
**Comal (County)**—*pop pl* TX-5
Comal County Courthouse—*hist pl* TX-5
Comales Campground—*locale* NM-5
Comales Canyon—*valley* NM-5
Comales Trail (Pack)—*trail* NM-5
Comal Hotel and Klein-Kuse House—*hist pl* TX-5
Comal North (CCD)—*cens area* TX-5
*Comal River* TX-5
Comal River—*stream* TX-5
Coman Cem—*cemetery* MI-6
Comanche—*locale* CO-8
**Comanche**—*pop pl* MT-8
**Comanche**—*pop pl* OK-5
**Comanche**—*pop pl* TX-5
Comanche, Lake—*lake* TX-5
Comanche, Lake—*reservoir* TX-5
Comanche Archeol Site—*hist pl* KS-7
Comanche Artesian Well—*well* TX-5
*Comanche Basin* MT-8
Comanche Bluff—*cliff* TX-5
Comanche Branch—*stream* TN-4
Comanche Branch—*stream* TX-5
Comanche Campground—*locale* CO-8
Comanche Canal—*canal* CO-8
Comanche Canyon—*valley* (3) NM-5
Comanche Canyon—*valley* UT-8
Comanche (CCD)—*cens area* OK-5
Comanche (CCD)—*cens area* TX-5
Comanche Cem—*cemetery* MT-8
Comanche Cem—*cemetery* OK-5
Comanche Cem—*cemetery* TX-5
Comanche Cemeteries—*cemetery* TX-5
Comanche County—*civil* KS-7
**Comanche (County)**—*pop pl* OK-5
**Comanche (County)**—*pop pl* TX-5
*Comanche Creek* TX-5
Comanche Creek—*stream* AZ-5
Comanche Creek—*stream* (2) CA-9
Comanche Creek—*stream* CO-8
Comanche Creek—*stream* (2) MT-8
Comanche Creek—*stream* (3) NM-5
Comanche Creek—*stream* (9) TX-5
Comanche Creek—*stream* UT-8
Comanche Crossing—*locale* TX-5
Comanche Crossing of the Kansas Pacific RR—*hist pl* CO-8
Comanche Draw—*valley* CO-8
Comanche Draw—*valley* (2) NM-5
Comanche Flat—*flat* MT-8
Comanche Flats—*flat* TX-5
Comanche Gulch—*valley* CA-9
Comanche Gulch—*valley* CO-8
Comanche Hill—*summit* NM-5
Comanche Hill—*summit* OK-5
Comanche Hills—*other* TX-5
Comanche (historical)—*locale* KS-7
Comanche Indian Cem—*cemetery* OK-5
Comanche Indian Mission—*church* OK-5
Comanche Lake—*lake* (2) CO-8
Comanche Lake—*lake* TX-5
Comanche Lake—*reservoir* (2) OK-5
Comanche Lateral—*canal* CA-9
Comanche Lookout—*locale* TX-5
Comanche Meadow—*flat* CA-9
Comanche Mine—*mine* CA-9
*Comanche Mountain* CO-8
Comanche Natl Grassland—*forest* CO-8
Comanche Park—*park* AZ-5
Comanche Park—*park* TX-5
Comanche Pass—*gap* (2) NM-5
Comanche Peak—*summit* (2) CO-8
Comanche Peak—*summit* (2) NM-5
Comanche Peak—*summit* (3) TX-5
Comanche Point—*cape* CA-9
Comanche Point—*cape* NM-5
Comanche Point—*summit* AZ-5
*Comanche Point Oil Field* CA-9
Comanche Ranch—*locale* NM-5
Comanche Ridge—*ridge* NM-5
Comanche Rim—*cliff* NM-5
Comancheros Creek—*stream* NM-5
Comanche Rsvr—*reservoir* CO-8
Comanche Sch—*school* TX-5
Comanche Spring—*spring* CA-9
Comanche Spring—*spring* NM-5
Comanche Spring—*spring* (3) TX-5
Comanche Spring—*spring* UT-8
Comanche Springs—*spring* TX-5
Comanche Springs Cem—*cemetery* TX-5
Comanche Springs Reservoir (Abandoned)—*locale* NM-5
Comanche Stadium—*other* TX-5
**Comanche Subdivision**—*pop pl* TN-4
Comanche Tank—*reservoir* NM-5
Comanche Tank—*reservoir* TX-5
**Comanche Township**—*pop pl* KS-7
Comanche Trail Camp—*locale* NM-5
Comanche Trail City Park—*park* TX-5
Comanche Trails Camp—*locale* TX-5
Comanche Waterhole—*lake* TX-5
Comanche Well—*well* NM-5
Comanche Wells—*well* NM-5
Comanche Windmill—*locale* TX-5
Coman House—*hist pl* WI-6
Coman Mtn—*summit* NY-2
Coman Pond—*lake* CT-1
Comans Well—*locale* VA-3
Comar—*locale* WA-9
Comargo—*locale* KY-4
Comar Lake—*lake* IA-7
Comar Spring—*spring* AZ-5
*Comar Springs* AZ-5
Comasa, Canada Del —*valley* CA-9
Comas Sch (historical)—*school* AL-4
Coma Tank—*reservoir* (3) TX-5
Comatchie Island—*island* FL-3
*Comate* AZ-5
Coma Well—*well* TX-5
Coma Windmill—*locale* (3) TX-5
Combahee Ferry—*locale* SC-3
Combahee River—*stream* SC-3
Combat Creek—*stream* MT-8
**Combate**—*pop pl* PR-3
Combat Village—*locale* VA-3
Comb Butte—*summit* MT-8
Comb Cem—*cemetery* AR-4
Comb Creek—*stream* CA-9
Comb Creek—*stream* (2) ID-8
Comb Creek—*stream* MT-8
*Combe Canyon* ID-8
Combe Canyon—*valley* ID-8
Combee Park—*park* FL-3
Combee Sch—*school* FL-3
Combee Settlement—*CDP* FL-3
Combellack Adobe Row House—*hist pl* NV-8
Combellack-Blair House—*hist pl* CA-9
Comber Inn—*locale* ME-1
Comber Island—*island* MN-6
Comber Point—*cape* MN-6
Combe Rsvr—*reservoir* ID-8
**Combes**—*pop pl* TX-5
Combes Cem—*cemetery* IL-6
Combes Cem—*cemetery* IN-6
Combes Dam—*dam* MA-1
Combes Dan—*dam* MA-1
Combes Pond—*reservoir* MA-1
**Combest**—*pop pl* NM-5
Combest Creek—*stream* MT-8
Combest Peak—*summit* MT-8
*Comb Ferry* TN-4
Combie, Lake—*reservoir* CA-9
Combie Ophir Canal—*canal* CA-9
Combination Baggage and Mail Car No. 5403—*hist pl* PA-2
Combination Creek—*stream* ID-8
Combination Ditch—*canal* NE-7
Combination Mill (Ruins)—*locale* NV-8
Combination Mine—*mine* AZ-5
Combination Ridge—*ridge* ID-8
Combination Sch—*school* MD-2
Combination Shaft—*mine* NV-8
Combination Spring—*spring* NV-8
Combination Trail Number 3—*trail* MT-8
**Combine**—*pop pl* TX-5
Combine Canyon—*valley* OR-9
Combined La Union Lateral—*canal* TX-5
**Combined Locks**—*pop pl* WI-6
Combine Flat—*bar* AK-9
Comb Peak—*summit* NV-8
*Combpest Creek* MT-8
Comb Ranch—*locale* WY-8
Comb Ridge—*ridge* AZ-5
Comb Ridge—*ridge* TN-4
Comb Ridge—*ridge* (2) UT-8
Comb Rock—*summit* MT-8
Comb Rocks—*summit* CA-9
Comb Run Ditch—*canal* IN-6
*Combs* GA-3
*Combs* TX-5
Combs—*locale* IL-6
Combs—*locale* TN-4
Combs—*locale* WV-2
**Combs**—*pop pl* AR-4
**Combs**—*pop pl* KY-4
Combs, H. B., House—*hist pl* TX-5
Combs, Nathan, House—*hist pl* AR-4
**Combs Addition**—*pop pl* WV-2
Combs Branch—*stream* IN-6
Combs Branch—*stream* (8) KY-4
Combs Branch—*stream* MO-7
Combs Branch Sch—*school* KY-4
Combs Bridge—*bridge* OK-5
Combs Brook—*stream* NY-2
Combs Canyon—*valley* (2) NV-8
Combs Cattle County Ranch—*locale* TX-5
Combs Cem—*cemetery* AR-4
Combs Cem—*cemetery* IL-6
Combs Cem—*cemetery* (5) KY-4
Combs Cem—*cemetery* (2) MO-7
Combs Cem—*cemetery* NC-3
Combs Cem—*cemetery* OK-5
Combs Cem—*cemetery* (2) TN-4
Combs Cem—*cemetery* (3) VA-3
Combs Ch—*church* AR-4
Combs Creek—*stream* IN-6
Combs Creek—*stream* MD-2
Combs Creek—*stream* NV-8
Combs Creek—*stream* (2) OR-9
Combs Creek—*stream* PA-2
Combs Ditch Number Two—*canal* MT-8
*Combs Ferry* TN-4
Combs Flat—*flat* OR-9
Combs Ford—*locale* KY-4
Combs Fork—*locale* NC-3
Combs Fork—*stream* (2) KY-4
Combs Hollow—*valley* PA-2
Combs HQ Ranch—*locale* TX-5
Combs Island—*island* ME-1
Combs Knob—*summit* NC-3
Combs Knob—*summit* OH-6
Combs Knob—*summit* TN-4
Combs Lake—*lake* NY-2
Combs Northeast Oil Field—*oilfield* KS-7
Combs Oil Field—*oilfield* KS-7
Combs Peak—*summit* CA-9
Combs Peak—*summit* NV-8
Combs Pond—*lake* TN-4
Combs Post Office (historical)—*building* TN-4
Comb Spur—*ridge* CA-9
Combs Ranch—*locale* MT-8
Combs Ranch—*locale* (2) WY-8
Combs Ridge—*ridge* KY-4
Combs Ridge—*ridge* VA-3
Combs Ridge Sch—*school* VA-3
Combs Riffle—*rapids* OR-9
Combs Run—*stream* WV-2
Combs Sch—*school* IN-6
Combs Sch—*school* NE-7
Combs Sch—*school* NC-3
Combs Shoals—*bar* TN-4
Combs Spring—*spring* KY-4
Combs Springhole—*bend* NY-2
Combs Station Prospect—*mine* TN-4
**Combs Switch**—*pop pl* IL-6
**Combs Township**—*pop pl* MO-7
Combs Trail—*trail* PA-2
Combs Trail—*trail* VA-3
Combs Valley—*basin* VA-3
Comb Wash—*valley* UT-8
*Comby Ridge* TN-4
Comby Ridge—*ridge* TN-4
Comcomly, Lake—*lake* WA-9
Com Creek—*stream* KY-4
Come-alive Ridge—*ridge* NM-5
Come Along Lode Mine—*mine* SD-7
Come And See Ch—*church* LA-4
*Come and See Church Number One* MS-4
Comeau Pass—*gap* MT-8
Comeaux, Lake—*lake* LA-4
Comeaux House—*hist pl* LA-4
Comeaux Park—*park* LA-4
Comeback Creek—*stream* AK-9
Comeback Mine—*mine* ID-8
**Comeby (historical)**—*pop pl* MS-4
Comeby Post Office (historical)—*building* MS-4
Comedor Crossing—*locale* TX-5
*Comegy Bight* MD-2
*Comegy Creek* MD-2
Comegys, Lake—*lake* DE-2
*Comegy's Bight* MD-2
Comegys Bight—*bay* MD-2
*Comegy's Creek* MD-2
Comegys Creek—*stream* MD-2
Comegys Lake—*lake* OR-9
Comegys Sch—*school* PA-2
*Comely* AZ-5
Comely Cem—*cemetery* LA-4
Comelys Branch—*stream* OK-5
Comenius Sch—*school* NE-7
Comeouter Hill—*summit* ME-1
Comer—*locale* CO-8
Comer—*locale* IL-6
Comer—*locale* KY-4
**Comer**—*pop pl* (2) AL-4
**Comer**—*pop pl* GA-3
Comer Ave Industrial Park—*locale* AL-4
Comer Branch—*stream* AR-4
Comer Branch—*stream* TN-4
Comer Branch—*stream* WV-2
Comer Bridge—*bridge* AL-4
Comer Brook—*stream* OR-9
Comer Canyon—*valley* NE-7
Comer (CCD)—*cens area* GA-3
Comer Cem—*cemetery* KY-4
Comer Cem—*cemetery* (2) OH-6
Comer Cem—*cemetery* TN-4
Comer Cem—*cemetery* (2) VA-3
Comer Cem—*cemetery* WV-2
Comer Chapel—*church* AL-4
Comer Creek—*stream* (2) OR-9
**Comerdale**—*pop pl* AL-4
*Comer Elementary School* AL-4
Comerer Ranch—*locale* CO-8
Comer Field—*park* AL-4
Comerford Theater—*hist pl* PA-2
**Comer (historical)**—*pop pl* OR-9
Comer Hollow—*valley* (2) TN-4
Comer HS—*school* AL-4
Comerio—*CDP* PR-3
**Comerio**—*pop pl* PR-3
Comerio (Municipio)—*civil* PR-3
Comerio (Pueblo)—*fmr MCD* PR-3
Comer Key—*island* FL-3
Comer Memorial Baptist Ch—*church* AL-4
Comer Memorial Methodist Ch—*church* AL-4
*Comer P.O.* AL-4
Comer Pond—*lake* NY-2
Comer Ranch—*locale* WY-8
Comers Branch—*stream* GA-3
Comers Branch—*stream* (2) VA-3
Comers Butte—*summit* MT-8
Comers Cem—*cemetery* AL-4
*Comer Sch* AL-4
Comer Sch—*school* (2) AL-4
Comer Sch—*school* MO-7
Comers Chapel—*church* NC-3
Comers Chapel Methodist Ch (historical)—*church* TN-4
Comers Chapel Sch (historical)—*school* TN-4
Comer Scout Reservation—*locale* AL-4
Comers Creek—*stream* VA-3
Comers Creek Ch—*church* VA-3
Comers Grave Ch—*church* GA-3
*Comer's Lake* MI-6
Comers Pond—*reservoir* AL-4
**Comers Rock**—*pop pl* VA-3
Comers Rock—*summit* VA-3
Comers Rock Branch—*stream* VA-3
Comers Rock Rec Area—*park* VA-3
Comertown—*locale* VA-3
**Comertown**—*pop pl* MT-8
*Comes Creek* PA-2
*Comet* IN-6
Comet—*locale* AK-9
Comet—*locale* AR-4
Comet—*locale* NC-3
Comet—*locale* VA-3
**Comet**—*pop pl* MO-7
**Comet**—*pop pl* MT-8
**Comet**—*pop pl* (2) OH-6
Cometa—*locale* CA-9
Cometa—*locale* TX-5
**Cometa**—*pop pl* PR-3
Cometa Cem—*cemetery* TX-5
Cometa Lateral—*canal* CA-9
Cometa Tank—*reservoir* TX-5
Comet Ch—*church* WV-2
Comet Creek—*stream* AK-9
Comet Creek—*stream* (2) ID-8
Comet Creek—*stream* MT-8
Comet Creek—*stream* OK-5
Comet Creek—*stream* WI-6
Comet Falls—*falls* WA-9
Comet Hill—*summit* MA-1
Comet (historical)—*locale* AL-4
Comet (historical)—*locale* KS-7
Comet Island—*island* MN-6
Comet Lake—*lake* MN-6
Comet Lake—*lake* MT-8
Comet Lake—*reservoir* OH-6
Comet Lake—*reservoir* PA-2
Comet Lake Dam—*dam* PA-2
Comet Mine—*mine* (4) CA-9
Comet Mine—*mine* NV-8
Comet Mine (Abandoned)—*mine* CA-9
Comet Mines—*mine* AK-9
Comet Mtn—*summit* MT-8
Comet Peak—*summit* AZ-5
*Comet Pond* MA-1
*Comets Peak* AZ-5
Comet Spring, The—*spring* AZ-5
Comet Swamp—*stream* VA-3
**Comettsburg**—*pop pl* PA-2
Comet Tungsten Mine—*mine* WY-8
Comet Tunnel—*mine* CO-8
*Comeva* AZ-5
Comeys Lake—*lake* NJ-2
Comeys Pond—*lake* MA-1
Comfort—*locale* TN-4
Comfort—*locale* WI-6
**Comfort**—*pop pl* (2) NC-3
**Comfort**—*pop pl* TX-5
**Comfort**—*pop pl* WV-2
Comfort, Lake—*reservoir* TN-4
Comfort, Point—*cape* ME-1
Comfort, Point—*cape* MI-6
Comfort, Point—*cape* NJ-2
Comfort, Point—*cape* NY-2
Comfort, Point—*cape* OR-9
Comfort, Point—*cape* (2) TX-5
Comfort, Point—*cemetery* NY-2
**Comfort, Point**—*pop pl* WI-6
Comfort, Point—*stream* SD-7
Comfort Cabin Springs—*spring* CA-9
Comfort Canal—*canal* FL-3
Comfort Canal Number C-5—*canal* FL-3
Comfort (CCD)—*cens area* TX-5
Comfort Cem—*cemetery* VA-3
Comfort Ch—*church* NC-3
Comfort Ch—*church* WV-2
Comfort Cove—*bay* AK-9
Comfort Creek—*stream* MN-6
Comfort Elem Sch—*school* NC-3
Comforter Mtn—*summit* CO-8
Comfort Hill—*summit* NY-2
Comfort Hist Dist—*hist pl* TX-5
Comfort Island—*island* LA-4
Comfort Island—*island* NY-2
Comfort Lake—*dam* PA-2
Comfort Lake—*lake* (2) MN-6
Comfort Lake—*reservoir* PA-2
Comfort Lookout Tower—*locale* NC-3
*Comfort Pond* PA-2
Comfort Post Office (historical)—*building* TN-4
Comfort Ridge—*ridge* GA-3
**Comfort (RR name Joe Creek)**—*pop pl* WV-2
Comfort Run—*locale* PA-2
Comfort Run—*stream* PA-2
Comfort Run—*stream* WV-2
Comfort Station—*hist pl* MA-1
Comfort Station No. 68—*hist pl* OR-9
Comfort Station No. 72—*hist pl* OR-9
**Comfort (Township of)**—*pop pl* MN-6
Comfort Trail—*trail* NY-2
**Comfrey**—*pop pl* MN-6
Comfy Creek—*stream* ID-8
**Comical Corners**—*pop pl* NJ-2
Comical Turn—*locale* ID-8
Comier Cem—*cemetery* LA-4
Coming Day Butte—*summit* MT-8
Coming Nation Mine—*mine* CO-8
Coming Portage Lake—*lake* AK-9
Comings Cabin—*locale* CA-9
Comings Creek—*stream* CA-9
Comingtee—*locale* SC-3
Comingtee Creek—*stream* SC-3
**Comins**—*pop pl* MI-6
Comins Cem—*cemetery* MI-6
Comins Creek—*stream* MI-6
Comins Flats—*flat* MI-6
Comins Lake—*lake* NV-8
Comins Marsh—*swamp* MI-6
Comins Meadow—*flat* NV-8
Comins Pond—*reservoir* MA-1
Comins Pond Dam—*dam* MA-1
**Comins (Township of)**—*pop pl* MI-6
**Cominsville**—*pop pl* MA-1
Cominto—*locale* AR-4
Cominto (Township of)—*fmr MCD* AR-4
Comiskey Field—*park* IA-7
Comiskey (historical)—*locale* KS-7
Comiskey Park—*park* IL-6
Comisky Cem—*cemetery* KS-7
Comitas Lake—*lake* TX-5
Comitas Tank—*reservoir* TX-5
**Comite**—*pop pl* LA-4
Comite Ch—*church* LA-4
Comite Creek—*stream* LA-4
Comite Creek—*stream* MS-4
Comite River—*stream* LA-4
*Comleysville* PA-2
Comly—*locale* PA-2
Comly—*other* OH-6
Comly, Watson, Sch—*hist pl* PA-2
Comly Sch—*school* PA-2
*Comlyville* PA-2
*Commac* NY-2
**Commack**—*pop pl* NY-2
Commack Cem—*cemetery* NY-2
Commack Hills Country Club—*other* NY-2
Commack HS—*school* NY-2
Commack Methodist Church and Cemetery—*hist pl* NY-2
Commack Park—*park* NY-2
Commack Road Sch—*school* NY-2
Comma Island—*island* AK-9
Comma Lake—*lake* OR-9
Commanche Creek—*stream* TX-5
Commanche Gap—*gap* TX-5
Commandant's House—*hist pl* NC-3
Commandant's Office, Washington Navy Yard—*hist pl* DC-2
Commandant's Quarters—*hist pl* MI-6
Commandant's Quarters—*hist pl* OK-5
Commandant's Quarters—*hist pl* PA-2
Commandant's Residence, Quarters Number One, Fort Adams—*hist pl* RI-1
Commandant's Residence Home—*hist pl* WI-6
Command Ch—*church* NC-3
Command Control—*locale* FL-3
Commander Airpark Inc—*airport* AL-4
Commander Creek—*stream* FL-3
Commander Mine—*mine* CO-8
Commanders House Park—*park* TX-5
Commanding Officer's Quarters, Watertown Arsenal—*hist pl* MA-1
Command Lake—*lake* MN-6
Commandment Keeping Ch—*church* GA-3
Commando Creek—*stream* NJ-2
Command Point—*cape* WA-9
*Commasskumkanit* MA-1
*Commatri Creek* CA-9
*Commatta Creek* CA-9
*Commatti Creek* CA-9
*Commatti Ranch* CA-9
Commemorative Cem—*cemetery* FL-3
Commencement Bay—*bay* WA-9
*Commencement City* WA-9
Commencement Creek—*stream* MI-6
Commencement Oil Field—*oilfield* MS-4
*Commerce* MN-6
Commerce—*locale* AL-4
**Commerce**—*pop pl* GA-3
**Commerce**—*pop pl* IA-7
**Commerce**—*pop pl* MI-6
**Commerce**—*pop pl* MS-4
**Commerce**—*pop pl* MO-7
**Commerce**—*pop pl* OK-5
**Commerce**—*pop pl* TN-4
**Commerce**—*pop pl* TX-5
Commerce—*uninc pl* AZ-5
Commerce—*uninc pl* PA-2
Commerce—*uninc pl* SD-7
Commerce Building/Hancock Bldg—*hist pl* OK-5
Commerce (CCD)—*cens area* GA-3
Commerce (CCD)—*cens area* TX-5
Commerce Cem—*cemetery* MI-6
Commerce Cem—*cemetery* MO-7
Commerce Cem—*cemetery* TN-4
**Commerce City**—*pop pl* CO-8
**Commerce (City of Commerce Post Office)**—*pop pl* CA-9
Commerce Country Club—*other* GA-3
Commerce Court Shop Ctr—*locale* MS-4
Commerce Cutoff—*channel* MS-4
Commerce Cut Off (1874)—*bend* AR-4
Commerce HS—*school* NY-2
Commerce Industrial Park—*locale* NC-3
Commerce Landing—*locale* KY-4
Commerce Landing—*locale* MS-4
Commerce Park RR Station—*locale* FL-3
Commerce Plaza Shop Ctr—*locale* MS-4
Commerce Post Office (historical)—*building* TN-4
Commerce Revetment—*levee* MS-4
Commerce Sch (historical)—*school* TN-4
Commerce Spur Junction RR Station—*locale* FL-3
Commerce Street Residential Hist Dist—*hist pl* AL-4
*Commerce Tower* MO-7
*Commerce Town Derby* CO-8
Commerce Township—*civil* MO-7
**Commerce (Township of)**—*pop pl* MI-6
Commerce Waterworks—*other* GA-3
*Commercial* MO-7
Commercial and Savings Bank—*hist pl* CA-9
Commercial Bank and Banker's House—*hist pl* MS-4
Commercial Bank Bldg—*hist pl* MN-6
Commercial Banking & Trust Co.—*hist pl* OH-6
Commercial Basin—*bay* CA-9
Commercial Bldg—*hist pl* IN-6
Commercial Bldg—*hist pl* LA-4
Commercial Bldg—*hist pl* (2) OH-6
Commercial Bridge—*bridge* FL-3
Commercial Canal—*canal* LA-4
Commercial Club-Stuckey, S. C., Bldg—*hist pl* OR-9
Commercial Coll—*school* MA-1
*Commercial Corner* DE-2
Commercial District—*hist pl* (2) MT-8
Commercial Hist Dist—*hist pl* ID-8
Commercial Hist Dist—*hist pl* KY-4
Commercial (historical)—*locale* AL-4
Commercial Hotel—*hist pl* (2) AR-4
Commercial Hotel—*hist pl* (2) MN-6
Commercial Hotel—*hist pl* PA-2
Commercial Hotel-Hart Hotel—*hist pl* AL-4
Commercial HS—*school* GA-3
Commercial Incline—*mine* NM-5
Commercial Park—*park* IL-6
*Commercial Place* IN-6
Commercial Point—*cape* MA-1
**Commercial Point**—*pop pl* OH-6
Commercial Sch—*school* MO-7
Commercial Shop Ctr—*locale* NC-3
Commercial Street Bridge—*hist pl* CO-8
Commercial Street Hist Dist—*hist pl* MO-7
Commercial Street Hist Dist—*hist pl* OH-6
**Commercial (Township of)**—*pop pl* NJ-2
Commercial Wharf—*locale* MA-1
Commerford Springs—*spring* ID-8
*Commerical Canal* LA-4
Commerical Community Hist Dist—*hist pl* MO-7
Commerical House—*hist pl* IL-6
Commertown Sch—*school* MO-7
*Commie Thomas Ditch* IN-6
Commins Corners—*locale* NY-2
Commisary Ch—*church* AR-4
**Commiskey**—*pop pl* IN-6
Commissary Branch—*stream* KY-4
Commissary Brook—*stream* VT-1
Commissary Canyon—*valley* (2) NM-5
Commissary Corner—*locale* KY-4
Commissary Creek—*stream* MT-8
Commissary Creek—*stream* NM-5
Commissary Creek—*stream* NY-2
Commissary Creek—*stream* (2) UT-8
Commissary Fork—*stream* UT-8
Commissary Gulch—*valley* CO-8
Commissary Gulch Campground—*locale* CO-8
Commissary Hill—*locale* GA-3
Commissary Hill—*summit* NC-3
Commissary Hill—*summit* WY-8
Commissary Hollow—*valley* KY-4
Commissary Hollow—*valley* (2) TN-4
Commissary Hollow Access Point—*park* TN-4
Commissary Park—*flat* CO-8
Commissary Park—*park* WY-8
Commissary Point—*cape* LA-4
Commissary Point—*cape* ME-1
Commissary Point—*cape* SD-7
Commissary Ridge—*ridge* ID-8
Commissary Ridge—*ridge* MT-8
Commissary Ridge—*ridge* NC-3
Commissary Ridge—*ridge* TN-4
Commissary Ridge—*ridge* WY-8
Commissary Sch—*school* TN-4
Commissary Spring—*spring* CA-9
Commissary Spring—*spring* MT-8
Commissary Spring—*spring* UT-8
Commissary Spring—*spring* WY-8
Commissary Springs—*spring* MT-8
*Commissarytown* IL-6
Commission Creek—*stream* OK-5
Commission Creek—*stream* TX-5
Commission Ditch—*canal* NY-2
Commissioner Creek—*stream* GA-3
Commissioner Creek—*stream* NC-3
Commissioner Ditch—*canal* CO-8
Commissioner Gap—*gap* NC-3
Commissioner Run—*stream* PA-2
Commissioner Run Trail—*trail* (2) PA-2
*Commissioners Creek* GA-3
Commissioners Creek—*stream* MS-4
Commissioners Creek—*stream* TX-5
Commissioners Ledge—*rock* MA-1
Commissioner's Office—*hist pl* MH-9
Commissioners Rock—*other* GA-3
Commissioners Run—*stream* PA-2
Committee Creek—*stream* OR-9
Committee Tank—*reservoir* AZ-5
**Commodore**—*pop pl* PA-2
Commodore Apartment Bldg—*hist pl* KY-4
Commodore Apartment Bldg—*hist pl* OH-6
Commodore Bainbridge Sch—*school* WA-9
Commodore Creek—*stream* OK-5
Commodore D Loveless Bridge—*bridge* TN-4
Commodore Downs—*other* PA-2
Commodore Foods Company Dam—*dam* MA-1
Commodore Gulch—*valley* CO-8
Commodore Gun Club—*other* CA-9
Commodore Hotel—*hist pl* OR-9
Commodore Hull Sch—*hist pl* CT-1
Commodore Hull Sch—*school* CT-1
Commodore Island—*island* GA-3
Commodore Jones Point—*cape* CA-9
*Commodore Key* FL-3
Commodore Lake—*lake* MN-6
Commodore Lake—*lake* OR-9
Commodore Macdonogh Elem Sch—*school* DE-2
Commodore Marina—*locale* NC-3

Commodore Mine—*mine* (2) ... CA-9
Commodore Mine—*mine* ... CO-8
Commodore Mine—*mine* ... ID-8
Commodore Mine—*mine* ... KY-4
**Commodore Park**—*pop pl* ... VA-3
Commodore Pass—*gap* ... UT-8
Commodore Point—*cape* ... FL-3
Commodore Post Office (historical)—*building* ... MS-4
Commodore Ridge—*ridge* ... OR-9
Commodore Trail—*trail* ... CA-9
*Common* ... RI-1
*Common, The* ... MA-1
Common Bedground Waterhole—*reservoir* ... OR-9
Common Burying Ground and Island Cemetery—*hist pl* ... RI-1
Common Burying Ground at Sandy Bank—*hist pl* ... MA-1
*Common Creek* ... PA-2
Common Fence Point—*cape* ... RI-1
**Common Fence Point**—*pop pl* ... RI-1
Common Field Archeol Site—*hist pl* ... MO-7
Common Flat—*flat* ... MA-1
Common Hill—*summit* ... ME-1
Common Hill—*summit* ... MA-1
Common Hill Ch—*church* ... AR-4
Common Hist Dist—*hist pl* ... MA-1
Common Lake—*lake* ... SC-3
Common Pond—*lake* ... NH-1
Common Run—*stream* ... IN-6
**Commons**—*pop pl* ... RI-1
Commons, John R., House—*hist pl* ... WI-6
*Commons, The* (2) ... RI-1
Commons, The—*flat* ... ME-1
Commons, The—*park* ... AL-4
Commons, The—*park* ... IL-6
Commons, The—*park* ... MA-1
Commons Branch—*stream* ... TN-4
Commons Brook—*stream* ... MA-1
Commons Cem—*cemetery* ... TN-4
Common Sch No. 10—*hist pl* ... NY-2
Common Sch Number 1—*school* ... NY-2
Commons Creek—*stream* ... OR-9
*Common Sense Point* ... RI-1
Common Sense Sch (historical)—*school* (2) ... MO-7
Commons Hill—*summit* ... CT-1
Commons Island—*island* ... NH-1
Commons Store (historical)—*locale* ... MS-4
**Commons (subdivision), The**—*pop pl* ... MS-4
Common Street Cem—*cemetery* ... MA-1
Common Street District—*hist pl* ... AL-4
Commonwealth—*CDP* ... VA-3
Commonwealth—*locale* ... KS-7
**Commonwealth**—*pop pl* ... WI-6
Commonwealth—*uninc pl* ... CA-9
Commonwealth Ave Sch—*school* ... CA-9
Commonwealth Club Hist Dist—*hist pl* ... VA-3
Commonwealth Creek—*stream* ... WA-9
Commonwealth Forest Camp—*locale* ... WA-9
Commonwealth Lake—*lake* ... OR-9
Commonwealth Mine—*mine* ... AZ-5
Commonwealth Mine—*mine* ... CA-9
Commonwealth Mine—*mine* ... ID-8
Commonwealth Mine—*mine* ... NV-8
Commonwealth Mine—*mine* ... UT-8
Commonwealth Mine—*mine* ... WA-9
*Commonwealth Natl Bank Airport* ... PA-2
Commonwealth of Massachusetts—*civil* ... MA-1
Commonwealth Pier—*locale* ... MA-1
Commonwealth Sch—*school* ... CA-9
Commonwealth Shopper—*locale* ... MA-1
**Commonwealth Square Condominium**—*pop pl* ... UT-8
**Commonwealth Square Subdivision**—*pop pl* ... UT-8
**Commonwealth (Town of)**—*pop pl* ... WI-6
Commonwealth Water Company Rsvr Number Three—*reservoir* ... NJ-2
Comm/Scope Company—*facility* ... NC-3
Comm Scope Dam—*dam* ... NC-3
Comm Scope Lake—*reservoir* ... NC-3
Commston Lake—*lake* ... FL-3
Communia—*locale* ... IA-7
Communia Cem—*cemetery* ... IA-7
Communion Butte—*summit* ... MT-8
Communion Cem—*cemetery* ... ND-7
**Communipaw**—*pop pl* ... NJ-2
*Communi Point* ... NJ-2
*Communipon Farmes* ... NJ-2
*Communipon Farms* ... NJ-2
**Community**—*pop pl* ... VA-3
Community and Adult Education Center—*school* ... FL-3
*Community Baptist Ch* ... MS-4
*Community Baptist Ch* ... TN-4
Community Baptist Ch—*church* (3) ... AL-4
Community Baptist Ch—*church* (8) ... FL-3
Community Baptist Ch—*church* ... IN-6
Community Baptist Ch—*church* ... KS-7
Community Baptist Ch—*church* ... MS-4
Community Baptist Ch—*church* ... TN-4
Community Baptist Ch (Moab)—*church* ... UT-8
Community Baptist Ch (St. George)—*church* ... UT-8
Community Beach Park—*park* ... IL-6
Community Bible Ch—*church* ... AL-4
Community Bible Ch—*church* ... MS-4
Community Bible Ch—*church* ... SC-3
Community Bible Ch of Seminole—*church* ... FL-3
Community Bldg—*hist pl* ... IA-7
Community Bldg—*hist pl* ... NY-2
Community Bldg—*hist pl* ... NC-3
Community Camp (historical)—*locale* ... AL-4
Community Cem—*cemetery* (3) ... AL-4
Community Cem—*cemetery* ... KS-7
Community Cem—*cemetery* (2) ... NC-3
Community Cem—*cemetery* ... WI-6
Community Center—*hist pl* ... TX-5
Community Center—*locale* ... CA-9
Community Center—*park* ... FL-3
Community Center and War Memorial Bldg—*hist pl* ... WA-9
Community Center Baptist Ch—*church* ... AL-4
Community Center Bldg—*building* ... MO-7
Community Center Cem—*cemetery* ... MS-4
Community Center Ch—*church* (2) ... AL-4
Community Center Ch—*church* ... MS-4
Community Center Park—*park* ... AL-4
Community Center Park—*park* ... MI-6
Community Center Sch—*school* ... NE-7
*Community Ch* ... AL-4
*Community Ch* ... MS-4
*Community Ch* ... PA-2
Community Ch—*church* (7) ... AL-4
Community Ch—*church* ... AR-4
Community Ch—*church* ... CT-1
Community Ch—*church* (3) ... IN-6
Community Ch—*church* (2) ... KS-7
Community Ch—*church* (2) ... LA-4
Community Ch—*church* ... ME-1
Community Ch—*church* ... MA-1
Community Ch—*church* (4) ... MI-6
Community Ch—*church* (2) ... MN-6
Community Ch—*church* (5) ... MS-4
Community Ch—*church* (7) ... MO-7
Community Ch—*church* ... MT-8
Community Ch—*church* (5) ... NY-2
Community Ch—*church* (10) ... NC-3
Community Ch—*church* (2) ... TN-4
Community Ch—*church* (2) ... VA-3
Community Ch—*church* (7) ... WV-2
Community Ch—*church* (2) ... WI-6
*Community Chapel* ... TN-4
Community Chapel—*church* (2) ... MO-7
Community Chapel—*church* ... TN-4
Community Chapel—*church* ... TX-5
Community Chapel—*church* ... WV-2
Community Chapel Ch—*church* ... AL-4
Community Chapel Ch of God—*church* ... AL-4
Community Chapel Ch of God—*church* ... MS-4
Community Ch of God—*church* ... FL-3
Community Ch of God in Christ—*church* ... AL-4
Community Ch of God in Christ—*church* ... KS-7
Community Ch of Keystone Heights—*church* ... FL-3
Community Ch of the Brethren—*church* ... FL-3
Community Christian Ch—*church* ... KS-7
Community Christian Ch—*church* ... PA-2
Community Christian Sch—*school* ... CA-9
Community Christian Sch—*school* (2) ... FL-3
Community Christian Sch of LaBelle—*school* ... FL-3
Community Church (historical)—*locale* ... MO-7
Community Church of Gonzales—*hist pl* ... CA-9
Community Club Cem—*cemetery* ... MS-4
Community Club Ch—*church* ... MS-4
Community Coll—*school* ... OR-9
Community Coll Of Allegheny County—*school* ... PA-2
Community Congregational Ch—*church* ... KS-7
Community Congregational Ch (Provo)—*church* ... UT-8
Community Congregational Holiness Ch—*church* ... AL-4
Community Congregational United Ch of Christ—*church* ... FL-3
Community Ditch—*canal* ... CA-9
Community Ditch—*canal* ... CO-8
Community Ditch—*canal* ... NM-5
Community Education Center—*school* ... FL-3
Community Farm Center—*other* ... CA-9
Community Full Gospel Ch—*church* ... NY-2
Community General Osteopathic Hosp—*hospital* ... PA-2
Community Gospel Ch—*church* ... WV-2
Community Gospel Chapel—*church* ... MI-6
Community Grove Ch—*church* ... GA-3
Community Grove Ch—*church* ... TN-4
Community Hall—*building* ... MO-7
Community Hall Rockland Cem—*cemetery* ... CO-8
Community Holiness Ch—*church* ... AL-4
Community Holy Tabernacle of Deliverance—*church* ... DE-2
Community Hosp—*hospital* ... IN-6
Community Hosp—*hospital* ... MA-1
Community Hosp—*hospital* ... MI-6
Community Hosp (historical)—*hospital* ... MS-4
Community Hospital Airp—*airport* ... IN-6
Community Hosp of Anaconda—*hospital* ... MT-8
Community Hosp of Bunnell—*hospital* ... FL-3
Community Hosp of Calhoun County—*hospital* ... MS-4
*Community Hosp of Lancaster* ... PA-2
Community Hosp of New Port Richey—*hospital* ... FL-3
Community House, First Congregational Church—*hist pl* ... WI-6
Community House of Prayer—*church* ... GA-3
Community HS—*school* ... FL-3
Community Lake—*lake* ... CT-1
Community Lake—*lake* ... ID-8
Community Life Ch—*church* ... NC-3
Community Memorial Garden—*cemetery* ... NC-3
Community Memorial Hosp—*hospital* ... OR-9
*Community Methodist Ch* ... AL-4
Community Missionary Baptist Ch—*church* ... FL-3
Community Missionary Baptist Ch—*church* ... MS-4
Community Mission Ch—*church* ... WV-2
Community Outreach Center—*school* ... FL-3
Community Park—*locale* ... NY-2
Community Park—*park* ... NE-7
**Community Park**—*pop pl* ... MA-1
Community Pasture Trail (Pack)—*trail* ... NM-5
Community Place—*hist pl* ... NY-2
Community Plaza (Shop Ctr)—*locale* (2) ... FL-3
Community Pond—*reservoir* ... MS-4
Community Presbyterian Ch—*church* ... DE-2
Community Presbyterian Ch—*church* ... FL-3
Community Presbyterian Ch—*church* ... UT-8
Community Presbyterian Ch (American Fork)—*church* ... UT-8
Community Presbyterian Ch (Cedar City)—*church* ... UT-8
Community Presbyterian Ch (Myton)—*church* ... UT-8
Community Reformed Ch—*church* ... FL-3
Community Reformed Ch of Clearwater—*church* ... FL-3
Community Relief Cem—*cemetery* ... TX-5
Community Reseeding Waterhole—*reservoir* ... OR-9
Community Rest Cem—*cemetery* ... NC-3
Community Sch—*school* ... AR-4
Community Sch—*school* ... NY-2
Community Sch (historical)—*school* ... TN-4
Community Sch of Naples—*school* ... FL-3
Community Service Center and Sch—*school* ... AZ-5
**Community Siding**—*pop pl* ... SC-3
Community Spring—*spring* ... TN-4
Community Tank—*reservoir* (2) ... AZ-5
Community Temple—*church* ... NY-2
Community Theatre—*hist pl* ... NY-2
Community Training Center—*school* ... VA-3
Community United Methodist Ch—*church* (3) ... FL-3
Community United Methodist Ch—*church* ... UT-8
Community Vine Ch—*church* ... FL-3
*Comnuck Island* ... RI-1
*Como* ... MN-6
Como—*locale* ... CA-9
Como—*locale* ... MO-7
Como—*locale* ... MT-8
Como—*locale* ... NV-8
Como—*locale* ... NY-2
Como—*locale* ... WY-8
**Como**—*pop pl* ... CO-8
**Como**—*pop pl* ... IL-6
**Como**—*pop pl* ... IN-6
**Como**—*pop pl* ... KY-4
**Como**—*pop pl* ... LA-4
**Como**—*pop pl* ... MS-4
**Como**—*pop pl* ... NC-3
**Como**—*pop pl* ... TN-4
**Como**—*pop pl* ... TX-5
**Como**—*pop pl* ... WI-6
Como, Bayou—*stream* ... AL-4
Como, Lake—*lake* (2) ... CO-8
Como, Lake—*lake* ... CT-1
Como, Lake—*lake* ... DE-2
Como, Lake—*lake* (2) ... FL-3
Como, Lake—*lake* ... ME-1
Como, Lake—*lake* (2) ... MN-6
Como, Lake—*lake* ... NY-2
Como, Lake—*lake* ... OR-9
Como, Lake—*lake* ... TX-5
**Como, Lake**—*pop pl* ... WI-6
Como, Lake—*reservoir* ... DE-2
Como, Lake—*reservoir* ... MA-1
Como, Lake—*reservoir* ... MT-8
Como, Lake—*reservoir* ... NJ-2
Como, Lake—*reservoir* ... PA-2
Como, Lake—*reservoir* ... TX-5
Como, Lake—*reservoir* (2) ... WI-6
Como, Lake (historical)—*lake* ... SD-7
Como, Mount—*summit* ... NV-8
**Comobabi**—*pop pl* ... AZ-5
Comobabi Pass—*gap* ... AZ-5
*Comobabi Peak* ... AZ-5
*Comobabi Wash* ... AZ-5
Comobabi Wash—*stream* ... AZ-5
Comobabi Well—*well* ... AZ-5
Comobari Mountains—*range* ... AZ-5
*Comobavi Mountains* ... AZ-5
*Comobavi Wash* ... AZ-5
Como Bayou—*stream* ... LA-4
Como Bluff—*hist pl* ... WY-8
Como Bluff Fish Hatchery—*locale* ... WY-8
Como Bluffs—*cliff* ... WY-8
Como Cem—*cemetery* ... CO-8
Como Cem—*cemetery* ... MS-4
Como Ch—*church* ... AR-4
Como Ch—*church* ... MS-4
*Comochechebbee Creek* ... GA-3
*Comock* ... NY-2
Como Creek—*stream* ... CO-8
Como Creek—*stream* (2) ... WI-6
*Como Depot.* ... MS-4
Como Diversion—*dam* ... UT-8
Como Elem Sch—*school* ... MS-4
Como Farm—*hist pl* ... PA-2
*Como-Friendship Cemetery* ... MS-4
Como-Harriet Streetcar Line and Trolley—*hist pl* ... MN-6
Como (historical)—*locale* ... KS-7
*Comojelano Creek* ... TX-5
*Como Lake* ... WI-6
Como Lake—*lake* ... CO-8
Como Lake—*lake* (2) ... FL-3
Como Lake—*lake* ... MI-6
Como Lake—*lake* ... WY-8
Como Lake (historical)—*reservoir* ... MS-4
Como Lake Park—*park* ... NY-2
Como Landing—*locale* ... LA-4
**Comolli**—*pop pl* ... GA-3
Como Oil Field—*oilfield* ... TX-5
Como Park—*park* ... MN-6
Como Park—*park* ... OH-6
Como Park Conservatory—*hist pl* ... MN-6
Como Park JHS—*school* ... MN-6
Como Park Sch—*school* ... MN-6
Como Park Sch—*school* ... NY-2
*Como Peak* ... NV-8
Como Peaks—*summit* ... MT-8
Como Post Office—*building* ... TN-4
Comorant Island—*island* ... AK-9
Como Ridge—*ridge* ... WY-8
Comorn—*locale* ... VA-3
*Comoro Canyon* ... AZ-5
*Comoro Fresno Canyon* ... AZ-5
Como Roundhouse, RR Depot and Hotel Complex—*hist pl* ... CO-8
Como Run—*stream* ... IN-6
Como Sch—*school* ... MS-4
Como Sch—*school* ... SD-7
Como Springs—*locale* ... UT-8
*Comot* ... AZ-5
*Comote* ... AZ-5
*Comoti* ... AZ-5
Como Township—*civil* ... MO-7
**Como Township**—*pop pl* ... SD-7
**Como (Township of)**—*pop pl* ... MN-6
*Comova* ... AZ-5
*Comovo* ... AZ-5
*Comovo Valley* ... AZ-5
Como Windmill—*locale* ... TX-5
Compaanen Kill—*stream* ... NY-2
Compadre Mine—*mine* ... AZ-5
Compania Tank—*reservoir* ... TX-5
Companion Lake—*lake* ... MT-8
Company Branch—*stream* ... KY-4
Company Brook—*stream* ... MA-1
Company Butte—*summit* ... OR-9
Company Canal—*canal* (2) ... LA-4
Company Cem—*cemetery* ... GA-3
Company Cem—*cemetery* (2) ... KY-4
Company Cem—*cemetery* (2) ... VA-3
Company Creek—*stream* ... OR-9
Company Creek—*stream* ... WA-9
Company Creek—*stream* ... WY-8
Company Creek Campground—*locale* ... WA-9
*Company Creek Glacier* ... WA-9
Company Ditch—*canal* (2) ... CO-8
Company Ditch—*canal* (2) ... MT-8
**Company Farm**—*pop pl* ... NC-3
Company Glacier—*glacier* ... WA-9
Company Gulch—*valley* ... MT-8
*Company Hill* ... MA-1
Company Hollow—*valley* ... KY-4
Company Hollow—*valley* ... MO-7
Company Hollow—*valley* ... OR-9
Company Hollow—*valley* ... PA-2
Company Hollow Spring—*spring* ... OR-9
Company Lake—*lake* ... WI-6
Company Lake—*reservoir* ... OR-9
Company Meadows—*flat* ... CA-9
Company Pond—*reservoir* ... LA-4
Company Pond—*reservoir* ... SC-3
Company Ranch—*locale* ... WY-8
*Company Shops* ... NC-3
Company Slough—*swamp* ... FL-3
Company Spring—*spring* (2) ... NV-8
Company Spring—*spring* ... OR-9
Company Springs—*spring* ... OR-9
Company Swamp—*swamp* ... PA-2
Company Tank—*reservoir* ... AZ-5
Company Tank—*reservoir* ... TX-5
Company Trough—*spring* ... OR-9
Company Well—*well* ... NV-8
Company Windmill—*locale* ... TX-5
Company 40 Spring—*spring* ... NV-8
Compartidero, Arroyo del—*valley* ... AZ-5
Compartidero Flats—*flat* ... AZ-5
Compartment Creek—*stream* ... WY-8
**Compass**—*pop pl* ... PA-2
*Compass Creek* ... NC-3
Compass Creek—*stream* (2) ... NC-3
Compass Creek—*stream* ... OR-9
Compass Harbor—*bay* ... ME-1
Compass Island—*island* ... ME-1
Compass Lake—*lake* (2) ... FL-3
**Compass Lake**—*pop pl* ... FL-3
Compass Lake Tower (fire tower)—*tower* ... FL-3
Compass Point—*cape* ... FL-3
Compass Point—*cape* ... VI-3
Compass Point Creek—*stream* ... FL-3
Compass Pond—*lake* ... ME-1
Compass Rock—*summit* ... ME-1
Compass Rose—*military* ... CA-9
Compass Run—*stream* ... MD-2
Compass Sch—*school* ... PA-2
Compass Tank—*reservoir* ... AZ-5
*Compassville* ... PA-2
*Compbest Creek* ... MT-8
*Compbest Peak* ... MT-8
Compeau Creek—*stream* ... MI-6
*Compensating Reservoir* ... CT-1
Compere Ch—*church* ... TX-5
Compers Lake Dam—*dam* ... MS-4
Competine—*locale* ... IA-7
Competine Cem—*cemetery* ... IA-7
Competine Creek—*stream* ... IA-7
Competine (historical P.O.)—*locale* ... IA-7
Competine Township—*fmr MCD* ... IA-7
**Competition**—*pop pl* ... MO-7
Compground Rsvr—*reservoir* ... OR-9
*Compher* ... OH-6
**Complete**—*pop pl* ... MS-4
Complex—*locale* ... NC-3
Complex Drain—*stream* ... MI-6
Complexion Canyon—*valley* ... CA-9
Complexion Spring—*spring* ... CA-9
Complex Lake—*lake* ... FL-3
**Compo**—*pop pl* ... CT-1
Compo Beach—*beach* ... CT-1
**Compo Beach**—*pop pl* ... CT-1
Compo Cove—*bay* ... CT-1
Compo Creek—*stream* ... NY-2
**Compo Hill**—*pop pl* ... CT-1
Compo Hill—*summit* ... CT-1
Compolindo HS—*school* ... CA-9
Compoodie Creek—*stream* ... NV-8
*Compoodle Creek* ... CA-9
Compos Canyon—*valley* ... NM-5
*Compos Creek* ... NY-2
Compos Creek—*stream* ... NY-2
Composite Island—*island* ... AK-9
Compo Swamp—*swamp* ... NY-2
Compounce Lake—*reservoir* ... CT-1
Compounce Mtn—*summit* ... CT-1
Compound Draw—*valley* ... TX-5
Compound Hollow—*valley* ... PA-2
Comprehensive JHS—*school* ... FL-3
*Compressed Cliffs* ... MH-9
Compressor Gulch—*valley* ... CA-9
Compressor Station—*locale* ... MO-7
Compressor Station Bench—*beach* ... ID-8
Compressor Station Number 10 Airstrip—*airport* ... OR-9
Compressor Station Number 11 Airstrip—*airport* ... OR-9
Compressor Station Number 8 Stolport—*airport* ... WA-9
Compressor Station Number 9—*other* ... OR-9
Compressor Station Ruin (LA 5658)—*hist pl* ... NM-5
Compressor Station 14 Airstrip—*airport* ... OR-9
Compressor Tank—*reservoir* ... AZ-5
Compress Slough—*stream* ... TX-5
Compro—*locale* ... IL-6
Compromise—*locale* ... MS-4
Compromise Ch—*church* (2) ... TN-4
Compromise Gulch—*valley* ... MT-8
Compromise Landing—*locale* ... TN-4
Compromise Sch—*school* ... IL-6
Compromise Sch (historical)—*school* (2) ... MS-4
Compromise Sch (historical)—*school* ... TN-4
**Compromise (Township of)**—*pop pl* ... IL-6
Compro-Wittmer Ditch—*canal* ... IN-6
Comps Crossroads—*locale* ... PA-2
**Comptche**—*pop pl* ... CA-9
*Compti* ... TX-5
*Compton* ... RI-1
Compton—*hist pl* ... MD-2
Compton—*locale* ... AL-4
Compton—*locale* ... AR-4
Compton—*locale* ... OK-5
Compton—*locale* ... VA-3
**Compton**—*pop pl* ... CA-9
**Compton**—*pop pl* ... IL-6
**Compton**—*pop pl* ... MD-2
**Compton**—*pop pl* (2) ... PA-2
**Compton**—*pop pl* ... TN-4
Compton, Alma, House—*hist pl* ... UT-8
Compton, Arthur H., House—*hist pl* ... IL-6
Compton, Dr. James, House—*hist pl* ... MO-7
Compton and Bloomfield—*hist pl* ... PA-2
Compton Ave Sch—*school* ... CA-9
Compton Bassett—*hist pl* ... MD-2
Compton Branch—*stream* ... IN-6
Compton Branch—*stream* (2) ... KY-4
Compton Branch—*stream* (2) ... MO-7
Compton Branch—*stream* ... TN-4
Compton Branch—*stream* ... TX-5
Compton Canyon—*valley* ... CO-8
Compton (CCD)—*cens area* ... CA-9
Compton Cem—*cemetery* ... AL-4
Compton Cem—*cemetery* ... IL-6
Compton Cem—*cemetery* ... KY-4
Compton Cem—*cemetery* ... MN-6
Compton Cem—*cemetery* ... OH-6
Compton Cem—*cemetery* ... TN-4
Compton Cem—*cemetery* (6) ... VA-3
Compton Cem—*cemetery* (2) ... WV-2
Compton Ch—*church* ... MN-6
Compton Ch—*church* ... TX-5
Compton Coll—*school* ... CA-9
*Compton Commons* ... RI-1
*Compton Creek* ... AL-4
*Compton Creek* ... NJ-2
Compton Creek—*stream* ... CA-9
Compton Creek—*stream* ... MS-4
Compton Creek—*stream* ... MO-7
Compton Creek—*stream* ... NJ-2
Compton Creek—*stream* ... OH-6
Compton Dam—*dam* ... PA-2
Compton Ditch—*canal* (2) ... IN-6
Compton Drain—*canal* ... MI-6
Compton Draw—*valley* ... NM-5
**Compton East (census name East Compton)**—*pop pl* ... CA-9
Compton (Election Precinct)—*fmr MCD* ... IL-6
Compton Fork—*stream* ... KY-4
Compton Gap—*gap* ... VA-3
Compton Gap Site—*hist pl* ... VA-3
Compton Hill—*ridge* ... MO-7
Compton Hill Rsvr—*reservoir* ... MO-7
Compton Hill Water Tower—*hist pl* ... MO-7
Compton (historical)—*locale* ... AL-4
Compton Hollow—*valley* ... IN-6
Compton Hollow—*valley* ... MO-7
Compton Hollow—*valley* ... OK-5
Compton Hollow—*valley* ... TN-4
Compton Hollow—*valley* ... VA-3
Compton HS—*school* ... CA-9
Compton JHS—*school* ... CA-9
Compton Lake—*lake* ... IN-6
Compton Lake—*swamp* ... LA-4
Compton Lake Canal—*canal* ... LA-4
Compton Landing—*locale* ... AL-4
Compton Landing—*locale* ... CA-9
Compton Lookout Tower—*locale* ... AR-4
*Compton Mill* ... AL-4
Compton Mtn—*summit* ... VA-3
Compton Park—*park* ... DE-2
Compton Park—*park* ... IL-6
Compton Park—*park* ... MI-6
**Compton Park**—*pop pl* ... OH-6
Compton Peak—*summit* ... VA-3
Compton Plaza (Shop Ctr)—*locale* ... FL-3
Compton Ranch—*locale* ... NM-5
Compton Ranch (historical)—*locale* ... SD-7
Compton Rec Area—*park* ... MO-7
Compton Ridge—*ridge* ... MO-7
Comptons—*locale* ... TX-5
Compton Sch—*school* (2) ... IL-6
Compton Sch—*school* ... MO-7
Compton Sch—*school* ... NE-7
Compton Sch—*school* ... OK-5
Compton Sch (abandoned)—*school* ... PA-2
Comptons Corner—*locale* ... VA-3
*Comptons Creek* ... NJ-2
Compton-Short House—*hist pl* ... MS-4
*Comptons Landing* ... AL-4
*Comptons Mill* ... PA-2
Compton Spring—*spring* ... CA-9
Compton Spring—*spring* ... OR-9
Compton Spring—*spring* ... SD-7
Compton Spring Branch—*stream* ... AR-4
Compton Spring Hollow—*valley* ... MO-7
Comptons Ranch (historical)—*locale* ... SD-7
Compton (Township of)—*fmr MCD* ... AR-4
**Compton (Township of)**—*pop pl* ... MN-6
*Comptonville* ... CA-9
Compton West (census name West Compton)—*uninc pl* ... CA-9
Compton-Wood House—*hist pl* ... AR-4
*Compton Woods* ... OH-6
**Compton Woods**—*pop pl* ... OH-6
Compuerta—*channel* ... TX-5
Comrade Cem—*cemetery* ... LA-4
Comrade Ch—*church* ... LA-4
Comrade Creek—*stream* ... LA-4
*Comroy Creek* ... OR-9
*Comroy Spring* ... OR-9
Comsewogue Sch—*school* ... NY-2
*Comslo* ... GA-3
*Comstock* ... ND-7
Comstock—*locale* ... NY-2
Comstock—*locale* ... ND-7
Comstock—*locale* ... OR-9
**Comstock**—*pop pl* ... MI-6
**Comstock**—*pop pl* ... MN-6
**Comstock**—*pop pl* ... NE-7
**Comstock**—*pop pl* ... NV-8
**Comstock**—*pop pl* ... TX-5
**Comstock**—*pop pl* ... UT-8
**Comstock**—*pop pl* ... WI-6
Comstock—*summit* ... WA-9
Comstock, Elias, Cabin—*hist pl* ... MI-6
Comstock, Solomon Gilman, House—*hist pl* ... MN-6
Comstock, Zephnia, Farmhouse—*hist pl* ... NY-2
Comstock Basin—*basin* ... OR-9
Comstock Bay—*bay* ... MI-6
Comstock Branch—*stream* ... TN-4
*Comstock Brook* ... RI-1
Comstock Brook—*stream* ... CT-1
Comstock Brook—*stream* (2) ... ME-1
Comstock Campground—*locale* ... CO-8
Comstock Canyon—*valley* ... CA-9
Comstock Cem—*cemetery* ... IN-6
Comstock Cem—*cemetery* ... MN-6
Comstock Cem—*cemetery* (2) ... NY-2
Comstock Cem—*cemetery* ... TN-4
Comstock Cem—*cemetery* ... WI-6
Comstock-Cheney Hall—*hist pl* ... CT-1
Comstock Childrens Hosp—*hospital* ... AZ-5
**Comstock Corners**—*pop pl* ... NY-2
Comstock Covered Bridge—*hist pl* ... VT-1
Comstock Creek—*stream* ... AK-9
Comstock Creek—*stream* ... ID-8
Comstock Creek—*stream* ... IA-7
Comstock Creek—*stream* (2) ... MI-6
Comstock Creek—*stream* ... MO-7
Comstock Creek—*stream* ... TN-4
Comstock-Dexter Mine—*mine* ... AZ-5
Comstock Ditch—*canal* ... ID-8
Comstock Ditch—*canal* ... OH-6
Comstock Ditch—*canal* ... WY-8
Comstock Fire Tower—*locale* ... MI-6
*Comstock Gardens* ... RI-1
**Comstock Gardens**—*pop pl* ... RI-1
Comstock (Great Meadows Correctional Institution)—*building* ... NY-2
Comstock Gulch—*valley* ... CO-8
Comstock Hall—*hist pl* ... NY-2
Comstock-Harris House—*hist pl* ... FL-3
Comstock Hill—*summit* ... AZ-5
Comstock Hill—*summit* (2) ... CT-1
Comstock Hill—*summit* ... NH-1
Comstock Hills—*summit* ... MI-6
Comstock (historical P.O.)—*locale* ... IA-7
Comstock Hollow—*valley* ... NY-2
Comstock Homestead—*locale* ... WY-8
Comstock HS—*school* ... MI-6
Comstock Knoll—*summit* ... CT-1
Comstock Lake—*lake* ... MI-6
Comstock Lake—*lake* ... MN-6
Comstock Lake—*lake* ... WI-6
Comstock Mine—*mine* ... CO-8
Comstock Mine—*mine* ... ID-8
Comstock Mine—*mine* ... UT-8
Comstock Mines—*mine* ... WY-8
Comstock Mtn—*summit* ... ME-1
Comstock Park—*flat* ... WA-9
Comstock Park—*park* ... MI-6
**Comstock Park**—*pop pl* ... MI-6
Comstock Park Sch—*school* ... MI-6
Comstock Playground—*park* ... MI-6
Comstock Point—*cape* ... ME-1
Comstock Pond—*reservoir* ... CT-1
Comstock Public Sch—*hist pl* ... MN-6
Comstock Riverside Park—*park* ... MI-6
Comstock's Bridge—*hist pl* ... CT-1
Comstock Sch—*school* ... FL-3
Comstock Sch—*school* (2) ... MI-6
Comstock Sch—*school* ... NE-7
Comstock Sch—*school* ... WA-9
Comstock Slide—*slope* ... CA-9
Comstock Station (historical)—*locale* ... IA-7
Comstock Tobogan Slide—*other* ... MI-6
**Comstock Township**—*pop pl* ... NE-7
**Comstock (Township of)**—*pop pl* ... MI-6
**Comstock (Township of)**—*pop pl* ... MN-6
Comstock (Township of)—*unorg* ... ME-1
**Comstock Tract**—*pop pl* ... NY-2
Comstock Vly—*swamp* ... NY-2
Comstock Wash—*stream* ... AZ-5
Comstock Windmill—*locale* ... TX-5
Comtois Hill—*summit* ... VT-1
**Comunas**—*pop pl* ... PR-3
Comus—*locale* ... MD-2
Comus—*locale* ... MN-6
Comus—*locale* ... NV-8
Comus Lake—*reservoir* ... WI-6
Comyn—*locale* ... TX-5
Comynie Bayou—*stream* ... MS-4
Conabeer Chrysler Bldg—*hist pl* ... NC-3
Conaby Creek—*stream* ... NC-3
**Conalco**—*pop pl* ... TN-4
**Conalco Junction**—*pop pl* ... TN-4
Conally Branch—*stream* ... SC-3
Conan Coulee—*valley* ... MT-8
Conanicut Battery—*hist pl* ... RI-1
Conanicut Island—*island* ... RI-1
Conanicut Island Lighthouse—*hist pl* ... RI-1
**Conanicut Park**—*pop pl* ... RI-1
Conanicut Point—*cape* ... RI-1
Conant—*locale* ... AR-4
Conant—*locale* ... CA-9
Conant—*locale* ... FL-3
**Conant**—*pop pl* ... IL-6
**Conant**—*pop pl* ... OH-6
Conant, Samuel B., House—*hist pl* ... RI-1
Conant Basin—*basin* ... OR-9
Conant Basin—*basin* ... WY-8
Conant Brook—*stream* ... CT-1
Conant Brook—*stream* (3) ... ME-1
Conant Brook—*stream* ... MA-1
Conant Brook Dam—*dam* ... MA-1
Conant Brook Rsvr—*reservoir* ... MA-1
Conant Cem—*cemetery* ... ME-1
Conant Creek—*stream* (2) ... ID-8
Conant Creek—*stream* ... MT-8
Conant Creek—*stream* ... OR-9
Conant Creek—*stream* (2) ... WY-8
Conant Hill—*summit* ... ME-1
Conant Hill—*summit* (2) ... MA-1
Conant Hill—*summit* ... NH-1
Conant Marsh—*swamp* ... MI-6
Conant Pass—*gap* ... WY-8
Conant Playground—*park* ... MA-1
Conant Pond—*lake* ... MA-1
Conant Public Library—*hist pl* ... NH-1
Conant Sch—*school* ... MI-6
Conants Park—*park* ... IA-7
Conant Stream—*stream* ... ME-1
Conant Swamp—*swamp* ... VT-1
Conant Thread-Coats & Clark Mill Complex District—*hist pl* ... RI-1
Conant Valley—*valley* ... ID-8
**Conantville**—*pop pl* ... CT-1
Conantville Brook—*stream* ... CT-1
*Conaquenessing* ... PA-2
*Conaquenessing Creek* ... PA-2

Coneeto ... NC-3
Coneeto Creek ... NC-3
Conegal Creek ... AL-4
Cone Glacier—glacier ... AK-9
Conegocheague Criver ... MD-2
Conegocheek Creek ... MD-2
conegocheige Creek ... MD-2
Conegochiegh Creek ... MD-2
Conegoge Creek ... MD-2
Conegogee Creek ... MD-2
Conegogeek Creek ... MD-2
**Conehatta**—pop pl ... MS-4
Conehatta Church ... MS-4
Conehatta Creek—stream ... MS-4
Conehatta Day School ... MS-4
Conehatta HS—school ... MS-4
Conehatta Indian Sch ... MS-4
Conehatta Institute (historical)—school ... MS-4
Conehatta Missionary Baptist Ch—church ... MS-4
Conehatta Sch—school ... MS-4
Cone Hill—pillar ... NM-5
Cone Hill—summit ... AK-9
Cone Hill—summit ... CA-9
Cone Hill—summit ... ME-1
Cone Hill—summit ... MA-1
Cone Hill Cem—cemetery ... MA-1
Cone Hill Ch—church ... MS-4
Cone Hill Tank—reservoir ... NM-5
Conehoma Creek—stream ... MS-4
Conehoma Sch (historical)—school ... MS-4
Conehurst Sch—school ... VA-3
Cone Island ... ME-1
Cone Island—island (3) ... AK-9
Cone Island—island ... TX-5
Cone Islands—island ... WA-9
Cone Islands State Park—park ... WA-9
Coneja Wells—locale ... NM-5
**Conejo**—pop pl ... CA-9
Conejo, Arroyo—stream ... CA-9
Conejo, Arroyo Del—stream ... CA-9
Conejo Basin—basin ... NM-5
Conejo Canyon—valley ... CO-8
Conejo Canyon—valley ... NV-8
Conejo Canyon—valley ... NM-5
Conejo Creek—stream (2) ... CA-9
Conejo Creek—stream (2) ... NM-5
Conejohela Valley—valley ... PA-2
Conejo Mesa—summit ... NM-5
Conejo Mtn—summit ... CA-9
**Conejos**—pop pl ... CO-8
Conejos Campground—locale ... CO-8
Conejos Cem—cemetery ... CO-8
Conejo Sch—school (2) ... CA-9
Conejos Creek—stream ... CA-9
Conejos Creek—stream ... TX-5
Conejos Peak—summit ... CO-8
Conejo Spring—spring (2) ... NM-5
Conejos River—stream ... CO-8
Conejos River Diversion—channel ... CO-8
Conejos Stock Driveway—trail ... CO-8
Conejos Trail—trail ... CO-8
Conejos Valley—valley ... CA-9
Conejos West—cens area ... CO-8
Conejos Windmill—locale ... TX-5
Conejo Tank—reservoir ... AZ-5
Conejo Valley—post sta ... CA-9
Conejo Valley—valley ... CA-9
Conejo Well—well ... CA-9
Conejo Well—well ... TX-5
Conejo Windmill—locale ... TX-5
Cone Kimball Ditch—canal ... CA-9
Cone Lake—lake ... CA-9
Cone Lake—lake ... IA-7
Cone Lake—lake ... MI-6
Cone Lake—lake ... NM-5
Cone Lake—reservoir ... NC-3
Cone Lake Dam—dam ... NC-3
Conelly Cem—cemetery ... NC-3
Conelway Sch—school ... PA-2
Conelys Point ... MI-6
Cone Marsh State Wildlife Mngmt Area—park ... IA-7
**Conemaugh**—pop pl ... PA-2
Conemaugh Cem—cemetery ... PA-2
Conemaugh Ch (historical)—church ... PA-2
Conemaugh (corporate name East Conemaugh) ... PA-2
Conemaugh Dam—dam ... PA-2
Conemaugh Furnace—locale ... PA-2
Conemaugh Gorge—valley ... PA-2
Conemaugh Lake—lake ... PA-2
Conemaugh Lake Natl Rec Area—park ... PA-2
Conemaugh Reservoir ... PA-2
Conemaugh River ... PA-2
Conemaugh River—stream ... PA-2
Conemaugh River Lake—reservoir ... PA-2
**Conemaugh (Township of)**—pop pl (3) ... PA-2
Conemaugh Township Rsvr—reservoir ... PA-2
Conemaugh Twp Impounding Dam—dam ... PA-2
Conemaugh Valley Elem Sch—school ... PA-2
Conemaugh Valley Junior Senior HS—school ... PA-2
Conemaugh Water Gap—gap ... PA-2
Cone Memorial Hosp—hospital ... NC-3
Cone Mill—locale ... OR-9
Cone Mills Lake—reservoir ... NC-3
Cone Mills Lake Dam—dam ... NC-3
Cone Mine—mine ... AZ-5
Cone Mountain Burn—area ... CA-9
Cone Mtn ... CA-9
Cone Mtn—summit (5) ... AK-9
Cone Mtn—summit ... CA-9
Cone Mtn—summit (3) ... CO-8
Cone Mtn—summit ... NH-1
Cone Mtn—summit ... TX-5
Cone Mtn—summit ... WA-9
Cone Mtn—summit ... WY-8
Cone Peak—summit (2) ... AK-9
Cone Peak—summit (2) ... CA-9
Cone Peak—summit ... ID-8
Cone Peak—summit (2) ... MT-8
Cone Peak—summit ... NV-8
Cone Peak—summit ... OR-9
Cone Peak—summit ... TX-5
Cone Pinnacle—summit ... CO-8
Cone Pinnade ... CO-8
Cone Point ... VT-1
Cone Point—cape (2) ... AK-9
Cone Point—cape ... CA-9
Cone Point—summit ... AR-4
Cone Point Trail—trail ... CA-9
Cone Pond—lake ... CT-1
Cone Pond—lake ... NH-1
Conequenessing ... PA-2
Conequenessing Creek ... PA-2
**Conerby (historical)**—pop pl ... MS-4
Cone Reef—bar ... OH-6
Cone Reservoir Dam—dam ... AL-4
Cone Ridge—ridge ... NM-5
Cone Ridge—ridge ... OR-9
Cone River ... CA-9
Conerly—locale ... MS-4
Conerly Cem—cemetery ... MS-4
Conerly House—hist pl ... LA-4
Conerlys Post Office ... MS-4
Cone Rock ... CA-9
Cone Rock—bar ... CA-9
Cone Rock—island (2) ... CA-9
Cone Rock—rock ... MA-1
**Coneross**—pop pl ... SC-3
Coneross Ch—church ... SC-3
Coneross Creek—stream ... SC-3
Coneross Creek Rsvr—reservoir ... SC-3
Cone RR Station—locale ... FL-3
Cone Rsvr—reservoir ... AL-4
Cone Rsvr—reservoir ... CA-9
Cone Rsvr—reservoir ... CO-8
Cone Rsvr—reservoir ... OR-9
Cone (Ruins)—locale ... NM-5
**Cones**—pop pl ... NH-1
Cone Sch—school ... ME-1
Cone Sch—school ... NH-1
Cones HQ (Site)—locale ... CA-9
Cones Lake—lake ... NC-3
Cones Point—cape ... CT-1
Cones Point—cape ... VT-1
Cone Spring—spring ... NV-8
Cone Springs ... UT-8
Conesquit River ... NY-2
**Conestee**—pop pl ... SC-3
Conestee Lake—reservoir ... SC-3
Conestoga—locale ... PA-2
**Conestoga**—pop pl ... PA-2
Conestoga Camp—locale ... MI-6
Conestoga Camp—locale ... PA-2
Conestoga Center ... PA-2
Conestoga Ch—church ... PA-2
Conestoga Country Club—other ... PA-2
Conestoga Creek ... PA-2
Conestoga Creek Dam ... PA-2
Conestoga Falls—falls ... PA-2
**Conestoga Farms**—pop pl ... PA-2
**Conestoga Gardens**—pop pl ... PA-2
Conestoga Girl Scout Camp—locale ... IA-7
Conestoga HS—school ... PA-2
Conestoga Lake—reservoir ... NE-7
Conestoga Memorial Park (Cemetery)—cemetery ... PA-2
Conestoga Pines Park—park ... PA-2
Conestoga Post Office (historical)—building ... PA-2
Conestoga River—stream ... PA-2
Conestoga Sch—school (2) ... PA-2
Conestoga Sch (abandoned)—school ... MO-7
Conestoga Senior HS ... PA-2
Conestoga Town—hist pl ... PA-2
**Conestoga (Township of)**—pop pl ... PA-2
Conestoga Valley JHS—school ... PA-2
Conestoga Valley Senior HS—school ... PA-2
Conestoga View Sch—school ... PA-2
**Conestoga Woods**—pop pl ... PA-2
Conestogo Creek ... PA-2
Conestogoe Creek ... PA-2
**Conesus**—pop pl ... NY-2
Conesus Creek—stream ... NY-2
Conesus Inlet—stream ... NY-2
Conesus Lake—lake ... NY-2
Conesus Lake Junction—locale ... NY-2
**Conesus (Town of)**—pop pl ... NY-2
**Conesville**—pop pl ... IA-7
**Conesville**—pop pl ... NY-2
**Conesville**—pop pl ... OH-6
**Conesville (Town of)**—pop pl ... NY-2
Coneto ... NC-3
Coneto Creek ... NC-3
**Conetoe**—pop pl ... NC-3
Conetoe Creek—stream ... NC-3
Conety Run—stream ... PA-2
Conevllle—locale ... PA-2
Conewago—locale ... PA-2
Conewago Chapel—church ... PA-2
Conewago Chapel—hist pl ... PA-2
Conewago Ch Number 1—church ... PA-2
Conewago Ch Number 2—church ... PA-2
Conewago Creek—stream (2) ... PA-2
Conewago Elementary School ... PA-2
Conewago Falls—falls (2) ... PA-2
**Conewago Heights**—pop pl ... PA-2
Conewago Hill—summit ... PA-2
Conewago Industrial Park—locale ... PA-2
Conewago Lake—lake ... PA-2
Conewago Lake—reservoir ... PA-2
Conewago Mass House—hist pl ... PA-2
Conewago Mtn—range ... PA-2
Conewago Narrows Creek ... PA-2
Conewago Sch—school (2) ... PA-2
**Conewago (Township of)**—pop pl (3) ... PA-2
**Conewango**—pop pl ... NY-2
Conewango Country Club—other ... PA-2
Conewango Creek—stream ... NY-2
Conewango Creek—stream ... PA-2
Conewango (RR name for Conewango Valley)—other ... NY-2
Conewango Station ... NY-2
Conewango Swamp—swamp ... NY-2
**Conewango (Town of)**—pop pl ... NY-2
**Conewango (Township of)**—pop pl ... PA-2
**Conewango Valley (Conewango Station)**—pop pl ... NY-2
**Conewango Valley (RR name Conewango)**—pop pl ... NY-2
C One Wash—stream ... AZ-5
Cone Wash—valley ... AZ-5
**Coney**—pop pl ... GA-3
Coney Basin—basin ... WA-9
Coney Bayou—stream ... LA-4
Coney Branch ... GA-3
Coney Branch—stream ... SC-3
Coney Brook—stream ... RI-1
Coney Cem—cemetery ... MS-4
Coney Creek ... AR-4
Coney Creek ... CO-8
Coney Creek ... GA-3
Coney Creek ... OK-5
Coney Creek ... WA-9
Coney Creek—stream ... CO-8
Coney Creek—stream (2) ... WA-9
Coney Creek—stream ... WY-8
Coneyhoe Creek ... NC-3
Coney Island—island ... AK-9
Coney Island—island (2) ... CA-9
Coney Island—island ... IN-6
Coney Island—island ... MA-1
Coney Island—ISLAND ... MN-6
Coney Island—island ... TN-4
Coney Island—island ... WV-2
Coney Island—locale ... CA-9
**Coney Island**—pop pl (2) ... NY-2
Coney Island Amusement Park—park ... OH-6
Coney Island Beach—beach ... NY-2
Coney Island Channel—channel ... NY-2
Coney Island Creek—stream ... NY-2
Coney Island Fire Station Pumping Station—hist pl ... NY-2
Coney Island Hosp—hospital ... NY-2
Coney Island Lighthouse—locale ... NY-2
Coney Island of the West—hist pl ... MN-6
Coney Island Rock—rock ... MA-1
Coney Lake—lake ... GA-3
Coney Lake—lake ... MT-8
Coney Lake—lake (3) ... WA-9
Coney Lake—lake ... WY-8
Coney Ledge—bar ... MA-1
Coney Mtn—summit ... NY-2
Coney Pass—gap ... WA-9
Coney Peak—summit ... MT-8
Coney River—stream ... WI-6
Coneys Creek—stream ... NC-3
Coneys Temple—church ... GA-3
Confederate—locale ... KY-4
Confederate Armory Site—hist pl ... MS-4
Confederate Ave Brick Arch Bridge—hist pl ... MS-4
Confederate Ave Sch—school ... GA-3
Confederate Branch—stream ... KY-4
Confederate Breastworks—hist pl ... NC-3
Confederate Bridge—bridge ... GA-3
Confederate Cem—cemetery (2) ... AR-4
Confederate Cem—cemetery (2) ... GA-3
Confederate Cem—cemetery (2) ... IL-6
Confederate Cem—cemetery (2) ... KY-4
Confederate Cem—cemetery (4) ... MS-4
Confederate Cem—cemetery ... OH-6
Confederate Cem—cemetery (2) ... OK-5
Confederate Cem—cemetery ... SC-3
Confederate Cem—cemetery (3) ... TN-4
Confederate Cem—cemetery (4) ... VA-3
Confederate Cemetery at Lewisburg—hist pl ... WV-2
Confederate Chapel, Cemetery and Cottage—hist pl ... MO-7
**Confederate Corners**—pop pl ... CA-9
Confederate Creek—stream ... AK-9
Confederate Earthworks—hist pl ... MS-4
Confederate Field—airport ... NC-3
Confederate Grove Sch (historical)—school ... MS-4
Confederate Gulch—valley ... AK-9
Confederate Gulch—valley ... ID-8
Confederate Gulch—valley ... MT-8
**Confederate Heights**—pop pl ... VA-3
Confederate Heights Country Club—locale ... MS-4
Confederate Heights Golf Club Dam—dam ... MS-4
Confederate Heights Golf Club Number 2 Dam—dam ... MS-4
**Confederate Hill Estates**—pop pl ... AL-4
Confederate Home—other ... MO-7
Confederate Memorial Cem—cemetery ... TN-4
Confederate Memorial Cemetery ... AL-4
Confederate Memorial Chapel—hist pl ... VA-3
Confederate Memorial Hall—hist pl ... LA-4
Confederate Memorial Park—cemetery ... TN-4
Confederate Memorial Park—park ... AL-4
Confederate Mine (underground)—mine ... AL-4
Confederate Monmt—hist pl ... TN-4
Confederate Park—hist pl (2) ... AL-4
**Confederate Park (subdivision)**—pop pl ... MS-4
Confederate Pass—bay ... AL-4
Confederate Printing Plant—hist pl ... SC-3
Confederate Prison Site—park ... NC-3
Confederate Rest Cem—cemetery ... AL-4
**Confederate Ridge**—pop pl ... VA-3
Confederate Soldiers Home—building ... VA-3
Confederate State Capitol—hist pl ... AR-4
Confederate Unknow Memorial Cem—cemetery ... VA-3
**Confer**—pop pl ... FL-3
Conference Grounds—locale ... CA-9
Conference Grounds—locale ... WA-9
Conference House—hist pl ... NY-2
Conference Point ... RI-1
Conference Point—cape ... WI-6
Confer Sag—valley ... PA-2
Confer Valley ... PA-2
Confidence—locale ... IL-6
**Confidence**—pop pl ... CA-9
**Confidence**—pop pl ... IA-7
**Confidence**—pop pl ... WV-2
Confidence Cem—cemetery ... OH-6
Confidence Ch—church (2) ... GA-3
Confidence Ch—church ... NC-3
Confidence Hall—hist pl ... CA-9
Confidence Hills—range ... CA-9
Confidence Mill—locale ... CA-9
Confidence Mine—mine ... NV-8
Confidence Mine—mine ... NM-5
Confidence Mine—mine ... SD-7
Confidence Mines—mine ... NM-5
Confidence Peak—summit ... AZ-5
Confidence Ravine—valley ... NV-8
Confidence Wash—stream ... CA-9
Confluence—locale ... KY-4
**Confluence**—pop pl ... AL-4
**Confluence**—pop pl ... PA-2
Confluence, The—area ... UT-8
Confluence Borough—civil ... PA-2
Confluence Ch—church ... AL-4
Confluence Methodist Ch ... AL-4
Confluence Oakland Junction Station—locale ... PA-2
Confluence Overlook—locale ... UT-8
Confluence Sch—school ... AL-4
Confucius Sch—school ... CA-9
Confucius Temple—summit ... AZ-5
Confusion, Lake—lake ... FL-3
Confusion Cave—cave ... AL-4
Confusion Creek—stream ... AK-9
Confusion Hills—summit ... NV-8
Confusion Hills Rsvr—reservoir ... UT-8
Confusion Lake—lake ... ID-8
Confusion Mine—mine ... CO-8
Confusion Range—range ... UT-8
Confusion Ridge—ridge ... WA-9
Confusion Rsvr—reservoir ... MT-8
Confusion Run—stream ... OH-6
Conga—area ... GU-9
Congahbuna Lake—lake ... AK-9
**Congamond**—pop pl ... MA-1
Congamond Lakes—lake ... MA-1
**Congamond Lakes**—pop pl ... CT-1
Congamond Lakes Middle Dike—dam ... MA-1
Congamond Lakes Middle Pond—reservoir ... MA-1
Congamond Lakes North Dike—dam ... MA-1
Congamond Lakes North Pond—reservoir ... MA-1
Congamond Lakes South Dike—dam ... MA-1
Congamond Lakes South Pond—reservoir ... MA-1
Congamuck Lakes ... MA-1
Congamunck River ... NY-2
Congaree ... SC-3
Congaree—locale ... SC-3
Congaree Boat Creek—gut ... SC-3
Congaree Ch—church (2) ... SC-3
Congaree Creek—stream ... SC-3
Congaree River—stream ... SC-3
Congaree Spring Branch—stream ... SC-3
"Congarees" Site—hist pl ... SC-3
Congaree Swamp Natl Monmt—park ... SC-3
Congar Sch—school ... WI-6
**Congdon**—pop pl ... WA-9
Congdon—ridge ... AZ-5
Congdon Canal—canal ... WA-9
Congdon Cove—bay ... RI-1
Congdon Creek ... MT-8
Congdon Creek—stream ... MT-8
Congdon Creek—stream ... OR-9
Congdon Hill—summit ... RI-1
Congdon Mine—mine ... MT-8
Congdon Park—park ... MN-6
Congdon Park Sch—school ... MN-6
Congdon Peak—summit ... MT-8
Congdon River ... RI-1
Congdon River—stream ... RI-1
Congdon Sch—school ... MA-1
Congdons Cove ... RI-1
Congdons Creek—bay ... NY-2
Congdon Shoal—bar ... MI-6
Congdons Mill Brook ... RI-1
Congdons Point—cape ... NY-2
Congdon Street Baptist Church—hist pl ... RI-1
Congdon Trail (Camp)—locale ... NY-2
Congdon Well—locale ... NM-5
Conger ... PA-2
Conger—locale ... AZ-5
Conger—locale ... IA-7
Conger—locale ... PA-2
**Conger**—pop pl ... MN-6
Conger, Isaac, House—hist pl ... TN-4
Conger, J. Newton, House—hist pl ... IL-6
Conger, Jonathan Clark, House—hist pl ... IA-7
Conger Bay ... MI-6
Conger Bay—bay ... NY-2
Conger Brook—stream ... NY-2
Conger Cem—cemetery ... KS-7
Conger Cem—cemetery ... LA-4
Conger Cem—cemetery ... TN-4
**Conger Corners**—pop pl ... NY-2
Conger Creek—stream ... AZ-5
Conger Creek—stream ... IN-6
Conger Creek—stream ... MT-8
Conger Creek—stream ... OR-9
Conger Creek—stream ... WA-9
Conger Creek Trail—trail ... MT-8
Conger Dam—dam ... AZ-5
Conger Draw—valley ... TX-5
Conger Hill—summit ... NY-2
**Conger (historical)**—pop pl ... OR-9
Conger Island—island ... NY-2
Conger Lake—lake ... WA-9
Conger Lake—reservoir ... NM-5
Conger Mesa—bench ... NM-5
Conger Mine—mine ... AZ-5
Conger Mine—mine ... CO-8
Conger Mtn—summit ... NY-2
Conger Mtn—summit ... OR-9
Conger Mtn—summit ... UT-8
Conger Point—summit ... MT-8
Conger Point Trail—trail ... MT-8
Conger Pond—lake ... WA-9
Conger Ranch—locale ... TX-5
Conger Range ... UT-8
Conger Range—range ... UT-8
Conger Rsvr—reservoir ... UT-8
**Congers**—pop pl ... NY-2
Conger Sch—school ... OH-6
Congers Creek—stream ... VA-3
Congers Lake—lake ... NY-2
Congers Marsh—swamp ... MN-6
Conger Spring—spring ... AZ-5
Conger Spring—spring ... UT-8
Conger Tank—reservoir (2) ... AZ-5
**Congerville**—pop pl ... IL-6
Congerville Ch—church ... IL-6
Conger Water Spring—spring ... AZ-5
Conger Windmill—locale ... TX-5
Congeto ... NC-3
Congeto Creek ... NC-3
Congin river ... ME-1
Congleton—locale (2) ... KY-4
Congleton—locale ... NC-3
**Congleton**—pop pl ... NC-3
Congleton Cem—cemetery ... KY-4
Congleton Ch—church ... KY-4
Congleton Mtn—summit ... KY-4
Conglin Lakes—lake ... NY-2
Conglomerate Bay—bay ... MI-6
Conglomerate Canyon—valley ... ID-8
Conglomerate Cave—cave ... PA-2
Conglomerate Creek—stream (4) ... AK-9
Conglomerate Falls ... MI-6
Conglomerate Mesa—summit ... CA-9
Conglomerate Mtn—summit ... AK-9
Conglomerate Point—cape ... WA-9
Congo—locale ... AL-4
Congo—locale ... AR-4
Congo—locale ... NC-3
**Congo**—pop pl ... OH-6
**Congo**—pop pl ... PA-2
**Congo**—pop pl ... WV-2
Congo Bottom—bend ... TN-4
Congo Cay—island ... VI-3
Congo Cay Archeol District—hist pl ... VI-3
Congo Ch—church ... AR-4
Congo Ch—church ... NC-3
Congo Creek—stream ... AL-4
Congo Creek—stream ... LA-4
Congo Creek—stream ... OH-6
Congo Gulch—valley ... OR-9
Congo Helistop—airport ... NJ-2
Congo Hill Ch—church ... NC-3
Congo Island—island ... LA-4
Congo Lake—lake ... MS-4
Congoon Hill ... RI-1
Congo Point—cape ... VI-3
Congo Post Office (historical)—building ... AL-4
Congor Mesa—summit ... CO-8
Congo Run—stream ... WV-2
Congo Sch (abandoned)—school ... MO-7
Congo Sch (historical)—school ... PA-2
Congo Spring—spring ... AL-4
Congo Square—locale ... AL-4
Congotekatel ... PW-9
Congree Boat Creek ... SC-3
Congregational Cem—cemetery ... IL-6
Congregational Cem—cemetery ... KS-7
Congregational Cem—cemetery ... MN-6
Congregational Cem—cemetery ... NE-7
Congregational Cem—cemetery ... ND-7
Congregational Cem—cemetery (3) ... SD-7
Congregational Center—building ... NH-1
Congregational Ch ... MA-1
Congregational Ch—church ... GA-3
Congregational Ch—church ... MA-1
Congregational Ch—church ... MI-6
Congregational Ch—church ... MS-4
Congregational Ch—church (2) ... SD-7
Congregational Ch (historical)—church ... SD-7
Congregational Christian Ch—church (2) ... AL-4
Congregational Christian Ch—church ... FL-3
Congregational Church ... SD-7
Congregational Church—hist pl ... CO-8
Congregational Church—hist pl ... NH-1
Congregational Church—hist pl ... NJ-2
Congregational Church, The—church ... MA-1
Congregational Church and Manse—hist pl ... NE-7
Congregational Church of Ada—hist pl ... MN-6
Congregational Church Of Austinburg—hist pl ... OH-6
Congregational Church of Blair—hist pl ... NE-7
Congregational Church of Chelsea—hist pl ... VT-1
Congregational Church of Christ—hist pl ... OH-6
Congregational Church of Edgecomb—hist pl ... ME-1
Congregational Church of Faribault—hist pl ... MN-6
Congregational Church of Iowa City—hist pl ... IA-7
Congregational Church of Medway—hist pl ... ME-1
Congregational Holiness Campground—locale ... AL-4
Congregational Holiness Church ... AL-4
Congregational Methodist Ch—church ... AL-4
Congregational-Presbyterian Church—hist pl ... OH-6
Congregational Store—hist pl ... PA-2
Congregation Bayt Shalom—church ... NC-3
Congregation Bet Breira Preschool—school ... FL-3
Congregation Bethel of Ansonia Cem—cemetery ... CT-1
Congregation Beth-El Zedeck—church ... IN-6
Congregation Beth Israel—church ... NJ-2
Congregation Beth Israel Synagogue—hist pl ... ID-8
Congregation Beth Sholem Synagogue—church ... UT-8
Congregation Beth Sholum—church ... NJ-2
Congregation B'nai B'rith—hist pl ... CA-9
Congregation B'Nai Israel—church ... MT-8
Congregation Bnai-Sholom—church ... AL-4
Congregation B'nai Torah—church ... IN-6
Congregation B'rith Sholem Synagogue—hist pl ... UT-8
Congregation Cem—cemetery ... ND-7
Congregation House ... NC-3
Congregation Kol Ami Synagogue—church ... UT-8
Congregation Mercy and Truth Cem—cemetery ... PA-2
Congregation Montefiore—hist pl ... UT-8
Congregation of Notre Dame Sch—school ... NY-2
Congregation Sharey Tzedek Synagogue—hist pl ... UT-8
Congregration Mishkan Israel Synagogue ... AL-4
**Congress**—pop pl ... AZ-5
**Congress**—pop pl ... OH-6
Congress Ave—uninc pl ... FL-3
Congress Ave Hist Dist—hist pl ... TX-5
Congress Bldg—hist pl ... FL-3
Congress Canyon—valley ... NV-8
Congress (CCD)—cens area ... AZ-5
Congress Cem—cemetery ... AZ-5
Congress Ch ... MS-4
Congress Ch—church ... MS-4
Congress Community MS—school ... FL-3
Congress Green—swamp ... IN-6
Congress Group—summit ... CA-9
Congress Hall—building ... PA-2
**Congress Heights**—pop pl ... DC-2
Congress Heights Sch—school ... DC-2
**Congress Hill**—pop pl ... PA-2
Congress Hill Cem—cemetery ... PA-2
Congress Hill Ch—church ... PA-2
Congress Hill Sch—school ... PA-2
Congress Hill Sch (historical)—school ... PA-2
**Congress (historical)**—pop pl ... MS-4
Congress (historical P.O.)—locale ... IA-7
Congressional Cemetery—hist pl ... DC-2
Congressional Ch—church ... AL-4
Congressional Ch (historical)—church ... SD-7
Congressional Country Club—other ... MD-2
**Congressional Estates**—pop pl ... NJ-2
**Congressional Forest Estates (Congressional Manor)**—pop pl ... MD-2
**Congressional Manor**—pop pl ... MD-2
Congressional Sch—school ... MD-2
Congressional Sch—school ... VA-3
Congressional Shopping Plaza—locale ... MD-2
Congress Junction ... AZ-5
Congress Junction—locale ... AZ-5
Congress Knob—summit ... ID-8
Congress Lake—lake ... OH-6
**Congress Lake**—pop pl ... OH-6
Congress Lake Golf Club—other ... OH-6
Congress Lake Outlet ... OH-6
Congress Lake Outlet—stream ... OH-6
Congress Mine—mine ... AZ-5
Congress Mine—mine ... NV-8
Congress Mountain ... ME-1
Congress Park ... IL-6
Congress Park—park ... CO-8
Congress Park—park ... NY-2
**Congress Park**—pop pl ... DC-2
Congress Park Sch—school ... IL-6
Congress Post Office—building ... AZ-5
Congress Post Office (historical)—building ... MS-4
Congress RR Station—building ... AZ-5
Congress Run—stream (3) ... OH-6
Congress Sch—school ... AZ-5
Congress Sch—school ... MI-6
Congress Sch—school ... WI-6
Congress School ... MS-4
Congress Springs Canyon—valley ... CA-9
Congress Square—post sta ... TX-5
Congress Street—hist pl ... CT-1
Congress Street Bridge—bridge ... MA-1
Congress Street Fire Station—hist pl ... MA-1
Congress Street Interchange—crossing ... AZ-5
Congress Street Sch—school ... MI-6
**Congress (Township of)**—pop pl (2) ... OH-6
Congress Valley—valley ... CA-9
Congrove Cem—cemetery ... KY-4
Congrove Cem—cemetery ... WV-2
**Congruity**—pop pl ... PA-2
Conhocton River ... NY-2
Con Hook—cape ... NY-2
Conical Butte—summit ... UT-8
Conical Hill—summit ... NV-8
Conical Peak ... MT-8
Conical Peak—summit ... MT-8
Conical Peak—summit ... WY-8
Conical Red Hill—summit ... AK-9
Conical Rock ... CA-9
Conical Rock—island ... CA-9
Conical Rock—island ... OR-9
Conical Sink—basin ... MO-7
Conical White Rock—island ... OR-9
Conic Lake—lake ... ME-1
Conic Lake—lake ... MN-6
Conic Peak ... AZ-5
Conic Stream—stream ... ME-1
Conicula Windmill—locale ... TX-5
Conicville—locale ... VA-3
Conie Creek—stream ... ID-8
Conifer—locale ... PA-2
**Conifer**—pop pl ... AL-4
**Conifer**—pop pl ... CO-8
**Conifer**—pop pl ... NY-2
Conifer Box Spring—spring ... UT-8
Conifer Cem—cemetery ... PA-2
**Conifer Mountain**—pop pl ... CO-8
**Conifer Park**—pop pl ... CO-8
Conifer Ridge—ridge ... CA-9
**Conifer View**—pop pl ... WA-9
Coniff Creek—stream ... MT-8
Conigochego Cree ... MD-2
Conihasset ... MA-1
Coniho Creek ... NC-3
Conimicut ... RI-1
**Conimicut**—pop pl ... RI-1
Conimicut Lighthouse—hist pl ... RI-1
Conimicut Point—cape ... RI-1
Conim Lake—lake ... OR-9
Conine, Lake—lake ... FL-3
Conine Bend—bend ... NC-3
Conine Cem—cemetery ... AR-4
Conine Creek—stream ... NC-3
Conine Island—island ... NC-3
Conines Mill Dam ... NJ-2
Conines Millpond—reservoir ... NJ-2
Coning Inlet—bay ... AK-9
Coning Point—cape ... AK-9
**Conings**—pop pl ... WV-2
Coniott Creek—stream ... NC-3
Coniott Landing—locale ... NC-3
Con Island—island ... MN-6
Coniston—locale ... GA-3
Coniston, Lake—lake ... NH-1
Conium ... IA-7
Coniza Mesa ... AZ-5
Conjada Mountains—summit ... OK-5
Conjecture Mine—mine ... ID-8
Conkelley—locale ... MT-8
Con Kelley Mtn—summit ... MT-8
Conkepot River ... MA-1
Conkey Branch—stream ... IL-6
Conkey Branch—stream ... NY-2
Conkey Cem—cemetery ... IL-6
Conkey Cove—bay ... LA-4
Conkey Cove Pass—channel ... LA-4
Conkey Drain—canal ... MI-6
Conkey Hill—summit ... VT-1
Conkey-Stevens House—hist pl ... MA-1
Conk Hollow—valley ... MO-7
Conkill Bay (Carolina Bay)—swamp ... NC-3
Conkin Cem—cemetery ... TN-4
Conkintown—locale ... TN-4
Conkle Cem—cemetery ... MO-7
Conkle Cem—cemetery ... WI-6
Conkles Hollow—valley ... OH-6
Conklin—locale ... MO-7
Conklin—locale ... TN-4
Conklin—locale ... VA-3

**Conklin**—*pop pl* (2) MI-6
**Conklin**—*pop pl* NY-2
Conklin, David, House—*hist pl* NY-2
Conklin, Nathaniel, House—*hist pl* NY-2
Conklin Bay—*bay* IN-6
Conklin Brook—*stream* NY-2
Conklin Canyon—*valley* CA-9
Conklin Canyon—*valley* NM-5
Conklin Cem—*cemetery* IN-6
Conklin Cem—*cemetery* NY-2
Conklin Cem—*cemetery* ND-7
Conklin Cem—*cemetery* TN-4
**Conklin Center**—*pop pl* NY-2
**Conklin Cove**—*pop pl* NY-2
*Conklin Creek* TX-5
Conklin Creek—*stream* AZ-5
Conklin Creek—*stream* CA-9
Conklin Creek—*stream* (2) OR-9
Conklin Creek Campgrounds—*park* AZ-5
*Conklin Dam* ND-7
Conklin Drain—*stream* MI-6
Conkline Creek—*stream* TX-5
**Conklin Forks**—*pop pl* NY-2
Conkling—*locale* IA-7
Conkling—*locale* KY-4
Conkling, Roscoe, House—*hist pl* NY-2
Conkling (historical)—*locale* KS-7
**Conkling Park**—*pop pl* ID-8
Conkling Point—*cape* ID-8
Conkling Point—*cape* NY-2
Conkling Pond—*lake* NJ-2
Conkling Post Office (historical)—*building* TN-4
Conkling Sch—*school* NY-2
*Conkling's Point* NY-2
**Conkling Township**—*pop pl* KS-7
Conklin Gully—*valley* NY-2
**Conklingville**—*pop pl* NY-2
Conklingville Dam—*dam* NY-2
Conklin Hill—*locale* PA-2
Conklin Hill—*summit* (2) NY-2
Conklin Hollow—*valley* OH-6
Conklin Hollow—*valley* PA-2
Conklin House—*hist pl* OK-5
Conklin HS—*school* MI-6
Conklin Island—*island* NJ-2
Conklin Island—*island* NY-2
Conklin Lake—*lake* MN-6
Conklin Lake—*lake* MT-8
Conklin Lake—*lake* WA-9
Conklin Lake—*reservoir* OK-5
Conklin Meadow—*flat* WA-9
Conklin-Montgomery House—*hist pl* IN-6
Conklin Mtn—*summit* NY-2
Conklin Orchard—*locale* CA-9
Conklin Park Campground—*locale* CA-9
Conklin Point—*cape* NY-2
*Conklin Pond* NJ-2
Conklin Ridge—*ridge* AZ-5
Conklin Run—*stream* (3) PA-2
Conklin Sch—*school* (2) IL-6
Conklin Sch—*school* KY-4
Conklin Sch—*school* MI-6
Conklins Crossing—*trail* NY-2
Conklin Spring—*spring* AZ-5
Conklin Spring—*spring* CA-9
Conklin Spring—*spring* OR-9
**Conklin Station**—*pop pl* NY-2
Conklintown—*uninc pl* NJ-2
**Conklin (Town of)**—*pop pl* NY-2
**Conklin Township**—*pop pl* ND-7
Conko Lake—*lake* MT-8
Conkwright Ranch—*locale* TX-5
Conlan Creek—*stream* WI-6
Conlan Spring—*spring* CA-9
*Conlans Ranch* NV-8
Conlee Sch—*school* NM-5
Conlen—*locale* TX-5
Conley—*locale* GA-3
Conley—*locale* KY-4
Conley—*locale* OR-9
Conley, John D., House—*hist pl* WY-8
Conley, Lake—*lake* FL-3
Conley, Sanford F., House—*hist pl* MO-7
Conley Bend—*bend* AR-4
Conley Bluff—*ridge* GA-3
Conley Bottom Dock—*locale* KY-4
Conley Branch—*stream* GA-3
Conley Branch—*stream* (4) KY-4
Conley Branch—*stream* MO-7
Conley Branch—*stream* NC-3
Conley Branch—*stream* (2) TN-4
Conley Branch—*stream* (3) WV-2
Conley Camp Branch—*stream* NC-3
Conley Canyon—*valley* NM-5
Conley Cem—*cemetery* (2) AL-4
Conley Cem—*cemetery* (2) AR-4
Conley Cem—*cemetery* (7) KY-4
Conley Cem—*cemetery* MI-6
Conley Cem—*cemetery* (2) MO-7
Conley Cem—*cemetery* NE-7
Conley Cem—*cemetery* NC-3
Conley Cem—*cemetery* OH-6
Conley Cem—*cemetery* WV-2
Conley Cemeterys—*cemetery* WV-2
Conley Ch—*church* GA-3
Conley Chapel—*church* AL-4
Conley Chapel—*church* IL-6
Conley Chapel—*church* (2) NC-3
Conley Chapel Cem—*cemetery* AL-4
*Conley Chapel Church* AL-4
*Conley Chapel CME Church* AL-4
**Conley Chapel Village (trailer park)**—*pop pl* DE-2
Conley Creek—*stream* AR-4
Conley Creek—*stream* CA-9
Conley Creek—*stream* (2) GA-3
Conley Creek—*stream* NC-3
Conley Creek—*stream* (3) OR-9
Conley Creek Ch—*church* NC-3
**Conley Crossroads (historical)**—*pop pl* TN-4
Conley Ditch—*canal* AR-4
Conley Draw—*valley* (2) WY-8
Conley Fork—*stream* (2) KY-4
Conley Fork—*stream* WV-2
Conley-Greene Rockshelter (15EL4)—*hist pl* KY-4
Conley Grove Ch—*church* MO-7
Conley Hills Sch—*school* GA-3
Conley Hole—*cave* TN-4
Conley Hollow—*valley* MO-7
Conley Hollow—*valley* OK-5
Conley Hollow—*valley* TN-4
Conley Hollow—*valley* WV-2
Conley HS—*school* NC-3
Conley Lake—*lake* MN-6
Conley Lake—*lake* OR-9
Conley Lake—*lake* WI-6
Conley Lakes—*reservoir* CO-8
Conley Memorial Ch—*church* NC-3
Conley Points—*summit* AZ-5
Conley Pond—*lake* RI-1
Conley Ranch—*locale* AZ-5
Conley Ridge—*ridge* NC-3
Conley Rsvr—*reservoir* WY-8
*Conley Run* VA-3
Conley Run—*stream* WV-2
Conley Sch—*school* CA-9
Conley Sch—*school* IL-6
Conley Sch—*school* KY-4
Conley Sch—*school* MA-1
Conley Sch—*school* MI-6
Conley Sch—*school* OK-5
Conley Sch—*school* SD-7
Conley Sch—*school* WV-2
Conley Sch (abandoned)—*school* MO-7
Conley Sch Number 1—*school* PA-2
Conley's Ford Bridge—*hist pl* IN-6
Conleys Ford Covered Bridge—*bridge* IN-6
Conleys Golf Course—*locale* PA-2
**Conleys Grove**—*pop pl* NH-1
Conleys Lake—*lake* MT-8
*Conley Smith Creek* WI-6
Conley Spring—*spring* NM-5
Conley Spring—*spring* OR-9
Conley Spring Wash—*stream* AZ-5
Conley Swamp—*stream* VA-3
Conley Tank—*reservoir* AZ-5
**Conley Township**—*pop pl* NE-7
Conlin, Lake—*lake* FL-3
Conlin Drain—*canal* MI-6
Conlin Gulch—*valley* MT-8
Conlin Hill—*summit* MA-1
Conlogue—*locale* IL-6
**Conlogue**—*pop pl* IL-6
Conlogue Sch—*school* IL-6
Conlogue Sch—*school* ME-1
Conlon Arm—*canal* IN-6
Conlon Camp—*locale* NV-8
Conly Cem—*cemetery* IL-6
Conly Mills (historical)—*locale* MS-4
Conn—*locale* LA-4
Conn—*locale* MS-4
Conn, Adrian Edwards, House—*hist pl* TX-5
Conn, John P., House—*hist pl* PA-2
Connahanee Sch—*school* TN-4
*Connahasset, Town of* MA-1
Connally, Roy, House—*hist pl* TX-5
Connally Cem—*cemetery* AL-4
Connally Cem—*cemetery* GA-3
Connally Cem—*cemetery* MS-4
Connally Ch—*church* NC-3
Connally Cove—*bay* GA-3
Connally Heights Park—*park* TX-5
*Connally Hollow* MO-7
Connally Peak—*summit* TX-5
Connally Point—*summit* AZ-5
Connally Point Tank—*reservoir* AZ-5
Connally Ranch—*locale* TX-5
Connally Sch—*school* GA-3
Connally Sch—*school* TX-5
Connally School (Abandoned)—*locale* MN-6
Connally Spring—*spring* OR-9
**Connarista**—*pop pl* NC-3
**Connaritsa**—*pop pl* NC-3
Connaritsa Ch—*church* NC-3
Connaritsa Pocosin—*swamp* NC-3
Connaritsa Swamp—*stream* NC-3
Connary Brook—*stream* NH-1
*Connasana Creek* GA-3
*Connasauga* TN-4
*Connasauga Creek* TN-4
*Connasauga River* GA-3
*Connasauga River* TN-4
*Connasene Creek* GA-3
**Connaughton**—*pop pl* PA-2
**Connaughtown**—*pop pl* PA-2
*Connawai Creek* WA-9
Conn Branch—*stream* (2) KY-4
Conn Brown Harbor—*harbor* TX-5
Conn Cem—*cemetery* AL-4
Conn Cem—*cemetery* IN-6
Conn Cem—*cemetery* MS-4
Conn Ch—*church* OH-6
Conn Cove—*bay* CT-1
*Conn Creek* AL-4
Conn Creek—*stream* CA-9
Conn Creek—*stream* CO-8
Conn Creek—*stream* GA-3
Conn Creek—*stream* MS-4
Conn Creek—*stream* MT-8
Conn Creek—*stream* OR-9
Conn Creek—*stream* TX-5
Conn Creek—*stream* WA-9
Conn Creek Ch—*church* GA-3
Conn Creek Sch—*school* CO-8
Conn Dam—*dam* CA-9
Conn Ditch—*canal* IN-6
Conn Ditch—*canal* MT-8
Conn Ditch—*canal* OR-9
Conn Dock—*locale* TN-4
**Conneaut**—*pop pl* OH-6
**Conneaut Center**—*pop pl* PA-2
Conneaut Center Cem—*cemetery* PA-2
Conneaut Creek—*stream* OH-6
Conneaut Creek—*stream* PA-2
*Conneaut Harbor* OH-6
Conneaut Harbor—*bay* OH-6
Conneaut Lake—*lake* PA-2
**Conneaut Lake**—*pop pl* PA-2
Conneaut Lake Airp—*airport* PA-2
Conneaut Lake Borough—*civil* PA-2
*Conneaut Lake Creek* PA-2
Conneaut Lake HS—*school* PA-2
Conneaut Lake Kame—*summit* PA-2
**Conneaut Lake Park**—*pop pl* PA-2
Conneaut Marsh—*swamp* PA-2
Conneaut Marsh Dam—*dam* PA-2
Conneaut Marsh Rsvr—*reservoir* PA-2
Conneaut Outlet—*stream* PA-2
*Conneaut Outlet Creek* PA-2
Conneaut Park—*park* OH-6
Conneaut Sch—*school* OH-6
*Conneaut Swamp* PA-2
*Conneautte Creek* PA-2
Conneauttee Creek—*stream* PA-2
*Conneauttee Lake* PA-2
*Conneautte Lake* PA-2
Conneaut (Township of)—*other* OH-6
**Conneaut (Township of)**—*pop pl* (2) PA-2
Conneaut Valley Elem Sch—*school* PA-2
Conneaut Valley HS—*school* PA-2
**Conneautville**—*pop pl* PA-2
Conneautville Borough—*civil* PA-2
**Conneautville Station**—*pop pl* PA-2
Conneaut Works—*hist pl* OH-6
Connecticut Agricultural Experiment Station—*hist pl* CT-1
**Connecticut Ave Estates**—*pop pl* MD-2
**Connecticut Ave Hills**—*pop pl* MD-2
**Connecticut Ave Park**—*pop pl* MD-2
Connecticut Ave Park Sch—*school* MD-2
Connecticut Coll—*school* CT-1
Connecticut Creek—*stream* AK-9
Connecticut Farms Sch—*school* NJ-2
**Connecticut Gardens**—*pop pl* MD-2
Connecticut General Hosp for the Insane—*hist pl* CT-1
Connecticut Hall, Yale Univ—*hist pl* CT-1
Connecticut Hill—*summit* NY-2
Connecticut Hill State Game Mngmt Area—*park* NY-2
*Connecticut Lake* NH-1
Connecticut Lake—*lake* CO-8
Connecticut Land Company Office—*hist pl* OH-6
Connecticut Mine—*mine* AZ-5
Connecticut Railway and Lighting Company Car Barn—*hist pl* CT-1
Connecticut Ridge—*ridge* ME-1
*Connecticut River* NY-2
Connecticut River—*stream* CT-1
Connecticut River—*stream* MA-1
Connecticut River—*stream* NH-1
Connecticut River—*stream* VT-1
Connecticut River Rsvr—*reservoir* (2) MA-1
Connecticut State Capitol—*hist pl* CT-1
Connecticut Statehouse—*hist pl* CT-1
Connecticut State Library and Supreme Court Bldg—*hist pl* CT-1
Connecticut State Prison—*building* CT-1
Connecticut Valley Hosp—*hospital* CT-1
Connecting Ridge—*ridge* OH-6
Connecting Slough—*gut* CA-9
Connection Hill Ch—*church* TN-4
Connection Pass—*channel* AK-9
Connection Slough—*gut* CA-9
*Connecuh River* AL-4
*Connecuh River* FL-3
Connel Ditch—*canal* CO-8
Conneley Ditch—*canal* IN-6
Connell—*locale* KS-7
Connell—*locale* TX-5
**Connell**—*pop pl* WA-9
Connell, William M., Sch—*hist pl* MA-1
Connell Bayou—*stream* LA-4
Connell Branch—*stream* GA-3
Connell Bridge—*bridge* GA-3
Connell (CCD)—*cens area* WA-9
Connell Cem—*cemetery* IN-6
Connell Cem—*cemetery* LA-4
Connell Cem—*cemetery* ND-7
Connell Cem—*cemetery* (2) TN-4
Connell Cem—*cemetery* WA-9
Connell City Airp—*airport* WA-9
Connell Creek—*stream* GA-3
Connell Creek—*stream* TN-4
Connell Creek—*stream* TX-5
Connell Creek Cave—*cave* TN-4
Connell Dam—*dam* PA-2
Connellee Millpond—*reservoir* VA-3
*Connelle Mill Run* VA-3
Connelley Cem—*cemetery* KY-4
*Connelley Run* PA-2
Connell Gulch—*valley* AZ-5
Connell JHS—*school* TX-5
Connell Lake—*lake* FL-3
Connell Lake—*reservoir* AK-9
Connell Mansion—*hist pl* PA-2
Connell Mountains—*range* AZ-5
Connell Park—*park* PA-2
Connell Pond—*reservoir* (2) PA-2
Connell Ranch—*locale* (3) NE-7
Connell Run—*stream* PA-2
Connells Cem—*cemetery* AR-4
Connell Sch—*school* MA-1
Connell Sch—*school* MI-6
Connell Sch (historical)—*school* TN-4
Connells Cow Camp—*locale* CA-9
*Connells Dam* PA-2
Connell Seep—*spring* AZ-5
*Connell Seep Spring* AZ-5
**Connells Point**—*pop pl* AR-4
Connells Prairie—*flat* WA-9
**Connellsville**—*pop pl* PA-2
Connellsville Airp—*airport* PA-2
Connellsville Area Senior HS—*school* PA-2
Connellsville City—*civil* PA-2
Connellsville (historical)—*locale* AL-4
Connellsville Junction (historical)—*locale* AL-4
Connellsville Mine (underground)—*mine* (2) AL-4
Connellsville Township Elem Sch—*school* PA-2
**Connellsville (Township of)**—*pop pl* PA-2
Connell Well—*well* NM-5
**Connelly**—*pop pl* NY-2
Connelly, Clifford B., Trade Sch—*hist pl* PA-2
Connelly Branch—*stream* TN-4
Connelly Branch—*stream* WV-2
Connelly Brook—*stream* MA-1
Connelly Cave—*basin* IN-6
Connelly Cem—*cemetery* IL-6
Connelly Cem—*cemetery* TN-4
*Connelly Creek* NC-3
Connelly Creek—*stream* WA-9
*Connelly Ditch* IN-6
Connelly Ford—*locale* IL-6
*Connelly Gap* PA-2
Connelly-Harrington House—*hist pl* AR-4
Connelly Hill—*summit* MA-1
Connelly HS—*school* CA-9
Connelly JHS—*school* TN-4
Connelly Lake—*lake* KY-4
Connelly Mill Branch—*stream* DE-2
Connelly Mill Branch—*stream* MD-2
Connelly Mtn—*summit* NC-3
**Connelly Park**—*pop pl* NY-2
Connelly Run—*stream* PA-2
Connelly Sch—*school* IL-6
Connelly Sch—*school* PA-2
Connelly Sch—*school* WV-2
*Connellys Creek* NC-3
*Connelly Springs* NC-3
Connelly Springs (RR name for Connelly Springs)—*other* NC-3
Connellys Run—*stream* VA-3
**Connellys Springs**—*pop pl* NC-3
**Connellys Springs (RR name Connelly Springs)**—*pop pl* NC-3
**Connelly (Township of)**—*pop pl* MN-6
**Connelsville**—*pop pl* MO-7
Connel Tank—*reservoir* NM-5
*Connelville* OH-6
Connel Well—*locale* NM-5
Connel Well—*well* NM-5
*Connely Creek* NC-3
Connely Creek—*stream* MT-8
Connely Davis Lake Dam—*dam* MS-4
Connely Field—*island* FL-3
Connely Gulch—*valley* CA-9
*Connemosset Pond* MA-1
*Conner* ID-8
*Conner* KS-7
*Conner* MI-6
Conner—*locale* AR-4
Conner—*locale* FL-3
Conner—*locale* KY-4
**Conner**—*pop pl* CA-9
**Conner**—*pop pl* MT-8
Conner, Alexander, House—*hist pl* OH-6
Conner, Mount—*summit* MT-8
Conner, Wesley O., House—*hist pl* GA-3
Conner, William, House—*hist pl* IN-6
Conner Basin—*basin* UT-8
Conner Bay—*bay* NY-2
*Conner Branch* IL-6
Conner Branch—*stream* IA-7
Conner Branch—*stream* (2) MO-7
Conner Branch—*stream* OH-6
Conner Branch—*stream* (3) TX-5
Conner Brook—*stream* ME-1
Conner Cabin Spring—*spring* CA-9
Conner Cem—*cemetery* AL-4
Conner Cem—*cemetery* FL-3
Conner Cem—*cemetery* GA-3
Conner Cem—*cemetery* (2) IN-6
Conner Cem—*cemetery* IA-7
Conner Cem—*cemetery* MS-4
Conner Cem—*cemetery* NC-3
Conner Cem—*cemetery* TN-4
Conner Cem—*cemetery* (4) TX-5
Conner Cem—*cemetery* WV-2
Conner Ch—*church* MT-8
Conner Ch—*church* TN-4
*Conner City* KS-7
Conner Coulee—*valley* MT-8
*Conner Creek* ID-8
*Conner Creek* OR-9
Conner Creek—*stream* AK-9
Conner Creek—*stream* CA-9
Conner Creek—*stream* ID-8
Conner Creek—*stream* MO-7
Conner Creek—*stream* (2) OR-9
Conner Creek—*stream* SC-3
Conner Creek—*stream* (2) TN-4
Conner Creek—*stream* (3) TX-5
**Conner Creek (historical)**—*pop pl* OR-9
Conner Creek Sch (historical)—*school* TX-5
Conner Elem Sch—*school* IN-6
**Conner Estates (subdivision)**—*pop pl* AL-4
*Conner Flat* ID-8
Conner-Green Cem—*cemetery* FL-3
**Conner Grove**—*pop pl* VA-3
Conner Gulch—*valley* ID-8
Conner Gulch—*valley* WA-9
**Conner Heights**—*pop pl* TN-4
**Conner Heights (subdivision)**—*pop pl* MS-4
Conner Hill—*summit* ME-1
Conner Hill—*summit* WI-6
Conner Hollow—*valley* AR-4
Conner Hollow—*valley* MO-7
Conner House—*hist pl* VA-3
Conner HS—*school* AR-4
Conner JHS—*school* TX-5
*Conner Lake* MS-4
Conner Lake—*reservoir* TX-5
Conner Lake—*reservoir* VA-3
Conner Landing—*locale* FL-3
Connerley Cem—*cemetery* LA-4
Connerly Bayou—*gut* AR-4
Connerly Brook—*stream* ME-1
Conner Mill Branch—*stream* NC-3
Conner Mtn—*summit* GA-3
*Conneross Creek* SC-3
Conner Park—*park* AZ-5
Conner Park—*park* (2) TX-5
Conner Playground—*park* MI-6
*Conner Point* ME-1
Conner Pond—*lake* NH-1
Conner Post Office (historical)—*building* PA-2
Conner Prairie Museum—*building* IN-6
Conner Ranch—*locale* NE-7
*Conner Ridge* ID-8
Conner Ridge—*ridge* OH-6
Conner Ridge Ch—*church* OH-6
Conner Run—*stream* (2) WV-2
*Conner's* MI-6
Conner's Bookstore—*hist pl* IN-6
*Conners Branch* GA-3
Conners Branch—*stream* IL-6
Conners Brook—*stream* (4) ME-1
Conners Cabin—*locale* OR-9
Conners Cave—*cave* MO-7
Conner Sch—*school* MI-6
Conners Chapel—*church* IL-6
Conners Chapel—*church* TX-5
Conners Corner—*locale* MD-2
*Conners Creek* WI-6
Conners Creek—*harbor* MI-6
Conners Creek—*stream* (2) NV-8
Conners Creek—*stream* VA-3
Conners Ford—*crossing* FL-3
**Conners Ford**—*pop pl* FL-3
Conners Grove—*locale* VA-3
Conners Hump—*summit* AZ-5
Conners Island—*island* MN-6
*Conners Lake* MN-6
Conners Lake—*lake* WI-6
Conners Lake—*reservoir* AL-4
Conners Landing (historical)—*locale* AL-4
Conner Slough—*swamp* SD-7
Conners Marsh—*swamp* MI-6
Conners Mill—*locale* PA-2
Conners Mill (historical)—*locale* MS-4
Conners Notch—*gap* NY-2
Conners Nubble—*summit* ME-1
*Conners Pass* NV-8
Conners Place—*locale* OR-9
Conners Point—*cape* MI-6
Conner Spring—*spring* ID-8
Conner Spring—*spring* MO-7
Conner Spring—*spring* OR-9
Conner Spring—*spring* TN-4
Conner Spring Branch—*stream* TX-5
Conners Rock—*pillar* SD-7
Conners Sch (historical)—*school* TN-4
Conners Spring—*spring* ID-8
Conners Spur—*ridge* VA-3
*Conners Store* AL-4
**Conners Valley**—*pop pl* VA-3
Conners View Ch—*church* VA-3
Connersville—*locale* FL-3
**Connersville**—*pop pl* FL-3
**Connersville**—*pop pl* IN-6
**Connersville**—*pop pl* KY-4
**Connersville**—*pop pl* PA-2
Connersville Area Vocational Sch—*school* IN-6
Connersville Junior High North—*school* IN-6
Connersville Senior HS—*school* IN-6
Connersville (Township of)—*civ div* IN-6
**Connerton**—*pop pl* PA-2
Conner Trail—*trail* PA-2
**Conner Village (subdivision)**—*pop pl* NC-3
**Connerville**—*pop pl* OK-5
Connerville Run—*stream* PA-2
Connery Pond—*lake* NY-2
Connery Sch—*school* MA-1
*Connesauga* TN-4
*Connesauga Creek* TN-4
*Connesauga River* GA-3
*Connesauga River* TN-4
Connesena Ch—*church* GA-3
Connesena Creek—*stream* GA-3
Connesena Mtn—*summit* GA-3
Connesena Spring—*spring* GA-3
Conness, Mount—*summit* CA-9
Conness Creek—*stream* CA-9
Conness Glacier—*lake* CA-9
Conness Lakes—*lake* CA-9
Conness Sch—*school* IL-6
**Connestee**—*pop pl* NC-3
Connestee Falls—*falls* NC-3
**Connestee Falls (subdivision)**—*pop pl* NC-3
Connetquot Brook—*stream* NY-2
Connetquot HS—*school* NY-2
Connetquot River—*stream* NY-2
Connetquot Sch—*school* NY-2
Connett—*locale* OH-6
Connett, Point—*cape* MA-1
Connett Cem—*cemetery* OH-6
*Connett Point* MA-1
Connewah Bottom—*valley* MS-4
*Connewango* NY-2
*Connewango Creek* NY-2
Conneway Hill—*summit* MD-2
*Connewong* NY-2
*Connewongo Creek* NY-2
Conn Fred Ditch—*canal* IN-6
Connia Slough—*lake* ND-7
Connick Creek—*stream* (2) CA-9
Connie, Lake—*lake* FL-3
Connie, Lake—*lake* WA-9
Connie, Lake—*reservoir* GA-3
Connie Glacier—*glacier* WY-8
Connie Knob—*summit* KY-4
Connie Mack Island—*island* FL-3
Connie Mack Stadium—*other* PA-2
Conniff Sch—*school* CA-9
Conningham Ditch—*canal* IN-6
*Connings* WV-2
Conning Towers-Nautilus Park—*CDP* CT-1
Conn Island—*island* MD-2
Conniston JHS—*school* FL-3
Connley Cem—*cemetery* KY-4
Connley Creek—*stream* TN-4
Connley Ditch—*canal* WY-8
Connley Draw—*valley* WY-8
Connley Gulch—*valley* CO-8
Connley Hills—*summit* OR-9
Conn Mtn—*summit* MT-8
*Connohasset* MA-1
Connoisarauley Creek—*stream* NY-2
Connoley Lake—*reservoir* NJ-2
*Connolly* ND-7
Connolly Basin—*basin* OR-9
Connolly Basin Spring—*spring* OR-9
Connolly Cove—*bay* MD-2
Connolly Creek—*stream* AK-9
Connolly Field—*park* AZ-5
Connolly Intermediate Sch—*school* AZ-5
*Connolly JHS* AZ-5
Connolly Lake—*reservoir* TX-5
Connolly Park—*park* IL-6
Connolly Point—*cape* MD-2
Connoly Mine—*mine* AK-9
Connoly Spring—*spring* NV-8
Connoly Wash—*stream* NV-8
**Connoquenessing**—*pop pl* PA-2
Connoquenessing Borough—*civil* PA-2
Connoquenessing Creek—*stream* PA-2
**Connoquenessing (Township of)**—*pop pl* PA-2
Connoquenessing Valley Sch—*school* PA-2
*Connor* KS-7
*Connor* MT-8
*Connor* OH-6
Connor—*locale* ID-8
Connor—*locale* NC-3
Connor—*locale* OH-6
Connor—*locale* PA-2
Connor—*locale* TX-5
**Connor**—*pop pl* AR-4
**Connor**—*pop pl* SC-3
Connor Arroyo—*stream* NM-5
*Connor Basin* UT-8
Connor Battlefield—*hist pl* WY-8
Connor Bayou—*gut* MI-6
Connor-Bovie House—*hist pl* ME-1
Connor Brook—*stream* NH-1
Connor Cabin—*locale* CA-9
Connor Canyon—*valley* AZ-5
Connor Canyon—*valley* OR-9
Connor Cem—*cemetery* IL-6
Connor Cem—*cemetery* IN-6
Connor Cem—*cemetery* MS-4
Connor Cem—*cemetery* (2) NC-3
Connor Cem—*cemetery* (2) OH-6
Connor Cem—*cemetery* OK-5
Connor Cem—*cemetery* TX-5
*Connor Creek* CA-9
*Connor Creek* TX-5
*Connor Creek* WI-6
Connor Creek—*stream* CA-9
Connor Creek—*stream* ID-8
Connor Creek—*stream* KS-7
Connor Creek—*stream* LA-4
Connor Creek—*stream* MI-6
Connor Creek—*stream* MT-8
Connor Creek—*stream* OR-9
Connor Creek—*stream* TX-5
Connor Creek—*stream* WA-9
Connor Creek Mine—*mine* OR-9
Connor Creek Rsvr—*reservoir* OR-9
Connor Drain—*canal* MI-6
Connor Flat—*flat* ID-8
Connor Gulch—*valley* MT-8
Connor Hall—*hist pl* NM-5
Connor Hollow—*valley* WV-2
Connor House—*hist pl* AZ-5
Connor House—*hist pl* IL-6
*Connor Lake* MI-6
*Connor Lake* WI-6
Connor Lake—*lake* MI-6
Connor Lake—*lake* OR-9
Connor Lake—*lake* WA-9
Connor Lake—*lake* WI-6
Connor Lakes—*lake* MI-6
Connor Point—*cape* ME-1
Connor Pond—*lake* MA-1
Connor Pond—*reservoir* MA-1
Connor Pond—*reservoir* SC-3
Connor Pond Dam—*dam* MA-1
Connor Ridge—*ridge* ID-8
Connor Ridge—*ridge* NC-3
Connor Rsvr—*reservoir* MA-1
*Connors* CO-8
*Connor's* MI-6
Connors And Sessions Drain—*canal* MI-6
*Connors Branch* IL-6
Connors Canyon—*valley* ID-8
Connors Canyon—*valley* NV-8
Connors Ch—*church* GA-3
Connor Sch—*school* NY-2
Connor Sch (abandoned)—*school* PA-2
Connor Sch Number 1—*school* ND-7
**Connors Corner**—*pop pl* ME-1
Connors Creek—*stream* AL-4
Connors Creek—*stream* (2) MI-6
Connors Creek—*stream* TX-5
Connors Creek—*stream* (2) WI-6
Connors Gulch—*valley* MT-8
Connors Gulch—*valley* WA-9
Connors House—*hist pl* ME-1
Connors Lake—*lake* AK-9
Connors Lake—*lake* MN-6
Connors Lake—*lake* MT-8
Connors Lake—*lake* SD-7
Connors Lake—*lake* WI-6
Connors Lake Lookout Tower—*locale* WI-6
Connors Lookout Tower—*locale* MI-6
Connors Mine—*mine* CO-8
Connors Pass—*gap* NV-8
Connors Pass Well—*well* NV-8
*Connors Point* ME-1
Connors Point—*cape* WI-6
Connors Point—*uninc pl* WI-6
Connors Point (historical)—*cape* ND-7
*Connor Spring* UT-8
Connor Spring—*spring* NV-8
Connor Springs—*spring* UT-8
Connors Reef—*ridge* MT-8
Connors Spring—*spring* ID-8
Connors Spring—*spring* WI-6
Connors State Agricultural Coll—*school* OK-5
*Connors StatiOn* KS-7
*Connorsville* OH-6
**Connorsville**—*pop pl* WI-6
Connor Toll House—*hist pl* TN-4
**Connor Township**—*pop pl* ND-7
Connor (Township of)—*unorg* ME-1
Connor (Unorganized Territory of)—*unorg* ME-1
Connor Valley—*valley* VA-3
**Connorville**—*pop pl* MI-6
**Connorville**—*pop pl* OH-6
Connor Wash—*stream* AZ-5
Connor Well—*well* NM-5
*Connotten Creek* OH-6
*Connotton Creek* OH-6
*Connover Ranch* MT-8
*Conn Point* MI-6
Conn Post Office (historical)—*building* MS-4
Conn Ranch—*locale* CA-9
Conn Ranch—*locale* MT-8
Conn Ranch—*locale* TX-5
Conn Run—*stream* WV-2
Conn Sch—*school* MO-7
Conn Sch—*school* NC-3
Conn Sch (abandoned)—*school* PA-2
Conn Sch (historical)—*school* MO-7
Conns Coulee—*valley* MT-8
*Conns Creek* CA-9
*Conns Creek* IN-6
Conns Creek—*stream* (2) IN-6
Conns Creek—*stream* MO-7
Conns Point—*cape* MI-6
Connundrum Hot Springs—*spring* CO-8
Conn Valley—*valley* CA-9
*Conob Pond* RI-1
Conocido Park—*park* AZ-5
Conocka Shoal—*bar* LA-4

*Conockonoquit Island* RI-1
**Conococheague**—*pop pl* MD-2
*Conococheague Creek* PA-2
Conococheague Creek—*stream* MD-2
Conococheague Creek—*stream* PA-2
Conococheague Island—*island* PA-2
Conococheague Mtn—*summit* PA-2
Conococheague Trail—*trail* PA-2
*Conococheaque Creek* PA-2
Conocodell Golf Course—*locale* PA-2
Conoconnara Swamp—*stream* NC-3
Conoconnara (Township of)—*fmr MCD* NC-3
Conodoguinet Cave—*cave* PA-2
Conodoguinet Creek—*stream* PA-2
Conodoquinet Dam—*dam* PA-2
Conoe Creek—*stream* KY-4
Conoe Lake—*lake* NY-2
*Conohasset* MA-1
Conoho Bend—*bend* NC-3
Conoho Creek—*stream* NC-3
Conoley—*locale* TX-5
**Conologue**—*pop pl* IN-6
Conologue Ch—*church* IN-6
*Conologue Post Office* IN-6
Conoloway—*locale* KY-4
Conoloway Creek—*stream* KY-4
*Conolton Creek* OH-6
Conoly (historical)—*locale* AL-4
*Conomly Lagoon* OR-9
**Conomo**—*pop pl* MA-1
Conomo Point—*cape* MA-1
Cononut Grove Metrorail Station—*locale* FL-3
*Conoquenessing* PA-2
*Conoquenessing Creek* PA-2
Conordale Park—*park* OR-9
Cono Township—*fmr MCD* IA-7
**Conotton**—*pop pl* OH-6
Conotton Creek—*stream* OH-6
Conotton Valley HS—*school* OH-6
Conover—*locale* IL-6
**Conover**—*pop pl* IL-6
**Conover**—*pop pl* IA-7
**Conover**—*pop pl* NC-3
**Conover**—*pop pl* OH-6
**Conover**—*pop pl* WI-6
Conover Archaeol Site—*hist pl* VA-3
Conover Bldg—*hist pl* OH-6
Conover Branch—*stream* IL-6
Conover Canyon—*valley* NV-8
Conover Cem—*cemetery* IL-6
Conover Cem—*cemetery* IN-6
Conover Cem—*cemetery* WI-6
Conover Channel—*channel* NJ-2
Conover Gulch—*valley* OR-9
Conover Hollow—*valley* PA-2
Conover Lake—*lake* MI-6
Conover Lake—*lake* TX-5
Conover Pond—*reservoir* NY-2
Conover Ranch—*locale* ID-8
Conover Ranch—*locale* (2) MT-8
Conover Sch—*school* IL-6
*Conovers Channel* NJ-2
Conover Special Education
Center—*school* NC-3
**Conovertown**—*pop pl* NJ-2
**Conover (Town of)**—*pop pl* WI-6
Conoves Creek—*stream* NM-5
*Conowago Creek* PA-2
*Conoway* VA-3
Conoway Ch—*church* IN-6
*Conoway Church* AL-4
Conoway Knob—*summit* NC-3
Conoway (RR name for Conaway)—*other* VA-3
*Conowingo* MD-2
Conowingo Ch—*church* MD-2
Conowingo Creek—*stream* MD-2
Conowingo Creek—*stream* PA-2
Conowingo Dam—*dam* MD-2
*Conowingo (Kilby Corner)* MD-2
Conowingo ( P O)—*locale* MD-2
Conowingo Rsvr—*reservoir* MD-2
Conowingo Rsvr—*reservoir* PA-2
*Conowingo Station* MD-2
Conowingo Station—*locale* MD-2
**Conowingo Village**—*pop pl* MD-2
Conoy, Lake—*lake* MD-2
Conoy Ch—*church* PA-2
Conoy Creek—*stream* PA-2
**Conoy (Township of)**—*pop pl* PA-2
Conoy Township Park—*park* PA-2
Conpitt Junction—*locale* PA-2
Conqueror Mine—*mine* NM-5
Conqueror Mines—*mine* CO-8
Conquer Point—*cape* AK-9
**Conquest**—*pop pl* NY-2
Conquest Mine—*mine* NV-8
**Conquest (Town of)**—*pop pl* NY-2
*Con Quien* AZ-5
Conquista Creek—*stream* TX-5
Conquista Crossing—*locale* TX-5
Conquistador Aisle—*gap* AZ-5
*Conquistador Isle* AZ-5
Conrad—*locale* IL-6
Conrad—*locale* OK-5
**Conrad**—*pop pl* FL-3
**Conrad**—*pop pl* IN-6
**Conrad**—*pop pl* IA-7
**Conrad**—*pop pl* MT-8
**Conrad**—*pop pl* PA-2
**Conrad**—*pop pl* SC-3
Conrad, Charles E., Mansion—*hist pl* MT-8
Conrad, Hair, Cabin—*hist pl* TN-4
Conrad Branch—*stream* IN-6
Conrad Butte—*summit* MT-8
Conrad Camp—*locale* MT-8
Conrad Cem—*cemetery* (2) IN-6
Conrad Cem—*cemetery* KY-4
Conrad Cem—*cemetery* LA-4
Conrad Cem—*cemetery* OH-6
Conrad Cem—*cemetery* PA-2
Conrad Cem—*cemetery* WV-2
Conrad Cemeteries—*cemetery* OH-6
Conrad City Hall—*hist pl* MT-8
Conrad Coal Mine—*mine* CO-8
*Conrad Creek* NV-8
Conrad Creek—*bay* FL-3
Conrad Creek—*stream* AL-4
Conrad Creek—*stream* ID-8
Conrad Creek—*stream* MO-7
Conrad Creek—*stream* NV-8
Conrad Creek—*stream* OR-9
Conrad Creek—*stream* SC-3
Conrad Creek—*stream* (2) WA-9
Conrad Crossing Campground—*locale* ID-8
Conrad Ditch—*canal* (2) IN-6
Conrad Field—*park* FL-3
Conrad Fork—*stream* WV-2
Conrad Gap Run—*stream* WV-2
Conrad Glacier—*glacier* WA-9
Conrad Gulch—*valley* CA-9
*Conrad Hill* NC-3
Conrad Hill—*summit* GA-3
Conrad Hill (Township of)—*fmr MCD* NC-3
Conrad (historical)—*locale* MS-4
*Conrad HS* DE-2
Conrad HS—*school* CT-1
Conrad HS—*school* DE-2
**Conrad (Hull)**—*pop pl* PA-2
Conrad Island—*island* VA-3
Conrad JHS—*school* CA-9
Conrad Lake—*lake* WA-9
Conrad Lake—*reservoir* NC-3
Conrad Lake Dam—*dam* NC-3
Conrad Meadows—*flat* WA-9
Conrad Meadows Ranch—*locale* TX-5
Conrad Memorial Cem—*cemetery* MT-8
Conrad Memorial Ch—*church* NC-3
Conrad Mound Archeol Site—*hist pl* OH-6
Conrad MS—*school* DE-2
Conrad Peak—*summit* ID-8
Conrad Place—*locale* OR-9
*Conrad Point* LA-4
Conrad Point—*cape* MT-8
Conrad Pond—*lake* NJ-2
Conrad Pond—*reservoir* VA-3
Conrad Ranch—*locale* CA-9
Conrad Ranch—*locale* MT-8
Conrad Ranch—*locale* TX-5
Conrad Rice Mill—*hist pl* LA-4
Conrad Ridge—*ridge* PA-2
Conrad Ridge—*ridge* TN-4
Conrad Rsvr—*reservoir* MT-8
Conrad Run—*stream* (2) WV-2
Conrads Bridge—*bridge* PA-2
Conrads Cem—*cemetery* TX-5
Conrad Sch—*school* OH-6
Conrad Sch (abandoned)—*school* MO-7
Conrad Sch (historical)—*school* PA-2
Conrads Mill—*locale* MO-7
Conrad Stadium—*park* NC-3
Conradts Landing—*locale* NV-8
Conrad Weiser—*park* PA-2
Conrail Franklin Bridge—*bridge* PA-2
**Conran**—*pop pl* MO-7
Conran Dike—*levee* MO-7
Conran Dike Hole—*lake* MO-7
Conrard—*locale* KY-4
**Conrath**—*pop pl* WI-6
Conrey Ch—*church* KY-4
Conring Ranch—*locale* TX-5
**Conrock**—*pop pl* FL-3
**Conroe**—*pop pl* TX-5
Conroe, Lake—*reservoir* TX-5
Conroe Bridge—*hist pl* KS-7
Conroe Ch—*church* IN-6
*Conroe Lake* TX-5
Conroe Memorial Park—*cemetery* TX-5
Conroe Normal and Industrial
Coll—*school* TX-5
Conroe Number One—*building* TX-5
Conroe Oil Field—*oilfield* TX-5
Conroe Townsite Oil Field—*oilfield* TX-5
Conrow Creek—*stream* MT-8
Conrow Spring Number One—*spring* MT-8
Conrow Spring Number Two—*spring* MT-8
Conroy—*locale* OR-9
**Conroy**—*pop pl* IA-7
*Conroy Canyon* CO-8
Conroy Canyon—*valley* NE-7
Conroy Canyon—*valley* OR-9
Conroy Canyon Rsvr—*reservoir* OR-9
Conroy Creek—*stream* (2) OR-9
*Conroy Educational Center* PA-2
Conroy Gulch—*valley* CO-8
Conroy JHS—*hist pl* PA-2
Conroy Lake—*lake* ME-1
Conroy Lake—*reservoir* WY-8
Conroy Lateral—*canal* ID-8
Conroy Mine—*mine* WY-8
Conroy Ranch—*locale* NE-7
Conroy Spring—*spring* CA-9
Conroy Spring—*spring* OR-9
Con Rsvr—*reservoir* OR-9
Consalus Creek—*stream* ID-8
Consalus Creek—*stream* WA-9
Consalus Vly—*summit* NY-2
Consant Sch—*school* NH-1
Consavvy Lake—*lake* TX-5
Conscience Bay—*bay* NY-2
Conscience Hill—*summit* MA-1
*Conscience Hills* MA-1
Conscience Point—*cape* NY-2
Consejo (Barrio)—*fmr MCD* (2) PR-3
Conselyeas Pond—*lake* NY-2
Consentino Sch—*school* MA-1
*Consequit River* NY-2
**Conser**—*pop pl* OK-5
Conser, Jacob, House—*hist pl* OR-9
Conser, Peter, House—*hist pl* OK-5
Conser Creek—*stream* OK-5
**Conser (historical)**—*pop pl* OR-9
Conser Run—*stream* OH-6
Conser Run Lake—*reservoir* OH-6
Conservation Camp Thirtyseven—*locale* CA-9
Conservation (CCD)—*cens area* FL-3
Conservation Island—*island* PA-2
Conservation Lake—*reservoir* AL-4
Conservation Lake—*reservoir* IL-6
Conservation Lake Dam—*dam* AL-4
Conservation Lake Dam—*dam* MS-4
Conservation League Dam—*dam* TN-4
Conservation League Lake—*lake* MS-4
Conservation League Lake—*reservoir* TN-4
Conservation Park Site
(20GR33)—*hist pl* MI-6
Conservation Spring—*spring* UT-8
Conservatory of Music of Puerto
Rico—*school* PR-3
**Conshal**—*pop pl* FL-3
Con Shea Basin—*basin* ID-8
Conshea Creek—*stream* CA-9
**Conshel**—*pop pl* NC-3
**Conshohocken**—*pop pl* PA-2
Conshohocken Borough—*civil* PA-2
Conshohocken Elem Sch—*school* PA-2
Conshohocken Station—*building* PA-2
**Conshohocken Station**—*pop pl* PA-2
Conshohocken United Methodist
Ch—*church* PA-2
Cons Hole—*basin* UT-8
*Con's Hood* NY-2
Conshul RR Station—*locale* FL-3
**Considine**—*pop pl* ND-7
Considine, Lake—*lake* IA-7
Consignee Creek—*stream* CA-9
Consistory Field—*park* PA-2
Cons Knoll—*summit* UT-8
**Consol**—*pop pl* IA-7
Consolata Mission Seminary—*school* NY-2
**Consolation**—*pop pl* KY-4
Consolation Cem—*cemetery* (2) AL-4
Consolation Ch—*church* AL-4
Consolation Ch—*church* GA-3
Consolation Mine—*mine* NM-5
Consolation Mission Ch—*church* KY-4
*Consolation Primitive Baptist Ch* AL-4
Consolation Primitive Baptist Ch—*church* AL-4
Consolation Sch—*school* KY-4
Console Springs—*spring* CA-9
Consolidated Bldg—*hist pl* SC-3
Consolidated Canal—*canal* AZ-5
Consolidated Canal—*canal* CA-9
Consolidated Canal East Branch—*canal* AZ-5
Consolidated Die Cast
Corporation—*facility* MI-6
Consolidated Ditch—*canal* (2) CO-8
Consolidated Ditch—*canal* OR-9
Consolidated Extension Ditch—*canal* CO-8
Consolidated Farmers Canal—*canal* ID-8
Consolidated Gulch—*valley* NV-8
Consolidated HS—*school* KY-4
Consolidated Law Ditch—*canal* CO-8
Consolidated Lookout Tower—*locale* WI-6
Consolidated Mine—*mine* (2) CA-9
Consolidated Mines—*mine* WA-9
Consolidated Oil Field—*oilfield* TX-5
Consolidated Peoples Ditch—*canal* CA-9
Consolidated Presbyterian Ch
(historical)—*church* AL-4
Consolidated Rsvr—*reservoir* CO-8
Consolidated Sch—*school* GA-3
Consolidated Sch—*school* (2) IN-6
Consolidated Sch—*school* (2) KY-4
Consolidated Sch—*school* MA-1
Consolidated Sch—*school* NE-7
Consolidated Sch—*school* TN-4
Consolidated Sch—*school* WI-6
Consolidated Sch (abandoned)—*school* PA-2
Consolidated Sch (historical)—*school* MS-4
Consolidated Sch Number 1—*school* NY-2
Consolidated Sch Number 1
(abandoned)—*school* MO-7
Consolidated Sch Number 2—*school* NV-8
*Consolidated School* PA-2
Consolidated Schools—*school* TX-5
Consolidated Slip—*harbor* CA-9
Consolidated Slough—*stream* CO-8
Consolidation Coal Water Supply
Lake—*reservoir* TN-4
Consolidation Creek—*stream* WA-9
Consolidation Freight Locomotive No.
1187—*hist pl* PA-2
Consolidation Freight Locomotive No.
2846—*hist pl* PA-2
Consolidation Freight Locomotive No.
7688—*hist pl* PA-2
Consolli Gulch—*valley* CA-9
**Consol No 9**—*pop pl* WV-2
Conspiracy Island—*island* MA-1
*Constabals Hoek* NJ-2
**Constable**—*pop pl* NY-2
Constable Creek—*stream* NY-2
Constable Hall—*hist pl* NY-2
Constable Hook—*cape* NJ-2
Constable Hook—*uninc pl* NJ-2
Constable Hook Reach—*channel* NJ-2
Constable Hook Reach—*channel* NY-2
*Constable Point* NJ-2
Constable Pond—*lake* NY-2
*Constables Hoeek* NJ-2
**Constable (Town of)**—*pop pl* NY-2
**Constableville**—*pop pl* NY-2
Constableville Village Hist Dist—*hist pl* NY-2
*Constance* MN-6
Constance—*locale* NE-7
**Constance**—*pop pl* KY-4
**Constance**—*pop pl* MN-6
Constance, Lake—*lake* NH-1
Constance, Lake—*lake* WA-9
Constance, Lake—*reservoir* PA-2
Constance, Mount—*summit* WA-9
Constance Bayou—*stream* LA-4
Constance Bayou Gas Field—*oilfield* LA-4
Constance Creek—*stream* AK-9
Constance Creek—*stream* TX-5
Constance Creek—*stream* WA-9
Constance Dam—*dam* PA-2
Constance Ditch—*canal* LA-4
Constance Lake—*lake* CA-9
Constance Lake—*lake* (2) MN-6
Constance Lake—*lake* WI-6
Constance Lake—*reservoir* GA-3
Constance Pass—*gap* WA-9
Constance Peak—*summit* CA-9
Constance Rsvr—*reservoir* OR-9
**Constancia**—*pop pl* (2) PR-3
Cons Tank—*reservoir* AZ-5
Constans Hotel—*hist pl* MN-6
*Constant* KS-7
Constant, Lake—*lake* AK-9
Constant Cem—*cemetery* IL-6
Constant Creek—*stream* KS-7
Constant Flow Gulch—*valley* CA-9
**Constant Friendship**—*pop pl* MD-2
Constantia—*other* OH-6
**Constantia**—*pop pl* NY-2
**Constantia Center**—*pop pl* NY-2
**Constantia (Town of)**—*pop pl* NY-2
**Constantine**—*pop pl* KY-4
**Constantine**—*pop pl* MI-6
Constantine, Lake—*lake* CO-8
Constantine Bay—*bay* AK-9
Constantine Branch—*stream* LA-4
Constantine Canyon—*valley* UT-8
Constantine Cove—*bay* AK-9
Constantine Creek—*stream* AK-9
Constantine Creek—*stream* OR-9
*Constantine Elementary School* AL-4
Constantine Harbor—*bay* (2) AK-9
Constantine Historic Commercial
District—*hist pl* MI-6
Constantine Point—*cape* AK-9
Constantine Rock—*bar* CA-9
Constantine Sch—*school* AL-4
Constantines Pond—*reservoir* AL-4
Constantines Pond Dam—*dam* AL-4
**Constantine (Township of)**—*pop pl* MI-6
Constant Run—*stream* WV-2
**Constanza**—*pop pl* PR-3
**Constellation**—*pop pl* AZ-5
Constellation Lake—*lake* WI-6
Constellation Mine—*mine* NM-5
Constellation Park—*park* AZ-5
Constellation Shaft—*mine* UT-8
Constien Cem—*cemetery* OK-5
Constine Bridge—*locale* NY-2
Constitution—*locale* GA-3
Constitution—*locale* MD-2
Constitution—*locale* OH-6
Constitution—*locale* PA-2
*Constitution Arch* UT-8
Constitution Hall—*hist pl* KS-7
Constitution Hall (Daughters of the American
Revolution)—*hist pl* DC-2
Constitution Hall Park—*park* AL-4
Constitution Hill—*locale* VI-3
Constitution Hill—*summit* MA-1
Constitution Hist Dist—*hist pl* KY-4
Constitution Island—*island* NY-2
Constitution JHS—*school* TN-4
Constitution Lake—*lake* GA-3
Constitution Mtn—*summit* NY-2
Constitution Museum—*building* MA-1
Constitution Park—*park* CA-9
Constitution Park—*park* FL-3
Constitution Park—*park* MD-2
Constitution Park—*park* OH-6
Constitution Sch—*school* AZ-5
Constitution Sch—*school* KY-4
Constitution Square Hist Dist—*hist pl* KY-4
Constitution (Township of)—*other* OH-6
Constitution Wharf—*locale* MA-1
Construction Creek—*stream* OR-9
Construction Products Dam—*dam* TN-4
Construction Products Lake—*reservoir* TN-4
Construction Rsvr—*reservoir* UT-8
**Consuella**—*pop pl* LA-4
Consuelo Hill—*summit* TX-5
Consuelo Tank—*reservoir* TX-5
Consul—*locale* AL-4
Consultation Lake—*lake* CA-9
**Consumers**—*pop pl* UT-8
Consumers Powder Companys
Mill—*building* PA-2
*Consumers Switch* IA-7
Consumers Wash—*valley* UT-8
*Consumnes River* CA-9
**Consumo**—*pop pl* PR-3
Cons Virg Shaft—*mine* NV-8
Contact—*locale* MT-8
Contact—*mine* AZ-5
**Contact**—*pop pl* NV-8
Contact Canyon—*valley* AZ-5
Contact Canyon—*valley* CA-9
Contact Canyon—*valley* UT-8
Contact Creek—*stream* (6) AK-9
Contact Creek—*stream* (2) MT-8
Contact Glacier—*glacier* (2) AK-9
Contact Gulch—*valley* AK-9
Contact Hill—*summit* CO-8
Contact Lake—*lake* AK-9
Contact Mine—*mine* (2) CA-9
Contact Mine—*mine* NV-8
Contact Mtn—*summit* MT-8
Contact Mtn—*summit* WA-9
Contact Nunatak—*summit* AK-9
Contact Pass—*gap* CA-9
Contact Pass—*gap* NV-8
Contact Peak *summit* (2) AK-9
Contact Point—*cape* AK-9
Contact Sch—*school* NV-8
Contact Spring—*spring* AZ-5
Contact Trick Tank—*reservoir* AZ-5
**Contadora Estates
Subdivision**—*pop pl* UT-8
Container Corporation Dam—*dam* AL-4
Container Corporation Lake—*reservoir* (2) AL-4
Container Corporation Lake Dam—*dam* AL-4
Container Corporation of America—*facility* IL-6
Container Corporation of
America—*facility* KY-4
Container Corporation Treatment
Dam—*dam* AL-4
Container Corporation Treatment
P—*reservoir* AL-4
**Contant**—*pop pl* (2) VI-3
Contant Point—*cape* VI-3
Contant Ranch—*locale* NV-8
**Contee**—*pop pl* MD-2
Contee Lake—*lake* TX-5
Contees Wharf—*locale* MD-2
Contemporary Plaza (Shop Ctr)—*locale* FL-3
Contempo Tempe (trailer park)—*locale* AZ-5
**Contempo Tempe (trailer
park)**—*pop pl* AZ-5
*Contennial Creek* OR-9
Contennial Sch—*school* PA-2
Content—*hist pl* (2) MD-2
Content—*locale* MT-8
Content—*locale* PA-2
Content—*locale* TX-5
Content, Lake—*lake* WI-6
Content Brook—*stream* MA-1
Contentea Campground—*locale* NC-3
*Contention* OR-9
Contention—*locale* AZ-5
Contention Cove—*bay* ME-1
Contention Hill—*summit* WA-9
Contention Mine—*mine* CA-9
Contention Mine—*mine* NV-8
Contention Pond—*lake* NH-1
Contention Ridge—*ridge* CA-9
Content Keys—*island* FL-3
Contentment—*hist pl* WV-2
Contentment—*locale* VI-3
Contentment Bluff—*cliff* GA-3
Contentment Island—*island* CT-1
Contentment Lake—*lake* MN-6
**Contentnea**—*pop pl* (2) NC-3
Contentnea Ch—*church* NC-3
Contentnea Creek—*stream* NC-3
Contentnea Elem Sch—*school* NC-3
Contentnea Junction—*locale* NC-3
Contentnea Neck (Township
of)—*fmr MCD* NC-3
Content Passage—*channel* FL-3
**Content (Tokeen)**—*pop pl* TX-5
Conterra—*locale* NE-7
Contest Lake—*lake* (2) MN-6
Contest Point—*cape* ID-8
**Continental**—*pop pl* AZ-5
**Continental**—*pop pl* OH-6
Continental—*uninc pl* PA-2
Continental Adit—*mine* NM-5
Continental Airp—*airport* AZ-5
Continental Army Encampment
Site—*hist pl* DE-2
Continental Bank Bldg—*hist pl* UT-8
Continental Camp—*locale* UT-8
Continental Camp—*park* IN-6
Continental Camp of America Dam Number
1—*dam* MA-1
Continental Can Company
Lake—*reservoir* NC-3
Continental Can Company Lake
Dam—*dam* NC-3
Continental Can of America Dam
A—*dam* MA-1
Continental Chief Mine—*mine* CO-8
Continental Clay Brick Plant—*hist pl* WV-2
Continental Creek—*stream* ID-8
Continental Creek—*stream* MT-8
Continental Dam Number Three—*dam* AZ-5
Continental Ditch—*canal* CO-8
Continental Ditch—*canal* WY-8
Continental Divide—*locale* NM-5
Continental Divide—*locale* WY-8
Continental Divide—*ridge* AK-9
Continental Divide—*ridge* CO-8
Continental Divide—*ridge* ID-8
Continental Divide—*ridge* MT-8
Continental Divide—*ridge* NM-5
Continental Divide—*ridge* WY-8
Continental Divide Ditch—*canal* WY-8
Continental Divide Raceway—*other* CO-8
Continental Divide Tank—*reservoir* NM-5
Continental Divide Trail—*trail* CO-8
Continental Divide Well—*well* NM-5
**Continental Estates**—*pop pl* UT-8
**Continental Estates
(subdivision)**—*pop pl* UT-8
**Continental Estates
Subdivision**—*pop pl* UT-8
Continental Gin Company—*hist pl* AL-4
Continental Gin Company—*hist pl* TX-5
Continental Glacier—*glacier* WY-8
Continental Golf Course—*other* AZ-5
Continental Hotel—*hist pl* MO-7
Continental Interchange—*crossing* AZ-5
Continental Lake—*lake* ID-8
Continental Lake—*lake* MN-6
Continental Lake—*lake* MT-8
Continental Lake—*lake* NV-8
Continental Military Institute—*school* FL-3
Continental Mill Housing—*hist pl* ME-1
Continental Mine—*mine* (2) AZ-5
Continental Mine—*mine* CO-8
Continental Mine—*mine* ID-8
Continental Mine—*mine* (2) OR-9
Continental Mtn—*summit* AZ-5
Continental Mtn—*summit* ID-8
Continental No. 2—*other* PA-2
Continental Number One Dam—*dam* AZ-5
Continental Number Two Dam—*dam* AZ-5
**Continental Number 2**—*pop pl* PA-2
Continental Park—*park* FL-3
Continental Peak—*summit* WY-8
Continental Plaza (Shop Ctr)—*locale* UT-8
Continental Pond—*lake* RI-1
Continental Ranch—*locale* (2) TX-5
Continental Ravine—*valley* CA-9
Continental Rsvr—*reservoir* CO-8
Continental Rsvr No 1—*reservoir* WY-8
Continental Rsvr No 2—*reservoir* WY-8
Continental Sch—*school* AZ-5
Continental Sch—*school* NJ-2
Continental Sch—*school* NY-2
Continental Sch—*school* PA-2
Continental Shaft—*mine* NM-5
Continental Shaft—*mine* PA-2
Continental Shopping Plaza—*locale* AZ-5
Continental Spring—*spring* AZ-5
Continental Spring—*spring* (2) MT-8
Continental Stove Works—*hist pl* PA-2
Continental Tank—*reservoir* AZ-5
**Continental Tempe (subdivision)**—*pop pl*
(2) AZ-5
**Continental Townhouse
Condominium**—*pop pl* UT-8
Continental Trust Company Bldg—*hist pl* MD-2
Continental Tunnel—*mine* AZ-5
*Continental Village* IL-6
Continental Village—*locale* NY-2
**Continental Village (subdivision)**—*pop pl*
(2) AZ-5
Continent Lake—*lake* UT-8
Continuation HS—*school* WA-9
Continuation Sch—*school* CA-9
Conto Gulch—*valley* WA-9
**Contoocook**—*pop pl* NH-1
Contoocook Lake—*lake* NH-1
Contoocook Mills Industrial
District—*hist pl* NH-1
Contoocook Mills Industrial District (Boundary
Increase)—*hist pl* NH-1
Contoocook River—*stream* NH-1
Contoocook State For—*forest* NH-1
*Contoohatchee River* FL-3
Contorno (Barrio)—*fmr MCD* PR-3
Contorta Point Campground—*park* OR-9
Contos, Lake—*lake* MI-6
**Contoy Estates (subdivision)**—*pop pl* UT-8
Contra—*locale* VA-3
Contra Acequia—*canal* NM-5
Contraband, Bayou—*stream* LA-4
Contrabando Canyon—*valley* TX-5
Contrabando Creek—*stream* TX-5
Contrabando Mtn—*summit* TX-5
Contrabando Waterhole—*lake* TX-5
Contra Costa Canal—*canal* CA-9
**Contra Costa (County)**—*pop pl* CA-9
Contra Costa County Boys Ranch—*locale* CA-9
Contra Costa County Jail Farm—*other* CA-9
Contra Costa Golf Club—*other* CA-9
Contractors Creek—*stream* WA-9
Contractors Point—*cape* WA-9
Contract Point—*cape* CA-9
Contra Loma Rsvr—*reservoir* CA-9
Contrariete Island—*island* LA-4
Contrariete Pass—*channel* LA-4
Contrary, Lake—*lake* MO-7
Contrary Bend—*bend* OR-9
Contrary Branch—*stream* KY-4
Contrary Brook—*stream* (2) ME-1
Contrary Brook Bog—*swamp* ME-1
Contrary Creek—*stream* ID-8
Contrary Creek—*stream* IL-6
Contrary Creek—*stream* IA-7
Contrary Creek—*stream* KY-4
Contrary Creek—*stream* (2) MO-7
Contrary Creek*—*stream* NE-7
Contrary Creek—*stream* (3) TX-5
Contrary Creek—*stream* (2) VA-3
Contrary Creek—*stream* WV-2
Contrary Knob—*summit* MD-2
Contrary Lake—*gut* TX-5
Contrary Run—*stream* PA-2
Contrary Sch—*school* IL-6
Contrary Sch—*school* VA-3
Contrary Spring—*spring* TX-5
Contrary Swamp—*stream* NC-3
Contrary Swamp—*stream* VA-3
Contrary Swamp—*swamp* SC-3
Contrary Tank—*reservoir* AZ-5
*Contras* OH-6
Contrayerba Canyon—*valley* NM-5
**Contrell**—*pop pl* MS-4
Contrell Ch—*church* MS-4
*Contrell Methodist Ch* MS-4
*Contreras* LA-4
Contreras—*locale* OH-6
**Contreras**—*pop pl* IN-6
**Contreras**—*pop pl* LA-4
**Contreras**—*pop pl* NM-5
Contreras, Lake—*reservoir* AL-4
Contreras Canyon—*valley* AZ-5
Contreras Mesa—*summit* AZ-5
Contreras Ranch—*locale* AZ-5
Contreras Spring—*spring* AZ-5
Contreras Tank—*reservoir* TX-5
Contreras Wash—*stream* (2) AZ-5
Contreville—*locale* VA-3
Control Creek—*stream* (2) AK-9
Control Creek—*stream* ID-8
Control Creek—*stream* MT-8
Control House on 72nd Street—*hist pl* NY-2
Control Lake—*lake* AK-9
Controller Bay—*bay* AK-9
Contury Rsvr—*reservoir* CA-9
Contux Creek—*stream* ID-8
Contwell—*locale* AL-4
Contzen Pass—*gap* AZ-5
Conundrum Basin—*basin* CO-8
Conundrum Creek—*stream* CO-8
Conundrum Creek—*stream* (2) OR-9
Conundrum Guard Station—*locale* CO-8
*Conundrum Pass* CO-8
Conundrum Peak—*summit* CO-8
Convalescent Hosp—*hospital* (2) CA-9
Convalescent Hosp for Children—*hospital* NY-2
*Convas Creek* SD-7
Convenant Ch—*church* PA-2
Convenant Cove Camp—*locale* MI-6
**Convene**—*pop pl* ME-1
Convenience Cem—*cemetery* AR-4
Convenience (Township of)—*fmr MCD* AR-4
Convenient Cove—*bay* AK-9
**Convent**—*pop pl* LA-4
**Convent**—*pop pl* NC-3
Convent Assembly of God Ch—*church* AL-4
Convent Cem—*cemetery* MN-6
Convent Cem—*cemetery* NJ-2
Convent Ch—*church* SC-3
*Convent (Convent Station)* NJ-2
*Convent Hill* MA-1
Convent Immaculate Conception Hist
Dist—*hist pl* IN-6
Convention Hall—*hist pl* OK-5
**Convento**—*pop pl* PR-3
Convento de Porta Coeli—*hist pl* PR-3
Convent of Mercy—*church* AL-4
Convent of Saint Helena—*church* NY-2
Convent of the Cenacle—*church* MA-1
Convent of the Good Shepherd—*church*
(2) CA-9
Convent of the Good Shepherd—*church* CO-8
Convent of the Good Shepherd—*church* TX-5
Convent of the Holy Ghost—*church* TX-5
Convent of the Holy Spirit—*church* IL-6
Convent of the Immaculate
Conception—*school* IN-6
Convent Of The Sacred Heart—*church* CT-1
Convent of the Sacred Heart—*school* CA-9
Convent of the Sisters of St. Joseph
Carondelet—*hist pl* MO-7
Convent of the Visitation—*church* MN-6
Convento Nuestra Senora de
Fatima—*locale* PR-3
Convent Sch—*school* SD-7
Convent School, The—*school* NY-2
Convent Station—*locale* NJ-2
**Convent Station (Convent)**—*pop pl* NJ-2
Convent Township (historical)—*civil* SD-7
Conventual Church of St. Mary and St.
John—*hist pl* MA-1
Converse—*locale* MO-7
Converse—*locale* NY-2
**Converse**—*pop pl* (2) IN-6
**Converse**—*pop pl* LA-4
**Converse**—*pop pl* (2) OH-6

Converse—pop pl SC-3
Converse—pop pl TX-5
Converse Airp—airport IN-6
Converse Basin—basin CA-9
Converse Basin Grove—woods CA-9
Converse Bay—bay VT-1
Converse Cem—cemetery MA-1
Converse Cem—cemetery MO-7
Converse Cem—cemetery OH-6
Converse City Park—park TX-5
Converse Coll—school SC-3
Converse College Hist Dist—hist pl SC-3
Converse Cottage—hist pl NJ-2
Converse County Park—park WY-8
Converse Creek—stream (2) CA-9
Converse-Dalton House—hist pl GA-3
Converse Ditch—canal OH-6
Converse Elem Sch—school IN-6
Converse Farm Landing Strip—airport KS-7
Converse Flats—flat CA-9
Converse Forest Service Station—locale CA-9
Converse Hall—hist pl UT-8
Converse Heights—pop pl SC-3
Converse House and Barn—hist pl CT-1
Converse Lake AL-4
Converse Lake—lake CT-1
Converse Lake—reservoir NY-2
Converse Lateral—canal AZ-5
Converse Meadow Pond—lake NH-1
Converse Memorial Bldg—hist pl MA-1
Converse-Mertz Apartments—hist pl OH-6
Converse Mine—mine CO-8
Converse Mountain Grove—woods CA-9
Converse Mtn—summit CA-9
Converse Point—cape MA-1
Converse Pond—lake NH-1
Converse Pond Brook—stream CT-1
Converse Ranch—locale MT-8
Converse Sch—school WI-6
Converset Ditch—canal IN-6
Converseville—pop pl NH-1
Convers Flat CA-9
Convert Creek—stream AK-9
Convert Sch—school AZ-5
Conves Cem—cemetery IL-6
Convest Subdivision—pop pl UT-8
Convey Creek—stream IA-7
Conveyors Goose Neck—cape MD-2
Convict Branch—stream TN-4
Convict Branch—stream TX-5
Convict Creek—stream CA-9
Convict Hollow—valley VA-3
Convict Lake—lake CA-9
Convict Lake—lake TN-4
Convict Lake (Carson Camp)—pop pl CA-9
Convict Pond—swamp TX-5
Convicts' Bread Oven—hist pl CO-8
Convict Spring—spring CA-9
Convict Spring—spring FL-3
Convict Tank—reservoir AZ-5
Con-Virginia Mine—mine OR-9
Convis (Township of)—pop pl MI-6
Convoy—pop pl OH-6
Convoy Gut—stream NC-3
Convoy Point—cape FL-3
Convoy Union JHS—school OH-6
Convulsion Canyon—valley UT-8
Conwa IA-7
Conway—locale KY-4
Conway—locale TN-4
Conway—pop pl AR-4
Conway—pop pl FL-3
Conway—pop pl IA-7
Conway—pop pl KS-7
Conway—pop pl LA-4
Conway—pop pl MA-1
Conway—pop pl MI-6
Conway—pop pl MS-4
Conway—pop pl MO-7
Conway—pop pl NH-1
Conway—pop pl NC-3
Conway—pop pl ND-7
Conway—pop pl OR-9
Conway—pop pl PA-2
Conway—pop pl SC-3
Conway—pop pl TX-5
Conway—pop pl WA-9
Conway, Bayou—stream LA-4
Conway, Lake—lake FL-3
Conway, Lake—reservoir AR-4
Conway Addition—pop pl OH-6
Conway Baptist Ch—church MS-4
Conway Bay—bay MI-6
Conway Bayou AL-4
Conway Bayou—stream LA-4
Conway Bldg—hist pl IL-6
Conway Bluff—cliff TX-5
Conway Borough—civil PA-2
Conway Branch—stream NE-7
Conway Branch—stream SC-3
Conway Bridge—bridge TN-4
Conway (CCD)—cens area KY-4
Conway (CCD)—cens area SC-3
Conway (CCD)—cens area WA-9
Conway Cem—cemetery AL-4
Conway Cem—cemetery IA-7
Conway Cem—cemetery (3) MI-6
Conway Cem—cemetery MS-4
Conway Cem—cemetery (3) MO-7
Conway Cem—cemetery PA-2
Conway Cemetery—hist pl AR-4
Conway Center (Shop Ctr)—locale FL-3
Conway Centre (Center Conway) NH-1
Conway Ch—church AL-4
Conway Ch—church IL-6
Conway Ch—church MI-6
Conway Ch—church MO-7
Conway Cohoctah Union Drain—canal MI-6
Conway Compact (census name Conway)—pop pl NH-1
Conway Corral—locale AZ-5
Conway (County)—pop pl AR-4
Conway County Library—hist pl AR-4
Conway Creek—gut MI-6
Conway Creek—stream AL-4
Conway Creek—stream WY-8
Conway Dam—dam VT-1
Conway Ditch—canal IN-6
Conway Drain No 1—canal MI-6
Conway Draw—valley CO-8
Conway East (CCD)—cens area SC-3
Conway Electric Dam—dam MA-1
Conway Electric Rsvr—reservoir MA-1
Conway Elem Sch—school FL-3
Conway First Baptist Ch—church FL-3
Conway Fish Pond Number One—reservoir AL-4
Conway Gulch—valley ID-8
Conway Hill—summit NY-2
Conway (historical)—pop pl OR-9
Conway Hollow—valley KY-4
Conway Hollow—valley (2) MO-7
Conway Hollow—valley OH-6
Conway Hollow—valley PA-2
Conway Hosp—hospital LA-4
Conway Hotel—hist pl AR-4
Conway House—hist pl ME-1
Conway House—hist pl MT-8
Conway JHS—school FL-3
Conway JHS—school NC-3
Conway Lake—lake CA-9
Conway Lake—lake (2) MI-6
Conway Lake—lake NE-7
Conway Lake—lake NH-1
Conway Methodist Ch—church MS-4
Conway Methodist Church, 1898 and 1910 Sanctuaries—hist pl SC-3
Conway Playground—park MA-1
Conway Playground—park MN-6
Conway Point—cape ME-1
Conway Point—cape MI-6
Conway Post Office (historical)—building AL-4
Conway Post Office (historical)—building MS-4
Conway Presbyterian Ch—church FL-3
Conway Ranch—locale AZ-5
Conway Ranch—locale (2) CA-9
Conway Recreation Dam—dam MA-1
Conway Ridge—ridge MT-8
Conway River—stream VA-3
Conway-Robinson Memorial State For—forest VA-3
Conway (RR name Fir)—pop pl WA-9
Conway Rsvr—reservoir OR-9
Conway Sch—school CA-9
Conway Sch—school MO-7
Conway Sch—school (2) TN-4
Conway Sch—school WA-9
Conways Chapel—church NC-3
Conway Sch (historical)—school TN-4
Conways Lake—lake AL-4
Conway Slough—stream MS-4
Conways Point MI-6
Conway Spring—spring AZ-5
Conway Spring—spring CO-8
Conway Springs—pop pl KS-7
Conway Springs Cem—cemetery KS-7
Conway Springs HS—school KS-7
Conway Stage Station (Site) (historical)—locale NV-8
Conway State For—forest MA-1
Conway State Forest—park NH-1
Conway Street Sch—school MA-1
Conway Summit—gap CA-9
Conway Swamp—swamp VT-1
Conway-Thomastown School MS-4
Conway (Town of)—pop pl MA-1
Conway (Town of)—pop pl NH-1
Conway Township—pop pl KS-7
Conway (Township of)—pop pl MI-6
Conway United Methodist Ch—church FL-3
Conway Valley—valley WI-6
Conway Village Cem—cemetery NH-1
Conway Yard—locale PA-2
Conwell, Elias, House—hist pl IN-6
Conwell, Russell H., Sch—hist pl PA-2
Conwell Cem—cemetery TN-4
Conwell Ditch—canal CO-8
Conwell Ditch—canal MT-8
Conwell Pond—lake DE-2
Conwell Pond—lake MA-1
Conwell Sch—school (2) MA-1
Conwell Sch—school PA-2
Conwells Landing DE-2
Conwells Mills IN-6
Conwill Cem—cemetery AL-4
Conwill Cem—cemetery (2) MS-4
Cony, Gov. Samuel, House—hist pl ME-1
Cony Basin—basin WY-8
Cony Cem—cemetery ME-1
Cony Crags—ridge CA-9
Cony Creek—stream CO-8
Conyer Creek—stream ID-8
Conyer Lake—lake SC-3
Conyer Lake Island—island SC-3
Conyers—pop pl GA-3
Conyers Bay—swamp SC-3
Conyers Branch—stream TN-4
Conyers (CCD)—cens area GA-3
Conyers Cem—cemetery (2) AR-4
Conyers Cem—cemetery GA-3
Conyers Cem—cemetery IA-7
Conyers Cem—cemetery KY-4
Conyers Cem—cemetery MO-7
Conyer Sch—school CA-9
Conyers Commercial Hist Dist—hist pl GA-3
Conyers Creek—stream OR-9
Conyers Lake—lake GA-3
Conyers-Rosenwald Sch—school AL-4
Conyers Spring Sch—school AR-4
Conyersville—locale TN-4
Conyersville Post Office (historical)—building TN-4
Conyers Waterworks—other GA-3
Cony HS—hist pl ME-1
Cony Lake—lake CO-8
Cony Lake—lake ID-8
Cony Lake—lake WY-8
Cony Mtn—summit AK-9
Cony Mtn—summit WY-8
Conyngham—pop pl PA-2
Conyngham Borough—civil PA-2
Conyngham-Hacker House—hist pl PA-2
Conyngham Station—locale PA-2
Conyngham (Township of)—pop pl (2) PA-2
Cony Pass—gap CO-8
Cony Pass—gap WY-8
Cony Peak—summit ID-8
Conzemius Park—park MN-6
Cooch—pop pl DE-2
Coocheyville—locale VA-3
Coochie Brake—swamp LA-4
Coochs Bridge—locale DE-2
Cooch's Bridge Hist Dist—hist pl DE-2
Cocksey Branch—stream FL-3
Coody Creek—stream GA-3
Coody Creek—stream OK-5
Coody Crossing—locale TX-5
Coodys Bluff—cliff OK-5
Coodys Bluff—locale OK-5
Cooeg Pond—lake FL-3
Cooey Field—island FL-3
Coogan Creek—stream WA-9
Coogan Park—park MI-6
Coogan Ranch—locale CA-9
Coogler Pond—lake FL-3
Cooglers Beach—locale FL-3
Cook IN-6
Cook PA-2
Cook—locale KS-7
Cook—locale OH-6
Cook—locale OK-5
Cook—locale SC-3
Cook—pop pl FL-3
Cook—pop pl IN-6
Cook—pop pl MN-6
Cook—pop pl NE-7
Cook—pop pl OR-9
Cook—pop pl TX-5
Cook, A. E., House—hist pl MA-1
Cook, Alexander, House—hist pl WI-6
Cook, Amos, House—hist pl OR-9
Cook, Anthony Wayne, Mansion—hist pl PA-2
Cook, Asa M., House—hist pl MA-1
Cook, Bayou—gut LA-4
Cook, Charles, House—hist pl TX-5
Cook, Clarissa, Home for the Friendless—hist pl IA-7
Cook, Clarissa C., Library/Blue Ribbon News Bldg.—hist pl IA-7
Cook, Col. Edward, House—hist pl PA-2
Cook, Ellis, House—hist pl NJ-2
Cook, Fayette, House—hist pl SD-7
Cook, Grace, House—hist pl HI-9
Cook, Harold J., Homestead Cabin—hist pl NE-7
Cook, James, House—hist pl NM-5
Cook, J.M., House—hist pl OH-6
Cook, John, Farm—hist pl OH-6
Cook, John, House—hist pl CT-1
Cook, John W., Hall—hist pl IL-6
Cook, Joseph, House—hist pl ID-8
Cook, Maj. George Beecher, House—hist pl CA-9
Cook, Merlyn G., Sch—hist pl GU-9
Cook, Mount—summit AK-9
Cook, Thomas, House—hist pl WI-6
Cook, William, House—hist pl MA-1
Cook, William H., Water Tank House—hist pl ID-8
Cook, Will Marion, House—hist pl NY-2
Cook, Zimri, House—hist pl OH-6
Cook Acres—pop pl IN-6
Cook Airfield—airport KS-7
Cook Allen Brook—stream MA-1
Cook and Duncan Drain—canal MI-6
Cook and Green Butte—summit CA-9
Cook and Green Campground—locale CA-9
Cook and Green Creek—stream CA-9
Cook and Green Pass—gap CA-9
Cook and Thorburn Drain—stream MI-6
Cook and White Lake—lake MI-6
Cook Arroyo—stream NM-5
Cook Ave Sch—school IL-6
Cook-Bateman Farm—hist pl RI-1
Cook Bay—bay AK-9
Cook Bay—bay FL-3
Cook Bay—bay NY-2
Cook Blacksmith Shop—hist pl NE-7
Cook Bldg—hist pl OH-6
Cook Bluff—cliff AL-4
Cook Bog—swamp ME-1
Cook Branch—stream (3) AL-4
Cook Branch—stream (2) AR-4
Cook Branch—stream GA-3
Cook Branch—stream (3) KY-4
Cook Branch—stream (5) NC-3
Cook Branch—stream SC-3
Cook Branch—stream (2) TN-4
Cook Branch—stream (4) TX-5
Cook Branch—stream VA-3
Cook Bridge—bridge AL-4
Cook Bridge—other IL-6
Cook Brook MA-1
Cook Brook—stream (3) ME-1
Cook Brook—stream MA-1
Cook Brook—stream NH-1
Cook Brook—stream (3) NY-2
Cook Brook—stream VT-1
Cook Burn—area OR-9
Cook Camp—locale TX-5
Cook Canal—canal ID-8
Cook Canyon TX-5
Cook Canyon—valley AZ-5
Cook Canyon—valley (3) CA-9
Cook Canyon—valley CO-8
Cook Canyon—valley NV-8
Cook Canyon—valley (2) NM-5
Cook Canyon—valley TX-5
Cook Canyon—valley (3) UT-8
Cook Canyon—valley WY-8
Cook Cave—cave AL-4
Cook Cave—cave AR-4
Cook Cave—cave TN-4
Cook Cave Hollow—valley AR-4
Cook Cem TN-4
Cook Cem—cemetery (3) AL-4
Cook Cem—cemetery (3) AR-4
Cook Cem—cemetery (3) GA-3
Cook Cem—cemetery (7) IL-6
Cook Cem—cemetery (3) IN-6
Cook Cem—cemetery (2) IA-7
Cook Cem—cemetery (7) KY-4
Cook Cem—cemetery (3) LA-4
Cook Cem—cemetery MN-6
Cook Cem—cemetery (5) MS-4
Cook Cem—cemetery (10) MO-7
Cook Cem—cemetery NE-7
Cook Cem—cemetery (4) NY-2
Cook Cem—cemetery (5) NC-3
Cook Cem—cemetery (4) OH-6
Cook Cem—cemetery OK-5
Cook Cem—cemetery PA-2
Cook Cem—cemetery SC-3
Cook Cem—cemetery (15) TN-4
Cook Cem—cemetery (4) TX-5
Cook Cem—cemetery VT-1
Cook Cem—cemetery (3) VA-3
Cook Cem—cemetery (4) WV-2
Cook Center Cem—cemetery IA-7
Cook Ch AL-4
Cook Ch—church AL-4
Cook Ch—church LA-4
Cook Chapel AL-4
Cook Chapel—church (2) GA-3
Cook Chapel—church MI-6
Cook Chapel—church SC-3
Cook Chapel Sch—school AL-4
Cook Corner—locale SC-3
Cook Corner—locale UT-8
Cook Corners NY-2
Cook Corners—locale NY-2
Cook Corners—pop pl (3) NY-2
Cook Coulee—valley MT-8
Cook (County)—pop pl GA-3
Cook (County)—pop pl IL-6
Cook (County)—pop pl MN-6
Cook County Courthouse—hist pl MN-6
Cook County Criminal Court Bldg—hist pl IL-6
Cook County Lake—lake MN-6
Cook Cove—bay ME-1
Cook Creek ID-8
Cook Creek OR-9
Cook Creek PA-2
Cook Creek—stream AL-4
Cook Creek—stream CA-9
Cook Creek—stream (3) CO-8
Cook Creek—stream FL-3
Cook Creek—stream GA-3
Cook Creek—stream (4) ID-8
Cook Creek—stream IA-7
Cook Creek—stream (2) KY-4
Cook Creek—stream (2) LA-4
Cook Creek—stream (3) MS-4
Cook Creek—stream MO-7
Cook Creek—stream (4) MT-8
Cook Creek—stream (2) NE-7
Cook Creek—stream NY-2
Cook Creek—stream (2) NC-3
Cook Creek—stream (10) OR-9
Cook Creek—stream (2) PA-2
Cook Creek—stream TN-4
Cook Creek—stream (3) TX-5
Cook Creek—stream VA-3
Cook Creek—stream (4) WA-9
Cook Creek—stream (2) WI-6
Cook Creek Butte—summit MT-8
Cook Creek Rsvr—reservoir MT-8
Cook Creek Trail—trail OR-9
Cook Ditch—canal CO-8
Cook Ditch—canal (4) IN-6
Cook Ditch—canal MT-8
Cook Ditch—canal OR-9
Cook Ditch—canal SD-7
Cook Ditch—canal WY-8
Cook Ditch No 9—canal WY-8
Cook Drain—canal (3) MI-6
Cook Drain—stream MI-6
Cook Draw—valley WA-9
Cook Draw—valley (2) WY-8
Cooke RI-1
Cooke, Amos, House—hist pl RI-1
Cooke, Charles Montague, Jr., House—hist pl HI-9
Cooke, Clarence H., House—hist pl HI-9
Cooke, Eleutheros, House—hist pl OH-6
Cooke, E. V., House—hist pl ID-8
Cooke, Frederick William, Residence—hist pl NJ-2
Cooke, Jay, House—hist pl OH-6
Cooke, Jay, JHS—hist pl PA-2
Cooke, Noah, House—hist pl NH-1
Cooke, Peyton , House—hist pl KY-4
Cooke, Wm. L., House—hist pl GA-3
Cooke Basin MI-6
Cooke Canyon—valley WA-9
Cooke Cem—cemetery MS-4
Cooke Cem—cemetery ND-7
Cooke Cem—cemetery SC-3
Cooke Cem—cemetery (2) TN-4
Cooke Cem—cemetery WI-6
Cooke Cemetery MO-7
Cooke City—pop pl MT-8
Cooke City Store—hist pl MT-8
Cooke (County)—pop pl TX-5
Cooke County Junior Coll—school TX-5
Cooke Creek—stream TX-5
Cooke Creek—stream WA-9
Cooke Crossroads—pop pl SC-3
Cooke Dam—dam MI-6
Cooke Dam Basin MI-6
Cooke Dam Pond—reservoir MI-6
Cooke Drain TX-5
Cooke House—hist pl NC-3
Cooke JHS—school MI-6
Cooke JHS—school PA-2
Cooke Knob—summit TN-4
Cooke Lake—reservoir KY-4
Cooke Lake Dam—dam MS-4
Cooke Landing—locale TN-4
Cooke Memorial Ch—church MS-4
Cooke Mtn—summit WA-9
Cooke Park—park WI-6
Cooke Pass MT-8
Cooke Peak—summit NM-5
Cooke Point—cape LA-4
Cooke Post Office (historical)—building MS-4
Cooke Ranch—flat IL-6
Cooke Ranger Station—locale (2) MT-8
Cooker Branch—stream AR-4
Cooke Reservoir MI-6
Cooke-Robertson House—hist pl OH-6
Cooke Sch—school DC-2
Cooke Sch—school IL-6
Cooke Sch—school MI-6
Cooke Sch—school NY-2
Cooke Sch—school TX-5
Cookes House—hist pl PA-2
Cookes Landing (historical)—locale MS-4
Cookes Peak NM-5
Cookes Pond NJ-2
Cookes Subdivision—pop pl UT-8
Cooke (Township of)—pop pl PA-2
Cooke Tunnel—tunnel HI-9
Cooke Valley—valley WI-6
Cookeville—pop pl TN-4
Cookeville Armory—building TN-4
Cookeville (CCD)—cens area TN-4
Cookeville Ch of Christ—church TN-4
Cookeville Christian Sch—school TN-4
Cookeville City Hall—building TN-4
Cookeville Division—civil TN-4
Cookeville Filtration Plant—building TN-4
Cookeville First Baptist Ch—church TN-4
Cookeville General Hosp—hospital TN-4
Cookeville Golf and Country Club—locale TN-4
Cookeville HS—school TN-4
Cookeville Mall Shop Ctr—locale TN-4
Cookeville Post Office—building TN-4
Cookeville RR Depot—hist pl TN-4
Cook Farm—hist pl IA-7
Cook Ferry TN-4
Cook Ferry (historical)—locale AL-4
Cookfield Branch—stream AR-4
Cook Flat—flat TX-5
Cook Ford—locale AR-4
Cook Forest Cem—cemetery PA-2
Cook Forest State Park—park PA-2
Cook Forest State Park Indian Cabin District—hist pl PA-2
Cook Forest State Park River Cabin District—hist pl PA-2
Cook Forest Tower—tower PA-2
Cook Fork—stream KY-4
Cook Fork—stream VA-3
Cook Gap—gap NC-3
Cook Gap Mtn—summit AL-4
Cook Gulch—valley CA-9
Cook Gulch—valley OR-9
Cook Harbor—bay IL-6
Cook Hill—summit CT-1
Cook Hill—summit ME-1
Cook Hill—summit (2) NH-1
Cook Hill—summit (2) NY-2
Cook Hill—summit RI-1
Cook Hill—summit (2) VT-1
Cook Hill—summit (2) WA-9
Cook Hills—summit MI-6
Cook Hill Sch—school CT-1
Cook-Holland Cem—cemetery TX-5
Cook Hollow—valley (2) AR-4
Cook Hollow—valley (2) KY-4
Cook Hollow—valley (4) MO-7
Cook Hollow—valley NY-2
Cook Hollow—valley (2) OH-6
Cook Hollow—valley OK-5
Cook Hollow—valley PA-2
Cook Hollow—valley (9) TN-4
Cook Hollow—valley VT-1
Cook Hollow—valley VA-3
Cook-Hormel House—hist pl MN-6
Cook House—hist pl LA-4
Cook House—hist pl MS-4
Cook House—hist pl WV-2
Cookhouse Creek—stream NY-2
Cookhouse Creek—stream OR-9
Cookhouse Gulch—valley (2) CA-9
Cookhouse Gulch—valley ID-8
Cook HS—school GA-3
Cook HS—school TN-4
Cookie Jar, The UT-8
Cookie Jar Butte—summit UT-8
Cookietown—locale OK-5
Cookingham Hill—summit NY-2
Cook Inlet—bay AK-9
Cook Island—island AK-9
Cook Island—island IN-6
Cook Island—island IA-7
Cook Island—island ME-1
Cook JHS—school CA-9
Cook JHS—school GA-3
Cook JHS—school MS-4
Cook Kindergarten—school FL-3
Cook Knob ID-8
Cook Knob—summit NC-3
Cook-Koster Lateral—canal ID-8
Cook Lake MI-6
Cook Lake—lake AK-9
Cook Lake—lake (2) FL-3
Cook Lake—lake IN-6
Cook Lake—lake KS-7
Cook Lake—lake (6) MI-6
Cook Lake—lake (3) MN-6
Cook Lake—lake MS-4
Cook Lake—lake MT-8
Cook Lake—lake NE-7
Cook Lake—lake (3) TX-5
Cook Lake—lake UT-8
Cook Lake—lake WA-9
Cook Lake—lake (3) WI-6
Cook Lake—lake (2) WY-8
Cook Lake—reservoir AL-4
Cook Lake—reservoir GA-3
Cook Lake—reservoir TX-5
Cook Lake Dam—dam AL-4
Cook Lake Dam—dam (3) MS-4
Cook Lakes—lake WY-8
Cook Landing—locale FL-3
Cook Landing—locale SC-3
Cook Landing—locale VA-3
Cook Landing Cem—cemetery SC-3
Cook Landing Field—airport SD-7
Cook Landing Site—hist pl WA-9
Cook Lick Hollow—valley VA-3
Cook Lougheed Wildlife Pond—reservoir IN-6
Cook Lougheed Wildlife Pond Dam—dam IN-6
Cookman Ch—church PA-2
Cookman Fork—stream WV-2
Cookman Sch—school FL-3
Cook-Martin Cemetery MS-4
Cook Meadow Brook—stream ME-1
Cook Memorial Baptist Ch—church FL-3
Cook Memorial Baptist Church MS-4
Cook Memorial Cem—cemetery TN-4
Cook Memorial Hosp—hospital TX-5
Cook Memorial Library—hist pl NH-1
Cook Memorial Park—park CO-8
Cook Mill—locale TN-4
Cook Mill—pop pl TN-4
Cook Mills—pop pl ME-1
Cook Mine—mine AL-4
Cook Mine—mine (2) AZ-5
Cook Mine—mine MT-8
Cook-Morrow House—hist pl AR-4
Cook Mountain MA-1
Cook Mountain—ridge AR-4
Cook Mtn—summit AR-4
Cook Mtn—summit CO-8
Cook Mtn—summit (2) GA-3
Cook Mtn—summit ID-8
Cook Mtn—summit (2) MT-8
Cook Mtn—summit (2) NY-2
Cook Mtn—summit NC-3
Cook Mtn—summit VA-3
Cook Mtn—summit WA-9
Cook Mtn—summit WV-2
Cook Number One Mine (underground)—mine AL-4
Cook Number Two Mine (underground)—mine AL-4
Cookoosh Lake—lake MN-6
Cook Park—park (2) IA-7
Cook Park—park (2) MI-6
Cook Park—park (2) MN-6
Cook Park—park OH-6
Cook Pasture—flat UT-8
Cook Path—trail NH-1
Cook Peak—summit CA-9
Cook Peak—summit WY-8
Cook Place Post Office (historical)—building TN-4
Cook Playground—park MI-6
Cook Point—cape CT-1
Cook Point—cape HI-9
Cook Point—cape MD-2
Cook Point—cape MN-6
Cook Point—cape NY-2
Cook Point Cove—bay MD-2
Cook Point Range Channel—channel OR-9
Cook Pond MA-1
Cook Pond—lake AL-4
Cook Pond—lake (2) GA-3
Cook Pond—lake (2) MA-1
Cook Pond—lake NY-2
Cook Pond—lake VT-1
Cook Pond—reservoir AZ-5
Cook Pond—reservoir MA-1
Cook Pond Dam—dam MA-1
Cook Pond (historical)—lake TN-4
Cook Pond Outlet—stream NY-2
Cookport—pop pl PA-2
Cook Ranch—locale AZ-5
Cook Ranch—locale ID-8
Cook Ranch—locale (3) NE-7
Cook Ranch—locale NM-5
Cook Ranch—locale (3) TX-5
Cook Ranch—locale UT-8
Cook Ridge—ridge CA-9
Cook Ridge—ridge TN-4
Cook Ridge—ridge WA-9
Cook (RR name Cooks)—pop pl WA-9
Cook Rsvr—reservoir AZ-5
Cook Rsvr—reservoir CA-9
Cook Rsvr—reservoir MT-8
Cook Rsvr—reservoir (2) OR-9
Cook Rsvr—reservoir UT-8
Cook Run PA-2
Cook Run—stream PA-2
Cook Run—stream SC-3
Cook Run—stream WV-2
Cook-Rutledge House—hist pl WI-6
Cooks—locale PA-2
Cooks—pop pl AL-4
Cooks—pop pl MI-6
Cooks—pop pl OH-6
Cooks and Davenport Cemetery AL-4
Cooks Bay—bay MI-6
Cooks Bay—bay MN-6
Cooks Bay—bay NY-2
Cooks Bayou—stream FL-3
Cooks Bayou—stream MS-4
Cooks Beach—beach CA-9
Cooks Bend—bend AL-4
Cooks Bend—bend AK-9
Cooks Bend Cut Off—channel AL-4
Cooks Brake AR-4
Cooks Brake—swamp AR-4
Cooks Branch AL-4
Cooks Branch PA-2
Cooks Branch—stream (2) AL-4
Cooks Branch—stream AR-4
Cooks Branch—stream GA-3
Cooks Branch—stream KY-4
Cooks Branch—stream LA-4
Cooks Branch—stream MD-2
Cooks Branch—stream MS-4
Cooks Branch—stream MO-7
Cooks Branch—stream NC-3
Cooks Branch—stream (2) TN-4
Cooks Branch—stream TX-5
Cooks Branch—stream (3) VA-3
Cooks Bridge—bridge ME-1
Cooks Bridge—bridge NJ-2
Cooks Bridge—bridge SC-3
Cooks Brook MA-1
Cooks Brook—stream ME-1
Cooks Brook—stream VT-1
Cooks Brook Beach—pop pl MA-1
Cooksburg—locale KY-4
Cooksburg—pop pl NY-2
Cooksburg—pop pl PA-2
Cooksburg (Cook State Forest Park)—pop pl PA-2
Cooks Butte—summit OR-9
Cooks Cabin—locale UT-8
Cooks Cabin—locale WA-9
Cooks Canyon—valley (2) CA-9
Cooks Canyon—valley NM-5
Cooks Canyon—valley OR-9
Cooks Canyon—valley WY-8
Cooks Canyon Channel—canal CA-9
Cooks Cave—cave MO-7
Cooks Cem—cemetery AL-4
Cooks Cem—cemetery AR-4
Cooks Cem—cemetery GA-3
Cooks Cem—cemetery IN-6
Cooks Cem—cemetery MI-6
Cooks Cem—cemetery (2) MS-4
Cooks Cem—cemetery SC-3
Cooks Cem—cemetery TN-4
Cooks Cem—cemetery VT-1

Cooks Cem—cemetery ... WV-2
Cooks Ch—church ... TN-4
Cook Sch—school ... AL-4
Cook Sch—school (2) ... AR-4
Cook Sch—school (5) ... CA-9
Cook Sch—school ... DC-2
Cook Sch—school ... FL-3
Cook Sch—school ... GA-3
Cook Sch—school (7) ... IL-6
Cook Sch—school ... MA-1
Cook Sch—school (3) ... MI-6
Cook Sch—school ... MN-6
Cook Sch—school ... MO-7
Cook Sch—school ... NE-7
Cook Sch—school ... NC-3
Cook Sch—school ... OR-9
Cook Sch—school ... PA-2
Cook Sch—school ... UT-8
Cook Sch—school (3) ... VA-3
Cook Sch—school (2) ... WI-6
Cook Sch (abandoned)—school ... MO-7
Cooks Chapel ... MS-4
Cooks Chapel—church ... GA-3
Cooks Chapel—church (2) ... IN-6
Cooks Chapel—church ... KY-4
Cooks Chapel—church ... MS-4
Cooks Chapel—church ... MO-7
Cooks Chapel—church ... NC-3
Cooks Chapel—church (2) ... WV-2
Cooks Chapel—locale ... AL-4
Cooks Chapel Ch—church ... AL-4
Cooks Chapel Number 2 Ch—church ... AL-4
Cooks Chapel School ... AL-4
Cooks Chasm—bay ... OR-9
Cook Sch (historical)—school ... AL-4
Cooks Corner—locale ... ME-1
Cooks Corner—locale ... RI-1
**Cooks Corner**—pop pl ... ME-1
**Cooks Corner**—pop pl ... MA-1
**Cooks Corner**—pop pl ... VA-3
Cooks Corner Elem Sch—school ... IN-6
Cooks Corners—locale ... NY-2
Cooks Corners—locale ... PA-2
**Cooks Corners**—pop pl ... MI-6
Cooks Cove—basin ... GA-3
Cooks Cove—bay ... WA-9
Cooks Cove Branch—stream ... GA-3
Cooks Creek ... AL-4
Cooks Creek ... IN-6
Cooks Creek ... MS-4
Cooks Creek ... NY-2
Cooks Creek ... SC-3
Cooks Creek ... VA-3
Cooks Creek—gut ... NJ-2
Cooks Creek—gut ... SC-3
Cooks Creek—stream ... AR-4
Cooks Creek—stream ... CA-9
Cooks Creek—stream ... ID-8
Cooks Creek—stream ... IN-6
Cooks Creek—stream ... KY-4
Cooks Creek—stream ... MI-6
Cooks Creek—stream ... MO-7
Cooks Creek—stream ... MT-8
Cooks Creek—stream ... NV-8
Cooks Creek—stream (2) ... NC-3
Cooks Creek—stream ... PA-2
Cooks Creek—stream ... SC-3
Cooks Creek—stream ... TX-5
Cooks Creek—stream (2) ... VA-3
Cooks Creek—stream ... WA-9
Cooks Creek Ch—church ... VA-3
Cooks Crossing—locale ... GA-3
**Cooks Crossing**—pop pl ... NH-1
**Cooks Crossing**—pop pl ... NC-3
Cooks Crossroads—locale ... AL-4
**Cooks Crossroads**—pop pl ... SC-3
Cooks Dam—dam ... AL-4
Cooks Dam—dam ... SD-7
Cook-Sellers House—hist pl ... MS-4
Cookses Branch ... MS-4
Cookses Creek ... MS-4
Cooksey ... MD-2
Cooksey Cem—cemetery ... KY-4
Cooksey Cem—cemetery ... MO-7
Cooksey Cem—cemetery ... TN-4
Cooksey Fork—stream ... KY-4
Cooksey Hill—summit ... IN-6
Cooksey Island—island ... MD-2
Cooksey Oil Field—oilfield ... TX-5
Cooksey Point—cape ... MD-2
Cooksey Run—stream ... MD-2
Cooksey Well (Flowing)—well ... TX-5
**Cooks Falls**—pop pl ... NY-2
Cooks Farm—locale ... MO-7
Cooks Ferry Bridge (historical)—bridge ... AL-4
Cooks Ferry (historical)—locale ... MS-4
Cooks Ferry (historical)—locale ... PA-2
Cooks Ferry (historical)—locale ... TN-4
Cooks Flat—flat ... CA-9
Cooks Flat—flat ... MT-8
Cooks Ford ... KS-7
Cooks Gap—gap ... CT-1
Cooks Gulch—valley ... MT-8
Cook Shack, The—locale ... TX-5
Cooks Hammock—locale ... FL-3
Cook Sheep Ranch—locale ... MT-8
Cooks Heiau—locale ... HI-9
Cooks Hill—summit ... CT-1
Cooks Hill—summit ... IN-6
Cooks Hill—summit ... MA-1
Cooks Hill—summit ... NH-1
Cooks Hill—summit ... NY-2
Cooks Hill—summit ... VT-1
Cooks Hollow—valley ... NY-2
Cooks Hollow—valley ... TN-4
Cooks Hollow—valley ... VA-3
Cooks Hollow—valley ... WV-2
Cook Shop Ctr—locale ... MS-4
Cooksie Canyon—valley ... CA-9
Cooksie Creek ... CA-9
Cooksie Dam—dam ... AZ-5
Cooksie Gulch—valley ... OR-9
Cook Sink—basin ... FL-3
Cooks Island—island ... FL-3
Cooks Island—island ... GA-3
Cooks Island—island ... TX-5
Cooks Island—island ... WA-9
Cooks Junction (historical)—locale ... AL-4
Cooks Knob—summit ... MO-7
Cooks Knob—summit ... VA-3
Cooks Lake ... MI-6
Cooks Lake ... NJ-2
Cooks Lake ... TX-5
Cooks Lake—lake (2) ... AR-4
Cooks Lake—lake (2) ... ID-8
Cooks Lake—lake (3) ... MI-6
Cooks Lake—lake ... MN-6
Cooks Lake—lake ... MS-4
Cooks Lake—lake ... MT-8
Cooks Lake—lake (2) ... TX-5
Cooks Lake—lake ... WA-9
Cooks Lake—lake (2) ... WI-6
Cooks Lake—reservoir ... AL-4
Cooks Lake—reservoir ... MS-4
Cooks Lake—reservoir ... TX-5
Cooks Lake—swamp ... AZ-5
Cooks Lake Dam—dam ... MS-4
Cooks Landing—locale ... MS-4
Cooks Landing Field—airport ... SD-7
Cooks Landing (historical)—locale ... AL-4
Cooks Ledge—summit ... MA-1
Cooksley Cem—cemetery ... LA-4
Cooksley Creek—stream ... IA-7
Cooksley Lake—reservoir ... CA-9
Cooks Lookout Tower—locale ... MI-6
Cook Slough—gut ... OR-9
Cook Slough—stream ... IA-7
Cook Slough—stream ... WA-9
Cooks Meadow—flat ... OR-9
Cooks Memorial Ch—church ... NC-3
Cooks Mesa—summit ... AZ-5
Cooks Mesa—summit ... UT-8
Cooks Mesa Tank Number One—reservoir ... AZ-5
Cooks Mill ... MS-4
Cooks Mill ... TN-4
Cooks Mill—locale ... MI-6
Cooks Mill—locale ... NY-2
Cooks Mill (historical)—locale ... AL-4
Cooks Mill (historical)—locale ... TN-4
Cooks Mill Pond—lake ... GA-3
Cooks Mill Pond—reservoir ... FL-3
Cooks Millpond—reservoir ... VA-3
Cooks Mills ... NJ-2
Cooks Mills—locale ... PA-2
**Cooks Mills**—pop pl ... IL-6
**Cooks Mills**—pop pl ... ME-1
**Cooks Mills**—pop pl ... NJ-2
Cooks Mine (underground)—mine ... AL-4
Cook-Smith Cem—cemetery ... KY-4
Cooks Monument—locale ... HI-9
Cooks Mount—summit ... SC-3
Cooks Mtn—summit ... CA-9
Cooks Mtn—summit ... MA-1
Cooks Mtn—summit ... NY-2
Cooks Mtn—summit ... OR-9
Cooks Mtn—summit (2) ... WA-9
Cookson—locale ... OK-5
Cookson Bend Public Use Area—park ... OK-5
Cookson Bluff—cliff ... OK-5
Cookson Bluff Public Use Area—park ... OK-5
Cookson Branch—stream ... TN-4
Cookson Cem—cemetery ... OK-5
Cookson Creek—stream ... TN-4
Cookson Creek Ch—church ... TN-4
Cookson Creek Sch (historical)—school ... TN-4
Cookson Dam—dam ... MA-1
Cookson Field—park ... MA-1
Cookson Hills Sch—school ... OK-5
Cookson Hills State Game Ref—park ... OK-5
Cookson Lake—lake (2) ... MI-6
Cookson State For—forest ... MA-1
Cooks Park—park ... NE-7
Cooks Pass—gap ... ID-8
Cooks Peak—locale ... NM-5
Cooks Peak—summit (2) ... CA-9
Cooks Peak—summit ... ID-8
Cooks Peak—summit ... NM-5
Cooks Peak—summit ... ND-7
Cooks Point ... MD-2
Cooks Point—area ... AR-4
Cooks Point—cape ... CT-1
Cooks Point—cape ... NH-1
Cooks Point—locale ... TX-5
Cooks Point (CCD)—cens area ... TX-5
Cooks Point Ch—church ... TX-5
Cooks Point Cove ... MD-2
Cooks Point Creek ... MD-2
Cooks Point Sch—school ... TX-5
Cooks Pond ... MA-1
Cooks Pond ... NH-1
Cooks Pond ... NJ-2
Cooks Pond ... SC-3
Cooks Pond—lake (2) ... CT-1
Cooks Pond—lake ... ME-1
Cooks Pond—lake ... NH-1
Cooks Pond—lake ... UT-8
Cooks Pond—lake (2) ... VT-1
Cooks Pond—reservoir ... AL-4
Cooks Pond—reservoir ... AR-4
Cooks Pond—reservoir ... GA-3
Cooks Pond—reservoir ... MD-2
Cooks Pond—reservoir ... MA-1
Cooks Pond—reservoir (3) ... NJ-2
Cooks Pond—reservoir ... NY-2
Cooks Pond—reservoir (2) ... PA-2
Cooks Pond—reservoir (2) ... SC-3
Cooks Pond Dam—dam ... MA-1
Cooks Pond Dam—dam ... NJ-2
Cooks Pond Dam—dam ... PA-2
Cooks Prairie Ch—church ... MI-6
Cook Spring—spring ... ID-8
Cook Spring—spring ... KY-4
Cook Spring—spring ... MT-8
Cook Spring—spring ... NV-8
Cook Spring—spring ... NM-5
Cook Spring—spring (2) ... OR-9
Cook Spring—spring ... TN-4
Cook Spring—spring ... UT-8
Cook Spring—spring ... WA-9
Cook Spring Branch—stream ... KY-4
Cook Spring Ch—church ... TX-5
Cook Springs Baptist Ch—church ... AL-4
Cooks Ramp—locale ... AR-4
Cooks Ranch—locale ... AZ-5
Cooks Range—range ... NM-5
Cooks Ridges—ridge ... CA-9
Cooks (RR name for Cook)—other ... WA-9
Cooks Rsvr—reservoir ... NY-2
Cooks Run ... PA-2
**Cooks Run**—pop pl ... PA-2
Cooks Run—stream ... MI-6
Cooks Run—stream ... MT-8
Cooks Run—stream ... OH-6
Cooks Run—stream (3) ... PA-2
Cooks Run—stream (2) ... WV-2
Cooks Run River ... MI-6
Cooks Run Trail—trail ... PA-2
Cooks Run Trout Feeding Station—hist pl ... MI-6
Cooks Sch—school ... MI-6
Cooks Sch—school ... TN-4
Cooks Sch—school ... VT-1
Cooks Sch (historical)—school ... AL-4
Cooks Shop Ctr—locale ... NC-3
Cooks Slough ... OR-9
Cooks Slough—stream ... TX-5
Cooks Spring—spring ... KY-4
Cooks Spring—spring (2) ... MO-7
Cooks Spring—spring ... UT-8
Cooks Spring—spring ... WY-8
Cooks Springs—locale ... AL-4
Cooks Springs—spring ... CA-9
Cooks Spring Station (Ruins)—locale ... NM-5
Cooks Springs Tunnel—tunnel ... AL-4
Cooks Stand—locale ... AL-4
Cooks State Wildlife Mngmt Area—park ... MN-6
Cooks Station—locale ... CA-9
Cooks Station Ridge—ridge ... CA-9
Cooks Still—locale ... GA-3
**Cooks Store**—pop pl ... TX-5
Cooks Store (historical)—locale ... AL-4
Cooks Store (historical)—locale ... MS-4
**Cooks Summit**—pop pl ... PA-2
**Cook Station**—pop pl ... MO-7
Cookston Branch—stream ... TN-4
Cookston Cave—cave ... TN-4
Cookston Cave Creek—stream ... TN-4
Cookston Cem—cemetery (2) ... TN-4
Cookston Ranch—locale ... WY-8
Cook Stove Basin—basin ... OR-9
Cook Stove Basin—basin ... WY-8
Cook Stove Basin Rsvr ... OR-9
Cook Stove Canyon—valley ... MT-8
Cookstove Creek—stream ... ID-8
Cookstove Draw—valley ... AZ-5
Cookstove Prong Olmstead Creek—stream ... WY-8
Cook Stove Rsvr—reservoir ... OR-9
Cookstove Tank—reservoir ... AZ-5
Cookstown—locale ... PA-2
Cookstown—locale ... VA-3
**Cookstown**—pop pl ... NJ-2
Cookstown Pond—reservoir ... NJ-2
Cook Street—unincorporated pl ... MA-1
Cook Street Sch—school ... CA-9
Cook Street Station (historical)—locale ... MA-1
Cooks Trick Tank—reservoir ... AZ-5
**Cook Subdivision**—pop pl ... UT-8
Cooks Union Ch—church ... GA-3
**Cooks Valley**—pop pl ... CA-9
Cooks Valley Branch—stream ... TN-4
Cooks Valley Cem—cemetery ... WI-6
**Cooks Valley (Town of)**—pop pl ... WI-6
Cooks Vee—flat ... WY-8
Cooksville ... TN-4
Cooksville—locale ... GA-3
Cooksville—locale ... KY-4
Cooksville—locale ... MS-4
**Cooksville**—pop pl ... IL-6
**Cooksville**—pop pl ... MD-2
**Cooksville**—pop pl ... NC-3
**Cooksville**—pop pl ... WI-6
Cooksville Cem—cemetery ... MS-4
Cooksville Cem—cemetery ... OK-5
Cooksville Cheese Factory—hist pl ... WI-6
Cooksville Hist Dist—hist pl ... WI-6
Cooksville Methodist Ch—church ... MS-4
Cooksville Mill and Mill Pond Site—hist pl ... WI-6
Cooksville Post Office (historical)—building ... MS-4
Cooks Wall—cliff ... NC-3
Cooks Wall Trail—trail ... NC-3
Cook Swamp ... VA-3
Cook Swamp—stream ... VA-3
Cooks Well—well ... CA-9
Cook Tank—reservoir (2) ... AZ-5
**Cook Terrace Annex**—pop pl ... VA-3
**Cook Tomb**—pop pl ... PA-2
Cooktown—locale ... GA-3
Cooktown—locale ... KY-4
Cooktown—locale ... TN-4
**Cooktown**—pop pl ... GA-3
**Cooktown**—pop pl ... NC-3
**Cooktown**—pop pl ... VA-3
Cooktown Sch (historical)—school ... TN-4
Cook Township—fmr MCD ... IA-7
**Cook Township**—pop pl ... KS-7
**Cook (Township of)**—pop pl ... PA-2
Cook Tunnel ... HI-9
Cook Valley ... WI-6
Cook Valley—flat ... MN-6
Cook Valley—valley ... TN-4
Cook Valley—valley ... WI-6
Cook Valley Ch—church ... AL-4
Cook Valley Sch—school ... WI-6
Cookville ... TN-4
Cookville—locale ... MO-7
Cookville—locale ... NY-2
**Cookville**—pop pl ... KS-7
**Cookville**—pop pl ... TX-5
Cookville Brook—stream ... VT-1
Cookville (CCD)—cens area ... TX-5
**Cookville (Corinth Post Office)**—pop pl ... VT-1
Cookville Dock—locale ... TN-4
Cook Well—well ... NM-5
Cooky Hat Point—summit ... TX-5
Cookys Hollow—valley ... UT-8
Cool—locale ... CA-9
**Cool**—pop pl ... IA-7
**Cool**—pop pl ... TX-5
Coo Lake—lake ... AK-9
Coo Lake—lake ... MN-6
Coolaw Lakes—lake ... MI-6
Coolbaugh—locale ... PA-2
**Coolbaugh**—pop pl ... PA-2
Coolbaugh Creek ... MI-6
Coolbaugh Lake—lake ... PA-2
Coolbaugh Pond ... PA-2
**Coolbaughs**—pop pl ... PA-2
**Coolbaugh (Township of)**—pop pl ... PA-2
Cool Boiler Bayou—stream ... MS-4
Coolbough Creek ... MI-6
Cool Branch—locale ... SC-3
Cool Branch—stream ... AL-4
Cool Branch—stream ... DE-2
Cool Branch—stream ... GA-3
Cool Branch—stream ... KY-4
Cool Branch—stream ... MS-4
Cool Branch—stream ... NC-3
Cool Branch—stream (5) ... TN-4
Cool Branch—stream ... VA-3
Cool Branch Rec Area—locale ... GA-3
Coolbranch Run—stream ... MD-2
Cool Branch Sch (historical)—school ... TN-4
Cool Brook—stream ... IN-6
Cool Brook—stream ... ME-1
Cool Brook Country Club—locale ... PA-2
Coolbroth Canyon—valley ... CO-8
Cool Camp—locale ... OR-9
Cool Camp Trail—trail ... OR-9
Cool Creek ... IN-6
Cool Creek ... WA-9
Cool Creek—stream ... CO-8
Cool Creek—stream (2) ... ID-8
Cool Creek—stream ... IN-6
Cool Creek—stream ... KS-7
Cool Creek—stream ... KY-4
Cool Creek—stream ... LA-4
Cool Creek—stream (2) ... MI-6
Cool Creek—stream (2) ... MT-8
Cool Creek—stream ... OK-5
Cool Creek—stream ... OR-9
Cool Creek—stream ... WA-9
Cool Creek Trail—trail ... OR-9
Cool Easy Creek ... AR-4
Cool Easy Creek—stream ... AR-4
Cooledge Brook—stream ... MA-1
Cooleemee—hist pl ... NC-3
**Cooleemee**—pop pl ... NC-3
Cooleemee Dam—dam ... NC-3
Cooleemee Elem Sch—school ... NC-3
Cooleemee Junction—locale ... NC-3
Cooleewahee Creek—stream ... GA-3
Cooler Branch—stream ... GA-3
Cooleridge ... NE-7
Cooler Pond—lake ... NY-2
Coolers Knob—summit ... KY-4
Coolers Knob Mtn—summit ... NC-3
Cooley—locale ... LA-4
**Cooley**—pop pl ... MN-6
**Cooley**—pop pl ... NY-2
Cooley, Eli R., House—hist pl ... WI-6
Cooley, G. B., House—hist pl ... LA-4
Cooley, George C., House—hist pl ... OR-9
Cooley, Lake—lake ... FL-3
Cooley Bay—swamp ... NC-3
Cooley Branch—stream (2) ... KY-4
Cooley Branch—stream ... LA-4
Cooley Bridge—bridge ... SC-3
Cooley Bridge—other ... MI-6
Cooley Brook—stream (3) ... MA-1
Cooley Brook—stream ... NJ-2
Cooley Butte—summit ... TX-5
Cooley Camp Branch—stream ... VA-3
Cooley Canyon—valley ... ID-8
Cooley Canyon—valley ... NM-5
Cooley Cave—cave ... TN-4
Cooley Cem—cemetery ... AL-4
Cooley Cem—cemetery ... CT-1
Cooley Cem—cemetery ... IL-6
Cooley Cem—cemetery (3) ... MS-4
Cooley Cem—cemetery ... SC-3
Cooley Cem—cemetery ... TN-4
Cooley Ch—church ... WV-2
Cooley Covered Bridge—hist pl ... VT-1
Cooley Creek ... IN-6
Cooley Creek ... LA-4
Cooley Creek—stream ... AL-4
Cooley Creek—stream ... AR-4
Cooley Creek—stream ... ID-8
Cooley Creek—stream ... IN-6
Cooley Creek—stream ... KY-4
Cooley Creek—stream ... LA-4
Cooley Creek—stream ... NY-2
Cooley Creek—stream (3) ... OR-9
Cooley Creek—stream ... PA-2
Cooley Creek—stream ... UT-8
Cooley Crossroads—locale ... AL-4
Cooley Dam ... MA-1
Cooley Dam—dam ... AZ-5
Cooley Dickinson Hosp—hospital ... MA-1
Cooley Drain—canal ... MI-6
Cooley Draw—valley ... TX-5
Cooley Draw—valley ... WY-8
Cooley Farms—hist pl ... OH-6
Cooley Ford—locale ... TN-4
Cooley Ford Bridge—bridge ... TN-4
Cooley Gap—gap ... KY-4
Cooley Glen Shelter—locale ... VT-1
Cooley Glen Trail—trail ... VT-1
Cooley Goffena Ditch—canal ... MT-8
Cooley Gulch—valley ... MT-8
Cooley Gulch—valley ... UT-8
Cooley-Hawkins Cem—cemetery ... MS-4
Cooley Hill—summit ... AR-4
Cooley Hill—summit ... MA-1
Cooley Hill—summit ... NH-1
Cooley Hill—summit ... TN-4
Cooley Hill Sch—school ... CT-1
Cooley Hollow—valley ... TN-4
Cooley HS—school ... MI-6
Cooley Kill—stream ... NY-2
Cooley Knob—summit ... KY-4
Cooley Knoll—summit ... AZ-5
Cooley Lake—lake ... AR-4
Cooley Lake—lake ... MS-4
Cooley Lake—lake ... NM-5
Cooley Lake—lake ... SD-7
Cooley Lake—lake (3) ... WI-6
Cooley Lake—reservoir ... AZ-5
Cooley Lake—reservoir ... MA-1
Cooley Lake—reservoir ... MO-7
Cooley Lake—reservoir ... OK-5
Cooley Lake Campground—park ... AZ-5
Cooley Lake Dam—dam ... MA-1
Cooley Landing—locale ... CA-9
Cooley Lateral—canal ... ID-8
Cooley Mtn—summit ... AZ-5
Cooley Number 3 Mine ... AL-4
Cooley Park—park ... MO-7
Cooley Pass—gap ... UT-8
Cooley Pond—reservoir ... CT-1
Cooley Post Office—building ... MN-6
Cooley Post Office (historical)—building ... MS-4
Cooley Ranch—locale ... AZ-5
Cooleys Brook ... MA-1
Cooleys Cabin—locale ... NV-8
Cooley Sch—school ... LA-4
Cooley Sch—school (2) ... MI-6
Cooley Sch—school ... MO-7
Cooley Sch—school (2) ... TX-5
Cooley Sch—school ... VA-3
Cooley Sch (historical)—school ... PA-2
Cooley School—locale ... MI-6
Cooleys Corner—locale ... NJ-2
Cooleys Crossroads—locale ... NC-3
Cooleys Landing (historical)—locale ... AL-4
Cooleys Landing (historical)—locale ... TN-4
Cooleys Pond—lake ... AL-4
Cooleys Pond—lake ... MD-2
Cooley Spring—spring ... AZ-5
Cooley Spring—spring ... TN-4
**Cooley Springs**—pop pl ... MS-4
**Cooley Springs**—pop pl ... SC-3
Cooley Springs Cem—cemetery ... MS-4
Cooley Springs Ch—church ... MS-4
Cooley Springs Sch (historical)—school ... MS-4
Cooleys Slough—stream ... UT-8
Cooley Valley—valley ... WI-6
Cooleyville—locale ... AR-4
**Cooleyville**—pop pl ... MA-1
Cooley Vocational HS—school ... IL-6
Cooley Well—well ... UT-8
Cooley-Whitney House—hist pl ... IA-7
Coolfield Branch—stream ... KY-4
Cool Gap—gap ... NC-3
Coolgardie Camp—locale ... CA-9
Cool Glacier—glacier ... WA-9
Cool Gulch—valley ... ID-8
Cool Hill—summit ... OH-6
Cool (historical)—locale ... KS-7
Cool Hollow—valley ... TN-4
Cool Hollow—valley ... WV-2
Coolico Creek—stream ... NC-3
Coolidge ... MT-8
Coolidge—locale ... MT-8
Coolidge—locale ... NM-5
**Coolidge**—pop pl ... AZ-5
**Coolidge**—pop pl ... GA-3
**Coolidge**—pop pl ... KS-7
**Coolidge**—pop pl ... KY-4
**Coolidge**—pop pl ... TX-5
Coolidge, Calvin, Homestead District—hist pl ... VT-1
Coolidge, Calvin, House—hist pl ... MA-1
Coolidge, Josiah, House—hist pl ... MA-1
Coolidge, Orlando, House—hist pl ... OR-9
Coolidge Arroyo—stream ... NM-5
**Coolidge Beach**—pop pl ... NY-2
Coolidge Brook—stream ... MA-1
Coolidge Brook—stream ... NH-1
Coolidge Canal—canal ... WY-8
Coolidge (CCD)—cens area ... AZ-5
Coolidge (CCD)—cens area ... GA-3
Coolidge (CCD)—cens area ... TX-5
Coolidge Cem—cemetery ... KS-7
Coolidge Cem—cemetery ... MA-1
Coolidge Cem—cemetery ... NH-1
Coolidge Cem—cemetery ... TX-5
Coolidge Corner—locale ... ME-1
**Coolidge Corner (subdivision)**—pop pl ... MA-1
Coolidge Creek—stream ... IL-6
Coolidge Creek—stream ... MN-6
Coolidge Dam—dam ... AZ-5
Coolidge Dam—hist pl ... AZ-5
**Coolidge Dam**—pop pl ... AZ-5
Coolidge Ditch—canal ... WY-8
Coolidge Drain—canal ... MI-6
Coolidge Florence Municipal Airp—airport ... AZ-5
Coolidge Hill—summit (3) ... MA-1
Coolidge Hollow—lake ... PA-2
Coolidge House—hist pl ... AR-4
Coolidge HS—school ... AZ-5
Coolidge HS—school ... DC-2
Coolidge JHS—school (2) ... IL-6
Coolidge JHS—school (2) ... MA-1
Coolidge Lake—lake ... WI-6
Coolidge Mine—mine ... AZ-5
Coolidge Municipal Airp—airport ... AZ-5
Coolidge Navajo Ch—church ... NM-5
Coolidge Park—park ... CA-9
Coolidge Park—park ... FL-3
Coolidge Park—park ... MA-1
Coolidge Park—park ... NJ-2
Coolidge Park—park ... TN-4
Coolidge Playground—park ... MA-1
Coolidge Point ... MA-1
Coolidge Point—cape ... MA-1
Coolidge Pond—reservoir ... MA-1
Coolidge Range—range ... VT-1
Coolidge Reservoir ... AZ-5
Coolidge Ridge—ridge ... TN-4
Coolidge-Rising House—hist pl ... WA-9
Coolidge RR Station—building ... AZ-5
Coolidge Sch—school (2) ... CA-9
Coolidge Sch—school (2) ... IL-6
Coolidge Sch—school ... ME-1
Coolidge Sch—school (3) ... MA-1
Coolidge Sch—school (3) ... MI-6
Coolidge Sch—school (3) ... NJ-2
Coolidge Sch—school (2) ... NY-2
Coolidge Sch—school ... OH-6
Coolidge Sch—school (2) ... OK-5
Coolidge Sch—school ... SD-7
Coolidge Sch (historical)—school ... TN-4
Coolidge Springs—locale ... CA-9
Coolidge Square Shop Ctr—locale ... AZ-5
Coolidge Swamp—swamp ... MA-1
Coolidge Sylvan Theatre—hist pl ... SD-7
**Coolidge Township**—pop pl ... KS-7
Coolidge Turnout—locale ... WY-8
Coolie Creek ... WI-6
Coolie Spring—spring ... OR-9
Coolies Rift—basin ... TN-4
Coolie Valley ... WI-6
Cooliks Lake—lake ... GA-3
**Coolin**—pop pl ... ID-8
Cooling Lake—reservoir ... NC-3
Cooling Lake Dam—dam ... NC-3
Cooling Pond—reservoir ... PA-2
Cooling Pond Dam—dam ... PA-2
Coolin Mtn—summit ... ID-8
**Coolin Township**—pop pl ... ND-7
Cool Kell Lake—lake ... FL-3
Cool Lake—lake ... AK-9
Cool Lake—lake ... MI-6
Cool Lake—reservoir ... WV-2
Cool Lakes—lake ... ND-7
Coolmoor—locale ... PA-2
Coolmore Plantation—hist pl ... NC-3
Cool Mtn—summit ... NY-2
Cooloska Branch—stream ... NC-3
Coolot Company Bldg—hist pl ... CA-9
Cool Point—cape ... NC-3
Coolride Park—park ... MA-1
**Cool Ridge**—pop pl ... WV-2
Cool Ridge Ch—church ... WV-2
**Cool Ridge Heights**—pop pl ... OH-6
Cool Rock—bar ... ME-1
Cool Run—locale ... NC-3
Cool Run—stream ... NJ-2
Cool Run—stream ... NC-3
Cool Sch—school ... IA-7
Cool Slough—stream ... LA-4
Cool Spring ... NC-3
Cool Spring ... PA-2
Coolspring ... SC-3
Cool Spring ... WV-2
Cool Spring—locale ... DE-2
Cool Spring—locale ... VA-3
**Cool Spring**—pop pl ... GA-3
**Cool Spring**—pop pl ... NC-3
**Coolspring**—pop pl (2) ... PA-2
**Cool Spring**—pop pl ... PA-2
**Cool Spring**—pop pl ... SC-3
**Coolspring**—pop pl ... VA-3
Cool Spring—spring ... AZ-5
Cool Spring—spring ... CA-9
Cool Spring—spring ... GA-3
Cool Spring—spring ... OR-9
Cool Spring—spring (2) ... PA-2
Cool Spring—spring ... SD-7
Cool Spring—spring ... UT-8
Cool Spring—spring ... VA-3
Cool Spring Branch ... DE-2
Cool Spring Branch—stream ... MD-2
Coolspring Branch—stream ... MD-2
Cool Spring Branch—stream ... NC-3
Coolspring Branch—stream ... WV-2
Cool Spring Cem ... MO-7
Cool Spring Cem ... PA-2
Cool Spring Cem—cemetery ... FL-3
Cool Spring Cem—cemetery ... GA-3
Cool Spring Cem—cemetery ... KY-4
Cool Spring Cem—cemetery ... MO-7
Cool Spring Cem—cemetery ... TN-4
Coolspring Cemeteries—cemetery ... PA-2
Cool Spring Ch—church (3) ... GA-3
Cool Spring Ch—church ... KY-4
Cool Spring Ch—church ... MD-2
Cool Spring Ch—church (2) ... MS-4
Cool Spring Ch—church (2) ... NC-3
Cool Spring Ch—church ... PA-2
Cool Spring Ch—church ... SC-3
Cool Spring Ch—church (2) ... TN-4
Cool Spring Ch—church (7) ... VA-3
Cool Spring Church ... AL-4
Cool Spring Church ... DE-2
Cool Spring Cove—bay ... MD-2
Cool Spring Creek ... DE-2
Cool Spring Creek—stream ... CA-9
Cool Spring Creek—stream ... MD-2
Cool Spring Creek—stream ... PA-2
Cool Spring Dam Number Two—dam ... PA-2
Coolspring Elem Sch—school ... IN-6
**Cool Spring Farms**—pop pl ... DE-2
Cool Spring Fork ... WV-2
Cool Spring Grange—locale ... DE-2
Cool Spring (historical)—locale ... DC-2
Cool Spring Hollow—valley (2) ... KY-4
Cool Spring Hollow—valley ... VA-3
Cool Spring House (ruins)—locale ... UT-8
Cool Spring HS—school ... NC-3
Cool Spring Island—island ... VA-3
Cool Spring Knob—summit ... WV-2
**Cool Spring Manor (subdivision)**—pop pl ... DE-2
Cool Spring Missionary Baptist Ch ... MS-4
Cool Spring Park—park ... DE-2
Cool Spring Park Hist Dist—hist pl ... DE-2
Cool Spring Place—hist pl ... NC-3
Cool Spring Pond—lake ... FL-3
Cool Spring Presbyterian Ch—church ... DE-2
Cool Spring Presbyterian Church—hist pl ... DE-2
Cool Spring Rsvr—reservoir ... DE-2
Coolspring Run—stream ... PA-2
Coolspring Run—stream ... WV-2
Cool Spring Run—stream ... WV-2
Cool Springs ... SC-3
Cool Springs—hist pl ... NC-3
Cool Springs—locale ... AL-4
Cool Springs—locale ... KY-4
Cool Springs—locale ... TN-4
Cool Springs—locale ... WV-2
**Cool Springs**—pop pl ... GA-3
**Cool Springs**—pop pl (2) ... NC-3
Cool Springs—spring ... TX-5
Cool Springs Baptist Ch—church ... TN-4
Cool Springs Baptist Church ... AL-4
Cool Springs Branch—stream ... GA-3
Cool Springs Branch—stream ... KY-4
Cool Springs Branch—stream ... MS-4
Cool Springs Branch—stream ... TN-4
Cool Springs Campground—locale ... CA-9
Cool Springs Cem—cemetery ... AL-4
Cool Springs Cem—cemetery ... MS-4
Cool Springs Cem—cemetery ... NC-3
Cool Springs Cem—cemetery ... OH-6
Cool Springs Cem—cemetery (2) ... TN-4
Cool Springs Cem—cemetery ... TX-5
Cool Springs Ch—church (6) ... AL-4
Cool Springs Ch—church (8) ... GA-3
Cool Springs Ch—church ... LA-4
Cool Springs Ch—church ... MS-4
Cool Springs Ch—church ... MO-7
Cool Springs Ch—church (5) ... NC-3
Cool Springs Ch—church ... SC-3
Cool Springs Ch—church (3) ... TN-4
Cool Springs Ch—church ... TX-5

Cooters Pond Park—*park* AL-4
Cooter Terrell Spring—*spring* AL-4
Cooter Township—*civil* MO-7
**Cooterville**—*pop pl* LA-4
Cootes Store—*locale* VA-3
Coot Hill—*summit* (2) NY-2
Coot Hill—*summit* PA-2
Coot Hollow—*valley* MO-7
*Coot Island* ME-1
*Coot Islands* ME-1
Coot Islands—*island* ME-1
Coot Lake—*lake* LA-4
Coot Lake—*lake* MN-6
Coot Mtn—*summit* MO-7
Coots Branch—*stream* TX-5
Coots Cem—*cemetery* AR-4
*Coots Creek* IN-6
*Coots Creek* LA-4
Coots Creek—*stream* MO-7
Coots Gap—*gap* NC-3
Coots Lake—*reservoir* GA-3
Coot Slough—*gut* TN-4
Coots Ranch—*locale* TX-5
Coots Slough—*gut* UT-8
Coots Well—*well* TX-5
*Cooty Brook* VT-1
Cooty Canyon—*valley* NM-5
Coover Hollow—*valley* NY-2
Coover Island—*island* NJ-2
Coover Run—*stream* PA-2
Coovert Ditch—*canal* OH-6
*Cooyehuttee Creek* GA-3
*Cooyehuttee Creek* TN-4
Copacia Lake—*lake* OH-6
Copahee Sound—*bay* SC-3
**Copake**—*pop pl* NY-2
**Copake Falls**—*pop pl* NY-2
Copake Lake—*lake* NY-2
**Copake Lake**—*pop pl* NY-2
**Copake (Town of)**—*pop pl* NY-2
**Copalis Beach**—*pop pl* WA-9
**Copalis Crossing**—*pop pl* WA-9
**Copalis Crossing (Copalis)**—*pop pl* WA-9
Copalis Head—*cliff* WA-9
Copalis Natl Wildlife Ref—*park* WA-9
Copalis River—*stream* WA-9
Copalis Rock—*pillar* WA-9
Copalis Rock Natl Wildlife Ref—*park* WA-9
Copalis (RR name for Copalis Crossing)—*other* WA-9
Copalis State Airp—*airport* WA-9
Copalis Station—*locale* WA-9
**Copan**—*pop pl* OK-5
Copan (CCD)—*cens area* OK-5
Copan Lake—*reservoir* KS-7
Copan Lake—*reservoir* OK-5
Copano Artesian Well—*well* TX-5
Copano Bay—*bay* TX-5
Copano Bay Causeway State Park—*park* TX-5
Copano Bay Oil And Gas Field—*oilfield* TX-5
Copano Creek—*stream* TX-5
Copano Reef—*bar* TX-5
**Copano Village**—*pop pl* TX-5
Copan Wildlife Area—*park* KS-7
**Copas**—*pop pl* MN-6
Copas, John, House—*hist pl* MN-6
*Copasaw* MS-4
Copasaw, Bayou—*stream* LA-4
Copasaw Canal—*canal* LA-4
Copas Cem—*cemetery* OH-6
Copas Cem—*cemetery* (2) TN-4
Copassaw—*locale* AL-4
Copasville Ch—*church* OH-6
*Copaum Pond* MA-1
Copa Windmill—*locale* (2) TX-5
**Copco**—*pop pl* (2) CA-9
Copco Lake—*reservoir* CA-9
Cop Cop, Bayou—*stream* LA-4
Copco Powerhouse—*other* OR-9
Copco Substation—*other* CA-9
Copcutt,John,Mansion—*hist pl* NY-2
Cope—*mine* CA-9
**Cope**—*pop pl* CO-8
**Cope**—*pop pl* IN-6
**Cope**—*pop pl* SC-3
Cope, Edward Drinker, House—*hist pl* PA-2
Copebranch—*locale* KY-4
Cope Branch—*stream* KY-4
Cope Branch—*stream* MO-7
Cope Branch—*stream* NC-3
Cope Branch—*stream* TX-5
Cope Butte—*summit* AZ-5
Cope Canyon—*valley* OR-9
Cope Canyon—*valley* UT-8
Cope (CCD)—*cens area* SC-3
Cope Cem—*cemetery* AL-4
Cope Cem—*cemetery* KS-7
Cope Cem—*cemetery* KY-4
Cope Cem—*cemetery* MO-7
Cope Cem—*cemetery* (4) TN-4
Cope Cem—*cemetery* (2) TX-5
Cope Ch—*church* MO-7
*Cope Creek* SC-3
Cope Creek—*stream* AL-4
Cope Creek—*stream* KY-4
Cope Creek—*stream* MI-6
Cope Creek—*stream* NC-3
Cope Creek—*stream* TN-4
Cope Creek—*stream* TX-5
*Copecut Hill* MA-1
*Copecut River.* MA-1
Cope Dam—*dam* SD-7
Copeechan Pond—*reservoir* PA-2
Cope Fork—*stream* KY-4
Cope Hill—*summit* GA-3
Cope Hollow—*valley* IN-6
Cope Hollow—*valley* MO-7
Cope Hollow—*valley* TN-4
Cope Impoundment—*swamp* MS-4
Cope JHS—*school* CA-9
*Copeka* AZ-5
*Copeka Mountains* AZ-5
*Copeke Mtn* AZ-5
Cope Knob—*summit* NC-3
Cope Lake—*lake* MI-6
*Copeland* GA-3
*Copeland* IN-6
*Copeland* KY-4
Copeland—*locale* AR-4
Copeland—*locale* FL-3
Copeland—*locale* GA-3
Copeland—*locale* ID-8
Copeland—*locale* MD-2
Copeland—*locale* OK-5
Copeland—*locale* TX-5
Copeland—*locale* VA-3
**Copeland**—*pop pl* (2) AL-4
**Copeland**—*pop pl* KS-7
**Copeland**—*pop pl* NC-3
Copeland, Austin, House I—*hist pl* TX-5
Copeland, Austin, House II—*hist pl* TX-5
Copeland, George, House—*hist pl* IA-7
Copeland, Henry, House—*hist pl* AR-4
Copeland, Lake—*lake* FL-3
Copeland, Lake—*reservoir* OH-6
Copeland, Samuel, House—*hist pl* MA-1
Copeland, Wesley, House—*hist pl* AR-4
*Copeland Airport* KS-7
Copeland Assembly of God Ch—*church* AL-4
Copeland Baptist Ch (historical)—*church* AL-4
Copeland Baptist Mission Parsonage—*church* FL-3
Copeland Bar—*bar* CA-9
Copeland Basin—*basin* MT-8
Copeland Bay—*swamp* FL-3
Copeland Bend—*bend* AL-4
Copeland Bluff—*cliff* KY-4
*Copeland Branch* AL-4
Copeland Branch—*stream* AL-4
Copeland Branch—*stream* GA-3
Copeland Branch—*stream* MS-4
Copeland Branch—*stream* OK-5
Copeland Branch—*stream* (3) TN-4
Copeland Branch—*stream* TX-5
Copeland Branch—*stream* WV-2
Copeland Bridge—*other* IL-6
**Copeland Bridge**—*pop pl* AL-4
Copeland Brook—*stream* ME-1
Copeland Brook—*stream* NH-1
Copeland Butte—*summit* (2) OR-9
Copeland Canyon—*valley* (2) NM-5
Copeland Canyon—*valley* OR-9
Copeland Cave—*cave* AL-4
Copeland Caves—*cave* MS-4
Copeland Cem—*cemetery* (2) AL-4
Copeland Cem—*cemetery* (2) GA-3
Copeland Cem—*cemetery* ID-8
Copeland Cem—*cemetery* IN-6
Copeland Cem—*cemetery* KY-4
Copeland Cem—*cemetery* (2) MO-7
Copeland Cem—*cemetery* OH-6
Copeland Cem—*cemetery* (7) TN-4
Copeland Ch—*church* (3) AL-4
Copeland Ch—*church* FL-3
Copeland Ch—*church* IL-6
Copeland Chapel—*church* TN-4
*Copeland Ch of God* AL-4
Copeland Corner—*locale* MI-6
Copeland Cove—*valley* AL-4
Copeland Cove—*valley* TN-4
*Copeland Creek* AL-4
*Copeland Creek* OR-9
*Copeland Creek* TN-4
*Copeland Creek* TX-5
Copeland Creek—*stream* (4) AL-4
Copeland Creek—*stream* (2) AK-9
Copeland Creek—*stream* CA-9
Copeland Creek—*stream* (2) GA-3
Copeland Creek—*stream* ID-8
Copeland Creek—*stream* MT-8
Copeland Creek—*stream* NC-3
Copeland Creek—*stream* (2) OR-9
Copeland Creek—*stream* (4) TN-4
Copeland Creek—*stream* (3) TX-5
Copeland Creek Ch (historical)—*church* TN-4
Copeland Creek Rec Area—*park* TX-5
Copeland Creek Trail—*trail* (2) OR-9
Copeland Crossing—*locale* GA-3
Copeland Dam—*dam* AL-4
Copeland Ditch—*canal* TX-5
Copeland Divide—*ridge* TN-4
Copeland Drain—*swamp* SC-3
Copeland Draw—*valley* AZ-5
Copeland Elem Sch—*school* KS-7
Copeland Elem Sch—*school* NC-3
Copeland Elk Creek Ditch—*canal* CO-8
Copeland Falls—*falls* CO-8
Copeland Ferry—*locale* ID-8
Copeland Ferry Bridge—*bridge* AL-4
Copeland Ferry Ch—*church* AL-4
Copeland Ferry (historical)—*locale* AL-4
Copeland Flats—*flat* (2) ID-8
Copeland Ford—*locale* (2) AL-4
Copeland Gap—*gap* AL-4
**Copeland Gap**—*pop pl* AL-4
Copeland Gap Missionary Baptist Ch—*church* AL-4
Copeland Hill—*summit* IN-6
Copeland Hill—*summit* ME-1
Copeland Hill—*summit* MA-1
Copeland Hill—*summit* NH-1
Copeland Hill—*summit* NY-2
Copeland Hill—*summit* TN-4
Copeland Hill Cem—*cemetery* ME-1
Copeland (historical)—*locale* KS-7
**Copeland (historical)**—*pop pl* TN-4
Copeland Hollow—*valley* MO-7
Copeland Hollow—*valley* (2) TN-4
Copeland House—*hist pl* TN-4
Copeland HS—*school* KS-7
Copeland Island—*island* AL-4
Copeland Island—*island* OH-6
Copeland Knob—*summit* WV-2
Copeland Lake—*lake* AR-4
Copeland Lake—*lake* MT-8
Copeland Lake—*lake* TX-5
Copeland Lake—*reservoir* (2) CO-8
Copeland Lakes—*lake* TX-5
Copeland Lake Trail—*trail* WY-8
Copeland Landing—*locale* LA-4
Copeland Landing Strip—*airport* KS-7
Copeland Macedonia Ch—*church* TX-5
Copeland Manor Sch—*school* IL-6
Copeland Mine—*mine* NM-5
Copeland Moraine—*ridge* CO-8
Copeland Mtn—*summit* CO-8
Copeland Mtn—*summit* TN-4
Copeland Park—*park* IA-7
Copeland Park—*park* OH-6
Copeland Park—*park* VA-3
Copeland Park—*park* WI-6
Copeland Pit—*cave* TN-4
Copeland Place—*locale* OR-9
Copeland Pond—*lake* NY-2
Copeland Pond Dam—*dam* MS-4
Copeland Post Office (historical)—*building* TN-4
Copeland Prairie—*flat* FL-3
*Copeland Presbyterian Church* AL-4
Copeland Ranch—*locale* NE-7
Copeland Ranch—*locale* NM-5
Copeland Ranch—*locale* TX-5
Copeland Ridge—*ridge* IN-6
Copeland Ridge—*ridge* (2) TN-4
Copeland Ridge Branch—*stream* AR-4
Copeland Ridge Cem—*cemetery* AR-4
Copeland Ridge Community Hall—*locale* AR-4
Copeland Rsvr—*reservoir* OR-9
Copeland Rsvrs—*reservoir* OR-9
Copeland Salteter Cave—*cave* TN-4
*Copelands Bridge* AL-4
Copeland Sch—*school* AL-4
Copeland Sch—*school* IL-6
Copeland Sch—*school* MA-1
Copeland Sch—*school* MN-6
Copeland Sch—*school* (2) PA-2
Copeland Sch—*school* (2) VA-3
Copeland Sch (historical)—*school* (2) AL-4
Copeland Sch Number 1—*school* ND-7
**Copeland Settlement**—*pop pl* FL-3
*Copelands Ferry* AL-4
Copeland Shoals—*bar* TN-4
Copeland Sink—*basin* FL-3
Copelands Landing—*locale* FL-3
Copeland Slough—*stream* AR-4
Copelands Mill (historical)—*locale* TN-4
Copelands Pond—*reservoir* (2) AL-4
Copeland Spring—*spring* MS-4
Copeland Spring—*spring* OR-9
Copeland Spring Trail—*trail* PA-2
Copeland State Wildlife Mngmt Area—*park* MN-6
Copeland Street Pentecostal/Holiness Ch—*church* FL-3
Copeland Swamp—*swamp* GA-3
Copeland Tank—*reservoir* (2) TX-5
Copeland Tannery Brook—*stream* MA-1
Copeland Tower—*tower* FL-3
**Copeland Township**—*pop pl* KS-7
Copeland & Tracht Service Station—*hist pl* AZ-5
Copeland Trap—*basin* TX-5
*Copeland Valley* KY-4
Copeleys Rock—*pillar* OR-9
Copelin Cem—*cemetery* IN-6
Copelin Cem—*cemetery* KY-4
Copelin Valley—*valley* KY-4
**Copella**—*pop pl* PA-2
Copelle Creek—*stream* TX-5
*Copello* PA-2
*Copely* OH-6
*Copemans Tomb* WY-8
**Copemish**—*pop pl* MI-6
Cope Mtn—*summit* AK-9
Cope Mtn—*summit* NC-3
Cope Mtn—*summit* TN-4
Copen—*locale* WV-2
Copena Skull Pit—*cave* TN-4
Copenbarger Gulch—*valley* ID-8
Copen Branch—*stream* WV-2
*Copenhagen* TN-4
*Copenhagen* UT-8
**Copenhagen**—*pop pl* LA-4
**Copenhagen**—*pop pl* MI-6
**Copenhagen**—*pop pl* NE-7
**Copenhagen**—*pop pl* NY-2
Copenhagen Basin—*basin* ID-8
**Copenhagen Beach**—*pop pl* MI-6
Copenhagen Canyon—*valley* ID-8
Copenhagen Canyon—*valley* NV-8
Copenhagen Cem—*cemetery* MO-7
Copenhagen Creek—*stream* AK-9
Copenhagen (historical)—*locale* AL-4
**Copenhagen (historical)**—*pop pl* NC-3
Copenhagen Lake—*lake* MN-6
Copenhagen Mine—*mine* WY-8
*Copenhagen Post Office* TN-4
Copenhagen Sch—*school* NE-7
*Copenhagen Slough* LA-4
Copenhague—*locale* LA-4
Copenhaven Cem—*cemetery* MO-7
**Copenhaver**—*pop pl* MD-2
**Copenhaver**—*pop pl* VA-3
*Copenhaver Basin* ID-8
Copenhaver Cem—*cemetery* VA-3
Copenhaver Gulch—*valley* CO-8
Copenhaver Park—*park* MT-8
Copenhaver Ranch—*locale* MT-8
Copenhavers—*locale* VA-3
Copening Bridge—*other* MO-7
Copening Ch—*church* MO-7
Copening Ch—*church* NC-3
*Copen Run* WV-2
Copen Run—*stream* WV-2
Copen Run Ch—*church* WV-2
Cope Oil Field—*oilfield* TX-5
Copepod Lake—*lake* OR-9
Cope Pond—*lake* PA-2
Cope Post Office (historical)—*building* TN-4
*Coperas Cove* TX-5
Coperas Creek—*stream* MO-7
*Copergard Creek* WI-6
Copernicus Park—*park* TX-5
Copernicus Peak—*summit* CA-9
Copernicus Sch—*school* IL-6
Copernicus Sch—*school* MI-6
Cope Row Houses—*hist pl* CA-9
Copes Basin—*basin* UT-8
Cope's Bridge—*hist pl* PA-2
**Copes Bridge**—*pop pl* PA-2
Cope Sch (abandoned)—*school* (2) MO-7
Copes Corner—*locale* NY-2
Copes Dugway—*trail* UT-8
Copes Gin (historical)—*locale* AL-4
*Copes Lake* ND-7
Copes Lake—*lake* OH-6
*Copessuatuxett Cove* RI-1
Copesville—*locale* PA-2
Copet Creek—*stream* ID-8
**Copeville**—*pop pl* TX-5
Cope Williams Sch—*school* SC-3
*Cop Fork* AR-4
**Copiague**—*pop pl* NY-2
Copiague HS—*school* NY-2
Copiague JHS—*school* NY-2
Copiague Neck—*cape* NY-2
Copiah, Lake—*reservoir* MS-4
**Copiah County**—*pop pl* MS-4
Copiah County Airp—*airport* MS-4
*Copiah County Game Mngmt Area* MS-4
Copiah County State Wildlife Mngmt Area—*park* MS-4
*Copiah Creek* MS-4
Copiah Creek—*stream* MS-4
Copiah Lincoln Junior Coll—*school* MS-4
Copic—*locale* CA-9
Copic Bay—*other* CA-9
Copic Ch—*church* OK-5
Copic Slab—*locale* OK-5
*Copicut* MA-1
Copicut Hill—*summit* MA-1
Copicut Neck—*cape* MA-1
Copicut River—*stream* MA-1
Copicut Rsvr—*reservoir* MA-1
Copicut Swamp—*swamp* MA-1
Copinger Rsvr—*reservoir* CO-8
Copita Cem—*cemetery* TX-5
Copita Well—*well* TX-5
Copita Windmill—*locale* TX-5
Coplan Chapel Cem—*cemetery* TX-5
*Coplan Church* AL-4
Copland—*locale* KY-4
*Copland Butte* OR-9
Copland Cem—*cemetery* GA-3
Copland Cem—*cemetery* IL-6
*Copland Post Office* TN-4
Coplar Creek—*stream* WA-9
**Coplay**—*pop pl* PA-2
Coplay Borough—*civil* PA-2
Coplay Cement Company Kilns—*hist pl* PA-2
Coplay Creek—*stream* PA-2
Coplay Lake—*lake* WA-9
Cople (Magisterial District)—*fmr MCD* VA-3
Cople-Montross Sch—*school* VA-3
*Coplen* TX-5
Cople Sch—*school* VA-3
Copleston, Mount—*summit* AK-9
*Copley* PA-2
Copley—*locale* LA-4
Copley—*locale* WV-2
**Copley**—*pop pl* OH-6
Copley, Col. Ira C., Mansion—*hist pl* IL-6
Copley Branch—*stream* TN-4
Copley Branch—*stream* WV-2
Copley Canyon—*valley* UT-8
Copley Cem—*cemetery* (2) TN-4
Copley Cem—*cemetery* WV-2
**Copley Center**—*pop pl* OH-6
Copley Country Club—*other* VT-1
*Copley Creek* PA-2
Copley Creek—*stream* UT-8
Copley Hosp—*hospital* IL-6
Copley HS—*school* OH-6
Copley Junction—*locale* OH-6
Copley Lake—*lake* CO-8
Copley Lake—*lake* MI-6
Copley Mtn—*summit* CA-9
Copley Place (Shop Ctr)—*locale* MA-1
Copley Playground—*park* IL-6
Copley Saltpeter Cave—*cave* TN-4
Copleys Cove Picnic Area—*locale* UT-8
Copley Square—*park* MA-1
**Copley (Township of)**—*pop pl* IL-6
**Copley (Township of)**—*pop pl* MN-6
**Copley (Township of)**—*pop pl* OH-6
Copley Trace Sch—*school* WV-2
*Coplin Branch* TX-5
Coplin Branch—*stream* KY-4
Coplin Branch—*stream* TX-5
Coplin Ch—*church* WV-2
*Coplinger Creek* OR-9
*Copling Ridge* TN-4
Copling Ridge—*ridge* TN-4
Coplin Hollow—*valley* TN-4
Coplin (Plantation of)—*civ div* ME-1
Coplin Post Office (historical)—*building* AL-4
Coplin Run—*stream* (2) WV-2
Coplin Sch—*school* ME-1
Coplyn Spring Cem—*cemetery* TX-5
Coply Reef—*bar* AK-9
Copmans Tomb—*ridge* WY-8
Copneconic Lake—*lake* MI-6
*Copopa* OH-6
Copopa—*other* OH-6
Coposo Island—*island* AK-9
**Copp**—*pop pl* AR-4
Coppage, Rhodin, Spring House—*hist pl* KY-4
*Coppage Spring* MO-7
Coppahaunk Swamp—*stream* VA-3
Coppas Branch—*stream* GA-3
*Copp Brook* NH-1
Copp Brook—*stream* (2) NH-1
Copp Cem—*cemetery* WI-6
Copp Chapel—*church* MO-7
Coppedge Creek—*stream* MO-7
Coppedge Gulch—*valley* MT-8
Coppei—*locale* WA-9
*Coppei Creek* WA-9
Coppei Creek—*stream* WA-9
Coppei Spring—*spring* WA-9
**Coppell**—*pop pl* TX-5
Coppell Sch—*school* TX-5
Coppenger Cem—*cemetery* TN-4
*Coppenger Cove* TN-4
Coppens Corner—*locale* WI-6
Copper—*locale* OR-9
Copper Age Mine—*mine* AZ-5
Copper and Gold Mine—*mine* AZ-5
Copperas Bald—*summit* NC-3
Copperas Bluff—*cliff* TN-4
Copperas Branch—*stream* (2) AL-4
Copperas Branch—*stream* (2) KY-4
Copperas Branch—*stream* MS-4
Copperas Branch—*stream* (4) TN-4
Copperas Branch—*stream* (6) TX-5
Copperas Branch Park—*park* TX-5
Copperas Branch Prospect—*mine* TN-4
Copperas Branch Sch—*school* TX-5
Copperas Brook—*stream* VT-1
Copperas Canyon—*valley* AZ-5
Copperas Cove—*cave* AL-4
Copperas Cove—*cave* (2) TN-4
Copperas Cem—*cemetery* (2) TX-5
**Copperas Cove**—*pop pl* TX-5
Copperas Cove (CCD)—*cens area* TX-5
Copperas Cove Stagestop and Post Office—*hist pl* TX-5
*Copperas Creek* IL-6
*Copperas Creek* TX-5
Copperas Creek—*stream* AL-4
Copperas Creek—*stream* AR-4
Copperas Creek—*stream* (3) IL-6
Copperas Creek—*stream* (3) KY-4
Copperas Creek—*stream* NM-5
Copperas Creek—*stream* TN-4
Copperas Creek—*stream* (10) TX-5
Copperas Creek Chapel—*church* IL-6
Copperas Creek Dam—*dam* IL-6
Copperas Creek Park—*park* TX-5
Copperas Falls—*falls* (2) TN-4
Copperas Fork—*stream* KY-4
Copperas Gap—*gap* AL-4
Copperas Gap—*gap* AR-4
Copperas Hill—*summit* TN-4
Copperas Hill—*summit* (2) VT-1
Copperas Lake—*swamp* AR-4
Copperas Lick Branch—*stream* KY-4
Copperas Mine Fork—*stream* WV-2
Copperas Mountain—*ridge* OH-6
Copperas Mtn—*range* NC-3
Copperas Mtn—*summit* NJ-2
Copperas Peak—*summit* NM-5
Copperas Point—*cape* (2) TX-5
*Copperas Pond* NY-2
Copperas Pond—*lake* (2) NY-2
Copperas Rock—*cliff* NC-3
*Copperas Rock Branch* WV-2
Copperas Rock Hollow—*valley* OH-6
Copperas Sch—*school* IL-6
Copperas Sch—*school* TN-4
Copperas Sch—*school* WV-2
Copperas Spring—*spring* AZ-5
Copperas Spring—*spring* (2) TN-4
Copperas Spring Hollow—*valley* AR-4
Copperas Springs—*spring* AL-4
Copperas Springs Branch—*stream* TX-5
Copperas Springs Cem—*cemetery* AR-4
Copperas Springs Ch—*church* AR-4
Copperas Spring Sch (historical)—*school* TX-5
Copperas Springs Missionary Baptist Ch—*church* TX-5
Copperas Tank—*reservoir* AZ-5
Copperas Tank—*reservoir* NM-5
Copperas Vista—*locale* NM-5
*Copper Bald* NC-3
Copper Basin—*basin* (2) AZ-5
Copper Basin—*basin* (2) CA-9
Copper Basin—*basin* CO-8
Copper Basin—*basin* (2) ID-8
Copper Basin—*basin* (2) NV-8
Copper Basin—*basin* TN-4
Copper Basin—*basin* UT-8
**Copper Basin**—*pop pl* NV-8
Copper Basin Cow Camp—*locale* ID-8
Copper Basin Flat—*flat* ID-8
Copper Basin Guard Station—*locale* ID-8
Copper Basin HS—*school* TN-4
Copper Basin Knob—*summit* ID-8
Copper Basin Med Ctr—*hospital* TN-4
Copper Basin Mine—*mine* CA-9
Copper Basin Mine—*mine* ID-8
Copper Basin Road Spring—*spring* AZ-5
Copper Basin Rsvr—*reservoir* CA-9
Copper Basin Spring—*spring* AZ-5
Copper Basin Spring—*spring* UT-8
Copper Basin Tunnel—*tunnel* CA-9
Copper Basin Wash—*stream* AZ-5
Copper Basin Wash—*stream* CA-9
Copper Bay—*bay* AK-9
Copper Bayou—*stream* TX-5
Copper Bell Mine—*mine* NV-8
Copperbelt Mine—*mine* WA-9
Copperbelt Mine—*mine* WY-8
Copper Belt Peak—*summit* UT-8
Copper Belt Trail—*trail* UT-8
Copper Blossom Mine—*mine* UT-8
Copper Bottom Mine—*mine* AZ-5
Copper Bottom Pass—*gap* AZ-5
Copper Bottom Tank—*reservoir* NM-5
Copper Branch—*stream* AR-4
Copper Branch—*stream* DE-2
Copper Branch—*stream* MS-4
Copper Branch—*stream* NC-3
Copper Branch—*stream* (2) TN-4
Copper Branch—*stream* (3) TX-5
Copper Butte—*summit* (2) AZ-5
Copper Butte—*summit* (2) CA-9
Copper Butte—*summit* CO-8
Copper Butte—*summit* ID-8
Copper Butte—*summit* MT-8
Copper Butte—*summit* WA-9
Copper Butte Creek—*stream* CA-9
Copper Butte Mine—*mine* AZ-5
Copper Buttes—*summit* OR-9
*Copper Camp* AZ-5
Copper Camp—*locale* AZ-5
Copper Camp—*locale* ID-8
Copper Camp—*locale* MT-8
Copper Camp Creek—*stream* AZ-5
**Copper Camp (historical)**—*pop pl* SD-7
*Copper Canyon* CA-9
*Copper Canyon* OR-9
**Copper Canyon**—*pop pl* TX-5
Copper Canyon—*valley* (8) AZ-5
Copper Canyon—*valley* (3) CA-9
Copper Canyon—*valley* ID-8
Copper Canyon—*valley* (8) NV-8
Copper Canyon—*valley* (2) NM-5
Copper Canyon—*valley* OR-9
Copper Canyon—*valley* UT-8
Copper Canyon—*valley* WA-9
Copper Canyon Mine—*mine* NV-8
Copper Canyon Placer Camp—*locale* NV-8
Copper Canyon Spring—*spring* AZ-5
Copper Canyon Substation—*locale* AZ-5
Copper Canyon Well—*well* NM-5
Copper Cave—*cave* IL-6
Copper Cave Hollow—*valley* TN-4
Copper Cem—*cemetery* CA-9
Copper Cem—*cemetery* LA-4
Copper Cem—*cemetery* NC-3
**Copper Center**—*pop pl* AK-9
Copper Center ANV764—*reserve* AK-9
Copper Center Lake—*lake* AK-9
Copper Chief Mine—*mine* (2) AZ-5
Copper Chief Mine—*mine* NV-8
Copper Chief Spring—*spring* AZ-5
Copper Cities Tailings Dam Number Eight—*dam* AZ-5
Copper Cities Tailings Dam Number Nine—*dam* AZ-5
Copper Cities Tailings Dam Number Ten—*dam* AZ-5
Copper Cities Tailings Dam Number Two—*dam* AZ-5
*Copper City* AK-9
Copper City—*locale* (2) CA-9
Copper City—*locale* MT-8
**Copper City**—*pop pl* MI-6
Copper City (Aban'd)—*locale* AK-9
Copper City (historical)—*locale* AZ-5
Copper City (Site)—*locale* WA-9
**Copper City Subdivision**—*pop pl* UT-8
Copper Cliff—*cliff* TN-4
Copper Cliff—*locale* MT-8
Copper Cliff Mine—*mine* MT-8
Copper Cliff Mine—*mine* WA-9
**Copper Cove Condominium**—*pop pl* UT-8
**Copper Cove Subdivision**—*pop pl* UT-8
*Copper Creek* AZ-5
*Copper Creek* CO-8
*Copper Creek* ID-8
*Copper Creek* IL-6
*Copper Creek* IA-7
*Copper Creek* KY-4
*Copper Creek* MI-6
*Copper Creek* WA-9
Copper Creek—*locale* AZ-5
Copper Creek—*stream* AL-4
Copper Creek—*stream* (4) AK-9
Copper Creek—*stream* (7) AZ-5
Copper Creek—*stream* (9) CA-9
Copper Creek—*stream* (5) CO-8
Copper Creek—*stream* (15) ID-8
Copper Creek—*stream* IN-6
Copper Creek—*stream* IA-7
Copper Creek—*stream* KS-7
Copper Creek—*stream* (2) KY-4
Copper Creek—*stream* (2) MI-6
Copper Creek—*stream* (10) MT-8
Copper Creek—*stream* (2) NV-8
Copper Creek—*stream* NJ-2
Copper Creek—*stream* NM-5
Copper Creek—*stream* NY-2
Copper Creek—*stream* (2) NC-3
Copper Creek—*stream* (11) OR-9
Copper Creek—*stream* (3) TX-5
Copper Creek—*stream* (3) UT-8
Copper Creek—*stream* VA-3
Copper Creek—*stream* (14) WA-9
Copper Creek—*stream* (6) WI-6
Copper Creek—*stream* (3) WY-8
Copper Creek Benches—*bench* UT-8
Copper Creek Bluff—*cliff* VA-3
Copper Creek Cabin—*locale* AZ-5
Copper Creek Camp—*locale* ID-8
Copper Creek Campground—*locale* (2) MT-8
Copper Creek Falls—*falls* OR-9
Copper Creek Knob—*range* VA-3
Copper Creek Lakes—*lake* MT-8
Copper Creek Mesa—*summit* AZ-5
Copper Creek Mine—*mine* CA-9
*Copper Creek Ranger Station* ID-8
Copper Creek Rapids—*rapids* ID-8
Copper Creek Spring—*spring* AZ-5
Copper Creek Tank—*reservoir* AZ-5
Copper Creek Trail—*trail* (2) ID-8
Copper Creek Trail—*trail* MT-8
Copper Creek Trail—*trail* OR-9
Copper Creek Well—*well* NM-5
Copper Creek Windmill—*locale* AZ-5
Copper Crown Mine—*mine* AZ-5
Copper Culture Mounds State Park—*park* WI-6
Copperdahl Hill—*summit* ND-7
Copperdale—*locale* CO-8
Copper Dick Mine—*mine* NM-5
Copper Ditch—*canal* IN-6
Copper Duke Mine—*mine* AZ-5
Coppereid—*locale* NV-8
Copper Falls—*falls* ID-8
Copper Falls—*falls* WI-6
**Copper Falls**—*pop pl* MI-6
Copper Falls Lake—*lake* MI-6
Copper Falls State Park—*park* WI-6
*Copperfield* OR-9
**Copperfield**—*pop pl* NV-8
**Copperfield**—*pop pl* OR-9
**Copperfield**—*pop pl* VT-1
Copperfield Draw—*valley* OR-9
Copperfield-Homestead Cem—*cemetery* OR-9
Copperfields Lateral—*canal* UT-8
Copper Flat—*flat* NV-8
Copper Flat—*flat* (2) NM-5
Copper Flat—*locale* VT-1
**Copper Flat**—*pop pl* NV-8
Copper Flat No 2 Shaft—*mine* NM-5
Copper Flat No 4 Shaft—*mine* NM-5
Copper Flats—*flat* NM-5
Copper Flat Well—*well* NV-8
Copper Ford—*locale* NC-3
Copper Fork—*stream* WV-2
Copper Fork Tank—*reservoir* AZ-5
Copper Gap—*gap* NC-3
Copper Gap—*gap* TN-4
Copper Giant Mine—*mine* (2) AZ-5
Copper Glacier—*glacier* AK-9
Copper Glance Creek—*stream* WA-9
Copper Glance Lake—*lake* WA-9
Copper Glance Mine—*mine* (2) AZ-5
Copper Glance Shaft—*mine* NM-5
Copper Glance Trail One Hundred Seventeen—*trail* AZ-5
Copper Globe—*bench* UT-8
Copper Golbe Mine—*mine* UT-8
*Copper Gulch* AZ-5
*Copper Gulch* ID-8
Copper Gulch—*valley* AZ-5
Copper Gulch—*valley* CA-9
Copper Gulch—*valley* (7) CO-8
Copper Gulch—*valley* ID-8

Copper Gulch—*valley* (2) MT-8
Copper Gulch—*valley* (2) UT-8
Copper Gulch Divide—*gap* CO-8
Copper Gulf Shaft—*mine* NM-5
Copper Harbor—*bay* AK-9
Copper Harbor—*bay* MI-6
**Copper Harbor**—*pop pl* MI-6
Copper Harbor Lighthouse—*locale* MI-6
Copperhead Branch—*stream* AL-4
Copperhead Branch—*stream* KY-4
Copperhead Branch—*stream* TN-4
Copperhead Branch—*stream* VA-3
Copperhead Branch—*stream* WV-2
Copperhead Cave—*cave* AL-4
Copperhead Cave—*cave* PA-2
Copperhead Creek—*stream* CA-9
Copperhead Creek—*stream* (2) OR-9
Copperhead Gap—*gap* VA-3
Copperhead Hollow—*valley* KY-4
Copperhead Hollow—*valley* OH-6
Copperhead Hollow—*valley* PA-2
Copperhead Hollow—*valley* TX-5
Copperhead Lookout Tower—*locale* OH-6
Copperhead Mine—*mine* AR-4
Copperhead Peak—*summit* ID-8
Copperhead Ridge—*ridge* TN-4
*Copper Hill* MO-7
Copper Hill—*locale* AZ-5
Copper Hill—*locale* NJ-2
Copper Hill—*locale* VA-3
**Copperhill**—*pop pl* TN-4
Copper Hill—*summit* AZ-5
Copper Hill—*summit* (2) CA-9
Copper Hill—*summit* NM-5
Copper Hill Cem—*cemetery* CT-1
Copper Hill Ch—*church* CT-1
Copperhill Ch—*church* NC-3
Copper Hill Country Club—*other* NJ-2
**Copper Hill Heights Subdivision 11**—*pop pl* UT-8
**Copper Hill Heights Subdivision 12**—*pop pl* UT-8
**Copper Hill Heights Subdivision 9-10**—*pop pl* UT-8
Copper Hill Mine—*mine* CA-9
Copperhill Post Office—*building* TN-4
Copperhill Sch (historical)—*school* TN-4
**Copper Hills Heights**—*pop pl* UT-8
Copper Hills Sch—*school* UT-8
Copper Hills Tank—*reservoir* AZ-5
Copper Hill Tank—*reservoir* AZ-5
Copper Hill Wash—*stream* AZ-5
**Copper (historical)**—*pop pl* OR-9
Copper Hollow—*valley* KY-4
Copper Hollow—*valley* MO-7
Copper Hollow—*valley* TN-4
*Copper Island* CT-1
Copper Jack Mine—*mine* UT-8
Copper Kettle Canyon—*valley* NV-8
Copper Kettle Canyon—*valley* NM-5
Copperkettle Creek—*stream* CO-8
Copper Kettle Trailer Villa—*locale* AZ-5
Copper Kettle Well—*well* NM-5
Copper King—*mine* AZ-5
Copper King Campground—*locale* MT-8
Copper King Canyon—*valley* AZ-5
Copper King Canyon—*valley* CO-8
Copper King Hill—*summit* AZ-5
Copper King Mine—*mine* AZ-5
Copper King Mine—*mine* (3) CA-9
Copper King Mine—*mine* CO-8
Copper King Mine—*mine* (2) ID-8
Copper King Mine—*mine* (2) MT-8
Copper King Mine—*mine* (2) NV-8
Copper King Mine—*mine* UT-8
Copper King Mine—*mine* (3) WA-9
Copper King Mine—*mine* WY-8
*Copper King Mountain* ID-8
Copper King Mtn—*summit* AZ-5
Copper King Natl Mansion Historic Place—*park* MT-8
Copper King No 2 Mine—*mine* WA-9
Copper Knob—*summit* NC-3
*Copper Lake* MN-6
Copper Lake—*lake* AK-9
Copper Lake—*lake* CO-8
Copper Lake—*lake* ID-8
Copper Lake—*lake* MI-6
Copper Lake—*lake* MN-6
Copper Lake—*lake* (3) MT-8
Copper Lake—*lake* NY-2
Copper Lake—*lake* (2) OR-9
Copper Lake—*lake* VA-3
Copper Lake—*lake* (3) WA-9
Copper Lake—*lake* WI-6
Copper Lakes—*lake* WA-9
Copper Lakes—*lake* WY-8
Copper Leaf—*mine* UT-8
Copper (Magisterial District)—*fmr MCD* WV-2
Copper Mill Bayou—*stream* LA-4
Copper Mill Brook—*stream* CT-1
*Coppermill Creek* MS-4
Coppermill Creek—*stream* MS-4
Copper Mine—*locale* AZ-5
Copper Mine—*mine* MT-8
**Copper Mine**—*pop pl* AR-4
**Copper Mine (abandoned)**—*pop pl* MO-7
Copper Mine Branch—*stream* KY-4
Copper Mine Branch—*stream* (2) NC-3
Coppermine Branch—*stream* SC-3
Copper Mine Branch—*stream* VA-3
Copper Mine Brook—*stream* CT-1
Coppermine Brook—*stream* NH-1
Copper Mine Brook—*stream* NY-2
*Copper Mine Creek* WI-6
Copper Mine Creek—*stream* MO-7
Coppermine Creek—*stream* NC-3
Copper Mine Creek—*stream* NC-3
Coppermine Gap—*gap* GA-3
Copper Mine Gulch—*valley* (2) CA-9
*Copper Mine Hill* RI-1
Copper Mine Hill—*summit* RI-1
Copper Mine Hollow—*valley* AR-4
Copper Mine Hollow—*valley* MO-7
Coppermine Hollow—*valley* MO-7
Copper Mine Pass—*gap* CA-9
Copper Mines Ch—*church* MO-7
Copper Mine Sch (abandoned)—*school* MO-7
Copper Mines Post Office (historical)—*building* TN-4
Copper Mine Spring—*spring* NV-8
**Copper Mines (Trading Post)**—*pop pl* AZ-5
Copper Mine Tank—*reservoir* AZ-5
Coppermine Tank—*reservoir* TX-5
Coppermount (Aban'd)—*locale* AK-9
Copper Mountain—*post sta* CO-8
Copper Mountain Bar—*bar* AK-9
Copper Mountain Dam—*dam* AZ-5
Copper Mountain Mine—*mine* (2) AZ-5
Copper Mountain Mine—*mine* OR-9
Copper Mountain Mine—*mine* UT-8
Copper Mountain Peninsula—*cape* AK-9
Copper Mountain Points Tank—*reservoir* AZ-5
Copper Mountains—*range* AZ-5
Copper Mountain Tank—*reservoir* (2) AZ-5
Copper Mountain Trail—*trail* ID-8
Copper Mtn—*summit* (3) AK-9
Copper Mtn—*summit* (5) AZ-5
Copper Mtn—*summit* (4) CA-9
Copper Mtn—*summit* (5) CO-8
Copper Mtn—*summit* (5) ID-8
Copper Mtn—*summit* MO-7
Copper Mtn—*summit* (2) MT-8
Copper Mtn—*summit* (4) NV-8
Copper Mtn—*summit* NM-5
Copper Mtn—*summit* OR-9
Copper Mtn—*summit* SD-7
Copper Mtn—*summit* UT-8
Copper Mtn—*summit* (4) WA-9
Copper Mtn—*summit* WY-8
Copper Mtns—*range* NV-8
Copper Neck—*cape* NC-3
Coppernoll Sch—*school* MI-6
*Copperopolis* AZ-5
Copperopolis—*locale* AZ-5
**Copperopolis**—*pop pl* CA-9
Copperopolis Creek—*stream* AZ-5
Copperopolis Creek—*stream* UT-8
Copperopolis Mine—*mine* AZ-5
Copperopolis Mine—*mine* OR-9
Copperopolis Mtn—*summit* CA-9
Copperopolis Rsvr—*reservoir* CA-9
*Copperosity* AZ-5
Copperosity Hills—*summit* AZ-5
Copperosity Mine—*mine* AZ-5
Copperous Branch—*stream* IL-6
Copper Park—*flat* NM-5
Copper Pass—*gap* CO-8
Copper Pass—*gap* (2) WA-9
Copper Peak—*hist pl* MI-6
Copper Peak—*summit* AZ-5
Copper Peak—*summit* MI-6
Copper Peak—*summit* WA-9
Copper Penny—*airport* NJ-2
*Copper Pit* NV-8
Copperplate Gulch—*valley* AZ-5
Copper Point—*cape* (2) AK-9
Copper Point—*summit* ID-8
Copper Point—*summit* UT-8
Copper Pond—*lake* MI-6
Copper Pond—*lake* NY-2
Copper Prince Mine—*mine* AZ-5
Copper Queen—*mine* AZ-5
Copper Queen—*uninc pl* AZ-5
Copper Queen Canyon—*valley* CA-9
Copper Queen Mine—*mine* (2) AZ-5
Copper Queen Mine—*mine* (2) CA-9
Copper Queen Mine—*mine* ID-8
Copper Queen Mine—*mine* MT-8
Copper Queen Mine—*mine* (2) NV-8
Copper Queen Mine—*mine* NM-5
Copper Queen Mine—*mine* OR-9
Copper Queen Mine—*mine* WA-9
Copper Queen Shaft—*mine* NM-5
Copper Queen Smelter—*other* AZ-5
Copper Ranch Mine—*mine* UT-8
Copper Range—*summit* MI-6
**Copper Range Junction (Dupont Jct.)**—*pop pl* MI-6
Copper Rapids—*rapids* OR-9
Copper Reef Mine—*mine* AZ-5
Copper Reef Mtn—*summit* AZ-5
**Copper Ridge**—*pop pl* TN-4
Copper Ridge—*range* (2) TN-4
Copper Ridge—*ridge* AZ-5
Copper Ridge—*ridge* CO-8
Copper Ridge—*ridge* (3) ID-8
Copper Ridge—*ridge* MI-8
Copper Ridge—*ridge* (2) NC-3
Copper Ridge—*ridge* UT-8
Copper Ridge—*ridge* VA-3
Copper Ridge Bald—*summit* NC-3
Copper Ridge Branch—*stream* (2) TN-4
Copper Ridge Ch—*church* (2) TN-4
Copper Ridge Ch—*church* VA-3
*Copper Ridge Elementary School* TN-4
Copper Ridge Mine—*mine* NV-8
Copper Ridge Point—*cape* TN-4
Copper River—*stream* (2) AK-9
Copper River—*stream* WI-6
Copper River and Northwestern Railway—*hist pl* AK-9
Copper River Bay—*bay* AK-9
Copper River (Census Subarea)—*cens area* AK-9
Copper River Delta—*area* AK-9
Copper Rivet Mine—*mine* CO-8
Copper Rock Falls—*falls* NY-2
Copper Rock Mine—*mine* MT-8
Copper RR Station—*building* AZ-5
Copper Run—*stream* PA-2
Copperrun Branch—*stream* AL-4
*Coppersalt Creek* AL-4
Copper Salt Creek—*stream* AL-4
Copper Sands—*bar* AK-9
Copper Sandy Creek—*stream* GA-3
Coppers Branch—*stream* (2) AL-4
Coppers Branch—*stream* KY-4
Coppers Branch—*stream* (5) TX-5
Coppersburgh (historical)—*locale* KS-7
*Coppers Creek* AL-4
*Coppers Creek* TX-5
Coppers Creek—*stream* IA-7
Coppers Creek—*stream* MO-7
Coppers Creek—*stream* (2) TX-5
Coppers Fork—*stream* KY-4
*Coppers Gap* AL-4
Coppers Grove—*woods* CA-9
Coppers Hill—*summit* MO-7
Coppershop Hollow—*valley* OH-6
Copper Siding—*locale* VA-3
Coppers Knob—*summit* AR-4
Copper Slick Hollow—*valley* KY-4
Copper Slough—*gut* IL-6
Copper Slough—*stream* IL-6
Coppersmith Branch—*stream* NC-3
Coppersmith Hills—*range* CA-9
Coppersmith Lake—*lake* MN-6
Coppersmith Mine—*mine* MT-8
*Copper Spring* UT-8
Copper Spring—*locale* IA-7
Copper Spring—*spring* AL-4
Copper Spring—*spring* AZ-5
Copper Spring—*spring* AR-4
Copper Spring—*spring* MO-7
Copper Spring—*spring* NV-8
Copper Spring—*spring* (2) UT-8
Copper Spring Branch—*stream* KY-4
Copper Spring Hollow—*valley* AL-4
Copper Spring Hollow—*valley* (2) AR-4
Copper Spring Mtn—*summit* AR-4
**Copper Springs**—*pop pl* AL-4
Copper Springs—*spring* AZ-5
Copper Springs Canyon—*valley* AZ-5
Copper Springs Ch—*church* AL-4
Copper Spring Sch (abandoned)—*school* MO-7
Copper Springs Creek—*stream* TN-4
Copper Springs Hollow—*valley* AR-4
**Copper Spur**—*pop pl* CO-8
Coppers Rock Creek—*stream* AL-4
Copperstain Cliff—*cliff* CO-8
Copper Standard Mine—*mine* AZ-5
Copper State Mine—*mine* MT-8
Copper Strand Mine—*mine* CA-9
Copper Substation—*locale* AZ-5
Copper Substation—*other* CA-9
Copper Tank—*reservoir* (2) AZ-5
Copperton—*locale* NM-5
Copperton—*locale* WY-8
**Copperton**—*pop pl* NM-5
**Copperton**—*pop pl* UT-8
*Copperton City Cemetery* UT-8
Copperton Hist Dist—*hist pl* UT-8
**Copperton Subdivision**—*pop pl* UT-8
Copper Trail—*trail* CA-9
Copperus Spring—*spring* KY-4
Copper Valley—*basin* NV-8
Copper Valley—*locale* VA-3
Copper Valley—*valley* AZ-5
Copper Valley—*valley* CT-1
Copper Valley Ch—*church* VA-3
Copper Vault Tunnel—*mine* AZ-5
**Copper View Estates (subdivision)**—*pop pl* UT-8
Copperview Sch—*school* UT-8
**Copperview Subdivision**—*pop pl* UT-8
**Copperview Village Condominium**—*pop pl* UT-8
Copperville—*locale* ID-8
Copperville—*locale* NH-1
**Copperville**—*pop pl* (2) MD-2
Copperville Sch—*school* NE-7
*Copper Wash* AZ-5
Copper Wash—*stream* AZ-5
*Copperwater* CA-9
Copper Well—*well* AZ-5
**Copper Works**—*pop pl* MA-1
Copper World Mine—*mine* AZ-5
Copper World Mine—*mine* (2) CA-9
Coppes Ditch—*canal* IN-6
Coppes Lake—*lake* WI-6
Coppess, Benjamin Franklin House—*hist pl* OH-6
Coppess Cem—*cemetery* OH-6
**Coppess Corner**—*pop pl* IN-6
*Coppess Ditch* IN-6
Copp Hill—*summit* (2) NH-1
Copp Hollow—*valley* PA-2
Copp Hollow—*valley* TN-4
*Coppick Knob* TN-4
*Coppier Creek* MI-6
Coppin African Methodist Episcopal Chapel—*church* IN-6
Coppin Cem—*cemetery* ND-7
Coppinger Cave—*cave* TN-4
Coppinger Chapel—*church* TN-4
Coppinger Cove—*valley* TN-4
Coppinger Creek—*stream* TN-4
Coppinger Rsvr—*reservoir* CO-8
Coppinger Sch (historical)—*school* TN-4
Coppinger Well—*well* NM-5
Coppins Meadow—*flat* CA-9
Coppin State Teachers Coll—*school* MD-2
**Coppinville**—*pop pl* AL-4
Coppinville HS—*school* AL-4
*Copp Island* CT-1
Copp Landing—*locale* SC-3
Copple, Simpson, House—*hist pl* OR-9
Copple Butte—*summit* OR-9
Copple Butte Trail (pack)—*trail* OR-9
Copple Creek—*stream* (2) OR-9
Copple Crown Mtn—*summit* NH-1
Copple Place—*locale* CA-9
Coppler Creek—*stream* MI-6
**Coppock**—*pop pl* IA-7
*Coppock Bay* CA-9
Coppock Cave—*cave* TN-4
Coppock Cem—*cemetery* TN-4
*Coppock Gap* TN-4
Coppola House—*hist pl* NY-2
Copp Rsvr—*reservoir* OR-9
Copps Branch—*stream* MD-2
Copps Branch—*stream* TN-4
Copps Bridge—*bridge* ME-1
Copps Bridge—*bridge* NH-1
*Copps Brook* NH-1
Copps Brook—*stream* CT-1
Copp Sch—*school* SD-7
Copps Creek—*stream* MI-6
Copps Draw—*valley* WY-8
Copps Hill—*summit* MA-1
Copps Hill Burial Ground—*cemetery* MA-1
Copp's Hill Burial Ground—*hist pl* MA-1
*Copps Hill Cemetery* MA-1
*Copp's Island* CT-1
Copps Island—*island* CT-1
Copps Lookout Tower—*locale* MI-6
Copps Pond—*lake* NH-1
Copps Rocks—*island* CT-1
**Copps Spurr**—*pop pl* MI-6
Copse Road Sch—*school* CT-1
Copsey Camp—*locale* OR-9
*Copsey Creek* CA-9
Copsey Creek—*stream* CA-9
Copsey Creek—*stream* OR-9
Copsey Sch—*school* NE-7
Copter-Barness Airp—*airport* PA-2
Copter-Borden Airp—*airport* PA-2
Copter-Liberty Bell Airp—*airport* PA-2
Copter Peak—*summit* AK-9
Copter-PNB-Bristol Airp—*airport* PA-2
Copter Pnb Philadelphia Airp—*airport* PA-2
Copter Ridge—*ridge* CA-9
Coptown—*locale* TN-4
Copts Brook—*stream* CT-1
Copus Hollow—*valley* TN-4
Copy Run—*stream* IN-6
*Coq d'Inde* AL-4
Coquat Gas Field—*oilfield* TX-5
Coquelin Run—*stream* MD-2
Coquette, Bay—*bay* LA-4
Coquette, Bayou—*gut* LA-4
Coquette Creek—*stream* CA-9
Coquette Falls—*falls* CA-9
Coqui—*CDP* PR-3
**Coqui**—*pop pl* PR-3
Coquillard Park—*park* IN-6
*Coquillard School* IN-6
**Coquille**—*pop pl* OR-9
Coquille, Bayou—*gut* LA-4
Coquille, Lake—*lake* LA-4
Coquille (CCD)—*cens area* OR-9
*Coquille City* OR-9
Coquille Harbor—*harbor* FM-9
*Coquille Island* MP-9
Coquille Myrtle Grove State Park—*park* OR-9
Coquille Point—*cape* LA-4
Coquille Point—*cape* (2) OR-9
Coquille River—*stream* OR-9
Coquille River Falls—*falls* OR-9
Coquille River Life Boat Station—*hist pl* OR-9
Coquille River Light—*hist pl* OR-9
Coquille Rock—*island* OR-9
*Coquille Rsvr* OR-9
Coquille Valley—*valley* OR-9
Coquille Valley Hosp—*hospital* OR-9
Coquille Valley MS—*school* OR-9
Coquina Beach—*beach* NC-3
Coquina Bench—*bench* NC-3
Coquina Elem Sch—*school* FL-3
**Coquina Gables**—*pop pl* FL-3
Coquina Key—*island* FL-3
Coquina Lake—*lake* ID-8
Cora—*locale* ID-8
Cora—*locale* KS-7
Cora—*locale* LA-4
Cora—*locale* MO-7
Cora—*locale* OH-6
Cora—*locale* OK-5
Cora—*locale* WY-8
Cora—*other* GA-3
**Cora**—*pop pl* FL-3
**Cora**—*pop pl* IL-6
**Cora**—*pop pl* IA-7
**Cora**—*pop pl* LA-4
**Cora**—*pop pl* WV-2
Cora, Lake—*lake* FL-3
Cora, Lake—*lake* MI-6
Cora, Lake—*reservoir* GA-3
Corabelle Lake—*lake* MN-6
Cora Belle Mine—*mine* CO-8
Cora Bridge—*bridge* WA-9
Cora Butte—*summit* WY-8
Cora Cem—*cemetery* FL-3
Cora Ch—*church* FL-3
*Cora City* KS-7
Cora Clark Park—*park* PA-2
Cora Creek—*stream* (2) AK-9
Cora Creek—*stream* CA-9
Cora Creek—*stream* MT-8
Cora Crew—*locale* NM-5
Cora Davis Sch (abandoned)—*school* MO-7
**Co Rae Subdivision**—*pop pl* UT-8
Cora Gulch—*valley* ID-8
Cora Island—*island* AK-9
Cora Island—*island* MO-7
Cora Island Chute—*gut* MO-7
Cora Kelly Sch—*school* VA-3
Coral—*locale* MS-4
**Coral**—*pop pl* IL-6
**Coral**—*pop pl* MI-6
**Coral**—*pop pl* PA-2
*Cora Lake* MI-6
Cora Lake—*lake* CA-9
Cora Lake—*lake* MN-6
Cora Lake—*lake* WA-9
Cora Lakes—*lake* CA-9
Coral Baptist Ch Mission—*church* FL-3
Coral Bay—*bay* FL-3
Coral Bay—*bay* VI-3
Coral Bay—*locale* VI-3
**Coral Bay**—*pop pl* FL-3
**Coral Bay**—*pop pl* NC-3
Coral Bay (Census Subdistrict)—*cens area* VI-3
Coral Cem—*cemetery* IL-6
Coral Cem—*cemetery* MI-6
Coral Ch—*church* FL-3
**Coral City**—*pop pl* WI-6
Coral Cove—*bay* FL-3
Coral Cove—*CDP* FL-3
*Coral Creek* MT-8
Coral Creek—*stream* AK-9
Coral Creek—*stream* FL-3
Coral Creek—*stream* NE-7
Coral Creek—*stream* WA-9
Coral Creek Country Club—*locale* FL-3
Coral Creek Inlet—*gut* FL-3
Coral Creek Reef—*rapids* OR-9
Cora Lee, Lake—*lake* FL-3
**Coral Estates**—*pop pl* FL-3
Coral Estates Park—*park* FL-3
Coral Fountain Chapel—*church* MO-7
*Coral Gable* IL-6
**Coral Gables**—*pop pl* FL-3
Coral Gables Canal—*canal* (2) FL-3
Coral Gables City Hall—*hist pl* FL-3
Coral Gables Congregational Church—*hist pl* FL-3
Coral Gables Elem Sch—*hist pl* FL-3
Coral Gables Elem Sch—*school* FL-3
Coral Gables Hosp—*hospital* FL-3
Coral Gables House—*hist pl* FL-3
Coral Gables Police and Fire Station—*hist pl* FL-3
Coral Gables Sch—*school* FL-3
Coral Gables Senior HS—*school* FL-3
**Coral Gables (sta.)**—*pop pl* FL-3
Coral Gables Waterway—*channel* FL-3
Coral Gables Wayside Park—*park* FL-3
Coral Gables Youth Center—*locale* FL-3
**Coral Gardens**—*pop pl* FL-3
**Coral Gardens**—*pop pl* HI-9
Coral Gate Park—*park* FL-3
Coral Gate Park Preschool—*school* FL-3
Coral Gate Shop Ctr—*locale* (2) FL-3
Coral Harbor—*bay* VI-3
**Coral Heights**—*pop pl* FL-3
**Coral Heights Subdivision**—*pop pl* UT-8
*Coral Hill* ID-8
Coral Hill—*locale* KY-4
**Coral Hills**—*pop pl* FL-3
**Coral Hills**—*pop pl* MD-2
Coral Hollow—*valley* WV-2
Coralina Ranch—*locale* TX-5
Coral Isles Ch—*church* (2) FL-3
*Coral Lake* MA-1
Coral Lake—*lake* AK-9
Coral Lake—*lake* FL-3
Coral Lake—*lake* MI-6
*Corall Creek* CA-9
**Coral Manor**—*pop pl* FL-3
Coral Meadow—*flat* WA-9
*Coral Park* FL-3
Coral Park Baptist Ch—*church* FL-3
Coral Park Center (Shop Ctr)—*locale* FL-3
Coral Park Day School/ Kindergarten—*school* FL-3
Coral Park Mission—*church* NC-3
Coral Park Sch—*school* FL-3
Coral Pine Park—*park* FL-3
Coral Pink Sand Dunes Campground—*locale* UT-8
*Coral Pink Sand Dunes State Park* UT-8
Coral Pink Sand Dunes State Res—*park* UT-8
Coral Point—*uninc pl* FL-3
Coral Pointe Shop Ctr—*locale* FL-3
Coral Reef Elem Sch—*school* FL-3
Coral Reef Hosp—*hospital* FL-3
Coral Reef Park—*park* FL-3
*Coral Ridge* KY-4
Coral Ridge—*post sta* FL-3
Coral Ridge—*ridge* KY-4
Coral Ridge—*uninc pl* KY-4
Coral Ridge Baptist Ch of Cape Coral—*church* FL-3
Coral Ridge Country Club—*locale* FL-3
Coral Ridge Gardens—*cemetery* FL-3
**Coral Ridge Isles**—*pop pl* FL-3
Coral Ridge Presbyterian Ch—*church* FL-3
Coral Ridge Psychiatric Hosp—*hospital* FL-3
Coral Ridge Shopping Plaza—*locale* FL-3
**Coral Ridge (sta.)**—*pop pl* KY-4
Coral Run—*stream* PA-2
Coral Sands Mobile Estates—*locale* AZ-5
Coral Shores Sch—*school* FL-3
Coral Spring—*spring* NM-5
**Coral Springs**—*pop pl* FL-3
Coral Springs Alpha Day—*school* FL-3
Coral Springs Christian Sch—*school* FL-3
Coral Springs Community Ch—*church* FL-3
Coral Springs Country Day Sch—*school* FL-3
Coral Springs Elem Sch—*school* FL-3
Coral Springs HS—*school* FL-3
Coral Springs Mall—*locale* FL-3
Coral Springs MS—*school* FL-3
Coral Square Mall—*locale* FL-3
Coral Square (Shop Ctr)—*locale* FL-3
Coral Sunset Elem Sch—*school* FL-3
Coral Terrace—*CDP* FL-3
Coral Terrace Sch—*school* FL-3
**Coral (Township of)**—*pop pl* IL-6
Coral Villa Christian Acad—*school* FL-3
Coral Village Ch—*church* FL-3
**Coral Villas (subdivision)**—*pop pl* FL-3
**Coralville**—*pop pl* IA-7
Coralville Dam—*dam* IA-7
Coralville Public Sch—*hist pl* IA-7
Coralville Rsvr—*reservoir* IA-7
Coralville Union Ecclesiastical Church—*hist pl* IA-7
Coral Wash—*stream* CA-9
Coral Way Elem Sch—*school* FL-3
Coral Way Hispanic United Methodist Ch—*church* FL-3
Coral Way Park—*park* FL-3
Coral Way Sch—*school* FL-3
Coral Way Shop Ctr—*locale* FL-3
Coral Way Shopping Plaza—*locale* FL-3
Coral Way United Methodist Ch—*church* FL-3
**Coral Way Village**—*pop pl* FL-3
Coralwood—*post sta* FL-3
Coralwood Mall—*locale* FL-3
**Coral Woods**—*pop pl* FL-3
Coram—*locale* CA-9
**Coram**—*pop pl* MT-8
**Coram**—*pop pl* NY-2
Coram Cem—*cemetery* CT-1
Coram Hill—*summit* CT-1
Cora Miller Mine—*mine* NM-5
Cora Mine—*mine* CO-8
Cora Mine—*mine* SD-7
Coram Sch—*school* NY-2
Coran—*locale* TN-4
*Corano Ranch* NV-8
**Coraopolis**—*pop pl* PA-2
Coraopolis Borough—*civil* PA-2
Coraopolis Bridge—*hist pl* PA-2
**Coraopolis Heights**—*pop pl* PA-2
Coraopolis Heights Golf Course—*other* PA-2
Coraopolis RR Station—*hist pl* PA-2
**Corapeake**—*pop pl* NC-3
Corapeake Ditch—*canal* NC-3
Corapeake Swamp—*stream* NC-3
Cora Point—*cape* AK-9
*Cora School* SD-7
Coras Grove Ch—*church* NC-3
Corashire Cem—*cemetery* MA-1
Cora Spring—*spring* ID-8
Cora Township—*civil* SD-7
**Cora Township**—*pop pl* KS-7
Coraville—*locale* KY-4
*Coray Creek* PA-2
Corazon—*CDP* PR-3
**Corazon**—*pop pl* NM-5
**Corazon**—*pop pl* PR-3
Corazon Creek—*stream* NM-5
Corazon de Trinidad—*hist pl* CO-8
Corazones Peaks—*summit* TX-5
Corazon Hill—*summit* NM-5
*Corbaley Canyon* WA-9
Corbaley Canyon—*valley* WA-9
Corbandale—*locale* TN-4
Corbandale Post Office (historical)—*building* TN-4
Corbat Drain—*canal* MI-6
Corbeal Butte—*summit* NV-8
Corbeal Well—*well* NV-8
Corbeau Creek—*stream* NY-2
Corbeds Landing (historical)—*locale* TN-4
Corbell Butte—*summit* OR-9
Corbell Cem—*cemetery* AL-4
Corbell Ditch—*canal* OR-9
Corbell Park—*park* AZ-5
Corbell Spring—*spring* OR-9
*Corbens Neck* VA-3
*Corbet* MD-2
Corbet—*locale* TX-5
Corbet Branch—*stream* AL-4
Corbet Cem—*cemetery* OH-6
Corbet Creek—*stream* (2) CA-9
*Corbett* KS-7
Corbett—*locale* MD-2
Corbett—*locale* PA-2
**Corbett**—*pop pl* NY-2
**Corbett**—*pop pl* NC-3
**Corbett**—*pop pl* OK-5
**Corbett**—*pop pl* OR-9
Corbett—*uninc pl* MD-2
Corbet Tank—*reservoir* AZ-5
Corbett Branch—*stream* FL-3
Corbett Branch—*stream* VA-3
Corbett Cabin—*locale* OR-9
Corbett Canal—*canal* NV-8
*Corbett Canyon* CA-9
Corbett (CCD)—*cens area* OR-9
Corbett Cem—*cemetery* LA-4
Corbett Cem—*cemetery* NC-3
Corbett Creek—*stream* AL-4
Corbett Creek—*stream* CO-8
Corbett Creek—*stream* ID-8
Corbett Creek—*stream* OR-9
Corbett Creek—*stream* UT-8
Corbett Creek—*stream* WA-9
Corbett Cross Road—*locale* AL-4
Corbett Dam—*dam* AZ-5
Corbett Dam—*dam* WY-8
Corbett Dam Rsvr—*reservoir* AZ-5
Corbett Ditch—*canal* KY-4
Corbett Draw—*valley* WA-9
Corbett Estate Pond—*lake* FL-3
Corbett Hill—*summit* FL-3
Corbett Hist Dist—*hist pl* MD-2
Corbett Hollow—*valley* VT-1
Corbett Lake—*lake* CA-9
Corbett Lake—*lake* CO-8
Corbett Lake—*lake* MI-6
Corbett Lake—*lake* WI-6
Corbett Memorial State Park—*park* OR-9
Corbett Mine—*mine* CA-9
Corbettown—*locale* PA-2
Corbett Peak—*summit* CO-8
Corbett Point—*cape* NY-2
Corbett Pond—*reservoir* FL-3
Corbett Ranch—*locale* NM-5
Corbett Ridge—*ridge* NC-3
Corbett Run—*stream* WV-2
Corbett Sch—*school* (2) NV-8
Corbett Sch—*school* OR-9
Corbett's/Eby's Mill Bridge—*hist pl* IA-7
Corbett Sink—*basin* FL-3
Corbetts Lake—*reservoir* AL-4
Corbett Slough Canal—*canal* ID-8
*Corbetts Pond* NH-1
Corbetts Pond Number One—*reservoir* NC-3
Corbetts Pond Number One Dam—*dam* NC-3
Corbett Spring—*spring* UT-8
Corbett Spring No 1—*spring* ID-8
*Corbett State Wildlife Mngmt Area* FL-3
**Corbett Station**—*pop pl* OR-9
**Corbettsville**—*pop pl* NY-2
Corbett Tunnel—*tunnel* WY-8
*Corbin* ID-8
Corbin—*locale* GA-3
Corbin—*locale* MD-2
Corbin—*locale* MO-7
**Corbin**—*pop pl* AL-4
**Corbin**—*pop pl* KS-7
**Corbin**—*pop pl* KY-4
**Corbin**—*pop pl* LA-4
**Corbin**—*pop pl* MT-8
**Corbin**—*pop pl* VA-3
Corbin, Lake—*reservoir* VA-3
Corbin Bank Bldg—*hist pl* KY-4
Corbin Branch—*stream* MD-2
Corbin Branch—*stream* MS-4
Corbin Branch—*stream* WV-2
Corbin Bridge—*bridge* VA-3
Corbin Cabin—*locale* VA-3
Corbin Cabin Trail—*trail* VA-3
Corbin Canyon—*valley* CO-8
Corbin (CCD)—*cens area* (2) KY-4
Corbin Cem—*cemetery* AR-4
Corbin Cem—*cemetery* MA-1
Corbin Cem—*cemetery* (2) NY-2
Corbin Cem—*cemetery* PA-2
Corbin Cem—*cemetery* TN-4
Corbin Cem—*cemetery* WV-2
Corbin Ch—*church* MO-7
**Corbin City**—*pop pl* NJ-2
*Corbin City Grounds* NJ-2
Corbin Corner—*locale* NY-2
Corbin Covered Bridge—*hist pl* NH-1
Corbin Creek—*stream* AK-9
Corbin Creek—*stream* CA-9
Corbin Creek—*stream* GA-3
Corbin Creek—*stream* IN-6
Corbin Creek—*stream* (2) NC-3
Corbin Creek—*stream* OH-6
Corbin Creek—*stream* OR-9
Corbin Creek—*stream* PA-2

Corbin Creek—stream SC-3
Corbin Creek—stream VA-3
Corbindale PA-2
Corbin Dam—dam TN-4
Corbin Drain MI-6
Corbin Drain—canal MI-6
**Corbin Estates**—pop pl TN-4
Corbin Ferry Ch—church LA-4
Corbing Creek PA-2
Corbin Glacier—glacier AK-9
Corbin Gulch—valley CO-8
Corbin Hall—hist pl VA-3
**Corbin Hill**—pop pl TN-4
Corbin Hill—summit IN-6
Corbin Hill—summit (2) NY-2
Corbin Hill—summit TN-4
Corbin Hill Sch—school NY-2
Corbin Hills Golf Course—locale NC-3
**Corbin Hills (subdivision)**—pop pl NC-3
Corbin (historical)—locale KS-7
**Corbin (historical)**—pop pl OR-9
Corbin Hollow—valley VA-3
Corbin Horse Stamp—summit GA-3
Corbin Hosp—hospital CT-1
Corbin House—locale WA-9
Corbin Junction—locale ID-8
Corbin Knob—summit NC-3
Corbin Lake—lake (2) MI-6
Corbin Lake—reservoir TN-4
Corbin Lake (historical)—lake TN-4
Corbin Ledge—bench NY-2
Corbin Mine (Aban'd)—mine AK-9
Corbin Mountain Trail—trail VA-3
Corbin Mtn—summit NC-3
Corbin Mtn—summit SC-3
Corbin Mtn—summit VA-3
Corbin Neck VA-3
Corbin Oil Field—other NM-5
Corbin Park—park ID-8
Corbin Park—park WA-9
Corbin Point—cape AK-9
Corbin Pond—lake FL-3
Corbin Pond—lake VA-3
Corbin Pond—reservoir VA-3
Corbin Ranch—locale CA-9
Corbins Airp—airport PA-2
Corbin Sch (abandoned)—school PA-2
Corbin Sch (historical)—school AL-4
Corbins Creek VA-3
Corbins Island Fishing Access—area PA-2
Corbins Neck—cape VA-3
Corbin Swamp—swamp NY-2
Corbin Village—post sta CA-9
**Corbinville**—pop pl AL-4
Corbinville Sch (historical)—school AL-4
Corbin Work Center—locale CA-9
Corbit—locale DE-2
Corbit Branch—stream FL-3
Corbit Canyon—valley CA-9
Corbit Cem—cemetery DE-2
Corbit Sch—school DE-2
Corbit-Sharp House—hist pl DE-2
Corbitt KS-7
Corbitt Branch—stream LA-4
Corbitt Ditch—canal CO-8
Corbitt Ditch—canal OH-6
Corbitt Ranch—locale WY-8
Corbitts Millpond—reservoir SC-3
Corbley PA-2
Corbley, John, Farm—hist pl PA-2
Corbly Creek MT-8
Corbly Gulch—valley MT-8
Corbran Cem—cemetery MS-4
Corbus Creek—stream ID-8
Corbusier Slough—stream AK-9
Corbus Lake—lake ID-8
Corbutt Island—island OH-6
Corby-Forsee Bldg—hist pl MO-7
Corby Gulch MT-8
Corbyn—locale TX-5
Corby Swamp—swamp PA-2
Cor Campbell School (historical)—locale MO-7
**Corcega**—pop pl (3) PR-3
**Corcoran**—pop pl AL-4
**Corcoran**—pop pl CA-9
**Corcoran**—pop pl MN-6
Corcoran, Mount—summit CA-9
Corcoran Canyon—valley NV-8
Corcoran (CCD)—cens area CA-9
Corcoran Creek—stream NV-8
Corcoran Creek—stream OK-5
Corcoran Divide Spring—spring NV-8
Corcoran Flat—flat CA-9
Corcoran Gallery of Art—hist pl DC-2
Corcoran HS—school NY-2
Corcoran Lagoon—lake CA-9
Corcoran Lake—lake AK-9
Corcoran Memorial Park—cemetery CA-9
Corcoran Mine—mine CO-8
Corcoran Mountain CA-9
Corcoran Peak—summit CO-8
Corcoran Point—cliff CO-8
Corcoran Rsvr—reservoir OR-9
Corcoran Sch—school MA-1
Corcoran Sch—school MN-6
Corcoran Substation—other CA-9
Corcoran Wash—stream CO-8
Corcoraque Butte AZ-5
Corcovada (Barrio)—fmr MCD PR-3
**Corcovado**—pop pl PR-3
Corcovado (Barrio)—fmr MCD PR-3
**Corcys Subdivision**—pop pl UT-8
**Cord**—pop pl AR-4
Corda Creek—stream AK-9
**Cordage**—pop pl MA-1
Cordage Park Marketplace—building MA-1
Cordal Creek Mine (surface)—mine AL-4
Cordal Creek Mine (underground)—mine AL-4
Cordana Ranch NV-8
Cordano Ranch—locale NV-8
Cordano Well—well NV-8
**Cordaville**—pop pl MA-1
Cord Branch VA-3
Cord Cem—cemetery MI-6
Cordeal FL-3
Cordele—locale TX-5
**Cordele**—pop pl GA-3
Cordele (CCD)—cens area GA-3
Cordele Fish Hatchery—other GA-3
Cordele Oil Field—oilfield TX-5
Cordelia—locale PA-2
**Cordelia**—pop pl CA-9
Cordelia Club—other CA-9
Cordelia Flat—flat OR-9
**Cordelia Junction**—pop pl CA-9
Cordelia Park—park NC-3
Cordelia Slough—stream CA-9
Cordelia Station—locale PA-2
**Cordelia Township**—pop pl ND-7
Cordell—locale KY-4
Cordell—locale MI-6
Cordell—locale TN-4
Cordell—locale WA-9
**Cordell**—pop pl OK-5
**Cordell**—pop pl SC-3
Cordell Branch—stream TN-4
Cordell Bridge—bridge TN-4
Cordell Canyon—valley NM-5
Cordell Cem—cemetery AL-4
Cordell Cem—cemetery OK-5
Cordell Cem—cemetery (3) TN-4
Cordell (corporate name New Cordell) OK-5
Cordell Creek—stream AL-4
Cordell Creek—stream AR-4
Cordell Creek—stream TN-4
Cordell Creek—stream (2) TX-5
Cordell (historical)—locale AL-4
Cordell Hull Birthplace—building TN-4
Cordell Hull Bridge—bridge TN-4
Cordell Hull Dam—dam TN-4
Cordell Hull Lake—reservoir TN-4
Cordell Hull Lock and Dam—dam TN-4
Cordell Hull Rsvr—reservoir KY-4
Cordell Hull Rsvr—reservoir (2) TN-4
Cordell Lake OK-5
Cordell Lane Branch—stream TN-4
Cordell Mtn—summit GA-3
Cordell Mtn—summit TN-4
Cordello Ave Sch—school NY-2
Cordell Post Office (historical)—building TN-4
Cordell Reservoir OK-5
Cordell Sch (historical)—school TN-4
Cordell Well—well NM-5
Cordell Windmill—locale NM-5
**Corder**—pop pl MO-7
Corder Bldg—hist pl CA-9
Corder Bottom Lake VA-3
Corder Branch—stream TN-4
Corder Branch—stream VA-3
Corder Cem—cemetery MO-7
Corder Cem—cemetery (2) VA-3
Corder Creek—stream ID-8
Corder Creek—stream KY-4
Corder Creek—stream WY-8
Corder Crossing—locale WV-2
**Corder Crossroads**—pop pl TN-4
**Corder Cross Roads**—pop pl TN-4
Corder Hollow—valley MO-7
Corder Hollow—valley VA-3
Corder Lake—lake TX-5
Corder Lake—reservoir KS-7
Corder Log Pond—reservoir OR-9
Corder Log Pond Dike—dam OR-9
**Cordero**—pop pl NV-8
Cordero Junction—locale CA-9
Cordero Mine—mine NV-8
Cordero Sch—school NV-8
Corder Ranch—locale TX-5
Corders Crossroads Sch (historical)—school TN-4
Corder Spring—spring AL-4
Corder Spring Branch—stream TN-4
Corders Rsvr—reservoir CA-9
Cordery Creek—stream NJ-2
Cordery Thorofare—channel NJ-2
Cordes—locale AZ-5
Cordes—locale IL-6
Cordes—locale OR-9
Cordes Cem—cemetery IL-6
Cordes Chapel—church NY-2
Cordes Junction—locale AZ-5
Cordes Junction Interchange—crossing AZ-5
Cordes Lake—lake MI-6
Cordes Lake—lake SC-3
**Cordes Lakes**—pop pl AZ-5
Cordes Landing Strip—airport AZ-5
Cordes-Oberlander Ranch—locale CO-8
Cordes Oil Field—other IL-6
Cordes Peak—summit AZ-5
Cordes Tank—reservoir AZ-5
**Cordesville**—pop pl SC-3
Cordesville (CCD)—cens area SC-3
Cordesville Sch—school SC-3
Cordey Cem—cemetery TX-5
Cord Hollow—valley MO-7
Cord Hollow—valley TN-4
Cordia—locale KY-4
Cordia Branch—stream MO-7
Cordia Cem—cemetery KS-7
Cordiality Ch—church NC-3
**Cordillera**—pop pl NM-5
Cordillera (Barrio)—fmr MCD PR-3
Cordillera Central—range PR-3
Cordillera Del Tule AZ-5
Cordillera Ditch—canal NM-5
Cordillera Jaicoa—range PR-3
Cordillera Sabana Alta—range PR-3
Cordilleras Creek—stream CA-9
Cordi Marian Villa Convent and Chapel—church TX-5
Cordingly Canyon—valley UT-8
Cordingly Dam—dam MA-1
Cording Sch—school IL-6
Cordle Branch—stream KY-4
Cordle Cem—cemetery KY-4
Cordle Cem—cemetery OH-6
Cordle Cem—cemetery VA-3
Cordle Lake—reservoir GA-3
Cordley Elem Sch—school KS-7
Cordley Lake—lake MI-6
Cordner Pond—reservoir PA-2
Cordones, The—summit AZ-5
Cordonices Creek CA-9
Cordonier Sch—school KS-7
Cordory Hollow—valley NY-2
Cordova CO-8
Cordova—locale CA-9
Cordova—locale MT-8
Cordova—locale WV-2
**Cordova**—pop pl AL-4
**Cordova**—pop pl AK-9
**Cordova**—pop pl IL-6
**Cordova**—pop pl IA-7
**Cordova**—pop pl KY-4
**Cordova**—pop pl MD-2
**Cordova**—pop pl MN-6
**Cordova**—pop pl NE-7
**Cordova**—pop pl NM-5
**Cordova**—pop pl NY-2
**Cordova**—pop pl NC-3
**Cordova**—pop pl SC-3
**Cordova**—pop pl TN-4
**Cordova**—pop pl VA-3
**Cordova, Plaza**—pop pl CO-8
Cordova Bay—bay AK-9
Cordova Bend TX-5
Cordova Bend—bend TX-5
Cordova Canyon—valley CO-8
Cordova Canyon—valley (2) NM-5
Cordova (CCD)—cens area AL-4
Cordova Cem—cemetery CO-8
Cordova (Census Subarea)—cens area AK-9
Cordova Ch—church AL-4
Cordova Ch—church NC-3
Cordova Creek—stream NM-5
**Cordova Davila**—pop pl (2) PR-3
Cordova Ditch—canal CO-8
Cordova Division—civil AL-4
Cordova Elem Sch—school AL-4
Cordova Elem Sch—school NC-3
Cordova Gardens Sch—school CA-9
Cordova Glacier—glacier AK-9
Cordova Hollow—valley TX-5
Cordova House—hist pl AZ-5
Cordova HS—school AL-4
Cordova HS—school CA-9
Cordova Lake—reservoir CO-8
Cordova Lake—reservoir NM-5
Cordova Lane Sch—school CA-9
Cordova Mall—post sta FL-3
Cordova Meadows Sch—school CA-9
Cordova Mesa—summit (2) CO-8
Cordova-Mile 13 Airp—airport AK-9
Cordova Mine (underground)—mine (2) AL-4
Cordova Mountain TX-5
Cordova Number 1 Mine (surface)—mine AL-4
Cordova Park Sch—school FL-3
Cordova Pass—gap CO-8
Cordova Peak TX-5
Cordova Peak—summit AK-9
**Cordova Plaza**—pop pl CO-8
Cordova Plazza CO-8
Cordova Post Office—building AL-4
Cordova Post Office and Courthouse—hist pl AK-9
Cordova Sch—school AZ-5
Cordova Slough—stream IA-7
Cordovas Spring—spring NM-5
Cordovas Tank—reservoir NM-5
**Cordova (Steeles Mill)**—pop pl NC-3
Cordova Tank—reservoir AZ-5
Cordova Tank—reservoir CO-8
Cordova Tank—reservoir NM-5
**Cordova (Township of)**—pop pl IL-6
**Cordova (Township of)**—pop pl MN-6
**Cordova Town West**—pop pl CA-9
Cordova Villa Sch—school CA-9
Cordova Well—locale NM-5
Cordova Windmill—locale CO-8
Cordoza Canyon—valley CA-9
Cordoza Ridge—ridge CA-9
Cord Pond MA-1
Cord Pond—lake PA-2
Cordray Ch—church GA-3
Cordrays Mill—locale GA-3
Cordrays Pond—lake GA-3
Cordreys Beach—beach VA-3
Cordrey Windmill—locale CO-8
Cord Run—stream IN-6
**Cordry Lake**—pop pl IN-6
Cordry Lake—reservoir IN-6
Cords, Erwin, House—hist pl WI-6
Cords Marsh VA-3
Cord's Marshes VA-3
Cord Spring—spring TX-5
Cord Spring Draw—valley TX-5
Cordua Canal—canal CA-9
Cordua Sch—school CA-9
Corduroy—locale AL-4
**Corduroy**—pop pl PA-2
Corduroy, The—flat CA-9
Corduroy Basin—basin NV-8
Corduroy Canyon—valley (2) NM-5
Corduroy Creek ID-8
Corduroy Creek—stream (2) AZ-5
Corduroy Creek—stream CO-8
Corduroy Creek—stream (3) ID-8
Corduroy Creek—stream (2) MT-8
Corduroy Creek—stream OK-5
Corduroy Creek—stream UT-8
Corduroy Creek—stream WA-9
Corduroy Creek—stream WY-8
Corduroy Creek Bridge—hist pl AZ-5
Corduroy Gulch—valley CO-8
Corduroy Hollow—valley WV-2
Corduroy Meadows—flat (2) ID-8
Corduroy Mountains NV-8
Corduroy Mtn—summit NV-8
Corduroys, The—swamp ME-1
Corduroy Spring—spring CO-8
Corduroy Spring—spring ID-8
Corduroy Station AL-4
Corduroy Swamp—stream NC-3
Corduroy Wash—stream AZ-5
Cordwood Bottom—bend WY-8
Cordwood Branch—stream TN-4
Cordwood Canyon—valley OR-9
Cordwood Creek—stream AK-9
Cordwood Creek—stream TX-5
Cordwood Creek—stream UT-8
Cordwood Hill—summit ME-1
Cordwood Point MA-1
Cordwood Point—cape MI-6
Cordy Brake—gut MS-4
Cordy Branch—stream TX-5
**Core**—pop pl WV-2
Corea—locale GA-3
**Corea**—pop pl ME-1
Corea Cem—cemetery ME-1
Corea Creek—stream AK-9
Corea Harbor—bay ME-1
Core Bank NC-3
Core Banks—bar NC-3
Core Beach NC-3
Core Branch—stream KY-4
Core Brook MA-1
Core Cem—cemetery TN-4
Core Cem—cemetery TX-5
Core Cem—cemetery (2) WV-2
Core Creek NC-3
Core Creek OR-9
Core Creek—bay NC-3
Core Creek—locale NC-3
Core Creek—stream MO-7
Core Creek—stream NC-3
Core Creek—stream PA-2
Core Creek Ch—church NC-3
Core Creek Dam—dam PA-2
Core Creek Landing—locale NC-3
Core Creek Rsvr—reservoir PA-2
**Corega**—pop pl PR-3
Core Hill—summit OH-6
Core Hollow—valley MO-7
Core Hollow—valley WI-6
Core Island—island FL-3
Corell Creek—stream NY-2
Core Log Canyon—valley NM-5
**Core Point**—pop pl NC-3
Core Point Chapel—church NC-3
Core Point Shoal—bar NC-3
Corer PW-9
Core Road Sch—school WV-2
Core Run—stream WV-2
Cores Creek—stream VA-3
Core Site—hist pl CA-9
Core Sound—bay NC-3
Core Springs—spring NV-8
Cores Sch (historical)—school PA-2
Coreta Mine (underground)—mine AL-4
Coretue MA-1
Corey AL-4
Corey—locale IA-7
Corey—locale LA-4
Corey—mine OR-9
**Corey**—pop pl FL-3
**Corey**—pop pl MI-6
Corey, Timothy, House No. 1—hist pl MA-1
Corey, Timothy, House No. 2—hist pl MA-1
Corey Bar—bar ID-8
Corey Branch—stream LA-4
Corey Branch—stream TX-5
Corey Butte—summit SD-7
Corey Cem—cemetery IN-6
Corey Cem—cemetery KY-4
Corey Cove—bay MI-6
Corey Cove Resort—locale MI-6
Corey Creek—bay NY-2
Corey Creek—stream MN-6
Corey Creek—stream NV-8
Corey Creek—stream NY-2
Corey Creek—stream PA-2
Corey Creek Golf Course—other PA-2
Corey Drain—canal AZ-5
Corey Farm—hist pl NH-1
Corey Gulch—valley (2) OR-9
Corey Gully—valley NY-2
Corey Hill—locale OR-9
Corey Hill—summit MA-1
Corey House—hist pl MT-8
Corey House/Hotel—hist pl OK-5
Corey Island—island NY-2
Corey Lake—lake (3) MI-6
**Corey Lake**—pop pl MI-6
Corey Lake Sch—school MI-6
Corey Marsh—swamp MI-6
Corey Peak—summit NV-8
Corey Point—cape MN-6
Corey Pond—lake NH-1
Corey Pond—lake NY-2
Corey Ranch—locale SD-7
Corey Ridge—ridge ID-8
Corey Run—stream IN-6
Corey Run—stream OH-6
**Coreys**—pop pl NY-2
Corey Sch—school IL-6
Corey Sch—school MI-6
Corey Sch—school MN-6
Corey Sch (historical)—school AL-4
Coreys Creek NY-2
**Coreys Crossroads**—pop pl NC-3
Corey's Hill MA-1
Coreys Hill—summit NH-1
**Corey's Lane**—pop pl RI-1
Corey Spring—spring MT-8
Coreytown FL-3
Coreytown—other FL-3
Coreyville Cem—cemetery NH-1
**Coreze**—pop pl PA-2
Corez Pond—lake VT-1
Corfeine Bayou—gut LA-4
Corfu—locale WA-9
**Corfu**—pop pl NY-2
Corfu Station—locale NY-2
Corgett Wash—stream AZ-5
Corgey Cem—cemetery TX-5
Corgiat Wash AZ-5
Cories, Lake—lake AK-9
Cori House—hist pl MO-7
Corilla Lake—lake PA-2
Corination Drop Cave—cave AL-4
Corinda Los Trancos—ridge CA-9
Corinda Los Trancos Creek—stream CA-9
Corine Sch—school TX-5
**Corinna**—pop pl ME-1
Corinna Cem—cemetery MN-6
Corinna Center—locale ME-1
Corinna Stream ME-1
**Corinna (Town of)**—pop pl ME-1
**Corinna (Township of)**—pop pl MN-6
Corinne—locale OK-5
Corinne—locale PA-2
**Corinne**—pop pl MI-6
**Corinne**—pop pl UT-8
**Corinne**—pop pl WV-2
Corinne Canal—canal UT-8
Corinne Cem—cemetery OK-5
Corinne Cem—cemetery UT-8
Corinne Gas Field—oilfield MS-4
Corinne Key—island FL-3
Corinne Methodist Episcopal Church—hist pl UT-8
Corinne Sch—school ND-7
Corinne Sch—school UT-8
**Corinne Township**—pop pl ND-7
Corinth NC-3
Corinth—locale (2) AL-4
Corinth—locale AR-4
Corinth—locale KS-7
Corinth—locale KY-4
Corinth—locale MS-4
Corinth—locale MT-8
Corinth—locale OH-6
Corinth—locale (3) TX-5
Corinth—locale (2) VA-3
**Corinth**—pop pl (3) AL-4
**Corinth**—pop pl AR-4
**Corinth**—pop pl GA-3
**Corinth**—pop pl IL-6
**Corinth**—pop pl KY-4
**Corinth**—pop pl LA-4
**Corinth**—pop pl MI-6
**Corinth**—pop pl MS-4
**Corinth**—pop pl NY-2
**Corinth**—pop pl (3) NC-3
**Corinth**—pop pl ND-7
**Corinth**—pop pl SC-3
**Corinth**—pop pl (2) TN-4
**Corinth**—pop pl (2) TX-5
**Corinth**—pop pl VT-1
**Corinth**—pop pl WV-2
**Corinth**—pop pl WI-6
Corinth Arsenal (historical)—building MS-4
Corinth Baptist Ch MS-4
Corinth Baptist Ch—church MS-4
Corinth Baptist Ch (historical)—church TN-4
Corinth Baptist Church AL-4
Corinth Branch—stream (2) TN-4
Corinth (CCD)—cens area KY-4
Corinth Cem—cemetery (4) AL-4
Corinth Cem—cemetery (3) AR-4
Corinth Cem—cemetery (5) GA-3
Corinth Cem—cemetery KS-7
Corinth Cem—cemetery KY-4
Corinth Cem—cemetery LA-4
Corinth Cem—cemetery (5) MS-4
Corinth Cem—cemetery (4) MO-7
Corinth Cem—cemetery (3) TN-4
Corinth Cem—cemetery (4) TX-5
**Corinth Center**—pop pl VT-1
Corinth Ch AL-4
Corinth Ch GA-3
Corinth Ch—church (33) AL-4
Corinth Ch—church (15) AR-4
Corinth Ch—church (8) FL-3
Corinth Ch—church (27) GA-3
Corinth Ch—church IL-6
Corinth Ch—church (5) IN-6
Corinth Ch—church (15) KY-4
Corinth Ch—church (4) LA-4
Corinth Ch—church (15) MS-4
Corinth Ch—church (9) MO-7
Corinth Ch—church (18) NC-3
Corinth Ch—church (2) OH-6
Corinth Ch—church OK-5
Corinth Ch—church (4) SC-3
Corinth Ch—church (13) TN-4
Corinth Ch—church (14) TX-5
Corinth Ch—church (12) VA-3
Corinth Ch—church WV-2
Corinth Chapel—church TN-4
Corinth Chapel—church VA-3
Corinth Ch (historical)—church (4) AL-4
Corinth Ch (historical)—church MO-7
Corinth Ch of Christ AL-4
Corinth Ch of God—church AR-4
Corinth Ch (reduced usage)—church TX-5
Corinth City Cem—cemetery MS-4
Corinth City Hall—building MS-4
Corinth City Park—park MS-4
**Corinth (Clifty)**—pop pl AL-4
Corinth Community Hall—locale AR-4
**Corinth Corner**—pop pl VT-1
**Corinth Corners**—pop pl VT-1
Corinth (Election Precinct)—fmr MCD IL-6
Corinth Elem Sch—school KS-7
Corinth Female Coll (historical)—school MS-4
Corinth Fork—locale VA-3
Corinth General Ch—church MO-7
Corinth Holder HS—school NC-3
Corinth Holders NC-3
Corinth Holders Elem Sch NC-3
Corinthia—hist pl KY-4
Corinthian Baptist Ch—church IN-6
Corinthian Cem—cemetery AR-4
Corinthian Cem—cemetery ME-1
Corinthian Cem—cemetery MN-6
Corinthian Cem—cemetery ND-7
Corinthian Ch—church AR-4
Corinthian Ch—church GA-3
Corinthian Ch—church MO-7
Corinthian Island—island CA-9
Corinthian Missionary Baptist Ch—church AL-4
Corinthian Yacht Club—other NY-2
Corinth Industrial Park—locale MS-4
Corinth Junior-Senior HS—school MS-4
Corinth Lake—reservoir KY-4
Corinth-Leefield Cem—cemetery GA-3
Corinth Missionary Baptist Ch of Christ AL-4
Corinth Missionary Baptist Church MS-4
Corinth Municipal Park MS-4
Corinth Number 2 Ch—church (2) SC-3
Corinth-O'Neil Cem—cemetery AR-4
Corinth Post Office (historical)—building (2) TN-4
Corinth Public Library—building MS-4
**Corinth (Ray)**—pop pl KY-4
Corinth Rec Area—locale AL-4
Corinth Run—stream IN-6
Corinth Sanitarium (historical)—hospital MS-4
Corinth Sch—school GA-3
Corinth Sch—school IL-6
Corinth Sch—school KY-4
Corinth Sch—school MS-4
Corinth Sch—school SC-3
Corinth Sch—school WI-6
Corinth Sch (abandoned)—school (3) MO-7
Corinth Sch (historical)—school (2) AL-4
Corinth Sch (historical)—school MS-4
Corinth Sch (historical)—school (5) TN-4
Corinth Square—locale KS-7
Corinth Street Viaduct—bridge TX-5
Corinth Tabernacle—church LA-4
**Corinth (Town of)**—pop pl ME-1
**Corinth (Town of)**—pop pl NY-2
**Corinth (Town of)**—pop pl VT-1
Corinth Township—fmr MCD IA-7
**Corinth Township**—pop pl KS-7
Corinth United Ch—church NC-3
Corinth United Methodist Ch—church TN-4
Corinth Village—hist pl ME-1
Corinth West Ch—church AL-4
Corioman Bay VA-3
Corita Windmill—locale TX-5
Cor Jesu HS—school LA-4
Cork—locale AZ-5
Cork—locale GA-3
Cork—locale KY-4
Cork—locale NY-2
**Cork**—pop pl OH-6
**Cork**—pop pl PA-2
Cork, The—summit AZ-5
Cork Academy—locale FL-3
Cork Branch—stream TN-4
Cork Brook—stream RI-1
Cork Canyon TX-5
Cork Cem—cemetery OH-6
Cork Center Rsvr—reservoir NY-2
Cork Colored Sch (historical)—school MS-4
Cork Cove—bay ME-1
Cork Creek—gut SC-3
Cork Drain—canal MI-6
Cork Draw—valley NM-5
Cork Draw—valley TX-5
Cork Elem Sch—school FL-3
Corkem Cem—cemetery LA-4
Corken Cem—cemetery LA-4
Corken Lake LA-4
Corkenson Creek—stream NC-3
Corker Canyon—valley MT-8
Corker Creek—stream ID-8
Corkern Cem—cemetery LA-4
Corkern Lake—lake LA-4
Corkers Creek—stream MD-2
Corkers Knob—summit VA-3
Corker Springs—spring ID-8
Corkery—locale MO-7
Corkery Sch—school IL-6
Cork Hill—summit PA-2
Cork Hill Creek—stream NY-2
Cork Hill Creek—stream PA-2
Cork Hill District—hist pl IA-7
Corkindale—locale WA-9
Corkindale Creek—stream WA-9
Corkin Hill—summit NY-2
Corkin Lodge—locale NM-5
Corkin Ranch—locale NE-7
Corkins Lake—reservoir FL-3
Corkish Apartments—hist pl OR-9
Cork Island—island FL-3
Cork Island—island MI-6
Cork Island—island NY-2
Cork Key—island FL-3
Cork Lake MN-6
Cork Lake—lake MN-6
Corklan Branch—stream FL-3
**Cork Lane**—pop pl PA-2
Corkplain—flat NH-1
Cork Prairie—flat FL-3
Cork Ridge—ridge UT-8
Cork Rsvr Number Seven—reservoir OR-9
Cork Sch (historical)—school MS-4
Corkscrew—locale FL-3
Corkscrew Canyon—valley CA-9
Corkscrew Canyon—valley NV-8
Corkscrew Canyon—valley NM-5
Corkscrew Canyon—valley (2) WA-9
Corkscrew Cave—cave AL-4
Corkscrew Creek—stream AK-9
Corkscrew Creek—stream MT-8
Corkscrew Draw—valley NM-5
Corkscrew Gulch—valley CO-8
Corkscrew Lookout Tower—tower FL-3
Corkscrew Marsh FL-3
Corkscrew Mtn—summit ID-8
Corkscrew Peak—summit CA-9
Corkscrew River FL-3
Corkscrew Sanctuary Camp—locale FL-3
Corkscrew Slough—gut CA-9
Corkscrew Swamp—swamp FL-3
Corkscrew Swamp Sanctuary—park FL-3
Cork Slough—gut FL-3
Corks Point Ditch—stream DE-2
Cork Spring—spring AZ-5
Corktown Hist Dist—hist pl MI-6
Corktown Sch—school MI-6
**Corkwell**—pop pl IN-6
Corkwood Pond—lake FL-3
Corky Lake—lake ID-8
Corky Lake—lake WI-6
Corky Row Hist Dist—hist pl MA-1
Corl Acres PA-2
Corlaer Bay—bay NY-2
Corlaer Kill—stream NY-2
Corlear Bay NY-2
Corlear Kill NY-2
Corlears Hook—cape NY-2
Corlely Cave—cave TN-4
Corlena—locale TX-5
Corless Dam—dam OR-9
Corless Flat OR-9
Corless Rsvr—reservoir OR-9
Corless Spring—spring OR-9
Corlett Creek WY-8
Corlett Creek—stream WY-8
Corlett Sch—school OH-6
Corlett Sch—school WY-8
Corlew Bend—bend TN-4
Corlew Cem—cemetery TN-4
Corlew Meadows—flat CA-9
Corlew Mtn—summit CA-9
Corley AL-4
Corley MS-4
Corley—locale AR-4
Corley—locale TX-5
Corley—locale WV-2
**Corley**—pop pl IA-7
**Corley**—pop pl WV-2
Corley, C. E., House—hist pl SC-3
Corley Branch AR-4

**Cornpropst**—pop pl PA-2
*Cornpropst Mill* PA-2
Cornpropst Mills—locale PA-2
Corn Ranch—locale (5) NM-5
Corn Ranch—locale TX-5
Corn Ridge—ridge GA-3
Corn Rock—summit AZ-5
Corn Run—stream IN-6
Corn Run—stream PA-2
Corn Sage Point—cape NC-3
Corns Cem—cemetery IL-6
Cornsheller Rapids—rapids WI-6
Cornsilk—hist pl TN-4
Cornsilk Branch—stream NC-3
Corns Lake—lake MO-7
Corn Spring—spring CA-9
Corn Springs Wash—stream CA-9
Corns Ranch—locale NM-5
Corns Ridge—ridge IN-6
Corns Run—stream OH-6
Cornstalk—locale WV-2
Cornstalk Branch—stream AR-4
*Cornstalk Creek* WA-9
Cornstalk Creek—stream IN-6
Cornstalk Creek—stream KY-4
Cornstalk Creek—stream WA-9
Cornstalk Flat—flat AZ-5
Cornstalk Flat Tank—reservoir AZ-5
**Cornstalk (historical)**—pop pl IN-6
Cornstock Ditch—canal OR-9
Cornstock Mine—mine CO-8
Corn Tank—reservoir NM-5
Corntassel Branch—stream TN-4
Corntassel Ch—church TN-4
*Cornucopia* IN-6
Cornucopia—hist pl DE-2
**Cornucopia**—pop pl OR-9
**Cornucopia**—pop pl WI-6
Cornucopia Creek—stream AK-9
Cornucopia Diversion Dam—dam NM-5
Cornucopia Draw—valley NM-5
Cornucopia Hills—range NM-5
Cornucopia Mine—mine AZ-5
Cornucopia Mine—mine CA-9
Cornucopia Mine—mine (2) MT-8
Cornucopia Mine—mine NV-8
Cornucopia Mines—mine OR-9
*Cornucopia Mountains* OR-9
Cornucopia Peak—summit OR-9
Cornucopia Ranch—locale NM-5
Cornucopia Ridge—ridge NV-8
Cornudas—locale TX-5
Cornudas Draw—valley NM-5
Cornudas Draw—valley TX-5
Cornudas Mountains—range NM-5
Cornudas Mountains—range TX-5
Cornudas Mtn—summit NM-5
Cornudas Ranch—locale NM-5
Cornudas Ranch—locale TX-5
Cornudas Tank—reservoir NM-5
Cornutt—locale OR-9
Corn Valley—locale VA-3
Cornville—locale ME-1
**Cornville**—pop pl AZ-5
Cornville Ch—church ME-1
Cornville Ditch—canal AZ-5
Cornville Post Office—building AZ-5
**Cornville (Town of)**—pop pl ME-1
*Cornwall* NY-2
Cornwall—locale ID-8
**Cornwall**—pop pl CT-1
**Cornwall**—pop pl MO-7
**Cornwall**—pop pl NC-3
**Cornwall**—pop pl PA-2
**Cornwall**—pop pl VT-1
**Cornwall**—pop pl VA-3
Cornwall—uninc pl WA-9
Cornwall, Mason, House—hist pl ID-8
Cornwall Acad—school MA-1
Cornwall and Brown Houses—hist pl KY-4
Cornwall Apartments—hist pl CO-8
Cornwall Basin—basin AZ-5
Cornwall Basin—basin NV-8
Cornwall Basin Spring—spring AZ-5
Cornwall Borough—civil PA-2
**Cornwall Bridge**—pop pl CT-1
Cornwall Bridge RR Station—hist pl CT-1
Cornwall Brothers' Store—hist pl NY-2
Cornwall Canyon—valley AZ-5
Cornwall Cem—cemetery CT-1
Cornwall Cem—cemetery IL-6
Cornwall Cem—cemetery NY-2
Cornwall Cem—cemetery PA-2
**Cornwall (census name Firthcliffe)**—pop pl NY-2
Cornwall Center—locale CT-1
**Cornwall Center**—pop pl PA-2
Cornwall Ch—church (2) MO-7
Cornwall Ch—church PA-2
Cornwall Consolidated Sch—school CT-1
**Cornwall (corporate name for Cornwall-on-Hudson)**—pop pl NY-2
Cornwall Creek—stream ID-8
Cornwall Creek—stream MI-6
Cornwall Creek—stream NV-8
Cornwall Friends Meeting House—hist pl NY-2
Cornwall Furnace—hist pl AL-4
Cornwall Furnace—locale AL-4
Cornwall Furnace—locale PA-2
Cornwall Furnace Memorial Park—park AL-4
Cornwall Hill—summit NY-2
Cornwall Hollow—locale CT-1
*Cornwall Iron Furnace* PA-2
Cornwall Iron Furnace—hist pl PA-2
*Cornwallis* MP-9
Cornwallis—locale WV-2
**Cornwallis Hills (subdivision)**—pop pl NC-3
Cornwallis Neck—cape MD-2
Cornwallis Point—cape AK-9
Cornwallis Rsvr—reservoir CO-8
Cornwall Junction—locale PA-2
Cornwall Lake—lake (2) MI-6
**Cornwall Landing**—pop pl NY-2
Cornwall & Lebanon RR Station—hist pl PA-2
Cornwall Lookout Tower—tower PA-2
Cornwall Memorial Park—cemetery WA-9
Cornwall Mtn—summit CO-8
Cornwall Mtn—summit NV-8
**Cornwall-on-Hudson (corporate name Cornwall)**—pop pl NY-2
*Cornwall-on-the-Hudson* NY-2
Cornwall Pass—gap NV-8
Cornwall Point—cape OR-9
Cornwall Point—summit ID-8
*Cornwall Pond* CT-1
Cornwall Pond—lake KY-4
Cornwall Rsvr—reservoir PA-2
Cornwall Sch—school NC-3
Cornwall Sch—school SD-7
Cornwalls Nose—pillar CO-8
**Cornwall (subdivision)**—pop pl AL-4
Cornwall Tailings Dam—dam PA-2
Cornwall-Tilden Cem—cemetery NY-2
*Cornwall Tower* PA-2
Cornwall Town Hall—hist pl VT-1
**Cornwall (Town of)**—pop pl CT-1
**Cornwall (Town of)**—pop pl NY-2
**Cornwall (Town of)**—pop pl VT-1
**Cornwall Township**—pop pl SD-7
**Cornwall (Township of)**—pop pl IL-6
**Cornwallville**—pop pl NY-2
Cornwallville Creek—stream NY-2
*Corn Wash* AZ-5
Cornwater Spring—spring AZ-5
*Cornwell* PA-2
Cornwell—locale FL-3
Cornwell—locale KY-4
Cornwell—locale VA-3
**Cornwell**—pop pl PA-2
**Cornwell**—pop pl SC-3
**Cornwell**—pop pl WV-2
Cornwell Ave Sch—school NY-2
Cornwell Branch—stream KY-4
Cornwell Branch—stream NC-3
Cornwell Cem—cemetery MS-4
Cornwell Chapel—church TN-4
Cornwell Drain—canal MI-6
Cornwell Farm—hist pl VA-3
Cornwell Field—park KY-4
*Cornwell Heights Maud* PA-2
Cornwell Hollow—valley TN-4
Cornwell Lake—lake WA-9
Cornwell Mtn—summit PA-2
Cornwell Post Office (historical)—building MS-4
Cornwell Rsvr—reservoir MT-8
Cornwell Run—stream NJ-2
Cornwells Ch—church PA-2
Cornwell Sch—school WV-2
Cornwells Elem Sch—school PA-2
**Cornwells Heights**—pop pl PA-2
Cornwells Heights Post Office (historical)—building PA-2
Corny Coulee—valley MT-8
Corny Coulee Rsvr—reservoir MT-8
Corny Lake—lake MN-6
Corodope Spring—spring AZ-5
*Corog* FM-9
**Coro Lake**—pop pl TN-4
Coro Lake—reservoir TN-4
Coro Lake Dam—dam TN-4
Coro Lake Sch—school TN-4
**Corolla**—pop pl NC-3
Corolla C G Station 166—locale NC-3
Coromar—locale CA-9
*Corona* MS-4
Corona—locale CO-8
Corona—locale MN-6
Corona—locale NM-5
Corona—locale TN-4
**Corona**—pop pl AL-4
**Corona**—pop pl CA-9
**Corona**—pop pl NM-5
**Corona**—pop pl NY-2
**Corona**—pop pl SD-7
Corona, The—summit CO-8
Corona-A—post sta NY-2
Corona Ave Sch—school CA-9
Corona Ave Sch—school NY-2
Corona Bar—bar TN-4
Corona Bar Dikes—levee TN-4
**Coronaca**—pop pl SC-3
Coronaca Creek—stream SC-3
Corona (CCD)—cens area CA-9
Corona (CCD)—cens area NM-5
Corona Cem—cemetery SD-7
Corona Ch—church AL-4
Corona Christian Sch—school CA-9
**Coronaco**—pop pl SC-3
Corona Creek—stream MT-8
**Coronada Foothills Estates**—pop pl AZ-5
Coronada Sch—school AZ-5
**Corona del Mar**—pop pl CA-9
Corona del Mar HS—school CA-9
Corona Del Mar Sch—school CA-9
Corona del Sol High School Tennis and Racquetball Courts—other AZ-5
Corona del Sol HS—school AZ-5
**Corona de Tucson**—pop pl AZ-5
Corona Divide—ridge MT-8
Coronado—hist pl IL-6
Coronado—locale AZ-5
Coronado—locale KS-7
**Coronado**—pop pl CA-9
**Coronado**—pop pl CO-8
**Coronado**—pop pl VA-3
Coronado—uninc pl AZ-5
Coronado—uninc pl NM-5
Coronado—uninc pl TX-5
Coronado, Lake—reservoir AR-4
Coronado Apartments—hist pl MI-6
Coronado Beach Bridge—bridge FL-3
Coronado Beach Elem Sch—school FL-3
Coronado Butte—summit AZ-5
Coronado Camp—locale AZ-5
Coronado Cem—cemetery KS-7
Coronado (Coronado Beach)—uninc pl FL-3
Coronado Elem Sch—school AZ-5
**Coronado Estates (subdivision)**—pop pl AL-4
Coronado Evaporation Rsvr—reservoir AZ-5
Coronado Generating Station Dam—dam AZ-5
Coronado Golf Course—other AZ-5
Coronado Gulch—valley AZ-5
Coronado Heights Park—park KS-7
Coronado Heights Sch—school OK-5
**Coronado Hills**—pop pl TX-5
Coronado Hosp—hospital CA-9
Coronado Hotel—hist pl AZ-5
Coronado HS—school CA-9
Coronado Incline—slope AZ-5
Coronado JHS—school CA-9
Coronado JHS—school CO-8
Coronado JHS—school KS-7
Coronado JHS—school TX-5
Coronado Lake—reservoir OH-6
Coronado Lodge—locale NM-5
Coronado Memorial HQ—building AZ-5
*Coronado Mesa* AZ-5
Coronado Mesa—summit AZ-5
Coronado Mesa (historical)—summit AZ-5
Coronado Mine—mine AZ-5
Coronado Mine—mine CA-9
Coronado Mobile Home Park—locale AZ-5
Coronado Mountains (historical)—summit AZ-5
Coronado Mtn—summit AZ-5
Coronado Natl For—forest AZ-5
Coronado Natl Memorial—hist pl AZ-5
Coronado Natl Memorial—park AZ-5
Coronado Naval Amphibious Base—military CA-9
Coronado Neighborhood Hist Dist—hist pl AZ-5
Coronado Park—park AZ-5
Coronado Park—park KS-7
Coronado Park—park NM-5
Coronado Peak—summit AZ-5
Coronado Peak Trail—trail AZ-5
*Coronado Plateau* AZ-5
Coronado Post Office—building AZ-5
Coronado Post Office (historical)—building AL-4
Coronado Ridge—ridge AZ-5
Coronado Sch—school (2) AZ-5
Coronado Sch—school (2) CA-9
Coronado Sch—school (2) NM-5
Coronado Sch—school (3) TX-5
**Coronado Shores**—pop pl OR-9
Coronados Islands—area AK-9
Coronado Spring—spring AZ-5
Coronado State Monument Kuaua Ruins—locale NM-5
Coronado Substation—locale AZ-5
*Coronado Summit* AZ-5
Coronado Summit (historical)—summit AZ-5
Coronado Tank—reservoir AZ-5
Coronado Trail—trail AZ-5
**Coronado Village**—pop pl AZ-5
Coronado Village Shop Ctr—locale AZ-5
Coronado Wash—stream AZ-5
Coronado Well—well AZ-5
Coronado Wye—dam CA-9
Corona-Elmhurst—uninc pl NY-2
Corona Female Coll (historical)—school MS-4
Corona Female Institute (historical)—school TN-4
Corona Gulch—valley MT-8
Corona Heights Playground—school CA-9
Corona Hill—summit NM-5
Corona HS—school CA-9
Corona Lake—lake CO-8
Corona Lake—lake MN-6
Corona Lake—lake MT-8
Corona Lake—lake TN-4
Corona La Laja—bar PR-3
Corona Mine—mine (3) CA-9
Corona Mine (surface)—mine AL-4
Corona Mine (underground)—mine AL-4
Corona Number 12 Mine (underground)—mine AL-4
Corona Number 13 Mine (underground)—mine AL-4
Corona Number 15 Mine (underground)—mine AL-4
Corona Number 20 Mine (underground)—mine AL-4
Corona Park—park CA-9
*Corona Peak* CO-8
Corona Post Office (historical)—building AL-4
Corona Post Office (historical)—building TN-4
Corona Range Study Plot—other CO-8
Corona Sch—school CA-9
Corona Shoal—bar MI-6
Corona Speedway—locale AZ-5
Corona Tank—reservoir (3) NM-5
*Coronation Brook* CT-1
Coronation Island—island AK-9
Coronation of Our Lady Sch—school MO-7
*Coronation Peak* AZ-5
**Corona Village (subdivision)**—pop pl (2) AZ-5
Corona Wash—stream AZ-5
Corona Well—well AZ-5
Corona Well—well NM-5
**Coronet**—pop pl FL-3
**Coronet**—pop pl VA-3
Coronet—uninc pl CA-9
Coronet Junction (railroad junction)—locale FL-3
Coronet Lake—lake CA-9
Coronet Lake—reservoir NY-2
Coroni, Lake—lake FL-3
Coronia Sch—school TN-4
Coronilla Canyon—valley NM-5
**Coronita**—pop pl CA-9
Coronita Sch—school CA-9
*Coroteros* AZ-5
Corothers Sch Number 36—school SD-7
Corotoman—hist pl VA-3
**Corozal**—pop pl (2) PR-3
Corozal (Municipio)—civil PR-3
Corozal (Pueblo)—fmr MCD PR-3
**Corozo**—pop pl PR-3
Corpe Creek—stream WY-8
Corpe Draw—valley WY-8
Corpening Branch—stream NC-3
Corpening Bridge—bridge NC-3
**Corpening Hills (subdivision)**—pop pl TN-4
Corpening Ranch—locale (2) WY-8
Corpening Sch—school NC-3
Corper Lake Dam—dam MS-4
**Corpers Homes**—pop pl PA-2
Corpier Cem—cemetery TN-4
Corp Mound Bayou—stream LA-4
Corporal—locale CA-9
Corporal Creek—stream MT-8
Corporal Mine—mine CO-8
Corporation Beach—beach MA-1
Corporation Brook—stream VT-1
Corporation Canal—canal LA-4
Corporation Guard Station—locale OR-9
Corporation Gulch—valley NE-7
Corporation Lake—flat OR-9
Corporation Meadow—flat CA-9
Corporation Mtn—summit VT-1
Corporation Rim—ridge OR-9
Corprew Sch—school TX-5
Corpse Pond—lake MI-6
Corps Sch—school MI-6
**Corpus Christi**—pop pl TX-5
Corpus Christi, Lake—reservoir TX-5
Corpus Christi Acad—school TX-5
Corpus Christian Sch—school CA-9
Corpus Christi Army Depot—other TX-5
Corpus Christi Bay—bay TX-5
Corpus Christi Bayou—channel TX-5
Corpus Christi Beach—beach TX-5
Corpus Christi Catholic Ch—church AL-4
Corpus Christi Catholic Ch—church FL-3
Corpus Christi (CCD)—cens area TX-5
Corpus Christi Cem—cemetery IA-7
Corpus Christi Cem—cemetery KS-7
Corpus Christi Ch—church AL-4
Corpus Christi Ch—church FL-3
Corpus Christi Ch—church MN-6
Corpus Christi Ch—church NJ-2
Corpus Christi Ch—church NY-2
Corpus Christi Ch—church OH-6
Corpus Christi Ch—church PA-2
Corpus Christi Ch—church WI-6
Corpus Christi Channel—channel TX-5
Corpus Christi Church—hist pl IA-7
Corpus Christi Filtration Plant—other TX-5
Corpus Christi Golf Center—other TX-5
Corpus Christi Home—building MN-6
*Corpus Christi Inlet* TX-5
Corpus Christi International Airp—airport TX-5
Corpus Christi Minor Seminary—school TX-5
Corpus Christi Monastery—church NY-2
Corpus Christi Naval Air Station—military TX-5
Corpus Christi Naval Regional Med Ctr—hospital TX-5
Corpus Christi Pass—channel TX-5
Corpus Christi Sch—school AL-4
Corpus Christi Sch—school CA-9
Corpus Christi Sch—school CT-1
Corpus Christi Sch—school FL-3
Corpus Christi Sch—school (2) IN-6
Corpus Christi Sch—school KS-7
Corpus Christi Sch—school LA-4
Corpus Christi Sch—school MI-6
Corpus Christi Sch—school (2) NJ-2
Corpus Christi Sch—school (3) NY-2
Corpus Christi Sch—school OH-6
Corpus Christi Sch—school (2) PA-2
Corpus Christi Sch—school TX-5
Corpus Christi Sch—school WV-2
Corpus Christi West (CCD)—cens area TX-5
Corpus Cristi Catholic Sch—school PA-2
Corpus Cristi Ch—church SD-7
*Corra* PW-9
**Corrado Corners**—pop pl NY-2
Corra Harris Home—building GA-3
Corrailsen Creek—stream ID-8
Corral—locale ID-8
Corral—locale NM-5
Corral, Arroyo Del—stream CA-9
Corral, Canada Del —valley CA-9
Corral, Lake—lake WA-9
Corral Basin—basin ID-8
Corral Basin—basin (2) OR-9
Corral Basin Creek—stream ID-8
Corral Basin Creek—stream OR-9
Corral Beach—beach CA-9
Corral Bluffs—cliff CO-8
Corral Bottom—bend CA-9
Corral Butte—summit ID-8
Corral Butte—summit MT-8
Corral Butte—summit OR-9
Corral Butte—summit WA-9
Corral Camp—locale OR-9
*Corral Campground* OR-9
*Corral Canyon* UT-8
Corral Canyon—valley (5) AZ-5
Corral Canyon—valley (6) CA-9
Corral Canyon—valley CO-8
Corral Canyon—valley (6) ID-8
Corral Canyon—valley NE-7
Corral Canyon—valley (12) NV-8
Corral Canyon—valley (13) NM-5
Corral Canyon—valley (2) OR-9
Corral Canyon—valley (16) UT-8
Corral Canyon—valley (3) WA-9
Corral Canyon—valley (3) WY-8
Corral Canyon Bench—bench UT-8
Corral Canyon Forest Station—locale CA-9
Corral Canyon Point—cape UT-8
Corral Canyon Spring—spring AZ-5
Corral Canyon Spring—spring UT-8
Corral Canyon Wash—valley UT-8
Corral Cave—cave AL-4
Corral Cem—cemetery ID-8
**Corral City**—pop pl TX-5
Corral Coulee—valley (5) MT-8
*Corral Crater* UT-8
*Corral Creek* AZ-5
*Corral Creek* CO-8
*Corral Creek* ID-8
*Corral Creek* MT-8
*Corral Creek* NV-8
*Corral Creek* OR-9
*Corral Creek* TX-5
*Corral Creek* WY-8
Corral Creek—stream (2) AZ-5
Corral Creek—stream (10) CA-9
Corral Creek—stream (13) CO-8
Corral Creek—stream (36) ID-8
Corral Creek—stream KS-7
Corral Creek—stream (27) MT-8
Corral Creek—stream (5) NV-8
Corral Creek—stream (3) ND-7
Corral Creek—stream (18) OR-9
Corral Creek—stream SD-7
Corral Creek—stream (6) TX-5
Corral Creek—stream (4) UT-8
Corral Creek—stream (7) WA-9
Corral Creek—stream (23) WY-8
Corral Creek Campground—locale CA-9
Corral Creek Campground—locale WA-9
Corral Creek Canyon—valley ID-8
Corral Creek Cow Camp—locale ID-8
Corral Creek Guard Station—locale ID-8
Corral Creek Guard Station—locale WY-8
Corral Creek Lake—lake WY-8
Corral Creek Ranch—locale MT-8
Corral Creek Rsvr—reservoir ID-8
Corral Creek Rsvr—reservoir MT-8
Corral Creek Summit—summit ID-8
Corral Creek Trail—trail OR-9
Corral Creek Well—well MT-8
Corral Crossing—locale OK-5
Corral Del Tierra (McCobb)—civil CA-9
Corral De Piedra—civil CA-9
Corral de Piedra—hist pl CA-9
Corral De Quati—civil CA-9
Corral De Tierra (Palomares)—civil CA-9
Corral de Tierra Valley—valley CA-9
Corral De Tierra (Vasquez)—civil CA-9
Corral Ditch—canal OR-9
*Corral Draw* CO-8
Corral Draw—valley (3) CO-8
Corral Draw—valley ND-7
Corral Draw—valley OR-9
Corral Draw—valley TX-5
Corral Draw—valley WY-8
**Corrales**—pop pl NM-5
**Corrales**—pop pl PR-3
Corrales (Barrio)—fmr MCD PR-3
Corrales Canyon—valley CA-9
Corrales Canyon—valley NM-5
Corrales Creek—stream NM-5
**Corrales Heights**—pop pl NM-5
Corrales Lateral—canal NM-5
Corrales Main Canal—canal NM-5
Corrales Riverside Drain—canal NM-5
**Corrales (Sandoval PO)**—pop pl NM-5
**Corrales South**—pop pl NM-5
Corrales Windmill—locale (2) TX-5
Corral Flat—flat (2) CA-9
Corral Flat—flat ID-8
Corral Flat—flat (2) OR-9
Corral Flat—flat UT-8
Corral Flat Rsvr—reservoir UT-8
Corral Fork—stream (2) UT-8
Corral Fork Little Creek—stream CO-8
*Corral Gulch* CO-8
Corral Gulch—valley (5) CA-9
Corral Gulch—valley (6) CO-8
Corral Gulch—valley (2) ID-8
Corral Gulch—valley (2) MT-8
Corral Gulch—valley (4) OR-9
Corral Gulch—valley WY-8
Corral Hill—summit CA-9
Corral Hill—summit ID-8
Corral Hill—summit NM-5
Corral Hill—summit OK-5
Corral Hole—basin UT-8
Corral Hollow—valley (2) CA-9
Corral Hollow—valley ID-8
Corral Hollow—valley OR-9
Corral Hollow—valley (8) UT-8
Corral Hollow Creek—stream CA-9
*Corralillos Canyon* CA-9
**Corralitos**—pop pl CA-9
Corralitos Canyon—valley CA-9
*Corralitos Creek* CA-9
Corralitos Creek—stream CA-9
Corralitos Creek—stream (2) NM-5
Corralitos Lagoon—lake CA-9
Corralitos Ranch—hist pl TX-5
Corralitos Ranch—locale CA-9
Corralitos Side Camp—locale NM-5
Corralitos Tank—reservoir NM-5
Corralitos Union Sch—school CA-9
Corralitos Valley—valley CA-9
Corral Junction Number Two Rsvr—reservoir MT-8
*Corral Knoll* UT-8
Corral Knoll—summit UT-8
Corral Lake—basin NV-8
Corral Lake—flat OR-9
Corral Lake—lake AZ-5
Corral Lake—lake (2) CO-8
Corral Lake—lake ID-8
Corral Lake—lake MN-6
Corral Lake—lake OR-9
Corral Lake—lake (2) WA-9
Corral Lake—lake WY-8
Corral Lake Butte—summit NV-8
Corral Lake Rsvr—reservoir NV-8
Corral Lake Well—well NV-8
*Corral Meadow* CA-9
Corral Meadow—flat (5) CA-9
Corral Meadow—flat NV-8
Corral Meadows—flat UT-8
Corral Mtn—summit AZ-5
Corral Mtn—summit (2) CA-9
Corral Mtn—summit CO-8
Corral Mtn—summit OR-9
Corral Mtn—summit UT-8
Corral No 9—other NM-5
*Corral Nueva Spring* AZ-5
Corral Nuevo—locale AZ-5
Corral Park—flat (4) CO-8
Corral Park—flat UT-8
Corral Park Cow Camp—locale CO-8
Corral Park Trail—trail CO-8
Corral Pass—gap WA-9
Corral Peaks—summit CO-8
Corral Point—cape CA-9
Corral Point—cape UT-8
Corral Point—summit UT-8
Corral Pond—reservoir AZ-5
Corral Pond—reservoir SD-7
Corral Reservoir—lake ID-8
Corral Ridge—ridge UT-8
Corral Ridge—ridge WA-9
Corral Rsvr—reservoir MT-8
Corral Rsvr—reservoir (2) OR-9
Corral Spring—spring (5) AZ-5
Corral Spring—spring (2) CA-9
Corral Spring—spring (2) ID-8
Corral Spring—spring (8) NV-8
Corral Spring—spring (4) OR-9
Corral Spring—spring UT-8
Corral Spring—spring WA-9
Corral Spring—spring (2) WY-8
*Corral Spring Mountain* AZ-5
Corral Spring No 1—spring CO-8
Corral Spring No 2—spring CO-8
Corral Springs—spring CA-9
Corral Springs Creek—stream NV-8
Corral Springs Draw—valley CO-8
Corral Springs Trail—trail OR-9
Corral Swamp—swamp OR-9
Corral Swamp Trail—trail OR-9
Corral Tank—reservoir (5) AZ-5
Corral Tank—reservoir (3) NM-5
Corral Tank—reservoir (3) TX-5
Corral Tanks—reservoir AZ-5
Corral Valley—basin (2) CA-9
Corral Valley—valley AZ-5
Corral Valley—valley CA-9
Corral Valley Creek—stream CA-9
Corral Valley Trail (historical)—trail CA-9
**Corral Viejo**—pop pl PR-3
Corral Viejo Canyon—valley CA-9
Corral Wash—stream NV-8
Corral Wash—valley UT-8
Corral Waterhole—reservoir OR-9
*Corral Well* OR-9
Corral Well—well (3) AZ-5
Corral Well—well NM-5
Corral Well—well TX-5
Corral Windmill—locale NM-5
Corral Windmill—locale (2) TX-5
Correco Canyon—valley CA-9
**Correct**—pop pl IN-6
Correction Creek—stream WI-6
Correction Hosp—hospital NY-2
Correction Rsvr—reservoir ID-8
**Correctionville**—pop pl IA-7
Correctionville Cem—cemetery IA-7
**Corregidor (subdivision)**—pop pl NC-3
Corregimiento Plaza Theater—hist pl PR-3
Correhuella, Arroyo—valley TX-5
Correhuella Tank—reservoir TX-5
*Correis Branch* VA-3
Correjo Crossing—locale AZ-5
Correl Cem—cemetery OH-6
**Correll**—pop pl MN-6
Correll Branch—stream NC-3
Correll Branch—stream OK-5
Correll Cem—cemetery TN-4
Correll Creek—stream IN-6
Correll Ditch—canal OR-9
Correllos House (historical)—locale AZ-5
**Correll Park (subdivision)**—pop pl NC-3
Correll Ranch—locale NE-7
Correll Ridge—ridge TN-4
*Correll Run* WV-2
Corrells Branch—stream VA-3
Correll's Farm and Lawn Supply—hist pl DE-2
*Corrells Ferry* NJ-2
Corren Knob—summit WV-2
*Corren Mountain* ID-8
Correo—locale NM-5
Correo Spring—spring NM-5
Corre Valley Country Club—other AZ-5
Corr Hill—summit VT-1
**Corridon**—pop pl MO-7
Corridon Hollow—valley MO-7
Corridon-Reynolds Cem—cemetery MO-7
Corridon-Reynolds Sch—school MO-7
Corridor Bayou—gut LA-4
Corrie Cem—cemetery IL-6
Corriedale Ranch—locale WY-8
Corrier, Lake—reservoir NC-3
Corrigall Drain—canal MI-6
Corrigal Spring—spring (2) OR-9
Corrigal Spring Campground—park OR-9
**Corrigan**—pop pl TX-5
Corrigan, Bernard, House—hist pl MO-7
Corrigan, Thos., Bldg—hist pl MO-7
Corrigan (CCD)—cens area TX-5
Corrigan Hill—summit NY-2
Corrigan Hole—lake TX-5
Corrigan Lake—lake OR-9
Corrigan Lake—reservoir KS-7
Corrigan Mtn—summit MT-8
*Corrigan Peak* AZ-5
Corrigan Playground—park MI-6
Corrigan Reef—bar FL-3
Corrigan Ridge—ridge ID-8
Corrigan Sch—school NE-7
**Corriganville**—pop pl MD-2
Corrigenda Guard Station—locale WA-9
*Corrigen Hill* NY-2
Corriher, Lake—reservoir NC-3
Corriher Field—park NC-3
Corriher Grange Hall—hist pl NC-3
**Corriher Heights**—pop pl NC-3
Corriher Lipe JHS—school NC-3
*Corrila Lake* PA-2
**Corrine**—pop pl PA-2
Corrine, Lake—lake FL-3
Corrine Drive Baptist Ch—church FL-3
**Corrine (historical)**—pop pl MS-4
Corrine Lake—lake WI-6
Corrine Lake—reservoir CA-9
**Corrinne**—pop pl WV-2
Corrin Sch—school SD-7
*Corrinth* ND-7
Corrizalillo Spring—spring NM-5
Corrode Run—stream IN-6
**Corrona**—pop pl MS-4
*Corror* PW-9
*Corrora* PW-9
Corrotoman Cem—cemetery VA-3
Corrotoman Ch—church VA-3
Corrotoman Point—cape VA-3
*Corrotoman River* VA-3
Corrotoman River—stream VA-3
Corrowaugh Swamp—stream VA-3
*Corrs Church* AL-4
*Corrugated Ridge* MT-8
Corrugate Ridge—ridge MT-8
Corrumpa Cem—cemetery NM-5
Corrumpa Creek—stream NM-5
Corrumpa Creek—stream OK-5
Corry—locale MO-7
Corry—locale TX-5
**Corry**—pop pl PA-2
*Corry Area High School* PA-2
Corry Branch—stream MO-7
Corry City—civil PA-2
Corry City Mine—mine CO-8
**Corry Field**—pop pl FL-3
Corry Field Shopping Mart—locale FL-3
Corry JHS—school GA-3
Corry JHS—school TN-4

Corry Junior-Senior HS—*school* ... PA-2
*Corry-Lawrence Airport* ... PA-2
Corry Point—*cape* ... UT-8
*Corry State Fish Hatchery* ... PA-2
Corry Station Naval Technical Training Center—*military* ... FL-3
**Corryton**—*pop pl* ... TN-4
Corryton Baptist Ch—*church* ... TN-4
Corryton (CCD)—*cens area* ... TN-4
Corryton Division—*civil* ... TN-4
Corryton Post Office—*building* ... TN-4
Corryton Sch—*school* ... TN-4
*Corryville* ... OH-6
**Corryville**—*pop pl* (2) ... OH-6
Corryville Playground—*park* ... OH-6
Corsair Canyon—*valley* ... MA-1
*Corsair Gorge* ... MA-1
Corsepius Island—*island* ... IA-7
Corser Brook—*stream* ... NH-1
*Corser Crook* ... MI-6
Corser Hill—*summit* ... NH-1
Corser Hill Cem—*cemetery* ... NH-1
Corser Lake—*lake* ... AK-9
Corse Sch—*school* ... IA-7
Corset Creek—*stream* ... OR-9
Corset Island—*island* ... FL-3
Corset Lake—*lake* ... MN-6
Corsey Creek—*stream* ... MD-2
Corsey Creek—*stream* ... TX-5
Corsey Grove Ch—*church* ... GA-3
**Corsica**—*pop pl* ... PA-2
**Corsica**—*pop pl* ... SD-7
Corsica Borough—*civil* ... PA-2
Corsica Furnace—*locale* ... PA-2
Corsica Lake—*reservoir* ... SD-7
Corsica Lake Dam—*dam* ... SD-7
Corsica Landing—*locale* ... MD-2
Corsicana—*locale* ... MO-7
**Corsicana**—*pop pl* ... TX-5
Corsicana, Lake—*reservoir* ... TX-5
Corsicana (CCD)—*cens area* ... TX-5
Corsicana Country Club—*other* ... TX-5
Corsicana Junction—*uninc pl* ... TX-5
Corsicana Oil Field—*oilfield* ... TX-5
Corsicana Oil Field Discovery Well—*hist pl* ... TX-5
Corsicana Township—*civil* ... MO-7
Corsica Neck—*cape* ... MD-2
Corsica Post Office (historical)—*building* ... PA-2
Corsica River—*stream* ... MD-2
Cors Island—*island* ... WA-9
*Corske Creek* ... CO-8
Corske Creek—*stream* ... CO-8
**Corso**—*pop pl* ... MO-7
**Corson**—*pop pl* ... SD-7
Corson, Alan W., Homestead—*hist pl* ... PA-2
Corson Bay—*swamp* ... NC-3
Corson Branch—*stream* ... NE-7
Corson Brook—*stream* ... ME-1
Corson Corner—*locale* ... ME-1
Corson County—*civil* ... SD-7
Corson Inlet—*bay* ... NJ-2
Corson Peak—*summit* ... UT-8
Corson Place—*locale* ... CO-8
Corsons—*locale* ... PA-2
Corson Sch—*school* ... KS-7
Corsons Corner—*locale* ... ME-1
**Corson Siding**—*pop pl* ... NJ-2
*Corsons Inlet* ... NJ-2
Corson Sound—*bay* ... NJ-2
Corson Township—*civil* ... SD-7
Corssbill Lake—*lake* ... MI-6
Corsser Creek—*stream* ... NV-8
Corstone Sales Company—*hist pl* ... TX-5
*Corstons Inlet* ... NJ-2
**Cort**—*pop pl* ... MN-6
**Corta**—*pop pl* ... AZ-5
**Cortableau**—*pop pl* ... LA-4
Corta Creek—*stream* ... OK-5
**Cortada**—*pop pl* ... PR-3
Cortada Sch—*school* ... CA-9
Cortado Canyon—*valley* ... NM-5
Corta Junction—*locale* ... AZ-5
Corta Ranch—*locale* ... NV-8
Cortaro—*locale* ... AZ-5
Cortaro Road Interchange—*crossing* ... AZ-5
Cortaro RR Station—*building* ... AZ-5
Corta Rsvr rosorvoir ... OR-9
Corta Sacate Windmill—*locale* ... TX-5
Corta Spring—*spring* ... ID-8
Corta Spring—*spring* ... NV-8
*Corta Waterhole* ... OR-9
Corta Well Number One—*well* ... NV-8
Corta Well Number Two—*well* ... NV-8
Cort Creek—*stream* ... MT-8
*Corte De Madera Creek* ... CA-9
Corte De Madera Del Presidio—*civil* ... CA-9
**Cortelyou**—*pop pl* ... AL-4
*Cortelyou Baptist Church* ... AL-4
Cortelyou Ch—*church* ... AL-4
Cortelyou Elem Sch (historical)—*school* ... AL-4
Cortelyou Spring—*spring* ... CA-9
**Corte Madera**—*pop pl* ... CA-9
Corte Maderaa Channel—*channel* ... CA-9
Corte Madera Creek—*stream* (2) ... CA-9
Corte Madera Del Rprsidio, Arroyo—*stream* ... CA-9
Corte Madera De Novato—*civil* ... CA-9
Corte Madera Mtn—*summit* ... CA-9
Corte Madera Ridge—*ridge* ... CA-9
Corte Madera Sch—*school* ... CA-9
Corte Madera Trail—*trail* ... CA-9
Corte Madera Valley—*valley* ... CA-9
Cortena—*locale* ... CA-9
**Corten Torres**—*pop pl* ... GU-9
Corteo Peak—*summit* ... WA-9
Cortes, Cape—*cape* ... CA-9
**Cortese**—*pop pl* ... IL-6
Cortes Lake—*lake* ... MN-6
*Cortex Creek* ... WY-8
*Cortez* ... FL-3
Cortez—*locale* ... CA-9
Cortez—*locale* ... PA-2
**Cortez**—*pop pl* ... CO-8
**Cortez**—*pop pl* ... FL-3
**Cortez**—*pop pl* ... NV-8
**Cortez**—*pop pl* ... PA-2
Cortez, Lake—*lake* ... FL-3
Cortez, Lake—*lake* ... WA-9
Cortez Airstrip Airp—*airport* ... NV-8
*Cortez Beach* ... FL-3
Cortez Bridge—*bridge* ... FL-3
Cortez Canyon—*valley* ... CA-9
Cortez Canyon—*valley* ... NV-8
Cortez Cem—*cemetery* ... TX-5
Cortez Creek—*stream* ... KS-7
Cortez Creek—*stream* ... WY-8
**Cortez Estates (subdivision)**—*pop pl* ... FL-3
Cortez Filtration Plant—*other* ... CO-8
Cortez HS—*school* ... AZ-5
Cortez Mine—*mine* ... NV-8
Cortez-Montezuma County Airport—*airport* ... CO-8
Cortez Mtns—*range* ... NV-8
Cortez Park—*park* ... AZ-5
Cortez Park—*park* ... FL-3
Cortez Peak—*summit* ... AZ-5
Cortez Plaza (Shop Ctr)—*locale* ... FL-3
Cortez Road—*post sta* ... FL-3
Cortez Road Baptist Ch—*church* ... FL-3
Cortez Road Plaza (Shop Ctr)—*locale* ... FL-3
Cortez Sch—*school* (3) ... CA-9
Cortez Sch—*school* ... NM-5
Cortez Sch (historical)—*school* ... PA-2
Cortez Spring—*spring* ... CA-9
**Corticelli**—*pop pl* ... MO-7
Corticelli Ch—*church* ... MO-7
Cortina Creek—*stream* ... CA-9
**Cortina Rancheria**—*pop pl* ... CA-9
Cortina Ridge—*ridge* ... CA-9
*Cortland* ... SD-7
Cortland—*locale* ... WV-2
**Cortland**—*pop pl* ... IL-6
**Cortland**—*pop pl* ... IN-6
**Cortland**—*pop pl* ... NE-7
**Cortland**—*pop pl* ... NY-2
**Cortland**—*pop pl* ... OH-6
Cortland Cem—*cemetery* ... IN-6
Cortland Cem—*cemetery* ... WI-6
Cortland Country Club—*other* ... NY-2
**Cortland (County)**—*pop pl* ... NY-2
Cortland County Courthouse—*hist pl* ... NY-2
Cortland County Poor Farm—*hist pl* ... NY-2
Cortland Elem Sch—*school* ... IN-6
Cortland Fire HQ—*hist pl* ... NY-2
Cortland Fork—*stream* ... KY-4
Cortland Lake—*reservoir* ... NY-2
Cortland Natl Fish Hatchery—*other* ... NY-2
Cortland Post Office (historical)—*building* ... TN-4
Cortland Sch—*school* ... KY-4
*Cortlandt* ... SD-7
*Cortland Township* ... KS-7
**Cortland (Township of)**—*pop pl* ... IL-6
**Cortlandt (Town of)**—*pop pl* ... NY-2
**Cortlandt Township**—*pop pl* ... SD-7
**Cortlandville (Town of)**—*pop pl* ... NY-2
Cortland West—*CDP* ... NY-2
**Cortner**—*pop pl* ... TN-4
Cortner Branch—*stream* ... TN-4
Cortner Cem—*cemetery* (2) ... TN-4
Cortner Lake—*reservoir* ... TN-4
Cortner Lake Dam—*dam* ... TN-4
Cortner Post Office (historical)—*building* ... TN-4
Cortners Mill—*locale* ... TN-4
Cortney Lake Dam—*dam* ... MS-4
Corto, Arroyo—*stream* ... CA-9
Corto Creek—*stream* ... ID-8
**Corton**—*pop pl* ... WV-2
Cortright Creek—*stream* ... WA-9
Cortright Creek Trail—*trail* ... WA-9
Cortright Point—*cape* ... WA-9
Cortright-Van Patten Mill—*hist pl* ... MI-6
**Cortsville**—*pop pl* ... OH-6
Cort Well—*well* ... AZ-5
**Coruco**—*pop pl* ... NM-5
Coruick Lake—*lake* ... WI-6
**Corum**—*pop pl* ... OK-5
Corum Branch—*stream* ... TN-4
Corum Cem—*cemetery* ... AL-4
Corum Cem—*cemetery* ... OK-5
Corum Cem—*cemetery* ... TN-4
Corum Chapel—*church* ... AL-4
*Corum Chapel Missionary Baptist Ch* ... AL-4
Corum Creek—*stream* ... KS-7
Corum Hill Ch—*church* ... TN-4
Corum (historical)—*locale* ... AL-4
Corum Hollow—*valley* ... AL-4
*Corumoran Sho* ... PW-9
Corum Post Office (historical)—*building* ... TN-4
*Corun* ... AL-4
*Corundel Stream* ... ME-1
Corundum Hill—*summit* ... NC-3
Corundum Point—*cape* ... MN-6
**Corunna**—*pop pl* ... IN-6
**Corunna**—*pop pl* ... KY-4
**Corunna**—*pop pl* ... MI-6
Corunna Cem—*cemetery* ... IN-6
Corunna Sch—*school* ... MD-2
Coruth Branch—*stream* ... KY-4
Corva—*locale* ... AZ-5
Corva Hill—*summit* ... AZ-5
*Corvallis* ... KS-7
**Corvallis**—*pop pl* ... MT-8
**Corvallis**—*pop pl* ... OR-9
Corvallis Arts Center—*hist pl* ... OR-9
Corvallis Canal—*canal* ... MT-8
Corvallis (CCD)—*cens area* ... OR-9
Corvallis Cem—*cemetery* ... MT-8
Corvallis Country Club—*other* ... OR-9
Corvallis (historical)—*locale* ... KS-7
Corvallis Hotel—*hist pl* ... OR-9
Corvallis HS—*school* ... CA-9
Corvallis Junction—*locale* ... OR-9
Corvallis Municipal Airp—*airport* ... OR-9
Corvallis Rsvr—*reservoir* ... OR-9
Corvallis Sch—*school* (2) ... CA-9
Corvallis Siding—*locale* ... MT-8
Corvallis Watershed Wild Animal Ref—*park* ... OR-9
Corva Tank—*reservoir* ... AZ-5
*Corvel Lake* ... NE-7
Corvell Park—*park* ... NE-7
Corver Ranches Recreation Center—*park* ... FL-3
Corvette Ledge—*bar* ... ME-1
Corvie Bay—*bay* ... AK-9
Corvin Cem—*cemetery* ... TN-4
Corvin Hollow—*valley* ... TN-4
Corvus Creek—*stream* ... ID-8
**Corvuso**—*pop pl* ... MN-6
Corwells Millpond—*reservoir* ... NC-3
**Corwin**—*pop pl* (2) ... IN-6
**Corwin**—*pop pl* ... KS-7
**Corwin**—*pop pl* ... NY-2
**Corwin**—*pop pl* ... OH-6
Corwina Park—*park* ... CO-8
Corwin Bluff—*cliff* ... AK-9
Corwin-Bolin House—*hist pl* ... OH-6
Corwin Branch—*stream* ... IL-6
Corwin Cem—*cemetery* ... NY-2
Corwin Creek—*stream* ... AK-9
Corwin Ditch—*canal* ... IN-6
Corwine Cem—*cemetery* ... OH-6
Corwin House—*hist pl* ... OH-6
Corwin JHS—*school* ... CO-8
Corwin Mine—*mine* ... AK-9
Corwin Ridge—*ridge* ... WI-6
Corwin Rock—*bar* ... ME-1
Corwin Rock—*island* ... AK-9
Corwin Sch—*school* ... IL-6
Corwin Sch—*school* ... MI-6
Corwin Sch Number 3—*school* ... MI-6
**Corwins Corners**—*pop pl* ... PA-2
*Corwins Lake* ... PA-2
**Corwin Springs**—*pop pl* ... MT-8
Corwin Township—*fmr MCD* ... IA-7
**Corwin Township**—*pop pl* ... ND-7
**Corwin (Township of)**—*pop pl* ... IL-6
*Corwith* ... IL-6
**Corwith**—*pop pl* ... IA-7
Corwith Cem—*cemetery* ... IA-7
**Corwith (Township of)**—*pop pl* ... MI-6
Cory—*locale* ... CA-9
Cory—*locale* ... KY-4
**Cory**—*pop pl* ... CO-8
**Cory**—*pop pl* ... IN-6
Cory, Ambrose, House—*hist pl* ... OH-6
Cory Branch—*stream* (2) ... KY-4
Cory Branch—*stream* ... TN-4
Cory Brook—*stream* ... CT-1
Cory Brook—*stream* ... MN-6
Cory Canyon—*valley* ... CA-9
Cory Cem—*cemetery* ... IN-6
Cory Cem—*cemetery* (2) ... MS-4
Cory Cem—*cemetery* ... SC-3
Cory Ch—*church* ... OH-6
Cory Corners—*locale* ... NY-2
*Cory Creek* ... NV-8
*Cory Creek* ... PA-2
Coryden Run—*stream* ... IN-6
Cory Ditch—*canal* ... CA-9
Cory Ditch—*canal* ... OR-9
**Corydon**—*pop pl* ... IN-6
**Corydon**—*pop pl* ... IA-7
**Corydon**—*pop pl* ... KY-4
Corydon Battle Site—*hist pl* ... IN-6
Corydon Bridge (historical)—*bridge* ... IA-7
Corydon (CCD)—*cens area* ... KY-4
Corydon Cem—*cemetery* ... IA-7
Corydon Cem—*cemetery* ... KY-4
Corydon City Hall—*building* ... IA-7
Corydon Country Club—*other* ... IN-6
*Corydon Creek - in part* ... PA-2
Corydon Hist Dist—*hist pl* ... IN-6
**Corydon (historical)**—*pop pl* ... IA-7
**Corydon (historical)**—*pop pl* ... PA-2
*Corydon Junction* ... IN-6
**Corydon Junction**—*pop pl* ... IN-6
Corydon Pike Sch—*school* ... IN-6
Corydon Township—*fmr MCD* ... IA-7
*Corydon (Township of)* ... PA-2
**Corydon (Township of)**—*pop pl* ... PA-2
Corydon Water Works Dam Number 1—*dam* ... IN-6
Corydon Water Works Dam Number 2—*dam* ... IN-6
**Coryell**—*pop pl* ... TX-5
Coryell Cem—*cemetery* ... IN-6
Coryell Ch—*church* ... TX-5
Coryell Chapel—*church* ... NE-7
*Coryell City* ... TX-5
**Coryell (County)**—*pop pl* ... TX-5
Coryell County Courthouse—*hist pl* ... TX-5
Coryell Creek—*stream* ... KS-7
Coryell Creek—*stream* ... TX-5
Coryell Island—*island* ... MI-6
**Coryell Islands**—*pop pl* ... MI-6
Coryell Pass—*gap* ... OR-9
*Coryell's* ... MI-6
*Coryells* ... PA-2
*Coryells Ferry* ... NJ-2
*Coryells Ferry* ... PA-2
Coryell Valley Ch—*church* ... TX-5
Coryeon Point—*cape* ... MI-6
Cory Flat—*flat* ... MT-8
Cory Grove Cem—*cemetery* ... IA-7
Cory Grove Ch—*church* ... IA-7
Cory Hill—*summit* ... NY-2
Cory Lake—*lake* ... IN-6
Coryland—*locale* ... PA-2
Cory Marsh State Game Mngmt Area—*park* ... IA-7
*Cory Middle School* ... AL-4
Cory Mine—*mine* ... CA-9
*Cory Peak* ... NV-8
Cory Peak—*summit* ... CA-9
*Cory Post Office* ... CO-8
Cory-Rawson HS—*school* ... OH-6
Cory Rsvr—*reservoir* ... OR-9
**Corys**—*pop pl* ... NC-3
Corys Brook—*stream* ... NJ-2
Cory Sch—*school* ... AL-4
Cory Sch—*school* ... CA-9
Cory Sch—*school* ... CO-8
Cory Sch—*school* ... IA-7
*Corys Creek* ... IN-6
Corys Island—*island* ... MA-1
*Coryville* ... IN-6
**Coryville**—*pop pl* ... OH-6
**Coryville**—*pop pl* ... PA-2
Corzine Cem—*cemetery* ... KS-7
*Cosa* ... AL-4
Cosby—*locale* ... TN-4
**Cosby**—*pop pl* ... MO-7
Cosby Acad (historical)—*school* ... TN-4
Cosby Bridge—*bridge* ... TN-4
Cosby Bridge—*bridge* ... VA-3
Cosby Cem—*cemetery* ... AR-4
Cosby Cem—*cemetery* ... IL-6
Cosby Cem—*cemetery* ... TN-4
Cosby Ch—*church* ... KY-4
Cosby Creek—*stream* ... TN-4
Cosby Ford—*crossing* ... TN-4
*Cosby Gap* ... NC-3
*Cosby Gap* ... TN-4
Cosby Hollow—*valley* ... AL-4
Cosby Hollow—*valley* ... TN-4
Cosby Knob—*summit* ... NC-3
Cosby Knob—*summit* ... TN-4
Cosby Memorial Ch—*church* ... VA-3
Cosby Post Office—*building* ... TN-4
Cosby Sch—*school* ... TN-4
Cosbys Corners—*locale* ... VA-3
Cosbys Lake—*reservoir* ... VA-3
Cosby Spring—*spring* ... TX-5
**Cos Cob**—*pop pl* ... CT-1
Cos Cob Harbor—*bay* ... CT-1
Cos Cob Pond—*lake* ... CT-1
Coscorie Branch—*stream* ... VA-3
Cosden Bldg—*hist pl* ... OK-5
Cosden Lake—*reservoir* ... TX-5
Cosden Refinery—*other* ... TX-5
Cosden West Oil Field—*oilfield* ... TX-5
Cosena Spring—*spring* ... OR-9
*Coseta* ... AL-4
Cosey Branch—*stream* ... SC-3
Cosey Ch—*church* ... AL-4
*Coseys Old Field* ... AL-4
**Coseytown**—*pop pl* ... PA-2
**Cosfort (historical)**—*pop pl* ... NC-3
*Cosgrave* ... NV-8
Cosgrave Canyon—*valley* ... NV-8
Cosgrave Hill—*summit* ... WA-9
Cosgriff Memorial Sch—*school* ... UT-8
Cosgriff Ranch—*locale* ... MT-8
Cosgrove—*locale* ... AR-4
Cosgrove—*locale* ... NV-8
**Cosgrove**—*pop pl* ... IA-7
**Cosgrove**—*pop pl* ... MO-7
**Cosgrove**—*pop pl* ... PA-2
Cosgrove, Carson H., House—*hist pl* ... MN-6
Cosgrove Aqueduct—*canal* ... MA-1
Cosgrove Brook—*stream* ... NY-2
Cosgrove Canyon—*valley* ... CO-8
Cosgrove Cem—*cemetery* ... TX-5
Cosgrove Creek—*stream* ... CA-9
Cosgrove Lake—*lake* ... WI-6
Cosgrove Sch—*school* ... NY-2
Cosgrove Shoal—*bar* ... FL-3
*Coshaqua Creek* ... NY-2
Coshatte Agricultural Society Hall—*locale* ... TX-5
Coshatte Cem—*cemetery* ... TX-5
*Coshattee* ... AL-4
*Coshattee* ... TX-5
**Coshocton**—*pop pl* ... OH-6
**Coshocton (County)**—*pop pl* ... OH-6
Coshocton County Courthouse—*hist pl* ... OH-6
Coshocton (Township of)—*other* ... OH-6
Cosho Peak—*summit* ... WA-9
*Coshow Flat* ... OR-9
*Coshow Spring* ... OR-9
*Cosiens Inlet* ... NJ-2
Cosio Knob—*summit* ... CA-9
Coskakat—*locale* ... AK-9
**Coskata**—*pop pl* ... MA-1
Coskata Beach—*beach* ... MA-1
Coskata Pond—*lake* ... MA-1
*Coskaty* ... MA-1
*Coskaty Beach* ... MA-1
*Coskaty Pond* ... MA-1
Coski Creek—*stream* ... ID-8
Cosklos Elkview Airp—*airport* ... PA-2
Cosley Lake—*lake* ... MT-8
Cosley Lake Cutoff Trail—*trail* ... MT-8
Cosley Ridge—*ridge* ... MT-8
Cosman Cem—*cemetery* ... NY-2
Cosme—*locale* ... FL-3
Cosme Tank—*lake* ... NM-5
Cosmic Cavern—*cave* ... AR-4
Cosmit Ind Res—*reserve* ... CA-9
Cosmit Peak—*summit* ... CA-9
**Cosmo**—*pop pl* ... FL-3
Cosmo Cem—*cemetery* ... FL-3
Cosmo Mine (underground)—*mine* ... AL-4
Cosmo Park—*park* ... MO-7
**Cosmopolis**—*pop pl* ... WA-9
Cosmopolitan Community Ch—*church* ... NC-3
Cosmopolitan Creek—*stream* ... ID-8
Cosmopolitan Mine—*mine* ... NV-8
Cosmus—*locale* ... OH-6
**Cosmos**—*pop pl* ... MN-6
*Cosmosa* ... KS-7
Cosmos Cem—*cemetery* ... MN-6
Cosmos Club—*hist pl* ... DC-2
Cosmos Cove—*bay* ... AK-9
*Cosmos Creek* ... ID-8
Cosmos Creek—*stream* ... AK-9
**Cosmos Heights**—*pop pl* ... NY-2
Cosmos Hill—*summit* ... NY-2
Cosmos Mtn—*summit* ... AK-9
Cosmos Pass—*channel* ... AK-9
Cosmos Peak—*summit* ... AK-9
Cosmos Playground—*park* ... CA-9
Cosmos Point—*cape* ... AK-9
Cosmos Range—*other* ... AK-9
**Cosmos (Township of)**—*pop pl* ... MN-6
**Cosmo Township**—*pop pl* ... NE-7
Cosmus—*locale* ... PA-2
Cosna—*locale* ... AK-9
Cosna Bluff—*cliff* ... AK-9
Cosnahan Cem—*cemetery* ... GA-3
Cosna River—*stream* ... AK-9
Cosna Slough—*stream* ... AK-9
Cosner Branch—*stream* ... IN-6
Cosner Cem—*cemetery* ... IL-6
Cosner Gap—*gap* ... WV-2
Cosner Ranch—*locale* ... WY-8
*Cosners* ... WV-2
*Cosners Branch* ... IN-6
Cosner Sch—*school* ... IL-6
Cosnino—*locale* ... AZ-5
Cosnino Interchange—*crossing* ... AZ-5
Cosnino Overpass—*crossing* ... AZ-5
Cosnino RR Station—*building* ... AZ-5
Cosnino Tank—*reservoir* ... AZ-5
*Coso* ... CA-9
Coso—*locale* (2) ... CA-9
Coso Basin—*basin* ... CA-9
Coso Hot Springs—*hist pl* ... CA-9
Coso Hot Springs—*spring* ... CA-9
Coso Junction—*locale* ... CA-9
Coso Peak—*summit* ... CA-9
Coso Range—*range* ... CA-9
Coso Springs—*spring* ... CA-9
Coso Wash—*stream* ... CA-9
Cosper—*locale* ... AZ-5
**Cosper**—*pop pl* ... OR-9
Cosper Bend—*bend* ... AL-4
Cosper Cem—*cemetery* ... IN-6
Cosper Cem—*cemetery* ... LA-4
Cosper Creek—*stream* ... OR-9
*Cospers Bend* ... AL-4
**Cospers Bend (subdivision)**—*pop pl* ... AL-4
**Cosperville**—*pop pl* ... IN-6
*Cosquitt* ... MA-1
Coss, V. R., House—*hist pl* ... OK-5
Cossa Boones Branch—*stream* ... NJ-2
Cossack Tunnel—*tunnel* ... ID-8
Cossaduck Hill—*summit* ... CT-1
Cossalman Lake—*lake* ... WA-9
Cossar State Park—*park* ... MS-4
Cossart—*locale* ... PA-2
Cossatot Cem—*cemetery* ... AR-4
Cossatot Mountains—*ridge* ... AR-4
Cossatot River—*stream* ... AR-4
**Cossayuna**—*pop pl* ... NY-2
Cossayuna Cem—*cemetery* ... NY-2
Cossayuna Lake—*lake* ... NY-2
**Cossayuna Lake**—*pop pl* ... NY-2
**Coss Corners**—*pop pl* ... NY-2
Cossell Lake—*reservoir* ... KS-7
Cossell Lake Dam—*dam* ... KS-7
*Cosser Creek* ... NV-8
*Cosset Creek* ... OH-6
Cossett Creek—*stream* ... OH-6
Cossey Branch—*stream* ... AL-4
Cossey Sch—*school* ... AR-4
Coss Ferry (historical)—*locale* ... AL-4
Cossiers Creek—*stream* ... FL-3
Cossin Cem—*cemetery* ... WV-2
Cossitt, Frederick H., Library—*hist pl* ... CT-1
*Cossitt Cemetery* ... MS-4
Cossitt Sch—*school* ... IL-6
Cosson Mill—*locale* ... FL-3
Cosson Mill—*stream* ... FL-3
**Cossville**—*pop pl* ... MO-7
**Cost**—*pop pl* ... TX-5
Costa, Cayo—*island* ... FL-3
Costa (Barrio)—*fmr MCD* ... PR-3
Costa Creek—*stream* ... CA-9
Costa Del Sol Golf Course—*locale* ... FL-3
Costa Fork—*stream* ... AK-9
Costa Gulch—*valley* ... CA-9
**Costa (historical)**—*pop pl* ... AL-4
Costain Hill—*summit* ... OK-5
**Costa Mesa**—*pop pl* ... CA-9
Costa Mesa Air Natl Guard Station—*building* ... CA-9
Costa Mesa HS—*school* ... CA-9
Costa Mesa (sta.)—*uninc pl* ... CA-9
Costano Sch—*school* ... CA-9
Costapia, Bayou—*stream* ... MS-4
*Costapla Creek* ... MS-4
Costa Plente, Rancho—*locale* ... AZ-5
Costa Rica, Arroyo—*valley* ... TX-5
**Costa (RR name Brushton)**—*pop pl* ... WV-2
Costas Lake—*reservoir* ... MS-4
Costas Lake Dam—*dam* ... MS-4
Costa Verde Plaza (Shop Ctr)—*locale* ... FL-3
Cost Cem—*cemetery* ... IL-6
Cost Cem—*cemetery* ... OH-6
Costeau Park—*park* ... CA-9
Costella Coulee—*valley* ... MT-8
**Costello**—*pop pl* ... PA-2
Costello Cem—*cemetery* ... PA-2
Costello Coulee—*valley* ... MT-8
Costello Creek—*stream* ... AK-9
Costello Creek—*stream* ... MI-6
Costello Ditch—*canal* ... IN-6
*Costello Island* ... NY-2
Costello Island—*island* ... TX-5
Costello Park—*park* ... MA-1
Costello Place—*locale* ... NV-8
Costello Point—*cape* ... SD-7
Costello Recreation Center—*park* ... CA-9
Costello Sch—*school* ... IL-6
Costello Spring—*spring* ... AZ-5
Costello Spring—*spring* ... MN-6
Costello Tank—*reservoir* ... AZ-5
Costelow—*locale* ... KY-4
Costel Windmill—*locale* ... NM-5
Costen—*locale* ... MD-2
Costen, William, House—*hist pl* ... MD-2
Costen Branch—*stream* ... MD-2
Costen Drain—*canal* ... MI-6
Costen House—*hist pl* ... MD-2
Coster—*locale* ... IA-7
Coster—*locale* ... MD-2
Coster—*uninc pl* ... TN-4
*Coster Blanches* ... KS-7
Coster Cove—*bay* ... MD-2
**Coster Yards**—*pop pl* ... TN-4
**Costigan**—*pop pl* ... ME-1
Costigan Brook—*stream* ... ME-1
Costigan Creek—*stream* ... MI-6
Costigan Slough—*lake* ... SD-7
**Costilla**—*pop pl* ... NM-5
Costilla Canal—*canal* ... CO-8
Costilla Canyon—*valley* ... NM-5
Costilla Creek—*stream* ... CO-8
Costilla Creek—*stream* (2) ... NM-5
*Costilla Creek Number One* ... CO-8
Costilla Crossing Bridge—*hist pl* ... CO-8
Costilla Lodge—*locale* ... NM-5
*Costilla Number One Creek* ... CO-8
*Costilla Peak* ... CO-8
Costilla Peak—*summit* ... NM-5
*Costilla River* ... CO-8
Costilla Rsvr—*reservoir* ... NM-5
Costilla Tank—*reservoir* ... TX-5
*Costilleia Lake* ... CO-8
Costilow Lake—*reservoir* ... MS-4
*Costin* ... IL-6
Costin—*locale* ... NE-7
Costin—*locale* ... NC-3
Costin Pond—*reservoir* ... VA-3
Costley Millpond—*lake* ... GA-3
Costner Lake—*reservoir* ... MS-4
Costner Post Office (historical)—*building* ... TN-4
Costner Sch—*school* ... NC-3
Costo Lake—*lake* ... CO-8
Coston Hill—*summit* ... AL-4
**Costonia**—*pop pl* ... OH-6
*Costons Corner* ... ME-1
**Costons Corner**—*pop pl* ... ME-1
*Costons Inlet* ... NJ-2
Costons Pond—*reservoir* ... AL-4
Cost Sch—*school* ... TX-5
Cosuata (historical)—*civil* ... MA-1
Cosumne—*locale* ... CA-9
*Cosumnes* ... CA-9
Cosumnes—*civil* ... CA-9
Cosumnes Copper Mine—*mine* ... CA-9
Cosumnes Mine—*mine* ... CA-9
Cosumnes River—*stream* ... CA-9
Cosumnes River Overflow—*stream* ... CA-9
Cosumnes River Sch—*school* ... CA-9
**Cosunme**—*pop pl* ... CA-9
Coswell Bayou—*stream* ... LA-4
Cosy Dell—*locale* ... CA-9
Cosy Dell—*valley* ... CA-9
**Cosytown**—*pop pl* ... PA-2
*Cota* ... LA-4
Cota Brook—*stream* ... VT-1
Cotaco Ch—*church* ... AL-4
*Cotaco County* ... AL-4
Cotaco Creek—*stream* ... AL-4
*Cotaco High School* ... AL-4
*Cotaco Landing* ... AL-4
Cotaco Opera House—*hist pl* ... AL-4
Cotaco Post Office (historical)—*building* ... AL-4
Cotaco Sch—*school* ... AL-4
Cotaco Shoals Cave—*cave* ... AL-4
Cotaco Valley—*valley* ... AL-4
**Cotaco (Woodland Mills)**—*pop pl* ... AL-4
Cota Creek—*stream* ... AK-9
Cota Creek—*stream* ... IA-7
*Cotahaga Creek* ... AL-4
Cotahaga Landing (historical)—*locale* ... AL-4
*Cotahager Creek* ... AL-4
Cotahoma Creek—*stream* ... AL-4
Cotal—*area* ... GU-9
*Cotamy* ... MA-1
*Cotamy Bay* ... MA-1
*Cotamy Point* ... MA-1
*CO Tank* ... AZ-5
Cota Round Barns—*hist pl* ... MN-6
*Cotaska Mountain* ... TN-4
Cotas Lake—*lake* ... WI-6
Cotate—*civil* ... CA-9
**Cotati**—*pop pl* ... CA-9
Cotati (Siding)—*locale* ... CA-9
Cot Creek—*stream* ... OR-9
**Cote**—*pop pl* ... KY-4
Cote, Mount—*summit* ... AK-9
**Coteau**—*pop pl* (2) ... LA-4
**Coteau**—*pop pl* ... ND-7
Coteau, Bayou—*stream* ... LA-4
**Coteau Bourgeois**—*pop pl* ... LA-4
Coteau Charles—*area* ... LA-4
Coteau Chevreuil—*area* ... LA-4
Coteau des Prairies—*plain* ... SD-7
Coteau du Missouri—*plain* ... ND-7
*Coteau Frene* ... LA-4
Coteau Frene—*area* ... LA-4
**Coteau Holmes**—*pop pl* ... LA-4
*Coteau Island Lake* ... SD-7
Coteau Island State Public Shooting Area—*park* ... SD-7
*Coteau Lake* ... SD-7
Coteau Mission—*church* ... LA-4
Coteau Pistolet—*area* ... LA-4
**Coteau Rodaire**—*pop pl* ... LA-4
Coteaus, The—*ridge* ... SD-7
Cote Bas—*locale* ... SC-3
Cote Bas Landing—*locale* ... SC-3
Cote Blanche Island—*island* ... LA-4
Cote Blanche Island Oil and Gas Field—*oilfield* ... LA-4
Cote Blanche Landing—*locale* ... LA-4
Cote Bonneville—*hist pl* ... OH-6
Cote Corner—*locale* ... ME-1
Cote Dame Marie—*summit* ... MI-6
Cote Grade—*locale* ... OR-9
Cote House—*hist pl* ... NH-1
Cote Lake—*lake* ... IL-6
Cote Lake—*lake* ... OR-9
*Coteman Lake* ... MI-6
Cote Pond—*reservoir* ... CT-1
Coterell Lake—*lake* ... PA-2
Coterell Lake Dam—*dam* ... PA-2
Coters Tank—*reservoir* ... AZ-5
Cote Sandy—*other* ... MO-7
Cote Sans Dessein—*ridge* ... MO-7
Cote Sans Dessein Archeol Site—*hist pl* ... MO-7
Cote Sans Dessein Township—*civil* ... MO-7
*Cotes Branch* ... WV-2
Cotes Camp—*locale* ... ME-1
Cotes Cem—*cemetery* ... NY-2
Cote Sch Number 2—*school* ... ND-7
**Cotesfield**—*pop pl* ... NE-7
Cotesfield Cem—*cemetery* ... NE-7
Cote Slough—*stream* ... OR-9
Cotes Mill (historical)—*locale* ... MS-4
Cotesworth—*hist pl* ... MS-4
Cotey Branch—*stream* ... AL-4
Coteys Corner—*locale* ... NY-2
Cotham Cem—*cemetery* ... AR-4
Cotham Cem—*cemetery* ... TN-4
Cotham Hill—*summit* ... TN-4
**Cotham (historical)**—*pop pl* ... TN-4
Cotham Hollow—*valley* ... TN-4
Cotham Pond—*lake* ... MO-7
Cothell Meadow Brook—*stream* ... ME-1
Cother Clanton Dam—*dam* ... SD-7
Cotherman Lake—*lake* ... MI-6
Cothern Ch—*church* ... AR-4
Cothern Sch—*school* ... IL-6
Cothern Well—*well* ... NM-5
Cothers Ferry (historical)—*locale* ... MS-4
Cothran Bend—*bend* ... TN-4
Cothran Bridge—*bridge* ... SC-3
Cothran Cem—*cemetery* ... KY-4
Cothran Cem—*cemetery* ... TN-4
Cothran Hill—*summit* ... TN-4
Cothrin Cove—*basin* ... CA-9
Cothrum Ranch—*locale* ... TX-5
Cothwell Branch—*stream* ... MO-7
Cotigo Lake—*reservoir* ... WV-2
Cotile Lake—*reservoir* ... LA-4
Cotillion Hall—*hist pl* ... OR-9

Cottonwood Bayou—*stream* ... LA-4
Cottonwood Bayou—*stream* (2) ... TX-5
Cottonwood Beach—*beach* ... AK-9
**Cottonwood Beach**—*pop pl* ... WA-9
Cottonwood Bench—*bench* ... MT-8
Cottonwood Bench—*bench* ... WY-8
Cottonwood Bend—*bend* ... OR-9
Cottonwood Bend—*bend* ... TX-5
Cottonwood Bottom—*basin* ... MT-8
Cottonwood Bottom—*bend* ... UT-8
Cottonwood Box Spring—*spring* ... AZ-5
Cottonwood Branch—*stream* (6) ... MO-7
Cottonwood Branch—*stream* (15) ... TX-5
Cottonwood Branch Post Office—*building* ... UT-8
Cottonwood Bridge—*bridge* ... OR-9
*Cottonwood Bridge State Park* ... OR-9
Cottonwood Butte—*summit* (2) ... ID-8
*Cottonwood Buttes* ... ID-8
Cottonwood Buttes—*summit* ... OR-9
Cottonwood Cabin—*locale* ... AZ-5
Cottonwood Cabin Spring—*spring* ... OR-9
Cottonwood Camp—*locale* (2) ... AZ-5
Cottonwood Camp—*locale* ... CA-9
Cottonwood Camp—*locale* ... CO-8
Cottonwood Camp—*locale* ... MT-8
Cottonwood Camp—*locale* (2) ... OR-9
Cottonwood Camp—*locale* (2) ... TX-5
Cottonwood Camp—*locale* ... WA-9
Cottonwood Campground—*locale* (2) ... CA-9
Cottonwood Campground—*locale* ... CO-8
Cottonwood Campground—*locale* ... ID-8
Cottonwood Campground—*locale* ... NM-5
Cottonwood Campground—*locale* ... ND-7
Cottonwood Campground—*locale* ... TX-5
Cottonwood Campground—*locale* (2) ... UT-8
Cottonwood Campground—*locale* ... WA-9
Cottonwood Campground—*park* ... OR-9
Cottonwood Canal—*canal* ... LA-4
Cottonwood Canal—*canal* ... WY-8
Cottonwood Canon—*valley* ... NV-8
*Cottonwood Canyon* ... AZ-5
*Cottonwood Canyon* ... CA-9
*Cottonwood Canyon* ... UT-8
Cottonwood Canyon—*valley* (36) ... AZ-5
Cottonwood Canyon—*valley* (17) ... CA-9
Cottonwood Canyon—*valley* (7) ... CO-8
Cottonwood Canyon—*valley* ... MT-8
Cottonwood Canyon—*valley* (4) ... NE-7
Cottonwood Canyon—*valley* (28) ... NV-8
Cottonwood Canyon—*valley* (36) ... NM-5
Cottonwood Canyon—*valley* ... OK-5
Cottonwood Canyon—*valley* (3) ... OR-9
Cottonwood Canyon—*valley* (8) ... TX-5
Cottonwood Canyon—*valley* (40) ... UT-8
Cottonwood Canyon—*valley* (2) ... WA-9
Cottonwood Canyon—*valley* ... WY-8
Cottonwood Canyon Cliff Dwelling—*hist pl* ... UT-8
Cottonwood Canyon Narrows—*gap* ... UT-8
Cottonwood Canyon Trail Two Hundred Sixtysix—*trail* ... AZ-5
Cottonwood Cave—*cave* ... NM-5
Cottonwood (CCD)—*cens area* ... AL-4
Cottonwood Cem—*cemetery* (2) ... AR-4
Cottonwood Cem—*cemetery* ... CA-9
Cottonwood Cem—*cemetery* (2) ... ID-8
Cottonwood Cem—*cemetery* ... IL-6
Cottonwood Cem—*cemetery* (2) ... IA-7
Cottonwood Cem—*cemetery* ... KS-7
Cottonwood Cem—*cemetery* ... LA-4
Cottonwood Cem—*cemetery* (2) ... MN-6
Cottonwood Cem—*cemetery* (2) ... MT-8
Cottonwood Cem—*cemetery* (2) ... NE-7
Cottonwood Cem—*cemetery* (3) ... OK-5
Cottonwood Cem—*cemetery* ... SD-7
Cottonwood Cem—*cemetery* (11) ... TX-5
Cottonwood Cem—*cemetery* ... WY 8
Cottonwood Ch—*church* ... AR-4
Cottonwood Ch—*church* ... IL-6
Cottonwood Ch—*church* ... IN-6
Cottonwood Ch—*church* ... IA-7
Cottonwood Ch—*church* ... KS-7
Cottonwood Ch—*church* ... ND-7
Cottonwood Ch—*church* ... TN-4
Cottonwood Ch—*church* (8) ... TX-5
Cottonwood Chute—*gut* ... MS-4
Cottonwood Chute—*lake* ... AR-4
Cottonwood Chute—*lake* ... LA-4
Cottonwood Chute—*stream* ... MO-7
Cottonwood Circle Two Hundred Thirtythree—*trail* ... AZ-5
*Cottonwood City* ... ND-7
Cottonwood Cliffs—*cliff* ... AZ-5
Cottonwood Community Center—*hist pl* ... OK-5
Cottonwood Community Ch—*church* ... NM-5
Cottonwood Community Hall—*locale* ... MT-8
Cottonwood Community Hall—*locale* ... WY-8
**Cottonwood Condominium, The**—*pop pl* ... UT-8
Cottonwood Corner—*locale* (2) ... AR-4
**Cottonwood Corner**—*pop pl* ... AR-4
Cottonwood Corner Sch—*school* ... NE-7
*Cottonwood Corral Spring* ... AZ-5
*Cottonwood Coulee* ... MT-8
Cottonwood Coulee—*stream* ... MT-8
Cottonwood Coulee—*valley* (7) ... MT-8
Cottonwood Country Club—*other* ... MT-8
Cottonwood Country Club Golf Course—*other* ... AZ-5
**Cottonwood (County)**—*pop pl* ... MN-6
Cottonwood County Courthouse—*hist pl* ... MN-6
Cottonwood Cove—*bay* (2) ... NV-8
Cottonwood Cove—*locale* ... NV-8
**Cottonwood Cove**—*pop pl* ... NY-2
Cottonwood Cove—*valley* ... AZ-5
Cottonwood Cove Spring—*spring* ... AZ-5
**Cotton Wood Cove Subdivision**—*pop pl* ... UT-8
Cottonwood Cow Camp—*locale* ... NM-5
*Cottonwood Creek* ... AL-4
*Cottonwood Creek* ... AZ-5
*Cottonwood Creek* ... CA-9
*Cottonwood Creek* ... CO-8
*Cottonwood Creek* ... ID-8
*Cottonwood Creek* ... KS-7
*Cottonwood Creek* ... MT-8
*Cottonwood Creek* ... NV-8
*Cottonwood Creek* ... NM-5
*Cottonwood Creek* ... OR-9
*Cottonwood Creek* ... SD-7
*Cottonwood Creek* ... TX-5
*Cottonwood Creek* ... UT-8
*Cottonwood Creek* ... WA-9
*Cottonwood Creek* ... WY-8
Cottonwood Creek—*arroyo* ... NV-8
Cottonwood Creek—*stream* ... AL-4
Cottonwood Creek—*stream* (8) ... AK-9
Cottonwood Creek—*stream* (21) ... AZ-5
Cottonwood Creek—*stream* (41) ... CA-9
Cottonwood Creek—*stream* (28) ... CO-8
Cottonwood Creek—*stream* (50) ... ID-8
Cottonwood Creek—*stream* (4) ... IL-6
Cottonwood Creek—*stream* (3) ... IA-7
Cottonwood Creek—*stream* (11) ... KS-7
Cottonwood Creek—*stream* ... MI-6
Cottonwood Creek—*stream* (2) ... MN-6
Cottonwood Creek—*stream* (14) ... MO-7
Cottonwood Creek—*stream* (68) ... MT-8
Cottonwood Creek—*stream* (5) ... NE-7
Cottonwood Creek*—*stream* ... NE-7
Cottonwood Creek—*stream* (6) ... NE-7
Cottonwood Creek—*stream* (37) ... NV-8
Cottonwood Creek—*stream* (9) ... NM-5
Cottonwood Creek—*stream* (5) ... ND-7
Cottonwood Creek—*stream* (20) ... OK-5
Cottonwood Creek—*stream* (31) ... OR-9
Cottonwood Creek—*stream* (23) ... SD-7
Cottonwood Creek—*stream* (105) ... TX-5
Cottonwood Creek—*stream* (28) ... UT-8
Cottonwood Creek—*stream* (16) ... WA-9
Cottonwood Creek—*stream* (64) ... WY-8
Cottonwood Creek—*valley* ... MT-8
Cottonwood Creek Archeol Site—*hist pl* ... NE-7
Cottonwood Creek Basin—*valley* ... SD-7
Cottonwood Creek Canyon—*valley* ... NV-8
Cottonwood Creek Cem—*cemetery* ... AZ-5
Cottonwood Creek Dam—*dam* ... ND-7
Cottonwood Creek Huntington Canal—*canal* ... UT-8
Cottonwood Creek Meadows—*flat* ... CA-9
Cottonwood Creek Oil And Gas Field—*oilfield* ... WY-8
Cottonwood Creek Oil Field—*oilfield* ... TX-5
Cottonwood Creek Sch—*school* ... AZ-5
**Cottonwood Creek Subdivision**—*pop pl* ... UT-8
Cottonwood Creek Trail—*trail* ... OR-9
Cottonwood Creek Turnout—*locale* ... WY-8
Cottonwood Crossing—*locale* ... CO-8
Cottonwood Cutoff—*bend* ... MO-7
Cottonwood Dam—*dam* (2) ... OR-9
Cottonwood Dam—*dam* ... TX-5
Cottonwood Day Sch—*school* ... AZ-5
*Cottonwood Ditch* ... IN-6
Cottonwood Ditch—*canal* ... AZ-5
Cottonwood Ditch—*canal* ... CA-9
Cottonwood Ditch—*canal* (2) ... CO-8
Cottonwood Ditch—*canal* ... IN-6
Cottonwood Ditch—*canal* ... IA-7
Cottonwood Ditch—*canal* ... OH-6
Cottonwood Divide—*ridge* ... CO-8
Cottonwood Divide—*ridge* ... WY-8
Cottonwood Divide Site (LA 55829)—*hist pl* ... NM-5
Cottonwood Division—*civil* ... AL-4
Cottonwood Division—*civil* ... UT-8
Cottonwood Drain—*stream* ... IA-7
Cottonwood Drain—*stream* ... WY-8
*Cottonwood Draw* ... CO-8
*Cottonwood Draw* ... WY-8
Cottonwood Draw—*valley* ... AZ-5
Cottonwood Draw—*valley* (2) ... CO-8
Cottonwood Draw—*valley* ... ID-8
Cottonwood Draw—*valley* ... MT-8
Cottonwood Draw—*valley* ... NV-8
Cottonwood Draw—*valley* (5) ... NM-5
Cottonwood Draw—*valley* ... OR-9
Cottonwood Draw—*valley* ... SD-7
Cottonwood Draw—*valley* (3) ... TX-5
Cottonwood Draw—*valley* (2) ... UT-8
Cottonwood Draw—*valley* (14) ... WY-8
Cottonwood Draw Mesa—*summit* ... NM-5
Cottonwood Elem Sch—*school* ... AZ-5
**Cottonwood Estates**—*pop pl* ... TN-4
**Cottonwood Estates Number One (subdivision)**—*pop pl* ... UT-8
**Cottonwood Estates Subdivision**—*pop pl* ... UT-8
Cottonwood Extension Ditch—*canal* ... CO-8
*Cotton Wood Falls* ... KS-7
Cottonwood Falls—*falls* ... AR-4
Cottonwood Falls—*falls* ... WY-8
**Cottonwood Falls**—*pop pl* ... KS-7
Cottonwood Falls Elem Sch—*school* ... KS-7
Cottonwood Falls Spring—*spring* ... WY-8
Cottonwood Field—*flat* ... NV-8
Cottonwood Field Station Dam—*dam* ... SD-7
Cottonwood Fire Break—*dam* ... CA-9
Cottonwood Flat—*flat* (3) ... CA-9
Cottonwood Flat—*flat* ... TX-5
Cottonwood Flat Cem—*cemetery* ... TX-5
Cottonwood Flats—*flat* ... ID-8
Cottonwood Flats—*flat* ... NM-5
Cottonwood Forest Service Administrative Site—*locale* ... NV-8
Cottonwood Fork—*stream* ... MO-7
Cottonwood Glade—*flat* ... CA-9
Cottonwood Glades—*flat* ... OR-9
**Cottonwood Glade Subdivision**—*pop pl* ... UT-8
Cottonwood Glen—*locale* ... CA-9
*Cottonwood Grove* ... KS-7
**Cottonwood Grove**—*pop pl* ... TN-4
Cottonwood Grove Baptist Ch—*church* ... TN-4
**Cottonwood Grove Condominium**—*pop pl* ... UT-8
Cottonwood Grove Sch—*school* ... KS-7
Cottonwood Grove Sch—*school* (3) ... NE-7
Cottonwood Guard Station—*locale* ... CO-8
Cottonwood Guard Station—*locale* ... UT-8
Cottonwood Guard Station—*locale* ... WA-9
*Cottonwood Gulch* ... MT-8
Cottonwood Gulch—*valley* (2) ... AZ-5
Cottonwood Gulch—*valley* (3) ... CA-9
Cottonwood Gulch—*valley* (13) ... CO-8
Cottonwood Gulch—*valley* ... ID-8
Cottonwood Gulch—*valley* (4) ... MT-8
Cottonwood Gulch—*valley* (6) ... OR-9
Cottonwood Gulch—*valley* (2) ... UT-8
Cottonwood Gulch—*valley* ... WA-9
Cottonwood Gulch Camp—*locale* ... NM-5
Cottonwood Gully—*valley* ... NY-2
Cottonwood Gun Club—*other* ... CA-9
**Cottonwood Heights**—*pop pl* ... UT-8
Cottonwood Heights Sch—*school* ... UT-8
**Cottonwood Heights Subdivision**—*pop pl* (3) ... UT-8
Cottonwood Hill—*summit* ... AZ-5
Cottonwood Hill—*summit* ... NE-7
Cottonwood Hill—*summit* ... UT-8
Cottonwood Hills—*other* ... AK-9
Cottonwood Hills—*range* ... NM-5
**Cottonwood Hills Condo**—*pop pl* ... UT-8
**Cottonwood Hills Subdivision**—*pop pl* ... UT-8
Cottonwood Hist Dist—*hist pl* ... CA-9
**Cottonwood (historical)**—*pop pl* ... OR-9
Cottonwood Holes—*spring* ... UT-8
Cottonwood Hollow—*valley* ... AR-4
Cottonwood Hollow—*valley* ... IA-7
Cottonwood Hollow—*valley* ... MO-7
Cottonwood Hollow—*valley* ... MT-8
Cottonwood Hollow—*valley* (4) ... TX-5
Cottonwood Hollow—*valley* ... UT-8
Cottonwood Hollow—*valley* ... WY-8
Cottonwood Hollows—*valley* ... TX-5
Cottonwood Hosp—*hospital* ... UT-8
Cottonwood Hospital Heliport—*airport* ... UT-8
*Cottonwood Hospital Med Ctr* ... UT-8
Cottonwood Hot Springs—*spring* ... CO-8
Cottonwood HS—*school* ... AL-4
Cottonwood HS—*school* ... UT-8
Cottonwood Island—*island* ... IL-6
Cottonwood Island—*island* ... MO-7
Cottonwood Island—*island* ... NE-7
Cottonwood Island—*island* ... WA-9
Cottonwood Island (historical)—*island* ... SD-7
Cottonwood Island Lower Range—*channel* ... OR-9
Cottonwood Island Lower Range—*channel* ... WA-9
Cottonwood Islands—*area* ... AK-9
Cottonwood Island Upper Range—*channel* ... OR-9
Cottonwood Island Upper Range—*channel* ... WA-9
Cottonwood Job Corps Center—*locale* ... ID-8
Cottonwood Kids Park—*park* ... AZ-5
*Cottonwood Lake* ... CO-8
*Cottonwood Lake* ... MT-8
Cottonwood Lake—*lake* (3) ... AK-9
Cottonwood Lake—*lake* ... CA-9
Cottonwood Lake—*lake* ... ID-8
Cottonwood Lake—*lake* ... IL-6
Cottonwood Lake—*lake* (6) ... MN-6
Cottonwood Lake—*lake* ... MO-7
Cottonwood Lake—*lake* (2) ... MT-8
Cottonwood Lake—*lake* (3) ... NE-7
Cottonwood Lake—*lake* ... NM-5
Cottonwood Lake—*lake* (9) ... ND-7
Cottonwood Lake—*lake* (2) ... OR-9
Cottonwood Lake—*lake* (8) ... SD-7
Cottonwood Lake—*lake* ... TX-5
Cottonwood Lake—*lake* ... UT-8
Cottonwood Lake—*lake* ... WA-9
Cottonwood Lake—*lake* ... WY-8
Cottonwood Lake—*reservoir* ... CA-9
Cottonwood Lake—*reservoir* (3) ... CO-8
Cottonwood Lake—*reservoir* ... TX-5
Cottonwood Lakebed—*flat* ... MN-6
Cottonwood Lake Campground—*locale* ... WY-8
Cottonwood Lake Ch—*church* ... ND-7
Cottonwood Lake (historical)—*lake* ... IL-6
Cottonwood Lake Natl Wildlife Ref—*park* ... ND-7
Cottonwood Lake No. 1—*reservoir* ... CO-8
Cottonwood Lake No. 2—*reservoir* ... CO-8
Cottonwood Lake No. 4—*reservoir* ... CO-8
Cottonwood Lake No. 5—*reservoir* ... CO-8
Cottonwood Lakes—*lake* ... CA-9
Cottonwood Lakes—*lake* ... MT-8
Cottonwood Lakes Foot Trail—*trail* ... CO-8
Cottonwood Lake State Public Shooting Area—*park* ... SD-7
Cottonwood Lake State Wildlife Mngmt Area—*park* ... SD-7
Cottonwood Lake State Wildlife Ref—*park* ... SD-7
**Cottonwood Lake Township**—*pop pl* ... ND-7
**Cottonwood Lake Township**—*pop pl* ... SD-7
Cottonwood Landing—*locale* ... MS-4
Cottonwood Landing Field—*airport* ... AZ-5
Cottonwood Lateral—*canal* ... CO-8
Cottonwood Mall Shop Ctr—*locale* ... UT-8
**Cottonwood Manor Subdivision**—*pop pl* ... UT-8
Cottonwood Marina—*locale* ... NE-7
Cottonwood Maxwell Ditch—*canal* ... CO-8
Cottonwood Meadow—*flat* ... CA-9
Cottonwood Meadow—*flat* ... MT-8
Cottonwood Meadow Dam—*dam* ... OR-9
Cottonwood Meadow Lake—*reservoir* ... OR-9
Cottonwood Meadows—*flat* ... OR-9
Cottonwood Meadows—*locale* ... UT-8
**Cottonwood Meadows Condominium**—*pop pl* ... UT-8
**Cottonwood Meadows Estates Subdivision**—*pop pl* ... UT-8
**Cottonwood Meadows Subdivision**—*pop pl* (2) ... UT-8
Cottonwood Meadows Trail—*trail* ... OR-9
**Cottonwood Meadows Twin Homes Condominium**—*pop pl* ... UT-8
Cottonwood Mesa—*summit* ... AZ-5
Cottonwood Mesa—*summit* ... CO-8
Cottonwood Mine—*mine* ... WY-8
*Cottonwood Mountains* ... AZ-5
Cottonwood Mountains—*other* ... CA-9
Cottonwood Mountains—*range* ... AZ-5
Cottonwood Mountains—*range* (3) ... CA-9
Cottonwood Mountain Trail Sixty six—*trail* ... AZ-5
Cottonwood Mtn—*summit* (3) ... AZ-5
Cottonwood Mtn—*summit* ... CA-9
Cottonwood Mtn—*summit* ... MT-8
Cottonwood Mtn—*summit* ... OR-9
Cottonwood Mtn—*summit* ... TX-5
Cottonwood Mtn—*summit* ... UT-8
Cottonwood Mtn—*summit* ... WY-8
Cottonwood Natural Area—*reserve* ... MT-8
Cottonwood Number One Spring—*spring* ... NV-8
Cottonwood Number Two Spring—*spring* ... NV-8
Cottonwood Number Two Tank—*reservoir* ... AZ-5
Cottonwood-Oak Creek Sch—*school* ... AZ-5
Cottonwood Park—*flat* (2) ... WY-8
Cottonwood Park—*park* ... AZ-5
**Cottonwood Park (subdivision)**—*pop pl* ... AL-4
**Cottonwood Park Subdivision**—*pop pl* ... UT-8
Cottonwood Pass—*gap* ... AZ-5
Cottonwood Pass—*gap* (3) ... CA-9
Cottonwood Pass—*gap* (3) ... CO-8
Cottonwood Pass—*gap* (2) ... NV-8
Cottonwood Pass—*gap* ... SD-7
Cottonwood Pass—*gap* ... UT-8
Cottonwood Pass—*gap* ... WY-8
*Cottonwood Peak* ... UT-8
Cottonwood Peak—*summit* ... AZ-5
Cottonwood Peak—*summit* (2) ... CA-9
Cottonwood Peak—*summit* (2) ... CO-8
Cottonwood Peak—*summit* (2) ... ID-8
Cottonwood Peak—*summit* ... NV-8
Cottonwood Peak—*summit* ... UT-8
Cottonwood Peak—*summit* ... WY-8
Cottonwood Pens—*locale* ... TX-5
Cottonwood Pens Draw—*valley* ... TX-5
Cottonwood Picnic Area—*locale* ... UT-8
Cottonwood Plantation (historical)—*locale* ... MS-4
Cottonwood Point—*cape* (2) ... AK-9
Cottonwood Point—*cape* (2) ... AR-4
Cottonwood Point—*cape* ... IA-7
Cottonwood Point—*cape* ... WA-9
Cottonwood Point—*cliff* ... AZ-5
Cottonwood Point—*cliff* ... CO-8
**Cottonwood Point**—*pop pl* ... MO-7
**Cottonwood Point**—*pop pl* ... NY-2
Cottonwood Point—*summit* ... ID-8
Cottonwood Point—*summit* (2) ... UT-8
Cottonwood Point Dikes—*levee* ... TN-4
Cottonwood Point Eagle Bar—*bar* ... TN-4
Cottonwood Point Ferry (historical)—*locale* ... TN-4
Cottonwood Point Landing—*locale* ... MO-7
Cottonwood Point Public Use Area—*park* ... KS-7
Cottonwood Pond—*lake* ... AL-4
Cottonwood Pond—*lake* ... CO-8
Cottonwood Pond—*lake* ... IL-6
Cottonwood Pond—*lake* ... NV-8
Cottonwood Pond—*reservoir* ... OR-9
*Cotton Wood Post Office* ... AL-4
Cottonwood Post Office—*building* ... AL-4
Cottonwood Post Office—*building* ... AZ-5
Cottonwood Power Plant—*other* ... CA-9
Cottonwood Presbytarian Ch—*church* ... UT-8
Cottonwood Prong—*stream* ... WY-8
Cottonwood Pumping Station—*other* ... CA-9
Cottonwood Ranch—*locale* ... AZ-5
Cottonwood Ranch—*locale* ... CO-8
Cottonwood Ranch—*locale* ... NV-8
Cottonwood Ranch—*locale* (2) ... NM-5
Cottonwood Ranch—*locale* ... TX-5
Cottonwood Ranch—*locale* ... WY-8
Cottonwood Ranch Landing Strip—*airport* ... SD-7
**Cottonwood Ranch (subdivision)**—*pop pl* (2) ... AZ-5
Cottonwood Ranch Windmill—*locale* ... NM-5
Cottonwood Ranger Station—*locale* ... ID-8
Cottonwood Ranger Station—*locale* ... WY-8
Cottonwood Rec Area—*park* ... SD-7
Cottonwood Resrvoir—*reservoir* ... AZ-5
Cottonwood Revetment—*levee* ... MS-4
Cottonwood Ridge—*ridge* (2) ... AZ-5
Cottonwood Ridge—*ridge* ... CA-9
Cottonwood Ridge—*ridge* ... CO-8
Cottonwood Ridge—*ridge* ... ID-8
Cottonwood Ridge—*ridge* ... OR-9
Cottonwood Ridge—*ridge* (4) ... UT-8
Cottonwood Ridge Spring—*spring* ... ID-8
**Cottonwood Ridge Subdivision**—*pop pl* ... UT-8
Cottonwood Rim—*cliff* (2) ... WY-8
*Cottonwood River* ... KS-7
*Cottonwood River* ... MN-6
Cottonwood River—*stream* ... KS-7
Cottonwood River—*stream* ... MN-6
Cottonwood River Bridge—*hist pl* ... KS-7
Cottonwood Row Sch—*school* ... NE-7
Cottonwood Rsvr—*reservoir* (2) ... CO-8
Cottonwood Rsvr—*reservoir* (4) ... MT-8
Cottonwood Rsvr—*reservoir* ... NV-8
Cottonwood Rsvr—*reservoir* (2) ... OR-9
Cottonwood Rsvr—*reservoir* ... UT-8
Cottonwood Rsvr—*reservoir* (2) ... WY-8
Cottonwoods, The—*area* ... ID-8
Cottonwoods, The—*locale* ... WA-9
Cottonwoods, The—*woods* (2) ... UT-8
Cottonwood Saddle—*gap* ... AZ-5
Cottonwood Sawmill—*locale* ... CA-9
Cottonwood Sch—*hist pl* ... MT-8
Cottonwood Sch—*school* ... AR-4
Cottonwood Sch—*school* (2) ... CA-9
Cottonwood Sch—*school* ... CO-8
Cottonwood Sch—*school* (6) ... IL-6
Cottonwood Sch—*school* (2) ... KS-7
Cottonwood Sch—*school* ... MO-7
Cottonwood Sch—*school* (5) ... MT-8
Cottonwood Sch—*school* (5) ... NE-7
Cottonwood Sch—*school* ... NM-5
Cottonwood Sch—*school* ... ND-7
Cottonwood Sch—*school* (6) ... SD-7
Cottonwood Sch—*school* (2) ... TX-5
Cottonwood Sch—*school* (2) ... UT-8
Cottonwood Sch (abandoned)—*school* ... SD-7
Cottonwood Sch (historical)—*school* (3) ... MO-7
Cottonwood School—*locale* ... ID-8
Cottonwood School—*locale* ... MT-8
**Cottonwoods Condominium, The**—*pop pl* ... UT-8
Cottonwood Seep—*spring* (2) ... AZ-5
**Cottonwood Shores**—*pop pl* ... TX-5
**Cottonwood Slopes Subdivision**—*pop pl* ... UT-8
Cottonwood Slough—*gut* (2) ... AK-9
Cottonwood Slough—*gut* ... MO-7
Cottonwood Slough—*gut* ... SD-7
Cottonwood Slough—*gut* ... TX-5
Cottonwood Slough—*lake* ... SD-7
Cottonwood Slough—*stream* ... AK-9
Cottonwood Slough—*stream* (3) ... AR-4
Cottonwood Slough—*stream* ... CA-9
Cottonwood Slough—*stream* ... ID-8
Cottonwood Slough—*stream* ... IL-6
Cottonwood Slough—*stream* ... LA-4
Cottonwood Slough—*stream* ... NV-8
Cottonwood Slough—*stream* ... SD-7
**Cottonwoods of Holladay Subdivision**—*pop pl* ... UT-8
*Cottonwood Spring* ... AZ-5
*Cottonwood Spring* ... CA-9
Cottonwood Spring—*reservoir* ... AZ-5
Cottonwood Spring—*spring* (68) ... AZ-5
Cottonwood Spring—*spring* (17) ... CA-9
Cottonwood Spring—*spring* (7) ... CO-8
Cottonwood Spring—*spring* (4) ... ID-8
Cottonwood Spring—*spring* (2) ... MT-8
Cottonwood Spring—*spring* (31) ... NV-8
Cottonwood Spring—*spring* (21) ... NM-5
Cottonwood Spring—*spring* ... OK-5
Cottonwood Spring—*spring* (20) ... OR-9
Cottonwood Spring—*spring* (6) ... TX-5
Cottonwood Spring—*spring* (30) ... UT-8
Cottonwood Spring—*spring* (3) ... WA-9
Cottonwood Spring—*spring* (3) ... WY-8
Cottonwood Spring Campground—*locale* ... CA-9
*Cottonwood Spring Canyon* ... AZ-5
Cottonwood Spring Gulch—*valley* ... CA-9
Cottonwood Spring (historical)—*spring* ... NV-8
Cottonwood Spring Hollow—*valley* ... UT-8
Cottonwood Spring Number One—*spring* ... AZ-5
Cottonwood Spring Number One—*spring* ... NV-8
Cottonwood Spring Number Three—*spring* ... AZ-5
Cottonwood Spring Number Two—*spring* ... NV-8
Cottonwood Spring Rsvr—*reservoir* ... OR-9
Cottonwood Springs—*spring* (2) ... AZ-5
Cottonwood Springs—*spring* (3) ... CA-9
Cottonwood Springs—*spring* ... CO-8
Cottonwood Springs—*spring* ... ID-8
Cottonwood Springs—*spring* (4) ... NV-8
Cottonwood Springs—*spring* (3) ... NM-5
Cottonwood Springs—*spring* (3) ... OR-9
Cottonwood Springs—*spring* ... TX-5
Cottonwood Springs—*spring* (2) ... UT-8
Cottonwood Springs Branch—*stream* ... TX-5
Cottonwood Springs Creek—*stream* ... CA-9
Cottonwood Springs Creek—*stream* ... SD-7
Cottonwood Springs Dam—*dam* ... SD-7
Cottonwood Springs Lake—*reservoir* ... SD-7
*Cottonwood Springs Reservoir* ... SD-7
Cottonwoods Slough—*swamp* ... AR-4
Cottonwoods Spring—*spring* ... AZ-5
*Cottonwood Station* ... KS-7
**Cottonwood Station**—*pop pl* ... AZ-5
Cottonwood Stomp—*flat* ... CO-8
**Cottonwood (subdivision)**—*pop pl* ... AL-4
**Cottonwood Subdivision**—*pop pl* ... UT-8
Cottonwood Substation—*locale* ... AZ-5
Cottonwood Substation—*other* ... CA-9
Cottonwood Swale—*stream* ... OH-6
Cottonwood Tailings Pond—*reservoir* ... AZ-5
Cottonwood Tank—*lake* ... NM-5
Cottonwood Tank—*locale* ... AZ-5
Cottonwood Tank—*reservoir* (15) ... AZ-5
Cottonwood Tank—*reservoir* (7) ... NM-5
Cottonwood Tank—*reservoir* (5) ... TX-5
Cottonwood Tanks—*reservoir* ... UT-8
**Cottonwood Township**—*pop pl* ... KS-7
**Cottonwood Township**—*pop pl* (3) ... NE-7
**Cottonwood Township**—*pop pl* ... ND-7
**Cottonwood Township**—*pop pl* (3) ... SD-7
Cottonwood Township (historical)—*civil* ... SD-7
**Cottonwood (Township of)**—*pop pl* ... IL-6
**Cottonwood (Township of)**—*pop pl* ... MN-6
Cottonwood Trail—*trail* ... CA-9
Cottonwood Trail—*trail* ... CO-8
Cottonwood Trail—*trail* ... WY-8
Cottonwood Trail Canyon—*valley* ... NM-5
Cottonwood Trail Pond—*reservoir* ... ID-8
Cottonwood Trail Rsvr—*reservoir* ... WY-8
Cottonwood Trap Windmill—*locale* ... TX-5
Cottonwood Tree Lakes—*reservoir* ... MT-8
Cottonwood Tree Windmill—*locale* ... CO-8
Cottonwood Tunnel—*tunnel* ... CA-9
Cottonwood Valley—*basin* ... NV-8
Cottonwood Valley—*valley* ... AZ-5
Cottonwood Valley—*valley* ... CA-9
Cottonwood Valley—*valley* ... CO-8
Cottonwood Valley—*valley* ... ID-8
Cottonwood Valley—*valley* ... NE-7
Cottonwood Valley—*valley* ... NV-8
Cottonwood Valley Township—*civil* ... SD-7
*Cottonwood Valy* ... AZ-5
Cottonwood Village (Shop Ctr)—*locale* ... UT-8
**Cottonwood Village Subdivision**—*pop pl* ... UT-8
*Cottonwood Wash* ... AZ-5
*Cottonwood Wash* ... UT-8
Cottonwood Wash—*stream* (9) ... AZ-5
Cottonwood Wash—*stream* ... CA-9
Cottonwood Wash—*stream* (3) ... NV-8
Cottonwood Wash—*stream* ... NM-5
Cottonwood Wash—*stream* ... UT-8
Cottonwood Wash—*valley* (4) ... AZ-5
Cottonwood Wash—*valley* ... CO-8
Cottonwood Wash—*valley* ... TX-5
Cottonwood Wash—*valley* (19) ... UT-8
Cottonwood Wash Bridge—*bridge* ... AZ-5
Cottonwood Wash Dam—*dam* ... AZ-5
Cottonwood Wash Spring—*spring* ... AZ-5
Cottonwood Wash (42 MD 183)—*hist pl* ... UT-8
Cottonwood Well—*locale* ... NM-5
Cottonwood Well—*well* (6) ... AZ-5
Cottonwood Well—*well* ... CA-9
Cottonwood Well—*well* ... MT-8
Cottonwood Well—*well* (7) ... NM-5
Cottonwood Well—*well* ... TX-5
Cottonwood Windmill—*locale* (3) ... AZ-5
Cottonwood Windmill—*locale* (5) ... NM-5
Cottonwood Windmill—*locale* (7) ... TX-5
**Cottrell**—*pop pl* ... OR-9
Cottrell Branch—*stream* ... TN-4
Cottrell Cem—*cemetery* ... AL-4
Cottrell Cem—*cemetery* ... OH-6
Cottrell Cem—*cemetery* ... TN-4
**Cottrell Corners**—*pop pl* ... NJ-2
Cottrell Creek—*stream* ... NY-2
Cottrell Drain—*canal* ... MI-6
Cottrell Drain—*stream* ... MI-6
Cottrell Family Cem—*cemetery* ... MS-4
Cottrell-Johnson Cem—*cemetery* ... TN-4
Cottrell Key—*island* ... FL-3
Cottrell Knob—*summit* ... NC-3
*Cottrell Lake* ... PA-2
Cottrell Lake—*reservoir* ... AL-4
*Cottrell Lake Dam* ... PA-2
Cottrell Lake Dam—*dam* ... AL-4
Cottrell Ponds—*lake* ... TN-4
Cottrell Ranch—*locale* ... CA-9
Cottrell Ridge—*ridge* ... WV-2
Cottrell Run—*stream* ... WV-2
Cottrells Blowout—*crater* ... ID-8
Cottrell Sch—*school* ... OR-9
Cottrells Mission—*church* ... OK-5
Cottrell Spring—*spring* ... TN-4
Cottrell Spring Branch—*stream* ... TN-4
Cottrellville Oil And Gas Field—*other* ... MI-6
Cottrellville (Township of)—*civ div* ... MI-6
Cottrel Spring—*spring* ... ID-8
Cottrill, Matthew, House—*hist pl* ... ME-1
Cottrill Cem—*cemetery* ... WV-2
Cottrill Opera House—*hist pl* ... WV-2
Cottrill Run—*stream* (2) ... WV-2
Cotts Creek—*stream* ... AL-4
Cotts Creek—*stream* ... TN-4
*Cottsville* ... MA-1
*Cottsville* ... VA-3
Cott Tank—*reservoir* ... AZ-5
Cotui (Barrio)—*fmr MCD* ... PR-3
*Cotuit* ... MA-1
**Cotuit**—*pop pl* ... MA-1
Cotuit Anchorage—*harbor* ... MA-1
Cotuit Bay—*bay* ... MA-1
*Cotuit Harbor* ... MA-1
**Cotuit Highlands**—*pop pl* ... MA-1
Cotuit Hist Dist—*hist pl* ... MA-1
*Cotuit Lake* ... MA-1
*Cotuit Pond* ... MA-1
*Cotuit Ponds* ... MA-1
*Cotuitport* ... MA-1
*Cotuit River* ... MA-1
**Cotula**—*pop pl* ... TN-4
Cotula Post Office (historical)—*building* ... TN-4
**Cotulla**—*pop pl* ... TX-5
Cotulla (CCD)—*cens area* ... TX-5
Cotulla Windmill—*locale* ... TX-5
*Cotutlogee Creek* ... AL-4
Coty Corners—*locale* ... NY-2
Coty Cox Branch—*stream* ... MD-2
Couba, Bayou—*channel* ... LA-4
Couba Island—*island* ... LA-4
Couba Island Oil Field—*oilfield* ... LA-4
Couba Oil Field Canal, Bayou—*canal* ... LA-4
Coubers Brook—*stream* ... ME-1
Couble Cem—*cemetery* ... TX-5
Couble Creek—*stream* ... NE-7
Couborn Creek—*stream* ... CA-9
Couch—*locale* ... WV-2
**Couch**—*pop pl* ... AL-4
**Couch**—*pop pl* ... FL-3
**Couch**—*pop pl* ... MO-7
Couchanda Lake—*swamp* ... LA-4
Couch-Artrip House—*hist pl* ... WV-2
Couchatana Creek—*stream* ... TX-5
Couch Branch—*stream* (2) ... KY-4
Couch Branch—*stream* ... MO-7
Couch Branch—*stream* ... TN-4
Couch Branch—*stream* ... TX-5
Couch Brook—*stream* ... MA-1
Couch Canyon—*valley* ... UT-8
*Couch Cem* ... TN-4
Couch Cem—*cemetery* ... KY-4
Couch Cem—*cemetery* (3) ... TN-4
Couch Cem—*cemetery* (2) ... VA-3
Couch Ch—*church* ... MO-7
Couch Cove—*valley* ... GA-3
*Couch Creek* ... GA-3
Couch Creek—*stream* ... CA-9
Couch Creek—*stream* ... OR-9
Coucher Ditch—*canal* ... IN-6
Couches Creek—*stream* (2) ... NC-3
Couches Creek—*stream* ... VA-3
Couches Mill (historical)—*locale* ... AL-4
Couches Pond—*reservoir* ... VA-3
Couch Family Investment Development—*hist pl* ... OR-9
Couch Ford (historical)—*crossing* ... TN-4
Couch Fork—*stream* (2) ... KY-4
Couch Hill—*summit* ... NH-1
**Couch (historical)**—*pop pl* ... TN-4
Couch Hollow—*valley* ... MO-7
Couch Hollow—*valley* ... NY-2
*Couch Island* ... FL-3
Couch Lake—*reservoir* ... GA-3
Couchman Draw—*valley* ... CO-8
Couchman House—*hist pl* ... KY-4
Couch Mansion—*building* ... OR-9
Couch Mine—*mine* ... TN-4
Couch Mtn—*summit* (2) ... NC-3
Couch Mtn—*summit* ... TX-5
Couch Oil Field—*oilfield* ... KS-7
*Couchon Bay* ... LA-4
Couch Park—*park* ... OK-5
Couch Ranch—*school* ... SD-7
Couch Run—*stream* ... PA-2
Couchsachraga Peak—*summit* ... NY-2
Couch Sch—*school* ... GA-3
Couch Sch—*school* ... OR-9
Couch Sch (abandoned)—*school* ... PA-2
*Couch School* ... MO-7
Couch Schools—*school* ... MO-7
Couchs Knob—*summit* ... VA-3
Couch Summit—*summit* ... ID-8
Couchtown—*locale* ... PA-2
**Couchtown**—*pop pl* ... SC-3
Couch Township—*civil* ... MO-7
Couchville—*uninc pl* ... TN-4
Couchwood—*hist pl* ... AR-4
**Couchwood**—*pop pl* ... LA-4
**Couderay**—*pop pl* ... WI-6
Couderay River—*stream* ... WI-6
**Couderay (Town of)**—*pop pl* ... WI-6
**Coudersport**—*pop pl* ... PA-2
Coudersport and Port Allegany RR Station—*hist pl* ... PA-2
Coudersport and Port Allegheny RR Historic Site—*locale* ... PA-2
Coudersport Area Elem Sch—*school* ... PA-2
Coudersport Area Junior Senior HS—*school* ... PA-2
Coudersport Borough—*civil* ... PA-2
Coudersport Country Club—*other* ... PA-2

Coudersport Court House Historic Site—locale ... PA-2
Coudersport Hist Dist—hist pl ... PA-2
Coudley—locale (2) ... PA-2
Coudray Lake—lake ... WI-6
Cou-e-lis-ke Pass ... WA-9
Coues, Elliott, House—hist pl ... DC-2
Coueta, Lake—reservoir ... GA-3
Couey Field ... FL-3
Cou Falls—locale ... IA-7
Coufal Site—hist pl ... NE-7
Coufal-Warren Airp—airport ... KS-7
Cougar—locale ... CA-9
**Cougar**—pop pl (2) ... WA-9
Cougar Basin—basin (2) ... ID-8
Cougar Basin—basin ... OR-9
Cougar Basin—basin ... UT-8
Cougar Basin Trail—trail ... ID-8
Cougar Bay—bay ... ID-8
Cougar Bench—bench ... UT-8
Cougar Bend—bend ... OR-9
Cougar Bluffs—cliff ... OR-9
Cougar Branch—stream ... TX-5
Cougar Butte—summit ... CA-9
Cougar Butte—summit (2) ... OR-9
Cougar Buttes—ridge ... CA-9
Cougar Camp—locale ... CA-9
Cougar Camp—locale (2) ... OR-9
Cougar Camp—locale ... WA-9
Cougar Canyon—valley (2) ... AZ-5
Cougar Canyon—valley (2) ... CA-9
Cougar Canyon—valley ... CO-8
Cougar Canyon—valley (2) ... ID-8
Cougar Canyon—valley (3) ... NV-8
Cougar Canyon—valley (3) ... OR-9
Cougar Canyon—valley (5) ... UT-8
Cougar Canyon—valley (7) ... WA-9
Cougar Canyon Rsvr—reservoir ... OR-9
Cougar Canyon Tank—reservoir ... AZ-5
Cougar Club Athletic Field—park ... NM-5
Cougar Creek ... OR-9
Cougar Creek ... WA-9
Cougar Creek—stream ... CA-9
Cougar Creek—stream (21) ... ID-8
Cougar Creek—stream (6) ... MT-8
Cougar Creek—stream ... NV-8
Cougar Creek—stream (32) ... OR-9
Cougar Creek—stream ... UT-8
Cougar Creek—stream (23) ... WA-9
Cougar Creek—stream (3) ... WY-8
Cougar Creek Campground—park ... OR-9
Cougar Creek Guard Station—locale ... WA-9
Cougar Creek Patrol Cabin—locale ... WY-8
Cougar Creek Ranch—locale ... ID-8
Cougar Creek Shelter—locale ... WA-9
Cougar Creek Summit—summit ... ID-8
Cougar Creek Trail—trail ... OR-9
Cougar Creek Trail—trail ... WY-8
Cougar Dam—dam (2) ... OR-9
Cougar Divide—ridge ... WA-9
Cougar Falls—falls ... WA-9
Cougar Flat—flat ... ID-8
Cougar Flat—flat (2) ... OR-9
Cougar Flat—flat (2) ... WA-9
Cougar Flat Airstrip Airp—airport ... WA-9
Cougar Flat Campground—locale ... WA-9
Cougar Flat Grange—locale ... WA-9
Cougar Flats—flat ... WA-9
Cougar Forest Camp—locale ... OR-9
Cougar Fork—stream ... WV-2
Cougar Gap—gap ... OR-9
Cougar Gap—gap (2) ... WA-9
Cougar Gulch—valley ... CA-9
Cougar Gulch—valley (3) ... ID-8
Cougar Gulch—valley ... MT-8
Cougar Gulch—valley (4) ... OR-9
Cougar Gulch—valley ... WA-9
Cougar Gulch Sch III—hist pl ... ID-8
Cougar Heliport—airport ... WA-9
Cougar Hollow ... UT-8
Cougar Hollow—valley ... TX-5
Cougar Hollow—valley (2) ... UT-8
Cougar Island ... ID-8
Cougar Island—island ... ID-8
Cougar Island—island ... WA-9
Cougar Knoll—summit ... UT-8
Cougar Lake ... OR-9
Cougar Lake—lake ... AZ-5
Cougar Lake—lake ... ID-8
Cougar Lake—lake ... MI-6
Cougar Lake—lake ... MN-6
Cougar Lake—lake ... MT-8
Cougar Lake—lake (2) ... OR-9
Cougar Lake—lake (5) ... WA-9
Cougar Lakes—lake ... ID-8
Cougar Lookout—locale ... ID-8
Cougar Meadow—flat ... OR-9
Cougar Meadow—flat ... WA-9
Cougar Meadows—flat ... ID-8
Cougar Meadows—flat ... OR-9
Cougar Mine ... OR-9
Cougar Mine—mine (2) ... AZ-5
Cougar Mine—mine ... ID-8
Cougar Mine—mine (2) ... OR-9
Cougar Mountain Airfield Airp—airport ... WA-9
Cougar Mountian—summit ... ID-8
Cougar Mtn—summit ... ID-8
Cougar Mtn—summit ... NM-5
Cougar Mtn—summit (7) ... OR-9
Cougar Mtn—summit ... TX-5
Cougar Mtn—summit ... UT-8
Cougar Mtn—summit (6) ... WA-9
Cougar Park—flat ... AZ-5
Cougar Pass—gap (2) ... OR-9
Cougar Pass—gap ... UT-8
Cougar Pass—gap ... WY-8
Cougar Pass Tank—reservoir ... CA-9
Cougar Pass Trail—trail ... WY-8
Cougar Peak—summit (2) ... ID-8
Cougar Peak—summit ... MT-8
Cougar Peak—summit ... NV-8
Cougar Peak—summit ... OR-9
Cougar Point—cape ... NV-8
COUGAR POINT CAMP ... ID-8
Cougar Point Recreation Site—locale ... ID-8
Cougar Pond—lake ... OR-9
Cougar Rapids—rapids ... OR-9
Cougar Rapids Bar—bar ... ID-8
Cougar Ridge—ridge (6) ... OR-9
Cougar Ridge—ridge ... UT-8
Cougar Ridge—ridge ... WA-9
Cougar Ridge Mine—mine ... OR-9
Cougar Ridge Trail—trail ... ID-8
Cougar Ridge Trail (pack)—trail ... OR-9
Cougar Rock—cape ... OR-9
Cougar Rock—pillar (2) ... OR-9
Cougar Rock—summit ... ID-8
Cougar Rock—summit (2) ... OR-9
Cougar Rock—summit (2) ... WA-9
Cougar Rock Campground—locale ... WA-9
Cougar Rocks—summit ... WA-9
Cougar Rock Trail—trail ... ID-8
Cougar Rsvr—reservoir ... ID-8
Cougar Rsvr—reservoir (2) ... OR-9
Cougar Run—stream ... PA-2
Cougar Saddle—gap ... ID-8
Cougar Spar Mine—mine ... UT-8
Cougar Spit—bar ... WA-9
Cougar Spring—spring ... AZ-5
Cougar Spring—spring (2) ... ID-8
Cougar Spring—spring ... NV-8
Cougar Spring—spring (4) ... OR-9
Cougar Spring—spring (5) ... UT-8
Cougar Spring—spring ... WA-9
Cougar Springs—spring ... NV-8
Cougar Tank—reservoir (2) ... AZ-5
Cougar Trail—trail ... OR-9
Cougar Valley—locale ... WA-9
Cougar Valley Trail—trail ... WA-9
Cougar Way—trail ... WA-9
Couger Mtn ... TX-5
Coughanour Apartment Block—hist pl ... ID-8
Coughanour Ditch—canal ... OR-9
Coughenour Ridge—ridge ... PA-2
Coughenour Sch (abandoned)—school ... PA-2
Cougher Creek ... VA-3
Coughlin—locale ... IL-6
Coughlin—locale ... TX-5
Coughlin Brook—stream ... NY-2
Coughlin Campanile—hist pl ... SD-7
Coughlin Mound—summit ... MS-4
Coughlin Sch—hist pl ... MA-1
Coughlin Sch—school ... MA-1
Coughran—locale ... TX-5
Coughran, Edward, House—hist pl ... SD-7
Coughran Canyon—valley ... AZ-5
Coughran Cem—cemetery ... MI-6
Coughran Ranch—locale ... AZ-5
Coughron Sch (historical)—school ... TN-4
Cou Head Spring ... CA-9
Coulam—locale (2) ... ID-8
Coulbourn Millpond—reservoir ... MD-2
Coulby, Harry, Mansion—hist pl ... OH-6
Coulee ... ND-7
**Coulee**—pop pl ... ND-7
Coulee, Bayou—stream ... LA-4
Coulee, The—stream ... LA-4
Coulee, The—valley ... ND-7
Coulee a Elphege, La —stream ... LA-4
Coulee Andre—stream ... LA-4
Coulee Baton—stream ... LA-4
Coulee Baton Canal—canal ... LA-4
Coulee Bayou ... LA-4
Coulee Bayou—stream ... LA-4
Coulee Canyon—valley ... CA-9
Coulee Center ... WA-9
**Coulee City**—pop pl ... WA-9
Coulee City Airp—airport ... WA-9
Coulee City (CCD)—cens area ... WA-9
Coulee City Cem—cemetery ... WA-9
Coulee Cocodrie—stream ... LA-4
Coulee Community Hospital Heliport—airport ... WA-9
Coulee Coteau Holmes—stream ... LA-4
Coulee Creek—stream ... IA-7
Coulee Creek—stream (4) ... LA-4
Coulee Creek—stream ... MT-8
Coulee Creek—stream ... OR-9
Coulee Creek—stream ... UT-8
Coulee Creek—stream (2) ... WA-9
Coulee Croche—stream ... LA-4
Coulee Crow—stream ... LA-4
**Coulee Dam**—pop pl ... WA-9
Coulee Dam Natl Rec Area—park ... WA-9
Coulee Datider—stream ... LA-4
Coulee De John ... LA-4
Coulee de Marks—stream ... LA-4
Coulee des Grues ... LA-4
Coulee Des Iles—stream ... LA-4
Coulee des Poches—stream ... LA-4
Coulee Dessaule ... LA-4
Coulee Drain—canal ... ID-8
Coulee Drain—canal ... WA-9
Coulee du Cimentiere—stream ... LA-4
Coulee du Pecheur—stream ... LA-4
Coulee du Portage—stream ... LA-4
Coulee Galleque—stream ... LA-4
Coulee Garrigue—valley ... LA-4
Coulee Heights ... WA-9
Coulee Hollow—valley ... TX-5
Coulee Kennys ... LA-4
Coulee Kinney ... LA-4
Coulee Lake—lake ... WA-9
Coulee Lantier—stream ... LA-4
Coulee Malam—stream ... LA-4
Coulee Manuel—stream ... LA-4
Coulee Mesa ... WY-8
Coulee Michel—stream ... LA-4
Coulee Mine—stream ... LA-4
Coulee Nicole Guidry—stream ... LA-4
Coulee Noir ... LA-4
Coulee Noire —lake ... LA-4
Coulee Polete ... LA-4
Coulee Portage—stream ... LA-4
Coulee Ridge—ridge ... WI-6
Coulee Rouge—stream ... LA-4
Coulee Sch—school ... ND-7
Coulee State Experimental For—forest ... WI-6
Coulee Tank—reservoir ... AZ-5
Coulee Teal—stream ... LA-4
**Coulee Township**—pop pl ... ND-7
Coulee Valentine—stream ... LA-4
Couler Valley—valley ... IA-7
Couley Ch—church ... LA-4
Couley Creek—stream ... LA-4
Couley Sch—school ... LA-4
Coulie des Grues ... LA-4
Couller Creek—stream ... TX-5
Couloir Peak—summit ... AK-9
Coulombe Creek—stream ... NY-2
Coulon Cem—cemetery ... LA-4
Coulon Cem—cemetery ... NY-2
**Coulon Plantation**—pop pl ... LA-4
Coulsen Hughes Draw—valley ... SD-7
**Coulson**—pop pl ... VA-3
Coulson Bayou—stream ... MS-4
Coulson Ch—church ... VA-3
Coulson Ditch—canal ... MT-8
Coulson Gulch—valley ... CO-8
Coulson Lake—reservoir ... CO-8
Coulson Pond—lake ... MD-2
Coulsontown Cottages Hist Dist—hist pl ... PA-2
Coulstone—locale ... MO-7
**Coulstone**—pop pl ... MO-7
Coulston Elem Sch—school ... IN-6
Coulston Mine—mine ... MT-8
Coultas Sch—school ... IL-6
Coult Cem—cemetery ... CT-1
Coulter ... MS-4
Coulter—locale ... OH-6
Coulter—locale ... PA-2
**Coulter**—pop pl ... IA-7
**Coulter**—pop pl ... PA-2
**Coulter**—pop pl ... TN-4
Coulter, George, House—hist pl ... AL-4
Coulter Basin—lake ... FL-3
Coulter Branch—stream ... AR-4
Coulter Branch—stream (2) ... GA-3
Coulter Branch—stream (2) ... TN-4
Coulter Brook—stream ... NY-2
Coulter Cabin—locale ... AZ-5
Coulter Canyon—valley ... MT-8
Coulter Cem—cemetery ... AL-4
Coulter Cem—cemetery ... AR-4
Coulter Cem—cemetery ... GA-3
Coulter Cem—cemetery ... MS-4
Coulter Cem—cemetery (2) ... OH-6
Coulter Cem—cemetery ... SC-3
Coulter Chapel—church ... WV-2
Coulter Corral—locale ... ID-8
Coulter Creek—stream ... CO-8
Coulter Creek—stream ... GA-3
Coulter Creek—stream (2) ... WA-9
Coulter Creek—stream ... WY-8
Coulter Creek Trail—trail ... WY-8
Coulter Gap—gap ... KY-4
Coulter Gulch—valley ... ID-8
Coulter Hill—summit ... AZ-5
Coulter Hollow—valley ... WI-6
Coulter House—hist pl ... CA-9
Coulter Island—island ... TX-5
Coulter Lake ... MN-6
Coulter Lake—reservoir ... CO-8
Coulter Lake—reservoir ... MS-4
Coulter Lateral—canal ... NM-5
Coulter Mesa—summit ... CO-8
Coulter Mtn—summit ... AZ-5
Coulter Park—flat ... AZ-5
Coulter Park Tank—reservoir ... AZ-5
Coulter Pass ... MT-8
Coulter Peak ... WY-8
Coulter Ridge—ridge ... AZ-5
Coulter (RR name for Coulters)—other ... PA-2
Coulter Rsvr Number One—reservoir ... OR-9
Coulter Rsvr Number Two—reservoir ... OR-9
Coulter Run—stream ... WV-2
Coulter Sch—school ... IL-6
Coulter Sch—school ... MI-6
Coulter Sch—school ... NE-7
Coulter Sch (historical)—school ... PA-2
Coulters Corner ... IN-6
Coulters Grove Ch—church ... NC-3
Coulter Shoals—bar ... TN-4
**Coulter Shoals**—pop pl ... TN-4
Coulters Hollow—valley ... IN-6
Coulters Island ... TN-4
Coulters Lake—reservoir ... GA-3
Coulter Slough—channel ... WI-6
Coulters Pond Dam—dam ... MS-4
Coulter Spring—spring ... OR-9
**Coulters (RR name Coulter;Twp name South Versailles)**—pop pl ... PA-2
Coulters Run—stream ... OH-6
Coulters Shoals—bar ... TN-4
Coulter Summit—summit ... ID-8
Coulter Tank—reservoir (2) ... AZ-5
Coulterville—locale ... TN-4
**Coulterville**—pop pl ... CA-9
**Coulterville**—pop pl ... IL-6
Coulterville (CCD)—cens area ... CA-9
Coulterville (Election Precinct)—fmr MCD ... IL-6
Coulterville Main Street Hist Dist—hist pl ... CA-9
Coulter Well—well ... NM-5
Coulthurst Flat—flat ... CA-9
Coulton Creek—stream ... CO-8
Coulton Creek Campground—locale ... CO-8
Coultown ... PA-2
Coultrap JHS—school ... IL-6
Coults Hole—bay ... CT-1
**Coulwood**—pop pl ... VA-3
**Coulwood Hills (subdivision)**—pop pl ... NC-3
Coulwood JHS—school ... NC-3
Coulwood MS ... NC-3
**Coulwood (RR name Finney)**—pop pl ... VA-3
**Coulwood (subdivision)**—pop pl ... NC-3
Coumbe Bluff—cliff ... NE-7
Coumbe Cem—cemetery ... WI-6
Coumbe Island—island ... WI-6
**Counce**—pop pl ... TN-4
Council—locale ... AR-4
Council—locale ... FL-3
Council—locale ... VA-3
**Council**—pop pl ... AK-9
**Council**—pop pl ... GA-3
**Council**—pop pl (2) ... ID-8
**Council**—pop pl ... NC-3
Council—uninc pl ... OK-5
Council Baptist Church ... TN-4
Council Bar—bar ... AR-4
**Council Bay**—pop pl ... WI-6
Council Bear Creek—stream ... SD-7
Council Bear Draw—valley ... SD-7
Council Bend—bend ... IA-7
Council Bend—bend ... MS-4
Council Bend—bend ... NE-7
Council Bend—bend ... TN-4
Council Bend Plantation (historical)—locale ... MS-4
Council Bluff—cliff ... AL-4
Council Bluff—cliff ... WA-9
Council Bluff—locale ... AL-4
Council Bluff Ch—church ... MO-7
Council Bluff Lake—lake ... MO-7
**Council Bluffs**—pop pl ... IA-7
Council Bluff Sch—school ... PA-2
Council Bluff Sch (historical)—school ... AL-4
Council Branch—stream ... TX-5
Council Butte—summit ... OR-9
Council Campground—locale ... CA-9
Council Cem—cemetery ... AR-4
Council Cem—cemetery ... FL-3
Council Cem—cemetery ... GA-3
Council Cem—cemetery ... TN-4
Council Ch—church ... NE-7
Council Ch—church ... TN-4
Council Christian Acad—school ... NC-3
Council Chute ... AR-4
Council City ... KS-7
Council Corner—locale ... KS-7
Council Corner Ch—church ... KS-7
Council Corner Sch (historical)—school ... MO-7
Council Cove—bay ... OK-5
Council Creek—stream ... NE-7
Council Creek—stream (2) ... OK-5
Council Creek—stream (2) ... OR-9
Council Creek—stream ... TX-5
Council Creek—stream ... WI-6
Council Creek Cem—cemetery ... OK-5
Council Creek Ch—church ... OK-5
Council Creek Sch—school ... WI-6
Council Creek Spring—spring ... WI-6
**Council Creek Township**—pop pl ... NE-7
**Council Crest**—pop pl ... OR-9
**Council Crest**—pop pl ... PA-2
Council Crest—ridge ... PA-2
Council Crest Park—park ... OR-9
Council Cup—summit ... PA-2
Council Cup Scenic Overlook—locale ... PA-2
Council Gap—gap ... NC-3
Council Grounds State Park—park ... WI-6
**Council Grove**—pop pl ... KS-7
Council Grove Airport ... KS-7
Council Grove Carnegie Library—hist pl ... KS-7
Council Grove Ch—church ... OK-5
Council Grove Dam—dam ... KS-7
Council Grove Hist Dist—hist pl ... KS-7
Council Grove (historical)—locale ... AL-4
Council Grove HS—school ... KS-7
Council Grove Lake—reservoir ... KS-7
Council Grove Methodist Church—hist pl ... AR-4
Council Grove Municipal Airp—airport ... KS-7
Council Grove Natl Bank—hist pl ... KS-7
Council Grove Reservoir ... KS-7
Council Grove Wildlife Area—park ... KS-7
Council Hall—hist pl ... UT-8
**Council Heights (subdivision)**—pop pl ... NC-3
Council High School ... AL-4
Council Hill ... IL-6
Council Hill—locale ... IL-6
**Council Hill**—pop pl ... OK-5
Council Hill—summit ... MT-8
Council Hill—summit ... NE-7
Council Hill Cem—cemetery ... IL-6
Council Hill Cem—cemetery ... IA-7
Council Hill Cem—cemetery ... OK-5
Council Hill Ch—church ... KS-7
Council Hill Station—locale ... IL-6
Council Hill (Township of)—civ div ... IL-6
Council Hollow—valley ... OK-5
Council House—locale ... SD-7
Council House Ch—church ... OK-5
Council Island—island ... MS-4
Council Island—island ... MT-8
Council Island—island ... TX-5
Council Lake ... AR-4
Council Lake ... MS-4
Council Lake—lake ... CA-9
Council Lake—lake ... MI-6
Council Lake—lake ... WA-9
Council Landing—locale ... AK-9
Council Lookout—locale ... ID-8
Councillors Point—cape ... MD-2
Councilmans Run—stream ... MD-2
Council Millpond—reservoir ... NC-3
Council Mill Pond Dam—dam ... NC-3
Council Mtn—summit ... ID-8
**Council Oaks (subdivision)**—pop pl ... NC-3
Council Ridge—ridge ... NC-3
Council Ridge (historical)—locale ... MS-4
Council Rock—area ... NM-5
Council Rock—pillar ... AZ-5
Council Rock Arroyo—stream ... NM-5
Council Rock Cem—cemetery ... NY-2
Council Rock HS—school ... PA-2
Council Rock JHS ... PA-2
Council Rock Ranch—locale ... NM-5
Council Rocks Archaeol District—hist pl ... AZ-5
Council Rock Sch—school ... NY-2
Council Rock Sch—school ... PA-2
Council Rsvr—reservoir ... OR-9
Council Run—stream ... PA-2
Council Sch—school (4) ... AL-4
Council Spring—spring ... NM-5
Council Spring—spring ... TN-4
Council Swamp—stream ... VA-3
Council (Township of)—fmr MCD ... AR-4
Council Valley Ch—church ... OK-5
Coundly Lake—lake ... WA-9
Counsellor Sch—school ... NE-7
Counselman Run—stream ... PA-2
Counselor—locale ... NM-5
Counselor Creek—stream ... SD-7
Counselor Creek Rec Area—park ... SD-7
Counsman—locale ... CA-9
Count Branch—stream ... VA-3
Count Chute Ridge—ridge ... WA-9
Count Creek—stream ... OR-9
Count Creek—stream ... VA-3
Count Creek—stream (2) ... WY-8
Count Draw—valley ... TX-5
Counterfeit Branch—stream ... NC-3
Counterfeit Branch—stream ... WV-2
Counterfeit Creek—stream ... WA-9
Counterfeit Hill—summit ... CA-9
Counterfeit Hollow—valley ... AL-4
Counterfeit Lake—lake ... FL-3
Counterfeit Mill Creek—stream ... FL-3
Counterfeit Pass—gut ... LA-4
Counterfeit Ridge—ridge ... AR-4
Counterline Ch—church ... MS-4
Counter Pen—locale ... TN-4
Counter Ridge Sch—school ... VA-3
Counters Branch—stream ... AL-4
Countess Branch ... AL-4
Countess Cem—cemetery ... AL-4
Countess Gulch—valley ... ID-8
Countess Moore HS—school ... NY-2
Count Heiden Island ... MP-9
Count Heiden Islands ... MP-9
Counties Creek ... AR-4
Counting Chute Spring—spring ... ID-8
Counting Station Rsvr—reservoir ... UT-8
**Countis Corner (Fleenors Spring)**—pop pl ... VA-3
Countis Creek—stream ... AR-4
**Countiss**—pop pl ... AR-4
Countiss Ridge—ridge ... VA-3
Count Peak—summit ... MT-8
**Country Acres**—pop pl ... IL-6
**Country Acres**—pop pl ... OH-6
**Country Acres**—pop pl ... PA-2
Country Acres Baptist Ch—church ... KS-7
**Country Acres (subdivision)**—pop pl ... AL-4
**Country Acres (subdivision)**—pop pl ... NC-3
**Country Acres (subdivision)**—pop pl ... SD-7
Country Aire ... IL-6
**Countrybrook (subdivision)**—pop pl ... TN-4
**Country Campus**—pop pl ... TX-5
Country Ch—church ... MN-6
Country Ch—church ... MS-4
Country Chapel—church ... KS-7
Country Church ... AL-4
Country Church, The—church ... OH-6
Country Club ... MO-7
Country Club—CDP ... CA-9
**Country Club**—pop pl ... MO-7
**Country Club**—pop pl (2) ... PR-3
Country Club—uninc pl ... FL-3
Country Club—uninc pl ... VA-3
Country Club, The—locale ... MA-1
Country Club, The—locale ... TN-4
**Country Club Acres**—pop pl ... AL-4
**Country Club Acres**—pop pl ... FL-3
**Country Club Acres**—pop pl ... OH-6
Country Club Acres—uninc pl ... MD-2
**Country Club Acres (subdivision)**—pop pl ... AL-4
**Country Club Acres (subdivision)**—pop pl (2) ... NC-3
**Country Club Acres (subdivision)**—pop pl ... UT-8
Country Club Airp—airport ... MS-4
Country Club Annex Park—park ... AZ-5
Country Club Bayou—stream ... TX-5
Country Club Branch—stream ... CA-9
Country Club Branch—stream ... KY-4
Country Club Branch—stream ... TN-4
Country Club Cem—cemetery ... OH-6
Country Club Centre Shop Ctr—locale ... CA-9
**Country Club Colony (subdivision)**—pop pl ... NC-3
Country Club Creek—stream ... GA-3
Country Club Creek—stream ... TX-5
Country Club Dam ... ND-7
Country Club Dam ... SD-7
Country Club Dam—dam ... AL-4
**Country Club East (subdivision)**—pop pl ... NC-3
Country Club Estates ... OH-6
Country Club Estates—other ... FL-3
**Country Club Estates**—pop pl (2) ... AL-4
**Country Club Estates**—pop pl ... CA-9
**Country Club Estates**—pop pl ... CO-8
**Country Club Estates**—pop pl ... DE-2
**Country Club Estates**—pop pl (2) ... FL-3
**Country Club Estates**—pop pl ... NM-5
**Country Club Estates**—pop pl ... NC-3
**Country Club Estates**—pop pl (4) ... PA-2
**Country Club Estates**—pop pl ... SC-3
Country Club Estates—uninc pl ... SC-3
Country Club Estates—uninc pl ... TN-4
Country Club Estates—uninc pl ... TX-5
**Country Club Estates (subdivision)**—pop pl (3) ... AL-4
**Country Club Estates (subdivision)**—pop pl ... MS-4
**Country Club Estates (subdivision)**—pop pl (4) ... NC-3
**Country Club Estates (subdivision)**—pop pl (2) ... TN-4
**Country Club Estates Subdivision**—pop pl ... UT-8
**Country Club Forest (subdivision)**—pop pl ... NC-3
**Country Club Gables (subdivision)**—pop pl ... AL-4
**Country Club Gardens**—pop pl ... IN-6
**Country Club Gardens (subdivision)**—pop pl ... AL-4
**Country Club Grove**—pop pl ... VA-3
**Country Club Heights**—pop pl ... CT-1
**Country Club Heights**—pop pl ... IN-6
**Country Club Heights**—pop pl ... KY-4
**Country Club Heights**—pop pl ... PA-2
Country Club Heights—uninc pl ... NM-5
**Country Club Heights Addition (subdivision)**—pop pl ... UT-8
**Country Club Highlands**—pop pl ... AL-4
**Country Club Highlands**—pop pl ... OH-6
Country Club Hills—locale ... GA-3
**Country Club Hills**—pop pl ... IL-6
**Country Club Hills**—pop pl ... MO-7
**Country Club Hills**—pop pl (2) ... VA-3
**Country Club Hills (subdivision)**—pop pl ... AL-4
**Country Club Hills (subdivision)**—pop pl (5) ... NC-3
Country Club Hist Dist—hist pl ... CO-8
Country Club Hist Dist—hist pl ... MN-6
Country Club Hist Dist (Boundary Increase)—hist pl ... CO-8
**Country Club Houses (subdivision)**—pop pl ... NC-3
**Country Club Isles**—pop pl ... FL-3
Country Club Lake—CDP ... VA-3
Country Club Lake—lake ... LA-4
Country Club Lake—lake ... TX-5
Country Club Lake—reservoir ... MS-4
Country Club Lake—reservoir (2) ... NC-3
Country Club Lake—reservoir (3) ... OK-5
Country Club Lake—reservoir ... SC-3
Country Club Lake—reservoir (3) ... TX-5
Country Club Lake Dam—dam (2) ... MS-4
Country Club Lake Dam—dam (2) ... NC-3
Country Club Manor ... ID-8
Country Club Manor ... IL-6
**Country Club Manor**—pop pl ... FL-3
**Country Club Manor**—pop pl ... VA-3
**Country Club Meadows**—pop pl ... IN-6
**Country Club North (subdivision)**—pop pl ... NC-3
Country Club of Asheville—locale ... NC-3
Country Club of Fairfax—other ... VA-3
Country Club Of Maryland—other ... MD-2
Country Club of Northampton County ... PA-2
Country Club Of Virginia—other ... VA-3
Country Club of York—locale ... PA-2
Country Club Park—park ... KS-7
**Country Club Park**—pop pl ... CO-8
**Country Club Park**—pop pl ... MD-2
**Country Club Park (subdivision)**—pop pl ... AL-4
**Country Club Park (subdivision)**—pop pl ... NC-3
**Country Club Place**—pop pl ... IL-6
Country Club Plaza—locale ... MO-7
Country Club Plaza Shop Ctr—locale ... CA-9
Country Club Plaza (Shop Ctr)—locale (3) ... FL-3
**Country Club Point (subdivision)**—pop pl ... NC-3
Country Club Ponds—lake ... NJ-2
**Country Club Ridge**—pop pl ... NJ-2
Country Club Ridge Sch—school ... NJ-2
Country Club Sch—school ... CA-9
Country Club Sch—school ... NM-5
Country Club Shop Ctr—locale ... AL-4
Country Club Shop Ctr—locale ... MA-1
Country Club Spring—spring ... AL-4
**Country Club Subdivision**—pop pl ... LA-4
**Country Club Subdivision**—pop pl ... MS-4
**Country Club Subdivison**—pop pl ... MS-4
Country Club Terrace ... ID-8
**Country Club Terrace**—pop pl ... IL-6
**Country Club Terrace**—pop pl ... TX-5
Country Club Terrace—uninc pl ... TX-5
Country Club Trailer Grove—locale ... AZ-5
**Country Club View**—pop pl ... VA-3
**Country Club View (subdivision)**—pop pl ... NC-3
**Country Club Village**—pop pl ... AL-4
**Country Club Village**—pop pl ... MD-2
**Country Club Village**—pop pl ... MI-6
**Country Club Village**—pop pl ... MO-7
Country Club Village Mobile Home Park—other ... AZ-5
Country Club Village Shop Ctr—locale ... MS-4
**Country Club West**—pop pl ... PA-2
**Country Club Woods (subdivision)**—pop pl ... MS-4
**Country Corners Condominium**—pop pl ... UT-8
Country Corner Shop Ctr—locale ... AL-4
**Country Courts**—pop pl ... IL-6
Country Cousins Mobile Mecca—locale ... AZ-5
**Country Cove (subdivision)**—pop pl ... NC-3
**Country Creek Estates Subdivision**—pop pl ... UT-8
**Country Creek Estates Subdivision Five**—pop pl ... UT-8
**Country Creek Estates Subdivision 1, Two**—pop pl ... UT-8
**Country Creek Subdivision**—pop pl ... UT-8
**Country Crossing Subdivision**—pop pl ... UT-8
Country Day Sch—school ... CA-9
Country Day Sch—school ... CT-1
Country Day Sch—school ... KY-4
Country Day Sch—school ... MO-7
Country Day Sch—school ... NJ-2
Country Day Sch—school ... WV-2
Country Day School, The—school ... CA-9
**Country Esquire**—pop pl ... IL-6
**Country Estate**—pop pl ... OR-9
**Country Estates**—pop pl ... AL-4
**Country Estates**—pop pl ... FL-3
**Country Estates Park Subdivision**—pop pl ... UT-8
Country Estates Sch—school ... OK-5
**Country Estates (subdivision)**—pop pl ... AL-4
**Country Estates (subdivision)**—pop pl (2) ... AZ-5
**Country Estates (subdivision)**—pop pl ... NC-3
**Country Estates (subdivision)**—pop pl ... PA-2
**Country Estates Subdivision**—pop pl (2) ... UT-8
**Country Estates Subdivision (subdivision)**—pop pl ... SD-7
Country Fair Shop Ctr—locale ... AZ-5
Country Farm Cem—cemetery ... IN-6
Country Gable Park—park ... AZ-5
Country Gables Park—park ... AZ-5
**Country Gables Subdivision (subdivision)**—pop pl ... SD-7
**Country Garden Estates Subdivision**—pop pl ... UT-8
Country Gardens ... IL-6
**Country Gardens**—pop pl ... PA-2
Country Gardens Sch—school ... CA-9
**Country Greens at Villa de Paz (subdivision)**—pop pl (2) ... AZ-5
**Country Haven**—pop pl ... TN-4
**Country Haven Estates (subdivision)**—pop pl ... TN-4
**Country Heights**—pop pl ... IL-6
Country Hill—summit ... MA-1
**Country Hills**—pop pl ... PA-2
**Country Hills Addition Subdivision**—pop pl ... UT-8
Country Hill Shop Ctr—locale ... KS-7
**Country Hills Manor Condominiums**—pop pl ... UT-8
Country Hills Mobile Estates—locale ... AZ-5
**Country Hills of Farmington Subdivision**—pop pl ... UT-8
Country Hills Plaza (Shop Ctr)—locale ... UT-8
**Country Hills Square Condominium**—pop pl ... UT-8
**Country Hills (subdivision)**—pop pl ... AL-4
**Country Hills (subdivision)**—pop pl ... MS-4
**Country Hills Subdivision**—pop pl (2) ... UT-8
**Country Hollow Subdivision**—pop pl ... UT-8

Country Home Cem—cemetery ........ KY-4
Country Home Cem—cemetery ........ MS-4
Country Home Cem—cemetery ........ TN-4
**Country Homes**—pop pl ........ WA-9
Country Homes Park—park ........ MI-6
**Country Homes Subdivision**—pop pl ........ UT-8
**Country Horizons (subdivision)**—pop pl (2) ........ AZ-5
Country Knob—summit ........ TX-5
Country Knolls ........ IL-6
Country Knolls—CDP ........ NY-2
**Country Lake**—pop pl ........ IL-6
Country Lake—reservoir ........ IN-6
Country Lake—reservoir ........ NJ-2
Country Lake Camp Dam—dam ........ IN-6
**Country Lake Estates**—pop pl ........ NJ-2
**Country Lane Estates**—pop pl ........ OH-6
**Country Lane Estates (subdivision)**—pop pl ........ NC-3
Country Lane Park—park ........ IL-6
Country Lane Park—park ........ OR-9
Country Lane Sch—school ........ CA-9
**Country Lane (subdivision)**—pop pl ........ NC-3
**Country Lane Subdivision**—pop pl (3) ........ UT-8
Country Lane Woods—woods ........ IL-6
**Country Life Acres**—pop pl ........ MO-7
**Country Life Estates (subdivision)**—pop pl ........ NC-3
Country Life Press—uninc pl ........ NY-2
Country Life Sch—school ........ FL-3
**Country Life (Trailer Park)**—pop pl ........ AZ-5
Country Line Cem—cemetery ........ IL-6
Country Line Cem—cemetery ........ NY-2
Countryline Creek ........ VA-3
Country Line Creek—stream ........ NC-3
Country Line Creek—stream ........ VA-3
Country Line Interchange—crossing ........ AZ-5
**Country Living Subdivision**—pop pl ........ UT-8
**Country Living (trailer park)**—pop pl ........ DE-2
Countryman—locale ........ NY-2
Countryman Basin—basin ........ WY-8
Countryman Cem—cemetery ........ OH-6
Countryman Creek—stream ........ MT-8
Countryman Creek Sch—school ........ MT-8
Countryman House—hist pl ........ TX-5
Countryman Kill—stream ........ NY-2
**Country Manor**—pop pl ........ IL-6
**Country Manor Subdivision**—pop pl ........ UT-8
Country Manor Subdivision Mini Park—park ........ AZ-5
Country Manor Subdivision Water Retention Basin—reservoir ........ AZ-5
Countryman Peak—summit ........ WY-8
Countryman Ranch—locale ........ WY-8
Countrymans Bluff—cliff ........ MT-8
Countryman Sch—school ........ WY-8
Countrymans Creek ........ MT-8
Country Meadows Golf Course—other ........ AZ-5
**Country Meadows (subdivision)**—pop pl (2) ........ AZ-5
**Country Meadows (subdivision)**—pop pl ........ MS-4
**Country Meadows (subdivision)**—pop pl ........ NC-3
**Country Meadows Subdivision**—pop pl (3) ........ UT-8
**Country Modern**—pop pl ........ CA-9
**Country Oak Estates**—pop pl ........ MS-4
**Country Oaks Condominium**—pop pl ........ UT-8
Country Oaks Lakes—lake ........ FL-3
**Country Oaks Subdivision**—pop pl ........ UT-8
**Country Park Acres (subdivision)**—pop pl ........ NC-3
**Country Park Subdivision**—pop pl ........ UT-8
**Country Place**—pop pl ........ NJ-2
**Country Place (subdivision)**—pop pl ........ MS-4
**Country Place (subdivision)**—pop pl (2) ........ NC-3
**Country Place Subdivision**—pop pl ........ UT-8
Country Plaza Golf Course—other ........ OR-9
Country Pond—lake ........ NH-1
Country Post Office (historical)—building ........ AL-4
**Country Ridge Estates**—pop pl ........ NY-2
**Country Ridge (subdivision)**—pop pl ........ AZ-5
**Country Ridge (subdivision)**—pop pl ........ NC-3
**Country Roads (subdivision)**—pop pl ........ NC-3
**Country Roads Subdivision**—pop pl ........ UT-8
Country Run—stream ........ IN-6
Country Sch—school ........ CT-1
Country Sch—school ........ FL-3
Country School, The—school ........ MA-1
Countryside ........ IL-6
Countryside ........ MO-7
**Countryside**—pop pl (2) ........ IL-6
**Countryside**—pop pl ........ KS-7
**Countryside**—pop pl ........ MA-1
**Countryside**—pop pl ........ TN-4
Country Side—school ........ GA-3
Countryside—uninc pl ........ FL-3
**Countryside Acres Subdivision**—pop pl ........ UT-8
Countryside Airp—airport ........ PA-2
Countryside Baptist Ch—church ........ FL-3
Countryside Beach—beach ........ WA-9
Countryside Cathedral Ch of God—church ........ FL-3
Country Side Ch—church ........ OK-5
Countryside Ch—church ........ OK-5
Countryside Chapel—church ........ FL-3
Countryside Christian Ch—church ........ KS-7
**Countryside Condominium**—pop pl ........ UT-8
Countryside Elem Sch—school ........ KS-7
**Countryside Estates**—pop pl ........ IN-6
**Countryside Estates**—pop pl (2) ........ TN-4
Country Side Estates Park Site—park ........ AZ-5
**Country Side Estates (subdivision)**—pop pl ........ MS-4
**Countryside Estates (subdivision)**—pop pl ........ UT-8
Countryside Evangelical Covenant Ch—church ........ FL-3
**Countryside Farms (subdivision)**—pop pl ........ DE-2
Countryside Golf Club—other ........ IL-6
Countryside Golf Club—other ........ WI-6
Countryside Lake—lake ........ IL-6
**Countryside Lake**—pop pl ........ IL-6
Countryside Mall—locale ........ FL-3
**Countryside Manor**—pop pl ........ IL-6
Countryside Memorial Gardens—area ........ MO-7
Countryside Mobile Home Park—locale ........ AZ-5
Countryside Park—park ........ MN-6
Countryside Plaza—post sta ........ TX-5
Countryside Plaza (Shop Ctr)—locale ........ FL-3
Countryside Sch—school (2) ........ IL-6
Countryside Sch—school (3) ........ KS-7
Countryside Sch—school ........ MA-1
Countryside Sch—school ........ MN-6
Countryside Senior HS—school ........ FL-3
Countryside United Methodist Ch—church ........ KS-7
**Countryside Village**—pop pl ........ TN-4
Countryside Village Square (Shop Ctr)—locale ........ FL-3
Country Square Shop Ctr—locale ........ PA-2
Country Square (Shop Ctr)—locale ........ UT-8
**Country Squire Acres Subdivision**—pop pl ........ UT-8
Country Squire Airpark—airport ........ OR-9
**Country Squire Estates (subdivision)**—pop pl ........ AL-4
**Country Squire Estates (subdivision)**—pop pl ........ UT-8
Country Squire Lake—reservoir ........ IN-6
Country Squire Lake Dam—dam ........ IN-6
**Country Station Condominium**—pop pl ........ UT-8
**Country (subdivision), The**—pop pl ........ NC-3
**Country Terrace**—pop pl ........ IN-6
Country Terrace Acres—locale ........ PA-2
**Country Trace (subdivision)**—pop pl (2) ........ AZ-5
**Country View Estates**—pop pl ........ IL-6
**Country View Estates**—pop pl ........ MA-1
**Country View Lane PUD Subdivision**—pop pl ........ UT-8
Country View Nursing Home—hospital ........ IL-6
Country View Sch—school ........ UT-8
**Country Village Mobile Park (subdivision)**—pop pl ........ SD-7
**Country Village (subdivision)**—pop pl (2) ........ AL-4
**Country Village (subdivision)**—pop pl ........ DE-2
**Country Village Subdivision**—pop pl ........ UT-8
Country Villa (trailer park)—locale ........ AZ-5
**Country Villa (trailer park)**—pop pl ........ AZ-5
**Country West Subdivision**—pop pl ........ UT-8
**Country Willows Subdivision**—pop pl ........ UT-8
Countrywood Sch—school ........ NY-2
**Country Woods (subdivision)**—pop pl ........ MS-4
**Country Woods (subdivision)**—pop pl ........ NC-3
**Country Wood (subdivision)**—pop pl ........ TN-4
Counts—locale ........ OK-5
Counts—locale (2) ........ VA-3
**Counts**—pop pl ........ MS-4
Counts Branch ........ NJ-2
Counts Branch—stream ........ MS-4
Counts Butte—summit ........ WA-9
Counts Cem—cemetery ........ AL-4
Counts Cem—cemetery ........ OH-6
Counts Cem—cemetery ........ TX-5
Counts Cem—cemetery (5) ........ VA-3
Counts Cem—cemetery ........ WV-2
Counts Ch—church ........ VA-3
Count Sch—school ........ AR-4
Counts Chapel—church ........ MS-4
Counts Chapel—church ........ VA-3
Counts Cove—valley ........ VA-3
Counts Creek—stream ........ MT-8
Counts Creek—stream ........ TX-5
**Counts Cross Roads**—pop pl ........ KY-4
**Counts Crossroads**—pop pl ........ KY-4
Counts Gulch—valley ........ CA-9
Counts Hill Prairie—area ........ CA-9
Counts Hollow—valley ........ MO-7
Counts Hotel—hist pl ........ TN-4
Count's House—hist pl ........ IL-6
Counts Island—island ........ SC-3
Counts Ridge—ridge ........ VA-3
Counts Run—stream ........ OH-6
Counts Sch—school ........ VA-3
Counts Spur ........ MS-4
Countsville—locale ........ WV-2
Countsville Ch—church ........ SC-3
Count Tank—reservoir (2) ........ TX-5
County Acad—school ........ VA-3
**County Acres**—pop pl ........ KS-7
County Acres—uninc pl ........ KS-7
**County Acres (subdivision)**—pop pl ........ NC-3
County Airp—airport ........ CO-8
County Airport Dam ........ AL-4
County and City Hall—hist pl ........ NY-2
County Ave Ch—church ........ AR-4
County Beagle Club—other ........ WV-2
County Boys Home—other ........ MO-7
County Boys Sch—school ........ MN-6
County Bridge No. 101—hist pl ........ PA-2
County Bridge No. 124—hist pl ........ PA-2
County Bridge No. 148—hist pl ........ PA-2
County Bridge No. 171—hist pl ........ PA-2
County Bridge No. 36—hist pl ........ PA-2
County Bridge No. 54—hist pl ........ PA-2
County Bridge Picnic Area—locale ........ PA-2
County Brook—stream ........ IN-6
County Brook—stream ........ MA-1
County Camp—locale ........ NJ-2
County Camp Fifteen—locale ........ CA-9
County Camp Number Three—locale ........ SC-3
County Canal—canal ........ CO-8
County Canyon—valley ........ UT-8
County Cem—cemetery ........ CA-9
County Cem—cemetery ........ IL-6
County Center of Technology and Education—school ........ NY-2
County Ch—church ........ VA-3
County Childrens Home—building ........ OH-6
**County Club Acres**—pop pl ........ FL-3
County Community Junior Coll—school ........ KS-7
County Corner—locale ........ TN-4
County Corners—locale ........ TN-4
County Corners Cem—cemetery ........ IA-7
County Corners Sch—school ........ WI-6
**County Cove (subdivision)**—pop pl ........ UT-8
County Creek—stream ........ ID-8
County Creek—stream (2) ........ OK-9
County Creek—stream ........ WA-9
County Creek—stream ........ WY-8
County Day Sch—school ........ NY-2
County Day Sch—school ........ VA-3
County Detention Camp Number One—locale ........ CA-9
County Detention Home—building ........ TX-5
County Ditch ........ IN-6
County Ditch—canal ........ IN-6
County Ditch No. Fifteen—canal ........ MI-6
County Ditch No. Fifty-seven—canal ........ MI-6
County Ditch No. Fourty-nine—canal ........ MI-6
County Ditch No. One Hundred Seventy-two—canal ........ MI-6
County Ditch No. One Hundred Sixty-three—canal ........ MI-6
County Ditch No. One Hundred Thirty-one—canal ........ MI-6
County Ditch No. Seven—canal ........ MI-6
County Ditch No. Three Hundred Twenty-four—canal ........ MI-6
County Ditch No 1—canal ........ IL-6
County Ditch No. 17 ........ OH-6
County Ditch No 2—canal ........ IL-6
County Ditch No 53—canal ........ IA-7
County Ditch No 7 canal ........ MN-6
County Ditch Number B Five—canal (2) ........ MN-6
County Ditch Number B Four—canal ........ MN-6
County Ditch Number B Seven—canal ........ MN-6
County Ditch Number B Six—canal ........ MN-6
County Ditch Number B Three—canal ........ MN-6
County Ditch Number Eight—canal (17) ........ MN-6
County Ditch Number Eight A—canal ........ MN-6
County Ditch Number Eight And Fiftythree—canal ........ MN-6
County Ditch Number Eighteen—canal (16) ........ MN-6
County Ditch Number Eighty—canal (4) ........ MN-6
County Ditch Number Eightyeight—canal ........ MN-6
County Ditch Number Eightyfive—canal (4) ........ MN-6
County Ditch Number Eightyfour—canal ........ MN-6
County Ditch Number Eightynine—canal (2) ........ MN-6
County Ditch Number Eightyone—canal (3) ........ MN-6
County Ditch Number Eightyseven—canal (2) ........ MN-6
County Ditch Number Eightysix—canal ........ MN-6
County Ditch Number Eightythree—canal (4) ........ MN-6
County Ditch Number Eleven—canal (22) ........ MN-6
County Ditch Number Fifteen—canal (17) ........ MN-6
County Ditch Number Fifteen-two—canal ........ MN-6
County Ditch Number Fifty—canal (4) ........ MN-6
County Ditch Number Fiftyeight—canal (6) ........ MN-6
County Ditch Number Fiftyfive—canal (4) ........ MN-6
County Ditch Number Fiftyfour—canal (2) ........ MN-6
County Ditch Number Fiftynine—canal (6) ........ MN-6
County Ditch Number Fiftyone—canal (7) ........ MN-6
County Ditch Number Fiftyseven—canal (8) ........ MN-6
County Ditch Number Fiftysix—canal (5) ........ MN-6
County Ditch Number Fiftythree—canal (7) ........ MN-6
County Ditch Number Fiftytwo—canal (3) ........ MN-6
County Ditch Number Five ........ MN-6
County Ditch Number Five—canal (17) ........ MN-6
County Ditch Number Five A—canal ........ MN-6
County Ditch Number Five And Thirtyseven—canal ........ MN-6
County Ditch Number Forty—canal (7) ........ MN-6
County Ditch Number Forty A—canal ........ MN-6
County Ditch Number Fortyeight—canal (6) ........ MN-6
County Ditch Number Fortyfive—canal (9) ........ MN-6
County Ditch Number Fortyfour—canal (8) ........ MN-6
County Ditch Number Fortynine—canal (7) ........ MN-6
County Ditch Number Fortyone—canal (9) ........ MN-6
County Ditch Number Fortyseven—canal (7) ........ MN-6
County Ditch Number Fortyseven A—canal ........ MN-6
County Ditch Number Fortysix—canal (8) ........ MN-6
County Ditch Number Fortysix A—canal ........ MN-6
County Ditch Number Fortythree—canal (7) ........ MN-6
County Ditch Number Fortytwo—canal (9) ........ MN-6
County Ditch Number Four—canal (19) ........ MN-6
County Ditch Number Four A—canal ........ MN-6
County Ditch Number Fourteen—canal (13) ........ MN-6
County Ditch Number Nine—canal (17) ........ MN-6
County Ditch Number Ninteen—canal (15) ........ MN-6
County Ditch Number Ninty—canal (3) ........ MN-6
County Ditch Number Nintyeight—canal ........ MN-6
County Ditch Number Nintyfive—canal ........ MN-6
County Ditch Number Nintyfour—canal ........ MN-6
County Ditch Number Nintyone—canal (2) ........ MN-6
County Ditch Number Nintysix—canal (2) ........ MN-6
County Ditch Number Nintythree—canal (2) ........ MN-6
County Ditch Number Nintytwo—canal (2) ........ MN-6
County Ditch Number One—canal (18) ........ MN-6
County Ditch Number One-a—canal ........ MN-6
County Ditch Number One-b—canal ........ MN-6
County Ditch Number One Hundred—canal (4) ........ MN-6
County Ditch Number One Hundred Eight—canal ........ MN-6
County Ditch Number One Hundred Eighteen—canal (2) ........ MN-6
County Ditch Number One Hundred Eleven—canal ........ MN-6
County Ditch Number One Hundred Fifteen—canal ........ MN-6
County Ditch Number One Hundred Fiftyeight—canal ........ MN-6
County Ditch Number One Hundred Five—canal ........ MN-6
County Ditch Number One Hundred Forty—canal (2) ........ MN-6
County Ditch Number One Hundred Fortyeight—canal ........ MN-6
County Ditch Number One Hundred Fortyfour—canal ........ MN-6
County Ditch Number One Hundred Fortythree—canal ........ MN-6
County Ditch Number One Hundred Four—canal (2) ........ MN-6
County Ditch Number One Hundred Fourteen—canal ........ MN-6
County Ditch Number One Hundred Ninteen—canal (2) ........ MN-6
County Ditch Number One Hundred One—canal ........ MN-6
County Ditch Number One Hundred Seven—canal (2) ........ MN-6
County Ditch Number One Hundred Seventeen—canal ........ MN-6
County Ditch Number One Hundred Six—canal (2) ........ MN-6
County Ditch Number One Hundred Sixteen—canal (2) ........ MN-6
County Ditch Number One Hundred Sixtynine—canal ........ MN-6
County Ditch Number One Hundred Sixtyone—canal ........ MN-6
County Ditch Number One Hundred Sixtysix—canal ........ MN-6
County Ditch Number One Hundred Sixtythree—canal ........ MN-6
County Ditch Number One Hundred Ten—canal ........ MN-6
County Ditch Number One Hundred Thirteen—canal ........ MN-6
County Ditch Number One Hundred Thirty—canal ........ MN-6
County Ditch Number One Hundred Thirtyeight—canal ........ MN-6
County Ditch Number One Hundred Thirtyfive—canal ........ MN-6
County Ditch Number One Hundred Thirtyfour—canal (2) ........ MN-6
County Ditch Number One Hundred Thirtynine—canal ........ MN-6
County Ditch Number One Hundred Thirtyone—canal ........ MN-6
County Ditch Number One Hundred Thirtythree—canal (3) ........ MN-6
County Ditch Number One Hundred Thirtytwo—canal ........ MN-6
County Ditch Number One Hundred Three—canal (2) ........ MN-6
County Ditch Number One Hundred Tweleve—canal ........ MN-6
County Ditch Number One Hundred Twenty—canal ........ MN-6
County Ditch Number One Hundred Twentyfour—canal ........ MN-6
County Ditch Number One Hundred Twentynine—canal ........ MN-6
County Ditch Number One Hundred Twentysix—canal ........ MN-6
County Ditch Number One Hundred Twentythree—canal ........ MN-6
County Ditch Number One Hundred Two—canal (2) ........ MN-6
County Ditch Number Seven—canal (12) ........ MN-6
County Ditch Number Seven A—canal ........ MN-6
County Ditch Number Seventeen—canal (10) ........ MN-6
County Ditch Number Seventeen A—canal ........ MN-6
County Ditch Number Seventy—canal (2) ........ MN-6
County Ditch Number Seventyeight—canal (4) ........ MN-6
County Ditch Number Seventyfive—canal (4) ........ MN-6
County Ditch Number Seventyfour—canal ........ MN-6
County Ditch Number Seventynine—canal (2) ........ MN-6
County Ditch Number Seventyone—canal (3) ........ MN-6
County Ditch Number Seventyseven—canal (3) ........ MN-6
County Ditch Number Seventysix—canal (2) ........ MN-6
County Ditch Number Seventythree—canal (3) ........ MN-6
County Ditch Number Seventytwo—canal (2) ........ MN-6
County Ditch Number Six—canal (12) ........ MN-6
County Ditch Number Six-a—canal ........ MN-6
County Ditch Number Six a—canal ........ MN-6
County Ditch Number Sixteen—canal (16) ........ MN-6
County Ditch Number Sixty—canal (7) ........ MN-6
County Ditch Number Sixtyeight—canal (4) ........ MN-6
County Ditch Number Sixtyfive—canal (4) ........ MN-6
County Ditch Number Sixtyfour—canal (9) ........ MN-6
County Ditch Number Sixtynine—canal (4) ........ MN-6
County Ditch Number Sixtyone—canal (3) ........ MN-6
County Ditch Number Sixtyseven—canal (4) ........ MN-6
County Ditch Number Sixtysix—canal (4) ........ MN-6
County Ditch Number Sixtythree—canal (8) ........ MN-6
County Ditch Number Sixtytwo—canal ........ MN-6
County Ditch Numbers 20 and 66—canal ........ ND-7
County Ditch Number Ten—canal (16) ........ MN-6
County Ditch Number Ten A—canal ........ MN-6
County Ditch Number Thirteen—canal (18) ........ MN-6
County Ditch Number Thirteen A—canal ........ MN-6
County Ditch Number Thirty—canal (4) ........ MN-6
County Ditch Number Thirty A—canal ........ MN-6
County Ditch Number Thirty Eight—canal ........ MN-6
County Ditch Number Thirtyeight—canal (10) ........ MN-6
County Ditch Number Thirtyfive—canal (11) ........ MN-6
County Ditch Number Thirtyfive A—canal ........ MN-6
County Ditch Number Thirtyfive C—canal ........ MN-6
County Ditch Number Thirtyfive D—canal ........ MN-6
County Ditch Number Thirtyfour—canal (6) ........ MN-6
County Ditch Number Thirtynine—canal (9) ........ MN-6
County Ditch Number Thirtynine A—canal ........ MN-6
County Ditch Number Thirtyone—canal (16) ........ MN-6
County Ditch Number Thirtyseven—canal (15) ........ MN-6
County Ditch Number Thirtysix—canal (9) ........ MN-6
County Ditch Number Thirtysix A—canal ........ MN-6
County Ditch Number Thirtythree—canal (10) ........ MN-6
County Ditch Number Thirtythree A—canal ........ MN-6
County Ditch Number Thirtytwo—canal (9) ........ MN-6
County Ditch Number Thirtytwo A—canal ........ MN-6
County Ditch Number Three—canal (16) ........ MN-6
County Ditch Number Twelve—canal (14) ........ MN-6
County Ditch Number Twenty—canal (17) ........ MN-6
County Ditch Number Twentyeight—canal (12) ........ MN-6
County Ditch Number Twentyeight-one—canal ........ MN-6
County Ditch Number Twentyfive—canal (12) ........ MN-6
County Ditch Number Twentyfour—canal (8) ........ MN-6
County Ditch Number Twentynine—canal (11) ........ MN-6
County Ditch Number Twentynine A—canal ........ MN-6
County Ditch Number Twentyone—canal (16) ........ MN-6
County Ditch Number Twentyseven—canal (12) ........ MN-6
County Ditch Number Twentyseven A—canal ........ MN-6
County Ditch Number Twentysix—canal (15) ........ MN-6
County Ditch Number Twentythree—canal (11) ........ MN-6
County Ditch Number Twentythree A—canal ........ MN-6
County Ditch Number Twentythree B—canal ........ MN-6
County Ditch Number Twentytwo—canal (13) ........ MN-6
County Ditch Number Two—canal (17) ........ MN-6
County Ditch Number 1—canal ........ ND-7
County Ditch Number 11—canal (2) ........ ND-7
County Ditch Number 12—canal ........ ND-7
County Ditch Number 13—canal (2) ........ ND-7
County Ditch Number 14—canal ........ SD-7
County Ditch Number 16—canal ........ ND-7
County Ditch Number 16—canal ........ SD-7
County Ditch Number 16A—canal ........ ND-7
County Ditch Number 17—canal ........ ND-7
County Ditch Number 19—canal ........ ND-7
County Ditch Number 21—canal ........ SD-7
County Ditch Number 26—canal ........ ND-7
County Ditch Number 27—canal ........ ND-7
County Ditch Number 29—canal ........ ND-7
County Ditch Number 3—canal (3) ........ ND-7
County Ditch Number 30—canal (2) ........ ND-7
County Ditch Number 32—canal ........ ND-7
County Ditch Number 33—canal ........ ND-7
County Ditch Number 34—canal (2) ........ ND-7
County Ditch Number 35—canal ........ ND-7
County Ditch Number 39—canal ........ ND-7
County Ditch Number 4—canal ........ SD-7
County Ditch Number 42—canal ........ ND-7
County Ditch Number 5—canal ........ ND-7
County Ditch Number 55—canal (2) ........ ND-7
County Ditch Number 58—canal ........ ND-7
County Ditch Number 6—canal ........ ND-7
County Ditch Number 64—canal ........ ND-7
County Ditch Number 67A—canal ........ ND-7
County Ditch Number 67D—canal ........ ND-7
County Ditch Number 7—canal ........ ND-7
County Ditch Number 7—canal ........ SD-7
County Ditch Number 8—canal ........ SD-7
County Ditch Number 9—canal ........ ND-7
County Drain Number Twentyseven—canal ........ MN-6
County Drain Number 20—canal ........ ND-7
County Drain Number 33—canal ........ ND-7
County Drain Number 42—canal ........ ND-7
County East Shop Ctr—locale ........ CA-9
County Fairground—park ........ IL-6
County Fairgrounds—locale ........ NY-2
**County Fair West (subdivision)**—pop pl (2) ........ AZ-5
**County Farm**—pop pl ........ WV-2
County Farm Bridge—hist pl (2) ........ NH-1
County Farm Brook ........ MA-1
County Farm Cem—cemetery ........ AL-4
County Farm Cem—cemetery (5) ........ IL-6
County Farm Cem—cemetery ........ IN-6
County Farm Cem—cemetery ........ KS-7
County Farm Cem—cemetery ........ MO-7
County Farm Cem—cemetery (3) ........ TN-4
County Farm Cem—cemetery ........ VA-3
County Farm Cem—cemetery ........ WI-6
County Farm Ditch ........ IN-6
County Farm Ditch—canal (2) ........ IN-6
County Farm Pond—reservoir ........ MI-6
County Farm Sch—school ........ MI-6
County Farm Sch—school ........ WI-6
County Fire Station Number Seventynine—locale ........ CA-9
County Fish Holding Pond—reservoir ........ NV-8
County Ford—locale ........ AL-4
County Foundation Sch—school ........ MS-4
County F S Camp—locale ........ CA-9
County General Hosp—hospital ........ IN-6
County Grove Ch—church ........ SC-3
County Hill—summit ........ WI-6
County Hollow—valley ........ MO-7
County Home and Infirmary—hospital ........ NY-2
County Home Cove—cave ........ PA-2
County Home Cem—cemetery ........ KY-4
County Home Cem—cemetery ........ MS-4
County Home Cem—cemetery (2) ........ NJ-2
County Home Cem—cemetery (2) ........ NY-2
County Home Cem—cemetery (2) ........ NC-3
County Home Cem—cemetery (5) ........ OH-6
County Home Cem—cemetery ........ OK-5
County Home Cem—cemetery (2) ........ PA-2
County Home Cem—cemetery ........ SD-7
County Home Cem—cemetery ........ TX-5
County Home Cem—cemetery ........ WI-6
County Hosp—hospital ........ NE-7
County House Branch—stream ........ MO-7
County House Hill—summit ........ TN-4
County House Mtn—summit ........ NJ-2
County HS—school ........ CO-8
County HS—school (5) ........ GA-3
County HS—school ........ TN-4
County HS—school (2) ........ VA-3
County HS—school ........ WV-2
County Industrial Farm—locale ........ CA-9
County Industrial Road Camp—locale ........ CA-9
County Industrial Sch—school ........ VA-3
County Infirmary Cem—cemetery ........ OH-6
County Infirmary Farm—hospital ........ OH-6
County Island—island ........ NJ-2
County JHS—school (2) ........ VA-3
**County Junction**—pop pl ........ PA-2
County Junction Resort—locale ........ TN-4
County Juvenile Center—other ........ IN-6
County Lake—lake ........ IL-6
County Lake—lake ........ MN-6
County Lake—lake ........ MS-4
County Lake—reservoir (4) ........ AL-4
County Lake—reservoir ........ KY-4
County Lake—reservoir (2) ........ MS-4
County Lake—swamp ........ TX-5
County Lake Dam ........ AL-4
County Lake Park—park ........ IA-7
County Lake State Wildlife Mngmt Area—park ........ MO-7
County Landing—locale ........ LA-4
County Line ........ AL-4
County Line—locale ........ AL-4
County Line—locale ........ AR-4
County Line—locale (2) ........ GA-3
County Line—locale ........ PA-2
County Line—locale (4) ........ TX-5
**County Line**—pop pl (3) ........ AL-4
**County Line**—pop pl ........ MS-4
**County Line**—pop pl ........ NY-2
**Countyline**—pop pl ........ NC-3
**Countyline**—pop pl ........ OK-5
**County Line**—pop pl (2) ........ PA-2
**County Line**—pop pl ........ TN-4
**Countyline**—pop pl ........ TN-4
**County Line**—pop pl (2) ........ TX-5
**County Line**—pop pl (2) ........ WI-6
County Line Baptist Ch ........ MS-4
County Line Baptist Ch—church ........ MS-4
County Line Baptist Ch (historical)—church ........ AL-4
County Line Baptist Church ........ AL-4
County Line Baptist Church—hist pl ........ AL-4
County Line Branch—stream (3) ........ AL-4
County Line Branch—stream ........ AR-4
County Line Branch—stream ........ GA-3
County Line Branch—stream ........ IL-6
County Line Branch—stream ........ IN-6
County Line Branch—stream ........ LA-4
County Line Branch—stream ........ NC-3
County Line Branch—stream (2) ........ PA-2
County Line Branch—stream ........ VA-3
Countyline Bridge—other ........ IL-6
County Line Bridge—other (2) ........ IL-6
County Line Brook—stream ........ NY-2
County Line Canal—canal ........ FL-3
County Line Canyon—valley ........ CA-9
County Line Canyon—valley ........ NV-8
County Line Cem ........ AL-4
County Line Cem ........ MS-4
County Line Cem—cemetery (4) ........ AL-4
County Line Cem—cemetery (2) ........ AR-4
County Line Cem—cemetery (2) ........ GA-3
County Line Cem—cemetery ........ IL-6
County Line Cem—cemetery ........ IN-6
County Line Cem—cemetery ........ IA-4
County Line Cem—cemetery (2) ........ MI-6
County Line Cem—cemetery (2) ........ MN-6
County Line Cem—cemetery (11) ........ MS-4
County Line Cem—cemetery ........ MO-7
County Line Cem—cemetery (2) ........ NY-2
County Line Cem—cemetery ........ NC-3
County Line Cem—cemetery ........ OH-6
Countyline Cem—cemetery ........ OK-5
County Line Cem—cemetery ........ TN-4
County Line Cem—cemetery (3) ........ TX-5
County Line Cem—cemetery (2) ........ WI-6
County Line Ch ........ AL-4
County Line Ch ........ TN-4
County Line Ch—church (19) ........ AL-4
County Line Ch—church (7) ........ AR-4
County Line Ch—church (29) ........ GA-3
County Line Ch—church ........ IL-6
County Line Ch—church (2) ........ IN-6
County Line Ch—church ........ LA-4
County Line Ch—church ........ MI-6
County Line Ch—church (14) ........ MS-4
County Line Ch—church (3) ........ MO-7
County Line Ch—church (2) ........ OH-6
County Line Ch—church ........ OK-5
Countyline Ch—church ........ OK-5
County Line Ch—church ........ TN-4
County Line Ch—church (2) ........ TX-5
County-Line Ch—church ........ TX-5
County Line Ch—church (12) ........ TX-5
County Line Ch—church (7) ........ VA-3
County Line Ch—church ........ WI-6
County Line Ch (historical)—church ........ AL-4
County Line Ch (historical)—church ........ MS-4
County Line Ch (historical)—church ........ TN-4
County Line Ch Number 2—church ........ AL-4
County Line Ch of Christ ........ AL-4
County Line Ch of Christ ........ TN-4
County Line Community Ch—church ........ TX-5
County Line Community Club—building ........ MS-4
County Line Creek ........ AL-4
County Line Creek ........ NC-3

*County Line Creek* .... VA-3
County Line Creek—*stream* (2) .... AL-4
County Line Creek—*stream* .... CA-9
County Line Creek—*stream* .... KS-7
County Line Creek—*stream* .... MD-2
County Line Creek—*stream* (2) .... MI-6
County Line Creek—*stream* .... OK-5
County Line Creek—*stream* .... TX-5
County Line Creek—*stream* .... WA-9
County Line Creek—*stream* .... WI-6
County Line Creek—*stream* .... WY-8
County Line Cross Roads—*locale* .... VA-3
County Line Dam—*dam* .... SD-7
County Line Ditch—*canal* .... IN-6
County Line Ditch*—*canal* .... IA-7
County Line Ditch—*canal* .... NE-7
County Line Ditch—*canal* .... NC-3
County Line Ditch Lateral No 1—*canal* .... MO-7
County Line Drain—*canal* .... MI-6
County Line Drain—*stream* .... MI-6
County Line Draw—*valley* .... TX-5
County Line Draw—*valley* .... WY-8
County Line Flow—*lake* .... NY-2
County Line Ford—*locale* .... MO-7
County Line Fork—*locale* .... VA-3
County Line Gap—*gap* .... TN-4
County Line Gin—*locale* .... TX-5
County Line Hill—*summit* .... AL-4
County Line Hill—*summit* .... CA-9
County Line Hill—*summit* .... TX-5
County Line Hollow—*valley* .... PA-2
County Line HS—*school* .... AR-4
County Line Inlet—*bay* .... TX-5
County Line Island—*island* .... NY-2
County Line Island—*island* .... TN-4
County Line Knob—*summit* .... AR-4
*County Line Lake* .... MI-6
*County Line Lake* .... WI-6
County Line Lake—*lake* (4) .... MI-6
County Line Lake—*lake* .... NY-2
County Line Lake—*lake* .... WI-6
County Line Lake—*reservoir* .... IN-6
County Line Lakes—*reservoir* .... TX-5
County Line Landing—*locale* .... FL-3
County Line Marsh—*swamp* .... NE-7
*County Line Missionary Baptist Church* .... AL-4
County Line Mtn—*summit* (2) .... NY-2
County Line Mtn—*summit* .... VA-3
County Line Pasture—*flat* .... KS-7
County Line Picnic Area—*area* .... PA-2
County Line Pit—*mine* .... NM-5
County Line Pond—*lake* .... NV-8
*County Line Post Office* .... TN-4
Countyline Post Office (historical)—*building* .... TN-4
*County Line Primitive Baptist Church* .... AL-4
County Line Public Use Area—*park* .... NC-3
County Line Rec Area—*park* .... AR-4
County Line Ridge—*ridge* .... CA-9
County Line Ridge—*ridge* .... NC-3
County Line Ridge—*ridge* (2) .... UT-8
County Line Rsvr—*reservoir* .... CO-8
County Line Rsvr—*reservoir* .... OR-9
County Line Run—*stream* (3) .... PA-2
County Line Sch—*school* .... FL-3
County Line Sch—*school* .... GA-3
County Line Sch—*school* .... ID-8
Countyline Sch—*school* .... IL-6
County Line Sch—*school* .... IA-7
County Line Sch—*school* (2) .... MI-6
County Line Sch—*school* .... MO-7
County Line Sch—*school* .... TN-4
County Line Sch—*school* .... TX-5
County Line Sch—*school* .... WI-6
County Line Sch and Lodge—*hist pl* .... AR-4
County Line Sch (historical)—*school* (3) .... AL-4
County Line Sch (historical)—*school* (7) .... MS-4
County Line Sch (historical)—*school* .... TN-4
County Line Shop Ctr—*locale* .... PA-2
County Line Spring—*spring* .... WA-9
County Line State Wildlife Mngmt Are—*park* .... MN-6
County Line Station—*locale* .... PA-2
County Line Swamp—*swamp* .... GA-3
County Line Tank—*reservoir* .... AZ-5
County Line Tank—*reservoir* (2) .... NM-5
County Line Tank—*reservoir* (5) .... TX-5
County Line (Township of)—*fmr MCD* .... AR-4
County Line Trail—*trail* .... CA-9
County Line Trail—*trail* .... FL-3
County Line Trail—*trail* .... MD-2
County Line Trail—*trail* .... PA-2
County Line Trail—*trail* .... WA-9
County Line Trail—*trail* .... WV-2
*County Line Waterhole* .... OR-9
County Line Windmill—*locale* .... TX-5
County Memorial Airp—*airport* .... MO-7
County Memorial Cem—*cemetery* .... NC-3
County Memorial Cem—*cemetery* .... SC-3
County Memorial Cem—*cemetery* .... TX-5
County Memorial Hosp—*hospital* .... CA-9
County Memorial Hosp—*hospital* (2) .... IN-6
County Memorial Hosp—*hospital* .... VA-3
County Memorial Park—*cemetery* .... MO-7
County Memorial Park—*cemetery* .... NC-3
County Memorial Park Cem—*cemetery* .... MO-7
County Memorial Park Cem—*cemetery* .... PA-2
County Memory Gardens—*cemetery* .... AL-4
County Memory Gardens—*cemetery* .... SC-3
County Mine—*mine* .... CA-9
County Mission Ch—*church* .... IA-7
County Park Campgrounds—*locale* .... TX-5
County Park Dock—*locale* .... TN-4
County Peak—*summit* .... WY-8
County Plaza Shop Ctr—*locale* .... TN-4
County Pond—*reservoir* .... MS-4
County Pond—*reservoir* .... VA-3
County Pond Dam—*dam* .... MS-4
County Poor Farm—*other* .... GA-3
**County Prison Spur**—*pop pl* .... GA-3
*County Regional Airport* .... NC-3
County Road Ditch—*canal* .... CA-9
County Road Drain—*canal* .... UT-8
*County Road Hollow* .... MO-7
County Road Hollow—*valley* .... MO-7
County Road Lake—*lake* .... ME-1
County Road Trail—*trail* .... MA-1
County Rsvr—*reservoir* .... PA-2
County Run—*stream* .... IN-6
County Sanitarium—*hospital* .... IL-6
County Sch—*school* .... MA-1
County Sch—*school* .... TN-4
County Sch No 1—*school* .... KY-4
County Sch No 2—*school* .... GA-3
County Sch No 2—*school* .... KY-4
County Sch No 3—*school* .... KY-4
County Sch Number One Hundred—*school* .... MN-6
County School Administration—*locale* .... NC-3
**County Seat Gardens (trailer park)**—*pop pl* .... DE-2
County South Cem—*cemetery* .... TX-5
County Spring—*spring* .... OR-9
*County Spur* .... MI-6
**County Square Estates (subdivision)**—*pop pl* .... NC-3
County Street Hist Dist—*hist pl* .... MA-1
**County Strip**—*pop pl* .... CA-9
County Subsidiary Prison No 056—*locale* .... NC-3
County Tank—*reservoir* .... AZ-5
County Tank—*reservoir* .... TX-5
County Technical Education Center—*school* .... SC-3
County Training Sch—*school* .... AL-4
County Training Sch—*school* .... FL-3
County Training Sch—*school* .... MI-6
County Trough Spring—*spring* .... OR-9
County Vocational Sch—*school* .... GA-3
County Voc-Tech Sch—*school* .... MS-4
County War Memorial Fairgrounds—*other* .... KY-4
County Well—*well* .... AZ-5
County Well (Dry)—*well* .... CA-9
County Well Windmill—*locale* .... TX-5
County Windmill—*locale* (3) .... TX-5
**County Wood Subdivision**—*pop pl* .... UT-8
County Youth Camp—*locale* .... WY-8
*Coup* .... FM-9
Couparle Ch—*church* .... MS-4
Coupe Colin—*channel* .... LA-4
Coupe Creuse—*channel* .... LA-4
Coupeland Branch—*stream* .... TX-5
Coupe Nouvelle—*bay* .... LA-4
Coupe Ranch—*locale* .... TX-5
Coupe Ridge—*ridge* .... LA-4
Couperle (historical)—*locale* .... MS-4
**Coupeville**—*pop pl* .... WA-9
Coupeville Sch—*school* .... WA-9
**Coupland**—*pop pl* .... TX-5
Coupland Cem—*cemetery* .... TN-4
Coupland Ranch—*locale* (2) .... NM-5
Coupland Tank—*reservoir* .... NM-5
Coupland Well—*well* .... NM-5
Couples Run—*stream* .... PA-2
Couples Store (historical)—*locale* .... TN-4
Coupling Field—*flat* .... NV-8
Coupling Spring—*spring* .... NV-8
**Coupon**—*pop pl* .... PA-2
Coupon Bight—*bay* .... FL-3
Coupon Bight Aquatic Preserve—*park* .... FL-3
Coupon Tank—*reservoir* .... AZ-5
Coup Point—*cape* .... LA-4
Coupville Airpark Airp—*airport* .... WA-9
Courage, Bayou—*gut* .... LA-4
Courant, Bayou—*gut* (2) .... LA-4
Courbet Mine—*mine* .... NV-8
Courchene Cem—*cemetery* .... MT-8
Courchesne—*locale* .... TX-5
Courchesne Sch—*school* .... TX-5
*Courcy Point* .... MD-2
Courdin, David W., House—*hist pl* .... MO-7
*Courdoroy Meadows* .... ID-8
Courier Field—*park* .... FL-3
Courier Gulch—*valley* .... ID-8
Courier Mine—*mine* .... ID-8
Courier Mine—*mine* .... OR-9
Courney Cem—*cemetery* .... LA-4
Cournoyer Pond—*reservoir* .... MA-1
Course Brook—*stream* .... MA-1
*Course Gold Creek* .... CA-9
Coursen Grove Cem—*cemetery* .... KS-7
Coursen Grove Shcool Number Two—*school* .... KS-7
Coursens Grove (historical)—*locale* .... KS-7
*Coursenville* .... NJ-2
Course Point—*cape* .... AK-9
Courses Landing—*locale* .... NJ-2
Coursey Lake—*reservoir* .... GA-3
Coursey Lookout Tower—*locale* .... MS-4
Coursey Point—*cape* .... MD-2
Coursey Pond—*reservoir* .... DE-2
Coursey Pond Dam—*dam* .... DE-2
Coursey Rsvr No. 1—*reservoir* .... CO-8
*Courseys Point* .... MD-2
Coursey Springs State Fish Hatchery—*locale* .... VA-3
Courson Cem—*cemetery* .... IL-6
Courson Eddy—*bay* .... PA-2
Courson Island—*island* .... PA-2
Courson Lake—*lake* .... MI-6
*Court* .... MI-6
Court—*hist pl* .... CA-9
Court—*uninc pl* .... CA-9
**Courtableau**—*pop pl* .... LA-4
Courtableau, Bayou—*stream* .... LA-4
Courtableau Outlet Channel, Bayou—*canal* .... LA-4
Courtade School—*locale* .... MI-6
Court at King of Prussia—*locale* .... PA-2
Court Bldg (Furniture Building)—*hist pl* .... IN-6
Court Branch—*stream* .... TX-5
Court Clerk's Office-County & Circuit—*hist pl* .... KY-4
Court Creek—*stream* .... IL-6
**Courtdale**—*pop pl* .... PA-2
Courtdale Borough—*civil* .... PA-2
Courtemanche Ranch—*locale* .... SD-7
**Courtenay**—*pop pl* .... FL-3
**Courtenay**—*pop pl* .... ND-7
**Courtenay**—*pop pl* .... SC-3
Courtenay Cem—*cemetery* .... MS-4
Courtenay Cem—*cemetery* .... ND-7
Courtenay Sch—*school* .... SC-3
**Courtenay Township**—*pop pl* .... ND-7
Courteney, James, House—*hist pl* .... KY-4
Courte Oreilles, Lac—*lake* .... WI-6
**Courter**—*pop pl* .... IN-6
Courter Cem—*cemetery* .... IN-6
Courter Drain—*canal* .... MI-6
Courter Prairie—*flat* .... OR-9
Courter-Ritchey Cem—*cemetery* .... KS-7
Court Exchange Building-National Casket Company—*hist pl* .... NY-2
Court Ground—*locale* .... GA-3
Courthey Cem—*cemetery* .... MS-4
Court Hill—*summit* .... MA-1
Court Hill (historical)—*locale* .... AL-4
Court Hill P.O. (historical)—*locale* .... AL-4
*Court House* .... NC-3
Courthouse—*locale* .... GA-3
**Court House**—*pop pl* .... VA-3
Courthouse—*uninc pl* .... MD-2
Court House—*uninc pl* .... NC-3
Court House, The—*arch* .... TN-4
Courthouse and Jail House Rocks—*hist pl* .... NE-7
Courthouse and Lawyers' Row—*hist pl* .... LA-4
Courthouse Bald—*summit* .... NC-3
Courthouse Bay—*bay* .... NC-3
Courthouse Branch—*stream* .... GA-3
Court House Branch—*stream* .... KY-4
Courthouse Branch—*stream* .... VA-3
*Court House Butte* .... AZ-5
Courthouse Butte—*summit* .... AZ-5
Courthouse Butte—*summit* .... WY-8
Courthouse Butte Rsvr—*reservoir* .... WY-8
Courthouse Cave—*cave* .... MO-7
Courthouse Center—*hist pl* .... OH-6
*Courthouse Creek* .... VA-3
Courthouse Creek—*stream* .... CO-8
Courthouse Creek—*stream* .... MS-4
Courthouse Creek—*stream* .... NC-3
Courthouse Creek—*stream* .... OK-5
Courthouse Creek—*stream* (3) .... VA-3
Courthouse Falls—*falls* .... NC-3
Courthouse Fork—*stream* .... KY-4
Courthouse Gap—*gap* .... GA-3
Courthouse Gap—*gap* .... OK-5
Courthouse Green—*locale* .... NC-3
Courthouse Hill Hist Dist—*hist pl* .... WI-6
Courthouse Hollow—*valley* .... MO-7
Courthouse Hollow—*valley* .... OK-5
Courthouse Hollow—*valley* .... TN-4
Courthouse Hollow Cave—*cave* .... TN-4
Courthouse Hollow Creek—*stream* .... TN-4
*Courthouse Knob* .... NC-3
Courthouse Knob—*summit* .... NC-3
Courthouse Landing—*locale* .... VA-3
Court House (Magisterial District)—*fmr MCD* .... VA-3
Courthouse (Magisterial District)—*fmr MCD* .... VA-3
Court House (Magisterial District)—*fmr MCD* .... VA-3
Court House (Magisterial District)—*fmr MCD* .... WV-2
Courthouse Millpond—*reservoir* .... VA-3
Courthouse Mountain—*ridge* .... VA-3
*Courthouse Mtn* .... AZ-5
Courthouse Mtn—*summit* .... AZ-5
Courthouse Mtn—*summit* .... CO-8
Courthouse Mtn—*summit* .... MT-8
Courthouse Mtn—*summit* .... TX-5
Courthouse of American Samoa—*hist pl* .... AS-9
Courthouse Pasture—*flat* .... UT-8
Courthouse Point—*cape* .... ME-1
Courthouse Point—*cape* .... MD-2
Courthouse Pond—*swamp* .... FL-3
Courthouse Prairie—*flat* .... OK-5
Courthouse Residential Hist Dist—*hist pl* .... MI-6
Courthouse Ridge—*ridge* .... NC-3
Courthouse Road—*post sta* .... MS-4
*Court House Rock* .... AZ-5
Courthouse Rock—*cliff* .... WV-2
Courthouse Rock—*pillar* .... CA-9
Courthouse Rock—*pillar* .... CO-8
Courthouse Rock—*pillar* .... OR-9
Courthouse Rock—*summit* .... AZ-5
Courthouse Rock—*summit* .... KY-4
Courthouse Rock—*summit* (2) .... OR-9
Courthouse Rock—*summit* .... UT-8
Courthouse Rock Canal—*canal* .... NE-7
Courthouse Rock Sch—*school* .... NE-7
Courthouse Rock Trail—*trail* .... KY-4
Courthouse Sch—*school* .... VA-3
Courthouse Slough—*gut* .... AR-4
Courthouse Spring—*spring* .... TN-4
Courthouse Spring—*spring* .... UT-8
Courthouse Square—*hist pl* .... OR-9
Courthouse Square and Mechanics' Row Hist Dist—*hist pl* .... KY-4
Courthouse Square Hist Dist—*hist pl* .... IN-6
Courthouse Square Hist Dist—*hist pl* .... MI-6
Courthouse Swamp—*stream* .... VA-3
Courthouse Towers—*pillar* .... UT-8
Court House (Township of)—*fmr MCD* .... NC-3
Courthouse Trail—*trail* .... CO-8
Courthouse Wash—*valley* .... UT-8
Courthouse Wash Bridge—*bridge* .... UT-8
Courthouse Wash Pictographs—*hist pl* .... UT-8
Courthouse Well—*well* (2) .... AZ-5
Courtis Sch—*school* .... MI-6
Court JHS—*school* .... NM-5
Court Lake—*lake* .... ND-7
Courtland—*locale* .... AZ-5
**Courtland**—*pop pl* .... AL-4
**Courtland**—*pop pl* .... CA-9
**Courtland**—*pop pl* .... KS-7
**Courtland**—*pop pl* .... MN-6
**Courtland**—*pop pl* .... MS-4
**Courtland**—*pop pl* .... TN-4
**Courtland**—*pop pl* .... VA-3
**Courtland Acres (subdivision)**—*pop pl* .... NC-3
Courtland Airfield—*airport* .... AL-4
Courtland Baptist Ch—*church* .... MS-4
Courtland Bay—*swamp* .... MN-6
Courtland Bennett Sch—*school* .... WI-6
Courtland Birchard Pond—*reservoir* .... PA-2
Courtland Canal—*canal* .... KS-7
Courtland Canal—*canal* .... NE-7
Courtland Cem—*cemetery* .... KS-7
Courtland Cem—*cemetery* .... MI-6
Courtland Cem—*cemetery* .... MN-6
Courtland Ch—*church* .... MS-4
Courtland Ch—*church* .... TX-5
Courtland Community Hosp—*hospital* .... AL-4
*Courtland Elementary School* .... AL-4
Courtland Flats—*hist pl* .... OH-6
Courtland HS—*school* .... AL-4
Courtland Lake—*lake* .... WI-6
Courtland (Magisterial District)—*fmr MCD* .... VA-3
Courtland Mtn—*summit* .... AL-4
Courtland Oil Field—*oilfield* .... MS-4
**Courtland Park**—*pop pl* .... VA-3
**Courtland Park (subdivision)**—*pop pl* .... NC-3
Courtland Place—*locale* .... TN-4
Courtland Playground—*park* .... WA-9
Courtland Post Office—*building* .... AL-4
Courtland Sch (historical)—*school* .... MS-4
**Courtland (Town of)**—*pop pl* .... WI-6
Courtland Township—*civil* .... KS-7
**Courtland (Township of)**—*pop pl* .... MI-6
**Courtland (Township of)**—*pop pl* .... MN-6
Courtlandt Place Hist Dist—*hist pl* .... TX-5
Courtland West Canal—*canal* .... KS-7
**Courtleigh**—*pop pl* .... MD-2
Courtleys Run—*stream* .... PA-2
Court Martial Lake—*lake* .... FL-3
Courtney—*locale* .... TX-5
**Courtney**—*pop pl* .... MO-7
**Courtney**—*pop pl* .... NC-3
**Courtney**—*pop pl* .... OK-5
**Courtney**—*pop pl* .... PA-2
**Courtney**—*pop pl* .... TX-5
**Courtney**—*pop pl* .... VA-3
**Courtney**—*pop pl* .... WV-2
Courtney Branch—*stream* .... MS-4
Courtney Branch—*stream* .... TN-4
Courtney Branch—*stream* .... WV-2
Courtney Butte—*summit* .... OR-9
Courtney Cabin—*hist pl* .... WA-9
Courtney Canyon—*valley* .... WA-9
Courtney Cem—*cemetery* .... AR-4
Courtney Cem—*cemetery* .... LA-4
Courtney Cem—*cemetery* .... MS-4
Courtney Cem—*cemetery* .... MO-7
Courtney Cem—*cemetery* .... OK-5
Courtney Cem—*cemetery* .... PA-2
Courtney Cem—*cemetery* .... SC-3
Courtney Cem—*cemetery* (3) .... TN-4
Courtney Cem—*cemetery* .... WV-2
**Courtney Corner**—*pop pl* .... IN-6
Courtney Creek—*stream* (2) .... MS-4
Courtney Creek—*stream* .... OK-5
Courtney Creek—*stream* (2) .... OR-9
Courtney Creek—*stream* .... TX-5
Courtney Creek Sch—*school* .... OR-9
Courtney Ditch—*canal* .... OR-9
*Courtney Elementary School* .... NC-3
Courtney Hollow—*valley* .... AR-4
Courtney Hollow—*valley* .... NY-2
Courtney Hollow—*valley* .... VA-3
Courtney House—*hist pl* .... KY-4
Courtney HS—*school* .... NC-3
Courtney Island—*island* .... SC-3
Courtney Lake—*lake* .... MI-6
Courtney Lake—*lake* .... MN-6
Courtney Millpond—*reservoir* .... VA-3
Courtney Mine—*mine* .... NM-5
Courtney Peak—*summit* .... WA-9
Courtney Point—*cape* .... FL-3
Courtney Pond—*lake* .... NY-2
Courtney Ponds—*lake* .... NJ-2
*Courtney Post Office* .... OK-5
Courtney Ranch—*locale* .... NM-5
Courtney Ridge—*ridge* (2) .... WV-2
Courtney Run—*stream* .... WV-2
Courtney Sch (abandoned)—*school* .... PA-2
Courtneys Creek—*stream* .... MT-8
Courtneys Mills—*locale* .... PA-2
Courtneys Old Bay—*lake* .... FL-3
Court of the Patriarchs—*valley* .... UT-8
*Courtoi Creek* .... MO-7
**Courtois**—*pop pl* .... MO-7
Courtois Cem—*cemetery* .... MO-7
Courtois Church (historical)—*locale* .... MO-7
*Courtois Creek* .... MO-7
Courtois Creek—*stream* .... MO-7
*Courtois Pond* .... WI-6
Courtois Township—*civil* .... MO-7
*Court Oreilles Lake* .... WI-6
*Court Oreilles River* .... WI-6
**Court Park (subdivision)**—*pop pl* .... MA-1
**Courtright**—*pop pl* .... WV-2
Courtright Canyon—*valley* .... WA-9
Courtright Corners—*locale* .... NY-2
Courtright Rsvr—*reservoir* (2) .... CA-9
Courtright Sch—*school* .... OH-6
Court Rock—*pillar* .... NV-8
**Courtrock**—*pop pl* .... OR-9
Courtrock Post Office Bldg—*building* .... OR-9
Courtrock Sch—*school* .... OR-9
Courts Cem—*cemetery* .... OK-5
Courts Creek—*stream* .... NC-3
Court Sheriff Rec Area—*locale* .... MT-8
*Courtside School* .... KS-7
Court Spring—*spring* .... OR-9
Court Square—*uninc pl* .... GA-3
Court Square-Dexter Ave Hist Dist (Boundary Increase)—*hist pl* .... AL-4
Court Square Hist Dist—*hist pl* .... AL-4
Court Square Hist Dist—*hist pl* .... KY-4
Court Square Hist Dist—*hist pl* .... MA-1
Court Square Hist Dist—*hist pl* .... TN-4
Court Square Hist Dist (Boundary Increase)—*hist pl* .... KY-4
Court Square Plaza Shop Ctr—*locale* .... AL-4
Court Street Baptist Ch—*church* .... RI-1
Court Street Baptist Church—*hist pl* .... VA-3
Court Street Bridge—*hist pl* .... NY-2
Court Street Cem—*cemetery* .... ME-1
Court Street-Chemeketa Street Hist Dist—*hist pl* .... OR-9
Court Street Firehouse—*hist pl* .... OH-6
Court Street Hist Dist—*hist pl* .... MS-4
Court Street Hist Dist—*hist pl* (2) .... NY-2
Court Street Methodist Ch—*church* .... AL-4
Court Street Methodist Church—*hist pl* .... WI-6
Court Street Sch—*school* .... NY-2
Court Street Sch—*school* .... OH-6
Court Street United Methodist Ch—*church* .... MS-4
Court Tennis Bldg—*hist pl* .... SC-3
Courtview—*hist pl* .... AL-4
Courtview Sch—*school* .... NY-2
Courtville Cem—*cemetery* .... LA-4
**Courtyard Condominium, The**—*pop pl* .... UT-8
Courtyard Shoppes—*locale* .... FL-3
*Courtyard Townhome Condominiums Phase 2* .... UT-8
County Center Number Three—*other* .... CA-9
Courville, Bayou—*stream* .... LA-4
Courville Creek—*stream* .... MT-8
Courville Sch—*school* .... MI-6
**Coury Heights**—*pop pl* .... MA-1
*Coury Park* .... AZ-5
*Cousaia Marsh* .... VA-3
*Cousaic Marsh* .... VA-3
Cousatin Bayou—*stream* .... AR-4
Couse—*pop pl* .... NY-2
Couse Creek—*stream* .... OR-9
Couse Creek—*stream* .... WA-9
Couse Hill—*summit* .... NY-2
Couser Barn—*hist pl* .... NE-7
Couser Canyon—*valley* .... CA-9
**Coushatta**—*pop pl* .... LA-4
Coushatta Bank Bldg—*hist pl* .... LA-4
Coushatta Bayou—*gut* .... LA-4
Coushatta Country Club—*other* .... LA-4
Coushatta Creek—*stream* .... TX-5
**Coushatta Ind Res**—*pop pl* .... LA-4
Coushatta Oil Field—*oilfield* .... LA-4
**Coushatta Village**—*pop pl* .... TX-5
Cousiac Marsh—*swamp* .... VA-3
Cousin Canal—*canal* .... LA-4
Cousin Cem—*cemetery* .... LA-4
Cousin Cem—*cemetery* .... MS-4
Cousineau Lake—*lake* .... MI-6
Cousino—*locale* .... MI-6
Cousino Drain—*stream* .... MI-6
Cousino HS—*school* .... MI-6
Cousin Point—*cape* .... AK-9
*Cousin River* .... ME-1
Cousins—*island* .... OR-9
Cousins Brook—*stream* .... ME-1
Cousins Cabin—*locale* .... WA-9
Cousins Canal—*canal* .... LA-4
Cousins Cem—*cemetery* .... GA-3
Cousins Cem—*cemetery* .... OH-6
*Cousins Creek* .... TX-5
Cousins Draw—*valley* .... WY-8
Cousins Gulch—*valley* .... CA-9
Cousins House—*hist pl* .... SC-3
Cousins HS—*school* .... GA-3
Cousins Island—*island* .... ME-1
**Cousins Island**—*pop pl* .... ME-1
Cousins Point—*cape* .... TX-5
*Cousins River* .... ME-1
Cousins River—*stream* .... ME-1
Coutant Creek—*stream* .... WY-8
Couter Rsvr—*reservoir* .... OR-9
Couters Neck—*locale* .... LA-4
Couthard, Lake—*lake* .... ND-7
Couts Ditch—*canal* .... WY-8
Cout Lake—*lake* .... NM-5
Coutlerville Post Office (historical)—*building* .... TN-4
Coutolenc (Site)—*locale* .... CA-9
*Coutre* .... MO-7
Couts Cem—*cemetery* .... TN-4
Coutta Cem—*cemetery* .... TN-4
Couturier Lake—*lake* .... SC-3
Couvent Sch—*school* .... LA-4
Couverden Island—*island* .... AK-9
Couverden Rock—*island* .... AK-9
Couzens Sch—*school* .... MI-6
Covach Lake—*lake* .... MI-6
Covada—*locale* .... WA-9
*Covajea Mountains* .... AZ-5
Covalt—*locale* .... PA-2
Covanter Cem—*cemetery* .... PA-2
Covas Creek—*stream* .... FL-3
Cov Branch—*stream* .... MO-7
*Cove* .... MA-1
*Cove* .... NC-3
Cove—*locale* .... GA-3
Cove—*locale* .... MD-2
Cove—*locale* .... OH-6
Cove—*locale* .... PA-2
**Cove**—*pop pl* .... AZ-5
**Cove**—*pop pl* .... AR-4
**Cove**—*pop pl* .... FL-3
**Cove**—*pop pl* .... MN-6
**Cove**—*pop pl* .... MO-7
**Cove**—*pop pl* .... NC-3
**Cove**—*pop pl* .... OR-9
**Cove**—*pop pl* .... PA-2
**Cove**—*pop pl* (2) .... TX-5
**Cove**—*pop pl* (2) .... UT-8
**Cove**—*pop pl* .... WA-9
Cove, Fort (historical)—*locale* .... UT-8
*Cove, The* .... AL-4
*Cove, The* .... CA-9
*Cove, The* .... CT-1
*Cove, The* .... NY-2
Cove, The—*area* .... ID-8
Cove, The—*basin* .... CA-9
Cove, The—*basin* .... GA-3
Cove, The—*basin* .... MA-1
Cove, The—*basin* (2) .... NV-8
Cove, The—*basin* .... OR-9
Cove, The—*basin* (6) .... UT-8
Cove, The—*basin* .... VA-3
Cove, The—*bay* .... CA-9
Cove, The—*bay* (2) .... NY-2
Cove, The—*bay* .... NC-3
Cove, The—*bay* (2) .... PA-2
Cove, The—*bay* .... RI-1
Cove, The—*bay* .... SC-3
Cove, The—*bay* .... TX-5
Cove, The—*bend* .... NV-8
Cove, The—*civil* .... UT-8
Cove, The—*cove* (2) .... MA-1
Cove, The—*flat* .... CA-9
Cove, The—*flat* (2) .... PA-2
Cove, The—*lake* .... AL-4
**Cove, The**—*pop pl* .... FL-3
Cove, The—*slope* .... NV-8
Cove, The—*valley* (2) .... AZ-5
Cove, The—*valley* .... ID-8
Cove, The—*valley* (2) .... PA-2
Cove, The—*valley* .... TX-5
Cove, The—*valley* (6) .... UT-8
Cove Arch—*arch* .... UT-8
**Cove at Hidden Valley, The**—*pop pl* .... UT-8
*Cove at Tiburon, The* .... AZ-5
Cove Baptist Ch—*church* .... FL-3
Cove Bay—*bay* .... MN-6
Cove Bayou—*gut* .... TX-5
Cove Beach—*beach* .... OR-9
Cove Boat Ramp—*locale* .... NC-3
*Cove Branch* .... NC-3
Cove Branch—*stream* .... AL-4
Cove Branch—*stream* (2) .... AR-4
Cove Branch—*stream* .... GA-3
Cove Branch—*stream* (2) .... KY-4
Cove Branch—*stream* (2) .... NC-3
Cove Branch—*stream* (5) .... TN-4
Cove Branch—*stream* .... TX-5
Cove Branch—*stream* (5) .... VA-3
Cove Branch—*stream* .... WV-2
*Cove Brook* .... ME-1
*Cove Brook* .... MA-1
Cove Brook—*stream* .... ME-1
Cove Brook—*stream* .... MA-1
Cove Brook—*stream* .... NY-2
Coveburg—*locale* .... PA-2
Cove Burying Ground—*cemetery* .... MA-1
Cove Camp—*locale* .... ID-8
Cove Camp—*locale* .... MD-2
Cove Camp—*locale* .... NV-8
Cove Camp—*locale* .... OR-9
Cove Campground—*locale* .... CA-9
Cove Campground—*locale* .... CO-8
Cove Canal—*canal* .... ID-8
Cove Canyon—*valley* (3) .... AZ-5
Cove Canyon—*valley* .... CA-9
Cove Canyon—*valley* .... CO-8
Cove Canyon—*valley* .... NV-8
Cove Canyon—*valley* (3) .... UT-8
Cove (CCD)—*cens area* .... OR-9
Cove Cem—*cemetery* (3) .... AR-4
Cove Cem—*cemetery* .... CA-9
Cove Cem—*cemetery* .... CT-1
Cove Cem—*cemetery* .... ME-1
Cove Cem—*cemetery* (2) .... MO-7
Cove Cem—*cemetery* .... OR-9
Cove Cem—*cemetery* .... TX-5
Cove Center (Shop Ctr)—*locale* .... FL-3
*Cove Ch* .... TN-4
Cove Ch—*church* .... AL-4
Cove Ch—*church* .... AR-4
Cove Ch—*church* (2) .... GA-3
Cove Ch—*church* .... PA-2
Cove Ch—*church* .... VA-3
Cove Ch—*church* .... WV-2
Cove Ch (abandoned)—*church* .... MO-7
Cove Chapel—*church* .... AR-4
Cove Chapel—*church* .... TN-4
Cove Chapel—*church* (2) .... WV-2
Cove Ch (historical)—*church* .... AL-4
**Cove City**—*pop pl* (2) .... NC-3
Cove City—*uninc pl* .... TX-5
Cove City (Township of)—*fmr MCD* .... AR-4
**Cove Colony**—*pop pl* .... VA-3
*Cove Creek* .... AL-4
*Cove Creek* .... AR-4
*Cove Creek* .... NC-3
*Cove Creek* .... PA-2
*Cove Creek* .... TN-4
*Cove Creek* .... UT-8
*Cove Creek* .... VA-3
*Cove Creek* .... WV-2
Cove Creek—*gap* .... NC-3
Cove Creek—*locale* .... NC-3
Cove Creek—*locale* .... VA-3
**Cove Creek**—*pop pl* (2) .... TN-4
**Cove Creek**—*pop pl* .... VA-3
**Cove Creek**—*pop pl* .... WV-2
Cove Creek—*stream* (2) .... AL-4
Cove Creek—*stream* (2) .... AK-9
Cove Creek—*stream* (12) .... AR-4
Cove Creek—*stream* .... CA-9
Cove Creek—*stream* .... GA-3
Cove Creek—*stream* (8) .... ID-8
Cove Creek—*stream* .... MD-2
Cove Creek—*stream* (2) .... MO-7
Cove Creek—*stream* (2) .... MT-8
Cove Creek—*stream* .... NV-8
Cove Creek—*stream* (7) .... NC-3
Cove Creek—*stream* (12) .... OR-9
Cove Creek—*stream* (2) .... PA-2
Cove Creek—*stream* .... SC-3
Cove Creek—*stream* (7) .... TN-4
Cove Creek—*stream* .... TX-5
Cove Creek—*stream* (3) .... UT-8
Cove Creek—*stream* (9) .... VA-3
Cove Creek—*stream* .... WA-9
Cove Creek—*stream* (4) .... WV-2
Cove Creek Boat Ramp—*locale* .... TN-4
Cove Creek Bridge—*bridge* .... ID-8
**Cove Creek Cascades**—*pop pl* .... TN-4
**Cove Creek Cascades (Cornpone)**—*pop pl* .... TN-4
Cove Creek Cave—*cave* .... TN-4
Cove Creek Cem—*cemetery* .... MO-7
Cove Creek Cem—*cemetery* .... NC-3
Cove Creek Ch—*church* .... AR-4
Cove Creek Ch—*church* .... MO-7
Cove Creek Ch—*church* (2) .... NC-3
Cove Creek Ch—*church* .... TN-4
Cove Creek Ch—*church* .... WV-2
Cove Creek Cumberland Presbyterian Ch (historical)—*church* .... AL-4
*Cove Creek Dam* .... TN-4
*Cove Creek Elementary School* .... NC-3
Cove Creek Mill—*locale* .... TN-4
Cove Creek P.O. (historical)—*building* .... AL-4
Cove Creek Rec Area—*park* .... TN-4
Cove Creek Ridge—*ridge* .... NC-3
*Cove Creek Sch* .... TN-4
Cove Creek Sch—*school* .... NC-3
Cove Creek Sch—*school* .... TN-4
Cove Creek Sch (historical)—*school* .... TN-4
Cove Creek Shoals—*bar* .... TN-4
Cove Creek (Township of)—*fmr MCD* .... AR-4
Cove Creek (Township of)—*fmr MCD* .... NC-3
Cove Creek View Sch (historical)—*school* .... TN-4
Cove Creek Wildlife Mngmt Area—*park* .... TN-4
Covedale—*locale* .... KY-4
Covedale—*locale* .... OH-6
**Covedale**—*pop pl* .... PA-2
Covedale Cem—*cemetery* .... OH-6
Covedale Sch—*school* .... OH-6
*Coveda Mission* .... OK-5
Cove Detention Dam—*dam* .... AZ-5
Cove Ditch—*canal* .... MT-8
Cove Draw—*valley* .... AZ-5
Cove Draw—*valley* .... WY-8
Cove Field Branch—*stream* .... NC-3
Covefield Branch—*stream* .... NC-3
Cove Field Branch—*stream* (2) .... TN-4

Cowart—*locale* VA-3
**Cowart**—*pop pl* MS-4
*Cowart Baptist Church* MS-4
Cowart Bend—*bend* TX-5
Cowart Branch—*stream* AL-4
Cowart Branch—*stream* MS-4
Cowart Cem—*cemetery* GA-3
Cowart Cem—*cemetery* LA-4
Cowart Cem—*cemetery* MS-4
Cowart Ch—*church* MS-4
Cowart Creek—*stream* TX-5
*Cowart Elementary School* AL-4
Cowart Gap—*gap* GA-3
Cowart Lake—*reservoir* GA-3
Cowart Lake Dam—*dam* MS-4
Cowarts—*locale* NC-3
**Cowarts**—*pop pl* AL-4
Cowarts Baptist Ch—*church* AL-4
Cowarts Cem—*cemetery* AL-4
Cowart Sch—*school* TX-5
Cowarts Creek—*stream* AL-4
Cowarts Creek—*stream* FL-3
Cowarts Creek Cem—*cemetery* AL-4
Cowarts Creek Ch—*church* AL-4
*Cowarts Creek Freewill Baptist Ch* AL-4
Cowarts Lake—*lake* FL-3
Cowarts Post Office—*building* AL-4
Cowarts Town Hall—*building* AL-4
Cowaselon Creek—*stream* NY-2
Cowassock Brook—*stream* MA-1
Cow Bar—*bar* MO-7
Cow Barn Sch (historical)—*school* MS-4
Cow Bay—*bay* MN-6
Cow Bay—*swamp* FL-3
Cow Bay—*swamp* NC-3
Cow Bay Knoll—*summit* UT-8
Cow Bayou—*gut* AR-4
Cow Bayou—*gut* (2) LA-4
Cow Bayou—*gut* TX-5
Cow Bayou—*stream* AR-4
Cow Bayou—*stream* (10) LA-4
Cow Bayou—*stream* (4) TX-5
Cow Bayou Bar—*bar* AR-4
Cow Bayou Cove—*bay* LA-4
Cowbay Swamp—*swamp* SC-3
Cow Beach Point—*cape* ME-1
Cowbell Branch—*stream* SC-3
**Cowbell Corners**—*pop pl* NH-1
Cowbell Creek—*stream* KY-4
Cowbell Creek—*stream* OK-5
Cowbell Hollow—*valley* NC-3
Cowbell Hollow—*valley* PA-2
Cowbell Hollow—*valley* TN-4
Cowbell Hollow Trail—*trail* PA-2
Cowbell Hollow Trail—*trail* TN-4
Cowbell Lake—*lake* AZ-5
Cowbell Mtn—*summit* OR-9
Cow Bell Strand—*swamp* FL-3
Cow Bog—*swamp* SC-3
Cow Bog Branch—*stream* NC-3
Cow Bog Hollow—*valley* OK-5
Cowbone Branch—*stream* VA-3
Cow Bone Cave—*cave* AL-4
Cowbone Creek—*swamp* FL-3
Cowbone Hammock—*island* FL-3
Cow Bone Island—*island* FL-3
Cowbone Lake—*lake* MT-8
Cowbone Marsh—*swamp* FL-3
Cowbone Ridge—*ridge* VA-3
Cowbones, The—*flat* TN-4
Cowboy Basin—*basin* ID-8
Cowboy Bench—*bench* UT-8
Cowboy Brook—*stream* NH-1
Cowboy Butte—*summit* (2) AZ-5
Cowboy Cabin Park—*park* WY-8
Cowboy Camp—*locale* (2) UT-8
Cowboy Camp—*locale* WY-8
Cowboy Canyon—*valley* (2) AZ-5
Cowboy Canyon—*valley* MT-8
Cowboy Canyon—*valley* (2) UT-8
Cowboy Caves—*hist pl* UT-8
Cowboy Cem—*cemetery* OK-5
Cowboy Cem—*cemetery* TX-5
*Cowboy Creek* OR-9
Cowboy Creek—*stream* ID-8
Cowboy Creek—*stream* MT-8
Cowboy Creek—*stream* NE-7
Cowboy Creek—*stream* NM-5
Cowboy Creek—*stream* SD-7
Cowboy Creek—*stream* TX-5
Cowboy Creek—*stream* UT-8
Cowboy Draw—*valley* NM-5
Cowboy Flat—*flat* AZ-5
Cowboy Gulch—*valley* SD-7
Cowboy Hall of Fame—*building* OK-5
Cowboy Hat—*pillar* UT-8
Cowboy Hill—*summit* NE-7
Cowboy Hill—*summit* SD-7
Cowboy Hill Cem—*cemetery* OK-5
Cowboy (historical)—*locale* KS-7
Cowboy Junior Tank—*reservoir* AZ-5
Cowboy Lake—*lake* CA-9
Cowboy Lake—*lake* CO-8
Cowboy Lake—*lake* MI-6
Cowboy Lake—*lake* NM-5
Cowboy Mesa—*summit* CO-8
Cowboy Mine—*locale* WY-8
Cowboy Mine—*mine* (2) AZ-5
Cowboy Mine—*mine* NV-8
Cowboy Mine—*mine* SD-7
Cowboy Mine—*mine* UT-8
Cowboy Mtn—*summit* WA-9
Cowboy Parking Lot—*locale* WA-9
Cowboy Pass—*gap* NM-5
Cowboy Pass—*gap* (2) UT-8
Cowboy Pasture—*flat* UT-8
Cowboy Peaks—*summit* AZ-5
Cowboy Pen Windmill—*locale* TX-5
Cowboy Rest—*locale* NV-8
Cowboy Rest Creek—*stream* NV-8
Cowboy Run—*stream* IN-6
Cowboy Shaft—*mine* NM-5
Cowboys Heaven—*locale* MT-8
Cowboy Sinkhole—*cave* AL-4
Cowboy Spring—*spring* (3) AZ-5
Cowboy Spring—*spring* (2) ID-8
Cowboy Spring—*spring* NM-5
Cowboy Spring—*spring* (2) OR-9
Cowboy Spring—*spring* UT-8
Cowboy Spring (Dry)—*spring* UT-8
Cowboy Springs—*spring* OK-5
*Cowboy Springs Wash* CO-8
*Cowboy Springs Wash* UT-8
*Cowboy Steele Creek* MT-8
Cowboy Swimming Hole—*spring* AZ-5
Cowboy Tank—*reservoir* (7) AZ-5
Cowboy Tank—*reservoir* (2) NM-5
Cowboy Trail (Pack)—*trail* NM-5
Cowboy Wash—*stream* AZ-5
Cowboy Wash—*stream* CO-8
Cowboy Wash—*valley* UT-8
Cowboy Well—*well* (2) NM-5
Cowboy Windmill—*locale* TX-5
*Cow Branch* FL-3
*Cow Branch* LA-4
Cow Branch—*stream* (3) AL-4
Cow Branch—*stream* AR-4
Cow Branch—*stream* (2) FL-3
Cow Branch—*stream* (2) GA-3
Cow Branch—*stream* IA-7
Cow Branch—*stream* (15) KY-4
Cow Branch—*stream* (2) LA-4
Cow Branch—*stream* (2) MS-4
Cow Branch—*stream* (2) MO-7
Cow Branch—*stream* (5) NC-3
Cow Branch—*stream* (8) SC-3
Cow Branch—*stream* (3) TN-4
Cow Branch—*stream* (3) TX-5
Cow Branch—*stream* (2) VA-3
Cow Branch Sch—*school* KY-4
Cow Bridge—*locale* DE-2
Cow Bridge Branch—*stream* DE-2
*Cow Bridge Brook* DE-2
Cow Bridge Brook—*stream* MA-1
Cow Brook—*stream* (2) ME-1
Cow Brook—*stream* (2) NH-1
Cow Brook Trail—*trail* NH-1
*Cow Butte* OR-9
Cow Butte—*summit* AZ-5
Cow Butte—*summit* CO-8
Cow Butte—*summit* ND-7
Cow Butte—*summit* WY-8
Cow Butte Tank—*reservoir* AZ-5
Cow Cabin Creek—*stream* (2) MT-8
Cow Camp—*hist pl* CA-9
Cow Camp—*locale* AZ-5
Cow Camp—*locale* CA-9
Cow Camp—*locale* CO-8
Cow Camp—*locale* (2) FL-3
Cow Camp—*locale* (2) ID-8
Cow Camp—*locale* (4) MT-8
Cow Camp—*locale* (4) NV-8
Cow Camp—*locale* NM-5
Cow Camp—*locale* (3) OR-9
Cow Camp—*locale* UT-8
Cow Camp—*locale* WA-9
Cow Camp, The—*locale* CO-8
Cow Camp Campground—*park* OR-9
Cowcamp Creek—*stream* CA-9
Cow Camp Creek—*stream* NC-3
Cow Camp Creek—*stream* (2) WY-8
Cow Camp Dam—*dam* CA-9
Cow Camp Gap—*gap* NC-3
Cowcamp Gap—*gap* VA-3
Cow Camp Gulch—*valley* CO-8
Cow Camp Lead—*ridge* TN-4
Cow Camp Meadows—*flat* MT-8
Cow Camp Meadows—*flat* OR-9
Cow Camp No 1—*locale* NM-5
Cow Camp No. 2—*locale* NM-5
Cow Camp No 5—*locale* NM-5
Cowcamp Ridge—*ridge* TN-4
Cow Camp Rsvr—*reservoir* CO-8
*Cow Camp Spring* NV-8
Cow Camp Spring—*spring* ID-8
Cow Camp Spring—*spring* (2) MT-8
Cow Camp Spring—*spring* NV-8
Cow Camp Spring—*spring* (2) OR-9
Cow Camp Spring—*spring* (2) WY-8
Cow Camp Tank—*reservoir* TX-5
Cow Camp Trail—*trail* TN-4
Cow Camp Well—*well* UT-8
*Cow Canyon* AZ-5
Cow Canyon—*valley* (6) AZ-5
Cow Canyon—*valley* (8) CA-9
Cow Canyon—*valley* (6) CO-8
Cow Canyon—*valley* ID-8
Cow Canyon—*valley* (9) NV-8
Cow Canyon—*valley* (3) NM-5
Cow Canyon—*valley* (6) OR-9
Cow Canyon—*valley* TX-5
Cow Canyon—*valley* (12) UT-8
Cow Canyon—*valley* (3) WA-9
Cow Canyon—*valley* WY-8
*Cow Canyon Creek* OR-9
Cow Canyon Saddle—*gap* CA-9
Cow Canyon Safety Rest Area—*park* OR-9
Cow Canyon Springs—*spring* OR-9
Cow Canyon Tank—*reservoir* NM-5
Cow Castle Creek—*stream* SC-3
Cowcatcher Ridge—*ridge* ID-8
*Cow Cave* OR-9
Cow Cave—*cave* AL-4
Cow Cave Bluff—*cliff* TX-5
Cow Channel—*channel* NC-3
Cow Chip Spring—*spring* CA-9
Cow Cliff—*cliff* KY-4
Cow Coulee—*valley* MT-8
Cow Cove—*bay* AR-4
Cow Cove—*bay* MD-2
Cow Cove—*bay* RI-1
Cow Cove—*valley* (2) CA-9
Cow Cove Spring—*spring* CA-9
*Cow Creek* CA-9
*Cow Creek* CO-8
*Cow Creek* FL-3
*Cow Creek* ID-8
*Cow Creek* KS-7
*Cow Creek* LA-4
*Cow Creek* MD-2
*Cow Creek* MT-8
*Cow Creek* NV-8
*Cow Creek* NC-3
*Cow Creek* OR-9
*Cow Creek* TX-5
*Cow Creek* WA-9
*Cow Creek* WY-8
Cow Creek—*bay* (2) NC-3
Cow Creek—*locale* FL-3
Cow Creek—*locale* ID-8
Cowcreek—*locale* KY-4
Cow Creek—*locale* OR-9
**Cow Creek**—*pop pl* CA-9
**Cow Creek**—*pop pl* KY-4
**Cow Creek**—*pop pl* MT-8
**Cow Creek**—*pop pl* WY-8
Cow Creek—*spring* NV-8
Cow Creek—*stream* (3) AL-4
Cow Creek—*stream* (3) AK-9
Cow Creek—*stream* (4) AZ-5
Cow Creek—*stream* (7) AR-4
Cow Creek—*stream* (18) CA-9
Cow Creek—*stream* (12) CO-8
Cow Creek—*stream* (13) FL-3
Cow Creek—*stream* (2) GA-3
Cow Creek—*stream* (31) ID-8
Cow Creek—*stream* IN-6
Cow Creek—*stream* (7) KS-7
Cow Creek—*stream* (11) KY-4
Cow Creek—*stream* (4) LA-4
Cow Creek—*stream* (2) MD-2
Cow Creek—*stream* MI-6
Cow Creek—*stream* MN-6
Cow Creek—*stream* (2) MS-4
Cow Creek—*stream* (3) MO-7
Cow Creek—*stream* (31) MT-8
Cow Creek—*stream* (3) NE-7
Cow Creek—*stream* (9) NV-8
Cow Creek—*stream* (3) NM-5
Cow Creek—*stream* NY-2
Cow Creek—*stream* (2) NC-3
Cow Creek—*stream* ND-7
Cow Creek—*stream* (10) OK-5
Cow Creek—*stream* (20) OR-9
Cow Creek—*stream* (2) SD-7
Cow Creek—*stream* (3) TN-4
Cow Creek—*stream* (23) TX-5
Cow Creek—*stream* (4) UT-8
Cow Creek—*stream* (2) VA-3
Cow Creek—*stream* (7) WA-9
Cow Creek—*stream* (5) WV-2
Cow Creek—*stream* (15) WY-8
Cow Creek Breaks—*range* WY-8
Cow Creek Bridge—*bridge* OR-9
Cow Creek Butte—*summit* WY-8
Cow Creek Buttes—*summit* WY-8
Cow Creek Campground—*locale* MT-8
Cowcreek (CCD)—*cens area* KY-4
Cow Creek Cem—*cemetery* KY-4
Cow Creek Cem—*cemetery* ND-7
Cow Creek Cem—*cemetery* TX-5
Cowcreek Ch—*church* KY-4
Cow Creek Ch—*church* WV-2
*Cow Creek Craters* OR-9
Cow Creek Ditch—*canal* CO-8
Cow Creek Forebay—*lake* CA-9
Cow Creek Forest Camp—*locale* ID-8
Cow Creek Game Ref—*park* OR-9
Cow Creek Highland Ditch—*canal* WY-8
**Cow Creek (historical)**—*pop pl* MS-4
*Cow Creek Lava Flow* OR-9
*Cow Creek Meadows* CA-9
Cow Creek Meadows—*swamp* WA-9
Cow Creek Mountain—*ridge* AR-4
Cow Creek Mtn—*summit* OK-5
Cow Creek Mtn—*summit* WY-8
Cow Creek Park—*park* MO-7
Cow Creek Petroglyphs—*hist pl* CA-9
Cow Creek Pond—*reservoir* VA-3
Cow Creek Powerhouse—*other* CA-9
Cow Creek Public Use Area—*locale* MO-7
Cow Creek Ranch—*locale* (2) WY-8
Cow Creek Rec Area—*park* SD-7
Cow Creek Rest Area—*park* OR-9
Cow Creek Ridge—*ridge* CA-9
Cow Creek Road Rsvr—*reservoir* OR-9
Cow Creek Rsvr—*reservoir* ID-8
Cow Creek Rsvr—*reservoir* MT-8
Cow Creek Rsvr—*reservoir* (2) WY-8
Cow Creek Saddle—*gap* ID-8
Cow Creek Sch—*school* ID-8
Cow Creek Sch—*school* KY-4
Cow Creek Sch—*school* MT-8
Cow Creek Sch—*school* WY-8
Cow Creek Sink—*basin* OR-9
Cow Creek Spring—*spring* AZ-5
Cow Creek Spring—*spring* MT-8
Cow Creek State Park—*park* OR-9
Cow Creek Tank—*reservoir* TX-5
**Cow Creek Township**—*pop pl* ND-7
Cow Creek Trail—*trail* (2) CO-8
Cow Creek Trail—*trail* MT-8
Cow Creek Valley—*valley* OR-9
Cow Creek Wall—*ridge* WY-8
*Cow Crossing Tank* AZ-5
Cow Crossing Tank—*reservoir* AZ-5
Cowcumber Creek—*stream* LA-4
Cowcumber Hill—*summit* AL-4
Cowcumber Hollow—*valley* AR-4
Cow Cut—*gut* SC-3
Cowdell, Enoch E., House—*hist pl* UT-8
Cowdell Waste Water Ditch—*canal* WY-8
*Cowden* AL-4
Cowden—*locale* SC-3
Cowden—*locale* TN-4
**Cowden**—*pop pl* IL-6
**Cowden**—*pop pl* OK-5
**Cowden**—*pop pl* PA-2
Cowden, Lake—*lake* MI-6
Cowden Bridge—*other* IL-6
Cowden Canyon—*valley* NV-8
Cowden Cem—*cemetery* AL-4
Cowden Cem—*cemetery* VA-3
Cowden City Park—*park* AZ-5
Cowden Coll (historical)—*school* TN-4
Cowden Ditch—*canal* CA-9
Cowden Gap—*gap* AL-4
Cowden Gap Mine (underground)—*mine* AL-4
Cowden Hollow—*valley* TN-4
Cowden JHS—*school* TX-5
Cowden Junction—*locale* OK-5
Cowden Lake—*lake* MI-6
Cowden Lake Ch—*church* MI-6
Cowden Mine—*mine* NV-8
Cowden Oil Field—*oilfield* TX-5
**Cowden (Pitco)**—*pop pl* PA-2
Cowden Place—*locale* TX-5
Cowden Ranch—*locale* AZ-5
Cowden Ranch—*locale* NM-5
Cowden Ranch—*locale* (2) TX-5
Cowden Rsvr—*reservoir* WY-8
Cowden Sch—*school* MO-7
Cowdens Corner—*locale* NY-2
Cowdens Creek—*stream* SC-3
Cowden Spring—*spring* AR-4
**Cowdensville**—*pop pl* MD-2
Cowdery Cem—*cemetery* OH-6
Cowdevil Creek—*stream* FL-3
Cowdin Ranch—*locale* NE-7
Cow Draw—*valley* KS-7
Cow Draw—*valley* WY-8
Cowdray Hill—*summit* MA-1
**Cowdrey**—*pop pl* CO-8
Cowdrey, George, House—*hist pl* MA-1
Cowdrey, Lake—*lake* MN-6
Cowdrey Enlargement—*canal* CO-8
Cowdrey House—*hist pl* AR-4
Cowdrey Outlook—*summit* VT-1
Cowdrey Rsvr—*reservoir* CO-8
Cowdrey Rsvr No 2—*reservoir* CO-8
Cowdry, William D., Plantation—*hist pl* GA-3
Cowdry Cem—*cemetery* IL-6
Cowdry Hill—*summit* (2) MA-1
Cowdry Hollow—*valley* NY-2
*Cowdry Lake* MN-6
*Cowecha* WA-9
*Cowecha Creek* WA-9
Cowee—*locale* NC-3
Cowee Bald—*summit* NC-3
Cowee Ch—*church* NC-3
Cowee Creek—*stream* AK-9
Cowee Creek—*stream* NC-3
*Cowee Gap* NC-3
Cowee Gap—*gap* NC-3
Coweeman Lake—*lake* WA-9
Coweeman Ranger Station—*locale* WA-9
Coweeman River—*stream* WA-9
Cowee Mound and Village Site—*hist pl* NC-3
Cowee Mountain Mine—*mine* NC-3
Cowee Mountains—*range* NC-3
Cowee Pond—*reservoir* MA-1
Cowee Pond Dam—*dam* MA-1
Cowee Sch—*school* NC-3
Coweeset Brook—*stream* MA-1
Coweeset Cem—*cemetery* MA-1
Cowees Hill—*summit* MA-1
Coweeta Ch—*church* NC-3
Coweeta Creek—*stream* NC-3
Coweeta Experiment Station—*locale* NC-3
Coweeta Gap—*gap* NC-3
Cowee (Township of)—*fmr MCD* NC-3
Cowee Tunnel—*tunnel* NC-3
*Cowe Island* NC-3
*Coweliske River* WA-9
**Cowell**—*pop pl* AR-4
**Cowell**—*pop pl* CA-9
Cowell Battery—*locale* VI-3
Cowell Beach—*beach* CA-9
Cowell Cem—*cemetery* PA-2
Cowell Cem—*cemetery* TN-4
*Cowell Chapel School* TN-4
Cowell Creek—*stream* MT-8
Cowell Ditch—*canal* CA-9
*Cowell Draw* WY-8
Cowell Mine—*mine* CA-9
Cowell Point—*cape* VI-3
Cowell Ranch—*locale* CA-9
Cowell Sch—*school* CA-9
Cowell Sch—*school* CO-8
Cowells Chapel—*church* TN-4
Cowells Chapel Cem—*cemetery* TN-4
Cowells Chapel Sch (historical)—*school* TN-4
Cowells Creek—*stream* NC-3
Cowell Spring—*spring* AZ-5
Cowells Run—*stream* WV-2
*Coweman Lake* WA-9
*Coweman River* WA-9
*Cowen* IN-6
*Cowen* MI-6
**Cowen**—*pop pl* WV-2
Cowen, Mount—*summit* MT-8
Cowen Branch—*stream* TN-4
Cowen Chapel Cem—*cemetery* MS-4
**Cowen Corner**—*pop pl* MA-1
Cowen Cove—*bay* ME-1
*Cowen Creek* NC-3
Cowen Creek—*stream* SC-3
Cowen Creek—*stream* WA-9
Cowen Gulch—*valley* ID-8
Cowen Hill—*summit* ME-1
Cowen Hill—*summit* NH-1
Cowen Hill Camp—*locale* NH-1
Cowenhoven Tunnel—*mine* CO-8
Cowen Knob—*summit* TN-4
*Cowen Landing* NC-3
Cowen Mtn—*summit* AL-4
Cowen Park Bridge—*hist pl* WA-9
Cowen Point—*cape* TN-4
Cowen Rocks—*bar* MA-1
Cowen Rocks—*summit* TX-5
Cowen Run—*stream* MD-2
Cowen Run—*stream* OH-6
Cowen Sch—*school* IL-6
Cowen Sch—*school* SD-7
*Cowens Corner* MA-1
*Cowens Creek* NC-3
Cowens Gap Dam—*dam* PA-2
Cowens Gap Lake—*reservoir* PA-2
Cowen Spit—*bar* SC-3
**Cowentown**—*pop pl* MD-2
**Cowenville**—*pop pl* TN-4
Cowern Sch—*school* MN-6
Cowerts Branch—*stream* MS-4
*Coweserr Brook* MA-1
*Cowesett* RI-1
**Cowesett**—*pop pl* RI-1
*Cowesett Bay* RI-1
*Cowesett Pond* RI-1
Cowesett Pound—*hist pl* RI-1
**Coweta**—*pop pl* OK-5
Coweta (CCD)—*cens area* OK-5
**Coweta (County)**—*pop pl* GA-3
Coweta County Courthouse—*hist pl* GA-3
*Coweta Creek* NC-3
Coweta Creek—*stream* OK-5
*Cowetah* OK-5
Cowett Hill—*summit* ME-1
Cow Face Hill—*summit* MT-8
Cow Flat—*flat* (3) AZ-5
Cow Flat—*flat* (2) CA-9
Cow Flat—*flat* CO-8
Cow Flat—*flat* NM-5
Cow Flat—*flat* SD-7
Cow Flat—*flat* UT-8
Cow Flat Creek—*stream* CA-9
Cow Flat Mtn—*summit* AZ-5
Cow Flat Rsvr—*reservoir* UT-8
Cow Flats—*flat* ID-8
Cow Flats—*flat* UT-8
*Cowford* FL-3
Cow Ford—*crossing* TN-4
Cow Ford—*locale* AL-4
Cow Ford—*locale* TN-4
Cow Ford Bar—*bar* AL-4
Cow Ford Bar (historical)—*bar* AL-4
Cowford Branch—*stream* NC-3
Cow Ford Bridge—*bridge* FL-3
Cow Ford Bridge—*bridge* SC-3
Cowford Ch—*church* GA-3
Cowford Ferry—*locale* FL-3
Cow Ford Hollow—*valley* KY-4
Cow Ford Hollow—*valley* MO-7
Cowford Island—*island* FL-3
*Cowford Lakes* FL-3
*Cowford Swamp* NC-3
Cowford Swamp—*stream* NC-3
Cowford Swamp—*stream* SC-3
Cow Fork—*stream* (4) KY-4
Cow Fork—*stream* TX-5
Cow Fork—*stream* UT-8
Cow Fork—*stream* VA-3
Cow Fork Ch—*church* KY-4
Cow Fork Eightmile Creek—*stream* ID-8
Cowfort—*beach* MA-1
Cow Gallus Creek—*stream* (2) NC-3
Cow Gap—*gap* AL-4
Cow Gap—*gap* TX-5
Cow Gap Creek—*bay* MD-2
Cow Gap Island—*island* MD-2
Cow Gap Landing—*locale* TN-4
Cowger Cem—*cemetery* WV-2
Cowger Hill Ch—*church* WV-2
Cowger Lake—*lake* AR-4
Cowger Mtn—*summit* WV-2
Cowger Ridge—*ridge* VA-3
*Cowghran Canyon* AZ-5
*Cowgill* DE-2
**Cowgill**—*pop pl* MO-7
Cowgill Cem—*cemetery* MO-7
Cowgill Cem—*cemetery* TN-4
*Cowgill Corner* DE-2
Cowgill Cut—*gap* TX-5
Cowgill-Roemer Airp—*airport* MO-7
Cowgills Corner—*locale* DE-2
Cowgill Well—*well* OR-9
Cow Glade—*flat* CA-9
Cow Gulch—*stream* MT-8
Cow Gulch—*valley* (3) CA-9
Cow Gulch—*valley* (4) CO-8
Cow Gulch—*valley* ID-8
Cow Gulch—*valley* (3) MT-8
Cow Gulch—*valley* OR-9
Cow Gulch—*valley* WY-8
*Cowgulch Creek* MT-8
Cow Gulch Spring—*spring* ID-8
Cow Gut—*gut* NC-3
Cow Gut—*gut* VA-3
Cow Gut Flat—*flat* VA-3
Cow Hammock—*island* FL-3
Cow Hammock Lake—*lake* LA-4
Cowham Sch—*school* WI-6
Cowhand Ranch—*locale* MI-6
Cow Haul Swamp—*stream* NC-3
*Cowhead* AL-4
Cowhead Bayou—*gut* LA-4
Cowhead Bayou—*stream* (2) LA-4
Cowhead Branch—*stream* KY-4
Cow Head Branch—*stream* SC-3
Cowhead Creek—*stream* AL-4
Cow Head Creek—*stream* AR-4
Cowhead Creek—*stream* FL-3
Cowhead Creek—*stream* NC-3
Cowhead Creek—*stream* OR-9
Cowhead Divide—*gap* OK-5
Cowhead Hill—*summit* UT-8
Cow Head Hollow—*valley* TX-5
Cow Head Lake—*lake* CA-9
*Cowhead Lake Basin* CA-9
Cow Head Landing—*locale* SC-3
Cowhead Mtn—*summit* OK-5
Cowhead Potrero—*flat* CA-9
Cow Head Saddle—*gap* AZ-5
Cow Head Slough—*stream* CA-9
Cow Head Slough—*stream* OR-9
Cow Head Spring—*spring* CA-9
Cowhead Tank—*reservoir* (4) AZ-5
Cow Head Tank—*reservoir* CA-9
Cow Head Trail Spring—*spring* AZ-5
Cowhead Well—*well* AZ-5
Cowhea Reach—*channel* SC-3
Cow Heaven Bay—*swamp* FL-3
Cow Heaven Canyon—*valley* CA-9
Cow Heaven Mtn—*summit* TX-5
Cow Heaven Spring—*spring* CA-9
Cow Heaven Spring—*spring* TX-5
Cow Heaven Spring (Dry)—*spring* NV-8
Cow Heaven Tank—*reservoir* TX-5
Cow Hell Swamp—*swamp* GA-3
Cowherd, Francis, House—*hist pl* KY-4
Cowherd, Jonathan, Jr., House—*hist pl* KY-4
Cowherd Cem—*cemetery* KY-4
Cowherd Mtn—*summit* VA-3
*Cowher Run* PA-2
*Cowhide Bayou* LA-4
Cowhide Bayou—*stream* LA-4
Cowhide Branch—*stream* GA-3
Cowhide Cove Public Use Area—*park* AR-4
Cowhide Creek—*stream* AR-4
Cowhide Creek—*stream* FL-3
Cowhide Creek—*stream* WV-2
Cowhide Slough—*stream* KY-4
Cow Hill—*summit* AZ-5
Cow Hill—*summit* CA-9
Cow Hill—*summit* ME-1
Cow Hill—*summit* MA-1
Cow Hill—*summit* MO-7
Cow Hill—*summit* VT-1
Cow Hill Tank—*reservoir* AZ-5
Cow Hill Tank—*reservoir* TX-5
Cow Hill Trail—*trail* PA-2
Cowhold, The—*cave* TN-4
Cow Hole—*valley* PA-2
Cow Hole Bay—*bay* NC-3
Cow Hole Branch—*stream* NC-3
Cowhole Branch—*stream* NC-3
Cowhole Mtn—*summit* CA-9
*Cow Hollow* UT-8
Cow Hollow—*locale* WY-8
Cow Hollow—*valley* ID-8
Cow Hollow—*valley* (3) KY-4
Cow Hollow—*valley* MD-2
Cow Hollow—*valley* MO-7
Cow Hollow—*valley* (3) OR-9
Cow Hollow—*valley* PA-2
Cow Hollow—*valley* (4) TN-4
Cow Hollow—*valley* (2) TX-5
Cow Hollow—*valley* (9) UT-8
Cow Hollow—*valley* VA-3
Cow Hollow—*valley* (2) WV-2
Cow Hollow Branch—*stream* TN-4
Cow Hollow Branch Stream—*stream* TN-4
Cow Hollow Creek—*stream* TX-5
Cow Hollow Creek—*stream* WY-8
Cow Hollow Recreation Site—*locale* UT-8
Cow Hollow Run—*stream* WV-2
Cow Hollow Siphon—*locale* OR-9
Cow Hollow Spring—*spring* (2) OR-9
Cow Hollow Spring—*spring* TN-4
Cow Hollow Tank—*reservoir* TX-5
Cow Hollow Trap—*reservoir* TX-5
Cow Hollow Well—*well* UT-8
Cow Hollow Windmill—*locale* TX-5
Cow Hoof Branch—*stream* KY-4
Cow Horn Branch—*stream* GA-3
Cowhorn Branch—*stream* NC-3
Cowhorn Branch—*stream* TN-4
Cowhorn Creek—*stream* KY-4
Cowhorn Creek—*stream* OR-9
Cowhorn Creek—*stream* TX-5
*Cowhorne Hollow* TN-4
Cowhorn Hollow—*valley* KY-4
Cowhorn Hollow—*valley* TX-5
Cow Horn Lake—*lake* MN-6
Cowhorn Mtn—*summit* OR-9
Cowhorn Pond—*lake* NY-2
Cowhorn Swamp—*stream* NC-3
Cowhorn Trail—*trail* OR-9
Cowhorn Valley—*valley* CA-9
Cowhouse Bay—*swamp* FL-3
Cowhouse Bay—*swamp* GA-3
Cowhouse Branch—*stream* DE-2
Cowhouse Branch—*stream* GA-3
Cow House Creek—*stream* FL-3
Cow House Creek—*stream* SC-3
Cowhouse Creek—*stream* TX-5
Cowhouse Flats—*swamp* GA-3
Cowhouse Island—*island* GA-3
Cowhouse Mtn—*summit* TX-5
*Cow House Pond* FL-3
Cowhouse Prairie—*swamp* GA-3
Cowhy Drain—*canal* MI-6
**Cowiche**—*pop pl* WA-9
Cowiche Basin—*basin* WA-9
Cowiche Canyon—*valley* WA-9
Cowiche Creek—*stream* WA-9
*Cowiche Mtn* WA-9
Cowiche Mtn—*summit* WA-9
Cowiche Sch—*school* WA-9
Cowie Cem—*cemetery* VA-3
Cowie Corner—*locale* VA-3
Cowikee Creek—*stream* (2) AL-4
Cowikee Rec Area—*park* AL-4
*Cowikee River* AL-4
Cowing, Thomas F., House—*hist pl* MN-6
Cowing Park—*park* IN-6
Cowing Sch—*school* MA-1
**Cowin (historical)**—*pop pl* NC-3
*Cow Island* ME-1
*Cow Island* TX-5
*Cow Island* FM-9
Cow Island—*bend* AR-4
Cow Island—*flat* AR-4
Cow Island—*island* (2) FL-3
Cow Island—*island* GA-3
Cow Island—*island* (3) LA-4
Cow Island—*island* (7) ME-1
Cow Island—*island* MD-2
Cow Island—*island* MT-8
Cow Island—*island* NH-1
Cow Island—*island* NY-2
Cow Island—*island* (3) NC-3
Cow Island—*island* VA-3
Cow Island—*island* WY-8
Cow Island—*locale* LA-4
**Cow Island**—*pop pl* TX-5
Cow Island Bayou—*stream* LA-4
Cow Island Bayou—*stream* TX-5
Cow Island Bend—*bend* AR-4
Cow Island Bend—*bend* MS-4
Cow Island Bend—*bend* TN-4
Cow Island Bend Revetment—*dam* AR-4
Cow Island Cut-Off—*stream* LA-4
*Cow Island Dry Ledges* ME-1
Cow Island Dry Ledges—*bar* ME-1
Cow Island (historical)—*island* FL-3
Cow Island (historical)—*island* NC-3
Cow Island Lake—*lake* LA-4
Cow Island Ledge—*bar* ME-1
Cow Island Ledges—*bar* ME-1
Cow Island Number Forty-eight—*island* TN-4
Cow Island Number Forty-seven—*island* TN-4
Cow Island Number One Canal—*canal* LA-4
Cow Island Number Two Canal—*canal* LA-4
Cow Island Pond—*lake* MA-1
Cow Islands—*island* MS-4
Cow Island Sunken Ledges—*bar* ME-1
Cow Island Trail—*trail* MT-8
*Cowitchee* WA-9
*Cowitchee Creek* WA-9
Cow Key—*island* (2) FL-3
Cow Key Channel—*channel* FL-3
*Cow Keys* FL-3
Cow-Killer Archeol Site—*hist pl* KS-7
Cow Knob—*summit* KY-4
Cow Knob—*summit* VA-3
Cow Knob—*summit* WV-2
Cow Knoll Ridge—*ridge* MO-7
*Cow Lake* FL-3
Cow Lake—*lake* (3) AK-9
Cow Lake—*lake* (2) AZ-5

Crabapple Creek—stream .......... PA-2
Crabapple Creek—stream (2) .......... TX-5
Crabapple Dam—dam .......... PA-2
Crabapple Gap—gap .......... PA-2
Crab Apple Hill—summit .......... SC-3
Crabapple Hollow—valley .......... PA-2
Crabapple Hollow—valley .......... TN-4
Crabapple Island—island .......... IL-6
Crabapple Lake—lake .......... OR-9
Crabapple Lake—lake .......... WA-9
Crabapple Path—trail .......... PA-2
Crabapple Point—cape .......... AR-4
Crab Apple Point Site—hist pl .......... WI-6
Crabapple Prairie—flat .......... OR-9
Crabapple Ridge—ridge .......... NV-8
Crabapple Run—stream (2) .......... PA-2
Crabapple Run—stream .......... WV-2
Crabapple Sch—school .......... IL-6
Crab Apple Sch—school .......... IA-7
Crabapple Valley—valley .......... AL-4
Crabb—locale .......... TX-5
Crab Bank—island .......... SC-3
Crab Bay—bay (3) .......... AK-9
Crab Bay—bay .......... KY-4
**Crab Bay**—pop pl .......... AK-9
Crab Bayou—channel .......... TX-5
Crabb Cem—cemetery .......... IA-7
Crabb Creek—stream .......... KS-7
Crabb Creek—stream .......... TX-5
Crabb Ditch—canal .......... IN-6
Crabbe Mill—locale .......... VA-3
Crabbe Mill Stream—stream .......... VA-3
Crabbe Sch—school .......... KY-4
Crabbing Creek—stream .......... NC-3
Crabbing Marsh—swamp .......... VA-3
Crabbing Point .......... MD-2
Crabb Kill—stream .......... NY-2
Crab Bottom .......... VA-3
Crab Branch—stream .......... NC-3
Crab Branch—stream .......... OH-6
Crab Brook—stream .......... NJ-2
Crabbs Branch—stream .......... MD-2
Crabbs Ferry (historical)—locale .......... AL-4
**Crabbs (Peawee)**—pop pl .......... MO-7
Crabbs Prairie—locale .......... TX-5
Crab Butte—summit .......... MT-8
Crab Cem—cemetery .......... MO-7
Crab Claw Spit—cape .......... NC-3
Crab Cove—bay .......... AK-9
Crab Cove—bay .......... NC-3
Crab Cove—cove .......... MA-1
Crab Creek .......... KS-7
Crab Creek .......... NJ-2
Crab Creek .......... NC-3
Crab Creek .......... VA-3
Crab Creek .......... WA-9
Crab Creek—bay .......... MD-2
Crab Creek—bay .......... NY-2
Crab Creek—gut .......... VA-3
Crab Creek—stream .......... AL-4
Crab Creek—stream (2) .......... AK-9
Crab Creek—stream .......... CA-9
Crab Creek—stream (3) .......... FL-3
Crab Creek—stream .......... GA-3
Crab Creek—stream (3) .......... ID-8
Crab Creek—stream (2) .......... KY-4
Crab Creek—stream .......... MN-6
Crab Creek—stream (2) .......... NC-3
Crab Creek—stream .......... OH-6
Crab Creek—stream .......... OR-9
Crab Creek—stream .......... TX-5
Crab Creek—stream .......... UT-8
Crab Creek—stream (3) .......... VA-3
Crab Creek—stream (2) .......... WA-9
Crab Creek—stream .......... WV-2
Crab Creek Basin—basin .......... ID-8
Crab Creek Cem—cemetery .......... KY-4
Crab Creek Ch—church (2) .......... NC-3
Crab Creek Grange Hall—locale .......... WA-9
Crab Creek Lateral—canal .......... WA-9
Crab Creek Point—cape .......... NY-2
Crab Creek (Township of)—fmr MCD .......... NC-3
Crabe, Bay—bay .......... LA-4
Crab Flats—flat .......... CA-9
Crab Fork—stream .......... NC-3
Crab Glacier—glacier .......... AK-9
Crab Grass Creek .......... FL-3
Crabgrass Creek—stream .......... FL-3
Crabgrass Creek—stream .......... MS-4
Crabgrass Pond—lake .......... FL-3
Crab Gully—stream .......... LA-4
Crab Harbor—bay .......... OR-9
Crab Haul Creek—stream .......... SC-3
Crab Hill .......... MA-1
Crab Hollow—valley .......... NY-2
Crab Hollow—valley (2) .......... TN-4
Crabill, David, House—hist pl .......... OH-6
Crabill Sch (historical)—school .......... MO-7
Crab Island—island .......... AK-9
Crab Island—island .......... CA-9
Crab Island—island .......... FL-3
Crab Island—island .......... GA-3
Crab Island—island .......... ME-1
Crab Island—island .......... MD-2
Crab Island—island .......... MI-6
Crab Island—island .......... NJ-2
Crab Island—island (4) .......... NY-2
Crab Island—island .......... TN-4
Crab Island—island .......... WA-9
Crab Island—island .......... WV-2
Crab Island Point .......... MI-6
Crab Island Reach—channel .......... NJ-2
Crab Island Shoal—bar .......... MI-6
Crab Key .......... FL-3
Crab Key—island .......... FL-3
Crab Key Bight—bay .......... FL-3
Crab Keys—island .......... FL-3
Crab Lagoon—bay .......... AK-9
Crab Lake .......... MN-6
Crab Lake—lake .......... AR-4
Crab Lake—lake .......... FL-3
Crab Lake—lake .......... LA-4
Crab Lake—lake (2) .......... MN-6
Crab Lake—lake (2) .......... TX-5
Crab Lake—lake (2) .......... WI-6
Crab Lake Gas Field—oilfield .......... LA-4
Crab Ledge—bar .......... ME-1
Crab Lice Bayou—stream .......... LA-4
Crablouse Ravine—valley .......... CA-9
**Crab Meadow**—pop pl .......... NY-2
Crab Meadow—swamp .......... NY-2
Crab Meadow Park—park .......... NY-2
Crab Mountain .......... MA-1
Crabneck .......... VA-3
Crab Neck—cape (2) .......... VA-3
Crab Orchard .......... AL-4
Craborchard .......... IL-6
Craborchard .......... WV-2
**Crab Orchard**—pop pl .......... IL-6
**Crab Orchard**—pop pl .......... KY-4
**Crab Orchard**—pop pl .......... NE-7
**Crab Orchard**—pop pl .......... TN-4
**Crab Orchard**—pop pl .......... VA-3
**Crab Orchard**—pop pl .......... WV-2
Crab Orchard Branch—stream .......... VA-3
Crab Orchard (CCD)—cens area .......... KY-4
Crab Orchard (CCD)—cens area .......... TN-4
Crab Orchard Cem—cemetery .......... IL-6
Craborchard Cem—cemetery .......... MO-7
Crab Orchard Cem—cemetery .......... NE-7
Craborchard Ch—church .......... IL-6
Crab Orchard Ch—church .......... NC-3
Crab Orchard Ch—church .......... TN-4
Craborchard Ch (historical)—church .......... MO-7
Crab Orchard Creek—stream .......... IL-6
Craborchard Creek—stream (2) .......... KY-4
Crab Orchard Creek—stream .......... KY-4
Craborchard Creek—stream .......... NC-3
Craborchard Creek—stream .......... OH-6
Crab Orchard Creek—stream .......... TN-4
Crab Orchard Creek—stream .......... VA-3
Craborchard Creek—stream .......... VA-3
Crab Orchard Creek—stream .......... VA-3
Crab Orchard Creek—stream .......... WV-2
Crab Orchard Division—civil .......... TN-4
Crab Orchard (Election Precinct)—fmr MCD .......... IL-6
Crab Orchard Elem Sch—school .......... TN-4
**Crab Orchard Estates**—pop pl .......... IL-6
Crab Orchard Fields—ridge .......... NC-3
Crab Orchard Gap—gap .......... TN-4
Crab Orchard Golf Club—other .......... IL-6
Crab Orchard JHS—school .......... IL-6
Crab Orchard Lake—reservoir .......... IL-6
Crab Orchard Mountains—summit .......... TN-4
Crab Orchard Post Office—building .......... TN-4
Crab Orchard Run—stream .......... WV-2
Crab Orchard Sch (abandoned)—school .......... MO-7
Crab Orchard Sch (historical)—school .......... MO-7
Crab Park—park .......... CA-9
Crab Place—locale .......... TN-4
Crab Point—cape .......... AK-9
Crab Point—cape .......... FL-3
Crab Point—cape (2) .......... MD-2
Crab Point—cape .......... NJ-2
Crab Point—cape (3) .......... NC-3
Crab Point—cape .......... VA-3
**Crab Point**—pop pl .......... NC-3
Crab Point Bay .......... NC-3
Crab Point Bay—bay .......... NC-3
Crab Point Cove—bay .......... MD-2
Crab Point Neck—cape .......... NC-3
Crab Point Thorofare—channel .......... NC-3
**Crab Point Village**—pop pl .......... NC-3
Crab Pond—lake (2) .......... NY-2
Crab Ridge—ridge .......... UT-8
Crab Rock—island .......... OR-9
Crab Rock—pillar .......... OR-9
Crab Run .......... MD-2
Crab Run .......... VA-3
Crab Run—stream .......... KY-4
Crab Run—stream .......... MD-2
Crab Run—stream .......... OH-6
Crab Run—stream (4) .......... PA-2
Crab Run—stream (3) .......... VA-3
Crab Run—stream (2) .......... WV-2
Crab Run Cem—cemetery .......... WV-2
Crab Run Ch—church .......... WV-2
Crabs Branch—stream .......... TX-5
Crabs Corners—locale .......... PA-2
Crab Spring—spring .......... ID-8
Crab Spring Butte—summit .......... ID-8
Crab Town—locale .......... IA-7
Crabtown Creek—channel .......... NJ-2
Crab Trap Cove—bay .......... AK-9
Crab Tree .......... MD-2
Crabtree—locale .......... AR-4
Crabtree—locale .......... CA-9
Crabtree—locale .......... OH-6
Crabtree—locale .......... TN-4
Crabtree—locale .......... WA-9
**Crabtree**—pop pl .......... MD-2
**Crabtree**—pop pl .......... NC-3
**Crabtree**—pop pl .......... OR-9
**Crabtree**—pop pl .......... PA-2
**Crabtree**—pop pl .......... VA-3
Crabtree, Lake—lake .......... NC-3
Crabtree Bald—summit .......... NC-3
Crabtree Bay—bay .......... NC-3
Crabtree-Blackwell Farm—hist pl .......... VA-3
Crabtree Bog—swamp .......... ME-1
Crabtree Branch—stream .......... AR-4
Crabtree Branch—stream (2) .......... KY-4
Crabtree Branch—stream .......... MO-7
Crab Tree Branch—stream .......... OK-5
Crabtree Branch—stream (3) .......... TN-4
Crabtree Butte—summit .......... AZ-5
Crabtree Cabin (ruins - historical)—locale .......... CA-9
Crabtree Campsite—locale .......... CA-9
Crabtree Canyon—valley .......... CA-9
Crabtree Cem—cemetery .......... AR-4
Crabtree Cem—cemetery .......... IL-6
Crabtree Cem—cemetery (2) .......... KY-4
Crabtree Cem—cemetery (2) .......... MO-7
Crabtree Cem—cemetery .......... OH-6
Crabtree Cem—cemetery .......... TN-4
Crabtree Cem—cemetery (5) .......... VA-3
Crabtree Cem—cemetery .......... WV-2
Crabtree Cem Number 1—cemetery .......... OH-6
Crabtree Ch—church .......... AR-4
Crabtree Ch—church .......... FL-3
Crabtree Ch—church .......... NC-3
Crabtree Ch—church .......... TN-4
Crabtree Chapel—church .......... NC-3
Crabtree Chapel—church .......... VA-3
Crabtree Cove—basin .......... TN-4
Crabtree Cove—bay .......... MO-7
Crabtree Cove Cave—cave .......... TN-4
Crabtree Cove Public Use Area—park .......... MO-7
Crabtree Cove Sch (historical)—school .......... TN-4
Crabtree Creek—stream .......... AZ-5
Crabtree Creek—stream .......... CA-9
Crabtree Creek—stream .......... MD-2
Crabtree Creek—stream (3) .......... NC-3
Crabtree Creek—stream .......... OR-9
Crabtree Creek—stream .......... PA-2
Crabtree Creek—stream .......... TN-4
Crabtree Creek—stream .......... TX-5
Crabtree Creek—stream .......... VA-3
Crabtree Creek-Hoffman Covered Bridge—hist pl .......... OR-9
Crabtree Creek State Park .......... NC-3
Crabtree Creek W/S—reservoir .......... NC-3
Crabtree Creek W/S Number Eighteen—reservoir .......... NC-3
Crabtree Creek W/S Number Eighteen Dam—dam .......... NC-3
Crabtree Creek W/S Structure Number One Dam—dam .......... NC-3
Crabtree Creek W/S Structure Number Three .......... NC-3
Crabtree Creek W/S Structure Number Two Dam—dam .......... NC-3
Crabtree Cree W/S—reservoir .......... NC-3
Crabtree Falls—falls .......... NC-3
Crabtree Falls—falls .......... VA-3
Crabtree Fork—stream .......... VA-3
Crabtree Gap—gap .......... NC-3
Crabtree Gap—gap .......... VA-3
Crabtree Gurad Station—locale .......... OR-9
Crabtree Hill—summit .......... OR-9
**Crabtree Hills**—pop pl .......... TN-4
Crabtree (historical)—locale .......... AL-4
**Crabtree Hollow**—pop pl .......... PA-2
Crabtree Hollow—valley (2) .......... MO-7
Crabtree Hollow—valley (3) .......... TN-4
Crabtree Hot Springs—spring .......... CA-9
Crabtree-Ironduff HS .......... NC-3
Crabtree Iron Duff HS—school .......... NC-3
Crabtree Lake—lake .......... CA-9
Crabtree Lake—lake .......... IL-6
Crab Tree Lake—lake .......... IA-7
Crabtree Lake—lake .......... OR-9
Crabtree Lakes—lake .......... CA-9
Crab Tree Lakes—lake .......... ND-7
Crabtree Lake Trail—trail .......... OR-9
Crabtree Ledge—bar .......... ME-1
Crabtree Lodge—locale .......... CA-9
Crabtree Meadow—flat .......... CA-9
Crabtree Mtn—summit .......... NC-3
Crabtree Mtn—summit .......... OR-9
Crabtree Neck—cape .......... ME-1
Crabtree Park—park .......... AZ-5
Crabtree Park—park .......... CA-9
Crabtree Park—park .......... FL-3
Crabtree Place—locale .......... CA-9
Crabtree Point .......... ME-1
Crabtree Point—cape .......... ME-1
Crabtree Point—cape .......... OR-9
Crabtree Ranger Station—locale .......... CA-9
Crabtree Sch—school .......... OR-9
Crabtree Sch—school .......... VA-3
Crabtree Sch (historical)—school .......... TN-4
Crabtree's Ledge .......... ME-1
Crabtree Slough—gut .......... AL-4
Crabtree Spring—spring (2) .......... AZ-5
Crabtree Spring—spring .......... TN-4
Crab Tree Swamp—stream .......... SC-3
Crabtree (Township of)—fmr MCD (2) .......... NC-3
Crabtree Trail Twenty-two—trail .......... AZ-5
Crabtree Valley—post sta .......... NC-3
Crabtree Wash—stream .......... AZ-5
Craciosa Canyon—valley .......... CA-9
Crack, The—ridge .......... NV-8
Crackatuxet Cove—lake .......... MA-1
Crackaway .......... IN-6
Crack Canyon—valley .......... CA-9
Crack Canyon—valley .......... UT-8
Cracked Crag—summit .......... CA-9
Cracked Spring—spring .......... TX-5
Crackenport .......... PA-2
**Cracker**—pop pl .......... KY-4
Cracker—summit .......... MT-8
Crackerbox Canyon .......... AZ-5
Crackerbox Canyon—valley .......... AZ-5
Cracker Box Creek .......... MT-8
Crackerbox Creek—stream .......... MT-8
Crackerbox Ridge—ridge .......... CA-9
Crackerbox Ridge—ridge .......... TN-4
Crackerbox Sch—school .......... NE-7
Crackerbox Spring—spring .......... AZ-5
Cracker Box Tank—reservoir .......... AZ-5
Cracker Branch—stream (2) .......... FL-3
Cracker Bridge Trail—trail .......... PA-2
Cracker Camp (site)—locale .......... OR-9
Cracker Canyon—valley .......... CA-9
**Cracker City (historical)**—pop pl .......... OR-9
Cracker Creek—stream .......... OR-9
Cracker Creek—stream (2) .......... TN-4
Cracker Creek—stream .......... WY-8
Cracker Flats—flat .......... MT-8
Cracker Grove—woods .......... UT-8
**Cracker Jack**—pop pl .......... PA-2
Cracker Jack Draw—valley .......... TX-5
Crackerjack Mesa—summit .......... AZ-5
Crackerjack Mine—mine .......... AZ-5
Crackerjack Mine—mine .......... ID-8
Crackerjack Ridge—ridge .......... AZ-5
Cracker Jack Tank .......... AZ-5
Crackerjack Tank—reservoir (2) .......... AZ-5
Cracker Jack Windmill—locale .......... TX-5
Cracker Johnson Spring Number One—spring .......... NV-8
Cracker Johnson Spring Number Two—spring .......... NV-8
Cracker Lake—lake .......... MT-8
Cracker Lake Trail—trail .......... MT-8
Cracker Landing—locale .......... FL-3
Cracker Meadow .......... CA-9
Cracker Meadows—area .......... CA-9
Cracker Mine—mine .......... MT-8
Cracker Neck—cape .......... VA-3
**Cracker Neck**—pop pl .......... VA-3
Cracker Neck—valley .......... TX-5
Cracker Neck Branch .......... MO-7
Cracker Neck Branch—stream .......... MO-7
Cracker Neck Ch—church .......... VA-3
Crackerneck Country Club—other .......... MO-7
Cracker Neck Hollow—valley .......... MO-7
Cracker Neck Valley—valley .......... TN-4
Cracker Point—cliff .......... VA-3
Cracker Pond—lake .......... NY-2
Crackers Neck—locale .......... TN-4
Crackers Neck—locale .......... VA-3
**Crackers Neck**—pop pl .......... VA-3
Crackers Neck—valley .......... VA-3
Crackersneck Ridge—ridge .......... WV-2
Crackers Port .......... PA-2
**Crackersport**—pop pl .......... PA-2
Cracker Swamp—swamp .......... FL-3
**Crackertown**—pop pl .......... FL-3
Crackerville—locale .......... MT-8
Crackilukent Cove .......... MA-1
Crack in Rock Ruins—locale .......... AZ-5
Crack in Rock Trail—trail .......... AZ-5
Crackle Ditch—canal .......... IL-6
Crack Rock—pillar .......... RI-1
Crackrock—summit .......... MA-1
Crackrock Pond—reservoir .......... MA-1
Crackrock Pond Dam—dam .......... MA-1
Crackstill Branch—stream .......... KY-4
Crack Tank—reservoir (2) .......... AZ-5
Cracktop—summit .......... CO-8
Cracktuxet Pond .......... MA-1
Crack Whip Furnace Trail—trail .......... WV-2
Cracky Ridge—ridge .......... IN-6
Craddock .......... VA-3
Craddock—locale .......... MO-7
Craddock—locale .......... WV-2
Craddock Bottom—bend .......... KY-4
Craddock Branch—stream .......... VA-3
Craddock Cem—cemetery .......... KY-4
Craddock Cem—cemetery .......... MO-7
Craddock Cem—cemetery .......... VA-3
Craddock Cem—cemetery .......... WV-2
Craddock Creek—stream .......... ID-8
Craddock Creek—stream .......... TX-5
Craddock Creek—stream (2) .......... VA-3
Craddock Crewes Pond—lake .......... MA-1
Craddock Drain—canal .......... MI-6
Craddock Fork—stream .......... WV-2
Craddock Hist Dist—hist pl .......... VA-3
Craddock Lake—lake .......... MO-7
Craddock Meadows—flat .......... OR-9
Craddock Neck—cape .......... VA-3
Craddock Peak—summit .......... ID-8
Craddock Sch—school .......... MO-7
Craddock Sch—school .......... TX-5
Craddock Spring—spring .......... OR-9
**Craddock Subdivision**—pop pl .......... TN-4
Craddock Swamp—stream .......... NC-3
**Craddockville**—pop pl .......... VA-3
Craddockville Ch—church .......... VA-3
Craddy Creek—stream .......... KY-4
Crader Cem—cemetery .......... MO-7
**Cradick Corner**—pop pl .......... IN-6
Cradit Cem—cemetery .......... MI-6
Cradle, The—summit .......... WA-9
Cradlebaugh Bridge—bridge .......... NV-8
Cradlebow Branch—stream .......... KY-4
Cradlebow Cem—cemetery .......... KY-4
Cradle Butte—summit .......... WY-8
Cradle Cove—bay .......... ME-1
Cradle Creek—stream .......... FL-3
Cradle Creek—stream .......... ID-8
Cradle Gap—gap .......... PA-2
Cradle Gut—stream .......... NC-3
Cradle Lake—lake .......... WA-9
Cradle Lakes—lake .......... MT-8
Cradle Mesa—summit .......... NM-5
Cradle Mesa Tank Number One .......... NM-5
Cradle Mesa Tank Number Two .......... NM-5
Cradle Nursery—school .......... FL-3
Cradle of Forestry in America Visitor Center—locale .......... NC-3
Cradle Park—park .......... OH-6
Cradle Point—cape .......... NC-3
Cradle Point—cape .......... VA-3
Cradle Point Light—other .......... VA-3
Cradle Rock Ridge—ridge .......... NY-2
Cradle Tank—reservoir .......... AZ-5
Cradle Valley—basin .......... CA-9
Cradnick Corner .......... IN-6
**Cradock**—pop pl .......... VA-3
Cradock HS—school .......... VA-3
Cradock Sch—school .......... VA-3
Cradock Slough—stream .......... LA-4
Crady Creek—stream .......... KY-4
Craemer Rsvr—reservoir .......... CA-9
Craemer Springs—spring .......... CA-9
**Craf**—pop pl .......... CA-9
Craft—locale .......... MO-7
Craft—locale .......... NE-7
Craft—locale .......... TX-5
Craft, Gershom, House—hist pl .......... PA-2
Craft Branch—stream .......... TN-4
Craft Brook—stream .......... PA-2
Craft Canyon—valley .......... OR-9
Craft Cem—cemetery .......... AL-4
Craft Cem—cemetery .......... KY-4
Craft Cem—cemetery (2) .......... LA-4
Craft Cem—cemetery .......... MS-4
Craft Cem—cemetery .......... OH-6
Craft Creek—stream .......... AR-4
Craft Creek—stream .......... OR-9
Craft Ditch—canal .......... MT-8
Craft Draw—valley .......... WY-8
Craft Fire Tower .......... AL-4
Craft Hill—summit .......... MA-1
Craft Hill—summit .......... TN-4
Craft Hollow—valley .......... AR-4
Craft Hollow—valley .......... TN-4
Craft Hollow—valley (2) .......... VA-3
Craft Island—island .......... WA-9
Craft Lake—lake .......... LA-4
Craft Lake Dam—dam .......... MS-4
Craft Memorial Ch—church .......... TN-4
Craft Mill—locale .......... VA-3
Craft Mine (underground)—mine .......... AL-4
Craft Neck .......... MD-2
Crafton—locale .......... CA-9
Crafton—locale .......... VA-3
**Crafton**—pop pl .......... PA-2
**Crafton**—pop pl .......... TX-5
Crafton, John, House—hist pl .......... TN-4
Crafton Borough—civil .......... PA-2
Crafton Cem—cemetery .......... SC-3
Crafton Cem—cemetery .......... TN-4
Crafton Cem—cemetery .......... TX-5
Crafton Creek .......... OR-9
Crafton Elem Sch—school .......... PA-2
Crafton Gate—locale .......... VA-3
Crafton Golf Course—other .......... PA-2
Crafton Hills—range .......... CA-9
Crafton Island—island .......... AK-9
Crafton Landing—locale .......... AR-4
Crafton Public Golf Course .......... PA-2
Crafton Rsvr—reservoir .......... CA-9
Crafton Sch—school .......... CA-9
Craft Point—cape .......... TX-5
Craft Point—cliff .......... OR-9
Craft Pond—lake .......... SC-3
Craft Pond—reservoir (2) .......... PA-2
Craft Pond Dam—dam .......... PA-2
Craft Pour-Off—stream .......... AL-4
Craft Run—stream .......... PA-2
**Crafts**—pop pl .......... NY-2
Crafts Airp—airport .......... NC-3
**Craftsbury**—pop pl .......... VT-1
Craftsbury Common—other .......... VT-1
**Craftsbury (Town of)**—pop pl .......... VT-1
Crafts Canyon—valley .......... UT-8
Crafts Cem—cemetery .......... KY-4
Crafts Ch—church .......... VA-3
Craft Sch—school .......... AL-4
Craft Sch—school .......... IL-6
Craft Sch—school (2) .......... MI-6
Craft Sch—school .......... TX-5
Craft Sch (historical)—school .......... MS-4
Crafts Colly Creek—stream .......... KY-4
Crafts Creek—stream .......... NJ-2
Crafts Creek—stream .......... PA-2
Crafts-Farrow State Hosp—hospital .......... SC-3
**Crafts-Farrow (State Hospital)**—pop pl .......... SC-3
Crafts Fork—stream .......... CA-9
Crafts Fork—stream .......... KY-4
Crafts Fork Sch—school .......... KY-4
Crafts Hill—summit .......... MA-1
Crafts Hill—summit .......... NH-1
Crafts Island—island .......... PA-2
Crafts Lake—lake .......... UT-8
Crafts Peak—summit .......... CA-9
Crafts Prairie—flat .......... TX-5
Craft Spring—locale .......... TN-4
Craft Spring—spring .......... OR-9
Crafts Run .......... PA-2
Crafts Run—stream .......... WV-2
Crafts William H., House—hist pl .......... OH-6
Crag—locale .......... AZ-5
Crag—locale .......... WV-2
Crag, Mount—summit .......... NH-1
Crag, Mount—summit .......... WA-9
Cragar Cem—cemetery .......... AR-4
Crag Branch—stream .......... MO-7
Crag Creek .......... WY-8
Crag Creek—stream .......... AK-9
Crag Creek—stream .......... CA-9
Crag Creek—stream .......... OR-9
Crag Creek—stream .......... WA-9
Crag Crest Trail—trail .......... CO-8
Cragdale Ch—church .......... AL-4
Cragdale Mill .......... AL-4
Crager Branch—stream .......... KY-4
Crager Fork—stream .......... KY-4
Crager Ridge—ridge .......... NM-5
Cragfont—hist pl .......... TN-4
Cragfoot Hill—summit .......... NY-2
Cragford—locale .......... AL-4
Cragford JHS (historical)—school .......... AL-4
Cragg Branch—stream .......... MO-7
Cragged Branch—stream .......... VA-3
Cragged Mountain Farm—locale .......... NH-1
Cragged Mtn—summit .......... NH-1
Craggie Creek—stream .......... OR-9
Craggie Fork .......... OR-9
**Craggie Hope**—pop pl .......... TN-4
Craggie Hope Post Office (historical)—building .......... TN-4
Craggie Hope United Methodist Ch—church .......... TN-4
Cragg Mtn .......... MA-1
Craggs—locale .......... FL-3
Craggs Run—stream .......... PA-2
**Craggy**—pop pl .......... NC-3
Craggy Canyon .......... UT-8
Craggy Creek—stream .......... OR-9
Craggy Dam—dam .......... NC-3
Craggy Dam Rsvr—reservoir .......... NC-3
Craggy Dome—summit .......... NC-3
Craggy Flats—swamp .......... NC-3
Craggy Gardens—ridge .......... NC-3
Craggy Knob—summit .......... NC-3
Craggy Mtn—summit .......... CA-9
Craggy Mtn—summit .......... OR-9
Craggy Peak—summit .......... CA-9
Craggy Peak—summit .......... WA-9
Craggy Pinnacle—summit .......... NC-3
Craggy Point—cape .......... AS-9
Craggy Prison—locale .......... NC-3
Craggy Rock—pillar .......... OR-9
Craghead Branch—stream .......... MO-7
Crag Hollow—valley .......... VA-3
Cragies Bridge .......... MA-1
Cragin .......... IL-6
Cragin, Daniel, Mill—hist pl .......... NH-1
Cragin Junction .......... IL-6
Cragin Playground—park .......... IL-6
Cragin Sch—school .......... AZ-5
Crag Lake .......... ID-8
Crag Lake—lake .......... CA-9
Crag Lake—lake .......... ID-8
Crag Lake—lake .......... MN-6
Crag Lake—lake (2) .......... MT-8
Crag Lake—lake .......... WA-9
**Cragmere Park**—pop pl .......... NJ-2
**Cragmere (subdivision)**—pop pl .......... DE-2
**Cragmere Woods (subdivision)**—pop pl .......... DE-2
Cragmont—uninc pl .......... CA-9
Cragmont Park—park .......... CA-9
Cragmont Primary Sch—school .......... CA-9
Cragmont Sch—school .......... CA-9
Cragmor—uninc pl .......... CO-8
Cragmor Sanatorium—hospital .......... CO-8
Crag Mtn—summit .......... CT-1
Crag Mtn—summit .......... MA-1
Crag Mtn—summit .......... WA-9
Cragnola Gap—gap .......... NC-3
Crago .......... MI-6
Crago, Lake—lake .......... FL-3
**Crag O Lea**—pop pl .......... MO-7
Crago Ranch—locale .......... WY-8
Crag Peak—summit .......... AK-9
Crag Peak—summit .......... CA-9
Crag Peak—summit .......... ID-8
Crag Point—cape .......... AK-9
Crags, Lake—lake .......... CO-8
Crags, Lake Of The—lake .......... WY-8
Crags, The—cliff .......... NY-2
Crags, The—pillar (2) .......... CO-8
Crags, The—summit .......... ID-8
Crags, The—summit .......... MA-1
Crags, The—summit .......... WY-8
Crags Campground—locale .......... ID-8
Crags Island—island .......... VA-3
Crags Lake—lake .......... CA-9
**Cragsmoor**—pop pl .......... NY-2
Crags Mountain .......... ID-8
Crags Mountains .......... ID-8
Crags Mountains, The .......... ID-8
Cragston Dependencies—hist pl .......... NY-2
Cragston Lakes—reservoir .......... NY-2
Crags Trail—trail .......... ID-8
Crag View—summit .......... WA-9
Craham Cem—cemetery .......... SC-3
**Crahen (historical)**—pop pl .......... MS-4
Craig .......... AZ-5
Craig .......... IL-6
Craig .......... WV-2
Craig—fmr MCD .......... NE-7
Craig—locale .......... CA-9
Craig—locale .......... KS-7
Craig—locale .......... OK-5
Craig—locale .......... PA-2
Craig—locale .......... VA-3
Craig—other .......... IL-6
**Craig**—pop pl .......... AK-9
**Craig**—pop pl .......... CO-8
**Craig**—pop pl .......... FL-3
**Craig**—pop pl .......... IN-6
**Craig**—pop pl .......... IA-7
**Craig**—pop pl .......... MS-4
**Craig**—pop pl .......... MO-7
**Craig**—pop pl .......... MT-8
**Craig**—pop pl .......... NE-7
**Craig**—pop pl .......... OK-5
**Craig**—pop pl .......... TX-5
Craig, Lake—dam .......... NC-3
Craig, Mount—summit .......... CO-8
Craig, Newton, House and Penitentiary Buildings Complex—hist pl .......... KY-4
Craig AFB—military .......... AL-4
Craig Arroyo—stream .......... NM-5
Craig Ave Sch—school .......... VA-3
Craig Bayou—stream .......... LA-4
**Craig Beach**—pop pl .......... OH-6
Craig Branch .......... OR-9
Craig Branch—stream .......... FL-3
Craig Branch—stream .......... KY-4
Craig Branch—stream .......... PA-2
Craig Branch—stream .......... TN-4
Craig Branch—stream .......... VA-3
Craig Branch—stream (2) .......... WV-2
Craig Bridge—bridge .......... TN-4
Craig Bridge—bridge .......... TX-5
Craig Bridge—bridge .......... VA-3
Craig Brook—stream .......... ME-1
Craig-Bryan House—hist pl .......... AR-4
Craig Camp—locale .......... ID-8
Craig Campground—locale .......... CO-8
Craig Canal—canal .......... MS-4
Craig Canyon—valley (3) .......... CA-9
Craig Canyon—valley (2) .......... NV-8
Craig Cave—cave .......... CA-9
Craig Cem—cemetery (3) .......... AL-4
Craig Cem—cemetery .......... AR-4
Craig Cem—cemetery .......... GA-3
Craig Cem—cemetery (3) .......... IL-6
Craig Cem—cemetery .......... IN-6
Craig Cem—cemetery (5) .......... KY-4
Craig Cem—cemetery .......... NE-7
Craig Cem—cemetery .......... NC-3
Craig Cem—cemetery .......... OH-6
Craig Cem—cemetery (2) .......... PA-2
Craig Cem—cemetery .......... SC-3
Craig Cem—cemetery (2) .......... TN-4
Craig Cem—cemetery (2) .......... TX-5
Craig Cem—cemetery (2) .......... WV-2
Craig Cemeteries—cemetery .......... WV-2
Craig Chapel—church .......... AL-4
Craig Chapel—church .......... TN-4
Craig Chapel (historical)—church .......... TN-4
Craig Chapel Methodist Ch (historical)—church .......... AL-4
Craig City (historical)—locale .......... KS-7
Craig Coulee—valley .......... MT-8
**Craig (County)**—pop pl .......... OK-5
**Craig (County)**—pop pl .......... VA-3
Craig County Courthouse—hist pl .......... OK-5
Craig Cove—valley .......... NC-3
Craig Creek .......... MD-2
Craig Creek .......... OR-9
Craig Creek—stream .......... AK-9
Craig Creek—stream .......... AR-4
Craig Creek—stream .......... CA-9
Craig Creek—stream .......... CO-8
Craig Creek—stream .......... FL-3
Craig Creek—stream .......... GA-3
Craig Creek—stream .......... ID-8
Craig Creek—stream .......... KS-7
Craig Creek—stream (4) .......... KY-4
Craig Creek—stream (2) .......... NC-3
Craig Creek—stream (2) .......... OR-9
Craig Creek—stream (3) .......... VA-3
Craig Creek Valley—valley .......... VA-3
Craig Ditch—canal .......... CO-8
Craig Ditch—canal .......... IN-6
Craig Drain—canal (2) .......... MI-6
Craig Draw—valley (2) .......... CO-8
Craig Draw Rsvr—reservoir .......... CO-8
**Craige**—pop pl .......... WA-9
Craige Cem—cemetery .......... WA-9
Craigel Island—island .......... IL-6
Craigel Slough—gut .......... IL-6
Craigen Tunnel—tunnel .......... VA-3
Craiger Branch—stream .......... KY-4
Craiger Hollow—valley .......... VA-3
Craigfield—locale .......... TN-4
Craig Field (airport)—airport .......... AL-4
Craigfield Cem—cemetery .......... TN-4

Craig Field Lake Dam—dam AL-4
Craigfield Post Office (historical)—building TN-4
Craig-Flowers House—hist pl MS-4
Craig Fork—stream PA-2
Craig Gap—gap GA-3
Craig Grave—cemetery OR-9
Craig Gulch—valley OR-9
Craig Harbor—bay NY-2
**Craighead**—pop pl PA-2
Craighead Caverns—cave TN-4
Craighead Caverns—park TN-4
Craighead Cem—cemetery MO-7
Craighead Cem—cemetery VA-3
**Craighead (County)**—pop pl AR-4
Craighead Creek—stream (2) TN-4
Craighead Dam—dam TN-4
Craighead Forest Park—park AR-4
Craighead-Jackson House—hist pl TN-4
Craighead Lake—lake TN-4
Craighead Lake—reservoir TN-4
Craighead Pond—lake LA-4
Craigheads PA-2
**Craigheads**—pop pl PA-2
Craighead Sch—school AL-4
Craigheads Shoals—rapids TN-4
Craighead Tunnel—tunnel PA-2
Craig Healing Spring VA-3
Craig Healing Springs VA-3
Craig Healing Springs—hist pl VA-3
**Craig Heights (subdivision)**—pop pl NC-3
**Craig Highlands**—pop pl IN-6
Craig Highway—channel MI-6
Craig Hill—summit AR-4
Craig Hill—summit GA-3
Craig Hill—summit (2) NY-2
Craig Hill—summit OK-5
Craig Hill—summit PA-2
Craig Hill—summit TX-5
Craig Hill Cem—cemetery WV-2
Craighill Channel—channel MD-2
Craig Hill Country Club—other NY-2
Craig Hill Sch—school NY-2
Craig (historical)—locale AL-4
Craig Hollow—valley MO-7
Craig Hollow—valley (4) TN-4
Craig Hollow—valley WV-2
Craig Horse Creek—stream CO-8
Craig HS—school WI-6
Craig-Hudson Cem—cemetery TN-4
Craigie Arms—hist pl MA-1
**Craigie Clair**—pop pl NY-2
Craigie Creek—stream AK-9
Craigie Point—ridge OR-9
Craigin Brook—stream ME-1
Craigin Gilbert Lake Dam—dam MS-4
Craig Island—island ME-1
Craig-Johnson Mill Dam and Mill Sites—hist pl KY-4
Craig Junction—locale ID-8
Craig Key—island FL-3
Craig Lake ID-8
Craig Lake MN-6
Craig Lake—dam MS-4
Craig Lake—lake AK-9
Craig Lake—lake (2) MI-6
Craig Lake—lake MN-6
Craig Lake—lake (3) OR-9
Craig Lake—lake UT-8
Craig Lake—reservoir TN-4
Craig Lake Dam—dam TN-4
Craig Lake Dam Number Two—dam TN-4
Craig Lake Number Two—reservoir TN-4
Craig Landing—locale LA-4
Craig Manor IL-6
**Craigmar (historical)**—pop pl TN-4
Craig Meadows—flat CO-8
Craig Memorial Ch—church AL-4
Craig Memorial Ch—church NC-3
Craig Memorial United Methodist Ch AL-4
Craigmile Ditch—canal IN-6
Craigmiles, P. M., House—hist pl TN-4
Craigmiles Hall—hist pl TN-4
Craig Mine—mine NV-8
**Craigmont**—pop pl ID-8
**Craigmont (subdivision)**—pop pl TN-4
**Craigmoor**—pop pl WV-2
Craig Mountain Lookout Tower—locale AL-4
Craig Mountains ID-8
Craig Mtn—summit AL-4
Craig Mtn—summit AK-9
Craig Mtn—summit ID-8
Craig Mtn—summit NC-3
Craig Mtn—summit (3) OR-9
Craig Mtn—summit VA-3
Craig Municipal Airp—airport CO-8
Craig Park—flat CO-8
Craig Park—park IN-6
Craig Pass—gap SD-7
Craig Pass—gap WY-8
Craig Pass Spring—spring SD-7
Craig Peak—summit CA-9
Craig Peak—summit CO-8
Craig Place IL-6
Craig Place—locale CO-8
Craig Plantation (historical)—locale MS-4
Craig Point CA-9
Craig Point—cape AK-9
Craig Point—cape NY-2
Craig Point—cape NC-3
Craig Point—cliff CO-8
Craig Pond—lake ME-1
Craig Pond—lake MA-1
Craig Pond Brook—stream ME-1
Craig Private Airstrip—airport ND-7
Craig Quarry—mine (2) TN-4
Craig Ranch—locale AZ-5
Craig Ranch Country Club—locale NV-8
Craig Rehabilitation Hosp—hospital CO-8
Craig Ridge—ridge TN-4
Craig Ridge—ridge WV-2
Craig Road Speedway—locale NV-8
Craig Rock—other AK-9
Craig Run PA-2
Craig Run—stream (4) PA-2
Craig Run—stream (2) VA-3
Craig Run—stream (2) WV-2
Craigs—locale NY-2
Craigs—locale PA-2
Craigs Cabin—locale OR-9
Craigs Cave—cave AL-4
Craigs Ch—church VA-3
Craig Sch—school GA-3
Craig Sch—school (3) IL-6
Craig Sch—school IA-7
Craig Sch—school ME-1
Craig Sch—school MI-6
Craig Sch—school NV-8
Craig Sch—school NJ-2
Craig Sch—school NY-2
Craig Sch—school PA-2
Craig Sch—school WI-6
Craig Sch (abandoned)—school SD-7
Craigs Chapel—church WV-2
Craig Sch (historical)—school TN-4
Craigs Creek KS-7
Craigs Creek TN-4
Craigs Creek VA-3
Craigs Creek—stream CA-9
Craigs Creek—stream KY-4
Craigs Creek Mtn—summit CA-9
Craig-Seay House—hist pl MS-4
Craigs Ferry (historical)—locale AL-4
Craigs Flat—flat CA-9
Craigs Ford Post Office (historical)—building TN-4
Craigs Hill—summit WA-9
**Craigside**—pop pl MS-4
Craigside Landing MS-4
Craigs Island (historical)—island PA-2
Craigs Knoll—summit AZ-5
Craigs Landing—locale MS-4
Craigs Landing (historical)—locale AL-4
**Craigs Meadow**—pop pl PA-2
**Craigs Meadow (Birch Acres)**—pop pl PA-2
Craigsmere—locale MI-6
Craigs Mill—locale DE-2
Craigs Mill—locale VA-3
Craigs Mills VA-3
**Craigs Mills**—pop pl VA-3
**Craig South Highlands**—pop pl CO-8
Craigs Pond—lake DE-2
Craig Spring—spring (2) CA-9
Craig Spring—spring ID-8
**Craig Springs**—pop pl MS-4
**Craig Springs**—pop pl VA-3
Craig Springs Cem—cemetery MS-4
Craig Springs Ch—church VA-3
Craigs Run PA-2
Craigs Run—stream PA-2
Craigs Shoals—bar AL-4
Craigs Store Landing (historical)—locale MS-4
Craig State Sch—school NY-2
Craig State School Cem—cemetery NY-2
Craig Station (Site)—locale NV-8
Craig Street Shops—locale PA-2
Craigsville NY-2
**Craigsville**—pop pl NY-2
**Craigsville**—pop pl PA-2
**Craigsville**—pop pl VA-3
**Craigsville**—pop pl WV-2
Craigsville Rsvr—reservoir VA-3
Craigsville Sch—hist pl VA-3
Craig Tabernacle—church LA-4
**Craigton**—pop pl OH-6
Craig Tower—locale LA-4
**Craigtown**—pop pl MD-2
Craigtown Cem—cemetery IL-6
Craigtown Sch—school IL-6
**Craig Township**—pop pl NE-7
Craig (Township of)—fmr MCD AR-4
**Craig (Township of)**—pop pl IN-6
Craig-Tyler (CCD)—cens area AL-4
Craig-Tyler Division—civil AL-4
Craigville WV-2
**Craigville**—pop pl IN-6
**Craigville**—pop pl MA-1
**Craigville**—pop pl MN-6
**Craigville**—pop pl NY-2
Craigville Beach—beach MA-1
**Craigville Beach**—pop pl MA-1
Craigville Brach Junction Station—locale PA-2
Craigville Depot—hist pl IN-6
Craigville Hist Dist—hist pl MA-1
Craigville Marshes—swamp MA-1
Craik-Patton House—hist pl WV-2
**Craik Spur**—pop pl WA-9
Crail Creek—stream MT-8
Crailhope—locale KY-4
Crail Ranch—locale MT-8
Crail Ranch Buildings—hist pl MT-8
Crain—locale IL-6
Crain, F. H., House—hist pl TX-5
Crain, W. H., House—hist pl TX-5
Crain Camp—locale WY-8
Crain Cem—cemetery AR-4
Crain Cem—cemetery IL-6
Crain Cem—cemetery KS-7
Crain Cem—cemetery KY-4
Crain Cem—cemetery (2) LA-4
Crain Cem—cemetery MO-7
Crain Cem—cemetery NY-2
Crain Cem—cemetery TN-4
Crain Cem—cemetery TX-5
Crain City—locale AR-4
**Crain Creek**—pop pl IA-7
Crain Creek—stream KS-7
Craine Ch—church FL-3
Craine Creek NV-8
Craine Creek—stream NV-8
Crainer Creek—stream MI-6
Craine Spring NV-8
Craine Spring—spring NV-8
Crainesville Post Office (historical)—building TN-4
Crain Hill Cem—cemetery TN-4
Crain Hill Ch—church TN-4
Crain Hill Sch and Church—hist pl TN-4
Crain Hill Sch (historical)—school TN-4
Crainhoek DE-2
Crain Lake—lake LA-4
Crain Lake—reservoir IN-6
Crain Lake Dam—dam IN-6
Crain Lake Dam—dam MS-4
Crain Mill (Site)—locale CA-9
Crain Mine—mine SD-7
Crain Park—park TX-5
Crain Place—locale MT-8
Crain Pond—lake FL-3
Crain Prairie Trail—trail OR-9
Crain Prairie Way OR-9
Crain Ranch—locale WY-8
Crain Sch—school WY-8
Crains Corners—locale NY-2
Crains Creek NC-3
Crains Creek VA-3
Crains Creek—stream LA-4
Crains Creek Ch—church LA-4
Crains Island—island IL-6
Crains Lake—reservoir TX-5
**Crains Mills**—pop pl NY-2
Crains Run—stream OH-6
Crains Store (historical)—locale MS-4
Crain's Wholesale and Retail Store—hist pl KY-4
Craintown—locale KY-4
**Craintown**—pop pl KY-4
Craintown Branch—stream KY-4
**Crainville**—pop pl IL-6
Crainville (historical)—locale KS-7
Craker Meadows—flat CA-9
Cral Coulee—valley MT-8
Crale—locale OR-9
Crale Creek—stream OR-9
**Craley**—pop pl PA-2
Crall Hollow—valley WA-9
**Cram**—pop pl AR-4
Cramberry Bog Rsvr Number One—reservoir MA-1
Cramberry Pond MA-1
Cramberry Slough—gut AK-9
Cramblet Ranch—locale CO-8
Cram Brook—stream ME-1
Cram Brook—stream VT-1
Cram Creek—stream KY-4
Cram Creek—stream (2) OR-9
Cram Creek Sch—school KY-4
Cram Ditch—canal OR-9
Cramer PA-2
Cramer—locale MN-6
**Cramer**—pop pl IL-6
**Cramer**—pop pl (2) PA-2
Cramer, Frederick, House—hist pl NY-2
Cramer, Martin, House—hist pl MT-8
Cramer, Mount—summit ID-8
Cramer Brook PA-2
Cramer Canyon—valley OR-9
Cramer Cem—cemetery AL-4
Cramer Corners—locale NY-2
Cramer Creek—stream CO-8
Cramer Creek—stream ID-8
Cramer Creek—stream KS-7
Cramer Creek—stream MI-6
Cramer Creek—stream (2) MT-8
Cramer Creek—stream NJ-2
Cramer Creek—stream NM-5
Cramer Creek—stream PA-2
Cramer Creek—stream TX-5
Cramer Creek—stream WI-6
Cramer Ditch MT-8
Cramer Ditch—canal MT-8
Cramer Ditch—canal OH-6
Cramer Ditch—canal WY-8
Cramer Gut—gut MD-2
**Cramer Hill**—pop pl NJ-2
Cramer Hollow—valley AL-4
Cramer Hollow—valley PA-2
Cramer Homestead Lake—lake MN-6
Cramer House—hist pl UT-8
Cramer Island—island MN-6
Cramer Lake—lake MN-6
Cramer Lake—lake WA-9
Cramer Lake—lake WI-6
Cramer Lake Trail—trail WA-9
Cramer Mine—mine AZ-5
Cramer Mountain Country Club—locale NC-3
**Cramer Mountain (subdivision)**—pop pl NC-3
Cramer Mtn—summit WA-9
Cramer Park—park VI-3
Cramer Point—cape NY-2
Cramer Pond PA-2
Cramer Ranch—locale NE-7
Cramer (RR name for Stump Creek)—other PA-2
Cramer Sch—school MI-6
Cramer Sch—school NE-7
Cramer Sch—school NJ-2
**Cramers (Cramer)**—pop pl IL-6
Cramers Creek—stream NJ-2
Cramer Shaft—mine NM-5
Cramer Spring—spring CA-9
Cramer Tank—reservoir AZ-5
**Cramerton**—pop pl NC-3
Cramerton Christian Acad—school NC-3
Cramerton Elementary and JHS—school NC-3
Cramer Woods—woods WA-9
Cramford Hall Nursing Home—hospital NJ-2
Cram Gulch—valley CA-9
Cram Hill—summit VT-1
**Cram (historical)**—pop pl OR-9
Cram Lake WI-6
Crammeys Run—stream WV-2
Cramm Mtn—summit AZ-5
Cramond—hist pl PA-2
Cramp Cem—cemetery OK-5
Cramp Drain—canal MI-6
Cram Peak—summit CA-9
Cramps Bay ID-8
Cramps Bay—bay ID-8
Cramp Sch—school PA-2
Cramp Spring—spring MT-8
Crampton IL-6
**Crampton**—pop pl IL-6
Crampton Cem—cemetery VT-1
Crampton Ditch—canal IN-6
Crampton Gap—gap MD-2
Crampton Lake—lake WI-6
Crampton Mountain CO-8
Crampton Mtn—summit CO-8
Crampton Ranch—locale MT-8
Crampton Rsvr—reservoir OR-9
**Crampton Spur**—pop pl SD-7
Crampton Troughs—spring NV-8
Cram Ranch—locale AZ-5
Cram Ranch—locale WY-8
Cram Rsvr—reservoir OR-9
Crams Brook VT-1
Cram Sch—school CA-9
**Crams Corner**—pop pl ME-1
Crams Point—cape ME-1
Crams Point—cape MN-6
Cram Spring—spring OR-9
Cramton Bowl—basin AL-4
Cramton Park—park MI-6
Cranberry MD-2
Cranberry NJ-2
Cranberry WV-2
Cranberry—locale MD-2
**Cranberry**—pop pl NC-3
**Cranberry**—pop pl (2) PA-2
**Cranberry**—pop pl WV-2
Cranberry Area HS—school PA-2
Cranberry Area Junior Senior HS PA-2
Cranberry Bay—bay MN-6
Cranberry Bog MA-1
Cranberry Bog—lake NH-1
Cranberry Bog—swamp (2) NY-2
Cranberry Bog—swamp RI-1
Cranberry Bog—swamp VT-1
Cranberry Bog, The—swamp CT-1
**Cranberry Bog Corner**—pop pl MA-1
Cranberry Bog Dam—dam MA-1
Cranberry Bog Dam Number 1—dam MA-1
Cranberry Bog Notch—gap NH-1
Cranberry Bog Pond—lake NH-1
Cranberry Bog Rsvr—reservoir MA-1
Cranberry Bogs—swamp MI-6
Cranberry Bottoms—bend CT-1
Cranberry Branch DE-2
Cranberry Branch—stream MD-2
Cranberry Branch—stream NJ-2
Cranberry Branch—stream NC-3
Cranberry Brook MA-1
Cranberry Brook NJ-2
Cranberry Brook—stream (4) ME-1
Cranberry Brook—stream MA-1
Cranberry Brook—stream NJ-2
Cranberry Brook—stream NY-2
Cranberry Brook—stream RI-1
Cranberry Campground—locale WV-2
Cranberry Cem—cemetery NC-3
Cranberry Ch—church MD-2
Cranberry Ch—church (3) NC-3
Cranberry Ch—church VA-3
Cranberry Chute—gut MO-7
Cranberry Cove—bay (2) ME-1
Cranberry Cove Plaza (Shop Ctr)—locale MA-1
Cranberry Creek MI-6
**Cranberry Creek**—pop pl NY-2
Cranberry Creek—stream AK-9
Cranberry Creek—stream (2) ID-8
Cranberry Creek—stream (5) MI-6
Cranberry Creek—stream (2) MN-6
Cranberry Creek—stream (2) NY-2
Cranberry Creek—stream (5) NC-3
Cranberry Creek—stream (3) OH-6
Cranberry Creek—stream (2) PA-2
Cranberry Creek—stream VT-1
Cranberry Creek—stream (2) VA-3
Cranberry Creek—stream (3) WA-9
Cranberry Creek—stream WV-2
Cranberry Creek—stream (7) WI-6
Cranberry Creek Archeol District—hist pl WI-6
Cranberry Dam—dam NC-3
Cranberry Drain—stream MI-6
Cranberry Elem Sch—school PA-2
Cranberry Flat—flat PA-2
Cranberry Flat—flat WV-2
Cranberry Flowage—reservoir WI-6
Cranberry Gap—gap PA-2
**Cranberry Gap**—pop pl NC-3
Cranberry Glade Dam—dam PA-2
Cranberry Glade Lake—reservoir PA-2
Cranberry Glade Run—stream PA-2
Cranberry Glades—swamp WV-2
Cranberry Glades Overlook—locale WV-2
Cranberry Gulch—valley CA-9
Cranberry Gut—gut NJ-2
Cranberry Hall—locale NJ-2
Cranberry Harbor—bay ME-1
Cranberry Hill—summit CT-1
Cranberry Hill—summit ME-1
Cranberry Hill—summit MA-1
Cranberry Hill—summit NJ-2
Cranberry Hill—summit NY-2
Cranberry Hill—summit RI-1
Cranberryhorn ME-1
Cranberryhorn Cem—cemetery ME-1
Cranberryhorn Hill—summit ME-1
Cranberryhorn Mtn ME-1
Cranberry HS—school NC-3
Cranberry Island ME-1
Cranberry Island—island (3) ME-1
Cranberry Island—island MN-6
Cranberry Island—island NC-3
Cranberry Island Passage ME-1
**Cranberry Isles**—pop pl ME-1
**Cranberry Isles (Town of)**—pop pl ME-1
Cranberry Junction—locale PA-2
Cranberry Knob—summit NC-3
Cranberry Lake MI-6
Cranberry Lake MN-6
Cranberry Lake MO-7
Cranberry Lake WA-9
Cranberry Lake WI-6
Cranberry Lake—lake IL-6
Cranberry Lake—lake (36) MI-6
Cranberry Lake—lake (19) MN-6
Cranberry Lake—lake (2) NY-2
Cranberry Lake—lake ND-7
Cranberry Lake—lake (6) WA-9
Cranberry Lake—lake (19) WI-6
**Cranberry Lake**—pop pl NJ-2
**Cranberry Lake**—pop pl NY-2
**Cranberry Lake**—pop pl WI-6
Cranberry Lake—reservoir NJ-2
Cranberry Lake—reservoir (2) NY-2
Cranberry Lake—reservoir NC-3
Cranberry Lake—reservoir PA-2
Cranberry Lake Biological Station—other NY-2
Cranberry Lake Bog—swamp MI-6
Cranberry Lake Campground—locale NY-2
Cranberry Lake Cem—cemetery NY-2
Cranberry Lake Dam—dam NJ-2
Cranberry Lake Dam—dam PA-2
Cranberry Lake Oil And Gas Storage Field—other MI-6
Cranberry Lake Ridge—ridge ME-1
Cranberry Lakes—lake MI-6
Cranberry Lakes—lake NY-2
Cranberry Ledge—bench CT-1
Cranberry Mall (Shop Ctr)—locale MA-1
Cranberry Marsh—area AK-9
**Cranberry Marsh**—pop pl WI-6
Cranberry Marsh—swamp IN-6
Cranberry Marsh—swamp (3) NY-2
Cranberry Marsh—swamp OH-6
Cranberry Marsh—swamp (3) WA-9
Cranberry Marsh—swamp WI-6
Cranberry Marsh Drain—canal MI-6
Cranberry Marsh Drain—stream MI-6
Cranberry Meadow—swamp ME-1
Cranberry Meadow Brook CT-1
Cranberry Meadow Brook—stream (2) CT-1
Cranberry Meadow Pond—lake NH-1
Cranberry Meadow Pond—lake VT-1
Cranberry Meadow Pond—reservoir MA-1
Cranberry Meadow Pond Dam—dam MA-1
Cranberry Memorial Ch—church VA-3
Cranberry Mines—mine NC-3
Cranberry Mountain—ridge WV-2
Cranberry Mtn—summit ME-1
Cranberry Mtn—summit (4) NY-2
Cranberry Narrows—channel WI-6
Cranberry Peak CA-9
Cranberry Peak—summit AK-9
Cranberry Peak—summit ME-1
Cranberry Plaza (Shop Ctr)—locale MA-1
Cranberry Point—cape (2) ME-1
Cranberry Point—cliff IN-6
Cranberry Pond MA-1
Cranberry Pond—lake (4) CT-1
Cranberry Pond—lake (12) ME-1
Cranberry Pond—lake (6) MA-1
Cranberry Pond—lake (3) NH-1
Cranberry Pond—lake (15) NY-2
Cranberry Pond—lake (2) PA-2
Cranberry Pond—reservoir (2) MA-1
Cranberry Pond—reservoir NY-2
Cranberry Pond—swamp NY-2
Cranberry Pond Brook—stream (2) MA-1
Cranberry Pond Dam—dam (2) MA-1
Cranberry Pond (historical)—lake MA-1
Cranberry Post Office (historical)—building PA-2
**Cranberry Prairie**—pop pl OH-6
Cranberry Reservoir NJ-2
Cranberry Ridge—ridge NC-3
Cranberry Ridge—ridge (2) PA-2
Cranberry Ridge—ridge WV-2
**Cranberry Ridge (Old Cranberry)**—pop pl PA-2
Cranberry Ridge Overlook—locale NC-3
Cranberry Ridge Trail—trail WV-2
Cranberry River MN-6
Cranberry River—stream MA-1
Cranberry River—stream MI-6
Cranberry River—stream WV-2
Cranberry River—stream WI-6
Cranberry Rock Lookout Tower—locale WI-6
Cranberry Run PA-2
Cranberry Run—stream MD-2
Cranberry Run—stream (3) OH-6
Cranberry Run—stream (3) PA-2
Cranberry Run—stream WV-2
Cranberry Sch—school (3) PA-2
Cranberry Sch (abandoned)—school PA-2
Cranberry Shoal—bar MI-6
Cranberry Springs Gulch—valley WY-8
Cranberry State Park—park NJ-2
Cranberry Station NJ-2
Cranberry Station—locale MD-2
Cranberry Stream—stream ME-1
Cranberry Summit WV-2
Cranberry Swamp MA-1
Cranberry Swamp—swamp CT-1
Cranberry Swamp—swamp ME-1
Cranberry Swamp—swamp MD-2
Cranberry Swamp—swamp MA-1
Cranberry Swamp—swamp (6) PA-2
Cranberry Swamp—swamp VT-1
Cranberry Swamp Natural Area—area PA-2
Cranberry (Township of)—fmr MCD (2) NC-3
**Cranberry (Township of)**—pop pl OH-6
**Cranberry (Township of)**—pop pl (2) PA-2
Cranberry Valley—valley PA-2
Cranberry Village PA-2
Cranberry Vly Creek—stream NY-2
Cranberry World Visitors Center—park MA-1
Cranbrook DE-2
Cranbrook MI-6
Cranbrook—hist pl MI-6
Cranbrook Lake—lake MI-6
Cranbrook River DE-2
Cranbrook Sch—school MI-6
Cranbrook Sch—school OH-6
Cranbury CT-1
**Cranbury**—pop pl CT-1
**Cranbury**—pop pl NJ-2
Cranbury Brook—stream NJ-2
Cranbury (census name for Cranbury Center)—CDP NJ-2
Cranbury Center (census name Cranbury)—other NJ-2
Cranbury Hist Dist—hist pl NJ-2
**Cranbury Station**—pop pl NJ-2
**Cranbury (Township of)**—pop pl NJ-2
Crance Brook—stream PA-2
C Ranch—locale TX-5
Cranch Park—locale PA-2
Cranch Sch—hist pl MA-1
Cranch Sch—school MA-1
Cranch Sch (abondoned)—school DC-2
Crandal Hill—summit PA-2
Crandall—locale FL-3
Crandall—locale IL-6
**Crandall**—pop pl GA-3
**Crandall**—pop pl IN-6
**Crandall**—pop pl MS-4
**Crandall**—pop pl SD-7
**Crandall**—pop pl TX-5
Crandall, Lake—reservoir SC-3
Crandall, Lorenzo, House—hist pl RI-1
Crandall, Prudence, House—hist pl CT-1
Crandall Branch—stream IN-6
Crandall Brook CT-1
Crandall Brook—stream NY-2
Crandall Canyon—valley (3) UT-8
Crandall (CCD)—cens area TX-5
Crandall Cem—cemetery IL-6
Crandall Cem—cemetery KS-7
Crandall Cem—cemetery KY-4
Crandall Cem—cemetery MI-6
Crandall Cem—cemetery MN-6
Crandall Cem—cemetery OH-6
Crandall Cem—cemetery SD-7
Crandall Cem—cemetery TN-4
Crandall Cem—cemetery VT-1
**Crandall Corners**—pop pl NY-2
Crandall Creek IN-6
Crandall Creek MT-8
Crandall Creek WY-8
Crandall Creek—stream CA-9
Crandall Creek—stream MT-8
Crandall Creek—stream NY-2
Crandall Creek—stream OR-9
Crandall Creek—stream WA-9
Crandall Creek—stream WY-8
Crandall Dam—dam WY-8
Crandall Ditch—canal WY-8
Crandall Drain—canal MI-6
Crandall Drain—stream MI-6
Crandall-Eton (CCD)—cens area GA-3
Crandall Falls—falls NY-2
Crandall Farm Complex—hist pl NY-2
Crandall Hill—summit CT-1
Crandall (historical)—locale KS-7
Crandall Hollow—valley PA-2
Crandall Houses—hist pl UT-8
Crandall Lake—lake MN-6
Crandall Lake—lake WI-6
Crandall Mtn—summit NY-2
Crandall Park—park NY-2
Crandall Park—park OH-6
Crandall Peak—summit CA-9
Crandall Pond Brook CT-1
Crandall Post Office (historical)—building MS-4
Crandall Ranger Station—locale WY-8
Crandall Rsvr—reservoir MT-8
Crandalls Bay—reservoir WI-6
Crandalls Beach—beach IA-7
Crandall Sch—school AL-4
Crandall Sch—school IL-6
Crandall Sch—school MI-6
Crandall Sch (historical)—school SD-7
Crandalls Corners NY-2
Crandalls Lodge—building IA-7
**Crandalls Lodge**—pop pl IA-7
Crandalls Mills RI-1
Crandall Spit—cape WA-9
Crandall Spring—spring ID-8
Crandall Station IN-6
Crandall Town Trail PA-2
Crandalltown Trail—trail PA-2
Crandall Trail—trail WY-8
Crandell Cem—cemetery KS-7
Crandell Corneers NY-2
Crandell Creek—stream NY-2
Crandells Corners NY-2
**Crandenbrook**—pop pl OH-6
C R And H Trail—trail CA-9
Crandic IA-7
Crandon—locale SD-7
Crandon—locale VA-3
**Crandon**—pop pl WI-6
Crandon Cem—cemetery SD-7
Crandon Cem—cemetery WI-6
Crandon County Park—park FL-3
Crandon Lakes—CDP NJ-2
Crandon Lakes—reservoir NJ-2
Crandon Marina—harbor FL-3
Crandon Park—park FL-3
Crandon Park Arcade (Shop Ctr)—locale FL-3
**Crandon (Town of)**—pop pl WI-6
**Crandon Township**—pop pl SD-7
Crandon Township (historical)—civil SD-7
Crandull—locale TN-4
Crandull Mine TN-4
Crandull Post Office (historical)—building TN-4
Crandull Sch (historical)—school TN-4
Crane IN-6
Crane—locale KS-7
Crane—locale OR-9
Crane—locale VA-3
Crane—locale WA-9
Crane—locale WY-8
**Crane**—pop pl AZ-5
**Crane**—pop pl IN-6
**Crane**—pop pl MO-7
**Crane**—pop pl MT-8
**Crane**—pop pl TX-5
Crane, Gerard, House—hist pl NY-2
Crane, Israel, House—hist pl NJ-2
Crane, Jonathan, Farm—hist pl OH-6
Crane, Ross, House—hist pl GA-3
Crane, Thomas, Public Library—hist pl MA-1
Crane Ammunition Depot, U S Naval Reserv—other IN-6
Crane and Chase Creek—stream WI-6
Crane and Chase Lake—lake WI-6
Crane and Company—hist pl MA-1
Crane Basin—basin ID-8
Crane Bay—swamp FL-3
Crane Bayou—bay TX-5
Crane Beach—beach MA-1
Crane-Bethune Sch—school TX-5
Crane Black Ditch—canal OH-6
Crane Bldg—hist pl TN-4
Crane Bottom—bend AR-4
Crane Branch KY-4
Crane Branch VA-3
Crane Branch—stream (2) FL-3
Crane Branch—stream (2) KY-4
Crane Branch—stream NC-3
Crane Branch—stream TN-4
Crane Branch—stream TX-5
Crane Bridge—bridge NE-7
Cranebrook DE-2
Crane Brook—stream ME-1
Crane Brook—stream (2) MA-1
Crane Brook—stream NH-1
Crane Brook—stream NY-2
Crane Brook Bog Dam—dam MA-1
Crane Brook Bog Rsvr—reservoir MA-1
Cranebrook Cem—cemetery NY-2
Crane Brook Rsvr—reservoir MA-1
Crane Butte—summit OR-9
Crane Camp Run—stream WV-2
Crane Canyon—valley (2) CA-9

Craven Cem—*cemetery* TN-4
Craven Cor Ch—*church* NC-3
Craven Corner—*locale* SD-7
**Craven Corner**—*pop pl* NC-3
**Craven County**—*pop pl* NC-3
*Craven Creek* VA-3
Craven Creek—*stream* KY-4
Craven Creek—*stream* NE-7
Craven Creek—*stream* (2) SC-3
Craven Creek—*stream* SD-7
Craven Creek—*stream* WY-8
Craven Creek Meadows—*flat* WY-8
Craven Creek Rsvr (Franklin Reservoir)—*reservoir* WY-8
Craven Creek Sch—*school* NE-7
Craven Ditch—*canal* IN-6
Craven Ditch—*canal* MO-7
Craven Field—*airport* NC-3
Craven Gap—*gap* NC-3
Craven (historical)—*locale* SD-7
Craven Park—*park* MI-6
Craven Ranch—*locale* SD-7
Craven Rock—*summit* WA-9
Craven Run—*stream* WV-2
*Cravens* TN-4
Cravens—*locale* AR-4
Cravens—*locale* KY-4
**Cravens**—*pop pl* LA-4
**Cravens**—*pop pl* OK-5
Cravens Bay—*bay* KY-4
Cravens Cem—*cemetery* IL-6
Cravens Cem—*cemetery* IN-6
Cravens Cem—*cemetery* KY-4
Cravens Cem—*cemetery* MO-7
Cravens Ch—*church* OK-5
*Cravens Creek* KY-4
*Cravens Creek* MS-4
Cravens Creek—*stream* AR-4
Cravens Creek—*stream* KY-4
Cravens Creek—*stream* MO-7
Cravens Hammock—*island* GA-3
Cravens (historical)—*locale* PA-2
Cravens House—*locale* TN-4
Cravens Island—*island* GA-3
Cravens Landing—*locale* TN-4
Cravens Oil Field—*oilfield* TX-5
Cravens Sch—*school* KY-4
**Cravenstown**—*pop pl* TN-4
Cravenstown Sch (historical)—*school* TN-4
Cravens (Township of)—*fmr MCD* AR-4
Cravensville—*locale* KS-7
Cravens Yards—*locale* TN-4
Craven Tank—*reservoir* NM-5
**Craven Terrace**—*pop pl* NC-3
Craven Township—*civil* SD-7
Craven Well—*well* CO-8
Craven Well—*well* NM-5
Craver—*locale* MT-8
**Craver**—*pop pl* OH-6
Craver Creek—*stream* CO-8
Craver Creek—*stream* MT-8
Craver Lake—*lake* NC-3
Cravero House—*hist pl* FL-3
Cravero Lake—*lake* FL-3
*Craves Landing* VA-3
**Cravey**—*pop pl* GA-3
Cravey Bridge—*bridge* AL-4
Cravey Hill—*summit* AL-4
Cravey Ponds—*lake* AL-4
Cravey Well—*well* AZ-5
Cravins Cem—*cemetery* MO-7
Cravy Lakes—*lake* FL-3
*Cravy Ponds* FL-3
Crawar Oil Field—*oilfield* TX-5
Crawbuckie Point—*cape* NY-2
Craw Cem—*cemetery* IL-6
Craw Cem—*cemetery* NY-2
Craw Creek—*stream* NV-8
Craw Creek Well—*well* NV-8
Crawdad Creek—*stream* WA-9
Crawdad Slough—*gut* IL-6
Craw Drain—*canal* MI-6
Crawfin Lake—*lake* MI-6
Crawfis Cem—*cemetery* OH-6
Crawfish Branch—*stream* KY-4
Crawfish Branch—*stream* (2) TN-4
*Crawfish Creek* WY-8
Crawfish Creek—*stream* AL-4
Crawfish Creek—*stream* (3) GA-3
Crawfish Creek—*stream* IL-6
Crawfish Creek—*stream* (2) OR-9
Crawfish Creek—*stream* TN-4
Crawfish Creek—*stream* TX-5
Crawfish Creek—*stream* WY-8
Crawfish Draw—*valley* TX-5
Crawfish Gulch—*valley* CA-9
Crawfish Hollow—*valley* MO-7
Crawfish Inlet—*bay* AK-9
Crawfish Key—*island* FL-3
*Crawfish Lake* MN-6
Crawfish Lake—*lake* (2) OR-9
Crawfish Lake—*lake* WA-9
Crawfish Meadow—*flat* OR-9
Crawfish Pond—*lake* AL-4
Crawfish River—*stream* WI-6
Crawfish Rock—*bar* CA-9
Crawfish Spring Lake—*lake* GA-3
Crawfish Tank—*reservoir* TX-5
Crawfish Valley—*valley* GA-3
Crawfish Valley—*valley* VA-3
Crawfish Valley Community Center—*building* TN-4
Crawfis Institute—*hist pl* OH-6
*Crawford* AL-4
*Crawford* IN-6
Crawford—*locale* AR-4
Crawford—*locale* FL-3
Crawford—*locale* KS-7
Crawford—*locale* KY-4
Crawford—*locale* ME-1
Crawford—*locale* MI-6
Crawford—*locale* MO-7
Crawford—*locale* NY-2
Crawford—*locale* OH-6
Crawford—*locale* WA-9
**Crawford**—*pop pl* (2) AL-4
**Crawford**—*pop pl* CO-8
**Crawford**—*pop pl* GA-3
**Crawford**—*pop pl* IN-6
**Crawford**—*pop pl* (2) KY-4
**Crawford**—*pop pl* MS-4
**Crawford**—*pop pl* NE-7
**Crawford**—*pop pl* OH-6
**Crawford**—*pop pl* OK-5
**Crawford**—*pop pl* PA-2
**Crawford**—*pop pl* TN-4
**Crawford**—*pop pl* TX-5
**Crawford**—*pop pl* WV-2
**Crawford**—*pop pl* WI-6
Crawford, A. Jackson, Bldg—*hist pl* KY-4
Crawford, Col., Burn Site Monmt—*hist pl* OH-6
Crawford, Col. William, Capture Site—*hist pl* OH-6
Crawford, David, House—*hist pl* NY-2
Crawford, Elias, House—*hist pl* MA-1
Crawford, James L., House—*hist pl* PA-2
Crawford, Lake—*reservoir* NE-7
Crawford, Lake—*reservoir* SC-3
Crawford, Mount—*summit* NH-1
Crawford Assembly of God Ch—*church* AL-4
Crawford Attendance Center—*school* MS-4
Crawford Ave Sch—*school* KS-7
Crawford Baptist Ch—*church* AL-4
Crawford Bayou—*stream* LA-4
Crawford Bend—*bend* TX-5
Crawford Bldg—*hist pl* KS-7
Crawford Branch—*stream* AL-4
Crawford Branch—*stream* (2) KY-4
Crawford Branch—*stream* (2) MS-4
Crawford Branch—*stream* (6) NC-3
Crawford Branch—*stream* OR-9
Crawford Branch—*stream* (2) PA-2
Crawford Branch—*stream* (2) SC-3
Crawford Branch—*stream* (3) TN-4
Crawford Branch—*stream* TX-5
Crawford Branch—*stream* VA-3
Crawford Branch—*stream* WV-2
Crawford Brandeis Ditch—*canal* IN-6
Crawford Bridge—*bridge* AL-4
Crawford Bridge—*bridge* OH-6
Crawford Bridge—*other* MO-7
Crawford Brook—*stream* (2) NH-1
Crawford Brook—*stream* NY-2
Crawford Brothers Pond Dam—*dam* MS-4
Crawford Butte—*summit* OR-9
Crawford Camp—*locale* CA-9
Crawford Canal—*canal* LA-4
Crawford Canyon—*valley* (2) CA-9
Crawford Canyon—*valley* ID-8
Crawford Canyon—*valley* NM-5
Crawford Canyon—*valley* (2) UT-8
Crawford Cave—*cave* TN-4
Crawford (CCD)—*cens area* AL-4
Crawford (CCD)—*cens area* TN-4
Crawford (CCD)—*cens area* TX-5
Crawford Cem—*cemetery* (4) AL-4
Crawford Cem—*cemetery* (3) AR-4
Crawford Cem—*cemetery* CO-8
Crawford Cem—*cemetery* GA-3
Crawford Cem—*cemetery* (2) IL-6
Crawford Cem—*cemetery* (2) IN-6
Crawford Cem—*cemetery* KY-4
Crawford Cem—*cemetery* MI-6
Crawford Cem—*cemetery* (6) MS-4
Crawford Cem—*cemetery* MO-7
Crawford Cem—*cemetery* NE-7
Crawford Cem—*cemetery* NH-1
Crawford Cem—*cemetery* (2) NY-2
Crawford Cem—*cemetery* (2) NC-3
Crawford Cem—*cemetery* (3) OH-6
Crawford Cem—*cemetery* PA-2
Crawford Cem—*cemetery* (6) TN-4
Crawford Cem—*cemetery* (5) TX-5
Crawford Cem—*cemetery* VA-3
Crawford Cem—*cemetery* WV-2
Crawford Ch—*church* AL-4
Crawford Ch—*church* IN-6
Crawford Ch—*church* NY-2
Crawford Ch—*church* TN-4
Crawford Ch—*church* VA-3
Crawford Chute—*basin* AL-4
Crawford City Hall—*building* MS-4
Crawford Clipper Ditch—*canal* CO-8
**Crawford Corners**—*pop pl* NJ-2
**Crawford Corners**—*pop pl* OH-6
**Crawford Corners**—*pop pl* PA-2
**Crawford Countryside**—*pop pl* IL-6
Crawford County—*civil* KS-7
**Crawford (County)**—*pop pl* AR-4
**Crawford (County)**—*pop pl* GA-3
**Crawford (County)**—*pop pl* IL-6
**Crawford County**—*pop pl* IN-6
**Crawford (County)**—*pop pl* MI-6
**Crawford County**—*pop pl* MO-7
**Crawford (County)**—*pop pl* OH-6
**Crawford County**—*pop pl* PA-2
**Crawford (County)**—*pop pl* WI-6
Crawford County Area Vocational Technical Sch—*school* PA-2
Crawford County Courthouse—*hist pl* GA-3
Crawford County Courthouse—*hist pl* IA-7
Crawford County Courthouse—*hist pl* WI-6
Crawford County Home for the Aged—*building* IA-7
Crawford County State Park Number One—*park* KS-7
Crawford Cove—*valley* NC-3
Crawford Covered Bridge—*hist pl* PA-2
*Crawford Creek* MS-4
*Crawford Creek* MO-7
Crawford Creek—*gut* FL-3
Crawford Creek—*stream* (2) AL-4
Crawford Creek—*stream* AK-9
Crawford Creek—*stream* (5) CA-9
Crawford Creek—*stream* CO-8
Crawford Creek—*stream* FL-3
Crawford Creek—*stream* (4) GA-3
Crawford Creek—*stream* ID-8
Crawford Creek—*stream* (2) IL-6
Crawford Creek—*stream* (2) IN-6
Crawford Creek—*stream* IA-7
Crawford Creek—*stream* (2) MI-6
Crawford Creek—*stream* (3) MS-4
Crawford Creek—*stream* (2) MO-7
Crawford Creek—*stream* MT-8
Crawford Creek—*stream* NY-2
Crawford Creek—*stream* (3) NC-3
Crawford Creek—*stream* (4) OR-9
Crawford Creek—*stream* (2) TX-5
Crawford Creek—*stream* UT-8
Crawford Creek—*stream* (3) VA-3
Crawford Creek—*stream* (2) WA-9
Crawford Creek—*stream* (3) WI-6
Crawford Creek—*stream* WY-8
Crawford Creek Forest Service Station—*locale* CA-9
Crawford Creek Gap—*gap* NC-3
Crawford Crossing—*locale* WI-6
Crawford Dam—*dam* CO-8
Crawford Dam—*dam* NC-3
Crawford-De Forest Ditch—*canal* NM-5
Crawford Depot—*hist pl* GA-3
Crawford Depot—*hist pl* NH-1
Crawford Ditch—*canal* CA-9
Crawford Ditch—*canal* ID-8
Crawford Ditch—*canal* IN-6
Crawford Ditch—*canal* OH-6
Crawford Ditch—*canal* UT-8
Crawford Ditch—*stream* WA-9
Crawford Division—*civil* AL-4
Crawford Division—*civil* TN-4
Crawford-Dorsey House and Cemetery—*hist pl* GA-3
Crawford Drain—*canal* (3) MI-6
Crawford Draw—*valley* UT-8
Crawford Draw—*valley* WY-8
Crawford Field—*park* MS-4
Crawford Fire Tower—*locale* PA-2
Crawford Flats—*basin* NC-3
Crawford Forest Work Center—*locale* ID-8
**Crawford Fork**—*pop pl* AL-4
Crawford Gap—*gap* NC-3
Crawford Gap—*gap* VA-3
Crawford-Gardner House—*hist pl* WV-2
Crawford General Store—*hist pl* TN-4
Crawford Grove Ch—*church* (2) GA-3
*Crawford Guard Station* ID-8
Crawford Gulch—*valley* CA-9
Crawford Gulch—*valley* CO-8
Crawford Gulch—*valley* OR-9
Crawford Heights Memorial Cem—*cemetery* IA-7
Crawford Hill—*summit* AZ-5
Crawford Hill—*summit* FL-3
Crawford Hill—*summit* NJ-2
Crawford Hill—*summit* SD-7
Crawford Hill—*summit* TX-5
Crawford Hill—*summit* VT-1
Crawford Hill Historic Residential District—*hist pl* AZ-5
Crawford Hills—*ridge* WI-6
Crawford (historical)—*locale* SD-7
**Crawford (historical)**—*pop pl* (2) OR-9
**Crawford (historical)**—*pop pl* TN-4
Crawford Holes—*spring* UT-8
Crawford Hollow—*valley* KY-4
Crawford Hollow—*valley* NM-5
Crawford Hollow—*valley* OR-9
Crawford Hollow—*valley* (2) PA-2
Crawford Hollow—*valley* (6) TN-4
Crawford Hollow—*valley* TX-5
Crawford Hollow—*valley* VA-3
Crawford House—*hist pl* IA-7
Crawford House—*hist pl* (2) KY-4
Crawford House—*hist pl* NJ-2
Crawford House—*hist pl* OK-5
Crawford House—*locale* NH-1
Crawford House Artist's Studio—*hist pl* NH-1
Crawford HS—*school* CA-9
Crawford Irrigation Canal—*hist pl* UT-8
Crawford Island—*island* ME-1
Crawford Island—*island* MN-6
Crawford Island—*island* NY-2
Crawford Island—*island* OH-6
Crawford JHS—*school* KY-4
Crawford Junction—*locale* PA-2
Crawford Knob—*summit* (2) VA-3
Crawford Knob Trail—*trail* VA-3
*Crawford Lake* MI-6
*Crawford Lake* MS-4
Crawford Lake—*lake* CO-8
Crawford Lake—*lake* (2) FL-3
Crawford Lake—*lake* (2) KY-4
Crawford Lake—*lake* ME-1
Crawford Lake—*lake* (3) MI-6
Crawford Lake—*lake* MN-6
Crawford Lake—*lake* MS-4
Crawford Lake—*lake* WA-9
Crawford Lake—*lake* (2) WI-6
Crawford Lake—*reservoir* GA-3
Crawford Lake—*reservoir* MS-4
Crawford Lake—*reservoir* (2) NC-3
Crawford Lake—*reservoir* TX-5
Crawford Lake—*swamp* MN-6
Crawford Lake Ch—*church* FL-3
Crawford Lake Dam—*dam* (3) MS-4
Crawford Lake Dam—*dam* (2) NC-3
Crawford Lake Drain—*canal* MI-6
Crawford Lakes—*reservoir* GA-3
Crawford Lake Sch—*school* MN-6
Crawford Landing—*locale* LA-4
Crawford Landing—*locale* MO-7
Crawford Lateral—*canal* ID-8
Crawford Lateral—*canal* NM-5
Crawford Lookout Tower—*locale* AL-4
Crawford Lookout Tower—*locale* MS-4
Crawford Marsh—*swamp* WA-9
Crawford Meadow—*flat* OR-9
Crawford Meadow Spring—*spring* OR-9
Crawford Memorial Gardens—*cemetery* NC-3
Crawford Mesa—*summit* CO-8
Crawford Mill Run—*stream* NC-3
Crawford Mine—*mine* ID-8
Crawford Mountain Trail—*trail* VA-3
Crawford Mtn—*summit* AR-4
Crawford Mtn—*summit* (2) NC-3
Crawford Mtn—*summit* (2) TX-5
Crawford Mtn—*summit* (2) VA-3
Crawford Mtn—*summit* WA-9
Crawford Mtns—*range* WY-8
Crawford Mtns—*summit* UT-8
Crawford Municipal Golf Course—*other* NE-7
*Crawford Notch* NH-1
Crawford Notch—*valley* NH-1
*Crawford Notch (Crawford House)* NH-1
Crawford Notch State Reservation—*reserve* NH-1
Crawford Oil Field—*oilfield* KS-7
Crawford Park—*park* AL-4
Crawford Park—*park* OK-5
Crawford Pass—*gap* UT-8
Crawford Path—*trail* NH-1
Crawford-Pettyjohn House—*hist pl* SD-7
Crawford Place (site)—*locale* ID-8
Crawford Point—*cape* AR-4
Crawford Point—*cape* FL-3
Crawford Point—*cape* LA-4
Crawford Point—*cape* OR-9
Crawford Point—*summit* AL-4
Crawford Pond—*lake* (2) ME-1
Crawford Pond Dam—*dam* MS-4
Crawford Post Office—*building* MS-4
Crawford Post Office—*building* TN-4
Crawford Post Office (historical)—*building* TN-4
Crawford Pumping Station—*building* PA-2
*Crawford Purchase* NH-1
Crawford Ranch—*locale* CA-9
Crawford Ranch—*locale* MT-8
Crawford Ranch—*locale* NE-7
Crawford Ranch—*locale* (3) NM-5
Crawford Rec Area—*park* CO-8
Crawford Ridge—*ridge* VA-3
Crawford Road Baptist Ch—*church* AL-4
Crawford Road Ch—*church* AL-4
Crawford Rsvr—*reservoir* CO-8
Crawford Rsvr—*reservoir* OR-9
Crawford Run—*stream* OH-6
Crawford Run—*stream* (4) PA-2
Crawford Run—*stream* (2) WV-2
*Crawfords* PA-2
Crawfords Bar—*bar* AL-4
Crawfords Cem—*cemetery* IN-6
Crawford Sch—*school* AR-4
Crawford Sch—*school* CO-8
Crawford Sch—*school* GA-3
Crawford Sch—*school* IL-6
Crawford Sch—*school* IA-7
Crawford Sch—*school* (2) MI-6
Crawford Sch—*school* MO-7
Crawford Sch—*school* NY-2
Crawford Sch—*school* (2) OH-6
Crawford Sch—*school* (2) PA-2
Crawford Sch—*school* SC-3
Crawford Sch (abandoned)—*school* PA-2
Crawford Sch (historical)—*school* (2) AL-4
Crawford Sch (historical)—*school* MS-4
Crawford Sch (historical)—*school* MO-7
Crawford Sch (historical)—*school* PA-2
Crawford Sch (historical)—*school* TN-4
Crawfords Cove—*valley* AL-4
Crawfords Dam—*dam* NC-3
Crawfords Ferry (historical)—*locale* MS-4
Crawford-Shirley House—*hist pl* GA-3
Crawfords Island (historical)—*island* AL-4
Crawford Site—*hist pl* MS-4
Crawfords Lake—*reservoir* NC-3
Crawford Slide—*cliff* TX-5
Crawford Slough—*stream* TX-5
Crawfords Mill (historical)—*locale* TN-4
Crawford Sog—*swamp* FL-3
Crawford Spring—*spring* OR-9
Crawford Spring—*spring* (2) TN-4
Crawford Spring Number 1—*spring* AL-4
Crawford Spring Number 2—*spring* AL-4
Crawford Spring Number 3—*spring* AL-4
Crawford Spring Number 4—*spring* AL-4
Crawford Springs—*spring* PA-2
Crawfords Purchase—*civil* NH-1
Crawfords Store—*locale* VA-3
Crawford State Fishing Lake Number One—*park* KS-7
Crawford State Park—*park* KS-7
Crawford State Wildlife Mngmt Area—*park* SD-7
Crawford Street Sch—*school* GA-3
Crawford Street United Methodist Ch—*church* MS-4
*Crawfordsville* GA-3
*Crawfordsville* KS-7
**Crawfordsville**—*pop pl* AR-4
**Crawfordsville**—*pop pl* IN-6
**Crawfordsville**—*pop pl* IA-7
**Crawfordsville**—*pop pl* OR-9
Crawfordsville Bridge—*hist pl* (2) OR-9
Crawfordsville Municipal Airp—*airport* IN-6
Crawfordsville Senior HS—*school* IN-6
Crawfordsville Union Cem—*cemetery* OR-9
Crawford-Talmadge House—*hist pl* GA-3
Crawford Thompson Canal—*canal* UT-8
Crawford-Tilden Apartments—*hist pl* OH-6
Crawfordton Post Office (historical)—*building* TN-4
Crawford Top—*summit* GA-3
Crawford Towhead—*island* IL-6
**Crawfordtown**—*pop pl* PA-2
Crawfordtown Delancey PO (historical)—*building* PA-2
**Crawford (Town of)**—*pop pl* ME-1
**Crawford (Town of)**—*pop pl* NY-2
Crawford Township—*civil* (2) MO-7
Crawford Township—*fmr MCD* (2) IA-7
**Crawford Township**—*pop pl* (2) KS-7
**Crawford Township**—*pop pl* NE-7
**Crawford Township**—*pop pl* ND-7
Crawford (Township of)—*fmr MCD* (2) AR-4
Crawford (Township of)—*fmr MCD* NC-3
**Crawford (Township of)**—*pop pl* (2) OH-6
**Crawford (Township of)**—*pop pl* PA-2
Crawford Trail—*trail* CO-8
Crawford Trail—*trail* PA-2
Crawford Valley Ch—*church* NE-7
**Crawfordville**—*pop pl* FL-3
**Crawfordville**—*pop pl* GA-3
Crawfordville (CCD)—*cens area* GA-3
Crawfordville Elem Sch—*school* FL-3
Crawfordville Lookout Tower—*tower* FL-3
Crawfordville Road Ch—*church* FL-3
Crawford Wash—*valley* UT-8
Crawford Windmill—*locale* (3) TX-5
Crawford Windmills—*locale* TX-5
Crawford Woods—*park* OH-6
Crawforth, Charles, Farmstead—*hist pl* UT-8
Crawl Cave—*cave* AL-4
Crawl Cave—*cave* TN-4
Crawl Creek—*stream* SC-3
**Crawley**—*pop pl* GA-3
**Crawley**—*pop pl* WV-2
Crawley Branch—*stream* (2) NC-3
Crawley Cem—*cemetery* GA-3
*Crawley Creek* VA-3
Crawley Creek—*stream* NC-3
Crawley Creek—*stream* WV-2
Crawley Creek Ch—*church* WV-2
Crawley Gap—*gap* GA-3
*Crawley Hill* PA-2
Crawley Mtn—*summit* GA-3
Crawley Pond—*lake* NC-3
Crawley Pond—*lake* TN-4
Crawley Ridge—*ridge* TN-4
Crawleys Creek—*stream* VA-3
Crawleys Pond—*reservoir* NC-3
Crawleys Pond Dam—*dam* NC-3
Crawley Swamp—*swamp* NC-3
**Crawleyville**—*pop pl* IN-6
Crawling Cave—*cave* TN-4
Crawling Stone Lake—*lake* WI-6
*Crawl Key* FL-3
Crawl Key—*island* (4) FL-3
Crawl Key Number Two—*island* FL-3
Crawl Sch—*school* IL-6
Craw Pond—*reservoir* AL-4
Craw Sch—*school* NY-2
Crawson Lake—*lake* AK-9
Craw Spring—*spring* NV-8
*Crawther Lake* NE-7
*Crawthner Cow Camp* NM-5
Crawthner Cow Camp—*locale* NM-5
**Cray**—*pop pl* MN-6
Cray, Lorin, House—*hist pl* MN-6
*Craybill Creek* IA-7
Craycraft—*locale* KY-4
Craycraft Branch—*stream* KY-4
Craycroft—*locale* AZ-5
Craycroft Diggings—*mine* CA-9
Craycroft Ridge—*ridge* CA-9
Craycroft Sch—*school* AZ-5
C Ray Greene Bridge—*bridge* FL-3
Cray House—*hist pl* MD-2
Cray Mill—*locale* CA-9
*Craynars Run* PA-2
**Crayne**—*pop pl* KY-4
Crayne Cem—*cemetery* KY-4
Crayne Hill—*summit* KY-4
*Crayne Island* VA-3
Crayne Knob—*summit* KY-4
Craynes Run—*stream* PA-2
Craynor—*locale* KY-4
**Crayold**—*pop pl* CA-9
Crayon—*locale* OH-6
**Crayton**—*pop pl* PA-2
Crayton Cem—*cemetery* TX-5
Crayton Cove—*bay* FL-3
Crayton Hollow Run—*stream* PA-2
Crayton JHS—*school* SC-3
**Crayton Manor Apartments**—*pop pl* SC-3
Crayton Station—*locale* PA-2
**Craytonville**—*pop pl* SC-3
Craze Bend—*cape* AL-4
Crazy Basin Creek—*stream* AZ-5
Crazy Bayou—*gut* AR-4
Crazy Bear Pass—*gap* CA-9
*Crazy Bess Bayou* TX-5
Crazy Branch—*stream* LA-4
Crazy Branch—*stream* TX-5
Crazy Canyon—*valley* (2) CA-9
Crazy Canyon—*valley* ID-8
Crazy Canyon—*valley* MT-8
Crazy Canyon—*valley* TX-5
Crazycat Mtn—*summit* TX-5
Crazy Corners—*locale* RI-1
Crazy Cow Creek—*stream* WA-9
Crazy Cow Tank—*reservoir* AZ-5
Crazy Creek—*stream* AK-9
Crazy Creek—*stream* AZ-5
Crazy Creek—*stream* AR-4
Crazy Creek—*stream* CA-9
Crazy Creek—*stream* ID-8
Crazy Creek—*stream* (2) IN-6
Crazy Creek—*stream* MI-6
Crazy Creek—*stream* (4) MT-8
Crazy Creek—*stream* NY-2
Crazy Creek—*stream* OK-5
Crazy Creek—*stream* (7) OR-9
Crazy Creek—*stream* TN-4
Crazy Creek—*stream* UT-8
Crazy Creek—*stream* WA-9
Crazy Creek—*stream* (2) WY-8
Crazy Creek Bridge—*bridge* AZ-5
Crazy Creek Campground—*locale* MT-8
Crazy Creek Campground—*locale* WY-8
Crazy Creek Cave—*cave* AL-4
*Crazy Creek Spring* OR-9
*Crazy Crow Creek* WA-9
*Crazy Fish Lake* MT-8
Crazy Fish Lake—*lake* MT-8
Crazy Fork—*valley* OR-9
Crazy Girl Shaft—*mine* CO-8
Crazy Gulch—*valley* CO-8
Crazy Gully—*stream* LA-4
Crazy Harry Gulch—*valley* CA-9
*Crazy Head Creek* MT-8
Crazy Head Creek—*stream* MT-8
Crazy Head Fork—*stream* MT-8
Crazy Head Spring—*spring* MT-8
*Crazy Hill* AL-4
Crazy Hills—*range* WA-9
Crazy Hole Creek—*stream* SD-7
Crazy Hollow—*valley* MO-7
Crazy Hollow—*valley* OK-5
Crazy Hollow—*valley* OR-9
Crazy Hollow—*valley* UT-8
Crazy Hollow Spring—*spring* UT-8
*Crazy Hollow Springs* UT-8
**Crazy Horse**—*pop pl* SD-7
Crazy Horse Campark—*locale* UT-8
Crazy Horse Canyon—*valley* CA-9
Crazy Horse Canyon—*valley* SD-7
*Crazy Horse Carving* SD-7
*Crazy Horse Creek* MT-8
Crazy Horse Creek—*stream* AZ-5
Crazy Horse Creek—*stream* (2) MT-8
Crazy Horse Creek—*stream* (2) WI-6
Crazy Horse Creek—*stream* (2) WY-8
Crazy Horse Ditch—*canal* WY-8
*Crazy Horse Monument* SD-7
*Crazy Horse Mountain* SD-7
Crazy Horse Post Office—*locale* SD-7
Crazy Horse Spring—*spring* AZ-5
Crazy Horse Spring—*spring* MT-8
Crazy Horse Wash—*stream* AZ-5
Crazy John Spring—*spring* OR-9
Crazy John Stream—*stream* VT-1
Crazy Jug Canyon—*valley* AZ-5
Crazy Jug Point—*cape* AZ-5
Crazy Jug Spring—*spring* AZ-5
Crazy K Ranch—*locale* NV-8
Crazy Lake—*lake* CA-9
Crazy Lake—*lake* MT-8
*Crazy Lakes* MT-8
Crazy Lakes—*lake* MT-8
Crazy Lakes—*lake* WY-8
Crazy Lakes Trail—*trail* WY-8
Crazyman Coulee—*valley* MT-8
Crazy Man Coulee—*valley* ND-7
Crazyman Creek—*stream* MT-8
Crazy Man Creek—*stream* MT-8
Crazyman Creek—*stream* OR-9
Crazyman Flat—*flat* OR-9
Crazy Man Mtn—*summit* WA-9
Crazy Man Pass—*gap* WA-9
Crazy Mountains—*range* AK-9
Crazy Mountain Trail—*trail* WY-8
Crazy Mtn—*summit* CO-8
Crazy Mtn—*summit* MT-8
Crazy Mtns—*range* MT-8
Crazy Mule Gulch—*valley* CA-9
Crazy Nance Hollow—*valley* OK-5
Crazy Notch—*gap* AK-9
Crazy Park—*flat* AZ-5
Crazy Park Canyon—*valley* AZ-5
Crazy Park Tank—*reservoir* AZ-5
*Crazy Peak* NM-5
Crazy Peak—*summit* CA-9
Crazy Peak—*summit* MT-8
Crazy Quilt Rsvr—*reservoir* WY-8
Crazy Rapids—*rapids* WA-9
Crazy Run—*stream* PA-2
Crazy Slough—*stream* AK-9
Crazy Spring—*spring* CA-9
Crazy Spring—*spring* (2) OR-9
Crazy Spring—*spring* UT-8
Crazy Spring Hollow—*valley* MO-7
Crazy Springs Creek—*stream* MT-8
Crazy Swede Creek—*stream* MT-8
Crazy Water Spring—*spring* AZ-5
*Crazy Woman* WY-8
Crazy Woman Battlefield Historical Mark—*locale* WY-8
*Crazy Woman Butte* NM-5
Crazy Woman Campground—*locale* WY-8
Crazy Woman Canyon—*valley* NM-5
Crazy Woman Creek—*stream* CO-8
Crazy Woman Creek—*stream* WY-8
Crazy Woman Mtn—*summit* WY-8
Crazy Woman Ranch—*locale* WY-8
Crazy Woman Wash—*stream* AZ-5
Crazy Women Gulch—*valley* CO-8
Creach Cem—*cemetery* MO-7
Creacy Cem—*cemetery* KY-4
Creacy Lake—*lake* KY-4
**Creadmore (subdivision)**—*pop pl* NC-3
Creager Bridge—*bridge* NY-2
Creager Cem—*cemetery* OH-6
Creager Rsvr—*reservoir* CO-8
**Creagerstown**—*pop pl* MD-2
Creagerstown Station—*locale* MD-2
Creagh, Patrick, House—*hist pl* MD-2
**Creagleville**—*pop pl* TX-5
Creagleville Ch—*church* TX-5
Creaky Creek—*stream* ID-8
**Creal**—*pop pl* CA-9
**Creal**—*pop pl* KY-4
*Crealey Creek* ID-8
Creal Field Branch—*stream* MS-4
**Creal Springs**—*pop pl* IL-6
Creal Springs Cem—*cemetery* IL-6
Creal Springs (Election Precinct)—*fmr MCD* IL-6
Creal Store—*hist pl* KY-4
Cream—*locale* PA-2
**Cream**—*pop pl* WI-6
Cream Alley Branch—*stream* KY-4
Cream Brook—*stream* NH-1
Cream Can Junction—*locale* ID-8
Cream Can Lake—*lake* ID-8
*Cream City* OH-6
**Cream City**—*pop pl* OH-6
Cream City Point—*cape* MI-6
Cream Colored Rock—*summit* NM-5
Cream Creek—*stream* (2) MT-8
Creamer Brook—*stream* ME-1
Creamer Cem—*cemetery* ME-1
Creamer Cem—*cemetery* OH-6
Creamer Creek—*stream* TX-5
Creamer Hollow—*valley* IN-6
Creamer Pond—*lake* RI-1
Creamers Field State Game Ref—*park* AK-9
Creamery—*locale* WV-2
**Creamery**—*pop pl* IA-7
**Creamery**—*pop pl* MA-1
**Creamery**—*pop pl* PA-2
Creamery Bay—*bay* CA-9
Creamery Bridge—*hist pl* KS-7
Creamery Brook—*stream* (4) CT-1
Creamery Brook—*stream* MA-1
Creamery Brook—*stream* NY-2
Creamery Canyon—*valley* AZ-5
Creamery Covered Bridge—*hist pl* VT-1
Creamery Creek—*stream* OR-9
Creamery Ditch—*canal* CO-8
Creamery Gulch—*valley* CO-8
Creamery Hill—*summit* MT-8
Creamery Package—*locale* AR-4
*Creamery Pond* CT-1
Creamery Pond—*lake* CT-1
Creamery Pond—*lake* NY-2
Creamery Pond—*lake* PA-2
**Cream Hill**—*pop pl* VT-1
Cream Hill—*summit* CT-1
Cream Hill—*summit* NY-2
Cream Hill—*summit* PA-2
Cream Hill Agricultural Sch—*hist pl* CT-1
Cream Hill Lake—*lake* CT-1
*Cream Hill Pond* CT-1
Cream Hill Shelter—*hist pl* CT-1
Cream Hollow—*valley* CT-1
Cream Lake—*lake* MN-6
Cream Lake—*lake* OR-9
Cream Lake—*lake* WA-9
Cream Lake—*lake* WI-6
Cream Lake Creek—*stream* WA-9

Crescent Park—*flat* ... MT-8
Crescent Park—*park* ... IL-6
Crescent Park—*park* ... NJ-2
Crescent Park—*park* ... TX-5
**Crescent Park**—*pop pl* ... CT-1
**Crescent Park**—*pop pl* ... KY-4
**Crescent Park**—*pop pl* ... NY-2
**Crescent Park**—*pop pl* ... WI-6
Crescent Park—*uninc pl* ... NJ-2
Crescent Park Carousel—*hist pl* ... RI-1
Crescent Park Sch—*school* ... CA-9
Crescent Park Sch—*school* ... IA-7
Crescent Park Sch—*school* ... ME-1
Crescent Park Sch—*school* ... NJ-2
Crescent Peak—*summit* ... NV-8
Crescent Plantation—*hist pl* ... LA-4
*Crescent Pond* ... RI-1
Crescent Pond—*lake* (2) ... ME-1
Crescent Pond—*lake* ... MI-6
Crescent Pond Outlet—*stream* ... MI-6
Crescent Quarry Archeol Site—*hist pl* ... MO-7
Crescent Ranch—*locale* ... CO-8
Crescent Ranch—*locale* ... TX-5
Crescent Ranch—*locale* ... WY-8
Crescent Range—*ridge* ... NH-1
Crescent Ravine—*valley* ... AZ-5
Crescent Retarding Basin—*reservoir* ... CA-9
Crescent Ridge—*ridge* ... AZ-5
Crescent Ridge—*ridge* ... MS-4
Crescent Ridge—*ridge* ... OR-9
Crescent Ridge—*ridge* ... UT-8
Crescent Ridge—*ridge* ... WA-9
**Crescent Ridge Subdivision**—*pop pl* ... UT-8
Crescent River—*stream* ... AK-9
Crescent River—*stream* ... GA-3
Crescent Rock—*summit* ... VA-3
Crescent Rock Overlook—*locale* ... VA-3
Crescent Rock Trail—*trail* ... VA-3
Crescent Roller Mills—*hist pl* ... WI-6
Crescent Rsvr—*reservoir* ... NV-8
Crescent Rsvr—*reservoir* ... OR-9
Crescent Sail Yacht Club—*other* ... MI-6
Crescent Sch—*school* ... CA-9
Crescent Sch—*school* ... GA-3
Crescent Sch—*school* ... IL-6
Crescent Sch—*school* ... KS-7
Crescent Sch—*school* ... MO-7
Crescent Sch—*school* ... TN-4
Crescent Sch—*school* ... TX-5
Crescent Sch—*school* ... UT-8
Crescent Sch—*school* ... WA-9
Crescent Sch—*school* ... WV-2
Crescent Sch—*school* (2) ... WI-6
Crescent Sch (abandoned)—*school* ... MO-7
Crescent Sch (historical)—*school* ... PA-2
Crescent Sch (historical)—*school* ... TN-4
*Crescent School* ... PA-2
Crescent (siding)—*locale* ... OR-9
Crescent (Site)—*locale* ... NV-8
Crescent Spring—*spring* ... AZ-5
Crescent Spring—*spring* (2) ... NV-8
**Crescent Springs**—*pop pl* ... KY-4
**Crescent Springs**—*pop pl* ... OK-5
**Crescent (sta)**—*pop pl* ... OR-9
*Crescent Station* ... PA-2
**Crescent Station**—*pop pl* ... NY-2
Crescent Street Dam—*dam* ... MA-1
Crescent Surf—*beach* ... ME-1
Crescent Tank—*reservoir* (3) ... AZ-5
Crescent Tank—*reservoir* ... NM-5
Crescent Tank—*reservoir* ... TX-5
Crescent Top—*summit* ... WY-8
**Crescent (Town of)**—*pop pl* ... WI-6
Crescent Township—*CDP* ... PA-2
Crescent Township—*fmr MCD* ... IA-7
**Crescent (Township of)**—*pop pl* ... IL-6
**Crescent (Township of)**—*pop pl* ... PA-2
Crescent Trail—*trail* ... WY-8
Crescent Tunnel—*mine* ... MT-8
Crescent Tunnel—*mine* ... UT-8
Crescent Valley—*basin* ... NV-8
**Crescent Valley**—*pop pl* ... NV-8
**Crescent Valley**—*pop pl* ... WA-9
Crescent Valley—*valley* ... WA-9
Crescent Valley Airp—*airport* ... NV-8
Crescent Valley Ch—*church* ... OK-5
Crescent Valley Ch—*church* ... TX-5
Crescent Valley HS—*school* ... OR-9
Crescent View—*locale* ... TN-4
Crescent View MS—*school* ... UT-8
**Crescent Village**—*pop pl* ... CO-8
*Crescentville* ... OH-6
Crescentville—*locale* ... PA-2
**Crescentville**—*pop pl* ... OH-6
*Crescent Villiage* ... CO-8
*Crescent Wash* ... UT-8
Crescent Wash—*valley* ... UT-8
Crescent Wash Dam—*dam* ... UT-8
Crescent Wash Rsvr—*reservoir* ... UT-8
Crescent Weir—*dam* ... CA-9
Crescent Well—*well* ... NV-8
Crescentwood Sch—*school* ... MI-6
**Cresceus Farms**—*pop pl* ... OH-6
**Cresco**—*pop pl* ... IN-6
**Cresco**—*pop pl* ... IA-7
**Cresco**—*pop pl* ... PA-2
Cresco Cem—*cemetery* ... KS-7
Cresco Heights—*summit* ... PA-2
Cresco (historical)—*locale* ... KS-7
Cresco Opera House—*hist pl* ... IA-7
Cresco Township—*fmr MCD* ... IA-7
Cresecent Hill Ch—*church* ... GA-3
Cresecent Lake—*lake* ... UT-8
Cresenta Park—*park* ... AZ-5
Cresent Beach—*beach* ... OR-9
Cresent City Lighthouse—*hist pl* ... CA-9
**Cresent (Cresent City Post Office and Station)**—*pop pl* ... IL-6
**Cresent Estates (subdivision)**—*pop pl* ... MS-4
**Cresent Heights (subdivision)**—*pop pl* ... AL-4
Cresent Hill—*summit* ... OR-9
Cresent Hill Sch—*school* ... AL-4
*Cresent Lake* ... PA-2
Cresent Lake Dam—*dam* ... OR-9
Cresent Lake Dam—*dam* ... PA-2
Cresent Lake Rsvr—*reservoir* ... OR-9
Cresent Plaza Shop Ctr—*locale* ... TN-4
*Creseys Creek* ... TN-4
Creseys Island (historical)—*island* ... TN-4
Creseys Shoals—*bar* ... TN-4
Creshaw Spring—*spring* ... NM-5
Cresheim Creek—*stream* ... PA-2
Cresheim Valley—*valley* ... PA-2
Creslane Sch—*school* ... OR-9
Creslenn Camp—*locale* ... TX-5
Creslenn Park—*park* ... TX-5
Creslenn Ranch (Headquarters)—*locale* ... TX-5
**Creslo**—*pop pl* ... PA-2
**Creslo (sta.)**—*pop pl* ... PA-2
*Creslo Station* ... PA-2
Cresmont—*locale* ... PA-2
**Creson**—*pop pl* ... TN-4
Creson Cem—*cemetery* ... TN-4
Creson Hollow—*valley* ... TN-4
Cresote Slough—*stream* ... MS-4
Crespi JHS—*school* ... CA-9
Crespin, Gregorio, House—*hist pl* ... NM-5
Crespin Cem—*cemetery* ... CO-8
Crespin Tank—*reservoir* ... NM-5
Crespi Park—*park* ... FL-3
Crespi Sch—*school* ... CA-9
Cresprin Well—*well* ... NM-5
Cress—*locale* ... PA-2
*Cressaps* ... WV-2
Cress Branch—*stream* (2) ... TN-4
Cress Brook—*stream* ... MA-1
Cressbrook Farm—*hist pl* ... PA-2
Cress Brook Pond—*lake* ... MA-1
Cress Camp—*locale* ... WA-9
Cress Cem—*cemetery* ... IN-6
Cress Cem—*cemetery* ... TX-5
Cress Cem—*cemetery* ... VA-3
*Cress Creek* ... IL-6
Cress Creek—*stream* ... IL-6
Cress Creek—*stream* ... KS-7
Cress Creek—*stream* ... LA-4
Cress Creek—*stream* ... OR-9
Cress Creek—*stream* ... WY-8
Cresse Creek—*stream* ... NJ-2
Cresse Island—*island* ... NJ-2
Cresset Ch—*church* ... NC-3
Cresse Thorofare—*channel* ... NJ-2
Cressey—*locale* ... MI-6
**Cressey**—*pop pl* ... CA-9
Cressey Brook—*stream* ... NH-1
Cressey Cem—*cemetery* ... MI-6
Cressey Hill—*summit* ... ME-1
Cressey Lateral—*canal* ... CA-9
Cressey Lateral East—*canal* ... CA-9
Cressey Park Fire Station—*park* ... CA-9
Cressey Point—*cape* ... NH-1
*Cresseys Island* ... TN-4
*Cresseys Shoals* ... TN-4
Cress Falls—*falls* ... WA-9
Cress Field—*airport* ... CO-8
Cress Hill—*summit* ... IL-6
Cress Hill Cem—*cemetery* (2) ... IL-6
Cressie Branch—*stream* ... AL-4
**Cresskill**—*pop pl* ... NJ-2
Cresskill Brook—*stream* ... NJ-2
Cressler Cave—*cave* ... PA-2
Cressler Creek—*stream* ... OR-9
*Cressman* ... PA-2
Cressman Hill—*summit* ... PA-2
Cressmans Gulch—*valley* ... CO-8
Cressmer Lodge—*locale* ... NM-5
Cressmont—*locale* ... KY-4
Cressmont—*locale* ... WV-2
Cressmont (Post Office)—*locale* ... KY-4
Cressmont Sch—*school* ... KY-4
Cressmoor Country Club—*other* ... IN-6
*Cresson* ... KS-7
Cresson—*locale* ... MN-6
**Cresson**—*pop pl* ... PA-2
**Cresson**—*pop pl* ... TX-5
Cresson, Mount—*summit* ... NH-1
**Cressona**—*pop pl* ... MS-4
**Cressona**—*pop pl* ... PA-2
Cressona Borough—*civil* ... PA-2
Cressona Mall—*locale* ... PA-2
Cresson Borough—*civil* ... PA-2
Cresson Cem—*cemetery* ... TX-5
Cresson Dam—*dam* ... PA-2
Cresson (historical)—*locale* ... KS-7
Cresson Lake—*reservoir* ... PA-2
Cresson Mine—*mine* ... CO-8
Cresson Ranch—*locale* ... TX-5
Cresson Sch—*school* ... CA-9
*Cresson State School and Hospital* ... PA-2
**Cresson State School And Hospital**—*pop pl* ... PA-2
**Cresson (Township of)**—*pop pl* ... PA-2
Cress Outing Club Lake—*reservoir* ... AL-4
Cress Pond—*reservoir* ... TN-4
Cress Prospect—*mine* ... TN-4
*Cress Run* ... IN-6
Cress Spring—*spring* ... MO-7
Cress Spring—*spring* (2) ... NV-8
Cressville Creek—*stream* ... TN-4
*Cresswell* ... NC-3
Cresswell, George, Furnace—*hist pl* ... MO-7
Cresswell Association Cem—*cemetery* ... OR-9
Cresswell Cem—*cemetery* ... AR-4
Cresswell Draw—*valley* ... WY-8
Cresswell Petroglyph Archeol Site—*hist pl* ... MO-7
Cresswell Stuart Sch—*school* ... NJ-2
Cresswell Well—*well* ... WA-9
Cresswood Lake Dam—*dam* ... IN-6
Cressy—*locale* ... KY-4
Cressy Beach—*beach* ... MA-1
*Cressy Creek* ... TN-4
Cressy Creek—*stream* ... VA-3
Cressy Number 1 Dam—*dam* ... SD-7
Cressy Number 2 Dam—*dam* ... SD-7
Cressy Number 3 Dam—*dam* ... SD-7
*Cressys Beach* ... MA-1
Crest—*locale* ... AR-4
Crest—*locale* ... CA-9
Crest—*locale* ... KY-4
Crest—*locale* ... MO-7
Crest—*locale* ... VA-3
**Crest**—*pop pl* ... AL-4
**Crest**—*pop pl* ... CO-8
**Crest**—*pop pl* ... GA-3
**Crest**—*pop pl* ... TX-5
**Crest**—*pop pl* ... WA-9
Crest, Lake—*lake* ... LA-4
Cresta—*locale* ... CA-9
Cresta Dam—*dam* ... CA-9
Crest Airpark Airp—*airport* ... WA-9
Cresta Powerhouse—*other* ... CA-9
Cresta Tunnel—*tunnel* ... CA-9
Crest Ave Elem Sch—*school* ... PA-2
*Crest Ave Sch* ... PA-2
Cresta Vista—*uninc pl* ... CO-8
Crest Branch—*stream* ... IN-6
Crest Cave One—*cave* ... AL-4
Crest Cave Three—*cave* ... AL-4
Crest Cave Two—*cave* ... AL-4
Crest Ch—*church* ... FL-3
Crest Ch—*church* ... GA-3
Crest Creek—*stream* ... CA-9
Crest Creek—*stream* ... MT-8
**Crestdale (subdivision)**—*pop pl* ... AL-4
Crest Ditch—*canal* ... MT-8
Crest Drive Sch—*school* ... OR-9
Crest East Elem Sch—*school* ... KS-7
**Crested Butte**—*pop pl* ... CO-8
Crested Butte—*summit* ... CO-8
Crested Buttes—*summit* ... WA-9
*Crested Point* ... AK-9
Crested Rsvr—*reservoir* ... OR-9
Crested Wheatgrass Windmill—*locale* ... WY-8
Crested Wheat Patch—*flat* ... NV-8
Crested Wheat Ridge—*ridge* ... NV-8
**Crestfield**—*pop pl* ... TN-4
Crestfield Hosp—*hospital* ... CT-1
**Crestfield (subdivision)**—*pop pl* ... DE-2
**Crestfield Subdivision**—*pop pl* ... UT-8
**Crest Forest (census name Crestline)**—*pop pl* ... CA-9
Crest Forest Sch—*school* ... CA-9
Crest Garden Tank—*reservoir* ... NM-5
Cresthaven—*hist pl* ... FL-3
**Cresthaven**—*pop pl* ... FL-3
**Crest Haven**—*pop pl* ... IL-6
**Crest Haven**—*pop pl* ... MD-2
**Cresthaven**—*pop pl* ... MD-2
Cresthaven—*uninc pl* ... TX-5
Crest Haven Cem—*cemetery* ... IL-6
Crest Haven Cem—*cemetery* ... IN-6
Cresthaven Country Club—*other* ... IL-6
Cresthaven County Home—*building* ... NJ-2
Crest Haven Memorial Park (Cemetery)—*cemetery* ... NJ-2
Crest Haven Sch—*school* ... CA-9
Cresthaven Sch—*school* ... FL-3
Cresthaven Sch—*school* ... IA-7
Cresthaven Sch—*school* ... MD-2
**Cresthaven (subdivision)**—*pop pl* ... FL-3
Cresthill—*locale* ... VA-3
**Cresthill**—*pop pl* ... GA-3
**Crest Hill**—*pop pl* ... IL-6
Cresthill Ch—*church* ... GA-3
Crest Hill Ch—*church* ... WV-2
**Cresthill Circle Subdivision**—*pop pl* ... UT-8
**Crest Hill Gardens**—*pop pl* ... GA-3
**Cresthomes Addition Subdivision**—*pop pl* ... UT-8
Crest HS—*school* ... KS-7
Crest HS—*school* ... NC-3
Crest Island—*island* ... WA-9
Crest JHS—*school* ... NC-3
Crest Lake—*lake* ... FL-3
Crest Lake—*lake* ... MN-6
Crest Lake Park—*park* ... FL-3
Crestland Community Sch—*school* ... IA-7
*Crestlawn* ... IN-6
**Crestlawn**—*pop pl* ... IN-6
Crestlawn Cem—*cemetery* ... AL-4
Crest Lawn Cem—*cemetery* ... FL-3
Crestlawn Cem—*cemetery* (2) ... GA-3
Crestlawn Cem—*cemetery* ... TN-4
Crest Lawn Gardens—*cemetery* ... KY-4
Crestlawn Memorial Garden—*cemetery* ... MN-6
*Crestlawn Memorial Gardens* ... AL-4
Crestlawn Memorial Gardens—*cemetery* ... GA-3
Crestlawn Memorial Gardens—*cemetery* ... NC-3
Crest Lawn Memorial Park—*park* ... AR-4
Crestlawn Memorial Park (Cemetery)—*cemetery* ... CA-9
**Crest Leigh**—*pop pl* ... MD-2
Crestley Branch—*stream* ... KY-4
Crestley Hollow—*valley* ... KY-4
**Crestline**—*pop pl* ... CA-9
**Crestline**—*pop pl* ... KS-7
**Crestline**—*pop pl* ... NV-8
**Crestline**—*pop pl* ... OH-6
Crestline—*uninc pl* ... AL-4
Crestline Camp—*locale* ... CA-9
Crestline (census name for Crest Forest)—*CDP* ... CA-9
Crestline Ch—*church* ... OK-5
Crestline City Hall—*hist pl* ... OH-6
Crestline Draw—*valley* ... UT-8
**Crestline Gardens**—*pop pl* ... AL-4
Crestline Gardens—*uninc pl* ... KS-7
**Crestline Heights**—*pop pl* ... AL-4
**Crestline Park**—*pop pl* ... AL-4
Crestline Rsvr—*reservoir* ... UT-8
Crestline Sch—*school* ... AL-4
Crestline Sch—*school* ... CA-9
Crestline Trail—*trail* (2) ... ID-8
Crest Lookout Tower—*locale* ... GA-3
**Crestlyn Court**—*pop pl* ... PA-2
*Crest Manor* ... IN-6
**Crest Manor Addition**—*pop pl* ... IN-6
Crestmere Lake—*lake* ... NJ-2
**Crestmont**—*pop pl* ... LA-4
**Crestmont**—*pop pl* (3) ... PA-2
Crestmont Country Club—*other* ... NJ-2
*Crestmont Elem Sch* ... AL-4
Crestmont Park—*park* ... PA-2
Crestmont Park—*park* ... TX-5
Crestmont Sch—*school* ... AL-4
Crestmont Sch—*school* ... CA-9
Crestmont Shop Ctr—*locale* ... PA-2
**Crestmont (subdivision)**—*pop pl* ... AL-4
**Crestmont Village**—*pop pl* ... PA-2
*Crestmoor* ... CO-8
**Crestmoor**—*pop pl* ... IN-6
**Crestmoor**—*pop pl* ... KY-4
**Crestmoor**—*pop pl* ... NJ-2
Crestmoore—*locale* ... NJ-2
Crestmoor HS—*school* ... CA-9
Crestmoor Park—*park* ... CO-8
Crestmoor Sch—*school* ... CA-9
Crestmore—*locale* ... CA-9
**Crestmore**—*pop pl* ... CA-9
**Crestmore Heights**—*pop pl* ... CA-9
Crestmore Quarry—*mine* ... CA-9
Crestmore Sch—*school* ... CA-9
Crest of Montezuma—*ridge* ... NM-5
*Creston* ... IN-6
Creston—*locale* ... CA-9
Creston—*locale* ... KY-4
Creston—*locale* ... OR-9
Creston—*locale* ... SD-7
**Creston**—*pop pl* ... CA-9
**Creston**—*pop pl* ... IL-6
**Creston**—*pop pl* (2) ... IN-6
**Creston**—*pop pl* ... IA-7
**Creston**—*pop pl* ... LA-4
**Creston**—*pop pl* ... MT-8
**Creston**—*pop pl* ... NE-7
**Creston**—*pop pl* ... NJ-2
**Creston**—*pop pl* ... NC-3
**Creston**—*pop pl* ... OH-6
**Creston**—*pop pl* ... OR-9
**Creston**—*pop pl* ... SC-3
**Creston**—*pop pl* ... TN-4
**Creston**—*pop pl* ... WA-9
**Creston**—*pop pl* ... WV-2
**Creston**—*pop pl* ... WY-8
Creston—*ridge* ... NM-5
Creston, The—*ridge* ... NM-5
Creston Baptist Ch—*church* ... TN-4
Creston-Bigfork—*cens area* ... MT-8
Creston Butte—*summit* ... WA-9
Creston Cem—*cemetery* ... TN-4
Creston Ch—*church* ... MT-8
Creston Ch—*church* ... WV-2
Creston City Hall—*building* ... IA-7
Creston Creek—*stream* ... AK-9
Creston Draw—*valley* ... WY-8
**Crestone**—*pop pl* ... CO-8
Crestone Creek—*stream* ... CO-8
Crestone Ditch—*canal* ... CO-8
*Crestone Goup* ... CO-8
*Crestone Group* ... CO-8
Crestone Needle—*summit* ... CO-8
Crestone Peak—*summit* ... CO-8
*Crestone Peaks* ... CO-8
Crestone Peaks—*summit* ... CO-8
*Crestone Ridge* ... CO-8
*Crestones Creek* ... CO-8
Creston Hill—*uninc pl* ... OK-5
Creston Hill Ch—*church* ... MS-4
Creston Hills Baptist Ch—*church* ... MS-4
Creston Hill Sch—*school* ... OK-5
Creston HS—*school* ... MI-6
**Creston Junction**—*pop pl* ... WY-8
*Creston Needles* ... CO-8
Creston Park—*park* ... OR-9
Creston Pioneer Cem—*cemetery* ... NE-7
Creston Post Office (historical)—*building* ... TN-4
Creston Sch—*school* ... MI-6
Creston Sch—*school* ... OR-9
**Creston Township**—*pop pl* ... NE-7
Creston (Township of)—*fmr MCD* ... NC-3
Creston Waterhole—*lake* ... OR-9
Cresto Ranch—*locale* ... CO-8
Cresto Ranch—*locale* ... NM-5
Cresto Rsvr—*reservoir* ... CO-8
Cresto Spring—*spring* ... CO-8
**Crest Park**—*pop pl* ... CA-9
Crest Park Ch of God—*church* ... MS-4
Crest Plaza Shop Ctr—*locale* ... PA-2
Crest Ridge Sch (historical)—*school* ... TN-4
Crest Sch—*school* ... PA-2
Crest Spring—*spring* ... ID-8
Creststone Sch—*hist pl* ... CO-8
Crest Summit—*summit* ... CA-9
**Crest (Suncrest)**—*pop pl* ... CA-9
Crest Trail—*trail* ... AZ-5
Crest Trail—*trail* ... NM-5
Crest Trail Number One Hundred Three—*trail* ... AZ-5
Crest Trail (Pack)—*trail* (4) ... NM-5
Crest Trail Two Hundred Seventy—*trail* ... AZ-5
*Crestview* (2) ... OH-6
Crestview—*CDP* ... SC-3
Crestview—*locale* ... GA-3
**Crestview**—*pop pl* ... CA-9
**Crestview**—*pop pl* (2) ... FL-3
**Crestview**—*pop pl* ... HI-9
**Crestview**—*pop pl* (2) ... IN-6
**Crestview**—*pop pl* ... KY-4
**Crestview**—*pop pl* ... MD-2
**Crestview**—*pop pl* ... NJ-2
**Crestview**—*pop pl* ... NY-2
**Crestview**—*pop pl* (3) ... PA-2
**Crest View**—*pop pl* ... TN-4
**Crestview**—*pop pl* ... TN-4
**Crestview**—*pop pl* ... VA-3
**Crestview**—*pop pl* (2) ... WI-6
Crestview—*uninc pl* ... AZ-5
**Crestview Acres (subdivision)**—*pop pl* ... NC-3
**Crest View Acrs Subdivision**—*pop pl* ... UT-8
*Crestview Baptist Ch* ... MS-4
Crestview Baptist Ch—*church* ... AL-4
Crestview Baptist Ch—*church* ... FL-3
Crestview (CCD)—*cens area* ... FL-3
Crestview Cem—*cemetery* ... AL-4
Crestview Cem—*cemetery* ... OH-6
Crestview Cem—*cemetery* ... TN-4
Crestview Cem—*cemetery* ... TX-5
*Crestview Ch* ... IN-6
Crestview Ch—*church* ... AL-4
Crestview Ch—*church* ... FL-3
Crestview Ch—*church* ... GA-3
Crestview Ch—*church* ... MS-4
Crestview Ch—*church* (3) ... NC-3
Crestview Ch—*church* ... OH-6
Crestview Ch—*church* ... SC-3
*Crestview Ch of Christ* ... AL-4
Crestview Christian Ch—*church* ... IN-6
Crestview Community Hosp—*hospital* ... FL-3
Crestview Conservation Club—*other* ... IN-6
Crestview Country Club—*locale* ... FL-3
Crestview Country Club—*other* ... KS-7
*Crestview Elementary School* ... UT-8
Crestview Elem Sch—*school* ... IN-6
Crestview Elem Sch—*school* (2) ... KS-7
Crestview Elem Sch—*school* ... PA-2
**Crestview Estates (subdivision)**—*pop pl* ... AL-4
**Crestview Estates Subdivision**—*pop pl* ... UT-8
**Crestview Gardens**—*pop pl* ... AL-4
Crestview Golf Course—*other* ... MI-6
**Crestview Heights**—*pop pl* ... IN-6
**Crestview Heights**—*pop pl* ... NY-2
**Crestview Hills**—*pop pl* ... AL-4
**Crestview Hills**—*pop pl* ... KY-4
Crestview JHS—*school* ... IN-6
Crest View Lake—*lake* ... NY-2
Crestview Lake—*reservoir* ... IN-6
Crestview Lake Dam—*dam* ... IN-6
Crestview Lodge—*locale* ... NE-7
**Crestview Manor**—*pop pl* ... MD-2
**Crestview Manor (subdivision)**—*pop pl* ... PA-2
Crestview Memorial Cem—*cemetery* ... AL-4
Crestview Memorial Cem—*cemetery* ... NC-3
Crestview Memorial Garden—*cemetery* ... CO-8
Crestview Memorial Gardens—*cemetery* ... SC-3
Crestview Memorial Park—*cemetery* ... TN-4
Crestview Memorial Park—*cemetery* ... VA-3
Crestview Memorial Park Cem—*cemetery* ... TX-5
Crestview Nursing Home—*building* ... OH-6
Crestview Park—*hist pl* ... AR-4
Crestview Park—*park* ... AL-4
Crestview Park—*park* ... KS-7
Crestview Park—*park* ... MI-6
Crestview Park—*park* ... MO-7
Crestview Plaza (Shop Ctr)—*locale* ... FL-3
Crestview Post Office (historical)—*building* ... TN-4
Crestview Sch—*school* ... CA-9
Crest View Sch—*school* ... CA-9
Crestview Sch—*school* ... CA-9
Crestview Sch—*school* ... FL-3
Crestview Sch—*school* ... IN-6
Crestview Sch—*school* ... MI-6
Crestview Sch—*school* (2) ... MN-6
Crestview Sch—*school* ... MO-7
Crestview Sch—*school* (2) ... OH-6
Crestview Sch—*school* (2) ... TX-5
Crestview Sch—*school* (2) ... UT-8
Crestview Sch—*school* ... VA-3
Crestview Senior HS—*school* ... FL-3
Crestview Shop Ctr—*locale* ... AL-4
Crestview Shop Ctr—*locale* ... MO-7
**Crestview (subdivision)**—*pop pl* (2) ... AL-4
**Crestview (subdivision)**—*pop pl* ... AZ-5
**Crestview (subdivision)**—*pop pl* ... NC-3
**Crest View (subdivision)**—*pop pl* ... PA-2
**Crestview Subdivision**—*pop pl* ... UT-8
*Crestview Terrace* ... IL-6
**Crestview Terrace**—*pop pl* ... PA-2
Crestview United Methodist Ch—*church* ... KS-7
Crestview Vocational-Technical Center—*school* ... FL-3
Crestway Ch—*church* ... AL-4
Crestway Free Methodist Ch—*church* ... KS-7
Crestwell Farm—*locale* ... AL-4
**Crestwell Heights**—*pop pl* ... GA-3
Crest West Elem Sch—*school* ... KS-7
*Crestwood* ... IA-7
*Crestwood* ... VA-3
Crestwood—*hist pl* ... GA-3
**Crestwood**—*pop pl* ... DC-2
**Crestwood**—*pop pl* ... GA-3
**Crestwood**—*pop pl* ... IL-6
**Crestwood**—*pop pl* ... IN-6
**Crestwood**—*pop pl* ... IA-7
**Crestwood**—*pop pl* (2) ... KY-4
**Crestwood**—*pop pl* (2) ... MD-2
**Crestwood**—*pop pl* ... MO-7
**Crestwood**—*pop pl* ... NY-2
**Crestwood**—*pop pl* (2) ... NC-3
**Crestwood**—*pop pl* ... PA-2
**Crestwood**—*pop pl* ... TN-4
**Crestwood**—*pop pl* ... VA-3
Crestwood—*uninc pl* ... AL-4
Crestwood—*uninc pl* ... KY-4
Crestwood—*uninc pl* ... TX-5
*Crestwood Acres* ... IA-7
**Crestwood Acres**—*pop pl* ... MD-2
**Crestwood Acres**—*pop pl* ... OH-6
**Crestwood Acres Subdivision**—*pop pl* ... UT-8
*Crestwood Baptist Ch* ... MS-4
Crestwood Baptist Ch—*church* ... MS-4
Crestwood Cem—*cemetery* ... OK-5
Crestwood Ch—*church* ... GA-3
Crestwood Ch—*church* ... KY-4
Crestwood Ch—*church* ... MS-4
Crestwood Ch—*church* ... NC-3
Crestwood Community MS—*school* ... FL-3
Crestwood Country Club—*locale* ... MA-1
**Crestwood East**—*pop pl* ... PA-2
*Crestwood Elementary School* ... MS-4
Crestwood Elem Sch—*school* ... FL-3
**Crestwood Estates**—*pop pl* ... IL-6
*Crestwood Forest* ... TN-4
**Crestwood Gardens**—*pop pl* ... NY-2
Crestwood Golf Club—*other* ... IA-7
**Crestwood Hills**—*pop pl* ... OH-6
**Crestwood Hills**—*pop pl* ... TN-4
Crestwood Hills Park—*park* ... CA-9
Crestwood Hosp—*hospital* ... AL-4
Crestwood HS—*school* ... MI-6
Crestwood HS—*school* ... OH-6
Crestwood HS—*school* ... VA-3
**Crestwood (Industrial Park)**—*pop pl* ... PA-2
Crestwood JHS—*school* ... IA-7
Crestwood JHS—*school* ... VA-3
Crestwood Lake—*lake* ... NY-2
Crestwood Lake—*reservoir* ... NJ-2
**Crestwood Manor**—*pop pl* ... VA-3
**Crestwood Manor (Crestwood)**—*pop pl* ... VA-3
Crestwood Memorial Cem—*cemetery* ... AL-4
Crestwood Memorial Gardens—*cemetery* ... GA-3
Crestwood Memorial Gardens—*cemetery* ... MI-6
Crestwood Memorial Park—*cemetery* ... KS-7
Crestwood Memorial Park—*park* ... NC-3
Crestwood Park—*park* ... FL-3
Crestwood Plaza (Shop Ctr)—*locale* ... MO-7
Crestwood Professional Plaza Subdivision—*locale* ... UT-8
Crestwood Rest Home—*hospital* ... TN-4
Crestwood Sch—*school* ... AR-4
Crestwood Sch—*school* (2) ... IL-6
Crestwood Sch—*school* ... MI-6
Crestwood Sch—*school* ... MN-6
Crestwood Sch—*school* ... MS-4
Crestwood Sch—*school* ... NV-8
Crestwood Sch—*school* ... OH-6
Crestwood Sch—*school* ... TX-5
Crestwood Sch—*school* ... VA-3
Crestwood Sch—*school* (2) ... WI-6
Crestwood Shop Ctr—*locale* ... AL-4
Crestwood Shop Ctr—*locale* ... AZ-5
Crestwood Shop Ctr—*locale* ... MO-7
Crestwood (sta.)—*uninc pl* ... NY-2
Crestwood Station—*locale* ... PA-2
Crestwood Street Sch—*school* ... CA-9
**Crestwood (subdivision)**—*pop pl* ... AL-4
**Crestwood Subdivision**—*pop pl* (2) ... UT-8
**Crestwood Village**—*pop pl* ... NJ-2
**Crestwyck**—*pop pl* ... PA-2
*Creswell* ... IN-6
*Creswell* ... KS-7
*Creswell* ... OH-6
Creswell—*locale* ... AL-4
Creswell—*locale* ... AR-4
Creswell—*locale* ... KY-4
Creswell—*locale* ... MI-6
Creswell—*locale* ... PA-2
Creswell—*locale* ... VA-3
**Creswell**—*pop pl* ... IA-7
**Creswell**—*pop pl* ... MD-2
**Creswell**—*pop pl* ... NC-3
**Creswell**—*pop pl* ... OR-9
Creswell Branch—*stream* ... KY-4
Creswell Butte—*summit* ... OR-9
Creswell Canyon—*valley* ... OR-9
Creswell (CCD)—*cens area* ... OR-9
Creswell Cem—*cemetery* ... AL-4
Creswell Cem—*cemetery* ... LA-4
Creswell Cem—*cemetery* ... TN-4
Creswell Ch—*church* ... KY-4
Creswell Elem Sch—*school* ... NC-3
**Creswell Heights**—*pop pl* ... WA-9
Creswell (historical)—*locale* ... KS-7
Creswell (historical), Lake—*lake* ... MS-4
Creswell (historical P.O.)—*locale* ... IA-7
Creswell HS—*school* ... NC-3
Creswell HS—*school* ... OR-9
Creswell Island—*island* ... AR-4
Creswell Lake Number Thirty-eight—*reservoir* ... TN-4
Creswell Lake Number Thirty-eight Dam—*dam* ... TN-4
Creswell Lake Number Thirty-five—*reservoir* ... TN-4
Creswell Lake Number Thirty-five Dam—*dam* ... TN-4
Creswell Lake Number Thirty-four—*reservoir* ... TN-4
Creswell Lake Number Thirty-four Dam—*dam* ... TN-4
Creswell Lake Number Thirty-one—*reservoir* ... TN-4
Creswell Lake Number Thirty-one Dam—*dam* ... TN-4
Creswell Lake Number Thirty-three—*reservoir* ... TN-4
Creswell Lake Number Thirty-three Dam—*dam* ... TN-4
Creswell Lake Number Thirty-two—*reservoir* ... TN-4
Creswell Lake Number Thirty-two Dam—*dam* ... TN-4
Creswell Lake Number Twenty-eight—*reservoir* ... TN-4
Creswell Lake Number Twenty-eight Dam—*dam* ... TN-4
Creswell Lake Number Twenty-five—*reservoir* ... TN-4
Creswell Lake Number Twenty-five Dam—*dam* ... TN-4
Creswell Lake Number Twenty-four—*reservoir* ... TN-4
Creswell Lake Number Twenty-four Dam—*dam* ... TN-4
Creswell Lake Number Twenty-nine—*reservoir* ... TN-4
Creswell Lake Number Twenty-nine Dam—*dam* ... TN-4
Creswell Lake Number Twenty-one—*reservoir* ... TN-4
Creswell Lake Number Twenty-one Dam—*dam* ... TN-4
Creswell Lake Number Twenty-three—*reservoir* ... TN-4
Creswell Lake Number Twenty-three Dam—*dam* ... TN-4
Creswell Mansion—*hist pl* ... CO-8
Creswell Methodist Ch—*church* ... NC-3
Creswell MS—*school* ... OR-9
Creswell Mtn—*summit* ... AR-4
Creswell Ridge—*ridge* ... WV-2
Creswell Sch—*school* ... LA-4
Creswell Sch—*school* ... PA-2
Creswell Station (abandoned)—*locale* ... PA-2
Creswell Tank—*reservoir* ... AZ-5
**Creswell Township**—*pop pl* ... KS-7
Creswell Trick Tank—*reservoir* ... AZ-5
**Creta**—*pop pl* ... OK-5
Cretaceous Mtn—*summit* ... WY-8
*Creta Station* ... OK-5
Cretcheloe Hill—*summit* ... KY-4
**Cretcher**—*pop pl* ... MO-7
Cretcher Ditch—*canal* ... IN-6
*Crete* ... PA-2
*Crete* ... WV-2
Crete—*locale* ... NE-7
Crete—*locale* ... PA-2
**Crete**—*pop pl* (2) ... IL-6
**Crete**—*pop pl* ... IN-6
**Crete**—*pop pl* ... NE-7
**Crete**—*pop pl* ... ND-7
**Crete**—*pop pl* ... PA-2
Crete Creek—*stream* ... AK-9
Crete Drain—*stream* ... IN-6
**Crete Junction**—*pop pl* ... NE-7
**Crete (Township of)**—*pop pl* ... IL-6
*Crethers Spring* ... NV-8
Crethers Springs—*spring* ... NV-8
Cretin HS—*school* ... MN-6
Creto Site—*hist pl* ... GU-9
*Creums Lake* ... CA-9
Crevasse Cayon—*valley* ... NM-5
Crevasse Pond—*reservoir* ... GA-3
Crevasses, The—*valley* ... WY-8
**Creve Coeur**—*pop pl* ... IL-6

**Creve Coeur**—pop pl MO-7
Creve Coeur Airp—airport MO-7
Creve Coeur Creek—stream MO-7
Creve Coeur Golf Club—other MO-7
Creve Coeur Lake—lake MO-7
Creve Coeur (OPlaza (Shop Ctr)—locale MO-7
Creve Coeur Plaza—locale MO-7
Creve Coeur Township—civil MO-7
Creveling Hill—summit PA-2
Creveling Lake—reservoir PA-2
Creveling Lake Dam—dam PA-2
Creveling Sch—school OH-6
Crevice, The—locale ID-8
Crevice Cave—cave AL-4
Crevice Creek—stream (3) AK-9
Crevice Creek—stream (2) MT-8
Crevice Creek—stream (2) OR-9
Crevice Creek—stream WA-9
Crevice Gulch MT-0
Crevice Lake—lake (2) MT-8
Crevice Mtn—summit MT-8
Crevice Point—cliff AZ-5
Crevice Ruin (LA 13218)—hist pl NM-5
Crevice Spring—spring UT-8
Crevice Station—locale MT-8
**Crevi (historical)**—pop pl MS-4
Creviosur Cem—cemetery MO-7
Crevi P.O. (historical)—building MS-4
Crevis Creek—stream CA-9
Crevison Peak—summit CA-9
Crevis Well—well AZ-5
Crew, Bayou—stream LA-4
Crew Bayou—gut LA-4
Crew Canyon—valley OR-9
Crew Creek AR-4
Crew Creek—stream CA-9
Crew Creek—stream ID-8
Crew Cut Trail—trail NH-1
**Crewe**—pop pl VA-3
Crewes Channel—stream VA-3
Crewes House—building VA-3
Crewey Branch—stream VA-3
Crew Lake—lake (2) LA-4
**Crew Lake**—pop pl LA-4
Crew Point MD-2
**Crewport (Labor Camp)**—pop pl WA-9
Crews—locale CO-8
Crews—locale LA-4
Crews—locale TX-5
Crews—other TX-5
**Crews**—pop pl AL-4
Crews, Lake—lake FL-3
Crews Branch—stream MO-7
Crews Branch—stream SC-3
Crews Branch—stream TN-4
Crews Branch—stream VA-3
Crews Cem—cemetery (2) IL-6
Crews Cem—cemetery (2) KY-4
Crews Cem—cemetery TN-4
Crews Cem—cemetery TX-5
Crews Ch—church AL-4
Crews Ch—church NC-3
Crew Sch (abandoned)—school MO-7
Crews Coll (historical)—school AL-4
Crews Creek—stream (2) GA-3
Crews Creek—stream OR-9
Crews Crossing—locale GA-3
Crews Depot AL-4
Crews Depot Post Office (historical)—building AL-4
Crews Ditch—canal IN-6
Crews Hill—summit TN-4
Crews (historical)—locale MS-4
Crews Hollow—valley (2) TN-4
Crews Island—island FL-3
Crews Island—island GA-3
Crews Lake—lake (3) FL-3
Crews Methodist Church AL-4
Crews Mill Branch—stream AL-4
Crews Mill (historical)—locale AL-4
Crews Mine—mine TN-4
Crews Normal College AL-4
Crews Point—cape GA-3
Crews Pond MA-1
Crews Post Office (historical)—building MS-4
**Crews Spur**—pop pl MS-4
Crews Square—park MO-7
Crews Store—locale TN-4
**Crewstown**—pop pl TN-4
Crewstown Ch of Christ—church TN-4
Crewsville—locale AL-4
Crewsville—locale FL-3
Crews Well—well NM-5
Crex Meadows State Wildlife Area—park WI-6
C R Fortenberry Pond Dam—dam MS-4
**Cribb**—pop pl PA-2
Cribb Bay—swamp GA-3
Cribb Cem—cemetery NC-3
**Cribb Crossroads**—pop pl SC-3
Cribbins Hill—summit OR-9
Crib Branch—stream KY-4
Cribbs Cem—cemetery PA-2
Cribbs Corner—locale NY-2
Cribbs Creek AL-4
Cribbs Creek NC-3
Cribbs Mill Creek—stream AL-4
Cribbs Mill (historical)—locale AL-4
Cribbs Pond—lake AL-4
Cribbs Sch (abandoned)—school PA-2
Cribb Station Creek—stream TX-5
Cribb Town—locale NC-3
Cribby Creek—stream AK-9
Crib Creek—stream LA-4
Crib Creek—stream TX-5
Crib Gap—gap TN-4
Crib Hollow—valley AR-4
Crib Point—cape AK-9
Crib Point—summit OR-9
Crib Reef—bar OH-6
Cribs Creek—stream NC-3
Crib Spring—spring CO-8
Crib Spring—spring (3) ID-8
Crib Spring—spring UT-8
Crib Station Creek TX-5
Crichfield Cem—cemetery WV-2
Crichton—locale LA-4
**Crichton**—pop pl AL-4
**Crichton**—pop pl WV-2
Crichton Assembly of God Ch—church AL-4
Crichton Bridge—bridge VA-3
Crichton Ch of God—church AL-4
Crichton Lake—lake LA-4
Crichton McCormick Park—park PA-2
Crichton Pentecostal Full Gospel Ch—church AL-4
Crichton Sch—school AL-4
Crichton Shop Ctr—locale AL-4
Cricker Brook—stream CT-1
Cricket—locale AR-4
**Cricket**—pop pl IA-7
**Cricket**—pop pl NC-3
Cricket Branch—stream TN-4
Cricket Canyon—valley NV-8
Cricket Cave—cave AL-4
Cricket Cave—cave TN-4
Cricket Cave Number Two—cave AL-4
Cricket Ch—church NC-3
Cricket Corner—locale NH-1
Cricket Corner Cem—cemetery NH-1
Cricket Creek—stream AR-4
Cricket Creek—stream NV-8
Cricket Creek—stream NJ-2
Cricket Creek—stream (2) OR-9
Cricket Creek—stream TN-4
Cricket Creek Public Use Area—park AR-4
Cricket Dam—dam NM-5
Cricket Field—park MA-1
Cricket Field Airp—airport WA-9
Cricket Flat—flat OR-9
Cricket Flat Grange Hall—locale OR-9
Cricket Hill IL-6
Cricket Hill—locale VA-3
**Cricket Hill**—pop pl DE-2
Cricket Hill—summit (2) MA-1
Cricket Hill—summit NH-1
Cricket Hill Cem—cemetery MA-1
Cricket Hill Golf Course—locale PA-2
Cricket Hill Southern Baptist Ch—church IN-6
Cricket Holler Camp—locale OH-6
Cricket Hollow—valley VA-3
Cricket Hollow—valley WV-2
Cricket Island—island NC-3
Cricket Island Point—cape NC-3
Cricket Lake—lake NE-7
Cricket Mine—mine MT-8
Cricket Mtns—range UT-8
**Cricket (Omaha)**—pop pl AR-4
**Cricket Park (subdivision)**—pop pl NC-3
Cricket River OR-9
Cricket Rock—island VI-3
Cricket Rsvr—reservoir UT-8
Cricket Rsvr No 2—reservoir UT-8
Cricket Seeps—spring UT-8
Cricket Spicket Cave—cave AL-4
Cricket Spring—spring (2) NV-8
Cricket Swamp—stream NC-3
Crickett Creek AR-4
Crickett Creek—stream OR-9
Crickett Hill MA-1
**Crickmer**—pop pl WV-2
Cricks Run—stream NY-2
Criddle Cem—cemetery MO-7
Criddlin Swamp—swamp VA-3
Cridebring Canyon—valley NM-5
Cridebring Spring—spring NM-5
**Crider**—pop pl KY-4
**Crider**—pop pl MO-7
Crider Cem—cemetery AR-4
Crider Cem—cemetery IN-6
Crider Cem—cemetery (2) KY-4
Crider Cem—cemetery MO-7
Crider Creek—stream GA-3
Crider Creek—stream MO-7
Crider Creek—stream TN-4
Crider Hill—summit KY-4
Crider Hollow—valley MO-7
Crider Island—island IL-6
Crider Pond—lake OR-9
Criders—locale VA-3
Criders Ch—church VA-3
Crider School (historical)—locale MO-7
**Criders Corners**—pop pl PA-2
**Cridersville**—pop pl OH-6
Crider Valley—valley WA-9
Cridleys Ferry (historical)—locale AL-4
**Criehaven**—pop pl ME-1
Criehaven Harbor—bay ME-1
Criehaven (Unorganized Territory of)—unorg ME-1
Crier Creek TX-5
Crier Creek—stream TX-5
Crier Park—park TX-5
Cries Creek—stream OR-9
Crietz Creek—stream IN-6
Crieve Hall—uninc pl TN-4
Crieve Hall Ch—church TN-4
Crieve Hall Sch—school TN-4
Crievewood Ch—church TN-4
Crig Chapel—church KY-4
Crigger—other KY-4
Crigger Cem—cemetery TN-4
Crigger Creek—stream VA-3
Criggers Mill—other VA-3
Crighton School ND-7
Crigler—locale AR-4
Crigler Branch—stream MO-7
Crigler Cem—cemetery MS-4
Crigler Cem—cemetery MO-7
Crigler Mound Group Archeol Site—hist pl MO-7
**Criglersville**—pop pl VA-3
Crileys Branch—stream IL-6
Crill Ave Shop Ctr—locale FL-3
Crillon, Mount—summit AK-9
Crillon Inlet—bay AK-9
Crillon Lake—lake AK-9
Crillon River—stream AK-9
Crill Place—locale ID-8
Crilly Gap—gap WY-8
Crim, J. N. B., House—hist pl WV-2
Crimbo Point—cape CT-1
Crim Cem—cemetery CO-8
Crim Cem—cemetery MO-7
Crim Cem—cemetery NY-2
Crim Creek—stream SC-3
Crim Creek—stream WA-9
**Crimcrest**—pop pl TX-5
Crimea—locale LA-4
Crimea House—locale CA-9
Crimes Chapel AL-4
Crimes Creek SC-3
Crimfield Creek GA-3
Criminal Courts Bldg—hist pl LA-4
Criminal Creek—stream OR-9
Criminal Lake—lake TX-5
Criminal Point CA-9
Crim Lake—lake AL-4
Crim Lake Dam—dam AL-4
Crimm Cem—cemetery OH-6
**Crimora**—pop pl VA-3
Crimora Lake—reservoir VA-3
Crimora Lake Overlook—locale VA-3
Crimora Sch—hist pl VA-3
Crimper Creek—stream ID-8
Crim Pond—reservoir SC-3
Crimpville MA-1
Crim Sch—school OH-6
Crims Chapel—locale TX-5
Crims Creek—stream SC-3
**Crims Crossroads**—pop pl NC-3
Crims Island—island OR-9
**Crimson**—pop pl OH-6
Crimson Creek—stream MT-8
Crimson Dawn—locale WY-8
Crimson Lake—lake ID-8
Crimson Lake—lake MT-8
Crimson Peak—summit MT-8
Crimson Spring Ch—church WV-2
Crimson Springs—locale WV-2
Crim Sublateral Lateral—canal ID-8
Crim Tank—reservoir NM-5
Crim-Tice House—hist pl NJ-2
**Criner**—pop pl OK-5
Criner Cem—cemetery OK-5
Criner Cem—cemetery WV-2
Criner Creek—stream OK-5
Criner Creek—stream TN-4
Criner Hills—range OK-5
Crinerville Ch—church OK-5
Crinkley Post Office (historical)—building TN-4
Criotz Park—park IN-6
Cripe Cem—cemetery IN-6
Cripe Run—stream IN-6
Cripe Sandlin Ditch—canal IN-6
**Crippen**—pop pl ID-8
Crippen, Henry J., House—hist pl NH-1
Crippen Branch—stream MD-2
Crippen Canyon—valley NV-8
Crippen Cem—cemetery OH-6
Crippen Creek—stream NY-2
Crippen Creek—stream VA-3
Crippen Drain—stream MI-6
Crippen Gap—gap TN-4
**Crippen Gap**—pop pl TN-4
Crippen Hill—summit PA-2
Crippen Hollow—valley PA-2
Crippen Point—cape MS-4
Crippen Run—stream (2) PA-2
Crippen's Brook ME-1
Crippens Brook—stream ME-1
Crippin Corners—locale IA-7
Cripple Branch—stream AR-4
Cripple Brush Creek—stream VT-1
Cripplebush Creek—stream NY-2
Cripple Cat Tank—reservoir AZ-5
Cripple Childrens Hosp—hospital TX-5
Cripple Creek AL-4
Cripple Creek TN-4
**Cripple Creek**—pop pl CO-8
**Cripple Creek**—pop pl VA-3
Cripple Creek—stream (2) AL-4
Cripple Creek—stream (7) AK-9
Cripple Creek—stream CA-9
Cripple Creek—stream CO-8
Cripple Creek—stream (4) KY-4
Cripple Creek—stream MI-6
Cripple Creek—stream MO-7
Cripple Creek—stream MT-8
Cripple Creek—stream NY-2
Cripple Creek—stream (2) NC-3
Cripple Creek—stream OK-5
Cripple Creek—stream (3) OR-9
Cripple Creek—stream (3) TN-4
Cripple Creek—stream UT-8
Cripple Creek—stream (3) VA-3
Cripple Creek—stream WA-9
Cripple Creek—stream WY-8
Cripple Creek Cem—cemetery AL-4
Cripple Creek Ch—church AL-4
Cripple Creek Ch—church TN-4
Cripple Creek Forest Camp—locale OR-9
Cripple Creek Hist Dist—hist pl CO-8
Cripple Creek Mine—mine AK-9
Cripple Creek Mine—mine CO-8
Cripple Creek Mine (underground)—mine AL-4
Cripple Creek Mountains—other AK-9
Cripple Creek Ranch—locale OR-9
**Cripple Creek (subdivision)**—pop pl DE-2
Cripple Creek Trail—trail OR-9
Crippled Children Clinic—hospital AL-4
Crippled Childrens Clinic and Rehabilitation Center—hospital AL-4
Crippled Childrens Sch—school ND-7
Crippled Deer Creek MS-4
Crippled Deer Lake—lake MN-6
Cripple Deer Creek—stream AL-4
Cripple Deer Creek—stream MS-4
Cripple Deer Sch (historical)—school MS-4
Crippled Horse Spring—spring (2) OR-9
Crippled Jack Well—well NV-8
Cripple Goose Windmill—locale TX-5
Cripple Gulch—valley OR-9
Cripple Horse Canyon—valley UT-8
Cripple Horse Creek—stream MT-8
Cripple Horse Mtn—summit MT-8
Cripple Lake—lake MN-6
Cripple Landing—locale AK-9
Cripple Mountains—other AK-9
Cripple Mountain Trail—trail OK-5
Cripple River—stream (2) AK-9
Cripple Rocks—bar MA-1
Cripple Spring—spring NV-8
Cripple Tank—reservoir AZ-5
Cripple T Farm—locale TX-5
Cripps Bend—bend IL-6
Cripps Cem—cemetery TN-4
Cripps Cem—cemetery WI-6
Cripps Mill Cave—cave TN-4
Cripps Mill (historical)—locale TN-4
Crips Hole—flat UT-8
Crip Tank—reservoir NM-5
C R I Ranch—locale WY-8
Crisafulli Lake—reservoir MT-8
Crisawn Cem—cemetery NC-3
Crisawn Knob—summit NC-3
Cris Bow Ranch MT-8
Cris Brown Creek—stream MI-6
Cris Brown Lake—lake MI-6
C R I Sch—school WY-8
Criscillis Branch—stream KY-4
Crisco Branch—stream NC-3
Criscoe Cem—cemetery AL-4
Cris Creek—stream KS-7
Crisel Cem—cemetery (2) IL-6
Crisenberry Dam—dam IL-6
Crise Run—stream PA-2
Crisfield—locale KS-7
**Crisfield**—pop pl MD-2
Crisfield Armory—hist pl MD-2
Crisfield Cem—cemetery KS-7
Crisfield Country Club—other MD-2
Cris Hollow—valley TN-4
Crisholm Swamp GA-3
Crishook Canyon—valley OR-9
Cris Lee Draw—valley CO-8
Crislip Run—stream WV-2
Crisman IN-6
Crisman—locale CO-8
**Crisman**—pop pl IN-6
Crisman Cem—cemetery MO-7
Crisman Elem Sch—school IN-6
Crisman Hill—summit OR-9
Crisman Hollow—valley VA-3
Crisman Mill Sch—school KY-4
Crisman Park—park OH-6
Crisman Rsvr—reservoir WA-9
Crisman, Canal (historical)—canal AZ-5
Crismond VA-3
Crisp—locale MO-7
Crisp—locale TX-5
Crisp—other PA-2
**Crisp**—pop pl IL-6
**Crisp**—pop pl IA-7
**Crisp**—pop pl MI-6
**Crisp**—pop pl NC-3
Crisp—uninc pl MD-2
Crisp Acad—school GA-3
Crisp Branch—stream KY-4
Crisp Bridge—other MO-7
Crisp Cem—cemetery MO-7
Crisp Cem—cemetery TX-5
**Crisp (County)**—pop pl GA-3
Crisp County Hydro-Electric Plant—other GA-3
Crisp Creek—stream NC-3
Crisp Creek—stream WA-9
Crispell Lake—lake MI-6
Crispen Island—island GA-3
**Crisp (historical)**—pop pl OR-9
**Crisp (historical)**—pop pl TN-4
Crisp Hollow—valley KY-4
Crisp Hollow—valley TX-5
Crispin Cem—cemetery OH-6
Crispin Island GA-3
Crispin Sch—school PA-2
Crisp Memorial Ch—church MD-2
Crisp Point—cape MI-6
Crisp Post Office (historical)—building TN-4
Crisp Quarry—mine TN-4
Crisp Ranch—locale NM-5
Crisp Sch—school TN-4
Crisps Crossroads (historical)—locale IN-6
Crisp Spring—locale TN-4
**Crisp Spring**—pop pl TN-4
Crisp Spring—spring TN-4
**Crisp Subdivision**—pop pl UT-8
Crispus Attucks HS—school IN-6
Crispus Attucks Sch—school TX-5
Crispy Tank—reservoir NM-5
Criss Brook—stream NJ-2
Criss Creek UT-8
Criss Cross—hist pl VA-3
Criss Cross—locale VA-3
Crisscross Cave—cave AL-4
**Crissey**—pop pl OH-6
Crissey Pond—lake CT-1
Crissman Gap—gap PA-2
Crissman Knob—summit PA-2
Crissman Spring—spring AZ-5
Criss Spring—spring NV-0
Criss Sch—school NE-7
Criss Sch—school WV-2
Crisswell Spring—spring AL-4
Crist, Henry, House—hist pl KY-4
Crist, J. W., House—hist pl WI-6
Crist Airp—airport KS-7
Crist Cabin—locale ID-8
Cristholm's Cristholm's Creek VA-3
Cristian Creek MI-6
Cristian Hill—cemetery MA-1
Cristianitos Canyon—valley CA-9
Cristianitos Creek—stream CA-9
**Cristina**—pop pl PR-3
Cristina Island—island AK-9
**Cristine Manor**—pop pl DE-2
Cristo Rey Cem—cemetery NM-5
Cristo Rey Ch—church NM-5
Cristoval De La Serna—civil NM-5
Crist Point—cape AK-9
Crist Ridge—ridge PA-2
Cristy Canyon—valley KS-7
Cristy Creek—stream WA-9
Cristy Park—park TX-5
Criswell Basin—basin CO-8
Criswell Branch KY-4
Criswell Cem—cemetery (2) KY-4
Criswell Cem—cemetery MO-7
Criswell Cem—cemetery PA-2
Criswell Cem—cemetery TX-5
Criswell Cemetery MS-4
Criswell Ch—church TX-5
Criswell City—locale PA-2
Criswell Cliff—cliff KY-4
Criswell Coulee—valley MT-8
Criswell Creek—stream CO-8
Criswell Creek—stream (2) TX-5
Criswell Ditch—canal MT-8
Criswell (historical)—locale MS-4
Criswell Hollow—valley (2) KY-4
Criswell Mtn—summit KY-4
Criswell Park—park FL-3
Criswell Ranch—locale (2) MT-8
Criswell Ranch—locale TX-5
Criswell Sch—school IL-6
Criswell Sch—school IA-7
Criswell Sch—school PA-2
Criswell Tank—reservoir NM-5
Criswell Windmill—locale NM-5
**Criswood Manor**—pop pl MD-2
Critchell—locale CO-8
**Critchfield**—pop pl IN-6
Critchfield Sch (abandoned)—school PA-2
Critchfield Stone Ch—church PA-2
Critchlow Cem—cemetery IL-6
Critchlow Flat—flat AZ-5
Critchlow Spring—spring TN-4
**Critco**—pop pl AR-4
Criterion—locale OR-9
Criterion Summit—summit OR-9
Criterion Theatre—hist pl ME-1
Crites—locale WV-2
Crites Cem—cemetery MO-7
Crites Ch—church WV-2
Crites Corner—locale MO-7
Crites Creek—stream MO-7
Crites Hall—hist pl NE-7
Crites Mountain Sch—school WV-2
Crite Spring—spring WA-9
Critian Hollow—valley UT-8
Critical Bayou—bay FL-3
Critical Creek—stream FL-3
Critical Fork—stream VA-3
Critie Mine—mine AZ-5
Crit May Pond—reservoir TN-4
Critmore Cem—cemetery KY-4
Critnan Creek—stream WY-8
Critnan Springs—spring WY-8
Crits Mtn—summit VA-3
Crittenden Bridge—bridge VA-3
Crittenberger Sch—school KY-4
Crittende Cem—cemetery OK-5
**Crittenden**—pop pl AR-4
**Crittenden**—pop pl KY-4
**Crittenden**—pop pl (2) NY-2
**Crittenden**—pop pl VA-3
Crittenden, Florena, House—building DC-2
Crittenden Bldg—hist pl AL-4
Crittenden Branch—stream TN-4
Crittenden Campground—locale MT-8
Crittenden (CCD)—cens area KY-4
Crittenden Cem—cemetery OK-5
**Crittenden (County)**—pop pl AR-4
**Crittenden (County)**—pop pl KY-4
Crittenden County Bank and Trust Company—hist pl AR-4
Crittenden County Courthouse—hist pl AR-4
Crittenden County HS—school KY-4
Crittenden Creek NV-8
Crittenden Creek—stream AK-9
Crittenden Creek—stream IN-6
Crittenden Creek—stream LA-4
Crittenden Creek—stream MT-8
Crittenden Creek—stream NV-8
Crittenden Drain—stream MI-6
Crittenden East (CCD)—cens area KY-4
Crittenden Farm—hist pl OH-6
Crittenden Fork Baptist Church TN-4
Crittenden Gulch—valley MT-8
Crittenden Hist Dist—hist pl MO-7
Crittenden Home—hospital NC-3
Crittenden Island—island MT-8
Crittenden Memorial Hosp—hospital AR-4
Crittenden Memorial Park—cemetery AR-4
Crittenden Peak—summit ID-8
Crittenden Ranch—locale NV-8
Crittenden Rsvr—reservoir NV-8
Crittenden Sch—school CA-9
Crittenden Sch—school NY-2
Crittenden (site)—locale AZ-5
Crittenden South (CCD)—cens area KY-4
Crittenden Spring—spring KY-4
Crittenden Springs—spring NV-8
Crittenden Spring Sch—school KY-4
**Crittenden (Township of)**—pop pl IL-6
Crittenden West (CCD)—cens area KY-4
Crittendon VA-3
Crittendon Cem—cemetery LA-4
Crittendon Gas Field—oilfield TX-5
Crittendon Hollow—valley TX-5
**Critten Ridge**—pop pl AR-4
Critter Branch—stream TN-4
Crittle Creek—stream GA-3
Critton Run—stream WV-2
**Critz**—pop pl VA-3
Critz, Jacob, House—hist pl TN-4
Critz, Thomas L., House—hist pl TN-4
Critzer—locale KS-7
Critzers Shop—locale VA-3
**Crivitz**—pop pl WI-6
Crix Ridge—ridge KY-4
Crizaba Mine—mine AZ-5
Croaker—locale VA-3
Croaker Hole—bay TX-5
Croaker Hole Cove—bay FL-3
Croaker Island—island GA-3
Croaker Landing—locale VA-3
Croaker Landing Archaeol Site (44JC70)—hist pl VA-3
Croakes—locale KY-4
Crooks Gulch—valley CA-9
Croasdaile Country Club—locale NC-3
Croatamung NC-3
**Croatan**—pop pl NC-3
Croatan Beach—locale VA-3
Croatan Lookout Tower—locale NC-3
Croatan Natl For—forest NC-3
Croatan Shores NC-3
**Croatan Shores**—pop pl NC-3
Croatan Sound—bay NC-3
Croatan (Township of)—fmr MCD NC-3
**Crocheron**—pop pl MD-2
Crocheron-McDowall House—hist pl TX-5
Crocheron Park—park NY-2
Crochet Canal—canal LA-4
Crochet Mountain NH-1
Crockard Junction—locale AL-4
Crock Cave—cave AL-4
Crocked Branch—stream VA-3
Crockelt Lake—lake MT-8
Crockenburg Pond—lake PA-2
Crocker NC-3
Crocker—locale AR-4
Crocker—locale NM-5
**Crocker**—pop pl IN-6
**Crocker**—pop pl IA-7
**Crocker**—pop pl MO-7
**Crocker**—pop pl SD-7
**Crocker**—pop pl WA-9
Crocker, Benomi and Barnabas, House—hist pl MA-1
Crocker, Capt. Alexander, House—hist pl MA-1
Crocker, E. B., Art Gallery—hist pl CA-9
Crocker, Ebenezer, Jr., House—hist pl MA-1
Crocker, F. W., and Company Steam Cracker Factory—hist pl CO-8
Crocker, Lot, House—hist pl MA-1
Crocker, Mount—summit CA-9
Crocker Amazon Playground—park CA-9
Crocker Branch TN-4
Crocker Branch—stream SC-3
Crocker Brook—stream (2) ME-1
Crocker Camp (historical)—locale ME-1
Crocker Canyon—valley CA-9
Crocker Cem—cemetery IA-7
Crocker Cem—cemetery KS-7
Crocker Cem—cemetery ME-1
Crocker Cem—cemetery MA-1
Crocker Cem—cemetery MO-7
Crocker Cem—cemetery TN-4
Crocker Cemeteries—cemetery NC-3
Crocker Center Sch—school IA-7
Crocker Ch—church AL-4
Crocker Creek FL-3
Crocker Creek—stream AK-9
Crocker Creek—stream (4) CA-9
Crocker Creek—stream ID-8
Crocker Creek—stream KS-7
Crocker Creek—stream MI-6
Crocker Creek—stream NY-2
Crocker Cut—canal CA-9
Crocker Dam—dam AL-4
Crocker Dam—dam CA-9
Crocker Ditch IA-7
Crocker Ditch—canal CO-8
Crocker Drift Mine (underground)—mine AL-4
Crocker Flat—flat CA-9
Crocker Guard Station—locale CA-9
Crocker Highlands Sch—school CA-9
Crocker Hill—summit AL-4
Crocker Hill—summit (2) ME-1
Crocker Hill—summit MA-1
Crocker Hollow—valley TN-4
Crocker Island—island NY-2
Crocker Junction—locale AL-4
Crocker Lake MN-6
Crocker Lake—lake CA-9
Crocker Lake—lake MI-6
Crocker Lake—lake WA-9
Crocker Lake—reservoir AL-4
Crocker Lake—reservoir UT-8
Crocker Marsh—swamp UT-8
Crocker Meadow—flat CA-9
Crocker Mtn—summit AL-4
Crocker Mtn—summit CA-9
Crocker Mtn—summit ME-1
Crocker Neck—cape MA-1
Crocker Park—park CA-9
Crocker Park—park MA-1
Crocker Place—locale CA-9
Crocker Point—cape ME-1
Crocker Point—cliff CA-9
Crocker Pond MA-1
Crocker Pond—lake (3) ME-1
Crocker Pond—lake (2) MA-1
Crocker Pond—reservoir (3) MA-1
Crocker Pond Dam—dam (3) MA-1
Crocker Post Office (historical)—building AL-4
Crocker Ranch—hist pl KS-7
Crocker Ranch—locale CO-8
Crocker Reef—bar FL-3
Crocker Reef Buoy 16—locale FL-3
Crocker Ridge—ridge CA-9
Crocker Sch—school (3) CA-9
Crocker Sch—school MA-1
Crocker Sch—school MI-6
Crocker Sch (abandoned)—school PA-2
Crockers Crossroads TN-4
Crockers Curve—bend CA-9
Crocker Site—hist pl ME-1
**Crockers Nub**—pop pl NC-3
Crockers Point—cliff WY-8
Crocker Spring—spring AZ-5
Crocker Spring—spring OR-9
Crocker Spring Branch—stream TN-4
Crocker Springs—spring MT-8
Crocker Springs Dam—dam TN-4
Crocker Springs Lake—reservoir TN-4
Crocker Spur—canal IA-7
Crocker State Public Shooting Area—park SD-7
Crocker Tavern—building MA-1
**Crockertown**—pop pl AL-4
**Crockertown**—pop pl ME-1
Crocker Township—fmr MCD IA-7
Crocker Turn—locale ME-1
Crockerville MA-1
Crockerville—locale MO-7
Crocker Woods Park—park IA-7
Crockery Chapel—church MI-6
Crockery Creek TX-5
Crockery Creek—stream MI-6
Crockery Creek—stream TX-5
Crockery Lake—lake MI-6
**Crockery (Township of)**—pop pl MI-6
Crocket TX-5
Crocket Branch—stream GA-3
Crocket Canyon—valley NM-5
Crocket Cem—cemetery MS-4
Crocket Cove—basin VA-3
Crocket Creek Church TN-4
Crocket Furnace (historical)—locale TN-4
Crocket Hill—summit ME-1
Crocket Lake—lake MN-6
Crocket Meadow—flat MA-1
Crockets Bayou—gut LA-4
Crocket Sch—school TX-5
Crockets Landing—locale TN-4
Crockets Landing (historical)—locale TN-4
Crockets Point Ch—church LA-4
Crocket Spring—spring NV-8
Crockett KY-4
Crockett—locale KY-4

Crockett—locale OR-9
Crockett—locale WV-2
Crockett—pop pl AR-4
Crockett—pop pl CA-9
Crockett—pop pl MS-4
Crockett—pop pl TN-4
Crockett—pop pl TX-5
Crockett—pop pl VA-3
Crockett, Andrew, House—hist pl TN-4
Crockett, David, Fire Hall and Pumper—hist pl LA-4
Crockett, John, House—hist pl NH-1
Crockett, John Edward, House—hist pl KY-4
Crockett, Judge Joseph, House—hist pl KY-4
Crockett, Lake—reservoir TX-5
Crockett, Samuel, House—hist pl TN-4
Crockett And Gambogy Labor Camp—locale CA-9
Crockett and Gambogy Ranch—locale CA-9
Crockett Bay—bay TN-4
Crockett Bluff AR-4
Crockett Branch—stream ME-1
Crockett Branch—stream (2) TN-4
Crockett Brook—stream (2) ME-1
Crockett Cabin—locale AZ-5
Crockett (CCD)—cens area TX-5
Crockett Cem—cemetery AR-4
Crockett Cem—cemetery GA-3
Crockett Cem—cemetery IL-6
Crockett Cem—cemetery (2) IN-6
Crockett Cem—cemetery LA-4
Crockett Cem—cemetery (2) MS-4
Crockett Cem—cemetery NH-1
Crockett Cem—cemetery NM-5
Crockett Cem—cemetery (10) TN-4
Crockett Cem—cemetery (2) VA-3
Crockett Cem—cemetery (2) WV-2
Crockett Ch—church KY-4
Crockett Ch—church MS-4
Crockett Chapel—church VA-3
Crockett Ch of Christ MS-4
Crockett Corner—pop pl ME-1
Crockett Corner—pop pl NH-1
Crockett County—pop pl TN-4
Crockett (County)—pop pl TX-5
Crockett County Courthouse—building TN-4
Crockett County Courthouse—hist pl TX-5
Crockett Cove—basin VA-3
Crockett Cove—bay (2) ME-1
Crockett Cove—valley VA-3
Crockett Creek—stream GA-3
Crockett Creek—stream MO-7
Crockett Creek—stream (5) TN-4
Crockett Creek—stream TX-5
Crockett Creek Ch (historical)—church TN-4
Crockett Creek Drainage Ditch—canal TN-4
Crockett Creek Sch (historical)—school TN-4
Crockett Ditch—canal MT-8
Crockett Drain—canal MI-6
Crockett Drain Branch—canal WY-8
Crockett Draw—valley (2) NM-5
Crockett Fork—stream WV-2
Crockett Gardens—area TX-5
Crockett General Hosp—hospital TN-4
Crockett Heights—pop pl TX-5
Crockett HS—school (2) TX-5
Crockett JHS—school TX-5
Crockett Junction—pop pl AL-4
Crockett Knob—summit OR-9
Crockett Knob—summit VA-3
Crockett Lake—lake AR-4
Crockett Lake—lake IN-6
Crockett Lake—lake WA-9
Crockett Lake Ranger Station—locale MT-8
Crockett Main Drain—canal WY-8
Crockett McKinney Cem—cemetery AL-4
Crockett Meadows—flat WY-8
Crockett Memorial AME Zion Ch—church AL-4
Crockett Mills—pop pl TN-4
Crockett Mills Post Office—building TN-4
Crockett Mountains—range SD-7
Crockett Mtn—summit ME-1
Crockett Oil Field—oilfield TX-5
Crockett Park—park SD-7
Crockett Peak—summit CA-9
Crockett Point—cape (3) ME-1
Crockett Pond—lake ME-1
Crockett Post Office (historical)—building MS-4
Crockett Post Office (historical)—building TN-4
Crockett Ranch—locale (2) NM-5
Crockett Ridge—ridge (2) ME-1
Crockett Ridge—ridge (2) TN-4
Crockett Ridge (subdivision)—pop pl TN-4
Crockett (RR name for Field)—other KY-4
Crockett Run—stream VA-3
Crocketts NH-1
Crocketts—pop pl NY-2
Crocketts Bluff—pop pl AR-4
Crocketts Brook—stream ME-1
Crocketts Cem—cemetery TN-4
Crockett Sch—school AZ-5
Crockett Sch—school CA-9
Crockett Sch—school (15) TX-5
Crocketts Chapel—church TN-4
Crockett Sch (historical)—school TN-4
Crocketts Corner—pop pl ME-1
Crocketts Crossing—pop pl NH-1
Crocketts Crossroad—pop pl SC-3
Crocketts Estates—pop pl IL-6
Crocketts Neck—cape ME-1
Crocketts Neck—pop pl ME-1
Crockett Spring—spring AZ-5
Crockett Spring—spring ID-8
Crockett Spring—spring NM-5
Crockett Spring—spring OR-9
Crockett Spring—spring TN-4
Crockett Spring—spring VA-3
Crockett Spring Branch—stream TN-4
Crockett Springs—pop pl VA-3
Crockett Springs Lake—reservoir TN-4
Crockett Springs Lake Dam—dam TN-4
Crockett Square—park TX-5
Crockettsville AL-4
Crockettsville—locale KY-4
Crockettsville Sch—school TN-4
Crockett Tank—reservoir AZ-5
Crockett Tank—reservoir NM-5
Crockett Town—locale VA-3
Crockett Town Creek VA-3
Crockett (Township of)—fmr MCD (2) AR-4
Crockett Well—well NM-5
Crocketville—pop pl SC-3
Crockson OH-6
Crocodile, Bayou—gut LA-4
Crocodile Bayou—stream LA-4
Crocodile Dragover—bar FL-3
Crocodile Lake—lake FL-3
Crocodile Lake—lake MN-6
Crocodile Lake Natl Wildlife Ref—park FL-3
Crocodile Mtn—summit UT-8
Crocodile Point—cape FL-3
Crocodile Point Trail—trail FL-3
Crocodile River—stream MN-6
Croco House—hist pl OH-6
Crocon du Nez—cliff MT-8
Cro Creek—stream ID-8
Crocus—locale KY-4
Crocus—locale ND-7
Crocus Creek—stream KY-4
Crocus (historical)—pop pl OR-9
Crocus Hollow—valley TN-4
Crocus Lake MN-6
Crocus Park—park MN-6
Crocus Township—pop pl ND-7
Crodson Creek—stream KY-4
Crodson Spring—spring KY-4
Crody Lake—lake MN-6
Croesus Canyon—valley TX-5
Croesus Gulch—valley ID-8
Croesus Mine—mine ID-8
Croesus Mine—mine NV-8
Croesus Pass—channel LA-4
Croesus Peak—summit ID-8
Croetan NC-3
Croff—locale ND-7
Croff Farm Brook—stream CT-1
Croff Farm Brook—stream RI-1
Croff Lake MT-8
Croff Sch—school ND-7
Croffs Lake—lake MT-8
Croff Wren Sch—school MT-8
Crofoot Lake—lake MI-6
Crofoot Point—summit ID-8
Crofoot Ranch—locale ID-8
Crofoot Sch—school MI-6
Croft—locale CA-9
Croft—locale IL-6
Croft—locale KS-7
Croft—locale PA-2
Croft—locale SC-3
Croft—pop pl NC-3
Croft—pop pl PA-2
Croft Cem TN-4
Croft Cem—cemetery KY-4
Croft Cem—cemetery TN-4
Croft Cem—cemetery VA-3
Croft Ch—church AR-4
Croft Chapel—church TN-4
Croft Dam—dam OR-9
Croft Ditch—canal IN-6
Crofte Township—pop pl ND-7
Croft Ferry—locale AL-4
Croft Forest Camp—locale OR-9
Croft Hollow—valley PA-2
Croft Lake—lake MI-6
Croft Lake—lake OR-9
Croft Lateral—canal AZ-5
Croft Mine—mine MN-6
Crofton—locale MI-6
Crofton—pop pl KY-4
Crofton—pop pl MD-2
Crofton—pop pl NE-7
Crofton Butte—summit WA-9
Crofton (CCD)—cens area KY-4
Crofton Cem—cemetery AR-4
Crofton Cem—cemetery NE-7
Crofton Creek—stream MI-6
Crofton Creek—stream WA-9
Crofton Lookout Tower—locale KY-4
Crofton Prairie—flat WA-9
Crofton Ridge—ridge WA-9
Crofton Rsvr—reservoir KY-4
Crofton Sch—school CO-8
Crofton Spring—spring CA-9
Crofton Swamp—swamp MI-6
Crofton United Ch—church NE-7
Croft Place (historical)—locale AL-4
Croft Pond—lake FL-3
Croft Ranch—locale WY-8
Croft Rsvr—reservoir OR-9
Crofts—pop pl KS-7
Croft Sch—school CT-1
Crofts Corners—pop pl NY-2
Crofts Ferry AL-4
Croft Tank—reservoir NM-5
Croftville—pop pl MN-6
Crogan Creek—stream CA-9
Crogan Hole—basin CA-9
Crogan Lake—lake MN-6
Crogen, Ole, Farm District—hist pl ND-7
Croghan—pop pl NY-2
Croghan—uninc pl SC-3
Croghan Rsvr—reservoir NY-2
Croghan Sch—school OH-6
Croghan (Town of)—pop pl NY-2
Crogman Sch—school GA-3
Croil Island—island NY-2
Croisan Creek—stream OR-9
Croisan Ridge—ridge OR-9
Croisant Airp—airport KS-7
Croissant Park Sch—school FL-3
Croix, Bayou—stream LA-4
Croke Canal—canal CO-8
Croke Lake—reservoir CO-8
Croke-Patterson-Campbell Mansion—hist pl CO-8
Croker IN-6
Croker—locale WA-9
Croker—pop pl AR-4
Croker Flat—flat WA-9
Croker Lake—lake WI-6
Croker Spur AR-4
Croke Rsvr—reservoir CO-8
Croke (Township of)—pop pl MN-6
Crokscrew Christian Acad—school FL-3
Croley—pop pl KY-4
Croley Bend—bend KY-4
Croley Cem—cemetery KY-4
Croley-Evans Site (15KX24)—hist pl KY-4
Croll Bldg—hist pl CA-9
Crolls Mills—locale PA-2
Cromack Draw—valley WY-8
Cromack Sch—school TX-5
Cromakill Creek NJ-2
Cromakill Creek—stream NJ-2
Croman Sch—school PA-2
Cromanton—locale FL-3
Cromartie Arm—bay FL-3
Cromartie Hill Ch—church NC-3
Cromartie Marsh—swamp NC-3
Cromartie Sch—school FL-3
Cromberg—pop pl CA-9
Cromberg Cem—cemetery CA-9
Cromberg Spring—spring CA-9
Crombie Street District—hist pl MA-1
Cromby—locale PA-2
Crome CA-9
Crome—pop pl CA-9
Cromeans Creek—stream TX-5
Cromecraft Lake—reservoir MS-4
Cromeenes Hollow—valley IL-6
Crom Elbow Creek NY-2
Crom Elbow Kill NY-2
Crome Park—park CO-8
Cromer, Mount—summit ME-1
Cromer Crossroads—locale SC-3
Cromer Lake MN-6
Cromers—locale GA-3
Cromers—pop pl OH-6
Cromer's Mill Covered Bridge—hist pl GA-3
Cromer Top—gap WV-2
Cromeset Ledge—bar MA-1
Cromeset Neck—cape MA-1
Cromeset Point—cape MA-1
Cromesett Ledge MA-1
Cromesett Point MA-1
Cromey Ditch—canal IN-6
Cromie Creek—stream MT-8
Cromie Sch—school MI-6
Cromir—locale CA-9
Crom Lake—reservoir CO-8
Cromley Bench—bench MT-8
Cromley Cem—cemetery IN-6
Cromley Cem—cemetery OH-6
Cromley Ditch—canal IN-6
Cromline Creek—stream NY-2
Crommelin Lake—reservoir AL-4
Crommelin Lake Dam—dam AL-4
Crommertown Sch (historical)—school MO-7
Crommet Creek—stream NH-1
Crommett Brook—stream ME-1
Cromo Creek MT-8
Cromona—pop pl KY-4
Crom Pond—lake NY-2
Crompond—pop pl NY-2
Crompton—pop pl RI-1
Crompton Ditch—canal WY-8
Crompton Free Library—hist pl RI-1
Crompton Hill—pop pl IN-6
Crompton Lake—reservoir SD-7
Crompton Loom Works—hist pl MA-1
Crompton Lower Dam—dam RI-1
Crompton Park—park (2) MA-1
Crompton Rsvr—reservoir WY-8
Crompton Spring—spring WY-8
Cromwell—locale AL-4
Cromwell—locale VA-3
Cromwell—locale WA-9
Cromwell—pop pl (2) CT-1
Cromwell—pop pl IN-6
Cromwell—pop pl IA-7
Cromwell—pop pl KY-4
Cromwell—pop pl MN-6
Cromwell—pop pl OK-5
Cromwell—uninc pl VA-3
Cromwell Baptist Ch—church TN-4
Cromwell Branch—stream TN-4
Cromwell Bridge—bridge MD-2
Cromwell Brook—stream ME-1
Cromwell Canal—canal NC-3
Cromwell Canyon—valley ID-8
Cromwell Cem TN-4
Cromwell Cem—cemetery TN-4
Cromwell Cem—cemetery WV-2
Cromwell Centre—locale IA-7
Cromwell Ch—church PA-2
Cromwell Ch—church TN-4
Cromwell Chapel (historical)—church TN-4
Cromwell Cove—bay ME-1
Cromwell Creek—stream (2) MT-8
Cromwell Crossroads—locale TN-4
Cromwell Crossroads Cem—cemetery TN-4
Cromwell Ditch—canal IN-6
Cromwell-Dixon Picnic Ground—locale MT-8
Cromwell Elem Sch—school IN-6
Cromwell Heights (subdivision)—pop pl NC-3
Cromwell Hill—summit IN-6
Cromwell (historical)—pop pl OR-9
Cromwell Island—island MT-8
Cromwell Lake—lake NY-2
Cromwell Lake—reservoir NJ-2
Cromwell Lake Dam—dam NJ-2
Cromwell Oil Field—oilfield OK-5
Cromwell Park—park OH-6
Cromwell Sch—school TN-4
Cromwells Run—stream VA-3
Cromwell State Wildlife Mngmt Area—park MN-6
Cromwell Station—locale AL-4
Cromwell Township—pop pl ND-7
Cromwell (Township of)—pop pl MN-6
Cromwell (Township of)—pop pl PA-2
Cromwood—pop pl MD-2
Cronan Gulch CA-9
Cronan Gulch—valley CA-9
Cronan Park—park OK-5
Cronanville—pop pl TN-4
Cronanville Cem—cemetery TN-4
Cronanville Cumberland Presbyterian Ch—church TN-4
Cronanville Post Office (historical)—building TN-4
Cronberg Pit Rsvr No 1—reservoir WY-8
Cronberg Pit Rsvr No 2—reservoir WY-8
Cronberg Spring—spring WY-8
Cronce Brook PA-2
Crondall Creek—stream NY-2
Cron Drain—canal MI-6
Crone Gulch—valley ID-8
Crone Gulch—valley NV-8
Crone Island—island AK-9
Crone Island—island MN-6
Crone Lake Dam—dam MS-4
Cronenwett, Georg, House—hist pl OH-6
Crone Ranch—locale WY-8
Cronese Mountains CA-9
Cronese Valley CA-9
Cronese Valley—locale CA-9
Crones Pond—reservoir TX-5
Croney Cem—cemetery TN-4
Croney Creek—stream CA-9
Croney Hollow—valley ID-8
Croney Hollow Spring—spring ID-8
Croney Ridge—ridge CA-9
Cronhardt—pop pl MD-2
Cronican Slough—gut MO-7
Cronice Brook PA-2
Cronie Creek MT-8
Cronin—locale TX-5
Cronin Brook—stream MA-1
Cronin Creek—stream (2) OR-9
Cronin Ditch—canal IN-6
Cronin Draw—valley WY-8
Cronin Gulch—valley CA-9
Cronin Hollow—valley IL-6
Cronin Hollow—valley OH-6
Cronin Island—island (2) AK-9
Cronin Lake—lake WI-6
Cronin Rsvr—reservoir OR-9
Cronin Slough—stream AK-9
Cronin Spring—spring OR-9
Cronin Well—well OR-9
Cronise Lake CA-9
Cronise Mountains—ridge CA-9
Cronise Valley—basin CA-9
Cronk Cem—cemetery MI-6
Cronk Cem—cemetery NY-2
Cronk Corners—locale NY-2
Cronk Drain—canal MI-6
Cronkhite Ranch House—hist pl OK-5
Cronks Canyon—valley ID-8
Cronley Wash—stream AZ-5
Cronninger Cem—cemetery IL-6
Cronomer Hill—summit NY-2
Cronomer Valley—pop pl NY-2
Cronquist Field—airport ND-7
Cronyn, William B., House—hist pl NY-2
Crony Pond Branch—stream DE-2
Crooed Esses, Th—area CT-1
Crook SD-7
Crook—locale MO-7
Crook—pop pl CO-8
Crook, Gen. George, House—hist pl NE-7
Crook, John, House—hist pl UT-8
Crook, Lake—reservoir TX-5
Crook All Bayou—stream LA-4
Crook Branch—stream IN-6
Crook Branch—stream KY-4
Crook Branch—stream VA-3
Crook Brook—stream (2) NY-2
Crook Brook—stream VT-1
Crook Canyon—valley UT-8
Crook Cem—cemetery GA-3
Crook Cem—cemetery TX-5
Crook Cem—cemetery VA-3
Crook Chene, Bayou—stream LA-4
Crook Chene Cove—lake LA-4
Crook City—locale SD-7
Crook County—pop pl OR-9
Crook County HS—school OR-9
Crook Creek CA-9
Crook Creek—stream OR-9
Crook Cut MI-6
Crook Dam—dam SD-7
Crooked MI-6
Crooked Anger Creek—stream NE-7
Crooked Arm—ridge TN-4
Crooked Arm Branch—stream TN-4
Crooked Arm Coulee—valley MT-8
Crooked Arm Ridge TN-4
Crooked Arm Ridge—ridge TN-4
Crooked Arroyo—stream CO-8
Crooked Auger Creek—stream KS-7
Crooked Bar—bar CA-9
Crooked Bay—swamp SC-3
Crooked Bay Branch—stream NC-3
Crooked Bayou LA-4
Crooked Bayou—gut AR-4
Crooked Bayou—gut (9) LA-4
Crooked Bayou—gut (2) MS-4
Crooked Bayou—stream AR-4
Crooked Bayou—stream (9) LA-4
Crooked Bayou—stream TX-5
Crooked Bayou Ch—church AR-4
Crooked Billet Elem Sch—school PA-2
Crooked Branch TX-5
Crooked Branch—gut TX-5
Crooked Branch—stream (3) AL-4
Crooked Branch—stream (3) AR-4
Crooked Branch—stream (4) GA-3
Crooked Branch—stream IN-6
Crooked Branch—stream (5) KY-4
Crooked Branch—stream (2) LA-4
Crooked Branch—stream MS-4
Crooked Branch—stream (3) MO-7
Crooked Branch—stream NE-7
Crooked Branch—stream NC-3
Crooked Branch—stream OK-5
Crooked Branch—stream SC-3
Crooked Branch—stream (4) TN-4
Crooked Branch—stream (5) TX-5
Crooked Branch—stream (7) VA-3
Crooked Branch Hunting Club—locale AL-4
Crooked Bridge Creek—stream OR-9
Crooked Bridge Hollow—valley PA-2
Crooked Brook—stream (4) CT-1
Crooked Brook—stream (2) ME-1
Crooked Brook—stream MI-6
Crooked Brook—stream MN-6
Crooked Brook—stream NH-1
Crooked Brook—stream (6) NY-2
Crooked Brook—stream RI-1
Crooked Brook Flowage—lake ME-1
Crooked Brook Lake—lake ME-1
Crooked Canyon—valley (2) CO-8
Crooked Canyon—valley (2) ID-8
Crooked Canyon—valley (2) NV-8
Crooked Canyon—valley (5) NM-5
Crooked Canyon—valley OR-9
Crooked Canyon—valley (6) UT-8
Crooked Canyon—valley (2) WY-8
Crooked Cave—cave PA-2
Crooked Coulee MT-8
Crooked Coulee—valley (3) MT-8
Crooked Creek AL-4
Crooked Creek AZ-5
Crooked Creek AR-4
Crooked Creek GA-3
Crooked Creek ID-8
Crooked Creek IL-6
Crooked Creek IN-6
Crooked Creek IA-7
Crooked Creek KS-7
Crooked Creek KY-4
Crooked Creek LA-4
Crooked Creek MI-6
Crooked Creek MN-6
Crooked Creek MS-4
Crooked Creek MO-7
Crooked Creek MT-8
Crooked Creek OH-6
Crooked Creek PA-2
Crooked Creek TN-4
Crooked Creek TX-5
Crooked Creek VA-3
Crooked Creek—gut FL-3
Crooked Creek—gut NJ-2
Crooked Creek—gut NY-2
Crooked Creek—locale AK-9
Crooked Creek—pop pl AK-9
Crooked Creek—pop pl (2) PA-2
Crooked Creek—pop pl TN-4
Crooked Creek—pop pl WV-2
Crooked Creek—stream (12) AL-4
Crooked Creek—stream (10) AK-9
Crooked Creek—stream AZ-5
Crooked Creek—stream (10) AR-4
Crooked Creek—stream (2) CA-9
Crooked Creek—stream (6) CO-8
Crooked Creek—stream DE-2
Crooked Creek—stream (7) FL-3
Crooked Creek—stream (24) GA-3
Crooked Creek—stream (15) ID-8
Crooked Creek—stream (16) IL-6
Crooked Creek—stream (17) IN-6
Crooked Creek—stream (9) IA-7
Crooked Creek—stream (11) KS-7
Crooked Creek—stream (12) KY-4
Crooked Creek—stream (5) LA-4
Crooked Creek—stream MD-2
Crooked Creek—stream (5) MI-6
Crooked Creek—stream (5) MN-6
Crooked Creek—stream (8) MS-4
Crooked Creek—stream (19) MO-7
Crooked Creek—stream (13) MT-8
Crooked Creek—stream (7) NE-7
Crooked Creek—stream (2) NV-8
Crooked Creek—stream NJ-2
Crooked Creek—stream (3) NM-5
Crooked Creek—stream (3) NY-2
Crooked Creek—stream (13) NC-3
Crooked Creek—stream (6) ND-7
Crooked Creek—stream (8) OH-6
Crooked Creek—stream (10) OK-5
Crooked Creek—stream (16) OR-9
Crooked Creek—stream (8) PA-2
Crooked Creek—stream (7) SC-3
Crooked Creek—stream (5) SD-7
Crooked Creek—stream (13) TN-4
Crooked Creek—stream (17) TX-5
Crooked Creek—stream (5) UT-8
Crooked Creek—stream (7) VA-3
Crooked Creek—stream (4) WA-9
Crooked Creek—stream (5) WV-2
Crooked Creek—stream (3) WI-6
Crooked Creek—stream (13) WY-8
Crooked Creek and Sheets Ditch IN-6
Crooked Creek and Sheets Main Creek IN-6
Crooked Creek ANV767—reserve AK-9
Crooked Creek Baptist Ch—church IN-6
Crooked Creek Baptist Church MS-4
Crooked Creek Bay—bay KY-4
Crooked Creek Boat Dock—locale TN-4
Crooked Creek Campground—locale MO-7
Crooked Creek Cem—cemetery (2) AL-4
Crooked Creek Cem—cemetery IN-6
Crooked Creek Cem—cemetery KS-7
Crooked Creek Cem—cemetery TN-4
Crooked Creek Ch—church (2) GA-3
Crooked Creek Ch—church IL-6
Crooked Creek Ch—church (2) IN-6
Crooked Creek Ch—church (2) KY-4
Crooked Creek Ch—church MS-4
Crooked Creek Ch—church MO-7
Crooked Creek Ch—church NC-3
Crooked Creek Ch—church (2) PA-2
Crooked Creek Ch—church (2) TN-4
Crooked Creek Ch—church VA-3
Crooked Creek Ch (historical)—church TN-4
Crooked Creek Dam—dam NC-3
Crooked Creek Dam—dam PA-2
Crooked Creek Ditch—canal AR-4
Crooked Creek Ditch—canal CO-8
Crooked Creek Ditch—canal NE-7
Crooked Creek Drain—canal MI-6
Crooked Creek Drainage—canal TN-4
Crooked Creek Drainage Ditch—canal NE-7
Crooked Creek Elem Sch—school IN-6
Crooked Creek Falls—falls WA-9
Crooked Creek Golf Course—locale NC-3
Crooked Creek Gut—gut MD-2
Crooked Creek Hill—summit WY-8
Crooked Creek (historical)—locale (2) AL-4
Crooked Creek (Holiday)—pop pl PA-2
Crooked Creek Hollow—valley TN-4
Crooked Creek Lake—lake TX-5
Crooked Creek Lake—reservoir IN-6
Crooked Creek Lake—reservoir NC-3
Crooked Creek Lake—reservoir PA-2
Crooked Creek Lake Dam—dam IN-6
Crooked Creek Lake Rec Area—park PA-2
Crooked Creek Marina—locale TN-4
Crooked Creek Meadows—flat OR-9
Crooked Creek Mine (surface)—mine AL-4
Crooked Creek No 1 Ditch—canal CO-8
Crooked Creek No. 25 Township—civ div SD-7
Crooked Creek Park—flat CO-8
Crooked Creek Pass—gap CO-8
Crooked Creek Point FL-3
Crooked Creek Post Office (historical)—building AL-4
Crooked Creek Ranch—locale NM-5
Crooked Creek Ranch—locale OR-9
Crooked Creek Ridge—ridge TN-4
Crooked Creek Rsvr—reservoir CO-8
Crooked Creek Sch—school KY-4
Crooked Creek Sch (historical)—school TN-4
Crooked Creek Siphon—other MT-8
Crooked Creek Spring—spring OR-9
Crooked Creek Spring Roadside Rest Area—park OR-9
Crooked Creek Spring Safety Rest Area OR-9
Crooked Creek Springs Roadside Rest Area OR-9
Crooked Creek State Forest—park MO-7
Crooked Creek State Park—park PA-2
Crooked Creek State Wayside—park OR-9
Crooked Creek (subdivision)—pop pl AL-4
Crooked Creek (subdivision)—pop pl NC-3
Crooked Creek Supply Ditch—canal CO-8
Crooked Creek Township—civil MO-7
Crooked Creek Township—civil SD-7
Crooked Creek Township—pop pl KS-7
Crooked Creek (Township of)—civ div (2) IL-6
Crooked Creek (Township of)—civ div MN-6
Crooked Creek (Township of)—fmr MCD (2) AR-4
Crooked Creek (Township of)—fmr MCD NC-3
Crooked Creek Trail Camp—locale NM-5
Crooked Creek Valley—valley OR-9
Crooked Creek Watershed Dam Number 16—dam AL-4
Crooked Creek Watershed Dam Number 2—dam AL-4
Crooked Creek Watershed Dam Number 3—dam AL-4
Crooked Creek Watershed Dam Number 5—dam AL-4
Crooked Creek Well—well NM-5
Crooked Creek Woods—woods IL-6
Crooked Dam—dam SD-7
Crooked Ditch DE-2
Crooked Ditch—canal CO-8
Crooked Ditch—canal VA-3
Crooked Dogwood Gap—gap GA-3
Crooked Drain—stream FL-3
Crooked Draw—valley TX-5
Crooked Draw—valley (2) WY-8
Crooked Elm Creek—stream SD-7
Crooked Falls—falls MT-8
Crooked Finger Sch—school OR-9
Crooked Finger Spring—spring AZ-5
Crooked Ford Post Office TN-4
Crookedford Post Office (historical)—building TN-4
Crooked Fork NC-3
Crooked Fork TN-4
Crooked Fork VA-3
Crooked Fork—stream ID-8
Crooked Fork—stream KY-4
Crooked Fork—stream NC-3
Crooked Fork—stream TN-4
Crooked Fork—stream VA-3
Crooked Fork—stream (6) WV-2
Crooked Fork Ch—church WV-2
Crooked Fork Creek ID-8
Crookedfork (historical)—pop pl TN-4
Crooked Gap—gap AL-4
Crooked Gulch—valley (2) CA-9
Crooked Gut—gut DE-2
Crooked Hollow—valley TN-4
Crooked Hollow—valley (2) TX-5
Crooked Hollow—valley UT-8
Crooked Hollow—valley WV-2
Crooked Intention—hist pl MD-2
Crooked Island—island (2) AK-9
Crooked Island—island FL-3
Crooked Island—island LA-4
Crooked Island—island ME-1
Crooked Island—island MI-6
Crooked Island—swamp FL-3
Crooked John Branch—stream LA-4
Crooked John Creek—stream MT-8
Crooked Knee Lake—lake WA-9
Crooked Lake MI-6
Crooked Lake MN-6
Crooked Lake NJ-2
Crooked Lake NY-2
Crooked Lake PA-2
Crooked Lake TX-5
Crooked Lake WA-9
Crooked Lake WI-6
Crooked Lake—lake (3) AK-9
Crooked Lake—lake AR-4
Crooked Lake—lake (4) FL-3
Crooked Lake—lake (2) GA-3
Crooked Lake—lake (2) IL-6
Crooked Lake—lake (2) IN-6
Crooked Lake—lake KY-4
Crooked Lake—lake (22) MI-6
Crooked Lake—lake (25) MN-6
Crooked Lake—lake (5) NY-2
Crooked Lake—lake (2) ND-7
Crooked Lake—lake SC-3
Crooked Lake—lake SD-7
Crooked Lake—lake TX-5
Crooked Lake—lake (14) WI-6
Crooked Lake—pop pl IL-6
Crooked Lake—pop pl IN-6
Crooked Lake—pop pl (2) MI-6
Crooked Lake—reservoir MI-6
Crooked Lake Bayou—stream AR-4
Crooked Lakebed—flat MN-6
Crooked Lake Ditch—canal MN-6
Crooked Lake Golf Club—other IN-6
Crooked Lake Number One MI-6
Crooked Lake Number 2 MI-6
Crooked Lake Oaks—pop pl IL-6
Crooked Lake Park—pop pl FL-3
Crooked Lakes MN-6
Crooked Lakes—lake CA-9
Crooked Lake Sch Number 1—school ND-7
Crooked Lake Sch Number 3—school ND-7
Crooked Lake Sch Number 4—school ND-7
Crooked Lake (Township of)—civ div MN-6
Crooked Lead—channel NY-2
Crookedleg Creek—stream IL-6
Crooked Leg Tank—reservoir AZ-5
Crooked Lookout (historical)—locale MO-7
Crooked Marsh—swamp TX-5

**Crossgate**—*pop pl* ... KY-4
**Crossgates**—*pop pl* ... DE-2
**Crossgates**—*pop pl* ... MS-4
Crossgates Baptist Ch—*church* ... MS-4
Crossgates Lake—*reservoir* ... MS-4
Crossgates Lake Dam—*dam* ... MS-4
Crossgates Park—*park* ... MS-4
Crossgates Plaza Shop Ctr—*locale* ... MS-4
**Crossgates (subdivision)**—*pop pl* ... NC-3
Crossgates United Methodist Ch—*church* ... MS-4
Crossgates Village Shop Ctr—*locale* ... MS-4
Crossgrain Valley—*basin* ... NV-8
Crossgrove—*locale* ... PA-2
Cross Gulch—*valley* ... CO-8
Cross Gut—*gut* ... VA-3
Cross H Cow Camp—*locale* ... WY-8
Cross H Creek—*stream* ... WY-8
**Cross Heights (subdivision)**—*pop pl* ... NC-3
**Cross Hill**—*pop pl* ... SC-3
Cross Hill—*summit* ... AZ-5
Cross Hill—*summit* ... ME-1
Cross Hill—*summit* ... NH-1
Cross Hill—*summit* ... NY-2
Cross Hill—*summit* ... OR-9
Cross Hill (CCD)—*cens area* ... SC-3
Cross Hill Sch—*school* ... NY-2
Cross (historical P.O.)—*locale* ... IA-7
*Cross Hollow* ... OR-9
Cross Hollow—*locale* ... AR-4
Cross Hollow—*valley* ... AR-4
Cross Hollow—*valley* ... MO-7
Cross Hollow—*valley* ... OH-6
Cross Hollow—*valley* ... OR-9
Cross Hollow—*valley* (3) ... TN-4
Cross Hollow—*valley* ... UT-8
Cross Hollow Hills—*summit* ... UT-8
Cross Hollows—*locale* ... OR-9
Cross Hollow School (historical)—*locale* ... MO-7
Crosshouse Hollow—*valley* ... TN-4
Cross H Ranch—*locale* ... TX-5
Cross HS—*school* ... CT-1
Cross HS—*school* ... SC-3
Crossinade Cem—*cemetery* ... LA-4
*Crossing* ... MS-4
*Crossing, The* ... ND-7
Crossing, The—*locale* ... CA-9
Crossing, The—*locale* ... ME-1
Crossing, The—*locale* ... NV-8
Crossing Cave—*cave* ... AL-4
Crossing Cove—*lake* ... LA-4
Crossing Hollow—*valley* ... MO-7
Crossing Knob—*summit* ... NC-3
Crossing Lake—*lake* ... ID-8
*Crossing of the Fathers, The* ... UT-8
Crossing Sch—*school* ... IL-6
Crossings Country Club, The—*locale* ... FL-3
Crossings Shop Ctr, The—*locale* ... FL-3
*Crossing Station* ... PA-2
**Crossingville**—*pop pl* ... PA-2
Crossing Way—*trail* ... OR-9
*Cross Island* ... MA-1
Cross Island—*island* (2) ... AK-9
Cross Island—*island* ... FL-3
Cross Island—*island* ... ME-1
Cross Island—*summit* ... MA-1
Cross Island Coast Guard Station—*locale* ... ME-1
Cross Island Head—*cliff* ... ME-1
*Cross Island Ledge* ... ME-1
Cross Island Ledge—*bar* ... ME-1
Cross Island Narrows—*channel* ... ME-1
Cross JHS—*school* ... AZ-5
Cross J Ranch—*locale* ... CO-8
Cross Junction—*locale* ... VA-3
Cross Junction (historical)—*locale* ... PA-2
Cross J Windmill—*locale* ... AZ-5
*Cross Katy* ... MA-1
*Cross Key* ... TN-4
Cross Key—*island* ... FL-3
Cross Key—*locale* ... AL-4
*Cross Key Canal* ... FL-3
Cross Key Cem—*cemetery* ... AL-4
Cross Key Cem—*cemetery* ... TN-4
Cross Key Ch—*church* (3) ... AL-4
Cross Key Chapel (historical)—*church* ... TN-4
Cross Key Ch (historical)—*church* ... AL-4
*Cross Keys* ... AL-4
*Crosskeys* ... NJ-2
*Cross Keys* ... PA-2
*Cross Keys* ... TN-4
Cross Keys—*airport* ... NJ-2
Cross Keys—*locale* ... AL-4
Cross Keys—*locale* ... DE-2
Cross Keys—*locale* ... LA-4
Crosskeys—*locale* ... LA-4
Cross Keys—*locale* ... PA-2
Cross Keys—*locale* ... TN-4
Cross Keys—*locale* ... VA-3
**Cross Keys**—*pop pl* ... GA-3
**Cross Keys**—*pop pl* ... MO-7
**Cross Keys**—*pop pl* ... NJ-2
**Cross Keys**—*pop pl* (3) ... PA-2
**Cross Keys**—*pop pl* ... SC-3
**Cross Keys**—*pop pl* ... VA-3
**Crosskeys**—*pop pl* ... VA-3
Cross Keys Battle Monmt—*park* ... VA-3
**Cross Keys (Beryl)**—*pop pl* ... PA-2
Cross Keys (CCD)—*cens area* ... SC-3
Cross Keys Cem—*cemetery* ... LA-4
Cross Key Sch (historical)—*school* ... AL-4
**Cross Keys (historical)**—*pop pl* ... OR-9
Cross Keys House—*hist pl* ... SC-3
Cross Keys Path—*trail* ... PA-2
Cross Keys P.O. (historical)—*locale* ... AL-4
Cross Keys Post Office (historical)—*building* ... TN-4
Cross Keys Run—*stream* ... PA-2
Cross Keys Tavern Kitchen and Quarters—*hist pl* ... KY-4
*Cross Key Waterway* ... FL-3
*Cross Kill Creek* ... PA-2
Crosskill Creek—*stream* ... PA-2
*Cross Kill Creek - in part* ... PA-2
**Crosskill Mills**—*pop pl* ... PA-2
Cross Lake—*lake* ... GA-3
Cross Lake—*lake* ... IL-6
Cross Lake—*lake* ... LA-4
Cross Lake—*lake* (2) ... ME-1
Cross Lake—*lake* (2) ... MI-6
Cross Lake—*lake* (2) ... MN-6
Cross Lake—*lake* ... NE-7
Cross Lake—*lake* ... NY-2
Cross Lake—*lake* ... SC-3
Cross Lake—*lake* ... WI-6
Cross Lake—*lake* (2) ... WY-8
**Cross Lake**—*pop pl* ... MN-6
**Crosslake**—*pop pl* ... MN-6
**Cross Lake**—*pop pl* ... WI-6
Cross Lake—*reservoir* ... LA-4
Cross Lake—*reservoir* (2) ... MN-6
Cross Lake—*reservoir* (2) ... TX-5
Cross Lake Cem—*cemetery* ... MN-6
Cross Lake Ch—*church* ... MN-6
Crosslake Post Office—*building* ... MN-6
Cross Lake Sch—*school* ... MN-6
Crossland—*locale* ... PA-2
**Crossland**—*pop pl* ... KY-4
**Crossland**—*pop pl* ... TN-4
Cross Land and Fruit Company Orchards and Ranch—*hist pl* ... CO-8
Crossland Ave Baptist Ch—*church* ... TN-4
Crossland Cem—*cemetery* ... KY-4
Crossland Creek—*stream* ... SC-3
Crossland Hill—*summit* ... OK-5
Crossland Hill—*summit* ... WA-9
Crossland (historical)—*locale* ... AL-4
Crossland HS—*school* ... MD-2
Cross Landing—*locale* ... NC-3
Cross Landing Ch—*church* ... NC-3
Cross Landing Strip—*airport* ... KS-7
Crosslands Mission—*church* ... NM-5
*Crosslanes* ... WV-2
Cross Lanes—*locale* ... AR-4
**Cross Lanes**—*pop pl* ... TN-4
**Cross Lanes**—*pop pl* ... WV-2
Cross Lane Sch—*school* ... IL-6
Cross Lane Sch (abandoned)—*school* ... MO-7
Cross Lane School (Abandoned)—*locale* ... MO-7
Crosslay Slough—*swamp* ... AR-4
Cross Ledge—*bar* ... NJ-2
Cross Ledge Range—*channel* ... NJ-2
*Crossleg Lake* ... MT-8
Crossley—*locale* ... FL-3
Crossley Hollow—*valley* ... ID-8
*Crossley Lake* ... MT-8
Crossley Reflector—*other* ... CA-9
*Crossley Ridge* ... MT-8
Crossley Sch—*school* ... TX-5
**Crossley Siding**—*pop pl* ... MD-2
Crossley 99 Ranch—*locale* ... NV-8
Crosslin Branch—*stream* ... TN-4
Crosslin Cem—*cemetery* ... TN-4
Crosslin Hollow—*valley* ... TN-4
Cross Lookout Tower—*locale* ... SC-3
Cross L Ranch—*locale* ... NM-5
Cross L Ranch—*locale* ... TX-5
Cross L Ranch—*locale* ... WY-8
Cross L Spring—*spring* ... CO-8
Crossman, Mount—*summit* ... CA-9
**Crossman Corner**—*pop pl* ... ME-1
Crossman Corners—*locale* ... NY-2
Crossman Coulee—*valley* ... MT-8
Crossman Creek—*stream* ... WI-6
Cross Manor—*hist pl* ... MD-2
Crossman Peak—*summit* ... AZ-5
Crossman Point—*cape* ... MN-6
Crossman Pond—*lake* ... MA-1
Crossman Ridge—*ridge* ... AK-9
Crossman Run—*stream* ... PA-2
Crossmans—*locale* ... NJ-2
Crossman Sch—*school* ... LA-4
*Crossman School* ... SD-7
*Crossmans Pond* ... MA-1
Crossmans Run—*stream* ... PA-2
Crossman Stream—*stream* ... ME-1
Crossman Well—*well* ... NM-5
Cross Memorial Ch—*church* ... NC-3
*Cross Mesa* ... WY-8
Cross Mill—*locale* ... PA-2
**Cross Mill**—*pop pl* ... NC-3
*Cross Mill Brook* ... RI-1
*Cross Mill Pond* ... RI-1
**Cross Mills**—*pop pl* ... RI-1
Cross Mills Pond—*lake* ... RI-1
Cross Mine—*mine* ... MT-8
*Cross Mountain* ... CO-8
Cross Mountain—*locale* ... CO-8
Cross Mountain Branch—*stream* ... GA-3
Cross Mountain Canyon—*valley* ... CO-8
*Cross Mountain Creek* ... GA-3
Cross Mountain Dam—*dam* ... AZ-5
Cross Mountain Hollow—*valley* ... NY-2
Cross Mountain Number 1 Mine (underground)—*mine* ... TN-4
Cross Mountain Prospect—*mine* ... TN-4
Cross Mountain Run—*stream* ... VA-3
Cross Mountains—*ridge* ... AR-4
Cross Mtn—*summit* ... AZ-5
Cross Mtn—*summit* (2) ... CA-9
Cross Mtn—*summit* (5) ... CO-8
Cross Mtn—*summit* (2) ... MT-8
Cross Mtn—*summit* (2) ... NM-5
Cross Mtn—*summit* (3) ... NY-2
Cross Mtn—*summit* (2) ... NC-3
Cross Mtn—*summit* ... OK-5
Cross Mtn—*summit* ... PA-2
Cross Mtn—*summit* (4) ... TN-4
Cross Mtn—*summit* (2) ... TX-5
Cross Mtn—*summit* ... VA-3
Cross Mtn—*summit* ... WV-2
*Crossmus Pond* ... MA-1
Crossno Cem—*cemetery* ... TN-4
Crossnoe Cem—*cemetery* ... TN-4
Crossnoe Lake—*reservoir* ... TN-4
Crossnoe Lake Dam—*dam* ... TN-4
Crossnoe Slough—*stream* ... TN-4
**Crossnore**—*pop pl* ... NC-3
Crossnore Creek—*stream* ... NC-3
Crossnore Elem Sch—*school* ... NC-3
Crossnore-Newland MS—*school* ... NC-3
Crossno Ridge—*ridge* ... TN-4
Cross O Canyon—*valley* ... NM-5
Cross of Calvary Ch—*church* ... SC-3
Cross of Christ Lutheran Ch—*church* ... TN-4
Cross of Christ Lutheran Ch—*church* ... UT-8
Cross of Christ Lutheran Church—*hist pl* ... MN-6
Cross of Glory Ch—*church* ... MN-6
Cross-O Mtn—*summit* ... NM-5
Crosson, Mount—*summit* ... AK-9
Crosson Cem—*cemetery* ... OH-6
Crosson Field—*airport* ... CO-8
**Crossons**—*pop pl* ... CO-8
Cross O Peak—*summit* ... NM-5
Cross O Spring—*spring* ... NM-5
Crossout Waste—*canal* ... CA-9
Crossover Canyon—*valley* ... NV-8
Crossover Island—*island* ... NY-2
Crossover Mtn—*summit* ... MT-8
*Cross-over Passage* ... VA-3
Crossover Trail—*trail* ... CO-8
Cross Over Trail—*trail* ... KY-4
Cross O Well—*well* ... NM-5
Cross Paths—*locale* ... TN-4
*Cross Plains* ... AL-4
Cross Plains—*locale* ... GA-3
**Cross Plains**—*pop pl* ... IN-6
**Cross Plains**—*pop pl* ... SC-3
**Cross Plains**—*pop pl* ... TN-4
**Cross Plains**—*pop pl* ... TX-5
**Cross Plains**—*pop pl* ... WI-6
Cross Plains (CCD)—*cens area* ... TN-4
Cross Plains (CCD)—*cens area* ... TX-5
Cross Plains Cem—*cemetery* ... KS-7
Cross Plains Cem—*cemetery* ... TN-4
Cross Plains Ch—*church* (2) ... GA-3
Cross Plains Division—*civil* ... TN-4
Cross Plains Oil Field—*oilfield* ... TX-5
*Crossplains Post Office* ... TN-4
Cross Plains Post Office—*building* ... TN-4
**Cross Plains (Town of)**—*pop pl* ... WI-6
**Cross Plains Township**—*pop pl* ... SD-7
Cross Plaza—*locale* ... TX-5
*Cross Point* ... AL-4
Cross Point—*cape* (3) ... AK-9
Cross Point—*cape* ... ME-1
**Crosspointe Condo**—*pop pl* ... UT-8
*Cross Pond* ... NY-2
Cross Pond—*lake* ... ME-1
Cross Pond—*lake* ... MA-1
Cross Pond—*lake* (2) ... NY-2
Cross Pond—*reservoir* ... MA-1
Cross Pond—*reservoir* ... NC-3
Cross Pond—*stream* ... TN-4
Cross Pond—*swamp* ... AR-4
Crosspond Bayou—*gut* ... AR-4
Cross Pond Dam—*dam* ... MA-1
Cross Pond Dam—*dam* ... NC-3
Crossport—*locale* ... ID-8
Cross Post Office (historical)—*building* ... AL-4
Cross P Ranch—*locale* ... AZ-5
Cross Prong—*stream* ... TN-4
Cross Pump Station—*other* ... PA-2
Cross Ranch—*locale* ... MT-8
Cross Ranch—*locale* ... NE-7
Cross Ranch—*locale* ... NV-8
Cross Ranch—*locale* ... ND-7
Cross Ranch—*locale* ... OR-9
Cross Ranch—*locale* ... TX-5
Cross Ranch—*locale* ... WY-8
Cross Ranch Archeol District—*hist pl* ... ND-7
Cross Ranch Ditch—*canal* ... MT-8
Cross Range, The—*summit* ... ME-1
*Cross Ridge* ... MS-4
*Cross Rip* ... MA-1
Cross Rip Channel (reduced usage)—*channel* ... MA-1
Cross Rip Shoal—*bar* ... MA-1
**Cross River**—*pop pl* ... NY-2
Cross River—*stream* ... ME-1
Cross River—*stream* (3) ... MN-6
Cross River—*stream* ... NY-2
Cross River Hall—*locale* ... MN-6
Cross River Lake—*lake* ... MN-6
Cross River Rsvr—*reservoir* ... NY-2
*Crossroad* ... AR-4
Crossroad—*locale* ... AL-4
Crossroad—*locale* (2) ... AR-4
Crossroad—*locale* ... KY-4
Cross Road—*locale* ... KY-4
Crossroad—*locale* ... MS-4
Cross Road—*locale* ... TX-5
**Crossroad**—*pop pl* ... AR-4
**Cross-road**—*pop pl* ... LA-4
**Crossroad**—*pop pl* ... MS-4
**Cross Road**—*pop pl* ... NC-3
Crossroad Baptist Ch—*church* ... FL-3
Crossroad Cem—*cemetery* ... AL-4
Crossroad Cem—*cemetery* (3) ... AR-4
Crossroad Cem—*cemetery* ... IL-6
Crossroad Cem—*cemetery* ... IN-6
Cross Road Cem—*cemetery* ... MS-4
Crossroad Cem—*cemetery* ... TX-5
*Cross Road Ch* ... AL-4
*Cross Road Ch* ... MS-4
Crossroad Ch—*church* (6) ... AL-4
Crossroad Ch—*church* ... AR-4
Cross Road Ch—*church* (2) ... AR-4
Crossroad Ch—*church* (2) ... AR-4
Crossroad Ch—*church* (3) ... GA-3
Cross Road Ch—*church* ... GA-3
Crossroad Ch—*church* ... GA-3
Crossroad Ch—*church* ... IN-6
Crossroad Ch—*church* (2) ... LA-4
Crossroad Ch—*church* (2) ... MS-4
Cross Road Ch—*church* ... MS-4
Crossroad Ch—*church* ... MS-4
Crossroad Ch—*church* (2) ... MO-7
Crossroad Ch—*church* ... PA-2
Crossroad Ch—*church* (3) ... SC-3
Crossroad Ch—*church* ... TN-4
Crossroad Ch—*church* ... TX-5
Cross Road Ch—*church* ... VA-3
Crossroad Ch—*church* (2) ... VA-3
Crossroad Chapel—*church* ... KY-4
*Crossroad CME Ch* ... MS-4
Crossroad Lake—*lake* ... ID-8
Crossroad Plaza—*locale* ... IN-6
Crossroad Plaza (Shop Ctr)—*locale* ... UT-8
Cross Road Rsvr—*reservoir* ... ID-8
*Crossroads* ... AL-4
*Crossroads* ... AR-4
*Cross Roads* ... DE-2
*Cross Roads* ... IN-6
*Crossroads* ... MS-4
*Cross Roads* ... MO-7
*Cross Roads* ... NC-3
*Cross Roads* ... PA-2
*Crossroads* ... TN-4
*Crossroads* ... TX-5
Crossroads—*locale* ... AL-4
Cross Roads—*locale* ... AR-4
Crossroads—*locale* ... AR-4
Cross Roads—*locale* ... AR-4
Crossroads—*locale* ... AR-4
Cross Roads—*locale* ... AR-4
Crossroads—*locale* ... AR-4
Cross Roads—*locale* (2) ... AR-4
Crossroads—*locale* ... AR-4
Cross Roads—*locale* ... AR-4
Crossroads—*locale* (2) ... GA-3
Cross Roads—*locale* (2) ... GA-3
Crossroads—*locale* ... GA-3
Crossroads—*locale* ... IL-6
Crossroads—*locale* ... MD-2
Crossroads—*locale* ... MS-4
Cross Roads—*locale* (2) ... MO-7
Crossroads—*locale* ... NV-8
Cross Roads—*locale* ... NY-2
Cross Roads—*locale* ... OK-5
Crossroads—*locale* ... OK-5
Crossroads—*locale* ... TN-4
Cross Roads—*locale* ... TN-4
Crossroads—*locale* (3) ... TN-4
Cross Roads—*locale* ... TN-4
Cross Roads—*locale* ... TX-5
Crossroads—*locale* ... TX-5
Cross Roads—*locale* ... TX-5
Crossroads—*locale* ... TX-5
Cross Roads—*locale* (2) ... TX-5
Crossroads—*locale* ... TX-5
Crossroads—*locale* (4) ... VA-3
**Cross Roads**—*pop pl* ... AL-4
**Crossroads**—*pop pl* ... AL-4
**Crossroads**—*pop pl* ... AR-4
**Cross Roads**—*pop pl* ... AR-4
**Crossroads**—*pop pl* ... AR-4
**Cross Roads**—*pop pl* ... AR-4
**Crossroads**—*pop pl* ... AR-4
**Cross Roads**—*pop pl* ... AR-4
**Crossroads**—*pop pl* ... AR-4
**Cross Roads**—*pop pl* ... CA-9
**Crossroads**—*pop pl* ... FL-3
**Crossroads**—*pop pl* (2) ... GA-3
**Crossroads**—*pop pl* ... IL-6
**Cross Roads**—*pop pl* (2) ... IN-6
**Cross Roads**—*pop pl* ... KY-4
**Cross Roads**—*pop pl* ... LA-4
**Crossroads**—*pop pl* (2) ... MS-4
**Cross Roads**—*pop pl* (2) ... MS-4
**Cross Roads**—*pop pl* ... MO-7
**Crossroads**—*pop pl* ... NJ-2
**Crossroads**—*pop pl* ... NM-5
**Crossroads**—*pop pl* ... OH-6
**Cross Roads**—*pop pl* ... PA-2
**Crossroads**—*pop pl* ... PA-2
**Cross Roads**—*pop pl* ... SC-3
**Crossroads**—*pop pl* (3) ... TN-4
**Cross Roads**—*pop pl* (4) ... TN-4
**Crossroads**—*pop pl* ... TN-4
**Cross Roads**—*pop pl* (2) ... TX-5
**Crossroads**—*pop pl* ... TX-5
**Cross Roads**—*pop pl* (2) ... TX-5
**Crossroads**—*pop pl* ... UT-8
**Cross Roads**—*pop pl* ... VA-3
**Crossroads**—*pop pl* ... VA-3
**Crossroads**—*pop pl* (2) ... WV-2
Crossroads—*post sta* ... WA-9
Crossroads—*uninc pl* ... FL-3
Crossroads—*uninc pl* ... MS-4
Crossroads, The—*locale* ... IL-6
Crossroads, The—*locale* ... TN-4
Crossroads, The—*locale* ... TX-5
Cross Roads, The—*locale* ... VA-3
Cross Roads Airp—*airport* ... NC-3
*Crossroads Assembly of God Church* ... AL-4
Crossroads Baptist Ch—*church* ... FL-3
Crossroads Baptist Ch—*church* ... TN-4
Cross Roads Baptist Ch—*church* ... TN-4
*Cross Roads Baptist Church* ... MS-4
Crossroads Bay—*swamp* ... GA-3
Cross Roads Borough—*civil* ... PA-2
Crossroads Branch—*stream* ... AL-4
Crossroads Branch—*stream* ... TN-4
*Cross Roads Cem* ... MS-4
Cross Roads Cem—*cemetery* ... AL-4
Crossroads Cem—*cemetery* (3) ... AL-4
Crossroads Cem—*cemetery* (2) ... AR-4
Cross Roads Cem—*cemetery* ... AR-4
Crossroads Cem—*cemetery* ... FL-3
Crossroads Cem—*cemetery* ... IL-6
Crossroads Cem—*cemetery* ... IA-7
Cross Roads Cem—*cemetery* ... MS-4
Crossroads Cem—*cemetery* ... MS-4
Cross Roads Cem—*cemetery* (2) ... MS-4
Crossroads Cem—*cemetery* ... MS-4
Cross Roads Cem—*cemetery* ... MS-4
Cross Roads Cem—*cemetery* ... NC-3
Crossroads Cem—*cemetery* (2) ... OH-6
Crossroads Cem—*cemetery* ... OK-5
Crossroads Cem—*cemetery* (2) ... PA-2
Crossroads Cem—*cemetery* ... SC-3
Crossroads Cem—*cemetery* (6) ... TN-4
Crossroads Cem—*cemetery* (2) ... TX-5
*Cross Roads Ch* ... AL-4
*Cross Roads Ch* ... MS-4
*Cross Roads Ch* ... PA-2
*Crossroads Ch* ... TN-4
Crossroads Ch—*church* ... AL-4
Cross Roads Ch—*church* ... AL-4
Crossroads Ch—*church* ... AL-4
Cross Roads Ch—*church* ... AL-4
Crossroads Ch—*church* (5) ... AL-4
Cross Roads Ch—*church* ... AR-4
Crossroads Ch—*church* (9) ... AR-4
Cross Roads Ch—*church* ... AR-4
Crossroads Ch—*church* ... AR-4
Cross Roads Ch—*church* ... AR-4
Crossroads Ch—*church* ... FL-3
Cross Roads Ch—*church* ... GA-3
Crossroads Ch—*church* (3) ... GA-3
Cross Roads Ch—*church* (2) ... GA-3
Crossroads Ch—*church* ... GA-3
Cross Roads Ch—*church* ... GA-3
Crossroads Ch—*church* ... GA-3
Cross Roads Ch—*church* ... IL-6
Cross Roads Ch—*church* ... IN-6
Crossroads Ch—*church* (3) ... IN-6
Crossroads Ch—*church* ... KY-4
Crossroads Ch—*church* (5) ... LA-4
Cross Roads Ch—*church* ... LA-4
Crossroads Ch—*church* ... MN-6
Cross Roads Ch—*church* ... MS-4
Crossroads Ch—*church* (4) ... MS-4
Cross Roads Ch—*church* (2) ... MS-4
Crossroads Ch—*church* (3) ... MS-4
Cross Roads Ch—*church* (2) ... MS-4
Crossroads Ch—*church* (7) ... MS-4
Crossroads Ch—*church* (11) ... MO-7
Cross Roads Ch—*church* ... NC-3
Crossroads Ch—*church* (2) ... NC-3
Cross Roads Ch—*church* ... NC-3
Crossroads Ch—*church* ... NC-3
Cross Roads Ch—*church* ... NC-3
Crossroads Ch—*church* ... NC-3
Crossroads Ch—*church* ... OH-6
Crossroads Ch—*church* (2) ... OK-5
Crossroads Ch—*church* (3) ... PA-2
Cross Roads Ch—*church* ... PA-2
Crossroads Ch—*church* (4) ... SC-3
Cross Roads Ch—*church* (2) ... SC-3
Crossroads Ch—*church* (4) ... SC-3
Cross Roads Ch—*church* ... TN-4
Crossroads Ch—*church* (8) ... TN-4
Crossroads Ch—*church* (2) ... TX-5
Cross Roads Ch—*church* ... TX-5
Crossroads Ch—*church* (5) ... TX-5
Cross Roads Ch—*church* ... TX-5
Crossroads Ch—*church* ... VA-3
Cross Roads Ch—*church* ... VA-3
Crossroads Ch—*church* ... WV-2
Crossroads Ch—*church* ... WI-6
Crossroad Sch—*school* (2) ... AL-4
Cross Road Sch—*school* ... AR-4
Cross Road Sch—*school* ... FL-3
Crossroad Sch—*school* ... PA-2
Crossroad Sch—*school* ... SC-3
Crossroad Sch (abandoned)—*school* ... MO-7
Crossroad Sch (abandoned)—*school* ... PA-2
Crossroads Chapel—*church* ... TN-4
Crossroads Ch (historical)—*church* (2) ... AL-4
Cross Roads Ch (historical)—*church* ... AL-4
Crossroads Ch (historical)—*church* ... MS-4
Crossroads Ch (historical)—*church* (2) ... TN-4
Crossroad Sch (historical)—*school* ... AL-4
Cross Road Sch (historical)—*school* ... MS-4
Cross Road Sch (historical)—*school* ... TN-4
*Crossroads Ch of Christ* ... AL-4
Crossroads Ch of Christ—*church* ... FL-3
*Cross Roads Christian Church* ... MS-4
Cross Roads Church—*hist pl* ... MD-2
Crossroads Community Centery—*locale* ... TX-5
Crossroads Elem Sch—*school* ... TN-4
**Cross Roads Estates**—*pop pl* ... NY-2
*Crossroads Free Pentecostal Ch* ... MS-4
Crossroads Freewill Baptist Ch—*church* ... TN-4
Cross Roads Grange—*locale* ... PA-2
Crossroads Grave Site—*hist pl* ... NE-7
Crossroads (historical)—*locale* ... AL-4
Cross Roads (historical)—*locale* ... MS-4
**Crossroads (historical)**—*pop pl* ... IN-6
**Cross Roads (historical)**—*pop pl* ... MS-4
Crossroads Independent Baptist Ch—*church* ... IN-6
Crossroads Mall (Shop Ctr)—*locale* ... IA-7
Crossroads Mall Shop Ctr—*locale* ... VA-3
Crossroads Memoria Ch—*church* ... GA-3
*Cross Roads Methodist Ch* ... MS-4
Cross Roads Methodist Ch—*church* ... MS-4
*Cross Roads Methodist Church* ... AL-4
*Crossroads Missionary Baptist Ch* ... MS-4
Cross Roads Missionary Ch—*church* ... NC-3
Crossroads Mtn—*summit* ... SC-3
**Cross Roads (New Hope)**—*pop pl* ... TX-5
Crossroads Number 2 Ch—*church* ... SC-3
Crossroads of America Industrial Park—*locale* ... AL-4
Crossroads of Life Ch—*church* ... FL-3
Cross Roads of Life Ch—*church* ... NC-3
Crossroads of the World—*hist pl* ... CA-9
Crossroads Oil Field—*other* ... NM-5
**Cross Roads (Poco)**—*pop pl* ... VA-3
Crossroads Post Office—*building* ... MS-4
Cross Roads Post Office (historical)—*building* ... TN-4
Cross Roads Presbyterian Church and Cemetery and Stainback Store—*hist pl* ... NC-3
Crossroads Rsvr—*reservoir* ... ID-8
Crossroads Rsvr—*reservoir* ... OR-9
*Crossroads Sch* ... PA-2
Crossroads Sch—*school* (2) ... AL-4
Cross Roads Sch—*school* ... AL-4
Cross Roads Sch—*school* ... AR-4
Crossroads Sch—*school* (2) ... AR-4
Crossroads Sch—*school* ... FL-3
Crossroads Sch—*school* ... GA-3
Crossroads Sch—*school* (5) ... IL-6
Cross Roads Sch—*school* ... IL-6
Cross Roads Sch—*school* ... MO-7
Crossroads Sch—*school* ... MO-7
Cross Roads Sch—*school* ... NE-7
Crossroads Sch—*school* ... PA-2
Cross Roads Sch—*school* ... PA-2
Crossroads Sch—*school* (2) ... PA-2
Crossroads Sch—*school* ... SC-3
Cross Roads Sch—*school* ... TX-5
Crossroads Sch—*school* ... TX-5
Crossroads Sch—*school* ... VA-3
Cross Roads Sch—*school* ... VA-3
Crossroads Sch—*school* ... WV-2
Crossroads Sch (abandoned)—*school* ... MO-7
Cross Roads Sch (abandoned)—*school* ... MO-7
Crossroads Sch (abandoned)—*school* ... MO-7
Crossroads Sch (abandoned)—*school* (3) ... PA-2
Crossroads Sch (historical)—*school* (9) ... AL-4
Cross Roads Sch (historical)—*school* ... MS-4
Crossroads Sch (historical)—*school* (2) ... MS-4
Cross Roads Sch (historical)—*school* (3) ... MS-4
Crossroads Sch (historical)—*school* (2) ... MO-7
Crossroads Sch (historical)—*school* (6) ... PA-2
Cross Roads Sch (historical)—*school* (2) ... TN-4
Crossroads Sch (historical)—*school* ... TN-4
Cross Roads Sch (historical)—*school* ... TN-4
Crossroads Sch (historical)—*school* ... TN-4
Cross Roads Sch (historical)—*school* (5) ... TN-4
Cross Roads Sch (historical)—*school* ... TX-5
*Cross Roads School* ... MS-4
*Crossroads School* ... TN-4
Crossroads School (abandoned)—*church* ... PA-2
Crossroads School(Abandoned)—*locale* ... IA-7
Crossroads School (Abandoned)—*locale* ... MO-7
Crossroads School (Abandoned)—*locale* ... TX-5
Crossroads (Shop Ctr)—*locale* ... FL-3
Crossroads Shop Ctr—*locale* (2) ... FL-3
Cross Roads Shop Ctr—*locale* ... MA-1
Crossroads Shop Ctr—*locale* (2) ... MO-7
Cross Roads Shop Ctr—*locale* ... NC-3
Cross Roads Shopping Plaza—*locale* ... MA-1
Crossroads Spring—*spring* ... ID-8
Crossroads Store—*locale* ... MO-7
Crossroads Store—*locale* ... VA-3
Crossroads Tavern—*hist pl* ... VA-3
Crossroad Store—*locale* ... TX-5
Cross Roads (Township of)—*fmr MCD* (2) ... NC-3
Crossroads Union Ch—*church* ... KY-4
Crossroads Union Chapel—*church* ... VA-3
*Cross Roads United Methodist Church* ... TN-4
Crossroads West—*locale* (2) ... MO-7
**Cross Roads (Wilkins)**—*pop pl* ... AR-4
Crossroad Tank—*reservoir* ... AZ-5
*Crossroad Temple* ... IN-6
Crossroad Temple—*church* ... IN-6
**Crossroad Temple**—*pop pl* ... IN-6
Cross Road Trail—*trail* ... MD-2
Crossroad Well—*well* ... ID-8
Cross Rock—*bar* ... NC-3
Crossrock Ch—*church* ... NC-3
*Cross Rock Rapids* ... ME-1
Cross Rock Rapid Sluice—*hist pl* ... NC-3
Cross Rock Sch—*school* ... ME-1
Cross Rsvr *reservoir* ... OR-9
Cross Run—*stream* (2) ... PA-2
Cross Run—*stream* ... WV-2
Cross Sch—*hist pl* ... IN-6
Cross Sch—*school* (2) ... CT-1
Cross Sch—*school* ... IL-6
Cross Sch—*school* (2) ... MI-6
Cross Sch—*school* ... NE-7
Cross Sch—*school* ... NY-2
Cross Sch—*school* ... SC-3
Cross Sch—*school* ... WV-2
Cross Sch—*school* ... WI-6
Cross Sch (abandoned)—*school* ... MO-7
Cross Sch (historical)—*school* ... MO-7
Cross Sch (historical)—*school* ... TN-4
Cross S Creek—*stream* ... MT-8
*Cross Shoal* ... NC-3
Cross Shoal Beacon (C)—*tower* ... NC-3
Cross Shoal Channel—*channel* ... NC-3
Cross Slough—*canal* ... KY-4
Cross Slough—*gut* ... AK-9
Cross Slough—*gut* ... CA-9
Cross Slough—*gut* ... KY-4
Cross Slough—*gut* ... TX-5
Cross Slough—*gut* ... WI-6
Cross Slough—*stream* ... AR-4
Cross Slough—*stream* ... GA-3
Cross Sound—*bay* ... AK-9
Cross Spring—*spring* ... CA-9
Cross Spring—*spring* ... KY-4
Cross Spring—*spring* ... TN-4
Cross S Sch—*school* ... MT-8
*Cross State Canal* ... FL-3
*Cross-State Waterway* ... FL-3
*Cross Station* ... PA-2
Cross Street Bog Rsvr—*reservoir* ... MA-1
Cross Street Number 2 Dam—*dam* ... MA-1
Cross Street Sch—*school* ... CT-1
Cross Street Sch—*school* ... NY-2
**Cross Subdivision**—*pop pl* ... UT-8
Cross Swamp—*stream* ... GA-3
Cross Swamp—*stream* ... NC-3
Cross Swamp—*stream* ... SC-3
Cross Swamp—*swamp* (2) ... GA-3
Cross Swamp—*swamp* ... NC-3
Cross Swamp—*swamp* ... SC-3
Cross Swamp—*swamp* ... VA-3
Cross Swamp Ch—*church* ... SC-3
Cross Swamp Sch—*school* ... SC-3
Cross Tank—*reservoir* (2) ... AZ-5
Cross Tank—*reservoir* ... NM-5
Cross Tide Creek—*channel* ... GA-3
Crosstie Lake—*swamp* ... SC-3
Crosstie Slough—*gut* ... AR-4
*Cross Timber Creek* ... TX-5
Crosstimber Creek—*stream* ... TX-5
Cross Timber Creek—*stream* ... TX-5
**Cross Timbers**—*pop pl* ... MO-7
**Cross Timbers**—*pop pl* ... TN-4
Crosstimbers Ch—*church* ... TX-5
Cross Timbers Natl Grassland Field HQ—*locale* ... TX-5
Cross Timbers Public Use Area—*park* ... MO-7
Cross Timbers Township—*civil* ... MO-7
**Crosston**—*pop pl* ... AL-4
*Crosstown* ... MS-4
*Crosstown* ... TN-4
Crosstown—*locale* ... WV-2
**Crosstown**—*pop pl* ... MO-7
**Crosstown**—*pop pl* ... OH-6
**Crosstown**—*pop pl* ... TN-4
Crosstown—*uninc pl* ... TN-4
**Cross (Town of)**—*pop pl* ... WI-6
Crosstown Sch—*school* ... MO-7
Crosstown Sch (historical)—*school* ... TN-4
Cross Township—*civil* ... SD-7
Cross (Township of)—*fmr MCD* ... AR-4
Cross Tracks Tank—*reservoir* ... TX-5
Cross Track Well—*well* ... NM-5
Cross Trail—*trail* (2) ... PA-2
Cross Trail Cem—*cemetery* ... AR-4
Cross Trail Center (Shop Ctr)—*locale* ... FL-3
Crosstrail Lake—*lake* ... AK-9
*Cross Trails* ... AL-4
Cross Trails—*locale* ... GA-3
Cross Trails—*locale* ... ID-8
Crosstrails Wayside Park—*park* ... NE-7
Cross Triangle Ranch—*locale* (2) ... AZ-5
Cross Union Ch—*church* ... IN-6
Crossuntic Stream—*stream* ... ME-1
Cross U Ranch—*locale* ... AZ-5
Cross Valley—*valley* ... TN-4
Crossview Baptist Ch—*church* ... MS-4
**Cross Village**—*pop pl* ... MI-6
**Cross Village**—*pop pl* ... PA-2
Cross Village (Township of)—*civ div* ... MI-6
*Crossville* ... WI-6
**Crossville**—*pop pl* (2) ... AL-4
**Crossville**—*pop pl* ... IL-6
**Crossville**—*pop pl* ... TN-4
Crossville Branch—*stream* ... MO-7
Crossville (CCD)—*cens area* ... AL-4

Crossville (CCD)—cens area ... TN-4
Crossville-Creston Sch—school ... TN-4
Crossville Division—civil ... AL-4
Crossville Division—civil ... TN-4
Crossville Elem Sch—school ... TN-4
**Crossville Estates**—pop pl ... TN-4
Crossville (historical)—locale ... NC-3
Crossville (historical P.O.)—locale ... AL-4
Crossville HS—school ... AL-4
Crossville Lake—lake ... MI-6
Crossville Memorial Airp—airport ... TN-4
Crossville Mtn—summit ... TX-5
Crossville Municipal Airp ... TN-4
Crossville North (CCD)—cens area ... TN-4
Crossville North Division—civil ... TN-4
Crossville Post Office—building ... TN-4
Crossville Sch (abandoned)—school ... MO-7
Crossville Seventh Day Adventist Ch—church ... TN-4
Cross Vine, Bayou—stream ... LA-4
Cross V Ranch—locale ... NM-5
Cross Water Island ... PA-2
Crossway ... NC-3
Crossway—bar ... AK-9
Cross Way—locale ... MO-7
**Crossway**—pop pl ... NC-3
Crossway Baptist Ch—church ... FL-3
Crossway Branch—stream ... AL-4
Crossway Branch—stream ... FL-3
Crossway Branch—stream ... GA-3
Cross Way Creek—gut ... NC-3
Crossway Creek—stream ... AL-4
Crossway Creek—stream ... NJ-2
Crossway Field—park ... NY-2
Cross Way Island—island ... NC-3
Cross Way Lake—lake ... FL-3
Crossway Mission Ch—church ... GA-3
Crossway Mtn—summit ... NY-2
Crossways Lake—lake ... MN-6
Crossway Slough—gut ... LA-4
Crossway Slough—stream ... LA-4
**Crosswell**—pop pl ... SC-3
Crosswell Ch—church ... SC-3
Crosswell Ford—locale ... TN-4
Crosswell Ford Bridge—bridge ... TN-4
Crosswell Home—building ... SC-3
Crosswell Sch—school (2) ... SC-3
Crosswhite Butte—summit ... OR-9
Crosswhite Canyon—valley ... OR-9
Crosswhite Cem—cemetery (2) ... TN-4
Crosswhite Creek—stream ... OR-9
Crosswhite Sch (historical)—school ... MO-7
Crosswick—locale ... OH-6
Crosswicks—hist pl ... NJ-2
Crosswicks—locale ... PA-2
**Crosswicks**—pop pl ... NJ-2
Crosswicks Creek—stream ... NJ-2
**Cross William MHP (subdivision)**—pop pl ... NC-3
Crosswind Airfield—airport ... KS-7
Crosswind Lake (Charley Lake)—lake ... AK-9
Cross Windmill—locale ... TX-5
**Crosswinds**—pop pl ... VA-3
Cross Winds Airp—airport ... WA-9
Crosswinds Shop Ctr—locale ... FL-3
Crosswise Islands—area ... AK-9
Cross X Ranch—locale ... AZ-5
Cross Y Ranch Airstrip—airport ... AZ-5
Cross Y Tank—reservoir ... AZ-5
Crostick Millpond—reservoir ... VA-3
Croston Sch—school ... WV-2
**Croswell**—pop pl ... MI-6
**Croswell**—pop pl ... OH-6
Croswell, Gov. Charles, House—hist pl ... MI-6
Croswell-Lexington HS—school ... MI-6
Croswell Sch—school ... MI-6
Croswells Pond ... MA-1
Crotch, The—cape ... ME-1
Crotch Camp Brook—stream ... ME-1
Crotched Lake—lake ... MI-6
Crotched Meadow—flat ... ME-1
Crotched Mtn—summit ... NH-1
Crotched Pond ... ME-1
Crotched Pond—lake ... NY-2
Crotched Pond Island—island ... NY-2
Crotched Pond Mtn—summit ... NY-2
Crotchet Mtn ... NH-1
Crotch Hill—summit ... ME-1
Crotch Island ... ME-1
Crotch Island—island (3) ... ME-1
Crotch Island Ledge ... ME-1
Crotch Island Ledges—bar ... ME-1
Crotch Islands—island ... ME-1
Crotch Lake ... MI-6
Crotch Lake—lake ... MI-6
**Crotch Lake**—pop pl ... MI-6
Crotchline Saddle—gap ... OR-9
Crotch Run—stream ... PA-2
Crote Mac Lake—reservoir ... MO-7
Crothers—locale ... PA-2
Crothers Ditch—canal ... IN-6
Crothers Hill—summit ... NH-1
Crothers Sch—school ... MI-6
Crothers Sch—school ... PA-2
**Crothersville**—pop pl ... IN-6
Crothersville Cem—cemetery ... IN-6
Croton—locale ... TX-5
Croton—locale ... WY-8
**Croton**—pop pl ... IA-7
**Croton**—pop pl ... MI-6
**Croton**—pop pl ... NJ-2
**Croton**—pop pl ... NY-2
Crotona Park—park ... NY-2
Croton Aqueduct Gate House—hist pl ... NY-2
Croton Bay—bay ... NY-2
Croton Bench—bench ... UT-8
Croton Breaks—summit ... TX-5
Croton Camp—locale ... TX-5
Croton Canyon—valley ... UT-8
Croton Cem—cemetery ... MI-6
Croton (corporate name Hartford) ... OH-6
Croton Creek ... UT-8
Croton Creek—stream ... OK-5
Croton Creek—stream ... TX-5
Croton Dam—dam ... MI-6
Croton Dam Pond—reservoir ... MI-6
Croton Elem Sch ... PA-2
Croton Elem Sch—school ... FL-3
**Croton Falls**—pop pl ... NY-2
Croton Falls Rsvr—reservoir ... NY-2

Croton-harmon (RR name for Croton-on-Hudson)—other ... NY-2
**Croton Heights**—pop pl ... MI-6
**Croton Heights**—pop pl ... NY-2
Croton Hydroelectric Plant—hist pl ... MI-6
Croton Lookout Tower—locale ... MI-6
**Croton North**—pop pl ... NY-2
Croton North RR Station—hist pl ... NY-2
**Croton-On-Hudson**—pop pl ... NY-2
**Croton-on-Hudson (Croton-Harmon)**—pop pl ... NY-2
Croton Peak—summit ... TX-5
Croton Pens—locale ... TX-5
Croton Point—cape ... NY-2
Croton Point Park—park ... NY-2
Croton Pond ... MI-6
Croton Post Office (historical)—building ... TN-4
Croton Ridge—ridge ... ME-1
Croton River—stream ... NY-2
Croton Sch—school ... NY-2
Croton Sch—school ... PA-2
Crotons Mine—mine ... UT-8
Croton Spring—spring ... TX-5
Croton Springs—spring ... AZ-5
**Croton (Township of)**—pop pl ... MI-6
Croton Union Cem—cemetery ... NY-2
**Crotonville**—pop pl ... NY-2
Croton Windmill—locale (2) ... TX-5
Crotte Creek—stream ... WI-6
Crott Lake—lake ... WI-6
**Crotts**—pop pl ... MS-4
Crottstown ... MS-4
Crottstown Post Office (historical)—building ... MS-4
Crotty ... IL-6
Crotty—other ... IL-6
Crotty Brook ... WI-6
Crouce Drain—canal ... MI-6
Crouch—locale ... VA-3
**Crouch**—pop pl ... ID-8
**Crouch**—pop pl ... SC-3
Crouch Branch—stream ... TN-4
Crouch Cem—cemetery ... GA-3
Crouch Cem—cemetery ... IL-6
Crouch Cem—cemetery ... IN-6
Crouch Cem—cemetery (3) ... KY-4
Crouch Cem—cemetery ... TN-4
Crouch Cem—cemetery ... WV-2
Crouch Chapel—church ... MD-2
Crouch Creek ... OR-9
Crouch Creek—stream ... AZ-5
Crouch Creek—stream ... VA-3
Crouch Creek—stream ... WA-9
Crouch Creek—stream ... WY-8
**Crouch Crossroad**—pop pl ... TN-4
Crouch Ditch—canal ... IN-6
Crouch Elem Sch—school ... IN-6
Crouches Creek—stream ... MS-4
Crouches Creek—stream ... TN-4
Crouches Creek Cem—cemetery ... TN-4
Crouches Station—locale ... PA-2
Crouche Valley ... WI-6
Crouch Hollow—valley ... AR-4
Crouch Hollow—valley ... IN-6
Crouch Hollow—valley ... WV-2
Crouching Lion—summit ... HI-9
Crouch Knob—summit ... WV-2
Crouch Lake—lake ... LA-4
Crouch Lateral—canal ... CA-9
Crouch Mesa—reservoir ... AZ-5
Crouch Mesa—summit ... AZ-5
Crouch-Perkins House—hist pl ... TX-5
Crouch Pond ... MA-1
Crouch Pond Dam—dam ... AL-4
Crouch Ranch—locale ... CA-9
Crouch Ranch—locale ... SD-7
Crouch Ranch—locale ... WY-8
Crouch Ravine—valley ... CA-9
Crouch Ridge Trail—trail ... WV-2
Crouch Run—stream ... WV-2
Crouch Sch—school ... IL-6
Crouch Sch—school ... VA-3
Crouch Spring—spring ... CO-8
**Crouch Subdivision**—pop pl ... UT-8
**Crouch (Township of)**—pop pl ... IL-6
Crouch Valley—valley ... CA-9
Crouch Valley—valley ... WI-6
Croudip Lake—lake ... MS-4
Crough Ditch—canal ... CA-9
Crouix, Bayou—gut ... LA-4
Crouix, Bayou—stream ... LA-4
Croul-Palms House—hist pl ... MI-6
Croupon Bayou—stream ... LA-4
**Crouse**—pop pl ... NC-3
Crouse, Elbert, Farmstead—hist pl ... NC-3
Crouse, Frederick, House—hist pl ... NY-2
Crouse, Jacob, Inn—hist pl ... NY-2
Crouse, John and Henry, Farm Complex—hist pl ... NY-2
Crouse Airp—airport ... PA-2
Crouse Canyon—valley ... UT-8
Crouse Cem—cemetery ... IN-6
Crouse Cem—cemetery ... MS-4
Crouse Cem—cemetery ... OH-6
Crouse Cem—cemetery ... TN-4
Crouse Cem—cemetery ... VA-3
Crouse Chapel—church ... OH-6
Crouse College, Syracuse Univ—hist pl ... NY-2
Crouse Company Airp—airport ... PA-2
Crouse Creek—stream ... UT-8
Crouse Dam—dam ... UT-8
Crouse Elem Sch—school ... IN-6
Crouse House—hist pl ... FL-3
Crouse Lake—reservoir ... IN-6
Crouse Lake Dam—dam ... IN-6
Crouse Mill—locale ... MD-2
Crouse Mtn—summit ... NC-3
Crouse Ranch—locale ... NE-7
Crouser Sch (abandoned)—school ... PA-2
Crouse Rsvr—reservoir ... UT-8
Crouse Run ... PA-2
Crouse Run—stream ... PA-2
Crouses Store—locale ... NY-2
**Crouseville**—pop pl ... ME-1
Crouseville Cem—cemetery ... ME-1
Crout Creek—stream ... MS-4
Crout Ditch No 1—canal ... WY-8
Crout Ditch No 2—canal ... WY-8
Crout Pond—reservoir ... SC-3
Croutslot Hollow—valley ... PA-2

Crow—island ... PA-2
Crow—locale (2) ... TX-5
**Crow**—pop pl ... MS-4
**Crow**—pop pl ... OR-9
**Crow**—pop pl ... WV-2
Crow, Lake—reservoir ... AL-4
Crow, William, House—hist pl ... KY-4
**Crow Agency**—pop pl ... MT-8
Crow Agency Cem—cemetery ... MT-8
Crowan Cottage—hist pl ... AL-4
Crow Arm—bay ... AK-9
**Crow (Baker)**—pop pl ... TN-4
Crow Bar—bar ... AL-4
Crow Bar—cape ... VA-3
Crow-Barbee House—hist pl ... KY-4
Crowbar Canyon—valley ... CA-9
Crowbar Creek—stream ... CO-8
Crowbar Dam—dam ... MT-8
Crowbar Point—cape ... NY-2
Crowbar Point—cliff ... AZ-5
Crowbar Ranch—locale ... HI-9
Crowbar Ranch—locale ... TX-5
Crowbar Spring—spring ... NV-8
Crowbar Springs—spring ... OR-9
Crow Bay—bay ... VA-3
Crow Bay—swamp ... SC-3
Crow Bayou—stream ... LA-4
Crowberry Creek—stream ... MD-2
Crowbill Point—cape ... AK-9
Crow Bottom—bend ... CO-8
Crow Branch—stream ... AL-4
Crow Branch—stream ... GA-3
Crow Branch—stream ... IL-6
Crow Branch—stream ... MD-2
Crow Branch—stream ... MO-7
Crow Branch—stream (2) ... NC-3
Crow Branch—stream ... TN-4
Crow Branch—stream (2) ... TX-5
Crow Branch—stream ... WI-6
Crow Bridge—bridge ... AL-4
Crow Bridge—bridge ... IN-6
Crow Brook—stream ... ME-1
Crow Brook—stream ... MA-1
Crowburg—locale ... SC-3
Crow Butte ... MT-8
Crow Butte—summit ... NE-7
Crow Butte—summit ... WA-9
Crow Butte Cem—cemetery ... NE-7
Crow Buttes—range ... SD-7
Crow Cabin—locale ... CO-8
Crowcamp Creek—stream ... OR-9
Crowcamp Mtn—summit ... OR-9
Crowcamp Rsvr—reservoir ... OR-9
Crow Canyon—valley (2) ... AZ-5
Crow Canyon—valley (3) ... CA-9
Crow Canyon—valley ... CO-8
Crow Canyon—valley (3) ... NV-8
Crow Canyon—valley (8) ... NM-5
Crow Canyon—valley ... TX-5
Crow Canyon—valley ... UT-8
Crow Canyon—valley (2) ... WA-9
Crow Canyon Archeol District—hist pl ... NM-5
Crow Canyon Site (LA 20219)—hist pl ... NM-5
Crow Cem—cemetery (5) ... AL-4
Crow Cem—cemetery ... AR-4
Crow Cem—cemetery ... GA-3
Crow Cem—cemetery ... IN-6
Crow Cem—cemetery (2) ... KY-4
Crow Cem—cemetery (3) ... LA-4
Crow Cem—cemetery (2) ... OH-6
Crow Cem—cemetery ... OK-5
Crow Cem—cemetery (2) ... TN-4
Crow Cem—cemetery (4) ... TX-5
Crow Ch—church (2) ... MO-7
Crow Church (abandoned)—locale ... MO-7
Crow Coulee—valley (3) ... MT-8
Crow Coulee Bar—island ... MT-8
Crow Cove—bay ... ME-1
Crow Creek ... ID-8
Crow Creek ... OR-9
Crow Creek ... PA-2
Crow Creek ... SD-7
Crow Creek ... TN-4
Crow Creek ... WV-2
Crow Creek—gut ... MI-6
**Crow Creek**—pop pl ... AR-4
Crow Creek—stream (2) ... AL-4
Crow Creek—stream (2) ... AK-9
Crow Creek—stream (3) ... AR-4
Crow Creek—stream (4) ... CA-9
Crow Creek—stream (2) ... CO-8
Crow Creek—stream ... GA-3
Crow Creek—stream (5) ... ID-8
Crow Creek—stream (2) ... IL-6
Crow Creek—stream (5) ... IA-7
Crow Creek—stream (3) ... KS-7
Crow Creek—stream (2) ... KY-4
Crow Creek—stream ... MI-6
Crow Creek—stream (3) ... MN-6
Crow Creek—stream (2) ... MS-4
Crow Creek—stream ... MO-7
Crow Creek—stream (10) ... MT-8
Crow Creek—stream ... NE-7
Crow Creek—stream ... NV-8
Crow Creek—stream (2) ... NJ-2
Crow Creek—stream (2) ... NM-5
Crow Creek—stream ... NY-2
Crow Creek—stream (2) ... NC-3
Crow Creek—stream ... OH-6
Crow Creek—stream (3) ... OK-5
Crow Creek—stream (6) ... OR-9
Crow Creek—stream ... SC-3
Crow Creek—stream (7) ... SD-7
Crow Creek—stream ... TN-4
Crow Creek—stream (5) ... TX-5
Crow Creek—stream (2) ... UT-8
Crow Creek—stream (3) ... WA-9
Crow Creek—stream (9) ... WY-8
Crow Creek—unorg reg (3) ... SD-7
Crow Creek Basin—basin (2) ... WY-8
Crow Creek Canyon—valley ... WY-8
Crow Creek Cave—cave ... AL-4
Crow Creek Cem—cemetery ... SD-7
Crow Creek Ch—church ... SC-3
Crow Creek Ch—church ... SD-7
Crow Creek Church ... AL-4
Crow Creek Consolidated Gold Mining Company—hist pl ... AK-9
Crow Creek Dam—dam ... OR-9
Crow Creek Dam—dam ... SD-7

Crow Creek Ditch—canal ... SD-7
Crow Creek Drainage Ditch—canal ... SD-7
Crow Creek Falls—falls ... MT-8
**Crow Creek Ind Res**—pop pl ... SD-7
Crow Creek Island—island ... AL-4
Crow Creek Lake—lake ... WA-9
Crow Creek Lakes—lake ... MT-8
Crow Creek Lakes—lake ... WY-8
Crow Creek Pass ... MT-8
Crow Creek Pass—gap ... WY-8
Crow Creek Rsvr—reservoir ... OR-9
Crow Creek Sch—school ... MT-8
Crow Creek Site—hist pl ... SD-7
Crow Creek Spring—spring ... NV-8
Crow Creek Trail—trail (2) ... MT-8
Crow Creek Valley—valley ... TN-4
Crow Creek Wildlife Mngmt Area—park ... AL-4
Crowcroft Pond—lake ... NH-1
Crowdabout Creek—stream ... AL-4
Crowd Canyon—valley ... UT-8
Crowded Fish Slough—gut ... AK-9
Crowden Cemetery ... PA-2
**Crowder**—pop pl ... MD-2
**Crowder**—pop pl ... MS-4
**Crowder**—pop pl ... MO-7
**Crowder**—pop pl ... OK-5
Crowder, Mount—summit ... WA-9
Crowder, William Leonard, Home Place—hist pl ... GA-3
Crowder Bluff—cliff ... NC-3
Crowder Bluff—cliff ... TN-4
Crowder Branch—stream ... AL-4
Crowder Branch—stream (3) ... TN-4
Crowder Branch Trail—trail ... TN-4
Crowder Canyon—valley ... CA-9
Crowder Canyon Archeol District—hist pl ... CA-9
Crowder Cem—cemetery ... AR-4
Crowder Cem—cemetery ... FL-3
Crowder Cem—cemetery ... MS-4
Crowder Cem—cemetery ... MO-7
Crowder Cem—cemetery ... NC-3
Crowder Cem—cemetery (4) ... TN-4
Crowder Ch—church ... AR-4
Crowder Ch—church ... FL-3
Crowder Ch—church ... VA-3
Crowder Coll—school ... MO-7
Crowder Creek ... OK-5
Crowder Creek ... TN-4
Crowder Creek ... VA-3
Crowder Creek—stream (2) ... MS-4
Crowder Creek—stream ... OK-5
Crowder Dam—dam ... AZ-5
Crowder Elem Sch—school ... MS-4
Crowder Flat Ranger Station—locale ... CA-9
Crowder Holes—lake ... FL-3
Crowder Hollow—valley ... MO-7
Crowder Hollow—valley ... VA-3
Crowder HS—school ... MS-4
Crowder Lake ... LA-4
Crowder Lake—reservoir ... MO-7
Crowder Lake—reservoir ... OK-5
Crowder Lick—summit ... GA-3
Crowder Mountain Rsvr—reservoir ... CA-9
Crowder Mountain Spring—spring ... CA-9
Crowder Mountain (Township of)—fmr MCD ... NC-3
Crowder Mtn—summit ... CA-9
Crowder Mtn—summit ... KY-4
Crowder Mtn—summit ... OK-5
Crowder Point East Rec Area—park ... OK-5
Crowder Point West Rec Area—park ... OK-5
Crowder Prairie Sch—school ... OK-5
Crowder Ranch—locale ... CA-9
Crowder Rsvr—reservoir ... OK-5
Crowder Run—stream ... NJ-2
**Crowders**—pop pl ... NC-3
Crowders Branch—stream ... VA-3
Crowder Sch—school ... FL-3
Crowder Sch—school ... NE-7
Crowders Creek ... NC-3
Crowders Creek—stream ... NC-3
Crowders Creek—stream ... SC-3
Crowders Creek Ch—church ... NC-3
Crowders Crossing—locale ... GA-3
Crowders Ferry ... TN-4
**Crowders (historical)**—pop pl ... NC-3
Crowder Shoals (historical)—bar ... AL-4
Crowders Lake—lake ... LA-4
Crowder Slough—stream ... AL-4
Crowders Mountain—other ... NC-3
Crowders Mountain State Park—park ... NC-3
Crowders Mtn ... NC-3
Crowders Mtn—summit ... NC-3
Crowder Springs Sch—school ... OK-5
Crowder State Park—park ... MO-7
Crowder State Park Vehicle Bridge—hist pl ... MO-7
Crowder Tank—reservoir ... AZ-5
Crowder Tank—reservoir ... NM-5
Crowder Tank—reservoir ... TX-5
Crowdertown—locale ... VA-3
Crowder Well—well ... AZ-5
Crowding Pens Well—well ... NM-5
Crow Drive Creek—stream ... KY-4
Crowduck Island—island ... MN-6
Crowe ... KS-7
Crow Eagle Creek—stream ... SD-7
**Croweburg**—pop pl ... KS-7
Crowe Cem—cemetery ... KY-4
Crowe Cem—cemetery ... LA-4
Crowe Drain—canal ... MI-6
Crowe Falls—falls ... IN-6
Crowe-Garritt House—hist pl ... IN-6
Crowe Hill Rsvr—reservoir ... AR-4
Crowe Hollow—valley (3) ... KY-4
Crowe Hollow—valley ... OH-6
Crowe Hollow Ch—church ... OH-6
Crowe Lake—reservoir ... GA-3
**Crowell**—pop pl ... NE-7
**Crowell**—pop pl ... TX-5
Crowell, C. C., Jr., House—hist pl ... NE-7
Crowell, J. B., and Son Brick Mould Mill Complex—hist pl ... NY-2
Crowell, Lake—lake ... FL-3
Crowell-Bourne Farm—hist pl ... MA-1
Crowell Branch—stream ... AL-4
Crowell Branch—stream (2) ... TN-4
Crowell (CCD)—cens area ... TX-5
Crowell Cem—cemetery ... AL-4
Crowell Cem—cemetery ... AR-4

Crowell Cem—cemetery (3) ... KY-4
Crowell Cem—cemetery ... ME-1
Crowell Cem—cemetery ... MA-1
Crowell Cem—cemetery (3) ... TN-4
Crowell Cem—cemetery ... TX-5
Crowell Ch ... TN-4
Crowell Ch—church ... AR-4
Crowell Ch—church ... NC-3
Crowell Chapel—church ... TN-4
Crowell Chapel Cem—cemetery ... TN-4
Crowell Chapel Methodist Ch (historical)—church ... TN-4
Crowell Creek—stream ... AR-4
Crowell Creek—stream ... MT-8
Crowell Gap—gap ... VA-3
Crowell Hill—summit ... KY-4
Crowell Hollow—valley ... PA-2
Crowell Hollow—valley (4) ... TN-4
Crowell Hollow Trail—trail ... PA-2
Crowell House—hist pl ... NY-2
Crowell House—hist pl ... NC-3
Crowell Lake—lake ... WI-6
Crowell Landing—locale ... KY-4
Crowell Mine—mine ... NV-8
Crowell Mtn—summit ... AR-4
Crowell Mtn—summit ... MT-8
Crowell Mtn—summit ... WA-9
Crowell Pinnacle—summit ... AR-4
Crowell Point—cape ... AK-9
Crowell Pond—lake ... ME-1
Crowell Pond—lake ... MA-1
Crowell Post Office (historical)—building ... TN-4
Crowell Ridge—ridge ... WA-9
Crowell Rock—bar ... ME-1
**Crowells**—pop pl ... NC-3
Crowells Ch—church ... GA-3
Crowells Ch—church ... NC-3
Crowell Sch—school ... CA-9
Crowell Sch—school ... IL-6
Crowell Sch—school ... LA-4
Crowell Sch—school ... MA-1
Crowell Sch—school ... SD-7
Crowell Sch—school ... TN-4
Crowells Corner—locale ... VA-3
**Crowells Crossroads**—pop pl ... NC-3
Crowells Pond ... MA-1
Crowell Spring—spring ... MT-8
Crowell Swamp—swamp ... MI-6
Crowell Water Supply—other ... TX-5
Crowe Neck ... ME-1
Crowers Canyon—valley ... ID-8
Crowe Rsvrs ... OR-9
Crowes—dam ... AL-4
Crowes Crossing Public Use Area—park ... MO-7
Crowe Shell Midden (15McL109)—hist pl ... KY-4
Crowes Neck ... ME-1
Crowes Point ... MA-1
Crowes Pond—reservoir ... AL-4
Crowe Tank—reservoir ... AZ-5
Crowfeet Mtn—summit ... MT-8
Crowfield Hist Dist—hist pl ... RI-1
Crow-Fish-High Indian Agency (historical)—locale ... ND-7
Crow Flat—flat ... CA-9
Crow Flat—flat ... OR-9
Crow Flat Lake—lake ... NM-5
Crow Flats—flat (2) ... NM-5
Crow Flats—flat (2) ... TX-5
Crow Flies High Butte Historic Site—park ... ND-7
Crow Fly High Hill—summit ... ND-7
Crowfoot—locale ... NJ-2
**Crow Foot**—pop pl ... NJ-2
**Crowfoot**—pop pl ... OR-9
Crowfoot Bog—swamp ... ME-1
Crowfoot Branch—stream ... TN-4
Crowfoot Brook—stream ... MA-1
Crowfoot Brook—stream ... NY-2
Crowfoot Cem—cemetery ... OH-6
Crowfoot Creek—stream ... CO-8
Crowfoot Creek—stream ... OR-9
**Crowfoot (historical)**—pop pl ... OR-9
Crowfoot Lake—lake ... AR-4
Crowfoot Lake—lake ... MI-6
Crowfoot Lake—lake ... WA-9
Crowfoot Point—cape ... CA-9
Crowfoot Rapids—rapids ... ME-1
Crowfoot Ridge—ridge ... WY-8
Crowfoot Rsvr—reservoir ... MT-8
Crowfoots Brook—stream ... MA-1
Crowfoot Sch—school ... ND-7
Crow Foot Springs—spring ... OR-9
**Crowfoot Township**—pop pl ... ND-7
Crow Gap—gap ... AL-4
Crow Gap—gap (2) ... GA-3
Crowgeys—locale ... VA-3
Crow Glacier—glacier ... AK-9
Crow Gulch—valley (2) ... CA-9
Crow Gulch—valley ... CO-8
Crow Hanging ... AZ-5
Crow Harbor Island—island ... GA-3
Crow Harbor Reach—channel ... GA-3
Crow Head—cliff ... NY-2
Crow Head Creek ... SD-7
Crowheart—locale ... WY-8
Crowheart Butte—summit ... WY-8
Crow Hill ... DE-2
Crow Hill ... MA-1
Crow Hill ... ND-7
Crow Hill—summit ... CA-9
Crow Hill—summit (2) ... CO-8
Crow Hill—summit (4) ... CT-1
Crow Hill—summit ... IL-6
Crow Hill—summit (3) ... ME-1
Crow Hill—summit ... MA-1
Crow Hill—summit ... MO-7
Crow Hill—summit (5) ... NY-2
Crow Hill—summit ... ND-7
Crow Hill—summit ... VT-1
Crow Hill—summit ... WA-9
Crow Hill Brook—stream ... CT-1
Crow Hill Brook—stream (2) ... MA-1
Crow Hill Cem—cemetery ... AR-4
Crow Hills—summit ... MA-1
Crow Hill Sch—school ... NY-2
Crow Hill Sch—school ... WI-6
Crow Hills Pond—reservoir ... MA-1
Crow (historical)—locale ... KS-7
**Crow (historical)**—pop pl ... MS-4
Crow Hollow ... OH-6
Crow Hollow—valley (2) ... KY-4
Crow Hollow—valley ... MO-7

Crow Hollow—valley ... OH-6
Crow Hollow—valley (2) ... TN-4
Crow Hollow—valley ... TX-5
Crow Hollow—valley (2) ... VA-3
Crow Hollow—valley ... WI-6
Crow Hollow Brook—stream ... CT-1
Crow Hollow Creek—stream ... OK-5
Crow Hop—gut ... GA-3
Crow House—hist pl ... AR-4
**Crow Ind Res**—pop pl ... MT-8
Crow Inlet ... NC-3
Crow Island ... ME-1
Crow Island ... OR-9
Crow Island—cape ... MA-1
Crow Island—island (3) ... AK-9
Crow Island—island ... AR-4
Crow Island—island ... CT-1
Crow Island—island ... GA-3
Crow Island—island (2) ... ID-8
Crow Island—island ... LA-4
Crow Island—island (17) ... ME-1
Crow Island—island ... MA-1
Crow Island—island (2) ... MI-6
Crow Island—island ... NY-2
Crow Island—island ... NC-3
Crow Island—island ... SC-3
Crow Island—locale ... MI-6
Crow Island (historical)—island ... PA-2
Crow Island Lead—channel ... NY-2
Crow Island Ledge—bar ... ME-1
Crow Island Ledges—bar ... ME-1
Crow Island Park—park ... IL-6
Crow Island Rock—rock ... MA-1
Crow Islands—island ... ME-1
Crow Island Sch—school ... IL-6
Crow Island State Game Area—park ... MI-6
Crow Key—island ... FL-3
Crow Knoll—summit ... UT-8
Crowl ... PA-2
Crow Lake ... WI-6
Crow Lake—lake ... AK-9
Crow Lake—lake ... AR-4
Crow Lake—lake ... ID-8
Crow Lake—lake (2) ... MI-6
Crow Lake—lake (2) ... MN-6
Crow Lake—lake ... MT-8
Crow Lake—lake (2) ... NM-5
Crow Lake—lake (3) ... ND-7
Crow Lake—lake (2) ... WA-9
Crow Lake—lake ... WI-6
Crow Lake—locale ... SD-7
Crow Lake Ch—church ... MN-6
Crow Lake Ch—church ... SD-7
**Crow Lake Township**—pop pl ... SD-7
**Crow Lake (Township of)**—pop pl ... MN-6
Crow Lake Trail—trail ... WA-9
Crowl Branch—stream ... TN-4
Crowle Rapids—rapids ... WI-6
Crowley ... IN-6
Crowley—locale ... CA-9
Crowley—locale (2) ... OR-9
**Crowley**—pop pl ... CO-8
**Crowley**—pop pl ... LA-4
**Crowley**—pop pl ... TX-5
Crowley—uninc pl ... CA-9
Crowley, Lake—reservoir ... CA-9
Crowley Airstrip—airport ... OR-9
Crowley Bight—bay ... AK-9
Crowley Branch—stream ... KY-4
Crowley Branch—stream ... ME-1
Crowley Brook ... CT-1
Crowley Brook—stream ... CT-1
Crowley Canyon—valley ... CA-9
Crowley Cem—cemetery ... GA-3
Crowley Cem—cemetery (3) ... MO-7
Crowley Cem—cemetery ... TX-5
Crowley Cheese Factory—hist pl ... VT-1
Crowley Corner—locale ... CT-1
Crowley Creek—stream ... AK-9
Crowley Creek—stream ... MO-7
Crowley Creek—stream ... NV-8
Crowley Creek—stream (3) ... OR-9
Crowley Dam—dam ... OR-9
Crowley Dam—dam ... WI-6
Crowley Ditch—canal ... LA-4
Crowley Ditch—canal ... MT-8
Crowley Drain Canal—canal ... CO-8
Crowley Guard Station—locale ... OR-9
Crowley Hill—summit ... MO-7
Crowley Hist Dist—hist pl ... LA-4
Crowley Hollow—valley ... PA-2
Crowley House—hist pl ... AZ-5
Crowley House—hist pl ... MA-1
Crowley Island—island ... ME-1
Crowley Island—island ... TN-4
**Crowley Lake**—pop pl ... CA-9
Crowley Lateral—canal ... CO-8
Crowley Mine—mine ... MT-8
Crowley Mine Creek—stream ... OR-9
Crowley Oil and Gas Field—oilfield ... LA-4
Crowley Park—flat ... AZ-5
Crowley Park—park ... MI-6
Crowley Ranch—locale ... OR-9
Crowley Resort Airstrip—airport ... ND-7
Crowley Ridge—ridge (2) ... AR-4
Crowley Ridge—ridge ... WI-6
Crowley Rock—bar ... AK-9
Crowley Rsvr—reservoir ... OR-9
Crowleys ... ME-1
Crowley Sand—well ... NM-5
Crowley Sch—school ... CA-9
Crowley Sch—school ... MA-1
Crowley Sch—school ... MI-6
Crowley Sch—school ... MN-6
Crowley Sch—school ... SD-7
Crowley School ... MS-4
Crowleys Corner—locale ... CT-1
Crowleys Junction ... ME-1
Crowleys Pond ... AL-4
Crowley Spring—spring ... SD-7
Crowleys Ridge—ridge ... AR-4
Crowleys Ridge—ridge ... MO-7
Crowleys Ridge State Park—park ... AR-4
Crowleys Run ... PA-2
Crowley Station ... TN-4
**Crowley Store**—pop pl ... TN-4
Crowley Tank—reservoir ... AZ-5
Crowley Tank—reservoir ... TX-5
**Crowleytown**—pop pl ... NJ-2
Crowley (Township of)—fmr MCD ... AR-4

Crowley Trail—trail PA-2
Crowleyville IN-6
Crowl Hill—summit MA-1
Crowl Post Office (historical)—building PA-2
Crowly Lake Dam—dam MS-4
Crow-Mag Airfield—airport OR-9
Crow Meadow Cem—cemetery IL-6
Crow Mesa—summit (2) NM-5
Crow Mine—mine MT-8
Crow Mountain Petroglyph—hist pl AR-4
Crow Mtn—summit AL-4
Crow Mtn—summit (4) GA-3
Crow Mtn—summit MS-4
Crow Mtn—summit (2) MT-8
Crow Mtn—summit UT-8
Crow Mtn—summit VA-3
Crow Mtn—summit (2) WY-8
Crow Mtn Cave AL-4
Crown—locale IA-7
Crown—locale PA-2
Crown—locale TX-5
Crown—pop pl CA-9
Crown—pop pl KY-4
Crown—pop pl MN-6
Crown—pop pl MO-7
Crown—pop pl (2) WV-2
Crown, The—ridge CO-8
Crown Basin—basin CA-9
Crown Bay—bay VI-3
Crown Butte—summit (7) MT-8
Crown Butte—summit NE-7
Crown Butte—summit ND-7
Crown Butte Canal—canal MT-8
Crown Butte Creek—stream MT-8
Crown Butte Creek—stream ND-7
Crown Butte Dam—dam ND-7
Crown Butte Lake—reservoir ND-7
Crown Butte State Game Mngmt Area—park ND-7
Crown Center—pop pl IN-6
Crown Center Cem—cemetery IN-6
Crown Center Shops—locale MO-7
Crown City—locale WV-2
Crown City—pop pl OH-6
Crown City Ferry WV-2
Crown Colony—pop pl IN-6
Crown Colony Subdivision—pop pl UT-8
Crown Cove—bay CA-9
Crown C Ranch—locale AZ-5
Crown Creek—stream CA-9
Crown Creek—stream ID-8
Crown Creek—stream IN-6
Crown Creek—stream MN-6
Crown Creek—stream MT-8
Crown Creek—stream OR-9
Crown Creek—stream PA-2
Crown Creek—stream WA-9
Crown Crest Memorial Park—cemetery PA-2
Crowndam Dam—dam SD-7
Crown Ditch—canal (2) WY-8
Crow Neck—cape ME-1
Crow Neck Sch—school ME-1
Crowned Creek—stream MI-6
Crowner Brook—stream NY-2
Crowner Creek—stream CO-8
Crowner Rsvr—reservoir CO-8
Crowner Run PA-2
Crowners Run PA-2
Crown Estates IL-6
Crownest Creek TX-5
Crow Nest Creek—stream AK-9
Crow Nest Rock—summit AK-9
Crownest Spring—spring TX-5
Crown Heights—CDP NY-2
Crown Heights Park—park OK-5
Crown Hill—pop pl WA-9
Crown Hill—pop pl WV-2
Crown Hill—summit NH-1
Crown Hill Cem—cemetery CO-8
Crown Hill Cem—cemetery GA-3
Crown Hill Cem—cemetery IL-6
Crown Hill Cem—cemetery (9) IN-6
Crown Hill Cem—cemetery (2) IA-7
Crown Hill Cem—cemetery KS-7
Crown Hill Cem—cemetery MN-6
Crown Hill Cem—cemetery (2) MO-7
Crown Hill Cem—cemetery MT-8
Crown Hill Cem—cemetery NE-7
Crownhill Cem—cemetery OH-6
Crown Hill Cem—cemetery (4) OH-6
Crown Hill Cem—cemetery (2) OK-5
Crown Hill Cem—cemetery PA-2
Crown Hill Cem—cemetery VA-3
Crown Hill Cem—cemetery WA-9
Crown Hill Cem—cemetery WI-6
Crown Hill Cem—cemetery WY-8
Crown Hill Cemetery—hist pl IN-6
Crown Hill Ditch—canal CO-8
Crown Hill (historical)—locale SD-7
Crown Hill Lake—lake CO-8
Crown Hill Memorial Park—cemetery NY-2
Crown Hill Memorial Park—cemetery TX-5
Crown Hill Mine (historical)—mine SD-7
Crown Hill Sch—school (2) WA-9
Crown Hill Sch—school WV-2
Crown Hill Township—pop pl ND-7
Crowningshield—pop pl NY-2
Crowninshield House—hist pl MA-1
Crowninshield Point—cape ME-1
Crown Island—island NY-2
Crown Jewel—locale CA-9
Crown Jewel Mine—mine CO-8
Crown King—pop pl AZ-5
Crown King Cem—cemetery AZ-5
Crown King Elem Sch—school AZ-5
Crown King Mine—mine AZ-5
Crown King Post Office—building AZ-5
Crown King Ranger Station—locale AZ-5
Crown Lake—lake (2) CA-9
Crown Lake—lake (2) MN-6
Crown Lake—lake OR-9
Crownland Cem—cemetery IN-6
Crown Mill Hist Dist—hist pl GA-3
Crown Mine SD-7
Crown Mine—mine OR-9
Crown Mine—mine SD-7
Crown Mine—pop pl IL-6
Crown Mine No 1—mine IL-6
Crown Mine No 2—mine IL-6
Crown Mountain Trail—trail MT-8
Crown Mtn TX-5
Crown Mtn—summit AK-9
Crown Mtn—summit CO-8
Crown Mtn—summit GA-3
Crown Mtn—summit MT-8
Crown Mtn—summit (2) TX-5
Crown Mtn—summit VI-3
Crown of Glory Lutheran Ch (WELS)—church FL-3
Crownover Branch—stream TX-5
Crownover Cem—cemetery TN-4
Crownover Mill—locale OH-6
Crownover Saltpeter Cave—cave TN-4
Crownover Spring—spring AL-4
Crownover Trail—trail PA-2
Crown Park—park TX-5
Crown Park—park WA-9
Crown Peak—summit AK-9
Crown Peak—summit CO-8
Crown Peak—summit NV-8
Crown Point NV-8
Crown Point OH-6
Crown Point—cape AK-9
Crown Point—cape CO-8
Crown Point—cape FL-3
Crown Point—cape ID-8
Crown Point—cape MN-6
Crown Point—cape NY-2
Crown Point—cape RI-1
Crown Point—cliff (2) ID-8
Crown Point—cliff WA-9
Crown Point—locale FL-3
Crown Point—mine UT-8
Crown Point—pop pl AK-9
Crown Point—pop pl IN-6
Crown Point—pop pl LA-4
Crown Point—pop pl NE-7
Crownpoint—pop pl NM-5
Crown Point—pop pl NY-2
Crown Point—pop pl OH-6
Crown Point—pop pl OR-9
Crown Point—pop pl VT-1
Crown Point—summit CA-9
Crown Point—summit (2) CO-8
Crown Point—summit NM-5
Crown Point—summit (2) OR-9
Crown Point—summit WA-9
Crown Point—uninc pl CA-9
Crown Point Bay—bay NY-2
Crownpoint Boarding Sch—school NM-5
Crownpoint (CCD)—cens area NM-5
Crown Point Cem—cemetery CO-8
Crown Point Cem—cemetery (2) IN-6
Crown Point Cem—cemetery KS-7
Crown Point Center—pop pl NY-2
Crown Point Center (Crown Point Centre)—pop pl NY-2
Crown Point Centre—other NY-2
Crown Point Ch—church IL-6
Crown Point Ch—church MS-4
Crown Point Country Club—other VT-1
Crown Point Elem Sch—school FL-3
Crown Point Falls—falls WA-9
Crown Point Gulch—valley AZ-5
Crown Point Gulch—valley CO-8
Crown Point Hill—summit TN-4
Crown Point (historical)—locale KS-7
Crown Point HS—school IN-6
Crown Point Mine—mine AK-9
Crown Point Mine—mine AZ-5
Crown Point Mine—mine OR-9
Crown Point No 2—mine UT-8
Crown Point No 3—mine UT-8
Crown Point Plaza—locale NC-3
Crown Point Post Office (historical)—building TN-4
Crown Point Ravine—valley NV-8
Crown Point Sch—school CA-9
Crown Point Sch—school NH-1
Crown Point Sch (historical)—school TN-4
Crown Point Shop Ctr—locale TN-4
Crown Point State Park—park OR-9
Crown Point (Town of)—pop pl NY-2
Crown Point Vista—locale WA-9
Crown Point Well—well AZ-5
Crown Reefer Point—cape AK-9
Crown Ridge—ridge CA-9
Crown Ridge, The—ridge NY-2
Crownridge Estates (subdivision)—pop pl MA-1
Crown Rock—pillar CA-9
Crown Rock—pillar NE-7
Crown Rock—summit OR-9
Crown Rock (historical)—pop pl OR-9
Crown Rock Ruin—locale AZ-5
Crown (RR name Lax)—pop pl WV-2
Crown Sch—school CA-9
Crown Sch—school GA-3
Crown Sch—school IL-6
Crown Sch (abandoned)—school MO-7
Crowns Creek FL-3
Crownshield-Bentley House—building MA-1
Crowns Nest Hollow—valley PA-2
Crown Subdivision—pop pl UT-8
Crownsville—locale MD-2
Crownsville State Hosp—hospital MD-2
Crown Valley—basin (2) CA-9
Crown Valley Guard Station—locale CA-9
Crown Valley Sch—school CA-9
Crown Village—pop pl NY-2
Crown Z Lake—lake OR-9
Crow Pass MT-8
Crow Pass—gap AK-9
Crow Peak—summit MT-8
Crow Peak—summit SD-7
Crow Peak—summit TX-5
Crow Peak—summit UT-8
Crow Peak—summit WY-8
Crow Pen Branch—stream LA-4
Crow Point—cape AK-9
Crow Point—cape (2) ME-1
Crow Point—cape (2) MA-1
Crow Point—cape (2) MI-6
Crow Point—cape MN-6
Crow Point—cape NY-2
Crow Point—cape NC-3
Crow Point—cliff CT-1
Crow Point—cliff NM-5
Crow Point—ridge MA-1
Crow Point Dam—dam NM-5
Crow Point Flats—bar MA-1
Crow Point Island—island NC-3
Crow Point Pier Light—locale MA-1
Crow Point (subdivision)—pop pl MA-1
Crow Poison—locale AZ-5
Crow Pond AL-4
Crow Pond—lake FL-3
Crow Pond—lake TN-4
Crow Pond Cem—cemetery MO-7
Crow Post Office (historical)—building AL-4
Crow Rapids—rapids WI-6
Crow Reef—bar AK-9
Crow Reservation—cens area MT-8
Crow Ridge—ridge OR-9
Crow River MN-6
Crow River—locale MN-6
Crow River—stream MI-6
Crow River—stream MN-6
Crow River Cem—cemetery MN-6
Crow River Ch—church (2) MN-6
Crow River (Township of)—pop pl MN-6
Crow Road Coulee—valley MT-8
Crow Rock—locale MT-8
Crow Rock—pillar MT-8
Crow Rock Creek—stream MT-8
Crow Rookery Slough—gut FL-3
Crow Roost Canyon—valley UT-8
Crow Rsvr—reservoir (2) OR-9
Crow Run—stream OH-6
Crow Run—stream PA-2
Crow Run—stream VA-3
Crow Run—stream WV-2
Crows—locale GA-3
Crows—pop pl AR-4
Crows—pop pl VA-3
Crows Bluff—locale FL-3
Crows Camp (historical)—locale AL-4
Crows Cem—cemetery TN-4
Crow Sch—school MI-6
Crow Sch—school MO-7
Crow Sch—school TX-5
Crow Sch (abandoned)—school MO-7
Crow Sch (historical)—school MS-4
Crow School (historical)—locale MO-7
Crows Creek—stream (2) MO-7
Crows Creek—stream NC-3
Crow Seep—spring UT-8
Crowser Hollow—valley WV-2
Crowser Ranch—locale SD-7
Crow's-Foot Brook MA-1
Crowsfoot Campground—locale CA-9
Crowsfoot Creek—stream OR-9
Crows Fork Ch—church MO-7
Crows Fork Creek—stream MO-7
Crowsheart Cem—cemetery ND-7
Crowshill Creek NJ-2
Crow Shoal—bar NJ-2
Crow Shoal—bar NY-2
Crow Shoals—bar KY-4
Crows Hollow—locale NY-2
Crows Lake—reservoir GA-3
Crows Landing—pop pl CA-9
Crows Landing Bridge—bridge CA-9
Crows Mill Creek—stream NJ-2
Crows Mills—locale PA-2
Crows Neck ME-1
Crows Neck Recreation and Environmental Center—park MS-4
Crow's Nest NY-2
Crows Nest—area ID-8
Crows Nest—basin WY-8
Crows Nest—cliff CO-8
Crows Nest—flat ID-8
Crows Nest—island NY-2
Crows Nest—locale ID-8
Crows Nest—locale ME-1
Crows Nest—locale MD-2
Crows Nest—locale NV-8
Crows Nest—pop pl IN-6
Crows Nest—summit CA-9
Crows Nest—summit (2) NV-8
Crows Nest—summit NH-1
Crows Nest—summit NY-2
Crows Nest—summit OR-9
Crows Nest—summit UT-8
Crows Nest—summit (2) WY-8
Crows Nest Basin—basin ID-8
Crows Nest Brook—stream NY-2
Crows Nest Butte SD-7
Crows Nest Camp—locale MT-8
Crows Nest Campground ME-1
Crows Nest Campsite—locale ME-1
Crows Nest Canyon—valley ID-8
Crows Nest Creek—stream ID-8
Crows Nest Creek—stream MT-8
Crows Nest Creek—stream OK-5
Crows Nest Creek—stream TX-5
Crows Nest Creek—stream WY-8
Crows Nest Gate—gap NV-8
Crows Nest Gulch—valley WY-8
Crows Nest Hammock—island FL-3
Crows Nest Hill—summit TX-5
Crows Nest (historical)—summit SD-7
Crows Nest Lookout—locale WY-8
Crows Nest Mountain NY-2
Crows Nest Peak—summit SD-7
Crows Nest Point—cape VA-3
Crows Nest Point—cliff AZ-5
Crows Nest Resort—pop pl IA-7
Crows Nest Rsvr—reservoir ID-8
Crows Nest Rsvr—reservoir OR-9
Crows Nest Slough—swamp FL-3
Crows Nest Spring—spring AZ-5
Crows Nest Spring—spring ID-8
Crows Nest Spring—spring UT-8
Crows Nest Tank—reservoir TX-5
Crows Nest Valley—valley AZ-5
Crows Nest Windmill—locale AZ-5
Crows Nest Windmill—locale NM-5
Crows Nest Windmill—locale (2) TX-5
Crowson TN-4
Crowson—locale LA-4
Crowson Cave—cave AL-4
Crowson Cem—cemetery TN-4
Crowson Creek—stream TN-4
Crowson Hill Cem—cemetery AL-4
Crowson Post Office (historical)—building TN-4
Crows Point MA-1
Crows Point Sch—school IL-6
Crows Pond—cove MA-1
Crow Spring NV-8
Crow Spring—spring AZ-5
Crow Spring—spring CA-9
Crow Spring—spring GA-3
Crow Spring—spring (2) NV-8
Crow Spring—spring TX-5
Crow Spring—stream MN-6
Crow Spring Canyon—valley CA-9
Crow Springs—spring MT-8
Crow Springs—spring NV-8
Crow Springs—spring NM-5
Crow Springs Ch—church GA-3
Crows Roost—summit CO-8
Crows Run—stream PA-2
Crowsshot Creek MS-4
Crows Swamp—swamp RI-1
Crow Summit—locale WV-2
Crow Swamp—swamp ME-1
Crow Tank—reservoir (2) AZ-5
Crow Tank—reservoir TX-5
Crowtexas—locale TN-4
Crowther—locale TX-5
Crowther, Mount—summit AK-9
Crowther Cow Camp—pop pl NM-5
Crowther House—hist pl NY-2
Crowther Lake—lake NE-7
Crowther Oil Field—oilfield KS-7
Crowthers Rsvr—reservoir ID-8
Crowther Subdivision—pop pl UT-8
Crow Timber Creek—stream SD-7
Crowton AL-4
Crowton Post Office (historical)—building AL-4
Crowton Sch (historical)—school AL-4
Crowtown—locale AL-4
Crowtown—pop pl KY-4
Crowtown Island AL-4
Crowtown Sch—school PA-2
Crow Township—pop pl SD-7
Crow Trace Park—park TX-5
Crow Trace Point Park—park TX-5
Crow Valley—locale KY-4
Crow Valley—valley GA-3
Crow Valley—valley WA-9
Crow Valley Creek—stream GA-3
Crow Valley Park—flat CO-8
Crow Valley Sch—hist pl WA-9
Crowville—locale GA-3
Crowville—pop pl LA-4
Crowville (historical P.O.)—locale IN-6
Crowville Windmill—locale NM-5
Crow Wash—stream AZ-5
Crow Windmill—locale AZ-5
Crow Windmill—locale (2) NM-5
Crow Windmill—locale (2) TX-5
Crow Wing—pop pl MN-6
Crow Wing Ch—church MN-6
Crow Wing (County)—pop pl MN-6
Crow Wing County Courthouse and Jail—hist pl MN-6
Crow Wing Lake MN-6
Crow Wing Lake—lake (2) MN-6
Crow Wing Lake Number Five MN-6
Crow Wing Lake (Township of)—civ div MN-6
Crow Wing River—stream MN-6
Crow Wing Sch—school MN-6
Crow Wing State For—forest MN-6
Crow Wing State Park—hist pl MN-6
Crow Wing (Township of)—pop pl MN-6
Croxford Mtn—summit ME-1
Croxson House—hist pl AR-4
Crox Spring—spring TN-4
Croxton—locale NJ-2
Croxton, Thomas, House—hist pl OR-9
Croxton Airp—airport KS-7
Croxton Crossroads—locale GA-3
Croxton Mine—mine MN-6
Croxton Pond—lake MN-6
Croxton Run—stream OH-6
Croxton Stream—stream VA-3
Croy Creek—stream CA-9
Croy Creek—stream ID-8
Croyden Park—park TX-5
Croydon—pop pl NH-1
Croydon—pop pl PA-2
Croydon—pop pl UT-8
Croydon Acres—pop pl PA-2
Croydon Branch NH-1
Croydon Cem—cemetery UT-8
Croydon Crest—pop pl PA-2
Croydon Flat—pop pl NH-1
Croydon Four Corners—locale NH-1
Croydon Hall Sch—school NJ-2
Croydon Heights—pop pl PA-2
Croydon Manor—pop pl PA-2
Croydon Mtn—summit NH-1
Croydon Park—pop pl MD-2
Croydon Park—pop pl PA-2
Croydon Peak—summit NH-1
Croydon Post Office (historical)—building PA-2
Croydon River NH-1
Croydon (Town of)—pop pl NH-1
Croy Gulch—valley CA-9
Croy (historical)—pop pl OR-9
Croy Lake—lake MI-6
Croyland—locale PA-2
Croyle Cem—cemetery PA-2
Croyle Island—school NY-2
Croyle Run—stream PA-2
Croyle (Township of)—pop pl PA-2
Croy Ridge—ridge CA-9
Croys Creek IN-6
Croys Creek—stream IN-6
Croys Creek Ch—church IN-6
Crozar Terrace—uninc pl PA-2
Crozer, George K., Mansion—hist pl PA-2
Crozer, John P., II, Mansion—hist pl PA-2
Crozer, Mount—summit FM-9
Crozer Chester Medical Sch—school PA-2
Crozer Park Gardens—uninc pl PA-2
Crozer Seminary (abandoned)—school PA-2
Crozer Theological Seminary-abandoned- PA-2
Crozerville PA-2
Crozet—pop pl VA-3
Crozet House—hist pl VA-3
Crozier—locale AZ-5
Crozier—locale IA-7
Crozier—locale VA-3
Crozier—pop pl LA-4
Crozier Canyon Spring—spring AZ-5
Crozier Cem—cemetery LA-4
Crozier Creek—stream IL-6
Crozier Creek—stream MT-8
Crozier Draw—valley KS-7
Crozier Hill—summit NY-2
Crozier Hollow—valley PA-2
Crozier JHS—school CA-9
Crozier Park—park PA-2
Crozier Peak—summit AZ-5
Crozier Ridge—ridge OH-6
Crozier RR Station—building AZ-5
Crozier Run Branch Junction—pop pl PA-2
Crozier Run Branch Junction Station (historical)—building PA-2
Croziers Lake—lake MI-6
Crozier Spring—spring AZ-5
Croziers Run—stream PA-2
Crozier Tank—reservoir (2) AZ-5
Crozier Technical HS—school TX-5
Crozierville—locale PA-2
Crozier Wash—stream AZ-5
Crozier Well—well AZ-5
Crozler Spring—spring TN-4
C R Smith Dam—dam NC-3
Cruce Branch—stream KY-4
Cruce Cem—cemetery KY-4
Cruce Davila—pop pl (2) PR-3
Cruce Magueyes—pop pl PR-3
Crucero—locale CA-9
Crucero Hill—summit CA-9
Cruces, Canada De Las —valley CA-9
Cruces (Barrio)—fmr MCD (2) PR-3
Cruces Creek—stream NM-5
Crucible—pop pl PA-2
Crucible Elem Sch—school PA-2
Crucifer—pop pl TN-4
Crucifer Post Office (historical)—building TN-4
Crucifixion Cem—cemetery MN-6
Crucifixion Creek—stream MT-8
Crucifix Monument—locale VA-3
Crudington Creek—stream AR-4
Crudo—uninc pl OK-5
Crudos Tank—reservoir TX-5
Crudo Windmill—locale TX-5
Crudup—pop pl AL-4
Crudup, Josiah, House—hist pl NC-3
Cruess Post Office (historical)—building AL-4
Cruey Branch—stream KY-4
Crugar Cave—cave AL-4
Cruger—locale IL-6
Cruger—pop pl MS-4
Cruger Baptist Ch—church MS-4
Cruger Island—island NY-2
Crugers—pop pl NY-2
Cruger (Township of)—pop pl IL-6
Cruice RR Station—building AZ-5
Cruich Creek WA-9
Cruickshank Knob—summit TN-4
Cruickshank Rsvr—reservoir ID-8
Cruie Creek—stream LA-4
Cruien Creek—stream MT-8
Cruikshank Butte—summit OR-9
Cruikshank Cem—cemetery LA-4
Cruikshank Creek—stream ID-8
Cruikshank Creek—stream WI-6
Cruikshank Creek—stream WY-8
Cruikshank Flat—flat MT-8
Cruikshanks PA-2
Cruikshanks Mill PA-2
Cruikshank Spring—spring OR-9
Cruise—locale KY-4
Cruise—locale MO-7
Cruise—pop pl VA-3
Cruise Cem—cemetery MS-4
Cruise Mill—locale MO-7
Cruiser, Mount—summit WA-9
Cruiser Butte—summit OR-9
Cruiser Creek—stream (2) OR-9
Cruiser Gulch—valley ID-8
Cruiser Lake—lake MN-6
Cruiser Lake—lake WI-6
Cruiser Mtn—summit MT-8
Cruiser Point—ridge NV-8
Cruiser Spring—spring OR-9
Cruise Sch—school MO-7
Cruises Creek—stream KY-4
Crukh Creek WA-9
Crukleton Cem—cemetery GA-3
Crukleton Ridge—ridge GA-3
Crukshanks PA-2
Crulch Creek WA-9
Crulls Island—island PA-2
Crum—locale KY-4
Crum—pop pl WA-9
Crum—pop pl WV-2
Crumarine Creek—stream ID-8
Crumb—locale PA-2
Crumbacher Lake—lake WA-9
Crumbaker Run OH-6
Crumbaugh Lake—lake CA-9
Crumbaugh Spring—spring KY-4
Crumb Canyon—valley UT-8
Crumb Cem—cemetery NY-2
Crumb Corner—pop pl IN-6
Crumb Creek NE-7
Crumb Creek—stream MO-7
Crumb Creek—stream OK-5
Crumb Creek Trail—trail OK-5
Crumb Gulch—valley AK-9
Crumb Hill—summit (3) NY-2
Crumb Hill Cem—cemetery NY-2
Crumb Hollow—valley TN-4
Crumbie AL-4
Crumbie Post Office AL-4
Crumble Island—island ME-1
Crumbley Bethel Baptist Ch—church AL-4
Crumbley Lake—reservoir GA-3
Crumbleys Chapel—church AL-4
Crumbleys Chapel Ch AL-4
Crumbly Hollow—valley MO-7
Crumbly Knob—summit GA-3
Crumbly Mtn—summit GA-3
Crumbly Spring—spring MO-7
Crumblys Store (historical)—locale MS-4
Crumbo Lake CA-9
Crumb Ranch—locale MT-8
Crum Branch—stream (2) KY-4
Crum Branch—stream SC-3
Crum Branch Sch—school KY-4
Crum Bridge—bridge (2) MS-4
Crumby Creek GA-3
Crum Canyon WA-9
Crum Canyon—valley NV-8
Crum Canyon—valley WA-9
Crum Canyon Spring No 2—spring WA-9
Crum Cem—cemetery AL-4
Crum Cem—cemetery FL-3
Crum Cem—cemetery GA-3
Crum Cem—cemetery (2) IL-6
Crum Cem—cemetery KS-7
Crum Church Cem—cemetery NY-2
Crum Creek—pop pl NY-2
Crum Creek—stream MS-4
Crum Creek—stream NE-7
Crum Creek—stream (3) NY-2
Crum Creek—stream PA-2
Crum Creek Dam—dam PA-2
Crum Creek Manor—pop pl PA-2
Crum Creek Rsvr—reservoir PA-2
Crum Creek Storage Dam PA-2
Crum Ditch—canal IN-6
Crume Gin—locale TX-5
Crum Elbow—bend NY-2
Crum Elbow Cem—cemetery NY-2
Crum Elbow Creek—stream NY-2
Crumes Lake—lake CA-9
Crum Gulch—valley MT-8
Crum Hill—summit MA-1
Crum Hill—summit MI-6
Crumhorn Lake—lake NY-2
Crumhorn Mtn—summit NY-2
Crumkill Creek—stream NY-2
Crum Lake—lake MN-6
Crum Lake Dam—dam MS-4
Crumley Branch—stream MO-7
Crumley Cem—cemetery (3) TN-4
Crumley Chapel—pop pl AL-4
Crumley Chapel Community Center—building AL-4
Crumley Chapel Elem Sch—school AL-4
Crumley Chapel Methodist Ch—church AL-4
Crumley Creek—stream GA-3
Crumley Creek—stream MI-6
Crumley Crossing—pop pl IN-6
Crumley Gulch—valley ID-8
Crumley Hollow—valley TN-4
Crumleys Chapel AL-4
Crumling Airp—airport PA-2
Crum Lynne—locale PA-2
Crum Lynne (Leiperville)—pop pl PA-2
Crum Lynne (sta.)—uninc pl PA-2
Crumlynn Station—building PA-2
Crummell Sch—school DC-2
Crummet Creek NH-1
Crummet Run WV-2
Crummett Brook—stream ME-1
Crummett Ch—church WV-2
Crummett Creek NH-1
Crummett Mtn—summit ME-1
Crummett Run—stream WV-2
Crummetts Creek NH-1
Crummies—pop pl KY-4
Crummies Creek—stream KY-4
Crummis Creek—stream WV-2
Crum Mtn—summit MS-4
Crump AL-4
Crump—pop pl MI-6
Crump—pop pl MS-4
Crump—pop pl MO-7
Crump—pop pl TN-4
Crump, E. H., House—hist pl TN-4
Crumpacker Arm—canal IN-6
Crumpacker Cem—cemetery MO-7
Crump and Field Grocery Company—hist pl KY-4
Crum Park—park MI-6
Crump Branch—stream (2) AL-4
Crump Brook—stream NY-2
Crump Cave—cave AL-4
Crump Cave Number One—cave AL-4
Crump Cave Number Two—cave AL-4
Crump Cem—cemetery (2) AL-4
Crump Cem—cemetery KY-4
Crump Cem—cemetery MS-4
Crump Cem—cemetery MO-7
Crump Cem—cemetery TX-5
Crump Ch—church MI-6
Crump Ch—church MS-4
Crump Creek—stream AR-4
Crump Creek—stream GA-3
Crump Creek—stream TX-5
Crump Creek—stream VA-3
Crump Dam—dam OR-9
Crump Ditch—canal OR-9
Crump Drain—stream MI-6
Crump Draw—valley NM-5
Crump Elem Sch—school AL-4
Crumper Sch (historical)—school AL-4
Crump Estates IN-6
Crump Gap—gap AL-4
Crump Geyser—geyser OR-9
Crump Hill—summit AL-4
Crump (historical)—pop pl OR-9
Crump Hollow—valley AR-4
Crump Island—island KY-4
Crump Lake NE-7
Crump Lake—lake OR-9
Crump Landing—locale TN-4
Crumpler—pop pl NC-3
Crumpler—pop pl WV-2
Crumpler Millpond—reservoir NC-3
Crumplers Crossroads—pop pl NC-3
Crumplers Peak—summit AL-4
Crumply Creek—stream AL-4
Crump Neck—cape VA-3
Crum Point—cliff IN-6
Crump Park—park AL-4
Crump Park—park TN-4
Crump Park—park TX-5
Crump Ranch—locale OR-9
Crump Ranch—locale TX-5
Crump Rsvr—reservoir OR-9
Crumps Bank—levee VA-3
Crumps Bottom—bend WV-2
Crumps Bottom—locale WV-2
Crump Sch—school IL-6
Crumps Creek—stream MS-4
Crumps Knob—summit KY-4
Crumps Lower Landing—locale MS-4
Crumps Mill—locale VA-3
Crump Spring—spring OR-9

Crump Spring—spring TN-4
Crumps Swamp—stream VA-3
Crump Stadium—park TN-4
Crumps Upper Landing—locale MS-4
Crump Swamp VA-3
Crump Tank—reservoir NM-5
Crump Tank—reservoir TX-5
Crump Tanks—reservoir NM-5
Crumpton AL-4
**Crumpton**—pop pl MD-2
Crumpton Cem—cemetery AL-4
Crumpton Cem—cemetery MD-2
Crumpton Creek—stream SC-3
Crumpton Creek—stream TN-4
Crumpton Golf Club—locale FL-3
Crumptonia—locale AL-4
Crumpton Lake—reservoir GA-3
Crumpton Lake Dam—dam (2) MS-4
**Crump Town**—pop pl NC-3
Crumpy Gulch—valley CA-9
Crum Ridge Ch—church OH-6
Crum Road Bridge—hist pl MD-2
**Crumrod**—pop pl AR-4
Crum Rsvr—reservoir CA-9
Crum Rsvr—reservoir CO-8
Crum Run—stream PA-2
Crums Ch—church VA-3
Crums Chapel—church IL-6
Crum Sch (historical)—school (2) MS-4
**Crums Corners**—pop pl PA-2
Crums Lane Sch—school KY-4
Crums Point IN-6
**Crumstown**—pop pl IN-6
Crumtown—locale MS-4
Crum Town—locale NY-2
Cruncleton Cem—cemetery MO-7
Crunigen Creek CA-9
**Crunk**—pop pl TN-4
Crunk Cem—cemetery TN-4
Crunk Ditch—canal IN-6
Crupe Run—stream PA-2
Crupe Run—stream WV-2
**Crupp**—pop pl MS-4
Crupper Run—stream VA-3
**Cruppers Corner**—pop pl KS-7
Crusade Ch—church OH-6
Crusader Camp—locale NC-3
Crusader Mine—mine CA-9
Crusade Sch—school IN-6
Crusade Sch—school KY-4
Crusatte's River WA-9
Cruse—locale IL-6
Cruse—locale PA-2
**Cruse**—pop pl GA-3
Cruse Cem—cemetery AR-4
Cruse Cem—cemetery IL-6
Cruse Cem—cemetery MO-7
Cruse-Hossington House—hist pl NJ-2
Crusenberry Hollow—valley VA-3
Crusenberry Meadow—stream VA-3
Cruser Brook—stream NJ-2
Cruse Ridge—ridge KY-4
Cruse Ridge Sch—school KY-4
Crusers Brook NJ-2
Cruse Wash—stream CO-8
Crusher—locale OK-5
Crusher—locale TX-5
Crusher Branch—stream NC-3
Crusher Canyon—valley (2) WA-9
Crusher Creek—stream (2) OR-9
Crusher Hill—summit MT-8
Crusher Hill—summit NY-2
Crusher Hollow—valley OK-5
Crusher Mica Quarry—mine AZ-5
Crusher Ridge Trail—trail VA-3
Crusher Sink—reservoir AZ-5
Crusher Spring—spring OR-9
Crusher Tank—reservoir NM-5
Crush Lake—reservoir TX-5
Crush Park—park PA-2
Crush Run—stream VA-3
**Cruso**—pop pl NC-3
Cruso Cabin Creek—stream CA-9
Crusoe NC-3
Crusoe Cem—cemetery NY-2
Crusoe Community Hall—locale NC-3
Crusoe Creek—stream NY-2
Crusoe Island NC-3
**Crusoe Island**—pop pl NC-3
Crusoe Island—summit NY-2
Crusoe Island (historical)—island AL-4
Crusoe Lake—lake NY-2
Cruson Slough—gut WI-6
**Crus Subdivision**—pop pl UT-8
Crutch Creek—stream WA-9
Crutcher—uninc pl CA-9
Crutcher Bench—bench OR-9
Crutcher Branch—stream MO-7
Crutcher Canyon—valley NV-8
Crutcher Cem—cemetery AL-4
Crutcher Cem—cemetery AR-4
Crutcher Cem—cemetery MO-7
Crutcher Crossing—locale ID-8
Crutcher Ditch—canal OR-9
Crutcher Fork—stream KY-4
Crutcher Hollow—valley (2) TN-4
Crutcher House—hist pl KY-4
Crutcher Lake—lake (2) TN-4
Crutcher Lake—reservoir TN-4
Crutcher Lake Dam—dam TN-4
Crutchers Creek—stream TX-5
Crutcher Shop Ctr—locale AL-4
Crutcher Slough—canal KY-4
Crutcher Springs—spring NV-8
Crutchet Ranch—locale WY-8
**Crutchfield**—pop pl KY-4
**Crutchfield**—pop pl NC-3
Crutchfield Bar—bar TN-4
Crutchfield Branch—stream NC-3
Crutchfield Branch—stream OK-5
Crutchfield Branch—stream VA-3
Crutchfield Cem—cemetery OK-5
Crutchfield Cem—cemetery TN-4
Crutchfield Creek—stream OR-9
**Crutchfield Crossroads**—pop pl NC-3
Crutchfield Playground—park OK-5
Crutchfield-Rowlett Cem—cemetery TN-4
Crutchfield Sch—school TX-5
Crutchlow Bay—swamp SC-3
Crutchlow Branch—stream SC-3
Crutchman Island—island FL-3
Crutchmer Hollow—valley KY-4
Crutcho Creek—stream OK-5
Crutcho Sch—school OK-5
Crutch Pond—lake AL-4
Cruthers Butte—summit ID-8
Cruthers Creek—stream CA-9
Cruthers Gap PA-2
Cruthins Cem—cemetery MS-4
Cruthoff Sch—school SD-7
Crutsinger Cem—cemetery MO-7
Crutts Well—well CA-9
Cruver Pond—lake PA-2
**Cruz**—pop pl UT-8
Cruz, Cerro de la—summit TX-5
Cruz, Loma la—summit TX-5
Cruz, Puerto de la—summit AZ-5
Cruzane Gulch—valley MT-8
Cruzane Mtn—summit MT-8
Cruzan Mesa—summit CA-9
**Cruzatt**—pop pl WA-9
Cruzatte—locale OR-9
Cruz (Barrio)—fmr MCD PR-3
Cruz Bay—bay VI-3
**Cruz Bay**—pop pl VI-3
Cruz Bay (Census Subdistrict)—cens area VI-3
Cruz Calle—locale TX-5
**Cruz Calle (Santa Cruz)**—pop pl TX-5
Cruz Canyon—valley NM-5
Cruz Canyon Tank—reservoir AZ-5
Cruze Cem—cemetery TN-4
Cruze Creek—stream TN-4
Cruze Lake—lake TX-5
Cruzen Ditch—canal ID-8
Cruzen Pond—lake ID-8
Cruzen Springs CO-8
Cruze Spring—spring TN-4
Cruz Islands—area AK-9
Cruz Oil Field—other NM-5
Cruzon Lake—lake MI-6
Cruz Pass AZ-5
Cruz Pass—channel AK-9
Cruz-Sayreville—airport NJ-2
Cruz Tank—reservoir TX-5
Cruz Trading Post—hist pl AZ-5
Cruzville—locale NM-5
Cruz Wash—stream AZ-5
Cruz Windmill—locale TX-5
C R Wise Pond—lake FL-3
Cry Cem—cemetery TN-4
Cry Creek—stream GA-3
Cry Creek—stream OR-9
Cry Creek—stream WY-8
Cry Creek Post Office (historical)—building TN-4
Cryder Butte—summit OR-9
Cryder Cem—cemetery IL-6
Cryder Creek NY-2
Cryder Creek—stream NY-2
Cryder Creek—stream PA-2
Cryder Hollow—valley AL-4
Cryderman Lake—lake MI-6
Cryderman Lake Drain—canal MI-6
Cryder School PA-2
Cryders Point—cape NY-2
Cryder Trail—trail PA-2
Cryer Cem—cemetery LA-4
Cryer Creek—locale TX-5
Cryer Creek—stream TX-5
Cryer Creek Cem—cemetery TX-5
Cryers Branch—stream TX-5
Cryer Slough—stream LA-4
Cryer Spring—spring AL-4
Crying Bog—swamp RI-1
Crying Child Island—island FL-3
Crying Creek—stream TN-4
Crymes Corner VA-3
Crymes Store—locale VA-3
Crysler Island NY-2
Crysler Island Shoal NY-2
Crysler Shoal—bar NY-2
Crystal MS-4
Crystal PA-2
Crystal—locale (2) ID-8
Crystal—locale KY-4
Crystal—locale NV-8
Crystal—locale NM-5
Crystal—locale OK-5
**Crystal**—pop pl CO-8
**Crystal**—pop pl IN-6
**Crystal**—pop pl ME-1
**Crystal**—pop pl MI-6
**Crystal**—pop pl MN-6
**Crystal**—pop pl NH-1
**Crystal**—pop pl ND-7
**Crystal**—pop pl (2) PA-2
**Crystal**—pop pl TN-4
**Crystal**—pop pl WV-2
Crystal, Lake—lake FL-3
Crystal, Lake—lake MN-6
Crystal, Lake—lake MT-8
Crystal, Lake—reservoir GA-3
Crystal Acres—uninc pl VA-3
Crystalaire Country Club—other CA-9
Crystal Arch—arch UT-8
Crystal Basin—basin OR-9
Crystal Basin—basin UT-8
Crystal Bay MN-6
Crystal Bay—bay FL-3
Crystal Bay—bay (2) MN-6
Crystal Bay—bay NV-8
Crystal Bay—bay TX-5
Crystal Bay—bay UT-8
**Crystal Bay**—pop pl MN-6
**Crystal Bay**—pop pl NV-8
Crystal Bay Lake—lake WI-6
Crystal Bayou—gut MI-6
**Crystal Bay (Township of)**—pop pl MN-6
Crystal Beach MD-2
Crystal Beach—beach MI-6
Crystal Beach—island OH-6
**Crystal Beach**—pop pl FL-3
**Crystal Beach**—pop pl (2) MD-2
**Crystal Beach**—pop pl (2) MI-6
**Crystal Beach**—pop pl NY-2
**Crystal Beach**—pop pl TX-5
**Crystal Beach**—pop pl VT-1
**Crystal Beach**—pop pl VA-3
Crystal Beach Lake—reservoir OK-5
Crystal Beach Manor MD-2
**Crystal Beach Manor**—pop pl MD-2
**Crystal Beach (Patton)**—pop pl TX-5
Crystal Beach Plaza (Shop Ctr)—locale FL-3
**Crystal Block**—pop pl WV-2
Crystal Blue Lake—reservoir MO-7
Crystal Bowl—lake FL-3
**Crystal Brook**—pop pl NY-2
Crystal Brook—stream ME-1
Crystal Brook—stream MA-1
Crystal Brook—stream MI-6
Crystal Brook—stream (2) NH-1
Crystal Brook—stream (5) NY-2
Crystal Brook—stream PA-2
Crystal Brook—stream (2) VT-1
Crystal Brook—stream WI-6
Crystal Butte—summit ID-8
Crystal Canyon—valley CO-8
Crystal Canyon—valley NV-8
Crystal Canyon—valley UT-8
Crystal Cascades—spring MT-8
Crystal Castle Spring—spring OR-9
Crystal Cave AL-4
Crystal Cave SD-7
Crystal Cave—cave AL-4
Crystal Cave—cave (3) AZ-5
Crystal Cave—cave AR-4
Crystal Cave—cave CA-9
Crystal Cave—cave KY-4
Crystal Cave—cave MO-7
Crystal Cave—cave MT-8
Crystal Cave—cave OK-5
Crystal Cave—cave PA-2
Crystal Cave—cave SD-7
Crystal Cave—cave (2) TN-4
Crystal Cave—cave UT-8
Crystal Cave—cave WI-6
Crystal Cave (historical)—locale SD-7
Crystal Caverns—cave MO-7
Crystal Caverns—cave VA-3
Crystal Cave Spring—spring MT-8
Crystal Cem—cemetery IA-7
Crystal Cem—cemetery OK-5
Crystal Center (Shop Ctr)—locale FL-3
Crystal Ch—church MI-6
Crystal Ch—church OK-5
Crystal Chasm—cave AL-4
**Crystal City**—pop pl MO-7
**Crystal City**—pop pl TX-5
Crystal City—post sta VA-3
Crystal City (CCD)—cens area TX-5
Crystal Clear Creek—stream CA-9
Crystal Cliff—cliff NY-2
Crystal Cliffs—cliff CA-9
Crystal Cove—bay FL-3
Crystal Cove—bay ME-1
Crystal Cove—bay MI-6
Crystal Cove—cove MA-1
**Crystal Cove**—pop pl CA-9
Crystal Cove Hist Dist—hist pl CA-9
Crystal Crag—summit CA-9
Crystal Creek CO-8
Crystal Creek KS-7
Crystal Creek MT-8
Crystal Creek NE-7
Crystal Creek TN-4
Crystal Creek TX-5
Crystal Creek—gut UT-8
Crystal Creek—stream (6) AK-9
Crystal Creek—stream (2) AZ-5
Crystal Creek—stream (10) CA-9
Crystal Creek—stream (10) CO-8
Crystal Creek—stream (6) ID-8
Crystal Creek—stream IL-6
Crystal Creek—stream (2) IA-7
Crystal Creek—stream KS-7
Crystal Creek—stream KY-4
Crystal Creek—stream LA-4
Crystal Creek—stream (2) MI-6
Crystal Creek—stream (4) MN-6
Crystal Creek—stream (9) MT-8
Crystal Creek—stream (2) NE-7
Crystal Creek—stream (2) NM-5
Crystal Creek—stream (3) NY-2
Crystal Creek—stream OK-5
Crystal Creek—stream (9) OR-9
Crystal Creek—stream TN-4
Crystal Creek—stream (2) TX-5
Crystal Creek—stream (3) UT-8
Crystal Creek—stream (7) WA-9
Crystal Creek—stream WI-6
Crystal Creek—stream (5) WY-8
Crystal Creek Campground—locale WY-8
Crystal Creek Conservation Camp—locale CA-9
Crystal Creek County Park—park OR-9
Crystal Creek Ditch—canal CO-8
Crystal Creek Rock—pillar CA-9
Crystal Creek Rsvr—reservoir CO-8
Crystal Creek Spring—spring UT-8
Crystal Cross Mtn—summit MT-8
Crystal Dale—locale NY-2
Crystal Dam—dam ND-7
Crystal Dam—dam PA-2
**Crystal Fall**—pop pl AK-9
Crystal Falls—falls CO-8
Crystal Falls—falls TN-4
Crystal Falls—falls WA-9
Crystal Falls—falls WY-8
Crystal Falls—locale TX-5
**Crystal Falls**—pop pl MI-6
Crystal Falls Creek—stream CO-8
Crystal Falls Dam and Power Plant—hist pl MI-6
Crystal Falls (Township of)—civ div MI-6
Crystal Farms Ch—church TX-5
Crystal Fissure Flow—lava ID-8
Crystal For—area AZ-5
Crystal Ford—locale MT-8
**Crystal Gardens**—pop pl IL-6
Crystal Geyser—spring UT-8
Crystal Glacier—glacier WA-9
Crystal Glen Creek—stream IL-6
Crystal Grottoes—cave MD-2
Crystal Gulch—valley (2) ID-8
Crystal Heights Sch—school MN-6
**Crystal Heights (subdivision)**—pop pl FL-3
Crystal Hill—locale VA-3
**Crystal Hill**—pop pl AR-4
Crystal Hill—summit AZ-5
Crystal Hill—summit AR-4
Crystal Hill—summit CA-9
Crystal Hill—summit PA-2
Crystal Hill—summit WY-8
Crystal Hill Cem—cemetery GA-3
Crystal Hill Ch—church (5) AR-4
Crystal Hill Ch—church VA-3
**Crystal Hills Subdivision**—pop pl UT-8
Crystal (historical)—locale IA-7
**Crystal (historical)**—pop pl OR-9
Crystal Hollow—valley UT-8
Crystal Hot Springs UT-8
**Crystalia**—pop pl MI-6
Crystal Ice Cave—cave ID-8
Crystal Ice Company Bldg—hist pl FL-3
Crystal Inn—hist pl MI-6
Crystal Island—cape FL-3
Crystal Island Marina—locale AL-4
Crystal Knob—summit CA-9
Crystal Lake AL-4
Crystal Lake IA-7
Crystal Lake MA-1
Crystal Lake MI-6
Crystal Lake NH-1
Crystal Lake RI-1
Crystal Lake TX-5
Crystal Lake WI-6
Crystal Lake—CDP NE-7
Crystal Lake—lake AL-4
Crystal Lake—lake (4) AK-9
Crystal Lake—lake (9) CA-9
Crystal Lake—lake (6) CO-8
Crystal Lake—lake CT-1
Crystal Lake—lake (14) FL-3
Crystal Lake—lake GA-3
Crystal Lake—lake (4) ID-8
Crystal Lake—lake (3) IL-6
Crystal Lake—lake (2) IN-6
Crystal Lake—lake (2) IA-7
Crystal Lake—lake KY-4
Crystal Lake—lake (3) ME-1
Crystal Lake—lake (7) MA-1
Crystal Lake—lake (13) MI-6
Crystal Lake—lake (15) MN-6
Crystal Lake—lake (10) MT-8
Crystal Lake—lake (3) NE-7
Crystal Lake—lake (4) NH-1
Crystal Lake—lake NJ-2
Crystal Lake—lake NM-5
Crystal Lake—lake (16) NY-2
Crystal Lake—lake (2) NC-3
Crystal Lake—lake ND-7
Crystal Lake—lake (3) OH-6
Crystal Lake—lake (2) OR-9
Crystal Lake—lake PA-2
Crystal Lake—lake (2) SD-7
Crystal Lake—lake TN-4
Crystal Lake—lake UT-8
Crystal Lake—lake VT-1
Crystal Lake—lake (8) WA-9
Crystal Lake—lake WV-2
Crystal Lake—lake (20) WI-6
Crystal Lake—lake (4) WY-8
Crystal Lake—locale CA-9
Crystal Lake—locale FL-3
**Crystal Lake**—pop pl CT-1
**Crystal Lake**—pop pl (2) IL-6
**Crystal Lake**—pop pl IA-7
**Crystal Lake**—pop pl KY-4
**Crystal Lake**—pop pl (2) NJ-2
**Crystal Lake**—pop pl (2) NY-2
**Crystal Lake**—pop pl PA-2
**Crystal Lake**—pop pl TX-5
**Crystal Lake**—pop pl WV-2
Crystal Lake—reservoir (4) AL-4
Crystal Lake—reservoir AR-4
Crystal Lake—reservoir CA-9
Crystal Lake—reservoir (4) CO-8
Crystal Lake—reservoir (4) CT-1
Crystal Lake—reservoir (2) GA-3
Crystal Lake—reservoir IN-6
Crystal Lake—reservoir (2) KS-7
Crystal Lake—reservoir KY-4
Crystal Lake—reservoir (3) MA-1
Crystal Lake—reservoir MI-6
Crystal Lake—reservoir MS-4
Crystal Lake—reservoir MO-7
Crystal Lake—reservoir (4) NJ-2
Crystal Lake—reservoir (2) NC-3
Crystal Lake—reservoir (2) OH-6
Crystal Lake—reservoir (2) OK-5
Crystal Lake—reservoir OR-9
Crystal Lake—reservoir (3) PA-2
Crystal Lake—reservoir (2) SC-3
Crystal Lake—reservoir TN-4
Crystal Lake—reservoir (3) TX-5
Crystal Lake—reservoir (2) VA-3
Crystal Lake and Pleasant Street Hist Dist—hist pl MA-1
Crystal Lake Brook—stream CT-1
Crystal Lake Brook—stream NH-1
Crystal Lake Canal—canal ID-8
Crystal Lake Cave—cave (2) IA-7
Crystal Lake Cem—cemetery MA-1
Crystal Lake Cem—cemetery MI-6
Crystal Lake Cem—cemetery MN-6
Crystal Lake Cem—cemetery NY-2
Crystal Lake (census for Lake Holloway)—CDP FL-3
Crystal Lake Ch—church AL-4
Crystal Lake Ch—church FL-3
Crystal Lake Ch—church MN-6
Crystal Lake Ch—church WI-6
Crystal Lake Corners—locale WI-6
Crystal Lake Country Club—other IL-6
Crystal Lake Country Club—other MO-7
Crystal Lake Creek—stream CO-8
Crystal Lake Dam AL-4
Crystal Lake Dam—dam (2) AL-4
Crystal Lake Dam—dam (2) MA-1
Crystal Lake Dam—dam (3) NJ-2
Crystal Lake Dam—dam (2) NC-3
Crystal Lake Dam—dam (2) PA-2
Crystal Lake Dam—dam TN-4
Crystal Lake Dike—dam MA-1
Crystal Lake Elem Sch—school CT-1
**Crystal Lake Estates**—pop pl IL-6
**Crystal Lake (Greenhead)**—pop pl FL-3
Crystal Lake Guard Station—locale CA-9
Crystal Lake Guard Station—locale MT-8
Crystal Lake (historical)—lake ND-7
Crystal Lake JHS—school FL-3
Crystal Lake Masonic Cem—cemetery OR-9
Crystal Lake Memorial Park—cemetery IL-6
Crystal Lake MS—school FL-3
Crystal Lake Park—park (2) IL-6
Crystal Lake Park—park IA-7
Crystal Lake Park—park MA-1
Crystal Lake Park—park NH-1
Crystal Lake Park—park NJ-2
Crystal Lake Park—park WI-6
**Crystal Lake Park**—pop pl MO-7
Crystal Lake Rec Area—park CA-9
Crystal Lake Reservoir CT-1
Crystal Lake Rsvr—reservoir MA-1
Crystal Lake Rsvr—reservoir WY-8
Crystal Lakes—lake AK-9
Crystal Lakes—lake CO-8
Crystal Lakes—locale OK-5
**Crystal Lakes**—pop pl (2) OH-6
**Crystal Lakes**—pop pl OK-5
Crystal Lakes—reservoir CO-8
Crystal Lakes—reservoir OH-6
Crystal Lake Sch—school FL-3
Crystal Lake Shop Ctr—locale FL-3
**Crystal Lake Shores (subdivision)**—pop pl FL-3
Crystal Lake State Game Mgt Area—park IA-7
Crystal Lake State Public Shooting Area—park SD-7
Crystal Lake State Rec Area—locale NE-7
Crystal Lake Stock Farm—hist pl OH-6
Crystal Lakes Trout Farm—locale NV-8
**Crystal Lake (Town of)**—pop pl (2) WI-6
**Crystal Lake Township**—pop pl ND-7
**Crystal Lake Township**—pop pl SD-7
Crystal Lake (Township of)—civ div MI-6
Crystal Lake Trail Head—locale UT-8
**Crystal Lawns**—pop pl IL-6
**Crystallia**—pop pl MI-6
Crystal Light Ch—church AL-4
Crystalline Hills—other AK-9
Crystalline Spring—spring OR-9
Crystal Lookout Tower—locale MI-6
**Crystal Manor**—pop pl IL-6
**Crystal Manor Condominium**—pop pl UT-8
Crystal Marsh—swamp NV-8
Crystal Mill—hist pl CO-8
Crystal Mine—mine (4) CA-9
Crystal Mine—mine CO-8
Crystal Mine—mine IL-6
Crystal Mine—mine NM-5
Crystal Mine (historical)—mine AZ-5
Crystal Mineral Springs—locale PA-2
Crystal Mines—mine KY-4
**Crystal Mountain**—pop pl WA-9
Crystal Mountain—ridge AR-4
Crystal Mountain Mine—mine MT-8
Crystal Mountains—ridge AR-4
Crystal Mtn WA-9
Crystal Mtn—summit (4) AR-4
Crystal Mtn—summit CO-8
Crystal Mtn—summit ID-8
Crystal Mtn—summit NH-1
Crystal Mtn—summit SD-7
Crystal Mtn—summit WA-9
Crystal Onyx Cave—cave KY-4
Crystal Palace Gulch—valley OR-9
Crystal Palace Mine—mine OR-9
Crystal Park—flat CO-8
Crystal Park—flat MT-8
Crystal Park—park PA-2
Crystal Park Picnic Area—locale MT-8
**Crystal Park (subdivision)**—pop pl NC-3
Crystal Pass—gap NV-8
Crystal Peak—cliff WY-8
Crystal Peak—summit AK-9
Crystal Peak—summit AZ-5
Crystal Peak—summit (4) CA-9
Crystal Peak—summit (4) CO-8
Crystal Peak—summit ID-8
Crystal Peak—summit MT-8
Crystal Peak—summit (2) UT-8
Crystal Peak—summit WA-9
Crystal Peak Guard Station—locale CA-9
Crystal Peak Hills UT-8
Crystal Peak Park—park NV-8
Crystal Peak Ranch—locale CO-8
Crystal Pier—locale CA-9
Crystal Pit—basin ID-8
Crystal Pit—cave PA-2
Crystal Plains Ch—church KS-7
Crystal Plains (historical)—locale KS-7
**Crystal Plains Township**—pop pl KS-7
Crystal Point—cape MT-8
Crystal Point—cape PA-2
Crystal Point—cliff AR-4
Crystal Point—locale MT-8
**Crystal Point (subdivision)**—pop pl FL-3
Crystal Pond MA-1
Crystal Pond—lake (4) ME-1
Crystal Pond—lake (2) MA-1
Crystal Pond—lake NY-2
Crystal Pond—lake VT-1
Crystal Pond—reservoir (2) CT-1
Crystal Pond—reservoir MA-1
Crystal Pond Brook—stream CT-1
Crystal Pool—lake VT-1
Crystal Pool—spring NV-8
Crystal Post Office (historical)—building TN-4
Crystal Prong—stream AR-4
Crystal Queen Mine—mine NV-8
Crystal Ranch—locale UT-8
Crystal Range—range CA-9
Crystal Rapids—rapids AZ-5
Crystal Rec Area—park AR-4
Crystal Reef—bar FL-3
Crystal Reservoir CO-8
Crystal Ridge PA-2
Crystal Ridge—ridge AZ-5
Crystal Ridge—ridge TN-4
Crystal Ridge—ridge WA-9
Crystal Ridge Ch—church MS-4
Crystal Ridge Ind Res—reserve MS-4
Crystal Ridge Sch (historical)—school TN-4
**Crystal River**—pop pl FL-3
Crystal River—stream CO-8
Crystal River—stream FL-3
Crystal River—stream MI-6
Crystal River—stream WI-6
Crystal River (CCD)—cens area FL-3
Crystal River Christian Acad—school FL-3
Crystal River Historic Memorial—park FL-3
Crystal River HS—school FL-3
Crystal River Indian Mounds—hist pl FL-3
Crystal River MS—school FL-3
Crystal River Primary Sch—school FL-3
Crystal River Ranch—locale CO-8
Crystal River Tower—tower FL-3
**Crystal Rock**—pop pl OH-6
**Crystal Rock Park**—pop pl OH-6
Crystal Rsvr—reservoir NV-8
Crystal Rsvr—reservoir OR-9
Crystal Rsvr—reservoir PA-2
Crystal Run—locale NY-2
Crystal Run—stream DE-2
Crystal Run—stream PA-2
**Crystal Run Farm (subdivision)**—pop pl DE-2
Crystal Sch—school CA-9
Crystal Sch—school MI-6
Crystal Sch—school WV-2
Crystal School (Abandoned)—locale ID-8
Crystal Spring AZ-5
Crystal Spring NV-8
Crystal Spring TN-4
Crystal Spring WV-2
Crystal Spring—locale MN-6
Crystal Spring—locale NY-2
**Crystal Spring**—pop pl MI-6
**Crystal Spring**—pop pl PA-2
Crystal Spring—spring (4) AZ-5
Crystal Spring—spring (3) CA-9
Crystal Spring—spring (2) CO-8
Crystal Spring—spring FL-3
Crystal Spring—spring (3) ID-8
Crystal Spring—spring MA-1
Crystal Spring—spring MN-6
Crystal Spring—spring (3) MO-7
Crystal Spring—spring MT-8
Crystal Spring—spring (3) NV-8
Crystal Spring—spring NC-3
Crystal Spring—spring (9) OR-9
Crystal Spring—spring (4) PA-2
Crystal Spring—spring (4) TN-4
Crystal Spring—spring (7) UT-8
Crystal Spring—spring WA-9
Crystal Spring—spring WI-6
Crystal Spring—spring (2) WY-8
Crystal Spring Branch—stream TN-4
Crystal Spring/Butterfly Trail—trail AZ-5
Crystal Spring Camp—locale (2) PA-2
Crystal Spring Ch—church MS-4
Crystal Spring Creek—stream (2) CO-8
Crystal Spring Creek—stream MI-6
Crystal Spring Creek—stream OR-9
Crystal Spring Dam—dam CA-9
Crystal Spring Draw—valley WY-8
Crystal Spring Fish Hatchery—other WI-6
Crystal Spring Forest Camp—locale WA-9
**Crystal Spring Knolls**—pop pl VA-3
Crystal Spring Lake—reservoir NJ-2
Crystal Spring Lake Dam—dam NJ-2
Crystal Spring Resort—locale UT-8
Crystal Springs PA-2
Crystal Springs—locale UT-8
Crystal Springs—locale WA-9
**Crystal Springs**—pop pl AL-4
**Crystal Springs**—pop pl AR-4
**Crystal Springs**—pop pl FL-3
**Crystal Springs**—pop pl (2) GA-3
**Crystal Springs**—pop pl KS-7
**Crystal Springs**—pop pl MD-2
**Crystal Springs**—pop pl MS-4
**Crystal Springs**—pop pl ND-7
**Crystal Springs**—pop pl OH-6
**Crystal Springs**—pop pl PA-2
**Crystal Springs**—pop pl TN-4
**Crystal Springs**—pop pl VA-3
**Crystal Springs**—pop pl WA-9
**Crystal Springs**—pop pl (2) WV-2
Crystal Springs—spring (2) AL-4
Crystal Springs—spring (2) CA-9
Crystal Springs—spring (2) ID-8
Crystal Springs—spring (2) NV-8
Crystal Springs—spring ND-7
Crystal Springs—spring (2) OR-9
Crystal Springs—spring UT-8
Crystal Springs Air Force Station—other MS-4
Crystal Springs Baptist Ch—church MS-4
Crystal Springs Branch—stream TN-4
Crystal Springs Campground—locale (2) CA-9
Crystal Springs Campground—locale MI-6
Crystal Springs Canyon—valley CA-9
Crystal Springs Canyon—valley UT-8
Crystal Springs Cem—cemetery AL-4
Crystal Springs Cem—cemetery FL-3
Crystal Springs Cem—cemetery LA-4
Crystal Springs Cem—cemetery MI-6
Crystal Springs Cem—cemetery (3) MS-4
Crystal Springs Cem—cemetery ND-7
Crystal Springs Ch MS-4
Crystal Springs Ch—church GA-3
Crystal Springs Ch—church KS-7
Crystal Springs Ch—church LA-4
Crystal Springs Ch—church MS-4
Crystal Springs Ch—church NC-3
Crystal Spring School MS-4
Crystal Springs Coulee—valley WI-6
Crystal Springs Creek—stream OR-9
Crystal Springs Elementary School MS-4
Crystal Springs Golf Club—locale MA-1
Crystal Springs Golf Club (historical P.O.)—locale IA-7
Crystal Springs Golf Course—other CA-9
Crystal Springs HS—school MS-4
Crystal Springs Lake CA-9
Crystal Springs Lake—lake WI-6
Crystal Springs Lake—reservoir AL-4
Crystal Springs Lake—reservoir NC-3
Crystal Springs Lake—reservoir OR-9
Crystal Springs Lake—reservoir SC-3
Crystal Springs Lake—reservoir TX-5
Crystal Springs Lake Dam—dam NC-3
Crystal Springs Landing—locale AR-4
Crystal Springs Lookout Tower—locale MS-4
Crystal Springs Mine—mine CA-9
Crystal Springs Park—park AL-4
Crystal Springs Park—park FL-3
Crystal Springs Park—park NE-7
Crystal Springs Plantation (historical)—locale AL-4

Crystal Springs Ranch—*locale* .......... CO-8
Crystal Springs Sch—*school* .......... MA-1
Crystal Springs Sch—*school* .......... MS-4
Crystal Springs Sch—*school* .......... NY-2
Crystal Springs Sch—*school* .......... VA-3
Crystal Springs Sch for Girls—*school* .......... CA-9
Crystal Springs Speedway—*other* .......... AL-4
Crystal Springs State Public Shooting Area—*park* .......... SD-7
Crystal Spring Station (historical)—*locale* . MA-1
Crystal Spring Steam Pumping Station—*hist pl* .......... VA-3
**Crystal Springs Township**—*pop pl* .......... ND-7
Crystal Springs United Methodist Ch—*church* .......... MS-4
Crystal Springs Youth Camp—*locale* .......... ND-7
Crystal Station Bridge—*bridge* .......... IN-6
Crystal Stream Cem—*cemetery* .......... NJ-2
Crystal Street Sch—*school* .......... LA-4
Crystal Swamp—*swamp* .......... WI-6
**Crystal (Town of)**—*pop pl* .......... ME-1
**Crystal (Town of)**—*pop pl* .......... WI-6
*Crystal Township* .......... KS-7
Crystal Township—*fmr MCD* (2) .......... IA-7
**Crystal Township**—*pop pl* .......... KS-7
**Crystal Township**—*pop pl* .......... ND-7
Crystal Township (historical)—*civil* .......... ND-7
Crystal (Township of)—*civ div* .......... MI-6
**Crystal (Township of)**—*pop pl* (2) .......... MI-6
Crystal Valley—*locale* .......... GA-3
**Crystal Valley**—*pop pl* .......... MI-6
Crystal Valley—*valley* .......... AR-4
Crystal Valley—*valley* (2) .......... CO-8
Crystal Valley—*valley* .......... NY-2
Crystal Valley—*valley* .......... WI-6
Crystal Valley Cemetery—*hist pl* .......... CO-8
Crystal Valley Ch—*church* .......... AR-4
Crystal Valley Ditch—*canal* .......... CO-8
**Crystal Vista**—*pop pl* .......... IL-6
Crystal Vly—*swamp* .......... NY-2
Crystal Wash—*stream* .......... NV-8
Crystal Waterhole—*lake* .......... CA-9
Crystal Waters Dam—*dam* .......... MA-1
Crystal Waters Rsvr—*reservoir* .......... MA-1
Crystal Well—*well* (2) .......... AZ-5
*Crystal Windmill* .......... AZ-5
Crystal Windmill—*locale* .......... TX-5
Crystella, Lake—*lake* .......... PA-2
*Cryster Lake* .......... MN-6
Crystle Lake—*lake* .......... ID-8
*Crystleys Run* .......... VA-3
**Crystola**—*pop pl* (2) .......... CO-8
Crystola Creek—*stream* .......... CO-8
*Crystoval* .......... AZ-5
Crysup, J. T., House—*hist pl* .......... TX-5
Crysup Lake—*reservoir* .......... TX-5
C S Canyon—*valley* .......... AZ-5
C Sch—*school* .......... PA-2
C Schultz Ranch—*locale* .......... NE-7
C S Creek—*stream* .......... MT-8
C S Creek—*stream* .......... ND-7
C S Dam—*dam* .......... NV-8
C S Doak Sch—*school* .......... TN-4
C Serrano Cabin—*locale* .......... NM-5
C Shaft Hill—*summit* .......... MI-6
C Shuptrine Dam—*dam* .......... AL-4
C Shurley Ranch—*locale* .......... TX-5
*C Smith Ditch* .......... IN-6
C S Mott Lake—*reservoir* .......... MI-6
C Snow Hinton Park—*park* .......... AL-4
C.S.P.S. Hall—*hist pl* .......... IA-7
C.S.P.S. Hall—*hist pl* .......... MN-6
CSPS Lodge-Griesser Bakery—*hist pl* .......... TX-5
C S Ranch—*locale* .......... NM-5
C S Ranch—*locale* .......... WY-8
CSS GEORGIA (ironclad)—*hist pl* .......... GA-3
C.S.S. MUSCOGEE AND CHATTAHOOCHEE (gunboats)—*hist pl* .......... GA-3
C S Stirling Junior Dam—*dam* .......... AL-4
C Steen Dam—*dam* .......... SD-7
C Surplus—*unorg* .......... ME-1
C Swanson Ranch—*locale* .......... WY-8
C Tank—*reservoir* .......... TX-5
C-Three Pool—*reservoir* .......... MI-6
C T Rsvr—*reservoir* .......... OR-9
C T Spring—*spring* .......... AZ-5
C T Spring—*spring* .......... OR-9
C-Two Pool—*reservoir* .......... MI-6
**Cuadrilla**—*pop pl* .......... TX-5
Cuadrilla Lateral—*canal* .......... TX-5
Cuadro Wash—*stream* .......... AZ-5
Cuarta, Canada De La —*valley* .......... CA-9
*Cuarta Canyon* .......... CA-9
**Cuarta de Tierra**—*pop pl* .......... PR-3
Cuarto (Barrio)—*fmr MCD* .......... PR-3
**Cuarto De Tierra**—*pop pl* .......... PR-3
Cuarto Esquinas Well—*well* .......... TX-5
*Cuarzo Canyon* .......... AZ-5
Cuaslui Creek—*stream* .......... CA-9
Cuatas Windmill—*locale* .......... TX-5
Cuate Canyon—*valley* .......... NM-5
Cuates Butte—*summit* .......... AZ-5
Cuates Creek—*stream* .......... CO-8
Cuates Lake—*lake* .......... TX-5
Cuates Sch—*school* .......... NM-5
Cuates Tank—*reservoir* .......... TX-5
Cuates Windmill—*locale* .......... TX-5
Cuate Tank—*reservoir* .......... NM-5
Cuate Tank—*reservoir* .......... TX-5
Cuatites Well (Windmill)—*locale* .......... TX-5
Cuatralvo Ranch (Bigford Ranch)—*locale* .... TX-5
Cuatro Caballo, Lake—*lake* .......... LA-4
Cuatro Calles—*locale* .......... PR-3
**Cuatro Calles**—*pop pl* (3) .......... PR-3
Cuatro Caminos—*locale* .......... TX-5
**Cuatro Caminos**—*pop pl* .......... PR-3
*Cuatro Creek* .......... CO-8
Cuatro de Julio Waterhole—*lake* .......... TX-5
Cuatro de Julio Windmill—*locale* (4) .......... TX-5
Cuatro Esquinas Windmill—*locale* (2) .......... TX-5
Cuatrojulio Tank—*reservoir* .......... TX-5
Cuatus Tank—*reservoir* .......... TX-5
Cuave Lake Dam—*dam* .......... MS-4
*Cuba* .......... AL-4
*Cuba* .......... IN-6
Cuba—*locale* .......... GA-3
Cuba—*locale* .......... IL-6
Cuba—*locale* .......... ND-7
Cuba—*locale* .......... TN-4
Cuba—*locale* .......... TX-5
Cuba—*locale* .......... WV-2
**Cuba**—*pop pl* .......... AL-4
**Cuba**—*pop pl* .......... IL-6
**Cuba**—*pop pl* (3) .......... IN-6
**Cuba**—*pop pl* .......... KS-7
**Cuba**—*pop pl* .......... KY-4
**Cuba**—*pop pl* .......... MS-4
**Cuba**—*pop pl* .......... MO-7
**Cuba**—*pop pl* .......... NM-5
**Cuba**—*pop pl* .......... NY-2
**Cuba**—*pop pl* (2) .......... OH-6
**Cuba**—*pop pl* .......... TN-4
**Cuba**—*pop pl* .......... PR-3
Cuba Bluff—*cliff* .......... MO-7
Cuba Bottom—*bend* .......... AR-4
Cuba Branch—*stream* .......... FL-3
Cuba Branch—*stream* .......... KY-4
Cuba Canyon—*valley* .......... WA-9
Cuba (CCD)—*cens area* .......... AL-4
Cuba (CCD)—*cens area* .......... NM-5
Cuba Cem—*cemetery* .......... IA-7
Cuba Cem—*cemetery* .......... KY-4
Cuba Cem—*cemetery* .......... OH-6
Cuba Ch—*church* .......... GA-3
Cuba Ch—*church* (2) .......... LA-4
Cuba Ch—*church* .......... MO-7
Cuba Ch—*church* .......... NE-7
Cuba Ch—*church* (2) .......... TX-5
**Cuba City**—*pop pl* .......... WI-6
Cuba Creek—*stream* .......... MS-4
Cuba Creek—*stream* .......... MT-8
Cuba Dam—*dam* .......... ND-7
Cuba Ditch—*canal* .......... NM-5
Cuba Division—*civil* .......... AL-4
Cuba Elem Sch—*school* .......... AL-4
**Cubage**—*pop pl* .......... KY-4
Cubage Creek—*stream* .......... KY-4
*Cubages Pond* .......... NH-1
Cuba Gulch—*valley* .......... CO-8
*Cubahatchee* .......... AL-4
*Cubahatchee Baptist Church* .......... AL-4
Cubahatchee Ch—*church* .......... AL-4
Cubahatchee Creek—*stream* .......... AL-4
Cubahatchee Lookout Tower—*locale* .......... AL-4
Cubahatchie Post Office (historical)—*building* .......... AL-4
Cuba Head Start Sch—*school* .......... AL-4
Cuba Hill—*summit* .......... NY-2
Cuba Hill Lookout Tower—*locale* .......... MN-6
Cuba Hill Sch—*school* .......... NY-2
Cuba Hollow—*valley* .......... TN-4
Cuba HS—*school* .......... KS-7
Cuba HS—*school* .......... KY-4
Cuba Interchange—*crossing* .......... ND-7
Cuba Island—*island* .......... ME-1
Cuba Island—*island* (2) .......... NY-2
Cuba Island—*island* .......... TX-5
Cuba Island—*island* .......... VA-3
Cuba Lake—*lake* (2) .......... MN-6
Cuba Lake—*reservoir* .......... NY-2
Cuba Lake Outlet—*stream* .......... NY-2
Cuba Landing—*locale* .......... AL-4
Cuba Landing—*locale* .......... TN-4
Cuba Landing Marina—*locale* .......... TN-4
Cuba Landing Post Office (historical)—*building* .......... TN-4
*Cuba Mill* .......... PA-2
**Cuba Mills**—*pop pl* .......... PA-2
Cuba Mine—*mine* .......... AZ-5
Cuba Mine—*mine* .......... NV-8
Cuba Mine (historical)—*mine* .......... PA-2
**Cuba Mines (subdivision)**—*pop pl* .......... PA-2
Cuba Municipal Airp—*airport* .......... MO-7
Cubana—*locale* .......... WV-2
Cuban Branch—*stream* .......... FL-3
Cuban Creek—*stream* .......... ID-8
Cuban Embassy Bldg—*building* .......... DC-2
Cuban Gulch—*valley* .......... AK-9
Cuban Hill—*summit* .......... ID-8
Cuban Ledge—*bar* .......... NY-2
Cuba Post Office (historical)—*building* .......... MS-4
Cuba Ranger Station—*locale* .......... NM-5
*Cuba Rock* .......... DE-2
**Cuba (Sand Flat)**—*pop pl* .......... TX-5
Cuba Sch—*school* .......... IL-6
Cuba Sch—*school* .......... KY-4
Cuba Sch—*school* .......... LA-4
*Cuba School* .......... TN-4
Cuba Shoals—*bar* .......... AL-4
Cuba State Wildlife Mngmt Area—*park* ... MN-6
*Cuba Station* .......... AL-4
Cuba Towhead—*island* .......... KY-4
Cuba Town Hall—*building* .......... ND-7
**Cuba (Town of)**—*pop pl* .......... NY-2
**Cuba Township**—*pop pl* .......... ND-7
**Cuba (Township of)**—*pop pl* .......... IL-6
**Cuba (Township of)**—*pop pl* .......... MN-6
Cubbage Cem—*cemetery* .......... KY-4
Cubbage Chapel—*church* .......... IL-6
Cubbage Creek—*stream* .......... GA-3
Cubbage Hollow—*valley* .......... VA-3
Cubbage Island—*island* .......... GA-3
Cubbage Mtn—*summit* .......... VA-3
Cubbage Pond—*reservoir* .......... DE-2
Cubbage Pond Dam—*dam* .......... DE-2
Cubbage Sch—*school* .......... KY-4
*Cub Basin* .......... ID-8
Cub Basin—*basin* .......... ID-8
Cub Basin Spring—*spring* .......... ID-8
*Cubb Canyon* .......... AZ-5
Cubb Creek—*stream* .......... GA-3
Cub Bear Creek—*stream* .......... AK-9
Cub Bear Creek—*stream* .......... MI-6
Cub Bear Mine—*mine* .......... CA-9
Cubberley HS—*school* .......... CA-9
Cubberley Sch—*school* (2) .......... CA-9
Cubberly Pond—*lake* .......... FL-3
Cubbington Hollow—*valley* .......... TN-4
Cubbins Hollow—*valley* .......... TN-4
Cubbison Coulee—*valley* .......... MT-8
Cubbison Ridge—*ridge* .......... OH-6
Cubbler Place—*locale* .......... CA-9
Cub Branch—*stream* .......... IL-6
Cub Branch—*stream* .......... IN-6
Cub Branch—*stream* (2) .......... KY-4
Cub Branch—*stream* .......... NC-3
Cub Branch—*stream* (2) .......... TN-4
Cub Branch—*stream* .......... VA-3
Cub Branch—*stream* (6) .......... WV-2
Cub Branch Gap—*gap* .......... WV-2
Cub Brook—*stream* .......... NJ-2
*Cubbs Creek* .......... AL-4
Cubbs Creek Shoals—*bar* .......... AL-4
*Cubb Spring* .......... UT-8
Cubby Cove—*valley* .......... KY-4
Cubby Hole—*bay* .......... ME-1
Cubby House Hill—*summit* .......... IN-6
Cub Canal—*canal* .......... ID-8
Cub Canyon—*valley* .......... AZ-5
Cub Canyon—*valley* .......... CA-9
Cub Canyon—*valley* (2) .......... ID-8
Cub Cem—*cemetery* .......... TN-4
*Cub Church* .......... TN-4
**Cub City**—*pop pl* .......... WV-2
Cub Cliff—*cliff* .......... OR-9
*Cub Creek* .......... WV-2
Cub Creek—*fmr MCD* .......... NE-7
**Cub Creek**—*pop pl* .......... TN-4
Cub Creek—*stream* .......... AL-4
Cub Creek—*stream* (4) .......... AK-9
Cub Creek—*stream* (3) .......... AR-4
Cub Creek—*stream* (4) .......... CA-9
Cub Creek—*stream* (3) .......... CO-8
Cub Creek—*stream* (8) .......... ID-8
Cub Creek—*stream* .......... IA-7
Cub Creek—*stream* (2) .......... KY-4
Cub Creek—*stream* .......... LA-4
Cub Creek—*stream* (2) .......... MO-7
Cub Creek—*stream* (6) .......... MT-8
Cub Creek—*stream* (3) .......... NE-7
Cub Creek—*stream* .......... NM-5
Cub Creek—*stream* (8) .......... NC-3
Cub Creek—*stream* (3) .......... OR-9
Cub Creek—*stream* (7) .......... TN-4
Cub Creek—*stream* (2) .......... UT-8
Cub Creek—*stream* (5) .......... VA-3
Cub Creek—*stream* (6) .......... WA-9
Cub Creek—*stream* .......... WV-2
Cub Creek—*stream* (4) .......... WY-8
Cub Creek Campground—*locale* .......... CO-8
Cub Creek Cem—*cemetery* .......... KY-4
Cub Creek Cem—*cemetery* .......... TN-4
Cub Creek Ch—*church* .......... KY-4
Cub Creek Ch—*church* (2) .......... NC-3
Cub Creek Cove—*bay* .......... TN-4
Cub Creek Dam—*dam* .......... TN-4
*Cub Creek Hall Baptist Church* .......... TN-4
*Cub Creek Hall Church* .......... TN-4
Cub Creek Island (historical)—*island* .......... TN-4
**Cub Creek Junction**—*pop pl* .......... WV-2
Cub Creek Lake—*reservoir* .......... TN-4
Cub Creek Lake Dam Number One—*dam* .. TN-4
Cub Creek Lake Dam Number Three—*dam* .......... TN-4
Cub Creek Lake Number One—*reservoir* ... TN-4
Cub Creek Lake Number Three—*reservoir* . TN-4
Cub Creek Lake Number Two A—*reservoir* .......... TN-4
Cub Creek Number Two A Dam—*dam* .......... TN-4
Cub Creek Park—*park* .......... CO-8
Cub Creek Park—*park* .......... NC-3
Cub Creek Rsvr—*reservoir* .......... MT-8
Cub Creek Sch (historical)—*school* .......... TN-4
Cub Creek Shoals—*bar* .......... TN-4
Cub Creek Trail—*trail* .......... OR-9
Cub Creek Tree Farm Dam—*dam* .......... TN-4
Cub Creek Tree Farm Lake—*reservoir* .......... TN-4
Cub Creek Well—*well* .......... MT-8
Cube Cove—*bay* .......... AK-9
Cube Iron Mtn—*summit* .......... MT-8
Cubelow Hollow—*valley* .......... TN-4
Cube Point—*cape* .......... AK-9
Cube Point—*cape* .......... MI-6
Cuberant Lake—*lake* .......... UT-8
**Cubero**—*pop pl* .......... NM-5
Cube Rock Pass—*gap* .......... WY-8
Cubero Grant—*civil* .......... NM-5
*Cube's* .......... MI-6
Cube Spring—*spring* .......... OR-9
Cub Gulch—*valley* .......... MT-8
Cub Headland—*cliff* .......... AZ-5
*Cub Hill* .......... UT-8
**Cub Hill**—*pop pl* .......... MD-2
Cub Hill—*summit* .......... CA-9
Cub Hill—*summit* .......... MA-1
Cub Hollow—*valley* .......... TN-4
Cub Hollow—*valley* (2) .......... TX-5
Cubhunt Branch—*stream* .......... TX-5
*Cubia Landing* .......... TN-4
Cubilo Hollow—*valley* .......... KY-4
Cub Island—*island* .......... AK-9
Cub Island—*island* .......... GA-3
Cub Island—*island* .......... UT-8
Cubitis—*locale* .......... FL-3
Cubits Gap—*gap* .......... LA-4
Cubitt Creek—*stream* .......... VA-3
Cub Knob—*summit* .......... TN-4
Cub Lake—*lake* .......... AZ-5
Cub Lake—*lake* .......... CA-9
Cub Lake—*lake* .......... CO-8
Cub Lake—*lake* .......... FL-3
Cub Lake—*lake* .......... ID-8
Cub Lake—*lake* (3) .......... MI-6
Cub Lake—*lake* .......... MN-6
Cub Lake—*lake* .......... NJ-2
Cub Lake—*lake* .......... TX-5
Cub Lake—*lake* .......... UT-8
Cub Lake—*lake* (2) .......... WA-9
Cub Lake—*lake* (2) .......... WI-6
Cub Lake—*lake* .......... WY-8
**Cub Lake**—*pop pl* .......... MS-4
Cub Lake—*reservoir* .......... ID-8
Cub Lake—*reservoir* .......... IN-6
Cub Lake—*reservoir* .......... TN-4
Cub Lake Bayou—*stream* .......... MS-4
Cublake Post Office (historical)—*building* .. MS-4
Cub Lake Slough—*stream* .......... MS-4
Cub Lee Well—*well* .......... CA-9
Cubleigh Hill—*summit* .......... NH-1
Cubley Park—*park* .......... NY-2
Cub Mesa—*summit* .......... NM-5
Cub Mine—*mine* .......... UT-8
Cub Mtn—*summit* .......... AR-4
Cub Mtn—*summit* (2) .......... NM-5
Cub Mtn—*summit* .......... TN-4
*Cubo* .......... AZ-5
*Cubo Hills* .......... AZ-5
Cub Pass—*gap* .......... WA-9
*Cub Peak* .......... OR-9
Cub Point—*cape* .......... AK-9
Cub Point—*cape* .......... OR-9
Cub Point—*cliff* .......... ID-8
Cub Pond—*lake* .......... NH-1
Cub Prairie Cem—*cemetery* .......... IL-6
Cub Ridge—*ridge* .......... WV-2
Cub River—*stream* .......... ID-8
Cub River—*stream* .......... UT-8
Cub River Worm Creek Canal—*canal* .......... ID-8
*Cub Run* .......... VA-3
*Cub Run* .......... WV-2
Cub Run—*locale* .......... KY-4
**Cub Run**—*pop pl* .......... KY-4
Cub Run—*stream* (2) .......... KY-4
Cub Run—*stream* .......... OH-6
Cub Run—*stream* .......... PA-2
Cub Run—*stream* (4) .......... VA-3
Cub Run—*stream* (2) .......... WV-2
Cub Run Cave—*cave* .......... KY-4
Cub Run Ch—*church* .......... VA-3
Cub Spring—*spring* .......... AZ-5
Cub Spring—*spring* .......... CA-9
Cub Spring—*spring* .......... CO-8
Cub Spring—*spring* .......... ID-8
Cub Spring—*spring* .......... NM-5
Cub Spring—*spring* (2) .......... OR-9
Cub Spring—*spring* .......... TX-5
Cub Spring—*spring* (2) .......... UT-8
Cub Springs—*spring* .......... AZ-5
Cub Swamp—*swamp* .......... NJ-2
Cub Tank—*reservoir* .......... NM-5
Cubtown Brook—*stream* .......... NY-2
Cub Trace Branch—*stream* .......... WV-2
Cubuy (Barrio)—*fmr MCD* .......... PR-3
Cub Valley—*basin* .......... UT-8
Cub Valley—*valley* .......... CA-9
Cub Wallow—*basin* .......... CA-9
Cuca—*civil* .......... CA-9
Cucamonga—*civil* .......... CA-9
**Cucamonga**—*pop pl* .......... CA-9
Cucamonga Canyon—*valley* .......... CA-9
Cucamonga Creek—*stream* .......... CA-9
Cucamonga Creek—*stream* .......... OR-9
Cucamonga JHS—*school* .......... CA-9
Cucamonga Junction—*locale* .......... AZ-5
Cucamonga Peak—*summit* .......... CA-9
Cucamonga Peak Trail—*trail* .......... CA-9
Cucamonga Sch—*school* .......... CA-9
Cucamonga Wilderness—*park* .......... CA-9
Cucamonga Winery (Historical Landmark)—*park* .......... CA-9
Cucchi Fork—*stream* .......... UT-8
**Cuchara**—*pop pl* .......... CO-8
Cuchara Campground—*locale* .......... CO-8
*Cuchara Camps* .......... CO-8
Cuchara Creek—*stream* .......... TX-5
Cuchara Junction—*locale* .......... CO-8
*Cucharas Camps* .......... CO-8
Cucharas Creek—*stream* .......... CO-8
*Cucharas Junction* .......... CO-8
Cucharas Pass—*gap* .......... CO-8
Cucharas River—*stream* .......... CO-8
Cucharas Rsvr—*reservoir* .......... CO-8
**Cucharillas**—*pop pl* .......... PR-3
Cuchila el Asomante—*ridge* .......... PR-3
Cuchilla, Loma la—*summit* .......... TX-5
Cuchilla Alta—*ridge* .......... CO-8
Cuchilla Alta Creek—*stream* .......... CO-8
Cuchilla Arroyo—*stream* .......... NM-5
Cuchilla Blanca Hill—*ridge* .......... NM-5
Cuchilla Buena Vista—*ridge* .......... PR-3
Cuchilla De Bucarabones—*ridge* .......... PR-3
Cuchilla de Escala—*ridge* .......... NM-5
Cuchilla De Hato Nuevo—*ridge* .......... PR-3
Cuchilla de Juan Gonzalez—*ridge* .......... PR-3
Cuchilla Del Ojo—*summit* .......... NM-5
Cuchilla de Monte Llano—*ridge* .......... PR-3
Cuchilla de Panduras—*ridge* .......... PR-3
Cuchilla de San Francisco—*ridge* .......... NM-5
Cuchilla de Santa Ines—*ridge* .......... PR-3
Cuchilla El Duque—*ridge* .......... PR-3
Cuchilla Los Matos—*ridge* .......... PR-3
Cuchilla Lupe—*ridge* .......... NM-5
Cuchilla Naranjo—*ridge* .......... PR-3
Cuchilla Pasture—*flat* .......... TX-5
Cuchilla Ranchera—*ridge* .......... PR-3
Cuchillas—*ridge* .......... NM-5
Cuchillas Aceitunas—*ridge* .......... PR-3
Cuchillas (Barrio)—*fmr MCD* (3) .......... PR-3
Cuchillas Peladas—*bench* .......... NM-5
**Cuchillo**—*pop pl* .......... NM-5
Cuchillo Community Allotment Rsvr—*reservoir* .......... NM-5
Cuchillo Community Ditch—*canal* .......... NM-5
Cuchillo de Fernando—*summit* .......... NM-5
Cuchillo del Medio—*summit* .......... NM-5
Cuchillo Mtn—*summit* .......... NM-5
Cuchillo Negro Creek—*stream* .......... NM-5
Cuchillo Tank No 2—*reservoir* .......... NM-5
Cuchillo Windmill—*locale* .......... TX-5
Cucho Mesa—*summit* .......... NM-5
Cuch Spring—*spring* .......... UT-8
Cuchudas Canyon—*valley* .......... CA-9
**Cuckelbur (Cucklebur)**—*pop pl* .......... AZ-5
Cuckels Brook—*stream* .......... NJ-2
**Cuckhold Creek**—*pop pl* .......... MD-2
Cucklebur—*other* .......... AZ-5
Cuckle Creek—*stream* .......... OH-6
Cuckle Creek—*stream* .......... TN-4
*Cucklemaer Creek* .......... NC-3
Cucklemaker Creek—*stream* .......... NC-3
*Cucklemaker Swamp* .......... NC-3
*Cuckles Brook* .......... NJ-2
Cucko Lake—*lake* .......... MN-6
Cuckold Creek—*bay* (2) .......... MD-2
Cuckold Point—*cape* .......... MD-2
Cuckolds, The—*island* .......... ME-1
*Cuckolds Brook* .......... NJ-2
Cuckolds Creek—*stream* .......... NC-3
Cuckolds Creek—*stream* .......... SC-3
*Cuckoldstown* .......... DE-2
**Cuckoo**—*pop pl* .......... VA-3
Cuckoo, The—*gap* .......... VA-3
Cuckoo (Magisterial District)—*fmr MCD* .......... VA-3
Cuckoo Pond—*lake* .......... TX-5
Cuckoo Ridge—*ridge* .......... CA-9
Cucomungo Canyon—*valley* .......... CA-9
Cucomungo Canyon—*valley* .......... NV-8
Cucomungo Spring—*spring* .......... NV-8
Cuculus Island—*island* .......... MN-6
**Cucumber**—*pop pl* .......... WV-2
Cucumber Branch—*stream* .......... KY-4
Cucumber Creek—*stream* .......... AK-9
Cucumber Creek—*stream* .......... CO-8
Cucumber Creek—*stream* .......... NC-3
Cucumber Creek—*stream* .......... OK-5
Cucumber Creek—*stream* .......... WV-2
Cucumber Falls—*falls* .......... PA-2
Cucumber Gap—*gap* .......... TN-4
Cucumber Gulch—*valley* .......... CO-8
Cucumber Hill—*summit* .......... RI-1
Cucumber Hollow—*valley* .......... MD-2
Cucumber Hollow—*valley* (2) .......... TN-4
Cucumber Island—*island* .......... FL-3
Cucumber Lake—*lake* (2) .......... MI-6
Cucumber Lake—*lake* (2) .......... MN-6
Cucumber Reef—*bar* .......... AK-9
Cucumber Ridge—*ridge* .......... WV-2
Cucumber Run—*stream* (2) .......... PA-2
Cucumber Slough—*gut* .......... FL-3
Cudahay Mine—*mine* .......... KS-7
**Cudahy**—*pop pl* .......... CA-9
**Cudahy**—*pop pl* .......... WI-6
Cudahy—*uninc pl* .......... CA-9
Cudahy Camp—*locale* .......... CA-9
Cudahy Drain—*canal* .......... UT-8
Cudahy Mine—*mine* .......... UT-8
Cudahy Park—*park* .......... WI-6
Cudahy Rsvr—*reservoir* .......... CO-8
Cudahys Old Dutch Cleanser Mine—*mine* .. CA-9
**Cudai**—*pop pl* .......... NM-5
*Cuddahunka Island* .......... MA-1
Cudd Cem—*cemetery* .......... AR-4
Cudd Creek—*stream* .......... AR-4
Cuddeback Creek—*stream* .......... CA-9
Cuddeback Hill—*summit* .......... NY-2
Cuddeback Lake—*flat* .......... CA-9
Cuddeback Lake Air Force Range—*military* .......... CA-9
Cuddeback Sch—*school* .......... CA-9
**Cuddebackville**—*pop pl* .......... NY-2
Cuddigan Gulch—*valley* .......... CO-8
Cuddihy Fork—*stream* .......... CA-9
Cuddihy Lakes—*lake* .......... CA-9
Cuddihy Landing Strip—*airport* .......... NJ-2
Cuddihy Valley—*valley* .......... CA-9
Cuddleback Flat—*flat* .......... CA-9
Cudd Sch (abandoned)—*school* .......... MO-7
Cudds Creek—*stream* .......... SC-3
Cuddyback Lake—*lake* .......... UT-8
Cuddybum Branch—*stream* .......... NC-3
Cuddy Cabin—*locale* .......... CA-9
Cuddy Canyon—*valley* .......... CA-9
Cuddy Creek—*stream* .......... CA-9
Cuddy Creek—*stream* .......... OK-5
**Cuddy Hill**—*pop pl* .......... PA-2
Cuddy Mine—*mine* .......... ID-8
Cuddy Mtn—*summit* .......... ID-8
Cuddy Mtns—*range* .......... ID-8
*Cuddy Peak* .......... CA-9
Cuddy Ranch—*locale* .......... CA-9
Cuddy Ranch—*locale* .......... CO-8
**Cuddy (Treveskyn)**—*pop pl* .......... PA-2
Cuddy Valley—*valley* .......... CA-9
*Cude* .......... MS-4
Cude Cem—*cemetery* .......... MO-7
Cude Cem—*cemetery* (2) .......... TN-4
Cude Crossing Windmill—*locale* .......... TX-5
Cude Hollow—*valley* .......... TN-4
Cudejarre, Point—*cape* .......... VI-3
Cudell Park—*park* .......... OH-6
Cude Tank—*reservoir* .......... TX-5
Cude Windmill—*locale* .......... TX-5
Cud Gap—*gap* .......... NC-3
Cudge Hollow—*valley* .......... TN-4
Cudgetown Cem—*cemetery* .......... IL-6
Cudio Cave—*cave* .......... VA-3
Cudjo Cem—*cemetery* .......... OK-5
Cudjo Creek—*stream* .......... OK-5
**Cudjoe**—*pop pl* .......... FL-3
Cudjoe Basin—*bay* .......... FL-3
Cudjoe Bay—*bay* .......... FL-3
Cudjoe Channel—*channel* .......... FL-3
Cudjoe Key—*island* .......... FL-3
**Cudjoe Key**—*pop pl* .......... FL-3
Cudjoe Key Air Force Site—*military* .......... FL-3
Cudjoe Key Air Force Station—*military* .......... FL-3
Cudler Creek—*stream* .......... KY-4
Cudney Draw—*valley* .......... MT-8
Cud Swamp—*stream* .......... SC-3
*Cudworth Brook* .......... MA-1
Cudworth Cem—*cemetery* .......... MO-7
*Cudzu Cave* .......... AL-4
**Cuebas**—*pop pl* .......... PR-3
Cuebas (Barrio)—*fmr MCD* .......... PR-3
Cue Creek—*stream* .......... AK-9
Cue Creek—*stream* .......... MO-7
Cue Lake—*lake* .......... FL-3
**Cuelen Acres (subdivision)**—*pop pl* .......... DE-2
Cuelho Ranch—*locale* .......... CA-9
Cuellar Park—*park* .......... TX-5
Cuenin Creek—*stream* .......... WI-6
Cuenin Lake—*lake* .......... WI-6
Cuerbo, Point—*cape* .......... AK-9
Cuerda de Lena—*stream* .......... AZ-5
*Cuerda de Lena Wash* .......... AZ-5
**Cuerna Verde Park**—*pop pl* .......... CO-8
*Cuerno Verde* .......... CO-8
Cuernudo Hills—*summit* .......... NM-5
**Cuero**—*pop pl* .......... TX-5
Cuero (CCD)—*cens area* .......... TX-5
Cuero Commercial Hist Dist—*hist pl* .......... TX-5
Cuero Creek—*stream* .......... TX-5
Cuero de Venada Windmill—*locale* .......... TX-5
Cuero Gin—*hist pl* .......... TX-5
Cuero HS—*hist pl* .......... TX-5
Cuero Hydroelectric Plant—*hist pl* .......... TX-5
Cuero I Archeol District—*hist pl* .......... TX-5
Cuero Windmill—*locale* .......... TX-5
Cuerton Dial Branch—*stream* .......... TN-4
Cuerva Pen Windmill—*locale* .......... TX-5
Cuerva Tank—*reservoir* .......... TX-5
Cuervito Creek—*stream* .......... NM-5
Cuervito Peak—*summit* .......... NM-5
Cuervitos Windmill—*locale* .......... TX-5
**Cuervo**—*pop pl* .......... NM-5
Cuervo Canyon—*valley* .......... NM-5
Cuervo Cem—*cemetery* .......... NM-5
Cuervo Creek—*stream* .......... NM-5
Cuervo Creek—*stream* (2) .......... TX-5
Cuervo Crossing—*locale* .......... NM-5
Cuervo Draw—*valley* .......... TX-5
Cuervo Hill—*summit* .......... NM-5
Cuervo Mesa—*summit* .......... NM-5
Cuervo Tank—*lake* .......... NM-5
Cuervo Well—*well* .......... TX-5
Cuervo Windmill—*locale* .......... TX-5
Cuesta—*locale* .......... CA-9
Cuesta Blanca—*summit* .......... TX-5
**Cuesta-by-the-Sea**—*pop pl* .......... CA-9
Cuesta Canyon County Park—*park* .......... CA-9
Cuesta de la McBride—*summit* .......... NM-5
**Cuesta de las Piedras**—*pop pl* .......... PR-3
Cuesta de la Yuca—*summit* .......... PR-3
Cuesta Del Burro—*ridge* .......... TX-5
Cuesta Navajo—*ridge* .......... NM-5
Cuesta Pass—*gap* .......... CA-9
Cuesta Sch—*school* .......... FL-3
**Cueston Plaza (condominium)**—*pop pl* .. UT-8
*Cueter Creek* .......... OR-9
Cueto Well—*well* .......... AZ-5
Cueva Canyon—*valley* .......... CA-9
Cueva Canyon—*valley* .......... NM-5
Cueva de Frio—*cave* .......... PR-3
Cueva de la Julia—*bay* .......... PR-3
Cueva de Los Indios—*hist pl* .......... PR-3
Cueva de los Novios—*locale* .......... NM-5
Cueva Escarpment—*ridge* .......... NM-5
Cueva La Mora—*hist pl* .......... PR-3
Cueva Manahena—*cave* .......... PR-3
Cueva Pajita—*cave* .......... PR-3
Cueva Pintada—*hist pl* .......... CA-9
**Cuevas**—*pop pl* .......... MS-4
Cuevas (Barrio)—*fmr MCD* .......... PR-3
Cuevas Creek—*stream* .......... TX-5
Cuevas Lake Dam—*dam* .......... MS-4
Cuevas Post Office (historical)—*building* ... MS-4
Cueva Tank—*reservoir* .......... NM-5
Cueva Valdaze—*cave* .......... CA-9
Cuevitas—*locale* .......... TX-5
**Cuevitas**—*pop pl* .......... TX-5
Cuevitas Banco Number 96—*levee* .......... TX-5
Cuevitas Camp—*locale* .......... NM-5
Cuevo Canyon—*valley* .......... NM-5
Cuevo Ranch—*locale* .......... NM-5
Cuffawa Creek—*stream* .......... MS-4
Cuff Brook—*stream* .......... CT-1
Cuff Button Spring—*spring* .......... AZ-5
Cuff Cem—*cemetery* .......... AR-4
Cuff Creek—*stream* .......... MT-8
Cuffe, Paul, Farm—*hist pl* .......... MA-1
*Cuffees Cove* .......... CA-9
Cuffey Branch—*stream* .......... SC-3
*Cuffey Cove* .......... CA-9
Cuffey Hill—*summit* .......... MA-1
*Cuffey Inlet* .......... CA-9
Cuffeys Cove—*bay* .......... CA-9
Cuffeys Inlet—*bay* .......... CA-9
Cuffeys Point—*cape* .......... CA-9
Cuff Hollow—*valley* .......... TN-4
Cuffie Creek—*stream* .......... SC-3
Cuffietown—*locale* .......... GA-3
Cuff Lake—*lake* .......... WI-6
**Cuffman's Switch**—*pop pl* .......... AR-4
**Cuff Siding**—*pop pl* .......... MI-6
Cuffs Lake—*lake* .......... MN-6
Cuffs Pond—*lake* .......... MA-1
Cuffs Run—*stream* .......... PA-2
Cuff Tarkiln Creek—*stream* .......... NC-3
*Cuffy Cove* .......... CA-9
Cuffy Knob—*summit* .......... WI-6
Cuffytown Creek—*stream* .......... SC-3
**Cufty Heights**—*pop pl* .......... IL-6
*Cuggins Brook* .......... MA-1
Cughan Cem—*cemetery* .......... IL-6
Cuheca, Lake—*lake* .......... CT-1
*Cuidado Mountain* .......... CA-9
*Cuidow Mountain* .......... CA-9
*Cuillicoga* .......... AL-4
Cuiper Park—*park* .......... TX-5
Cuisanto Well—*well* .......... AZ-5
Cuitan Creek—*stream* .......... OR-9
Cuitin, Lake—*lake* .......... WA-9
Cuitin Creek—*stream* (2) .......... WA-9
Cuivre Creek—*stream* .......... MO-7
Cuivre Island—*island* .......... MO-7
*Cuivre River* .......... MO-7
Cuivre River—*stream* .......... MO-7
*Cuivre River Rec Area* .......... MO-7
Cuivre River State Park—*park* .......... MO-7
Cuivre River State Park Administrative Area Hist Dist—*hist pl* .......... MO-7
Cuivre Slough—*stream* .......... MO-7
Cuivre Township—*civil* (2) .......... MO-7
*Cukiisenuk* .......... FM-9
*Cukucap* .......... FM-9
*Cukune* .......... FM-9
*Cukusamaw* .......... FM-9
*Cukusoow* .......... FM-9
*Cukuwen* .......... FM-9
Cula Creek—*stream* .......... AK-9
Culbartson Cem—*cemetery* .......... MO-7
Culberhouse Cem—*cemetery* .......... AR-4
**Culberson**—*pop pl* .......... NC-3
Culberson Cem—*cemetery* .......... MI-6
**Culberson (County)**—*pop pl* .......... TX-5
*Culberson Creek* .......... WV-2
Culberson Ranch—*locale* .......... NM-5
Culberston Hills Golf Course—*locale* .......... PA-2
Culbert Branch—*stream* .......... NC-3
Culbert Bridge, The—*bridge* .......... TN-4
Culbert Canyon—*valley* .......... UT-8
*Culbert Hollow* .......... AL-4
Culbert Hollow Spring—*spring* .......... AL-4
Culbert Lake—*lake* .......... MS-4
Culbert Ridge—*ridge* .......... NC-3
Culbert Sch—*school* .......... PA-2
**Culbertson**—*pop pl* .......... KY-4
**Culbertson**—*pop pl* .......... MT-8
**Culbertson**—*pop pl* .......... NE-7
**Culbertson**—*pop pl* .......... PA-2
Culbertson, Cordelia A., House—*hist pl* .......... CA-9
Culbertson, Robert, House—*hist pl* .......... OH-6
Culbertson, William, House—*hist pl* .......... OH-6
Culbertson Branch—*stream* .......... KY-4
Culbertson Canal—*canal* .......... NE-7
Culbertson Cem—*cemetery* .......... MO-7
Culbertson Cem—*cemetery* (3) .......... VA-3
Culbertson Chapel—*church* .......... VA-3
Culbertson Creek—*stream* .......... MT-8
Culbertson Creek—*stream* .......... VA-3

Culbertson Creek—stream WY-8
Culbertson Dam—dam NE-7
Culbertson Ditch—canal IN-6
Culbertson Elem Sch—school PA-2
Culbertson Extension Canal—canal NE-7
Culbertson-Harbison Farm—hist pl PA-2
Culbertson Heights OH-6
Culbertson Hills Airp—airport PA-2
Culbertson House—hist pl KY-4
Culbertson Kiln—hist pl AR-4
Culbertson Lake—lake WI-6
Culbertson Lake—reservoir CA-9
Culbertson Mansion—hist pl IN-6
Culbertson Memorial Ch—church AZ-5
Culbertson Mine—mine MO-7
Culbertson Point—summit AR-4
Culbertson Ranch—locale NM-5
Culbertson Run—stream PA-2
Culbertson Sch—school GA-3
Culbertson Sch—school IL-6
Culbertson Sch—school LA-4
Culbertson Sch—school NJ-2
Culbertson School PA-2
Culbertsons Corners Sch—school OH-6
Culbertson Station—locale PA-2
Culbertson Trail—trail PA-2
Culb Lake—reservoir TX-5
Culbreath Bayou—bay FL-3
**Culbreth**—pop pl NC-3
Culbreth Bridge—bridge GA-3
Culbreth Cem—cemetery SC-3
Culbreth JHS—school NC-3
Culbreth Marsh Ditch—stream DE-2
Culbreth Memorial Ch—church NC-3
Culbutson Cem—cemetery VA-3
Cul-car-mac Falls—falls TN-4
Culclosure Pond—reservoir SC-3
Culdee Ch—church NC-3
Cul de Sac—locale MO-7
**Culdesac**—pop pl ID-8
Culdesac Creek—stream ID-8
Cul-De-Sac Glacier—glacier AK-9
Culdesac Hill—summit ID-8
Cul de Sac Island SD-7
Culdrum State Wildlife Mngmt Area—park MN-6
**Culdrum (Township of)**—pop pl MN-6
Culebra—locale AL-4
Culebra—locale NM-5
**Culebra**—pop pl PR-3
Culebra Bluff—cliff NM-5
Culebra Creek CO-8
Culebra Creek—stream CO-8
Culebra Creek—stream TX-5
Culebra Hill—summit TX-5
Culebra Islands—area AK-9
Culebra (Municipio)—civil PR-3
Culebra Peak—summit CO-8
Culebra (Pueblo)—fmr MCD PR-3
Culebras Alto (Barrio)—fmr MCD PR-3
Culebras Bajo (Barrio)—fmr MCD PR-3
Culebrina Island—island AK-9
Culebrinas (Barrio)—fmr MCD PR-3
Culebrino, Arroyo—stream CA-9
Culebron Banco Number 153—levee TX-5
Culex Basin—basin WY-8
Culhane Brook—stream NH-1
Culhane Creek—stream MI-6
Culhane Lake—lake MI-6
**Culkin**—pop pl MS-4
Culkin, Lake—lake MN-6
Culkin Acad—school MS-4
Culkin Lake MN-6
Culkin Sch MS-4
Cull—locale KY-4
Cull—locale MO-7
Cullabrella Creek MS-4
Cullaby Creek—stream OR-9
Cullaby Lake—lake OR-9
Cullaby Slough—stream OR-9
Cullage Branch—stream TN-4
Cullasagee NC-3
Cullasagee Creek NC-3
**Cullasaja**—pop pl NC-3
Cullasaja Branch—stream NC-3
Cullasaja Falls—falls NC-3
Cullasaja River—stream NC-3
Cull Canyon Regional Rec Area—park CA-9
Cull Cem—cemetery KY-4
Cull Creek—stream CA-9
Cull Creek Dam—dam CA-9
Cullegan Branch AL-4
Cullen—locale KY-4
Cullen—locale WI-6
**Cullen**—pop pl LA-4
**Cullen**—pop pl NY-2
**Cullen**—pop pl VA-3
Cullen, Ezekiel, House—hist pl TX-5
Cullen, Victor, Sch Power House—hist pl MD-2
Cullen Branch DE-2
Cullen Brothers Dam—dam ND-7
Cullen Cabin—locale OR-9
Cullen Cem—cemetery GA-3
Cullen Cem—cemetery IN-6
Cullen Cem—cemetery KY-4
Cullen Cem—cemetery WI-6
Cullen Creek IN-6
Cullen Creek—stream OR-9
Cullen Creek—stream UT-8
**Cullendale**—pop pl AR-4
Cullendale Cem—cemetery AR-4
Cullen Grimes Sch—school TX-5
Cullen Grove Ch—church GA-3
Cullen JHS—school TX-5
Cullen Mall—post sta TX-5
Cullen Park—park OH-6
Cullen Park—park TX-5
Cullen Place JHS—school TX-5
Cullen Ridge—ridge OH-6
Cullen Sch—school CA-9
Cullen Sch (historical)—school MS-4
Cullens Rsvr—reservoir OR-9
Cullen Tank—reservoir NM-5
Cullen Thomas Dam—dam AL-4
Cullen-Thompson Rsvr—reservoir TX-5
Cullen Township—civil MO-7
Cullen (Victor Cullen State School)—school MD-2
**Cullen Village**—pop pl KS-7
Cullen Village—uninc pl KS-7
Cullen Wash AZ-5
Cullen Windmill—locale NM-5
**Culleoka**—pop pl TN-4
**Culleoka**—pop pl TX-5
Culleoka (CCD)—cens area TN-4
Culleoka Division—civil TN-4
Culleoka Methodist Episcopal Church, South—hist pl TN-4
**Culleoka (RR name Pleasant Grove)**—pop pl TN-4
Culler Cem—cemetery NC-3
Culler Hollow—valley KY-4
Culler JHS—school NE-7
Culler Lake—lake MD-2
**Culler Mill**—pop pl OH-6
Culler Millpond—reservoir SC-3
Cullerot Park—park NH-1
Culler Ponds—reservoir SC-3
Culler Run WV-2
Cullers Cem—cemetery TX-5
Cullers Run—stream WV-2
Culletts Ferry (historical)—locale IN-6
Culley, Bogue—stream MS-4
Culley Creek—stream MS-4
Culley Creek—stream MO-7
Culley Hill—summit WV-2
Culley Hollow—valley TN-4
Culley-Holt Cem—cemetery TN-4
Culley Lake—reservoir MS-4
Culley Run—stream PA-2
Culley Sch—school NV-8
Cull Hollow—valley KY-4
Cullie Creek—stream NC-3
Culliers Run—stream NJ-2
Culligan, Incorporated—facility IL-6
Culligans Flats—flat WY-8
Culling Pond—lake ME-1
Cullings Well AZ-5
Cullin Lake OR-9
Cullins-Baker House—hist pl NC-3
Cullins Hollow—valley AR-4
Cullins Well AZ-5
Cullins Windmill—locale NM-5
**Cullison**—pop pl KS-7
Cullison Lake—lake NE-7
Cull Lake—reservoir IN-6
Cull Lake Dam—dam IN-6
**Cullman**—pop pl AL-4
Cullman (CCD)—cens area AL-4
Cullman College AL-4
**Cullman County**—pop pl AL-4
Cullman County Club—locale AL-4
Cullman County Courthouse—building AL-4
Cullman County Vocational Center—school AL-4
Cullman Division—civil AL-4
Cullman Downtown Commercial Hist Dist—hist pl AL-4
Cullman First Baptist Ch—church AL-4
Cullman Hist Dist—hist pl AL-4
Cullman HS—school AL-4
Cullman JHS AL-4
Cullman MS—school AL-4
Cullman Post Office—building AL-4
Cullman Public Sch (historical)—school AL-4
**Culloden**—pop pl GA-3
**Culloden**—pop pl WV-2
CULLODEN, H.M.S., Shipwreck Site—hist pl NY-2
Culloden-Dolingbroke (CCD)—cens area GA-3
Culloden Cem—cemetery WV-2
Culloden Hist Dist—hist pl GA-3
Culloden Point—cape NY-2
Cullom IL-6
Cullom—locale NE-7
**Cullom**—pop pl IL-6
Cullom, Frances, Jr., House—hist pl KY-4
Cullom Baptist Church AL-4
Cullomberg AL-4
**Cullomburg**—pop pl AL-4
Cullomburg Baptist Ch—church AL-4
Cullomburg United Methodist Ch—church AL-4
**Cullom (historical)**—pop pl TN-4
Cullom Hollow—valley TN-4
Cullom Post Office (historical)—building TN-4
Cullom Sch—school NE-7
Cullom Springs—locale AL-4
Cullom Street-Twelfth Street South Hist Dist—hist pl AL-4
Cullop Branch—stream VA-3
Cullor Cem—cemetery MO-7
**Cullowhee**—pop pl NC-3
Cullowhee Creek—stream NC-3
Cullowhee Gap—gap NC-3
Cullowhee Mountain—ridge NC-3
Cullowhee (Township of)—fmr MCD NC-3
Culls—locale VA-3
Cullum—locale MS-4
Cullum Branch—stream MS-4
Cullum Branch—stream MO-7
Cullum Cem—cemetery SC-3
Cullum Hollow—valley TN-4
Cullum Lake—reservoir IL-6
Cullum Mansion—hist pl TN-4
Cullum Mtn—summit AR-4
Cullum Post Office (historical)—building MS-4
Cullums Pond—lake SC-3
Cull Watt Park—flat WY-8
Cully—CDP OR-9
Cully Cem—cemetery OK-5
Cully Draw—valley TX-5
Cully Memorial Cem—cemetery WA-9
Cullys Branch—stream NC-3
Cullywaugh Rocks—pillar RI-1
Cully Windmill—locale TX-5
Culmer, William, House—hist pl UT-8
**Culmerville**—pop pl PA-2
Culmerville Airp—airport PA-2
**Culmore**—pop pl VA-3
Culong—hist pl NC-3
Culotches Bayou AR-4
Culotches Bay Slough—stream AR-4
Culp—locale AR-4
Culp—locale CO-8
**Culp**—pop pl CA-9
**Culp**—pop pl PA-2
Culp, The—summit WY-8
Culp Branch—stream MO-7
Culp Branch—stream TX-5
Culp Canyon—valley CA-9
Culp Canyon—valley NM-5
Culp Cem—cemetery (2) OH-6
Culp Cem—cemetery (3) TN-4
Culp Chapel TN-4
**Culp Creek**—pop pl OR-9
Culp Creek—stream KY-4
Culp Creek—stream OR-9
Culp Creek Chapel—church KY-4
Culp Draw—valley WY-8
Culpeper—hist pl KY-4
Culpeper—locale AL-4
**Culpeper**—pop pl AR-4
**Culpeper**—pop pl VA-3
Culpeper Branch—stream AR-4
Culpeper Branch—stream VA-3
**Culpeper (County)**—pop pl VA-3
Culpeper Creek—stream AL-4
Culpeper Hist Dist—hist pl VA-3
Culpeper Island—island NC-3
Culpeper Lookout Tower—locale VA-3
Culpepper AL-4
Culpepper—locale AR-4
**Culpepper**—pop pl TN-4
Culpepper Branch—stream AL-4
Culpepper Branch—stream TN-4
Culpepper Brook—stream IN-6
Culpepper Cem—cemetery AL-4
Culpepper Cem—cemetery (2) GA-3
Culpepper Cem—cemetery MO-7
Culpepper Cem—cemetery TN-4
Culpepper Cem—cemetery TX-5
Culpepper Creek—stream GA-3
Culpepper Creek—stream NC-3
Culpepper Hollow—valley KY-4
Culpepper Mtn—summit AR-4
Culpepper-Pummil Site (23SH14/55)—hist pl MO-7
Culpeppers Bridge—bridge NC-3
Culpepper Spring—spring GA-3
Culpepper (Township of)—fmr MCD AR-4
**Culpepper Woods**—pop pl PA-2
Culp Flat—flat WY-8
Culp Ford—locale MO-7
Culp Gulch—valley MT-8
Culp (historical)—building TN-4
Culp Hollow—valley MO-7
Culp Hollow—valley TN-4
Culp House—hist pl SC-3
Culp Island—island SC-3
Culpitt Coulee—valley WI-6
Culp Lake—lake MN-6
Culp Lake—reservoir GA-3
Culp Lake—reservoir SC-3
Culp Lake Dam—dam MS-4
Culp Mtn—summit TX-5
Culp Peak—summit NM-5
Culp Ranch—locale (2) NM-5
Culp Ranch—locale OR-9
Culp Ridge—ridge PA-2
Culp Run—stream OH-6
Culp Sch—school MI-6
Culps Chapel TN-4
Culps Chapel Cemetery TN-4
Culp Sch (historical)—school TN-4
Culp School (Abandoned)—locale TX-5
Culps Hill—summit PA-2
Culps Island TN-4
Culp Tank—reservoir TX-5
Culp Valley—valley (2) CA-9
Culp Well—well NM-5
Culross Bay—bay AK-9
Culross Island—island AK-9
Culross Passage—channel AK-9
Culstigh Creek—stream AL-4
Cultas Creek—stream AK-9
Cultas Lake OR-9
Cultivator Canyon—valley CA-9
Culton, Charles L., House—hist pl WI-6
Culton Cem—cemetery TX-5
Culton Creek—stream TN-4
Cultural Center Hist Dist—hist pl MI-6
Cultus Bay—bay WA-9
Cultus Creek—stream ID-8
Cultus Creek—stream (4) OR-9
Cultus Creek—stream (2) WA-9
Cultus Creek Station—locale WA-9
Cultus Hole—area WA-9
Cultus Lake—lake (2) OR-9
Cultus Lake—lake WA-9
Cultus Lake Trail—trail OR-9
Cultus Mountains—range WA-9
Cultus Mtn—summit OR-9
Cultus Mtn—summit WA-9
Cultus River—stream OR-9
**Culvahouse**—pop pl TN-4
Culvahouse Cem—cemetery TN-4
Culvahouse House—hist pl TN-4
Culver IA-7
Culver NJ-2
Culver—locale IL-6
Culver—locale KY-4
**Culver**—pop pl ID-8
**Culver**—pop pl IN-6
**Culver**—pop pl KS-7
**Culver**—pop pl MN-6
**Culver**—pop pl OR-9
Culver, C. Z., House—hist pl CA-9
Culver-Bear Mine—mine CA-9
Culver Branch—stream IN-6
Culver Branch—stream WI-6
Culver Brook—stream CT-1
Culver Cave—cave AL-4
Culver (CCD)—cens area OR-9
Culver Cem—cemetery IA-7
Culver Cem—cemetery MN-6
Culver Cem—cemetery NY-2
Culver Cem—cemetery VT-1
Culver Cem—cemetery WI-6
**Culver City**—pop pl CA-9
Culver City HS—school CA-9
Culver City Junior Acad—school CA-9
Culver Community Junior-Senior HS—school IN-6
Culver Creek—stream AR-4
Culver Creek—stream ID-8
Culver Creek—stream MI-6
Culver Creek—stream NE-7
Culver Creek—stream (2) NY-2
Culver Creek—stream OH-6
Culver Creek—stream OR-9
Culver Creek—stream PA-2
Culver Cut—channel TX-5
Culver Dam ND-7
Culver Ditch—canal CO-8
Culver Elem Sch—school IN-6
Culver Gulch—valley CO-8
Culver Gulch—valley WA-9
Culver Hist Dist—hist pl IN-6
Culver Hollow—valley AL-4
Culver Hollow—valley PA-2
Culverhouse Branch—stream TN-4
Culver Island—island PA-2
**Culver Junction**—pop pl CA-9
Culver Lake—lake MI-6
Culver Lake—lake MN-6
Culver Lake—lake OR-9
Culver Lateral—canal CO-8
Culver Military Academy IN-6
**Culver Military Academy**—pop pl IN-6
Culver Military and Girls Acad—school IN-6
Culver Pond—reservoir CT-1
Culver Ranch—locale NV-8
Culver Ranch (abandoned)—locale MT-8
Culver Run—stream OH-6
Culver Run—stream PA-2
Culver Sch IN-6
Culver Sch—school CA-9
Culver Sch—school FL-3
Culver Sch—school IN-6
Culver Sch—school (2) MI-6
Culver Sch—school NJ-2
Culver Sch—school NY-2
Culver Sch—school ND-7
Culver Sch (historical)—school PA-2
Culvers Creek—stream NJ-2
Culvers Gap—gap NJ-2
Culvers (historical)—locale AL-4
Culvers Inlet—locale NJ-2
Culvers Lake—CDP NJ-2
Culvers Lake—reservoir NJ-2
Culvers Lake Dam—dam NJ-2
Culverson Creek—stream WV-2
Culver Spring—spring AZ-5
Culver Spring—spring UT-8
Culver Spring Creek WA-9
Culver Springs—spring MT-8
Culver Springs Creek—stream WA-9
Culver Springs Gulch WA-9
Culver Stockton Coll—school MO-7
Culver Studio—hist pl MT-8
Culvert Branch—stream NC-3
Culvert Branch—stream TN-4
Culvert Creek GA-3
Culvert Creek—stream MT-8
Culvert Creek—stream OR-9
Culvert Hollow—valley MD-2
Culvert Hollow—valley UT-8
Culvert Hollow—valley WV-2
Culvert Lake—lake SD-7
**Culverton**—pop pl GA-3
Culvertown—locale KY-4
Culvertown—locale NY-2
**Culver Township**—pop pl KS-7
**Culver (Township of)**—pop pl MN-6
Culvert Spring—spring OR-9
Culvert Street Baptist Ch—church AL-4
Culvert Swamp—swamp GA-3
Culvert Tank—reservoir (2) AZ-5
Culvert Waterhole OR-9
Culver Union Cem—cemetery KS-7
Culverwell Ranch—locale CO-8
Culverwell Rsvr—reservoir NV-8
Culver West Park—park CA-9
Culwell Cem—cemetery AR-4
Culwell School (abandoned)—locale MO-7
Cumahauti—locale AZ-5
Cumaro Canyon—valley AZ-5
Cumaro Spring—spring AZ-5
Cumaro Wash—stream AZ-5
**Cumback**—pop pl IN-6
**Cumbee**—pop pl FL-3
Cumbee Bay—swamp NC-3
Cumbee Cem—cemetery SC-3
Cumbee Drain—stream FL-3
Cumbee Mill—locale AL-4
Cumbee Park—park GA-3
Cumbee RR Station—locale FL-3
Cumbeland Plateau AL-4
Cumber—locale MI-6
Cumber Cem—cemetery TX-5
Cumberland IL-6
Cumberland IN-6
Cumberland ME-1
Cumberland NJ-2
Cumberland—hist pl MI-6
**Cumberland**—pop pl IN-6
**Cumberland**—pop pl IA-7
**Cumberland**—pop pl KY-4
**Cumberland**—pop pl MD-2
**Cumberland**—pop pl MS-4
**Cumberland**—pop pl NJ-2
**Cumberland**—pop pl NC-3
**Cumberland**—pop pl OH-6
**Cumberland**—pop pl OK-5
**Cumberland**—pop pl SC-3
**Cumberland**—pop pl VA-3
**Cumberland**—pop pl WA-9
**Cumberland**—pop pl WI-6
**Cumberland**—post sta GA-3
Cumberland, Lake—reservoir (2) KY-4
Cumberland Acad—school TN-4
Cumberland and Oxford Canal—hist pl ME-1
Cumberland Basin—basin (2) CO-8
Cumberland Bay—bay NY-2
Cumberland Bay State Park—park NY-2
Cumberland Branch IN-6
**Cumberland (Br. P.O.)**—pop pl RI-1
Cumberland Camp Ground—locale TN-4
Cumberland Caverns—cave TN-4
Cumberland (CCD)—cens area KY-4
Cumberland Cem—cemetery (2) AL-4
Cumberland Cem—cemetery KS-7
Cumberland Cem—cemetery KY-4
Cumberland Cem—cemetery (2) MS-4
Cumberland Cem—cemetery NC-3
Cumberland Cem—cemetery (2) OH-6
Cumberland Cem—cemetery (3) PA-2
Cumberland Cem—cemetery WY-8
**Cumberland Center**—pop pl ME-1
**Cumberland Center Station**—pop pl ME-1
Cumberland Ch AL-4
Cumberland Ch MS-4
Cumberland Ch MO-7
Cumberland Ch TN-4
Cumberland Ch—church (7) AL-4
Cumberland Ch—church (3) AR-4
Cumberland Ch—church GA-3
Cumberland Ch—church (2) IL-6
Cumberland Ch—church KS-7
Cumberland Ch—church (5) KY-4
Cumberland Ch—church LA-4
Cumberland Ch—church MS-4
Cumberland Ch—church (2) MO-7
Cumberland Ch—church (2) NC-3
Cumberland Ch—church OK-5
Cumberland Ch—church (3) SC-3
Cumberland Ch—church (6) TN-4
Cumberland Ch—church (2) VA-3
Cumberland Chapel—church MO-7
Cumberland Ch (historical)—church (3) TN-4
**Cumberland City**—pop pl KY-4
**Cumberland City**—pop pl TN-4
Cumberland City-Carlisle (CCD)—cens area TN-4
Cumberland City-Carlisle Division—civil TN-4
Cumberland City (CCD)—cens area KY-4
Cumberland City Ferry (historical)—locale TN-4
Cumberland City Post Office—building TN-4
Cumberland City Reservoir PA-2
Cumberland City Steam Plant—building TN-4
Cumberland Coll—school KY-4
Cumberland Country Club—other MD-2
**Cumberland (County)**—pop pl IL-6
**Cumberland (County)**—pop pl KY-4
**Cumberland (County)**—pop pl ME-1
**Cumberland County**—pop pl NJ-2
**Cumberland County**—pop pl NC-3
**Cumberland County**—pop pl PA-2
**Cumberland County**—pop pl TN-4
**Cumberland (County)**—pop pl VA-3
Cumberland County Coll—school NJ-2
Cumberland County Courthouse—hist pl IL-6
Cumberland County Courthouse—hist pl NC-3
Cumberland County Courthouses—hist pl TN-4
Cumberland County Home PA-2
Cumberland County Home Cem—cemetery PA-2
Cumberland County HS—school TN-4
Cumberland County Nursing Home—hospital PA-2
Cumberland County Park—park NC-3
Cumberland County Playhouse—building TN-4
Cumberland Covered Bridge—hist pl IN-6
Cumberland Creek NV-8
Cumberland Creek NC-3
Cumberland Creek—stream AK-9
Cumberland Creek—stream (2) IN-6
Cumberland Creek—stream MI-6
Cumberland Creek—stream NV-8
Cumberland Creek—stream NC-3
Cumberland Creek—stream (2) WA-9
Cumberland Creek—stream WY-8
Cumberland Dam—dam AL-4
Cumberland Ditch—canal CO-8
Cumberland Entrance FL-3
Cumberland Escarpment—cliff TN-4
**Cumberland Estates**—pop pl TN-4
Cumberland Estates Shop Ctr—locale TN-4
Cumberland Fair Grounds locale MD-2
Cumberland Falls—falls KY-4
Cumberland Falls (CCD)—cens area KY-4
Cumberland Falls (sta.) (RR name for Parkers Lake)—other KY-4
Cumberland Falls State Park—park KY-4
**Cumberland Falls (State Park)**—pop pl KY-4
Cumberland Farmers Club—other ME-1
Cumberland Farm Sch (historical)—school TN-4
Cumberland First Baptist Ch—church IN-6
Cumberland Flats—flat WY-8
**Cumberland Foreside**—pop pl ME-1
**Cumberland Furnace**—pop pl TN-4
Cumberland Furnace Hist Dist (40DS22)—hist pl TN-4
Cumberland Gap—gap KY-4
Cumberland Gap—gap NC-3
Cumberland Gap—gap VA-3
Cumberland Gap—gap WY-8
**Cumberland Gap**—pop pl TN-4
Cumberland Gap (CCD)—cens area TN-4
Cumberland Gap Division—civil TN-4
Cumberland Gap Hist Dist—hist pl KY-4
Cumberland Gap Hist Dist—hist pl TN-4
Cumberland Gap Hist Dist—hist pl VA-3
Cumberland Gap Natl Historical Park—park VA-3
Cumberland Gap Natl Historical Park (Also KY)—park TN-4
Cumberland Gap Natl Historic Park (Also TN)—park KY-4
Cumberland Gap Post Office—building TN-4
Cumberland Golf Course—locale PA-2
Cumberland Green IL-6
**Cumberland Grove**—pop pl TN-4
Cumberland Gulch—valley CO-8
Cumberland Gulch—valley ID-8
Cumberland Gulch—valley WY-8
Cumberland Head—cape NY-2
Cumberland Head Sch—school NY-2
Cumberland Heights IL-6
**Cumberland Heights**—pop pl (3) TN-4
**Cumberland Heights**—pop pl WV-2
Cumberland Heights (CCD)—cens area TN-4
Cumberland Heights Clinic—hospital TN-4
Cumberland Heights Division—civil TN-4
Cumberland Heights Sch—school TN-4
**Cumberland Heights (subdivision)**—pop pl TN-4
Cumberland Highlands IL-6
**Cumberland Hill**—pop pl RI-1
**Cumberland Hills (subdivision)**—pop pl (2) TN-4
Cumberland (historical)—locale KS-7
Cumberland Homestead Ch—church TN-4
**Cumberland Homesteads**—pop pl TN-4
Cumberland Homesteads Hist Dist—hist pl TN-4
Cumberland Hosp—hospital NY-2
Cumberland HS—school TN-4
Cumberland Iron Works (historical)—locale TN-4
Cumberland Iron Works Post Office (historical)—building TN-4
Cumberland Island—island GA-3
Cumberland Island—island KY-4
Cumberland Island Natl Seashore—park GA-3
Cumberland Junction—locale AL-4
Cumberland Knob—summit NC-3
Cumberland Knob Rec Area—park NC-3
Cumberland Lake AL-4
Cumberland Levee—levee OK-5
Cumberland (Magisterial District)—fmr MCD VA-3
Cumberland Male and Female Coll (historical)—school MS-4
Cumberland Med Ctr—hospital TN-4
Cumberland Memorial Gardens—cemetery KY-4
Cumberland Mill—locale ID-8
Cumberland Mill Ruins—locale CO-8
Cumberland Mills ME-1
**Cumberland Mills**—pop pl ME-1
Cumberland Mills Elem Sch—school NC-3
Cumberland Mills Hist Dist—hist pl ME-1
Cumberland Mine—mine MT-8
Cumberland Mine—mine NV-8
Cumberland Mines—mine MT-8
Cumberland Mine (underground)—mine TN-4
Cumberland Missionary Baptist Ch—church TN-4
Cumberland Mountain AL-4
Cumberland Mountain—ridge (2) TN-4
Cumberland Mountain Camp Ground TN-4
Cumberland Mountain Farm Colony (historical)—locale AL-4
Cumberland Mountain Lake—lake TN-4
Cumberland Mountain Lake—reservoir TN-4
Cumberland Mountain Lake Dam—dam TN-4
Cumberland Mountain Retreat—locale TN-4
Cumberland Mountain Retreat Lake—reservoir TN-4
Cumberland Mountain Retreat Lake Number One—reservoir TN-4
Cumberland Mountain Retreat Lake Number Three—reservoir TN-4
Cumberland Mountains AL-4
Cumberland Mountain Saltpeter Cave—cave TN-4
Cumberland Mountain Sch (historical)—school TN-4
Cumberland Mountain Sd Company Lake—reservoir TN-4
Cumberland Mountain State Park—park TN-4
Cumberland Mountain Tunnel—hist pl TN-4
Cumberland Mtn—summit CO-8
Cumberland Mtn—summit KY-4
Cumberland Mtn—summit VA-3
Cumberland Mtn—summit WA-9
Cumberland Normal Institute (historical)—school MS-4
Cumberland Oil Field—oilfield OK-5
Cumberland Overlook—locale KY-4
Cumberland Park—park OH-6
**Cumberland Park**—pop pl PA-2
**Cumberland Park (subdivision)**—pop pl AL-4
Cumberland Pass—gap CO-8
Cumberland Peak CO-8
Cumberland Pike Ch—church IN-6
Cumberland Pines TN-4
Cumberland Plateau—flat AL-4
Cumberland Plateau—plain AL-4
Cumberland Plateau—plain TN-4
Cumberland Plateau (CCD)—cens area TN-4
Cumberland Plateau Division—civil TN-4
Cumberland Plateau Observatory—building TN-4
Cumberland Point—cape KY-4
Cumberland Point—cape MI-6
Cumberland Point Rec Area—park KY-4
Cumberland Pond—reservoir NJ-2
Cumberland Pond—reservoir NC-3
Cumberland Pond Dam—dam NJ-2
Cumberland Pond Dam—dam NC-3
**Cumberland (Poor Fork)**—pop pl KY-4
Cumberland Post Office (historical)—building MS-4
Cumberland Prairie Park—park IL-6
Cumberland Presbyterian Camp—locale TN-4
Cumberland Presbyterian Ch AL-4
Cumberland Presbyterian Ch—church AL-4
Cumberland Presbyterian Church MS-4
Cumberland Presbyterian Church—hist pl AR-4
Cumberland Presbyterian Church—hist pl IL-6
Cumberland Presbyterian Church—hist pl MO-7
Cumberland Presbyterian Church of Loudon—hist pl TN-4
Cumberland Reef—bar MI-6
Cumberland Ridge—ridge KY-4
Cumberland Ridge Ch—church MO-7
Cumberland River KY-4
Cumberland River—channel GA-3
Cumberland River—stream KY-4
Cumberland River—stream TN-4
Cumberland Road Elem Sch—school NC-3
Cumberland Rolling Mill Landing (historical)—locale TN-4
Cumberland Run—stream OH-6
Cumberland Sch—school CA-9
Cumberland Sch—school IL-6
Cumberland Sch—school MI-6
Cumberland Sch—school NY-2
Cumberland Sch—school (2) TN-4
Cumberland Sch—school WI-6
Cumberland Sch (historical)—school TN-4
Cumberland Sch Of Medical Technology—school TN-4
Cumberland School MS-4
Cumberland Shed Cem—cemetery TN-4
Cumberland Shed Ch (historical)—church TN-4
Cumberland Shop Ctr—locale TN-4
Cumberland Shores—locale KY-4
Cumberland Sound—bay FL-3
Cumberland Sound—bay GA-3
Cumberland South (CCD)—cens area KY-4
Cumberland Spring—locale TN-4
Cumberland Spring—spring NV-8
Cumberland Springs—locale TN-4
**Cumberland Springs**—pop pl TN-4
Cumberland Springs Lake—reservoir TN-4

Cumberland Springs Lake Dam—*dam* ... TN-4
Cumberland Stand Ch—*church* ... TN-4
Cumberland State For—*forest* ... VA-3
**Cumberland (subdivision)**—*pop pl* ... NC-3
Cumberland Thorofare—*gut* ... VA-3
**Cumberland (Town of)**—*pop pl* ... ME-1
**Cumberland (Town of)**—*pop pl* ... RI-1
**Cumberland (Town of)**—*pop pl* ... WI-6
**Cumberland (Township of)**—*pop pl* (2) ... PA-2
*Cumberland Trail* ... PA-2
Cumberland Union Ch—*church* ... NC-3
Cumberland Univ—*school* ... TN-4
Cumberland Valley—*basin* ... PA-2
Cumberland Valley Airstrip—*airport* ... PA-2
Cumberland Valley Car—*hist pl* ... PA-2
Cumberland Valley Ch—*church* ... TN-4
Cumberland Valley Elem Sch—*school* ... PA-2
Cumberland Valley HS—*school* ... PA-2
Cumberland Valley RR Station and Station Master's House—*hist pl* ... PA-2
Cumberland Valley Run—*stream* ... PA-2
Cumberland Valley State Normal Sch Hist Dist—*hist pl* ... PA-2
**Cumberland Valley (Township of)**—*pop pl* ... PA-2
**Cumberland View**—*pop pl* (2) ... TN-4
Cumberland View Cem—*cemetery* (2) ... TN-4
Cumberland View Ch—*church* ... TN-4
**Cumberland View Estates**—*pop pl* ... TN-4
Cumberland View Sch (historical)—*school* ... TN-4
**Cumberland Village**—*pop pl* ... PA-2
**Cumberland Village (subdivision)**—*pop pl* ... NC-3
*Cumberland Works* ... NJ-2
Cumberledge Cem—*cemetery* ... WV-2
*Cumberry Pond* ... MA-1
*Cumbers* ... CO-8
Cumberstone—*locale* ... MD-2
*Cumbery Pond* ... MA-1
Cumbess Creek—*stream* ... SC-3
Cumbest, Bayou—*stream* ... MS-4
Cumbest Bluff—*cliff* ... MS-4
Cumbies Pond—*reservoir* ... AL-4
Cumbie Windmill—*locale* ... TX-5
Cumble Draw—*valley* ... TX-5
**Cumbo**—*pop pl* ... WV-2
Cumbo Branch—*stream* ... NC-3
Cumbo Ch—*church* ... VA-3
Cumbo Chapel—*church* ... NC-3
Cumbo Flat—*flat* ... WA-9
**Cumbola**—*pop pl* ... PA-2
Cumbow Cem—*cemetery* ... VA-3
Cumbo Yard—*locale* ... WV-2
Cumbres—*locale* ... CO-8
Cumbres and Toltec Scenic RR—*hist pl* ... CO-8
Cumbres and Toltec Scenic RR—*hist pl* ... NM-5
Cumbres Creek—*stream* ... CO-8
Cumbres Pass—*gap* ... CO-8
*Cumbry Pond* ... MA-1
**Cumby**—*pop pl* ... TX-5
Cumby (CCD)—*cens area* ... TX-5
Cumby Spring Branch—*stream* ... GA-3
Cumbyville Bar—*bar* ... MS-4
*Cumero Canyon* ... AZ-5
Cumero Canyon—*valley* ... AZ-5
Cumero Mtn—*summit* ... AZ-5
*Cumero Spring* ... AZ-5
Cumi—*locale* ... AR-4
Cuming, Dr. John, House—*hist pl* ... MA-1
Cuming City Cem—*cemetery* ... NE-7
Cuming City Sch—*school* ... NE-7
Cuming Creek—*stream* ... NE-7
*Cumings* ... ND-7
**Cuming Township**—*pop pl* (2) ... NE-7
Cumiskey—*locale* ... PA-2
Cumley Creek—*stream* ... OR-9
*Cumliffs Pond* ... RI-1
**Cummaquid**—*pop pl* ... MA-1
Cummer Drain—*canal* ... MI-6
Cummin Creek—*stream* ... MT-8
**Cumming**—*pop pl* ... GA-3
**Cumming**—*pop pl* ... IA-7
Cumming, Mtn—*summit* ... OK-5
Cumming (CCD)—*cens area* ... GA-3
Cumming Cem—*cemetery* ... IL-6
Cumming Cem—*cemetery* ... OH-6
Cumming Gulch—*valley* ... OR-9
Cummingham Bridge—*bridge* ... TN-4
Cummingham Cem—*cemetery* ... IN-6
Cummingham Cem—*cemetery* ... TN-4
Cumming Ranch—*locale* ... AZ-5
Cummings—*locale* ... CA-9
Cummings—*locale* ... FL-3
**Cummings**—*pop pl* ... KS-7
**Cummings**—*pop pl* ... ME-1
**Cummings**—*pop pl* ... ND-7
**Cummings**—*pop pl* ... PA-2
**Cummings**—*pop pl* ... SC-3
**Cummings**—*pop pl* ... TN-4
Cummings, Byron, House—*hist pl* ... UT-8
cummings, e.e., House—*hist pl* ... MA-1
Cummings, Judge Will, House—*hist pl* ... TN-4
Cummings, Lake—*lake* ... FL-3
Cummings, Wilson S., House—*hist pl* ... OH-6
Cummings Art Sch—*school* ... ME-1
Cummings Bench—*bench* ... MT-8
Cummings Bog—*swamp* ... ME-1
*Cummings Branch* ... TN-4
Cummings Branch—*stream* ... MS-4
Cummings Branch—*stream* ... TN-4
Cummings Bridge—*bridge* ... AL-4
Cummings Bridge—*locale* ... NY-2
*Cummings Brook* ... ME-1
Cummings Brook—*stream* ... MA-1
Cummings Brook—*stream* ... NH-1
Cummings Cabins—*locale* ... MI-6
Cummings Canyon—*valley* ... CA-9
Cummings Canyon—*valley* ... CO-8
Cummings Canyon—*valley* ... UT-8
Cummings Canyon—*valley* ... WA-9
Cummings Cem—*cemetery* (3) ... AR-4
Cummings Cem—*cemetery* ... GA-3
Cummings Cem—*cemetery* ... IL-6
Cummings Cem—*cemetery* ... IN-6
Cummings Cem—*cemetery* ... KS-7
Cummings Cem—*cemetery* ... ME-1
Cummings Cem—*cemetery* ... MI-6
Cummings Cem—*cemetery* ... MS-4
Cummings Cem—*cemetery* ... NY-2
Cummings Cem—*cemetery* ... ND-7
Cummings Cem—*cemetery* (4) ... TN-4
Cummings Cem—*cemetery* ... TX-5
Cummings Cem—*cemetery* ... VA-3
Cummings Cem—*cemetery* (2) ... WV-2
Cummings Cem—*cemetery* ... WI-6
*Cummings Ch* ... TN-4
Cummings Ch—*church* ... TN-4
Cummings Chapel—*church* ... AR-4
Cummings Chapel—*church* ... SC-3
Cummings Chapel Sch (historical)—*school* ... TN-4
Cummings Corners—*locale* ... NY-2
*Cummings Cove* ... ME-1
Cummings Cove Branch—*stream* ... TN-4
Cummings Cove Cave—*cave* ... TN-4
*Cummings Creek* ... MS-4
*Cummings Creek* ... NY-2
*Cummings Creek* ... TX-5
Cummings Creek—*bay* ... MD-2
Cummings Creek—*stream* ... AK-9
Cummings Creek—*stream* (3) ... CA-9
Cummings Creek—*stream* ... MS-4
Cummings Creek—*stream* ... MT-8
Cummings Creek—*stream* ... NY-2
Cummings Creek—*stream* ... OH-6
Cummings Creek—*stream* (3) ... OR-9
Cummings Creek—*stream* ... PA-2
Cummings Creek—*stream* (2) ... TN-4
Cummings Creek—*stream* ... UT-8
Cummings Creek—*stream* ... WA-9
Cummings Creek—*stream* ... WV-2
Cummings Creek—*stream* (2) ... WY-8
Cummings Creek—*valley* ... CA-9
Cummings Creek Ch—*church* ... WV-2
Cummings Crossing—*locale* ... NY-2
**Cummings Crossroads**—*pop pl* ... TN-4
Cummings Dam—*dam* ... PA-2
Cummings Dam—*dam* ... WI-6
Cummings Ditch—*canal* ... MT-8
Cummings Ditch—*canal* ... OR-9
Cummings Ditch—*canal* ... WY-8
Cummings Drain—*canal* (2) ... MI-6
Cummings Draw—*valley* ... ND-7
Cummings Flat—*flat* ... UT-8
Cummings Ford (historical)—*crossing* ... TN-4
Cummings Gap—*gap* ... TN-4
Cummings Gulch—*valley* ... CO-8
*Cummings Head* ... ME-1
**Cummings Heights**—*pop pl* ... VA-3
Cummings Hill—*summit* (2) ... ME-1
Cummings Hill—*summit* ... VT-1
Cummings Hill Summit—*gap* ... OR-9
Cummings (historical)—*locale* ... MS-4
Cummings Hollow—*valley* ... KY-4
Cummings Hollow—*valley* ... OH-6
Cummings House—*hist pl* ... TX-5
Cummings HS—*school* ... NC-3
Cummings Island Shoals—*bar* ... TN-4
Cummings JHS—*school* ... TX-5
*Cummings Lake* ... NY-2
*Cummings Lake* ... OR-9
*Cummings Lake* ... PA-2
Cummings Lake—*lake* (2) ... MI-6
Cummings Lake—*lake* (2) ... MN-6
Cummings Lake—*lake* ... TN-4
Cummings Lake—*lake* ... WA-9
Cummings Lakes—*lake* ... MI-6
Cummings Lateral—*canal* ... AZ-5
Cummings Ledge—*bar* ... ME-1
Cummings Meadow—*flat* ... NH-1
Cummings Meadows—*flat* ... MT-8
Cummings Memorial Ch—*church* ... NC-3
Cummings Mesa—*summit* (2) ... AZ-5
Cummings Mesa—*summit* ... UT-8
Cummings Mtn—*summit* ... CA-9
Cummings Mtn—*summit* ... ME-1
Cummings Mtn—*summit* ... NH-1
Cummings Park—*flat* ... WY-8
Cummings Park—*park* ... CT-1
Cummings Park—*park* ... MI-6
Cummings Park Sch—*school* ... NE-7
Cummings Pit—*cave* ... TN-4
Cummings Place—*locale* ... NM-5
Cummings Point—*cape* ... FL-3
Cummings Point—*cape* ... NY-2
Cummings Point—*cape* ... SC-3
Cummings Point—*cape* ... WA-9
*Cummings Pond* ... CT-1
*Cummings Pond* ... MA-1
Cummings Pond—*lake* ... NY-2
Cummings Pond—*lake* ... PA-2
Cummings Pond—*reservoir* ... PA-2
Cummings Ranch—*locale* ... CA-9
Cummings Ranch—*locale* ... NV-8
Cummings Ranch—*locale* ... TX-5
Cummings Research Park—*locale* ... AL-4
Cummings Research Park West—*locale* ... AL-4
Cummings Reservoir Dam—*dam* ... AZ-5
Cummings Rsvr—*reservoir* ... AZ-5
Cummings Rsvr—*reservoir* ... PA-2
Cummings Run—*stream* ... PA-2
Cummings Run Spring—*stream* ... VA-3
Cummings Sch—*school* ... IL-6
Cummings Sch—*school* ... ME-1
Cummings Sch—*school* ... MA-1
Cummings Sch—*school* (2) ... MI-6
Cummings Sch—*school* ... NH-1
Cummings Sch—*school* ... OH-6
Cummings Sch—*school* ... OR-9
Cummings Sch—*school* ... PA-2
Cummings Sch—*school* (2) ... TN-4
Cummings Sch (abandoned)—*school* ... PA-2
Cummings Spring—*spring* ... CA-9
Cummings Spring—*spring* ... CO-8
Cummings Spring—*spring* ... OR-9
Cummings Spring—*spring* ... PA-2
Cummings Spring—*spring* ... TN-4
Cummings Springs—*locale* ... AR-4
Cummings Square—*park* ... IL-6
Cummings Store—*locale* ... VA-3
**Cummings Subdivision**—*pop pl* ... UT-8
Cummings Tank—*reservoir* ... AZ-5
Cummingston Park—*park* ... MI-6
**Cummingstown**—*pop pl* ... PA-2
Cummings Township—*civil* ... PA-2
**Cummings (Township of)**—*pop pl* ... PA-2
Cummings Valley—*valley* ... CA-9
Cummings Valley Sch—*school* ... CA-9
*Cummingsville* ... KS-7
*Cummingsville* ... NY-2
Cummingsville—*locale* ... MN-6
Cummingsville—*locale* ... TN-4
**Cummingsville**—*pop pl* ... MA-1
**Cummingsville**—*pop pl* ... NY-2
Cummingsville Cem—*cemetery* ... TN-4
Cummingsville Chapel Methodist Ch (historical)—*church* ... TN-4
Cummingsville Post Office (historical)—*building* ... TN-4
Cummingsville Sch (historical)—*school* (2) ... TN-4
Cummings Well—*well* ... UT-8
Cummingswood Park—*park* ... PA-2
**Cummington**—*pop pl* ... MA-1
Cummington Fairgrounds—*locale* ... MA-1
Cummington Farm Village—*park* ... MA-1
**Cummington (Town of)**—*pop pl* ... MA-1
**Cumming (Township of)**—*pop pl* ... MI-6
Cumming Twin Lakes—*reservoir* ... GA-3
Cummins, Albert Baird, House—*hist pl* ... IA-7
Cummins, David, Octagon House—*hist pl* ... OH-6
Cummins, David J., House—*hist pl* ... DE-2
Cummins, John R., Farmhouse—*hist pl* ... MN-6
Cummins, Timothy, House—*hist pl* ... DE-2
Cummins Bar—*bar* ... AR-4
Cummins Branch—*stream* ... TN-4
*Cummins Bridge* ... TX-5
*Cummins Brook* ... ME-1
Cummins Cem—*cemetery* ... AL-4
Cummins Cem—*cemetery* ... IL-6
Cummins Cem—*cemetery* ... OK-5
Cummins Chapel—*church* ... TN-4
Cummins Charleston, Incorporated—*facility* ... SC-3
*Cummins Creek* ... WV-2
Cummins Creek—*stream* (2) ... OR-9
Cummins Creek—*stream* ... PA-2
Cummins Creek—*stream* (2) ... TX-5
Cummins Creek Bridge—*hist pl* ... TX-5
Cummins Crossing—*locale* ... TX-5
Cummins Ditch—*canal* ... OH-6
Cummins Falls—*falls* ... TN-4
Cummins Gulch—*valley* ... WY-8
Cummins-Heard Cem—*cemetery* ... TX-5
Cummins Hollow—*valley* ... MO-7
Cummins Hollow—*valley* ... TN-4
Cummins Hollow—*valley* ... TX-5
Cummins Lake—*lake* ... CA-9
Cummins Memorial Church—*hist pl* ... MD-2
Cummins Mill Baptist Ch—*church* ... TN-4
Cummins Mill (historical)—*locale* ... TN-4
*Cummins Mountain* ... ME-1
Cummins Peak—*summit* ... OR-9
Cummins Pond—*lake* ... NH-1
Cummins Ridge—*ridge* ... OR-9
Cummins Sch—*hist pl* ... OH-6
Cummins Sch—*school* ... IL-6
Cummins Spring—*spring* ... MO-7
Cummins State Prison—*other* ... AR-4
Cummins Station—*hist pl* ... TN-4
Cummins Tank—*reservoir* ... TX-5
Cummins Township—*fmr MCD* ... IA-7
*Cumminsville* ... NJ-2
Cumminsville—*locale* ... KY-4
**Cumminsville**—*pop pl* ... NE-7
**Cumminsville**—*pop pl* ... NY-2
**Cumminsville**—*pop pl* ... OH-6
**Cumminsville**—*pop pl* ... PA-2
*Cumminsville (Northside)* ... OH-6
Cumminsville Sch—*school* ... PA-2
Cummins Well—*well* ... TX-5
Cummins Windmill—*locale* ... TX-5
Cummins Woods Park—*park* ... IA-7
Cummiskey Creek—*stream* ... CA-9
*Cummoc Island* ... RI-1
Cummock Island—*island* ... RI-1
**Cumnock**—*pop pl* ... NC-3
Cumnor—*locale* ... VA-3
Cumorah, Hill—*summit* ... NY-2
Cumples Woods—*forest* ... DE-2
Cumpressco—*locale* ... FL-3
Cumpton Branch—*stream* ... MO-7
Cumro—*locale* ... NE-7
Cumru Elem Sch—*school* ... PA-2
**Cumru (Township of)**—*pop pl* ... PA-2
Cumslo—*locale* ... GA-3
Cumston Hall—*hist pl* ... ME-1
Cumulus, Mount—*summit* ... CO-8
Cumulus Ridge—*airport* ... NJ-2
Cunard—*locale* ... CA-9
**Cunard**—*pop pl* ... MI-6
**Cunard**—*pop pl* ... WV-2
Cunard Cem—*cemetery* ... GA-3
Cunard Gulch—*valley* ... ID-8
Cunard Lake—*lake* ... WI-6
Cunard Rest Area—*locale* ... MI-6
Cunavea Basin—*basin* ... NM-5
Cundall Post Office (historical)—*building* ... TN-4
Cundall Ranch—*locale* ... WY-8
*Cundalls Mill Post Office* ... TN-4
Cundiff—*locale* ... KY-4
**Cundiff**—*pop pl* ... TX-5
Cundiff, C. C., House—*hist pl* ... NC-3
Cundiff Cem—*cemetery* ... IL-6
Cundiff Cem—*cemetery* (3) ... KY-4
*Cundiff Creek* ... TX-5
Cundiff Ford Island—*island* ... TN-4
Cundiff Hill—*summit* ... KY-4
Cundiff (historical)—*locale* ... KS-7
Cundiff Island—*island* ... TN-4
Cundiff Slough—*stream* ... OR-9
**Cundiyo**—*pop pl* ... NM-5
*Cundiz Ledge* ... ME-1
Cundy Creek—*stream* ... WY-8
*Cundy Harbor* ... ME-1
Cundy Harbor—*bay* ... ME-1
*Cundy Ledge* ... ME-1
Cundy Mine—*mine* ... MI-6
Cundy Rsvr—*reservoir* ... SD-7
*Cundy's Harbor* ... ME-1
**Cundys Harbor**—*pop pl* ... ME-1
*Cuneo* ... PA-2
**Cuneo**—*pop pl* ... PA-2
Cuneo Camp—*locale* ... CA-9
Cuneo Campground—*locale* ... CA-9
Cuneo Creek—*stream* (2) ... CA-9
Cuneo Hosp—*hospital* ... IL-6
Cuneo Point—*summit* ... ID-8
Cuneo Ridge—*ridge* ... CA-9
**Cuney**—*pop pl* ... TX-5
Cuney Acad—*school* ... TX-5
Cuney Sch—*school* ... TX-5
*Cungermuck River* ... NY-2
Cunha Canyon—*valley* ... OR-9
Cunhingham Cem—*cemetery* ... IA-7
Cuniff Basin—*basin* ... MT-8
Cuniff Creek—*stream* ... MT-8
Cuniff Ditch—*canal* ... MT-8
Cuningham Windmill—*locale* ... NM-5
*Cunio Tubbi Creek* ... OK-5
Cunjer Channel—*channel* ... VA-3
Cunliff Cem—*cemetery* ... MS-4
Cunliffe Brook—*stream* (2) ... ME-1
Cunliffe Depot Camp—*locale* ... ME-1
Cunliffe Islands—*island* ... ME-1
*Cunliffe Lake* ... RI-1
Cunliffe Lake—*lake* ... ME-1
Cunliffe Pond—*lake* ... ME-1
Cunliff Lake—*lake* ... RI-1
Cunliff Park—*park* ... IL-6
*Cunliff Pond* ... RI-1
Cunliff Pond Dam—*dam* ... RI-1
*Cunneotubby Creek* ... OK-5
Cunneo Tubby Creek—*stream* ... OK-5
*Cunner Creek* ... IN-6
Cunniff Creek—*stream* ... OR-9
Cunnigan Cem—*cemetery* ... KY-4
Cunning Bluff Landing—*locale* ... NC-3
Cunning Ford Creek—*stream* ... SC-3
*Cunningham* ... AL-4
Cunningham—*locale* ... AL-4
Cunningham—*locale* ... GA-3
Cunningham—*locale* ... NC-3
Cunningham—*locale* ... OH-6
Cunningham—*locale* ... PA-2
Cunningham—*locale* ... VA-3
Cunningham—*locale* ... WV-2
**Cunningham**—*pop pl* (2) ... AL-4
**Cunningham**—*pop pl* ... CA-9
**Cunningham**—*pop pl* ... KS-7
**Cunningham**—*pop pl* ... KY-4
**Cunningham**—*pop pl* (2) ... MO-7
**Cunningham**—*pop pl* ... SC-3
**Cunningham**—*pop pl* ... TN-4
**Cunningham**—*pop pl* ... TX-5
**Cunningham**—*pop pl* ... WA-9
Cunningham, Andrew, Farm—*hist pl* ... IL-6
Cunningham, John F., House—*hist pl* ... UT-8
Cunningham, Lake—*lake* ... AK-9
Cunningham, Samuel, House—*hist pl* ... WV-2
Cunningham, Thomas, House—*hist pl* ... UT-8
Cunningham Archeol Site—*hist pl* ... NE-7
Cunningham Bar—*bar* ... AL-4
Cunningham Bar—*bar* ... ID-8
Cunningham Bend—*bend* ... AL-4
Cunningham Bluff—*cliff* ... AL-4
Cunningham Brake—*swamp* ... LA-4
*Cunningham Branch* ... AL-4
Cunningham Branch—*stream* ... AL-4
Cunningham Branch—*stream* ... GA-3
Cunningham Branch—*stream* ... MS-4
Cunningham Branch—*stream* (2) ... MO-7
Cunningham Branch—*stream* (3) ... TN-4
Cunningham Bridge—*bridge* ... TN-4
Cunningham Broadbent Lake—*reservoir* ... TN-4
Cunningham Broadbent Lake Dam—*dam* ... TN-4
Cunningham Brook—*stream* ... ME-1
Cunningham Brook—*stream* ... NH-1
Cunningham Brook—*stream* ... VT-1
Cunningham Cabin—*hist pl* ... WY-8
Cunningham Cabin—*locale* ... WY-8
Cunningham Canyon—*valley* ... AZ-5
Cunningham Canyon—*valley* ... CA-9
Cunningham Canyon—*valley* ... OR-9
Cunningham Cave—*cave* ... AL-4
Cunningham (CCD)—*cens area* ... KY-4
Cunningham Cem—*cemetery* (4) ... AL-4
Cunningham Cem—*cemetery* (2) ... AR-4
Cunningham Cem—*cemetery* ... IL-6
Cunningham Cem—*cemetery* (2) ... IN-6
Cunningham Cem—*cemetery* ... KS-7
Cunningham Cem—*cemetery* (3) ... MO-7
Cunningham Cem—*cemetery* (9) ... TN-4
Cunningham Cem—*cemetery* ... TX-5
Cunningham Cem—*cemetery* (2) ... VA-3
Cunningham Cem—*cemetery* (5) ... WV-2
Cunningham Ch—*church* ... MS-4
Cunningham Ch—*church* ... TN-4
Cunningham Chapel—*church* ... TX-5
Cunningham Ch of God in Christ—*church* ... MS-4
Cunningham-Coleman House—*hist pl* ... GA-3
Cunningham Corner—*locale* ... GA-3
Cunningham Coulee—*valley* ... MT-8
Cunningham Coulee—*valley* ... WA-9
*Cunningham Courts* ... IL-6
*Cunningham Cove* ... TN-4
Cunningham Cove—*basin* ... OR-9
Cunningham Cove—*bay* ... TX-5
Cunningham Creek—*stream* (2) ... AL-4
Cunningham Creek—*stream* (2) ... AK-9
Cunningham Creek—*stream* ... AZ-5
Cunningham Creek—*stream* (2) ... AR-4
Cunningham Creek—*stream* (2) ... CA-9
Cunningham Creek—*stream* (3) ... CO-8
Cunningham Creek—*stream* ... FL-3
Cunningham Creek—*stream* ... ID-8
Cunningham Creek—*stream* ... MI-6
Cunningham Creek—*stream* ... MO-7
Cunningham Creek—*stream* ... NE-7
Cunningham Creek—*stream* ... NM-5
Cunningham Creek—*stream* ... NY-2
Cunningham Creek—*stream* ... NC-3
Cunningham Creek—*stream* ... OH-6
Cunningham Creek—*stream* (2) ... OR-9
Cunningham Creek—*stream* ... SC-3
Cunningham Creek—*stream* ... TX-5
Cunningham Creek—*stream* ... VA-3
Cunningham Creek—*stream* (2) ... WA-9
Cunningham Creek—*stream* ... WI-6
Cunningham Crossroads—*locale* ... GA-3
Cunningham Dam—*dam* ... AL-4
Cunningham District Sch—*school* ... VA-3
Cunningham Ditch—*canal* ... CA-9
Cunningham Ditch—*canal* ... CO-8
Cunningham Ditch—*canal* (2) ... IN-6
Cunningham Ditch—*canal* ... NM-5
Cunningham Ditch—*canal* ... OH-6
Cunningham Elem Sch—*school* ... IN-6
Cunningham Elem Sch—*school* ... KS-7
**Cunningham Estates**—*pop pl* ... FL-3
Cunningham Falls—*falls* ... MD-2
Cunningham Farm—*locale* ... AR-4
Cunningham Fork—*stream* ... WV-2
Cunningham Gap—*gap* ... AL-4
Cunningham Grove—*woods* ... CA-9
Cunningham Gulch—*valley* ... CO-8
Cunningham Gulch—*valley* (2) ... NM-5
Cunningham-Hall Pt-6,Nc-692W—*hist pl* ... AK-9
**Cunningham Heights (subdivision)**—*pop pl* ... MS-4
Cunningham-Hevener House—*hist pl* ... WV-2
Cunningham Highlands—*uninc pl* ... KS-7
Cunningham Hill—*locale* ... UT-8
Cunningham Hill—*summit* ... GA-3
Cunningham Hill—*summit* ... NH-1
Cunningham Hill—*summit* ... NM-5
Cunningham Hill—*summit* ... TX-5
Cunningham Hollow—*valley* (2) ... MO-7
Cunningham Hollow—*valley* (3) ... TN-4
Cunningham House—*hist pl* ... NY-2
Cunningham House and Outbuildings—*hist pl* ... WV-2
Cunningham HS—*school* ... KS-7
Cunningham Island—*island* ... ME-1
Cunningham Island—*island* ... TN-4
Cunningham JHS—*school* ... TX-5
Cunningham Key—*island* ... FL-3
Cunningham Knob—*summit* ... WV-2
*Cunningham Lake* ... TN-4
Cunningham Lake—*lake* ... CA-9
Cunningham Lake—*lake* (3) ... MI-6
Cunningham Lake—*lake* ... MS-4
Cunningham Lake—*lake* ... OR-9
Cunningham Lake—*reservoir* ... AL-4
Cunningham Lake—*reservoir* ... MD-2
Cunningham Lake—*reservoir* ... NC-3
Cunningham Lake—*reservoir* ... TX-5
Cunningham Lake Dam—*dam* ... NC-3
Cunningham Landing—*locale* ... AL-4
Cunningham Lateral—*canal* ... ID-8
Cunningham Ledge—*island* ... MA-1
**Cunningham (Lone Oak)**—*pop pl* ... TN-4
Cunningham (Magisterial District)—*fmr MCD* ... VA-3
Cunningham-Maier House—*hist pl* ... OH-6
Cunningham Memorial Park—*cemetery* ... WV-2
Cunningham Mine—*mine* ... AZ-5
Cunningham Mine (underground)—*mine* ... AL-4
Cunningham Mountains—*summit* ... ME-1
*Cunningham Mtn* ... ME-1
Cunningham Mtn—*summit* ... AK-9
Cunningham Mtn—*summit* ... AZ-5
Cunningham Mtn—*summit* (2) ... ME-1
Cunningham Mtn—*summit* ... NC-3
Cunningham Number 1 Dam—*dam* ... AL-4
Cunningham Oil Field—*oilfield* ... KS-7
Cunningham Park—*flat* ... WY-8
Cunningham Park—*park* ... MI-6
Cunningham Park—*park* ... MO-7
Cunningham Park—*park* ... NY-2
Cunningham Park—*park* ... VA-3
Cunningham Park Sch—*school* ... VA-3
Cunningham Pass—*gap* ... AZ-5
Cunningham Pond—*lake* ... AR-4
Cunningham Pond—*lake* ... ME-1
Cunningham Pond—*lake* ... MA-1
Cunningham Pond—*lake* (2) ... NH-1
Cunningham Pond—*reservoir* ... AL-4
Cunningham Pond—*reservoir* ... CT-1
Cunningham Post Office—*building* ... TN-4
Cunningham-Pyles Cem—*cemetery* ... AL-4
Cunningham Ranch—*locale* ... CA-9
Cunningham Ranch—*locale* ... UT-8
Cunningham Ravine—*valley* ... CA-9
Cunningham Ridge—*ridge* ... AK-9
Cunningham Ridge—*ridge* (2) ... TN-4
Cunningham Ridge—*ridge* ... WV-2
Cunningham Rsvr—*reservoir* ... CO-8
Cunningham Rsvr—*reservoir* ... OR-9
Cunningham Run—*stream* ... PA-2
Cunningham Run—*stream* (4) ... WV-2
Cunningham Saddle—*gap* ... OR-9
Cunninghams Canyon—*valley* ... AZ-5
Cunningham Sch—*school* ... AL-4
Cunningham Sch—*school* (2) ... CA-9
Cunningham Sch—*school* ... CO-8
Cunningham Sch—*school* (2) ... IL-6
Cunningham Sch—*school* ... NJ-2
Cunningham Sch—*school* ... OH-6
Cunningham Sch—*school* ... TN-4
Cunningham Sch—*school* (3) ... TX-5
Cunningham Sch—*school* ... WI-6
Cunningham Sch (abandoned)—*school* ... MO-7
Cunningham Sch (historical)—*school* (2) ... PA-2
Cunningham Sch (historical)—*school* ... TN-4
*Cunninghams Cove* ... TN-4
*Cunninghams Creek* ... VA-3
Cunninghams Creek—*stream* ... VA-3
Cunninghams Ford—*locale* ... AL-4
Cunninghams Ford (historical)—*crossing* ... TN-4
*Cunningham Sink* ... AL-4
Cunningham Sinks—*basin* ... AL-4
Cunninghams Island—*island* ... VA-3
Cunninghams Landing (historical)—*locale* ... AL-4
Cunningham Slough—*gut* ... OR-9
Cunninghams Mill (historical)—*locale* ... AL-4
Cunningham Spring—*spring* ... AZ-5
*Cunningham Station* ... GA-3
Cunningham Swamp—*swamp* ... MD-2
Cunningham Swamp—*swamp* ... WI-6
*Cunninghams Woodyard Landing* ... AL-4
Cunningham Tank—*reservoir* (2) ... TX-5
Cunningham Township—*civil* ... SD-7
**Cunningham Township**—*pop pl* ... MO-7
Cunningham (Township of)—*fmr MCD* ... NC-3
**Cunningham (Township of)**—*pop pl* ... IL-6
Cunningham Tunnel—*mine* ... UT-8
*Cunningham Valley* ... AZ-5
Cunningham Wash—*stream* ... AZ-5
Cunningham Wash—*valley* ... UT-8
Cunning Harbor Bay—*bay* ... NC-3
Cunning Harbor Island—*island* ... NC-3
Cunninghill Cove—*bay* ... MD-2
Cunnington Cem—*cemetery* ... MO-7
*Cunninham Pass* ... AZ-5
Cunny Lake—*lake* ... TX-5
Cuno Creek—*stream* ... FL-3
**Cunot**—*pop pl* ... IN-6
Cuny Table—*summit* ... SD-7
Cuny Table Sch—*school* ... SD-7
*Cuop* ... FM-9
Cup, The—*summit* ... NM-5
*Cupahica* ... FL-3
Cup and Saucer—*ridge* ... CA-9
Cup and Saucer Hills—*range* ... KS-7
*Cupaum Pond* ... MA-1
Cup Bayou—*gut* ... AR-4
Cupboard Creek—*stream* ... ID-8
Cupboard Creek—*stream* ... SC-3
Cupboard Pond—*lake* ... DE-2
Cup Butte—*summit* ... UT-8
*Cup-Cake Islands* ... RI-1
Cupco Ch—*church* ... OK-5
Cupco Church—*hist pl* ... OK-5
Cup Cove—*bay* ... AK-9
Cup Creek—*stream* (3) ... ID-8
Cup Creek—*stream* ... IN-6
Cup Creek—*stream* ... MT-8
Cup Creek Ch—*church* ... IN-6
Cupel Mine—*mine* ... AZ-5
**Cupertino**—*pop pl* ... CA-9
*Cupertino Creek* ... CA-9
Cupertino Friary—*church* ... NY-2
Cupertino HS—*school* ... CA-9
Cupertino Sch—*school* ... CA-9
Cupe Seep—*spring* ... AZ-5
Cupey (Barrio)—*fmr MCD* ... PR-3
Cup Fields—*flat* ... TN-4
Cup Gap—*gap* ... TN-4
Cup Gulch—*valley* ... OR-9
C Uphoff Ranch—*locale* ... NE-7
Cup Hollow—*valley* ... TN-4
*Cupia Hatchee Creek* ... AL-4
Cupid Lake—*lake* ... MN-6
Cupido Draw—*valley* ... NM-5
Cupido Tank—*reservoir* ... NM-5
Cupids Heart—*rock* ... MT-8
Cupids Knoll—*summit* ... OR-9
Cupio—*locale* ... KY-4
Cupio Hill—*summit* ... KY-4
Cupit Cem—*cemetery* ... MS-4
Cupit Mary Meadow—*flat* ... OR-9
Cupit Mary Meadow Trail—*trail* ... OR-9
Cupit Mary Mtn—*summit* ... OR-9
Cupit Mary Trail—*trail* ... OR-9
Cup Lake—*lake* ... CA-9
Cup Lake—*lake* ... MI-6
Cup Lake—*lake* (2) ... MN-6
Cup Lake—*lake* ... MT-8
Cup Lake—*lake* (3) ... WA-9
Cupler Sloughs—*gut* ... NC-3
Cupola—*locale* ... PA-2
Cupola Cem—*cemetery* ... NE-7
Cupola House—*building* ... NC-3
Cupola House—*hist pl* ... MN-6
Cupola House—*hist pl* ... NC-3
Cupola House—*hist pl* ... WI-6
Cupola Mtn—*summit* ... TX-5
Cupola Peak—*summit* ... AK-9
Cupola Point—*cape* ... VA-3
Cupola Pond—*lake* ... MO-7
Cupola Rock—*pillar* ... OR-9
*Cuppame Pond* ... MA-1
Cupp Branch—*stream* (2) ... TN-4
Cupp Cem—*cemetery* (2) ... MO-7
Cupp Cem—*cemetery* ... TN-4
Cupp Ch—*church* ... IN-6
Cupp Corral—*locale* ... ID-8
Cupp Creek—*stream* ... ID-8
Cupp Creek—*stream* ... TN-4
Cupper Canyon—*valley* ... OR-9
*Cupper Creek* ... AL-4
Cupp Hollow—*valley* ... OH-6
Cupp Lake—*reservoir* ... TN-4
Cupples, Samuel, House—*hist pl* ... MO-7
**Cupp Mill**—*pop pl* ... TN-4
Cup Post Office (historical)—*building* ... AL-4
Cupp Post Office (historical)—*building* ... TN-4
Cupp Ridge—*ridge* ... TN-4
Cupp Run—*stream* ... WV-2
Cupps Cem—*cemetery* ... OH-6
Cupp Sch—*school* ... TN-4
Cupps Chapel—*church* ... KY-4
Cupps Hill—*summit* ... AK-9
*Cupps Mill* ... TN-4
Cuppy Butte—*summit* ... CA-9
Cuppy Cave—*hist pl* ... CA-9
Cuppy Cem—*cemetery* ... OH-6
Cuppy Gulch—*valley* ... CA-9
*Cupress Fork* ... TX-5
Cupric Mine—*mine* ... UT-8
Cuprite—*locale* ... NV-8
Cuprite Hills—*ridge* ... NV-8
Cuprite Hills—*summit* ... NV-8
Cuprite Mine—*mine* (2) ... AZ-5
**Cuprum**—*pop pl* ... ID-8
Cup Run—*stream* (2) ... WV-2
Cups, The—*locale* ... CA-9
Cupsaw Brook—*stream* ... NJ-2
Cupsaw Lake—*reservoir* ... NJ-2
Cupsoque Beach—*beach* ... NY-2
Cup Spring—*spring* ... CA-9
Cup Spring—*spring* (2) ... OR-9
**Cupsuptic**—*pop pl* ... ME-1
Cupsuptic Lake—*lake* ... ME-1
Cupsuptic Mtn—*summit* ... ME-1
Cupsuptic Nursery (historical)—*locale* ... ME-1
Cupsuptic Pond—*lake* ... ME-1
Cupsuptic River—*stream* ... ME-1
Cupsuptic Sporting Camp (historical)—*locale* ... ME-1
Cup Tank—*reservoir* ... AZ-5
Cup Tank—*reservoir* ... NM-5
Curacao Reef—*bar* ... AK-9
Curatole Island—*island* ... CT-1
**Curb**—*pop pl* ... KY-4
Curbow Cem—*cemetery* ... TN-4
**Curbville**—*pop pl* ... AL-4
Curbville Post Office (historical)—*building* ... AL-4
Curbville Sch (historical)—*school* ... AL-4
**Curby**—*pop pl* ... IN-6
Curby Branch—*stream* ... VA-3
**Curchece**—*pop pl* ... OK-5
Cur Creek—*stream* ... OR-9
Curd Cem—*cemetery* ... KY-4
Curd Cem—*cemetery* ... TN-4
Curd Garden Ridge—*ridge* ... KY-4
Curd House—*hist pl* ... KY-4
Curd-Moss House—*hist pl* ... KY-4
Curd Sch (historical)—*school* ... TN-4
Curdsville—*locale* ... VA-3

**Curdsville**—*pop pl* ... KY-4
Curdsville (Magisterial District)—*fmr MCD* ... VA-3
Curdton—*locale* ... MO-7
Cure-al Branch—*stream* ... TN-4
**Cureall**—*pop pl* ... MO-7
Cureall Cem—*cemetery* ... MO-7
Cureall School (abandoned)—*locale* ... MO-7
Cureall Spring—*spring* ... MO-7
Cure-all Spring—*spring* ... TN-4
Curecanti Archeol District—*hist pl* ... CO-8
Curecanti Creek—*stream* ... CO-8
Curecanti Natl Recreation Area—*park* ... CO-8
Curecanti Needle—*pillar* ... CO-8
Curecanti Pass—*gap* ... CO-8
Cure D'Ars Chapel—*church* ... LA-4
Cure d'Ars Sch—*school* ... CO-8
*Cure Island* ... HI-9
Curentons Ferry (historical)—*locale* ... TN-4
Cure of Ars Convent—*church* ... KS-7
Cure of Ars Sch *school* ... KS 7
Cure of Ars Sch—*school* ... NY-2
Cureranti Pass Trail—*trail* ... CO-8
Cureton Canyon—*valley* ... NM-5
Cureton Cem—*cemetery* (2) ... SC-3
Cureton-Huff House—*hist pl* ... SC-3
Cureton Ranch—*locale* ... NM-5
Curetons Bridge Post Office (historical)—*building* ... AL-4
Cureton Sch—*school* ... CA-9
Curey Canyon—*valley* ... OR-9
**Curfew**—*pop pl* ... PA-2
Curfew Hunting Lodge—*building* ... CA-9
Curfman Run—*stream* ... PA-2
*Curger Channel* ... VA-3
Curia Creek—*stream* ... AR-4
Curia Creek Ditch—*canal* ... AR-4
Curia Lake—*lake* ... AR-4
*Curia Old River* ... AR-4
Curias, Aljibe las—*reservoir* ... PR-3
Curiel Elem Sch Annex—*school* ... AZ-5
Curiel Sch—*school* ... AZ-5
Curiel School Mini Park Site—*park* ... AZ-5
Curie Park—*park* ... MI-6
Curie Spring—*spring* ... CO-8
Curio Canyon—*valley* ... NM-5
Curiosity Branch—*stream* ... AL-4
Curiosity Creek—*stream* (2) ... FL-3
Curiosity Spring—*spring* ... OR-9
Curis Landing (historical)—*locale* ... TN-4
Curitan Creek—*stream* ... WY-8
Curits Corner—*locale* ... NH-1
*Curl* ... AL-4
*Curlan* ... GA-3
Curlane Run—*stream* ... OH-6
Curl Cem—*cemetery* ... AL-4
Curl Cem—*cemetery* ... AR-4
Curl Creek—*stream* ... AR-4
Curl Creek—*stream* ... CA-9
Curl Creek—*stream* ... IL-6
Curl Creek—*stream* ... OK-5
Curl Creek—*stream* ... OR-9
**Curlee**—*pop pl* ... TN-4
Curlee Cem—*cemetery* ... IL-6
Curlee Cem—*cemetery* ... TN-4
Curlee Ch of Christ—*church* ... TN-4
Curlee Museum—*building* ... MS-4
Curlee Sch (historical)—*school* ... TN-4
*Curlees Church* ... TN-4
Curler Lake—*lake* ... UT-8
Curles Creek—*stream* ... VA-3
Curles Neck—*cape* ... VA-3
Curles Neck Mansion Wharf—*locale* ... VA-3
Curles Neck Plantation—*locale* ... VA-3
Curles Neck Swamp—*swamp* ... VA-3
Curless Cem—*cemetery* ... IL-6
Curless Prairie—*flat* ... CA-9
Curletts Point—*cape* ... VA-3
Curlew—*locale* ... CA-9
Curlew—*locale* ... KY-4
**Curlew**—*pop pl* ... FL-3
**Curlew**—*pop pl* ... IA-7
**Curlew**—*pop pl* ... WA-9
Curlew Airp—*airport* ... WA-9
Curlew Bay—*bay* ... VA-3
Curlew Bridge—*hist pl* ... WA-9
Curlew Buttes—*summit* ... ND-7
Curlew Campground—*locale* ... ID-8
Curlew (CCD)—*cens area* ... WA-9
Curlew Creek—*stream* ... FL-3
Curlew Creek—*stream* ... ID-8
Curlew Creek—*stream* ... MT-8
Curlew Creek—*stream* ... WA-9
Curlew Creek Elem Sch—*school* ... FL-3
Curlew Dam—*dam* ... SD-7
Curlew Gulch—*valley* ... ID-8
Curlew Hill—*summit* ... WY-8
Curlew Hills Memory Gardens—*cemetery* ... FL-3
Curlew Islands—*island* ... LA-4
Curlew Junction—*locale* ... UT-8
Curlew Key—*island* ... FL-3
Curlew Lake—*lake* ... AK-9
Curlew Lake—*lake* ... NM-5
Curlew Lake—*lake* ... WA-9
Curlew Lake—*reservoir* ... SD-7
Curlew Lake State Park—*park* ... WA-9
Curlew Ledge—*bay* ... AK-9
Curlew Mines—*mine* ... MT-8
Curlew Natl Grassland—*plain* ... ID-8
Curlew Point—*cape* ... AK-9
Curlew Pond—*lake* ... MA-1
Curlew Pool—*reservoir* ... UT-8
*Curlew Reservoir* ... ID-8
Curlew Rock—*island* ... ME-1
Curlew Sch—*hist pl* ... WA-9
Curlew Sch—*school* ... MT-8
Curlew Sch Number 1—*school* ... ND-7
Curlew Sch Number 3—*school* ... ND-7
Curlew Township—*civ div* ... ND-7
**Curlew Township**—*pop pl* ... SD-7
*Curlew Valley* ... ID-8
Curlew Valley—*valley* ... ID-8
Curlew Valley—*valley* ... ND-7
Curlew Valley—*valley* ... UT-8
*Curlew Valley Reservoir* ... ID-8
Curlew Well—*well* ... TX-5
*Curley Bear Mountain* ... MT-8
Curley Branch—*stream* ... AR-4
Curley Canyon—*valley* ... SD-7
*Curley Creek* ... MS-4
Curley Creek—*stream* ... ID-8
Curley Creek—*stream* ... MT-8
Curley Creek—*stream* ... OR-9
Curley Creek—*stream* ... WA-9
**Curley Hill**—*pop pl* ... PA-2
Curley Hill Acres—*locale* ... PA-2
Curley Hollow—*valley* ... VA-3
Curley Hollow Rsvr—*reservoir* ... UT-8
Curley Jack Campground—*locale* ... CA-9
Curley Jack Creek—*stream* ... CA-9
*Curley Lake* ... MN-6
Curley Maple Gap—*gap* ... TN-4
Curley Park—*park* ... ID-8
Curley Peak—*summit* ... CO-8
Curley Sage Flat—*flat* ... UT-8
Curley Sch—*school* ... AZ-5
Curley Sch (historical)—*school* ... PA-2
Curley Seep—*spring* ... AZ-5
Curley Seep Tank—*reservoir* ... AZ-5
Curleys Run—*stream* ... PA-2
Curley State Public Shooting Area *park* ... SD 7
Curley Tank—*reservoir* ... TX-5
*Curley Valley* ... ID-8
*Curley Valley* ... UT-8
Curley Wallace Tank—*reservoir* ... AZ-5
*Curlie Creek Canyon* ... NE-7
Curlin Cem—*cemetery* ... KY-4
Curlis Lake—*reservoir* ... NJ-2
Curliss Meadows Guard Station—*locale* ... CA-9
Curl Lake—*lake* ... MT-8
Curl Lake—*lake* ... WA-9
**Curllsville**—*pop pl* ... PA-2
Curlow Flat—*flat* ... NV-8
Curlow Pond—*lake* ... WA-9
Curl Ridge—*ridge* ... CA-9
Curl Ridge Jeep Trail—*trail* ... CA-9
*Curls* ... AL-4
*Curl's Neck* ... VA-3
*Curls Station* ... AL-4
Curl Station—*locale* ... AL-4
Curl Tail Creek—*stream* ... NC-3
Curly Bear Mtn—*summit* (2) ... MT-8
*Curly Canyon* ... OR-9
Curly Cow Creek—*stream* ... CA-9
*Curly Creek* ... ID-8
*Curly Creek* ... MT-8
Curly Creek—*stream* ... MT-8
Curly Creek—*stream* ... WA-9
Curly Creek Campground—*locale* ... WA-9
Curly Fork—*stream* ... KY-4
Curly Gulch—*valley* ... MT-8
Curly Head Canyon—*valley* ... MT-8
Curly Hill—*summit* ... TX-5
Curly Hill Acres—*locale* ... PA-2
Curly Hollow Wash—*valley* ... UT-8
Curly Jack Flat—*flat* ... ID-8
Curly Jack Spring—*spring* ... ID-8
Curly Lake—*lake* ... MT-8
Curly Mapel Ridge—*ridge* ... NC-3
Curly Tank—*reservoir* ... AZ-5
*Curnes Creek* ... IN-6
Curnow Canyon—*valley* ... NV-8
Curnow Spring—*spring* ... NV-8
Curns Well (historical)—*locale* ... AL-4
Curnutte Branch—*stream* ... KY-4
Curnutte Cem—*cemetery* ... KY-4
Curop Ditch—*canal* ... OR-9
Curp Cem—*cemetery* ... OH-6
Currahee Ch—*church* ... GA-3
Currahee Mtn—*summit* ... GA-3
Curran—*locale* ... WI-6
**Curran**—*pop pl* ... IL-6
**Curran**—*pop pl* ... MI-6
Curran, John, House—*hist pl* ... MS-4
Curran Branch—*stream* ... IA-7
Curran Branch—*stream* ... VA-3
Curran Cem—*cemetery* ... MI-6
Curran Cem—*cemetery* ... MS-4
Curran Cem—*cemetery* ... WI-6
Curran Coulee—*valley* ... WI-6
Curran Creek—*stream* ... ID-8
Curran Creek—*stream* ... OR-9
Curran Gulch—*valley* ... CO-8
Curran Gulch—*valley* ... ID-8
Curran Hall—*hist pl* ... AR-4
Curran JHS—*school* ... CA-9
Curran Lake—*lake* ... MN-6
Curran Lookout Tower (historical)—*locale* ... MI-6
Curran Lower Reservoir Dam—*dam* ... RI-1
Curran Lower Rsvr—*reservoir* ... RI-1
Curran Mountain Spring—*spring* ... OR-9
Curran Sch—*school* ... NE-7
Curran Sch—*school* ... WI-6
Currant—*locale* ... NV-8
Currant Canyon—*valley* ... NV-8
Currant Canyon—*valley* (2) ... UT-8
*Currant Creek* ... OR-9
*Currant Creek* ... UT-8
Currant Creek—*stream* ... AK-9
Currant Creek—*stream* (2) ... CO-8
Currant Creek—*stream* (2) ... ID-8
Currant Creek—*stream* (3) ... MT-8
Currant Creek—*stream* (2) ... NV-8
Currant Creek—*stream* ... OK-5
Currant Creek—*stream* ... OR-9
Currant Creek—*stream* (7) ... UT-8
Currant Creek—*stream* ... WA-9
Currant Creek—*stream* (2) ... WY-8
Currant Creek Canal—*canal* ... UT-8
Currant Creek Dam—*dam* ... OR-9
Currant Creek Dam—*dam* ... UT-8
Currant Creek Feeder Canal—*canal* ... UT-8
Currant Creek Forest Service Recreation Site—*locale* ... NV-8
*Currant Creek Forest Service Station* ... UT-8
Currant Creek Guard Station—*locale* ... ID-8
Currant Creek Guard Station—*locale* ... UT-8
Currant Creek Mtn—*summit* ... UT-8
Currant Creek No 2 Ditch—*canal* ... CO-8
Currant Creek Pass—*gap* ... CO-8
Currant Creek Peak—*summit* ... UT-8
Currant Creek Ranch—*locale* ... WY-8
Currant Creek Ridge—*ridge* ... WY-8
Currant Creek Rsvr—*reservoir* ... OR-9
Currant Creek Rsvr—*reservoir* ... UT-8
Currant Creek Sch—*school* ... NV-8
*Currant Creek Summit* ... NV-8
Currant Creek Trail—*trail* ... MT-8
Currant Creek Tunnel (proposed)—*canal* ... UT-8
Currant Creek Wildlife Mngmt Area—*park* ... UT-8
Currant Draw—*valley* ... WY-8
Currant Hollow—*valley* ... ID-8
Currant Island—*island* ... ME-1
*Currant Lake* ... MN-6
Currant Mtn—*summit* ... NV-8
Currant Mtn—*summit* ... VA-3
**Curran (Town of)**—*pop pl* ... WI-6
**Curran (Township of)**—*pop pl* ... IL-6
*Currant Peak* ... UT-8
Currant Peak—*summit* ... OR-9
Currant Ranch Airp—*airport* ... NV-8
Currant Spring—*spring* ... NV-8
Currant Spring—*spring* ... OR-9
Currant Spring—*spring* (2) ... UT-8
Currant Springs Ranch—*locale* ... CO-8
Currant Summit—*summit* ... NV-8
Curran Upper Reservoir Dam—*dam* ... RI-1
Curran Upper Rsvr Dam—*reservoir* ... RI-1
**Curranville**—*pop pl* ... KS-7
*Curratuch Creek* ... VA 3
Curratuck Creek—*stream* ... VA-3
Curr Creek—*stream* ... LA-4
*Currean Branch* ... IA-7
*Currecanti Needle* ... CO-8
Currell Cove—*bay* ... VA-3
*Curren Branch* ... IA-7
Curren Brook—*stream* ... NY-2
Currence Cem—*cemetery* ... KY-4
Curren Ditch—*canal* ... ID-8
Curren Mtn—*summit* ... ID-8
Curren Mtn—*summit* ... NY-2
Curren Sch—*school* ... MN-6
Current, Bayou—*stream* (2) ... LA-4
Current Canyon—*valley* ... CO-8
Current Cem—*cemetery* ... MN-6
Current Cem—*cemetery* ... WV-2
*Current Creek* ... UT-8
Current Creek—*stream* ... CO-8
Current Creek—*stream* ... ID-8
*Current Creek Dam* ... UT-8
*Current Creek Reservoir* ... UT-8
Curren Terrace—*uninc pl* ... PA-2
Current Hole—*channel* ... VI-3
Current Lake—*lake* (2) ... MN-6
Current Lake—*locale* ... MN-6
Current Lake State Wildlife Mngmt Area—*park* ... MN-6
*Current River* ... UT-8
Current River—*stream* ... AR-4
Current River—*stream* ... LA-4
Current River—*stream* ... MO-7
Current River Country Club—*building* ... MO-7
Current River Township—*civil* ... MO-7
Current River (Township of)—*fmr MCD* ... AR-4
Current Rock—*island* ... VI-3
Current Sch (historical)—*school* ... TN-4
Currents Landing—*locale* ... TN-4
Current Spring Ditch—*canal* ... UT-8
**Currentsville**—*pop pl* ... KY-4
Current Township—*civil* ... MO-7
**Current Township**—*pop pl* ... MO-7
*Currentview* ... MO-7
**Current View**—*pop pl* ... AR-4
**Current View**—*pop pl* ... MO-7
**Currentview**—*pop pl* ... MO-7
Currey Canyon—*valley* ... OR-9
Currey Canyon Rsvr—*reservoir* ... OR-9
Currey Creek—*stream* ... TX-5
Currey Farms Airp—*airport* ... KS-7
Currey Flowage—*swamp* ... WI-6
Currey Lake—*lake* ... MI-6
Currey Pond—*reservoir* ... TN-4
Currey Rsvr—*reservoir* ... OR-9
*Curreys Ford* ... TN-4
*Curreys Fork* ... KY-4
Currey Spring—*spring* ... OR-9
*Curricanti Needle* ... CO-8
Currie—*locale* ... TX-5
**Currie**—*pop pl* ... MN-6
**Currie**—*pop pl* (2) ... MS-4
**Currie**—*pop pl* ... NV-8
**Currie**—*pop pl* ... NC-3
**Currie**—*pop pl* ... TN-4
Currie Airp—*airport* ... NV-8
Currie Bay (Carolina Bay)—*swamp* ... NC-3
Currie Bennett Park—*park* ... MI-6
Currie Canyon—*valley* ... NV-8
Currie Canyon—*valley* ... OR-9
Currie Cem—*cemetery* ... MS-4
Currie Cem—*cemetery* ... TN-4
Currie Coulee—*valley* ... MT-8
*Currie Creek* ... MS-4
Currie Creek—*stream* ... CO-8
Currie Creek—*stream* ... GA-3
Currie Creek—*stream* ... MS-4
Currie Gardens—*spring* ... NV-8
Currie Hill—*summit* ... NC-3
Currie Hills—*range* ... NV-8
Currie Lake—*lake* ... WI-6
Currie Lake—*reservoir* ... TX-5
Currie Maintenance Station—*locale* ... NV-8
Currie Oil Field—*oilfield* (2) ... TX-5
Currie Park—*park* ... WI-6
Currie Pond—*reservoir* ... NC-3
Currie Pond Dam—*dam* ... NC-3
Currie Post Office (historical)—*building* ... TN-4
Currier, Capt. Jonathan, House—*hist pl* ... NH-1
Currie Ranch—*locale* (3) ... TX-5
Currier Bay—*bay* ... MN-6
Currier Brook—*stream* (2) ... ME-1
Currier Brook—*stream* (3) ... NH-1
Currier Brook—*stream* ... VT-1
Currier Camp—*locale* ... NH-1
Currier Canyon—*valley* ... WA-9
Currier Cem—*cemetery* ... MS-4
Currier Cem—*cemetery* ... TN-4
Currier Creek—*stream* (2) ... OR-9
Currier Creek—*stream* ... WA-9
Currier Gallery of Art—*hist pl* ... NH-1
Currier Gurad Station—*locale* ... OR-9
Currier Hill—*summit* ... ME-1
Currier Hill—*summit* (2) ... NH-1
Currier Hill—*summit* ... VT-1
Currier House—*hist pl* ... IA-7
Currier House—*hist pl* ... MI-6
*Currie Ridge Church* ... MS-4
Currier Lake—*lake* ... WI-6
Currier Mtn—*summit* ... NH-1
Currier Point—*cape* ... NH-1
Currier Ranch—*locale* ... MT-8
Currier Rsvr—*reservoir* ... CO-8
Currie RR Turntable—*hist pl* ... MN-6
**Curriers**—*pop pl* ... NY-2
Currier Sch—*school* (2) ... MA-1
Currier Sch (abandoned)—*school* ... PA-2
Currier Spring—*spring* ... OR-9
Currie Rsvr—*reservoir* ... TX-5
Curries Branch—*stream* ... NC-3
Currie Sch—*school* ... NC-3
Currie Sch—*school* ... ND-7
Curries Chapel—*church* ... AL-4
Curries Ferry (historical)—*locale* ... PA-2
Curries Pond—*reservoir* ... NC-3
Currie Spring—*spring* ... MT-8
Currie Summit—*summit* ... NV-8
**Currie Township**—*pop pl* ... ND-7
Currie Well—*well* ... NV-8
Currin Bridge—*hist pl* ... OR-9
Currin Creek—*stream* ... OR-9
Currington Cem *cemetery* ... OH 6
Currin Gulch—*valley* ... ID-8
Currin Lake—*reservoir* ... NC-3
Currin Lake Dam—*dam* ... NC-3
Currin Slough—*stream* ... AK-9
Currins Sch—*school* ... TN-4
**Currinsville**—*pop pl* ... OR-9
Currin Valley—*valley* ... VA-3
Currioman Bay—*bay* ... VA-3
Currioman Cem—*cemetery* ... VA-3
Currioman Creek—*stream* ... VA-3
Currioman Landing—*locale* ... VA-3
*Currioman Wharf* ... VA-3
**Currituck**—*pop pl* ... NC-3
Currituck Banks—*island* ... NC-3
Currituck Beach—*beach* ... NC-3
Currituck Beach Lighthouse—*hist pl* ... NC-3
Currituck Beach Lighthouse—*locale* ... NC-3
**Currituck County**—*pop pl* ... NC-3
Currituck County Airp—*airport* ... NC-3
Currituck County Courthouse and Jail—*hist pl* ... NC-3
Currituck County HS—*school* ... NC-3
Currituck County Schools Administrative Office—*building* ... NC-3
*Currituck Creek* ... NC-3
**Currituck Farms**—*pop pl* ... VA-3
Currituck Light—*locale* ... NC-3
*Currituck Narrows* ... NC-3
Currituck Point—*cape* ... NC-3
Currituck Shooting Club—*hist pl* ... NC-3
Currituck Sound—*bay* ... NC-3
**Currituck (subdivision)**—*pop pl* ... NC-3
Currituck (Township of)—*fmr MCD* ... NC-3
*Currumpa River* ... OK-5
*Currumpaw River* ... OK-5
*Curry* ... PA-2
Curry—*locale* (2) ... AL-4
Curry—*locale* ... LA-4
Curry—*locale* ... MT-8
Curry—*locale* ... PA-2
Curry—*locale* ... WA-9
**Curry**—*pop pl* ... AL-4
**Curry**—*pop pl* ... AK-9
**Curry**—*pop pl* ... ID-8
**Curry**—*pop pl* ... NE-7
**Curry**—*pop pl* ... NY-2
Curry, Abraham, House—*hist pl* ... NV-8
Curry, J. L. M., House—*hist pl* ... AL-4
Curry, Lake—*lake* ... LA-4
Curry, Lake—*reservoir* ... CA-9
Curry, Lewis, House—*hist pl* ... UT-8
Curry, Nathaniel, House—*hist pl* ... OR-9
Curry, Solomon S., House—*hist pl* ... MI-6
Curry Archeol Site—*hist pl* ... KS-7
Curry Basin—*basin* ... AZ-5
Curry Branch—*canal* ... MI-6
Curry Branch—*stream* ... AL-4
Curry Branch—*stream* ... AR-4
Curry Branch—*stream* (2) ... KY-4
Curry Branch—*stream* ... LA-4
Curry Branch—*stream* (2) ... SC-3
Curry Branch—*stream* (3) ... TN-4
Curry Branch—*stream* (4) ... WV-2
Curry Branch Sch—*school* ... KY-4
Curry Brook—*stream* ... ME-1
Curry Camp—*locale* ... AZ-5
Currycamp Fork—*stream* ... WV-2
Curry Canyon—*valley* ... CA-9
Curry Canyon—*valley* ... NM-5
Curry Canyon—*valley* ... UT-8
Curry Canyon—*valley* ... WA-9
Curry Cave—*cave* ... AL-4
Curry Cem—*cemetery* (2) ... AL-4
Curry Cem—*cemetery* ... FL-3
Curry Cem—*cemetery* ... GA-3
Curry Cem—*cemetery* ... IL-6
Curry Cem—*cemetery* (2) ... KS-7
Curry Cem—*cemetery* (2) ... KY-4
Curry Cem—*cemetery* (2) ... OH-6
Curry Cem—*cemetery* ... PA-2
Curry Cem—*cemetery* ... TN-4
Curry Cem—*cemetery* (4) ... WV-2
Curry Ch—*church* ... AL-4
Curry Chapel—*church* ... IN-6
Curry Chapel—*church* ... TN-4
Curry Chapel—*church* ... WV-2
Curry Chapel (historical)—*church* ... MO-7
Curry Chapel Sch—*school* ... WV-2
Curry-Chucovich House—*hist pl* ... CO-8
Curry Coll—*school* ... MA-1
Currycomb Branch—*stream* ... TX-5
Currycomb Cem—*cemetery* ... WV-2
*Curry-Compton Cemetery* ... AL-4
Curry Coulee—*valley* ... MT-8
**Curry (County)**—*pop pl* ... NM-5
**Curry County**—*pop pl* ... OR-9
Curry County Courthouse—*hist pl* ... NM-5
Curry Creek—*stream* ... AL-4
Curry Creek—*stream* ... CA-9
Curry Creek—*stream* ... FL-3
Curry Creek—*stream* (2) ... GA-3
Curry Creek—*stream* ... IA-7
Curry Creek—*stream* ... KY-4
Curry Creek—*stream* ... LA-4
Curry Creek—*stream* ... MS-4
Curry Creek—*stream* ... MT-8
Curry Creek—*stream* (3) ... TX-5
Curry Creek—*stream* ... VA-3
Curry Creek—*stream* (2) ... WY-8
Curry Crossing—*locale* ... TX-5
Curry Drain—*canal* ... MI-6
Curry Draw—*valley* ... TX-5
Curry Draw—*valley* ... WY-8
*Curry Elem Sch* ... AL-4
Curry Elem Sch—*school* ... AL-4
Curry Elem Sch—*school* ... AZ-5
Curry Ferry—*locale* ... FL-3
Curry Ford—*locale* ... AL-4
Curry Ford—*locale* ... TN-4
Curry Ford East (Shop Ctr)—*locale* ... FL-3
Curry Ford United Methodist Ch—*church* ... FL-3
Curry Fork—*stream* ... WV-2
Curry Gap—*gap* ... TN-4
Curry Gap—*gap* ... VA-3
Curry Gap—*gap* ... WA-9
*Curry Gordan Creek* ... OR-9
Curry Gordon Creek—*stream* ... OR-9
Curry Grove Cem—*cemetery* ... AL-4
Curry Gulch—*valley* ... OR-9
Curry Ho Mtn *summit* ... TN 4
Curry Hill—*locale* ... GA-3
**Curry Hill**—*pop pl* ... PA-2
Curry Hill—*summit* ... GA-3
Curry Hill Ch—*church* ... GA-3
Curry Hill Plantation—*hist pl* ... GA-3
Curry Hollow—*valley* ... KY-4
Curry Hosp—*hospital* ... OK-5
Curry HS—*school* ... AL-4
*Curry Island* ... FL-3
Curry Island—*island* ... AL-4
Curry Island—*island* (2) ... FL-3
Curry Key—*island* ... FL-3
Curry Lake—*lake* ... FL-3
Curry Lake—*lake* ... MI-6
Curry Lake—*lake* ... MS-4
Curry Lake—*lake* ... MO-7
Curry Lake—*lake* ... NE-7
Curry Lake—*lake* ... OR-9
Curry Lake—*reservoir* ... MO-7
Curry Lake—*swamp* ... IL-6
Curry Lookout—*locale* ... AK-9
Curry (Magisterial District)—*fmr MCD* ... WV-2
Curry Memorial Ch—*church* ... TN-4
Curry Memorial Home—*building* ... PA-2
Curry Mine—*mine* ... MI-6
Curry Mountain—*ridge* ... CA-9
Curry Oil And Gas Field—*oilfield* ... AR-4
Curry Oil Field—*oilfield* ... TX-5
Curry Peak—*summit* ... UT-8
Curry Pond—*lake* ... NY-2
Curry Pond—*reservoir* ... MS-4
Curry Prairie—*flat* ... IN-6
Curry Prairie Creek—*stream* ... IN-6
Curry Prong—*stream* ... TN-4
Curry Ranch—*locale* (2) ... NE-7
Curry Ranch—*locale* ... WY-8
Curry Rapids—*rapids* ... UT-8
Curry Ridge—*ridge* ... AK-9
Curry Ridge—*ridge* (2) ... WV-2
Curry (RR name for Curryville)—*other* ... PA-2
**Curry Run**—*pop pl* ... PA-2
Curry Run—*stream* (3) ... PA-2
Curry Run—*stream* ... WV-2
Curry Run Camp—*locale* ... PA-2
Curry Run Ch—*church* ... PA-2
*Currys* ... AL-4
**Currys**—*pop pl* ... AL-4
Curry Sch—*school* ... AL-4
Curry Sch—*school* ... CA-9
Curry Sch—*school* ... IL-6
Curry Sch—*school* ... KY-4
Curry Sch—*school* ... NC-3
Curry Sch—*school* ... SD-7
Currys Chapel—*church* ... TX-5
Curry Sch (historical)—*school* ... PA-2
**Currys Corner**—*pop pl* ... AZ-5
Currys Corners—*locale* ... OH-6
*Currys Ferry* ... AL-4
*Currys Fisher* ... MN-6
Currys Fork—*stream* ... KY-4
Curry She Mtn—*summit* ... TN-4
Currys Island—*island* ... FL-3
Currys Island—*island* ... MN-6
Currys Lake—*reservoir* ... SC-3
Currys Lake—*swamp* ... FL-3
Curry Slough—*lake* ... MN-6
Currys Mills—*locale* ... PA-2
*Currys Point* ... FL-3
Currys Pond—*reservoir* ... NC-3
Curry Spring—*spring* ... OR-9
*Currys Run* ... PA-2
*Currys Station* ... AL-4
*Currys Store* ... AL-4
*Currysville* ... IN-6
Curry Tank—*reservoir* (2) ... AZ-5
**Currytown**—*pop pl* ... AL-4
**Currytown**—*pop pl* ... NY-2
**Currytown**—*pop pl* ... NC-3
**Curry (Township of)**—*pop pl* ... IN-6
*Curry Trick Tank* ... AZ-5
*Curry Tuck Post Office* ... TN-4
**Curry Village**—*pop pl* ... CA-9
*Curryville* ... PA-2
**Curryville**—*pop pl* ... GA-3
**Curryville**—*pop pl* (2) ... IN-6
**Curryville**—*pop pl* ... MO-7
**Curryville**—*pop pl* ... PA-2
**Curryville (RR name Curry)**—*pop pl* ... PA-2
Curry Well—*well* ... TX-5
Curry Woods—*woods* ... WA-9
*Cursin Chapel Church* ... AL-4
Cursing Hollow—*valley* ... VA-3
*Curso Siding* ... KS-7
Cursten Creek—*stream* ... MI-6
**Curt**—*pop pl* ... AL-4
**Curt**—*pop pl* ... KY-4
Curtain Falls—*falls* ... MN-6
Curtain Ponds—*lake* ... CO-8
*Curtains* ... PA-2
Curtain Sch—*school* ... IL-6
Curtain Sch—*school* ... WI-6
Curt Branch—*stream* ... TN-4
*Curt Creek* ... AR-4
Curte Oreilles, Lac—*lake* ... WI-6
Curteys Chapel—*church* ... NC-3
Curt Hollow—*valley* ... KY-4
Curt Hollow—*valley* ... TN-4
**Curtice**—*pop pl* ... OH-6
Curtice Cem—*cemetery* ... MI-6
Curtice Mine—*mine* ... AZ-5
Curtin—*locale* ... PA-2
Curtin—*locale* ... WV-2
**Curtin**—*pop pl* ... OR-9
**Curtin**—*pop pl* ... WV-2
Curtin, Jeremiah, House—*hist pl* ... WI-6
*Curtin Creek* ... AL-4
*Curtin Creek* ... PA-2
Curtin Creek—*stream* ... OR-9
Curtin Ditch—*canal* ... CO-8
*Curtin Elementary School* ... PA-2
Curtin Gap—*gap* ... PA-2
*Curtin Narrows* ... PA-2
Curtin Pond—*lake* ... MA-1
**Curtin (RR name Barton)**—*pop pl* ... WV-2
Curtin Rsvr—*reservoir* ... CO-8
Curtin Run—*stream* ... WV-2
Curtin Sch—*school* (2) ... PA-2
**Curtin (Township of)**—*pop pl* ... PA-2
Curtin Village—*hist pl* ... PA-2
*Curtis* ... IN 6
Curtis—*locale* ... CA-9
Curtis—*locale* ... GA-3
Curtis—*locale* ... IL-6
Curtis—*locale* ... KY-4
Curtis—*locale* ... LA-4
Curtis—*locale* ... NY-2
Curtis—*locale* ... OK-5
Curtis—*locale* ... OR-9
Curtis—*locale* ... TX-5
Curtis—*locale* ... VA-3
Curtis—*locale* ... WA-9
Curtis—*locale* ... WY-8
**Curtis**—*pop pl* ... AL-4
**Curtis**—*pop pl* ... AR-4
**Curtis**—*pop pl* ... CO-8
**Curtis**—*pop pl* ... FL-3
**Curtis**—*pop pl* (2) ... MI-6
**Curtis**—*pop pl* ... NE-7
**Curtis**—*pop pl* ... NY-2
**Curtis**—*pop pl* ... UT-8
**Curtis**—*pop pl* ... VA-3
Curtis—*uninc pl* ... TX-5
Curtis, Allen Crocker, House-Pillar House—*hist pl* ... MA-1
Curtis, Charles, House—*hist pl* ... KS-7
Curtis, Elijah P., House—*hist pl* ... IL-6
Curtis, George M., House—*hist pl* ... IA-7
Curtis, Lake—*reservoir* ... NC-3
Curtis, Mount—*summit* ... AK-9
Curtis, Nathaniel, House—*hist pl* ... CT-1
Curtis, Paul, House—*hist pl* ... MA-1
Curtis, Uri B., House—*hist pl* ... NV-8
Curtis, Uri B., House/Tasker L. Oddie House—*hist pl* ... NV-8
Curtis, Walter, House—*hist pl* ... OH-6
Curtis, Walter W. House—*hist pl* ... GA-3
Curtis, William, House—*hist pl* ... MA-1
Curtis, William D., House—*hist pl* ... OH-6
Curtis, William E., House—*hist pl* ... FL-3
Curtis Airp—*airport* ... WA-9
Curtis Arboretum—*park* ... PA-2
Curtis Bar Creek—*stream* ... AK-9
Curtis Bay—*bay* ... MD-2
**Curtis Bay**—*pop pl* ... MD-2
Curtis Bay Channel—*channel* ... MD-2
Curtis Bay Sch—*school* ... MD-2
Curtis Bldg—*hist pl* ... MA-1
Curtis Bog—*swamp* ... ME-1
Curtis Branch—*stream* (3) ... KY-4
Curtis Branch—*stream* (2) ... MS-4
Curtis Branch—*stream* ... NC-3
Curtis Branch—*stream* ... WV-2
*Curtis Brook* ... CT-1
Curtis Brook—*stream* ... CT-1
Curtis Brook—*stream* ... ME-1
Curtis Brook—*stream* ... NH-1
Curtis Brook—*stream* ... NY-2
Curtis Camp—*locale* ... AL-4
Curtis Camp—*locale* ... NM-5
Curtis Canal—*canal* ... AZ-5
Curtis Canyon—*valley* (3) ... NM-5
Curtis Canyon—*valley* ... WY-8
Curtis Canyon Campground—*locale* ... WY-8
Curtis Canyon Dam—*reservoir* ... NM-5
Curtis Canyon Overlook—*locale* ... WY-8
Curtis Cem—*cemetery* ... AL-4
Curtis Cem—*cemetery* (4) ... AR-4
Curtis Cem—*cemetery* ... CO-8
Curtis Cem—*cemetery* (3) ... GA-3
Curtis Cem—*cemetery* ... IL-6
Curtis Cem—*cemetery* (2) ... ME-1
Curtis Cem—*cemetery* (5) ... MI-6
Curtis Cem—*cemetery* (3) ... MS-4
Curtis Cem—*cemetery* (2) ... MO-7
Curtis Cem—*cemetery* ... NE-7
Curtis Cem—*cemetery* (2) ... NY-2
Curtis Cem—*cemetery* ... OK-5
Curtis Cem—*cemetery* ... PA-2
Curtis Cem—*cemetery* ... SC-3
Curtis Cem—*cemetery* (2) ... TN-4
Curtis Cem—*cemetery* ... TX-5
Curtis Cem—*cemetery* ... VA-3
Curtis Cem—*cemetery* ... WV-2
Curtis Cem—*cemetery* ... WI-6
Curtis Ch—*church* ... MD-2
Curtis Ch—*church* ... MO-7
Curtis Ch—*church* (2) ... WV-2
Curtis-Champa Streets District—*hist pl* ... CO-8
Curtis-Champa Streets Hist Dist (Boundary Increase)—*hist pl* ... CO-8
Curtis Chapel—*church* ... MS-4
Curtis Chapel—*church* ... MO-7
Curtis Chapel—*church* ... TN-4
Curtis Chapel Cem—*cemetery* ... MS-4
Curtis Chapel Cem—*cemetery* ... TN-4
*Curtis Chapel Methodist Episcopal Church* ... MS-4
Curtis Clearing—*flat* ... NY-2
Curtis Corner—*locale* ... ME-1
Curtis Corner—*locale* ... NH-1
Curtis Corner—*locale* ... NY-2
**Curtis Corner**—*pop pl* ... RI-1
Curtis Cove—*bay* (3) ... ME-1
Curtis Cove—*valley* ... NC-3
*Curtis Creek* ... CO-8
*Curtis Creek* ... MI-6
*Curtis Creek* ... UT-8
Curtis Creek—*stream* ... AK-9
Curtis Creek—*stream* (3) ... AR-4
Curtis Creek—*stream* ... CA-9
Curtis Creek—*stream* ... CO-8

Curtis Creek—*stream* (2) ... GA-3
Curtis Creek—*stream* (3) ... ID-8
Curtis Creek—*stream* ... IL-6
Curtis Creek—*stream* ... IN-6
Curtis Creek—*stream* ... KS-7
Curtis Creek—*stream* (2) ... LA-4
Curtis Creek—*stream* ... ME-1
Curtis Creek—*stream* ... MD-2
Curtis Creek—*stream* ... MN-6
Curtis Creek—*stream* ... MS-4
Curtis Creek—*stream* ... NM-5
Curtis Creek—*stream* ... NY-2
Curtis Creek—*stream* (5) ... NC-3
Curtis Creek—*stream* ... OK-5
Curtis Creek—*stream* (3) ... OR-9
Curtis Creek—*stream* ... TX-5
Curtis Creek—*stream* ... UT-8
Curtis Creek—*stream* ... WA-9
Curtis Creek—*stream* (2) ... WY-8
Curtis Creek Canyon—*valley* ... NE-7
Curtis Creek Cem—*cemetery* ... MS-4
Curtis Creek Ch—*church* ... MS-4
Curtis Creek Ch—*church* ... NC-3
*Curtis Creek Forest Service Station* ... UT-8
Curtis Creek Guard Station—*locale* ... UT-8
**Curtis Crossing**—*pop pl* ... MA-1
Curtis Crossing Dam—*dam* ... MA-1
Curtis Crossroads—*locale* ... AL-4
Curtis Dam—*dam* ... PA-2
Curtis Ditch—*canal* ... IN-6
Curtis Ditch—*canal* ... OR-9
Curtis Drain—*canal* ... MI-6
Curtis Drain—*stream* ... MI-6
Curtis Draw—*valley* ... SD-7
Curtis Draw—*valley* ... WY-8
Curtis Field Airp—*airport* ... MO-7
Curtis Forest Camp—*locale* ... WA-9
*Curtis Glacier* ... WA-9
Curtis Grove Cem—*cemetery* ... AR-4
Curtis Gulch—*valley* ... AK-9
Curtis Gulch—*valley* ... MT-8
Curtis Gulch—*valley* ... WY-8
Curtis Gulch Campground—*locale* ... WY-8
Curtis Hall—*hist pl* ... AZ-5
Curtis Hall Cem—*cemetery* ... AR-4
Curtis Hill—*summit* ... ME-1
Curtis Hill—*summit* (3) ... MA-1
Curtis Hill—*summit* ... NH-1
Curtis Hill—*summit* ... VT-1
Curtis Hill Cem—*cemetery* ... ME-1
Curtis Hill Cem—*cemetery* ... TN-4
Curtis Hill Ch—*church* ... TN-4
**Curtis Hills**—*pop pl* ... PA-2
Curtis Hills—*summit* ... AK-9
**Curtis (historical)**—*pop pl* ... IA-7
Curtis Hole—*cave* ... AL-4
*Curtis Hollow* ... TN-4
Curtis Hollow—*valley* (2) ... AR-4
Curtis Hollow—*valley* (2) ... TN-4
Curtis Hollow—*valley* ... UT-8
Curtis Hollow—*valley* ... VT-1
Curtis House—*hist pl* ... AL-4
Curtis HS—*school* ... NY-2
Curtis Island—*island* ... ME-1
Curtis Island Light—*hist pl* ... ME-1
Curtis JHS—*school* ... CA-9
Curtis JHS—*school* (2) ... KS-7
Curtis JHS—*school* ... MA-1
Curtis JHS—*school* ... WA-9
Curtis-Kittleson House—*hist pl* ... WI-6
Curtis Knob—*summit* ... NC-3
*Curtis Lake* ... MN-6
*Curtis Lake* ... PA-2
Curtis Lake—*lake* ... AK-9
Curtis Lake—*lake* ... CA-9
Curtis Lake—*lake* ... ID-8
Curtis Lake—*lake* ... IL-6
Curtis Lake—*lake* (5) ... MI-6
Curtis Lake—*lake* (4) ... MN-6
Curtis Lake—*lake* ... NY-2
Curtis Lake—*lake* ... OR-9
Curtis Lake—*lake* ... PA-2
Curtis Lake—*lake* (2) ... WA-9
Curtis Lake—*lake* (2) ... WI-6
Curtis Lake—*reservoir* ... CO-8
Curtis Lake—*reservoir* ... MS-4
Curtis Lateral—*canal* ... CO-8
Curtis (Magisterial District)—*fmr MCD* ... WV-2
Curtis Mansion—*hist pl* ... DE-2
Curtis Meadows—*flat* ... CA-9
Curtis Memorial Library—*hist pl* ... CT-1
Curtis Mill—*locale* ... FL-3
Curtis Mill Creek—*stream* ... AL-4
Curtis Millpond—*reservoir* ... SC-3
Curtis Mtn—*summit* ... AR-4
Curtis Mtn—*summit* ... CA-9
Curtis Mtn—*summit* ... KY-4
Curtis Mtn—*summit* ... NY-2
Curtis Mtn—*summit* ... TN-4
Curtis Paper Mill Workers' Houses—*hist pl* ... DE-2
Curtis Park—*park* ... CA-9
Curtis Park—*park* ... CO-8
Curtis Park—*park* ... TX-5
Curtis Park—*uninc pl* (2) ... PA-2
*Curtis Park Manor* ... NV-8
Curtis Park Station—*locale* ... PA-2
Curtis Point—*cape* ... ME-1
Curtis Point—*cape* ... MD-2
Curtis Point—*cape* ... MA-1
Curtis Point—*cape* ... NJ-2
Curtis Point—*cape* (2) ... VA-3
*Curtis Pond* ... MA-1
Curtis Pond—*lake* ... ME-1
Curtis Pond—*lake* (2) ... MA-1
Curtis Pond—*lake* ... NY-2
Curtis Pond—*lake* ... VT-1
Curtis Pond—*reservoir* ... CT-1
Curtis Pond—*reservoir* ... PA-2
Curtis Pond Brook—*stream* ... CT-1
Curtis Ponds—*reservoir* ... MA-1
Curtis Ponds Dam—*dam* ... MA-1
Curtis Ranch—*locale* (2) ... CO-8
Curtis Ranch—*locale* ... NE-7
Curtis Ravine—*valley* ... CA-9
Curtis Ridge—*ridge* ... OH-6
Curtis Ridge—*ridge* ... UT-8
Curtis Ridge—*ridge* ... WA-9
Curtis Ridge Cem—*cemetery* ... OH-6
Curtis RR Station—*building* ... AZ-5
Curtis Rsvr—*reservoir* ... ID-8
Curtis Rsvr—*reservoir* ... PA-2
Curtis Run—*stream* ... PA-2
Curtis Run—*stream* (2) ... WV-2
*Curtiss* ... MS-4
Curtiss—*locale* ... AZ-5
**Curtiss**—*pop pl* ... WI-6
Curtiss, Louis, Studio Bldg—*hist pl* ... MO-7
Curtiss, Lua, House I—*hist pl* ... FL-3
Curtiss, Lua, House II—*hist pl* ... FL-3
Curtiss, Marcus, Inn—*hist pl* ... OH-6
Curtiss Brook—*stream* ... CT-1
Curtiss Cem—*cemetery* ... MO-7
Curtiss Cem—*cemetery* ... NY-2
Curtiss Cem—*cemetery* ... TX-5
Curtiss Cem—*cemetery* ... WI-6
Curtis Sch—*school* ... CA-9
Curtis Sch—*school* ... CO-8
Curtis Sch—*school* (2) ... FL-3
Curtis Sch—*school* ... IA-7
Curtis Sch—*school* (2) ... LA-4
Curtis Sch—*school* ... MA-1
Curtis Sch—*school* (2) ... MO-7
Curtis Sch—*school* ... NJ-2
Curtis Sch—*school* (2) ... SD-7
Curtis Sch—*school* ... TX-5
Curtis Sch—*school* ... UT-8
Curtis Sch—*school* ... VA-3
Curtis Sch (abandoned)—*school* ... PA-2
Curtis Sch (historical)—*school* ... MO-7
*Curtis School* ... TN-4
*Curtiss Creek* ... UT-8
Curtiss Ditch—*canal* (2) ... IN-6
Curtiss Dogwood State Park—*park* ... NH-1
**Curtiss Heights**—*pop pl* ... CA-9
*Curtiss Hill* ... MA-1
Curtiss Knob—*summit* ... NC-3
*Curtiss Lake* ... LA-4
*Curtiss Lake* ... MI-6
Curtiss Lake—*lake* ... NE-7
Curtis Slough—*stream* ... AK-9
Curtis Slough—*stream* ... OR-9
*Curtiss Mill Pond* ... MA-1
Curtis Smith Lake—*reservoir* ... TX-5
*Curtiss Mountain* ... NY-2
Curtiss Park—*park* ... MI-6
Curtiss Park—*park* ... NY-2
*Curtiss Pond* ... VT-1
Curtis Spring—*spring* ... AZ-5
Curtis Spring—*spring* ... NV-8
Curtis Spring—*spring* ... OR-9
Curtis Spring—*spring* ... TN-4
Curtis Spring—*spring* ... WY-8
Curtiss Sch—*school* ... CT-1
Curtiss Spring Branch—*stream* ... TX-5
*Curtiss Station* ... MS-4
**Curtis (sta.)**—*pop pl* ... WA-9
Curtiss Tank—*reservoir* ... TX-5
Curtis State Public Shooting Area—*park* ... SD-7
**Curtis Station**—*pop pl* ... MS-4
**Curtis Subdivision**—*pop pl* ... UT-8
Curtis Swamp—*swamp* ... NY-2
*Curtis Tank* ... TX-5
Curtis Tank—*reservoir* ... AZ-5
**Curtiston**—*pop pl* ... AL-4
Curtiston Elem Sch—*school* ... AL-4
Curtiston Methodist Ch—*church* ... AL-4
Curtistown—*locale* ... TN-4
**Curtis (Township of)**—*pop pl* ... MI-6
Curtis Union Cem—*cemetery* ... OH-6
Curtis Valley Sch—*school* ... PA-2
*Curtisville* ... MA-1
**Curtisville**—*pop pl* ... IN-6
**Curtisville**—*pop pl* ... MA-1
**Curtisville**—*pop pl* ... MI-6
**Curtisville**—*pop pl* ... PA-2
**Curtisville**—*pop pl* ... WV-2
Curtisville Cem—*cemetery* ... MI-6
Curtisville Civic Center—*locale* ... MI-6
Curtis Wash—*stream* ... AZ-5
Curtis Waterhole—*lake* ... CA-9
Curtis Way—*trail* ... ID-8
Curtis Well—*well* ... AZ-5
Curtis Well—*well* ... NM-5
Curtis Wharf—*hist pl* ... WA-9
Curtis Williams Lake—*reservoir* ... AL-4
Curtis Williams Lake Dam—*dam* ... AL-4
Curtis Williams Upper Dam—*dam* ... AL-4
Curtis Williams Upper Lake—*reservoir* ... AL-4
Curtis Windmill—*locale* ... AZ-5
Curtis Windmill—*locale* ... TX-5
**Curtiswood (subdivision)**—*pop pl* ... TN-4
Curtner—*locale* ... CA-9
Curtner Lateral—*canal* ... CA-9
Curtner Sch—*school* ... CA-9
Curton Well—*well* ... TX-5
Curt P O—*locale* ... KY-4
Curtright Cem—*cemetery* ... MO-7
Curt- Roy Oil Field—*oilfield* ... TX-5
Curts Ranch—*locale* ... OK-5
Curty Run—*valley* ... WY-8
Curtz Lake—*lake* ... CA-9
Curtz Mine—*mine* ... CA-9
Curup Spring—*spring* ... OR-9
Curutchet Spring—*spring* ... WY-8
Curve—*locale* ... VA-3
**Curve**—*pop pl* ... TN-4
Curve Baptist Ch—*church* ... TN-4
Curve Branch—*stream* ... VA-3
Curve Bridge Picnic Area—*park* ... MO-7
Curve Creek—*stream* ... AK-9
Curve Creek—*stream* ... ID-8
Curve Lake—*lake* ... FL-3
Curve Lake—*lake* (2) ... WI-6
Curve Mtn—*summit* ... AK-9
Curve Mtn—*summit* ... PA-2
Curven Creek—*stream* ... ID-8
Curve of the RR Bay—*swamp* ... NC-3
Curve Post Office (historical)—*building* ... TN-4
Curve Rsvr—*reservoir* ... AZ-5
Curve Sch (historical)—*school* ... TN-4
Curve Slough—*stream* ... AK-9
Curve Tank—*reservoir* ... NM-5
Curve Trestle Hollow—*valley* ... MO-7
Curve Wash—*stream* ... AZ-5
*Curview* ... FL-3
*Curvitas* ... TX-5
**Curvitas**—*pop pl* ... TX-5
Curvo—*locale* ... UT-8
Curvo, Arroyo—*stream* ... CA-9
*Curvy Creek* ... MS-4
**Curwensville**—*pop pl* ... PA-2
*Curwensville Boro* ... PA-2
Curwensville Borough—*civil* ... PA-2
Curwensville Dam—*dam* ... PA-2
Curwensville Lake—*reservoir* ... PA-2
Curwensville Rsvr—*reservoir* (2) ... PA-2
Curwood, Mount—*summit* ... MI-6
Curwood Castle—*hist pl* ... MI-6
**Curzon Mill**—*pop pl* ... MA-1
*Curzons Mill* ... MA-1
**Cusaac Crossroads**—*pop pl* ... SC-3
Cusaac Sch—*school* ... IL-6
Cusac Crossroads—*locale* ... SC-3
**Cusator Township**—*pop pl* ... ND-7
Cuscadian Park—*park* ... FL-3
*Cuscowilla* ... FL-3
Cusco Willa—*locale* ... VA-3
**Cuscowilla**—*pop pl* ... VA-3
**Cuscowilla (historical)**—*pop pl* ... FL-3
*Cuse Hill* ... NH-1
Cuselich Bay—*bay* ... LA-4
Cuselich Canal—*canal* ... LA-4
Cusenbary Draw—*valley* ... TX-5
Cush—*locale* ... PA-2
Cushaw Branch—*stream* ... KY-4
**Cush Creek**—*pop pl* ... PA-2
Cush Creek—*stream* ... PA-2
Cush Creek Junction—*locale* ... PA-2
Cush Creek Sch (abandoned)—*school* ... PA-2
Cush Cushion—*locale* ... PA-2
*Cush-Cushion Creek* ... PA-2
Cush Cushion Creek—*stream* ... PA-2
Cush Cushion Crossing—*locale* ... PA-2
Cushenbury—*locale* ... CA-9
Cushenbury Canyon—*valley* ... CA-9
Cushenbury Pit—*mine* ... CA-9
Cushenbury Springs—*spring* ... CA-9
Cusher Arm—*bay* ... IN-6
Cushetunk—*locale* ... NJ-2
Cushetunk Lake—*reservoir* ... NJ-2
Cushetunk Mtn—*summit* ... NJ-2
*Cushey Creek* ... MI-6
*Cushian Creek* ... PA-2
*Cushietunk* ... NJ-2
*Cushing* ... AL-4
*Cushing* ... MA-1
Cushing—*locale* ... CA-9
Cushing—*locale* ... MA-1
**Cushing**—*pop pl* ... IA-7
**Cushing**—*pop pl* ... ME-1
**Cushing**—*pop pl* ... MN-6
**Cushing**—*pop pl* ... NE-7
**Cushing**—*pop pl* ... OK-5
**Cushing**—*pop pl* ... TX-5
**Cushing**—*pop pl* ... UT-8
**Cushing**—*pop pl* ... WI-6
Cushing, Caleb, House—*hist pl* ... MA-1
Cushing, Caleb, House and Farm—*hist pl*. MA-1
Cushing Acad—*school* ... MA-1
**Cushing Briggs**—*pop pl* ... ME-1
Cushing Brook—*stream* ... MA-1
Cushing (CCD)—*cens area* ... OK-5
Cushing Cem—*cemetery* ... IA-7
Cushing Cem—*cemetery* ... MA-1
Cushing Corners Sch—*school* ... MI-6
Cushing Country Club—*other* ... OK-5
Cushing Creek—*stream* ... CA-9
Cushing Creek—*stream* ... FL-3
Cushing Ditch—*canal* ... MT-8
Cushing-Douglass (CCD)—*cens area* ... TX-5
Cushing Falls—*falls* ... OR-9
Cushing Glacier—*glacier* ... AK-9
Cushing Hall—*school* ... MA-1
Cushing Hill—*summit* ... VT-1
Cushing Hollow—*valley* ... PA-2
Cushing Homestead—*hist pl* ... MA-1
Cushing Hosp—*hospital* ... KS-7
Cushing Hotel—*hist pl* ... MN-6
*Cushing Island* (2) ... ME-1
Cushing Island—*island* (2) ... ME-1
Cushing Island—*locale* ... ME-1
Cushing Lake—*reservoir* ... OK-5
Cushing Lookout Tower—*locale* ... TX-5
Cushing Memorial Park—*park* ... GA-3
Cushing Memorial State Park—*park* ... MA-1
Cushing Memorial State Park—*park* ... WI-6
Cushing Point—*cape* (2) ... ME-1
Cushing Pond—*lake* (2) ... MA-1
Cushing Pond—*reservoir* ... MA-1
Cushing Pond Dam—*dam* ... MA-1
*Cushing Rsvr* ... OK-5
Cushing Run—*stream* ... OH-6
Cushing Sch—*school* ... MA-1
Cushing Sch—*school* ... WI-6
*Cushing's Island* ... ME-1
Cushings Peaks—*summit* ... MN-6
*Cushings Pond* ... MA-1
Cushing Swamp—*swamp* ... MA-1
**Cushing (Town of)**—*pop pl* ... ME-1
**Cushing (Township of)**—*pop pl* ... MN-6
*Cushion* ... PA-2
**Cushion**—*pop pl* ... AL-4
Cushion Branch—*stream* ... NC-3
*Cushion Creek* ... AL-4
Cushion Creek—*stream* ... FL-3
Cushion Peak—*summit* ... PA-2
Cushion Spring—*spring* ... AL-4
Cushion Swamp—*swamp* ... SC-3
*Cushman* ... ND-7
Cushman—*locale* ... IL-6
Cushman—*locale* ... MT-8
Cushman—*locale* ... OR-9
**Cushman**—*pop pl* ... AR-4
**Cushman**—*pop pl* ... MA-1
**Cushman**—*pop pl* ... NE-7
**Cushman**—*pop pl* ... NH-1
Cushman, Charles L., House—*hist pl* ... ME-1
Cushman, Lake—*reservoir* ... WA-9
Cushman, Mount—*summit* ... NH-1
Cushman, Mount—*summit* ... VT-1
Cushman Bayou—*stream* ... TX-5
Cushman Branch—*stream* ... PA-2
Cushman Brook—*stream* ... ME-1
Cushman Brook—*stream* (2) ... MA-1
Cushman Brook—*stream* ... NH-1
Cushman Camp—*locale* ... CA-9
Cushman Canyon—*valley* ... OR-9
Cushman Cem—*cemetery* ... VT-1
Cushman Cem—*cemetery* ... WI-6
Cushman Ch—*church* ... MA-1
Cushman Cove—*bay* ... ME-1
Cushman Creek—*stream* ... AK-9
Cushman Creek—*stream* ... CO-8
Cushman Creek—*stream* (2) ... MI-6
Cushman Creek—*stream* ... WY-8
Cushman Crest—*ridge* ... WA-9
**Cushman Dam**—*pop pl* ... WA-9
*Cushman Falls* ... WA-9
Cushman Gulch—*valley* ... CO-8
Cushman Hill—*summit* ... CA-9
Cushman Hill—*summit* (2) ... ME-1
Cushman Hill—*summit* ... VT-1
Cushman Hill—*summit* ... WA-9
Cushman House—*hist pl* ... MA-1
Cushman Junction—*locale* ... AR-4
Cushman Lake—*lake* ... CA-9
Cushman Lake—*lake* ... CO-8
Cushman Lake—*reservoir* ... NJ-2
Cushman Lake—*reservoir* ... TX-5
Cushman Lake Dam—*dam* ... NJ-2
Cushman Mill Sch—*school* ... WI-6
Cushman No. 1 Hydroelectric Power Plant—*hist pl* ... WA-9
Cushman No. 2 Hydroelectric Power Plant—*hist pl* ... WA-9
Cushman Park—*park* (2) ... MA-1
*Cushman Point* ... WA-9
Cushman Point—*cape* ... ME-1
Cushman Pond—*lake* (2) ... ME-1
Cushman Pond—*reservoir* ... WI-6
*Cushman Reservoir* ... WA-9
*Cushman Ridge* ... WA-9
Cushman Ridge—*ridge* ... ME-1
*Cushman's Brook* ... ME-1
Cushman Sch—*school* ... FL-3
Cushman Sch—*school* ... ME-1
Cushman Sch—*school* ... MA-1
*Cushmans Lake* ... NJ-2
Cushmans Landing—*locale* ... VA-3
Cushmans Pond—*lake* ... MA-1
Cushman Tavern—*hist pl* ... ME-1
Cushman (Township of)—*fmr MCD* ... AR-4
Cushman Trail—*trail* ... PA-2
Cushman Well—*well* ... NM-5
Cushner Pond—*swamp* ... GA-3
Cushtusha (historical)—*locale* ... MS-4
Cushtusia Canal—*canal* ... MS-4
Cushtusia Creek—*stream* ... MS-4
Cushwa Cem—*cemetery* ... MD-2
Cushway, Benjamin, House—*hist pl* ... MI-6
Cusick—*locale* ... TN-4
**Cusick**—*pop pl* ... TN-4
**Cusick**—*pop pl* ... WA-9
Cusick Creek—*stream* ... ID-8
Cusick Creek—*stream* (2) ... OR-9
Cusick Creek—*stream* ... WA-9
Cusick Lake—*lake* ... MI-6
Cusick Lake Grange Hall—*locale* ... MI-6
Cusick Mtn—*summit* ... OR-9
**Cusicks Crossing**—*pop pl* ... WV-2
Cusino—*locale* ... MI-6
Cusino Lake—*lake* ... MI-6
Cuskers House—*locale* ... MT-8
Cusky Pond—*reservoir* ... MA-1
Cuss Creek—*stream* ... AL-4
Cuss Creek—*stream* ... AK-9
Cussed Hollow—*valley* ... WA-9
Cusseta—*locale* ... TX-5
**Cusseta**—*pop pl* ... AL-4
**Cusseta**—*pop pl* ... GA-3
Cusseta (CCD)—*cens area* ... GA-3
Cusseta Cem—*cemetery* ... AL-4
Cussetah Creek—*stream* ... OK-5
Cusseta Mountains—*summit* ... TX-5
Cusseta Road Elem Sch—*school* ... GA-3
Cusseta Sch—*school* ... AL-4
Cussetaw (historical)—*locale* ... AL-4
Cussewago Creek—*stream* ... PA-2
Cussewago Creek Access Area—*other* ... PA-2
*Cussewago School* ... PA-2
**Cussewago (Township of)**—*pop pl* ... PA-2
Cussewago Township Sch—*school* ... PA-2
Cussgutter Brook—*stream* ... CT-1
Cussicks Spring—*spring* ... ND-7
Cusson—*locale* ... MN-6
Cusson Creek—*stream* ... MN-6
**Custar**—*pop pl* ... OH-6
Custard Apple Hammock—*island* ... FL-3
Custard Cem—*cemetery* ... OH-6
Custard Cem—*cemetery* ... TN-4
Custard Drain—*stream* ... IN-6
Custard Hollow—*valley* ... TN-4
Custard Hollow Cave—*cave* ... TN-4
Custard Massacre Site—*locale* ... WY-8
Custard Run—*stream* ... PA-2
**Custards**—*pop pl* ... PA-2
Custards Dam—*dam* ... PA-2
Custenborder Field—*park* ... OH-6
Custer—*fmr MCD* ... NE-7
Custer—*locale* ... ID-8
Custer—*locale* ... IL-6
**Custer**—*pop pl* ... KY-4
**Custer**—*pop pl* ... MI-6
**Custer**—*pop pl* ... MO-7
**Custer**—*pop pl* ... MT-8
**Custer**—*pop pl* ... ND-7
**Custer**—*pop pl* ... PA-2
**Custer**—*pop pl* ... SD-7
**Custer**—*pop pl* (2) ... WA-9
**Custer**—*pop pl* ... WI-6
Custer, Mount—*summit* ... MT-8
**Custer Addition**—*pop pl* ... WV-2
Custer Battlefield Natl Monmt—*hist pl* ... MT-8
Custer Battlefield Natl Monument—*park* ... MT-8
Custer Bayou—*bay* ... FL-3
Custer Bluff—*summit* ... KY-4
Custer Branch—*stream* ... MO-7
Custer Cabins—*locale* ... CO-8
Custer Canyon—*valley* ... NE-7
Custer Cem—*cemetery* ... IA-7
Custer Cem—*cemetery* ... KS-7
Custer Cem—*cemetery* ... PA-2
Custer Cem—*cemetery* ... VA-3
Custer Center Ch—*church* ... NE-7
Custer Center Sch—*school* ... NE-7
*Custer City* ... SD-7
Custer City—*locale* ... TX-5
**Custer City**—*pop pl* ... OK-5
**Custer City**—*pop pl* ... PA-2
Custer City (CCD)—*cens area* ... OK-5
**Custer City (corporate and RR name for Custer)**—*pop pl* ... OK-5
Custer City Elem Sch—*school* ... PA-2
Custer City HS—*school* ... OK-5
*Custer (corporate and RR name Custer City)* . OK-5
Custer Coulee—*stream* ... MT-8
Custer Coulee—*valley* ... MT-8
Custer County—*civil* ... SD-7
**Custer (County)**—*pop pl* ... OK-5
Custer County Airfield—*airport* ... SD-7
Custer County Courthouse—*hist pl* ... SD-7
Custer County Courthouse and Jail—*hist pl* ... NE-7
Custer County Drain—*canal* ... MI-6
Custer County Jail—*hist pl* ... ID-8
*Custer Creek* ... MT-8
Custer Creek—*stream* ... CO-8
Custer Creek—*stream* ... ID-8
Custer Creek—*stream* ... MI-6
Custer Creek—*stream* (2) ... MT-8
Custer Creek—*stream* ... TX-5
Custer Creek—*stream* ... WA-9
Custer Dam—*dam* ... CO-8
Custer Ditch—*canal* ... CO-8
Custer Draw—*valley* ... CO-8
Custer Flats—*flat* ... ND-7
Custer Group Mine—*mine* ... SD-7
Custer Gulch—*valley* ... NV-8
Custer Gulch—*valley* ... SD-7
Custer-Herron Cem—*cemetery* ... AR-4
Custer Hill—*summit* ... KS-7
Custer Hill—*summit* ... SD-7
Custer Hist Dist—*hist pl* ... ID-8
Custer (historical)—*locale* ... KS-7
**Custer (historical)**—*pop pl* ... TN-4
Custer Hollow—*valley* ... MD-2
Custer Hollow—*valley* ... WV-2
Custer HS—*school* ... WI-6
Custer Island—*island* ... ID-8
Custer Island Park—*park* ... KS-7
Custer JHS—*school* ... MI-6
Custer Lake—*lake* ... MI-6
Custer Lake—*lake* ... MO-7
Custer Lookout—*locale* ... ID-8
Custer Lookout—*summit* ... ND-7
Custer Lookout Tower—*locale* ... MI-6
Custer Lookout Tower—*locale* ... SD-7
Custer Mica Lodes Numbers 1 and 2 Mine—*mine* ... SD-7
Custer Mine—*mine* ... ID-8
Custer Mine—*mine* ... SD-7
Custer Mine State Game Mngmt Area—*park* ... ND-7
Custer Mountain Lode Mine—*mine* ... SD-7
Custer Mtn—*summit* ... CO-8
Custer Mtn—*summit* ... NM-5
Custer Mtn—*summit* ... SD-7
Custer Natl Cem—*cemetery* ... MT-8
Custer No 1 Campground—*locale* ... ID-8
Custer Park—*park* ... IL-6
Custer Park—*park* ... ND-7
Custer Park—*park* ... OR-9
Custer Peak—*summit* ... ID-8
Custer Peak—*summit* ... SD-7
Custer Post Office (historical)—*building* ... TN-4
Custer Reservoir—*reserve* ... CO-8
Custer Ridge—*ridge* ... WA-9
**Custer Road Terrace**—*pop pl* ... GA-3
Custer Run—*stream* ... PA-2
*Custers* ... PA-2
Custer Sch—*hist pl* ... WA-9
Custer Sch—*school* ... IL-6
Custer Sch—*school* (2) ... MI-6
Custer Sch—*school* ... NE-7
Custer Sch—*school* ... ND-7
Custer Sch—*school* ... PA-2
Custer Sch—*school* ... SD-7
Custer Slaughter House—*hist pl* ... ID-8
Custers Lookout—*summit* ... MT-8
Custers Point—*cape* ... OH-6
Custer State Game Lodge—*hist pl* ... SD-7
Custer State Park—*park* ... SD-7
Custer State Park Airstrip—*airport* ... SD-7
Custer State Park HQ—*locale* ... SD-7
Custer State Park Museum—*hist pl* ... SD-7
Custers Wash—*stream* ... ND-7
Custer Terrace—*uninc pl* ... GA-3
Custer Terrace Sch—*school* ... GA-3
**Custer Township**—*pop pl* (2) ... KS-7
**Custer Township**—*pop pl* (2) ... NE-7
**Custer Township**—*pop pl* (2) ... SD-7
**Custer (Township of)**—*pop pl* ... IL-6
**Custer (Township of)**—*pop pl* (3) ... MI-6
**Custer (Township of)**—*pop pl* ... MN-6
Custer Trail Ranch—*locale* ... ND-7
*Custig Creek* ... AL-4
Custis Channel—*channel* ... VA-3
Custis Cove—*bay* ... VA-3
Custis Creek—*stream* ... VA-3
Custis Lee Mansion—*building* ... VA-3
Custis Neck—*cape* ... VA-3
Custis Point—*cape* ... VA-3
Custis Pond—*lake* ... VA-3
Custis Pond—*reservoir* ... VA-3
Custis Sch—*school* ... VA-3
Custis Tombs—*hist pl* ... VA-3
**Custis Woods**—*pop pl* ... PA-2
Custom Commerce Center (Shop Ctr)—*locale* ... FL-3
Custom House—*building* ... MA-1
Custom House—*uninc pl* ... LA-4
Customhouse—*uninc pl* ... VA-3
Customhouse and Post Office—*hist pl* ... DC-2
Customhouse Bay—*bay* ... LA-4
Customhouse Cove—*bay* ... AK-9
Customhouse District—*hist pl* ... MA-1
Customhouse Hist Dist—*hist pl* ... RI-1
Custom Mill—*locale* ... WY-8
Customs Bldg—*building* ... TX-5
Custom Service Bldg—*building* ... DC-2
Customs House—*building* ... DC-2
Customs House—*hist pl* ... NY-2
*Custusha Creek* ... MS-4
Cut—*locale* ... TX-5
*Cut, The* ... CA-9
Cut, The—*bend* ... KY-4
Cut, The—*channel* ... AL-4
Cut, The—*gap* ... VA-3
Cut, The—*gap* ... WY-8
Cut, The—*stream* ... MI-6
Cut, The (historical)—*isthmus* ... MA-1
Cutalong—*locale* ... VA-3
**Cut and Shoot**—*pop pl* ... TX-5
Cut Around Bayou—*gut* ... LA-4
Cut Around Canal—*canal* ... TX-5
Cutaway Creek—*stream* ... AK-9
Cutaway Lake—*lake* (2) ... MN-6
Cutaway Mtn—*summit* ... MT-8
Cutaway Pass—*gap* ... MT-8
Cut A West Range Light—*locale* ... TX-5
Cutawhiskie Creek—*stream* ... NC-3
Cut B—*canal* ... CA-9
*Cutbank* ... MT-8
Cut Bank—*cliff* ... MT-8
**Cut Bank**—*pop pl* ... MT-8
Cutbank Bridge—*bridge* ... VA-3
Cut Bank Campground—*locale* ... MT-8
Cutbank Ch—*church* ... VA-3
Cut Bank Coulee—*valley* (2) ... MT-8
*Cut Bank Creek* ... MT-8
*Cutbank Creek* ... ND-7
Cut Bank Creek—*stream* ... AL-4
Cut Bank Creek—*stream* ... MT-8
Cutbank Creek—*stream* ... MT-8
Cut Bank Creek—*stream* (3) ... ND-7
Cut Bank Greasewood Canal—*canal* ... MT-8
Cut Bank John Coulee—*valley* ... MT-8
*Cut Bank Pass* ... MT-8
Cut Bank Pass—*gap* ... MT-8
Cut Bank Pass Trail—*trail* ... MT-8
Cut Bank Ranger Station—*locale* ... MT-8
Cut Bank Refinery—*other* ... MT-8
Cutbank Ridge—*ridge* ... MT-8
Cut Bank Ridge—*ridge* ... MT-8
*Cut Bank River* ... MT-8
Cutbank Spring—*spring* ... MT-8
**Cut Bank Township**—*pop pl* ... ND-7
Cut B East Lead Light—*locale* ... TX-5
Cut B East Range Light—*locale* ... TX-5
Cutbert—*locale* ... TX-5
*Cutbert Bayou* ... FL-3
*Cutberth Bayou* ... FL-3
*Cutberths Bayou* ... FL-3
Cut Bluff Slough—*gut* ... AR-4
Cut Brook—*stream* ... ME-1
Cutcane—*locale* ... GA-3
Cutcane Creek—*stream* ... GA-3
Cutcane Ridge—*ridge* ... GA-3
Cutcane Sch—*school* ... GA-3
Cut Canyon—*valley* ... NE-7
Cutca Trail—*trail* ... CA-9
Cutca Valley—*valley* ... CA-9
Cutca Valley Truck Trail—*trail* ... CA-9
Cutcheon—*locale* ... MI-6
**Cutchogue**—*pop pl* ... NY-2
Cutchogue Harbor—*bay* ... NY-2
Cutchogue-New Suffolk—*CDP* ... NY-2
Cutchogue Sch—*school* ... NY-2
**Cutchogue Station**—*pop pl* ... NY-2
Cutcomb Lake Sch—*school* ... NE-7
Cutcomb Valley—*basin* ... NE-7
Cut Coulee—*valley* (2) ... MT-8
Cut Coulee—*valley* ... WY-8
Cut Creek—*stream* ... FL-3
Cut Creek—*stream* ... OR-9
Cut Creek—*stream* ... SD-7
Cut Creek—*stream* ... WY-8
Cut Cypress Creek—*gut* ... NC-3
**Cute (historical)**—*pop pl* ... TN-4
Cute Post Office (historical)—*building* ... TN-4
Cuter Place Tank—*reservoir* ... AZ-5
Cuter Tank—*reservoir* ... AZ-5
Cut Eye Fosters Bar—*bar* ... CA-9
Cut Face Creek—*stream* ... MN-6
Cutfinger Creek—*stream* ... CA-9
Cut Foot Sioux Lake—*lake* ... MN-6
Cutfoot Sioux Trail—*trail* ... MN-6
Cutfoot Wash—*stream* ... AZ-5
Cutgrass Coulee—*stream* ... LA-4
Cuthand—*locale* ... TX-5
Cuthand Creek—*stream* ... TX-5
Cuthbert—*locale* ... SD-7
**Cuthbert**—*pop pl* ... GA-3
**Cuthbert**—*pop pl* ... TX-5
Cuthbert, John A., House—*hist pl* ... SC-3
*Cuthbert Bight* ... FL-3
Cuthbert (CCD)—*cens area* ... GA-3
Cuthbert First Methodist Ch—*church* ... SD-7
Cuthbert Hist Dist—*hist pl* ... GA-3
Cuthbert Lake—*lake* ... FL-3
**Cuthbert Manor**—*pop pl* ... NJ-2
Cuthbertson Cem—*cemetery* ... NC-3
Cuthbertson Mtn—*summit* ... MO-7
Cuthbert Switch—*locale* ... TN-4
Cuthbert Switch Sch—*school* ... TN-4
*Cuthead Creek* ... SD-7
**Cuthi Uckehaca (historical)**—*pop pl* ... MS-4
Cuthrie Run—*stream* ... NY-2
Cut In Two Island—*island* ... CT-1
Cutknife Mtn—*summit* ... NY-2
*Cut Lake* ... MN-6
Cut Lake—*lake* ... ME-1
Cut Lake—*lake* ... MN-6
Cut Lake Stream—*stream* ... ME-1
Cut Laurel Branch—*stream* ... TN-4
Cut Laurel Creek—*stream* ... NC-3
Cut Laurel Gap—*gap* ... NC-3
Cut Laurel Gap—*gap* ... TN-4
Cut Laurel Knob—*summit* ... NC-3
Cut Laurel Knob—*summit* ... TN-4
*Cutler* ... UT-8
Cutler—*locale* ... WI-6
**Cutler**—*pop pl* ... CA-9
**Cutler**—*pop pl* ... FL-3
**Cutler**—*pop pl* ... IL-6
**Cutler**—*pop pl* ... IN-6
**Cutler**—*pop pl* ... ME-1
**Cutler**—*pop pl* ... OH-6
**Cutler**—*pop pl* ... UT-8
Cutler, Bayou—*gut* ... LA-4
Cutler, Morris, House—*hist pl* ... WI-6
Cutler, Mount—*summit* ... CO-8
Cutler, Mount—*summit* ... ME-1
Cutler, Thomas R., Mansion—*hist pl* ... UT-8
Cutler Acad—*school* ... CA-9
Cutler and Porter Block—*hist pl* ... MA-1
Cutler and Walker Drain—*canal* ... MI-6
Cutler Brook—*stream* ... RI-1
Cutler Canyon—*valley* ... UT-8

Cutler Cem—cemetery IN-6
Cutler Cem—cemetery OH-6
Cutler Cem—cemetery (2) VT-1
Cutler Ch—church MA-1
Cutler Chapel—church OH-6
Cutler City OR-9
**Cutler City**—pop pl OR-9
Cutler Cove—bay ME-1
Cutler Cove Sch—school FL-3
Cutler Creek WY-8
Cutler Creek—stream (2) CO-8
Cutler Creek—stream ID-8
Cutler Creek—stream NY-2
Cutler Creek—stream UT-8
Cutler Creek—stream WY-8
Cutler Dam—dam SD-7
Cutler Dam—dam UT-8
Cutler Ditch—canal WI-6
Cutler-Donahue Covered Bridge—hist pl IA-7
Cutler Drain—canal (2) MI-6
Cutler Drain Canal FL-3
Cutler Drain Canal C-100—canal FL-3
Cutler Drain Canal C-100A—canal FL-3
Cutler Drain Canal C-100B—canal FL-3
Cutler Drain Canal Number C-100—canal (2) FL-3
Cutler Drain Canal Number C-100 A—canal FL-3
Cutler Drain Canal Number C-100 C—canal FL-3
Cutler Draw—valley CO-8
Cutler Draw—valley WY-8
Cutler (Election Precinct)—fmr MCD IL-6
Cutler Gulch—valley CO-8
Cutler Gulch—valley WY-8
Cutler Hall—hist pl CO-8
Cutler-Hammer, Incorporated (Warehouse)—facility GA-3
Cutler Harbor ME-1
Cutler Harbor—bay ME-1
Cutler Hill—summit WY-8
Cutler Homestead—hist pl NJ-2
Cutler Lake—lake MT-8
Cutler Memorial Library—hist pl ME-1
Cutler Mill Brook—stream VT-1
Cutler Mine—mine CO-8
Cutler Mound Group—hist pl WI-6
Cutler Naval Communications Unit—military ME-1
Cutler Park—park CA-9
Cutler Park—park MA-1
Cutler Park—park NM-5
Cutler Park—park WI-6
Cutler Pockets—basin (2) AZ-5
Cutler Point—cape UT-8
Cutler Pond—lake MA-1
Cutler Pond—lake VT-1
**Cutler Ridge**—pop pl FL-3
Cutler Ridge Christian Acad—school FL-3
Cutler Ridge Elem Sch—school FL-3
Cutler Ridge JHS—school FL-3
Cutler Ridge Mall—locale FL-3
Cutler Ridge Methodist Ch—church FL-3
Cutler Ridge Park—park FL-3
Cutler Ridge Shop Ctr—locale FL-3
Cutler River—stream AK-9
Cutler River—stream NH-1
Cutler Rsvr—reservoir CO-8
Cutler Rsvr—reservoir NV-8
Cutler Rsvr—reservoir UT-8
Cutlers—locale FL-3
Cutler Savage Ch—church MI-6
Cutler Sch—school (2) MA-1
Cutler Sch—school OH-6
Cutler Sch (abandoned)—school PA-2
Cutlers Farm Cem—cemetery CT-1
Cutlers Pond MA-1
Cutler Spring—spring (2) CO-8
Cutler Spring—spring UT-8
**Cutler Summit**—pop pl PA-2
Cutler Thicker—area CA-9
**Cutler (Town of)**—pop pl ME-1
**Cutler (Town of)**—pop pl WI-6
**Cutler Township**—pop pl KS-7
**Cutlerville**—pop pl MI-6
Cutlip Branch—stream WV-2
Cutlip Cem—cemetery (2) WV-2
Cutlip Ch—church WV-2
Cutlipp Hollow—valley OH-6
Cutlips—locale WV-2
Cutlips Fork WV-2
Cutlips Fork—stream WV-2
Cut Locust Gap—gap GA-3
Cut Locust Ridge—ridge GA-3
Cut Lookout Tower—locale MO-7
Cutmaptico Creek—stream MD-2
Cut Meat Creek—stream SD-7
Cut Meat Issue Station (historical)—locale SD-7
Cutmer—locale IL-6
Cutno Bay—swamp SC-3
Cutnoe Creek AL-4
Cut Nose Creek AL-4
Cutnose Creek—stream AL-4
Cut 'N Shoot TX-5
Cutocache Creek AL-4
Cutocoche Creek AL-4
Cutoe Bank—bar FL-3
Cutoe Key—island FL-3
Cutoff FL-3
Cut-Off IN-6
Cut-Off LA-4
Cutoff—gut AR-4
Cut-Off—locale TN-4
**Cutoff**—pop pl GA-3
**Cutoff**—pop pl LA-4
**Cut Off**—pop pl LA-4
Cut Off—uninc pl LA-4
Cut Off, Bayou—stream LA-4
Cut-Off, The AL-4
Cutoff, The CA-9
Cutoff, The—area KY-4
Cutoff, The—bend AL-4
Cutoff, The—bend LA-4
Cutoff, The—bend OR-9
Cutoff, The—channel AL-4
Cutoff, The—channel (4) FL-3
Cutoff, The—channel TX-5
Cutoff, The—gap KY-4
Cutoff, The—gut AL-4
Cutoff, The—gut (2) TX-5
Cutoff, The—stream OK-5
Cutoff, The—stream SC-3
Cut Off, The—stream TX-5
Cutoff, The—stream TX-5
Cutoff Bayou AR-4
Cut Off Bayou TX-5
Cutoff Bayou—gut (3) LA-4
Cut-off Bayou—gut LA-4
Cutoff Bayou—gut LA-4
Cutoff Bayou—gut MS-4
Cut-off Bayou—stream AR-4
Cutoff Bayou—stream (6) LA-4
Cutoff Bayou—stream MS-4
Cutoff Branch—stream AL-4
Cutoff Branch—stream GA-3
Cutoff Branch—stream (2) KY-4
Cutoff Canal—canal (3) LA-4
Cutoff Canyon—valley AZ-5
Cutoff Canyon—valley UT-8
Cutoff Canyon Spring—spring UT-8
Cutoff Ch—church AR-4
Cut Off Creek VA-3
Cut Off Creek—bay FL-3
Cutoff Creek—gut SC-3
Cutoff Creek—stream AK-9
Cut-Off Creek—stream AR-4
Cutoff Creek—stream AR-4
Cutoff Creek—stream ID-8
Cutoff Creek—stream (2) MT-8
Cutoff Creek—stream TX-5
Cutoff Creek—stream VA-3
Cutoff Ditch—canal OH-6
Cut-off Gap—gap GA-3
Cutoff Gap—gap TX-5
Cutoff Gulch—valley CO-8
Cutoff Gulch—valley MT-8
Cutoff Gulch Campground—locale MT-8
Cutoff Island—island FL-3
Cutoff Island—island (2) LA-4
Cutoff Island—swamp FL-3
Cut-off Junction LA-4
Cut-off Junction—locale LA-4
**Cut Off Junction**—pop pl LA-4
Cutoff Knob—summit KY-4
Cut Off Lagoon LA-4
Cutoff Lagoon—lake LA-4
Cut-Off Lake AR-4
Cutoff Lake NE-7
Cut-off Lake—lake (2) AR-4
Cutoff Lake—lake ID-8
Cutoff Lake—lake (2) LA-4
Cut-off Lake—lake MN-6
Cutoff Lake—lake (2) MS-4
Cut-Off Lake—lake MO-7
Cutoff Lake—lake OK-5
Cutoff Lake—lake TN-4
Cutoff Lake—lake TX-5
Cut Off Landing—locale LA-4
Cutoff Mtn—summit KY-4
Cutoff Mtn—summit MT-8
Cutoff Mtn—summit (3) TX-5
Cutoff No 7a—bend GA-3
Cutoff No. 7-A—bend SC-3
Cutoff Number Nine—bend SC-3
Cut-Off Number One—bend LA-4
Cutoff Number Ten—bend SC-3
Cut-Off Number Two—bend LA-4
Cut Off Oil and Gas Field—oilfield LA-4
Cut Off Park—park TX-5
Cutoff Peak MT-8
Cutoff Peak—summit ID-8
Cutoff Point—cape LA-4
Cutoff Pond—lake IL-6
Cutoff Pond (historical)—lake TX-5
Cutoff Post Office Site—locale NC-3
Cutoff Reach—channel SC-3
Cutoff Ridge—ridge NM-5
Cut-Off Ridge—ridge NC-3
Cutoff Ridge—ridge TX-5
Cutoff Ridge—ridge UT-8
Cutoff Rock Tank—reservoir TX-5
Cut Off Rsvr—reservoir ID-8
Cutoff Run—stream WV-2
Cut Off Sch—school LA-4
Cut-off Slough WA-9
Cutoff Slough—gut (2) CA-9
Cutoff Slough—gut IL-6
Cutoff Slough—gut MO-7
Cutoff Slough—gut (3) TX-5
Cutoff Slough—stream AK-9
Cut-Off Slough—stream AR-4
Cutoff Slough—stream AR-4
Cutoff Spring—spring TX-5
Cut Off (Township of)—fmr MCD AR-4
Cutoff Trail—trail (2) MT-8
Cut Off Trail—trail (2) PA-2
Cut- off Well—well TX-5
Cut Out Rsvr OR-9
Cutout Rsvr—reservoir OR-9
Cutover Island—island MN-6
Cut Pond—lake ME-1
Cut Pond Brook—stream ME-1
Cutreef Creek—stream MT-8
Cutrer Branch—stream LA-4
Cutrer Cem—cemetery LA-4
Cutrer Cem—cemetery MS-4
Cut Ridge—ridge TN-4
Cutright Ch—church WV-2
Cutright Run—stream WV-2
Cut River—channel MA-1
Cut River—stream MI-6
Cut Rock—gap OH-6
Cutrock Creek—stream MT-8
Cut Rsvr—reservoir WY-8
Cuts Canyon—valley UT-8
Cutsforth Corner—locale OR-9
Cutsforth Dam—dam OR-9
Cutsforth Park—park OR-9
Cutsforth Pond—lake OR-9
Cutsforth Rsvr—reservoir OR-9
Cutshall Branch—stream NC-3
Cutshall Cem—cemetery TN-4
Cutshall Ditch—canal OH-6
Cutshalltown—locale NC-3
Cutshaw Gap—gap TN-4
Cutshaw Spring—spring CO-8
Cutshin—locale KY-4
Cutshin (CCD)—cens area KY-4
Cutshin Creek—stream KY-4
Cutshin Hollow—valley KY-4
Cutship Ch—church KY-4
Cutsinger Cem—cemetery TN-4
Cutsinger Ditch—canal IN-6
Cut Spring—spring CA-9
Cuttacoochee Creek AL-4
Cuttalosa Creek—stream PA-2
Cuttchechoe River NH-1
**Cutten**—pop pl CA-9
Cutter—locale AZ-5
Cutter—locale NM-5
Cutter—locale WI-6
Cutter, B. O., House—hist pl MN-6
Cutter, Ephraim, House—hist pl MA-1
Cutter, Jefferson, House—hist pl MA-1
Cutter, Judson C., House—hist pl WI-6
Cutter, Second, A. P., House—hist pl MA-1
Cutter Bank—bar FL-3
**Cutter Bank**—pop pl FL-3
Cutterbank Spring—spring CA-9
Cutter Butte—summit CA-9
Cutter Canyon—valley NM-5
Cutter Cem—cemetery NM-5
Cutter Cem—cemetery NY-2
Cutter Creek ID-8
Cutter Creek—stream VA-3
**Cutter Hill**—pop pl NH-1
Cutter HS—school OH-6
Cutter Laboratories—facility NC-3
Cutter Meadow—flat CA-9
Cutter Mill Park—park NY-2
Cutter Mill Sch—school NY-2
Cutter Place Campground—locale CA-9
Cutter Point—cape AK-9
Cutter Pond—lake VT-1
Cutter Ranch—locale AZ-5
Cutter Rocks—area AK-9
Cutter Sch—school MA-1
**Cutters Creek (subdivision)**—pop pl NC-3
Cutters Nubble—island ME-1
Cutters Pond—lake MA-1
Cutters Pond—lake MI-6
Cutter Square—locale MA-1
Cutter Tank—reservoir (2) AZ-5
Cutter Tank—reservoir NM-5
Cuttes Creek NC-3
Cutthoat Lake—lake WY-8
Cutthroat Castle Group Ruins—locale CO-8
Cut Throat Coulee—valley MT-8
Cutthroat Creek—stream WA-9
Cutthroat Draw—valley WY-8
Cutthroat Gap NC-3
Cut-Throat Gulch—valley CA-9
Cutthroat Gulch—valley CA-9
Cutthroat Lake WY-8
Cutthroat Lake—lake (2) ID-8
Cutthroat Lake—lake UT-8
Cutthroat Lake—lake WA-9
Cut Throat Lake—reservoir OK-5
Cutthroat Lakes—lake WY-8
Cutthroat Pass—gap WA-9
Cutthroat Peak—pillar WA-9
Cutthroat Shoal—bar MA-1
Cutthroat Trout Bay—bay CO-8
Cut Through—channel NJ-2
Cut Through—channel (2) NC-3
**Cutting**—pop pl GA-3
**Cutting**—pop pl NY-2
Cutting, Bayard, Estate—hist pl NY-2
Cutting and Damon Lakes—lake MI-6
Cutting Bone Creek—stream GA-3
Cutting Brook—stream NY-2
Cutting Brook—stream VT-1
Cutting Cem—cemetery (2) VT-1
Cutting Creek—stream ME-1
Cutting Drain—canal MI-6
Cutting Flat Windmill—locale TX-5
Cutting Hill—summit VT-1
Cutting Hollow—valley MO-7
Cutting Pen Draw—valley TX-5
Cuttings Camp—locale NY-2
Cutting Sedge Creek—stream NC-3
Cutting Shed Coulee—valley MT-8
Cuttings Mtn—summit NH-1
**Cuttingsville**—pop pl VT-1
**Cuttings Wharf**—pop pl CA-9
Cuttington Creek—stream IL-6
Cuttle Creek—stream MI-6
Cuttle Drain—canal MI-6
Cuttler Rock WA-9
Cuttock Butte—summit OR-9
Cutt Off, The—channel AL-4
Cutton Lake MN-6
Cutts KS-7
Cutts Cem—cemetery VT-1
Cutts Creek—stream OH-6
Cutts Drain—canal MI-6
Cutt's Grant NH-1
Cutts Grant—civil NH-1
Cutts (historical)—locale KS-7
Cutts Island—island ME-1
Cutts Island—island WA-9
**Cutts Island**—pop pl ME-1
Cutts Meadow—flat CA-9
Cutts Peak—summit VT-1
Cutts Pond—lake ME-1
Cutts Ridge—ridge ME-1
Cutts Ridge Brook—stream ME-1
Cuttsville AL-4
**Cuttyhunk**—pop pl MA-1
Cuttyhunk Harbor—bay MA-1
Cuttyhunk Harbor North Jetty Light—locale MA-1
Cuttyhunk Island—island MA-1
Cuttyhunk Light—locale MA-1
Cuttyhunk Pond—harbor MA-1
Cuttys Ark Mine—mine SD-7
Cuttywaug Rocks RI-1
Cuttywow of Longfellows Poem Rocks RI-1
Cutuno—locale KY-4
**Cutuno (Gent)**—pop pl KY-4
Cut Wash—stream CA-9
Cuvacan Cove—bay AK-9
Cuvier Press Club—hist pl OH-6
Cuxabexis Cove—bay ME-1
Cuxabexis Lake—lake ME-1
Cuxabexis Stream—stream ME-1
**Cuyahoga (County)**—pop pl OH-6
**Cuyahoga Falls**—pop pl OH-6
Cuyahoga Falls (Township of)—other OH-6
**Cuyahoga Heights**—pop pl OH-6
Cuyahoga Heights Sch—school OH-6
Cuyahoga Lake Outlet OH-6
Cuyahoga Mine—mine MI-6
Cuyahoga Peak—summit MI-6
Cuyahoga River OH-6
Cuyahoga River—stream OH-6
Cuyahoga Valley Natl Rec Area—park OH-6
Cuyahoga Mine—mine SD-7
**Cuyama**—pop pl CA-9
Cuyamaca—civil CA-9
Cuyamaca, Lake—reservoir CA-9
Cuyamaca Dam—dam CA-9
Cuyamaca Lodge—locale CA-9
Cuyamaca Mountains—range CA-9
Cuyamaca Peak—summit CA-9
Cuyamaca Reservoir CA-9
Cuyamaca Sch—school CA-9
Cuyamaca State Park—park CA-9
Cuyamaca State Park HQ—locale CA-9
Cuyama (CCD)—cens area CA-9
Cuyama (heirs of Cesario Lataillade)—civil CA-9
Cuyama (Maria Antonio De La Guerra Y Lataii—civil CA-9
Cuyama Peak—summit CA-9
Cuyama Ranch—locale CA-9
Cuyama Ranger Station—locale CA-9
Cuyama River—stream CA-9
Cuyama Valley—valley CA-9
Cuyama Valley HS—school CA-9
**Cuyamungue**—pop pl NM-5
Cuyamungue Grant—civil NM-5
**Cuyapaipe Ind Res**—pop pl CA-9
Cuyapaipe Rsvr—reservoir CA-9
Cuyhoga Creek—stream MO-7
Cuyler—locale TX-5
**Cuyler**—pop pl NY-2
Cuyler Harbor—bay CA-9
Cuyler (historical)—locale KS-7
Cuyler Island NY-2
**Cuyler (Town of)**—pop pl NY-2
**Cuylerville**—pop pl NY-2
Cuyon—post sta PR-3
Cuyon (Barrio)—fmr MCD (2) PR-3
**Cuyuna**—pop pl MN-6
Cuyuna Lookout Tower—locale MN-6
Cuyuna Range—range MN-6
**Cuzco**—pop pl IN-6
Cuzick—locale KY-4
**Cuzick**—pop pl TN-4
Cuzick Ch—church KY-4
**Cuzzart**—pop pl WV-2
Cuzzie—locale WV-2
C Valliant Ranch—locale TX-5
C V Junction—locale PA-2
**Cv Spur Junction**—pop pl UT-8
C W A Well—well OR-9
C Wayne Collier Elem Sch—school NC-3
CW Bonham—locale TX-5
C W Bucher Elementary School PA-2
C W Bulow Grant—civil FL-3
C W Clarke Grant—civil FL-3
C. W. Cullen Bridge—bridge DE-2
C W Downer Pond Dam—dam MS-4
C W Gaston Dam—dam AL-4
C Wilson Ranch—locale ND-7
C W Ladow Center—school AL-4
C W McLemore Pond Dam—dam MS-4
C W Murphy Pond Dam—dam MS-4
C.W. Post College NY-2
C W Rice Middle School PA-2
C W Ruckel JHS—school FL-3
C W Shipley Sch—school WV-2
C W Stewart Dam—dam SD-7
C W Thomas Lake—lake FL-3
C W Trenholm Sch AL-4
C Wulff Stockwater Dam—dam SD-7
CX Ranch—locale ID-8
Cy—post sta WY-8
Cyanamid-Hannibal Heliport—airport MO-7
Cyanes Creek KS-7
Cyanide Creek—stream MT-8
Cyanide Gulch—valley ID-8
Cyanide Mtn—summit MT-8
Cyanide Rsvr—reservoir NV-8
Cyanide Shaft—mine NV-8
CYA Reception Center and Clinic—building CA-9
C Y A Reception Center and Clinic—other CA-9
Cy Beedes Ledge—bench NY-2
Cy Bend—bend KY-4
Cy Bingham Park OR-9
Cy Branch—stream KY-4
**Cybur**—pop pl MS-4
Cycad MH-9
Cycadia Cem—cemetery FL-3
Cyclamen Lake—lake CA-9
Cyclane Rsvr—reservoir OR-9
**Cycle**—pop pl NC-3
Cycleham Gap—gap NC-3
Cycle Lake—lake WI-6
Cyclone TN-4
Cyclone—locale KY-4
Cyclone—locale MO-7
Cyclone—locale TX-5
**Cyclone**—pop pl IN-6
**Cyclone**—pop pl MS-4
**Cyclone**—pop pl PA-2
**Cyclone**—pop pl WV-2
Cyclone Bar—bar WY-8
Cyclone Bar Creek—stream WY-8
Cyclone Basin—basin WY-8
Cyclone Bend—bend TX-5
Cyclone Branch—stream IN-6
Cyclone Branch—stream TX-5
Cyclone Canyon—basin UT-8
Cyclone Canyon—valley OR-9
Cyclone Canyon—valley WY-8
Cyclone Cem—cemetery MO-7
Cyclone Ch—church WV-2
Cyclone Co-op Rsvr—reservoir UT-8
Cyclone Creek—stream (2) CO-8
Cyclone Creek—stream (4) MT-8
Cyclone Creek—stream OK-5
Cyclone Creek—stream SD-7
Cyclone Creek—stream WA-9
Cyclone Dam—dam AZ-5
Cyclone Ditch—canal SD-7
Cyclone Draw—valley UT-8
Cyclone Draw—valley WY-8
Cyclone Flat—flat UT-8
Cyclone Gap—gap CA-9
Cyclone Gulch—valley MT-8
Cyclone Heights Sch—school IL-6
Cyclone Hill—summit AZ-5
Cyclone Hill—summit KY-4
Cyclone Hill—summit TX-5
**Cyclone (historical)**—pop pl TN-4
Cyclone Hollow—valley (2) MO-7
Cyclone Hollow—valley WV-2
Cyclone Knoll—summit UT-8
Cyclone Knoll Rsvr—reservoir UT-8
Cyclone Lake—lake MT-8
Cyclone Lake—lake UT-8
Cyclone Lake—lake WA-9
Cyclone Lake—lake WI-6
Cyclone Lake Campground—park AZ-5
Cyclone Meadow—flat CA-9
Cyclone Mine—mine MT-8
Cyclone Mtn—summit (3) CO-8
Cyclone Mtn—summit OK-5
Cyclone Park—flat (2) CO-8
Cyclone Park—flat MT-8
Cyclone Park—park MI-6
Cyclone Pass—gap UT-8
Cyclone Pass—gap WY-8
Cyclone Peak—summit MT-8
Cyclone Pens—locale TX-5
Cyclone Post Office (historical)—building PA-2
Cyclone Post Office (historical)—building TN-4
Cyclone Ridge—ridge WY-8
Cyclone Rim—cliff WY-8
Cyclone Saddle—gap NM-5
Cyclone Sch (abandoned)—school MO-7
Cyclone Sch (historical)—school MO-7
Cyclone Tank—reservoir AZ-5
Cyclopic—locale AZ-5
Cyclopic Pumping Station—building AZ-5
Cyclops AZ-5
Cyclops Cove—cove MO-7
Cyclops Ditch—canal WY-8
Cyclops Mine—mine MI-6
Cyclorama Bldg—hist pl MA-1
**Cyclorama Heights**—pop pl OH-6
Cyclorama of the Battle of Atlanta—hist pl GA-3
Cyco AL-4
Cy Creek—stream MT-8
Cy Creek—stream WA-9
Cycuan Peak CA-9
Cydonia, Mount—summit PA-2
Cy Draw—valley WY-8
Cyduan Ind Res CA-9
Cyer Cem—cemetery LA-4
Cy-Fair HS—school TX-5
Cy-Fair Park—park TX-5
**Cygnet**—pop pl OH-6
Cygnet Island—island AK-9
Cygnet Lake—lake (2) AK-9
Cygnet Lake—lake MT-8
Cygnet Lakes—lake WY-8
Cygnet Pond—lake WY-8
Cygnus—locale CA-9
Cygnus Cone—summit AK-9
Cy Hoskins Branch—stream KY-4
Cylburn House and Park District—hist pl MD-2
Cylburn Park—park MD-2
**Cylinder**—pop pl IA-7
Cylinder Creek—stream IA-7
Cyllacogga AL-4
**Cylon**—pop pl WI-6
Cylon Ch—church WI-6
Cylone Cem—cemetery AL-4
Cylone Spring—spring NV-8
Cylon State Public Hunting Grounds—park WI-6
**Cylon (Town of)**—pop pl WI-6
**Cymbling Branch**—pop pl AL-4
Cymbria—locale PA-2
**Cymbria Mine**—pop pl PA-2
Cymric Oil Field CA-9
Cymulga AL-4
Cyner Hollow—valley AR-4
Cynosure Forest Camp—locale OR-9
Cynth Creek—stream GA-3
Cyntheanne Ch—church IN-6
Cynthia—locale MS-4
Cynthia, Lake—reservoir SC-3
Cynthia Bayou—stream LA-4
Cynthia Bayou Ch—church LA-4
Cynthia Branch—stream NC-3
Cynthia Branch—stream WV-2
Cynthia Chapel—church KY-4
Cynthia Ch of Christ Holiness—church MS-4
Cynthia Creek—stream MO-7
Cynthia Falls—falls AK-9
Cynthia Heights Elementary and JHS—school IN-6
Cynthia Heights Sch IN-6
Cynthia Hollow—valley (3) TN-4
Cynthia Knob—summit GA-3
Cynthia Lake—lake MN-6
Cynthiana IN-6
Cynthiana TN-4
**Cynthiana**—pop pl IN-6
**Cynthiana**—pop pl KY-4
**Cynthiana**—pop pl OH-6
Cynthiana (CCD)—cens area KY-4
Cynthiana Ch—church IN-6
Cynthiana Ch (historical)—church TN-4
Cynthiana Commercial District—hist pl KY-4
Cynthiana Post Office (historical)—building TN-4
Cynthian Cem—cemetery OH-6
Cynthiann IN-6
**Cynthian (Township of)**—pop pl OH-6
Cynthia Park Cem—cemetery MA-1
Cynthia Post Office (historical)—building MS-4
Cynthia Slough—gut WI-6
Cynthia Street Sch—school IL-6
Cynwyd PA-2
**Cyn-Wyd**—pop pl NJ-2
**Cynwyd Estates**—pop pl PA-2
**Cynwyd Hills**—pop pl PA-2
Cynwyd Park—park PA-2
Cynwyd (RR name for Bala-Cynwyd)—other PA-2
Cynwyd Station—building PA-2
Cynwyd Station—locale PA-2
CYO Camp—locale NY-2
Cyokamo Camp—locale MO-7
Cy Orr Spring—spring CO-8
Cy Peak—summit AK-9
Cyper Creek—stream SC-3
Cyper Creek Picnic Grounds—locale SC-3
**Cypert**—pop pl AR-4
Cypert Cem—cemetery AR-4
Cypert Ch—church AR-4
Cypert-Copeland-Lay Cem—cemetery TN-4
Cypert Mtn—summit AR-4
Cypert Park—park ND-7
Cypert-Thornton Cem—cemetery TN-4
Cypert (Township of)—fmr MCD AR-4
**Cypher**—pop pl PA-2
Cypher Cem—cemetery IL-6
Cypher Cove—basin GA-3
Cyphers Lake—lake MN-6
Cypher Station—other PA-2
Cyphus Pond Ch—church GA-3
Cypre, Bayou—stream LA-4
Cypremort LA-4
**Cypremort**—pop pl LA-4
Cypremort, Bayou—stream (2) LA-4
cypremort bayou LA-4
Cypremort Crevasse—basin LA-4
**Cypremort (Louisa)**—pop pl LA-4
Cypremort Point—cape LA-4
Cypremort Point Beach—beach LA-4
Cypremort Post Office LA-4
Cypre-Mort Station LA-4
Cypres, Bayou des—stream LA-4
Cypres, Lac A—lake LA-4
Cypresmore Point LA-4
Cypres Mort Point LA-4
Cypress KY-4
Cypress MS-4
Cypress—locale (2) TN-4
Cypress—locale TX-5
**Cypress**—pop pl (2) AL-4
**Cypress**—pop pl CA-9
**Cypress**—pop pl FL-3
**Cypress**—pop pl IL-6
**Cypress**—pop pl IN-6
**Cypress**—pop pl (2) LA-4
**Cypress**—pop pl TX-5
Cypress—post sta FL-3
Cypress, Bayou—gut (2) LA-4
Cypress, Point of—locale FL-3
Cypress Ave East Hist Dist—hist pl NY-2
Cypress Ave West Hist Dist—hist pl NY-2
Cypress Bank Landing—locale VA-3
Cypress Bay LA-4
Cypress Bay—swamp GA-3
Cypress Bay—swamp (6) NC-3
Cypress Bay—swamp (4) SC-3
Cypress Bay Ch—church GA-3
Cypress Bayou LA-4
Cypress Bayou TX-5
Cypress Bayou—canal LA-4
Cypress Bayou—gut (2) AR-4
Cypress Bayou—gut (3) LA-4
Cypress Bayou—gut MS-4
Cypress Bayou—stream (4) AR-4
Cypress Bayou—stream (12) LA-4
Cypress Bayou—stream (3) MS-4
Cypress Bayou Dam—dam LA-4
Cypress Bayou Oil Field—oilfield LA-4
Cypress Bayou Rsvr—reservoir LA-4
Cypress Bay Resort—locale TN-4
Cypress Bend—bend KY-4
Cypress Bend—bend (2) MS-4
**Cypress Bend**—pop pl AR-4
**Cypress Bend**—pop pl TX-5
Cypress Bog—swamp MD-2
Cypress Borough—civil VA-3
Cypress Bottom—basin TN-4
Cypress Bottom—flat KY-4
Cypress Brake LA-4
Cypress Brake—swamp (3) AR-4
Cypress Brake—swamp (3) LA-4
Cypress Brake—woods TX-5
Cypress Brake (historical)—swamp MS-4
Cypress Branch AL-4
Cypress Branch LA-4
Cypress Branch—stream (3) AL-4
Cypress Branch—stream AR-4
Cypress Branch—stream (2) DE-2
Cypress Branch—stream (2) FL-3
Cypress Branch—stream GA-3
Cypress Branch—stream (4) LA-4
Cypress Branch—stream MD-2
Cypress Branch—stream (4) MS-4
Cypress Branch—stream (7) NC-3
Cypress Branch—stream (6) SC-3
Cypress Branch—stream TN-4
Cypress Branch—stream (3) TX-5
Cypress Branch—swamp NC-3
Cypress Branch Ch—church NC-3
Cypress Brook—stream NH-1
Cypress Butte—summit AZ-5
Cypress Campground—locale CA-9
Cypress Campground—locale SC-3
Cypress Camp Trail—trail CA-9
Cypress Canyon—valley AZ-5
Cypress Canyon—valley CA-9
Cypress Canyon—valley TX-5
Cypress Cathedral—church FL-3
Cypress (CCD)—cens area FL-3
Cypress Cem—cemetery (2) CT-1
Cypress Cem—cemetery KY-4
Cypress Cem—cemetery MS-4
Cypress Cem—cemetery SC-3
Cypress Ch—church AR-4
Cypress Ch—church LA-4
Cypress Ch—church NC-3
Cypress Ch—church SC-3
Cypress Ch—church (2) TX-5
Cypress Chapel—church MS-4
Cypress Chapel—church NC-3
Cypress Chapel—church SC-3
Cypress Chapel—church TX-5
Cypress Chapel—church VA-3
Cypress Chapel—uninc pl VA-3
Cypress Ch (historical)—church MS-4
Cypress City Lake—lake AR-4
Cypress Corner—locale AR-4
**Cypress Corner**—pop pl MS-4
Cypress Court—hist pl CA-9
Cypress Cove—bay CA-9

# D


D, Lateral—canal AZ-5
Daabaab—locale FM-9
**Daabach**—pop pl FM-9
Daablyuch FM-9
Daabiyuch—cape FM-9
Daabyuch FM-9
Daag Sch—school MO-7
Daaquam—locale ME-1
Daaquam River—stream ME-1
Daarpum—summit FM-9
Daaruku MP-9
Daaruku To MP-9
Daawoch FM-9
Daawoch—summit FM-9
Dabaang—summit FM-9
Dabaar—summit FM-9
Dabaat'—cape FM-9
Dabab FM-9
Dabach FM-9
Daball Corners—locale NY-2
Dabanawa, Lake—reservoir KS-7
Dabang FM-9
Dabar FM-9
Dabat FM-9
Dabb Bend—bend LA-4
Dabbler Lake—lake AK-9
Dabbs Branch—stream TX-5
Dabbs Cem—cemetery (2) TN-4
Dabbs Cem—cemetery TX-5
Dabbs Creek TX-5
Dabbs Creek—stream MS-4
Dabbs Creek—stream MO-7
Dabbs Creek—stream TN-4
Dabbs Creek—stream TX-5
Dabbs Ford—locale TN-4
Dabbs Ford Bridge—bridge TN-4
Dabbs Hollow—valley (2) TN-4
Dabbs Lake Dam—dam MS-4
Dabbs Post Office (historical)—building TN-4
Dabbs Store—hist pl AR-4
Dabdeben—island MP-9
Dabel OH-6
Dabeycheeg—summit FM-9
Dabeyicheg FM-9
Dabill Creek—stream MN-6
Dabiyuch FM-9
Dabiyuuch FM-9
Dab Keele Spring—spring UT-8
Dabler Dam—dam MT-8
Dablon Monument—other NY-2
Dablon Point—cape NY-2
Dablow State Wildlife Mngmt Area—park MN-6
Dabner Hill Ch—church TX-5
Dabney MS-4
Dabney—locale AR-4
Dabney—locale KY-4
Dabney—locale TX-5
Dabney—locale WV-2
**Dabney**—pop pl IN-6
**Dabney**—pop pl NC-3
**Dabney**—pop pl VA-3
Dabney Brake—woods MS-4
Dabney Branch—stream TN-4
Dabney Canyon—valley CA-9
Dabney Cem—cemetery AR-4
Dabney Cem—cemetery (3) TN-4
Dabney Cem—cemetery VA-3
Dabney Creek—stream AL-4
Dabney Creek—stream AR-4
Dabney Crossroads—locale MS-4
Dabney-Green House—hist pl MS-4
Dabney (historical)—locale MS-4
Dabney Lake—reservoir VA-3
Dabney Point—cape WA-9
Dabney Post Office—hist pl KY-4
Dabney Post Office (historical)—building MS-4
Dabneys—locale VA-3
Dabney Sch—school FL-3
Dabney Sch (historical)—school AL-4
Dabneys Millpond—reservoir VA-3
Dabney State Park—park OR-9
Dabney-Thompson House—hist pl VA-3
Dabney (Township of)—fmr MCD NC-3
Dabob—locale WA-9
Dabob Bay—bay WA-9
Dabob Sch—school WA-9
Daboll Corners—locale NY-2
**Dabolt**—pop pl KY-4
Dabolt Seven Pines Sch—school KY-4
Dabop WA-9
Dabop Bay WA-9
Dabreed FM-9
Dabrowski Playground—park MI-6
**Dabscook**—pop pl ME-1
Dabscook Crossover—locale ME-1
Dabured FM-9
Dabureed—bay FM-9
Daby Island—island CA-9
Daby Mtn—summit NY-2
**Dacada**—pop pl WI-6
D A C Country Club—other TX-5
Dace Eddy—bay MS-4
Dace Hollow—valley OH-6
Dace Lake—lake MS-4
Dacetown Sch (historical)—school MS-4
Dacey Mountain ME-1
Dacey Rsvr—reservoir NV-8
Dacey Sch (historical)—school PA-2
Dachafir—summit FM-9
Dachangar—locale FM-9
Dachfir FM-9
Dachikjowaruk Cove—bay AK-9
Dachirowruk Cove—bay AK-9
Dachingur FM-9
Dach Ridge—ridge WI-6
Dachthul—cape FM-9
Dacies Creek NV-8
Dacies Pass NV-8
Dacite Cliffs—ridge AZ-5
Dacite Cliffs Mine—mine AZ-5
Dacite Hills—summit NV-8
**Dacoma**—pop pl OK-5
Dacoma Park SD-7
**Dacono**—pop pl CO-8
D A Cook Pond Dam—dam MS-4
Dacosta NJ-2
**Da Costa**—pop pl NJ-2
**Da Costa**—pop pl TX-5
Dacotah Saint Sch—school CA-9
Dacotah State Wildlife Mngmt Area—park MN-6
Dacres Hotel—hist pl WA-9
**Dacula**—pop pl GA-3
Dacula-Rocky Creek (CCD)—cens area GA-3
**Dacus**—pop pl TX-5
Dacus (Braggs)—uninc pl AR-4
Dacus Cem—cemetery AR-4
Dacus Cem—cemetery MS-4
**Dacusville**—pop pl SC-3
Dacy Cem—cemetery AL-4
Dacy Gulch—valley AK-9
**Dacy (historical)**—pop pl SD-7
Dad—locale WY-8
D Adam Ranch—locale NE-7
Dad Canyon—valley TX-5
Dad Clark Gulch—valley CO-8
Dad Creek—stream (2) MT-8
Dad Creek—stream OK-5
Dad Creek Lake—lake MT-8
Dad Dail Rsvr—reservoir WY-8
Dadd Gulch—valley CO-8
Dadd Gulch Trail—trail CO-8
Daddy Canyon—valley UT-8
Daddy Frye Hill—summit MA-1
Daddy Frye's Hill Cemetery—hist pl MA-1
Daddy Haynes Well—well NM-5
Daddy Hole—lake FL-3
Daddy Jim Spring, Lake—lake AL-4
Daddy Knob—summit TN-4
Daddy Lode Mine—mine OR-9
Daddy Miller Spring—spring OK-5
Daddy Ridge—ridge TN-4
Daddy Run—stream VA-3
**Daddys Creek**—pop pl TN-4
Daddys Creek—stream TN-4
Daddys Creek Post Office (historical)—building TN-4
Daddy Spring—spring UT-8
Daddys Ridge—ridge ME-1
Daddy Stump Ridge—ridge UT-8
**Daddysville**—pop pl NC-3
Daddy Williams Bridge—bridge CO-8
**Dade**—pop pl KY-4
Dade, Mount—summit CA-9
Dade Battlefield Historic Memorial—hist pl FL-3
Dade Battlefield Memorial State Park—park FL-3
Dade Branch—stream NC-3
Dade-Broward Levee—levee FL-3
**Dade City**—pop pl FL-3
Dade City (CCD)—cens area FL-3
**Dade City East**—pop pl FL-3
Dade City North—CDP FL-3
Dade City Plaza (Shop Ctr)—locale FL-3
Dade City Shopping Plaza—locale FL-3
Dade Correctional Institute—building FL-3
Dade Correctional Institution (State Prison)—locale FL-3
**Dade County**—pop pl FL-3
**Dade (County)**—pop pl GA-3
**Dade County**—pop pl MO-7
Dade County Courthouse—hist pl GA-3
Dade County Department of Youth and Family Development—locale FL-3
Dade County Fire and Rescue HQ—building FL-3
Dade County Fire Control HQ—locale FL-3
Dade County Stockade Pretrial Detention Center—building FL-3
Dade Lake—lake CA-9
Dade Lake—lake FL-3
Dade Lake—lake MN-6
Dadeland—post sta FL-3
Dadeland Mall—locale FL-3
Dadeland Square (Shop Ctr)—locale FL-3
D A Deloney Lake AL-4
D A Deloney Lake Dam No. 1 AL-4
D A Deloney Lake Dam Number 1 AL-4
D A Deloney Lake Dam Number 2—dam AL-4
D A Deloney Lake Number One—reservoir AL-4
D A Deloney Lake Number Two—reservoir AL-4
D A Delony Dam—dam AL-4
Dade Memorial Park—cemetery FL-3
Dade Sch—school FL-3
Dade South Memorial Park—cemetery FL-3
Dade Village (Shop Ctr)—locale FL-3
Dadeville AL-4
**Dadeville**—pop pl AL-4
**Dadeville**—pop pl MO-7
Dadeville Baptist Ch—church AL-4
Dadeville (CCD)—cens area AL-4
Dadeville Division—civil AL-4
Dadeville Elem Sch—school AL-4
Dadeville Grammar Sch (historical)—school AL-4
Dadeville HS—school AL-4
Dadeville Methodist Episcopal Church AL-4
Dadi Beach—beach GU-9
Dadina Glacier—glacier AK-9
Dadina Lake—lake AK-9
Dadina River—stream AK-9
Dad Island—island FL-3
Dad Jones Tank—reservoir AZ-5
Dad Jones Tank Number Two—reservoir AZ-5
Dad Knob—summit WV-2
Dad Lofton Spring—spring CA-9
Dad Mill (historical)—locale TN-4
Dadmuns Pond MA-1
Dad Patterson Tank—reservoir AZ-5
Dad Peak—summit MT-8
**D'adrian Gardens**—pop pl IL-6
Dad Rock—other AK-9
Dads Bay—bay FL-3
Dads Corner—locale MN-6
Dads Corner—locale TX-5
Dads Creek—locale OR-9
Dads Creek—stream AK-9
Dads Creek—stream GA-3
Dads Creek—stream NV-8
Dads Creek—stream (2) OR-9
Dads Creek—stream (2) TX-5
Dads Creek—stream UT-8
Dads Creek—stream WY-8
Dads Flat—flat CO-8
Dads Gulch—valley CA-9
Dads Hill Number 2 Mine (underground)—mine AL-4
Dads Hill Slope Mine (underground)—mine AL-4
Dads Hump—summit ID-8
Dads Lake—lake MS-4
Dads Lake—lake (2) NE-7
Dads Lake—lake WI-6
Dads Lake—lake (2) WY-8
Dads Lake—swamp AR-4
Dads Lookout—summit AZ-5
Dads Pocket—basin CA-9
Dad Spring—spring OR-9
Dads Ridge—ridge GA-3
Dads Rsvr—reservoir CO-8
Dads Spring—spring UT-8
Dads Tank—reservoir AZ-5
**Dadsville**—pop pl OH-6
Dadu FM-9
Dadum FM-9
**Dadville**—pop pl NY-2
Dad Youngs Spring—spring CA-9
Daede-Shima FM-9
Daerur—channel PW-9
Daes Chapel Methodist Church—hist pl GA-3
Daescher Bldg—hist pl IN-6
Daeufers Valley Sch (abandoned)—school PA-2
Daew' FM-9
Daew—cape FM-9
Dafer (historical)—locale KS-7
Daffan—locale VA-3
**Daffan**—pop pl TX-5
**Daffenville**—pop pl KY-4
Daffer Sch—school KS-7
**Daffin Heights**—pop pl GA-3
Daffin House—hist pl MD-2
Daffin Park—park GA-3
Daffodil Canal—canal CA-9
Daffodil Island—island MD-2
Daffodil Mine—mine CA-9
Daffod Mine—mine OR-9
Dafford Mine (underground)—mine AL-4
Daffron Mtn—summit MO-7
Daffy Run PA-2
Dafoe Ranch—locale MT-8
Dafor Dam—dam NC-3
Dafor Lake—reservoir NC-3
Dafoste Park—park TX-5
Dafron Hollow—valley MO-7
Daft Block—hist pl UT-8
**Dafter**—pop pl MI-6
**Dafter (Township of)**—pop pl MI-6
Dagany Gap—gap CA-9
Dagaya MP-9
Dagaya—island MP-9
Dagaya Island MP-9
Dagaya-To MP-9
Dagelet, Mount—summit AK-9
Dagelet River—stream AK-9
Dagett Hollow—valley IL-6
Dagg Cem—cemetery TX-5
Dagger—locale AZ-5
Dagger Basin—basin AZ-5
Dagger Camp—locale TX-5
Dagger Canyon—valley AZ-5
Dagger Creek—stream ID-8
Dagger Dam No 1—dam NM-5
Dagger Dam No 2—dam NM-5
Dagger Dam No 3—dam NM-5
Dagger Draw—valley (3) NM-5
Dagger Draw—valley (2) TX-5
Dagger Falls—falls ID-8
Dagger Flat—flat CA-9
Dagger Flat—flat (2) TX-5
Dagger Flat Canyon—valley CA-9
Dagger Flat Draw—valley TX-5
Dagger Flat Trail (Pack)—trail CA-9
Dagger Hill—summit TX-5
Dagger Island—island ME-1
Dagger Island—island TX-5
Dagger Lake—lake (2) NM-5
Dagger Lake—lake (2) WA-9
Dagger Ledge—bar ME-1
Dagger Mtn—summit TX-5
Dagger Peak—summit AZ-5
Dagger Point—cape (2) TX-5
Dagger Spring—spring (2) AZ-5
Dagger Springs—spring AZ-5
Daggers Springs—spring VA-3
Daggert IL-6
Dagger Tank—reservoir (2) NM-5
Dagger Tank—reservoir (5) TX-5
Daggert Bog ME-1
Dagger Wash—stream AZ-5
Dagger Well—well TX-5
Dagger Windmill—locale (2) TX-5
Dagget County Airport UT-8
Dagget Creek NY-2
Dagget Creek OR-9
Dagget Creek—stream NV-8
Dagget Flat—flat UT-8
Dagget Lake UT-8
Dagget Lake—lake MI-6
Daggets Creek—stream WI-6
Dagget Spring—spring NV-8
Daggett ME-1
Daggett—locale PA-2
**Daggett**—pop pl AR-4
**Daggett**—pop pl CA-9
**Daggett**—pop pl IN-6
**Daggett**—pop pl MI-6
Daggett, Nathaniel, House—hist pl RI-1
Daggett and Parker Ditch—canal CO-8
Daggett Bog—lake ME-1
Daggett Brook—stream (3) ME-1
Daggett Brook—stream (2) MN-6
Daggett Brook Town Hall—locale MN-6
Daggett Brook (Township of)—civ div MN-6
Daggett Canyon—valley (2) NM-5
Daggett Cem—cemetery CA-9
Daggett Ch—church MI-6
Daggett Coulee—valley WI-6
Daggett County—civil UT-8
Daggett Creek NY-2
Daggett Creek PA-2
Daggett Creek—stream CA-9
Daggett Creek—stream CO-8
Daggett Creek—stream ID-8
Daggett Creek—stream MN-6
Daggett Creek—stream MT-8
Daggett Creek—stream NV-8
Daggett Creek—stream OR-9
Daggett Creek—stream TX-5
Daggett Hill—summit ME-1
Daggett Hollow—valley MO-7
Daggett Hollow—valley (2) PA-2
Daggett Island—island FL-3
Daggett JHS—school TX-5
Daggett Lake—lake MN-6
Daggett Lake—lake UT-8
Daggett Lake Dam—dam UT-8
Daggett Lookout Tower—locale MI-6
Daggett Meadow—flat ID-8
Daggett Mtn—summit CA-9
Daggett Pass—gap NV-8
Daggett Point—cape OR-9
Daggett Pond—lake ME-1
Daggett Pond—lake NY-2
Daggett (reduced usage)—locale IL-6
Daggett Ridge—ridge CA-9
Daggett Ridge—ridge ME-1
**Daggetts**—pop pl IL-6
Daggetts Brook MA-1
Daggett Sch—school IL-6
Daggett Sch—school NE-7
Daggett Sch—school TX-5
Daggetts Ford (historical)—locale MO-7
Daggetts Mills PA-2
**Daggett (Township of)**—pop pl MI-6
Daggett Wash—stream CA-9
Daggs Branch—stream MO-7
Daggs Dam—dam AZ-5
Daggs Rsvr AZ-5
Daggs Rsvr—reservoir AZ-5
Daggs Tank—reservoir AZ-5
Daggs Wash—stream AZ-5
Daggy Camp Hollow—valley VA-3
Daggy Hollow—valley VA-3
Dag Hammarskjold JHS—school CT-1
Dag Hammarskjold Sch—school CA-9
Dagislakhna Creek—stream AK-9
Dagitli River—stream AK-9
Dagle Lake—lake MN-6
Dagley Creek—stream WY-8
Daglia Canyon—valley CA-9
**Daglum**—pop pl ND-7
Daglum Cem—cemetery ND-7
Daglum Ch—church ND-7
Dagmar—locale AR-4
**Dagmar**—pop pl MT-8
Dagmar Ch—church MT-8
Dagmar Mine—mine UT-8
Dagmar State Game Area—park AR-4
Dago MH-9
Dago Cliffs MH-9
Dago Creek ID-8
Dago Creek—stream ID-8
Dago Creek—stream MN-6
Dago Creek—stream WY-8
Dagody Hill—summit NH-1
Dago Gulch—valley MT-8
Dago Gulch—valley OR-9
Dago Hill—summit IL-6
Dago Joe Spring—spring NV-8
Dago Lake—lake MN-6
Dagon—locale CA-9
Dagonia Ch—church MO-7
Dago Pass NV-8
Dago Peak ID-8
Dago Peak—summit ID-8
Dago Peak Gulch—valley ID-8
Dago Slough—stream IL-6
Dago Spring—spring AZ-5
Dago Spring—spring OR-9
D'Agostini Ranch—locale CA-9
D A Green Bridge—bridge TN-4
Dagret Creek—stream MT-8
**Dagsboro**—pop pl DE-2
Dagsboro Ch—church DE-2
Dagsboro Hundred—civil DE-2
Dagsborough DE-2
Dagsbury DE-2
Dag Tank—reservoir AZ-5
Dagu—basin MH-9
Dagu, Laderan—cliff (2) MH-9
**Daguao**—pop pl PR-3
Daguao (Barrio)—fmr MCD (2) PR-3
**Dague**—pop pl OH-6
Dague Lake—lake FL-3
Daguerra Dam—dam CA-9
Daguerra Point—cape CA-9
Daguey (Barrio)—fmr MCD PR-3
Dagunahi AL-4
**Dagus**—pop pl PA-2
**Daguscahonda**—pop pl PA-2
Daguscahonda Run—stream PA-2
**Dagus Mines**—pop pl PA-2
Dahar Creek UT-8
Dahdayla—island WA-9
Dahdayla Island WA-9
Daheim-Kirchof Cem—cemetery MI-6
Dahigren Peak—summit AK-9
D A Hill School MS-4
**Dahinda**—pop pl IL-6
Dahinden, Edward J., House—hist pl WI-6
Dahistrom Meadow—flat WA-9
Dahl—locale (2) AK-9
Dahl—locale KY-4
Dahl, Martin K., House—hist pl WI-6
Dahl, Peder, Farm—hist pl TX-5
Dahl, William, House—hist pl MN-6
Dahlberg—locale FL-3
Dahlberg—locale SD-7
Dahlberg Lake—lake (2) MN-6
Dahlbero Mtn—summit WA-9
Dahlbero Ponds—lake WA-9
Dahl Cem—cemetery KS-7
Dahl Cem—cemetery MO-7
Dahl Cem—cemetery TX-5
Dahl Cem—cemetery VA-3
Dahl Creek—stream (2) AK-9
Dahl Creek—stream OR-9
Dahl Ditch IN-6
Dahle Hollow—valley UT-8
Dahlem Ranch—locale CA-9
Dahlem Ranch—locale WY-8
**Dahlen**—pop pl ND-7
Dahlenburg Sch—school SD-7
**Dahlen Township**—pop pl ND-7
Dahle Park—park IA-7
Dahler Island—island MN-6
Dahler Lake—lake MN-6
Dahle Spring—spring OR-9
Dahl Fork—stream OR-9
Dahlgreen Creek—stream UT-8
Dahlgren—locale MN-6
**Dahlgren**—pop pl IL-6
**Dahlgren**—pop pl VA-3
Dahlgren Junction—locale VA-3
Dahlgren Lake—reservoir OK-5
Dahlgren Ridge—ridge AK-9
Dahlgren River—stream MN-6
Dahlgrens Corner—locale VA-3
Dahlgren Slough—lake MN-6
**Dahlgren (Township of)**—pop pl IL-6
**Dahlgren (Township of)**—pop pl MN-6
Dahl Hollow—valley AR-4
Dahlia—locale NM-5
Dahlia—locale VA-3
Dahlia—locale WA-9
**Dahlia**—pop pl NY-2
Dahlia Canal—canal (2) CA-9
Dahlia Canyon CA-9
Dahlia Ch—church NM-5
Dahlia Drain—canal CA-9
Dahlia Heights Sch—school CA-9
Dahlia Lateral—canal CA-9
Dahlia Lateral Eight—canal CA-9
Dahlia Pumping Station—other NM-5
Dahlia Sch—school NM-5
Dahlia Shoal—bar MI-6
Dahlin Arm—bay OR-9
Dahlin Creek—stream OR-9
Dahlinghaus Ditch—canal OH-6
Dahling Slough—lake SD-7
Dahlin Ranch—locale NE-7
Dahlizin Mesa AZ-5
Dahl Lake—lake MT-8
Dahl Lake—lake WI-6
Dahl Log Pond—reservoir OR-9
Dahlman Creek—stream ID-8
Dahlman Gulch—valley MT-8
**Dahlonega**—pop pl GA-3
**Dahlonega**—pop pl IA-7
Dahlonega (CCD)—cens area GA-3
Dahlonega Commercial Hist Dist—hist pl GA-3
Dahlonega Consolidated Gold Mine—hist pl GA-3
Dahlonega Courthouse Gold Museum—hist pl GA-3
Dahlonega Creek—stream ID-8
Dahlonegah Lake—reservoir OK-5
Dahlonegah Mtn—summit OK-5
Dahlonegah Park—park OK-5
Dahlonegah Sch—school OK-5
Dahlonega Township—fmr MCD IA-7
Dahloongamiut Lagoon—lake AK-9
Dahloongamiut River—stream AK-9
Dahloongamiut (Summer Camp)—locale AK-9
Dahl Park—park WA-9
**Dahl Pine**—pop pl OR-9
Dahl Place—locale MT-8
Dahl Placer—mine NV-8
Dahl Placer Mine—mine AK-9
Dahl Private Airstrip—airport ND-7
Dahlsborg SD-7
Dahl Sch—school MN-6
Dahls Lake—lake MN-6
Dahl Slough—gut ND-7
Dahl Spring—spring MT-8
Dahlstrom Branch—stream WI-6
Dahl Well—well NV-8
Dahmer—locale WV-2
Dahmer Lake Dam—dam MS-4
Dahm House—hist pl AL-4
Dahm Lake—lake MI-6
Dahnerts Lake—lake NJ-2
Dahn Lake—lake MN-6
Dahoga—locale PA-2
Dahoma—locale FL-3
**Dahomey**—pop pl MS-4
**Dahomy**—pop pl MS-4
Dahomy Post Office (historical)—building MS-4
Dahs Ditch—canal OH-6
Dahteh—locale AK-9
Dahtkit Cove—bay AK-9
Daiat FM-9
Daicey Mountain ME-1
Daicey Pond—lake ME-1
**Daigle**—pop pl ME-1
Daigle Brook—stream (3) ME-1
Daigle House—hist pl LA-4
Daigle Lake—lake MN-6
Daigle Mill—locale ME-1
Daigle Pond—lake ME-1
Daigles Eddy—bay MT-8
Daigleville—uninc pl LA-4
Daigleville Sch—school LA-4
Daigneau Hill—summit VT-1
Daigneau Pond—lake NY-2
Daigre Rsvr—reservoir CO-8
Dail Cem—cemetery AR-4
Dailey ND-7
Dailey—locale IL-6
Dailey—locale MT-8
**Dailey**—pop pl CO-8
**Dailey**—pop pl MI-6
**Dailey**—pop pl WV-2
Dailey Branch—stream MO-7
Dailey Brook ME-1
Dailey Brook MA-1
Dailey Cem—cemetery IN-6
Dailey Cem—cemetery MS-4
Dailey Cem—cemetery PA-2
Dailey Cem—cemetery TN-4
Dailey Chapel—church VA-3
Dailey Creek—stream AL-4
Dailey Creek—stream IA-7
Dailey Creek—stream MT-8
Dailey Creek—stream OR-9
Dailey Creek—stream SC-3
Dailey Creek—stream TN-4
Dailey Dam—dam OR-9
Dailey Hill—summit GA-3
Dailey (historical)—locale AL-4
Dailey Hollow—valley TN-4
Dailey Hollow—valley VT-1
Dailey Lake—lake IN-6
Dailey Lake—lake LA-4
Dailey Lake—lake MT-8
Dailey Lake—lake WA-9
Dailey Lateral—canal ID-8
Dailey Oil Field—oilfield CO-8
Dailey Park—park CO-8
Dailey Prairie—flat WA-9
Dailey Ranch—locale OR-9
Dailey Ridge Ch—church NY-2
Daileys Bottom AL-4
Dailey Sch—school CA-9
Dailey Sch—school CO-8
Dailey Sch—school MI-6
Dailey Sch—school NC-3
Dailey Sch (abandoned)—school MO-7
Daileys Chapel NC-3
Daileys Chapel—church (2) AL-4
Daileys Chapel Ch AL-4
Daileys Chapel Methodist Ch AL-4

Daileys Creek NC-3
Dailey Spring—spring MO-7
Daileys Store VA-3
Daileys Store—locale VA-3
Dailey Street Baptist Ch—church AL-4
**Dailey (Township of)**—pop pl MN-6
Dailland Park Shop Ctr—locale FL-3
Dailman Lake—lake WA-9
Dails Pond—reservoir NC-3
Dailsville—locale MD-2
Daily—locale ND-7
Daily Branch—stream NE-7
Daily Branch Cem—cemetery NE-7
Daily Brook ME-1
Daily Cem—cemetery MO-7
Daily Chapel—church IN-6
Daily Creek OR-9
Daily Creek—stream AR-4
Daily Creek—stream (2) MT-8
Daily Creek—stream NM-5
Daily Creek—stream PA-2
Daily Creek—stream TN-4
Daily Creek Spring—spring MT-8
Daily Ditch—canal IN-6
Daily East Shaft—mine NV-8
Daily Hill—summit TX-5
Daily Mine Group—mine AZ-5
Daily News Bldg—hist pl NY-2
Daily Northwestern Bldg—hist pl WI-6
Daily Rsvr—reservoir (2) MT-8
Daily Run—stream PA-2
Daily Sch—school MS-4
Dailys Creek NC-3
Daily Tank—reservoir TX-5
**Daily Township**—pop pl NE-7
**Dailyville**—pop pl OH-6
Daimechesengel PW-9
Daimechesengel—channel PW-9
Daimwood Branch TN-4
Daimwood Cem—cemetery TN-4
Dain WV-2
Dain Arroyo—stream NM-5
Dainel Cem—cemetery VA-3
**Daingerfield**—pop pl TX-5
Daingerfield (CCD)—cens area TX-5
Daingerfield Island—island VA-3
Daingerfield Landing—locale VA-3
Daingerfield State Park—park TX-5
Dainty Island—island AK-9
Dair Creek—stream MI-6
Dairy—locale IA-7
**Dairy**—pop pl AK-9
**Dairy**—pop pl OH-6
**Dairy**—pop pl OR-9
Dairy, The—flat UT-8
Dairy Branch—stream NC-3
Dairy Branch—stream (2) SC-3
Dairy Branch—stream TN-4
Dairy Brook—stream ME-1
Dairy Canyon—valley AZ-5
Dairy Canyon—valley ID-8
Dairy Canyon—valley NV-8
Dairy Canyon—valley (4) UT-8
Dairy Canyon—valley WA-9
Dairy Center—locale WI-6
**Dairy City**—pop pl CA-9
Dairy Creek ID-8
Dairy Creek—locale ID-8
Dairy Creek—stream AL-4
Dairy Creek—stream (5) CA-9
Dairy Creek—stream (4) ID-8
Dairy Creek—stream MI-6
Dairy Creek—stream (5) OR-9
Dairy Creek—stream UT-8
Dairy Creek—stream WA-9
Dairy Creek Campground—park (2) OR-9
Dairy Creek Guard Station—locale OR-9
Dairy Crossing—locale TX-5
Dairy Draw—valley WY-8
Dairy Farm Mine (Inactive)—mine CA-9
Dairy Field Ditch—canal CA-9
Dairy Field Ditch Number One—canal CA-9
Dairy Field Drain Number Two—canal CA-9
Dairy Flat—flat (2) CA-9
Dairy Fork—stream UT-8
Dairy Fork Wildlife Mngmt Area—park UT-8
Dairygrove Cem—cemetery IA-7
Dairy Gulch—valley (2) CA-9
Dairy Hill—summit NY-2
Dairy Hill—summit UT-8
Dairy Hill Sch—school NY-2
Dairy Hill Sch—school VT-1
Dairy (historical P.O.)—locale IA-7
Dairy Hollow—valley ID-8
Dairy Hollow—valley UT-8
Dairy Hollow—valley WV-2
Dairy Knoll—summit UT-8
Dairy Lake—lake ID-8
Dairy Lake—lake MI-6
**Dairyland**—pop pl (2) CA-9
**Dairyland**—pop pl NY-2
**Dairyland**—pop pl WI-6
Dairyland Cem—cemetery WI-6
Dairyland Flowage WI-6
Dairyland Lateral—canal CA-9
Dairyland Lookout Tower—locale WI-6
Dairyland Rsvr—reservoir WI-6
**Dairyland (Town of)**—pop pl WI-6
Dairy Meadow—flat OR-9
**Dairy Meadows Subdivision**—pop pl UT-8
Dairy Mtn—summit AZ-5
Dairy Mtn—summit ID-8
Dairy Mtn—summit TX-5
Dairy Point—cape UT-8
Dairy Point—summit OR-9
Dairy Pond—lake MO-7
Dairy Pump—other OR-9
Dairy Ridge—ridge CA-9
Dairy Ridge—ridge ID-8
Dairy Ridge—ridge UT-8
Dairy Ridge Rsvr—reservoir UT-8
Dairy Run—stream OH-6
Dairy Siding—locale OR-9
Dairy Spring—spring (2) AZ-5
Dairy Spring—spring (2) CA-9
Dairy Spring—spring ID-8
Dairy Springs—spring ID-8
Dairy Springs—spring UT-8
Dairy Springs Campground—park AZ-5
Dairy Tank—reservoir AZ-5
Dairy Trail—trail UT-8
**Dairy Valley**—pop pl CA-9
Dairy Valley—valley NV-8
**Dairy Valley (Cerritos)**—pop pl CA-9
Dairy Valley Creek—stream NV-8
Dairy Valley Creek—stream UT-8
Dairy Valley Springs—spring NV-8
Dairyville—locale CA-9
**Dairyville**—pop pl IA-7
**Dairyville (local name Los Robles)**—pop pl CA-9
**Daisetta**—pop pl TX-5
Daisetta (CCD)—cens area TX-5
Daisetta Swamp—swamp TX-5
**Daisey City**—pop pl AL-4
Daisey Mountain ME-1
Daisey Pond—lake ME-1
Daiseys Goose Pond DE-2
Daisu—island MP-9
Daisy TN-4
Daisy MP-9
Daisy—locale AL-4
Daisy—locale MD-2
Daisy—locale OK-5
Daisy—locale VA-3
Daisy—locale WA-9
**Daisy**—pop pl AL-4
**Daisy**—pop pl AR-4
**Daisy**—pop pl GA-3
**Daisy**—pop pl KY-4
**Daisy**—pop pl MO-7
**Daisy**—pop pl NY-2
**Daisy**—pop pl SC-3
**Daisy**—pop pl TN-4
**Daisy**—pop pl WV-2
Daisy—uninc pl NC-3
Daisy, Lake—lake FL-3
Daisy Basin—basin OR-9
Daisy Basin Spring—spring OR-9
Daisy Bay—bay MN-6
Daisy Blue Mine (Inactive)—mine CA-9
Daisy Canyon—valley (2) CA-9
Daisy Canyon—valley CO-8
Daisy (CCD)—cens area KY-4
Daisy Chapel—church TN-4
Daisy Chapel—church WV-2
Daisy City Mine (underground)—mine AL-4
Daisy Congregational Ch—church TN-4
Daisy Creek MT-8
Daisy Creek—stream (3) AK-9
Daisy Creek—stream AR-4
Daisy Creek—stream FL-3
Daisy Creek—stream ID-8
Daisy Creek—stream (5) MT-8
Daisy Creek—stream NV-8
Daisy Creek—stream OR-9
Daisy Creek—stream WA-9
Daisy Creek Pass—gap MT-8
Daisy Creek Trail—trail MT-8
Daisy Dean Creek—stream (2) MT-8
Daisy Dean Spring—spring CA-9
Daisy Dee Creek MT-8
Daisydell Post Office (historical)—building TN-4
Daisy Dell Sch—school WI-6
Daisy Ditch—canal CO-8
Daisy Elem Sch—school TN-4
Daisy Falls Dam—dam AL-4
Daisy Falls Lake—reservoir AL-4
Daisy Farm Campground—locale MI-6
Daisy Flour Mill, Inc.—hist pl NY-2
Daisy Gap—gap AL-4
Daisy Glacier—glacier AK-9
Daisy Grove Sch—school LA-4
Daisy Guard Station—locale MT-8
Daisy Gulch—valley (3) ID-8
Daisy Gulch—valley NM-5
Daisy Hill—locale KS-7
**Daisy Hill**—pop pl IN-6
Daisy Hill—summit IN-6
Daisy Hill Ch—church IN-6
Daisy (historical)—locale MS-4
Daisy Interchange—other OK-5
Daisy Island—island AK-9
Daisy Island—island MN-6
Daisy Knob—summit KY-4
Daisy Knob—summit VA-3
Daisy Lake WI-6
Daisy Lake—lake MI-6
Daisy Lake—lake MN-6
Daisy Lake—locale FL-3
Daisy Lodge—locale AR-4
Daisy Marsh—swamp DE-2
Daisy Mine—mine AZ-5
Daisy Mine—mine CA-9
Daisy Mine—mine (2) CO-8
Daisy Mine—mine OR-9
Daisy Mine—mine TN-4
Daisy Mine—mine WA-9
Daisy Mine (historical)—mine SD-7
Daisy Mtn—summit AZ-5
Daisy Mtn—summit OK-5
Daisy Narrows—gap MT-8
Daisy Notch—gap MT-8
Daisy Pass—gap CA-9
Daisy Pass—gap NV-8
Daisy Peak—summit MT-8
Daisy Post Office—building TN-4
Daisy Sch—school KY-4
Daisy Sch (historical)—school AL-4
Daisy Shaft—mine AZ-5
Daisy Spring—spring CO-8
Daisy Spring—spring MT-8
Daisy Spring—spring OR-9
Daisy State Park—park AR-4
Daisy Swamp—swamp SC-3
Daisy Swift Creek—stream AK-9
Daisy Tank—reservoir AZ-5
**Daisytown**—pop pl (2) PA-2
Daisytown Borough—civil PA-2
Daisy Trail—trail WA-9
Daisy Valley—valley MN-6
Daisy Vein Mine—mine MT-8
**Daisy-Vestry**—pop pl MS-4
Daisy Vestry Sch (historical)—school MS-4
Daisy Windmill—locale TX-5
Daiton Mountain CA-9
Daiye AK-9
Dajaos (Barrio)—fmr MCD PR-3
Daka MP-9
Dakah De'nin's Village Site—hist pl AK-9
Dakain Brook ME-1
Dakai Well—well NM-5
Dakaneek Bay—bay AK-9
Dakan Mtn—summit CO-8
Dakavak Bay—bay AK-9
Dakavak Lake—lake AK-9
Dake Branch—stream TN-4
Dake Cem—cemetery AR-4
Dake Cem—cemetery IN-6
Dake Creek—stream (2) MO-7
Dakeekalik Creek—stream AK-9
Dakeekathlrimjingia Point—cape AK-9
Dake Lake—lake MI-6
Dake Lake—lake WI-6
Dakemei—bar FM-9
Dakeneyuch—summit FM-9
Daken Flat—flat CA-9
Dake Rsvr—reservoir NV-8
Dake Sch—school NY-2
Dakin Bay—bay NY-2
Dakin Brook—stream ME-1
Dakin Creek—stream NY-2
Dakin Creek—stream WI-6
Dakin Hill—summit NH-1
Dakin Park—park ME-1
Dakins Brook—stream MA-1
Dakin Sch—school WI-6
Dakin Shoal—bar NY-2
Dakins Lake—reservoir IA-7
Dakins Lake Park—park IA-7
Dakins Run—stream OH-6
Dakiy FM-9
Dak'iy—summit FM-9
Dakli River—stream AK-9
Dakoma Siding WY-8
Dakomin—locale MN-6
Dakoming—locale WY-8
Dakota IA-7
Dakota—fmr MCD NE-7
Dakota—locale GA-3
**Dakota**—pop pl IL-6
**Dakota**—pop pl MN-6
**Dakota**—pop pl WV-2
**Dakota**—pop pl WI-6
Dakota Apartments—hist pl NY-2
Dakota Block—hist pl ND-7
**Dakota Boys Ranch**—pop pl ND-7
Dakota Calmet Mine—mine SD-7
Dakota Cem—cemetery IL-6
Dakota Ch—church GA-3
Dakota Christian HS—school SD-7
**Dakota City**—pop pl IA-7
**Dakota City**—pop pl NE-7
Dakota City Cem—cemetery SD-7
Dakota City (historical)—locale SD-7
Dakota City Post Office (historical)—building SD-7
**Dakota (County)**—pop pl MN-6
Dakota County Courthouse—hist pl MN-6
Dakota Creek WA-9
Dakota Creek—stream AK-9
Dakota Creek—stream MI-6
Dakota Creek—stream MN-6
Dakota Creek—stream WA-9
Dakota Divide—ridge WY-8
Dakota Farmer Bldg—hist pl SD-7
Dakotah IA-7
Dakota Hill—summit CO-8
Dakota Hill—summit UT-8
Dakota Hills Park—park MN-6
Dakota Junction—locale MN-6
Dakota Junction—locale NE-7
Dakota Lake—reservoir ND-7
Dakota Lake Dam—dam ND-7
Dakota Lake Natl Wildlife Ref—park ND-7
Dakota Mine—mine NM-5
Dakota Mine—mine SD-7
Dakota Playground—park DC-2
**Dakota Point**—pop pl IA-7
Dakota Range Sch—school SD-7
Dakota Ridge WY-8
Dakota River ND-7
Dakota River SD-7
Dakota Sch (historical)—school PA-2
Dakota Square—locale ND-7
**Dakota (Town of)**—pop pl WI-6
**Dakota (Township of)**—pop pl IL-6
Dakota Wesleyan Univ—hist pl SD-7
Dakota Wesleyan Univ—school SD-7
Dakota Zoo—park ND-7
Dal—locale KY-4
Dalaach—summit FM-9
Dalaap'—summit FM-9
Dalach FM-9
Dalander Cem—cemetery IA-7
Dalap FM-9
Dalap—island MP-9
Dalap Island MP-9
**Dalark**—pop pl AR-4
Dalasuga Island—island AK-9
Dalbec Lake—lake MN-6
Dalbey—locale KS-7
Dalbey Memorial Park—park WY-8
D'Albini Ranch—locale AZ-5
**Dalbo**—pop pl MN-6
Dalbom Airp—airport MO-7
**Dalbo (Township of)**—pop pl MN-6
Dalby KS-7
Dalby—locale IA-7
Dalby Creek—stream TX-5
Dalby Creek—stream WA-9
Dalby Lake—lake TX-5
Dalbys—locale VA-3
Dalby Springs—locale TX-5
Dalby Springs-Simms (CCD)—cens area TX-5
Dalby State Wildlife Mngmt Area—park MN-6
Dalco, Point—cape WA-9
Dalco Mine—mine NM-5
Dalco Passage—channel WA-9
**Dalcour**—pop pl LA-4
Dale WY-8
Dale—locale KS-7
Dale—locale KY-4
Dale—locale MN-6
Dale—locale MO-7
Dale—locale OH-6
Dale—locale OR-9
Dale—locale PA-2
**Dale**—pop pl IL-6
**Dale**—pop pl (2) IN-6
**Dale**—pop pl IA-7
**Dale**—pop pl MI-6
**Dale**—pop pl MS-4
**Dale**—pop pl NY-2
**Dale**—pop pl NC-3
**Dale**—pop pl OK-5
**Dale**—pop pl (2) PA-2
**Dale**—pop pl SC-3
**Dale**—pop pl TX-5
**Dale**—pop pl WV-2
**Dale**—pop pl WI-6
**Dale**—pop pl WY-8
Dale, Felix, Stone House—hist pl PA-2
Dale, John, House—hist pl KY-4
Dale, Lake—reservoir VA-3
Dale, Samuel F., House—hist pl PA-2
**Dale Acres**—pop pl TN-4
Dale and Demkos Mine—mine NC-3
Dale and Leonard Eriksen Dam—dam SD-7
Dale Bend (historical)—bend TN-4
Dale Borough—civil PA-2
Dale Branch—stream GA-3
Dale Branch—stream MS-4
Dale Branch—stream (2) TN-4
Dale Branch—stream VA-3
Dale Canyon—valley NV-8
Dale Canyon—valley OR-9
**Dalecarlia**—pop pl IN-6
Dalecarlia, Lake—reservoir IN-6
**Dalecarlia Reservoir**—pop pl MD-2
Dalecarlia Rsvr—reservoir DC-2
Dalecarlia Rsvr—reservoir MD-2
Dale Cem—cemetery (2) IN-6
Dale Cem—cemetery (2) IA-7
Dale Cem—cemetery MN-6
Dale Cem—cemetery (2) MO-7
Dale Cem—cemetery NE-7
Dale Cem—cemetery (2) NY-2
Dale Cem—cemetery ND-7
Dale Cem—cemetery OK-5
Dale Cem—cemetery (2) TN-4
Dale Cem—cemetery TX-5
Dale Cem—cemetery VA-3
Dale Cem—cemetery WI-6
Dale Center Sch (historical)—school MO-7
Dale Ch—church MN-6
Dale Ch—church PA-2
Dale Chapel—church TN-4
**Dale City**—pop pl VA-3
Dale Corfield Ranch—locale NE-7
**Dale County**—pop pl AL-4
Dale County Christian Sch—school AL-4
Dale County Hosp—hospital AL-4
Dale County Public Lake—reservoir AL-4
Dale County Public Lake Dam—dam AL-4
Dale Court House AL-4
Dale Covenant Cem—cemetery MN-6
**Dale Creek**—pop pl WY-8
Dale Creek—stream AR-4
Dale Creek—stream CA-9
Dale Creek—stream CO-8
Dale Creek—stream ID-8
Dale Creek—stream (3) MT-8
Dale Creek—stream TX-5
Dale Creek—stream WA-9
Dale Creek—stream WI-6
Dale Creek—stream (2) WY-8
Dale Creek Crossing (48AB145)—hist pl WY-8
**Dale Crest**—pop pl TX-5
**Dalecrest**—pop pl VA-3
Dale Crest Ch—church TX-5
Dale Ditch—canal CO-8
Dale Ellis Dam—dam SD-7
**Dale Enterprise**—pop pl VA-3
Dale Ferry Landing—locale AL-4
Dale Gulf—valley NY-2
Dale (historical)—locale AL-4
Dalehite Lake—lake MS-4
**Dale Hollow**—pop pl TN-4
Dale Hollow—valley TN-4
Dale Hollow—valley TX-5
Dale Hollow Boat Dock—locale TN-4
Dale Hollow Dam—dam (2) TN-4
Dale Hollow Dam Rec Area—park TN-4
Dale Hollow Fish Hatchery—locale TN-4
Dale Hollow Lake—reservoir KY-4
Dale Hollow Lake—reservoir (2) TN-4
Dale Hollow Rsvr KY-4
Dale Hollow Rsvr TN-4
Dale HS—school VA-3
Dale Industrial Sch (historical)—school AL-4
Dale JHS—school CA-9
Dale Knob—summit MO-7
Dale Lake—flat CA-9
Dale Lake—lake CA-9
Dale Lake—lake (2) MN-6
Dale Lake—lake UT-8
Dale Lake—lake WY-8
Dale Landing Strip—airport MS-4
Dale Mabry Shop Ctr—locale FL-3
Dale Maffit Rsvr—reservoir IA-7
Dale (Magisterial District)—fmr MCD VA-3
Dale McCauley Ranch—locale NM-5
Dale Memorial Park—cemetery VA-3
Dale Mtn—summit NM-5
Dale Mtn—summit VA-3
Dale Neely Branch—stream TN-4
**Dalen Township**—pop pl ND-7
Dale Oil Field—oilfield TX-5
Dale Oil Field—other IL-6
Dale Park—park OH-6
Dale Place—locale AR-4
Dale Playground—park MN-6
Dale Powell Ditch—canal IN-6
Dale Ranch—locale (2) SD-7
Dale Ranger Station—locale OR-9
Dale Resler Camp—locale NM-5
Dale Ridge TN-4
**Dale Ridge**—pop pl VA-3
Dale Ridge—ridge TN-4
Dale Ridge Ch—church TN-4
Dale Ridge Hollow—valley VA-3
**Dalerose**—pop pl CO-8
Dalerose Mesa—summit CO-8
Dale Rsvr—reservoir CO-8
Dale Rsvr—reservoir IN-6
Dale Run—stream (2) PA-2
**Dales**—pop pl CA-9
Dale's, USB Market—hist pl NC-3
Dalesberg SD-7
Dales Bluff Creek—stream OR-9
Dales Branch—stream MO-7
Dales Branch—stream WV-2
Dalesburg—locale (2) KY-4
Dalesburg—locale SD-7
Dalesburg Baptist Church SD-7
Dalesburg Ch—church SD-7
Dalesburg Sch—school SD-7
Dalesburg School Number 35 SD-7
Dale Sch—school IL-6
Dale Sch—school KY-4
Dale Sch—school MO-7
Dale Sch—school NE-7
Dale Sch—school OH-6
Dale Sch—school OK-5
Dale Sch—school WI-6
Dale Sch (abandoned)—school PA-2
Dales Chapel—church LA-4
Dales Chapel—church TN-4
Dale Sch (historical)—school (2) MO-7
Dales Creek NC-3
Dales Creek—stream NC-3
Dales Ford—locale IA-7
Dales Hill—summit MA-1
Dales Lake—lake CA-9
Dales Mills PA-2
Dales Point—cape MS-4
Dales Pond—lake NY-2
Dale Spring—spring CA-9
Dale Springs—spring NM-5
Dale's Right—hist pl MD-2
Dales (RR name for Dale)—other IL-6
Dale State Public Shooting Area—park SD-7
Dale Street Sch—school MA-1
**Dale Summit**—pop pl PA-2
Dalesville IN-6
Dalesville MD-2
Dale Swedland Number 1 Dam—dam SD-7
Dales Well—well NV-8
**Dale Terrace (subdivision)**—pop pl TN-4
Daletown AL-4
Dale Townhall—building IA-7
**Dale (Town of)**—pop pl WI-6
Dale Township—civil MO-7
Dale Township—fmr MCD (2) IA-7
**Dale Township**—pop pl KS-7
**Dale Township**—pop pl ND-7
**Dale Township**—pop pl SD-7
**Dale (Township of)**—pop pl IL-6
**Dale (Township of)**—pop pl MN-6
Dale Valley—valley NE-7
Dale Valley—valley WI-6
Dale Valley Ranch—locale TX-5
Daleva Post Office (historical)—building AL-4
Daleview—locale MT-8
Daleview Sch—school MO-7
Dale Villa Park—park MN-6
Daleville—locale PA-2
**Daleville**—pop pl AL-4
**Daleville**—pop pl AR-4
**Daleville**—pop pl CT-1
**Daleville**—pop pl IN-6
**Daleville**—pop pl MS-4
**Daleville**—pop pl PA-2
**Daleville**—pop pl VA-3
Daleville (CCD)—cens area AL-4
Daleville Cem—cemetery MS-4
Daleville Cem—cemetery OH-6
Daleville Ch—church AL-4
Daleville Division—civil AL-4
Daleville Elem Sch—school IN-6
Daleville HS—school AL-4
Daleville HS—school IN-6
Daleville Memorial Gardens—cemetery AL-4
Daleville Methodist Ch—church MS-4
Daleville Post Office (historical)—building MS-4
Daleville Station (historical)—locale AL-4
**Dalevue**—pop pl PA-2
**Dalewood**—pop pl OH-6
**Dalewood**—pop pl SC-3
**Dalewood**—pop pl TN-4
Dalewood Baptist Ch—church TN-4
Dalewood JHS—school TN-4
Dalewood Shore Lake—reservoir (2) MS-4
Dalewood Shores Lake Dam—dam MS-4
Daley—locale (2) KY-4
**Daley**—pop pl PA-2
Daley Bay—bay MN-6
Daley Branch—stream SC-3
Daley Brook ME-1
Daley Brook—stream MA-1
Daley Brook—stream MN-6
Daley Brook—stream (2) VT-1
Daley Canyon—valley CA-9
Daley Cem—cemetery OH-6
Daley Cemetery—cemetery AR-4
Daley Con Mines—mine ID-8
**Daley Corner**—pop pl MA-1
Daley Creek—stream AL-4
Daley Creek—stream AR-4
Daley Creek—stream GA-3
Daley Creek—stream MN-6
Daley Creek—stream (2) OR-9
Daley Creek Picnic Ground—park OR-9
Daley Draw—valley WY-8
Daley Flat—flat CA-9
Daley Gulch—valley CA-9
Daley Gulch—valley CO-8
Daley Hollow—valley TN-4
Daley Hollow—valley TX-5
Daley Island NY-2
Daley Lake OR-9
Daley Lake—lake WY-8
Daley Lake—reservoir OR-9
Daley Mill—locale CA-9
Daley Park—park AZ-5
Daley Prairie—flat OR-9
Daley Ranch—locale WY-8
Daley Road Truck Trail—trail CA-9
Daley Run—stream PA-2
Daley Run—stream WV-2
Daleys MT-8
Daleys Island NY-2
Daleys Post Office (historical)—building TN-4
Daley Spring—spring OR-9
**Daley's Ranch**—pop pl WY-8
Daley Tank—reservoir CO-8
Daley Valley—basin NE-7
**Daleyville**—pop pl OH-6
**Daleyville**—pop pl WI-6
Daleyville Branch WI-6
Dalgain—hist pl WV-2
Dalgren Ranch—locale NE-7
**Dalhart**—pop pl TX-5
**Dalhart**—pop pl VA-3
Dalhart (CCD)—cens area TX-5
Dalhke Ranch Number 1 Dam—dam SD-7
Dalhke Ranch Number 2 Dam—dam SD-7
Dalhke Ranch Number 3 Dam—dam SD-7
Dalhke Ranch Number 4 Dam—dam SD-7
Dalhke Ranch Number 5 Dam—dam SD-7
Dalhke Ranch Number 6 Dam—dam SD-7
Dalhman Island—island MN-6
Dalhousie, Lake—lake FL-3
Dalhousie Acres—locale FL-3
Daliby Hollow—valley TX-5
Dali-Dona—summit CA-9
**Dalies**—pop pl NM-5
Dalies Oil Well (Abandoned)—well NM-5
Dalimalook Creek—stream AK-9
Dalimalook Mtn—summit AK-9
Dalipebinau FM-9
Dalipebinau (Municipality)—civ div FM-9
Dalipebinaw FM-9
Dalipebinaw Municipality FM-9
Dalipeebinaew—civil FM-9
Dalipeebinaew Sch—school FM-9
Dalkai Spring—spring AZ-5
Dalkeith—hist pl NC-3
Dalkeith—locale FL-3
**Dalkena**—pop pl WA-9
Dalker Buttes NV-8
Dalkey Ridge—ridge WI-6
Dalkhorn Ch—church MS-4
Dalkhorn Sch—school MS-4
Dall, Andrew, Jr. and James, Houses—hist pl OH-6
Dall, Mount—summit AK-9
Dallam—locale TX-5
**Dallam (County)**—pop pl TX-5
Dallam Creek—stream KY-4
Dallam-Merritt House—hist pl CA-9
**Dallams Creek**—pop pl KY-4
Dallan Spring—spring SD-7
Dallara Park—park MN-6
**Dallardsville**—pop pl TX-5
Dallas IN-6
Dallas IA-7
Dallas KS-7
Dallas MO-7
Dallas ND-7
Dallas PA-2
Dallas—locale CO-8
Dallas—locale ME-1
Dallas—mine AZ-5
Dallas—other OH-6
**Dallas**—pop pl (2) AL-4
**Dallas**—pop pl AR-4
**Dallas**—pop pl FL-3
**Dallas**—pop pl GA-3
**Dallas**—pop pl IA-7
**Dallas**—pop pl MO-7
**Dallas**—pop pl NC-3
**Dallas**—pop pl OR-9
**Dallas**—pop pl PA-2
**Dallas**—pop pl SD-7
**Dallas**—pop pl TX-5
**Dallas**—pop pl WV-2
**Dallas**—pop pl WI-6
Dallas, Mount—summit WA-9
Dallas, The (historical)—rapids OR-9
Dallas Academy AL-4
**Dallas Acres**—pop pl PA-2
Dallas And Bengal Drain—canal MI-6
**Dallasania**—pop pl IL-6
Dallas Bank—bar WA-9
Dallas Bay—bay TN-4
Dallas Bay Sky Park—airport TN-4
Dallas Borough—civil PA-2
**Dallas Branch**—pop pl TN-4
Dallas Branch—stream (2) AL-4
Dallas Branch—stream TX-5
**Dallasburg**—pop pl OH-6
Dallas Carnegie Library—hist pl SD-7
Dallas (CCD)—cens area GA-3
Dallas (CCD)—cens area OR-9
Dallas Cem—cemetery AL-4
Dallas Cem—cemetery AR-4
Dallas Cem—cemetery IA-7
Dallas Cem—cemetery OR-9
Dallas Cem—cemetery SD-7
Dallas Cem—cemetery WI-6
**Dallas Center**—pop pl IA-7
Dallas Center Cem—cemetery IA-7
Dallas Center Sch—school IA-7
Dallas Center Sch (historical)—school MO-7
Dallas Ch—church AL-4
Dallas Ch—church GA-3
Dallas Ch—church TN-4
**Dallas City**—pop pl IL-6
**Dallas City**—pop pl PA-2
Dallas City Cem—cemetery TX-5
**Dallas City (Township of)**—pop pl IL-6
Dallas Country Club—other TX-5
**Dallas County**—pop pl AL-4
**Dallas (County)**—pop pl AR-4
**Dallas County**—pop pl MO-7
**Dallas (County)**—pop pl TX-5
Dallas County Area Vocational Sch—school AL-4
Dallas County Care Facility—building IA-7
Dallas County Community Ch—church MO-7
Dallas County Courthouse—building AL-4
Dallas County Courthouse—hist pl AL-4
Dallas County Courthouse—hist pl AR-4
Dallas County Courthouse—hist pl IA-7
Dallas County Courthouse—hist pl TX-5
Dallas County Courthouse (Boundary Increase)—hist pl IA-7
Dallas County HS—school AL-4
Dallas County Lake—reservoir AL-4
Dallas County Public Lake AL-4
Dallas County Public Lake—reservoir AL-4
Dallas County Public Lake Dam—dam AL-4
Dallas Creek MT-8
Dallas Creek—stream AR-4
Dallas Creek—stream CO-8
Dallas Creek—stream WY-8

Damrel Creek—stream LA-4
Dam Ridge—ridge ID-8
Dam Ridge—ridge ME-1
Damriscove Island ME-1
Dam Rock—summit WY-8
Damrock Point WA-9
Damron Branch—stream (3) KY-4
Damron Cem—cemetery GA-3
Damron Cem—cemetery (2) KY-4
Damron Cem—cemetery (3) TN-4
Damron Cem—cemetery (3) WV-2
Damron Creek—stream KY-4
Damron Hollow—valley TN-4
Damron Sch—school CA-9
Damron Sch—school WV-2
Damron Spring—spring TN-4
**Damron Way Subdivision**—pop pl UT-8
Dam Run—stream PA-2
Dams Canyon—valley OR-9
Damsch School SD-7
**Dams Corner**—pop pl NY-2
Damsel—locale MO-7
Damsite Campground—locale CA-9
Damsite Canyon—valley CA-9
Dam Site East Bank Access Area—park MS-4
Damsite Eastbank Access Area—park MS-4
Damsite East Bank Public Use Area—park AL-4
Damsite Eastbank Public Use Area—park AL-4
Dam Site East Public Use Area—park OK-5
Damsite Left Bank Public Use Area AL-4
Damsite Left Bank Rec Area—park AL-4
Dam Site Marina—locale AR-4
Dam Site North Public Use Area—park AR-4
Damsite Public Use Area—park AL-4
Dam Site Public Use Area—park MO-7
Dam Site Public Use Area—park OK-5
Dam Site Rec Area—park AR-4
Damsite Rec Area—park MS-4
Damsite Right Bank AL-4
Dam Site Rsvr—reservoir OR-9
Dam Site South Public Use Area—park AR-4
Damsite Trail—trail OR-9
Dam Site West Bank Access Area—park MS-4
Damsite Westbank Access Area—park MS-4
Damsite West Bank Public Use Area—park (2) AL-4
Dam Site West Public Use Area—park OK-5
Dams Meadow—flat OR-9
Damson Brook MA-1
Dam Swamp—stream SC-3
Dam Tank—reservoir (2) AZ-5
Damtown—locale VA-3
Damundtali Lake—lake AK-9
**Dam View (Trailer Park)**—pop pl AZ-5
Damworth Hollow TN-4
Dam 149—dam CA-9
Dam 194—dam CA-9
Dam 6-2020—dam MS-4
Dam 67—dam LA-4
Dam 68—dam LA-4
Dam 69—dam LA-4
Dam 71—dam LA-4
Dam 72—dam LA-4
Dam 73—dam LA-4
Dam 76—dam LA-4
Dam 78—dam LA-4
Dam 80—dam LA-4
Dan KS-7
Dan—locale KY-4
Dan—locale VA-3
**Dan**—pop pl GA-3
**Dan**—pop pl KY-4
**Dan**—pop pl WV-2
Dan, Bayou—stream (2) LA-4
Dan, Lake—lake FL-3
Dan, Mount—summit MA-1
Dana KS-7
Dana MA-1
Dana—locale KY-4
Dana—locale ND-7
Dana—locale WY-8
**Dana**—pop pl CA-9
**Dana**—pop pl FL-3
**Dana**—pop pl IL-6
**Dana**—pop pl IN-6
**Dana**—pop pl IA-7
**Dana**—pop pl NC-3
Dana, James Dwight, House—hist pl CT-1
Dana, Lake—lake ND-7
Dana, Marcus, House—hist pl OH-6
Dana, Mount—summit AK-9
Dana, Mount—summit CA-9
Dana, Mount—summit WA-9
Dana, Richard Henry, Branch—hist pl CA-9
Dana, Susan Lawrence, House—hist pl IL-6
Dana Adobe—hist pl CA-9
Dana Butte—summit AZ-5
Dana Cem—cemetery OH-6
**Dana Center**—pop pl MA-1
Dana Centre MA-1
Dana Ch—church NH-1
Dana Coll—school NE-7
Dana Coulee—valley MT-8
Dana Cove—bay CA-9
Dana Cove—bay TX-5
Dana Fork—stream CA-9
Dana Glacier—glacier WA-9
Dana Gray Sch—school CA-9
Dana Hall Sch—school MA-1
Dana Heights—summit PA-2
Danaher—locale MI-6
Danaher, Mount—summit CA-9
Danaher Creek—stream MI-6
Danaher Creek—stream MT-8
Danaher Guard Station—locale MT-8
Danaher Hahn Creek Trail—trail MT-8
Danaher Lake—reservoir MI-6
Danaher Meadows—flat MT-8
Danaher Mtn—summit MT-8
Dana Hill—summit MA-1
Dana Hill—summit NY-2
Dana Hill—summit (3) VT-1
**Dana Hills**—pop pl TN-4
Dana (historical)—civil MA-1
Dana Island—island OH-6
Dana JHS—school (2) CA-9
Dana Junction IN-6
**Danak**—pop pl MI-6
Dana Lake—lake CA-9
Dana Lake—lake IL-6
Dana Lake—lake MI-6
Dan Allens Shoals—bar TN-4
Dana Meadows—flat CA-9
Dana Meadows—flat WY-8
Dana Meeting House—hist pl NH-1
Dana Memorial Park—park PA-2
Dan and Hannah McLean Graves—cemetery TX-5
Dana-Palmer House—hist pl MA-1
Dana Park—park CA-9
Dana park—park MA-1
Dana Passage—channel WA-9
Dana Peak—summit AK-9
Dana Peak—summit TX-5
Dana Plateau—plain CA-9
Dana Point—cape CA-9
**Dana Point**—pop pl CA-9
Dana Point Harbor—harbor CA-9
Dana Pond WI-6
Dana Ranch—locale (2) CA-9
Dana Ranch—locale MT-8
Dana Ridge—ridge WY-8
Danas Bar—bar MT-8
Danascara Creek—stream NY-2
Dana Sch—school (2) CA-9
Dana Sch—school NC-3
Dana Sch—school OH-6
Dana Slough—gut CA-9
Dana South Fork CA-9
Dana Spring—spring MT-8
Dana Spring—spring NV-8
Dana Springs Creek—stream WY-8
Danas Run—stream OH-6
**Dana (sta.) (Wabash River Ordnance Works)**—pop pl IN-6
Danas Trailer Ranch—locale AZ-5
Dan Baker Cove—cove MA-1
Dan Barr Hollow—valley PA-2
Dan Bay—bay AK-9
Dan Bay—bay LA-4
Dan Beard, Mount—summit AK-9
Dan Beard Trail Camp—locale NM-5
Dan Bias Sch—school WV-2
Dan Bland Bay—swamp GA-3
Dan Blough Cove—bay CA-9
Dan Blough Creek—stream CA-9
**Danboro**—pop pl PA-2
Danboro Post Office (historical)—building PA-2
Danborough PA-2
Danbow Creek—stream KY-4
Dan Bowling Sch—school KY-4
Dan Branch—stream KY-4
Dan Branch—stream LA-4
Dan Branch—stream MO-7
Dan Branch—stream (4) TN-4
Dan Branch—stream TX-5
Dan Branch—stream VA-3
Dan Branch—stream WV-2
Dan Brewers Mountain ME-1
Dan Brook—stream NY-2
**Danbrooke Park (subdivision)**—pop pl NC-3
Danbrook Sch—school CA-9
Danburg—locale GA-3
Danburg Beach—beach CA-9
Danburg Sch—school GA-3
**Danbury**—pop pl CT-1
**Danbury**—pop pl IA-7
**Danbury**—pop pl NE-7
**Danbury**—pop pl NH-1
**Danbury**—pop pl NC-3
**Danbury**—pop pl OH-6
**Danbury**—pop pl TX-5
**Danbury**—pop pl WI-6
Danbury Bay—bay CT-1
Danbury Cem—cemetery IA-7
Danbury Cem—cemetery WI-6
Danbury Ch—church NC-3
Danbury Creek—stream NC-3
Danbury Dam—dam WI-6
Danbury Dome Oil Field—oilfield TX-5
Danbury Fairgrounds—locale CT-1
**Danbury Forest**—pop pl VA-3
Danbury Hist Dist—hist pl NC-3
Danbury Hosp—hospital CT-1
Danbury HS—school CT-1
**Danbury Lane Condominium**—pop pl UT-8
Danbury Lookout Tower—locale WI-6
Danbury-Marion Cem—cemetery NE-7
**Danbury Quarter**—pop pl CT-1
Danbury Quarter Cem—cemetery CT-1
Danbury (Town of)—civ div CT-1
**Danbury (Town of)**—pop pl NH-1
Danbury Town Park—park CT-1
**Danbury Township**—pop pl ND-7
Danbury (Township of)—fmr MCD NC-3
**Danbury (Township of)**—pop pl OH-6
Danby—locale CA-9
Danby—locale KY-4
**Danby**—pop pl MO-7
**Danby**—pop pl NY-2
**Danby**—pop pl VT-1
Danby Cem—cemetery MI-6
**Danby Corners (Danby Four Corners)**—pop pl VT-1
Danby Creek—stream NY-2
**Danby Four Corners**—pop pl VT-1
Danby Hill—summit VT-1
Danby (historical)—locale KS-7
Danby Lake—lake CA-9
Danby Park—flat SD-7
Danby Pond—lake VT-1
Danby Ridge—ridge ID-8
Danby Rural Cem—cemetery NY-2
Danby Sch—school NY-2
Danbys Mill (historical)—locale AL-4
Danby State For—forest NY-2
**Danby (Town of)**—pop pl NY-2
**Danby (Town of)**—pop pl VT-1
**Danby (Township of)**—pop pl MI-6
Danby Village Hist Dist—hist pl VT-1
Dan Casey Slough—stream CA-9
Dan Cauthorn Ranch—locale TX-5
Dan Cave—cave AL-4
Dance Bay—bay NC-3
Dance Bayou—stream TX-5
Dance Branch—stream AL-4
Dance Branch—stream GA-3
Dance Branch—stream TN-4
Dance Cave—cave TN-4
Dance Cem—cemetery TN-4
Dance Creek ND-7
Dance Creek VA-3
Dance Creek—stream OK-5
Danceground Cem—cemetery KS-7
Dancehall Flats—flat WY-8
Dance Hall Rock—pillar UT-8
Dance Hall Rock (historical)—locale UT-8
Dancehall Spring—spring UT-8
Dancehall Spring—spring WY-8
Dance Hollow TN-4
Dance Nichols Cem—cemetery KY-4
Dancer Branch—stream TN-4
Dancer Cem—cemetery TX-5
Dancer Flats—flat TX-5
Dancer Peak—summit TX-5
Dancer Ranch—locale (2) NE-7
Dance Tank—reservoir (2) AZ-5
Danceyard Creek—stream MO-7
Dancey Branch—stream KY-4
Dancey Flat—flat FL-3
Dancey Point—cape FL-3
Danceys FL-3
**Danceys Corner**—pop pl NJ-2
Danceys Flat FL-3
Danceys Point FL-3
Dan Charles Pond—lake ME-1
**Danci**—pop pl TX-5
**Danciger**—pop pl TX-5
Dancing Branch—stream NC-3
Dancing Branch Post Office (historical)—building TN-4
Dancing Creek MT-8
Dancing Creek—stream TN-4
Dancing Creek—stream (2) VA-3
Dancing Creek Overlook—locale VA-3
Dancing Fern Cave—cave TN-4
Dancing Gap—gap TN-4
Dancing Lady Lake—lake WA-9
Dancing Marsh—swamp VA-3
Dancing Point—cape VA-3
Dancing Rabbit Creek—stream (2) MS-4
Dancing Rabbit Creek—stream (2) OK-5
Dancing Rabbit Creek Treaty Site—hist pl MS-4
Dancing Rabbit Springs—spring MS-4
Dancing Ridge—ridge PA-2
Dancing Ridge Lookout—tower PA-2
Dancing Ridge Run—stream PA-2
Dancing Rocks—pillar AZ-5
Dan Clayton Pond Dam—dam MS-4
Dan Cold Spring—spring OR-9
Dan Cole Spring OR-9
Dan Cook Canyon—valley CA-9
Dan Covey Butte—summit CA-9
Dan Creek—stream (4) AK-9
Dan Creek—stream (2) ID-8
Dan Creek—stream TX-5
Dan Creek—stream WA-9
Dan Creek Camp—locale AK-9
**Dancy**—pop pl AL-4
**Dancy**—pop pl MS-4
**Dancy**—pop pl WI-6
Dancy, Col. Francis, House—hist pl AL-4
Dancy Cem—cemetery AL-4
Dancy Ch—church AL-4
Dancy Chapel—church AL-4
Dancy Memorial Cem—cemetery NC-3
Dancy Mtn—summit NC-3
Dancy Point—cape FL-3
Dancy Post Office (historical)—building MS-4
Dancy Quarters—locale AL-4
**Dancyville**—pop pl (2) TN-4
Dancyville Cem—cemetery TN-4
Dancyville Post Office (historical)—building TN-4
Dancyville Sch (historical)—school TN-4
Dandan—area GU-9
Dandan—slope MH-9
Dandan, Laderan—cliff MH-9
Dandan, Puntan—cape MH-9
Dandan, Sabanan—slope MH-9
Dandan, Unai—beach MH-9
Dandan Beach MH-9
Dandan Cliffs MH-9
Dan Day Hollow—valley PA-2
Dan Day Rsvr—reservoir UT-8
D And B Airpark Airp—airport WA-9
Dandee Mine—mine NM-5
Dandelion Canal—canal CA-9
Dandelion Creek—stream OR-9
Dandelion Flat—flat (3) UT-8
Dandelion Hollow—valley OH-6
Danden WV-2
Dandenai AR-4
D and GW Ditch—canal NV-8
D and H Green Ridge Bridge—bridge PA-2
Dan Dick Creek—stream MN-6
D and J Farms Lake—reservoir NC-3
D and J Farms Lake Dam—dam NC-3
**D and K Mobile Home Park**—pop pl DE-2
D and M Junction—locale PA-2
D and M Warehousing Units 1-3—locale UT-8
D and R Airp—airport IN-6
Dan Draw—valley WY-8
Dandrea—locale AZ-5
Dandrea Spring—spring AZ-5
**Dandridge**—pop pl TN-4
Dandridge (CCD)—cens area TN-4
Dandridge City Hall—building TN-4
Dandridge Division—civil TN-4
Dandridge Dock—locale TN-4
Dandridge Elem Sch—school TN-4
Dandridge Golf and Country Club—locale TN-4
Dandridge Hist Dist—hist pl TN-4
Dandridge Hist Dist—locale TN-4
Dandridge Municipal Park—park TN-4
Dandridge Post Office—building TN-4
Dandron Highway—channel MI-6
D and Winter Park—park OR-9
D and W Mine—mine CA-9
Dandy—locale VA-3
Dandy Creek—stream MI-6
Dandy Creek—stream WA-9
Dandy Creek—stream WI-6
Dandy Creek Flowage—reservoir WI-6
Dandy Crossing (inundated)—locale UT-8
Dandy Gulch—valley AK-9
Dandy Lake—lake ID-8
Dandy Mine—mine AZ-5
Dandy Mine—mine ID-8
Dandy Mine—mine (2) MT-8
Dandy Mine, The—mine MT-8
Dandy Pass—gap WA-9
Dandy Point—cape VA-3
Dandy Tank—reservoir AZ-5
Dandy Wire Spring—spring AZ-5
D and Z Ramp Station—locale PA-2
Dane—locale OK-5
**Dane**—pop pl WI-6
Dan East Cabin (Site)—locale CA-9
Dan East Creek—stream CA-9
Dan East Trail—trail CA-9
Danebo—locale OR-9
Danebod—hist pl MN-6
Danebod Cem—cemetery MN-6
**Daneborg Estates Subdivision**—pop pl UT-8
Danebo Sch—school OR-9
Dane Brook—stream ME-1
Dane Canyon—valley AZ-5
Dane Cem—cemetery IA-7
Dane Cem—cemetery KS-7
Dane Ch—church NE-7
Dane Ch—church SD-7
Dane Corner—locale ME-1
Dane Coulee—valley MT-8
**Dane (County)**—pop pl WI-6
Dane County Regional Airp (Truax Field)—airport WI-6
Dane Creek—stream NE-7
Danefield Sch—school SD-7
Danefield School Number 51 SD-7
Danefield Seventh Day Advent Cem—cemetery SD-7
**Dane (historical)**—pop pl MS-4
Daneilson Airpstrip—airport OR-9
Daneka Lake—lake AK-9
Dane Lake—lake MI-6
Dane Lake—lake (2) MN-6
Dane Lake—lake TX-5
Dane Lakebed—flat MN-6
Danella Park—park MS-4
Danelle Plaza Shop Ctr—locale AZ-5
Dan Emmett Sch—school OH-6
Dan Emmett (Township of)—other OH-6
Danenman Point—cape FL-3
Dane Prairie (Township of)—civ div MN-6
Dane Ridge—ridge AZ-5
**Danes**—pop pl IN-6
Danes Corners—locale NY-2
Danes Dam—dam AZ-5
**Danese**—pop pl WV-2
Danese Sch—school WV-2
Danes Hall—hist pl WI-6
Danes Mills KS-7
Dane Spring—spring AZ-5
Dane Spring—spring UT-8
Dane Street Beach—beach MA-1
Danesville—locale MN-6
Dane Tank—reservoir AZ-5
**Dane (Town of)**—pop pl WI-6
Dane Valley—basin NE-7
**Danevang**—pop pl TX-5
Danevang Ch—church TX-5
Danevang Sch—school TX-5
Daneville ND-7
Daneville SD-7
Daneville (historical)—locale SD-7
Daneville Sch—school WI-6
**Daneville Township**—pop pl ND-7
**Daneville Township**—pop pl SD-7
Daneville Township (historical)—civil SD-7
Daneville Valley—valley WI-6
Danewood Cem—cemetery MN-6
Danewood Creek—stream OR-9
Daney Canyon—valley CA-9
Daney Canyon—valley NV-8
Daney Mine—mine NV-8
Daney Point—cape NY-2
Daneys Chapel AL-4
**Danfield Acres (subdivision)**—pop pl DE-2
Danfield Creek—stream CA-9
Danfield Ridge—ridge CA-9
Danford TN-4
Danford, Samuel, Farm, Church and Cemetery—hist pl OH-6
Danford Bay—swamp FL-3
Danford Branch SC-3
Danford Branch—stream SC-3
Danford Canyon—valley CA-9
Danford Cem—cemetery (2) OH-6
Danford Cove—bay ME-1
Danford Post Office (historical)—building TN-4
Danforth—locale IA-7
Danforth—locale MS-4
Danforth—locale MO-7
Danforth—locale SD-7
**Danforth**—pop pl IL-6
**Danforth**—pop pl ME-1
Danforth Brook—stream (3) MA-1
Danforth Brook—stream NH-1
Danforth Cem—cemetery IL-6
Danforth Cem—cemetery (2) ME-1
Danforth Cem—cemetery MN-6
Danforth Cem—cemetery TX-5
Danforth Ch—church MO-7
Danforth Cove ME-1
Danforth Creek—stream FL-3
Danforth Ditch—canal OR-9
Danforth Falls—falls MA-1
Danforth Hill—summit ME-1
Danforth Hills—range CO-8
Danforth (historical)—locale SD-7
Danforth (historical P.O.)—locale IA-7
Danforth Memorial Library—hist pl NJ-2
Danforth Ponds—lake NH-1
Danforths Brook MA-1
Danforth Sch—school MN-6
Danforth Sch—school NY-2
Danforth Sch—school TX-5
Danforth Sch (abandoned)—school MO-7
Danforth Spring—spring CO-8
**Danforth (Town of)**—pop pl ME-1
**Danforth (Township of)**—pop pl IL-6
**Danforth (Township of)**—pop pl MN-6
Danforts Chapel—church MS-4
**Dan (Friedaland)**—pop pl KY-4
Danga Lake—reservoir NC-3
Danga Lake Dam—dam NC-3
Dan Gap—gap (2) GA-3
Dan Gap—gap NC-3
Dangberg Camp—locale CA-9
Dangel Oil Field—oilfield TX-5
Dan George Lake—lake FL-3
Danger Bay—bay OR-9
Danger Branch—stream KY-4
Danger Cave—cave AL-4
Danger Cave—cave UT-8
Danger Cave—hist pl UT-8
Danger Cave State Historical Monmt—park UT-8
Danger Creek—stream AK-9
Danger Creek—stream CA-9
Dangerfield MA-1
Danger Island—island (3) AK-9
Dangerous Branch—stream MO-7
Dangerous Cape—cape (2) AK-9
Dangerous Cape Reef—bay AK-9
Dangerous Park—park NM-5
Dangerous Park Canyon—valley NM-5
Dangerous Passage—channel AK-9
Dangerous River—stream AK-9
Dangerous Shoals AL-4
Danger Pass—gap AK-9
Danger Passage—channel AK-9
Danger Point—cape (3) AK-9
Danger Point—cape VA-3
Danger Point—cliff CA-9
Danger Point—cliff NV-8
Danger Point—cliff WA-9
Danger Point Reef—bar AK-9
Danger Reef—bar AK-9
Danger Rock—bar WA-9
Danger Run—stream WV-2
Danger Shoal—bar WA-9
Danger Slit—cave TN-4
Danger Spring—spring AZ-5
Danger Wash—stream AZ-5
Dan Gillam Hollow—valley KY-4
Dangkolo, Unai—beach MH-9
Dangkolo, Unai—slope MH-9
Dangkulo MH-9
Dangling Rope Canyon—valley UT-8
Dangling Rope Marina Site—locale UT-8
Dang Post Office (historical)—building TN-4
Dan Green Slough—lake IA-7
Dan Green Slough State Game Mngmt Area—park IA-7
Dan Hall Branch—stream KY-4
Danhauser Reservoir CA-9
Dan Henry Spring—spring AR-4
Dan Hill—summit TX-5
Dan Hill Brook—stream (2) ME-1
Dan (historical)—locale AL-4
Dan (historical P.O.)—locale IA-7
Dan Hole Pond—lake NH-1
Dan Hole River—stream NH-1
Dan Holland Creek—stream NC-3
Dan Hollow—valley AR-4
Dan Hollow—valley (3) TN-4
Dan Hough Mine—mine UT-8
Dan House Prairie—flat FL-3
Dan Hunt Meadows—flat CA-9
Dan Hunt Mtn—summit CA-9
**Dania**—pop pl FL-3
Dania Bridge—bridge FL-3
Dania Cem—cemetery MN-6
Dania Cut-Off Canal—canal FL-3
Dania Elem Sch—school FL-3
Dania Hall—hist pl MN-6
Dania Heights Baptist Ch—church FL-3
Dania Heights Ch—church FL-3
Dania Ind Res—other FL-3
Danials, Bayou—stream LA-4
Danials-Davis Dam—dam NC-3
Danialson Island NE-7
Dania Shopping Plaza—locale FL-3
Dania Sound FL-3
Dania Town Canal—canal FL-3
Daniel MD-2
Daniel UT-8
Daniel—locale GA-3
Daniel—locale MS-4
Daniel—locale VA-3
**Daniel**—pop pl MD-2
**Daniel**—pop pl MS-4
**Daniel**—pop pl TX-5
**Daniel**—pop pl UT-8
**Daniel**—pop pl WY-8
Daniel, Benjamin, House—hist pl KY-4
Daniel, Dr. James W., House—hist pl GA-3
Daniel, James and Cunningham, House—hist pl GA-3
Daniel, J. M., House—hist pl NE-7
Daniel, J. M., School-District #3—hist pl NE-7
Daniel, J. M. and Emily, House—hist pl TX-5
Daniel, Lake—reservoir TX-5
Daniel, Mount—summit WA-9
Daniel Arthur Rehabilitation Center TN-4
Daniel Band Ch—church MI-6
Daniel Baptist Ch—church MS-4
Daniel Bay—swamp MS-4
Daniel-Belview Sch—school TX-5
Daniel Boone—locale KY-4
**Daniel Boone (Albert)**—pop pl VA-3
Daniel Boone Bridge—other MO-7
Daniel Boone Camp—locale NC-3
Daniel Boone Cave—cave KY-4
Daniel Boone Home—building MO-7
Daniel Boone Homestead—building PA-2
Daniel Boone Hotel—hist pl NC-3
Daniel Boone Hotel—hist pl WV-2
Daniel Boone HS—school TN-4
Daniel Boone Lake—reservoir MO-7
Daniel Boone Lake—reservoir PA-2
Daniel Boone Memorial State For—forest MO-7
Daniel Boone Monument—other MO-7
Daniel Boone Natl For—forest KY-4
Daniel Boones Cave—cave KY-4
Daniel Boone Sch—school CA-9
Daniel Boone Sch—school IL-6
Daniel Boone Sch—school KY-4
Daniel Boone Sch—school MO-7
Daniel Boone Scout Trail—trail NC-3
Daniel Boone State Park—park NC-3
Daniel Boone Theater—locale NC-3
Daniel Boone Trail—trail VA-3
Daniel Boone Wildlife Mngmt Area—park NC-3
Daniel Branch—stream AL-4
Daniel Branch—stream (3) KY-4
Daniel Branch—stream LA-4
Daniel Branch—stream MS-4
Daniel Branch—stream SC-3
Daniel Branch—stream (2) TN-4
Daniel Branch—stream TX-5
Daniel Branch—stream VA-3
Daniel Branch—stream WV-2
Daniel Bridge—bridge GA-3
Daniel Broc Ch—church MI-6
Daniel-Caldwell Cem—cemetery AL-4
Daniel Camp Gap—gap GA-3
Daniel Cave—cave AL-4
Daniel Cave—cave (2) TN-4
Daniel Caves—cave MO-7
Daniel Cem TN-4
Daniel Cem—cemetery (2) AL-4
Daniel Cem—cemetery AR-4
Daniel Cem—cemetery (4) GA-3
Daniel Cem—cemetery IN-6
Daniel Cem—cemetery KY-4
Daniel Cem—cemetery MS-4
Daniel Cem—cemetery (4) TN-4
Daniel Cem—cemetery WV-2
Daniel Ch—church AL-4
Daniel Chapel TX-5
Daniel Chapel—church AL-4
Daniel Church MS-4
Daniel Clarke Grant—civil FL-3
Daniel C Lincoln Elem Sch—school AZ-5
Daniel Corner—locale VA-3
Daniel Creek MT-8
Daniel Creek TX-5
Daniel Creek—stream AL-4
Daniel Creek—stream (2) GA-3
Daniel Creek—stream IN-6
Daniel Creek—stream MS-4
Daniel Creek—stream OR-9
Daniel Creek—stream (2) TN-4
Daniel Creek—stream TX-5
Daniel Creek—stream WY-8
Daniel Creek Mine (underground)—mine AL-4
Daniel Creek Public Use Area—park AL-4
**Danieldale**—pop pl TX-5
Daniel D Bray Lake—reservoir IN-6
Daniel D Bray Lake Dam—dam IN-6
Daniel Flat—flat UT-8
Daniel Gap—gap AL-4
Daniel Grindstone Butte—summit WY-8
Daniel Grove Cem—cemetery KY-4
Daniel Grove Ch—church (5) GA-3
Daniel Hale Williams Elem Sch—school IN-6
Daniel Hill—summit TN-4
Daniel (historical)—building MO-7
Daniel Hole Branch—stream SC-3
Daniel Hollow—valley (7) TN-4
Daniel Hollow—valley WV-2
Daniel HS—school MS-4
Daniel Huegel Ditch—canal IN-6
Daniel Island MP-9
Daniel Island—island NJ-2
Daniel Island—island SC-3
Daniel Island—island VA-3
Daniel Island Bend—bend SC-3
Daniel Islands MP-9
Daniel J Flood Elem Sch—school PA-2
Daniel Junction—locale WY-8
Daniel Lake MN-6
Daniel Lake—lake LA-4
Daniel Lake—lake MN-6
Daniel Lake—reservoir MS-4
Daniel Landing—locale GA-3
Daniel Lateral—canal AZ-5
Daniell Cem—cemetery MS-4
Daniell Sch—school WV-2
Daniells Well—well AZ-5
Daniel Lumber Company Lake—reservoir NC-3
Daniel Lumber Company Lake Dam—dam NC-3
Daniel Memorial Baptist Ch—church MS-4
Daniel Memorial Childrens Home—building TX-5
Daniel M Pounds Cemetery MS-4
Daniel Mtn—summit NY-2
Daniel Pratt Cem—cemetery AL-4
Daniel Pratt Hist Dist—hist pl AL-4
Daniel Ranch—locale TX-5
Daniel Ridge—ridge NC-3
Daniel Ridge—ridge WV-2
Daniel Ridge Creek—stream NC-3
Daniel Run—stream KY-4
Daniel Run—stream VA-3
Daniels—locale GA-3
Daniels—locale ID-8
Daniels—locale NC-3
Daniels—locale (2) TX-5
**Daniels**—pop pl (2) MD-2
**Daniels**—pop pl NC-3
**Daniels**—pop pl UT-8
**Daniels**—pop pl WV-2
Daniels, Blake, Cottage—hist pl MA-1
Daniels, Charles, House—hist pl CT-1
Daniels, Charles A., Sch—hist pl MA-1
Daniels, Frederick, House—hist pl MA-1
Daniels, Josephus, House—hist pl NC-3
Daniels, Mount—summit MA-1
Daniels, O. J., House—hist pl ID-8
Daniels Acad—school NH-1
Daniels and Fisher Tower—hist pl CO-8
Daniels Arroyo—valley AZ-5
Daniels Band Ch—church MI-6
Daniels Branch—stream FL-3
Daniels Branch—stream GA-3
Daniels Branch—stream (7) KY-4
Daniels Branch—stream NJ-2
Daniels Branch—stream NC-3
Daniels Branch—stream VA-3
Daniels Bridge—locale NJ-2
Daniels Brook—stream CT-1
Daniels Brook—stream MA-1
Daniels Brook—stream NH-1
Daniels Camp Canyon—valley AZ-5
Daniels Canyon—valley (4) UT-8
Daniels Cem—cemetery AL-4
Daniels Cem—cemetery AR-4
Daniels Cem—cemetery FL-3
Daniels Cem—cemetery (4) GA-3
Daniels Cem—cemetery IL-6
Daniels Cem—cemetery (2) KY-4
Daniels Cem—cemetery MI-6

Daniels Cem—*cemetery* ....MS-4
Daniels Cem—*cemetery* ....MO-7
Daniels Cem—*cemetery* ....NH-1
Daniels Cem—*cemetery* ....NY-2
Daniels Cem—*cemetery* ....NC-3
Daniels Cem—*cemetery* ....OH-6
Daniels Cem—*cemetery* ....SC-3
Daniels Cem—*cemetery* (5) ....TN-4
Daniels Cem—*cemetery* ....TX-5
Daniels Cem—*cemetery* ....VA-3
Daniels Cem—*cemetery* ....WV-2
Daniels Ch—*church* ....PA-2
Daniel Sch—*school* ....IL-6
Daniels Chapel—*church* (2) ....AL-4
Daniels Chapel—*church* (2) ....AR-4
Daniels Chapel—*church* (2) ....MS-4
Daniels Chapel—*church* (3) ....NC-3
Daniels Chapel—*church* (2) ....TX-5
Daniels Chapel—*locale* ....TX-5
*Daniels Chapel Baptist Ch* ....AL-4
Daniels Chapel Cem—*cemetery* ....AL-4
Daniels Chapel Sch (historical)—*school* (2) ....TN-4
Daniel Sch (historical)—*school* ....AL-4
Daniel Sch (historical)—*school* (2) ....MS-4
Daniel Sch (historical)—*school* ....TN-4
Daniels Cove—*valley* ....NC-3
Daniels Cow Camp—*locale* ....MT-8
*Daniels Creek* ....AL-4
*Daniels Creek* ....TN-4
Daniels Creek—*stream* (2) ....AK-9
Daniels Creek—*stream* ....AR-4
Daniels Creek—*stream* (2) ....CA-9
Daniels Creek—*stream* ....GA-3
Daniels Creek—*stream* ....ID-8
Daniels Creek—*stream* (4) ....KY-4
Daniels Creek—*stream* ....MS-4
Daniels Creek—*stream* ....MT-8
Daniels Creek—*stream* ....NC-3
Daniels Creek—*stream* (3) ....OR-9
Daniels Creek—*stream* (3) ....TX-5
Daniels Creek—*stream* (2) ....UT-8
Daniels Creek—*stream* ....VA-3
Daniels Creek—*stream* ....WA-9
Daniels Creek—*stream* ....WV-2
Daniels Creek—*stream* (2) ....WY-8
**Daniels Creek (Odds)**—*pop pl* ....KY-4
Daniels Creek Sch—*school* (2) ....KY-4
Daniels Creek Shoal (historical)—*bar* ....AL-4
Daniels Cut—*channel* ....LA-4
Daniels Dam—*dam* ....ID-8
Daniels Ditch—*canal* ....IN-6
Daniels Ditch—*stream* ....TX-5
Daniels Farm Cem—*cemetery* ....CT-1
Daniels Farm Sch—*school* ....CT-1
Daniels Field—*airport* ....OR-9
Daniels Field—*locale* ....CA-9
Daniels Fork—*stream* ....KY-4
Daniels Gap—*gap* ....AL-4
Daniels Gap—*gap* ....NC-3
Daniels Gift Cem—*cemetery* ....GA-3
Daniels Gulch—*valley* ....AZ-5
Daniels Hill—*summit* ....CO-8
Daniels Hill—*summit* ....MA-1
Daniel's Hill Hist Dist—*hist pl* ....VA-3
Daniels (historical P.O.)—*locale* ....AL-4
Daniel Shoals—*bar* ....GA-3
Daniels Hollow—*valley* ....TN-4
Daniels House—*hist pl* ....AR-4
*Daniels Island* ....ME-1
*Daniels Island* ....SC-3
Daniels Island—*cape* ....MA-1
Daniels Island—*island* ....ME-1
Daniels JHS—*school* ....NC-3
*Daniels Lake* ....IN-6
Daniels Lake—*lake* ....AK-9
Daniels Lake—*lake* ....MN-6
Daniels Lake—*lake* ....NH-1
Daniels Lake—*lake* ....TX-5
Daniels Lake—*reservoir* ....NC-3
Daniels Lake—*reservoir* ....TN-4
Daniels Lake—*swamp* ....FL-3
Daniels Lake Dam—*dam* ....NC-3
Daniels Lake Dam—*dam* ....TN-4
Daniels Landing—*locale* ....TN-4
Daniels Landing Post Office (historical)—*building* ....TN-4
Daniels Memorial Ch—*church* ....NC-3
Daniels Mill—*hist pl* ....MD-2
Daniels Mill—*locale* ....VA-3
Daniels Mill Branch—*stream* ....AL-4
Daniels Mill Creek—*stream* ....GA-3
Daniels Mill (historical)—*locale* (3) ....AL-4
Daniels Mill (historical)—*locale* ....TN-4
Daniels Millpond—*reservoir* ....GA-3
Daniels Mine—*mine* ....AZ-5
Daniels Mtn—*summit* ....AR-4
Daniels Mtn—*summit* ....NH-1
Daniels Mtn—*summit* ....VA-3
Daniels North—*cens area* ....MT-8
Daniels Notch—*gap* ....VT-1
Danielson—*locale* ....CA-9
**Danielson**—*pop pl* ....CT-1
**Danielson**—*pop pl* ....MI-6
Danielson Basin—*basin* ....ID-8
Danielson Creek—*stream* ....ID-8
Danielson Dam—*dam* ....ND-7
Danielson Ditch—*canal* ....IN-6
Danielson Island—*island* ....NE-7
*Danielson Lake* ....OK-5
Danielson Lake—*reservoir* ....OK-5
Danielson Lateral—*canal* ....WI-6
Danielson Pond—*lake* ....MA-1
Danielson Ranch—*locale* ....MT-8
**Danielson (Township of)**—*pop pl* ....MN-6
*Danielsonville* ....CT-1
Daniels Park—*park* ....CO-8
Daniels Park—*park* ....IA-7
Daniels Park—*park* ....MO-7
Daniels Park—*park* ....OH-6
**Daniels Park**—*pop pl* ....MD-2
Daniels Pass—*gap* (2) ....UT-8
Daniels Peak—*summit* ....MA-1
*Daniels Point* ....FL-3
Daniels Point—*cape* ....AR-4
Daniels Point—*cape* ....FL-3
Daniels Point—*cape* ....MT-8
Daniels Point—*cape* ....NC-3
Daniels Point—*cape* ....WI-6
Daniels Point Landing—*locale* ....TN-4
Daniels Point Revetment—*levee* ....TN-4
*Daniels Pond* ....MA-1
Daniels Pond—*lake* (2) ....GA-3
Daniels Pond—*lake* ....TX-5
Daniels Pond—*lake* ....VT-1
Daniels Pond—*reservoir* (2) ....GA-3
Daniels Prairie—*area* ....AL-4
Daniel Spring—*spring* (2) ....AL-4
Daniel Spring—*spring* (3) ....OR-9
Daniel Spring—*spring* (2) ....TN-4
Daniel Springs—*locale* ....GA-3
Daniel Springs—*spring* ....FL-3
Daniel Springs—*spring* ....GA-3
Daniels Ranch—*locale* (3) ....MT-8
Daniels Ranch—*locale* ....NE-7
Daniels Ranch—*locale* (2) ....NM-5
Daniels Ranch—*locale* ....UT-8
Daniels Ranch (historical)—*locale* ....UT-8
Daniels Reed Brake—*stream* ....MS-4
**Daniels-Rhyne**—*pop pl* ....NC-3
Daniels Ridge—*ridge* ....KY-4
Daniels Ridge—*ridge* ....WV-2
Daniels Rsvr—*reservoir* ....ID-8
Daniels Run—*stream* ....OK-5
Daniels Run—*stream* ....PA-2
Daniels Run—*stream* (2) ....VA-3
Daniels Run—*stream* (4) ....WV-2
Daniels Run Sch—*school* ....WV-2
Daniels Sch—*school* ....AR-4
Daniels Sch—*school* (2) ....CO-8
Daniels Sch—*school* ....IL-6
Daniels Sch—*school* ....MA-1
Daniels Sch—*school* ....NY-2
Daniels Sch—*school* ....SC-3
Daniels Sch—*school* ....TX-5
Daniels Sch—*school* ....VA-3
Daniels Sch (abandoned)—*school* ....MO-7
Daniels Sch (historical)—*school* ....PA-2
Daniels School (abandoned)—*locale* ....CA-9
Daniels Sinkhole—*basin* ....MO-7
Daniels Spring—*spring* ....AZ-5
Daniels Tank—*reservoir* ....AZ-5
Danielstown—*locale* ....NY-2
**Daniels (Town of)**—*pop pl* ....WI-6
**Daniels Tract**—*pop pl* ....DE-2
Daniels Trail—*trail* ....UT-8
Daniel Street Sch—*school* ....NY-2
*Daniels Villa* ....AL-4
Daniel's Village Archeol Site—*hist pl* ....CT-1
*Danielsville* ....UT-8
Danielsville—*locale* ....MT-8
**Danielsville**—*pop pl* ....AL-4
**Danielsville**—*pop pl* ....GA-3
**Danielsville**—*pop pl* ....PA-2
Danielsville (CCD)—*cens area* ....GA-3
Danielsville Ch—*church* ....AL-4
Danielsville Sch (historical)—*school* ....AL-4
Daniel Swash—*bay* ....NC-3
Daniels Well—*locale* ....NM-5
Danieltown—*locale* ....VA-3
**Danieltown**—*pop pl* ....NC-3
Daniel Wash—*stream* ....NM-5
Daniel Webster Birthplace—*building* ....NH-1
Daniel Webster Elem Sch—*school* (3) ....IN-6
Daniel Webster Historical Monmt—*pillar* ....VT-1
Daniel Webster Home for Children—*building* ....NH-1
Daniel Webster Inn—*building* ....MA-1
Daniel Webster JHS—*school* ....IL-6
Daniel Webster Mine—*mine* ....CA-9
Daniel Webster Sch—*school* ....CA-9
Daniel Webster Sch—*school* ....MA-1
Daniel Webster Sch—*school* ....PA-2
Daniel Webster Trail—*trail* ....NH-1
Daniel Wertz Elem Sch—*school* ....IN-6
Daniel Windmill—*locale* ....NM-5
Daniher Rsvr—*reservoir* ....CO-8
**Danipei**—*pop pl* ....FM-9
*Dani Ridge* ....CA-9
Danish Baptist Ch—*church* ....SD-7
Danish Bench—*bench* ....UT-8
Danish Canyon—*valley* ....ID-8
Danish Cem—*cemetery* ....IL-6
Danish Cem—*cemetery* ....IA-7
Danish Cem—*cemetery* (6) ....MN-6
Danish Cem—*cemetery* ....NE-7
Danish Cem—*cemetery* ....ND-7
Danish Cem—*cemetery* ....OR-9
Danish Cem—*cemetery* ....SD-7
Danish Cem—*cemetery* ....WA-9
Danish Cem—*cemetery* (3) ....WI-6
Danish Ch—*church* ....KS-7
Danish Ch—*church* (2) ....MI-6
Danish Ch—*church* ....ND-7
Danish Ch (historical)—*church* ....SD-7
Danish Creek—*stream* ....CA-9
Danish Field Creek—*stream* ....UT-8
Danish Flat—*flat* ....ID-8
Danish Flat—*flat* ....UT-8
Danish Hill—*summit* ....UT-8
**Danish Hills PUD Subdivision**—*pop pl* ....UT-8
Danish Hollow—*valley* ....AZ-5
Danish Hollow—*valley* ....UT-8
Danish Home for the Aged—*building* ....NY-2
Danish Knoll—*summit* (2) ....UT-8
**Danish Landing**—*pop pl* ....MI-6
Danish Legation Bldg—*building* ....DC-2
Danish Lutheran Ch (historical)—*church* ....SD-7
*Danish Lutheran Church* ....SD-7
Danish Meadows—*flat* ....UT-8
Danish Pass—*gap* ....ID-8
Danish Ranch—*locale* ....UT-8
Danish Rsvr—*reservoir* ....UT-8
Danish Sch—*school* ....IL-6
*Danish Trinity Lutheran Church* ....SD-7
Danish Wash—*valley* ....UT-8
Danish Wash Gas and Oil Field—*oilfield* ....UT-8
Danish West India and Guinea Company Warehouse—*hist pl* ....VI-3
Danisi Cem—*cemetery* ....SD-7
*Daniss Mountain* ....MD-2
*Daniss Rock* ....MD-2
Danite Mine—*mine* ....NV-8
Dan Jenkins Creek—*stream* ....TX-5
Dankel Chapel—*church* ....GA-3
Dankes Lake—*lake* ....WI-6
*Dankes Pond* ....MA-1
Dan Kirk Branch—*stream* ....TN-4
Dan Knob—*summit* (3) ....NC-3
Dan Knob Ridge—*ridge* ....NC-3
**Dankowske Central Subdivision**—*pop pl* ....UT-8
Danks—*locale* ....LA-4
Danks Corner—*locale* ....FL-3
Danks JHS—*school* ....CA-9
Danks Pond—*lake* ....MA-1
Dankwardt Coulee—*valley* ....MN-6
Dankwardt Memorial Park—*cemetery* ....IA-7
Dankworth Canyon—*valley* ....NE-7
Dankworth Lake—*reservoir* ....AZ-5
*Dan Lake* ....WI-6
Dan Lake—*lake* ....ID-8
Dan Lake—*lake* ....MN-6
Danlboone Yard—*locale* ....VA-3
Dan Lee Creek—*stream* ....ID-8
Dan Lee Ridge—*ridge* ....ID-8
Dan Leigh Hollow—*valley* ....UT-8
*Danley* ....AL-4
Danley—*locale* ....IL-6
**Danley**—*pop pl* ....AL-4
Danley—*uninc pl* ....TN-4
Danley Branch—*stream* ....FL-3
Danley Branch—*stream* ....GA-3
Danley Canyon—*valley* ....NM-5
Danley Cem—*cemetery* ....GA-3
Danley Cem—*cemetery* ....MI-6
**Danley Corners**—*pop pl* ....NY-2
Danley Covered Bridge—*hist pl* ....PA-2
Danley Cross Roads Cem—*cemetery* ....AL-4
Danley Cross Roads Ch—*church* ....AL-4
Danley Estates Lake Dam—*dam* ....AL-4
Danley Hill—*summit* ....FL-3
Danley Park Lake—*reservoir* ....AL-4
Danley Pond—*lake* ....FL-3
**Danleys Crossroads**—*pop pl* ....AL-4
Danleys Mill Branch—*stream* ....AL-4
Danley Tank—*reservoir* (2) ....NM-5
Danleyton—*locale* ....KY-4
Danleyton Ch—*church* ....KY-4
Danleyton Sch—*school* ....KY-4
**Danleytown**—*pop pl* ....KY-4
Danley (Township of)—*fmr MCD* ....AR-4
Dan Little Brook—*stream* ....NH-1
Dan Maddox Dam—*dam* ....TN-4
Dan Maddox Fishing Lake—*reservoir* ....TN-4
Dan Maddox Fishing Lake Dam—*dam* ....TN-4
Dan Maddox Lake—*reservoir* ....TN-4
Dan Mahan Ditch—*canal* ....CO-8
Dan May Creek—*stream* ....FL-3
Dan McCarty MS—*school* ....FL-3
Dan Miller Sch (historical)—*school* ....AL-4
Dan Mini Sch—*school* ....CA-9
Dan Morgan Hollow—*valley* ....KY-4
Dan Morris Lake Dam—*dam* ....AL-4
Dan Mtn—*summit* ....GA-3
Dannart Corners—*locale* ....PA-2
Dannavang Cem—*cemetery* ....WI-6
Dannavang Ch—*church* ....WI-6
Dann Cem—*cemetery* ....MO-7
Dann Corner—*locale* ....NY-2
Dan Neal Spring—*spring* ....AZ-5
**Dannebrog**—*pop pl* ....NE-7
Danneel Sch Number 1—*school* ....LA-4
Danneel Sch Number 2—*school* ....LA-4
Danneffel Lake—*lake* ....MI-6
Dannel Chapel—*church* ....NC-3
Dannelly Field (airport)—*airport* ....AL-4
Dannelly Field (Airport)—*airport* ....AL-4
Dannelly Sch—*school* ....AL-4
**Dannemora**—*pop pl* ....NY-2
Dannemora Crossing—*locale* ....NY-2
Dannemora Mtn—*summit* ....NY-2
**Dannemora (Town of)**—*pop pl* ....NY-2
Danner—*locale* ....OR-9
Danner—*locale* ....TX-5
Danner Branch—*stream* ....TN-4
Danner Cem—*cemetery* (2) ....AL-4
Danner Cem—*cemetery* ....NC-3
Danner Creek—*stream* ....AL-4
Danner Creek—*stream* ....AR-4
Danner Ditch—*canal* ....IN-6
Danner-Fletcher House—*hist pl* ....WV-2
Danner Hill—*summit* ....KY-4
Danner Lake—*lake* ....AR-4
Danner Meadow—*flat* ....CA-9
Danners Cem—*cemetery* ....IN-6
*Danners Chapel* ....AL-4
*Danners Pond* ....PA-2
Danner Spring—*spring* ....NV-8
Dannersville—*locale* ....PA-2
Danner Valley—*valley* ....OR-9
*Dannerville* ....MO-7
**Dannevirke**—*pop pl* ....NE-7
Dannevirke Cem—*cemetery* ....NE-7
Dannhauser Rsvr—*reservoir* ....CA-9
**Dannich Estates (subdivision)**—*pop pl* ....UT-8
Dan Nicholas Lake—*reservoir* ....NC-3
Dan Nicholas Lake Dam—*dam* ....NC-3
Dan Nicholas Park—*park* ....NC-3
Dannie O'Connell Dam—*dam* ....SD-7
**Danniey Pines (subdivision)**—*pop pl* ....AL-4
Danns Spring—*spring* ....OR-9
Dann Valley—*flat* ....CA-9
Danny Austin Park—*park* ....MT-8
Danny Boy Spring—*spring* ....OR-9
Danny Burr Hollow—*valley* ....IN-6
Danny Creek—*stream* ....OR-9
Danny Davis Lake—*reservoir* ....AL-4
Danny Davis Lake Dam—*dam* ....AL-4
Danny Fulford Lake—*reservoir* ....AL-4
Danny Fulford Number 1 Dam—*dam* ....AL-4
Danny Fulford Number 2 Dam—*dam* ....AL-4
Danny Hole—*lake* ....FL-3
Danny O'Brien Gulch—*valley* ....MT-8
Dannys Lower Spring—*spring* ....AZ-5
Danny Walker Creek—*stream* ....WA-9
Dan Oak Dam—*dam* ....MS-4
**Danoby (historical)**—*pop pl* ....SD-7
Danoe Branch—*stream* ....AL-4
Dan O'Neal Lake Dam—*dam* ....MS-4
Danover Cem—*cemetery* ....MS-4
Dan Patch Mine—*mine* ....SD-7
Dan Payne Mtn—*summit* ....NC-3
Dan Post Office (historical)—*building* ....AL-4
Dan Price Creek—*stream* ....CA-9
Danquist Trail—*trail* ....ID-8
Dan Rice Creek—*stream* ....CA-9
Dan Ridge—*ridge* ....GA-3
Dan Ridge—*ridge* ....ID-8
Danripple—*locale* ....VA-3
Dan River—*stream* ....MO-7
Dan River—*stream* ....NC-3
Dan River—*stream* ....VA-3
Dan River Bethel Ch—*church* ....VA-3
Dan River Ch—*church* (3) ....NC-3
Dan River Ch—*church* (2) ....VA-3
Dan River HS—*school* ....VA-3
Dan River (Magisterial District)—*fmr MCD* (2) ....VA-3
Dan River Sch—*school* ....VA-3
**Dan River Shores**—*pop pl* ....NC-3
Dan River Textile Sch—*school* ....VA-3
Dan River (Township of)—*fmr MCD* ....NC-3
Dan River View Ch—*church* ....VA-3
*Danrlelle Gulch* ....OR-9
Dan Rsvr—*reservoir* ....MT-8
Dan Ryan Place—*locale* ....CA-9
Dan Ryan Woods—*woods* ....IL-6
**Dans**—*pop pl* ....MD-2
Dan Saddle—*gap* ....AZ-5
Dans Branch—*stream* (2) ....NC-3
Dans Branch—*stream* ....WV-2
Dans Bridge—*bridge* ....NJ-2
Dans Bridge Branch—*stream* ....NJ-2
Dansbury Reef—*bar* ....ME-1
**Dansby**—*pop pl* ....AR-4
Dansby Cem—*cemetery* ....AL-4
Dansby Cem—*cemetery* ....AR-4
Dansby Cem—*cemetery* ....TX-5
Dans Craw Cave—*cave* ....AL-4
*Dans Creek* ....NC-3
Dans Creek—*stream* ....CA-9
Dans Creek—*stream* ....NC-3
Dans Creek—*stream* (4) ....OR-9
Dans Creek—*stream* ....WY-8
Dans Creek Sch—*school* ....SC-3
Dansereau House—*hist pl* ....LA-4
Dans Fork—*stream* ....KY-4
Dans Gulch—*valley* ....WY-8
Dan S Hagood Lake—*reservoir* ....AL-4
Dan S Hagood Lake Dam—*dam* ....AL-4
Dan's Hill—*hist pl* ....VA-3
Dans Hole Spring—*spring* ....CO-8
Dans Hollow—*valley* ....UT-8
Dansie, George Henry, Farmstead—*hist pl* ....UT-8
Dansill Canyon—*valley* ....AZ-5
Dan Sill Creek—*stream* ....UT-8
Dan Sill Hill—*summit* ....UT-8
Dansil Spring—*spring* ....AZ-5
Dans Island—*island* ....AL-4
Danskammer Point—*cape* ....NY-2
Dansk Evangelical Lutheran Kirke—*hist pl* ....WI-6
Danskin Canal—*canal* ....ID-8
Danskin Creek—*stream* ....ID-8
Danskin Guard Station—*locale* ....ID-8
Danskin Lake—*lake* ....ID-8
Danskin Mtns—*range* ....ID-8
Danskin Peak—*summit* ....ID-8
Dans Lake—*lake* ....MN-6
Dan Slater Hollow—*valley* ....WV-2
Dan Slide—*bay* ....LA-4
*Dan's Mtn* ....MD-2
Dans Mtn—*summit* ....MD-2
Dans Nipple—*summit* ....WY-8
Danson Brook—*stream* ....MA-1
*Dansons Brook* ....MA-1
Dans Place—*locale* ....ID-8
*Dans Point* ....WI-6
Dans Point—*cape* ....MI-6
Dan Spring—*spring* ....ID-8
Dan Spring—*spring* ....UT-8
Dans Pulpit—*summit* ....PA-2
Dans Ridge—*ridge* ....LA-4
*Dan's Rock* ....MD-2
Dans Rock—*summit* ....MD-2
Dans Run—*locale* ....WV-2
Dans Run—*stream* ....PA-2
Dans Run—*stream* ....WV-2
Dans Spring—*spring* ....AZ-5
Dan Stevens—*flat* ....CA-9
Danstone Springs—*spring* ....AZ-5
Danstown—*locale* ....WV-2
Dan Sullivan Gulch—*valley* ....CA-9
**Dansville**—*pop pl* ....MI-6
**Dansville**—*pop pl* ....NY-2
Dansville Library—*hist pl* ....NY-2
Dansville Station—*locale* ....NY-2
**Dansville (Town of)**—*pop pl* ....NY-2
Dant—*locale* ....TX-5
**Dant**—*pop pl* ....OR-9
Dan Tank—*reservoir* (2) ....AZ-5
Dan Tank—*reservoir* ....TX-5
Dant (Dants Sta)—*locale* ....KY-4
*Dante* ....IN-6
**Dante**—*pop pl* ....SD-7
**Dante**—*pop pl* ....TN-4
**Dante**—*pop pl* ....VA-3
Dante, Lake—*reservoir* ....SD-7
Dante B Fassell Park—*park* ....FL-3
Dante Dale Sch (historical)—*school* ....TN-4
Dante Lake Dam—*dam* ....SD-7
*Dante Orphanage* ....PA-2
Dante Post Office (historical)—*building* ....TN-4
Dante River—*stream* ....GU-9
**Dante Scale**—*pop pl* ....VA-3
Dante Sch—*school* ....TN-4
Dantes View—*summit* ....CA-9
Dante United Methodist Ch—*church* ....TN-4
D'Antignac House—*hist pl* ....GA-3
Danton—*locale* ....VA-3
Dantoni—*locale* ....CA-9
**Dantoni Junction**—*pop pl* ....CA-9
Danton Town Hall—*building* ....ND-7
**Danton Township**—*pop pl* ....ND-7
Danton Township (historical)—*civil* ....ND-7
Dan Top—*summit* ....TN-4
**Dantown**—*pop pl* ....PA-2
**Dants**—*pop pl* ....KY-4
Dantuma Place—*locale* ....CA-9
Dantz Creek—*stream* ....ND-7
Dantzler—*locale* ....MS-4
Dantzler, A. F., House—*hist pl* ....MS-4
Dantzler, Col. Olin M., House—*hist pl* ....SC-3
*Dantzler Bay* ....SC-3
Dantzler Cem—*cemetery* ....MS-4
Dantzler-Hart Cem—*cemetery* ....SC-3
Dantzler Memorial First United Methodist Ch—*church* ....MS-4
Dantzler Pond—*lake* ....MS-4
Dantzler Post Office (historical)—*building* ....MS-4
*Dantz Ranch* ....WA-9
Dantz Run—*stream* ....PA-2
Dantz Tavern Sch—*school* ....WI-6
*Danube* ....KS-7
**Danube**—*pop pl* ....MN-6
Danube Ave Sch—*school* ....CA-9
Danube Cem—*cemetery* ....MN-6
Danube Mine—*mine* ....MN-6
Danuber Ch—*church* ....VA-3
**Danube (Town of)**—*pop pl* ....NY-2
Danuser Valley—*valley* ....WI-6
*Dan Valley* ....CA-9
**Dan Valley**—*pop pl* ....NC-3
Dan Valley—*valley* ....NM-5
Dan Valley Ch—*church* ....NC-3
Dan Valley Spring—*spring* ....NM-5
**Danvers**—*pop pl* ....IL-6
**Danvers**—*pop pl* ....MA-1
**Danvers**—*pop pl* ....MN-6
**Danvers**—*pop pl* ....MT-8
**Danvers Center**—*pop pl* ....MA-1
*Danvers Centre* ....MA-1
Danvers Centre (historical P.O.)—*locale* ....MA-1
Danvers HS—*school* ....MA-1
*Danvers Insane Asylum* ....MA-1
*Danvers New Mills* ....MA-1
*Danvers Plains* ....MA-1
Danvers Plaza (Shop Ctr)—*locale* ....MA-1
*Danvers Port* ....MA-1
**Danversport**—*pop pl* ....MA-1
Danvers Port (historical P.O.)—*locale* ....MA-1
Danversport Sch—*school* ....MA-1
Danvers Port Station (historical)—*locale* ....MA-1
Danvers Reservoir (historical)—*lake* ....MA-1
Danvers River—*bay* ....MA-1
Danvers State Hosp—*hospital* ....MA-1
Danvers State Wildlife Mngmt Areas—*park* ....MN-6
Danvers Townhall—*building* ....MA-1
**Danvers (Town of)**—*pop pl* ....MA-1
**Danvers (Township of)**—*pop pl* ....IL-6
Dan View Cem—*cemetery* ....NC-3
Danvik Place—*locale* ....NM-5
*Danville* ....IN-6
*Danville* ....KS-7
*Danville* ....MS-4
*Danville* ....NJ-2
*Danville* ....PA-2
Danville—*locale* ....FL-3
Danville—*locale* ....NV-8
Danville—*locale* ....TX-5
**Danville**—*pop pl* (2) ....AL-4
**Danville**—*pop pl* ....AR-4
**Danville**—*pop pl* ....CA-9
**Danville**—*pop pl* ....GA-3
**Danville**—*pop pl* ....IL-6
**Danville**—*pop pl* (2) ....IN-6
**Danville**—*pop pl* ....IA-7
**Danville**—*pop pl* ....KS-7
**Danville**—*pop pl* (2) ....KY-4
**Danville**—*pop pl* ....LA-4
**Danville**—*pop pl* (2) ....MD-2
**Danville**—*pop pl* ....MO-7
**Danville**—*pop pl* ....NH-1
**Danville**—*pop pl* ....NY-2
**Danville**—*pop pl* (3) ....OH-6
**Danville**—*pop pl* ....PA-2
**Danville**—*pop pl* ....VT-1
**Danville**—*pop pl* ....WA-9
**Danville**—*pop pl* ....WV-2
**Danville**—*pop pl* ....WI-6
Danville Acad (historical)—*school* ....MS-4
Danville Airp—*airport* ....AL-4
Danville Airp—*airport* ....PA-2
Danville Area Senior HS—*school* ....PA-2
Danville Borough—*civil* ....PA-2
Danville Branch—*stream* ....AL-4
Danville Canyon—*valley* ....NV-8
Danville (CCD)—*cens area* ....AL-4
Danville (CCD)—*cens area* ....KY-4
Danville Cem—*cemetery* ....LA-4
Danville Cem—*cemetery* ....MN-6
Danville Cem—*cemetery* ....NH-1
**Danville Center**—*pop pl* ....IA-7
**Danville Center**—*pop pl* ....VT-1
Danville Ch—*church* ....AL-4
Danville Ch—*church* ....MS-4
Danville Ch—*church* ....WV-2
Danville Commercial District—*hist pl* ....KY-4
Danville Community Coll—*school* ....VA-3
Danville Community HS—*school* ....IN-6
Danville Conservation Club Lake—*reservoir* ....IN-6
Danville Conservation Club Lake Dam—*dam* ....IN-6
*Danville Corner* ....ME-1
**Danville Corner**—*pop pl* ....ME-1
Danville Country Club—*other* ....IL-6
Danville Country Club—*other* ....KY-4
Danville Creek—*stream* ....AR-4
Danville Creek—*stream* ....NV-8
**Danville (Danville Junction)**—*pop pl* ....ME-1
Danville Division—*civil* ....AL-4
**Danville East (census name Mechanicsville)**—*pop pl* ....PA-2
Danville Elem Sch—*school* ....PA-2
Danville Ferry (historical)—*locale* ....TN-4
*Danville Green* ....VT-1
Danville Hill—*summit* ....VT-1
Danville Hist Dist—*hist pl* ....VA-3
Danville (historical)—*locale* ....MS-4
**Danville (historical)**—*pop pl* ....TN-4
Danville HS—*school* ....AL-4
**Danville (ind. city)**—*pop pl* ....VA-3
Danville Industrial Development Area—*locale* ....VA-3
*Danville Junction* ....IL-6
Danville Junction (RR name for Danville)—*other* ....ME-1
Danville Junior Coll—*school* ....IL-6
Danville Landing (historical)—*locale* ....TN-4
Danville Meetinghouse—*hist pl* ....NH-1
Danville Memorial Gardens—*cemetery* ....KY-4
Danville Memorial Gardens—*cemetery* ....VA-3
*Danville Mountain* ....AR-4
Danville Mountain—*ridge* ....AR-4
Danville MS—*school* ....PA-2
Danville Mtn—*summit* ....NJ-2
Danville Municipal Airp—*airport* ....VA-3
Danville-Neel Rec Area—*park* ....AL-4
Danville Pass—*gap* ....NV-8
Danville Pike Cave—*cave* ....PA-2
Danville Pond—*lake* ....AL-4
*Danville Post Office* ....TN-4
Danville Post Office—*building* ....AL-4
Danville Post Office (historical)—*building* ....TN-4
Danville Public Library—*hist pl* ....IL-6
Danville Public Library—*hist pl* ....VA-3
Danville River Terminal (historical)—*locale* ....TN-4
*Danville (RR name Danville Junction)* ....ME-1
Danville Rsvr—*reservoir* ....VT-1
Danville Sch—*school* ....TX-5
Danville State Hosp—*hospital* ....PA-2
Danville State Wildlife Area—*park* ....MO-7
Danville Technical Institute—*school* ....VA-3
Danville Tobacco Warehouse and Residential District—*hist pl* ....VA-3
**Danville (Town of)**—*pop pl* ....NH-1
**Danville (Town of)**—*pop pl* ....VT-1
Danville Township—*civil* ....MO-7
Danville Township—*fmr MCD* (2) ....IA-7
Danville (Township of)—*fmr MCD* ....AR-4
**Danville (Township of)**—*pop pl* ....IL-6
**Danville (Township of)**—*pop pl* ....MN-6
Danville West Market Street Hist Dist—*hist pl* ....PA-2
Dan Wallace Cem—*cemetery* ....WV-2
Danway—*locale* ....AL-4
Danway—*locale* ....IL-6
Danway Cem—*cemetery* ....IA-7
Dan White Hollow—*valley* ....OH-6
*Dan Wiley Branch* ....TN-4
Dan Witt Park—*park* ....FL-3
**Danwood**—*pop pl* ....SC-3
Danwood (CCD)—*cens area* ....SC-3
Dan Wright Brook—*stream* ....NY-2
Danz Basten Sch—*school* ....WI-6
Danzel Slough—*gut* ....MN-6
Danzey—*locale* ....AL-4
Danzey Cem—*cemetery* ....AL-4
**Danzig**—*pop pl* ....ND-7
Danzig Ch—*church* ....SD-7
Danzig Dam—*dam* ....ND-7
Danzler—*locale* ....AL-4
Danz Park—*park* ....WI-6
Danz Ranch—*locale* ....TX-5
Danz Ranch—*locale* ....WA-9
Danzy Cem—*cemetery* ....AL-4
Dao Channel—*channel* ....FM-9
Da'ok, Kannat I—*stream* ....MH-9
Da'ok, Laderan I—*cliff* ....MH-9
Daou Tank—*reservoir* ....AZ-5
**Daphane**—*pop pl* ....TX-5
Dapheny Branch—*stream* ....AL-4
Daphine—*locale* ....TX-5
Daphna—*locale* ....VA-3
Daphna Creek—*stream* ....VA-3
**Daphne**—*pop pl* ....AL-4
Daphne (CCD)—*cens area* ....AL-4
*Daphne City Park* ....AL-4
**Daphnedale Park**—*pop pl* ....CA-9
Daphne Division—*civil* ....AL-4
Daphne Elem Sch—*school* ....AL-4
Daphne Grove Campground—*park* ....OR-9
Daphne JHS—*school* ....AL-4
Daphne Lake—*lake* ....WY-8
Daphne Park—*park* ....MS-4
Daphne Shop Ctr—*locale* ....AL-4
Daphnia Lake—*lake* ....WY-8
Dapp Cem—*cemetery* ....OH-6
Dapper Cem—*cemetery* ....OH-6
*Dapping Brook* ....MA-1
Dapping Brook Swamp—*swamp* ....MA-1
Dapplegray Sch—*school* ....CA-9
Daprakmiut (Summer Camp)—*locale* ....AK-9
Daqabyuch—*bay* ....FM-9
Daque Lake—*lake* ....FL-3
Dar—*locale* ....MD-2
Darachaq—*locale* ....FM-9
Darain Ch—*church* ....AL-4
*Darait Anchorage* ....MP-9
*Darap* ....FM-9
Darb Branch—*stream* ....NC-3
Darbey Hollow—*valley* ....KY-4
Darb Fork—*stream* ....KY-4
*Darbo Island* ....GA-3
*Darbon* ....MS-4
D'Arbonne—*locale* ....LA-4
Darbonne—*locale* ....LA-4
**Darbonne**—*pop pl* ....LA-4
D'Arbonne, Bayou—*stream* ....LA-4
Darbonne Bay—*stream* ....LA-4
*Darbonne Bayou* ....LA-4
D'Arbonne Ch—*church* ....LA-4
D'Arbonne Lookout Tower—*locale* ....LA-4
**Darboy**—*pop pl* ....WI-6
Darbs Branch—*stream* (2) ....KY-4
Darbs Hollow—*valley* ....TX-5
Darbui, Bayou—*stream* ....LA-4
**Darbun**—*pop pl* ....MS-4
Darbun Cem—*cemetery* (2) ....MS-4
Darbun Ch—*church* ....MS-4
Darbun Creek—*stream* ....MS-4
*Darbun Methodist Church* ....MS-4
*Darby* ....KY-4
*Darby* ....MA-1
Darby—*locale* ....FL-3
Darby—*locale* ....NC-3
Darby—*locale* ....ND-7
Darby—*other* ....WV-2
**Darby**—*pop pl* ....ID-8
**Darby**—*pop pl* ....KY-4
**Darby**—*pop pl* ....LA-4
**Darby**—*pop pl* ....MT-8
**Darby**—*pop pl* ....NC-3
**Darby**—*pop pl* ....PA-2
Darby, Bayou—*stream* ....LA-4
Darby, Mount—*summit* ....MA-1
Darby, Mount—*summit* ....WY-8
Darby Acres Shop Ctr—*locale* ....NC-3
**Darby Acres (subdivision)**—*pop pl* ....NC-3
Darby Arroyo—*valley* ....AZ-5
Darby Bend—*bend* ....MI-6
Darby Bluff—*cliff* ....MO-7
Darby Borough—*civil* ....PA-2
Darby Branch—*stream* ....AL-4
Darby Branch—*stream* ....MO-7

Darby Brook—*stream* ... CT-1
Darby Brook—*stream* ... NH-1
Darby Brook—*stream* ... VT-1
Darby Buttes—*summit* ... MT-8
Darby Canyon—*valley* ... WY-8
Darby Cem—*cemetery* ... MO-7
Darby Cem—*cemetery* ... TN-4
Darby Center Cem—*cemetery* ... VT-1
Darby Ch—*church* ... MO-7
Darby Ch—*church* ... OH-6
Darby Corners—*locale* ... NY-2
Darby Coulee—*stream* ... LA-4
*Darby Creek* ... OH-6
Darby Creek—*locale* ... PA-2
Darby Creek—*stream* (2) ... CO-8
Darby Creek—*stream* ... ID-8
Darby Creek—*stream* ... KY-4
Darby Creek—*stream* (2) ... OH-6
Darby Creek—*stream* ... OR-9
Darby Creek—*stream* ... PA-2
Darby Creek—*stream* ... TX-5
Darby Creek—*stream* (2) ... WY-8
Darby Creek Cem—*cemetery* ... OH-6
Darby Creek Metropolitan Park—*park* ... OH-6
**Darby Crest**—*pop pl* ... OH-6
**Darbydale**—*pop pl* ... OH-6
Darby Ditch—*canal* ... CO-8
Darby Ditch—*canal* ... IN-6
Darby Draw—*valley* ... WA-9
Darby Drive Ch of Christ—*church* ... AL-4
Darby Fork—*stream* ... KY-4
Darby Girls Camp—*locale* ... WY-8
*Darby High School* ... PA-2
Darby Hill—*summit* ... MA-1
Darby Hill—*summit* ... TX-5
Darby Hill—*summit* ... VT-1
Darby Hill—*summit* ... VI-3
Darby Hill Ch—*church* ... TX-5
Darby Hollow—*valley* (2) ... MO-7
Darby House—*hist pl* ... LA-4
Darby JHS—*school* ... AR-4
Darby Junction—*locale* ... MN-6
Darby Knob—*summit* ... CA-9
Darby Knob Firebreak—*trail* ... CA-9
Darby Lake—*lake* (2) ... MI-6
Darby Lake—*reservoir* ... AR-4
Darby Meeting—*hist pl* ... PA-2
Darby Memorial Park—*park* ... CA-9
Darby Mountains—*other* ... AK-9
Darby Plantation—*hist pl* ... LA-4
Darby Plantation—*hist pl* ... SC-3
Darby Point—*cape* ... NC-3
Darby Pond—*basin* ... CA-9
Darby Pond—*lake* ... AL-4
Darby Pond—*reservoir* ... MA-1
Darby Pond Outlet—*dam* ... MA-1
Darby Pond West Outlet Dam—*dam* ... MA-1
Darbys Branch Sch—*school* ... KY-4
Darby Sch (historical)—*school* ... AL-4
Darby Sch (historical)—*school* ... TN-4
Darbys Lake—*lake* ... AL-4
Darbys Nose—*summit* ... WV-2
*Darbys Pond* ... MA-1
Darby Spring—*spring* ... AL-4
Darby Station—*locale* ... PA-2
**Darbyton**—*pop pl* ... KY-4
**Darbytown**—*pop pl* ... PA-2
Darbytown Branch—*stream* ... TN-4
Darbytown Falls—*falls* ... PA-2
Darby Township—*CDP* ... PA-2
Darby Township Elem Sch—*school* ... PA-2
**Darby (Township of)**—*pop pl* (3) ... OH-6
**Darby (Township of)**—*pop pl* ... PA-2
**Darbyville**—*pop pl* ... IA-7
**Darbyville**—*pop pl* ... OH-6
**Darbyville**—*pop pl* ... VA-3
Darby Well—*well* ... AZ-5
*Darcey Crossing* ... FL-3
Darcey Sch—*school* ... CT-1
*Darcha'* ... FM-9
Darco—*locale* ... TX-5
Darco Mine—*mine* ... TX-5
**Darcy**—*pop pl* ... AR-4
Darcy Ditch—*canal* ... CO-8
**Darcy Estates**—*pop pl* ... MD-2
Darcy's Air Strip Airp—*airport* ... WA-9
**Dardanelle**—*pop pl* ... AR-4
**Dardanelle**—*pop pl* ... CA-9
Dardanelle, Lake—*reservoir* ... AR-4
Dardanelle Lock And Dam—*dam* ... AR-4
Dardanelle Mtn—*summit* ... AR-4
Dardanelle Rock—*pillar* ... AR-4
Dardanelles, The—*summit* ... CA-9
Dardanelles Cone—*summit* ... CA-9
Dardanelles Creek—*stream* (2) ... CA-9
Dardanelles Lake—*lake* ... CA-9
Dardanelles Mine—*mine* ... AZ-5
*Dardanelles Mountain* ... CA-9
Dardanelle (Township of)—*fmr MCD* ... AR-4
Dardeau Bldg—*hist pl* ... LA-4
*Darden* ... NC-3
Darden—*locale* ... TX-5
Darden—*other* ... TX-5
**Darden**—*pop pl* ... MS-4
**Darden**—*pop pl* ... TN-4
Darden Baptist Ch—*church* ... TN-4
Darden Branch—*stream* ... AL-4
Darden Branch—*stream* ... GA-3
Darden Branch—*stream* ... TN-4
Darden Camp—*locale* ... VA-3
Darden Canyon—*valley* ... TX-5
Darden (CCD)—*cens area* ... TN-4
Darden Cem—*cemetery* ... AL-4
Darden Cem—*cemetery* (2) ... MS-4
Darden Cem—*cemetery* (3) ... TN-4
Darden Cem—*cemetery* ... TX-5
Darden Chapel—*church* ... MS-4
*Darden Chapel Baptist Ch* ... MS-4
Darden Dam—*dam* ... AL-4
**Darden (Dardens)**—*pop pl* ... NC-3
Darden Division—*civil* ... TN-4
Darden Elem Sch—*school* ... IN-6
Darden-Gifford House—*hist pl* ... AR-4
Darden Hills—*summit* ... MS-4
Darden (historical)—*locale* ... AL-4
Darden Hotel—*hist pl* ... NC-3
Darden HS—*school* ... AL-4
Darden HS—*school* ... NC-3
Darden Lake—*reservoir* ... MS-4
Darden Lake Dam—*dam* ... MS-4
Darden Landing (historical)—*locale* ... NC-3
Darden Millpond—*reservoir* ... VA-3
Darden Mill Run—*stream* ... VA-3
**Dardenne**—*pop pl* ... MO-7
Dardenne Cem—*cemetery* ... MO-7
Dardenne Ch—*church* ... MO-7
Dardenne Creek—*stream* ... MO-7
Dardenne Island—*island* ... MO-7
Dardenne Lake—*swamp* ... MO-7
Dardenne Township—*civil* ... MO-7
Darden Palestine Sch—*school* ... TX-5
Darden Pond—*reservoir* ... VA-3
Darden Post Office—*building* ... TN-4
Darden Post Office (historical)—*building* ... MS-4
*Darden Ridge* ... MS-4
**Dardens**—*pop pl* ... NC-3
Darden Sch (historical)—*school* ... TN-4
Dardens Lake—*reservoir* ... AL-4
Dardens Pond—*lake* ... VA-3
Darden-Thomas Sch—*school* ... GA-3
*Darden-Vick Middle School* ... NC-3
Darden Windmill—*locale* ... TX-5
*Dardis Lake* ... WI-6
Dardon Canyon—*valley* ... CA-9
Dardy Branch—*stream* ... KY-4
Dardy Windmill—*locale* ... TX-5
Dare—*locale* ... VA-3
Dareach—*cape* ... FM-9
Dare Branch—*stream* ... TN-4
*Darech* ... FM-9
**Dare County**—*pop pl* ... NC-3
Dare County Airp—*airport* ... NC-3
*Dare County Aycock Brown Welcome Center* ... NC-3
Dare County Bombing Range—*military* ... NC-3
*Dare County Range Military Reservation* ... NC-3
Dare Creek—*stream* ... AR-4
Dare Gulch—*valley* ... ID-8
Dare Mine Knob—*summit* ... AR-4
*Dare Naval Weapons Complex* ... NC-3
Darent (RR name for Lemont
Furnace)—*other* ... PA-2
Dare Run—*stream* ... OH-6
Dares—*locale* ... MD-2
**Dares Beach**—*pop pl* ... MD-2
Dare Sch—*school* ... MA-1
Dare Sch—*school* ... MO-7
*Dares Whart* ... MD-2
Dare Tank—*reservoir* ... NM-5
**Daretown**—*pop pl* ... NJ-2
*Daretown Lake* ... NJ-2
Daretown Lake—*reservoir* ... NJ-2
Daretown Lake Dam—*dam* ... NJ-2
*Daretown Mill Pond* ... NJ-2
**Dareville**—*pop pl* ... IL-6
*Dare Wharf* ... MD-2
**Darex**—*pop pl* ... KY-4
**Darfork**—*pop pl* ... KY-4
**Darfur**—*pop pl* ... MN-6
**Darg**—*pop pl* ... NC-3
**Dargan**—*pop pl* ... MD-2
Dargan, Julius A., House—*hist pl* ... SC-3
Dargan Creek—*stream* ... TX-5
Dargan Park—*park* ... GA-3
Dargans Bay—*basin* ... SC-3
Dargatz Park—*park* ... KS-7
*Darghtys Ferry* ... TN-4
**Dargin**—*pop pl* ... AL-4
Dargin Cem—*cemetery* ... AL-4
Dargin Community Center—*building* ... AL-4
*Dargon* ... MD-2
Dargon Cem—*cemetery* ... SC-3
Dargot Canyon—*valley* ... NM-5
Darian Cem—*cemetery* ... AL-4
*Darian Primitive Baptist Church* ... AL-4
Darien—*CDP* ... CT-1
**Darien**—*pop pl* ... CT-1
**Darien**—*pop pl* ... GA-3
**Darien**—*pop pl* ... IL-6
**Darien**—*pop pl* ... MO-7
**Darien**—*pop pl* ... NY-2
**Darien**—*pop pl* ... WI-6
Darien (CCD)—*cens area* ... GA-3
**Darien Center**—*pop pl* ... NY-2
Darien Ch—*church* (2) ... AL-4
Darien Ch—*church* ... GA-3
Darien Ch—*church* ... SC-3
Darien Creek—*stream* ... GA-3
Darien (historical P.O.)—*locale* ... IA-7
Darien HS—*school* ... CT-1
*Darien River* ... CT-1
Darien River—*stream* ... GA-3
**Darien (Town of)**—*pop pl* ... NY-2
**Darien (Town of)**—*pop pl* ... WI-6
Dariikaan—*locale* ... FM-9
*Darikan* ... FM-9
Darilek—*locale* ... TX-5
**Daris Crossing**—*pop pl* ... MO-7
Darity Branch—*stream* ... MO-7
Darius Creek—*stream* ... OR-9
Darius James Brook—*stream* ... VT-1
Darius Post Office (historical)—*building* ... TN-4
Dark Angel—*arch* ... UT-8
Dark Bay—*bay* ... MO-7
Dark Bay—*bay* (3) ... NY-2
Dark Bay—*stream* ... GA-3
Dark Bay—*swamp* ... FL-3
Dark Bay—*swamp* ... NC-3
Dark Betsy Canyon—*valley* ... NM-5
Dark Bottom Hollow—*valley* ... MO-7
Dark Branch—*stream* ... KY-4
Dark Branch—*stream* ... MD-2
Dark Branch—*stream* ... NJ-2
Dark Branch—*stream* (3) ... NC-3
Dark Branch—*stream* ... SC-3
Dark Branch—*stream* ... VT-1
*Dark Brook* ... MA-1
Dark Brook—*reservoir* ... MA-1
Dark Brook—*stream* ... ME-1
Dark Brook—*stream* (2) ... MA-1
Dark Brook Reservoir Dam—*dam* ... MA-1
Dark Brook Reservoir Dike—*dam* ... MA-1
Dark Brown Slough—*gut* ... AL-4
Dark Butte—*summit* ... MT-8
*Darkcabin Creek* ... OR-9
Dark Canyon—*valley* (5) ... AZ-5
Dark Canyon—*valley* (26) ... CA-9
Dark Canyon—*valley* (7) ... CO-8
Dark Canyon—*valley* (2) ... MT-8
Dark Canyon—*valley* (12) ... NM-5
Dark Canyon—*valley* (7) ... OR-9
Dark Canyon—*valley* ... SD-7
Dark Canyon—*valley* (6) ... TX-5
Dark Canyon—*valley* (6) ... UT-8
Dark Canyon—*valley* ... WA-9
Dark Canyon—*valley* (2) ... WY-8
Dark Canyon Camp—*locale* ... CA-9
Dark Canyon Creek—*stream* (2) ... CA-9
Dark Canyon Creek—*stream* (2) ... OR-9
Dark Canyon Creek—*stream* ... TX-5
Dark Canyon Draw—*valley* ... NM-5
Dark Canyon Lake—*lake* ... UT-8
Dark Canyon Plateau—*plateau* ... UT-8
Dark Canyon Primitive Area—*area* ... UT-8
Dark Canyon Rapids—*rapids* ... UT-8
Dark Canyon Spring—*spring* ... AZ-5
Dark Canyon Spring—*spring* ... CO-8
Dark Canyon Spring—*spring* ... TX-5
Dark Canyon Tank—*reservoir* (2) ... NM-5
Dark Canyon Tank—*reservoir* ... TX-5
Dark Canyon Trail—*trail* (2) ... CA-9
Dark Canyon Trail—*trail* ... OR-9
Dark Canyon Well—*well* ... NM-5
Dark Canyon Wells—*well* ... NM-5
*Dark Canyon Wilderness Area* ... UT-8
Dark Cave Hollow—*valley* ... KY-4
Dark Cave Run—*stream* ... OH-6
Dark Chute—*stream* ... IL-6
Dark Chute—*stream* ... IA-7
Dark Cliff Passage—*locale* ... UT-8
Dark Cliffs—*cliff* ... AK-9
*Dark Corner* ... AL-4
Dark Corner Cem—*cemetery* ... TX-5
Dark Corners Ch—*church* ... AR-4
Dark Corners (historical)—*locale* ... AL-4
Dark County Lake Wildlife Area—*park* ... OH-6
Dark Cove—*bay* ... AK-9
Dark Cove—*bay* (4) ... ME-1
Dark Cove—*locale* ... ME-1
Dark Cove—*valley* (2) ... NC-3
Dark Cove Mtn—*summit* ... ME-1
Dark Creek—*stream* ... GA-3
Dark Creek—*stream* ... MO-7
Dark Creek—*stream* ... MT-8
Dark Creek—*stream* ... OR-9
Dark Creek—*stream* ... WA-9
Dark Cypress Swamp—*swamp* ... MO-7
Dark Cypress Swamp State Wildlife
Area—*park* ... MO-7
Dark Dam—*dam* ... MA-1
Dark Day Canyon—*valley* ... CA-9
*Darke* ... OH-6
*Darke* ... WV-2
Darke—*other* ... WV-2
**Darke (County)**—*pop pl* ... OH-6
Darke County Courthouse, Sheriff's House, And
Jail—*hist pl* ... OH-6
Dark Entry—*swamp* ... FL-3
Dark Entry Brook—*stream* ... RI-1
*Dark Entry Creek* ... GA-3
Dark Entry Creek—*stream* ... GA-3
**Darkesville**—*pop pl* ... WV-2
Darkesville Hist Dist—*hist pl* ... WV-2
Darkey Creek—*stream* ... CA-9
Darkey Creek—*stream* ... OR-9
Darkeys Marsh—*swamp* ... MI-6
Darkey Springs—*locale* ... TN-4
Darkey Springs Branch—*stream* ... TN-4
Darkey Springs Post Office
(historical)—*building* ... TN-4
Dark Glacier—*glacier* ... WA-9
Dark Gulch—*valley* (6) ... CA-9
Dark Gulch—*valley* (2) ... CO-8
Dark Gulch—*valley* ... MT-8
Dark Hammock—*island* ... FL-3
Dark Hammock—*island* ... TX-5
Dark Harbor—*bay* ... ME-1
**Dark Harbor**—*pop pl* ... ME-1
Dark Head Creek—*stream* ... MD-2
Dark Hole—*basin* ... CA-9
Dark Hole—*channel* ... MT-8
Dark Hole, The—*valley* ... CA-9
Dark Hole Hollow—*valley* ... AR-4
Dark Hole Wind Cave—*cave* ... OR-9
*Dark Hollow* ... TN-4
*Dark Hollow* ... VA-3
Dark Hollow—*channel* ... NY-2
Dark Hollow—*flat* ... AR-4
**Dark Hollow**—*pop pl* ... IN-6
Dark Hollow—*valley* (5) ... AL-4
Dark Hollow—*valley* ... AK-9
Dark Hollow—*valley* (4) ... AR-4
Dark Hollow—*valley* ... CT-1
Dark Hollow—*valley* ... IL-6
Dark Hollow—*valley* ... IN-6
Dark Hollow—*valley* ... IA-7
Dark Hollow—*valley* (8) ... KY-4
Dark Hollow—*valley* (2) ... MS-4
Dark Hollow—*valley* (6) ... MO-7
Dark Hollow—*valley* (2) ... MT-8
Dark Hollow—*valley* ... NH-1
Dark Hollow—*valley* (3) ... NY-2
Dark Hollow—*valley* (4) ... NC-3
Dark Hollow—*valley* (3) ... OH-6
Dark Hollow—*valley* ... OR-9
Dark Hollow—*valley* (15) ... PA-2
Dark Hollow—*valley* (23) ... TN-4
Dark Hollow—*valley* ... UT-8
Dark Hollow—*valley* (13) ... VA-3
Dark Hollow—*valley* (5) ... WV-2
Dark Hollow—*valley* ... WI-6
Dark Hollow Branch—*stream* ... AL-4
Dark Hollow Branch—*stream* (2) ... KY-4
Dark Hollow Branch—*stream* ... NC-3
Dark Hollow Branch—*stream* ... OK-5
Dark Hollow Branch—*stream* (3) ... TN-4
Dark Hollow Branch—*stream* ... TX-5
Dark Hollow Brook—*stream* (3) ... CT-1
Dark Hollow Ch—*church* ... OH-6
Dark Hollow Ch—*church* ... TN-4
Dark Hollow Creek—*stream* ... CA-9
Dark Hollow Creek—*stream* ... OK-5
Dark Hollow Dam—*dam* ... PA-2
Dark Hollow Drift Mine
(underground)—*mine* ... AL-4
Dark Hollow Falls—*falls* ... VA-3
Dark Hollow Interchange—*other* ... AR-4
Dark Hollow Picnic Area—*park* ... VA-3
Dark Hollow Pond—*lake* ... MA-1
Dark Hollow Run—*stream* (3) ... PA-2
Dark Hollow Sch—*school* ... KY-4
Dark Hollow Trail—*trail* (2) ... PA-2
Dark Hollow Vista—*locale* ... PA-2
Dark Horse and General Grant
Mine—*mine* ... SD-7
Darkhorse Creek—*stream* ... MT-8
Darkhorse Lake—*lake* ... MT-8
Darkies Creek—*stream* ... IL-6
*Dark Island* ... NY-2
Dark Island—*island* ... AK-9
Dark Island—*island* ... FL-3
*Dark Lake* ... WI-6
Dark Lake—*lake* ... AK-9
Dark Lake—*lake* ... CA-9
Dark Lake—*lake* ... GA-3
Dark Lake—*lake* (4) ... MI-6
Dark Lake—*lake* (4) ... MN-6
Dark Lake—*lake* ... MO-7
Dark Lake—*lake* (2) ... OR-9
Dark Lake—*lake* (3) ... WI-6
*Dark Lake Swamp* ... MA-1
Dark Lick Hollow—*valley* ... OH-6
Dark Meadow—*flat* ... WA-9
Dark Meadows Trail—*trail* ... WA-9
**Darkmont**—*pop pl* ... KY-4
Dark Mtn—*summit* ... CO-8
Dark Mtn—*summit* (2) ... NC-3
Dark Mtn—*summit* ... WA-9
Dark-Nea Cem—*cemetery* ... LA-4
Darknell—*locale* ... WA-9
Dark Passage—*channel* ... AK-9
Dark Peak—*summit* ... NV-8
Dark Peak—*summit* ... WA-9
*Darkplains* ... NH-1
Dark Point—*cape* ... AK-9
Dark Point—*cape* ... FL-3
Dark Point—*cape* ... ME-1
Dark Pond—*lake* ... NH-1
Dark Prong—*stream* ... NC-3
Dark Range Peak—*summit* ... CA-9
Dark Ravine—*valley* (2) ... CA-9
Dark Ridge—*ridge* ... KY-4
Dark Ridge—*ridge* (2) ... NC-3
Dark Ridge Branch—*stream* ... TN-4
Dark Ridge Creek—*stream* ... NC-3
**Darkridge (Dark Ridge)**—*pop pl* ... NC-3
Dark River—*stream* ... MN-6
Dark Run—*stream* ... IN-6
Dark Run—*stream* (2) ... PA-2
Dark Run—*stream* (2) ... VA-3
Darks Creek—*stream* ... LA-4
Dark Shade Creek—*stream* ... PA-2
Dark Shrum Branch—*stream* ... TN-4
Dark Slough—*gut* ... MN-6
Dark Slough—*stream* ... MN-6
Dark Slough—*stream* ... TX-5
Dark Slough—*stream* ... WI-6
Darks Mill—*locale* ... TN-4
Dark Strand—*swamp* ... FL-3
**Darksville**—*pop pl* ... MO-7
Dark Swamp—*stream* (2) ... VA-3
Dark Swamp—*swamp* ... CT-1
Dark Swamp—*swamp* (2) ... PA-2
Dark Swamp—*swamp* ... RI-1
Dark Swamp Sch (historical)—*school* ... PA-2
Dark Thick—*swamp* (2) ... GA-3
Dark Thunder Canyon—*valley* ... NM-5
*Darktown* ... OH-6
Dark Valley—*valley* ... UT-8
Dark Valley Creek—*stream* ... TX-5
Dark Valley Draw—*valley* ... UT-8
Dark Valley Lake—*lake* ... UT-8
Dark Valley Shelf—*bench* ... UT-8
**Dark Water**—*pop pl* ... PA-2
Darkwater Lake—*lake* ... FL-3
Darkwood Ditch—*canal* ... IN-6
Darky Branch—*stream* ... TN-4
Darky Knob—*summit* ... KY-4
Darky Mine—*mine* ... WA-9
Darky Tom Branch—*stream* ... TN-4
Darky Tom Hollow—*valley* ... TN-4
Darky Tom Mine—*mine* ... TN-4
Darla Don—*building* ... NC-3
Darland Cem—*cemetery* ... OK-5
Darland Mtn—*summit* ... WA-9
Darland Ridge—*ridge* ... WA-9
Darlan Sch—*school* ... SC-3
**Darlco**—*pop pl* ... SC-3
**Darleigh Manor**—*pop pl* ... MD-2
Darlene Lake—*lake* ... OR-9
Darlet Lake—*lake* ... MN-6
Darley—*locale* ... LA-4
Darley House—*hist pl* ... DE-2
Darley Road Elem Sch—*school* ... DE-2
*Darley Road Sch* ... DE-2
**Darley Woods**—*pop pl* ... DE-2
Darline, Mount—*summit* ... CO-8
Darling—*locale* ... AZ-5
Darling—*locale* ... PA-2
Darling—*locale* ... TX-5
**Darling**—*pop pl* ... MN-6
**Darling**—*pop pl* ... MS-4
Darling, Frederick L., House—*hist pl* ... WI-6
Darling, Henry, House—*hist pl* ... RI-1
Darling, Lake—*lake* ... ID-8
Darling, Lake—*lake* ... MN-6
Darling, Lake—*reservoir* ... IA-7
Darling, Lake—*reservoir* (2) ... ND-7
Darling, Thomas, House and
Tavern—*hist pl* ... CT-1
Darling Branch—*stream* ... MS-4
Darling Brook—*stream* ... MA-1
Darling Canyon—*valley* ... OR-9
Darling Cem—*cemetery* ... GA-3
Darling Cem—*cemetery* ... KY-4
Darling Cem—*cemetery* ... ND-7
Darling Cem—*cemetery* ... PA-2
Darling Cinder Pit—*basin* ... AZ-5
Darling Coulee—*valley* ... WI-6
Darling Creek—*stream* (2) ... AK-9
Darling Creek—*stream* (2) ... CO-8
Darling Creek—*stream* ... ID-8
Darling Creek—*stream* ... LA-4
Darling Creek—*stream* ... MS-4
Darling Creek—*stream* ... NM-5
Darling Creek—*stream* ... NY-2
Darling Creek—*stream* (3) ... OR-9
Darling Creek—*stream* ... SD-7
Darling Creek Trail—*trail* ... CO-8
Darling Ditch—*canal* ... CO-8
Darling Drain—*canal* ... CA-9
Darling Draw—*valley* ... MT-8
Darling Draw Spring—*spring* ... MT-8
*Darling Elementary School* ... MS-4
*Darlinghaus Ditch* ... OH-6
Darling Hill—*summit* ... NY-2
Darling Hill—*summit* ... VT-1
Darling Hollow—*valley* ... NY-2
Darling Inn—*hist pl* ... VT-1
Darling Island—*island* ... ME-1
Darling Key—*island* ... FL-3
Darling Lake—*lake* ... CO-8
Darling Lake—*lake* ... WA-9
Darling Landing—*locale* ... AL-4
Darling Mine—*mine* ... AZ-5
Darling Mine—*mine* ... CA-9
*Darling Mountain* ... WA-9
Darling Mtn—*summit* ... NY-2
Darling Mtn—*summit* ... OR-9
Darling Observatory—*building* ... MN-6
Darling Pond—*lake* ... CT-1
Darling Pond—*reservoir* ... RI-1
Darling Pool—*lake* ... IA-7
Darling Ranch—*locale* ... CO-8
*Darling Ravine* ... CA-9
Darling Ridge—*ridge* ... CA-9
Darling Ridge—*ridge* ... CO-8
Darling Road Trail—*trail* ... PA-2
Darling RR Station—*building* ... AZ-5
Darling Rsvr—*reservoir* ... CO-8
Darling Run—*stream* ... OH-6
Darling Run—*stream* (2) ... PA-2
Darling Run Ch—*church* ... OH-6
Darling Run Trail—*trail* ... PA-2
Darling Sch—*school* ... CA-9
Darling Sch—*school* ... MI-6
Darling Sch—*school* ... MS-4
*Darlings Landing* ... AL-4
*Darlings Pond* ... RI-1
Darling Spring—*spring* ... AR-4
Darling Spring—*spring* ... GA-3
**Darling Springs Township**—*pop pl* ... ND-7
Darling State For—*forest* ... VT-1
Darling Switch—*locale* ... MN-6
*Darlington* ... AL-4
*Darlington* ... PA-2
*Darlington* ... RI-1
*Darlington* ... SD-7
Darlington—*locale* ... AL-4
Darlington—*locale* ... CA-9
**Darlington**—*pop pl* ... FL-3
**Darlington**—*pop pl* ... ID-8
**Darlington**—*pop pl* ... IN-6
**Darlington**—*pop pl* ... LA-4
**Darlington**—*pop pl* ... MD-2
**Darlington**—*pop pl* ... MO-7
**Darlington**—*pop pl* ... NJ-2
**Darlington**—*pop pl* ... NC-3
**Darlington**—*pop pl* (2) ... OH-6
**Darlington**—*pop pl* (3) ... PA-2
**Darlington**—*pop pl* ... RI-1
**Darlington**—*pop pl* ... SC-3
**Darlington**—*pop pl* ... WA-9
**Darlington**—*pop pl* ... WI-6
Darlington, Lyde Irby, House—*hist pl* ... SC-3
Darlington Agency Site—*hist pl* ... OK-5
Darlington Borough—*civil* ... PA-2
Darlington Brook—*stream* ... NJ-2
Darlington Brothers Ranch—*locale* ... MT-8
Darlington (CCD)—*cens area* ... SC-3
Darlington Cem—*cemetery* ... AL-4
Darlington Cem—*cemetery* ... ID-8
Darlington Cem—*cemetery* ... MD-2
Darlington Cem—*cemetery* ... SD-7
Darlington Ch—*church* ... AL-4
Darlington Ch—*church* ... LA-4
Darlington Ch—*church* ... NC-3
*Darlington Corner* ... PA-2
**Darlington Corners**—*pop pl* ... PA-2
Darlington Country Club—*other* ... SC-3
**Darlington (County)**—*pop pl* ... SC-3
Darlington County Park—*park* ... NJ-2
Darlington Creek—*stream* ... SC-3
Darlington Ditch—*canal* ... CO-8
Darlington Ditch—*canal* ... ID-8
Darlington Ditch—*canal* ... MT-8
Darlington Drain—*canal* ... MI-6
Darlington Draw—*valley* (2) ... WY-8
Darlington Elementary and JHS—*school* ... IN-6
Darlington Flat—*flat* ... CA-9
Darlington Heights—*locale* ... VA-3
**Darlington Heights**—*pop pl* ... NJ-2
**Darlington Heights
(subdivision)**—*pop pl* ... TN-4
Darlington Hist Dist—*hist pl* ... MD-2
Darlington (historical)—*locale* ... SD-7
**Darlingtonia**—*pop pl* ... CA-9
Darlington Industrial Hist Dist—*hist pl* ... SC-3
Darlington Lake—*lake* ... MI-6
Darlington Lake—*lake* ... PA-2
Darlington Lake—*reservoir* ... NJ-2
Darlington Lake Dam—*dam* ... NJ-2
Darlington Raceway—*other* ... SC-3
Darlington Sch—*school* ... GA-3
Darlington Sch—*school* ... OK-5
Darlington Sch—*school* ... WY-8
Darlington Shaft—*mine* ... ID-8
Darlington Sinks—*basin* ... ID-8
Darlington State Game Bird
Hatchery—*other* ... OK-5
Darlington State Park—*park* ... OR-9
Darlington Station—*building* ... PA-2
Darlington Swamp—*swamp* ... SC-3
**Darlington (Town of)**—*pop pl* ... WI-6
**Darlington Township**—*pop pl* ... KS-7
**Darlington Township**—*pop pl* (2) ... SD-7
Darlington Township Hall—*building* ... SD-7
**Darlington (Township of)**—*pop pl* ... PA-2
Darlington Trail—*trail* ... PA-2
**Darlington Woods**—*pop pl* ... IN-6
**Darling (Township of)**—*pop pl* ... MN-6
*Darling Trail* ... PA-2
*Darlin Mountain* ... WA-9
Darl Jones Sch—*school* ... KY-4
Darlngton Plantation—*locale* ... SC-3
**Darlove**—*pop pl* ... MS-4
*Darlove Baptist Church* ... MS-4
Darlove Ch—*church* ... MS-4
**Darlow**—*pop pl* ... CO-8
**Darlow**—*pop pl* ... KS-7
Darly Mine Group—*mine* ... AZ-5
Darlyn Lake—*lake* ... MI-6
D A R Memorial State For—*forest* ... MN-6
Darmer Post Office (historical)—*building* ... AL-4
D'Armond Post Office
(historical)—*building* ... TN-4
Darms Mine—*mine* ... NV-8
**Darmstadt**—*pop pl* ... IL-6
**Darmstadt**—*pop pl* ... IN-6
Darmstadt Cem—*cemetery* ... IL-6
Darmstadt Creek—*stream* ... TX-5
Darmstatter Cem—*cemetery* ... IL-6
Darnall—*locale* ... MD-2
**Darnall (historical)**—*pop pl* ... MS-4
Darnall Landing—*locale* ... TN-4
Darnall Place—*hist pl* ... MD-2
Darnall P.O. (historical)—*building* ... MS-4
Darnall Point—*cliff* ... TN-4
Darnall Post Office (historical)—*building* ... TN-4
Darnall Sch—*school* ... CA-9
*Darnalls Landing* ... TN-4
Darnall Towhead—*bar* ... TN-4
**Darndanelles (historical)**—*pop pl* ... OR-9
Darneille Gap—*gap* ... GA-3
Darnell—*locale* ... KY-4
**Darnell**—*pop pl* ... LA-4
**Darnell**—*pop pl* ... OH-6
Darnell, Rowland J., House—*hist pl* ... TN-4
Darnell Branch—*stream* ... TX-5
Darnell Canyon—*valley* ... NM-5
Darnell Cem—*cemetery* ... IL-6
Darnell Cem—*cemetery* ... MO-7
Darnell Cem—*cemetery* ... TN-4
Darnell Cem—*cemetery* ... VA-3
Darnell Cem—*cemetery* ... WV-2
Darnell Creek—*stream* ... CA-9
Darnell Creek—*stream* ... CO-8
Darnell Creek—*stream* (2) ... GA-3
Darnell Creek—*stream* ... KY-4
Darnell Creek—*stream* ... NC-3
**Darnell Estates (subdivision)**—*pop pl* ... TN-4
Darnell Gap—*gap* ... GA-3
Darnell Hollow—*valley* ... NC-3
Darnell Hollow—*valley* ... WV-2
*Darnell Landing* ... TN-4
Darnell Peak—*summit* ... AZ-5
Darnell Rsvr—*reservoir* ... CO-8
Darnell Run—*stream* ... WV-2
*Darnells Branch* ... KS-7
Darnell Sch (historical)—*school* ... TN-4
Darnells Creek—*stream* ... KS-7
**Darnell Town**—*pop pl* ... VA-3
**Darnen (Township of)**—*pop pl* ... MN-6
**Darnestown**—*pop pl* ... MD-2
Darniell Gulch—*valley* ... OR-9
Darning Needle, The—*summit* ... VT-1
Darning Needle Pond—*lake* ... NY-2
Darnit Brook—*stream* ... ME-1
*Darnstadt* ... IN-6
Darn Swamp—*swamp* ... SC-3
*Daroan* ... MP-9
*Daron Island* ... WA-9
*Daros Hollow* ... TX-5
Daroyan—*island* ... MP-9
Darpo, Lake—*reservoir* ... SC-3
*Darpum* ... FM-9
*Darr* ... MP-9
**Darr**—*pop pl* ... NE-7
**Darracott**—*pop pl* ... MS-4
*Darracott Crossroads* ... MS-4
Darracott HS (historical)—*school* ... MS-4
Darragh—*locale* ... MI-6
**Darragh**—*pop pl* ... PA-2
Darragh House—*hist pl* ... AR-4
**Darragh (RR name Madison
(sta.))**—*pop pl* ... PA-2
Darrah—*locale* ... AL-4
Darrah—*locale* ... CA-9
**Darrah**—*pop pl* ... UT-8
Darrah, Ben, Water Tank and Well
House—*hist pl* ... ID-8
Darrah, Lydia, Sch—*hist pl* ... PA-2
Darrah House and Water Tank
House—*hist pl* ... ID-8
Darrah Pond—*lake* ... NH-1
Darrah Rsvr—*reservoir* ... ID-8
Darrah Sch—*school* ... PA-2
Darrah Springs State Fish
Hatchery—*locale* ... CA-9
Darraugh—*locale* ... SC-3
Darr Bayou—*stream* ... MS-4
Darr Branch—*stream* ... MO-7
Darr Branch—*stream* ... TX-5
Darr Bridge—*bridge* (2) ... NE-7
Darr Canyon—*valley* ... OR-9
Darr Cave—*cave* ... TN-4
Darr Cem—*cemetery* ... AR-4
*Darr Cove* ... GA-3
Darr Cove—*valley* ... GA-3
Darr Creek—*stream* ... KS-7
Darr Creek—*stream* ... OR-9
Darr Creek—*stream* ... TN-4
Darr Ditch—*canal* ... CO-8
Darr Ditch—*canal* ... WY-8
Darrell Airp (reduced usage)—*airport* ... TX-5
Darrell Creek—*stream* ... SC-3
*Darrell Parker Dam* ... AL-4
Darrell Parker Pond—*reservoir* ... AL-4
Darrell Ranch—*locale* ... NM-5
Darrell Sch—*school* ... TX-5
Darrell Springs—*spring* ... WY-8
*Darrells Run* ... VA-3
Darrell Tully Stadium—*other* ... TX-5
Darrels Peak—*summit* ... TX-5
*Darrels Run* ... VA-3
Darrel Thompson Lake Dam—*dam* ... MS-4
*Darren Creek* ... OR-9
Darr Field—*airport* ... NC-3
Darr Flats—*flat* ... OR-9
Darr Grave—*cemetery* ... OR-9
Darr Hollow—*valley* ... PA-2
Darrigans Creek—*stream* ... MN-6
Darrington—*locale* ... MS-4
**Darrington**—*pop pl* ... WA-9
Darrington Muni Airp—*airport* ... WA-9
Darrington State Prison Farm—*other* ... TX-5
Darrington Substation—*other* ... WA-9
*Darrit Anchorage* ... MP-9
*Darrit Island* ... MP-9
Darr Lake—*lake* ... MS-4
Darr Lateral—*canal* ... NE-7

Darroch Cem—cemetery NC-3
Darroch Creek—stream MT-8
Darroch Ditch—canal IN-6
**Darrough Chapel**—pop pl IN-6
Darrough Hot Springs NV-8
Darroughs Hot Springs—locale NV-8
**Darrouzett**—pop pl TX-5
Darrow—locale IL-6
Darrow—locale OK-5
**Darrow**—pop pl LA-4
Darrow, Bayou—stream LA-4
Darrow, Clarence, Octagon House—hist pl OH-6
Darrow, George, Round Barn—hist pl IA-7
Darrow Bar—bar OR-9
Darrow Branch—stream MO-7
Darrow Brook—stream NY-2
Darrow Brook—stream PA-2
Darrow Cem—cemetery MO-7
Darrow Chute—channel OK-9
Darrow Creek—stream WI-6
Darrow Drain—stream MI-6
Darrow Hollow—valley TN-4
Darrow Island—island WI-6
Darrow Mill—locale TN-4
Darrow Oil Field—oilfield LA-4
Darrow Pond—lake CT-1
Darrow Pond—reservoir PA-2
Darrow Rocks—cliff OR-9
Darrow Rocks—island CT-1
Darrow Sch (historical)—school IA-7
Darrows Creek—stream PA-2
Darrows Islands—island OR-9
Darrowsville—locale NY-2
Darrowville LA-4
Darrowville OH-6
Darrowville—locale OH-6
Darrs Creek—stream TX-5
Darrs Run—stream OH-6
Darrs Spring—spring OR-9
**Darrtown**—pop pl (2) OH-6
Darr Trail—trail PA-2
Darr Valley MO-7
Darr Valley—valley MO-7
**Darryl Gardens**—pop pl MD-2
Darrynane, Lake—reservoir KS-7
D A R Sch—school AL-4
**Darsey**—pop pl FL-3
Darsey Cem—cemetery AL-4
Darsey Cem—cemetery GA-3
Darsey Cem—cemetery MS-4
Darsey Mill Branch—stream GA-3
Darsey Pond—reservoir GA-3
Darsey Private Cem AL-4
Dars Sch—school PA-2
Darst Bottoms—bend MO-7
Darst Branch—stream AR-4
Darst Creek—stream TX-5
Darst Oil Field—oilfield TX-5
Darsyville IN-6
Dart—locale OH-6
**Dart**—pop pl AL-4
D'Artaguette Battlefield—locale MS-4
Dart Brook—stream NH-1
Dart Brook—stream NY-2
Dart Cem—cemetery OR-9
Dart Creek—stream CA-9
Dart Creek—stream MT-8
Dart Creek—stream OR-9
Darter Cem—cemetery TX-5
Darter Cem—cemetery VA-3
**Dartford**—pop pl WA-9
Dartford Bay—bay WI-6
Dartford Creek—stream WA-9
Dart Hill—summit WA-9
Darthula Ch—church VA-3
Dartigo Cem—cemetery LA-4
Dartigo Creek—stream LA-4
Dart Island State Park—park CT-1
Dartja FM-9
Dart Lake—lake MN-6
Dart Lake—lake NY-2
Dartlett Creek MO-7
**Dartmont**—pop pl WV-2
**Dartmont (Darkmont)**—pop pl KY-4
**Dartmoor**—pop pl (2) WV-2
Dartmouth MA-1
Dartmouth—hist pl IN-6
Dartmouth—locale KS-7
**Dartmouth**—pop pl MA-1
Dartmouth, Mount—summit NH-1
Dartmouth, Town of MA-1
Dartmouth Brook—stream NH-1
Dartmouth Coll—school NH-1
Dartmouth College Grant NH-1
Dartmouth College Grant—other NH-1
Dartmouth Creek—stream OR-9
Dartmouth Glacier—glacier AK-9
**Dartmouth Hills**—pop pl PA-2
Dartmouth HS—school MA-1
Dartmouth MS—school MA-1
Dartmouth Outing Club Trail—trail NH-1
Dartmouth Outing Club Trail—trail VT-1
Dartmouth Park—park FL-3
Dartmouth Park—park MI-6
Dartmouth Range—ridge NH-1
Dartmouth Rock—rock MA-1
Dartmouth Sch—school CA-9
Dartmouth Station MA-1
Dartmouth Street Sch—hist pl MA-1
Dartmouth Street Sch—school MA-1
**Dartmouth (Town of)**—pop pl MA-1
Dartmouth Trail—trail NH-1
**Dartmouth Woods**—pop pl DE-2
Darton Dome—summit AZ-5
Darton Peak—summit WY-8
Dart P.O. AL-4
Dart Ranch—locale AZ-5
Darts Corners—locale NY-2
Dart's Mill Hist Dist—hist pl NJ-2
**Darts Mills**—pop pl NJ-2
Darts Point—cape SC-3
Dart Tank—reservoir AZ-5
Dart Settlement Cem—cemetery PA-2
Dartts Park—park MN-6
Darty Gap—gap KY-4
Darty Gap—gap VA-3
Darty Mine (underground)—mine TN-4
Darty Windmill—locale TX-5
Daruchi-to MP-9
Darudou Island MP-9
Darudou Island—island MP-9
Darudou-To MP-9
Daruku MP-9
Daruma Canyon OR-9
Daruma Ridge OR-9
Darus Cem—cemetery MO-7
Daruuchi MP-9
Daruuchi Passage MP-9
Daruuchi To MP-9
Darvassy Airp—airport PA-2
**Dar Verda Subdivision**—pop pl UT-8
Darveys Chapel—church GA-3
Darvills—locale VA-3
Darvills Community Center—building VA-3
Darvills (Magisterial District)—fmr MCD VA-3
Darvin Island—island AK-9
Darvis Mine—mine MA-1
Darwin (2) IN-6
Darwin IN-4
Darwin—locale IA-7
Darwin—locale NV-8
Darwin—locale OK-5
Darwin—locale VA-3
**Darwin**—pop pl CA-9
**Darwin**—pop pl IL-6
**Darwin**—pop pl MN-6
**Darwin**—pop pl OH-6
**Darwin**—pop pl OK-5
Darwin, Lake—lake MN-6
Darwin, Mary, House—hist pl IA-7
Darwin, Mount—summit CA-9
Darwin Branch—stream TN-4
Darwin Canyon—valley (2) CA-9
Darwin Cave—cave AL-4
Darwin Cem—cemetery IL-6
Darwin Cem—cemetery TN-4
Darwin Cem—cemetery TX-5
Darwin Ch—church OK-5
Darwin Ch—church TN-4
**Darwin Downs**—pop pl AL-4
Darwin Falls—falls CA-9
Darwin Ferry—locale IL-6
Darwin Ferry—locale IN-6
Darwin Field—park TN-4
Darwin Glacier—glacier CA-9
Darwin Hills—summit CA-9
Darwin (historical)—locale KS-7
Darwin HS—school TN-4
**Darwin Mines**—pop pl CA-9
**Darwin Park (subdivision)**—pop pl TN-4
Darwin Peak—summit WY-8
Darwin Plateau—plain AZ-5
Darwin Plateau—plain CA-9
Darwin Ranch—locale NE-7
Darwin Ranch—locale WY-8
Darwin Rsvr—reservoir CO-8
Darwin Sch—school IL-6
**Darwin (Township of)**—pop pl IL-6
**Darwin (Township of)**—pop pl MN-6
Darwin Wash—stream CA-9
Dary Creek KS-7
Daryls Well—well AZ-5
Darysaw (Township of)—fmr MCD AR-4
Dascher Pond—lake NY-2
Daschers Sch (abandoned)—school PA-2
Dascher Valley—valley WI-6
Dascomb House—hist pl MA-1
Das Coulee MT-8
Dasha Island—island AK-9
Dasha Landing—locale GA-3
Dash Cem—cemetery ND-7
Dash Creek—stream ID-8
**Dasher**—pop pl GA-3
Dasher Creek—stream GA-3
Dasher HS—hist pl GA-3
Dasher Meadow—area OR-9
Dasher Sch—school GA-3
Dasher Sch—school MI-6
Dashers Lake—reservoir GA-3
Dasher-Stevens House—hist pl GA-3
Dashields Creek—stream CA-9
Dashields Dam—dam PA-2
Dashields Locks And Dam—dam PA-2
Dashields Pool—reservoir PA-2
Dashiell Creek—stream CA-9
Dashikekao MH-9
Dashoga Ridge—ridge NC-3
Dashonga Ridge NC-3
Dash Point—cape WA-9
**Dash Point**—pop pl WA-9
Dash Point State Park—park WA-9
**Dash Township**—pop pl ND-7
Dashville—locale NY-2
Dashwa Lake—lake MI-6
Dasinger Cem—cemetery AL-4
D A Smith Hollow—valley PA-2
**Daspit**—pop pl LA-4
**Dassel**—pop pl MN-6
**Dassel (Township of)**—pop pl MN-6
Dassori Pond—lake NY-2
Dassow Sch—school IL-6
**D'aste**—pop pl MT-8
D'Aste Ch—church MT-8
Dastrup Canyon—valley UT-8
Data Fold Forms Company—facility IL-6
Data (historical)—locale AL-4
D A Tank Number One—reservoir AZ-5
D A Tank Number Two—reservoir AZ-5
Datch Ridge WI-6
Date—locale AZ-5
**Date**—pop pl SD-7
Date Canal—canal CA-9
**Date City**—pop pl CA-9
**Date Creek**—pop pl AZ-5
Date Creek—stream AZ-5
Date Creek Mountains—range AZ-5
Date Creek Ranch—locale AZ-5
Date Creek Well—well AZ-5
**Date (Date Creek)**—pop pl AZ-5
Date Drain—canal CA-9
Date Drain One—canal CA-9
Date Drain Three—canal CA-9
Date Drain Three A—canal CA-9
Date Drain Three D—canal CA-9
Date Flat—flat CA-9
**Dateland**—pop pl AZ-5
Dateland Airfield—airport AZ-5
Dateland Highway Yard—locale AZ-5
Dateland Interchange—crossing AZ-5
Dateland Radar Tower—tower AZ-5
Dateland Sch—school AZ-5
Dateland Sch—school CA-9
Date Lateral Eight—canal CA-9
Date Lateral Five—canal CA-9
Date Lateral Nine—canal CA-9
Date Lateral Seven—canal CA-9
Date Lateral Seven A—canal CA-9
Date Lateral Six—canal CA-9
Date Lateral Ten—canal CA-9
Date Palm Beach CA-9
Dater Creek—stream WY-8
Date RR Station—building AZ-5
Daters Mtn—summit NY-2
Date Sch—school SD-7
Dates Creek—stream NC-3
Dates Millpond—lake WI-6
**Date Township**—pop pl MO-7
Datha—locale KY-4
Datha Island—island SC-3
Datheekook Point—cape AK-9
Dathlalmund Lake—lake AK-9
**Datil**—pop pl NM-5
Datil Mountains—range NM-5
Datjumur FM-9
Datkokan Creek—stream AK-9
Datkokan Lake—lake AK-9
Datolite Mine—mine MI-6
Daton Chapel—church KY-4
Daton Gulch—valley CO-8
Daton Peak—summit CO-8
Dators Pond—lake NJ-2
Datrallo landing—locale TN-4
Datry Spring—spring AZ-5
**Datto**—pop pl AR-4
Datton Lake—reservoir SD-7
Datura—locale TX-5
Datura Post Office (historical)—building TN-4
Datz, Walter, House—hist pl OH-6
Datzkoo Harbor—bay AK-9
Datzkoo Islands—area AK-9
Datzkoo Point—cape AK-9
**Daub**—pop pl LA-4
Daub Dam—dam ND-7
Daubenheyer Cem—cemetery IN-6
Daubenspeck Knob—summit WV-2
Daubenspeck Sch (historical)—school PA-2
**Dauberville**—pop pl PA-2
Dauberville Bridge—hist pl PA-2
Dauberville Lake—reservoir PA-2
Dauberville Lake Dam—dam PA-2
Daubney, John, House—hist pl MN-6
Daubs Lake—lake MN-6
Daubs Lake State Wildlife Mngmt Area—park MN-6
Dauchite Bayou AR-4
Dauchite Bayou LA-4
Daue, Alexander, House—hist pl OR-9
Dauenand—gut FM-9
Dauenieng FM-9
Dauen Nan Rohi FM-9
Dauenne—gut FM-9
Dauen Neu—gut FM-9
Dauen Neu, Pillen—stream FM-9
Dauenpei—gut FM-9
Dauenwoauwoa—gut FM-9
Dauers Slough—gut ND-7
Daufen Park—park WI-6
Daufuskie Island—island SC-3
Daufuskie Island—locale SC-3
Daufuskie Island Hist Dist—hist pl SC-3
Daugamah Cem—cemetery OK-5
Daugdrill Cem—cemetery MS-4
Daugharty, Lake—lake FL-3
Daugharty Cem—cemetery TN-4
Daugharty Gap—gap TN-4
Daugharty Tank—reservoir NM-5
Daughdrill Cem MS-4
Daughdrill Dead Lake—lake MS-4
Daugherly Landing (historical)—locale TN-4
Daugherty TX-5
**Daugherty**—pop pl MO-7
**Daugherty**—pop pl VA-3
Daugherty Baptist Ch—church TX-5
Daugherty Bend—bend MO-7
Daugherty Branch—stream FL-3
Daugherty Branch—stream KY-4
Daugherty Branch—stream PA-2
Daugherty Branch—stream TN-4
Daugherty Branch—stream TX-5
Daugherty Canyon—valley OR-9
Daugherty Cave—cave TN-4
Daugherty Cem—cemetery IL-6
Daugherty Cem—cemetery (2) IN-6
Daugherty Cem—cemetery (3) KY-4
Daugherty Cem—cemetery (2) TN-4
Daugherty Cem—cemetery (2) TX-5
Daugherty Cem—cemetery VA-3
Daugherty Chapel—church VA-3
Daugherty Corners MI-6
**Daugherty Corners**—pop pl MI-6
Daugherty Creek—channel (2) MD-2
Daugherty Creek—stream CA-9
Daugherty Creek—stream IA-7
Daugherty Creek—stream KY-4
Daugherty Creek—stream TN-4
Daugherty Creek Canal—canal MD-2
Daugherty (Dougherty)—other TX-5
**Daugherty Estates**—pop pl TN-4
Daugherty Gulch—valley ID-8
Daugherty Hill—summit CA-9
Daugherty Hill—summit ID-8
Daugherty (historical)—locale AL-4
Daugherty Hollow—valley PA-2
Daugherty Hollow—valley TN-4
Daugherty Hollow Trail—trail PA-2
Daugherty Knob—summit TN-4
Daugherty Lake TX-5
Daugherty Lake—lake TX-5
Daugherty Lake—reservoir OH-6
Daugherty Lateral—canal TX-5
Daugherty-Monroe Archaeolgical Site (12SU13)—hist pl IN-6
Daugherty Mtn—summit WV-2
Daugherty Oil Field—other NM-5
Daugherty Ranch—locale NV-8
Daugherty Ranch—locale TX-5
Daugherty Ridge—ridge ME-1
Daugherty Ridge—ridge NM-5
Daugherty Ridge—ridge TN-4
Daugherty Run—stream (4) PA-2
Daugherty Run—stream WV-2
Daughertys Cave—cave VA-3
Daugherty's Cave and Breeding Site—hist pl VA-3
Daugherty Sch—school TX-5
Daugherty's Creek MD-2
Daughertys Creek Canal MD-2
Daughertys Mill (historical)—locale TN-4
Daugherty Spring—spring ID-8
Daugherty Spring—spring NM-5
Daugherty Spring—spring TN-4
Daughertys Run PA-2
**Daugherty Town**—pop pl MD-2
**Daugherty (Township of)**—pop pl PA-2
Daugherty Trail—trail PA-2
Daughett Pit Number Two—cave AL-4
Daught Cem—cemetery TN-4
Daughter-In-Law Island FM-9
Daughter of Messiah Ch—church SC-3
Daughter of the Sun Mtn—summit MT-8
Daughters Cem—cemetery TX-5
Daughters' College—hist pl KY-4
Daughters of Jacob Hosp—hospital NY-2
Daughters of Saint Joseph Sch—school TX-5
Daughters of the American Revolution Campground—locale CO-8
Daughters of the American Revolution State For—forest MA-1
Daughters of Utah Pioneers Museum—building UT-8
Daughters of Zion Ch—church MS-4
Daughters of Zion Ch—church SC-3
Daughters Temple—church MS-4
**Daughtery**—pop pl VA-3
Daughtery Spring ID-8
Daughtrey, E. M., House—hist pl TX-5
Daughtrey Bluff—cliff MO-7
Daughtrey Cem—cemetery MO-7
Daughtrey Cem—cemetery TN-4
Daughtrey Creek—stream FL-3
Daughtry Bayou—bay FL-3
Daughtry Bridge—bridge NC-3
Daughtry Cem—cemetery GA-3
Daughtry Pond—lake AL-4
Daughtys Ferry TN-4
Daughty Well—well NM-5
Daukatau, Dolen—ridge FM-9
Dauko—channel FM-9
Daulain—gut FM-9
Daulam FM-9
Daule, E. A., House—hist pl TX-5
Daulton—locale CA-9
Daulton Creek—stream (2) CA-9
Daulton Ditch—canal CA-9
Daulton Hollow—valley IN-6
Daulton Mine—mine CA-9
Daulton Sch—school KY-4
Daulton Spring—spring CA-9
Daulton Station—locale CA-9
Daults Creek—stream MI-6
Daults River MI-6
Dauman Park—park OK-5
Daum Brothers Dam—dam SD-7
Daum Brothers Number 1 Dam—dam SD-7
Daum Brothers Number 2 Dam—dam SD-7
Daum Brothers Number 3 Dam—dam SD-7
Daum Brothers Number 4 Dam—dam SD-7
Daum Creek CO-8
Daum Draw—valley CO-8
Daume Oil Field—oilfield TX-5
Daumler Park—park AZ-5
Dau Mwaokote—channel FM-9
Dauness Lake MN-6
Daunt Branch—canal MI-6
Dauntless Mine—mine CO-8
Dauphin—locale TX-5
**Dauphin**—pop pl PA-2
Dauphin Bay AL-4
Dauphin Beach—beach AL-4
Dauphin Borough—civil PA-2
**Dauphin County**—pop pl PA-2
Dauphin County Area Vocational Technical Sch—school PA-2
Dauphine, Bayou—gut LA-4
Dauphine Hotel—hist pl MO-7
Dauphin Island—island AL-4
**Dauphin Island**—pop pl AL-4
Dauphin Island Air Force Station—military AL-4
Dauphin Island Airp—airport AL-4
Dauphin Island Bay—bay AL-4
Dauphin Island Bridge—bridge AL-4
Dauphin Island Sch—school AL-4
Dauphin Island Sealab—school AL-4
Dauphin Island Spit—bar AL-4
Dauphin Playlot—park IL-6
Dauphin Plaza—locale PA-2
Dauphin Rapids—rapids MT-8
Dauphin Way Baptist Ch—church AL-4
Dauphin Way Methodist Ch—church AL-4
Dauphiny Creek—stream CA-9
Daupwelmatak FM-9
DAur—island MP-9
**Daus**—pop pl TN-4
Daus Addition Lake—reservoir IN-6
Daus Addition Lake Dam—dam IN-6
Daus Drain—stream MI-6
Dausman Creek WA-9
Dausman Ditch—canal IN-6
Dausokele—bay FM-9
Dau Sokole—bay FM-9
Daus Post Office (historical)—building TN-4
Daus Sch (historical)—school TN-4
Dauss Fork—stream WV-2
Dautch Ditch—canal OH-6
Dauterive Lake—lake LA-4
Dauterive Landing—locale LA-4
Dau-Webbenhorst Barn—hist pl ID-8
Davana Cem—cemetery TN-4
**Davant**—pop pl LA-4
Davchport Cem—cemetery AL-4
Dave—locale AR-4
**Dave**—pop pl LA-4
**Dave**—pop pl WY-8
Dave Allen Point—summit WV-2
Dave Barrett Creek—stream NC-3
Dave Bellew Top—summit NC-3
Dave Blue Creek—stream OK-5
Dave Bluff—cliff TN-4
Dave Boggs Cem—cemetery KY-4
Dave Boyer Lake—reservoir OK-5
Dave Branch—stream (2) FL-3
Dave Branch—stream KY-4
Dave Branch—stream MO-7
Dave Branch—stream NC-3
Dave Branch—stream VA-3
Dave Branch—stream (3) WV-2
Dave Bright Cove—valley NC-3
Dave Busenbark County Park—park OR-9
Dave Canyon—valley UT-8
Dave Cave—cave AL-4
Dave Cem—cemetery TN-4
Dave Cobb Mine (underground)—mine AL-4
Dave Conley Sch—school KY-4
Dave Creek GA-3
Dave Creek ID-8
Dave Creek—stream AR-4
Dave Creek—stream ID-8
Dave Creek—stream NV-8
Dave Creek—stream WY-8
Dave Dear Well—well TX-5
Davee Gardens—uninc pl VA-3
Dave Flyinghawk Ranch (historical)—locale SD-7
Dave Fork—stream WV-2
Dave Foy Bank—bar FL-3
Dave Gap—gap NC-3
Daveggio Creek—stream ID-8
Daveggio Knob—summit ID-8
Daveggio Meadows—flat ID-8
Dave Gill Canal—canal TX-5
Dave Gill Tank—reservoir TX-5
Dave Green Hollow—valley AR-4
Dave Gross Gap—gap PA-2
Dave Gulch—valley AK-9
Dave Gulch—valley MT-8
Dave Harris Windmill—locale TX-5
Dave Harvey Canyon—valley KS-7
Dave Hill—summit MO-7
Dave Hollow—valley IN-6
Dave Hollow—valley KY-4
Dave Hollow—valley TN-4
Dave Ike Spring—spring OR-9
Dave Ingram Creek—stream ID-8
Dave Inside Pond—bay LA-4
Dave Johnson Creek—stream MT-8
Dave Jones Catfish Ponds Dam—dam (2) MS-4
Dave Joy Point—cliff AZ-5
Dave Jude Sch—school KY-4
Dave Keane Mtn—summit NV-8
Dave Keane Spring—spring NV-8
Dave Lake—lake AK-9
Dave Lake—lake WI-6
Dave Lay Hollow—valley TN-4
Dave Lee Lake—lake NM-5
Dave Lewis Branch—stream KY-4
Dave Lewis Peak—summit ID-8
Davella—locale KY-4
Davella Ch—church KY-4
Davell Airp—airport TX-5
Davella Mills County Park—park NJ-2
Dave Mack Branch—stream TX-5
Dave Mackie County Park—park WA-9
Dave McCain Spring (Dry)—spring CA-9
Dave McCloud Pond—lake FL-3
Dave Miller Hollow—valley TN-4
Dave Millsaps Hollow—valley AR-4
Dave Mills Cemetery MS-4
Dave Moore Point—cape NC-3
Daven Hill—summit CT-1
Davenpoint AL-4
Davenport KY-4
Davenport MS-4
Davenport TN-4
Davenport—locale VA-3
**Davenport**—pop pl AL-4
**Davenport**—pop pl AR-4
**Davenport**—pop pl CA-9
**Davenport**—pop pl FL-3
**Davenport**—pop pl IA-7
**Davenport**—pop pl KY-4
**Davenport**—pop pl NE-7
**Davenport**—pop pl NY-2
**Davenport**—pop pl ND-7
**Davenport**—pop pl OK-5
**Davenport**—pop pl TX-5
**Davenport**—pop pl WA-9
**Davenport**—pop pl WV-2
Davenport, Deacon John, House—hist pl CT-1
Davenport, Isaiah, House—hist pl GA-3
Davenport, Lake—lake (2) FL-3
Davenport, Lake—reservoir OK-5
Davenport, T. D., Forge (40LR7)—hist pl TN-4
Davenport, William H., House—hist pl MI-6
Davenport Airp—airport WA-9
Davenport Apartments—hist pl SC-3
Davenport Art Gallery—building IA-7
Davenport Bay—bay KY-4
Davenport Bayou MS-4
Davenport Bayou—bay FL-3
**Davenport (Beverly)**—pop pl MS-4
Davenport-Bradfield House—hist pl IN-6
Davenport Branch—stream GA-3
Davenport Branch—stream KY-4
Davenport Branch—stream NJ-2
Davenport Branch—stream (2) NC-3
Davenport Branch—stream SC-3
Davenport Branch—stream TX-5
Davenport Bridge—bridge VA-3
Davenport Bridge—other IL-6
Davenport Brook NJ-2
Davenport Brook—stream MA-1
Davenport Brook Rsvr—reservoir MA-1
Davenport Cabin—locale CO-8
Davenport Cabin (historical)—locale OR-9
Davenport Canyon—valley NV-8
Davenport Canyon—valley (2) NM-5
Davenport Canyon—valley UT-8
Davenport Canyon Spring—spring UT-8
Davenport Cave—cave TN-4
Davenport (CCD)—cens area WA-9
Davenport Cem—cemetery (3) AL-4
Davenport Cem—cemetery FL-3
Davenport Cem—cemetery (2) KY-4
Davenport Cem—cemetery MO-7
Davenport Cem—cemetery NC-3
Davenport Cem—cemetery ND-7
Davenport Cem—cemetery (2) TN-4
Davenport Cem—cemetery (3) TX-5
**Davenport Center**—pop pl NY-2
Davenport Chapel—church OK-5
Davenport Chapel Sch—school AL-4
Davenport City Hall—building IA-7
Davenport City Hall—hist pl IA-7
Davenport City Township—fmr MCD IA-7
Davenport Coulee—valley MT-8
Davenport Country Club And Golf Course—other IA-7
Davenport Cove—bay ME-1
**Davenport Cove**—pop pl ME-1
Davenport Creek KY-4
Davenport Creek—stream AR-4
Davenport Creek—stream CA-9
Davenport Creek—stream CO-8
Davenport Creek—stream FL-3
Davenport Creek—stream MI-6
Davenport Creek—stream NC-3
Davenport Creek—stream OK-5
Davenport Creek—stream TN-4
Davenport Creek—stream UT-8
Davenport Creek Swamp—swamp FL-3
Davenport Crematorium—hist pl IA-7
Davenport Drain—canal MI-6
Davenport Draw TX-5
Davenport Draw—valley MT-8
Davenport Draw—valley UT-8
Davenport Elem Sch—school FL-3
Davenport Elem Sch—school NC-3
Davenport Elem Sch—school TN-4
Davenport Forks—locale NC-3
Davenport Gap—gap NC-3
Davenport Gap—gap TN-4
Davenport Glacier—glacier WA-9
Davenport Gulch—valley CO-8
Davenport Harbor—bay IA-7
Davenport Hill MA-1
Davenport Hill—summit AZ-5
Davenport Hill—summit TX-5
Davenport Hill—summit UT-8
Davenport (historical)—locale MS-4
**Davenport (historical)**—pop pl NC-3
Davenport Hollow—valley MO-7
Davenport Hollow—valley (3) TN-4
Davenport Hollow—valley UT-8
Davenport Hose Station No. 3—hist pl IA-7
Davenport Hotel—hist pl IA-7
Davenport Hotel—hist pl WA-9
Davenport House—hist pl NY-2
Davenport HS—school SC-3
Davenport Knob—summit GA-3
Davenport Knoll—summit AZ-5
Davenport Lake—lake AZ-5
Davenport Lake—lake MN-6
Davenport Landing—locale KY-4
**Davenport Landing**—pop pl CA-9
Davenport Library—hist pl NY-2
Davenport Lookout Tower—locale NM-5
Davenport Memorial Park—park IA-7
Davenport Mine—mine KY-4
Davenport Mine—mine NM-5
Davenport Mine—mine TN-4
Davenport Mtn—summit (2) GA-3
Davenport Mtn—summit NC-3
Davenport Neck—cape NY-2
Davenport Oil Field—oilfield TX-5
Davenport Park—park OH-6
Davenport Peak—summit AZ-5
Davenport Peak—summit NM-5
Davenport Picnic Area—locale CO-8
Davenport Point—cape CT-1
Davenport Point—cape ME-1
Davenport Point—cape MA-1
Davenport Pond—lake OH-6
Davenport Pond—reservoir AL-4
Davenport Pond—reservoir MA-1
Davenport Pond—reservoir OR-9
Davenport Pond—reservoir VA-3
Davenport Ranch—locale CO-8
Davenport Sch—school KS-7
Davenport Sch—school (3) MA-1
Davenport Sch—school MI-6
Davenport Sch—school TX-5
Davenport Sch Number 1—school TX-5
Davenport Sch Number 2—school TX-5
Davenports Creek NJ-2
Davenport's Island NY-2
Davenports Millpond—reservoir GA-3
Davenport Spring—spring NM-5
Davenport Spring—spring OR-9
Davenport Spring—spring TX-5
Davenport Spring—spring UT-8
Davenports Run NJ-2
Davenports Tavern Branch NJ-2
Davenport Table—summit NE-7
Davenport Tank—reservoir AZ-5
Davenport Tower (fire tower)—tower FL-3
**Davenport (Town of)**—pop pl NY-2
**Davenport Township**—pop pl ND-7
Davenport Village—hist pl IA-7
Davenport Wash—stream AZ-5
Davenport Water Co. Pumping Station No. 2—hist pl IA-7
Daven Sch—school IL-6
Daventon Ch—church SC-3
Dave Outside Pond—bay LA-4
Dave Peterson Number 3 Dam—dam SD-7
Dave Peterson Number 4 Dam—dam SD-7
Dave Phelps Ridge—ridge CA-9
Dave Pointer Pond Dam—dam MS-4
Dave Pond—reservoir AZ-5
Daveport Ranch—locale NM-5
Dave Rains Cemetery TN-4
Davereux Rocks—bar MA-1
Dave Ridge—ridge GA-3
Davern, William and Catherine, Farm House—hist pl MN-6
Daves Ave Sch—school CA-9
Daves Bayou—stream LA-4
Daves Branch—stream (2) KY-4
Daves Branch—stream VA-3
Daves Branch—stream WV-2
Daves Canyon—valley UT-8
Daves Cave—cave AL-4
Daves Cave—cave PA-2
Daves Cemetery TN-4
Daves Coulee—valley MT-8
Daves Cove—valley NC-3
Daves Creek—stream AK-9

Daves Creek—*stream* GA-3
Daves Creek—*stream* ID-8
Daves Creek—*stream* NY-2
Daves Creek Ch—*church* GA-3
Daves Falls Park—*park* WI-6
Daves Fork—*stream* WV-2
Daves Gap—*locale* PA-2
Dave Shea Spring—*spring* ID-8
Daves Hill—*summit* MD-2
Daves Hollow—*valley* UT-8
Daves Hollow Forest Service Station—*locale* UT-8
*Daves Hollow Ranger Station* UT-8
*Daves Island* ME-1
Daves Island—*island* LA-4
Dave Smith Branch—*stream* KY-4
Dave Smith Windmill—*locale* NM-5
Daves Mtn—*summit* NC-3
Daves Pass—*gap* ID-8
Daves Pass Spring—*spring* ID-8
Daves Peak—*summit* VT-1
Daves Pit—*cave* AL-4
Dave Spring—*spring* OR-9
Daves Ravine—*valley* CA-9
*Daves Ridge* WA-9
Daves Ridge—*ridge* CA-9
Daves Ridge—*ridge* VA-3
Daves Rock—*summit* NC-3
Daves Rsvr—*reservoir* (2) ID-8
Daves Run—*stream* (2) WV-2
Daves Slough—*gut* OR-9
Daves Spring—*spring* CA-9
Daves Tank—*reservoir* (3) AZ-5
Daves Well—*well* AZ-5
Dave Teeples Spring—*spring* UT-8
Dave Well—*well* NM-5
*Dave West Creek* OR-9
Dave Wright Hill—*summit* CO-8
**Davey**—*pop pl* NE-7
Davey, Harvey M., House—*hist pl* ID-8
Davey, John, House—*hist pl* OH-6
Davey, Randall, House—*hist pl* NM-5
Davey Butte—*summit* MT-8
Davey Coulee—*valley* MT-8
Davey Creek—*stream* MT-8
*Davey Gulch* MT-8
Davey Hill—*summit* VA-3
Davey Hill Sch (abandoned)—*school* PA-2
Davey Hollow Cove—*bay* MO-7
Davey JHS—*school* NJ-2
*Davey Johns Dam* PA-2
Davey Lake—*lake* CO-8
Davey Lake—*lake* OR-9
Davey Lake—*reservoir* TX-5
Davey Land Branch—*stream* VA-3
Davey Land Ridge—*ridge* VA-3
Davey Park—*park* TX-5
*Davey Reservoir* CO-8
Davey Run—*stream* PA-2
Davey Sch—*school* MT-8
Davey Sch—*school* WI-6
Daveys Hollow—*valley* MO-7
Daveys Lake—*lake* NJ-2
Daveys Spring—*spring* ID-8
Davey Station—*locale* PA-2
Davey Switch—*locale* IL-6
*Davey Town* NV-8
Daveytown—*locale* NV-8
Daveytown Flat—*flat* NV-8
Daveytown Spring—*spring* NV-8
*David* VA-3
*David* MP-9
**David**—*pop pl* GA-3
**David**—*pop pl* KY-4
David, Lake—*lake* AR-4
David, Lake—*lake* (2) FL-3
David, Lake—*lake* MI-6
David, Lake—*lake* NM-5
David, Lake—*reservoir* AL-4
David, Lake—*reservoir* GA-3
David, Lake—*reservoir* MS-4
David, Lake—*reservoir* NC-3
David, Leopold, House—*hist pl* AK-9
David, Mount—*summit* ME-1
David, Mount—*summit* WA-9
David, William, House—*hist pl* KY-4
David and Marshall Cave—*cave* AL-4
David Ave Sch—*school* CA-9
*David Ball Creek* NY-2
David Bayou—*stream* MS-4
David Beck Cem—*cemetery* PA-2
*David Bell Church* TN-4
David Blevins Branch—*stream* TN-4
David B Oliver Senior HS—*school* PA-2
David Bottom—*bend* TX-5
David Bradford House—*building* PA-2
David Branch—*stream* IN-6
David Branch—*stream* WV-2
David Brewer Elem Sch—*school* KS-7
David Canyon—*valley* NM-5
David Castle—*bar* ME-1
David Cem—*cemetery* IN-6
David Cem—*cemetery* NM-5
David Cem—*cemetery* OH-6
David Cem—*cemetery* TN-4
David Ch—*church* IA-7
David Ch—*church* (2) NC-3
David Chapel—*church* AR-4
David Chapel—*church* NC-3
David Chapel Cem—*cemetery* TX-5
**David City**—*pop pl* NE-7
David City Cem—*cemetery* NE-7
*David C Lincoln Elementary School* AZ-5
David Corckett Elem Sch—*school* TN-4
David Craigs Fort (historical)—*locale* TN-4
*David Craigs Station* TN-4
David Cravey Lake Dam—*dam* AL-4
*David Creek* MT-8
David Creek—*stream* (2) AK-9
David Creek—*stream* (2) MT-8
David Creek—*stream* (2) OR-9
David Creek—*stream* VA-3
David Creek—*stream* WA-9
David Creek Trail—*trail* TN-4
David Crockett HS—*school* TN-4
David Crockett HS—*school* TX-5
David Crockett JHS—*school* (2) TX-5
David Crockett Lake—*reservoir* TN-4
David Crockett Lake Dam—*dam* TN-4
David Crockett Mine—*mine* TN-4
David Crockett Sch—*school* (2) TX-5
David Crockett State Park—*park* TN-4
David Crockett Visit Lions Club Park—*park* AL-4
David Dam—*dam* AL-4
David Ditch—*canal* IN-6
David Douglas, Mount—*summit* OR-9
David Douglas State Park—*park* OR-9
David Drain—*canal* MI-6
David Drain—*stream* IN-6
David D Terry Lock and Dam—*dam* AR-4
David D Terry Public Use Area—*park* AR-4
*David Duck Cemetery* MS-4
David E Jones Pond Dam—*dam* MS-4
David E Miller Hill—*summit* UT-8
Davider Sch—*school* MI-6
David E Williams JHS—*school* PA-2
David Farm Trail—*trail* PA-2
David Fork—*stream* KY-4
David Fork Ch—*church* KY-4
David Gam Bay—*swamp* NC-3
David Garriott Lake—*reservoir* IN-6
David Garriott Lake Dam—*dam* IN-6
Davidge Brook—*stream* CT-1
Davidge Hall, Univ of Maryland—*hist pl* MD-2
Davidge Pond—*lake* CT-1
David Gourley Sch—*school* UT-8
David Gulch—*valley* CA-9
David Hill—*ridge* OR-9
David Hill—*summit* NM-5
David Hill Cem—*cemetery* OR-9
David Hill Sch—*school* OR-9
David (historical)—*locale* AL-4
David (historical)—*locale* MS-4
Davidhizer Ditch—*canal* IN-6
David Horse Camp—*locale* MT-8
David Island—*island* AK-9
David Island—*island* FL-3
David Island—*island* ME-1
David Jones Dam—*dam* SD-7
David Kent Dam—*dam* OR-9
David Kent Rsvr—*reservoir* OR-9
David Kernop Lake Dam—*dam* MS-4
David Kessler Memorial State Wildlife Area—*park* MO-7
David Key—*island* FL-3
David Kinker Ditch—*canal* WY-8
David Kitterman Dam—*dam* SD-7
David Knob—*summit* KY-4
David Lake—*lake* AL-4
David Lake—*lake* MN-6
David Lake—*lake* WI-6
David Lake Dam—*dam* MS-4
David Lawrence Convention Center—*building* PA-2
David Lindsay Cem—*cemetery* AL-4
David Lipscomb Coll—*school* TN-4
David L Swartz Intermediate Sch—*school* PA-2
David Lubin Sch—*school* CA-9
**David Manor (subdivision)**—*pop pl* PA-2
David McCarthy Ranch—*locale* WY-8
David Memorial Ch—*church* NC-3
David O Dodd Sch—*school* AR-4
David O Duncan Elem Sch—*school* IN-6
Davidof Island—*island* AK-9
Davidof Lake—*lake* AK-9
Davidof Lake Trail—*trail* AK-9
David Oil Field—*oilfield* KS-7
David Olson Dam—*dam* SD-7
David Park—*park* FL-3
*David Peterson Lake* PA-2
David Point—*cape* VI-3
David Pond—*lake* GA-3
David Pond—*lake* KY-4
David Pond—*lake* ME-1
David Ridge—*ridge* OR-9
David River—*stream* AK-9
David Rock—*rock* MA-1
David Run—*stream* IN-6
David Run—*stream* VA-3
**Davids**—*pop pl* LA-4
Davids' Bldg—*hist pl* ID-8
**Davidsburg**—*pop pl* PA-2
Davidsburg Run—*stream* PA-2
Davids Caves—*cave* AL-4
David Sch (historical)—*school* MO-7
*David School* PA-2
*Davids Creek* MS-4
Davids Creek—*stream* IL-6
Davids Creek—*stream* IA-7
Davids Creek—*stream* TN-4
Davids Crossroads—*locale* VA-3
David Scurry Grant—*civil* FL-3
Davids Drain—*stream* MI-6
Davids Grove Ch—*church* SC-3
Davids Home Ch—*church* GA-3
*Davids Island* GA-3
Davids Island—*island* MA-1
Davids Island—*island* NY-2
Davids Knob—*summit* TN-4
Davids Millpond—*reservoir* SC-3
**David Smith Subdivision**—*pop pl* UT-8
Davidson—*locale* AR-4
Davidson—*locale* ID-8
Davidson—*locale* MN-6
Davidson—*locale* TN-4
Davidson—*locale* TX-5
**Davidson**—*pop pl* IN-6
**Davidson**—*pop pl* NC-3
**Davidson**—*pop pl* OH-6
**Davidson**—*pop pl* OK-5
**Davidson**—*pop pl* OR-9
**Davidson**—*pop pl* (2) PA-2
**Davidson**—*pop pl* SC-3
**Davidson**—*pop pl* TN-4
Davidson, A. C., House—*hist pl* KY-4
Davidson, Benjamin W., House—*hist pl* NC-3
Davidson, Dr. John E. and Mary D., House—*hist pl* OR-9
Davidson, G. W., House and Bank—*hist pl* KY-4
Davidson, Mount—*summit* CA-9
Davidson, Mount—*summit* NV-8
Davidson, Sam, House—*hist pl* AR-4
Davidson, Tyler, Fountain—*hist pl* OH-6
Davidson, Wilbur F., House—*hist pl* MI-6
Davidson Acad—*school* TN-4
Davidson Bank—*bar* AK-9
**Davidson (Barretts Ferry)**—*pop pl* KY-4
Davidson Bay—*bay* AK-9
**Davidson Beach**—*pop pl* NY-2
Davidson Bldg—*hist pl* MO-7
Davidson Bldg—*hist pl* MT-8
Davidson Branch—*stream* (2) KY-4
Davidson Branch—*stream* NE-7
Davidson Branch—*stream* NC-3
Davidson Branch—*stream* (3) TN-4
Davidson Bridge—*bridge* OR-9
Davidson Brook—*stream* ME-1
Davidson Camp—*locale* AR-4
Davidson Canyon—*valley* (2) AZ-5
Davidson Canyon—*valley* OR-9
Davidson Canyon—*valley* TX-5
Davidson Canyon—*valley* UT-8
Davidson Cave—*cave* AL-4
Davidson (CCD)—*cens area* OK-5
Davidson Cem—*cemetery* (5) AL-4
Davidson Cem—*cemetery* AR-4
Davidson Cem—*cemetery* IL-6
Davidson Cem—*cemetery* (3) KY-4
Davidson Cem—*cemetery* (3) LA-4
Davidson Cem—*cemetery* (5) MO-7
Davidson Cem—*cemetery* (2) OH-6
Davidson Cem—*cemetery* OK-5
Davidson Cem—*cemetery* (9) TN-4
Davidson Cem—*cemetery* (4) TX-5
Davidson Cem—*cemetery* VT-1
Davidson Cem—*cemetery* (2) VA-3
Davidson Cem—*cemetery* (2) WV-2
Davidson Ch—*church* AR-4
Davidson Ch—*church* GA-3
Davidson Ch—*church* KY-4
Davidson Ch—*church* NC-3
Davidson Ch—*church* PA-2
Davidson Chapel—*church* (2) TN-4
Davidson Chapel—*church* TX-5
Davidson Chapel Cem—*cemetery* TN-4
Davidson Chapel Christian Methodist Episcopal Ch—*church* MS-4
Davidson Chapel Sch (historical)—*school* TN-4
*Davidson City* CA-9
*Davidson Coll* NC-3
Davidson Coll—*school* NC-3
Davidson Corners—*locale* PA-2
Davidson Coulee—*valley* (2) MT-8
*Davidson (County)* TN-4
Davidson County—*civil* TN-4
**Davidson County**—*pop pl* NC-3
Davidson County Courthouse—*hist pl* TN-4
Davidson County Developmental Center—*building* NC-3
Davidson County Extended Day Sch—*school* NC-3
*Davidson Cove* AL-4
Davidson Cove—*stream* TN-4
Davidson Cove—*valley* NC-3
Davidson Cove Branch—*stream* TN-4
*Davidson Creek* AL-4
*Davidson Creek* MT-8
Davidson Creek—*stream* AL-4
Davidson Creek—*stream* AK-9
Davidson Creek—*stream* GA-3
Davidson Creek—*stream* IL-6
Davidson Creek—*stream* MI-6
Davidson Creek—*stream* (2) MS-4
Davidson Creek—*stream* (2) MT-8
Davidson Creek—*stream* NC-3
Davidson Creek—*stream* (2) TN-4
Davidson Creek—*stream* (2) TX-5
Davidson Creek—*stream* VA-3
Davidson Creek—*stream* WI-6
Davidson Creek—*stream* WY-8
*Davidson-Cutler Cemetery* TX-5
*Davidson Ditch* IN-6
Davidson Ditch—*canal* AK-9
Davidson Ditch—*canal* CO-8
Davidson Ditch—*canal* IN-6
Davidson Drain—*canal* IN-6
Davidson Draw—*valley* MT-8
Davidson Elem Sch—*school* NC-3
Davidson Flat—*flat* SD-7
Davidson Flats—*flat* WY-8
Davidson Fork—*stream* KY-4
Davidson Gap—*gap* (2) NC-3
Davidson Glacier—*glacier* AK-9
Davidson Grove Ch—*church* SC-3
Davidson Gulch—*valley* OR-9
Davidson Hall—*hist pl* WI-6
Davidson Hall, Coker College—*hist pl* SC-3
*Davidson Head* WA-9
Davidson Heights—*locale* PA-2
**Davidson Heights**—*pop pl* PA-2
Davidson Hester Cem—*cemetery* TN-4
Davidson Hill—*summit* AR-4
Davidson Hill—*summit* CT-1
Davidson Hill—*summit* GA-3
Davidson Hill—*summit* OK-5
Davidson Hill—*summit* OR-9
Davidson Hill—*summit* PA-2
Davidson Hill—*summit* (2) TN-4
Davidson Hill—*summit* (2) VT-1
**Davidson (historical)**—*pop pl* ME-1
**Davidson (historical)**—*pop pl* MS-4
Davidson Hollow—*valley* AL-4
Davidson Hollow—*valley* AR-4
Davidson Hollow—*valley* OH-6
Davidson Hollow—*valley* (5) TN-4
Davidson Hollow—*valley* VA-3
Davidson House—*hist pl* LA-4
Davidson House—*hist pl* NC-3
Davidson House—*hist pl* WA-9
Davidson Inlet—*bay* AK-9
Davidson Island—*island* MI-6
Davidson JHS—*school* MI-6
*Davidson Lake* MI-6
Davidson Lake—*lake* AK-9
Davidson Lake—*lake* IN-6
Davidson Lake—*lake* MI-6
Davidson Lake—*lake* MN-6
Davidson Lakes—*reservoir* GA-3
Davidson Lookout Tower—*locale* GA-3
Davidson Marsh—*swamp* DE-2
Davidson Memorial Ch—*church* NC-3
Davidson Memorial Gardens—*cemetery* KY-4
Davidson Mesa—*summit* CO-8
Davidson Mountains—*range* AK-9
Davidson Number Three Mine—*mine* MI-6
Davidson Oil Field—*oilfield* KS-7
Davidson Oil Field—*oilfield* TX-5
Davidson Park—*park* IL-6
Davidson Park—*park* MO-7
Davidson Park—*park* OR-9
Davidson Peak—*summit* NV-8
Davidson Peak—*summit* TX-5
Davidson Plantation (historical)—*locale* TN-4
Davidson Plaza Shop Ctr—*locale* NC-3
Davidson Pond—*lake* MA-1
Davidson Pond—*reservoir* ME-1
Davidson Post Office (historical)—*building* SD-7
Davidson Post Office (historical)—*building* TN-4
Davidson Ranch—*locale* AZ-5
Davidson Ranch—*locale* CO-8
Davidson Ranch—*locale* ID-8
Davidson Ranch—*locale* (2) NM-5
Davidson Ranch—*locale* TX-5
Davidson Ranch—*locale* (2) WY-8
Davidson Ranch Airstrip—*airport* OR-9
Davidson Ridge—*ridge* VA-3
Davidson Ridge—*ridge* WV-2
**Davidson River**—*pop pl* NC-3
Davidson River—*stream* NC-3
Davidson River Cem—*cemetery* NC-3
Davidson River Rec Area—*locale* NC-3
*Davidson River Recreation Site* NC-3
Davidson Rock Light—*locale* WA-9
Davidson Rsvr—*reservoir* OR-9
Davidson Run—*stream* (2) PA-2
Davidson Run—*stream* VA-3
Davidsons Blue Spring—*spring* MO-7
Davidson Sch—*school* AZ-5
Davidson Sch—*school* (2) CA-9
Davidson Sch—*school* (2) MS-4
Davidson Sch—*school* MO-7
Davidson Sch—*school* PA-2
Davidson Sch (historical)—*school* (2) TN-4
Davidsons Corner—*locale* CT-1
*Davidsons Creek* NC-3
Davidsons Cross Roads (historical)—*locale* AL-4
*Davidson's Island* ID-8
Davidsons Landing—*locale* TN-4
**Davidsons Landing**—*pop pl* AK-9
Davidsons Landing (historical)—*locale* AL-4
Davidsons Mill (historical)—*locale* (2) TN-4
Davidsons Millpond—*reservoir* NJ-2
Davidsons Millpond Dam—*dam* NJ-2
Davidson-Smitherman House—*hist pl* AL-4
Davidson Spring—*spring* AL-4
Davidson Spring—*spring* AZ-5
Davidson Spring—*spring* CO-8
Davidson Spring—*spring* (2) OR-9
Davidson Spring—*spring* SD-7
Davidsons Slough—*stream* AK-9
*Davidsons Store* AL-4
Davidsons Store (historical)—*locale* AL-4
Davidson Station—*locale* KY-4
Davidson Tank—*reservoir* AZ-5
Davidson Tank—*reservoir* TX-5
Davidson (Township of)—*fmr MCD* (2) AR-4
Davidson (Township of)—*fmr MCD* NC-3
**Davidson (Township of)**—*pop pl* PA-2
Davidson Tunnel—*tunnel* NM-5
Davidson (Unorganized Territory of)—*unorg* MN-6
**Davidsonville**—*pop pl* MD-2
Davidsonville Branch—*stream* MD-2
Davidson Well—*well* AZ-5
Davidson Windmill—*hist pl* WI-6
Davids Point—*cape* NY-2
Davids Point—*cape* NC-3
*Davids Ridge* WA-9
Davids Run—*stream* OH-6
Davids Spring—*spring* VA-3
David Stand Ch—*church* SC-3
Davids Tank—*reservoir* TX-5
David Star Ch—*church* WI-6
*Davidstown* NJ-2
**David Street Subdivision**—*pop pl* UT-8
*Davidsville* PA-2
**Davidsville**—*pop pl* PA-2
Davids Well—*well* NV-8
Davids Windmill—*locale* TX-5
David Tank—*reservoir* AZ-5
David Temple Ch—*church* AL-4
David Thomas Cem—*cemetery* MS-4
David Thomas Jones Bridge—*bridge* TN-4
David Thompson Memorial—*locale* ND-7
David Thompson State Game Preserve—*park* ID-8
David Tod Memorial Park—*park* OH-6
David Turnham Educational Center—*school* IN-6
David Watts Bluff (historical)—*cliff* ND-7
David West Dam—*dam* AL-4
David West Lake—*reservoir* AL-4
David W Griffith JHS—*school* CA-9
David W. Harlan Elem Sch—*school* DE-2
David W Taylor R&D Center—*military* MD-2
**Davie**—*pop pl* FL-3
**Davie**—*pop pl* NC-3
Davie, William R., House—*hist pl* NC-3
Davie Academy Corners—*locale* NC-3
Davie Apostolic Ch—*church* FL-3
Davie Ave Sch—*school* NC-3
Davie Branch—*stream* NC-3
Davie (CCD)—*cens area* FL-3
Davie Cem—*cemetery* AL-4
**Davie Circle**—*pop pl* NC-3
Davie Country Stores Shop Ctr—*locale* FL-3
**Davie County**—*pop pl* NC-3
Davie County Courthouse—*hist pl* NC-3
Davie County Hosp—*hospital* NC-3
Davie County HS—*school* NC-3
Davie County Jail—*hist pl* NC-3
**Davie Crossroads**—*pop pl* NC-3
Davie Ditch—*canal* CO-8
Davie Elem Sch—*school* FL-3
**Davie Gardens (subdivision)**—*pop pl* NC-3
*Davie Lake* MI-6
Davie MS—*school* NC-3
Davie Mtn—*summit* NC-3
*Davies* OR-9
Davies—*locale* MN-6
**Davies**—*pop pl* WA-9
Davies, Charles E., House—*hist pl* UT-8
Davies, Dr. James, House—*hist pl* ID-8
Davies Bldg—*hist pl* KS-7
Davies Branch—*stream* VA-3
Davies Canyon—*valley* CA-9
Davies Canyon—*valley* WA-9
Davies Cem—*cemetery* AR-4
Davies Cem—*cemetery* MS-4
Davies Cem—*cemetery* NY-2
Davie Sch—*hist pl* FL-3
Davie Sch—*school* IL-6
*Davies Creek* CA-9
*Davies Creek* TN-4
Davies Creek—*stream* AK-9
Davies Creek—*stream* CA-9
Davies Creek—*stream* ID-8
Davies Creek—*stream* MI-6
Davies Grove Ch—*church* WV-2
Davies Gulch—*valley* OR-9
Davies Hosp (historical)—*hospital* AL-4
Davies Hotel—*hist pl* CO-8
Davies House—*hist pl* PA-2
Davies Island—*island* TN-4
Davies Junction—*locale* OR-9
*Davies Lake* MI-6
*Davies Lake* NJ-2
Davies Lake—*lake* MI-6
Davies Lake—*lake* MN-6
Davies Lake—*lake* WI-6
*Davies Lake Flowage* WI-6
Davies Manor—*hist pl* TN-4
Davies Orchard—*locale* CA-9
Davies Park—*park* MI-6
Davies Pass—*gap* ID-8
Davies Pass—*gap* WA-9
Davies Place—*locale* NM-5
Davies Ranch—*locale* UT-8
*Davies Reservoir* CO-8
Davies Sch—*school* OH-6
**Daviess County**—*pop pl* IN-6
**Daviess (County)**—*pop pl* KY-4
**Daviess County**—*pop pl* MO-7
Daviess County Airp—*airport* IN-6
Daviess County Courthouse—*hist pl* MO-7
Daviess East (CCD)—*cens area* KY-4
Davies Spring—*spring* NV-8
Davies Spring—*spring* OR-9
Davies State Wildlife Mngmt Area—*park* MN-6
Daviess West (CCD)—*cens area* KY-4
Davie Stadium—*other* CA-9
Davies Tank—*reservoir* NM-5
Davies Valley—*valley* CA-9
Davies Well—*well* UT-8
Davie Youth Park—*park* NC-3
Davignon Pond—*reservoir* NY-2
Davila Well—*well* NM-5
**Davilla**—*pop pl* TX-5
Davilla (CCD)—*cens area* TX-5
Davilla Cem—*cemetery* TX-5
*Davills Brook* RI-1
*Davils Brook* RI-1
Davin—*locale* WA-9
**Davin**—*pop pl* IN-6
**Davin**—*pop pl* WV-2
DaVinci Institute—*school* FL-3
Davin Ranch—*locale* WA-9
*Davions Rock* MS-4
*Davis* AR-4
*Davis* DE-2
*Davis* IN-6
*Davis* MO-7
*Davis* NJ-2
*Davis* PA-2
Davis—*locale* AL-4
Davis—*locale* GA-3
Davis—*locale* IL-6
Davis—*locale* KY-4
Davis—*locale* PA-2
Davis—*locale* TN-4
Davis—*locale* TX-5
Davis—*locale* VA-3
Davis—*locale* WA-9
Davis—*locale* WY-8
Davis—*other* PA-2
**Davis**—*pop pl* CA-9
**Davis**—*pop pl* IL-6
**Davis**—*pop pl* IN-6
**Davis**—*pop pl* MI-6
**Davis**—*pop pl* MN-6
**Davis**—*pop pl* (3) MS-4
**Davis**—*pop pl* (2) MO-7
**Davis**—*pop pl* (2) NH-1
**Davis**—*pop pl* NC-3
**Davis**—*pop pl* OK-5
**Davis**—*pop pl* SD-7
**Davis**—*pop pl* (2) WV-2
Davis—*uninc pl* TN-4
Davis, Alexander, Cabin—*hist pl* OH-6
Davis, Alexander, House—*hist pl* OH-6
Davis, Anson, House—*hist pl* OH-6
Davis, Anson, Springhouse—*hist pl* OH-6
Davis, Archibald H., Plantation—*hist pl* NC-3
Davis, Attoway R., Home—*hist pl* AL-4
Davis, Cyrus-Davis Brothers Farmhouse—*hist pl* WI-6
Davis, Daniel, House—*hist pl* KY-4
Davis, Daniel, House and Barn—*hist pl* PA-2
Davis, David, III & IV, House—*hist pl* IL-6
Davis, E. C., House—*hist pl* MN-6
Davis, E. F., House—*hist pl* ID-8
Davis, E. M., Farm—*hist pl* KY-4
Davis, George C., Site—*hist pl* TX-5
Davis, George C., Site (Boundary Increase)—*hist pl* TX-5
Davis, George W., House—*hist pl* TX-5
Davis, Grobin, Mound Group—*hist pl* OK-5
Davis, H. L., House—*hist pl* TX-5
Davis, Horn, Overholtzer Bridge—*hist pl* PA-2
Davis, H. R., House—*hist pl* WI-6
Davis, Isaac, House—*hist pl* MA-1
Davis, Isaac, Trail—*hist pl* MA-1
Davis, James, Barn—*hist pl* OH-6
Davis, James, Farm—*hist pl* OH-6
Davis, Jefferson, Capture Site—*hist pl* GA-3
Davis, Jefferson, Hotel—*hist pl* AL-4
Davis, Jefferson, Monmt—*hist pl* KY-4
Davis, J. M., House—*hist pl* AK-9
Davis, John, House—*hist pl* ME-1
Davis, John, House—*hist pl* NC-3
Davis, John A., House—*hist pl* GA-3
Davis, John T., House—*hist pl* GA-3
Davis, Joseph, House—*hist pl* MA-1
Davis, Joshua, House—*hist pl* FL-3
Davis, Josiah, House—*hist pl* GA-3
Davis, Lake—*lake* (2) FL-3
Davis, Lake—*reservoir* CA-9
Davis, Lake—*reservoir* TX-5
Davis, Mary Lee, House—*hist pl* AK-9
Davis, Mount—*summit* (2) AZ-5
Davis, Mount—*summit* (2) CA-9
Davis, Mount—*summit* NH-1
Davis, Mount—*summit* NC-3
Davis, Mount—*summit* PA-2
Davis, Mount—*summit* TN-4
Davis, Reuben, House—*hist pl* MS-4
Davis, R. K., House—*hist pl* ID-8
Davis, Robert, Farmhouse—*hist pl* DE-2
Davis, Robert S., House—*hist pl* MA-1
Davis, Rufus, Site—*hist pl* MS-4
Davis, Sam, House—*hist pl* TN-4
Davis, Samuel, House—*hist pl* OH-6
Davis, Samuel Henry, House—*hist pl* OH-6
Davis, Seth, House—*hist pl* MA-1
Davis, Theodore, Site—*hist pl* NE-7
Davis, Thomas, House—*hist pl* DE-2
Davis, Thomas Aspinwall, House—*hist pl* MA-1
Davis, Timothy, House—*hist pl* IA-7
Davis, William and Anna, House—*hist pl* TX-5
Davis, William Charles, House—*hist pl* AZ-5
Davis, William Morris, House—*hist pl* MA-1
Davis, Winnie, Hall—*hist pl* SC-3
Davis Acad—*school* GA-3
Davis Acad—*school* TN-4
Davis Academy (CCD)—*cens area* GA-3
Davis Acad (historical)—*school* TN-4
*Davis Access* IA-7
*Davis Acres* ID-8
**Davis Acres (subdivision)**—*pop pl* AL-4
Davis Airfield—*airport* KS-7
Davis Airp—*airport* PA-2
Davis Air Ranch—*airport* MO-7
Davis Airstrip—*airport* (3) OR-9
Davis And Company Ditch—*canal* WY-8
Davis and Dague Grocery Store, Old—*hist pl* OH-6
Davis And Elkins Coll—*school* WV-2
Davis Arroyo—*valley* TX-5
Davis Arroyo Tank—*reservoir* TX-5
Davis Ave Branch, Mobile Public Library—*hist pl* AL-4
Davis Ave Ch—*church* FL-3
Davis Bald—*summit* NC-3
Davis Bar—*bar* WA-9
Davis Barn—*hist pl* AR-4
Davis Basin—*basin* CO-8
Davis Basin—*basin* ID-8
Davis Bay—*bay* NY-2
Davis Bay—*bay* (2) NC-3
Davis Bay—*bay* WA-9
Davis Bay—*bay* WY-8
Davis Bay (Carolina Bay)—*swamp* NC-3
Davis Bayou—*gut* LA-4
Davis Bayou—*stream* AR-4
Davis Bayou—*stream* LA-4
Davis Bayou—*stream* MS-4
Davis Bayou—*stream* TX-5
Davis Beach—*beach* ME-1
Davis Beach—*beach* VA-3
Davis Beach—*beach* VI-3
Davis Beach—*cape* MA-1
**Davis Beach**—*pop pl* FL-3
Davis Bell Oil Field—*oilfield* TX-5
Davis Bench—*bench* MT-8
Davis Bend—*bend* AL-4
Davis Bend—*bend* KY-4
Davis Bend—*bend* (2) TN-4
Davis-Besse Nuclear Power Plant—*facility* OH-6
Davis Biggs Farm—*locale* AR-4
Davis Bluff—*cliff* AL-4
Davis Bluff—*cliff* AR-4
Davis Bluff—*cliff* FL-3
Davis Bluff—*cliff* KY-4
Davis Boat Landing—*locale* FL-3
Davis Boat Landing—*locale* GA-3
**Davisboro**—*pop pl* GA-3
Davisboro (CCD)—*cens area* GA-3
Davis Bottom—*bend* WY-8
*Davis Branch* AL-4
*Davis Branch* MS-4
**Davis Branch**—*pop pl* KY-4
Davis Branch—*stream* (6) AL-4
Davis Branch—*stream* (4) AR-4
Davis Branch—*stream* (2) FL-3
Davis Branch—*stream* (3) GA-3
Davis Branch—*stream* (3) IN-6
Davis Branch—*stream* (16) KY-4
Davis Branch—*stream* (3) LA-4
Davis Branch—*stream* (2) MD-2
Davis Branch—*stream* (2) MS-4
Davis Branch—*stream* (7) MO-7
Davis Branch—*stream* (6) NC-3
Davis Branch—*stream* (2) OK-5
Davis Branch—*stream* (4) SC-3
Davis Branch—*stream* (23) TN-4
Davis Branch—*stream* (9) TX-5
Davis Branch—*stream* VA-3
Davis Branch—*stream* (5) WV-2
Davis Branch—*stream* WY-8
Davis Branch Ch—*church* (2) KY-4
Davis-Braun Pond—*reservoir* NC-3
Davis-Braun Pond Dam—*dam* NC-3
Davis Bridge—*bridge* (2) AL-4
Davis Bridge—*bridge* IN-6
Davis Bridge—*bridge* MS-4
Davis Bridge—*bridge* NC-3
Davis Bridge—*bridge* (2) SC-3
Davis Bridge—*other* MI-6
**Davis Bridge**—*pop pl* NJ-2
Davis Bridge Access Point—*bridge* GA-3
*Davis Bridge Reservoir* VT-1
Davis Brook—*stream* (2) CT-1
Davis Brook—*stream* (8) ME-1
Davis Brook—*stream* MA-1
Davis Brook—*stream* (7) NH-1
Davis Brook—*stream* NY-2
Davis Brook—*stream* VT-1
Davis Brook Bog—*swamp* ME-1
Davis Brothers Ditch—*canal* CO-8
Davis Brothers Ditch No 1—*canal* WY-8
Davisburg—*locale* KY-4
**Davisburg**—*pop pl* MI-6
Davisburg Cem—*cemetery* MI-6
Davisburg Park—*park* MI-6
Davisburg Sch—*school* KY-4

Davisburg Trout Pond—*lake* ... MI-6
Davis Butte—*summit* ... ID-8
Davis Buttes—*range* ... ND-7
Davis Buttes—*range* ... SD-7
Davis Cabin—*locale* (2) ... CA-9
Davis Cabin—*locale* ... WY-8
Davis Cabin Hollow—*valley* ... PA-2
Davis Camp—*locale* ... AL-4
Davis Camp—*locale* ... FL-3
Davis Camp—*locale* ... ME-1
Daviscamp Branch—*stream* ... NC-3
Davis Campground—*locale* ... CA-9
*Davis Canyon* ... CO-8
Davis Canyon—*valley* (2) ... AZ-5
Davis Canyon—*valley* (6) ... CA-9
Davis Canyon—*valley* ... CO-8
Davis Canyon—*valley* (5) ... ID-8
Davis Canyon—*valley* (3) ... NV-8
Davis Canyon—*valley* (2) ... NM-5
Davis Canyon—*valley* ... OR-9
Davis Canyon—*valley* (2) ... TX-5
Davis Canyon—*valley* (5) ... UT-8
Davis Canyon—*valley* (5) ... WA-9
Davis Canyon—*valley* ... WY-8
Davis Carriage House—*hist pl* ... MI-6
Davis-Cate Cem—*cemetery* ... NH-1
Davis Cave—*cave* ... AL-4
Davis Cave—*cave* ... TX-5
Davis (CCD)—*cens area* ... CA-9
*Davis Cem* ... TN-4
Davis Cem—*cemetery* (16) ... AL-4
Davis Cem—*cemetery* (12) ... AR-4
Davis Cem—*cemetery* ... CA-9
Davis Cem—*cemetery* ... CT-1
Davis Cem—*cemetery* ... DE-2
Davis Cem—*cemetery* (9) ... GA-3
Davis Cem—*cemetery* (6) ... IL-6
Davis Cem—*cemetery* (7) ... IN-6
Davis Cem—*cemetery* (4) ... IA-7
Davis Cem—*cemetery* (14) ... KY-4
Davis Cem—*cemetery* (4) ... LA-4
Davis Cem—*cemetery* (3) ... ME-1
Davis Cem—*cemetery* ... MA-1
Davis Cem—*cemetery* (18) ... MS-4
Davis Cem—*cemetery* (24) ... MO-7
Davis Cem—*cemetery* ... NH-1
Davis Cem—*cemetery* (2) ... NY-2
Davis Cem—*cemetery* (16) ... NC-3
Davis Cem—*cemetery* (7) ... OH-6
Davis Cem—*cemetery* (4) ... OK-5
Davis Cem—*cemetery* (2) ... SC-3
Davis Cem—*cemetery* ... SD-7
Davis Cem—*cemetery* (46) ... TN-4
Davis Cem—*cemetery* (15) ... TX-5
Davis Cem—*cemetery* ... VT-1
Davis Cem—*cemetery* (18) ... VA-3
Davis Cem—*cemetery* ... WA-9
Davis Cem—*cemetery* (7) ... WV-2
Davis Cem—*cemetery* ... WI-6
*Davis Ch* ... AL-4
Davis Ch—*church* (2) ... AR-4
Davis Ch—*church* ... GA-3
Davis Ch—*church* ... IN-6
Davis Ch—*church* ... KY-4
Davis Ch—*church* ... MD-2
Davis Ch—*church* (2) ... MO-7
Davis Ch—*church* ... TX-5
Davis Ch—*church* ... VA-3
Davis Channel—*channel* ... NC-3
Davis Chapel—*church* (6) ... AL-4
Davis Chapel—*church* (6) ... GA-3
Davis Chapel—*church* (2) ... KY-4
Davis Chapel—*church* (3) ... MS-4
Davis Chapel—*church* ... MO-7
Davis Chapel—*church* (8) ... NC-3
Davis Chapel—*church* ... PA-2
Davis Chapel—*church* ... SC-3
Davis Chapel—*church* (4) ... TN-4
Davis Chapel—*church* ... TX-5
Davis Chapel—*church* (5) ... VA-3
Davis Chapel—*church* ... WV-2
**Davis Chapel**—*pop pl* (2) ... TN-4
Davis Chapel Baptist Ch—*church* ... TN-4
Davis Chapel Cem—*cemetery* ... AL-4
Davis Chapel Cem—*cemetery* ... GA-3
Davis Chapel Cem—*cemetery* ... KY-4
Davis Chapel Cem—*cemetery* ... MS-4
Davis Chapel Cem—*cemetery* (3) ... TN-4
Davis Chapel Ch—*church* ... NC-3
*Davis Chapel Church* ... AL-4
Davis Chapel (historical)—*church* ... AL-4
Davis Chapel (historical)—*church* ... TN-4
Davis Chapel Sch (historical)—*school* (2) ... TN-4
**Davis City**—*pop pl* ... IA-7
Davis Community Center,
Mount—*building* ... AL-4
Davis Community Park—*park* ... CA-9
Davis Corner—*locale* ... DE-2
Davis Corner—*locale* (2) ... VA-3
**Davis Corner**—*pop pl* ... ME-1
*Davis Corners* ... PA-2
Davis Corners—*locale* (2) ... NY-2
Davis Corners—*locale* ... WI-6
**Davis Corners**—*pop pl* ... IA-7
**Davis Corners**—*pop pl* ... NY-2
*Davis Coulee* ... MT-8
Davis Coulee—*valley* ... MT-8
*Davis County* ... KS-7
*Davis County* ... MS-4
Davis County—*civil* ... UT-8
Davis County Courthouse—*hist pl* ... IA-7
Davis County Heliport—*airport* ... UT-8
Davis County Home—*building* ... IA-7
Davis County Mosquito Abatement
Airstrip—*airport* ... UT-8
Davis County Poor Farm
(historical)—*locale* ... IA-7
Davis County Roadshop—*locale* ... UT-8
Davis Cove—*basin* ... AL-4
Davis Cove—*bay* ... FL-3
Davis Cove—*bay* ... ME-1
Davis Cove—*bay* ... NJ-2
Davis Cove—*valley* (2) ... NC-3
Davis Cove—*valley* ... TN-4
Davis Cove Cave—*cave* ... AL-4
Davis Covered Bridge—*hist pl* ... PA-2
*Davis Creek* ... AL-4
*Davis Creek* ... CO-8
*Davis Creek* ... GA-3
*Davis Creek* ... ID-8
*Davis Creek* ... KS-7
*Davis Creek* ... MS-4
*Davis Creek* ... MO-7
*Davis Creek* ... MT-8
*Davis Creek* ... NV-8
*Davis Creek* ... NC-3
*Davis Creek* ... TN-4
Davis Creek—*gut* ... FL-3
Davis Creek—*locale* ... IA-7
**Davis Creek**—*pop pl* ... CA-9
**Davis Creek**—*pop pl* ... WV-2
Davis Creek—*stream* (6) ... AL-4
Davis Creek—*stream* (6) ... AK-9
Davis Creek—*stream* ... AZ-5
Davis Creek—*stream* (3) ... AR-4
Davis Creek—*stream* (16) ... CA-9
Davis Creek—*stream* (2) ... CO-8
Davis Creek—*stream* (6) ... GA-3
Davis Creek—*stream* (6) ... ID-8
Davis Creek—*stream* (2) ... IL-6
Davis Creek—*stream* (2) ... IN-6
Davis Creek—*stream* (2) ... IA-7
Davis Creek—*stream* (4) ... KS-7
Davis Creek—*stream* (5) ... KY-4
Davis Creek—*stream* (3) ... LA-4
Davis Creek—*stream* (2) ... MD-2
Davis Creek—*stream* (4) ... MI-6
Davis Creek—*stream* (10) ... MS-4
Davis Creek—*stream* (8) ... MO-7
Davis Creek—*stream* (15) ... MT-8
Davis Creek—*stream* (3) ... NE-7
Davis Creek—*stream* (3) ... NV-8
Davis Creek—*stream* ... NM-5
Davis Creek—*stream* ... NY-2
Davis Creek—*stream* (6) ... NC-3
Davis Creek—*stream* ... ND-7
Davis Creek—*stream* ... OH-6
Davis Creek—*stream* ... OK-5
Davis Creek—*stream* (19) ... OR-9
Davis Creek—*stream* ... SD-7
Davis Creek—*stream* (7) ... TN-4
Davis Creek—*stream* (9) ... TX-5
Davis Creek—*stream* ... UT-8
Davis Creek—*stream* (6) ... VA-3
Davis Creek—*stream* (9) ... WA-9
Davis Creek—*stream* (2) ... WV-2
Davis Creek—*stream* (2) ... WI-6
Davis Creek—*stream* (2) ... WY-8
*Davis Creek Baptist Church* ... AL-4
Davis Creek Camping Area—*locale* ... WV-2
Davis Creek Cem—*cemetery* ... AL-4
Davis Creek Cem—*cemetery* ... NE-7
Davis Creek Ch—*church* ... AL-4
Davis Creek Ch—*church* ... MO-7
Davis Creek Ch—*church* (2) ... TN-4
Davis Creek County Park—*park* ... NV-8
Davis Creek Ditch—*stream* ... MO-7
Davis Creek Mine (surface)—*mine* ... AL-4
Davis Creek Picnic Area—*locale* ... WV-2
Davis Creek P. O. (historical)—*locale* ... AL-4
Davis Creek Rapids—*rapids* ... ID-8
Davis Creek Rapids—*rapids* ... OR-9
Davis Creek Rec Area—*park* ... TN-4
Davis Creek Sch—*school* ... NE-7
Davis Creek Sch—*school* ... WV-2
Davis Creek Sch (historical)—*school* ... MS-4
*Davis Creek School* ... MO-7
Davis Creek Springs—*spring* ... OR-9
Davis Creek Township—*civ div* ... NE-7
Davis Creek Trail—*trail* ... OR-9
Davis Crevasse (1884)—*basin* ... LA-4
Davis Crossing—*locale* ... NY-2
Davis Crossing Ch—*church* ... LA-4
*Davis Cross Roads* ... AL-4
*Davis Cross Roads* ... DE-2
Davis Crossroads—*locale* ... AL-4
Davis Crossroads—*locale* (2) ... GA-3
Davis Crossroads—*locale* ... KY-4
**Davis Cross Roads**—*pop pl* ... KY-4
**Davis Crossroads**—*pop pl* ... SC-3
*Davis Cross Roads Post Office* ... AL-4
Davis Cutoff—*stream* ... MO-7
Davis Dam—*dam* ... AL-4
Davis Dam—*dam* (3) ... AZ-5
Davis Dam—*dam* ... NV-8
Davis Dam—*dam* ... ND-7
Davis Dam—*dam* ... OR-9
Davis Dam—*dam* ... PA-2
**Davis Dam**—*pop pl* ... AZ-5
Davis Dam Number One—*dam* ... NC-3
Davis Dam Number Two—*dam* ... NC-3
**Davis (Davis Station)**—*pop pl* ... NJ-2
Davis Dead River—*lake* (2) ... MS-4
*Davis Ditch* ... IN-6
Davis Ditch—*canal* (2) ... CA-9
Davis Ditch—*canal* ... CO-8
Davis Ditch—*canal* (8) ... IN-6
Davis Ditch—*canal* ... MD-2
Davis Ditch—*canal* (3) ... MT-8
Davis Dome—*locale* ... AK-9
Davis Dome—*summit* ... NM-5
Davis Drain—*canal* (3) ... MI-6
Davis Drain—*canal* ... TX-5
Davis Drain—*stream* (2) ... MI-6
Davis Draw—*valley* ... CO-8
Davis Draw—*valley* (2) ... SD-7
Davis Draw—*valley* ... TX-5
Davis Draw—*valley* (4) ... WY-8
Davis Draw Rsvr—*reservoir* ... SD-7
Davis Dunkirk Mine—*mine* ... AZ-5
Davis Eddy—*bay* ... MS-4
Davis-Edwards House—*hist pl* ... GA-3
Davis Elbow—*locale* ... ID-8
Davis Elementary—*school* ... NC-3
*Davis Elementary School* ... MS-4
Davis Elem Sch—*school* ... AL-4
Davis Elem Sch—*school* ... PA-2
Davis Enlow Ditch—*canal* ... IN-6
*Davises* ... TX-5
Davis-Exchange Bank Bldg—*hist pl* ... GA-3
Davis Exit—*crossing* ... SD-7
Davis Falls—*falls* ... AL-4
Davis Falls Cem—*cemetery* ... AL-4
Davis Family Cem—*cemetery* (2) ... MS-4
Davis Family Cem—*cemetery* ... TX-5
Davis Farm (historical)—*locale* ... ME-1
Davis-Felton Plantation—*hist pl* ... GA-3
Davis Ferry—*locale* (2) ... AL-4
Davis Ferry—*locale* ... TN-4
Davis Ferry (historical)—*locale* ... MS-4
Davis Field—*airport* ... NJ-2
Davis Field—*other* ... MO-7
Davis Field Airp—*airport* ... WA-9
Davis Flat—*flat* (4) ... CA-9
Davis Flat—*flat* ... ID-8
Davis Flat—*flat* ... UT-8
Davis Flat—*swamp* ... OR-9
Davis Flat Creek—*stream* ... CA-9
Davis Folsom And Brewer Ditch—*canal* ... WY-8
Davis Ford—*locale* ... AR-4
Davis Ford—*locale* ... MO-7
Davis Ford—*locale* (2) ... TN-4
Davis Ford—*locale* ... WV-2
Davis Forest Service Station—*locale* ... CA-9
*Davis Fork* ... KY-4
Davis Fork—*stream* (3) ... KY-4
Davis Fork—*stream* (2) ... WV-2
Davis Gap—*gap* (2) ... AL-4
Davis Gap—*gap* ... GA-3
Davis Gap—*gap* ... KY-4
Davis Gap—*gap* ... NC-3
Davis Gifford Post Office
(historical)—*building* ... PA-2
Davis Grove—*locale* ... PA-2
Davis Grove Ch—*church* ... GA-3
*Davis Gulch* ... CO-8
*Davis Gulch* ... MT-8
Davis Gulch—*valley* ... AK-9
Davis Gulch—*valley* ... CA-9
Davis Gulch—*valley* (3) ... CO-8
Davis Gulch—*valley* (2) ... ID-8
Davis Gulch—*valley* (3) ... MT-8
Davis Gulch—*valley* (2) ... OR-9
Davis Gulch—*valley* ... UT-8
Davis Gulch Pictograph Panel—*hist pl* ... UT-8
Davis-Guttenberger-Rankin
House—*hist pl* ... GA-3
*Davis Head* ... ME-1
**Davis Heights**—*pop pl* ... TN-4
*Davis Hill* ... MA-1
Davis Hill—*locale* ... KY-4
**Davis Hill**—*pop pl* ... SC-3
Davis Hill—*summit* ... AL-4
Davis Hill—*summit* ... AR-4
Davis Hill—*summit* ... CT-1
Davis Hill—*summit* (2) ... GA-3
Davis Hill—*summit* ... IN-6
Davis Hill—*summit* (2) ... ME-1
Davis Hill—*summit* (6) ... MA-1
Davis Hill—*summit* ... MS-4
Davis Hill—*summit* (6) ... NH-1
Davis Hill—*summit* ... NY-2
Davis Hill—*summit* ... OR-9
Davis Hill—*summit* ... PA-2
Davis Hill—*summit* (2) ... TN-4
Davis Hill—*summit* (2) ... TX-5
Davis Hill—*summit* ... UT-8
Davis Hill—*summit* ... VT-1
Davis Hill—*summit* ... WA-9
Davis Hill—*summit* ... WY-8
Davis Hill Brook—*stream* ... VT-1
Davis Hill Ch—*church* ... GA-3
Davis Hill Ch—*church* ... MS-4
Davis-Hill House—*hist pl* ... TX-5
**Davis Hills**—*pop pl* ... AL-4
*Davis Hills Elementary School* ... AL-4
**Davis Hills Estates**
**(subdivision)**—*pop pl* ... AL-4
Davis Hills Sch—*school* ... AL-4
Davis (historical)—*locale* ... AL-4
Davis (historical P.O.)—*locale* ... MA-1
*Davis Hollow* ... UT-8
Davis Hollow—*valley* ... AL-4
Davis Hollow—*valley* (3) ... AR-4
Davis Hollow—*valley* (6) ... KY-4
Davis Hollow—*valley* (4) ... MO-7
Davis Hollow—*valley* (2) ... NY-2
Davis Hollow—*valley* (2) ... OH-6
Davis Hollow—*valley* ... OK-5
Davis Hollow—*valley* (2) ... PA-2
Davis Hollow—*valley* (13) ... TN-4
Davis Hollow—*valley* (2) ... TX-5
Davis Hollow—*valley* (3) ... UT-8
Davis Hollow—*valley* (3) ... VA-3
Davis Hollow—*valley* ... WA-9
Davis Hollow—*valley* (2) ... WV-2
Davis Hollow Rsvr—*reservoir* ... UT-8
Davis Hosp—*hospital* ... NC-3
Davis House—*hist pl* ... AR-4
Davis House—*hist pl* ... MS-4
Davis House—*hist pl* ... NM-5
Davis House—*hist pl* ... SC-3
Davis House—*hist pl* ... TX-5
Davis HS—*school* ... CA-9
Davis HS—*school* ... GA-3
Davis HS—*school* ... IL-6
Davis HS—*school* ... NY-2
Davis HS—*school* ... TX-5
Davis HS—*school* ... UT-8
Davis HS—*school* ... WA-9
Davis-Hull House—*hist pl* ... TN-4
Davis Irrigation Dam—*dam* ... SD-7
*Davis Island* ... FL-3
*Davis Island* ... ME-1
*Davis Island* ... MI-6
*Davis Island* ... MO-7
*Davis Island* ... NH-1
Davis Island—*area* ... MS-4
Davis Island—*island* ... CT-1
Davis Island—*island* (2) ... FL-3
Davis Island—*island* ... LA-4
Davis Island—*island* (2) ... ME-1
Davis Island—*island* ... NC-3
Davis Island—*island* ... PA-2
Davis Island—*island* (3) ... TN-4
**Davis Island**—*pop pl* ... ME-1
Davis Island Bend—*bend* ... MS-4
Davis Island Lock and Dam Site—*hist pl* ... PA-2
Davis Island Point—*cape* ... NC-3
Davis Islands—*island* ... FL-3
Davis Islands Playground—*park* ... FL-3
Davis JHS—*school* ... OH-6
Davis JHS—*school* ... UT-8
**Davis Junction**—*pop pl* ... IL-6
Davis Key—*island* ... FL-3
Davis Knob—*summit* ... AR-4
Davis Knob—*summit* ... MO-7
Davis Knob—*summit* ... OH-6
Davis Knob—*summit* ... TN-4
Davis Knob—*summit* ... VA-3
Davis Knob—*summit* ... WV-2
Davis Knolls—*summit* ... UT-8
Davis Lagoon—*stream* ... TN-4
*Davis Lake* ... IN-6
*Davis Lake* ... MI-6
*Davis Lake* ... MN-6
*Davis Lake* ... WA-9
*Davis Lake* ... WI-6
Davis Lake—*lake* ... AK-9
Davis Lake—*lake* (4) ... CA-9
Davis Lake—*lake* (2) ... FL-3
Davis Lake—*lake* ... GA-3
Davis Lake—*lake* ... ID-8
Davis Lake—*lake* ... IN-6
Davis Lake—*lake* ... LA-4
Davis Lake—*lake* (9) ... MI-6
Davis Lake—*lake* (4) ... MN-6
Davis Lake—*lake* ... MS-4
Davis Lake—*lake* ... MT-8
Davis Lake—*lake* (2) ... NY-2
Davis Lake—*lake* ... ND-7
Davis Lake—*lake* (3) ... OR-9
Davis Lake—*lake* ... TN-4
Davis Lake—*lake* (2) ... TX-5
Davis Lake—*lake* (6) ... WA-9
Davis Lake—*lake* (4) ... WI-6
Davis Lake—*reservoir* (5) ... AL-4
Davis Lake—*reservoir* ... AR-4
Davis Lake—*reservoir* (2) ... GA-3
Davis Lake—*reservoir* (2) ... MS-4
Davis Lake—*reservoir* (2) ... NC-3
Davis Lake—*reservoir* (2) ... TN-4
Davis Lake—*swamp* ... AR-4
Davis Lake—*swamp* ... LA-4
Davis Lake Dam—*dam* (7) ... MS-4
Davis Lake Dam—*dam* ... NC-3
Davis Lake Dam—*dam* (2) ... TN-4
Davis Lake Dam Number Two—*dam* ... AL-4
Davis Lake Dam Number Two—*dam* ... TN-4
*Davis Lake Front Acres* ... AL-4
Davis Lake Guard Station—*locale* ... OR-9
Davis Lake No 1—*reservoir* ... ID-8
Davis Lake No 2—*reservoir* ... ID-8
Davis Lake No 3—*reservoir* ... ID-8
Davis Lake Number One—*reservoir* ... NC-3
Davis Lake Number Two—*reservoir* ... AL-4
Davis Lake Number Two—*reservoir* ... NC-3
Davis Lake Number Two—*reservoir* ... TN-4
*Davis Lake Number 2* ... AL-4
Davis Lakes—*lake* ... CA-9
Davis Lakes—*lake* ... UT-8
Davis Lakes Dam—*dam* ... MS-4
Davis Lake Slough—*gut* ... LA-4
Davis Lakes Number One—*reservoir* ... AL-4
Davis Landing—*locale* (2) ... AL-4
Davis Landing—*locale* ... DE-2
Davis Landing—*locale* ... GA-3
Davis Landing—*locale* ... LA-4
Davis Landing—*locale* ... MS-4
Davis Landing—*locale* (3) ... NC-3
Davis Landing—*locale* ... SC-3
Davis Landing—*locale* ... VA-3
Davis Landing (historical)—*locale* ... AL-4
Davis Lane Ch—*church* ... FL-3
Davis Lateral—*canal* ... CA-9
Davis Lateral—*canal* ... TX-5
Davis Ledge—*bar* (2) ... MA-1
Davis Levee—*levee* ... CA-9
Davis Library—*building* ... MS-4
Davis Lick—*stream* ... WV-2
*Davis Log Branch* ... SC-3
Davis (Magisterial District)—*fmr MCD* ... VA-3
Davis (Magisterial District)—*fmr MCD* ... WV-2
Davis Marsh—*swamp* ... NC-3
Davis Meadow—*flat* ... CO-8
Davis Meadow—*flat* ... NV-8
*Davis Meadows* ... NV-8
Davis Meetinghouse—*locale* ... NH-1
Davis Memorial—*hist pl* ... KS-7
Davis Memorial Ch—*church* ... NC-3
Davis Memorial Ch—*church* ... TN-4
Davis Memorial Ch—*church* ... VA-3
Davis Memorial Chapel—*church* (2) ... KY-4
Davis Memorial Lookout Tower—*locale* ... GA-3
Davis Memorial Presbyterian
Church—*hist pl* ... WV-2
Davis Memorial Tower—*locale* ... NH-1
Davis Mesa—*summit* ... AZ-5
Davis Mesa—*summit* (2) ... CO-8
Davis Mesa—*summit* ... NM-5
Davis Mill—*hist pl* ... OH-6
Davis Mill—*locale* ... GA-3
Davis Mill—*locale* ... NJ-2
Davis Mill—*locale* ... VA-3
Davis Mill Creek—*stream* ... AL-4
Davis Mill Creek—*stream* (3) ... FL-3
Davis Mill Creek—*stream* ... GA-3
Davis Mill Creek—*stream* ... TN-4
Davis Mill Creek—*stream* ... VA-3
Davis Mill Dam—*dam* ... AL-4
Davis Mill (historical)—*locale* ... MS-4
Davis Mill (historical)—*locale* ... TN-4
Davis Millpond—*lake* ... NC-3
Davis Millpond—*reservoir* ... NJ-2
Davis Millpond—*reservoir* ... NC-3
Davis Millpond—*reservoir* ... VA-3
Davis Millpond Branch—*stream* ... MD-2
Davis Millpond Dam—*dam* ... NJ-2
Davis Millpond Dam—*dam* ... NC-3
*Davis Mills* ... MS-4
*Davis Mills* ... RI-1
Davis' Mills Battle Site—*hist pl* ... MS-4
Davis Mill (underground)—*mine* ... TN-4
Davis Mine—*mine* ... CA-9
Davis Mine—*mine* ... NV-8
Davis Mine—*mine* ... TN-4
Davis Mine Brook—*stream* ... MA-1
Davis Mine Creek—*stream* ... NC-3
Davis Mines (underground)—*mine* ... AL-4
Davis Mine (underground)—*mine* ... AL-4
Davis-Mitchell House—*hist pl* ... MS-4
Davis-Monthan AFB—*military* ... AZ-5
Davis Monthan Hosp—*hospital* ... AZ-5
Davis Motor Mine—*mine* ... CA-9
Davis Mountains—*range* ... TX-5
Davis Mountains State Park—*park* ... TX-5
Davis Mountain Trail—*trail* ... WA-9
Davis MS—*school* ... AL-4
*Davis Mtn* ... WA-9
Davis Mtn—*summit* ... AL-4
Davis Mtn—*summit* ... AZ-5
Davis Mtn—*summit* ... AR-4
Davis Mtn—*summit* (3) ... CA-9
Davis Mtn—*summit* ... CO-8
Davis Mtn—*summit* (2) ... GA-3
Davis Mtn—*summit* ... ID-8
Davis Mtn—*summit* (3) ... ME-1
Davis Mtn—*summit* (2) ... MT-8
Davis Mtn—*summit* ... NV-8
Davis Mtn—*summit* (2) ... NY-2
Davis Mtn—*summit* ... NC-3
Davis Mtn—*summit* (2) ... OK-5
Davis Mtn—*summit* ... OR-9
Davis Mtn—*summit* ... TN-4
Davis Mtn—*summit* ... UT-8
Davis Mtn—*summit* (2) ... VA-3
Davis Mtn—*summit* ... WA-9
*Davis Neck* ... MA-1
Davis Neck—*cape* (2) ... MA-1
*Davis New South Shoal* ... MA-1
Davis Number One Dam—*dam* ... AL-4
Davis Number 1 Dam—*reservoir* ... AL-4
Davis Number 2 Dam—*dam* ... AL-4
Davis Number 3 Dam—*dam* ... AL-4
Davis Number 4 Dam—*dam* ... AL-4
Davis Number 5 Dam—*dam* ... AL-4
Davis-Oak Grove District—*hist pl* ... AL-4
Davis Oil Field—*oilfield* ... MS-4
Davis Oil Field—*oilfield* ... OK-5
Davis Oil Field—*oilfield* ... TX-5
*Davis Old Field* ... MS-4
**Davison**—*pop pl* ... MI-6
Davison, Abner, House—*hist pl* ... IA-7
Davison, Frank B., House—*hist pl* ... TX-5
Davison Ave Sch—*school* ... NY-2
Davison Bay—*bay* ... AK-9
Davison Bayou—*stream* ... TX-5
*Davison Branch* ... NE-7
Davison Branch—*stream* ... KY-4
Davison Butte—*summit* ... OR-9
Davison Canyon—*valley* ... UT-8
*Davison Cem* ... AL-4
Davison Cem—*cemetery* ... AL-4
Davison Cem—*cemetery* ... IL-6
Davison Cem—*cemetery* ... MI-6
Davison Cem—*cemetery* ... WV-2
Davison Coulee—*valley* ... MT-8
Davison Country Club—*other* ... MI-6
Davison County—*civil* ... SD-7
Davison Creek—*stream* ... AK-9
Davison Creek—*stream* ... MI-6
*Davison Ditch* ... IN-6
Davison Ditch—*canal* ... IN-6
Davison Drain—*canal* ... MI-6
Davison Gulch—*valley* ... AK-9
Davison Head—*cape* ... WA-9
Davison Lake—*lake* ... MI-6
Davison Landing Field—*airport* ... KS-7
Davison Mtn—*summit* ... AK-9
Davison Ranch—*locale* ... WY-8
*Davison Ridge* ... TN-4
Davison Sch—*school* ... GA-3
Davison Sch—*school* (3) ... MI-6
Davisons Creek—*stream* ... IA-7
Davison Silo—*hist pl* ... OK-5
Davison Spring—*spring* ... CA-9
Davison Spring Branch—*stream* ... TN-4
**Davison (Township of)**—*pop pl* ... MI-6
Davis Overlook—*locale* ... CO-8
Davis Park—*flat* ... UT-8
Davis Park—*park* ... CA-9
Davis Park—*park* ... IA-7
Davis Park—*park* ... MO-7
Davis Park—*park* ... NE-7
Davis Park—*park* (3) ... NC-3
Davis Park—*park* ... TN-4
Davis Park—*park* (3) ... TX-5
**Davis Park**—*pop pl* ... GA-3
**Davis Park**—*pop pl* ... NY-2
Davis Park Elem Sch—*school* ... IN-6
Davis Park Ferry—*trail* ... NY-2
*Davis Parks Sch* ... IN-6
*Davis Pass* ... ID-8
Davis Pass—*gap* ... WY-8
Davis Path—*trail* (2) ... NH-1
Davis Peak—*summit* ... CO-8
Davis Peak—*summit* ... MT-8
Davis Peak—*summit* (3) ... WA-9
Davis Peak—*summit* ... WY-8
Davis Peak Lookout Trail—*trail* ... WA-9
Davis Pit—*cave* ... AL-4
Davis Plain—*plain* ... AZ-5
Davis Plantation—*hist pl* ... SC-3
Davis Plantation—*locale* ... AL-4
Davis Pocket—*basin* ... UT-8
Davis Point—*cape* ... CA-9
Davis Point—*cape* (3) ... FL-3
Davis Point—*cape* ... ME-1
Davis Point—*cape* ... MD-2
Davis Point—*cape* ... MO-7
Davis Point—*cape* (2) ... TN-4
Davis Point—*cape* ... WA-9
Davis Point—*cape* ... WI-6
Davis Point—*ridge* ... CO-8
Davis Point—*summit* ... CO-8
Davis Point—*summit* ... MT-8
Davis Point—*summit* ... OR-9
Davis Point—*summit* ... UT-8
*Davis Pond* ... AL-4
*Davis Pond* ... MA-1
Davis Pond—*lake* (2) ... CT-1
Davis Pond—*lake* (2) ... FL-3
Davis Pond—*lake* (3) ... GA-3
Davis Pond—*lake* ... IN-6
Davis Pond—*lake* ... LA-4
Davis Pond—*lake* (7) ... ME-1
Davis Pond—*lake* (3) ... MA-1
Davis Pond—*lake* (2) ... NH-1
Davis Pond—*lake* ... NY-2
Davis Pond—*lake* ... NC-3
Davis Pond—*lake* ... TN-4
Davis Pond—*reservoir* ... AL-4
Davis Pond—*reservoir* ... DE-2
Davis Pond—*reservoir* ... FL-3
Davis Pond—*reservoir* (3) ... GA-3
Davis Pond—*reservoir* ... MA-1
Davis Pond—*reservoir* ... NY-2
Davis Pond—*reservoir* ... NC-3
Davis Pond—*reservoir* (2) ... SC-3
Davis Pond—*reservoir* ... TX-5
Davis Pond—*reservoir* (3) ... VA-3
*Davis Pond Dam* ... AL-4
Davis Pond Dam—*dam* ... DE-2
Davis Pond Dam—*dam* ... NC-3
Davis Ponds—*reservoir* ... SC-3
Davisport—*locale* (2) ... KY-4
Davisport Sch—*school* ... KY-4
Davis Prairie—*locale* ... TX-5
Davis Prairie Ch—*church* ... IL-6
Davis Prong—*stream* ... MT-8
Davis Ranch—*locale* (3) ... AZ-5
Davis Ranch—*locale* (2) ... CA-9
Davis Ranch—*locale* (2) ... CO-8
Davis Ranch—*locale* (2) ... MT-8
Davis Ranch—*locale* (3) ... NE-7
Davis Ranch—*locale* (6) ... NM-5
Davis Ranch—*locale* ... ND-7
Davis Ranch—*locale* ... OR-9
Davis Ranch—*locale* (4) ... SD-7
Davis Ranch—*locale* (5) ... TX-5
Davis Ranch—*locale* ... WA-9
Davis Ranch—*locale* (5) ... WY-8
Davis Ranch Number 1 Dam—*dam* ... SD-7
Davis Ranch Oil Field—*oilfield* ... KS-7
Davis Range Camp—*locale* ... WY-8
Davis Recreation Center—*building* ... NC-3
*Davis-Redd Cemetery* ... TN-4
Davis Reef—*bar* ... FL-3
Davis Reef Light 14—*locale* ... FL-3
Davis Rich Ditch—*canal* ... IN-6
Davis Ridge—*ridge* ... AL-4
Davis Ridge—*ridge* ... GA-3
Davis Ridge—*ridge* ... ME-1
Davis Ridge—*ridge* ... NC-3
Davis Ridge—*ridge* (3) ... TN-4
Davis Ridge—*ridge* ... TX-5
Davis Ridge—*ridge* ... VA-3
Davis Ridge—*ridge* ... WV-2
Davis Ridge Cem—*cemetery* ... WV-2
Davis Ridges—*ridge* ... OR-9
Davis Ridge Sch—*school* ... WV-2
Davis Ripple—*rapids* ... TN-4
Davis River—*stream* ... AK-9
Davis Roadside Park—*park* ... LA-4
Davis Roadside Park—*park* (2) ... MO-7
Davis Rock—*island* ... AK-9
Davis Rsvr—*reservoir* (3) ... CO-8
Davis Rsvr—*reservoir* ... ID-8
Davis Rsvr—*reservoir* ... NM-5
Davis Rsvr—*reservoir* (2) ... OR-9
Davis Rsvr—*reservoir* ... WY-8
Davis Rsvr Four—*reservoir* ... OR-9
Davis Rsvr No 2—*reservoir* ... WY-8
Davis Rsvr Three—*reservoir* ... OR-9
*Davis Run* ... PA-2
Davis Run—*stream* ... KY-4
Davis Run—*stream* (3) ... OH-6
Davis Run—*stream* (5) ... PA-2
Davis Run—*stream* ... VA-3
Davis Run—*stream* (6) ... WV-2
Davis Salt Ground—*flat* ... CA-9
Davis Sch—*school* (2) ... AL-4
Davis Sch—*school* (2) ... AZ-5
Davis Sch—*school* ... AR-4
Davis Sch—*school* (5) ... CA-9
Davis Sch—*school* ... DC-2
Davis Sch—*school* (4) ... FL-3
Davis Sch—*school* (3) ... GA-3
Davis Sch—*school* (6) ... IL-6
Davis Sch—*school* ... IA-7
Davis Sch—*school* ... LA-4
Davis Sch—*school* ... ME-1
Davis Sch—*school* (5) ... MA-1
Davis Sch—*school* ... MI-6
Davis Sch—*school* (2) ... MN-6
Davis Sch—*school* (2) ... MS-4
Davis Sch—*school* (3) ... MO-7
Davis Sch—*school* ... NE-7
Davis Sch—*school* ... NH-1
Davis Sch—*school* ... NJ-2
Davis Sch—*school* ... NY-2
Davis Sch—*school* ... OH-6
Davis Sch—*school* ... OK-5
Davis Sch—*school* (3) ... PA-2
Davis Sch—*school* ... SC-3
Davis Sch—*school* (3) ... SD-7
Davis Sch—*school* (3) ... TN-4
Davis Sch—*school* (4) ... TX-5
Davis Sch—*school* ... UT-8
Davis Sch—*school* (3) ... VA-3
Davis Sch—*school* (2) ... WA-9
Davis Sch—*school* ... WV-2
Davis Sch—*school* (2) ... WI-6
Davis Sch—*school* ... WY-8
Davis Sch (abandoned)—*school* (3) ... MO-7
Davis Sch (abandoned)—*school* (2) ... PA-2
Davis Sch (historical)—*school* (3) ... AL-4
Davis Sch (historical)—*school* ... MS-4
Davis Sch (historical)—*school* ... MO-7
Davis Sch (historical)—*school* ... PA-2
Davis Sch (historical)—*school* (2) ... TN-4
*Davis School* ... OR-9
Davis School—*locale* (2) ... MI-6
Davis School (Aban'd)—*locale* ... MO-7
**Davis Sharp and Stringer**
**Subdivision**—*pop pl* ... UT-8
Davis Sheep Camp—*locale* ... CO-8
*Davis Shoal* ... MA-1
Davis Shoal—*bar* ... ME-1
Davis Shoals—*bar* ... TN-4
Davis Shop (historical)—*locale* ... TN-4
**Davis Shores**—*pop pl* ... FL-3
Davis Siding—*locale* ... IL-6
*Davis's Ledge* ... MA-1
*Davis Slough* ... NC-3
Davis Slough—*gut* ... IL-6
Davis Slough—*gut* ... LA-4
Davis Slough—*gut* ... MI-6
Davis Slough—*gut* ... ND-7
Davis Slough—*gut* ... SD-7
Davis Slough—*gut* ... WA-9
Davis Slough—*stream* ... AR-4
Davis Slough—*stream* ... OR-9
Davisson Chapel—*church* ... WV-2
*Davisson Ditch* ... IN-6
Davisson Ditch—*canal* ... IN-6
Davisson Run—*stream* ... WV-2
Davisson Run Ch—*church* ... WV-2
Davisson Sch—*school* ... NE-7
Davis South Shoal—*bar* ... MA-1

Davis Spring—*spring* AL-4
Davis Spring—*spring* (3) AZ-5
Davis Spring—*spring* AR-4
Davis Spring—*spring* CA-9
Davis Spring—*spring* (2) ID-8
Davis Spring—*spring* (2) MO-7
Davis Spring—*spring* (2) NV-8
Davis Spring—*spring* (3) OR-9
Davis Spring—*spring* (2) TN-4
Davis Spring—*spring* (2) UT-8
Davis Spring—*spring* (2) WY-8
Davis Spring Branch—*stream* AL-4
Davis Spring Branch—*stream* TX-5
Davis Spring Ch—*church* LA-4
Davis Spring Number Two—*spring* AZ-5
Davis Spring Rsvr—*reservoir* OR-9
*Davis Springs* TN-4
Davis Springs—*locale* TN-4
Davis Springs—*spring* ID-8
Davis Spring Trail Twenty-eight—*trail* AZ-5
**Davis Spur**—*pop pl* AR-4
Davis Square—*locale* MA-1
Davis Square—*park* IL-6
Davis State Sch—*school* MO-7
Davis Station—*locale* OH-6
**Davis Station**—*pop pl* PA-2
**Davis Station**—*pop pl* SC-3
*Davis Store* MS-4
**Davis Store**—*pop pl* MO-7
Davis Store (historical)—*locale* MS-4
Davis Strait—*channel* ME-1
Davis Stream—*stream* ME-1
Davis Street Sch—*school* CT-1
Davis Street Sch—*school* GA-3
**Davis Subdivision**—*pop pl* AL-4
**Davis Subdivision**—*pop pl* UT-8
Davis Swale—*stream* MI-6
Davis Swamp—*swamp* GA-3
Davis Swamp—*swamp* NY-2
Davis Tank—*reservoir* (2) AZ-5
Davis Tank—*reservoir* NM-5
Davis Tank—*reservoir* (2) TX-5
Davis Tavern—*hist pl* KY-4
Davis Temple—*church* AL-4
*Davis Temple Baptist Ch* AL-4
Davis Temple Cem—*cemetery* AL-4
Davis Temple Ch of God in Christ—*church* MS-4
*Davis Temple Church* AL-4
**Davis Terrace**—*pop pl* WA-9
Davis-Thomas Cem—*cemetery* TN-4
**Daviston**—*pop pl* AL-4
Daviston Cem—*cemetery* AL-4
Daviston HS—*school* AL-4
Daviston Methodist Ch—*church* AL-4
Davis Top—*summit* NH-1
Davis Top—*summit* NC-3
Davistown—*locale* AL-4
Davis Town—*locale* ME-1
Davistown—*locale* NC-3
Davistown—*locale* PA-2
**Davistown**—*pop pl* (2) KY-4
**Davistown**—*pop pl* NC-3
**Davistown**—*pop pl* (2) PA-2
**Davistown**—*pop pl* SC-3
Davistown Cem—*cemetery* AL-4
Davistown Sch (historical)—*school* AL-4
Davis-Townsend Sch—*school* NC-3
Davis Township—*civil* MO-7
**Davis Township**—*pop pl* (2) MO-7
Davis (Township of)—*fmr MCD* (2) AR-4
Davis (Township of)—*fmr MCD* NC-3
**Davis (Township of)**—*pop pl* (2) IN-6
**Davis (Township of)**—*pop pl* MN-6
Davis (Township of)—*unorg* ME-1
Davis Trace Branch—*stream* WV-2
Davis Trail—*trail* OR-9
Davis Trail—*trail* WA-9
Davis Trailer Court and RV Campground—*locale* UT-8
Davis-Tucker Cem—*cemetery* MS-4
Davis Tunnel—*tunnel* MD-2
Davis Tunnel—*tunnel* NV-8
*Davis Twin Lakes* AL-4
Davis Valley—*valley* VA-3
*Davisville* AL-4
*Davisville* DE-2
*Davisville* NJ-2
Davisville—*locale* KY-4
Davisville—*locale* NJ-2
Davisville—*locale* TX-5
**Davisville**—*pop pl* AL-4
**Davisville**—*pop pl* MA-1
**Davisville**—*pop pl* MO-7
**Davisville**—*pop pl* (2) NH-1
**Davisville**—*pop pl* NJ-2
**Davisville**—*pop pl* OH-6
**Davisville**—*pop pl* PA-2
**Davisville**—*pop pl* RI-1
**Davisville**—*pop pl* TX-5
**Davisville**—*pop pl* WV-2
Davisville Campground—*locale* MO-7
Davisville Cem—*cemetery* NH-1
Davisville Ch—*church* TX-5
**Davisville (community)**—*pop pl* RI-1
Davisville Hist Dist—*hist pl* RI-1
**Davisville (historical)**—*pop pl* MS-4
Davisville Hollow—*valley* MO-7
Davisville Methodist Ch (historical)—*church* AL-4
*Davisville Mill Pond* RI-1
Davisville State For—*forest* NH-1
Davisville Station—*locale* TX-5
Davis Wash—*stream* AZ-5
Davis-Weber Canal—*canal* UT-8
Davis Well—*well* AZ-5
Davis Well—*well* CA-9
Davis Well—*well* MT-8
Davis Well—*well* (5) NM-5
Davis Well—*well* OR-9
**Davis Wharf**—*pop pl* VA-3
Davis-Whitehead-Harriss House—*hist pl* NC-3
Davis Windmill—*locale* CO-8
Davis Windmill—*locale* (3) NM-5
Davis Windmill—*locale* TX-5
Davis Windmills—*locale* TX-5
Davis Woods—*woods* WA-9
Davis Woody Ditch—*canal* MT-8
Davis Works—*hist pl* OH-6
Davitt Pond—*lake* NY-2

Davo—*locale* MS-4
Davol, William C., Jr., House—*hist pl* MA-1
Davol Mills—*locale* MA-1
*Davol Pond* MA-1
Davol Pond—*lake* RI-1
Davol Rubber Company—*hist pl* RI-1
Davol Sch—*hist pl* MA-1
Davol Sch—*school* MA-1
*Davols Pond* MA-1
*Davotj* FM-9
D A V Park—*park* CO-8
*Davy* TX-5
**Davy**—*pop pl* IN-6
**Davy**—*pop pl* WV-2
*Davy Branch* WV-2
Davy Branch—*stream* TN-4
Davy Branch—*stream* (3) WV-2
Davy Branch Ch—*church* WV-2
Davy Brown Campground—*locale* CA-9
*Davy Brown Canyon* CA-9
Davy Brown Creek—*stream* CA-9
Davy Cain Run—*stream* WV-2
*Davy Community* TX-5
*Davy Cook Branch* WV-2
Davy Creek—*stream* ID-8
Davy Creek—*stream* WI-6
Davy Crockett—*uninc pl* TN-4
Davy Crockett Lake—*reservoir* TN-4
Davy Crockett Memorial Park—*park* TX-5
Davy Crockett Mtn—*summit* AR-4
Davy Crockett Natl For—*forest* TX-5
Davy Crockett Park—*park* TN-4
*Davy Crockett Reservoir* TX-5
Davy Crockett Sch—*school* TN-4
Davy Crockett Sch—*school* TX-5
Davy Ditch—*canal* CO-8
Davy High Ranch—*locale* MT-8
Davy Hill—*summit* PA-2
Davy Hill Ch—*church* PA-2
Davy Knob—*summit* WV-2
Davy Mtn—*summit* NC-3
Davy Park—*park* OK-5
Davy Run—*stream* KY-4
Davy Run—*stream* (2) WV-2
Davy Sch—*school* KS-7
Davys Corners—*locale* NY-2
Davy Valley—*valley* WI-6
Davy Windmill—*locale* NM-5
*Daw* FM-9
Daw—*locale* VA-3
*Dawach* FM-9
*Dawahk Island* FM-9
Da Wa Ke—*summit* AZ-5
Daw Branch—*stream* LA-4
Dawe Drain—*canal* MI-6
Dawes—*locale* OK-5
**Dawes**—*pop pl* AL-4
**Dawes**—*pop pl* WV-2
Dawes—*uninc pl* TX-5
Dawes, Charles Gates, House—*hist pl* IL-6
Dawes Brook—*stream* VT-1
Dawes Cem—*cemetery* MA-1
Dawes Cem—*cemetery* OH-6
Dawes Cem—*cemetery* OK-5
Dawes Chapel—*church* GA-3
Dawes Coulee—*valley* MT-8
Dawes Creek—*stream* ID-8
Dawes Creek—*stream* MT-8
Dawes Creek—*stream* WI-6
Dawes Glacier—*glacier* AK-9
Dawes Hill—*summit* NY-2
Dawes Hill—*summit* TN-4
Dawes JHS—*school* NE-7
Dawes Park—*park* IL-6
**Dawes Point (subdivision)**—*pop pl* AL-4
Dawes Ridge—*ridge* MO-7
Dawes Sch—*school* (2) IL-6
Dawes Sch—*school* MA-1
**Dawes Township**—*pop pl* NE-7
Dawes-Union Sch—*school* AL-4
Dawesville—*locale* GA-3
*Dawfuskie Island* SC-3
Dawho Bridge—*bridge* SC-3
Dawhoo Lake—*lake* SC-3
*Dawhoo River* SC-3
Dawho River—*stream* SC-3
*Dawings Pass* AZ-5
*Daw Island* SC-3
Dawkins—*locale* SC-3
**Dawkins**—*pop pl* KY-4
Dawkins, Judge Thomas, House—*hist pl* SC-3
Dawkins Branch—*stream* MT-8
Dawkins Branch—*stream* VA-3
Dawkins Chapel—*church* SC-3
Dawkins Creek—*stream* MN-6
*Dawkins Lake* MN-6
Dawkins Lake—*lake* MN-6
Dawkins Lake Dam—*dam* MS-4
Dawkins Oil Field—*oilfield* TX-5
Dawkins Pond—*lake* FL-3
Dawkins Post Office (historical)—*building* AL-4
Dawkins Sch—*school* SD-7
Dawkins Springs—*spring* MT-8
Dawlegs Corners—*uninc pl* VA-3
Dawley Brook—*stream* RI-1
Dawley Canyon—*valley* NV-8
Dawley Cem—*cemetery* KY-4
Dawley Cem—*cemetery* OH-6
**Dawley Corners**—*pop pl* VA-3
Dawley Ditch—*canal* OH-6
Dawley House—*hist pl* IA-7
Dawley Pond—*lake* CT-1
Dawley Pond—*reservoir* RI-1
Dawleys—*locale* IL-6
Dawleys Creek—*stream* NV-8
Dawley Swamp—*swamp* RI-1
**Dawmont**—*pop pl* WV-2
Dawn—*locale* VA-3
**Dawn**—*pop pl* (2) MO-7
**Dawn**—*pop pl* OH-6
**Dawn**—*pop pl* TX-5
Dawn, Lake—*lake* WA-9
**Dawn Acres (subdivision)**—*pop pl* PA-2
Dawn Branch—*stream* NC-3
**Dawnbury**—*pop pl* IN-6
Dawn Cem—*cemetery* (2) TN-4
**Dawn Circle Subdivision**—*pop pl* UT-8
*Dawn Creek* CO-8
Dawn Creek—*stream* AK-9
Dawndale Ch—*church* TX-5

**Dawn Developement Subdivision**—*pop pl* UT-8
Dawn Hill Country Club—*other* AR-4
**Dawn (historical)**—*pop pl* TN-4
Dawnings Sch—*school* OH-6
Dawn Lake—*lake* AK-9
Dawn Lake—*lake* AZ-5
Dawn Lake—*lake* MI-6
Dawn Lake—*lake* WI-6
Dawn Lake Dam—*dam* IN-6
Dawn Marie Beach—*beach* ME-1
Dawn Memory Garden—*cemetery* NC-3
Dawn Mine—*mine* NV-8
Dawn Mist Falls—*falls* MT-8
Dawn o'Day Canyon—*valley* CA-9
Dawn of Ages Memorial Park—*cemetery* IL-6
*Dawn River Golf Course* PA-2
Dawn Sch—*school* TN-4
*Dawn Spring* OR-9
Dawn Station—*locale* MO-7
Dawn Valley Memorial Park—*cemetery* MN-6
Dawnville—*locale* GA-3
Dawnwood JHS—*school* NY-2
*Dawoch* FM-9
**Daws**—*pop pl* NY-2
Daws Branch—*stream* KY-4
Dawsett Sch—*school* OH-6
Dawsey Ch—*church* AL-4
Dawsey Swamp—*swamp* SC-3
Daws Hollow—*valley* KY-4
Daws Island—*island* SC-3
Daws-Keys House—*hist pl* NM-5
Daws Knob—*summit* GA-3
*Dawson* KY-4
*Dawson* MO-7
*Dawson* MP-9
Dawson—*locale* IA-7
Dawson—*locale* MD-2
Dawson—*locale* NM-5
Dawson—*locale* NC-3
**Dawson**—*pop pl* AL-4
**Dawson**—*pop pl* GA-3
**Dawson**—*pop pl* IL-6
**Dawson**—*pop pl* IA-7
**Dawson**—*pop pl* MA-1
**Dawson**—*pop pl* MN-6
**Dawson**—*pop pl* MO-7
**Dawson**—*pop pl* NE-7
**Dawson**—*pop pl* ND-7
**Dawson**—*pop pl* OH-6
**Dawson**—*pop pl* OK-5
**Dawson**—*pop pl* OR-9
**Dawson**—*pop pl* (2) PA-2
**Dawson**—*pop pl* TX-5
**Dawson**—*pop pl* WV-2
Dawson, Alfred, House—*hist pl* OR-9
Dawson, Dr., House—*hist pl* DE-2
Dawson, Lake—*lake* MS-4
Dawson, Lake—*reservoir* CT-1
Dawson, Lake—*reservoir* TX-5
Dawson, T. H. B., House—*hist pl* WV-2
Dawson, Thomas, House—*hist pl* KY-4
Dawson Arroyo—*stream* CO-8
Dawson Arroyo—*valley* NM-5
*Dawson Atoll* MP-9
Dawson Bayou—*stream* MS-4
Dawson Bend—*bend* LA-4
Dawson Bldg—*hist pl* MA-1
Dawson Borough—*civil* PA-2
Dawson Bradford Cem—*cemetery* AL-4
Dawson Branch—*stream* KY-4
Dawson Branch—*stream* LA-4
Dawson Branch—*stream* MD-2
Dawson Branch—*stream* MO-7
Dawson Branch—*stream* SC-3
Dawson Branch—*stream* TN-4
Dawson Branch—*stream* (2) WV-2
Dawson Brothers Plant—*hist pl* IL-6
Dawson-bryant Sch—*school* OH-6
Dawson Bryant Sch—*school* OH-6
Dawsonburg—*locale* IA-7
Dawson Butte—*summit* CO-8
Dawson Canal—*canal* FL-3
Dawson Canyon—*valley* CA-9
Dawson Canyon—*valley* NM-5
Dawson Canyon—*valley* TX-5
Dawson Canyon—*valley* WA-9
Dawson Carnegie Library—*hist pl* MN-6
Dawson (CCD)—*cens area* GA-3
Dawson (CCD)—*cens area* TX-5
Dawson Cem—*cemetery* AL-4
Dawson Cem—*cemetery* (2) AR-4
Dawson Cem—*cemetery* GA-3
Dawson Cem—*cemetery* (2) IL-6
Dawson Cem—*cemetery* IA-7
Dawson Cem—*cemetery* (4) KY-4
Dawson Cem—*cemetery* (2) LA-4
Dawson Cem—*cemetery* (4) MS-4
Dawson Cem—*cemetery* (3) MO-7
Dawson Cem—*cemetery* NE-7
Dawson Cem—*cemetery* TX-5
Dawson Cem—*cemetery* (3) WV-2
Dawson Cem—*cemetery* WI-6
Dawson Cemetary—*cemetery* AR-4
Dawson Ch—*church* AL-4
Dawson Ch—*church* KY-4
Dawson Ch—*church* MD-2
Dawson Ch—*church* WV-2
Dawson Chapel—*church* OK-5
Dawson Corners—*locale* NY-2
Dawson Coulee—*valley* MT-8
**Dawson (County)**—*pop pl* GA-3
**Dawson (County)**—*pop pl* TX-5
Dawson County Canal—*canal* NE-7
Dawson County Courthouse—*hist pl* GA-3
Dawson County Drainage Ditch—*canal* NE-7
Dawson County Drain No 1—*canal* NE-7
Dawson County Junior Coll—*school* MT-8
Dawson Couty Jail—*hist pl* GA-3
*Dawson Creek* OR-9
Dawson Creek—*stream* (2) AK-9
Dawson Creek—*stream* AR-4
Dawson Creek—*stream* CO-8
Dawson Creek—*stream* ID-8
Dawson Creek—*stream* KS-7
Dawson Creek—*stream* KY-4
Dawson Creek—*stream* LA-4
Dawson Creek—*stream* MI-6
Dawson Creek—*stream* MS-4
Dawson Creek—*stream* (2) MT-8

Dawson Creek—*stream* NC-3
Dawson Creek—*stream* OR-9
Dawson Creek—*stream* SD-7
Dawson Creek—*stream* TN-4
Dawson Creek—*stream* (2) TX-5
Dawson Creek—*stream* WI-6
Dawson Creek Sch (historical)—*school* TN-4
**Dawson Crossroads**—*pop pl* NC-3
Dawson Dam—*dam* ND-7
Dawson Day Dam—*dam* AL-4
Dawson Ditch—*canal* CA-9
Dawson Ditch—*canal* IN-6
Dawson Drain—*canal* MI-6
Dawson Drain—*stream* MI-6
*Dawson Draw* CO-8
Dawson Draw—*valley* (2) CO-8
Dawson Draw—*valley* WY-8
Dawson Eddy—*bay* PA-2
*Dawson Elementay School* MS-4
Dawson Falls—*falls* MT-8
Dawson Farm—*hist pl* MD-2
Dawson Fork—*stream* WV-2
Dawson Grove Ch—*church* NC-3
Dawson (historical)—*locale* MS-4
Dawson (historical)—*locale* MT-8
Dawson Hole—*lake* MO-7
Dawson Hollow—*valley* KY-4
Dawson Hollow—*valley* TN-4
Dawson House—*hist pl* TX-5
*Dawson Inseln* MP-9
Dawson Island—*island* FL-3
Dawson Island—*island* MN-6
Dawson Island—*island* SC-3
Dawson Knob—*summit* (2) KY-4
Dawson LaForge School (historical)—*locale* MO-7
*Dawson Lake* MS-4
*Dawson Lake* MT-8
Dawson Lake—*lake* FL-3
Dawson Lake—*lake* ID-8
Dawson Lake—*lake* (2) MI-6
Dawson Lake—*lake* TX-5
Dawson Lake—*lake* WI-6
Dawson Lake—*reservoir* CA-9
Dawson Lake—*reservoir* IN-6
Dawson Lake—*reservoir* KS-7
Dawson Lake Dam—*dam* KS-7
**Dawson Manor**—*pop pl* PA-2
Dawson Massacre Historical Monmt—*park* TX-5
Dawson Memorial Baptist Ch—*church* AL-4
Dawson Memorial Ch—*church* KY-4
Dawson Mill—*locale* AL-4
Dawson Mill—*locale* VA-3
Dawson Mine—*mine* AK-9
Dawson Mine—*mine* CA-9
Dawson Mine—*mine* OR-9
*Dawson Mountain* VA-3
Dawson Mtn—*summit* CO-8
Dawson North—*cens area* MT-8
Dawson Oil Field—*oilfield* NE-7
Dawson Park—*flat* CO-8
Dawson Park—*park* IL-6
Dawson Park—*park* OR-9
Dawson Pass—*gap* MT-8
Dawson Pass Trail—*trail* MT-8
Dawson Peak—*summit* CA-9
Dawson Place—*locale* CA-9
Dawson Playfield—*park* WA-9
Dawson Pond—*lake* NY-2
Dawson Pond—*reservoir* MA-1
Dawson Ranch—*locale* MT-8
*Dawson Reservoir* TX-5
Dawson Ridge—*island* SC-3
**Dawson Ridge**—*pop pl* PA-2
Dawson Ridge—*ridge* CO-8
Dawson Ridge—*ridge* ID-8
Dawson Ridge—*ridge* OK-5
Dawson Run—*locale* PA-2
Dawson Run—*stream* (2) PA-2
Dawson Run—*stream* (2) WV-2
**Dawsons**—*pop pl* AL-4
Dawson Saddle—*gap* CA-9
Dawsons Brook—*stream* NJ-2
Dawson Sch—*school* IL-6
Dawson Sch—*school* KS-7
Dawson Sch—*school* LA-4
Dawson Sch—*school* MI-6
Dawson Sch—*school* MS-4
Dawson Sch—*school* MO-7
Dawson Sch—*school* NC-3
Dawson Sch—*school* TX-5
Dawson Sch (historical)—*school* MO-7
Dawson Sch No 7—*school* IA-7
Dawson School (historical)—*locale* MO-7
*Dawsons Creek* MS-4
Dawsons Creek—*stream* VA-3
**Dawsons Crossroads**—*pop pl* NC-3
Dawson Shoals—*bar* VA-3
Dawsons Island—*island* MI-6
*Dawsons Lake* MT-8
Dawson Slough—*stream* AR-4
Dawsons Millpond—*reservoir* MI-6
Dawson Spring—*spring* AL-4
Dawson Spring—*spring* CA-9
Dawson Spring—*spring* OR-9
*Dawsonsprings* KY-4
**Dawson Springs**—*pop pl* KY-4
Dawson Springs (CCD)—*cens area* KY-4
Dawson Springs Hist Dist—*hist pl* KY-4
Dawson Stand (historical)—*locale* TN-4
Dawson State Game Mngmt Area—*park* ND-7
Dawson Station (historical)—*locale* PA-2
Dawson Street Residential Hist Dist—*hist pl* GA-3
Dawson Street Sch—*school* GA-3
Dawson Swamp—*stream* VA-3
Dawsons Waterhole—*stream* ND-7
**Dawson Switch**—*pop pl* LA-4
Dawson Tank—*reservoir* AZ-5
Dawson Township—*civil* MO-7
Dawson Township—*fmr MCD* IA-7
**Dawson (Township of)**—*pop pl* IL-6
Dawson Valley Sch (historical)—*school* TN-4
Dawson-Vanderbilt Sch—*school* PA-2
Dawson-Vanderhorst House—*hist pl* SC-3
Dawsonville—*locale* VA-3
**Dawsonville**—*pop pl* GA-3
**Dawsonville**—*pop pl* MD-2
**Dawsonville**—*pop pl* MO-7
Dawsonville (CCD)—*cens area* GA-3

Dawson Waterhole—*lake* TX-5
Dawson Windmill—*locale* TX-5
Dawson Windmills—*locale* TX-5
Dawson Woman's Clubhouse—*hist pl* GA-3
Daws Ridge—*ridge* KY-4
Dawt—*locale* MO-7
*Dawtaw Island* SC-3
Dawt Mill—*locale* MO-7
Dawt Township—*civil* MO-7
Daxton Lake—*lake* MN-6
Day—*locale* AR-4
Day—*locale* CA-9
Day—*locale* KY-4
Day—*locale* VA-3
**Day**—*pop pl* FL-3
**Day**—*pop pl* LA-4
**Day**—*pop pl* MD-2
**Day**—*pop pl* MN-6
**Day**—*pop pl* MO-7
**Day**—*pop pl* PA-2
Day, Amasa, House—*hist pl* CT-1
Day, Anna, House—*hist pl* MA-1
Day, Calvin, House—*hist pl* CT-1
Day, C. C., House—*hist pl* MS-4
Day, Edwin and Hattie, House—*hist pl* TX-5
Day, Erastus, House—*hist pl* OH-6
Day, Fred Holland, House—*hist pl* MA-1
Day, Holman, House—*hist pl* ME-1
Day, Ivan W., House—*hist pl* ID-8
Day, John W., House—*hist pl* MI-6
Day, Josiah, House—*hist pl* MA-1
Day, Judge William T., House—*hist pl* AZ-5
Day, Mount—*summit* CA-9
**Day Acres (subdivision)**—*pop pl* NC-3
*Dayay* AK-9
Day Basin—*basin* OR-9
Daybeacon Stoll Memorial—*other* MI-6
Dayberry Creek—*stream* AR-4
Day Bethel Ch—*church* MI-6
Day Bible Ch—*church* MI-6
Day Bldg—*hist pl* OR-9
**Day Book**—*pop pl* NC-3
Day Branch—*stream* AL-4
Day Branch—*stream* AR-4
Day Branch—*stream* (2) KY-4
Day Branch—*stream* LA-4
Day Branch—*stream* TN-4
Daybreak Canyon—*valley* WA-9
Daybreak Chapel—*church* MS-4
Daybreak Plantation (historical)—*locale* MS-4
**Daybreak Subdivision**—*pop pl* UT-8
*Daybrook* NC-3
**Daybrook**—*pop pl* WV-2
Day Brook—*stream* CT-1
Day Brook—*stream* (2) ME-1
Day Brook—*stream* (2) MA-1
Day Brook—*stream* MN-6
Day Brook—*stream* (2) NH-1
Day Brook—*stream* VT-1
Daybrook Pond—*reservoir* NY-2
Day Brown Draw—*valley* SD-7
Dayburg Ch—*church* MI-6
Day Butte—*summit* WY-8
Daycamp Branch—*stream* WV-2
Day Canyon—*valley* CA-9
Day Canyon—*valley* ID-8
Day Canyon—*valley* NM-5
Day Canyon—*valley* OR-9
Day Canyon—*valley* (2) UT-8
Day Canyon Station—*locale* CA-9
Day Canyon Wash—*stream* CA-9
Day (CCD)—*cens area* FL-3
Day Cem—*cemetery* AL-4
Day Cem—*cemetery* CT-1
Day Cem—*cemetery* GA-3
Day Cem—*cemetery* IL-6
Day Cem—*cemetery* IN-6
Day Cem—*cemetery* (2) IA-7
Day Cem—*cemetery* KS-7
Day Cem—*cemetery* (5) KY-4
Day Cem—*cemetery* LA-4
Day Cem—*cemetery* (2) ME-1
Day Cem—*cemetery* MI-6
Day Cem—*cemetery* (3) MS-4
Day Cem—*cemetery* MO-7
Day Cem—*cemetery* NE-7
Day Cem—*cemetery* (4) OH-6
Day Cem—*cemetery* OR-9
Day Cem—*cemetery* PA-2
Day Cem—*cemetery* (2) TN-4
Day Cem—*cemetery* (2) TX-5
Day Cem—*cemetery* VT-1
Day Cem—*cemetery* (2) VA-3
Day Cem—*cemetery* (2) WV-2
**Day Center**—*pop pl* NY-2
Day Center Mtn—*summit* NY-2
Day Ch—*church* LA-4
Day Ch—*church* MO-7
*Day Chapel* TX-5
Daychild Creek—*stream* MT-8
*Day-cho-lah* WI-6
Day Church Creek—*stream* LA-4
Day Cliffs—*cliff* KY-4
Dayco Corporation—*facility* NC-3
Day Coulee—*valley* MT-8
Day County—*civil* SD-7
Day Cove—*bay* ME-1
Day Covered Bridge—*hist pl* PA-2
Daycrain Lake—*lake* LA-4
*Day Creek* OR-9
Day Creek—*locale* WA-9
Day Creek—*stream* AK-9
Day Creek—*stream* CA-9
Day Creek—*stream* CO-8
Day Creek—*stream* GA-3
Day Creek—*stream* (2) ID-8
Day Creek—*stream* KS-7
Day Creek—*stream* MN-6
Day Creek—*stream* MT-8
Day Creek—*stream* NY-2
Day Creek—*stream* OK-5
Day Creek—*stream* (5) OR-9
Day Creek—*stream* VA-3
Day Creek—*stream* (4) WA-9
Day Creek—*stream* WI-6
Day Creek Cem—*cemetery* TX-5
Day Dawn Ch—*church* SC-3
Day Ditch—*canal* MT-8
Day Draw—*valley* WY-8
Dayebas Creek—*stream* AK-9

Dayett Station—*locale* DE-2
Day Family Cem—*cemetery* AL-4
**Dayfield**—*pop pl* IA-7
Dayfoot Brook—*stream* NY-2
Dayforth Sch—*school* IL-6
Day Gap—*gap* AL-4
Daygo Cem—*cemetery* MS-4
Day Gulch—*valley* (2) MT-8
Day Gulch—*valley* WY-8
Day Harbor—*bay* AK-9
**Day Heights**—*pop pl* OH-6
Day Hill—*summit* CT-1
Day Hill—*summit* ME-1
Day Hill—*summit* MN-6
Day Hill—*summit* NY-2
Day (historical)—*locale* KS-7
**Day (historical)**—*pop pl* OR-9
Dayhoff Ditch—*canal* IN-6
Dayhoff Slough—*gut* FL-3
**Dayhoit (RR name Wilhoit)**—*pop pl* KY-4
Day Hollow—*valley* MO-7
Day Hollow—*valley* (2) TN-4
Day Homestead—*locale* (2) WY-8
Day House—*hist pl* AZ-5
Day House—*hist pl* CT-1
Day House—*hist pl* MO-7
Day Inlet—*bay* OR-9
*Day Island* WA-9
Day Island—*island* CA-9
**Day Island**—*pop pl* WA-9
Day JHS—*school* MA-1
Day Kimball Hosp—*hospital* CT-1
**Daykin**—*pop pl* NE-7
Day Knob—*summit* GA-3
Day Knob—*summit* WV-2
Daykoo Islands—*area* AK-9
*Day Lake* MN-6
Day Lake—*lake* IL-6
Day Lake—*lake* MI-6
Day Lake—*lake* (3) MN-6
Day Lake—*lake* TX-5
Day Lake—*lake* (2) WA-9
Day Lake—*lake* (2) WI-6
Day Lake—*reservoir* TN-4
Day Lake Dam—*dam* TN-4
Day Lake Lookout Tower—*locale* MN-6
*Day Lake Outlet* TX-5
Day Lake Slough—*gut* TX-5
*Dayle* MN-6
**Dayle Acres (subdivision)**—*pop pl* VA-3
Dayle Creek—*stream* CA-9
**Daylesford**—*pop pl* PA-2
Dayley Creek—*stream* ID-8
Daylight—*locale* TN-4
**Daylight**—*pop pl* IN-6
**Daylight**—*pop pl* KY-4
Daylight Bay—*lake* LA-4
Daylight Branch—*stream* KY-4
Daylight Creek—*stream* MT-8
Daylight Harbor—*bay* AK-9
Daylight Hill—*summit* WI-6
Daylight Lake—*reservoir* KY-4
Daylight Pass—*gap* CA-9
Daylight Post Office (historical)—*building* TN-4
Daylight Spring—*spring* CA-9
Daylis Stadium—*other* MT-8
Daylo—*locale* NC-3
Daymark Island—*island* GA-3
Day Meadow—*flat* (2) CA-9
Day Meadow Brook—*stream* CT-1
Day Memorial Ch—*church* GA-3
Day Memorial Park—*park* OR-9
Day Mesa—*summit* NM-5
Day Millpond—*lake* MA-1
Day Mine (underground)—*mine* AL-4
Day Mine Wash—*stream* AZ-5
Day Mine Windmill—*locale* AZ-5
Daymond Pond—*lake* ME-1
Day Mountain Pond—*lake* ME-1
*Day Mtn* ME-1
*Day Mtn* WA-9
Day Mtn—*summit* (2) ME-1
Day Mtn—*summit* MA-1
Day Mtn—*summit* TN-4
Day Mtn—*summit* (2) WA-9
Day Mtn—*summit* WV-2
Daynes Lake—*lake* UT-8
Day Number 1 Mine (surface)—*mine* AL-4
Day Ona Heights Ch—*church* TN-4
Day Opening—*flat* CA-9
Day Opening Mine (underground)—*mine* AL-4
**Day Park Estates (subdivision)**—*pop pl* UT-8
**Day Park Subdivision**—*pop pl* UT-8
Day Peaks—*summit* AZ-5
*Day Point* VA-3
Day Point—*cape* NY-2
Day Pond—*lake* CT-1
Day Pond—*lake* ME-1
Day Pond—*lake* NH-1
Day Pond—*lake* PA-2
Day Pond—*reservoir* AL-4
Day Pond Brook—*stream* CT-1
Day-Radcliff Cem—*cemetery* TX-5
Day Ranch—*locale* (2) AZ-5
Day Ranch—*locale* CA-9
Day Ranch—*locale* CO-8
Day Ranch—*locale* WY-8
**Day Ranch**—*pop pl* NE-7
Day Ridge—*ridge* KY-4
Day Ridge—*ridge* OR-9
Day Ridge—*ridge* WA-9
Day Ridge Sch—*school* KY-4
Day Rock—*pillar* CA-9
Day Rock—*pillar* WI-6
Day Run—*stream* PA-2
Day Run—*stream* WV-2
Day Run Campground—*locale* WV-2
Days—*locale* MS-4
Days—*locale* WY-8
Days—*other* MS-4
Days Academy Grant—*unorg* ME-1
Days Bar—*bar* AL-4
Days Bend—*bend* AL-4
Daysboro—*locale* KY-4
Days Branch—*stream* FL-3
Days Branch—*stream* KY-4
*Days Brook* MA-1
Days Canyon—*valley* UT-8
Days Cem—*cemetery* KY-4

Days Cem—cemetery TN-4
Day Sch—school IL-6
Day Sch—school KY-4
Day Sch—school LA-4
Day Sch—school MI-6
Day Sch—school MN-6
Day Sch—school MT-8
Day Sch—school TX-5
Day Sch—school (2) VT-1
Days Chapel—church TN-4
Days Chapel—church TX-5
Days Chapel (historical)—church TN-4
Day School—locale MI-6
Day School Wash—stream AZ-5
**Days Corners**—pop pl NY-2
Days Cove—bay ME-1
Days Cove—bay MD-2
Days Creek GA-3
Days Creek OK-5
Days Creek OR-9
Days Creek—cove MA-1
Days Creek—gut FL-3
**Days Creek**—pop pl OR-9
Days Creek—stream AR-4
Days Creek—stream IN-6
Days Creek—stream KY-4
Days Creek—stream MS-4
Days Creek—stream NC-3
Days Creek—stream OR-9
Days Creek—stream TN-4
Days Creek—stream TX-5
Days Creek Cutoff—bend OR-9
Days Creek (Township of)—fmr MCD AR-4
Days Crossroads—locale AL-4
Days Crossroads—locale GA-3
Days Crossroads—locale TN-4
**Days Crossroads**—pop pl NC-3
Days Crossroads Baptist Ch—church TN-4
**Daysen Heights Subdivision**—pop pl UT-8
**Days Ferry**—pop pl ME-1
Days Ferry Hist Dist—hist pl ME-1
Days Fork—stream UT-8
Days Gap AL-4
Days Gap—gap (2) NC-3
Days Gap—gap TN-4
Days Gap Drift Mine (underground)—mine AL-4
Days Gap Post Office AL-4
Days Gulch—valley OR-9
Days Head—summit ME-1
**Days High Landing**—pop pl MN-6
Days Hill MA-1
Days Island—island MD-2
Days Island—island WA-9
Days Lake—lake MN-6
Days Lake—lake TX-5
Days Lake—reservoir AL-4
Days Memorial Church TN-4
Days Mill—locale ME-1
Days Mill Ch (historical)—church TN-4
Days Mill (historical)—locale MS-4
Days Mine AL-4
Days of the Week Islands FM-9
Dayson—locale LA-4
Days Park—park NY-2
Days Pass—gap CA-9
Days Pit—cave AL-4
Days Point—cape MD-2
Days Point—cape NJ-2
Days Point—cape VA-3
Days Post Office (historical)—building MS-4
Day Spring—spring AL-4
Day Spring—spring AZ-5
Day Spring—spring OR-9
Day Spring—spring TN-4
Day Spring—spring UT-8
Dayspring Baptist Ch—church TN-4
Dayspring Haven Camp—locale IA-7
Dayspring Waldorf Sch—school FL-3
Days Ridge—ridge ME-1
Days River—stream MI-6
**Days Rock**—pop pl NY-2
Days Roundtop—summit PA-2
Days Rsvr—reservoir WY-8
Days Run—stream PA-2
Days Run—stream WV-2
Days Sch—school NY-2
Days Store (historical)—locale TN-4
Daystar Private Sch of Orange County—school FL-3
Daystown TX-5
Day Street Baptist Ch—church AL-4
Daystrom NC-3
Daystrom—other NC-3
Daysville—locale MD-2
Daysville—locale NY-2
Daysville—locale WV-2
**Daysville**—pop pl FL-3
**Daysville**—pop pl IL-6
**Daysville**—pop pl KY-4
**Daysville**—pop pl TN-4
Daysville Baptist Ch—church TN-4
Daysville Cem—cemetery NY-2
Daysville Corner—locale NY-2
Daysville Post Office (historical)—building TN-4
Daysville Sch (historical)—school TN-4
Days Woods SD-7
Day Tank—reservoir AZ-5
Day Tank—reservoir (2) NM-5
Day Tanks—reservoir NM-5
Day-Taylor House—hist pl CT-1
Daytoe, Bayou—gut LA-4
Dayton CO-8
Dayton MS-4
Dayton TN-4
Dayton—locale MI-6
Dayton—locale NM-5
Dayton—locale WA-9
**Dayton**—pop pl AL-4
**Dayton**—pop pl AR-4
**Dayton**—pop pl CA-9
**Dayton**—pop pl (2) ID-8
**Dayton**—pop pl (2) IL-6
**Dayton**—pop pl IN-6
**Dayton**—pop pl (2) IA-7
**Dayton**—pop pl KY-4
**Dayton**—pop pl MD-2
**Dayton**—pop pl MI-6
**Dayton**—pop pl MN-6
**Dayton**—pop pl MO-7
**Dayton**—pop pl MT-8
**Dayton**—pop pl NV-8
**Dayton**—pop pl NJ-2
**Dayton**—pop pl NY-2
**Dayton**—pop pl OH-6
**Dayton**—pop pl OR-9
**Dayton**—pop pl (2) PA-2
**Dayton**—pop pl TN-4
**Dayton**—pop pl TX-5
**Dayton**—pop pl VA-3
**Dayton**—pop pl WA-9
**Dayton**—pop pl WV-2
**Dayton**—pop pl WI-6
**Dayton**—pop pl WY-8
Dayton, Daniel, House—hist pl MN-6
Dayton, James, House—hist pl OH-6
Dayton, James, House, II—hist pl OH-6
**Daytona**—pop pl MI-6
Daytona, Lake—lake FL-3
**Daytona Beach**—pop pl FL-3
Daytona Beach Baptist Ch—church FL-3
Daytona Beach (CCD)—cens area FL-3
Daytona Beach Ch of Christ—church FL-3
Daytona Beach Community Coll—school FL-3
Daytona Beach Community College, Mary Karl Memorial Library—building FL-3
Daytona Beach Drive-In Christian Ch—church FL-3
Daytona Beach General Hosp—hospital FL-3
Daytona Beach Outlet Mall—locale FL-3
Daytona Beach Regional Airp—airport FL-3
**Daytona Beach Shores**—pop pl FL-3
Daytona Branch—locale MI-6
Daytona Christian Ch—church FL-3
**Daytona Highbridge Estates**—pop pl FL-3
**Daytona Hills (subdivision)**—pop pl TN-4
Dayton Airp—airport WA-9
Daytona Mall—locale FL-3
Dayton-Amity (CCD)—cens area OR-9
**Daytona Park Estates**—pop pl FL-3
Dayton Apartment Bldg—hist pl OR-9
Dayton Arcade—hist pl OH-6
Dayton Art Institute—hist pl OH-6
Dayton Art Institute—school OH-6
Dayton Auto and Transfer Company Bldg—hist pl OR-9
**Dayton Ave**—pop pl CA-9
Daytona Wash—stream AZ-5
Dayton Bayou—stream AR-4
Dayton Bend Ch—church NC-3
Dayton Borough—civil PA-2
Dayton Boys Club—building OH-6
Dayton Branch—stream AL-4
Dayton Branch Gowanda Central Sch—school NY-2
Dayton Brook—stream CT-1
Dayton Cabin—locale MT-8
Dayton-Campbell Hist Dist—hist pl OH-6
Dayton Canal—canal TX-5
Dayton Canyon—valley CA-9
Dayton (CCD)—cens area TN-4
Dayton (CCD)—cens area WA-9
Dayton Cem—cemetery (2) IL-6
Dayton Cem—cemetery IA-7
Dayton Cem—cemetery KS-7
Dayton Cem—cemetery LA-4
Dayton Cem—cemetery MD-2
Dayton Cem—cemetery WI-6
Dayton Center—locale MI-6
**Dayton Center**—pop pl MI-6
Dayton Center Cem—cemetery (2) MI-6
Dayton Center Ch—church MI-6
Dayton City Hall—building TN-4
Dayton Common Sch—hist pl OR-9
Dayton Corners Ch—church WI-6
Dayton Correction Farm—locale OH-6
Dayton Country Club—other OH-6
Dayton Cove—bay NC-3
Dayton Creek—stream CA-9
Dayton Creek—stream MT-8
Dayton Creek—stream NJ-2
Dayton Creek—stream NY-2
Dayton Creek—stream ND-7
Dayton - Crow Creek Ditch—canal SD-7
Dayton Daily News Bldg—hist pl OH-6
Dayton Dam—dam IL-6
Dayton Dam—dam PA-2
Dayton Depot—hist pl WA-9
Dayton Division—civil TN-4
Dayton Elem Sch—school IN-6
Dayton Fire Department Station No. 16—hist pl OH-6
Dayton Fire Station No. 14—hist pl OH-6
Dayton Golf and Country Club—locale TN-4
Dayton-Grant Well—well OR-9
Dayton Gulch—valley CO-8
Dayton Gulch—valley WY-8
Dayton Heights Sch—school CA-9
Dayton Hist Dist—hist pl VA-3
Dayton (historical)—locale (2) KS-7
Dayton (historical)—locale SD-7
**Dayton (historical)**—pop pl IA-7
Dayton (historical P.O.)—locale IA-7
Dayton Hollow—valley IL-6
Dayton Hollow Dam—dam MN-6
Dayton Hollow Rsvr—reservoir MN-6
Dayton HS—hist pl KY-4
Dayton HS—hist pl OR-9
Dayton HS—school PA-2
Dayton Island—island ME-1
Dayton Island—island NY-2
Dayton Knob—summit WV-2
Dayton Lake—lake MI-6
Dayton Lake Estates—lake TX-5
**Dayton Lakes**—pop pl TX-5
Dayton Lateral—canal CO-8
Dayton Masonic Coll (historical)—school TN-4
Dayton Memorial Park—cemetery OH-6
Dayton Methodist Episcopal Church—hist pl OR-9
Dayton Mine NV-8
Dayton Mine—mine NV-8
Dayton Motor Car Company Hist Dist—hist pl OH-6
Dayton Municipal Airp—airport OH-6
Dayton Municipal Park—park TN-4
Dayton Number 3 Mine (surface)—mine TN-4
Dayton Number 4 Mine (surface)—mine TN-4
Dayton Opera House—hist pl OR-9
Dayton Park—park MI-6
Dayton Park—park WV-2
Dayton Peak—summit WA-9
Dayton Plaza Shop Ctr—locale (2) TN-4
Dayton Pond—lake CT-1
Dayton Post Office—building TN-4
Dayton Power And Light Company Mound—hist pl OH-6
Dayton Prairie—flat OR-9
Dayton Public Library—building TN-4
Dayton Quarry Cave—cave TN-4
Dayton Rsvr—reservoir TN-4
Dayton Rsvr—reservoir WY-8
Daytons Bluff MN-6
Dayton Sch—hist pl OK-5
Dayton Sch—school CA-9
Dayton Sch—school MI-6
Dayton Sch—school NJ-2
Dayton Sch—school SC-3
Dayton Speedway—other OH-6
Dayton Spur—locale TN-4
Dayton (sta.) MN-6
**Dayton (sta)**—pop pl OR-9
Dayton State Hosp—hospital OH-6
Dayton State Hospital Farm—locale OH-6
Dayton Station TX-5
Dayton Station—locale OR-9
Dayton-Stena Ditch—canal SD-7
Dayton Stove and Cornice Works—hist pl OH-6
Dayton Street Hist Dist—hist pl OH-6
Dayton Street Sch—school NJ-2
Dayton Terra-Cotta Hist Dist—hist pl OH-6
Dayton Tire & Rubber Company—facility OH-6
Dayton Town Ditch—canal NV-8
Dayton Town Hall—building ND-7
**Dayton (Town of)**—pop pl ME-1
**Dayton (Town of)**—pop pl NY-2
**Dayton (Town of)**—pop pl (2) WI-6
Dayton Township—civil (2) MO-7
Dayton Township—fmr MCD (7) IA-7
Dayton Township—inact MCD NV-8
**Dayton Township**—pop pl (2) KS-7
**Dayton Township**—pop pl ND-7
**Dayton Township**—pop pl (2) SD-7
Dayton (Township of)—fmr MCD AR-4
Dayton (Township of)—other MN-6
**Dayton (Township of)**—pop pl IL-6
**Dayton (Township of)**—pop pl (2) MI-6
Dayton Valley Cem—cemetery IA-7
Dayton View OH-6
Dayton View Hist Dist—hist pl OH-6
**Daytonville**—pop pl IA-7
**Daytonville**—pop pl NY-2
Dayton Woman's Club—hist pl OH-6
Dayton Young Men's Christian Association Bldg—hist pl OH-6
**Daytown**—pop pl MO-7
**Day (Town of)**—pop pl NY-2
**Day (Town of)**—pop pl WI-6
Daytown Sch (abandoned)—school PA-2
**Day Township**—pop pl SD-7
**Day (Township of)**—pop pl MI-6
Day Tunnel—cave CA-9
Day Valley—valley CA-9
Day Valley Church AL-4
Day-Vandevander Mill—hist pl WV-2
Dayville FL-3
**Dayville**—pop pl CT-1
**Dayville**—pop pl IN-6
**Dayville**—pop pl MA-1
**Dayville**—pop pl OR-9
Dayville Brook—stream CT-1
Dayville Cem—cemetery OR-9
Dayville Hist Dist—hist pl CT-1
**Daywalt**—pop pl CA-9
Day Wash—stream AZ-5
Day Windmill—locale (2) TX-5
Day Windmill Flats—flat TX-5
Daze—locale AZ-5
Daze Canyon—valley AZ-5
Daze Lake—lake AZ-5
Dazen Canyon—valley AZ-5
Daze RR Station—building AZ-5
Daze Tank—reservoir (2) AZ-5
**Dazey**—pop pl ND-7
Dazey Cem—cemetery ND-7
Dazey Dam—dam ND-7
**Dazey Township**—pop pl ND-7
D Baker Ranch—locale TX-5
D Bar A Scout Ranch—locale MI-6
D Bar Basin—basin ID-8
D Bar Coulee—valley MT-8
D Bar H Tank—reservoir AZ-5
D Bar Ranch—locale NM-5
D Bar Rsvr—reservoir ID-8
D Bloodworth Grant—civil FL-3
D Booth Dam—dam SD-7
D Booth Number 2 Dam—dam SD-7
D Booth Number 3 Dam—dam SD-7
D Briggs Lake—lake NE-7
DBS Airp PA-2
Dbs Airp—airport PA-2
D B Walker Shoe Company Dam—dam NC-3
D B West Mine TN-4
D Camp—locale CA-9
D Canal—canal CA-9
D Canal—canal (2) MT-8
D Canal—canal NV-8
D Canal—canal NC-3
D Canal—canal OR-9
D Canal - in part NV-8
D Candelaria Place—locale NM-5
D Carmichael lake Dam—dam MS-4
D Carmichael Pond Dam—dam MS-4
D C Barksdale Lake Dam—dam MS-4
D C Beville Lake—reservoir AL-4
D C Beville Lake Dam AL-4
D.C.C. & P. Inscription "B"—hist pl UT-8
D C Ewing Dam—dam NC-3
D C General Hosp—hospital DC-2
D C Gulch—valley ID-8
DCH Regional Med Ctr AL-4
D C Leach Lake Dam—dam MS-4
D C Obraint Dam—dam MS-4
D Cox Ranch—locale NE-7
D C P Ditch—canal WY-8
D Creek OR-9
D Creek—stream CO-8
D Crighton Ranch—locale ND-7
D Cross Mtn—summit NM-5
D Cross Ranch—locale WY-8
D C Suther Lake Dam—dam MS-4
D C Tank—reservoir TX-5
D C Village—locale DC-2
D C Virgo JHS—school NC-3
D C Wedgeworth Cem—cemetery MS-4
DD-Antelope Tank—reservoir NM-5
D D Eisenhower Elem Sch—school FL-3
D Devaney Ranch—locale NM-5
DD Hollow UT-8
D D Hollow—valley UT-8
DD Hollow - in part UT-8
**D & D Ideal Acres Subdivision**—pop pl UT-8
DDI Electric Locomotive No. 36—hist pl PA-2
D Drain—canal CA-9
D D Ranch—locale NM-5
DD Spring—spring MT-8
D Dunn Dam—dam SD-7
DDZ Bridge over New Fork River—hist pl. WY-8
D D 100 Main Drain—canal CA-9
Deabach—summit FM-9
Deabreach—summit FM-9
**Deacon**—pop pl IN-6
Deacon Branch PA-2
Deacon Brook—stream PA-2
Deacon Cem—cemetery TN-4
Deacon Creek—stream CA-9
Deacon Creek—stream OH-6
Deacon Creek—stream TN-4
Deacon Creek Cem—cemetery OH-6
Deacon Creek Corner—locale OH-6
Deaconess Hosp—hospital MI-6
Deaconess Hosp—hospital MN-6
Deaconess Hosp—hospital MO-7
Deaconess Hosp—hospital (3) MT-8
Deaconess Hosp—hospital NE-7
Deaconess Hosp—hospital NY-2
Deaconess Hosp—hospital ND-7
Deaconess Hosp—hospital (2) OH-6
Deaconess Hosp—hospital OK-5
Deaconess Hosp—hospital WA-9
Deaconess Hospital Airp—airport IN-6
Deaconess Hospital Heliport—airport MO-7
Deaconess Med Ctr Heliport—airport WA-9
Deacon Flat—flat OR-9
Deacon Flat—flat WY-8
Deacon Gulch—valley (2) CO-8
Deacon Hill—summit MA-1
Deacon Hill Ch (historical)—church AL-4
Deacon Hutchins House—hist pl ME-1
Deacon Jones Gulch—valley CO-8
Deacon Lake—lake FL-3
Deacon Lake—lake MI-6
Deacon Lake—lake WY-8
Deacon Lee Place—locale CA-9
Deacon Lee Trail—trail CA-9
Deacon Long Ravine—valley CA-9
Deacon Meadows—flat WY-8
Deacon Pinnacle—summit ME-1
Deacon Pond MA-1
Deacon Pond—lake FL-3
Deacon Ridge—ridge TN-4
Deacon Ridge Public Use Area—park MS-4
Deacon Run—stream WV-2
**Deacons**—pop pl NJ-2
Deacons Cem—cemetery VA-3
Deacons Hill MA-1
Deacons Neck—cape VA-3
Deacons Pond Harbor MA-1
Deacons Rock—island AK-9
Deacon Store—locale TN-4
Deacon Street Cem—cemetery IL-6
**Deacons Walk**—pop pl DE-2
Deacon Thomas Lake—lake WI-6
Deacon Wright Lode Mine—mine SD-7
Deacoresd Institute—locale NE-7
Dead Alligator Point—cape LA-4
Dead and Bones Cove—bay VA-3
Dead Backwater—lake NC-3
Dead Bayou LA-4
Dead Bear Hollow—valley PA-2
Dead Beaver Lake—lake MN-6
Dead Boy Cove—bay AL-4
Dead Boy Creek—stream FL-3
Dead Boy Creek—stream MT-8
Dead Boy Divide—ridge MT-8
Dead Boy Point—cliff AZ-5
Dead Brake—swamp AR-4
Dead Branch—glacier AK-9
Dead Branch—stream MA-1
Dead Branch—stream OH-6
Dead Brier Creek—stream IA-7
Deadbroke Mine—mine SD-7
Dead Brook—stream (18) ME-1
Dead Brook Deadwater—lake ME-1
Dead Buffalo Dam—dam SD-7
Dead Buffalo Lake—lake ND-7
Dead Bull Canyon—valley NV-8
Dead Bull Creek—stream NV-8
Dead Bull Mine—mine AZ-5
Deadbull Waterhole—lake OR-9
Dead Calf Draw—valley WY-8
Dead Cambridge River—stream ME-1
Dead Camel Mtns—range NV-8
Dead Caney Lake—lake TX-5
Dead Can Gulch—valley CO-8
Dead Canyon—valley (2) WA-9
Dead Cat Canyon—valley ID-8
Dead Cedar Mine—mine NV-8
Dead Cedar Rsvr—reservoir MT-8
Dead Cedar Spring—spring NV-8
Dead Cedar Wash—stream NV-8
Dead Cedar Wash—valley UT-8
Dead Chicken Pit—cave TN-4
Dead Colt Creek—stream ND-7
Dead Coon Lake—lake MN-6
Dead Cottonwood Spring—spring NM-5
Dead Cow Canyon AZ-5
Dead Cow Canyon—valley AZ-5
Dead Cow Canyon—valley NM-5
Dead Cow Cave—cave AL-4
Dead Cow Creek—stream CA-9
Dead Cow Creek—stream OR-9
Dead Cow Creek—stream WY-8
Dead Cow Gulch—valley AZ-5
Dead Cow Gulch—valley OR-9
Dead Cow Lake—lake CA-9
Dead Cow Lake—lake NE-7
Dead Cow Point—cliff UT-8
Dead Cow Rsvr—reservoir MT-8
Dead Cow Rsvr—reservoir WY-8
Dead Cow Spring—spring AZ-5
Dead Cow Spring—spring CA-9
Dead Cow Spring—spring ID-8
Dead Cow Spring—spring OR-9
Dead Cow Spring—spring UT-8
Dead Cow Tank—reservoir (4) AZ-5
Dead Cow Tank—reservoir TX-5
Dead Cow Windmill—locale NM-5
Dead Creek AZ-5
Dead Creek CO-8
Dead Creek MI-6
Dead Creek—gut NY-2
Dead Creek—stream AK-9
Dead Creek—stream GA-3
Dead Creek—stream IL-6
Dead Creek—stream KY-4
Dead Creek—stream MA-1
Dead Creek—stream (6) MI-6
Dead Creek—stream MN-6
Dead Creek—stream NE-7
Dead Creek—stream (9) NY-2
Dead Creek—stream PA-2
Dead Creek—stream TX-5
Dead Creek—stream (3) VT-1
Dead Creek—stream (3) WI-6
Dead Creek Flow—bay NY-2
Dead Creek (historical)—stream MO-7
Dead Cypress Lake—lake FL-3
Dead Cypress Point—cape LA-4
Dead Deer Canyon—valley NV-8
Dead Deer Tank—reservoir AZ-5
Dead Diamond River—stream NH-1
Dead Dog Canyon—valley NM-5
Dead Dog Canyon—valley (2) OR-9
Dead Dog Cave—cave AL-4
Dead Dog Creek—stream ID-8
Deaddog Creek—stream OR-9
Dead Dog Creek—stream WY-8
Dead Dog Den—cave TN-4
Dead Dog Draw—valley CO-8
Dead Dog Draw—valley WY-8
Dead Dog Gulch—valley OR-9
Dead Dog Rsvr—reservoir CO-8
Dead Dog Slough—lake ND-7
Dead Duck Creek—stream WA-9
Dead Duck Pass—channel LA-4
Dead Duck Point—cape NC-3
Dead Dutchman Hollow MO-7
Dead Dutchman Hollow—valley MO-7
Dead Elk Creek—stream ID-8
Dead Elk Point—cliff ID-8
Deaden Branch—stream GA-3
Dead End Cabin—locale CA-9
Deadend Canyon—valley ID-8
Dead End Cave—cave TN-4
Dead End Creek—stream FL-3
Dead End Rsvr—reservoir OR-9
Dead End Rsvr—reservoir WY-8
Dead End Spring—spring OR-9
Dead End Trail—trail OK-5
Dead End Trail—trail OR-9
Deadening, The—flat TN-4
Deadening, The—lake FL-3
Deadening Branch—stream (3) KY-4
Deadening Branch—stream TN-4
Deadening Branch—stream VA-3
Deadening Cem—cemetery FL-3
Deadening Creek WV-2
Deadening Fork—stream (3) KY-4
Deadening Hollow—valley (2) KY-4
Deadening Hollow—valley WV-2
Deadening Knob—summit NC-3
Deadening Lake FL-3
Deadening Lakes FL-3
Deadening Lakes, The FL-3
Deadening Mtn—summit AL-4
Deadening Run—stream WV-2
Deadennen Mtn—summit GA-3
Deaden Top—summit NC-3
Deaden Tree Gap—gap NC-3
Deadeye Rsvr—reservoir (2) ID-8
Deadeye Spring—spring ID-8
Dead Eye Tank—reservoir NM-5
Deadfall Branch—stream KY-4
Deadfall Branch—stream TN-4
Dead Fall Creek NC-3
Deadfall Creek—stream AK-9
Deadfall Creek—stream CA-9
Deadfall Creek—stream FL-3
Deadfall Creek—stream ID-8
Deadfall Creek—stream MT-8
Deadfall Creek—stream NC-3
Deadfall Creek—stream SC-3
Deadfall Creek—stream WA-9
Deadfall Crossroads—locale SC-3
Deadfall Lakes—lake CA-9
Deadfall Run—stream WV-2
Deadfall Swamp—stream SC-3
Deadfall Trail—trail WA-9
Deadfish Lake—lake AK-9
Dead Fish Lake—lake MN-6
Deadfoot Canyon—valley CA-9
Dead Forest Tank—reservoir NM-5
Dead Goat Gulch—valley CO-8
Dead Goose Lake—lake WI-6
Deadhead Creek—stream WY-8
Deadhead Lake—lake WA-9
Deadhead Spring—spring WA-9
Dead Heart Slough—gut ND-7
Dead Heifer Gap—gap NC-3
Dead Heifer Spring—spring NV-8
Dead Hill—summit MA-1
Dead Hole—bend WA-9
Dead Hole Brook—stream ME-1
Dead Hollow—valley MO-7
Dead Hollow—valley TN-4
Deadhorse—locale AK-9
Deadhorse Airp—airport AK-9
Dead Horse Basin—basin OR-9
Dead Horse Bay—bay NY-2
Dead Horse Bay—bay WI-6
Dead Horse Branch—stream IN-6
Dead Horse Butte—ridge OR-9
Deadhorse Butte—summit OR-9
Dead Horse Butte—summit OR-9
Dead Horse Butte—summit SD-7
Deadhorse Campground—park OR-9
Dead Horse Canon NV-8
Dead Horse Canyon CA-9
Dead Horse Canyon CO-8
Dead Horse Canyon—valley (3) CA-9
Deadhorse Canyon—valley CA-9
Dead Horse Canyon—valley (2) CA-9
Deadhorse Canyon—valley CA-9
Dead Horse Canyon—valley (2) CA-9
Dead Horse Canyon—valley (2) CO-8
Deadhorse Canyon—valley (2) ID-8
Dead Horse Canyon—valley (2) NV-8
Dead Horse Canyon—valley (2) NM-5
Deadhorse Canyon—valley NM-5
Dead Horse Canyon—valley (4) OR-9
Deadhorse Canyon—valley SD-7
Dead Horse Canyon—valley UT-8
Deadhorse Canyon—valley UT-8
Dead Horse Canyon—valley UT-8
Deadhorse Canyon—valley WA-9
Deadhorse Canyon—valley (2) WY-8
Dead Horse Canyon Creek—stream OR-9
Dead Horse Cave—cave ID-8
Deadhorse Corral—locale OR-9
Deadhorse Coulee—valley MT-8
Dead Horse Coulee—valley MT-8
Dead Horse Creek CO-8
Deadhorse Creek MT-8
Deadhorse Creek OR-9
Dead Horse Creek WY-8
Deadhorse Creek—stream AK-9
Dead Horse Creek—stream (5) CA-9
Deadhorse Creek—stream (3) CA-9
Dead Horse Creek—stream (2) CO-8
Deadhorse Creek—stream CO-8
Dead Horse Creek—stream CO-8
Deadhorse Creek—stream (3) CO-8
Deadhorse Creek—stream (2) ID-8
Dead Horse Creek—stream (4) ID-8
Deadhorse Creek—stream ID-8
Deadhorse Creek—stream MI-6
Dead Horse Creek—stream MI-6
Dead Horse Creek—stream MN-6
Dead Horse Creek—stream (4) MT-8
Deadhorse Creek—stream (2) MT-8
Dead Horse Creek—stream MT-8
Deadhorse Creek—stream MT-8
Dead Horse Creek—stream (2) NE-7
Dead Horse Creek—stream NV-8
Dead Horse Creek—stream ND-7
Deadhorse Creek—stream (2) OR-9
Dead Horse Creek—stream OR-9
Deadhorse Creek—stream (6) OR-9
Dead Horse Creek—stream (4) OR-9
Deadhorse Creek—stream OR-9
Dead Horse Creek—stream (2) OR-9
Deadhorse Creek—stream OR-9
Dead Horse Creek—stream (3) TX-5
Dead Horse Creek—stream (2) WA-9
Deadhorse Creek—stream WA-9
Dead Horse Creek—stream WI-6
Dead Horse Creek—stream (3) WY-8
Deadhorse Creek—stream WY-8
Dead Horse Creek—stream WY-8
Dead Horse Creek Oil Field—oilfield WY-8
Dead Horse Cut—canal CA-9
Dead Horse Dam—dam AZ-5
Dead Horse Dam—dam MT-8
Dead Horse Draw—valley AZ-5
Dead Horse Draw—valley (2) CO-8
Deadhorse Draw—valley NV-8
Dead Horse Draw—valley SD-7
Dead Horse Draw—valley UT-8
Dead Horse Draw—valley WY-8
Deadhorse Falls—falls CA-9
Dead Horse Flat—flat AZ-5
Dead Horse Flat—flat (2) CA-9
Dead Horse Flat—flat (2) NV-8
Deadhorse Flat—flat OR-9
Deadhorse Flat Rsvr—reservoir CA-9
Dead Horse Flats—flat SD-7
Dead Horse Flats—flat WA-9
Dead Horse Gap—gap OR-9
Dead Horse Gulch—valley (3) CA-9
Deadhorse Gulch—valley (2) CO-8
Dead Horse Gulch—valley CO-8
Deadhorse Gulch—valley (2) ID-8
Dead Horse Gulch—valley ME-1
Dead Horse Gulch—valley MT-8
Deadhorse Gulch—valley SD-7
Dead Horse Gulch—valley WY-8
Dead Horse Hill—summit CO-8
Deadhorse Hill—summit MA-1
Deadhorse Hill—summit (2) NM-5
Deadhorse Hill—summit WA-9
Deadhorse Hollow—basin KY-4
Dead Horse Hollow—valley (2) KY-4
Dead Horse Hollow—valley (2) MO-7
Dead Horse Hollow—valley (3) PA-2
Deadhorse Hollow—valley TN-4
Dead Horse Inlet NY-2
Dead Horse Island—island CA-9
Dead Horse Knob—summit KY-4
Deadhorse Lake UT-8
Deadhorse Lake—lake CA-9
Dead Horse Lake—lake CO-8
Dead Horse Lake—lake (6) MN-6
Dead Horse Lake—lake NM-5
Dead Horse Lake—lake OR-9
Deadhorse Lake—lake OR-9
Dead Horse Lake—lake TN-4
Dead Horse Lake—lake (2) UT-8
Dead Horse Lake—lake WA-9
Dead Horse Lake—lake WI-6
Dead Horse Lake—lake (2) WY-8
Dead Horse Lake Campground—park OR-9
Dead Horse Lake Golf Course—locale TN-4
Dead Horse Lakes—lake MT-8
Dead Horse Meadow—flat (2) CA-9
Deadhorse Meadow—flat WA-9
Dead Horse Mesa NM-5
Dead Horse Mesa—summit AZ-5
Dead Horse Mesa—summit CO-8
Deadhorse Mtn—summit CO-8
Deadhorse Mtn—summit ID-8
Dead Horse Mtn—summit NY-2
Dead Horse Mtn—summit OR-9
Dead Horse Park—flat UT-8
Deadhorse Park—flat UT-8
Dead Horse Park—park WY-8
Dead Horse Pass—gap (2) UT-8
Deadhorse Pass—gap WA-9
Dead Horse Pass—gap WY-8

Dead Women Bend—bay ....LA-4
Dead Women Creek....OK-5
Dead Women Crossing—locale....OK-5
Dead Women Inside Pond—bay....LA-4
Dead Women Outside Pond—bay....LA-4
Dead Women Pass—channel....LA-4
Deadwood—locale (3)....CA-9
Deadwood—locale....ID-8
Deadwood—locale....TX-5
**Deadwood**—pop pl....OR-9
**Deadwood**—pop pl....SD-7
Deadwood Campground—locale....ID-8
Deadwood Canyon—valley (2)....CA-9
Deadwood Cem—cemetery....OR-9
Deadwood Ch—church....TX-5
Deadwood City....SD-7
Deadwood Cove—bay....MD-2
Deadwood Creek....CO-8
Deadwood Creek....OR-9
Deadwood Creek—stream (2)....AK-9
Deadwood Creek—stream (7)....CA-9
Deadwood Creek—stream....CO-8
Deadwood Creek—stream (6)....ID-8
Deadwood Creek—stream (2)....NV-8
Deadwood Creek—stream (6)....OR-9
Deadwood Creek—stream....SD-7
Deadwood Creek—stream....TX-5
Deadwood Creek—stream....WA-9
Deadwood Creek—stream (2)....WY-8
Deadwood Creek Bridge—hist pl....OR-9
Deadwood Diggings—mine....CA-9
Deadwood Ditch—canal....CA-9
Deadwood Draw—valley....AZ-5
Deadwood Draw Tank Number One—reservoir....AZ-5
Deadwood Draw Tank Number Two—reservoir....AZ-5
Deadwood Falls—falls....MT-8
Deadwood Gulch....CO-8
Deadwood Gulch—valley (2)....CA-9
Deadwood Gulch—valley (3)....CO-8
Deadwood Gulch—valley....ID-8
Deadwood Gulch—valley (2)....MT-8
Deadwood Gulch—valley....NM-5
Deadwood Gulch—valley....OR-9
Deadwood Gulch—valley....SD-7
Deadwood-Heidelberg Mine....SD-7
Deadwood Hist Dist—hist pl....SD-7
Deadwood Hollow—valley....TX-5
Deadwood Hollow—valley....WV-2
Deadwood Jim Creek—stream....ID-8
Deadwood Junction—locale....OR-9
Deadwood Lake—lake....AK-9
Deadwood Lake—lake....CA-9
Deadwood Lake—lake....MN-6
Deadwood Lake—lake....WI-6
Deadwood Lakes—lake....WA-9
Deadwood landing—locale....OR-9
Deadwood Lodge—locale....ID-8
Deadwood Lookout—locale....CA-9
Deadwood Meadow—flat....CA-9
Deadwood Mine—mine....ID-8
Deadwood Mine—mine....NM-5
Deadwood Mountain—ridge....OR-9
Deadwood Mtn—summit....CO-8
Deadwood Mtn—summit....ID-8
Deadwood Mtn—summit....NY-2
Deadwood Peak—summit (3)....CA-9
Deadwood Point—cape....WI-6
Deadwood Point—cliff....AZ-5
Deadwood Ravine—valley....CA-9
Deadwood Ridge—ridge....CA-9
Deadwood Ridge—ridge (2)....ID-8
Deadwood River—stream....ID-8
Deadwood River Trail—trail....ID-8
Deadwood Rsvr—reservoir....ID-8
Deadwood Saddle—gap....CA-9
Deadwood Sch—school....OR-9
Deadwood (Site)—locale (2)....CA-9
Deadwood (site)—locale....OR-9
Deadwood Spring—spring....CA-9
Deadwood Spring—spring....MT-8
Deadwood Spring—spring....OR-9
Deadwood Summit—summit....ID-8
Dead Wood Swamp—swamp....CT-1
Deadwood Tank—reservoir....AZ-5
Deadwood Terra Mine—mine....SD-7
Deadwood Trail—trail....AZ-5
Deady—locale....OR-9
Deady Hall—hist pl....OR-9
Deady JHS—school....TX-5
Deafenbough Rsvr....OR-9
Deafenbough Rsvr Number One—reservoir....OR-9
Deaf Jim Creek—stream....MT-8
Deaf Jim Knob—summit....MT-8
Deaf Joe Spring—spring....ID-8
Deafqorean—locale....FM-9
Deaf Run Trail—trail....PA-2
Deaf Smith Canyon—valley....UT-8
**Deaf Smith (County)**—pop pl....TX-5
Deaf Smith Sch—school....TX-5
Deafy Creek—stream....MT-8
Deafy Creek—stream....OR-9
Deafy Glade—flat....CA-9
Deafy Ridge—ridge....CA-9
Deafy Tank—reservoir....NM-5
Deahna Island—island....FM-9
Deaker Cem—cemetery....MO-7
Deakin Gulch—valley....CO-8
Deakin Island—island....WI-6
Deakin Ridge—ridge....MO-7
Deakins Cem—cemetery....GA-3
Deakins Cem—cemetery....WV-2
Deakle Creek—stream....AL-4
Deakyne Landing....DE-2
Deakynesville....DE-2
Deakyneville—locale....DE-2
Deal....MD-2
Deal....VA-3
Deal—locale....ID-8
Deal—locale....TX-5
**Deal**—pop pl (2)....NJ-2
**Deal**—pop pl....PA-2
Deal Beach....NJ-2
Deal Branch—stream....GA-3
Deal Branch—stream....KY-4
Deal Branch—stream....SC-3
Deal Canyon—valley....CA-9
Deal Cem—cemetery....AR-4
Deal Cem—cemetery....OH-6
Deal Cem—cemetery....OK-5
Deal Cem—cemetery....VT-1
Deal Creek....TX-5
Deal Creek—gut....VA-3
Deal Creek—stream (2)....AL-4
Deal Creek—stream....OR-9
Deal Creek—stream....SC-3
Deal Dam—dam....NJ-2
**Deale**—pop pl....MD-2
**Deale Beach**—pop pl....MD-2
Deale Mission—church....MD-2
Dealey, Lake—reservoir....TX-5
Dealey Cem—cemetery....OH-6
Dealey Sch—school....TX-5
Deal Fork—stream....WV-2
Deal Golf and Country Club—other....NJ-2
Deal Gulch—valley....CO-8
Deal Hollow—valley....AR-4
Deal Hollow—valley....TN-4
Deal Island—island....MD-2
Deal Island—island....MS-4
Deal Island—island....NC-3
**Deal Island**—pop pl....MD-2
Deal Island Marsh—swamp....MD-2
Deal Islands....MD-2
Deal Island State Wildlife Mngmt Area—park....MD-2
Deal JHS—school....DC-2
Deal Lake—reservoir....NJ-2
Deal Mtn—summit....VA-3
Dealno....MI-6
**Dealno**—pop pl....MI-6
Deal Park—park....NC-3
**Deal Park**—pop pl....NJ-2
Deal Point—cape....MD-2
Deal Ranch—locale....TX-5
Deal Ridge—ridge....VA-3
Deals Branch—stream....MD-2
Deals Branch—stream....NC-3
Deal Sch (historical)—school....AL-4
Deal School....PA-2
Deals Creek—stream....NC-3
Deals Flat—flat....CA-9
Deals Gap—gap....NC-3
Deals Gap—gap....TN-4
Deals Island....MD-2
De Alvarez Creek—stream....CA-9
Deal Windmill—locale....CO-8
Dealy Meadows—swamp....OR-9
Dealys Well—well....OR-9
Dealy Way—trail....OR-9
Deam Lake—reservoir....IN-6
Deam Lake State Rec Area—park....IN-6
Dean (2)....MI-6
Dean....SC-3
Dean....TN-4
Dean—locale....AR-4
Dean—locale....IA-7
Dean—locale....LA-4
Dean—locale....MI-6
Dean—locale....MO-7
Dean—locale....NY-2
**Dean**—pop pl....IL-6
**Dean**—pop pl....MT-8
**Dean**—pop pl....NC-3
**Dean**—pop pl....PA-2
**Dean**—pop pl....TN-4
**Dean**—pop pl (2)....TX-5
**Dean**—pop pl....WV-2
Dean, Abiezar, House—hist pl....MA-1
Dean, A. J., House—hist pl....MT-8
Dean, Dr. Edgar Everett, House—hist pl....MA-1
Dean, Erastus, Farmstead—hist pl....WI-6
Dean, George, House—hist pl....MA-1
Dean, James Heber, House—hist pl....UT-8
Dean, Jonathon, House—hist pl....MA-1
Dean, Joseph, & Son Woolen Mill—hist pl....DE-2
Dean, Lake—lake....LA-4
Dean, Lloyd, House—hist pl....MA-1
Dean, Nathaniel W., House—hist pl....WI-6
Dean, Silas, House—hist pl....MA-1
Dean, Theodore, House—hist pl....MA-1
**Dean Acres (subdivision)**—pop pl....MS-4
Dean-Barstow House—hist pl....MA-1
Dean Basin—basin....MT-8
Dean Bay—swamp....MS-4
Dean Bayou—stream....LA-4
Dean Broke—swamp....AR-4
Dean Branch....VA-3
Dean Branch—stream (2)....AR-4
Dean Branch—stream (3)....KY-4
Dean Branch—stream....MS-4
Dean Branch—stream (2)....TN-4
Dean Branch—stream (2)....TX-5
Dean Branch—stream (2)....VA-3
Dean Bridge—bridge....VT-1
Dean Brook....CT-1
Dean Brook—stream (3)....ME-1
Dean Brook—stream....MA-1
Dean Brook—stream....MN-6
Dean Brook—stream....NH-1
Dean Brook—stream....NY-2
Dean Brook Deadwater—swamp....ME-1
Dean Burd Leach Ditch—canal....MT-8
**Deanburg**—pop pl....TN-4
Deanburg Hills Dam—dam....TN-4
Deanburg Hills Lake—reservoir....TN-4
Deanburgh Post Office....TN-4
Deanburg Post Office (historical)—building....TN-4
Deanburg Sch (historical)—school....TN-4
Dean Camp—locale....ID-8
Dean Camp—locale....ME-1
Dean Canyon—valley....NV-8
Dean Canyon—valley....NM-5
Dean Cave—cave....PA-2
Dean Cem—cemetery (3)....AL-4
Dean Cem—cemetery....AR-4
Dean Cem—cemetery....FL-3
Dean Cem—cemetery....GA-3
Dean Cem—cemetery (2)....IL-6
Dean Cem—cemetery....KS-7
Dean Cem—cemetery (2)....LA-4
Dean Cem—cemetery (3)....MS-4
Dean Cem—cemetery (3)....MO-7
Dean Cem—cemetery....NY-2
Dean Cem—cemetery (3)....TN-4
Dean Cem—cemetery (4)....TX-5
Dean Cem—cemetery (2)....VA-3
Dean Cem—cemetery (2)....WV-2
Dean Ch—church....AL-4
Dean Ch—church....TX-5
Dean Chapel—church....AL-4
Dean Chapel—church....LA-4
Dean Chapel—church....VA-3
**Dean Chapel**—pop pl....LA-4
Dean Chapel Cem—cemetery....AL-4
Dean Corners—locale....CT-1
Dean Cove—bay....NY-2
Dean Cove—valley....GA-3
Dean Covered Bridge—hist pl....VT-1
Dean Creek....GA-3
Dean Creek—stream (2)....AL-4
Dean Creek—stream (2)....AK-9
Dean Creek—stream (3)....CA-9
Dean Creek—stream....FL-3
Dean Creek—stream (4)....GA-3
Dean Creek—stream....MS-4
Dean Creek—stream (3)....MT-8
Dean Creek—stream (3)....NY-2
Dean Creek—stream....OK-5
Dean Creek—stream (6)....OR-9
Dean Creek—stream (2)....TX-5
Dean Creek—stream (3)....WA-9
Dean Creek Campsite—locale....MT-8
Dean Dale....OH-6
Dean Dale....TX-5
Dean Dale—other....TX-5
**Deandale**—pop pl....OH-6
Dean Davis State Wildlife Area—park....MO-7
Dean Dead River—gut....FL-3
**Dean (Dean Dale)**—pop pl....TX-5
De Andreis HS—school....MO-7
Deane—locale....AR-4
Deane—locale....KY-4
Deane, Francis, Cottage—hist pl....MA-1
Deane, Silas, House—hist pl....CT-1
Deane Brook—stream....CT-1
**Deane Brothers Subdivision**—pop pl....CA-9
Deane Canal—canal....CA-9
Deane Creek—stream....MO-7
Deane Drain—canal....CA-9
Deanefield—locale....KY-4
Deanefield (RR name for Reynolds Station)—other....KY-4
**Deane Hill**—pop pl....TN-4
Deane Hill—summit....NY-2
Deane Hill Golf and Country Club—locale....TN-4
**Deane (historical)**—pop pl....MS-4
Deane House—hist pl....AR-4
Deane House—hist pl....NC-3
Deane Mountain....AR-4
Deane Peak....AZ-5
Deane Pond—lake....ME-1
Deane Pond—lake....MA-1
Deaner Lake—lake....MI-6
Deaner Oil Field—oilfield....OK-5
Deanes—locale....VA-3
Deanes Branch—stream....VA-3
Deane Sch—school....MN-6
Deanes Den—cave....TN-4
Deanes Valley—basin....CA-9
**Deanetta Subdivision**—pop pl....UT-8
Deane-Williams House—hist pl....MA-1
**Deanewood**—pop pl....DC-2
Deaneyville....AR-4
**Deaneyville**—pop pl....AR-4
Dean Factory Pond....MA-1
Dean Falls—falls....MT-8
Dean Family Farm—hist pl....OH-6
Dean Farm—hist pl....NC-3
Dean Ford—locale (2)....MO-7
Dean Forest Ch—church....GA-3
Dean Gap—gap....AL-4
Dean Gap—gap....GA-3
Dean Gap—gap....PA-2
Dean Gap—gap....WV-2
Dean Griffin Memorial Airp—airport....MS-4
Dean Griner Lake Dam—dam (2)....MS-4
Dean Gulch—valley....CO-8
Dean Gulch—valley....MT-8
Dean Gulf—valley....AL-4
Dean Gulf—valley....GA-3
Dean Hall—locale....SC-3
Dean-Hartshorn House—hist pl....MA-1
Dean-Highland Sch—school....TX-5
Dean Hill—summit....CT-1
Dean Hill—summit....ME-1
Dean Hill—summit (2)....PA-2
Dean Hill—summit....TN-4
Dean Hill Cem—cemetery....OH-6
Dean Hill Ch—church....MS-4
Dean Hills—summit....IL-6
Dean Hill Sch (historical)—school....TN-4
Dean (historical)—locale....AL-4
Dean (historical)—locale....SD-7
Dean Hollow—valley....MO-7
Dean Hollow—valley....OH-6
Dean Hollow—valley....TN-4
Dean Hollow—valley....WV-2
Dean House—hist pl (2)....AR-4
Dean Hunt Landing Strip—airport....SD-7
Dean Island—island....AR-4
Dean Island—island....ME-1
Dean Island—island....MA-1
Dean Island—island....MI-6
Dean Island—island....NC-3
Dean Island—island....VT-1
Dean Island Bar—bar....TN-4
Dean Island Landing—locale....AR-4
Dean Island Revetment—dam....AR-4
Dean Johnes Gulch....CO-8
Dean Jones Gulch—valley....CO-8
Dean Junior Coll—school....MA-1
Dean Junior College Hist Dist—hist pl....MA-1
Dean Lake....MI-6
Dean Lake....MN-6
Dean Lake....MO-7
Dean Lake—lake....IA-7
Dean Lake—lake....MI-6
Dean Lake—lake (2)....MN-6
Dean Lake—lake....MO-7
Dean Lake—lake....MT-8
Dean Lake—lake (2)....UT-8
Dean Lake—lake....WY-8
Dean Lake—reservoir....AL-4
Dean Lake Dam—dam....MS-4
Dean Lake (historical)—lake....MO-7
**Dean Lake (Township of)**—pop pl....MN-6
Dean Landing—locale....MS-4
Dean-McNairy Cem—cemetery....AL-4
Dean Memorial Park—cemetery....TX-5
Dean Mill (historical)—locale....AL-4
Dean Mine—mine....AZ-5
Dean Mine—mine....NV-8
Dean Mine—mine....TN-4
Dean Morgan JHS—school....WY-8
Dean Mountain Gap—gap....VA-3
Dean Mtn—summit (2)....AR-4
Dean Mtn—summit....GA-3
Dean Mtn—summit....ME-1
Dean Mtn—summit....NY-2
Dean Mtn—summit....VA-3
De Ann—locale....AR-4
DeAnn Cem—cemetery....AR-4
De Ann Creek—stream....AR-4
Dean Park—park (2)....MA-1
Dean Pass—gap....OR-9
Dean Peak—summit....AZ-5
Dean Peak—summit....CO-8
Dean Place—locale....CA-9
Dean Playground—park....IL-6
Dean Point—cape....LA-4
Dean Point—cape....OR-9
Dean Point—summit....AR-4
Dean Pond....MA-1
Dean Pond—lake....FL-3
Dean Pond—lake....GA-3
Dean Pond—lake (3)....MA-1
Dean Pond—lake (2)....NY-2
Dean Pond—reservoir (2)....MA-1
Dean Pond Dam—dam....MA-1
Dean Ranch—locale....NV-8
Dean Ranch—locale (7)....NM-5
Dean Ranch—locale....SD-7
Dean Ranch—locale....TX-5
Dean Ravine—valley....CT-1
Dean Reid Knob—summit....AR-4
Dean Ridge—ridge....AL-4
Dean Ridge—ridge....KY-4
Dean Ridge—ridge (2)....MT-8
Dean Ridge—ridge....TN-4
Dean Ridge Cem—cemetery....MS-4
**Dean (Roach Creek)**—pop pl....TN-4
Dean Road Baptist Ch—church....FL-3
Dean Road Bridge—hist pl....OH-6
Dean Road Cemetery....AL-4
Dean Road Chapel—church....FL-3
Dean Road Sch—school....AL-4
Dean (RR name for Colbert)—other....WA-9
Deans—locale....AL-4
Deans—locale....NJ-2
**Deans**—pop pl....AL-4
**Deans**—pop pl....ME-1
**Deans**—pop pl....SC-3
**Deans**—pop pl....TN-4
Deans—uninc pl....VA-3
Deans Blue Hole—lake....MO-7
Deans Bluff....MS-4
**Deansboro**—pop pl....NY-2
Deans Branch—stream....AR-4
Deans Branch—stream....IN-6
Deans Branch—stream....KY-4
Deans Branch—stream....VA-3
Deans Bridge—bridge....NY-2
Deans Cem—cemetery....AR-4
Deans Cem—cemetery....MS-4
Dean Sch—school (2)....IL-6
Dean Sch—school....KS-7
Dean Sch—school....KY-4
Dean Sch—school....MI-6
Dean Sch—school....NY-2
Dean Sch—school....NC-3
Dean Sch—school....PA-2
Dean Sch—school....VA-3
Deans Chapel....AL-4
Deans Chapel—church....NC-3
Deans Chapel—church....SC-3
Deans Chapel Ch—church....AL-4
Dean Sch (historical)—school....AL-4
Dean Sch (historical)—school....MO-7
Dean Sch (historical)—school....TN-4
Dean Sch Number 3 (historical)—school....SD-7
Deans Community....NC-3
Deans Corner—locale....NY-2
**Deans Corner**—pop pl....MS-4
Deans Corners locale....NY 2
**Deans Corners**—pop pl....NY-2
Deans Cove....MA-1
Deans Creek—stream....NY-2
Deans Creek—stream....TX-5
Deans Crossing....MS-4
Deans Crossing—locale....GA-3
Deans Factory Pond....MA-1
Deans Ferry Bridge—bridge....AL-4
Deans Fork—stream....OH-6
Deans Gap—gap....PA-2
Deans Gulf—stream....NY-2
**Deans Heights (subdivision)**—pop pl....NC-3
Deans Hill—summit....ME-1
Deans Hole—bay....DE-2
Dean Simpson Ranch—locale....NE-7
Dean's Island....AR-4
Dean's Island Landing....AR-4
Deans Lake....MI-6
Deans Lake—lake....MN-6
Deans Lake—lake....SD-7
Deans Lake—lake....WI-6
Deans Lake—reservoir....GA-3
Deans Lake—reservoir....MS-4
Deans Lake—stream....MS-4
Deans Lake Dam—dam....MS-4
Deans Landing—locale....AL-4
**Deans Market**—pop pl....AR-4
Deans Meadow—flat....CA-9
Deans Mill—locale....NY-2
**Deans Mill**—pop pl....NC-3
Deans Mills Dam—dam....NJ-2
Dean Sparrows Pond....MA-1
Deans Pass—gap....UT-8
Deans Point....OR-9
Deans Point—cape....MA-1
Deans Pond—lake....MA-1
Deans Pond—reservoir....NJ-2
Dean Spring....AR-4
**Dean Spring**—pop pl....AR-4
Dean Spring—spring....ID-8
Dean Spring—spring....NV-8
Dean Spring—spring (2)....OR-9
Dean Spring—spring....WY-8
Dean Springs—locale....AR-4
Dean Springs—spring....WY-8
Dean Springs Draw—valley....WY-8
Dean Springs (Township of)—fmr MCD....AR-4
Dean Spring Valley—valley....NV-8
Dean Spur—ridge....VA-3
Deans Ravine—valley....CA-9
Deans Ridge—ridge....CA-9
Deans Sandstone Cave—cave....AL-4
Deans Sch (historical)—school....NC-3
Deans Spring—spring....AL-4
Deans Spur....MS-4
Deans Station....AL-4
Deans Store—locale....NC-3
Dean Stone, Mount—summit....MT-8
Dean Street Shop Ctr—locale....MA-1
Dean Street Station (historical)—locale....MA-1
Deans Valley—basin....NE-7
Deansville....AL-4
**Deansville**—pop pl....WV-2
**Deansville**—pop pl....WI-6
Deansville Cem—cemetery....WI-6
Deansville Marsh—swamp....WI-6
Dean Swamp....SC-3
Dean Swamp—stream (2)....SC-3
Dean Swamp Ch—church....SC-3
Dean Swamp Creek—stream....SC-3
Dean Tank—reservoir....AZ-5
Dean Tank—reservoir (2)....NM-5
Dean Tank—reservoir....TX-5
Dean Terrace—uninc pl....LA-4
Deanton Cemetery....MS-4
Dean Town Hall—building....ND-7
**Dean Township**—pop pl....ND-7
**Dean (Township of)**—pop pl....PA-2
Dean Trail—trail....PA-2
Deanville—locale....FL-3
**Deanville**—pop pl....PA-2
**Deanville**—pop pl....TX-5
**Deanville**—pop pl (2)....WV-2
Deanville Cem—cemetery....MI-6
Deanville (historical)—locale....MA-1
Deanville Sch—school....MI-6
Dean Well—well....NM-5
Dean Windmill—locale....NM-5
Deanwood....DC-2
Deanwood—locale....KY-4
Deanwood—locale....VA-3
Deanwood Metro Station—locale....DC-2
**Deanwood Park**—pop pl....MD-2
Deanwright—locale....TX-5
Deanyville—locale....AR-4
De Anza Coll—school....CA-9
De Anza Cove—bay....CA-9
De Anza Desert Country Club—other....CA-9
De Anza Hotel—hist pl....CA-9
De Anza HS—school....CA-9
De Anza JHS—school....CA-9
De Anza Park—park....AZ-5
De Anza Peak—summit....CO-8
De Anza Point—cape....CA-9
De Anza Sch—school (4)....CA-9
De Anza Trail Monmt—pillar....CA-9
**De Anza Village**—pop pl....AZ-5
Deapolis Cem—cemetery....ND-7
Deapolis Post Office (historical)—building....ND-7
**Dearborn**—pop pl....IN-6
**Dearborn**—pop pl....LA-4
**Dearborn**—pop pl....MI-6
**Dearborn**—pop pl....MO-7
**Dearborn**—pop pl....MT-8
Dearborn, Mount—summit....NH-1
Dearborn Acad—school....NH-1
Dearborn Brook—stream....ME-1
Dearborn Brook—stream....NH-1
Dearborn Canal—canal....MT-8
Dearborn Cem—cemetery (2)....MT-8
Dearborn Community Center—building....AL-4
Dearborn Country Club—other....IN-6
Dearborn Country Club—other....MI-6
**Dearborn County**—pop pl....IN-6
Dearborn County Courthouse—hist pl....IN-6
Dearborn Creek....MT-8
Dearborn Creek—stream....MO-7
Dearborn Creek—stream....MT-8
Dearborn Ditch—canal....CO-8
Dearborn Gulch—valley....MT-8
Dearborn Heights....IL-6
**Dearborn Heights**—pop pl....MI-6
Dearborn Hill—summit....ME-1
Dearborn Hills Golf Club—other....MI-6
Dearborn Inn and Colonial Homes—hist pl....MI-6
Dearborn Memorial Park—cemetery....CA-9
Dearborn Mtn—summit....ME-1
Dearborn Park—park....WA-9
**Dearborn Park**—pop pl....CA-9
Dearborn Ranch—locale....MT-8
Dearborn River—stream....MT-8
Dearborn RR Station—locale....FL-3
Dearborn Rsvr—reservoir....MO-7
Dearborn Sch—school....IL-6
Dearborn Sch—school....ME-1
Dearborn Station—hist pl....IL-6
Dearborn Station—locale....IL-6
**Dearborn Township**—pop pl....SD-7
Dear Cem—cemetery....MS-4
Dear Creek....ID-8
Dear Creek—stream....OR-9
Dear Creek Canyon—valley....NE-7
De Arcy Branch—stream....IL-6
Dearden Fill Hollow—valley....TN-4
Dearden Ranch—locale....UT-8
Deardens Knoll—summit....UT-8
Deardoff, Daniel L., House—hist pl....OH-6
Deardorf Cem—cemetery....OR-9
Deardorff Cem—cemetery....PA-2
Deardorff Creek—stream....OR-9
Deardorff Mine—mine....IL-6
Deardorff Mtn—summit....OR-9
Deardorffs Mill—locale....PA-2
Deardorffs Mills....PA-2
Deardorf Ponds—lake....OR-9
Deardroff Creek....OR-9
Dearduff Ditch—canal (2)....IN-6
Dearfield—locale....CO-8
Dearing....OH-6
**Dearing**—pop pl (2)....GA-3
**Dearing**—pop pl....KS-7
Dearing, Albin P., House—hist pl....GA-3
Dearing Branch—stream....GA-3
Dearing Brook—stream....ME-1
Dearing (CCD)—cens area....GA-3
Dearing Cem—cemetery....TX-5
**Dearing Downs (subdivision)**—pop pl....AL-4
Dearing Elem Sch—school....KS-7
Dearinger Ditch—canal....IN-6
Dearing House—hist pl....AR-4
**Dearing Place (subdivision)**—pop pl....AL-4
Dearing Street Hist Dist—hist pl....GA-3
**Dearington**—pop pl....VA-3
**Dearman**—pop pl....AR-4
Dearman Branch—stream....AL-4
Dearman Ch (historical)—church....MS-4
De Armand Spring—spring (2)....NM-5
Dearman House—hist pl....MS-4
Dearman Sch (historical)—school....AL-4
**De Armanville**—pop pl....AL-4
**DeArmanville**—pop pl....AL-4
DeArmanville Ch—church....AL-4
DeArmanville First Baptist Ch....AL-4
DeArmanville JHS—school....AL-4
DeArmanville United Methodist Ch—church....AL-4
DeArment Sch (historical)—school....PA-2
Dearmin—locale....PA-2
**Dearmin**—pop pl....PA-2
Dearmin Lake—reservoir....IN-6
**DeArmond**—pop pl....TN-4
De Armond Bald—summit....NC-3
Dearmond Cem—cemetery....KY-4
De Armond Cem—cemetery....LA-4
DeArmond Cem—cemetery (2)....TN-4
De Armond Ditch—canal....IN-6
Dearmond Gap—gap....AR-4
De Armond Lake—lake....LA-4
De Armond Mtn—summit....OR-9
DeArmond Park—park....OR-9
De Armond Ridge—ridge....NC-3
Dearmond Sch (historical)—school....PA-2
DeArmond Spring—spring....TN-4
DeArmond Spring Branch—stream....TN-4
Dear Mtn—summit....OR-9
Dear Ranch—locale....MT-8
Dear Ranch (reduced usage)—locale....MT-8
Dear Rsvr—reservoir....OR-9
Dears Ferry (historical)—locale....MS-4
Dearth....PA-2
**Dearth**—pop pl....PA-2
Dearth Brook—stream....NH-1
Dearth Hill—summit....MA-1
Dearth Hill—summit....NH-1
Dearthtown....PA-2
**Deary**—pop pl....ID-8
Deary-Bovill—cens area....ID-8
Deary Cove—bay....VA-3
Deary Dam—dam....OR-9
Deary Pasture—flat....OR-9
Deary Rsvr—reservoir....OR-9
Deas—locale....AL-4
Deas, Edmund H., House—hist pl....SC-3
Deas Branch—stream....AL-4
Dease Inlet—channel....AK-9
Deasey Mtn—summit....ME-1
Deasey Ponds—lake....ME-1
Deas Mill—locale....SC-3
**Deason**—pop pl....TN-4
Deason, Amos, House—hist pl....MS-4
Deason Branch....TN-4
Deason Branch—stream....FL-3
Deason Ch of Christ—church....TN-4
Deason Cochran Cem—cemetery....KY-4
Deason Creek—stream....TN-4
**Deason Hill**—pop pl....AL-4
Deason Hill Ch—church....AL-4
Deason Post Office (historical)—building....TN-4
Deason Sch (historical)—school....AL-4
Deasons Lake—basin....AR-4
**Deasonville**—pop pl....MS-4
Deasonville Post Office (historical)—building....MS-4
Deasy Sch—school....NY-2
Deater Dam—dam....NC-3
Death Age Cem—cemetery....GA-3
Deathball Mtn—summit....OR-9
Deathball Rock—pillar....OR-9
Death Brook—stream....NY-2
Death Canyon....UT-8
Death Canyon—valley....CA-9
Death Canyon—valley....ID-8
Death Canyon—valley (3)....UT-8
Death Canyon—valley....WY-8
Death Canyon Pass....UT-8
Death Canyon Point—cliff....UT-8
Death Canyon Shelf—ridge....WY-8
Death Canyon Wash—valley....UT-8
Death Creek—stream....ID-8
Death Creek—stream....MS-4
Death Creek—stream....NE-7
Death Creek—stream....NV-8
Death Creek—stream....OH-6
Death Creek—stream....OK-5
Death Creek—stream (2)....UT-8
Death Creek Rsvr—reservoir....UT-8
Deathdoor Bluff—cliff....WI-6
Deatherage Cem—cemetery (2)....TN-4
Death Gulch—valley....WY-8
Death Hollow—valley (8)....UT-8
Death Hollow Rsvr—reservoir....UT-8
Death Hollow Rsvr No 1—reservoir....UT-8
Death Hollow Rsvr No 2—reservoir....UT-8
Death Hollow Spring—spring....UT-8
Death Mtn—summit....NY-2
Death of James Meadow—flat....UT-8
Death Point—cape....NY-2
Death Point—cape....UT-8
Death Ridge—ridge....OR-9
Death Ridge—ridge (2)....UT-8
Death Ridge Rsvr—reservoir....UT-8
Death Rock—pillar....NY-2
Death Run—stream....OH-6
Death's Door....WI-6
Deaths Door Bluff....WI-6
Death Trap Canyon—valley....AZ-5
Deathtrap Canyon—valley....UT-8
Death Trap Canyon—valley....UT-8
Death Trap Spring—spring....AZ-5
Death Valley—area....AK-9

Death Valley—basin ... AK-9
Death Valley—basin (2) ... CA-9
Death Valley—basin ... ME-1
Death Valley—valley ... AK-9
Death Valley—valley (2) ... CO-8
Death Valley—valley ... NV-8
Death Valley—valley ... PA-2
Death Valley—valley ... TX-5
Death Valley—valley (3) ... UT-8
Death Valley—valley ... WV-2
Death Valley Buttes—summit ... CA-9
Death Valley Canyon—valley ... CA-9
Death Valley (CCD)—cens area ... CA-9
Death Valley Creek—stream ... AK-9
Death Valley Creek—stream ... CA-9
Death Valley Creek—stream ... CO-8
Death Valley Creek—stream ... UT-8
Death Valley Draw—valley ... UT-8
**Death Valley (Furnace Creek Ranch)**—pop pl ... CA-9
**Death Valley Junction**—pop pl ... CA-9
**Death Valley Junction (Amargosa)**—pop pl ... CA-9
Death Valley Junction Hist Dist—hist pl ... CA-9
Death Valley Lake—lake ... AZ-5
Death Valley Mine—mine ... CA-9
Death Valley Natl Monmt—park ... NV-8
Death Valley Natl Monmt (Also NV)—park ... CA-9
Death Valley Natl Monument—park (2) ... NV-8
Death Valley Party Monmt—pillar ... UT-8
Death Valley Scotty Hist Dist—hist pl ... CA-9
Death Valley Scottys Castle ... CA-9
Death Valley Spring—spring ... AZ-5
Death Valley Spring—spring ... UT-8
Death Valley Wash—stream ... CA-9
Death Valley Wash—valley ... UT-8
De Atley Ranch—locale ... MT-8
Deaton, Lake—lake ... FL-3
Deaton Bridge—bridge ... FL-3
Deaton Cabin—hist pl ... AR-4
Deaton Cem—cemetery ... KY-4
Deaton Cem—cemetery ... MS-4
Deaton Cem—cemetery ... TX-5
Deaton Creek—stream ... GA-3
Deaton Draw—valley ... TX-5
Deaton Hollow—valley (2) ... TN-4
Deaton Mtn—summit ... TX-5
Deaton Ranch—locale ... TX-5
Deaton Sch—school ... NC-3
Deatons Ranch—locale ... NM-5
Deatonville—locale ... VA-3
Deaton Well—well ... TX-5
Deats Creek ... GA-3
**Deatsville**—pop pl ... AL-4
**Deatsville**—pop pl ... KY-4
Deatsville (CCD)—cens area ... AL-4
Deatsville Ch—church ... AL-4
Deatsville Division—civil ... AL-4
Deatsville Elem Sch (historical)—school ... AL-4
Deauville Beach—locale ... DE-2
**Deauville Beach**—pop pl ... NJ-2
Deauville Gardens Sch—school ... NY-2
**Deaver**—pop pl ... WY-8
Deaver, William, House—hist pl ... NC-3
Deaver Bay—swamp ... NC-3
Deaver Branch—stream ... NC-3
Deaver Canal—canal ... WY-8
Deaver Cem—cemetery ... MO-7
Deaver Cem—cemetery ... NE-7
Deaver Cem—cemetery ... WY-8
Deaver Creek—stream ... TX-5
Deaver Fork—stream ... WV-2
Deaver Rsvr—reservoir ... WY-8
Deaver Run—stream ... PA-2
Deavers Branch—stream ... AL-4
Deavers Branch—stream ... VA-3
Deavers Cem—cemetery ... TN-4
Deavers Chapel—church ... NC-3
Deavers Pond—reservoir ... NC-3
Deavers Springs (historical)—locale ... AL-4
Deavers Town—locale ... AL-4
**Deavertown**—pop pl ... AL-4
**Deavertown**—pop pl ... OH-6
**Deaver View**—pop pl ... NC-3
Deaver View Ch—church ... NC-3
Deaver View Mtn—summit ... NC-3
Deavor Powell Pond Dam—dam ... MS-4
**De Baca (County)**—pop pl ... NM-5
De Baca County Courthouse—hist pl ... NM-5
De Baca Tank—reservoir ... NM-5
Debar Brook—stream ... NY-2
**Debardeleben**—pop pl ... AL-4
**De Bardeleben**—pop pl ... AL-4
DeBardeleben Armory—military ... AL-4
De Bardeleben Landing—locale ... AL-4
Debar Mtn—summit ... NY-2
Debar Pond—lake ... NY-2
**DeBarr Vista**—pop pl ... AK-9
De Barr Vista—uninc pl ... AK-9
DeBarry Creek—stream ... FL-3
De Bary—CDP ... FL-3
**DeBary**—pop pl ... FL-3
DeBary Hall—hist pl ... FL-3
Debary Millpond—reservoir ... NC-3
Debary Millpond Dam—dam ... NC-3
De Bary-Orange City (CCD)—cens area ... FL-3
**De Bary (sta.)**—pop pl ... FL-3
De Bastrop (Township of)—fmr MCD ... AR-4
DeBatty Prong—stream ... IN-6
Debauch Gulch—valley ... MT-8
Debauch Mtn—summit ... AK-9
Debaun, Isaac, House—hist pl ... NJ-2
DeBaun Cem—cemetery (2) ... IN-6
Debaun-Demarest House—hist pl ... NJ-2
**Debbie**—pop pl ... TX-5
Debbie Sch—school ... FL-3
Debbies Cove—bay ... NV-8
Debbies Creek—stream ... NJ-2
Debbitt Basin—basin ... ID-8
Debbs Canyon—valley ... NV-8
Debbs Creek—stream ... ID-8
Debbs Creek—stream ... NV-8
Debby Hill—summit ... VT-1
Debebekid Lake—lake ... AZ-5
Debec Pond—lake ... ME-1
Debed, Elechol Ra—beach ... PW-9
Debeker Hollow—valley ... MO-7
De Bell Municipal Golf Course—other ... CA-9
Debello Cem—cemetery ... WI-6
Debello Ridge—ridge ... WI-6
Debenger Gap—gap ... OR-9
Debenham, I. N., House—hist pl ... MI-6
DeBenneyville House—building ... PA-2
**De Beque**—pop pl ... CO-8
De Beque Canyon—valley ... CO-8
De Beque Rsvr—reservoir ... CO-8
De Berard Draw—valley ... CO-8
De Berard Peak Ranch—locale ... CO-8
De Berard Ranch—locale ... CO-8
De Berniere ... AL-4
Deberrie—locale ... AR-4
Deberrie Cem—cemetery ... AR-4
**De Berry**—pop pl ... TX-5
DeBerry Branch—stream ... AR-4
DeBerry Cem—cemetery ... TN-4
De Berry Ch—church ... GA-3
De Berry Creek ... MO-7
Deberry Creek—stream ... MO-7
De Berry-Deadwood (CCD)—cens area ... TX-5
**Deberry Heights (subdivision)**—pop pl ... TN-4
Deberry-Hurt House—hist pl ... TN-4
DeBerry Ranch—locale ... TX-5
De Berry Sch—school ... TX-5
Deberrys Mill Pond—reservoir ... NC-3
**Deberry Subdivision**—pop pl ... TN-4
De Berry Swamp—swamp ... TN-4
Debidue Beach—beach ... SC-3
Debidue Creek—stream ... SC-3
Debidue Island—island ... SC-3
DeBinder Sch—school ... PA-2
**Debing Township**—pop pl ... ND-7
Debisadero Windmill—locale ... TX-5
Deblanc Coulee—stream ... LA-4
De Blieu Creek—gut ... FL-3
**Deblois**—pop pl ... ME-1
De Blois Point—cape ... FM-9
**Deblois (Town of)**—pop pl ... ME-1
**De Bloois Subdivision**—pop pl ... UT-8
**Deblyn Park (subdivision)**—pop pl ... NC-3
De Board Branch—stream ... KY-4
Deboch ... FM-9
Deboe Branch—stream ... KY-4
Deboe Cem—cemetery ... KY-4
De Boer Lake—lake ... AK-9
De Boer Park—park ... CO-8
Debois Creek—stream ... NJ-2
De Bois Hollow—valley ... PA-2
Deboldin Creek—stream ... TX-5
Debol Sch—school ... MO-7
Debolt ... KS-7
**Debolt**—pop pl ... NE-7
Debolt Cem—cemetery ... IL-6
Debolt Cem—cemetery ... OK-5
Debolt Place ... NE-7
**Debon**—pop pl ... CA-9
De Boose Creek—stream ... MT-8
Deborah, Lake—reservoir ... GA-3
Deborah, Mount—summit ... AK-9
Deborah Sanatorium—hospital ... NJ-2
Deborahs Run—stream ... PA-2
Debord—locale ... KY-4
DeBord Branch—stream ... KY-4
Debord Cem—cemetery ... IL-6
De Bord Cem—cemetery ... TN-4
DeBord Cem—cemetery ... TN-4
De Borde Ranch—locale ... AZ-5
DeBord Hollow—valley ... OH-6
Debordieu Beach ... SC-3
Debordieu Island ... SC-3
DeBord Peaks—summit ... OR-9
De Bord Post Office (historical)—building ... TN-4
Deborgia ... MT-8
**De Borgia**—pop pl ... MT-8
DeBorgia Schoolhouse—hist pl ... MT-8
Debose Chapel—church ... FL-3
De Bose JHS—school ... TX-5
De Bott ... NE-7
Deboullie Mtn—summit ... ME-1
Deboullie Pond—lake ... ME-1
DeBow, James R., House—hist pl ... TN-4
Debows Ch—church ... NJ-2
Deboy Ranch—locale ... OR-9
Deboy Rsvr—reservoir ... OR-9
DeBraine Lake—lake ... NY-2
Debra-Nell Cem—cemetery ... FL-3
DeBree—uninc pl ... VA-3
Debrick Cem—cemetery ... KS-7
Debris Cave—cave ... AL-4
Debris Creek—stream ... MT-8
Debris Dam—dam ... CA-9
De Broeck Landing—locale ... LA-4
**De Bruce**—pop pl ... GA-3
**Debruce**—pop pl ... NY-2
Debruhl-Marshall House—hist pl ... SC-3
Debruhls Landing—locale ... NC-3
Debrum House—hist pl ... MP-9
**Debs**—pop pl ... MN-6
Debs, Eugene V., House—hist pl ... IN-6
Debs Chapel—church ... MN-6
Debs Community Hall—locale ... CO-8
Debsconeag Deadwater—lake ... ME-1
Debsconeag Falls—falls ... ME-1
Debs Hill ... MA-1
Debs Island—island ... MI-6
Debtors' Prison—hist pl ... VA-3
Debtor's Prison—hist pl ... VA-3
Debuel Road Baptist Ch—church ... FL-3
Debu Island—island ... MP-9
Debuji-to ... MP-9
Debumaru—island ... MP-9
D E Burt Lake Dam—dam ... MS-4
**DeBusk**—pop pl ... TN-4
De Busk Cem—cemetery ... KS-7
DeBusk Hollow—valley ... VA-3
DeBusk Mill—locale ... VA-3
**De Busk Mill**—pop pl ... VA-3
DeBusk Sch—school ... TN-4
DeBussey Cem—cemetery ... WV-2
Debutant Creek—stream ... MI-6
Debutary Creek—stream ... SC-3
De Butte Creek—stream (2) ... LA-4
Debuu—island ... MP-9
Debuu Island ... MP-9
Debuuji To ... MP-9
**De Buys**—pop pl ... MS-4
Debuys Lake Dam—dam ... AL-4
**Deby**—pop pl ... KY-4
De Camp—locale ... IL-6
De Camp, John, House—hist pl ... NJ-2
**De Camp Gardens**—pop pl ... IN-6
De Camp Rsvr—reservoir ... CO-8
DeCamps Island—island ... NY-2
De Camp Tank—reservoir ... CA-9
Decan Hollow—valley ... OH-6
DeCanizares, F.A., House—hist pl ... FL-3
Decapolis—locale ... VA-3
Decarbo Ambulance Service Airp—airport ... PA-2
Decas Sch—school ... MA-1
Decathon Canyon—valley ... NV-8
Decathon Spring—spring ... NV-8
Decatur ... IA-7
Decatur ... OH-6
Decatur ... PA-2
Decatur—locale ... KY-4
Decatur—locale ... MO-7
Decatur—locale ... VA-3
**Decatur**—pop pl ... AL-4
**Decatur**—pop pl ... AR-4
**Decatur**—pop pl ... GA-3
**Decatur**—pop pl ... IL-6
**Decatur**—pop pl ... IN-6
**Decatur**—pop pl ... MI-6
**Decatur**—pop pl ... MS-4
**Decatur**—pop pl ... NE-7
**Decatur**—pop pl ... NY-2
**Decatur**—pop pl ... OH-6
**Decatur**—pop pl ... PA-2
**Decatur**—pop pl ... TN-4
**Decatur**—pop pl ... TX-5
**Decatur**—pop pl ... WA-9
Decatur, Lake—reservoir ... IL-6
Decatur Acad (historical)—school ... TN-4
Decatur Airp—airport ... IL-6
Decatur and Wheeler Basin Regional Library—building ... AL-4
Decatur Attendance Center—school ... MS-4
Decatur Bend Park—park ... IA-7
Decatur Branch—stream ... AR-4
Decatur Branch—stream ... MS-4
Decatur Branch—stream ... TN-4
Decatur Cave—cave ... AL-4
Decatur (CCD)—cens area ... AL-4
Decatur (CCD)—cens area ... TN-4
Decatur (CCD)—cens area ... TX-5
Decatur Cem—cemetery ... AL-4
Decatur Cem—cemetery ... GA-3
Decatur Cem—cemetery ... MS-4
Decatur Cem—cemetery ... NY-2
Decatur Cem—cemetery ... TN-4
Decatur Cem—cemetery ... WI-6
Decatur Central HS—school ... IN-6
Decatur Ch—church ... OH-6
Decatur Chapel—church ... OH-6
Decatur Ch of God—church ... TN-4
**Decatur City**—pop pl ... IA-7
Decatur City Cem—cemetery ... IA-7
Decatur City Hall—building ... AL-4
Decatur Coll—school ... TX-5
Decatur Community HS—school ... KS-7
Decatur Community JHS—school ... KS-7
Decatur Country Club—other ... IL-6
Decatur County—civil ... KS-7
**Decatur (County)**—pop pl ... GA-3
**Decatur County**—pop pl ... IN-6
**Decatur County**—pop pl ... TN-4
Decatur County Courthouse—building ... TN-4
Decatur County Courthouse—hist pl ... GA-3
Decatur County Courthouse—hist pl ... IN-6
Decatur County Courthouse—hist pl ... IA-7
Decatur County Fairground—locale ... IA-7
Decatur County General Hosp—hospital ... TN-4
Decatur County Home—building ... IA-7
Decatur County Hosp—hospital ... IA-7
Decatur County Training Sch (historical)—school ... TN-4
Decatur Creek—stream ... NY-2
Decatur Creek—stream ... TN-4
Decatur Day Use Park—park ... AL-4
Decatur Division—civil ... AL-4
Decatur Division—civil ... TN-4
Decatur Downtown Hist Dist—hist pl ... IL-6
Decatur First Baptist Ch—church ... TN-4
Decatur Furnace—locale ... TN-4
Decatur Furnace (40DR84)—hist pl ... TN-4
Decatur General Hosp—hospital ... AL-4
Decatur Golf and Country Club—other ... AL-4
Decatur Harbor—harbor ... AL-4
Decatur Head—summit ... WA-9
Decatur Heights—uninc pl ... MD-2
**Decatur Hills**—pop pl ... TN-4
Decatur Hist Dist—hist pl ... IL-6
Decatur (historical)—locale ... KS-7
Decatur Hi-Way Airp—airport ... IN-6
Decatur House—hist pl ... DC-2
Decatur HS—school ... AL-4
Decatur Island—island ... WA-9
Decatur /Jones/ Airp—airport ... WA-9
Decatur Junction—locale ... AL-4
**Decatur Junction**—pop pl ... IL-6
Decatur Lake—reservoir ... WI-6
Decatur Male and Female Institute ... AL-4
Decatur Methodist Church—hist pl ... TN-4
Decatur Mtn—summit ... CO-8
Decatur Municipal Boat Harbor ... AL-4
Decatur Negro High School ... AL-4
Decatur Post Office—building ... TN-4
Decatur Ridge—ridge ... TN-4
Decatur Road Shop Ctr—locale ... IN-6
Decatur Rock—rock ... MA-1
Decatur Sch—school ... IL-6
Decatur Sch—school ... PA-2
Decatur Sch—school ... WI-6
Decatur School ... IN-6
Decatur School ... TN-4
Decatur Shop Ctr—locale ... AL-4
Decatur Shores Airp—airport ... WA-9
Decatur State Docks—locale ... AL-4
Decatur Store—locale ... VA-3
Decatur Street Sch (historical)—school ... AL-4
**Decatur (Town of)**—pop pl ... NY-2
**Decatur (Town of)**—pop pl ... WI-6
Decatur Township—fmr MCD ... IA-7
**Decatur Township**—pop pl ... NE-7
Decatur Township JHS—school ... IN-6
Decatur (Township of)—fmr MCD ... AR-4
**Decatur (Township of)**—pop pl ... IL-6
**Decatur (Township of)**—pop pl ... IN-6
**Decatur (Township of)**—pop pl ... MI-6
**Decatur (Township of)**—pop pl (2) ... OH-6
**Decatur (Township of)**—pop pl (2) ... PA-2
Decatur United Methodist Ch—church ... TN-4
**Decaturville**—pop pl ... MO-7
**Decaturville**—pop pl ... OH-6
**Decaturville**—pop pl ... PA-2
**Decaturville**—pop pl ... TN-4
Decaturville Acad (historical)—school ... TN-4
Decaturville (CCD)—cens area ... TN-4
Decaturville Division—civil ... TN-4
Decaturville Elem Sch—school ... TN-4
Decaturville First Baptist Ch—church ... TN-4
Decaturville HS (historical)—school ... TN-4
Decaturville Post Office—building ... TN-4
Decatur Waterworks—other ... GA-3
Decautur—locale ... WA-9
De Cavasos Tank—reservoir ... TX-5
Decedar Ch—church ... MS-4
Decedar Missionary Baptist Ch ... MS-4
Deceiper Creek—stream ... AR-4
Deceiper Lake—lake ... AR-4
Deceitful Gulch—valley ... ID-8
Deceit Point—cape ... AK-9
DeCelis Cem—cemetery ... MO-7
December Creek—stream ... AK-9
December Point—cape ... AK-9
December 69 Cave—cave ... AL-4
Deception, Mount—summit ... AK-9
Deception, Mount—summit ... CO-8
Deception, Mount—summit ... NH-1
Deception, Mount—summit ... WA-9
Deception Basin—basin ... WA-9
Deception Brook ... NH-1
Deception Brook—stream ... NH-1
Deception Butte—summit ... OR-9
Deception Creek—stream (2) ... AK-9
Deception Creek—stream ... CO-8
Deception Creek—stream ... ID-8
Deception Creek—stream ... KS-7
Deception Creek—stream ... MT-8
Deception Creek—stream (3) ... OR-9
Deception Creek—stream (5) ... WA-9
Deception Creek—stream ... WY-8
Deception Creek Campground—locale ... WA-9
Deception Falls—falls ... WA-9
Deception Falls Picnic Area—locale ... WA-9
Deception Gulch—valley ... AZ-5
Deception Gulch—valley ... ID-8
Deception Hills—other ... AK-9
Deception Hollow—valley ... IA-7
Deception Hollow Public Fishing Site—park ... IA-7
Deception Island—island ... AK-9
Deception Island—island ... WA-9
Deception Lake—lake ... WA-9
Deception Lakes—lake ... WA-9
Deception Pass—channel ... WA-9
Deception Pass—gap (3) ... WA-9
Deception Pass—hist pl ... WA-9
Deception Pass State Park—park ... WA-9
Deception Peak ... OR-9
Deception Point—cape ... AK-9
Deception Point—summit ... ID-8
Deception Pup—stream ... AK-9
Deception Rock—summit ... OR-9
Deception Trail—trail ... NH-1
Deception Way—trail ... OR-9
D E C Farms Pond Dam—dam (2) ... MS-4
Dechambeau Creek—stream ... CA-9
Dechambeau Ranch—locale ... CA-9
DeChamps Creek—stream ... WI-6
Dechamur ... FM-9
Dechard ... TN-4
De Cheau Lake ... MI-6
DeCheau Lake—lake ... MI-6
**Decherd**—pop pl ... TN-4
Decherd City Cem—cemetery ... TN-4
Decherd City Hall—building ... TN-4
Decherd Elem Sch—school ... TN-4
Decherd Family Cem—cemetery ... TN-4
Decherd Nazarene Ch—church ... TN-4
Decherd Negro Cem—cemetery ... TN-4
Decherd Post Office—building ... TN-4
Decherd Presbyterian Ch—church ... TN-4
Decherds Bend ... OK-5
Decherds Cem—cemetery ... OK-5
Dechior ... FM-9
Dechmur ... FM-9
Dechor—bar ... PW-9
**Dechumur**—pop pl ... FM-9
Dechuter Sch—school ... WA-9
Decide—locale ... KY-4
Decie Ranch—locale ... TX-5
Decimal M Allen Sch—school ... CA-9
Decision Passage—channel ... AK-9
Decision Point—cape ... AK-9
**Deck**—pop pl ... NY-2
Deck Airpark—airport ... NC-3
**Deckard**—pop pl ... PA-2
Deckard Branch—stream ... AR-4
Deckard Cem—cemetery ... IN-6
Deckard Ch—church ... IN-6
Deckard Flats—flat ... MT-8
Deckard Hollow—valley ... MO-7
Deckard Hollow—valley ... VA-3
Deckard Mtn—summit ... AR-4
Deckard Ridge—ridge ... IN-6
Deckard Run—stream ... PA-2
Deckards ... PA-2
Deckards Run ... PA-2
**Deckard-Y**—pop pl ... MO-7
Deckbar Sch—school ... LA-4
Deck Cem—cemetery ... IL-6
Deck Cem—cemetery (2) ... MO-7
Deck Cem—cemetery (2) ... TN-4
Deck Cove—valley ... TN-4
Decke Canyon—valley ... CA-9
Deckelman Ridge—ridge ... WY-8
Decker ... MN-6
Decker—locale ... KY-4
Decker—locale ... MT-8
Decker—locale ... WI-6
**Decker**—pop pl ... IN-6
**Decker**—pop pl ... MI-6
**Decker**—pop pl ... OH-6
**Decker**—pop pl (2) ... TX-5
Decker, Dean, Site (48FR916; 48SW541)—hist pl ... WY-8
Decker, James Bean, House—hist pl ... UT-8
Decker, Johannes, Farm—hist pl ... NY-2
Decker, Stephen, Rowhouse—hist pl ... OH-6
Decker, William, House—hist pl ... NY-2
Decker Bayou ... AR-4
Decker Bayou—stream ... AR-4
Decker Bob Creek—stream ... NV-8
Decker Bog—swamp ... ME-1
Decker Branch—stream ... IN-6
Decker Branch—stream ... MO-7
Decker Branch—stream ... TX-5
Decker Brook—stream ... CT-1
Decker Brook—stream (2) ... ME-1
Decker Canyon—valley ... CA-9
Decker Canyon—valley ... CO-8
Decker Canyon—valley ... WA-9
Decker Cave Archeol Site—hist pl ... MO-7
Decker Cem—cemetery ... IL-6
Decker Cem—cemetery (2) ... KY-4
Decker Cem—cemetery ... MI-6
Decker Cem—cemetery ... MO-7
Decker Cem—cemetery ... NJ-2
Decker Cem—cemetery ... NC-3
Decker Cem—cemetery ... OH-6
Decker Cem—cemetery ... PA-2
Decker Cem—cemetery (2) ... TX-5
Decker Chapel—church ... IN-6
Decker Chapel—church ... PA-2
**Decker Chapel**—pop pl ... IN-6
Decker Chapel Cem—cemetery ... IN-6
Decker Chapel School ... IN-6
Decker Corner—locale ... ME-1
**Decker Corner**—pop pl ... WI-6
Decker Cove—valley ... UT-8
Decker Creek—stream ... CA-9
Decker Creek—stream (3) ... CO-8
Decker Creek—stream (3) ... ID-8
Decker Creek—stream ... MI-6
Decker Creek—stream ... NE-7
Decker Creek—stream ... NV-8
Decker Creek—stream ... NY-2
Decker Creek—stream ... ND-7
Decker Creek—stream ... PA-2
Decker Creek—stream ... SD-7
Decker Creek—stream (2) ... TX-5
Decker Creek—stream (2) ... UT-8
Decker Creek—stream ... WA-9
Decker Creek Reservoir ... TX-5
Decker Dam—dam ... NM-5
Decker Ditch—canal ... WY-8
Decker Drain—stream ... MI-6
Decker Draw—valley ... NM-5
Decker Drive Ch—church ... TX-5
Decker Elem Sch—school ... IN-6
Decker Farm Airp—airport ... TN-4
Decker Flat—flat ... ID-8
Decker Flats—flat ... MT-8
Decker Free Church Cem—cemetery ... TX-5
Decker Gulch—valley ... ID-8
Decker Gulch—valley (4) ... MT-8
**Decker Heights (subdivision)**—pop pl ... NC-3
Decker Hill—summit ... AR-4
Decker Hollow—valley ... KY-4
Decker Hollow—valley ... MO-7
Decker Hollow—valley ... PA-2
Decker Hollow—valley ... TX-5
Decker House Hotel—hist pl ... IA-7
Decker Island—island ... CA-9
Decker Lake ... TX-5
Decker Lake—lake ... MI-6
Decker Lake—lake (2) ... MN-6
Decker Lake—lake ... UT-8
Decker Lake—lake ... WI-6
Decker Lake—reservoir ... OH-6
Decker Lake—reservoir ... TX-5
Decker Library—other ... CO-8
Decker Meadows—flat ... CO-8
Decker Memorial County Park—park ... WI-6
Decker Park—park ... KS-7
Decker Park—park ... OH-6
Decker Path—trail ... PA-2
Decker Peak—summit ... ID-8
Decker - Pierce Rsvr—reservoir ... CO-8
Decker Point—cape ... ME-1
Decker Pond ... NJ-2
Decker Pond ... UT-8
Decker Pond—reservoir ... PA-2
Decker Ponds—lake ... ME-1
Decker Ponds—lake ... MI-6
**Decker Prairie**—pop pl ... TX-5
Decker Prairie Cem—cemetery ... TX-5
Decker Prairie Oil Field—oilfield ... TX-5
Decker Ranch—locale ... MT-8
Decker Ranch—locale ... UT-8
Decker Ranch Airstrip—airport ... OR-9
Decker Road Sch—school ... MI-6
Decker Run—stream (2) ... PA-2
Deckers ... IN-6
**Deckers**—pop pl ... CO-8
Deckers Brook—stream ... CT-1
Decker Sch—school ... CA-9
Decker Sch—school ... KS-7
Decker Sch—school ... KY-4
Decker Sch—school ... NE-7
Decker Sch—school ... OH-6
Decker Sch (abandoned)—school ... PA-2
**Deckers Corner**—pop pl ... WI-6
Deckers Cove—bay ... ME-1
Deckers Creek—stream ... WV-2
Deckers Creek - in part ... PA-2
Deckers Dam—dam ... PA-2
Deckers Ferry (historical)—locale ... PA-2
Deckers Gulch—valley ... NE-7
Deckers Hill—summit ... VA-3
Deckers Lake—lake ... CO-8
Deckers Point—cape ... MO-7
**Deckers Point**—pop pl ... PA-2
Decker Spring—spring ... IL-6
Decker Spring—spring (2) ... UT-8
Deckers Ridge—ridge ... MO-7
Decker Swamp—swamp ... NY-2
Decker Swamp Dam—dam ... PA-2
Deckert, Ludwig, House—hist pl ... SD-7
Decker Tank—reservoir (3) ... AZ-5
Deckert Lateral—canal ... CA-9
Deckertown ... IN-6
Deckertown ... NJ-2
**Deckertown**—pop pl (2) ... NY-2
**Deckertown**—pop pl ... PA-2
Deckertown Cem—cemetery ... NJ-2
Deckertown Cem—cemetery ... PA-2
**Decker (Township of)**—pop pl ... IL-6
**Decker (Township of)**—pop pl ... IN-6
Decker Valley—valley ... MN-6
Decker Valley—valley ... PA-2
Deckerville—locale ... AR-4
**Deckerville**—pop pl ... MI-6
**Deckerville**—pop pl ... WA-9
Deckerville Ch—church ... MI-6
Deckerville Rsvr—reservoir ... MI-6
Decker Wash—stream ... AZ-5
Deck Hill—summit ... NC-3
Deck Landing Strip—airport ... ND-7
Deck Lane Trail—trail ... PA-2
Deck Lateral—canal ... NM-5
Deck Mtn—summit ... TX-5
Deck Point—cape ... VI-3
Deck Ridge—ridge ... TN-4
Deck Ridge—ridge ... VA-3
Deck Run—stream ... IN-6
Decks Creek—stream ... NY-2
Deck Spring—spring ... TX-5
Deck Valley—valley ... TN-4
Declaration Creek—stream ... ID-8
Declaration Mine (Sand Pit)—mine ... CA-9
**Declare**—pop pl ... VA-3
De Clark, William, House—hist pl ... NJ-2
Declezville—locale ... CA-9
**DeCliff**—pop pl ... OH-6
Decline Creek—stream ... WA-9
**Declo**—pop pl ... ID-8
Declo Cem—cemetery ... ID-8
Decner Creek ... AR-4
Deco—locale ... MO-7
Deco—locale ... TX-5
**Deco**—pop pl ... MO-7
Decon Creek—stream ... AK-9
De Cora Gulch—valley ... CO-8
**Decorah**—pop pl ... IA-7
**Decorah Beach**—pop pl ... WI-6
Decorah Cem—cemetery ... WI-6
Decorah City Hall—building ... IA-7
Decorah Ice Cave—hist pl ... IA-7
Decorah Mound—summit ... WI-6
Decorah Peak—summit ... WI-6
Decorah Prairie—flat ... WI-6
**Decorah Prairie**—pop pl ... WI-6
Decorah Prairie Cem—cemetery ... WI-6
Decorah Sch—school ... WI-6
Decorah Township—fmr MCD ... IA-7
Decorative Arts Bldg—building ... MA-1
Decorator Square Shop Ctr—locale ... AZ-5
De Corde Peak ... TX-5
DeCordova and Dana Museum—building ... MA-1
De Cordova Bend—bend ... TX-5
Decoria Cem—cemetery ... MN-6
**Decoria (Township of)**—pop pl ... MN-6
Decorra—locale ... IL-6
**Decorum**—pop pl ... PA-2
De Costa ... NJ-2
De Coster Trail—trail ... ID-8
DeCoster Trail—trail ... WY-8
**Decota**—pop pl ... WV-2
Decoto—uninc pl ... CA-9
Decoto Sch—school ... CA-9
Decou Pond—lake ... NJ-2
Decourcey ... KY-4
Decourcey Creek ... KY-4
DeCourcy Mountain Mine—mine ... AK-9
DeCourcy Mtn—summit ... AK-9
De Courcy Point ... MD-2
**DeCoursey**—pop pl ... KY-4
**Decoursey**—pop pl ... KY-4
DeCoursey Bridge—bridge ... MD-2
DeCoursey Cove—bay ... MD-2
DeCoursey Creek—stream ... KY-4
DeCoursey Island—island ... MD-2
**De Cou Village**—pop pl ... NJ-2
Decoy—locale ... KY-4
Decoy—locale ... NV-8
De Coy Ch—church ... FL-3
Decoy Lake—lake ... AK-9
Decoy Lake—lake ... MO-7
Decoy Sch—school ... KY-4
Decros Point—cape ... TX-5
**Decrow Corners**—pop pl ... OH-6
Decrow's Point ... TX-5
Decul Brook—stream ... NH-1
Decy Canyon—valley ... CA-9
Dedan Cem—cemetery ... FL-3
Dedan Ch—church ... FL-3
**Dedeaux**—pop pl (2) ... MS-4
Dedeaux Cem—cemetery ... MS-4
Dedeaux Lake Dam—dam ... MS-4
Dedeaux Sch (historical)—school ... MS-4
Dedeckera Canyon—valley ... CA-9
**Dededo**—pop pl ... GU-9
Dededo (Election District)—fmr MCD ... GU-9
**Dederick**—pop pl ... MO-7
Dederman Sch—school ... NE-7
Dedham ... TN-4
Dedham—locale ... WI-6
**Dedham**—pop pl ... IA-7
**Dedham**—pop pl ... ME-1
**Dedham**—pop pl ... MA-1
Dedham, Town of ... MA-1
Dedham Bald Mountain ... ME-1
Dedham Cem—cemetery ... IA-7
Dedham Country Club—locale ... MA-1
Dedham Creek—stream ... IA-7
Dedham (historical P.O.)—locale ... MA-1
Dedham HS—school ... MA-1
**Dedham Island (subdivision)**—pop pl ... MA-1
Dedham JHS—school ... MA-1
Dedham Mall—locale ... MA-1
Dedham Plaza—locale ... MA-1
Dedham Post Office ... TN-4
Dedham Station (historical)—locale ... MA-1
Dedham Townhall—building ... MA-1
**Dedham (Town of)**—pop pl ... ME-1
**Dedham (Town of)**—pop pl ... MA-1
Dedham Village ... MA-1
Dedicar Mtn—summit ... AL-4
Dedication Island—island ... CA-9
Dedic Site—hist pl ... MA-1
Dedie—uninc pl ... TN-4
**De Diego**—pop pl ... PR-3
Dedin Hollow—valley ... TN-4
Dedisse Park—park ... CO-8
Dedman Branch—stream ... TN-4
Dedman Canyon—valley ... OR-9
Dedman Cem—cemetery ... AL-4
Dedman Cem—cemetery ... AR-4

*Deep Spring Pond* ... RI-1
*Deep Spring Post Office* ... TN-4
Deepspring Post Office (historical)—building ... TN-4
Deep Springs—locale ... CA-9
Deep Springs—locale ... TN-4
**Deep Springs**—pop pl ... KY-4
**Deep Springs**—pop pl ... TN-4
**Deep Springs**—pop pl ... VA-3
Deep Springs—spring ... GA-3
Deep Springs Baptist Ch—church ... TN-4
Deep Springs Cem—cemetery ... OH-6
Deep Springs Cem—cemetery ... TN-4
Deep Springs Ch—church ... GA-3
Deep Springs Ch—church ... NC-3
Deep Springs Cow Camp—locale ... CA-9
Deep Springs Hollow—valley ... TN-4
Deep Springs Lake—lake ... CA-9
Deep Springs Maintenance Station—other ... CA-9
Deep Springs Sch—school ... KY-4
Deep Springs Sch (historical)—school (2) ... TN-4
Deep Springs Valley—basin ... CA-9
*Deep Spring Valley* ... CA-9
**Deep Spring Woods**—pop pl ... IL-6
**Deepstep**—pop pl ... GA-3
Deep Step Branch—stream ... SC-3
Deepstep (CCD)—cens area ... GA-3
*Deepstep Creek* ... SC-3
Deep Step Creek—stream ... AL-4
Deepstep Creek—stream ... GA-3
Deep Step Creek—stream (2) ... SC-3
Deepstep Sch—school ... GA-3
Deep Swamp Branch—stream ... NC-3
Deep Tank—reservoir (4) ... AZ-5
Deep Tank—reservoir (5) ... NM-5
Deep Tank—reservoir (6) ... TX-5
Deep Tank Rsvr—reservoir ... CA-9
Deep Tank Windmill—locale ... NM-5
Deep Thorofare—channel ... NJ-2
Deep Throat Cave—cave ... AL-4
Deep Tunnel Mine—mine ... NM-5
**Deep Valley**—pop pl ... PA-2
**Deep Valley**—pop pl (2) ... WV-2
Deep Valley Camp—locale ... PA-2
*Deep Valley Golf Course* ... PA-2
Deep Valley Mine—mine ... IL-6
Deep Valley Sch—school ... WV-2
*Deep Vol Brook* ... NJ-2
Deep Ward Lake—reservoir ... CO-8
Deep Wash Canyon—valley ... CA-9
Deepwater—airport ... NJ-2
**Deepwater**—pop pl ... MO-7
**Deepwater**—pop pl ... NJ-2
**Deepwater**—pop pl ... TX-5
**Deepwater**—pop pl ... WV-2
*Deepwater Bay* ... WA-9
Deep Water Bay—bay ... AK-9
Deepwater Bay—bay ... WA-9
Deepwater Bayou—stream ... LA-4
Deepwater Bend—bend ... AZ-5
Deepwater Black Creek Mine (underground)—mine ... AL-4
Deep Water Bridge—bridge ... NC-3
**Deepwater Bridge**—pop pl ... WV-2
Deepwater Cem—cemetery ... MO-7
Deepwater Ch—church ... MO-7
*Deep Water Channel* ... CA-9
*Deepwater Creek* ... MO-7
Deepwater Creek—stream ... MO-7
Deepwater Creek—stream ... ND-7
Deepwater Creek—stream ... SC-3
Deepwater Creek—stream ... VA-3
Deepwater Creek Bay—bay ... ND-7
Deepwater Creek Public Use Area—park ... ND-7
Deepwater Creek State Game Mngmt Area—park ... ND-7
Deep Water Draw—valley ... NM-5
Deep Waterhole—lake ... CA-9
Deepwater Island—island ... PA-2
Deepwater JHS—school ... TX-5
Deepwater Lake—lake (2) ... MN-6
Deep Water Pass—channel ... LA-4
*Deep Water Point* ... DE-2
*Deep Water Point* ... NJ-2
Deepwater Point—cape ... AK-9
Deepwater Point—cape ... DE-2
Deepwater Point—cape ... LA-4
Deepwater Point—cape ... MD-2
Deepwater Point—cape ... MA-1
Deepwater Point—cape (2) ... MI-6
Deepwater Point—cape ... NJ-2
Deep Water Point—cape (2) ... NC-3
Deepwater Point—cape ... NC-3
Deepwater Point—cape ... SC-3
Deepwater Point—cape ... WA-9
**Deepwater Point (Dupont Works)**—pop pl ... NJ-2
**Deep Water Point Estates**—pop pl ... TX-5
Deepwater Point Range—channel ... DE-2
Deepwater Power Plant—other ... TX-5
Deep Water Rec Area—park ... NE-7
**Deep Water (RR name Deepwater)**—pop pl ... WV-2
Deepwater (RR name for Deep Water)—other ... WV-2
Deepwater Sch—school ... TX-5
Deep Water Sch (abandoned)—school ... MO-7
Deepwater Slough—gut ... CA-9
Deepwater Slough—stream ... WA-9
Deepwater Station—airport ... NJ-2
**Deepwater Terrace**—pop pl ... TX-5
**Deepwater Township**—pop pl (2) ... MO-7
**Deepwater Township**—pop pl ... ND-7
Deep Wear Point—cape ... NC-3
Deep Well—fmr MCD ... NE-7
Deep Well—locale (3) ... NM-5
Deep Well—locale ... TX-5
Deepwell—locale ... WV-2
Deep Well—well (10) ... AZ-5
Deep Well—well (2) ... NV-8
Deep Well—well (14) ... NM-5
Deep Well—well ... OR-9
Deep Well—well ... TX-5
Deep Well Canyon—valley ... AZ-5
Deep Well Canyon—valley ... CA-9
Deep Well Canyon—valley (2) ... NM-5
Deep Well Crossing—locale ... TX-5
Deepwell Ranch—locale ... AZ-5
Deep Well Ranch—locale (2) ... AZ-5
Deepwell Ranch—locale ... CA-9
Deep Well Ranch—locale ... NM-5
Deep Well Ranch—locale ... TX-5
Deep Wells—other ... NM-5
Deep Wells—well ... AZ-5
Deep Wells—well ... CA-9
Deep Wells—well ... NM-5
Deep Wells Ditch—canal ... CA-9
Deep Wells Ranch—locale ... CA-9
Deep Well Tank—reservoir ... AZ-5
Deep Well Tank—reservoir ... NM-5
Deep Well Windmill—locale ... AZ-5
Deep Well Windmill—locale ... NM-5
Deep Well Windmill—locale (4) ... TX-5
Deep White Pond—swamp ... TX-5
Deep Windmill—locale (3) ... NM-5
Deep Windmill—locale (4) ... TX-5
Deepwood Cem—cemetery ... MO-7
Deepwood Golf Course—other ... WI-6
Deep Wood Lake—lake ... WI-6
*Deep Woods* ... IL-6
Deep Woods Dam—dam ... NC-3
Deep Woods Lake—reservoir ... NC-3
**Deep Wood (subdivision)**—pop pl ... AL-4
Deer—locale ... MO-7
Deer—locale ... NM-5
**Deer**—pop pl ... AR-4
Deer, Lake—lake ... FL-3
Deer Arm—bay ... OR-9
Deer Back Lake—lake ... FL-3
Deer Basin—basin ... AZ-5
Deer Basin—basin ... CA-9
Deer Bay—bay ... AK-9
Deer Bay—bay ... LA-4
Deer Bay—bay ... NY-2
Deer Bay—bay ... WA-9
*Deer Bayou* ... MS-4
Deer Bayou—gut (2) ... LA-4
Deer Bayou—stream ... AR-4
Deer Bayou—stream ... LA-4
Deer Beaver Creek—stream ... CO-8
Deer Bog—lake ... ME-1
Deer Bone Pit—cave ... TN-4
Deerborne—uninc pl ... VA-3
Deer Branch—stream (2) ... AL-4
Deer Branch—stream ... AK-9
Deer Branch—stream ... IL-6
Deer Branch—stream ... IN-6
Deer Branch—stream ... KY-4
Deer Branch—stream ... NE-7
Deer Branch—stream ... NJ-2
Deer Branch—stream (3) ... NC-3
*Deer Brook* ... MN-6
**Deerbrook**—pop pl ... MS-4
**Deerbrook**—pop pl ... WI-6
Deer Brook—stream (4) ... ME-1
Deer Brook—stream ... MA-1
Deer Brook—stream (3) ... NH-1
Deer Brook—stream ... NY-2
Deer Brook—stream ... VT-1
Deerbrook Cem—cemetery ... MS-4
Deer Brook Cove—bay ... ME-1
Deerbrook Lookout Tower—locale ... MS-4
Deerbrook Post Office (historical)—building ... MS-4
Deer Brook Trail—trail ... NH-1
Deer Butte—summit ... MT-8
Deer Butte—summit (6) ... OR-9
Deer Butte—summit ... WA-9
Deer Butte—summit ... WY-8
Deer Butte Rsvr—reservoir ... OR-9
Deer Butte Rsvr Number One—reservoir ... OR-9
Deer Butte Rsvr Number Two—reservoir ... OR-9
Deer Butte Spring—spring ... OR-9
Deer Butte Trail—trail ... OR-9
Deer Cabin Brook—stream ... VT-1
Deer Camp—locale ... AZ-5
Deer Camp—locale (2) ... CA-9
Deer Camp—locale ... OR-9
Deer Camp—locale ... TX-5
Deer Camp Branch—stream ... TN-4
*Deer Canyon* ... CA-9
*Deer Canyon* ... UT-8
*Deer Canyon* ... WY-8
Deer Canyon—valley (2) ... AZ-5
Deer Canyon—valley (12) ... CA-9
Deer Canyon—valley (5) ... CO-8
Deer Canyon—valley (4) ... ID-8
Deer Canyon—valley ... MT-8
Deer Canyon—valley (4) ... NV-8
Deer Canyon—valley (10) ... NM-5
Deer Canyon—valley ... OR-9
Deer Canyon—valley (2) ... TX-5
Deer Canyon—valley (4) ... UT-8
Deer Canyon—valley ... WA-9
Deer Canyon—valley (3) ... WY-8
Deer Canyon Creek—stream ... MT-8
Deer Canyon Spring—spring ... AZ-5
Deer Canyon Spring—spring ... MT-8
Deer Canyon Spring—spring ... UT-8
Deer Canyon Wash—stream ... CA-9
Deer Canyon Well—well ... AZ-5
Deer Cave Canyon—valley ... OR-9
Deer Cem—cemetery ... IN-6
Deer Cem—cemetery ... MS-4
Deer Chase—hist pl ... VA-3
**Deer Chase Manor**—pop pl ... NJ-2
Deer Corner—valley ... IN-6
*Deer Corn Spring Creek* ... WY-8
Deercorn Spring Creek—stream ... WY-8
Deer Corral Spring—spring ... WY-8
Deer Coulee—valley (4) ... MT-8
**Deercourt**—pop pl ... GA-3
Deercourt Ch—church ... GA-3
Deer Cove—basin ... CA-9
Deer Cove—bay ... AK-9
Deer Cove—bay ... AR-4
Deer Cove—bay ... MO-7
Deer Cove—bay ... NH-1
Deer Cove—valley ... UT-8
Deer Cove Creek—stream ... CA-9
*Deer Creek* ... AZ-5
*Deer Creek* ... CA-9
*Deer Creek* ... CO-8
*Deer Creek* ... FL-3
*Deer Creek* ... ID-8
*Deer Creek* ... KS-7
*Deer Creek* ... MD-2
*Deer Creek* ... MI-6
*Deer Creek* ... MN-6
*Deer Creek* ... MO-7
*Deer Creek* ... MT-8
*Deer Creek* ... NV-8
*Deer Creek* ... NM-5
*Deer Creek* ... NY-2
*Deer Creek* ... NC-3
*Deer Creek* ... ND-7
*Deer Creek* ... OH-6
*Deer Creek* ... OK-5
*Deer Creek* ... OR-9
*Deer Creek* ... TX-5
*Deer Creek* ... UT-8
*Deer Creek* ... WA-9
*Deer Creek* ... WI-6
*Deer Creek* ... WY-8
Deer Creek—bay ... NC-3
Deer Creek—fmr MCD ... NE-7
Deer Creek—locale ... CA-9
Deer Creek—locale ... IA-7
Deer Creek—locale ... MI-6
Deer Creek—locale ... TX-5
Deer Creek—locale ... WV-2
**Deer Creek**—pop pl ... ID-8
**Deer Creek**—pop pl ... IL-6
**Deer Creek**—pop pl (3) ... IN-6
**Deer Creek**—pop pl ... MN-6
**Deer Creek**—pop pl ... OK-5
Deer Creek—stream (2) ... AL-4
Deer Creek—stream (7) ... AK-9
Deer Creek—stream (11) ... AZ-5
Deer Creek—stream (3) ... AR-4
Deer Creek—stream (42) ... CA-9
Deer Creek—stream (20) ... CO-8
Deer Creek—stream (2) ... FL-3
Deer Creek—stream (5) ... GA-3
Deer Creek—stream (48) ... ID-8
Deer Creek—stream (13) ... IL-6
Deer Creek—stream (14) ... IN-6
Deer Creek—stream (17) ... IA-7
Deer Creek—stream (16) ... KS-7
Deer Creek—stream (3) ... KY-4
Deer Creek—stream (3) ... LA-4
Deer Creek—stream ... MD-2
Deer Creek—stream (14) ... MI-6
Deer Creek—stream (13) ... MN-6
Deer Creek—stream (4) ... MS-4
Deer Creek—stream (10) ... MO-7
Deer Creek—stream (43) ... MT-8
Deer Creek—stream (5) ... NE-7
Deer Creek*—stream ... NE-7
Deer Creek—stream (9) ... NE-7
Deer Creek—stream (10) ... NV-8
Deer Creek—stream (9) ... NM-5
Deer Creek—stream (5) ... NY-2
Deer Creek—stream (2) ... NC-3
Deer Creek—stream (2) ... ND-7
Deer Creek—stream (6) ... OH-6
Deer Creek—stream (17) ... OK-5
Deer Creek—stream (54) ... OR-9
Deer Creek—stream (6) ... PA-2
Deer Creek—stream ... SC-3
Deer Creek—stream (8) ... SD-7
Deer Creek—stream (3) ... TN-4
Deer Creek—stream (18) ... TX-5
Deer Creek—stream (10) ... UT-8
Deer Creek—stream (28) ... WA-9
Deer Creek—stream (2) ... WV-2
Deer Creek—stream (11) ... WI-6
Deer Creek—stream (31) ... WY-8
Deer Creek Arm—bay ... MO-7
Deer Creek Bar—bar ... ID-8
Deer Creek Breaks—range ... WY-8
Deer Creek Buttes—spring ... MT-8
Deer Creek Cabin—locale ... AZ-5
Deer Creek Camp—locale ... CA-9
Deer Creek Camp—locale ... WA-9
*Deer Creek Campground* ... NV-8
Deer Creek Campground—locale ... CO-8
Deer Creek Campground—locale (2) ... UT-8
Deer Creek Campground—locale ... WY-8
Deer Creek Campground—park ... OR-9
*Deer Creek Canon* ... UT-8
Deer Creek Canyon—valley ... CO-8
Deer Creek Canyon—valley (2) ... NE-7
Deer Creek Canyon—valley (2) ... UT-8
Deer Creek Cem—cemetery ... IL-6
Deer Creek Cem—cemetery ... IN-6
Deer Creek Cem—cemetery ... KS-7
Deer Creek Cem—cemetery ... MN-6
Deer Creek Cem—cemetery (3) ... MO-7
Deer Creek Cem—cemetery ... NE-7
Deer Creek Cem—cemetery (2) ... OR-9
Deer Creek Cem—cemetery (2) ... PA-2
Deer Creek Cem—cemetery ... SD-7
Deer Creek Cem—cemetery (2) ... TX-5
Deer Creek Ch—church (2) ... IN-6
Deer Creek Ch—church ... IA-7
Deer Creek Ch—church ... KY-4
Deer Creek Ch—church (2) ... MD-2
Deer Creek Ch—church (2) ... OK-5
Deer Creek Ch—church (2) ... PA-2
Deer Creek Ch—church ... TN-4
Deer Creek Ch—church ... TX-5
Deer Creek Chapel—church ... IA-7
**Deer Creek Colony**—pop pl ... CA-9
Deer Creek Community Hall—locale ... OK-5
Deer Creek Conservation Club—other ... IN-6
Deer Creek Crossing—locale ... CA-9
Deer Creek Cut-off—bend ... LA-4
Deer Creek Dam—dam ... UT-8
Deer Creek Dam—dam ... WY-8
Deer Creek Ditch—canal (2) ... CA-9
Deer Creek Drainage Ditch—canal ... IL-6
Deer Creek-Dry Creek Divide—ridge ... WY-8
Deer Creek Falls—falls ... AZ-5
Deer Creek Falls—falls ... CA-9
Deer Creek Flat—flat ... WA-9
Deer Creek Flat Trail—trail ... CA-9
Deer Creek Friends Meetinghouse—hist pl ... MD-2
Deer Creek Gap—gap ... NC-3
Deer Creek Gap—gap ... TN-4
Deer Creek General Merchandise Store—hist pl ... OK-5
Deer Creek Golf Course—locale ... AL-4
Deer Creek Grove—woods ... CA-9
Deer Creek Guard Station—locale ... OR-9
Deer Creek Guard Station—locale ... UT-8
Deer Creek Guard Station—locale ... WY-8
Deer Creek (historical P.O.)—locale ... IA-7
Deer Creek Hollow—valley ... AR-4
Deer Creek Hollow—valley ... OH-6
Deer Creek Ind Res—reserve ... MN-6
*Deer Creek - in part* ... PA-2
Deer Creek Irrigation Ditch—canal ... CA-9
Deer Creek Lake—lake ... UT-8
Deer Creek Lake—reservoir ... OH-6
Deer Creek Lake—reservoir ... OR-9
*Deer Creek Lakes* ... CO-8
Deer Creek Landing—locale ... NM-5
Deer Creek Lateral—canal ... SD-7
Deer Creek Lookout—locale ... WY-8
Deer Creek Marsh—swamp ... NY-2
Deer Creek Meadows—flat ... CA-9
Deer Creek Mine—mine ... ID-8
Deer Creek Mine—mine ... UT-8
Deer Creek Mine (underground)—mine (2) ... AL-4
Deer Creek Oil Field—oilfield ... OK-5
Deer Creek Oil Field—oilfield (2) ... TX-5
Deer Creek Park—flat ... WY-8
Deer Creek Park—park ... OR-9
Deer Creek Park Campground—locale ... UT-8
Deer Creek Pass—gap (2) ... CA-9
Deer Creek Pass—gap (2) ... ID-8
Deer Creek Pass—gap (2) ... WA-9
Deer Creek Pass—gap ... WY-8
*Deer Creek Peak* ... ID-8
Deer Creek Peak—summit ... NV-8
Deer Creek Picnic Area—locale ... NV-8
Deer Creek Picnic Area—park ... ID-8
Deer Creek Point—cape ... MT-8
Deer Creek Powerhouse—other ... CA-9
Deer Creek Ranch—locale ... AZ-5
Deer Creek Ranch—locale ... CA-9
Deer Creek Ranch—locale ... ID-8
Deer Creek Ranch—locale ... NV-8
Deer Creek Range—range ... WY-8
Deer Creek Rec Area—area ... UT-8
Deer Creek Rec Area—locale ... CA-9
*Deer Creek Rsvr* ... OH-6
Deer Creek Rsvr—reservoir ... CA-9
Deer Creek Rsvr—reservoir ... NV-8
Deer Creek Rsvr—reservoir ... OH-6
Deer Creek Rsvr—reservoir ... UT-8
Deer Creek Rsvr Number One—reservoir ... MT-8
Deer Creek Rsvr Number Three—reservoir ... MT-8
Deer Creek Rsvr Number Two—reservoir ... MT-8
Deer Creek Sch—school ... CA-9
Deer Creek Sch—school ... IL-6
Deer Creek Sch—school (3) ... KS-7
Deer Creek Sch—school (2) ... MO-7
Deer Creek Sch—school ... MT-8
Deer Creek Sch—school (2) ... NE-7
Deer Creek Sch—school ... OK-5
Deer Creek Sch—school ... WY-8
Deer Creek Sch (historical)—school ... PA-2
Deer Creek Sch (historical)—school ... TN-4
Deer Creek School—locale ... ID-8
Deer Creek Site—hist pl ... OK-5
Deer Creek Slough—stream ... NV-8
Deer Creek Spring—spring ... MT-8
Deer Creek Spring—spring ... NV-8
Deer Creek Spring—spring ... WY-8
Deer Creek State Park—park ... MD-2
Deer Creek State Park—park ... UT-8
Deer Creek State Wildlife Area—park ... WI-6
Deer Creek Station—locale ... CA-9
**Deer Creek (subdivision)**—pop pl (2) ... AZ-5
**Deer Creek (subdivision)**—pop pl ... DE-2
Deer Creek Tank—reservoir ... AZ-5
**Deer Creek (Town of)**—pop pl (2) ... WI-6
Deer Creek Township—fmr MCD (3) ... IA-7
**Deer Creek Township**—pop pl (2) ... KS-7
**Deer Creek Township**—pop pl (2) ... MO-7
Deer Creek Township Hall—other ... IA-7
**Deer Creek (Township of)**—pop pl ... IL-6
**Deer Creek (Township of)**—pop pl (3) ... IN-6
**Deer Creek (Township of)**—pop pl ... MN-6
**Deer Creek (Township of)**—pop pl (2) ... OH-6
**Deer Creek (Township of)**—pop pl ... PA-2
Deer Creek Trail—trail ... CO-8
Deer Creek Trail—trail ... NV-8
Deer Creek Trail—trail ... UT-8
Deer Creek Truck Trail—trail ... WA-9
Deer Creek Union Ch—church ... MO-7
Deer Creek Valley—valley ... WV-2
Deer Creek Valley Ch—church ... MN-6
**Deer Creek Valley Ranchos**—pop pl ... CO-8
Deer Creek Wells—locale ... NM-5
Deercrest Country Club—other ... CT-1
**Deercroft**—pop pl ... PA-2
**Deer Crossing**—pop pl ... CA-9
Deer Dam—dam ... SD-7
Deer Dam Tank—reservoir ... AZ-5
Deer Ditch—canal ... CO-8
Deer Drain—stream ... MI-6
*Deer Draw* ... WY-8
Deer Draw—valley ... OR-9
Deer Draw—valley ... SD-7
Deer Draw—valley ... WY-8
Deer Draw Rsvr—reservoir ... WY-8
Deer Draw Sch—school ... ND-7
Deer Drive Hollow—valley ... AR-4
**Deere**—pop pl ... IL-6
Deere, John, Dubuque Tractor Works—facility ... IA-7
Deere, John, House and Shop—hist pl ... IL-6
Deere and Company—facility ... GA-3
*Deere Creek* ... LA-4
*Deere Creek* ... WY-8
Deere Creek—stream ... SD-7
Deere Creek—stream ... WY-8
*Deer Falls Creek* ... NY-2
Deer Farm Creek—stream ... MI-6
Deer Fence Canal—canal ... FL-3
*Deerfield* ... FL-3
*Deerfield* ... IN-6
*Deerfield* ... MD-2
Deerfield—fmr MCD ... NE-7
Deerfield—locale ... IA-7
Deerfield—locale ... MN-6
Deerfield—locale ... NH-1
Deerfield—locale ... NY-2
Deerfield—locale ... SC-3
Deerfield—locale ... SD-7
**Deerfield**—pop pl ... AR-4
**Deerfield**—pop pl ... CT-1
**Deerfield**—pop pl ... IL-6
**Deerfield**—pop pl (2) ... IN-6
**Deerfield**—pop pl ... KS-7
**Deerfield**—pop pl ... KY-4
**Deerfield**—pop pl (2) ... MD-2
**Deerfield**—pop pl ... MA-1
**Deerfield**—pop pl ... MI-6
**Deerfield**—pop pl ... MO-7
**Deerfield**—pop pl ... NH-1
**Deerfield**—pop pl ... NJ-2
**Deerfield**—pop pl ... NY-2
**Deerfield**—pop pl ... NC-3
**Deerfield**—pop pl ... OH-6
**Deerfield**—pop pl (2) ... TN-4
**Deerfield**—pop pl ... VA-3
**Deerfield**—pop pl ... WV-2
**Deerfield**—pop pl ... WI-6
Deerfield Acad—school ... MA-1
**Deerfield Acres**—pop pl ... TN-4
Deerfield Baptist Ch—church ... TN-4
**Deerfield Beach**—pop pl ... FL-3
Deerfield Beach Bridge—bridge ... FL-3
Deerfield Beach (CCD)—cens area ... FL-3
Deerfield Beach Elem Sch—school ... FL-3
Deerfield Beach HS—school ... FL-3
Deerfield Beach MS—school ... FL-3
Deerfield (CCD)—cens area ... TN-4
Deerfield Cem—cemetery ... IL-6
Deer Field Cem—cemetery ... KS-7
Deerfield Cem—cemetery ... MN-6
Deerfield Cem—cemetery (2) ... OH-6
Deerfield Cem—cemetery ... TN-4
Deerfield Center—locale ... MI-6
**Deerfield Center**—pop pl ... MI-6
**Deerfield Center**—pop pl ... NH-1
Deerfield Center Cem—cemetery ... MI-6
*Deerfield Centre* ... MA-1
Deerfield Ch—church ... MI-6
Deerfield Ch—church ... NJ-2
Deerfield Ch—church ... OH-6
Deerfield Ch of Christ—church ... MI-6
Deerfield Ch of Christ—church ... TN-4
**Deerfield Colony**—pop pl ... MT-8
**Deerfield Condominium Subdivision**—pop pl ... UT-8
Deerfield Corner—locale ... NE-7
**Deerfield Cove Subdivision**—pop pl ... UT-8
Deerfield Dam—dam ... SD-7
Deerfield Division—civil ... TN-4
Deerfield Elem Sch—school ... IN-6
Deerfield Elem Sch—school ... KS-7
**Deerfield Estates**—pop pl ... VA-3
Deerfield Fairgrounds—locale ... NH-1
**Deerfield Heights**—pop pl ... NY-2
Deerfield HS—school ... IL-6
Deerfield HS—school ... KS-7
Deerfield Island Park—park ... FL-3
Deerfield Lake—reservoir ... SD-7
Deerfield Locks—other ... FL-3
Deerfield Meadows—flat ... MA-1
**Deerfield Meadows Subdivision**—pop pl ... UT-8
*Deerfield Mountain* ... MA-1
Deerfield Mtn—summit ... NY-2
Deerfield Oil Field—oilfield ... MS-4
*Deerfield Parade* ... NH-1
**Deerfield Parade**—pop pl ... NH-1
Deerfield Park—park ... MI-6
Deerfield Park JHS—school ... FL-3
Deerfield Park Sch—school ... FL-3
Deerfield Pike Tollgate House—hist pl ... NJ-2
Deerfield Post Office (historical)—building ... AL-4
Deerfield Presbyterian Church—hist pl ... NJ-2
Deerfield River—stream ... MA-1
Deerfield River—stream ... VT-1
Deerfield River Rsvr—reservoir (2) ... MA-1
Deerfield Sch—hist pl ... VA-3
Deerfield Sch—school ... IL-6
Deerfield Sch—school ... MA-1
Deerfield Sch—school ... MI-6
Deerfield Sch—school ... SD-7
Deerfield Sch (historical)—school ... TN-4
Deerfield-Schuyler Cem—cemetery ... NY-2
Deer Field Shores—beach ... NC-3
**Deerfield (Smithfield)**—pop pl ... MD-2
*Deerfield Street* ... NJ-2
**Deerfield Street (Deerfield)**—pop pl ... NJ-2
**Deerfield (subdivision)**—pop pl ... AL-4
**Deerfield (subdivision)**—pop pl ... MS-4
**Deerfield (subdivision)**—pop pl (5) ... NC-3
**Deerfield (subdivision)**—pop pl ... TN-4
**Deerfield Subdivision**—pop pl (2) ... UT-8
**Deerfield Subdivision - Plat III**—pop pl ... UT-8
Deerfield Swamp—swamp ... MA-1
**Deerfield (Town of)**—pop pl ... MA-1
**Deerfield (Town of)**—pop pl ... NH-1
**Deerfield (Town of)**—pop pl ... NY-2
**Deerfield (Town of)**—pop pl (2) ... WI-6
Deerfield Township—fmr MCD ... IA-7
**Deerfield Township**—pop pl ... KS-7
**Deerfield Township**—pop pl ... MO-7
**Deerfield (Township of)**—pop pl (2) ... IL-6
**Deerfield (Township of)**—pop pl (5) ... MI-6
**Deerfield (Township of)**—pop pl (2) ... MN-6
**Deerfield (Township of)**—pop pl ... NJ-2
**Deerfield (Township of)**—pop pl (4) ... OH-6
**Deerfield (Township of)**—pop pl (2) ... PA-2
Deerfield Trail—trail ... MN-6
Deerfield Trail—trail ... VT-1
Deerfield Valley—valley ... VA-3
Deer Fire Tower—locale ... AR-4
*Deer Flat* ... OR-9
Deer Flat—flat (2) ... AZ-5
Deer Flat—flat (6) ... CA-9
Deer Flat—flat (2) ... ID-8
Deer Flat—flat ... NM-5
Deer Flat—flat ... OR-9
Deer Flat—flat (3) ... UT-8
Deer Flat—flat ... WA-9
Deer Flat Caldwell Canal—canal ... ID-8
Deer Flat Campground—locale ... CA-9
Deer Flat Campground—locale ... ID-8
Deer Flat Creek—stream ... CA-9
Deer Flat High Line Canal—canal (2) ... ID-8
Deer Flat Low Line Canal—canal ... ID-8
Deer Flat Nampa Canal—canal ... ID-8
Deer Flat Natl Wildlife Ref—park ... OR-9
Deer Flat Natl Wildlife Refuge—area ... ID-8
Deer Flat North Canal—canal ... ID-8
*Deer Flat Reservoir* ... ID-8
Deer Flats—flat ... ID-8
Deer Flats Spring—spring ... NM-5
Deer Flat Tank—reservoir (2) ... AZ-5
Deerfly Bay—bay ... FL-3
Deer Fly Camp—locale ... WA-9
Deer Fly Hollow—valley ... UT-8
Deerfly Pond—lake ... NY-2
Deer Fly Trail—trail ... WI-6
Deerfoot Cave—cave ... AL-4
*Deer Foot Lake* ... WI-6
Deerfoot Lake—lake (2) ... MI-6
Deerfoot Lake—lake ... WI-6
Deerfoot Ridge—ridge ... ID-8
**Deerford**—pop pl ... LA-4
Deer Gallus Island—island ... GA-3
Deer Gap—gap ... AL-4
Deer Gap—gap ... NC-3
**Deer Grove**—pop pl ... IL-6
Deer Grove Cem—cemetery ... IL-6
Deer Grove For Preserve—forest ... IL-6
*Deer Gulch* ... MT-8
Deer Gulch—valley ... AK-9
Deer Gulch—valley (2) ... CA-9
Deer Gulch—valley (5) ... CO-8
Deer Gulch—valley (7) ... ID-8
Deer Gulch—valley (3) ... MT-8
Deer Gulch—valley ... NV-8
Deer Gulch—valley (6) ... OR-9
Deer Gulch—valley ... UT-8
Deer Gulch—valley ... WA-9
Deer Gulch—valley (3) ... WY-8
Deer Gully—valley ... TX-5
Deer Harbor—bay (2) ... WA-9
Deer Harbor—locale ... WA-9
**Deerhaven**—pop pl ... NJ-2
Deer Haven Camp—locale ... WI-6
Deer Haven Campground—locale ... UT-8
Deerhaven Campgrounds—locale ... FL-3
Deerhaven Lake—lake ... FL-3
Deer Haven Lodge—locale ... WY-8
*Deer Head* ... KS-7
Deerhead—locale ... KS-7
Deerhead—locale ... NY-2
Deer Head—summit ... OR-9
Deer Head—valley ... FL-3
Deer Head Bluff—cliff ... TX-5
Deerhead Campground—locale ... NM-5
Deerhead Canyon—valley ... NV-8
Deerhead Canyon—valley ... NM-5
Deer Head Ch—church ... AL-4
Deer Head Cove—valley ... AL-4
*Deer Head Cove Cemetery* ... AL-4
Deerhead Creek—stream ... AZ-5
Deerhead Dam—dam ... TN-4
*Deerhead Drift Mine* ... AL-4
Deer Head Farm—locale ... ME-1
Deerhead Lake—lake ... MT-8
Deer Head Lake—reservoir ... NJ-2
Deerhead Lake—reservoir ... TN-4
Deer Head Lake Dam—dam ... NJ-2
Deer Head Lodge—locale ... SD-7
Deerhead North Oil and Gas Field—oilfield ... KS-7
Deer Head Point—cape ... OR-9
Deer Head Spring—spring ... AZ-5
Deerhead Spring—spring ... AZ-5
Deer Head Spring—spring ... OR-9
Deer Head Spring Cave—cave ... AL-4
**Deerhead Township**—pop pl ... KS-7
Deerheart Creek—stream ... CA-9
Deerheart Lake—lake ... CA-9
Deerheart Lodge—locale ... ND-7
**Deerheart Valley**—pop pl ... MI-6
Deer Heaven—summit ... UT-8
Deer Heaven Creek—stream ... ID-8
Deer Heaven Mtn—summit ... ID-8
*Deer Hill* ... MA-1
Deer Hill—hist pl ... NY-2
Deer Hill—summit ... AZ-5
Deer Hill—summit (2) ... CA-9
Deer Hill—summit ... CO-8
Deer Hill—summit (8) ... ME-1
Deer Hill—summit (3) ... MA-1
Deer Hill—summit (2) ... NH-1
Deer Hill—summit (4) ... NM-5
Deer Hill—summit ... NY-2
Deer Hill—summit ... TX-5
Deer Hill—summit (3) ... VT-1
Deer Hill—summit (2) ... WY-8
Deer Hill Branch—stream ... KY-4
Deer Hill Branch—stream ... TN-4
Deer Hill Cem—cemetery ... ME-1
Deer Hill Draw—valley ... WY-8
Deer Hill Sch—school ... MA-1
Deer Hill Spring—spring ... ME-1
Deer Hill State Reservation—park ... MA-1
Deer Hill Tank—reservoir ... CA-9
Deer Hill Trail—trail ... MA-1
Deer Hill Trail—trail ... PA-2
Deerhobble Branch—stream ... TN-4
Deerhobble Ridge—ridge ... TN-4
*Deer Hole Run* ... PA-2
*Deer Hollow* ... AR-4
*Deer Hollow* ... UT-8
Deer Hollow—valley ... AZ-5
Deer Hollow—valley ... ID-8
Deer Hollow—valley ... MT-8
Deer Hollow—valley ... NY-2
Deer Hollow—valley ... TN-4
Deer Hollow—valley (3) ... TX-5
Deer Hollow—valley (5) ... UT-8
Deer Hollow Branch—stream ... TN-4
Deer Hollow Brook—stream ... VT-1
Deer Hollow Trail—trail ... PA-2
**Deerhorn**—pop pl ... OR-9
Deerhorn Camp—locale ... CA-9
Deerhorn Campground—locale ... OR-9
Deerhorn Cem—cemetery ... MN-6
Deerhorn Ch—church ... MN-6
*Deerhorn Creek* ... MN-6
Deerhorn Creek—stream ... AK-9
Deerhorn Creek—stream ... CA-9
Deerhorn Creek—stream ... CO-8
Deer Horn Creek—stream ... ID-8
Deerhorn Creek—stream ... MN-6
Deerhorn Creek—stream ... MT-8
Deerhorn Creek—stream (2) ... OR-9
Deerhorn Creek—stream (3) ... WA-9
*Deerhorn Flat* ... CA-9
Deer Horn Hill—summit ... MA-1

Deerhorn Mtn—summit CA-9
Deerhorn Mtn—summit MT-8
Deerhorn Park—park OR-9
Deerhorn Pass—gap ID-8
Deerhorn Point—summit WY-8
Deerhorn Ridge—ridge OR-9
Deerhorn Spring—spring CA-9
Deer Horn Spring—spring CA-9
**Deerhorn (Township of)**—pop pl MN-6
Deerhorn Valley—valley CA-9
Deer House Spring—spring ID-8
Deer Hunting Slough—gut AK-9
Deerhurst—locale AL-4
**Deerhurst**—pop pl DE-2
Deerhurst Cem—cemetery AL-4
**Deerhurst (subdivision)**—pop pl NC-3
Deering IL-6
Deering KS-7
Deering (2) ME-1
**Deering**—pop pl AK-9
**Deering**—pop pl KY-4
**Deering**—pop pl ME-1
**Deering**—pop pl MO-7
**Deering**—pop pl NH-1
**Deering**—pop pl ND-7
**Deering**—pop pl OH-6
Deering, Charles, Estate—hist pl FL-3
Deering, J. G., House—hist pl ME-1
Deering Bldg—hist pl TN-4
Deering Brook—stream (2) ME-1
Deering Canyon—valley CA-9
Deering Cem—cemetery ME-1
Deering Cem—cemetery ND-7
Deering Channel—channel FL-3
**Deering City**—pop pl IL-6
Deering Community Center—locale NH-1
Deering Creek ID-8
Deering Creek—stream NV-8
Deering Drain—canal WY-8
Deering Estate—park (2) FL-3
Deering Gulch—valley CA-9
**Deering Heights**—pop pl KY-4
Deering Hollow—valley PA-2
Deering Hollow—valley (2) TN-4
Deering HS—school ME-1
Deering Island—island MN-6
Deering Junction ME-1
Deering Junction—locale ME-1
Deering Junction—locale MO-7
Deering Lake ME-1
Deering Lake NH-1
Deering Lake—lake CO-8
Deering Milliken Dam—dam NC-3
Deering Milliken Lake—reservoir NC-3
Deering Oaks Park—park ME-1
**Deering Park Estates**—pop pl AZ-5
Deering Place—locale NM-5
Deering Pond—lake CT-1
Deering Pond—lake ME-1
Deering Ridge—ridge ME-1
Deering Rsvr—reservoir NH-1
Deering Run—stream PA-2
Deerings Meadow—flat OR-9
Deerings Pond—lake ME-1
Deering Spring—spring AZ-5
Deering Street Hist Dist—hist pl ME-1
**Deering (Town of)**—pop pl NH-1
**Deering Township**—pop pl ND-7
Deering Valley—valley MN-6
Deer in Water Creek—stream OK-5
Deer Island TN-4
Deer Island—area LA-4
Deer Island—cape MA-1
Deer Island—island (2) AK-9
Deer Island—island AZ-5
Deer Island—island (3) CA-9
Deer Island—island CO-8
Deer Island—island (2) CT-1
Deer Island—island (3) FL-3
Deer Island—island IN-6
Deer Island—island (4) LA-4
Deer Island—island (4) ME-1
Deer Island—island MA-1
Deer Island—island MN-6
Deer Island—island MS-4
Deer Island—island MT-8
Deer Island—island (3) NY-2
Deer Island—island OR-9
Deer Island—island SC-3
Deer Island—island TX-5
Deer Island—island VA-3
Deer Island—island (3) WI-6
**Deer Island**—pop pl CT-1
**Deer Island**—pop pl OR-9
Deer Island—uninc pl MA-1
Deer Island Bayou—gut (2) LA-4
Deer Island Bayou—stream (2) LA-4
Deer Island Creek—gut FL-3
Deer Island Flats—flat MA-1
Deer Island Lake—lake MI-6
Deer Island Light—locale MA-1
Deer Island Oil and Gas Field—oilfield LA-4
Deer Island Pass—gut LA-4
Deer Island Point—cape OR-9
Deer Island Slough—gut OR-9
Deer Island State Game Mngmt
Area—park IA-7
Deer Island Thorofare—channel ME-1
Deer Isle—island ME-1
**Deer Isle**—pop pl ME-1
**Deer Isle (Town of)**—pop pl ME-1
Deer Key—island (3) FL-3
Deerkill Branch—stream TN-4
Deer Knob—summit CA-9
Deer Knoll—summit CA-9
Deer Knoll—summit VT-1
Deer Lagoon—lake WA-9
Deer Lake MI-6
Deer Lake MN-6
Deer Lake NV-8
Deer Lake OR-9
Deer Lake WI-6
Deer Lake—lake AK-9
Deer Lake—lake (2) AZ-5
Deer Lake—lake (5) CA-9
Deer Lake—lake CO-8
Deer Lake—lake (7) FL-3
Deer Lake—lake (2) ID-8
Deer Lake—lake IL-6
Deer Lake—lake (2) IN-6
Deer Lake—lake (2) LA-4
Deer Lake—lake (2) ME-1
Deer Lake—lake (26) MI-6
Deer Lake—lake (17) MN-6
Deer Lake—lake MS-4
Deer Lake—lake (2) MT-8
Deer Lake—lake (2) NE-7
Deer Lake—lake NM-5
Deer Lake—lake (5) NY-2
Deer Lake—lake (3) ND-7
Deer Lake—lake (2) OR-9
Deer Lake—lake (2) PA-2
Deer Lake—lake TX-5
Deer Lake—lake (3) UT-8
Deer Lake—lake (10) WA-9
Deer Lake—lake (30) WI-6
Deer Lake—lake WY-8
**Deer Lake**—pop pl NM-5
**Deer Lake**—pop pl (2) PA-2
**Deer Lake**—pop pl WA-9
Deer Lake—reservoir (2) CA-9
Deer Lake—reservoir CT-1
Deer Lake—reservoir IL-6
Deer Lake—reservoir IN-6
Deer Lake—reservoir MI-6
Deer Lake—reservoir MN-6
Deer Lake—reservoir NM-5
Deer Lake—reservoir OK-5
Deer Lake—reservoir (4) PA-2
Deer Lake—reservoir UT-8
Deer Lake—swamp WI-6
Deer Lake Bayou—gut MI-6
Deer Lake Borough—civil PA-2
Deer Lake Camp—locale CT-1
Deer Lake Campground—locale CO-8
Deer Lake Canyon—valley AZ-5
Deer Lake Cem—cemetery MI-6
Deer Lake Creek—stream MS-4
Deer Lake Cutoff—trail WA-9
Deer Lake Dam—dam (3) PA-2
Deer Lake Dam—dam UT-8
Deer Lake Farm—locale AR-4
Deer Lake Flowage—lake WI-6
Deer Lake Fossil Site—park PA-2
**Deer Lake Highlands**—pop pl CA-9
Deer Lake Mesa—summit NM-5
Deer Lake Mtn—summit WA-9
**Deer Lake Park**—pop pl NJ-2
Deer Lake Pond—reservoir PA-2
Deer Lakes—lake CA-9
Deer Lakes—lake ID-8
Deer Lakes—lake UT-8
Deer Lakes—lake WA-9
Deer Lakes—reservoir CO-8
Deer Lakes County Regional Park—park PA-2
Deer Lake Shelter—locale WA-9
Deer Lake Slough—gut MS-4
**Deer Lake Township**—pop pl ND-7
Deer Lake Trail—trail WA-9
Deer Lake (Unorganized Territory
of)—unorg MN-6
Deerland—locale FL-3
**Deerland**—pop pl GA-3
**Deer Land**—pop pl MO-7
**Deerland**—pop pl NY-2
Deerland Branch—stream FL-3
Deerland Camp—locale NY-2
**Deer Lane**—pop pl MN-6
Deer Leap—cliff MO-7
Deer Leap—cliff NY-2
Deer Leap Falls—falls PA-2
Deer Leap Mtn—summit NY-2
Deer Leap Mtn—summit VT-1
Deer Leap Rec Area—park MO-7
Deer Leap Rock—pillar OR-9
Deer Leap Rock—summit VT-1
Deer Ledge—summit NH-1
Deer Leg Windmill—locale TX-5
Deerlick PA-2
Deer Lick—locale (2) KY-4
Deer Lick—locale PA-2
Deerlick—locale WV-2
Deer Lick—stream WV-2
Deerlick Bend—bend TN-4
Deer Lick Bluff—cliff AL-4
Deer Lick Branch—stream (2) AL-4
Deerlick Branch—stream (2) AL-4
Deerlick Branch—stream IL-6
Deer Lick Branch—stream (2) KY-4
Deerlick Branch—stream KY-4
Deer Lick Branch—stream KY-4
Deerlick Branch—stream KY-4
Deer Lick Branch—stream (3) KY-4
Deerlick Branch—stream NC-3
Deerlick Branch—stream NC-3
Deerlick Branch—stream VA-3
Deer Lick Brook—stream NY-2
Deerlick Brook—stream NY-2
Deer Lick Brook—stream VT-1
Deer Lick Cabin—locale WA-9
Deer Lick Camp—locale PA-2
Deer Lick Canyon—valley AZ-5
Deer Lick Ch—church MO-7
Deerlick Ch—church TN-4
Deer Lick Creek CO-8
Deer Lick Creek LA-4
Deerlick Creek PA-2
Deer Lick Creek—stream AR-4
Deerlick Creek—stream AR-4
Deer Lick Creek—stream (6) CA-9
Deer Lick Creek—stream (2) CO-8
Deer Lick Creek—stream IL-6
Deer Lick Creek—stream (2) KY-4
Deerlick Creek—stream KY-4
Deer Lick Creek—stream LA-4
Deer Lick Creek—stream MI-6
Deerlick Creek—stream MI-6
Deer Lick Creek—stream MO-7
Deerlick Creek—stream MT-8
Deer Lick Creek—stream MT-8
Deerlick Creek—stream (2) NY-2
Deerlick Creek—stream OR-9
Deer Lick Creek—stream (3) PA-2
Deer Lick Creek—stream WA-9
Deerlick Creek Public Use Area—park AL-4
Deer Lick Drain—canal MI-6
Deerlick Draw—valley CO-8
Deer Lick Draw—valley TX-5
Deer Lick Falls—falls OR-9
Deer Lick Falls—falls TN-4
Deerlick Farm—hist pl OH-6
Deerlick Gap—gap GA-3
Deer Lick Gap—gap NC-3
Deer Lick Guard Station—locale CA-9
Deer Lick Gulch—valley ID-8
Deer Lick Hollow PA-2
Deer Lick Hollow—valley AR-4
Deer Lick Hollow—valley IL-6
Deer Lick Hollow—valley (2) KY-4
Deer Lick Hollow—valley (3) MO-7
Deerlick Hollow—valley NY-2
Deer Lick Hollow—valley (2) PA-2
Deerlick Hollow—valley (2) TN-4
Deer Lick Hollow Run—stream PA-2
Deerlick Knob—summit NC-3
Deer Lick Knob—summit OH-6
Deer Lick Lake—lake CA-9
Deer Lick Lake—lake WI-6
Deer Lick Point—cape MO-7
Deerlick Rapids—rapids NY-2
Deerlick Ridge—ridge MO-7
Deer Lick Ridge—ridge MO-7
Deerlick Ridge—ridge NC-3
Deerlick Rock—pillar NY-2
Deerlick Rsvr—reservoir PA-2
Deer Lick Rsvr—reservoir UT-8
Deer Lick Run—stream NY-2
Deer Lick Run—stream PA-2
Deerlick Run—stream PA-2
Deer Lick Run—stream (3) PA-2
Deer Lick Saddle—gap CA-9
Deerlick Sch—school MI-6
Deerlick Sch—school MS-4
Deer Lick Sch (historical)—school TN-4
Deer Lick Spring—spring AZ-5
Deer Lick Spring—spring MO-7
Deer Lick Spring—spring (2) OR-9
**Deer Lick Springs**—pop pl CA-9
Deer Lick Springs—spring CA-9
Deer Lick Station—locale CA-9
Deerlick Trail—trail VA-3
Deer Lick Woods—woods AR-4
Deerlodge MT-8
Deer Lodge—locale AZ-5
Deer Lodge—locale (2) CA-9
Deer Lodge—locale NV-8
Deer Lodge—locale SD-7
**Deer Lodge**—pop pl MT-8
**Deer Lodge**—pop pl TN-4
Deer Lodge Acad—school TN-4
Deer Lodge American Women's League Chapter
House—hist pl MT-8
Deerlodge Basin—basin MT-8
Deer Lodge Canyon—valley (2) NV-8
Deer Lodge Canyon—valley UT-8
Deer Lodge Country Club—other MT-8
Deer Lodge County MT-8
Deer Lodge County Courthouse—hist pl MT-8
Deer Lodge Elem Sch—school TN-4
Deer Lodge First Baptist Ch—church TN-4
Deer Lodge Lake WI-6
Deer Lodge Mtn—summit MT-8
Deerlodge Natl For—forest MT-8
Deerlodge Park—flat CO-8
Deer Lodge Park—park CA-9
Deerlodge Park Campground—locale CO-8
Deerlodge Post Office TN-4
Deer Lodge Post Office—building TN-4
deer Lodge River ID-8
Deer Lodge River WA-9
**Deer Lodge Summer Home
Area**—pop pl UT-8
Deer Lodge Valley—cens area MT-8
Deerman Chapel—church AL-4
Deerman Chapel Cem—cemetery AL-4
Deermans Chapel AL-4
Deer Marsh—swamp NY-2
Deer Meadow—flat (2) CA-9
Deer Meadow—flat WA-9
Deer Meadow Brook—stream ME-1
Deer Meadow Brook—stream NH-1
Deer Meadow Creek—stream WA-9
Deer Meadow Grove—woods CA-9
Deer Meadow Pond—lake ME-1
Deer Meadows—flat MT-8
Deer Meadows—swamp OR-9
Deer Mesa—summit NM-5
**Deer Mill**—pop pl IN-6
Deer Min Stream—stream ME-1
Deermont—locale TN-4
**Deermont**—pop pl CO-8
Deermont Post Office
(historical)—building TN-4
Deermont Sch (historical)—school TN-4
Deer Mound—summit MO-7
Deer Mountains MT-8
Deer Mountains—summit AK-9
Deer Mountain Tank—reservoir AZ-5
Deer Mountain Trail—trail CO-8
Deer Mountain Wash—arroyo AZ-5
Deer Mtn NC-3
Deer Mtn—summit AK-9
Deer Mtn—summit (3) AZ-5
Deer Mtn—summit (5) CA-9
Deer Mtn—summit (5) CO-8
Deer Mtn—summit ID-8
Deer Mtn—summit ME-1
Deer Mtn—summit (3) MT-8
Deer Mtn—summit NV-8
Deer Mtn—summit (3) NH-1
Deer Mtn—summit (4) NM-5
Deer Mtn—summit (2) NY-2
Deer Mtn—summit NC-3
Deer Mtn—summit OR-9
Deer Mtn—summit PA-2
Deer Mtn—summit SD-7
Deer Mtn—summit (3) TX-5
Deer Mtn—summit (2) UT-8
Deer Mtn—summit (2) VT-1
Deer Mtn—summit (4) WA-9
Deer Mtn—summit WY-8
Deer Neck—cape NH-1
Deer Neck Mesa UT-8
Deerneck Mesa—summit UT-8
Dee Road IL-6
**Deerock**—pop pl VA-3
Deerpark MO-7
Deer Park—flat (3) CA-9
Deer Park—flat (4) CO-8
Deer Park—flat ID-8
Deer Park—flat (3) MT-8
Deer Park—flat (2) NM-5
Deer Park—flat TX-5
Deer Park—flat UT-8
Deer Park—flat (2) WY-8
Deer Park—locale MT-8
Deer Park—locale VT-1
Deer Park—locale WA-9
Deer Park—park ID-8
Deer Park—park IL-6
Deer Park—park MT-8
Deer Park—park NV-8
Deer Park—park TN-4
Deer Park—park VA-3
Deer Park—park WA-9
Deer Park—park WY-8
**Deer Park**—pop pl AL-4
**Deer Park**—pop pl CO-8
**Deer Park**—pop pl (2) FL-3
**Deer Park**—pop pl IL-6
**Deer Park**—pop pl IN-6
**Deer Park**—pop pl LA-4
**Deer Park**—pop pl (3) MD-2
**Deerpark**—pop pl MD-2
**Deer Park**—pop pl MD-2
**Deer Park**—pop pl MI-6
**Deer Park**—pop pl MN-6
**Deer Park**—pop pl MO-7
**Deer Park**—pop pl NJ-2
**Deer Park**—pop pl NY-2
**Deer Park**—pop pl OH-6
**Deer Park**—pop pl PA-2
**Deer Park**—pop pl SC-3
**Deer Park**—pop pl TX-5
**Deer Park**—pop pl (2) VA-3
**Deer Park**—pop pl WA-9
**Deer Park**—pop pl WI-6
Deer Park Airp—airport WA-9
Deer Park Ave Sch—school NY-2
Deer Park Bar—bar ID-8
Deer Park Branch—stream CA-9
Deer Park Branch—stream NJ-2
Deer Park Camp—locale WA-9
Deer Park Canal—canal ID-8
Deer Park Canyon—valley (2) CA-9
Deer Park Canyon—valley NM-5
Deer Park (CCD)—cens area WA-9
Deer Park Cem—cemetery AL-4
Deer Park Cem—cemetery MN-6
Deer Park Cem—cemetery MS-4
Deer Park Ch—church AL-4
Deer Park Ch—church IL-6
Deer Park Ch—church MD-2
Deerpark Ch—church MD-2
Deer Park Ch—church MS-4
Deer Park Ch—church SC-3
Deer Park Ch (historical)—church MS-4
Deer Park Community Hall—locale ID-8
Deer Park Country Club—other IL-6
Deer Park Creek CO-8
Deer Park Creek—stream CA-9
Deer Park Creek—stream CO-8
Deer Park Creek—stream (2) ID-8
Deer Park Creek—stream WA-9
**Deer Park (Deer Park
Village)**—pop pl MD-2
Deer Park Farm—hist pl DE-2
Deer Park Grove—uninc pl VA-3
Deer Park Guard Station—locale ID-8
Deer Park Gulch—valley CO-8
**Deer Park Heights**—pop pl MD-2
Deer Park Hollow—valley KY-4
Deer Park Hotel—hist pl DE-2
**Deer Park Hotel**—pop pl MD-2
Deer Park JHS (historical)—school AL-4
Deer Park Lake MI-6
Deer Park Lake—lake MN-6
Deer Park Lake—reservoir NC-3
Deer Park Lake Dam—dam NC-3
Deer Park Methodist Church AL-4
Deer Park Mine—mine NC-3
Deer Park Mountain Trail Shelter—locale NC-3
Deer Park Mtn—summit NC-3
Deer Park Oil Field—oilfield LA-4
Deer Park Plantation (historical)—locale MS-4
Deer Park Pond—reservoir NJ-2
Deer Park Pond Dam—dam NJ-2
Deer Park Ridge—ridge CA-9
Deer Parks—flat ID-8
Deer Park (Sanitarium)—CDP CA-9
Deer Park Sch—school AL-4
Deer Park Sch—school CA-9
Deer Park Sch—school IL-6
Deer Park Sch—school (2) MS-4
Deer Park Sch—school MT-8
Deer Park Sch—school VA-3
Deer Park Sch (abandoned)—school MO-7
Deer Park Spring—spring NM-5
Deer Park Spring—spring WA-9
**Deerpark (Town of)**—pop pl NY-2
Deer Park (Township of)—other OH-6
**Deer Park (Township of)**—pop pl IL-6
**Deer Park (Township of)**—pop pl MN-6
Deer Park Trail—trail CO-8
Deer Park Trail—trail WA-9
Deer Park Village (Deer Park) MD-2
Deer Pass CA-9
Deer Pass—gap MT-8
Deer Pass—gap NV-8
Deer Pass—gap NY-2
Deer Passage—channel AK-9
Deer Pass Gulch—valley ID-8
Deer Pass Ranch—locale AZ-5
Deer Pasture—area UT-8
Deer Pasture—flat CA-9
Deer Pasture—meadow NV-8
**Deerpath**—pop pl IL-6
Deer Path Hill—summit PA-2
Deerpath Sch—school IL-6
Deer Peak—summit (3) CA-9
Deer Peak—summit CO-8
Deer Peak—summit (2) MT-8
Deer Peak—summit NM-5
Deer Peak—summit TX-5
Deer Peak—summit UT-8
Deer Pen—basin UT-8
Deer Pen Creek—stream CA-9
Deerpen Hollow—valley MO-7
Deerpen Pond—swamp FL-3
Deer Plain—locale IL-6
Deer Plain Ferry—locale IL-6
Deerplay Gap—gap NC-3
Deer Plot Tank—reservoir NM-5
Deer Point—cape (2) AK-9
Deer Point—cape (2) FL-3
Deer Point—cape (2) ME-1
Deer Point—cape OR-9
Deer Point—cape (3) WA-9
Deer Point—cliff (2) UT-8
Deer Point—summit ID-8
Deer Point Airp—airport WA-9
Deer Point Campground—locale TN-4
Deerpoint Campground—locale VA-3
Deer Point Islands—island MN-6
Deer Point Lake FL-3
Deerpoint Lake—lake FL-3
Deer Point Lake Assembly of God
Ch—church FL-3
Deer Point Mine—mine NV-8
Deer Pond IN-6
Deer Pond—bay NC-3
Deer Pond—lake CT-1
Deer Pond—lake (2) FL-3
Deer Pond—lake (6) ME-1
Deer Pond—lake (2) MA-1
Deer Pond—lake NH-1
Deer Pond—lake (16) NY-2
Deer Pond—lake PA-2
Deer Pond—lake TN-4
Deer Pond—lake TX-5
Deer Pond—reservoir NJ-2
Deer Pond—reservoir NY-2
Deer Pond Brook—stream NJ-2
Deer Pond Dam—dam NJ-2
Deer Pond Hollow—valley MO-7
Deer Pond Marsh—swamp NY-2
Deer Ponds NH-1
Deer Prairie Creek—stream FL-3
Deer Prairie Slough—stream FL-3
Deer Print Lake WI-6
Deer Print Lake—lake WI-6
Deer Range AL-4
Deer Range UT-8
Deer Range—locale LA-4
Deer Range—range (2) UT-8
Deer Range Canal—canal LA-4
Deer Range Canyon UT-8
Deer Range Canyon—valley (2) UT-8
Deer Range Cem—cemetery LA-4
Deer Range Point—cliff UT-8
Deer Range (Range) AL-4
Deer Ridge—locale MO-7
Deer Ridge—ridge (5) CA-9
Deer Ridge—ridge (2) CO-8
Deer Ridge—ridge (2) ID-8
Deer Ridge—ridge MA-1
Deer Ridge—ridge NH-1
Deer Ridge—ridge NY-2
Deer Ridge—ridge NC-3
Deer Ridge—ridge OK-5
Deer Ridge—ridge OR-9
Deer Ridge—ridge UT-8
Deer Ridge—ridge (2) WA-9
Deer Ridge—ridge WY-8
Deer Ridge Camp—locale CA-9
Deer Ridge School—locale MO-7
Deer Ridge Spring—spring UT-8
Deer Rips Dam—dam ME-1
Deer River MN-6
**Deer River**—pop pl MN-6
**Deer River**—pop pl NY-2
Deer River—stream AL-4
Deer River—stream LA-4
Deer River—stream MI-6
Deer River—stream (2) MN-6
Deer River—stream NH-1
Deer River—stream (2) NY-2
Deer River Flow—reservoir NY-2
Deer River Picnic Area—locale NY-2
Deer River Point—cape AL-4
Deer River Station—locale NY-2
**Deer River (Township of)**—pop pl MN-6
Deer Rsvr—reservoir CO-8
Deer Rsvr—reservoir ID-8
Deer Run PA-2
Deer Run—locale CO-8
Deer Run—locale MO-7
Deer Run—locale WV-2
Deer Run—stream CO-8
Deer Run—stream NM-5
Deer Run—stream OH-6
Deer Run—stream (2) PA-2
Deer Run—stream WV-2
Deer Run, Lake—lake GA-3
Deer Run, Lake—reservoir GA-3
Deer Run Campground—locale UT-8
**Deer Run Estates Subdivision**—pop pl UT-8
Deer Run Golf Club—other MI-6
Deer Run Golf Course—other MI-6
Deer Run Lake—reservoir IL-6
Deer Run Lake—reservoir MO-7
Deer Run Lookout Tower—locale MO-7
Deer Run Sch—school CT-1
Deer Run Sch (historical)—school PA-2
**Deer Run Shores**—pop pl CT-1
Deer Run State For—forest MO-7
**Deer Run (subdivision)**—pop pl DE-2
**Deer Run (subdivision)**—pop pl NC-3
Deer Run Trailer Park—locale PA-2
Deers—locale IL-6
Deer Scaffold Spring—spring OR-9
Deer School—locale AL-4
Deers Ears Butte—summit SD-7
Deer Seep Tank—reservoir AZ-5
Deer Shanty Brook—stream NY-2
**Deers Head**—pop pl MD-2
Deer Shelter Rock—pillar WI-6
Deershorns (historical)—locale MA-1
Deer Sink Spring—spring UT-8
Deerskin Branch—stream WV-2
Deerskin Creek—stream NY-2
Deerskin Lake—lake WI-6
Deerskin Lake—reservoir IN-6
Deerskin Lake Dam—dam IN-6
Deerskin Pond—lake NY-2
Deerskin River—stream WI-6
Deer Skull Cave—cave AL-4
Deers Leap Hill—summit MO-7
Deer Slough WA-9
Deer Slough—gut (2) MO-7
**Deers Mills**—pop pl IN-6
Deer Spring UT-8
Deer Spring—spring (15) AZ-5
Deer Spring—spring (15) CA-9
Deer Spring—spring CO-8
Deer Spring—spring ID-8
Deer Spring—spring MT-8
Deer Spring—spring (13) NV-8
Deer Spring—spring (4) NM-5
Deer Spring—spring (12) OR-9
Deer Spring—spring SD-7
Deer Spring—spring TX-5
Deer Spring—spring (8) UT-8
Deer Spring—spring WA-9
Deer Spring—spring (4) WY-8
Deer Spring Campground—locale CA-9
Deer Spring Canyon—valley (2) NM-5
Deer Spring Canyon—valley TX-5
Deer Spring Canyon—valley UT-8
Deer Spring Creek—stream AZ-5
Deer Spring Draw UT-8
Deer Spring Draw—valley UT-8
Deer Spring Mtn—summit AZ-5
Deer Spring Point—cape UT-8
Deer Spring Ridge—ridge CA-9
Deer Springs—spring (2) CA-9
Deer Springs—spring NV-8
Deer Springs—spring NM-5
Deer Springs—spring WA-9
Deer Springs Canyon UT-8
Deer Springs Canyon—valley (2) AZ-5
Deer Springs Canyon—valley NM-5
Deer Springs Ch—church AL-4
**Deer Springs Country Club Estates
(subdivision)**—pop pl NC-3
Deer Springs Creek—stream AZ-5
**Deer Springs Estates
(subdivision)**—pop pl AL-4
Deer Springs Guard Station—locale AZ-5
Deer Springs Lookout Complex—hist pl AZ-5
Deer Springs Ranch Airp—airport UT-8
Deer Springs Wash UT-8
Deer Springs Wash—stream NM-5
Deer Spring Wash—valley UT-8
Deers Sch (historical)—school TN-4
Deerstand Creek—stream NC-3
Deerstand Hill—summit TN-4
Deer Stop Keys—island FL-3
Deer Study Plot—area UT-8
**Deersville**—pop pl OH-6
Deersville Cem—cemetery OH-6
Deers Wood Yard Landing
(historical)—locale AL-4
Deer Tail Creek—stream WI-6
Deertail Lake—lake WI-6
Deer Tank—reservoir (15) AZ-5
Deer Tank—reservoir (2) NM-5
Deer Tank—reservoir (8) TX-5
Deer Tanks—reservoir AZ-5
Deer Tank Wash—stream AZ-5
Deerton KS-7
**Deerton**—pop pl MI-6
Deerton Cem—cemetery MI-6
Deertown Gully—stream FL-3
**Deer (Township of)**—pop pl MN-6
Deer Track Lake—reservoir MS-4
Deer Track Spring—spring NV-8
Deer Trail—locale WI-6
**Deer Trail**—pop pl CO-8
Deer Trail—trail (2) PA-2
Deer Trail—trail TN-4
Deertrail Basin—basin CO-8
Deer Trail Canyon—valley NM-5
Deer Trail Creek CO-8
Deer Trail Creek WI-6
Deer Trail Creek—stream MT-8
Deer Trail Creek—stream NM-5
Deer Trail Creek—stream WY-8
**Deer Trail Lake**—pop pl NJ-2
Deer Trail Lake—reservoir NJ-2
Deer Trail Lake Dam—dam NJ-2
Deer Trail Logde—locale UT-8
Deer Trail Mine—mine AZ-5
Deer Trail Mine—mine CA-9
Deer Trail Mine—mine UT-8
Deer Trail Mine—mine WA-9
Deer Trail Mtn—summit UT-8
Deer Trails—area UT-8
Deer Trail Tank—reservoir AZ-5
Deer Trap—gap UT-8
Deertrap Mtn—summit UT-8
Deer Trap Tank—reservoir (2) TX-5
Deer Tunnel—tunnel PA-2
Dee Run—stream PA-2
Dee Run Ch—church VA-3
Deer Valley UT-8
Deer Valley—basin (3) CA-9
Deer Valley—locale WA-9
**Deer Valley**—pop pl AZ-5
Deer Valley—valley AK-9
Deer Valley—valley AZ-5
Deer Valley—valley (2) CA-9
Deer Valley—valley CO-8
Deer Valley—valley (2) UT-8
Deer Valley—valley (2) WA-9
Deer Valley Airport AZ-5
Deer Valley Branch—stream NC-3
Deer Valley Camp—locale PA-2
Deer Valley Campground—locale CA-9
Deer Valley (CCD)—cens area AZ-5
Deer Valley Creek CA-9
Deer Valley Dam—dam UT-8
Deer Valley Filtration Plant—building AZ-5
Deer Valley Interchange—crossing AZ-5
Deer Valley Lake—reservoir PA-2
Deer Valley Lake Dam PA-2
Deer Valley Meadow—flat UT-8
Deer Valley Motorcycle Park—park AZ-5
Deer Valley Plaza Shop Ctr—locale AZ-5
Deer Valley Rsvr—reservoir UT-8
Deer Valley Sch—school AZ-5
Deer Valley Sch—school CA-9
Deer Valley Shop Ctr—locale AZ-5
Deer Valley Ski Area—locale UT-8
Deer Valley Substation—locale AZ-5
Deer View—locale CA-9
**Deer Walk**—pop pl WV-2
**Deerwalk**—pop pl WV-2
**Deerwalk Single Unit
Condominium**—pop pl UT-8

Deer Water—*spring* ID-8
Deer Watering Point—*cape* NC-3
Deerwater Lake—*lake* MI-6
*Deer Water Spring* ID-8
Deer Water Well—*well* AZ-5
Deer Well—*well* AZ-5
Deer Windmill—*locale* TX-5
Deerwood—*locale* WY-8
**Deerwood**—*pop pl* MN-6
**Deerwood**—*pop pl* NC-3
**Deerwood**—*pop pl* TN-4
Deerwood—*post sta* FL-3
Deerwood Cem—*cemetery* MN-6
Deerwood Ch—*church* MN-6
Deerwood Club—*locale* FL-3
Deerwood Elem Sch—*school* FL-3
Deerwood Farm—*hist pl* OH-6
**Deerwood Forest**—*pop pl* TN-4
Deerwood Lake—*reservoir* AL-4
Deerwood Lake—*reservoir* IN-6
Deerwood Lake Dam—*dam* AL-4
Deerwood Lake Dam—*dam* IN-6
Deerwood Park—*park* FL-3
**Deerwood Park**—*pop pl* GA-3
**Deerwoods**—*pop pl* NJ-2
**Deerwoods Estates (subdivision)**—*pop pl* NC-3
**Deerwood (subdivision)**—*pop pl* AL-4
**Deerwood (subdivision)**—*pop pl* DE-2
**Deerwood (subdivision)**—*pop pl* NC-3
**Deerwood (subdivision)**—*pop pl* TN-4
Deerwood Town Center (Shop Ctr)—*locale* FL-3
**Deerwood (Township of)**—*pop pl* (2) MN-6
Deerwood Village (Shop Ctr)—*locale* FL-3
*Deer Yard Creek* MN-6
Deeryard Lake—*lake* MI-6
Deer Yard Lake—*lake* MN-6
Deery Family Homestead—*hist pl* PA-2
Dees—*locale* IL-6
**Dees**—*pop pl* AL-4
Dees Branch—*stream* LA-4
Dees Branch—*stream* TX-5
Dees Cem—*cemetery* (2) AL-4
Dees Cem—*cemetery* AR-4
Dees Cem—*cemetery* KY-4
Dees Cem—*cemetery* LA-4
Dees Cem—*cemetery* MS-4
Dees Cem—*cemetery* MO-7
Dees Ch—*church* VA-3
Dee Sch—*school* MN-6
Dee Sch—*school* UT-8
Dees Chapel—*church* MO-7
Dees Creek—*stream* AL-4
**Deese**—*pop pl* KY-4
Deese Creek—*stream* FL-3
Dees Lake—*reservoir* AL-4
Dees Landing—*locale* MS-4
**Deeson**—*pop pl* MS-4
Deeson, Lake—*lake* FL-3
Dees Peak—*summit* CA-9
Dees Pond—*reservoir* MS-4
Dees Ranch—*locale* TX-5
Dees Well—*well* NM-5
Dee Tank—*reservoir* NM-5
Deetee Creek—*stream* OR-9
Deeter Cem—*cemetery* IA-7
Deeter Cem—*cemetery* OH-6
Deeter Sch—*school* PA-2
Deeters Gap—*locale* PA-2
*Deeters Run* PA-2
**Deeth**—*pop pl* NV-8
Deeth Interchange—*locale* NV-8
Deetler Ch—*church* NC-3
Deets Creek—*stream* NC-3
Deetz—*locale* CA-9
**Deevaan Villa Development (subdivision)**—*pop pl* SD-7
Deever Run—*stream* WV-2
*Deeversville* KS-7
Deevert—*locale* KY-4
Dee Wright Observatory—*building* OR-9
De Farges Bar—*bar* VA-3
Defas Dude Ranch—*locale* UT-8
*Defas Park* UT-8
**Defas Park**—*pop pl* UT-8
Defeat Branch—*stream* NC-3
Defeat Branch—*stream* WV-2
*Defeat Butte* OR-9
Defeat Butte—*summit* OR-9
**Defeated**—*pop pl* TN-4
**Defeated Creek**—*pop pl* KY-4
Defeated Creek—*stream* (2) KY-4
Defeated Creek—*stream* (2) TN-4
Defeated Creek Cave—*cave* TN-4
Defeated Creek Rec Area—*park* TN-4
Defeated Creek Sch—*school* (2) KY-4
Defeated Creek Sch (historical)—*school* TN-4
**Defeated (Edgefield)**—*pop pl* TN-4
Defeated Elem Sch—*school* TN-4
Defeated Post Office—*building* TN-4
Defeat Hollow—*valley* TX-5
Defeat Knob—*summit* NC-3
Defeat Ridge—*ridge* ID-8
Defeat Ridge—*ridge* TN-4
Defelder Rsvr—*reservoir* WY-8
Defenbaugh Cem—*cemetery* IL-6
Defenbaugh Sch—*school* IL-6
Defender Mine—*mine* CO-8
Defender Mine—*mine* IL-6
Defender Mine—*mine* NV-8
**Defense**—*pop pl* TX-5
Defense Construction Supply Center—*military* OH-6
Defense Depot—*military* TN-4
Defense Depot, Mechanicsburg—*other* PA-2
Defense Depot, Tracy—*military* CA-9
Defense Depot Memphis—*locale* TN-4
*Defense Depot Ogden* UT-8
Defense Depot Ogden—*military* UT-8
Defense Electronics Supply Center—*military* OH-6
Defense General Supply Center—*military* VA-3
**Defense Heights**—*pop pl* (2) MD-2
Defense Mapping Agency Aerospace Center—*military* MO-7
Defense Mapping Agency Hydro/Topo Center—*military* MD-2
Defense Mine—*mine* CA-9
Defense Personnel Support Center—*military* PA-2
**Deferiet**—*pop pl* NY-2
Deferred Pasture Windmill—*locale* TX-5
Defer Sch—*school* MI-6
Deffenbaugh—*locale* PA-2
Deffenbaugh, George, Mound—*hist pl* OH-6
Deffenbaugh Site (36FA57)—*hist pl* PA-2
*Defiance* NC-3
Defiance—*locale* KY-4
Defiance—*locale* NM-5
Defiance—*other* MI-6
**Defiance**—*pop pl* IA-7
**Defiance**—*pop pl* MO-7
**Defiance**—*pop pl* OH-6
**Defiance**—*pop pl* PA-2
Defiance, Lake—*lake* AR-4
Defiance, Mount—*summit* CA-9
Defiance, Mount—*summit* NJ-2
Defiance, Mount—*summit* OR-9
Defiance, Mount—*summit* TN-4
Defiance, Mount—*summit* WA-9
Defiance, Point—*cape* WA-9
*Defiance Canyon* UT-8
Defiance Cem—*cemetery* ND-7
Defiance Claim—*mine* NV-8
Defiance Coll—*school* OH-6
**Defiance (County)**—*pop pl* OH-6
Defiance Draw—*valley* NM-5
Defiance Elem Sch—*school* PA-2
Defiance (historical)—*locale* KS-7
Defiance House—*hist pl* UT-8
*Defiance Junction* OH-6
Defiance Lake—*lake* IL-6
Defiance Mine—*mine* NM-5
Defiance Public Library—*hist pl* OH-6
Defiance Sch—*school* IL-6
**Defiance (Township of)**—*pop pl* OH-6
Defiance-Vicco (CCD)—*cens area* KY-4
Defiant, Mount—*summit* AK-9
**Defoe**—*pop pl* (2) KY-4
Defoe Camp (historical)—*locale* TN-4
DeFoe Hollow—*valley* TN-4
Defoe Island—*island* MI-6
Defoe Park—*park* MI-6
Defond, Bayou—*channel* LA-4
DeFoor—*locale* AL-4
DeFoor Ch—*church* GA-3
DeFoor Sch—*school* AL-4
**Deford**—*pop pl* MI-6
DeFord Creek—*stream* OR-9
Deford Post Office (historical)—*building* TN-4
Deford State Game Area—*park* MI-6
Defore Cem—*cemetery* IN-6
Defore Cem—*cemetery* MO-7
*Def O'ren* FM-9
**De Forest**—*pop pl* MN-6
**DeForest**—*pop pl* OH-6
**De Forest**—*pop pl* OH-6
**De Forest**—*pop pl* WI-6
DeForest, Lake—*reservoir* TN-4
**Deforest Corners**—*pop pl* NY-2
DeForest Creek—*stream* WA-9
DeForest Junction—*locale* OH-6
**De Forest Junction**—*pop pl* OH-6
DeForest Lake—*lake* FL-3
Deforest Lake—*reservoir* NY-2
De France Hollow—*valley* PA-2
DeFrance Rsvr—*reservoir* CO-8
Defreest Homestead—*hist pl* NY-2
**Defreestville**—*pop pl* NY-2
Defriece Park—*park* TN-4
Defries—*locale* KY-4
Defries Ditch—*canal* IN-6
**Defries Landing**—*pop pl* IN-6
**De Fries Landing**—*pop pl* IN-6
Defue Spring—*spring* NV-8
DeFuniak, Lake—*reservoir* FL-3
DeFuniak Spring Country Club—*locale* FL-3
**De Funiak Springs**—*pop pl* FL-3
**DeFuniak Springs**—*pop pl* FL-3
De Funiak Springs (CCD)—*cens area* FL-3
DeFuniak Square (Shop Ctr)—*locale* FL-3
Degan Mtn—*summit* ID-8
Degano Pond—*lake* MA-1
Degan Ranch—*locale* ID-8
Degans Butte—*summit* WY-8
Degantown Sch—*school* WI-6
De Garcia, Tomasa Griego, House—*hist pl* NM-5
De Garmo Canyon—*valley* OR-9
Degel Israel Cem—*cemetery* NY-2
Degel Israel Cem—*cemetery* PA-2
**Degelow**—*pop pl* AR-4
Degel Yehudo Cem—*cemetery* NJ-2
**Degen**—*pop pl* KY-4
Degeneres—*locale* LA-4
Degenhardt, Mount—*summit* WA-9
Degenhart Sch—*school* IN-6
DeGeorge Sch—*school* WI-6
Dege Peak—*summit* WA-9
DeGerlia Hollow—*valley* IL-6
Degetau, Plaza—*park* PR-3
**DeGiorgio Subdivision**—*pop pl* UT-8
Degits Creek—*stream* ID-8
Degive's Grand Opera House—*hist pl* GA-3
**Deglow**—*pop pl* AR-4
*Degman Lake* PA-2
Degnan—*locale* OK-5
Degnan Sch—*hist pl* OK-5
Degner Canyon—*valley* OR-9
Degner Cem—*cemetery* MN-6
Degner Spring—*spring* OR-9
Degner Well—*well* OR-9
Degognia—*locale* IL-6
Degognia Creek—*stream* IL-6
**Degognia (Township of)**—*pop pl* IL-6
Degolia—*locale* PA-2
*Degolier* PA-2
DeGolyer Estate—*hist pl* TX-5
*Degonia* IL-6
**De Gonia (De Gonia Springs)**—*pop pl* IN-6
*Degonia Springs* IN-6
**De Gonia Springs**—*pop pl* IN-6
*DeGraff* KS-7
*De Graff* NY-2
**De Graff**—*pop pl* KS-7
**De Graff**—*pop pl* MN-6
**De Graff**—*pop pl* OH-6
DeGraff Bldg—*hist pl* CO-8
Degraff Creek—*stream* NY-2
DeGraffenreidt-Johnson House—*hist pl* NC-3
**DeGraffenried Park**—*pop pl* NC-3
De Graff Memorial Hosp—*hospital* NY-2
*De Graft* OH-6
DeGrant Cem—*cemetery* MO-7
**Degrasse**—*pop pl* NY-2
*De Grasse River* NY-2
Degrasse State For—*forest* NY-2
Degraves Creek—*stream* MI-6
DeGraw—*locale* NE-7
**De Graw**—*pop pl* NE-7
DeGraw Drain—*stream* NE-7
DeGraw Spring—*spring* WY-8
De Gray—*locale* AR-4
**Degray**—*pop pl* AR-4
DeGray Ch—*church* AR-4
De Gray Creek—*stream* AR-4
De Gray Dam—*dam* AR-4
DeGrayes Brook—*stream* CT-1
De Gray House—*hist pl* NJ-2
*DeGray Lake* AR-4
*De Gray Rsvr* AR-4
De Gray Rsvr—*reservoir* AR-4
**De Grays**—*pop pl* LA-4
De Gray State Park—*park* AR-4
De Grey—*locale* SD-7
De Grey Post Office (historical)—*building* SD-7
De Grey Rec Area—*park* SD-7
De Grey Sch—*school* SD-7
De Grey Township—*civil* SD-7
Degroat—*locale* OK-5
**De Groat Township**—*pop pl* ND-7
*De Groff* NY-2
Degroff—*locale* NY-2
DeGroff Bay—*bay* AK-9
De Groff Lateral—*canal* TX-5
DeGroote Folk House—*hist pl* MS-4
DeGroote Lake—*lake* MI-6
*Degroves Creek* MI-6
Degrow Branch—*stream* MI-6
Degrow Drain—*canal* MI-6
Degruy, Bayou—*stream* LA-4
Degusa—*beach* MH-9
Deguynos Canyon—*valley* CA-9
Dehaan Ditch—*canal* IN-6
De Haas Creek—*stream* KS-7
DeHaas Creek—*stream* MI-6
DeHaas Run—*stream* PA-2
D E Hall County Park—*park* WI-6
Dehany Cem—*cemetery* LA-4
Dehart—*locale* KY-4
**Dehart**—*pop pl* NC-3
DeHart Bald—*summit* NC-3
DeHart Branch—*stream* NC-3
Dehart Branch—*stream* NC-3
De Hart Branch—*stream* NC-3
De Hart Cem—*cemetery* NC-3
Dehart Ch—*church* NC-3
DeHart Creek—*stream* NC-3
Dehart Dam—*dam* PA-2
Dehart Draw—*valley* SD-7
Dehart Lake—*lake* MN-6
De Hart Lake—*lake* WA-9
De Hart Mill—*locale* NC-3
DeHart Mountian—*summit* VA-3
Dehart Rsvr—*reservoir* PA-2
De Hart Sch—*school* IL-6
*De Hass Creek* MI-6
DeHaven—*locale* CA-9
De Haven—*locale* VA-3
**DeHaven**—*pop pl* PA-2
DeHaven, Harry, House—*hist pl* PA-2
DeHaven Cem—*cemetery* WV-2
DeHaven Creek—*stream* CA-9
De Haven Ditch—*canal* IN-6
Dehaven Gulch—*valley* CA-9
De Haven Gulch—*valley* (2) CA-9
De Haven Sch—*school* PA-2
De Hay Sch (abandoned)—*school* PA-2
Dehd—*locale* FM-9
DeHeck, Albert, House—*hist pl* OH-6
De Herrera Lake—*lake* CO-8
Dehesa Sch—*school* CA-9
Dehesa Valley—*valley* CA-9
De Heur Ditch—*canal* IN-6
**Dehlco**—*pop pl* LA-4
Dehlco Oil Field—*oilfield* LA-4
Dehlin—*locale* ID-8
Dehlinger—*locale* OR-9
Dehlinger Rsvr—*reservoir* OR-9
Dehlin Sch—*school* ID-8
*Dehlmans Camp* CO-8
Dehmer Pond Dam—*dam* MS-4
Dehm Sch—*school* IL-6
Dehn, Arthur, House—*hist pl* MN-6
Dehner Cem—*cemetery* IN-6
Dehner Cem—*cemetery* PA-2
Dehne Sch—*school* IL-6
Dehon Mtn—*summit* NC-3
Dehon Seminary—*school* MA-1
Dehorn—*locale* AZ-5
DeHose Spring—*spring* AZ-5
Dehpehk—*island* FM-9
Dehpehk, Dolen—*summit* FM-9
Dehr Creek—*stream* CA-9
**Dehue**—*pop pl* WV-2
Deibert—*locale* MI-6
Deibert Sch—*school* PA-2
*Deibertsville* PA-2
Deible Branch—*stream* MO-7
Deibler—*locale* PA-2
**Deiblers**—*pop pl* PA-2
Deibler Station Ch—*church* PA-2
Deible Run—*stream* PA-2
Deicel Hollow—*valley* MO-7
Deichman Island—*island* AK-9
Deichman Oil Field—*oilfield* KS-7
Deichman Rock—*other* AK-9
**Deicke**—*pop pl* MO-7
*Deidelbwij* MP-9
Deidrich Cem—*cemetery* GA-3
*Deigel Lake* MO-7
*Deignault Hill* VT-1
Deike Ranch—*locale* TX-5
*Deils's Island* MD-2
Deimar—*locale* MO-7
Deindorfer Woods—*woods* MI-6
Deiner Ditch—*canal* MI-6
Deinhammer Creek—*stream* WI-6
Deirth Hollow—*valley* VA-3
Deis, John, House—*hist pl* OH-6
**Deisem**—*pop pl* ND-7
Deise Sch (abandoned)—*school* PA-2
Deisher, H. K., Knitting Mill—*hist pl* PA-2
Deisher Branch—*stream* VA-3
Deisher Cem—*cemetery* VA-3
Deisher Mtn—*summit* VA-3
Deister Archeol Site—*hist pl* MO-7
Deitch Pond—*lake* CT-1
Deiter Ditch—*canal* IN-6
Deiter Landing Strip—*airport* SD-7
Deiter Sch (abandoned)—*school* SD-7
Deitrich Flat—*flat* AR-4
Deitz Cem—*cemetery* OH-6
Deitz Lake—*lake* MS-4
*Dejah* AK-9
DeJarnate Cem—*cemetery* MS-4
Dejarnatt Dam—*dam* UT-8
**DeJarnett**—*pop pl* VA-3
DeJarnett Cem—*cemetery* AL-4
DeJarnett Cem—*cemetery* IN-6
DeJarnette—*locale* VA-3
DeJarnette, Lake—*reservoir* VA-3
DeJarnette Mill Run—*stream* VA-3
De Jarnette State Sanatorium—*hospital* VA-3
De Jean House—*hist pl* WI-6
DeJean Slough—*stream* LA-4
Dejolie Tank—*reservoir* AZ-5
Dejonah Creek—*stream* CA-9
Dejonah Creek Mine—*mine* CA-9
DeJong Brothers Number 1 Dam—*dam* SD-7
DeJong Brothers Number 2 Dam—*dam* SD-7
DeJong Brothers Number 3 Dam—*dam* SD-7
DeJong Brothers Number 4 Dam—*dam* SD-7
DeJong Brothers Number 5 Dam—*dam* SD-7
DeJong Brothers 12 Dam—*dam* SD-7
DeJong Brothers 7 Dam—*dam* SD-7
Dejong Dam—*dam* OR-9
DeJong House—*hist pl* SD-7
De Jong Rsvr—*reservoir* OR-9
DeJongs Brothers 8 Dam—*dam* SD-7
*DeJong School* SD-7
Dekairu—*channel* MH-9
*Dekalb* IN-6
*Dekalb* MO-7
*DeKalb* WV-2
De Kalb—*locale* IA-7
De Kalb—*locale* WV-2
**De Kalb**—*pop pl* IL-6
**De Kalb**—*pop pl* MS-4
**De Kalb**—*pop pl* MO-7
**De Kalb**—*pop pl* NY-2
**Dekalb**—*pop pl* OH-6
**De Kalb**—*pop pl* SC-3
**De Kalb**—*pop pl* TX-5
De Kalb Annex Sch—*school* AL-4
DeKalb Avenue-Clifton Road Archeol Site—*hist pl* GA-3
DeKalb Baptist Ch—*church* MS-4
De Kalb (CCD)—*cens area* TX-5
DeKalb Cem—*cemetery* MS-4
De Kalb Cem—*cemetery* MO-7
De Kalb Cem—*cemetery* TX-5
*Dekalb County* AL-4
**De Kalb County**—*pop pl* AL-4
**De Kalb (County)**—*pop pl* GA-3
**De Kalb (County)**—*pop pl* IL-6
**De Kalb County**—*pop pl* IN-6
**De Kalb County**—*pop pl* MO-7
**De Kalb County**—*pop pl* TN-4
DeKalb County Courthouse—*building* AL-4
De Kalb County Courthouse—*building* TN-4
De Kalb County Health Clinic—*hospital* AL-4
Dekalb County Home and Barn—*hist pl* IN-6
De Kalb County Hosp—*hospital* AL-4
De Kalb County HS—*school* TN-4
De Kalb County Library—*building* AL-4
De Kalb County Public Lake—*reservoir* AL-4
Dekalb County Public Lake Dam—*dam* AL-4
DeKalb County Water Works—*other* GA-3
*DeKalb Fellowship Church* MS-4
De Kalb General Hosp—*hospital* TN-4
Dekalb HS—*school* IN-6
Dekalb JHS—*school* IN-6
**DeKalb Junction**—*pop pl* NY-2
De Kalb (Magisterial District)—*fmr MCD* VA-3
De Kalb (Magisterial District)—*fmr MCD* WV-2
De Kalb Memorial Gardens—*cemetery* AL-4
Dekalb Memorial Hosp—*hospital* IN-6
DeKalb Park No 2—*park* GA-3
Dekalb-Peachtree Airp—*airport* GA-3
De Kalb Post Office (historical)—*building* TN-4
De Kalb Sch—*school* MO-7
**De Kalb (Town of)**—*pop pl* NY-2
Dekalb (Township of)—*fmr MCD* AR-4
**De Kalb (Township of)**—*pop pl* IL-6
De Kalb Vocational Sch—*school* AL-4
DeKalb Youth Camp—*locale* GA-3
DeKane Cem—*cemetery* MS-4
DeKays—*locale* NJ-2
*Deke* FM-9
Deke—*island* FM-9
*Dekehn* FM-9
Dekehn Awak—*bar* FM-9
Dekehn Iap—*locale* FM-9
Dekehtik—*island* FM-9
Dekein—*flat* FM-9
Dekekapw—*bar* FM-9
**Dekemont Downs (subdivision)**—*pop pl* TN-4
Dekeni, Dauen—*gut* FM-9
Deke Sokehs—*island* FM-9
Dekkas Creek—*stream* CA-9
Dekkas Creek Saddle—*gap* CA-9
**Dekle Beach**—*pop pl* FL-3
Dekle Cem—*cemetery* FL-3
Dekle Cem—*cemetery* GA-3
Dekles Millpond—*swamp* FL-3
**Dekorra**—*pop pl* WI-6
Dekorra Cem—*cemetery* WI-6
Dekorra Ch—*church* WI-6
Dekorra Sch—*school* WI-6
**Dekorra (Town of)**—*pop pl* WI-6
*De Koven* KY-4
**Dekoven**—*pop pl* KY-4
**De Koven (DeKoven)**—*pop pl* KY-4
DeKoven Foundation—*other* WI-6
De Krruse Canyon—*valley* CA-9
Dekum, The—*hist pl* OR-9
Dekyns Ferry—*locale* MO-7
Dekyns Gage—*other* MO-7
Dela—*locale* OK-5
Delabarre Creek—*stream* WA-9
**Delabole**—*pop pl* PA-2
Delack Point—*cape* NY-2
**Delaco**—*pop pl* FL-3
Delacombe Point—*cape* WA-9
Delacorte Park—*park* FL-3
Delacroix—*locale* LA-4
**Delacroix**—*pop pl* LA-4
Delacroix Canal—*canal* LA-4
Delacroix Island—*island* LA-4
Delacroix Oil and Gas Field—*oilfield* LA-4
De Lacy Creek—*stream* WY-8
De Lacy Creek Trail—*trail* WY-8
*De Lacy Lake* WY-8
De Lacy Lakes—*lake* WY-8
De Lacy Park—*park* WY-8
De La Farge Corners—*locale* NY-2
**Delafield**—*pop pl* IL-6
**Delafield**—*pop pl* KY-4
**Delafield**—*pop pl* WI-6
Delafield Cem—*cemetery* MN-6
Delafield Ch—*church* MN-6
Delafield Fish Hatchery—*hist pl* WI-6
Delafield Hosp—*hospital* NY-2
Delafield Point—*cape* NY-2
Delafield Pond—*reservoir* NY-2
**Delafield (Town of)**—*pop pl* WI-6
**Delafield (Township of)**—*pop pl* MN-6
De La Fontaine Mine—*mine* AZ-5
Delafosse Cem—*cemetery* LA-4
De LaFosse Lake—*reservoir* TX-5
De la Garza Cem—*cemetery* TX-5
De La Garza Tank—*reservoir* TX-5
De Lago, Lake—*reservoir* KS-7
Delagoon Park—*park* MN-6
Delagua—*locale* CO-8
Del Agua, Canyon—*valley* CO-8
*Delaguay Canyon* CO-8
De la Guerra Camp—*locale* CA-9
Delahoussaye Canal—*canal* LA-4
De La Howe State Sch—*school* SC-3
De La Howe Tomb—*cemetery* SC-3
Delahunty Lake—*lake* CA-9
Delahunty Pond—*lake* AL-4
**Delair**—*pop pl* NJ-2
*Delair Division Mark Twain Natl Forest - in part* MO-7
Del Aire—*CDP* CA-9
**Delaire**—*pop pl* DE-2
Del Aire Park—*park* CA-9
Delair Junction—*locale* NJ-2
Delair Range—*channel* NJ-2
Delair Range—*channel* PA-2
*De Lake* OR-9
**Delake**—*pop pl* OR-9
De Lake (CCD)—*cens area* OR-9
Delake Sch—*school* OR-9
De La Laguna, Arroyo—*stream* CA-9
Del Alto Windmill—*locale* TX-5
De la Luz Cem—*cemetery* CO-8
DeLamar—*locale* ID-8
Delamar—*locale* NV-8
De La Mar Apartments—*hist pl* WA-9
DeLamar Cem—*cemetery* AR-4
Delamar Creek—*stream* NC-3
Delamar Flat—*flat* NV-8
Delamar Flat Rsvr—*reservoir* NV-8
Delamar Hist Dist—*hist pl* ID-8
Delamar Lake—*lake* NV-8
DeLamar Mansion—*hist pl* NY-2
De Lamar Mine—*mine* ID-8
Delamar Mtn—*summit* CA-9
DeLamar Mtn—*summit* ID-8
Delamar Mtns—*range* NV-8
*Delamar Range* NV-8
Delamar Spring—*spring* CA-9
De Lamar Spring—*spring* ID-8
Delamar Valley—*valley* NV-8
Delamar Wash—*stream* NV-8
Delamar Windmill—*locale* TX-5
Delamater, Henry, House—*hist pl* NY-2
Delamater-Bevin Mansion—*hist pl* NY-2
**Delamater Corners**—*pop pl* PA-2
Delamater Sch (historical)—*school* PA-2
De La Matyr and Anderson Ditch—*canal* CO-8
**De Lamere**—*pop pl* ND-7
Delameter Creek—*stream* WA-9
Delameter Valley—*valley* WA-9
**Del Amo**—*pop pl* CA-9
Del Amo Junior Seminary—*school* CA-9
Delamore Park—*park* DE-2
Del Amo Senior Seminary—*school* CA-9
Del Amo Shop Ctr—*locale* CA-9
Delana Township—*fmr MCD* IA-7
*De Lancey* PA-2
**De Lancey**—*pop pl* NY-2
**De Lancey (Adrian Mines)**—*pop pl* PA-2
Delancey Cove—*bay* NY-2
Delancey Point—*cape* NY-2
*Delancey's Point* NY-2
**Delanco**—*pop pl* NJ-2
Delanco Sch—*school* NJ-2
**Delanco (Township of)**—*pop pl* NJ-2
Delancy, Lake—*lake* FL-3
Delancy Ridge—*ridge* WA-9
*Deland* FL-3
*Deland* ND-7
**De Land**—*pop pl* FL-3
**De Land**—*pop pl* IL-6
DeLand, Henry, House—*hist pl* NY-2
Deland, Lake—*reservoir* GA-3
De Land (CCD)—*cens area* FL-3
DeLand Ch—*church* MI-6
*De Land Creek* FL-3
*Deland Ditch* IN-6
Deland Drain—*canal* MI-6
Deland Draw—*valley* TX-5
DeLand Hall—*hist pl* FL-3
**De Land Highlands**—*pop pl* FL-3
DeLand JHS—*school* FL-3
Deland JHS—*school* NY-2
**De Land Junction**—*pop pl* FL-3
DeLand Marine Park—*park* FL-3
DeLand Memorial Gardens—*cemetery* FL-3
Deland Park—*park* WI-6
Deland (RR name for De Land)—*other* IL-6
DeLand Senior HS—*school* FL-3
De Land Southwest—*CDP* FL-3
Deland-Weldon HS—*school* IL-6
Delane House—*hist pl* CA-9
Delaney—*locale* MO-7
Delaney—*locale* WA-9
**Delaney**—*pop pl* AR-4
Delaney Bay—*bay* NY-2
*Delaney Branch* MS-4
*Delaney Branch* TN-4
*Delaney Branch* TX-5
Delaney Branch—*stream* AR-4
Delaney Branch—*stream* LA-4
Delaney Branch—*stream* TN-4
Delaney Butte—*summit* CO-8
Delaney Canyon—*valley* (2) WY-8
Delaney Cem—*cemetery* TN-4
*Delaney Cemetery* TX-5
Delaney Ch—*church* IN-6
Delaney Complex—*dam* (2) MA-1
*Delaney Corner* DE-2
*Delaney Corners* DE-2
Delaney Coulee—*valley* MT-8
Delaney Creek—*stream* AR-4
Delaney Creek—*stream* CA-9
Delaney Creek—*stream* (2) FL-3
Delaney Creek—*stream* (2) ID-8
Delaney Creek—*stream* IN-6
Delaney Creek—*stream* MI-6
Delaney Creek—*stream* VA-3
Delaney Creek—*stream* WY-8
Delaney Creek Structure Number 1—*dam* IN-6
*Delaney Dam* MA-1
Delaney Ditch—*canal* WY-8
Delaney Drain—*canal* MI-6
Delaney Elem Sch—*school* FL-3
Delaney Gulch—*valley* CO-8
Delaney Hollow—*valley* OH-6
Delaney Hollow—*valley* PA-2
Delaney Mount—*summit* LA-4
Delaney Mtn—*summit* TN-4
Delaney Pond—*reservoir* MA-1
Delaney Prairie—*flat* FL-3
Delaney Rim—*ridge* WY-8
Delaney River—*stream* FL-3
*Delaneys* DE-2
Delaney Sch—*school* MI-6
Delaney Sch—*school* MO-7
Delaney Sch—*school* NY-2
Delaneys Corner—*locale* DE-2
*Delaneys Creek* FL-3
*De Laneys Creek* IN-6
De Laneys Creek (historical P.O.)—*locale* IN-6
Delaney Slough—*stream* CA-9
Delaneys Methodist Ch—*church* DE-2
Delaney Spring—*spring* WA-9
Delaney Spring—*spring* WY-8
Delaney Street Baptist Ch—*church* FL-3
Delaney Street Playground—*park* FL-3
Delaney Swamp—*swamp* NY-2
Delaney Tank—*reservoir* AZ-5
**Delaney Township**—*pop pl* SD-7
*Delaney Valley* IN-6
Delaney Wash—*stream* AZ-5
Delaney Well—*well* AZ-5
De Lange Sch (historical)—*school* SD-7
De Langle Mtn—*summit* AK-9
*Delann Subdivision* UT-8
**Del Ann Subdivision**—*pop pl* UT-8
Delano—*locale* MI-6
Delano—*locale* OH-6
**Delano**—*pop pl* CA-9
**Delano**—*pop pl* MN-6
**Delano**—*pop pl* PA-2
**Delano**—*pop pl* TN-4
Delano—*uninc pl* KS-7
Delano, Clayton H., House—*hist pl* NY-2
Delano, Lake—*reservoir* GA-3
Delano, Mount—*summit* MT-8
Delano, William S., House—*hist pl* MI-6
Delano Baptist Ch—*church* TN-4
Delano Beach—*locale* WA-9
Delano Cem—*cemetery* MN-6
Delano Cem—*cemetery* MO-7
Delano Cem—*cemetery* TN-4
Delano Ch—*church* MI-6
Delano County (historical)—*civil* SD-7
Delano Cove—*bay* ME-1
Delano Creek—*stream* MT-8
Delano Drain—*canal* MI-6
**Delano Heights**—*pop pl* WA-9
Delano Hill—*summit* ME-1
Delano Hill—*summit* VT-1
Delano (historical)—*locale* NV-8
Delano-Hitch Park—*park* NY-2
De Lano HS—*school* MO-7
Delano Island—*island* NY-2
*Delano Junction* PA-2
**Delano Junction**—*pop pl* NY-2
Delano Lake—*lake* ME-1
Delano Lake—*lake* WI-6
Delano McFarland District Cem—*cemetery* CA-9
Delano Mill Pond—*lake* TN-4
Delano Mines—*mine* NV-8
Delano Mining District—*civil* NV-8
Delano Mtns—*range* NV-8
Delano Park—*park* AL-4
**Delano Park**—*pop pl* ME-1
Delano Peak—*summit* NV-8
Delano Peak—*summit* UT-8
Delano Place—*locale* MT-8
Delano Post Office—*building* TN-4
Delano Ranch—*locale* WY-8
Delano Ranger Station—*locale* UT-8
Delano Run—*stream* OH-6
Delano Sch—*school* IL-6
Delano Sch—*school* PA-2
Delano Sch—*school* TN-4
Delano Sch—*school* VT-1
Delano Sch (historical)—*school* TN-4
Delano Spring—*spring* MT-8
Delano Station (historical)—*locale* TN-4
Delano's Wharf—*locale* MA-1
Delano Terrace Sch—*school* CA-9
**Delano Township**—*pop pl* KS-7
**Delano (Township of)**—*pop pl* PA-2
Delano Trailer Park—*locale* UT-8
Delano Village Hall—*hist pl* MN-6
Delano Well—*well* NV-8
**Delanson**—*pop pl* NY-2
Delanson Hist Dist—*hist pl* NY-2
Delanson Rsvr—*reservoir* NY-2
Delanty Lake—*lake* WA-9

Delany Branch—*stream* ... LA-4
Delany Branch—*stream* ... TX-5
Delany Cem—*cemetery* ... TX-5
Delany Creek Structure Number 2—*dam* ... IN-6
Delany Gulch—*valley* ... CO-8
*Delanys Creek* ... FL-3
Delany Spring—*spring* ... WA-9
De La Ossa Well—*well* ... AZ-5
*Delap* ... MP-9
**De Lap**—*pop pl* ... TN-4
De Lap Cem—*cemetery* ... TN-4
Delap-Clenıant Cem—*cemetery* ... AL-4
de la Pena, Silverio, Drugstore and Post Office—*hist pl* ... TX-5
Delaplain—*locale* ... NV-8
**Delaplain**—*pop pl* ... KY-4
*Delaplaine* ... VA-3
**Delaplaine**—*pop pl* ... AR-4
Delap Lake—*lake* ... MI-6
Delaplane—*locale* ... VA-3
**Delaplane Manor**—*pop pl* ... DE-2
*Delapole* ... PA-2
De Lappe Ditch—*canal* ... CO-8
De Lappe Henderson Ditch—*canal* ... CO-8
**Delapre Township**—*pop pl* ... SD-7
Delaps Cave—*cave* ... TN-4
Del Aqua Arroyo—*stream* ... CO-8
De la Questa Canyon—*valley* ... CA-9
Delario Hill—*summit* ... GA-3
Delaroche Creek—*stream* ... GA-3
Delarof Harbor—*bay* ... AK-9
Delarof Islands—*island* ... AK-9
De La Ronde Canal—*canal* ... LA-4
De Lar Ware HS—*school* ... DE-2
De La Salle Coll—*school* ... MD-2
DeLaSalle HS—*school* ... CA-9
De LaSalle HS—*school* ... LA-4
De LaSalle HS—*school* ... MN-6
De La Salle Institute—*school* ... IL-6
De La Salle Sch—*school* ... CA-9
De La Salle Sch—*school* ... MI-6
Delashaw Sch (historical)—*school* ... AL-4
Delashment, Elias, House—*hist pl* ... OH-6
Delashmitt Road Ch—*church* ... TN-4
*DeLassus* ... MO-7
**De Lassus**—*pop pl* ... MO-7
Delate Creek—*stream* ... ID-8
Delate Creek—*stream* ... WA-9
Delatour Ranch—*locale* ... NE-7
Delaura JHS—*school* ... FL-3
*Delavan* ... CA-9
**Delavan**—*pop pl* ... IL-6
**Delavan**—*pop pl* ... KS-7
**Delavan**—*pop pl* ... MN-6
**Delavan**—*pop pl* ... WI-6
Delavan Cem—*cemetery* ... KS-7
Delavan Cem—*cemetery* ... NY-2
*Delavan Creek* ... NJ-2
*Delavan (Delevan)* ... CA-9
*Delavan Lake* ... WI-6
Dela Van Lake—*lake* ... NM-5
Delavan Lake—*lake* ... WI-6
**Delavan Lake**—*pop pl* ... WI-6
Delavan Prairie Sch—*school* ... WI-6
Delavan Terrace Hist Dist—*hist pl* ... NY-2
**Delavan (Town of)**—*pop pl* ... WI-6
**Delavan (Township of)**—*pop pl* ... IL-6
**Delavan (Township of)**—*pop pl* ... MN-6
De Laveaga Park—*park* ... CA-9
**Delawanna**—*pop pl* ... NJ-2
Delawanna Creek—*stream* ... NJ-2
Delawanna Station—*locale* ... NJ-2
*Delawar Bay* ... DE-2
*De La War Bay* ... NJ-2
*Delaware* ... IN-6
Delaware—*fmr MCD* ... NE-7
Delaware—*locale* ... AR-4
Delaware—*locale* ... LA-4
Delaware—*locale* ... MO-7
Delaware—*locale* ... VA-3
**Delaware**—*pop pl* ... IN-6
**Delaware**—*pop pl* ... IA-7
**Delaware**—*pop pl* ... KY-4
**Delaware**—*pop pl* ... MI-6
**Delaware**—*pop pl* ... NJ-2
**Delaware**—*pop pl* ... OH-6
**Delaware**—*pop pl* ... OK-5
**Delaware**—*pop pl* ... PA-2
Delaware—*uninc pl* ... NY-2
Delaware, Lackawanna and Western RR Station—*hist pl* ... NJ-2
Delaware, Lackawanna and Western RR Station—*hist pl* ... PA-2
Delaware, Lake—*reservoir* ... NY-2
Delaware Acad and Central Sch—*school* ... NY-2
Delaware Airpark—*airport* ... DE-2
Delaware And Hudson Canal—*canal* ... NY-2
Delaware and Hudson Canal—*hist pl* ... NY-2
Delaware and Hudson Canal—*hist pl* ... PA-2
Delaware and Hudson RR Company Bldg—*hist pl* ... NY-2
Delaware and Hudson RR Passenger Station—*hist pl* ... NY-2
Delaware and Raritan Canal—*canal* ... NJ-2
Delaware and Raritan Canal—*hist pl* ... NJ-2
Delaware and Raritan Canal State Park—*park* ... NJ-2
Delaware and Wallace Park—*park* ... PA-2
Delaware Aqueduct—*canal* ... NY-2
Delaware Aqueduct—*hist pl* ... NY-2
Delaware Aqueduct—*hist pl* ... PA-2
Delaware Ave Hist Dist—*hist pl* ... DE-2
Delaware Ave Hist Dist—*hist pl* ... NY-2
Delaware Ave Hist Dist (Boundary Increase)—*hist pl* ... DE-2
Delaware Ave Sch—*school* ... NJ-2
Delaware Bay—*bay* ... DE-2
Delaware Bay—*bay* ... NJ-2
*Delaware Beach* ... DE-2
Delaware Bend—*bend* ... KS-7
Delaware Bldg—*hist pl* ... IL-6
Delaware Boundary Markers—*hist pl* ... DE-2
Delaware Breakwater and Lewes Harbor—*hist pl* ... DE-2
Delaware Camp—*park* ... IN-6
Delaware Cem—*cemetery* ... IN-6
Delaware Cem—*cemetery* ... MI-6
Delaware Cem—*cemetery* ... MO-7
Delaware Cem—*cemetery* (2) ... PA-2
Delaware Ch—*church* ... FL-3
Delaware Ch—*church* ... MO-7
Delaware Ch—*church* ... NE-7
Delaware Ch—*church* (2) ... OK-5
Delaware Ch—*church* ... PA-2
Delaware Ch—*church* ... SD-7
Delaware Chapel—*church* ... IN-6
*Delaware City* ... KS-7
**Delaware City**—*pop pl* ... DE-2
*Delaware City Branch Canal* ... DE-2
Delaware City Branch Channel—*canal* ... DE-2
Delaware City Elem Sch—*school* ... DE-2
Delaware City Hist Dist—*hist pl* ... DE-2
Delaware City (historical)—*locale* ... KS-7
Delaware City Presbyterian Ch—*church* ... DE-2
Delaware Co. AVTS - Aston—*school* ... PA-2
Delaware Colony State Training Sch—*school* ... DE-2
Delaware Corporate Center—*locale* ... DE-2
Delaware Correctional Center—*locale* ... DE-2
Delaware Country Club—*other* ... IN-6
**Delaware County**—*pop pl* ... IN-6
**Delaware (County)**—*pop pl* ... NY-2
**Delaware (County)**—*pop pl* ... OH-6
**Delaware (County)**—*pop pl* ... OK-5
**Delaware County**—*pop pl* ... PA-2
Delaware County Area Vocational-Technical School-Folcroft—*school* ... PA-2
*Delaware County Campus Pennsylvania State Univ* ... PA-2
Delaware County Community Coll—*school* ... PA-2
Delaware County Courthouse—*hist pl* ... IA-7
Delaware County Courthouse—*hist pl* ... OH-6
Delaware County Courthouse Square District—*hist pl* ... NY-2
Delaware County Home—*building* ... IA-7
Delaware County-Johnson Field Airp—*airport* ... IN-6
Delaware County Juvenile Detention Center—*building* ... PA-2
Delaware County Memorial Hosp—*hospital* ... PA-2
Delaware County Natl Bank—*hist pl* ... PA-2
Delaware County Prison—*building* ... PA-2
Delaware Court—*hist pl* ... IN-6
*Delaware Creek* ... MO-7
*Delaware Creek* ... TX-5
Delaware Creek—*stream* ... AR-4
Delaware Creek—*stream* ... IN-6
Delaware Creek—*stream* ... KY-4
Delaware Creek—*stream* ... MO-7
Delaware Creek—*stream* ... MT-8
Delaware Creek—*stream* ... NV-8
Delaware Creek—*stream* ... NY-2
Delaware Creek—*stream* ... OH-6
Delaware Creek—*stream* (5) ... OK-5
Delaware Creek—*stream* ... PA-2
Delaware Creek—*stream* (6) ... TX-5
Delaware Creek Ch—*church* ... KY-4
Delaware Division of the Pennsylvania Canal—*hist pl* ... PA-2
Delaware Elementary and JHS—*school* ... IN-6
Delaware Elem Sch—*school* ... KS-7
Delaware Elem Sch—*school* ... PA-2
Delaware Falls—*falls* ... PA-2
Delaware Flats—*flat* ... CO-8
Delaware Flats—*hist pl* ... IN-6
Delaware Gap—*gap* ... ME-1
**Delaware Gardens**—*pop pl* ... NJ-2
**Delaware Grove**—*pop pl* ... PA-2
**Delaware Heights**—*pop pl* ... DE-2
Delaware Hosp—*hospital* ... DE-2
Delaware Industrial Park—*locale* ... DE-2
*Delaware Island* ... KS-7
Delaware Island—*island* ... OH-6
Delaware Junction—*locale* ... DE-2
Delaware Junction—*locale* ... TX-5
*Delaware Key* ... FL-3
Delaware Lackawanna and Western RR Station—*hist pl* ... NJ-2
Delaware Lake—*lake* ... NY-2
Delaware Lake—*reservoir* ... NJ-2
Delaware Lake—*reservoir* ... OH-6
Delaware Lake Dam—*dam* ... NJ-2
Delaware Learning Center—*school* ... DE-2
Delaware-Lehigh State Experimental For—*forest* ... PA-2
Delaware Memorial Bridge—*bridge* ... NJ-2
Delaware Memorial Bridges—*bridge* ... DE-2
Delaware Memorial Bridges—*bridge* ... NJ-2
Delaware Mine—*mine* ... AZ-5
Delaware Mine—*mine* ... NV-8
**Delaware Mine**—*pop pl* ... MI-6
Delaware Motor Club—*locale* ... DE-2
Delaware Mountains—*range* ... TX-5
Delaware Mtn—*summit* ... ME-1
Delaware Museum Airp—*airport* ... DE-2
Delaware Natl Scenic River (Also NJ)—*park* ... PA-2
Delaware Natl Scenic River (Also PA)—*park* ... NJ-2
Delaware Natl Scenic River (Also PA)—*park* ... NY-2
Delaware Park—*park* ... NY-2
**Delaware Park**—*pop pl* ... NJ-2
Delaware Park-Front Park System—*hist pl* ... NY-2
Delaware Park Race Track—*other* ... DE-2
Delaware Park Sch—*school* ... NJ-2
Delaware Point—*cape* ... DE-2
Delaware Preschool Association—*school* ... DE-2
Delaware Public Library—*hist pl* ... OH-6
Delaware Ranch—*locale* ... NM-5
Delaware Ranch Tank—*reservoir* ... TX-5
*Delaware Reservoir* ... OH-6
Delaware Reservoir Wildlife Area—*park* ... OH-6
Delaware River—*stream* ... DE-2
Delaware River—*stream* ... KS-7
Delaware River—*stream* ... NJ-2
Delaware River—*stream* ... NM-5
Delaware River—*stream* ... NY-2
Delaware River—*stream* ... PA-2
Delaware River—*stream* ... TX-5
Delaware River Gorge—*valley* ... PA-2
**Delaware River Pier**—*pop pl* ... DE-2
Delaware River Ranch—*locale* ... TX-5
*Delaware Run* ... PA-2
**Delaware Run**—*pop pl* ... PA-2
Delaware Run—*stream* ... MD-2
Delaware Run—*stream* ... OH-6
Delaware Run—*stream* ... PA-2
*Delaware Sch* ... IN-6
Delaware Sch—*school* ... MO-7
Delaware Sch—*school* (2) ... NY-2
Delaware Sch (abandoned)—*school* ... PA-2
*Delaware School* ... PA-2
Delaware Seashore State Park—*park* ... DE-2
Delaware Spring—*spring* (2) ... TX-5
Delaware Springs—*spring* ... KS-7
Delaware State Coll—*school* ... DE-2
Delaware State College Farm—*locale* ... DE-2
Delaware State Fairgrounds—*locale* ... DE-2
Delaware State Fire Sch—*school* ... DE-2
Delaware State For—*forest* ... NY-2
Delaware State Forest—*park* (2) ... PA-2
Delaware State Hosp—*hospital* ... DE-2
*Delaware State Hospital* ... DE-2
Delaware State Museum Buildings—*hist pl* ... DE-2
*Delaware State Park* ... KS-7
Delaware State Park—*park* ... KS-7
Delaware State Police Airp—*airport* ... DE-2
*Delaware Station* ... IN-6
*Delaware Station* ... NJ-2
Delaware Street Missionary Baptist Ch—*church* ... AL-4
Delaware Technical and Community Coll—*school* ... DE-2
*Delaware Town* ... DE-2
**Delaware (Town of)**—*pop pl* ... NY-2
*Delaware Township* ... NJ-2
Delaware Township—*civil* ... KS-7
Delaware Township—*civil* ... MO-7
Delaware Township—*fmr MCD* (3) ... IA-7
**Delaware Township**—*pop pl* (2) ... KS-7
**Delaware Township**—*pop pl* ... SD-7
Delaware (Township of)—*fmr MCD* ... AR-4
**Delaware (Township of)**—*pop pl* (3) ... IN-6
**Delaware (Township of)**—*pop pl* ... MI-6
**Delaware (Township of)**—*pop pl* ... MN-6
**Delaware (Township of)**—*pop pl* ... NJ-2
**Delaware (Township of)**—*pop pl* (3) ... OH-6
**Delaware (Township of)**—*pop pl* (4) ... PA-2
Delaware Trail Park—*park* ... TX-5
*Delaware Trails* ... IN-6
**Delaware Trails**—*pop pl* ... IN-6
Delaware Trail Sch—*school* ... IN-6
Delaware Valley Central Sch—*school* ... NY-2
Delaware Valley College—*uninc pl* ... PA-2
Delaware Valley College Station—*locale* ... PA-2
Delaware Valley Coll of Science and Agr—*school* ... PA-2
Delaware Valley HS—*school* ... PA-2
*Delaware Valley Interchange* ... PA-2
Delaware Valley Junior Acad—*school* ... NJ-2
Delaware Wash—*stream* ... AZ-5
*Delaware Watergap* ... PA-2
Delaware Water Gap—*gap* ... NJ-2
Delaware Water Gap—*gap* ... PA-2
**Delaware Water Gap**—*pop pl* ... PA-2
Delaware Water Gap Borough—*civil* ... PA-2
Delaware Water Gap Natl Rec Area (Also PA)—*park* ... NJ-2
Delaware Water Gap Natl Recreation Area(Also NJ)—*park* ... PA-2
Delaware Water Gap Station (historical)—*building* ... PA-2
Delaware Water Gap Toll Bridge—*bridge* ... PA-2
Delaware Windmill—*locale* ... TX-5
*De La War River* ... DE-2
*Delawar River* ... NJ-2
*De Lay* ... MS-4
**Delay**—*pop pl* ... MS-4
**De Lay**—*pop pl* ... MS-4
Delay Camp—*locale* ... CA-9
Delay Cem—*cemetery* ... GA-3
Delay Cem—*cemetery* ... IN-6
Delay Creek—*stream* ... KS-7
Delay Lake—*lake* ... MN-6
Delay Pass—*gap* ... AK-9
Delay Post Office (historical)—*building* ... MS-4
Delba—*locale* ... TX-5
Delba Creek—*stream* ... TX-5
**Delbarton**—*pop pl* ... WV-2
Delbarton Sch—*school* ... NJ-2
Delbert L. Atkinson—*uninc pl* ... TX-5
Del Bonita—*locale* ... MT-8
Delbos Bay—*stream* ... GA-3
Delbridge—*locale* ... MO-7
Delbridge Dam—*dam* ... SD-7
Delbridge Island—*island* ... IL-6
**Del Bueno Park**—*pop pl* ... LA-4
Del Buffalo Seminary—*school* ... MO-7
*Delby* ... TX-5
**Delcambre**—*pop pl* ... LA-4
Delcambre Canal—*canal* ... LA-4
Del Campo HS—*school* ... CA-9
Del Campo Peak—*summit* ... WA-9
*Del Carbo* ... IN-6
Delcarbon—*locale* ... CO-8
Delcardo Bay—*cape* ... ID-8
Delcardo Creek—*stream* ... ID-8
Del Carmen, Sierra—*range* ... TX-5
Delcer Buttes—*summit* ... NV-8
Del Cerro Park—*park* ... CA-9
**Delchamps**—*pop pl* ... AL-4
Delchamps Bayou—*stream* ... AL-4
Delchar Theater—*hist pl* ... ND-7
Delchay Butte—*summit* ... AZ-5
**Del City**—*pop pl* ... OK-5
**Delco**—*pop pl* ... NC-3
Delco Creek—*stream* ... OR-9
Delco Plaza Shop Ctr—*locale* ... MS-4
Delco Plaza Shop Ctr—*locale* ... PA-2
*Delco Shop Ctr* ... PA-2
Delcour Cem—*cemetery* ... MO-7
Del Creek—*stream* ... IN-6
**Delcrest**—*pop pl* ... NJ-2
Delcrest JHS—*school* ... OK-5
Delcroft Elem Sch—*school* ... PA-2
*Delcroft Sch* ... PA-2
Del Cuerto Spring—*spring* ... NM-5
Del Curto Ranch—*locale* ... NM-5
Del Dayo Sch—*school* ... CA-9
**Del Dios**—*pop pl* ... CA-9
Del Dios Sch—*school* ... CA-9
Deldorado Creek—*stream* ... CO-8
**Deldot**—*pop pl* (2) ... DE-2
*Delebog* ... PW-9
*Delectable Hill* ... IN-6
Delectable Mtn—*summit* (2) ... VT-1
*Delectable Point* ... MS-4
*Delectible* ... IN-6
Delegal Creek—*stream* ... GA-3
Delegan Brook—*stream* ... NY-2
Delehanty Ditch—*canal* ... IN-6
*Delehide Cove* ... TX-5
Deleissigues Creek—*stream* ... CA-9
Delemar Bayou—*stream* ... LA-4
Delemar Crossroads—*locale* ... SC-3
de Lemos, Pedro, House—*hist pl* ... CA-9
**Delena**—*pop pl* ... OR-9
DeLendrecie's Department Store—*hist pl* ... ND-7
Delene Lake—*lake* ... MI-6
Delenia Island—*island* ... AK-9
**De Leon**—*pop pl* ... TX-5
De Leon (CCD)—*cens area* ... TX-5
De Leon Cem—*cemetery* ... TX-5
DeLeon (historical)—*locale* ... IA-7
De Leon Lookout Tower—*tower* ... FL-3
DeLeon Park—*locale* ... TX-5
DeLeon Plaza and Bandstand—*hist pl* ... TX-5
DeLeon Pumping Station—*other* ... TX-5
*Deleon Springs* ... FL-3
**De Leon Springs**—*pop pl* ... FL-3
**De Leon Springs Heights**—*pop pl* ... FL-3
De Leon Springs Methodist Ch—*church* ... FL-3
*Delepebai* ... PW-9
*Delepebai Island* ... PW-9
Delery Canal—*canal* ... LA-4
Delesag—*island* ... FM-9
**Delespine**—*pop pl* ... FL-3
Delespine Grant—*civil* ... FL-3
DeLette Ridge—*ridge* ... ME-1
Deleur—*summit* ... FM-9
Deleurlap—*locale* ... FM-9
Delevan—*locale* ... CA-9
**Delevan**—*pop pl* ... NY-2
Delevan Baptist Church—*hist pl* ... VA-3
**Delevan (Delavan)**—*pop pl* ... CA-9
Delevan Drive Sch—*school* ... CA-9
Delevoe Park—*park* (2) ... FL-3
*Deleware River Bridge Exchange* ... PA-2
*Deleware Run* ... PA-2
*Delewares Bay* ... DE-2
Delezene Creek—*stream* ... WA-9
*Delezenne Creek* ... WA-9
Del Fair—*post sta* ... OH-6
Del-Fair Shop Ctr—*locale* ... AL-4
Delf Cem—*cemetery* ... KY-4
Delfelder—*locale* ... WY-8
Delfelder Hall—*locale* ... WY-8
Delfelder Schoolhouse—*hist pl* ... WY-8
Delfino Windmill—*locale* ... TX-5
Del Fondo Windmill—*locale* ... TX-5
Delfongos Pond—*reservoir* ... NY-2
*Delford* ... NJ-2
**Delfore**—*pop pl* ... AR-4
*Delft* ... CA-9
**Delft**—*pop pl* ... MN-6
Delft Cem—*cemetery* ... MN-6
**Delft Colony**—*pop pl* ... CA-9
Delft State Wildlife Mngmt Area—*park* ... MN-6
Delgada Canyon—*valley* ... CA-9
Delgadito Canyon—*valley* ... NM-5
Delgadito Mesa—*summit* ... NM-5
Delgadito Pueblito (LA 5649)—*hist pl* ... NM-5
Delgado, Arroyo—*stream* ... CA-9
Delgado Cem—*cemetery* ... TX-5
**Delgado (subdivision)**—*pop pl* ... NC-3
Delgado Technical Institute—*school* ... LA-4
**Delger Township**—*pop pl* ... ND-7
Del Gulch—*valley* ... WY-8
Delhaas HS—*school* ... PA-2
Del Harleson Camp—*locale* ... CA-9
Delhart—*locale* ... VA-3
**Del Haven**—*pop pl* ... NJ-2
**Del Haven Estates**—*pop pl* ... DE-2
**Del Haven Estates (subdivision)**—*pop pl* ... DE-2
*Delhi* ... OH-6
Delhi—*locale* ... CO-8
Delhi—*locale* ... GA-3
Delhi—*locale* ... TX-5
**Delhi**—*pop pl* ... CA-9
**Delhi**—*pop pl* ... IL-6
**Delhi**—*pop pl* ... IA-7
**Delhi**—*pop pl* ... LA-4
**Delhi**—*pop pl* (2) ... MN-6
**Delhl**—*pop pl* ... NY-2
**Delhi**—*pop pl* (2) ... OH-6
**Delhi**—*pop pl* ... OK-5
Delhi Cem—*cemetery* ... KS-7
Delhi Ch—*church* ... TX-5
Delhi Compressor Station—*other* ... LA-4
Delhi Coronet Band Hall—*hist pl* ... MN-6
**Delhi (Delhi Mills)**—*pop pl* ... MI-6
*Delhi Drain* ... MI-6
**Delhi Hills**—*pop pl* ... OH-6
Delhi (historical)—*locale* ... KS-7
**Delhill Corners**—*pop pl* ... PA-2
Delhi Metropolitan Park—*park* ... MI-6
**Delhi Mills**—*pop pl* ... MI-6
Delhi Plantation—*locale* ... LA-4
Delhi Post Office (historical)—*building* ... SD-7
Delhi Refining Company—*other* ... LA-4
Delhi Rsvr—*reservoir* ... NY-2
Delhi Sch—*school* ... IL-6
Delhi Sch—*school* ... MO-7
Delhi Sch—*school* ... OH-6
Delhi Silver Lake County Park—*park* ... IA-7
**Delhi (Town of)**—*pop pl* ... NY-2
Delhi Township—*fmr MCD* ... IA-7
**Delhi Township**—*pop pl* ... KS-7
**Delhi Township**—*pop pl* ... ND-7
**Delhi (Township of)**—*pop pl* ... MI-6
**Delhi (Township of)**—*pop pl* ... MN-6
**Delhi (Township of)**—*pop pl* ... OH-6
**Delhoste**—*pop pl* ... LA-4
Del Howe Coulee—*valley* ... MT-8
Deihurst Lake—*reservoir* ... OH-6
Delia—*locale* ... KY-4
**Delia**—*pop pl* ... KS-7
**Delia**—*pop pl* ... MT-8
**Delia**—*pop pl* ... TX-5
Delia Cem—*cemetery* ... KS-7
Delia Cem—*cemetery* ... TX-5
Delia Hill—*summit* ... MD-2
Delia Plantation—*locale* ... LA-4
*Delias Creek* ... MI-6
Delias Run—*stream* ... MI-6
*Delias Run Creek* ... MI-6
Delia Well—*well* ... AZ-5
Delicate Arch—*arch* ... UT-8
Delicate Arch Trail—*trail* ... UT-8
Delicate Arch Viewpoint—*locale* ... UT-8
**Delicias**—*pop pl* (2) ... PR-3
Delicias Park—*park* ... AZ-5
Deli Dell, The—*basin* ... UT-8
**Delight**—*pop pl* ... AR-4
**Delight**—*pop pl* ... MD-2
**Delight**—*pop pl* ... NC-3
Delight, Mount—*summit* ... ME-1
Delight, Mount—*summit* (2) ... NH-1
Delight Cem—*cemetery* ... WA-9
Delight Creek—*stream* ... IN-6
**Delightful**—*pop pl* ... OH-6
**Delight Junction**—*pop pl* ... AR-4
Delight Lake—*lake* ... AK-9
*Delight Nixon Crossroads* ... NC-3
Delight Nixon Crossroads—*locale* ... NC-3
*Delight Ridge* ... ME-1
Delight Sch—*school* ... NE-7
Delight Sch—*school* ... VA-3
**Delight Township**—*pop pl* ... NE-7
Delight Valley Sch—*school* ... OR-9
Delila—*locale* ... VA-3
Delilah Creek—*stream* ... CA-9
Delilah Lookout—*locale* ... CA-9
Delilah Peak—*summit* ... CO-8
*Delile Bayou* ... MS-4
DeLima Coll—*school* ... MI-6
**Delina**—*pop pl* ... TN-4
Delina Post Office (historical)—*building* ... TN-4
Deline Ditch—*canal* ... OH-6
Deline Drain—*canal* ... MI-6
Deline Drain—*stream* ... MI-6
Delino Cem—*cemetery* ... LA-4
Delintment Creek—*stream* ... OR-9
Delintment Lake—*lake* ... OR-9
Delintment Lake Dam—*dam* ... OR-9
Delio Creek—*stream* ... AK-9
Delirium Canyon—*valley* ... NV-8
Delirium Pond—*lake* ... MI-6
*Delirium Tremens* ... CA-9
**De Lisle**—*pop pl* ... MS-4
**Delisle**—*pop pl* ... OH-6
De Lisle Bayou—*stream* ... MS-4
DeLisle Creek—*stream* ... AR-4
DeLisle Hills—*ridge* ... AR-4
Delita Cem—*cemetery* ... MS-4
Deliverance, Mount—*summit* ... AK-9
Deliverance Center Ch—*church* ... GA-3
Deliverance Ch—*church* ... GA-3
Deliverance Ch—*church* ... VA-3
Deliverance Evangelistic Ch—*church* ... FL-3
Deliverance Miracle Revival Center—*church* ... FL-3
Deliverance Tabernacle—*church* ... NC-3
Deliverance Tabernacle—*church* ... SC-3
*Deliverance Tabernacle Church* ... AL-4
Deliverance Temple—*church* ... FL-3
Delk Bend—*bend* ... TN-4
Delk Bluff—*cliff* ... TN-4
Delk Branch—*stream* ... KY-4
Delk Cem—*cemetery* (2) ... TN-4
Delk Creek—*stream* ... TN-4
Delk Crossroads—*locale* ... VA-3
**Delkena**—*pop pl* ... WA-9
*Delker Buttes* ... NV-8
Delker Canyon—*valley* ... CA-9
**Delkern (Greenfield Corners)**—*pop pl* ... CA-9
*Delker Ranch* ... NV-8
*Delker Spring* ... NV-8
Delk Hollow—*valley* ... TN-4
Delk Island—*island* ... TN-4
Delks Bluff Bridge—*bridge* ... FL-3
Delk Sch—*school* ... KY-4
Delk Sch (historical)—*school* ... MS-4
Dell—*locale* ... CO-8
Dell—*locale* ... FL-3
Dell—*locale* ... MN-6
Dell—*locale* ... MO-7
Dell—*locale* ... MT-8
Dell—*locale* ... OH-6
Dell—*locale* ... WI-6
**Dell**—*pop pl* ... AR-4
**Dell**—*pop pl* ... MA-1
Dell, Lake—*lake* ... FL-3
Dell, Luke—*luke* ... ND-7
Dell, The—*basin* (2) ... UT-8
Dell, The—*locale* ... ID-8
**Dell, The**—*pop pl* ... KS-7
Dell, The—*valley* ... CA-9
*Della* ... KS-7
**Della**—*pop pl* ... MI-6
Della Basin—*basin* ... ID-8
Dell Abbey—*locale* ... IL-6
*Della Bella Lake* ... CT-1
Dellahunt Draw—*valley* ... TX-5
Dellahunty Cem—*cemetery* ... TN-4
Dellamater Hollow—*valley* ... WI-6
Dellamont—*summit* ... CA-9
Della Mtn—*summit* ... ID-8
Della Plain Sch—*school* ... TX-5
Dellaplane—*locale* ... NC-3
Della Ramsey Hollow—*valley* ... MO-7
Dellar Creek—*stream* ... CA-9
Dellar Meadow—*flat* ... CA-9
Dellar Trail—*trail* ... CA-9
Dellas Peak—*summit* ... ID-8
Dellas Towhead—*bar* ... TN-4
Della Tank—*reservoir* ... AZ-5
*Dellawar Bay* ... DE-2
*Dell Branch* ... TN-4
Dell Bullion Mound (22TI998)—*hist pl* ... MS-4
Dell Canyon—*valley* ... UT-8
Dell Cem—*cemetery* ... OR-9
*Dell City* ... OK-5
*Dell City* ... SD-7
**Dell City**—*pop pl* (2) ... TX-5
Dell City (CCD)—*cens area* ... TX-5
Dell Creek—*stream* ... MI-6
Dell Creek—*stream* ... NV-8
Dell Creek—*stream* (2) ... OR-9
Dell Creek—*stream* (2) ... WA-9
Dell Creek—*stream* ... WI-6
Dell Creek—*stream* (2) ... WY-8
Dell Creek State Wildlife Area—*park* ... WI-6
Dellcrest Park—*park* ... TX-5
Dellcrest Plaza—*locale* ... TX-5
Dell Cut—*canal* ... MT-8
Dell Delight Legion Park—*park* ... PA-2
Dell Dick Windmill—*locale* ... ID-8
Dell Ditch—*canal* ... MT-8
Delle—*locale* ... UT-8
Delle, The—*basin* ... UT-8
**Delleker**—*pop pl* ... CA-9
Dellemont-Wemple Farm—*hist pl* ... NY-2
Dellenbaugh, Mount—*summit* ... AZ-5
Dellenbaugh Butte—*summit* ... UT-8
Delle Ranch—*locale* ... UT-8
Deller Spring—*spring* ... CA-9
Delles Creek—*stream* ... OR-9
Delles Creek Camp—*locale* ... OR-9
Delle Springs—*stream* ... UT-8
**Dellesta Park**—*pop pl* ... WA-9
Dellette—*locale* ... NJ-2
Delle Well—*well* ... UT-8
Dell Frenzi Park—*park* ... NV-8
Dell Grove Ch—*church* ... MN-6
Dell Grove Post Office (historical)—*building* ... TN-4
**Dell Grove (Township of)**—*pop pl* ... MN-6
Dell Gulch—*valley* ... CO-8
Dellhalf Ch—*church* ... MO-7
Dell-High Mine—*mine* ... KY-4
Dell (historical)—*locale* ... KS-7
**Dell (historical)**—*pop pl* ... OR-9
Dell Hollow—*valley* ... MO-7
Dellies Lake—*lake* ... MI-6
Dellinger Branch—*stream* ... NC-3
Dellinger Cem—*cemetery* ... NC-3
Dellinger Creek—*stream* ... NC-3
Dellinger Gap—*gap* ... VA-3
Dellinger Hollow—*valley* ... NC-3
Dellinger Run—*stream* ... PA-2
Dellinger Sch—*school* ... PA-2
Dellingham Branch—*stream* ... SC-3
Dellinory Ch—*church* ... GA-3
Dell Island—*island* ... AK-9
**Dell Junction**—*pop pl* ... MO-7
Dell Lake—*lake* ... PA-2
Dell Lake—*lake* ... WI-6
Dell Lott Hollow—*valley* ... UT-8
*Dellman* ... MO-7
Dellmonell Post Office (historical)—*building* ... TN-4
**Dellmoor (historical)**—*pop pl* ... OR-9
Dellmoor Station—*locale* ... OR-9
Dell Oliver Dam—*dam* ... SD-7
**Del Loma**—*pop pl* ... CA-9
Del Loma Cane—*cave* ... CA-9
Dellona, Lake—*reservoir* ... WI-6
Dellona Center Cem—*cemetery* ... WI-6
**Dellona (Town of)**—*pop pl* ... WI-6
Dell Park Cem—*cemetery* ... MA-1
Dell Pond—*lake* ... NY-2
**Dell Prairie (Town of)**—*pop pl* ... WI-6
Dell Ranch—*locale* ... TX-5
**Dell Rapids**—*pop pl* ... SD-7
Dell Rapids Hist Dist—*hist pl* ... SD-7
**Dell Rapids Township**—*pop pl* ... SD-7
Dell Rapids Water Tower—*hist pl* ... SD-7
**Dellrose**—*pop pl* ... TN-4
Dellrose Ch of God—*church* ... KS-7
Dellrose Post Office—*building* ... TN-4
**Dellrose (RR name Delrose)**—*pop pl* ... TN-4
Dellrose Sch—*school* ... TN-4
*Dell Roy* ... OH-6
**Dellroy**—*pop pl* ... OH-6
Dellroy Creek—*stream* ... OH-6
Dells, Lake of the—*lake* ... WI-6
Dells, The—*area* ... WI-6
Dells Camp—*locale* ... WI-6
Dells Canyon—*valley* ... UT-8
Dells Canyon—*valley* ... WY-8
Dell Sch—*school* ... CA-9
Dell Sch—*school* ... GA-3
Dell Sch—*school* ... MO-7
Dell Sch Campus—*hist pl* ... NC-3
Dells Dam—*dam* ... WI-6
Dells Dam Cem—*cemetery* ... WI-6
Dell Seep—*spring* ... UT-8
Dells Fork—*stream* ... UT-8
*Dells Lake* ... AL-4
Dells Lake—*lake* ... WI-6
**Dellslow**—*pop pl* ... WV-2
Dells Mill—*hist pl* ... WI-6
*Dells Mill Pond* ... WI-6
Dells Millpond—*reservoir* ... WI-6
Dells Of The Eau Claire Park—*park* ... WI-6
Dells of the Sioux River—*cliff* ... SD-7
*Dells Pond* ... WI-6
Dells Pond—*lake* ... NH-1
Dells Pond—*reservoir* ... WI-6
Dell Spring—*spring* ... OR-9
Dells Run—*stream* ... PA-2
Dells Siding—*locale* ... WI-6
*Dellstow* ... WV-2
**Dell (subdivision), The**—*pop pl* ... MS-4
**Dells Vista Shores**—*pop pl* ... AL-4
Dellvale—*locale* ... KS-7
*Dell Valle* ... CA-9
Dellview—*locale* ... NC-3
Dellview Cem—*cemetery* ... KY-4
Dellview Cem—*cemetery* ... WY-8
Dellview Park—*park* ... TX-5
Dellview Sch—*school* ... TX-5
*Dellville* ... KY-4
**Dellville**—*pop pl* ... KY-4
**Dellville**—*pop pl* ... PA-2
Dellville Ch—*church* ... PA-2
Dellville Covered Bridge—*hist pl* ... PA-2
Dellwater Lake—*lake* ... MN-6
Dellwood—*locale* ... FL-3
Dellwood—*locale* ... NY-2
Dellwood—*locale* ... OR-9
**Dellwood**—*pop pl* ... FL-3
**Dellwood**—*pop pl* ... GA-3
**Dellwood**—*pop pl* ... MN-6
**Dellwood**—*pop pl* ... MO-7
**Dellwood**—*pop pl* ... NC-3
**Dellwood**—*pop pl* ... OR-9
**Dellwood**—*pop pl* ... PA-2
**Dellwood**—*pop pl* ... SC-3
**Dellwood**—*pop pl* ... TN-4
**Dellwood**—*pop pl* (2) ... WI-6
Dellwood—*uninc pl* ... FL-3
Dell Wood Branch—*canal* ... IN-6
Dell Wood Brook—*stream* ... IN-6

Dellwood Cem—*cemetery* VT-1
Dellwood Cem—*cemetery* WI-6
Dellwood Country Club—*other* NY-2
**Dellwood Highlands**—*pop pl* IL-6
Dellwood Lake—*reservoir* NC-3
Dellwood Park—*park* GA-3
Dellwood Park—*park* IL-6
Dellwood Park—*park* TX-5
**Dellwood Park (subdivision)**—*pop pl* NC-3
**Dellwood (subdivision)**—*pop pl* AL-4
**Dellwood (subdivision)**—*pop pl* (2) NC-3
Delly Hole—*bay* TN-4
Delma—*locale* AL-4
Delma Ch—*church* AL-4
Delmae—*CDP* SC-3
Delmage (historical)—*locale* SD-7
Delmage Ridge—*ridge* ID-8
*Delmar* SC-3
Delmar—*locale* AR-4
Delmar—*locale* GA-3
Delmar—*locale* IL-6
Delmar—*locale* MO-7
Delmar—*locale* NC-3
Delmar—*locale* OR-9
Delmar—*locale* SC-3
Del Mar—*locale* TX-5
**Delmar**—*pop pl* AL-4
**Del Mar**—*pop pl* (2) CA-9
**Delmar**—*pop pl* DE-2
**Delmar**—*pop pl* IA-7
**Delmar**—*pop pl* MD-2
**Delmar**—*pop pl* MO-7
**Delmar**—*pop pl* NY-2
**Del Mar**—*pop pl* TX-5
**Delmar**—*pop pl* VA-3
**Delmar**—*pop pl* WV-2
Delmar Apartments—*hist pl* PA-2
Delmar Bay—*bay* NV-8
Del Mar Beach—*beach* TX-5
Delmar Butte—*summit* NV-8
Delmar Calaboose—*hist pl* IA-7
Delmar Cem—*cemetery* MO-7
Delmar Ch—*church* AL-4
Del Mar Coll—*school* TX-5
Delmar Community Hall—*building* KS-7
Delmar Creek—*stream* OR-9
**Delmar Downs Subdivision**—*pop pl* UT-8
Del-Mar Golf Course—*locale* PA-2
**Del Mar Heights**—*pop pl* (2) CA-9
Del Mar Heights Sch—*school* CA-9
**Del Mar Hills**—*pop pl* TX-5
Del Mar HS—*school* CA-9
Delmar HS—*school* TX-5
Delmar Junior-Senior HS—*school* DE-2
Del Mar Landing—*locale* CA-9
Delmar Loop-Parkview Gardens Hist Dist—*hist pl* MO-7
Del Mar Mesa—*summit* CA-9
Delmar Mine (surface)—*mine* AL-4
Delmar Mine (underground)—*mine* AL-4
Del Mar Park—*park* CO-8
Del Mar Point—*cape* CA-9
Del Mar Race Track—*other* CA-9
Delmar Ranch (Headquarters)—*locale* TX-5
Delmar Rsvr—*reservoir* NY-2
Del Mar Sch—*school* (4) CA-9
Delmar Sch—*school* SC-3
Delmar Sch—*school* TX-5
Del Mar Shop Ctr—*locale* FL-3
Delmar Shop Ctr—*locale* FL-3
Delmar Stadium—*other* TX-5
Delmar State Game Farm—*park* NY-2
Delmar State Line Airp—*airport* DE-2
Del Mar Technical Institute—*school* TX-5
*Delmarter Bay* NY-2
**Delmar (Town of)**—*pop pl* WI-6
Delmar (Township of)—*fmr MCD* AR-4
**Delmar (Township of)**—*pop pl* PA-2
Delmarva Camp—*locale* DE-2
*Del-Mar-Va Peninsula* DE-2
Delmarva Peninsula—*cape* DE-2
Delmarva Power and Light Bldg—*hist pl* DE-2
Delmarva Raceway—*other* DE-2
**Del Mar Woods**—*pop pl* IL-6
Delmas Bayou—*gut* MS-4
Delmas Mine—*mine* NV-8
Delma Williams Pond Dam—*dam* MS-4
Delmer—*locale* KY-4
Delmer—*locale* TX-5
Delmer Ch—*church* KY-4
**Del Mesa**—*pop pl* CA-9
Del Mexico Mine—*mine* CA-9
Delmita—*locale* TX-5
**Delmo**—*pop pl* MO-7
Delmoe Ditch—*canal* MT-8
Delmoe Lake—*reservoir* MT-8
Delmoe Park—*flat* MT-8
Delmonica Gulch—*valley* CO-8
Delmonico Place—*locale* CA-9
**Delmont**—*pop pl* MD-2
**Delmont**—*pop pl* NJ-2
**Delmont**—*pop pl* OH-6
**Delmont**—*pop pl* PA-2
**Delmont**—*pop pl* SD-7
Delmont Borough—*civil* PA-2
Delmont Boy Scout Camp—*locale* PA-2
Delmont Cem—*cemetery* SD-7
Delmont Ch—*church* KY-4
Delmont Ch—*church* MD-2
Delmont Country Club—*locale* SD-7
DelMonte—*locale* ID-8
Del Monte—*locale* NV-8
**Del Monte**—*pop pl* CA-9
**Del Monte**—*pop pl* TX-5
Del Monte Canyon—*valley* NV-8
Del Monte Draw—*valley* WY-8
Del Monte Draw Rsvr—*reservoir* WY-8
**Del Monte Forest**—*pop pl* CA-9
Del Monte Golf Course—*other* CA-9
Del Monte Gulch—*valley* AZ-5
**Del Monte Heights**—*pop pl* CA-9
*Del Monte Junction* CA-9
Del Monte Lake—*lake* CA-9
Delmonte Lake—*reservoir* WI-6
Del Monte Lateral—*canal* TX-5
Del Monte Mine—*mine* MT-8
Del Monte Mine—*mine* OR-9
**Del Monte Park**—*pop pl* CA-9
Del Monte Peak—*summit* AK-9
Del Monte Ranch—*locale* NM-5
Del Monte Ridge—*ridge* WY-8
Del Monte Shop Ctr—*locale* AZ-5
Del Monte (site)—*locale* NV-8
Delmont Mine—*mine* TN-4
Del Mont Mine—*mine* UT-8
Delmont Mine Refuse Bank Dam—*dam* PA-2
**Delmont Place**—*pop pl* LA-4
Delmont Ridge—*ridge* CA-9
Delmont Sch—*school* KY-4
Delmont Sch—*school* LA-4
**Delmoor**—*pop pl* OR-9
Delmore (historical)—*locale* KS-7
*Delmore Labor Home* MO-7
**Delmore Township**—*pop pl* KS-7
Delmorma Sch—*school* CA-9
*Delmount* OH-6
Delmue Ranch—*locale* NV-8
*Del Muerto* AZ-5
**Del Muerto**—*pop pl* AZ-5
*Del Muerto Canyon* AZ-5
Del Muerto Creek—*stream* NM-5
Delmues Ranch—*locale* NV-8
*Delno Mines* NV-8
**Del Norte**—*pop pl* CO-8
Del Norte—*uninc pl* NM-5
**Del Norte Acres**—*pop pl* TX-5
Del Norte Cem—*cemetery* CO-8
Delnorte Cem—*cemetery* OK-5
Del Norte Coast Redwoods State Park—*park* CA-9
**Del Norte (County)**—*pop pl* CA-9
*Del Norte Gap* TX-5
Del Norte Golf Course—*other* CA-9
**Del Norte Heights**—*pop pl* TX-5
Del Norte Mountains—*range* TX-5
Del Norte Municipal and County Airp—*airport* CO-8
*Del Norte Peak* CO-8
Del Norte Peak—*summit* CO-8
Del Norte Sch—*school* (3) CA-9
Del Norte Sch—*school* NM-5
Del Norte Shop Ctr—*locale* AZ-5
Del North HS—*school* CA-9
Delnor-Wiggins State Rec Area—*park* FL-3
Delno Sch—*school* IL-6
Delno Sch (historical)—*school* TN-4
**De Loach**—*pop pl* LA-4
**DeLoach**—*pop pl* SC-3
DeLoach, George W., House—*hist pl* GA-3
De Loach And Moore Cem—*cemetery* GA-3
De Loach Branch—*stream* GA-3
Deloach Branch—*stream* NC-3
DeLoach Cem—*cemetery* SC-3
De Loach Cem—*cemetery* TN-4
Deloach Cem—*cemetery* TN-4
De Loach Ch—*church* GA-3
De Loach Creek—*stream* TN-4
DeLoach Lake—*reservoir* GA-3
De Loach Lower Pond—*reservoir* GA-3
*DeLoach Pond* GA-3
De Loach Pond—*reservoir* (2) GA-3
De Loach Upper Pond—*reservoir* GA-3
Deloche, Lake—*lake* AR-4
Deloche Canyon—*valley* NM-5
Deloche Trail (Pack)—*trail* NM-5
Delodo Draw—*valley* AZ-5
Delodo Tank—*reservoir* AZ-5
Deloges Bluff—*cliff* LA-4
Deloges Cem—*cemetery* LA-4
Deloit—*locale* NE-7
**Deloit**—*pop pl* IA-7
**Deloit Township**—*pop pl* NE-7
Delombre—*locale* LA-4
Delome Creek—*stream* AK-9
*Delonde* CO-8
Delonde Creek—*stream* CO-8
Delonde Gulch—*valley* CO-8
Delonegha Creek—*stream* CA-9
Delonegha Hot Springs—*spring* CA-9
*Delonegha Springs* CA-9
Deloney Canyon—*valley* WY-8
*De Long* IN-6
De Long—*locale* IL-6
DeLong—*locale* WV-2
**DeLong**—*pop pl* IL-6
**Delong**—*pop pl* IL-6
**Delong**—*pop pl* IN-6
DeLong, Homer B., House—*hist pl* WI-6
Delong, Zopher, House—*hist pl* NY-2
DeLong Agricultural Implements Warehouse—*hist pl* KY-4
DeLong Cem—*cemetery* OH-6
DeLong Cem—*cemetery* TX-5
De Long Creek—*stream* CA-9
DeLong Creek—*stream* IN-6
Delong Creek—*stream* UT-8
Delong Ditch—*canal* IN-6
De Long Hill—*summit* VT-1
DeLong Hollow—*valley* WV-2
DeLong Islands—*area* AK-9
*DeLong Lake* AK-9
DeLong Lake—*lake* AK-9
Delong Lake—*lake* MN-6
DeLong Memorial Sch—*school* PA-2
De Long Mountains—*range* AK-9
De Long Peak—*summit* AK-9
Delong Ranch—*locale* AZ-5
De Long Ranch—*locale* TX-5
De Long Ridge—*ridge* NV-8
**Delongs Addition Subdivision**—*pop pl* UT-8
DeLong Sch—*school* NY-2
DeLongs Creek—*stream* IA-7
DeLong Spring—*spring* NV-8
De Long Windmill—*locale* NV-8
Delores Draw—*valley* WY-8
Delores Mine—*mine* CA-9
*Delores Point* CO-8
*Delores Point* UT-8
Delorme—*locale* MN-6
**Delorme (Edgarton Post Office)**—*pop pl* WV-2
**Delorme (RR name for Edgarton)**—*pop pl* WV-2
Delorme Sch—*school* MN-6
Del Oro HS—*school* CA-9
Del Orto Camp—*locale* CA-9
Delos—*locale* VA-3
Delos Lake—*reservoir* VA-3
DeLoss Creek—*stream* OH-6
Deloss Island—*island* SC-3
Deloss Point—*cape* (2) SC-3
De Loutre—*locale* LA-4
De Loutre Basin—*basin* LA-4
Delowe—*uninc pl* GA-3
Deloy Hollow—*valley* PA-2
De Lozier Branch—*stream* TN-4
Delozier Cem—*cemetery* TN-4
DeLozier Gap—*gap* NC-3
Delozier Spring—*spring* TN-4
**Delp**—*pop pl* IN-6
**Delpark Manor**—*pop pl* DE-2
Del Pasco Mine—*mine* AZ-5
Del Paso—*civil* CA-9
Del Paso—*locale* CA-9
Del Paso Country Club—*other* CA-9
**Del Paso Heights**—*pop pl* CA-9
Del Paso JHS—*school* CA-9
Del Paso Manor Sch—*school* CA-9
Del Paso Park—*park* CA-9
Delp Cem—*cemetery* TN-4
Delp Cem—*cemetery* WV-2
Delp Creek—*stream* OR-9
Delp Creek Shelter—*locale* OR-9
Delph Branch—*stream* GA-3
*Delph Creek* TN-4
Delph Creek—*stream* MD-2
Delph Creek—*stream* OR-9
Delphene—*locale* PA-2
Delphey Island—*island* IA-7
Delphi—*locale* PA-2
Delphi—*locale* WA-9
Delphi—*locale* WV-2
**Delphi**—*pop pl* IN-6
**Delphi**—*pop pl* OH-6
Delphia—*locale* MT-8
**Delphia**—*pop pl* KY-4
**Delphia**—*pop pl* SC-3
Delphi Acad—*school* FL-3
Delphia Ch—*church* VA-3
Delphia Creek—*stream* MS-4
Delphia Melstone Ditch—*canal* MT-8
Delphi Baptist Church—*hist pl* NY-2
Delphi Brook—*stream* CT-1
Delphi Brook—*stream* MA-1
Delphi Cem—*cemetery* IN-6
Delphi Cem—*cemetery* NY-2
Delphic Sch—*school* CA-9
Delphi Falls—*falls* NY-2
**Delphi Falls**—*pop pl* NY-2
Delphi Municipal Airp—*airport* IN-6
Delphin Bay—*bay* AK-9
Delphine Place—*uninc pl* LA-4
Delphin Island—*island* AK-9
*Delphinium* MP-9
Delphin Point—*cape* AK-9
*Delphi Post Office* TN-4
Delphi (Site)—*locale* NV-8
Delphi Station—*locale* NY-2
Delphit Branch—*stream* LA-4
Delphi Village Sch—*hist pl* NY-2
Delphos—*locale* CA-9
Delphos—*locale* NM-5
**Delphos**—*pop pl* IA-7
**Delphos**—*pop pl* KS-7
**Delphos**—*pop pl* OH-6
Delphos Cem—*cemetery* KS-7
Delphos Country Club—*other* OH-6
Delphos Elem Sch—*school* KS-7
Delphus Kill—*stream* NY-2
**Delpine**—*pop pl* MT-8
Del Ponte Ridge—*ridge* CA-9
Del Prat Spring—*spring* CA-9
**Delpro**—*pop pl* AR-4
Delpro Company—*locale* DE-2
*Delps* PA-2
Delps—*locale* PA-2
*Delpsburg* PA-2
*Delpsburgh* PA-2
Delps Cem—*cemetery* PA-2
*Delps & Delpsburg* PA-2
Del Puent, Bayou—*stream* LA-4
Del Puerto and Saint Marys Cem—*cemetery* CA-9
Del Puerto Canyon—*valley* CA-9
Del Puerto Creek—*stream* CA-9
Del Puerto Creek—*stream* TX-5
Del Puerto Fire Control Station—*locale* CA-9
Del Puerto Hosp—*hospital* CA-9
*Delran* NJ-2
**Delran**—*pop pl* NJ-2
Del Rancho—*post sta* OK-5
Del Rancho Park—*park* CA-9
**Delran (Township of)**—*pop pl* NJ-2
*Del Ray* KS-7
*Delray* MI-6
Delray—*locale* GA-3
Delray—*locale* TX-5
Delray—*locale* WV-2
**Delray**—*pop pl* NY-2
**Del Ray**—*pop pl* VA-3
Delray—*post sta* FL-3
**Delray Beach**—*pop pl* FL-3
Delray Beach Country Club—*locale* FL-3
Delray Beach Elem Sch—*school* FL-3
Delray Beach Public Library—*building* FL-3
Delray Community Hosp—*hospital* FL-3
**Delray Gardens**—*pop pl* FL-3
Delray Mall—*locale* FL-3
Delrayno Ch—*church* NC-3
**Delray Park Estates (subdivision)**—*pop pl* TN-4
**Delray Shores**—*pop pl* FL-3
Delray Square (Shop Ctr)—*post sta* FL-3
**Del Rey**—*pop pl* CA-9
**Delrey**—*pop pl* IL-6
**Del Rey (Delrey)**—*pop pl* IL-6
Del Rey Lagoon—*lake* CA-9
**Del Rey Oaks**—*pop pl* CA-9
Del Rey Park—*park* CA-9
Del Rey Sch—*school* (3) CA-9
Del Rey Woods Sch—*school* CA-9
*Del Rey Yacht Harbor* CA-9
**Delridge**—*pop pl* WA-9
Delridge Run—*stream* VA-3
Del Rio—*CDP* FL-3
Del Rio—*locale* AZ-5
**Del Rio**—*pop pl* FL-3
**Del Rio**—*pop pl* TN-4
**Del Rio**—*pop pl* TX-5
Del Rio Baptist Ch—*church* TN-4
Del Rio (CCD)—*cens area* TN-4
Del Rio (CCD)—*cens area* TX-5
Del Rio Ch—*church* AL-4
Del Rio Country Club—*other* CA-9
Del Rio Dam—*dam* AZ-5
Del Rio Division—*civil* TN-4
Del Rio Drain—*canal* NM-5
Del Rio Elem Sch—*school* TN-4
Del Rio Golf and Country Club—*other* CA-9
Del Rio Grange Hall—*locale* WA-9
Del Rio Lateral—*canal* NM-5
Del Rio Mine—*mine* AZ-5
Del Rio Mine—*mine* ID-8
Del Rio Northeast (CCD)—*cens area* TX-5
Del Rio Northwest (CCD)—*cens area* TX-5
*Delrio Post Office* TN-4
Del Rio Post Office—*building* TN-4
Del Rio Ranch—*locale* AZ-5
Del Rio RR Station—*building* AZ-5
Del Rio Rsvr—*reservoir* OR-9
Del Rio Sacramento—*uninc pl* CA-9
Del Rio School (Abandoned)—*locale* WA-9
Del Rio Springs—*spring* AZ-5
**Del Rio Woods**—*pop pl* CA-9
**Del Rosa**—*pop pl* CA-9
Del Rosa Depot—*locale* CA-9
Del Rosa Sch—*school* CA-9
Delrose—*locale* TX-5
Delrose Ch—*church* TN-4
Delrose (RR name for Dellrose)—*other* TN-4
*Delroy* OH-6
**Delroy**—*pop pl* PA-2
**Del Ruby Subdivision**—*pop pl* UT-8
Del Ruth Resort—*locale* MI-6
**Delsea**—*pop pl* TN-4
Delsea Regional HS—*school* NJ-2
**Delser**—*pop pl* IN-6
Del Shay Basin—*basin* AZ-5
Del Shay Creek—*stream* AZ-5
Del Shay Spring—*spring* AZ-5
Del Shay Trail—*trail* AZ-5
Delshazer Spring—*spring* OR-9
**Del Shire**—*pop pl* DE-2
**Delshire (subdivision)**—*pop pl* DE-2
Del Stengl Lake—*lake* WI-6
Del Sur—*locale* CA-9
Del Sur Ridge—*ridge* CA-9
Del Sur Sch—*school* CA-9
*Delta* IN-6
*Delta* KS-7
*Delta* MI-6
Delta—*hist pl* KY-4
Delta—*locale* AR-4
Delta—*locale* CA-9
Delta—*locale* FL-3
Delta—*locale* ID-8
Delta—*locale* IL-6
Delta—*locale* KY-4
Delta—*locale* MS-4
Delta—*locale* WI-6
**Delta**—*pop pl* AL-4
**Delta**—*pop pl* CA-9
**Delta**—*pop pl* CO-8
**Delta**—*pop pl* IA-7
**Delta**—*pop pl* MS-4
**Delta**—*pop pl* MO-7
**Delta**—*pop pl* NC-3
**Delta**—*pop pl* OH-6
**Delta**—*pop pl* PA-2
**Delta**—*pop pl* SC-3
**Delta**—*pop pl* UT-8
**Delta**—*pop pl* VA-3
Delta—*uninc pl* CA-9
Delta, Lake—*lake* WI-6
Delta, The—*area* MS-4
Delta, The—*flat* CO-8
Delta Air Base—*airport* NC-3
*Delta Airp* NC-3
Delta Airp—*airport* PA-2
*Delta Basin* ID-8
Delta Basin—*harbor* NJ-2
Delta Bend—*bay* LA-4
Delta Blues Museum—*building* MS-4
Delta Borough—*civil* PA-2
Delta Branch Experimental Station Airp—*airport* MS-4
*Deltabridge* LA-4
Delta Bridge—*hist pl* CO-8
Delta Bridge—*locale* LA-4
Delta Canal—*canal* CA-9
Delta Canyon—*valley* CA-9
*Delta Cattle Corp Dam* MS-4
Delta (CCD)—*cens area* CA-9
Delta Cem—*cemetery* KS-7
Delta Cem—*cemetery* MS-4
Delta Cem—*cemetery* NY-2
**Delta Center**—*pop pl* MI-6
Delta Center Mound—*hist pl* MO-7
Delta Center Sch—*school* MI-6
**Delta City**—*pop pl* MS-4
Delta City Cem—*cemetery* MS-4
Delta City Cem—*cemetery* UT-8
Delta City Post Office—*building* MS-4
Delta Coll—*school* MI-6
Delta Community Med Ctr—*hospital* UT-8
Delta Community Med Ctr Heliport—*airport* UT-8
Delta Community Presbyterian Ch—*church* UT-8
Delta Company Pond Dam—*dam* MS-4
**Delta (County)**—*pop pl* MI-6
**Delta (County)**—*pop pl* TX-5
Delta County Airp—*airport* MI-6
Delta Covered Bridge—*hist pl* IA-7
*Delta Creek* TX-5
Delta Creek—*stream* (3) AK-9
Delta Creek—*stream* MI-6
Delta Creek—*stream* (2) OR-9
Delta Creek—*stream* WA-9
Delta Creek Pool—*reservoir* MI-6
Delta Crest Subdivision Lake Dam—*dam* MS-4
Delta Cross Channel—*canal* CA-9
Delta Cut—*gut* LA-4
Delta C-7 Sch—*school* MO-7
**Delta (Delta Point Station)**—*pop pl* LA-4
Delta Division—*civil* UT-8
Delta Drain—*canal* CA-9
Delta Drive—*uninc pl* MS-4
Delta Duck Oil Field—*oilfield* LA-4
Delta Experimental For—*forest* MS-4
Delta Experimental Station Pond Dam—*dam* MS-4
Delta Farm—*hist pl* NC-3
Delta Farms—*locale* LA-4
Delta Farms Oil and Gas Field—*oilfield* LA-4
Delta Fish Protective Facility—*other* CA-9
Delta-Friars Point Revetment—*levee* MS-4
Delta Heights Memorial Gardens—*cemetery* MS-4
Delta Hills of Pritchard Sch—*school* MS-4
Delta Hist Dist—*hist pl* PA-2
Delta HS—*school* UT-8
*Delta Industrial Institute* MS-4
Delta Island—*island* AK-9
Delta Island—*island* OR-9
Delta Islands—*area* AK-9
Delta Island Sch—*school* CA-9
Delta JHS (historical)—*school* AL-4
Delta Junction—*locale* WA-9
**Delta Junction**—*pop pl* AK-9
DELTA KING—*hist pl* CA-9
Delta Lake—*lake* CA-9
Delta Lake—*lake* MN-6
Delta Lake—*lake* MS-4
Delta Lake—*lake* WA-9
Delta Lake—*lake* WY-8
Delta Lake—*reservoir* NC-3
Delta Lake—*reservoir* TX-5
Delta Lake Dam—*dam* NC-3
*Delta Land Canal* UT-8
Delta Landing—*locale* NC-3
Delta Landing (historical)—*locale* MS-4
Delta Lookout Tower—*locale* WI-6
**Delta Manor**—*pop pl* PA-2
Delta Mart Shop Ctr—*locale* MS-4
Delta Meadows Site—*hist pl* CA-9
Delta Med Ctr—*hospital* MS-4
Delta Memorial Cem—*cemetery* TX-5
Delta-Mendota Canal—*canal* CA-9
*Delta Migratory Waterfowl Refuge* LA-4
**Delta Mills**—*pop pl* MI-6
Delta Mine—*mine* IL-6
Delta MS—*school* UT-8
Delta Municipal Airp—*airport* UT-8
Delta Natl Fish Hatchery—*park* CO-8
Delta Natl For—*forest* MS-4
Delta Natl Forest—*park* MS-4
Delta Natl Wildlife Ref—*park* LA-4
Delta North Sch—*school* UT-8
Delta Number One Canal—*canal* CA-9
Delta Park—*park* MN-6
Delta Park—*park* OR-9
**Delta Park Subdivision**—*pop pl* UT-8
Delta Pass—*channel* LA-4
Delta Plaza Shop Ctr—*locale* AL-4
Delta Point—*cape* AK-9
Delta Point—*cape* CA-9
Delta Point—*cape* LA-4
Delta Point (RR name for Delta)—*other* LA-4
Delta Post Office—*building* UT-8
Delta Post Office (historical)—*building* MS-4
Delta Processing Pond Dam—*dam* MS-4
*Delta Pumping Plant* CA-9
Delta Queen—*post sta* OH-6
DELTA QUEEN (Steamboat)—*hist pl* OH-6
Delta Ranch—*locale* CA-9
*Delta Reservoir* UT-8
Delta River—*stream* AK-9
*Delta Rocks* WA-9
**Delta (RR name Delta Point)**—*pop pl* LA-4
Delta Rsvr—*reservoir* CO-8
Delta Rsvr—*reservoir* NY-2
Delta Rsvr—*reservoir* OH-6
Delta Sch—*school* IL-6
Delta Sch (historical)—*school* MS-4
Delta Shoal—*bar* FL-3
Delta Shop Ctr—*locale* NC-3
Delta South Sch—*school* UT-8
Delta State Coll—*school* MS-4
Delta State Golf Course—*locale* MS-4
Delta State Junior Coll—*school* MS-4
*Delta State Teachers Coll* MS-4
Delta State University—*uninc pl* MS-4
Delta Tank—*reservoir* AZ-5
Delta Tau Delta Founders House—*hist pl* WV-2
Delta Theta Tau Sch—*school* KY-4
**Delta (Town of)**—*pop pl* WI-6
**Delta (Township of)**—*pop pl* MI-6
Deltaven Station—*locale* PA-2
Delta View Sch—*school* CA-9
Delta Village Shop Ctr—*locale* NC-3
*Deltaville* AL-4
**Deltaville**—*pop pl* VA-3
Delta Well No 1—*well* UT-8
Delta Well No 5—*well* UT-8
**Delta Yard**—*pop pl* OH-6
Deltlot Hill—*summit* ND-7
**Delton**—*pop pl* MI-6
**Delton**—*pop pl* VA-3
Delton, Lake—*reservoir* WI-6
**Deltona**—*pop pl* FL-3
Deltona Alliance Ch—*church* FL-3
Deltona (CCD)—*cens area* FL-3
Deltona Country Club—*locale* FL-3
Deltona JHS—*school* FL-3
Deltona Lakes Elem Sch—*school* FL-3
Deltona Memorial Gardens—*cemetery* FL-3
Delton Cem—*cemetery* MN-6
**Delton (Town of)**—*pop pl* WI-6
**Delton (Township of)**—*pop pl* MN-6
Delto Sch—*school* MO-7
De Luca Field—*park* MI-6
DeLuca Field—*park* PA-2
*Delucan* FM-9
Delucci Ridge—*ridge* CA-9
Deluce—*locale* AR-4
**De Luce**—*pop pl* AR-4
Deluce-Prairie Union Ch—*church* AR-4
Deluge Creek—*stream* CO-8
Deluge Lake—*lake* CO-8
Deluge Lake Trail—*trail* CO-8
Deluge Wash—*stream* AZ-5
Deluna Ranch—*locale* CO-8
Delusion Creek—*stream* AK-9
Delusion Lake—*lake* WY-8
Delutaoch—*harbor* PW-9
*Delutaog* PW-9
Delux—*locale* GA-3
DeLuxe Trailer Court—*locale* AZ-5
DeLuz—*locale* CA-9
De Luz—*locale* CA-9
De Luz Creek—*stream* CA-9
De Luz Sch—*school* CA-9
**De Luz (sta.)**—*pop pl* CA-9
Delvada Canyon—*valley* NV-8
Delvada Spring—*spring* NV-8
Delvale—*locale* VA-3
Del Valle—*locale* CA-9
**Del Valle**—*pop pl* TX-5
Del Valle HS—*school* TX-5
Del Vallejo JHS—*school* CA-9
*Del Valle Oil And Gas Field* CA-9
Del Valle Sch—*school* (2) CA-9
Del Valle State Rec Area—*park* CA-9
Del Valley Sch—*school* CA-9
Delvan Bay—*bay* AL-4
Delvas Pond—*lake* MA-1
*Delvecchio Cemetery* AL-4
Del Venado Ranch—*locale* TX-5
Delvic Bldg—*hist pl* MN-6
*Delville* PA-2
Delville—*locale* KY-4
Delvinta—*locale* KY-4
Delvinta Ch—*church* KY-4
Delvinta Sch—*school* KY-4
**Delway**—*pop pl* NC-3
Delwein City Park—*park* IA-7
Delwein Lake—*lake* IA-7
Delwin—*locale* TX-5
**Delwin**—*pop pl* MI-6
*Delwood* PA-2
**Delwood**—*pop pl* IL-6
**Delwood**—*pop pl* NJ-2
Delwood Beach—*locale* FL-3
Delwood Ch—*church* GA-3
Delwood Run—*stream* OH-6
**Delwoods (subdivision)**—*pop pl* DE-2
**Delwood (subdivision)**—*pop pl* NC-3
Delworth Spring—*spring* NM-5
**Delwynn (subdivision)**—*pop pl* DE-2
Delydia Hill Ch—*church* MS-4
Delyle Campground (historical)—*locale* ID-8
Delyle Creek—*stream* ID-8
Delyle Ridge—*ridge* ID-8
*Delyndia Lake* AK-9
Delyndia Lake—*lake* AK-9
Delzell Cem—*cemetery* TN-4
Delzer Falls—*falls* WA-9
Delzer Lake—*lake* WI-6
Delzer Number 1 Dam—*dam* SD-7
Delzer Number 2 Dam—*dam* SD-7
Delzer Number 3 Dam—*dam* SD-7
Delzer Sch—*school* SD-7
Dema—*locale* KY-4
**Dema**—*pop pl* KY-4
Demailei—*summit* PW-9
Demajagua (Barrio)—*fmr MCD* PR-3
De Malorie-Sowder Oil Field—*oilfield* KS-7
Demamang—*bay* FM-9
Demand-Gest House—*hist pl* OH-6
Demaray Point—*cliff* AZ-5
Demar Brook—*stream* NY-2
Demarcation Bay—*bay* AK-9
Demarcation Point—*cape* AK-9
DeMarcay Hotel—*hist pl* FL-3
De Marce Lake—*lake* WI-6
Demarchant Brook—*stream* ME-1
**Demarco**—*pop pl* TX-5
Demar Creek—*stream* AK-9
DeMarcus Cave—*cave* TN-4
Demaree, Abram, House—*hist pl* NJ-2
Demaree Canyon—*valley* CO-8
**Demarest**—*pop pl* NJ-2
Demarest, Cornelius, House—*hist pl* NJ-2
Demarest, Daniel, House—*hist pl* NJ-2
Demarest, Jacobus, House—*hist pl* NJ-2
Demarest, John R., House—*hist pl* NJ-2
Demarest, Samuel R., House—*hist pl* NJ-2
Demarest, Thomas, House—*hist pl* NJ-2
Demarest-Atwood House—*hist pl* NJ-2
Demarest-Bloomer House—*hist pl* NJ-2
Demarest Brook—*stream* NJ-2
Demarest-Hopper House—*hist pl* NJ-2
Demarest House—*hist pl* (2) NJ-2
Demarest Lloyd Memorial State Park—*park* MA-1
Demarest-Lyle House—*hist pl* NJ-2
Demarest Ranch—*locale* MT-8
Demarest Sch—*school* (2) NJ-2
**Demarest (subdivision)**—*pop pl* AL-4
Demargo Lake—*reservoir* AL-4
Demargo Lake Dam—*dam* AL-4
De Marillac Sch—*school* IL-6
Demaris Cabin—*locale* OR-9
Demaris Ch—*church* AL-4
Demaris Ditch—*canal* WA-9
Demaris Lake—*lake* OR-9
De Maris Spring—*spring* WY-8
DeMars Bridge—*bridge* ND-7
*DeMascio Airport* PA-2
Demasters Ch (historical)—*church* MS-4
De Matha HS—*school* MD-2
*Demay Creek* NV-8
Demazie Hollow—*valley* OH-6
Demby Park—*park* MI-6
Demchek Lake—*lake* CO-8
*Demechui* FM-9
De Mello Rsvr—*reservoir* HI-9
De Mello Sch—*school* MA-1
*Demembers Creek* KY-4
*Dememer Creek* KY-4
Demens Canyon—*valley* CA-9
Demens-Rumbough-Crawley House—*hist pl* NC-3
Dement Branch—*stream* AL-4
Dement Branch—*stream* TX-5
Dement Bridge—*bridge* TN-4
Dement Cem—*cemetery* (3) AL-4
Dement Creek—*stream* AL-4
Dement Creek—*stream* MS-4
Dement Creek—*stream* OR-9
Dement Creek—*stream* TX-5
Dement House—*hist pl* TN-4
Dement Printing Company—*hist pl* MS-4
Dement Ranch—*locale* OR-9
**Dement (Township of)**—*pop pl* IL-6
Demeree Branch—*stream* KY-4
Demeree Creek—*stream* IN-6
Demere Key—*hist pl* FL-3
Demere Key—*island* FL-3

Demere Landing—*locale* FL-3
Demere Park—*park* GA-3
Demeries Creek—*stream* GA-3
Demeris Spring—*spring* OR-9
Demeritt Cem—*cemetery* NH-1
Demeritt Hill—*summit* NH-1
Demeritt Pond—*lake* NH-1
Demerritt Cem—*cemetery* ME-1
Demers Ridge—*ridge* MT-8
Demersville Cem—*cemetery* MT-8
Demersville Sch—*school* MT-8
Demery Creek—*stream* LA-4
Demerys Lake—*reservoir* TN-4
Demerys Lake Dam—*dam* TN-4
Demesio Spring—*spring* CA-9
Demesio Tank—*reservoir* NM-5
Demetrie Wash—*stream* AZ-5
Demetrie Well—*well* AZ-5
Demian, Mount—*summit* AK-9
*Demick Lake* OR-9
Demicks Lake—*lake* ND-7
Demijohn Bend—*bend* (2) TX-5
Demijohn Creek—*stream* MT-8
Demijohn Creek—*stream* OK-5
Demijohn Flat—*flat* MT-8
Demijohn Flat Archeol District—*hist pl* MT-8
Demijohn Gulch—*valley* MT-8
Demijohn Hollow—*valley* MT-8
Demijohn Key—*island* FL-3
Demijohn Lake—*lake* MI-6
Demijohn Lake—*lake* TX-5
*Demijohn Mountain* CO-8
Demijohn Peak—*summit* CO-8
Demijohn Spring—*spring* CA-9
De Mille JHS—*school* CA-9
*De Mille Peak* UT-8
De Mille Peak—*summit* UT-8
De Mille Sch—*school* CA-9
**Deming**—*pop pl* IN-6
**Deming**—*pop pl* NM-5
**Deming**—*pop pl* WA-9
Deming, Col. Simeon, House—*hist pl* OH-6
Deming, Richard Henry, House—*hist pl* RI-1
Deming Armory—*hist pl* NM-5
Deming Brook—*stream* CT-1
Deming Cem—*cemetery* OH-6
Deming Creek—*stream* NY-2
Deming Creek—*stream* OR-9
Deming Elem Sch—*school* IN-6
Deming Glacier—*glacier* WA-9
Deming Gulch—*valley* OR-9
Deming Heights Park—*park* MN-6
Deming Hill—*summit* CT-1
Deming Hill—*summit* NY-2
Deming Lake—*lake* MN-6
Deming Lookout Tower—*locale* WA-9
Deming North (CCD)—*cens area* NM-5
Deming Park—*park* IN-6
Deming Park—*park* MA-1
Demings Arbor Lake—*lake* OH-6
Deming Sch—*school* NY-2
Deming Sch—*school* WI-6
Deming Sch—*school* WY-8
Demings Lake—*lake* MI-6
Demings Lake Ch—*church* MI-6
Deming South (CCD)—*cens area* NM-5
*Deming Woods* IN-6
**Deming Woods**—*pop pl* IN-6
DeMint Hollow—*valley* AL-4
*Demis Point* OR-9
Demit Island—*cape* TX-5
Demitro Flores Well—*well* NM-5
Demke Lateral—*canal* ID-8
Demke Pipeline—*other* ID-8
Demlow Lake State Fishery Area—*park* WI-6
**Demlytown**—*pop pl* KY-4
Demmel Lake Rsvr No. 2—*reservoir* CO-8
Demmer Cem—*cemetery* TX-5
*Demmeron Marsh* VA-3
*Demmick* AL-4
Demmick Hill—*ridge* NH-1
Demming Draw—*valley* WY-8
Demmitt Sch—*school* OH-6
*Demmittville* MO-7
**Demmler**—*pop pl* PA-2
**Demmler Transfer**—*pop pl* PA-2
Demo Brook—*stream* ME-1
*Demock Point* WA-9
*Democracy* OH-6
Democracy—*other* OH-6
*Democrat* AL-4
Democrat—*locale* ID-8
Democrat—*locale* KY-4
Democrat—*locale* TX-5
**Democrat**—*pop pl* AR-4
**Democrat**—*pop pl* NC-3
**Democrat**—*pop pl* TX-5
Democrat, Mount—*summit* CO-8
Democrat Basin—*basin* CO-8
Democrat Bldg—*hist pl* IA-7
*Democrat Bluff* AL-4
Democrat Cem—*cemetery* TX-5
Democrat Ch—*church* NC-3
Democrat Creek—*stream* AK-9
Democrat Creek—*stream* MO-7
Democrat Creek—*stream* NC-3
Democrat Crossing—*locale* TX-5
Democrat Gulch—*valley* CA-9
Democrat Gulch—*valley* (2) ID-8
Democrat Gulch—*valley* (2) MT-8
Democrat Gulch—*valley* OR-9
Democrat Hill—*summit* CO-8
Democrat (historical)—*locale* AL-4
Democrat Hollow—*valley* AR-4
**Democrat Hot Springs**—*pop pl* CA-9
Democrat Hot Springs—*spring* CA-9
Democratic Mtn—*summit* CO-8
Democrat Lake—*lake* MS-4
Democrat Landing—*locale* AL-4
Democrat Mesa—*summit* AZ-5
Democrat Mine—*mine* AZ-5
Democrat Mine—*mine* (2) ID-8
*Democrat Mountain* CO-8
Democrat Mtn—*summit* CA-9
Democrat Mtn—*summit* CO-8
Democrat Mtn—*summit* ID-8
Democrat Peak—*summit* CA-9
Democrat Point—*cape* NY-2
*Democrat Post Office* AL-4
Democrat Ridge—*ridge* CO-8
Democrat Ridge—*ridge* ME-1
Democrat Ridge—*ridge* MO-7
Democrat Rock—*island* CT-1
Democrat Sch—*school* MO-7
Democrat Spring—*locale* IL-6
Democrat Spring—*spring* CA-9
*Democrat Springs* CA-9
Democrat Tank—*reservoir* TX-5
**Democrat (Township of)**—*pop pl* IN-6
*DeMoisy Peak* UT-8
De Moisy Peak—*summit* UT-8
Demonbreun's Cave—*hist pl* TN-4
Demon Creek—*stream* AK-9
**Demond**—*pop pl* KY-4
Demond Hill Lookout Tower—*locale* MI-6
Demond Pond—*reservoir* MA-1
De Mongo Creek—*stream* MI-6
Demons, Lake—*lake* NY-2
*Demons Pond* MA-1
Demonstration Hill—*summit* AZ-5
Demont Arm—*canal* IN-6
Demont Creek—*stream* MT-8
Demont Creek—*stream* NY-2
de Montel, Charles, House—*hist pl* TX-5
Demont Lake—*lake* MI-6
De Montreville, Lake—*lake* MN-6
Demont Sch—*school* NE-7
*Demont's Island* ME-1
*De Monty Branch* OR-9
Demoore Ridge—*ridge* GA-3
**Demopolis**—*pop pl* AL-4
Demopolis, Lake—*reservoir* AL-4
Demopolis Access Area—*park* AL-4
Demopolis (CCD)—*cens area* AL-4
Demopolis Country Club Dam—*dam* AL-4
Demopolis Country Club Lake—*reservoir* AL-4
Demopolis Division—*civil* AL-4
Demopolis Historic Business District—*hist pl* AL-4
Demopolis Lake—*reservoir* AL-4
*Demopolis Lake Dam* AL-4
Demopolis Lock And Dam—*dam* AL-4
Demopolis Lower Landing (historical)—*locale* AL-4
Demopolis Municipal Airp—*airport* AL-4
Demopolis Public Sch—*hist pl* AL-4
Demopolis State Wildlife Mngmt Area—*park* AL-4
Demopolis Upper Landing—*locale* AL-4
*Demopolis Waterfowl Mngmt Area* AL-4
Demo Pond—*lake* ME-1
*De Mores* SD-7
De Mores—*locale* ND-7
De Mores Packing Plant Ruins—*hist pl* ND-7
**Demorest**—*pop pl* GA-3
Demorest Cem—*cemetery* MI-6
Demorest Creek—*stream* ID-8
Demorest Glacier—*glacier* AK-9
Demorest Lake—*reservoir* GA-3
Demoret Mound—*hist pl* OH-6
Demoreux Creek—*stream* MI-6
Demorst Ranch—*locale* WY-8
**Demory**—*pop pl* TN-4
Demory Ch—*church* TN-4
Demory Creek—*stream* (2) FL-3
Demory Gap—*channel* FL-3
*Demory Hill* FL-3
Demory Hill—*other* FL-3
Demory Sch (historical)—*school* TN-4
Demory Spring—*spring* CA-9
De Moss—*post sta* TX-5
DeMoss Branch—*stream* MO-7
DeMoss Branch—*stream* TN-4
DeMoss Canyon—*valley* OR-9
Demoss Cem—*cemetery* AR-4
De Moss Cem—*cemetery* OR-9
DeMoss Ch—*church* MO-7
DeMoss Creek—*stream* TN-4
Demoss Hollow—*valley* TN-4
Demoss Northeast- Strawn Oil Field—*oilfield* TX-5
De Moss Spring—*spring* CO-8
DeMoss Springs—*locale* OR-9
De Moss Springs Cem—*cemetery* OR-9
Demoss- Strawn Oil Field—*oilfield* TX-5
**DeMossville**—*pop pl* KY-4
**De Mossville (RR name Demossville)**—*pop pl* KY-4
Demossville (RR name for De Mossville)—*other* KY-4
Demotropolis Park—*park* AL-4
Demott Draw—*valley* WY-8
*De Motte* IN-6
**Demotte**—*pop pl* IN-6
De Motte Airp—*airport* IN-6
DeMotte Campground—*park* AZ-5
*Demotte (corporate and RR name De Motte)* IN-6
**De Motte (corporate and RR name for Demotte)**—*pop pl* IN-6
Demotte Elem Sch—*school* IN-6
De Motte Park—*flat* AZ-5
Demott-Westervelt House—*hist pl* NJ-2
De Moulin Drain—*canal* CA-9
*DeMount Church* AL-4
Demourelles Island—*island* LA-4
Demoure Sch—*school* IL-6
Dempcy Draw—*valley* NE-7
Dempcy Sch—*school* NE-7
Demple Draw—*valley* WY-8
Demplytown—*locale* KY-4
*Dempo Mountain* GA-3
Dempsay Farm Airp—*airport* KS-7
Demps Creek—*stream* GA-3
*Dempsey* MT-8
Dempsey—*locale* AK-9
Dempsey—*locale* OK-5
**Dempsey**—*pop pl* AL-4
**Dempsey**—*pop pl* MT-8
**Dempsey**—*pop pl* WV-2
Dempsey, Mount—*summit* PA-2
Dempsey Basin—*basin* MT-8
Dempsey Basin—*basin* WY-8
*Dempsey Branch* WV-2
Dempsey Branch—*stream* WV-2
Dempsey Branch Ch—*church* WV-2
Dempsey Canal—*canal* WY-8
Dempsey Cem—*cemetery* AL-4
Dempsey Cem—*cemetery* LA-4
Dempsey Cem—*cemetery* NM-5
Dempsey Cem—*cemetery* OK-5
Dempsey Cem—*cemetery* (2) TN-4
Dempsey Cem—*cemetery* (2) WV-2
Dempsey Ch—*church* GA-3
Dempsey Creek—*stream* AK-9
Dempsey Creek—*stream* CA-9
Dempsey Creek—*stream* ID-8
Dempsey Creek—*stream* MN-6
Dempsey Creek—*stream* MT-8
Dempsey Creek—*stream* OR-9
Dempsey Creek—*stream* TX-5
Dempsey Creek—*stream* (2) WA-9
Dempsey Creek—*stream* WY-8
Dempsey Dam—*dam* AL-4
Dempsey Dome—*summit* CO-8
Dempsey Flat—*flat* ID-8
Dempsey Hollow—*valley* AR-4
Dempsey Lake—*lake* FL-3
Dempsey Lake—*lake* LA-4
Dempsey Lake—*lake* MN-6
Dempsey Landing—*locale* CT-1
Dempsey Meadows—*flat* CO-8
Dempsey Meadows—*flat* ID-8
Dempsey Mtn—*summit* WV-2
Dempsey Park—*park* OH-6
Dempsey Parks—*flat* CO-8
Dempsey Peak—*summit* OK-5
Dempsey-Reynolds-Taylor House—*hist pl* NC-3
Dempsey Ridge—*ridge* WY-8
Dempsey Run—*stream* (2) PA-2
Dempsey Sch—*school* IL-6
Dempsey Sch—*school* NY-2
Dempsey Spring—*spring* AR-4
Dempsey Spring—*spring* CA-9
Dempsey Spring—*spring* (2) OR-9
Dempsey Spring Branch—*stream* AL-4
*Dempsey Station* MT-8
Dempsey Station (historical)—*locale* MT-8
**Dempseytown**—*pop pl* PA-2
Demps Hollow—*valley* KY-4
Dempsie Brewster Sch—*school* FL-3
Dempski Drain—*stream* MI-6
Demps Mtn—*summit* GA-3
Dempster—*locale* KY-4
**Dempster**—*pop pl* SD-7
**Dempster Beach**—*pop pl* NY-2
**Dempster Corners**—*pop pl* NY-2
Dempster Ditch—*canal* MT-8
Dempster JHS—*school* IL-6
**Dempster Township**—*pop pl* SD-7
Dempster Well—*well* NM-5
Dempster Windmill—*locale* NM-5
Dempster Windmill—*locale* TX-5
*Dempsy* AL-4
Dempsy Creek—*stream* AL-4
Demro Lake—*lake* MN-6
**Demster**—*pop pl* NY-2
**Demster Beach**—*pop pl* NY-2
Demster Creek—*stream* WI-6
Demster Grove Camp Ground—*locale* NY-2
Demster Windmill—*locale* TX-5
Demul Iou—*bay* PW-9
De Mull Creek—*stream* MI-6
Demumbers Bay—*bay* KY-4
Demumbers Creek—*stream* KY-4
Demumbers Point Rec Area—*park* KY-4
*Demumer Creek* KY-4
*De Mums Creek* KS-7
Demunbruns Store—*locale* KY-4
**Demunds Corners**—*pop pl* PA-2
Demun (Township of)—*fmr MCD* AR-4
Demuro Park—*park* NJ-2
Demuth—*locale* CA-9
Demuth Brook—*stream* ME-1
Demuth Hill—*summit* ME-1
De Muth Ranch—*locale* NM-5
*Denabeto Spring* AZ-5
*Denabeto Wash* AZ-5
Denagiemina Lake—*lake* AK-9
*Denahatso* AZ-5
**Denair**—*pop pl* CA-9
Denair Cem—*cemetery* CA-9
Denali—*locale* AK-9
Denali Natl Park—*park* AK-9
Denali Pass—*gap* AK-9
Denali Sch—*school* AK-9
Denali State Park—*park* AK-9
Denamrk Ch—*church* MS-4
Denard Branch—*stream* LA-4
Denaro—*locale* VA-3
Denaud—*locale* FL-3
**Denaud (Fort Denaud)**—*pop pl* FL-3
**Denault Corners**—*pop pl* NY-2
Denay Creek—*stream* NV-8
Denay Valley—*valley* NV-8
De-na-zin Wash—*stream* NM-5
**Denbeau Heights**—*pop pl* PA-2
**Denbigh**—*pop pl* ND-7
**Denbigh**—*pop pl* VA-3
Denbigh Ch—*church* VA-3
Denbigh Plantation Site—*hist pl* VA-3
**Denbigh Township**—*pop pl* ND-7
**Denbo**—*pop pl* PA-2
Denbo Cem—*cemetery* IN-6
*Denbo Heath* ME-1
Denbow Heath—*swamp* ME-1
Denbow Island—*island* ME-1
Denbow Neck—*cape* ME-1
Denbow Point—*cape* ME-1
Den Branch—*stream* NC-3
Den Branch—*stream* WV-2
Den Brock Park—*park* MA-1
Den Brook—*stream* NJ-2
Denby—*locale* SD-7
Denby Cem—*cemetery* IL-6
Denby Creek—*stream* AR-4
Denby Dam—*dam* SD-7
Denby House—*hist pl* AL-4
Denby HS—*school* MI-6
Denby Island—*island* WI-6
Denby Lake—*reservoir* SD-7
Denby Memorial Childrens Home—*building* MI-6
Denby Park—*park* IL-6
**Denby Park**—*pop pl* VA-3
Denby Point—*cape* AR-4
Denby Point Rec Area—*park* AR-4
**Dencer (historical)**—*pop pl* OR-9
*Dences Quarters* NC-3
Den Creek—*stream* KS-7
Den Creek—*stream* MD-2
Den Creek—*stream* VA-3
*Denden Island* MP-9
Dendinger Cem—*cemetery* LA-4
Dendora Ranch—*locale* AZ-5
Dendora Substation—*locale* AZ-5
Dendora Valley—*valley* AZ-5
Dendron—*locale* NC-3
**Dendron**—*pop pl* VA-3
Dendy Sch—*school* SC-3
De Neal Branch—*stream* IL-6
Deneault Springs State Fishery Area—*park* WI-6
*Denebito Wash* AZ-5
Deneen Dam—*dam* NC-3
Deneen Dam—*reservoir* NC-3
Deneen Gap—*gap* PA-2
Deneen Sch—*school* IL-6
Deneen Sch—*school* WI-6
*Denehotso* AZ-5
Deneki Lakes—*lake* AK-9
*Denent Creek* AL-4
Denesse Pass—*gut* LA-4
Denest Spring—*spring* OR-9
Deneth Chahis Spring—*spring* AZ-5
DeNeuville Heights Sch—*school* TN-4
De Neve, Felipe, Branch—*hist pl* CA-9
De Neve Square—*park* CA-9
De Neveu Creek—*stream* WI-6
DeNeveu Lake—*lake* WI-6
*Denevitz* ND-7
Denezipi Spring—*spring* AZ-5
*Denfey Hill* RI-1
Denfield HS—*school* MN-6
Dengate—*locale* ND-7
Dengel Bay—*bay* WI-6
*Dengel's Bay* WI-6
Denger Lake—*lake* MN-6
Denges—*channel* PW-9
*Denges Durchfahrt* PW-9
*Denges Einfahrt* PW-9
*Denges Passage* PW-9
*Dengisu Suido* PW-9
Den Gulch—*valley* MT-8
Den Gulch Spring—*spring* MT-8
Denham—*locale* MS-4
**Denham**—*pop pl* FL-3
**Denham**—*pop pl* IN-6
**Denham**—*pop pl* MN-6
Denham, Lake—*lake* FL-3
Denham Bayou—*stream* FL-3
Denham Branch—*stream* AL-4
Denham Branch—*stream* GA-3
Denham Cem—*cemetery* MN-6
Denham Creek—*stream* MS-4
Denham Knob—*summit* KY-4
Denham-Lacy House—*hist pl* FL-3
Denham Levee—*levee* IL-6
Denham Post Office (historical)—*building* MS-4
Denham Sch—*school* LA-4
Denham Sch (historical)—*school* MS-4
**Denham Springs**—*pop pl* LA-4
Denhart—*locale* IA-7
Denhart—*locale* LA-4
*Denhawkee* TX-5
**Denhawken**—*pop pl* TX-5
Denhawken Cem—*cemetery* TX-5
Den Hill—*summit* MA-1
Den Hill—*summit* RI-1
Den Hill—*summit* VA-3
Den Hill Cem—*cemetery* VA-3
**Denhoff**—*pop pl* ND-7
Denhoff Adventist Cem—*cemetery* ND-7
Denhoff Cemeteries—*cemetery* ND-7
**Denhoff Township**—*pop pl* ND-7
Den Hollow—*valley* UT-8
**Denholm**—*pop pl* PA-2
Denholms Bldg—*building* MA-1
*Denice* AL-4
Denick Cem—*cemetery* KS-7
**Denie**—*pop pl* TN-4
*Denigal* FM-9
Denike Ranch—*locale* MT-8
Deniktaw Ridge—*ridge* AK-9
Denikuio Agingan, Unai—*beach* MH-9
Denim Hill—*summit* AR-4
*Deningal* FM-9
**Denio**—*pop pl* NV-8
Denio Branch—*stream* TX-5
Denio Camp—*locale* NV-8
Denio Camp Springs—*spring* NV-8
*Denio Canyon* NV-8
Denio Canyon—*valley* NV-8
Denio Cem—*cemetery* OR-9
Denio Creek—*stream* OR-9
Denio Draw—*valley* WY-8
Denio Junction—*locale* NV-8
Denios Creek—*stream* IN-6
Denio Summit—*summit* NV-8
Denis—*locale* CA-9
Denis Bay—*bay* VI-3
*Denis Bayou* MS-4
Denis Cabin—*locale* OR-9
Denison—*locale* WA-9
**Denison**—*pop pl* IA-7
**Denison**—*pop pl* KS-7
**Denison**—*pop pl* (2) KY-4
**Denison**—*pop pl* PA-2
**Denison**—*pop pl* TX-5
Denison, Lake—*lake* MA-1
Denison, Mount—*summit* AK-9
Denison, William, House—*hist pl* OH-6
Denison Brook—*stream* CT-1
Denison Cem—*cemetery* IL-6
Denison Cem—*cemetery* MN-6
Denison Cem—*cemetery* OH-6
Denison Cem—*cemetery* OK-5
Denison Cem—*cemetery* TX-5
*Denison Cemetery* MS-4
Denison Commercial Hist Dist—*hist pl* TX-5
**Denison Corner**—*pop pl* NY-2
*Denison Cove* TN-4
Denison Dam—*dam* OK-5
Denison Dam—*dam* TX-5
Denison Draw—*valley* CO-8
Denison Elem Sch—*school* KS-7
Denison Fork—*stream* WV-2
Denison House—*hist pl* PA-2
Denison HS—*school* IA-7
Denison JHS—*school* FL-3
Denison JHS—*school* IA-7
*Denison Lake* MA-1
Denison Park—*park* NY-2
Denison Park—*park* (2) OH-6
*Denison Reservoir* OK-5
Denison Rsvr—*reservoir* OR-9
*Denison Run* WV-2
Denison Sch—*school* CO-8
Denison Sch—*school* OH-6
Denison Sch—*school* OK-5
Denison Tank—*reservoir* NM-5
Denison Tank—*reservoir* TX-5
Denison Township—*fmr MCD* IA-7
**Denison (Township of)**—*pop pl* IL-6
Denison Univ—*school* OH-6
Denis Ranch—*locale* TX-5
Deniston Cem—*cemetery* VA-3
Deniston Chapel—*church* VA-3
Denke Ranch—*locale* SD-7
Denker Ave Sch—*school* CA-9
Denkmann-Hauberg House—*hist pl* IL-6
Denkman Sch—*school* IL-6
Den Lake—*lake* CA-9
Den Lake—*lake* ND-7
**Den Lee Acres**—*pop pl* MD-2
Denley Brothers Dam—*dam* OR-9
Denley Cem—*cemetery* MS-4
Denley Creek—*stream* MN-6
Denley Lake—*lake* MN-6
Denley Rsvr—*reservoir* OR-9
**Denlow**—*pop pl* MO-7
Denman—*locale* OK-5
**Denman**—*pop pl* NE-7
**Denman**—*pop pl* OK-5
Denman Branch—*stream* MS-4
Denman Bridge—*bridge* AL-4
Denman Brook—*stream* CT-1
Denman Cabin—*locale* OR-9
Denman Cem—*cemetery* IL-6
Denman Cem—*cemetery* IN-6
Denman Cem—*cemetery* OK-5
Denman Creek—*stream* CA-9
Denman Creek—*stream* IL-6
Denman Crossroads—*locale* TX-5
Denman Falls—*falls* WA-9
Denman Flat—*flat* CA-9
Denman JHS—*school* CA-9
Denman JHS—*school* MS-4
Denman Lake—*lake* MS-4
Denman Lake—*reservoir* NY-2
Denman Mtn—*summit* NY-2
Denman Peak—*summit* WA-9
Denmans Creek—*stream* GA-3
Denmans Ferry (historical)—*locale* MS-4
Denmans Island—*island* NY-2
Denman Spring—*spring* AL-4
Denman Woods—*forest* IA-7
Denmar—*locale* WV-2
**Den-Mar Condominium**—*pop pl* UT-8
*Denmark* OH-6
Denmark—*locale* IL-6
Denmark—*locale* OR-9
Denmark—*locale* TN-4
Denmark—*locale* VA-3
**Denmark**—*pop pl* AR-4
**Denmark**—*pop pl* GA-3
**Denmark**—*pop pl* IN-6
**Denmark**—*pop pl* IA-7
**Denmark**—*pop pl* KS-7
**Denmark**—*pop pl* KY-4
**Denmark**—*pop pl* ME-1
**Denmark**—*pop pl* MS-4
**Denmark**—*pop pl* (2) NY-2
**Denmark**—*pop pl* OH-6
**Denmark**—*pop pl* SC-3
**Denmark**—*pop pl* TN-4
**Denmark**—*pop pl* WI-6
Denmark, Lake—*lake* NJ-2
Denmark, Lake—*reservoir* NJ-2
Denmark (CCD)—*cens area* SC-3
Denmark Cem—*cemetery* SC-3
Denmark Cem—*cemetery* WI-6
Denmark Center—*locale* OH-6
Denmark Congregational Church—*hist pl* IA-7
Denmark Cove—*bay* AK-9
Denmark Creek—*stream* OK-5
Denmark Elem Sch—*school* TN-4
Denmark Female Institute (historical)—*school* TN-4
*Denmark Firetower* MS-4
Denmark Hall—*locale* WA-9
Denmark Hill—*summit* NY-2
Denmark Island—*island* IL-6
Denmark Junction—*locale* MI-6
Denmark Lake—*reservoir* MS-4
Denmark Lake—*swamp* GA-3
Denmark Landing—*locale* LA-4
Denmark Lookout Tower—*locale* MS-4
Denmark Male Acad (historical)—*school* TN-4
Denmark Manor Cem—*cemetery* PA-2
Denmark Manor Ch—*church* PA-2
Denmark-Olar HS—*school* SC-3
Denmark-Olar JHS—*school* SC-3
*Denmark Pond* GA-3
Denmark Post Office—*building* TN-4
Denmark Post Office (historical)—*building* MS-4
Denmark Post Office (historical)—*building* SD-7
Denmark Presbyterian Ch—*church* TN-4
Denmark Presbyterian Church—*hist pl* TN-4
Denmark Sch—*school* KY-4
Denmark Sch—*school* MS-4
Denmark Sch—*school* NE-7
Denmark Sch—*school* WA-9
Denmark Sch (historical)—*school* MO-7
Denmark Sch (historical)—*school* TN-4
Denmark Sch Number 1—*school* ND-7
Denmark Spring Branch—*stream* AL-4
**Denmark (Town of)**—*pop pl* ME-1
**Denmark (Town of)**—*pop pl* NY-2
Denmark Township—*fmr MCD* (2) IA-7
**Denmark Township**—*pop pl* ND-7
Denmark (Township of)—*fmr MCD* AR-4
**Denmark (Township of)**—*pop pl* MI-6
**Denmark (Township of)**—*pop pl* MN-6
**Denmark (Township of)**—*pop pl* OH-6
Denmark Wash—*valley* UT-8
Denmark Wash Dam—*dam* UT-8
**Denmar State Hospital**—*pop pl* WV-2
**Den-Mar Subdivision**—*pop pl* UT-8
Denmeo—*island* MP-9
Denmoe Cove—*basin* TX-5
*Denmon* OK-5
Denmon Cutoff—*channel* MS-4
*Denmor* OK-5
**Denmore Park**—*pop pl* MD-2
Denna Mora Campground—*locale* MT-8
Denna Mora Creek—*stream* MT-8
**Dennard**—*pop pl* AR-4
Dennard Ch—*church* AR-4
Denn Branch—*stream* NJ-2
Denne', I—*summit* MH-9
Denne', Saddok I—*stream* MH-9
**Dennehotso**—*pop pl* AZ-5
Dennehotso Canyon—*valley* AZ-5
Dennehotso (CCD)—*cens area* AZ-5
**Dennehotso (Dinnehotso)**—*pop pl* AZ-5
Dennehotso Rec Area—*park* AZ-5
Denner Ridge—*ridge* CA-9
Dennery Canyon—*valley* CA-9
Dennery Lake Dam—*dam* MS-4
Dennery Pond Dam—*dam* MS-4
Dennet—*locale* FL-3
*Dennet Creek* AL-4
Dennett Brook—*stream* (2) ME-1
Dennett Canyon—*valley* UT-8
Dennett Creek—*stream* ID-8
Dennett Garrison—*hist pl* ME-1
Dennett Sch—*school* MA-1
Dennetts Pond—*reservoir* MA-1
Dennetts Pond Dam—*dam* MA-1
Dennewitz Cem—*cemetery* SD-7
Denney—*locale* KY-4
Denney Branch—*stream* MD-2
Denney Cem—*cemetery* KY-4
Denney Cem—*cemetery* MO-7
Denney Cem—*cemetery* OH-6
Denney Cem—*cemetery* TN-4
Denney Cliff—*cliff* KY-4
*Denney Creek* CA-9
Denney Creek—*stream* CA-9
Denney Creek—*stream* KY-4
Denney Gap—*gap* KY-4
Denney Hollow—*valley* (2) KY-4
Denney Hollow Sch—*school* KY-4
Denneys Post Office (historical)—*building* TN-4
Denney Trail—*trail* WA-9
Dennick Lake—*lake* ID-8
Dennie Ahl Hill—*summit* WA-9
Dennie Hollow—*valley* MO-7
*Dennie Kiln* AL-4
**Dennies Crossing**—*pop pl* NY-2
**Dennies Hollow**—*pop pl* NY-2
Dennin Brook—*stream* ME-1
Dennin Cem—*cemetery* OH-6
Denning—*locale* NY-2
Denning—*locale* TX-5
**Denning**—*pop pl* AR-4
Denning Brook—*stream* ME-1
Denning Cem—*cemetery* AR-4
Denning Cem—*cemetery* IL-6
Denning Creek—*stream* AR-4
Denning Creek—*stream* NY-2
Denning Hill—*summit* NY-2
Denning Hollow—*valley* MO-7
Denning Point—*cape* NY-2
Dennings—*locale* MD-2
Denning Spring—*spring* CA-9
Denning Spring—*spring* OR-9
Denning Spring—*spring* TX-5
*Denningsville* PA-2
**Denning (Town of)**—*pop pl* NY-2
**Denning (Township of)**—*pop pl* IL-6
Dennin Swamp—*swamp* ME-1
*Dennis* MS-4
Dennis—*locale* (2) GA-3
Dennis—*locale* KS-7
Dennis—*locale* KY-4
Dennis—*locale* OK-5
Dennis—*locale* OR-9
Dennis—*locale* SD-7
Dennis—*locale* UT-8
Dennis—*locale* WV-2
**Dennis**—*pop pl* GA-3
**Dennis**—*pop pl* MA-1
**Dennis**—*pop pl* MS-4
**Dennis**—*pop pl* MT-8
**Dennis**—*pop pl* NC-3
**Dennis**—*pop pl* TX-5
Dennis, Foster S., House—*hist pl* AZ-5
Dennis, James, House—*hist pl* RI-1
Dennis, Josiah, House—*hist pl* MA-1
**Dennis Acres**—*pop pl* MO-7
Dennis Airp—*airport* IN-6
Dennis and State Streets Hist Dist—*hist pl* MI-6
Dennis and State Streets Hist Dist (Boundary Increase)—*hist pl* MI-6
Dennis Ave Sch—*school* MD-2
Dennis Bay—*bay* NC-3
Dennis Bay Hist Dist—*hist pl* VI-3
*Dennis Bear Creek Bridge* MS-4
Dennis Best Lots—*locale* NC-3
Dennis Blackledge Cem—*cemetery* MS-4
Dennis Branch—*stream* MS-4
Dennis Branch—*stream* NC-3
Dennis Branch—*stream* TN-4
Dennis Branch—*stream* TX-5
Dennis Bridge—*bridge* MS-4
Dennis Brook—*stream* ME-1
Dennis Canyon—*valley* CA-9
Dennis Canyon—*valley* CO-8
Dennis Cem—*cemetery* AR-4
Dennis Cem—*cemetery* ME-1
Dennis Cem—*cemetery* MI-6
Dennis Cem—*cemetery* MS-4
Dennis Cem—*cemetery* (2) MO-7
Dennis Cem—*cemetery* OH-6
Dennis Cem—*cemetery* PA-2
Dennis Cem—*cemetery* (2) TN-4
Dennis Cem—*cemetery* TX-5
Dennis Cem—*cemetery* UT-8
Dennis Ch—*church* KY-4
Dennis Ch—*church* MO-7
Dennis Ch—*church* NC-3
Dennis Ch—*church* TX-5
Dennis Chapel—*church* KY-4
Dennis Chapel—*church* OH-6
Dennis Chapel—*church* TX-5
Dennis Chapel (historical)—*church* MS-4

Dennis Corners—*locale* NY-2
Dennis Cove—*locale* TN-4
Dennis Cove Sch (historical)—*school* TN-4
Dennis-Coxetter House—*hist pl* FL-3
*Dennis Creek* MT-8
*Dennis Creek* NJ-2
Dennis Creek—*stream* (3) AL-4
Dennis Creek—*stream* (2) AK-9
Dennis Creek—*stream* AZ-5
Dennis Creek—*stream* FL-3
Dennis Creek—*stream* GA-3
Dennis Creek—*stream* (2) ID-8
Dennis Creek—*stream* (2) MD-2
Dennis Creek—*stream* MI-6
Dennis Creek—*stream* NJ-2
Dennis Creek—*stream* NY-2
Dennis Creek—*stream* NC-3
Dennis Creek—*stream* (2) OR-9
Dennis Creek—*stream* PA-2
Dennis Creek Fish and Wildlife Mngmt Area—*park* NJ-2
*Dennis Crossroads* SC-3
Dennis Crossroads—*locale* MS-4
Dennis David Worth JHS—*school* IN-6
Dennis Ditch—*canal* IN-6
Dennis Ditch—*canal* (2) OH-6
Dennises Well—*well* UT-8
Dennis Flats—*flat* NV-8
Dennis Flats Pipeline—*locale* NV-8
Dennis Flats Well—*well* NV-8
Dennis Fork—*stream* WV-2
Dennis Gap—*gap* GA-3
Dennis Hill—*summit* CT-1
Dennis Hill—*summit* ME-1
Dennis Hill—*summit* (2) NY-2
Dennis Hill—*summit* PA-2
Dennis Hill—*summit* UT-8
Dennis Hill Cem—*cemetery* ME-1
Dennis Hill State Park—*park* CT-1
Dennis (historical)—*locale* IA-7
Dennis (historical P.O.)—*locale* IA-7
Dennis Hollow—*valley* IL-6
Dennis Hollow—*valley* UT-8
Dennis Hotel—*hist pl* FL-3
*Dennis HS* SC-3
Dennis HS—*school* SC-3
Dennis Hump—*cliff* CO-8
Dennis Klippel Ditch—*canal* IN-6
Dennis Knob—*summit* ID-8
*Dennis Lake* MI-6
Dennis Lake—*lake* AL-4
Dennis Lake—*lake* AK-9
Dennis Lake—*lake* (2) NE-7
Dennis Lake—*lake* OR-9
Dennis Lake—*lake* WY-8
Dennis Lakes—*lake* ID-8
Dennis Landing—*locale* MS-4
Dennis Lookout Tower—*locale* MS-4
**Dennis Manor**—*pop pl* AK-9
Dennis Memorial Camp—*locale* NJ-2
Dennis Methodist Ch—*church* MS-4
*Dennis Mills* PA-2
Dennis Mills—*locale* LA-4
Dennis Mills—*locale* PA-2
Dennis Mills (historical)—*locale* AL-4
Dennis Mtn—*summit* ID-8
Dennis Murphy Hollow—*valley* IN-6
*Dennison* TX-5
Dennison—*locale* AZ-5
**Dennison**—*pop pl* IL-6
**Dennison**—*pop pl* LA-4
**Dennison**—*pop pl* MI-6
**Dennison**—*pop pl* MN-6
**Dennison**—*pop pl* OH-6
Dennis O'Nan Ditch—*canal* KY-4
Dennison Bog—*swamp* ME-1
Dennison Bottoms—*bend* AR-4
Dennison Canyon—*valley* UT-8
Dennison Cap—*summit* WY-8
Dennison Cem—*cemetery* NE-7
Dennison Cem—*cemetery* NY-2
Dennison Cem—*cemetery* OH-6
Dennison Ch—*church* WV-2
**Dennison Corners**—*pop pl* (2) NY-2
Dennison Creek—*stream* NY-2
Dennison Ditch—*stream* OH-6
Dennison Ferry—*locale* KY-4
Dennison Fork—*stream* AK-9
Dennison Fork—*stream* PA-2
Dennison Fork—*stream* WV-2
**Dennison Heights**—*pop pl* AR-4
Dennison Hill—*summit* MA-1
Dennison Hill—*summit* NY-2
Dennison Hollow—*valley* IL-6
Dennison Hollow—*valley* OK-5
Dennison Hollow—*valley* PA-2
Dennison Interchange—*crossing* AZ-5
Dennison Mtn—*summit* CA-9
Dennison Park—*park* CA-9
Dennison Peak—*summit* CA-9
Dennison Picnic Ground—*park* AZ-5
Dennison Place—*locale* NM-5
Dennison Playground—*park* MA-1
Dennison Point—*cape* ME-1
Dennison Pond—*lake* NH-1
Dennison Portage—*locale* ME-1
Dennison Ridge—*ridge* CA-9
Dennison Ridge—*ridge* IN-6
Dennison Rsvr—*reservoir* OR-9
Dennison Run—*stream* (2) PA-2
Dennison Run—*stream* WV-2
Dennison Sch—*school* NE-7
Dennison Sch—*school* WI-6
*Dennisons Run* PA-2
Dennison Swamp—*swamp* WI-6
Dennison Tank—*reservoir* NM-5
**Dennison (Township of)**—*pop pl* PA-2
Dennison Well—*well* AZ-5
Dennison Well—*well* NM-5
**Dennis Park**—*pop pl* CA-9
Dennis Pass—*gut* LA-4
Dennis Pines Golf Club—*locale* MA-1
Dennis Point—*cape* MD-2
Dennis Pond—*lake* MA-1
Dennis Pond—*lake* VT-1
Dennis Pond—*reservoir* CT-1
Dennis Pond Brook—*stream* VT-1
*Dennisport* MA-1
**Dennis Port**—*pop pl* MA-1
Dennis Ranch—*locale* CA-9
Dennis Ranch—*locale* NE-7
Dennis Ranch—*locale* NM-5
Dennis Ranch—*locale* TX-5
Dennis Revetment—*levee* MS-4
Dennis Ridge—*ridge* ID-8
Dennis Ridge—*ridge* TN-4
Dennis Run—*stream* OH-6
Dennis Run—*stream* (2) PA-2
Dennis Sch—*school* (2) IL-6
Dennis Sch—*school* MS-4
Dennis Sch—*school* OH-6
Dennis Sch—*school* SC-3
Dennis Sch (historical)—*school* PA-2
*Dennis School* IN-6
Dennis Settlement—*locale* MS-4
Dennis Shoal—*bar* WA-9
Dennis Slough—*canal* AR-4
Dennis Slough—*gut* IL-6
Dennis Spring—*spring* AZ-5
Dennis Spring—*spring* CA-9
Dennis Tank—*reservoir* AZ-5
Dennis the Menace Park—*park* CA-9
Dennis The Menace Park—*park* TX-5
Denniston—*locale* KY-4
Denniston—*locale* NY-2
Denniston—*locale* VA-3
Denniston Cem—*cemetery* KY-4
Denniston Creek—*stream* CA-9
Denniston House—*hist pl* WI-6
Denniston Park—*park* OK-5
**Dennistown**—*pop pl* ME-1
**Dennis (Town of)**—*pop pl* MA-1
Dennistown Sch—*school* MS-4
**Dennis (Township of)**—*pop pl* NJ-2
**Dennisville**—*pop pl* NJ-2
Dennisville Hist Dist—*hist pl* NJ-2
Dennis Wagner Ditch—*canal* IN-6
Dennis Weaver Park—*park* AZ-5
Dennitt Brook—*stream* ME-1
Denn John MS—*school* FL-3
Dennson Branch—*stream* GA-3
*Denntt Creek* ID-8
*Denny* ND-7
Denny—*locale* CA-9
Denny—*locale* IL-6
Denny—*locale* OK-5
Denny—*locale* PA-2
**Denny**—*pop pl* NC-3
**Denny**—*pop pl* SC-3
**Denny**—*pop pl* TX-5
Denny, Professor Charles O., House—*hist pl* IA-7
Denny, T. H., House—*hist pl* DE-2
Denny Bldg—*building* NC-3
Denny Bluff—*cliff* TN-4
Denny Branch—*stream* GA-3
Denny Branch—*stream* KS-7
Denny Branch—*stream* KY-4
Denny Branch—*stream* MS-4
Denny Branch—*stream* TN-4
Denny Brook—*stream* MA-1
Denny Cave—*cave* TN-4
Denny Cem—*cemetery* AR-4
Denny Cem—*cemetery* IN-6
Denny Cem—*cemetery* IA-7
Denny Cem—*cemetery* NE-7
Denny Cem—*cemetery* NC-3
Denny Cem—*cemetery* OK-5
Denny Cem—*cemetery* PA-2
Denny Cem—*cemetery* (2) TN-4
Denny Ch—*church* AR-4
Denny Chimes—*other* AL-4
Denny Corner—*locale* SC-3
**Denny Corner**—*pop pl* IN-6
Denny Cove—*valley* TN-4
Denny Cove Branch—*stream* TN-4
**Denny Creek**—*pop pl* WA-9
Denny Creek—*stream* AK-9
Denny Creek—*stream* (2) CA-9
Denny Creek—*stream* CO-8
Denny Creek—*stream* GA-3
Denny Creek—*stream* ID-8
Denny Creek—*stream* MT-8
Denny Creek—*stream* OH-6
Denny Creek—*stream* (3) OR-9
Denny Creek—*stream* WA-9
**Denny Creek (Forest Service Camp Ground)**—*pop pl* WA-9
Denny Creek Historic Monument—*other* OR-9
*Denny Crossroads* SC-3
Denny Draw—*valley* WY-8
Denny Dunn Park—*park* AZ-5
Denny Ferry (historical)—*crossing* TN-4
Denny Ferry (historical)—*locale* AL-4
Denny Field—*park* IN-6
Denny Flat—*flat* OR-9
Denny Ford—*locale* AR-4
Denny Ford (historical)—*crossing* TN-4
Denny Guard Station—*locale* CA-9
Denny Gulch—*valley* CO-8
Denny Hill—*summit* MA-1
Denny Hill—*summit* NH-1
Denny Hill—*summit* NM-5
Denny Hill Ch—*church* TN-4
**Denny Hills (subdivision)**—*pop pl* TN-4
**Denny (historical)**—*pop pl* OR-9
Denny Hollow—*valley* (2) MO-7
Denny Hollow—*valley* NC-3
*Denny Horn* WA-9
Denny JHS—*school* WA-9
Denny Knob—*summit* KY-4
Denny Lake—*lake* CO-8
Denny Lake—*lake* MI-6
Denny Lake—*lake* WA-9
Denny Lake—*lake* WI-6
Denny Lake—*reservoir* AL-4
Denny Lake—*reservoir* CO-8
Denny Mill Creek—*stream* MS-4
*Denny Mills* PA-2
*Denny Mountain* TN-4
Denny Mountian—*summit* WA-9
Denny Mtn—*summit* AZ-5
Denny Mtn—*summit* AR-4
Denny Mtn—*summit* TX-5
Denny Mtn—*summit* WA-9
Denny Park—*park* CO-8
Denny Park—*park* WA-9
Denny Place—*hist pl* KY-4
Denny Pond—*lake* ME-1
Denny Pond—*lake* OR-9
Denny Ranch—*locale* NM-5
Denny Reed Point—*cape* ME-1
Denny Ridge—*ridge* KY-4
Denny Ridge—*ridge* OK-5
Denny Run—*stream* MO-7
Dennys—*uninc pl* VA-3
Dennys Bay—*bay* ME-1
Denny Sch—*school* IL-6
Denny Sch—*school* MO-7
Denny Sch—*school* OR-9
Denny Sch (historical)—*school* PA-2
**Dennys Corners**—*pop pl* PA-2
*Dennys Creek* NJ-2
*Dennys Crossroads* SC-3
Denny Seminary Ch—*church* TN-4
Denny Seminary (historical)—*school* TN-4
Dennys Gulch—*valley* AK-9
**Dennys Mill**—*pop pl* PA-2
**Dennys Mills**—*pop pl* PA-2
Denny Spring—*spring* NM-5
Denny Spring—*spring* OR-9
Denny Spring Branch—*stream* AR-4
Denny Spring Branch—*stream* MO-7
Dennys Ranch—*locale* AZ-5
Dennys River—*stream* ME-1
*Dennys Store* NC-3
**Dennys Store**—*pop pl* NC-3
Dennys Store (historical)—*locale* AL-4
*Denny Stadium* AL-4
**Denny Store**—*pop pl* NC-3
**Dennysville**—*pop pl* ME-1
Dennysville Cem—*cemetery* ME-1
Dennysville Hist Dist—*hist pl* ME-1
Dennysville Station—*locale* ME-1
**Dennysville (Town of)**—*pop pl* ME-1
**Denny Terrace**—*pop pl* SC-3
*Denny Tooth* WA-9
Dennytown—*locale* NY-2
*Dennyville* MA-1
Dennyville Ch—*church* NC-3
Denny Waite Bridge (historical)—*bridge* TN-4
Denny Walte Cave—*cave* TN-4
Deno Creek—*stream* MT-8
*Denois Creek* IN-6
De Nolda, Lake—*lake* CO-8
Denomie Creek—*stream* MI-6
Denomie Creek—*stream* WI-6
Denom Sch—*school* NY-2
Denonville JHS—*school* NY-2
Denoon—*uninc pl* WI-6
Denoon, Lake—*lake* WI-6
Denoon Sch—*school* WI-6
Deno Sch—*school* WA-9
De-No-To Cultural District—*hist pl* CA-9
**Denova**—*pop pl* IA-7
DeNova Club—*other* CA-9
**Denoya**—*pop pl* OK-5
Den Ranch—*locale* NE-7
Den Ridge—*ridge* NC-3
Denrock—*locale* IL-6
Den Run—*stream* WV-2
Densch Cem—*cemetery* IL-6
Dense Creek—*stream* MT-8
Densford Bar—*bar* TN-4
Densford Dikes—*levee* TN-4
Dens Ford Ditch—*canal* IN-6
Densford Revetment—*levee* TN-4
Denshore Gully—*valley* NY-2
*Densinyama* MH-9
**Densley Estates Subdivision**—*pop pl* UT-8
Denslow Drain—*canal* MI-6
Denslow Lake—*lake* AK-9
Denslow Sch (historical)—*school* MO-7
**Densmore**—*pop pl* KS-7
Densmore Bay—*bay* NY-2
Densmore Bay Ch—*church* NY-2
Densmore Brook—*stream* VT-1
Densmore Cem—*cemetery* MI-6
Densmore Cem—*cemetery* VT-1
Densmore Creek—*stream* ID-8
Densmore Creek—*stream* NY-2
Densmore Hill—*summit* VT-1
Densmore Lake—*lake* IA-7
Densmore Methodist Church of the Thousand Islands—*hist pl* NY-2
Densmore Mine—*mine* CA-9
Densmore Mtn—*summit* VT-1
Densmore Pond—*lake* NY-2
Densmore Sch—*school* MI-6
Denson—*locale* AL-4
**Denson**—*pop pl* LA-4
**Denson**—*pop pl* OH-6
Denson, Mount—*summit* AK-9
Denson, William H., House—*hist pl* GA-3
Denson Branch—*stream* TX-5
Denson Canyon—*valley* OR-9
*Denson Cem* TN-4
Denson Cem—*cemetery* IL-6
Denson Cem—*cemetery* (2) TN-4
Denson Cem—*cemetery* TX-5
Denson Cove—*basin* TN-4
Denson Creek—*stream* TX-5
Denson Dock Creek—*stream* MD-2
Denson Island—*island* TN-4
Denson Island (historical)—*island* AL-4
Denson Marsh—*swamp* GA-3
Denson Ranch—*locale* MT-8
Densons Creek—*stream* NC-3
Densons Landing—*locale* TN-4
Densons Landing Post Office (historical)—*building* TN-4
**Denson Spring**—*pop pl* TX-5
Den Spring—*spring* WY-8
*Den Stream* MA-1
*Dent* AL-4
Dent—*locale* CO-8
Dent—*locale* ID-8
Dent—*locale* WV-2
**Dent**—*pop pl* KY-4
**Dent**—*pop pl* MN-6
**Dent**—*pop pl* OH-6
**Dent Acres**—*pop pl* TN-4
Dent and Sayer Ranch (historical)—*locale* AZ-5
Dent and Sayer Tank—*reservoir* (2) AZ-5
Dentan Ranch—*locale* CO-8
Dentaybow Lookout Tower—*locale* MN-6
Dent Branch—*stream* MO-7
Dent Bridge—*bridge* ID-8
Dent Bridge—*bridge* MT-8
Dent Cem—*cemetery* AR-4
Dent Cem—*cemetery* (2) MO-7
Dent Cem—*cemetery* VA-3
**Dent County**—*pop pl* MO-7
Dent County Courthouse—*hist pl* MO-7
Dent County Fairground—*locale* MO-7
Dent County Farm—*locale* MO-7
Dent Creek—*stream* (2) ID-8
Dent Creek—*stream* (2) OR-9
Dent Creek—*stream* WI-6
*Dentdale* NJ-2
Dent Ditch—*canal* OH-6
Dentel Lake—*lake* MI-6
Denten Cem—*cemetery* OK-5
Denten Creek—*stream* CA-9
Dentene Creek—*stream* ID-8
Dent Ford—*locale* MO-7
Dent Fork—*stream* WV-2
Dent Hardware Company Factory Complex—*hist pl* PA-2
Dentist Parlor Ridge—*ridge* ID-8
Dent Lake—*lake* (2) MN-6
Dent Lake—*lake* MS-4
Dent Mine—*mine* CA-9
Dent Mtn—*summit* WA-9
*Denton* ID-8
Denton—*locale* AR-4
Denton—*locale* KY-4
Denton—*locale* MS-4
Denton—*locale* MO-7
Denton—*locale* OK-5
Denton—*locale* TX-5
**Denton**—*pop pl* GA-3
**Denton**—*pop pl* KS-7
**Denton**—*pop pl* MD-2
**Denton**—*pop pl* (2) MI-6
**Denton**—*pop pl* MO-7
**Denton**—*pop pl* MT-8
**Denton**—*pop pl* NE-7
**Denton**—*pop pl* NY-2
**Denton**—*pop pl* NC-3
**Denton**—*pop pl* PA-2
**Denton**—*pop pl* TN-4
**Denton**—*pop pl* TX-5
Denton, George W., House—*hist pl* NY-2
Denton, Lake—*lake* FL-3
**Denton Acres (subdivision)**—*pop pl* AL-4
Denton Airp—*airport* NC-3
Denton Armory—*hist pl* MD-2
Denton Ave Sch—*school* NY-2
Denton Baptist Ch—*church* TN-4
Denton Branch—*stream* AL-4
Denton Branch—*stream* KY-4
*Denton Brook* GA-3
Denton Camp—*locale* NM-5
Denton Canyon—*valley* CO-8
Denton Canyon—*valley* NV-8
Denton (CCD)—*cens area* GA-3
Denton (CCD)—*cens area* TX-5
Denton Cem—*cemetery* AR-4
Denton Cem—*cemetery* KS-7
Denton Cem—*cemetery* (2) KY-4
Denton Cem—*cemetery* MI-6
Denton Cem—*cemetery* MS-4
Denton Cem—*cemetery* OK-5
Denton Cem—*cemetery* (4) TN-4
Denton Cem—*cemetery* TX-5
Denton Cem—*cemetery* (3) VA-3
*Denton Cemetery* MO-7
Denton Ch—*church* OK-5
Denton Ch—*church* TX-5
Denton Clark Estate Dam—*dam* NJ-2
*Denton Community* TX-5
Denton Corners—*locale* NY-2
Denton Country Club—*other* TX-5
**Denton (County)**—*pop pl* TX-5
Denton County Courthouse—*hist pl* TX-5
Denton Cove—*valley* AR-4
Denton Cove—*valley* NC-3
Denton Creek—*stream* AL-4
Denton Creek—*stream* (2) AR-4
Denton Creek—*stream* GA-3
Denton Creek—*stream* (4) MI-6
Denton Creek—*stream* MO-7
Denton Creek—*stream* NY-2
Denton Creek—*stream* PA-2
Denton Creek—*stream* (7) TX-5
Denton Creek Cem—*cemetery* TX-5
Denton Creek Flooding—*reservoir* MI-6
**Denton Crossroads**—*pop pl* TN-4
*Denton Ditch* IN-6
Denton Ditch—*canal* IN-6
Denton Elem Sch—*school* NC-3
Denton Falls—*falls* NY-2
*Denton Gap* TN-4
Denton Gulch—*valley* MT-8
Denton Hill—*locale* PA-2
**Denton Hills**—*pop pl* NY-2
Denton Hill (ski area)—*locale* PA-2
Denton Hill State Park—*park* PA-2
Denton Hist Dist—*hist pl* MD-2
Denton (historical)—*locale* AL-4
Denton (historical)—*locale* SD-7
*Denton Hollow* TN-4
Denton Hollow—*valley* AL-4
Denton Hollow—*valley* OH-6
Denton Hollow—*valley* (2) TN-4
Denton Hollow—*valley* TX-5
Denton Hollow Cem—*cemetery* AL-4
Denton House—*hist pl* MD-2
Denton HS—*school* NC-3
Dentonia—*locale* KS-7
Dentonio Sch—*school* TX-5
Denton Island—*island* IL-6
Denton Island—*locale* AR-4
Denton Island Cem—*cemetery* AR-4
Denton Knob—*summit* TN-4
Denton Lake—*lake* (3) MI-6
Denton Lake—*lake* (2) WI-6
Denton Lake—*reservoir* NY-2
Denton L 7 Ranch—*locale* NM-5
**Denton Manor (subdivision)**—*pop pl* DE-2
Denton Marsh—*swamp* WA-9
**Denton-Mcworter Addition**—*pop pl* KS-7
Denton Mills (historical)—*locale* TN-4
**Denton Mills (subdivision)**—*pop pl* DE-2
Denton Mound and Village Archeol Site—*hist pl* MO-7
Denton Mtn—*summit* MT-8
Denton Oil Field—*other* NM-5
Denton Park—*park* AL-4
Denton Park—*park* (2) MI-6
Denton Plaza Shop Ctr—*locale* MS-4
*Denton Presbyterian Church* SD-7
Denton Ranch—*locale* NE-7
Denton Ranch (The Buzzard Roost)—*locale* NM-5
Denton Rsvr—*reservoir* WY-8
Denton Run—*stream* MD-2
Dentons—*locale* NC-3
Dentons Camp Branch—*stream* AL-4
Denton Sch—*school* AR-4
Denton Sch—*school* (2) TX-5
Dentons Chapel—*church* NC-3
Denton Sch (historical)—*school* (2) TN-4
Dentons Corner—*locale* VA-3
Denton Site—*hist pl* MS-4
Denton Slough—*gut* ID-8
Dentons Point—*cape* MT-8
**Dentons Point**—*pop pl* MT-8
Denton Spring—*spring* (2) AL-4
Denton Spring—*spring* CO-8
Denton Spring—*spring* ID-8
Denton Spring—*spring* TN-4
Dentons Shoals—*bar* TN-4
Denton State Sch—*school* TX-5
Denton Summit—*gap* NV-8
Denton Tank—*reservoir* NM-5
**Denton Terrace**—*pop pl* PA-2
**Dentontown**—*pop pl* MS-4
Denton (Township of)—*fmr MCD* AR-4
**Denton (Township of)**—*pop pl* MI-6
Denton Trail—*trail* AZ-5
Denton Trough Spring—*spring* AZ-5
Denton Valley—*basin* VA-3
Denton Valley Branch—*stream* TX-5
Denton Valley Ch—*church* VA-3
Denton Valley School (Abandoned)—*locale* TX-5
*Dentonville* KS-7
*Dentonville* SD-7
Dentonville—*locale* OK-5
Denton Windmills—*locale* NM-5
**Denton Woods (trailer park)**—*pop pl* DE-2
Dent-Phelps R-3 Sch—*school* MO-7
Dent Point—*cape* AK-9
Dent Pond Branch—*stream* GA-3
*Dent Post Office* AL-4
Dent Ranch—*locale* NM-5
Dent Ridge—*ridge* ID-8
Dent Ridge—*ridge* OH-6
*Dents* MD-2
*Dents* SC-3
Dents Bridge—*bridge* KY-4
Dent Sch—*school* DC-2
Dents Channel—*channel* FL-3
Dents Chapel—*church* GA-3
*Dents Creek* GA-3
*Dents (Dentsville)* SC-3
Dent Spring—*spring* OR-9
Dent Spur—*locale* KS-7
**Dents Run**—*pop pl* PA-2
Dents Run—*stream* PA-2
Dents Run—*stream* (2) WV-2
Dents Run Ch—*church* WV-2
Dents Run Covered Bridge—*hist pl* WV-2
**Dentsville**—*pop pl* MD-2
**Dentsville**—*pop pl* SC-3
Dentsville Bridge—*bridge* MD-2
Dentsville (Dents)—*CDP* SC-3
Dent Tank—*reservoir* (2) AZ-5
**Dent Terrace**—*pop pl* LA-4
*Dent Township* KS-7
Dent Township—*civil* MO-7
Dent (Township of)—*fmr MCD* (2) AR-4
Dent Union Sch—*school* CA-9
Dentville—*locale* TN-4
**Dentville**—*pop pl* MS-4
Dentville Post Office (historical)—*building* MS-4
Dentville Post Office (historical)—*building* TN-4
Dent Windmill—*locale* NM-5
*Dentzler* MS-4
Dentzler Sch—*school* OH-6
Denude Lake—*lake* OR-9
Denuser Cem—*cemetery* MO-7
*Denver* SD-7
*Denver* TN-4
Denver—*locale* AL-4
Denver—*locale* GA-3
Denver—*locale* ID-8
Denver—*locale* KY-4
Denver—*locale* NY-2
**Denver**—*pop pl* AR-4
**Denver**—*pop pl* CO-8
**Denver**—*pop pl* FL-3
**Denver**—*pop pl* IL-6
**Denver**—*pop pl* IN-6
**Denver**—*pop pl* IA-7
**Denver**—*pop pl* MO-7
**Denver**—*pop pl* NC-3
**Denver**—*pop pl* OH-6
**Denver**—*pop pl* OK-5
**Denver**—*pop pl* PA-2
**Denver**—*pop pl* SC-3
**Denver**—*pop pl* (2) TN-4
**Denver**—*pop pl* WV-2
Denver, Boulder and Western Railway Hist Dist—*hist pl* CO-8
Denver, Northwestern and Pacific Railway Hist Dist—*hist pl* CO-8
Denver and Rio Grande Depot—*hist pl* CO-8
Denver and Rio Grande Lime Kiln—*hist pl* UT-8
Denver and Rio Grande RR Station—*hist pl* UT-8
Denver and Rio Grande Western Railway Depot—*hist pl* NM-5
Denver and Rio Grande Western RR Business Car No. 101—*hist pl* WA-9
Denver Athletic Club—*hist pl* CO-8
Denver Ave Sch—*school* TX-5
**Denver (Bellton)**—*pop pl* WV-2
Denver Borough—*civil* PA-2
Denver Bridge—*bridge* CO-8
Denver Brook—*stream* ME-1
Denver Cem—*cemetery* AR-4
Denver Cem—*cemetery* ID-8
Denver Cem—*cemetery* IL-6
Denver Cem—*cemetery* OK-5
Denver Cem—*cemetery* TX-5
Denver Cem—*cemetery* WV-2
Denver Ch—*church* AL-4
Denver Childrens Home—*other* CO-8
Denver Church Campground—*locale* CA-9
**Denver City**—*pop pl* TX-5
Denver City Cable Railway Bldg—*hist pl* CO-8
Denver City (CCD)—*cens area* TX-5
Denver City Mine—*mine* CO-8
Denver City Railway Company Bldg—*hist pl* CO-8
**Denver City Subdivision**—*pop pl* UT-8
Denver Colony Lateral—*canal* CO-8
Denver Country Club—*other* CO-8
*Denver County* CO-8
*Denver Creek* IA-7
Denver Creek—*stream* AK-9
Denver Creek—*stream* CO-8
Denver Creek—*stream* ID-8
Denver Creek Campground—*locale* CO-8
Denver Dock—*locale* TN-4
Denver-Douglas Landing Strip—*airport* CO-8
Denver Dry Goods Company Bldg—*hist pl* CO-8
Denver Elem Sch—*school* AZ-5
Denver Elevator-Grain Elevator—*hist pl* CO-8
Denver Federal Center—*civil* CO-8
Denver General Hosp—*hospital* CO-8
Denver Glacier—*glacier* AK-9
Denver Harbor—*uninc pl* TX-5
Denver Harbor Park—*park* TX-5
Denver Heights—*locale* WV-2
Denver Heights Park—*park* TX-5
Denver Hill—*summit* AZ-5
Denver Hill—*summit* CO-8
**Denver (historical)**—*pop pl* OR-9
Denver-Hudson Canal—*canal* CO-8
Denver Jake Dam—*dam* WY-8
Denver Jake Draw—*valley* WY-8
Denver Junction (historical)—*locale* IA-7
Denver Lake—*reservoir* CO-8
**Denver Merchandise Mart**—*pop pl* CO-8
Denver Mine—*mine* NV-8
Denver Mint—*hist pl* CO-8
Denver Mountain Parks Emergency HQ—*other* CO-8
Denver Mountain Park Site—*park* CO-8
Denver Municipal Aqueduct—*canal* CO-8
*Denver Neres Canal* CO-8
Denver Pass—*gap* CO-8
Denver Place Sch—*school* OH-6
**Denver Place (subdivision)**—*pop pl* UT-8
Denver Point—*cape* OR-9
*Denver Post Office* SD-7
Denver Post Office—*building* TN-4
Denver Post Office (historical)—*building* MS-4
Denver Road Park—*park* TN-4
Denver Sch—*school* IL-6
Denver Sch—*school* MI-6
Denver Sch—*school* NY-2
Denver Sch—*school* ND-7
Denver Sch—*school* TN-4
Denver Sch—*school* TX-5
Denver Shaft—*mine* NM-5
Denvers Prong—*stream* MT-8
Denver Tank—*reservoir* TX-5
Denver Technological Center—*school* CO-8
Denverton—*locale* CA-9
Denverton Creek—*stream* CA-9
Denverton Slough—*stream* CA-9
**Denver Township**—*pop pl* NE-7
**Denver Township**—*pop pl* ND-7
**Denver Township**—*pop pl* SD-7
**Denver (Township of)**—*pop pl* IL-6
**Denver (Township of)**—*pop pl* (2) MI-6
**Denver (Township of)**—*pop pl* MN-6
Denver Tunnel—*tunnel* CO-8
Denver Union Stockyard—*other* CO-8
Denver University Research Institute—*other* CO-8
*Denville* NJ-2
**Denville**—*pop pl* NJ-2
**Denville (Township of)**—*pop pl* NJ-2
Denwiddie Bayou—*stream* TX-5
Denwiddie Ch of Christ—*church* MS-4
Den Williams Spring—*spring* WA-9
**Denwood**—*pop pl* AR-4
Denworth—*locale* TX-5
Deny—*uninc pl* TX-5
**Denzer**—*pop pl* WI-6
Denzer Bridge—*locale* OR-9
**Denzer (historical)**—*pop pl* OR-9
Denzer Lake—*lake* MI-6
*Denzer Range* OR-9
Denzer Ridge—*ridge* OR-9
*Deo Creek* OR-9
**Deodate**—*pop pl* PA-2
*Deonkook Hill* MA-1
*Deonkook Mtn* MA-1
Deon Lake—*lake* FL-3
Deora—*locale* CO-8
*De Orvilles Head* ME-1
De Osso Sch—*school* TX-5
Deovolente—*locale* MS-4
Deovolente Sch—*school* MS-4
Deowongo Island—*island* NY-2
DePadua HS—*school* WI-6
De Paoli Canyon—*valley* NV-8
Depaolo JHS—*school* CT-1
Departee Creek—*stream* AR-4
Departee (Township of)—*fmr MCD* AR-4
Departmental Auditorium—*building* DC-2
Department of Agriculture Administration Bldg—*building* DC-2
Department of Agriculture Bldg—*building* DC-2
Department of Agriculture Experimental Area—*area* NM-5
Department of Agriculture Extensible Bldg—*building* DC-2
Department of Agriculture South Bldg—*building* DC-2
Department of Commerce Bldg—*building* DC-2
Department of Conservation Training Sch—*school* MI-6
Department of Corrections Pre-Release Center—*building* MA-1
Department of Corrections Youth Camp No 2—*locale* MN-6
Department of Game Fish Parks Dam—*dam* (2) SD-7

Department of Health and Human Services Bldg—*building* ... DC-2
Department of Health Indian Hosp—*hospital* ... AZ-5
Department of Health Rehabilative Services—*building* ... FL-3
Department of Housing and Urban Development—*building* ... DC-2
Department of Justice Bldg—*building* ... DC-2
Department of Labor Bldg—*building* ... DC-2
Department of State Bldg—*building* ... DC-2
Department of the Interior Bldg—*building* ... DC-2
Department of the Interior South Bldg—*building* ... DC-2
Department of the Treasury Bldg—*building* ... DC-2
Department Of Transportation—*airport* ... NJ-2
Department of Transportation—*building* ... DC-2
Depas Creek—*stream* ... MI-6
De Pass—*gap* ... WY-8
Depaul Health Center Heliport—*airport* ... MO-7
DePaul Hosp—*hist pl* ... MO-7
DePaul Hosp—*hospital* ... LA-4
DePaul Hosp—*hospital* ... MO-7
DePaul Hosp—*hospital* ... WY-8
DePaul Institute—*school* ... PA-2
DePaul Sch of Northeast Florida—*school* ... FL-3
DePaul Univ—*school* ... IL-6
**Depauville**—*pop pl* ... NY-2
**Depauw**—*pop pl* ... IN-6
De Pauw Ch—*church* ... IN-6
*De Pauw Univ* ... IN-6
DePauw Univ—*school* ... IN-6
*Depaw* ... IN-6
Depe—*locale* ... FM-9
DePelchin Faith Home—*hist pl* ... TX-5
Dependency on Mulberry Creek—*hist pl* ... KY-4
**De Pere**—*pop pl* ... WI-6
De Pere Dam—*dam* ... WI-6
**De Pere (Town of)**—*pop pl* ... WI-6
Depew—*locale* ... OH-6
**Depew**—*pop pl* ... IA-7
**Depew**—*pop pl* ... NY-2
**Depew**—*pop pl* ... OK-5
**Depew Addition (subdivision)**—*pop pl* ... TN-4
Depew Chapel—*church* ... TN-4
Depew Chapel Cem—*cemetery* ... TN-4
Depew Creek—*stream* ... FL-3
Depew Creek—*stream* ... OR-9
Depew Island—*island* ... NJ-2
Depew Lake—*lake* ... IN-6
Depew-Lancaster Camp—*locale* ... NY-2
Depew Park—*park* ... NY-2
De Peyster—*locale* ... NY-2
**De Peyster (Town of)**—*pop pl* ... NY-2
Depler Park—*flat* ... CO-8
*Deplers Park* ... CO-8
Depler Springs—*locale* ... IL-6
*Deplymton* ... KY-4
*De Poe Bay* ... OR-9
Depoe Bay—*bay* ... OR-9
**Depoe Bay**—*pop pl* ... OR-9
Depoe Bay (CCD)—*cens area* ... OR-9
*Depoe Bay Creek* ... OR-9
Depoe Bay Creek—*stream* ... OR-9
Depoe Bay Wayside Ocean State Park—*park* ... OR-9
*Depoe Creek* ... OR-9
*Depoe Slough* ... OR-9
De Poo Hosp—*hospital* ... FL-3
DePorres Hosp—*hospital* ... AL-4
DePorres Sch—*school* ... OH-6
Deporres Sch—*school* ... SC-3
**Deport**—*pop pl* ... TX-5
Deport (CCD)—*cens area* ... TX-5
Deposit—*locale* ... AL-4
**Deposit**—*pop pl* ... NY-2
*Deposit Creek* ... AL-4
*Deposit Ferry* ... AL-4
Deposit Guarnty Bank Lake Dam—*dam* ... MS-4
**Deposit (historical)**—*pop pl* ... MS-4
Deposit Lake—*lake* ... MN-6
Deposit Landing (historical)—*locale* ... AL-4
Deposito Creek—*stream* ... NM-5
Deposit Post Office (historical)—*building* ... AL-4
Deposit Post Office (historical)—*building* ... TN-4
Deposit Rsvr—*reservoir* ... NY-2
**Deposit (Town of)**—*pop pl* ... NY-2
Depot—*hist pl* ... MS-4
**Depot**—*pop pl* ... OH-6
Depot Bar—*bar* ... ME-1
*Depot Bay* ... OR-9
Depot Branch—*stream* ... TN-4
Depot Brook—*stream* ... ME-1
Depot Brook—*stream* ... MA-1
Depot Brook—*stream* ... VT-1
Depot Business Buildings—*hist pl* ... GA-3
Depot Camp—*locale* ... ME-1
Depot Camp—*locale* ... NH-1
Depot-Compress Hist Dist—*hist pl* ... MS-4
Depot Covered Bridge—*hist pl* ... VT-1
*Depot Creek* ... CA-9
*Depot Creek* ... OR-9
Depot Creek—*stream* ... AR-4
Depot Creek—*stream* ... FL-3
Depot Creek—*stream* ... MS-4
Depot Creek—*stream* ... MT-8
Depot Creek—*stream* ... OR-9
Depot Creek—*stream* ... WA-9
Depot Drain—*canal* ... CA-9
Depot Flat—*flat* ... CA-9
Depot Hill—*summit* ... CT-1
Depot Hill—*summit* ... IN-6
Depot Hill—*summit* ... NY-2
Depot (historical)—*locale* ... AL-4
Depot Hollow—*valley* ... TN-4
Depot Hollow—*valley* ... WV-2
Depot Lake—*lake* ... ME-1
Depot Lake—*lake* ... WI-6
Depot Mtn—*summit* ... ME-1
Depot Pond—*lake* ... ME-1
Depot Pond—*lake* ... MA-1
Depot Pond—*reservoir* ... MD-2
Depot Pond—*reservoir* ... MA-1
Depot (RR name Navy) (McAlester Naval Ammun. Depot)—*other* ... OK-5
Depot Sch—*school* ... NY-2
Depot Slough—*stream* ... OR-9
Depot Square Hist Dist—*hist pl* ... VT-1
Depot Square Shop Ctr—*locale* ... TN-4
Depot Stream—*stream* ... ME-1
Depot Tank—*reservoir* ... AZ-5
**Depoy**—*pop pl* ... KY-4
Depoyster Ch (abandoned)—*church* ... MO-7
Depoyster Lake Dam—*dam* ... MS-4
Depoyster Sch (abandoned)—*school* ... MO-7
Deppe—*locale* ... NC-3
Deppe Landing Strip—*airport* ... NC-3
Depperschmidt Draw—*valley* ... KS-7
Deppmann Lake—*lake* ... MI-6
Deppy Creek—*stream* (2) ... OR-9
*Deprece Creek* ... MS-4
Depressed Lake—*lake* ... CA-9
Depression Canyon—*valley* ... AZ-5
Depression Mines—*mine* ... CO-8
Depression Pond—*lake* ... NY-2
Depression Rsvr—*reservoir* ... MT-8
Depression Storage Area Dam—*dam* ... PA-2
Depression Sump—*basin* ... OR-9
Depression Tank—*reservoir* ... AZ-5
De Prez Ditch—*canal* ... IN-6
De Priest, Oscar Stanton, House—*hist pl* ... IL-6
**DePriest Bend**—*pop pl* ... TN-4
**De Priest Bend**—*pop pl* ... TN-4
DePriest Branch—*stream* (2) ... TN-4
DePriest Branch Cave—*cave* ... TN-4
DePriest Cem—*cemetery* (2) ... AR-4
DePriest Cem—*cemetery* (2) ... TN-4
DePriest Ch—*church* ... MS-4
*DePriest Free Will Baptist Ch* ... MS-4
De Priest Hollow—*valley* ... MO-7
DePriest Hollow—*valley* ... TN-4
DePriest Sch—*school* ... TX-5
DePriest Sch (historical)—*school* ... TN-4
*Depriests Creek* ... MS-4
*Deptford* ... TN-4
**Deptford**—*pop pl* ... NJ-2
Deptford—*uninc pl* ... GA-3
**Deptford Terrace**—*pop pl* ... NJ-2
**Deptford (Township of)**—*pop pl* ... NJ-2
Deptmer Ditch—*canal* ... IN-6
Dept Of Natural Resources Helipad Heliport—*airport* ... WA-9
Depue—*locale* ... WV-2
**Depue**—*pop pl* ... IL-6
DePue, Grace Blair, House and Indian Museum—*hist pl* ... CA-9
Depue Cem—*cemetery* ... IL-6
Depue Cem—*cemetery* (2) ... WV-2
DePue Creek—*stream* ... WA-9
*Depue Ferry* ... PA-2
Depue Island—*island* ... PA-2
*Depue Junction* ... IL-6
Depue Lake—*lake* ... IL-6
Depue Ridge—*ridge* ... WV-2
Depue Run—*stream* ... OH-6
*Depui Ferry* ... PA-2
**Deputy**—*pop pl* ... IN-6
Deputy Elem Sch—*school* ... IN-6
Deputy Lookout Tower—*locale* ... IL-6
Depuy Creek—*stream* ... MT-8
Depuy Dam—*dam* ... ND-7
Depuy Dam Lake—*reservoir* ... ND-7
Depuy Ferry (historical)—*locale* ... PA-2
**De Queen**—*pop pl* ... AR-4
De Queen Dam—*dam* ... AR-4
*DeQueen Lake* ... AR-4
De Queen Lake—*reservoir* ... AR-4
*De Queen Rsvr* ... AR-4
De Queen Sch—*school* ... TX-5
**De Quincy**—*pop pl* ... LA-4
De Quincy Lookout Tower—*locale* ... LA-4
De Quincy Oil Field—*oilfield* ... LA-4
*Derak* ... FM-9
Deramus Park—*park* ... KS-7
De Ranch—*locale* ... WY-8
Deranof Island—*island* ... AK-9
Deranof Rock—*bar* ... AK-9
*Deray* ... TN-4
*De Ray Post Office* ... TN-4
Deray Post Office (historical)—*building* ... TN-4
Derbec Spring—*spring* ... CA-9
Derbey Lake—*reservoir* ... MO-7
Derbin Bay—*bay* ... AK-9
Derbin Island—*island* ... AK-9
Derbin Strait—*channel* ... AK-9
*Derbishire Gulch* ... CO-8
Derbonne, Bayou—*gut* ... LA-4
*Derby* ... CO-8
*Derby* ... VT-1
Derby—*locale* ... AL-4
Derby—*locale* (2) ... IL-6
Derby—*locale* ... KY-4
Derby—*locale* ... TX-5
**Derby**—*pop pl* ... CT-1
**Derby**—*pop pl* ... IN-6
**Derby**—*pop pl* ... IA-7
**Derby**—*pop pl* ... KS-7
**Derby**—*pop pl* ... ME-1
**Derby**—*pop pl* ... MI-6
**Derby**—*pop pl* ... MS-4
**Derby**—*pop pl* ... MO-7
**Derby**—*pop pl* ... NY-2
**Derby**—*pop pl* ... NC-3
**Derby**—*pop pl* ... OH-6
**Derby**—*pop pl* ... VA-3
Derby, H. W., Bldg—*hist pl* ... OH-6
Derby, James Daniel, House—*hist pl* ... CA-9
Derby, Lake—*lake* ... VT-1
Derby Acad—*school* ... MA-1
**Derby Acres**—*pop pl* ... CA-9
Derby Baptist Ch—*church* ... MS-4
Derby Bay—*bay* ... VT-1
Derby Brook—*stream* (2) ... NY-2
Derby Canyon—*valley* ... WA-9
Derby Cem—*cemetery* ... IN-6
Derby Cem—*cemetery* ... IA-7
Derby Cem—*cemetery* ... MI-6
Derby Cem—*cemetery* ... TX-5
**Derby Center (Derby Post Office)**—*pop pl* ... VT-1
*Derby (corporate name Derby Center)* ... VT-1
Derby Cove—*bay* ... AK-9
Derby Creek—*stream* ... AK-9
Derby Creek—*stream* ... CO-8
Derby Creek—*stream* ... OR-9
Derby Dam—*dam* ... NV-8
Derby Diversion Dam—*hist pl* ... NV-8
Derby Dome Oil Field—*oilfield* ... WY-8
Dcrbydown Homestead—*hist pl* ... PA-2
Derby Downs—*other* ... TX-5
Derby Field—*airport* ... NV-8
Derby Field Airp—*airport* ... NV-8
Derby Flats—*flat* ... CO-8
**Derby Glen (subdivision)**—*pop pl* ... TN-4
Derby Grade Sch—*school* ... KS-7
Derby Grange Sch—*school* ... IA-7
Derby Guard Station—*locale* ... CO-8
Derby Gulch—*valley* ... MT-8
Derby Hill—*summit* ... NH-1
Derby Hill—*summit* ... NY-2
Derby (historical)—*locale* ... MS-4
**Derby (historical)**—*pop pl* ... OR-9
**Derby (historical)**—*pop pl* ... TN-4
Derby House—*building* ... MA-1
Derby HS—*school* ... KS-7
Derby JHS—*school* ... MI-6
**Derby Junction**—*pop pl* ... CO-8
Derby Lake—*lake* ... MI-6
Derby Lake—*reservoir* ... CO-8
**Derby Line**—*pop pl* ... VT-1
Derby Mesa—*summit* ... CO-8
Derby Mine—*mine* ... AZ-5
Derby Mine—*mine* ... CA-9
Derby Mtn—*summit* ... ME-1
Derby Mtn—*summit* ... MT-8
Derby Mtn—*summit* ... NH-1
Derby Peak—*summit* ... CO-8
Derby Plaza (Shop Ctr)—*locale* ... FL-3
Derby Point—*cape* ... AK-9
*Derby Pond* ... VT-1
Derby Pond—*lake* ... IN-6
Derby Pond—*lake* ... NH-1
Derby Pond—*reservoir* ... DE-2
Derby Pond Dam—*dam* ... DE-2
Derby Post Office (historical)—*building* ... MS-4
Derby Ranch—*locale* ... WY-8
Derby Ridge—*ridge* ... CA-9
Derby Ridge—*ridge* ... MT-8
Derby Sch—*school* ... CO-8
Derby School (abandoned)—*locale* ... OR-9
Derbys Corners—*locale* ... NY-2
Derbyshire Baptist Ch—*church* ... FL-3
Derbyshire Creek—*stream* ... IN-6
Derbyshire Falls—*falls* ... IN-6
Derbyshire Gulch—*valley* ... CO-8
Derbyshire Lee Branch—*stream* ... MI-6
**Derby Shores**—*pop pl* ... DE-2
Derby Spring—*spring* ... WY-8
Derby Springs Draw—*valley* ... WY-8
*Derby Station* ... KS-7
Derby Station—*locale* ... OR-9
Derby Summerhouse—*hist pl* ... MA-1
*Derby's Wharf* ... MA-1
Derby Switch—*locale* ... NY-2
Derby (Town of)—*civ div* ... CT-1
**Derby (Town of)**—*pop pl* ... VT-1
Derby Tract—*uninc pl* ... AK-9
Derby Waterfront District—*hist pl* ... MA-1
**Derby Wharf**—*pop pl* ... MA-1
Derby Wharf Light—*locale* ... MA-1
Derby Wharf Light Station—*hist pl* ... MA-1
*Derch Meadow* ... CA-9
Derden—*locale* ... TX-5
*Derdens Creek* ... MS-4
*Derdens Ferry* ... AL-4
Derder Landing—*locale* ... AL-4
*Derdonnai* ... AR-4
Dereco—*uninc pl* ... OK-5
Dereemer Ranch—*locale* ... WY-8
Dereemer Ranch Hist Dist—*hist pl* ... WY-8
Derelict Flow—*lava* ... ID-8
Derelict Key—*island* ... FL-3
DeRemer, Joseph Bell, House—*hist pl* ... ND-7
De Remer Lakes—*reservoir* ... CO-8
Deremer Sch—*school* ... WI-6
Deremo Point—*cape* ... NY-2
Derenburger Cem—*cemetery* ... WV-2
Derenburger Hollow—*valley* ... WV-2
Derenne Sch—*school* ... GA-3
DeReno Windmill—*locale* ... NM-5
DeRevey, Lake—*reservoir* ... IL-6
Derfield Hollow—*valley* ... KY-4
Dergy Well—*well* ... NM-5
DeRham Farm—*hist pl* ... NY-2
Derham Hall and Our Lady of Victory Chapel, College of St. Catherine—*hist pl* ... MN-6
Derham JHS—*school* ... LA-4
**Derian Subdivision (subdivision)**—*pop pl* ... SD-7
Deriar Creek—*stream* ... ID-8
*Derick City* ... PA-2
Derickson Bay—*bay* ... AK-9
Derickson Island—*island* ... AK-9
*Derickson Point* ... DE-2
Derickson Point—*cape* ... DE-2
**De Ridder**—*pop pl* ... LA-4
DeRidder Commercial Hist Dist—*hist pl* ... LA-4
DeRidder Homestead—*hist pl* ... NY-2
Derifield Hollow—*valley* ... OH-6
*Derikan* ... FM-9
Derinda Center—*locale* ... IL-6
**Derinda (Township of)**—*pop pl* ... IL-6
**Deringer**—*pop pl* ... PA-2
Dering Harbor—*bay* ... NY-2
**Dering Harbor**—*pop pl* ... NY-2
Dering Point—*cape* ... NY-2
**Derita**—*pop pl* ... NC-3
Derita Creek—*stream* ... NC-3
Derita Crossroads—*locale* ... NC-3
Derita Mineral Spring—*spring* ... NC-3
**Derita Woods (subdivision)**—*pop pl* ... NC-3
Derk—*other* ... PA-2
Derks Field—*park* ... UT-8
Derleth Park—*park* ... WI-6
**Derma**—*pop pl* ... MS-4
Derma Post Office (historical)—*building* ... MS-4
Dermo Bayou—*bay* ... MI-6
Dermo Island—*island* ... MI-6
Dermon Bldg—*hist pl* ... TN-4
**Dermont**—*pop pl* ... KY-4
**Dermont (Dermot)**—*pop pl* ... KY-4
*Dermot* ... KY-4
Dermot—*other* ... KY-4
**Dermot**—*pop pl* ... KS-7
Dermot Cem—*cemetery* ... KS-7
Dermot Elem Sch—*school* ... KS-7
Dermot (historical)—*locale* ... KS-7
**Dermott**—*pop pl* ... AR-4
**Dermott**—*pop pl* ... TX-5
Dernal—*locale* ... TX-5
Dern Draw—*valley* ... MT-8
Dernieres, Isles—*island* ... LA-4
Dern Mine—*mine* ... AZ-5
De Roan (Township of)—*fmr MCD* ... AR-4
**De Roche**—*pop pl* ... AR-4
*DeRoche Bayou* ... AR-4
De Roche Cem—*cemetery* ... AR-4
De Roche Ch—*church* ... AR-4
De Roche Creek—*stream* ... AR-4
*Derocher Creek* ... MI-6
DeRocher Creek—*stream* ... MI-6
De Roche (Township of)—*fmr MCD* ... AR-4
Deroin Creek—*stream* ... NE-7
**Deronda**—*pop pl* ... WI-6
Deronda Bay—*bay* ... MN-6
Derose Pond—*reservoir* ... NC-3
Derose Pond Dam—*dam* ... NC-3
*De Rosier Lake* ... WI-6
Derosier Lake—*lake* ... WI-6
**De Rossett**—*pop pl* ... TN-4
Derossett Branch—*stream* ... KY-4
Derossett Cem—*cemetery* ... TN-4
De Rossett Ch of Christ—*church* ... TN-4
De Rossett Post Office (historical)—*building* ... TN-4
Derossett Sch—*school* ... KY-4
Derossitt Sch—*school* ... AR-4
**Derouen**—*pop pl* ... LA-4
DeRoux Creek—*stream* ... WA-9
DeRoux Forest Camp—*locale* ... WA-9
Deroy Hill—*summit* ... CT-1
DeRozier Creek—*stream* ... MT-8
Derraak—*locale* ... FM-9
Derrahs—*locale* ... MO-7
Derrahs Branch—*stream* ... MO-7
*Derrak* ... FM-9
Derramadero—*locale* ... NM-5
Derramadero Creek—*stream* ... TX-5
Derramadero de Machos—*stream* ... TX-5
Derr Camp—*locale* ... OR-9
Derr Cem—*cemetery* ... IL-6
Derr Creek—*stream* ... ID-8
Derreberry Branch—*stream* ... NC-3
Derreberry Gap—*gap* ... NC-3
Derrett Creek—*stream* ... TX-5
Derr Guard Station—*locale* ... OR-9
Derr Hill—*summit* ... MD-2
Derrick—*locale* ... NY-2
Derrick—*locale* ... ND-7
**Derrick**—*pop pl* ... CO-8
Derrick Bend—*bend* ... TN-4
Derrick Canyon—*valley* ... AZ-5
Derrick Canyon—*valley* ... TX-5
Derrick Cave—*cave* ... OR-9
Derrick Cem—*cemetery* ... MS-4
Derrick Cem—*cemetery* ... TN-4
**Derrick City**—*pop pl* ... PA-2
Derrick City Elem Sch—*school* ... PA-2
Derrick Creek—*stream* ... ID-8
Derrick Creek—*stream* ... WV-2
Derrick Creek Ridge—*ridge* ... WV-2
Derrick Draw—*valley* (2) ... NM-5
Derrick Draw—*valley* ... TX-5
Derrick Draw—*valley* ... WY-8
*Derrick Hollow* ... VA-3
Derrick Hollow—*valley* (2) ... AL-4
Derrick Key—*island* ... FL-3
Derrick Key Gap—*channel* ... FL-3
*Derrick Knob* ... NC-3
*Derrick Knob* ... TN-4
Derrick Knob Shelter—*locale* ... TN-4
*Derrick Lake* ... OR-9
Derrick Lake—*lake* ... OR-9
Derrick Lake—*lake* ... WA-9
Derrick Pocket—*basin* ... AZ-5
Derrick Ranch—*locale* ... NM-5
Derrick Ranch—*locale* (2) ... TX-5
Derrickson Ditch—*stream* ... DE-2
Derrickson Point—*cape* ... DE-2
Derrick Spring—*spring* ... TN-4
Derrick Trail—*trail* ... AZ-5
Derrieusseaux Creek—*stream* ... AR-4
*Derringer* ... WA-9
Derringer—*locale* ... PA-2
Derringer Cem—*cemetery* ... IN-6
Derringer Colliery—*building* ... PA-2
**Derringer Corners**—*pop pl* ... PA-2
Derringer Peak—*summit* ... CO-8
Derringer Spring—*spring* ... OR-9
Derringer Windmill—*locale* ... CO-8
Derring Gully—*bay* ... TX-5
*Derring Point* ... NY-2
Derrings Mill—*locale* ... VA-3
Derrio Canyon—*valley* ... AZ-5
*Derriseaux Creek* ... AR-4
Derr Island—*island* ... ID-8
Derritt Island—*island* ... GA-3
Derr Meadows—*swamp* ... OR-9
Derromel—*locale* ... PW-9
**Derromel**—*pop pl* ... PW-9
Derrow, Margaret, House—*hist pl* ... PA-2
Derr Point—*summit* ... ID-8
Derr Run—*stream* ... PA-2
Derrs—*locale* ... PA-2
Derrs Chapel—*locale* ... TX-5
**Derrs (Derks)**—*pop pl* ... PA-2
Derruder Dam—*dam* ... ND-7
Derrumba Ridge—*summit* ... AK-9
*Derry* ... NH-1
Derry—*locale* ... OR-9
Derry—*locale* ... PA-2
**Derry**—*pop pl* ... LA-4
**Derry**—*pop pl* ... NH-1
**Derry**—*pop pl* ... NM-5
**Derry**—*pop pl* ... PA-2
Derry Area JHS—*school* ... PA-2
Derry Area Senior HS—*school* ... PA-2
Derryberry Branch—*stream* (2) ... TN-4
Derryberry Cem—*cemetery* ... AR-4
Derryberry Cem—*cemetery* (3) ... TN-4
Derry Borough—*civil* ... PA-2
Derry Borough HS (historical)—*school* ... PA-2
Derry Ch—*church* ... PA-2
**Derry Church**—*pop pl* ... PA-2
Derry Compact (census name Derry)—*other* ... NH-1
Derrydale Creek—*stream* ... CA-9
*Derry Depot* ... NH-1
Derrydown P. O. (historical)—*building* ... PA-2
Derry Elem Sch—*school* (2) ... PA-2
Derry Farm—*locale* ... IL-6
Derryfield Country Club—*other* ... NH-1
Derryfield Park—*park* ... NH-1
Derryfield Sch—*school* ... NH-1
**Derryhale**—*pop pl* ... WV-2
*Derry Heights Cemetery* ... PA-2
Derry Hill—*summit* (2) ... NH-1
Derry Hill Sch—*school* ... NH-1
Derry HS—*school* ... PA-2
Derry Lake—*lake* ... WA-9
Derry Lateral—*canal* ... NM-5
Derry Mtn—*summit* ... ME-1
**Derrynane (Township of)**—*pop pl* ... MN-6
Derry No. 1 Ditch—*canal* ... CO-8
Derry One-Room Sch (historical)—*school* ... PA-2
Derry Robert Number 1 Dam—*dam* ... SD-7
Derry Rod And Gun Club Dam—*dam* ... PA-2
Derry Rod And Gun Club Lake—*reservoir* ... PA-2
**Derry (Town of)**—*pop pl* ... NH-1
*Derry Township High School* ... PA-2
**Derry (Township of)**—*pop pl* ... IL-6
**Derry (Township of)**—*pop pl* (4) ... PA-2
**Derry Village**—*pop pl* ... NH-1
Dersam Gulf—*valley* ... NY-2
Dersch Meadows—*flat* (2) ... CA-9
Dersch-Taylor Petroglyphs—*hist pl* ... CA-9
*Derstein* ... PA-2
Derstines—*locale* ... PA-2
Derudder Dam—*dam* ... ND-7
**DeRusk**—*pop pl* ... TN-4
De Ruwe Farm—*locale* ... WA-9
*De Ruyter* ... NY-2
**DeRuyter**—*pop pl* ... NY-2
*De Ruyter Rsvr* ... NY-2
DeRuyter Rsvr—*reservoir* ... NY-2
**DeRuyter (Town of)**—*pop pl* ... NY-2
Dervend Airp—*airport* ... PA-2
Dervin Cem—*cemetery* ... TX-5
Derway Island—*island* ... VT-1
**Derwent**—*pop pl* ... OH-6
Derwent Creek—*stream* ... AK-9
**Derwood**—*pop pl* ... MD-2
Derwood Ch—*church* ... MD-2
Derwood Experimental Laboratory—*other* ... MD-2
Derwood Park—*uninc pl* ... PA-2
**Derwyn**—*pop pl* ... PA-2
DeSabla—*locale* ... CA-9
Des Acre Hollow—*valley* ... MO-7
Desague Aguita—*stream* ... NM-5
Desair, Lake—*lake* ... WI-6
*Desaki Mesa* ... AZ-5
**De Sale**—*pop pl* ... PA-2
DeSale Cem—*cemetery* ... OH-6
DeSales Athletic Field—*park* ... NY-2
De Sales Hall—*school* ... MD-2
DeSales HS—*school* ... KY-4
DeSales HS—*school* ... NY-2
DeSales HS—*school* ... WA-9
DeSales Sch—*school* ... OH-6
DeSales Seminary—*school* ... WI-6
**Des Allemands**—*pop pl* ... LA-4
Des Allemands (census name for Allemands)—*CDP* ... LA-4
*Des Allemands Lake* ... LA-4
Desane Lake—*lake* ... OR-9
**Des Arc**—*pop pl* ... AR-4
**Des Arc**—*pop pl* ... MO-7
Des Arc, Bayou—*stream* ... AR-4
Des Arc Mtn—*summit* ... AR-4
Des Arc Mtn—*summit* ... MO-7
Des Arc (Township of)—*fmr MCD* (2) ... AR-4
De Sart—*locale* ... ND-7
DeSart Cem—*cemetery* ... ND-7
Desatoya Mtns—*range* ... NV-8
Desatoya Peak—*summit* ... NV-8
Desbrough Canyon—*valley* ... UT-8
**Desbrough Park**—*pop pl* ... NY-2
**Descalabrado**—*pop pl* ... PR-3
Descalabrado (Barrio)—*fmr MCD* ... PR-3
Descalso Windmill—*locale* ... TX-5
Descano Eterno Cem—*cemetery* ... TX-5
**Descanso**—*pop pl* ... CA-9
Descanso Bay—*bay* ... CA-9
Descanso Campground—*locale* ... CA-9
Descanso Creek—*stream* ... CA-9
Descanso Gardens—*park* ... CA-9
**Descanso Junction**—*pop pl* ... CA-9
Descanso Valley—*valley* ... CA-9
Descariso Cem—*cemetery* ... NM-5
*Descent Lake* ... MN-6
Des Champs Branch—*stream* ... SC-3
*Deschamps Lake* ... MI-6
Deschamps Pond—*reservoir* ... SC-3
*Deschee River* ... IN-6
Descher Sch (historical)—*school* ... MO-7
Deschutes—*locale* ... OR-9
*Deschutes Basin* ... WA-9
Deschutes Bridge Guard Station—*locale* ... OR-9
Deschutes Canyon—*valley* ... OR-9
**Deschutes County**—*pop pl* ... OR-9
Deschutes Falls—*falls* ... WA-9
**Deschutes (historical)**—*pop pl* ... OR-9
Deschutes Junction—*locale* ... OR-9
Deschutes Memorial Gardens (cemetery)—*cemetery* ... OR-9
Deschutes Natl For—*forest* ... OR-9
Deschutes River—*stream* ... OR-9
Deschutes River—*stream* ... WA-9
Deschutes River Rec Area—*park* ... OR-9
*Deschutes River Scenic Waterway* ... OR-9
*Deschutes River State Park* ... OR-9
Desconocida Reef—*bar* ... AK-9
Des Cyprie—*gut* ... MO-7
Desda—*locale* ... KY-4
*Desdamona* ... TX-5
Desda Ridge—*ridge* ... KY-4
**Desdemona**—*pop pl* ... TX-5
Desdemona Sands—*bar* ... OR-9
Desdemona Sands Light—*locale* ... OR-9
*Desdemonia* ... TX-5
*Desdimonia* ... TX-5
Dese Creek—*stream* ... AK-9
**De Selle**—*pop pl* ... LA-4
**Deselm**—*pop pl* ... IL-6
Deselm Cem—*cemetery* ... IL-6
**Desembarcadero Mosquito**—*pop pl* ... PR-3
Desenberg Bldg—*hist pl* ... MI-6
Desenburg Cem—*cemetery* ... OH-6
**Desengano**—*pop pl* ... PR-3
Desengong—*stream* ... PW-9
Deserama Mobile Ranch—*locale* ... AZ-5
**Deseret**—*pop pl* ... UT-8
Deseret at Lake Hills Cem—*cemetery* ... UT-8
Deseret Cabin—*locale* ... ID-8
Deseret Canal—*canal* ... UT-8
Deseret City Cem—*cemetery* ... UT-8
Deseret Peak—*summit* ... UT-8
*Deseret Ranch* ... NV-8
*Deseret Ranch* ... UT-8
Deseret Ranch—*locale* (2) ... UT-8
Deseret Reservoirs—*reservoir* ... UT-8
**Deseret Subdivision**—*pop pl* (2) ... UT-8
*Deserette Cabin* ... ID-8
Deseret Telegraph and Post Office—*hist pl* ... UT-8
Deseret Well—*well* ... UT-8
Deseret (42 MD 55)—*hist pl* ... UT-8
Desert—*locale* ... CA-9
Desert—*locale* ... NM-5
Desert—*locale* ... OR-9
Desert—*locale* ... UT-8
**Desert**—*pop pl* ... TX-5
Desert—*post sta* ... AZ-5
Desert, Bayou—*gut* ... LA-4
Desert, Lake in the—*lake* ... AZ-5
*Desert, The* ... NC-3
*Desert, The* ... VA-3
Desert, The—*area* ... AK-9
Desert, The—*swamp* ... NC-3
Desert, The—*swamp* ... VA-3
Desert Aire Park—*park* ... AZ-5
Desert Airp—*airport* ... WA-9
Desert Angel—*summit* ... CA-9
**Desert Beach**—*pop pl* ... CA-9
**Desert Bell Estates II (subdivision)**—*pop pl* (2) ... AZ-5
Desert Botanical Gardens—*park* ... AZ-5
Desert Branch—*stream* ... WV-2
Desert Butte—*summit* ... CA-9
**Desert Camp**—*pop pl* ... CA-9
**Desert Carmel**—*pop pl* ... AZ-5
Desert Cem—*cemetery* ... TX-5
**Desert Center**—*pop pl* ... CA-9
Desert Christ Park—*park* ... CA-9
Desert Claim—*flat* ... CO-8
Desert Claim Arroyo—*valley* ... CO-8
Desert Claim Ditch—*canal* ... CO-8
Desert Cold Spring—*spring* ... CA-9
Desert Cone—*summit* ... OR-9
Desert Coulee—*valley* ... MT-8
Desert Cove—*bay* ... VA-3
Desert Cove Sch—*school* ... AZ-5
*Desert Creek* ... ID-8
*Desert Creek* ... UT-8
Desert Creek—*stream* ... CA-9
Desert Creek—*stream* ... ID-8
Desert Creek—*stream* ... MS-4
Desert Creek—*stream* ... MT-8
Desert Creek—*stream* ... NV-8
Desert Creek—*stream* ... NY-2
Desert Creek—*stream* (2) ... OR-9
Desert Creek—*stream* ... TX-5
Desert Creek—*stream* ... UT-8
Desert Creek—*stream* ... WY-8
Desert Creek Peak—*summit* ... NV-8
Desert Creek Ranch—*locale* ... NV-8
Desert Crystal Salt Works (historical)—*mine* ... NV-8
Desert Dam—*dam* ... MT-8
Desert Dells—*uninc pl* ... AZ-5
Desert Divide Trail—*trail* ... CA-9
*Deserted Camp* ... OH-6
Deserted Glacier—*glacier* ... AK-9
Deserted Park Rsvr—*reservoir* ... CO-8
Desert Empire Fairgrounds—*locale* ... CA-9
Deserter Baygall—*swamp* ... TX-5
Deserter Creek—*stream* ... FL-3
Deserter Creek—*stream* ... KY-4
Deserter Creek—*stream* ... WA-9
Deserter Island—*island* ... TX-5
Deserter Lake—*lake* ... GA-3
Deserter Run—*stream* ... PA-2
Deserters Hammock—*island* ... FL-3
Deserters Island (historical)—*locale* ... MS-4
*Desert Experimental Range* ... UT-8
Desert Experimental Range—*forest* ... UT-8
Desert Facade—*cliff* ... AZ-5
Desert Farms Well One—*well* ... AZ-5
Desert Farms Well Two—*well* ... AZ-5
Desert Field—*flat* ... OR-9
Desert Foothills Amphitheater—*locale* ... AZ-5
Desert Forest Golf Course—*other* ... AZ-5
Desert Fork—*stream* ... WV-2
Desert Gem Mobile Home Park—*locale* ... AZ-5
Desert Gulch—*valley* ... CO-8
Desert Haven Sch—*school* ... CA-9
**Desert Heights**—*pop pl* ... CA-9
**Desert Highlands**—*pop pl* ... AZ-5
Desert Hill Cem—*cemetery* ... NV-8
*Desert Hills* ... UT-8
**Desert Hills**—*pop pl* ... AZ-5
Desert Hills—*range* ... NV-8
Desert Hills—*summit* ... NV-8
Desert Hills Ch—*church* ... NM-5
Desert Hills Golf Course—*other* ... AZ-5
Desert Hills Interchange—*crossing* ... AZ-5
Desert-Ho Ranch—*locale* ... AZ-5
Desert Horizon Elem Sch—*school* ... AZ-5
**Desert Hot Springs**—*pop pl* ... CA-9
Desert Hot Springs (CCD)—*cens area* ... CA-9
Desert Hound Mine—*mine* ... CA-9
Desert HS—*school* ... CA-9
Desert Inn Park—*park* ... NV-8
Desertion Point—*summit* ... WY-8
Desert Island—*island* ... LA-4
Desert King Spring—*spring* ... CA-9
Desert Knob—*summit* ... WV-2
Desert Knolls Wash—*stream* ... CA-9
Desert Laboratory—*hist pl* ... AZ-5
Desert Lake—*flat* ... NV-8
Desert Lake—*lake* ... OR-9
Desert Lake—*lake* ... UT-8
**Desert Lake**—*pop pl* ... CA-9
Desert Lake North Ditch—*canal* ... UT-8
Desert Lake Tank—*reservoir* ... AZ-5
Desert Lake Wash—*valley* ... UT-8

Desert Lake Waterfowl Mngmt Area—*park* ... UT-8
*Desert Lake Waterfowl Reserve* ... UT-8
Desert Lawn Cem—*cemetery* ... AZ-5
Desert Lawn Memorial Park—*cemetery* ... AZ-5
Desert Lawn Memorial Park—*cemetery* ... WA-9
**Desert Lodge**—*pop pl* ... CA-9
Desert Meadow—*flat* ... OR-9
Desert Memorial Park—*park* ... CA-9
Desert Mine—*mine* ... AZ-5
Desert Mound—*locale* ... UT-8
Desert Mound—*summit* ... UT-8
*Desert Mountain* ... UT-8
Desert Mountain Pass—*gap* ... UT-8
Desert Mountain Rsvr—*reservoir* ... UT-8
Desert Mountain Well—*well* ... UT-8
Desert Mtn—*summit* ... MT-8
Desert Mtn—*summit* ... UT-8
Desert Mtns—*range* ... NV-8
Desert Natl Wildlife Range—*park* ... NV-8
Desert Overlook—*locale* ... UT-8
Desert Peak—*summit* ... AZ-5
Desert Peak—*summit* ... NV-8
Desert Peak—*summit* ... UT-8
**Desert Pines (subdivision)**—*pop pl* (2) ... AZ-5
Desert Plantation—*hist pl* ... MS-4
Desert Pond—*lake* ... ME-1
Desert Pond—*lake* ... NY-2
Desert Power & Water Co., Electric Power Plant—*hist pl* ... AZ-5
Desert Proving Grounds—*locale* ... AZ-5
Desert Proving Grounds—*military* ... AZ-5
Desert Queen—*mine* ... NV-8
Desert Queen Mine—*hist pl* ... CA-9
Desert Queen Mine—*mine* (3) ... AZ-5
Desert Queen Mine—*mine* (2) ... CA-9
Desert Queen Mine—*mine* ... NV-8
Desert Queen Well—*well* ... CA-9
Desert Queen Well—*well* ... NV-8
Desert Ranch—*locale* ... NV-8
Desert Ranch Rsvr—*reservoir* ... NV-8
Desert Ranch Rsvr—*reservoir* ... UT-8
*Desert Range* ... UT-8
Desert Range—*range* ... NV-8
Desert Range Experimental Station—*military* ... UT-8
Desert Range Experimental Station HQ—*locale* ... UT-8
*Desert Range Experiment Station* ... UT-8
Desert Rest—*cemetery* ... AZ-5
Desert Ridge—*ridge* ... OR-9
**Desert Ridge (subdivision)**—*pop pl* (2) ... AZ-5
Desert Rock, Mount—*island* ... ME-1
*Desert Rock Airport* ... NV-8
Desert Rock Airstrip—*airport* ... NV-8
Desert Rose Mine—*mine* ... AZ-5
Desert Rose Mine—*mine* ... NM-5
Desert Rsvr—*reservoir* ... CO-8
Desert Rsvr No 1—*reservoir* ... WY-8
Desert Rsvr No 2—*reservoir* ... UT-8
Desert Rsvr No 2—*reservoir* ... WY-8
Desert Rsvr No 3—*reservoir* ... WY-8
Desert Rsvr No 4—*reservoir* ... WY-8
Desert Rsvr No 5—*reservoir* ... WY-8
Desert Rsvr No 6—*reservoir* ... WY-8
*Desert Sage* (2) ... AZ-5
Desert Sage Mobile Manor—*locale* ... AZ-5
Desert Sage Post Office—*building* ... AZ-5
Desert Samaritan Hosp—*hospital* ... AZ-5
Desert Samaritan Hospital Heliport—*airport* ... AZ-5
Desert Sands Golf Course—*other* ... AZ-5
Desert Sands JHS—*school* ... AZ-5
Desert Sands Mobile Home Park—*locale* ... AZ-5
**Desert Sands (Trailer Park)**—*pop pl* ... AZ-5
Desert Scheelite Mine—*mine* ... NV-8
Desert Seep Wash—*valley* ... UT-8
Desert Shadows Sch—*school* ... AZ-5
**Desert Shores**—*pop pl* ... CA-9
*Desert Siding* ... UT-8
Desert Siding—*locale* ... NV-8
Desert Spring—*spring* ... CA-9
Desert Spring—*spring* ... NV-8
Desert Spring—*spring* ... OR-9
Desert Spring—*spring* (2) ... UT-8
*Desert Springs* ... CA-9
**Desert Springs**—*pop pl* ... CA-9
Desert Springs—*spring* ... UT-8
Desert Springs—*spring* ... WY-8
*Desert Springs Park* ... AZ-5
Desert Spring Wash—*valley* ... UT-8
Desert Square Shop Ctr—*locale* ... AZ-5
*Desert Station* ... AZ-5
Desert Station—*locale* ... AZ-5
Desert Steppes—*uninc pl* ... AZ-5
Desert Sun Sch—*school* ... CA-9
Desert Swamp—*swamp* ... NY-2
Desert Tank—*reservoir* (2) ... AZ-5
*Desert Valley* ... NV-8
Desert Valley—*valley* (2) ... NV-8
**Desert Valley Estates (subdivision)**—*pop pl* (2) ... AZ-5
*Desert View* ... NV-8
*Desert View* ... UT-8
Desert View—*locale* ... AZ-5
Desert View—*locale* ... CA-9
Desert View Area—*locale* ... UT-8
Desert View Campground—*park* ... AZ-5
Desert View Highlands—*CDP* ... CA-9
Desert View Natural Environment Area—*park* ... NV-8
Desert View Point—*locale* ... NV-8
Desert Viewpoint—*locale* ... NV-8
Desert View Point—*summit* ... AZ-5
Desert View Sch—*school* ... AZ-5
Desert View Sch—*school* ... CA-9
Desert View Tower—*hist pl* ... CA-9
Desert View Trailhead—*locale* ... NV-8
Desert Village Mobile Home Park—*locale* ... AZ-5
**Desert Villas (subdivision)**—*pop pl* (2) ... AZ-5
**Desert Vista Estates III (subdivision)**—*pop pl* (2) ... AZ-5
*Desert Well* ... AZ-5
Desert Well—*well* (2) ... AZ-5
Desert Well—*well* (4) ... NV-8
Desert Well (Flowing)—*well* ... NV-8
Desert Well No 1—*well* ... WY-8
Desert Well No 2—*well* ... WY-8
Desert Well Number One—*well* ... AZ-5
Desert Well Number Two—*well* ... AZ-5
*Desert Wells* ... AZ-5
**Desert Wells**—*pop pl* ... AZ-5
**Desert Wind II (subdivision)**—*pop pl* (2) ... AZ-5
Des Fosse, Dr. Jules Charles, House—*hist pl* ... LA-4
Des Glaise—*locale* ... LA-4
Desha—*locale* ... TN-4
Desha—*locale* ... VA-3
**Desha**—*pop pl* ... AR-4
Desha, Franklin, House—*hist pl* ... AR-4
Desha Canyon—*valley* ... UT-8
Desha Central HS—*school* ... AR-4
**Desha (County)**—*pop pl* ... AR-4
Desha County Courthouse—*hist pl* ... AR-4
Desha Creek—*stream* ... UT-8
Desha Mine (underground)—*mine* ... AL-4
DeShano Drain—*canal* ... MI-6
Deshaw Ditch—*canal* ... WY-8
De Shazer Creek—*stream* ... KS-7
**Deshazo Corner**—*pop pl* ... VA-3
De Shazoo Mill Ford—*locale* ... AL-4
Deshea Creek—*stream* ... TN-4
Deshee, River—*stream* ... IN-6
*Deshee River* ... IN-6
Deshgish Butte—*summit* ... AZ-5
Deshield Cem—*cemetery* ... AR-4
Deshield Fork—*stream* ... AR-4
Deshiell Cem—*cemetery* ... TX-5
**Deshler**—*pop pl* ... NE-7
**Deshler**—*pop pl* ... OH-6
Deshler HS—*school* ... AL-4
Deshler Institute (historical)—*school* ... AL-4
*Deshler Island* ... NY-2
Deshler-Morris House—*hist pl* ... PA-2
Deshler Sch—*school* ... OH-6
Deshler Sewage Disposal—*other* ... OH-6
Deshon-Allyn House—*hist pl* ... CT-1
Deshon General Hospital—*other* ... PA-2
Deshong Park—*park* ... PA-2
**Deshon Manor**—*pop pl* ... PA-2
Deshon Veterans Administration Hosp—*hospital* ... PA-2
Deshotel—*locale* ... LA-4
Deshotel Cem—*cemetery* ... LA-4
*Deshotels* ... LA-4
**Deshotels**—*pop pl* ... LA-4
Deshu Isthmus—*civil* ... AK-9
**De Siard (reduced usage)**—*pop pl* (2) ... LA-4
*Desiderata Canyon* ... OR-9
*Desierta* ... MH-9
*Desierto de Altar* ... AZ-5
*Desierto Grande* ... AZ-5
Desierto Windmill—*locale* ... TX-5
Desilt Wash—*valley* ... CA-9
Desilu Studios—*other* (2) ... CA-9
DeSilva Sch—*school* ... HI-9
**Desire**—*pop pl* ... PA-2
Desire, Lake—*lake* ... FL-3
Desire, Lake—*lake* ... WA-9
Desire Plantation House—*hist pl* ... LA-4
*Des Islet Lake* ... KY-4
De Sisto Sch—*school* ... FL-3
Desjarlis Lake—*lake* ... ND-7
Deskin Branch—*stream* ... KY-4
Deskin Cem—*cemetery* ... MO-7
Deskin Creek—*stream* ... VA-3
Deskin Mtn—*summit* ... VA-3
Deskins—*locale* ... VA-3
Deskins Addition—*other* ... WV-2
Deskins Branch—*stream* ... KY-4
Deskins Cem—*cemetery* ... WV-2
Deskins Ch—*church* ... VA-3
Desko Post Office (historical)—*building* ... AL-4
**Deskys Addition Five (subdivision)**—*pop pl* ... UT-8
**Deskys Addition Three and Four (subdivision)**—*pop pl* ... UT-8
**Deskys Subdivision**—*pop pl* ... UT-8
**Des Lacs**—*pop pl* ... ND-7
Des Lacs Cem—*cemetery* ... ND-7
Des Lacs City Dam—*dam* ... ND-7
Des Lacs Migratory Bird Ref—*park* ... ND-7
Des Lacs River—*stream* ... ND-7
Des Lacs Rsvr—*reservoir* ... ND-7
**Des Lacs Township**—*pop pl* ... ND-7
Deslatte—*locale* ... LA-4
Des Lauriens Island (historical)—*island* ... SD-7
Des Liz—*area* ... NM-5
**Desloge**—*pop pl* ... MO-7
Desmans Camp—*locale* ... AL-4
DesMarest, Jacobus, House—*hist pl* ... NJ-2
*Desmet* ... ID-8
*DeSmet* ... SD-7
*De Smet* ... WY-8
De Smet—*locale* ... ID-8
De Smet—*locale* ... MT-8
**De Smet**—*pop pl* ... SD-7
De Smet, Lake—*lake* ... WY-8
De Smet Cem—*cemetery* ... SD-7
De Smet Creek—*stream* ... SD-7
De Smet (historical)—*civil* ... ND-7
*De Smet Mission* ... ID-8
DeSmet Sch—*school* ... MT-8
**De Smet Township**—*pop pl* ... SD-7
**Des Moines**—*pop pl* ... CA-9
**Des Moines**—*pop pl* ... IA-7
**Des Moines**—*pop pl* ... NM-5
**Des Moines**—*pop pl* ... WA-9
Des Moines Beach—*beach* ... IA-7
Des Moines Ch—*church* ... IA-7
Des Moines Creek—*stream* ... AK-9
Des Moines Creek—*stream* ... CA-9
Des Moines Ditch—*canal* ... WY-8
*Desmoines Lake* ... WI-6
Des Moines Lake—*lake* ... MN-6
Des Moines Lake—*lake* ... ND-7
Des Moines Lake—*lake* ... WI-6
Des Moines Municipal Airp—*airport* ... IA-7
Des Moines River—*stream* ... IA-7
Des Moines River—*stream* ... MN-6
Des Moines River—*stream* ... MO-7
Des Moines River Locks No. 5 and No. 7—*hist pl* ... IA-7
Des Moines River (Township of)—*civ div* ... MN-6
Des Moines Saddlery Company Bldg—*hist pl* ... IA-7
Des Moines Sch—*school* ... WI-6
Des Moines Township—*civil* ... MO-7
Des Moines Township—*fmr MCD* (8) ... IA-7
**Des Moines (Township of)**—*pop pl* ... MN-6
Desmond, Lake—*reservoir* ... NC-3
Desmond Able Lake—*reservoir* ... IN-6
Desmond Able Lake Dam—*dam* ... IN-6
Desmond Creek—*stream* ... MI-6
Desmond Ditch—*canal* ... CA-9
Desmond Mine—*mine* ... CA-9
Desmond Park—*park* ... NJ-2
Desmond Ranch—*locale* ... NV-8
Desmond Valley—*valley* ... NH-1
*Desmont* ... CA-9
*Des Monts Mountain* ... ME-1
*Des Morts* ... IA-7
Desnoyer Park Sch—*school* ... MN-6
Desobry Bldg—*hist pl* ... LA-4
Desolate Branch—*stream* ... WV-2
Desolate Brook—*stream* ... NY-2
Desolate Hill—*summit* ... NY-2
Desolate Swamp—*swamp* ... NY-2
Desolation, Lake—*lake* ... NY-2
Desolation, Lake—*lake* ... UT-8
Desolation Branch—*stream* ... NC-3
Desolation Brook—*stream* ... ME-1
Desolation Butte—*summit* ... OR-9
*Desolation Canyon* ... CA-9
Desolation Canyon—*hist pl* ... UT-8
Desolation Canyon—*valley* ... CA-9
Desolation Canyon—*valley* ... OR-9
Desolation Canyon—*valley* ... UT-8
Desolation Canyon Historical Landmark—*park* ... UT-8
*Desolation Canyon Historic Landmark* ... UT-8
Desolation Creek—*stream* ... AK-9
Desolation Creek—*stream* ... OR-9
Desolation Glacier—*glacier* ... AK-9
Desolation Guard Station—*locale* ... OR-9
Desolation Gulch—*valley* ... CA-9
Desolation Lake—*lake* (2) ... CA-9
Desolation Lake—*lake* ... MT-8
Desolation Meadows—*flat* ... OR-9
*Desolation Peak* ... WA-9
Desolation Peak—*summit* ... CA-9
Desolation Peak—*summit* ... MT-8
Desolation Peak—*summit* ... WA-9
Desolation Peak—*summit* ... WY-8
Desolation Peaks—*summit* ... CO-8
Desolation Point—*cape* ... MI-6
Desolation Pond—*lake* ... ME-1
Desolation Pond—*lake* ... NH-1
Desolation Saddle—*gap* ... OR-9
Desolation Swamp—*swamp* ... OR-9
Desolation Trail—*trail* ... NH-1
Desolation Valley—*basin* ... CA-9
Desolation Valley—*valley* ... AK-9
*Desolation Valley Primitive Area* ... CA-9
*Desolation Valley Wild Area* ... CA-9
Desolation Wilderness—*park* ... CA-9
Desomel—*cape* ... PW-9
Desomel—*island* ... PW-9
Desor, Lake—*lake* ... MI-6
Desor, Mount—*summit* ... MI-6
DeSota Sch—*school* ... FL-3
*De Soto* ... GA-3
*Desoto* ... MO-7
*De Soto* ... TX-5
**DeSoto**—*pop pl* ... GA-3
**De Soto**—*pop pl* ... GA-3
**De Soto**—*pop pl* ... IL-6
**Desoto**—*pop pl* ... IN-6
**De Soto**—*pop pl* ... IA-7
**De Soto**—*pop pl* ... KS-7
**De Soto**—*pop pl* ... MS-4
**De Soto**—*pop pl* ... MO-7
**De Soto**—*pop pl* ... NE-7
**De Soto**—*pop pl* ... TX-5
**De Soto**—*pop pl* ... WI-6
DeSoto, Lake—*reservoir* ... AR-4
DeSoto, Lake—*reservoir* ... FL-3
De Soto Baptist Ch—*church* ... MS-4
DeSoto Bay—*bay* ... WI-6
*Desoto Caverns* ... AL-4
DeSoto Cem—*cemetery* ... AR-4
De Soto Cem—*cemetery* ... KS-7
De Soto Cem—*cemetery* ... MS-4
De Soto Center Northwest Mississippi Junior Coll—*school* ... MS-4
DeSoto Center (Shop Ctr)—*locale* ... FL-3
**De Soto City**—*pop pl* ... FL-3
DeSoto Correctional Institute—*building* ... FL-3
DeSoto Correctional Institute of Adult Education—*school* ... FL-3
**De Soto County**—*pop pl* ... FL-3
**De Soto County**—*pop pl* ... MS-4
DeSoto County Adult Education Center—*school* ... FL-3
DeSoto Cutoff—*bend* ... NE-7
*De Soto (Desoto)* ... IN-6
De Soto Falls—*falls* ... AL-4
DeSoto Falls—*falls* ... GA-3
*Desoto Falls Dam* ... AL-4
De Soto Front (historical)—*locale* ... MS-4
Desoto Front Post Office (historical)—*building* ... MS-4
Desoto (historical)—*locale* ... AL-4
DeSoto HS—*school* ... FL-3
De Soto HS—*school* ... MO-7
De Soto Indian Fortification (historical)—*locale* ... AL-4
De Soto Island—*island* ... LA-4
De Soto Junction (Shop Ctr)—*locale* ... FL-3
De Soto Lake—*lake* ... IA-7
DeSoto Lake—*lake* ... NE-7
DeSoto Lake—*reservoir* ... MO-7
Desoto Lakes—*CDP* ... FL-3
Desoto Lakes—*lake* ... FL-3
DeSoto Landing—*locale* ... AR-4
Desoto Landing—*locale* ... MS-4
DeSoto Lookout Tower—*locale* ... LA-4
DeSoto Manor Sch—*school* ... AL-4
**De Soto Manor (subdivision)**—*pop pl* ... AL-4
DeSoto Memorial—*hospital* ... FL-3
DeSoto Memorial Speedway—*locale* ... FL-3
De Soto Mine—*mine* ... AZ-5
DeSoto Mine—*mine* ... NV-8
DeSoto Monmt—*park* ... FL-3
DeSoto Monument—*locale* ... TN-4
DeSoto MS—*school* ... FL-3
De Soto Natl Forest—*park* ... MS-4
DeSoto Natl Memorial—*hist pl* ... FL-3
De Soto Natl Memorial—*park* ... FL-3
De Soto Natl Wildlife Ref—*park* ... IA-7
De Soto Natl Wildlife Ref—*park* ... NE-7
DeSoto Natl Wildlife Ref—*park* ... NE-7
**De Soto Parish**—*pop pl* ... LA-4
DeSoto Parish Courthouse—*hist pl* ... LA-4
DeSoto Park—*park* ... AR-4
Desoto Park—*park* ... IN-6
DeSoto Park—*park* ... MO-7
De Soto Park—*park* ... TN-4
**De Soto Park**—*pop pl* ... GA-3
DeSoto Park Ch—*church* ... GA-3
DeSoto Park Mission—*church* ... GA-3
*De Soto Peninsula* ... LA-4
*De Soto Point* ... LA-4
DeSoto Point—*cape* ... FL-3
De Soto Point—*cape* ... FL-3
*De Soto River* ... AL-4
*De Soto River* ... GA-3
Desoto Shop Ctr—*locale* ... FL-3
Desoto Shop Ctr—*locale* ... MS-4
De Soto Square Mall—*post sta* ... FL-3
DeSoto Square (Shop Ctr)—*locale* ... FL-3
DeSoto Start Center—*school* ... FL-3
De Soto State Park—*park* ... AL-4
Desoto State Park Lake—*reservoir* ... AL-4
De Soto Tank—*reservoir* ... AZ-5
De Soto Tower—*tower* ... FL-3
De Soto Township—*civ div* ... NE-7
De Soto (Township of)—*fmr MCD* ... AR-4
**De Soto (Township of)**—*pop pl* ... IL-6
Desoto Trail—*trail* ... MN-6
**De Soto Village (subdivision)**—*pop pl* ... MS-4
*De Sotoville* ... AL-4
De Soto Vocational Technical Center—*school* ... MS-4
Des Ourses Swamp—*swamp* ... LA-4
Despain Gulch—*valley* ... OR-9
Despain Gulch Cem—*cemetery* ... OR-9
Despain Hollow—*valley* ... MO-7
De Spain Ranch—*locale* ... TX-5
Despain Rsvr—*reservoir* ... OR-9
DeSpain Spring—*spring* ... WA-9
DeSpain Tank—*reservoir* ... AZ-5
De Spain Tank—*reservoir* ... TX-5
Despair, Bayou—*stream* ... LA-4
Despair, Mount—*summit* ... MT-8
Despair, Mount—*summit* ... WA-9
Despair Island—*island* ... ME-1
Despair Island—*island* ... RI-1
Despair Lake—*lake* ... LA-4
**Despard**—*pop pl* ... WV-2
Desperado Spring—*spring* ... OK-5
Desperation Hollow—*valley* ... PA-2
Desperation Lake—*lake* ... AK-9
Desper Creek—*stream* ... AK-9
Desper Creek—*stream* ... VA-3
**Des Peres**—*pop pl* ... MO-7
Des Peres Presbyterian Church—*hist pl* ... MO-7
Des Peres Sch—*hist pl* ... MO-7
Des Peres Square—*locale* ... MO-7
Des Peres Square (Shop Ctr)—*locale* ... MO-7
**Des Plaines**—*pop pl* ... IL-6
Des Plaines Lake—*lake* ... IL-6
*Des Plaines Manor* ... IL-6
*Des Plaines River* ... WI-6
Des Plaines River—*stream* ... IL-6
Des Plaines River—*stream* ... WI-6
*Des Plaines Terrace* ... IL-6
Des Plaines Wildlife Conservation Area—*park* ... IL-6
Des Plaines Wildlife HQ—*locale* ... IL-6
Despoblado, El—*plain* ... AZ-5
Desprez Branch—*stream* ... AL-4
*Desrosier Lake* ... WI-6
**Dess**—*pop pl* ... LA-4
**Dessa**—*pop pl* ... MO-7
Dessaint, Marie Clare, House—*hist pl* ... IA-7
**Dessard**—*pop pl* ... MD-2
Dessau—*locale* ... TX-5
*Dess Cemetery* ... LA-4
Desser—*locale* ... GA-3
Desserette—*hist pl* ... NC-3
Dessert, Joseph, Library—*hist pl* ... WI-6
Dess Fire Lookout Tower—*locale* ... LA-4
Dessie—*locale* ... WV-2
Dessie Ranch—*locale* ... TX-5
Dessie Scott Childrens Home—*building* ... KY-4
Dessum Well—*well* ... NM-5
Destanella Flat—*flat* ... CA-9
De Stazo Hill—*summit* ... CA-9
*Dester* ... FL-3
Destiladera, Canada De La —*valley* ... CA-9
**Destin**—*pop pl* ... FL-3
Destin Harbor—*bay* ... FL-3
**Destino**—*pop pl* ... PR-3
Destin Sch—*school* ... FL-3
Destiny, Lake—*lake* ... FL-3
**Destrehan**—*pop pl* ... LA-4
Destrehan HS—*school* ... LA-4
Destrehan Plantation—*hist pl* ... LA-4
Destroyer Rock—*summit* ... CA-9
Destruction Brook—*stream* ... MA-1
Destruction Creek—*stream* ... OR-9
Destruction Island—*island* ... WA-9
Destruction Landing (historical)—*locale* ... MS-4
**Desvio Dolores**—*pop pl* ... PR-3
**Desvio Valdes**—*pop pl* ... PR-3
Deswood Spring—*spring* ... AZ-5
*Des Zyace Wash, The* ... AZ-5
Detache, Point—*cape* ... MI-6
Detached Glacier—*glacier* ... AK-9
Detached Mail—*post sta* ... KS-7
Detachment Meadow—*flat* ... CA-9
Detail Rsvr—*reservoir* ... MT-8
Detain Branch—*stream* ... AL-4
Detamore Ditch—*canal* ... IN-6
*Detamore Drain* ... IN-6
Detborn Draw—*valley* ... MT-8
Detborn Rsvr—*reservoir* ... MT-8
Detention Basin—*basin* ... AZ-5
Detention Basin Number One—*reservoir* ... PA-2
Detention Basin Number Two—*reservoir* ... PA-2
Detention Camp Fourteen—*locale* ... CA-9
Detention Dam No 1—*dam* ... NM-5
Detention Dam No 2—*dam* ... NM-5
Detention Dam No 5—*dam* ... NM-5
Detention Hosp—*hist pl* ... MT-8
Detention Number Five—*reservoir* ... AZ-5
Detention Number Four—*reservoir* ... AZ-5
Detention Number One—*reservoir* ... AZ-5
Detention Number Six—*reservoir* ... AZ-5
Detention Number Three—*reservoir* ... AZ-5
Detention Number Two—*reservoir* ... AZ-5
Deterding Sch—*school* ... CA-9
Determination Towers—*pillar* ... UT-8
Determination Towers—*summit* ... UT-8
Deter Spring—*spring* ... CA-9
Detert Rsvr—*reservoir* ... CA-9
Detgen Creek—*stream* ... MT-8
Detherage Cem—*cemetery* ... KY-4
Detherage Ch—*church* ... MO-7
Detherage Sch (abandoned)—*school* ... MO-7
Detheridge Branch—*stream* ... TN-4
*Deth Hill* ... MA-1
Dethloff Cem—*cemetery* ... TX-5
Dethloff Slough—*gut* ... MN-6
*Detianar* ... FM-9
*De Tilla Gulch* ... CO-8
De Tilla Gulch—*valley* ... CO-8
Detimer Run—*stream* ... WV-2
Detling Creek—*stream* ... MN-6
Detling Hollow—*valley* ... PA-2
Detmer, A. M., House—*hist pl* ... OH-6
Detmold—*locale* ... MD-2
Detmold—*locale* ... TX-5
**Detmold**—*pop pl* ... MO-7
Detmold Hill—*summit* ... MD-2
Detmold Township—*civil* ... SD-7
Detner Bridge—*other* ... MO-7
Deton Creek—*stream* ... OR-9
Detonti—*locale* ... AR-4
De Tonti Square Hist Dist—*hist pl* ... AL-4
*De Tour* ... MI-6
Detour—*locale* ... OR-9
Detour—*locale* ... UT-8
**Detour**—*pop pl* ... MD-2
De Tour, Point—*cape* ... MI-6
Detour, Point—*cape* ... MI-6
Detour, Point—*cape* ... WI-6
**De Tour (corporate name for De Tour Village)**—*pop pl* ... MI-6
De Tour Lighthouse—*locale* ... MI-6
De Tour Passage—*channel* ... MI-6
De Tour Shoal—*bar* ... MI-6
De Tour State Park—*park* ... MI-6
**De Tour Village**—*pop pl* ... MI-6
*De Tour Village (corporate name De Tour)* ... MI-6
De Tour Village (Township of)—*civ div* ... MI-6
Detrich Canal—*canal* ... ID-8
Detrick—*locale* ... VA-3
*Detrick Dreek* ... MI-6
Detrick Ranch—*locale* ... OR-9
Detrital Reefs—*bar* ... AZ-5
Detrital Valley—*valley* ... AZ-5
Detrital Wash—*stream* ... AZ-5
De Trobriand Bay—*bay* ... ND-7
De Trobriand State Game Mngmt Area—*park* ... ND-7
Detroit—*locale* ... ME-1
Detroit—*locale* ... TN-4
**Detroit**—*pop pl* ... AL-4
**Detroit**—*pop pl* ... IL-6
**Detroit**—*pop pl* ... KS-7
**Detroit**—*pop pl* ... MI-6
**Detroit**—*pop pl* ... OR-9
**Detroit**—*pop pl* ... TX-5
Detroit Arsenal (U.S. Army)—*military* ... MI-6
Detroit Ave Bridge—*hist pl* ... OH-6
Detroit-Bay City RR Company Columbiaville Depot—*hist pl* ... MI-6
**Detroit Beach**—*pop pl* ... MI-6
Detroit Boat Club—*other* ... MI-6
Detroit Camp—*locale* ... MI-6
Detroit (CCD)—*cens area* ... TX-5
Detroit Cem—*cemetery* ... SD-7
Detroit Cem—*cemetery* ... TX-5
Detroit Ch—*church* ... AL-4
Detroit City Airp—*airport* ... MI-6
Detroit Coast Guard Base—*military* ... MI-6
Detroit Cornice and Slate Company Bldg—*hist pl* ... MI-6
Detroit Country Club—*other* ... MI-6
Detroit County Sch—*school* ... MI-6
Detroit Cove—*valley* ... VA-3
Detroit Dam—*dam* ... OR-9
Detroit Dragway—*other* ... MI-6
Detroit Elem Sch—*school* ... AL-4
Detroit Golf Club—*other* ... MI-6
Detroit Harbor—*bay* ... WI-6
**Detroit Harbor**—*pop pl* ... WI-6
Detroit (historical)—*locale* ... SD-7
Detroit House of Correction—*other* ... MI-6
Detroit Institute of Technology—*school* ... MI-6
Detroit Island—*island* ... WI-6
Detroit Island Passage—*channel* ... WI-6
*Detroit Lake* ... OR-9
Detroit Lake—*lake* ... MN-6
**Detroit Lakes**—*pop pl* ... MN-6
Detroit Lakes Carnegie Library—*hist pl* ... MN-6
Detroit Lake State Park—*park* ... OR-9
Detroit Masonic Temple—*hist pl* ... MI-6
Detroit Metropolitan Wayne County Airp—*airport* ... MI-6
Detroit Mine—*mine* ... NV-8
Detroit Mtn—*summit* ... MN-6
Detroit Mtns—*range* ... UT-8
Detroit Observatory—*hist pl* ... MI-6
**Detroit Park (subdivision)**—*pop pl* ... AL-4
Detroit Point—*cape* ... MI-6
Detroit Police Acad—*school* ... MI-6
Detroit Post Office—*building* ... AL-4
Detroit Post Office (historical)—*building* ... SD-7
Detroit Post Office (historical)—*building* ... TN-4
Detroit Race Course—*other* ... MI-6
*Detroit River* ... MI-6
Detroit River—*stream* ... MI-6
Detroit River Light Station—*hist pl* ... MI-6
*Detroit Rsvr* ... OR-9
Detroit Rsvr—*reservoir* ... OR-9
Detroit Sch (historical)—*school* ... TN-4
Detroit-Superior High Level Bridge—*hist pl* ... OH-6
**Detroit (Town of)**—*pop pl* ... ME-1
Detroit Township (historical)—*civil* ... SD-7
**Detroit (Township of)**—*pop pl* ... IL-6
**Detroit (Township of)**—*pop pl* ... MN-6
Detroit Univ Sch—*school* ... MI-6
Detroit-Warren Bldg—*hist pl* ... OH-6
Detroit Waterworks—*other* ... MI-6
Detroit Well—*well* ... NM-5
Detroit Windsor Tunnel—*tunnel* ... MI-6
Detroit Yacht Club—*other* ... MI-6
Detroit Zoological Park—*park* ... MI-6
Detrow Hill—*summit* ... GA-3
Dets Sch—*school* ... PA-2
*Dett Creek* ... WY-8
Detters Lake—*lake* ... NE-7
**Detters Mill**—*pop pl* ... PA-2
Detters Trail—*trail* ... PA-2
Dettinger Ditch—*canal* ... WY-8
Dettmer Hosp—*hospital* ... OH-6
Dettroy Cem—*cemetery* ... MO-7
Dett Sch—*school* ... IL-6
Dett Tank—*reservoir* ... TX-5
Detty Creek—*stream* ... TX-5
Deturks Bridge—*bridge* ... PA-2
De Turksville—*locale* ... PA-2
**De Turksville**—*pop pl* ... PA-2
*De Turkville* ... PA-2
Detweiler Gap—*gap* ... PA-2
Detweiler Run—*stream* ... PA-2
Detweiler Run Natural Area—*park* ... PA-2
Detweiller Park—*park* ... IL-6
*Detweller Run* ... PA-2
Detwiler Cem—*cemetery* ... PA-2
Detwiler Ditch—*canal* ... OH-6
Detwiler House—*hist pl* ... AZ-5
Detwiler Park—*park* ... OH-6
Detwiler Sch—*school* ... MD-2
Detwiller Rsvr—*reservoir* ... CO-8
**Detwood**—*pop pl* ... PA-2
Deubendorff Rapids—*rapids* ... AZ-5
Deuce Island—*island* ... AK-9
Deuce Mine—*mine* ... NV-8
*Deuces Quarters* ... NC-3
*Deuchara* ... IN-6
**Deuchars**—*pop pl* ... IN-6
Deucher—*locale* ... OH-6
*Deuchers* ... IN-6
Deudeu—*island* ... MP-9
*Deudeu-to* ... MP-9
Deuel and Snyder Canal—*canal* ... CO-8
*Deuel Center* ... SD-7
Deuel County—*civil* ... SD-7
Deuel County Courthouse and Jail—*hist pl* ... SD-7
Deuel Creek—*stream* ... PA-2
**Deuel Creek Estates (subdivision)**—*pop pl* ... UT-8
**Deuel Creek Heights (subdivision)**—*pop pl* ... UT-8
Deuel Hollow Brook—*stream* ... NY-2
Deuel Post Office (historical)—*building* ... SD-7
*Deuels Corners* ... NY-2
**Deuels Corners**—*pop pl* ... NY-2
Deuel Vocational Institution—*school* ... CA-9
*Deumbers Creek* ... KY-4
**Deunquat**—*pop pl* ... OH-6
Deurell Pond—*lake* ... FL-3
Deuscher, Henry P., House—*hist pl* ... OH-6
Deusch Lake—*lake* ... MN-6
Deuser Cem—*cemetery* ... IA-7
Deuses Pond—*lake* ... CT-1
Deus Lake—*lake* ... CO-8
Deuson Draw—*valley* ... NM-5
*Deuthat* ... OK-5
Deutschburg Sch—*school* ... TX-5
Deutsche Bisch Cem—*cemetery* ... WI-6
Deutsche Evangelisch Lutherische Zion Kirche—*hist pl* ... NE-7
Deutsche Ev. Luth. St. Johannes Kirche—*hist pl* ... NE-7
Deutsch Evangelische St. Paul's Kirche—*hist pl* ... IN-6
Deutschtown Hist Dist—*hist pl* ... PA-2
Deux Bouts, lac a —*lake* ... LA-4
De Vaca Terrace—*bench* ... AZ-5
**Deval**—*pop pl* ... IL-6
**Devall**—*pop pl* ... LA-4
Devall Branch—*stream* ... FL-3
Devall Cem—*cemetery* (2) ... LA-4
Devall Drain—*canal* ... MI-6
De Valle Sch—*school* ... MA-1
**Devalls**—*pop pl* ... LA-4
**DeValls Bluff**—*pop pl* ... AR-4
**De Valls Bluff (Devallsbluff)**—*pop pl* ... AR-4
Devall Sch—*school* ... LA-4
DeVan Cem—*cemetery* ... AL-4
De Vance Pond—*lake* ... LA-4
Devane Branch—*stream* ... NC-3
Devane-MacQueen House—*hist pl* ... NC-3
Devaney Campground—*locale* ... NV-8
*Devaney Canyon* ... CA-9
Devaney Cem—*cemetery* ... AL-4
DeVaney Cem—*cemetery* ... TN-4
Devaney Creek—*stream* ... CO-8
Devaney Mtn—*summit* ... NV-8
Devaney Ranch—*locale* ... NM-5
Devaney Sch—*school* ... SD-7
Devanney Site—*hist pl* ... OH-6
D Evans Farm Airp—*airport* ... PA-2
Devany Canyon—*valley* ... CA-9
De Vargas Sch—*school* ... CA-9
Devasier Valley—*basin* ... NE-7
Devastation Trail—*trail* ... HI-9
*Devateertha Rock* ... OR-9
Deva Temple—*summit* ... AZ-5
Devaughn Lake Dam—*dam* ... AL-4
DeVaughn-Lewis House—*hist pl* ... GA-3
DeVaughn Sch—*school* ... FL-3
DeVaul Canyon—*valley* ... CA-9
Devaul Dam—*dam* ... OR-9
DeVaul Lake—*lake* ... OR-9
Devaul Ranch—*locale* ... OR-9
Devauls Creek—*stream* ... NJ-2
**Devault**—*pop pl* ... PA-2
DeVault, Valentine, House—*hist pl* ... TN-4
Devault Bend—*bend* ... TN-4
Devault Bridge—*bridge* (2) ... TN-4
Devault Cem—*cemetery* ... TN-4
De Vault Cem—*cemetery* ... TN-4
Devault Ford (historical)—*locale* ... TN-4
DeVault-Masengill House—*hist pl* ... TN-4
Devault Run—*stream* ... IN-6
De Vault Sch—*school* ... IN-6
*Devaults Poind* ... NY-2
DeVault Tavern—*hist pl* ... TN-4
Deveaux Bank—*bar* ... SC-3
Deveaux Park Sch—*school* ... OH-6
De Veaux Sch—*school* ... NY-2

Deveaux Sch Hist Dist—*hist pl* NY-2
Develin Brook—*stream* NY-2
Develin Cem—*cemetery* NY-2
Develing—*locale* PA-2
Develin House—*hist pl* TX-5
Develle Cem—*cemetery* AL-4
Developmental Resource Center Day Sch—*school* FL-3
**Deven Dale (subdivision)**—*pop pl* AL-4
Devener Airp—*airport* PA-2
DeVenoge, Lake—*lake* NY-2
*Devenport* AL-4
**Devenport**—*pop pl* AL-4
**Devenport**—*pop pl* TN-4
Devenport Post Office (historical)—*building* TN-4
**Devenscrest**—*pop pl* MA-1
Devens Island—*island* NH-1
Devens Sch—*school* MA-1
Deventer—*locale* MO-7
Deventer Ch (historical)—*church* MO-7
Deveny Coulee—*valley* MT-8
DeVeny Place—*locale* ID-8
Dever—*locale* OR-9
Deveraux Sch—*school* MN-6
Dever Cem—*cemetery* OH-6
Dever Creek—*stream* CO-8
Dever Cut—*channel* GA-3
Devereau Sch—*school* PA-2
**Devereaux**—*pop pl* MI-6
**Devereaux**—*pop pl* NY-2
Devereaux Branch—*stream* NY-2
Devereaux Cove—*bay* ME-1
Devereaux Ferry (historical)—*locale* NC-3
Devereaux House—*hist pl* UT-8
Devereaux Lake—*lake* MI-6
Devereaux Lake—*lake* TX-5
Devereaux Lake—*lake* WA-9
Devereaux Landing—*locale* NC-3
Devereaux Ranch Sch—*school* CA-9
Devereaux (Township of)—*unorg* ME-1
Devere Dam—*dam* AL-4
De Vere Field Airp—*airport* WA-9
Deverell Spring—*spring* TN-4
*Devereux* NY-2
D'Evereux—*hist pl* MS-4
**Devereux**—*pop pl* GA-3
**Devereux**—*pop pl* MA-1
**Devereux**—*pop pl* NY-2
*Devereux Beach* MA-1
Devereux Beach—*beach* MA-1
Devereux Camps—*locale* ME-1
Devereux (CCD)—*cens area* GA-3
*Devereux Heights* IL-6
**Devereux Heights**—*pop pl* IL-6
Devereux Sch—*school* (3) PA-2
Devereux Station (historical)—*locale* MA-1
Deverick Cem—*cemetery* (2) WV-2
Deverick Ridge—*ridge* WV-2
Deverman Sch—*school* IL-6
Devernia, Lake—*lake* TX-5
Devernois Ranch—*locale* CA-9
Dever Park—*park* MA-1
**Deverre**—*pop pl* NE-7
**Devers**—*pop pl* TX-5
Devers Bay—*bay* VI-3
Devers Branch—*stream* KY-4
Devers Canal—*canal* TX-5
Dever Sch—*school* IL-6
Dever Sch—*school* OR-9
Devers Cove—*valley* AL-4
Devers Cove Saltpeter Cave—*cave* AL-4
Devers Creek—*stream* TX-5
Devers East Canal—*canal* TX-5
Devers Gut—*gut* DE-2
Dever-Sherborn HS—*school* MA-1
Devers Hill—*summit* CA-9
Deversky Pond—*reservoir* CT-1
Devers Main Canal—*canal* TX-5
Deverson Lake—*reservoir* NJ-2
*Deverson Lake Dam* NJ-2
Devers Run—*stream* OH-6
Devers Run—*stream* WV-2
Dever State Sch—*school* (2) MA-1
Devers Woods—*woods* TX-5
Dever Valley—*valley* OH-6
Devess Slough—*lake* IL-6
Deviation Peak—*summit* AK-9
Devies Mtn—*summit* PA-2
**DeView**—*pop pl* AR-4
DeView, Bayou—*stream* AR-4
De View (Township of)—*fmr MCD* AR-4
*Devil* ID-8
Devil Alex Hollow—*valley* PA-2
*Devil Alexs Hollow* PA-2
Devilbiss Bridge—*bridge* MD-2
DeVilbiss Ranch—*locale* CA-9
Devilbliss HS—*school* OH-6
Devil Branch—*stream* LA-4
Devil Branch—*stream* (2) TN-4
Devil Branch—*stream* VA-3
*Devil Brook* MA-1
Devil Camp—*locale* CA-9
Devil Canyon—*valley* (7) CA-9
Devil Canyon—*valley* CO-8
Devil Canyon—*valley* ID-8
Devil Canyon—*valley* (2) MT-8
Devil Canyon—*valley* NV-8
Devil Canyon—*valley* NM-5
Devil Canyon—*valley* (2) OR-9
Devil Canyon—*valley* SD-7
Devil Canyon—*valley* UT-8
Devil Canyon—*valley* WY-8
Devil Canyon Station—*locale* CA-9
Devil Canyon Trail—*trail* CA-9
Devil Club Creek—*stream* WA-9
Devil Country—*area* HI-9
*Devil Creek* IA-7
*Devil Creek* MI-6
*Devil Creek* OR-9
Devil Creek—*stream* AK-9
Devil Creek—*stream* (3) CA-9
Devil Creek—*stream* (2) CO-8
Devil Creek—*stream* (4) ID-8
Devil Creek—*stream* (2) KY-4
Devil Creek—*stream* MN-6
Devil Creek—*stream* (2) MT-8
Devil Creek—*stream* NV-8
Devil Creek—*stream* OR-9
Devil Creek—*stream* TN-4
Devil Creek—*stream* (2) UT-8
Devil Creek—*stream* VA-3
Devil Creek—*stream* WA-9
Devil Creek—*stream* WV-2
Devil Creek—*stream* WI-6
Devil Creek Butte—*summit* ID-8
Devil Creek Falls—*falls* WA-9
Devil Creek Spring—*spring* UT-8
Devil Creek State Wildlife Area—*park* CO-8
Devil Creek Trail—*trail* MT-8
Devil Den Branch—*stream* AL-4
Devil Den Branch—*stream* MS-4
Devil Den Cove—*valley* AL-4
Devil Den Hollow—*valley* MO-7
Devil Den Ridge—*ridge* NC-3
Devil Dog Canyon—*valley* AZ-5
Devil Dog Interchange—*crossing* AZ-5
Devil Dog Tank—*reservoir* AZ-5
Devilfish Bay—*bay* AK-9
Devilfish Key—*island* FL-3
Devilfish Lake—*lake* MN-6
Devilfish Lookout Tower—*locale* MN-6
Devilfish Point—*cape* AK-9
Devil Fork—*stream* (2) TN-4
Devil Fork—*stream* VA-3
Devil Fork—*stream* WV-2
Devil Fork Creek—*stream* SC-3
Devil Fork Gap—*gap* NC-3
Devil Fork Gap—*gap* TN-4
Devil Gap—*valley* MT-8
Devil Gulch—*valley* (2) CA-9
Devil Gulch—*valley* CO-8
Devil Harbor—*ridge* KY-4
Devil Head—*summit* PA-2
Devil Hill—*summit* CA-9
Devil Hills—*summit* AZ-5
Devil Hole Branch—*stream* SC-3
Devilhole Creek—*stream* WV-2
Devil Hole Run—*stream* PA-2
Devil Hole Run—*stream* (2) WV-2
Devil Hollow—*valley* (2) KY-4
Devil Hollow—*valley* TX-5
*Devil Horn* WA-9
Devilhouse Branch—*stream* KY-4
Devilin Branch—*stream* AL-4
Devil Inlet—*bay* AK-9
Devil Island—*island* AK-9
Devil Island—*island* ME-1
Devil Island—*island* MD-2
Devil Island—*island* WI-6
Devil Jump Hollow—*valley* AR-4
*Devil Key* FL-3
*Devil Knob* CO-8
Devil Knob—*summit* NC-3
*Devil Lake* IN-6
*Devil Lake* MI-6
Devil Lake—*lake* AK-9
Devil Lake—*lake* (2) IN-6
Devil Lake—*lake* MI-6
Devil Lake—*lake* MN-6
Devil Lake—*lake* WA-9
Devil Lake—*reservoir* OR-9
Devil Lake Campground—*locale* MN-6
Devil Lake Ditch—*canal* MI-6
**Deville**—*pop pl* LA-4
**De Ville Acres Subdivision**—*pop pl* UT-8
Deville Cem—*cemetery* LA-4
Deville Ch—*church* LA-4
Deville Plaza Shop Ctr—*locale* MS-4
De Viller Cem—*cemetery* LA-4
De Villo—*locale* ND-7
De Villo Town Hall—*building* ND-7
De Villo Township—*civil* ND-7
**Devillo Township**—*pop pl* ND-7
Devil Mesa—*summit* UT-8
Devil Mountain Lakes—*lake* AK-9
Devil Mountain Trail—*trail* CO-8
Devil Mtn—*summit* AK-9
Devil Mtn—*summit* CO-8
Devil Mtn—*summit* MT-8
Devil Neck—*locale* AL-4
Devil Pass Well—*well* NM-5
Devilpaw Mtn—*summit* AK-9
Devil Peak—*summit* (2) CA-9
Devil Peak—*summit* ID-8
Devil Peak—*summit* NV-8
*Devil Point* FL-3
Devil Point—*cape* WA-9
Devil Point—*cliff* CO-8
*Devil Pond Devols Pond* MA-1
*Devil Postpile* CA-9
Devil Ridge—*ridge* MO-7
Devil Ridge—*ridge* TX-5
*Devil River* MI-6
*Devil River* WI-6
Devil River—*stream* OR-9
Devil Rock—*pillar* NV-8
Devil Rock Springs—*spring* NV-8
Devil Run—*stream* MT-8
Devil Run—*stream* WV-2
Devils Alley—*valley* MD-2
Devils Armchair—*summit* NV-8
Devils Armchair—*summit* WY-8
Devils Armchair, The—*basin* UT-8
Devils Back—*bar* ME-1
Devils Back—*bar* MA-1
**Devil's Backbone**—*pop pl* CT-1
Devils Backbone—*ridge* (2) AL-4
Devils Backbone—*ridge* (3) AR-4
Devils Backbone—*ridge* (5) CA-9
Devils Backbone—*ridge* CO-8
Devils Backbone—*ridge* (11) IN-6
Devils Backbone—*ridge* KS-7
Devils Backbone—*ridge* (4) KY-4
Devils Backbone—*ridge* (11) MO-7
Devils Backbone—*ridge* NE-7
Devils Backbone—*ridge* NM-5
Devils Backbone—*ridge* (3) OK-5
Devils Backbone—*ridge* (7) OR-9
Devils Backbone—*ridge* (6) TN-4
Devils Backbone—*ridge* (5) TX-5
Devils Backbone—*ridge* (3) VA-3
Devils Backbone—*ridge* (3) WA-9
Devils Backbone—*ridge* (4) WV-2
Devils Backbone—*summit* IL-6
Devils Backbone—*summit* MD-2
Devils Backbone—*summit* NY-2
Devils Backbone—*summit* OH-6
Devils Backbone—*summit* PA-2
Devils Backbone, The—*ridge* MT-8
Devils Backbone Mtn—*summit* TX-5
Devils Backbone Overlook—*locale* VA-3
Devils Backbone Ridge—*ridge* AR-4
Devils Ball Diamond—*flat* OR-9
*Devils Basin* CA-9
Devils Basin—*basin* (3) CA-9
Devils Basin—*basin* ID-8
Devils Basin Creek—*stream* WY-8
Devils Bathtub—*lake* CA-9
Devils Bathtub—*lake* NY-2
Devils Bathtub—*reservoir* AZ-5
Devils Bathtub—*spring* AZ-5
Devils Bathtub Spring—*spring* TX-5
Devils Bay—*bay* (2) AK-9
Devils Bay—*bay* LA-4
Devils Bay—*swamp* FL-3
Devils Bay—*swamp* (2) GA-3
Devils Bayou—*stream* LA-4
Devils Bayou—*stream* TX-5
Devils Bedstead, The—*summit* ID-8
Devils Bench—*bench* TN-4
Devils Bench Branch—*stream* TN-4
Devils Bend—*bend* AL-4
Devils Blackbone—*ridge* MO-7
Devils Bluff—*cliff* TX-5
Devils Bog—*swamp* ME-1
Devils Bog Brook—*stream* ME-1
Devils Bottom—*bend* MT-8
Devils Bowl Lake—*lake* MI-6
Devils Brake—*swamp* LA-4
Devils Branch—*stream* AL-4
Devils Branch—*stream* FL-3
Devils Branch—*stream* (3) GA-3
Devils Branch—*stream* KY-4
Devils Branch—*stream* MO-7
Devils Branch—*stream* NC-3
Devils Branch—*stream* SC-3
Devils Branch—*stream* (2) TN-4
Devils Branch—*stream* (3) VA-3
Devils Breakfast Table—*locale* TN-4
Devils Bridge—*bar* MA-1
Devils Bridge—*bridge* AZ-5
Devils Bridge—*bridge* VA-3
Devils Brook—*stream* MA-1
Devils Brook—*stream* NJ-2
Devils Butte—*summit* OR-9
Devils Butte—*summit* WA-9
*Devils Cache* AZ-5
*Devils Canon* CO-8
*Devils Canyon* AZ-5
*Devils Canyon* CA-9
*Devils Canyon* ID-8
Devil's Canyon—*hist pl* OK-5
Devils Canyon—*valley* AK-9
Devils Canyon—*valley* (7) AZ-5
Devils Canyon—*valley* AR-4
Devils Canyon—*valley* (20) CA-9
Devils Canyon—*valley* (9) CO-8
Devils Canyon—*valley* ID-8
Devils Canyon—*valley* (2) KS-7
Devils Canyon—*valley* (3) MT-8
Devils Canyon—*valley* NE-7
Devils Canyon—*valley* (2) NV-8
Devils Canyon—*valley* (8) NM-5
Devils Canyon—*valley* (2) OK-5
Devils Canyon—*valley* (8) OR-9
Devils Canyon—*valley* SD-7
Devils Canyon—*valley* (5) TX-5
Devils Canyon—*valley* (4) UT-8
Devils Canyon—*valley* (7) WA-9
Devils Canyon—*valley* (2) WY-8
Devil's Canyon Bridge—*hist pl* AZ-5
Devils Canyon Campground—*locale* UT-8
Devils Canyon (historical)—*locale* KS-7
Devils Canyon Spring—*spring* SD-7
Devils Canyon Spring—*spring* UT-8
Devils Canyon Tank—*reservoir* AZ-5
Devils Canyon Trail—*trail* OR-9
Devils Canyon Well—*well* AZ-5
Devils Canyon 237—*trail* AZ-5
Devils Cascade—*falls* MN-6
Devils Cash Box—*ridge* AZ-5
Devils Castle—*cliff* UT-8
Devils Castle—*rock* UT-8
Devils Castle Flat—*flat* UT-8
Devils Cauldron—*area* CA-9
Devils Cauldron—*bay* OR-9
Devils Cauldron—*bay* WI-6
Devils Causeway—*ridge* CO-8
Devils Cave—*cave* MS-4
Devils Cave—*cave* PA-2
Devils Cave Ridge—*ridge* NV-8
*Devils Cavern* MA-1
Devils Cellar Hollow—*valley* AL-4
Devils Center Table—*summit* TX-5
Devils Chair—*basin* AZ-5
Devils Chair—*basin* CO-8
Devils Chair—*pillar* ID-8
Devils Chair—*summit* CA-9
Devils Chair—*summit* WI-6
Devils Chair, The—*spring* MT-8
Devils Chair Bridge—*bridge* DC-2
*Devils Channel* TN-4
Devils Chasm—*valley* AZ-5
Devils Chimney—*pillar* WI-6
Devils Chimney—*summit* MT-8
Devils Chimney—*summit* NC-3
Devils Churn—*bay* OR-9
Devils Chute Cave—*cave* MT-8
Devils Clay Hole—*basin* FL-3
Devils Club Canyon—*valley* OR-9
Devils Club Creek—*stream* ID-8
Devils Club Creek—*stream* MT-8
Devils Club Creek—*stream* OR-9
Devils Club Creek—*stream* WA-9
Devils Corkscrew Creek—*stream* MT-8
Devils Corner—*locale* MI-6
Devils Corner—*locale* WI-6
Devil's Corner Cliff Walk—*hist pl* WA-9
Devils Cornfield—*flat* CA-9
Devils Corral—*basin* CA-9
Devils Corral—*locale* CA-9
Devils Corral—*locale* ID-8
Devils Corral—*locale* NV-8
*Devils Corral Creek* CA-9
Devils Cotton Patch—*swamp* SC-3
*Devils Course* PA-2
*Devils Court House* NC-3
Devils Courthouse—*ridge* NC-3
Devils Courthouse—*summit* TN-4
Devils Courthouse—*swamp* NC-3
Devils Courthouse Peak—*summit* TX-5
Devils Court House Ridge—*ridge* NC-3
Devils Cove—*bay* AK-9
Devils Cove—*bay* NV-8
Devils Cove—*valley* GA-3
Devils Cradle Creek—*stream* NC-3
Devils Crags—*summit* CA-9
*Devils Creek* CO-8
*Devil's Creek* IA-7
*Devils Creek* MT-8
*Devils Creek* TN-4
Devils Creek—*stream* (2) AK-9
Devils Creek—*stream* AR-4
Devils Creek—*stream* (4) CA-9
Devils Creek—*stream* (2) CO-8
Devils Creek—*stream* (2) ID-8
Devils Creek—*stream* IA-7
Devils Creek—*stream* KS-7
Devils Creek—*stream* KY-4
Devils Creek—*stream* (2) LA-4
Devils Creek—*stream* (2) MI-6
Devils Creek—*stream* (3) MT-8
Devils Creek—*stream* NV-8
Devils Creek—*stream* (2) NM-5
Devils Creek—*stream* NC-3
Devils Creek—*stream* OK-5
Devils Creek—*stream* (2) OR-9
Devils Creek—*stream* TN-4
Devils Creek—*stream* (3) TX-5
Devils Creek—*stream* (4) WA-9
Devils Creek—*stream* (3) WI-6
Devils Creek—*stream* WY-8
Devils Creek—*swamp* FL-3
Devils Creek Campground—*locale* MT-8
Devils Creek Gap—*gap* NC-3
Devils Creek Gap—*gap* TN-4
Devils Creek State Wildlife Mngmt Area—*park* WI-6
Devils Creek Swamp—*swamp* FL-3
Devils Creek Trail—*trail* AK-9
Devils Creek Well—*well* NM-5
Devils Cup and Saucer Island—*island* FL-3
*Devils Cut* NC-3
Devils Dance Floor—*flat* UT-8
Devils Dancehall—*valley* MT-8
Devils Darning Needle—*pillar* WV-2
Devils Darning Needle Hollow—*valley* GA-3
*Devils Den* CA-9
Devils Den—*area* CT-1
Devils Den—*basin* (3) AL-4
Devils Den—*basin* CA-9
Devils Den—*basin* (2) MO-7
Devils Den—*basin* NH-1
Devils Den—*basin* TN-4
Devils Den—*basin* TX-5
Devils Den—*basin* (2) VT-1
Devils Den—*cave* NY-2
Devils Den—*cave* (3) TN-4
Devils Den—*cave* VA-3
Devils Den—*flat* CA-9
Devils Den—*flat* OR-9
Devils Den—*gap* NY-2
Devils Den—*gap* VT-1
Devils Den—*lake* GA-3
Devils Den—*locale* CA-9
Devils Den—*locale* GA-3
Devils Den—*locale* PA-2
Devils Den—*locale* WY-8
Devils Den—*other* CA-9
Devils Den—*other* IN-6
Devils Den—*other* OK-5
Devils Den—*other* PA-2
Devils Den—*pillar* CA-9
Devils Den—*summit* ME-1
Devils Den—*summit* NY-2
Devils Den—*summit* (2) PA-2
Devils Den—*summit* TN-4
Devils Den—*summit* VA-3
Devils Den—*swamp* GA-3
Devils Den—*valley* MA-1
Devils Den—*valley* MO-7
Devils Den—*valley* UT-8
Devil's Den, McClurg Covered Bridge—*hist pl* PA-2
Devils Den Bay—*swamp* MS-4
*Devils Den Branch* MS-4
Devils Den Branch—*stream* AL-4
Devilsden Branch—*stream* GA-3
Devils Den Branch—*stream* GA-3
Devils Den Branch—*stream* KY-4
Devils Den Branch—*stream* WV-2
*Devils Den Canon* CO-8
*Devils Den Canyon* CO-8
Devils Den Canyon—*valley* AZ-5
Devils Den Canyon—*valley* CA-9
Devils Den Canyon—*valley* NE-7
Devils Den Canyon—*valley* (3) NM-5
Devils Den Canyon—*valley* TX-5
Devils Den Cave—*cave* AL-4
Devils Den Cave—*cave* PA-2
Devils Den Cave—*cave* TN-4
*Devils Den Creek* CO-8
Devils Den Creek—*stream* FL-3
Devils Den Creek—*stream* SC-3
Devils Den Hollow—*valley* AL-4
Devils Den Hollow—*valley* AR-4
Devils Den Hollow—*valley* (3) MO-7
Devils Den Hollow—*valley* OH-6
Devils Den Hollow—*valley* TX-5
Devils Den Hollow—*valley* WV-2
Devils Den Lookout Tower—*locale* NH-1
Devils Den Mtn—*summit* NH-1
Devils Den Mtn—*summit* NC-3
*Devils Den Oil Field* CA-9
*Devils Den Ridge* NC-3
Devils Den Spring—*spring* NM-5
Devils Den State Park—*park* AR-4
Devils Desk—*summit* AK-9
Devils Dining Room—*area* AZ-5
Devils Dip Creek—*stream* WY-8
Devils Dishfull Pond—*reservoir* MA-1
Devils Dishfull Pond Dam—*dam* MA-1
Devils Ditch—*gut* VA-3
Devils Ditch—*stream* KS-7
Devils Ditch—*stream* VA-3
Devils Dive—*locale* ID-8
Devils Dive Creek—*stream* ID-8
Devils Dome—*summit* WA-9
Devils Draw—*valley* TX-5
Devils Dream Creek—*stream* WA-9
Devils Dump Run—*stream* WV-2
Devils Dungeon Cave—*cave* AL-4
Devils Dutch Oven—*summit* UT-8
Devils Elbow—*bar* ME-1
Devils Elbow—*bay* AK-9
Devils Elbow—*bay* KY-4
Devils Elbow—*bend* AK-9
Devils Elbow—*bend* (2) AR-4
Devils Elbow—*bend* (5) CA-9
Devils Elbow—*bend* (6) FL-3
Devils Elbow—*bend* ID-8
Devils Elbow—*bend* (2) IN-6
Devils Elbow—*bend* (2) KY-4
Devils Elbow—*bend* (2) LA-4
Devils Elbow—*bend* ME-1
Devils Elbow—*bend* MN-6
Devils Elbow—*bend* MS-4
Devils Elbow—*bend* MT-8
Devils Elbow—*bend* NY-2
Devils Elbow—*bend* (5) NC-3
Devils Elbow—*bend* OR-9
Devils Elbow—*bend* (5) PA-2
Devils Elbow—*bend* (3) SC-3
Devils Elbow—*bend* (2) TN-4
Devils Elbow—*bend* (3) TX-5
Devils Elbow—*bend* (2) VA-3
Devils Elbow—*bend* (3) WA-9
Devils Elbow—*bend* (2) WI-6
Devils Elbow—*cape* (2) OR-9
Devils Elbow—*channel* AK-9
Devils Elbow—*channel* FL-3
Devils Elbow—*cliff* CO-8
Devils Elbow—*cliff* NY-2
Devils Elbow—*cliff* PA-2
Devils Elbow—*flat* NV-8
Devils Elbow—*gap* TN-4
Devils Elbow—*lake* FL-3
Devils Elbow—*locale* CA-9
**Devils Elbow**—*pop pl* MI-6
**Devils Elbow**—*pop pl* MO-7
Devils Elbow—*ridge* CA-9
Devils Elbow—*summit* PA-2
Devils Elbow Bayou—*gut* MS-4
Devils Elbow Campground—*locale* ID-8
Devils Elbow Creek—*stream* CA-9
Devils Elbow Hollow—*valley* PA-2
*Devils Elbow Landing* NC-3
Devils Elbow State Park—*park* OR-9
Devils Elbow Swamp—*swamp* FL-3
Devils Eye—*arch* WA-9
Devils Eyebrow—*ridge* WA-9
Devils Farm—*locale* ID-8
Devils Farm Creek—*stream* ID-8
Devils Feather Bed—*other* PA-2
Devils Fence—*ridge* MT-8
Devils Finger—*island* AK-9
Devils Flat Guard Station—*locale* OR-9
Devil's Foot Cemetery Archeol Site, RI-694—*hist pl* RI-1
Devils Foot Island—*island* MA-1
Devilsfoot Island—*island* MA-1
Devils Footstool—*summit* MT-8
Devils Ford Creek—*stream* TX-5
*Devils Fork* WV-2
Devils Fork—*stream* (2) AR-4
Devils Fork—*stream* IA-7
Devils Fork—*stream* KY-4
Devils Fork—*stream* (2) NC-3
Devils Fork—*stream* SC-3
Devils Fork—*stream* WV-2
*Devils Fork Creek* TX-5
Devils Fork Creek—*stream* (2) SC-3
Devils Fork Gas Field—*other* NM-5
Devils Fork Little Red River—*stream* AR-4
Devils Fork Mtn—*summit* NC-3
Devils Fork Rec Area—*park* AR-4
*Devils Gap* OR-9
Devils Gap—*gap* (2) AL-4
Devils Gap—*gap* (2) AR-4
Devils Gap—*gap* (3) CA-9
Devils Gap—*gap* CO-8
Devils Gap—*gap* ID-8
Devils Gap—*gap* NV-8
Devils Gap—*gap* OR-9
Devils Gap—*gap* UT-8
Devils Gap—*gap* VT-1
Devils Gap—*gap* WA-9
Devils Gap—*gap* WY-8
Devils Gap—*locale* NE-7
*Devils Gap Creek* MT-8
Devils Gap Sch—*school* NE-7
Devils Gap Spring—*spring* WY-8
*Devils Garden* UT-8
Devils Garden—*area* KY-4
Devils Garden—*area* (4) OR-9
Devils Garden—*area* UT-8
Devils Garden—*area* WV-2
Devils Garden—*cliff* NC-3
Devils Garden—*flat* CA-9
Devils Garden—*locale* FL-3
Devils Garden—*locale* ID-8
Devils Garden—*ridge* PA-2
Devils Garden—*rock* UT-8
Devils Garden—*summit* MA-1
Devils Garden—*summit* NM-5
Devils Garden—*summit* OR-9
Devils Garden—*swamp* FL-3
Devils Garden, The—*area* OR-9
Devils Garden Branch—*stream* KY-4
Devils Garden Campground—*locale* (2) UT-8
Devils Garden Forest Camp—*locale* OR-9
Devils Garden Outstanding Natural Area—*area* UT-8
Devils Garden Overlook—*locale* NC-3
Devils Garden Ridge—*ridge* WV-2
Devils Gardens—*area* WA-9
Devils Garden Slough—*gut* FL-3
Devils Garden Spring—*spring* OR-9
Devils Garden Trailhead—*locale* UT-8
Devils Gate—*cape* CA-9
Devils Gate—*channel* CA-9
Devils Gate—*flat* NV-8
Devils Gate—*gap* (7) CA-9
Devils Gate—*gap* (10) NV-8
Devils Gate—*gap* OR-9
Devils Gate—*gap* (4) UT-8
Devils Gate—*gap* WY-8
Devils Gate—*locale* (2) CA-9
Devils Gate—*valley* WI-6
Devils Gate Basin—*basin* UT-8
Devils Gate Canyon—*valley* (2) NV-8
Devils Gate Canyon—*valley* UT-8
Devils Gate Creek—*stream* WY-8
Devils Gate Interchange—*crossing* NV-8
Devils Gate Narrows—*gap* UT-8
Devils Gate Pass—*gap* CA-9
Devils Gate Ranch—*locale* NV-8
Devils Gate Rock—*island* CA-9
Devils Gate Rsvr—*reservoir* CA-9
Devils Gate Valley—*valley* UT-8
Devils Gateway—*gap* CA-9
Devils Gate Well—*well* NV-8
Devils Glen—*stream* CA-9
Devils Glen—*valley* MT-8
Devils Glen Brook—*stream* VT-1
Devils Glen Park—*park* IA-7
Devils Golf Ball—*pillar* UT-8
Devils Golf Course—*area* CA-9
Devils Gorge—*valley* ID-8
Devils Grave Hill—*summit* SD-7
Devils Grave Mesa—*summit* CO-8
Devils Graveyard—*area* OR-9
Devils Graveyard—*summit* WY-8
*Devils Gulch* CA-9
Devils Gulch—*basin* CA-9
Devils Gulch—*valley* AK-9
Devils Gulch—*valley* (10) CA-9
Devils Gulch—*valley* (3) CO-8
Devils Gulch—*valley* MT-8
Devils Gulch—*valley* NE-7
Devils Gulch—*valley* NM-5
Devils Gulch—*valley* ND-7
Devils Gulch—*valley* (3) OR-9
Devils Gulch—*valley* SD-7
Devils Gulch—*valley* (2) TX-5
Devils Gulch—*valley* WA-9
Devils Gulch—*valley* WV-2
Devils Gulch Trail—*trail* WA-9
Devils Gut—*gut* CA-9
Devils Gut—*gut* NJ-2
Devils Gut—*stream* NC-3
*Devils Half Acre* AL-4
Devils Half Acre—*area* SD-7
Devils Half Acre—*locale* CA-9
Devils Half Acre—*plain* CA-9
Devils Half Acre—*summit* OR-9
Devils Halfacre—*summit* OR-9
Devils Half Acre Meadow—*flat* OR-9
Devils Hall—*other* TX-5
Devils Hammock—*swamp* FL-3
Devils Head—*cape* ME-1
Devils Head—*cliff* WA-9
Devils Head—*summit* AZ-5
Devils Head—*summit* CO-8
Devils Head—*summit* (3) ME-1
Devils Head Campground—*locale* CO-8
Devils Head Golf Course—*other* WI-6
*Devil's Head Lake* MI-6
Devils Head Lake—*lake* MI-6
Devils Head Lodge—*building* WI-6
Devils Head Peak—*summit* CA-9
Devils Heart Butte—*summit* ND-7
Devils Heart Peak—*summit* CA-9
Devils Heel—*pillar* OR-9
Devils Hill—*summit* ID-8
Devils Hill—*summit* OR-9
Devils Hill—*summit* TX-5
Devils Hill—*summit* (2) VT-1
Devil Shoals—*bar* (2) NC-3
*Devils Hole* AL-4
*Devils Hole* WY-8
Devils Hole—*area* CA-9
Devils Hole—*area* NE-7
Devils Hole—*area* WA-9
Devils Hole—*basin* AZ-5
Devils Hole—*basin* CA-9
Devils Hole—*basin* (4) CO-8
Devils Hole—*basin* (2) ID-8
Devils Hole—*basin* MI-6
Devils Hole—*basin* MT-8
Devils Hole—*basin* (3) UT-8
Devils Hole—*bay* MI-6
Devils Hole—*bend* MT-8
Devils Hole—*bend* NM-5
Devils Hole—*bend* PA-2
Devils Hole—*bend* TX-5
Devils Hole—*bend* WY-8
Devils Hole—*cave* PA-2
Devils Hole—*gap* NY-2
Devils Hole—*lake* AL-4
Devils Hole—*locale* UT-8
Devils Hole—*other* CA-9
Devils Hole—*spring* ID-8
Devils Hole—*spring* NV-8
Devils Hole—*valley* (2) CA-9
Devils Hole—*valley* CO-8
Devils Hole, The—*bay* PA-2
Devils Hole Boulder Caves—*cave* PA-2
Devils Hole Canyon—*valley* CO-8
Devils Hole Canyon—*valley* UT-8
Devils Hole Cave—*cave* TN-4
Devils Hole Creek—*stream* CO-8
Devils Hole Creek—*stream* ID-8
Devils Hole Creek—*stream* (2) MT-8
Devils Hole Creek—*stream* NC-3
Devils Hole Creek—*stream* PA-2
Devils Hole Creek—*stream* SC-3
Devils Hole Creek—*stream* WY-8
Devils Hole Gulch—*valley* CA-9
Devils Hole Gulch—*valley* (2) CO-8
Devils Hole Lake—*lake* CA-9
Devils Hole Lakes—*lake* WY-8
Devils Hole Mountain—*ridge* WV-2
Devils Hole Mtn—*summit* CO-8
Devils Hole Mtn—*summit* VA-3
Devils Hole Prairie—*flat* CA-9
Devils Hole Ridge—*ridge* CA-9
Devils Holes—*rapids* NY-2
Devils Hole Trail—*trail* CO-8
Devils Hole Trail—*trail* WY-8
Devils Hollow—*valley* (2) AL-4
Devils Hollow—*valley* (3) AR-4
Devils Hollow—*valley* ID-8
Devils Hollow—*valley* IN-6
Devils Hollow—*valley* (2) IA-7
Devils Hollow—*valley* MO-7
Devils Hollow—*valley* (2) OK-5
Devils Hollow—*valley* (9) TX-5
Devils Hollow—*valley* (2) UT-8

Devils Hollow Creek—*stream* TX-5
Devils Hollow Lake—*lake* MI-6
Devils Homestead—*lake* CA-9
Devils Hopper, The—*basin* VA-3
Devils Hopyard State Park—*park* CT-1
Devils Hopyard Stream—*stream* NH-1
Devils Hopyard Swamp—*swamp* CT-1
Devils Horn—*summit* MO-7
Devils Horn—*summit* OR-9
Devils Horn—*valley* MO-7
Devils Horns—*summit* WA-9
Devils Hump—*summit* AZ-5
Devils Hump—*summit* MT-8
Devils Hump—*summit* PA-2
Devils Hump Tank—*reservoir* AZ-5
Devils Icebox—*other* MO-7
*Devil's Island* MD-2
Devils Island—*island* DE-2
Devils Island—*island* IL-6
Devils Island—*island* IA-7
Devils Island—*island* LA-4
Devils Island—*island* NJ-2
Devils Island—*island* WI-6
Devils Island (historical)—*island* SD-7
Devils Islands—*island* MN-6
Devils Island Shoal—*bar* WI-6
Devils Isle—*island* CA-9
Devils Jawbone Tank—*reservoir* AZ-5
Devils Jump—*cliff* KY-4
Devils Jump Branch—*stream* KY-4
Devils Jump Creek—*stream* TX-5
Devils Jumpoff—*locale* CA-9
*Devils Kitchen* UT-8
Devils Kitchen—*area* AZ-5
Devils Kitchen—*area* UT-8
Devils Kitchen—*basin* MO-7
Devils Kitchen—*basin* (2) MT-8
Devils Kitchen—*basin* NY-2
Devils Kitchen—*basin* OR-9
Devils Kitchen—*basin* (2) TX-5
Devils Kitchen—*basin* UT-8
Devils Kitchen—*basin* WY-8
Devils Kitchen—*bay* TX-5
Devils Kitchen—*flat* (4) CA-9
Devils Kitchen—*flat* GA-3
Devils Kitchen—*locale* VA-3
Devils Kitchen—*other* CA-9
Devils Kitchen—*other* OR-9
Devils Kitchen—*other* WA-9
Devils Kitchen—*pillar* CO-8
Devils Kitchen—*summit* CA-9
Devils Kitchen—*summit* CO-8
Devils Kitchen—*swamp* MI-6
Devils Kitchen—*valley* CA-9
Devils Kitchen, The—*basin* MT-8
Devils Kitchen Branch—*stream* TN-4
Devils Kitchen Cave—*cave* AR-4
Devils Kitchen Lake—*reservoir* IL-6
Devils Kitchen Mine—*mine* MO-7
Devils Kitchen Picnic Area—*locale* CO-8
Devils Kitchen Rsvr—*reservoir* UT-8
Devils Knob—*pillar* CO-8
Devils Knob—*summit* (3) AR-4
Devils Knob—*summit* KY-4
Devils Knob—*summit* OH-6
Devils Knob—*summit* VA-3
Devils Knob Creek—*stream* OR-9
Devils Knob Lookout—*locale* OR-9
Devils Ladder—*cliff* ID-8
Devils Ladder—*locale* ID-8
*Devils Lake* IN-6
*Devil's Lake* MI-6
*Devils Lake* MN-6
*Devils Lake* ND-7
*Devils Lake* OR-9
*Devils Lake* WI-6
*Devils Lake* WY-8
Devils Lake—*lake* (2) AK-9
Devils Lake—*lake* (2) CA-9
Devils Lake—*lake* CO-8
Devils Lake—*lake* (2) ID-8
Devils Lake—*lake* IN-6
Devils Lake—*lake* (3) LA-4
Devils Lake—*lake* (3) MI-6
Devils Lake—*lake* (6) MN-6
Devils Lake—*lake* NY-2
Devils Lake—*lake* ND-7
Devils Lake—*lake* (3) OR-9
Devils Lake—*lake* (2) TX-5
Devils Lake—*lake* (4) WA-9
Devils Lake—*lake* (9) WI-6
Devils Lake—*lake* WY-8
**Devils Lake**—*pop pl* (2) MI-6
**Devils Lake**—*pop pl* ND-7
**Devil's Lake**—*pop pl* OR-9
**Devils Lake**—*pop pl* WI-6
Devils Lake—*reservoir* MI-6
Devils Lake—*reservoir* OR-9
Devils Lake—*swamp* MI-6
*Devils Lake Creek* OR-9
Devils Lake Dam—*dam* NC-3
Devils Lake Drive-in Ch—*church* MI-6
Devils Lake Fork—*stream* OR-9
*Devils Lake Fork of Wilson River* OR-9
Devils Lake Golf Course—*other* OR-9
Devils Lake Mtn—*summit* ND-7
Devils Lake Municipal Airp—*airport* ND-7
Devils Lake State Park—*park* OR-9
Devils Lake State Park (Ice Age Natl Scientific Reserve)—*park* WI-6
Devils Lake Trail—*trail* MI-6
Devils Lane—*basin* UT-8
Devils Leap—*cliff* WY-8
Devil Slide—*basin* WY-8
Devils Limb—*bar* ME-1
Devils Lodge Branch—*stream* SC-3
Devils Looking Glass—*summit* TN-4
Devils Lookout—*cliff* CO-8
Devils Marbleyard—*rock* VA-3
Devils Marsh—*swamp* WI-6
Devils Meadow Campground—*park* OR-9
Devils Mesa—*summit* NM-5
Devils Mill Hopper—*basin* FL-3
Devils Mill Hopper State Geological Site—*locale* FL-3
Devils Monmt—*pillar* UT-8
Devils Monmt—*pillar* WI-6
Devils Monmt—*pillar* WY-8
Devils Mountain Lodge—*locale* AK-9
Devils Mtn—*summit* AK-9
Devils Mtn—*summit* CA-9
Devils Mtn—*summit* WA-9
Devils Neck—*cape* AR-4
Devils Neck—*cape* TN-4
Devils Nest—*basin* MD-2
Devils Nest—*flat* CA-9
Devils Nest—*summit* NC-3
Devils Nest—*summit* ND-7
Devils Nest—*swamp* NC-3
Devils Nest Creek—*stream* NE-7
Devils Nest Creek—*stream* TN-4
Devils Nest Mine—*mine* AZ-5
Devils Nest Rec Area—*park* NE-7
Devils Nose—*cape* NY-2
Devils Nose—*cliff* WI-6
Devils Nose—*ridge* WV-2
Devils Nose—*summit* CA-9
Devils Nose—*summit* CO-8
Devils Nose—*summit* TN-4
Devils Nose, The—*ridge* WV-2
Devils Nose Branch—*stream* TN-4
Devils Nose Valley—*valley* TN-4
Devils Old Field Swamp—*swamp* FL-3
Devils Orchard—*lava* ID-8
Devils Orchard—*swamp* SC-3
Devils Oven Island—*island* NY-2
Devils Oven Lake—*lake* CA-9
Devils Parade Ground—*area* CA-9
Devils Park—*flat* (2) CO-8
Devils Park—*flat* NM-5
Devils Park—*flat* WA-9
Devils Park Shelter—*locale* WA-9
Devils Park Tank—*reservoir* NM-5
Devils Pass—*gap* AK-9
Devils Pass—*gap* NV-8
Devils Pass—*gap* ND-7
Devils Pass—*gap* WA-9
Devils Pass—*gap* WY-8
Devils Pass Lake—*lake* AK-9
Devils Paw—*summit* AK-9
*Devils Peak* CA-9
Devils Peak—*summit* (3) CA-9
Devils Peak—*summit* MA-1
Devils Peak—*summit* OK-5
Devils Peak—*summit* (3) OR-9
Devils Peak—*summit* UT-8
Devils Peak—*summit* (3) WA-9
Devils Peak Trail—*trail* OR-9
Devils Pit—*cape* CA-9
Devils Playground—*area* MT-8
Devils Playground—*area* UT-8
Devils Playground—*area* WY-8
Devils Playground—*flat* CA-9
Devils Playground—*locale* ID-8
Devils Playground—*park* WY-8
Devils Playground—*rock* UT-8
Devils Playground Tank—*reservoir* AZ-5
Devils Playground Wash—*valley* CA-9
Devils Playground Windmill—*locale* TX-5
Devils Pocket—*basin* AZ-5
Devils Pocket—*basin* CA-9
Devils Pocket—*basin* TX-5
Devils Pocket—*basin* UT-8
Devils Pocket—*basin* WA-9
Devils Pocket—*valley* AR-4
Devils Pocket—*valley* TN-4
Devils Pocket—*valley* UT-8
Devils Point—*cape* FL-3
Devils Point—*cliff* NM-5
Devils Point—*summit* ID-8
Devils Point Rec Area—*park* TN-4
*Devils Pond* MA-1
Devils Pond—*lake* NY-2
Devils Pond—*lake* VT-1
Devils Pool—*lake* PA-2
Devils Pool—*spring* MO-7
*Devils Post Pile* CA-9
Devils Postpile—*cliff* CA-9
Devils Post Pile—*summit* CA-9
Devils Postpile Natl Monmt—*park* CA-9
Devils Potato Patch—*area* PA-2
Devils Potrero—*flat* CA-9
Devils Promenade Bridge—*bridge* OK-5
Devils Prong—*stream* NC-3
Devils Prongs—*pillar* AK-9
Devils Pulpit—*other* CA-9
Devils Pulpit—*pillar* PA-2
Devils Pulpit—*summit* ID-8
Devils Pulpit—*summit* OR-9
Devils Punchbowl—*basin* (3) CA-9
Devils Punchbowl—*basin* CO-8
Devils Punch Bowl—*basin* OR-9
Devils Punch Bowl—*basin* WY-8
Devils Punch Bowl—*lake* AK-9
Devils Punchbowl—*lake* (2) CA-9
Devils Punch Bowl—*lake* PA-2
Devils Punch Bowl—*lake* WA-9
Devils Punch Bowl—*locale* OR-9
Devils Punch Bowl County Park—*park* WI-6
Devils Punch Bowl Lake—*lake* NE-7
Devils Punch Bowl State Park—*park* OR-9
Devils Race Course—*area* PA-2
Devils Racecourse—*area* PA-2
Devils Race Course—*channel* TN-4
Devils Race Course—*stream* PA-2
*Devils Race Ground* TN-4
Devils Race Patch—*summit* NC-3
Devils Racepath—*gap* VA-3
Devils Racepath—*ridge* TN-4
Devils Race Track—*locale* TN-4
Devils Race Track—*summit* AL-4
*Devils Racetrack, The* UT-8
Devils Race Track (Diabase Dike)—*other* NM-5
Devils Reach—*area* MD-2
Devils Reach—*channel* (2) VA-3
Devils Reach—*gut* NJ-2
Devils Reservation Mtn—*summit* TX-5
Devils Rest—*summit* OR-9
Devils Ribs—*summit* CA-9
*Devils Ridge* WA-9
*Devils River* MI-6
*Devils River* TX-5
Devils River—*stream* MI-6
Devils River—*stream* (2) TX-5
Devils River—*stream* WI-6
*Devils River Canyon* TX-5
Devils River Draw—*valley* TX-5
Devils River Windmill—*locale* TX-5
Devils Rock—*pillar* CA-9
Devils Rock—*summit* MA-1
Devils Rock Garden—*area* CA-9
Devils Rock Garden—*ridge* CA-9
*Devils Rock House* UT-8
Devils Rocking Chair—*pillar* CO-8
Devils Rockpile—*pillar* CO-8
Devils Rockpile—*summit* CA-9
Devils Rock Pile—*summit* MO-7
Devils Rock Yard—*island* FL-3
Devils Run—*stream* (2) IA-7
Devils Run—*stream* MN-6
Devils Run—*stream* (2) MO-7
Devils Run—*stream* (2) PA-2
Devils Run—*stream* TX-5
Devils Run—*stream* VA-3
Devils Run—*stream* WV-2
Devils Run—*stream* WY-8
Devils Run Creek—*stream* OR-9
Devils Saddle—*gap* UT-8
Devils Saltcellar Ridge—*ridge* AL-4
**Devils Shores**—*pop pl* TX-5
Devils Sinkhole—*cave* TX-5
*Devils Sinkhole Cavern* TX-5
Devils Slack Tub—*basin* FL-3
*Devils Slide* OR-9
Devils Slide—*cape* WA-9
Devils Slide—*cliff* CO-8
Devils Slide—*cliff* ID-8
Devils Slide—*cliff* (2) MT-8
Devils Slide—*cliff* (3) OR-9
Devils Slide—*cliff* (3) WA-9
Devils Slide—*cliff* (2) WY-8
**Devils Slide**—*pop pl* UT-8
Devils Slide—*ridge* CO-8
Devils Slide—*slope* (3) CA-9
Devils Slide—*slope* (2) UT-8
Devils Slide—*slope* WA-9
Devils Slide—*valley* CA-9
Devils Slide Canyon—*valley* NV-8
Devils Slide Creek—*stream* CO-8
Devils Slide Lake—*lake* WA-9
Devils Slide Rapids—*rapids* AZ-5
Devils Slough—*gut* (2) CA-9
Devils Slough—*stream* TX-5
Devils Smoke Stack—*summit* WA-9
Devils Speedway—*area* CA-9
Devils Spring—*spring* CA-9
Devils Spring—*spring* (2) OR-9
Devils Spring—*stream* TX-5
Devils Spring Cave—*cave* AL-4
Devils Spring Mesa—*summit* NM-5
*Devils Staircase* OR-9
*Devils Stairs* VA-3
Devils Stairs—*locale* WY-8
Devils Stairs—*rapids* OR-9
Devils Stair Step Cave—*cave* AL-4
Devils Stairsteps—*ridge* CO-8
Devils Stairway—*cliff* CO-8
Devils Stairway—*cliff* OR-9
Devils Stairway—*cliff* WA-9
Devils Step—*cliff* TN-4
Devils Steps, The—*slope* UT-8
Devils Swamp—*swamp* (2) FL-3
Devils Swamp—*swamp* (3) LA-4
Devils Swamp—*swamp* MS-4
Devils Table—*summit* CA-9
Devils Table—*summit* WA-9
Devils Table Rock—*summit* MT-8
Devils Tailbone Ridge—*ridge* WA-9
*Devil Stairs* VA-3
Devils Tank—*reservoir* NM-5
Devils Tank—*reservoir* (2) TX-5
Devils Tanyard—*summit* VA-3
Devils Tater Patch—*summit* NC-3
Devils Tater Patch—*summit* TN-4
Devils Tater Patch Branch—*stream* TN-4
Devils Tea Table—*cliff* NJ-2
Devils Tea Table—*locale* OH-6
Devils Tea Table—*summit* WV-2
Devils Teeth Creek—*stream* ID-8
Devils Teeth Rapids—*rapids* ID-8
Devilstep Hollow—*valley* TN-4
Devilstep Hollow Cave—*cave* TN-4
Devils Throat—*crater* HI-9
Devils Throat—*reservoir* NV-8
Devils Throne—*cliff* NM-5
Devils Thumb—*cape* AK-9
Devils Thumb—*cliff* CO-8
Devils Thumb—*pillar* CA-9
Devils Thumb—*pillar* (2) CO-8
Devils Thumb—*pillar* NV-8
Devils Thumb—*ridge* CA-9
Devils Thumb—*summit* AK-9
Devils Thumb—*summit* ND-7
Devils Thumb—*summit* WA-9
Devils Thumb Lake—*lake* CO-8
Devils Thumb Park—*flat* CO-8
Devils Thumb Pass—*gap* CO-8
Devils Thumbs—*pillar* AK-9
Devils Thumb Trail—*trail* CO-8
Devils Toe Creek—*stream* ID-8
Devils Toenail—*summit* TX-5
Devils Tollgate—*other* MO-7
Devils Tombstone—*cliff* NY-2
Devils Tombstone—*pillar* TX-5
Devils Tooth—*summit* ID-8
Devils Tooth—*summit* WY-8
Devils Top—*summit* CA-9
**Devils Tower**—*pop pl* WY-8
Devils Tower—*summit* MT-8
Devils Tower—*summit* WY-8
Devils Tower Natl Monument—*park* WY-8
Devils Tower Natl Monument—*summit* WY-8
Devilstrace Branch—*stream* WV-2
*Devils Track Lake* MN-6
*Devils Track River* MN-6
*Devils Tract River* MN-6
Devils Turnip Patch—*flat* PA-2
Devils Twist—*cliff* UT-8
Devils Wall—*summit* ME-1
Devil Swamp—*swamp* (2) LA-4
*Devil's Wash Basin* MI-6
Devils Wash Basin—*basin* NM-5
Devils Washbasin—*basin* WA-9
Devils Washbasin—*lake* MI-6
Devils Wash Basin—*lake* NM-5
Devils Washbasin—*locale* ID-8
Devils Washbasin—*other* NE-7
Devils Washboard—*area* IL-6
Devils Washboard—*cliff* AZ-5
Devils Washboard Falls—*falls* ID-8
Devils Washbowl—*basin* CA-9
Devils Washbowl—*basin* WI-6
Devils Washbowl—*lake* NH-1
Devils Washdish—*lake* NY-2
Devils Wash Pan—*basin* MO-7
Devils Washtub—*locale* WY-8
Devils Waterhole—*lake* TX-5
Devils Waterhole Creek—*stream* TX-5
Devils Waterhole Hills—*range* TX-5
Devils Waterhole Tank—*reservoir* TX-5
Devils Wedge—*cape* NJ-2
Devils Well—*basin* NM-5
Devils Well—*cave* MO-7
Devils Well—*well* WA-9
Devils Well Cave—*cave* AL-4
Devils Well Creek—*stream* OR-9
Devils Well Hollow—*valley* MO-7
Devils Window—*gap* UT-8
*Devils Windpipe* AZ-5
Devils Windpipe—*valley* AZ-5
Devils Woodyard—*swamp* FL-3
Devils Woodyard—*swamp* NC-3
Devils Woodyard—*woods* DE-2
Devils Woodyard Bay—*basin* SC-3
Devil Tank—*reservoir* AZ-5
Devil Tank—*reservoir* NM-5
Devil Tank—*reservoir* TX-5
**Devil Town**—*pop pl* OH-6
Devil Track Lake—*lake* MN-6
Devil Track River—*stream* MN-6
Devil Tree, The—*locale* TX-5
Devilwater Creek—*stream* CA-9
Devin, Lake—*reservoir* NC-3
**Devine**—*pop pl* CO-8
**Devine**—*pop pl* TX-5
Devine, Ed and Lottie, House—*hist pl* AZ-5
Devine, Mount—*summit* AZ-5
Devine Bethel Ch—*church* AL-4
Devine Brook—*stream* CT-1
Devine Canyon—*valley* ID-8
Devine Canyon—*valley* OR-9
Devine Cem—*cemetery* MI-6
Devine Cem—*cemetery* MO-7
Devine Ch—*church* VA-3
Devine Creek—*stream* MT-8
Devine Flat—*flat* OR-9
Devine Flat Springs—*spring* OR-9
Devine Lake—*lake* MI-6
Devine Lake—*lake* MN-6
Devine Lake—*lake* WI-6
Devine Monument—*other* OR-9
Devine-Natalia (CCD)—*cens area* TX-5
Devine Opera House—*hist pl* TX-5
Devine Park—*park* NJ-2
Devine Peak—*summit* MT-8
Devine Ridge—*ridge* OR-9
Devine Ridge—*ridge* PA-2
Devine Ridge Cem—*cemetery* PA-2
Devine Ridge Spring—*spring* OR-9
Devine Rock—*summit* OR-9
Devine Sch—*school* MA-1
Devine Sch—*school* MS-4
Devine Sch—*school* NE-7
Devine Sch—*school* NY-2
Devine Sch Number 24 (historical)—*school* SD-7
Devines Knob—*summit* WV-2
Devine Spring—*spring* TX-5
Devine Well—*well* OR-9
Devine World Seminary—*school* IA-7
De Viney Bayou—*stream* MS-4
Deviney Lake Dam—*dam* MS-4
Deviney Lake Number Two Dam—*dam* MS-4
Devington Ch—*church* IN-6
Devington Shop Ctr—*locale* IN-6
Devinne Press Bldg—*hist pl* NY-2
De Vinney Canyon—*valley* CO-8
Devinny Cottage Sch—*school* CO-8
Devinny Sch—*school* CO-8
Devir Park—*park* MA-1
Devisadero Peak—*summit* NM-5
Devisadero Peak Loop Trail (Pack)—*trail* NM-5
Devisadero Windmill—*locale* TX-5
Devisadores Windmill—*locale* TX-5
Devish Lake—*lake* AK-9
Devitt—*locale* OR-9
*Devitt Camp* PA-2
*Devitt Camp Tuberculosis Sanitarium* PA-2
Devitt Creek—*stream* MT-8
Devitt Creek—*stream* ND-7
Devitt Creek—*stream* OR-9
DeVitte Military Acad—*school* NJ-2
Devitt Home—*locale* PA-2
Devizes—*locale* KS-7
Devizes Cem—*cemetery* KS-7
Devlin Channel—*channel* NJ-2
Devlin Channel—*channel* PA-2
Devlin Creek—*stream* MN-6
Devlin Falls—*falls* ID-8
Devlin Ranch—*locale* MT-8
Devlin Sch—*school* MT-8
DeVoa Run—*stream* OH-6
Devoe—*locale* SD-7
**Devoe**—*pop pl* MS-4
Devoe Brook—*stream* ME-1
Devoe Canyon—*valley* WY-8
Devoe Cem—*cemetery* MS-4
Devoe Cem—*cemetery* SD-7
DeVoe Community Building—*locale* SD-7
Devoe Ditch No 1—*canal* WY-8
Devoe Draw—*valley* WY-8
Devoe Lake—*lake* AR-4
Devoe Lake—*lake* (2) MI-6
DeVoe Lake—*reservoir* NJ-2
DeVoe Lake Dam—*dam* NJ-2
Devoe Park—*park* NY-2
Devoe Sch (historical)—*school* MS-4
**Devoe Township**—*pop pl* SD-7
Devoice Corners—*locale* NY-2
DeVoignes Spur—*locale* ID-8
*Devol* OH-6
**Devol**—*pop pl* OH-6
**Devol**—*pop pl* OK-5
*De Vola* OH-6
**Devola**—*pop pl* OH-6
Devol Cem—*cemetery* OH-6
Devol Cem—*cemetery* OK-5
*Devolente* MS-4
Devol Field—*park* IN-6
Devoll Ch—*church* TN-4
*Devolls Pond* MA-1
*Devol Pond* MA-1
Devol Pond—*lake* MA-1
Devol Run—*stream* OH-6
De Vol Sch—*school* SD-7
Devon—*locale* CA-9
Devon—*locale* IA-7
Devon—*locale* NY-2
Devon—*locale* WV-2
**Devon**—*pop pl* CT-1
**Devon**—*pop pl* (2) DE-2
**Devon**—*pop pl* KS-7
**Devon**—*pop pl* KY-4
**Devon**—*pop pl* MT-8
**Devon**—*pop pl* PA-2
Devon, Mount—*summit* MO-7
Devon Aire Elem Sch—*school* FL-3
Devon Aire Park—*park* FL-3
Devon-Berwyn—*CDP* PA-2
Devon Creek—*stream* FL-3
Devon Creek—*stream* IN-6
*Devondale* KY-4
**Devondale**—*pop pl* KY-4
Devon Drain—*stream* CA-9
*Devon Elementary School* PA-2
Devon Farm—*hist pl* TN-4
Devon Gas Field—*oilfield* MT-8
*Devonia* TN-4
Devonian Sch—*school* TX-5
Devonia Post Office—*building* TN-4
**Devonia (RR name Morco)**—*pop pl* TN-4
Devon Manor—*uninc pl* VA-3
Devonnaire Shop Ctr—*locale* FL-3
*Devon Park* IN-6
**Devon Park**—*pop pl* VA-3
**Devon Park (subdivision)**—*pop pl* NC-3
Devon Peak—*summit* NV-8
Devon Sch—*school* OH-6
Devon Sch—*school* PA-2
*Devonshire* IL-6
*Devonshire* IN-6
Devonshire—*hist pl* IN-6
**Devonshire**—*pop pl* DE-2
**Devonshire**—*pop pl* IN-6
**Devonshire**—*pop pl* NJ-2
Devonshire Ch—*church* NC-3
**Devonshire Crest (subdivision)**—*pop pl* PA-2
Devonshire Downs—*other* CA-9
*Devonshire Elementary School* NC-3
**Devonshire Estates (subdivision)**—*pop pl* PA-2
**Devonshire Forest**—*pop pl* MD-2
**Devonshire Gardens**—*pop pl* VA-3
Devonshire Golf Course—*other* CA-9
**Devonshire Heights (subdivision)**—*pop pl* PA-2
**Devonshire Hills (subdivision)**—*pop pl* PA-2
**Devonshire Manor**—*pop pl* TN-4
Devonshire Park—*park* IL-6
Devonshire Park—*park* (2) MI-6
Devonshire Sch—*school* (2) IL-6
Devonshire Sch—*school* NC-3
Devonshire Sch—*school* OH-6
Devonshire Sch—*school* VA-3
**Devonshire Square (subdivision)**—*pop pl* NC-3
**Devonshire (subdivision)**—*pop pl* NC-3
**Devonshire Woods (subdivision)**—*pop pl* DE-2
Devorak Sch—*school* SD-7
De vorak State Wildlife Mngmt Area—*park* MN-6
Devore—*locale* CA-9
**Devore**—*pop pl* IN-6
**De Vore**—*pop pl* OR-9
Devore, Lake—*lake* CO-8
Devore Arm—*bay* OR-9
Devore Campground—*locale* CA-9
Devore Cem—*cemetery* KS-7
Devore Creek—*stream* WA-9
Devore Drain—*canal* MI-6
**Devore Heights**—*pop pl* CA-9
Devore Hollow—*valley* TN-4
DeVore Mtn—*summit* OR-9
Devore Peak—*summit* WA-9
Devore Sch—*school* IL-6
DeVore Spring—*spring* AZ-5
DeVore Wash—*stream* AZ-5
DeVore Well—*well* AZ-5
Devorse Creek—*stream* NY-2
DeVoss Pond—*lake* OR-9
De Voss Sch—*school* CA-9
Devotion—*locale* NC-3
Devotion, Edward, House—*hist pl* MA-1
Devotional Gardens—*cemetery* NC-3
Devotional Gardens Cem—*cemetery* NC-3
*Devotion Island* CT-1
Devotion Sch—*school* (2) MA-1
Devouge Spring—*spring* CA-9
Devou Park—*park* KY-4
Devoys Canyon—*valley* NM-5
Devoys Peak—*summit* NM-5
Devreaux Ridge—*ridge* MO-7
Devrick Hollow—*valley* VA-3
DeVries Ditch—*canal* MT-8
DeVries Drain—*canal* MI-6
De Vries Palisade—*hist pl* DE-2
De Vry Technical Institute—*school* IL-6
**Devue**—*pop pl* AR-4
**Dew**—*pop pl* TX-5
Dewald Airp—*airport* WA-9
Dewald Sch—*school* SD-7
Dewald State Wildlife Mngmt Area—*park* MN-6
**Dewald (Township of)**—*pop pl* MN-6
*Dewal Springs* UT-8
**Dewalt**—*pop pl* TX-5
Dewalt Bldg—*hist pl* OH-6
Dewalt Cem—*cemetery* TX-5
De Walt Sch—*school* TX-5
*Dewampsh River* WA-9
Dew And Duffield Ditch—*canal* WY-8
**Dewar**—*pop pl* IA-7
**Dewar**—*pop pl* OK-5
Deward—*locale* MI-6
Deward Lookout Tower—*locale* MI-6
Dewarren Creek—*stream* CA-9
*Dewar Reservoir* NV-8
Dewar Ridge—*ridge* IN-6
Dewar Rsvr—*reservoir* NV-8
Dewars Pond—*reservoir* NC-3
Dewars Pond Dam—*dam* NC-3
**Dewart**—*pop pl* PA-2
Dewart Lake—*lake* IN-6
Dewatto—*locale* WA-9
Dewatto Bay—*bay* WA-9
Dewatto Cem—*cemetery* WA-9
*Dewatto Creek* WA-9
Dewatto River—*stream* WA-9
Dew Barn—*hist pl* SC-3
**Dewberry**—*pop pl* (2) GA-3
**Dewberry**—*pop pl* IN-6
Dewberry, Col. John, House—*hist pl* TX-5
*Dewberry Access* AL-4
Dewberry Branch—*stream* (2) AL-4
Dewberry Branch—*stream* TX-5
Dewberry Ch—*church* (2) GA-3
Dewberry Ch No 1—*church* GA-3
Dewberry Ch No 2—*church* GA-3
*Dewberry Creek* TX-5
*Dewberry Dam* SD-7
Dewberry Ferry (historical)—*locale* MS-4
Dewberry Hollow—*valley* TN-4
Dewberry Hollow—*valley* (3) TX-5
Dewberry Island—*island* TX-5
Dewberry Landing (historical)—*locale* MS-4
Dewberry Rec Area—*park* AL-4
Dew Cem—*cemetery* IN-6
Dew Cem—*cemetery* MS-4
Dew Cem—*cemetery* NC-3
Dew Cem—*cemetery* (2) OH-6
Dew Creek—*stream* MI-6
Dew Creek—*stream* MS-4
*Dew Drop* (2) AR-4
Dew Drop—*locale* ID-8
Dewdrop—*locale* KY-4
Dew Drop—*locale* PA-2
**Dew Drop**—*pop pl* CA-9
**Dewdrop**—*pop pl* LA-4
Dewdrop Brook—*stream* NH-1
Dewdrop Campground—*locale* PA-2
Dewdrop Cave—*cave* ID-8
*Dew Drop Creek* AR-4
Dew Drop Creek—*stream* TX-5
Dew Drop Fire Control Station—*locale* CA-9
Dewdrop (historical)—*locale* PA-2
Dew Drop Inn—*hist pl* AR-4
Dewdrop Lake—*lake* MN-6
Dewdrop Lake—*lake* WY-8
Dew Drop Landing (historical)—*locale* MS-4
Dewdrop Pool—*lake* FL-3
Dew Drop Post Office (historical)—*building* TN-4
Dewdrop Rsvr—*reservoir* OR-9
Dewdrop Run—*stream* PA-2
Dewdrop Sch—*school* NE-7
Dewdrop Spring—*spring* AZ-5
Dewdrop Springs—*spring* CO-8
Dewdrop Trail—*trail* PA-2
Dewees—*locale* TX-5
Dewees Creek—*stream* SC-3
DeWeese—*locale* MS-4
**Deweese**—*pop pl* NE-7
**Deweese**—*pop pl* NC-3
Deweese Branch—*stream* IN-6
De Weese Branch—*stream* NC-3
Deweese Cem—*cemetery* KY-4
DeWeese Creek—*stream* KY-4
Deweese Creek—*stream* TN-4
Deweese Creek—*stream* WY-8
Deweese Ditch—*canal* IN-6
De Weese Dye Ditch—*canal* CO-8
*De Weese-dye Reservoir* CO-8
Deweese Lake Dam—*dam* MS-4
Deweese Mtn—*summit* NC-3
Deweese Park—*park* OH-6
DeWeese Rsvr—*reservoir* CO-8
Deweese Sch—*school* MS-4
DeWeese Shell Mound (15BT6)—*hist pl* KY-4
Dewees Inlet—*bay* SC-3
Dewees Island—*island* SC-3
Dewees Mtn—*summit* AR-4
DeWees Playground—*park* MD-2
Dewees-Preston-Smith House—*hist pl* IN-6
Dewees Ranch—*locale* TX-5
Dewees Tank—*reservoir* (2) TX-5
Dewees Windmill—*locale* TX-5
Dewelle Cem—*cemetery* OH-6
Dewell Garden—*flat* CA-9
Dewell Lake—*lake* CA-9
*Dewells Corners* NY-2
Dewenlam—*gut* FM-9
Dewes, Francis J., House—*hist pl* IL-6
Dewes Cem—*cemetery* IL-6
*Dewey* AZ-5
*Dewey* KS-7
*Dewey* ME-1
*Dewey* MS-4
*Dewey* NE-7
*Dewey* UT-8
Dewey—*fmr MCD* NE-7
Dewey—*locale* AZ-5
Dewey—*locale* AR-4
Dewey—*locale* IA-7
Dewey—*locale* UT-8
Dewey—*locale* VA-3
Dewey—*locale* WA-9
Dewey—*locale* WI-6
**Dewey**—*pop pl* AL-4
**Dewey**—*pop pl* AR-4
**Dewey**—*pop pl* IL-6
**Dewey**—*pop pl* IN-6
**Dewey**—*pop pl* MT-8
**Dewey**—*pop pl* OK-5
**Dewey**—*pop pl* OR-9
**Dewey**—*pop pl* SD-7
**Dewey**—*pop pl* TX-5
**Dewey**—*pop pl* VA-3
**Dewey**—*pop pl* WA-9
Dewey—*uninc pl* FL-3
Dewey—*uninc pl* NY-2
Dewey, Chester, Sch No. 14—*hist pl* NY-2
Dewey, E. H., Stores—*hist pl* ID-8
Dewey, Mount—*summit* MT-8
Dewey & Almy Chemical Company—*facility* KY-4
Dewey Anchorage—*bay* AK-9
Dewey Ave Ch—*church* PA-2
Dewey Bald—*summit* MO-7

Dewey Bay—*bay* WI-6
Dewey Beach—*beach* NH-1
**Dewey Beach**—*pop pl* DE-2
Dewey Bridge—*bridge* UT-8
Dewey Bridge—*hist pl* UT-8
**Dewey Bridge**—*pop pl* NY-2
Dewey Bridge—*stream* AR-4
Dewey Canyon—*valley* UT-8
Dewey Cave—*cave* TN-4
Dewey Cem—*cemetery* IL-6
Dewey Cem—*cemetery* LA-4
Dewey Cem—*cemetery* MT-8
Dewey Cem—*cemetery* OK-5
Dewey Cem—*cemetery* TX-5
Dewey Ch—*church* GA-3
Dewey Ch—*church* MI-6
Dewey Ch—*church* (2) TX-5
Dewey Cone—*summit* HI-9
Dewey Corner—*locale* PA-2
Dewey Corners—*locale* NY-2
Dewey Corners—*locale* PA-2
Dewey County—*civil* SD-7
**Dewey (County)**—*pop pl* OK-5
Dewey County Courthouse—*hist pl* OK-5
Dewey Cove—*stream* AR-4
*Dewey Creek* MT-8
*Dewey Creek* NY-2
*Dewey Creek* OR-9
Dewey Creek—*stream* (5) AK-9
Dewey Creek—*stream* (3) ID-8
Dewey Creek—*stream* MT-8
Dewey Creek—*stream* NE-7
Dewey Creek—*stream* OH-6
Dewey Creek—*stream* (2) OR-9
Dewey Creek—*stream* WA-9
Dewey Creek—*stream* WI-6
Dewey Crossroads—*locale* GA-3
*Dewey Dam* SD-7
Dewey Dam—*dam* KY-4
Dewey Dann Creek—*stream* NV-8
Dewey Dann Ranch—*locale* NV-8
Dewey Ditch—*canal* IN-6
Dewey Ditch—*canal* WY-8
Dewey Durant Park—*park* MI-6
*Dewey Flat* MT-8
Dewey Flat—*flat* AZ-5
Dewey Flat Dam—*dam* AZ-5
Dewey Flat Well—*well* AZ-5
Dewey Francis, House—*hist pl* MA-1
Dewey Grade Tank—*reservoir* AZ-5
Dewey Gulch—*valley* CA-9
Dewey Gulch—*valley* ID-8
Dewey Heights—*locale* PA-2
Dewey Heights Ch—*church* AL-4
Dewey Hill—*summit* AK-9
Dewey Hill—*summit* ID-8
Dewey Hill—*summit* MA-1
Dewey Hill—*summit* NY-2
Dewey Hill—*summit* PA-2
Dewey Hollow—*valley* PA-2
Dewey Hollow Trail—*trail* PA-2
Dewey Hotel—*hist pl* OK-5
Dewey House—*building* DC-2
Dewey House—*hist pl* IL-6
Dewey JHS—*school* CO-8
Dewey JHS—*school* WA-9
Dewey JHS—*school* WI-6
Dewey Lake—*lake* (3) MI-6
Dewey Lake—*lake* (3) MN-6
Dewey Lake—*lake* MT-8
Dewey Lake—*lake* NE-7
Dewey Lake—*lake* TX-5
Dewey Lake—*lake* WA-9
Dewey Lake—*lake* WI-6
Dewey Lake—*reservoir* CO-8
Dewey Lake—*reservoir* KY-4
Dewey Lake Trail—*trail* WA-9
*Dewey Landing Strip* KS-7
Dewey Lateral—*canal* ID-8
Dewey Lode Mine—*mine* NM-5
Dewey Mahone Spring—*spring* AZ-5
Dewey Marsh—*swamp* WI-6
**Dewey Mill**—*pop pl* AR-4
Dewey Mine—*mine* CA-9
Dewey Mine—*mine* (3) ID-8
Dewey Mine—*mine* SD-7
Dewey Mine—*mine* UT-8
Dewey Mine—*mine* WY-8
Dewey M Johnson Bridge—*bridge* FL-3
Dewey Mound—*summit* KS-7
Dewey Mound Group—*hist pl* WI-6
Dewey Mtn—*summit* NY-2
Dewey Mtn—*summit* VT-1
Dewey Oil and Gas Field—*oilfield* KS-7
Dewey Park—*flat* CO-8
**Dewey Park**—*pop pl* FL-3
**Dewey Park**—*pop pl* IL-6
Dewey Park Gulch—*valley* CO-8
Dewey Park Spring—*spring* CO-8
Dewey Peak—*summit* ID-8
Dewey Pier—*locale* NC-3
Dewey Place—*hist pl* MA-1
Dewey Playground—*park* NY-2
*Dewey Point* PA-2
Dewey Point—*cape* CA-9
Dewey Point—*cape* NC-3
Dewey Post Office—*building* AZ-5
Dewey Post Office (historical)—*building* AL-4
Dewey Ranch—*locale* KS-7
*Dewey Resrvoir* KY-4
Dewey Rocks—*area* AK-9
Dewey Rose (RR name for Dewy Rose)—*other* GA-3
Dewey RR Station—*locale* FL-3
Deweys Bay—*bay* MT-8
Deweys Cave—*cave* AL-4
Dewey Sch—*school* AR-4
Dewey Sch—*school* CA-9
Dewey Sch—*school* GA-3
Dewey Sch—*school* ID-8
Dewey Sch—*school* (5) IL-6
Dewey Sch—*school* KS-7
Dewey Sch—*school* (3) MI-6
Dewey Sch—*school* MO-7
Dewey Sch—*school* NE-7
Dewey Sch—*school* NH-1
Dewey Sch—*school* OH-6
Dewey Sch—*school* OK-5
Dewey Sch—*school* WI-6
Dewey Sch (abandoned)—*school* MO-7
Dewey Sch (historical)—*school* TN-4
Dewey Sch Number 1—*school* ND-7
Dewey Sch Number 2—*school* (2) ND-7
Dewey Sch Number 3—*school* ND-7
Dewey Sch Number 4—*school* ND-7
Deweys Corners—*locale* NY-2
Dewey Seep—*spring* UT-8
Deweys Gateway—*gap* WY-8
**Deweys Hill**—*pop pl* SC-3
Dewey Short Visitor Center—*locale* MO-7
Dewey (Site)—*locale* ID-8
**Dewey's Mills**—*pop pl* VT-1
Dewey South (CCD)—*cens area* OK-5
Deweys Pasture State Game Mngmt Area—*park* IA-7
Deweys Pond—*reservoir* VT-1
Dewey Spring—*spring* (2) UT-8
Dewey Sulphur Mine (Abandoned)—*locale* ID-8
Dewey-Sumner Sch (historical)—*school* MO-7
Dewey Tabor—*fmr MCD* NE-7
Dewey Tank—*reservoir* AZ-5
**Dewey (Town of)**—*pop pl* (3) WI-6
Dewey Township—*civil* (2) SD-7
**Dewey Township**—*pop pl* ND-7
**Dewey Township**—*pop pl* SD-7
**Dewey (Township of)**—*pop pl* IN-6
**Dewey (Township of)**—*pop pl* MN-6
Dewey Tunnel—*tunnel* NM-5
Deweyville—*locale* AK-9
**Deweyville**—*pop pl* OH-6
**Deweyville**—*pop pl* TX-5
Deweyville (CCD)—*cens area* TX-5
Deweyville Cem—*cemetery* UT-8
**Deweyville (Dewey Station)**—*pop pl* UT-8
Dewey Well—*well* NM-5
Deweze Airp—*airport* KS-7
**Dew Field (subdivision)**—*pop pl* NC-3
Dew Hope Ch—*church* CO-8
Dew House—*hist pl* OH-6
**Dewhurst (Town of)**—*pop pl* WI-6
Dewien Lemwir, Pilen—*stream* FM-9
Dewies Canyon—*valley* OR-9
Dewill Cem—*cemetery* LA-4
*Dewing* NE-7
**Dewing**—*pop pl* NE-7
Dewing Creek—*stream* PA-2
Dewing Gap—*gap* KY-4
De Wint House—*hist pl* NY-2
*Dewit Run* PA-2
*Dewitt* AL-4
*De Witt* KS-7
*Dewitt* MO-7
*De Witt* VA-3
DeWitt—*locale* GA-3
Dewitt—*locale* KY-4
Dewitt—*locale* WV-2
**De Witt**—*pop pl* AR-4
**De Witt**—*pop pl* IL-6
**De Witt**—*pop pl* IA-7
**De Witt**—*pop pl* MI-6
**DeWitt**—*pop pl* MI-6
**De Witt**—*pop pl* MO-7
**De Witt**—*pop pl* NE-7
**DeWitt**—*pop pl* NY-2
**DeWitt**—*pop pl* VA-3
Dewitt—*post sta* VA-3
Dewitt, Benjamin, House—*hist pl* IL-6
Dewitt, Lake—*reservoir* AL-4
Dewitt, Zachariah Price, Cabin—*hist pl* OH-6
*Dewitt (alternate and RR name De Witt)* IL-6
DeWitt Bluff—*cliff* SC-3
Dewitt Campground—*locale* UT-8
Dewitt Canal—*canal* LA-4
Dewitt Canyon—*valley* CA-9
DeWitt Canyon—*valley* ID-8
Dewitt Cave—*cave* AL-4
Dewitt Cave—*cave* MO-7
Dewitt (CCD)—*cens area* KY-4
Dewitt Cem—*cemetery* IN-6
Dewitt Cem—*cemetery* KS-7
Dewitt Cem—*cemetery* KY-4
DeWitt Cem—*cemetery* KY-4
Dewitt Cem—*cemetery* (2) NE-7
DeWitt Cem—*cemetery* NY-2
DeWitt Cem—*cemetery* TX-5
DeWitt Cem—*cemetery* WV-2
Dewitt C Fenton Elem Sch—*school* PA-2
DeWitt Ch—*church* TN-4
DeWitt Clinton HS—*school* NY-2
Dewitt Clinton Sch—*school* NY-2
*Dewitt (corporate name De Witt)* MO-7
de Witt Cottage—*hist pl* VA-3
**De Witt (County)**—*pop pl* IL-6
**De Witt (County)**—*pop pl* TX-5
De Witt County Courthouse—*hist pl* TX-5
DeWitt Creek—*stream* ID-8
DeWitt Creek—*stream* IN-6
DeWitt Creek—*stream* OR-9
DeWitt D Barlow Sch—*school* NJ-2
Dewitt-Deweese Memorial Park—*park* MS-4
De Witt Drain—*stream* MI-6
Dewitt Field—*airport* ME-1
DeWitt Flour Mills and King Iron Bridge—*hist pl* NE-7
Dewitt Gulch—*valley* CA-9
DeWitt Hill—*summit* PA-2
Dewitt (historical)—*locale* KS-7
DeWitt (historical)—*locale* SD-7
Dewitt Hollow—*valley* AL-4
DeWitt Hosp—*hospital* VA-3
De Witt HS—*school* AR-4
DeWitt HS—*school* MI-6
DeWitt Lake—*lake* NY-2
Dewitt Mill—*locale* NV-8
DeWitt Mill (historical)—*locale* TN-4
**DeWitt Mills**—*pop pl* NY-2
Dewitt Mine—*mine* NV-8
De Witt Park Hist Dist—*hist pl* NY-2
Dewitt Peak—*summit* CA-9
Dewitt Point—*cape* NY-2
Dewitt Pond—*lake* (2) NY-2
Dewitt Pond—*reservoir* NC-3
Dewitt Pond Dam—*dam* NC-3
Dewitt Pool—*reservoir* MN-6
Dewitt Ranch—*locale* (2) WY-8
Dewitt Road Sch—*school* NY-2
DeWitt Run—*stream* OH-6
DeWitt Run—*stream* PA-2
Dewitt Run—*stream* PA-2
DeWitt Sch—*school* MI-6
Dewitt Sch—*school* SD-7
De Witt Sch—*school* TX-5
DeWitt Sch—*school* VA-3
DeWitt Sch (historical)—*school* TN-4
DeWitt Scrub—*woods* FL-3
DeWitt-Seitz Bldg—*hist pl* MN-6
Dewitts Landing (historical)—*locale* AL-4
Dewitt-Smith-Jobe Cem—*cemetery* TN-4
Dewitt S Morgan Elem Sch—*school* IN-6
Dewitts Pit—*cave* AL-4
De Witts Sch—*school* IL-6
Dewitt State Hosp—*hospital* CA-9
**De Witt (Town of)**—*pop pl* NY-2
De Witt Township—*fmr MCD* IA-7
**De Witt Township**—*pop pl* MO-7
**De Witt Township**—*pop pl* ND-7
**De Witt Township**—*pop pl* SD-7
**De Witt (Township of)**—*pop pl* IL-6
**De Witt (Township of)**—*pop pl* MI-6
**Dewittville**—*pop pl* NY-2
Dewittville Bay—*bay* NY-2
Dewittville Cem—*cemetery* NY-2
Dewittville Creek—*stream* NY-2
DeWitt Yards—*locale* NY-2
Dew Lake—*lake* OR-9
Dewlen-Spohnhauer Bridge—*hist pl* KS-7
**Dewmaine**—*pop pl* IL-6
DeWoff—*locale* ID-8
*Dewogibito* AZ-5
De Wolf Bight—*bay* WA-9
DeWolf Run—*stream* PA-2
DeWolf Sch—*school* NJ-2
Dew Point—*cape* AK-9
Dew Pond Hollow—*valley* MO-7
*Dewright* OK-5
Dews Creek—*stream* NC-3
Dews Ditch—*canal* OH-6
Dews Island—*island* NC-3
Dews Lake—*reservoir* GA-3
Dew Spring—*spring* AR-4
Dews Run—*stream* OH-6
Dew Valley—*locale* OR-9
Dew Valley—*valley* OR-9
Dewville—*locale* TX-5
Dewville Cem—*cemetery* TX-5
*De Wyckoff Lake Sch* NJ-2
**Dewy Rose**—*pop pl* GA-3
**Dewy Rose (RR name Dewey Rose)**—*pop pl* GA-3
*Dex Creek* MO-7
*Dexter* CT-1
Dexter—*locale* AK-9
Dexter—*locale* AR-4
Dexter—*locale* IL-6
Dexter—*locale* MS-4
Dexter—*locale* PA-2
Dexter—*locale* WI-6
**Dexter**—*pop pl* AL-4
**Dexter**—*pop pl* GA-3
**Dexter**—*pop pl* IN-6
**Dexter**—*pop pl* IA-7
**Dexter**—*pop pl* KS-7
**Dexter**—*pop pl* KY-4
**Dexter**—*pop pl* ME-1
**Dexter**—*pop pl* MI-6
**Dexter**—*pop pl* MN-6
**Dexter**—*pop pl* MO-7
**Dexter**—*pop pl* NM-5
**Dexter**—*pop pl* NY-2
**Dexter**—*pop pl* NC-3
**Dexter**—*pop pl* OH-6
**Dexter**—*pop pl* OR-9
**Dexter**—*pop pl* TX-5
Dexter, David, House—*hist pl* NH-1
Dexter, Edward, House—*hist pl* RI-1
Dexter, Jeremiah, House—*hist pl* RI-1
Dexter, Lake—*lake* (2) FL-3
Dexter, Lake—*reservoir* WI-6
Dexter Asylum—*building* RI-1
Dexter Attendance Center—*school* MS-4
Dexter Ave Baptist Ch—*church* AL-4
Dexter Ave Baptist Church—*hist pl* AL-4
Dexter Ave Methodist Ch—*church* AL-4
Dexter Basin—*basin* MT-8
Dexter Bog—*swamp* MA-1
Dexter Branch—*stream* GA-3
**Dexter By The Sea**—*pop pl* WA-9
Dexter Cabin—*hist pl* CO-8
Dexter Canyon—*valley* (2) CA-9
Dexter Canyon—*valley* OR-9
Dexter (CCD)—*cens area* GA-3
Dexter (CCD)—*cens area* NM-5
Dexter Cem—*cemetery* IA-7
Dexter Cem—*cemetery* MI-6
Dexter Cem—*cemetery* MN-6
Dexter Cem—*cemetery* MO-7
Dexter Cem—*cemetery* NY-2
Dexter Cem—*cemetery* SD-7
Dexter Center (census name Dexter)—*other* ME-1
**Dexter City**—*pop pl* (2) OH-6
Dexter Community House—*hist pl* IA-7
**Dexter Corner**—*pop pl* NH-1
Dexter Corners—*locale* DE-2
Dexter Corners—*locale* NY-2
*Dexter Creek* OR-9
Dexter Creek—*stream* (3) AK-9
Dexter Creek—*stream* (2) CA-9
Dexter Creek—*stream* (2) CO-8
Dexter Creek—*stream* MI-6
Dexter Creek—*stream* MO-7
Dexter Creek—*stream* (2) MT-8
Dexter Creek—*stream* OR-9
Dexter Dam—*dam* OR-9
*Dexter Ditch* IN-6
Dexter Ditch—*canal* IN-6
Dexter Elementary and JHS—*school* IN-6
Dexter Elem Sch—*school* KS-7
*Dexter Estate* MA-1
Dexter Federal Fish Hatchery—*other* NM-5
Dexter Gate—*locale* AR-4
Dexter Grist Mill—*hist pl* ME-1
Dexter Grist Mill—*locale* MA-1
Dexter Gulch—*valley* CA-9
Dexter Gulch—*valley* ID-8
Dexter Gulch—*valley* (2) MT-8
Dexter Hardin Ch—*church* KY-4
Dexter Hill Sch (historical)—*school* AL-4
Dexter (historical)—*locale* (2) SD-7
Dexter Hollow—*valley* PA-2
Dexter Hollow—*valley* UT-8
Dexter House—*hist pl* TX-5
Dexter House No. 1—*hist pl* WA-9
Dexter House No. 2—*hist pl* WA-9
Dexter HS—*school* KS-7
Dexter Huron Metropolitan Park—*park* MI-6
Dexter Island—*island* FL-3
**Dexter Junction**—*pop pl* MO-7
*Dexter Lake* OR-9
Dexter Lake—*lake* MI-6
Dexter Lake—*lake* (2) NY-2
Dexter Lake Dam—*dam* MS-4
Dexter Lake Outlet—*stream* NY-2
Dexter Memorial Hospital Heliport—*airport* MO-7
Dexter Mill Pond—*lake* ME-1
Dexter Mine—*mine* MI-6
Dexter Mine—*mine* MT-8
Dexter Mtn—*summit* NY-2
Dexter Municipal Airp—*airport* MO-7
Dexter Oil And Gas Field—*oilfield* MS-4
Dexter Park—*flat* CO-8
Dexter Park—*park* CA-9
Dexter Park—*park* KS-7
Dexter Park—*park* NV-8
Dexter Peak—*summit* AK-9
Dexter Peak—*summit* CA-9
Dexter Peak—*summit* WY-8
Dexter P. O. (historical)—*locale* AL-4
Dexter Point—*cape* FL-3
Dexter Point—*summit* MT-8
*Dexter Pond* ME-1
Dexter Pond—*lake* ME-1
Dexter Pond—*lake* MA-1
Dexter Pond—*lake* RI-1
Dexter Post Office (historical)—*building* MS-4
Dexter Ridge—*ridge* OR-9
Dexter Ridge—*ridge* WA-9
*Dexter River* MA-1
Dexter Rsvr—*reservoir* OR-9
Dexter Run—*stream* OH-6
*Dexter Sch* IN-6
Dexter Sch—*school* AZ-5
Dexter Sch—*school* CA-9
Dexter Sch—*school* IL-6
Dexter Sch—*school* IN-6
Dexter Sch—*school* (2) MA-1
*Dexter School* MS-4
Dexter Sewage Disposal Plant—*other* NM-5
Dexter Siding—*locale* OR-9
Dexter Spring—*spring* WA-9
Dexter Springs—*spring* CO-8
Dexters Terrace Sch—*school* NY-2
*Dexter Stream* ME-1
Dexter Town Hall—*building* ND-7
**Dexter (Town of)**—*pop pl* ME-1
**Dexter (Town of)**—*pop pl* WI-6
**Dexter Township**—*pop pl* KS-7
**Dexter Township**—*pop pl* ND-7
**Dexter Township**—*pop pl* SD-7
**Dexter (Township of)**—*pop pl* MI-6
**Dexter (Township of)**—*pop pl* MN-6
Dexter Universalist Church—*hist pl* ME-1
Dexterville—*locale* KY-4
**Dexterville**—*pop pl* NY-2
**Dexterville**—*pop pl* WI-6
Dexter Well (historical)—*oilfield* IN-6
Dextra—*locale* TX-5
DeYampert Cem—*cemetery* AL-4
DeYampert Plantation (historical)—*locale* AL-4
DeYarmon, Joseph L. House—*hist pl* OH-6
**Deyarmonville**—*pop pl* OH-6
Dey Cem—*cemetery* KY-4
Dey Cove—*bay* VA-3
Dey Draw—*valley* WY-8
Deyerle Hollow—*valley* VA-3
Dey Mansion—*hist pl* NJ-2
Deyo Cem—*cemetery* NY-2
Deyo Cem—*cemetery* OH-6
Deyo Cem—*cemetery* OK-5
Deyoe Creek—*stream* OR-9
De Yoe Pond—*reservoir* NJ-2
Deyo Hill—*summit* NY-2
Deyo Memorial Chapel—*church* OK-5
*Deyoung* PA-2
DeYoung Museum—*building* CA-9
DeYoung PO (historical)—*building* PA-2
**De Young (RR name Russell City)**—*pop pl* PA-2
Dey Sch—*school* VA-3
Deyton Camp—*locale* NC-3
*Deyton Primary* NC-3
*Deyugoru* FM-9
Deza Bluffs—*summit* NM-5
Dezarn Cem—*cemetery* KY-4
DeZarns Fork—*stream* KY-4
De Zavala Sch—*school* (2) TX-5
DeZavala Sch—*school* TX-5
DeZavalla Cem—*cemetery* TX-5
DeZavalla Park—*park* TX-5
DeZavalla Sch—*school* (2) TX-5
*Dezel Lake* WI-6
Dezellem Lake—*lake* WA-9
Dezengremel, Remy, House—*hist pl* NY-2
**Dezera**—*pop pl* SD-7
Dezern Sch (historical)—*school* TN-4
D Faulstich Dam—*dam* SD-7
D-five Spring—*spring* AZ-5
D-five Tank—*reservoir* AZ-5
D F Miller Ditch—*canal* CO-8
DFU Elk Mountain Bridge—*hist pl* WY-8
*D F Walker High School* NC-3
D Gifford Number 1 Dam—*dam* SD-7
D Gifford Number 2 Dam—*dam* SD-7
D Graham Lake Dam—*dam* MS-4
D Greenwood Ranch—*locale* ND-7
Dhahedse Ridge—*ridge* AK-9
**D'Hanis**—*pop pl* TX-5
D'Hanis (CCD)—*cens area* TX-5
D'Hanis Hist Dist—*hist pl* TX-5
D Hanna Ranch—*locale* NE-7
*Dharma Ridge* OR-9
D Havin—*locale* TX-5
D H Canyon—*valley* ID-8
*D H Conley High School* NC-3
D H Day State Park—*park* MI-6
**Dheinsville**—*pop pl* WI-6
D Henderson Ranch—*locale* NE-7
D Henriod Ranch—*locale* NV-8
D H Havin—*locale* TX-5
D H H Lengel MS—*school* PA-2
*Dhiensville* WI-6
D Hill—*summit* AZ-5
D & H RR Complex—*hist pl* NY-2
D H S Creek—*stream* MT-8
D H Spring—*spring* ID-8
D. H. Springhouse—*hist pl* MD-2
Dhuey Hill—*summit* WI-6
*Diabase Creek* WA-9
*Diablito Mtn* AZ-5
Diablito Mtn—*summit* AZ-5
Diablito Spring—*spring* AZ-5
Diablito Tank—*reservoir* AZ-5
**Diablo**—*pop pl* CA-9
**Diablo**—*pop pl* WA-9
Diablo, Arroyo—*valley* TX-5
Diablo, Canada Del —*valley* CA-9
Diablo, Canon—*valley* CO-8
Diablo, Canyon—*valley* (3) AZ-5
Diablo, Canyon—*valley* CO-8
Diablo, Cerro—*summit* TX-5
Diablo, Mount—*summit* AK-9
Diablo, Mount—*summit* CA-9
Diablo, Sierra—*range* TX-5
Diablo Anchorage—*bay* CA-9
*Diablo Arroyo* TX-5
Diablo Artesian Well—*well* TX-5
*Diablo Canyon* CA-9
Diablo Canyon—*valley* (2) AZ-5
Diablo Canyon—*valley* (2) CA-9
Diablo Canyon—*valley* (5) NM-5
Diablo Canyon—*valley* TX-5
**Diablock**—*pop pl* KY-4
Diablo Creek—*stream* NM-5
*Diablo Dam* CA-9
Diablo Dam—*dam* WA-9
*Diablo Grande* NV-8
Diablo Gulch—*valley* CA-9
Diablo Lake—*reservoir* MO-7
Diablo Lake—*reservoir* WA-9
Diablo Lateral—*canal* TX-5
*Diablo Mountain* OR-9
Diablo Mountains—*summit* AZ-5
Diablo Mtn—*summit* AZ-5
Diablo Mtn—*summit* ID-8
Diablo Pass—*gap* AZ-5
Diablo Peak—*summit* OR-9
*Diablo Plateau* TX-5
Diablo Point—*cape* CA-9
Diablo Range—*other* NM-5
Diablo Range—*range* (2) CA-9
Diablo Range (CCD)—*cens area* CA-9
Diablo Rim—*cliff* TX-5
*Diablo Rsvr* WA-9
Diablo Rsvr Number One—*reservoir* TX-5
Diablo Rsvr Number Two—*reservoir* TX-5
Diablo Spring—*spring* ID-8
Diablo Spring—*spring* NM-5
*Diablo Stadium* AZ-5
Diablo Tank—*reservoir* (3) AZ-5
Diablo Tank—*reservoir* (2) NM-5
Diablo Valley Coll—*school* CA-9
Diablo Valley Girl Scout Camp—*locale* CA-9
Diablo Vista Sch—*school* CA-9
Diablo Wash—*stream* AZ-5
Diablo Well—*well* (2) AZ-5
Diabold Canyon—*valley* CA-9
Diack Playground—*park* MI-6
*Diadama* VT-1
Diadi—*civil* FM-9
Diadi—*locale* FM-9
Diagnostic Center Hosp—*hospital* TN-4
**Diagonal**—*pop pl* IA-7
*Diagonal Creek* KS-7
*Diagonal Ditch* NC-3
Diagonal Drain—*canal* NV-8
Dial—*locale* GA-3
Dial—*locale* TX-5
**Dial**—*pop pl* TX-5
Dial, Allen, House—*hist pl* SC-3
Dial Bay—*swamp* SC-3
Dial Branch—*stream* (2) KY-4
Dial Branch—*stream* TN-4
Dial Branch—*stream* WV-2
Dial Canyon—*valley* AZ-5
Dial Cem—*cemetery* (2) TN-4
Dial Cem—*cemetery* WV-2
Dial Creek—*stream* NC-3
Dial-Dickey Ranch—*locale* TX-5
Dial Gas Field—*oilfield* TX-5
Dial-Goza House—*hist pl* FL-3
**Dial Heights Subdivision**—*pop pl* UT-8
Dial (historical)—*locale* AL-4
Dial (historical)—*locale* KS-7
Dial House—*hist pl* MS-4
**Dialion**—*pop pl* AR-4
Dial JHS—*school* AR-4
Dial Mill—*hist pl* GA-3
Dial Mtn—*summit* NY-2
Dial Oil Field—*oilfield* TX-5
*Dial P.O.* AL-4
Dial Pond—*lake* FL-3
Dial Pond—*lake* NY-2
Dial Ranch—*locale* TX-5
*Dial Rock* PA-2
Dial Rock—*summit* VA-3
Dials Bay—*swamp* SC-3
Dials Ch—*church* SC-3
Dial Sch—*school* WV-2
Dials Creek—*stream* AR-4
Dials Knob—*summit* UT-8
Dials Millpond—*lake* GA-3
Dial Spring—*spring* AZ-5
Dial Tank—*reservoir* AZ-5
**Dialton**—*pop pl* OH-6
**Dialtown**—*pop pl* GA-3
**Dialville**—*pop pl* TX-5
Dial Wash—*stream* AZ-5
Dial Well—*well* NM-5
Dial-Williamson House—*hist pl* TX-5
Dial Windmill—*locale* CO-8
Diamante Mill—*locale* NM-5
Diamante Tract—*civil* NM-5
Diamanti Canyon—*valley* UT-8
Diame Artesian Well—*well* TX-5
Diameter, The—*summit* NY-2
Diamond—*locale* AL-4
Diamond—*locale* AK-9
Diamond—*locale* GA-3
Diamond—*locale* ID-8
Diamond—*locale* NY-2
Diamond—*locale* PA-2
Diamond—*locale* SD-7
Diamond—*locale* UT-8
Diamond—*locale* WY-8
Diamond—*locale* VI-3
**Diamond**—*pop pl* FL-3
**Diamond**—*pop pl* IL-6
**Diamond**—*pop pl* (2) IN-6
**Diamond**—*pop pl* IA-7
**Diamond**—*pop pl* KY-4
**Diamond**—*pop pl* LA-4
**Diamond**—*pop pl* MO-7
**Diamond**—*pop pl* OH-6
**Diamond**—*pop pl* OR-9
**Diamond**—*pop pl* PA-2
**Diamond**—*pop pl* TN-4
**Diamond**—*pop pl* VA-3
**Diamond**—*pop pl* WA-9
**Diamond**—*pop pl* (2) WV-2
**Diamond**—*pop pl* VI-3
Diamond—*uninc pl* CA-9
Diamond, Lake—*lake* FL-3
**Diamond Acres Subdivision**—*pop pl* UT-8
Diamond A Desert—*desert* ID-8
Diamond A Desert—*plain* NV-8
*Diamondale* MI-6
Diamond and a Half Ranch—*locale* NM-5
Diamond A Ranch—*hist pl* NM-5
Diamond a Ranch—*locale* NM-5
Diamond A Ranch—*locale* (3) NM-5
Diamond A Trail—*trail* NV-8
Diamond A Windmill—*well* AZ-5
**Diamond Bar**—*pop pl* (2) CA-9
Diamond Bar Canyon—*valley* AZ-5
Diamond Bar Canyon—*valley* NM-5
Diamond Bar Cow Camp—*locale* WY-8
Diamond Bar Creek—*stream* CA-9
Diamond Bar Lake—*lake* NE-7
Diamond Bar Peak—*summit* AZ-5
Diamond Bar Ranch—*locale* (2) AZ-5
Diamond Bar Ranch—*locale* (3) NE-7
Diamond Bar Ranch—*locale* NM-5
Diamond Bar Ranch—*locale* OK-5
Diamond Bar Ranch—*locale* WY-8
Diamond Bar Spring—*spring* AZ-5
Diamond Bar X Ranch—*locale* MT-8
Diamond Basin—*basin* ID-8
Diamond Basin Well—*well* ID-8
Diamond Battle Historical Monmt—*park* UT-8
**Diamond Bell Ranch**—*pop pl* AZ-5
**Diamond Bluff**—*pop pl* WI-6
Diamond Bluff Cem—*cemetery* WI-6
Diamond Bluff Site-Mero Mound Group—*hist pl* WI-6
**Diamond Bluff (Town of)**—*pop pl* WI-6
Diamond Boulder Creek—*stream* ID-8
Diamond Boulder Flat—*flat* ID-8
Diamond Branch—*stream* (2) KY-4
Diamond Branch—*stream* TN-4
*Diamond Branch Shoals* TN-4
Diamond Brook—*stream* NJ-2
Diamond Brook—*stream* NY-2
Diamond Brook—*stream* RI-1
Diamond Butte—*summit* (3) AZ-5
Diamond Butte—*summit* (2) MT-8
Diamond Butte—*summit* (2) OR-9
Diamond Butte—*summit* WA-9
Diamond Butte Rsvr Number One—*reservoir* MT-8
Diamond Butte Rsvr Number Two—*reservoir* MT-8
Diamond Camp—*locale* OR-9
Diamond Campground—*locale* CA-9
Diamond Campground—*locale* UT-8
Diamond Canal—*canal* OR-9
*Diamond Canyon* AZ-5
*Diamond Canyon* ID-8
Diamond Canyon—*valley* AZ-5
Diamond Canyon—*valley* NV-8
Diamond Canyon—*valley* UT-8
Diamond Canyon Rsvr—*reservoir* NV-8
Diamond Cave—*cave* (2) AL-4
Diamond Cave—*cave* NM-5
Diamond Cave—*cave* PA-2
Diamond Cave—*cave* TN-4
Diamond Cave—*cave* TX-5
**Diamond Cave**—*pop pl* AR-4
Diamond Caverns—*cave* KY-4
Diamond (CCD)—*cens area* OR-9
Diamond Cem—*cemetery* GA-3
Diamond Cem—*cemetery* IA-7
Diamond Cem—*cemetery* MS-4
Diamond Cem—*cemetery* MO-7
Diamond Cem—*cemetery* OK-5
Diamond Cem—*cemetery* TN-4
Diamond Cem—*cemetery* VT-1
Diamond Cem—*cemetery* VA-3
Diamond Cemetery*—*cemetery* IA-7
Diamond Cemetery—*hist pl* UT-8
**Diamond Center**—*pop pl* IA-7
Diamond Ch—*church* AL-4
Diamond Ch—*church* LA-4
Diamond Chapel—*church* MI-6
*Diamond City* KS-7
*Diamond City* UT-8
Diamond City—*locale* MT-8
Diamond City—*locale* WA-9
**Diamond City**—*pop pl* AR-4
**Diamond City**—*pop pl* IL-6
Diamond City Cem—*cemetery* MT-8
Diamond City Hills—*summit* NC-3
**Diamond City (historical)**—*pop pl* SD-7
Diamond Corner—*locale* MN-6
Diamond Counting Corral—*locale* UT-8
Diamond Cove—*bay* ME-1
Diamond Craters—*crater* OR-9
*Diamond Creek* UT-8
Diamond Creek—*stream* (4) AK-9
Diamond Creek—*stream* (2) AZ-5
Diamond Creek—*stream* AR-4
Diamond Creek—*stream* (4) CA-9
Diamond Creek—*stream* (2) CO-8
Diamond Creek—*stream* FL-3
Diamond Creek—*stream* (5) ID-8
Diamond Creek—*stream* IL-6
Diamond Creek—*stream* IN-6
Diamond Creek—*stream* (2) KS-7
Diamond Creek—*stream* MA-1
Diamond Creek—*stream* MI-6

**Dickerson—pop pl** NC-3
Dickerson Arm—bay MS-4
Dickerson Bay—bay FL-3
*Dickerson Branch* DE-2
Dickerson Branch—stream MS-4
Dickerson Branch—stream MO-7
Dickerson Branch—stream TN-4
Dickerson Brook—stream NH-1
Dickerson Canyon—valley NM-5
Dickerson Cem—cemetery IL-6
Dickerson Cem—cemetery IN-6
Dickerson Cem—cemetery (4) KY-4
Dickerson Cem—cemetery MI-6
Dickerson Cem—cemetery (4) MS-4
Dickerson Cem—cemetery MO-7
Dickerson Cem—cemetery OK-5
Dickerson Cem—cemetery (4) TN-4
Dickerson Cem—cemetery (3) TX-5
Dickerson Cem—cemetery VA-3
Dickerson Ch—church OH-6
Dickerson Channel—channel NY-2
Dickerson Chapel—church MS-4
Dickerson Chapel—church (2) TN-4
Dickerson Ch (historical)—church TN-4
**Dickerson City—pop pl** FL-3
Dickerson Corner—locale NJ-2
Dickerson Creek—bay NY-2
Dickerson Creek—stream CA-9
Dickerson Creek—stream MI-6
Dickerson Creek—stream MS-4
Dickerson Creek—stream MO-7
Dickerson Creek—stream TX-5
Dickerson Creek—stream VA-3
Dickerson Creek—stream WA-9
Dickerson Dam—dam MT-8
Dickerson Ditch—canal OH-6
Dickerson Ditch—canal WY-8
Dickerson Draw—valley WY-8
*Dickerson Elementary School* MS-4
**Dickerson Estates (subdivision)—pop pl** NC-3
*Dickerson Hollow* TN-4
Dickerson Hollow—valley KY-4
Dickerson HS—school GA-3
Dickerson Island—island SC-3
*Dickerson Lake* NC-3
Dickerson Lake—lake MI-6
Dickerson Lake—lake MS-4
Dickerson Lake—reservoir KY-4
Dickerson Lake—reservoir NC-3
Dickerson Lake Dam—dam NC-3
Dickerson Manor—locale DE-2
Dickerson Mill—locale GA-3
Dickerson Millpond—reservoir GA-3
Dickerson Mtn—summit NY-2
Dickerson Park—park MO-7
Dickerson Park—park NC-3
*Dickerson Point* NJ-2
*Dickerson Point* WA-9
Dickerson Pond—reservoir NY-2
Dickerson Post Office (historical)—building MS-4
Dickerson Ranch Cem—cemetery OR-9
Dickerson Regional Park—park MD-2
Dickerson Ridge—ridge KY-4
Dickerson Rocks—summit OR-9
**Dickerson Run—pop pl** PA-2
Dickerson Run—stream OH-6
Dickerson Run—stream PA-2
Dickerson Run-Union Cem—cemetery PA-2
Dickerson Sch—school CA-9
Dickerson Sch—school GA-3
Dickerson School (historical)—locale MO-7
Dickerson Site (22CO502)—hist pl MS-4
Dickerson Slough—stream IL-6
Dickersons Mill (historical)—locale MS-4
Dickerson Swamp—stream VA-3
Dickerson Tank—reservoir NM-5
Dickerson Township—civil MO-7
Dickerson (Township of)—fmr MCD AR-4
**Dickersonville—pop pl** NY-2
Dickert—locale FL-3
**Dickert—pop pl** AL-4
Dickerville Creek—stream CO-8
*Dickes Creek* GA-3
Dickes Tank—reservoir TX-5
Dickey—locale GA-3
Dickey—locale ID-8
Dickey—locale ME-1
Dickey—locale PA-2
**Dickey—pop pl** GA-3
**Dickey—pop pl** ND-7
**Dickey—pop pl** PA-2
Dickey, Alfred E., Free Library—hist pl ND-7
Dickey, C. W., House—hist pl HI-9
Dickey, Mount—summit AK-9
Dickey, Walter, House—hist pl SD-7
Dickey Ave Sch—school OH-6
Dickey Bluff—cliff TN-4
Dickey Bluff Peninsula—locale TN-4
Dickey Bottom—basin TN-4
*Dickey Branch* KY-4
Dickey Branch—stream AL-4
Dickey Branch—stream GA-3
Dickey Branch—stream IA-7
Dickey Branch—stream NC-3
Dickey Branch—stream TX-5
Dickey Bridge—bridge OR-9
Dickey Bridge—bridge TN-4
Dickey Brook—stream (4) ME-1
Dickey Brook—stream (2) NY-2
Dickey Camp—locale WA-9
Dickey Canyon—valley CA-9
Dickey Canyon—valley NM-5
Dickey Cave—cave AL-4
Dickey Cem—cemetery AR-4
Dickey Cem—cemetery MS-4
Dickey Cem—cemetery NC-3
Dickey Cem—cemetery ND-7
Dickey Cem—cemetery OH-6
Dickey Cem—cemetery (2) TN-4
Dickey Cem—cemetery WV-2
Dickey Ch—church (2) OH-6
Dickey Chapel—church SC-3
Dickey County—civil ND-7
Dickey County Courthouse—hist pl ND-7
*Dickey Creek* MO-7
*Dickey Creek* WA-9
Dickey Creek—stream AL-4
Dickey Creek—stream IN-6
Dickey Creek—stream MS-4
Dickey Creek—stream (2) MT-8
Dickey Creek—stream (2) OR-9
Dickey Creek—stream (3) TX-5
Dickey Creek—stream VA-3
Dickey Creek—stream WA-9
Dickey Creek—stream WI-6
Dickey Creek—stream WY-8
Dickey Creek Trail—trail WA-9
Dickey Ditch—canal IN-6
Dickey Ditch—canal MT-8
Dickey Draw—valley WY-8
Dickey Farm Branch—stream VA-3
Dickey Fork—stream KY-4
*Dickey Hill* VA-3
Dickey Hill—summit NH-1
Dickey Hill—summit VA-3
*Dickey Hills* MT-8
Dickey Hill Trail—trail VA-3
Dickey Hoko Summit—summit WA-9
*Dickey Hollow* AL-4
Dickey Hollow—valley (3) TN-4
Dickey Island—island TN-4
Dickey Junction—locale AR-4
Dickey Knob—summit PA-2
Dickey Knob—summit VA-3
Dickey Lake—lake AK-9
Dickey Lake—lake (2) MT-8
Dickey Lake—lake WA-9
Dickey Lake—lake WI-6
Dickey Lake—reservoir TX-5
Dickey Lake Dam—dam MS-4
Dickey Landing—locale LA-4
Dickey Landing—locale (2) TN-4
Dickey Mill Creek—stream GA-3
Dickey Mine—mine TN-4
Dickey Mine (underground)—mine AL-4
Dickey Mtn—summit GA-3
Dickey Mtn—summit NH-1
Dickey Mtn—summit NC-3
Dickey Mtn—summit VA-3
Dickey Notch—gap NH-1
*Dickey Peak* MT-8
Dickey Peak—summit ID-8
Dickey Peak—summit NV-8
Dickey Pond—lake ME-1
Dickey Poppell Millpond—reservoir GA-3
Dickey Prairie—flat OR-9
**Dickey Prairie—pop pl** OR-9
Dickey Prairie Sch—school OR-9
Dickey Ridge—ridge TN-4
Dickey Ridge—ridge (2) VA-3
Dickey Ridge Visitor Center—locale VA-3
Dickey River—stream WA-9
Dickeys—locale IL-6
Dickeys Branch—stream TX-5
Dickey Sch—school IL-6
Dickey Sch—school PA-2
Dickey School Ch—church TN-4
Dickeys Ditch—stream NJ-2
*Dickeys Handing* ND-7
Dickeys Hill—summit VA-3
Dickeys Lake—lake MN-6
Dickey's Landing—other TN-4
Dickeys Mountain—locale PA-2
Dickeys Mountain—ridge PA-2
*Dickeys Mountains* PA-2
Dickey's Octagonal Barbershop—hist pl TN-4
Dickey Spring—spring AL-4
Dickey Spring—spring AZ-5
Dickey Spring—spring TN-4
Dickeys Sch (historical)—school TN-4
*Dickeys Siding* IL-6
Dickeys Swamp—stream VA-3
Dickey Swamp—stream SC-3
Dickey Top—summit NC-3
Dickey Towhead—island TN-4
Dickey Valley—valley TN-4
**Dickeyville—pop pl** IN-6
**Dickeyville—pop pl** MD-2
**Dickeyville—pop pl** WI-6
Dickeyville Hist Dist—hist pl MD-2
Dickeyville (historical)—locale KS-7
Dickeyville Sch—school WI-6
Dickey Wash—stream AZ-5
Dickey Water Mill (historical)—locale MS-4
*Dick Faldy Creek* MT-8
Dick Fork—stream KY-4
Dick Fork—stream WV-2
Dick Gap—gap KY-4
Dick Gulch—valley MT-8
Dick Gut Branch—stream AL-4
Dick Hart Draw—valley AZ-5
Dick Hart Ridge—ridge AZ-5
*Dick Hart Tank* AZ-5
Dick Hart Tank—reservoir (2) AZ-5
Dick Hill—summit NY-2
Dick Hill Cem—cemetery AR-4
Dick Hollow—valley TN-4
Dick Hollow—valley TX-5
Dick Hollow—valley UT-8
Dick Hollow—valley VA-3
Dick Hooten Branch—stream TX-5
**Dickie—pop pl** WY-8
Dickie Branch—stream AR-4
Dickie Bridge—bridge MT-8
Dickiebusch Lake—lake NY-2
Dickie Canyon—valley NM-5
Dickie Hills—range MT-8
Dickie Peak—summit MT-8
Dickie Ranch—locale (2) WY-8
Dickierville—locale IA-7
Dickies Creek—stream NC-3
Dickies Grove Ch—church NC-3
Dickie Shearing Sheds—locale WY-8
Dickie Springs—spring WY-8
Dickie Springs Creek—stream WY-8
Dickinson—locale VA-3
**Dickinson—pop pl** NY-2
**Dickinson—pop pl** ND-7
**Dickinson—pop pl** PA-2
**Dickinson—pop pl** TX-5
Dickinson, Edward, House—hist pl AR-4
Dickinson, Emily, House—hist pl MA-1
Dickinson, Gen. Philemon, House—hist pl NJ-2
Dickinson, John, House—hist pl DE-2
Dickinson, Mount—summit CO-8
Dickinson Air Force Station*—other ND-7
Dickinson Baptist Ch—church AL-4
Dickinson Bay—bay MD-2
Dickinson Bay—bay TX-5
Dickinson Bayou—stream TX-5
*Dickinson Branch* MA-1
Dickinson Branch—stream TN-4
Dickinson Branch—stream VA-3
*Dickinson Brook* CT-1
Dickinson Brook—stream MA-1
Dickinson Brook—stream (2) NH-1
Dickinson Cem—cemetery AL-4
Dickinson Cem—cemetery GA-3
Dickinson Cem—cemetery MS-4
Dickinson Cem—cemetery ND-7
**Dickinson Center—pop pl** NY-2
**Dickinson Center (Dickinson)—pop pl** NY-2
Dickinson Ch—church AR-4
Dickinson Ch—church PA-2
Dickinson Chapel Methodist Ch (historical)—church AL-4
Dickinson Coll—school PA-2
Dickinson Country Club—other TX-5
Dickinson County—civil KS-7
**Dickinson (County)—pop pl** MI-6
Dickinson County Courthouse—hist pl IA-7
Dickinson County Courthouse and Jail—hist pl MI-6
Dickinson County Home for the Aged—locale IA-7
Dickinson Creek—stream CT-1
Dickinson Creek—stream GA-3
Dickinson Creek—stream MI-6
Dickinson Creek—stream WA-9
Dickinson Creek—stream WI-6
Dickinson Creek—stream (2) WY-8
Dickinson Creek Campground—locale WY-8
Dickinson Dam—dam ND-7
**Dickinson (Dickenson)—pop pl** AL-4
**Dickinson (Dickenson Station)—pop pl** AL-4
*Dickinson Dike* ND-7
Dickinson Drain—canal MI-6
Dickinson Falls—falls NY-2
Dickinson Family Cem—cemetery AL-4
Dickinson Field—park MI-6
Dickinson Gap—gap VA-3
Dickinson Gap—gap WV-2
Dickinson Gillock Oil Field—oilfield TX-5
Dickinson Glacier—glacier AK-9
Dickinson Hill—locale WY-8
Dickinson Hill—summit NH-1
Dickinson Hill—summit NY-2
Dickinson Hill—summit UT-8
Dickinson Hist Dist—hist pl MA-1
Dickinson Hollow—valley WV-2
Dickinson House—hist pl AL-4
Dickinson House—hist pl NJ-2
Dickinson HS—school NJ-2
Dickinson Island—island MI-6
Dickinson Island—island NY-2
Dickinson Island—island TN-4
Dickinson JHS—school MI-6
Dickinson Lake—lake MI-6
Dickinson Lake—reservoir WV-2
Dickinson Law Sch—school PA-2
Dickinson Mansion—locale DE-2
Dickinson Memorial Park—park CT-1
Dickinson Mountain—ridge WV-2
Dickinson Mtn—summit OR-9
Dickinson Municipal Airp—airport ND-7
Dickinson North—unorg reg ND-7
Dickinson No 1 Ditch—canal WY-8
Dickinson Park—flat WY-8
Dickinson Park—park IN-6
Dickinson Park—park MI-6
Dickinson Park Guard Station—locale WY-8
Dickinson Playground—park IL-6
Dickinson Point—cape NY-2
Dickinson Pond—lake NH-1
**Dickinson (Quincy Post Office)—pop pl** WV-2
Dickinson Ranch—locale NM-5
*Dickinson Reservoir* MA-1
*Dickinson Reservoir* ND-7
**Dickinson (RR name for Quincy)—pop pl** WV-2
Dickinson Run—stream OH-6
*Dickinsons Brook* CT-1
Dickinson Sch—school CA-9
Dickinson Sch—school (2) MI-6
Dickinson Sch—school MT-8
Dickinson Sch—school NY-2
Dickinson Sch—school VA-3
Dickinson Sch—school (2) WI-6
Dickinsons Corner—locale VA-3
*Dickinsons Mill Run* PA-2
Dickinson South—unorg reg ND-7
Dickinson Square—park PA-2
Dickinson Store—locale VA-3
**Dickinson Store—pop pl** VA-3
**Dickinson (Town of)—pop pl (2)** NY-2
**Dickinson (Township of)—pop pl** PA-2
Dickins Peak—summit AK-9
Dickinson Cem—cemetery MO-7
Dick Island—island FL-3
Dick Island—island TX-5
Dickison Cem—cemetery IL-6
Dickison Run—stream IL-6
Dick Johnson Cut-Off—bend OK-5
Dick Johnson (Township of)—civ div IN-6
Dick Knob—summit NC-3
Dick-Kobel Homestead—hist pl MO-7
*Dick Lake* MN-6
Dick Lake—lake FL-3
Dick Lake—lake (2) MN-6
Dick Landing Strip—airport KS-7
Dickle Mill (historical)—locale AL-4
Dickman Bay—bay AK-9
Dickman Cem—cemetery IA-7
Dickman Cem—cemetery MO-7
Dickman Draw—valley CO-8
Dickman Lake—lake WI-6
Dickman Oil Field—oilfield KS-7
Dickman Park—park MN-6
*Dickman Point* FL-3
Dickmans Island—island FL-3
Dickmans Point—cape FL-3
Dick McCarthy Lake—lake AK-9
Dick Mesa—summit WA-9
Dick Messer Spring—spring CO-8
Dick Mill Creek—stream AL-4
Dick Miller Canyon—valley OR-9
Dick Moffet—locale TX-5
Dick Moore Canyon—valley TX-5
Dick Nickolas Spring—spring OR-9
*Dickodochtedar* WA-9
*Dickodochtedar Creek* WA-9
Dickoff Coulee—valley MT-8
Dickoff Creek—stream MT-8
Dick Palmer Wash—valley UT-8
Dick Path Hollow—valley MO-7
Dick Peak—summit AZ-5
Dick Point—cape NC-3
Dick Point—cape OR-9
Dick Pond—lake IL-6
Dick Pond—lake MI-6
Dick Pond—lake SC-3
Dick Pond—lake TN-4
Dick Ridge—ridge CO-8
Dick Ridge—ridge GA-3
Dick Ridge—ridge VA-3
*Dick River* KY-4
Dick Rock—island CT-1
Dick Rock—pillar RI-1
Dick Rocks—island CT-1
Dick Ross Creek—stream ID-8
Dick Rsvr—reservoir NV-8
Dick Rsvr—reservoir OR-9
Dick Run—stream IN-6
Dick Run—stream PA-2
Dicks, John, House—hist pl MS-4
Dicks Arm—bay AK-9
*Dicks Branch* VA-3
Dicks Branch—stream AR-4
Dicks Branch—stream KY-4
Dicks Branch—stream MO-7
Dicks Branch—stream (3) NC-3
Dicks Branch—stream TN-4
Dicks Branch—stream VA-3
Dicks Branch—stream WV-2
Dicks Bridge—other MO-7
*Dicks Brook* NJ-2
Dicks Brook—stream MA-1
Dicks Brook—stream NJ-2
Dicksburg Hills—range IN-6
Dicks Butte—summit CA-9
Dicks Camp—locale NC-3
Dicks Camp Spring—spring OR-9
Dicks Canyon—valley UT-8
Dicks Cem—cemetery SD-7
Dick Sch—school (2) IL-6
Dick Sch—school KS-7
Dick Sch—school (2) PA-2
*Dicks Chapel* MS-4
*Dicks Creek* AL-4
*Dicks Creek* CA-9
Dicks Creek—locale NC-3
Dicks Creek—stream AL-4
Dicks Creek—stream AR-4
Dicks Creek—stream CO-8
Dicks Creek—stream (4) GA-3
Dicks Creek—stream ID-8
Dicks Creek—stream IL-6
Dicks Creek—stream KY-4
Dicks Creek—stream (2) MS-4
Dicks Creek—stream MO-7
Dicks Creek—stream MT-8
Dicks Creek—stream (4) NC-3
Dicks Creek—stream (3) OH-6
Dicks Creek—stream OR-9
Dicks Creek—stream (2) VA-3
Dicks Creek—stream WA-9
Dicks Creek—stream WV-2
Dicks Creek Cem—cemetery NC-3
Dicks Creek Cem—cemetery OH-6
Dicks Creek Ch—church NC-3
Dicks Creek Cove—bay GA-3
Dicks Creek Dam—dam NC-3
Dicks Creek Gap—gap GA-3
Dicks Creek Post Office (historical)—building AL-4
Dicks Ferry (historical)—locale MS-4
Dicks Fork—stream (3) KY-4
Dicks Fork—stream MO-7
Dicks Fork—stream OR-9
Dicks Fork Creek—stream TN-4
Dicks Gap—gap AR-4
Dicks Gap—gap (3) NC-3
Dicks Gap Bridge—bridge NC-3
Dicks Gulch—valley MT-8
*Dicks Hill* PA-2
Dicks Hill—locale GA-3
Dick Shoal—bar ME-1
Dicks Hollow Windmill—locale TX-5
Dickshooter—locale ID-8
Dickshooter Creek—stream ID-8
Dickshooter Ridge—ridge ID-8
Dickshooter Rsvr—reservoir ID-8
Dick Simon Number 1 Dam—dam SD-7
Dicks Island—island GA-3
Dicks Islands—island NY-2
Dicks Knob—summit GA-3
Dicks Knob—summit KY-4
Dicks Knob—summit VA-3
Dicks Lake—lake CA-9
Dicks Lake—lake FL-3
Dick Slough—stream AK-9
Dicks Mine—mine CO-8
Dicks Mtn—summit NC-3
*Dickson* AL-4
*Dickson* MS-4
*Dickson* PA-2
Dickson—locale AK-9
Dickson—locale GA-3
Dickson—locale WV-2
**Dickson—pop pl** OK-5
**Dickson—pop pl** TN-4
**Dickson—pop pl** WV-2
Dickson, James, House—hist pl TN-4
Dickson, Roger, Farm—hist pl NC-3
Dickson, Samuel Thompson, House—hist pl MN-6
Dickson Airp—airport KS-7
*Dickson Bay* FL-3
Dickson Bay—bay FL-3
Dickson Bay—swamp FL-3
Dickson Bend—bend AR-4
Dickson Bluff—cliff (2) TN-4
Dickson Bluff Ridge—ridge TN-4
*Dickson Branch* DE-2
*Dickson Branch* MS-4
Dickson Branch—stream AR-4
Dickson Branch—stream IA-7
Dickson Branch—stream KY-4
**Dicksonburg—pop pl** PA-2
Dicksonburg Cem—cemetery PA-2
Dickson Butte—summit CA-9
Dickson Cave—cave AL-4
Dickson Cave—cave TN-4
Dickson (CCD)—cens area TN-4
Dickson Cem—cemetery (2) AL-4
Dickson Cem—cemetery AR-4
Dickson Cem—cemetery GA-3
Dickson Cem—cemetery IL-6
Dickson Cem—cemetery (2) IA-7
Dickson Cem—cemetery LA-4
Dickson Cem—cemetery MI-6
Dickson Cem—cemetery MS-4
Dickson Cem—cemetery MO-7
Dickson Cem—cemetery OH-6
Dickson Cem—cemetery (3) TN-4
Dickson Cem—cemetery WI-6
Dickson Chapel Rec Area—park TN-4
**Dickson City—pop pl** PA-2
Dickson City Borough—civil PA-2
**Dickson County—pop pl** TN-4
**Dickson Cove—pop pl** TX-5
*Dickson Creek* CO-8
Dickson Creek—stream AK-9
Dickson Creek—stream CA-9
Dickson Creek—stream CO-8
Dickson Creek—stream IL-6
Dickson Creek—stream MT-8
Dickson Creek—stream NC-3
Dickson Dam—dam OR-9
Dickson Division—civil TN-4
Dickson-Dodson Cem—cemetery MS-4
Dickson Elem Sch—school PA-2
Dickson Farm—locale NM-5
Dickson Flat—flat CA-9
Dickson Ford—locale AL-4
Dickson Golf and Country Club—locale TN-4
Dickson Grove Ch—church TN-4
Dickson Gulch—valley CO-8
Dickson Gulch—valley UT-8
Dickson Gulf—valley GA-3
Dickson Hollow—valley AL-4
Dickson Hollow—valley TN-4
*Dickson-Hopewell Cemetery* TX-5
Dickson HS—school PA-2
Dickson Lake—lake MI-6
Dickson Lake—reservoir GA-3
Dickson Lake—reservoir SC-3
Dickson Lake—reservoir TN-4
Dickson Lake Dam—dam TN-4
Dickson Landing (historical)—locale MS-4
Dickson Landing Strip—airport CO-8
Dickson Mounds—hist pl IL-6
Dickson Mounds State Park—park IL-6
Dickson Municipal Airp—airport TN-4
Dickson-Palmer Center—building NC-3
*Dickson Park* WY-8
Dickson Park—park AL-4
Dickson Park (subdivision)—park NC-3
Dickson Pass—gap UT-8
*Dickson Point* NY-2
Dickson Point—cape VA-3
*Dickson Ridge* UT-8
Dickson Rsvr—reservoir OR-9
Dicksons Cem—cemetery GA-3
*Dickson Sch* PA-2
*Dickson Sch* TN-4
Dickson Sch—school TN-4
Dickson Sch—school TX-5
Dickson Shaft—mine PA-2
Dickson Sink Cave—cave AL-4
Dicksons Mill Creek—stream GA-3
Dicksons Millpond—reservoir GA-3
*Dicksons Mills* IN-6
Dickson Spring—spring GA-3
Dickson Spring—spring TN-4
Dickson Station—locale PA-2
Dickson Tank—reservoir AZ-5
Dickson Timber County Park—park IA-7
**Dickson Town—pop pl** TN-4
Dickson (Township of)—fmr MCD AR-4
**Dickson (Township of)—pop pl** MI-6
Dickson Valley—valley MO-7
*Dicksonville* TN-4
Dickson-Walker Mtn—summit TX-5
Dickson Well—well NM-5
Dickson Works—hist pl PA-2
Dicks Pass—gap CA-9
Dicks Peak—summit AZ-5
Dicks Peak—summit CA-9
Dicks Peak—summit CO-8
Dicks Peak Tank—reservoir AZ-5
Dicks Point—cape AK-9
Dicks Point—cape FL-3
Dicks Point—cape (2) MD-2
Dicks Point—cape VA-3
Dicks Point—cliff AR-4
Dicks Point—summit KY-4
Dicks Pond—lake MA-1
Dicks Pond—lake (2) OR-9
Dicks Pond—reservoir OK-5
Dicks Pond—reservoir SC-3
Dicks Post Office (historical)—building MS-4
Dick Spring—spring AZ-5
Dick Spring—spring CA-9
Dick Spring—spring OR-9
Dick Spring Canyon—valley AZ-5
Dick Spring Creek—stream AZ-5
*Dick Spring Wash* AZ-5
Dicks Ridge—ridge OR-9
Dicks Ridge—ridge PA-2
*Dick's River* KY-4
Dicks Rsvr—reservoir OR-9
Dicks Run—stream (2) PA-2
Dicks Run—stream WV-2
Dicks Run Ch—church PA-2
Dicks Sch—school SD-7
*Dicks Spring* AZ-5
Dicks Spring—spring OR-9
*Dicks Spring Canyon* AZ-5
*Dicks Spring Creek* AZ-5
Dicks Swamp—stream SC-3
Dicks Swift—channel GA-3
Dicks Tank—reservoir AZ-5
Dicks Well—well NM-5
Dicks Well—well OR-9
Dick Swift Creek—stream GA-3
Dick Tank—reservoir NM-5
Dick Tank—reservoir TX-5
Dick Taylor Landing—locale NC-3
Dick Thomas Pond—reservoir IN-6
Dick Thomas Pond Dam—dam IN-6
Dicktown—locale NJ-2
**Dick-Urban—pop pl** NY-2
Dick-Urban Plaza Shop Ctr—locale NY-2
Dickvale—locale ME-1
**Dickville—pop pl** PA-2
Dick Williams Creek—stream AZ-5
Dickwood Lake—lake ME-1
Dick Woods Branch—stream IL-6
Dick Woods Windmill—locale TX-5
Dickworsham—locale TX-5
Dick Wright Spring—spring CA-9
Dicky Branch—stream KY-4
Dicky Creek—stream AL-4
Dicky Creek—stream AK-9
Dicky Creek—stream MO-7
Dicky Creek—stream WA-9
Dicky Creek Campground—locale WA-9
*Dicky Lake* MT-8
*Dicky Peak* MT-8
Dicky Playground—park CA-9
Dictator Creek—stream AK-9
Dictator Ledge—bar ME-1
Dictator Mine—mine NM-5
Dictator Number One Mine—mine CA-9
Dictionary Hill—summit CA-9
Dictum Ridge—ridge VA-3
Dictum Ridge Trail—trail VA-3
*Dicus* TX-5
Dicus—locale AR-4
Dicus Cem—cemetery KY-4
Dicus Cem—cemetery TN-4
Dicus Hollow—valley TN-4
Dicus Slough—stream CA-9
Dicycope Chapel—church KY-4
Didall—bridge PW-9
Didallas Creek—stream CA-9
Diddell—locale NY-2
Diddle Hill—summit MO-7
*Diddlers Beach* OR-9
Diddy Wells Fire Control Station—locale CA-9
*Didell* NY-2
Diden Cem—cemetery TN-4
Didero Spring—spring CO-8
Didi—island MP-9
**Didier—pop pl** PA-2
Didier, Lac—lake LA-4
**Didier Minor Subdivision—pop pl** UT-8
Didigue—area GU-9
*Didi Point* FL-3
Didi Point—cape FL-3
**Didlake (subdivision)—pop pl** MS-4
Dido—locale LA-4
**Dido—pop pl** TX-5
Dido Ch—church TX-5
Dido (historical)—locale MS-4
Dido (historical P.O.)—locale AL-4
Dido Post Office (historical)—building MS-4
Did Post Office (historical)—building TN-4
Didrickson Bay—bay AK-9
Diebel-Hyak House—hist pl TX-5
Die Bend—bend NC-3
Diebenow Gulch—valley ID-8
Diebert Spring—spring NV-8
Diebertsville—locale PA-2
Diebold, Anton, House—hist pl KY-4
Diebold, J. W., Jr. House—hist pl KY-4
Diechland Point—cliff PA-2
Dieders Fork—stream MT-8
Diedrich Park—park IL-6
Diedrichs Point—cape VI-3
**Diefenbach Corners—pop pl** WI-6
Dieffenbach—locale PA-2
Dieffenbacher Sch—school IL-6
Diegel Hollow—valley PA-2
Diego Coulee—valley MT-8
Diego Hernandez (Barrio)—fmr MCD PR-3
Diego Plains—flat FL-3
Diego Tank—reservoir NM-5
**Diehl—pop pl** PA-2
Diehl, George, Homestead—hist pl PA-2
Diehl Cem—cemetery IN-6
Diehl Ditch—canal IN-6
Diehl Drain—canal CA-9
Diehl Elem Sch—school PA-2
Diehl Hollow—valley IN-6
Diehl Hollow—valley TN-4
Diehl Lake—reservoir NE-7
Diehl Point—cape NJ-2
Diehl Point—ridge CO-8
Diehl Run—stream OH-6
*Diehl Sch* PA-2
Diehl Sch—school PA-2
Diehl Sch (abandoned)—school (2) PA-2
Diehls Covered Bridge—hist pl PA-2
Diehls Crossroads Ch—church PA-2
Diehl-Seitters House—hist pl OR-9
Diehls Hollow—valley PA-2
Diehl Spring—spring PA-2
**Diehlstadt—pop pl** MO-7
Diehltown—locale PA-2
Diehm Creek—stream AK-9
Diehr Lake—reservoir OH-6
Diekbrader Lake—reservoir OH-6
*Die Klee Kaft* PA-2
*Die Kleine Kaft* PA-2
Diekman Sch—school IL-6
Diekow Lake—lake MN-6
Diele, Ernest, House—hist pl MI-6
Dielman Ditch—canal IN-6
Dielman Lake—lake MN-6
Diem, John, House—hist pl UT-8
Diemer Lake—lake CO-8
*Diemers* PA-2
Diemer Sch—school KS-7
*Dien* FM-9
Dien—cape FM-9
Dien—civil FM-9
Diendoar—cape FM-9
Diene Lake—lake WI-6
Diener—locale NM-5
**Diener—pop pl** NM-5
Diener Canyon—valley NM-5
Diener Ditch—canal CA-9
Diener Ditch—canal IN-6
Diener Mine—mine CA-9
Diener Ranch—locale CA-9

**Dieners Hall**—*pop pl* PA-2
**Dieners Hill**—*pop pl* PA-2
Dienger, Joseph, Bldg—*hist pl* TX-5
Dieniepw—*cape* FM-9
Dien Kara—*bar* FM-9
Dienpako—*bar* FM-9
Dien Pei—*locale* FM-9
Dienpo—*locale* FM-9
Dienpwalek—*island* FM-9
Dienrar—*locale* FM-9
Dienslake Lake—*lake* SD-7
Dienst Ranch Airp—*airport* KS-7
*Die Pearl-und Hermesbank* HI-9
*Die Pond* RI-1
Diera Mtn—*summit* AR-4
Dierich Creek—*stream* CO-8
Dieringer—*locale* WA-9
Dierking Branch—*stream* MO-7
**Dierks**—*pop pl* AR-4
Dierks Cem—*cemetery* IA-7
Dierks Dam—*dam* AR-4
Dierks Lake—*reservoir* AR-4
Dierks Pond—*lake* MA-1
*Dierks Rsvr* AR-4
*Dieruff High School* PA-2
*Dies* TX-5
Dies—*locale* TX-5
**Dies**—*pop pl* TX-5
**Dies Community**—*pop pl* TX-5
Diesel-Moore Cem—*cemetery* MO-7
Dies Lake—*lake* TX-5
Dies Slough—*gut* MS-4
Dietch Creek—*stream* OR-9
**Dieter and Johnson Main Street Addition (subdivision)**—*pop pl* UT-8
Dieter Ditch—*canal* IN-6
Dieter Hollow—*valley* WI-6
**Dieterich**—*pop pl* IL-6
Dieterich Cem—*cemetery* IL-6
Dieterich Creek—*stream* IL-6
Dieterich Pond—*lake* NY-2
Dieterich Sch—*school* IL-6
Dieters Airp—*airport* PA-2
Dieter Sch—*school* IL-6
*Dieters Run* PA-2
**Dieter (Township of)**—*pop pl* MN-6
Dietline Drain—*canal* MI-6
**Dietrich**—*pop pl* ID-8
**Dietrich**—*pop pl* PA-2
Dietrich Allotment Well—*well* ID-8
Dietrich-Bowen House—*hist pl* IN-6
Dietrich Butte—*summit* ID-8
Dietrich Butte Well—*well* ID-8
Dietrich Cabin—*hist pl* KS-7
Dietrich Camp—*locale* AK-9
*Dietrich Creek* MI-6
Dietrich Lange State Wildlife Mngmt Are—*park* MN-6
Dietrich Main Canal—*canal* ID-8
Dietrich Ranch—*locale* CO-8
Dietrich Ranch—*locale* OR-9
Dietrich River—*stream* AK-9
Dietrich Sch—*school* MO-7
Dietrichs Mill Bridge—*bridge* PA-2
Dietrich Spring—*spring* OR-9
**Dietrichtown**—*pop pl* PA-2
*Dietrichville* PA-2
Dietrich Well—*well* TX-5
Dietrick Cem—*cemetery* OH-6
Dietz, Robert, Farmhouse—*hist pl* NM-5
**Dietz Acres**—*pop pl* KY-4
Dietz Airp—*airport* OR-9
Dietz Cem—*cemetery* GA-3
Dietz Cem—*cemetery* KS-7
Dietz Cem—*cemetery* NE-7
Dietz Creek—*arroyo* TX-5
Dietz Creek—*stream* MI-6
Dietz Creek—*stream* OR-9
Dietz Draw—*valley* ND-7
Dietz Gulch—*valley* CA-9
*Dietz Lake* MN-6
Dietz Lake—*lake* IN-6
Dietz Lake—*lake* MN-6
Dietz Lakes—*lake* WI-6
Dietz Sch—*school* AZ-5
Dietz Sch—*school* IL-6
*Die Wind Kapf* PA-2
*Diff* IA-7
*Diffee* GA-3
Diffenbacher, Aaron, Farmhouse—*hist pl* MN-6
Diffen Hill—*summit* OH-6
Different Drum Dam—*dam* NC-3
Different Drum Lake—*reservoir* NC-3
**Difficult**—*pop pl* TN-4
Difficult Campground—*locale* CO-8
Difficult Canyon—*valley* CA-9
Difficult Creek—*stream* AK-9
Difficult Creek—*stream* (2) CO-8
Difficult Creek—*stream* KY-4
Difficult Creek—*stream* (2) VA-3
Difficult Creek—*stream* WV-2
Difficult Hill—*summit* WV-2
Difficult Post Office—*building* TN-4
*Difficult Run* VA-3
Difficult Run—*stream* VA-3
Difficult Run Stream Valley Park—*park* VA-3
Difficult Spring—*spring* CA-9
Difficulty—*locale* WY-8
Difficulty Branch—*stream* AL-4
Difficulty Canyon—*valley* WY-8
Difficulty Creek—*stream* CO-8
Difficulty Creek—*stream* (2) KY-4
Difficulty Creek—*stream* MT-8
Difficulty Creek—*stream* WY-8
*Difficulty Rsvr, The* OR-9
Difficulty Spring—*spring* WY-8
Diffin—*locale* MI-6
Diffley Landing Strip—*airport* ND-7
Diffly Park—*park* AL-4
Diffucult Sch (historical)—*school* TN-4
Diffy Creek—*stream* TX-5
Diffy Mtn—*summit* AR-4
Difjakamiut (Summer Camp)—*locale* AK-9
Difrises Arroyo—*stream* NM-5
Digbey—*locale* GA-3
**Digbey**—*pop pl* GA-3
Digbey (CCD)—*cens area* GA-3
Digby—*locale* OH-6
Digby Cem—*cemetery* IL-6
Digby (historical)—*locale* KS-7
Dig Cave—*cave* TN-4
Digel Block—*hist pl* MO-7
Digger Basin—*basin* UT-8
Digger Bay—*bay* CA-9
Digger Bend—*bend* CA-9
Digger Bend Ranch—*locale* CA-9
Digger Butte—*summit* CA-9
*Digger Creek* AZ-5
Digger Creek—*stream* (10) CA-9
Digger Creek—*stream* OR-9
Digger Gulch—*valley* (2) CA-9
*Digger Jones Mountain* CA-9
Digger Mtn—*summit* OR-9
Digger Pine Campground—*locale* CA-9
Digger Pine Flat—*flat* (2) CA-9
Digger Pine Hill—*summit* CA-9
Digger Ravine—*valley* (2) CA-9
Digger Ridge—*ridge* CA-9
Digger Wash—*stream* AZ-5
Digger Windmill—*locale* TX-5
Digges Canyon—*valley* CA-9
Diggie Creek—*stream* ID-8
Diggings Creek—*stream* MI-6
Diggings Pit, The—*cave* AL-4
*Diggins* CA-9
**Diggins**—*pop pl* MO-7
Diggins Creek—*stream* CA-9
Diggins Creek—*stream* MT-8
Diggins Gap—*gap* GA-3
Diggins Knob—*summit* GA-3
Diggins Slough—*stream* IA-7
Diggles Gulch—*valley* CA-9
Diggs—*locale* NC-3
Diggs—*locale* VA-3
Diggs Chapel—*church* KY-4
Diggs Chapel—*church* NC-3
Diggs Creek—*stream* VA-3
Diggs Gap—*gap* TN-4
Diggs Hollow—*valley* TN-4
Diggs Mine (underground)—*mine* TN-4
Diggs Mtn—*summit* (2) VA-3
Diggs Park—*uninc pl* VA-3
Diggs Park Sch—*school* VA-3
Diggs Wharf—*locale* VA-3
Dighans Hill—*summit* MT-8
Dighton—*locale* OK-5
**Dighton**—*pop pl* KS-7
**Dighton**—*pop pl* MA-1
**Dighton**—*pop pl* MI-6
Dighton Airp—*airport* KS-7
**Dighton (Bartlett)**—*pop pl* OK-5
Dighton Cem—*cemetery* KS-7
Dighton City Wells—*well* KS-7
Dighton Grade Sch—*school* KS-7
Dighton HS—*school* KS-7
Dighton Rock—*hist pl* MA-1
Dighton Rock—*rock* MA-1
Dighton Rock State Park—*park* MA-1
Dighton Sch—*school* MI-6
Dighton Town Cem—*cemetery* MA-1
**Dighton (Town of)**—*pop pl* MA-1
**Dighton Township**—*pop pl* KS-7
**Di Giorgio**—*pop pl* CA-9
Di Giorgio County Park—*park* CA-9
Di Giorgio Sch—*school* CA-9
Digit Lake—*lake* MN-6
Digit Point Campground—*park* OR-9
Digman Lake—*reservoir* AR-4
Digman Sch—*school* WV-2
Digneo-Valdes House—*hist pl* NM-5
Di Gob Creek—*stream* TX-5
Digwood Swamp—*swamp* VA-3
Di Hill—*summit* CA-9
Dike—*locale* NV-8
Dike—*locale* OR-9
**Dike**—*pop pl* IN-6
**Dike**—*pop pl* IA-7
**Dike**—*pop pl* TX-5
Dike, The—*cliff* ID-8
Dike, The—*dam* NV-8
Dike, The—*levee* NM-5
Dike, The—*other* GA-3
Dike, The—*summit* TX-5
Dike, The—*summit* UT-8
Dike Branch—*stream* KY-4
Dike Canyon—*valley* NM-5
Dike Cem—*cemetery* CT-1
Dike Creek—*stream* (2) AK-9
Dike Creek—*stream* CA-9
Dike Creek—*stream* (2) WY-8
Dike Ditch—*canal* CO-8
Dike Ditch—*canal* IN-6
Dike Eight—*dam* CA-9
Dike Eight Picnic Area—*park* CA-9
Dike Five—*dam* CA-9
Dike Four—*dam* CA-9
Dike Hollow—*valley* AL-4
*Dike Lake* UT-8
Dike Lake—*lake* ID-8
Dike Lake—*lake* UT-8
Dikeman Airp—*airport* KS-7
Dikeman Ranch—*locale* NE-7
Dikeman (Site)—*locale* AK-9
Dike Mine—*mine* SD-7
*Dike Mountain* CO-8
*Dike Mountain* WY-8
Dike Mtn—*summit* AK-9
Dike Mtn—*summit* (2) WY-8
Dike Pit Tank—*reservoir* NM-5
Dike Pond—*lake* MA-1
Dike Pond—*reservoir* AZ-5
Dike Rock Ridge—*ridge* NM-5
*Dikes Brook Reservoir* MA-1
Dikes Canyon—*valley* TX-5
Dike Sch—*school* ME-1
Dike Sch—*school* OH-6
*Dikes Creek* GA-3
Dikes Creek—*stream* TX-5
Dike Seven—*dam* CA-9
Dike Six—*dam* CA-9
*Dikes Meadow Pond* MA-1
*Dikes Meadow Reservor* MA-1
Dikes Mill (historical)—*locale* TN-4
*Dikes Pond* MA-1
Dikes Sch (historical)—*school* AL-4
Dikes Shoals—*bar* TN-4
Dike Tank—*reservoir* AZ-5
Dike Tank—*reservoir* NM-5
Dike Windmill—*locale* NM-5
Dike 10 Dam—*dam* SD-7
Dikike'Agingan, Unai—*beach* MH-9
Dikike'Matuis, Unai—*beach* MH-9
Dilabaugh Buttes—*summit* WY-8
Dilabaugh Spring—*spring* WY-8
Dilaeg—*locale* FM-9
*Dilag* FM-9
Dilar Cove—*bay* OK-5
Dilbeck—*locale* VA-3
Dilbeck Cem—*cemetery* TX-5
Dilboy Field—*park* MA-1
*Dilburg Pates Lake Dam* AL-4
Dilce Combs HS—*school* KY-4
*Dilcon* AZ-5
Dilcon Sch—*school* AZ-5
Dildas Grove Ch—*church* NC-3
Dilday Cem—*cemetery* TN-4
Dilday Hollow—*valley* AR-4
Dilday Landing (historical)—*locale* TN-4
Dilday Mill—*hist pl* MO-7
Dilday Mill—*locale* MO-7
*Dildays Landing* TN-4
*Dildays Landing Post Office* TN-4
Dildays Post Office (historical)—*building* TN-4
*Dildicks Creek* MD-2
Dildine Ch—*church* MI-6
Dildine Creek—*stream* SC-3
Dildine Ditch—*canal* OH-6
Dildine Island—*island* NJ-2
Dildine Sch—*school* IN-6
Dildine Sch—*school* WY-8
Dildo Key—*island* FL-3
Dildo Key Bank—*bar* FL-3
Dildys Chapel—*church* NC-3
Dildys Mill—*locale* NC-3
Dildys Mills (historical)—*locale* NC-3
*Dileg* FM-9
Dilemma Pit—*cave* AL-4
Diles Creek—*stream* AR-4
Diles Creek—*stream* MO-7
Diles Creek Ch—*church* AR-4
Diley Trail—*trail* WV-2
Dilger Store—*hist pl* OH-6
**Dilhast**—*pop pl* NC-3
**Dilia**—*pop pl* NM-5
Dilia (CCD)—*cens area* NM-5
Di Lido Island—*island* FL-3
Dilkesboro—*locale* NJ-2
*Dilkesborough* NJ-2
*Dilkes Mill Pond* NJ-2
Dilkes Mills—*locale* NJ-2
Dilkon—*locale* AZ-5
Dilkon Hill—*summit* AZ-5
Dilkon Indian Mission—*school* AZ-5
**Dilkon (Trading Post)**—*pop pl* AZ-5
Dilky Ranch—*locale* CO-8
*Dill* OK-5
**Dill**—*pop pl* AL-4
**Dill**—*pop pl* AR-4
**Dill**—*pop pl* TN-4
Dill, Charles W., House—*hist pl* ID-8
Dill, Richard E., House—*hist pl* NE-7
Dillabaugh Rsvr—*reservoir* CO-8
Dillaberry Branch—*stream* FL-3
Dillaborough Cem—*cemetery* NY-2
Dillabough Creek—*stream* MI-6
Dillacort Canyon—*valley* WA-9
Dillahunty Cem—*cemetery* AL-4
Dillan Creek—*stream* WV-2
Dillant-Hopkins Airp—*airport* NH-1
Dillard—*locale* AL-4
Dillard—*locale* CA-9
Dillard—*locale* OK-5
**Dillard**—*pop pl* GA-3
**Dillard**—*pop pl* MO-7
**Dillard**—*pop pl* NC-3
**Dillard**—*pop pl* OR-9
**Dillard**—*pop pl* VA-3
Dillard, James H., House—*hist pl* LA-4
Dillard, William, Homestead—*hist pl* AR-4
Dillard Airp—*airport* NC-3
Dillard and Anderson Mines (underground)—*mine* TN-4
Dillard Bend—*bend* AR-4
*Dillard - Bibb Cemetery* AL-4
Dillard Branch—*stream* (2) AL-4
Dillard Branch—*stream* GA-3
Dillard Bridge—*bridge* VA-3
Dillard Canyon—*valley* NC-3
Dillard Cem—*cemetery* (2) AL-4
Dillard Cem—*cemetery* AR-4
Dillard Cem—*cemetery* MO-7
Dillard Cem—*cemetery* SC-3
Dillard Cem—*cemetery* TN-4
Dillard Cem—*cemetery* TX-5
Dillard Chapel Cem—*cemetery* GA-3
*Dillard Creek* TX-5
Dillard Creek—*stream* AR-4
Dillard Creek—*stream* GA-3
Dillard Creek—*stream* IN-6
Dillard Creek—*stream* MO-7
Dillard Creek—*stream* NC-3
Dillard Creek—*stream* SC-3
Dillard Creek—*stream* (2) TN-4
Dillard Creek—*stream* (3) TX-5
Dillard Creek—*stream* VA-3
Dillard Creek—*stream* WA-9
Dillard Creek Ch—*church* TN-4
**Dillard Crossroads**—*pop pl* SC-3
Dillard Cut off—*stream* AR-4
Dillard Draw—*valley* NM-5
Dillard Elem Sch—*school* FL-3
Dillard Elem Sch—*school* NC-3
Dillard-Gamble Houses—*hist pl* NC-3
Dillard HS—*school* FL-3
Dillard JHS—*school* NC-3
Dillard Log Pond—*reservoir* OR-9
Dillard Mesa—*summit* CO-8
Dillard Millpond—*reservoir* NC-3
Dillard Park Day Care Center—*school* FL-3
Dillard Pond—*lake* FL-3
Dillard Post Office (historical)—*building* MS-4
Dillard Post Office (historical)—*building* TN-4
*Dillards* AL-4
Dillard Sch—*school* CA-9
Dillard Sch—*school* FL-3
Dillard Sch—*school* TN-4
Dillard Sch (historical)—*school* (2) MS-4
*Dillard's Creek* GA-3
Dillard Street Sch—*school* FL-3
Dillard Tank—*reservoir* (2) NM-5
Dillard Top—*summit* NC-3
Dillard (Township of)—*fmr MCD* AR-4
Dillard Univ—*school* LA-4
Dillard Well—*well* NM-5
Dillard Wharf—*locale* VA-3
Dillard-Whitmore Well—*well* NM-5
Dillar Windmill—*locale* TX-5
Dillashaw Branch—*stream* AL-4
Dillashaw Mountain—*ridge* AL-4
Dillavou Cem—*cemetery* IA-7
*Dillawar Bay* NJ-2
Dillaway Sch—*hist pl* MA-1
*Dillberry Gulch* CA-9
Dillberry Windmill—*locale* TX-5
Dill Bldg—*hist pl* MA-1
Dill Branch—*stream* AR-4
Dill Branch—*stream* (2) NC-3
Dill Branch—*stream* TN-4
Dill Brook—*stream* ME-1
Dillburg—*locale* AL-4
Dill Butte—*summit* CA-9
Dill Camp Fork—*stream* KY-4
Dill Canyon—*valley* TX-5
Dill Cem—*cemetery* LA-4
Dill Cem—*cemetery* NC-3
Dill Cem—*cemetery* TN-4
**Dill City**—*pop pl* OK-5
Dill Creek—*stream* GA-3
Dill Creek—*stream* ID-8
Dill Creek—*stream* NY-2
Dill Creek—*stream* SC-3
Dill Creek—*stream* TX-5
Dill Creek—*stream* WA-9
Dill Creek—*stream* WI-6
Dilldear, Lake—*reservoir* IN-6
Dill Ditch—*canal* IN-6
Dilldown Creek—*stream* PA-2
*Dille* OH-6
**Dille**—*pop pl* WV-2
Dille Bottom—*bend* OH-6
**Dille (Dilles Bottom)**—*pop pl* OH-6
Dillehay Branch—*stream* TN-4
Dillehay Hollow—*valley* (2) TN-4
Dillen—*locale* AR-4
Dillen—*locale* NY-2
Dillen Airp—*airport* PA-2
Dillen Airp (private)—*airport* PA-2
Dillenback Cem—*cemetery* NY-2
Dillenbaugh Creek—*stream* WA-9
Dillenbeck Bay—*bay* VT-1
Dillenbeck Corners—*locale* NY-2
Dillen Cem—*cemetery* MO-7
**Diller**—*pop pl* NE-7
Diller, Anna C., Opera House—*hist pl* NE-7
Diller, Mount—*summit* CA-9
Diller Branch—*stream* NC-3
Diller Canyon—*valley* CA-9
Diller Cem—*cemetery* TX-5
Diller Ch—*church* PA-2
Diller Glacier—*glacier* OR-9
Diller Lake—*reservoir* TX-5
Diller Tank—*reservoir* TX-5
Dille Run—*stream* PA-2
Dille Run—*stream* (2) WV-2
*Dillerville* PA-2
*Dille's* OH-6
**Dilles Bottom**—*pop pl* OH-6
Dille Tunnel—*tunnel* CO-8
*Dilley* WI-6
**Dilley**—*pop pl* OR-9
**Dilley**—*pop pl* TN-4
**Dilley**—*pop pl* TX-5
Dilley (CCD)—*cens area* TX-5
Dilley Creek—*stream* OR-9
Dilley Ditch—*canal* IN-6
Dilley Hollow—*valley* TN-4
Dilley House—*hist pl* AR-4
Dilley Island—*island* ID-8
Dilley Ranch—*locale* CO-8
Dilley Run—*stream* WV-2
Dilleys Mill—*locale* WV-2
Dill Falls—*falls* NC-3
Dill Farm—*hist pl* NY-2
Dill Farm Site—*hist pl* DE-2
Dill Field—*flat* CA-9
Dill Gulch—*valley* CO-8
Dill Hill—*summit* ME-1
Dill Hill—*summit* PA-2
Dill Hollow—*valley* KY-4
Dill Hollow—*valley* MO-7
Dill Hollow—*valley* TN-4
Dill House—*hist pl* GA-3
Dilliard Creek—*stream* AL-4
*Dillie* OH-6
Dillie Lake—*lake* NE-7
*Dillies* OH-6
Dillihunt Hollow—*valley* TX-5
*Dillin* NY-2
Dillin Cem—*cemetery* IN-6
Dilliner—*locale* PA-2
Dilliner Hollow—*valley* AR-4
Dilling Cem—*cemetery* PA-2
*Dillinger* PA-2
**Dillinger**—*pop pl* PA-2
Dillinger Cem—*cemetery* IL-6
Dillinger Creek—*stream* ID-8
Dillinger Divide—*ridge* ND-7
*Dillinger Meadow* ID-8
Dillinger Meadows—*flat* ID-8
Dillinger Mine—*mine* ID-8
Dillinger Ranch—*locale* WY-8
Dillinger Ranch Oil Field—*oilfield* WY-8
Dillinger River—*stream* AK-9
*Dillingers* PA-2
Dillinger Station—*locale* PA-2
*Dillingersville* PA-2
**Dillingersville**—*pop pl* PA-2
Dillingersville Union Sch and Church—*hist pl* PA-2
Dillingerville—*locale* PA-2
**Dillingham**—*pop pl* AK-9
**Dillingham**—*pop pl* NC-3
Dillingham Airp—*airport* AK-9
Dillingham Cem—*cemetery* MA-1
Dillingham Cem—*cemetery* NC-3
*Dillingham (Census Area)* AK-9
Dillingham (Census Subarea)—*cens area* AK-9
Dillingham Ch—*church* IL-6
Dillingham Creek—*stream* MI-6
Dillingham Creek—*stream* NC-3
Dillingham Creek—*stream* TX-5
Dillingham Hill—*summit* ME-1
Dillingham House—*building* MA-1
Dillingham House—*hist pl* MA-1
*Dillingham Island* NY-2
Dillingham Lake—*lake* MI-6
Dillingham Ledge—*bar* ME-1
Dillingham Point—*cape* ME-1
Dillingham Ranch—*locale* HI-9
Dillingham Transportation Bldg—*hist pl* HI-9
Dilling Lake—*lake* ME-1
Dillings Lake—*lake* NE-7
*Dillion* MS-4
**Dillion**—*pop pl* IA-7
Dillion Branch—*stream* KY-4
Dillion Cove—*valley* CA-9
Dillion Creek—*stream* MO-7
Dillion Hollow—*valley* TN-4
Dillion HS—*school* LA-4
Dillion Lake—*lake* CA-9
Dillion Lake—*lake* OR-9
Dillion Ridge—*locale* NC-3
Dillion Sch—*school* MA-1
**Dillionvale**—*pop pl* OH-6
Dill Knob—*summit* NC-3
Dill Lake—*lake* SC-3
Dill Landing (historical)—*locale* TN-4
**Dillman**—*pop pl* IN-6
**Dillman**—*pop pl* MO-7
Dillman, Lake—*reservoir* IN-6
Dillman Cem—*cemetery* IL-6
Dillman Cem—*cemetery* VA-3
Dillman Ch—*church* IN-6
Dillman Creek—*stream* NM-5
Dillman Sch—*school* MI-6
Dillmans Lake—*lake* NE-7
Dillman Tank—*reservoir* NM-5
Dill Mine—*mine* TN-4
Dillock Hollow—*valley* MO-7
Dilloe Run—*stream* PA-2
Dill Oil Field—*oilfield* OK-5
*Dillon* OH-6
Dillon—*locale* GA-3
Dillon—*locale* KS-7
Dillon—*locale* MS-4
Dillon—*locale* NM-5
Dillon—*locale* VA-3
Dillon—*locale* WV-2
Dillon—*locale* WY-8
**Dillon**—*pop pl* CO-8
**Dillon**—*pop pl* IL-6
**Dillon**—*pop pl* IN-6
**Dillon**—*pop pl* IA-7
**Dillon**—*pop pl* KY-4
**Dillon**—*pop pl* MO-7
**Dillon**—*pop pl* MT-8
**Dillon**—*pop pl* SC-3
Dillon, George C., House—*hist pl* TX-5
Dillon, James W., House—*hist pl* SC-3
Dillon Bay—*bay* CO-8
**Dillon Beach**—*pop pl* CA-9
Dillon Bend—*bend* IL-6
Dillon Bldg—*hist pl* CT-1
Dillon Branch—*stream* IL-6
Dillon Branch—*stream* KY-4
Dillon Branch—*stream* TN-4
Dillon Branch—*stream* WV-2
Dillon Bridge—*bridge* SC-3
Dillon Brook—*stream* NY-2
Dillon Butte—*summit* OR-9
Dillon Camp—*locale* CA-9
Dillon Campground—*park* SD-7
Dillon Canal—*canal* MT-8
Dillon Canyon—*valley* CA-9
Dillon Canyon—*valley* NM-5
Dillon (CCD)—*cens area* SC-3
Dillon Cem—*cemetery* CO-8
Dillon Cem—*cemetery* IL-6
Dillon Cem—*cemetery* KY-4
Dillon Cem—*cemetery* (2) MS-4
Dillon Cem—*cemetery* MO-7
Dillon Cem—*cemetery* NY-2
Dillon Cem—*cemetery* OH-6
Dillon Cem—*cemetery* (3) VA-3
Dillon Cem—*cemetery* (2) WV-2
Dillon Ch—*church* AL-4
Dillon Ch—*church* GA-3
Dillon Chapel—*church* OH-6
Dillon City Library—*hist pl* MT-8
**Dillon (County)**—*pop pl* SC-3
Dillon County Country Club—*other* SC-3
Dillon County Courthouse—*hist pl* SC-3
Dillon Cove—*bay* CA-9
Dillon Creek—*stream* AK-9
Dillon Creek—*stream* (2) CA-9
Dillon Creek—*stream* IL-6
Dillon Creek—*stream* (2) IN-6
Dillon Creek—*stream* MS-4
Dillon Creek—*stream* MO-7
Dillon Creek—*stream* NJ-2
Dillon Creek—*stream* OR-9
Dillon Ditch—*canal* OR-9
Dillon Divide—*gap* CA-9
Dillon Divide—*ridge* CA-9
Dillon Drain—*stream* MI-6
Dillon Draw—*valley* SD-7
Dillon Draw—*valley* WY-8
Dillon Falls—*falls* OR-9
**Dillon Falls**—*pop pl* OH-6
Dillon Falls Campground—*park* OR-9
Dillon Farm Cem—*cemetery* TN-4
Dillon Ferry—*locale* AR-4
Dillon Ferry (historical)—*crossing* TN-4
Dillon Field—*flat* AZ-5
Dillon Ford (historical)—*crossing* TN-4
Dillon Gulch—*valley* CO-8
Dillon Gulch—*valley* MT-8
Dillon Gulf—*valley* NY-2
Dillon Hill—*summit* IN-6
**Dillon (historical)**—*pop pl* OR-9
Dillon Hollow—*valley* KY-4
Dillon Hollow—*valley* TN-4
Dillon Island—*island* IL-6
Dillon Lake—*reservoir* OH-6
Dillon Memorial—*hist pl* IA-7
Dillon Mesa—*summit* CO-8
Dillon Mtn—*summit* CA-9
Dillon Mtn—*summit* NM-5
Dillon Mtn—*summit* NY-2
Dillon Municipal Golf Course—*other* MT-8
Dillon Overlook—*locale* CO-8
**Dillon Park**—*pop pl* MD-2
Dillon Pass—*gap* SD-7
Dillon Point—*cape* CA-9
Dillon Pond—*lake* NY-2
Dillon Pond—*lake* TN-4
Dillon Ranch—*locale* CA-9
Dillon Relaid Drain—*canal* MI-6
Dillon Ridge—*ridge* OH-6
Dillon Rsvr—*reservoir* CO-8
Dillon Rsvr—*reservoir* MT-8
*Dillon's* OH-6
Dillon Sch—*school* MI-6
Dillon Sch—*school* (3) MO-7
Dillon Sch—*school* NY-2
Dillon Sch—*school* NC-3
Dillon Sch—*school* WV-2
Dillon Sch (abandoned)—*school* MO-7
Dillons Chapel—*church* VA-3
Dillon School (historical)—*locale* MO-7
*Dillons Falls* OH-6
**Dillons Fork**—*pop pl* VA-3
*Dillon's Furnace* OH-6
Dillons Hill Ch—*church* MS-4
*Dillon Slough* OR-9
Dillons Mill—*locale* VA-3
Dillons Mill Branch—*stream* VA-3
Dillons Mtn—*summit* WV-2
Dillon Spring—*spring* MO-7
Dillon Spring—*spring* SD-7
Dillons Run—*stream* WV-2
Dillons Stand (historical)—*locale* MS-4
Dillons Twin Lakes—*reservoir* NC-3
Dillon Tank—*reservoir* AZ-5
Dillontown—*locale* PA-2
Dillon Township—*civil* MO-7
**Dillon (Township of)**—*pop pl* IL-6
Dillon Trail—*trail* PA-2
**Dillonvale**—*pop pl* (2) OH-6
Dillon Wash—*stream* AZ-5
Dillon Well—*well* NV-8
Dillonwood Grove—*woods* CA-9
Dillow Sch—*school* TX-5
Dill Pond—*lake* ME-1
Dill Ridge—*ridge* ME-1
Dill Ridge—*ridge* MO-7
Dills—*locale* FL-3
**Dills**—*pop pl* OH-6
Dills, Harrison, House—*hist pl* WA-9
**Dillsboro**—*pop pl* IN-6
**Dillsboro**—*pop pl* NC-3
Dillsboro, Lake—*reservoir* NC-3
Dillsboro Dam—*dam* NC-3
Dillsboro Elem Sch—*school* IN-6
**Dillsboro Station**—*pop pl* IN-6
Dillsboro (Township of)—*fmr MCD* NC-3
*Dillsborough* IN-6
*Dillsborough Station* IN-6
Dills Branch—*stream* GA-3
Dillsburg—*locale* IL-6
**Dillsburg**—*pop pl* IL-6
**Dillsburg**—*pop pl* PA-2
Dillsburg Borough—*civil* PA-2
Dillsburg Cem—*cemetery* PA-2
Dillsburg Junction—*locale* PA-2
Dills Cem—*cemetery* NC-3
Dills Cem—*cemetery* TN-4
Dill Sch—*school* TN-4
Dill Sch—*school* TX-5
Dills Cove—*valley* NC-3
Dills Creek—*stream* (2) NC-3
Dills Draw—*valley* WY-8
*Dills Ferry* PA-2
Dills Ferry (historical)—*locale* PA-2
Dills Gap—*gap* NC-3
Dills Knob—*summit* NC-3
Dills Lakes—*lake* AR-4
Dills Landing (historical)—*locale* AL-4
Dills Lemon Lateral—*canal* WA-9
Dill Slough—*gut* ND-7
Dill Slough—*stream* CA-9
Dills Mills—*locale* AR-4
Dills Mound—*summit* WI-6
**Dills (Sheffield)**—*pop pl* FL-3
Dills Site—*hist pl* KY-4
Dills Spring—*spring* AL-4
Dills Spring—*spring* VA-3
Dillsworth Ditch—*canal* CO-8
**Dillton**—*pop pl* TN-4
**Dilltown**—*pop pl* PA-2
Dill Well—*well* AZ-5
Dillworth—*uninc pl* NC-3
*Dillworth Bench* WY-8
Dillworth Bench—*ridge* WY-8
Dillworth Creek—*stream* WY-8
Dillwyn—*locale* KS-7
**Dillwyn**—*pop pl* VA-3
Dillwyn Ch—*church* VA-3
Dillwyn Lake—*reservoir* VA-3
Dilly—*locale* WI-6
Dilly, Lake—*lake* WA-9
Dilly Branch—*stream* VA-3
Dilly Canyon—*valley* UT-8
Dilly Cem—*cemetery* WV-2
Dilly Creek—*stream* IN-6
Dilly Creek—*stream* WI-6
Dilly Fork—*stream* WV-2
Dilly Island—*island* MA-1
*Dilly Lake* CO-8
Dilly Lake—*lake* FL-3
Dilly Lake—*lake* WA-9
Dilly Lake—*lake* WI-6
Dilly Marsh—*swamp* FL-3
Dilly Pond—*lake* AR-4
*Dilly Run* WV-2
*Dilly's* OH-6
Dilly Sch (historical)—*school* MO-7
Dillys Corners—*locale* IL-6
Dilman Meadows—*swamp* OR-9
*Dilmat* FM-9
Dilmeet'—*island* FM-9
Dilnow Brook—*stream* ME-1
**Dilong**—*pop pl* PW-9
Diloreto Sch—*school* CT-1
Dilo Sch—*school* MT-8
Dils-Downer House—*hist pl* IA-7
Dilse Branch—*stream* KY-4
Dilse Branch—*stream* VA-3
*Dilton* TN-4
Dilts Anstis Ditch—*canal* IN-6

**Dilts Corner**—*pop pl* ... NJ-2
Dilts Flat—*flat* ... WY-8
*Dilts Ranch* ... WY-8
Dilts Ranch—*locale* ... WY-8
Dilts Sch—*school* ... WY-8
Dilts Sch (abandoned)—*school* ... PA-2
Diltz Mine—*mine* ... CA-9
Diluches Meded—*bar* ... PW-9
Di Lulo Mine—*mine* ... MT-8
Dilworth—*locale* ... AR-4
Dilworth—*locale* ... OK-5
Dilworth—*locale* ... TX-5
Dilworth—*locale* ... WA-9
**Dilworth**—*pop pl* ... AL-4
**Dilworth**—*pop pl* ... MN-6
**Dilworth**—*pop pl* ... OH-6
**Dilworth**—*pop pl* ... TX-5
Dilworth, Thomas F., House—*hist pl* ... MS-4
Dilworth Bench—*bench* ... MT-8
Dilworth Cem—*cemetery* ... MS-4
Dilworth Cem—*cemetery* (2) ... TX-5
Dilworth Cemeteries—*cemetery* ... MS-4
Dilworth Ch—*church* ... AL-4
Dilworth Ch—*church* ... AR-4
Dilworth Ch—*church* ... TX-5
Dilworth Creek—*stream* ... MT-8
Dilworth Drift Mine (underground)—*mine* ... AL-4
Dilworth Elem Sch—*hist pl* ... PA-2
Dilworth Hist Dist—*hist pl* ... NC-3
Dilworth House—*hist pl* ... DE-2
Dilworth JHS—*school* ... NV-8
Dilworth Memorial Ch—*church* ... AL-4
Dilworth Oil And Gas Field—*oilfield* ... OK-5
Dilworth Ranch Sch—*school* ... TX-5
Dilworth Run—*stream* ... PA-2
*Dilworth Sch* ... PA-2
Dilworth Sch—*school* ... CA-9
Dilworth Sch—*school* ... NC-3
Dilworth Sch—*school* ... PA-2
Dilworth Sch—*school* ... UT-8
Dilworth Sch (historical)—*school* ... MS-4
Dilworth Spr—*ridge* ... TX-5
Dilworth Store (historical)—*locale* ... MS-4
**Dilworth (subdivision)**—*pop pl* ... NC-3
**Dilworthtown**—*pop pl* ... PA-2
Dilworthtown Hist Dist—*hist pl* ... PA-2
**Dilworth Traditional Academy**—*pop pl* ... PA-2
Diman Vocational Sch—*school* ... MA-1
Dimario Place—*locale* ... AZ-5
*DiMascio Airport* ... PA-2
Dimascio Field—*airport* ... PA-2
Dimcher Hollow—*valley* ... MO-7
Dime—*locale* ... AL-4
**Dime**—*pop pl* ... PA-2
Dime Bank Bldg—*hist pl* ... PA-2
**Dime Box**—*pop pl* ... TX-5
Dime Branch—*stream* ... AL-4
Dime Canyon—*valley* ... CA-9
Dime Creek—*stream* (2) ... AK-9
Dime Creek—*stream* ... ID-8
Dime Creek—*stream* ... WY-8
Dime Drain—*stream* ... MI-6
Dime Gulch—*valley* ... AZ-5
Dime Hill—*summit* ... MT-8
Dime Lake—*lake* ... MN-6
Dime Lake—*lake* ... UT-8
**Dime Landing**—*pop pl* ... AK-9
Dimeling—*locale* ... PA-2
Dimeling Hotel—*hist pl* ... PA-2
Dime Methodist Ch—*church* ... AL-4
Dime Pond—*lake* ... AZ-5
Dime Post Office (historical)—*building* ... PA-2
*Dimers* ... PA-2
**Dimes**—*pop pl* ... PW-9
Dime Savings and Trust Company—*hist pl* ... PA-2
Dime Sch (historical)—*school* ... AL-4
Dimes Ferry (historical)—*locale* ... MS-4
Dime Spring—*spring* ... CO-8
Dime Spring Branch—*stream* ... AL-4
Dimick—*fmr MCD* ... NE-7
Dimick Brook—*stream* (2) ... VT-1
Dimick Gulch—*valley* ... CO-8
Dimicks Ferry—*locale* ... NJ-2
Dim'iingoeg—*cape* ... FM-9
*Dimingog* ... FM-9
Dimis Spring—*spring* ... NM-5
*Dim'iyngog* ... FM-9
*Dim Lake* ... MN-6
**Dimmette**—*pop pl* ... NC-3
Dimmich Sch—*school* ... OR-9
Dimmick—*locale* ... IL-6
Dimmick—*locale* ... OR-9
Dimmick Cem—*cemetery* (2) ... NY-2
Dimmick Cem—*cemetery* ... OR-9
Dimmick Corners—*locale* ... NY-2
Dimmick Creek—*stream* ... OR-9
Dimmick Hollow—*valley* ... NY-2
Dimmick Hollow—*valley* ... PA-2
Dimmick Hollow Sch—*school* ... NY-2
Dimmick Meadow Brook—*stream* ... PA-2
Dimmick Memorial Grove State Park—*park* ... CA-9
Dimmick Mine—*mine* ... CA-9
Dimmick Mtn—*summit* ... ME-1
*Dimmick Pond* ... MA-1
Dimmick Sch—*school* ... IL-6
Dimmicks Point—*cape* ... MI-6
Dimmick Stream—*stream* ... ME-1
**Dimmick (Township of)**—*pop pl* ... IL-6
**Dimmit (County)**—*pop pl* ... TX-5
Dimmit County Courthouse—*hist pl* ... TX-5
**Dimmitt**—*pop pl* ... TX-5
Dimmitt Cem—*cemetery* ... MO-7
Dimmitt Cem—*cemetery* ... TX-5
Dimmitt Lake—*lake* ... NE-7
Dimmitt Lake—*lake* ... NM-5
Dimmitt North (CCD)—*cens area* ... TX-5
Dimmitt South (CCD)—*cens area* ... TX-5
Dimmock—*locale* ... WV-2
Dimmock, Mount—*summit* ... ME-1
Dimmock Brook—*stream* ... MA-1
Dimmock Pond—*lake* ... MA-1
**Dimmocks Mill (subdivision)**—*pop pl* ... NC-3
**Dimmsville**—*pop pl* ... PA-2
Dimmsville Covered Bridge—*hist pl* ... PA-2
Dimnick Creek—*stream* ... OR-9
**Dimock**—*pop pl* ... PA-2
**Dimock**—*pop pl* ... SD-7
Dimock, Lake—*reservoir* ... SD-7
Dimock Brook—*stream* ... ME-1
Dimock Community Health Center Complex—*hist pl* ... MA-1
Dimock Corners—*locale* ... PA-2
Dimock Dam—*dam* ... SD-7
**Dimock (historical)**—*pop pl* ... ND-7
Dimock Station—*locale* ... PA-2
**Dimock (Township of)**—*pop pl* ... PA-2
*Dimond* ... WV-2
Dimond—*locale* ... NH-1
Dimond—*uninc pl* ... CA-9
**Dimondale**—*pop pl* ... MI-6
Dimondale Cem—*cemetery* ... MI-6
Dimond Canyon—*valley* ... CA-9
Dimond Canyon Park—*park* ... CA-9
Dimond Creek—*stream* ... AK-9
Dimond Grove—*woods* ... CA-9
Dimond Hill—*summit* ... NH-1
Dimond Memorial Sch—*school* ... FL-3
*Dimond Oaks* ... UT-8
**Dimond Oaks**—*pop pl* ... UT-8
Dimond Reef—*bar* ... NY-2
**Dimond Township**—*pop pl* ... ND-7
Dimon Sch—*school* ... IL-6
Dimple—*locale* ... AR-4
Dimple—*locale* ... KY-4
**Dimple**—*pop pl* ... TX-5
Dimple Creek—*stream* ... PA-2
**Dimple Dell Heights Subdivision**—*pop pl* ... UT-8
**Dimple Dell Lane Subdivision**—*pop pl* ... UT-8
**Dimple Dell Oaks Subdivision**—*pop pl* ... UT-8
**Dimple Dell Oaks Subdivision #2**—*pop pl* ... UT-8
**Dimple Dell Ranchettes Subdivision**—*pop pl* ... UT-8
**Dimple Dell Village Subdivision**—*pop pl* ... UT-8
*Dimpled Hills* ... TX-5
Dimple Hill—*summit* ... OR-9
Dimple Hills—*summit* ... TX-5
Dimple Mine—*mine* ... AZ-5
Dimpson Hollow—*valley* ... KY-4
Din, Bayou—*stream* ... TX-5
Dina Branch—*stream* ... NC-3
Dina Campground—*locale* ... UT-8
Dinaey—*locale* ... FM-9
Dinaey—*summit* ... FM-9
Dinah, Lake—*lake* ... MT-8
Dinah Cem—*cemetery* ... MS-4
Dinah Hollow—*valley* ... MO-7
Dinah Landing—*locale* ... NC-3
Dinah - mo Peak—*summit* ... OR-9
Dinah Point—*cape* ... ME-1
*Dinahs* ... DE-2
Dinahs Corner—*locale* ... DE-2
*Dinahs Crossroads* ... DE-2
Dinahs Pond—*lake* ... MA-1
Dinan—*locale* ... MS-4
Dinan Baptist Ch—*church* ... MS-4
Dinan Post Office (historical)—*building* ... MS-4
Dina Pond—*swamp* ... TX-5
Dinas Ch—*church* ... KS-7
*Dinay* ... FM-9
**Dinber**—*pop pl* ... SC-3
Dinca—*locale* ... MI-6
Dindy, Bayou—*stream* ... LA-4
*Dine Bito Spring* ... AZ-5
*Dine Bito Wash* ... AZ-5
Dineen Hill—*summit* ... MT-8
Dineen Park—*park* ... WI-6
Dinehart-Holt House—*hist pl* ... MN-6
Dineharts—*locale* ... NY-2
Dine Lake—*lake* ... IN-6
Dine Lake—*lake* ... UT-8
**Dinero**—*pop pl* ... TX-5
Dinero Tunnel—*mine* ... CO-8
Dines—*locale* ... WY-8
Dines Lake—*lake* ... CO-8
Dines Point—*cape* ... WA-9
**Dines Point**—*pop pl* ... WA-9
Dines Ranch—*locale* ... NM-5
Dines Tank—*reservoir* ... AZ-5
Diney Grove Cem—*cemetery* ... MA-1
*Dinfield Creek* ... NC-3
Dingbat Creek—*stream* ... WA-9
Ding Branch—*stream* ... VA-3
Ding Dong—*locale* ... TX-5
Dingdong Creek—*stream* ... WI-6
Dingee, Jacob, House—*hist pl* ... DE-2
Dingee, Obadiah, House—*hist pl* ... DE-2
Dingee Rsvr—*reservoir* ... CA-9
Dinger Creek—*stream* ... OR-9
Dinger Creek Trail—*trail* ... OR-9
Dinger Lake—*lake* ... OR-9
Dinger Lake—*lake* ... WI-6
Dinger Sch—*school* ... MI-6
Dinger Sch (abandoned)—*school* ... PA-2
Dinger Sch (abandoned)—*school* ... SD-7
Dingerville—*locale* ... TX-5
**Dingess**—*pop pl* ... WV-2
Dingess Branch—*stream* (2) ... WV-2
Dingess Camp Branch—*stream* ... WV-2
Dingess Cem—*cemetery* (2) ... WV-2
Dingess Fork—*stream* (2) ... WV-2
Dingess Run—*stream* (2) ... WV-2
Dingess Sch—*school* ... WV-2
Dingess Trace Branch—*stream* ... WV-2
Dingey Pond—*lake* ... ME-1
Dingfork Creek—*stream* ... WA-9
Dingiin—*locale* ... FM-9
*Dingin* ... FM-9
Dingit Corner—*locale* ... NH-1
Dingle—*locale* ... ID-8
**Dingle**—*pop pl* ... ID-8
Dingle Basin—*basin* ... WA-9
Dingleberry Lake—*lake* ... CA-9
*Dingle Brook* ... MA-1
Dingle Brook—*stream* ... CT-1
Dingle Cem—*cemetery* ... ID-8
Dingle Creek—*stream* ... NC-3
Dingle Creek—*stream* ... OR-9
Dingle Creek—*stream* ... WI-6
Dingle Hill—*summit* ... NY-2
Dingle Meadow Heath—*swamp* ... ME-1
Dingle Pond—*reservoir* ... SC-3
Dingler—*locale* ... AL-4
Dingler Chapel—*church* ... AL-4
Dingler Crossroads—*locale* ... GA-3
Dingler Lake—*reservoir* ... IN-6
Dingler Lake Dam—*dam* ... IN-6
*Dingle's Bay* ... WI-6
Dingle Sch—*school* ... CA-9
Dinglestadt Glacier—*glacier* ... AK-9
Dingle Swamp—*swamp* ... ID-8
Dingleton Hill—*summit* ... NH-1
Dingleton Hill Covered Bridge—*hist pl* ... NH-1
Dingletown Ch—*church* ... CT-1
Dinglewood—*hist pl* ... GA-3
**Dinglewood**—*pop pl* ... GA-3
Dingley, Frank L., House—*hist pl* ... ME-1
Dingley Cem—*cemetery* ... MA-1
Dingley Cove—*bay* ... ME-1
Dingley Creek—*stream* ... CA-9
Dingley Creek—*stream* ... MT-8
**Dingley Dell**—*pop pl* ... MA-1
Dingley Island—*island* ... ME-1
Dingley Islands—*island* ... ME-1
Dingley Lakes—*lake* ... MT-8
Dingley Pond—*lake* ... ME-1
Dingley Sch (abandoned)—*school* ... MO-7
Dinglishna Hill—*summit* ... AK-9
*Dingman Creek* ... MI-6
Dingman Creek—*stream* ... CA-9
Dingman Delaware Elem Sch—*school* ... PA-2
Dingman Drain—*canal* ... MI-6
Dingman Hill—*summit* ... NY-2
Dingman Point—*cape* ... NY-2
Dingman Ridge—*ridge* (2) ... CA-9
Dingman River—*stream* ... MI-6
Dingman Run—*stream* ... PA-2
Dingman Run Sch (abandoned)—*school* ... PA-2
Dingmans Creek—*stream* ... PA-2
Dingmans Falls—*falls* ... PA-2
Dingmans Ferry—*locale* ... NJ-2
**Dingmans Ferry**—*pop pl* ... PA-2
Dingman's Ferry Dutch Reformed Church—*hist pl* ... PA-2
Dingman Spring—*spring* ... PA-2
Dingman Township—*civil* ... PA-2
**Dingman (Township of)**—*pop pl* ... PA-2
Ding Pot Lake—*lake* ... MN-6
Dingus—*locale* ... KY-4
Dingus Branch—*stream* ... KY-4
Dingus Branch—*stream* ... VA-3
Dingus Cem—*cemetery* (4) ... VA-3
Dingus Gap—*gap* ... VA-3
Dingus Memorial Ch—*church* ... VA-3
Dingus Spring—*spring* ... OR-9
Dingy—*locale* ... WV-2
Dinham Lake—*lake* ... MN-6
Dinihanian Rsvr—*reservoir* ... OR-9
Dining Creek—*stream* ... SC-3
Dininger Cem—*cemetery* ... OH-6
Dining Fork—*stream* ... OH-6
Dininny, Harper J., House—*hist pl* ... UT-8
Dink—*locale* ... WV-2
Dinkel Lake—*lake* ... AK-9
Dinkelman Canyon—*valley* ... WA-9
Dinkelman Ridge—*ridge* ... WA-9
Dinken Bayou—*lake* ... FL-3
Dinken Creek—*stream* ... IN-6
Dinkerderry Landing (historical)—*locale* ... NC-3
**Dinkey Creek**—*pop pl* ... CA-9
Dinkey Creek—*stream* ... CA-9
Dinkey Creek Ranger Station—*locale* ... CA-9
Dinkey Dome—*summit* ... CA-9
Dinkey Meadow—*flat* ... CA-9
Dinkey Meadow Creek—*stream* ... CA-9
Dinkey Memorial Ch—*church* ... PA-2
Dinkey Mtn—*summit* ... CA-9
Dinkhorse Branch—*stream* ... TX-5
Dinkin Cove Creek—*stream* ... NC-3
Dinkins—*locale* ... TX-5
**Dinkins**—*pop pl* ... FL-3
**Dinkins**—*pop pl* ... SC-3
Dinkins Bay—*swamp* ... GA-3
Dinkins Cem—*cemetery* ... NC-3
Dinkins House—*hist pl* ... NC-3
**Dinkins Mill**—*pop pl* ... SC-3
Dinkins Sch—*school* ... GA-3
Dinkins Tank—*reservoir* ... TX-5
Dinkins Training Sch (historical)—*school* ... AL-4
Dinkle Hill—*summit* ... CO-8
Dinkle Lake—*lake* ... CO-8
*Dinkleman Canyon* ... WA-9
Dinkle Well—*well* ... TX-5
Dink Ridge—*ridge* ... KY-4
Dinkum Point—*cape* ... AK-9
Dinkum Rocks—*island* ... AK-9
Dinkum Sands—*island* ... AK-9
Dinky Creek—*stream* ... WY-8
Dinky Pit—*cave* ... AL-4
Dinky Spring—*spring* ... CA-9
Dinkytown—*post sta* ... MN-6
Din Lake—*lake* ... MN-6
*Dinnebito* ... AZ-5
Dinnebito Spring—*spring* ... AZ-5
*Dinnebito Trading Post* ... AZ-5
Dinnebito Trading Post—*locale* ... AZ-5
Dinnebito Wash—*arroyo* ... AZ-5
*Dinnehotso* (2) ... AZ-5
*Dinne Mesa* ... AZ-5
Dinner Bay—*swamp* ... FL-3
Dinner Branch—*stream* ... CO-8
Dinner Branch—*stream* ... GA-3
Dinner Branch—*stream* (2) ... TN-4
Dinner Branch—*stream* (3) ... TX-5
Dinner Camp, Lake—*lake* ... WI-6
Dinner Canyon—*valley* (2) ... AZ-5
Dinner Canyon—*valley* ... NM-5
*Dinner Creek* ... AZ-5
Dinner Creek—*stream* ... AL-4
Dinner Creek—*stream* ... AZ-5
Dinner Creek—*stream* (2) ... CA-9
Dinner Creek—*stream* ... ID-8
Dinner Creek—*stream* ... KS-7
Dinner Creek—*stream* (4) ... MN-6
Dinner Creek—*stream* (6) ... OR-9
Dinner Creek—*stream* (5) ... TX-5
Dinner Creek—*stream* ... VA-3
Dinner Creek Camp—*locale* ... TX-5
Dinner Creek Rsvr Number One—*reservoir* ... OR-9
Dinner Creek Rsvr Number Three—*reservoir* ... OR-9
Dinner Creek Rsvr Number Two—*reservoir* ... OR-9
Dinner Flat—*flat* ... AZ-5
Dinner Fork—*stream* ... OH-6
Dinner Gulch—*valley* (2) ... CA-9
Dinner Hammock—*island* ... FL-3
Dinner Hill—*summit* ... NM-5
Dinner Hill—*summit* ... TX-5
Dinner Island—*island* ... FL-3
Dinner Island—*island* ... ME-1
Dinner Island—*island* ... WA-9
Dinner Island—*locale* ... FL-3
Dinner Key—*island* ... FL-3
Dinner Key Channel—*channel* ... FL-3
Dinner Key Picnic Islands—*park* ... FL-3
*Dinner Lake* ... MN-6
Dinner Lake—*lake* (3) ... FL-3
Dinner Lake—*lake* (2) ... MI-6
Dinner Lake—*lake* ... MN-6
Dinner Pail Lake—*lake* ... MN-6
Dinner Park—*flat* ... CO-8
Dinner Park—*flat* ... NM-5
Dinner Pocket—*basin* ... AZ-5
Dinner Pockets Canyon—*valley* ... AZ-5
Dinner Pockets Trick Tank—*reservoir* ... AZ-5
Dinner Point—*cape* ... FL-3
Dinner Point—*cape* ... NJ-2
Dinner Point Creek—*stream* ... NJ-2
Dinner Pond—*lake* (2) ... FL-3
Dinner Pond—*lake* ... GA-3
Dinner Pond—*lake* ... UT-8
Dinner Ridge Way—*trail* ... OR-9
Dinner Saddle Tank—*reservoir* ... AZ-5
Dinner Sink Pond—*swamp* ... FL-3
Dinners Pond—*lake* ... FL-3
Dinner Spring—*spring* ... AZ-5
Dinner Spring—*spring* ... TX-5
Dinner Spring—*spring* ... WA-9
Dinner Springs—*spring* ... NV-8
**Dinner Station**—*pop pl* ... NV-8
Dinner Station Campground—*locale* ... CO-8
Dinner Tree—*locale* ... CA-9
Dinnie Block—*hist pl* ... ND-7
Dinning Post Office (historical)—*building* ... TN-4
Dinn Ranch—*locale* ... TX-5
**Dinosaur**—*pop pl* ... CO-8
Dinosaur, Lake—*lake* ... CO-8
Dinosaur Bluff—*cliff* ... WI-6
*Dinosaur City* (2) ... AZ-5
*Dinosaur City Airport* ... AZ-5
Dinosaur Dam—*dam* ... MT-8
Dinosaur Gardens—*locale* ... UT-8
Dinosaur Lake—*reservoir* ... CA-9
Dinosaur Mtn—*summit* ... AZ-5
Dinosaur Natl Monument—*park* ... CO-8
Dinosaur Natl Monument—*park* ... UT-8
*Dinosaur Natl Monument Visitor Center and Quarry* ... UT-8
*Dinosaur Natural History Museum* ... UT-8
Dinosaur Park—*park* ... SD-7
Dinosaur Quarry—*locale* ... UT-8
Dinosaur Rock—*pillar* ... PA-2
Dinosaur Rock—*summit* ... NM-5
Dinosaur Tank—*reservoir* ... NM-5
Dinosaur Tank—*reservoir* ... TX-5
Dinosaur Tracks—*area* ... AZ-5
Dinosaur Tracks—*other* ... UT-8
Dinosaur Valley State Park—*park* ... TX-5
Dino Tank—*reservoir* ... TX-5
Din Point—*cape* ... VI-3
**Dinsdale**—*pop pl* ... IA-7
Dinsdale Cem—*cemetery* ... IA-7
Dinsmoor-Hale House—*hist pl* ... NH-1
Dinsmore—*locale* ... AR-4
Dinsmore—*locale* ... MS-4
Dinsmore—*locale* ... PA-2
**Dinsmore**—*pop pl* ... CA-9
**Dinsmore**—*pop pl* ... CO-8
**Dinsmore**—*pop pl* ... FL-3
**Dinsmore**—*pop pl* ... TX-5
Dinsmore Brook—*stream* ... NH-1
*Dinsmore Canyon* ... CA-9
Dinsmore Cem—*cemetery* ... IN-6
Dinsmore Cem—*cemetery* ... KY-4
Dinsmore Cem—*cemetery* ... ME-1
Dinsmore Cem—*cemetery* ... VA-3
Dinsmore Cove—*bay* ... ME-1
Dinsmore Creek—*stream* ... AK-9
Dinsmore Elem Sch—*school* ... FL-3
Dinsmore Grain Company Mill—*hist pl* ... ME-1
Dinsmore House—*hist pl* ... KY-4
Dinsmore Lookout Tower—*tower* ... FL-3
Dinsmore Mtn—*summit* ... NH-1
*Dinsmore Point* ... NY-2
Dinsmore Pond—*lake* (2) ... NH-1
Dinsmore Post Office (historical)—*building* ... MS-4
Dinsmore Rsvr—*reservoir* ... PA-2
*Dinsmores* ... CA-9
Dinsmores—*locale* ... CA-9
Dinsmore Sch—*school* ... TX-5
Dinsmore Slough—*gut* ... AL-4
Dinsmores Shoals—*bar* ... TN-4
Dinsmore Storage Number Two Dam—*dam* ... PA-2
**Dinsmore (Township of)**—*pop pl* ... OH-6
Dinty, Lake—*lake* ... AK-9
Dinty Moore Park—*park* ... TX-5
Dinty Moore Rsvr—*reservoir* ... WY-8
**Dinuba**—*pop pl* ... CA-9
Dinuba (CCD)—*cens area* ... CA-9
Dinuba Junior Acad—*school* ... CA-9
*Dinuba Mountain* ... CA-9
Dinuba Town Ditch—*canal* ... CA-9
**Dinwiddie**—*pop pl* ... IN-6
**Dinwiddie**—*pop pl* ... VA-3
Dinwiddie Arm—*valley* ... CA-9
Dinwiddie Cem—*cemetery* ... TN-4
Dinwiddie Ch—*church* ... VA-3
**Dinwiddie (County)**—*pop pl* ... VA-3
Dinwiddie County Courthouse—*hist pl* ... VA-3
*Dinwiddie Creek* ... WY-8
**Dinwiddie Gardens**—*pop pl* ... VA-3
Dinwiddie Lake—*lake* ... WY-8
*Dinwiddie Lakes* ... WY-8
Dinwiddie Memorial Park—*cemetery* ... VA-3
Dinwiddie Ranch—*locale* ... AZ-5
Dinwiddie Ranch—*locale* ... NM-5
Dinwiddie Ranch—*locale* ... TX-5
Dinwiddie Sch (abandoned)—*school* ... MO-7
Dinwiddie Store (historical)—*locale* ... TN-4
Dinwiddie Tanks—*reservoir* ... NM-5
Dinwiddie Valley—*valley* ... OR-9
*Dinwiddle Valley* ... OR-9
**Dinwood (Alphoretta)**—*pop pl* ... KY-4
*Dinwoodie Creek* ... WY-8
*Dinwoodie Lakes* ... WY-8
Dinwoody, Henry, House—*hist pl* ... UT-8
Dinwoody Canal—*canal* ... WY-8
Dinwoody Creek—*stream* ... WY-8
Dinwoody Glacier—*glacier* ... WY-8
Dinwoody Glaciers—*glacier* ... WY-8
Dinwoody Lake—*lake* ... WY-8
Dinwoody Lakes—*lake* (2) ... WY-8
Dinwoody Mill (historical)—*locale* ... TN-4
Dinwoody Park—*park* ... UT-8
*Dinwoody Pass* ... WY-8
Dinwoody Peak—*summit* (2) ... WY-8
Dinwoody Ridge—*ridge* ... WY-8
Dinwoody Trail—*trail* ... WY-8
Diobsud Buttes—*summit* ... WA-9
Diobsud Creek—*stream* ... WA-9
Diocesan Sch—*school* ... IL-6
Diocese of Central Florida-Episcopal—*church* ... FL-3
Diocese of Orlando-Catholic—*church* ... FL-3
Diocese of Pensacola-Tallahassee—*church* ... FL-3
Diomede—*locale* ... AK-9
Diomede Islands—*island* ... AK-9
**Diomede (native name: Inalik)**—*pop pl* ... AK-9
Diona—*locale* ... IL-6
Dione—*locale* ... KY-4
Dione Rsvr—*reservoir* ... MT-8
Diongradid—*stream* ... PW-9
Dionis Beach—*beach* ... MA-1
Dion Lake—*lake* ... ND-7
Dionne Cornel—*locale* ... ME-1
**Diorite**—*pop pl* ... MI-6
Diorite Peak—*summit* ... CO-8
Dios Bay—*swamp* ... FL-3
*Diosub Creek* ... WA-9
*Dip* ... GA-3
Dip, The—*basin* ... NV-8
Dip, The—*locale* ... NV-8
Dip, The—*spring* ... NV-8
Dip Creek—*stream* ... CA-9
Dip Creek—*stream* (3) ... ID-8
Dip Creek—*stream* (2) ... NV-8
Dip Creek—*stream* ... NC-3
Dip Creek—*stream* ... UT-8
Dip Creek—*stream* (2) ... WY-8
*Dip Hollow* ... ID-8
Dip Hollow—*valley* (3) ... UT-8
Diplomat Country Club—*locale* ... FL-3
Diplomat Mall—*post sta* ... FL-3
Diplomat Mall Shop Ctr—*locale* ... FL-3
Diplomat Plaza—*post sta* ... IN-6
Diplomat Presidential Golf Course—*locale* ... FL-3
**Dippel Manor**—*pop pl* ... PA-2
Dippen Rig Creek—*stream* ... OR-9
Dipper—*lake* ... NY-2
Dipper, The—*locale* ... WY-8
Dipper, The—*valley* ... OR-9
Dipper Canyon—*valley* ... AZ-5
Dipper Cove—*bay* ... ME-1
Dipper Cove Ledges—*bar* ... ME-1
Dipper Creek—*stream* ... ID-8
Dipper Creek—*stream* ... MD-2
Dipper Gap—*gap* ... CO-8
Dipper Gulch—*valley* ... ID-8
Dipper Hill—*summit* ... CO-8
Dipper Lake—*lake* ... AK-9
Dipper Lake—*lake* ... IN-6
Dipper Lake—*lake* (2) ... MI-6
Dipper Lake—*lake* ... MN-6
Dipper Lake—*lake* ... WY-8
Dipper Mine—*mine* ... WA-9
Dipper Point—*cape* ... NJ-2
Dipper Pond—*lake* (2) ... ME-1
Dipper Pond—*lake* ... NY-2
Dipper Pond Mtn—*summit* ... NY-2
Dipper Spring—*spring* ... AZ-5
Dipper Spring—*spring* ... CO-8
Dippikill Mtn—*summit* ... NY-2
Dippikill Pond—*lake* ... NY-2
Dipping Bucket Valley—*valley* ... AZ-5
Dipping Corral Spring—*spring* ... UT-8
Dipping Corral Tank—*reservoir* ... AZ-5
Dipping Creek—*stream* ... OR-9
Dipping Lakes—*lake* ... CO-8
Dipping Pen Creek—*stream* ... UT-8
*Dipping Pen Wash* ... UT-8
Dipping Pond Run—*stream* ... MD-2
Dipping Spring Canyon—*valley* ... WY-8
Dipping Tank Creek—*stream* ... SD-7
Dipping Tank Spring—*spring* ... NV-8
Dipping Vat—*locale* ... UT-8
Dipping Vat Branch—*stream* ... TX-5
Dipping Vat Canyon—*valley* ... OR-9
Dipping Vat Canyon—*valley* ... WA-9
Dipping Vat Coulee—*valley* ... MT-8
Dipping Vat Creek—*stream* ... AL-4
Dipping Vat Creek—*stream* (2) ... CO-8
Dipping Vat Creek—*stream* ... MT-8
Dipping Vat Creek—*stream* ... NC-3
Dipping Vat Creek—*stream* (3) ... OR-9
Dipping Vat Creek—*stream* ... SD-7
Dipping Vat Creek—*stream* ... WY-8
Dipping Vat Draw—*valley* ... NM-5
Dipping Vat Draw—*valley* ... SD-7
Dipping Vat Draw—*valley* ... UT-8
Dipping Vat Flat—*flat* ... CA-9
Dipping Vat Hill—*summit* ... NM-5
Dipping Vat Hollow—*valley* ... AL-4
Dipping Vat Hollow—*valley* ... AR-4
Dipping Vat Hollow—*valley* ... UT-8
Dipping Vat Lake—*lake* ... NE-7
Dipping Vat Lake—*lake* ... NM-5
Dipping Vat Meadow—*swamp* ... NE-7
Dipping Vat Ponds—*lake* ... TX-5
Dipping Vat Spring—*spring* (2) ... AZ-5
Dipping Vat Spring—*spring* ... MT-8
Dipping Vat Spring—*spring* (2) ... NM-5
Dipping Vat Spring—*spring* (4) ... OR-9
Dipping Vat Spring—*spring* (2) ... TX-5
Dipping Vat Spring—*spring* (4) ... UT-8
Dipping Vat Springs—*spring* ... WY-8
Dipping Vat Tank—*reservoir* (2) ... NM-5
Dipping Vat Tank—*reservoir* ... TX-5
Dipping Vat Well—*well* ... NM-5
Dipping Vat Well—*well* (2) ... TX-5
Dipping Vat Windmill—*locale* ... NM-5
Dipping Vat Windmill—*locale* ... TX-5
Dipping Water Well—*locale* ... AZ-5
Dipple—*locale* ... OH-6
Dipple Drain—*canal* ... ND-7
**Dipple Manor**—*pop pl* ... PA-2
Dippold Basin—*basin* ... CO-8
Dippy Creek—*stream* ... WA-9
Dippy Island—*island* ... AK-9
Dipsea Trail—*trail* ... CA-9
Dips Hollow—*valley* ... UT-8
Dip Spring—*spring* ... CA-9
Dip Spring—*spring* (2) ... NV-8
Dip Spring—*spring* ... OR-9
Dip Vat Branch—*stream* ... FL-3
Dip Vat Creek—*stream* ... UT-8
Dip Vat Hollow—*valley* ... UT-8
Dipwilap—*unknown* ... FM-9
Dipwilap, Pilen—*stream* ... FM-9
Dipyramid—*summit* ... AK-9
*Dire Creek* ... OK-5
**Direct**—*pop pl* ... TX-5
Direct Sch—*school* ... TX-5
**Dirego Park**—*pop pl* ... FL-3
*Dire Mountain* ... OK-5
Dirgin—*locale* ... TX-5
Dirgylot Hill—*summit* ... NY-2
*Dirickson Creek* ... DE-2
Dirickson Creek—*stream* ... DE-2
Dirickson Neck—*cape* ... DE-2
**Diricksons**—*pop pl* ... MD-2
**Dirigo**—*pop pl* ... CA-9
**Dirigo**—*pop pl* ... KY-4
Dirigo Cem—*cemetery* ... ME-1
Dirigo Corner—*locale* ... ME-1
Dirigo Gulch—*valley* ... CO-8
Dirigo Hill—*summit* ... CO-8
Dirigo Sch—*school* ... ME-1
Dirk Goodin Sch (historical)—*school* ... MO-7
Dirkman Lake—*lake* ... MI-6
Dirk Sch (historical)—*school* ... MO-7
Dirksen Branch—*stream* ... KY-4
Dirksen JHS—*school* ... IL-6
Dirksen Sch—*school* ... SD-7
Dirksen Senate Office Bldg—*building* ... DC-2
Dirks Lake—*lake* ... KS-7
Dirks Oil Field—*oilfield* ... TX-5
Dirks Sch—*school* ... WY-8
Dirkstown (historical)—*locale* ... SD-7
Dirl Coulee—*valley* ... MT-8
Dirovati Point—*cape* ... AK-9
Dirreen Creek—*stream* ... NY-2
Dirt Bridge—*locale* ... VA-3
Dirt Bridge Run—*stream* ... VA-3
Dirt Cave—*cave* ... TN-4
*Dirt Cellar Mountain* ... AL-4
*Dirt Creek* ... OH-6
Dirt Creek—*stream* ... MT-8
Dirtdobber Cem—*cemetery* ... TN-4
Dirt Glacier—*glacier* ... AK-9
Dirt House Branch—*stream* ... TX-5
Dirt House Hollow—*valley* ... MO-7
*Dirt Lake* ... MI-6
Dirt Lodge Creek—*stream* ... SD-7
Dirt Oven Campground—*locale* ... ID-8
Dirt Rsvr—*reservoir* ... OR-9
Dirtseller Mountain—*ridge* ... AL-4
Dirtseller Mtn—*summit* ... GA-3
Dirt Slough—*gut* ... MO-7
Dirt Tank—*reservoir* (3) ... AZ-5
Dirt Tank—*reservoir* (5) ... NM-5
Dirt Tank, The—*reservoir* ... TX-5
Dirt Tank No 2—*reservoir* ... NM-5
Dirt Tank Well—*locale* ... NM-5
*Dirt Town* ... VA-3
*Dirttown Creek* ... GA-3
Dirty Butter Creek—*stream* ... OK-5
*Dirty Creek* ... MI-6
*Dirty Creek* ... MT-8
Dirty Creek—*stream* ... AR-4
Dirty Creek—*stream* (2) ... MT-8
Dirty Creek—*stream* ... NE-7
Dirty Creek—*stream* ... OK-5
Dirty Creek—*stream* ... SC-3
Dirty Devil—*rock* ... UT-8
*Dirty Devil Mountains* ... UT-8
*Dirty Devil River* ... UT-8
Dirty Devil River—*stream* ... UT-8
Dirty Dick Creek—*stream* ... MT-8
Dirty Face Creek—*stream* ... IA-7
Dirtyface Creek—*stream* ... MT-8
Dirtyface Creek—*stream* ... OH-6
Dirtyface Lake—*lake* ... WA-9
Dirtyface-Logan Creek Trail—*trail* ... MT-8
Dirtyface Lookout—*locale* ... WA-9
Dirty Face Mtn—*summit* ... WA-9
Dirtyface Peak—*summit* ... WA-9
Dirty Face Ridge—*ridge* ... WA-9
Dirty Face Trail—*trail* ... WA-9
*Dirty Fork* ... MO-7
Dirty Fork—*stream* ... OH-6
Dirty Gap—*gap* ... WY-8
Dirty George Creek—*stream* ... CO-8
Dirty George Creek and Doughspoon Aqueduct—*canal* ... CO-8
Dirty George Creek Aqueduct—*canal* ... CO-8
Dirty Glacier—*glacier* ... AK-9
Dirty Gulch—*valley* (2) ... CA-9
Dirty Gulch—*valley* ... CO-8
Dirty Gulch—*valley* ... MT-8
Dirty Head—*flat* ... UT-8
Dirty Head—*summit* ... ID-8
Dirty Hollow—*valley* ... UT-8
Dirty House Lake—*lake* ... MN-6
Dirty Ike Creek—*stream* ... MT-8
Dirty Jim Creek—*stream* ... NE-7
Dirty John Creek—*stream* ... NC-3
Dirtyman Draw—*valley* ... WY-8
Dirtyman Fork—*stream* ... WY-8
Dirty Meadow Brook—*stream* ... MA-1
Dirty Meadow Hill—*summit* ... MA-1
Dirty Meadow Swamp—*swamp* ... MA-1
Dirty Mike Lake—*lake* ... MN-6
Dirty Mtn—*summit* ... WY-8
Dirtyneck Canyon—*valley* ... AZ-5
Dirty Neck Cove—*bay* ... NV-8
Dirtyneck Tank—*reservoir* ... AZ-5
Dirty Nose Lake—*lake* ... MN-6
Dirty Point—*summit* ... NM-5
*Dirty River* ... TX-5
Dirty Shirt—*summit* ... WA-9

Dirty Smith Tank—*reservoir* AZ-5
Dirty Socks (Hot Spring)—*spring* CA-9
Dirty Spring—*spring* CA-9
*Dirtywater Lake* MN-6
Dirty Woman Creek—*stream* CO-8
Dirty Woman Creek—*stream* MT-8
Dirty Woman Draw—*valley* WY-8
Dirty Womans Creek—*stream* SD-7
Disabel Rsvr—*reservoir* NV-8
Disalto Creek—*stream* ID-8
Disappearing Creek—*stream* CA-9
Disappearing Lake—*lake* AK-9
*Disappearing Sand Beach* HI-9
Disappearing Sands Beach—*beach* HI-9
Disappearing Spring Wash—*stream* NM-5
Disappointment, Cape—*cape* WA-9
Disappointment, Mount—*summit* CA-9
Disappointment Bar—*bar* ID-8
Disappointment Cave—*cave* (2) AL-4
Disappointment Cleaver—*ridge* WA-9
*Disappointment Creek* AZ-5
Disappointment Creek—*stream* (3) AK-9
Disappointment Creek—*stream* CO-8
Disappointment Creek—*stream* ID-8
Disappointment Creek—*stream* KS-7
Disappointment Creek—*stream* KY-4
Disappointment Creek—*stream* (3) WA-9
Disappointment Draw—*valley* CO-8
Disappointment Hills—*summit* UT-8
*Disappointment Island* UT-8
Disappointment Lake—*lake* CA-9
Disappointment Lake—*lake* CO-8
Disappointment Lake—*lake* ID-8
Disappointment Lake—*lake* MN-6
Disappointment Lake—*lake* MT-8
Disappointment Mine—*mine* AK-9
Disappointment Mtn—*summit* MN-6
Disappointment Peak—*summit* CA-9
Disappointment Peak—*summit* WA-9
Disappointment Peak—*summit* WY-8
Disappointment Rsvr Number 1—*reservoir* CO-8
Disappointment Rsvr Number 2—*reservoir* CO-8
Disappointment Slough—*gut* CA-9
Disappointment Valley—*valley* CO-8
Disaster Creek—*stream* CA-9
Disaster Creek—*stream* ID-8
Disaster Creek—*stream* WA-9
Disaster Peak—*summit* CA-9
Disaster Peak—*summit* NV-8
**Disautel**—*pop pl* WA-9
Disbrow Creek—*stream* MT-8
Disbrow Drain—*stream* MI-6
Disbrow Pond—*lake* CT-1
Disbrow School—*locale* IL-6
Disbrows Hill—*summit* NJ-2
Discalced Carmelite Monastery—*church* TX-5
Discharge, The—*stream* IL-6
Discharge Bayou—*stream* LA-4
Disch Field—*park* TX-5
Disciple Cem—*cemetery* OH-6
Disciple Ch—*church* OH-6
Disciple-Christian Church—*hist pl* OH-6
Disciples Cem—*cemetery* PA-2
Disco—*locale* TN-4
**Disco**—*pop pl* IL-6
**Disco**—*pop pl* MI-6
**Disco**—*pop pl* WI-6
Disco Drain—*stream* MI-6
Disco Harbor—*harbor* AL-4
Discontented Pup—*stream* AK-9
Disco Post Office (historical)—*building* TN-4
*Discord* KS-7
Discord—*locale* IA-7
Disco Sch—*school* MI-6
Discoverer Bay—*bay* AK-9
Discovery—*CDP* MD-2
**Discovery**—*pop pl* AK-9
Discovery, Lake—*lake* MS-4
Discovery, Mount—*summit* NY-2
Discovery Bay—*bay* WA-9
Discovery Bay—*CDP* CA-9
**Discovery Bay**—*pop pl* WA-9
Discovery Bay Camp Meeting—*locale* WA-9
Discovery Bay (CCD)—*cens area* WA-9
Discovery Butte—*summit* MT-8
*Discovery Creek* CA-9
*Discovery Creek* WA-9
Discovery Creek—*stream* (6) AK-9
Discovery Creek—*stream* CA-9
Discovery Creek—*stream* (2) WA-9
Discovery Fork—*stream* AK-9
Discovery Gulch—*valley* AK-9
Discovery Gulch—*valley* OR-9
Discovery Hill—*summit* (2) MA-1
Discovery Island—*island* AK-9
Discovery Junction—*locale* WA-9
Discovery Lake—*lake* MN-6
Discovery Mine—*mine* CA-9
Discovery Mine—*mine* MT-8
Discovery Park—*park* CA-9
Discovery Peak—*summit* WA-9
Discovery Picnic Area—*park* ID-8
Discovery Pinnacle—*summit* CA-9
Discovery Plaza (Shop Ctr)—*locale* FL-3
Discovery Point—*cape* AK-9
Discovery Point—*cape* OR-9
Discovery Pup—*stream* AK-9
Discovery Pup—*valley* AK-9
Discovery Ridge—*ridge* CA-9
Discovery Rocks—*bar* AK-9
Discovery Saloon—*hist pl* AK-9
Discovery Sch—*school* UT-8
Discovery Tunnel—*mine* CO-8
Discovery Well Prudhoe Bay State No 1—*well* AK-9
Disenchantment Bay—*bay* AK-9
Disgrace Butte—*summit* ID-8
Disgrace Creek—*stream* ID-8
Disgust Creek—*stream* OR-9
Disharoon Cove—*valley* GA-3
Disharoon Creek—*stream* GA-3
Disharoon Gap—*gap* GA-3
*Disharoon Lake* LA-4
Disharoon Mtn—*summit* GA-3
Disharoon Plantation (historical)—*locale* MS-4
Dishaw—*locale* NY-2
Dishaw Lake—*lake* MI-6
Dish Bay—*swamp* FL-3
Disher Ditch—*canal* (2) OH-6
Dishinaw Creek—*stream* MI-6
*Dish Island* FM-9
*Dish Island Channel* FM-9
Dishkakat (Abandoned)—*locale* AK-9
*Dish Lake* MN-6
Dish Lake—*lake* WY-8
**Dishman**—*pop pl* WA-9
Dishman Cem—*cemetery* IN-6
Dishman Cem—*cemetery* (3) KY-4
Dishman Cem—*cemetery* MO-7
Dishman Hills Natural Area—*park* WA-9
Dishman-McGinnis Sch—*school* KY-4
Dishman Sch—*school* TX-5
Dishman Sch—*school* WA-9
Dishman Springs—*locale* KY-4
Dish Mill Brook—*stream* VT-1
Dishmon Creek—*stream* NC-3
Dishna River—*stream* AK-9
**Dishneau Pit**—*pop pl* MI-6
Dishner Cem—*cemetery* TN-4
Dishner Cem—*cemetery* (3) VA-3
Dishner Valley—*basin* VA-3
Dishno Creek—*stream* MI-6
Dishno Lake—*lake* MI-6
Dishongh Cem—*cemetery* AR-4
Dishongh Spring—*spring* TN-4
Dishopan Hill—*summit* UT-8
Dishpan Butte—*summit* (2) WY-8
Dishpan Gap—*gap* WA-9
Dishpan Hollow—*valley* PA-2
Dishpan Lake—*lake* AR-4
Dishpan Lake—*lake* ID-8
Dishpan Lake—*lake* (3) MI-6
Dishpan Lake—*lake* MN-6
Dishpan Spring—*spring* CA-9
Dishpan Spring—*spring* ID-8
Dishpan Spring—*spring* OR-9
Dishpan Tank—*reservoir* TX-5
Dishpan Valley—*basin* NE-7
Dishrag Canyon—*valley* OR-9
Dishrag Pond—*lake* NY-2
Dishrag Spring—*spring* ID-8
Dishrag Spring—*spring* OR-9
Dishroon Lake—*lake* LA-4
Dishrown Creek—*stream* AR-4
Dishwash Creek—*stream* MI-6
*Dishwashee Creek* MI-6
Dishwater Branch—*stream* AR-4
Dishwater Creek—*stream* MO-7
*Dishwater Pond* NH-1
*Disiguoy Creek* NV-8
*Disiguoy Hill* NV-8
Disk Island—*island* AK-9
**Disko**—*pop pl* IN-6
D Island—*island* NC-3
*Dislocate Creek* MT-8
Dislocation Lake—*lake* MN-6
*Dislon Valley* IL-6
*Dislon Valley School* IL-6
*Dislyn Valley* IL-6
*Dislyn Valley School* IL-6
Dismal—*locale* TN-4
Dismal, Falls of—*falls* VA-3
Dismal, The—*ridge* NC-3
Dismal Bay—*cove* MA-1
Dismal Bay—*swamp* (4) NC-3
Dismal Bay (Carolina Bay)—*swamp* NC-3
Dismal Branch—*stream* AL-4
Dismal Branch—*stream* KY-4
Dismal Branch—*stream* LA-4
Dismal Branch—*stream* NC-3
Dismal Branch—*stream* (3) TN-4
Dismal Branch—*stream* VA-3
Dismal Brook—*stream* CT-1
Dismal Brook—*stream* MA-1
Dismal Camp—*locale* ID-8
Dismal (carolina bay), The—*swamp* NC-3
Dismal Cove—*valley* GA-3
Dismal Cove—*valley* NC-3
Dismal Creek—*stream* AL-4
Dismal Creek—*stream* AR-4
Dismal Creek—*stream* CA-9
Dismal Creek—*stream* FL-3
Dismal Creek—*stream* GA-3
Dismal Creek—*stream* (2) ID-8
Dismal Creek—*stream* IL-6
Dismal Creek—*stream* (2) IN-6
Dismal Creek—*stream* KY-4
Dismal Creek—*stream* MN-6
Dismal Creek—*stream* (2) NC-3
Dismal Creek—*stream* (2) OH-6
Dismal Creek—*stream* (2) OR-9
Dismal Creek—*stream* TN-4
Dismal Creek—*stream* (2) VA-3
Dismal Creek—*stream* WA-9
**Dismal Creek Branch Junction**—*pop pl.* VA-3
Dismal Falls—*falls* NC-3
*Dismal Flats* AZ-5
Dismal Fork—*stream* VA-3
Dismal Gap—*gap* GA-3
Dismal Gap—*gap* TN-4
Dismal Hollow—*valley* AR-4
Dismal Hollow—*valley* TN-4
Dismal Hollow—*valley* (2) VA-3
**Dismal Key**—*pop pl* FL-3
Dismal Key Pass—*channel* FL-3
Dismal Knob—*summit* GA-3
Dismal Lake—*lake* (2) ID-8
Dismal Mtn—*summit* GA-3
Dismal Mtn—*summit* ID-8
Dismal Mtn—*summit* VA-3
Dismal Pond—*lake* NY-2
Dismal Ridge—*ridge* VA-3
Dismal River—*stream* NE-7
Dismal River Ranch—*locale* NE-7
Dismal Rock—*summit* KY-4
Dismal Run—*stream* PA-2
Dismal Sch (historical)—*school* TN-4
Dismal Spring—*spring* OR-9
Dismal Spring Branch—*stream* SC-3
*Dismal Swamp* NC-3
*Dismal Swamp* VA-3
Dismal Swamp—*swamp* AR-4
Dismal Swamp—*swamp* CA-9
Dismal Swamp—*swamp* CT-1
Dismal Swamp—*swamp* FL-3
Dismal Swamp—*swamp* ID-8
Dismal Swamp—*swamp* IA-7
Dismal Swamp—*swamp* LA-4
Dismal Swamp—*swamp* ME-1
Dismal Swamp—*swamp* MN-6
Dismal Swamp—*swamp* NY-2
Dismal Swamp—*swamp* OR-9
Dismal Swamp—*swamp* TN-4
*Dismal Swamp, The* VA-3
Dismal Swamp Canal—*canal* NC-3
Dismal Swamp Canal—*hist pl* NC-3
Dismal Swamp Canal—*hist pl* VA-3
Dismal Swamp State Wildlife Mngmt Area—*park* MN-6
Dismals Wonder Gardens—*park* AL-4
Dismal (Township of)—*fmr MCD* NC-3
**Dismal Yard**—*pop pl* VA-3
Dismant Cem—*cemetery* PA-2
*Dismero Slough* TX-5
Dismukes, Robert E., Sr., House—*hist pl* GA-3
Dismukes Branch—*stream* AR-4
Dismukes-Farmer Cem—*cemetery* MS-4
Dismukes Pond—*lake* AL-4
**Disney**—*pop pl* OK-5
**Disney**—*pop pl* TN-4
Disney, Mount—*summit* CA-9
Disney, Point—*cape* WA-9
Disney, Walt, House, and Garage—*hist pl* MO-7
Disney Cem—*cemetery* MD-2
Disney Cem—*cemetery* (3) TN-4
Disney Drift Mine (underground)—*mine* AL-4
Disney Hollow—*valley* TN-4
Disney Lake—*lake* WI-6
Disneyland—*locale* CA-9
Disney Sch—*school* CA-9
Disney Sch—*school* MO-7
Disney Spring—*spring* TN-4
Disney Studios—*other* CA-9
Disons Creek—*stream* NC-3
**Dispatch**—*pop pl* KS-7
Dispatch Creek—*stream* FL-3
Displacement Point—*cliff* UT-8
Disputant—*locale* KY-4
**Disputanta**—*pop pl* KY-4
**Disputanta**—*pop pl* VA-3
Disputas Windmill—*locale* TX-5
Disque—*locale* WA-9
Disque JHS—*school* AL-4
*Disque MS* AL-4
Disquiba Canyon—*valley* AZ-5
Disrud Lake—*lake* MN-6
Disseau Dam 2—*dam* SD-7
Dissel Creek—*stream* OR-9
**Dissen**—*pop pl* MO-7
Dissmore Canyon—*valley* WA-9
Dissmore Coulee—*valley* WI-6
**Disston**—*pop pl* OR-9
Disston, Hamilton, Sch—*hist pl* PA-2
Disston, Lake—*lake* (2) FL-3
Disston, Mary, Sch—*hist pl* PA-2
Disston Canal—*canal* FL-3
Disston JHS—*school* FL-3
Disston Park—*park* PA-2
Disston Plaza (Shop Ctr)—*locale* FL-3
Disston Recreation Center—*locale* PA-2
Disston Sch—*school* PA-2
Distaff Mine—*mine* AZ-5
Distall—*locale* MS-4
**Distant**—*pop pl* PA-2
Distant Island—*island* SC-3
Distant Island Creek—*stream* SC-3
Distant Point—*cape* AK-9
Distant View Overlook—*locale* CO-8
Distik, Mount—*summit* AK-9
Distillery Bay—*bay* ID-8
Distillery Branch—*stream* LA-4
Distillery Branch—*stream* VA-3
Distillery Canyon—*valley* AZ-5
Distillery Canyon Spring—*spring* AZ-5
Distillery Hollow—*valley* IL-6
Distill Spring—*spring* NM-5
Distin, Mount—*summit* AK-9
Distin Lake—*lake* AK-9
Distin Lake Trail—*trail* AK-9
Distin Peak—*summit* AK-9
Distlers Corners—*locale* PA-2
Distress Creek—*stream* AR-4
Distribute Branch—*stream* TN-4
Distributing Rsvr—*reservoir* MA-1
Distribution Centers of Detroit—*facility* MI-6
Distribution Tank—*reservoir* AZ-5
District A—*hist pl* NH-1
*District Agricultural Sch* AL-4
District B—*hist pl* NH-1
*District Bldg* DC-2
District Bldg—*hist pl* DC-2
District Boundary Lake—*lake* ID-8
District Branch—*stream* GA-3
District Branch—*stream* MD-2
District C—*hist pl* NH-1
District Courthouse—*hist pl* PR-3
District Courthouse and Police Station—*hist pl* HI-9
District D—*hist pl* NH-1
District Dam—*dam* PA-2
District E—*hist pl* NH-1
District Elem Sch 33—*school* NE-7
District Four Sanatorium—*hospital* AL-4
**District Heights**—*pop pl* MD-2
District Heights-Forestville—*post sta* MD-2
District Heights Sch—*school* MD-2
District Hill Cem—*cemetery* GA-3
District Hollow Branch—*stream* GA-3
District Hosp—*hospital* IL-6
District HS—*school* (2) WV-2
District I—*hist pl* MO-7
District II—*hist pl* MO-7
District III—*hist pl* MO-7
District Line Ch—*church* GA-3
District No. 1 (Magisterial District)—*fmr MCD* WV-2
District No. 1 Schoolhouse—*hist pl* ME-1
District No. 10 Sch—*hist pl* NE-7
District No. 2 (Magisterial District)—*fmr MCD* WV-2
District No. 2 Schoolhouse—*hist pl* NH-1
District No. 20 Sch—*hist pl* MN-6
District No. 3 (Magisterial District)—*fmr MCD* WV-2
District No 32 Sch—*school* MN-6
District No. 35 Sch—*school* CO-8
District No. 8 Sch—*school* CO-8
District No. 9 School—*locale* CO-8
District Number Fifty-Nine Rsvr—*reservoir* PA-2
District Number One Sanatorium—*hospital* AL-4
District Number 1 Central Sch—*school* NY-2
District Number 1 Sch—*school* (3) NY-2
District Number 1 Union Free Sch—*school* NY-2
District Number 103 Sch—*school* MN-6
District Number 104 Sch—*school* MN-6
District Number 112 And 148 Sch—*school* MN-6
District Number 121 Sch—*school* MN-6
District Number 123 Sch—*school* MN-6
District Number 132 Sch—*hist pl* MN-6
District Number 134 Sch—*school* MN-6
District Number 149 Sch—*school* MN-6
District Number 17 Cem—*cemetery* KS-7
District Number 18 Sch—*school* MN-6
District Number 19 Sch—*school* MN-6
District Number 2 Sch—*school* NY-2
District Number 28 Sch—*hist pl* MN-6
District Number 3 Sch—*school* (2) NY-2
District Number 36 Sch—*school* MN-6
District Number 39 Sch—*school* MN-6
District Number 40 Sch—*hist pl* MN-6
District Number 49 Sch—*school* MN-6
District Number 55 Sch—*hist pl* MN-6
District Number 55 Sch—*school* MN-6
District Number 66 Sch—*school* MN-6
District Number 7 Elem Sch—*school* NC-3
District Number 71 Sch—*school* MN-6
District Number 72 Sch—*hist pl* MN-6
District Number 8 Sch—*hist pl* MN-6
District Number 84 Sch—*school* MN-6
District Number 87 Sch—*school* MN-6
District Number 89 Sch—*school* MN-6
District Number 9 Sch—*school* NY-2
District Number 90 Sch—*school* MN-6
District Number 92 Sch—*hist pl* MN-6
District of Capoli Sch (historical)—*school* IA-7
District of Columbia Chapter American Red Cross Bldg—*building* DC-2
*District of Columbia (County-equivalent)* DC-2
District of Columbia Department of Corrections—*building* VA-3
District of Columbia Municipal Center—*building* DC-2
District of Columbia Tree Nursery (historical)—*locale* DC-2
District of Columbia War Memorial—*park* DC-2
District Office Forest Service - USDA—*building* MO-7
*District of Marshpee* MA-1
**District Path**—*pop pl* GA-3
District Pond—*lake* (2) GA-3
District Pond—*lake* UT-8
District Sch—*school* NY-2
District Sch—*school* VA-3
District Sch—*school* WV-2
District Sch No. 1—*hist pl* VT-1
District Sch No. 13—*hist pl* MN-6
District Sch No 206—*school* NE-7
District Sch No. 3—*hist pl* IN-6
District Sch No 5—*school* NH-1
District Sch No 60—*school* NE-7
District Sch No 77—*school* NE-7
District Sch No. 9—*hist pl* NY-2
District Sch Number 15—*school* VT-1
District Sch Number 7—*school* NY-2
District Sch Number 77—*school* NE-7
District Sch Number 8—*school* NY-2
*District School Forty* AL-4
District Schoolhouse No. 2—*hist pl* RI-1
District Six Schoolhouse—*hist pl* VT-1
*District Smoke Ditch* IN-6
District Ten Store—*locale* CA-9
**District (Township of)**—*pop pl* PA-2
District Two Community Hosp—*hospital* MS-4
District #1—*hist pl* KY-4
District 1 (Abingdon)(Election District)—*fmr MCD* MD-2
District 1 (Assessment District)—*fmr MCD* MD-2
District 1 (Barren Creek)(Election District)—*fmr MCD* MD-2
District 1 (Buckeystown)(Election District)—*fmr MCD* MD-2
District 1 (Cecilton)(Election District)—*fmr MCD* MD-2
District 1 (Dixon)(Election District)—*fmr MCD* MD-2
District 1 (Easton)(Election District)—*fmr MCD* MD-2
District 1 (Election District)—*fmr MCD* MD-2
District 1 (Elk Ridge)(Election District)—*fmr MCD* MD-2
District 1 (Fork)(Election District)—*fmr MCD* MD-2
District 1 (Henderson)(Election District)—*fmr MCD* MD-2
District 1 (La Plata)(Election District)—*fmr MCD* MD-2
District 1 (Laytonsville)(Election District)—*fmr MCD* MD-2
District 1 (Magisterial District)—*fmr MCD* (3) WV-2
District 1 (Masseys)(Election District)—*fmr MCD* MD-2
District 1 (Orleans)(Election District)—*fmr MCD* MD-2
District 1 (Pocomoke)(Election District)—*fmr MCD* MD-2
District 1 (Sharpsburg)(Election District)—*fmr MCD* MD-2
District 1 (Solomons Island)(Election District)—*fmr MCD* MD-2
District 1 (St. Ignigoes)(Election District)—*fmr MCD* MD-2
District 1 (Supervisor District)—*civil* (82) MS-4
District 1 (Swanton)(Election District)—*fmr MCD* MD-2
District 1 (Taneytown)(Election District)—*fmr MCD* MD-2
District 1 (Vansville)(Election District)—*fmr MCD* MD-2
District 1 (West Princess Anne)(Election District)—*fmr MCD* MD-2
District 10 (Deer Park)(Election District)—*fmr MCD* MD-2
District 10 (Election District)—*fmr MCD* MD-2
District 10 (Funkstown)(Election District)—*fmr MCD* MD-2
District 10 (Hauvers)(Election District)—*fmr MCD* MD-2
District 10 (Laurel)(Election District)—*fmr MCD* MD-2
District 10 (Lonaconing)(Election District)—*fmr MCD* MD-2
District 10 (Marbury)(Election District)—*fmr MCD* MD-2
District 10 (Middleburg)(Election District)—*fmr MCD* MD-2
District 10 (Ocean City)(Election District)—*fmr MCD* MD-2
District 10 (Potomac)(Election District)—*fmr MCD* MD-2
District 10 (Sharptown)(Election District)—*fmr MCD* MD-2
District 10 (Smiths Island)(Election District)—*fmr MCD* MD-2
District 10 (Straits)(Election District)—*fmr MCD* MD-2
District 11 (Barnesville)(Election District)—*fmr MCD* MD-2
District 11 (Brandywine)(Election District)—*fmr MCD* MD-2
District 11 (Dames Quarter)(Election District)—*fmr MCD* MD-2
District 11 (Delmar)(Election District)—*fmr MCD* MD-2
District 11 (Drawbridge)(Election District)—*fmr MCD* MD-2
District 11 (Election District)—*fmr MCD* MD-2
District 11 (Frostburg)(Election District)—*fmr MCD* MD-2
District 11 (New Windsor)(Election District)—*fmr MCD* MD-2
District 11 (Sandy Hook)(Election District)—*fmr MCD* MD-2
District 11 (The Elbow)(Election District)—*fmr MCD* MD-2
District 11 (Woodsboro)(Election District)—*fmr MCD* MD-2
District 12 (Asbury)(Election District)—*fmr MCD* MD-2
District 12 (Bittinger)(Election District)—*fmr MCD* MD-2
District 12 (Damascus)(Election District)—*fmr MCD* MD-2
District 12 (East Frostburg)(Election District)—*fmr MCD* MD-2
District 12 (Election District)—*fmr MCD* MD-2
District 12 (Fairplay)(Election District)—*fmr MCD* MD-2
District 12 (Nanticoke)(Election District)—*fmr MCD* MD-2
District 12 (Oxon Hill)(Election District)—*fmr MCD* MD-2
District 12 (Petersville)(Election District)—*fmr MCD* MD-2
District 12 (Union Bridge)(Election District)—*fmr MCD* MD-2
District 12 (Williamsburg)(Election District)—*fmr MCD* MD-2
District 13 (Bucktown)(Election District)—*fmr MCD* MD-2
District 13 (Camden)(Election District)—*fmr MCD* MD-2
District 13 (Election District)—*fmr MCD* MD-2
District 13 (Kent)(Election District)—*fmr MCD* MD-2
District 13 (Kitzmillerville)(Election District)—*fmr MCD* MD-2
District 13 (Mauganville)(Election District)—*fmr MCD* MD-2
District 13 (Mount Airy)(Election District)—*fmr MCD* MD-2
District 13 (Mount Pleasant)(Election District)—*fmr MCD* MD-2
District 13 (Mount Savage)(Election District)—*fmr MCD* MD-2
District 13 Police Station—*hist pl* MA-1
District 13 (Westover)(Election District)—*fmr MCD* MD-2
District 13 (Wheaton)(Election District)—*fmr MCD* MD-2
District 14 (Berrett)(Election District)—*fmr MCD* MD-2
District 14 (Bowie)(Election District)—*fmr MCD* MD-2
District 14 (Central)(Election District)—*fmr MCD* MD-2
District 14 (Deal Island)(Election District)—*fmr MCD* MD-2
District 14 (Election District)—*fmr MCD* MD-2
District 14 (Jefferson)(Election District)—*fmr MCD* MD-2
District 14 (Linkwood)(Election District)—*fmr MCD* MD-2
District 14 (Ringgold)(Election District)—*fmr MCD* MD-2
District 14 (West Oakland)(Election District)—*fmr MCD* MD-2
District 14 (Willards)(Election District)—*fmr MCD* MD-2
District 15 (Avilton)(Election District)—*fmr MCD* MD-2
District 15 (East Princess Anne)(Election District)—*fmr MCD* MD-2
District 15 (Election District)—*fmr MCD* MD-2
District 15 (Hebron)(Election District)—*fmr MCD* MD-2
District 15 (Hurlock)(Election District)—*fmr MCD* MD-2
District 15 (Indian Spring)(Election District)—*fmr MCD* MD-2
District 15 (Mellwood)(Election District)—*fmr MCD* MD-2
District 15 (Thurmont)(Election District)—*fmr MCD* MD-2
District 16 (Beaver Creek)(Election District)—*fmr MCD* MD-2
District 16 (Fruitland)(Election District)—*fmr MCD* MD-2
District 16 (Hyattsville)(Election District)—*fmr MCD* MD-2
District 16 (Jackson)(Election District)—*fmr MCD* MD-2
District 16 (Madison)(Election District)—*fmr MCD* MD-2
District 16 (Mountain Lake)(Election District)—*fmr MCD* MD-2
District 16 (North Branch)(Election District)—*fmr MCD* MD-2
District 17 (Chillum)(Election District)—*fmr MCD* MD-2
District 17 (Hagerstown)(Election District)—*fmr MCD* MD-2
District 17 (Johnsville)(Election District)—*fmr MCD* MD-2
District 17 (Salem)(Election District)—*fmr MCD* MD-2
District 17 (Vale Summit)(Election District)—*fmr MCD* MD-2
District 18 (Chewsville)(Election District)—*fmr MCD* MD-2
District 18 (Elliott)(Election District)—*fmr MCD* MD-2
District 18 (Ocean)(Election District)—*fmr MCD* MD-2
District 18 (Seat Pleasant)(Election District)—*fmr MCD* MD-2
District 18 (Woodville)(Election District)—*fmr MCD* MD-2
District 19 (Borden Shaft)(Election District)—*fmr MCD* MD-2
District 19 (Keedysville)(Election District)—*fmr MCD* MD-2
District 19 (Riverdale)(Election District)—*fmr MCD* MD-2
District 19 (Unganore)(Election District)—*fmr MCD* MD-2
District #2—*hist pl* KY-4
District 2 (Assessment District)—*fmr MCD* MD-2
District 2 (Bladensburg)(Election District)—*fmr MCD* MD-2
District 2 (Chesapeake)(Election District)—*fmr MCD* MD-2
District 2 (Church Hill)(Election District)—*fmr MCD* MD-2
District 2 (Clarksburg)(Election District)—*fmr MCD* MD-2
District 2 (East New Market)(Election District)—*fmr MCD* MD-2
District 2 (Election District)—*fmr MCD* MD-2
District 2 (Ellicott City)(Election District)—*fmr MCD* MD-2
District 2 (Frederick)(Election District)—*fmr MCD* MD-2
District 2 (Friendsville)(Election District)—*fmr MCD* MD-2
District 2 (Greensboro)(Election District)—*fmr MCD* MD-2
District 2 (Halls Cross Roads)(Election District)—*fmr MCD* MD-2
District 2 (Hill Top)(Election District)—*fmr MCD* MD-2
District 2 (Kennedyville)(Election District)—*fmr MCD* MD-2
District 2 (Magisterial District)—*fmr MCD* (3) WV-2
District 2 (Old Town)(Election District)—*fmr MCD* MD-2
District 2 (Prince Frederick)(Election District)—*fmr MCD* MD-2
District 2 (Quantico)(Election District)—*fmr MCD* MD-2
District 2 (Snow Hill)(Election District)—*fmr MCD* MD-2
District 2 (St. Michaels)(Election District)—*fmr MCD* MD-2
District 2 (St. Peters)(Election District)—*fmr MCD* MD-2
District 2 (Supervisor District)—*civil* (82) MS-4
District 2 (Uniontown)(Election District)—*fmr MCD* MD-2
District 2 (Valley Lee)(Election District)—*fmr MCD* MD-2
District 2 (Williamsport)(Election District)—*fmr MCD* MD-2
District 20 (Downsville)(Election District)—*fmr MCD* MD-2
District 20 (Ellerslie)(Election District)—*fmr MCD* MD-2
District 20 (Lanham)(Election District)—*fmr MCD* MD-2
District 20 (Lewistown)(Election District)—*fmr MCD* MD-2
District 21 (Berwyn)(Election District)—*fmr MCD* MD-2
District 21 (Gross)(Election District)—*fmr MCD* MD-2
District 21 (Hagerstown)(Election District)—*fmr MCD* MD-2
District 21 (Tuscarora)(Election District)—*fmr MCD* MD-2
District 22 (Burkittsville)(Election District)—*fmr MCD* MD-2
District 22 (Hagerstown)(Election District)—*fmr MCD* MD-2
District 22 (Union)(Election District)—*fmr MCD* MD-2
District 23 (Ballenger)(Election District)—*fmr MCD* MD-2
District 23 (Decatur)(Election District)—*fmr MCD* MD-2
District 23 (Eckhart)(Election District)—*fmr MCD* MD-2
District 23 Elem Sch—*school* NE-7
District 23 (Wilsons)(Election District)—*fmr MCD* MD-2
District 24 (Braddock)(Election District)—*fmr MCD* MD-2
District 24 (Cedar Lawn)(Election District)—*fmr MCD* MD-2
District 25 (Brunswick)(Election District)—*fmr MCD* MD-2
District 25 (Hagerstown)(Election District)—*fmr MCD* MD-2
District 26 (Frostburg)(Election District)—*fmr MCD* MD-2
District 26 (Halfway)(Election District)—*fmr MCD* MD-2
District 26 (Walkersville)(Election District)—*fmr MCD* MD-2
District 27 (Fountain Head)(Election District)—*fmr MCD* MD-2

Divide Island—*island* ... AK-9
*Divide Lake* ... UT-8
Divide Lake—*lake* (2) ... AK-9
Divide Lake—*lake* ... CA-9
Divide Lake—*lake* (2) ... MN-6
Divide Lake—*lake* (2) ... UT-8
Divide Lake—*lake* ... WA-9
Divide Lake—*lake* (5) ... WY-8
Divide Lakes—*reservoir* ... CO-8
Divide Lode Mine—*mine* ... SD-7
Divide Mine—*mine* ... NV-8
Divide Mines—*mine* ... NV-8
*Divide Mountain* ... CO-8
Divide Mtn—*summit* (2) ... AK-9
Divide Mtn—*summit* ... AR-4
Divide Mtn—*summit* (2) ... MT-8
Divide Mtn—*summit* (2) ... NC-3
Divide Mtn—*summit* ... TN-4
**Dividend**—*pop pl* ... UT-8
Dividend Bar—*locale* ... OR-9
Dividend Brook—*stream* ... CT-1
*Dividend Creek* ... VA-3
Dividend Miner's Dry—*hist pl* ... UT-8
Dividend Point—*cape* ... MA-1
Dividend Pond—*lake* ... CT-1
Dividened Mine (historical)—*mine* ... SD-7
Divide Number Two Rsvr—*reservoir* ... MT-8
Divide Oil Field—*other* ... IL-6
Divide Overlook Area—*park* ... MS-4
Divide Park—*flat* ... CO-8
Divide Park Springs—*spring* ... CO-8
Divide Peak—*summit* ... CA-9
Divide Peak—*summit* ... ID-8
Divide Peak—*summit* (2) ... MT-8
Divide Peak—*summit* ... NV-8
Divide Peak—*summit* ... WA-9
Divide Peak—*summit* ... WY-8
Divide Pond—*lake* ... OR-9
Divide Ridge—*ridge* ... CA-9
Divide Ridge—*ridge* ... MD-2
Divide Ridge—*ridge* ... MO-7
Divide Ridge—*ridge* (3) ... VA-3
Divide Ridge—*ridge* (2) ... WA-9
Divide Ridge—*ridge* ... WV-2
Divider Mountain—*ridge* ... AK-9
Divider Sch—*school* ... TN-4
Divide Rsvr—*reservoir* ... CO-8
Divide Rsvr—*reservoir* ... ID-8
Divide Rsvr—*reservoir* ... MT-8
Divide Rsvr—*reservoir* ... NV-8
Divide Rsvr—*reservoir* ... OR-9
*Divider Well* ... AZ-5
Divide Sch—*school* (2) ... MT-8
Divide Sch—*school* ... ND-7
Divide Sch—*school* ... SD-7
Divide Sch—*school* ... TX-5
Divide Sch—*school* ... WY-8
Divide Sch (abandoned)—*school* ... PA-2
Divide Sheep Camp—*hist pl* ... WY-8
Divide Spring—*spring* ... AZ-5
Divide Spring—*spring* ... NV-8
Divide Spring—*spring* (2) ... OR-9
Divide Spring—*spring* ... SD-7
Divide Spring—*spring* ... UT-8
Divide Springs—*spring* ... CA-9
Divide Station—*locale* ... AL-4
Divide Substation—*other* ... CA-9
Divide Tank—*reservoir* (6) ... AZ-5
Divide Tank—*reservoir* (3) ... NM-5
Divide Tanks—*reservoir* ... AZ-5
Divide Town Hall—*building* ... ND-7
**Divide Township**—*pop pl* (2) ... NE-7
**Divide Township**—*pop pl* ... ND-7
Divide Trading Post—*locale* ... NM-5
Divide Trail—*trail* ... CA-9
Divide Trail—*trail* (2) ... CO-8
Divide Trail—*trail* ... ID-8
Divide Trail—*trail* (4) ... MT-8
Divide Trail—*trail* ... PA-2
Divide Trail—*trail* ... VA-3
Divide Trail—*trail* ... WA-9
Divide Trail—*trail* ... WV-2
Divide Trail—*trail* ... WY-8
Divide Trail (pack)—*trail* ... MT-8
Divide Trail (Pack)—*trail* ... NM-5
Divide Waterhole—*reservoir* ... OR-9
Divide Well—*well* ... AZ-5
Divide Well—*well* ... OR-9
Divide Well—*well* (2) ... TX-5
Divide Well Campground—*park* ... OR-9
Divide Well Draw—*valley* ... TX-5
Divide Windmill—*locale* ... NM-5
Divide Windmill—*locale* (11) ... TX-5
Dividing—*ridge* ... TN-4
Dividing Branch—*stream* ... OH-6
Dividing Branch—*stream* (2) ... VA-3
Dividing Canal—*canal* ... NC-3
Dividing Canyon—*arroyo* ... AZ-5
Dividing Canyon—*valley* ... AZ-5
Dividing Canyon Tank—*reservoir* ... AZ-5
*Dividing Creek* ... MD-2
*Dividing Creek* ... NC-3
Dividing Creek—*bay* ... MD-2
Dividing Creek—*gut* ... SC-3
**Dividing Creek**—*pop pl* ... NJ-2
Dividing Creek—*stream* (2) ... MD-2
Dividing Creek—*stream* ... NJ-2
Dividing Creek—*stream* ... VA-3
*Dividing Creek, The* ... NC-3
Dividing Creek Station—*locale* ... NJ-2
*Dividing Fork* ... KY-4
Dividing Hollow—*valley* ... PA-2
Dividing Hollow—*valley* ... TN-4
*Dividing Mountain* ... PA-2
Dividing Point—*cape* ... AK-9
Dividing Ridge—*locale* ... KY-4
Dividing Ridge—*locale* ... PA-2
Dividing Ridge—*ridge* (3) ... AL-4
Dividing Ridge—*ridge* ... GA-3
Dividing Ridge—*ridge* ... IL-6
Dividing Ridge—*ridge* (2) ... KY-4
Dividing Ridge—*ridge* (2) ... MO-7
Dividing Ridge—*ridge* (4) ... NC-3
Dividing Ridge—*ridge* ... OH-6
Dividing Ridge—*ridge* (2) ... PA-2
Dividing Ridge—*ridge* (5) ... TN-4
Dividing Ridge—*ridge* (3) ... VA-3
Dividing Ridge—*ridge* ... WV-2
Dividing Ridge—*ridge* ... WI-6
*Dividing Ridge Baptist Church* ... MS-4
Dividing Ridge Cem—*cemetery* ... MS-4
Dividing Ridge Ch—*church* ... MS-4
Dividing Ridge Ch—*church* (2) ... TN-4
Dividing Ridge Sch (abandoned)—*school* ... PA-2
Dividing Ridge Trail—*trail* ... NY-2
Dividing Ridge Trail—*trail* ... VA-3
*Dividing Swamp* ... VA-3
Dividing Waters Trail—*trail* ... PA-2
*Divils Race Course* ... PA-2
Divil Tank—*reservoir* (2) ... AZ-5
Divine—*locale* ... IL-6
Divine, John, Law Office/Moore Public Library—*hist pl* ... MI-6
Divine Ch (historical)—*church* ... AL-4
Divine Child HS—*school* ... MI-6
**Divine Corners**—*pop pl* ... NY-2
Divine Heart Seminary—*school* ... IN-6
Divine Hollow—*valley* ... PA-2
Divine Infant of Prague Ch—*church* ... MI-6
Divine Lake—*lake* ... MI-6
Divine Lake—*lake* ... NM-5
Divine Master Convent—*church* ... CA-9
Divine Mercy Catholic Sch—*school* ... FL-3
*Divine Peak* ... MT-8
Divine Peak—*summit* ... NV-8
Divine Place—*locale* ... WA-9
Divine Post Office (historical)—*building* ... TN-4
Divine Providence Hosp—*hospital* (2) ... PA-2
Divine Providence Sch—*school* ... IL-6
Divine Rapids—*rapids* ... WI-6
Divine Rsvr—*reservoir* ... WY-8
Divine Savior HS—*school* ... WI-6
Divine Savior Sch—*school* ... CA-9
Divine Savior Sch—*school* ... WI-6
Divine Savior Seminary—*school* ... MD-2
Divine Spring—*spring* ... NV-8
Divine Word Seminary—*church* ... OH-6
Divine Word Seminary—*school* ... CA-9
Divine Word Seminary—*school* ... PA-2
Divine Word Seminary—*school* ... WI-6
Diving Board—*cliff* ... CA-9
Diving Board Tank—*reservoir* ... TX-5
Diving Board Tanks—*reservoir* ... AZ-5
Diving Island—*island* ... CT-1
Diving Rock Fisherman Access (projected)—*locale* ... UT-8
Divinie Draw—*valley* ... WY-8
Divining Creek—*stream* ... AK-9
*Divinity Creek* ... OR-9
Divinity Hall—*hist pl* ... MA-1
**Divinity Hill**—*pop pl* ... NY-2
Divins Creek—*stream* ... MO-7
Divisadero—*summit* ... TX-5
Divisadero, Loma del—*summit* ... TX-5
Division—*locale* ... CA-9
Division Ave HS—*school* ... NY-2
Division Ave Pumping Station—*hist pl* ... OH-6
Division Canyon—*valley* ... NV-8
Division Canyon—*valley* ... OR-9
Division Creek—*stream* ... AK-9
Division Creek—*stream* (2) ... CA-9
Division Creek—*stream* ... MN-6
Division Creek—*stream* ... NJ-2
Division Creek Powerhouse—*other* ... CA-9
Division D Stock Trail—*trail* ... ID-8
Division Fence Rsvr—*reservoir* ... OR-9
Division Four Canal—*canal* ... WA-9
Division Gulch—*valley* ... OR-9
Division Island—*island* ... AK-9
Division Knoll—*summit* ... CA-9
Division Lake—*lake* ... CA-9
Division Lake—*lake* ... TX-5
Division Lake—*reservoir* ... NV-8
Division Lake—*reservoir* ... UT-8
Division of St. John Hist Dist—*hist pl* ... LA-4
*Division Peak* ... NV-8
Division Peak—*summit* ... NV-8
Division Pens Spring—*spring* ... TX-5
Division Point—*cape* (2) ... AK-9
Division Point—*cape* ... FL-3
Division Point—*cape* ... ME-1
Division Pond—*lake* ... NY-2
Division-Powell Park—*park* ... OR-9
Division Ridge—*ridge* ... PA-2
Division Rock—*pillar* ... WA-9
*Division Rsvr* ... OR-9
Division Spring—*spring* ... AZ-5
Division Spring—*spring* ... OR-9
Division Spring—*spring* ... WA-9
*Division Street* ... IL-6
Division Street—*uninc pl* ... MA-1
Division Street Baptist Ch—*church* ... MS-4
Division Street Bridge—*hist pl* ... RI-1
Division Street Community Center—*building* ... MS-4
Division Street Hist Dist—*hist pl* ... CT-1
Division Street JHS—*school* ... IL-6
Division Street Sch—*school* ... NY-2
Division Tank—*reservoir* (4) ... AZ-5
Division Tank—*reservoir* (2) ... NM-5
Division Tank—*reservoir* (7) ... TX-5
Division Waterhole—*reservoir* ... OR-9
Division Well—*well* ... AZ-5
Division Well—*well* (5) ... TX-5
Division Windmill—*locale* ... CO-8
Division Windmill—*locale* (6) ... TX-5
Divison Rsvr—*reservoir* ... OR-9
**Divisoria**—*pop pl* ... PR-3
Divol Pond—*lake* ... NH-1
Divonia Ch—*church* ... FL-3
Divot—*locale* ... TX-5
Dix—*locale* ... TX-5
**Dix**—*pop pl* ... IL-6
**Dix**—*pop pl* ... NE-7
**Dix**—*pop pl* ... NY-2
Dix, James L., House—*hist pl* ... NY-2
**Dixacon**—*pop pl* ... AL-4
Dix Ave Sch—*school* ... NY-2
**Dixboro**—*pop pl* ... MI-6
Dixboro United Methodist Church—*hist pl* ... MI-6
Dix Branch—*stream* ... GA-3
Dix Branch—*stream* ... KY-4
Dix Branch—*stream* ... NC-3
Dix Bridge—*bridge* ... VA-3
Dix Brook—*stream* ... MA-1
Dix Canyon—*valley* ... CA-9
Dix Canyon—*valley* ... NM-5
Dix Cem—*cemetery* ... MO-7
Dix Cem—*cemetery* ... NE-7
Dix Cove—*bay* ... VA-3
*Dix Creek* ... AZ-5
*Dix Creek* ... ID-8
*Dix Creek* ... MS-4
*Dix Creek* ... MT-8
Dix Creek—*stream* ... AZ-5
Dix Creek—*stream* (2) ... NC-3
Dix Creek—*stream* ... UT-8
Dix Creek—*stream* ... VA-3
Dix Creek Chapel—*church* ... NC-3
Dix Creek Gap—*gap* ... NC-3
Dix Creek Post Office (historical)—*building* ... MS-4
Dix Dam—*dam* ... KY-4
Dixey Spring—*spring* ... ID-8
**Dixfield**—*pop pl* ... ME-1
Dixfield Center—*locale* ... ME-1
Dixfield Compact (census name Dixfield)—*other* ... ME-1
Dixfield (sta.) (RR name for West Peru)—*other* ... ME-1
**Dixfield (Town of)**—*pop pl* ... ME-1
Dix Fish and Wildlife Mngmt Area—*park* ... NJ-2
Dix Fork—*stream* ... KY-4
Dix Fork Ch—*church* ... KY-4
**Dix Fork (Crigger)**—*pop pl* ... KY-4
Dix Fork Sch—*school* ... KY-4
Dix Gap—*gap* ... NC-3
Dix Hammock—*island* ... VA-3
Dix Hill Conf Center Pond Dam—*dam* ... NC-3
Dix Hill Conference Center Pond—*reservoir* ... NC-3
Dix Hills—*CDP* ... NY-2
Dix Hills—*summit* ... NY-2
Dix Hills Park—*park* ... NY-2
Dix Hollow—*valley* ... TX-5
*Dixiana* ... AL-4
Dixiana—*locale* ... SC-3
Dixiana—*locale* ... VA-3
**Dixiana (Bradford)**—*pop pl* ... AL-4
Dixiana Ch—*church* ... SC-3
Dixiana Mine (underground)—*mine* ... AL-4
Dixico—*uninc pl* ... TX-5
*Dixie* ... MS-4
Dixie—*locale* ... AZ-5
Dixie—*locale* ... AR-4
Dixie—*locale* ... CA-9
Dixie—*locale* ... GA-3
Dixie—*locale* ... ID-8
Dixie—*locale* ... KY-4
Dixie—*locale* (2) ... MS-4
Dixie—*locale* ... MO-7
Dixie—*locale* ... NV-8
Dixie—*locale* ... OH-6
Dixie—*locale* (2) ... OR-9
Dixie—*locale* ... TN-4
Dixie—*locale* ... VA-3
**Dixie**—*pop pl* (3) ... AL-4
**Dixie**—*pop pl* (4) ... AR-4
**Dixie**—*pop pl* ... FL-3
**Dixie**—*pop pl* ... GA-3
**Dixie**—*pop pl* ... ID-8
**Dixie**—*pop pl* ... IN-6
**Dixie**—*pop pl* ... IA-7
**Dixie**—*pop pl* (2) ... KY-4
**Dixie**—*pop pl* ... LA-4
**Dixie**—*pop pl* ... MS-4
**Dixie**—*pop pl* (3) ... NC-3
**Dixie**—*pop pl* ... SC-3
**Dixie**—*pop pl* ... TX-5
**Dixie**—*pop pl* ... VA-3
**Dixie**—*pop pl* ... WA-9
**Dixie**—*pop pl* ... WV-2
Dixie—*post sta* ... KY-4
Dixie, Lake—*lake* ... FL-3
Dixie, Lake—*reservoir* ... AL-4
Dixie Acad—*school* ... AL-4
**Dixie Acres**—*pop pl* ... LA-4
Dixie Airp—*airport* ... MS-4
Dixie Baptist Ch—*church* ... MS-4
*Dixie Bar* ... AL-4
Dixie Bay—*bay* ... FL-3
Dixie Bayou—*gut* ... AR-4
Dixie Bayou—*stream* ... LA-4
Dixie Beach—*beach* ... FL-3
Dixie Bend—*bend* ... KY-4
Dixie Bluffs—*cliff* ... CO-8
Dixie Branch—*stream* ... AL-4
Dixie Branch—*stream* ... FL-3
Dixie Branch—*stream* ... LA-4
Dixie Branch—*stream* ... TX-5
Dixie Brook—*stream* ... NH-1
Dixie Butte—*summit* ... OR-9
Dixie Campground—*locale* ... OR-9
*Dixie Canyon* ... AZ-5
Dixie Canyon—*valley* ... AZ-5
Dixie Canyon—*valley* ... OR-9
Dixie Canyon Ave Sch—*school* ... CA-9
Dixie Canyon Ranch—*locale* ... AZ-5
Dixie Caverns—*cave* ... VA-3
Dixie (CCD)—*cens area* ... GA-3
Dixie (CCD)—*cens area* ... TN-4
Dixie Cem—*cemetery* ... MS-4
Dixie Cem—*cemetery* (3) ... OK-5
Dixie Ch—*church* ... GA-3
Dixie Ch—*church* ... LA-4
Dixie Ch—*church* ... MI-6
Dixie Ch—*church* ... TX-5
Dixie Church Cem—*cemetery* ... AL-4
Dixie Classics Fairgrounds—*park* ... NC-3
Dixie Coca-Cola Bottling Company Plant—*hist pl* ... GA-3
*Dixie College* ... UT-8
Dixie Community Ch—*church* ... TX-5
*Dixie Consolidated School* ... MS-4
Dixie Corner—*locale* ... ME-1
**Dixie County**—*pop pl* ... FL-3
Dixie County Adult Center—*school* ... FL-3
Dixie County Fire Control HQ—*locale* ... FL-3
Dixie County HS—*school* ... FL-3
Dixie Court Hotel—*hist pl* ... FL-3
*Dixie Creek* ... ID-8
Dixie Creek—*stream* ... AL-4
Dixie Creek—*stream* (2) ... AK-9
Dixie Creek—*stream* (2) ... CA-9
Dixie Creek—*stream* ... CO-8
Dixie Creek—*stream* ... GA-3
Dixie Creek—*stream* (2) ... ID-8
Dixie Creek—*stream* ... KY-4
Dixie Creek—*stream* ... LA-4
Dixie Creek—*stream* ... MT-8
Dixie Creek—*stream* ... NV-8
Dixie Creek—*stream* ... NM-5
Dixie Creek—*stream* (5) ... OR-9
Dixie Crossing—*locale* ... CA-9
Dixie Crossing—*locale* ... SC-3
**Dixie Crossroads**—*pop pl* ... NC-3
Dixie Cut-Off—*channel* ... AL-4
Dixie Dam—*dam* ... NH-1
Dixie Daniel Sch—*school* ... GA-3
Dixie Deer Airp—*airport* ... UT-8
Dixie Delta Canal—*canal* ... LA-4
Dixie Division—*civil* ... TN-4
Dixie Drain—*canal* ... ID-8
Dixie Drain Five—*canal* ... CA-9
Dixie Drain Four—*canal* ... CA-9
Dixie Drain One—*canal* ... CA-9
Dixie Drain One A—*canal* ... CA-9
Dixie Drain Three—*canal* ... CA-9
Dixie Drain Three-A—*canal* ... CA-9
Dixie Drain Three-B—*canal* ... CA-9
Dixie Drain Two—*canal* ... CA-9
Dixie Draw—*valley* ... WY-8
Dixie Flat—*flat* ... OR-9
Dixie Flats—*flat* ... NV-8
*Dixie Forest Camp* ... OR-9
Dixie Fork—*stream* ... KY-4
Dixie Fork Trout Creek—*stream* ... NV-8
**Dixie Gardens**—*pop pl* ... LA-4
Dixie Gold Mine—*mine* ... AZ-5
Dixie Golf Club—*locale* ... MS-4
**Dixie Grove**—*pop pl* ... FL-3
Dixie Grove Ch—*church* ... AL-4
Dixie Gulch—*valley* (4) ... ID-8
Dixie Gulch—*valley* ... OR-9
Dixie H Drain—*stream* ... MI-6
*Dixie Heights* ... OH-6
**Dixie Heights**—*pop pl* ... OH-6
Dixie Heights—*uninc pl* ... GA-3
Dixie Highway Hist Dist—*hist pl* ... KY-4
Dixie Highway Racetrack—*other* ... MI-6
**Dixie Hill**—*pop pl* ... VA-3
Dixie Hill Ch—*church* ... GA-3
Dixie Hills Baptist Ch—*church* ... TN-4
Dixie Hills Ch—*church* ... GA-3
Dixie (historical)—*locale* ... MS-4
**Dixie (historical)**—*pop pl* ... MS-4
**Dixie (historical)**—*pop pl* (2) ... OR-9
**Dixie (historical)**—*pop pl* ... TN-4
Dixie Hollow—*valley* ... OH-6
Dixie Hollow—*valley* (2) ... UT-8
Dixie Hollow Springs—*spring* ... UT-8
Dixie Hosp—*hospital* ... VA-3
Dixie Hotel, Hotel Kelley—*hist pl* ... FL-3
Dixie Hot Springs—*spring* ... NV-8
Dixie Hot Springs—*spring* ... UT-8
Dixie House—*locale* ... ID-8
Dixie HS—*hist pl* ... WA-9
Dixie HS—*school* ... SC-3
Dixie HS—*school* ... UT-8
Dixie Hunt Hotel—*hist pl* ... GA-3
**Dixie Inn**—*pop pl* ... LA-4
Dixie Islands—*island* ... IL-6
Dixie Jett Gulch—*valley* ... OR-9
Dixie Junior Coll—*school* ... UT-8
Dixie Knoll—*summit* ... UT-8
Dixie Lake—*lake* ... FL-3
Dixie Lake—*lake* ... MI-6
Dixie Lake—*lake* ... NY-2
Dixie Lake—*lake* ... WA-9
Dixie Lake—*reservoir* ... TX-5
Dixie Lakes—*lake* ... GA-3
**Dixieland**—*pop pl* ... CA-9
Dixieland—*uninc pl* ... FL-3
Dixieland Ch—*church* ... FL-3
Dixieland Ditch—*canal* ... CA-9
**Dixieland (Dixieland Junction)**—*pop pl* ... AL-4
Dixie Landing—*locale* ... AL-4
Dixie Landing—*locale* ... LA-4
Dixie Landing—*locale* ... TN-4
Dixie Landing (historical)—*locale* ... TN-4
Dixieland Junction—*other* ... AL-4
Dixie Land Lake—*reservoir* ... GA-3
Dixieland Min-Mall—*locale* ... FL-3
Dixieland Oil Field—*oilfield* ... TX-5
Dixieland Sch—*school* ... CA-9
Dixieland Sch—*school* ... FL-3
**Dixieland (subdivision)**—*pop pl* ... TN-4
Dixie Lateral—*canal* ... ID-8
Dixie Lateral One—*canal* ... CA-9
**Dixie Lee**—*pop pl* ... TN-4
Dixie Lee Baptist Ch—*church* ... TN-4
**Dixie Lee Junction**—*pop pl* ... TN-4
Dixie Library Bldg—*hist pl* ... SC-3
Dixie Lookout Tower—*locale* ... AL-4
Dixie Meadows—*flat* (2) ... OR-9
Dixie Meadows—*swamp* ... NV-8
Dixie Meadows Mine—*mine* ... OR-9
Dixie Med Ctr—*hospital* ... UT-8
Dixie Methodist Ch—*church* ... AL-4
Dixie M Hollins Senior HS—*school* ... FL-3
*Dixie Mills* ... MS-4
Dixie Mills—*locale* ... TN-4
Dixie Mine—*mine* (2) ... AZ-5
Dixie Mine—*mine* ... CO-8
Dixie Mine (underground)—*mine* ... AL-4
Dixie Mound—*summit* ... TX-5
Dixie MS—*school* ... UT-8
Dixie Mtn—*summit* ... CA-9
Dixie Mtn—*summit* ... ID-8
Dixie Mtn—*summit* ... OR-9
Dixie Natl For—*forest* ... UT-8
Dixie Oil Field—*oilfield* ... LA-4
*Dixie Park* ... FL-3
Dixie Park—*park* ... FL-3
**Dixie Park**—*pop pl* ... OK-5
*Dixie Pass* ... OR-9
Dixie Pass—*gap* ... AK-9
Dixie Peak—*summit* ... AZ-5
Dixie Peak—*summit* ... CA-9
Dixie Peak—*summit* ... MT-8
**Dixie Pine**—*pop pl* ... MS-4
**Dixie Plantation**—*pop pl* ... KY-4
**Dixie Plantation**—*pop pl* ... LA-4
Dixie Plantation House—*hist pl* ... LA-4
Dixie Plaza (Shop Ctr)—*locale* ... FL-3
Dixie Plaza Shop Ctr—*locale* ... TN-4
*Dixie Pond* ... MA-1
Dixie Pond—*lake* ... MA-1
Dixie Pond—*reservoir* ... NC-3
Dixie Pond Dam—*dam* ... NC-3
Dixie Queen Mine—*mine* ... AZ-5
Dixie Queen Mine—*mine* (2) ... CA-9
Dixie Queen Mine (historical)—*mine* ... ID-8
Dixie Ranch—*locale* (2) ... CA-9
Dixie Ranch—*locale* ... FL-3
Dixie Ranch—*locale* ... ID-8
Dixie Ranch—*locale* ... OR-9
**Dixie Ranch Acres**—*pop pl* ... FL-3
Dixie Ranch Lookout Tower—*locale* ... LA-4
Dixie Royal Mine—*mine* ... ID-8
Dixie Run—*stream* ... PA-2
Dixie Sailing Club—*locale* ... AL-4
Dixie Sch—*school* ... AL-4
Dixie Sch—*school* (2) ... IL-6
Dixie Sch—*school* (2) ... KY-4
Dixie Sch—*school* ... MI-6
Dixie Sch—*school* ... MO-7
Dixie Sch—*school* ... OR-9
Dixie Sch—*school* ... SC-3
Dixie Sch—*school* (2) ... TX-5
Dixie Sch (historical)—*school* ... TN-4
Dixie Sch (ihstorical)—*school* ... TN-4
Dixie School (Abandoned)—*locale* ... TX-5
Dixie Schoolhouse—*hist pl* ... CA-9
Dixie Slough—*stream* ... ID-8
*Dixie Spring* ... AL-4
Dixie Spring—*spring* (2) ... CA-9
Dixie Spring—*spring* (2) ... OR-9
Dixie Spring—*spring* ... UT-8
Dixie Spring Post Office (historical)—*building* ... AL-4
Dixie Springs—*locale* ... AL-4
Dixie Springs—*spring* ... CA-9
Dixie Springs Lake—*reservoir* ... MS-4
Dixie Springs Lake Dam—*dam* ... MS-4
Dixie Springs Mine (surface)—*mine* ... AL-4
*Dixie State Park* ... UT-8
Dixie Summit—*gap* ... ID-8
Dixie Summit—*summit* ... ID-8
Dixie Summit—*summit* ... OR-9
**Dixietown**—*pop pl* ... FL-3
Dixie Trail Mine—*mine* ... OR-9
**Dixie Union**—*pop pl* ... GA-3
Dixie Union (CCD)—*cens area* ... GA-3
*Dixie Valley* ... NV-8
Dixie Valley—*basin* ... CA-9
Dixie Valley—*basin* ... NV-8
Dixie Valley—*locale* ... NV-8
Dixie Valley—*valley* ... CA-9
Dixie Valley Rsvr Number Two—*reservoir* ... NV-8
*Dixie Valley Settlement* ... NV-8
**Dixie Valley Subdivision**—*pop pl* ... UT-8
Dixie Valley Wash—*stream* ... NV-8
Dixie Village—*uninc pl* ... FL-3
Dixie Village Christian Acad—*school* ... FL-3
Dixie Village Shop Ctr—*locale* ... NC-3
Dixieville Post Office (historical)—*building* ... TN-4
*Dixie Wash* ... NV-8
Dixie Woodyard—*locale* ... ID-8
Dixie Work Center—*locale* ... ID-8
Dixie Youth Park—*park* ... MS-4
Dixie Youth Park—*park* ... TN-4
*Dix Inlet* ... VA-3
*Dix Island* ... NY-2
Dix Island—*island* (2) ... ME-1
Dix Island Harbor—*bay* ... ME-1
Dix Lake—*lake* ... MN-6
Dix Ledge—*rock* ... MA-1
Dix Mesa—*summit* ... AZ-5
Dix Mesa Number Two Tank—*reservoir* ... AZ-5
Dix Mine—*mine* (2) ... CA-9
Dix Mix Memorial Field—*park* ... NY-2
**Dixmont**—*pop pl* ... ME-1
**Dixmont**—*pop pl* ... PA-2
**Dixmont Center**—*pop pl* ... ME-1
Dixmont Corner Church—*hist pl* ... ME-1
*Dixmont State Hospital* ... PA-2
**Dixmont (State Hospital)**—*pop pl* ... PA-2
**Dixmont (Town of)**—*pop pl* ... ME-1
**Dixmoor**—*pop pl* ... IL-6
Dix Mtn—*summit* ... NY-2
Dix Oil Field—*other* ... IL-6
*Dixon* ... FL-3
*Dixon* ... WY-8
Dixon—*locale* ... CO-8
Dixon—*locale* ... MI-6
Dixon—*locale* ... MS-4
Dixon—*locale* ... OR-9
Dixon—*locale* ... PA-2
Dixon—*locale* ... TX-5
**Dixon**—*pop pl* ... CA-9
**Dixon**—*pop pl* ... FL-3
**Dixon**—*pop pl* ... IL-6
**Dixon**—*pop pl* (2) ... IN-6
**Dixon**—*pop pl* ... IA-7
**Dixon**—*pop pl* ... KS-7
**Dixon**—*pop pl* ... KY-4
**Dixon**—*pop pl* ... MS-4
**Dixon**—*pop pl* ... MO-7
**Dixon**—*pop pl* ... MT-8
**Dixon**—*pop pl* ... NE-7
**Dixon**—*pop pl* ... NM-5
**Dixon**—*pop pl* ... NC-3
**Dixon**—*pop pl* ... OH-6
**Dixon**—*pop pl* ... OK-5
**Dixon**—*pop pl* ... PA-2
**Dixon**—*pop pl* ... SC-3
**Dixon**—*pop pl* ... SD-7
**Dixon**—*pop pl* ... WY-8
Dixon, Christopher F., Jr., House—*hist pl* ... UT-8
Dixon, James, Farm—*hist pl* ... NJ-2
Dixon, John, House—*hist pl* ... UT-8
Dixon, Mount—*summit* ... AK-9
Dixon, S. P., Farm—*hist pl* ... DE-2
Dixona—*hist pl* ... TN-4
**Dixon Acres (subdivision)**—*pop pl* ... MS-4
Dixon and Lewis Ditch—*canal* ... IN-6
Dixon Ave Sch—*school* ... PA-2
Dixon Bar Creek—*stream* ... CA-9
Dixon Bay—*bay* ... LA-4
Dixon Bayou—*stream* ... AR-4
*Dixon Bend* ... AR-4
Dixon Bldg—*hist pl* ... MS-4
Dixon Branch—*stream* ... IL-6
Dixon Branch—*stream* ... IN-6
Dixon Branch—*stream* (4) ... KY-4
Dixon Branch—*stream* (2) ... NC-3
Dixon Branch—*stream* ... OH-6
Dixon Branch—*stream* ... OK-5
Dixon Branch—*stream* ... SC-3
Dixon Branch—*stream* (2) ... TN-4
Dixon Branch—*stream* (2) ... TX-5
Dixon Branch—*stream* (2) ... VA-3
Dixon Branch—*stream* ... WV-2
Dixon Branch Ch—*church* ... GA-3
Dixon Branch Sch—*school* ... KY-4
Dixon Bridge—*bridge* ... AL-4
Dixon Camp—*locale* ... AZ-5
Dixon Canal—*canal* ... CO-8
*Dixon Canyon* ... CO-8
Dixon Canyon—*valley* (2) ... CA-9
Dixon Canyon Dam—*dam* ... CO-8
Dixon Canyon Lateral—*canal* ... CO-8
Dixon Cave—*cave* ... KY-4
Dixon (CCD)—*cens area* ... CA-9
Dixon (CCD)—*cens area* ... KY-4
Dixon (CCD)—*cens area* ... NM-5
Dixon Cem—*cemetery* (2) ... AL-4
Dixon Cem—*cemetery* (3) ... AR-4
Dixon Cem—*cemetery* (5) ... GA-3
Dixon Cem—*cemetery* (2) ... IL-6
Dixon Cem—*cemetery* ... IN-6
Dixon Cem—*cemetery* (8) ... KY-4
Dixon Cem—*cemetery* (4) ... MS-4
Dixon Cem—*cemetery* (4) ... MO-7
Dixon Cem—*cemetery* ... MT-8
Dixon Cem—*cemetery* ... NY-2
Dixon Cem—*cemetery* ... NC-3
Dixon Cem—*cemetery* (2) ... OH-6
Dixon Cem—*cemetery* ... PA-2
Dixon Cem—*cemetery* (3) ... SD-7
Dixon Cem—*cemetery* (4) ... TN-4
Dixon Cem—*cemetery* (2) ... TX-5
Dixon Cem—*cemetery* (2) ... WV-2
Dixon Cemeteries—*cemetery* ... NM-5
Dixon Cem (reduced usage)—*cemetery* ... TX-5
Dixon Ch—*church* ... GA-3
Dixon Ch—*church* ... NC-3
Dixon Ch—*church* ... TN-4
Dixon Chapel—*church* ... IN-6
Dixon Chapel—*church* ... NC-3
Dixon Chapel—*church* ... OK-5
Dixon Chapel—*church* ... TN-4
Dixon Chapel—*church* ... WV-2
Dixon Chapel Cem—*cemetery* ... OK-5
Dixon Corner—*locale* ... ME-1
Dixon Corner—*locale* ... PA-2
**Dixon Corner**—*pop pl* ... AL-4
Dixon Corners—*locale* ... NY-2
Dixon Corrals—*locale* ... ID-8
Dixon Cove—*bay* ... CO-8
Dixon Cove—*valley* ... TN-4
Dixon Cow Camp—*locale* ... ID-8
*Dixon Creek* ... IL-6
*Dixon Creek* ... TX-5
Dixon Creek—*stream* (2) ... AL-4
Dixon Creek—*stream* ... AK-9
Dixon Creek—*stream* (2) ... CA-9
Dixon Creek—*stream* ... CO-8
Dixon Creek—*stream* ... FL-3
Dixon Creek—*stream* ... GA-3
Dixon Creek—*stream* (2) ... IN-6
Dixon Creek—*stream* ... KS-7
Dixon Creek—*stream* ... MD-2
Dixon Creek—*stream* ... MN-6
Dixon Creek—*stream* (2) ... MS-4
Dixon Creek—*stream* (2) ... MT-8
Dixon Creek—*stream* (5) ... NC-3
Dixon Creek—*stream* (5) ... OR-9
Dixon Creek—*stream* (2) ... TN-4
Dixon Creek—*stream* (6) ... TX-5
Dixon Creek—*stream* (2) ... VA-3
Dixon Creek—*stream* ... WA-9
Dixon Creek Ch—*church* ... TN-4
Dixon Creek Ch—*church* ... TX-5
Dixon Creek Point—*cape* ... NC-3
Dixon Crossroads—*locale* ... GA-3
**Dixon Crossroads**—*pop pl* ... SC-3
Dixon Dam—*dam* ... SD-7
*Dixon Depot* ... AL-4
*Dixon Ditch* ... IN-6
Dixon Ditch—*canal* (3) ... IN-6
Dixon Drain—*stream* ... MI-6
Dixon Draw—*valley* (2) ... WY-8
Dixon (Election Precinct)—*fmr MCD* ... IL-6
Dixon Elem Sch—*school* ... NC-3
Dixon Entrance—*channel* ... AK-9
Dixon Flat—*flat* (2) ... CA-9
Dixon Ford (historical)—*locale* ... NC-3
Dixon Forestry Center—*locale* ... AL-4
Dixon Gap—*gap* ... NC-3
Dixon Glacier—*glacier* ... AK-9
Dixon Glacier—*glacier* ... MT-8
Dixon Grove Cem—*cemetery* ... GA-3
Dixon Grove Ch—*church* (3) ... GA-3
Dixon Gulch—*valley* ... MT-8
Dixon Hall Apartments—*hist pl* ... OH-6
Dixon Harbor—*bay* ... AK-9
**Dixon Hill**—*pop pl* ... MD-2
Dixon Hill—*summit* (2) ... CA-9
Dixon Hill—*summit* ... NY-2
Dixon Hill—*summit* ... OH-6
Dixon Hill—*summit* ... VA-3
Dixon Hills—*ridge* ... VA-3
Dixon (historical)—*locale* ... KS-7
**Dixon (historical)**—*pop pl* ... TN-4
Dixon Hollow—*valley* ... AR-4
Dixon Hollow—*valley* ... IL-6
Dixon Hollow—*valley* ... MS-4
Dixon Hollow—*valley* (2) ... MO-7
Dixon Hollow—*valley* ... OK-5
Dixon Hollow—*valley* ... PA-2
Dixon Hollow—*valley* (2) ... TN-4
*Dixon-Hopewell Cemetery* ... TX-5
Dixon Hopewell Ch—*church* ... TX-5
Dixon House—*hist pl* ... NY-2
Dixon HS—*school* ... TX-5
Dixon HS (historical)—*school* ... MS-4
Dixon Indian Chapel—*church* ... MT-8
*Dixon Island* ... NY-2
Dixon Island—*island* ... PA-2
Dixon Island—*island* ... TN-4
Dixon Island—*island* ... WA-9
Dixon-Israel Township Sch—*school* ... OH-6
Dixon JHS—*school* ... UT-8
Dixon Knob—*summit* ... KY-4
*Dixon Lake* ... MI-6
*Dixon Lake* ... SC-3

Doc Rogers Trail—trail ... TN-4
Docs Cove—bay ... IA-7
Docs Draw—valley ... ND-7
Docs Lake—lake ... IN-6
Docs Lake—lake ... ND-7
Docs Lake—lake ... UT-8
Doc Smith Island—island ... TN-4
Doc Smith Run—stream ... PA-2
Doc Spangle Mine—mine ... TN-4
Docs Pass—gap ... NV-8
Docs Pass Canyon—valley ... NV-8
Docs Pass Canyon—valley ... UT-8
Docs Point—cape ... MD-2
Docs Spring—spring ... NV-8
Docs Spring Campground—locale ... CA-9
Doc Stewart Ridge—ridge ... NC-3
Docs Valley—valley ... UT-8
Docteur, Joseph, House—hist pl ... NY-2
Doc Tharpe Bay—swamp ... FL-3
Doctor Arroyo—stream ... NM-5
Doctor A T Goodwin Lake Dam—dam ... MS-4
Doctor Bay—swamp ... SC-3
Doctor Beaver Creek—stream ... AK-9
Doctor Bob Donald Catfish Ponds Dam—dam ... MS-4
Doctor Branch—stream ... NC-3
Doctor Branch—stream ... SC-3
Doctor Branch—stream ... VA-3
Doctor Brook—stream ... ME-1
Doctor Canyon—valley ... UT-8
Doctor Carlson Memorial Park—park ... CA-9
Doctor Cash Sch—school ... TX-5
Doctor Chandler Memorial Park—park ... AZ-5
Doctor Creek—stream ... MT-8
Doctor Creek—stream ... NJ-2
Doctor Creek—stream ... NM-5
Doctor Creek—stream ... WA-9
Doctor Creek Campground—locale ... UT-8
Doctor Creek Group Area—locale ... UT-8
**Doctor Creek Recreation Residences**—pop pl ... UT-8
Doctor David Douglas Historical Monument (Kaluakauka)—other ... HI-9
Doctor David Holmes Dam—dam ... MS-4
Doctor David Wilson Lake Dam—dam ... MS-4
Doctor David W Kistler Elem Sch—school ... PA-2
Doctor Dawson Pond Dam—dam ... MS-4
Doctor D. E. Jackson Memorial Hosp—hospital ... AL-4
Doctor Ditch—canal ... IN-6
Doctor Ditch—canal ... MT-8
Doctor Ditch—canal ... WY-8
Doctor E E Bramlitt Pond Dam—dam ... MS-4
Doctor Francis Museum—building ... AL-4
Doctor Graysons Mill (historical)—locale ... AL-4
Doctor Gulch—valley ... CO-8
Doctor Harris Spring Branch—stream ... AL-4
**Doctor Heights (subdivision)**—pop pl ... PA-2
Doctor Hill—summit ... NY-2
Doctor Hole—lake ... SC-3
Doctor Hollingsworth Dam—dam ... AL-4
Doctor Hollow—valley ... TN-4
Doctor Island—island ... AK-9
Doctor James Bruce Dam—dam ... AL-4
Doctor James Bruce Number 2 Dam—dam ... AL-4
Doctor James Bruce Number 3 Dam—dam ... AL-4
Doctor James Bruce Number 4 Dam—dam ... AL-4
Doctor J Cash King Lake Dam—dam ... MS-4
Doctor Jenkins Lake—reservoir ... AL-4
Doctor J H Gammon Bridge—bridge ... TN-4
Doctor Josephus Hall House—park ... NC-3
Doctor Kellys Private Cem—cemetery ... AL-4
Doctor Knob—summit ... AL-4
Doctor Knok Pit—cave ... AL-4
Doctor Laird Lake Dam—dam ... MS-4
Doctor Lake—lake ... AL-4
Doctor Lake—lake ... MN-6
Doctor Lake—lake ... MS-4
Doctor Lake—lake ... MT-8
Doctor Lake—lake ... WI-6
Doctor Lewis Pond—lake ... RI-1
Doctor L Rush Lake Dam—dam ... MS-4
Doctor Mathews Pond Dam—dam ... MS-4
Doctor Max McCord Junior Lake—reservoir ... AL-4
Doctor Max McCord Junior Lake Dam—dam ... AL-4
Doctor McElraths Mill (historical)—locale ... AL-4
Doctor Mennies Sch—school ... NJ-2
Doctor Mesa—summit ... CO-8
Doctor Mine—mine ... CO-8
Doctor Moore Lake Dam—dam ... MS-4
Doctor Morrison Ditch—canal ... CO-8
Doctor Park—flat ... CO-8
Doctor Pattons Lake Dam—dam ... AL-4
Doctor Pattons Lower Lake—reservoir ... AL-4
Doctor Pattons Lower Lake Dam—dam ... AL-4
Doctor Pattons Upper Lake—reservoir ... AL-4
Doctor Phillips—locale ... FL-3
Doctor Phillips Cem—cemetery (2) ... FL-3
Doctor Phillips Elem Sch—school ... FL-3
Doctor Point—cape ... AK-9
Doctor Point—cape ... NC-3
Doctor Point—cape (2) ... VA-3
Doctor Pond—lake ... ME-1
Doctor Pond—swamp ... SC-3
Doctor Pond Sch—school ... SC-3
Doctor Ranier Lake—reservoir ... AL-4
Doctor Rankins Place—locale ... OR-9
Doctor Richard Clark Pond Dam—dam ... MS-4
Doctor Rock—pillar ... CA-9
Doctors Arm—bay ... FL-3
Doctor Savages Hosp (historical)—hospital ... AL-4
Doctors Bay ... FL-3
Doctors Bayou ... LA-4
Doctors' Bldg—hist pl ... OH-6
Doctor's Bldg—hist pl ... TN-4
Doctor's Branch ... VA-3
Doctors Branch—stream ... AL-4
Doctors Branch—stream ... KY-4
Doctors Branch—stream ... SC-3
Doctors Brook ... NJ-2
Doctors Brook—stream ... NY-2
Doctor Sch—school ... IL-6
Doctors Creek ... GA-3
Doctors Creek ... NJ-2
Doctors Creek—stream ... AR-4
Doctors Creek—stream ... CA-9
Doctors Creek—stream ... GA-3
Doctors Creek—stream ... MD-2
Doctors Creek—stream ... NJ-2
Doctors Creek—stream ... NC-3
Doctors Creek—stream ... SC-3
Doctors Creek—stream ... TX-5
Doctors Creek—stream (3) ... VA-3
Doctors Creek—stream ... WV-2
Doctors Creek Ch—church ... SC-3
Doctors Creek Sch—school ... WV-2
**Doctors Crossing**—pop pl ... NY-2
Doctors Fork ... AR-4
Doctors Fork—stream ... AR-4
Doctors Fork—stream ... KY-4
Doctors Fork Ch—church ... KY-4
Doctors General Hosp—hospital ... FL-3
Doctors Hammock—island ... FL-3
Doctors Hill—summit ... MA-1
**Doctors (historical)**—pop pl ... TN-4
Doctors Hosp—hospital ... AL-4
Doctors Hosp—hospital ... AR-4
Doctors Hosp—hospital (3) ... CA-9
Doctors Hosp—hospital (2) ... FL-3
Doctors Hosp—hospital ... IL-6
Doctors Hosp—hospital ... LA-4
Doctors Hosp—hospital ... MD-2
Doctors Hosp—hospital ... MA-1
Doctors Hosp—hospital ... MI-6
Doctors Hosp—hospital ... MS-4
Doctors Hosp—hospital ... MO-7
Doctors Hosp—hospital ... NE-7
Doctors Hosp—hospital (2) ... NY-2
Doctors Hosp—hospital (2) ... OH-6
Doctors Hosp—hospital ... PA-2
Doctors Hosp—hospital (2) ... TN-4
Doctors Hosp—hospital ... TX-5
Doctors Hosp (historical)—hospital ... TN-4
Doctors Hospital ... AZ-5
Doctors Hosp of Hollywood—hospital ... FL-3
Doctors Hosp of Lake Worth—hospital ... FL-3
Doctors Hosp of Sarasota—hospital ... FL-3
Doctors Inlet—channel ... FL-3
**Doctors Inlet**—pop pl ... FL-3
Doctors Inlet Elem Sch—school ... FL-3
Doctors Island—cape ... MA-1
Doctors Island—island ... ME-1
Doctors Island—island ... NY-2
Doctors Islands ... FL-3
Doctors Lake—lake ... FL-3
Doctors Lake—reservoir ... FL-3
**Doctor's Lake Estates**—pop pl ... FL-3
Doctor Slaughter Lake Dam—dam ... MS-4
Doctor SMcCorkle Sch (historical)—school ... NC-3
Doctors Memorial Hosp—hospital ... FL-3
Doctor Smith Flat—flat ... CA-9
Doctor's Office—hist pl ... AL-4
Doctors Park—building ... NC-3
Doctors Park—park ... WI-6
Doctors Pass—channel ... FL-3
Doctors Point—cape ... FL-3
Doctors Point—cape ... MA-1
Doctors Point—cape ... MI-6
Doctors Point—cape ... NJ-2
Doctors Pond ... MA-1
Doctors Pond—lake ... MA-1
Doctors Pond—lake ... NY-2
Doctors Prairie—flat ... FL-3
Doctor Spring—spring ... AZ-5
Doctor Spring—spring ... NM-5
Doctors Ridge—ridge ... TN-4
Doctors Ridge—ridge ... VA-3
Doctors Ridge Trail—trail ... TN-4
Doctors' Row Hist Dist—hist pl ... KY-4
Doctors Run—stream ... VA-3
Doctor Steven H Everitt (historical monument)—park ... TX-5
Doctors Well—well ... NM-5
Doctortown—locale ... GA-3
Doctor Vincent Best Dam—dam ... AL-4
Doctor Vincent Best Pond—reservoir ... AL-4
Doctor Walter Nicholas Dam—dam ... AL-4
Doctor Walter Nicholas Lake—reservoir ... AL-4
Doctor Watkins Infirmary ... AL-4
Doctor W G Munn Lake Dam—dam ... MS-4
Doctor William S Anderson House—building ... NC-3
Doctor Wittmeier Lake Number Two Dam—dam ... AL-4
Doctor W J Creel Elem Sch—school ... FL-3
Doctor W M Pounds Lake Dam—dam ... MS-4
Doctor W T Griggs Elem Sch—school ... NC-3
Doc Valley Overlook—locale ... UT-8
Doc Watkins Windmill—locale ... CO-8
Doc Watson Spring—spring ... UT-8
Doc Wood Lake—lake ... IA-7
Doc Young Pond—reservoir ... TX-5
Dod, John, House and Tavern—hist pl ... NJ-2
**Dodamead (Buckingham)**—pop pl ... VA-3
Dodd—locale ... CO-8
Dodd—locale ... MO-7
Dodd—locale ... TX-5
**Dodd**—pop pl ... IN-6
Dodd, A. B. C., House—hist pl ... IA-7
Dodd Branch—stream ... AL-4
Dodd Branch—stream ... AR-4
Dodd Branch—stream (3) ... TN-4
Dodd Branch—stream ... TX-5
Dodd Canyon—valley ... WA-9
Dodd Cem—cemetery ... AL-4
Dodd Cem—cemetery ... GA-3
Dodd Cem—cemetery ... IL-6
Dodd Cem—cemetery ... IN-6
Dodd Cem—cemetery ... MS-4
Dodd Cem—cemetery ... MO-7
Dodd Cem—cemetery (3) ... TN-4
Dodd Cem—cemetery ... TX-5
Dodd Cem—cemetery ... VA-3
Dodd City—locale ... AR-4
**Dodd City**—pop pl ... TX-5
Dodd City (CCD)—cens area ... TX-5
Dodd City Cem—cemetery ... AR-4
Dodd City Cem—cemetery ... TX-5
**Dodd City (RR name Dodds)**—pop pl ... TX-5
Dodd City (Township of)—fmr MCD ... AR-4
Dodd College President's Home—hist pl ... LA-4
Dodd Creek ... ID-8
Dodd Creek ... IA-7
Dodd Creek—stream ... AR-4
Dodd Creek—stream ... GA-3
Dodd Creek—stream ... MS-4
Dodd Creek—stream ... TN-4
Dodd Creek—stream ... VA-3
Dodd Creek—stream ... WA-9
Dodd Ditch—canal ... CO-8
Dodd Ditch—canal ... UT-8
Dodd Drift Mine (underground)—mine ... AL-4
Doddehl Spring—spring ... OK-5
Dodder Cem—cemetery ... KS-7
Dodd Ford—locale ... AL-4
**Dodd Hill**—pop pl ... SC-3
Dodd Hill—summit ... OH-6
Dodd-Hinsdale House—hist pl ... NC-3
Dodd Hollow—valley ... KY-4
Dodd Hollow—valley (4) ... TN-4
Dodd Homestead—hist pl ... DE-2
Doddies Creek—stream ... SC-3
Dodd Island—island ... PA-2
Dodd JHS—school ... CT-1
Dodd JHS—school ... NY-2
Dodd Lake ... TX-5
Dodd Lake—lake ... TX-5
Dodd Marsh—swamp ... DE-2
Dodd Memorial Cem—cemetery ... AL-4
Dodd Mine—mine ... TN-4
Dodd Mtn—summit (2) ... AR-4
Dodd Ponds—lake ... OR-9
Dodd Ranch—locale ... WY-8
**Doddridge**—pop pl ... AR-4
Dodd Ridge—ridge ... AR-4
Doddridge Ch—church ... AR-4
Doddridge Chapel—church ... IN-6
**Doddridge (County)**—pop pl ... WV-2
Doddridge County Courthouse—hist pl ... WV-2
Dodd Rsvr—reservoir ... CO-8
Dodds—locale ... OH-6
**Dodds**—pop pl ... MS-4
**Dodds**—pop pl (2) ... MO-7
**Dodds Addition (subdivision)**—pop pl ... DE-2
Dodds And Allen Ditch—canal ... WY-8
Dodds Bay—bay ... AK-9
Dodds Branch—stream ... AL-4
Dodds Branch—stream ... IL-6
Dodds Branch—stream ... MS-4
**Dodds Bridge**—pop pl (2) ... IN-6
Dodds Cem—cemetery ... MS-4
Dodds Cem—cemetery ... MO-7
Dodds Cem—cemetery ... NY-2
Dodds Cem—cemetery ... TN-4
Dodd Sch—school ... GA-3
Dodd Sch—school ... SC-3
Dodd Sch—school ... WI-6
Dodd Sch (historical)—school ... TN-4
Dodds Corner—locale ... VA-3
Dodds Cove—valley ... AL-4
Dodds Creek ... GA-3
Dodds Creek ... OR-9
Dodds Creek ... TX-5
Dodds Creek—stream ... IL-6
Dodds Creek—stream ... KS-7
Dodds Creek—stream ... KY-4
Dodds Creek—stream ... NY-2
Dodds Creek—stream ... OR-9
Dodds Creek—stream ... TX-5
Dodds Ferry ... MS-4
Dodds Gap—gap ... AL-4
Dodds Hollow—valley ... MO-7
Dodds Hollow—valley ... OH-6
Dodds Hollow—valley ... OR-9
Dodds Hollow—valley ... UT-8
Dodds Hollow Spring—spring ... UT-8
Dodds Island—area ... MO-7
Dodds Lake—reservoir ... TX-5
Dodds Mill (historical)—locale ... TN-4
Dodds Millpond—reservoir ... NC-3
Dodds Mtn—summit ... MA-1
Dodds Pit—cave ... AL-4
Dodd Spring—spring ... TN-4
Dodd Spring Sch (historical)—school ... AL-4
Dodds Ranch—locale ... WY-8
Dodds Ridge—ridge ... PA-2
Dodds (RR name for Dodd City)—other ... TX-5
Dodds Sch—school (2) ... IL-6
Dodds Sch—school ... SD-7
Dodds School ... TN-4
Dodds Sink Cave—cave ... AL-4
Dodds Spring—spring ... OR-9
Dodds Store ... VA-3
Dodds Store—locale ... VA-3
Dodds Town Hall—building ... ND-7
**Dodds Township**—pop pl ... ND-7
**Dodds (Township of)**—pop pl ... IL-6
Dodd Street Sch—school ... GA-3
Doddsville ... IN-6
Doddsville—locale ... IL-6
Doddsville—locale ... TN-4
**Doddsville**—pop pl ... MS-4
Doddsville Cem—cemetery ... IL-6
Doddsville Industrial Institute (historical)—school ... MS-4
Dodd Tank ... AZ-5
Doddtown ... NJ-2
Doddtown—locale ... WV-2
Doddtown—uninc pl ... NJ-2
**Doddville (Dodd Hill)**—pop pl ... SC-3
**Doddy**—pop pl ... KY-4
Doddy Branch—stream ... KY-4
Doddy Ch—church ... KY-4
Doddy Creek—stream ... TN-4
Doddy Sch—school ... KY-4
Dode Lake—lake ... MN-6
Dodendorf Mountian ... PA-2
Doden Reef—bar ... MI-6
Dodes Creek—stream ... LA-4
Dodes Creek—stream ... OR-9
Dodes Island—island ... WI-6
Dodey Creek—stream ... AL-4
Dodge—locale ... IA-7
Dodge—locale ... NV-8
Dodge—locale ... NY-2
Dodge—locale ... OK-5
Dodge—locale ... WA-9
**Dodge**—pop pl ... MA-1
**Dodge**—pop pl ... NE-7
**Dodge**—pop pl ... ND-7
**Dodge**—pop pl ... OR-9
**Dodge**—pop pl ... TX-5
**Dodge**—pop pl ... WI-6
Dodge, Augustus Caesar, House—hist pl ... IA-7
Dodge, Edward, House—hist pl ... MA-1
Dodge, Edward, House—hist pl ... WI-6
Dodge, Grenville M., House—hist pl ... IA-7
Dodge, Lillian Sefton, Estate—hist pl ... NY-2
Dodge, Ruth Anne, Memorial—hist pl ... IA-7
Dodge, Thomas, Homestead—hist pl ... NY-2
Dodge, William E., House—hist pl ... NY-2
Dodge Basin—basin ... ID-8
Dodge Bay—bay ... SD-7
Dodge Bldg—hist pl ... MA-1
Dodge Branch—stream ... SC-3
Dodge Branch—stream ... WI-6
Dodge Bridge—bridge ... OR-9
Dodge Brook—stream (2) ... NH-1
Dodge Brook State For—forest ... NH-1
Dodge Brothers State Park No. 2—park ... MI-6
Dodge Brothers State Park No 8—park ... MI-6
Dodge Butte—summit ... WY-8
Dodge Canyon—valley ... CA-9
Dodge Canyon—valley (2) ... OR-9
Dodge Canyon—valley (2) ... UT-8
Dodge Canyon Creek—stream ... OR-9
Dodge Cem—cemetery ... MA-1
Dodge Cem—cemetery ... OH-6
Dodge Cem—cemetery ... OR-9
Dodge Cem—cemetery ... RI-1
Dodge Cem—cemetery ... TX-5
Dodge Cem—cemetery ... VT-1
Dodge Cem—cemetery ... WI-6
**Dodge Center**—pop pl ... MN-6
Dodge Center Cem—cemetery ... IA-7
Dodge Center Ch—church ... IA-7
Dodge Center Creek—stream ... MN-6
Dodge Ch—church ... OK-5
Dodge Chapel—church ... GA-3
Dodge Chute—stream ... WI-6
Dodge City—locale ... AR-4
**Dodge City**—pop pl ... KS-7
Dodge City Community Coll—school ... KS-7
Dodge City HS—school ... KS-7
Dodge City JHS—school ... KS-7
Dodge City Municipal Airp—airport ... KS-7
Dodge City Public Library—hist pl ... KS-7
Dodge Colliery Breaker—building ... PA-2
Dodge Corner ... MA-1
Dodge Corner—locale (2) ... ME-1
**Dodge Corner**—pop pl (2) ... MA-1
Dodge Coulee—valley ... MT-8
**Dodge (County)**—pop pl ... GA-3
**Dodge (County)**—pop pl ... MN-6
**Dodge (County)**—pop pl ... WI-6
Dodge County Courthouse—hist pl ... GA-3
Dodge County Courthouse—hist pl ... WI-6
Dodge County Historical Museum—hist pl ... WI-6
Dodge Creek ... WI-6
Dodge Creek—stream ... AK-9
Dodge Creek—stream ... CA-9
Dodge Creek—stream (5) ... ID-8
Dodge Creek—stream ... IN-6
Dodge Creek—stream ... MI-6
Dodge Creek—stream ... MO-7
Dodge Creek—stream (2) ... MT-8
Dodge Creek—stream (2) ... NY-2
Dodge Creek—stream ... OR-9
Dodge Creek—stream (2) ... WY-8
Dodge Ditch—canal ... MT-8
Dodge Ditch—canal ... WY-8
Dodge Draw—valley ... SD-7
Dodge Draw Rec Area—park ... SD-7
Dodge Elem Sch Number 2—school ... KS-7
Dodge Flat—flat ... NV-8
Dodge Gap—gap ... KY-4
Dodge Gulch—valley ... CA-9
**Dodge High**—pop pl ... GA-3
Dodge Hill—summit ... CA-9
Dodge Hill—summit ... KY-4
Dodge Hill—summit ... ME-1
Dodge Hill—summit ... MA-1
Dodge Hill—summit ... NH-1
Dodge Hill—summit ... OK-5
Dodge Hill—summit ... WA-9
Dodge Hill—summit ... WY-8
Dodge Hills—range ... KY-4
Dodge (historical)—locale ... SD-7
Dodge (historical P.O.)—locale ... IA-7
**Dodge Hollow**—pop pl ... NH-1
Dodge Hollow—valley ... MO-7
Dodge Hollow—valley ... NY-2
Dodge Hollow—valley (3) ... PA-2
Dodge Hollow Run—stream ... PA-2
Dodge House—hist pl ... IN-6
Dodge Island ... CT-1
Dodge Island—island (3) ... OR-9
Dodge JHS—school ... TX-5
Dodge Lake—lake ... ID-8
Dodge Lake—lake (3) ... MI-6
Dodge Lake—lake ... WI-6
Dodge Landing—locale ... TN-4
Dodge Lookout—locale ... TX-5
Dodge Lower Cove—bay ... ME-1
Dodge Mansion—hist pl ... MI-6
Dodge Meadow—flat ... CA-9
Dodge Meadows—flat ... WY-8
Dodge Mtn—summit ... ME-1
Dodge Mtn—summit ... SC-3
Dodgen Cem—cemetery ... GA-3
Dodgen Creek—stream ... NC-3
Dodge Nevada Canal—canal ... AZ-5
Dodgen Ridge—ridge ... NC-3
Dodgens Creek—stream ... SC-3
Dodge Park—locale ... MD-2
Dodge Park—park ... IA-7
Dodge Park—park ... MA-1
Dodge Park—park ... NE-7
Dodge Park—park ... OR-9
Dodge Peak—summit ... ID-8
Dodge Pockets—basin ... NV-8
Dodge Point ... ME-1
Dodge Point—cape (3) ... ME-1
Dodge Point—cape ... MI-6
Dodge Point—cliff ... UT-8
Dodge Point—cliff ... WA-9
Dodge Point Sch—school ... MO-7
Dodge Pond—lake ... CT-1
Dodge Pond—lake (2) ... ME-1
Dodge Pond—lake ... MA-1
Dodge Pond—lake (3) ... NH-1
Dodge Pond—lake (3) ... NY-2
Dodge Ponds—lake ... NH-1
Dodge Post Office (historical)—building ... TN-4
Dodge Ranch—locale ... CO-8
Dodge Ranch—locale ... MT-8
Dodge Ranch—locale ... WY-8
Dodge Ranch HQ—locale ... CO-8
Dodger Hole—lake ... MA-1
Dodge Ridge—ridge ... CA-9
Dodge Rim—cliff ... WY-8
Dodge Rock—rock ... MA-1
Dodge Rock Creek—stream ... TX-5
Dodger Point—summit ... WA-9
Dodger Stadium—other ... CA-9
Dodge Rsvr—reservoir ... CA-9
Dodge Run—stream ... OH-6
Dodge Run—stream (2) ... PA-2
Dodge Sch—school ... IL-6
Dodge Sch—school (2) ... MI-6
Dodge Sch—school ... NE-7
Dodge Sch—school ... NY-2
Dodge Sch—school ... SD-7
Dodge School (Abandoned)—locale ... WI-6
**Dodges Corners**—pop pl ... WI-6
Dodges Corner Sch—school ... WI-6
Dodges Cove ... AL-4
Dodges Creek—stream ... IA-7
Dodges Island—island ... CT-1
Dodge Site—hist pl ... OH-6
Dodges Lake Landing—locale ... GA-3
Dodge Slough—stream ... OR-9
Dodges Point ... ME-1
Dodges Point—cape ... IA-7
Dodges Point—cape ... ME-1
Dodge Spring—spring ... CA-9
Dodge Spring—spring ... UT-8
Dodge Spring—spring ... WA-9
Dodge Summit—locale ... MT-8
Dodge Tank—reservoir ... AZ-5
Dodge Tank Wash—stream ... AZ-5
**Dodge Tavern**—pop pl ... NH-1
Dodgeton Creek—stream ... CO-8
Dodgetown—locale ... NC-3
**Dodge (Town of)**—pop pl ... WI-6
Dodge Township—fmr MCD (4) ... IA-7
**Dodge Township**—pop pl ... KS-7
Dodge Upper Cove—bay ... ME-1
Dodge Valley—valley ... CA-9
Dodge Valley—valley ... WA-9
**Dodgeville**—pop pl ... IA-7
**Dodgeville**—pop pl ... MA-1
**Dodgeville**—pop pl ... MI-6
**Dodgeville**—pop pl ... OH-6
**Dodgeville**—pop pl ... WI-6
Dodgeville Cem—cemetery ... OH-6
Dodgeville Pond—reservoir ... MA-1
Dodgeville Pond Dam—dam ... MA-1
**Dodgeville (Town of)**—pop pl ... WI-6
Dodge Vocational HS—school ... NY-2
Dodge Warehouses—building ... DC-2
Dodge Wash—stream ... AZ-5
Dodge Well—well ... NV-8
Dodge Windmill—locale ... ND-7
Dodging Hill—summit ... NC-3
**Dodgingtown**—pop pl ... CT-1
Dodgson Creek ... MT-8
Dodgson Creek—stream ... MT-8
Dodier, Arroyo—valley ... TX-5
Dodkin Cem—cemetery ... MO-7
Dodling Hill—summit ... ME-1
Dodlyt—locale ... VA-3
Dodo ... TX-5
Dodo—island ... MP-9
Dodo—locale ... OH-6
Dodoburgh ... TN-4
**Dodoburg (historical)**—pop pl ... TN-4
Dodoburgh Post Office (historical)—building ... TN-4
Dodo Creek—stream ... AK-9
Dodo Creek—stream ... ID-8
Dodo Durchfahrt ... MP-9
Dodo Einfahrt ... MP-9
Dodo Lake—lake ... MN-6
**Dodon**—pop pl ... MD-2
Dodo Passage—channel ... MP-9
Dodo Rsvr—reservoir ... CO-8
Dodo Spring—spring ... CO-8
Dodrill—locale ... WV-2
Dodrill Creek—stream ... IN-6
Dods Creek ... OR-9
Dods Creek ... TX-5
Dodsen Creek—stream ... AL-4
Dodson ... MO-7
Dodson—locale ... AR-4
Dodson—locale ... OR-9
Dodson—locale ... TN-4
Dodson—locale ... VA-3
**Dodson**—pop pl ... LA-4
**Dodson**—pop pl ... MO-7
**Dodson**—pop pl ... MT-8
**Dodson**—pop pl ... OH-6
**Dodson**—pop pl ... TN-4
**Dodson**—pop pl ... TX-5
Dodson Ave Community Health Center—hospital ... TN-4
Dodson Branch—locale ... TN-4
Dodson Branch—stream ... AL-4
Dodson Branch—stream ... IN-6
Dodson Branch—stream ... MS-4
Dodson Branch—stream ... TN-4
Dodson Branch—stream ... VA-3
Dodson Branch—stream ... WV-2
Dodson Branch Ch—church ... TN-4
Dodson Branch Sch—school ... TN-4
Dodson Butte—summit ... OR-9
Dodson Canyon—valley ... NM-5
Dodson Cave—cave ... TN-4
Dodson Cem—cemetery (2) ... AR-4
Dodson Cem—cemetery ... IL-6
Dodson Cem—cemetery ... IN-6
Dodson Cem—cemetery (2) ... IA-7
Dodson Cem—cemetery (5) ... KY-4
Dodson Cem—cemetery ... MN-6
Dodson Cem—cemetery ... MS-4
Dodson Cem—cemetery (4) ... MO-7
Dodson Cem—cemetery ... PA-2
Dodson Cem—cemetery (7) ... TN-4
Dodson Cem—cemetery (2) ... TX-5
Dodson Cem—cemetery ... VA-3
Dodson Cemeteries—cemetery ... TN-4
Dodson Chapel—church ... TN-4
Dodson Chapel Cem—cemetery ... TN-4
Dodson Corner—locale ... VA-3
Dodson Corners—locale ... VA-3
Dodson Cove—valley ... TN-4
Dodson Creek ... WA-9
Dodson Creek—stream (3) ... AR-4
Dodson Creek—stream ... MT-8
Dodson Creek—stream ... NC-3
Dodson Creek—stream ... OH-6
Dodson Creek—stream ... OR-9
Dodson Creek—stream (2) ... TN-4
Dodson Creek Ch—church (2) ... TN-4
Dodson Dam—dam ... MT-8
**Dodson (Dodsonville)**—pop pl ... TX-5
Dodson Elementary School ... PA-2
Dodson Estates—uninc pl ... TN-4
Dodson Fork—stream ... OR-9
Dodson Fork—stream ... WV-2
Dodson Gap—gap ... TN-4
Dodson Hollow—valley ... IN-6
Dodson Hollow—valley (2) ... KY-4
Dodson Hollow—valley (2) ... TN-4
Dodson Hollow—valley ... WI-6
Dodson House—hist pl ... TN-4
Dodson JHS—school ... CA-9
**Dodson Junction**—pop pl ... WV-2
Dodson Lake—lake ... AR-4
Dodson Lake—lake ... TX-5
Dodson Lake—reservoir ... NC-3
Dodson Lake Dam—dam ... MS-4
Dodson Lake Dam—dam ... NC-3
Dodson Lake Park—park ... TX-5
Dodson Landing (historical)—locale ... TN-4
Dodson Memorial Presbyterian Ch—church ... AL-4
Dodson Mine (underground)—mine ... TN-4
Dodson Mountain ... OR-9
Dodson Mtn—summit ... AR-4
Dodson Mtn—summit ... TN-4
Dodson North Canal—canal ... MT-8
Dodson Pass—gap ... ID-8
Dodson Peak ... AZ-5
Dodson Point—cape ... MD-2
Dodson Post Office (historical)—building ... TN-4
Dodson Prairie Ch—church ... TX-5
Dodson Prairie Community Hall—locale ... TX-5
Dodson Pump Canal—canal ... MT-8
Dodson Run—stream ... WV-2
**Dodsons**—pop pl ... TN-4
Dodsons Bend (historical)—bend ... SD-7
Dodson Sch—school ... PA-2
Dodson Sch—school ... SC-3
Dodson Sch—school ... TN-4
Dodson Sch—school ... TX-5
**Dodsons Corner**—pop pl ... AR-4
**Dodsons Crossroads**—pop pl ... NC-3
Dodson Siding—locale ... TN-4
Dodsons Lake—reservoir ... NC-3
Dodson Slough—stream ... OR-9
Dodson South Canal—canal ... MT-8
Dodson Spring—spring (2) ... TN-4
Dodson Spring—spring ... TX-5
Dodson Street Sch—school ... LA-4
**Dodson (Township of)**—pop pl ... OH-6
Dodson Trail—trail ... TX-5
Dodsonville—other ... TX-5
**Dodsonville**—pop pl ... OH-6
Dodsonville (historical)—locale ... AL-4
Dodsonville Sch—school ... IL-6
Dodson Wash—stream (2) ... AZ-5
Dods Ridge ... GA-3
Dodsworth Spring—spring ... NC-3
Dodwell Rixon Pass—gap ... WA-9
Dody Branch—stream ... TX-5
Dody Brook—stream ... WI-6
Dody Spring ... SD-7
Doe, M. E., House—hist pl ... MT-8
Doebay ... WA-9
Doe Bay—bay ... WA-9
Doe Bay—locale ... WA-9
**Doebay**—pop pl ... WA-9
Doe Bay—swamp ... SC-3
Doe Bay General Store and Post Office—hist pl ... WA-9
Doe Bay Mountain ... WA-9
Doebay Village ... WA-9
Doebler Gap ... PA-2
Doeblin Sch—school ... MO-7
Doe Branch ... AL-4
Doe Branch—stream ... AL-4
Doe Branch—stream (2) ... FL-3
Doe Branch—stream (2) ... GA-3
Doe Branch—stream (3) ... KY-4
Doe Branch—stream (2) ... LA-4
Doe Branch—stream (3) ... NC-3
Doe Branch—stream ... TN-4
Doe Branch—stream (2) ... TX-5
Doe Branch—stream (2) ... VA-3
Doe Bridge Branch ... DE-2
DOE Bridge over Laramie River—hist pl ... WY-8
Doe Brook—stream ... IA-7
Doe Brook—stream ... ME-1
Doe Brook—stream ... NY-2
Doe Butte—summit ... OR-9
Doe Camp—locale ... OR-9
Doe Canyon—valley (3) ... CA-9
Doe Canyon—valley (2) ... CO-8
Doe Canyon—valley (2) ... NV-8
Doe Canyon—valley ... OR-9
Doe Canyon—valley (2) ... UT-8
Doe Cem—cemetery (2) ... NH-1
Doecher Cem—cemetery ... MO-7
Doe Creek ... AL-4
Doe Creek ... ID-8
Doe Creek ... OR-9
Doe Creek ... TN-4
Doe Creek ... WY-8
Doe Creek—bay ... NC-3
**Doe Creek**—pop pl ... KY-4
**Doe Creek**—pop pl ... NC-3
Doe Creek—stream (2) ... CA-9
Doe Creek—stream (2) ... CO-8
Doe Creek—stream (10) ... ID-8
Doe Creek—stream (2) ... IN-6
Doe Creek—stream ... IA-7
Doe Creek—stream ... KS-7
Doe Creek—stream ... KY-4
Doe Creek—stream (2) ... MI-6
Doe Creek—stream ... MO-7
Doe Creek—stream (3) ... MT-8
Doe Creek—stream (2) ... NC-3
Doe Creek—stream (4) ... OK-5

Doe Creek—stream (10) OR-9
Doe Creek—stream (5) TN-4
Doe Creek—stream (3) TX-5
Doe Creek—stream (2) VA-3
Doe Creek—stream (4) WA-9
Doe Creek Cem—cemetery IN-6
Doe Creek Ch—church TN-4
Doe Creek Lake—lake TN-4
Doe Creek Lake—reservoir TN-4
Doe Creek Lake Dam—dam TN-4
Doe Creek Sch—school KY-4
Doe Creek Sch (historical)—school TN-4
Doedyns Sch—school TX-5
Doe Eddy—bay GA-3
Doe Elem Sch—school TN-4
Doeface Branch—stream VA-3
Doe Flat UT-8
Doe Flat—flat (5) CA-9
Doe Flat—flat UT-8
Doefoot Mtn—summit VA-3
Doe Fork—stream NC-3
Doe Gap—gap MO-7
Doe Gap—gap OR-9
Doeg Island VA-3
Doe Gulch—valley (3) CA-9
Doe Gulch—valley CO-8
Doe Gulch—valley OR-9
Doe Gully—locale WV-2
Doe Hall Creek—stream SC-3
Doehead Bay—swamp NC-3
Doehead Mtn—summit OR-9
Doe Head Swamp—swamp FL-3
Doe Hill OR-9
Doe Hill—locale VA-3
Doe Hill—summit ME-1
Doe Hill—summit VA-3
Doe Hill Mtn—summit NC-3
Doe Hole—basin UT-8
Doe Hollow—valley MO-7
Doe Hollow—valley (2) OR-9
Doe Hollow—valley TN-4
Doe Island—island ME-1
Doe Island—island MN-6
Doe Island—island (2) OR-9
Doe Island—island WA-9
Doe Island Marine State Park—park WA-9
Doe Knob—summit (2) NC-3
Doe Knob—summit TN-4
Doe Knoll—summit UT-8
Doe Lake—lake AK-9
Doe Lake—lake (3) CA-9
Doe Lake—lake (2) FL-3
Doe Lake—lake GA-3
Doe Lake—lake (2) ID-8
Doe Lake—lake LA-4
Doe Lake—lake (2) MI-6
Doe Lake—lake (5) MN-6
Doe Lake—lake WA-9
Doe Lake—lake WI-6
Doe Lake—reservoir CA-9
Doe Lake Camp—locale FL-3
Doe Lake Creek—stream ID-8
Doelger Ranch—locale CA-9
Doelick Cove—valley VA-3
Doelick Ridge—ridge WV-2
Doelick Run—stream WV-2
Doelle Lakes—lake WA-9
Doelle Valley—valley WI-6
Doe Lookout Tower TN-4
Doe Meadow—flat CA-9
Doemel Point—cape WI-6
Doe Memorial Library—hist pl CA-9
Doe Mill Ridge—ridge CA-9
Doe Mountain (ski area)—locale PA-2
Doe Mtn—summit AK-9
Doe Mtn—summit AZ-5
Doe Mtn—summit CA-9
Doe Mtn—summit (3) OR-9
Doe Mtn—summit TN-4
Doe Mtn—summit VA-3
Doe Mtn—summit WA-9
Doe Mtn Lookout Tower TN-4
Doe Mtn Mine TN-4
Doeneck Branch—stream AL-4
Doenz Place—locale CO-8
Doe Peak—summit AZ-5
Doe Peak—summit (2) CA-9
Doe Peak—summit OR-9
Doe Point—cape AK-9
Doe Point—cape NH-1
Doe Point—cape OR-9
Doe Point—cape SC-3
Doe Point—cliff ID-8
Doe Point—summit ID-8
Doe Point—summit OR-9
Doe Point Creek—channel SC-3
Doe Point Rsvr—reservoir CO-8
Doe Pond—lake (3) FL-3
Doe Pond—lake ME-1
Doe Pond—lake MA-1
Doe Pond—lake (3) NY-2
Doe Pond Ch—church SC-3
Doe Pond Creek—stream TX-5
Doe Ponds—lake TX-5
Doe Prairie—flat FL-3
Doe Reseeding Rsvr—reservoir CO-8
Doerfler Lake—lake MN-6
Doerfler Sch—school WI-6
Doerhoefer, Basil, House—hist pl KY-4
Doerhoefer, Peter C., House—hist pl KY-4
Doerhoefer-Hampton House—hist pl KY-4
Doe Ridge—ridge (2) CA-9
Doe Ridge—ridge NC-3
Doe Ridge—ridge OK-5
Doe Ridge—ridge TN-4
Doe Ridge—ridge UT-8
Doe Ridge Ch—church NC-3
Doering—locale WI-6
Doering Ditch—canal IN-6
Doe River—stream TN-4
Doe River Ch—church TN-4
Doe River Gorge—valley TN-4
Doer Mine—mine ID-8
Doernbecher, Frank Silas, House—hist pl OR-9
Doerner Creek—stream OR-9
Doe Rock—pillar CA-9
Doe Rock—summit CA-9
Doerr-Brown House—hist pl MO-7
Doerr Creek—stream MT-8
Doerr Creek—stream OR-9
Doerr Drain—canal MI-6
Doerr Lake—lake MI-6
Doerr Sch—school MI-6
Doersom Airp—airport PA-2
Doe Rsvr—reservoir (2) OR-9
Doertler Lake MN-6
Doe Run MO-7
Doe Run—locale PA-2
**Doerun**—pop pl GA-3
**Doe Run**—pop pl KY-4
**Doe Run**—pop pl MO-7
Doe Run—stream IN-6
Doe Run—stream (3) KY-4
Doe Run—stream MO-7
Doe Run—stream (8) PA-2
Doe Run—stream TX-5
Doe Run—stream VA-3
Doe Run—stream (2) WV-2
Doerun (CCD)—cens area GA-3
Doe Run Cem—cemetery MO-7
Doe Run Ch—church PA-2
Doe Run Ch—church VA-3
Doe Run Creek TX-5
Doe Run Creek—stream KY-4
Doe Run Creek—stream (2) MO-7
Doe Run Creek—stream VA-3
Doe Run Creek Hist Dist—hist pl KY-4
Doe Run Gas Storage Field—oilfield IN-6
Doe Run Gas Storage Field—oilfield KY-4
Doe Run Memorial Cem—cemetery MO-7
Doe Run Mill—hist pl KY-4
Doe Run Mill—locale KY-4
Doe Run Sch (historical)—school MO-7
Doe Run Station—locale PA-2
Doe Run Trail—trail PA-2
Doe Run Village Hist Dist—hist pl PA-2
Doerzbach, George J., House—hist pl OH-6
Does Fork—stream KY-4
Does Hammock—island VA-3
Doeskin Butte—summit OR-9
Doeskin Creek—stream OR-9
Doeskin Hill—summit MA-1
Doeskin Tank—reservoir AZ-5
Doe Slough Canal—canal LA-4
Doe Spring—spring (3) CA-9
Doe Spring—spring (2) CO-8
Doe Spring—spring NM-5
Doe Spring—spring (2) OR-9
Doe Spring Guard Station—locale OR-9
Doe Station (historical)—locale TN-4
Doestock Creek—stream AK-9
Doe Swamp—swamp NY-2
Doe Swamp—swamp OR-9
Doe Tank—reservoir (6) AZ-5
Doe Tank—reservoir NM-5
Doe Valley Ch—church TN-4
**Doe Valley Estates**—pop pl KY-4
Doe Valley Mine—mine TN-4
Doe Valley Sch (historical)—school TN-4
Doeville—locale TN-4
Doeville Post Office (historical)—building TN-4
Doeville Sch (historical)—school TN-4
Doeweel'iil—summit FM-9
Doff Branch—stream GA-3
Doff City PA-2
Dofflemyer Point—cape WA-9
Dofflemyer's Point WA-9
Dofflemyer Windmill—locale TX-5
Doga—locale OK-5
Doga Creek—stream OK-5
Dog And Bitch Islands—island MD-2
Dogan Elem Sch—school TX-5
Dogan House—building VA-3
Dogan HS—school TX-5
Dogan Sch—school (2) TX-5
Dog Area—locale UT-8
Do'gas, Okso'—summit MH-9
Do'gas, Puntan—cape MH-9
Do'gas, Saddok—stream MH-9
Dogas Point MH-9
Dog Back Mtn NC-3
Dogback Mtn—summit NC-3
Dogback Mtn—summit PA-2
Dogback Spring Branch—stream NC-3
Dog Bar MA-1
Dog Bar—bar MA-1
Dog Bar Breakwater—dam MA-1
Dog Bar Bridge—bridge CA-9
Dog Bay AK-9
Dog Bay—bay AK-9
Dog Bay—bay MT-8
Dog Bay (Carolina Bay)—swamp NC-3
Dog Bend—bend TX-5
**Dog Bluff**—pop pl SC-3
Dog Bluff Landing—locale SC-3
Dogbone Branch—stream WV-2
Dog Bone Island—island TX-5
Dog Bone Lake—flat NV-8
Dogbone Lake—lake (2) AK-9
Dog Branch DE-2
Dog Branch LA-4
Dog Branch—stream AL-4
Dog Branch—stream (4) AR-4
Dog Branch—stream FL-3
Dog Branch—stream GA-3
Dog Branch—stream (2) KY-4
Dog Branch—stream LA-4
Dog Branch—stream MS-4
Dog Branch—stream (3) MO-7
Dog Branch—stream NC-3
Dog Branch—stream OK-5
Dog Branch—stream (7) TN-4
Dog Branch—stream (4) TX-5
Dog Branch—stream (3) VA-3
Dog Branch Cem—cemetery AR-4
Dog Branch Gap—gap VA-3
Dog Branch Sch—school VA-3
Dog Brook—stream (5) ME-1
Dog Butte—summit MT-8
Dog Butte—summit SD-7
Dog Butte Creek—stream SD-7
Dog Canal—canal FL-3
Dog Canon TX-5
Dog Canyon—gap TX-5
Dog Canyon—valley AZ-5
Dog Canyon—valley (5) NM-5
Dog Canyon—valley OR-9
Dog Canyon—valley (3) TX-5
Dog Canyon Creek—stream NM-5
Dog Canyon Draw—valley NM-5
**Dog Canyon Estates**—pop pl NM-5
Dog Canyon Ranger Station—locale TX-5
Dog Canyon Tank—reservoir AZ-5
Dog Canyon Well—well NM-5
Dog Canyon Windmill—locale TX-5
Dog Channel NY-2
Dog Cliff—cliff VA-3
Dog Collar Cave—cave AL-4
**Dog Corner**—pop pl ME-1
Dog Corners—locale ME-1
Dog Coulee—valley (2) MT-8
Dog Cove—bay NH-1
Dog Cove—valley NC-3
Dog Cove—valley TN-4
Dog Creek MT-8
Dog Creek TN-4
Dog Creek TX-5
Dogcreek—locale KY-4
Dog Creek—locale OK-5
Dog Creek—stream (2) AK-9
Dog Creek—stream AR-4
Dog Creek—stream (5) CA-9
Dog Creek—stream FL-3
Dog Creek—stream (8) ID-8
Dog Creek—stream IL-6
Dog Creek—stream IN-6
Dog Creek—stream IA-7
Dog Creek—stream (5) KS-7
Dog Creek—stream (3) KY-4
Dog Creek—stream MD-2
Dog Creek—stream MN-6
Dog Creek—stream (2) MS-4
Dog Creek—stream (3) MO-7
Dog Creek—stream (16) MT-8
Dog Creek—stream NE-7
Dog Creek—stream (2) NV-8
Dog Creek—stream NM-5
Dog Creek—stream (2) NC-3
Dog Creek—stream OH-6
Dog Creek—stream (8) OK-5
Dog Creek—stream (14) OR-9
Dog Creek—stream (2) SD-7
Dog Creek—stream (5) TN-4
Dog Creek—stream (2) TX-5
Dog Creek—stream VA-3
Dog Creek—stream (4) WA-9
Dog Creek—stream WV-2
Dog Creek—stream (3) WY-8
Dog Creek Campground—locale ID-8
Dog Creek Cem—cemetery OK-5
Dog Creek County Park—park IA-7
Dog Creek Dam—dam IA-7
Dog Creek Meadow—flat OR-9
Dog Creek Mtn—summit CA-9
Dog Creek Point ID-8
Dog Creek Rsvr—reservoir MT-8
Dog Creek Sch—hist pl OK-5
Dog Creek Sch (historical)—school MO-7
Dog Creek Spring—spring MT-8
Dog Crossing—locale GA-3
Dogden ND-7
Dogden Butte—summit ND-7
**Dogden Township**—pop pl ND-7
Dog Draw UT-8
Dogeagle Lake—lake SD-7
Dog Ear Cem—cemetery FL-3
Dog Ear Creek—stream SD-7
Dog Ear Lake—lake FL-3
Dog Ear Lake—lake SD-7
**Dog Ear Township**—pop pl SD-7
Dogenai MP-9
Doget Hollow—valley NY-2
Dog Eye Pond—lake NM-5
Dogfall Branch—stream NC-3
Dog Falls—falls ME-1
Dog Far Mtn—summit AK-9
Dog Fennel Prairie—swamp FL-3
Dogfish Bar—bar MA-1
Dogfish Bay AK-9
Dogfish Bay WA-9
Dogfish Bight—bay WA-9
Dogfish Cove—bay ME-1
Dogfish Head—cape ME-1
Dogfish Island—island AK-9
Dogfish Island—island CT-1
Dogfish Island—island ME-1
Dogfish Lake—lake MI-6
Dogfish Lake—lake (4) MN-6
Dogfish Ledge—rock MA-1
Dogfish Mtn—summit AK-9
Dogfish Point—cape ME-1
Dogfish Point—cape WA-9
Dogfish Rocks—island ME-1
Dogfish Rsvr—reservoir CO-8
Dogfish Slough—gut MO-7
Dogfish Village—locale AK-9
Dog Flat—flat (3) UT-8
Dog Flat Hollow—valley UT-8
Dog Flat Tank—reservoir AZ-5
Dog Fork CA-9
Dog Fork—stream CA-9
Dog Fork—stream (5) KY-4
Dog Fork—stream OH-6
Dog Fork—stream OR-9
Dog Fork—stream VA-3
Dog Fork—stream (4) WV-2
Dog Fork Creek CA-9
Doggan Drain—canal MI-6
Dog Gap—gap KY-4
Dog Gap—gap TN-4
Doggard Point—cape ME-1
Dogged Dead River—lake MS-4
Doggett Branch—stream NC-3
Doggett Branch—stream TN-4
Doggett Brook—stream MA-1
Doggett Castle—summit ME-1
Doggett Cave—cave TN-4
Doggett Cem—cemetery IA-7
Doggett Cem—cemetery KY-4
Doggett Chapel—church WV-2
Doggett Creek—stream CA-9
Doggett Gap—gap NC-3
Doggett Grove Ch—church NC-3
Doggett Hollow—valley TN-4
Doggett Knob—summit NC-3
Doggett Lake—reservoir NC-3
Doggett Lake Dam—dam NC-3
Doggett Ranch—locale MT-8
Doggett Rsvr—reservoir MT-8
Doggetts Brook MA-1
**Doggetts Fork**—pop pl VA-3
Doggetts Pond—lake MA-1
Doggett Spring—spring TX-5
Doggie Butte SD-7
Doggie Island—island SC-3
Doggie Windmill—locale TX-5
Dog Gulch—valley (2) CA-9
Dog Gulch—valley MT-8
Dog Gulch—valley NM-5
Dog Gun Lake—lake MT-8
Dog Hammock—island GA-3
Dog Hammock Spit—bar GA-3
Dog Head—pillar CO-8
Doghead Bay—swamp NC-3
Doghead Flat—flat VA-3
Doghead Gap—gap FL-3
Doghead Island—island LA-4
Doghead Mtn—summit CO-8
Doghead Peak—summit CA-9
Dog Head Pond—reservoir NV-8
Dog Hill—locale TN-4
Dog Hill—summit MA-1
Dog Hill—summit (3) NY-2
Dog Hill Architectural District—hist pl TN-4
**Dog Hill (Siloam)**—pop pl TN-4
Doghobble Branch—stream TN-4
Dog Hole—cave (2) TN-4
Dog Hole—lake FL-3
Dog Hole—locale NM-5
Doghole Basin—bay FL-3
Dog Hollow—valley AL-4
Dog Hollow—valley (2) AR-4
Dog Hollow—valley IL-6
Dog Hollow—valley (2) KY-4
Dog Hollow—valley (6) MO-7
Dog Hollow—valley NV-8
Dog Hollow—valley (2) NY-2
Dog Hollow—valley (3) OH-6
Dog Hollow—valley OK-5
Dog Hollow—valley (3) TN-4
Dog Hollow—valley TX-5
Dog Hollow—valley UT-8
Dog Hollow—valley WV-2
Dog Hollow—valley WI-6
Dog Hollow Creek—stream UT-8
Dog Hollow Dam—dam OR-9
Dog Hollow Rsvr—reservoir OR-9
Dog Hollow Rsvr—reservoir UT-8
Dog Hollow Run—stream OH-6
Dog Hollow Run—stream PA-2
Dog Hollow Sch—school NY-2
Doghouse, The—pillar AZ-5
Doghouse Cabin—locale AK-9
Doghouse Cave—cave AL-4
Doghouse Creek—stream CA-9
Doghouse Gulch—valley OR-9
Doghouse Junction—locale CA-9
Doghouse Lake—lake (2) AK-9
Dog House Spring—spring AZ-5
Doghouse Spring—spring OR-9
Dogie Butte—summit SD-7
Dogie Canyon—valley NM-5
Dogie Canyon Pumping Station—locale NM-5
Dogie Creek SD-7
Dogie Creek—stream (2) MT-8
Dogie Creek—stream SD-7
Dogie Creek—stream TX-5
Dogie Creek—stream WY-8
Dogie Draw—valley WY-8
Dogie Mtn—summit TX-5
Dogie Spring—spring AZ-5
Dogie Spring—spring NM-5
Dogies Well—well NV-8
Dogie Tank—reservoir (2) AZ-5
Dogie Tank—reservoir NM-5
Dogie Tank—reservoir TX-5
Dog Island NC-3
Dog Island FM-9
Dog Island—island (3) AK-9
Dog Island—island CT-1
Dog Island—island (5) FL-3
Dog Island—island GA-3
Dog Island—island IL-6
Dog Island—island KY-4
Dog Island—island (2) LA-4
Dog Island—island (2) ME-1
Dog Island—island MN-6
Dog Island—island MS-4
Dog Island—island NJ-2
Dog Island—island (2) NY-2
Dog Island—island TX-5
Dog Island—island VA-3
Dog Island—island VI-3
Dog Island Corner ME-1
**Dog Island Corner**—pop pl ME-1
Dog Island Cut—channel VI-3
Dog Island (historical)—island MS-4
Dog Island Lake—lake WI-6
Dog Island Pass—channel LA-4
Dog Island Reef—bar FL-3
Dog Island Reef—bar TX-5
Dog Islands—island ME-1
Dog Islands—island NC-3
Dog Key—island (2) FL-3
Dog Keys Pass—channel MS-4
Dog Knobs—summit AZ-5
Dog Knobs Lake—lake AZ-5
Dog Knobs Trick Tank—reservoir AZ-5
Dog Knoll—summit UT-8
Dog Knoll Draw—valley UT-8
Dog Lake—lake (3) AK-9
Dog Lake—lake AZ-5
Dog Lake—lake CA-9
Dog Lake—lake (2) FL-3
Dog Lake—lake ID-8
Dog Lake—lake IN-6
Dog Lake—lake LA-4
Dog Lake—lake (2) MI-6
Dog Lake—lake (5) MN-6
Dog Lake—lake MT-8
Dog Lake—lake (2) NM-5
Dog Lake—lake (2) OR-9
Dog Lake—lake SC-3
Dog Lake—lake (4) UT-8
Dog Lake—lake WA-9
Dog Lake—lake (5) WI-6
Dog Lake—swamp MN-6
Dog Lake Bayou—gut LA-4
Dog Lake Burn Spring—spring OR-9
Dog Lake Oil and Gas Field—oilfield LA-4
Dog Lake Rsvr—reservoir OR-9
Dog Lake Spring—spring OR-9
Dog Lake Well—locale NM-5
Dog Lake Work Center—locale OR-9
Dogle Canyon—valley TX-5
Dogleg Branch—stream TN-4
Dog Leg Canyon—valley UT-8
Dog Leg Key—island FL-3
Dogleg Lake—lake MN-6
Dog Lick Branch—stream AR-4
Dog Loser Knob—summit NC-3
Dogman Lake PA-2
Dog Monument Draw—valley MT-8
Dog Mountain Creek—stream OR-9
Dog Mountains—other NM-5
Dog Mtn—summit AR-4
Dog Mtn—summit CO-8
Dog Mtn—summit ID-8
Dog Mtn—summit MT-8
Dog Mtn—summit NC-3
Dog Mtn—summit (3) OR-9
Dog Mtn—summit TX-5
Dog Mtn—summit (2) WA-9
Dognash Gully—valley TX-5
Dogneck Branch—stream LA-4
Dogney Island VA-3
Dogpatch—locale AR-4
**Dogpatch**—pop pl AK-9
**Dog Patch**—pop pl WV-2
**Dogpatch (Marble Falls)**—pop pl AR-4
Dog Paw Gulch—valley CA-9
Dogpen Branch—stream VA-3
Dog Point—cape AK-9
Dog Point—cliff AZ-5
Dog Point—cliff ID-8
Dog Point—summit TX-5
Dog Pond FL-3
Dog Pond—lake AR-4
Dog Pond—lake CT-1
Dog Pond—lake FL-3
Dog Pond—lake NY-2
Dog Pond—reservoir OK-5
Dog Pond—swamp FL-3
Dog Pond Branch—stream NC-3
Dog Pond Clear Lake—lake FL-3
Dog Pond Mtn—summit NY-2
Dog Ponds—lake UT-8
Dog Pong VT-1
Dog Pool Branch—stream WV-2
Dog Prairie—flat (2) OR-9
Dog Prairie Creek—stream OR-9
Dog Prairie Shelter—locale OR-9
Dog Prairie Trail—trail OR-9
**Dogridge**—pop pl TX-5
**Dog Ridge**—pop pl TX-5
Dog Ridge—ridge IN-6
Dog Ridge—ridge NC-3
Dog Ridge—ridge OR-9
Dog Ridge—ridge TN-4
Dog Rincon—valley CO-8
Dog River MS-4
Dog River OR-9
Dog River—stream AL-4
Dog River—stream GA-3
Dog River—stream MS-4
Dog River—stream OR-9
Dog River—stream VT-1
Dog River Bar—bar AL-4
Dog River Bridge—bridge AL-4
Dog River Point—cape AL-4
Dog River Springs—spring OR-9
Dog River Trail—trail OR-9
Dog Rock—pillar CA-9
Dog Rock—summit AZ-5
Dog Rock—summit OR-9
Dog Rocks—island VI-3
Dog Run WV-2
Dog Run—stream IL-6
Dog Run—stream (2) IN-6
Dog Run—stream KS-7
Dog Run—stream (3) OH-6
Dog Run—stream (2) PA-2
Dog Run—stream (2) VA-3
Dog Run—stream (5) WV-2
Dog Run Hollow—valley OK-5
Dog Run Spring—spring CA-9
Dog Salmon Bay AK-9
Dog Salmon Creek—stream (2) AK-9
Dog Salmon Flats—flat AK-9
Dog Salmon River—stream AK-9
Dogsboro DE-2
**Dogs Corners**—pop pl NJ-2
Dogs Ear Corner DE-2
Dog Seep—spring NM-5
Dogs Head—island ME-1
Dogs Head—summit NM-5
Dogs Head—summit WA-9
Dogshead Creek—stream WY-8
Dogshead Glacier—glacier AK-9
Dogs Head Tank—reservoir NM-5
Dogskin Mtn—summit NV-8
Dogskin Run—stream OH-6
Dog Slaughter Creek—stream KY-4
Dog Slaughter Ridge—ridge KY-4
Dog Slaughter Ridge—ridge VA-3
Dogsled Pass—gap AK-9
Dogson Creek MT-8
Dog Spring—spring (2) AZ-5
Dog Spring—spring NV-8
Dog Spring—spring (2) NM-5
Dog Spring—spring (2) OR-9
Dog Spring—spring (2) UT-8
Dog Spring—spring WY-8
Dog Spring Canyon—valley (2) NM-5
Dog Spring Ranch—locale NM-5
Dog Springs—spring NM-5
Dog Springs Arroyo—stream CO-8
Dog Springs Canyon—valley NM-5
Dog Springs Wash WY-8
Dog Spring Wash WY-8
Dog Spring Wash—valley WY-8
Dog Square Ridge—ridge MN-6
Dog Star Mine—mine NV-8
Dog Swamp—swamp SC-3
**Dogtail Corners**—pop pl NY-2
Dogtail Creek—stream TN-4
Dog Tail Creek—stream TN-4
Dogtail Landing—locale MS-4
Dog Tank—reservoir TX-5
Dog Tanks Draw—valley UT-8
Dog Tank Springs UT-8
Dog Tanks Spring—spring UT-8
Dogteam Lake—lake AK-9
Dog Thresher Creek—stream OK-5
Dog Tooth ND-7
Dogtooth Bend—bend AK-9
Dogtooth Bend Mounds and Village Site—hist pl IL-6
Dog Tooth Buttes—range ND-7
Dog Tooth Creek ND-7
Dogtooth Creek—stream (2) ND-7
Dog Tooth Creek—stream SD-7
Dogtooth Hollow—valley ID-8
Dogtooth Island—island IL-6
Dogtooth Peak—summit CA-9
Dog Tooth Rock—pillar MT-8
Dog Tooth Rock—pillar OR-9
Dogtown IN-6
Dogtown NE-7
Dogtown OH-6
Dogtown—locale AR-4
Dogtown—locale (4) CA-9
Dogtown—locale FL-3
Dogtown—locale ME-1
Dogtown—locale MD-2
Dogtown—locale NY-2
Dogtown—locale NC-3
Dogtown—locale (3) PA-2
Dogtown—locale (2) TN-4
Dogtown—locale VA-3
Dogtown—locale WV-2
Dogtown—other OH-6
**Dog Town**—pop pl AL-4
**Dogtown**—pop pl (2) AL-4
**Dogtown**—pop pl KY-4
**Dog Town**—pop pl ME-1
**Dogtown**—pop pl MS-4
**Dogtown**—pop pl PA-2
**Dog Town**—pop pl PA-2
**Dogtown**—pop pl (2) PA-2
**Dogtown**—pop pl TN-4
**Dog Town**—pop pl TN-4
Dogtown—ridge ID-8
Dog Town Campground AZ-5
Dogtown Common MA-1
**Dogtown Commons**—pop pl MA-1
Dogtown Creek—stream CA-9
Dogtown Creek—stream OR-9
Dogtown Creek—stream WI-6
Dogtown Dam—dam AZ-5
Dog Town Draw—valley NM-5
Dogtown Draw—valley WY-8
Dogtown Ferry Public Fishing Site—park IN-6
Dogtown Flat NE-7
Dogtown Flats—flat CO-8
Dogtown Flats—flat NE-7
Dogtown Flats Sch—school NE-7
Dogtown Hills—summit IL-6
Dogtown Hollow—valley IL-6
Dogtown Landing—locale IL-6
Dogtown Mine—mine AZ-5
Dog Town Mountain Windmill—locale TX-5
Dog Town Mtn—summit TX-5
**Dogtown (Penn Avon)**—pop pl PA-2
Dogtown Picnic Ground—park AZ-5
Dogtown Ranch—locale NM-5
Dogtown Reservoir Recreation Site—park AZ-5
Dogtown Rsvr—reservoir AZ-5
Dogtown Rsvr—reservoir WY-8
Dogtown Rsvr Campground AZ-5
Dogtown Sch (historical)—school MS-4
Dogtown Sewer—stream MT-8
Dog Town State Game Mngmt Area—park ND-7
Dogtown Tank—reservoir (2) AZ-5
Dogtown Tank—reservoir NM-5
Dog Town Tank—reservoir NM-5
Dogtown Wash—stream AZ-5
Dogtown Well—well TX-5
Dog Town Windmill—locale NM-5
Dog Town Windmill—locale TX-5
Dogtown Windmill—locale (2) TX-5
Dogtrot KS-7
Dog Trot—hist pl LA-4
Dogtrot Branch—stream (2) KY-4
Dogtrot Cem—cemetery IN-6
Dog Trot Fork—stream KY-4
Dog Trot Hollow—valley MO-7
Dogtrot Lake—lake MN-6
**Dogue**—pop pl VA-3
Dogue Creek—stream VA-3
Dogue Island VA-3
Dogue Run—stream VA-3
Dog Valley—basin UT-8
Dog Valley—valley AZ-5
Dog Valley—valley CA-9
Dog Valley—valley (2) UT-8
Dog Valley Canyon UT-8
Dog Valley Creek—stream UT-8
Dog Valley Guard Station—locale CA-9
Dog Valley Mine—mine UT-8
Dog Valley Mtn—summit UT-8
Dog Valley Peak—summit UT-8
Dog Valley Rsvr—reservoir UT-8
Dog Valley Tank—reservoir AZ-5
Dog Valley Wash—valley (2) UT-8
Dog Valley Well—well AZ-5
Dogville Crossroads NC-3
Dogwalk—locale KY-4
Dogwalk—other IL-6
**Dog Walk**—pop pl IL-6
**Dog Walk**—pop pl KY-4
Dog Walk Branch—stream KY-4
Dog Walk Creek—stream KS-7
Dog Wash—stream CA-9
Dog Water Mine—mine AZ-5
Dogwater Well—well AZ-5
Dogway—locale WV-2
Dogway Camping Shelter—locale WV-2
Dogway Fork—stream WV-2
Dog Well—well AZ-5
Dog Windmill—locale NM-5
Dog Windmill—locale TX-5
Dogwood AL-4
Dogwood MS-4
Dogwood—locale AR-4
Dogwood—locale IL-6
Dogwood—locale KY-4
Dogwood—locale (2) TN-4
**Dogwood**—pop pl (3) AL-4

**Dogwood**—pop pl AR-4
**Dogwood**—pop pl IN-6
**Dogwood**—pop pl KY-4
**Dogwood**—pop pl (2) MO-7
**Dogwood**—pop pl TX-5
Dogwood Acres—locale TX-5
**Dogwood Acres**—pop pl AL-4
**Dogwood Acres**—pop pl (2) NC-3
**Dogwood Acres**—pop pl PA-2
Dogwood Acres—uninc pl NC-3
Dogwood Acres—uninc pl TX-5
Dogwood Acres Ch—church NC-3
**Dogwood Acres (subdivision)**—pop pl DE-2
**Dogwood Acres (subdivision)**—pop pl (4) NC-3
**Dogwood Acres (subdivision)**—pop pl TN-4
**Dogwood Acres Trailer Park**—pop pl DE-2
Dogwood Baptist Church TN-4
Dogwood Bayou AR-4
Dogwood Bayou—stream MS-4
Dogwood Bench—bench TN-4
Dogwood Branch—stream (3) AL-4
Dogwood Branch—stream AR-4
Dogwood Branch—stream DE-2
Dogwood Branch—stream FL-3
Dogwood Branch—stream GA-3
Dogwood Branch—stream KY-4
Dogwood Branch—stream LA-4
Dogwood Branch—stream MS-4
Dogwood Branch—stream NC-3
Dogwood Branch—stream (2) TN-4
Dogwood Branch—stream (3) TX-5
Dogwood Bridge—bridge TN-4
Dogwood Butte—summit CA-9
Dogwood Camp—locale AL-4
Dogwood Campground—locale CA-9
Dogwood Canal—canal CA-9
Dogwood Canyon—valley (2) CA-9
Dogwood Cave—cave AL-4
Dogwood Cem—cemetery AR-4
Dogwood Cem—cemetery GA-3
Dogwood Cem—cemetery MS-4
Dogwood Cem—cemetery TN-4
Dogwood Ch—church AL-4
Dogwood Ch—church AR-4
Dogwood Ch—church GA-3
Dogwood Ch—church NC-3
Dogwood Ch (historical)—church TN-4
Dogwood Cove—valley NC-3
Dogwood Creek WA-9
Dogwood Creek—stream AL-4
Dogwood Creek—stream (3) AR-4
Dogwood Creek—stream (2) CA-9
Dogwood Creek—stream IL-6
Dogwood Creek—stream MO-7
Dogwood Creek—stream NC-3
Dogwood Creek—stream OK-5
Dogwood Creek—stream (2) OR-9
Dogwood Creek—stream SC-3
Dogwood Creek—stream (6) TX-5
Dogwood Creek—stream WV-2
Dogwood Dam—dam TN-4
Dogwood Elem Sch (historical)—school AL-4
Dogwood Estates Lake TN-4
Dogwood Farm Airp—airport NC-3
Dogwood Flat—flat AR-4
Dogwood Flat—flat TN-4
Dogwood Flat—locale TN-4
Dogwood Flats—flat AR-4
Dogwood Flats—flat IL-6
Dogwood Flats—flat (2) NC-3
Dogwood Flats—flat (2) TN-4
Dogwood Flats—locale AL-4
**Dogwood Flats**—pop pl MD-2
Dogwood Flats Creek—stream NC-3
Dogwood Fork—stream KY-4
Dogwood Fork—stream VA-3
Dogwood Gap—gap KY-4
Dogwood Gap—gap (2) NC-3
Dogwood Gap—gap TN-4
Dogwood Gap—gap WV-2
Dogwood Grove Baptist Church AL-4
Dogwood Grove Ch—church AL-4
**Dogwood Grove (subdivision)**—pop pl NC-3
Dogwood Gulch—valley (2) CA-9
Dogwood Hammock—island FL-3
Dogwood Harbor—bay MD-2
Dogwood Head Branch—stream FL-3
**Dogwood Heights**—pop pl TN-4
**Dogwood Heights (subdivision)**—pop pl TN-4
**Dogwood Hill**—pop pl VA-3
Dogwood Hill Ch—church SC-3
**Dogwood Hills**—pop pl MD-2
**Dogwood Hills**—pop pl TN-4
Dogwood Hollow TN-4
**Dogwood Hollow**—pop pl PA-2
Dogwood Hollow—valley (3) MO-7
Dogwood Hollow—valley (3) TN-4
Dogwood Hollow—valley VA-3
Dogwood Hollow Lake—reservoir TX-5
Dogwood Island (historical)—locale MS-4
Dogwood Key FL-3
Dogwood Knob—summit GA-3
**Dogwood Knoll**—pop pl VA-3
Dogwood Knolls Country Club—other NY-2
Dogwood Lake MS-4
Dogwood Lake—lake CA-9
Dogwood Lake—lake LA-4
Dogwood Lake—lake MN-6
Dogwood Lake—reservoir (2) AL-4
Dogwood Lake—reservoir IN-6
Dogwood Lake—reservoir (2) MS-4
Dogwood Lake—reservoir NC-3
Dogwood Lake—reservoir SC-3
Dogwood Lake—reservoir TN-4
Dogwood Lake—reservoir WV-2
Dogwood Lake Dam AL-4
Dogwood Lake Dam IN-6
Dogwood Lake Dam—dam (2) MS-4
Dogwood Lake Dam—dam NC-3
**Dogwood Lake Estates**—pop pl FL-3
Dogwood Lakes—reservoir TN-4
Dogwood Landing—locale MS-4
Dogwood Landing (historical)—locale NC-3
Dogwood Lateral Eight—canal CA-9
Dogwood Lateral Six—spring CA-9
Dogwood Lateral Ten—canal CA-9
Dogwood Lateral Ten A—canal CA-9
Dogwood Lateral Two—canal CA-9
Dogwood Lateral 6—canal CA-9
Dogwood Level AL-4
Dogwood Lodge—building TN-4
Dogwood Mine (underground)—mine AL-4
Dogwood Mudhole—locale TN-4
Dogwood Neck Sch—school SC-3
Dogwood Number 1 Mine (underground)—mine AL-4
Dogwood Number 3 Mine (underground)—mine AL-4
Dogwood Park—park AL-4
Dogwood Park—park GA-3
Dogwood Park—park (2) OH-6
**Dogwood Park (trailer park)**—pop pl DE-2
Dogwood Peak—summit CA-9
**Dogwood Place (subdivision)**—pop pl MS-4
Dogwood Plantation MS-4
Dogwood Point—cape AL-4
Dogwood Pond—lake CT-1
Dogwood Pond—swamp SC-3
Dogwood Post Office (historical)—building TN-4
Dogwood Recreation Site—park OR-9
Dogwood Ridge OR-9
Dogwood Ridge—ridge NC-3
Dogwood Ridge—ridge (2) OH-6
Dogwood Ridge—ridge WV-2
Dogwood Ridge Campground—locale TN-4
Dogwood Ridge Plantation MS-4
Dogwood Run—stream (2) MD-2
Dogwood Run—stream NC-3
Dogwood Run—stream PA-2
Dogwood Sch—school IL-6
Dogwood Sch—school NY-2
Dogwood Sch (historical)—school AL-4
Dogwood Sch (historical)—school MO-7
Dogwood Sch (historical)—school (2) TN-4
Dogwood Shores—locale TN-4
Dogwood Side Main—canal CA-9
Dogwood Spring—spring AZ-5
Dogwood Spring—spring (2) OR-9
Dogwood Spring—spring TN-4
Dogwood Springs Lake—reservoir IN-6
Dogwood Springs Lake Dam—dam IN-6
Dogwood Stamp Mtn—summit NC-3
Dogwood Swamp VA-3
Dogwood Swamp—swamp NH-1
Dogwood Tower Site State Hunting Area—other MO-7
Dogwood (Township of)—fmr MCD AR-4
Dogwood Trail—trail NC-3
Dogwood Valley—valley GA-3
Dogwood Well—well TX-5
Dohammer Cem—cemetery MO-7
Do-help-me Hollow—valley TN-4
Doheney Sch—school MT-8
Doheny Estate/Greystone—hist pl CA-9
Doheny Park CA-9
**Doheny Park**—pop pl CA-9
Doheny Ranch—locale NV-8
Doheny State Beach—park CA-9
Doherty—locale OH-6
Doherty Brook—stream NY-2
Doherty Creek—stream AK-9
Doherty House—hist pl AR-4
Doherty Island—island NY-2
Doherty Lake—lake MN-6
Doherty Memorial HS—school MA-1
Doherty Mtn—summit MT-8
Doherty Pond—lake NY-2
Doherty Ranch—locale OR-9
Doherty Ridge NM-5
Doherty Ridge—ridge CA-9
Doherty Rsvr—reservoir OR-9
Doherty Slide—other OR-9
Doherty Spring—spring OR-9
Doherty Valley—basin NE-7
Doh Halian—spring AZ-5
Dohlberg SD-7
Dohner, Michael, Farmhouse—hist pl PA-2
Dohner Lake—lake OH-6
Dohners Ch—church PA-2
Dohner Tank—reservoir AZ-5
Dohn Lake MN-6
Dohoney Cem—cemetery KY-4
Dohrmann Bldg—hist pl CA-9
Dohrs Creek—stream MT-8
Doh Yai Nos Cly—spring AZ-5
Doiason Hill Prairie—area CA-9
Doieg Hill—summit AL-4
Doig Creek—stream NY-2
Doig Ranch—locale MT-8
Doig Sch—school CA-9
Doing Ditch—canal CO-8
Doins Point—cliff AR-4
Doke Ditch—canal IN-6
Doke Lake—reservoir OH-6
Doke Spring—spring WA-9
Dokken Cem—cemetery ND-7
Dokken Hollow—valley AR-4
Dokken-Nelson Funeral Home—hist pl MT-8
Doko SC-3
Doko—locale PW-9
**Doko**—pop pl PW-9
Dok Point—cape AK-9
Dokter State Public Shooting Area—park SD-7
**Dola**—pop pl OH-6
**Dola**—pop pl WV-2
Dola Cem—cemetery OH-6
Dolahite Lake TX-5
Dolan MS-4
Dolan ND-7
Dolan—locale TX-5
**Dolan**—pop pl IN-6
Dolan, Terence, House—hist pl MA-1
Dolan Branch—stream TN-4
Dolan Bridge—bridge OK-5
Dolan Canyon—valley CA-9
Dolanco Junction—locale CA-9
Dolan Creek—stream OR-9
Dolan Creek—stream TN-4
Dolan Creek—stream TX-5
Doland ND-7
**Doland**—pop pl SD-7
Dolan Davis Dam—dam AL-4
Dolan Davis Lake—reservoir AL-4
Doland Branch—stream TN-4
Doland Cem—cemetery SD-7
Doland Church (historical)—locale MO-7
Doland Dam SD-7
Doland Hollow MO-7
Dolan Ditch—canal IL-6
Doland Mine—mine AZ-5
Dolan Drain—canal TX-5
Doland Ridge—ridge SD-7
Doland Sch (abandoned)—school MO-7
Doland Township (historical)—civil SD-7
Dolan Falls—falls TX-5
Dolan Gap—gap TN-4
Dolan Gulch—valley CO-8
Dolan Hollow—valley (2) TN-4
Dolan HS—school CT-1
Dolan JHS—school MI-6
Dolan Lake WI-6
Dolan Lake—lake WI-6
Dolan Lake Dam—dam MS-4
Dolan Mesa—summit WY-8
Dolan Mine (Site)—locale CA-9
Dolan Mound—summit MO-7
Dolan Mountain AR-4
Dolan Park—park NY-2
Dolan Ranch—locale SD-7
Dolan Ridge Mission—church IN-6
Dolan Rock—island CA-9
Dolans AL-4
Dolans Fork—stream WV-2
Dolans Lake—reservoir NY-2
Dolan Spring—spring CO-8
Dolan Spring—spring NM-5
Dolan Springs TX-5
**Dolan Springs**—pop pl AZ-5
Dolan Springs—spring AZ-5
Dolan Springs—spring TX-5
Dolan Springs Post Office—building AZ-5
**Dolans Subdivision**—pop pl UT-8
Dolans Trap Canyon—valley NV-8
Dolans Trap Spring—spring NV-8
Dolan Tank—reservoir NM-5
Dolan Township—civil MO-7
Dolan Well—locale NM-5
Dolap—summit FM-9
Dolapampap—summit FM-9
Dolapwail—summit FM-9
Dolbeare Hill—summit CT-1
Dolbeare Sch—school MA-1
Dolbee Cem—cemetery IA-7
Dolbee Creek—stream IA-7
Dolberg—locale OK-5
Dolberg Ch—church OK-5
Dolberg Oil Field—oilfield OK-5
Dolberry Cem—cemetery AL-4
Dolberry Hollow—valley AL-4
Dolbia Hill—summit CT-1
Dolbier Hill—summit MA-1
Dolbow Island—island GA-3
Dolbow Lateral—canal ID-8
Dolby—locale ME-1
Dolby Creek IA-7
Dolby Ditch—canal IN-6
Dolby Pond—reservoir ME-1
Dolby Sch—school LA-4
**Dolcito**—pop pl AL-4
Dolcode Mine—mine SD-7
Dold Cem—cemetery OH-6
Dole—locale OR-9
**Dole**—pop pl WA-9
Dole, James D., Homestead—hist pl HI-9
Dole Brook—stream ME-1
Dole Brook (Township of)—unorg ME-1
Dole Cem—cemetery OH-6
Dole Corner MA-1
Dole Creek—stream (2) WA-9
Dole-Darrell House—hist pl OH-6
Doleful Pond—lake MA-1
Dole Hill—summit IL-6
Dole Hill—summit VT-1
Dolehtik—island FM-9
Dolehtik Island FM-9
Dole Island—island MA-1
**Dole Junction**—pop pl NH-1
Dolekei, Dolen—summit FM-9
Dolekole—summit FM-9
Dole Mweir—summit FM-9
Dolen MP-9
Dolen—locale TX-5
Dolen Awak FM-9
Dolen Branch—stream KY-4
Dolen Cem—cemetery TN-4
Dol En Eir—summit FM-9
Dolener FM-9
Dolen Mtn—summit KY-4
Dolen Pahnwell FM-9
Dolen Palikar FM-9
Dolen Sch—school KY-4
Dolen Sch—school NE-7
Dolen Sch—school TX-5
Dolensekir—summit FM-9
Dolente—ridge FM-9
Dole Playground—park HI-9
Dole Pond—reservoir ME-1
Dolepwel—summit FM-9
Dolereirei—summit FM-9
Doles—locale GA-3
Doles—locale ID-8
**Doles Addition (subdivision)**—pop pl UT-8
Doles Ch—church GA-3
Dole Sch—school HI-9
Dole Sch—school (2) IL-6
**Doles Corner**—pop pl MA-1
Doles Crossroads—locale VA-3
Dolesew—summit FM-9
Dolesewi Pah—locale FM-9
Dolesewi Powe—locale FM-9
Doles Point—cape NJ-2
Doles Pond—lake ME-1
Dole Spring—spring OR-9
Dolet Bayou—stream LA-4
Dolet Brake—swamp LA-4
Doletik—island FM-9
Doletikitik—summit FM-9
Dolezal John Number 7 Dam—dam SD-7
Dolezal Ranch—locale MT-8
Dolf—locale PA-2
Dolf Brook—stream NH-1
Dolf Creek—stream CA-9
Dolfinger Sch—school KY-4
Dolge Company Factory Complex—hist pl NY-2
**Dolgeville**—pop pl NY-2
Dolgeville Point—cape NY-2
Dolgeville Rsvr—reservoir NY-2
Dolgoi Cape—cape AK-9
Dolgoi Harbor—bay AK-9
Dolgoi Island—island (3) AK-9
Dolgoi Lake—lake AK-9
Dolhonde Sch—school LA-4
Dolick Ditch IN-6
Dolie Temple Ch of God—church AL-4
Dolietic—summit FM-9
Dolif Mtn—summit VT-1
Dolina Point—cape AK-9
Dolin Cem—cemetery WV-2
Doling Branch—stream MO-7
**Dolinger**—pop pl NC-3
Dolinger Cem—cemetery NC-3
Doling Park—park MO-7
Doling Sch—school MO-7
Dolington—locale PA-2
Dolington Post Office (historical)—building PA-2
Dolinton PA-2
Dolis Hill—summit WY-8
**Doliska**—pop pl AL-4
Do Little Creek—stream GA-3
Dolittle Creek—stream (2) VA-3
Do Little Flat OR-9
Dolittle Pond—reservoir AZ-5
Dolive AL-4
**D'Olive**—pop pl AL-4
D'Olive Bay—bay AL-4
D'Olive Cem—cemetery AL-4
Dolive Creek AL-4
D'Olive Creek—stream AL-4
Doliver Island—island ME-1
Dolives AL-4
D'Olives Bay AL-4
D'olives Creek AL-4
Dollahan Cem—cemetery IL-6
Dolland Sch—school CA-9
Dollan Rsvr—reservoir CO-8
Dollap—summit FM-9
Dollap Channel—channel MP-9
Dollap Grosse Einfahrt MP-9
Dollapwail—civil FM-9
Dollar—locale AL-4
Dollar—locale OR-9
**Dollar**—pop pl TN-4
Dollar, Lake—lake MI-6
Dollar, Robert, Estate—hist pl CA-9
Dollar Basin—basin OR-9
Dollar Basin Creek—stream OR-9
Dollar Bay—bay FL-3
Dollar Bay—bay MI-6
Dollar Bay—bay TX-5
**Dollar Bay**—pop pl MI-6
Dollar Bend—bend CA-9
Dollar Bill Mine—mine CA-9
Dollar Branch—stream KY-4
Dollar Branch—stream NC-3
Dollar Butte—summit ID-8
Dollar Cem—cemetery GA-3
**Dollar Corner**—pop pl WA-9
Dollar Creek—stream AL-4
Dollar Creek—stream (3) AK-9
Dollar Creek—stream (2) CA-9
Dollar Creek—stream (3) ID-8
Dollar Creek—stream TN-4
Dollar Creek—stream TX-5
Dollar Creek—stream WA-9
Dollar Creek—stream WI-6
Dollar Creek Meadow—flat ID-8
Dollar Creek Ridge Trail—trail ID-8
Dollar Creek Way—trail ID-8
Dollard Hill—summit ME-1
Dollar Downs Racetrack—other TX-5
Dollar Drain—canal MI-6
Dollard's Wharf VA-3
Dollar Gap—gap WV-2
Dollar Hide Bay—bay MN-6
Dollarhide Camp—locale AL-4
Dollarhide Camp Lake—reservoir AL-4
Dollarhide Cem—cemetery AR-4
Dollarhide Cem—cemetery OH-6
Dollarhide Cem—cemetery VA-3
Dollarhide Creek—stream AL-4
Dollar Hide Creek—stream IN-6
Dollarhide Cutoff—gut TX-5
Dollarhide Hunting Club Dams—dam AL-4
Dollarhide Hunting Lake—reservoir AL-4
Dollarhide Lake—lake TX-5
Dollarhide Mtn—summit ID-8
Dollarhide Oil Field—oilfield TX-5
Dollarhide Oil Field—other NM-5
Dollarhide Pond—reservoir OR-9
Dollarhide Spring—spring CO-8
Dollarhide Spring—spring OR-9
Dollarhide Summit—summit ID-8
Dollarhide Swamp—swamp AL-4
Dollar Hollow—valley AR-4
Dollar Island—island IA-7
Dollar Island—island (6) ME-1
Dollar Island—island MI-6
Dollar Island—island (2) MN-6
Dollar Island—island NH-1
Dollar Island—island NY-2
Dollar Island—island TN-4
Dollar Island—island WY-8
Dollar Junction—locale AR-4
Dollar Lake CA-9
Dollar Lake MI-6
Dollar Lake WI-6
Dollar Lake—lake CA-9
Dollar Lake—lake (4) CO-8
Dollar Lake—lake FL-3
Dollar Lake—lake ID-8
Dollar Lake—lake (4) IN-6
Dollar Lake—lake (22) MI-6
Dollar Lake—lake (6) MN-6
Dollar Lake—lake (2) MS-4
Dollar Lake—lake MO-7
Dollar Lake—lake (3) MT-8
Dollar Lake—lake ND-7
Dollar Lake—lake (2) OR-9
Dollar Lake—lake PA-2
Dollar Lake—lake SD-7
Dollar Lake—lake (2) UT-8
Dollar Lake—lake (7) WI-6
Dollar Lake—lake (3) WY-8
Dollar Lake—reservoir IN-6
Dollar Lake—reservoir MS-4
Dollar Lake—reservoir OH-6
Dollar Lakes—lake NV-8
Dollar Lake Saddle—gap CA-9
Dollar Lake Trail (Pack)—trail CA-9
Dollar Mark Tank—reservoir AZ-5
Dollar Meadows—flat CA-9
Dollar More Tank—reservoir AZ-5
Dollar Mtn—summit ID-8
Dollar Mtn—summit OR-9
Dollar Mtn—summit WA-9
Dollar Mtn—summit WY-8
Dollar Mud PA-2
Dollar Nine Lake—lake OR-9
Dollar Point—cape CA-9
Dollar Point—cape TX-5
Dollar Pond—lake AR-4
Dollar Pond—lake FL-3
Dollar Pond—lake (2) ME-1
Dollar Pond—lake MI-6
Dollar Prairie—flat FL-3
Dollar Ranch—locale CA-9
Dollar Ranch—locale WY-8
Dollar Ranch—uninc pl CA-9
Dollar Rsvr—reservoir CA-9
Dollar Savings Bank—hist pl PA-2
**Dollar Settlement**—pop pl MI-6
Dollar Settlement Cem—cemetery MI-6
Dollar Slough—swamp ND-7
Dollarson Creek KY-4
Dollar Spring—spring NV-8
Dollar Spring—spring OR-9
Dollar Spring—spring TN-4
Dollars Station (historical)—locale TN-4
Dollars Store (historical)—locale MS-4
Dollar Tank—reservoir NM-5
**Dollarville**—pop pl MI-6
Dollarville Dam—dam MI-6
Dollarville Flooding—reservoir MI-6
Dollar Watch Mtn—summit WA-9
Dollar Watch Pass—gap WA-9
Dollarway—uninc pl AR-4
Dollarway Road—hist pl AR-4
Dollarway Sch—school AR-4
Doll Baby Ranch—locale AZ-5
Dollbeer Mobile Home Ranch—locale AZ-5
Doll Branch—stream TN-4
Doll Camp—locale CA-9
Doll Canyon—valley TX-5
Doll Cem—cemetery OH-6
Doll Creek—bay NC-3
Doll Creek—stream CA-9
Doll Day Tank—reservoir NM-5
Dolleiso—summit FM-9
Dollekei—civil FM-9
Dollens Cem—cemetery KY-4
Dollens Elem Sch—school IN-6
Dollepwel—summit FM-9
Dolley Cem—cemetery ME-1
**Dolley Corner**—pop pl ME-1
Dolley Madison House PA-2
Doll Flats—flat NC-3
Doll Flats—flat TN-4
Doll Hill—summit NY-2
Doll Hill—summit PA-2
Doll House, The—area UT-8
Dolliber Cove—cove MA-1
Dolliber Point—cape MA-1
Dollie Hollow—valley OK-5
Dollie Sch—school WV-2
Dolliff Pond—lake ME-1
Dolling Mine—mine CA-9
Dolling Ranch—locale WY-8
Dollings Cem—cemetery IN-6
Dollington PA-2
Dollins Canyon—valley NM-5
Dollins Creek—stream VA-3
Dollins Spring—spring NM-5
Dollison Creek KY-4
Dollison Pond—lake AL-4
Dollisons Landing—locale NC-3
Dollisons Landing (historical)—locale NC-3
Dollisons Swamp—swamp NC-3
**Dolliver**—pop pl IA-7
Dolliver Beach Neck Marshes—swamp MA-1
Dolliver Branch—stream WV-2
Dolliver House—hist pl CA-9
Dolliver Memorial State Park—park IA-7
Dolliver Neck—cape MA-1
Dolliver Trail—trail PA-2
Doll Katar—summit FM-9
Doll Lake—lake UT-8
Doll Mountain Ch—church GA-3
Doll Mtn—summit MA-1
Doll Mtn—summit PA-2
Dolloff, Lake—lake WA-9
Dolloff Brook—stream NH-1
Dolloff Hill—summit ME-1
Dolloff Hill—summit NH-1
Dolloff Ponds—lake VT-1
Dollof Pond—lake NH-1
Doll Ranch—locale SD-7
Doll Ridge—ridge CA-9
Doll Ridge—ridge VA-3
Doll Run—stream DE-2
Doll Run—stream WV-2
Dolls Gap—gap WV-2
Dolls Gut—stream NC-3
Dolls Run DE-2
Dolls Run—stream WV-2
Doll Top—summit NC-3
**Dollville**—pop pl IL-6
Dolly, Mount—summit AK-9
Dolly Ann Hollow—valley VA-3
Dolly Bay—bay FL-3
Dolly Boamans Creek MD-2
Dolly Boarmans Creek—stream MD-2
Dolly Branch—stream MO-7
Dolly Branch—stream TN-4
Dolly Brook—stream AL-4
Dolly Brook—stream ME-1
Dolly Brook—stream PA-2
Dolly Clark Mine—mine UT-8
Dolly Cole Brook—stream RI-1
Dolly Copp Campground—locale NH-1
Dolly Creek—stream (2) CA-9
Dolly Creek—stream ID-8
Dolly Creek—stream NV-8
Dolly Creek—stream WA-9
Dolly Gordon Brook—stream ME-1
Dolly Hayden Spring—spring NV-8
Dolly Head—cape ME-1
Dolly Hill—summit ME-1
Dollyhyde Creek—stream MD-2
Dolly Lakes—lake FL-3
Dolly Madison House—building DC-2
Dolly Meadow—flat WY-8
**Dollymount (Township of)**—pop pl MN-6
Dolly Mtn—summit ME-1
Dolly Mtn—summit VA-3
Dolly Pond RI-1
Dolly Pond—reservoir TN-4
Dolly Pond Cem—cemetery TN-4
Dolly Ridge—ridge AL-4
Dolly Ridge—ridge WV-2
Dolly Run—stream PA-2
Dolly Run—stream WV-2
Dollys Hill ME-1
**Dolly Siding**—pop pl MO-7
Dollys Island—island ME-1
Dollys Knob—summit VA-3
Dolly Sods—flat WV-2
Dolly Sods Picnic Area—park WV-2
Dolly Spring—spring OR-9
Dolly Varden—locale NV-8
**Dolly Varden**—pop pl OH-6
Dolly Varden Basin—basin NV-8
Dolly Varden Campgound—locale WA-9
Dolly Varden Campground—park OR-9
Dolly Varden Canyon—valley NV-8
Dolly Varden Creek WA-9
Dolly Varden Creek—stream MT-8
Dolly Varden Flat—flat NV-8
Dolly Varden Gulch—valley CO-8
Dolly Varden (historical)—locale NV-8
Dolly Varden Lake—lake AK-9
Dolly Varden Mine—mine CO-8
Dolly Varden Mines—mine NV-8
Dolly Varden Mtn—summit CO-8
Dolly Varden Mtns—summit NV-8
Dolly Varden Spring—spring (2) NV-8
Dolly Vinsant Hosp—hospital TX-5
Dolly Warden Lake—lake NE-7
Dolman Island—island ID-8
Dolman Pond—lake IL-6
Dolman Rapids—rapids ID-8
Dolman Row—hist pl MO-7
Dolmweir—summit FM-9
Dolney Lake—lake MN-6
Dolneys Lake MN-6
Doloff Pond—lake ME-1
Dolohmwar—summit FM-9
Dolokole Peak FM-9
Dololab FM-9
Dolomi (Aban'd)—locale AK-9
Dolomi Bay—bay AK-9
Dolomi Mtn—summit AK-9
Dolomite—locale CA-9
Dolomite—locale TN-4
**Dolomite**—pop pl AL-4
**Dolomite**—pop pl FL-3
**Dolomite**—pop pl UT-8
**Dolomite**—pop pl WA-9
Dolomite, The—mine NV-8
Dolomite Campground—locale NV-8
Dolomite Canyon—valley CA-9
Dolomite Creek—stream AK-9
Dolomite Elem Sch—school AL-4
Dolomite Hill Drill Hole—well NV-8
Dolomite Mine—mine CA-9
Dolomite Mine (underground)—mine AL-4
Dolomite Mtn—summit WA-9
Dolomite Number 1 Slope Mine (underground)—mine AL-4
Dolomite Number 2 Mine (underground)—mine AL-4
Dolomite Plant—building UT-8
Dolomite Sch (historical)—school TN-4
**Dolonah**—pop pl AL-4
Dolonah Ch—church AL-4
Dolonah Quarry—mine AL-4
**Dolonar**—pop pl AL-4
Dolonar Junction—locale AL-4
Dolores—locale CA-9
**Dolores**—pop pl CO-8
Dolores, Arroyo—valley TX-5
Dolores, Desvio—locale PR-3
Dolores Canyon—valley (2) CO-8
Dolores Canyon Overlook Picnic Area—locale CO-8
Dolores Cem—cemetery TX-5
Dolores Creek—stream (2) CA-9
Dolores Creek—stream CO-8
Dolores Creek—stream (3) TX-5
Dolores Gulch—valley NM-5
Dolores Mine—mine CO-8
Dolores Mine—mine NV-8
Dolores Mine—mine NM-5
Dolores Mines—mine CO-8
Dolores Mission Sch—school CA-9
Dolores Mountain CO-8
Dolores Mtn—summit CO-8
Dolores Mtn—summit TX-5
Dolores Nuevo—hist pl TX-5
Dolores Peak CO-8
Dolores Peak—summit CO-8
Dolores Point—summit CO-8
Dolores Point—summit UT-8
Dolores Point Spring—spring CO-8
Dolores Ranch—locale NM-5
Dolores Ranch—locale TX-5
Dolores River—stream CO-8
Dolores River—stream UT-8
Dolores Sch—school TX-5
Dolores S Parrott JHS—school FL-3
Dolores Street Sch—school CA-9
Dolores Viejo—hist pl TX-5
Dolorosa Sch—school LA-4
**Doloroso**—pop pl MS-4
Dolotomw—summit FM-9
Dolotomw Peak FM-9
Dolph WV-2
Dolph—locale MI-6
Dolph—locale OR-9
**Dolph**—pop pl AR-4
Dolph Bldg—hist pl OR-9
Dolph Branch—stream NC-3
Dolph Bridge—other MI-6
Dolphburgh Sch—school NY-2
Dolph Corner—locale OR-9
Dolph Creek—stream ID-8

Dolph Creek—*stream* SD-7
Dolph Dias Lake—*lake* LA-4
Dolphees Island (historical)—*island* SD-7
Dolphin—*locale* VA-3
Dolphin—*uninc pl* NJ-2
Dolphin Bay—*bay* WA-9
**Dolphin Cove**—*pop pl* CT-1
Dolphin Creek—*stream* FL-3
Dolphin Head—*cape* SC-3
Dolphin Island—*summit* UT-8
Dolphin Point—*cape* AK-9
Dolphin Point—*cape* NY-2
Dolphin Point—*cape* WA-9
Dolphin Pond—*reservoir* CT-1
Dolphin Post Office (historical)—*building* MS-4
Dolphin Rock—*rock* MA-1
Dolphin Run—*stream* PA-2
Dolphin Sch Number 2—*school* ND-7
Dolphin Square (Shop Ctr)—*locale* FL-3
Dolphins Ridge—*ridge* OH-6
Dolphin Station—*locale* NJ-2
Dolphin Tank—*reservoir* AZ-5
**Dolphin Township**—*pop pl* NE-7
Dolphin Village (Shop Ctr)—*locale* FL-3
Dolphin Well—*well* AZ-5
Dolph Pond—*lake* NY-2
Dolph Post Office (historical)—*building* SD-7
Dolph Rock—*other* AK-9
Dolphs Breaker—*building* PA-2
Dolphus Peninsula—*cape* SD-7
*Dolpohmwar* FM-9
Dolrakied—*summit* FM-9
Dolsen—*locale* LA-4
Dolsen Sch—*school* MI-6
*Dolson* IL-6
Dolson Coulee—*valley* MT-8
Dolson Drain—*canal* CA-9
Dolson Drain Four—*canal* CA-9
Dolson Drain One—*canal* CA-9
Dolson Hill Sch—*school* MN-6
**Dolson (Township of)**—*pop pl* IL-6
**Dolton**—*pop pl* AR-4
**Dolton**—*pop pl* IL-6
**Dolton**—*pop pl* SD-7
Dolton, Lake—*reservoir* SD-7
Dolton Branch—*stream* AL-4
Dolton Park—*park* IL-6
Dolton Spring—*spring* OR-9
**Dolton Township**—*pop pl* SD-7
Dolus Creek—*stream* MT-8
Dolus Creek—*stream* WY-8
Dolus Hill—*summit* WY-8
Dolus Lakes—*lake* MT-8
Dolven State Wildlife Mngmt
Area—*park* MN-6
Dolves Mtn—*summit* NC-3
Dolvin Lake—*reservoir* GA-3
Dom, Lake—*lake* PA-2
Domaas—*locale* MN-6
Domaas Creek—*stream* MN-6
Domantle Lake—*lake* CO-8
Domaschofsky Rsvr—*reservoir* OR-9
**Domascus**—*pop pl* MS-4
*Dom'athing* FM-9
**Dombach Manor**—*pop pl* PA-2
Dombo—*summit* CA-9
Dombròski Lake—*lake* WI-6
*Dombrowski Lake* WI-6
Domby Ditch—*canal* OR-9
Dome—*other* AK-9
**Dome**—*pop pl* AZ-5
**Dome**—*pop pl* TX-5
Dome, Mount—*summit* CA-9
*Dome, The* WA-9
Dome, The—*summit* AK-9
Dome, The—*summit* (2) AZ-5
Dome, The—*summit* CO-8
Dome, The—*summit* ID-8
Dome, The—*summit* NM-5
Dome, The—*summit* (2) OR-9
Dome, The—*summit* UT-8
Dome, The—*summit* VT-1
Dome, The—*summit* WA-9
Dome Basin Mine—*mine* AZ-5
Dome Butte—*summit* SD-7
Dome Butte—*summit* WY-8
Dome Camp—*locale* AK-9
Dome Camp—*locale* WA-9
Dome Canal—*canal* AZ-5
Dome Canyon—*valley* (2) UT-8
Dome Canyon Pass—*gap* UT-8
*Dome Creek* CA-9
*Dome Creek* ID-8
Dome Creek—*locale* AK-9
Dome Creek—*stream* (7) AK-9
Dome Creek—*stream* (2) CA-9
Dome Creek—*stream* CO-8
Dome Creek—*stream* ID-8
Dome Creek—*stream* OR-9
Dome Creek—*stream* WA-9
Dome Creek Shelter Cabin—*locale* AK-9
Dome Glacier—*glacier* WA-9
Dome Hill—*summit* AK-9
Dome Hill—*summit* CA-9
Dome Hill—*summit* ID-8
Dome Hill—*summit* NV-8
Dome Hill—*summit* TX-5
Dome House Cave—*cave* KY-4
Domeier Sch—*school* IL-6
Dome Island—*island* MN-6
Dome Island—*island* NY-2
Dome Islets—*island* AK-9
*Dome Lake* WY-8
Dome Lake—*lake* CO-8
Dome Lake—*lake* ID-8
Dome Lake—*lake* MT-8
Dome Lake—*lake* WY-8
Dome Lake Rsvr—*reservoir* WY-8
Dome Land—*area* CA-9
Dome Lateral—*canal* AZ-5
Dome Lookout Tower—*locale* NM-5
Dome Mountain Camps—*locale* ME-1
*Dome Mountains* AZ-5
*Dome Mtn* AZ-5
*Dome Mtn* CA-9
Dome Mtn—*summit* (2) AK-9
Dome Mtn—*summit* AZ-5
Dome Mtn—*summit* (2) CA-9
Dome Mtn—*summit* CO-8
Dome Mtn—*summit* ID-8
Dome Mtn—*summit* ME-1
Dome Mtn—*summit* (2) MT-8
Dome Mtn—*summit* (2) NV-8
Dome Mtn—*summit* SD-7
Dome Mtn—*summit* (2) WY-8
Dom'em'ul—*bar* FM-9
Domengine Creek—*stream* CA-9
Domengine Ranch—*locale* CA-9
Domengine Spring—*spring* (2) CA-9
Domenicks Pond—*lake* CT-1
*Dom'enifiy* FM-9
Domenigoni Valley—*valley* CA-9
*Dome North of Mesquite* AZ-5
Domen Reef—*bar* MI-6
Dome Pass—*gap* AK-9
*Dome Peak* MA-1
Dome Peak—*summit* (3) AK-9
Dome Peak—*summit* (2) CO-8
Dome Peak—*summit* TX-5
Dome Peak—*summit* (2) WA-9
Dome Peak—*summit* (2) WY-8
Dome Plateau—*plateau* UT-8
Dome Pocket—*basin* AZ-5
Dome Point—*cape* AK-9
Dome Protective Channel—*canal* AZ-5
Domer—*bar* FM-9
Domer Ch—*church* PA-2
*Dome Reservoir* WY-8
Domerie Creek—*stream* WA-9
Domerie Flats—*flat* WA-9
Domerie Peak—*summit* WA-9
Domerie Peak Trail—*trail* WA-9
Dome Rock—*island* AK-9
Dome Rock—*pillar* (2) CO-8
Dome Rock—*pillar* NE-7
Dome Rock—*pillar* OR-9
Dome Rock—*pillar* WY-8
**Dome Rock**—*pop pl* CO-8
Dome Rock—*summit* (2) CA-9
Dome Rock—*summit* OR-9
Dome Rock—*summit* WY-8
Dome Rock Canyon—*valley* CO-8
Dome Rock Interchange—*crossing* AZ-5
Dome Rock Mountains—*range* AZ-5
*Dome Rock Range* AZ-5
Domer Ranch—*locale* MT-8
Domersville Cem—*cemetery* OH-6
Dome Shaped Mtn—*summit* MT-8
Dome Spring—*spring* AZ-5
Dome Spur—*locale* AK-9
**Domestic**—*pop pl* IN-6
Domestic Arts Hall And Flower
Hall—*hist pl* OH-6
Domestic Science Bldg—*hist pl* AL-4
Domestic Science Bldg—*hist pl* AR-4
Domestic Supply Ditch—*canal* CO-8
Dome Tank—*reservoir* NM-5
Dome Trail—*trail* AZ-5
Dome Two—*summit* CA-9
Dome Valley—*valley* AZ-5
Dome Well—*well* NM-5
Domeys Dome—*summit* VT-1
Domhoff Buildings—*hist pl* OH-6
Domick Ditch—*canal* WY-8
Domijohn Canyon—*valley* NM-5
Domijohn Well—*well* NM-5
Domin—*cape* FM-9
Domin Airp—*airport* PA-2
Domineguez Valley Hosp—*hospital* CA-9
Dominey Branch—*stream* GA-3
Domingas Mine—*mine* CA-9
**Domingo**—*pop pl* NM-5
Domingo, Bayou—*gut* LA-4
Domingo, Lake—*reservoir* CA-9
Domingo Acosta Grant—*civil* (2) FL-3
Domingo Cabin—*locale* NV-8
Domingo Creek—*stream* AK-9
Domingo Creek—*stream* (3) CA-9
Domingo Fernandez Grant—*civil* (3) FL-3
Domingo Flat—*flat* CA-9
Domingo Peak—*summit* CA-9
Domingo Ranch—*locale* NM-5
Domingo Reyes Grant—*civil* FL-3
**Domingo Ruiz**—*pop pl* (2) PR-3
Domingo Ruiz (Barrio)—*fmr MCD* PR-3
Domingos House—*hist pl* GA-3
Domingo Spring—*spring* (2) CA-9
Domingo Spring—*spring* NV-8
Domingo Tank—*reservoir* AZ-5
Domingo Well—*well* NV-8
Domingues Canyon—*valley* NM-5
Domingues Ranch—*locale* TX-5
Domingues Windmill—*locale* NM-5
Dominguez—*locale* CO-8
**Dominguez**—*pop pl* CA-9
Dominguez Butte—*summit* UT-8
Dominguez Campground—*locale* CA-9
Dominguez Campground—*locale* CO-8
Dominguez Canyon—*valley* CA-9
Dominguez Canyon—*valley* CO-8
Dominguez Channel—*canal* CA-9
Dominguez Golf Course—*other* CA-9
Dominguez Hill—*summit* UT-8
Dominguez Hills—*range* CA-9
Dominguez Hills—*uninc pl* CA-9
Dominguez HS—*school* CA-9
Dominguez Junction—*locale* CA-9
Dominguez Lake—*lake* CO-8
Dominguez Mtn—*summit* TX-5
Dominguez Ranch Adobe—*hist pl* CA-9
Dominguez Ridge—*ridge* CO-8
Dominguez Rim—*cliff* CO-8
Dominguez Rim Rsvr—*reservoir* CO-8
*Dominguez Rock* UT-8
Dominguez Spring Trail—*trail* TX-5
Dominguez Trail—*trail* CO-8
**Dominguito**—*pop pl* PR-3
Dominguito (Barrio)—*fmr MCD* PR-3
*Dominican* MI-6
Dominican Acad—*school* MA-1
Dominican Block—*hist pl* ME-1
Dominican Camp—*locale* NY-2
Dominican Camp for Girls—*locale* OH-6
Dominican Coll—*school* CA-9
Dominican Coll—*school* IL-6
Dominican Coll—*school* NY-2
Dominican Coll—*school* WI-6
Dominican Convent—*church* PA-2
Dominican House of Studies
(historical)—*school* MI-6
Dominican HS—*school* MI-6
Dominican HS—*school* WI-6
Dominican Legation Bldg—*building* DC-2
Dominican Monastery—*church* MA-1
Dominican Retreat—*church* PA-2
Dominican Retreat House—*church* NY-2
Dominican Sisters Convent—*church* NY-2
Dominicar Merlo Cem—*cemetery* TX-5
Dominic Buttes—*summit* MT-8
Dominic Creek—*gut* AL-4
**Dominic (historical)**—*pop pl* OR-9
**Dominick**—*pop pl* AL-4
Dominick Bayou—*stream* LA-4
Dominick Lake—*lake* NE-7
Dominick Rsvr—*reservoir* CO-8
Dominic Point—*summit* MT-8
Dominie Creek—*stream* CA-9
Dominion—*locale* CO-8
**Dominion**—*pop pl* MD-2
**Dominion**—*pop pl* VA-3
Dominion Creek—*stream* (4) AK-9
Dominion Creek—*stream* MT-8
**Dominion Heights**—*pop pl* VA-3
**Dominion Hills**—*pop pl* VA-3
Dominion Hotel—*hist pl* AZ-5
Dominion JHS—*school* OH-6
Dominion Montessori Sch—*school* TX-5
Dominion Peak—*summit* ID-8
Dominion Peak—*summit* MT-8
Dominion Point—*summit* ID-8
Dominique, Bayou—*gut* LA-4
**Domino**—*pop pl* TX-5
*Domino, The* UT-8
Domino Cem—*cemetery* TX-5
Domino Mine—*mine* AZ-5
Domino Number 2 Mine
(underground)—*mine* AL-4
*Dominquez Mountain* TX-5
Dominy Branch—*stream* GA-3
Dominy Lake—*lake* GA-3
Domke Lake—*lake* WA-9
Domke Mtn—*summit* WA-9
Domkirk Rock—*island* VI-3
Dommerich Elem Sch—*school* FL-3
Dommericks Pond—*lake* CT-1
Dommer Lake—*lake* MI-6
Domogalla Canyon—*valley* OR-9
Domogalla Ridge—*ridge* OR-9
*Domorest* GA-3
Dompier Creek—*stream* OR-9
Domsch Sch—*school* SD-7
Doms Rsvr—*reservoir* WY-8
*Domuchuy* FM-9
*Domus* KS-7
Don—*locale* ID-8
Don—*locale* WV-2
Don, Lake—*lake* FL-3
Dona—*locale* NM-5
**Dona**—*pop pl* LA-4
**Dona**—*pop pl* VA-3
**Dona Ana**—*pop pl* NM-5
Dona Ana, Quebrada—*valley* PR-3
Dona Ana Arroyo—*stream* NM-5
Dona Ana Bend Colony—*civil* NM-5
*Dona Ana County* AZ-5
**Dona Ana (County)**—*pop pl* NM-5
Dona Ana Drain—*canal* NM-5
Dona Ana- East Picacho—*school* NM-5
Dona Ana-Hill (CCD)—*cens area* NM-5
Dona Ana Lateral—*canal* NM-5
Dona Ana Mountains—*other* NM-5
Dona Ana Peak—*summit* NM-5
Dona Ana Range Camp—*locale* NM-5
Donabahba Yogee—*swamp* ID-8
Dona Bay—*bay* FL-3
Dona Brook—*stream* NY-2
Donaby Creek—*stream* MO-7
Donaby Sch (historical)—*school* MO-7
Donaca Creek—*stream* OR-9
Donaca Lake—*lake* OR-9
*Dona Cove* TX-5
*Dona Creek* DE-2
Dona Creek—*stream* CA-9
Dona Elena (Barrio)—*fmr MCD* PR-3
Donaghey State Park—*park* LA-4
**Donaghmore**—*pop pl* PA-2
Donaghy Sch—*school* MA-1
*Donahor Mountain* MT-8
*Donahoe* PA-2
Donahoe—*locale* TX-5
Donahoe, Daniel J., House—*hist pl* OK-5
Donahoe Creek—*stream* (3) TX-5
Donahoe Fork—*stream* WV-2
Donahoe Lake—*lake* AK-9
Donahoe Lake—*lake* TX-5
Donahoe Marsh—*swamp* TX-5
Donahoe Ridge—*ridge* AR-4
Donahoe Sch—*school* NJ-2
Donahoo, Lake—*reservoir* AL-4
Donahoo Cem—*cemetery* VA-3
Donahoo Dam—*dam* AL-4
Donahower, Frederick A., House—*hist pl* MN-6
Donahue—*locale* WA-9
**Donahue**—*pop pl* IA-7
Donahue Basin—*basin* ID-8
**Donahue Beach**—*pop pl* MI-6
Donahue Bldg—*hist pl* IA-7
Donahue Branch—*stream* TN-4
Donahue Brook—*stream* CT-1
Donahue Canyon—*valley* NM-5
Donahue Cem—*cemetery* IN-6
Donahue Cem—*cemetery* VA-3
Donahue Cem—*cemetery* WV-2
*Donahue Creek* TX-5
Donahue Creek—*stream* ID-8
Donahue Creek—*stream* KS-7
Donahue Creek—*stream* MT-8
Donahue Creek—*stream* OR-9
Donahue Creek—*stream* TX-5
Donahue Creek—*stream* WA-9
Donahue Crossing—*locale* TX-5
Donahue Ditch—*canal* WY-8
Donahue Flat—*flat* CA-9
Donahue Flat Creek—*stream* CA-9
**Donahue (historical)**—*pop pl* OR-9
*Donahue Hollow* TN-4
Donahue Hollow—*valley* TN-4
*Donahue Lake* WI-6
Donahue Lake—*lake* AR-4
Donahue Lake—*reservoir* IN-6
Donahue Lake Dam—*dam* IN-6
Donahue Mtn—*summit* AR-4
*Donahue Pass* CA-9
Donahue Ranch—*locale* NV-8
Donahue Ridge—*ridge* MO-7
Donahue Rsvr—*reservoir* WY-8
Donahue Sch—*school* IL-6
Donahue Sch—*school* IA-7
Donahue Sch—*school* MA-1
Donahue Sch—*school* MI-6
Donahue Slough—*stream* CA-9
Donahue Spring—*spring* TN-4
Donahue Spring—*spring* WY-8
Donahue Station (historical P.O.)—*locale* IA-7
Donahue Tank—*reservoir* AZ-5
Donahue Windmill—*locale* NM-5
*Dona Landing* DE-2
Donald—*locale* MT-8
Donald—*locale* WV-2
**Donald**—*pop pl* AL-4
**Donald**—*pop pl* GA-3
**Donald**—*pop pl* MT-8
**Donald**—*pop pl* OR-9
**Donald**—*pop pl* WA-9
**Donald**—*pop pl* WI-6
Donald, Lake—*lake* WA-9
Donald Branch—*stream* VA-3
Donald Cem—*cemetery* MS-4
Donald Cem—*cemetery* MO-7
Donald Cem—*cemetery* WI-6
*Donald Cemetery* AL-4
Donald Ch—*church* (2) AL-4
Donald Chapel—*church* LA-4
Donald Creek—*stream* WY-8
Donald Drain—*canal* MI-6
Donald Duck Gun Club—*other* CA-9
Donald Durks Lake Dam—*dam* MS-4
Donald E Gavit Middle/HS—*school* IN-6
Donald Farm—*hist pl* WI-6
Donald Farm Cem—*cemetery* NC-3
Donald Ferguson Dam—*dam* SD-7
Donald G. Trayer Museum—*building* MA-1
Donald Halters Dam—*dam* TN-4
Donald Halters Lake—*reservoir* TN-4
Donald Hesselman Lake—*reservoir* AL-4
Donald Hesselman Lake Dam—*dam* AL-4
Donald House—*hist pl* WA-9
Donald Kelly Dam—*dam* SD-7
Donald King Dam—*dam* SD-7
Donald King 1 Dam—*dam* SD-7
Donald King 2 Dam—*dam* SD-7
Donald King 3 Dam—*dam* SD-7
Donald King 4 Dam—*dam* SD-7
Donald Kitchens Lake Dam—*dam* MS-4
Donald Kunkle Ditch—*canal* IN-6
Donald Lake—*lake* IN-6
Donald Lake—*lake* ND-7
Donald Lake—*lake* WY-8
Donald Lake—*reservoir* AL-4
Donald L Rheem Sch—*school* CA-9
Donald MacDonald State Camp
Ground—*locale* FL-3
Donald Mcphail Ditch—*canal* WY-8
Donald Mill (historical)—*locale* TN-4
Donald Oil and Gas Field—*oilfield* KS-7
Donald Park—*flat* CO-8
Donald Peeples Pond—*lake* FL-3
Donald Post Office (historical)—*building* TN-4
Donald Ranch—*locale* CO-8
Donald Ridge—*ridge* AK-9
Donald Ridge—*ridge* AR-4
Donald Rock—*pillar* WI-6
Donald Rsvr—*reservoir* MT-8
**Donalds**—*pop pl* SC-3
*Donalds Assembly of God Church* AL-4
Donaldsburg—*locale* VA-3
Donalds (CCD)—*cens area* SC-3
Donald Sch—*school* TX-5
Donalds Day Care—*school* FL-3
Donalds Knoll—*summit* IN-6
Donalds Lake—*lake* MN-6
*Donalds Mill* TN-4
Donald Smith Lake—*reservoir* AL-4
Donald Smith Lake Dam—*dam* AL-4
Donaldson—*locale* KY-4
Donaldson—*locale* PA-2
Donaldson—*locale* WV-2
**Donaldson**—*pop pl* AR-4
**Donaldson**—*pop pl* IN-6
**Donaldson**—*pop pl* MI-6
**Donaldson**—*pop pl* MN-6
**Donaldson**—*pop pl* PA-2
**Donaldson**—*pop pl* WV-2
Donaldson—*uninc pl* OK-5
DONALDSON, LT. C. V.—*hist pl* AK-9
Donaldson, T. Q., House—*hist pl* SC-3
Donaldson, Widow, Place—*hist pl* PA-2
Donaldson AFB—*military* SC-3
Donaldson Branch—*stream* AL-4
Donaldson Branch—*stream* NC-3
Donaldson Branch—*stream* WV-2
Donaldson Canyon—*valley* OR-9
Donaldson Cave—*cave* IN-6
Donaldson Cem—*cemetery* (2) AL-4
Donaldson Cem—*cemetery* GA-3
Donaldson Cem—*cemetery* IL-6
Donaldson Cem—*cemetery* (2) IN-6
Donaldson Cem—*cemetery* LA-4
Donaldson Cem—*cemetery* MO-7
Donaldson Cem—*cemetery* TN-4
Donaldson Cem—*cemetery* WV-2
**Donaldson Center**—*pop pl* SC-3
Donaldson Ch—*church* (2) KY-4
Donaldson Court Apartments—*hist pl* MO-7
*Donaldson Creek* KY-4
*Donaldson Creek* MI-6
*Donaldson Creek* OR-9
*Donaldson Creek* TN-4
*Donaldson Creek* TX-5
Donaldson Creek—*stream* AK-9
Donaldson Creek—*stream* CA-9
Donaldson Creek—*stream* ID-8
Donaldson Creek—*stream* IA-7
Donaldson Creek—*stream* (3) KY-4
Donaldson Creek—*stream* MN-6
Donaldson Creek—*stream* MS-4
Donaldson Creek—*stream* MT-8
Donaldson Creek—*stream* OH-6
Donaldson Creek—*stream* (2) OR-9
Donaldson Creek—*stream* TN-4
Donaldson Creek—*stream* (3) WA-9
Donaldson Creek Ch—*church* KY-4
Donaldson Creek Public Use Area—*locale* KY-4
**Donaldson Crossroads**—*pop pl* PA-2
Donaldson Dam—*dam* AZ-5
Donaldson Draw—*valley* WA-9
Donaldson Grove Ch—*church* TN-4
Donaldson Gulch—*valley* WA-9
*Donaldson Lake* AL-4
Donaldson Lake—*lake* IN-6
Donaldson Lake—*lake* MI-6
Donaldson Lake—*lake* TX-5
Donaldson Lake Dam—*dam* AL-4
Donaldson Mill—*locale* AL-4
Donaldson Mine—*mine* AZ-5
Donaldson Mine—*mine* CO-8
Donaldson Mine—*mine* OR-9
Donaldson Mtn—*summit* NY-2
Donaldson Mtn—*summit* TX-5
Donaldson Number One Mine
(underground)—*mine* AL-4
Donaldson Park—*park* MN-6
Donaldson Park—*park* VA-3
**Donaldson Park**—*pop pl* NJ-2
Donaldson Park Rec Area—*park* TN-4
Donaldson Peak—*summit* ID-8
*Donaldson Point* FL-3
Donaldson Point—*cape* MO-7
Donaldson Point—*cape* VT-1
Donaldson Pond—*reservoir* (2) AL-4
Donaldson Ranch—*locale* AZ-5
Donaldson Ranch—*locale* WY-8
Donaldson Run—*stream* VA-3
Donaldson Sch—*school* AZ-5
Donaldson Sch—*school* AR-4
Donaldson Sch—*school* IL-6
Donaldson Sch—*school* MI-6
Donaldson Sch—*school* MS-4
**Donaldsons Crossroads**—*pop pl* PA-2
Donaldsons Crossroads Shop Ctr—*locale* PA-2
Donaldson-Simmons Cem—*cemetery* TN-4
Donaldsons Mill (historical)—*locale* TN-4
Donaldson Spring—*spring* OR-9
Donaldson Spring—*spring* WY-8
Donaldson Tank—*reservoir* AZ-5
**Donaldson (Township name
Frailey)**—*pop pl* PA-2
**Donaldsonville**—*pop pl* IN-6
**Donaldsonville**—*pop pl* LA-4
Donaldsonville Hist Dist—*hist pl* LA-4
Donaldson Way Sch—*school* CA-9
Donaldson Well—*well* NM-5
Donald Springs—*spring* TN-4
Donald Springs Branch—*stream* TN-4
*Donaldsville* SC-3
Donald (Township of)—*fmr MCD* AR-4
Donald Wall Place—*locale* CO-8
*Donald W. Waddell Dam* AZ-5
Don Alonso (Barrio)—*fmr MCD* PR-3
*Donalson Creek* TX-5
Donalson Creek—*stream* TX-5
Donalson Point—*cape* FL-3
**Donalsonville**—*pop pl* GA-3
Donalsonville (CCD)—*cens area* GA-3
*Don Amegus Mine* AZ-5
Don Andres Hill—*ridge* NM-5
Donansburg—*locale* KY-4
Donansburg (CCD)—*cens area* KY-4
*Dona River* DE-2
Donart HS—*school* OK-5
Donas Landing—*locale* DE-2
Donathan Branch—*stream* WV-2
Donathan Ridge—*ridge* AR-4
Donathan Rock—*summit* KY-4
Donathey Ch—*church* PA-2
Donath Lake—*lake* CO-8
*Donathon Fork* WV-2
**Donation**—*pop pl* PA-2
Donation Canyon—*valley* UT-8
Donation Hill Ch—*church* PA-2
Donation Sch (abandoned)—*school* PA-2
Donation Sch (historical)—*school* PA-2
*Donat Pig* PA-2
Donats Mtn—*summit* NY-2
*Donavan* MS-4
Donavan Lake—*lake* WI-6
*Donavan Mountain* WA-9
*Donavan Reservoir* CA-9
**Dona Vista**—*pop pl* FL-3
*Donavon Pond* CT-1
*Donavon Pond Brook* CT-1
*Donaway Hollow* TN-4
*Donaway Ridge* TN-4
Donaway Sch (historical)—*school* TN-4
Don Ball Lake Dam—*dam* MS-4
Don Benito Sch—*school* CA-9
Don Bosco, Mount—*summit* NY-2
Don Bosco Ch—*church* NY-2
Don Bosco Coll—*school* NJ-2
Don Bosco Institute—*school* NJ-2
Don Bosco Juniorate—*school* NY-2
Don Bosco Technical Institute—*school* CA-9
Don Bosco Technical Sch—*school* NJ-2
Don Bosco Youth Center—*building* TX-5
Don Box Windmill—*locale* TX-5
Don Canyon—*valley* UT-8
Don Carlos Court—*hist pl* CA-9
Don Carlos Hills—*other* NM-5
*Doncaster* NJ-2
Doncaster—*locale* MD-2
Doncaster State For—*forest* MD-2
Doncaster Town Site—*hist pl* MD-2
Don Castro Regional Rec Area—*park* CA-9
Don Castro Rsvr—*reservoir* CA-9
Don Cecil Trail—*trail* CA-9
Don Ce Sar Hotel—*hist pl* FL-3
*Don-ce-Sar Place* FL-3
Don-Ce-Sar Place—*uninc pl* FL-3
**Don Ce-Sar Place (historical)**—*pop pl* FL-3
Donchelok Creek—*stream* AK-9
Don Coleman Dam—*dam* TN-4
Don Coleman Lake—*reservoir* TN-4
Don Creek—*stream* ID-8
Don Cundall Ranch—*locale* WY-8
Don Dahvee Park—*park* CA-9
Don Delfino Tank—*reservoir* TX-5
Dondero HS—*school* MI-6
Dondero Park—*park* MI-6
Donders Lake—*lake* MN-6
Don Diego Tank—*reservoir* AZ-5
*Don Don Pass* NV-8
Don Drennen Dam Number 1—*dam* AL-4
Don Drennen Dam Number 2—*dam* AL-4
Dondy Bldg—*hist pl* AR-4
Done Creek—*stream* ID-8
Donegal—*locale* GA-3
Donegal—*locale* MS-4
Donegal—*locale* PA-2
**Donegal**—*pop pl* PA-2
Donegal, Lake—*reservoir* PA-2
*Donegal Airport* PA-2
Donegal Bay—*bay* MI-6
*Donegal Borough* PA-2
Donegal Borough—*civil* PA-2
Donegal Cave—*cave* PA-2
Donegal Creek—*stream* PA-2
**Donegal Heights**—*pop pl* PA-2
Donegal HS—*school* PA-2
*Donegal Interchange* PA-2
Donegal Mills Plantation—*hist pl* PA-2
Donegal Presbyterian Church
Complex—*hist pl* PA-2
Donegal Sch—*school* PA-2
*Donegal Senior HS* PA-2
Donegal Spring—*spring* PA-2
**Donegal Springs**—*pop pl* PA-2
*Donegal Springs Airpark* PA-2
**Donegal (Township of)**—*pop pl* (3) PA-2
Donegan Block—*hist pl* AL-4
Donegan Cem—*cemetery* AL-4
Donegan Cem—*cemetery* TN-4
Donegan Creek—*stream* OR-9
Donegan Creek—*stream* WA-9
Donegan Crossing—*locale* TN-4
Donegan Elem Sch—*school* PA-2
Donegan Prairies—*flat* OR-9
*Donegan Sch* PA-2
Donegan Slough—*stream* MT-8
Donegan Spring—*spring* TN-4
Donehew Head—*summit* TN-4
Donehew Hollow—*valley* TN-4
Donehoo Elem Sch—*school* AL-4
Donehower—*locale* MN-6
Donelly Creek—*stream* CA-9
Donelly Station—*locale* PA-2
*Donelson* IN-6
**Donelson**—*pop pl* TN-4
Donelson, Daniel Smith, House—*hist pl* TN-4
Donelson Branch—*stream* GA-3
Donelson Cem—*cemetery* IL-6
Donelson Ch—*church* TN-4
Donelson Ditch—*canal* CO-8
Donelson House—*hist pl* MS-4
Donelson Ranch—*locale* CO-8
Donelson Sch—*school* MI-6
Donelson Spring—*spring* TN-4
**Donelton**—*pop pl* TX-5
Donelton Cem—*cemetery* TX-5
Donelton Ch—*church* TX-5
Donerail—*locale* KY-4
Doneraile—*CDP* SC-3
Done Ridge—*ridge* UT-8
Doners Station—*locale* PA-2
**Donerville**—*pop pl* PA-2
D-One Spring—*spring* AZ-5
D One Tank—*reservoir* AZ-5
**Doney**—*pop pl* IL-6
Doney Bottoms—*bend* MT-8
Doney Branch—*stream* AL-4
Doney Coulee—*valley* MT-8
*Doney Crater* AZ-5
*Doney Craters* AZ-5
Doney Creek—*stream* CA-9
Doney Gulch—*valley* CA-9
*Doney Hill* AZ-5
Doney Hill—*summit* CA-9
Doney Hollow—*valley* NY-2
Doney Lake—*lake* (2) MT-8
Doney Meadows—*flat* MT-8
Doney Mountain Wash—*stream* AZ-5
Doney Mtn—*summit* AZ-5
Doney Park—*flat* AZ-5
*Doneys* OH-6
*Doneys Cone* AZ-5
Don Farlee Dam—*dam* SD-7
Donford Branch—*stream* SC-3
**Dongan Hills**—*pop pl* NY-2
Dongan Place—*park* NY-2
Don Gaspar Hist Dist—*hist pl* NM-5
*Don George Lake* TX-5
Donges Bay—*bay* WI-6
*Dongnay* MH-9
Dongola—*locale* KY-4
Dongola—*locale* SC-3
Dongola—*locale* VA-3
**Dongola**—*pop pl* AR-4
**Dongola**—*pop pl* IL-6
**Dongola**—*pop pl* IN-6
**Dongola**—*pop pl* MO-7
Dongola District No. 1 (Election
Precinct)—*fmr MCD* IL-6
Dongola District No. 2 (Election
Precinct)—*fmr MCD* IL-6
Dongola Hollow—*valley* IL-6
Dongola Sch—*school* WI-6
Dong Run—*stream* IN-6
Dongua—*area* GU-9
Dongua Point—*cape* GU-9
Donham Cem—*cemetery* (2) AL-4
Donham Cem—*cemetery* IN-6
Donham Cem—*cemetery* PA-2
Donibureeku Passage—*channel* FM-9
Donica Creek—*stream* IL-6
Donica Memorial Ch—*church* IN-6
Donica Mtn—*summit* CA-9
**Donie**—*pop pl* TX-5
Donie Rsvr—*reservoir* TX-5
Donigan Drain—*canal* MI-6
Donigoppin Passage—*channel* FM-9
Doniparo Passage—*channel* FM-9
Doniphan—*locale* ID-8
**Doniphan**—*pop pl* AR-4
**Doniphan**—*pop pl* KS-7
**Doniphan**—*pop pl* MO-7
**Doniphan**—*pop pl* NE-7
Doniphan, Lake—*reservoir* MO-7
Doniphan Archeol Site—*hist pl* KS-7
Doniphan Bend—*bend* MO-7
Doniphan Cem—*cemetery* KS-7
Doniphan County—*civil* KS-7

Doniphan County Courthouse—hist pl ... KS-7
Doniphan Hollow—valley ... MO-7
Doniphan HS—school ... MO-7
Doniphan Lake—lake ... AR-4
Doniphan Lookout Tower—tower ... MO-7
Doniphan Station (historical)—locale ... KS-7
Doniphan Township—civil ... MO-7
Doniphan Township—fmr MCD ... NE-7
Donis Cem—cemetery ... KY-4
**Donita Subdivision**—pop pl ... UT-8
Donithan Branch—stream ... KY-4
Donivan Creek—stream ... MS-4
Donivan Creek—stream ... OR-9
Donivan Mtn—summit ... OR-9
Don Jean Bay—bay ... WI-6
**Donjean Subdivision**—pop pl ... UT-8
Don Jose Corral—locale ... AZ-5
Don Jose Creek—stream ... OK-5
Don Juan Creek—stream ... CA-9
Don Juan Cross Banco Number 155—levee ... TX-5
Don Juan Flat ... AZ-5
Don Juan (historical P.O.)—locale ... IN-6
Don Juan Mine—mine ... OR-9
Don Julian Sch—school ... CA-9
Don Julio JHS—school ... CA-9
**Donken**—pop pl ... MI-6
Donken Lake—lake ... MI-6
**Donkey**—pop pl ... VA-3
Donkey Bay—bay ... AK-9
Donkey Canyon—valley ... AZ-5
Donkey Canyon—valley ... CA-9
Donkey Canyon—valley ... ID-8
Donkey Creek—stream ... AK-9
Donkey Creek—stream (2) ... ID-8
Donkey Creek—stream ... UT-8
Donkey Creek—stream ... WA-9
Donkey Creek—stream (2) ... WY-8
Donkey Creek Lake—lake ... AK-9
Donkey Creek Oil Field—oilfield ... WY-8
Donkey Creek Slough—stream ... AK-9
Donkey Dam—dam ... UT-8
Donkey Draw—valley ... ID-8
Donkey Flat—flat ... UT-8
Donkey Hill Cutoff—trail ... NH-1
Donkey Hills—range ... ID-8
Donkey Lake—lake ... AK-9
Donkey Lake—lake ... AZ-5
Donkey Lake—lake ... CA-9
Donkey Lake—lake ... UT-8
Donkey Meadows—flat ... UT-8
Donkey Mtn—summit ... TX-5
Donkey Point—cape ... CA-9
Donkey Point—cliff ... UT-8
Donkey Ridge—ridge ... UT-8
Donkey Rsvr—reservoir ... UT-8
Donkeys Corners—locale ... NJ-2
Donkey Spring—spring (2) ... AZ-5
Donkey Spring Canyon—valley ... AZ-5
Donkey Trace ... AL-4
Donkey Trail ... AL-4
Donkey Trail ... MS-4
Don K Ranch—locale ... CO-8
Don Lake—lake ... AR-4
Don Lake—lake ... LA-4
Don Lake—lake ... MN-6
Don Lake—lake ... OR-9
Don Lake—lake ... WA-9
Don Lake—lake ... WY-8
Donlan—locale ... MT-8
Donlan—locale ... WV-2
Donlan Canyon—valley ... CA-9
Don Landrum Lake Dam—dam ... MS-4
Donlan Flats—flat ... MT-8
Donlan Point—cape ... CA-9
Donlans Creek—stream ... WI-6
**Donleigh**—pop pl ... MD-2
Donlevy ... PA-2
Donley ... MS-4
Donley—locale ... PA-2
**Donley**—pop pl ... PA-2
Donley Camp—locale ... CO-8
Donley Cem—cemetery ... AL-4
Donley Cem—cemetery ... WV-2
**Donley (County)**—pop pl ... TX-5
Donley County Courthouse and Jail—hist pl ... TX-5
Donley Creek ... CA-9
Donley Creek—stream ... MT-8
Donley Fork—stream ... PA-2
Donley Fork—stream ... WV-2
Donley Hollow ... VA-3
Donley Hollow—valley ... VA-3
Donley Island—island ... PA-2
Donley Mtn—summit ... TN-4
Donley (reduced Usage)—locale ... MS-4
Donley Run—stream ... WV-2
Donley Sch—school (2) ... MI-6
Donleys Rsvr—reservoir ... MT-8
**Donley Station (historical)**—pop pl ... IA-7
Donlin Creek—stream ... AK-9
Donlin Drive Sch—school ... NY-2
Donlon—uninc pl ... CA-9
Donlontown—locale ... NJ-2
**Don Luis**—pop pl ... AZ-5
Don Luis Sch—school ... AZ-5
Don McKinsey Branch—stream ... KY-4
Donmeyer ... KS-7
Don Miller Hills—other ... AK-9
Donmyer Cem—cemetery ... KS-7
Donna ... OR-9
**Donna**—pop pl ... GR-9
**Donna**—pop pl ... TX-5
Donna Creek—stream ... NV-8
Donna Creek—stream ... OR-9
Donna Drain—canal ... TX-5
Donna Draw—valley ... WY-8
Donna Gas Field—oilfield ... TX-5
**Donnaha**—pop pl ... NC-3
Donnaha Ch—church ... NC-3
Donnaha Site—hist pl ... NC-3
Donna K Mine—mine ... CO-8
Donna Lake—lake ... OR-9
Donna Lake—reservoir ... MN-6
**Donna Lee Gardens**—pop pl ... VA-3
**Donnally Mills**—pop pl ... PA-2
Donna Loy Talc Mine—mine ... CA-9
Donna Main Canal—canal ... TX-5
**Donnan**—pop pl ... IA-7
Donnan-Asher Iron-Front Bldg—hist pl ... VA-3
Donnan Branch—stream ... GA-3
Donnan Cem—cemetery ... IL-6
Donna Pump—other ... TX-5
Donna Pumping Station—other ... TX-5
Donna Reservoirs—reservoir ... TX-5
Donna Rsvr—reservoir ... WY-8
Donna Schee Peak—summit ... NV-8
Donna Schee Spring—spring ... NV-8
Donnas Pit—cave ... AL-4
Donna V, Lake—reservoir ... TX-5
Donnay ... MH-9
Donnebroug Mine—mine ... CA-9
Donneby Branch—stream ... AL-4
Donneby Branch—stream ... TN-4
Donnegal Bay ... MI-6
Donnel Chapel—church ... TN-4
Donnell ... TN-4
**Donnell**—pop pl ... MO-7
Donnell, Harry E., House—hist pl ... NY-2
Donnell, Robert, House—hist pl ... AL-4
Donnell Cem—cemetery ... IA-7
Donnell Cem—cemetery ... MO-7
Donnell Cem—cemetery ... OK-5
Donnell Cem—cemetery (2) ... TN-4
Donnell Cem—cemetery ... TX-5
Donnell Ditch—canal ... IN-6
Donnelley—locale ... IA-7
Donnelley, R. R., & Sons Company (Dwight)—facility ... IL-6
Donnelley, R. R., & Sons Company (Matton)—facility ... IL-6
Donnelley Station ... IA-7
Donnell Hill—summit ... CA-9
Donnell (historical P.O.)—locale ... IA-7
Donnell JHS—school ... OH-6
Donnell Lake—lake ... LA-4
Donnell Lake—lake ... MI-6
Donnell Lake—reservoir ... CA-9
Donnell Pond—lake ... ME-1
Donnell Powerhouse—other ... CA-9
**Donnellson**—pop pl ... IL-6
**Donnellson**—pop pl ... IA-7
Donnellson Cem—cemetery ... IL-6
Donnell Tunnel—tunnel ... CA-9
Donnell Vista Point—locale ... CA-9
Donnelly—locale ... AK-9
Donnelly—locale ... MI-6
Donnelly—locale ... PA-2
**Donnelly**—pop pl ... ID-8
**Donnelly**—pop pl ... IA-7
**Donnelly**—pop pl ... MN-6
Donnelly Basin—basin ... OR-9
Donnelly Branch—stream ... TN-4
Donnelly Brook—stream ... NY-2
Donnelly Brook Sch—school ... ME-1
Donnelly Butte—summit ... OR-9
Donnelly Camp—locale ... OR-9
Donnelly Canyon ... AZ-5
Donnelly Canyon—valley ... UT-8
Donnelly Cem—cemetery ... OK-5
Donnelly Coll—school ... KS-7
Donnelly Creek—stream ... NV-8
Donnelly Creek—stream ... OR-9
Donnelly Dome—summit ... AK-9
Donnelly Flat—flat ... NV-8
Donnelly Gulch—valley (2) ... CA-9
Donnelly Gulch—valley ... ID-8
Donnelly Hill—summit ... OK-5
Donnelly House—hist pl ... FL-3
Donnelly Island—island ... ME-1
Donnelly Lake—lake ... LA-4
Donnelly Memorial Park—park ... NJ-2
Donnelly North Oil Field—oilfield ... TX-5
Donnelly Oil Field—oilfield ... TX-5
Donnelly Park—park ... FL-3
Donnelly Park—park ... IA-7
Donnelly Peak—summit ... NV-8
Donnelly Point—cape ... AK-9
Donnelly Ranch—locale ... AZ-5
Donnelly Spring—spring ... NV-8
Donnelly Spring—spring ... OR-9
Donnelly State Public Shooting Area—park ... SD-7
**Donnellytown**—pop pl ... PA-2
**Donnelly (Township of)**—pop pl (2) ... MN-6
Donnelly Trail—trail ... ID-8
Donnelly Wash—stream ... AZ-5
Donnel Point—cape ... TX-5
Donnel Reef—bar ... TX-5
**Donnels Chapel**—pop pl ... TN-4
Donnels Creek—stream ... OH-6
Donnels Creek Ch—church ... OH-6
**Donnelsville**—pop pl ... OH-6
Donnelsville Station—locale ... OH-6
Donnely Basin ... OR-9
Donnely Creek—stream ... OR-9
Donnely Gulch ... ID-8
Donnely Park—park ... CA-9
Donnely Pond—lake ... MA-1
Donnely Rsvr—reservoir ... CO-8
Donnely Sch—school ... SD-7
**Donner**—pop pl ... FL-3
**Donner**—pop pl ... LA-4
Donner—post sta ... CA-9
Donner and Blitzen River ... OR-9
Donner Camp—hist pl ... CA-9
Donner Canal—canal (2) ... LA-4
Donner Canyon—valley ... CA-9
Donner Canyon—valley ... UT-8
Donner (CCD)—cens area ... CA-9
Donner Creek ... TX-5
Donner Creek—stream (2) ... CA-9
**Donner Crossroads**—pop pl ... PA-2
Donner Dam—dam ... AL-4
Donner Hill Trail—trail ... CO-8
Donner Lake ... MT-8
Donner Lake—lake ... CA-9
**Donner Lake**—pop pl ... CA-9
Donner Lake—reservoir ... AL-4
Donner Memorial State Park—park ... CA-9
Donner Monument—other ... CA-9
Donner Oil Field—oilfield ... LA-4
Donner Park—park ... IN-6
Donner Pass—gap ... CA-9
Donner Pass—gap ... CO-8
Donner Peak ... CA-9
Donner Peak—summit ... CA-9
Donner Point—cape ... MI-6
Donner-Reed Pass—gap ... UT-8
Donner - Reed Trail—trail ... UT-8
Donner Ridge—ridge ... CA-9
Donner Sch—school ... CA-9
Donner Sch (abandoned)—school ... PA-2
Donners Landing (historical)—locale ... IN-6
Donner Spring—spring ... UT-8
Donner Summit Bridge—bridge ... CA-9
**Donnersville**—pop pl ... OH-6
Donner Trail Sch—school ... CA-9
Donner und Blitzen River—stream ... OR-9
Donner und Blitzen Valley ... OR-9
Donnerville ... PA-2
Donnerville State For—forest ... NY-2
Donnet-Fry Ranch—locale ... AZ-5
Donne Windmills—locale ... NM-5
Donney Tank—reservoir ... AZ-5
Donni ... MH-9
Donnick—locale ... AR-4
Donnii ... MH-9
Donnington Branch—stream ... SC-3
Donnis Tank—reservoir ... NM-5
Donni Stream ... MH-9
Donnivan ... MS-4
Donnoha ... NC-3
Donnors Landing ... IN-6
Donnybrook—locale ... OR-9
**Donnybrook**—pop pl ... MD-2
**Donnybrook**—pop pl ... ND-7
Donny Brook—stream ... PA-2
Donnybrooke Speedway—other ... MN-6
Donnybrook Forest Camp—locale ... WA-9
Donoe—locale ... VI-3
Donoghue, Thomas J., House—hist pl ... TX-5
Donoghue Beach ... MI-6
**Donoghue Beach**—pop pl ... MI-6
Donoho—locale ... TN-4
Donoho Branch—stream ... TN-4
Donoho Ch—church ... IL-6
Donoho Creek—stream ... NC-3
Donohoe—locale ... MS-4
**Donohoe**—pop pl ... PA-2
Donohoe Bay—swamp ... SC-3
Donohoe Mine—mine ... CA-9
Donohoe Mtn—summit ... CA-9
Donohoe Spring—spring ... CA-9
Donoho Hollow—valley ... TN-4
Donoho Hotel Hist Dist—hist pl ... TN-4
Donohoo Cem—cemetery ... TN-4
Donohoos Plantation ... AL-4
Donoho Peak—summit ... AK-9
Donoho Point—island ... WY-8
Donoho Post Office (historical)—building ... TN-4
Donoho Ranch—locale ... WA-9
Donoho Sch (historical)—school ... TN-4
Donoho School ... AL-4
Donohue ... PA-2
Donohue ... WV-2
Donohue Creek—stream ... IN-6
Donohue Pass—gap ... CA-9
Donohue Peak—summit ... CA-9
Donohue Run—stream ... IL-6
Donohue Spring—spring ... WA-9
Donomore Creek ... CA-9
Donomore Creek—stream ... CA-9
Donomore Meadows—flat ... CA-9
Donomore Peak—summit ... OR-9
**Donora**—pop pl ... PA-2
Donora Borough—civil ... PA-2
Donora Webster Bridge—bridge ... PA-2
Do Nothing Canyon—valley ... AZ-5
Do Nothing Tank—reservoir ... AZ-5
Donovan ... TN-4
**Donovan**—pop pl ... GA-3
**Donovan**—pop pl ... IL-6
Donovan, J. J., House—hist pl ... WA-9
Donovan Brook—stream ... NY-2
Donovan Cove—bay ... ME-1
Donovan Creek ... OR-9
Donovan Creek—stream ... AK-9
Donovan Creek—stream ... MT-8
Donovan Creek—stream ... WA-9
**Donovan Development (subdivision)**—pop pl (2) ... DE-2
Donovan Hill—summit ... CA-9
Donovan Hill—summit ... WA-9
**Donovan (historical)**—pop pl ... MS-4
Donovan Hollow—valley ... PA-2
Donovan Lake—lake ... MI-6
Donovan Lake—lake ... MN-6
Donovan Lateral—canal ... AZ-5
Donovan Mtn—summit ... NV-8
Donovan Playground—park ... IL-6
Donovan Post Office (historical)—building ... MS-4
Donovan Ranch—locale ... MT-8
Donovan Ridge—ridge ... CA-9
Donovan Rsvr—reservoir ... CA-9
Donovan Sch—school ... MA-1
Donovan Sch—school ... TN-4
Donovan Sch (abandoned)—school ... PA-2
Donovan School (historical)—locale ... MO-7
Donovans Corner—locale ... VA-3
Donovans Cove ... ME-1
**Donovans Pier**—pop pl ... MD-2
Donovan State Park—park ... WA-9
Donovan Tank—reservoir ... AZ-5
Donovan Valley—stream ... CA-9
Don Paul Draw—valley ... WA-9
**Don Pedro Camp**—pop pl ... CA-9
Don Pedro Island—island ... FL-3
Don Pedro Rsvr—reservoir ... CA-9
Don Pedro Sch—school ... CA-9
Don Quanella Sch—school ... PA-2
Don Quixote Key—island ... FL-3
Don Reid Lake—reservoir ... IN-6
Don Reid Lake Dam—dam ... IN-6
Don River—stream ... AK-9
Don Roberto Windmill—locale ... TX-5
Don Rsvr—reservoir ... ID-8
Dons Bayou—bay ... FL-3
Dons Branch—stream ... WV-2
Dons Butte—summit ... OR-9
Dons Camp—locale ... AZ-5
Dons Canyon—valley ... UT-8
Dons Chapel ... TN-4
Dons Creek ... OR-9
Dons Creek—stream ... ID-8
Dons Dump Tank ... NM-5
**Donsfort**—pop pl ... PA-2
Don Sheldon Amphitheater—basin ... AK-9
Dons Hollow ... UT-8
Donsill Canyon ... AZ-5
Dons Lake—lake ... UT-8
Don Smith Spring—spring ... AZ-5
Donsmore Spring—spring ... OR-9
Dons Place Airp—airport ... PA-2
Don Spring—spring ... CA-9
Don Spring—spring (2) ... UT-8
Don Spring Mtn—summit ... UT-8
Dons Spring—spring (2) ... OR-9
Dons Tank—reservoir (3) ... AZ-5
Dons Tank—reservoir ... NM-5
Dons Texaco Campground—locale ... UT-8
Don Tank—reservoir (2) ... AZ-5
Don Timoteo Sch—school ... CA-9
Don-Tol—locale ... TX-5
**Don Tol**—pop pl ... TX-5
Donton Island—island ... CA-9
Don Triste Artesian Well—well ... TX-5
Donugantamu—island ... FM-9
Donut Island—island ... MN-6
Donut Lake—lake ... MI-6
Donut Lake—lake ... MN-6
Donut Rock—summit ... CA-9
Don Victor Campground—locale ... CA-9
Don Victor Canyon—valley ... CA-9
Don Victor Valley—basin ... CA-9
Don Williams Lake Dam—dam ... IA-7
Don Williams Park—park ... IA-7
Don Williams Private Heliport—airport ... WA-9
**Donwood**—pop pl ... WV-2
**Dony**—pop pl ... KY-4
Donze Lake—reservoir ... MO-7
Donzelman And Tilton Ditch—canal ... WY-8
Doodlebug Branch—stream ... MO-7
Doodlebug Cave—cave ... AL-4
Doodlebug Diggings—mine ... AZ-5
Doodlebug Gulch—valley ... CA-9
Doodlebug Gulch—valley ... CO-8
Doodlebug Tank—reservoir ... AZ-5
Doodlebug Tank—reservoir ... TX-5
Doodlebug Well—well (2) ... NM-5
Doodle Bug Well—well ... TX-5
Doodlebug Windmill—locale (2) ... NM-5
Doodlebug Windmill—locale (2) ... TX-5
Doodle Bug Windmill—locale ... TX-5
Doodle Creek—stream ... OR-9
Doodle Hill Pond—reservoir ... SC-3
Doodle Hole Hollow—valley ... MO-7
Doodle Hollow—valley ... TN-4
Doodlelink Creek—stream ... ID-8
**Doodletown**—pop pl ... NY-2
Doodletown Bight—bay ... NY-2
Doodletown Brook—stream ... NY-2
Doodle Waterhole ... OR-9
Doody, Mount—summit ... MT-8
Doody Creek—stream ... SD-7
**Doogan**—pop pl ... GA-3
Doogan Hole—rapids ... GA-3
Doogan Mtn—summit ... GA-3
Doogen Mtn ... GA-3
Dooksook Lagoon—lake ... AK-9
Dooksook River—stream ... AK-9
Doolan Canyon—valley ... CA-9
Doolan Chute—stream ... MO-7
Doolan Hollow—valley ... TN-4
**Doolans**—pop pl ... AL-4
Doolans Hole Creek—stream ... CA-9
**Doole**—pop pl ... TX-5
Doolen Cem—cemetery ... IL-6
Dooles Creek—stream ... CA-9
Dooley—locale ... AR-4
Dooley—locale ... MS-4
**Dooley**—pop pl ... MT-8
**Dooley**—pop pl ... VA-3
Dooley Bayou—gut ... LA-4
Dooley Bedground Rsvr—reservoir ... OR-9
Dooley Bend—bend ... AR-4
Dooley Bend—bend ... MO-7
Dooley Bend Cem—cemetery ... MO-7
Dooley Bend Sch (abandoned)—school ... MO-7
Dooley Branch—stream ... AR-4
Dooley Branch—stream ... GA-3
Dooley Branch—stream ... LA-4
Dooley Canyon—valley ... CA-9
Dooley Canyon Spring—spring ... CA-9
Dooley Cem—cemetery (2) ... AL-4
Dooley Cem—cemetery ... IN-6
Dooley Cem—cemetery ... IA-7
Dooley Cem—cemetery ... MO-7
Dooley Cem—cemetery ... TN-4
Dooley Chapel—church ... MO-7
Dooley Creek ... OR-9
Dooley Creek—stream ... AR-4
Dooley Creek—stream (2) ... CA-9
Dooley Creek—stream ... GA-3
Dooley Creek—stream ... ID-8
Dooley Creek—stream ... LA-4
Dooley Creek—stream (2) ... TX-5
Dooley Ditch—canal ... MT-8
Dooley Ditch—canal ... UT-8
Dooley Draw—valley ... WY-8
Dooley Gulch—valley ... MT-8
Dooley Gulch—valley ... OR-9
Dooley Gulch Pond—lake ... OR-9
Dooley Hollow—valley ... MO-7
Dooley Hollow—valley ... TN-4
Dooley Hollow—valley ... VA-3
Dooley Homestead—locale ... MT-8
Dooley Lake—lake ... NE-7
Dooley Lake Dam—dam ... MS-4
Dooley Mtn—summit ... AL-4
Dooley Mtn—summit ... MT-8
Dooley Mtn—summit ... OR-9
Dooley Mtn—summit ... TX-5
Dooley Pond—reservoir ... CT-1
Dooley Run—stream ... PA-2
Dooley Run—stream ... WV-2
Dooley Sch (historical)—school ... TN-4
Dooleys Island—island ... MS-4
Dooley Slough—gut ... SD-7
Dooley Spring—spring ... GA-3
Dooley Spring—spring ... MT-8
Dooley Spring—spring ... NE-7
Dooleys Prong ... MD-2
**Dooley Station (historical)**—pop pl ... IN-6
Dooley Summit—gap ... OR-9
Dooley Tank—reservoir ... NM-5
**Dooleyville**—pop pl ... PA-2
Dooleyville Creek—stream ... KS-7
Dooley Windmill—locale ... TX-5
Dooley Wood Cem—cemetery ... MS-4
Dooley Wood Sch—school ... MS-4
**Doolie**—pop pl ... NC-3
Doolin—locale ... OK-5
Doolin Branch—stream ... KY-4
Doolin Cem—cemetery ... KY-4
Doolin Creek—stream ... CA-9
**Dooling**—pop pl ... GA-3
Dooling Chapel (historical)—church ... TN-4
Dooling Creek—stream ... MO-7
Dooling Spring Branch—stream ... TN-4
Doolin Hollow—valley ... MO-7
Doolin Knob—summit ... KY-4
Doolin Lake—lake ... KY-4
Doolin Run—stream ... WV-2
Doolin Sch—school ... KY-4
Doolins Crossing—locale ... NY-2
Doolin Windmill—locale ... NM-5
**Doolittle**—pop pl ... MO-7
Doolittle Branch—stream ... TN-4
Doolittle Brook—stream ... MA-1
Doolittle Butte—summit ... OR-9
Doolittle Cave—cave ... TN-4
Doolittle Chapel Black Sch ... MS-4
Doolittle Chapel Sch—school ... MS-4
Doolittle Confederate Cem—cemetery ... MS-4
Doolittle Creek ... ID-8
Doolittle Creek—stream (2) ... CA-9
Doolittle Creek—stream ... GA-3
Doolittle Creek—stream ... MS-4
Doolittle Creek—stream (2) ... MO-7
Doolittle Creek—stream ... MT-8
Doolittle Creek—stream ... NY-2
Doolittle Creek—stream ... OR-9
Doolittle Creek—stream ... SC-3
Doolittle Creek—stream ... WA-9
Doolittle Flat—flat ... OR-9
Doolittle Gulch—valley ... MT-8
Doolittle Hill—summit ... NY-2
Doolittle Hill—summit ... PA-2
**Doolittle (historical)**—pop pl ... MS-4
Doolittle Hollow—valley ... IN-6
Doolittle Lake ... NE-7
Doolittle Lake—lake ... CT-1
Doolittle Lake Brook—stream ... CT-1
Doolittle Mill Pond—reservoir ... NC-3
Doolittle Mill Pond Dam—dam ... NC-3
**Doolittle Mills**—pop pl ... IN-6
Doolittle Park—park ... CT-1
Doolittle Pond—reservoir ... GA-3
Doolittle Ranch—locale ... CO-8
Doolittle Run ... PA-2
Doolittle Sch—school ... CT-1
Doolittle Sch—school (2) ... IL-6
Doolittle Sch—school ... NY-2
Doolittle Sch (historical)—school ... MS-4
Doolittle Sch (historical)—school ... TN-4
Doolittle Tank No 1—reservoir ... NM-5
Dool Sch—school ... CA-9
Doolth Mtn—summit ... AK-9
Dooly, Frank E., House—hist pl ... OR-9
Dooly Campground—locale ... GA-3
**Dooly (County)**—pop pl ... GA-3
Dooly County Courthouse—hist pl ... GA-3
Dooly Creek—stream ... OR-9
Dooly Knob—summit ... UT-8
Dooly Med Ctr—hospital ... GA-3
Dooly Park—flat ... CO-8
Dooly Spring—spring ... UT-8
Doom, Col. Randolph C., House—hist pl ... TX-5
Doomas Creek ... NC-3
Doom'athing—cape ... FM-9
Doom Cem—cemetery ... KY-4
Doom Chapel—church ... KY-4
Doomchuy ... FM-9
Doom'eenifiy—summit ... FM-9
Doomes Creek ... NC-3
Doom Run—stream ... PA-2
**Dooms**—pop pl ... VA-3
Dooms Chapel—church ... KY-4
Dooms Den—cave ... TN-4
Dooms Island—island ... TX-5
Doom Spring—spring ... KY-4
Doom Spring Branch—stream ... KY-4
Dooms Spring—spring ... KY-4
**Doon**—pop pl ... CA-9
**Doon**—pop pl ... IA-7
Doonan Corners—locale ... NY-2
Doonan Gulch—valley ... MT-8
Doonan Peak—summit ... MT-8
Doonan Spring—spring ... MT-8
Doone Creek—stream ... AK-9
Doone Creek—stream ... MI-6
Doone Pond ... MA-1
Doonerak, Mount—summit ... AK-9
Doon Township—fmr MCD ... IA-7
Doonysio ... AZ-5
Door, The—gap ... UT-8
Doorbell Spring—spring ... OR-9
**Door (County)**—pop pl ... WI-6
Door Creek ... WA-9
Door Creek—locale ... WI-6
Door Creek—stream ... AK-9
Door Creek—stream ... WA-9
Door Creek—stream ... WI-6
Doore Sch—school ... ME-1
Door Mountains—ridge ... AK-9
Door Peninsula—cape ... WI-6
Door Point—cape ... LA-4
Door Point Bayou—gut ... LA-4
Door Point Lagoon—bay ... LA-4
Door Point Light—locale ... LA-4
Door Pond ... NH-1
Doorshutter Creek—stream ... FL-3
Doorshutter Lake—lake ... FL-3
Door Spring, The—spring ... AZ-5
Doortown ... WV-2
**Doortown**—pop pl ... WV-2
**Door Village**—pop pl ... IN-6
Door Village Elem Sch—school ... IN-6
Doorway—locale ... KY-4
Dootey Draw—valley ... WY-8
Doove Kill—stream ... NY-2
**Dooville**—pop pl ... IN-6
Dope Creek—stream ... OR-9
Dopf, John Dickinson, Mansion—hist pl ... MO-7
**Dopler**—pop pl ... FL-3
Dopler RR Station—locale ... FL-3
Dopp Cem—cemetery ... WI-6
Doppelberg Von ... PW-9
Doppelberg Von Ngamlungui ... PW-9
Dopp Hill—summit ... NY-2
Dopping Brook—stream ... MA-1
Dopple Brook ... MA-1
Dopps Hollow—valley ... PA-2
Dopson Branch—stream ... GA-3
Dopson Cem—cemetery ... GA-3
**Doqomchuuy**—pop pl ... FM-9
Dora—locale ... NC-3
Dora—locale ... PA-2
**Dora**—pop pl ... AL-4
**Dora**—pop pl ... AR-4
**Dora**—pop pl ... LA-4
**Dora**—pop pl ... MO-7
**Dora**—pop pl ... NM-5
**Dora**—pop pl ... OR-9
**Dora**—pop pl ... PA-2
**Dora**—pop pl ... TN-4
Dora, Lake—lake ... FL-3
Dora, Lake—lake ... MN-6
Dora, Mount—summit ... NM-5
Dora Bay—bay ... AK-9
Dorabell Ch—church ... AR-4
Dora Belle—locale ... CA-9
Dora Branch—stream (2) ... KY-4
Dora Canal—canal ... FL-3
Dora (CCD)—cens area ... AL-4
Dora (CCD)—cens area ... NM-5
Dorace Lake—lake ... MN-6
Dora Cem—cemetery ... OK-5
Dora Cem—cemetery ... TX-5
Dora Christian Ch—church ... IN-6
Dora Creek—stream (3) ... AK-9
Dora Creek—stream ... CA-9
Dora Creek—stream ... ID-8
Dora Creek—stream ... NV-8
Dorada Park—park ... CA-9
Dora Division—civil ... AL-4
**Dorado**—pop pl ... PR-3
Dorado Canyon—valley ... NM-5
Dorado (Municipio)—civil ... PR-3
Dorado Needle—pillar ... WA-9
Dorado (Pueblo)—fmr MCD ... PR-3
Dorado Wash, El—stream ... AZ-5
Dora Hi-Way Ch—church ... VA-3
Dora Hollow—valley ... MO-7
Dora HS—school ... AL-4
Dora Island—island (2) ... AK-9
**Dora Junction**—pop pl ... AL-4
**Dora Junction**—pop pl ... VA-3
Dora Keen Range—ridge ... AK-9
Dora Kennedy Sch—school ... TN-4
Dora Lake—lake ... AK-9
Dora Lake—lake ... MN-6
Dora Lake—lake ... NE-7
Dora Lake—locale ... MN-6
**Doraland**—pop pl ... GA-3
Doral Country Club—locale ... FL-3
**Doral Estates (subdivision)**—pop pl ... AL-4
Dorals Playground—park ... MI-6
Dora Mine (underground)—mine ... AL-4
Dora Mtn—summit (2) ... CO-8
Doran—locale ... WA-9
**Doran**—pop pl (2) ... MN-6
**Doran**—pop pl ... VA-3
Doran, Mount—summit ... AK-9
**Doran Addition**—pop pl ... TN-4
Doran Beach—beach ... CA-9
Doran Cem—cemetery ... KY-4
Doran Cem—cemetery ... NY-2
Doran Cem—cemetery ... TN-4
Doran County Park—park ... CA-9
Doran Cove—valley ... AL-4
Doran Cove—valley ... TN-4
Doran Cove Cave—cave ... AL-4
Doran Cove Ch—church ... AL-4
Doran Creek—stream ... CO-8
Doran Creek—stream ... MT-8
Doran Creek—stream ... SC-3
Doran Ditch—canal ... CO-8
Doran Ditch—canal ... OH-6
Doranew Holland State Rec Area—park ... IN-6
**Dorange**—pop pl ... SC-3
Doran (historical P.O.)—locale ... IA-7
Doran Hollow—valley ... TN-4
Doran Lake—lake ... MN-6
Doran Point—summit ... MT-8
Doran Ranch—locale ... SD-7
Dorans—locale ... PA-2
**Dorans**—pop pl ... IL-6
Doran Sch—school ... MA-1
Doran Sch—school ... MT-8
Doran Sch—school ... WI-6
Dorans Cove ... TN-4
Doran Slough—stream ... TN-4
Dorans Stand (historical)—locale ... TN-4
Doran State Wildlife Mngmt Area—park ... MN-6
Doran Strait—channel ... AK-9
Dora Passage—channel ... AK-9
Dora Peak—summit (2) ... AK-9
Dora Pit Mine (surface)—mine ... AL-4
Dora Pond—reservoir ... PA-2
Dora Reef—bar ... AK-9
Dora Roberts Oil Field—oilfield ... TX-5
Dora Sink—basin ... MO-7
Dora Spring—spring ... NV-8
Dora Thorn Lake—lake ... MT-8
Dora Thorn Ridge—ridge ... MT-8
Dora (Township of)—fmr MCD ... AR-4
**Dora (Township of)**—pop pl ... IL-6
**Dora (Township of)**—pop pl ... MN-6
**Doraville**—pop pl ... GA-3
**Doraville**—pop pl ... NY-2
Dorcas—locale ... FL-3
**Dorcas**—pop pl ... OH-6
**Dorcas**—pop pl ... VA-3
**Dorcas**—pop pl ... WV-2
Dorcas, Mount—summit ... ME-1
Dorcas Black Grant—civil ... FL-3
Dorcas Ch—church ... AL-4
Dorcester Village ... MA-1
**Dorceytown**—pop pl ... MD-2
Dorcheat—locale ... LA-4
Dorcheat, Bayou—stream ... AR-4
Dorcheat, Bayou—stream ... LA-4
Dorcheat Bayou ... AR-4
Dorcheat Bayou ... LA-4
Dorcheat Creek ... AR-4
Dorcheat Creek ... LA-4
Dorcheat Macedonia Oil Field—oilfield ... AR-4

Doss Windmill—*locale* ... AZ-5
*Dosten Bayou* ... FL-3
Doster—*locale* ... KS-7
Doster—*locale* ... MI-6
**Doster**—*pop pl* ... AL-4
Doster, Lake—*lake* ... MI-6
Doster Cem—*cemetery* ... AL-4
Doster Cem—*cemetery* ... GA-3
Doster Ch—*church* ... MI-6
Dosters Cem—*cemetery* ... GA-3
Dosters Creek—*stream* ... GA-3
**Dosterville**—*pop pl* ... AL-4
Dos Titos—*summit* ... AZ-5
Dostler Creek—*stream* ... OR-9
**Do Stop**—*pop pl* ... KY-4
Dos Tristes—*locale* ... NM-5
**Doswell**—*pop pl* ... VA-3
Doswell Post Office (historical)—*building* ... AL-4
Dot—*locale* ... GA-3
Dot—*locale* ... VA-3
Dot—*locale* ... WA-9
**Dot**—*pop pl* ... KY-4
**Dot**—*pop pl* ... TX-5
Dot, Lake—*lake* (4) ... FL-3
Dota—*locale* ... AR-4
Dota Creek—*stream* ... AR-4
Dota Old River—*lake* ... AR-4
Dota (Township of)—*fmr MCD* ... AR-4
Dotchikichiki Passage—*channel* ... FM-9
Dot Creek—*stream* ... CA-9
Dot Creek—*stream* ... ID-8
Dot Creek—*stream* (2) ... WA-9
Doten Brook—*stream* ... MA-1
Doten Hill—*summit* ... ME-1
Doten Sch—*school* ... NV-8
*Dotens Cliff* ... MA-1
**Dotham**—*pop pl* ... MO-7
Dothan—*locale* ... NC-3
**Dothan**—*pop pl* ... AL-4
**Dothan**—*pop pl* ... TX-5
**Dothan**—*pop pl* ... VT-1
**Dothan**—*pop pl* ... WV-2
Dothan Airp—*airport* (2) ... AL-4
Dothan Brook—*stream* ... VT-1
Dothan (CCD)—*cens area* ... AL-4
Dothan Cem—*cemetery* ... LA-4
Dothan Cem—*cemetery* ... TX-5
Dothan Ch—*church* ... NC-3
Dothan Ch—*church* (2) ... SC-3
Dothan City Cem—*cemetery* ... AL-4
Dothan City Hall—*building* ... AL-4
Dothan Civic Center—*building* ... AL-4
Dothan Coll Grammar Sch (historical)—*school* ... AL-4
*Dothan Community Center* ... AL-4
Dothan Country Club—*other* ... AL-4
Dothan Division—*civil* ... AL-4
**Dothan (historical)**—*pop pl* ... OR-9
Dothan HS—*school* ... AL-4
Dothan Opera House—*hist pl* ... AL-4
Dothan Post Office—*building* ... AL-4
Dothan Prison Camp—*other* ... AL-4
*Dothan Public School* ... AL-4
Dothan Run—*stream* ... PA-2
Dothan Service League Sch—*school* ... AL-4
Dothan Speedway—*other* ... AL-4
Dothan Valley—*valley* ... PA-2
*Dothen* ... AL-4
**Dotiki**—*pop pl* ... KY-4
Dot Island—*island* (2) ... AK-9
Dot Island—*island* (2) ... WA-9
Dot Island—*island* ... WY-8
*Dot Klish Canyon* ... AZ-5
*Dot Klish Wash* ... AZ-5
Dot Lake—*lake* ... AK-9
Dot Lake—*lake* ... MN-6
Dot Lake—*lake* ... WA-9
Dot Lake ANV773—*reserve* ... AK-9
Dot Lakes—*lake* ... WA-9
Dotmond—*locale* ... NC-3
Dot Mtn—*summit* ... WA-9
Dotons Point—*cape* ... CA-9
*Dotor Point* ... NJ-2
Dot Rock State Park—*park* ... WA-9
Dot Sch—*school* ... WA-9
Dotsero—*locale* ... CO-8
Dotsero Crater—*crater* ... CO-8
Dotsero Wildlife Area—*park* ... CO-8
Dots Island—*island* ... MD-2
Dots Lake—*lake* ... NY-2
Dotson—*locale* ... AR-4
Dotson—*locale* ... KY-4
Dotson—*locale* ... MN-6
Dotson—*locale* ... TN-4
Dotson—*locale* (2) ... TX-5
*Dotson Branch* ... TN-4
**Dotson Branch**—*pop pl* ... TN-4
Dotson Branch—*stream* ... NC-3
Dotson Branch—*stream* ... WV-2
Dotson Campground Ch—*church* ... TN-4
Dotson Cem—*cemetery* ... AL-4
Dotson Cem—*cemetery* ... GA-3
Dotson Cem—*cemetery* (2) ... KY-4
Dotson Cem—*cemetery* ... MO-7
Dotson Cem—*cemetery* ... OH-6
Dotson Cem—*cemetery* (6) ... TN-4
Dotson Cem—*cemetery* (3) ... VA-3
Dotson Cem—*cemetery* ... WV-2
Dotson Ch—*church* ... TN-4
Dotson Creek—*stream* ... OH-6
Dotson Creek—*stream* ... TN-4
Dotson Creek—*stream* ... VA-3
Dotson Drain—*canal* ... ID-8
Dotson Fork—*stream* ... KY-4
Dotson Fork—*stream* ... VA-3
Dotson Fork—*stream* ... WV-2
Dotson Point—*cape* ... TN-4
Dotson Ridge—*ridge* ... KY-4
Dotson Rsvr—*reservoir* ... CO-8
Dotson Run—*stream* ... WV-2
**Dotson's Camp Ground (Red Hill)**—*pop pl* ... TN-4
Dotson Sch—*school* ... VA-3
Dotson Sch (historical)—*school* ... TN-4
Dotson-Simpson Cem—*cemetery* ... WV-2
Dotson-Simson Ch—*church* ... WV-2
*Dotson Slough* ... OR-9
Dotson Spring—*spring* ... AZ-5
**Dotson Subdivision**—*pop pl* ... UT-8
Dotsontown—*locale* ... TN-4
**Dotsonville**—*pop pl* ... TN-4
Dotsonville Baptist Ch—*church* ... TN-4
Dotsonville Post Office (historical)—*building* ... TN-4
Dots Spot Airp—*airport* ... TN-4
Dots Tots Sch—*school* ... FL-3
*Dott* ... WV-2
Dott—*locale* ... TX-5
**Dott**—*pop pl* ... PA-2
Dotta Canyon—*valley* ... CA-9
Dotta Neck—*cape* ... CA-9
Dotta Saddle—*gap* ... CA-9
Dotta Spring—*spring* ... CA-9
Dotted Lake—*lake* ... AR-4
Dotter—*locale* ... PA-2
Dotterel Memorial Ch—*church* ... PA-2
Dotterer Cem—*cemetery* ... OH-6
*Dotters* ... PA-2
**Dotters Corners**—*pop pl* ... PA-2
Dotters Corners Cem—*cemetery* ... PA-2
Dotters Creek—*stream* ... PA-2
Dotters Run—*stream* ... PA-2
*Dottersville* ... PA-2
Dottie Branch—*stream* ... TX-5
Dottie Q Mine—*mine* ... CA-9
Dottie West Park—*park* ... TN-4
Dottle Brook—*stream* ... ME-1
**Dott (RR name Wenonah)**—*pop pl* ... WV-2
Dotts Hollow—*valley* ... PA-2
*Dotty Creek* ... OH-6
Dotty Lake—*lake* ... AR-4
Dotty Pond—*lake* ... NC-3
Dottys Store (historical)—*locale* ... TN-4
*Dottyville* ... WI-6
**Dotville (historical)**—*pop pl* ... OR-9
*Doty* ... MS-4
Doty—*locale* ... MI-6
Doty—*locale* ... TX-5
**Doty**—*pop pl* ... WA-9
Doty Branch—*stream* (2) ... KY-4
Doty Bridge—*hist pl* ... WA-9
Doty Brook—*stream* ... MI-6
Doty Cabin—*locale* ... CA-9
Doty Cem—*cemetery* (2) ... IL-6
Doty Cem—*cemetery* ... IN-6
Doty Cem—*cemetery* ... KY-4
Doty Cem—*cemetery* (2) ... MI-6
Doty Cem—*cemetery* ... TX-5
Doty Chapel—*church* ... TN-4
*Doty Chapel Baptist Church* ... MS-4
Doty Cove—*bay* ... AK-9
*Doty Creek* ... OR-9
Doty Creek—*stream* ... CA-9
Doty Creek—*stream* (2) ... KY-4
Doty Creek—*stream* ... NY-2
Doty Creek—*stream* ... OR-9
Doty Creek—*stream* ... TN-4
Doty Ditch—*canal* ... MT-8
Doty Draw—*valley* ... ID-8
Doty Flat—*flat* ... CA-9
Doty Glade—*stream* ... DE-2
Doty Highway—*channel* ... MI-6
Doty Hill—*summit* ... NY-2
Doty Hill—*summit* ... OR-9
Doty Hill—*summit* ... PA-2
Doty Hill—*summit* ... WY-8
Doty Hill Cem—*cemetery* ... PA-2
Doty Hills—*range* ... WA-9
Doty Hill Sch (historical)—*school* ... PA-2
Doty Hollow—*valley* ... MA-1
Doty Hollow—*valley* ... NY-2
Doty Hollow—*valley* ... TN-4
Doty House Branch—*stream* ... AL-4
Doty Island—*island* ... WI-6
Doty Island (47-WN-30)—*hist pl* ... WI-6
Doty Mtn—*summit* ... WY-8
Doty Oil Field—*oilfield* ... TX-5
Doty Park—*park* ... WI-6
Doty Post Office (historical)—*building* ... MS-4
Doty Ravine—*valley* ... CA-9
Doty Ravine North Canal—*canal* ... CA-9
Doty Ridge—*ridge* ... TN-4
Doty Roundtop—*locale* ... PA-2
Doty Run—*stream* ... IN-6
Doty Run—*stream* ... OH-6
Doty Run Lake Dam—*dam* ... IN-6
Dotys Camp (Site)—*locale* ... CA-9
Doty Sch—*school* (2) ... IL-6
Doty Sch—*school* ... KY-4
Doty Sch—*school* (2) ... MI-6
Doty Sch—*school* ... SD-7
Doty Sch—*school* ... VT-1
Dotys Chapel—*church* ... MS-4
Dotys Chapel Cem—*cemetery* ... MS-4
Doty Sch (historical)—*school* ... MO-7
Dotys Corners—*locale* ... NY-2
*Dotys Cove* ... FL-3
Doty Spring—*spring* ... CA-9
Doty Spring—*spring* ... SD-7
*Doty Springs Baptist Church* ... MS-4
Doty Springs Cem—*cemetery* ... MS-4
Doty Springs Ch—*church* ... MS-4
**Doty Springs (historical)**—*pop pl* ... MS-4
Doty Springs Sch (historical)—*school* ... MS-4
**Doty (Town of)**—*pop pl* ... WI-6
*Dotyville* ... IN-6
Dotyville—*locale* ... OK-5
Dotyville—*locale* ... PA-2
**Dotyville**—*pop pl* ... WI-6
**Dotyville (historical)**—*pop pl* ... OR-9
*Doub* ... MD-2
Doub Cem—*cemetery* ... NC-3
Doub Farm—*hist pl* ... MD-2
Doublas Milit Reservation—*military* ... AZ-5
**Doublea**—*pop pl* ... AZ-5
Double A Creek—*stream* ... ID-8
**Double Adobe**—*pop pl* ... AZ-5
Double Adobe Creek—*stream* ... NM-5
Double Adobes—*locale* ... NM-5
Double Adobe Site—*hist pl* ... AZ-5
Double A Knoll—*summit* ... AZ-5
Double A Lakes—*reservoir* ... TX-5
Double A Landing—*locale* ... ME-1
Double A Ranch—*locale* ... CA-9
Double A Ranch (historical)—*locale* ... AZ-5
*Double Arch* ... UT-8
Double Arch—*arch* ... KY-4
Double Arch—*arch* ... UT-8
Double Arch Canyon—*valley* ... AZ-5
Double-arch Sandstone Bridge—*hist pl* ... MA-1
Double Arch Trail—*trail* ... KY-4
Double Arrow Lookout—*locale* ... MT-8
Double Arrow Ranch—*locale* ... MT-8
*Double A RR Station* ... AZ-5
Double A (siding)—*building* ... AZ-5
Double A Tank—*reservoir* (2) ... AZ-5
Double Bar—*bar* (2) ... AL-4
Double Bar Bend—*bend* ... AR-4
Double Barn Cem—*cemetery* ... KY-4
Double Barrel Creek—*stream* (2) ... FL-3
Double Barrel Creek—*stream* ... OR-9
Double Barrel Creek—*stream* ... TX-5
Double Barrell Cave—*cave* ... AL-4
Double Barrel Spring—*spring* ... NM-5
Double Bar Two Ranch—*locale* ... WY-8
Double Basin—*lake* ... TN-4
Double Bay—*bay* ... AK-9
Double Bay—*swamp* ... MS-4
Double Bayou—*bay* (2) ... FL-3
Double Bayou—*gut* ... FL-3
Double Bayou—*gut* ... LA-4
Double Bayou—*gut* ... TX-5
Double Bayou—*locale* ... TX-5
Double Bayou—*stream* ... TX-5
Double Bayou Gas Field—*oilfield* ... TX-5
Double Bayou Lagoon—*lake* ... LA-4
Double Bayou Park—*park* ... TX-5
Double Bayou Pass—*gut* ... FL-3
Double Bayou Sch—*school* ... TX-5
**Double Beach**—*pop pl* ... CT-1
Double Blind Lick—*stream* ... KY-4
Double Bluff—*cliff* ... WA-9
Double Bluff Lake—*lake* ... FL-3
Double Bowknot—*flat* ... CA-9
*Double Branch* ... AL-4
*Double Branch* ... SC-3
*Double Branch* ... TX-5
Double Branch—*stream* (12) ... AL-4
Double Branch—*stream* ... AR-4
Double Branch—*stream* (7) ... FL-3
Double Branch—*stream* (11) ... GA-3
Double Branch—*stream* (2) ... LA-4
Double Branch—*stream* (5) ... MS-4
Double Branch—*stream* ... MO-7
Double Branch—*stream* (7) ... NC-3
Double Branch—*stream* (8) ... SC-3
Double Branch—*stream* (7) ... TN-4
Double Branch—*stream* (4) ... TX-5
Double Branch—*stream* (3) ... VA-3
*Double Branch Assembly of God Church* ... AL-4
Double Branch Bay—*bay* ... FL-3
Double Branch Bay—*swamp* ... NC-3
Double Branch Ch—*church* (2) ... AL-4
Double Branch Ch—*church* (2) ... GA-3
Double Branch Ch—*church* ... OK-5
Double Branch Ch—*church* ... SC-3
*Double Branch Creek* ... AL-4
Double Branch Creek—*stream* ... GA-3
Double Branch Creek—*stream* ... OK-5
Double Branch Creek—*stream* ... VA-3
Double Branches—*channel* ... FL-3
Double Branches—*locale* ... GA-3
Double Branches—*stream* (2) ... GA-3
Double Branches—*stream* ... LA-4
Double Branches—*stream* ... SC-3
Double Branches—*stream* ... TN-4
Doublebranches Cem—*cemetery* ... AL-4
Double Branches Ch—*church* ... AL-4
Double Branches Ch—*church* ... GA-3
Double Branches Ch—*church* ... SC-3
Double Branch Ford—*locale* ... AL-4
Double Branch Hole—*basin* ... IL-6
Double Branch Hollow—*valley* ... AL-4
Double Branch Pond—*lake* ... FL-3
Double Branch Sch—*school* ... MO-7
Double Branch Sch (historical)—*school* ... TN-4
Double Bridge—*bridge* ... VA-3
Double Bridge—*locale* ... VA-3
*Double Bridge Branch* ... MD-2
Double Bridge Branch—*stream* ... GA-3
Double Bridge Branch—*stream* ... MD-2
Double Bridge Branch—*stream* ... TX-5
*Double Bridge Creek* ... AL-4
Double Bridges—*bridge* (2) ... GA-3
Double Bridges—*bridge* ... TN-4
Double Bridges—*locale* (4) ... AL-4
Double Bridges—*locale* ... AR-4
Double Bridges—*locale* (3) ... TN-4
Double Bridges—*locale* ... VA-3
**Double Bridges**—*pop pl* (2) ... AL-4
**Double Bridges**—*pop pl* ... TN-4
Double Bridges Archeol Site—*hist pl* ... MO-7
Double Bridges Creek—*stream* (2) ... AL-4
Double Bridges Ferry (historical)—*locale* ... AL-4
Double Bridges (historical)—*bridge* ... TN-4
Double Bridges Park—*park* ... AL-4
Double Bridges Post Office (historical)—*building* ... TN-4
Double Bridges Sch (historical)—*school* ... TN-4
Double Brook—*stream* (2) ... MA-1
Double Brook Dam—*dam* ... MA-1
Double Brook Rsvr—*reservoir* ... MA-1
Double Bunk Creek—*stream* ... CA-9
Double Bunk Meadow—*flat* ... CA-9
*Double Butte* ... AZ-5
Double Butte—*summit* ... CA-9
Double Butte—*summit* ... WY-8
Double Butte Rsvr—*reservoir* ... WY-8
*Double Buttes* ... AZ-5
Double Buttes—*summit* ... AZ-5
Double Butte Tank—*reservoir* ... AZ-5
Double Cabin—*locale* ... AZ-5
Double Cabin—*locale* ... WY-8
Double Cabin Branch—*stream* ... WV-2
*Double Cabin Creek* ... OR-9
Double Cabin Creek—*stream* ... KY-4
Double Cabin Creek—*stream* ... MS-4
Double Cabin Creek—*stream* ... OR-9
Double Cabin Flat—*flat* ... CA-9
Double Cabin Forest Camp—*locale* ... OR-9
Double Cabin Lake—*lake* ... AR-4
Double Cabin Park—*flat* ... AZ-5
Double Cabins—*hist pl* ... GA-3
Double Cabins Park—*flat* ... CO-8
Double Cabin Spring—*spring* ... AZ-5
Double Cabins (Ruin)—*locale* ... CA-9
*Double Camp Branch* ... TN-4
Doublecamp Branch—*stream* (2) ... WV-2
Double Camp Creek—*stream* ... TN-4
Doublecamp Creek—*stream* ... TN-4
Double Camp Fork—*stream* ... WV-2
Double Camp Rec Area—*park* ... TN-4
Double Camp Run—*stream* ... WV-2
Double Camp Shelter—*locale* ... WA-9
Double Canyon—*other* ... NM-5
Double Canyon—*valley* (2) ... CA-9
Double Canyon—*valley* ... NV-8
Double Canyon—*valley* ... NM-5
Double Canyon Draw—*valley* ... NM-5
Double Cave—*cave* ... NM-5
Double Cave Branch—*stream* ... KY-4
Double Cellars—*basin* ... KY-4
Double Ch—*church* ... LA-4
Double Ch—*church* ... MS-4
Double Check Well—*well* ... NV-8
Double Chimney Sch (historical)—*school* ... NC-3
Double Churches—*church* ... GA-3
**Double Churches (historical)**—*pop pl* ... MS-4
Double Churches Sch—*school* ... GA-3
Double Cienega—*flat* ... AZ-5
Double Cienega Creek—*stream* ... AZ-5
Double Circle Ranch—*locale* ... AZ-5
Double Circle Ranch—*locale* ... NM-5
Double Circle Tank—*reservoir* (2) ... AZ-5
Double Cone Rock—*island* ... CA-9
Double Corral—*locale* ... OR-9
Double Corral Canyon—*valley* ... CA-9
Double Corral Creek—*stream* (2) ... MT-8
Double Corral Creek—*stream* ... OR-9
Double Corral Spring—*spring* ... AZ-5
Double Corral Tank—*reservoir* (2) ... AZ-5
Double Corral Trough—*well* ... AZ-5
Double Cove—*bay* ... AK-9
Double Cove Point—*cliff* ... OR-9
Double C Ranch Lake Dam—*dam* ... MS-4
Double Crater—*crater* ... AZ-5
*Double Creek* ... AL-4
*Double Creek* ... NC-3
*Double Creek* ... OR-9
Double Creek—*bay* ... KY-4
Double Creek—*stream* (3) ... AL-4
Double Creek—*stream* ... AK-9
Double Creek—*stream* ... AR-4
Double Creek—*stream* ... GA-3
Double Creek—*stream* ... ID-8
Double Creek—*stream* ... MS-4
Double Creek—*stream* ... NJ-2
Double Creek—*stream* (4) ... NC-3
Double Creek—*stream* ... OH-6
Double Creek—*stream* (2) ... OK-5
Double Creek—*stream* ... OR-9
Double Creek—*stream* ... TX-5
Double Creek—*stream* ... VA-3
Double Creek Cem—*cemetery* ... NC-3
Double Creek Ch—*church* ... MD-2
Double Creek Ch—*church* (2) ... NC-3
Double Creek Channel—*channel* ... NJ-2
Double Creek Sch—*school* ... KY-4
Double Creek Wide Place—*bay* ... NJ-2
*Double Cross Draw* ... WY-8
Double Crossing—*locale* ... NM-5
*Double Crossing Creek* ... WY-8
Double Crossing Creek—*stream* ... WY-8
Double Crossing Rsvr—*reservoir* ... MT-8
Double Culvert—*locale* ... KY-4
Double Culvert Branch—*stream* ... GA-3
Double Dam—*dam* ... SD-7
Double Dam Ditch—*canal* ... KY-4
Double Dam Golf Course—*locale* ... PA-2
Double Dam Tank—*reservoir* ... AZ-5
**Doubleday**—*pop pl* ... IA-7
Doubleday Cem—*cemetery* ... AR-4
Doubleday Creek—*stream* ... OR-9
Doubleday Glen—*valley* ... NY-2
Doubleday Mtn—*summit* ... VT-1
Doubledays Landing—*locale* ... TN-4
*Double Deck Arch* ... UT-8
Double Diamond Ranch—*locale* ... WY-8
Double Dick Mines—*mine* ... CO-8
Double Ditch—*canal* ... WA-9
Double Ditch—*canal* ... WY-8
Double Ditch Earth Lodge Village Site (32BL8)—*hist pl* ... ND-7
Double Ditches—*canal* ... VA-3
Double Ditch Indian Village—*locale* ... ND-7
Double Dives (Picnic Area)—*locale* ... WY-8
Double Dolan Windmill—*locale* ... TX-5
Double Dome Rock—*summit* ... CA-9
Doubledoor Cave—*cave* ... TN-4
Double D Ranch—*locale* ... WY-8
Double Drop Falls—*falls* ... TN-4
Double Duros Country Club—*other* ... OH-6
Double Eagle Mine—*mine* (2) ... AZ-5
Double Eagle Mine—*mine* ... NV-8
Double Eagle Quarries—*mine* ... WA-9
*Double E Coulee* ... MT-8
Double E Coulee—*valley* ... MT-8
*Double E Creek* ... MT-8
Double E Heliport—*airport* ... MO-7
Double E Tank—*reservoir* ... AZ-5
Double Falls—*falls* ... MT-8
Double Falls—*falls* ... OR-9
Double Falls—*falls* ... TN-4
Double Falls—*falls* ... UT-8
Double Fish Trap Shoals—*bar* ... TN-4
Double Ford—*locale* ... TX-5
Double Fork Branch—*stream* ... DE-2
Double Fork Branch—*stream* ... MS-4
Double Four Ranch—*locale* ... WY-8
Double F Tank—*reservoir* ... AZ-5
Double Gap—*gap* ... GA-3
Double Gap—*gap* (2) ... NC-3
Double Gap Branch—*stream* ... GA-3
Double Gap Branch—*stream* ... NC-3
Double Gap Mtn—*summit* ... TX-5
Double Gap Ridge—*ridge* ... NC-3
**Doublegate**—*pop pl* ... GA-3
Doublegate Country Club—*other* ... GA-3
Double Gate Ridge—*ridge* ... CA-9
Double Gates Ch—*church* ... TX-5
Double Gates Windmill—*locale* (2) ... TX-5
Double Glacier—*glacier* ... AK-9
Double Gourd Branch—*stream* ... TN-4
Double G Ranch—*locale* ... TN-4
Double Grantham Tank—*reservoir* ... AZ-5
Double Gulch—*valley* ... MT-8
Double Gum Island—*island* ... TX-5
Double Hammock Creek—*stream* ... FL-3
Doublehead—*locale* ... AL-4
Double Head—*summit* ... GA-3
Double Head—*summit* ... NC-3
Double Head—*summit* ... TN-4
Double Head Bay—*swamp* ... NC-3
Doublehead Bluff—*cliff* ... AR-4
Double Head Branch—*stream* ... FL-3
Doublehead Cem—*cemetery* ... OK-5
Double Head Creek—*stream* ... KY-4
Doublehead Creek—*stream* ... NC-3
*Double-headed Island* ... ME-1
Double Header Mine—*mine* ... AZ-5
Double Header Tank—*reservoir* ... NM-5
Double Header Tank—*reservoir* ... TX-5
Doublehead Fort (historical)—*locale* ... AL-4
Doublehead Gap—*gap* ... GA-3
Doublehead Gap—*gap* ... KY-4
Doublehead Gap—*gap* ... NC-3
Double Head Knob—*summit* ... MO-7
Double Head Lake—*lake* ... CA-9
Doublehead Mountain—*summit* ... CO-8
Double Head Mtn—*summit* ... CA-9
Doublehead Mtn—*summit* ... NH-1
Doublehead Mtn—*summit* (2) ... NC-3
Doublehead Mtn—*summit* ... OK-5
Doublehead Ridge—*ridge* ... KY-4
Double Heads Ch—*church* ... GA-3
*Double Head Shot Island* ... ME-1
Double Head Shot Islands—*island* ... ME-1
*Doublehead Spring* ... AL-4
Doublehead Spring—*spring* ... AL-4
*Doublehead Spring Branch* ... AL-4
*Double Heads Spring* ... AL-4
Doubleheads Village (historical)—*locale* ... AL-4
Double Heart Ranch—*locale* ... CO-8
Double Heart Ranch—*locale* ... TX-5
Double Hill—*ridge* ... CA-9
Double Hill—*summit* ... WA-9
Double Hitch Spring—*spring* ... OR-9
Double H Mtns—*range* ... NV-8
Double Hogpen—*basin* ... GA-3
Double H Oil Field—*oilfield* ... TX-5
Double Hollow—*gap* ... GA-3
Double Hollow—*valley* ... AL-4
Double Hollow—*valley* ... KY-4
Double Hollow—*valley* ... TX-5
Double Horn Creek—*stream* ... TX-5
Double Hot Springs—*spring* ... NV-8
Double House—*locale* ... CO-8
Double H Ranch—*locale* ... NM-5
Double Hump—*summit* ... WY-8
*Double Inn* ... PA-2
*Double Island* ... WA-9
Double Island—*island* (3) ... AK-9
Double Island—*island* ... LA-4
Double Island—*island* ... WA-9
**Double Island**—*pop pl* ... NC-3
Double Island Gully—*stream* ... LA-4
*Double Islands* ... WA-9
Double Islands—*area* ... AK-9
Double Islands—*island* ... GA-3
Double Islands—*island* ... TN-4
Double Kill—*stream* ... NJ-2
Double Knob—*summit* (4) ... GA-3
Double Knob—*summit* (2) ... NC-3
Double Knob Gap—*gap* ... NC-3
Double Knob Ridge—*ridge* ... GA-3
Double Knobs—*summit* ... AZ-5
Double Knobs—*summit* ... GA-3
Double Knobs—*summit* (2) ... NC-3
Double Knobs—*summit* (2) ... TX-5
Double Knobs Tank—*reservoir* ... AZ-5
Double Knolls—*summit* ... AZ-5
Double K Ranch—*locale* ... WY-8
*Double Lake* ... FL-3
Double Lake—*lake* (2) ... GA-3
Double Lake—*lake* ... MI-6
Double Lake—*lake* ... MN-6
Double Lake—*lake* (2) ... MT-8
Double Lake—*lake* ... WY-8
Double Lake—*reservoir* ... TX-5
Double Lake Branch—*stream* ... TX-5
Double Lake Creek—*stream* ... WY-8
Double Lake Rec Area—*park* ... TX-5
Double Lakes—*lake* (2) ... GA-3
Double Lakes—*lake* (2) ... TX-5
Double Lazy T Ranch—*locale* ... WY-8
Double Lick—*basin* ... VA-3
Double Lick—*stream* ... VA-3
Double Lick Branch—*stream* ... TN-4
Doublelick Branch—*stream* ... WV-2
Double Lick Creek—*stream* ... KY-4
Doublelick Run—*stream* ... IN-6
Double Lick Run—*stream* ... MD-2
Doublelick Run—*stream* ... OH-6
Double Log Cabin, The—*other* ... TX-5
Double Long Canyon Windmill—*locale* ... TX-5
Double L Ranch—*locale* ... TX-5
Double L Ranch—*locale* ... WY-8
Double L Site, RI-958—*hist pl* ... RI-1
Double Mac Mine—*mine* ... MT-8
Double Meadow—*flat* ... CA-9
Double Mill Draw—*valley* ... TX-5
*Double Mill Pond* ... MD-2
Double Mill Ranch—*locale* ... AZ-5
Double Mills—*locale* (2) ... NM-5
Double Mills Point—*cape* ... MD-2
Double Mills Rsvr—*reservoir* ... NM-5
Double Mounds—*summit* ... TX-5
Double Mountain—*locale* ... TX-5
Double Mountain—*ridge* ... AL-4
Double Mountain Branch—*stream* ... AL-4
Double Mountain Creek—*stream* ... NV-8
*Double Mountain Fork Brazos River* ... TX-5
Double Mountain Fork Brazos River—*stream* ... TX-5
*Double Mountain Fork of Brazos river* ... TX-5
*Double Mountain Fork of The Brazos River* ... TX-5
*Double Mountains* ... TX-5
Double Mountains—*summit* ... TX-5
Double Mountain Spring—*spring* ... NV-8
Double Mountain Well—*well* ... NV-8
Double Mount Spring—*spring* ... OR-9
Double Mouth Bayou—*stream* ... LA-4
Double Mouth Cave—*cave* ... TN-4
Double Mtn—*summit* (2) ... AK-9
Double Mtn—*summit* ... CA-9
Double Mtn—*summit* ... MT-8
Double Mtn—*summit* ... NV-8
Double Mtn—*summit* ... OR-9
Double Mtn—*summit* (2) ... TN-4
Double Mtn—*summit* (3) ... TX-5
Double Mtn—*summit* ... VA-3
Double Mtn—*summit* ... WY-8
*Double Mtn Draw* ... TX-5
*Double Mtn Fork* ... TX-5
Double Natural Bridge Cave—*cave* ... AL-4
Double Natural Bridges—*arch* ... AL-4
Double N Lake—*lake* ... MT-8
**Double Oak**—*pop pl* ... TX-5
Double Oak Cem—*cemetery* ... KY-4
Double Oak Lake—*reservoir* ... AL-4
Double Oak Mountain—*ridge* ... AL-4
Double Oak Mountain Lake Dam—*dam* ... AL-4
Double Oak Mtn—*summit* ... AL-4
Double Oak Sch—*school* ... TX-5
Double Oaks Gap—*gap* ... VA-3
Double Oaks Park—*park* ... NC-3
Double Oaks Sch—*school* ... NC-3
Double Oak Stand (historical)—*locale* ... TN-4
*Double-O Arch* ... UT-8
Double O Arch—*arch* ... UT-8
Double O Bay—*swamp* ... GA-3
Double O Cold Spring—*spring* ... OR-9
Double O Hunting Club—*locale* ... AL-4
Double Oil Field—*other* ... NM-5
Double O Mine—*mine* ... CA-9
Double O Mine—*mine* ... NV-8
Double O Ranch—*locale* ... AZ-5
Double-O Ranch Hist Dist—*hist pl* ... OR-9
Double O Tank—*reservoir* ... AZ-5
Double Peak—*summit* ... AK-9
Double Peak—*summit* ... AZ-5
Double Peak—*summit* (2) ... CA-9
Double Peak—*summit* ... OR-9
Double Peak—*summit* ... WA-9
*Double Peaks* ... AZ-5
Double Peaks—*summit* ... AZ-5
Double Peaks—*summit* ... OR-9
Double Peaks Lake—*lake* ... OR-9
Double Pines Ch—*church* ... GA-3
Double Pipe Creek—*stream* ... MD-2
Double Point—*cape* ... CA-9
Double Point—*cape* ... FL-3
Double Point Mtn—*summit* ... AK-9
Double Pond—*lake* (6) ... FL-3
Double Pond—*lake* ... KY-4
Double Pond—*lake* ... MD-2
Double Pond—*swamp* (2) ... TX-5
Double Pond Branch—*stream* ... FL-3
Double Pond Ch—*church* ... FL-3
Double Pond Ch—*church* ... SC-3
Double Ponds—*lake* ... FL-3
Double Ponds—*reservoir* ... AL-4
Double Pond Swamp—*swamp* ... FL-3
Double Poplar Top—*summit* ... GA-3
Double Portion Baptist Ch—*church* ... AL-4
Double Prong Creek—*gut* ... SC-3
Double Rainbow Mine—*mine* ... SD-7
Double R Canyon—*valley* ... AZ-5
Double R Creek—*stream* ... SD-7
Double Reed Brake Branch—*stream* ... MS-4
Doubler Hollow—*valley* ... PA-2
Double Ridge—*ridge* ... VA-3
Double Ridge Knob—*summit* ... VA-3
*Double Rock* ... CA-9
Double Rock—*island* (3) ... CA-9
Double Rock—*island* ... OR-9
Double Rock—*other* ... AK-9
Double Rock—*summit* ... CA-9
Double Rock Branch—*stream* ... KY-4
Double Round Tank Windmill—*locale* ... TX-5
Double R Springs—*spring* ... AZ-5
Double Run—*locale* ... GA-3
Double Run—*stream* ... DE-2
Double Run—*stream* ... NC-3
Double Run—*stream* (2) ... PA-2
Double Run Bay—*swamp* ... FL-3
Double Run Creek—*stream* ... FL-3
Double Run Creek—*stream* ... GA-3
Double Run Swamp—*swamp* ... FL-3
Double Run Swamp—*swamp* (2) ... GA-3
Double Run Trail—*trail* ... PA-2
Doubles, The—*gap* ... KY-4
Doubles, The—*ridge* ... TN-4
Doubles, The—*summit* (3) ... VA-3
Double S Bend—*bend* ... MO-7
Double S Bend—*bend* ... TN-4
Doubles Branch—*stream* ... NC-3
Double S Branch—*stream* ... TX-5
Doubles Branch—*stream* (2) ... VA-3
Double Sch (historical)—*school* ... AL-4
Double S Hill—*summit* ... KY-4
**Double Shoals**—*pop pl* ... NC-3
*Double Shot* ... ME-1
*Double Shot Island* ... ME-1
Double Shot Island—*island* ... ME-1
*Double Shot Islands* ... ME-1
Doubleside Knob—*summit* ... NC-3
Double Sink—*basin* ... FL-3
Double Sink—*locale* ... FL-3
*Double Sinks* ... KY-4
Double Sinks—*basin* ... KY-4
Double Slough—*gut* ... TX-5
Double Sloughs—*gut* ... FL-3
Double-Span Metal Pratt Truss Bridge—*hist pl* ... NY-2
Double-Span Whipple Bowstring Truss Bridge—*hist pl* ... NY-2
Double S Peaks—*summit* ... NM-5
Double Spearhead Bar Ranch—*locale* ... WY-8
Double Spillway Tank—*reservoir* ... TX-5
Double Spout Spring—*spring* ... NV-8
*Double Spring* ... MO-7
*Double Spring* ... TN-4
Double Spring—*spring* ... AL-4
Double Spring—*spring* (2) ... CA-9
Doublespring—*spring* ... ID-8
Double Spring—*spring* ... MO-7
Double Spring—*spring* (2) ... NV-8
Double Spring—*spring* ... NM-5
Double Spring—*spring* ... OR-9
Double Spring—*spring* ... PA-2
Double Spring—*spring* ... WA-9
Double Spring—*swamp* ... FL-3
Double Spring Bay—*swamp* ... FL-3
*Double Spring Branch* ... GA-3
*Double Spring Branch* ... TN-4
Double Spring Branch—*stream* ... GA-3
Double Spring Branch—*stream* ... NC-3
Double Spring Branch—*stream* ... OK-5
Double Spring Branch—*stream* ... TX-5

Douglas Sch—*school* (2) LA-4
Douglas Sch—*school* MI-6
Douglas Sch—*school* (2) MN-6
Douglas Sch—*school* (3) MO-7
Douglas Sch—*school* (2) NC-3
Douglas Sch—*school* (2) OH-6
Douglas Sch—*school* (4) OK-5
Douglas Sch—*school* PA-2
Douglas Sch—*school* (2) SC-3
Douglas Sch—*school* TN-4
Douglas Sch—*school* (9) TX-5
Douglas Sch—*school* UT-8
Douglas Sch—*school* WV-2
Douglas Sch—*school* WY-8
Douglas Sch (abandoned)—*school* MO-7
Douglas Sch (abandoned)—*school* PA-2
Douglass Chapel—*church* TN-4
Douglass Ch (historical)—*church* MS-4
Douglas Sch (historical)—*school* (2) MO-7
Douglas Sch (historical)—*school* TN-4
Douglas Sch (historical)—*school* TX-5
*Douglas School* IN-6
Douglas School (Aban'd)—*locale* CA-9
*Douglass City* CA-9
*Douglass County* KS-7
*Douglass Creek* KS-7
Douglass Creek—*stream* NY-2
Douglass Creek—*stream* TN-4
Douglass Crossroads—*locale* FL-3
Douglass Crossroads—*locale* GA-3
**Douglass Dwellings**—*pop pl* DC-2
Douglass Elem Sch—*school* KS-7
Douglass Falls—*falls* WA-9
Douglass Falls Grange Park—*park* WA-9
Douglas Shed—*locale* TN-4
Douglas Shed Ch—*church* TN-4
Douglas Shed Ridge—*ridge* TN-4
*Douglass Hill* ME-1
**Douglass Hills**—*pop pl* KY-4
Douglas Shoals—*bar* TN-4
Douglass Hollow—*valley* TN-4
Douglas Shop Ctr—*locale* FL-3
Douglas Shores Campground—*locale* TN-4
Douglass Hosp—*hospital* KS-7
Douglass House—*hist pl* MI-6
Douglass House—*hist pl* NJ-2
Douglass HS—*school* (2) MD-2
Douglass HS—*school* MO-7
Douglass HS—*school* NC-3
Douglass HS—*school* OK-5
Douglass HS—*school* TN-4
Douglass HS—*school* TX-5
Douglass HS—*school* VA-3
Douglass HS Auditorium—*hist pl* OK-5
*Douglass Island* MI-6
Douglas-Sixth Street Hist Dist—*hist pl* NM-5
Douglass JHS—*school* DC-2
Douglass JHS—*school* NY-2
Douglass JHS—*school* NC-3
Douglass Junior and Senior HS—*hist pl* WV-2
Douglass Lake—*lake* WA-9
Douglass Lake Rsvr No. 10—*reservoir* CO-8
Douglass Landing (historical)—*locale* MS-4
Douglas Slough—*gut* WA-9
Douglas Slough—*stream* FL-3
Douglass Memorial Home—*park* DC-2
Douglass Millpond—*reservoir* SC-3
*Douglass Mountain* ME-1
Douglass Oil Field—*oilfield* KS-7
Douglas Sonoran Hist Dist—*hist pl* AZ-5
Douglass Park—*park* TN-4
**Douglass Park**—*pop pl* VA-3
Douglass Park—*uninc pl* VA-3
Douglass-Pettus Cem—*cemetery* AL-4
Douglass Place—*hist pl* MD-2
*Douglass Point* MD-2
*Douglass Pond* ME-1
**Douglass (Port Douglas)**—*pop pl* NY-2
Douglas Spring—*spring* CA-9
Douglas Spring—*spring* ID-8
Douglas Spring—*spring* (2) NV-8
Douglas Spring—*spring* (2) UT-8
Douglass-Reams House—*hist pl* TN-4
**Douglass Ridge**—*pop pl* OR-9
Douglass Row House—*building* DC-2
Douglass Run—*stream* MD-2
Douglass Run—*stream* (2) PA-2
Douglass Sch—*school* MD-2
Douglass Sch—*school* MO-7
Douglass Sch—*school* OK-5
Douglass Sch—*school* PA-2
Douglass Sch—*school* (2) TN-4
Douglass Sch—*school* (2) VA-3
Douglass Sch (historical)—*school* MS-4
*Douglass School Number 19* IN-6
*Douglass Shed* TN-4
Douglass Shed Post Office (historical)—*building* TN-4
Douglass State For—*forest* MA-1
Douglass-Stevenson House—*hist pl* WI-6
Douglas State Fishing Lake—*park* KS-7
Douglass Township—*civil* KS-7
**Douglass Township**—*pop pl* KS-7
**Douglass (Township of)**—*pop pl* MI-6
**Douglass (Township of)**—*pop pl* (2) PA-2
Douglas Street Ch—*church* GA-3
Douglas Studs—*locale* MT-8
Douglas Substation—*locale* AZ-5
**Douglassville**—*pop pl* PA-2
**Douglassville**—*pop pl* TX-5
**Douglassville (historical)**—*pop pl* PA-2
Douglas Swamp—*stream* SC-3
Douglas Swamp—*swamp* CT-1
Douglas-Sweet Sch—*school* WY-8
Douglas Tabernacle—*church* AL-4
Douglas Tank—*reservoir* TX-5
Douglas Tomb State Memorial—*hist pl* IL-6
**Douglaston**—*pop pl* NY-2
Douglas T Orchard Sch—*school* UT-8
Douglas Townhall—*building* IA-7
**Douglas (Town of)**—*pop pl* MA-1
**Douglas (Town of)**—*pop pl* WI-6
Douglas Township—*civil* SD-7
Douglas Township—*fmr MCD* (17) IA-7
Douglas Township—*fmr MCD* KS-7
**Douglas Township**—*pop pl* KS-7
**Douglas Township**—*pop pl* NE-7
**Douglas Township**—*pop pl* ND-7
Douglas Township Cem—*cemetery* (2) IA-7
**Douglas (Township of)**—*pop pl* (3) IL-6
**Douglas (Township of)**—*pop pl* MN-6
Douglas Underpass—*hist pl* AZ-5
Douglas Valley Sch—*school* CO-8
Douglasville—*locale* GA-3
**Douglasville**—*pop pl* (2) AL-4
**Douglasville**—*pop pl* AR-4
**Douglasville**—*pop pl* GA-3
Douglasville Cem—*cemetery* AL-4
Douglasville Creek—*stream* TX-5
Douglasville HS (historical)—*school* AL-4
Douglasville Lookout—*locale* TX-5
Douglas Wash—*valley* UT-8
Douglas Well—*well* AZ-5
Douglas Well—*well* TX-5
Dougle Roof House—*hist pl* AZ-5
*Dougod Creek* WA-9
Dougren—*locale* OR-9
Doug Seale Cem—*cemetery* MS-4
Doug Young Dam Number Two—*dam* NC-3
Doug Young Lake Number Two—*reservoir* NC-3
Douhitt Mtn—*summit* WY-8
Douhty Creek—*stream* OR-9
**Doule**—*pop pl* TX-5
**Doull Brothers Subdivision**—*pop pl* UT-8
Doull Sch—*school* CO-8
Doulls Ranch—*locale* ID-8
Doullut Canal—*canal* LA-4
**Doulom**—*pop pl* NE-7
Doulton Tunnel—*tunnel* CA-9
Douluts Canal—*canal* LA-4
Doumecq Plains—*flat* ID-8
Dourine Canyon—*valley* AZ-5
Dourine Detention Dam—*dam* AZ-5
Dourine Pasture—*flat* AZ-5
Dourine Tank—*reservoir* AZ-5
Douro—*locale* TX-5
Douse Lake—*lake* MN-6
Dousette Tank—*reservoir* NM-5
Dousinbury Creek—*stream* MO-7
**Dousman**—*pop pl* WI-6
Dousman Creek—*stream* IA-7
Dousman Ditch—*canal* WI-6
Dousman Hotel—*hist pl* WI-6
Dousman Inn—*hist pl* WI-6
Doussoss Bay—*swamp* SC-3
Douthard Hollow—*valley* AR-4
Douthat—*locale* OK-5
**Douthat (Century)**—*pop pl* OK-5
Douthat Creek—*stream* WV-2
Douthat Lake—*lake* VA-3
Douthat State Park—*park* VA-3
Douthat State Park Hist Dist—*hist pl* VA-3
Douthett Tank—*reservoir* NM-5
Douthet Well—*well* NM-5
*Douthid Cemetery* TX-5
Douthit Branch—*stream* MO-7
Douthit Cem—*cemetery* AL-4
Douthit Cem—*cemetery* GA-3
Douthit Cem—*cemetery* TN-4
Douthit Cem—*cemetery* TX-5
Douthit Ch—*church* AL-4
Douthit Creek—*stream* OR-9
Douthit Methodist Ch (historical)—*church* AL-4
Douthit Place—*locale* NM-5
Douthit Sch (historical)—*school* AL-4
Douthit Spring—*spring* (2) OR-9
Douthitt Creek—*stream* KY-4
Douthrittville (historical)—*locale* AL-4
Douthys Spring Branch—*stream* AL-4
Doutre Henriod Well—*well* NV-8
*Doutre Ranch* NV-8
Doutre Ranch—*locale* NV-8
Doutres Mobile Home Park—*locale* UT-8
*Doutres Well* NV-8
Doutre Well—*well* NV-8
*Douty Brook* MA-1
Douty Canyon—*valley* WA-9
Douty Mill Trail—*trail* PA-2
**Doutyville**—*pop pl* PA-2
Douven Mine—*mine* KY-4
Dova Bay—*bay* AK-9
Do Val Sch—*school* AR-4
*Dove* TN-4
*Dove* MP-9
**Dove**—*pop pl* AL-4
**Dove**—*pop pl* IA-7
**Dove**—*pop pl* MO-7
Dove, The—*glacier* CO-8
Dove Airstrip—*airport* MO-7
Dove Bay—*bay* MN-6
Dove Branch—*stream* MS-4
Dove Branch—*stream* TX-5
Dove Canyon—*valley* AZ-5
Dove Canyon—*valley* CA-9
Dove Cem—*cemetery* KS-7
Dove Cem—*cemetery* TN-4
*Dove Cemetery* MS-4
Dove Chapel—*church* IN-6
Dove Chapel—*church* NC-3
*Dove Cove* MD-2
*Dove Creek* SD-7
*Dove Creek* TX-5
Dove Creek—*gut* FL-3
Dove Creek—*locale* GA-3
**Dove Creek**—*pop pl* CO-8
Dove Creek—*stream* AL-4
Dove Creek—*stream* CO-8
Dove Creek—*stream* (3) GA-3
Dove Creek—*stream* IN-6
Dove Creek—*stream* MO-7
Dove Creek—*stream* NE-7
Dove Creek—*stream* NV-8
Dove Creek—*stream* NJ-2
Dove Creek—*stream* NM-5
Dove Creek—*stream* NY-2
Dove Creek—*stream* (2) OR-9
Dove Creek—*stream* SD-7
Dove Creek—*stream* (3) TX-5
Dove Creek—*stream* UT-8
Dove Creek—*stream* WV-2
Dove Creek Baptist Church—*hist pl* GA-3
Dove Creek Ch—*church* GA-3
Dove Creek Draw—*valley* TX-5
Dove Creek Hills—*summit* UT-8
Dove Creek Mountains—*other* UT-8
Dove Creek Pass—*gap* UT-8
Dove Creek Pumping Station—*locale* CO-8
Dove Creek Well—*well* UT-8
Dove Dale Cem—*cemetery* LA-4
Dove Fork—*stream* VA-3
Dove Gulch—*valley* CO-8
Dove Hill Cem—*cemetery* NE-7
**Dove (historical)**—*pop pl* TN-4
Dove Hollow—*valley* OR-9
Dove Hollow—*valley* TN-4
Dove Hollow—*valley* WV-2
Dove Island—*island* (2) AK-9
Dove Island—*ISLAND* MN-6
Dove Island—*island* NJ-2
*Dove Islands* MN-6
Dove Key—*island* FL-3
*Dove Keys* FL-3
Dovel, J. H., Farm—*hist pl* OH-6
Dove Lake—*lake* PA-2
Dove Lakebed—*flat* MN-6
**Dove Landing**—*pop pl* LA-4
Dovelawik Bay—*bay* AK-9
Dovel Hollow—*valley* VA-3
Dovel Mtn—*summit* VA-3
*Dovel Run* VA-3
Dove Mill Branch—*stream* NJ-2
Dove Mountain Ranch (Stillwell)—*locale* TX-5
Dove Mountains—*other* MO-7
Dove Mtn—*summit* OR-9
Dove Mtn—*summit* TX-5
*Dovenport Spring* OR-9
Dove Oil Field—*oilfield* TX-5
Dove Playground—*park* OH-6
Dove Point—*cape* MN-6
Dove Pond—*lake* GA-3
Dove Post Office (historical)—*building* TN-4
*Dover* OH-6
Dover—*locale* CO-8
Dover—*locale* ME-1
Dover—*locale* MD-2
Dover—*locale* MI-6
Dover—*locale* MS-4
Dover—*locale* MO-7
Dover—*locale* MT-8
Dover—*locale* ND-7
Dover—*locale* OR-9
Dover—*locale* VA-3
Dover—*locale* WI-6
Dover—*other* OH-6
**Dover**—*pop pl* AR-4
**Dover**—*pop pl* DE-2
**Dover**—*pop pl* FL-3
**Dover**—*pop pl* GA-3
**Dover**—*pop pl* ID-8
**Dover**—*pop pl* IL-6
**Dover**—*pop pl* (2) IN-6
**Dover**—*pop pl* IA-7
**Dover**—*pop pl* KS-7
**Dover**—*pop pl* KY-4
**Dover**—*pop pl* MA-1
**Dover**—*pop pl* MI-6
**Dover**—*pop pl* MN-6
**Dover**—*pop pl* MS-4
**Dover**—*pop pl* MO-7
**Dover**—*pop pl* NH-1
**Dover**—*pop pl* NJ-2
**Dover**—*pop pl* (3) NC-3
**Dover**—*pop pl* OH-6
**Dover**—*pop pl* OK-5
**Dover**—*pop pl* PA-2
**Dover**—*pop pl* SC-3
**Dover**—*pop pl* (2) TN-4
**Dover**—*pop pl* VT-1
**Dover**—*pop pl* VA-3
Dover Acad Elem Sch—*school* DE-2
Dover Access Point—*park* TN-4
Dover AFB—*military* DE-2
Dover Air Force Base JHS—*school* DE-2
Dover Annex—*post sta* NJ-2
*Dover Area Elem Sch* PA-2
Dover Area Elem Sch—*school* PA-2
Dover Assembly Ch of God—*church* PA-2
Dover Ave Sch—*school* OH-6
Dover Base Hospital—*CDP* DE-2
Dover Bethel Chapel—*church* OH-6
Dover Bible Chapel—*church* DE-2
Dover Bluff—*cliff* ME-1
**Dover Bluff**—*pop pl* GA-3
*Dover Bluff Club* GA-3
Dover Borough—*civil* PA-2
Dover Bridge—*bridge* MD-2
Dover Brook—*stream* VT-1
**Doverbrook Gardens**—*pop pl* DE-2
Dover Brook Golf Club—*other* MD-2
Dover Canal—*canal* UT-8
Dover Canyon—*valley* CA-9
Dover (CCD)—*cens area* DE-2
Dover (CCD)—*cens area* TN-4
Dover Cem—*cemetery* AL-4
Dover Cem—*cemetery* GA-3
Dover Cem—*cemetery* IN-6
Dover Cem—*cemetery* KS-7
Dover Cem—*cemetery* MO-7
Dover Cem—*cemetery* OK-5
Dover Cem—*cemetery* (2) TX-5
Dover Cem—*cemetery* UT-8
Dover (census name for Dover Center)—*CDP* MA-1
*Dover Center* OH-6
Dover Center Cem—*cemetery* MI-6
Dover Center Cem—*cemetery* VT-1
Dover Center (census name Dover)—*other* MA-1
*Dover Centre* MA-1
Dover Ch—*church* FL-3
Dover Ch—*church* GA-3
Dover Ch—*church* (4) KY-4
Dover Ch—*church* MD-2
Dover Ch—*church* (3) MO-7
Dover Ch—*church* (2) NC-3
Dover Ch—*church* (2) OH-6
Dover Ch—*church* TN-4
Dover Ch—*church* VA-3
*Dover Chapel* NJ-2
Dover Chapel—*church* KY-4
Dover Christian Sch—*school* DE-2
*Dover Cliffs* MA-1
*Dover Common* VT-1
Dover Cranberry Bog—*swamp* NJ-2
Dover Creek—*stream* (2) GA-3
Dover Creek—*stream* (2) MI-6
Dover Creek—*stream* VA-3
*Dover Cumberland Presbyterian Ch* TN-4
Dover Dale Landing (historical)—*locale* TN-4
Dover Division—*civil* TN-4
Dover Downs—*other* DE-2
Dover Downs Helistop—*airport* DE-2
Dover Draw—*valley* SD-7
Doverel—*locale* GA-3
Dover Elem Sch—*school* FL-3
Dover Elem Sch—*school* TN-4
Dover Flat—*flat* WA-9
Dover Flint Quarries—*hist pl* TN-4
Dover Forge—*locale* NJ-2
Dover-Foxcroft—*CDP* ME-1
Dover-Foxcroft Gun Club—*other* ME-1
**Dover-Foxcroft (Town of)**—*pop pl* ME-1
*Dover Furnace* TN-4
**Dover Furnace**—*pop pl* NY-2
Dover Grange Hall—*building* KS-7
Dover Green Hist Dist—*hist pl* DE-2
*Doverhill* IN-6
**Dover Hill**—*pop pl* IN-6
**Dover Hill Condominium**—*pop pl* UT-8
**Dover Hills**—*pop pl* NJ-2
**Dover (historical)**—*pop pl* MS-4
Dover Hollow—*valley* MO-7
Dover Hollow—*valley* WV-2
Dover HS—*school* DE-2
*Dover Hundred* DE-2
Dover Island—*island* TN-4
Dover JHS—*school* MA-1
Dover Knob—*summit* NC-3
*Dover Lake* MI-6
Dover Lake—*lake* OH-6
Dover Lake—*reservoir* MO-7
Dover Lake—*reservoir* OH-6
Dover Lake—*reservoir* (2) VA-3
Dover Landing—*locale* MS-4
Dover Landing—*locale* TN-4
Dover Lookout Tower—*locale* TN-4
Dover (Magisterial District)—*fmr MCD* VA-3
*Dover Mill* NC-3
**Dover Mill**—*pop pl* NC-3
*Dover Mills* VA-3
**Dover Mills**—*pop pl* IA-7
Dover Mine—*mine* CO-8
Dover Municipal (Township of)—*civ div* OH-6
*Dover Neck* NH-1
Dove Roost Hill—*summit* AL-4
Dover Park—*park* CA-9
Dover Park—*park* MI-6
Dover Park—*park* OH-6
**Dover Plains**—*pop pl* NY-2
Doverplum Center (Shop Ctr)—*locale* FL-3
*Dover Point* NH-1
Dover Point—*cape* MA-1
Dover Point—*cape* NH-1
Dover Point—*cape* WA-9
Dover Pond A—*reservoir* NC-3
Dover Pond A Dam—*dam* NC-3
Dover Post Office—*building* TN-4
Dover Post Office (historical)—*building* MS-4
Dover Post Office (historical)—*building* SD-7
Dover Presbyterian Ch—*church* DE-2
*Dover Reservoir* OH-6
Dover Ridge—*ridge* OH-6
Dover Rsvr—*reservoir* NJ-2
Dover Rsvr No 2—*reservoir* WY-8
Dover Run—*stream* (2) IN-6
Doversberger Ditch—*canal* IN-6
Dovers Branch—*stream* NC-3
Dover Sch—*school* (3) CA-9
Dover Sch—*school* MO-7
Dover Sch—*school* NE-7
Dover Sch—*school* NC-3
Dover Sch—*school* (2) OH-6
Dover Sch—*school* TX-5
Dover Sch—*school* WI-6
Dover Sch (abandoned)—*school* MO-7
Dover Sch (historical)—*school* MO-7
**Dover Shores**—*pop pl* NJ-2
Dover Shores—*uninc pl* FL-3
Dover Shores Baptist Ch—*church* FL-3
Dover Shores Elem Sch—*school* FL-3
Dover Shores Shop Ctr—*locale* FL-3
Dovers Island—*island* MT-8
Dover South Mills—*locale* ME-1
Doverspike Creek—*stream* AK-9
*Doverspike Dam Number Two* PA-2
Doverspike Number One Dam—*dam* PA-2
Doverspike Number Two Dam—*dam* PA-2
*Dover Spring* AZ-5
Dovers Ridge—*ridge* NC-3
**Dover Station**—*pop pl* MO-7
**Dovers View**—*pop pl* IN-6
**Dovertown**—*pop pl* AL-4
Dovertown Ch—*church* AL-4
*Dovertown Freewill Baptist Ch* AL-4
Dover Town Hall—*building* ND-7
Dover Town Hall—*hist pl* VT-1
**Dover (Town of)**—*pop pl* MA-1
**Dover (Town of)**—*pop pl* NY-2
**Dover (Town of)**—*pop pl* VT-1
**Dover (Town of)**—*pop pl* (2) WI-6
Dover Township—*civil* MO-7
Dover Township—*fmr MCD* (2) IA-7
**Dover Township**—*pop pl* KS-7
**Dover Township**—*pop pl* MO-7
**Dover Township**—*pop pl* ND-7
**Dover (Township and local name Kelso)**—*pop pl* IN-6
Dover Township Cem—*cemetery* IA-7
Dover (Township of)—*fmr MCD* (2) AR-4
**Dover (Township of)**—*pop pl* IL-6
**Dover (Township of)**—*pop pl* (3) MI-6
**Dover (Township of)**—*pop pl* MN-6
**Dover (Township of)**—*pop pl* NJ-2
**Dover (Township of)**—*pop pl* (3) OH-6
**Dover (Township of)**—*pop pl* PA-2
Doves Bar—*bar* OR-9
*Dove's Cove* MD-2
Doves Cove—*bay* MD-2
Dove Sound—*bay* FL-3
*Doves Point* MN-6
Dove Spring—*spring* (6) AZ-5
Dove Spring—*spring* (2) CA-9
Dove Spring—*spring* (2) ID-8
Dove Spring—*spring* (2) NM-5
Dove Spring Canyon—*valley* CA-9
Dove Spring Canyon—*valley* NM-5
Dove Springs Canyon—*valley* NM-5
**Dovesville**—*pop pl* SC-3
Doves Waterholes—*lake* ID-8
**Dovetail**—*pop pl* MT-8
*Dovetail Creek* MT-8
Dovetail Creek—*stream* MT-8
Dove Tank—*reservoir* (5) AZ-5
Dove Tank—*reservoir* TX-5
**Doveville**—*pop pl* VA-3
Dove Well—*well* CA-9
Dove Windmill—*locale* TX-5
Dovillers-Manning-Magoffin House—*hist pl* SC-3
Dovolno Point—*cape* AK-9
*Dovovan Creek* MT-8
**Dovray**—*pop pl* MN-6
Dovray State Wildlife Mngmt Area—*park* MN-6
**Dovray (Township of)**—*pop pl* MN-6
Dovre Campground—*park* OR-9
Dovre Cem—*cemetery* MN-6
Dovre Cem—*cemetery* ND-7
Dovre Ch—*church* WI-6
Dovre Lake—*lake* MN-6
Dovre Municipal Landing Field—*airport* ND-7
Dovre Peak—*summit* OR-9
Dovre Sch Number 1—*school* ND-7
**Dovre (Town of)**—*pop pl* WI-6
**Dovre Township**—*pop pl* ND-7
**Dovre (Township of)**—*pop pl* MN-6
*Dow* ME-1
Dow—*locale* KY-4
Dow—*locale* ME-1
**Dow**—*pop pl* IL-6
**Dow**—*pop pl* OK-5
**Dow**—*pop pl* VA-3
Dow, Gen. Neal, House—*hist pl* ME-1
Dow, Herbert H., House—*hist pl* MI-6
Dow, J.B., House and Carpenter Douglas Barn—*hist pl* WI-6
Dow, John T., House—*hist pl* WI-6
Dow Acad—*hist pl* NH-1
Dowach—*cape* FM-9
*Dowagain* MP-9
*Dowagain-To* MP-9
**Dowagiac**—*pop pl* MI-6
*Dowagiac Creek* MI-6
Dowagiac Creek—*stream* MI-6
Dowagiac Drain—*canal* MI-6
Dowagiac River—*stream* MI-6
Dowagiac Swamp—*swamp* MI-6
Dowans Creek—*stream* WA-9
Dowarugui Channel—*channel* FM-9
Dowa Yalanne—*summit* NM-5
Dowa Yalanne Sch—*school* NM-5
Dow Barge Canal—*canal* TX-5
Dow Block—*hist pl* MA-1
Dow Brook—*stream* MA-1
Dow Brook Reservoir Dam—*dam* MA-1
Dow Brook Rsvr—*reservoir* (2) MA-1
Dow Butte—*summit* CA-9
Dow Canyon—*valley* NM-5
Dow Cem—*cemetery* AR-4
Dow Cem—*cemetery* MI-6
Dow Cem—*cemetery* (2) NH-1
Dow Chemical Company (Elwood)—*facility* IL-6
Dow Chemical Company (Minooka)—*facility* IL-6
**Dow City**—*pop pl* IA-7
Dow City Cem—*cemetery* IA-7
Dow Corner—*locale* ME-1
**Dow Corner**—*pop pl* ME-1
Dow Creek—*stream* KS-7
Dow Creek—*stream* MI-6
Dow Creek—*stream* WA-9
*Dowd* CO-8
Dowdall Creek—*stream* CA-9
Dowdall Sch—*school* MI-6
Dowd Brook—*stream* CT-1
Dowd Canyon—*valley* CA-9
Dowd Cem—*cemetery* AR-4
Dowd Cem—*cemetery* IL-6
Dowd Cem—*cemetery* MS-4
Dowd Creek—*stream* IA-7
Dowd Creek—*stream* MS-4
Dowd Creek—*stream* OH-6
Dowd Creek—*stream* UT-8
Dowd Dam—*dam* SD-7
Dowd Drain—*canal* MI-6
Dowdel Creek—*stream* MD-2
Dowdell Canyon—*valley* UT-8
Dowdell Cem—*cemetery* TX-5
Dowdell Creek—*stream* GA-3
Dowdell JHS—*school* FL-3
Dowdell Knob—*summit* GA-3
**Dowdel Settlement**—*pop pl* TX-5
**Dowden Acres**—*pop pl* IN-6
Dowden Branch—*stream* IN-6
Dowden Bridge—*bridge* CO-8
Dowden Cem—*cemetery* AR-4
Dowden Cem—*cemetery* (2) IN-6
Dowden Creek—*stream* LA-4
Dowden Gulch—*valley* CO-8
Dowden Run—*stream* WV-2
Dowden's Luck—*hist pl* MD-2
Dowden Tannery—*hist pl* NY-2
**Dowden Terrace**—*pop pl* VA-3
Dowdey Corner—*locale* VT-1
Dowd Hill—*summit* PA-2
Dowd Hollow Brook—*stream* CT-1
Dowdle—*locale* AL-4
Dowdle Branch—*stream* NC-3
Dowdle Branch—*stream* SC-3
*Dowdle Canyon* AZ-5
Dowdle Knob—*summit* NC-3
Dowdle Sch (historical)—*school* MS-4
Dowdle Tank—*reservoir* AZ-5
Dowd Mountain Overlook Picnic Area—*locale* UT-8
Dowd Mtn—*summit* UT-8
Dowd Plantation (historical)—*locale* MS-4
*Dowds* CO-8
Dowd Sch—*school* GA-3
Dowd Sch—*school* MS-4
Dowd Sch (historical)—*school* MO-7
**Dowd's Corner**—*pop pl* CT-1
Dowds Grave—*cemetery* UT-8
Dowds Hole—*lake* UT-8
Dowds Junction—*locale* CO-8
*Dowds Landing* MS-4
Dowd Spring—*spring* UT-8
**Dowdville**—*pop pl* MS-4
Dowdy—*locale* AR-4
Dowdy Bay—*bay* (2) NC-3
Dowdy Bluff—*cliff* WV-2
Dowdy Branch—*stream* GA-3
Dowdy Branch—*stream* LA-4
Dowdy Branch—*stream* MO-7
Dowdy Branch—*stream* TN-4
Dowdy Branch—*stream* TX-5
Dowdy Cem—*cemetery* AL-4
Dowdy Cem—*cemetery* GA-3
Dowdy Cem—*cemetery* MO-7
Dowdy Cem—*cemetery* TN-4
Dowdy Cem—*cemetery* VA-3
Dowdy Ch—*church* MS-4
Dowdy Chapel Sch (historical)—*school* AL-4
Dowdy Creek—*bay* NC-3
Dowdy Creek—*stream* AL-4
Dowdy Creek—*stream* TX-5
Dowdy Creek—*stream* WV-2
Dowdy Ditch—*canal* MT-8
Dowdy Field—*park* FL-3
Dowdy Hollow—*valley* TN-4
Dowdy Lake—*lake* CO-8
Dowdy Point—*cape* (2) NC-3
Dowdy Pond—*lake* AL-4
Dowdy Pond—*lake* FL-3
Dowdy Ranch—*locale* CA-9
*Dowdys Bay* NC-3
Dowdy Sch—*school* MS-4
Dowdy Sch—*school* TN-4
Dowdy Slough—*gut* AR-4
Dowdy Spring—*spring* TN-4
Dowe Cem—*cemetery* KY-4
Dowe Chapel—*church* TN-4
Dowe Ditch—*canal* OH-6
Dowe Flats—*flat* CO-8
Dowe Hist Dist—*hist pl* AL-4
*Dowel'il* FM-9
*Dowell* KS-7
**Dowell**—*pop pl* IL-6
**Dowell**—*pop pl* MD-2
**Dowell**—*pop pl* MS-4
Dowell, J. S., House—*hist pl* TX-5
Dowell Arm—*bay* OR-9
Dowell Branch—*stream* AR-4
Dowell Branch—*stream* TN-4
Dowell Branch—*stream* VA-3
Dowell Butte—*summit* OR-9
Dowell Cem—*cemetery* KY-4
Dowell Cem—*cemetery* MO-7
Dowell Cem—*cemetery* OH-6
Dowell Cem—*cemetery* TN-4
Dowell Cem—*cemetery* TX-5
Dowell Cove—*valley* AR-4
*Dowell Creek* GA-3
Dowell Creek—*stream* MT-8
Dowell Ditch—*canal* IN-6
Dowell Dock (Floating moorage)—*locale* NC-3
Dowell Gap—*gap* VA-3
Dowell Hill—*summit* IN-6
**Dowell (historical)**—*pop pl* TN-4
Dowell Homestead—*locale* CO-8
Dowell Mtn—*summit* VA-3
Dowell Ranch—*locale* OR-9
Dowell Rsvr—*reservoir* (2) OR-9
Dowell Sch (abandoned)—*school* MO-7
Dowells Deep Six Cave—*cave* AL-4
Dowells Draft—*valley* VA-3
Dowells Peninsula—*cape* OR-9
Dowell Spring—*spring* OR-9
Dowell Spring—*spring* SD-7
**Dowelltown**—*pop pl* TN-4
Dowelltown Baptist Ch—*church* TN-4
Dowelltown Post Office—*building* TN-4
Dowelltown Sch (historical)—*school* TN-4
*Dowell Township* KS-7
Dowell (Township of)—*fmr MCD* AR-4
Dowelltown United Methodist Ch—*church* TN-4
Dowel Town Ridges—*ridge* AR-4
Dowen Cem—*cemetery* LA-4
Dowe Pass—*gap* CO-8
Dowe Pond—*lake* ME-1
Dower Draw—*valley* MT-8
Dower House Pond—*reservoir* MD-2
Dower House Pond Branch—*stream* MD-2
Dower Lake—*lake* MN-6
Dowers Kill—*stream* NY-2
Dower State Wildlife Mngmt Area—*park* MN-6
Dow Flat—*flat* CA-9
Dowfords Chapel—*church* MS-4
*Dowfords Chapel Ch* MS-4
Dow Fork—*stream* WV-2
Dow Hill—*summit* VT-1
Dow Hollow—*valley* AR-4
Dow House—*hist pl* IA-7
Dow House—*hist pl* OH-6
Dow HS—*school* MI-6
Dowies Point—*cape* MI-6
Dowing Pond—*reservoir* MS-4
*Dowingsville* KY-4
Dowis Chapel—*church* KY-4
Dow Island—*island* NH-1
Dowis Sch—*school* KY-4
Dow Jones And Company—*airport* NJ-2
Dow Lake—*lake* (2) MI-6
Dow Lake—*lake* SC-3
Dow Lake—*lake* WA-9
Dow Lake—*reservoir* OH-6
Dow Lake—*reservoir* OK-5
Dow Lateral—*stream* IL-6
Dow Ledge—*bar* ME-1
Dowler, Charles, House—*hist pl* RI-1
**Dowler Heights**—*pop pl* TN-4
Dowler Junction—*locale* PA-2
*Dowler Junction Station* PA-2
Dowler Mill Sch (abandoned)—*school* MO-7
**Dowley Corners**—*pop pl* PA-2
Dowley-Taylor House—*hist pl* MA-1
Dowlin—*locale* PA-2
**Dowlin**—*pop pl* MT-8
Dowlin Cem—*cemetery* SD-7
Dowlin Ditch—*canal* WY-8
Dowling—*locale* TX-5
**Dowling**—*pop pl* MI-6
**Dowling**—*pop pl* OH-6
Dowling Bayou—*gut* MS-4
Dowling Bayou Greentree Rsvr—*reservoir* MS-4
Dowling Branch—*stream* AL-4
Dowling Cem—*cemetery* GA-3
Dowling Cem—*cemetery* MI-6
Dowling Cem—*cemetery* SD-7
*Dowling Creek* MI-6

Dozler Rsvr—*reservoir* OR-9
D P Canal—*canal* LA-4
D Phillips Ranch—*locale* NE-7
D P Murphy Lake Dam—*dam* MS-4
D Pool—*reservoir* MI-6
D-q Drain—*canal* ID-8
**Draayer Subdivision**—*pop pl* UT-8
*Drab* PA-2
Drab—*locale* PA-2
Drabbels Rsvr—*reservoir* MT-8
Drabb's Ranch—*locale* MT-8
Drace Hollow—*valley* OR-9
Dracena Park—*park* CA-9
Drachenburg Lake—*lake* MI-6
Drachman Sch—*school* AZ-5
Draco—*locale* NC-3
Draco—*locale* PA-2
Draco—*locale* TX-5
**Dracut**—*pop pl* MA-1
*Dracut Centre* MA-1
Dracut HS—*school* MA-1
Dracut JHS—*school* MA-1
**Dracut Junction**—*pop pl* MT-8
**Dracut (Town of)**—*pop pl* MA-1
Drady—*locale* ND-7
Draffen Branch—*stream* MO-7
**Draffenville**—*pop pl* KY-4
**Draffin**—*pop pl* KY-4
Draft Branch—*stream* NC-3
Drafts Pond—*reservoir* SC-3
*Drag* AL-4
Draga, Loma de la—*summit* TX-5
Drag A Ranch—*locale* NM-5
Drag A Spring—*spring* NM-5
Drag Brook—*stream* ME-1
Drag Channel—*channel* NJ-2
*Drag Channel Sedge* NJ-2
Drag Creek—*stream* MT-8
Drag Creek—*stream* VA-3
Drag Creek—*stream* WV-2
Drag Creek Sch—*school* WV-2
**Dragerton**—*pop pl* UT-8
Drager Well—*well* NM-5
Drag Hill—*summit* NJ-2
Draghi Mine—*mine* AZ-5
Drag Hollow—*valley* (2) UT-8
Drag Hollow Spring—*spring* UT-8
Dragin Creek—*stream* MT-8
Drag Island—*island* AK-9
Drag Island—*island* NJ-2
Drag Lake—*lake* (2) MN-6
Drag Line Pond—*lake* FL-3
Dragline Tank—*reservoir* TX-5
Drag Mtn—*summit* NY-2
Drag Mtn—*summit* VA-3
Drag Nasty Creek—*stream* GA-3
*Dragod Creek* MI-6
Dragon—*locale* MS-4
Dragon—*locale* UT-8
*Dragon, The* UT-8
Dragon, The—*ridge* AZ-5
Dragon Brook—*stream* MA-1
Dragon Brook—*stream* VT-1
*Dragon Canyon* UT-8
Dragon Canyon—*valley* (2) UT-8
*Dragon Creek* KS-7
*Dragon Creek* TX-5
*Dragon Creek* WA-9
Dragon Creek—*stream* AZ-5
Dragon Creek—*stream* DE-2
Dragon Douglas Trail—*trail* CO-8
Dragonfly Creek—*stream* AK-9
Dragonfly Lake—*lake* AK-9
*Dragon Ghost Town* UT-8
Dragon Gulch—*valley* CA-9
Dragon Head—*summit* AZ-5
Dragon Head Peak—*summit* WY-8
Dragon Hill—*summit* MA-1
*Dragon Island* FM-9
Dragon Lake—*lake* CA-9
Dragon Lake—*lake* MI-6
Dragon Lake—*lake* MN-6
Dragon Lake—*lake* WA-9
Dragon Meadow Brook—*stream* ME-1
Dragon Mine—*mine* AZ-5
Dragon Mine—*mine* (2) UT-8
Dragon Peak—*summit* CA-9
Dragon Point—*cape* AK-9
Dragon Point—*cape* FL-3
Dragon Point—*cliff* CO-8
Dragon Pond—*lake* MI-6
Dragon Ridge—*ridge* NM-5
Dragon Ridge—*ridge* UT-8
*Dragon Run* VA-3
Dragon Run—*stream* VA-3
Dragon Run Farm—*hist pl* DE-2
**Dragon Run Terrace (trailer park)**—*pop pl* DE-2
Dragons Egg Rock—*pillar* CO-8
Dragons Mouth Spring—*spring* WY-8
*Dragon Swamp* VA-3
Dragon Swamp—*stream* (2) VA-3
Dragon Swamp—*swamp* MD-2
*Dragon Tail* WA-9
Dragontail Peak—*summit* WA-9
Dragonville—*locale* VA-3
Dragon Wash—*stream* CA-9
Dragon Wash—*stream* NM-5
Dragon Z Mine—*mine* AZ-5
Dragoo Creek—*stream* MI-6
Dragoo Creek—*stream* TX-5
Dragoo Hollow—*valley* PA-2
Dragoo Hollow—*valley* TX-5
**Dragoon**—*pop pl* AZ-5
Dragoon Camp—*locale* AZ-5
Dragoon Camp Tank—*reservoir* AZ-5
Dragoon Cem—*cemetery* NY-2
Dragoon Commandant's Quarters—*hist pl* OK-5
*Dragoon Creek* AZ-5
Dragoon Creek—*stream* KS-7
Dragoon Creek—*stream* TX-5
Dragoon Creek—*stream* WA-9
Dragoon Creek State Park—*park* WA-9
Dragoon Fork—*stream* AZ-5
Dragoon (historical)—*locale* KS-7
Dragoon Hollow—*valley* TX-5
Dragoon Interchange—*crossing* AZ-5
Dragoon Lake—*lake* WA-9
Dragoon Mountains—*range* AZ-5
Dragoon Oil And Gas Field—*oilfield* TX-5
Dragoon Pass—*gap* AZ-5
Dragoon Peak—*summit* AZ-5
Dragoon Post Office—*building* AZ-5
*Dragoon Range* AZ-5
Dragoon Rec Area—*park* KS-7
Dragoon RR Station—*building* AZ-5
Dragoon Spring—*spring* AZ-5
Dragoon Spring—*spring* WA-9
Dragoon Springs Stage Station Site—*hist pl* AZ-5
**Dragoon Township**—*pop pl* KS-7
Dragoon Wash—*stream* AZ-5
Dragoo Ranch—*locale* TX-5
Drag Over—*locale* MO-7
Drag Road Canyon—*valley* NV-8
Dragroad Spring—*spring* ID-8
Dragsaw Spring—*spring* CA-9
Drag Sedge—*island* NJ-2
Dragslab Hollow—*valley* KY-4
Drag Spring—*spring* AZ-5
Dragston—*locale* NJ-2
*Dragstown* NJ-2
Drags Wolf Bay—*bay* ND-7
Drag Tank—*lake* TX-5
**Drain**—*pop pl* OR-9
Drain, Bay—*canal* MI-6
Drain, Charles D., Jr., House—*hist pl* OR-9
Drain, Lake—*canal* MI-6
Drain, Lake—*stream* NC-3
*Drain, The* NC-3
Drain, The—*bay* NC-3
Drain, The—*channel* NY-2
**Drainage**—*pop pl* SC-3
Drainage District Number 2—*area* LA-4
Drainage District Seven Ditch—*canal* OR-9
Drainage Ditch—*canal* IL-6
Drainage Ditch No 1—*canal* (4) IA-7
Drainage Ditch No 1—*canal* WA-9
Drainage Ditch No 10—*canal* IA-7
Drainage Ditch No 101—*canal* IA-7
Drainage Ditch No 102—*canal* IA-7
Drainage Ditch No 103—*canal* IA-7
Drainage Ditch No 107—*canal* IA-7
Drainage Ditch No 108—*canal* IA-7
Drainage Ditch No 11—*canal* IA-7
Drainage Ditch No 110—*canal* IA-7
Drainage Ditch No 114—*canal* IA-7
Drainage Ditch No 116—*canal* (2) IA-7
Drainage Ditch No 117—*canal* (2) IA-7
Drainage Ditch No 121—*canal* IA-7
Drainage Ditch No 129—*canal* IA-7
Drainage Ditch No 13—*canal* IA-7
Drainage Ditch No 164—*canal* IA-7
Drainage Ditch No 168—*canal* IA-7
Drainage Ditch No 169—*canal* IA-7
Drainage Ditch No 175—*canal* IA-7
Drainage Ditch No 177—*canal* IA-7
Drainage Ditch No 18—*canal* (2) IA-7
Drainage Ditch No 182—*canal* IA-7
Drainage Ditch No 183—*canal* IA-7
Drainage Ditch No 2—*canal* IL-6
Drainage Ditch No 2—*canal* IA-7
Drainage Ditch No 20—*canal* (2) IA-7
Drainage Ditch No 21—*canal* IA-7
Drainage Ditch No 219—*canal* IA-7
Drainage Ditch No 24—*canal* IA-7
Drainage Ditch No. 26—*canal* IA-7
Drainage Ditch No 29—*canal* (2) IA-7
Drainage Ditch No. 29—*canal* IA-7
Drainage Ditch No 3—*canal* (2) IA-7
Drainage Ditch No 33—*canal* IA-7
Drainage Ditch No 35—*canal* IA-7
Drainage Ditch No 37—*canal* IA-7
Drainage Ditch No 39—*canal* IA-7
Drainage Ditch No 4—*canal* IA-7
Drainage Ditch No 46—*canal* IA-7
Drainage Ditch No 47—*canal* IA-7
Drainage Ditch No 48—*canal* IA-7
Drainage Ditch No 54—*canal* IA-7
Drainage Ditch No 55—*canal* IA-7
Drainage Ditch No 57—*canal* (2) IA-7
Drainage Ditch No 6—*canal* IA-7
Drainage Ditch No 63—*canal* IA-7
Drainage Ditch No 64—*canal* IA-7
Drainage Ditch No 66—*canal* IA-7
Drainage Ditch No 67—*canal* IA-7
Drainage Ditch No 69—*canal* IA-7
Drainage Ditch No 7—*canal* IL-6
Drainage Ditch No 7—*canal* IA-7
Drainage Ditch No 74—*canal* IA-7
Drainage Ditch No 8—*canal* IA-7
Drainage Ditch No 80—*canal* IA-7
Drainage Ditch No 81—*canal* (2) IA-7
Drainage Ditch No 82—*canal* IA-7
Drainage Ditch No 84—*canal* IA-7
Drainage Ditch No 9—*canal* IA-7
Drainage Ditch No 90—*canal* IA-7
Drainage Ditch No 9-13—*canal* IA-7
Drainage Ditch No 92—*canal* IA-7
Drainage Ditch No 97—*canal* IA-7
*Drainage Ditch Number 17* IA-7
Drainage Ditch 10—*canal* IA-7
Drainage Ditch 102—*canal* IA-7
Drainage Ditch 121—*canal* IA-7
Drainage Ditch 125—*canal* IA-7
Drainage Ditch 13—*canal* IA-7
Drainage Ditch 157—*canal* IA-7
Drainage Ditch 171—*canal* IA-7
Drainage Ditch 183—*canal* IA-7
Drainage Ditch 19—*canal* IA-7
Drainage Ditch 198—*canal* IA-7
Drainage Ditch 25—*canal* IA-7
*Drainage Ditch 26* IA-7
Drainage Ditch 31—*canal* IA-7
Drainage Ditch 46—*canal* IA-7
Drainage Ditch 57—*canal* IA-7
Drainage Ditch 6—*canal* IA-7
Drainage Ditch 60—*canal* IA-7
Drainage Ditch 65—*canal* IA-7
Drainage Ditch 66—*canal* IA-7
Drainage Ditch 67—*canal* IA-7
Drainage Ditch 71—*canal* (2) IA-7
Drainage Ditch 73—*canal* IA-7
Drainage Ditch 79—*canal* IA-7
Drain Cem—*cemetery* OR-9
Drain Creek—*stream* OR-9
Drain E—*stream* MT-8
Drain Family Cem—*cemetery* MS-4
Drain Hill—*summit* OR-9
Drainie Lake—*lake* AR-4
Drain IOOF Cem—*cemetery* OR-9
Drain Islands—*island* NC-3
Drain Lake—*lake* LA-4
Drain Lake—*lake* MN-6
Drain Lake—*lake* TN-4
Drainland—*locale* SC-3
*Drain Lick* PA-2
Drain M—*stream* MT-8
Drain No. One Hundred Fourty-two—*canal* MI-6
Drain No. Two Hundred Two—*canal* MI-6
Drain No 2—*canal* NE-7
Drain Number One—*canal* NV-8
Drain One—*canal* CA-9
Drain Plywood Company Dam—*dam* OR-9
Drain Plywood Company Log Pond—*reservoir* OR-9
Drain Point—*cape* NC-3
Drain Pond—*lake* NY-2
Drain Ranch—*locale* NE-7
Drain Tunnel Creek—*stream* UT-8
Drain Tunnel No 1—*canal* UT-8
Drain Twenty—*canal* CA-9
Drain Twenty-A—*canal* CA-9
Drain Twentyone—*canal* CA-9
Drain Twentytwo—*canal* CA-9
Drain Two A—*canal* CA-9
Drain 1-A—*canal* CA-9
Drain 1 A—*canal* CA-9
Drain 2—*canal* WA-9
Drain 215—*canal* WA-9
Drain 3—*canal* WA-9
Drain 4—*canal* WA-9
*Drake* IL-6
Drake—*locale* AZ-5
Drake—*locale* CA-9
Drake—*locale* KY-4
Drake—*locale* OK-5
**Drake**—*pop pl* AZ-5
**Drake**—*pop pl* CO-8
**Drake**—*pop pl* IL-6
**Drake**—*pop pl* MO-7
**Drake**—*pop pl* NC-3
**Drake**—*pop pl* ND-7
**Drake**—*pop pl* OH-6
**Drake**—*pop pl* PA-2
**Drake**—*pop pl* SC-3
Drake, Alonzo, House—*hist pl* OH-6
Drake, Col. C. F., House—*hist pl* ID-8
Drake, Edwin S., Farmhouse—*hist pl* MN-6
Drake, Elam, House—*hist pl* OH-6
Drake, John and Amanda Bigler, House—*hist pl* IA-7
Drake, Mount—*summit* AK-9
Drake, Nathaniel, House—*hist pl* NJ-2
Drake Bay—*swamp* FL-3
Drake Branch—*stream* GA-3
Drake Branch—*stream* KY-4
Drake Branch—*stream* (2) TN-4
Drake Branch—*stream* VA-3
Drake Brook—*stream* (2) ME-1
Drake Brook—*stream* MA-1
Drake Butte—*summit* OR-9
Drake Canyon—*valley* NM-5
Drake Cem—*cemetery* (3) AL-4
Drake Cem—*cemetery* AR-4
Drake Cem—*cemetery* GA-3
Drake Cem—*cemetery* (2) IL-6
Drake Cem—*cemetery* MI-6
Drake Cem—*cemetery* (3) MO-7
Drake Cem—*cemetery* (2) OH-6
Drake Cem—*cemetery* (2) OK-5
Drake Cem—*cemetery* (5) TN-4
*Drake Church* MS-4
Drake Corner—*locale* ME-1
Drake Corners—*locale* PA-2
Drake Court Apartments and the Dartmore Apartments Hist Dist—*hist pl* NE-7
Drake Cove—*valley* AL-4
Drake Cove Branch—*stream* AL-4
*Drake Creek* KY-4
*Drake Creek* TN-4
Drake Creek—*stream* AL-4
Drake Creek—*stream* (2) ID-8
Drake Creek—*stream* IL-6
Drake Creek—*stream* KY-4
Drake Creek—*stream* LA-4
Drake Creek—*stream* (5) OR-9
Drake Creek—*stream* WA-9
Drake Creek—*stream* (2) WI-6
Drake Crossing—*locale* OR-9
Drake Drain—*canal* (2) MI-6
Drake Dune—*summit* OR-9
*Drake Eye* AL-4
Drake Falls—*falls* OR-9
Drake Field (Airport)—*airport* AR-4
**Drake Forest**—*pop pl* TN-4
Drake Fork Indian Guyan Creek—*stream* OH-6
Drake Gulch—*valley* MT-8
Drake Head—*cliff* AK-9
*Drake Hill* MA-1
Drake Hill—*ridge* AL-4
Drake Hill—*summit* IN-6
Drake Hill—*summit* (2) MA-1
Drake Hill—*summit* NH-1
Drake Hill Ch—*church* MS-4
Drake Hill Hist Dist—*hist pl* MS-4
Drake Hill Road Bridge—*hist pl* CT-1
Drake (historical)—*locale* KS-7
Drake Hollow—*valley* (2) PA-2
Drake Hollow—*valley* (2) TN-4
Drake Hollow—*valley* TX-5
Drake Hollow Trail—*trail* PA-2
Drake Hotel—*hist pl* IL-6
Drake Hotel—*hist pl* NM-5
Drake Hotel—*hist pl* PA-2
Drake House—*hist pl* AZ-5
Drake House—*hist pl* LA-4
Drake HS—*school* AL-4
Drake Island—*island* AL-4
Drake Island—*island* AK-9
Drake JHS—*school* CO-8
Drake Lake—*lake* AK-9
Drake Lake—*lake* CA-9
Drake Lake—*lake* ME-1
Drake Lake—*lake* (2) MI-6
Drake Lake—*lake* MN-6
Drake Lake—*reservoir* CO-8
Drake Lake—*reservoir* LA-4
Drake Log Cabin—*hist pl* PA-2
Drake Lookout—*locale* WA-9
Drake Lookout Tower—*locale* MO-7
Drake Loop—*locale* PA-2
Drake-Magruder Cem—*cemetery* MS-4
Drake Mine—*mine* TN-4
Drake Mtn—*summit* (2) AL-4
Drake Mtn—*summit* MA-1
Drake Mtn—*summit* NY-2
Drake Mtn—*summit* NC-3
Drake Municipal Airp—*airport* ND-7
Drake Oil Well—*hist pl* PA-2
Drake Oil Well—*well* PA-2
*Drake Park* NC-3
Drake Park—*park* CA-9
Drake Park—*park* IA-7
Drake Park—*park* NY-2
Drake Park—*park* OH-6
Drake Park—*park* OR-9
**Drake Park**—*pop pl* NC-3
Drake Peak—*summit* OR-9
Drake Peak Lookout—*locale* OR-9
Drake Place (historical)—*locale* ME-1
Drake Point—*cape* OR-9
Drake Pond—*lake* ME-1
Drake Pond Brook—*stream* CT-1
Drake Post Office (historical)—*building* TN-4
Drake Ranch—*locale* OR-9
Drake Ridge—*ridge* PA-2
Drake Road Sch—*school* OH-6
Drake RR Station—*building* AZ-5
Drake Run—*stream* OH-6
Drake Run—*stream* PA-2
Drakes—*locale* CO-8
**Drakes**—*pop pl* OH-6
Drake Saddle—*gap* ID-8
Drakesbad—*locale* CA-9
Drakes Bay—*bay* CA-9
Drakes Bay—*lake* LA-4
Drakes Bayou—*stream* MS-4
Drakes Beach—*beach* CA-9
**Drakesboro**—*pop pl* KY-4
Drakesboro (CCD)—*cens area* KY-4
*Drakes Branch* TN-4
**Drakes Branch**—*pop pl* VA-3
Drakes Branch—*stream* (2) KY-4
Drakes Branch—*stream* (2) TX-5
Drakes Branch—*stream* VA-3
Drakes Bridge—*bridge* NC-3
*Drakes Brook* ME-1
Drakes Brook—*stream* MA-1
Drakes Brook—*stream* NH-1
Drakes Brook—*stream* NJ-2
Drakes Brook Trail—*trail* NH-1
**Drakesburg**—*pop pl* OH-6
Drakesburg Cem—*cemetery* OH-6
Drakes Cem—*cemetery* MS-4
Drakes Ch—*church* MS-4
Drake Sch—*school* AL-4
Drake Sch—*school* (3) IL-6
Drake Sch—*school* MI-6
Drake Sch—*school* NV-8
Drake Sch—*school* NY-2
Drake Sch—*school* SD-7
Drake Sch (abandoned)—*school* MO-7
Drake Sch (abandoned)—*school* PA-2
Drakes Chapel—*church* GA-3
Drakes Chapel—*church* MO-7
Drake Sch (historical)—*school* MS-4
Drake School—*locale* MI-6
Drakes Corner—*locale* NY-2
Drakes Corner—*locale* OK-5
Drakes Corner—*locale* VA-3
Drakes Creek—*locale* AR-4
Drakes Creek—*locale* PA-2
Drakes Creek—*stream* AR-4
Drakes Creek—*stream* (5) KY-4
Drakes Creek—*stream* LA-4
Drakes Creek—*stream* (2) PA-2
Drakes Creek—*stream* TN-4
Drakes Creek Baptist Church—*hist pl* KY-4
*Drakes Creek Boat Dock* TN-4
Drakes Creek Ch—*church* AR-4
Drakes Creek Ch—*church* KY-4
Drakes Creek Marina—*locale* TN-4
Drakes Creek Park—*park* TN-4
Drakes Creek Sch (historical)—*school* PA-2
Drakes Estero—*bay* CA-9
Drakes Fork Cem—*cemetery* LA-4
Drakes Gap—*gap* VA-3
Drakes Head—*cape* CA-9
*Drakes Island* NH-1
Drakes Island—*island* ME-1
**Drakes Island**—*pop pl* ME-1
Drakes Island Beach—*beach* ME-1
Drakes Landing—*locale* AL-4
Drakes Landing—*locale* FL-3
Drakes Landing Ferry (historical)—*locale* AL-4
Drakes Lane Cem—*cemetery* TN-4
*Drakes Lick Creek* TN-4
Drakes Marsh—*swamp* VA-3
**Drakes Mills**—*pop pl* PA-2
Drakes Mill Shoals (historical)—*bar* AL-4
*Drakes Peak* CA-9
Drakes Point—*cape* TX-5
Drakes Point—*summit* CA-9
Drakes Pond—*lake* NJ-2
Drakes Pond—*reservoir* SC-3
Drake Spring—*spring* AL-4
Drake Spring—*spring* (2) OR-9
Drake Springs Branch—*stream* TX-5
Drakes Ridge—*ridge* IN-6
Drakes River—*stream* NH-1
*Drakes Run* PA-2
Drakes Run—*stream* NY-2
Drakes Run—*stream* WV-2
Drakes Seat—*other* VI-3
Drakes Still—*locale* GA-3
Drake Stand Cem—*cemetery* OK-5
*Drake Station* FL-3
*Drakes Town* NJ-2
**Drakestown**—*pop pl* NJ-2
*Drakes United Methodist Ch* MS-4
**Drakesville**—*pop pl* IA-7
Drakesville Cem—*cemetery* IA-7
Drakesville Township—*fmr MCD* IA-7
Drake Tank—*reservoir* AZ-5
Drake Tank—*reservoir* NM-5
Draketown—*locale* GA-3
**Draketown**—*pop pl* (3) PA-2
Drake Township—*civil* MO-7
Drake Univ—*school* IA-7
Drake Univ Campus Hist Dist—*hist pl* IA-7
Drake Valley—*basin* NE-7
*Drakeville* CT-1
*Drakeville* IA-7
Drakeville—*locale* CT-1
Drake Well State Park—*park* PA-2
Drakies Bluff—*cliff* GA-3
Drakies Cut—*channel* GA-3
Drakies Point—*cape* GA-3
Drakola (historical)—*locale* SD-7
*Drakut* MA-1
*Dramanville* MA-1
Dram Branch—*stream* FL-3
Dram Branch—*stream* GA-3
Dram Cup Hill—*summit* NH-1
Dram Island—*island* (2) ME-1
Drammen Ch—*church* WI-6
Drammen Farmers' Club—*hist pl* MN-6
**Drammen (Town of)**—*pop pl* WI-6
**Drammen (Township of)**—*pop pl* MN-6
Dram Rock—*island* ME-1
Dramus Cem—*cemetery* AL-4
D Ranch—*locale* CA-9
D Ranch—*locale* TX-5
D Ranch—*locale* WY-8
Dranchak Dam—*dam* PA-2
Drane—*locale* TX-5
**Drane**—*pop pl* PA-2
Drane, Col. James, House—*hist pl* MS-4
Drane, James, House—*hist pl* MD-2
Drane Branch—*stream* KY-4
Drane Cem—*cemetery* KY-4
Drane-Foust House—*hist pl* TN-4
Drane (historical)—*locale* AL-4
Drane House—*hist pl* AR-4
Drane JHS—*school* TX-5
Drane Lake—*reservoir* TN-4
Drane Park—*park* FL-3
Dranes—*lake* KY-4
*Dranes Lake* TN-4
Dranes Mills (historical)—*locale* MS-4
*Dranesville* GA-3
**Dranesville**—*pop pl* GA-3
**Dranesville**—*pop pl* VA-3
Dranesville (Magisterial District)—*fmr MCD* VA-3
Dranesville Tavern—*hist pl* VA-3
Draneville—*locale* GA-3
Draney Creek—*stream* ID-8
Draney Peak—*summit* ID-8
Dranishnikof, Mount—*summit* AK-9
Drano Lake—*lake* WA-9
*Draper* NC-3
Draper—*locale* PA-2
**Draper**—*pop pl* KY-4
**Draper**—*pop pl* NC-3
**Draper**—*pop pl* SD-7
**Draper**—*pop pl* UT-8
**Draper**—*pop pl* VA-3
**Draper**—*pop pl* WI-6
Draper, John W., House—*hist pl* NY-2
Draper, Mount—*summit* AK-9
Draper-Adkins House—*hist pl* DE-2
Draper Annex Mine—*mine* MN-6
Draper-Bennet Ditch—*canal* DE-2
Draper Branch—*stream* MO-7
Draper Canal—*canal* UT-8
Draper Canyon—*valley* AZ-5
Draper Canyon—*valley* OR-9
Draper Cave—*cave* TN-4
Draper Cem—*cemetery* AL-4
Draper Cem—*cemetery* IL-6
Draper Cem—*cemetery* LA-4
Draper Cem—*cemetery* MI-6
Draper Cem—*cemetery* OH-6
Draper Cem—*cemetery* SD-7
Draper Cem—*cemetery* (3) TN-4
Draper Cem—*cemetery* TX-5
**Draper Commercial Parkway**—*pop pl* UT-8
Draper Correctional Center—*building* AL-4
Draper Creek—*stream* CO-8
Draper Creek—*stream* (2) OR-9
**Draper Cross Roads**—*pop pl* TN-4
Draper Dam—*dam* SD-7
Draper Elem Sch—*school* NC-3
Draper Ferry (historical)—*locale* AL-4
**Draper (historical)**—*pop pl* OR-9
Draper Hollow—*valley* (2) UT-8
Draper House—*hist pl* DE-2
Draper Irrigation Canal—*canal* UT-8
Draper Irrigation Company Ditch—*canal* UT-8
Draper Island—*island* MI-6
Draper Lake—*lake* CA-9
Draper Lake—*lake* FL-3
Draper Lake—*lake* WA-9
Draper Lookout Tower—*locale* MN-6
Draper (Magisterial District)—*fmr MCD* VA-3
Draper Mill Creek—*stream* VA-3
Draper Mtn—*summit* VA-3
Draper-Naff Cem—*cemetery* TN-4
**Draper Oaks Subdivision**—*pop pl* UT-8
**Draper Old Farm Subdivision**—*pop pl* UT-8
Draper Park—*park* NY-2
Draper Park—*park* UT-8
Draper Park Sch—*hist pl* UT-8
Draper Playground—*park* MA-1
Draper Pond—*lake* (2) ME-1
Draper Post Office—*building* UT-8
Draper Ranch—*locale* CA-9
Draper Ridge—*ridge* PA-2
Drapers Bluff—*cliff* IL-6
Draper Sch—*school* DC-2
Draper Sch—*school* MT-8
Draper Sch—*school* (2) NY-2
Draper Sch—*school* UT-8
*Drapers Corner* DE-2
Drapers Corners—*locale* DE-2
*Drapers Creek* DE-2
**Drapers Crossroads**—*pop pl* TN-4
Drapers Hollow—*valley* TN-4
Drapers Inlet (historical)—*gut* DE-2
Draper Slaughter Chapel—*church* VA-3
*Drapers Pond* DE-2
Draper Spring—*spring* TX-5
**Draper Spring (Camp Draper)**—*pop pl* WA-9
Draper Springs—*spring* WA-9
Draper Springs Camp—*locale* WA-9
Drapers Run—*stream* OH-6
Drapers Sch (historical)—*school* TN-4
Drapersville—*locale* VA-3
**Draper (Town of)**—*pop pl* WI-6
**Draper Township**—*pop pl* SD-7
Draper Valley—*basin* VA-3
Draper Valley—*valley* OR-9
Draper Valley Ch—*church* (3) VA-3
**Draperville**—*pop pl* OR-9
**Draperville Subdivision**—*pop pl* UT-8
Draper Wash—*stream* CA-9
Drapper Branch—*stream* IL-6
Drasco—*locale* TX-5
**Drasco**—*pop pl* AR-4
Drashner Lake—*lake* AK-9
Draucker Ranch—*locale* NE-7
**Drauckers**—*pop pl* PA-2
Draughan Cem—*cemetery* (2) TN-4
Draughan Creek—*stream* LA-4
*Draughans Creek* LA-4
Draughn—*locale* NC-3
Draughn Hollow—*valley* KY-4
Draughn-Moore House—*hist pl* TX-5
*Draughns Mill Creek* MS-4
Draughon Library—*building* AL-4
Draughon-Miller Municipal Airp—*airport* TX-5
*Draughons College* TN-4
Draughons Junior Coll—*school* TN-4
Draughons Junior Coll-Palm Beach Center—*school* FL-3
Draught Creek—*stream* TN-4
Drauzenes Island—*gut* LA-4
Draves Cem—*cemetery* IL-6
Draville Sch—*school* MO-7
Dravo Cem—*cemetery* PA-2
Dravo Gravel Site—*hist pl* OH-6
**Dravosburg**—*pop pl* PA-2
Dravosburg Borough—*civil* PA-2
Dravosburg Cave—*cave* PA-2
*Draw* NC-3
Draw—*locale* TX-5
Draw, Lake—*valley* UT-8
Drawbar Hollow—*valley* AR-4
Drawbridge—*locale* DE-2
Drawbridge—*locale* MD-2
**Drawbridge**—*pop pl* CA-9
Drawbridge Sch—*school* DE-2
Draw Channel—*channel* NJ-2
Draw Channel—*channel* PA-2
Draw Creek—*stream* AR-4
Draw Creek—*stream* KS-7
Draw Creek—*stream* NV-8
Draw Creek—*stream* (2) OR-9
Draw Creek—*stream* UT-8
*Drawd* SC-3
Drawdy—*locale* SC-3
Drawdy, Lake—*lake* FL-3
Drawdy Bay—*swamp* FL-3
Drawdy Cem—*cemetery* WV-2
Drawdy Ch—*church* WV-2
Drawdy Creek—*stream* WV-2
Drawdy Creek Ch—*church* WV-2
Drawdy Falls Roadside Park—*park* WV-2
Drawdy Pond—*lake* FL-3
Drawe Cem—*cemetery* TX-5
*Drawer Creek* DE-2
*Drawers Creek* DE-2
Drawhorn Creek—*stream* GA-3
Drawing Bldg—*hist pl* CA-9
Drawing Channel—*channel* VA-3
*Drawjers Creek* DE-2
Drawn Boys Ledges—*bar* ME-1
Draw No 2—*valley* WY-8
Draw No 3—*valley* WY-8
Draw One Tank—*reservoir* TX-5
Draw Rock—*pillar* TN-4
Draw Tank—*reservoir* (2) NM-5
Draw Three Tank—*reservoir* TX-5
Draw Two Tank—*reservoir* TX-5
Draw Well—*well* (2) NM-5
Draw Windmill—*locale* NM-5
Draw Windmill—*locale* (7) TX-5
Drawyer Ch—*church* DE-2
Drawyer Creek—*stream* DE-2
*Drawyers Creek* DE-2
Drayden—*locale* MD-2
*Drayer Creek* DE-2
Drayer Creek—*stream* MN-6
*Drayers Creek* DE-2
Drayham Creek—*stream* AK-9
D Rayman Ranch—*locale* SD-7
Drays Mound—*summit* WA-9
Drayton—*locale* GA-3
**Drayton**—*pop pl* ND-7
**Drayton**—*pop pl* (2) SC-3
Drayton Cem—*cemetery* ND-7
Drayton Cem—*cemetery* SC-3
Drayton Ch—*church* GA-3
Drayton Dam—*dam* ND-7
*Drayton Hall* SC-3
Drayton Hall—*hist pl* SC-3
Drayton Hall—*locale* SC-3
Drayton Island—*island* FL-3
**Drayton Island**—*pop pl* FL-3
Drayton Light—*locale* WA-9
Drayton Municipal Airp—*airport* ND-7
Drayton Passage—*channel* WA-9
**Drayton Plains**—*pop pl* MI-6
Draytons Chapel—*church* AR-4
*Drayton Station* SC-3
Drayton Street Sch—*school* SC-3
Drayton Swamp—*swamp* SC-3
**Drayton Township**—*pop pl* ND-7
Drayton United Methodist Church—*hist pl* ND-7
**Draytonville**—*pop pl* SC-3
Draytonville Mtn—*summit* SC-3
D R Beeson Park—*park* TN-4
Dr. Buck-Stevens House—*hist pl* NY-2
*Dr. Buell Brook* CT-1
Drbuu—*island* MP-9
Dr Cook Lake—*lake* AK-9
*Dr Creek* NV-8
D R Dunlap Estate Dam—*dam* AL-4
Dr Durham—*locale* TX-5
Dread and Terror Ridge—*ridge* OR-9
Dreading Lake—*lake* GA-3
Dread Ledge—*rock* MA-1
Dreadnaught Hill—*summit* MT-8
Dreadnaught Mine—*mine* NM-5
Dreadnaught Mine (Inactive)—*mine* CA-9

Dreadnought Island—island ... OR-9
Dreahook—locale ... NJ-2
*Dreakers Creek* ... PA-2
Dream Creek—stream ... AK-9
Dream Creek—stream ... WY-8
Dream Gulch—valley ... AK-9
Dream Gulch—valley ... ID-8
**Dream Hill Estates**—pop pl ... TX-5
**Dream House Acres**—pop pl ... CO-8
Dreaming Creek—stream ... KY-4
Dreaming Creek—stream ... VA-3
Dream Island—island ... MT-8
*Dream Lake* ... CT-1
*Dream Lake* ... IN-6
Dream Lake—lake ... CA-9
Dream Lake—lake ... CO-8
Dream Lake—lake (2) ... FL-3
Dream Lake—lake (2) ... MI-6
Dream Lake—lake (2) ... NH-1
Dream Lake—lake (3) ... NY-2
Dream Lake—lake ... NC-3
Dream Lake—lake ... WA-9
Dream Lake—lake ... WY-8
Dream Lake—reservoir ... IN-6
Dream Lake Dam—dam ... IN-6
Dream Lake Dam Number One—dam ... AL-4
Dream Lake Dam Number Three—dam ... AL-4
Dream Lakes—lake ... AL-4
Dream Lake Sch—school ... FL-3
Dreamland—locale ... MI-6
Dreamland Cem—cemetery (2) ... TX-5
Dreamland Ch—church ... KY-4
Dreamland Creek—stream ... AK-9
Dreamland Lake—reservoir ... KY-4
Dreamland Park—park ... FL-3
Dreamland Park Sch—school ... NC-3
Dreamland-Velda Rose—CDP ... AZ-5
Dreamland Villa—locale ... AZ-5
Dreamland Villa Golf Course—other ... AZ-5
Dream Mine—mine (3) ... UT-8
Dream Pond—lake ... FL-3
Dreams, Lake of—lake ... WI-6
**Dreams End Subdivision**—pop pl ... UT-8
Dreams Landing—locale ... MD-2
Dream Tree Point—cape ... NC-3
Dream Valley—valley ... AR-4
Dream Valley Lake—reservoir ... OH-6
Dream Valley Ranch—locale ... CO-8
**Dreamwold Heights**—pop pl ... IN-6
**Dreamworld**—pop pl ... FL-3
Dreamworld—uninc pl ... FL-3
Dreamy Draw—arroyo ... AZ-5
Dreamy Draw Dam—dam ... AZ-5
Dreary Island—island ... LA-4
*Dreck Creek* ... DE-2
Dreck Creek—stream ... PA-2
Dreck Creek Rsvr—reservoir ... PA-2
Drectrah Coulee—valley ... WI-6
Dreddin Branch—stream ... AL-4
Dreden Cem—cemetery ... TN-4
Dredge Bayou (historical)—gut ... MS-4
Dredge Boat Creek Ditch No 1—canal ... AR-4
Dredge Boat Creek Ditch No 12—canal ... AR-4
Dredgeboat Slough—bay ... TX-5
Dredge Harbor—bay ... NJ-2
**Dredge (historical)**—pop pl ... MS-4
Dredge Lake—lake ... AK-9
Dredgers Key—island ... FL-3
Dr. Edmund A. Babler Memorial State Park Hist Dist—hist pl ... MO-7
Dreer Spring—spring ... VT-1
Dreese's Covered Bridge—hist pl ... PA-2
Dreguez Key—island ... FL-3
*Dreher* ... AL-4
Dreher, Jacob Wingard, House—hist pl ... SC-3
Dreher Island—island ... SC-3
Dreher Sch—school ... SC-3
Dreher Sch (historical)—school ... AL-4
**Drehersville**—pop pl ... PA-2
**Dreher (Township of)**—pop pl ... PA-2
Dreibelbis—locale ... PA-2
Dreibelbis Sch—school ... PA-2
Dreibelbis Station Bridge—hist pl ... PA-2
Drei Creek Cem—cemetery ... SD-7
Dreieinigkeit Cem—cemetery ... WI-6
Dreisbach Ch—church ... PA-2
Dreis Brothers Dam—dam ... SD-7
Dreiser Loop—post sta ... NY-2
Dreiss Creek—stream ... MI-6
Dreissner Branch—stream ... TX-5
*Dreka* ... TX-5
**Dreka**—pop pl ... TX-5
Drekatimon—island ... MP-9
Drenaenae—island ... MP-9
Drenan Cem—cemetery ... TN-4
Drench Branch—stream ... KY-4
Drenchwater Creek—stream ... AK-9
Drendell Sch—school ... CA-9
Drendel Sch—school ... IL-6
Drenn—locale ... VA-3
*Drennan* ... WV-2
Drennan Camp—locale ... CA-9
Drennan Cem—cemetery ... KY-4
Drennan Ditch—canal ... OH-6
Drennan Sch—school ... CO-8
Drennan Sch—school ... MI-6
**Drennen**—pop pl (2) ... PA-2
**Drennen**—pop pl ... WV-2
Drennen Lake Number 1—reservoir ... AL-4
Drennen Lake Number 2—reservoir ... AL-4
Drennen Lake Number 3—reservoir ... AL-4
Drennen Lake Number 4—reservoir ... AL-4
Drennen-Scott House—hist pl ... AR-4
Drenner Cem—cemetery ... WV-2
Drenner Hollow—valley ... WV-2
Drennin Spring—spring ... MT-8
*Drennon Cem* ... TN-4
Drennon Chapel—church ... KY-4
Drennon Creek—stream ... KY-4
Drennons Camp—locale ... MO-7
**Drennon Springs**—pop pl ... KY-4
**Drenthe**—pop pl ... MI-6
*Drepeiuen* ... MP-9
*Drerenbwij* ... MP-9
**Dresbach**—pop pl ... MN-6
Dresbach Cem—cemetery ... MN-6
Dresbach Ch—church ... OH-6
Dresbach Creek—stream ... OH-6
Dresbach-Hunt-Boyer House—hist pl ... CA-9
Dresbach Island—island ... MN-6
Dresbach Slough—channel ... MN-6
**Dresbach (Township of)**—pop pl ... MN-6
Drescher Ditch—canal ... OR-9
Drescher Island—island ... WI-6
Drescher Lateral—canal ... CO-8
Drescher Rsvr—reservoir ... OR-9
Drescher Sch—school ... WI-6
*Dresden* ... ME-1
Dresden—locale ... GA-3
Dresden—locale ... IA-7
Dresden—locale ... NY-2
Dresden—locale ... TX-5
**Dresden**—pop pl ... IN-6
**Dresden**—pop pl ... IA-7
**Dresden**—pop pl ... KS-7
**Dresden**—pop pl ... ME-1
**Dresden**—pop pl ... MO-7
**Dresden**—pop pl ... NY-2
**Dresden**—pop pl ... NC-3
**Dresden**—pop pl ... ND-7
**Dresden**—pop pl ... OH-6
**Dresden**—pop pl ... TN-4
Dresden Acad (historical)—school ... TN-4
**Dresden Acres**—pop pl ... IL-6
Dresden Bog—lake ... ME-1
Dresden Brick Sch House—hist pl ... ME-1
Dresden (CCD)—cens area ... TN-4
Dresden Cem—cemetery ... IL-6
Dresden Cem—cemetery ... IA-7
Dresden Cem—cemetery ... KS-7
Dresden Cem—cemetery ... MO-7
Dresden City Hall—building ... TN-4
Dresden Division—civil ... TN-4
**Dresden (Dresden Mills)**—pop pl ... ME-1
Dresden Elem Sch—school ... TN-4
Dresden Female Acad (historical)—school ... TN-4
Dresden First Baptist Ch—church ... TN-4
**Dresden Green**—pop pl ... MD-2
Dresden Heights Sch—school ... IL-6
Dresden (historical)—locale ... KS-7
Dresden HS—school ... TN-4
Dresden Industrial Park—locale ... TN-4
Dresden Island—island ... IL-6
Dresden Island Lock and Dam—dam ... IL-6
Dresden JHS—school ... TN-4
Dresden Lake—lake ... PA-2
Dresden Male Acad (historical)—school ... TN-4
**Dresden Mills**—pop pl ... ME-1
Dresden Nuclear Power Plant—facility ... IL-6
Dresden Post Office—building ... TN-4
Dresden Run—stream ... IL-6
**Dresden Station (Dresden)**—pop pl ... NY-2
Dresden Suspension Bridge—hist pl ... OH-6
**Dresden (Town of)**—pop pl ... ME-1
**Dresden (Town of)**—pop pl ... NY-2
Dresden Township—civil ... MO-7
Dresden Township—fmr MCD ... IA-7
**Dresden Township**—pop pl (2) ... KS-7
**Dresden Township**—pop pl ... ND-7
Dresden Training Sch (historical)—school ... TN-4
*Dresden Village* ... MI-6
*Dresdon* ... MO-7
Dresher—locale ... PA-2
Dresher Marsh—swamp ... WI-6
Dresher Rsvr—reservoir ... CO-8
*Dreshertown* ... PA-2
**Dreshertowne**—pop pl ... PA-2
Dressel Rsvr—reservoir ... CO-8
Dresselville Cem—cemetery ... MN-6
**Dressen**—pop pl ... KY-4
*Dresser* ... IN-6
Dresser—locale ... CA-9
**Dresser**—pop pl ... TX-5
**Dresser**—pop pl ... WI-6
Dresser, Paul, Birthplace—hist pl ... IN-6
Dresser Brook—stream ... MA-1
Dresser Camp—locale ... CA-9
Dresser Cem—cemetery ... MA-1
Dresser Creek—stream ... ID-8
Dresser Creek—stream ... NY-2
Dresser Hill—summit ... MA-1
Dresser Hill—summit ... PA-2
Dresser Hills—summit ... NH-1
Dresser Island—island ... MO-7
*Dresser Junction* ... WI-6
Dresser Memorial Park—park ... IN-6
Dresser Mtn—summit ... ME-1
*Dresser Pond* ... MA-1
Dresser Power Plant—other ... IN-6
Dresser Run—stream ... PA-2
*Dresser Run Dam* ... PA-2
Dressers Mtn—summit ... ME-1
*Dressers Pond* ... MA-1
Dresser Spring—spring ... WA-9
**Dresser (Taylorville)**—pop pl ... IN-6
**Dresserville**—pop pl ... NY-2
Dresserville Creek—stream ... NY-2
Dresserville Sch—school ... MI-6
Dressier Drain—canal ... MI-6
Dressing Apartments—hist pl ... AZ-5
Dressing Point—island ... TX-5
Dressler Cem—cemetery ... PA-2
Dressler Ditch—canal ... IN-6
Dressler Gulch—valley ... CO-8
Dressler Hammond Dead River—lake ... MS-4
Dressler Lake—lake ... MI-6
Dressler Ranch—locale ... NM-5
Dressler Run—stream ... PA-2
Dresslers Ch—church ... PA-2
Dresslers Ridge—ridge ... PA-2
**Dresslerville**—pop pl ... NV-8
**Dresslerville Colony**—pop pl ... NV-8
Dressor—locale ... IL-6
Dress Point—cape ... AK-9
Dressy Cem—cemetery ... TX-5
*Drew* ... FL-3
*Drew* ... IN-6
Drew—locale ... GA-3
Drew—locale ... LA-4
Drew—locale ... MI-6
Drew—locale ... MO-7
Drew—locale ... NC-3
Drew—locale ... OR-9
**Drew**—pop pl ... IN-6
**Drew**—pop pl ... IA-7
**Drew**—pop pl ... MI-6
**Drew**—pop pl ... MS-4
Drew—uninc pl ... LA-4
Drew, Charles Richard, House—hist pl ... VA-3
Drew, J. W., Grain Elevator—hist pl ... MT-8
Drew, The—ridge ... OR-9
*Drew Baptist Church* ... MS-4
Drew Branch—stream ... AL-4
Drew Branch—stream ... TN-4
Drew Brook—stream ... ME-1
Drew Brook—stream (2) ... NH-1
Drew Canal—canal ... LA-4
Drew Cem—cemetery ... ME-1
Drew Cem—cemetery ... MS-4
Drew Cem—cemetery ... NC-3
Drew Cem—cemetery ... OR-9
Drew Ch of Christ—church ... MS-4
*Drew Colored School* ... MS-4
**Drew (County)**—pop pl ... AR-4
Drew Cove—cove ... MA-1
*Drew Creek* ... WI-6
Drew Creek—stream (2) ... CA-9
Drew Creek—stream ... MT-8
Drew Creek—stream (2) ... OR-9
Drew Creek—stream (2) ... WI-6
**Drew Dell Acres**—pop pl ... IL-6
Drew Drain—canal ... ID-8
Drew (Drew Park)—uninc pl ... FL-3
Drewek Creek—stream ... WI-6
Drewel Cem—cemetery ... MO-7
Drewel Ford (historical)—locale ... MO-7
Drewell Hollow—valley ... MO-7
**Drewersburg**—pop pl ... IN-6
Drewersburg Ch—church ... IN-6
*Drewersburgh* ... IN-6
*Drewery* ... AL-4
Drewery Creek—stream ... MS-4
Drewery Lake—lake ... MN-6
Drewery Lake—reservoir ... MS-4
Drew Gulch—valley ... ID-8
Drew-Hamilton—uninc pl ... NY-2
Drew Health Clinic—hospital ... MS-4
Drew Hill—summit ... ME-1
Drew HS—school ... AR-4
Drew HS—school ... MS-4
Drew JHS—school ... AL-4
Drew JHS—school ... CA-9
Drew JHS—school (2) ... FL-3
Drew JHS—school ... TX-5
Drew Lagoon Dam—dam ... MS-4
*Drew Lake* ... ME-1
Drew Lake—lake ... CA-9
Drew Lake—lake ... NH-1
Drew Lake—lake ... OR-9
Drew Lake Rec Area—park ... NH-1
Drew Lateral—canal ... ID-8
Drew Mansion—building ... FL-3
Drew Meadow—flat ... CA-9
Drew Memorial Ch—church ... KY-4
Drew Mine—mine ... NV-8
Drew Mtn—summit ... NH-1
Drew Mtn—summit ... VT-1
Drewniany-Springmeadow Airp—airport ... PA-2
Drew Park—park ... FL-3
Drew Park—park ... SC-3
**Drew Park**—pop pl ... FL-3
Drew Park Baptist Temple—church ... FL-3
Drew (Plantation of)—civ div ... ME-1
Drew Playground—park ... FL-3
Drew Plaza (Shop Ctr)—locale ... FL-3
Drew Point—cape ... AK-9
*Drew Pond* ... NH-1
Drew Pond—lake ... IL-6
Drew Pond—lake ... ME-1
Drew Pond—lake ... NY-2
Drew Public Library—building ... MS-4
Drew Ranch—locale ... WY-8
*Drew Rsvr* ... OR-9
Drewry—locale ... AL-4
**Drewry**—pop pl ... NC-3
*Drewry Bluff* ... VA-3
Drewry Cem—cemetery ... MS-4
Drewry Creek—stream ... CA-9
**Drewry Hills (subdivision)**—pop pl ... NC-3
Drewry Mason HS—school ... VA-3
Drewry-Mitchell-Moorer House—hist pl ... AL-4
Drewry Point—cape ... VA-3
*Drewry's Bluff* ... VA-3
Drewrys Bluff—cliff ... VA-3
**Drewrys Bluff**—pop pl ... VA-3
Drewrys Bluff Ch—church ... VA-3
**Drewryville**—pop pl ... VA-3
Drewryville District Sch—school ... VA-3
Drewryville (Magisterial District)—fmr MCD ... VA-3
Drews Airstrip—airport ... OR-9
Drew Sch—school ... DC-2
Drew Sch—school (2) ... FL-3
Drew Sch—school ... IL-6
Drew Sch—school ... LA-4
Drew Sch—school (2) ... ME-1
Drew Sch—school ... MN-6
Drew Sch—school ... OR-9
Drew Sch—school ... VA-3
*Drew School* ... IN-6
Drewsclift Cem—cemetery ... NY-2
Drews Corner—locale ... NY-2
**Drews Corner**—pop pl ... NY-2
*Drews Creek* ... TX-5
**Drews Creek**—pop pl ... WV-2
Drews Creek—stream (2) ... OR-9
Drews Creek—stream ... WV-2
Drews Creek Campground—park ... OR-9
Drews Creek Slough—stream ... OR-9
Drews Dam—dam ... OR-9
**Drewsey**—pop pl ... OR-9
Drewsey (CCD)—cens area ... OR-9
*Drewsey Ditch* ... OR-9
Drewsey Reclamation Company Ditch—canal ... OR-9
Drewsey Table—summit ... OR-9
Drewsey Valley—valley ... OR-9
Drews Gap—gap ... OR-9
Drews Gap Summit—gap ... OR-9
Drews Hill—summit ... NH-1
Drew Siding—locale ... MI-6
Drews Island—island ... LA-4
*Drews Lake* ... ME-1
Drews Landing—locale ... TX-5
*Drews Landing Creek* ... TX-5
*Drews Mill Creek* ... TX-5
Drew Smith Sch—school ... VA-3
Drews Pass—channel ... LA-4
Drews Prairie—flat ... WA-9
Drew Spring Well—well ... AZ-5
Drews Ranch—locale ... OR-9
Drews Rsvr—reservoir ... OR-9
Drew Station RR Station—locale ... FL-3
Drews Valley—valley ... OR-9
**Drews Valley (historical)**—pop pl ... OR-9
Drews Valley Ranch—locale ... OR-9
**Drewsville**—pop pl ... NH-1
Drew-Syme Mine—mine ... MN-6
Drew Tank—reservoir ... AZ-5
Drew Tank—reservoir ... NM-5
Drew United Methodist Ch—church ... MS-4
Drew Univ—school ... NJ-2
**Drewville Heights**—pop pl ... NY-2
Drew Wash—stream ... AZ-5
Drew Well—well ... WY-8
Drewyer, Mount—summit ... MT-8
Drew 19 Shop Ctr—locale ... FL-3
Drexall Creek—stream ... ID-8
Drexall Spring—spring ... ID-8
*Drexel* ... IL-6
Drexel—locale ... MT-8
**Drexel**—pop pl ... FL-3
**Drexel**—pop pl ... GA-3
**Drexel**—pop pl ... MO-7
**Drexel**—pop pl ... NC-3
**Drexel**—pop pl ... OH-6
Drexel, Francis M., Sch—hist pl ... PA-2
Drexel and Company Bldg—hist pl ... PA-2
Drexel Ave Sch—school ... NY-2
**Drexelbrook**—pop pl ... PA-2
**Drexelbrook (subdivision)**—pop pl ... NC-3
Drexel Corner—locale ... KS-7
Drexel Development Hist Dist—hist pl ... PA-2
Drexel Estate—hist pl ... ME-1
*Drexel Gardens* ... IN-6
**Drexel Gardens**—pop pl ... IN-6
**Drexel Gardens**—pop pl ... PA-2
**Drexel Heights**—pop pl ... AZ-5
**Drexel Heights**—pop pl ... PA-2
**Drexel Hill**—pop pl ... PA-2
*Drexel Hill Junior High School* ... PA-2
Drexel Hill MS—school ... PA-2
**Drexel Hills**—pop pl ... PA-2
Drexel Institute of Technology—school ... PA-2
Drexel Lake—reservoir ... SC-3
**Drexel Lake Hills**—pop pl ... SC-3
Drexell Branch—stream ... MD-2
Drexell Landing—locale ... MD-2
**Drexel Manor**—pop pl ... PA-2
Drexel Park—park ... GA-3
Drexel Park—park ... PA-2
**Drexel Plaza**—pop pl ... PA-2
Drexel Run—stream ... IN-6
Drexel Sch—school ... AZ-5
Drexel Sch—school ... IL-6
Drexel Sch—school ... PA-2
Drexel (Township of)—fmr MCD ... NC-3
Drexler Tract—civil ... CA-9
**Dreyer**—pop pl ... TX-5
Dreyfoos—locale ... TX-5
*Dreyfus* ... MS-4
Dreyfus—other ... MS-4
**Dreyfus**—pop pl ... KY-4
**Dreyfus**—pop pl ... SC-3
Dreyfus JHS—school ... NY-2
Dreyfus Rsvr—reservoir ... CO-8
Dreyir Sch—school ... IA-7
D & RG Narrow Gauge Trestle—hist pl ... CO-8
Dr H E Atherton Lake—reservoir ... TN-4
Dr H E Athertons Lake Dam—dam ... TN-4
D R Houpt Pond Dam—dam ... MS-4
Dribble Spring—spring ... OR-9
*Drice* ... TN-4
*Drice Post Office* ... TN-4
Dried Indian Creek—stream ... GA-3
Dried Meat Rapids—rapids ... ID-8
Drier Bay—bay ... AK-9
Drier Creek—stream ... OR-9
Drier Offerman Park—park ... NY-2
Driesbach Lake—lake ... AL-4
Driest Point—cape ... AK-9
Drietz Lake—lake ... MN-6
Driffil Sch—school ... CA-9
**Drift**—pop pl ... KY-4
Drift Branch—stream ... AL-4
Drift Branch—stream (2) ... KY-4
Drift Branch—stream ... NC-3
Drift Branch—stream ... WV-2
Drift Campground—park ... OR-9
*Drift Canyon* ... TX-5
Drift Chute—stream ... IL-6
**Drift Creek**—pop pl ... OR-9
Drift Creek—stream ... CO-8
Drift Creek—stream ... ID-8
Drift Creek—stream ... MT-8
Drift Creek—stream ... OH-6
Drift Creek—stream (6) ... OR-9
Drift Creek—stream ... WA-9
Drift Creek Bridge—hist pl ... OR-9
Drift Creek Falls—falls ... OR-9
Drift Creek Shelter—locale ... OR-9
Drift Creek Trail—trail ... OR-9
Drift Fence Campground—park ... OR-9
Drift Fence Canyon—valley ... NM-5
Drift Fence Dam—dam ... AZ-5
Drift Fence Lake—reservoir ... AZ-5
Drift Fence Lake Campground—park ... AZ-5
Drift Fence Rsvr—reservoir ... CO-8
Drift Fence Spring—spring ... AZ-5
Drift Fence Spring—spring ... CO-8
Drift Fence Tank—reservoir (2) ... AZ-5
Drift Fence Tank—reservoir ... CA-9
Drift Fence Tank—reservoir ... NM-5
Drift Fence Waterhole—reservoir ... OR-9
Drift Fence Well—locale ... NM-5
Drift Fork—stream ... WV-2
Drift Hills—ridge ... AZ-5
**Drifting**—pop pl ... PA-2
Drifting Snow Creek—stream ... AK-9
Drift Island—island ... IL-6
Drift Lake—lake ... UT-8
Drift Lake—reservoir ... UT-8
Drift Lake Dam—dam ... UT-8
Driftmeyer Ditch—canal ... OH-6
Drifton—locale ... AL-4
**Drifton**—pop pl ... FL-3
**Drifton**—pop pl ... PA-2
Drifton Branch—stream ... FL-3
Drifton Mine (underground)—mine ... AL-4
Drifton Post Office (historical)—building ... AL-4
Drift Peak—summit ... MT-8
Drift Post Office (historical)—building ... TN-4
Drift River—stream ... AK-9
Drift River Lobe Double Glacier—glacier ... AK-9
Drift River Terminal—other ... AK-9
Drift Run—locale ... WV-2
Drift Run—stream ... KY-4
Drift Run—stream (4) ... WV-2
Drift Trail Canyon—valley ... UT-8
Driftwood—fmr MCD (2) ... NE-7
Driftwood—locale ... TX-5
**Driftwood**—pop pl ... AL-4
**Driftwood**—pop pl ... AR-4
**Driftwood**—pop pl ... NY-2
**Driftwood**—pop pl (2) ... OH-6
**Driftwood**—pop pl ... OK-5
**Driftwood**—pop pl ... PA-2
Driftwood—uninc pl ... FL-3
Driftwood Acad—school ... FL-3
**Driftwood Acres**—pop pl ... FL-3
Driftwood Bay—bay (2) ... AK-9
Driftwood Beach—beach ... CA-9
Driftwood Beach Wayside—locale ... OR-9
Driftwood Borough—civil ... PA-2
Driftwood Branch Sinnemahoning Creek—stream ... PA-2
Driftwood Canal—canal ... NE-7
Driftwood Canyon—valley ... AZ-5
Driftwood Canyon—valley ... SD-7
Driftwood Canyon—valley ... TX-5
Driftwood Canyon—valley ... UT-8
Driftwood Cave—cave ... AL-4
Driftwood Cem—cemetery ... IN-6
Driftwood Ch—church ... AL-4
Driftwood Ch—church ... IN-6
Driftwood Cove—bay ... AK-9
Driftwood Cove—bay ... NV-8
Driftwood Creek—stream ... AK-9
Driftwood Creek—stream ... KS-7
Driftwood Creek—stream ... NE-7
Driftwood Creek—stream ... OK-5
Driftwood Creek—stream ... SD-7
Driftwood Creek—stream ... VA-3
Driftwood Dock—locale ... TN-4
Driftwood Elem Sch—school ... FL-3
**Driftwood Estates (subdivision)**—pop pl ... AL-4
**Driftwood Estates (subdivision)**—pop pl ... FL-3
**Driftwood Estates Subdivision**—pop pl ... UT-8
*Driftwood Fork* ... IN-6
*Driftwood Fork White River* ... IN-6
**Driftwood Hills**—pop pl ... IN-6
Driftwood Island—island ... AZ-5
Driftwood JHS—school ... FL-3
Driftwood Mtn—summit ... NY-2
Driftwood Nursery Sch—school ... FL-3
**Driftwood Park (subdivision)**—pop pl ... TN-4
Driftwood Point—cape ... CT-1
Driftwood Point—cape ... ID-8
Driftwood Point—cape ... MN-6
Driftwood River—stream ... IN-6
Driftwood Shores—locale ... WA-9
Driftwood Slough—gut ... AK-9
Driftwood Spring—spring ... AZ-5
**Driftwood (subdivision)**—pop pl ... TN-4
**Driftwood Township**—pop pl ... KS-7
**Driftwood (Township of)**—pop pl ... IN-6
**Driftwood Village (trailer park)**—pop pl ... DE-2
Driftwood West Canal—canal ... NE-7
Drifwood Bay—bay ... AK-9
Drifwood Forest Camp—locale ... OR-9
Driger Ditch—canal ... IN-6
*Drigger Crossroad* ... SC-3
**Drigger Crossroads**—pop pl ... SC-3
Drigger Islands—island ... FL-3
Driggers Chapel—church ... SC-3
Driggers Pond—lake ... LA-4
Driggers Ridge—ridge ... FL-3
**Driggerstown**—pop pl ... SC-3
**Driggs**—pop pl ... AR-4
**Driggs**—pop pl ... ID-8
Driggs Cem—cemetery ... ID-8
Driggs-Darby Cem—cemetery ... ID-8
Driggs Lake—lake ... MI-6
Driggs Marsh—swamp ... MI-6
Driggs River—stream ... MI-6
Driggs Sch—school ... CT-1
**Driggs (Spur 88)**—pop pl ... MI-6
Driggs (Township of)—fmr MCD ... AR-4
Drill—locale ... VA-3
Drill Box Canyon—valley ... OR-9
Drill Creek—stream ... AK-9
Drill Draw Canyon—valley ... NM-5
Driller Lake—lake ... MN-6
Drillers Ridge—ridge ... CA-9
Drill Hole A-2—well ... NV-8
Drill Hole D—well ... NV-8
Drill Hole Gulch—valley ... CO-8
Drill Hole Me 1—well ... NV-8
Drill Hole Me 2—well ... NV-8
Drill Hole Me 3—well ... NV-8
Drill Hole Me 4—well ... NV-8
Drill Hole Sand Windmill—locale ... NM-5
Drill Hole Twenty Gallon Well—well ... NM-5
Drill Hole U 15-32—well ... NV-8
Drill Hole U 15-33—well ... NV-8
Drill Hole U 15-35—well ... NV-8
Drill Hole 2—well ... NV-8
Drill Hole 4—locale ... NV-8
Drill Hollow—valley ... TX-5
Drill Lake—lake ... AK-9
*Drill Ridge* ... NC-3
Drindarry Gulch—valley ... OR-9
Drinkard Cem—cemetery ... VA-3
Drinkard Oil Field—other ... NM-5
Drink Creek—stream ... CO-8
Drinkenberg's, F. H., First Home—hist pl ... MT-8
**Drinker**—pop pl ... PA-2
Drinker, John, House—hist pl ... WV-2
Drinker Creek—stream ... PA-2
Drinker Sch—school ... PA-2
Drinker's Court—hist pl ... PA-2
Drinker Tank—reservoir ... AZ-5
Drinkhall, The—hist pl ... NY-2
Drinking Branch—stream ... AL-4
Drinking Cove—bay ... ME-1
Drinking Cup Gulch—valley ... AK-9
Drinking Pond—swamp ... NC-3
Drinking Swamp—stream ... VA-3
Drinkle—locale ... OH-6
Drinklog Branch—stream ... NC-3
Drinks Canyon—valley ... UT-8
Drinks Run—stream ... MD-2
Drinkwater Canyon—valley ... CA-9
Drinkwater Cem—cemetery ... KS-7
Drinkwater Corner—locale ... ME-1
Drinkwater Creek—stream ... NC-3
Drinkwater Flat—flat ... CA-9
Drinkwater Gulch—valley ... CA-9
Drinkwater Gulch—valley ... MT-8
Drinkwater Hill—summit ... IN-6
Drinkwater Hill—summit ... VT-1
Drinkwater Lake—flat ... CA-9
Drinkwater Mine—mine ... NV-8
Drinkwater Pass—gap ... OR-9
Drinkwater Point—cape ... ME-1
Drinkwater River—stream ... MA-1
Drinkwater Rsvr—reservoir ... CA-9
Drinkwater Rsvr Number Two—reservoir ... OR-9
Drinkwater Sch—school ... ME-1
Drinkwater Spring—spring ... CA-9
Drinkwater Spring—spring ... MS-4
Drinkwine Creek—stream ... WI-6
**Drinnon Heights (subdivision)**—pop pl ... TN-4
Drip, The—spring ... KY-4
Drip Creek—stream ... AR-4
Drip Creek—stream ... MT-8
Drip Creek—stream ... OR-9
Drip Nose Mtn—summit ... GA-3
Dripoff Branch—stream ... NC-3
Dripoff Hollow—valley ... AR-4
Drip Pee Wee Dam—dam ... NM-5
Dripper Windmill—locale ... NM-5
Dripping Canyon—valley ... UT-8
Dripping Cave—cave ... TN-4
*Dripping Creek* ... TX-5
Dripping Hole Branch—stream ... TX-5
Dripping Hole Spring—spring ... MT-8
Dripping Point—ridge ... UT-8
Dripping Rock—pillar ... CO-8
Dripping Rock—summit ... VA-3
Dripping Rock Bluff—cliff ... TN-4
Dripping Rock Creek—stream ... CO-8
Dripping Rock Draw—valley ... WY-8
Dripping rock Hollow—valley ... TN-4
Dripping Rock Pit No 2—basin ... WY-8
Dripping Rock Rsvr—reservoir ... CO-8
Dripping Rock Rsvr—reservoir ... WY-8
Dripping Rocks—cliff ... GA-3
Dripping Rock Seep—spring ... UT-8
Dripping Rock Spring—spring ... CO-8
Dripping Rock Spring—spring ... WY-8
*Dripping Spring* ... AZ-5
Dripping Spring—locale ... KY-4
Dripping Spring—locale ... MO-7
Dripping Spring—locale ... NM-5
Dripping Spring—locale ... OK-5
Dripping Spring—spring (3) ... AL-4
Dripping Spring—spring (18) ... AZ-5
Dripping Spring—spring (2) ... AR-4
Dripping Spring—spring (3) ... CA-9
Dripping Spring—spring (2) ... CO-8
Dripping Spring—spring ... GA-3
Dripping Spring—spring ... KY-4
Dripping Spring—spring ... MO-7
Dripping Spring—spring ... MT-8
Dripping Spring—spring (4) ... NM-5
Dripping Spring—spring (6) ... TN-4
Dripping Spring—spring (8) ... TX-5
Dripping Spring—spring (8) ... UT-8
Dripping Spring Branch—stream ... AL-4
Dripping Spring Branch—stream ... KY-4
Dripping Spring Campground—locale ... UT-8
Dripping Spring Canyon—valley (2) ... NM-5
Dripping Spring Cave—cave ... AL-4
Dripping Spring Cem—cemetery ... MO-7
Dripping Spring Ch—church (2) ... KY-4
*Dripping Spring Cove* ... TN-4
Dripping Spring Cove Branch—stream ... TN-4
*Dripping Spring Creek* ... TN-4
Dripping Spring Creek—stream ... MT-8
Dripping Spring Creek—stream ... TX-5
*Dripping Spring Gap* ... AR-4
Dripping Spring Hollow—valley ... MO-7
Dripping Spring Hollow—valley (2) ... OK-5
*Dripping Spring Mountains* ... AZ-5
Dripping Spring Mountains—range ... AZ-5
Dripping Spring Mtn—summit ... TN-4
*Dripping Spring Quartzite* ... AZ-5
*Dripping Spring Ranch* ... AZ-5
*Dripping Spring Range* ... AZ-5
*Dripping Springs* ... AZ-5
Dripping Springs—locale ... AZ-5
Dripping Springs—locale ... AR-4
Dripping Springs—locale ... TN-4
**Dripping Springs**—pop pl ... AL-4
**Dripping Springs**—pop pl ... OK-5
**Dripping Springs**—pop pl ... TX-5
Dripping Springs—spring (4) ... AZ-5
Dripping Springs—spring ... AR-4
Dripping Springs—spring (3) ... CA-9
Dripping Springs—spring ... CO-8
Dripping Springs—spring ... KY-4
Dripping Springs—spring ... MO-7
Dripping Springs—spring (4) ... NM-5
Dripping Springs—spring ... OK-5
Dripping Springs—spring ... OR-9
Dripping Springs—spring (2) ... TN-4
Dripping Springs—spring (7) ... TX-5
Dripping Springs—stream ... TX-5
Dripping Springs Branch—stream ... KY-4
Dripping Springs Branch—stream ... OK-5
Dripping Springs Camp—locale ... OK-5
Dripping Springs Canyon—valley ... AZ-5
Dripping Springs Canyon—valley ... CO-8
Dripping Springs Canyon—valley ... NV-8
Dripping Springs Canyon—valley ... UT-8
Dripping Springs Cem—cemetery ... AR-4
Dripping Springs Cem—cemetery (2) ... OK-5
Dripping Springs Ch—church (2) ... AR-4
Dripping Springs Ch—church ... KY-4
Dripping Springs Ch—church ... MO-7
Dripping Springs Ch—church ... OK-5
Dripping Springs Ch—church ... TX-5
Dripping Spring Sch—school ... KY-4
Dripping Spring Sch (historical)—school ... AL-4
*Dripping Springs Creek* ... OK-5

Dry Boulder Gulch ... MT-8
Dry Branch ... AL-4
Dry Branch ... AR-4
Dry Branch ... GA-3
Dry Branch ... IN-6
Dry Branch ... MS-4
Dry Branch ... SC-3
Dry Branch ... TN-4
Dry Branch ... TX-5
Dry Branch ... VA-3
Dry Branch—locale ... VA-3
**Dry Branch**—pop pl ... GA-3
**Drybranch**—pop pl ... MD-2
**Dry Branch**—pop pl ... SC-3
**Dry Branch**—pop pl ... TN-4
**Dry Branch**—pop pl ... WV-2
**Drybranch**—pop pl ... WV-2
Dry Branch—stream (33) ... AL-4
Dry Branch—stream (14) ... AR-4
Dry Branch—stream (8) ... FL-3
Dry Branch—stream (21) ... GA-3
Dry Branch—stream (5) ... IL-6
Dry Branch—stream (19) ... IN-6
Dry Branch—stream (5) ... IA-7
Dry Branch—stream (4) ... KS-7
Dry Branch—stream (46) ... KY-4
Dry Branch—stream (11) ... LA-4
Dry Branch—stream ... MD-2
Dry Branch—stream (12) ... MS-4
Dry Branch—stream (24) ... MO-7
Dry Branch—stream (4) ... NE-7
Dry Branch—stream (2) ... NJ-2
Dry Branch—stream (12) ... NC-3
Dry Branch—stream ... ND-7
Dry Branch—stream ... OH-6
Dry Branch—stream (6) ... OK-5
Dry Branch—stream (12) ... SC-3
Dry Branch—stream ... SD-7
Dry Branch—stream (88) ... TN-4
Dry Branch—stream (35) ... TX-5
Dry Branch—stream (29) ... VA-3
Dry Branch—stream (19) ... WV-2
Dry Branch Cave—cave ... MO-7
Dry Branch Cem—cemetery ... TN-4
Dry Branch Cem—cemetery ... WV-2
Dry Branch Ch—church ... FL-3
Dry Branch Ch—church (2) ... GA-3
Dry Branch Ch—church ... NC-3
Dry Branch Ch—church ... TN-4
Dry Branch Ch (historical)—church ... TN-4
Dry Branch Ch of Christ ... TN-4
Dry Branch Church ... AL-4
Dry Branch Cove—bay ... MO-7
Dry Branch Creek ... GA-3
Dry Branch Creek—stream (2) ... GA-3
Dry Branch Gap—gap ... VA-3
Dry Branch Hollow—valley ... AR-4
Dry Branch Hollow—valley (2) ... TN-4
Dry Branch Kickapoo Creek—stream ... TX-5
Dry Branch Mine—mine ... TN-4
Dry Branch Pioneer Cem—cemetery ... NE-7
Dry Branch Sch—school ... IA-7
Dry Branch Sch—school ... MO-7
Dry Branch Sch—school (2) ... NE-7
Dry Branch Sch—school ... TN-4
Dry Branch Sch—school ... WV-2
Dry Branch Sch (historical)—school ... TN-4
**Dry Branch (Youley)**—pop pl ... GA-3
Dry Bread Branch—stream ... KY-4
Dry Bread Fork—stream ... KY-4
Dry Bread Hollow—valley ... UT-8
Dry Bread Island—island ... LA-4
Dry Bread Pond—lake ... UT-8
Dry Breakers—bar ... MA-1
Dry Bridge—bridge ... NY-2
Dry Bridge—locale ... VA-3
Dry Bridge Mtn—summit ... CA-9
Dry Brook ... NY-2
Dry Brook ... RI-1
Dry Brook—stream ... AL-4
Dry Brook—stream ... CT-1
Dry Brook—stream ... IN-6
Dry Brook—stream (2) ... ME-1
Dry Brook—stream (5) ... MA-1
Dry Brook—stream (4) ... NH-1
Dry Brook—stream ... NJ-2
Dry Brook—stream (24) ... NY-2
Dry Brook—stream (3) ... PA-2
Dry Brook—stream ... RI-1
Dry Brook—stream (2) ... VT-1
Dry Brook Ch—church ... NY-2
Dry Brook Hill—summit ... MA-1
Dry Brook Hollow—valley ... VT-1
Dry Brook Ridge—ridge ... NY-2
Dry Brushy Creek ... TX-5
Dry Brushy Creek—stream (2) ... TX-5
Dry Buck Creek—stream ... CO-8
Dry Buck Creek—stream (2) ... ID-8
Dry Buck Meadow—flat ... ID-8
Dry Buck Mtn—summit ... ID-8
Dry Buck School (Abandoned)—locale ... ID-8
Dry Buck Summit—summit ... ID-8
Dry Buck Valley—valley ... ID-8
Dry Buffalo Branch—stream ... TN-4
Dry Bullion Creek—stream ... ND-7
Dryburg—locale ... MI-6
Dryburg—locale ... VA-3
Dry Burn Canyon—valley ... UT-8
Dry Burney Creek—stream ... CA-9
Dry Burnt Canyon—valley ... NM-5
Dry Bush Creek—stream ... WY-8
Dry Butte—summit (3) ... OR-9
Dry Butte Gulch—valley ... ID-8
Dry Buttes—summit ... OR-9
Dry Cabin Creek—stream ... OR-9
Dry Cabin Creek—stream ... WY-8
Dry Cabin Creek Trail (pack)—trail ... OR-9
Dry California Creek—stream ... TX-5
Dry Camas Creek—stream ... OR-9
Dry Camp—locale ... AZ-5
Dry Camp—locale ... WA-9
Dry Camp Canyon—valley ... AZ-5
Dry Camp Hollow—valley ... MO-7
Dry Camp Mine—mine ... OR-9
Dry Camp Picnic Area—locale ... NM-5
Dry Camp Spring—spring ... AZ-5
Dry Camp Tank—reservoir ... TX-5
Dry Camp Valley Spring—spring ... UT-8
Dry Can Creek—stream ... ID-8
Dry Can Creek—stream ... TX-5
Dry Canyon ... CA-9
Dry Canyon ... ID-8
Dry Canyon ... NV-8
Dry Canyon ... UT-8
Dry Canyon ... WA-9
Dry Canyon—valley (10) ... AZ-5
Dry Canyon—valley (14) ... CA-9
Dry Canyon—valley (3) ... CO-8
Dry Canyon—valley (26) ... ID-8
Dry Canyon—valley (5) ... MT-8
Dry Canyon—valley ... NE-7
Dry Canyon—valley (35) ... NV-8
Dry Canyon—valley (12) ... NM-5
Dry Canyon—valley (2) ... OK-5
Dry Canyon—valley (5) ... OR-9
Dry Canyon—valley ... TX-5
Dry Canyon—valley (49) ... UT-8
Dry Canyon—valley ... WA-9
Dry Canyon—valley (7) ... WY-8
Dry Canyon Basin—basin ... UT-8
Dry Canyon Creek ... ID-8
Dry Canyon Creek—stream ... AK-9
Dry Canyon Creek—stream ... WY-8
Dry Canyon Mine—mine ... NV-8
Dry Canyon Mountains ... UT-8
Dry Canyon Mtn—summit ... UT-8
Dry Canyon Picnic Area—locale ... UT-8
Dry Canyon Ridge—ridge ... WA-9
Dry Canyon Rsvr—reservoir ... CA-9
Dry Canyon Rsvr—reservoir ... ID-8
Dry Canyon Spring ... UT-8
Dry Canyon Spring—spring (3) ... AZ-5
Dry Canyon Spring—spring ... CO-8
Dry Canyon Spring—spring ... ID-8
Dry Canyon Spring—spring (4) ... NV-8
Dry Canyon Spring—spring ... UT-8
Dry Canyon Spring—spring ... WY-8
Dry Canyon Summit—summit ... NV-8
Dry Canyon Tank—reservoir (2) ... AZ-5
Dry Canyon Wash—stream ... CO-8
Dry Canyon Wash—stream ... NV-8
Dry Canyon Wash—valley ... UT-8
Dry Canyon Well—well ... AZ-5
Dry Canyon Well—well ... NM-5
Dry Cave—cave ... AL-4
Dry Cave—cave ... AR-4
Dry Cave—cave (2) ... MO-7
Dry Cave—cave (6) ... TN-4
Dryce ... TN-4
Dry Cedar—fmr MCD ... NE-7
Dry Cedar Creek—stream ... AL-4
Dry Cedar Creek—stream ... CO-8
Dry Cedar Creek—stream ... NE-7
Dry Cedar Creek—stream ... TX-5
Dry Cem—cemetery ... AL-4
Dry Cem—cemetery ... IL-6
Dry Cem—cemetery ... OH-6
Dry Channel Big Lost River—stream ... ID-8
Dry Channel Pond—lake ... NY-2
Dry Cherry Creek—stream ... TX-5
Dry Cheyenne Creek—stream ... WY-8
Dry Choctaw Creek—stream ... LA-4
Dry Choteau Creek—stream ... SD-7
Dry Cibolo Creek—stream ... TX-5
Dry Cimarron Canyon ... AZ-5
Dry Cimarron River—stream ... NM-5
Dry Cimarron River—stream ... OK-5
Dry Clover Creek—stream ... CA-9
Dry Columbia Gulch—valley ... CO-8
Dry Comal Creek—stream ... TX-5
Dry Corner Spring—spring ... OR-9
Dry Cottonwood Creek ... MT-8
Dry Cottonwood Creek ... WY-8
Dry Cottonwood Creek—stream ... CO-8
Dry Cottonwood Creek—stream ... ID-8
Dry Cottonwood Creek—stream (4) ... MT-8
Dry Cottonwood Creek—stream (4) ... WY-8
Dry Cottonwood Guard Station—locale ... MT-8
Dry Cottonwood Rsvr—reservoir ... ID-8
Dry Coulee ... MT-8
Dry Coulee—valley (7) ... MT-8
Dry Coulee—valley ... ND-7
Dry Coulee—valley (2) ... WA-9
Dry Coulee—valley ... WI-6
Dry Cove—bay ... AK-9
Dry Cove—valley (2) ... AL-4
Dry Cove (historical)—locale ... AL-4
Dry Cow Creek—stream ... WY-8
Dry Cow House Prairie—flat ... FL-3
Dry Coyote Creek—stream ... WY-8
Dry Crane Creek—stream ... MO-7
Dry Creek ... AL-4
Dry Creek ... AZ-5
Dry Creek ... AR-4
Dry Creek ... CA-9
Dry Creek ... CO-8
Dry Creek ... FL-3
Dry Creek ... GA-3
Dry Creek ... ID-8
Dry Creek ... IN-6
Dry Creek ... KS-7
Dry Creek ... KY-4
Dry Creek ... LA-4
Dry Creek ... MS-4
Dry Creek ... MO-7
Dry Creek ... MT-8
Dry Creek ... NE-7
Dry Creek ... NV-8
Dry Creek ... NY-2
Dry Creek ... OH-6
Dry Creek ... OK-5
Dry Creek ... OR-9
Dry Creek ... SC-3
Dry Creek ... SD-7
Dry Creek ... TN-4
Dry Creek ... TX-5
Dry Creek ... UT-8
Dry Creek ... WA-9
Dry Creek ... WY-8
Dry Creek—locale ... IA-7
Dry Creek—locale ... KY-4
Dry Creek—locale ... OR-9
Dry Creek—locale ... WA-9
Dry Creek—locale ... WY-8
**Dry Creek**—pop pl ... CA-9
**Dry Creek**—pop pl ... LA-4
**Dry Creek**—pop pl (2) ... MS-4
**Dry Creek**—pop pl ... NC-3
**Dry Creek**—pop pl ... TN-4
**Drycreek**—pop pl ... TN-4
**Dry Creek**—pop pl ... WV-2
Dry Creek—stream (89) ... AL-4
Dry Creek—stream (9) ... AK-9
Dry Creek—stream (9) ... AZ-5
Dry Creek—stream (36) ... AR-4
Dry Creek—stream (64) ... CA-9
Dry Creek—stream (27) ... CO-8
Dry Creek—stream (4) ... FL-3
Dry Creek—stream (32) ... GA-3
Dry Creek—stream (39) ... ID-8
Dry Creek—stream (5) ... IL-6
Dry Creek—stream (2) ... IN-6
Dry Creek—stream (8) ... IA-7
Dry Creek—stream (40) ... KS-7
Dry Creek—stream (15) ... KY-4
Dry Creek—stream (23) ... LA-4
Dry Creek—stream (4) ... MI-6
Dry Creek—stream (5) ... MN-6
Dry Creek—stream (57) ... MS-4
Dry Creek—stream (27) ... MO-7
Dry Creek—stream (68) ... MT-8
Dry Creek—stream (17) ... NE-7
Dry Creek*—stream ... NE-7
Dry Creek—stream (17) ... NE-7
Dry Creek*—stream ... NE-7
Dry Creek—stream (14) ... NE-7
Dry Creek—stream (26) ... NV-8
Dry Creek—stream ... NM-5
Dry Creek—stream (6) ... NY-2
Dry Creek—stream (11) ... NC-3
Dry Creek—stream (9) ... ND-7
Dry Creek—stream (7) ... OH-6
Dry Creek—stream (31) ... OK-5
Dry Creek—stream (90) ... OR-9
Dry Creek—stream ... PA-2
Dry Creek—stream (8) ... SC-3
Dry Creek—stream (30) ... SD-7
Dry Creek—stream (57) ... TN-4
Dry Creek—stream (94) ... TX-5
Dry Creek—stream (21) ... UT-8
Dry Creek—stream (14) ... VA-3
Dry Creek—stream (39) ... WA-9
Dry Creek—stream (6) ... WV-2
Dry Creek—stream (3) ... WI-6
Dry Creek—stream (46) ... WY-8
Dry Creek—swamp ... OR-9
Dry Creek Archeol Site—hist pl ... AK-9
Dry Creek Arm—bay ... OK-5
Dry Creek Arm—bay ... OR-9
Dry Creek Baptist Church ... MS-4
Dry Creek Baptist Church ... TN-4
Dry Creek Basin—basin ... CA-9
Dry Creek Basin—basin (2) ... CO-8
Dry Creek Basin—basin ... MT-8
Dry Creek Basin—basin (2) ... WY-8
**Dry Creek Basin**—pop pl ... CO-8
Dry Creek Bayou ... MS-4
Dry Creek Bridge—bridge ... TN-4
Dry Creek Butte ... OR-9
Dry Creek Butte—locale ... OR-9
Dry Creek Buttes—summit ... OR-9
Dry Creek Buttes Rsvr—reservoir ... OR-9
Dry Creek Cabin—locale ... OR-9
Dry Creek Cabin Site—locale ... MT-8
Dry Creek Cabin Site Area—locale ... TN-4
Dry Creek Camp—locale ... CO-8
Dry Creek Camp—locale (2) ... OR-9
Dry Creek Camp—locale ... WA-9
Dry Creek Campground ... UT-8
Dry Creek Campground—locale ... CA-9
Dry Creek Campground—locale ... ID-8
Dry Creek Camp Ground—locale ... TN-4
Dry Creek Campground—park ... OR-9
Dry Creek Canal—canal ... CA-9
Dry Creek Canal—canal ... ID-8
Dry Creek Canal—canal (2) ... MT-8
Dry Creek Canal—canal ... WY-8
Dry Creek Canyon—valley (2) ... CO-8
Dry Creek Canyon—valley (2) ... UT-8
Dry Creek Canyon—valley ... WY-8
Dry Creek Cave—cave (2) ... AL-4
Dry Creek Cem—cemetery ... AL-4
Dry Creek Cem—cemetery (2) ... ID-8
Dry Creek Cem—cemetery ... KS-7
Dry Creek Cem—cemetery ... LA-4
Dry Creek Cem—cemetery (2) ... MS-4
Dry Creek Cem—cemetery (2) ... MO-7
Dry Creek Cem—cemetery ... MT-8
Dry Creek Cem—cemetery (3) ... NE-7
Dry Creek Cem—cemetery ... OR-9
Dry Creek Cem—cemetery ... TN-4
Dry Creek Cem—cemetery ... TX-5
Dry Creek Ch ... AL-4
Dry Creek Ch—church (3) ... AL-4
Dry Creek Ch—church (2) ... GA-3
Dry Creek Ch—church ... KY-4
Dry Creek Ch—church (2) ... MS-4
Dry Creek Ch—church ... MO-7
Dry Creek Ch—church ... MT-8
Dry Creek Ch—church ... NE-7
Dry Creek Ch—church ... NC-3
Dry Creek Ch—church ... OK-5
Dry Creek Ch—church ... SC-3
Dry Creek Ch—church (3) ... TN-4
Dry Creek Corral—locale ... CO-8
Dry Creek Cove—valley ... AL-4
Dry Creek Crossroads ... AL-4
Dry Creek Ditch—canal (3) ... CO-8
Dry Creek Ditch—canal ... MT-8
Dry Creek Ditch No 2—canal ... CO-8
Dry Creek Drain—canal ... NE-7
Dry Creek Drain Branch B—canal ... WY-8
Dry Creek Elbow—bend ... WA-9
**Dry Creek Estates**—pop pl ... TN-4
Dry Creek Falls—falls ... TN-4
Dry Creek Falls—falls ... WA-9
Dry Creek Gorge—valley ... OR-9
Dry Creek Guard Station—locale ... UT-8
Dry Creek Gulch—valley ... TN-4
Dry Creek Hill—summit ... CA-9
Dry Creek (historical)—locale ... KS-7
Dry Creek Hollow—valley ... OK-5
Dry Creek HS Bldg—hist pl ... LA-4
Dry Creek Island—island ... OR-9
Dry Creek Lake—lake ... WY-8
Dry Creek Lake—reservoir ... MS-4
Dry Creek Lake—reservoir ... TX-5
Dry Creek Lakes ... WY-8
Dry Creek Lateral—canal ... CA-9
Dry Creek Lateral Bench Canal—canal ... WY-8
Dry Creek Lookout Tower—locale ... WA-9
Dry Creek Mountain—ridge ... AL-4
Dry Creek Mountain—ridge ... AR-4
Dry Creek Mtn—summit ... NV-8
Dry Creek Number Two Dam—dam ... OR-9
Dry Creek Number Two Rsvr—reservoir ... OR-9
Dry Creek Number 1 Cave—cave ... AL-4
Dry Creek Number 2 Cave—cave ... AL-4
Dry Creek Oil Field—oilfield ... MS-4
Dry Creek Pass—gap ... OR-9
Dry Creek Pass—gap (2) ... WA-9
Dry Creek Peak—summit ... CA-9
Dry Creek Post Office (historical)—building ... AL-4
Dry Creek Post Office (historical)—building ... MS-4
Dry Creek Presbyterian Church ... MS-4
Dry Creek Ranch—locale (2) ... NV-8
Dry Creek Ranch—locale ... TX-5
Dry Creek Ranch Airp—airport ... NV-8
**Dry Creek Rancheria (Indian Reservation)**—pop pl ... CA-9
Dry Creek Rapids—rapids ... OR-9
Dry Creek Reservoir ... ID-8
Dry Creek Ridge—ridge ... OR-9
Dry Creek Ridge—ridge ... WY-8
Dry Creek Rim—cliff ... CA-9
Dry Creek Rim—cliff (2) ... OR-9
Dry Creek Rim—cliff ... WY-8
Dry Creek Rsvr ... OR-9
Dry Creek Rsvr—reservoir ... CO-8
Dry Creek Rsvr—reservoir ... ID-8
Dry Creek Rsvr—reservoir ... NV-8
Dry Creek Rsvr—reservoir (3) ... OR-9
Dry Creek Rsvr—reservoir ... SD-7
Dry Creek Rsvr—reservoir (2) ... WY-8
Dry Creek Rsvr No 10—reservoir ... ID-8
Dry Creek Rsvr No 11—reservoir ... ID-8
Dry Creek Rsvr No. 2 ... OR-9
Dry Creek Rsvr No 2—reservoir ... ID-8
Dry Creek Rsvr No 3—reservoir ... ID-8
Dry Creek Rsvr No 4—reservoir ... ID-8
Dry Creek Rsvr No 5—reservoir ... ID-8
Dry Creek Rsvr No 6—reservoir ... ID-8
Dry Creek Rsvr No 7—reservoir ... ID-8
Dry Creek Rsvr No 8—reservoir ... ID-8
Dry Creek Rsvr No 9—reservoir ... ID-8
Dry Creek Rsvrs—reservoir ... OR-9
Dry Creek Sch ... TN-4
Dry Creek Sch—hist pl ... MT-8
Dry Creek Sch—school ... AL-4
Dry Creek Sch—school ... AR-4
Dry Creek Sch—school (3) ... CA-9
Dry Creek Sch—school (2) ... CO-8
Dry Creek Sch—school ... GA-3
Dry Creek Sch—school (2) ... MT-8
Dry Creek Sch—school ... SD-7
Dry Creek Sch—school ... TN-4
Dry Creek Sch—school ... VA-3
Dry Creek Sch—school ... WA-9
Dry Creek Sch—school ... WY-8
Dry Creek Sch (historical)—school (4) ... MS-4
Dry Creek Sch (historical)—school (2) ... MO-7
Dry Creek Sch (historical)—school (5) ... TN-4
Dry Creek School—locale ... CO-8
Dry Creek School (Abandoned)—locale ... MT-8
Dry Creek School (Abandoned)—locale ... NE-7
Dry Creek Spring—spring ... AL-4
Dry Creek Spring—spring ... AZ-5
Dry Creek Spring—spring ... CA-9
Dry Creek Spring—spring ... ID-8
Dry Creek Spring—spring (2) ... NV-8
Dry Creek Spring—spring (3) ... OR-9
Dry Creek Spring—spring ... SD-7
Dry Creek Spring—spring ... UT-8
Dry Creek Spring No 1—spring ... ID-8
Dry Creek Spring No 2—spring ... ID-8
Dry Creek Spring Number One—spring ... AZ-5
Dry Creek Spring Number Two—spring ... AZ-5
Dry Creek Stock Driveway—trail ... CO-8
Dry Creek Structure 1 Dam—dam ... MS-4
Dry Creek Structure 2 Dam—dam ... MS-4
Dry Creek Structure 3 Dam—dam ... MS-4
**Dry Creek Subdivision**—pop pl ... TN-4
**Dry Creek Subdivision**—pop pl ... UT-8
Dry Creek Tank—reservoir (2) ... AZ-5
Dry Creek Tanks—reservoir ... AZ-5
Dry Creek Township—civil (2) ... MO-7
Dry Creek Trail—trail ... CO-8
Dry Creek Trail—trail ... ID-8
Dry Creek Trail—trail ... OR-9
Dry Creek Trail—trail ... WA-9
Dry Creek Trail—trail ... WY-8
Dry Creek Trough—reservoir ... AZ-5
Dry Creek Valley—valley ... GA-3
Dry Creek Valley—valley ... ID-8
Dry Creek Valley Ditch—canal ... CO-8
Dry Creek-Warm Springs Valleys Archeol District—hist pl ... CA-9
Dry Creek Waterhole—reservoir ... OR-9
Dry Creek Watershed 4 Dam—dam ... MS-4
Dry Creek Well—well ... AZ-5
Dry Creek Well—well ... MT-8
Dry Creek Well—well ... NV-8
Dry Curtis Creek—stream ... UT-8
Dry Cypress Bayou—gut ... LA-4
Dry Cypress Bayou—stream ... LA-4
Dry Cypress Canal—canal ... LA-4
Dry Cypress Creek ... TX-5
Dry Cypress Creek—stream ... TN-4
Dry Cypress Lake—swamp ... LA-4
Dry Dallas Creek—stream ... WY-8
Dry Dam—dam (2) ... AZ-5
Dry Dam Lake—lake ... WI-6
Dry Dam Rsvr—reservoir ... OR-9
Dryden—locale ... AR-4
Dryden—locale ... ID-8
Dryden—locale ... OR-9
**Dryden**—pop pl ... ME-1
**Dryden**—pop pl ... MI-6
**Dryden**—pop pl ... NY-2
**Dryden**—pop pl ... TX-5
**Dryden**—pop pl ... VA-3
**Dryden**—pop pl ... WA-9
Dryden, George B., House—hist pl ... IL-6
Dryden Branch—stream ... TN-4
Dryden Brook—stream ... NY-2
Dryden Cem—cemetery ... IL-6
Dryden Cem—cemetery ... MO-7
Dryden Center Cem—cemetery ... MI-6
Dryden Ch—church (2) ... OK-5
Dryden Community Ch—church ... NY-2
Dryden Creek ... NY-2
Dryden Creek—stream ... GA-3
Dryden Creek—stream ... ID-8
Dryden Creek—stream (2) ... MT-8
Dryden Creek—stream ... TX-5
Dryden Creek—stream ... WI-6
Dryden Crossing (Cable)—locale ... TX-5
Dryden Estates—locale ... KY-4
Dryden Heights ... RI-1
Dryden Hill—summit ... NY-2
Dryden Hist Dist—hist pl ... NY-2
Dryden (historical P.O.)—locale ... IA-7
Dryden Hollow—valley ... TN-4
Dryden Hollow—valley ... WV-2
Dryden HS—school ... NY-2
Dryden Lake—lake ... NY-2
Dryden-Louthan House—hist pl ... MO-7
Dryden Park—park ... IL-6
Dryden Park—park ... NE-7
Dryden Park Municipal Golf Course—other ... CA-9
Dryden Peak—summit ... ID-8
Dryden Research Center (NASA)—building ... CA-9
Dryden Rsvr—reservoir ... ID-8
Dryden Sch—school ... IL-6
Dryden Street Sch—school ... NY-2
**Dryden (Town of)**—pop pl ... NY-2
**Dryden Township**—pop pl ... SD-7
**Dryden (Township of)**—pop pl ... MI-6
**Dryden (Township of)**—pop pl ... MN-6
Dry Devils River—stream (2) ... TX-5
Dry Diamond Creek—stream ... NM-5
Dry Diamond Ridge—ridge ... UT-8
Dry Diggins Lookout—locale ... ID-8
Dry Diggins Ridge—ridge ... ID-8
Dry Ditch—canal ... IA-7
Dry Ditch—canal ... NE-7
Dry Ditch—stream ... WY-8
Drydock—locale ... KY-4
Dry Dock Gulch—valley ... CA-9
Dry Dock Island—cape ... GU-9
Drydock No. 1—hist pl ... VA-3
Dry Dock Number One—locale ... MA-1
Dry Dock Number Two—locale ... MA-1
Dry Doe Creek—stream ... WY-8
Dry Dog Ridge—ridge ... WI-6
Dry Donkey Creek—stream ... WY-8
Dry Draft—valley ... PA-2
Dry Draw—valley ... ID-8
Dry Draw—valley ... MT-8
Dry Draw—valley ... TX-5
Dry Draw—valley ... UT-8
Dry Draw—valley (10) ... WY-8
Dry Draw Dam—dam ... SD-7
Dry Duck Creek—stream (2) ... TX-5
Dry Dude Creek—stream ... AZ-5
Dry Duncan Creek—stream ... OR-9
Dry Duncan Creek Trail (pack)—trail ... OR-9
Drye Branch—stream ... KY-4
Dry Ecleto Creek—stream ... TX-5
Dry Elk Canyon—valley ... ID-8
Dry Elk Gulch—valley ... SD-7
Dry Elm Creek—stream ... SD-7
Dry Elm Creek—stream ... TX-5
Dryer ... TX-5
Dryer Creek ... AL-4
Dryer Ditch—canal ... CO-8
Dryer Glacier—glacier ... WA-9
Dryer Hollow—valley ... MO-7
Dryer Park—park ... KS-7
Dryer Place—locale ... MT-8
Dryer Sch—school ... SC-3
Dryers Creek ... TN-4
Dryers Creek Rec Area—park ... TN-4
Drye Sch—school ... NC-3
Dry Escondido Creek—stream ... TX-5
Dry Falls—falls ... NC-3
Dry Falls—falls ... WA-9
Dry Falls Dam—dam ... WA-9
Dry Falls Junction—locale ... WA-9
Dry Falls Lake—lake ... WA-9
Dry Farm—locale ... UT-8
Dry Farm Flat—flat ... UT-8
Dry Farm Rsvr—reservoir ... NV-8
Dry Farm Ruin—locale ... NV-8
Dry Farm Wash—stream ... AZ-5
Dry Fawn Creek—stream ... MT-8
Dry Fivemile Creek—stream ... OR-9
Dry Flat—flat ... CA-9
Dry Flat Spring—spring ... ID-8
Dry Flat Trail—trail ... CA-9
Dry Ford Branch—stream ... AL-4
Dry Ford Branch—stream ... FL-3
Dry Fork ... AR-4
Dry Fork ... CO-8
Dry Fork ... ID-8
Dry Fork ... IN-6
Dry Fork ... LA-4
Dry Fork ... MO-7
Dry Fork ... MT-8
Dry Fork ... OH-6
Dry Fork ... OR-9
Dry Fork ... TN-4
Dry Fork ... UT-8
Dry Fork ... WV-2
Dry Fork ... WY-8
Dryfork—locale ... AR-4
Dry Fork—locale ... KY-4
Dry Fork—locale ... UT-8
Dry Fork—locale ... VA-3
**Dryfork**—pop pl ... KY-4
**Dry Fork**—pop pl ... KY-4
**Dry Fork**—pop pl (2) ... VA-3
**Dryfork**—pop pl ... WV-2
Dry Fork—stream ... AK-9
Dry Fork—stream (16) ... AR-4
Dry Fork—stream (2) ... CA-9
Dry Fork—stream (2) ... GA-3
Dry Fork—stream (12) ... ID-8
Dry Fork—stream (9) ... IL-6
Dry Fork—stream (6) ... IN-6
Dry Fork—stream (40) ... KY-4
Dry Fork—stream (3) ... LA-4
Dry Fork—stream (2) ... MS-4
Dry Fork—stream (23) ... MO-7
Dry Fork—stream (13) ... MT-8
Dry Fork—stream (2) ... NC-3
Dry Fork—stream (5) ... OH-6
Dry Fork—stream ... OR-9
Dry Fork—stream (2) ... SC-3
Dry Fork—stream (19) ... TN-4
Dry Fork—stream (8) ... TX-5
Dry Fork—stream (24) ... UT-8
Dry Fork—stream (11) ... VA-3
Dry Fork—stream (15) ... WV-2
Dry Fork—stream (7) ... WY-8
Dry Fork—valley ... UT-8
Dry Fork Antelope Creek ... ID-8
Dry Fork Ash Creek ... UT-8
Dry Fork Ashley Creek ... UT-8
Dry Fork Badwater Creek—stream ... WY-8
Dry Fork Bay—bay ... TN-4
Dry Fork Belt Creek—stream ... MT-8
Dry Fork Big Dominguez Creek—stream ... CO-8
Dry Fork Bingham Canyon—valley ... UT-8
Dry Fork Blackwater Wash—stream ... CA-9
Dry Fork Boggy Creek—stream ... TX-5
Dry Fork Branch ... TN-4
Dry Fork Branch—stream (2) ... KY-4
Dry Fork Branch—stream (3) ... TN-4
Dry Fork Brown Creek—stream ... OR-9
Dry Fork Bull Canyon—valley ... UT-8
Dry Fork Cabin Creek—stream ... CO-8
Dry Fork Cabin Creek Trail—trail ... MT-8
Dry Fork Calf Creek—stream ... MT-8
Dry Fork Canyon—valley ... UT-8
Dry Fork Canyon Creek—stream ... NV-8
Dry Fork Canyon Indian Petroglyphs—locale ... UT-8
Dry Fork Cem—cemetery ... AR-4
Dry Fork Cem—cemetery ... KY-4
Dry Fork Cem—cemetery ... MO-7
Dry Fork Cem—cemetery ... TX-5
Dry Fork Cem—cemetery ... UT-8
Dry Fork Ch—church ... KY-4
Dry Fork Ch—church (2) ... MO-7
Dry Fork Ch—church (2) ... TN-4
Dry Fork Ch—church (2) ... VA-3
Dry Fork Cheyenne River—stream ... WY-8
Dry Fork Ch (historical)—church (2) ... TN-4
Dry Fork Choctaw Creek—stream ... AR-4
Dry Fork Clear Creek—stream ... OR-9
Dry Fork Clear Creek—stream ... WY-8
Dry Fork Community Ch—church ... KY-4
Dry Fork Corral Gulch—valley ... CO-8
Dry Fork Cottonwood Creek ... MT-8
Dry Fork Coulee—valley (6) ... MT-8
Dry Fork Coulee—valley ... WY-8
Dry Fork Cow Camp—locale ... CO-8
Dry Fork Coyote Gulch—valley ... UT-8
Dry Fork Creek ... AR-4
Dry Fork Creek ... CA-9
Dry Fork Creek ... ID-8
Dry Fork Creek ... IN-6
Dry Fork Creek ... MO-7
Dry Fork Creek ... MT-8
Dry Fork Creek ... SC-3
Dry Fork Creek ... TN-4
Dry Fork Creek ... UT-8
Dry Fork Creek—stream ... AR-4
Dry Fork Creek—stream (2) ... GA-3
Dry Fork Creek—stream ... ID-8
Dry Fork Creek—stream ... IL-6
Dry Fork Creek—stream (5) ... KY-4
Dry Fork Creek—stream ... LA-4
Dry Fork Creek—stream ... MS-4
Dry Fork Creek—stream (7) ... MT-8
Dry Fork Creek—stream ... ND-7
Dry Fork Creek—stream (2) ... SC-3
Dry Fork Creek—stream (8) ... TN-4
Dry Fork Creek—stream ... TX-5
Dry Fork Curecanti Creek—stream ... CO-8
Dry Fork Daisy Dean Creek ... MT-8
Dry Fork Daisy Dean Creek—stream ... MT-8
Dry Fork Ditch—canal (2) ... IN-6
Dry Fork Dota Creek—stream ... AR-4
Dry Fork Drainage Ditch—canal ... IL-6
Dry Fork Draney Creek—stream ... ID-8
Dry Fork Dry Creek—stream ... MT-8
Dry Fork Elkhead Creek ... CO-8
Dry Fork Elkhead Creek—stream ... CO-8
Dry Fork Escalante Creek—stream ... CO-8
Dry Fork Fire Gulch—valley ... MT-8
Dry Fork Flathead Divide—ridge ... MT-8
Dry Fork Franklin Canyon—valley ... UT-8
Dry Fork Fresno River ... CA-9
Dry Fork Goose Creek ... TN-4
Dry Fork Granite Creek—stream ... WY-8
Dry Fork Hawk Creek—stream ... MT-8
Dry Fork Hay Creek ... OR-9
Dry Fork Hay Creek—stream ... OR-9
Dry Fork Hickory Creek—stream ... TX-5
Dry Fork Hollow—stream ... MO-7
Dry Fork Horse Creek—stream ... WY-8
Dry Fork Jakes Creek—stream ... NV-8
Dry Fork Johnson Canyon—valley ... NV-8
Dry Fork Johnson Canyon—valley ... UT-8
Dry Fork Jordan Creek—stream ... OR-9
Dry Fork Katemcy Creek—stream ... TX-5
Dry Fork Kimball Creek—stream ... CO-8
Dry Fork Kiwa Creek ... ID-8
Dry Fork Lake—reservoir ... MO-7
Dry Fork La Prele Creek—stream ... WY-8
Dry Fork Leatherwood Creek ... TN-4
Dry Fork Lick Creek—stream ... WA-9
Dry Fork Lightner Creek—stream ... CO-8
Dry Fork Little Bear Creek—stream ... CO-8
Dry Fork Little Bighorn River—stream ... WY-8
Dry Fork Little Powder River—stream ... WY-8
Dry Fork Little Thunder Creek—stream ... WY-8
Dry Fork Little Wichita River—stream ... TX-5
Dry Fork (Magisterial District)—fmr MCD (2) ... WV-2
Dry Fork Marias River ... MT-8
Dry Fork Marias River—stream ... MT-8
Dry Fork Martin Creek ... TN-4
Dry Fork Marvine Creek—stream ... CO-8
Dry Fork Meramec Creek ... MO-7
Dry Fork Mesa Creek—stream ... CO-8
Dry Fork Michigan River—stream ... CO-8
Dry Fork Milk River—stream ... MT-8
Dry Fork Mill Creek ... TN-4
Dry Fork Mill Creek—stream ... UT-8
Dry Fork Minnesota Creek—stream ... CO-8
Dry Fork Mountain—ridge ... AR-4
Dry Fork Musselshell River—stream ... MT-8
Dry Fork North Fork Blackfoot River—stream ... MT-8

Dry Slough—gut CA-9
Dry Slough—gut TX-5
Dry Slough—stream AL-4
Dry Slough—stream CA-9
Dry Slough—stream LA-4
Dry Slough—stream WA-9
Dry Sluice Gap—gap NC-3
**Drys Mill (historical)**—pop pl NC-3
Dry Soap Creek—stream MT-8
Dry Soda Creek—stream OR-9
Dry Soda Gulch—valley OR-9
Dry Soda Lookout—locale OR-9
Dry Spadra Creek—stream AR-4
Dry Spottedtail Creek—stream NE-7
Dry Spring—spring NM-5
Dry Spring—spring OR-9
Dry Spring—spring UT-8
Dryspring Branch—stream NC-3
Dry Spring Cave—cave AL-4
Dry Spring Ch—church GA-3
Dry Springs Ch—church FL-3
Dry Spring Well—well AZ-5
Dry Spruce Bay—bay AK-9
Dry Spruce Island—island AK-9
Dry Starkweather Canyon—valley NM-5
Drystone Branch—stream TN-4
Drystone Ridge VA-3
Dry Strait—channel AK-9
Dry Straw Branch—stream MO-7
Dry Stream Cave—cave AL-4
Dry Susie Creek—stream NV-8
Dry Swale Creek—stream OR-9
Dry Swamp—stream (2) SC-3
Dry Swamp—swamp FL-3
Dry Swamp Creek—stream MS-4
Dry Swamp Lake—lake SC-3
Dry Swamp Sch—school SC-3
Dry Sweetwater Creek—stream CO-8
Dry Sycamore Creek—stream TX-5
Dry Tank—reservoir (11) AZ-5
Dry Tank—reservoir (5) NM-5
Dry Tank—reservoir (4) TX-5
Dry Tavern—locale PA-2
**Dry Tavern**—pop pl PA-2
Dry Tensleep Creek—stream WY-8
Dry Thirteenmile Creek—stream CO-8
Dry Timber Gulch—valley MT-8
Dry Timber Lake—lake NY-2
Dry Tok Creek—stream AK-9
Dry Top—locale PA-2
Dry Tortugas—island FL-3
Dry Tortugas Islands FL-3
Dry Tortugas Keys FL-3
Dry Tortugas Light—locale FL-3
Drytown—locale PA-2
Drytown—locale VA-3
**Drytown**—pop pl CA-9
**Drytown**—pop pl PA-2
Drytown (Township of)—fmr MCD AR-4
Dry Trail Creek—stream WY-8
Dry Trap Tank—reservoir AZ-5
Dry Trap Windmill—locale (2) TX-5
Dry Tree Point—cape OH-6
Dry Tripe Branch—stream VA-3
Dry Tugelo Branch AL-4
Dry Tugule Branch AL-4
Dry Turkey Creek—stream KS-7
Dry Twin Creek—stream (2) WY-8
Dry Union Gulch—valley CO-8
Dry Valley TN-4
Dry Valley—basin (3) NE-7
Dry Valley—basin OR-9
Dry Valley—basin (2) UT-8
Dry Valley—basin VA-3
Dry Valley—flat CA-9
Dry Valley—locale AL-4
Dry Valley—locale MO-7
Dry Valley—locale TX-5
**Dry Valley**—pop pl AL-4
**Dry Valley**—pop pl ID-8
**Dry Valley**—pop pl TN-4
Dry Valley—valley AL-4
Dry Valley—valley AZ-5
Dry Valley—valley (3) CA-9
Dry Valley—valley GA-3
Dry Valley—valley ID-8
Dry Valley—valley (2) KY-4
Dry Valley—valley (2) MO-7
Dry Valley—valley NE-7
Dry Valley—valley (4) NV-8
Dry Valley—valley OR-9
Dry Valley—valley PA-2
Dry Valley—valley (6) TN-4
Dry Valley—valley TX-5
Dry Valley—valley (5) UT-8
Dry Valley Alternative School TN-4
Dry Valley Branch—stream MO-7
Dry Valley Branch—stream TN-4
Dry Valley Cem—cemetery CA-9
Dry Valley Cem—cemetery MO-7
Dry Valley Cem—cemetery NE-7
Dry Valley Ch—church (2) GA-3
Dry Valley Ch—church KY-4
Dry Valley Ch—church MO-7
Dry Valley Ch—church (2) TN-4
Dry Valley Church AL-4
Dry Valley Corrals—locale NV-8
Dry Valley Creek CA-9
Dry Valley Creek—stream CA-9
Dry Valley Creek—stream ID-8
Dry Valley Creek—stream MO-7
Dry Valley Creek—stream NV-8
Dry Valley Creek—stream TX-5
Dry Valley Creek—stream UT-8
**Dry Valley Crossroads**—pop pl PA-2
Dry Valley Cumberland Presbyterian Ch TN-4
Dry Valley Gap—gap CA-9
Dry Valley Guard Station—locale ID-8
Dry Valley Lake—lake NE-7
Dry Valley Methodist Ch—church AL-4
Dry Valley Pits—cave PA-2
Dry Valley Post Office (historical)—building TN-4
Dry Valley Ridge—ridge CA-9
Dry Valley Rim—cliff OR-9
Dry Valley Rsvr—reservoir CA-9
Dry Valley Run—stream PA-2
Dry Valley Sch—school KY-4
Dry Valley Sch—school (3) NE-7
Dry Valley Sch—school TN-4
Dry Valley Tank—reservoir AZ-5
Dry Valley Trail—trail ID-8
Dry Valley Wash—valley UT-8
Dry Vee Cabin—locale WY-8
Dry Vee Slope—flat WY-8
Dry Vee Windmill—locale WY-8
**Dryville**—pop pl PA-2
Dryville Post Office (historical)—building PA-2
**Dryville (Stony Point)**—pop pl PA-2
Dry Walnut Creek KS-7
Dry Walnut Creek—stream KS-7
Dry Wash UT-8
Dry Wash—arroyo NV-8
Dry Wash—stream (3) AZ-5
Dry Wash—stream (2) CA-9
Dry Wash—valley AZ-5
Dry Wash—valley (17) UT-8
Dry Wash—valley (2) WY-8
Dry Wash, The—valley UT-8
Dry Wash Branch—stream GA-3
Dry Wash Creek—stream MI-6
Dry Wash Gulch—valley ID-8
Dry Wash Mineral Creek—stream AZ-5
Dry Wash Number Two Dam—dam UT-8
Dry Wash Number Two Rsvr—reservoir UT-8
Dry Wash Pond—lake UT-8
Dry Wash Reservoir UT-8
Dry Wash Rsvr—reservoir ID-8
Dry Wash Trail—trail UT-8
Dry Weakley Creek TN-4
Dry Weakley Creek—stream TN-4
Dry Weather Creek—stream MN-6
Dry Weather Ford Tank—reservoir AZ-5
Dryweed Island—island MN-6
Dry Well—well (4) AZ-5
Dry Well—well (2) CA-9
Dry Well—well (2) NV-8
Dry Well—well NM-5
Dry Well—well (2) OR-9
Dry Well Creek—stream OR-9
Dry Well Lake—lake WI-6
Dry Well Rsvr—reservoir WY-8
Dry Wells PA-2
Dry Wells—locale NC-3
Dry Wells—locale TX-5
Dry Well Spring—spring OR-9
Dry Wells (Township of)—fmr MCD NC-3
Dry Wild Horse Lake—lake CO-8
Dry Willow Creek—stream CO-8
Dry Willow Creek—stream WY-8
Dry Willow Peak—summit UT-8
Dry Willow Spring—spring UT-8
Dry Windmill—locale NM-5
Dry Windmill—locale TX-5
Dry Wolf Campground—locale MT-8
Dry Wolf Creek—stream (2) MT-8
Dry Wolf Ranger Station—locale MT-8
Dry Woman Canyon—valley CO-8
Dry Wood—locale KS-7
**Drywood**—pop pl WI-6
Dry Wood Creek SD-7
Dry Wood Creek—stream MN-6
Dry Wood Creek—stream MO-7
Drywood Creek—stream WI-6
Drywood Creek State Public Hunting Ground—park WI-6
Drywood Island—island MN-6
Dry Wood Lake—lake MN-6
Drywood Lakes—lake SD-7
**Dry Wood Lake Township**—pop pl SD-7
**Drywood Township**—pop pl KS-7
**Drywood Township**—pop pl MO-7
Dry Woody Creek—stream CO-8
Dry X Rsvr—reservoir UT-8
Drzewiceki Lake—lake WI-6
D's Camp—locale TX-5
D-S Canal—canal CA-9
Dschakarenkap FM-9
Dschalapuk FM-9
Dschaluit MP-9
Dschalut Spitze MP-9
Dschaniak FM-9
Dschaputik FM-9
Dschelatak FM-9
Dschokadsch FM-9
Dschokadsch Einfahrt FM-9
Dschokadsch Hafen FM-9
Dschokadsch Spitze FM-9
Dschountin Hamdel Station FM-9
Dschountin Handel Station FM-9
D Schrempp Dam—dam SD-7
Dschuniak FM-9
DSD Bridge over Cheyenne River—hist pl WY-8
D Sivertson Ranch—locale ND-7
D-Six Pond—reservoir AZ-5
D-Six Rsvr AZ-5
D S Keith Junior High School PA-2
D S Ranch—locale AZ-5
D S Ranch Tank—reservoir AZ-5
D. S. Tavern—hist pl VA-3
D Talley Dam—dam SD-7
D Tank—reservoir AZ-5
D Tank—reservoir TX-5
D T Blakeys Steam Mill (historical)—locale AL-4
D T Hannah Lake Dam—dam AL-4
D Timmons Dam—dam SD-7
Dtokoah Point—cape WA-9
D Trumble Dam—dam SD-7
DT TANK—reservoir AZ-5
DT Tank—reservoir AZ-5
Dual Creek—stream ID-8
Dual Head—summit AK-9
Dual Spring—spring TX-5
Dual Springs—spring UT-8
**Duan**—pop pl NC-3
Duane—locale ND-7
Duane—locale VA-3
Duane—other KY-4
**Duane**—pop pl NY-2
Duane, Lake—lake NY-2
Duane Bliss Peak—summit NV-8
Duane Block—hist pl OH-6
Duane Cem—cemetery MN-6
**Duane Center**—pop pl NY-2
Duane Fork—locale VA-3
Duane Lake—lake NY-2
Duane Mansion—hist pl NY-2
Duane Mansion—locale NY-2
Duane Pond—lake MA-1
**Duanesburg**—pop pl NY-2
Duanesburg Churches—church NY-2
Duanesburg-Florida Baptist Church—hist pl NY-2
**Duanesburg (Town of)**—pop pl NY-2
Duanespurg Reservoir—lake NY-2
Duane Stream—stream NY-2
Duane Street Sch—school NY-2
**Duane (Town of)**—pop pl NY-2
**Duane Yards**—pop pl IN-6
Duart—locale NC-3
**Duarte**—pop pl CA-9
Duarte Mine—mine CA-9
Duarte Park—park CA-9
Duarte Pond—lake MA-1
Duarte Ponds—lake MA-1
Duarte Sch—school CA-9
Duarts Pond MA-1
**Dub**—pop pl AR-4
**Dubach**—pop pl LA-4
Dubach, Fred B., House—hist pl LA-4
Dubachang, Rois—summit PW-9
Dubacher Canyon—valley AZ-5
Dubacher Gulch AZ-5
Dubach Meadows—flat CO-8
Dubakella Creek—stream CA-9
Dubakella Mtn—summit CA-9
Duban CO-8
Duban Lake—lake MN-6
**Dubard**—pop pl MS-4
Dubard Branch—stream MS-4
Dubard Post Office (historical)—building MS-4
DuBary Creek FL-3
Dubault Prospect—mine TN-4
Du Bay, Lake—reservoir WI-6
Dubay Creek—stream MT-8
Dubay Lake—lake ME-1
Du Bay Park—park WI-6
Dubay Point—cape ME-1
Du Bay Reservoir WI-6
Dubb Creek—stream AR-4
**Dubberly**—pop pl LA-4
Dubbers CA-9
**Dubbers**—pop pl CA-9
Dubber Spur—locale CA-9
Dubbe Rsvr—reservoir MT-8
Dubbistown PA-2
**Dubbs**—pop pl MS-4
Dubbs Creek—stream TX-5
Dubbs Ranch—locale NE-7
Dubbs Sch—school MS-4
Dub Day Arena—building TX-5
Dubeau Meadow—flat CO-8
Dube Brook—stream (2) NH-1
Dube Cem—cemetery TX-5
Dube Hill—summit NH-1
Dubel Bridge—bridge NE-7
Dubel Bridge—bridge SD-7
Duberry Ferry MS-4
Duberry Spring—spring AZ-5
Dubes Pond—lake NH-1
Du Bianons Creek—gut GA-3
DuBignon Hammock—island GA-3
Dubin, Henry, House—hist pl IL-6
Dubina—locale TX-5
Dubin Creek—stream OR-9
Dubinkey Spring UT-8
Dubinkey Wash—valley UT-8
Dubinky Well—well UT-8
Du Binnion Hammock GA-3
Dubin Point—cape AK-9
Dubius Creek—stream ID-8
Dubley Cem—cemetery GA-3
Dublin DE-2
Dublin IN-6
Dublin KS-7
Dublin MD-2
Dublin—fmr MCD NE-7
Dublin—locale FL-3
Dublin—locale IA-7
**Dublin**—pop pl AL-4
**Dublin**—pop pl AZ-5
**Dublin**—pop pl AR-4
**Dublin**—pop pl CA-9
**Dublin**—pop pl GA-3
**Dublin**—pop pl IN-6
**Dublin**—pop pl KY-4
**Dublin**—pop pl MD-2
**Dublin**—pop pl MI-6
**Dublin**—pop pl MS-4
**Dublin**—pop pl NH-1
**Dublin**—pop pl NY-2
**Dublin**—pop pl NC-3
**Dublin**—pop pl (2) OH-6
**Dublin**—pop pl PA-2
**Dublin**—pop pl TX-5
**Dublin**—pop pl VA-3
Dublin Acres—locale PA-2
Dublin Borough—civil PA-2
Dublin Branch—stream AL-4
Dublin Brook—stream NY-2
Dublin Canyon—valley CA-9
Dublin (CCD)—cens area GA-3
Dublin (CCD)—cens area TX-5
Dublin Cem—cemetery NE-7
Dublin Cem—cemetery NY-2
Dublin Cem—cemetery VA-3
Dublin Cem—cemetery WA-9
Dublin Cemetery Vaults—hist pl OH-6
Dublin Ch—church MS-4
Dublin Christian Church—hist pl OH-6
Dublin Church AL-4
Dublin Corners—locale NY-2
Dublin Country Club—other GA-3
Dublin Creek PA-2
Dublin Creek—stream CA-9
Dublin Creek—stream NY-2
Dublin Dutch Creek (historical P.O.)—locale IA-7
Dublin Elem Sch—school IN-6
Dublin Field—airport NC-3
Dubling Creek—stream NC-3
Dublin Golf Club—other NH-1
Dublin Grove Ch—church NC-3
Dublin Gulch—uninc pl MT-8
Dublin Gulch—valley MT-8
Dublin Gulch—valley NV-8
Dublin High Street Hist Dist—hist pl OH-6
Dublin Hill—locale DE-2
Dublin Hills—range CA-9
Dublin (historical)—locale KS-7
Dublin Hollow—valley NY-2
Dublin Jack Ravine—valley CA-9
Dublin Lake—lake OR-9
Dublin Lake—reservoir TX-5
Dublin Lake Hist Dist—hist pl NH-1
Dublin Memorial Gardens—cemetery GA-3
Dublin Mill PA-2
Dublin Millpond—reservoir VA-3
**Dublin Mills**—pop pl PA-2
Dublin P. O. (historical)—locale AL-4
Dublin Pond—lake NH-1
Dublin Post Office (historical)—building PA-2
Dublin Ranch—locale NM-5
Dublin Sch—school CA-9
Dublin Sch—school IL-6
Dublin Sch—school MI-6
Dublin Sch—school MS-4
Dublin Sch—school OH-6
Dublin Sch—school (2) WI-6
Dublin Sch (historical)—school MS-4
Dublin Spring—spring OR-9
Dublin Swamp—swamp MD-2
Dublin Tank—reservoir NM-5
Dublin Town Hall—hist pl NH-1
**Dublin (Town of)**—pop pl NH-1
**Dublin Township**—pop pl ND-7
**Dublin (Township of)**—pop pl MN-6
**Dublin (Township of)**—pop pl OH-6
**Dublin (Township of)**—pop pl (2) PA-2
**Dublin Town Subdivision**—pop pl (2) UT-8
Dublin Veterinary Clinic—hist pl OH-6
Dublin Village Green—locale PA-2
Dublin Village Hist Dist—hist pl NH-1
Dublin Village Shop Ctr—locale PA-2
Dublin Wash—valley UT-8
Dublin Waterworks—other VA-3
Dublin Well—well NM-5
**Dublin Woods (subdivision)**—pop pl NC-3
Dublon—island FM-9
Dublon (Municipality)—civ div FM-9
Du Bocage—hist pl AR-4
Duboce Park—park CA-9
Dubock Slough—stream CA-9
**Duboin**—pop pl LA-4
Duboin Plantation—locale LA-4
Dubois NE-7
DuBois PA-2
Dubois—locale GA-3
Dubois—locale MD-2
**Dubois**—pop pl ID-8
**Dubois**—pop pl IL-6
**Dubois**—pop pl IN-6
**Du Bois**—pop pl NE-7
**Du Bois**—pop pl PA-2
**Dubois**—pop pl WY-8
Dubois, Mount—summit CA-9
DuBois, W.E.B., Sch—hist pl OK-5
Du Bois, William E.B., Boyhood Homesite—hist pl MA-1
Du Bois Area JHS—school PA-2
Du Bois Battery—locale MO-7
Dubois Cem—cemetery IA-7
Dubois Cem—cemetery MA-1
Dubois Cem—cemetery (2) MI-6
Dubois Cem—cemetery MS-4
DuBois Cem—cemetery NE-7
Dubois Cem—cemetery NY-2
DuBois Center—locale IL-6
Du Bois City—civil PA-2
Dubois Community Club Lake—reservoir IN-6
Dubois Community Club Lake Dam—dam IN-6
Dubois (corporate name Du Bois; RR name Bois) IL-6
**Dubois County**—pop pl IN-6
Dubois Creek—stream IN-6
Dubois Creek—stream (2) MO-7
DuBois Creek—stream MT-8
Dubois Creek—stream NY-2
Dubois Creek—stream OR-9
DuBois Creek—stream PA-2
Dubois Creek Dam—dam PA-2
**Dubois Crossroads**—pop pl IN-6
Dubois Ditch—canal IN-6
Dubois Drain—canal CA-9
Dubois Drain—canal MI-6
Dubois Drain One—canal CA-9
Duboise Bay—swamp GA-3
Duboise Cem—cemetery AL-4
Duboise Corner—locale NY-2
Duboise Hollow—valley AL-4
Duboise Hollow—valley TN-4
Duboise Lake—reservoir AL-4
DuBois Gulch—valley MT-8
Dubois Hill—summit NM-5
Dubois Hollow AL-4
Dubois Hollow—valley AL-4
Dubois Hollow—valley AR-4
Du Bois-Jefferson County Airp—airport PA-2
Dubois Lake—lake WI-6
Dubois Lake Dam—dam AL-4
Dubois Lateral—canal ID-8
DuBois Lateral—canal ID-8
Dubois Lateral—canal ID-8
Dubois Mill (historical)—locale AL-4
Dubois Mine—mine CO-8
Dubois Mine—mine IL-6
Dubois Oil Field—oilfield KS-7
Du Bois Oil Field—other IL-6
DuBois Park—park FL-3
Dubois Pond—lake ME-1
Du Bois Regional Med Ctr—hospital PA-2
Dubois Ridge—ridge IN-6
Dubois Rsvr PA-2
Du Bois Rsvr—reservoir PA-2
Dubois Rsvr—reservoir PA-2
Dubois Sch—school IL-6
Duboiss Creek MO-7
Dubois Spring—spring CA-9
DuBois Swamp—swamp PA-2
**Duboistown**—pop pl PA-2
Duboistown Borough—civil PA-2
**Du Bois (Township of)**—pop pl IL-6
Du Bois Trick Tank—reservoir NM-5
Dubois Wash—stream NM-5
Dubois Well—well NM-5
Du Bon Lake MN-6
DuBon Lake—lake MN-6
Dubonnet, Lake—lake MI-6
Dubor Creek—stream WA-9
Du Bordieu Beach SC-3
DuBoris, Hendrikus, House—hist pl NY-2
**DuBose**—pop pl SC-3
Dubose Cem—cemetery GA-3
Dubose Cem—cemetery LA-4
DuBose Cem—cemetery SC-3
Dubose Cem—cemetery TX-5
Dubose Chapel—church AL-4
Dubose Crossroads—locale SC-3
**Du Bose Crossroads**—pop pl SC-3
Dubose Dam—dam AL-4
Dubose Lake—reservoir AL-4
Dubose Lake—reservoir NC-3
Dubose Landing—locale AL-4
DuBose Memorial Church Training Sch—hist pl TN-4
DuBose Memorial Training Sch (historical)—school TN-4
**DuBose Park**—pop pl SC-3
**Du Bose Park**—pop pl SC-3
Dubose Pond—reservoir SC-3
DuBose Ranch HQ—locale TX-5
DuBose Sch—school MS-4
Dubowich Bank Prospect—mine TN-4
Dubrague Sch—school MA-1
Dubray Coulee—valley MT-8
Dubre—locale KY-4
Dubre Cem—cemetery KY-4
Dubred FM-9
**Dubree**—pop pl WV-2
DuBroc, Bayou—stream LA-4
Dubs, Dr. Charles H., Townhouse—hist pl MS-4
Dubs Cem—cemetery PA-2
Dubs Deep Well—well NM-5
Dubsdread Country Club—locale FL-3
Dubs Picnic Grove—park PA-2
Dubstardt Sch (historical)—school PA-2
Dubugue Harbor—bay IA-7
**Dubuisson**—pop pl LA-4
Dubuisson Cem—cemetery LA-4
Dubuissons Landing—locale MS-4
Dubuque—locale KS-7
**Dubuque**—pop pl IA-7
Dubuque, Julien, Monmt—hist pl IA-7
Dubuque Cem—cemetery KS-7
Dubuque City Hall—hist pl IA-7
Dubuque Claim—mine SD-7
Dubuque Country Club—other IA-7
Dubuque County Courthouse—hist pl IA-7
Dubuque County Home—building IA-7
Dubuque County Jail—hist pl IA-7
Dubuque Creek—stream MI-6
Dubuque Creek—stream OR-9
Dubuque Creek—stream WA-9
Dubuque Freight House—hist pl IA-7
Dubuque Greyhound Park—park IA-7
**Dubuque Junction**—pop pl IA-7
Dubuque Memorial Gardens Cem—cemetery IA-7
Dubuque Mtn—summit AK-9
Dubuque Municipal Airp—airport IA-7
Dubuque Oil and Gas Field—oilfield KS-7
Dubuque Township—fmr MCD IA-7
Dubuque Trading Post-Village of Kettle Chief Archeol Distr—hist pl IA-7
**Dubwright**—pop pl TX-5
Ducan Slough—bay AK-9
Ducasse Rsvr—reservoir CA-9
**Ducat**—pop pl OH-6
**Ducat Settlement**—pop pl TX-5
**Ducat Town**—pop pl MD-2
**Duce**—pop pl AR-4
Duce Creek—stream MT-8
Ducette Island—island MN-6
Ducetts Lakes—lake WI-6
Ducey Creek—stream MI-6
**Duchamp**—pop pl LA-4
Ducharme Cem (historical)—cemetery SD-7
Ducharme Creek MT-8
Ducharme Creek—stream MT-8
Du Charme Creek—stream SD-7
Du Charme Creek—stream WI-6
Du Charme Ridge—ridge WI-6
Ducharm Lake—lake MT-8
Ducharts Creek NC-3
Duchein Place—uninc pl LA-4
Duchemin Lake IN-6
Duchene Cem—cemetery LA-4
Ducher Island—island MO-7
Duches Hole—bend UT-8
**Duchesne**—pop pl UT-8
Duchesne Cem—cemetery UT-8
Duchesne City Cemetery UT-8
Duchesne Coll—school NE-7
Duchesne County—civil UT-8
Duchesne County Hosp—hospital UT-8
Duchesne County Hospital Heliport—airport UT-8
Duchesne Division—civil UT-8
Duchesne Feeder Canal—canal UT-8
Duchesne HS—school UT-8
Duchesne Monmt—pillar UT-8
Duchesne Municipal Airp—airport UT-8
Duchesne Ridge—ridge UT-8
Duchesne River—stream UT-8
Duchesne Sch—school TX-5
Duchesne Sch—school UT-8
Duchesne Tunnel—tunnel UT-8
Duchess Canyon—valley CA-9
Duchess Company Superintendent's House—hist pl NY-2
Duchess Creek—stream OK-5
Duchess Creek—stream WI-6
Duchess Island—island AK-9
Duchess Quarry—mine NY-2
du Chien KY-4
Duchien Lake—lake WI-6
Duchikmiut River—stream AK-9
Duchikmiut (Summer Camp)—locale AK-9
Duchikthluk Bay—bay AK-9
**Duchouquet (Township of)**—pop pl OH-6
Duck MI-6
Duck—locale NC-3
**Duck**—pop pl WV-2
Duckabush—locale WA-9
Duckabush, Mount—summit WA-9
Duckabush River—stream WA-9
Duckabush River Bridge—hist pl WA-9
Duckabush Shelter—locale WA-9
Duck Bait Slough—gut NC-3
Duck Bar—bar AL-4
Duck Bar—bar CA-9
Duck Bay—bay AK-9
Duck Bay—bay ID-8
Duck Bay—bay MI-6
Duck Bay—bay MN-6
Duck Bay—bay (3) NY-2
Duck Bay—bay OR-9
Duck Bay—bay WA-9
Duck Bayou—gut AL-4
Duck Bayou—stream (3) LA-4
Duckbill—summit AZ-5
Duckbill Lake—lake AK-9
Duckbill Mtn—summit WA-9
Duck Bottom—bend TN-4
Duck Bottom Lake—lake SC-3
Duck Branch—stream (2) AL-4
Duck Branch—stream (2) GA-3
Duck Branch—stream IN-6
Duck Branch—stream KY-4
Duck Branch—stream (3) NC-3
Duck Branch—stream SC-3
Duck Branch—stream (2) TN-4
Duck Branch Ditch—canal AR-4
Duck Bridge—bridge MA-1
Duck Brook—stream (3) ME-1
Duck Brook—stream VT-1
Duck Brown Hollow—valley WV-2
Duck Butte OR-9
Duckcamp Branch—stream VA-3
Duck Canyon—valley NM-5
Duck Cape—cape AK-9
Duck Cave—cave AL-4
Duck Cem—cemetery (2) MS-4
Duck Cem—cemetery OK-5
Duck Chute—swamp MS-4
Duck Club—building WA-9
Duck Club—other OR-9
Duck Club Turn—channel OR-9
Duck Cove—bay (2) CA-9
Duck Cove—bay (4) ME-1
Duck Cove—bay (2) NY-2
Duck Cove—bay NC-3
Duck Cove—bay TX-5
Duck Cove—lake RI-1
Duck Cove Bridge—bridge TX-5
Duck Cove Brook—stream ME-1
Duck Creek AL-4
Duck Creek CA-9
Duck Creek CO-8
Duck Creek DE-2
Duck Creek GA-3
Duck Creek IN-6
Duck Creek KS-7
Duck Creek MI-6
Duck Creek MS-4
Duck Creek NV-8
Duck Creek NC-3
Duck Creek OH-6
Duck Creek SC-3
Duck Creek TX-5
Duck Creek UT-8
Duck Creek WI-6
Duck Creek WY-8
Duck Creek—bay MA-1
Duck Creek—channel NY-2
Duck Creek—civil KS-7
Duck Creek—gut LA-4
Duck Creek—gut NJ-2
Duck Creek—gut SC-3
Duck Creek—locale NC-3
Duck Creek—locale OH-6
Duck Creek—locale TN-4
**Duck Creek**—pop pl WI-6
Duck Creek—stream (3) AL-4
Duck Creek—stream (5) AK-9
Duck Creek—stream (2) AR-4
Duck Creek—stream (3) CA-9
Duck Creek—stream (4) CO-8
Duck Creek—stream (2) DE-2
Duck Creek—stream (2) GA-3
Duck Creek—stream (6) ID-8
Duck Creek—stream (2) IL-6
Duck Creek—stream (6) IN-6
Duck Creek—stream (3) IA-7
Duck Creek—stream (8) KS-7
Duck Creek—stream KY-4
Duck Creek—stream LA-4
Duck Creek—stream MD-2
Duck Creek—stream (6) MI-6
Duck Creek—stream (2) MN-6
Duck Creek—stream (4) MO-7
Duck Creek—stream (16) MT-8
Duck Creek—stream (4) NE-7
Duck Creek—stream (4) NV-8
Duck Creek—stream NM-5
Duck Creek—stream (9) NC-3
Duck Creek—stream (3) ND-7
Duck Creek—stream (7) OH-6
Duck Creek—stream (4) OK-5
Duck Creek—stream (3) OR-9
Duck Creek—stream (2) SC-3
Duck Creek—stream (3) SD-7
Duck Creek—stream TN-4
Duck Creek—stream (11) TX-5
Duck Creek—stream (2) UT-8
Duck Creek—stream (3) WA-9
Duck Creek—stream (3) WV-2
Duck Creek—stream (6) WI-6
Duck Creek—stream (9) WY-8
Duck Creek—uninc pl WI-6
Duck Creek—unorg reg SD-7
Duck Creek Baptist Ch—church TN-4
Duck Creek Breaks—range (2) WY-8
Duck Creek Butte—summit OR-9
Duck Creek Camp—locale WY-8
Duck Creek Campground—locale UT-8
Duck Creek Cem—cemetery (2) OH-6
Duck Creek Cem—cemetery TX-5
Duck Creek Ch—church AL-4
Duck Creek Ch—church MO-7
Duck Creek Ch—church OK-5
Duck Creek Ch—church TX-5
Duck Creek Ch—church WV-2
Duck Creek Cross Roads DE-2
Duck Creek Dam—dam NV-8
Duck Creek Dam—dam ND-7
Duck Creek Dam Number 2—dam SD-7
Duck Creek Falls—falls WY-8

Duck Creek Flat—*flat* OR-9
Duck Creek Flats—*flat* WY-8
Duck Creek Forest Service Station—*locale* UT-8
Duck Creek Hundred—*civil* DE-2
*Duck Creek - in part* NV-8
Duck Creek Island—*island* LA-4
Duck Creek Lakebed—*flat* OR-9
Duck Creek Lutheran Church and Cemetery—*hist pl* SD-7
Duck Creek Mall—*locale* IA-7
Duck Creek Marsh—*swamp* NY-2
Duck Creek Overflow Canal—*canal* NV-8
Duck Creek Park—*park* IA-7
Duck Creek Pass—*gap* MT-8
Duck Creek Point—*summit* ID-8
Duck Creek Pond—*reservoir* DE-2
Duck Creek Pond Dam—*dam* DE-2
Duck Creek Range—*range* NV-8
Duck Creek Red Spring—*spring* UT-8
*Duck Creek Reservoir* UT-8
Duck Creek Rsvr—*reservoir* (2) MT-8
Duck Creek Sch—*school* IL-6
Duck Creek Sch—*school* MT-8
Duck Creek Sch—*school* SD-7
Duck Creek Sch (historical)—*school* TN-4
Duck Creek School—*locale* MT-8
Duck Creek Sinks—*basin* UT-8
Duck Creek Spring—*spring* OR-9
*Duck Creek State Wildlife Area* MO-7
Duck Creek State Wildlife Mngmt Area—*park* MO-7
Duck Creek State Wildlife Ref—*park* MO-7
Duck Creek Stone Chapel—*church* IN-6
*Duck Creek Town* DE-2
Duck Creek Township—*civil* SD-7
**Duck Creek Township**—*pop pl* KS-7
**Duck Creek Township**—*pop pl* MO-7
**Duck Creek Township**—*pop pl* ND-7
**Duck Creek (Township of)**—*pop pl* IN-6
Duck Creek Valley—*valley* NV-8
Duck Creek Village—*hist pl* DE-2
Duck Creek Village Campground—*locale* UT-8
Duck Creek Wickiup Village—*hist pl* CO-8
Duck Dam—*dam* SD-7
Duck Eddy Run—*stream* PA-2
*Duckenfield Estate* NC-3
Ducker—*locale* GA-3
Ducker, William, House—*hist pl* NE-7
Ducker Bay—*bay* AL-4
Ducker Creek—*stream* CA-9
Ducker Creek—*stream* NC-3
Ducker Creek—*stream* VA-3
Ducker Mtn—*summit* NC-3
**Duckers**—*pop pl* KY-4
*Duckers Bay* AL-4
Ducket Creek—*stream* CA-9
Ducket Crossing—*locale* UT-8
Ducket Lake—*reservoir* GA-3
*Ducket Peak* CA-9
Ducket Peak—*summit* CA-9
Duckett, Charles H., House—*hist pl* SC-3
Duckett Bluff—*cliff* CA-9
Duckett Bridge—*bridge* AL-4
Duckett Cabin—*locale* UT-8
Duckett Cem—*cemetery* AR-4
Duckett Creek—*stream* CO-8
Duckett Creek—*stream* MO-7
Duckett Draw—*valley* CO-8
Duckett Ford—*locale* AR-4
Duckett Lookout Tower—*locale* NC-3
Duckett Mill Access Point—*locale* GA-3
Duckett Mine (underground)—*mine* AL-4
*Duckett Mountain* TN-4
Duckett Park—*flat* CO-8
Duckett Ranch—*locale* CO-8
Duckett Ridge—*ridge* TN-4
Duckett Ridge—*ridge* UT-8
Duckett Ridge Mine—*mine* TN-4
Duckett Sch—*school* WI-6
**Duckettsville**—*pop pl* MD-2
Duckett Top—*summit* NC-3
*Duckett Top Lookout* NC-3
Duckett (Township of)—*fmr MCD* AR-4
Duck Fire Department—*building* NC-3
Duck Flat—*flat* (2) NV-8
Duck Flats—*flat* AK-9
Duck Flat Wash—*stream* NV-8
Duckfoot Creek—*stream* CO-8
Duckfoot Island—*island* MN-6
Duckford Branch—*stream* SC-3
Duck Fork—*stream* KY-4
Duck Fork—*stream* UT-8
Duck Fork Dam—*dam* UT-8
Duck Fork Rsvr—*reservoir* (2) UT-8
*Duck Gap* PA-2
Duck Gut—*gut* NJ-2
Duck Hall Point—*cape* VA-3
Duck Harbor—*bay* (2) ME-1
Duck Harbor—*swamp* MA-1
**Duck Harbor (historical)**—*pop pl* MA-1
Duck Harbor Mtn—*summit* ME-1
Duck Harbor Pond—*reservoir* PA-2
Duck Harbor Pond Dam—*dam* PA-2
*Duck Head Creek* DE-2
Duckhead Lake—*lake* MT-8
Duck Head Point—*cape* MO-7
*Duckhill* MS-4
*Duck Hill* NV-8
**Duck Hill**—*pop pl* MS-4
Duck Hill—*summit* CT-1
Duck Hill—*summit* MA-1
Duck Hill—*summit* NV-8
Duck Hill—*summit* WI-6
Duck Hill Baptist Ch—*church* MS-4
Duck Hill Cem—*cemetery* MS-4
*Duck Hill Cemetery* TN-4
Duck Hill Ch—*church* MS-4
Duck Hill Ch (historical)—*church* TN-4
Duck Hill Elem Sch—*school* MS-4
Duck Hill HS—*school* MS-4
Duck Hill River—*stream* MA-1
Duck Hole—*bay* MO-7
Duck Hole—*bay* NY-2
Duck Hole—*bay* NC-3
Duck Hole—*lake* NH-1
Duck Hole—*lake* NY-2
Duck Hole Branch—*stream* KY-4
Duck Hole Lake—*lake* MI-6
Duck Hollow—*valley* IN-6
Duck Hollow—*valley* PA-2
Duck Hollow—*valley* (2) TN-4
Duck House—*hist pl* GA-3
Duck Hunters Lake—*lake* MO-7
Duckinghoe Creek—*stream* VA-3
*Ducking Pond* DE-2
Ducking Stool Point—*cape* VA-3
*Duck Island* MA-1
Duck Island—*island* (3) AK-9
Duck Island—*island* CT-1
Duck Island—*island* GA-3
Duck Island—*island* (2) IL-6
Duck Island—*island* (3) ME-1
Duck Island—*island* (2) MD-2
Duck Island—*island* MA-1
Duck Island—*island* (3) MI-6
Duck Island—*island* MT-8
Duck Island—*island* NE-7
Duck Island—*island* NJ-2
Duck Island—*island* (2) NY-2
Duck Island—*island* NC-3
Duck Island—*island* SC-3
Duck Island—*island* TN-4
Duck Island—*island* WI-6
Duck Island Bluff—*cliff* NY-2
Duck Island Channel—*channel* SC-3
Duck Island Cove—*bay* MD-2
Duck Island Creek—*stream* MD-2
Duck Island Harbor—*bay* NY-2
Duck Island Hunting Club—*other* IL-6
Duck Island Marsh—*swamp* MD-2
Duck Island Range—*channel* NJ-2
Duck Island Range—*channel* PA-2
Duck Island Roads—*bay* CT-1
Duck Islands—*area* AK-9
Duck Islands—*island* MA-1
*Duck Key* FL-3
Duck Key—*island* (3) FL-3
**Duck Key**—*pop pl* FL-3
Duck Key Channel—*channel* FL-3
Duck Key Point—*cape* FL-3
Duck Knob—*summit* GA-3
*Duck Lake* IN-6
*Duck Lake* LA-4
*Duck Lake* MI-6
*Duck Lake* MN-6
*Duck Lake* MT-8
*Duck Lake* UT-8
*Duck Lake* WI-6
Duck Lake—*bay* FL-3
Duck Lake—*flat* (2) NV-8
Duck Lake—*lake* AL-4
Duck Lake—*lake* (5) AK-9
Duck Lake—*lake* (2) AZ-5
Duck Lake—*lake* (2) AR-4
Duck Lake—*lake* (9) CA-9
Duck Lake—*lake* (5) CO-8
Duck Lake—*lake* (3) FL-3
Duck Lake—*lake* (2) GA-3
Duck Lake—*lake* (4) ID-8
Duck Lake—*lake* IL-6
Duck Lake—*lake* IN-6
Duck Lake—*lake* IA-7
Duck Lake—*lake* KY-4
Duck Lake—*lake* (8) LA-4
Duck Lake—*lake* (2) ME-1
Duck Lake—*lake* (28) MI-6
Duck Lake—*lake* (20) MN-6
Duck Lake—*lake* (4) MS-4
Duck Lake—*lake* MO-7
Duck Lake—*lake* (4) MT-8
Duck Lake—*lake* (4) NE-7
Duck Lake—*lake* (3) NY-2
Duck Lake—*lake* (2) ND-7
Duck Lake—*lake* OR-9
Duck Lake—*lake* SD-7
Duck Lake—*lake* (5) TX-5
Duck Lake—*lake* (3) UT-8
Duck Lake—*lake* (7) WA-9
Duck Lake—*lake* (15) WI-6
Duck Lake—*lake* (4) WY-8
**Duck Lake**—*pop pl* (2) MI-6
Duck Lake—*reservoir* AZ-5
Duck Lake—*reservoir* (2) CO-8
Duck Lake—*reservoir* NC-3
Duck Lake—*reservoir* TX-5
Duck Lake—*reservoir* (2) UT-8
Duck Lake—*spring* UT-8
Duck Lake—*swamp* MN-6
Duck Lake—*swamp* UT-8
Duck Lakebed—*flat* MN-6
Duck Lake Brook—*stream* ME-1
Duck Lake Cem—*cemetery* MI-6
Duck Lake Cove—*bay* ME-1
Duck Lake Creek—*stream* CA-9
Duck Lake Dam—*dam* UT-8
Duck Lake Ditch—*canal* MI-6
Duck Lake Drain—*stream* MI-6
Duck Lake Oil and Gas Field—*oilfield* LA-4
*Duck Lake on the Hill* MI-6
Duck Lake Pass—*channel* LA-4
Duck Lake Rsvr—*reservoir* ID-8
Duck Lake Sch—*school* MI-6
Duck Lake Sch—*school* NE-7
Duck Lake State Wildlife Mngmt Area—*park* MN-6
Duck Lake Station Site—*hist pl* WY-8
Duck Lake Swamp—*swamp* MI-6
Duck Lake Tank—*reservoir* AZ-5
**Duck Lake Woods**—*pop pl* IL-6
Duck Ledges—*bar* ME-1
*Duckles Ranch* SD-7
Duck Lick Creek—*stream* KY-4
Duckling Lake—*lake* AK-9
Duck Marsh—*swamp* (2) MI-6
Duck Marshes—*reservoir* PA-2
Duck Mill—*hist pl* MA-1
Duckmill Creek—*stream* NC-3
Duck Mill Dam—*dam* MA-1
Duck Mtn—*summit* AK-9
Duck Mtn—*summit* ME-1
Duck Mtn—*summit* NC-3
Duck Neck—*bay* IL-6
Ducknest Creek—*stream* WI-6
Duck Nest Creek—*stream* WY-8
Ducknest Falls—*falls* WI-6
Duck Nest Springs—*locale* AL-4
Duck-on-the-Rock—*pillar* UT-8
*Duck Pasture* NV-8
Duck Peak—*summit* ID-8
*Duck Point* NC-3
Duck Point—*cape* (2) AK-9
Duck Point—*cape* (2) FL-3
Duck Point—*cape* ME-1
Duck Point—*cape* MD-2
Duck Point—*cape* (3) NY-2
Duck Point—*cape* TN-4
Duck Point—*cape* WI-6
Duck Point Cove—*bay* MD-2
Duck Point Marshes—*swamp* NY-2
*Duck Pond* IL-6
*Duck Pond* LA-4
*Duck Pond* MA-1
*Duck Pond* NJ-2
*Duck Pond* NC-3
*Duck Pond* SC-3
Duck Pond—*bay* FL-3
Duck Pond—*lake* (5) AL-4
Duck Pond—*lake* (2) AR-4
Duck Pond—*lake* (2) CT-1
Duck Pond—*lake* (11) FL-3
Duck Pond—*lake* (4) GA-3
Duck Pond—*lake* IN-6
Duck Pond—*lake* (2) LA-4
Duck Pond—*lake* (15) ME-1
Duck Pond—*lake* (10) MA-1
Duck Pond—*lake* (4) MS-4
Duck Pond—*lake* (5) NH-1
Duck Pond—*lake* (2) NJ-2
Duck Pond—*lake* (13) NY-2
Duck Pond—*lake* NC-3
Duck Pond—*lake* OH-6
Duck Pond—*lake* (3) RI-1
Duck Pond—*lake* (3) TN-4
Duck Pond—*lake* (6) TX-5
Duck Pond—*lake* (6) VT-1
Duck Pond—*lake* (2) VA-3
Duck Pond—*lake* WY-8
Duck Pond—*locale* OR-9
Duck Pond—*reservoir* (2) MA-1
Duck Pond—*reservoir* (2) NJ-2
Duck Pond—*reservoir* (2) PA-2
Duck Pond—*reservoir* RI-1
Duck Pond—*swamp* AR-4
Duck Pond—*swamp* (3) FL-3
Duck Pond—*swamp* (3) GA-3
Duck Pond—*swamp* MS-4
Duck Pond—*swamp* SC-3
Duck Pond—*swamp* (2) TX-5
Duck Pond Bay—*swamp* SC-3
Duckpond Bayou—*gut* LA-4
Duck Pond Bayou—*stream* MS-4
Duck Pond Bottom—*bend* IN-6
Duck Pond Branch—*stream* AL-4
Duck Pond Branch—*stream* FL-3
Duck Pond Branch—*stream* MS-4
Duck Pond Branch—*stream* NC-3
Duck Pond Branch—*stream* (2) TX-5
Duck Pond Brook—*stream* (2) ME-1
Duck Pond Brook—*stream* MA-1
Duck Pond Brook—*stream* VT-1
Duck Pond Cem—*cemetery* GA-3
Duck Pond Cem—*cemetery* IL-6
Duck Pond Corner—*other* ME-1
Duck Pond Creek—*stream* OK-5
Duck Pond Creek—*stream* SC-3
Duck Pond Creek—*stream* TX-5
Duck Pond Dam—*dam* MS-4
Duck Pond Drain—*canal* MI-6
Duck Pond Gulch—*valley* CA-9
Duck Pond Hill—*summit* ME-1
Duck Pond (historical)—*lake* MS-4
Duck Pond Mtn—*summit* NH-1
Duck Pond Outlet—*stream* ME-1
Duck Pond Point—*cape* NY-2
Duck Pond Ridge—*ridge* OR-9
Duck Pond Rsvr—*reservoir* OR-9
Duck Pond Run—*stream* NJ-2
Duck Ponds—*lake* NY-2
Duck Ponds—*lake* NC-3
Duck Ponds—*lake* RI-1
Duck Pond Slough—*gut* MS-4
*Duck Pond Swamp* GA-3
Duck Pond Swamp—*swamp* MS-4
Duck Pond Swamp—*swamp* NC-3
Duck Pond Tank—*reservoir* NM-5
Duck Pond Tank—*reservoir* TX-5
Duck Puddle—*stream* KY-4
Duck Puddle—*swamp* FL-3
Duckpuddle Pond—*lake* ME-1
Duckpuddle Run—*stream* PA-2
Duck Puddles—*lake* FL-3
*Duck River* AL-4
*Duck River* MI-6
*Duckriver* TN-4
**Duck River**—*pop pl* TN-4
Duck River—*stream* AL-4
Duck River—*stream* AK-9
Duck River—*stream* AR-4
Duck River—*stream* CT-1
Duck River—*stream* TN-4
Duck River Bar—*bar* TN-4
Duck River Cave—*cave* TN-4
Duck River Cem—*cemetery* AL-4
Duck River Cem—*cemetery* CT-1
Duck River Ch—*church* AL-4
Duck River Dewatering Area—*basin* TN-4
*Duck River Islands* TN-4
Duck River Landing (historical)—*locale* TN-4
*Duckriver Post Office* TN-4
Duck River Post Office (historical)—*building* TN-4
Duck River Ridge—*ridge* TN-4
Duck River Suck—*rapids* TN-4
Duck River Unit Tennessee Natl Wildlife Ref—*park* TN-4
Duck Rock—*island* FL-3
Duck Rock—*island* ME-1
Duck Rock—*pillar* UT-8
Duck Rock Cove—*bay* FL-3
Duck Rocks—*island* ME-1
**Duckroost**—*pop pl* LA-4
Duck Roost—*summit* TX-5
Duck Roost—*swamp* MS-4
Duckroost Bayou—*stream* LA-4
Duckroost Cove—*bay* FL-3
Duck Roost Lake—*lake* AR-4
Duck Roost Lake—*lake* LA-4
Duck Roost Lake—*lake* MS-4
Duck Roost Lake—*swamp* LA-4
Duckroost Point—*cape* FL-3
Duck Roost Pond—*lake* GA-3
Duck Roost Slough—*gut* AR-4
**Duck (RR name Villa Nova)**—*pop pl* WV-2
*Duck Run* PA-2
Duckrun—*locale* KY-4
**Duckrun**—*pop pl* PA-2
Duck Run—*stream* KY-4
Duck Run—*stream* (3) OH-6
Duck Run—*stream* PA-2
Duck Run—*stream* (2) VA-3
Duck Run—*stream* WV-2
Duck Samford Park—*park* AL-4
*Duckschire Lake* ND-7
**Ducks Head**—*pop pl* NH-1
*Duck-shire Lake* ND-7
Duckshire Lake—*lake* ND-7
**Ducks Landing (subdivision)**—*pop pl* NC-3
Duck Slash—*swamp* TX-5
Duck Slough—*gut* (2) CA-9
Duck Slough—*gut* (3) FL-3
Duck Slough—*gut* IL-6
Duck Slough—*gut* LA-4
Duck Slough—*gut* MS-4
Duck Slough—*stream* (2) CA-9
Duck Slough—*stream* FL-3
Duck Slough—*stream* LA-4
Duck Slough—*stream* OR-9
Ducks Nest—*summit* TN-4
Ducks Nest Gap—*gap* GA-3
Ducksnest Lake—*lake* AZ-5
Ducks Nest Stream—*stream* NJ-2
Duck Spring—*spring* AZ-5
Duck Spring—*spring* ID-8
Duck Spring Branch—*stream* KY-4
**Ducksprings**—*pop pl* AL-4
**Duck Springs**—*pop pl* AL-4
Duck Springs—*spring* AL-4
Duck Springs Cem—*cemetery* AL-4
Duck Springs Ch—*church* AL-4
Duck Springs Ch (historical)—*church* TN-4
Duck Springs Covered Bridge (historical)—*bridge* AL-4
Duck Springs Ranch—*locale* ID-8
Duck Springs Sch—*school* AL-4
Ducks Store—*locale* VA-3
Ducks Swamp—*stream* VA-3
*Ducks Tank* AZ-5
Duck Swale—*swamp* TX-5
*Duck Swamp* VA-3
Ducktail Pond—*lake* ME-1
Duck Tank—*reservoir* (6) AZ-5
Duck Tank—*reservoir* (2) NM-5
Duck Tank—*reservoir* (3) TX-5
Duck Thorofare—*channel* NJ-2
*Ducktown* PA-2
*Duck Town* TN-4
Ducktown—*locale* TN-4
**Ducktown**—*pop pl* GA-3
**Ducktown**—*pop pl* NC-3
**Ducktown**—*pop pl* TN-4
*Ducktown Basin High School* TN-4
Ducktown (CCD)—*cens area* TN-4
Ducktown Cem—*cemetery* TN-4
Ducktown Ch—*church* TN-4
Ducktown Division—*civil* TN-4
Ducktown Elem Sch—*school* TN-4
Ducktown HS—*school* TN-4
Ducktown Post Office—*building* TN-4
Ducktown Sch—*school* GA-3
Ducktown (sta.) (RR name For Postelle)—*other* TN-4
*Ducktown Station* TN-4
**Ducktrap**—*pop pl* ME-1
Ducktrap Harbor—*bay* ME-1
Ducktrap Mtn—*summit* ME-1
Ducktrap River—*stream* ME-1
Duck Valley—*reserve* NV-8
Duck Valley—*valley* ID-8
Duck Valley—*valley* NV-8
Duck Valley Canal—*canal* NV-8
**Duck Valley Ind Res**—*pop pl* NV-8
Duck Valley Ind Res—*reserve* ID-8
*Duckville* MA-1
**Duckville**—*pop pl* MA-1
Duckville Gun Club—*other* UT-8
Duck Walk Tank—*reservoir* AZ-5
Duckwall Cem—*cemetery* OH-6
Duckwall Creek—*stream* CA-9
Duckwall Mtn—*summit* CA-9
Duck Wallow—*lake* GA-3
Duckwall Ridge—*ridge* CA-9
Duckwall Rsvr—*reservoir* OR-9
Duckwalls Ch—*church* WV-2
*Duck Wash* NV-8
*Duckwater* NV-8
Duckwater (Agency Headquarters)—*locale* NV-8
Duckwater Airp—*airport* NV-8
Duckwater Branch—*stream* FL-3
Duckwater Cem—*cemetery* NV-8
Duckwater Creek—*stream* NV-8
Duckwater Hills—*summit* NV-8
**Duckwater Ind Res**—*pop pl* NV-8
*Duckwater Mountain* NV-8
Duckwater Peak—*summit* (2) NV-8
Duckwater Sch—*school* NV-8
Duckwater Valley—*basin* NV-8
Duckwiller Cem—*cemetery* VA-3
Duckworth—*locale* WV-2
Duckworth Branch—*stream* TN-4
Duckworth Canyon—*valley* CA-9
Duckworth Cem—*cemetery* AR-4
Duckworth Cem—*cemetery* WV-2
Duckworth Creek—*stream* IA-7
Duckworth Ditch—*canal* IN-6
Duckworth (historical)—*locale* KS-7
Duckworth Hollow—*valley* (3) TN-4
Duckworth Park—*park* FL-3
Duckworth Park—*park* MS-4
Duckworth Ridge—*ridge* WV-2
Duckworth Ridge—*ridge* WI-6
Duckworth Sch—*school* IL-6
Duckworth-Williams House—*hist pl* AR-4
Ducky Ferrell Hollow—*valley* WV-2
Ducky Hollow—*valley* KY-4
Du Clos, Fourche a—*stream* MO-7
Duclos Run—*stream* PA-2
Duco—*locale* KY-4
Ducolon Drain—*canal* MI-6
**Ducor**—*pop pl* CA-9
Duco Sch—*school* KY-4
Ducrest Bldg—*hist pl* LA-4
Ducros, Bayou—*gut* (2) LA-4
Ducros, Louis, House—*hist pl* FL-3
Ducros Plantation House—*hist pl* LA-4
Ducroz Cem—*cemetery* TX-5
**Duda**—*pop pl* FL-3
Dudas Ford—*locale* MO-7
Dud Brook—*stream* ME-1
Dud Canyon—*valley* NM-5
Dud Cave—*cave* AL-4
Dud Creek—*stream* GA-3
Dudden Fork—*stream* WV-2
Duddington Pasture—*civil* DC-2
Dudd Lake—*lake* MI-6
Duddy Memorial Sch—*school* PA-2
Dude Branch—*stream* NC-3
Dude Canyon—*valley* CO-8
Dudeck Ridge—*ridge* OR-9
Dude Creek—*stream* AK-9
Dude Creek—*stream* AZ-5
Dude Creek—*stream* ID-8
Dude Creek—*stream* OK-5
Dude Creek—*stream* OR-9
Dude Creek—*stream* WY-8
Dude Hole—*valley* CO-8
Dude Lake—*lake* AK-9
Dude Lake—*lake* AZ-5
Dude Lake—*lake* MI-6
Dude Lake—*lake* MT-8
Dude Mesa—*summit* NM-5
Dude Mine—*mine* NM-5
Dude Mtn—*summit* AK-9
Dude Mtn—*summit* AZ-5
**Dudenville**—*pop pl* MO-7
**Dudeon**—*pop pl* WV-2
Dude Ranch Hill—*summit* OK-5
Dude Ridge—*ridge* AR-4
Dudes Canyon—*valley* OR-9
Dudes Lake—*lake* FL-3
Dude Tank—*reservoir* AZ-5
Dudgean Swamp—*swamp* MI-6
Dudgen Butte—*summit* CA-9
Dudgeon Ditch—*canal* OH-6
Dudgeon Lake State Wildlife Mgt Area—*park* IA-7
Dudgeon Sch—*school* MO-7
Dudgeon Sch—*school* WI-6
Dudie—*locale* VA-3
Dudlee Hill—*summit* OR-9
*Dudley* AL-4
*Dudley* MS-4
Dudley—*locale* AL-4
Dudley—*locale* CO-8
Dudley—*locale* ID-8
Dudley—*locale* IA-7
Dudley—*locale* MN-6
Dudley—*locale* OK-5
Dudley—*locale* TX-5
Dudley—*locale* VA-3
Dudley—*locale* WI-6
**Dudley**—*pop pl* CA-9
**Dudley**—*pop pl* GA-3
**Dudley**—*pop pl* (2) IL-6
**Dudley**—*pop pl* ME-1
**Dudley**—*pop pl* MA-1
**Dudley**—*pop pl* MO-7
**Dudley**—*pop pl* NC-3
**Dudley**—*pop pl* OH-6
**Dudley**—*pop pl* PA-2
**Dudley**—*pop pl* SC-3
**Dudley**—*pop pl* SD-7
Dudley, Charles B., House—*hist pl* PA-2
Dudley, Jedidiah, House—*hist pl* CT-1
Dudley, Lake—*reservoir* SD-7
Dudley Anderson Park—*park* MT-8
**Dudley (Barnett)**—*pop pl* PA-2
Dudley Bay—*bay* MI-6
Dudley Block—*hist pl* ME-1
Dudley Bluff—*cliff* TN-4
Dudley Bluffs—*cliff* CO-8
Dudley Borough—*civil* PA-2
Dudley Branch—*stream* IL-6
Dudley Branch—*stream* KY-4
Dudley Branch—*stream* MS-4
Dudley Branch—*stream* (2) TX-5
Dudley Brook—*stream* (4) ME-1
Dudley Brook—*stream* (2) MA-1
Dudley Brook—*stream* (3) NH-1
Dudley Brook—*stream* NY-2
Dudley Brook—*stream* VT-1
Dudley Brook Ridge—*ridge* ME-1
Dudley Canal—*canal* CA-9
Dudley Canyon—*valley* NM-5
Dudley Canyon—*valley* SD-7
Dudley (CCD)—*cens area* GA-3
Dudley Cem—*cemetery* IA-7
Dudley Cem—*cemetery* KS-7
Dudley Cem—*cemetery* ME-1
Dudley Cem—*cemetery* MO-7
Dudley Cem—*cemetery* NE-7
Dudley Cem—*cemetery* NH-1
Dudley Cem—*cemetery* OH-6
Dudley Cem—*cemetery* SD-7
Dudley Cem—*cemetery* (3) TN-4
Dudley Cem—*cemetery* TX-5
Dudley Cem—*cemetery* (2) VA-3
**Dudley (census name Merino Village)**—*pop pl* MA-1
*Dudley Centre* MA-1
Dudley Ch—*church* MO-7
Dudley Ch—*church* NC-3
**Dudley Corners**—*pop pl* MD-2
*Dudley Creek* AR-4
Dudley Creek—*stream* CA-9
Dudley Creek—*stream* (2) CO-8
Dudley Creek—*stream* CT-1
Dudley Creek—*stream* ID-8
Dudley Creek—*stream* KY-4
Dudley Creek—*stream* MO-7
Dudley Creek—*stream* (3) MT-8
Dudley Creek—*stream* NY-2
Dudley Creek—*stream* OR-9
Dudley Creek—*stream* SC-3
Dudley Creek—*stream* TN-4
Dudley Creek—*stream* WY-8
Dudley Cut—*gap* TN-4
Dudley Dam—*dam* AL-4
Dudley Dam—*dam* SD-7
*Dudley Ditch* MO-7
Dudley Ditch—*canal* OH-6
Dudley Ditch—*locale* CO-8
Dudley Field—*locale* TN-4
Dudley Field—*park* TX-5
Dudley Fork—*stream* WV-2
**Dudley Gap**—*pop pl* WV-2
Dudley Grange Park—*park* NJ-2
Dudley Gulch—*valley* CO-8
Dudley Gulch North—*valley* CO-8
**Dudley Heights (subdivision)**—*pop pl* NC-3
**Dudley Hill**—*pop pl* MA-1
Dudley Hill—*summit* CA-9
Dudley Hill—*summit* MA-1
Dudley Hill Ch (historical)—*church* TN-4
*Dudley Hill School* TN-4
Dudley (historical)—*locale* SD-7
**Dudley (historical)**—*pop pl* OR-9
Dudley (historical P.O.)—*locale* IA-7
Dudley Hollow—*valley* AL-4
Dudley Hollow—*valley* KY-4
Dudley Hollow—*valley* (3) TN-4
Dudley House—*hist pl* CA-9
Dudley House—*hist pl* NH-1
Dudley HS—*school* NC-3
*Dudley Island* WA-9
Dudley Island—*island* ME-1
Dudley Island—*island* MI-6
Dudley Island—*island* NC-3
Dudley JHS—*school* MA-1
Dudley Lake—*lake* AZ-5
Dudley Lake—*lake* AR-4
Dudley Lake—*lake* MN-6
Dudley Lake—*lake* MT-8
Dudley Lake—*lake* WI-6
Dudley Lake—*lake* WY-8
Dudley Lake—*reservoir* (2) AL-4
Dudley Lake Sch—*school* MN-6
Dudley Lake (Township of)—*fmr MCD* AR-4
Dudley Landing—*locale* NC-3
Dudley Main Ditch—*canal* MO-7
Dudley Mine—*mine* AZ-5
Dudley Mtn—*summit* NY-2
Dudley Mtn—*summit* OR-9
Dudley Mtn—*summit* VA-3
Dudley Nobel Pond Dam—*dam* MS-4
Dudley Oil Field—*oilfield* TX-5
Dudley Park—*park* GA-3
Dudley Park—*park* NY-2
Dudley Park—*park* OH-6
Dudley Park—*park* TN-4
Dudley Park N Shop—*locale* MA-1
Dudley Peak—*summit* ID-8
Dudley Place—*locale* NV-8
Dudley Plain Cem—*cemetery* ME-1
Dudley Plaza—*locale* MA-1
Dudley Point—*cape* MI-6
*Dudley Pond* AL-4
Dudley Pond—*basin* CA-9
Dudley Pond—*lake* AL-4
Dudley Pond—*lake* CT-1
Dudley Pond—*lake* NH-1
Dudley Pond—*lake* NY-2
Dudley Pond—*reservoir* AL-4
Dudley Pond—*reservoir* CO-8
Dudley Pond—*reservoir* (2) MA-1
Dudley Pond—*reservoir* NC-3
Dudley Pond Dam—*dam* (2) MA-1
Dudley Pond Dam—*dam* NC-3
Dudley Pond Mtn—*summit* AL-4
Dudley Ranch—*locale* (2) CA-9
Dudley Ranch—*locale* TX-5
Dudley Ridge—*ridge* AL-4
Dudley Ridge—*ridge* CA-9
Dudley Rips—*rapids* ME-1
Dudley Rsvr—*reservoir* MA-1
Dudley Run—*stream* OH-6
*Dudleys* MA-1
**Dudleys**—*pop pl* AL-4
Dudley Sch—*school* AL-4
Dudley Sch—*school* CA-9
Dudley Sch—*school* IL-6
Dudley Sch—*school* ME-1
Dudley Sch—*school* MA-1
Dudley Sch—*school* MI-6
Dudley Sch—*school* NC-3
Dudley Sch—*school* TX-5
Dudley Sch—*school* (2) VA-3
Dudley's Chapel—*hist pl* MD-2
Dudleys Club—*locale* MO-7
Dudleys Creek—*stream* TX-5
Dudley Settlement—*locale* NY-2
**Dudley Shoals**—*pop pl* NC-3
Dudley Sink Cave—*cave* AL-4
Dudleys Lake—*reservoir* AL-4
Dudley Slope Mine (underground)—*mine* AL-4
Dudley Slough—*swamp* MT-8
Dudleys Pond—*lake* MA-1
Dudley Spring—*spring* CA-9
Dudley Spring—*spring* MT-8
Dudleys Store (historical)—*locale* AL-4
Dudley State Public Shooting Area—*park* SD-7
Dudley Station Hist Dist—*hist pl* MA-1
Dudley Station (historical)—*locale* AL-4
Dudley Street Station (historical)—*locale* MA-1
*Dudleysville* AL-4
Dudley Swamp—*swamp* (2) ME-1
Dudley Tank—*reservoir* NM-5
Dudley Third Tank—*reservoir* TX-5
**Dudleytown**—*pop pl* IN-6
Dudleytown Conservation Club—*other* IN-6
Dudleytown Hill—*summit* CT-1
**Dudley (Town of)**—*pop pl* MA-1
Dudley Township—*civil* SD-7
**Dudley Township**—*pop pl* KS-7
**Dudley Township**—*pop pl* SD-7
**Dudley (Township of)**—*pop pl* IN-6
**Dudley (Township of)**—*pop pl* MN-6
**Dudley (Township of)**—*pop pl* OH-6
Dudley (Township of)—*unorg* ME-1
Dudley Trail—*trail* ME-1
*Dudleyville* AL-4
Dudleyville—*locale* AZ-5
Dudleyville—*locale* IL-6
**Dudleyville**—*pop pl* AL-4
**Dudleyville**—*pop pl* MA-1
Dudleyville Cem—*cemetery* (2) AL-4
*Dudleyville Pond* MA-1
Dudleyville Pond Dam—*dam* MA-1
Dudley Waterhole—*reservoir* OR-9
Dudley Williams Point—*cape* TX-5

Dudman Springs Ch—*church* MO-7
Dudmore—*locale* CA-9
Dudney Cem—*cemetery* (2) TN-4
**Dudney Hill**—*pop pl* TN-4
Dudneys Hill Sch (historical)—*school* TN-4
Dudo', As—*slope* MH-9
Duds Branch—*stream* TN-4
Duds Cave—*cave* TN-4
Duds Island—*island* NH-1
Duds Pond—*lake* ME-1
Dud Tank—*reservoir* NM-5
*Dudu* MH-9
Dudy Noble Field—*park* MS-4
Dueber Sch—*school* OH-6
*Duece Pond* CT-1
Dueitt—*locale* MS-4
**Duel**—*pop pl* MI-6
Duel Creek—*stream* OK-5
Duel Creek—*stream* OR-9
Duel Hollow—*valley* WY-8
*Duel Lake* MI-6
Duel Lake—*lake* MI-6
Duell Creek—*stream* WY-8
Duell Lake—*lake* MI-6
**Duells Corner**—*pop pl* NY-2
**Duell Spur**—*pop pl* MT-8
**Duell Township**—*pop pl* SD-7
**Duelm**—*pop pl* MN-6
Duel Sch—*school* MI-6
Duely Lake—*lake* IN-6
Duenler Sch (abandoned)—*school* MO-7
**Duenweg**—*pop pl* MO-7
Duer Cem—*cemetery* TN-4
**Duerden Subdivision**—*pop pl* UT-8
Duer Ditch—*canal* IN-6
Duerrs Run—*stream* WV-2
**Duerr Township**—*pop pl* ND-7
*Duers Neck* MD-2
Duers Neck—*cape* MD-2
Duers Neck Landing—*locale* MD-2
Duerson Slide—*cliff* MO-7
Duerson Store—*locale* VA-3
Duesler—*locale* MN-6
Duesler Creek—*stream* WI-6
Duessen Rsvr—*reservoir* TX-5
Duet—*locale* VA-3
Duett Branch Tank—*reservoir* AZ-5
Duette—*locale* FL-3
Duette Elem Sch—*school* FL-3
Duetts Eddy Lake—*lake* LA-4
Duett Tank—*reservoir* AZ-5
Due West—*locale* GA-3
**Due West**—*pop pl* SC-3
Due West—*uninc pl* TN-4
Due West (CCD)—*cens area* SC-3
Due West Chapel—*church* TN-4
*Due West Community* GA-3
Due West Plantation (historical)—*locale* MS-4
Duey Alto (Barrio)—*fmr MCD* PR-3
Duey Bajo (Barrio)—*fmr MCD* PR-3
Duey (Barrio)—*fmr MCD* PR-3
Duferene, Bayou—*gut* LA-4
Dufers Point—*cliff* NM-5
*Duff* IN-6
Duff—*locale* KY-4
Duff—*locale* NE-7
Duff—*locale* TX-5
**Duff**—*pop pl* AR-4
**Duff**—*pop pl* IN-6
**Duff**—*pop pl* TN-4
Duff, Mount—*summit* AK-9
**Duffau**—*pop pl* TX-5
Duffau Cem—*cemetery* TX-5
Duffau Creek—*stream* TX-5
Duff Bayou—*stream* LA-4
Duff Bldg—*hist pl* MI-6
Duff Branch—*stream* AL-4
Duff Branch—*stream* (2) KY-4
Duff Branch—*stream* TX-5
Duff Brown Tank—*reservoir* AZ-5
Duff Cem—*cemetery* AL-4
Duff Cem—*cemetery* IA-7
Duff Cem—*cemetery* (2) MS-4
Duff Cem—*cemetery* NE-7
Duff Cem—*cemetery* (2) VA-3
Duff Cem—*cemetery* (2) WV-2
Duff Chapel—*church* MS-4
**Duff City**—*pop pl* (2) PA-2
Duff Conservation Club—*other* IN-6
**Duff Creek**—*pop pl* NC-3
Duff Creek—*stream* CA-9
Duff Creek—*stream* MI-6
Duff Creek—*stream* (2) MT-8
Duff Creek—*stream* NV-8
Duff Creek—*stream* NC-3
Duff Creek—*stream* TX-5
Duff Drain—*stream* MI-6
**Duffee**—*pop pl* GA-3
**Duffee**—*pop pl* MS-4
Duffee Ch—*church* MS-4
Duffer Hollow—*valley* MO-7
Duffer Hollow—*valley* TN-4
Duffer Peak—*summit* NV-8
Duffey Creek—*stream* WA-9
Duffey Dome—*summit* CA-9
Duffey Park—*park* TX-5
Duff Flat—*flat* AZ-5
Duff Fork—*stream* KY-4
Duff Gulch—*valley* ND-7
Duff Hill—*summit* MT-8
Duff Hollow—*valley* KY-4
Duff Hollow—*valley* TN-4
Duffield—*locale* CO-8
**Duffield**—*pop pl* MI-6
**Duffield**—*pop pl* PA-2
**Duffield**—*pop pl* VA-3
Duffield Acad—*school* TN-4
Duffield Cem—*cemetery* WV-2
Duffield Creek—*stream* (2) ID-8
Duffield Creek—*stream* WA-9
Duffield Ditch—*canal* MT-8
Duffield Elem Sch—*school* PA-2
Duffield Library—*building* MI-6
Duffield Meadows—*flat* CO-8
Duffield Memorial Cem—*cemetery* OK-5
Duffield Peninsula—*cape* AK-9
Duffield Run—*stream* NJ-2
**Duffields**—*pop pl* WV-2
Duffield Sch—*school* IL-6
Duffield Sch—*school* MI-6
Duffield Sch—*school* VA-3
Duffield Sch (historical)—*school* MO-7
**Duffields (Darke)**—*pop pl* WV-2
**Duffies**—*pop pl* NC-3
Duffies Pond—*reservoir* SC-3
**Duffin Heights Subdivision**—*pop pl* UT-8
Duffin Substation—*other* ID-8
Duff Knob—*summit* VA-3
Duff Lake—*lake* FL-3
Duff Lake—*lake* IN-6
Duff Lake—*swamp* MN-6
Duffle Cem—*cemetery* TN-4
Duffle Sch—*school* IL-6
Duff Meadows—*flat* OR-9
*Duff Mesa* AZ-5
Duffner Creek—*stream* ID-8
Duffney Lake—*lake* MN-6
Dufford Cem—*cemetery* MT-8
Duff Park—*park* IA-7
Duff Post Office—*building* IN-4
Duff Ranch—*locale* NV-8
Duff Ranch—*locale* TX-5
**Duffryn Mawr (subdivision)**—*pop pl* PA-2
Duffs—*uninc pl* PA-2
Duffs Branch—*stream* SC-3
Duffs Cabin—*locale* CO-8
Duff Sch—*school* CA-9
Duff Sch—*school* IL-6
Duff Sch (historical)—*school* TN-4
Duffs Fork—*stream* OH-6
Duffs Junction—*uninc pl* PA-2
Duffs Junction Station—*building* PA-2
*Duff Spring* TX-5
Duff Spring—*spring* AZ-5
Duff Spring—*spring* NV-8
Duff Spring—*spring* TN-4
Duff Spring—*spring* WA-9
Duff Springs—*spring* TX-5
Duffs-Scully Junction Station—*building* PA-2
Duffs Station—*building* PA-2
Duff Tank—*reservoir* AZ-5
Duffurrena Pond Number Twenty-one—*reservoir* NV-8
Duffy—*locale* WV-2
**Duffy**—*pop pl* OH-6
Duffy, Lake—*reservoir* PA-2
Duffy Branch—*stream* TN-4
Duffy Branch—*stream* TX-5
Duffy Branch—*stream* VA-3
Duffy Branch—*stream* WV-2
Duffy Butte—*summit* OR-9
Duffy Cove—*bay* ME-1
Duffy Creek—*stream* CA-9
Duffy Creek—*stream* (2) ID-8
Duffy Creek—*stream* MD-2
Duffy Creek—*stream* OR-9
Duffy Creek—*stream* UT-8
Duffy Creek—*stream* (2) WA-9
Duffy Creek—*stream* WI-6
Duffy Ditch—*canal* MT-8
Duffy Gulch—*valley* CA-9
Duffy Hill—*summit* OH-6
Duffy Hill—*summit* VT-1
Duffy Hollow—*valley* MO-7
Duffy Hollow—*valley* NY-2
Duffy Island—*island* MN-6
Duffy Lake—*lake* (2) MN-6
Duffy Lake—*lake* MT-8
Duffy Lake—*lake* OR-9
Duffy Lake—*lake* WA-9
Duffy Lake—*reservoir* TN-4
Duffy Lake Dam—*dam* TN-4
Duffy Lake Trail—*trail* OR-9
Duffy Meadows—*flat* NV-8
Duffy Mtn—*summit* AL-4
Duffy Mtn—*summit* CO-8
Duffy Point—*cape* ME-1
Duffy Prairie—*flat* (2) OR-9
Duffy Ridge—*ridge* WV-2
Duffys Bend—*bend* AL-4
Duffy Sch—*school* AZ-5
Duffy Sch—*school* CT-1
Duffy Sch—*school* SC-3
Duffy Sch (historical)—*school* TN-4
Duffys Creek—*stream* TN-4
Duffy Site—*hist pl* IL-6
Duffys Mtn—*summit* TX-5
Duffys Mtn—*summit* WA-9
Duffys Ponds—*lake* AL-4
Duffy Spring—*spring* UT-8
Duffys Reef—*bar* CA-9
Duffys Tavern—*locale* AK-9
Duffy Trail—*trail* NC-3
Duffy Tunnel—*tunnel* CO-8
Dufoe Creek—*stream* OR-9
**Duford**—*pop pl* SC-3
Dufort—*locale* ID-8
Dufort Creek—*stream* OR-9
Du Forte Lake—*lake* MN-6
Dufour—*locale* CA-9
Dufour Creek—*stream* MI-6
Dufrene, Bayou—*gut* LA-4
Dufrene Camp—*locale* CA-9
Dufrene Ponds—*lake* LA-4
**Dufresne**—*pop pl* LA-4
Dufresne Gulch—*valley* CA-9
Dufresne Pond—*lake* VT-1
Dufroco Sch—*school* LA-4
Dufton Hollow—*valley* NY-2
Dufunny Creek—*stream* WY-8
**Dufur**—*pop pl* OR-9
Dufur (CCD)—*cens area* OR-9
Dufur City Rsvr—*reservoir* OR-9
Dufur Ditch—*canal* OR-9
Dufur Elem Sch-HS—*school* OR-9
Dufurenna Grade—*summit* NV-8
Dufur Hosp—*hospital* PA-2
Dufur Orchards Rsvr—*reservoir* OR-9
Dufur Ranger Station—*locale* OR-9
Dufurrena Pond Number Nineteen—*reservoir* NV-8
Dufurrena Ranch—*locale* NV-8
Duga Lake—*lake* MI-6
Dugals Loop—*locale* ID-8
Dugan—*locale* CA-9
**Dugan**—*pop pl* KY-4
Dugan Bayou—*stream* MS-4
Dugan Bench—*bench* WY-8
Dugan Branch—*stream* KY-4
Dugan Branch—*stream* (2) TN-4
Dugan Brook—*stream* MA-1
Dugan Cem—*cemetery* (2) AR-4
Dugan Cem—*cemetery* KY-4
Dugan Cem—*cemetery* (2) OH-6
Dugan Cem—*cemetery* PA-2
Dugan Cem—*cemetery* TN-4
Dugan Cem—*cemetery* (2) TX-5
Dugan Ch—*church* AR-4
Dugan Creek—*stream* AL-4
Dugan Creek—*stream* AK-9
Dugan Creek—*stream* MT-8
Dugan Creek—*stream* NY-2
Dugan Creek—*stream* SC-3
Dugan Creek—*stream* TX-5
Dugan Ditch—*canal* OH-6
Dugan Gap—*gap* OH-6
**Dugan Hill**—*pop pl* PA-2
Dugan Hills—*other* AK-9
Dugan Hollow—*valley* IN-6
Dugan Hollow—*valley* KY-4
Dugan Hollow—*valley* (4) MO-7
Dugan Hollow—*valley* PA-2
Dugan Hollow—*valley* (2) WV-2
Dugan JHS—*school* TX-5
Dugan Lake—*lake* WI-6
Dugan Lake—*reservoir* IN-6
Dugan Lake Dam—*dam* IN-6
Dugan Landing—*locale* LA-4
Dugan Mill (historical)—*locale* TN-4
Dugan Mine—*mine* AZ-5
Dugan Number 1 Dam—*dam* SD-7
Dugan Park—*flat* CO-8
Dugan Park—*park* SD-7
Dugan Point—*cape* GA-3
Dugan Pond—*lake* CA-9
Dugan Pond—*lake* FL-3
Dugan Ranch—*locale* AZ-5
Dugan Ridge—*ridge* OH-6
Dugan Rock Tank—*reservoir* AZ-5
Dugan Run—*stream* OH-6
Dugan Run—*stream* (2) PA-2
Dugan Run—*stream* WI-6
Dugans Branch—*stream* AL-4
Dugan Sch—*school* NE-7
Dugan Sch (historical)—*school* PA-2
Dugans Opening—*flat* CA-9
Dugans Pond—*lake* CA-9
Dugan Spring—*spring* TN-4
Dugansville—*locale* KY-4
Dugan Tank—*reservoir* (2) AZ-5
Dugan Trail—*trail* PA-2
Dugan Valley—*valley* WI-6
**Duganville**—*pop pl* KY-4
Dugan Wash—*stream* AZ-5
Dugar Brook—*stream* VT-1
Dugar Hollow—*valley* KY-4
Dugar Ridge—*ridge* KY-4
Dugas—*locale* AZ-5
Dugas Canal—*canal* LA-4
Dugas Cem—*cemetery* LA-4
Dugas Interchange—*crossing* AZ-5
Dugas Plantation—*locale* LA-4
Dugaway Hill—*summit* RI-1
Dug Bar—*bar* OR-9
*Dug Branch* TN-4
Dug Branch—*stream* LA-4
*Dug Brook* MA-1
Dug Brook—*stream* ME-1
*Dugchol* FM-9
Dug Creek—*gut* FL-3
Dug Creek—*stream* FL-3
Dug Creek—*stream* OR-9
Dug Creek Rapids—*rapids* ID-8
Dug Creek Rapids—*rapids* OR-9
Dugdale—*locale* MN-6
Dugdemona River—*stream* LA-4
*Dugdemonia River* LA-4
Dugdown—*locale* GA-3
*Dugdown Mtn* GA-3
Dugdown Mtn—*summit* GA-3
Duge'—*slope* MH-9
*Duger Creek* MS-4
Dug Ford—*locale* TX-5
Dugford Cem—*cemetery* OK-5
Dug Ford (historical)—*locale* TN-4
Dug Fork—*stream* (2) KY-4
*Duggan* IA-7
Duggan Branch—*stream* TN-4
Duggan Dam—*dam* OR-9
Duggan Hollow—*valley* (2) AR-4
Duggan JHS—*school* MA-1
Duggans Cem—*cemetery* TN-4
Duggan Sch—*school* CT-1
Duggan Spring—*spring* TN-4
Duggan Spur—*locale* NV-8
Dug Gap—*gap* (3) GA-3
Dug Gap—*gap* TN-4
Dug Gap Ch—*church* GA-3
Duggar Branch—*stream* KY-4
Duggar Dam—*dam* AL-4
**Duggar Farms (subdivision)**—*pop pl* AL-4
*Duggar Lake* AL-4
*Duggars* MS-4
Duggar Sch (historical)—*school* MS-4
Dugger—*locale* AR-4
**Dugger**—*pop pl* IN-6
*Dugger Branch* TN-4
Dugger Branch—*stream* GA-3
Dugger Branch—*stream* KY-4
Dugger Branch—*stream* (3) TN-4
Dugger Bridge (historical)—*bridge* TN-4
Dugger Cem—*cemetery* (2) AR-4
Dugger Cem—*cemetery* FL-3
Dugger Cem—*cemetery* IL-6
Dugger Cem—*cemetery* IN-6
Dugger Cem—*cemetery* KY-4
Dugger Cem—*cemetery* TN-4
Dugger Cem—*cemetery* TX-5
Dugger Cem—*cemetery* VA-3
*Dugger Creek* TN-4
Dugger Creek—*stream* MS-4
Dugger Creek—*stream* (2) NC-3
Dugger Creek—*stream* OR-9
Dugger Elem Sch—*school* IN-6
Dugger Hill—*summit* KY-4
Dugger Hill—*summit* TN-4
Dugger Hollow—*valley* MO-7
Dugger Hollow—*valley* (2) TN-4
Dugger Hollow Prospects—*mine* TN-4
Dugger Mountain—*ridge* AL-4
Dugger Mtn—*summit* NC-3
Dugger Park—*park* MA-1
Dugger Prospect—*mine* TN-4
Dugger Rsvr—*reservoir* CO-8
Dugger Sch—*school* NE-7
Duggers Ferry (historical)—*crossing* TN-4
Duggers Ferry Post Office (historical)—*building* TN-4
Duggers Forge (historical)—*locale* TN-4
*Duggers Mountain* AL-4
Dugger Spring—*spring* (2) AR-4
Dugger Spring—*spring* TN-4
Dugger Spring Hollow—*valley* AR-4
Dugget Creek—*stream* AR-4
*Duggeys Lake* TX-5
Duggin Cem—*cemetery* TN-4
Duggin Hollow—*valley* TN-4
Duggins Creek—*stream* UT-8
Duggins Sch (historical)—*school* MO-7
Dugginsville—*locale* MO-7
Duggins Well—*well* NM-5
Duggle Hollow—*valley* AR-4
*Dug Hill* PA-2
*Dughill* TN-4
Dug Hill—*locale* KY-4
**Dug Hill**—*pop pl* AL-4
**Dug Hill**—*pop pl* TN-4
Dug Hill—*summit* AR-4
Dug Hill—*summit* IL-6
Dug Hill—*summit* (2) IN-6
Dug Hill—*summit* (3) KY-4
Dug Hill—*summit* MA-1
Dug Hill—*summit* MO-7
Dug Hill—*summit* TN-4
Dug Hill, The—*summit* KY-4
Dug Hill Brook—*stream* ME-1
Dug Hill Cem—*cemetery* AL-4
*Dughill Ch* AL-4
Dug Hill Ch—*church* AL-4
Dug Hill Ch—*church* AR-4
Dughill Gap—*gap* TN-4
**Dughill (historical)**—*pop pl* TN-4
Dug Hill Hollow—*valley* AR-4
*Dug Hill Post Office* TN-4
Dughill Post Office (historical)—*building* TN-4
Dug Hill Ridge—*ridge* MD-2
Dughill Ridge—*ridge* NC-3
Dug Hill Ridge—*ridge* PA-2
Dughill Ridge—*ridge* SC-3
Dug Hill Ridge—*ridge* TN-4
Dug Hill Run—*stream* WV-2
Dug Hill Sch (historical)—*school* AL-4
Dughi Spring—*spring* CA-9
Dughman Cem—*cemetery* NE-7
Dug Hollow—*valley* AR-4
Dug Hollow—*valley* (4) TN-4
*Dugi* MH-9
Dugi Archeological Site—*hist pl* MH-9
Dug Knob—*summit* WV-2
Duglas Lake—*lake* MN-6
Duglay Ditch—*canal* IN-6
Dug Long Hill—*summit* MT-8
*Duglow Brook* CT-1
Dug Mountain Brook—*stream* NY-2
Dug Mountain Ponds—*lake* NY-2
Dug Mtn—*summit* GA-3
Dug Mtn—*summit* NY-2
Dug Mtn—*summit* SC-3
Dug Mtn—*summit* VA-3
Dugor—*cape* FM-9
**Dugor**—*pop pl* FM-9
Dugout, The—*gap* AL-4
Dugout, The—*locale* MT-8
Dugout, The—*locale* WY-8
Dugout Bench—*bench* UT-8
Dugout Bench Spring—*spring* UT-8
Dugout Butte—*summit* OR-9
Dugout Canyon—*valley* NV-8
Dugout Canyon—*valley* OR-9
Dugout Canyon—*valley* (2) UT-8
Dugout Coulee—*valley* (2) MT-8
*Dugout Creek* OK-5
Dugout Creek—*stream* AK-9
Dugout Creek—*stream* (3) CO-8
Dugout Creek—*stream* ID-8
Dugout Creek—*stream* (2) IL-6
Dugout Creek—*stream* (2) IA-7
Dugout Creek—*stream* KS-7
Dugout Creek—*stream* (5) MT-8
Dugout Creek—*stream* ND-7
Dugout Creek—*stream* (4) OK-5
Dugout Creek—*stream* (3) OR-9
Dugout Creek—*stream* SD-7
Dugout Creek—*stream* (5) TX-5
Dugout Creek—*stream* (3) UT-8
Dugout Creek—*stream* (4) WY-8
Dugout Dam—*dam* UT-8
Dugout Draw—*valley* CO-8
Dugout Draw—*valley* SD-7
Dugout Draw—*valley* (2) TX-5
Dugout Draw—*valley* (4) WY-8
Dugout Flat—*flat* UT-8
Dugout Gulch—*valley* MT-8
Dugout Gulch—*valley* WY-8
Dugout Hill—*summit* ID-8
Dugout Hill—*summit* TN-4
Dugout Hollow—*valley* TN-4
Dugout Lake—*lake* (2) MN-6
Dugout Lake—*lake* OR-9
Dugout Lake—*lake* WI-6
Dugout Lookout Trail—*trail* WA-9
Dugout Mine—*mine* UT-8
Dugout Mtn—*summit* AL-4
Dugout Mtn—*summit* AR-4
Dugout Mtn—*summit* TX-5
Dugout Mtn—*summit* WA-9
Dugout Ranch—*locale* MT-8
Dugout Ranch—*locale* UT-8
Dugout Ranch—*locale* WY-8
Dugout Rsvr—*reservoir* MT-8
Dugout Rsvr—*reservoir* OR-9
Dugout Rsvr—*reservoir* UT-8
Dugout Run—*stream* IL-6
Dugout Sch—*school* IL-6
Dugout Spring—*spring* ID-8
Dugout Spring—*spring* NE-7
Dugout Spring—*spring* NV-8
Dugout Spring—*spring* (2) OR-9
Dugout Spring—*spring* SD-7
Dugout Spring—*spring* UT-8
Dugout Spring—*spring* WY-8
Dugout Tank—*reservoir* (5) TX-5
Dugout Valley—*valley* (3) AL-4
Dugout Valley—*valley* AZ-5
Dugout Wash—*stream* CO-8
Dugout Wash—*valley* (2) UT-8
Dugout Wells—*well* TX-5
Dugout Windmill—*locale* (3) TX-5
*Dug P.O.* AL-4
Dug Pond—*lake* MA-1
Dug Ridge—*ridge* TN-4
Dug Road Creek—*stream* CA-9
Dug Road Creek—*stream* PA-2
Dug Road Hollow—*valley* KY-4
Dug Road Mtn—*summit* AZ-5
Dug Road Trail—*trail* (2) PA-2
Dug Rsvr—*reservoir* ID-8
Dug Run—*stream* OH-6
Dug Spring—*spring* ID-8
Dug Spring—*spring* MO-7
Dug Spring—*spring* OR-9
Dug Spring—*spring* TX-5
Dug Spring Canyon—*valley* TX-5
Dug Springs Stage Station Ruins—*locale* WY-8
Dug Springs Station Site—*hist pl* WY-8
Dugspur—*locale* VA-3
Dugspur Sch—*school* VA-3
Dugtown Cem—*cemetery* TN-4
Dug Trail—*trail* PA-2
Dugualla Bay—*bay* WA-9
Duguchoel—*summit* FM-9
Dugues Canal—*canal* LA-4
*Dugula Bay* WA-9
Dug Way—*channel* MA-1
Dugway—*locale* NY-2
**Dugway**—*pop pl* UT-8
Dugway Brook—*stream* NY-2
Dugway Camping Area—*locale* NH-1
Dugway Canyon—*valley* WY-8
Dugway Cem—*cemetery* NY-2
Dugway Creek—*stream* NY-2
*Dugway Dell* UT-8
Dugway Gorge—*valley* NY-2
*Dugway Hill* RI-1
Dugway Hill—*summit* MA-1
Dugway Hollow—*valley* UT-8
Dugway HS—*school* UT-8
Dugway Lake—*lake* WY-8
Dugway Military Clinic Heliport—*airport* UT-8
Dugway Mtn—*summit* (2) NY-2
Dugway Pass—*gap* UT-8
Dugway Pond—*lake* MA-1
Dugway Pony Express Station—*locale* UT-8
Dugway Proving Ground—*military* UT-8
Dugway Proving Ground HQ (Easy Area)—*military* UT-8
Dugway Proving Grounds-English Village Heliport—*airport* UT-8
Dugway Range—*range* UT-8
Dugway Ridge—*ridge* UT-8
Dugway Rim—*cliff* WY-8
Dugway Rsvr—*reservoir* UT-8
Dugway Sch—*school* UT-8
Dugway Spring—*spring* UT-8
*Dugway Station-Site* UT-8
Dugway Tank—*reservoir* AZ-5
Dugway Topaz Well—*well* UT-8
Dugway Valley—*valley* UT-8
Dugway-Wendover—*cens area* UT-8
Dugway-Wendover Division—*civil* UT-8
Dugwell—*locale* VA-3
Dug Well—*well* NM-5
Dugwell Canyon—*valley* AZ-5
Dugwell Canyon—*valley* TX-5
Duhaime Flat—*flat* OR-9
**Duhamel Corners**—*pop pl* MD-2
Duhamel Flat—*flat* SD-7
*Duhane Ranch* SD-7
Duhart Ch—*church* GA-3
Duhart Creek—*stream* GA-3
Duharts Creek—*stream* NC-3
Duhernal Dam—*dam* NJ-2
Duhernal Lake—*reservoir* NJ-2
Duhon Bayou—*stream* LA-4
**Duhring**—*pop pl* PA-2
**Duhring**—*pop pl* WV-2
Duhringe Pass—*locale* OK-5
Duhrsen, Carl H., House—*hist pl* HI-9
Duhuy, Bayou—*gut* (2) LA-4
*Duie Branch* FL-3
Duis Sch—*school* IL-6
Duitatuk Lake—*lake* AK-9
Duitelmans Lake—*lake* MI-6
*Duke* AL-4
Duke—*locale* IA-7
Duke—*locale* MS-4
Duke—*locale* OH-6
Duke—*locale* TX-5
**Duke**—*pop pl* AL-4
**Duke**—*pop pl* MO-7
**Duke**—*pop pl* OK-5
Duke—*uninc pl* NC-3
Duke, Green, House—*hist pl* NC-3
Duke, Holmes, House—*hist pl* TX-5
Duke, James B., Mansion—*hist pl* NY-2
Duke, James Buchanan, House—*hist pl* NC-3
Duke, Nathaniel W., House—*hist pl* CO-8
Duke Bar—*bar* OR-9
Duke Basin—*basin* CO-8
Duke Bayou—*stream* LA-4
Duke Branch—*stream* (2) TN-4
Duke Branch—*stream* TX-5
Duke Bridge—*bridge* TX-5
Duke Cave—*cave* TN-4
Duke Cem—*cemetery* (2) AL-4
Duke Cem—*cemetery* (2) IN-6
Duke Cem—*cemetery* KY-4
Duke Cem—*cemetery* (2) MS-4
Duke Cem—*cemetery* MO-7
Duke Cem—*cemetery* OK-5
Duke Cem—*cemetery* SC-3
Duke Cem—*cemetery* TX-5
Duke Cem—*cemetery* VA-3
**Duke Center**—*pop pl* PA-2
*Duke Centre* PA-2
Duke Ch—*church* AL-4
Duke Chapel—*church* TN-4
Duke City Logging Camp—*locale* AZ-5
Duke Creek—*stream* AZ-5
Duke Creek—*stream* AR-4
Duke Creek—*stream* CA-9
Duke Creek—*stream* GA-3
Duke Creek—*stream* IL-6
Duke Creek—*stream* MI-6
Duke Creek—*stream* (2) OR-9
Duke Creek—*stream* TN-4
Duke Crossing—*locale* TX-5
**Dukedale**—*pop pl* LA-4
Dukedall Creek—*stream* LA-4
**Dukedom**—*pop pl* KY-4
**Dukedom**—*pop pl* TN-4
Dukedom Post Office—*building* TN-4
Duke Family Cem—*cemetery* AL-4
**Duke Gardens**—*pop pl* VA-3
*Duke Harbor Pond* PA-2
Dukeharts Channel—*channel* MD-2
Dukeharts Creek—*bay* MD-2
Duke Hill—*summit* AK-9
Duke Hill—*summit* CO-8
Duke Hill—*summit* IN-6
Duke Hill—*summit* NH-1
Duke Hill Windmill—*locale* TX-5
**Duke (historical)**—*pop pl* TN-4
Duke Hollow—*valley* (2) MO-7
Duke Hollow—*valley* (2) TN-4
Duke Hollow—*valley* VA-3
Duke Homestead—*locale* NC-3
Duke Homestead and Tobacco Factory—*hist pl* NC-3
Dukehurst—*locale* KY-4
Duke Island—*island* AK-9
Duke Island Park—*park* NJ-2
Duke JHS—*school* AL-4
*Duke Lake* MI-6
Duke Lake—*lake* MN-6
Duke Lake—*lake* SC-3
Duke Lake—*reservoir* TX-5
Duke Lake Dam—*dam* (3) MS-4
Duke Landing—*locale* OR-9
Duke-Lawrence House—*hist pl* NC-3
Duke Lower, Lake—*reservoir* AL-4
Duke Memorial Ch—*church* NC-3
Duke Memorial United Methodist Ch—*hist pl* NC-3
Duke Mine (underground)—*mine* AL-4
*Duke Missionary Baptist Church* AL-4
*Duke Mountain* ME-1
Duke Mountain Branch—*stream* TX-5
Duke Mtn—*summit* AL-4
Duke Mtn—*summit* TX-5
Duke Park—*park* AL-4
Duke Park—*park* NC-3
Duke Peak—*summit* AZ-5
*Duke Plantation* MS-4
Duke Point—*cape* AK-9
Duke Pond—*lake* TN-4
Duke Pond—*swamp* TX-5
Duke Post Office (historical)—*building* MS-4
Duke Powder State Park—*park* NC-3
Duke Power Dam—*dam* SC-3
Duke Power Park Dam—*dam* NC-3
Duke Power Park Lake—*reservoir* NC-3
Duke Power Village—*facility* NC-3
Duke Power Village—*locale* NC-3
Duke Ranch—*locale* AZ-5
*Duke Rsvr* OR-9
**Dukerville**—*pop pl* NE-7
Dukes—*cape* ID-8
Dukes—*locale* FL-3
Dukes—*locale* KY-4
Dukes—*locale* MI-6
Dukes—*locale* NC-3
Dukes—*locale* WV-2
**Dukes**—*pop pl* SC-3
Dukes, The—*summit* AK-9
Dukes and Jobs Ditch—*stream* DE-2
Dukes Bay—*swamp* FL-3
*Dukes Branch* GA-3
Dukes Branch—*stream* AR-4
Dukes Branch—*stream* GA-3
Dukes Branch—*stream* VA-3
Dukes Bridge—*bridge* IN-6
**Dukes Bridge**—*pop pl* NJ-2
Dukes Brook—*stream* NJ-2
Dukes Canyon Creek—*stream* OR-9
Dukes Cem—*cemetery* FL-3
Dukes Cem—*cemetery* IL-6
Dukes Cem—*cemetery* MS-4
Dukes Cem—*cemetery* OH-6
Dukes Cem—*cemetery* (2) TN-4
Duke Sch—*school* SC-3
Dukes Chapel—*church* NC-3
Duke Sch (historical)—*school* AL-4
Duke Sch (historical)—*school* TN-4
**Dukes County**—*pop pl* MA-1
*Dukes Creek* AL-4
Dukes Creek—*stream* (2) GA-3
Dukes Creek—*stream* (2) ID-8
Dukes Creek—*stream* TN-4
Dukes Creek Ch—*church* GA-3
Dukes Creek Falls—*falls* GA-3
**Dukes Crossroads**—*pop pl* NC-3
Dukes Ditch—*stream* DE-2
Dukes Ferry (historical)—*locale* MS-4
Dukes Fork—*stream* MT-8
Dukes Gymnasium—*hist pl* SC-3
Dukes Hole—*valley* ID-8
Dukes Hollow—*valley* TX-5
Dukes Islands—*island* FL-3
Dukes Lake—*lake* FL-3
Dukes Lake—*lake* MI-6
Dukes Lake—*reservoir* NC-3
Dukes Lake—*reservoir* TN-4
Dukes Lodge—*locale* NC-3
Dukes Lookout Tower—*locale* MI-6
Dukes Memorial Hosp—*hospital* IN-6
Dukes Mill (historical)—*locale* (2) AL-4
Dukes Mtn—*summit* TN-4
Dukes Pond—*lake* AL-4
Dukes Pond—*swamp* GA-3
Duke's Private Airp—*airport* WA-9
**Duke Spur**—*pop pl* ND-7
Dukes Run—*stream* OH-6
*Dukes Station* AL-4
Dukes Valley—*basin* OR-9
**Dukes Valley**—*pop pl* OR-9
Dukes V Spring—*spring* ID-8
Duke Swamp—*stream* NC-3
Duke Tank Number One—*reservoir* AZ-5
Duke Tank Number Two—*reservoir* AZ-5

Duketon—*locale* AL-4
Duke (Township of)—*fmr MCD* NC-3
Duke Univ—*school* NC-3
Dukeville—*locale* NC-3
Duke Wilson Ranch—*locale* TX-5
Duke Windmill—*locale* NM-5
Duktoth Mtn—*summit* AK-9
Duktoth River—*stream* AK-9
*Dulac* TN-4
**Dulac**—*pop pl* LA-4
Dulac, Bayou—*gut* LA-4
Dula Canyon—*valley* NV-8
Dula Chapel—*church* NC-3
Dulac Post Office (historical)—*building* TN-4
Dulac Sch—*school* LA-4
Dulah—*locale* NC-3
**Dulah**—*pop pl* CA-9
Dula (historical)—*locale* MS-4
Dulah Mormon Ch—*church* NC-3
Dula Knob—*summit* NC-3
*Dulan* NC-3
Duland Sch—*school* OK-5
Dulaney—*locale* KY-4
Dulaney—*locale* WV-2
**Dulaney**—*pop pl* TN-4
Dulaney, Joe E., House—*hist pl* TX-5
Dulaney, Joseph Field, House—*hist pl* TX-5
Dulaney Branch—*stream* MD-2
Dulaney Branch—*stream* MS-4
Dulaney Branch—*stream* (2) TN-4
Dulaney Cem—*cemetery* TX-5
Du Laney Cem—*cemetery* TX-5
*Dulaney Church* AL-4
*Dulaney Creek* FL-3
*Dulaney Creek* TX-5
Dulaney Creek—*stream* TX-5
Dulaney Hollow—*valley* VA-3
Dulaney Lake—*reservoir* MS-4
Dulaney Mtn—*summit* VA-3
Dulaney-Ross Lake—*lake* MS-4
Dulaney Sch—*school* AL-4
Dulaney Sch—*school* MO-7
Dulaney Sch (abandoned)—*school* PA-2
*Dulaney School* PA-2
**Dulaney Village**—*pop pl* MD-2
Dulaney Well—*well* TX-5
*Dulany* TN-4
*Dulany Cave* PA-2
Dulany Ch—*church* AL-4
Du Large Gas Field—*oilfield* LA-4
Dula Spring—*spring* NV-8
**Dula Springs**—*pop pl* NC-3
Dula Thoroughfare—*stream* NC-3
Dulbatna Mtn—*summit* AK-9
Dulbi Flats—*area* AK-9
Dulbi River—*stream* AK-9
Dulbi Slough—*stream* AK-9
**Dulce**—*pop pl* NM-5
Dulce Canyon—*valley* NM-5
Dulce Creek—*stream* NM-5
Dulce Lake—*reservoir* NM-5
Dulce Mtn—*summit* NM-5
Dulce Ridge—*ridge* NM-5
Dulce Rock—*summit* NM-5
Dulces Nombres Windmill—*locale* TX-5
Dulce Spring—*spring* NM-5
Dulding Ranch—*locale* TX-5
Dulea Creek—*stream* MT-8
Duleke Mine—*mine* CA-9
Duley—*locale* MD-2
Duley Bluff—*cliff* KY-4
Duley Bluff Cem—*cemetery* KY-4
Duley Creek—*stream* OR-9
*Duley Lake* IN-6
Duley Lake—*lake* WA-9
Duley Pond—*lake* ME-1
*Dulfur* OR-9
Dulin—*locale* TX-5
**Dulin**—*pop pl* AL-4
Dulin, H. L., House—*hist pl* TN-4
Dulin Branch—*stream* AL-4
Dulin Branch—*stream* TN-4
Dulin Cem—*cemetery* IA-7
Dulin Ch—*church* NC-3
Dulin Chapel—*church* VA-3
Dulin Creek—*stream* KY-4
Dulin Creek—*stream* MO-7
Duling Canyon—*valley* WY-8
Duling Cem—*cemetery* WV-2
Duling Ch—*church* WV-2
Duling Creek—*stream* CO-8
Duling Hill—*summit* WY-8
Duling Lakes—*lake* CO-8
Duling Park—*flat* CO-8
Duling Ridge—*ridge* WV-2
Duling Sch—*school* MS-4
Dulin Ranch—*locale* CA-9
**Dulkaan**—*pop pl* FM-9
*Dulkan* FM-9
Dull—*locale* OH-6
Dull—*locale* TX-5
**Dull**—*pop pl* TN-4
Dullam Cem—*cemetery* IL-6
*Dullard Creek* TX-5
*Dull Axe* ID-8
Dull Axe Mtn—*summit* ID-8
Dull Ax Lake—*lake* AK-9
Dull Center (reduced usage)—*locale* WY-8
Dulles International Airp—*airport* VA-3
Dulles (Magisterial District)—*fmr MCD* VA-3
Dulles Sch—*school* CA-9
Dulles Sch—*school* IL-6
Dulles Sch—*school* IN-6
Dull Flats—*flat* TX-5
Dull Hoe Creek—*stream* TN-4
Dull Hunt Hollow—*valley* VA-3
Dull Hunt Trail—*trail* VA-3
Dullinger Lake—*lake* MN-6
Dullin Sch—*school* MA-1
Dull Knife Battlefield—*hist pl* WY-8
Dull Knife Creek—*stream* WY-8
Dull Knife Pass—*gap* WY-8
Dullknife Rsvr—*reservoir* WY-8
Dullnig Ranch—*locale* TX-5
Dull Rsvr—*reservoir* WY-8
Dulls Cem—*cemetery* AL-4
Dulls Corner—*locale* MD-2
*Dulls Creek* WV-2
Dulls Creek—*stream* WV-2
Dulls Creek Sch—*school* WV-2
Dulls Point—*cape* NC-3
Dulog Creek—*stream* OR-9
Dulog Riffle—*rapids* OR-9
D Ulrich Dam—*dam* SD-7
Dulton Branch—*stream* VA-3
*Dulucan* FM-9
*Dulukan* FM-9
*Dulukun* FM-9
Duluth—*locale* KY-4
Duluth—*locale* NE-7
**Duluth**—*pop pl* GA-3
**Duluth**—*pop pl* KS-7
**Duluth**—*pop pl* MN-6
Duluth Air Natl Guard Station—*building* MN-6
Duluth and Iron Range RR Company
Depot—*hist pl* MN-6
Duluth Cem—*cemetery* KS-7
Duluth Central HS—*hist pl* MN-6
Duluth Civic Center Hist Dist—*hist pl* MN-6
Duluth Harbor Basin—*bay* MN-6
*Duluth Heights* MN-6
**Duluth Heights**—*pop pl* MN-6
Duluth International Airport—*mil airp* MN-6
Duluth Junction—*locale* MN-6
Duluth Playground—*park* MN-6
Duluth Public Library—*hist pl* MN-6
Duluth Snowden Pond Dam—*dam* MS-4
Duluth South Breakwater Inner (Duluth Range
Rear) Lighthouse—*hist pl* MN-6
Duluth State Normal Sch Hist
Dist—*hist pl* MN-6
**Duluth (Township of)**—*pop pl* MN-6
Duluth Union Depot—*hist pl* MN-6
Dulweber—*locale* MS-4
*Dulweber Spur* MS-4
Dulwich—*locale* WA-9
**Dulworth**—*pop pl* KY-4
**Dulzura**—*pop pl* CA-9
Dulzura Community Cemetery—*locale* CA-9
Dulzura Creek—*stream* CA-9
*Dulzura Lake* CA-9
*Dulzural Lake* CA-9
Dulzura Summit—*gap* CA-9
Dumaines Lake—*reservoir* NC-3
**Dumais**—*pop pl* ME-1
Duman Lake—*reservoir* PA-2
Duman Lake Park—*park* PA-2
Duma Point—*summit* UT-8
Du Mar, Bayou—*stream* LA-4
Dumarce Lake—*lake* SD-7
**Dumarce Township**—*pop pl* SD-7
Dumarce Township (historical)—*civil* SD-7
*Dumas* AL-4
Dumas—*locale* GA-3
Dumas—*locale* WA-9
**Dumas**—*pop pl* AR-4
**Dumas**—*pop pl* MS-4
**Dumas**—*pop pl* NE-7
**Dumas**—*pop pl* PA-2
**Dumas**—*pop pl* TX-5
Dumas Acad (historical)—*school* AL-4
Dumas Baptist Ch—*church* MS-4
Dumas Bay—*bay* WA-9
Dumas Cave—*cave* TX-5
Dumas (CCD)—*cens area* TX-5
Dumas Cem—*cemetery* (2) MS-4
Dumas Cem—*cemetery* TN-4
Dumas Cem—*cemetery* TX-5
Dumas Ch—*church* MS-4
Dumas City—*locale* AR-4
Dumas Creek—*stream* MO-7
Dumas Creek—*stream* (2) NC-3
Dumas Gulch—*valley* OR-9
Dumas Hill—*summit* WA-9
Dumas Institute (historical)—*school* MS-4
Dumas Junction—*locale* TX-5
Dumas Lake—*lake* MS-4
*Dumas Lookout Tower* MS-4
Dumas Methodist Ch—*church* AL-4
Dumas Pond—*lake* MS-4
Dumas Presbyterian Ch
(historical)—*church* MS-4
Dumas Ranch—*locale* MT-8
Dumas Sch—*school* IL-6
Dumas Sch—*school* MS-4
Dumas Sch (abandoned)—*school* PA-2
Dumas Sch (historical)—*school* MS-4
Dumass Ferry (historical)—*locale* NC-3
Dumas Spring—*spring* TX-5
Dumas Tank—*reservoir* AZ-5
Dumas-Twin Lakes—*CDP* WA-9
Dumaw Creek—*stream* MI-6
Dumaw Creek Site—*hist pl* MI-6
Dumbald Cem—*cemetery* KS-7
Dumbar HS—*school* TX-5
Dum Barr, Bayou—*gut* LA-4
**Dumbarton**—*pop pl* MD-2
**Dumbarton**—*pop pl* NY-2
**Dumbarton**—*pop pl* VA-3
Dumbarton—*uninc pl* CA-9
Dumbarton Bridge—*bridge* CA-9
Dumbarton Bridge—*hist pl* DC-2
Dumbarton Bridge (toll)—*bridge* CA-9
**Dumbarton Heights**—*pop pl* MD-2
Dumbarton House—*building* DC-2
Dumbarton JHS—*school* MD-2
Dumbarton Oaks Park—*park* DC-2
Dumbarton Oaks Park and Montrose
Park—*hist pl* DC-2
Dumbarton Point—*cape* CA-9
*Dumb-bel Lake* MI-6
*Dumb-bell Lake* MI-6
Dumbbell Lake—*lake* AK-9
Dumbbell Lake—*lake* IA-7
Dumbbell Lake—*lake* MI-6
Dumbbell Lake—*lake* (2) MN-6
Dumbbell Lake—*lake* (2) OR-9
Dumbbell Lake—*lake* WA-9
Dumbbell Lakes—*lake* CA-9
*Dumbbell Mountain* WA-9
Dumbbell Ranch—*locale* AZ-5
Dumbbell Ranch—*locale* NE-7
Dumbbell River—*stream* MN-6
Dumb Betty Branch—*stream* KY-4
Dumb Brook—*stream* ME-1
**Dumbeck**—*pop pl* MO-7
Dumbell—*locale* WY-8
*Dumbell Lake* MN-6
*Dumbell Lake* WA-9
Dumbell Mtn—*summit* WA-9
*Dumbell River* MN-6
Dumbell Rock Draw—*valley* WY-8
Dumblane—*locale* MN-6
Dumbuk Ridge—*ridge* SD-7
*Dume Canyon* CA-9
*Dume Cove* CA-9
Dume Cove—*bay* CA-9
Dumesnil—*locale* LA-4
Dumesnil Street ME Church—*hist pl* KY-4
*Dum'et'uy* FM-9
Dumford Cem—*cemetery* KY-4
Dumford Hollow—*valley* KY-4
*Dumfounding Bay* FL-3
Dumfoundling Bay—*bay* FL-3
*Dumfoundling River* FL-3
Dumfries—*locale* IA-7
Dumfries—*locale* MN-6
**Dumfries**—*pop pl* VA-3
Dumfries (Magisterial District)—*fmr MCD* VA-3
Duming Brook—*stream* CT-1
Dumke Lake—*lake* WI-6
Dumke Sch—*school* WI-6
Dumler Oil Field—*oilfield* KS-7
Dumm Canyon—*valley* NM-5
Dummer Hill—*summit* NH-1
Dummer Lake—*lake* MN-6
Dummer Plain Sch—*school* NH-1
Dummer Ponds—*lake* NH-1
Dummer Spring—*spring* ID-8
**Dummerston Center**—*pop pl* VT-1
**Dummerston (Dummerston
Center)**—*pop pl* VT-1
Dummerston Hill—*summit* VT-1
**Dummerston (Town of)**—*pop pl* VT-1
**Dummer (Town of)**—*pop pl* NH-1
Dummit Branch—*stream* KY-4
Dummit Cove—*bay* FL-3
Dummit Creek—*gut* FL-3
Dummit Grove—*locale* FL-3
Dumm Mine—*mine* NV-8
Dummoor—*locale* NM-5
Dumm Ridge—*ridge* OH-6
Dummy Bottom—*bend* CO-8
Dummy Branch—*stream* LA-4
Dummy Branch—*stream* NC-3
Dummy Canyon—*valley* NV-8
Dummy Creek—*stream* AK-9
Dummy Creek—*stream* (2) ID-8
Dummy Hill—*summit* WY-8
*Dummy Lake* WI-6
Dummy Point—*cliff* TX-5
Dumolin Canal—*canal* LA-4
Dumond, Lake—*lake* AR-4
Dumond Sch—*school* ME-1
*Dumonnt Sand Dunes* CA-9
Dumont—*locale* CA-9
Dumont—*locale* SD-7
**Dumont**—*pop pl* CO-8
**Dumont**—*pop pl* IA-7
**Dumont**—*pop pl* MN-6
**Dumont**—*pop pl* NJ-2
**Dumont**—*pop pl* TX-5
Dumont Canyon—*valley* ID-8
Dumont Cem—*cemetery* TX-5
Dumont Creek—*stream* MI-6
Dumont Creek—*stream* OR-9
Dumont Creek Picnic Ground—*park* OR-9
Dumont Dunes—*summit* CA-9
Dumont Hills—*summit* CA-9
Dumont Horse Pasture Windmill—*locale* TX-5
Dumont Lake—*lake* MI-6
**Dumont Lake**—*pop pl* MI-6
Dumont Lake—*reservoir* CO-8
Dumont Oil Field—*oilfield* TX-5
Dumont Ranger Station—*locale* OR-9
Dumont (RR name for South
Houston)—*other* TX-5
Dumont Sand Dunes—*summit* CA-9
Dumont Sch (abandoned)—*school* SD-7
Dumonts Meadows—*flat* CA-9
Dumont Tank—*reservoir* TX-5
**Dumontville**—*pop pl* OH-6
Dumony Ridge—*ridge* TN-4
Dump Branch—*stream* KY-4
*Dump Canyon* CA-9
Dump Canyon—*valley* CA-9
Dump Cave—*cave* PA-2
Dump Creek—*bay* NC-3
Dump Creek—*stream* (3) ID-8
Dump Draw—*valley* SD-7
Dump Draw—*valley* WY-8
Dumpers Creek—*stream* SC-3
Dump Ground Lake—*lake* MN-6
Dump Ground Well—*well* TX-5
Dumpground Windmill—*locale* TX-5
Dump Hollow—*valley* AL-4
Dump Hollow—*valley* PA-2
Dumphy Hollow—*valley* WY-8
Dumping Rock—*summit* RI-1
Dump Island—*island* NC-3
Dump Keys—*island* FL-3
Dump Lake—*lake* MS-4
Dump Lake—*lake* WI-6
**Dumplin**—*pop pl* TN-4
Dumplin, Mount—*summit* MA-1
Dumplin Baptist Ch—*church* TN-4
Dumplin Branch—*stream* IN-6
Dumplin Branch—*stream* VA-3
Dumplin Brook—*stream* MA-1
Dumplin Cem—*cemetery* TN-4
Dumplin Creek—*stream* LA-4
Dumplin Creek—*stream* TN-4
*Dumpling* TN-4
Dumpling Cave—*cave* KY-4
*Dumpling Creek* TN-4
Dumpling Creek—*stream* MO-7
Dumpling Creek—*stream* NC-3
Dumpling Creek—*stream* OK-5
Dumpling Hill—*summit* NE-7
Dumpling Hill—*summit* OH-6
Dumpling Hill—*summit* VT-1
Dumpling Hill Cem—*cemetery* TN-4
Dumpling Hill Ch (historical)—*church* TN-4
Dumpling Hollow—*valley* KY-4
*Dumpling Island* ME-1
Dumpling Island—*island* ME-1
Dumpling Island—*island* VA-3
Dumpling Mtn—*summit* AK-9
Dumpling Mtn—*summit* TN-4
Dumpling Mtn—*summit* VA-3
Dumpling Neck—*cape* DE-2
*Dumpling Point* RI-1
Dumpling Pond—*lake* ME-1
*Dumpling Rock* MA-1
*Dumpling Rocks* RI-1
Dumpling Rocks—*bar* MA-1
Dumpling Rocks, The—*summit* KY-4
Dumpling Run—*stream* (3) WV-2
Dumplings, The—*cape* RI-1
Dumplings, The—*summit* RI-1
Dumpling Spring Run—*stream* WV-2
Dumplings Rocks Light—*locale* MA-1
Dumplingtown Hill—*summit* NH-1
Dumplin Gut—*stream* NC-3
*Dumplin Island* ME-1
Dumplin Mill—*locale* TN-4
Dumplin Point—*cape* NC-3
Dumplin Post Office (historical)—*building* TN-4
*Dumplins* RI-1
Dumplin Spring—*spring* TN-4
Dumplin Valley—*valley* TN-4
*Dumplin Valley Cemetery* TN-4
Dump Mtn—*summit* AR-4
Dump Mtn—*summit* CO-8
*Dump Reservoir, The* NH-1
*Dumpries* MN-6
Dump Run—*stream* PA-2
Dumps Creek—*stream* VA-3
*Dumps Spring, The* NV-8
Dump Tank—*reservoir* AZ-5
Dums Creek—*stream* IL-6
Dumtah (Indian Camp Ground
Site)—*locale* CA-9
*Dumy Old Lime Works and Quarry* AL-4
Dun, John, Homestead—*hist pl* OH-6
Dunagan—*locale* TX-5
Dunagan Bridge—*bridge* OR-9
Dunagan Canyon—*valley* CO-8
Dunagan Cem—*cemetery* AR-4
Dunagan Cem—*cemetery* MO-7
Dunagan Chapel—*church* GA-3
Dunagan Creek—*stream* NC-3
Dunagan Hill—*summit* AL-4
Dunagan Lake—*lake* TX-5
Dunagan Mtn—*summit* GA-3
Dunagan Park—*park* TX-5
*Dunagin Cemetery* TN-4
Dunahay Brake—*swamp* AR-4
**Dunaire**—*pop pl* GA-3
Dunanda Falls—*falls* WY-8
Dunathon Lake—*lake* MI-6
*Dunavan* MS-4
Dunavant—*locale* KS-7
Dunavant—*locale* VA-3
**Dunavant**—*pop pl* AL-4
Dunavant Cem—*cemetery* TN-4
Dunavant Lake—*reservoir* MS-4
Dunaway—*locale* OR-9
Dunaway Branch—*stream* GA-3
Dunaway Branch—*stream* KY-4
Dunaway Cem—*cemetery* AL-4
Dunaway Cem—*cemetery* AR-4
Dunaway Cem—*cemetery* KY-4
Dunaway Cem—*cemetery* (2) MO-7
Dunaway Ch—*church* KY-4
Dunaway Chapel—*church* TN-4
Dunaway Creek—*stream* TN-4
**Dunaway Farms (subdivision)**—*pop pl* AL-4
Dunaway Gap—*gap* GA-3
Dunaway Gardens—*locale* GA-3
Dunaway Hill—*summit* KY-4
Dunaway Hollow—*valley* AR-4
Dunaway Hollow—*valley* MO-7
Dunaway Hollow—*valley* (2) TN-4
Dunaway House—*hist pl* AR-4
Dunaway Island—*island* MN-6
Dunaway Landing (historical)—*locale* TN-4
Dunaway Mtn—*summit* AL-4
Dunaway Oil Field—*oilfield* KS-7
Dunaway Pumping Station—*other* OR-9
Dunaway Ridge—*ridge* TN-4
Dunbar—*locale* AL-4
Dunbar—*locale* AK-9
Dunbar—*locale* IA-7
Dunbar—*locale* KY-4
Dunbar—*locale* MN-6
Dunbar—*locale* NY-2
Dunbar—*locale* OK-5
Dunbar—*locale* TN-4
Dunbar—*locale* UT-8
**Dunbar**—*pop pl* IL-6
**Dunbar**—*pop pl* NE-7
**Dunbar**—*pop pl* OH-6
**Dunbar**—*pop pl* OK-5
**Dunbar**—*pop pl* PA-2
**Dunbar**—*pop pl* (2) SC-3
**Dunbar**—*pop pl* TX-5
**Dunbar**—*pop pl* VA-3
**Dunbar**—*pop pl* WV-2
**Dunbar**—*pop pl* WI-6
Dunbar, C. F., House—*hist pl* WI-6
Dunbar, George, House—*hist pl* AZ-5
Dunbar, Paul Lawrence, House—*hist pl* OH-6
Dunbar, Paul Lawrence, Sch—*hist pl* PA-2
Dunbar, William, House—*hist pl* ID-8
Dunbar Airp—*airport* PA-2
Dunbar Apartments—*hist pl* NY-2
Dunbar Bayou—*stream* MS-4
Dunbar Bluff—*cliff* KY-4
Dunbar Borough—*civil* PA-2
Dunbar Branch—*stream* (2) KY-4
Dunbar Branch—*stream* TN-4
Dunbar Bridge—*bridge* NC-3
Dunbar Brook—*stream* MA-1
Dunbar Brook—*stream* VT-1
Dunbar Brook Dam—*dam* MA-1
Dunbar Brook Rsvr—*reservoir* MA-1
Dunbar Brook Trail—*trail* MA-1
Dunbar Canal—*canal* NC-3
Dunbar Cave—*cave* TN-4
Dunbar Cave—*cave* TX-5
**Dunbar Cave**—*pop pl* TN-4
*Dunbar Cave State Natural Area* TN-4
Dunbar Cave State Park—*park* TN-4
Dunbar Cem—*cemetery* KY-4
Dunbar Cem—*cemetery* ME-1
Dunbar Cem—*cemetery* NE-7
Dunbar Cem—*cemetery* ND-7
Dunbar Cem—*cemetery* WV-2
Dunbar Cem—*cemetery* WI-6
Dunbar Chapel—*church* TN-4
Dunbar Covered Bridge—*bridge* IN-6
Dunbar Creek—*stream* AL-4
Dunbar Creek—*stream* GA-3
Dunbar Creek—*stream* IL-6
Dunbar Creek—*stream* MN-6
Dunbar Creek—*stream* MS-4
Dunbar Creek—*stream* PA-2
Dunbar Creek—*stream* TX-5
Dunbar Creek—*stream* VA-3
Dunbar-Creigh House—*hist pl* PA-2
Dunbar Dam—*dam* CO-8
Dunbar Drain—*canal* MI-6
*Dunbar Draw* TX-5
Dunbar Draw—*valley* TX-5
*Dunbar Elementary School* TN-4
Dunbar Gardens—*uninc pl* VA-3
Dunbar Gulch—*valley* OR-9
Dunbar Heights—*uninc pl* FL-3
Dunbar Hill—*locale* KY-4
Dunbar Hill—*summit* ME-1
Dunbar Hill—*summit* MA-1
Dunbar Hill—*summit* MT-8
Dunbar Hill—*summit* NH-1
Dunbar Hill—*summit* WI-6
Dunbar Hill Sch—*school* CT-1
Dunbar Hist Dist—*hist pl* OH-6
Dunbar (historical)—*locale* ND-7
Dunbar Hollow—*valley* KY-4
Dunbar Hollow—*valley* NY-2
Dunbar Hosp—*hist pl* MI-6
Dunbar HS—*school* (2) AL-4
Dunbar HS—*school* AR-4
Dunbar HS—*school* DC-2
Dunbar HS—*school* IL-6
Dunbar HS—*school* KY-4
Dunbar HS—*school* LA-4
Dunbar HS—*school* NC-3
Dunbar HS—*school* OH-6
Dunbar HS—*school* (5) TX-5
Dunbar HS—*school* VA-3
Dunbar Inlet—*bay* AK-9
*Dunbar Intermediate Sch* NC-3
*Dunbar JHS* AL-4
Dunbar JHS—*school* AR-4
Dunbar Junior and Senior HS and Junior
College—*hist pl* AR-4
Dunbar Junior High—*school* TX-5
Dunbar Junior-Senior High—*school* MD-2
Dunbar Lake—*lake* (2) MN-6
Dunbar Lake—*reservoir* TN-4
Dunbar Landing—*locale* SC-3
Dunbar Lookout Tower—*locale* WI-6
Dunbar Mine—*mine* AZ-5
Dunbar MS—*school* FL-3
Dunbar Mtn—*summit* GA-3
Dunbar Mtn—*summit* OK-5
Dunbar Park—*park* AL-4
Dunbar Park—*park* FL-3
Dunbar Park—*park* MI-6
Dunbar Park—*park* OK-5
Dunbar Park—*park* TX-5
Dunbar Plantation (historical)—*locale* MS-4
Dunbar Point—*cape* MA-1
*Dunbar Pond* CT-1
Dunbar Pond—*lake* NY-2
Dunbar Pond—*reservoir* AL-4
Dunbar Pond—*reservoir* SC-3
Dunbar Post Office (historical)—*building* TN-4
Dunbar-Pulaski MS—*school* IN-6
Dunbar Ranch—*locale* SD-7
Dunbar Riffle—*rapids* OR-9
Dunbar River—*stream* MN-6
Dunbar Sch—*hist pl* OK-5
Dunbar Sch—*school* AL-4
Dunbar Sch—*school* AZ-5
Dunbar Sch—*school* (3) FL-3
Dunbar Sch—*school* GA-3
Dunbar Sch—*school* IN-6
Dunbar Sch—*school* (3) KS-7
Dunbar Sch—*school* KY-4
Dunbar Sch—*school* LA-4
Dunbar Sch—*school* MA-1
Dunbar Sch—*school* (3) MO-7
Dunbar Sch—*school* NM-5
Dunbar Sch—*school* (3) NC-3
Dunbar Sch—*school* OH-6
Dunbar Sch—*school* (5) OK-5
Dunbar Sch—*school* (2) TN-4
Dunbar Sch—*school* (10) TX-5
Dunbar Sch—*school* VA-3
Dunbar Sch—*school* (2) WV-2
Dunbar Sch (historical)—*school* MO-7
Dunbar Sch (historical)—*school* TN-4
Dunbar School (Abandoned)—*locale* OK-5
Dunbar Shop Ctr—*locale* MA-1
Dunbars Landing—*locale* NC-3
Dunbars Landing (historical)—*locale* TN-4
Dunbar Slough—*gut* IA-7
Dunbar Slough State Wildlife Mngmt
Area—*park* IA-7
Dunbar Spring—*spring* MT-8
Dunbar Springs—*spring* MT-8
Dunbar Store—*locale* SC-3
Dunbar Tank—*reservoir* AZ-5
Dunbar Tank—*reservoir* TX-5
*Dunbarton* NH-1
Dunbarton—*locale* NJ-2
**Dunbarton**—*pop pl* LA-4
**Dunbarton**—*pop pl* SC-3
**Dunbarton**—*pop pl* WI-6
Dunbarton Cem—*cemetery* MS-4
**Dunbarton Center**—*pop pl* NH-1
**Dunbarton Centre**—*pop pl* NH-1
Dunbarton Coll—*school* DC-2
*Dunbarton (Dunbarton Centre)* NH-1
Dunbarton Landing (historical)—*locale* MS-4
**Dunbarton Oaks Apartments**—*pop pl* DE-2
Dunbarton Sch—*school* WI-6
**Dunbarton (Town of)**—*pop pl* NH-1
Dunbar Town Hall—*building* ND-7
**Dunbar (Town of)**—*pop pl* WI-6
**Dunbar Township**—*pop pl* ND-7
**Dunbar (Township of)**—*pop pl* MN-6
**Dunbar (Township of)**—*pop pl* PA-2
Dunbar Trail—*trail* PA-2
Dunbar Union Sch—*school* CA-9
**Dunbridge**—*pop pl* OH-6
Dunbrill Creek—*stream* WY-8
**Dunbrook**—*pop pl* MD-2
Dun Brook—*stream* NY-2
Dunbrooke—*locale* VA-3
Dun Brook Mtn—*summit* NY-2
**Dunbrook (subdivision)**—*pop pl* AL-4
Dunbury (historical P.O.)—*locale* MA-1
*Duncan* AL-4
*Duncan* MI-6
Duncan—*locale* AR-4
Duncan—*locale* CO-8
Duncan—*locale* KY-4
Duncan—*locale* MO-7
Duncan—*locale* OR-9
Duncan—*locale* PA-2
Duncan—*locale* TN-4
Duncan—*locale* VA-3
Duncan—*locale* WA-9
Duncan—*locale* WV-2
**Duncan**—*pop pl* (2) AL-4
**Duncan**—*pop pl* AZ-5
**Duncan**—*pop pl* (2) IL-6
**Duncan**—*pop pl* IN-6
**Duncan**—*pop pl* IA-7
**Duncan**—*pop pl* KY-4
**Duncan**—*pop pl* MI-6
**Duncan**—*pop pl* MS-4
**Duncan**—*pop pl* NE-7
**Duncan**—*pop pl* NC-3
**Duncan**—*pop pl* OK-5
**Duncan**—*pop pl* SC-3
**Duncan**—*pop pl* WY-8
Duncan, Bishop William Wallace,
House—*hist pl* SC-3
Duncan, Charles, House—*hist pl* KS-7
Duncan, Father William, House—*hist pl* AK-9
Duncan, John M., House—*hist pl* IA-7
Duncan, Joseph, House—*hist pl* IL-6
Duncan, J. W., House—*hist pl* KY-4
Duncan, Lake—*reservoir* OK-5
Duncan and Coans Mine
(underground)—*mine* TN-4
Duncan Ave Hist Dist—*hist pl* KY-4
Duncan Bald—*ridge* GA-3
Duncan Bar—*bar* AL-4
Duncan Bay—*bay* (2) MI-6
Duncan Bay Campground—*locale* MI-6
Duncan Bay Narrows Campground—*locale* MI-6
Duncan Bluff—*cliff* KY-4
Duncan Brake—*woods* AR-4
*Duncan Branch* MS-4
*Duncan Branch* TN-4
*Duncan Branch* TX-5
Duncan Branch—*stream* (3) AL-4
Duncan Branch—*stream* AR-4
Duncan Branch—*stream* IN-6
Duncan Branch—*stream* (2) KY-4
Duncan Branch—*stream* MS-4
Duncan Branch—*stream* (3) MO-7
Duncan Branch—*stream* NC-3
Duncan Branch—*stream* (6) TN-4
Duncan Branch—*stream* (2) VA-3
Duncan Branch—*stream* WV-2
Duncan Bridge—*bridge* GA-3
Duncan Butte—*summit* OR-9
Duncan Canal—*canal* (2) LA-4
Duncan Canal—*channel* AK-9
**Duncan Canal**—*pop pl* AK-9
Duncan Canal Portage—*trail* AK-9
Duncan Canyon—*valley* (5) CA-9
Duncan Canyon—*valley* NM-5
Duncan Canyon—*valley* (2) OR-9
Duncan Canyon—*valley* (2) UT-8
Duncan Canyon Trail—*trail* UT-8
Duncan Cave—*cave* AL-4
Duncan Cave—*cave* TN-4
Duncan (CCD)—*cens area* AZ-5
Duncan (CCD)—*cens area* OK-5
*Duncan Cem* TN-4
Duncan Cem—*cemetery* (2) AL-4
Duncan Cem—*cemetery* AZ-5
Duncan Cem—*cemetery* (4) AR-4
Duncan Cem—*cemetery* (3) GA-3
Duncan Cem—*cemetery* (4) IL-6
Duncan Cem—*cemetery* (2) IN-6
Duncan Cem—*cemetery* IA-7
Duncan Cem—*cemetery* (6) KY-4
Duncan Cem—*cemetery* LA-4
Duncan Cem—*cemetery* MI-6
Duncan Cem—*cemetery* (7) MS-4
Duncan Cem—*cemetery* (5) MO-7
Duncan Cem—*cemetery* OH-6
Duncan Cem—*cemetery* (3) OK-5
Duncan Cem—*cemetery* PA-2
Duncan Cem—*cemetery* (13) TN-4
Duncan Cem—*cemetery* TX-5
Duncan Cem—*cemetery* (2) VA-3
Duncan Cem—*cemetery* WV-2
*Duncan Ch* AL-4
Duncan Ch—*church* AL-4
Duncan Ch—*church* IN-6
Duncan Ch—*church* OH-6
Duncan Ch—*church* SD-7
Duncan Chapel—*church* AL-4
Duncan Chapel—*church* KY-4
Duncan Chapel—*church* MS-4
Duncan Chapel—*church* (2) TN-4
*Duncan Chapel Baptist Ch* TN-4
Duncan Chapel Ch—*church* VA-3
Duncan Community Center—*building* AL-4
Duncan Community Center—*locale* TX-5
Duncan Corral—*locale* CA-9
Duncan Coulee—*valley* MT-8
*Duncan Creek* AL-4
*Duncan Creek* GA-3
*Duncan Creek* MS-4
*Duncan Creek* MO-7
Duncan Creek—*stream* (3) AL-4
Duncan Creek—*stream* (3) AK-9
Duncan Creek—*stream* (5) CA-9
Duncan Creek—*stream* CO-8
Duncan Creek—*stream* (2) GA-3
Duncan Creek—*stream* ID-8
Duncan Creek—*stream* KS-7
Duncan Creek—*stream* (3) KY-4
Duncan Creek—*stream* MI-6
Duncan Creek—*stream* MS-4
Duncan Creek—*stream* (3) MO-7
Duncan Creek—*stream* (2) MT-8
Duncan Creek—*stream* (2) NC-3
Duncan Creek—*stream* (4) OR-9
Duncan Creek—*stream* (3) SC-3

**Dunkled Estates**—*pop pl* TN-4
Dunklee Pond—*lake* NH-1
Dunklee Pond—*lake* VT-1
Dunkle Hollow—*valley* VA-3
Dunkle Knob—*summit* WV-2
Dunkle Mine—*locale* AK-9
Dunkle Ranch—*locale* WY-8
Dunkle Run—*stream* OH-6
Dunkle Run—*stream* PA-2
Dunkle Sch—*school* IL-6
Dunkle Sch—*school* PA-2
Dunkle Trail—*trail* PA-2
*Dunkley and Sellers Reservoir* CO-8
*Dunkley Flat Tops* CO-8
Dunklin, James, House—*hist pl* SC-3
Dunklin, William A., House—*hist pl* MS-4
*Dunklin Cem* AL-4
Dunklin Cem—*cemetery* AL-4
**Dunklin County**—*pop pl* MO-7
Dunklin County Cut-off—*bend* MO-7
Dunklin Memorial Camp—*locale* FL-3
Dunk Pond—*lake* NY-2
Dunks Bar—*bar* NJ-2
**Dunksburg**—*pop pl* MO-7
*Dunks Ferry* NJ-2
Dunks Island—*island* CT-1
Dunks Point—*cape* NJ-2
*Dunksville* PA-2
Dunkwaden Flats—*flat* MT-8
Dunlan Cem—*cemetery* TN-4
**Dunlaney Village**—*pop pl* MD-2
*Dunlap* AZ-5
*Dunlap* TX-5
Dunlap—*locale* AR-4
Dunlap—*locale* GA-3
Dunlap—*locale* KY-4
Dunlap—*locale* NM-5
Dunlap—*locale* (2) PA-2
Dunlap—*locale* (2) TX-5
**Dunlap**—*pop pl* CA-9
**Dunlap**—*pop pl* IL-6
**Dunlap**—*pop pl* IN-6
**Dunlap**—*pop pl* IA-7
**Dunlap**—*pop pl* KS-7
**Dunlap**—*pop pl* MO-7
**Dunlap**—*pop pl* MT-8
**Dunlap**—*pop pl* OH-6
**Dunlap**—*pop pl* OK-5
**Dunlap**—*pop pl* TN-4
**Dunlap**—*pop pl* WA-9
Dunlap, Charles H., House—*hist pl* AZ-5
Dunlap, John, House—*hist pl* ME-1
Dunlap, Lake—*reservoir* TX-5
Dunlap, Thomas, Sch—*hist pl* PA-2
Dunlap, William B., Mansion—*hist pl* PA-2
Dunlap, William K., House—*hist pl* OH-6
**Dunlap Acres**—*pop pl* CA-9
Dunlap Archeol District—*hist pl* OH-6
*Dunlap Baptist Church* TN-4
Dunlap Beach—*beach* VA-3
*Dunlap Branch* TN-4
Dunlap Branch—*stream* MS-4
Dunlap Branch—*stream* (2) TN-4
Dunlap Branch—*stream* TX-5
Dunlap Branch—*stream* WV-2
Dunlap Bridge—*bridge* NC-3
*Dunlap Butte* WA-9
Dunlap Camp Tank—*reservoir* NM-5
Dunlap Canyon—*valley* NV-8
Dunlap Canyon—*valley* OR-9
Dunlap Cave—*cave* AL-4
Dunlap (CCD)—*cens area* TN-4
Dunlap Cem—*cemetery* AL-4
Dunlap Cem—*cemetery* GA-3
Dunlap Cem—*cemetery* (2) KS-7
Dunlap Cem—*cemetery* KY-4
Dunlap Cem—*cemetery* (2) MS-4
Dunlap Cem—*cemetery* MO-7
Dunlap Cem—*cemetery* OK-5
Dunlap Cem—*cemetery* (2) TN-4
Dunlap Cem—*cemetery* TX-5
Dunlap Cem—*cemetery* WI-6
Dunlap Ch—*church* IL-6
Dunlap Ch—*church* OH-6
Dunlap Ch—*church* SD-7
Dunlap Chapel—*church* WV-2
Dunlap City Hall—*building* TN-4
Dunlap Coke Ovens—*hist pl* TN-4
Dunlap Cove—*valley* AL-4
Dunlap Creek—*stream* AL-4
Dunlap Creek—*stream* KS-7
Dunlap Creek—*stream* MO-7
Dunlap Creek—*stream* (2) MT-8
Dunlap Creek—*stream* NE-7
Dunlap Creek—*stream* (3) OH-6
Dunlap Creek—*stream* (3) OR-9
Dunlap Creek—*stream* (2) PA-2
Dunlap Creek—*stream* (2) TN-4
Dunlap Creek—*stream* VA-3
Dunlap Creek—*stream* WI-6
Dunlap Creek Ch—*church* PA-2
**Dunlap Creek Junction**—*pop pl* PA-2
**Dunlap Creek Village**—*pop pl* PA-2
Dunlap Creek Watershed Rsvr—*reservoir* PA-2
Dunlap Creek Watershed Site Dam—*dam* PA-2
Dunlap Ditch—*canal* WY-8
Dunlap Division—*civil* TN-4
Dunlap Drain—*canal* MI-6
Dunlap Drain—*stream* MI-6
Dunlape Crossroads—*locale* SC-3
Dunlap Gulch—*valley* (2) CA-9
Dunlap Gulch—*valley* CO-8
Dunlap Hill—*summit* KY-4
Dunlap Hill—*summit* TX-5
Dunlap (historical)—*locale* SD-7
**Dunlap (historical)**—*pop pl* TN-4
*Dunlap Hollow* WI-6
Dunlap Hollow—*valley* KY-4
Dunlap Hollow—*valley* (2) TN-4
Dunlap Hollow—*valley* VA-3
Dunlap Hollow Creek—*stream* TN-4
Dunlap House—*hist pl* AR-4
Dunlap Island—*island* MN-6
*Dunlap Lake* NJ-2
Dunlap Lake—*lake* OR-9
Dunlap Lake—*lake* TX-5
**Dunlap Lake**—*pop pl* IL-6
Dunlap Lake—*reservoir* AL-4
Dunlap Lake—*reservoir* IL-6
Dunlap Landing (historical)—*locale* AL-4
Dunlap Meadow—*flat* CA-9
Dunlap Mine—*mine* AZ-5
Dunlap Mine—*mine* NV-8
Dunlap Oil Field—*oilfield* NE-7
Dunlap Oil Field—*oilfield* TX-5
*Dunlap Orphanage* TN-4
Dunlap Orphanage—*building* TN-4
Dunlap Pass—*gap* CA-9
Dunlap Place—*locale* CA-9
Dunlap Pond—*lake* NJ-2
Dunlap Pond—*reservoir* MA-1
Dunlap Pond Dam—*dam* MA-1
Dunlap Pond Dam—*dam* MS-4
Dunlap Post Office—*building* TN-4
Dunlap Ranch—*locale* (2) CO-8
Dunlap Ranch—*locale* NM-5
Dunlap Ranch—*locale* TX-5
Dunlap Reef—*bar* WI-6
Dunlap Run—*stream* OH-6
Dunlap Run—*stream* PA-2
*Dunlaps* IN-6
Dunlaps Cave Number One—*cave* TN-4
Dunlap Sch—*school* CA-9
Dunlap Sch—*school* GA-3
Dunlap Sch—*school* IL-6
Dunlap Sch—*school* IA-7
Dunlap Sch—*school* NE-7
Dunlap Sch (historical)—*school* (2) TN-4
*Dunlaps Creek* PA-2
Dunlap's Creek Bridge—*hist pl* PA-2
Dunlap Sill—*cliff* NM-5
*Dunlap's Island* MN-6
Dunlaps Lake—*reservoir* AL-4
Dunlap Spring—*spring* AL-4
Dunlap Spring—*spring* WA-9
Dunlap Spring Branch—*stream* AL-4
Dunlaps Slope Mine (underground)—*mine* AL-4
**Dunlapsville**—*pop pl* IN-6
Dunlapsville Causeway—*other* IN-6
Dunlap Tank—*reservoir* NM-5
Dunlap Tunnel Spring—*spring* NV-8
Dunlap Valley—*basin* NE-7
Dunlap Village Shop Ctr—*locale* AZ-5
Dunlavy Park—*park* TX-5
Dunlavy Ridge—*ridge* WV-2
Dunlawton (historical)—*locale* FL-3
Dunlawton Plantation-Sugar Mill Ruins—*hist pl* FL-3
Dunlawton Square (Shop Ctr)—*locale* FL-3
Dunlay—*locale* KS-7
**Dunlay**—*pop pl* TX-5
Dunlea Airpark—*airport* PA-2
Dunleary—*locale* KY-4
Dunleary Hollow—*valley* KY-4
Dunleavey Brook—*stream* MA-1
Dunleavey Pond—*reservoir* MA-1
Dunleith—*hist pl* MS-4
**Dunleith**—*pop pl* DE-2
**Dunleith**—*pop pl* MS-4
**Dunleith (Township of)**—*pop pl* IL-6
**Dunlevy**—*pop pl* PA-2
Dunlevy Bay—*bay* MI-6
Dunlevy Borough—*civil* PA-2
**Dunley**—*pop pl* KY-4
**Dunlinden Acres**—*pop pl* DE-2
Dunlin Lake—*lake* AK-9
**Dunlo**—*pop pl* PA-2
**Dunloggin**—*pop pl* MD-2
*Dunloop* WV-2
*Dunloop Creek* WV-2
Dunlop—*locale* VA-3
Dunlop, Mount—*summit* PA-2
Dunlop Brook—*stream* MA-1
Dunlop Hollow—*valley* OH-6
Dunlop Hollow—*valley* WV-2
Dunlop Lake—*lake* MI-6
**Dunlops Hills**—*pop pl* MD-2
*Dun Loup* WV-2
Dunloup—*locale* WV-2
*Dun Loup Creek* WV-2
Dunloup Creek—*stream* WV-2
Dunlovy Sch—*school* OH-6
**Dunlow**—*pop pl* WV-2
Dunman Creek—*stream* TX-5
Dunman Mtn—*summit* TX-5
**Dunminning**—*pop pl* PA-2
Dunmire Hollow—*valley* TN-4
Dunmire Ridge—*ridge* PA-2
Dunmon Sch—*school* NY-2
Dunmont Dunes—*summit* CA-9
**Dunmoor**—*pop pl* NM-5
**Dunmor**—*pop pl* KY-4
Dunmore—*locale* MT-8
**Dunmore**—*pop pl* PA-2
**Dunmore**—*pop pl* WV-2
Dunmore, Lake—*lake* VT-1
Dunmore Borough—*civil* PA-2
Dunmore Cem—*cemetery* LA-4
Dunmore Cem—*cemetery* PA-2
Dunmore Elem Sch—*school* PA-2
Dunmore Hill—*summit* NY-2
Dunmore HS—*school* PA-2
Dunmore Number One Dam—*dam* PA-2
*Dunmore Number One Reservoir* PA-2
Dunmore Number Three Dam—*dam* PA-2
*Dunmore Number Three Reservoir* PA-2
Dunmore Ridge—*ridge* WV-2
Dunmore Rsvr Number Four—*reservoir* PA-2
Dunmore Rsvr Number One—*reservoir* PA-2
Dunmore Rsvr Number Three—*reservoir* PA-2
*Dunmore Water Company Rsvr* PA-2
**Dunmovin**—*pop pl* CA-9
Dunmyer Cem—*cemetery* PA-2
*Dunn* GA-3
*Dunn* ND-7
*Dunn* UT-8
Dunn—*locale* CA-9
Dunn—*locale* GA-3
Dunn—*locale* IL-6
Dunn—*locale* PA-2
**Dunn**—*pop pl* AL-4
**Dunn**—*pop pl* AR-4
**Dunn**—*pop pl* IN-6
**Dunn**—*pop pl* LA-4
**Dunn**—*pop pl* MO-7
**Dunn**—*pop pl* NC-3
**Dunn**—*pop pl* TN-4
**Dunn**—*pop pl* TX-5
Dunn, Andrew C., House—*hist pl* MN-6
Dunn, Nathaniel, House—*hist pl* KY-4
Dunn, Patrick, Ranch—*hist pl* OR-9
Dunn, Robert C., House—*hist pl* MN-6
Dunn, Zaccheus, House—*hist pl* NJ-2
Dunnagan Branch—*stream* TX-5
Dunnagan Cem—*cemetery* TN-4
Dunnagin Creek—*stream* MS-4
Dunnahoo Hills—*area* NM-5
Dunn Airstrip—*airport* SD-7
**Dunnam**—*pop pl* TX-5
Dunnam Field—*flat* MS-4
Dunnam Sch (historical)—*school* MS-4
Dunnan—*uninc pl* TX-5
*Dunnavant* AL-4
Dunnavant Cem—*cemetery* TN-4
Dunnavant Community Cem—*cemetery* AL-4
Dunnavant Creek—*stream* VA-3
Dunnavant Faith Chapel—*church* AL-4
Dunnavant's Bldg—*hist pl* AL-4
Dunnavants Mall Shop Ctr—*locale* AL-4
Dunn Ave—*post sta* FL-3
Dunn Ave Sch—*school* TN-4
Dunnaway Canyon—*valley* NM-5
Dunnaway Creek—*stream* IN-6
Dunnaway Draw—*valley* NM-5
Dunnaway Lake Dam—*dam* NC-3
Dunnaway Pond—*reservoir* NC-3
Dunnaway Tank—*reservoir* NM-5
Dunn Bay—*bay* NY-2
Dunn Bayou—*gut* TX-5
Dunn Branch—*stream* (2) AL-4
Dunn Branch—*stream* FL-3
Dunn Branch—*stream* (2) GA-3
Dunn Branch—*stream* IL-6
Dunn Branch—*stream* ME-1
Dunn Branch—*stream* TN-4
Dunn Branch—*stream* TX-5
Dunn Bridge—*other* NM-5
Dunn Brook—*locale* NY-2
Dunn Brook—*stream* (3) ME-1
Dunn Brook—*stream* (2) MA-1
Dunn Brook—*stream* (2) NY-2
Dunn Brook—*stream* VT-1
Dunn Butte—*summit* AZ-5
Dunn Camp—*locale* ME-1
Dunn Canal—*canal* UT-8
*Dunn Canyon* NM-5
Dunn Canyon—*valley* (2) CA-9
Dunn Canyon—*valley* MT-8
Dunn Canyon—*valley* NV-8
Dunn Canyon—*valley* WA-9
Dunn Cem—*cemetery* (2) AL-4
Dunn Cem—*cemetery* (4) AR-4
Dunn Cem—*cemetery* IL-6
Dunn Cem—*cemetery* (2) IN-6
Dunn Cem—*cemetery* (6) KY-4
Dunn Cem—*cemetery* ME-1
Dunn Cem—*cemetery* (3) MS-4
Dunn Cem—*cemetery* MO-7
Dunn Cem—*cemetery* OH-6
Dunn Cem—*cemetery* PA-2
Dunn Cem—*cemetery* (12) TN-4
Dunn Cem—*cemetery* TX-5
Dunn Cem—*cemetery* VA-3
Dunn Cem—*cemetery* WV-2
**Dunn Center**—*pop pl* ND-7
Dunn Center Cem—*cemetery* ND-7
*Dunn Center Dam* ND-7
Dunn Ch—*church* KY-4
Dunn Ch—*church* TN-4
Dunn Chapel—*church* GA-3
Dunn Chapel—*church* OH-6
**Dunn Corner**—*pop pl* RI-1
*Dunn Corners* ME-1
Dunn County—*civil* ND-7
**Dunn (County)**—*pop pl* WI-6
Dunn County Courthouse—*hist pl* ND-7
*Dunn Creek* AR-4
*Dunn Creek* WA-9
**Dunn Creek**—*pop pl* FL-3
Dunn Creek—*stream* AL-4
Dunn Creek—*stream* (3) AR-4
Dunn Creek—*stream* (3) CA-9
Dunn Creek—*stream* (2) FL-3
Dunn Creek—*stream* GA-3
Dunn Creek—*stream* KY-4
Dunn Creek—*stream* LA-4
Dunn Creek—*stream* MD-2
Dunn Creek—*stream* (2) MI-6
Dunn Creek—*stream* (2) MS-4
Dunn Creek—*stream* (3) MT-8
Dunn Creek—*stream* NC-3
Dunn Creek—*stream* (2) OR-9
Dunn Creek—*stream* (2) SC-3
Dunn Creek—*stream* TN-4
Dunn Creek—*stream* (4) TX-5
Dunn Creek—*stream* (4) WA-9
Dunn Creek—*stream* WI-6
Dunn Creek—*stream* (2) WY-8
Dunn Creek (CCD)—*cens area* TN-4
Dunn Creek Cem—*cemetery* FL-3
Dunn Creek Ch—*church* AL-4
Dunn Creek Division—*civil* TN-4
Dunn Creek Park—*park* FL-3
**Dunn Crossroads**—*pop pl* NC-3
Dunn Dam—*dam* OR-9
Dunn Ditch—*canal* CO-8
Dunn Ditch—*canal* (2) IN-6
Dunn Ditch—*canal* WY-8
Dunn Drain—*stream* (2) MI-6
Dunn Draw—*valley* SD-7
**Dunn (Dunns Station)**—*pop pl* PA-2
Dunnean—*locale* OR-9
Dunnebacke Park—*park* MI-6
Dunn Eden Lake—*lake* OH-6
**Dunnegan**—*pop pl* MO-7
Dunnegan Cem—*cemetery* MO-7
Dunnegan Grove Ch—*church* MO-7
Dunnegan Park—*park* MO-7
Dunnegan Spring—*spring* MO-7
**Dunnell**—*pop pl* MN-6
**Dunnellon**—*pop pl* FL-3
*Dunnellon Backwater* FL-3
Dunnellon Boomtown Hist Dist—*hist pl* FL-3
Dunnellon (CCD)—*cens area* FL-3
Dunnellon Christian Sch—*school* FL-3
Dunnellon Elem Sch—*school* FL-3
Dunnellon HS—*school* FL-3
Dunnellon Lookout Tower—*tower* FL-3
Dunnellon Memorial Gardens—*cemetery* FL-3
Dunnellon MS—*school* FL-3
Dunnellon Plaza (Shop Ctr)—*locale* FL-3
Dunne Memorial Park—*park* CA-9
Dunne Ridge—*ridge* CA-9
Dunners Mtn—*summit* TX-5
Dunne Sch—*school* (2) IL-6
**Dunneville**—*pop pl* CA-9
**Dunneville Corners**—*pop pl* CA-9
**Dunnfield**—*pop pl* NJ-2
Dunnfield Creek—*stream* NJ-2
Dunn Gap—*gap* GA-3
Dunn Gap—*gap* TN-4
Dunn-Hefner Cem—*cemetery* MS-4
Dunn Hill—*summit* NY-2
Dunn Hollow—*valley* KY-4
Dunn Hollow—*valley* (4) TN-4
Dunn Hollow—*valley* WV-2
Dunn House—*hist pl* AR-4
Dunnie Branch—*stream* KY-4
Dunnie Burnout—*area* TX-5
**Dunnigan**—*pop pl* CA-9
Dunnigan Ch—*church* TX-5
Dunnigan Chapel—*church* MS-4
Dunnigan Coulee—*valley* WA-9
Dunnigan Creek—*stream* CA-9
Dunnigan Creek—*stream* ID-8
Dunnigan Gulch—*valley* MT-8
Dunnigan Hill—*summit* CA-9
Dunnigan Hills—*range* CA-9
*Dunnigan Hills Gas Field* CA-9
Dunnigan Lake—*lake* MN-6
*Dunnigan Mountain* WA-9
Dunnigan Spring—*spring* OR-9
Dunnihoes Cave—*cave* IN-6
*Dunning* IL-6
Dunning—*locale* PA-2
**Dunning**—*pop pl* IL-6
**Dunning**—*pop pl* NE-7
**Dunning**—*pop pl* ND-7
Dunning-Benedict House—*hist pl* CO-8
Dunning Brook—*stream* (2) ME-1
Dunning Cem—*cemetery* AL-4
Dunning Cem—*cemetery* (4) KY-4
Dunning Cem—*cemetery* (3) MO-7
Dunning Cove—*basin* PA-2
Dunning Creek—*stream* CO-8
Dunning Creek—*stream* NY-2
Dunning Creek—*stream* (2) OR-9
Dunning Creek—*stream* PA-2
Dunning Creek Ch—*church* PA-2
Dunning Field—*park* MN-6
Dunning Hill—*summit* KY-4
Dunning Lake—*lake* MN-6
Dunning Lake—*lake* WA-9
Dunning Mtn—*summit* PA-2
Dunning Point—*cape* NH-1
Dunning Pond—*lake* NY-2
Dunning Ranch—*locale* CO-8
Dunning Rsvr—*reservoir* (2) MT-8
*Dunnings* PA-2
Dunning Sch—*school* MA-1
**Dunnings Creek Junction**—*pop pl* PA-2
Dunning Slough—*gut* CA-9
Dunnings Pond—*reservoir* AL-4
Dunning Spring—*spring* MT-8
Dunning Street Cem—*cemetery* NY-2
**Dunningsville**—*pop pl* PA-2
Dunnington—*locale* AR-4
**Dunnington**—*pop pl* IN-6
Dunnington Post Office (historical)—*building* TN-4
Dunnington (Township of)—*fmr MCD* AR-4
**Dunningtown**—*pop pl* PA-2
Dunningville—*locale* MI-6
Dunn Island—*island* KY-4
Dunn Island—*island* ME-1
Dunn Island—*island* MN-6
*Dunn Lake* FL-3
*Dunn Lake* OR-9
Dunn Lake—*lake* (2) AL-4
Dunn Lake—*lake* LA-4
Dunn Lake—*lake* (2) MI-6
Dunn Lake—*lake* MN-6
Dunn Lake—*lake* TX-5
Dunn Lake—*lake* (2) WI-6
Dunn Lake—*lake* WY-8
Dunn Lake—*swamp* AR-4
Dunn Lakes—*lake* MI-6
Dunn Lakes—*reservoir* SC-3
Dunn Landing—*locale* RI-1
Dunn Ledge—*summit* ME-1
**Dunn Location**—*pop pl* MI-6
**Dunn Loring**—*pop pl* VA-3
Dunn Loring Sch—*school* VA-3
**Dunn Loring Woods**—*pop pl* VA-3
Dunn Memorial Ch—*church* TX-5
Dunn Memorial Hosp—*hospital* IN-6
*Dunn Methodist Church* TN-4
**Dunn Mill**—*pop pl* IN-6
*Dunn Mill Creek* GA-3
Dunn Mine (underground)—*mine* AL-4
Dunn Mountain Ch—*church* NC-3
Dunn MS—*school* NC-3
Dunn Mtn—*summit* MT-8
Dunn Mtn—*summit* NC-3
Dunn Mtn—*summit* VT-1
Dunn Mtn—*summit* (2) WA-9
Dunn Notch—*gap* ME-1
Dunnock Island—*island* MD-2
Dunnock Island Creek—*channel* MD-2
Dunnock Slough—*stream* MD-2
Dunno Creek—*stream* OR-9
Dunnovants Ferry (historical)—*locale* MS-4
Dunn Park—*park* MO-7
Dunn Park—*park* NY-2
*Dunn Peak* CA-9
*Dunn Peak* CO-8
Dunn Peak—*summit* CO-8
Dunn Peak—*summit* ID-8
Dunn Peak—*summit* MT-8
Dunn Peak Trail (historical)—*trail* ID-8
Dunn Pit—*cave* TN-4
Dunn Place—*locale* (2) NM-5
Dunn Plaza (Shop Ctr)—*locale* NC-3
*Dunn Point* ME-1
*Dunn Point* MT-8
Dunn Pond—*lake* PA-2
Dunn Pond—*reservoir* MA-1
Dunn Pond—*reservoir* SC-3
Dunn Pond Dam—*dam* MA-1
Dunn Post Office (historical)—*building* TN-4
Dunn Prairie—*area* CA-9
Dunn-Raley Cem—*cemetery* FL-3
Dunn Ranch—*locale* MT-8
Dunn Ranch—*locale* (2) OR-9
Dunn Ranch—*locale* SD-7
Dunn Ranch—*locale* (2) WY-8
Dunn Ranch, Novillo Line Camp—*hist pl* TX-5
Dunn Ridge—*ridge* (2) CA-9
Dunn Ridge—*ridge* TN-4
Dunn Riffle—*rapids* OR-9
Dunn Road Dam—*dam* SD-7
**Dunn (RR name Dunns)**—*pop pl* LA-4
Dunn Rsvr—*reservoir* CA-9
Dunn Rsvr—*reservoir* WY-8
Dunn Run—*stream* (2) PA-2
*Dunn's* ME-1
Dunns—*locale* AL-4
Dunns—*locale* ME-1
Dunns—*locale* WV-2
**Dunns**—*pop pl* WV-2
**Dunns Addition (subdivision)**—*pop pl* UT-8
Dunns Bend—*bend* AL-4
Dunns Block—*hist pl* CA-9
Dunns Bluff—*cliff* OR-9
Dunns Branch—*stream* AL-4
Dunns Bridge—*bridge* AL-4
**Dunns Bridge**—*pop pl* IN-6
Dunns Camp—*locale* AL-4
Dunns Camp Hollow—*valley* KY-4
Dunns Canyon—*valley* ID-8
Dunns Canyon—*valley* TX-5
Dunns Canyon—*valley* UT-8
Dunns Cem—*cemetery* ME-1
Dunn Sch—*school* (2) CA-9
Dunn Sch—*school* CO-8
Dunn Sch—*school* (2) IL-6
Dunn Sch—*school* LA-4
Dunn Sch—*school* MI-6
Dunn Sch—*school* OR-9
Dunn Sch—*school* SD-7
Dunn Sch—*school* WY-8
Dunn Sch (abandoned)—*school* MO-7
Dunns Chapel—*church* SC-3
Dunns Chapel—*church* TN-4
Dunns Chapel—*church* VA-3
Dunn Sch (historical)—*school* AL-4
Dunn Sch (historical)—*school* PA-2
Dunn Sch (historical)—*school* TN-4
Dunn School—*locale* MI-6
Dunn School (historical)—*locale* MO-7
*Dunns Corner* RI-1
Dunns Corner—*locale* ME-1
Dunns Corner—*locale* VA-3
**Dunns Corners**—*pop pl* RI-1
*Dunns Creek* AL-4
*Dunns Creek* FL-3
*Dunns Creek* ND-7
Dunns Creek—*stream* AL-4
Dunns Creek—*stream* FL-3
Dunns Creek—*stream* IA-7
Dunns Creek—*stream* (2) NC-3
Dunns Creek—*stream* SC-3
Dunns Creek Cem—*cemetery* AL-4
Dunns Creek Cem—*cemetery* SC-3
Dunns Creek Ch—*church* FL-3
Dunns Creek Ch—*church* NC-3
Dunns Creek Ch—*church* SC-3
*Dunns Creek Church* AL-4
*Dunns Creek Missionary Baptist Church* AL-4
Dunns Creek Sch (historical)—*school* AL-4
Dunns Draw—*valley* MT-8
**Dunns Eddy**—*pop pl* PA-2
Dunns Falls—*falls* MS-4
Dunns Fishery—*locale* NC-3
Dunns Fishery (historical)—*locale* NC-3
Dunns Fort—*locale* TX-5
Dunns Gap—*gap* PA-2
Dunns Gap—*gap* VA-3
Dunns Grove Ch—*church* NC-3
Dunns Gulch—*stream* CA-9
Dunns Hollow—*valley* UT-8
*Dunns Island* ME-1
*Dunns Lake* FL-3
*Dunns Lake* PA-2
Dunns Lake—*lake* GA-3
Dunns Lake—*lake* IL-6
Dunns Lake—*lake* LA-4
Dunns Lake—*lake* MN-6
Dunns Lake—*reservoir* GA-3
*Dunns Landing* RI-1
Dunns Landing—*locale* MS-4
Dunn Slough Creek—*stream* KY-4
Dunns Marsh—*stream* NC-3
*Dunns Mill Creek* AL-4
**Dunns Mills**—*pop pl* NJ-2
Dunns Mount—*summit* SC-3
Dunns Mtn—*summit* WA-9
Dunn Sound—*bay* SC-3
Dunn Sound Creek—*gut* SC-3
*Dunns Peak* CO-8
Dunns Peak—*summit* CA-9
*Dunns Point* MA-1
*Dunns Pond* MA-1
Dunns Pond—*lake* MA-1
Dunns Pond—*reservoir* OH-6
Dunns Pond Mound—*hist pl* OH-6
Dunn Spring—*spring* AZ-5
Dunn Spring—*spring* KY-4
Dunn Spring—*spring* TN-4
Dunn Spring Cem—*cemetery* KY-4
Dunn Spring Ch—*church* KY-4
Dunn Spring Creek—*stream* MO-7
Dunn Springs Cem—*cemetery* AR-4
Dunn Springs Mtn—*summit* AZ-5
Dunns Rock—*cliff* NC-3
Dunns Rock—*locale* NC-3
**Dunns Rock**—*pop pl* NC-3
Dunns Rock (Township of)—*fmr MCD* NC-3
Dunns (RR name for Dunn)—*other* LA-4
*Dunns Run* PA-2
Dunns Run—*stream* KY-4
Dunns Shanty Point—*cape* AR-4
*Dunns Sound* SC-3
*Dunns Sound Creek* SC-3
Dunns Spring—*spring* TN-4
*Dunns Station* ME-1
*Dunns Station* PA-2
Dunns Station—*locale* PA-2
Dunns Store—*locale* NC-3
Dunns Store (historical)—*building* MS-4
Dunns Store (historical)—*locale* TN-4
**Dunnstable (Township of)**—*pop pl* PA-2
**Dunn Store**—*pop pl* GA-3
**Dunnstown**—*pop pl* PA-2
*Dunns Trading Post* UT-8
Dunnsville—*locale* VA-3
**Dunnsville**—*pop pl* NY-2
Dunn Swamp—*swamp* (2) NY-2
Dunn Swamp—*swamp* NC-3
Dunns Well—*well* AZ-5
Dunn Tank—*reservoir* AZ-5
**Dunn (Town of)**—*pop pl* (2) WI-6
**Dunn (Township of)**—*pop pl* MN-6
Dunn Valley—*valley* PA-2
Dunn Valley Cem—*cemetery* PA-2
Dunn Valley Creek—*stream* PA-2
*Dunnville* VT-1
**Dunnville**—*pop pl* KY-4
**Dunnville**—*pop pl* WI-6
Dunnville (CCD)—*cens area* KY-4
Dunnville Cem—*cemetery* IA-7
Dunnville Ch—*church* IA-7
Dunnville State Public Hunting Grounds—*park* WI-6
Dunn-Watkins House—*hist pl* KY-4
Dunn Well—*locale* NM-5
Dunn Well—*well* SD-7
Dunn Well—*well* TX-5
Dunn Windmill—*locale* (2) NM-5
DuNoir—*locale* WY-8
Du Noir Creek—*stream* WY-8
DuNoir Glacier—*glacier* WY-8
DuNoir Trail—*trail* WY-8
Du Noir Trail—*trail* WY-8
Dunovan Canyon—*valley* NM-5
**Dunphy**—*pop pl* NV-8
Dunphy Pass—*gap* NV-8
Dunphy Ranch—*locale* NV-8
Dunphy Ridge—*ridge* ME-1
Dunphy Sch—*school* MA-1
Dun Ranch—*locale* TX-5
Dunraven—*locale* KY-4
Dunraven—*locale* NY-2
Dunraven, Lake—*lake* CO-8
Dunraven, Mount—*summit* CO-8
Dunraven Glade—*valley* CO-8
Dunraven Pass—*gap* WY-8
Dunraven Peak—*summit* WY-8
Dunraven Trail—*trail* CO-8
Dunreath—*locale* IA-7
Dunreath Cem—*cemetery* IA-7
**Dunreith**—*pop pl* IN-6
**Dunring**—*pop pl* PA-2
Dunroamin Farms Airp—*airport* NC-3
Dunroven House—*hist pl* WI-6
**Dunrovin Estates**—*pop pl* TN-4
Dunrovin Hatchery—*other* TX-5
**Dunrowin**—*pop pl* AL-4
Dunrud Peak—*summit* WY-8
Dun Run—*stream* OH-6
Dunsbach, Martin, House—*hist pl* NY-2
**Dunsbach Ferry**—*pop pl* NY-2
Dunschen Cem—*cemetery* IL-6
*Duns Creek* MD-2
**Dunseith**—*pop pl* ND-7
Dunseith Indian Sch—*school* ND-7
Dunseith Landing Field—*airport* ND-7
Dunsfort—*locale* PA-2
Dunshee Island—*island* NH-1
Dunsinane—*summit* CO-8
Dunsire Creek—*stream* MT-8
Dunsire Point—*summit* MT-8
Duns Mill (historical)—*locale* AL-4
Dunsmore Canyon—*valley* CA-9
Dunsmore Canyon Channel—*canal* CA-9
Dunsmore Coulee—*valley* MT-8
Dunsmore Cove—*valley* NC-3
Dunsmore House—*hist pl* IA-7
Dunsmore Mtn—*summit* GA-3
Dunsmore Mtn—*summit* NC-3
Dunsmore Post Office (historical)—*building* SD-7
Dunsmore Sch—*school* CA-9
Dunsmore Sch (abandoned)—*school* MO-7
**Dunsmuir**—*pop pl* CA-9
Dunsmuir (CCD)—*cens area* CA-9
Dunsmuir Historic Commercial District—*hist pl* CA-9
Dunsmuir House—*hist pl* CA-9
Dunson Cem—*cemetery* GA-3
Dunson Mills Sch—*school* GA-3
Duns Scotus Coll—*school* MI-6
**Dunstable**—*pop pl* MA-1
*Dunstable Centre* MA-1
**Dunstable (Town of)**—*pop pl* MA-1
*Dunstan* ME-1
Dunstan—*other* ME-1
**Dunstan**—*pop pl* TX-5
Dunstan Gulch—*valley* CO-8
Dunstan River—*stream* ME-1
*Dun Station* KS-7
Dunston Creek—*stream* OR-9
*Dunston River* ME-1
Dunsworth Park—*flat* CO-8
**Dunthorpe**—*pop pl* OR-9
**Dunton**—*pop pl* CO-8
Dunton, Minnie Preist, House—*hist pl* ID-8
Dunton Cove—*bay* (2) VA-3
Dunton Guard Station—*locale* CO-8
*Dunton Hill* NC-3
Dunton Hot Spring—*spring* CO-8
Dunton House—*hist pl* OH-6
Dunton Lake—*lake* IN-6
Dunton Lake—*reservoir* NY-2
Duntons Millpond—*reservoir* VA-3
*Duntze Island* WA-9
Dunukchavuk Slough—*stream* AK-9
Dunul—*locale* CO-8
Dunuletak Creek—*stream* AK-9
Dunulimjingia Point—*cape* AK-9
Dunvegan, The—*hist pl* MA-1
**Dunvilla**—*pop pl* MN-6
Dunville Hollow—*valley* VT-1
Dun Well—*well* AZ-5
**Dunwhite**—*pop pl* AR-4
Dunwiddie Sch—*school* WI-6
Dunwolters Oil Field—*oilfield* TX-5
**Dunwood**—*pop pl* MD-2
Dunwood Home—*building* PA-2
**Dunwoodie**—*pop pl* NY-2

Durling Park—*park* ... OH-6
Durling Sch—*school* ... OH-6
Durlin Hotel—*hist pl* ... AZ-5
Durloe Cays—*other* ... VI-3
Durloe Channel—*channel* ... VI-3
Durm Cem—*cemetery* ... KY-4
Durmid—*locale* ... CA-9
Durmid—*uninc pl* ... VA-3
Durnam Island—*island* ... MN-6
**Durnell**—*pop pl* ... MO-7
Durnell Chapel—*church* ... MO-7
Durnell Ditch—*canal* ... IN-6
Durney Lake—*lake* ... CA-9
Durnian Cem—*cemetery* ... NY-2
Duroc—*locale* ... OR-9
Duroc—*locale* ... WY-8
Duroc Bay—*bay* ... MO-7
Durose Cem—*cemetery* ... LA-4
Du Rosset Bayou—*gut* ... LA-4
**Duross Heights**—*pop pl* ... DE-2
**Duross Heights (subdivision)**—*pop pl* ... DE-2
Duroy Lake—*lake* ... WI-6
*Duroys Lake* ... WI-6
Durphee Lake—*lake* ... WI-6
Durphy Creek—*stream* ... CA-9
Durphy Gulch—*valley* ... WY-8
Durphys Fork—*stream* ... UT-8
Durrance Elem Sch—*school* ... FL-3
Durrant Cem—*cemetery* ... OK-5
Durrant Creek—*stream* ... AK-9
Durrant Sch—*school* ... UT-8
Durr Branch—*stream* ... KY-4
Durr Cem—*cemetery* ... IL-6
Durr Creek—*stream* ... CA-9
**Durrell**—*pop pl* ... PA-2
Durrell Brook—*stream* ... ME-1
Durrell Brook—*stream* ... NH-1
Durrell Hill—*summit* ... ME-1
Durrence Pond—*reservoir* (2) ... GA-3
*Durrett Cem* ... TN-4
Durrett Cem—*cemetery* ... TN-4
Durrett Cem—*cemetery* ... WV-2
**Durrett Grove (subdivision)**—*pop pl* ... AL-4
Durrett HS—*school* ... KY-4
Durrett Park—*park* ... TX-5
Durrett Town—*locale* ... VA-3
Durr Farm Pond Dam—*dam* ... MS-4
Durr Hill—*summit* ... IA-7
Durrigan Hollow—*valley* ... KY-4
Durrill Camp—*locale* ... TX-5
Durrough Branch—*stream* ... AR-4
Durrow Marsh—*swamp* ... MI-6
Durr Ranch—*locale* ... MT-8
Durrs Knob—*summit* ... PA-2
Durrstein Lake—*lake* ... SD-7
Durrwood Camp—*locale* ... CA-9
Durrwood Creek—*stream* ... CA-9
Durrwood Meadows—*flat* ... CA-9
Durse Canyon—*valley* ... UT-8
**Durso Corner**—*pop pl* ... NY-2
Durst-Bloedau Site—*hist pl* ... WI-6
Durst Cem—*cemetery* (2) ... TX-5
Durst Creek—*stream* ... MT-8
Durst Creek—*stream* ... UT-8
Durst Creek—*stream* ... WA-9
Durst Hollow—*valley* ... WI-6
Durst Mtn—*summit* ... UT-8
Durst Park—*park* ... MO-7
Durst Ranch—*locale* ... CA-9
Durst Ridge—*ridge* ... OH-6
Durst Spring—*spring* ... UT-8
Durst Windmill—*locale* ... TX-5
*Duruokowaru Island* ... PW-9
*Duruokowaru To* ... PW-9
Durupt—*locale* ... ND-7
Durussell Drain—*canal* ... MI-6
D'Urville Point—*cape* ... FM-9
Durvin Cem—*cemetery* ... AR-4
Durward—*locale* ... PA-2
Durward—*uninc pl* ... FL-3
Durward's Glen—*hist pl* ... WI-6
Durwards Glen—*locale* ... WI-6
Durward Station—*locale* ... PA-2
Durwood—*locale* ... OK-5
Durwood Ch—*church* ... OK-5
Durwood Owens Pond—*lake* ... FL-3
Durwood Sch—*school* ... OK-5
**Duryea**—*pop pl* ... PA-2
Duryea Borough—*civil* ... PA-2
**Duryea Junction**—*pop pl* ... PA-2
Du Sable, Jean Baptiste Point, Homesite—*hist pl* ... IL-6
Du Sable Sch—*school* ... IL-6
Duscham Creek—*stream* ... WI-6
Duschee Creek—*stream* ... MN-6
Dusenberry Glade—*stream* ... NM-5
Dusenberry Hollow—*valley* ... MO-7
Dusenberry House—*hist pl* ... NJ-2
Dusenberry Knob—*summit* ... VA-3
Dusenberry Lake—*lake* ... OR-9
*Dusenbery Peak* ... CA-9
Dusenbury—*locale* ... LA-4
Dusenbury Creek—*gut* ... FL-3
Dusenbury Peak—*summit* ... CA-9
*Dusewallips River* ... WA-9
Dushey Canyon—*valley* ... AZ-5
Dushey Tank—*reservoir* ... AZ-5
Dushkin Lagoon—*bay* ... AK-9
Dushkot Island—*island* ... AK-9
**Dushore**—*pop pl* ... PA-2
Dushore Borough—*civil* ... PA-2
Dusing Gulf—*valley* ... NY-2
Duskcamp Ch—*church* ... WV-2
Duskcamp Run—*stream* ... WV-2
Dusk Ch—*church* ... WV-2
**Dusk File (subdivision)**—*pop pl* (2) ... AZ-5
Duskin Creek—*stream* ... MO-7
Duskin Creek—*stream* ... TN-4
Duskins Branch—*stream* ... WV-2
Dusk Island—*island* ... AK-9
Dusk Lake—*lake* ... AK-9
*Dusk Peak* ... WA-9
Dusk Point—*summit* ... WA-9
Dusky Creek—*stream* ... OR-9
Dusky Rsvr—*reservoir* ... MT-8
Dusmal House—*hist pl* ... PA-2
Duso Marsh—*swamp* ... NY-2
**Duson**—*pop pl* ... LA-4
Duson Gas Field—*oilfield* ... LA-4
Duson Park—*park* ... LA-4
Dussar Spring—*spring* ... CO-8
Dustan, Mount—*summit* ... NH-1
Dustan Pond—*lake* ... NH-1
Dust Bowl—*basin* ... OR-9
Dust Bowl—*flat* ... OR-9
Dust Bowl Duck Club—*other* ... CA-9
Dust Bowl Lake—*lake* ... NV-8
Dust Bowl Tank—*reservoir* (2) ... AZ-5
Dust Bowl Tank—*reservoir* ... TX-5
Dustbox Spring—*spring* ... OR-9
Dust Cave—*cave* ... AL-4
Dust Creek—*stream* ... AK-9
Duster—*locale* ... TX-5
Dusterburgs Hill—*summit* ... UT-8
Dustin—*locale* ... NE-7
**Dustin**—*pop pl* ... OK-5
Dustin, Lake—*lake* ... MI-6
**Dustin Acres**—*pop pl* ... CA-9
Dustin Agricultural Bldg—*hist pl* ... OK-5
Dustin Cabin—*hist pl* ... OH-6
Dustin Cem—*cemetery* ... MO-7
Dustin Cem—*cemetery* ... OK-5
*Dustin Creek* ... WI-6
Dustin Creek—*stream* ... OR-9
Dustin Creek—*stream* ... WI-6
Dustin Gulch—*valley* ... CO-8
**Dustin (historical)**—*pop pl* ... TN-4
*Dustin Hollow* ... WA-9
Dustin Hollow—*valley* ... WA-9
Dustin Lake—*lake* ... MI-6
Dustin Lake—*reservoir* ... OK-5
Dustin Masonic Memorial Park—*cemetery* ... NM-5
Dustin Point—*cape* ... OR-9
Dustin Pond—*lake* ... AR-4
Dustin Post Office (historical)—*building* ... TN-4
Dustin Sch—*school* ... MA-1
Dustin Slough—*gut* ... AL-4
Dustin Spring—*spring* ... CA-9
**Dustin Township**—*pop pl* ... NE-7
Dustlick Creek—*stream* ... WV-2
Duston Cem—*cemetery* ... OH-6
Duston Country Club—*other* ... NH-1
Duston Creek—*stream* ... ID-8
*Dusty* ... OR-9
**Dusty**—*pop pl* ... NM-5
**Dusty**—*pop pl* ... WA-9
**Dusty Bend**—*pop pl* ... SC-3
Dusty Branch—*stream* ... AL-4
Dusty Camp Springs—*spring* ... OR-9
Dusty Cem—*cemetery* ... NM-5
Dusty Corners Sch—*school* ... KS-7
Dusty Creek—*stream* (2) ... ID-8
Dusty Creek—*stream* ... MT-8
Dusty Creek—*stream* ... WA-9
**Dusty Downs Estates**—*pop pl* ... UT-8
Dusty Downs Racetrack—*other* ... TX-5
Dusty Draw—*valley* ... TX-5
*Dusty Fork* ... KY-4
Dusty Fork—*stream* ... KY-4
*Dusty Glacier* ... WA-9
Dusty Glacier—*glacier* ... WA-9
Dusty Hill Golf Club—*other* ... SC-3
Dusty Hollow—*valley* ... PA-2
Dusty Lake—*lake* ... WA-9
Dusty Mine—*mine* ... CO-8
Dusty Mtn—*summit* ... AK-9
Dusty Peak—*summit* ... ID-8
Dusty Peak—*summit* ... MT-8
Dusty Ridge—*ridge* ... OR-9
Dusty Saddle—*gap* ... OR-9
Dusty Saddle Canyon—*valley* ... OR-9
Dusty Spring—*spring* ... OR-9
Dusty Star Mtn—*summit* ... MT-8
Dustys Waterhole—*lake* ... CA-9
Dusty Tank—*reservoir* ... AZ-5
Dusty Tank—*reservoir* ... TX-5
Dusuaus Canal—*canal* ... LA-4
Dusy Basin—*basin* ... CA-9
Dusy Branch—*stream* ... CA-9
Dusy Creek—*stream* ... CA-9
Dusy Meadow—*flat* ... CA-9
Dutard Creek—*stream* ... CA-9
Dutart Creek—*stream* ... SC-3
*Du Tartes Creek* ... SC-3
Dutch—*locale* ... TN-4
Dutch—*locale* ... WV-2
**Dutch Acres (subdivision)**—*pop pl* ... DE-2
**Dutch Bayou**—*pop pl* ... LA-4
Dutch Bayou—*stream* ... LA-4
Dutch Bayou—*stream* (2) ... MS-4
Dutch Bench—*bench* ... MT-8
Dutch Bend—*bend* ... AL-4
Dutch Bend—*bend* ... AR-4
Dutch Bend Ch—*church* ... AL-4
Dutch Bend Sch—*school* ... AL-4
Dutch Bethel Ch—*church* ... IN-6
Dutch Bill Creek—*stream* ... CA-9
Dutch Bill Lake—*lake* ... NV-8
Dutch Blue Creek—*stream* ... AZ-5
Dutch Bottoms—*flat* ... TN-4
*Dutch Botton* ... PA-2
Dutch Brake—*swamp* ... MS-4
Dutch Branch—*stream* ... IA-7
Dutch Branch—*stream* (2) ... KY-4
Dutch Branch—*stream* ... MS-4
Dutch Branch—*stream* (3) ... TX-5
Dutch Branch Park—*park* ... TX-5
Dutch Broadway Sch—*school* ... NY-2
Dutch Buffalo Creek—*stream* ... NC-3
*Dutch Buffaloe Creek* ... NC-3
Dutch Butte—*summit* ... AZ-5
Dutch Butte—*summit* ... CA-9
Dutch Cabin Spring—*spring* ... AZ-5
*Dutch Canyon* ... AZ-5
Dutch Canyon—*valley* ... CA-9
Dutch Canyon—*valley* ... ID-8
Dutch Canyon—*valley* ... NV-8
Dutch Canyon—*valley* ... OR-9
Dutch Canyon—*valley* ... TX-5
Dutchcap Cay—*island* ... VI-3
Dutchcap Passage—*channel* ... VI-3
Dutch Cem—*cemetery* ... AL-4
Dutch Cem—*cemetery* (3) ... NY-2
Dutch Cem—*cemetery* ... OH-6
Dutch Ch—*church* ... KY-4
Dutch Ch—*church* ... NY-2
Dutch Charles Draw—*valley* ... UT-8
Dutch Charley Creek—*stream* ... MN-6
Dutch Charlie Canyon—*valley* ... CA-9
Dutch Charlie Creek—*stream* ... CA-9
Dutch Charlie Creek—*stream* ... WY-8
Dutch Ch (historical)—*church* ... MO-7
*Dutch Colony* ... MS-4
Dutch Corner—*locale* ... PA-2
Dutch Corners—*locale* ... MI-6
**Dutch Corners**—*pop pl* ... OH-6
Dutch Cove—*valley* ... NC-3
Dutch Cove Canyon—*valley* ... TX-5
Dutch Cove Cem—*cemetery* ... LA-4
Dutch Cove Ch—*church* ... NC-3
Dutch Cove Creek—*stream* ... NC-3
*Dutch Creek* ... CA-9
*Dutch Creek* ... DE-2
*Dutch Creek* ... ID-8
*Dutch Creek* ... KS-7
*Dutch Creek* ... WY-8
Dutch Creek—*stream* ... AL-4
Dutch Creek—*stream* (2) ... AK-9
Dutch Creek—*stream* ... AR-4
Dutch Creek—*stream* (12) ... CA-9
Dutch Creek—*stream* (6) ... CO-8
Dutch Creek—*stream* (5) ... ID-8
Dutch Creek—*stream* (3) ... IL-6
Dutch Creek—*stream* ... IN-6
Dutch Creek—*stream* (3) ... IA-7
Dutch Creek—*stream* (5) ... KS-7
Dutch Creek—*stream* ... KY-4
Dutch Creek—*stream* ... MI-6
Dutch Creek—*stream* (2) ... MN-6
Dutch Creek—*stream* (2) ... MO-7
Dutch Creek—*stream* (4) ... MT-8
Dutch Creek—*stream* (3) ... NE-7
Dutch Creek—*stream* ... NV-8
Dutch Creek—*stream* ... NC-3
Dutch Creek—*stream* (2) ... OH-6
Dutch Creek—*stream* (3) ... OR-9
Dutch Creek—*stream* ... PA-2
Dutch Creek—*stream* ... SD-7
Dutch Creek—*stream* (2) ... TN-4
Dutch Creek—*stream* (3) ... TX-5
Dutch Creek—*stream* ... UT-8
Dutch Creek—*stream* ... VA-3
Dutch Creek—*stream* ... WA-9
Dutch Creek—*stream* (3) ... WI-6
Dutch Creek—*stream* (3) ... WY-8
Dutch Creek Cave—*cave* ... KY-4
Dutch Creek Ch—*church* ... KY-4
Dutch Creek Falls—*falls* ... NC-3
Dutch Creek Forest Service Station—*locale* ... ID-8
Dutch Creek Mine—*mine* ... CO-8
Dutch Creek Mountain—*ridge* ... AR-4
Dutch Creek Sch—*school* ... AR-4
Dutch Creek Sch—*school* ... IL-6
Dutch Creek Sch—*school* ... WY-8
Dutch Creek Shelter—*locale* ... OR-9
Dutch Creek Shoal—*bar* ... DE-2
Dutch Creek Township—*fmr MCD* ... IA-7
Dutch Creek (Township of)—*fmr MCD* ... AR-4
**Dutch Creek Woodlands**—*pop pl* ... IL-6
*Dutch Dams Gulch* ... WY-8
*Dutch Dan Gulch* ... WY-8
Dutch Dans Gulch—*valley* ... WY-8
Dutch Draw—*valley* ... TX-5
Dutch Draw—*valley* ... UT-8
Dutch Drift Mine (underground)—*mine* ... AL-4
Dutch Ed Gulch—*valley* ... CA-9
Dutcher Cove—*bay* ... WA-9
*Dutcher Creek* ... OR-9
Dutcher Creek—*stream* ... CA-9
Dutcher Creek—*stream* ... ID-8
Dutcher Creek—*stream* ... OR-9
Dutcher Dock—*locale* ... MA-1
Dutcher Hill—*summit* ... CT-1
*Dutcher Knob* ... TN-4
Dutcher Pond—*lake* ... NY-2
Dutcher Street Sch—*school* ... MA-1
Dutcherville—*locale* ... NY-2
Dutchess, Lake—*reservoir* ... NY-2
Dutchess Cave—*cave* ... AL-4
**Dutchess (County)**—*pop pl* ... NY-2
Dutchess County Court House—*hist pl* ... NY-2
Dutchess Golf and Country Club—*other* ... NY-2
**Dutchess Junction**—*pop pl* ... NY-2
Dutchess Manor—*hist pl* ... NY-2
Dutchess Mine—*mine* ... CA-9
Dutchess Quarry Cave Site—*hist pl* ... NY-2
Dutchess Sch—*school* ... NY-2
**Dutchess Village (subdivision)**—*pop pl* ... NC-3
Dutche Well—*well* ... NM-5
Dutch Fields—*flat* ... TN-4
Dutch Flat—*flat* ... AZ-5
Dutch Flat—*flat* (4) ... CA-9
Dutch Flat—*flat* ... CO-8
Dutch Flat—*flat* (2) ... ID-8
Dutch Flat—*flat* (3) ... NV-8
Dutch Flat—*flat* (3) ... OR-9
Dutch Flat—*flat* ... UT-8
Dutch Flat—*flat* ... WA-9
**Dutch Flat**—*pop pl* ... CA-9
Dutch Flat Canyon—*valley* (2) ... CA-9
Dutch Flat Cem—*cemetery* ... IL-6
Dutch Flat Creek—*stream* ... CA-9
Dutch Flat Creek—*stream* ... OR-9
Dutch Flat Ditch—*canal* ... UT-8
Dutch Flat Extension—*canal* ... WY-8
Dutch Flat Hist Dist—*hist pl* ... CA-9
Dutch Flat Lake—*lake* ... OR-9
Dutch Flat Mine—*mine* ... NV-8
Dutch Flat Powerhouse—*other* ... CA-9
Dutch Flat Rsvr—*reservoir* ... UT-8
Dutch Flats—*flat* ... NE-7
Dutch Flats—*flat* ... SD-7
Dutch Flats—*locale* ... NY-2
Dutch Flat Saddle—*gap* ... OR-9
Dutch Flats Gulch—*valley* ... CO-8
Dutch Flat Station—*locale* ... CA-9
Dutch Flat Tunnel—*tunnel* ... CA-9
Dutch Flat Well—*well* ... ID-8
*Dutch Fork* ... PA-2
**Dutch Fork**—*pop pl* ... SC-3
Dutch Fork—*stream* (2) ... KY-4
Dutch Fork—*stream* ... OH-6
Dutch Fork—*stream* ... PA-2
Dutch Fork—*stream* ... WV-2
Dutch Fork (CCD)—*cens area* ... SC-3
Dutch Fork Ch—*church* ... PA-2
Dutch Fork Dam—*dam* ... PA-2
Dutch Fork Lake—*reservoir* ... PA-2
Dutch Fork Sch—*school* ... SC-3
Dutch Fork Sch Number 2—*school* ... SC-3
Dutch Frank Creek—*stream* ... ID-8
Dutch Fred Gulch—*valley* ... CO-8
Dutch Fred Lake—*lake* ... MI-6
Dutch Gap—*gap* ... OH-6
Dutch Gap—*gap* ... VA-3
**Dutch Gap**—*pop pl* (2) ... VA-3
Dutch Gap Canal—*canal* ... IL-6
Dutch Gap Canal—*canal* ... WI-6
*Dutch Gap Channel* ... VA-3
Dutch George Creek—*stream* ... WY-8
Dutch George Flats—*flat* ... CO-8
Dutch Girl Lake—*lake* ... CO-8
Dutch Girl Tank—*reservoir* ... TX-5
Dutch Group—*island* ... AK-9
Dutch Gulch—*valley* (3) ... CA-9
Dutch Gulch—*valley* (3) ... CO-8
Dutch Gulch—*valley* ... MT-8
Dutch Gulch—*valley* (2) ... OR-9
Dutch Harbor—*bay* (2) ... AK-9
Dutch Harbor—*bay* ... CA-9
Dutch Harbor—*bay* ... WA-9
Dutch Harbor—*harbor* ... MD-2
Dutch Harbor—*harbor* ... WA-9
Dutch Harbor—*uninc pl* ... AK-9
Dutch Harbor Airp—*airport* ... AK-9
Dutch Harbor Naval Operating Base and Fort Mears, U.S. Army—*hist pl* ... AK-9
Dutch Henry Butte—*summit* ... ND-7
*Dutch Henry Canyon* ... CA-9
Dutch Henry Canyon—*valley* ... AZ-5
Dutch Henry Canyon—*valley* (2) ... CA-9
Dutch Henry Coulee—*valley* ... MT-8
Dutch Henry Creek—*stream* (4) ... CA-9
Dutch Henry Draw—*valley* ... WA-9
Dutch Henry Trail (historical)—*trail* ... OR-9
Dutch Henry Two hundred ninety seven Trail—*trail* ... AZ-5
Dutch Henry Well—*well* ... AZ-5
**Dutch Hill**—*pop pl* (3) ... PA-2
Dutch Hill—*spring* ... MT-8
Dutch Hill—*summit* (2) ... IL-6
Dutch Hill—*summit* (9) ... NY-2
Dutch Hill—*summit* (4) ... PA-2
Dutch Hill—*summit* ... TX-5
Dutch Hill—*summit* (2) ... VT-1
Dutch Hill Cem—*cemetery* ... IL-6
Dutch Hill Cem—*cemetery* ... NY-2
Dutch Hill Cem—*cemetery* (2) ... OH-6
Dutch Hill Ch—*church* ... MO-7
Dutch Hill Ch—*church* ... PA-2
Dutch Hill Mine—*mine* ... CA-9
Dutch Hills—*other* ... AK-9
Dutch Hill Sch—*school* (2) ... PA-2
Dutch Hill Sch (abandoned)—*school* ... PA-2
Dutch Hill Sch (historical)—*school* ... MO-7
Dutch Hill Sch (historical)—*school* ... PA-2
*Dutch Hollow* ... TX-5
*Dutch Hollow* ... UT-8
**Dutch Hollow**—*pop pl* ... IL-6
**Dutch Hollow**—*pop pl* (2) ... NY-2
Dutch Hollow—*valley* ... IL-6
Dutch Hollow—*valley* (2) ... IA-7
Dutch Hollow—*valley* ... KS-7
Dutch Hollow—*valley* ... MD-2
Dutch Hollow—*valley* (3) ... MO-7
Dutch Hollow—*valley* (2) ... MT-8
Dutch Hollow—*valley* ... NY-2
Dutch Hollow—*valley* (2) ... OH-6
Dutch Hollow—*valley* (3) ... PA-2
Dutch Hollow—*valley* ... UT-8
Dutch Hollow—*valley* (3) ... WV-2
Dutch Hollow—*valley* ... WI-6
Dutch Hollow Branch—*stream* ... VA-3
Dutch Hollow Brook—*stream* ... NY-2
Dutch Hollow Cem—*cemetery* ... WI-6
Dutch Hollow Cemeteries—*cemetery* ... OH-6
Dutch Hollow Creek—*stream* ... NY-2
Dutch Hollow Creek—*stream* ... WI-6
Dutch Hollow Lake—*reservoir* ... WI-6
Dutch Hollow Sch—*school* ... MD-2
Dutch Hollow Sch—*school* ... NE-7
Dutch Hollow Spring—*spring* ... MT-8
Dutch Hollow Wine Cellars—*hist pl* ... WV-2
Dutch House, The—*hist pl* ... MA-1
Dutch Island—*island* ... AL-4
Dutch Island—*island* ... GA-3
Dutch Island—*island* ... ME-1
Dutch Island—*island* ... RI-1
Dutch Island Harbor—*bay* ... RI-1
Dutch Island Lighthouse—*hist pl* ... RI-1
Dutch Joe Creek—*stream* (2) ... WY-8
Dutch Joe Draw—*valley* ... WY-8
Dutch Joe Guard Station—*locale* ... WY-8
Dutch Joe Lookout—*locale* ... AZ-5
Dutch Joe Ranch—*locale* ... AZ-5
**Dutch John**—*pop pl* ... UT-8
Dutch John Airp—*airport* ... UT-8
Dutch John Bay—*bay* ... NY-2
Dutch John Bench—*bench* ... UT-8
Dutch John Boat Ramp—*locale* ... UT-8
Dutch John Bottom—*bend* ... LA-4
Dutch John Branch—*stream* ... LA-4
Dutch John Cabin—*locale* ... OR-9
Dutch John Canyon—*valley* ... UT-8
Dutch John Coulee—*valley* ... MT-8
Dutch John Creek—*stream* ... NV-8
Dutch John Creek—*stream* ... NC-3
Dutch John Creek—*stream* ... OR-9
Dutch John Cut—*canal* ... CA-9
Dutch John Draw—*valley* ... UT-8
Dutch John Draw Campground—*locale* ... UT-8
Dutch John Flat—*flat* ... CA-9
Dutch John Flat—*flat* ... UT-8
Dutch John Gap—*gap* ... UT-8
Dutch John Guard Station—*locale* ... UT-8
Dutch John Helibase—*airport* ... UT-8
Dutch John Mtn—*summit* ... NV-8
Dutch John Mtn—*summit* ... UT-8
Dutch John Ravine—*valley* ... OR-9
Dutch John Section—*locale* ... OR-9
Dutch Johns Meadow—*flat* ... CA-9
Dutch Johns Point—*cape* ... MI-6
Dutch John Spring—*spring* ... AZ-5
Dutch John Spring—*spring* ... UT-8
Dutch John Well—*well* ... NV-8
Dutch John Windmill—*locale* ... NM-5
Dutch Kid Knoll—*summit* ... AZ-5
Dutch Kid Tank—*reservoir* (4) ... AZ-5
Dutch Kills—*harbor* ... NY-2
Dutch Lake—*lake* ... CA-9
Dutch Lake—*lake* ... ID-8
Dutch Lake—*lake* (3) ... MI-6
Dutch Lake—*lake* (3) ... MN-6
Dutch Lake—*lake* ... NM-5
Dutch Lake—*lake* ... TX-5
Dutch Lakes—*lake* ... MT-8
Dutch Lakes—*lake* ... NM-5
Dutch Lane Sch—*school* ... NY-2
Dutchler Mtn—*summit* ... ID-8
Dutch Louie Campground—*locale* ... CA-9
Dutchman—*locale* ... WV-2
**Dutchman**—*pop pl* ... SC-3
Dutchman Arch—*arch* ... UT-8
Dutchman Bay—*bay* ... GA-3
Dutchman Branch—*stream* ... KY-4
Dutchman Branch—*stream* ... TN-4
Dutchman Branch—*stream* (2) ... VA-3
Dutchman Butte—*summit* ... OR-9
Dutchman Camp—*locale* ... CA-9
Dutchman Canyon—*valley* (2) ... CA-9
Dutchman Canyon—*valley* (3) ... NM-5
Dutchman Canyon—*valley* ... OR-9
Dutchman Coulee—*valley* ... MN-6
Dutchman Coulee—*valley* (2) ... MT-8
Dutchman Cove—*basin* ... TX-5
*Dutchman Creek* ... MI-6
*Dutchman Creek* ... SC-3
Dutchman Creek—*stream* (2) ... CA-9
Dutchman Creek—*stream* ... CO-8
Dutchman Creek—*stream* ... ID-8
Dutchman Creek—*stream* ... IL-6
Dutchman Creek—*stream* ... KY-4
Dutchman Creek—*stream* ... LA-4
Dutchman Creek—*stream* ... MI-6
Dutchman Creek—*stream* (4) ... MT-8
Dutchman Creek—*stream* (4) ... NC-3
Dutchman Creek—*stream* (3) ... OR-9
Dutchman Creek—*stream* ... SC-3
Dutchman Creek—*stream* ... SD-7
Dutchman Creek—*stream* (3) ... TX-5
Dutchman Creek—*stream* ... VA-3
Dutchman Creek—*stream* (2) ... WI-6
Dutchman Creek W/S Number Five—*reservoir* ... NC-3
Dutchman Creek W/S Number Six—*reservoir* ... NC-3
Dutchman Creek W/S Number Ten—*reservoir* ... NC-3
Dutchman Creek W/S Number Two—*reservoir* ... NC-3
Dutchman Creek W/S Structure Number Five Dam—*dam* ... NC-3
Dutchman Creek W/S Structure Number Six Dam—*dam* ... NC-3
Dutchman Creek W/S Structure Number Two Dam—*dam* ... NC-3
Dutchman Draw—*valley* (2) ... AZ-5
Dutchman Falls—*falls* ... PA-2
Dutchman Flat—*flat* ... AZ-5
Dutchman Flat—*flat* (3) ... OR-9
Dutchman Flat—*flat* ... UT-8
Dutchman Flat Campground—*locale* ... ID-8
Dutchman Grave Spring—*spring* ... AZ-5
Dutchman Guard Station—*locale* ... UT-8
Dutchman Gulch—*valley* ... CA-9
Dutchman Hill—*summit* ... PA-2
Dutchman Hollow—*valley* (2) ... AR-4
Dutchman Hollow—*valley* ... TN-4
*Dutchman Island* ... FL-3
Dutchman Island—*island* ... IA-7
Dutchman Island—*island* ... NY-2
Dutchman Island—*island* ... SC-3
Dutchman Islands—*island* ... WI-6
Dutchman Key—*island* ... FL-3
Dutchman Lake—*lake* ... CO-8
Dutchman Lake—*lake* (2) ... MN-6
Dutchman Lake—*lake* ... MT-8
Dutchman Lake—*lake* ... WI-6
Dutchman Lakes—*lake* ... MI-6
Dutchman Lookout Tower—*locale* ... WI-6
Dutchman Mine—*mine* ... MT-8
Dutchman Mine—*mine* ... UT-8
Dutchman Mtn—*summit* ... MT-8
Dutchman Mtn—*summit* ... NC-3
Dutchman Pass—*channel* ... LA-4
Dutchman Pass—*gap* ... NV-8
*Dutchman Peak* ... UT-8
Dutchman Peak—*summit* ... CA-9
Dutchman Peak—*summit* ... MT-8
Dutchman Peak—*summit* ... OR-9
Dutchman Point—*cape* ... MD-2
Dutchman Point—*cape* (2) ... MI-6
Dutchman Point—*cape* ... VA-3
*Dutchman Pond* ... MA-1
Dutchman Pond—*lake* ... NH-1
Dutchman Prospect Spring—*spring* ... CA-9
Dutchman Ridge—*ridge* ... NC-3
Dutchman Ridge—*ridge* ... OK-5
Dutchman Ridge—*ridge* ... UT-8
Dutchman Rsvr—*reservoir* ... UT-8
Dutchman Run—*stream* (5) ... PA-2
Dutchman Run—*stream* ... WV-2
*Dutchmans, The* ... AZ-5
Dutchmans Bay—*bay* ... MI-6
Dutchmans Bend—*bend* ... FL-3
Dutchmans Bluff—*cliff* ... MN-6
Dutchmans Branch—*stream* ... NC-3
*Dutch Mans Butte* ... AZ-5
Dutchmans Camp—*locale* ... CA-9
*Dutchmans Creek* ... NC-3
Dutchmans Creek—*stream* ... IL-6
Dutchmans Creek—*stream* (2) ... NC-3
Dutchmans Creek—*stream* ... SC-3
Dutchmans Creek Ch—*church* ... NC-3
Dutchmans Creek Lake—*reservoir* ... NC-3
*Dutchmans Creek W/S Structure Number 15* ... NC-3
*Dutchmans Creek W/S Structure Number 8* ... NC-3
Dutchmans Flat—*flat* ... CA-9
Dutchmans Flat—*flat* ... UT-8
Dutchmans Hump—*summit* ... ID-8
Dutchmans Knob—*summit* ... TN-4
Dutchmans Knoll—*summit* ... CA-9
Dutchmans Lake—*lake* ... IL-6
Dutchman Slough—*gut* ... CA-9
*Dutchman Sound* ... GA-3
*Dutchmans Peak* ... OR-9
Dutchmans Point—*cape* ... NJ-2
Dutchman Spring—*spring* ... CA-9
Dutchman Spring—*spring* (2) ... MT-8
Dutchman Spring—*spring* ... OR-9
*Dutchmans Run* ... PA-2
Dutchmans Run—*stream* ... PA-2
Dutchmans Swamp—*swamp* ... NY-2
Dutchmans Trail—*trail* ... AZ-5
Dutchmans Trail—*trail* ... PA-2
Dutchman Summit—*gap* ... NV-8
Dutchman Swamp—*swamp* ... PA-2
Dutchmans Wash—*valley* ... UT-8
Dutchman Tank—*reservoir* (5) ... AZ-5
Dutchman Valley—*valley* ... NE-7
Dutchman Valley Sch—*school* ... NE-7
Dutchman Wash—*stream* ... AZ-5
Dutchman Windmill—*locale* ... TX-5
Dutch Meadow—*flat* ... CA-9
Dutch Mill—*hist pl* ... IL-6
Dutch Miller Gap—*gap* ... WA-9
Dutch Mills—*locale* ... AR-4
Dutch Mills—*locale* ... IL-6
**Dutch Mills**—*pop pl* ... AR-4
Dutch Mills (Township of)—*fmr MCD* ... AR-4
Dutch Mtn—*summit* ... AZ-5
Dutch Mtn—*summit* ... AR-4
Dutch Mtn—*summit* ... ME-1
Dutch Mtn—*summit* ... PA-2
Dutch Mtn—*summit* (2) ... TX-5
Dutch Mtn—*summit* ... UT-8
Dutch Neck—*cape* (2) ... DE-2
Dutch Neck—*cape* ... ME-1
Dutch Neck—*cape* ... NJ-2
**Dutch Neck**—*pop pl* ... NJ-2
Dutch Neck Canal—*canal* ... DE-2
Dutch Neck Crossroads—*locale* ... DE-2
**Dutch Neck Farms (subdivision)**—*pop pl* ... DE-2
Dutch Nick Flat—*flat* ... WY-8
Dutch Oven—*basin* ... ID-8
Dutch Oven—*basin* ... OR-9
Dutch Oven—*pillar* ... MT-8
Dutch Oven Campground—*locale* ... CA-9
Dutch Oven Canyon—*valley* ... CO-8
Dutch Oven Creek—*stream* (2) ... CA-9
Dutch Oven Creek—*stream* (4) ... ID-8
Dutch Oven Creek—*stream* ... MT-8
Dutch Oven Creek—*stream* ... OR-9
Dutch Oven Flat—*flat* ... OR-9
Dutch Oven Forest Camp—*locale* ... OR-9
Dutch Oven Gulch—*valley* ... ID-8
Dutch Oven Lake—*lake* ... WY-8
Dutch Oven Meadow—*flat* ... CA-9
Dutch Oven Pass—*gap* ... WY-8
Dutch Oven Rsvr—*reservoir* ... OR-9
Dutch Oven Spring—*spring* ... AZ-5
Dutch Oven Spring—*spring* ... ID-8
Dutch Park—*park* ... MT-8
Dutch Pasture Canyon—*valley* ... AZ-5
Dutch Pasture Tank—*reservoir* ... AZ-5
Dutch Pasture Well—*well* ... AZ-5
Dutch Peak—*summit* ... UT-8
Dutch Pete Spring—*spring* ... CA-9
Dutch Petes Ranch—*locale* ... CA-9
*Dutch Point* ... NY-2
Dutch Point—*cliff* ... OR-9
Dutch Post Office (historical)—*building* ... TN-4
Dutch Ravine—*valley* (3) ... CA-9
Dutch Reformed Cem—*cemetery* ... NY-2
Dutch Reformed Ch—*church* ... NY-2
Dutch Reformed Ch (historical)—*church* (2) ... SD-7
Dutch Reformed Ch of Old Platte and Castalia (historical)—*church* ... SD-7
*Dutch Reformed Church* ... SD-7
Dutch Reformed Church—*hist pl* ... KY-4
Dutch Reformed Church—*hist pl* ... NJ-2
Dutch Reformed Church—*hist pl* (2) ... NY-2
Dutch Reformed Church at Romopock—*hist pl* ... NJ-2
Dutch Ridge—*locale* ... OH-6
**Dutch Ridge**—*pop pl* ... WV-2
Dutch Ridge—*ridge* (2) ... IL-6
Dutch Ridge—*ridge* (2) ... IN-6
Dutch Ridge—*ridge* ... MT-8
Dutch Ridge—*ridge* ... NY-2
Dutch Ridge—*ridge* (2) ... OH-6
Dutch Ridge—*ridge* (5) ... WV-2
Dutch Ridge—*ridge* ... WI-6
Dutch Ridge Cem—*cemetery* (2) ... OH-6
Dutch Ridge Ch—*church* ... IL-6
Dutch Ridge Chapel—*church* ... WV-2
Dutch Ridge Lake—*lake* ... IN-6
Dutch Ridge Lookout Tower—*tower* ... IN-6
*Dutch Ridge Pond* ... IN-6
Dutch Row Sch—*school* ... IL-6
Dutch Rsvr—*reservoir* ... OR-9
Dutch Rsvr—*reservoir* ... WY-8
Dutch Run—*stream* (3) ... OH-6
Dutch Run—*stream* (5) ... PA-2
Dutch Run Cem—*cemetery* ... OH-6
Dutch Run Ch—*church* ... OH-6
Dutch Sch—*school* ... NE-7
*Dutch Second Creek* ... NC-3
Dutch Settlement—*locale* ... NY-2
Dutch Settlement—*locale* ... WA-9
**Dutch Settlement**—*pop pl* ... NY-2
**Dutch Settlement**—*pop pl* ... PA-2
Dutch Settlement Cem—*cemetery* ... MI-6
Dutch Settlement Creek—*stream* ... NY-2
*Dutch Ship Island* ... MD-2
Dutch Slough—*gut* ... CA-9
Dutch Slough—*stream* ... MN-6
*Dutch Slough Gas Field* ... CA-9
Dutch Smith Creek—*stream* ... TX-5
Dutchs Tank—*reservoir* (2) ... AZ-5
Dutch Street Cem—*cemetery* ... NY-2
*Dutch Tank* ... AZ-5
Dutch Tank—*reservoir* ... AZ-5
Dutch Tank—*reservoir* (2) ... NM-5
Dutch Tank—*reservoir* ... TX-5
*Dutchter Mountain* ... ID-8
*Dutch Town* ... IN-6
Dutchtown—*hist pl* ... CO-8
Dutchtown—*locale* ... IA-7
**Dutch Town**—*pop pl* ... LA-4
**Dutchtown**—*pop pl* ... MO-7
**Dutchtown**—*pop pl* (2) ... NJ-2
**Dutchtown**—*pop pl* ... NY-2
**Dutchtown**—*pop pl* ... PA-2

Dutchtown Ch—*church* IL-6
Dutchtown Ditch—*canal* MO-7
Dutchtown Sch—*school* NY-2
Dutch Trap Windmill—*locale* TX-5
Dutch Valley—*locale* TN-4
Dutch Valley—*valley* AZ-5
Dutch Valley—*valley* CA-9
Dutch Valley—*valley* OH-6
Dutch Valley—*valley* (3) TN-4
Dutch Valley—*valley* WI-6
Dutch Valley Baptist Ch—*church* TN-4
Dutch Valley Cem—*cemetery* OH-6
Dutch Valley Ch—*church* (2) TN-4
Dutch Valley Creek—*stream* TN-4
*Dutch Valley Elementary School* TN-4
Dutch Valley Post Office (historical)—*building* TN-4
Dutch Valley Sch—*school* TN-4
Dutch Valley Sch (historical)—*school* TN-4
Dutch Valley Tank—*reservoir* AZ-5
Dutchville (Township of)—*fmr MCD* NC-3
Dutch Waterhole—*lake* OR-9
Dutch Waterhole—*lake* TX-5
Dutch Windmill—*locale* NM-5
Dutch Windmill—*locale* TX-5
Dutchwoman Butte—*summit* AZ-5
Dutch Woman Draw—*valley* TX-5
Dutchwoman Tank—*reservoir* AZ-5
Dutch Woman Windmill—*locale* TX-5
*Dutchwomen Butte* AZ-5
Dutch Wonderland Amusement Park—*park* PA-2
*Dutchy Creek* OR-9
Dutchy Creek—*stream* OR-9
Dutchy Lake—*lake* OR-9
Dutemple Brook—*lake* RI-1
Dutes Pond—*reservoir* SC-3
Dutes Sch—*school* MI-6
Dutherage Spring—*spring* AR-4
Duthie—*locale* ID-8
Duthu Lake Dam—*dam* MS-4
*Dutil Church* PA-2
Dutile Sch—*school* MA-1
Dutilh Ch—*church* PA-2
DuToit, Frederick E., House—*hist pl* MN-6
Duton Creek—*stream* KY-4
**Dutotsburg (historical)**—*pop pl* PA-2
Dutour Sch—*school* IL-6
Dutoy Creek—*stream* VA-3
Dutra Creek—*stream* CA-9
Dutro Carter Creek—*stream* MO-7
Dutro Cem—*cemetery* KS-7
Dutro Ditch—*canal* IN-6
Dutschke Hill—*summit* CA-9
Dutson Canyon—*valley* WY-8
*Dutten Lake* TX-5
*Dutters Trail* PA-2
Dutton—*locale* AR-4
Dutton—*locale* CA-9
Dutton—*locale* IL-6
Dutton—*locale* OK-5
Dutton—*locale* VA-3
**Dutton**—*pop pl* AL-4
**Dutton**—*pop pl* MI-6
**Dutton**—*pop pl* MT-8
**Dutton**—*pop pl* OK-5
Dutton, James B., House—*hist pl* MI-6
Dutton, Mount—*summit* AK-9
Dutton, Mount—*summit* UT-8
Dutton (Aban'd)—*locale* AK-9
Dutton Basin—*basin* WY-8
Dutton Branch—*stream* AL-4
Dutton Branch—*stream* KY-4
Dutton Brook—*stream* NY-2
Dutton Brook—*stream* (3) VT-1
Dutton-Burton Mine (underground)—*mine* AL-4
Dutton Canal—*canal* MT-8
Dutton Canyon—*valley* AZ-5
Dutton Canyon—*valley* OR-9
Dutton Cem—*cemetery* AL-4
Dutton Cem—*cemetery* AR-4
Dutton Cem—*cemetery* IL-6
Dutton Cem—*cemetery* KY-4
Dutton Cem—*cemetery* MI-6
Dutton Cem—*cemetery* OH-6
Dutton Cem—*cemetery* VA-3
Dutton Cliff—*cliff* OR-9
Dutton Corners—*locale* NY-2
Dutton Coulee—*valley* MT-8
Dutton Creek—*stream* AL-4
Dutton Creek—*stream* CA-9
Dutton Creek—*stream* CO-8
Dutton Creek—*stream* OR-9
Dutton Creek—*stream* WA-9
Dutton Creek—*stream* WY-8
Dutton Creek Ditch—*canal* WY-8
Dutton Creek Oil Field—*oilfield* WY-8
Dutton Creek Reservoir Supply Ditch—*canal* WY-8
Dutton Creek Rsvr—*reservoir* WY-8
Dutton Ditch—*canal* CO-8
Dutton Ditch—*canal* IN-6
Dutton Ditch—*canal* MI-6
Dutton Ditch—*stream* DE-2
Dutton Gap—*gap* KY-4
Dutton Gap—*gap* VA-3
Dutton Gap—*gap* WV-2
Dutton Hill—*summit* AZ-5
Dutton Hill—*summit* ME-1
Dutton Hill—*summit* NY-2
Dutton Hill Ch—*church* AL-4
*Dutton Hill Missionary Baptist Ch* AL-4
Dutton Hollow—*valley* NY-2
Dutton Hollow—*valley* (2) PA-2
Dutton Hollow—*valley* TN-4
Dutton Hollow—*valley* VA-3
Dutton Homestead (abandoned)—*locale* MT-8
Dutton Hotel, Stagecoach Station—*hist pl* CA-9
*Dutton Island* NH-1
Dutton Island—*island* CA-9
*Dutton Lake* MN-6
Dutton Lake—*lake* IL-6
Dutton Lake—*lake* MN-6
Dutton Lake—*lake* TX-5
Dutton Lakes—*lake* WA-9
Dutton Landing—*locale* CA-9
Dutton Mill—*locale* PA-2
Dutton Mtn—*summit* CT-1
Dutton Mtn—*summit* NY-2
Dutton Park—*flat* CO-8
Dutton Pass—*gap* UT-8
Dutton Pines State Forest Park—*park* VT-1
**Dutton Place (subdivision)**—*pop pl* AL-4
Dutton Point—*cliff* AZ-5
Dutton Pond—*lake* (3) ME-1
Dutton Pond—*lake* VT-1
Dutton Pond—*reservoir* MA-1
Dutton-Power—*cens area* MT-8
Dutton Ranch—*locale* AZ-5
Dutton Ranch—*locale* MT-8
Dutton Ranch—*locale* TX-5
Dutton Ridge—*ridge* NY-2
Dutton Ridge—*ridge* OR-9
Dutton Run—*stream* PA-2
Duttons Cave Campground—*locale* IA-7
Dutton Sch—*school* MI-6
Dutton Sch—*school* MT-8
Dutton Sch—*school* WI-6
*Dutton's Island* NH-1
Dutton Slough—*gut* MN-6
Dutton Slough—*lake* ND-7
Duttons Mill—*locale* PA-2
Dutton Spring—*spring* AZ-5
Dutton Spring—*spring* OR-9
**Dutton Still**—*pop pl* FL-3
Dutton Swamp—*swamp* CT-1
Dutton Valley Ch—*church* AL-4
**Duttonville**—*pop pl* NJ-2
Duttonville Gulf—*valley* VT-1
*Dutty Gulch* CA-9
Duty—*locale* LA-4
**Duty**—*pop pl* VA-3
*Duty Branch* VA-3
Duty Branch—*stream* (2) KY-4
Duty Branch—*stream* VA-3
Duty Branch—*stream* WV-2
Duty Cem—*cemetery* AR-4
Duty Cem—*cemetery* (2) VA-3
Duty Cem—*cemetery* (3) WV-2
Duty Knob—*summit* KY-4
Dutys Creek—*stream* TX-5
Duty (Township of)—*fmr MCD* AR-4
**Dutzow**—*pop pl* MO-7
Dutzow Sch—*school* MO-7
*Duual Leach Wash* AZ-5
*Du Urees Creek* CA-9
*Duval* IL-6
Duval—*locale* AZ-5
Duval—*locale* KY-4
**Duval**—*pop pl* FL-3
Duval—*uninc pl* AL-4
Duval, Gen. I. H., Mansion—*hist pl* WV-2
Duval, Lake—*lake* FL-3
Duval, Mary, House—*hist pl* TX-5
Duval Acad—*school* FL-3
Duval Branch—*stream* (2) FL-3
Duval Cem—*cemetery* GA-3
Duval Cem—*cemetery* KY-4
Duval Cem—*cemetery* TN-4
Duval Christian Sch—*school* FL-3
*Duval (County)* FL-3
Duval County—*civil* FL-3
**Duval (County)**—*pop pl* TX-5
Duval Creek—*stream* MI-6
Duval Creek—*stream* MS-4
Duval Creek—*stream* MO-7
Duval Creek—*stream* MT-8
Duval Creek—*stream* OR-9
Duval Draw—*valley* WY-8
Duval Gulch—*valley* MT-8
DuVal HS—*school* MD-2
Duval HS—*school* WV-2
*Duval Interchange* AZ-5
Duval Island—*island* FL-3
Duvall—*locale* IL-6
**Duvall**—*pop pl* AL-4
**Duvall**—*pop pl* AR-4
**Duvall**—*pop pl* (2) OH-6
**Duvall**—*pop pl* WA-9
**Duvall**—*pop pl* WI-6
Duvall, Marene, House—*hist pl* KY-4
Duval Lake—*reservoir* AZ-5
Duvall and Steger Cem—*cemetery* KY-4
Duval Lateral—*canal* ID-8
Duvall Branch—*stream* AL-4
Duvall Branch—*stream* KY-4
Duvall Bridge—*bridge* MD-2
Duvall Cem—*cemetery* (2) MS-4
Duvall Cem—*cemetery* NY-2
Duvall Cem—*cemetery* WI-6
*Duvall Creek* MD-2
Duvall Creek—*bay* MD-2
Duvall Creek—*stream* KY-4
Duvall Creek—*stream* OR-9
Duval Leach Flood Dam Number One—*dam* AZ-5
Duvall Lake—*reservoir* CA-9
Duvall Pond—*lake* KY-4
Duvall Ponds—*lake* MD-2
Duvall Ranch Oil Field—*oilfield* WY-8
Duvall Ridge—*ridge* IN-6
Duvall Ridge—*ridge* PA-2
**Duvalls**—*pop pl* OH-6
Duvalls Cem—*cemetery* PA-2
Duvall Sch—*school* MI-6
Duvall Sch—*school* OH-6
Duvalls Landing—*locale* TN-4
Duvall Swamp—*swamp* WI-6
Duvall Trail—*trail* PA-2
Duvall Valley—*valley* KY-4
Duvall Valley Ch—*church* KY-4
Duval (Magisterial District)—*fmr MCD* WV-2
Duval Med Ctr—*hospital* FL-3
Duval Mine—*mine* AZ-5
Duval Mine Road Interchange—*crossing* AZ-5
Duval Pond—*lake* FL-3
Duval Pond—*reservoir* VA-3
Duval Ranch—*locale* TX-5
Duval Ridge—*ridge* WV-2
Duval Sch—*school* FL-3
Duval Sch—*school* IL-6
Duval Sch—*school* MO-7
Duval Spring—*spring* CA-9
Duval Township—*civil* MO-7
Duval Trail—*trail* VT-1
Duveneck—*locale* WI-6
Duvillard Mill—*hist pl* NY-2
Duvivier Place—*locale* NV-8
Duvoul Creek—*stream* CA-9
**Duwamish**—*pop pl* WA-9
Duwamish East Waterway—*channel* WA-9
Duwamish Head—*cliff* WA-9
Duwamish Light—*locale* WA-9
Duwamish Number 1 Site—*hist pl* WA-9
*Duwamish River* WA-9
Duwamish River—*stream* WA-9
*Duwamish River Waterway* WA-9
Duwamish Waterway—*channel* WA-9
Duwamish West Waterway—*channel* WA-9
Duwayne Slaathaug 1 Dam—*dam* SD-7
Duwee Falls—*falls* OR-9
Duwess Canyon—*valley* NM-5
Duwess Windmill—*locale* NM-5
*Duwuz libito* AZ-5
Duxberry Park Sch—*school* OH-6
DUX Bessemer Bend Bridge—*hist pl* WY-8
Duxbury—*locale* SD-7
**Duxbury**—*pop pl* MA-1
**Duxbury**—*pop pl* MN-6
**Duxbury**—*pop pl* VT-1
*Duxbury, Town of* MA-1
Duxbury Bay—*bay* MA-1
Duxbury Beach—*isthmus* MA-1
Duxbury (census name for Duxbury Center)—*CDP* MA-1
Duxbury Center (census name Duxbury)—*other* MA-1
Duxbury JHS—*school* MA-1
Duxbury Marsh—*swamp* MA-1
Duxbury Pier Light—*locale* MA-1
Duxbury Pier Lighthouse—*locale* MA-1
Duxbury Plaza (Shop Ctr)—*locale* MA-1
Duxbury Point—*cape* CA-9
Duxbury Reef—*bar* CA-9
Duxbury Town For—*forest* MA-1
**Duxbury (Town of)**—*pop pl* MA-1
**Duxbury (Town of)**—*pop pl* VT-1
*Duyer Gulch* CO-8
Duysard Ridge—*ridge* WV-2
Duzel Creek—*stream* CA-9
Duzel Rock—*pillar* CA-9
*Duzenberry Peak* CA-9
Duzine Sch—*school* NY-2
Dvarishkis Hunting Camp—*locale* WY-8
Dvorak Lake—*lake* WI-6
Dvorak Park—*park* IL-6
Dvorak Sch—*school* IL-6
*D V Partridge Estate Dam* MS-4
DVR Airp—*airport* AZ-5
**Dwaar Kill**—*pop pl* NY-2
**Dwaarkill**—*pop pl* NY-2
Dwaar Kill—*stream* (2) NY-2
*Dwaas Kill* NY-2
Dwaas Kill—*stream* NY-2
Dwale—*locale* VA-3
**Dwale**—*pop pl* KY-4
*Dwamish Bay* WA-9
*Dwamish Lake* WA-9
*Dwamish River* WA-9
Dwarf—*flat* UT-8
**Dwarf**—*pop pl* KY-4
Dwarf For—*forest* CA-9
*Dwarf Lake* MI-6
Dwarf Lake—*lake* FL-3
Dwarf Lake—*lake* MI-6
Dwarf Lakes Area—*area* OR-9
Dwarfs Kill—*stream* PA-2
Dwars Kill—*stream* NJ-2
Dwayne Spring—*spring* OR-9
Dwelley, William, House—*hist pl* WI-6
Dwelley Brook—*stream* ME-1
Dwelley Pond—*lake* ME-1
**Dwelly Corners**—*pop pl* NY-2
Dwelly Sch—*school* MA-1
**Dwenger Field**—*pop pl* IN-6
D W Field Park—*park* MA-1
*D W Forrest Cem* MS-4
D W G Universal Instrument Airp—*airport* PA-2
**Dwiggins**—*pop pl* MS-4
Dwiggins Post Office (historical)—*building* MS-4
Dwight—*locale* AL-4
Dwight—*locale* (2) VA-3
**Dwight**—*pop pl* ID-8
**Dwight**—*pop pl* IL-6
**Dwight**—*pop pl* KS-7
**Dwight**—*pop pl* MA-1
**Dwight**—*pop pl* NE-7
**Dwight**—*pop pl* ND-7
Dwight, Austin H., and Frankie A., Summer House—*hist pl* MI-6
Dwight Baity Dam—*dam* NC-3
Dwight Baptist Ch—*church* AL-4
Dwight Brandon Dam—*dam* AL-4
Dwight Brandon Lake—*reservoir* AL-4
Dwight Cem—*cemetery* KS-7
Dwight Cem—*cemetery* MA-1
Dwight Cem—*cemetery* OK-5
Dwight Chicago and Alton RR Depot—*hist pl* IL-6
Dwight Creek—*stream* CA-9
Dwight Creek—*stream* MT-8
Dwight Creek—*stream* OR-9
Dwight Creek—*stream* PA-2
Dwight Creek—*stream* SC-3
Dwight Creek Trail—*trail* MT-8
**Dwight Crossroads**—*pop pl* SC-3
Dwight Dam—*dam* MA-1
Dwight D Eisenhower Elem Sch—*school* FL-3
Dwight Drain—*canal* (2) MI-6
Dwight Elem Sch—*school* KS-7
Dwight Fields—*locale* LA-4
Dwight-Henderson House—*hist pl* MA-1
Dwight Hill—*summit* AL-4
Dwight (historical)—*locale* (2) NC-3
Dwight Hollow—*valley* PA-2
Dwight-Hooker Ave Hist Dist—*hist pl* NY-2
Dwight HS—*school* TX-5
Dwight Institute (historical)—*school* TN-4
Dwight JHS—*school* NJ-2
Dwight Manufacturing Company Housing District—*hist pl* MA-1
Dwight Mission—*church* OK-5
Dwight Mission—*hist pl* OK-5
Dwight Murphy Park—*park* CA-9
Dwight Pond—*lake* NY-2
Dwight Pond—*reservoir* SC-3
Dwight Sch—*school* AL-4
Dwight Sch—*school* (2) CT-1
Dwight Sch—*school* MA-1
Dwight Sch—*school* NJ-2
Dwights Point—*cape* WI-6
*Dwights Station* MA-1
*Dwight Station* MA-1
Dwight Street Hist Dist—*hist pl* CT-1
**Dwight Township**—*pop pl* ND-7
Dwight Township Hall—*building* ND-7
Dwight Township (historical)—*civil* ND-7
**Dwight (Township of)**—*pop pl* IL-6
**Dwight (Township of)**—*pop pl* MI-6
D Williams Ranch—*locale* NM-5
Dwina—*locale* VA-3
Dwina Hollow—*valley* VA-3
Dwinal Pond—*lake* ME-1
Dwina Station—*locale* VA-3
Dwinell Cem—*cemetery* MA-1
Dwinell Ditch—*canal* CO-8
Dwinell Ranch—*locale* CO-8
Dwinell Sch—*school* VT-1
*Dwinnell* CA-9
Dwinnell, George, House—*hist pl* WI-6
*Dwinnell Reservoir* CA-9
Dwire Valley—*basin* NE-7
D Woddell Dam—*dam* SD-7
D Wood Dam—*dam* SD-7
Dworshak Rsvr—*reservoir* ID-8
Dworshak Sch—*school* ID-8
D-W Ranch—*locale* AZ-5
D W Rutland Dam—*dam* AL-4
Dwyer—*locale* WY-8
**Dwyer**—*pop pl* MS-4
**Dwyer**—*pop pl* MO-7
**Dwyer**—*pop pl* NM-5
Dwyer Branch—*stream* MS-4
*Dwyer Canal* LA-4
Dwyer Canal—*canal* LA-4
Dwyer Cem—*cemetery* OH-6
Dwyer Cem—*cemetery* WY-8
Dwyer Creek—*stream* ID-8
Dwyer Creek—*stream* MT-8
Dwyer Creek—*stream* OR-9
Dwyer Dam—*dam* NV-8
Dwyer Dam—*dam* SD-7
Dwyer Gulch—*valley* CO-8
Dwyer Junction—*locale* WY-8
Dwyer Mesa—*summit* NM-5
Dwyer Mtn—*summit* NY-2
Dwyer Park—*park* IL-6
Dwyer Post Office (historical)—*building* MS-4
Dwyer Sch—*school* CA-9
Dwyer Sch—*school* MI-6
Dwyer Well—*well* AZ-5
DXN Bridge over Missouri River—*hist pl* WY-8
Dyal—*locale* FL-3
Dyal Cem—*cemetery* FL-3
Dyals Sch—*school* GA-3
Dyal-Upchurch Bldg—*hist pl* FL-3
Dyans Tank—*reservoir* TX-5
Dyar Rock—*pillar* OR-9
Dyar Spring—*spring* CA-9
Dyas—*locale* AL-4
Dyas—*locale* GA-3
Dyas Ch—*church* AL-4
*Dyas Creek* MS-4
Dyas Creek—*stream* AL-4
Dyas Hexagonal Barn—*hist pl* IA-7
Dyas Swamp—*swamp* AL-4
Dybdall Gristmill—*hist pl* WA-9
**Dyberry**—*pop pl* PA-2
Dyberry Cem—*cemetery* PA-2
Dyberry Creek—*stream* PA-2
**Dyberry (Township of)**—*pop pl* PA-2
Dybvig State Public Shooting Area—*park* SD-7
Dyce Creek—*stream* MT-8
Dyce Post Office (historical)—*building* SD-7
Dyche Cem—*cemetery* WV-2
Dyche Hall, Univ of Kansas—*hist pl* KS-7
Dyche Memorial Park—*cemetery* KY-4
Dyches Draw—*valley* UT-8
*Dyches Lake* SC-3
Dyches Lake—*lake* FL-3
Dyche Stadium—*other* IL-6
Dyche Valley—*valley* CA-9
**Dyckesville**—*pop pl* WI-6
Dyckman, William, House—*hist pl* NY-2
Dyckman Mtn—*summit* AK-9
Dyckman Park—*park* TX-5
*Dyck's River* KY-4
*Dycus* TN-4
Dycus—*other* TN-4
**Dycusburg**—*pop pl* KY-4
Dycusburg Cem—*cemetery* KY-4
Dycus Cem—*cemetery* KY-4
Dycus Landing—*locale* TN-4
Dycus Post Office (historical)—*building* TN-4
Dye—*locale* MO-7
Dye—*locale* TX-5
**Dye**—*pop pl* GA-3
**Dye**—*pop pl* VA-3
Dye, John Minor, Stone House—*hist pl* OH-6
Dyea—*locale* AK-9
Dyea Point—*cape* AK-9
Dye Branch—*stream* AL-4
Dye Branch—*stream* AR-4
Dye Branch—*stream* GA-3
Dye Branch—*stream* KY-4
Dye Branch—*stream* MS-4
Dye Branch—*stream* NC-3
Dye Branch—*stream* SC-3
Dye Branch—*stream* TN-4
Dye Brush Wash—*stream* NM-5
Dye Canyon—*valley* CA-9
Dye Cem—*cemetery* GA-3
Dye Cem—*cemetery* IN-6
Dye Cem—*cemetery* MI-6
Dye Cem—*cemetery* MS-4
Dye Cem—*cemetery* OH-6
Dye Cem—*cemetery* PA-2
Dye Cem—*cemetery* (3) TX-5
Dye Cem—*cemetery* (2) VA-3
Dye Ch—*church* (2) TX-5
*Dye Community* TX-5
*Dye Creek* AL-4
Dye Creek—*stream* AL-4
Dye Creek—*stream* AR-4
Dye Creek—*stream* CA-9
Dye Creek—*stream* IA-7
Dye Creek—*stream* MI-6
Dye Creek—*stream* NC-3
Dye Creek—*stream* OR-9
Dye Creek—*stream* (2) SC-3
Dye Creek—*stream* TX-5
Dye Dirt Hollow—*valley* TN-4
Dye Ditch—*canal* MS-4
Dye Hill—*summit* RI-1
Dye (historical P.O.)—*locale* IN-6
*Dye Inlet* WA-9
Dye JHS—*school* MI-6
Dye Knob—*summit* KY-4
Dye Lake—*lake* MI-6
Dye Leaf Branch—*stream* TN-4
Dyeleaf Mtn—*summit* NC-3
Dye Leaf Ridge—*ridge* TN-4
Dye Library—*building* MS-4
Dye Mill Branch—*stream* SC-3
*Dye Mound* TX-5
**Dye Mound**—*pop pl* TX-5
Dye Mound—*summit* TX-5
*Dye Mounds* TX-5
Dye Mtn—*summit* CA-9
Dye Pond—*lake* AL-4
Dyepot Branch—*stream* WV-2
**Dye (Pumpkin Center)**—*pop pl* VA-3
*Dyer* NM-5
Dyer—*locale* NE-7
Dyer—*locale* NV-8
Dyer—*locale* WA-9
**Dyer**—*pop pl* AR-4
**Dyer**—*pop pl* CA-9
**Dyer**—*pop pl* FL-3
**Dyer**—*pop pl* IN-6
**Dyer**—*pop pl* KY-4
**Dyer**—*pop pl* TN-4
**Dyer**—*pop pl* WV-2
Dyer, Nathaniel, House—*hist pl* ME-1
Dyer, Reuter, House—*hist pl* NY-2
Dyer Airp—*airport* NV-8
Dyer Amphitheater—*basin* CO-8
Dye Ranch—*locale* AZ-5
Dyer Bay—*bay* ME-1
Dyer Branch—*stream* GA-3
Dyer Branch—*stream* (6) KY-4
Dyer Branch—*stream* MO-7
Dyer Branch—*stream* PA-2
Dyer Branch—*stream* (3) TN-4
Dyer Branch—*stream* TX-5
Dyer Bridge—*bridge* GA-3
**Dyer Brook**—*pop pl* ME-1
Dyer Brook—*stream* (3) ME-1
Dyer Brook—*stream* (2) NH-1
*Dyer Brook Lake* RI-1
**Dyer Brook (Town of)**—*pop pl* ME-1
Dyer Canyon—*valley* CA-9
Dyer Canyon—*valley* NV-8
Dyer (CCD)—*cens area* TN-4
Dyer Cem—*cemetery* AR-4
Dyer Cem—*cemetery* GA-3
Dyer Cem—*cemetery* ME-1
Dyer Cem—*cemetery* MI-6
Dyer Cem—*cemetery* MS-4
Dyer Cem—*cemetery* (2) MO-7
Dyer Cem—*cemetery* NY-2
Dyer Cem—*cemetery* (8) TN-4
Dyer Cem—*cemetery* (2) WV-2
Dyer Ch—*church* AR-4
Dyer Chapel—*church* TN-4
Dyer Ch of Christ—*church* TN-4
Dyer City Hall—*building* TN-4
Dyer Corner—*locale* ME-1
**Dyer County**—*pop pl* TN-4
Dyer County Cem—*cemetery* TN-4
Dyer County Central Elem Sch—*school* (2) TN-4
Dyer County Courthouse—*building* TN-4
Dyer County Fairgrounds—*locale* TN-4
Dyer County Farm (historical)—*locale* TN-4
Dyer County HS—*school* TN-4
Dyer Cove—*bar* ME-1
Dyer Cove—*basin* GA-3
Dyer Cove—*bay* (3) ME-1
Dyer Cove—*bay* NJ-2
**Dyer Cove**—*pop pl* ME-1
Dyer Cove—*valley* NC-3
Dyer Cove—*valley* TN-4
Dyer Cove Point—*cape* ME-1
Dyer Cove Ridge—*ridge* ME-1
*Dyer Creek* TN-4
Dyer Creek—*stream* (4) CA-9
Dyer Creek—*stream* CO-8
Dyer Creek—*stream* GA-3
Dyer Creek—*stream* IN-6
Dyer Creek—*stream* KS-7
Dyer Creek—*stream* LA-4
Dyer Creek—*stream* MD-2
Dyer Creek—*stream* (2) MI-6
Dyer Creek—*stream* NJ-2
Dyer Creek—*stream* OK-5
Dyer Creek—*stream* OR-9
Dyer Creek—*stream* TN-4
Dyer Creek—*stream* TX-5
Dyer Creek—*stream* VA-3
Dyer Cumberland Presbyterian Ch—*church* TN-4
Dyer Ditch—*canal* CO-8
Dyer Ditch—*canal* IN-6
Dyer Ditch No 8—*canal* WY-8
Dyer Division—*civil* TN-4
Dyer Elem Sch—*school* TN-4
Dyer Field—*locale* GA-3
Dyer Flat Well—*well* NV-8
*Dyer Fork* CO-8
Dyer Fork Ditch—*canal* CO-8
Dyer Gap—*gap* GA-3
Dyer Gulch—*valley* CA-9
Dyer Gulch—*valley* TN-4
Dyer Gulch Creek—*stream* TN-4
Dyer Harbor—*bay* ME-1
Dyer Hill—*summit* KY-4
Dyer Hill—*summit* (2) ME-1
Dyer Hill—*summit* VT-1
Dyer Hill—*summit* WA-9
Dyer Hill Cem—*cemetery* ME-1
Dyer Hill Ch—*church* KY-4
Dyer Hill Creek—*stream* KY-4
Dyer Hill Mine—*mine* KY-4
Dyer Hills—*range* KY-4
Dyer Hill Spring—*spring* KY-4
Dyer Hollow—*valley* KY-4
Dyer HS—*school* TN-4
Dyer Ice Pond—*lake* ME-1
Dye Ridge—*ridge* AZ-5
Dye Ridge—*ridge* OH-6
Dyer Industrial Park—*locale* TN-4
Dyer Island—*island* (2) ME-1
Dyer Island—*island* RI-1
Dyer Island Narrows—*channel* ME-1
*Dyer Junior High School* IN-6
Dyer-Kelly Sch—*school* CA-9
Dyer Knob—*summit* NC-3
*Dyer Lake* MI-6
Dyer Lake—*lake* (5) MI-6
Dyer Lake—*reservoir* IN-6
Dyer Lake—*reservoir* (2) TN-4
Dyer Lake—*reservoir* WI-6
Dyer Lake Dam—*dam* IN-6
Dyer Lake Dam—*dam* (2) TN-4
Dyer Long Pond—*lake* ME-1
*Dyer Mine* UT-8
Dyer Mines—*mine* UT-8
Dyer MS—*school* IN-6
Dyer Mtn—*summit* CA-9
Dyer Mtn—*summit* CO-8
Dyer Mtn—*summit* (2) GA-3
Dyer Mtn—*summit* OK-5
Dyer Mtn—*summit* UT-8
Dyer Neck—*cape* ME-1
Dyer Park—*flat* UT-8
Dyer Park—*park* OH-6
Dyer Pike Trail—*trail* PA-2
Dyer Point—*cape* FL-3
Dyer Point—*cape* (3) ME-1
Dyer Point Riffles—*rapids* ME-1
Dyer Pond—*lake* IL-6
Dyer Pond—*lake* ME-1
Dyer Pond—*lake* MA-1
Dyer Pond—*lake* RI-1
Dyer Pond—*swamp* ME-1
Dyer Post Office—*building* TN-4
Dyer Postoffice—*locale* NV-8
Dyer Ranch—*locale* NV-8
Dyer Ranch—*locale* NM-5
Dyer Ridge—*ridge* TN-4
Dyer River—*stream* ME-1
*Dyer Rock* OR-9
Dyer Rock Creek—*stream* MO-7
Dyer Rosenwald Sch—*school* TN-4
Dyer RR Station—*locale* FL-3
Dyer Rsvr—*reservoir* OR-9
Dyer Run—*stream* PA-2
Dyers Branch—*stream* MO-7
Dyers Branch—*stream* TX-5
Dyers Bridge (historical)—*bridge* AL-4
**Dyersburg**—*pop pl* TN-4
Dyersburg (CCD)—*cens area* TN-4
Dyersburg City Hall—*building* TN-4
Dyersburg Division—*civil* TN-4
Dyersburg First Baptist Ch—*church* TN-4
*Dyersburgh* TN-4
*Dyersburgh Post Office* TN-4
Dyersburg HS—*school* TN-4
Dyersburg Industrial Park—*locale* TN-4
Dyersburg Male and Female Acad (historical)—*school* TN-4
Dyersburg MS—*school* TN-4
Dyersburg Municipal Airp—*airport* TN-4
Dyersburg Post Office—*building* TN-4
Dyersburg Second Baptist Ch—*church* TN-4
Dyersburg State Community Coll—*school* TN-4
Dyers Cave—*cave* WV-2
Dyers Cem—*cemetery* TN-4
Dyer Sch—*school* IL-6
Dyer Sch—*school* MA-1
Dyer Sch—*school* NV-8
Dyer Sch—*school* OH-6
Dyer Sch—*school* VT-1
Dyers Chapel—*church* KY-4
Dyers Chapel—*church* VA-3
*Dyers Chapel Church of Christ* TN-4
*Dyers Creek* TN-4
Dyers Creek—*stream* CO-8
Dyers Creek—*stream* GA-3
Dyers Creek—*stream* IN-6
Dyers Creek—*stream* KY-4
Dyers Creek—*stream* PA-2
Dyers Creek—*stream* TN-4
**Dyers Crossroads**—*pop pl* AL-4
**Dyersdale**—*pop pl* TX-5
Dyers Ferry (historical)—*crossing* TN-4
Dyers Fork—*stream* PA-2
Dyers Hill Ch—*church* SC-3
Dyers Hill Sch—*school* PA-2
*Dyers Island* RI-1
Dyers Knob—*summit* VA-3
Dyers Knob—*summit* WV-2
Dyers Lake—*lake* MN-6
Dyers Park—*flat* CO-8
Dyers Point—*cape* FL-3
*Dyers Pond* MA-1
*Dyers Pond* RI-1
Dyer Spring—*spring* AZ-5
Dyer Spring—*spring* WY-8
*Dyers Run* PA-2
Dyers Run—*stream* WV-2
Dyers Run Dam Number Three—*dam* PA-2
Dyers Slough—*gut* WI-6
*Dyers Station Post Office* TN-4
Dyers Store—*locale* (2) VA-3
Dyer State Wayside—*park* OR-9
*Dyer Station* TN-4
Dyerstown—*locale* PA-2
Dyerstown Hist Dist—*hist pl* PA-2
Dyer Street Sch—*school* CA-9
*Dyersville* TN-4
Dyersville—*locale* CO-8
**Dyersville**—*pop pl* IA-7
Dye Rsvr—*reservoir* CO-8
Dyer Top—*summit* NC-3
Dyer (Township of)—*fmr MCD* (2) AR-4
Dyer (Township of)—*unorg* ME-1
Dye Run—*stream* WV-2
*Dyerville* CA-9
*Dyerville* IA-7
*Dyerville* RI-1
Dyerville—*locale* ME-1
**Dyerville**—*pop pl* RI-1
Dyerville Giant—*locale* CA-9
Dyerville Mill—*hist pl* RI-1
Dyerville (Site)—*locale* CA-9
Dyer Well—*well* OR-9
Dyes Branch—*stream* TX-5

# E

*E* WA-9
*E* MH-9
E—*mine* OR-9
E, Ditch—*canal* AR-4
E, Ditch—*canal* MS-4
Ea, Loko—*lake* HI-9
E A A Chapter 453 Airp—*airport* MO-7
E Ables Lake—*reservoir* AL-4
E Ables Lake Dam—*dam* AL-4
Eacher Hollow—*valley* NY-2
*Eachpoquastsit Pond* MA-1
Eachus Lake—*lake* CA-9
*Eacker Creek* KS-7
Ead Creek—*stream* OR-9
Eaddy Big Lake—*lake* SC-3
*Eadendale Church* AL-4
Eader Sch—*school* CA-9
Eades Branch—*stream* AL-4
Eades Cem—*cemetery* MS-4
Eades Corners—*locale* PA-2
Eades Post Office (historical)—*building* MS-4
Eades Slope Mine (underground)—*mine* AL-4
Eades Spring—*spring* CA-9
Eades Tavern—*hist pl* KY-4
Ead Ferry Landing—*locale* AL-4
Eadie Ford (historical)—*crossing* TN-4
Eadl Hollow—*valley* AR-4
**Eads**—*pop pl* CO-8
**Eads**—*pop pl* TN-4
**Eads**—*pop pl* VA-3
Eads Bluff—*cliff* TN-4
Eads Bridge—*hist pl* IL-6
Eads Bridge—*hist pl* MO-7
Eads Bridge—*other* IL-6
Eads Bridge—*other* MO-7
Eads Cem—*cemetery* TN-4
*Eads Creek* OR-9
Eads Creek—*stream* MS-4
Eads Creek—*stream* MO-7
Eads Creek—*stream* TX-5
Eads Creek Cem—*cemetery* MO-7
Eads Ditch—*canal* IN-6
Eads Gap—*gap* NC-3
Eads Hill Trail—*trail* OR-9
Eads Hollow—*valley* IN-6
Eads Hollow—*valley* (2) KY-4
Eads Hollow—*valley* TN-4
*Eads Island* CA-9
Eads Mill—*locale* WV-2
Eads Municipal Airp—*airport* CO-8
Eadson Sch—*school* KY-4
Eadsons Spring—*spring* MO-7
Eads Ridge—*ridge* WV-2
Eads Sch—*school* TN-4
*Eads School* IN-6
Eads Spring—*spring* TN-4
Eads Springs—*spring* OR-9
Eadsville—*locale* KY-4
Eadsville—*locale* WI-6
Eadsville—*locale* WY-8
Eads Wash—*stream* AZ-5
Eady Cem—*cemetery* TN-4
**Eady City**—*pop pl* AL-4
Eady Hollow—*valley* MO-7
Eady Pond—*reservoir* GA-3
**Eadytown**—*pop pl* SC-3
Eaf Hollow—*valley* KY-4
Eagalite Cem—*cemetery* CO-8
Eagalite School—*locale* CO-8
*Eagan* AL-4
**Eagan**—*pop pl* MN-6
**Eagan**—*pop pl* TN-4
Eagan Baptist Ch—*church* TN-4
Eagan Cem—*cemetery* IL-6
Eagan Creek—*stream* ID-8
Eagan Creek—*stream* MO-7
**Eagandale**—*pop pl* MN-6
Eagan Ditch—*canal* IN-6
Eagan Point—*summit* ID-8
Eagan Post Office—*building* TN-4
*Eagans* TN-4
Eagans Branch—*stream* TX-5
Eagan Sch—*school* AL-4
Eagan Sch (historical)—*school* TN-4
Eagans Creek—*stream* TX-5
*Eagans Station* TN-4
*Eagans Store* TN-4
Eagan (Township of)—*other* MN-6
*Eaganville* TN-4
Eaganville Post Office (historical)—*building* TN-4
**Eagar**—*pop pl* AZ-5
Eagar Elem Sch—*school* AZ-5
Eagar-Slade Dam—*dam* AZ-5
Eagar-Springerville (CCD)—*cens area* AZ-5
**Eagarville (corporate name for Eagerville)**—*pop pl* IL-6
Eagel Mine (abandoned)—*locale* WY-8
*Eagel Tail* KS-7
Eagel View Springs Golf Course—*locale* PA-2
Eagen, Mount—*summit* ID-8
Eagen Lake—*lake* MN-6
Eager Ch—*church* KY-4
Eager Free Public Library—*hist pl* WI-6
Eager Inn—*hist pl* OH-6
Eagers Bay—*bay* NY-2
**Eagerville**—*pop pl* IL-6
*Eagerville (corporate name Eagarville)* IL-6
*Eagigen Island* MP-9
Eagin Cem—*cemetery* TN-4
*Eagle* CO-8
*Eagle* IN-6
*Eagle* KS-7
*Eagle* MS-4
Eagle—*locale* IL-6
Eagle—*locale* NJ-2
Eagle—*locale* PA-2
Eagle—*locale* SD-7
Eagle—*mine* UT-8
**Eagle**—*pop pl* AL-4
**Eagle**—*pop pl* AK-9
**Eagle**—*pop pl* CO-8
**Eagle**—*pop pl* (2) ID-8
**Eagle**—*pop pl* KS-7
**Eagle**—*pop pl* MI-6
**Eagle**—*pop pl* NE-7
**Eagle**—*pop pl* NY-2
**Eagle**—*pop pl* NC-3
**Eagle**—*pop pl* PA-2
**Eagle**—*pop pl* WV-2
**Eagle**—*pop pl* WI-6
Eagle—*post sta* DC-2
Eagle, Mount—*summit* VI-3
**Eagle Acres**—*pop pl* TX-5
Eagle Adventist Schoolhouse—*hist pl* ID-8
Eagle Airp—*airport* MS-4
Eagle Airstrip—*airport* OR-9
Eagle and Blue Bell Mine—*hist pl* UT-8
Eagle ANV775—*reserve* AK-9
Eagle Arroyo—*valley* TX-5
Eagle-Babb Mine—*mine* KY-4
Eagle Bank Landing (historical)—*locale* MS-4
Eagle Banners Ranch Lake Dam—*dam* MS-4
Eagle Bar—*bar* ID-8
Eagle Bar—*bar* MA-1
Eagle Bar (historical)—*bar* AL-4
Eagle Bar (historical)—*locale* AL-4
Eagle Basin—*basin* UT-8
*Eagle Basin Hideout Trail* UT-8
*Eagle Bay* NY-2
Eagle Bay—*bay* (5) AK-9
Eagle Bay—*bay* MI-6
Eagle Bay—*bay* NJ-2
Eagle Bay—*bay* NY-2
Eagle Bay—*bay* WI-6
Eagle Bay—*bay* WY-8
Eagle Bay—*lake* FL-3
**Eagle Bay**—*pop pl* NY-2
Eagle Bay Creek—*stream* AK-9
Eagle Bay Island—*island* AK-9
*Eagle Bayou* LA-4
Eagle Bayou—*stream* LA-4
**Eagle Beach**—*pop pl* OH-6
*Eaglebend* MS-4
Eagle Bend—*bend* TN-4
Eagle Bend—*bend* WV-2
**Eagle Bend**—*pop pl* MN-6
**Eagle Bend**—*pop pl* MS-4
Eagle Bend Cem—*cemetery* MN-6
Eagle Bend Cut-Off—*bend* TX-5
Eagle Bend Industrial Park—*locale* TN-4
Eagle Bend Lake—*lake* OK-5
Eagle Bend Landing—*locale* MS-4
Eagle Bend Point—*cape* LA-4
Eagle Bend Public Access Area—*park* TN-4
Eaglebird Mine—*mine* CA-9
Eagle Bird Mine—*mine* CO-8
Eagle Bird Mine—*mine* ID-8
Eagle Bird Mine—*mine* SD-7
Eagle Bird Mine (Abandoned)—*mine* CA-9
Eagle Bird Trail—*trail* CA-9
Eagle Bluff—*cliff* AL-4
Eagle Bluff—*cliff* (2) AK-9
Eagle Bluff—*cliff* ID-8
Eagle Bluff—*cliff* (2) ME-1
Eagle Bluff—*cliff* MN-6
Eagle Bluff—*cliff* MO-7
Eagle Bluff—*cliff* NY-2
Eagle Bluff—*cliff* (2) TX-5
Eagle Bluff—*cliff* (2) WI-6
Eagle Bluff—*summit* TN-4
Eagle Bluff Lake—*reservoir* TN-4
Eagle Bluff Landing (historical)—*locale* AL-4
Eagle Bluff Lighthouse—*hist pl* WI-6
Eagle Bluffs—*cliff* TX-5
Eagle Bluff Springs—*spring* TN-4
Eagle Borax Spring—*spring* CA-9
Eagle Borax Works—*hist pl* CA-9
Eagle Bottom Creek—*stream* VA-3
Eagle Brake—*swamp* AR-4
Eagle Brake—*swamp* MS-4
Eagle Branch—*stream* GA-3
Eagle Branch—*stream* IL-6
Eagle Branch—*stream* IN-6
Eagle Branch—*stream* MO-7
Eagle Branch—*stream* TN-4
Eagle Branch—*stream* (2) TX-5
Eagle Branch—*stream* (2) WV-2
Eagle Bridge—*bridge* ID-8
**Eagle Bridge**—*pop pl* NY-2
Eagle Brook—*stream* ME-1
Eagle Brook—*stream* MA-1
**Eaglebrook Estates Subdivision**—*pop pl* UT-8
Eaglebrook Gulch—*valley* CO-8
Eagle Brook Sch—*school* MA-1
*Eagle Butte* MT-8
**Eagle Butte**—*pop pl* SD-7
Eagle Butte—*summit* (2) MT-8
Eagle Butte—*summit* NV-8
Eagle Butte—*summit* (5) OR-9
Eagle Butte—*summit* SD-7
Eagle Butte Creek—*stream* OR-9
Eagle Butte Lake—*reservoir* SD-7
Eagle Buttes—*summit* MT-8
Eagle Buttes—*summit* WY-8
Eagle Butte Sch—*school* MT-8
Eagle Camp—*locale* OR-9
Eagle Camp—*locale* TX-5
Eagle Camp—*locale* WY-8
Eagle Campground—*locale* CA-9
*Eagle Canyon* NV-8
Eagle Canyon—*valley* AZ-5
Eagle Canyon—*valley* (4) CA-9
Eagle Canyon—*valley* MT-8
Eagle Canyon—*valley* NE-7
Eagle Canyon—*valley* NV-8
Eagle Canyon—*valley* (3) NM-5
Eagle Canyon—*valley* (2) OR-9
Eagle Canyon—*valley* (3) TX-5
Eagle Canyon—*valley* (2) UT-8
Eagle Canyon—*valley* WY-8
Eagle Canyon Channel—*canal* CA-9
Eagle Canyon Ditch—*canal* CA-9
Eagle Canyon Tank—*reservoir* TX-5
Eagle Cap—*summit* OR-9
Eagle Cape—*cape* AK-9
Eagle Cap Wilderness Area—*reserve* OR-9
Eagle Cave—*cave* WI-6
Eagle Cem—*cemetery* KS-7
Eagle Cem—*cemetery* NE-7
Eagle Cem—*cemetery* NY-2
Eagle Cem—*cemetery* ND-7
Eagle Cem—*cemetery* SD-7
Eagle Cem—*cemetery* WV-2
Eagle Center—*locale* NY-2
**Eagle Center**—*pop pl* IA-7
Eagle Ch—*church* IL-6
Eagle Ch—*church* MI-6
Eagle Ch—*church* PA-2
Eagle Ch—*church* VA-3
Eagle Ch—*church* WV-2
Eagle Chapel—*church* WV-2
**Eagle Chase (subdivision)**—*pop pl* NC-3
Eagle Chasing Draw—*valley* SD-7
Eagle Chief Cem—*cemetery* OK-5
Eagle Chief Creek—*stream* OK-5
Eagle Chief Creek—*stream* SD-7
Eagle Child Mtn—*summit* MT-8
Eagle Chute—*stream* LA-4
*Eagle City* OR-9
Eagle City—*locale* IA-7
Eagle City—*locale* UT-8
**Eagle City**—*pop pl* OH-6
**Eagle City**—*pop pl* OK-5
Eagle City Cem—*cemetery* OK-5
Eagle Cliff—*cliff* AL-4
Eagle Cliff—*cliff* AK-9
Eagle Cliff—*cliff* CO-8
Eagle Cliff—*cliff* GA-3
Eagle Cliff—*cliff* ID-8
Eagle Cliff—*cliff* MT-8
Eagle Cliff—*cliff* (3) NH-1
Eagle Cliff—*cliff* (2) NY-2
Eagle Cliff—*cliff* NC-3
Eagle Cliff—*cliff* TN-4
Eagle Cliff—*cliff* TX-5
Eagle Cliff—*cliff* VA-3
Eagle Cliff—*cliff* (3) WA-9
Eagle Cliff—*locale* GA-3
Eagle Cliff—*locale* WA-9
Eagle Cliff Cem—*cemetery* WA-9
Eagle Cliff Mtn—*summit* CO-8
Eagle Cliff Pit—*cave* TN-4
Eagle Club Lake—*reservoir* GA-3
Eagle Corners—*locale* WI-6
Eagle Coulee—*valley* MT-8
Eagle Cove—*basin* TX-5
Eagle Cove—*bay* OR-9
Eagle Cove—*bay* WA-9
Eagle Cove—*valley* ID-8
Eagle Crag—*pillar* NH-1
Eagle Crag—*summit* AZ-5
Eagle Crage—*summit* CA-9
Eagle Crag Lake—*lake* NY-2
Eagle Crag Ruin—*locale* AZ-5
Eagle Crags—*summit* CA-9
Eagle Crags—*summit* OR-9
Eagle Crags—*summit* UT-8
*Eagle Creek* AZ-5
*Eagle Creek* CA-9
*Eagle Creek* ID-8
*Eagle Creek* IN-6
*Eagle Creek* KS-7
*Eagle Creek* LA-4
*Eagle Creek* MT-8
*Eagle Creek* NC-3
*Eagle Creek* OH-6
*Eagle Creek* OK-5
*Eagle Creek* OR-9
*Eaglecreek* TN-4
*Eagle Creek* UT-8
*Eagle Creek* WA-9
*Eagle Creek* WI-6
*Eagle Creek* WY-8
Eagle Creek—*locale* TN-4
**Eagle Creek**—*pop pl* AL-4
**Eagle Creek**—*pop pl* AZ-5
**Eagle Creek**—*pop pl* OR-9
Eagle Creek—*stream* AL-4
Eagle Creek—*stream* (11) AK-9
Eagle Creek—*stream* AZ-5
Eagle Creek—*stream* (15) CA-9
Eagle Creek—*stream* (2) CO-8
Eagle Creek—*stream* FL-3
Eagle Creek—*stream* GA-3
Eagle Creek—*stream* (13) ID-8
Eagle Creek—*stream* (5) IL-6
Eagle Creek—*stream* (6) IN-6
Eagle Creek—*stream* IA-7
Eagle Creek—*stream* (4) KS-7
Eagle Creek—*stream* (5) KY-4
Eagle Creek—*stream* MI-6
Eagle Creek—*stream* (3) MN-6
Eagle Creek—*stream* MO-7
Eagle Creek—*stream* (15) MT-8
Eagle Creek—*stream* (2) NE-7
Eagle Creek—*stream* NV-8
Eagle Creek—*stream* (3) NM-5
Eagle Creek—*stream* NY-2
Eagle Creek—*stream* NC-3
Eagle Creek—*stream* (5) OH-6
Eagle Creek—*stream* (5) OK-5
Eagle Creek—*stream* (15) OR-9
Eagle Creek—*stream* SC-3
Eagle Creek—*stream* (2) SD-7
Eagle Creek—*stream* (4) TN-4
Eagle Creek—*stream* (6) TX-5
Eagle Creek—*stream* UT-8
Eagle Creek—*stream* (11) WA-9
Eagle Creek—*stream* (3) WI-6
Eagle Creek—*stream* (7) WY-8
Eagle Creek Airpark—*airport* IN-6
Eagle Creek Archeol Site—*hist pl* NE-7
Eagle Creek Baptist Ch—*church* TN-4
Eagle Creek Benches—*bench* CA-9
Eagle Creek Camp—*locale* CA-9
Eagle Creek Campground—*locale* CA-9
Eagle Creek Campground—*locale* WY-8
Eagle Creek Campground—*park* OR-9
Eagle Creek Canyon—*valley* OR-9
Eagle Creek Cem—*cemetery* AL-4
Eagle Creek Cem—*cemetery* OH-6
Eagle Creek Cem—*cemetery* TN-4
Eagle Creek Cem—*cemetery* TX-5
Eagle Creek Ch—*church* AL-4
Eagle Creek Ch—*church* IN-6
Eagle Creek Ch—*church* KY-4
Eagle Creek Ch—*church* (2) OH-6
Eagle Creek Covered Bridge—*hist pl* OH-6
Eagle Creek Cutoff—*trail* OR-9
Eagle Creek Dam—*dam* IN-6
Eagle Creek Forest Camp—*park* OR-9
**Eagle Creek (historical)**—*pop pl* TN-4
Eagle Creek Lodge—*locale* NM-5
Eagle Creek Lookout—*locale* OR-9
Eagle Creek Meadows—*flat* WY-8
Eagle Creek Park—*park* (2) IN-6
Eagle Creek Parks—*flat* WY-8
*Eagle Creek Peak* CA-9
*Eagle Creek Point* ID-8
*Eagle Creek Post Office* TN-4
Eaglecreek Post Office (historical)—*building* TN-4
Eagle Creek Pumping Station—*locale* AZ-5
Eagle Creek Ranch—*locale* CA-9
Eagle Creek Ranger Station—*locale* MT-8
Eagle Creek Recreation Site—*park* OR-9
Eagle Creek Rsvr—*reservoir* IN-6
Eagle Creek Sch—*school* MT-8
Eagle Creek Sch—*school* OR-9
Eagle Creek (Township of)—*other* MN-6
**Eagle Creek (Township of)**—*pop pl* IL-6
**Eagle Creek (Township of)**—*pop pl* IN-6
Eagle Creek Trail—*trail* (2) OR-9
Eagle Creek Upper Falls—*falls* OR-9
Eagle Creek Well—*well* NM-5
Eagle Crest Airp—*airport* DE-2
Eagle Crest Corner—*locale* OR-9
**Eagle Crest Corners**—*pop pl* OR-9
Eagle Crest Creek—*stream* IN-6
Eagle Crest Golf Course Dam—*dam* NC-3
Eagle Crest Rsvr—*reservoir* OR-9
Eagle Crest Spring—*spring* OR-9
**Eagledale**—*pop pl* WA-9
Eagledale Independent Baptist Ch—*church* IN-6
Eagledale Nazarene Ch—*church* IN-6
Eagledale Plaza—*locale* IN-6
Eagle Dam—*dam* AZ-5
Eagle Dell Peak—*summit* CA-9
*Eagle Ditch* IN-6
Eagle Ditch—*canal* CA-9
Eagle Ditch—*canal* CO-8
Eagle Ditch—*canal* IL-6
Eagle Ditch—*canal* WY-8
Eagle Drain—*canal* MI-6
Eagle Draw—*valley* NV-8
Eagle Draw—*valley* ND-7
Eagle Draw—*valley* (2) TX-5
Eagle Draw—*valley* (2) WY-8
Eagle Drive Sch—*school* NY-2
Eagle Eye Mesa—*summit* CO-8
Eagle Eye Mine—*mine* AZ-5
Eagle Eye Mtn—*summit* AZ-5
Eagle Eye Peak—*summit* AZ-5
Eagle Eye Peak—*summit* NM-5
Eagle Eye Ranch—*locale* AZ-5
Eagle Eye Sch—*school* PA-2
Eagle Eye Substation—*locale* (2) AZ-5
Eagle Eyrie—*summit* NY-2
Eagle Eyrie Virginia Baptist Assembly—*locale* VA-3
*Eagle Falls* WA-9
Eagle Falls—*falls* CA-9
Eagle Falls—*falls* CO-8
Eagle Falls—*falls* KY-4
Eagle Falls—*falls* TN-4
Eagle Falls—*falls* WA-9
Eagle Falls—*locale* NY-2
Eagle Falls Campground—*locale* CA-9
Eagle Falls Ch (historical)—*church* TN-4
Eagle Falls Sluice—*hist pl* NC-3
**Eagle Farms**—*pop pl* PA-2
*Eagle Feather Creek* SD-7
Eagle Feather Lake—*reservoir* SD-7
Eagle Feathers Creek—*stream* MT-8
Eagle Fern Park—*park* OR-9
Eagle Field—*airport* PA-2
Eagle Flat—*flat* NV-8
Eagle Flat—*flat* UT-8
Eagle Flat—*locale* TX-5
Eagle Flat Draw—*valley* TX-5
**Eagle Ford**—*pop pl* TX-5
Eagle Ford Sch—*school* TX-5
*Eagle Fork* OK-5
Eagle Fork Ch—*church* NC-3
*Eagle Fork Creek* OK-5
Eagle Fork Creek—*stream* NC-3
Eagle Forks Forest Campground—*park* OR-9
Eagle Foundary—*locale* PA-2
Eagle Foundry—*locale* PA-2
Eagle Foundry Ch—*church* PA-2
Eagle Furnace—*locale* VA-3
**Eagle Furnace**—*pop pl* TN-4
Eagle Furnace Ch—*church* TN-4
Eagle Furnace Post Office (historical)—*building* TN-4
Eagle Gap—*gap* AR-4
Eagle Gap—*gap* NC-3
Eagle Gap—*gap* OR-9
Eagle Gap—*gap* (2) TN-4
Eagle Gap Cem—*cemetery* AR-4
Eagle Gap Ranger Station—*locale* AR-4
Eagle Glacier—*glacier* (2) AK-9
**Eagle Gorge**—*pop pl* WA-9
Eagle Gorge—*valley* AK-9
Eagle Gorge—*valley* WA-9
*Eagle Gorge Reservoir* WA-9
*Eaglegrove* IA-7
Eagle Grove—*locale* GA-3
**Eagle Grove**—*pop pl* IA-7
Eagle Grove Ch—*church* AL-4
Eagle Grove Ch—*church* MS-4
Eagle Grove Ch—*church* OK-5
Eagle Grove City Hall—*building* IA-7
Eagle Grove Country Club—*other* IA-7
Eagle Grove (historical P.O.)—*locale* IA-7
Eagle Grove HS—*school* IA-7
Eagle Grove JHS*—*school* IA-7
*Eagle Grove Junction* IA-7
Eagle Grove Public Library—*hist pl* IA-7
Eagle Grove Township—*fmr MCD* IA-7
Eagle Gulch—*valley* (3) CA-9
Eagle Gulch—*valley* CO-8
Eagle Gulch—*valley* NV-8
Eagle Gulch—*valley* OR-9
Eagle Gully—*valley* TX-5
Eagle-Gypsum—*cens area* CO-8
Eagle Hall—*locale* MD-2
Eagle Harbor—*bay* (4) AK-9
Eagle Harbor—*bay* FL-3
Eagle Harbor—*bay* MI-6
Eagle Harbor—*bay* (2) WA-9
Eagle Harbor—*bay* WI-6
Eagle Harbor—*locale* AK-9
**Eagle Harbor**—*pop pl* MD-2
**Eagle Harbor**—*pop pl* MI-6
**Eagle Harbor**—*pop pl* NY-2
Eagle Harbor Lighthouse—*locale* MI-6
Eagle Harbor Light Station—*hist pl* MI-6
Eagle Harbor Schoolhouse—*hist pl* MI-6
**Eagle Harbor Station**—*pop pl* NY-2
Eagle Harbor (Township of)—*civ div* MI-6
Eagle Head—*cape* MA-1
Eaglehead Lookout Tower—*locale* MN-6
Eaglehead Mtn—*summit* (2) MT-8
Eaglehead Ranch Airp—*airport* KS-7
Eagle Head Rock—*summit* AZ-5
**Eagle Heights**—*pop pl* IL-6
**Eagle Heights**—*pop pl* PA-2
Eagle Heights—*uninc pl* WI-6
Eagle Heights Sch—*school* AR-4
**Eagle Heights (subdivision)**—*pop pl* NC-3
*Eagle Hill* CA-9
Eagle Hill—*cliff* MA-1
Eagle Hill—*locale* KY-4
**Eagle Hill**—*pop pl* MD-2
**Eagle Hill**—*pop pl* TN-4
Eagle Hill—*summit* CA-9
Eagle Hill—*summit* CO-8
Eagle Hill—*summit* LA-4
Eagle Hill—*summit* ME-1
Eagle Hill—*summit* MD-2
Eagle Hill—*summit* (2) MA-1
Eagle Hill—*summit* NY-2
Eagle Hill—*summit* TX-5
Eagle Hill—*summit* UT-8
Eagle Hill—*summit* WY-8
Eagle Hill Cem—*cemetery* NM-5
Eagle Hill Community Center—*locale* TN-4
Eagle Hill JHS—*school* NY-2
Eagle Hill Oil Field—*oilfield* TX-5
*Eaglehill River* MA-1
Eagle Hill River—*stream* MA-1
Eagle Hill River Marshes—*swamp* MA-1
Eagle Hill Sch—*school* MA-1
Eagle Hill Sch (historical)—*school* TN-4
Eagle Hist Dist—*hist pl* AK-9
Eagle (historical)—*locale* (2) SD-7
**Eagle Hollow**—*pop pl* IN-6
Eagle Hollow—*valley* IN-6
Eagle Hollow—*valley* MA-1
Eagle Hollow—*valley* OH-6
Eagle Hollow—*valley* OK-5
Eagle Hollow—*valley* TN-4
Eagle Hollow—*valley* UT-8
*Eagle Hol-low Creek* IN-6
Eagle Hollow Creek—*stream* IN-6
Eagle Hollow Notch—*gap* VT-1
Eagle Hotel—*hist pl* NH-1
Eagle Hotel—*hist pl* PA-2
Eagle Hotel—*locale* CA-9
Eagle House—*hist pl* AR-4
**Eaglehurst**—*pop pl* PA-2
Eagle Island—*hist pl* ME-1
Eagle Island—*island* (5) AK-9
Eagle Island—*island* (2) FL-3
Eagle Island—*island* ID-8
Eagle Island—*island* (3) IL-6
Eagle Island—*island* (2) IN-6
Eagle Island—*island* (3) LA-4
Eagle Island—*island* (7) ME-1
Eagle Island—*island* MD-2
Eagle Island—*island* (3) MA-1
Eagle Island—*island* (2) MI-6
Eagle Island—*island* MN-6
Eagle Island—*island* (2) MO-7
Eagle Island—*island* NH-1
Eagle Island—*island* (2) NJ-2
Eagle Island—*island* (4) NY-2
Eagle Island—*island* NC-3
Eagle Island—*island* OR-9
Eagle Island—*island* SC-3
Eagle Island—*island* SD-7
Eagle Island—*island* WA-9
Eagle Island—*island* (2) WI-6
Eagle Island—*locale* FL-3
**Eagle Island**—*pop pl* ME-1
Eagle Island Bayou—*stream* LA-4
Eagle Island Camp—*hist pl* NY-2
Eagle Island Channel—*channel* MA-1
Eagle Island Creek—*stream* OR-9
Eagle Island Gut—*gut* NJ-2
Eagle Island (historical)—*island* AL-4
Eagle Island Ledge—*bar* ME-1
Eagle Island Prison Farm—*area* ID-8
Eagle Island Reef—*bar* ME-1
Eagle Island Shoals—*bar* WI-6
Eaglek Bay—*bay* AK-9
Eagle Key—*island* FL-3
Eagle Key Pass—*channel* FL-3
Eaglek Glacier—*glacier* AK-9
Eagle King Mine—*mine* CA-9
Eaglek Island—*island* AK-9
Eagle Knob—*summit* GA-3
Eagle Knob—*summit* (2) NC-3
Eagle Knob—*summit* VA-3
Eagle Knob Branch—*stream* KY-4
*Eagle Lake* AR-4
*Eagle Lake* CA-9
*Eagle Lake* IL-6
*Eagle Lake* LA-4
*Eagle Lake* MI-6
*Eagle Lake* MS-4
*Eagle Lake* WA-9
*Eagle Lake* WI-6
Eagle Lake—*lake* (3) AK-9
Eagle Lake—*lake* (5) AR-4
Eagle Lake—*lake* (3) CA-9
Eagle Lake—*lake* (2) CO-8
Eagle Lake—*lake* (3) FL-3
Eagle Lake—*lake* (2) IL-6
Eagle Lake—*lake* (2) IN-6
Eagle Lake—*lake* (2) IA-7
Eagle Lake—*lake* KY-4
Eagle Lake—*lake* (3) LA-4
Eagle Lake—*lake* (4) ME-1
Eagle Lake—*lake* (12) MI-6
Eagle Lake—*lake* (19) MN-6
Eagle Lake—*lake* (3) MS-4
Eagle Lake—*lake* MO-7
Eagle Lake—*lake* MT-8
Eagle Lake—*lake* (2) NY-2
Eagle Lake—*lake* OK-5
Eagle Lake—*lake* OR-9
Eagle Lake—*lake* TN-4
Eagle Lake—*lake* TX-5
Eagle Lake—*lake* (3) WA-9
Eagle Lake—*lake* (11) WI-6
**Eagle Lake**—*pop pl* FL-3
**Eagle Lake**—*pop pl* IL-6
**Eagle Lake**—*pop pl* ME-1
**Eagle Lake**—*pop pl* (2) MI-6
**Eagle Lake**—*pop pl* MN-6
**Eagle Lake**—*pop pl* MS-4
**Eagle Lake**—*pop pl* NY-2
**Eagle Lake**—*pop pl* TX-5
**Eagle Lake**—*pop pl* WI-6
Eagle Lake—*reservoir* GA-3
Eagle Lake—*reservoir* IN-6
Eagle Lake—*reservoir* MA-1
Eagle Lake—*reservoir* (2) MN-6
Eagle Lake—*reservoir* NM-5
Eagle Lake—*reservoir* NY-2
Eagle Lake—*reservoir* NC-3

Eagle Lake—*reservoir* TX-5
Eagle Lake—*swamp* MS-4
Eagle Lake Basin—*basin* IL-6
Eagle Lake Bend—*bend* AR-4
Eagle Lake Boys Camp—*locale* CO-8
Eagle Lake Burn—*area* CA-9
Eagle Lake (CCD)—*cens area* TX-5
Eagle Lake Cem—*cemetery* FL-3
Eagle Lake Cem—*cemetery* IL-6
Eagle Lake Cem—*cemetery* MN-6
Eagle Lake Ch—*church* AR-4
Eagle Lake Ch—*church* (2) MN-6
Eagle Lake Ch—*church* MS-4
Eagle Lake Dam—*dam* IN-6
Eagle Lake Dam—*dam* NC-3
Eagle Lake Dam—*dam* OR-9
Eagle Lake Ditch—*canal* CA-9
Eagle Lake Drain—*stream* MI-6
Eagle Lake Elem Sch—*school* FL-3
Eagle Lake Ferry—*locale* MS-4
Eagle Lake (historical)—*lake* IA-7
Eagle Lake (historical)—*lake* LA-4
Eagle Lake (historical)—*lake* MS-4
Eagle Lake Landing (historical)—*locale* MS-4
**Eagle Lake Manor**—*pop pl* WI-6
Eagle Lake Park—*park* WI-6
Eagle Lake Pass—*gut* MS-4
*Eagle Lake Reservoir* SD-7
Eagle Lake Resort—*locale* CA-9
Eagle Lakes—*lake* CA-9
Eagle Lakes—*lake* NM-5
Eagle Lakes—*lake* (2) WA-9
Eagle Lake Sch—*school* MN-6
Eagle Lake State Game Mngmt Area—*park* IA-7
Eagle Lake State Park—*park* IA-7
Eagle Lake State Wildlife Mngmt Area—*park* MN-6
Eagle Lake Substation—*locale* WA-9
Eagle Lake Tote Road—*trail* ME-1
**Eagle Lake (Town of)**—*pop pl* ME-1
**Eagle Lake (Township of)**—*pop pl* MN-6
Eagle Lake (Township of)—*unorg* ME-1
Eagle Lake Trail—*trail* ME-1
*Eagle Landing* AZ-5
Eagle Landing—*locale* MS-4
Eagle Ledge—*bench* NH-1
Eagle Ledge—*bench* (2) VT-1
Eagle Link Trail—*trail* NH-1
Eagle Lodge—*hist pl* NC-3
Eagle Lodge—*locale* CA-9
Eagle Lodge—*locale* ID-8
Eagle Lodge—*locale* TN-4
Eagle Lodge Airp—*airport* MO-7
Eagle Lodge Golf Course—*locale* (2) PA-2
Eagle Lookout Tower—*locale* MO-7
Eagle Mans Butte—*summit* SD-7
Eagle Meadow—*flat* CA-9
Eagle Mesa—*summit* NM-5
Eagle Mesa—*summit* UT-8
Eagle Mill—*locale* TN-4
Eagle Mill Ford—*locale* KY-4
*Eagle Mills* MI-6
Eagle Mills—*locale* KY-4
Eagle Mills—*locale* NC-3
Eagle Mills—*locale* OH-6
**Eagle Mills**—*pop pl* AR-4
**Eagle Mills**—*pop pl* MI-6
**Eagle Mills**—*pop pl* NY-2
Eagle Mills (historical)—*locale* AL-4
Eagle Mills (historical)—*locale* MS-4
Eagle Mills (Township of)—*fmr MCD* NC-3
Eagle Mine—*locale* PA-2
Eagle Mine—*mine* AZ-5
Eagle Mine—*mine* (3) CA-9
Eagle Mine—*mine* (3) CO-8
Eagle Mine—*mine* NV-8
Eagle Mine—*mine* OR-9
Eagle Mine—*mine* WY-8
Eaglemount—*locale* WA-9
*Eagle Mountain* UT-8
**Eagle Mountain**—*pop pl* CA-9
**Eagle Mountain**—*pop pl* TX-5
Eagle Mountain—*ridge* MT-8
**Eagle Mountain Acres**—*pop pl* TX-5
Eagle Mountain Camp—*locale* VT-1
Eagle Mountain Creek—*stream* AK-9
Eagle Mountain Creek—*stream* ID-8
Eagle Mountain Lake—*lake* ID-8
Eagle Mountain Lake—*reservoir* TX-5
Eagle Mountain Mine—*mine* CA-9
Eagle Mountain Ranch—*locale* TX-5
*Eagle Mountains* OR-9
Eagle Mountains—*range* CA-9
Eagle Mountains—*range* TX-5
Eagle Mountain Sch—*school* TX-5
Eagle Mountains Wells—*well* NM-5
*Eagle Mtn* CA-9
*Eagle Mtn* ME-1
*Eagle Mtn* TX-5
Eagle Mtn—*summit* AK-9
Eagle Mtn—*summit* AZ-5
Eagle Mtn—*summit* (2) AR-4
Eagle Mtn—*summit* (3) CA-9
Eagle Mtn—*summit* (5) CO-8
Eagle Mtn—*summit* GA-3
Eagle Mtn—*summit* (2) ID-8
Eagle Mtn—*summit* (2) ME-1
Eagle Mtn—*summit* (3) MN-6
Eagle Mtn—*summit* NV-8
Eagle Mtn—*summit* NH-1
Eagle Mtn—*summit* (4) NY-2
Eagle Mtn—*summit* (3) OK-5
Eagle Mtn—*summit* (2) OR-9
Eagle Mtn—*summit* SD-7
Eagle Mtn—*summit* (3) TX-5
Eagle Mtn—*summit* VT-1
Eagle Mtn—*summit* WA-9
Eagle Mtn—*summit* (2) WY-8
Eagle Neck—*cape* GA-3
*Eagle Nest* CA-9
*Eagle Nest* CO-8
Eagle Nest—*bay* FL-3
Eagle Nest—*cliff* AZ-5
Eagle Nest—*cliff* NE-7
Eagle Nest—*hist pl* NC-3
Eagle Nest—*island* FL-3
Eagle Nest—*locale* MI-6
Eagle Nest—*locale* NM-5
Eagle Nest—*locale* NY-2
Eagle Nest—*locale* ND-7
**Eagle Nest**—*pop pl* AZ-5
**Eagle Nest**—*pop pl* ID-8
**Eagle Nest**—*pop pl* NM-5
Eagle Nest—*rock* AL-4
Eagle Nest—*stream* FL-3
Eagle Nest—*summit* CO-8
Eagle Nest—*summit* ID-8
Eagle Nest—*summit* NM-5
Eagle Nest—*summit* WY-8
Eagle Nest, The—*pillar* CO-8
Eagle Nest Arroyo—*stream* NM-5
Eaglenest Basin—*basin* WY-8
Eagle Nest Bay—*bay* NC-3
Eagle Nest Bayou—*stream* FL-3
Eagle Nest Branch—*stream* VA-3
*Eagle Nest Butte* SD-7
Eagle Nest Butte—*summit* CA-9
Eagle Nest Butte—*summit* ND-7
Eagle Nest Butte—*summit* SD-7
Eagle Nest Camp—*locale* NC-3
Eagle Nest Canyon—*valley* AZ-5
Eagle Nest Canyon—*valley* NV-8
Eagle Nest Coulee—*valley* MT-8
Eaglenest Creek—*stream* FL-3
Eaglenest Creek—*stream* NC-3
Eagle Nest Creek—*stream* SD-7
Eagle Nest Creek—*stream* TX-5
Eaglenest Creek—*stream* WY-8
Eagle Nest Dam—*hist pl* NM-5
Eagle Nest Draw—*valley* WY-8
Eagle Nest Farm Camp—*locale* NJ-2
Eagle Nest Flowage—*reservoir* WI-6
Eagle Nest Hill—*summit* KY-4
Eagle Nest Hill—*summit* OH-6
Eaglenest (Historical Stage Station)—*locale* WY-8
*Eagle Nest Homesites* CA-9
Eagle Nest House—*locale* CO-8
Eagle Nest Island—*island* FL-3
Eagle Nest Island—*island* MI-6
Eagle Nest Island—*island* TN-4
*Eaglenest Key* FL-3
Eagle Nest Lake—*lake* (4) AR-4
Eagle Nest Lake—*lake* GA-3
Eagle Nest Lake—*lake* LA-4
Eagle Nest Lake—*lake* TX-5
Eagle Nest Lake—*lake* WI-6
Eagle Nest Lake—*reservoir* NM-5
Eagle Nest Lodge—*locale* NM-5
Eagle Nest Marina—*locale* TN-4
Eagle Nest Mines—*mine* CA-9
*Eagle Nest Mountain* CO-8
*Eaglenest Mountain* WY-8
Eagle Nest Mtn—*summit* AZ-5
Eaglenest Mtn—*summit* NC-3
Eagle Nest Peak—*summit* MT-8
Eagle Nest Peak—*summit* NM-5
*Eagle Nest Point* MA-1
Eaglenest Point—*cape* FL-3
Eaglenest Point—*cape* MD-2
Eagle Nest Point—*cape* MN-6
Eagle Nest Point—*cape* NC-3
Eagle Nest Point—*cliff* AZ-5
Eagle Nest Pond—*lake* FL-3
Eaglenest Post Office (historical)—*building* MS-4
Eagle Nest Ranch—*locale* WY-8
Eagle Nest Ranch Airstrip—*airport* OR-9
Eagle Nest Rapids—*rapids* OR-9
Eagle Nest Ridge—*ridge* MA-1
Eaglenest Ridge—*ridge* NC-3
Eagle Nest Rock—*pillar* MT-8
Eagle Nest Rock—*pillar* ND-7
Eagle Nest RR Station—*building* AZ-5
Eagle Nest Rsvr—*reservoir* AZ-5
Eagle Nest Spring—*spring* NM-5
**Eagle Nest (Therma)**—*pop pl* NM-5
Eagle Nest Trail—*trail* ID-8
Eagle Nest Windmill—*locale* NM-5
Eagle Newspaper Office—*hist pl* MN-6
Eagle Park—*flat* (2) CO-8
Eagle Park—*flat* MT-8
Eagle Park—*flat* UT-8
Eagle Park—*park* MT-8
**Eagle Park**—*pop pl* IL-6
Eagle Park Country Club—*other* OH-6
*Eagle Pass* AZ-5
Eagle Pass—*gap* (3) AZ-5
Eagle Pass—*gap* (2) CA-9
Eagle Pass—*gap* CO-8
Eagle Pass—*gap* ID-8
Eagle Pass—*gap* MT-8
Eagle Pass—*gap* NV-8
Eagle Pass—*gap* NY-2
Eagle Pass—*gap* WA-9
Eagle Pass—*gap* WY-8
**Eagle Pass**—*pop pl* TX-5
Eagle Pass (CCD)—*cens area* TX-5
Eagle Pass Creek—*stream* MT-8
Eagle Pass Hill—*summit* TX-5
Eagle Pass Hollow—*valley* OK-5
Eagle Pass Rec Area—*park* CA-9
Eagle Pass Spring—*spring* NM-5
*Eagle Peak* WI-6
Eagle Peak—*summit* (2) AK-9
Eagle Peak—*summit* (3) AZ-5
Eagle Peak—*summit* (16) CA-9
Eagle Peak—*summit* (3) CO-8
Eagle Peak—*summit* MT-8
Eagle Peak—*summit* (3) NM-5
Eagle Peak—*summit* (2) OR-9
Eagle Peak—*summit* PA-2
Eagle Peak—*summit* TX-5
Eagle Peak—*summit* UT-8
Eagle Peak—*summit* (4) WA-9
Eagle Peak—*summit* WI-6
Eagle Peak—*summit* (3) WY-8
Eagle Peak Creek—*stream* CA-9
Eagle Peak Meadows—*flat* CA-9
Eagle Peak Spring—*spring* NM-5
Eagle Peak Tank—*reservoir* NM-5
Eagle Peak Trail—*trail* CO-8
Eagle Picher Mine—*mine* NV-8
Eagle Plantation Cem—*cemetery* MS-4
Eagle Plume Mtn—*summit* MT-8
Eagle Point—*cape* (4) AK-9
Eagle Point—*cape* AR-4
Eagle Point—*cape* (4) CA-9
Eagle Point—*cape* (2) FL-3
Eagle Point—*cape* GA-3
Eagle Point—*cape* IL-6
Eagle Point—*cape* (2) IN-6
Eagle Point—*cape* IA-7
Eagle Point—*cape* LA-4
Eagle Point—*cape* (2) ME-1
Eagle Point—*cape* MD-2
Eagle Point—*cape* (4) MI-6
Eagle Point—*cape* MT-8
Eagle Point—*cape* (2) NJ-2
Eagle Point—*cape* (4) NY-2
Eagle Point—*cape* (4) OR-9
Eagle Point—*cape* SC-3
Eagle Point—*cape* TX-5
Eagle Point—*cape* VT-1
Eagle Point—*cape* VA-3
Eagle Point—*cape* (7) WA-9
Eagle Point—*cape* (2) WI-6
Eagle Point—*cape* WY-8
Eagle Point—*cliff* MT-8
Eagle Point—*cliff* NE-7
Eagle Point—*cliff* TX-5
Eagle Point—*locale* IA-7
Eagle Point—*locale* MO-7
Eagle Point—*locale* WI-6
**Eagle Point**—*pop pl* IL-6
**Eagle Point**—*pop pl* IN-6
**Eagle Point**—*pop pl* MI-6
**Eagle Point**—*pop pl* NY-2
**Eagle Point**—*pop pl* OR-9
**Eagle Point**—*pop pl* PA-2
**Eagle Point**—*pop pl* TN-4
**Eagle Point**—*pop pl* VT-1
Eagle Point—*summit* AZ-5
Eagle Point—*summit* (4) ID-8
Eagle Point—*summit* (3) MT-8
Eagle Point—*summit* NM-5
Eagle Point—*summit* OR-9
Eagle Point—*summit* WA-9
Eagle Point—*summit* WI-6
**Eagle Point Bay**—*pop pl* IL-6
Eagle Point Boat Ramp—*locale* VA-3
Eagle Point Bridge—*bridge* IA-7
Eagle Point Bridge (toll)—*bridge* WI-6
**Eagle Point Cabin Area**—*pop pl* TN-4
Eagle Point (CCD)—*cens area* OR-9
Eagle Point Cem—*cemetery* OH-6
Eagle Point Cem—*cemetery* TX-5
Eagle Point Ch—*church* MN-6
*Eagle Point Colony* OH-6
**Eagle Point Colony**—*pop pl* OH-6
Eagle Point Colony Hist Dist—*hist pl* OH-6
**Eagle Point Heights**—*pop pl* TN-4
Eagle Point Hill—*summit* CO-8
Eagle Point Irrigation Canal—*canal* OR-9
Eagle Point Lake—*lake* MN-6
Eagle Point Lookout Tower—*locale* NE-7
Eagle Point Meadows—*flat* OR-9
Eagle Point Park—*park* (2) IA-7
Eaglepoint Ranch—*locale* CA-9
Eagle Point Range—*channel* NJ-2
Eagle Point Range—*channel* PA-2
Eagle Point Rec Area—*park* MO-7
Eagle Point Sch—*school* CO-8
Eagle Point Sch—*school* MN-6
Eagle Point Sch—*school* OH-6
Eagle Point Sch (historical)—*school* MO-7
**Eagle Point (Town of)**—*pop pl* WI-6
**Eagle Point (Township of)**—*pop pl* IL-6
**Eagle Point (Township of)**—*pop pl* MN-6
Eagle Point Well—*well* AZ-5
Eagle Pond—*lake* FL-3
Eagle Pond—*lake* (2) ME-1
Eagle Pond—*lake* (2) MA-1
Eagle Pond—*lake* NH-1
Eagle Pond—*lake* NY-2
Eagle Pond—*lake* VT-1
Eagle Pond—*locale* GA-3
Eagle Pond—*swamp* TX-5
Eagle Pool—*lake* MO-7
**Eagleport**—*pop pl* OH-6
Eagle Post Office (historical)—*building* AL-4
Eagle Prairie—*flat* FL-3
*Eagle Ranch* AZ-5
Eagle Ranch—*locale* (2) CA-9
Eagle Ranch—*locale* TX-5
*Eagle Range* TX-5
Eagle Rapids—*rapids* WA-9
Eagle Ravine—*valley* CA-9
Eagle Reef—*bar* AK-9
Eagle Rest Peak—*summit* CA-9
Eagle Rest Peak—*summit* WY-8
Eagle Ribs Mtn—*summit* MT-8
Eagle Ridge—*ridge* OH-6
Eagle Ridge—*ridge* (2) OR-9
Eagle Ridge Ch—*church* OH-6
Eagle Ridge Gliderport—*airport* PA-2
Eagle Riffle—*stream* AR-4
*Eagle River* MN-6
**Eagle River**—*pop pl* AK-9
**Eagle River**—*pop pl* MI-6
**Eagle River**—*pop pl* WI-6
Eagle River—*stream* (3) AK-9
Eagle River—*stream* CO-8
Eagle River—*stream* MI-6
Eagle River—*stream* (2) WI-6
Eagle River Cem—*cemetery* MI-6
Eagle River Flats—*flat* AK-9
Eagle River Hist Dist—*hist pl* MI-6
Eagle River Mine—*mine* AK-9
*Eagle Rock* CO-8
*Eagle Rock* ID-8
*Eagle Rock* OR-9
*Eagle Rock* UT-8
Eagle Rock—*bar* AK-9
Eagle Rock—*cliff* CA-9
Eagle Rock—*cliff* ID-8
Eagle Rock—*cliff* WV-2
Eagle Rock—*island* (3) AK-9
Eagle Rock—*island* CA-9
Eagle Rock—*pillar* (2) AZ-5
Eagle Rock—*pillar* (6) CA-9
Eagle Rock—*pillar* (4) CO-8
Eagle Rock—*pillar* ID-8
Eagle Rock—*pillar* IA-7
Eagle Rock—*pillar* (3) MT-8
Eagle Rock—*pillar* NE-7
Eagle Rock—*pillar* NV-8
Eagle Rock—*pillar* (2) NM-5
Eagle Rock—*pillar* NY-2
Eagle Rock—*pillar* (3) OR-9
Eagle Rock—*pillar* WA-9
Eagle Rock—*pillar* WI-6
Eagle Rock—*pillar* (3) WY-8
**Eagle Rock**—*pop pl* CA-9
**Eagle Rock**—*pop pl* MO-7
**Eagle Rock**—*pop pl* NC-3
**Eagle Rock**—*pop pl* PA-2
**Eagle Rock**—*pop pl* VA-3
Eagle Rock—*summit* (2) AZ-5
Eagle Rock—*summit* (10) CA-9
Eagle Rock—*summit* (4) CO-8
Eagle Rock—*summit* CT-1
Eagle Rock—*summit* (2) ID-8
Eagle Rock—*summit* MD-2
Eagle Rock—*summit* MA-1
Eagle Rock—*summit* (6) MT-8
Eagle Rock—*summit* NV-8
Eagle Rock—*summit* NH-1
Eagle Rock—*summit* NY-2
Eagle Rock—*summit* NC-3
Eagle Rock—*summit* (7) OR-9
Eagle Rock—*summit* (3) PA-2
Eagle Rock—*summit* UT-8
Eagle Rock—*summit* VT-1
Eagle Rock—*summit* VA-3
Eagle Rock—*summit* (5) WA-9
Eagle Rock—*summit* WV-2
Eagle Rock—*summit* (3) WY-8
Eagle Rock Branch Library—*hist pl* CA-9
Eagle Rock Camp—*locale* CA-9
Eagle Rock Camp—*locale* VT-1
Eagle Rock Campground—*locale* NM-5
Eagle Rock Campground—*park* OR-9
Eagle Rock Canal—*canal* ID-8
Eagle Rock Ch—*church* CT-1
Eagle Rock Cove—*valley* NC-3
Eagle Rock Creek—*stream* MT-8
Eagle Rock Creek—*stream* NV-8
Eagle Rock Ditch—*canal* CO-8
Eagle Rock Draw—*valley* CO-8
Eagle Rock Draw—*valley* WY-8
Eagle Rock Ferry—*hist pl* ID-8
Eagle Rock Flat Well—*well* NV-8
Eagle Rock HS—*school* CA-9
Eagle Rock Lake—*lake* NM-5
Eagle Rock Lakes—*lake* CO-8
Eagle Rock Mine—*mine* CA-9
Eagle Rock Mine—*mine* MT-8
*Eagle Rock Mountain* CA-9
Eagle Rock Public Use Area—*locale* MO-7
Eagle Rock Ranch—*locale* CA-9
Eagle Rock Ranch—*locale* CO-8
Eagle Rock Ranch—*locale* TX-5
Eagle Rock Recreation Center—*park* CA-9
Eagle Rock Reservation (County Park)—*park* NJ-2
Eagle Rock Ridge—*ridge* UT-8
Eagle Rock Rsvr—*reservoir* CA-9
Eagle Rock Rsvr—*reservoir* CO-8
Eagle Rock Rsvr—*reservoir* NV-8
Eagle Rocks—*area* AK-9
Eagle Rocks—*summit* CA-9
Eagle Rocks—*summit* TN-4
Eagle Rock Sch—*school* ID-8
Eagle Rock Sch—*school* MT-8
Eagle Rock Sch—*school* PA-2
Eagle Rock Spring—*spring* NV-8
Eagle Rocks Prong—*stream* TN-4
Eagle Rock Stage Station (reduced usage)—*locale* MT-8
Eagle Rock Trail—*trail* ID-8
Eagle Rock Wash—*valley* UT-8
Eagle Rock Well—*well* AZ-5
Eagle Rod and Gun Club—*other* NY-2
Eagle Roost—*cliff* CO-8
Eagle Roost Airstrip—*airport* AZ-5
Eagle Roost Radio Tower—*tower* NV-8
Eagle Rsvr—*reservoir* ID-8
Eagle Rsvr—*reservoir* OR-9
Eagle Run—*stream* IL-6
Eagle Run—*stream* IN-6
Eagle Run—*stream* PA-2
Eagle Run—*stream* WV-2
Eagles Auditorium Bldg—*hist pl* WA-9
Eagles Beak—*pillar* CO-8
Eagles Bldg—*hist pl* (2) OH-6
Eagles Bluff—*cliff* (2) OK-5
Eagles Camp—*locale* WV-2
Eagles Camp Trail—*trail* WV-2
Eagles Canyon—*valley* UT-8
Eagles Ch—*church* NC-3
Eagle Sch—*school* AR-4
Eagle Sch—*school* IL-6
Eagle Sch—*school* IA-7
Eagle Sch—*school* KY-4
Eagle Sch—*school* (3) MI-6
Eagle Sch—*school* NE-7
Eagle Sch—*school* ND-7
Eagle Sch—*school* OH-6
Eagle Sch—*school* TX-5
Eagle Sch (abandoned)—*school* PA-2
Eagle Sch (historical)—*school* MO-7
Eagle Sch (historical)—*school* TN-4
Eagle School (Abandoned)—*locale* IA-7
Eagles Cliff—*cliff* NE-7
Eagles Cliff—*summit* NY-2
Eagles Club—*hist pl* WI-6
Eagle Scout Creek—*stream* CA-9
Eagle Scout Peak—*summit* CA-9
Eagle Scout Trail—*trail* MN-6
EAgles Cove Marina—*locale* TN-4
Eagles Crag—*summit* ME-1
Eagles Eye—*area* NE-7
Eagles Eye, The—*summit* AZ-5
*Eagles Grove Church* AL-4
Eagles Grove Sch (historical)—*school* AL-4
Eagle Shaft (historical)—*mine* PA-2
Eagle Shaft No 1—*mine* NM-5
Eagle Shaft No 2—*mine* NM-5
Eagles Hall—*hist pl* CA-9
Eagles Hall Park—*park* TX-5
Eagle-Shawmut Mine—*mine* CA-9
Eagleshead—*summit* VT-1
Eagle Shoal—*bar* VI-3
Eagle Shoals—*bar* AL-4
Eagles Home—*hist pl* IN-6
Eagles House—*summit* NV-8
Eagle Sinkhole—*basin* CA-9
*Eagles Island* NC-3
Eagles Lair—*airport* NJ-2
Eagles Lake—*lake* NE-7
Eagles Lakes—*lake* NH-1
Eagles Landing Airp—*airport* MO-7
Eagle Slide—*valley* AK-9
Eagle Slough—*gut* IL-6
Eagle Slough—*stream* IL-6
Eagle Slough Drainage Ditch—*canal* IL-6
*Eaglesmere* PA-2
**Eagles Mere**—*pop pl* PA-2
Eagles Mere Borough—*civil* PA-2
*Eagles Mere Emergency Airport* PA-2
Eagles Mere Golf Course—*locale* PA-2
Eagles Mere Lake—*lake* PA-2
Eaglesmere Lakes—*lake* CO-8
Eagles Mere Municipal Airp—*airport* PA-2
Eagles Mere Park—*park* PA-2
Eagles Neck Point—*cape* NY-2
*Eagle's Nest* CO-8
*Eagles Nest* PA-2
Eagles Nest—*airport* NJ-2
Eagle's Nest—*hist pl* CT-1
Eagle's Nest—*hist pl* MD-2
Eagles Nest—*locale* (2) CA-9
Eagles Nest—*locale* CO-8
Eagles Nest—*locale* FL-3
Eagles Nest—*locale* MI-6
Eagles Nest—*locale* MN-6
**Eagles Nest**—*pop pl* MS-4
Eagles Nest—*spring* MT-8
Eagles Nest—*summit* (2) CA-9
Eagles Nest—*summit* (2) CO-8
Eagles Nest—*summit* ID-8
Eagles Nest—*summit* NH-1
Eagles Nest—*summit* NM-5
Eagles Nest—*summit* SC-3
Eagles Nest—*summit* (2) WY-8
*Eagles Nest Bay* NC-3
Eagles Nest Bay—*cove* MA-1
Eagles Nest Boat Landing—*locale* FL-3
Eagles Nest Brake—*stream* LA-4
Eagles Nest Butte—*summit* SD-7
Eagles Nest Canyon—*valley* NM-5
Eagles Nest Canyon—*valley* SD-7
Eagles Nest Canyon—*valley* (2) WY-8
Eagles Nest Ch—*church* FL-3
Eagles Nest Coulee—*valley* MT-8
*Eagles Nest Creek* SD-7
Eagles Nest Dam—*dam* NC-3
Eagles Nest Draw—*valley* WY-8
Eagles Nest Draw Rsvr No 1—*reservoir* WY-8
*Eagles Nest Island* TN-4
Eagles Nest Island—*island* IL-6
Eagles Nest Island—*island* WI-6
Eagles Nest Lake—*lake* AR-4
Eagles Nest Lake—*lake* NY-2
Eagles Nest Lake—*reservoir* NC-3
Eagles Nest Lake No 2—*lake* MN-6
Eagles Nest Lake Number Four—*lake* MN-6
Eagles Nest Lake Number One—*lake* MN-6
Eagles Nest Lake Number Three—*lake* MN-6
Eagles Nest Landing—*locale* DE-2
Eagles Nest Mine—*mine* AZ-5
Eagles Nest Mine—*mine* OR-9
Eagles Nest Mine—*mine* UT-8
*Eagles Nest Mountain* CO-8
*Eagles Nest Plantation* MS-4
Eagles Nest Point—*cape* MA-1
Eagles Nest Point—*cape* VA-3
Eagles Nest Pond—*lake* NY-2
Eagles Nest Private Sch—*school* FL-3
Eagles Nest Ranch—*locale* CO-8
*Eagles Nest Range* CO-8
Eagles Nest Rock—*summit* NV-8
Eagles Nest Spring—*spring* SD-7
Eagles Nest Spring—*spring* (2) WY-8
Eagles Nest Township—*obs name* ND-7
Eagles Nest Trail—*trail* TX-5
Eagleson Summit—*summit* ID-8
Eagles Park—*park* ND-7
Eagles Peak—*summit* WI-6
Eagles Peak Ski Area—*park* CA-9
Eagles Picnic Grounds—*park* IN-6
Eagles Point—*cape* MN-6
Eagles Point—*summit* TX-5
Eagles Point and Red Barn Village Airpark—*airport* MO-7
Eagle Spring—*spring* (4) AZ-5
Eagle Spring—*spring* (6) CA-9
Eagle Spring—*spring* (3) ID-8
Eagle Spring—*spring* (2) MT-8
Eagle Spring—*spring* (2) NV-8
Eagle Spring—*spring* NM-5
Eagle Spring—*spring* (3) OR-9
Eagle Spring—*spring* TX-5
Eagle Spring—*spring* UT-8
Eagle Spring—*spring* WA-9
Eagle Spring Creek—*stream* ID-8
*Eagle Spring Draw* TX-5
Eagle Spring Lake—*lake* WA-9
Eagle Spring Lake—*reservoir* WI-6
**Eagle Springs**—*pop pl* NC-3
Eagle Springs—*spring* MT-8
Eagle Springs—*spring* NV-8
Eagle Springs—*spring* OR-9
Eagle Springs—*spring* TX-5
Eagle Springs—*spring* UT-8
Eagle Springs Cem—*cemetery* TX-5
Eagle Springs Corral—*locale* OR-9
Eagle Springs Grange Hall—*building* IN-6
Eagle Springs (historical)—*locale* KS-7
*Eagle Springs Lake* WA-9
Eagle Spur—*ridge* CA-9
Eagle Square—*park* MA-1
Eagle's Rest—*hist pl* NY-2
Eagles Rest—*summit* OR-9
Eagles Rest Trail—*trail* OR-9
Eagles Roost—*summit* NM-5
Eagle's Roost Airp—*airport* WA-9
Eagles Roost Heliport—*airport* MO-7
Eagle's Store—*hist pl* MT-8
Eagle Stadium—*other* NM-5
Eagle Station—*building* PA-2
Eagle Station—*locale* KY-4
Eagles' Temple—*hist pl* OH-6
Eagles Temple—*hist pl* OH-6
Eagleston Cem—*cemetery* IL-6
Eagles Trap—*summit* WY-8
Eagle Stream—*stream* (2) ME-1
Eagle Street Sch—*school* NY-2
Eagle Summit—*gap* AK-9
*Eaglesville* OH-6
**Eaglesville**—*pop pl* MA-1
Eagle Swamp—*stream* NC-3
Eagles Windmill—*locale* NM-5
**Eagleswood (Township of)**—*pop pl* NJ-2
**Eaglet**—*pop pl* CA-9
*Eagle Tail* KS-7
*Eagletail, The* AZ-5
Eagle Tail Canal—*canal* (2) NM-5
*Eagle Tail Creek* KS-7
Eagletail Creek—*stream* KS-7
Eagle Tail Mesa—*summit* NM-5
Eagle Tail Mine—*mine* AZ-5
*Eagle Tail Mountains* AZ-5
*Eagle Tail Mountains* TX-5
Eagletail Mountains—*range* AZ-5
Eagle Tail Mtn—*summit* NM-5
*Eagle Tail Peak* AZ-5
Eagletail Peak—*summit* AZ-5
Eagletail Petroglyph Site—*hist pl* AZ-5
Eagletail Rock—*pillar* ID-8
Eagletail Tank—*reservoir* AZ-5
Eagle Tank—*reservoir* (5) AZ-5
Eagle Tank—*reservoir* CA-9
Eagle Tank—*reservoir* NM-5
Eagle Tank—*reservoir* (4) TX-5
Eagle Tanks—*reservoir* NM-5
Eagle Tank Well—*well* TX-5
Eagle Tanner Trail—*trail* OR-9
*Eagle Tavern* PA-2
Eagle Tavern—*hist pl* GA-3
Eagle Tavern—*hist pl* NC-3
Eagle Tavern—*hist pl* PA-2
Eagle Theater—*hist pl* MI-6
Eagletie—*locale* AR-4
*Eagleton* PA-2
Eagleton—*locale* AR-4
**Eagleton**—*pop pl* MT-8
**Eagleton**—*pop pl* NC-3
**Eagleton**—*pop pl* WI-6
Eagleton Cem—*cemetery* WI-6
*Eagleton Elementary School* TN-4
Eagleton Fields—*locale* PA-2
**Eagleton (historical)**—*pop pl* OR-9
Eagleton MS—*school* TN-4
Eagleton Point—*cape* NC-3
Eagleton Run—*stream* PA-2
Eagleton Run Trail—*trail* PA-2
Eagleton Sch—*school* CO-8
Eagleton Sch—*school* TN-4
**Eagleton Village**—*pop pl* TN-4
Eagle Top—*summit* WY-8
**Eagletown**—*pop pl* IN-6
**Eagletown**—*pop pl* NC-3
**Eagletown**—*pop pl* OK-5
Eagletown Cem—*cemetery* OK-5
**Eagle (Town of)**—*pop pl* NY-2
**Eagle (Town of)**—*pop pl* (2) WI-6
*Eagle Township* KS-7
Eagle Township—*civil* MO-7
Eagle Township—*civil* SD-7
Eagle Township—*fmr MCD* (3) IA-7
**Eagle Township**—*pop pl* (3) KS-7
**Eagle Township**—*pop pl* ND-7
**Eagle Township**—*pop pl* (2) SD-7
Eagle Township Cem—*cemetery* IA-7
Eagle (Township of)—*fmr MCD* (5) AR-4
**Eagle (Township of)**—*pop pl* IL-6
**Eagle (Township of)**—*pop pl* IN-6
**Eagle (Township of)**—*pop pl* MI-6
**Eagle (Township of)**—*pop pl* (3) OH-6
Eagle Township Works I Mound—*hist pl* OH-6
Eagle Trail—*trail* AK-9
Eagle Trail—*trail* PA-2
Eagle Trail Wayside—*locale* AK-9
**Eagle Tree**—*pop pl* CA-9
Eaglette—*locale* MO-7
Eaglette Ch—*church* AR-4
Eagle Valley—*basin* CA-9
Eagle Valley—*basin* NV-8
Eagle Valley—*locale* PA-2
**Eagle Valley**—*pop pl* NY-2
Eagle Valley—*valley* CO-8
Eagle Valley—*valley* NV-8
Eagle Valley—*valley* (2) OR-9
Eagle Valley—*valley* WI-6
Eagle Valley Canyon—*valley* NV-8
Eagle Valley (CCD)—*cens area* OR-9
Eagle Valley Cem—*cemetery* NY-2
Eagle Valley Cem—*cemetery* OR-9
Eagle Valley Cem—*cemetery* WI-6
Eagle Valley Ranch Childrens Foundation—*locale* NV-8
Eagle Valley Reservoir State Rec Area—*park* NV-8
Eagle Valley Rsvr—*reservoir* NV-8
Eagle Valley (Township of)—*civ div* MN-6
Eagle View—*locale* CA-9
Eagle View Springs Golf Course—*other* PA-2
**Eagle Village**—*pop pl* AK-9
**Eagle Village**—*pop pl* IN-6
**Eagle Village**—*pop pl* NY-2
*Eagleville* MA-1
*Eagleville* PA-2
Eagleville—*locale* CA-9
**Eagleville**—*pop pl* CA-9
**Eagleville**—*pop pl* CT-1
**Eagleville**—*pop pl* MA-1
**Eagleville**—*pop pl* MO-7
**Eagleville**—*pop pl* (2) NY-2
**Eagleville**—*pop pl* (2) OH-6
**Eagleville**—*pop pl* (2) PA-2
**Eagleville**—*pop pl* RI-1
**Eagleville**—*pop pl* TN-4
**Eagleville**—*pop pl* WI-6
Eagleville Brook—*stream* CT-1
Eagleville (CCD)—*cens area* TN-4
Eagleville Cem—*cemetery* CA-9
Eagleville Covered Bridge—*hist pl* NY-2
Eagleville Division—*civil* TN-4
**Eagleville (East Salem)**—*pop pl* NY-2
Eagleville Elem Sch—*school* PA-2
Eagleville Gap—*gap* PA-2
Eagleville (historical)—*locale* MA-1
Eagleville (historical)—*locale* NV-8
Eagleville Hosp Rehabilitation Center—*hospital* PA-2
*Eagleville Lake* CT-1
Eagleville Mine—*mine* NV-8

*Eagleville Pond* MA-1
Eagleville Pond—*lake* CT-1
Eagleville Sanitarium—*hospital* PA-2
Eagleville Sch—*school* TN-4
Eagle Wash—*stream* (2) AZ-5
Eagle Wash—*stream* (2) NV-8
Eagle Waterhole Canyon—*valley* TX-5
Eagle Well—*locale* NM-5
Eagle Well—*well* CA-9
Eagle Well—*well* (2) TX-5
Eagle Windmill—*locale* (2) NM-5
*Eaglewing Group* NY-2
Eagle Wing Group—*island* NY-2
*Eaglewing Island* NY-2
Eagle Wing Island—*island* NY-2
**Eaglewood Estates**—*pop pl* IN-6
**Eaglewood Estates (subdivision)**—*pop pl* AL-4
**Eaglewood Forest (subdivision)**—*pop pl* NC-3
Eaglewood Point—*cape* MN-6
**Eaglewood (subdivision)**—*pop pl* NC-3
Eaglin Ch—*church* IL-6
Eagloil—*uninc pl* NJ-2
Eagon Run—*stream* OH-6
*Eagte River* CO-8
*Eaharley Creek* GA-3
Eaheart Cem—*cemetery* IN-6
E A I Landing Strip—*airport* NJ-2
E A Juvenal—*locale* TX-5
Eaker Cem—*cemetery* MO-7
Eaker Cem—*cemetery* NC-3
Eakers Cem—*cemetery* MO-7
*Eakers Corner* NC-3
**Eakers Corner**—*pop pl* NC-3
Eaker Windmill—*locale* TX-5
Eakin—*locale* OR-9
Eakin—*locale* SD-7
Eakin Cabin—*locale* ID-8
Eakin Canyon—*valley* OR-9
Eakin Cem—*cemetery* PA-2
Eakin Corner—*locale* PA-2
Eakin Elem Sch—*school* TN-4
Eakin Grove Ch—*church* IL-6
Eakin Hill—*summit* PA-2
Eakin Knob—*summit* PA-2
Eakin Mill Covered Bridge—*hist pl* OH-6
Eakin Northwest Oil Field—*oilfield* KS-7
Eakin Park—*park* VA-3
Eakin Point—*summit* ID-8
Eakin Pumping Station—*locale* WY-8
Eakin Ridge—*ridge* ID-8
Eakins—*locale* NM-5
Eakins, Thomas, House—*hist pl* PA-2
Eakins Cem—*cemetery* KY-4
Eakin Sch—*school* OH-6
Eakin Sch—*school* TN-4
Eakin Sch (abandoned)—*school* PA-2
*Eakins Corners* PA-2
Eakle—*locale* WV-2
Eakle Cem—*cemetery* IL-6
Eakle Ch—*church* WV-2
Eakle Park—*park* TX-5
**Eakles Mill**—*pop pl* MD-2
Eakles Mills—*locale* MD-2
**Eakly**—*pop pl* OK-5
Eakly Cem—*cemetery* OK-5
Eako Lake—*reservoir* VA-3
Eakon Cem—*cemetery* MO-7
Eakpicada County Park—*park* IA-7
E Albemarle Sch—*school* NC-3
E Alderman—*locale* TX-5
Ealen Windmill—*locale* NM-5
Eales, James, House—*hist pl* KY-4
Eales Post Office (historical)—*building* SD-7
*Ealge Island* MS-4
Ealiah, Bogue—*stream* MS-4
Ealon Branch—*stream* AL-4
Ealon Branch—*stream* MS-4
**Ealum**—*pop pl* FL-3
Ealum Bay—*swamp* FL-3
Ealy Cem—*cemetery* VA-3
Ealy Hollow—*valley* TN-4
Ealy Sch—*school* MI-6
Ealy Sch—*school* MS-4
Ealy Sch (abandoned)—*school* PA-2
**Eaman Park**—*pop pl* NC-3
Eaman Sch—*school* MI-6
**Eames**—*pop pl* IN-6
**Eames**—*pop pl* MI-6
Eames, Philip, House—*hist pl* MA-1
Eames Brook—*stream* ME-1
Eames Brook—*stream* MA-1
Eames Cem—*cemetery* NY-2
Eames Cem—*cemetery* VT-1
Eames Creek—*stream* OR-9
Eames Hill—*summit* ME-1
Eames Hill—*summit* MA-1
Eames Knob—*summit* TN-4
Eames Pond—*lake* MA-1
Eames Pond—*reservoir* MA-1
Eames Pond Dam—*dam* MA-1
Eames Way Sch—*school* MA-1
E A Mtn—*summit* WY-8
E Andersons Dam—*dam* UT-8
**Eanes**—*pop pl* GA-3
Eanes, Lake—*reservoir* TX-5
Eanes Sch—*school* TX-5
*Eanning Springs* FL-3
*Eanon* AL-4
Eanon Ch—*church* AL-4
*Eanuel Creek* SD-7
*Eap* FM-9
E A Patterson Lake—*reservoir* ND-7
E A Ranch—*locale* WY-8
Earbob Ferry Rec Area—*park* OK-5
Ear Creek—*stream* ID-8
Ear Creek—*stream* MT-8
Ear Creek Sheep Corral—*locale* ID-8
*Eardley Canyon* UT-8
Eardley Canyon—*valley* UT-8
Eardley Spit—*bar* UT-8
Eardly Farm—*locale* (2) TX-5
Eargle Cem—*cemetery* SC-3
Eargle Sch—*school* AL-4
Earhart, Amelia, Birthplace—*hist pl* KS-7
Earhart Cem—*cemetery* OH-6
Earhart Cem—*cemetery* PA-2
Earhart Cem—*cemetery* VA-3
Earhart Creek—*stream* VA-3
Earhart Environment Elem Sch—*school* KS-7
Earhart Sch—*school* IL-6
Earhart Sch—*school* MT-8
Earhart Sch—*school* TX-5
Earheart Cem—*cemetery* MO-7
**Earheart (historical)**—*pop pl* TN-4
Earis Tank—*reservoir* AZ-5
Earkan Lake Dam—*dam* MS-4
*Earl* AR-4
*Earl* IN-6
Earl—*fmr MCD* NE-7
Earl—*locale* CO-8
Earl—*locale* MO-7
Earl—*locale* WA-9
**Earl**—*pop pl* NC-3
**Earl**—*pop pl* OK-5
**Earl**—*pop pl* WI-6
Earl, Lake—*lake* CA-9
Earl, Lake—*lake* FL-3
Ear Lake—*lake* LA-4
Ear Lake—*lake* MI-6
Earlakill Run—*stream* PA-2
*Earlaki Run* PA-2
Earl Bar—*bar* AL-4
Earl Beatty Hill—*summit* NY-2
Earl Bell Sch—*school* TX-5
Earl Boyles Park—*park* OR-9
Earl Brake—*swamp* AR-4
Earl Branch—*stream* AR-4
Earl Branch Drain—*canal* MI-6
Earl Burtz Number 1 Dam—*dam* SD-7
Earl Burtz Number 2 Dam—*dam* SD-7
Earl Canyon—*valley* (2) UT-8
Earl C. Davis Elem Sch—*school* PA-2
Earl Cem—*cemetery* IL-6
Earl Cem—*cemetery* KY-4
Earl Cem—*cemetery* OK-5
Earl Ch—*church* SC-3
**Earl (corporate name for Earl Station)**—*pop pl* NC-3
Earl Cove—*bay* AK-9
Earl Creek—*stream* AZ-5
Earl Creek—*stream* LA-4
Earl Creek—*stream* OR-9
Earl Davis Pond Dam—*dam* MS-4
**Earl D Grays Subdivision**—*pop pl* UT-8
Earl Draw—*valley* NM-5
**Earle**—*pop pl* AR-4
**Earle**—*pop pl* IN-6
**Earle**—*pop pl* NJ-2
**Earle**—*pop pl* SC-3
**Earle**—*pop pl* TX-5
Earle, Col. Elias, Hist Dist—*hist pl* SC-3
Earle, John M., House—*hist pl* MA-1
Earl-Eagle Mine—*mine* UT-8
Earle Ammun Depot—*military* NJ-2
Earle Branch—*stream* MO-7
Earle Bridge—*bridge* NC-3
Earle Brook—*stream* MI-6
Earle Chapter Ch—*church* MD-2
Earle Cove—*bay* AK-9
Earle Cove—*bay* (2) MD-2
Earle Creek—*stream* KY-4
Earle Creek—*stream* MD-2
Earle Creek—*stream* MS-4
**Earle Homes**—*pop pl* SC-3
Earle House—*hist pl* AR-4
Earlehurst—*locale* VA-3
**Earleigh Heights**—*pop pl* MD-2
Earle Lake—*lake* AK-9
Earle Lake—*lake* WA-9
Earle Landing—*locale* AL-4
Earle Landing—*locale* MD-2
Earle Mine—*mine* NV-8
Earle-Napier-Kinnard House—*hist pl* TX-5
Earle Naval Weapons Station—*military* NJ-2
*Earle Point* MH-9
Earle Pond—*lake* MA-1
Earle River—*stream* AK-9
Earles—*locale* KY-4
**Earles**—*pop pl* SC-3
Earles Branch—*stream* AR-4
Earles Bridge—*bridge* SC-3
Earle Sch—*school* IL-6
Earle Sch—*school* MA-1
Earle Sch—*school* SC-3
Earles Chapel—*church* TX-5
Earles Chapel—*locale* TX-5
*Earle School* IN-6
Earles Ferry (historical)—*locale* MS-4
**Earles Grove**—*pop pl* SC-3
Earles Lake—*lake* PA-2
*Earleton* KS-7
**Earleton**—*pop pl* FL-3
Earle Town House—*hist pl* SC-3
**Earleville**—*pop pl* MD-2
*Earley* PA-2
**Earley**—*pop pl* NC-3
Earley Branch—*stream* KY-4
Earley Ch—*church* KY-4
Earley Creek—*stream* OR-9
Earley Creek—*stream* WY-8
Earley-Hartzell House—*hist pl* OH-6
Earley Island (historical)—*island* TN-4
Earley JHS—*school* CT-1
Earley Lake—*lake* MN-6
Earley Landing—*locale* ME-1
Earley Ranch—*locale* CO-8
**Earleys**—*pop pl* NC-3
Earleys Landing (historical)—*locale* TN-4
Earleys Run—*stream* WV-2
Earleyville—*locale* TN-4
Earleyville Ch of Christ—*church* TN-4
Earleyville Post Office (historical)—*building* TN-4
Earl Fields Memorial Airp—*airport* MO-7
*Earlham* IN-6
**Earlham**—*pop pl* IA-7
Earlham Cem—*cemetery* IN-6
Earlham Coll—*school* IN-6
Earlham College Observatory—*hist pl* IN-6
Earlham Lake—*reservoir* IN-6
Earlham Lake Dam—*dam* IN-6
Earlham Public Sch—*hist pl* IA-7
Earl Hanrahan Dam—*dam* SD-7
Earl Hendrix Dam—*dam* NC-3
**Earl (historical)**—*pop pl* OR-9
*Earl Hollow* TN-4
Earl Hollow—*valley* MO-7
Earl Hollow—*valley* PA-2
Earl Hollow—*valley* TN-4
*Earlhurst* VA-3
**Earlhurst**—*pop pl* VA-3
Earlies Gap—*gap* NC-3
**Earlimart**—*pop pl* CA-9
Earlimart (CCD)—*cens area* CA-9
**Earling**—*pop pl* IA-7
**Earling**—*pop pl* WV-2
Earling Cem—*cemetery* SD-7
Earling (historical)—*locale* SD-7
**Earlington**—*pop pl* KY-4
**Earlington**—*pop pl* PA-2
Earlington—*uninc pl* WA-9
Earlington Heights Sch—*school* FL-3
**Earling Township**—*pop pl* SD-7
Earl Island—*island* NY-2
Earl Johnson Sch—*school* CO-8
Earl Kennel Dam—*dam* OR-9
Earl Kennel Rsvr—*reservoir* OR-9
Earl Laird Lake Dam—*dam* (2) MS-4
*Earl Lake* MI-6
Earl Lake—*lake* MI-6
*Earl Landing* AL-4
Earl Lode Mine—*mine* SD-7
Earl McPherson Dam Number 1—*dam* SD-7
Earlmont—*locale* WA-9
*Earlmount* WA-9
Earlmount—*uninc pl* WA-9
Earl Mtn—*summit* NC-3
**Earl Park**—*pop pl* IN-6
Earl Park Cem—*cemetery* IN-6
Earl Park Dam—*dam* AZ-5
Earl Park Lake—*reservoir* AZ-5
Earl Park Tank—*reservoir* AZ-5
Earl Patton Mine (underground)—*mine* TN-4
Earl Peak—*summit* WA-9
Earl Pinham Lake Dam—*dam* MS-4
Earl Point—*cape* TX-5
Earl Pond—*lake* AZ-5
Earl Prairie—*locale* AR-4
Earl Prairie District Sch No 66—*school* AR-4
Earl Pullins Dam—*dam* SD-7
Earl Ridge—*ridge* KY-4
Earl River—*stream* AK-9
Earl Rsvr—*reservoir* AZ-5
Earl Rsvr—*reservoir* NY-2
Earls—*locale* TX-5
Earls—*locale* VA-3
**Earlsboro**—*pop pl* OK-5
Earlsboro Cem—*cemetery* OK-5
Earlsboro Oil Field—*oilfield* OK-5
Earls Branch—*stream* KY-4
Earls Branch—*stream* VA-3
Earls Bridge—*bridge* SC-3
Earls Cem—*cemetery* MO-7
Earls Cem—*cemetery* TN-4
Earls Cem—*cemetery* VA-3
Earls Ch—*church* TN-4
Earl Sch—*school* IL-6
Earl Sch—*school* MI-6
Earl Sch—*school* NE-7
Earl Sch—*school* NV-8
Earl Sch—*school* WV-2
Earl Sch (abandoned)—*school* MO-7
*Earls Chapel* TX-5
Earls Chapel—*church* TN-4
Earlscourt Hist Dist—*hist pl* RI-1
Earls Creek—*stream* NY-2
Earls Draw—*valley* UT-8
Earls Ford—*locale* GA-3
Earls Gulch—*valley* MT-8
*Earls Hollow* TN-4
Earls Hollow—*valley* TN-4
**Earls Island**—*pop pl* OH-6
Earls Knob—*summit* KY-4
Earls Lake—*reservoir* SC-3
*Earls Landing* AL-4
Earl Smith Lake Dam—*dam* MS-4
Earl Snell Birthplace Historical Monument—*other* OR-9
Earl Spring—*spring* CO-8
Earl Spring—*spring* OR-9
Earl Spring—*spring* UT-8
Earl Springs—*spring* WI-6
Earls Sch (historical)—*school* TN-4
Earls Sch Number 8—*school* NY-2
Earls Tank—*reservoir* AZ-5
*Earl Station (corporate name Earl)* NC-3
**Earlston**—*pop pl* PA-2
Earl Tank—*reservoir* (2) NM-5
Earlton—*locale* MD-2
**Earlton**—*pop pl* KS-7
**Earlton**—*pop pl* NY-2
Earltown Cem—*cemetery* AL-4
**Earl (Township of)**—*pop pl* IL-6
**Earl (Township of)**—*pop pl* (2) PA-2
*Earl Travillion Attendance Center* MS-4
Earl Union Sch—*school* PA-2
**Earlville**—*pop pl* AL-4
**Earlville**—*pop pl* IL-6
**Earlville**—*pop pl* IA-7
**Earlville**—*pop pl* (3) NY-2
**Earlville**—*pop pl* OH-6
**Earlville**—*pop pl* PA-2
Earlville Cem—*cemetery* NY-2
Earlville Cem—*cemetery* SD-7
Earlville Hist Dist—*hist pl* NY-2
Earlville Lake—*lake* NY-2
Earlville Opera House—*hist pl* NY-2
Earlville Rsvr—*reservoir* NY-2
**Earlville (sta.)**—*pop pl* NY-2
Earl Ward Park—*park* OK-5
Earl Warren JHS—*school* CA-9
Earl Warren Sch—*school* (2) CA-9
Earl Well—*locale* NM-5
Earl Witte Number 1 Dam—*dam* SD-7
Earlwood Park—*park* SC-3
**Earlwood Park**—*pop pl* SC-3
Early—*locale* VA-3
**Early**—*pop pl* FL-3
**Early**—*pop pl* GA-3
**Early**—*pop pl* IA-7
**Early**—*pop pl* TX-5
Early, William W., House—*hist pl* MD-2
Early Advantage Kindergarten—*school* FL-3
Early Bird—*locale* FL-3
Early Bird Dam—*dam* CO-8
Early Bird Mine—*mine* CA-9
Early Bird Mine—*mine* CO-8
**Early Branch**—*pop pl* SC-3
Early Branch—*stream* AL-4
Early Branch—*stream* FL-3
Early Branch—*stream* MO-7
Early Branch—*stream* (2) SC-3
Early Bridge—*bridge* VA-3
Early Brook—*stream* CT-1
Early Canyon—*valley* NM-5
Early Cem—*cemetery* AL-4
Early Cem—*cemetery* FL-3
Early Cem—*cemetery* KY-4
Early Cem—*cemetery* (2) MO-7
Early Cem—*cemetery* (2) OH-6
Early Cem—*cemetery* (2) TN-4
Early Chapel—*church* IA-7
Early Ch (historical)—*church* AL-4
Early Childhood/Coral Gables Congregational—*school* FL-3
Early Childhood Education Center—*school* FL-3
Early Cotton Press—*hist pl* SC-3
Early Coulee—*valley* MT-8
**Early (County)**—*pop pl* GA-3
Early County Courthouse—*hist pl* GA-3
Early Creek—*stream* AL-4
Early Creek—*stream* CA-9
Early Creek—*stream* (2) ID-8
Early Creek—*stream* NC-3
Early Greek Revival Cottage—*hist pl* OH-6
Early Greek Revival House—*hist pl* OH-6
*Earlygrove* MS-4
Early Grove Cem—*cemetery* MS-4
Early Grove Creek—*stream* MS-4
Early Grove Creek—*stream* TN-4
**Earlygrove (Early Grove)**—*pop pl* MS-4
*Early Grove Methodist Church* MS-4
*Earlygrover* MS-4
Early Gulch—*valley* CO-8
Early Harvest Shaft—*mine* UT-8
Early Hill Park—*park* OH-6
**Early (historical)**—*pop pl* OR-9
Early Hollow—*valley* OH-6
Early Hope Ch—*church* GA-3
Early Indian Fish Traps—*other* CA-9
Early Intake Powerhouse—*other* CA-9
Early Intervention Center—*school* FL-3
Early Lake—*reservoir* VA-3
Early Lateral—*canal* ID-8
Early Memorial Hosp—*hospital* GA-3
Early Mine—*mine* CA-9
Early Mine—*mine* NM-5
Early Mine (underground)—*mine* AL-4
Early Post Office—*hist pl* ME-1
Early Prong West Prong Hanging Woman Creek—*stream* WY-8
*Early Rose Baptist Ch* AL-4
Early Rose Baptist Ch—*church* AL-4
Early Rose Ch—*church* AL-4
Earlys Chapel—*church* KY-4
Earlys Chapel—*church* VA-3
Early Sch (historical)—*school* MO-7
Early Schools—*school* TX-5
**Earlys Crossing**—*pop pl* NJ-2
Earlys Crossroads—*locale* SC-3
Earlys Flat—*flat* NY-2
Early Shakopee Houses—*hist pl* MN-6
Early Slough—*bay* TN-4
Earlys Point—*cape* VT-1
Early Spring—*spring* CA-9
**Early Station**—*pop pl* IN-6
Earlysville—*locale* VA-3
Early Times—*locale* KY-4
Early Tower—*locale* LA-4
**Earlytown**—*pop pl* AL-4
Earlytown Ch—*church* AL-4
Earlytown Sch (abandoned)—*school* PA-2
Early Union Cem—*cemetery* IA-7
Early View Ch—*church* AR-4
Earlyville—*locale* PA-2
**Earlyville**—*pop pl* MS-4
Earlyville Post Office (historical)—*building* MS-4
Early Weed Bench—*bench* UT-8
Earlywine—*locale* TX-5
Earlywine Cem—*cemetery* OH-6
Earlywine Cem—*cemetery* WV-2
Early Winters (CCD)—*cens area* WA-9
Early Winters Creek—*stream* WA-9
Early Winters Ranger Station—*locale* WA-9
Early Winters Ranger Station Work Center—*hist pl* WA-9
Early Winters Spires—*pillar* WA-9
Early Winters Trail—*trail* WA-9
Earman, George, House—*hist pl* VA-3
Earman River—*stream* FL-3
**Earmans**—*pop pl* VA-3
Ear Mountain Ranger Station—*locale* MT-8
Ear Mtn—*summit* AK-9
Ear Mtn—*summit* MT-8
Earmuff Spring—*spring* OR-9
*Earnes Hill* ME-1
*Earnest* AL-4
*Earnest* MS-4
**Earnest**—*pop pl* PA-2
Earnest, Lake—*lake* PA-2
Earnest Anderson Dam—*dam* MS-4
Earnest Branch—*stream* NC-3
Earnest Bridge—*bridge* TN-4
Earnest Butte—*summit* WY-8
Earnest Cem—*cemetery* AL-4
Earnest Cem—*cemetery* AR-4
Earnest C Gaston Steam Plant—*building* AL-4
Earnest Ch—*church* AL-4
*Earnest Chapel* AL-4
Earnest Chapel—*church* AR-4
*Earnest Chapel Church* AL-4
Earnest Corner—*locale* ME-1
Earnest Ditch—*canal* CO-8
Earnest Gully—*stream* LA-4
**Earnest (historical)**—*pop pl* TN-4
Earnest (historical P.O.)—*locale* IA-7
Earnest Mill Creek—*stream* FL-3
Earnest Owen Pond—*lake* FL-3
Earnest Post Office (historical)—*building* TN-4
Earnest Rsvr—*reservoir* OR-9
Earnests Chapel Cem—*cemetery* TN-4
Earnests Chapel Methodist Ch (historical)—*church* TN-4
*Earnest S Colliers Bridge* AL-4
Earnest Shopping Plaza—*locale* FL-3
Earnest Street Yard Station—*locale* PA-2
*Earnest United Methodist Ch* AL-4
Earnestville—*locale* KY-4
**Earnestville**—*pop pl* MO-7
**Earnestville**—*pop pl* PA-2
Earnest Windmill—*locale* TX-5
Earney Cem—*cemetery* MO-7
Earnhardt Lake—*reservoir* NC-3
Earnhardt Lake Dam—*dam* NC-3
*Earnharts* AR-4
**Earnharts**—*pop pl* AR-4
Earnheart—*locale* AR-4
Earnheart Island—*island* AR-4
Earnhearts Ferry—*locale* AR-4
Earn Knob—*summit* VA-3
Earns Branch—*stream* KY-4
**Earnshaw**—*pop pl* WV-2
Earnshaw Cem—*cemetery* IL-6
Earnshaw Cem—*cemetery* WV-2
Earnst Cem—*cemetery* KS-7
Earp—*locale* CA-9
Earp Cem—*cemetery* IL-6
Ear Peak—*summit* AK-9
Earp Pond Dam—*dam* NC-3
Earp Ranch—*locale* NM-5
**Earpsboro**—*pop pl* NC-3
Earp Spring—*spring* OR-9
Earring Cem—*cemetery* MT-8
Ear River—*stream* AK-9
Ear Rock—*pillar* NM-5
*Earskin Mountain* UT-8
Earson Hollow—*valley* WV-2
**Earth**—*pop pl* TX-5
Earth (CCD)—*cens area* TX-5
**Earth City**—*pop pl* MO-7
Earth Dam West—*dam* IN-6
*Earthenville* TX-5
Earthexn Tank—*reservoir* AZ-5
Earthman Fork—*stream* TN-4
*Earthquake Bay* CA-9
Earthquake Creek—*stream* ID-8
Earthquake Lake—*lake* MT-8
Earthquake Meadows—*flat* ID-8
Earthquake Memorial—*locale* MT-8
Earthquake Point—*cliff* WA-9
Earthquake Spring—*spring* CA-9
Earthquake Valley—*valley* CA-9
*Earth Resources Observation Data Center* SD-7
Earven Flat—*flat* AZ-5
Earven Ranch—*locale* AZ-5
Earwood Creek—*stream* TX-5
Earwood Draw—*valley* TX-5
Earwood Hollow—*valley* AL-4
Earwood Ranch—*locale* TX-5
Eary Ranch—*locale* NM-5
*Earystown* NJ-2
Easam Mill Seat Lake—*reservoir* TX-5
**Easby**—*pop pl* ND-7
**Easby Township**—*pop pl* ND-7
*Eascoheague Hill* RI-1
*Easdale* KS-7
Easdale—*locale* KS-7
Easely Mountain—*ridge* AR-4
Easen Hill—*summit* MS-4
Eash Cem—*cemetery* IA-7
*Easland Creek* MO-7
*Easle Island* NJ-2
Easley—*locale* AL-4
**Easley**—*pop pl* IA-7
**Easley**—*pop pl* MO-7
**Easley**—*pop pl* SC-3
**Easley**—*pop pl* WV-2
Easley, Oscar, Block—*hist pl* CA-9
Easley, S. A., House—*hist pl* TX-5
Easley Bend—*bend* TN-4
Easley Branch—*stream* AR-4
Easley Branch—*stream* MS-4
Easley Canyon—*valley* OK-5
Easley (CCD)—*cens area* SC-3
Easley Cem—*cemetery* AR-4
Easley Cem—*cemetery* GA-3
Easley Cem—*cemetery* IL-6
Easley Cem—*cemetery* LA-4
Easley Cem—*cemetery* MS-4
Easley Cem—*cemetery* MO-7
Easley Cem—*cemetery* (2) TN-4
Easley Cem—*cemetery* (2) TX-5
*Easley Cemetery* AL-4
Easley Ch—*church* AL-4
Easley Ch—*church* MS-4
**Easley Chapel**—*pop pl* TX-5
*Easley Ch of the Brethern* AL-4
Easley Covered Bridge—*hist pl* AL-4
Easley Creek—*stream* AK-9
Easley Creek—*stream* AR-4
Easley Creek—*stream* (2) ID-8
Easley Creek—*stream* TX-5
Easley Ditch—*canal* IL-6
Easley East (CCD)—*cens area* SC-3
**Easley Estates**—*pop pl* TN-4
Easley Ford (historical)—*locale* MO-7
Easley Gap—*gap* GA-3
Easley Gulch—*valley* ID-8
Easley Hollow—*valley* MO-7
**Easley Hot Springs**—*pop pl* ID-8
Easley Mines—*mine* TN-4
Easley Peak—*summit* ID-8
Easley Post Office (historical)—*building* TN-4
Easley Ridge—*ridge* TN-4
Easley Sch (historical)—*school* MO-7
Easley Tank—*reservoir* NM-5
Easley Township—*civil* MO-7
**Easleyville**—*pop pl* LA-4
**Easly**—*pop pl* WV-2
Easly Cem—*cemetery* AL-4
Easly Creek—*stream* KS-7
Easly Creek—*stream* NE-7
Eason—*locale* GA-3
Eason—*locale* OK-5
Eason, T. T., Mansion—*hist pl* OK-5
Eason Bend—*bend* TN-4
Eason Bluff—*locale* GA-3
Eason Branch—*stream* MS-4
**Easonburg**—*pop pl* NC-3
Eason Cem—*cemetery* (3) GA-3
Eason Cem—*cemetery* MO-7
Eason Cem—*cemetery* (2) NC-3
Eason Cem—*cemetery* (3) TN-4
Eason Cem—*cemetery* TX-5
Eason Ch—*church* MS-4
Eason Chapel—*church* GA-3
**Eason Crossroads**—*pop pl* NC-3
Eason Hill Ch—*church* GA-3
Eason Island Landing—*locale* NC-3
Eason Johnson Cem—*cemetery* AL-4
Eason Lake—*lake* NE-7
Eason Lake Club—*other* TX-5
Easons Cem—*cemetery* GA-3
Eason Sch (historical)—*school* MS-4
*Easons Crossroads* NC-3
**Easons Crossroads**—*pop pl* NC-3
*Easons Store* NC-3
**Easons Store**—*pop pl* NC-3
*Eason Store* TN-4
Eason Swamp—*stream* NC-3
*Easonville Academy* AL-4
Easonville Creek—*stream* AL-4
Easonville (historical)—*locale* AL-4
Easonville HS (historical)—*school* AL-4
Eassis Creek—*stream* AR-4
Easson Ditch—*canal* CO-8
*East* MA-1
East—*uninc pl* NJ-2
East—*uninc pl* NY-2
East—*uninc pl* TN-4
East, Canyon—*valley* CO-8
East, Nicholas, House—*hist pl* PA-2
**East Abeika (historical)**—*pop pl* MS-4
**East Aberdeen**—*pop pl* MS-4
**East Aberdeen**—*pop pl* WA-9
**East Aberdeen (Days)**—*pop pl* MS-4
East Aberdeen Gardens—*uninc pl* VA-3
*East Abington* MA-1
*Eastaboga* AL-4
**Eastaboga**—*pop pl* AL-4
Eastaboga Baptist Ch—*church* AL-4
Eastaboga Creek—*stream* AL-4
Eastaboga Sch—*school* AL-4
*Eastaboga Station* AL-4
*East Abolo Chitto Creek* MS-4
Eastabrook Lake—*lake* ME-1
**Eastabuchie**—*pop pl* (2) MS-4
Eastabuchie Cem—*cemetery* MS-4
East Abutment Rec Area—*locale* TX-5
East Access Area—*locale* IL-6
**East Acres**—*pop pl* CA-9
**East Acres**—*pop pl* TN-4
**East Acton**—*pop pl* MA-1
**East Acworth**—*pop pl* NH-1
East Adams—*cens area* CO-8
East Adams—*unorg reg* ND-7
East Adams Canal—*canal* CA-9
East Adams Cem—*cemetery* ND-7
East Adobe Creek—*stream* NV-8
East Adrian Windmill—*locale* TX-5
East Afton—*locale* NY-2
**East Afton**—*pop pl* TX-5
**East Agana**—*pop pl* GU-9
*East Aiabeka* MS-4
*East Akron* OH-6
**East Akron**—*pop pl* OH-6
East Akron Cem—*cemetery* OH-6
East Akron Oil Field—*oilfield* CO-8
East Alabama Bible Coll—*school* AL-4
East Alabama Hosp (historical)—*hospital* AL-4
*East Alabama Junction* AL-4
*East Alabama Male College* AL-4
East Alabama Masonic Institute (historical)—*school* AL-4
East Alabama Med Ctr—*hospital* AL-4
East Alabama Motor Speedway—*locale* AL-4
East Alabama Street Ch of Christ (historical)—*church* AL-4
**East Alachua**—*pop pl* FL-3
East Alamo Canyon—*valley* CO-8
East Alamocitos Windmill—*locale* TX-5
**East Alamosa**—*pop pl* CO-8
*East Alamosa Creek* TX-5
East Alapah Glacier—*glacier* AK-9
East Alarka Ch—*church* NC-3
East Alaska Lake—*lake* WI-6
East Albany—*cens area* WY-8
**East Albany**—*pop pl* GA-3
**East Albany**—*pop pl* VT-1
East Albemarle Sch—*school* NC-3
East Albert Creek—*stream* AK-9
**East Alburg**—*pop pl* VT-1
**East Alburgh**—*pop pl* VT-1
East Alcoa Baptist Ch—*church* TN-4
East Alden Creek—*stream* ID-8
East Alder Creek—*stream* CO-8
East Aldrich Creek—*stream* IA-7
East Aler Island—*island* NY-2
East Alexander—*locale* NY-2
East Algansee Ch—*church* MI-6
East Alkali Creek—*stream* WY-8
East Alkali Drain—*stream* ID-8
East Alkali Gulch—*valley* CO-8
East Alkali Lake Number One—*reservoir* NV-8
East Alkali Lake Number Two—*reservoir* NV-8
East Allegheny JHS—*school* PA-2
*East Allen Creek* WI-6
*East Allendale* MI-6
East Allen Lake—*lake* WY-8
**East Allen (Township of)**—*pop pl* PA-2
**East Allentown (subdivision)**—*pop pl* PA-2
**East Alliance**—*pop pl* NC-3
**East Alliance**—*pop pl* OH-6
**East Alma Township**—*pop pl* ND-7
East Alsek River—*stream* AK-9
**East Alstead**—*pop pl* NH-1
**East Alta Loma**—*pop pl* CA-9
**East Alton**—*pop pl* IL-6
**East Alton**—*pop pl* NH-1
East Alton Cem—*cemetery* IL-6
**East Altoona**—*pop pl* PA-2
East Alum Creek—*stream* WY-8
**East Amana**—*pop pl* IA-7
East Amarillo—*uninc pl* TX-5
East Amarillo Creek—*stream* TX-5
East Amatuli Island—*island* AK-9
East Amboy—*locale* NY-2
**East Americus**—*pop pl* GA-3
**East Amherst**—*pop pl* NY-2
**East Amherst (RR name Transit)**—*pop pl* NY-2
East Amite Creek Prong—*stream* LA-4
East Amory Missionary Baptist Ch—*church* MS-4
**Eastampton (Township of)**—*pop pl* NJ-2
**East Amwell (Township of)**—*pop pl* NJ-2
East Anacoco Creek—*stream* LA-4

East Anadarche Arm—bay ... OK-5
East Anadarche Creek—stream ... OK-5
Eastanalle Creek ... TN-4
Eastanallee Baptist Ch ... TN-4
Eastanallee Ch—church ... TN-4
Eastanallee Creek ... TN-4
Eastanalle Valley ... TN-4
Eastanaula Creek ... TN-4
East Anchor Cove—bay ... AK-9
East and Bodell Drain—canal ... MI-6
East Anderson Oil Field—other ... NM-5
East Andover—pop pl ... ME-1
East Andover (Halcyon Station)—pop pl ... NH-1
East and West Dollar Islands—island ... NY-2
East and West Goose Structure R-9-1 Dam—dam ... MS-4
East and West Goose Structure R-9-2 Dam—dam ... MS-4
East and West Junction ... AL-4
East and West Potomac Parks—hist pl ... DC-2
East and West Sch—school ... TN-4
East And West Truck Trail—trail ... WA-9
Eastanelle Creek ... TN-4
Eastanelle Valley ... TN-4
East Annalaide Lake—lake ... MN-6
East Ann Arbor ... MI-6
Eastanollee—pop pl ... GA-3
Eastanollee Creek—stream ... GA-3
East Antelope Creek ... CO-8
East Antelope Creek ... NE-7
East Antelope Creek ... WY-8
East Antelope Creek—stream ... AZ-5
East Antelope Creek—stream ... MT-8
East Antelope Creek—stream ... WY-8
East Antelope Gas Field—oilfield ... WY-8
East Antelope Mtn—summit ... CO-8
East Antelope Rsvr—reservoir ... UT-8
East Antioch—pop pl ... CA-9
East Antioch Ch—church ... MS-4
East Antioch Elem Sch—school ... KS-7
East Anvil Point—cliff ... CO-8
East Appanoose Creek—stream ... KS-7
East Applegate—pop pl ... CA-9
East Apple Lake—lake ... WI-6
East Apple Tank—reservoir ... NM-5
East Apple Tree Branch—stream ... KY-4
East Apple Tree Ch—church ... KY-4
East Aransas River ... TX-5
East Arapahoe—cens area ... CO-8
East Arapahoe Creek—stream ... WY-8
East Ararat—locale ... PA-2
East Ararat Sch (historical)—school ... PA-2
East Arbela Ch—church ... MI-6
East Arboga—locale ... CA-9
East Arcade—locale ... NY-2
East Arcadia—pop pl ... NC-3
Eastard Bay—bay ... NC-3
East Area Sch—school ... WI-6
East Arkansas Creek—stream ... WY-8
East Arkansas River ... TX-5
East Arkdale Cem—cemetery ... WI-6
East Arlington—pop pl ... VT-1
East Arlington JHS—school ... MA-1
East Arlington (subdivision)—pop pl ... AL-4
East Arlington (subdivision)—pop pl ... MA-1
East Arm—canal ... IN-6
East Arm Clifford Lake—lake ... ME-1
East Arm Grand Traverse Bay—bay ... MI-6
East Arm Holtz Bay—bay ... AK-9
East Arm Lake Itasca—lake ... MN-6
East Arm Nevidiskov Bay—bay ... AK-9
East Arm Nuka Bay ... AK-9
East Arm of Traverse Bay ... MI-6
East Arm Payne Ditch—canal ... IN-6
East Armuchee—locale ... GA-3
East Armuchee Creek ... GA-3
East Armuchee Creek—stream ... GA-3
East Armuchee Valley—valley ... GA-3
East Arm Uganik Bay—bay ... AK-9
East Arndell Windmill—locale ... TX-5
East Arsenicker Key—island ... FL-3
East Art Cem—cemetery ... TX-5
East Artifact Rsvr—reservoir ... ID-8
East Arvada JHS—school ... CO-8
Easta Saugus—pop pl ... MA-1
East Ash Creek—stream ... AZ-5
East Ash Creek—stream ... NE-7
East Ashe Lateral—canal ... CA-9
East Asher Creek—stream ... KS-7
East Ash Fork Interchange—crossing ... AZ-5
East Ashland Shopping Plaza—locale ... MA-1
East Ash Spring—spring ... AZ-5
East Ashtabula ... OH-6
East Ashtabula—pop pl ... OH-6
East Aspetuck River—stream ... CT-1
East Atchison ... MO-7
East Atchison Airp (historical)—airport ... MO-7
East Athens—pop pl ... PA-2
East Athens Baptist Church ... TN-4
East Athens Ch—church ... TN-4
East Atlanta—pop pl ... GA-3
East Atlanta Ch—church ... GA-3
East Atlantic Beach—beach ... NY-2
East Atlantic Beach—pop pl ... NY-2
Eastatoe—pop pl ... SC-3
Eastatoe Ch—church ... SC-3
Eastatoe Creek—stream ... NC-3
Eastatoe Creek—stream ... SC-3
Eastatoe Gap—gap ... NC-3
Eastatoe (Township of)—fmr MCD ... NC-3
East Attleborough ... MA-1
East Attleborough Acad—hist pl ... MA-1
East Auburn ... ME-1
East Auburn—pop pl ... ME-1
East Auburn—uninc pl ... WA-9
East Auburndale—CDP ... FL-3
East Auburn Elem Sch—school ... IN-6
East Au Gres River ... MI-6
Eastaunaula Creek ... TN-4
East Aurora—pop pl ... IL-6
East Aurora—pop pl ... NY-2
East Aurora Cem—cemetery ... IL-6
East Aurora Country Club—other ... NY-2
East Austin—uninc pl ... TX-5
East Austin Creek—stream ... CA-9
East Aux Sable Creek—stream ... IL-6
East Ave—uninc pl ... FL-3
East Ave Cem—cemetery ... OH-6
East Ave Hist Dist—hist pl ... NY-2
East Ave Park—park ... TX-5
East Ave Sch—school ... CA-9
East Ave Sch—school ... TX-5
East Avilas Tank—reservoir ... NM-5
East Avon—pop pl ... NY-2
East Avon Cem—cemetery ... NY-2
East Avondale School ... KS-7
East Babcock Canyon—valley ... AZ-5
East Bachelor Cemeteries—cemetery ... TX-5
East Back Creek—stream ... VA-3
East Badger Creek—stream ... CO-8
East Badger Creek—stream ... KS-7
East Badlands Creek—stream ... SD-7
East Bad Medicine Trail—trail ... MN-6
East Bahia Honda Channel—channel ... FL-3
East Bahia Honda Key—island ... FL-3
East Baker Bench—bench ... UT-8
East Baker Canal—canal ... FL-3
East Bakersfield—post sta ... CA-9
East Bakersfield HS—school ... CA-9
East Bald Peak Drain—canal ... NE-7
East Bald Peak Lateral—canal ... NE-7
East Baldwin Mattocks Station—pop pl ... ME-1
East Baldwin (RR name Mattocks)—pop pl ... ME-1
East Baldy Basin—basin ... MT-8
East Ball Mtn—summit ... CO-8
East Balsam Ch—church ... WI-6
East Bangor—pop pl ... ME-1
East Bangor—pop pl ... PA-2
East Bangor Borough—civil ... PA-2
Eastbank ... WV-2
East Bank—bar ... FL-3
East Bank—bar ... NY-2
East Bank—other ... LA-4
East Bank—pop pl ... WV-2
East Bank—post sta ... KS-7
East Bank Park—park ... MS-4
East Bank Public Use Area—park ... AL-4
East Bank Public Use Area—park ... GA-3
East Banks—bar ... AL-4
East Bank Trail—trail ... WA-9
East Banner Lake—lake ... WY-8
East Baptist Ch—church ... MS-4
East Baptist Hollow Mine—mine ... TN-4
East Baptist Sch (historical)—school ... MS-4
East Bardstown—locale ... KY-4
East Bare Creek ... WA-9
East Barge—island ... ME-1
East Barnard—pop pl ... VT-1
East Barnet—other ... VT-1
East Barnet Inwood Station—pop pl ... VT-1
East Barnitz Creek—stream ... OK-5
East Barnstable Cem—cemetery ... MA-1
East Barre—pop pl ... NY-2
East Barre—pop pl ... VT-1
East Barre Dam—dam ... VT-1
East Barrigada Sch—school ... GU-9
East Barrington ... NH-1
East Barrington—pop pl ... NH-1
East Barron Creek ... AR-4
East Barry Rsvr—reservoir ... OR-9
East Bartlett Oil Field—oilfield ... TX-5
East Barton—pop pl ... NE-7
East Basin—basin (2) ... CO-8
East Basin—basin ... OH-6
East Basin—basin ... TX-5
East Basin—basin ... UT-8
East Basin—harbor (3) ... CA-9
East Basin—harbor ... FL-3
East Basin—harbor ... NY-2
East Basin—harbor ... OR-9
East Basin Cem—cemetery ... OK-5
East Basin Channel—channel ... CA-9
East Basin Creek—stream ... ID-8
East Basin Creek—stream ... UT-8
East Basin Draw—valley ... WY-8
East Basin Lake—lake ... ID-8
East Basin Pass—gap ... UT-8
East Bass Creek—stream ... AR-4
East Bassetts Bar—bar ... AL-4
East Bassetts Creek ... AL-4
East Bassetts Landing—locale ... AL-4
East Bass Lake—lake ... MN-6
East Bass Lake—lake ... MT-8
East Bass Lake—pop pl ... OH-6
East Batavia—pop pl ... IL-6
East Batavia Cem—cemetery ... IL-6
East Batavia Heights—pop pl ... OH-6
East Batesville Ch—church ... MS-4
East Bates Well—well ... NM-5
East Bates Windmill—locale ... TX-5
East Bath Cem—cemetery ... OH-6
East Baton Rouge Parish—pop pl ... LA-4
East Battleground Ch—church ... AL-4
East Battle Lake—lake ... MN-6
East Bay ... FL-3
East Bay ... TX-5
East Bay—bay (4) ... FL-3
East Bay—bay ... IA-7
East Bay—bay (2) ... LA-4
East Bay—bay ... ME-1
East Bay—bay (3) ... MI-6
East Bay—bay (3) ... MN-6
East Bay—bay ... MT-8
East Bay—bay (4) ... NY-2
East Bay—bay ... NC-3
East Bay—bay ... TX-5
East Bay—bay ... UT-8
East Bay—bay ... VT-1
East Bay—bay (2) ... WA-9
East Bay—bay ... WI-6
East Bay—cove ... MA-1
East Bay—gut ... NY-2
East Bay—pop pl ... NY-2
East Bay—swamp ... FL-3
East Bayard—fmr MCD ... NE-7
East Bay Baptist Ch—church ... FL-3
East Bay Bayou—stream ... TX-5
East Bay Christian Sch—school ... FL-3
East Bay Fire Tower—tower ... FL-3
East Bay Harbor ... WA-9
East Bay HS—school ... FL-3
East Bay Junop—bay ... LA-4
East Bay Lake—lake ... MI-6
East Bay Little Saint Germain Lake—lake ... WI-6
East Bay Missionary Baptist Ch—church ... FL-3
East Bayou ... AR-4
East Bayou ... FL-3
East Bayou—bay ... FL-3
East Bayou—gut (2) ... LA-4
East Bayou—stream ... AR-4
East Bayou Grand Marais—stream ... LA-4
East Bayou Lacassine—stream ... LA-4
East Bayou Pigeon Gas Field—oilfield ... LA-4
East Bay Park—park ... MI-6
East Bay Park—pop pl ... NY-2
East Bay Playground—park ... SC-3
East Bay Plaza (Shop Ctr)—locale ... FL-3
East Bay Recreation Site—park ... OR-9
East Bay River—stream ... FL-3
East Bay Sch—school ... MI-6
East Bay Sch—school ... SC-3
East Bay Sch Number 15—school ... MI-6
East Bay Swamp—swamp ... FL-3
East Bay (Township of)—pop pl ... MI-6
East Bay Vista Park—park ... FL-3
East Beach ... NY-2
East Beach ... RI-1
East Beach ... WA-9
East Beach—beach ... CA-9
East Beach—beach ... FL-3
East Beach—beach (3) ... NY-2
East Beach—beach ... NC-3
East Beach—beach ... TX-5
East Beach—lake ... RI-1
East Beach Park—park ... WA-9
East Bear Canyon—valley ... AZ-5
East Bear Creek—stream ... CO-8
East Bear Creek—stream ... GA-3
East Bear Creek—stream ... MO-7
East Bear Creek—stream ... OR-9
East Bear Creek—stream ... WA-9
East Bearden Oil Field—oilfield ... OK-5
East Beards Creek—stream ... SC-3
East Bear Flat ... ID-8
East Bear Gulch—valley ... CO-8
East Bear Island—pop pl ... NH-1
East Bear Lake—lake ... MI-6
East Bearskin Campground—locale ... MN-6
East Bearskin Lake—lake ... MN-6
East Bear Springs Arroyo—stream ... CO-8
East Bear Trap Campground—locale ... NM-5
East Bear Valley Draw—valley ... CO-8
East Bear Wallow Gulch—valley ... CO-8
East Beaver Bay—pop pl ... MN-6
East Beaver Cem—cemetery ... IA-7
East Beaver Charlie Rsvr—reservoir ... OR-9
East Beaver Creek ... CO-8
East Beaver Creek ... OH-6
East Beaver Creek ... OK-5
East Beaver Creek ... WY-8
East Beaver Creek—stream (5) ... CO-8
East Beaver Creek—stream ... IA-7
East Beaver Creek—stream ... KS-7
East Beaver Creek—stream (2) ... OK-5
East Beaver Creek—stream ... OR-9
East Beaver Creek—stream ... TN-4
East Beaver Creek—stream ... WI-6
East Beaver Creek Canal—canal ... TN-4
East Beaver Creek Drainage Canal ... TN-4
East Beaver River ... MN-6
East Beaver Sch—school ... WI-6
East Beaver Sch (historical)—school ... IA-7
East Beaver Trap Creek—stream ... SD-7
East Beckley—pop pl ... WV-2
East Beckwith Mountain ... CO-8
East Beckwith Mtn—summit ... CO-8
East Bedico Creek—stream ... LA-4
East Bee Branch—stream ... MO-7
East Beech—locale ... PA-2
East Beech Creek Oil Field—oilfield ... TX-5
East Beecher Hill—summit ... NY-2
East Beecher Hill Community Club—other ... NY-2
East Beech Woods—woods ... PA-2
East Beekmantown—pop pl ... NY-2
East Bee Rock—other ... AK-9
East Belews Creek—stream ... NC-3
East Belfast Cem—cemetery ... ME-1
East Belfast Sch—school ... ME-1
East Belknap Creek—stream ... TX-5
East Bell (CCD)—cens area ... TX-5
East Bellows Creek—stream ... CO-8
East Bell Windmill—locale ... NM-5
East Belmont Cem—cemetery ... MN-6
East Belmont Sch—school ... NC-3
East Belmore Cem—cemetery ... OH-6
East Belt Mine (reduced usage)—mine ... MT-8
East Bench—bench ... MT-8
East Bench—bench ... OR-9
East Bench—bench (3) ... UT-8
East Bench at 29th Subdivision—pop pl ... UT-8
East Bench Canal—canal ... MT-8
East Bench Canal—canal (2) ... UT-8
East Bench Ditch—canal ... UT-8
East Bench Substation—other ... UT-8
East Bench Well Number One—well ... NV-8
Eastbend ... AL-4
East Bend—bend ... LA-4
East Bend—pop pl ... AL-4
East Bend—pop pl ... NC-3
East Bend Cem—cemetery ... IL-6
East Bend Ch—church ... IL-6
East Bend Ch—church ... KY-4
East Bend Ditch—canal ... CO-8
East Bend Elem Sch—school ... NC-3
East Bend Lake—lake ... NY-2
East Bend Park (census name Red Oak Mill)—pop pl ... NY-2
East Bend P.O. ... AL-4
East Bend (Township of)—fmr MCD ... NC-3
East Bend (Township of)—pop pl ... IL-6
East Bennett—unorg reg ... SD-7
East Bennett Canyon—valley ... SD-7
East Bennett Valley Cem—cemetery ... WI-6
East Bennington—locale ... NY-2
East Bens Hollow—valley ... UT-8
East Benton—pop pl ... ME-1
East Benton—pop pl ... PA-2
East Benton Cem—cemetery ... PA-2
East Benton (Jordan Hollow)—pop pl ... PA-2
East Benton Township—civil (2) ... MO-7
East Bergen—locale ... NY-2
East Berkshire—pop pl ... NY-2
East Berkshire—pop pl ... VT-1
East Berkshire United Methodist Church—hist pl ... NY-2
East Berlin—locale ... PA-2
East Berlin—pop pl ... CT-1
East Berlin—pop pl ... MA-1
East Berlin—pop pl ... NJ-2
East Berlin—pop pl ... PA-2
East Berlin Borough—civil ... PA-2
East Berlin Cem—cemetery ... MI-6
East Berlin Hist Dist—hist pl ... PA-2
East Berlin Sch—school ... OR-9
East Bernard—CDP ... TX-5
East Bernard—pop pl ... TX-5
East Bernard Creek—stream ... TX-5
East Berne—pop pl ... NY-2
East Bernstadt—pop pl ... KY-4
East Bernstadt (CCD)—cens area ... KY-4
East Berwick—pop pl ... PA-2
East Bethany—pop pl ... NY-2
East Bethel—pop pl ... ME-1
East Bethel—pop pl ... MN-6
East Bethel—pop pl ... VT-1
East Bethel Cem—cemetery ... IA-7
East Bethel Cem—cemetery ... MN-6
East Bethel Ch—church ... IL-6
East Bethel Ch—church ... NC-3
East Bethel Ch—church ... OH-6
East Bethlehem ... PA-2
East Bethlehem Ch—church ... PA-2
East Bethlehem Sch—school ... MI-6
East Bethlehem (Township of)—pop pl ... PA-2
East B Hill—summit ... ME-1
East Bicknell Sand Wash Pond—reservoir ... UT-8
East Big Canyon Creek—stream ... CA-9
East Big Creek—stream ... IA-7
East Big Creek—stream ... KS-7
East Big Flat Ridge—ridge ... PA-2
East Biggs—pop pl ... CA-9
East Bight—bay ... AK-9
East Bijou Creek—stream ... CO-8
East Bijou Sch—school ... CO-8
East Billerica—pop pl ... MA-1
East Billings—pop pl ... MT-8
East Billings Oil Field—oilfield ... OK-5
East Bills Creek—stream ... OK-5
East Billy Creek—stream ... OK-5
East Biltmore (subdivision)—pop pl ... NC-3
East Birch Creek—stream (2) ... OR-9
East Birmingham—pop pl ... AL-4
East Birmingham Baptist Church ... AL-4
East Bitter Creek ... TX-5
East Bitter Creek—stream ... KS-7
East Bitter Creek—stream (2) ... OK-5
East Bitter Creek—stream ... TX-5
East Blackburn Fork—stream ... TN-4
East Black Canyon Creek—stream ... ID-8
East Black Hills—summit ... TX-5
East Black Ledge—bar ... ME-1
East Black Oak—locale ... AR-4
East Black Rock—island ... ME-1
East Blackstone—pop pl ... MA-1
East Blacktail Creek—stream (2) ... MT-8
East Bladen HS—school ... NC-3
East Bloomfield—pop pl ... NY-2
East Bloomfield (Town of)—pop pl ... NY-2
East Bloomsburg—locale ... PA-2
East Blue Creek ... IA-7
East Blue Creek Meadow—flat ... WA-9
East Bluegrass Creek—stream ... WY-8
East Bluehill ... ME-1
East Blue Hill—pop pl ... ME-1
East Blue Mounds Ch—church ... WI-6
East Blue Mounds Creek ... WI-6
East Bluff—cliff ... IA-7
East Bluff—cliff ... WI-6
East Bluff—ridge ... MI-6
East Bluff Bay—bay ... NC-3
East Bluffport Landing ... AL-4
East Bluff Trail—trail ... WI-6
East Bluff Woods Trail—trail ... WI-6
East Blythe—pop pl ... CA-9
East Boardman Ch—church ... MI-6
East Boardman Lake—lake ... WA-9
East Bob Smith Creek—stream ... ID-8
East Boca Canyon—valley ... CA-9
East Boca Spring—spring ... CA-9
East Boga ... AL-4
East Boggy Bayou—stream ... AR-4
East Boggy Depot Oil Field—oilfield ... OK-5
East Bogue Chitto—stream ... LA-4
East Bogue Chitto—stream ... MS-4
East Bogue Chitto River ... MS-4
East Bogue Hasty—stream ... MS-4
East Bok Tuklo ... OK-5
East Boktuklo Creek—stream ... OK-5
East Boktukola Creek ... OK-5
East Boley Oil Field—oilfield ... OK-5
East Bologna Canyon—valley ... OR-9
East Bolton—pop pl ... MA-1
East Bolton Dam ... MA-1
East Bolton Sch—school ... KS-7
East Bonito Prairie Tank—reservoir ... AZ-5
East Bonne Terre—pop pl ... MO-7
East Bonus Cem—cemetery ... IL-6
East Boone—pop pl ... IA-7
East Boone Draw—valley ... CO-8
East Boone Prairie Cem—cemetery ... TX-5
East Boone Township—pop pl ... MO-7
East Booneville Baptist Ch—church ... MS-4
East Booth Bay ... ME-1
East Boothbay—pop pl ... ME-1
East Boot Lake—lake ... MN-6
Eastboro Shop Ctr—locale ... KS-7
Eastborough—pop pl ... KS-7
Eastborough Park—park ... KS-7
East Bosque Creek ... TX-5
East Bosque River—stream ... TX-5
East Bosshart Coulee—valley ... MT-8
East Boston—pop pl ... NY-2
East Boston Bridge ... MA-1
East Boston Hill—summit ... NY-2
East Boston (historical P.O.)—locale ... MA-1
East Boston HS—school ... MA-1
East Boston Pier Number One—locale ... MA-1
East Boston (subdivision)—pop pl ... MA-1
East Boulder Canyon—valley ... AZ-5
East Boulder Creek—stream ... AK-9
East Boulder Creek—stream ... CA-9
East Boulder Creek—stream ... ID-8
East Boulder Ditch—canal ... CO-8
East Boulder Draw—valley ... UT-8
East Boulder Lake—lake ... CA-9
East Boulder Lakes—lake ... UT-8
East Boulder Meadow—flat ... ID-8
East Boulder Plateau—plain ... MT-8
East Boulder River ... MT-8
East Boulder River—stream ... MT-8
East Boulder Sch—school ... MT-8
East Boulder Trail—trail ... AZ-5
East Bouldin Creek—stream ... TX-5
East Boundary—CDP ... GA-3
East Bound Brook—uninc pl ... NJ-2
East Bourland Mtn—summit ... TX-5
East Bow Creek—stream ... NE-7
East Bower Sch—school ... NE-7
East Bowie Interchange—crossing ... AZ-5
East Boxelder Creek ... NE-7
East Box Elder Creek—stream ... NE-7
East Box Elder Creek—stream ... WY-8
East Boxford—pop pl ... MA-1
East Boyer River—stream ... IA-7
East Boyer Township—fmr MCD ... IA-7
East Boyer Trail—trail ... PA-2
East Boyles—uninc pl ... AL-4
East Boylston—locale ... NY-2
East Boynton—locale ... GA-3
East Bradfield River—stream ... AK-9
East Bradford—uninc pl ... PA-2
East Bradford Boarding Sch for Boys—hist pl ... PA-2
East Bradford Station—locale ... PA-2
East Bradford (Township of)—pop pl ... PA-2
East Bradley Brook—stream ... CT-1
East Brady—pop pl ... PA-2
East Brady Borough—civil ... PA-2
East Brady Elem Sch—school ... PA-2
East Brady Junior-Senior HS—school ... PA-2
East Brainerd—pop pl ... TN-4
East Brainerd Elementary School ... TN-4
East Brainerd Sch—school ... TN-4
East Braintree—pop pl ... MA-1
East Braintree—pop pl ... VT-1
East Branch ... HI-9
East Branch ... IL-6
East Branch ... KS-7
East Branch ... ME-1
East Branch ... MD-2
East Branch ... MA-1
East Branch ... MI-6
East Branch ... MN-6
East Branch ... NY-2
East Branch ... NC-3
East Branch ... PA-2
East Branch—canal ... MI-6
East Branch—channel ... CT-1
East Branch—gut ... CA-9
East Branch—locale (2) ... PA-2
East Branch—pop pl ... NY-2
East Branch—stream ... AR-4
East Branch—stream ... MO-7
East Branch—stream (3) ... OH-6
East Branch—stream ... PA-2
East Branch Acoakset River ... MA-1
East Branch Acoaksett River ... MA-1
East Branch Allagash Stream—stream ... ME-1
East Branch Amity Creek—stream ... MN-6
East Branch Antietam Creek—stream ... PA-2
East Branch Anti Mason Drain—canal ... MI-6
East Branch Apple Creek—stream ... ND-7
East Branch Arcadia Wash—stream ... CA-9
East Branch Armstrong Brook—stream ... ME-1
East Branch Armstrong Creek—stream ... MI-6
East Branch Ash Creek ... NE-7
East Branch Ash Creek—stream ... SD-7
East Branch Ashtabula River—stream ... OH-6
East Branch Ashtabula River—stream ... PA-2
East Branch Atkins Brook—stream ... ME-1
East Branch Au Gres River ... MI-6
East Branch Au Gres River—stream ... MI-6
East Branch August Creek—stream ... OK-5
East Branch Au Sable River ... MI-6
East Branch Au Sable River—stream ... MI-6
East Branch Ausable River—stream ... NY-2
East Branch Baker River—stream ... NH-1
East Branch Baptism River—stream ... MN-6
East Branch Baraboo River ... WI-6
East Branch Barnetts Creek—stream ... GA-3
East Branch Barrett Brook—stream ... ME-1
East Branch Basket Creek—stream ... NY-2
East Branch Bass River—stream ... NJ-2
East Branch Battrick Creek ... IA-7
East Branch Bayou Hasouse ... LA-4
East Branch Bear Creek—stream ... KS-7
East Branch Bear Creek—stream ... MI-6
East Branch Bear Creek—stream ... TN-4
East Branch Beaver Brook—stream ... ME-1
East Branch Beaver Brook—stream ... NH-1
East Branch Beaverdam Creek—stream ... IA-7
East Branch Beaver Dam Creek—stream ... SD-7
East Branch Beaver River—stream ... MN-6
East Branch Big Creek—stream ... CA-9
East Branch Big Creek—stream (2) ... MI-6
East Branch Big Creek—stream ... WI-6
East Branch Big Dalton Wash—stream ... CA-9
East Branch Big Eau Pleine River—stream ... WI-6
East Branch Big Elk Creek—stream ... PA-2
East Branch Big Lost River ... ID-8
East Branch Big Mine Run (historical)—stream ... PA-2
East Branch Big Musquash Stream—stream ... ME-1
East Branch Big Rock Creek—stream ... IL-6
East Branch Big Run—stream ... PA-2
East Branch Big Salt Wash—stream ... CO-8
East Branch Big Sandy Creek—stream ... WI-6
East Branch Big Sewickley Creek—stream ... PA-2
East Branch Big Sous Creek—stream ... TX-5
East Branch Big Wea Creek ... IN-6
East Branch Biloxi Bayou ... LA-4
East Branch Birch Stream—stream ... ME-1
East Branch Black Creek—stream ... LA-4
East Branch Blackfoot Canal—canal ... ID-8
East Branch Black River—stream (2) ... MI-6
East Branch Black River—stream ... OH-6
East Branch Black Stream—stream ... ME-1
East Branch Blue Creek—stream ... IA-7
East Branch Blue Earth River ... KS-7
East Branch Blue Earth River—stream ... MN-6
East Branch Blue Mounds Creek ... WI-6
East Branch Blue Mounds Creek—stream ... WI-6
East Branch Bluff Creek—stream ... KS-7
East Branch Bog Brook—stream ... NH-1
East Branch Boone Creek—stream ... OK-5
East Branch Boone River—stream ... IA-7
East Branch Boyd Creek—stream ... SC-3
East Branch Brackett Creek—stream ... CO-8
East Branch Brandywine Creek—stream ... PA-2
East Branch Briar Creek—stream ... PA-2
East Branch Bronco Creek—stream ... TX-5
East Branch Bruce Lake Trail—trail ... PA-2
East Branch Brush Creek—stream ... MO-7
East Branch Buckatany Creek ... MS-4
East Branch Buckley Creek—stream ... IA-7
East Branch Buck Run—stream ... OH-6
East Branch Bucktooth Run—stream ... NY-2
East Branch Buffalo Creek—stream ... IA-7
East Branch Bull Creek—stream ... SD-7
East Branch Bullskin Creek—stream ... OH-6
East Branch Bunch Ditch—canal ... IN-6
East Branch Bush Kill Creek ... PA-2
East Branch Byram River—stream ... NY-2
East Branch Cahoochie Creek—stream ... MO-7
East Branch Caldwell Creek ... PA-2
East Branch Callicoon Creek—stream ... NY-2
East Branch Camp Creek—stream ... MT-8
East Branch Camp (historical)—locale ... ME-1
East Branch Canada Run—stream ... PA-2
East Branch Canal Creek—stream ... MD-2
East Branch Canasawacta Creek—stream ... NY-2
East Branch Canawacta Creek—stream ... PA-2
East Branch Caney Creek—stream ... LA-4
East Branch Caney Creek—stream ... OK-5
East Branch Carry Brook—stream ... ME-1
East Branch Cascade Creek—stream ... VA-3
East Branch Cass River ... MI-6
East Branch Cattail Creek—stream ... MD-2
East Branch Cazenovia Creek—stream ... NY-2
East Branch Cedar Creek—stream ... IL-6
East Branch Cedar Creek—stream ... TX-5
East Branch Cedar Run—stream ... PA-2
East Branch Cem—cemetery ... PA-2
East Branch Ch—church ... OH-6
East Branch Chagrin River—stream (2) ... OH-6
East Branch Chandler Brook—stream ... ME-1
East Branch Chandler River ... ME-1
East Branch Chandler River—stream ... ME-1
East Branch Chanta Peta Creek ... ND-7
East Branch Chelsea Creek ... MT-8
East Branch Chenango River ... NY-2
East Branch Chester Creek—stream ... MN-6
East Branch Chester Creek—stream ... PA-2
East Branch Chicod Creek ... NC-3
East Branch Chicot Creek ... NC-3
East Branch Chigley Sandy Creek—stream ... OK-5
East Branch Chillisquaque Creek—stream ... PA-2
East Branch Chippewa River ... WI-6
East Branch Chippewa River—stream ... MN-6
East Branch Chocolay River—stream ... MI-6
East Branch Choctawhatchee Creek ... AL-4
East Branch Christina River—stream ... DE-2
East Branch Christina River—stream ... MD-2
East Branch Christina River—stream ... PA-2
East Branch Clarion River—stream ... PA-2
East Branch Clarion River Lake—reservoir ... PA-2
East Branch Clarion Stream ... PA-2
East Branch Clay Creek—stream ... NE-7
East Branch Clear Creek—stream ... KS-7
East Branch Clear Creek—stream ... TX-5
East Branch Codorus Creek—stream ... PA-2
East Branch Cold Brook—stream (2) ... NY-2
East Branch Cold Spring Creek—stream ... NY-2
East Branch Collington Branch—stream ... MD-2
East Branch Comstock Brook—stream ... CT-1
East Branch Conestoga River—stream ... PA-2
East Branch Conneaut Creek—stream (2) ... PA-2
East Branch Converse Pond Brook—stream ... CT-1
East Branch Coon Creek ... WI-6
East Branch Coon Creek—stream ... MI-6
East Branch Coon Creek—stream ... MO-7
East Branch Cooper River—stream ... SC-3
East Branch Copperas Creek—stream ... IL-6
East Branch Coral Creek—stream ... FL-3
East Branch County Line Brook—stream ... NY-2
East Branch Cowley Run—stream ... PA-2
East Branch Coxes Creek—stream ... PA-2
East Branch Crawford Creek—stream ... MO-7
East Branch Cricker Brook—stream ... CT-1
East Branch Crooked Arroyo—stream ... CO-8
East Branch Crooked Creek ... MN-6
East Branch Cross Creek—stream (2) ... CA-9
East Branch Croton River—stream ... NY-2
East Branch Cupsuptic River—stream ... ME-1
East Branch Cuyahoga River—stream ... OH-6
East Branch Dam—dam ... CT-1
East Branch Dam—dam ... PA-2
East Branch Dayton Lateral—canal ... CO-8
East Branch Dead Creek—stream ... VT-1
East Branch Dead Diamond River—stream ... NH-1
East Branch Deadwater—lake ... ME-1
East Branch Dead Water Stream—stream ... NH-1
East Branch Deep Creek—stream ... KS-7
East Branch Deer Creek—stream ... MS-4
East Branch Deer Creek—stream ... NY-2
East Branch Deerfield River—stream ... VT-1
East Branch Deer River ... NY-2
East Branch Delaware River—stream ... NY-2
East Branch Des Moines River ... IA-7
East Branch Des Moines River ... MN-6
East Branch Devers Canal—canal ... TX-5
East Branch Ditch—canal ... CA-9
East Branch Douglas Creek—stream ... ND-7
East Branch Dowells Draft—valley ... VA-3
East Branch Downer Creek—stream ... KS-7
East Branch Dry Creek—stream ... KS-7
East Branch Duck Creek ... MI-6
East Branch Duck River ... MI-6
East Branch Duck River—stream ... MI-6
East Branch Du Page River—stream ... IL-6
East Branch Dyberry Creek—stream ... PA-2
East Branch Eagle Creek—stream ... NE-7
East Branch Eagle River—stream ... MI-6
East Branch East Branch Wolf Creek—stream ... OH-6
East Branch Eastern River—stream ... ME-1
East Branch East Fork North Fork Trinity River—stream ... CA-9
East Branch East Fork Pond River ... KY-4

East Branch East Weaver Creek—stream ... CA-9
East Branch Eau Claire River—stream ... WI-6
East Branch Eighteenmile Creek—stream ... NY-2
East Branch Eightmile River—stream ... CT-1
East Branch El Dorado Canyon—valley ... CA-9
East Branch Elk Creek—stream ... ND-7
East Branch Elk River ... WA-9
East Branch Elk River—stream ... WA-9
East Branch Elm Creek—stream ... KS-7
East Branch Embarras River—stream ... IL-6
East Branch Enchanted Stream—stream ... ME-1
East Branch Escanaba River ... MI-6
East Branch Escanaba River—stream ... MI-6
East Branch Esconawby River ... MI-6
East Branch Fall Creek—stream ... KS-7
East Branch Fall River—stream ... KS-7
East Branch Farmington River—stream ... CT-1
East Branch Fence River—stream ... MI-6
East Branch Ferguson Brook—stream ... ME-1
East Branch Fever Brook—stream ... MA-1
East Branch Field Brook—stream ... PA-2
East Branch Firesteel River—stream ... MI-6
East Branch Fish Creek—stream ... MI-6
East Branch Fish Creek—stream ... NY-2
East Branch Fishing Creek—stream (2) ... PA-2
East Branch Flandreau Creek—stream ... MN-6
East Branch Flat Creek—stream ... AR-4
East Branch Fond Du Lac River—stream ... WI-6
East Branch Fortythree Creek—stream ... MN-6
East Branch Fourmile Creek—stream ... FL-3
East Branch Fox Creek—stream ... OR-9
East Branch Fox River—stream ... MI-6
East Branch Freeman Run—stream ... PA-2
East Branch Furlong Creek—stream ... MI-6
East Branch Galien River—stream ... MI-6
East Branch Galloway Creek—stream ... MO-7
East Branch Galls Creek—stream ... OR-9
East Branch Glade Creek—stream ... WA-9
East Branch Glenn Brook ... MA-1
East Branch Goose Creek—stream ... ID-8
East Branch Gordon Creek—stream ... OR-9
East Branch Grant Creek—stream ... KS-7
East Branch Graveraet River—stream ... MI-6
East Branch Green Creek—stream ... IL-6
East Branch Green River—stream ... MA-1
East Branch Green Valley Creek—stream ... CA-9
East Branch Gulf Stream—stream ... ME-1
East Branch Gulliver Brook—stream ... ME-1
East Branch Gulpha Creek—stream ... AR-4
East Branch Hackensack River—stream ... NY-2
East Branch Halawa Gulch—valley ... HI-9
East Branch Handsome Brook—stream ... NY-2
East Branch Harbor Brook ... CT-1
East Branch Harraseeket River ... ME-1
East Branch Hat Creek—stream ... VA-3
East Branch Hay Creek—stream ... MN-6
East Branch Hay Creek—stream ... MT-8
East Branch Hay Creek—stream ... WI-6
East Branch Heald Creek—stream ... MI-6
East Branch Hellroaring Creek—stream ... MT-8
East Branch Hemlock Creek—stream (2) ... PA-2
East Branch Hemlock River—stream ... MI-6
East Branch Herbert Run—stream ... MD-2
East Branch Herman Creek—stream ... WA-9
East Branch Hersey Creek—stream ... MI-6
East Branch Hickory Creek ... PA-2
East Branch Hicks Run—stream ... PA-2
East Branch Highline Canal—canal ... CO-8
East Branch Hix Brook ... NH-1
East Branch Honey Creek—stream ... WI-6
East Branch Honokane Iki Stream—stream ... HI-9
East Branch Honokane Nui Stream—stream ... HI-9
East Branch Hopkins Creek—stream ... CA-9
East Branch Horse Creek—stream ... IL-6
East Branch Horsepen Creek—stream ... VA-3
East Branch Hot Brook—stream ... ME-1
East Branch Housatonic River ... MA-1
East Branch Housatonic River—stream ... MA-1
East Branch Housatonic River Rsvr—reservoir ... MA-1
East Branch Howe Brook—stream ... ME-1
East Branch Huerhuero Creek—stream ... CA-9
East Branch Humboldt Creek—stream ... KS-7
East Branch Hunger Kill—stream ... NY-2
East Branch Huron River—stream ... MI-6
East Branch Huron River—stream ... OH-6
East Branch Hurricane Creek—stream ... IL-6
East Branch Hurricane Creek—stream ... TN-4
East Branch Hyner Run—stream ... PA-2
East Branch Illinois River—gut ... IL-6
East Branch Indian Creek ... IA-7
East Branch Indian Creek—stream ... AL-4
East Branch Indian Creek—stream ... PA-2
East Branch Indian Hollow—valley ... AZ-5
East Branch Indian Stream—stream ... NH-1
East Branch Iowa River—stream ... IA-7
East Branch Jackson River—stream ... VA-3
East Branch Jelloway Creek—stream ... OH-6
East Branch Jenkintown Creek—stream ... PA-2
East Branch Jim Creek—stream ... KS-7
East Branch Jones Creek—stream ... NE-7
East Branch Jordan Creek—stream ... MI-6
East Branch Jumbo Creek ... MI-6
East Branch Kanaranzi Creek—stream ... MN-6
East Branch Keg Creek—stream ... IA-7
East Branch Kibby Stream—stream ... ME-1
East Branch Killbuck Creek ... IL-6
East Branch Killbuck Creek—stream ... IL-6
East Branch Kiser Creek—stream ... IL-6
East Branch Knob Creek—stream ... MO-7
East Branch Kokosing River—stream ... OH-6
East Branch Kunjamuk River—stream ... NY-2
East Branch Lackawanna River—stream ... PA-2
East Branch Lake—lake ... ME-1
East Branch Lake—reservoir ... PA-2
East Branch Lake Fork—stream ... IL-6
East Branch Lakeside Ditch—canal ... CA-9
East Branch Lamarsh Creek—stream ... IL-6
East Branch Lateral—canal ... CA-9
East Branch Laughing Water Creek—stream ... NE-7
East Branch Laurel Run—stream ... MD-2
East Branch Leadmine Brook—stream ... CT-1
East Branch LeBoeuf Creek—stream ... PA-2
East Branch Le Clerc Creek—stream ... WA-9
East Branch LeVasseur Creek—stream ... MI-6
East Branch Lick Creek—stream ... IA-7
East Branch Liddell Creek—stream ... CA-9
East Branch Lights Creek—stream ... CA-9
East Branch Lilttle Antietam Creek ... PA-2
East Branch Lily River—stream ... WI-6
East Branch Limestone Creek—stream ... NY-2
East Branch Little Black River—stream ... WI-6
East Branch Little Brokenstraw Creek—stream ... NY-2
East Branch Little Canyon Creek—stream ... CA-9
East Branch Little Creek—stream ... WY-8
East Branch Little Hocking River—stream ... OH-6
East Branch Little Kennebec Bay—bay ... ME-1
East Branch Little Mopang Stream—stream ... ME-1
East Branch Little Muddy Run—stream ... PA-2
East Branch Little Muskegon River—stream ... MI-6
East Branch Little North Fork—stream ... CA-9
East Branch Little Pine Creek—stream ... WI-6
East Branch Little Salmon River—stream ... NY-2
East Branch Little Sandy Creek—stream ... KS-7
East Branch Little Schuylkill River—stream ... PA-2
East Branch Little Silver Creek—stream ... IL-6
East Branch Little Spokane River ... WA-9
East Branch Little Walnut Creek—stream ... OH-6
East Branch Little Whiteoak Creek—stream ... NC-3
East Branch Little Yellow River—stream ... WI-6
East Branch Live Oak Creek—stream ... TX-5
East Branch Lockes Creek—stream ... MS-4
East Branch Long Swamp Creek—stream ... GA-3
East Branch Lost Creek ... AL-4
East Branch Lost Creek—stream ... OH-6
East Branch Lost River ... OR-9
East Branch Lost River—stream ... CA-9
East Branch Lost River—stream ... OR-9
East Branch Louse Creek—stream ... NE-7
East Branch Lowney Creek—stream ... MI-6
East Branch Luxapallila Creek—stream ... AL-4
East Branch Lyons Creek ... TN-4
East Branch Mad Island Slough—stream ... TX-5
East Branch Magurrewock Stream—stream ... ME-1
East Branch Mahoning Creek—stream ... PA-2
East Branch Maple River—stream ... MI-6
East Branch Maple Springs Brook—stream ... MA-1
East Branch Mare Creek—stream ... FL-3
East Branch Martin Canal—canal ... ID-8
East Branch Martins Creek ... PA-2
East Branch Martins Creek—stream ... PA-2
East Branch Mattakeunk Stream—stream ... ME-1
East Branch Mattawamkeag River—stream ... ME-1
East Branch McCullough Creek—stream ... OH-6
East Branch Medunkeunk Stream—stream ... ME-1
East Branch Methow River ... WA-9
East Branch Mianus River—stream ... CT-1
East Branch Mianus River—stream ... NY-2
East Branch Middle Branch Nimishillen Creek ... OH-6
East Branch Middle Brook—stream ... NJ-2
East Branch Middle Fork Little Beaver Creek—stream ... OH-6
East Branch Millard Canyon—valley ... CA-9
East Branch Millard Canyon Trail (Pack)—trail ... CA-9
East Branch Mill Brook—stream ... NH-1
East Branch Mill Creek—stream ... CA-9
East Branch Mill Creek—stream ... KS-7
East Branch Mill Creek—stream ... MI-6
East Branch Mill Creek—stream ... MO-7
East Branch Mill Creek—stream ... PA-2
East Branch Mill Creek—stream ... WI-6
East Branch Mill River ... MA-1
East Branch Mill River—stream ... MA-1
East Branch Millstone Creek—stream ... PA-2
East Branch Milwaukee River—stream ... WI-6
East Branch Mingamahone Brook—stream ... NJ-2
East Branch Missionary Baptist Ch—church ... KS-7
East Branch Mission Creek ... WA-9
East Branch Missisquoi River—stream (2) ... VT-1
East Branch Mohawk River—stream ... NH-1
East Branch Mohawk River—stream ... NY-2
East Branch Molunkus Stream—stream ... ME-1
East Branch Monocacy Creek—stream ... PA-2
East Branch Moose River—stream ... ME-1
East Branch Moose River—stream ... VT-1
East Branch Mosquito Creek—stream ... KS-7
East Branch Mosquito Creek—stream ... MN-6
East Branch mounds Creek ... WI-6
East Branch Mountain Creek—stream ... NC-3
East Branch Mount Hope River—stream ... CT-1
East Branch Mud Brook—stream (2) ... ME-1
East Branch Mud Creek ... CA-9
East Branch Mud Creek ... MI-6
East Branch Mud Creek ... OR-9
East Branch Mud Creek ... WA-9
East Branch Mud Creek—stream ... CA-9
East Branch Muddy Creek—stream ... NE-7
East Branch Muddy Creek—stream ... PA-2
East Branch Munkers Creek—stream ... KS-7
East Branch Munuscong River—stream ... MI-6
East Branch Murray Run—stream ... PA-2
East Branch Musquash River ... ME-1
East Branch Musquash Stream ... ME-1
East Branch Naaman Creek ... PA-2
East Branch Naaman Creek—stream ... PA-2
East Branch Naamans Creek ... PA-2
East Branch Naked Creek—stream ... VA-3
East Branch Naked Creek Trail—trail ... VA-3
East Branch Nanticoke Creek—stream ... NY-2
East Branch Narcelle Creek—stream ... SD-7
East Branch Nash Stream—stream ... NH-1
East Branch Naugatuck River—stream ... CT-1
East Branch Nekoma Coulee—valley ... ND-7
East Branch Neosho River ... KS-7
East Branch Neponset River—stream ... MA-1
East Branch Nescatunga Creek—stream ... KS-7
East Branch Net River—stream ... MI-6
East Branch Neversink Creek ... NY-2
East Branch Neversink River—stream ... NY-2
East Branch Newman Creek—stream ... WA-9
East Branch Nezinscot River—stream ... ME-1
East Branch Nimishillen Creek—stream ... OH-6
East Branch Norris Brook—stream ... ME-1
East Branch North Branch Nippersink Creek—stream ... WI-6
East Branch North Branch Patapsco River—stream ... MD-2
East Branch North Carrizo Creek ... CO-8
East Branch North Fork Big River—stream ... CA-9
East Branch North Fork Elkhorn River—stream ... NE-7
East Branch North Fork Feather River—stream ... CA-9
East Branch North Fork Jackass Creek—stream ... CA-9
East Branch North Fork Mattole River—stream ... CA-9
East Branch North River—stream ... MA-1
East Branch North River—stream ... VT-1
East Branch North Salmon Brook ... CT-1
East Branch Nulhegan River—stream ... VT-1
East Branch Oak Creek—stream ... KS-7
East Branch Octoraro Creek ... PA-2
East Branch Octoraro Creek—stream ... PA-2
East Branch Of Ausable River ... NY-2
East Branch of Bummet Brook ... MA-1
East Branch of Des Plaines River ... WI-6
East Branch of North Fork of Eel River ... CA-9
East Branch Of Perkiomen Creek ... PA-2
East Branch Of Shepang ... CT-1
East Branch Of The Ausable River ... NY-2
East Branch of the Esconawby river ... MI-6
East Branch of the Hou ... MA-1
East Branch of Tully River ... MA-1
East Branch Ogontz River—stream ... MI-6
East Branch Oil Creek—stream ... PA-2
East Branch Oil Creek - in part ... PA-2
East Branch Okannatie Creek—stream ... MS-4
East Branch Olentangy River ... OH-6
East Branch Ontonagon River—stream ... MI-6
East Branch Otsdawa Creek—stream ... NY-2
East Branch Otter Brook ... NH-1
East Branch Otter Creek ... IA-7
East Branch Owego Creek—stream ... NY-2
East Branch Owl Creek—stream ... IN-6
East Branch Oyster Bayou—gut ... LA-4
East Branch Oyster River—stream ... ME-1
East Branch Painter Creek—stream ... KY-4
East Branch Palmer River—stream ... MA-1
East Branch Panther Creek—stream ... IL-6
East Branch Panther Creek—stream ... IA-7
East Branch Parsons Creek—stream ... KS-7
East Branch Passadumkeag River—stream ... ME-1
East Branch Passumpsic River—stream ... VT-1
East Branch Paupack Creek ... PA-2
East Branch Paw Paw River—stream ... MI-6
East Branch Pecatonica River—stream ... WI-6
East Branch Pemigewasset River—stream ... NH-1
East Branch Penobscot River—stream ... ME-1
East Branch Peoples Ditch—canal ... CA-9
East Branch Perkiomen Creek—stream ... PA-2
East Branch Phillips Fork—stream ... KY-4
East Branch Pigeon River ... MI-6
East Branch Pine Arroyo—valley ... CO-8
East Branch Pine Creek—stream ... IA-7
East Branch Pine Log Creek—stream ... FL-3
East Branch Pine River—stream (2) ... MI-6
East Branch Pinnacles—pillar ... ME-1
East Branch Pinos Creek—stream ... CO-8
East Branch Piscataqua River—stream ... ME-1
East Branch Piscataquis River—stream ... ME-1
East Branch Pleasant River—stream (2) ... ME-1
East Branch Pocwock Stream—stream ... ME-1
East Branch Pond ... PA-2
East Branch Pond—lake ... ME-1
East Branch Pond—lake ... NJ-2
East Branch Pond River—stream ... KY-4
East Branch Poplar Creek—stream ... IL-6
East Branch Poquonock River ... CT-1
East Branch Potato Creek—stream ... PA-2
East Branch Prairie Creek ... KS-7
East Branch Pratt Creek—stream ... WI-6
East Branch Presque Isle River—stream ... MI-6
East Branch Presque Isle River—stream ... WI-6
East Branch Presque Isle Stream—stream ... ME-1
East Branch Price Creek—stream ... NC-3
East Branch Queens Run—stream ... PA-2
East Branch Rabbit Creek—stream ... CA-9
East Branch Raccoon Creek—stream ... OH-6
East Branch Raft Creek—stream ... AR-4
East Branch Rahway River—stream ... NJ-2
East Branch Rainey Brook—stream ... ME-1
East Branch Rainy River—stream ... MI-6
East Branch Rat Root River—stream ... MN-6
East Branch Rattling Creek—stream ... PA-2
East Branch Rausch Creek—stream (2) ... PA-2
East Branch Raven Creek—stream ... PA-2
East Branch Raven Stream—stream ... MN-6
East Branch Red Clay Creek—stream ... PA-2
East Branch Reed Wash—stream ... CO-8
East Branch Reservoir ... CT-1
East Branch Reservoir Dam—dam ... NJ-2
East Branch Richards Run—stream ... PA-2
East Branch Richland Creek—stream ... IL-6
East Branch Richland Creek—stream (2) ... WI-6
East Branch Ridge—ridge ... ME-1
East Branch Ripogenus Stream—stream ... ME-1
East Branch Roaring Brook—stream ... PA-2
East Branch Robbers Roost Creek—stream ... WY-8
East Branch Rock Creek—stream ... CA-9
East Branch Rock Creek—stream ... KS-7
East Branch Rock Creek—stream ... OH-6
East Branch Rock River—stream ... MN-6
East Branch Rock River—stream ... WI-6
East Branch Rock Run—stream ... PA-2
East Branch Rocky Fork—stream ... OH-6
East Branch Rocky River—stream ... OH-6
East Branch Rondout Creek ... NY-2
East Branch Root River Canal—canal ... WI-6
East Branch Rosebud Creek—stream ... SD-7
East Branch Ross Run—stream ... PA-2
East Branch Rousseau Creek—stream ... SD-7
East Branch Rsvr—reservoir ... NJ-2
East Branch Rsvr—reservoir ... NY-2
East Branch Rsvr—reservoir ... OH-6
East Branch Rush Creek—stream ... MI-6
East Branch Russian Gulch—valley ... CA-9
East Branch Sacandaga River—stream ... NY-2
East Branch Saco River—stream ... NH-1
East Branch Sage River—stream ... MI-6
East Branch Saint Joseph River—stream ... MI-6
East Branch Saint Joseph River—stream ... OH-6
East Branch Saint Regis River—stream ... NY-2
East Branch Salman Brook ... CT-1
East Branch Salmon Brook ... CT-1
East Branch Salmon Brook—stream ... CT-1
East Branch Salmon Brook—stream ... MA-1
East Branch Salmon Stream—stream ... ME-1
East Branch Salmon Trout River—stream ... MI-6
East Branch Salt Creek—stream ... IA-7
East Branch Salt Slough—gut ... CA-9
East Branch Sand Creek—stream ... KS-7
East Branch Sand Draw—valley ... WY-8
East Branch Sand River—stream ... MI-6
East Branch Sandy Creek—stream ... NY-2
East Branch Sandy Stream—stream ... ME-1
East Branch Saucon Creek—stream ... PA-2
East Branch Saugatuck River ... CT-1
East Branch Sch (historical)—school ... PA-2
East Branch Schneider Creek—stream ... CA-9
East Branch Sebasticook River—stream ... ME-1
East Branch Seboeis Stream—stream ... ME-1
East Branch Seboois Stream ... ME-1
East Branch Sees Creek—stream ... MO-7
East Branch Shade River—stream ... OH-6
East Branch Sharpes Creek—stream ... KS-7
East Branch Shavano Creek—stream ... CO-8
East Branch Shepaug River—stream ... CT-1
East Branch Sherman Creek—stream ... NV-8
East Branch Shioc River—stream ... WI-6
East Branch Shoal Creek ... IL-6
East Branch Shoal Creek—stream ... MO-7
East Branch Short Creek—stream ... KS-7
East Branch Short Creek—stream ... ND-7
East Branch Sideling Hill Creek—stream ... PA-2
East Branch Silver Creek—stream ... MN-6
East Branch Silvermine River—stream ... CT-1
East Branch Silvermine River—stream ... NY-2
East Branch Silver River—stream ... MI-6
East Branch Silver Springs Creek—stream ... WY-8
East Branch Simms Stream—stream ... NH-1
East Branch Sippican River—stream ... MA-1
East Branch Sippicon River ... MA-1
East Branch Skunk Creek—stream ... MI-6
East Branch Slate Creek—stream ... CA-9
East Branch Smith Ferry Canal—canal ... CA-9
East Branch Snake River Valley Canal—canal ... ID-8
East Branch Sneech Brook ... RI-1
East Branch Snow Creek—stream ... CA-9
East Branch Soda Creek—stream ... CA-9
East Branch Sopchoppy River—stream ... FL-3
East Branch South Branch Codorus Creek ... PA-2
East Branch South Branch Kishwaukee River—stream ... IL-6
East Branch South Branch Portage River—stream ... OH-6
East Branch South Elm Creek—stream ... KS-7
East Branch South Fork Big Creek—stream ... MT-8
East Branch South Fork Eel River—stream ... CA-9
East Branch South Fork Mad Creek—stream ... CO-8
East Branch South Fork South Eden Canyon—valley ... UT-8
East Branch South Fork Sugar Creek—stream ... OH-6
East Branch South Grand River—stream ... MO-7
East Branch Southwest Prong Slocum Creek—stream ... NC-3
East Branch Speaker and Maple Valley Drain—canal ... MI-6
East Branch Spencer Robinson Ditch—canal ... WI-6
East Branch Spring Creek—stream ... IA-7
East Branch Spring Creek—stream ... NE-7
East Branch Spring Creek—stream (2) ... PA-2
East Branch Squaw Creek—stream ... AZ-5
East Branch Squaw Creek—stream ... MO-7
East Branch Squaw Creek—stream ... SD-7
East Branch Standing Stone Creek—stream ... PA-2
East Branch Stonehouse Brook—stream ... CT-1
East Branch Stony Creek ... PA-2
East Branch Stony Fork—stream ... PA-2
East Branch Stony Run—stream ... IN-6
East Branch Stony Run Ditch ... IN-6
East Branch Stratford Bog Brook—stream ... NH-1
East Branch Strayhorn Creek—stream ... MS-4
East Branch Sturgeon River—stream ... MI-6
East Branch Sturgeon River—stream ... MN-6
East Branch Sugar Creek—stream ... KY-4
East Branch Sugar Creek—stream (2) ... PA-2
East Branch Sugar Works Run—stream ... PA-2
East Branch Sunday Creek—stream ... OH-6
East Branch Sweetwater Creek—stream ... IN-6
East Branch Swift Brook—stream ... ME-1
East Branch Swift Diamond River—stream ... NH-1
East Branch Swift River—stream ... ME-1
East Branch Swift River—stream ... MA-1
East Branch Tahquamenon River—stream ... MI-6
East Branch Teaspoon Creek—stream ... MI-6
East Branch Tegua Creek ... KS-7
East Branch Tenmile River—stream ... NY-2
East Branch Tequa Creek—stream ... KS-7
East Branch Third Creek—stream ... KS-7
East Branch Thirtymile Creek—stream ... MT-8
East Branch Thomas Creek—stream ... OR-9
East Branch Thomas Fork—stream ... OH-6
East Branch Thompson Creek—stream ... NE-7
East Branch Thoroughfare Brook—stream ... ME-1
East Branch Thoroughfare Stream ... ME-1
East Branch Thumb Run—stream ... VA-3
East Branch Tionesta Creek—stream ... PA-2
East Branch Tioughnioga Creek—stream ... NY-2
East Branch Tioughnioga River—stream ... NY-2
East Branch Tittabawassee River—stream ... MI-6
East Branch Tobyhanna Creek—stream ... PA-2
East Branch Toms Run—stream ... PA-2
East Branch Tortuga Creek—stream ... TX-5
**East Branch Township**—pop pl ... KS-7
East Branch Trail—trail (2) ... PA-2
East Branch Trail Creek—stream ... IN-6
East Branch Troublesome Creek—stream ... FL-3
East Branch Troublesome Creek—stream ... KS-7
East Branch Trout Brook—stream ... ME-1
East Branch Trout Brook—stream ... NY-2
East Branch Trout Creek - in part ... NV-8
East Branch Trout River—stream ... NY-2
East Branch Tuckahoe Creek—stream ... VA-3
East Branch Tulandic Stream ... ME-1
East Branch Tully River—stream ... MA-1
East Branch Tunkhannock Creek—stream ... PA-2
East Branch Tunungwant Creek—stream ... PA-2
East Branch Turkey Creek—stream ... NE-7
East Branch Turkey Creek—stream ... TX-5
East Branch Twelve Mile Creek—stream ... IN-6
East Branch Twelvemile Creek—stream ... KS-7
East Branch Twelvemile Creek—stream ... NY-2
East Branch Twin Creek ... MI-6
East Branch Two Hearted River—stream ... MI-6
East Branch Umbrella Creek—stream ... WA-9
East Branch Umcolcus Stream—stream ... ME-1
East Branch Umculcus Stream ... ME-1
East Branch Union River—stream ... ME-1
East Branch Upper Millecoquin River ... MI-6
East Branch Upper Pine Creek—stream ... WI-6
East Branch Ute Creek—stream ... CO-8
East Branch Verdigre Creek—stream ... NE-7
East Branch Vermilion River ... IL-6
East Branch Vermilion River—stream ... OH-6
East Branch Vermillion river ... IL-6
East Branch Victoria Canal—canal ... CA-9
East Branch Village Brook—stream ... NH-1
East Branchville Sch—school ... SC-3
East Branch Wading River ... NJ-2
East Branch Waiska River ... MI-6
East Branch Waiska River—stream ... MI-6
East Branch Wallace Branch—stream ... VA-3
East Branch Wallenpaupack Creek—stream ... PA-2
East Branch Wallis Run—stream ... PA-2
East Branch Walnut River ... KS-7
East Branch Wappinger Creek—stream ... NY-2
East Branch Wapsinonoc Creek ... IA-7
East Branch Wapsinonoc Creek—stream ... IA-7
East Branch Wapsipinicon River ... IA-7
East Branch War Creek—stream ... SD-7
East Branch Wards Fork Creek—stream ... VA-3
East Branch Ware River—stream ... MA-1
East Branch Warroad River—stream ... MN-6
East Branch Waterford Creek ... IN-6
East Branch Wea Creek—stream ... IN-6
East Branch Wedges Creek—stream ... WI-6
East Branch Weiser River—stream ... ID-8
East Branch Wesserunsett Stream—stream ... ME-1
East Branch West Branch Codorus Creek ... PA-2
East Branch West Creek—stream ... CO-8
East Branch Westfield River ... MA-1
East Branch West Nishnabotna River—stream ... IA-7
East Branch Westport River—stream ... MA-1
East Branch West Salt Creek—stream ... CO-8
East Branch Wheeler Creek—stream ... MI-6
East Branch Whetstone Creek—stream ... OH-6
East Branch Whiskey Creek—stream ... OR-9
East Branch White Clay Creek—stream ... PA-2
East Branch White Clay Creek—stream ... SD-7
East Branch Whiteface River—stream ... NH-1
East Branch Whitefish River—stream ... MI-6
East Branch White Oak Creek—stream ... TX-5
East Branch Whitewater Creek—stream ... KS-7
East Branch Whitewater River—stream ... KS-7
East Branch Wildhorse Creek—stream ... OR-9
East Branch Willow Creek ... SD-7
East Branch Willow Creek ... TX-5
East Branch Willow Creek—stream ... CO-8
East Branch Willow Creek—stream ... MI-6
East Branch Willow Creek—stream ... OR-9
East Branch Willow Creek—stream (2) ... WY-8
East Branch Willow River ... MI-6
East Branch Wilson Run—stream ... PA-2
East Branch Winters Run—stream ... MD-2
East Branch Wiscoggin Drain—stream ... MI-6
East Branch Wolf Creek—stream ... IA-7
East Branch Wolf Creek—stream ... MI-6
East Branch Wolf Creek—stream ... OH-6
East Branch Wolf Creek—stream ... OK-5
East Branch Wolf Creek—stream ... PA-2
East Branch Wolf Creek—stream ... TX-5
East Branch Wolfe Creek—stream ... AL-4
East Branch Wyalusing Creek—stream ... PA-2
East Branch Yellow River—stream ... WI-6
East Brandywine Ch—church ... PA-2
East Brandywine Hist Dist—hist pl ... DE-2
**East Brandywine (Township of)**—pop pl ... PA-2
East Bray Creek—stream ... AZ-5
East Breaks Tank—reservoir ... TX-5
East Breakwater—other ... CT-1
East Breedlove Well—well ... NM-5
**East Bremen**—pop pl ... GA-3
**East Bremerton**—pop pl ... WA-9
East Bremerton Sch—school ... WA-9
East Brent Baptist Ch—church ... FL-3
**East Brentwood**—pop pl ... NY-2
**East Brewster**—pop pl ... MA-1
**East Brewton**—pop pl ... AL-4
East Brianerd Ch of Christ—church ... TN-4
**East Bridge**—pop pl ... LA-4
East Bridge Creek—stream ... KS-7
East Bridgeport ... CT-1
**East Bridgeport**—pop pl ... CT-1
East Bridgeport Hist Dist—hist pl ... CT-1
East Bridger—locale ... MT-8
East Bridger Creek—stream ... MT-8
East Bridger Creek—stream ... WY-8
East Bridgeton—uninc pl ... NJ-2
**East Bridgewater**—pop pl ... MA-1
East Bridgewater Central Cem—cemetery ... MA-1
East Bridgewater Ch—church ... PA-2
East Bridgewater (historical P.O.)—locale ... MA-1
East Bridgewater HS—school ... MA-1
East Bridgewater JHS—school ... MA-1
East Bridgewater Sch—school ... PA-2
East Bridgewater Station (historical)—locale ... MA-1
East Bridgewater (Town of)—civil ... MA-1
**East Brighton**—pop pl ... AL-4
**East Brighton**—pop pl ... VT-1
**East Brightwood (historical)**—pop pl ... IN-6
**East Brimfield**—pop pl ... MA-1
East Brimfield Dam—dam ... MA-1
East Brimfield Lake—reservoir ... MA-1
East Brimfield Rsvr ... MA-1
**East Bristol**—pop pl ... CT-1
**East Bristol**—pop pl ... WI-6
East Broad Canyon—valley ... CO-8
East Broad Channel—channel ... NY-2
East Broad Street Commercial Bldg—hist pl ... OH-6
East Broad Street-Davie Ave Hist Dist—hist pl ... NC-3
East Broad Street Hist Dist—hist pl ... OH-6
East Broad Street Presbyterian Church—hist pl ... OH-6
East Broad Street Sch—school ... OH-6
East Broad Top RR—hist pl ... PA-2
East Broadway Sch—school ... NY-2
**Eastbronk (subdivision)**—pop pl ... NC-3
East Brook ... MA-1
East Brook ... NJ-2
East Brook ... NY-2
East Brook ... PA-2
Eastbrook ... VA-3
Eastbrook—locale ... NC-3
**Eastbrook**—pop pl ... FL-3
**Eastbrook**—pop pl ... ME-1
**Eastbrook**—pop pl ... PA-2
**Eastbrook**—pop pl ... TN-4
**East Brook**—pop pl ... VA-3
Eastbrook—post sta ... AL-4
East Brook—stream ... CT-1
East Brook—stream ... IN-6
East Brook—stream ... ME-1
East Brook—stream (4) ... MA-1
East Brook—stream ... NH-1
East Brook—stream (4) ... NY-2
East Brook—stream ... VT-1
Eastbrook Baptist Church and Eastbrook Town House—hist pl ... ME-1
Eastbrook Cem—cemetery ... WI-6
East Brook Ch—church ... MO-7
Eastbrook Ch—church ... PA-2
Eastbrook Ch of Christ—church ... AL-4
Eastbrook Elem Sch—school ... FL-3
Eastbrook Elem Sch—school ... IN-6
**East Brookfield**—pop pl ... MA-1
**East Brookfield**—pop pl ... VT-1
East Brookfield River ... MA-1
East Brookfield River—stream ... MA-1
**East Brookfield (Town of)**—pop pl ... MA-1
Eastbrook Ford (historical)—crossing ... TN-4
Eastbrook Hollow—valley ... TN-4
East Brook HS—school ... GA-3
East Brook Lakes ... CA-9
East Brookling Creek—stream ... OR-9
East Brooklyn—locale ... MD-2
**East Brooklyn**—pop pl ... CT-1
**East Brooklyn**—pop pl ... IL-6
East Brooklyn (Election Precinct)—fmr MCD ... IL-6
Eastbrook Plaza—locale ... IN-6
Eastbrook Post Office (historical)—building ... TN-4
Eastbrook Sch—school ... CA-9
East Brook Shop Ctr—locale ... AL-4
Eastbrook Shop Ctr—locale ... MI-6
Eastbrook Station (historical)—locale ... PA-2
**East Brook (subdivision)**—pop pl ... AL-4
**Eastbrook (Town of)**—pop pl ... ME-1
**East Brookwood**—pop pl ... AL-4
East Brookwood Free Will Baptist Ch—church ... AL-4
East Brookwood Mine (surface)—mine ... AL-4
East Brookwood Missionary Baptist Ch—church ... AL-4
East Broomy Valley Tank—reservoir ... AZ-5
East Brother Island—island ... AK-9
East Brother Island Light Station—hist pl ... CA-9
East Broussard Sch—school ... LA-4
East Brown Cow—island ... ME-1
**East Brownfield**—pop pl ... ME-1
East Brownington Sch—school ... VT-1
East Brownlee Creek—stream ... ID-8
East Brown Tank—reservoir ... AZ-5
East Brownville Cem—cemetery ... OH-6
East Brule Creek—stream ... SD-7
East Brunswick—airport ... NJ-2
**East Brunswick**—pop pl ... GA-3
**East Brunswick (sta.)**—pop pl ... NJ-2
**East Brunswick (Township of)**—pop pl ... NJ-2
**East Brunswick (Township of)**—pop pl ... PA-2
East Brush Creek—stream (2) ... CO-8
East Brush Creek—stream ... MO-7
East Brush Creek—stream ... OK-5
East Brushy Creek ... TX-5
East Brushy Creek—stream ... MO-7
East Brushy Sch—school ... IL-6
East Bryan (CCD)—cens area ... OK-5
East Buchanan Well—well ... TX-5
East Buck Creek—stream ... IA-7
East Buck Creek—stream ... OK-5
East Buck Creek Ditch—canal (2) ... IN-6
East Bucket Mountain Dam—dam ... AZ-5
East Buckeye Creek—stream ... KS-7
East Buckeye Creek—stream ... MT-8
East Buckfield—locale ... ME-1
East Buckhorn Draw—valley ... WY-8
East Buck Island ... MA-1
East Buck Point Gas Field—oilfield ... LA-4
East Buckskin Tank—reservoir ... AZ-5
East Bucksport—locale ... ME-1
East Bucksport Ch—church ... ME-1
East Buck Trap Windmill—locale ... NM-5
**East Buffalo**—pop pl ... NY-2
**East Buffalo**—pop pl ... PA-2
East Buffalo Cem—cemetery ... KS-7
East Buffalo Ch—church ... NC-3
East Buffalo Creek ... MT-8
East Buffalo Creek—stream ... CO-8
East Buffalo Creek—stream (2) ... KS-7
East Buffalo Creek—stream ... MT-8
East Buffalo Creek—stream (2) ... NE-7
East Buffalo Creek—stream ... NC-3
East Buffalo Creek—stream (2) ... TX-5
East Buffalo Ditch—canal ... CO-8
East Buffalo Peak—summit ... CO-8
East Buffalo Prairie Sch—school ... IL-6
East Buffalo Sch—school ... NE-7
East Buffalo Sch—school ... PA-2
East Buffalo Sch—school ... SD-7
East Buffalo Springs Windmills—locale ... NM-5
**East Buffalo (Township of)**—pop pl ... PA-2
East Buies Creek—stream ... NC-3
East Bull Canyon—valley ... CA-9
East Bull Creek—stream ... CO-8
East Bull Creek—stream ... WY-8

East Bull Gulch—*valley* CO-8
East Bull Pasture Windmill—*locale* TX-5
East Bulls Head Channel—*channel* CA-9
East Bunker Ledge—*bar* ME-1
East Bunker Peak Wash—*stream* NV-8
East Bunker Peak Wash—*valley* UT-8
East Bureau Creek—*stream* IL-6
Eastburg (historical)—*locale* MS-4
**East Burke**—*pop pl* VT-1
East Burke HS—*school* NC-3
East Burke JHS—*school* NC-3
East Burleigh—*unorg reg* ND-7
**East Burlington**—*pop pl* IL-6
**East Burlington**—*pop pl* NJ-2
East Burlington Extension Ditch—*canal* CO-8
Eastburn—*locale* IL-6
Eastburn, Davis, Farm—*hist pl* DE-2
Eastburn, J., Barn—*hist pl* DE-2
**Eastburn Acres**—*pop pl* DE-2
Eastburn Acres Park—*park* DE-2
Eastburn Ditch No 1—*canal* IL-6
Eastburn Ditch No 2—*canal* IL-6
**Eastburn Farms**—*pop pl* DE-2
**Eastburn Heights**—*pop pl* DE-2
Eastburn Hollow—*valley* IL-6
Eastburn-Jeanes Lime Kilns Hist Dist—*hist pl* DE-2
East Burns Valley—*valley* MN-6
East Burn Tank—*reservoir* AZ-5
East Burnt Corral Creek—*stream* OR-9
East Burnt Creek—*stream* MT-8
East Burnt Log Spring—*spring* OR-9
East Burr Oak Creek—*stream* IA-7
Eastbury Sch—*school* CT-1
*East Bush Lake* WI-6
East Buskirk—*locale* NY-2
**East Butler**—*pop pl* PA-2
East Butler Borough—*civil* PA-2
East Butler Chapel—*church* PA-2
**East Butte**—*pop pl* MT-8
East Butte—*summit* CA-9
East Butte—*summit* CO-8
East Butte—*summit* (2) ID-8
East Butte—*summit* (2) MT-8
East Butte—*summit* OR-9
East Butte—*unorg reg* SD-7
East Butte Creek—*stream* ID-8
East Butte Mine—*mine* MT-8
East Butterfly Lake—*lake* AK-9
East Buttke—*dam* NC-3
East Buttke Dam—*reservoir* NC-3
East Buttons—*other* AK-9
East Buttress—*ridge* AK-9
East Buttrick Creek—*stream* IA-7
East Buxton Ch—*church* ME-1
East Buzzard Point—*cliff* AZ-5
East Cabin Coulee—*valley* MT-8
*East Cabin Creek* CO-8
East Cabin Creek—*stream* CO-8
East Cabin Creek—*stream* MT-8
East Cabot—*locale* VT-1
East Cache Creek—*stream* OK-5
*East Cache Ditch* AR-4
East Cache River Ditch—*canal* AR-4
East Cactus Flat—*flat* CO-8
*East Caddo Butte* TX-5
East Caddo Creek—*stream* TX-5
*East Caddo Fork* TX-5
East Caddo Peak—*summit* TX-5
**East Cadiz**—*pop pl* OH-6
*East Cahaba* AL-4
**East Cairo**—*pop pl* KY-4
**East Calais**—*pop pl* VT-1
**East California**—*pop pl* PA-2
**East Caln (Township of)**—*pop pl* PA-2
*East Calumick River* IN-6
East Calvert Oil Field—*oilfield* TX-5
East Calvert Sch—*school* AL-4
East Camas—*cens area* ID-8
East Camas Creek—*stream* ID-8
*East Cambridge* OH-6
**East Cambridge**—*pop pl* OH-6
**East Cambridge**—*pop pl* VT-1
East Cambridge Cem—*cemetery* VT-1
East Cambridge Hist Dist—*hist pl* MA-1
East Cambridge Savings Bank—*hist pl* MA-1
**East Cambridge (subdivision)**—*pop pl* MA-1
**East Camden**—*pop pl* AR-4
**East Camden**—*pop pl* NJ-2
**East Camden (Industrial Park)**—*pop pl* AR-4
**East Camden (Shumaker Park)**—*pop pl* AR-4
East Cameron (CCD)—*cens area* TX-5
**East Cameron (Township of)**—*pop pl* PA-2
*East Camp* FL-3
*East Camp* NY-2
East Camp—*locale* FL-3
East Camp—*locale* (2) NM-5
**East Campbell**—*pop pl* NY-2
East Campbell Branch—*stream* TX-5
East Campbell Ditch—*canal* NV-8
East Campbell Gas Field—*oilfield* OK-5
East Campbell Sch—*school* SD-7
East Camp Clarke—*fmr MCD* NE-7
East Camp Creek—*stream* (2) OR-9
East Camp Creek—*stream* TN-4
East Camp Mine—*mine* NM-5
East Camp Tank—*reservoir* (2) NM-5
East Campus HS—*school* CA-9
East Camp Windmill—*locale* NM-5
East Camp Windmill—*locale* (2) TX-5
**East Canaan**—*pop pl* CT-1
East Canaan Cem—*cemetery* PA-2
East Canada Creek—*stream* NY-2
East Canada Lake—*reservoir* NY-2
East Canadian (CCD)—*cens area* OK-5
*East Canal* VA-3
East Canal—*canal* (2) CA-9
East Canal—*canal* CO-8
East Canal—*canal* FL-3
East Canal—*canal* (2) ID-8
East Canal—*canal* NV-8
East Canal—*canal* NM-5
East Canal—*canal* (2) NC-3
East Canal—*canal* (2) OR-9
East Canal Ancho (historical)—*canal* AZ-5
East Canal Gulch—*valley* ID-8
**East Candia**—*pop pl* NH-1
East Caneadea Ch—*church* NY-2
East Cane Island—*island* TX-5
East Caney—*locale* TX-5
East Caney Branch—*stream* LA-4
East Caney Ch—*church* TX-5
*East Caney Creek* TX-5
East Caney Creek—*stream* (2) TX-5
East Canfield Butte—*summit* ID-8
East Canfield Mtn—*summit* PA-2
East Cannal—*canal* NY-2
*East Canon* CO-8
**East Canon**—*pop pl* CO-8
East Canon Creek—*stream* NV-8
East Canon de Santa Rosa—*valley* NM-5
East Canon Escondido—*valley* CO-8
**East Canton**—*pop pl* IA-7
**East Canton**—*pop pl* OH-6
**East Canton**—*pop pl* PA-2
East Canton—*uninc pl* MS-4
East Canyon—*valley* AZ-5
East Canyon—*valley* (4) CA-9
East Canyon—*valley* (2) CO-8
East Canyon—*valley* ID-8
East Canyon—*valley* (2) NV-8
East Canyon—*valley* (4) NM-5
East Canyon—*valley* OR-9
East Canyon—*valley* TX-5
East Canyon—*valley* (7) UT-8
East Canyon—*valley* (2) WY-8
East Canyon Campground—*locale* UT-8
East Canyon Channel—*stream* CA-9
East Canyon Creek—*stream* CO-8
East Canyon Creek—*stream* UT-8
East Canyon Creek—*stream* WA-9
East Canyon Creek—*stream* WY-8
*East Canyon Creek Reservoir* UT-8
East Canyon Dam—*dam* UT-8
East Canyon Gas Field—*oilfield* UT-8
*East Canyon Lake State Park* UT-8
East Canyon Ridge—*ridge* WA-9
East Canyon Rsvr—*reservoir* CO-8
East Canyon Rsvr—*reservoir* UT-8
East Canyon Spring—*spring* NV-8
East Canyon State Park—*park* UT-8
East Canyon Wash—*valley* UT-8
East Canyon Windmill—*locale* CO-8
*East Cape* FL-3
East Cape—*cape* (2) AK-9
East Cape—*cape* FL-3
East Cape Canal—*canal* FL-3
East Cape (Election Precinct)—*fmr MCD* IL-6
**East Cape Girardeau**—*pop pl* IL-6
East Cape Girardeau Sch—*school* IL-6
East Cape Light 2—*locale* FL-3
East Cape Sch—*school* WI-6
East Capitol Drive Hist Dist—*hist pl* WI-6
East Capitol Street Bridge—*bridge* DC-2
East Capitol Street Carbarn—*hist pl* DC-2
East Capron Cem—*cemetery* IL-6
East Captain Creek—*stream* OK-5
East Carancahua Creek—*stream* TX-5
**East Carbon**—*pop pl* (2) UT-8
East Carbonate Tunnel—*mine* UT-8
**East Carbon City**—*pop pl* UT-8
East Carbon Division—*civil* UT-8
East Carbon HS—*school* UT-8
East Caribou Island—*island* MI-6
**East Carlisle**—*pop pl* OH-6
East Carlisle Sch—*school* OH-6
**East Carmel**—*pop pl* OH-6
**East Carnegie**—*pop pl* PA-2
East Caroga Lake—*lake* NY-2
East Caroga Lake Camping Area—*area* NY-2
East Carolina Creek—*stream* TX-5
East Carolina Univ—*school* NC-3
*East Carolina Univ Sch of Medicine* NC-3
**East Carondelet**—*pop pl* IL-6
East Carrizo Cone—*summit* NM-5
East Carrizo Creek—*stream* CO-8
East Carrol Lake—*lake* UT-8
**East Carroll Parish**—*pop pl* LA-4
East Carroll Prison Farm—*locale* LA-4
East Carroll (Township of)—*civ div* PA-2
East Carry Camps—*locale* ME-1
East Carry Pond—*lake* ME-1
*East Carson River* NV-8
East Carson Street Hist Dist—*hist pl* PA-2
East Cart Creek—*stream* WY-8
East Carthage Point Oil Field—*oilfield* MS-4
East Cart Hollow—*valley* UT-8
East Cart Hollow Rsvr—*reservoir* UT-8
**East Carver**—*pop pl* MA-1
East Carver (historical P.O.)—*locale* MA-1
East Cary JHS—*school* NC-3
*East Casco* MI-6
East Casitas Pass—*gap* CA-9
East Cass (Unorganized Territory of)—*unorg* MN-6
East Castle Oil Field—*oilfield* OK-5
East Castle Rock Gulch—*valley* CO-8
East Cat Canyon—*valley* NV-8
East Cathance Stream—*stream* ME-1
East Cathedral Peak—*summit* ID-8
East Catholic HS—*school* CT-1
East Catholic HS—*school* MI-6
East Cattle Creek—*stream* OK-5
East Cattron Sch—*school* SD-7
East Cayuga Heights—*CDP* NY-2
East Cedar Creek—*stream* AZ-5
East Cedar Creek—*stream* (2) AR-4
East Cedar Creek—*stream* IA-7
East Cedar Creek—*stream* (2) KS-7
East Cedar Hill Institute—*hist pl* KY-4
*East Cedar Lake* IN-6
East Cedar Mountain Spring—*spring* UT-8
East Cedar Mtn—*summit* AZ-5
East Cedar Mtn—*summit* UT-8
East Cedar Tank—*reservoir* AZ-5
East Cem—*cemetery* AL-4
East Cem—*cemetery* (4) CT-1
East Cem—*cemetery* IN-6
East Cem—*cemetery* IA-7
East Cem—*cemetery* KY-4
East Cem—*cemetery* LA-4
East Cem—*cemetery* MA-1
East Cem—*cemetery* (2) MI-6
East Cem—*cemetery* MN-6
East Cem—*cemetery* MS-4
East Cem—*cemetery* MO-7
East Cem—*cemetery* (2) NH-1
East Cem—*cemetery* ND-7
East Cem—*cemetery* (3) OH-6
East Cem—*cemetery* SD-7
East Cem—*cemetery* TX-5
East Cem—*cemetery* VT-1
East Cem—*cemetery* WI-6
East Cement Mtn—*summit* CO-8
East Center Canal—*canal* ID-8
East Center Ch—*church* MO-7
East Center Ch—*church* TX-5
East Center City Commercial Hist Dist—*hist pl* PA-2
East Center Sch—*school* IL-6
East Center Sch—*school* MO-7
East Center Tank—*reservoir* NM-5
East Central County Golf Course—*locale* MS-4
East Central County Park—*park* MS-4
East Central Drain—*canal* AZ-5
East Central Franklin (Unorganized Territory of)—*unorg* ME-1
East Central HS—*school* IN-6
East Central HS—*school* MS-4
East Central HS—*school* OK-5
East Central HS—*school* TX-5
East Central Pennington—*unorg reg* SD-7
East Central State Coll—*school* OK-5
East Central State Normal Sch—*hist pl* OK-5
East Central Washington (Unorganized Territory of)—*unorg* ME-1
East Ch—*church* MN-6
East Ch—*church* NY-2
East Chadron—*fmr MCD* NE-7
**East Chain**—*pop pl* MN-6
East Chain Ch—*church* MN-6
East Chain Lake—*lake* MN-6
East Chain Lake—*lake* OR-9
East Chain Sch—*school* MN-6
East Chain State Wildlife Mngmt Area—*park* MN-6
**East Chain (Township of)**—*pop pl* MN-6
East Chairback Pond—*lake* ME-1
East Champagne Bay—*bay* LA-4
East Champoeg Creek—*stream* OR-9
East Chance Sch—*school* SD-7
East Channel—*canal* WY-8
East Channel—*channel* (2) AK-9
East Channel—*channel* (4) FL-3
East Channel—*channel* GA-3
East Channel—*channel* MS-4
East Channel—*channel* NH-1
East Channel—*channel* (3) NY-2
East Channel—*channel* NC-3
East Channel—*channel* WA-9
East Channel—*channel* WI-6
East Channel—*channel* (3) MP-9
East Channel—*harbor* CA-9
East Channel Hayward Strait—*channel* AK-9
East Channel Island—*island* AK-9
East Channel Islands—*island* NY-2
East Channel Little Last Chance Creek—*stream* CA-9
East Channel (not verified)—*channel* MP-9
East Channel Of Humptulips River—*channel* WA-9
East Channel South Santiam River—*channel* OR-9
East Channel Uinta River—*stream* UT-8
East Channel Whitewater River—*stream* MO-7
East Channel Willamette River—*channel* OR-9
*East Chapel* TN-4
East Chapel—*church* AL-4
East Chapel—*church* (2) TX-5
**East Chapel Subdivision**—*pop pl* UT-8
**East Chapman**—*pop pl* AL-4
East Chapman Canyon—*valley* CA-9
East Chapman Sch (historical)—*school* AL-4
**East Charlemont**—*pop pl* MA-1
East Charlemont Ch—*church* MA-1
**East Charleroi**—*pop pl* PA-2
*East Charleston* PA-2
**East Charleston**—*pop pl* VT-1
East Charleston Ch—*church* PA-2
**East Charleston (Whitneyville)**—*pop pl* PA-2
*East Charley Creek* MT-8
East Charley Pond—*lake* NY-2
*East Charlie Creek* MT-8
East Charlie Creek—*stream* MT-8
**East Charlotte**—*pop pl* VT-1
East Charlotte—*uninc pl* NC-3
East Chatham—*locale* PA-2
**East Chatham**—*pop pl* NY-2
**East Chattanooga**—*pop pl* TN-4
East Chattanooga Baptist Ch—*church* TN-4
East Chattanooga Ch of Christ—*church* TN-4
East Chattanooga Elem Sch—*school* TN-4
East Chattanooga Post Office—*building* TN-4
East Chattanooga United Methodist Ch—*church* TN-4
East Chavez Windmill—*locale* NM-5
East Chavez Windmill—*locale* TX-5
East Cheatham Elem Sch—*school* TN-4
**East Chelmsford**—*pop pl* MA-1
East Chelsea Cem—*cemetery* IL-6
*East Chenango River* NY-2
East Cheney—*locale* WA-9
East Cherokee (CCD)—*cens area* OK-5
*East Cherokee Elem Sch* TN-4
East Cherry Creek—*stream* CO-8
East Cherry Ridge Sch—*school* PA-2
East Cherry Valley Well—*well* NM-5
East Chesapeake—*uninc pl* VA-3
Eastchester—*CDP* NY-2
**Eastchester**—*pop pl* NY-2
**East Chester**—*pop pl* NY-2
Eastchester—*uninc pl* AK-9
*East Chester Bay* NY-2
Eastchester Bay—*bay* NY-2
East Chester (CCD)—*cens area* TN-4
East Chester County Elem Sch—*school* TN-4
*Eastchester Creek* NY-2
East Chester Division—*civil* TN-4
East Chesterfield Ch—*church* OH-6
Eastchester HS—*school* NY-2
**Eastchester (Town of)**—*pop pl* NY-2
East Chestnut Hill—*summit* CT-1
East Cheyenne Creek—*stream* TX-5
East Cheyenne Oil And Gas Field—*oilfield* OK-5
**East Chicago**—*pop pl* IN-6
*East Chicago Heights* IL-6
**East Chicago Heights**—*pop pl* IL-6
East Chicago Street Hist Dist—*hist pl* MI-6
East Chickamauga Creek—*stream* GA-3
East Chicos Rsvr—*reservoir* CO-8
East Chihuahua Well—*well* NM-5
**East Chillisquaque (Township of)**—*pop pl* PA-2
East Chilocco Oil Field—*oilfield* OK-5
East Chimney—*pillar* CO-8
East China Creek—*stream* TX-5
East China Gulch—*valley* MT-8
East China Gulch—*valley* SD-7
East China Sch—*school* MI-6
East China Spring—*spring* OR-9
**East China (Township of)**—*pop pl* MI-6
East Chinook Sch—*school* MT-8
East Chippewa Ch—*church* OH-6
East Chippy Creek—*stream* MT-8
*East Choctaw HS* AL-4
East Choctaw Sch—*school* AL-4
*East Choctowhatchee River* AL-4
East Chop—*cape* MA-1
**East Chop**—*pop pl* MA-1
East Chop Beach Club—*locale* MA-1
East Chop Flats—*flat* MA-1
East Chop Light—*hist pl* MA-1
East Chop Light—*locale* MA-1
East Choteau Creek—*stream* OK-5
**East Choteau Township**—*pop pl* SD-7
East Christiania Cem—*cemetery* MN-6
East Chub Lake—*lake* MN-6
East Chugach Island—*island* AK-9
East Chunchula Sch—*school* AL-4
*East Church* MS-4
East Church Street Hist Dist—*hist pl* GA-3
East Chute—*stream* NE-7
East Cinnabar Creek—*stream* OR-9
**East Circle (subdivision)**—*pop pl* AL-4
East City Center (Shop Ctr)—*locale* UT-8
*East C Lake* IL-6
*East Clallam* WA-9
East Claremont—*summit* CA-9
East Claremont—*uninc pl* NJ-2
East Clarence—*locale* NY-2
**East Clarendon**—*pop pl* VT-1
**East Claridon**—*pop pl* OH-6
East Clark—*cens area* ID-8
East Clark Bench—*bench* UT-8
East Clark Sch—*school* OH-6
East Clarkson Well—*well* SD-7
East Clarno Sch—*school* WI-6
East Clavey Lateral—*canal* CA-9
East Clay Creek—*stream* CO-8
East Clay Creek—*stream* OK-5
East Clayton—*locale* OH-6
East Clayton Sch—*school* GA-3
*East Clear Creek* AZ-5
East Clear Creek—*stream* AZ-5
East Clear Creek—*stream* KY-4
East Clear Creek—*stream* NE-7
*East Clear Water Creek* AL-4
East Clermont Ch—*church* IA-7
**East Cleveland**—*pop pl* OH-6
**East Cleveland**—*pop pl* TN-4
East Cleveland (CCD)—*cens area* OK-5
East Cleveland Cem—*cemetery* OH-6
East Cleveland District 9 Sch—*hist pl* OH-6
*East Cleveland Elementary School* TN-4
East Cleveland Sch—*school* TN-4
**East Clifford**—*pop pl* IN-6
East Cliff Park—*park* TX-5
East Cliff Sch—*school* TX-5
East Clifty Creek—*stream* MO-7
**East Clinton**—*pop pl* IL-6
East Clinton Elem Sch—*school* AL-4
East Cloudy Sch—*school* OK-5
East Clover Creek—*stream* OR-9
East Clubhouse Lake—*lake* SD-7
East Clump—*bar* NY-2
East Clump—*island* AK-9
East Coal (CCD)—*cens area* OK-5
East Coal Creek—*stream* (2) CO-8
*East Coalinga Extension Oil Field* CA-9
East Cobb Windmill—*locale* TX-5
**East Cobleskill**—*pop pl* NY-2
**East Cocalico (Township of)**—*pop pl* PA-2
East Cochecton—*locale* NY-2
*East Cocopah Reservation* AZ-5
East Cod Ledge—*bar* ME-1
East Cod Ledge Rock—*bar* ME-1
*East Cody Lake* NE-7
East Coeur D'Alene Mine—*mine* MT-8
East Coffee Creek—*stream* TX-5
East Coffee Elem Sch—*school* TN-4
East Cohoctah—*other* MI-6
East Cokedale Mine—*mine* CO-8
East Colbert Ch—*church* AL-4
**East Coldenham**—*pop pl* NY-2
East Colebrook Ch—*church* NH-1
East Cole Creek—*stream* AR-4
East Colfax Airpark—*airport* CO-8
East College of DePauw Univ—*hist pl* IN-6
East Collinsville—*other* IL-6
East Coloma Sch—*school* IL-6
East Colrain Ch—*church* MA-1
**East Columbia**—*pop pl* TX-5
*East Columbia Baptist Church* MS-4
East Columbia Cem—*cemetery* MS-4
East Columbia Ch—*church* MS-4
East Columbia Ch—*church* NH-1
East Columbia Ch—*church* SC-3
**East Columbia Park**—*pop pl* MD-2
*East Columbus* IN-6
*East Columbus* OH-6
**East Columbus**—*pop pl* IN-6
East Columbus Ch—*church* IN-6
East Columbus Ch of Christ—*church* MS-4
East Colusa (CCD)—*cens area* CA-9
East Commencement Oil Field—*oilfield* MS-4
East Commerce Baptist Ch—*church* TN-4
East Commerce Street Hist Dist—*hist pl* AL-4
East Community Center—*locale* MT-8
East Community Well—*well* MT-8
East Compadre Shaft—*mine* AZ-5
East Compton—*CDP* CA-9
*East Compton (census name Compton East)* CA-9
**East Comstock**—*pop pl* MI-6
*East Concord* NH-1
**East Concord**—*pop pl* NH-1
**East Concord**—*pop pl* NY-2
**East Concord**—*pop pl* VT-1
**East Conemaugh**—*pop pl* PA-2
East Conemaugh Borough—*civil* PA-2
**East Conemaugh (corporate name for Conemaugh)**—*pop pl* PA-2
East Conemaugh Post Office (historical)—*building* PA-2
*East Conneaut* OH-6
**East Connellsville**—*pop pl* PA-2
*East Connersville* IN-6
East Conrad Creek—*bay* FL-3
East Constance Bayou—*stream* LA-4
East Constance Lake—*lake* LA-4
East Contra Costa (CCD)—*cens area* CA-9
East Conventry Ch—*church* PA-2
**East Conway**—*pop pl* NH-1
East Cook (Unorganized Territory of)—*unorg* MN-6
**East Coongetto (historical)**—*pop pl* MS-4
**East Cooper**—*pop pl* MI-6
East Cooper Cem—*cemetery* MI-6
East Cooper Cem—*cemetery* OK-5
East Cooper Creek—*stream* AR-4
East Cooper Sch—*school* OK-5
East Cooper Sch—*school* SD-7
**East Cooper Township**—*pop pl* KS-7
East Cooper Well—*well* NM-5
East Copeland Rsvr—*reservoir* OR-9
**East Copper**—*pop pl* MI-6
East Copperas Creek—*stream* TX-5
East Copper Creek—*stream* UT-8
East Copper Spring—*spring* AZ-5
East Coral Lake—*lake* FL-3
East Cora Sch—*school* SD-7
East Corazones Draw—*valley* TX-5
**East Cordele**—*pop pl* GA-3
**East Corinth**—*pop pl* ME-1
**East Corinth**—*pop pl* VT-1
East Corinth Ch—*church* NC-3
East Corinth Ch of Christ—*church* MS-4
*East Corinth Elementary School* MS-4
*East Corn Creek* UT-8
*East Cornell Creek* WA-9
East Corner—*other* DC-2
**East Corning**—*pop pl* NY-2
East Cornwall—*locale* CT-1
East Corporate Ch (historical)—*church* TN-4
East Corral de Piedra Creek—*stream* CA-9
East Corral Spring—*spring* OR-9
East Coteau Lake—*lake* SD-7
East Cote Blanche Bay—*bay* LA-4
East Cote Blanche Bay Oil and Gas Field—*oilfield* LA-4
*East Cottage Grove* MN-6
**East Cottage Grove**—*pop pl* MN-6
East Cottaquilla Springs—*spring* AL-4
East Cotter Ch—*church* AR-4
East Cottonwood Canyon—*valley* NV-8
East Cottonwood Canyon—*valley* UT-8
East Cottonwood Creek—*stream* MT-8
East Cottonwood Creek—*stream* OK-5
East Cottonwood Creek—*stream* (2) SD-7
East Cottonwood Creek—*stream* (2) TX-5
East Cottonwood Creek—*stream* (2) WY-8
East Cottonwood Draw—*valley* CO-8
**East Cottonwood Heights**—*pop pl* UT-8
East Cottonwood Park—*flat* WY-8
East Cottonwood Spring—*spring* NM-5
East Coulee Dam—*uninc pl* WA-9
East Coulter Creek—*stream* CO-8
East County Line Cem—*cemetery* MS-4
East County Line Ch—*church* (2) MS-4
*East Cove* ME-1
East Cove—*basin* UT-8
East Cove—*bay* AK-9
East Cove—*bay* FL-3
East Cove—*bay* NH-1
East Cove—*bay* NY-2
East Coventry Elem Sch—*school* PA-2
**East Coventry (Township of)**—*pop pl* PA-2
East Covington Sch—*school* VA-3
*East Cow Creek* CO-8
*East Cow Creek* OK-5
East Cow Creek—*stream* KS-7
East Cow Creek—*stream* MO-7
East Cow Creek—*stream* (2) OR-9
East Cow Creek—*stream* TX-5
East Cow Creek Rsvr—*reservoir* WY-8
East Coweta Sch—*school* GA-3
East Cow Hollow—*valley* OR-9
East Cow Hollow Rsvr—*reservoir* OR-9
East Cow Pasture Windmill—*locale* TX-5
East Cox Rsvr—*reservoir* CO-8
East Cox Windmill—*locale* CO-8
East Coyle Hollow—*valley* MO-7
East Coyote Hills—*range* CA-9
East Coyote Tank—*reservoir* TX-5
East Coyote Wash—*valley* UT-8
**East Craftsbury**—*pop pl* VT-1
East Cranberry Lake—*lake* MN-6
East Crater—*crater* AK-9
East Crater—*crater* WA-9
East Craters Sand Flat—*flat* CA-9
East Crater Trail—*trail* WA-9
*East Creek* AR-4
*East Creek* KS-7
*East Creek* MA-1
*East Creek* MN-6
*East Creek* MT-8
*East Creek* NY-2
*East Creek* NC-3
*East Creek* SD-7
*East Creek* UT-8
**East Creek**—*pop pl* NY-2
East Creek—*stream* (2) AL-4
East Creek—*stream* (2) AK-9
East Creek—*stream* (3) CA-9
East Creek—*stream* (4) CO-8
East Creek—*stream* (3) FL-3
East Creek—*stream* (2) ID-8
East Creek—*stream* (3) IL-6
East Creek—*stream* IN-6
East Creek—*stream* (3) KS-7
East Creek—*stream* MD-2
East Creek—*stream* (3) MI-6
East Creek—*stream* MN-6
East Creek—*stream* (3) MO-7
East Creek—*stream* (2) MT-8
East Creek—*stream* NE-7
East Creek—*stream* NV-8
East Creek—*stream* (2) NJ-2
East Creek—*stream* (7) NY-2
East Creek—*stream* (2) OH-6
East Creek—*stream* (3) OK-5
East Creek—*stream* (8) OR-9
East Creek—*stream* SD-7
East Creek—*stream* UT-8
East Creek—*stream* (2) VT-1
East Creek—*stream* (3) WA-9
East Creek—*stream* WI-6
East Creek—*stream* (2) WY-8
East Creek Campground—*locale* MT-8
East Creek Campground—*locale* NV-8
*East Creek Forest Service Recreation Site* NV-8
East Creek Gut—*gut* MD-2
*East Creek - in part* UT-8
*East Creek Lake* AL-4
East Creek Point—*cape* MD-2
East Creek Pond—*reservoir* NJ-2
East Crook Pond Dam *dam* NJ-2
East Creek Tioga River—*stream* PA-2
East Creek Trail—*trail* CA-9
East Creek Well—*well* TX-5
East Cresap Ranch—*locale* MO-7
**East Crest Estates Subdivision**—*pop pl* UT-8
**East Creston**—*pop pl* IA-7
Eastcrest Sch—*school* OH-6
East Crisp—*locale* GA-3
East Crocker Lake—*reservoir* UT-8
East Crockett Branch—*stream* OR-9
East Crockett (CCD)—*cens area* TX-5
East Cromo Creek—*stream* MT-8
East Cromwell—*locale* WA-9
East Cromwell Oil Field—*oilfield* OK-5
*East Cronese Lake* CA-9
East Cronise Lake—*flat* CA-9
East Crooked Creek—*stream* IL-6
East Crooked Lake—*lake* FL-3
East Crooked Lake—*lake* MI-6
East Crooked Lake—*lake* MN-6
East Cross Canyon—*valley* CO-8
East Cross Creek—*stream* (2) CO-8
East Crossing Camp—*locale* WA-9
East Crossing Strand—*swamp* FL-3
East Croton Creek—*stream* OK-5
East Crow Island—*island* NY-2
East Crown Point—*mine* UT-8
East Crystal Creek—*stream* CO-8
East C Streamline Lake—*lake* IL-6
*East Cullman Church of God* AL-4
*East Cumberland* RI-1
East Cumberland Ch—*church* WI-6
*East Cumminsville* OH-6
East Cundy Point—*cape* ME-1
*East Curecanti Creek* CO-8
*East Curry Creek* TX-5
East Curtis Canyon—*valley* NM-5
East Curtis Creek Canyon—*valley* NE-7
East Curtis Sch—*school* NE-7
East Curtis Spring—*spring* NM-5
East Custer—*unorg reg* SD-7
**East Custer Township**—*pop pl* NE-7
**East Cutchogue**—*pop pl* NY-2
East Cutoff—*channel* FL-3
East Cutoff Creek—*stream* FL-3
East Cypress Creek—*stream* MS-4
East Cypress Lake—*reservoir* MS-4
East Cyruston—*locale* TN-4
East Cyruston Cem—*cemetery* TN-4
East Cyruston Ch—*church* TN-4
East Daggett—*cens area* UT-8
East Daggett Division—*civil* UT-8
**East Dailey**—*pop pl* WV-2
East Dairy Fork—*stream* UT-8
Eastdale—*locale* CO-8
**Eastdale**—*pop pl* TN-4
Eastdale—*post sta* AL-4
Eastdale Acad—*school* TN-4
Eastdale Baptist Chapel—*church* AL-4
Eastdale Branch Cerro Canal—*canal* CO-8
Eastdale Canal No 2—*canal* CO-8
Eastdale Culebra Canal—*canal* CO-8
Eastdale Elem Sch—*school* TN-4
Eastdale Mall Shop Ctr—*locale* AL-4
Eastdale Mall (Shop Ctr)—*locale* IA-7
Eastdale Park—*park* WY-8
Eastdale Rsvr No 1—*reservoir* CO-8
*East Dale Sch* TN-4
Eastdale United Methodist Ch—*church* TN-4
**East Dallas**—*pop pl* TX-5
East Dallas Ch—*church* PA-2
East Dallas Sch—*school* AL-4
East Dallas Township—*civil* MO-7
*East Dam* SD-7
East Dam—*dam* AZ-5
East Dam—*dam* CO-8
East Damascus Ch—*church* GA-3
East Dam Creek—*stream* MT-8
East Dam Tailings Pond—*reservoir* AZ-5
*East Dandies Creek* TX-5
**East Danville**—*pop pl* OH-6
**East Danville**—*pop pl* VA-3
East Darian Run—*stream* PA-2
*East Davenport* IA-7
East Davidson HS—*school* NC-3
East Davis Lake—*lake* WI-6
East Davis Lake Campground—*park* OR-9
East Dawkins Lake—*lake* MN-6
East Days Creek—*stream* OK-5
*East Dayton* OH-6
East Dayton—*locale* MI-6
East Dayton Street Hist Dist—*hist pl* WI-6
*East Dead Lake* MN-6
East Deaton Windmill—*locale* TX-5
East De Baca (CCD)—*cens area* NM-5
**East Decatur**—*pop pl* IL-6
East Decatur Sch—*school* MI-6
East Deception Canyon—*valley* CA-9
**East Dedham (subdivision)**—*pop pl* MA-1
East Deep Creek—*stream* TX-5
East Deep Creek—*stream* UT-8
East Deer Creek—*stream* CO-8
East Deer Creek—*stream* IN-6
East Deer Creek—*stream* UT-8
East Deer Creek—*stream* WA-9
East Deer Creek Canyon—*valley* NE-7
**East Deerfield**—*pop pl* MA-1
East Deerfield Cem—*cemetery* MA-1

East Deerfield Ch—church ... MI-6
*East Deering* ... ME-1
**East Deering**—pop pl ... ME-1
**East Deering**—pop pl ... NH-1
East Deer Pond—lake ... IN-6
East Deer Tank—reservoir ... AZ-5
East Deer Township—CDP ... PA-2
**East Deer (Township of)**—pop pl ... PA-2
*East Defiance* ... OH-6
**East De Kalb**—pop pl ... NY-2
East DeKalb Cem—cemetery ... NY-2
East Delaney Lake—lake ... CO-8
**East Delavan**—pop pl ... WI-6
East Delaware Aqueduct—canal ... NY-2
**East Delhi**—pop pl ... NY-2
*East Delphos* ... OH-6
East Delta—locale ... TX-5
East Delta Canal—canal ... CA-9
East Dempsey Creek—stream ... ID-8
East Dempsey Gulch—valley ... CO-8
East Denison Sch—school ... OH-6
**East Denmark**—pop pl ... ME-1
**East Dennis**—pop pl ... MA-1
East Dennis—summit ... ID-8
East Denver Ch—church ... MI-6
East Depot Street Sch—school ... GA-3
*East Derby* ... CT-1
**East Derby**—pop pl ... CT-1
**East Derry**—pop pl ... NH-1
East Derry Hist Dist—hist pl ... NH-1
*East Desert Range* ... NV-8
East Desert Range—range ... NV-8
**East Des Moines**—pop pl ... IA-7
East Des Moines Access Public Hunting Area—area ... IA-7
*East Des Moines River* ... IA-7
*East Des Moines River* ... MN-6
East Des Moines Township—fmr MCD ... IA-7
**East Detroit**—pop pl ... MI-6
East Detroit HS—school ... MI-6
East Devils Lake—lake ... ND-7
**East DeWitt**—pop pl ... MI-6
East Dexter Oil Field—oilfield ... MS-4
**East Diamond**—pop pl ... KY-4
East Diamond Creek—stream ... NM-5
East Diamond Mine—mine ... KY-4
East Diamond Springs—spring ... AZ-5
East Diamond Springs—spring ... WY-8
East Diamond Springs Draw—valley ... WY-8
**East Dickinson**—pop pl ... NY-2
East Dietz Creek—arroyo ... TX-5
East Dike Ch—church ... TX-5
East Dipping Vat Coulee—valley ... MT-8
**East Direct**—pop pl ... TX-5
East Dismal Swamp—swamp ... NC-3
East District Sch—hist pl ... CT-1
East District Sch (historical)—school ... PA-2
East Ditch—canal ... NJ-2
East Ditch—canal ... NM-5
East Ditch—canal ... VA-3
East Divide Creek—stream ... CO-8
East Divide Creek Ditch—canal ... CO-8
East Divide Oil Field—other ... IL-6
East Divide Two hundred eighty seven Trail—trail ... AZ-5
East Dix—summit ... NY-2
**East Dixfield**—pop pl ... ME-1
East Dixmont—locale ... ME-1
East Dixon Creek—stream ... TX-5
East Dixon Sch—school ... CA-9
East Dobbin Creek—stream ... NV-8
East Dobbin Summit Spring—spring ... NV-8
East Dog Creek—stream ... FL-3
East Dog Fork—stream ... CA-9
East Dome—summit ... WA-9
East Donegal Cem—cemetery ... PA-2
**East Donegal (Township of)**—pop pl ... PA-2
East Donica Creek—stream ... IL-6
East Donica Sch—school ... IL-6
East Donna Sch—school ... TX-5
**East Dorset**—pop pl ... VT-1
East Double Bayou—gut ... LA-4
East Double Canyon—valley ... CA-9
East Double Creek—stream ... NC-3
**East Dougherty**—pop pl ... GA-3
East Dougherty (CCD)—cens area ... GA-3
**East Douglas**—pop pl ... MA-1
East Douglas Creek—stream ... CO-8
East Douglas HS—school ... MA-1
*East Douglass* ... MA-1
East Douglas Sch—school ... SD-7
**East Douglas Station**—pop pl ... MA-1
*East Douglas Village* ... MA-1
East Douthet Well—well ... NM-5
**East Dover**—pop pl ... ME-1
**East Dover**—pop pl ... VT-1
East Dover Hundred—civil ... DE-2
East Downer Windmill—locale ... CO-8
East Downey Creek—stream ... CO-8
East Drain—canal (2) ... AZ-5
East Drain—canal ... CA-9
East Drain—canal ... NM-5
East Drain—canal ... TX-5
East Drainage Canal—canal ... CA-9
East Drain Extension—canal ... AZ-5
East Draw—valley ... CO-8
East Draw—valley ... UT-8
East Draw—valley (2) ... WY-8
East Drenthe Cem—cemetery ... MI-6
East Drive Park—park ... FL-3
East Drumore Central Sch—school ... PA-2
**East Drumore (Township of)**—pop pl ... PA-2
East Dry Branch—stream ... VA-3
East Dry Canyon—valley ... ID-8
East Dry Canyon—valley ... UT-8
*East Dry Creek* ... FL-3
*East Dry Creek* ... TX-5
East Dry Creek—stream (2) ... CA-9
East Dry Creek—stream ... CO-8
East Dry Creek—stream (3) ... ID-8
East Dry Creek—stream (2) ... KS-7
East Dry Creek—stream ... TX-5
*East Dry Fork Coulee* ... MT-8
East Dry Gulch—valley ... CO-8
East Dry Lake Canyon—valley ... CO-8
East Dry Run—stream ... WV-2
East Dry Run Ch—church ... WV-2
East Dry Run Fork—stream ... VA-3
East Drywood Creek—stream ... MO-7
East Dubbs Ch—church ... MS-4
**East Dublin**—pop pl ... GA-3
East Dublin (CCD)—cens area ... GA-3
East Du Bois—uninc pl ... PA-2
East Dubois Junction—locale ... PA-2
East Du Bois Junction—uninc pl ... PA-2
**East Dubuque**—pop pl ... IL-6
East Dubuque Sch—hist pl ... IL-6
East Duck Creek—stream ... MT-8
East Due West—uninc pl ... TN-4
East Dugout Coulee—valley ... MT-8
East Dugway Rsvr—reservoir ... UT-8
**East Duke**—pop pl ... OK-5
**East Dummer**—pop pl ... NH-1
**East Dummerston**—pop pl ... VT-1
East Dunbarton Cem—cemetery ... NH-1
East Duncan Creek—stream ... OR-9
**East Dundee (Dundee Station)**—pop pl ... IL-6
East Du Noir Creek—stream ... WY-8
East Du Noir Trail—trail ... WY-8
East Duplin HS—school ... NC-3
East Duplin Memorial Gardens—cemetery ... NC-3
*East Durgy Lake* ... MI-6
**East Durham**—pop pl ... NY-2
East Durham—uninc pl ... NC-3
East Durham Well—well ... NM-5
East Durrance Island—island ... FL-3
East Dutch Woman Draw—valley ... TX-5
East Dyberry Cem—cemetery ... PA-2
East Eagle Creek—stream ... AZ-5
East Eagle Eye Mesa—summit ... CO-8
East Eagle Head Ranch—locale ... KS-7
East Eagle Mine—mine ... OR-9
East Eagle Mountain Tunnel—tunnel ... CA-9
East Eagle Trail Thirty-Three—trail ... AZ-5
**East Earl**—pop pl ... PA-2
**East Earl (Township of)**—pop pl ... PA-2
East Easy Canal—canal ... FL-3
East Eaton Canyon—valley ... AZ-5
East Echo Lake—lake ... WY-8
East Echols (CCD)—cens area ... GA-3
East Eckford Cem—cemetery ... MI-6
East Eckford Ch—church ... MI-6
**East Eddington**—pop pl ... ME-1
**East Eden**—pop pl ... NY-2
East Eden Sch—school ... NY-2
Eastedge—locale ... ND-7
East Edgecomb—locale ... ME-1
**East Edgewood**—pop pl ... GA-3
East Eighth Street Baptist Ch—church ... KS-7
East Eightmile Lake—lake ... WI-6
East Eight Section Windmill—locale ... TX-5
East E-K Oil Field—other ... NM-5
East Elba—locale ... NY-2
East Elbow Ditch—canal ... MT-8
East El Dorado—locale ... KS-7
East El Dorado—uninc pl ... KS-7
East Eldorado (Township of)—civ div ... IL-6
East Elementary Early Childhood Center—school ... DE-2
*East Elem Sch* ... MS-4
*East Elem Sch* ... TN-4
East Elem Sch—school ... AL-4
East Elem Sch—school ... DE-2
East Elem Sch—school ... FL-3
East Elem Sch—school ... IN-6
East Elem Sch—school ... KS-7
East Elem Sch—school ... MS-4
East Elem Sch—school (2) ... NC-3
East Elem Sch—school ... OH-6
East Elem Sch—school (2) ... TN-4
East Elevenmile Tank—reservoir ... TX-5
East Elfers Cem—cemetery ... FL-3
East Elim Cem—cemetery ... MN-6
East Eliot—locale ... ME-1
East Eliot Ch—church ... ME-1
**East Elizabeth**—pop pl ... PA-2
East Elizabeth Sch—school ... SC-3
East Elk Creek—stream (3) ... CO-8
East Elk Creek—stream ... KS-7
East Elk Fork—stream ... MO-7
East Elkhorn Creek—stream (2) ... KS-7
East Elk Mtn—summit ... NM-5
East Elk Peak—summit ... ID-8
*East Elkport* ... IA-7
East Elk Spring—spring ... AZ-5
East Ellerson Lake—lake ... WI-6
**East Ellijay**—pop pl ... GA-3
East Ellis Cem—cemetery ... SC-3
East Ellisville Sch—school ... SD-7
**East Ellsworth**—pop pl ... WI-6
East Ellsworth—uninc pl ... WI-6
**East Elma**—pop pl ... NY-2
East Elm Creek—stream ... OK-5
East Elm Creek—stream ... SD-7
East Elm Creek—stream (3) ... TX-5
East Elm Grove Sch (abandoned)—school ... MO-7
**East Elmhurst**—pop pl ... NY-2
East Elmira—locale ... NY-2
East Elm-North Macomb Street Hist Dist—hist pl ... MI-6
**East Elmore**—pop pl ... VT-1
**East Ely**—pop pl ... NV-8
East Ely Depot—hist pl ... NV-8
East Emanuel Ch—church ... WI-6
East Emerick Sch—school ... NE-7
East Emma Creek—stream ... KS-7
East Emmaus Ch—church ... MN-6
East Emmett Ch—church ... KS-7
East Emory Ch (historical)—church ... TN-4
East Emory Sch (historical)—school ... TN-4
*East End* ... CT-1
*East End* ... ME-1
*East End* ... MA-1
*East End* ... MN-6
*East End* (2) ... OH-6
East End—cliff ... TN-4
East End—flat ... CA-9
**East End**—pop pl ... AR-4
**East End**—pop pl ... ME-1
**East End**—pop pl ... MO-7
**East End**—pop pl ... OH-6
**East End**—pop pl (2) ... PA-2
**East End**—pop pl ... WI-6
**East End**—pop pl ... VI-3
East End—post sta ... FL-3
East End—post sta ... PA-2
East End—summit ... AZ-5
East End—uninc pl ... MD-2
East End—uninc pl ... PA-2
East End—uninc pl ... VA-3
East End—uninc pl ... WI-6
East End Baptist Ch—church ... MS-4
East End Bay—bay (2) ... VI-3
East End Beach—beach ... ME-1
East End Cem—cemetery ... NY-2
East End Cem—cemetery (2) ... TX-5
East End Cem—cemetery (2) ... VA-3
East End (Census Subdistrict)—cens area (3) ... VI-3
East End Ch—church ... AL-4
East End Ch—church ... AR-4
East End Ch—church ... PA-2
East End Ch—church ... TX-5
East End Ch—church ... VA-3
East End Ch of Christ—church ... TN-4
East End Community Center—building ... MS-4
East End Creek—stream ... CA-9
East End Draw—valley ... WY-8
East End Unive Ch of Christ—church ... TN-4
*East End Elementary School* ... PA-2
East End Elem Sch—school ... AL-4
*East End Estates* ... IL-6
East End Freight Yards—locale ... CT-1
East End Hist Dist—hist pl ... GA-3
East End Hist Dist—hist pl ... MA-1
East End Hist Dist—hist pl ... MS-4
East End Hist Dist—hist pl ... NY-2
East End Hist Dist—hist pl ... OH-6
East End Hist Dist—hist pl ... TX-5
East End Hist Dist—hist pl ... WV-2
East End HS—school ... AL-4
East End HS—school ... VA-3
*East End Lake* ... MI-6
East End Meetinghouse Ch—church ... MA-1
East End Meml Hospital Airp—airport ... AL-4
East End Memorial Hosp—hospital ... AL-4
East End Methodist Ch—church ... AL-4
East End Methodist Ch—church ... TN-4
*East End of Norton* ... MA-1
*East End of Taunton North Purchase* ... MA-1
East End Park—park ... IL-6
East End Point—cape ... VI-3
East End Rec Area—park ... AR-4
East End Sch—school ... AL-4
East End Sch—school ... LA-4
East End Sch—school ... ME-1
East End Sch—school ... MS-4
East End Sch—school ... NJ-2
East End Sch—school (3) ... NC-3
East End Sch—school (2) ... OH-6
East End Sch—school (5) ... PA-2
East End Sch—school (2) ... SC-3
East End Sch—school ... TX-5
East End Sch—school (2) ... VA-3
East End Sch—school (3) ... WV-2
East End Sch (abandoned)—school ... PA-2
East End Sch (historical)—school ... AL-4
East End Shop Ctr—locale ... VA-3
East End Spring—spring (2) ... UT-8
**East End (subdivision)**—pop pl ... AL-4
**East End (subdivision)**—pop pl ... PA-2
East End Trail—trail (2) ... PA-2
East End United Methodist Ch—church (2) ... MS-4
East Englewood—uninc pl ... GA-3
**East Enosburg**—pop pl ... VT-1
**East Enterprise**—pop pl ... IN-6
**East Enterprise**—pop pl ... MS-4
*East Entrance* ... PW-9
East Entrance—channel ... MI-6
East Entrance—other ... UT-8
East Entrance Checking Station—hist pl ... UT-8
East Entrance Colorado Natl Monument—locale ... CO-8
East Entrance Monument Canyon—valley ... CO-8
East Entrance Ranger Station—locale ... WY-8
East Entrance Residence—hist pl ... UT-8
East Entrance Sign—hist pl ... UT-8
East Entrance Trail—trail ... UT-8
Eastep Branch—stream ... KY-4
Eastep Ch—church ... WV-2
Eastep Hollow—valley ... KY-4
Easter—locale ... TX-5
Easter, Lake—reservoir ... IA-7
Easter, Mount—summit ... CT-1
Easter Branch—stream ... SC-3
Easter Branch Cem—cemetery ... SC-3
Easter Brook—stream ... MA-1
Easterbrook Pond—lake ... MA-1
Easterbrook Sch—school ... CA-9
Easter Cave—cave ... MO-7
Easter Cem—cemetery ... AL-4
Easter Cem—cemetery ... MS-4
Easter Cem—cemetery ... MO-7
Easter Cem—cemetery ... WV-2
Easter Ch—church ... KY-4
Easter Ch—church (2) ... VA-3
*Easter Creek* ... AR-4
*Easter Creek* ... VA-3
Easter Creek—stream (3) ... AK-9
Easter Creek—stream ... ID-8
Easter Creek—stream ... MO-7
Easter Creek—stream ... MT-8
Easter Creek—stream ... NC-3
Easter Creek—stream ... OR-9
Easter Creek—stream ... TX-5
Easter Creek—stream (2) ... VA-3
Easter Creek—stream ... WY-8
Easter Cross—locale ... CA-9
Easterday—locale ... KY-4
Easterday Dam—dam ... OR-9
Easterday Ditch—canal ... IN-6
Easterday Ditch—canal ... OR-9
*Easterday Ranch* ... OR-9
Easterday Rsvr—reservoir ... OR-9
Easter Ferry Bridge (historical)—bridge ... AL-4
Easter Fork—stream ... WV-2
Easter Hill—summit ... CT-1
Easter Hill—summit ... DE-2
Easter Hole Camp—locale ... FL-3
Easter Hollow—valley ... OH-6
Easter Hollow Cove—bay ... MO-7
East Erie Plaza—locale ... PA-2
*Easter Lake* ... CT-1
Easter Lily Mine—mine ... MT-8
Easterling Branch—stream ... KY-4
Easterling Branch—stream ... MS-4
Easterling Cem—cemetery (2) ... KY-4
Easterling Cem—cemetery ... VA-3
*Easterling Mill Pond* ... AL-4
Easterling Mill Pond Dam—dam ... AL-4
Easterling Pond—reservoir ... AL-4
Easterling Sch (historical)—school ... MS-4
Easterlings Fish Hatchery—other ... AL-4
Easterlings Pond—reservoir ... AL-4
Easterly—locale ... SD-7
**Easterly**—pop pl ... TX-5
Easterly Branch—stream ... TN-4
*Easterly Branch Home Creek* ... WA-9
Easterly Breakwater—other ... IL-6
Easterly Bridge—bridge ... TN-4
Easterly Cove—cave ... TN-4
Easterly Cem—cemetery ... OH-6
Easterly Cem—cemetery ... TX-5
Easterly Island—island ... AK-9
*Easterly Kettle Cove* ... MA-1
Easterly Parkway Sch—school ... PA-2
Easterly Pond—lake ... TN-4
Easterly Sch—school ... CA-9
Easterly Sch (historical)—school ... TN-4
Easter Mine—mine ... ID-8
Easter Mtn—summit ... AZ-5
Eastern—fmr MCD ... NE-7
**Eastern**—pop pl ... KY-4
Eastern—uninc pl ... OK-5
Eastern, Canal (historical)—canal ... AZ-5
**Eastern, The**—pop pl ... OH-6
Eastern Acad—school ... FL-3
**Eastern Addition Sandy Plat A**—pop pl ... UT-8
Eastern Arizona Junior Coll—school ... AZ-5
*Eastern Arizona Junior Coll Campus* ... AZ-5
Eastern Arm Third Machias Lake—bay ... ME-1
*Eastern Auxilary Canal* ... AZ-5
Eastern Ave Baptist Ch—church ... FL-3
Eastern Ave Sch—school (3) ... MA-1
Eastern Basham Lookout Tower—locale ... AL-4
Eastern Bay—bay (2) ... ME-1
Eastern Bay—bay ... MD-2
Eastern Beach Ledge—bar ... ME-1
Eastern Bend—bay ... NC-3
Eastern Bible Institute—school ... PA-2
*Eastern Branch* ... DC-2
*Eastern Branch* ... ME-1
*Eastern Branch* ... MD-2
Eastern Branch—stream ... ME-1
Eastern Branch—stream ... MD-2
Eastern Branch Carter Creek—stream ... VA-3
Eastern Branch Ch—church ... TX-5
Eastern Branch Corrotoman River—stream ... VA-3
Eastern Branch Elizabeth River—stream ... VA-3
Eastern Branch Johns River—stream ... ME-1
*Eastern Branch Lynnhaven Bay* ... VA-3
Eastern Branch Lynnhaven River—stream ... VA-3
*Eastern Branch of Lynnhaven River* ... VA-3
Eastern Brook Lake—lake ... CA-9
Eastern Brook Lake—lake ... OR-9
Eastern Brook Lakes—lake ... CA-9
Eastern Canal—canal ... AZ-5
Eastern Canal—canal ... MA-1
Eastern Canyon—valley ... CA-9
Eastern Caroline Islands—island ... FM-9
Eastern Cem—cemetery ... FL-3
Eastern Cem—cemetery ... IN-6
Eastern Cem—cemetery ... KY-4
Eastern Cem—cemetery (3) ... ME-1
Eastern Cem—cemetery ... MS-4
Eastern Cem—cemetery ... PA-2
Eastern Cem—cemetery ... VA-3
Eastern Cemetery—hist pl ... ME-1
Eastern Centennial Mtns—range ... MT-8
Eastern Ch—church ... NC-3
*Eastern Channel* ... VA-3
Eastern Channel—channel ... AK-9
Eastern Channel—channel ... ME-1
Eastern Channel—channel (2) ... NC-3
Eastern Channel—gut ... MA-1
Eastern Channel Light 24—locale ... SC-3
Eastern Channel Light 25 Upper Range Front—locale ... SC-3
**Eastern Cherokee Ind Res**—pop pl ... NC-3
Eastern Christian Institute—school ... NJ-2
Eastern Coll—school ... PA-2
Eastern Correctional Institution—building ... PA-2
Eastern Coulee—valley ... MT-8
*Eastern Cove* ... ME-1
Eastern Cove—bay ... ME-1
*Eastern Creek* ... CA-9
Eastern Creek—stream ... AK-9
Eastern Cross—stream ... NJ-2
*Eastern Cross Creek* ... NJ-2
Eastern (District)—civil ... AS-9
Eastern District HS—school ... NY-2
Eastern Drunkers Ledge—bar ... ME-1
Eastern Duck Rock—island ... ME-1
Eastern Ear Island—island ... ME-1
Eastern Egg Rock—island ... ME-1
*Eastern Elem Sch* ... NC-3
Eastern Elem Sch—school ... NC-3
Eastern Female HS—hist pl ... MD-2
*Eastern Fire Tower* ... AL-4
Eastern Gate Baptist Ch—church ... AL-4
Eastern Grazing Association Number 1 Dam—dam ... SD-7
Eastern Grazing Association Number 2 Dam—dam ... SD-7
Eastern Grazing Association Number 3 Dam—dam ... SD-7
Eastern Grazing Association Number 4 Dam—dam ... SD-7
Eastern Grazing Association Number 5 Dam—dam ... SD-7
Eastern Gulch—valley ... CO-8
Eastern Hancock Elem Sch—school ... IN-6
Eastern Hancock Junior-Senior HS—school ... IN-6
*Eastern Harbor* ... MA-1
Eastern Harbor—bay ... ME-1
*Eastern Head* ... ME-1
Eastern Head—summit (2) ... ME-1
Eastern Head Ledges—bar ... ME-1
*Eastern Heights* (2) ... IN-6
*Eastern Heights* ... MI-6
*Eastern Heights* ... MN-6
**Eastern Heights**—pop pl (2) ... IN-6
**Eastern Heights**—pop pl ... NC-3
Eastern Heights Ch—church (2) ... GA-3
Eastern Heights HS—school ... KS-7
Eastern Heights Sch—school ... MN-6
Eastern Heights Sch—school ... OH-6
Eastern Hights Chapel—church ... IN-6
Eastern Hill Baptist Ch—church ... AL-4
Eastern Hill HS—school ... TX-5
Eastern Hills Baptist Ch—church ... AL-4
Eastern Hills Ch—church ... NY-2
Eastern Hills Ch—church ... OH-6
Eastern Hills Country Club—other ... TX-5
Eastern Hills Golf Course—other ... MI-6
Eastern Hills Golf Course—other ... TX-5
Eastern Hills Sch—school ... OH-6
Eastern Hills Sch—school ... TX-5
**Eastern Hills (subdivision)**—pop pl ... AL-4
**Eastern Hills (subdivision)**—pop pl ... TN-4
Eastern HS—school ... CT-1
Eastern HS—school ... DC-2
Eastern HS—school ... KY-4
Eastern HS—school ... MD-2
Eastern HS—school (2) ... MI-6
Eastern HS—school ... NJ-2
Eastern HS—school (2) ... NC-3
Eastern HS—school ... OH-6
Eastern Idaho Slough—canal ... ID-8
Eastern Iowa Central Coll—school ... IA-7
*Eastern Island* ... MI-6
Eastern Island—island ... ME-1
Eastern Jackson Sch—school ... IN-6
Eastern JHS—school ... CT-1
Eastern JHS—school ... KY-4
Eastern JHS—school ... MD-2
Eastern JHS—school ... MA-1
Eastern JHS—school ... MI-6
Eastern Junior and Senior HS—school ... IN-6
Eastern Kentucky Univ—school ... KY-4
Eastern Kentucky Univ Hist Dist—hist pl ... KY-4
*Eastern Kettle Cove* ... MA-1
Eastern Knubble—summit ... ME-1
Eastern Ladle Ledge—bar ... ME-1
Eastern Lake—lake ... FL-3
Eastern Lake—lake (2) ... ME-1
Eastern Lead—gut ... VA-3
*Eastern Ledge* ... ME-1
Eastern Ledge—bar (3) ... ME-1
Eastern Ledges—bar ... ME-1
Eastern Lock of the Chesapeake and Delaware Canal—hist pl ... DE-2
Eastern (Magisterial District)—fmr MCD ... VA-3
Eastern (Magisterial District)—fmr MCD (2) ... WV-2
Eastern Maine Med Ctr—hospital ... ME-1
Eastern Market—hist pl ... DC-2
Eastern Market Hist Dist—hist pl ... MI-6
Eastern Mark Island—island ... ME-1
Eastern Marsh Brook—stream ... ME-1
**Eastern Meadows (subdivision)**—pop pl ... AL-4
Eastern Mennonite Coll—school ... VA-3
Eastern Michigan Asylum Hist Dist—hist pl ... MI-6
Eastern Michigan Univ—school ... MI-6
Eastern Michigan Univ Hist Dist—hist pl ... MI-6
Eastern Military Acad—school ... NY-2
Eastern Montana Bible Camp—locale ... MT-8
Eastern Montana Coll—school ... MT-8
Eastern Montana Fairground—locale ... MT-8
Eastern MS—school ... NC-3
Eastern Neck—cape ... MD-2
Eastern Neck—cape ... MA-1
Eastern Neck Island—island ... MD-2
*Eastern Neck Island Narrows* ... MD-2
Eastern Neck Narrows—channel ... MD-2
Eastern Neck Natl Wildlife Ref—park ... MD-2
Eastern New Mexico Univ—school ... NM-5
Eastern New York Hosp and School—hospital ... NY-2
Eastern North Carolina Hosp—hospital ... NC-3
Eastern North Carolina Sch for Deaf—school ... NC-3
**Eastern Oklahoma A&M College**—pop pl ... OK-5
Eastern Oklahoma State Coll—school ... OK-5
Eastern Oklahoma State Hosp—hospital ... OK-5
Eastern Oklahoma State Tuberculosis Sanatorium—other ... OK-5
Eastern Oregon Coll—school ... OR-9
Eastern Oregon Livestock Exposition Grounds—park ... OR-9
Eastern Oregon State Hosp—hospital ... OR-9
Eastern Pacific Mine—mine ... MT-8
Eastern Park—park ... MI-6
Eastern Park—uninc pl ... VA-3
Eastern Parkway—hist pl ... NY-2
**Eastern Parkway**—pop pl ... NY-2
*Eastern Passage* ... RI-1
Eastern Passage—channel (2) ... AK-9
Eastern Pennsylvania Psychiatric Institue—school ... PA-2
Eastern Pequot Ind Res—reserve ... CT-1
Eastern Pilgrim Coll—school ... PA-2
Eastern Pitch—cape ... ME-1
Eastern Plain—flat ... NY-2
Eastern Plain Point—cape ... NY-2
*Eastern Point* ... CT-1
*Eastern Point* ... ME-1
Eastern Point—cape ... AK-9
Eastern Point—cape ... CT-1
Eastern Point—cape (2) ... ME-1
Eastern Point—cape ... MA-1
Eastern Point—ridge ... MA-1
Eastern Point Harbor—bay ... ME-1
Eastern Point Ledge—bar ... MA-1
Eastern Point Light—locale ... MA-1
Eastern Point Lighthouse—locale ... MA-1
Eastern Point Light Station—hist pl ... MA-1
Eastern Point Sch—school ... CT-1
Eastern Prong Middle Swamp—stream ... NC-3
Eastern Pulaski Elem Sch—school ... IN-6
Eastern Randolph HS—school ... NC-3
Eastern Regional Jetport at Stallings Field—airport ... NC-3
Eastern River—stream ... ME-1
*Eastern Rocks* ... NC-3
Eastern Rocks—bar ... ME-1
*Eastern Sch* ... IN-6
Eastern Sch—school ... CA-9
Eastern Sch—school ... GA-3
Eastern Sch—school ... KY-4
Eastern Sch—school (2) ... MI-6
Eastern Sch—school ... NC-3
Eastern Shoal—bar ... TN-4
*Eastern Shore* ... NC-3
Eastern Shore—area ... DE-2
Eastern Shore Ch—church ... VA-3
*Eastern Shore Church* ... AL-4
Eastern Shore Expermintal For—forest ... MD-2
**Eastern Shores**—pop pl ... FL-3
Eastern Shore Shop Ctr—locale ... AL-4
Eastern Shore Yacht And Country Club—other ... VA-3
Eastern Sierra Madre Ridge Archeol District—hist pl ... CA-9
Eastern Slope Inn—hist pl ... NH-1
Eastern Slough—gut ... MO-7
Eastern Star Baptist Ch—church ... IN-6
Eastern Star Baptist Church—hist pl ... NC-3
Eastern Star Cem—cemetery ... OK-5
Eastern Star Cem—cemetery (2) ... TN-4
Eastern Star Ch—church ... AR-4
Eastern Star Ch—church (4) ... MS-4
Eastern Star Ch—church ... TN-4
Eastern Star Ch Number 1—church ... LA-4
*Eastern Star Freewill Baptist Ch* ... TN-4
Eastern Star Grange Hall—locale ... OR-9
Eastern Star Home—hospital ... OH-6
Eastern Star Mine—mine ... CA-9
Eastern Star Sanitorium—hospital ... IL-6
Eastern Star Sch—school ... MN-6
Eastern Star Sch—school ... OK-5
Eastern State Fairgrounds—locale ... ID-8
Eastern State Game Farm—park ... PA-2
Eastern State Hosp—hospital ... KY-4
Eastern State Hosp—hospital ... VA-3
Eastern State Hosp—hospital ... WA-9
*Eastern State Hospital* ... TN-4
Eastern State Hospital—other ... OK-5
Eastern State Hospital Farm—locale ... TN-4
Eastern State Hospital Rsvr—reservoir ... VA-3
*Eastern State Penitentiary* ... PA-2
Eastern State Penitentiary—hist pl ... PA-2
Eastern State Psychiatric Hosp—hospital ... TN-4
Eastern State School And Hosp—hospital ... PA-2
Eastern State Wildlife Mngmt Area—park ... TN-4
Eastern Stream—stream ... ME-1
**Eastern Summit**—pop pl ... MA-1
Eastern Tennessee State University Para-Medical Center—hospital ... TN-4
Eastern Theological Seminary—school ... PA-2
**Eastern Township**—pop pl ... NE-7
**Eastern (Township of)**—pop pl ... IL-6
**Eastern (Township of)**—pop pl ... MN-6
Eastern Township State Wildlife Mngmt—park ... MN-6
Eastern Union Cem—cemetery ... NJ-2
Eastern Univ Preparatory Sch—hist pl ... OK-5
**Eastern Valley**—pop pl ... AL-4
Eastern View—locale ... VA-3
Eastern Washington Coll of Education—school ... WA-9
Eastern Way—channel ... ME-1
Eastern Wayne Elem Sch—school ... NC-3
Easter Opening—channel ... MD-2
*Easter Pageant* ... OK-5
**Easter Pageant**—pop pl ... OK-5
Easter Pasture Canyon—valley ... UT-8
Easter Point—cape ... CT-1
Easter Point—cape ... MD-2
Easter Ridge—ridge ... OR-9
**Easter Rock**—pop pl ... WI-6
Easter Run—stream ... OH-6
Easter Sch—school ... TX-5
Easter Seal Demonstration Sch—school ... FL-3
Easter Seal Handicamp—locale ... CO-8
Easter Springs—spring ... NV-8
Easter Star Cem—cemetery ... LA-4
Easter Sunday Lake—lake ... WA-9
Easter Sunday Mine—mine ... AZ-5
Easter Sunday Mine—mine ... WA-9
Easter Tank—reservoir (2) ... AZ-5
Easter Temple Ch of God in Christ—church ... MS-4
**Easter Township**—pop pl ... SD-7
Easterville Sch (historical)—school ... MO-7
Easter Windmill—locale ... TX-5
Easterwood Archeol Site—hist pl ... OK-5
Easterwood Branch—stream ... AL-4
Easterwood Mountain—ridge ... AR-4
Easterwood Mtn—summit ... AL-4
Easterwood Park—park ... MD-2
Easterwood Spring—spring ... AL-4
East Escambia (CCD)—cens area ... AL-4
East Escambia Division—civil ... AL-4
Eastes Creek—stream ... MS-4
Eastes Ditch—canal ... IN-6
East Essex Sch—school ... MI-6
East Etiwanda Canyon—valley ... CA-9
East Etiwanda Creek—stream ... CA-9
**East Etowah**—pop pl ... TN-4
East Etowah Sch (historical)—school ... TN-4
East Evacuation Creek—stream ... CO-8
East Everett—uninc pl ... MA-1
East Everett Sch—school ... WA-9
East Evergreen Sch—school ... MT-8
**East Exeter**—pop pl ... ME-1
Eastex Oaks Ch—church ... TX-5
Eastex Oaks Village—uninc pl ... TX-5
East Face—cliff ... CO-8
**East Fairchance**—pop pl ... PA-2
East Fairfax (Magisterial District)—fmr MCD ... VA-3
**East Fairfield**—pop pl ... OH-6
**East Fairfield**—pop pl ... VT-1
East Fairfield Covered Bridge—hist pl ... VT-1
**East Fairfield (Township of)**—pop pl ... PA-2
**East Fairhaven**—pop pl ... MA-1
East Fairmont—uninc pl ... VA-3
East Fairmount—locale ... KS-7
**East Fairview**—pop pl ... ND-7
East Fairview Cem—cemetery ... IA-7
East Fairview Cem—cemetery ... OK-5
East Fairview Ch—church ... NE-7
East Fairview Ch—church ... PA-2
East Fairview Ch—church ... TN-4
East Fairview Oil Field—oilfield ... MS-4
East Fairview Sch (abandoned)—school ... MO-7
East Fairview School (historical)—locale ... MO-7
East Fallowfield Elem Sch—school ... PA-2
**East Fallowfield (Township of)**—pop pl (2) ... PA-2
*East Fall River* ... KS-7
**East Falls**—pop pl ... PA-2
**East Falls Church**—pop pl ... VA-3

East Fork East Branch Saco River—stream ... NH-1
East Fork East Branch South Grand River—stream ... MO-7
East Fork East Fork Creek ... ID-8
East Fork East Fork Creek ... MT-8
East Fork East Fork Whitewater River ... OH-6
East Fork East Fork Wind River—stream ... WY-8
East Fork East Nodaway River—stream ... IA-7
East Fork East Pass Creek—stream ... WY-8
East Fork East Plum River ... IL-6
East Fork East Plum River—stream ... IL-6
East Fork East Sandy Creek—stream ... TX-5
East Fork Ecleto Creek—stream ... TX-5
East Fork Eddy Gulch—valley ... CA-9
East Fork Eden Creek—stream ... NV-8
East Forked Gulch—valley ... CO-8
East Fork Eel River ... IN-6
East Fork Eightmile Creek—stream ... CO-8
East Fork Eightmile Creek—stream ... ID-8
East Fork Eightmile Creek—stream ... UT-8
East Fork Elk Creek—stream ... CA-9
East Fork Elk Creek—stream (5) ... ID-8
East Fork Elk Creek—stream ... MT-8
East Fork Elk Creek—stream (2) ... OR-9
East Fork Elk Creek—stream ... VA-3
East Fork Elkhorn Creek—stream ... WY-8
East Fork Elk Winter Pasture HQ—locale ... WY-8
East Fork Elliot Creek ... OR-9
East Fork Elliot Creek—stream ... OR-9
East Fork Elliott Creek—stream ... TX-5
East Fork Ellis Branch—stream ... AR-4
East Fork Ellis Branch—stream ... TX-5
East Fork Ellis Canyon—valley ... MT-8
East Fork Ellis Creek ... MT-8
East Fork Elm Branch—stream ... MO-7
East Fork Elm Creek—stream ... NE-7
East Fork Elm Creek—stream ... TX-5
East Fork Elochoman River—stream ... WA-9
East Fork Elokomin River ... WA-9
East Fork Emerald Creek—stream ... ID-8
East Fork Emigrant Creek—stream ... MT-8
East Fork Encampment River—stream ... WY-8
East Fork Englebaugh Creek—stream ... MT-8
East Fork English Bayou—stream ... LA-4
East Fork Eno River—stream ... NC-3
East Fork Erskine Creek—stream ... CA-9
East Fork Escalante Creek—stream ... CO-8
East Fork Eslick Creek—stream ... OR-9
East Fork Etivluk River—stream ... AK-9
East Fork Evans Creek ... OR-9
East Fork Evans Gulch—valley ... OR-9
East Fork Fall Branch—stream ... TN-4
East Fork Fall Creek—stream ... CO-8
East Fork Fall Creek—stream (3) ... ID-8
East Fork Falling River ... VA-3
East Fork Falls—falls ... CO-8
East Fork Falls Creek—stream ... MT-8
East Fork Fan Creek—stream ... WY-8
East Fork Farm Creek—stream ... UT-8
East Fork Farmers Creek—stream ... NE-7
East Fork Fawn Creek—stream ... CO-8
East Fork Fawn Creek—stream ... WA-9
East Fork Fence Forest Creek—stream ... OR-9
East Fork Fern Creek—stream ... CA-9
East Fork Fiddler Creek—stream ... MT-8
East Fork Finley Creek—stream ... MT-8
East Fork Firebox Creek ... CO-8
East Fork First Creek—stream ... OR-9
East Fork First Creek—stream ... WA-9
East Fork Fish Canyon—valley ... CA-9
East Fork Fish Creek—stream ... CA-9
East Fork Fish Creek—stream ... CO-8
East Fork Fish Creek—stream (2) ... ID-8
East Fork Fish Creek—stream ... IN-6
East Fork Fish Creek—stream ... UT-8
East Fork Fish Creek—stream ... WA-9
East Fork Fisher Creek—stream ... ID-8
East Fork Fisher Creek—stream ... MT-8
East Fork Fishhook Creek—stream ... AK-9
East Fork Fishhook Creek—stream ... ID-8
East Fork Fishing River—stream ... MO-7
East Fork Fishtrap Creek—stream ... MT-8
East Fork Fivemile Creek—stream ... ID-8
East Fork Fivemile Creek—stream ... OH-6
East Fork Fivemile Draw—valley ... NM-5
East Fork Flag Creek—stream ... CO-8
East Fork Flag River—stream ... WI-6
East Fork Flat Creek ... TN-4
East Fork Flat Creek—stream ... AK-9
East Fork Flat Creek—stream ... ID-8
East Fork Flat Creek—stream ... KY-4
East Fork Flint Creek—stream ... AL-4
East Fork Floodwood Creek ... ID-8
East Fork Floras Creek ... OR-9
East Fork Floras Creek—stream ... OR-9
East Fork Floyds Fork—stream ... KY-4
East Fork Flynn Creek—stream ... MT-8
East Fork Flynn Fork—stream ... KY-4
East Fork Foley Creek—stream ... OR-9
East Fork Fords Creek—stream ... MT-8
East Fork Forest Service Station—locale ... MT-8
East Fork Fork Run—stream ... PA-2
East Fork Fort Goff Creek—stream ... CA-9
East Fork Fortysix Creek—stream ... MT-8
East Fork Foss River—stream ... WA-9
East Fork Fourche Creek—stream ... MO-7
East Fork Fourmile Creek—stream ... KY-4
East Fork Four Mile Creek—stream ... OH-6
East Fork Fourteenmile Creek—stream ... IN-6
East Fork Fourteenmile Creek—stream ... WV-2
East Fork Fox River—stream ... IL-6
East Fork Francs Fork—stream ... WY-8
East Fork Fremont River ... UT-8
East Fork French Broad River—stream ... NC-3
East Fork French Creek ... ID-8
East Fork French Creek—stream ... ID-8
East Fork Friday Creek—stream ... WA-9
East Fork Froze To Death Creek—stream ... MT-8
East Fork Furnace Creek—stream ... TN-4
East Fork Galena River—stream ... IL-6
East Fork Gap—gap ... NC-3
East Fork Gar Creek—stream ... AR-4
East Fork Garden Creek—stream ... MT-8
East Fork Genito Creek—stream ... VA-3
East Fork George River—stream ... AK-9
East Fork Ghost Creek—stream ... WI-6
East Fork Gila River—stream ... NM-5
East Fork Gilbert Creek—stream ... OR-9
East Fork Gimlet Creek—stream ... OR-9
East Fork Glade Creek—stream ... TX-5
East Fork Glady Fork—stream ... WV-2
East Fork Glen Creek—stream ... AK-9
East Fork Glens Creek—stream ... KY-4
East Fork Globe Creek—stream ... TN-4
East Fork Glover Creek ... OK-5
East Fork Glover River—stream ... OK-5
East Fork Gold Creek—stream (2) ... ID-8
East Fork Golden Gulch Drain—canal ... ID-8
East Fork Gonzales Creek ... TX-5
East Fork Goose Creek ... NV-8
East Fork Goose Creek ... TN-4
East Fork Goose Creek ... WY-8
East Fork Goose Creek—stream ... CA-9
East Fork Goose Creek—stream (2) ... ID-8
East Fork Goose Creek—stream ... KY-4
East Fork Goose Creek—stream ... OR-9
East Fork Goose Creek—stream ... TX-5
East Fork Goose Creek - in part ... TN-4
East Fork Goose Creek—stream ... NC-3
East Fork Government Creek—stream ... MT-8
East Fork Graham Creek ... AR-4
East Fork Graham Creek—stream ... ID-8
East Fork Graham Draw—valley ... WY-8
East Fork Grande Ronde River—stream ... OR-9
East Fork Grand River ... CO-8
East Fork Grand River*—stream ... IA-7
East Fork Grand River—stream ... MO-7
East Fork Granite Boulder Creek—stream ... OR-9
East Fork Granite Creek—stream ... CA-9
East Fork Granite Creek—stream ... MT-8
East Fork Granite Creek—stream ... NV-8
East Fork Grant Creek—stream ... MT-8
East Fork Grants Bayou—stream ... LA-4
East Fork Grape Creek—stream ... TX-5
East Fork Grasshopper Creek—stream ... MT-8
East Fork Grassy Creek—stream ... NC-3
East Fork Grave Creek—stream ... MT-8
East Fork Gravelly Creek—stream ... TX-5
East Fork Grays River ... WA-9
East Fork Grays River—stream ... WA-9
East Fork Greasewood Creek—stream ... CO-8
East Fork Greasy Creek ... AR-4
East Fork Greenbrier River—stream ... WV-2
East Fork Green Creek—stream ... CA-9
East Fork Greenlick Creek—stream ... TN-4
East Fork Green Pole Canyon—valley ... MT-8
East Fork Green River—stream ... OR-9
East Fork Greens Creek—stream ... MS-4
East Fork Greys River—stream ... WY-8
East Fork Griffin Creek—stream ... WA-9
East Fork Griffith Draw—valley ... WY-8
East Fork Grizzley Creek—stream ... CA-9
East Fork Groat Creek—stream ... MT-8
East Fork Grouse Creek—stream ... WA-9
East Fork Grove—woods ... CA-9
East Fork Guard Station—locale ... WY-8
East Fork Gunsolus Creek—stream ... TX-5
East Fork Hall Canyon—valley ... CA-9
East Fork Hall Creek—stream ... VA-3
East Fork Halls Creek—stream ... WI-6
East Fork Hamann Creek ... WI-6
East Fork Hamilton Creek—stream ... TN-4
East Fork Hampton Creek ... AR-4
East Fork Hams Fork—stream ... WY-8
East Fork Hanging Woman Creek—stream ... MT-8
East Fork Hanks Creek ... NV-8
East Fork Hardin Creek—stream ... IA-7
East Fork Hardscrabble Creek ... AZ-5
East Fork Harmon Creek—stream ... TX-5
East Fork Hart Creek ... WV-2
East Fork Harts Creek ... WV-2
East Fork Harts Run—stream ... KY-4
East Fork Harveys Creek—stream ... PA-2
East Fork Hatcher Creek—stream ... KY-4
East Fork Hatchet Creek—stream ... AL-4
East Fork Hat Creek—stream ... CA-9
East Fork Hawkins Creek ... MT-8
East Fork Hawkwright Creek—stream ... SD-7
East Fork Hay Creek—stream ... SD-7
East Fork Hay Creek—stream ... WI-6
East Fork Hay Creek—stream (2) ... WY-8
East Fork Hayden Creek—stream (2) ... ID-8
East Fork Hayfork Creek—stream ... CA-9
East Fork Hay Gulch ... CO-8
East Fork Haymaker Creek ... MT-8
East Fork Haymaker Creek—stream ... MT-8
East Fork Hell Creek ... MT-8
East Fork Hell Creek—stream ... MT-8
East Fork Hellroaring Creek—stream ... MT-8
East Fork Hemlock Creek—stream ... CA-9
East Fork Hemlock Creek—stream ... WI-6
East Fork Henshaw Creek—stream ... AK-9
East Fork Henshaw (Sozhekla)—stream ... AK-9
East Fork Herd Creek ... ID-8
East Fork Herd Creek—stream ... ID-8
East Fork Herman Creek—stream ... OR-9
East Fork Hermosa Creek—stream ... CO-8
East Fork Hess Draw—valley ... AZ-5
East Fork Hewitt Creek—stream ... OR-9
East Fork Hicks Creek—stream ... TN-4
East Fork Higgins Creek—stream ... TN-4
East Fork Higgins Gulch—valley ... SD-7
East Fork High Prairie Creek—stream ... OR-9
East Fork High Rock Canyon ... NV-8
East Fork Hill—summit ... KY-4
East Fork Hills—other ... AK-9
East Fork Hilton Creek—stream ... ID-8
East Fork Hines Branch—stream ... TX-5
East Fork Hoe Ranch Arroyo—stream ... CO-8
East Fork Hog Creek ... TX-5
East Fork Holy Terror Creek—stream ... ID-8
East Fork Homestake Creek—stream ... CO-8
East Fork Honey Creek ... MO-7
East Fork Honey Creek—stream ... IN-6
East Fork Honey Creek—stream ... MO-7
East Fork Honey Creek—stream ... OH-6
East Fork Honeydew Creek—stream ... CA-9
East Fork Hood River—stream ... OR-9
East Fork Hoop Creek—stream ... TN-4
East Fork Hopkins Branch—stream ... VA-3
East Fork Hopley Creek—stream ... MT-8
East Fork Hoquiam River—stream ... WA-9
East Fork Horn Creek—stream ... ID-8
East Fork Horse Canyon ... UT-8
East Fork Horse Canyon—valley ... CA-9
East Fork Horse Canyon—valley ... CO-8
East Fork Horse Creek—stream ... CA-9
East Fork Horse Creek—stream ... ID-8
East Fork Horse Creek—stream (2) ... MT-8
East Fork Horse Creek—stream (2) ... OR-9
East Fork Horse Creek—stream ... TX-5
East Fork Horse Creek—stream ... WY-8
East Fork Horsefly Creek—stream ... CO-8
East Fork Horsehead Creek—stream ... AR-4
East Fork Horse Linto Creek—stream ... CA-9
East Fork Horse Ranch Creek—stream ... WY-8
East Fork Horseshoe Draw—valley ... WY-8
East Fork Horton Creek—stream ... AZ-5
East Fork Hotel Creek—stream ... ID-8
East Fork Hound Creek ... MT-8
East Fork Hound Creek—stream ... MT-8
East Fork Howard Creek—stream (2) ... OR-9
East Fork Howard Draw—valley ... TX-5
East Fork Hudlow Creek—stream ... ID-8
East Fork Hulsey Branch—stream ... TN-4
East Fork Humboldt River ... NV-8
East Fork Humboldt River - in part ... NV-8
East Fork Humptulips River—stream ... WA-9
East Fork Hundred And Two River ... IA-7
East Fork Hundred and Two River ... MO-7
East Fork Hunt Creek—stream ... UT-8
East Fork Hunters Creek—stream ... TX-5
East Fork Hurricane Creek—stream ... KY-4
East Fork Hurricane Creek—stream (2) ... TN-4
East Fork Huzzah Creek—stream ... MO-7
East Fork Hyalite Creek—stream ... MT-8
East Fork Illinois Bayou—stream ... AR-4
East Fork Illinois River—stream ... CA-9
East Fork Illinois River—stream ... OR-9
East Fork Immells Creek ... MT-8
East Fork Index Creek—stream ... WA-9
East Fork Indian Creek ... ID-8
East Fork Indian Creek ... IN-6
East Fork Indian Creek—stream (2) ... AK-9
East Fork Indian Creek—stream ... CA-9
East Fork Indian Creek—stream (3) ... ID-8
East Fork Indian Creek—stream ... KY-4
East Fork Indian Creek—stream (3) ... MT-8
East Fork Indian Creek—stream (4) ... OR-9
East Fork Indian Creek—stream ... TX-5
East Fork Indian Grave Creek—stream ... VA-3
East Fork Indigo Creek—stream ... OR-9
East Fork Institute (historical)—school ... MS-4
East Fork Iron Creek—stream ... AK-9
East Fork Iron River—stream ... WI-6
East Fork Irrigation District Canal ... OR-9
East Fork Irving Creek ... ID-8
East Fork Issaquah Creek—stream ... WA-9
East Fork Jack River—stream ... AK-9
East Fork James Creek—stream ... ID-8
East Fork James River ... TX-5
East Fork Jarbidge River—stream ... ID-8
East Fork Jarbidge River—stream ... NV-8
East Fork Jemez River—stream ... NM-5
East Fork Jenkins Creek—stream (2) ... MO-7
East Fork Jenkins Creek—stream ... NC-3
East Fork Jenkins Draw—valley ... WY-8
East Fork Jernigan Creek—stream ... TX-5
East Fork Jester Creek—stream ... KS-7
East Fork Joe Branch—stream ... TN-4
East Fork Joe Creek—stream ... WA-9
East Fork John Day Creek—stream ... ID-8
East Fork Johnson Creek—stream ... MT-8
East Fork Johnson Creek—stream ... VA-3
East Fork Jones Creek—stream ... OR-9
East Fork Jones Creek—stream ... TX-5
East Fork Jones Creek—stream ... WY-8
East Fork Jordan Branch—stream ... MO-7
East Fork Jordan Creek—stream ... WY-8
East Fork Joseph Creek ... OR-9
East Fork Jubb Creek—stream ... CO-8
East Fork Juniper Creek—stream ... CA-9
East Fork Juniper Creek—stream ... FL-3
East Fork Kahiltna Glacier—glacier ... AK-9
East Fork Kalaloch Creek ... WA-9
East Fork Kalaloch Creek—stream ... WA-9
East Fork Kane Creek—stream ... OR-9
East Fork Kaskaskia River—stream ... IL-6
East Fork Kate Creek—stream ... MT-8
East Fork Kate Creek Springs—spring ... MT-8
East Fork Kaweah River ... CA-9
East Fork Kaweah River—stream ... CA-9
East Fork Kawela Gulch—valley ... HI-9
East Fork Keechi Creek—stream ... TX-5
East Fork Keg Creek—stream ... IN-6
East Fork Kejulik River—stream ... AK-9
East Fork Kelly Bayou—stream ... AR-4
East Fork Kelsey Creek—stream ... OR-9
East Fork Kennally Creek—stream ... ID-8
East Fork Kenney Creek—stream ... OR-9
East Fork Kent Branch—stream ... VA-3
East Fork Kern River ... CA-9
East Fork Kiagna River—stream ... AK-9
East Fork Kimball Creek—stream ... WA-9
East Fork King Arroyo—stream ... CO-8
East Fork King Hill Creek—stream ... ID-8
East Fork Kingsbury Gulch—valley ... CA-9
East Fork Kirtley Creek—stream ... ID-8
East Fork Knoblick Creek—stream ... KY-4
East Fork Knownothing Creek—stream ... CA-9
East Fork Koontz Creek—stream ... OR-9
East Fork Koyuk River—stream ... AK-9
East Fork Kruse Creek—stream ... WY-8
East Fork Kuskokwim River—stream ... AK-9
East Fork Kutz Canyon—valley ... NM-5
East Fork Kuyukutuk River—stream ... AK-9
East Fork Lacamas Creek—stream ... WA-9
East Fork Ladd Canyon—valley ... CA-9
East Fork Lagunitas Creek—stream ... CA-9
East Fork Lake—reservoir ... OH-6
East Fork Lake Bayou ... LA-4
East Fork Lake Canyon—stream ... UT-8
East Fork Lake Creek—stream ... MT-8
East Fork Lake Creek—stream ... WY-8
East Fork Lake Fork—stream ... ID-8
East Fork Lakes—lake ... CA-9
East Fork La Marche Creek—stream ... MT-8
East Fork Lame Deer Creek—stream ... MT-8
East Fork La Moine River—stream ... IL-6
East Fork Langford Creek—stream ... MD-2
East Fork Larson Draw—valley ... AZ-5
East Fork Last Chance Creek—stream ... CA-9
East Fork Laurel Branch—stream ... TN-4
East Fork Laurel Creek—stream ... NC-3
East Fork Lawrence Creek—stream ... LA-4
East Fork Layng Creek—stream ... OR-9
East Fork Lazy Creek—stream ... MT-8
East Fork Leatherwood Creek—stream (2) ... TN-4
East Fork Lee Creek—stream ... MT-8
East Fork Lees Creek—stream ... WA-9
East Fork Lehman Creek—stream ... ID-8
East Fork Lemonweir River ... WI-6
East Fork Lemonweir River—stream ... WI-6
East Fork Lena Creek—stream ... WA-9
East Fork Leopard Creek—stream ... CO-8
East Fork LeRoy Creek—stream ... WI-6
East Fork Lewis Creek—stream ... CA-9
East Fork Lewis Creek—stream ... MS-4
East Fork Lewis Fork ... NC-3
East Fork Lewis River—stream ... WA-9
East Fork Lick Creek—stream ... TN-4
East Fork Lick Run—stream ... TN-4
East Fork Lightning Creek ... ID-8
East Fork Lightning Creek ... MT-8
East Fork Ligias Creek—stream ... TN-4
East Fork Ligias Creek - in part ... TN-4
East Fork Lion Canyon—valley ... CO-8
East Fork Lion Creek—stream ... MT-8
East Fork Little Barren River—stream ... KY-4
East Fork Little Bear Creek—stream ... MO-7
East Fork Little Bear River—stream ... UT-8
East Fork Little Bigby Creek—stream ... TN-4
East Fork Little Blue Creek—stream ... CO-8
East Fork Little Blue River—stream ... MO-7
East Fork Little Bogue Falaya—stream ... LA-4
East Fork Little Bremner River—stream ... AK-9
East Fork Little Buffalo Creek ... AR-4
East Fork Little Buffalo River—stream ... AR-4
East Fork Little Cane Creek—stream ... TN-4
East Fork Little Chariton River—stream ... MO-7
East Fork Little Cimarron River—stream ... CO-8
East Fork Little Clifty Creek ... AR-4
East Fork Little Colorado River—stream ... AZ-5
East Fork Little Cottonwood Creek—stream ... SD-7
East Fork Little Creek—stream ... NC-3
East Fork Little Creek—stream ... UT-8
East Fork Little Deer Creek—stream ... WY-8
East Fork Little Delta River—stream ... AK-9
East Fork Little Elk Creek—stream ... TN-4
East Fork Little Elkhart Creek ... TX-5
East Fork Little Goose Creek—stream ... WY-8
East Fork Little Gravois Creek—stream ... MO-7
East Fork Little Lusk Creek—stream ... IL-6
East Fork Little Miami River—stream ... OH-6
East Fork Little Muddy Creek ... ND-7
East Fork Little Muddy Creek—stream (2) ... CO-8
East Fork Little Muddy Gulch—valley ... CO-8
East Fork Little Muddy River—stream ... ND-7
East Fork Little North Fork Clearwater River ... ID-8
East Fork Little Pass Creek—stream ... WY-8
East Fork Little Pigeon Creek—stream ... IN-6
East Fork Little Pigeon River—stream ... TN-4
East Fork Little Porcupine Creek—stream (2) ... MT-8
East Fork Little Poteau Creek ... AR-4
East Fork Little Powder River ... MT-8
East Fork Little Powder River ... WY-8
East Fork Little Powder River—stream ... MT-8
East Fork Little Pumpkin Creek—stream ... MT-8
East Fork Little Reed Island Creek—stream ... VA-3
East Fork Little River ... SC-3
East Fork Little River—stream ... AL-4
East Fork Little River—stream (2) ... GA-3
East Fork Little Roanoke Creek ... VA-3
East Fork Little Sand Creek—stream ... UT-8
East Fork Little Sandy River—stream ... KY-4
East Fork Little Sheep Creek—stream ... MT-8
East Fork Little Soda Canyon—valley ... CO-8
East Fork Little Tarkio Creek—stream ... MO-7
East Fork Little Tongue River—stream ... WY-8
East Fork Little Tonzona River—stream ... AK-9
East Fork Little Washougal River—stream ... WA-9
East Fork Little Wichita River—stream ... TX-5
East Fork Little Wildcat Creek—stream ... IN-6
East Fork Lizard Canyon—valley ... CA-9
East Fork Lobster Creek—stream ... OR-9
East Fork L O Creek—stream ... MT-8
East Fork Lolo Creek ... ID-8
East Fork Lolo Creek—stream ... MT-8
East Fork Long Arroyo—stream ... NM-5
East Fork Long Branch Creek—stream ... MT-8
East Fork Long Creek—stream (2) ... WY-8
East Fork Longfork Creek—stream ... MT-8
East Fork Long Tom Creek—stream ... ID-8
East Fork Lookout—hist pl ... ID-8
East Fork Lookout Creek—stream ... AL-4
East Fork Lookout Creek—stream ... MT-8
East Fork Loon Creek ... ID-8
East Fork Los Pinos Creek—stream ... CO-8
East Fork Lost Creek ... MO-7
East Fork Lost Creek—stream ... AL-4
East Fork Lost Creek—stream (2) ... ID-8
East Fork Lost Creek—stream (2) ... MO-7
East Fork Lost River ... CA-9
East Fork Lost River ... OR-9
East Fork Love Creek—stream ... OR-9
East Fork Luce Creek—stream ... OR-9
East Fork Lukfata Creek—stream ... OK-5
East Fork Luna Creek—stream ... NM-5
East Fork Lunt Branch—stream ... TN-4
East Fork Lynn Camp Creek—stream ... KY-4
East Fork Lynn Creek—stream ... TN-4
East Fork Lyons Creek—stream ... TN-4
East Fork Lysite Creek—stream ... WY-8
East Fork Maclaren River—stream ... AK-9
East Fork Magruder Creek—stream ... ID-8
East Fork Main Canal—canal ... OR-9
East Fork Major Creek—stream ... WA-9
East Fork Manatee River—stream ... FL-3
East Fork Mancos River ... CO-8
East Fork Mansker Creek ... TN-4
East Fork Maple Creek—stream ... NE-7
East Fork Maria Ygnacio Creek—stream ... CA-9
East Fork Marsh Bog Brook—stream ... NJ-2
East Fork Martins Creek—stream ... PA-2
East Fork Marys Creek—stream ... WY-8
East Fork Marys Lake Creek ... WY-8
East Fork Marys River—stream ... NV-8
East Fork Marys River—stream ... OR-9
East Fork Massac Creek ... KY-4
East Fork Matanuska River—stream ... AK-9
East Fork Mayfield Creek—stream ... ID-8
East Fork Mazon River—stream ... IL-6
East Fork McAlester Creek—stream ... WA-9
East Fork McCabe Creek—stream ... MT-8
East Fork McCanyon—valley ... AZ-5
East Fork McCarthy Creek—stream ... AK-9
East Fork McClellan Creek—stream ... MT-8
East Fork McCoin Creek—stream ... OR-9
East Fork McConnell Run—stream ... KY-4
East Fork McCreedy Creek—stream ... WA-9
East Fork McDermotts Gulch—valley ... WY-8
East Fork McGrady Creek—stream ... KY-4
East Fork McKay Creek—stream ... MT-8
East Fork McKay Creek—stream ... OR-9
East Fork Mc Kenzie Creek—stream ... CO-8
East Fork Meacham Creek ... OR-9
East Fork Meadow Brook—stream ... OR-9
East Fork Meadow Creek ... ID-8
East Fork Meadow Creek—stream (5) ... ID-8
East Fork Meadow Creek—stream ... MT-8
East Fork Meadow Creek—stream ... WA-9
East Fork Medicine Bow River—stream ... WY-8
East Fork Medicine Creek ... MO-7
East Fork Medicine Creek*—stream ... IA-7
East Fork Medicine Creek—stream ... MO-7
East Fork Mendenhall Creek—stream ... MT-8
East Fork Merry Creek ... ID-8
East Fork Mica Creek—stream ... ID-8
East Fork Middle Cottonwood Creek—stream ... WY-8
East Fork Middle Creek—stream ... CA-9
East Fork Middle Fork Stewart Gulch—valley ... CO-8
East Fork Middle Sandy Creek—stream ... TX-5
East Fork Mikes Canyon—valley ... UT-8
East Fork Milk Creek—stream ... WA-9
East Fork Milk River ... MT-8
East Fork Millard Canyon—valley ... UT-8
East Fork Mill Creek ... TX-5
East Fork Mill Creek—stream ... AL-4
East Fork Mill Creek—stream ... CA-9
East Fork Mill Creek—stream ... IL-6
East Fork Mill Creek—stream (2) ... IN-6
East Fork Mill Creek—stream ... KY-4
East Fork Mill Creek—stream (2) ... MT-8
East Fork Mill Creek—stream ... NV-8
East Fork Mill Creek—stream ... OH-6
East Fork Mill Creek—stream ... OR-9
East Fork Miller Creek—stream ... MT-8
East Fork Miller Creek—stream ... WA-9
East Fork Miller River ... WA-9
East Fork Miller River—stream ... WA-9
East Fork Mill Hollow—valley ... UT-8
East Fork Millicoma River—stream ... OR-9
East Fork Milsap Creek—stream ... CO-8
East Fork Mimbres River—stream ... NM-5
East Fork Minam Creek ... OR-9
East Fork Mineral Creek—stream ... AK-9
East Fork Mineral Creek—stream ... MT-8
East Fork Miners Creek—stream ... OR-9
East Fork Mingamahone Brook—stream ... NJ-2
East Fork Mink Creek—stream ... ID-8
East Fork Minneconjou Creek—stream ... SD-7
East Fork Minnesota Creek—stream ... CO-8
East Fork Minnow Creek—stream ... OR-9
East Fork Mission Creek—stream (2) ... ID-8
East Fork Mission Creek—stream ... WA-9
East Fork Mission Sch—school ... AZ-5
East Fork Moffit Creek—stream ... UT-8
East Fork Monture Creek—stream ... MT-8
East Fork Moon Creek—stream ... MT-8
East Fork Moores Creek—stream ... ID-8
East Fork Moose Creek—stream ... AK-9
East Fork Moose Creek—stream ... ID-8
East Fork Moose River—stream ... WI-6
East Fork Morgan Creek—stream ... ID-8
East Fork Morgan Gulch—valley ... CO-8
East Fork Morro Creek—stream ... CA-9
East Fork Mosby Creek—stream ... OR-9
East Fork Moses Creek—stream ... NC-3
East Fork Mosetown Creek—stream ... OR-9
East Fork Mosier Creek ... OR-9
East Fork Mosquito River—stream ... AK-9
East Fork Mountain Home Creek—stream ... CA-9
East Fork Mtn—summit ... CA-9
East Fork Mud Creek—stream ... CO-8
East Fork Mud Creek—stream ... MT-8
East Fork Mudd Creek—stream ... MT-8
East Fork Muddy Creek ... WY-8
East Fork Muddy Creek—stream ... KS-7
East Fork Muddy Creek—stream ... MT-8
East Fork Muddy Creek—stream ... OR-9
East Fork Muir Creek—stream ... OR-9
East Fork Mujares Creek—stream ... TX-5
East Fork Mukewater Creek—stream ... TX-5
Eastfork Mulberry Creek ... AL-4
East Fork Mulberry Creek—stream ... TN-4
East Fork Mule Creek—stream ... SD-7
East Fork Muscatatuck River ... IN-6
East Fork Mustang Creek ... TX-5
East Fork Mustang Creek—stream ... TX-5
East Fork Myers Creek—stream ... WA-9
East Fork Nara Visa Arroyo—stream ... NM-5
East Fork Nasel Creek ... WA-9
East Fork Naselle River ... WA-9
East Fork Nasel River ... WA-9
East Fork Navajo Canyon—valley ... CO-8
East Fork Navajo River—stream ... CO-8
East Fork Navarre Creek—stream ... ID-8
East Fork Neal Creek ... OR-9
East Fork Nehalem River—stream ... OR-9
East Fork Nelson Creek—stream ... CA-9
East Fork Neosho River ... KS-7
East Fork Nettle Creek—stream ... IL-6
East Fork Newhalem Creek—stream ... WA-9
East Fork New River—stream ... CA-9
East Fork New Wood River—stream ... WI-6
East Fork Nianguo River—stream ... MO-7
East Fork Nicks Creek—stream ... VA-3
East Fork Ninemile Creek—stream ... CO-8
East Fork Ninemile Creek—stream ... ID-8
East Fork Ninuluk Creek—stream ... AK-9
East Fork No Mouth Creek—stream ... SD-7
East Fork Nookachamps Creek—stream ... WA-9
East Fork North Canyon—valley ... UT-8
East Fork North Canyon Creek—stream ... AZ-5
East Fork North Creek—stream ... UT-8
East Fork North Elk Creek—stream ... CO-8
East Fork North Fork Big Wood River—stream ... ID-8
East Fork North Fork Blackfoot River—stream ... MT-8
East Fork North Fork Embarrass River ... IL-6
East Fork North Fork Lewis River—stream ... CA-9
East Fork North Fork Mad River—stream ... CA-9
East Fork North Fork of North Fork American River—stream ... CA-9
East Fork North Fork Squaw Creek—stream ... CA-9
East Fork North Fork Teton River—stream ... MT-8
East Fork North Fork Trinity River—stream ... CA-9
East Fork North Mouse Creek—stream ... TN-4
East Fork North River—stream ... WA-9
East Fork No Two Draw—valley ... WY-8
East Fork No Water Creek ... WY-8
East Fork Nowater Creek—stream ... WY-8
East Fork Obey River—stream ... TN-4
East Fork O'Dell Creek—stream ... MT-8
East Fork O'Fallon Creek—stream ... MT-8
East Fork of Blue River ... KS-7
East Fork Of Blue River ... NE-7
East Fork of Canon Creek ... CA-9
East Fork of Chetco River ... OR-9
East Fork of Coast Fork of Willamette River ... OR-9
East Fork of East Fork Creek ... ID-8
East Fork Of East Fork Of Whitewater River ... OH-6
East Fork of Firehole River ... WY-8
East Fork of Hunter Creek ... ID-8
East Fork of Kaweah River ... CA-9
East Fork Of Nisqually River ... WA-9
East Fork of North Fork Desolation Creek—stream ... OR-9
East Fork of North Fork Trinity River ... CA-9
East Fork of North Fork Yuba River ... CA-9
East Fork of Point Remove Creek ... AR-4
East Fork of Right Prong Black Bayou—stream ... LA-4
East Fork of South Fork Saint Joe River ... ID-8
East Fork of South Fork Trask River ... OR-9
East Fork of Stuart Fork ... CA-9
East Fork of the Bear- Boy Scouts of America Camp ... UT-8
East Fork of the Cowlitz River ... WA-9
East Fork of The Forks—stream ... AK-9
East Fork of the San Jacinto River ... TX-5
East Fork of the Trinity River ... TX-5
East Fork of the Yellowstone River ... WY-8
East Fork of Trinity River ... TX-5
East Fork of Weaver Creek ... CA-9
East Fork of West Fork ... MT-8
East Fork of West Fork Cow Creek—stream ... OR-9
East Fork of White River ... IN-6
East Fork O'Hara Creek—stream ... ID-8
East Fork Oldman Creek—gut ... NJ-2
East Fork Old Mans Gulch—valley ... CO-8
East Fork Oliver Creek—stream ... CO-8
East Fork Olsen Bay Creek—stream ... AK-9
East Fork O'Neal Creek—stream ... TX-5
East Fork One Hundred and Two River—stream ... IA-7
East Fork One Hundred and Two River—stream ... MO-7
East Fork Oolamnagavik River—stream ... AK-9
East Fork Osier Creek ... ID-8
East Fork Oswego Creek—stream ... MT-8
East Fork Otter Creek—stream ... IL-6
East Fork Otter Creek—stream (2) ... KY-4
East Fork Otter Creek—stream ... MT-8
East Fork Overalls Creek—stream ... KY-4
East Fork Overflow Creek—stream ... NC-3
East Fork Owl Creek—stream ... ID-8
East Fork Owyhee River ... ID-8
East Fork Owyhee River ... NV-8
East Fork Owyhee River ... OR-9
East Fork Oyster Bayou—stream ... TX-5
East Fork Pacheco Creek—stream ... CA-9
East Fork Packer Creek—stream ... MT-8
East Fork Pahsimeroi River—stream ... ID-8
East Fork Paint Creek—stream ... OH-6
East Fork Painter Gulch—valley ... WY-8
East Fork Palisades Creek—stream ... ID-8
East Fork Palisades Creek—stream ... WY-8
East Fork Palm Canyon—valley ... CA-9
East Fork Panther Creek—stream ... FL-3
East Fork Panther Creek—stream ... OR-9
East Fork Panther Creek—stream ... TN-4
East Fork Panther Creek—stream ... VA-3
East Fork Papoose Creek—stream ... CA-9
East Fork Papoose Creek—stream ... ID-8
East Fork Parachute Creek—stream ... CO-8
East Fork Parashant Wash—valley ... AZ-5
East Fork Park—park ... TX-5
East Fork Park Creek—stream ... OR-9
East Fork Parks Creek—stream ... ID-8
East Fork Pasayten River—stream ... WA-9
East Fork Pass—gap ... MT-8
East Fork Pass—gap ... WY-8
East Fork Pass Creek—stream ... WY-8
East Fork Pasture Creek—stream ... MT-8
East Fork Pataha Creek ... WA-9
East Fork Patrick Bayou—stream ... TX-5
East Fork Patrick Creek—stream ... CA-9
East Fork Pats Creek—stream ... TX-5
East Fork Patterson Creek—stream ... ID-8
East Fork Peak—summit ... ID-8
East Fork Peak—summit ... MT-8
East Fork Peavine Creek—stream ... OR-9
East Fork Pecan Creek—stream ... TX-5
East Fork Pecwan Creek—stream ... CA-9
East Fork Peet Creek—stream ... MT-8
East Fork Pen Creek—stream ... TX-5
East Fork Pentagon Creek—stream ... MT-8
East Fork Peterson Creek—stream ... MT-8
East Fork Petty Creek—stream ... MT-8
East Fork Phoenix Park Canyon—valley ... AZ-5
East Fork Pickleweg Creek—stream ... UT-8
East Fork Piedra River—stream ... CO-8
East Fork Pierce Creek—stream ... ID-8
East Fork Pigeon River—stream ... NC-3
East Fork Pigeon Roost Branch—stream ... KY-4
East Fork Pike Run—stream ... OH-6
East Fork Pilgrim Creek—stream ... WY-8
East Fork Pilot Grove Creek—stream ... TX-5
East Fork Pine Branch—stream ... MO-7
East Fork Pine Creek ... CO-8
East Fork Pine Creek ... ID-8

East Fork Pine Creek—*stream* (2)............ ID-8
East Fork Pine Creek—*stream* (2)............ OR-9
East Fork Pine Swamp Creek—*stream* ...... NC-3
East Fork Piney Creek—*stream*.................. CA-9
East Fork Piney Creek—*stream*................ WY-8
East Fork Piney Fork—*stream*................. OH-6
East Fork Pinhook Creek—*stream* ............ AL-4
East Fork Pinos Creek—*stream* ................ CO-8
East Fork Pinto Lake Trail—*trail*..............UT-8
East Fork Pipe Creek—*stream* ..................MT-8
*East Fork Piquett Creek*...............................MT-8
*East Fork Pistol Creek* .................................OR-9
East Fork Pistol River—*stream*................ OR-9
*East Fork Pitman Creek* ...............................KY-4
East Fork Pit No 3—*basin*........................ WY-8
East Fork Platte Creek—*stream* ............... SD-7
East Fork Pleasant Bayou—*stream*..............TX-5
East Fork Pleasant Valley Creek—*stream* ... ID-8
East Fork Plumb Bush Creek—*stream*........ CO-8
East Fork Plum Creek—*stream*.................. SD-7
East Fork Point—*cliff*................................ WY-8
East Fork Point Remove Creek—*stream* ...... AR-4
East Fork Pole Creek—*stream* (2)..............MT-8
East Fork Pole Creek—*stream*....................NV-8
East Fork Pole Creek—*stream*................... OR-9
East Fork Pole Creek—*stream*.................. WY-8
East Fork Pollock Canyon—*valley* ............ CO-8
East Fork Pond Creek—*stream*.................. TN-4
East Fork Pond Creek—*stream*....................TX-5
East Fork Pond Fork—*stream*.................... GA-3
*East Fork Pond River* .................................. KY-4
East Fork Pond Run—*stream* ...................OH-6
East Fork Poole Creek—*stream*................. OR-9
East Fork Popes Head Creek—*stream* ........ VA-3
East Fork Poplar Creek—*stream*................ TN-4
*East Fork Poplar River*................................. WI-6
East Fork Poplar River—*stream*..................MT-8
East Fork Popple River—*stream*................. WI-6
East Fork Porcupine Creek—*stream*............MT-8
East Fork Portuguese Creek—*stream*.......... CA-9
*East Fork Postoak Creek*............................ MO-7
East Fork Post Oak Creek—*stream* .......... MO-7
East Fork Post Office
(historical)—*building* ........................... MS-4
East Fork Potato Patch Draw—*valley* ........ AZ-5
East Fork Poteau River—*stream*................ AR-4
East Fork Potlatch River—*stream* ............. ID-8
*East Fork Pouderhorn Creek*....................... CO-8
*East Fork Powderhorn Creek* ...................... CO-8
East Fork Powderhorn Creek—*stream* ........ CO-8
East Fork Powell Creek—*stream* ............... AR-4
*East Fork Prairie Creek* .............................. IN-6
East Fork Prairie Creek—*stream*.................LA-4
East Fork Prairie Elk Creek—*stream*...........MT-8
East Fork Prather Creek—*stream* .............. OR-9
East Fork Premo Creek—*stream*................. MI-6
East Fork Prince Creek—*stream* ................WA-9
*East Fork Pryor Creek*..................................MT-8
East Fork Pryor Creek—*stream* ................MT-8
East Fork Public Campground
(historical)—*locale* ................................ID-8
*East Fork Puckatunna Creek*.......................MS-4
East Fork Pumpkin Creek—*stream* .............TX-5
East Fork Pushepatapa Creek—*stream* .......LA-4
East Fork Pushepatapa Creek—*stream*........MS-4
East Fork Quanah Creek—*stream*............... OK-5
East Fork Quarry Creek—*stream*................ OR-9
East Fork Quartz Creek—*stream* ...............MT-8
East Fork Queer Creek—*stream*................ OH-6
*East Fork Quinault River*..............................WA-9
East Fork Quinn River—*stream* .................NV-8
East Fork Quinn River—*stream* ................ OR-9
East Fork Quitchupah Creek—*stream*..........UT-8
East Fork Raccoon Creek—*stream* ............ WI-6
East Fork Raft Creek—*stream*................... KY-4
East Fork Ranch Creek—*stream* .................TX-5
East Fork Ranger Branch—*stream* ..............TX-5
East Fork Rapid River—*stream* ................. MN-6
East Fork Rat Creek—*stream* .................... OR-9
*East Fork Rat Root River* ............................ MN-6
*East Fork Rattlesnake Creek* ........................UT-8
East Fork Rattlesnake Creek—*stream* ........ CA-9
East Fork Rattlesnake Creek—*stream* ......... ID-8
East Fork Rattlesnake Creek—*stream* ......... KS-7
East Fork Rattlesnake Creek—*stream*..........MT-8
East Fork Rattlesnake Creek—*stream*......... OH-6
East Fork Rattlesnake Creek—*stream* ........ OR-9
East Fork Rattlesnake Creek
(distributary)—*stream*........................... OR-9
East Fork Rattlesnake Gulch—*valley* ......... OR-9
East Fork Rawhide Creek—*stream* ............ OR-9
East Fork Razor Creek—*stream* .................MT-8
East Fork Rec Area—*park*.......................... WI-6
East Fork Red Canyon—*valley*.....................ID-8
East Fork Red Canyon—*valley* (2) ..............UT-8
East Fork Red Canyon Creek—*stream* ........ CO-8
East Fork Red Creek—*stream* ................... CO-8
East Fork Red Dirt Creek—*stream*.............. CO-8
*East Fork Red River* ....................................ID-8
East Fork Red River—*stream* .................... NM-5
East Fork Relief Creek—*stream*...................ID-8
East Fork Reservation Creek—*stream* .........MT-8
*East Fork Reservoir*.................................... OH-6
*East Fork Reservoir Creek*............................ ID-8
East Fork Revais Creek—*stream* ...............MT-8
East Fork Reynolds Creek—*stream* (2) ........ ID-8
East Fork Rhett Creek—*stream* ................. ID-8
East Fork Richland Creek—*stream* ............. TN-4
East Fork Ridge—*ridge*............................. CA-9
East Fork Ridge—*ridge*............................. OR-9
East Fork Ridge—*ridge*............................. TN-4
East Fork Rio Brazos—*stream*.................... NM-5
*East Fork Rio Chama* ................................. CO-8
East Fork Rio Chama—*stream* .................. CO-8
East Fork Rio Santa Barbara—*stream* ....... NM-5
*East Fork River* ......................................... SD-7
*East Fork River*..........................................WY-8
East Fork River—*stream*.......................... WY-8
East Fork Roaring Creek—*stream*.............. CO-8
East Fork Roaring Fork—*stream*................ NC-3
East Fork Roaring River—*stream*................ ID-8
*East Fork Roaring Run* ............................... WV-2
East Fork Roaring Run—*stream*................. PA-2
East Fork Roark Creek—*stream*................ MO-7
East Fork Roatcap Gulch—*valley*............... CO-8
East Fork Roberts Creek—*stream*...............MT-8
East Fork Roberts Creek—*stream*.............. VA-3
East Fork Robinson Canyon—*valley*........... NV-8
East Fork Roblas Canyon—*valley*................ AZ-5
East Fork Rock Canyon—*valley*.................. CO-8
*East Fork Rock Creek* ................................. KS-7
*East Fork Rock Creek*..................................MT-8
*East Fork Rock Creek* ................................. OR-9
*East Fork Rock Creek* .................................WA-9
*East Fork Rock Creek* ................................. WY-8
East Fork Rock Creek—*stream* .................. CA-9
East Fork Rock Creek—*stream* .................. CO-8
East Fork Rock Creek—*stream* (3) ............. ID-8
East Fork Rock Creek—*stream* ................. MO-7
East Fork Rock Creek—*stream* (3) .............MT-8
East Fork Rock Creek—*stream* ................. NV-8
East Fork Rock Creek—*stream* (2) ............ OR-9
East Fork Rock Creek—*stream* .................. TX-5
East Fork Rock Creek—*stream* .................. UT-8
East Fork Rock Creek—*stream* ................. WY-8
East Fork Rockhouse Creek—*stream*.......... KY-4
East Fork Rocky Creek—*stream* ................. TX-5
East Fork Rocky Draw—*valley* .................. AZ-5
East Fork Rollins Creek—*stream* .............. MO-7
East Fork Roseberry Ditch—*canal*.............. ID-8
East Fork Rosebud Gulch—*valley* .............. ID-8
*East Fork Rossman Creek* ........................... WI-6
East Fork Roubidoux Creek—*stream* ........ MO-7
East Fork Rough Creek—*stream* ................ TN-4
East Fork Round Corral Creek—*stream* ..... NV-8
East Fork Rsvr—*reservoir* (3)...................MT-8
East Fork Rsvr—*reservoir* (2)................... OR-9
East Fork Rsvr No 1—*reservoir* ................ WY-8
East Fork Rsvr No 3—*reservoir* ................ WY-8
East Fork Rsvr No 4—*reservoir* ................ WY-8
East Fork Rsvr No 5—*reservoir* ................ WY-8
East Fork Rsvr No 6—*reservoir* ................ WY-8
East Fork Ruby Creek—*stream*.................. SD-7
East Fork Ruby River—*stream* .................MT-8
East Fork Rum Creek—*stream* .................. OR-9
East Fork Run—*stream* ............................ PA-2
*East Fork Rush Creek* .................................. ID-8
East Fork Rush Creek—*stream* .................. IN-6
East Fork Russian River—*stream*................ CA-9
East Fork Sabino Canyon—*valley* ............. AZ-5
East Fork Sable Creek—*stream*.................. ID-8
East Fork Sabula Slough—*stream* ............. IA-7
East Fork Sackett Creek—*stream* .............. WY-8
East Fork Saddletree Draw—*valley* ............UT-8
East Fork Sage Creek—*stream*................... ID-8
East Fork Sage Hen Creek—*stream*........... WY-8
East Fork Sage Valley—*valley* ...................UT-8
East Fork Sain Creek—*stream* .................. OR-9
*East Fork Salmon River* ............................. ID-8
East Fork Salmon River—*stream*................ ID-8
East Fork Salmon River—*stream*............... NY-2
East Fork Salmon River—*stream*............... OR-9
East Fork Sals Creek—*stream* ................. MO-7
East Fork Salt Canyon—*valley*................... CA-9
East Fork Salt Creek—*stream* ................... IN-6
East Fork Salt Creek—*stream* ...................MT-8
East Fork Salt Creek—*stream* (2) ...............TX-5
East Fork Salt Creek—*stream* ....................UT-8
East Fork Salt Creek—*stream* ................. WY-8
East Fork Salt Pond Creek—*stream*.......... MO-7
East Fork Sams Canyon—*valley* .................UT-8
East Fork San Carlos Creek—*stream* ......... CA-9
East Fork Sand Coulee Creek—*stream* ......MT-8
East Fork Sand Creek—*stream*.................. CA-9
East Fork Sand Creek—*stream*.................. CO-8
East Fork Sand Creek—*stream*...................MT-8
East Fork Sand Creek—*stream*.................. OK-5
East Fork Sand Creek—*stream*....................TX-5
East Fork Sand Creek—*stream*.................. WY-8
East Fork Sand Draw—*valley* ................... WY-8
East Fork San Dimas Canyon—*valley*......... CA-9
East Fork Sandstone Creek—*stream*.......... OK-5
East Fork Sandy Creek—*stream* (2) ........... OK-5
East Fork San Francisco Creek—*stream*..... CO-8
*East Fork San Gabriel River*......................... CA-9
East Fork San Jacinto River—*stream*...........TX-5
*East Fork San Juan River* ........................... CO-8
East Fork San Juan River—*stream* ............ CO-8
East Fork Santa Anita Canyon—*valley*....... CA-9
East Fork Santa Cruz Creek—*stream*......... CA-9
East Fork Santa Paula Canyon—*valley*....... CA-9
East Fork Sarpy Creek—*stream*..................MT-8
East Fork Satsop River—*stream*................WA-9
East Fork Savannah Creek—*stream*........... NC-3
East Fork Savery Creek—*stream*............... WY-8
*East Fork Savoy Creek* .................................MT-8
East Fork Sawmill Canyon—*valley* ........... NM-5
East Fork Sawmill Creek—*stream* ............. AK-9
East Fork Sawmill Gulch—*valley*............... CO-8
East Fork Scarce Grease Branch—*stream*....AL-4
East Fork Scarp Canyon—*valley* ............... NV-8
East Fork Sch—*school* ............................. CA-9
East Fork Sch—*school* ..............................MT-8
East Fork Sch—*school* ............................. ND-7
East Fork School (historical)—*locale* ......... MO-7
East Fork Schoolhouse Canyon—*valley* ..... NM-5
East Fork Schwachheim Creek—*stream* ..... CO-8
East Fork Scott Creek—*stream*.................. OR-9
East Fork Scott River—*stream* .................. CA-9
East Fork Scouter Branch—*stream*............. SC-3
*East Fork Second Creek* ............................. TN-4
East Fork Seiad Creek—*stream*.................. CA-9
East Fork Sergeant Major Creek—*stream* .. OK-5
*East Fork Sevier River*..................................UT-8
East Fork Sevier River—*stream* ................UT-8
East Fork Shafer Canyon—*valley* ...............UT-8
East Fork Shane Creek—*stream*.................MT-8
East Fork Shannon Creek—*stream* (2)........ TN-4
East Fork Shawnee Creek—*stream* ............ WY-8
East Fork Shearer Creek—*stream*.............. CO-8
East Fork Sheenjek River—*stream* ............ AK-9
East Fork Sheep Creek—*stream* (2) ........... CO-8
East Fork Sheep Creek—*stream* (3) ........... ID-8
East Fork Sheep Creek—*stream* (2) ........... WY-8
East Fork Shell Creek—*stream* .................. ND-7
*East Fork Sheridan Creek* ........................... ID-8
East Fork Sheridan Creek—*stream* ........... ID-8
East Fork Shively Creek—*stream* .............. OR-9
East Fork Shoal Creek—*stream*....................IL-6
East Fork Shoal Creek—*stream* ................ MO-7
East Fork Shoal Creek—*stream* (2)............ TN-4
East Fork Shoofly Creek—*stream* .............. ID-8
East Fork Shop Creek—*stream*.................. AR-4
East Fork Short And Dirty Creek—*stream* ..WA-9
East Fork Short Creek—*stream* ................ AK-9
East Fork Shut-In Creek—*stream* ............. NC-3
East Fork Shutler Creek—*stream*............... OR-9
East Fork Sibley Creek—*stream*................WA-9
East Fork Siebert Creek—*stream* ..............WA-9
East Fork Sig Creek—*stream* .................... CO-8
*East fork Silver Butte Fisher River* .............MT-8
East Fork Silver Creek—*stream*....................IL-6
East Fork Silver Creek—*stream*................. KY-4
East Fork Silver Creek—*stream*................WA-9
East Fork Silvies River—*stream*................. OR-9
East Fork Simpson Creek—*stream* ............ KY-4
East Fork Sinker Creek—*stream* ................ ID-8
East Fork Sinking Fork—*stream*................ KY-4
East Fork Sinnemahoning Creek—*stream* ... PA-2
*East Fork Sipsey River* ................................AL-4
*East Fork Sister Creek*..................................TX-5
East Fork Site—*hist pl*............................. OH-6
*East Fork Six Mile Creek* .............................LA-4
East Fork Sixmile Creek—*stream*...............AL-4
East Fork Sixmile Creek—*stream*.............. AK-9
East Fork Sixmile Creek—*stream*...............LA-4
East Fork Sixmile Creek—*stream*............. WY-8
East Fork Skagway River—*stream* ............ AK-9
East Fork Skegg Creek—*stream*................ KY-4
East Fork Skeleton Creek—*stream* ............ ID-8
East Fork Skull Creek—*stream*.................. NV-8
East Fork Slabtown Branch—*stream* .......... TN-4
East Fork Slash Creek—*stream* ................. IN-6
East Fork Slate Creek—*stream* ................. KY-4
East Fork Slater Creek—*stream* ................ ID-8
East Fork Slaters Creek—*stream* .............. TN-4
East Fork Slough—*gut*............................. AK-9
East Fork Sly Run—*stream* ...................... IN-6
East Fork Small Creek—*stream*.................WA-9
*East Fork Smalle Creek* ...............................WA-9
East Fork Smith Canyon—*valley* .............. NM-5
*East Fork Smith Creek* .................................TX-5
East Fork Smith Creek—*stream* ................ GA-3
East Fork Smith Creek—*stream* ................ ID-8
East Fork Smith Creek—*stream* ................MT-8
East Fork Smith Creek—*stream* ................ SD-7
*East Fork Smith Fork* ...................................UT-8
East Fork Smiths Fork—*stream*.................UT-8
East Fork Smiths Fork—*stream*................. WY-8
East Fork Smoke Creek—*stream*................ NV-8
East Fork Smoky Creek—*stream*................ CA-9
East Fork Snag Creek—*stream*.................. AK-9
East Fork Sni-A-Bar Creek—*stream* .......... MO-7
East Fork Snow Coulee—*valley* ................MT-8
East Fork Snow Creek—*stream*.................. CA-9
*East Fork Snowshoe Creek* ........................... CO-8
*East Fork Soap Creek*................................... CO-8
East Fork Socagee Creek—*stream*...............TX-5
East Fork Soldier Creek—*stream*.............. WY-8
East Fork Solitaire Creek—*stream* ............ ID-8
East Fork Soloman River—*stream*............. AK-9
East Fork Somerset Creek—*stream* ........... KY-4
East Fork Sourdough Gulch—*valley*........... NV-8
East Fork South Fork Crystal
River—*stream*....................................... CO-8
East Fork South Fork McKenzie
River—*stream*....................................... OR-9
East Fork South Fork New River—*stream* .. NC-3
East Fork South Fork Salmon
River—*stream*....................................... CA-9
East Fork South Fork Salmon
River—*stream*........................................ ID-8
East Fork South Fork Trask River—*stream* . OR-9
East Fork South Fork Trinity
River—*stream*....................................... CA-9
East Fork South Fork Wood
River—*stream*...................................... WY-8
East Fork South Prairie Creek—*stream*......WA-9
East Fork South River—*stream*................. NC-3
East Fork South Spring Creek—*stream* ..... WY-8
East Fork South Tongue River—*stream*..... WY-8
East Fork Spanish Creek—*stream*.............. CA-9
East Fork Specimen Creek—*stream*...........MT-8
East Fork Split Creek—*stream* .................. ID-8
East Fork Spoon River—*stream*..................IL-6
East Fork Spotted Bear Creek—*stream* ..... SD-7
East Fork Spread Creek—*stream*...............MT-8
East Fork Spring—*spring* ......................... AZ-5
East Fork Spring—*spring* ......................... CA-9
East Fork Spring—*spring* .........................MT-8
East Fork Spring—*spring* ........................ NV-8
East Fork Spring—*stream* ........................ CO-8
East Fork Spring Branch—*stream* ............ MO-7
*East Fork Spring Creek* ............................... TN-4
East Fork Spring Creek—*stream* (2) .......... CO-8
East Fork Spring Creek—*stream*................ ID-8
East Fork Spring Creek—*stream* (3)..........MT-8
East Fork Spring Creek—*stream*............... NV-8
East Fork Spring Creek—*stream* (2)........... TN-4
East Fork Spring Creek—*stream*.................TX-5
East Fork Spring Creek—*stream*............... WY-8
East Fork Spring Hollow Creek—*stream* .... OR-9
East Fork Spruce Creek—*stream* ............... AK-9
East Fork Squaw Creek—*stream* ............... CA-9
East Fork Squaw Creek—*stream* (2) .......... ID-8
East Fork Squaw Creek—*stream* (3) .......... OR-9
East Fork Squaw Creek—*stream* .............. WY-8
East Fork Station—*locale* ........................ CA-9
*East Fork Steamboat Creek* ......................... ID-8
*East Fork Steamboat Creek* ........................ OR-9
East Fork Steamboat Creek—*stream* ......... ID-8
East Fork Steamboat Creek—*stream* ......... OR-9
East Fork Steller River—*stream* ............... AK-9
East Fork Steppes Creek—*stream* .............TX-5
East Fork Stewart Gulch—*valley*............... CO-8
East Fork Stewarts Creek—*stream* ............ NC-3
East Fork Stillwater Creek—*stream* .......... CA-9
East Fork Stiner Creek—*stream*................MT-8
East Fork Stinking Creek—*stream* .............AL-4
East Fork Stone Ch—*church* .................... IN-6
*East Fork Stone River* ................................. TN-4
East Fork Stones River—*stream* ................ TN-4
*East Fork Stones River Church* ...................... TN-4
East Fork Stony Flat Creek—*stream*........... TN-4
East Fork Stony Fork—*stream*................... VA-3
East Fork Story Gulch—*valley*................... CO-8
East Fork Stouts Creek—*stream* ............... OR-9
East Fork Strawberry Creek—*stream* .........MT-8
East Fork Strawberry Creek—*valley*.......... CO-8
East Fork Stuart Fork—*stream* ................. CA-9
East Fork Sturgill Creek—*stream* .............. ID-8
East Fork Sucker Creek Trail—*trail* ........... OR-9
East Fork Sugar Creek—*stream* ................ IN-6
East Fork Sugar Creek—*stream* ................ KY-4
East Fork Sugar Creek—*stream* ................ TN-4
East Fork Sugarloaf Creek—*stream* .......... CA-9
East Fork Sulphur Creek—*stream* ............. CA-9
East Fork Sulphur Creek—*stream* ............ MO-7
East Fork Sulphur Creek—*stream* ..............TX-5
East Fork Sumac Creek—*stream* ............... OR-9
*East Fork Summit Creek*.............................. CA-9
East Fork Sunbeam Creek—*stream* ........... ID-8
East Fork Sunday Creek—*stream*...............MT-8
East Fork Sunday Gulch—*valley* ............... CA-9
East Fork Sunshine Creek—*stream* ........... OR-9
*East Fork Surface Creek* .............................. CO-8
East Fork Susanna Canyon—*valley* ........... CA-9
East Fork Susitna River—*stream* .............. AK-9
*East Fork Sutton Creek* ............................... OR-9
East Fork Suwannee River—*stream*........... GA-3
East Fork Swamp Creek—*stream* ..............MT-8
East Fork Swanholm Creek—*stream* ......... ID-8
East Fork Swauger Creek—*stream* ............ CA-9
East Fork Swede George Creek—*stream* .... CA-9
East Fork Sweet Grass Creek—*stream*.......MT-8
*East Fork Sweetwater Creek* ....................... ID-8
East Fork Sweetwater Creek—*stream*........ ID-8
*East Fork Sweetwater River* ....................... WY-8
East Fork Swift Creek—*stream* .................MT-8
East Fork Sycamore Creek—*stream* (2)...... AZ-5
East Fork Sycamore Creek—*stream*........... CA-9
East Fork Sycamore Creek—*stream*............TX-5
East Fork Sylvia Creek—*stream* ...............WA-9
*East Fork Syrup Creek* ................................ ID-8
East Fork Tacoma Creek—*stream* .............WA-9
East Fork Taffner Creek—*stream*.............. WY-8
*East Fork Tallahala Creek*............................MS-4
*East Fork Tamarack Creek* ........................... OR-9
East Fork Tamarack Creek—*stream* .......... OR-9
East Fork Tank—*reservoir* (3) .................. AZ-5
East Fork Tanners Creek—*stream* ............ IN-6
East Fork Tanyard Branch—*stream*............AL-4
East Fork Tanyard Branch—*stream*.............TX-5
East Fork Targhee Creek—*stream*.............. ID-8
*East Fork Tarkio River*................................. IA-7
*East Fork Tarkio River*................................ MO-7
East Fork Tauy Creek—*stream*.................. KS-7
East Fork Tebo Creek—*stream* ................ MO-7
East Fork Tenmile Swamp—*stream*.............FL-3
*East Fork Tennessee Creek*........................... CO-8
East Fork Tepee Creek—*stream* ................MT-8
East Fork Terrapin Creek—*stream* ............ AR-4
East Fork Terrapin Creek—*stream*............. KY-4
East Fork Terror Creek—*stream*................ CO-8
East Fork The Forks—*stream*................... AK-9
East Fork Third Creek—*stream*..................MT-8
East Fork Thirsty Canyon—*valley*.............. NV-8
East Fork Thirtymile Creek—*stream*.......... OR-9
East Fork Thomas Creek—*stream*.............. ID-8
East Fork Thomas Creek—*stream*............. WY-8
East Fork Thompson Creek—*stream* .......... CA-9
East Fork Thompson Creek—*stream* ..........MT-8
East Fork Thompson Creek—*stream* ......... WY-8
*East Fork Thorobred Creek*.......................... ID-8
East Fork Thoroughbred Creek—*stream* ..... ID-8
East Fork Three Forks—*valley*...................UT-8
East Fork Three Licks Creek—*stream* ....... CO-8
East Fork Threemile Creek—*stream* .......... ID-8
East Fork Threemile Creek—*stream*............TX-5
East Fork Thumb River—*stream*................ AK-9
East Fork Tilton River—*stream*.................WA-9
East Fork Timber Creek—*stream* (2)..........MT-8
East Fork Timber Creek—*stream*.............. WY-8
East Fork T L Creek—*stream*....................MT-8
East Fork Todd Fork—*stream*.................. OH-6
East Fork Toklat River—*stream*................ AK-9
*East Fork Tombigbee River* .........................AL-4
*East Fork Tombigbee River* ..........................MS-4
East Fork Tonawanda Creek—*stream* ....... NY-2
East Fork Tonk Creek—*stream*...................TX-5
East Fork Tonowek Creek—*stream* ........... AK-9
*East Fork Torch River*.................................. WI-6
*East Fork Toroda Creek*...............................WA-9
*East Fork Touchet River*...............................WA-9
East Fork Tower Creek—*stream* ............... ID-8
East Fork Township—*inact MCD* .............. NV-8
**East Fork Township**—*pop pl* (2)............ ND-7
East Fork (Township of)—*civ div*................PA-2
East Fork (Township of)—*fmr MCD*........... AR-4
East Fork (Township of)—*fmr MCD*........... NC-3
**East Fork (Township of)**—*pop pl* (2)..........IL-6
East Fork Trail—*trail*................................ ID-8
East Fork Trail—*trail*............................... WV-2
East Fork Trail—*trail*............................... WY-8
*East Fork Trail Creek* ..................................MT-8
East Fork Trail Creek—*stream* ................. GA-3
East Fork Trail Creek—*stream* ................. ID-8
East Fork Trail (Pack)—*trail*.................... NM-5
East Fork Trapper Creek—*stream* ............. ID-8
*East Fork Trask River* ................................ OR-9
East Fork Trinity River—*stream* ............... CA-9
East Fork Trinity River—*stream*.................TX-5
East Fork Troublesome Creek—*stream*...... CO-8
*East Fork Trout Creek* .................................AL-4
*East Fork Trout Creek* ................................ OR-9
East Fork Trout Creek—*stream*................. ID-8
East Fork Trout Creek—*stream*.................MT-8
East Fork Trout Creek—*stream*................. OR-9
East Fork Trout Creek—*stream*................WA-9
East Fork Trout Creek—*stream*................ WY-8
*East Fork Trout Creek - in part*.................. NV-8
East Fork Tsivat River—*stream* ................ AK-9
East Fork Tucker Creek—*stream* .............. OR-9
East Fork Tulip Creek—*stream*................. AR-4
East Fork Tullock Creek—*stream* .............MT-8
East Fork Tuluga River—*stream* ............... AK-9
East Fork Tunitas Creek—*stream*.............. CA-9
East Fork Turkey Creek—*stream*............... CO-8
East Fork Turkey Creek—*stream* (2) ..........TX-5
East Fork Turtle Brook—*stream*................. NJ-2
*East Fork Twelve Mile Creek* ...................... NC-3
East Fork Twelvemile Creek—*stream*......... MN-6
East Fork Twelvemile Creek—*stream*......... NC-3
East Fork Twelvemile Creek—*stream*......... NC-3
East Fork Twelvepole Creek—*stream* ........ WV-2
East Fork Twentyfour Mile Creek—*stream* .. ID-8
East Fork Twentymile Creek—*stream* ........ WY-8
East Fork Twentyone Creek—*stream* ........ WY-8
East Fork Twin Canyon—*valley*..................UT-8
East Fork Twin Creek—*stream* ................. AK-9
East Fork Twin Creek—*stream* ................. AR-4
East Fork Twin Creek—*stream* ................. ID-8
East Fork Twin Creek—*stream* (2) ............ WY-8
East Fork Twin Lakes Creek—*stream*.........MT-8
East Fork Twomile Creek—*stream* ............ ID-8
East Fork Union River—*stream* ................WA-9
East Fork Upper Deer Creek—*stream* .......MT-8
East Fork Upper Twin Creek—*stream* ....... OH-6
East Fork Ute Canyon—*valley* .................. CO-8
East Fork Ute Creek—*stream*................... CO-8
East Fork Valley—*valley*.......................... TN-4
East Fork Valley Creek—*stream*................ ID-8
East Fork Valley Creek—*stream*................MT-8
East Fork Valley Creek—*stream*............... WY-8
*East Fork Vermilion Creek* .......................... CO-8
East Fork Vermilion River—*stream*........... OH-6
East Fork Vermillion River—*stream*........... SD-7
East Fork Vermillion River Rsvr—*reservoir* . SD-7
East Fork Vesta Creek—*stream* ...............WA-9
East Fork Virgin River—*stream* ................UT-8
East Fork Waggoner Creek—*stream* ..........MS-4
*East Fork Wagner Creek* ...............................MS-4
*East Fork Wagoner Creek*..............................MS-4
East Fork Wagonhound Creek—*stream* ...... WY-8
East Fork Wallace Creek—*stream*..............MT-8
East Fork Wallowa River—*stream*.............. OR-9
East Fork Walnut Creek—*stream*............... KS-7
East Fork Walnut Creek—*stream* .............. MO-7
East Fork Walnut Run—*stream*................ OH-6
East Fork Wapsipinicon River—*stream* ....... IA-7
East Fork Warm Springs Canyon—*valley* .... AZ-5
East Fork Warm Springs Creek—*stream* .... ID-8
East Fork Warm Springs Creek—*stream*
(2)..........................................................MT-8
East Fork Warrens Creek—*stream*............. OR-9
East Fork Wartrace Creek—*stream* ........... TN-4
East Fork Way—*trail*.............................. OR-9
East Fork Wayne Creek—*stream*................MT-8
East Fork Weakly Branch—*stream*..............TX-5
*East Fork Weaver Creek* ............................. CA-9
East Fork Weimer Canyon—*valley* ............ AZ-5
East Fork Weiser River—*stream* ............... ID-8
East Fork Weminuche Creek—*stream* ....... CO-8
*East Fork Wenatchee Creek*..........................WA-9
East Fork West Beaver Creek—*stream* ...... CO-8
East Fork West Boulder River—*stream* ......MT-8
East Fork West Branch Saint Joseph
River—*stream*........................................ MI-6
East Fork West Bridger Creek—*stream* ..... WY-8
East Fork West Creek—*stream*................. AR-4
East Fork West Eagle Creek—*stream* ........ OR-9
*East Fork West Fisher Creek* .......................MT-8
*East Fork West Fisher River* ........................MT-8
East Fork West Fork Little River—*stream* ...AL-4
East Fork West Fork Little River—*stream* .. GA-3
East Fork West Fork Mojave
River—*stream*........................................ CA-9
*East Fork West Fork Saint Maries River*........ ID-8
*East Fork West Fork Thomas Creek* ............. ID-8
East Fork West Red Lodge
Creek—*stream*......................................MT-8
East Fork Wetweather Creek—*stream* .........IL-6
East Fork Wheatridge Lateral—*canal* ........ CO-8
East Fork Wheeler Creek—*stream* .............UT-8
*East Fork Whetstone Creek* ..........................MT-8
*East Fork Whimpey Creek* ............................ ID-8
East Fork Whimstick Creek—*stream* ......... ID-8
East Fork Whisky Creek—*stream*.............. OR-9
East Fork Whitcomb Creek—*stream* ......... OR-9
*East Fork White Creek* ................................ IN-6
East Fork White Creek—*stream* ............... ID-8
East Fork White Creek—*stream* ............... IN-6
East Fork White Eyes Creek—*stream* ........ OH-6
*East Fork Whitefish Creek*............................MT-8
East Fork Whitehorse Creek—*stream*......... OR-9
East Fork White Lick Creek—*stream* ......... IN-6
East Fork White Oak Creek—*stream* ......... OH-6
East Fork White Oak Creek—*stream* ..........TX-5
*East Fork White River* ................................. IN-6
East Fork White River—*stream* ................ AZ-5
East Fork White River—*stream* ................ IN-6
East Fork White River—*stream* ................ WI-6
East Fork White Rock Creek—*stream* .........TX-5
East Fork Whiterocks River—*stream*...........UT-8
East Fork Whites Gulch—*valley* ............... CA-9
*Eastfork Whitewater Creek* ......................... OH-6
East Fork Whitewater Creek—*stream* ....... NM-5
East Fork Whitewater River—*stream* ........ CA-9
East Fork Whitewater River—*stream* ......... IN-6
East Fork Whitewater River—*stream*......... OH-6
East Fork Wickiup Canyon—*valley*............ CO-8
East Fork Wickiup Creek—*stream* ............ ID-8
*East Fork Wildcat Creek* ............................. NV-8
East Fork Wildcat Creek—*stream*..............WA-9
East Fork Wildhorse Creek—*stream*........... OK-5
East Fork Wild Horse Creek—*stream*......... WY-8
*East Fork Willamina Creek*........................... OR-9
East Fork Willard Creek—*stream* .............. CA-9
East Fork Williams Creek—*stream* (2)........ CO-8
East Fork Williams Creek—*stream* ............ KY-4
East Fork Williams Creek—*stream* ............ OR-9
East Fork Williams Creek—*stream* .............TX-5
East Fork Williams Fork—*stream*............... CO-8
*East Fork Willow Creek* ...............................MT-8
East Fork Willow Creek—*stream* .............. CA-9
East Fork Willow Creek—*stream* .............. CO-8
East Fork Willow Creek—*stream* .............. ID-8
East Fork Willow Creek—*stream* .............. NV-8
East Fork Willow Creek—*stream* .............. SD-7
East Fork Willow Creek—*stream* .............. WY-8
East Fork Willow Creek—*valley* ............... WY-8
East Fork Wilson Creek—*stream* .............. CO-8
East Fork Wimpey Creek—*stream* ............ ID-8
East Fork Winchuck River—*stream* ........... OR-9
East Fork Windham Canyon—*valley*.......... NM-5
East Fork Wind River—*stream*.................. WY-8
*East Fork Winnemucca Creek* ....................... CO-8
East Fork Wishkah River—*stream*.............WA-9
*East Fork Wolf Creek* ................................. OR-9
East Fork Wolf Creek—*stream* ................. CO-8
East Fork Wolf Creek—*stream* ................. IA-7
East Fork Wolf Creek—*stream* ................. KS-7
East Fork Wolf Creek—*stream* ................ MO-7
East Fork Wolf Creek—*stream* (2).............MT-8
East Fork Wolf Creek—*stream* ................. NM-5
East Fork Wolf Creek—*stream* ................. OR-9
East Fork Wolf Creek—*stream* (3)............. TN-4
East Fork Wolf Creek—*stream* ................. VA-3
East Fork Wolf Creek—*stream* ................. WY-8
East Fork Wood River—*stream*................. ID-8
East Fork Wood River—*stream*...................IL-6
East Fork Woods Canyon—*valley* ............. AZ-5
East Fork Woods Creek—*stream* ...............MT-8
East Fork Woody Creek—*stream*...............MT-8
*East Fork Wooley Creek*.............................. CA-9
East Fork Worswick Creek—*stream* .......... ID-8
East Fork Wright Canyon—*valley*.............. AZ-5
East Fork Yaak River—*stream*...................MT-8
East Fork Yanubbee Creek—*stream*.......... OK-5
East Fork Yellow Brook—*stream*................ NJ-2
East Fork Yellow Creek—*stream* (2).......... TN-4
*East Fork Yellow River*.................................AL-4
East Fork Yentna River—*stream* .............. AK-9
East Fork Yuba River—*stream* .................. ID-8
East Fork Yuki River—*stream*................... AK-9
East Fork Zena Creek—*stream*.................. ID-8
*East Forney Ridge* ...................................... NC-3
East Forrest HS—*school*............................MS-4
East Forrest Junior Senior HS—*school* ....... PA-2
East Forsyth HS—*school* .......................... NC-3
East Fort—*locale* ..................................... AZ-5
**East Fort Madison**—*pop pl*........................IL-6
East Fort Myers—*locale*.............................FL-3
East Fort Point—*cape*.............................. NY-2
East Forty Creek—*stream*..........................MT-8
East Foster Creek—*stream*........................WA-9
East Four Draw—*valley* ........................... WY-8
East Four Legged Lake—*lake* ................... MN-6
East Fourmile Creek—*stream*................... OH-6
East Fourmile Draw—*valley*...................... CO-8
*East Fourteenth Street*................................. IA-7
East Fourth Ave Parkway—*hist pl*.............. CO-8
East Fourth Street Hist Dist—*hist pl* (2).... OH-6
East Fourth Street Park—*park* .................. NC-3
East Fowl River—*stream*...........................AL-4
**East Foxboro**—*pop pl* ............................. MA-1
*East Foxborough*......................................... MA-1
East Fox Creek—*channel* ......................... NY-2
*East Fox Lake* ............................................ MN-6
East Fox Lake—*lake*..................................FL-3
East Fox Lake—*lake*................................ MN-6
East Fqrk Big Creek—*stream*......................IL-6
**East Frankfort**—*pop pl*............................ NY-2
East Frankfort—*uninc pl*........................... KY-4
**East Franklin**—*pop pl* ............................. ME-1
**East Franklin**—*pop pl* ............................. NC-3
**East Franklin**—*pop pl* ............................. PA-2
**East Franklin**—*pop pl* ...............................VT-1
East Franklin JHS—*school*.........................AL-4
East Franklin Sch—*school* ....................... OH-6
**East Franklin (Township of)**—*pop pl*......PA-2
East Franklin (Unorganized Territory
of)—*other*............................................ ME-1
**East Fredericktown**—*pop pl*..................... PA-2
East Fredlund Sch—*school* ....................... SD-7
**East Fredricktown**—*pop pl* ..................... PA-2
East Freeborn Ch—*church* ....................... MN-6
East Freedom—*locale*................................ NH-1
**East Freedom**—*pop pl* ............................. PA-2
East Freedom Ch—*church*......................... NC-3
East Freehold—*locale*................................ NJ-2
East Freehold County Park—*park* .............. NJ-2
**East Freetown**—*pop pl* ........................... MA-1
**East Freetown**—*pop pl* ............................ NY-2
East Fremont Sch—*school* ........................ WI-6
East French Oil Field—*oilfield*................... OK-5
East Fresno—*uninc pl* .............................. CA-9
East Frickey Spring—*spring* ..................... OR-9
**East Friendship**—*pop pl*.......................... ME-1
**East Friesland**—*pop pl*............................. WI-6
East Friesland Cem—*cemetery* .................. IA-7
East Friesland Ch—*church* ........................ IA-7
East Frio River—*stream*............................TX-5
**East Fryeburg**—*pop pl*.............................. ME-1
East F Tank—*reservoir* ..............................TX-5
East Fulton Baptist Ch—*church* .................MS-4
East Fulton Cem—*cemetery* ......................MS-4
**East Fulton (East Okie)**—*pop pl*................IL-6
**East Fultonham**—*pop pl*......................... OH-6
**East Fultonham Junction**—*pop pl* ........... OH-6
East Fulton Township—*civil* ..................... MO-7
**East Funston**—*pop pl*............................... KS-7
East Furnace Ridge—*ridge*........................ TN-4
East Furnace Ridge Mine—*mine* ............... TN-4
East Gab Court House—*building* ............... NC-3
**East Gadsden**—*pop pl* ..............................AL-4
East Gadsden Baptist Ch—*church* ..............AL-4
East Gadsden Ch of God—*church*...............AL-4
East Gadsden Ch of the
Nazarene—*church*..................................AL-4
East Gadsden Community
Center—*building*....................................AL-4
East Gadsden Cumberland Presbyterian
Ch—*church*............................................AL-4
East Gadsden Sch—*school* .........................AL-4
East Gadsden United Methodist
Ch—*church*............................................AL-4
**East Gaffney**—*pop pl*................................ SC-3
East Gafford Creek—*stream* ...................... AR-4
*East Gaffords Creek* ..................................... AR-4
**East Gaines**—*pop pl* ................................ NY-2
**East Galena (Township of)**—*pop pl*............IL-6
**East Galesburg**—*pop pl* ............................IL-6
East Galilee Ch—*church*............................MS-4
East Gallatin Cem—*cemetery*.....................MT-8
East Gallatin River—*stream*.......................MT-8
**East Galway**—*pop pl* ............................... NY-2
East Gambier Street District—*hist pl* ........ OH-6
**East Gantt**—*pop pl*................................... SC-3
*East Gap*...................................................... FL-3
East Gap—*gap* ........................................... CO-8
East Gap—*gap* ........................................... KY-4
East Garden Grove Wintersburg
Channel—*canal* ..................................... CA-9
*East Gardens*............................................. OH-6
East Garden Well—*well*............................ NM-5
**East Gardiner**—*pop pl* ............................ OR-9
**East Gardner**—*pop pl* .............................. MA-1
East Garland Cem—*cemetery* .....................UT-8
**East Garrison**—*pop pl*.............................. CA-9
*East Gary* .................................................... IN-6
**East Gastonia**—*pop pl*............................. NC-3
East Gaston Senior HS—*school*.................. NC-3
*Eastgate* (2) ................................................ IN-6
*East Gate* .................................................... IN-6
*Eastgate*...................................................... IN-6
*East Gate* .................................................... NV-8
*East Gate* .................................................... NC-3
Eastgate—*gap* ........................................... NV-8
East Gate—*locale* ...................................... AZ-5
Eastgate—*locale* .........................................TX-5
**East Gate**—*pop pl*.................................... CA-9
**Eastgate**—*pop pl* (2).................................FL-3
**Eastgate**—*pop pl* ...................................... IN-6
**East Gate**—*pop pl*..................................... IN-6
**Eastgate**—*pop pl* ..................................... NV-8
**Eastgate**—*pop pl* .....................................WA-9
Eastgate—*uninc pl* ................................... CA-9
Eastgate—*uninc pl* .....................................FL-3
Eastgate—*uninc pl* ...................................WA-9
Eastgate Baptist Ch—*church* .....................MS-4
East Gate Basin—*harbor* .......................... WI-6

East Gate Center—locale MO-7
Eastgate Ch—church MI-6
Eastgate Ch—church TX-5
East Gate Ch—church TX-5
Eastgate Christian Ch—church IN-6
**East Gate Estates (subdivision)**—pop pl AL-4
Eastgate JHS—school MO-7
Eastgate North (Shop Ctr)—locale FL-3
Eastgate Park—park CA-9
**East Gate Park**—pop pl FL-3
*Eastgate Plaza* NC-3
Eastgate Plaza—locale MO-7
East Gate Plaza Shop Ctr—locale AZ-5
Eastgate Plaza (Shop Ctr)—locale FL-3
Eastgate Plaza Shop Ctr—locale MA-1
Eastgate (P.O.)—uninc pl WA-9
East Gate Rsvr—reservoir UT-8
Eastgate Sch—school (2) OH-6
Eastgate Sch—school (2) WA-9
East Gate Shop Ctr—locale AZ-5
Eastgate Shop Ctr—locale FL-3
East Gate Shop Ctr—locale FL-3
Eastgate Shop Ctr—locale FL-3
Eastgate Shop Ctr—locale (2) IN-6
Eastgate Shop Ctr—locale KS-7
East Gate Shop Ctr—locale KS-7
East Gate Shop Ctr—locale MA-1
Eastgate Shop Ctr—locale MI-6
Eastgate Shop Ctr—locale MS-4
Eastgate Shop Ctr—locale MO-7
East Gate Shop Ctr—locale NC-3
Eastgate Shop Ctr—locale NC-3
East Gate Shop Ctr—locale OH-6
Eastgate Shop Ctr—locale PA-2
Eastgate Shop Ctr—locale (2) TN-4
Eastgate Shopping Plaza—locale PA-2
East Gate Square (Shop Ctr)—locale FL-3
**Eastgate (subdivision)**—pop pl NC-3
Eastgate Village Shop Ctr—locale MS-4
Eastgate Wash—stream NV-8
East Gavett Creek—stream TX-5
East Genesee Cem—cemetery IL-6
East Genesee Historic Business District—hist pl MI-6
**East Geneva**—pop pl NY-2
**East Genoa**—pop pl NY-2
East Georgia—locale VT-1
East German Cem—cemetery WI-6
**East Germantown**—pop pl IN-6
East Germantown—uninc pl PA-2
East Germantown Recreation Center—park PA-2
*East Geuda Springs* KS-7
East Gibraltar Peak—summit CO-8
East Gibson Ditch—canal IL-6
East Gibson Gas and Oil Field—oilfield LA-4
East Gift Ridge Ch—church OH-6
East Gilbert Creek—stream MT-8
East Gilbert Sch—school MI-6
**East Gilead**—pop pl MI-6
**East Gillespie**—pop pl IL-6
East Gimlet Creek—stream SD-7
*East Glacier* MT-8
East Glacier Creek—stream AK-9
**East Glacier Park**—pop pl MT-8
East Glacier Park Cem—cemetery MT-8
East Glacier Ranger Station Hist Dist—hist pl MT-8
East Glade—flat CA-9
**East Glastonbury**—pop pl CT-1
*East Glen* IN-6
East Glen Brook—stream MA-1
**East Glenn**—pop pl IN-6
**East Glenville**—pop pl NY-2
East Glenville Ch—church NY-2
East Glenwood Cem—cemetery IA-7
East Glenwood School—locale MT-8
East Globe Elem Sch—school AZ-5
*East Globe Sch* AZ-5
**East Gloucester (subdivision)**—pop pl MA-1
East Goat Mtn—summit MT-8
East Goat Peak—summit MT-8
East Godfrey Gulch—valley CO-8
East Goens Creek—stream TX-5
East Gold Brook—stream OR-9
East Gold Creek—stream OR-9
East Golden Pond—swamp MI-6
East Golden Valley—unorg reg ND-7
East Gold Lookout—locale ID-8
**East Goldsboro**—pop pl NC-3
East Goldsmith Oil Field—oilfield TX-5
*East Goodenough Creek* ID-8
East Goodland Drain—canal MI-6
*East Goose creek* WY-8
East Goose Creek—stream FL-3
East Goose Creek Pond—reservoir ID-8
*East Goosefare Rocks* ME-1
East Goose Lake—lake IA-7
East Goose Rock—island ME-1
East Goose Rocks—island ME-1
East Goose Valley—valley MS-4
East Gordon—fmr MCD NE-7
East Gordon Gulch—valley CO-8
East Gosage Creek—stream OR-9
**East Goshen**—pop pl OH-6
East Goshen Hole Ditch—canal WY-8
**East Goshen (Township of)**—pop pl PA-2
East Gospel Lake—lake ID-8
East Government Creek—stream UT-8
East Government Mtn—summit OK-5
East Grace Cem—cemetery MN-6
East Grade Sch—school MT-8
**East Grafton**—pop pl NH-1
**East Grafton**—pop pl NY-2
*East Graham Creek* AR-4
East Graham Lake—lake MN-6
East Grain Camp Canal—canal OR-9
**East Granby**—pop pl CT-1
East Granby Hist Dist—hist pl CT-1
**East Granby (Town of)**—pop pl CT-1
East Grand—uninc pl TX-5
East Granddaddy Mtn—summit UT-8
East Grand Ave Ch—church TX-5
East Grand Creek—stream IA-7
**East Grand Forks**—pop pl MN-6
East Grand Island Cem—cemetery NE-7
*East Grand Lake* ME-1
*East Grand Marais Ditch* LA-4
**East Grand Plains**—pop pl NM-5
**East Grand Rapids**—pop pl MI-6
East Grant—unorg reg ND-7
East Grantham—locale NH-1
East Grant-Pond Creek Oil Field—oilfield OK-5
East Grants Ridge—ridge NM-5
*East Granville* MA-1
**East Granville**—pop pl VT-1
East Granville Brook—stream VT-1
East Granville Sch—school WI-6
East Grassy Creek—stream IN-6
East Grassy Mountain Well—well UT-8
East Graveyard Windmill—locale NM-5
**East Gray**—pop pl ME-1
East Grayson (CCD)—cens area TX-5
East Greasy Creek—stream AR-4
East Greasy Sch—school IL-6
East Great Bend Sch (historical)—school PA-2
*East Great Plain* CT-1
East Great Plain—flat CT-1
East Great Works Pond—lake ME-1
East Greenacres—locale ID-8
East Greenacres East Ditch—canal ID-8
East Greenacres Main Ditch—canal ID-8
East Greenacres North Ditch—canal ID-8
East Greenacres Sch—school ID-8
**East Greenbush**—pop pl NY-2
East Greenbush Central Sch—school NY-2
East Greenbush Station—locale NY-2
**East Greenbush (Town of)**—pop pl NY-2
East Greene Cem—cemetery OH-6
East Greene Ch—church PA-2
**East Greenfield**—pop pl MA-1
East Green Mine—mine IL-6
East Greensboro—locale VT-1
**East Greenville**—pop pl NY-2
**East Greenville**—pop pl OH-6
**East Greenville**—pop pl PA-2
**East Greenville**—pop pl SC-3
East Greenville Borough—civil PA-2
*East Greenville Shopping Center* NC-3
**East Greenwich**—pop pl NY-2
**East Greenwich**—pop pl RI-1
East Greenwich Hist Dist—hist pl RI-1
**East Greenwich (Town of)**—pop pl RI-1
**East Greenwich (Township of)**—pop pl NJ-2
**East Greer**—pop pl SC-3
East Gregerie Channel—channel VI-3
East Gregory—unorg reg SD-7
East Gresham—uninc pl OR-9
East Gresham Sch—school OR-9
East Greynolds Park—park FL-3
**East Gridley**—pop pl CA-9
East Griever Creek—stream OK-5
**East Griffin**—pop pl GA-3
East Griffin Creek—stream FL-3
*East Grindstone Creek* TX-5
East Grindstone Spring—spring UT-8
East Grossman Creek—stream OR-9
East Gros Ventre Butte—summit WY-8
**East Groton**—pop pl MA-1
East Groton Cem—cemetery NY-2
*East Groton Station* MA-1
*East Grouse Creek* CO-8
East Grouse Peak—summit ID-8
East Grove Baptist Ch—church AL-4
East Grove Ch—church PA-2
**Eastgrove Condominium**—pop pl UT-8
**Eastgrove Condominium Phase 2-7**—pop pl UT-8
**East Groveland**—pop pl NY-2
East Grove Sch (historical)—school TN-4
East Grove Street District-Bloomington—hist pl IL-6
**East Grove (Township of)**—pop pl IL-6
East Guard Lock—other NY-2
**East Guernewood**—pop pl CA-9
**East Guilford**—pop pl NY-2
East Gulch—valley CA-9
East Gulch—valley (4) CO-8
East Gulch—valley (2) OR-9
East Gulch Waterhole—reservoir OR-9
*East Gulf* WV-2
**Eastgulf**—pop pl WV-2
East Gulfport HS—school MS-4
**Eastgulf (RR name East Gulf)**—pop pl WV-2
East Gulf (RR name for Eastgulf)—other WV-2
**East Gull Lake**—pop pl MN-6
East Gully Creek—stream MS-4
East Gum Creek—stream TX-5
East Gumlog Creek—stream GA-3
East Gumm Creek—stream OR-9
East Gunsight Mtn—summit TX-5
East Gustavus Cem—cemetery OH-6
East Gut—gut VA-3
East Guthrie Lake Gas And Oil Field—oilfield OK-5
East Gutter—gut MA-1
East Gypsum Bay—bay AZ-5
East Haakon—unorg reg SD-7
East Hackberry Oil Field—oilfield LA-4
East Hackerott Well—locale NM-5
**East Haddam**—pop pl CT-1
East Haddam Hist Dist—hist pl CT-1
**East Haddam Landing**—pop pl CT-1
East Haddam Sch—school CT-1
**East Haddam (Town of)**—pop pl CT-1
**East Hadley**—pop pl MA-1
**East Hale Township**—pop pl KS-7
East Hale Windmill—locale NM-5
**East Half Hollow Hills**—pop pl NY-2
East Hall—hist pl MI-6
East Hall—hist pl WV-2
East Hall HS—school GA-3
East Halls Creek—stream TX-5
Eastham—locale VA-3
**Eastham**—pop pl MA-1
Eastham, D. D., House—hist pl TX-5
**East Hamburg**—pop pl NY-2
Eastham Creek—stream NC-3
Eastham Creek Point—cape NC-3
Eastham Dunes—range MA-1
*Eastham Harbor* MA-1
East Hamilton—locale TX-5
**East Hamilton**—pop pl NY-2
East Hamilton Ch—church TX-5
East Hamilton Township—civil KS-7
Eastham Junction—locale MT-8
Eastham Lake—lake MN-6
**East Hamlet**—pop pl NC-3
East Hamlett—dam NC-3
East Hamlett Lake—reservoir NC-3
Eastham Mill, The—locale MA-1
East Hammond—CDP LA-4
East Hammond Creek—stream MT-8
East Hamongog—summit UT-8
**East Hampden**—pop pl ME-1
**East Hampstead**—pop pl NH-1
*East Hampton* MA-1
**East Hampton**—pop pl AL-4
**East Hampton**—pop pl CT-1
**Easthampton**—pop pl MA-1
**East Hampton**—pop pl NY-2
**East Hampton**—pop pl VA-3
East Hampton Beach—beach NY-2
**East Hampton Center**—pop pl CT-1
Easthampton Gun Club—other NY-2
Easthampton HS—school MA-1
Easthampton JHS—school MA-1
*East Hampton Pond* CT-1
Easthampton Townhall—building MA-1
**East Hampton (Town of)**—pop pl CT-1
**Easthampton (Town of)**—pop pl MA-1
**East Hampton (Town of)**—pop pl NY-2
East Hampton Village District—hist pl NY-2
East Hampton Village Hist Dist (Boundary Increase)—hist pl NY-2
*Easthampton Water Works Reservoir* MA-1
*Eastham River* VA-3
Eastham Sch—school OR-9
Eastham State Prison Farm—other TX-5
**Eastham (Town of)**—pop pl MA-1
Eastham 1869 Schoolhouse Museum—building MA-1
East Hanawana—civil HI-9
East Hanceville Baptist Ch—church AL-4
East Hancock Neighborhood Hist Dist—hist pl MI-6
East Hancock (Unorganized Territory of)—unorg ME-1
East Handley Sch—school TX-5
East Hanks Lake—lake OR-9
East Hanna Mtn—summit AR-4
East Hannibal—locale IL-6
East Hanover—locale PA-2
East Hanover Ch—church PA-2
*East Hanover Elem Sch* PA-2
East Hanover Elem Sch—school PA-2
East Hanover (Hanover)—CDP NJ-2
East Hanover Sch—school PA-2
**East Hanover (Township of)**—pop pl NJ-2
**East Hanover (Township of)**—pop pl (2) PA-2
East Hansen Fisk Ditch—canal CA-9
**East Hanson Township**—pop pl SD-7
*East Harbor* MA-1
*East Harbor* NY-2
East Harbor—bay (2) NY-2
East Harbor—bay OH-6
East Harbor—harbor CA-9
East Harbor Arm—harbor IN-6
East Harbor Key Channel—channel FL-3
East Harbor Keys—island FL-3
East Harbor State Park—park OH-6
East Hardin—locale IL-6
East Hardpan Rsvr—reservoir UT-8
*East Hardscrabble Creek* MT-8
East Hardscrabble Creek—stream MT-8
**East Hardwick**—pop pl VT-1
East Harney Creek—stream WY-8
East Harper Basin Spring—spring OR-9
East Harper Elem Sch—school NC-3
**East Harpswell**—pop pl ME-1
East Harpswell Free Will Baptist Church—hist pl ME-1
East Harrisburg Cem—cemetery PA-2
East Hartford—CDP CT-1
**East Hartford**—pop pl CT-1
**East Hartford**—pop pl NY-2
East Hartford Dike—levee CT-1
**East Hartford Gardens**—pop pl CT-1
**East Hartland**—pop pl CT-1
East Hartley Gulch—valley ID-8
East Hartsville (College Heights)—CDP SC-3
**East Harwich**—pop pl MA-1
*East Hastings* MN-6
East Hastings Brook—stream ME-1
*East Hat Creek* CA-9
East Hat Creek—stream NE-7
**East Hauppauge**—pop pl NY-2
*East Hauxhurst Creek* CO-8
East Haven—CDP CT-1
East Haven—harbor VA-3
**East Haven**—pop pl AL-4
**East Haven**—pop pl CT-1
**East Haven**—pop pl IN-6
**East Haven**—pop pl TX-5
**East Haven**—pop pl VT-1
Easthaven Baptist Ch—church (2) MS-4
Easthaven Cem—cemetery MS-4
East Haven Mtn—summit VT-1
East Haven Range—range VT-1
*East Haven River* CT-1
**East Haven (subdivision)**—pop pl AL-4
**Easthaven (subdivision)**—pop pl (3) MS-4
**Easthaven (subdivision)**—pop pl (2) NC-3
**East Haven (Town of)**—pop pl VT-1
**East Haverhill**—pop pl NH-1
East Haverhill (historical P.O.)—locale MA-1
East Haverhill Sch—school MA-1
*East Hawkhurst Creek* CO-8
East Hawksbill Creek—stream VA-3
*East Hawley* MA-1
East Hawxhurst Creek—stream CO-8
East Hayden Lake Sch II—hist pl ID-8
East Hay Draw Creek—stream ND-7
East Haynesville Oil and Gas Field—oilfield LA-4
East Hayshed Creek—stream CA-9
East Haystack Wash—valley WY-8
East Haywood Ch—church TN-4
**East Hazel Crest**—pop pl IL-6
East Head—cape AK-9
East Head—cliff AK-9
East Head—valley FL-3
East Head Bog Dam Number 1—dam MA-1
East Head Bog Dam Number 2—dam MA-1
East Head Bog Rsvr—reservoir MA-1
East Header Windmill—locale NM-5
East Head Pond—reservoir MA-1
East Head Pond Dam—dam MA-1
East Healy Draw—valley WY-8
East Hearn Lateral—canal AZ-5
*East Hebron* PA-2
**East Hebron**—pop pl ME-1
**East Hebron**—pop pl NH-1
**East Hebron**—pop pl NY-2
East Hebron Cem—cemetery NY-2
East Heidelberg Oil Field—oilfield MS-4
East Heights—post sta MS-4
East Heights Baptist Ch—church MS-4
East Heights Elem Sch—school KS-7
**East Helena**—pop pl MT-8
East Hemet—CDP CA-9
*East Hemlock Run* PA-2
East Hempfield Post Office (historical)—building PA-2
**East Hempfield (Township of)**—pop pl PA-2
**East Hempstead**—pop pl NY-2
East Henderson HS—school NC-3
East Hensley Windmill—locale TX-5
East Herd Windmill—locale (2) TX-5
**East Herkimer**—pop pl NY-2
East Herrick—locale PA-2
East Hersey Ch—church MI-6
East Hess Hills—range NM-5
**East Hess Township**—pop pl KS-7
**East Hibbard Township**—pop pl KS-7
**East Hickman**—pop pl (2) KY-4
East Hickman Canyon—valley UT-8
East Hickman Creek—stream KY-4
**East Hickory**—pop pl PA-2
**East Hickory (census name Hickory East)**—pop pl NC-3
East Hickory Creek—stream (2) KS-7
East Hickory Creek—stream OK-5
East Hickory Creek—stream PA-2
East Hickory Sch—school IL-6
**East Highgate**—pop pl VT-1
East Highgate Cem—cemetery VT-1
*East Highland* CA-9
**East Highland**—pop pl MI-6
*East Highland Baptist Church* AL-4
East Highland Ch—church AL-4
East Highland Ch—church SD-7
**East Highland Estates Subdivision**—pop pl UT-8
East Highland Lake—reservoir NJ-2
East Highland Lake Dam—dam NJ-2
East Highland MS—school AL-4
**East Highland Park**—pop pl VA-3
East Highland Rsvr—reservoir CA-9
**East Highlands**—pop pl CA-9
**East Highlands**—pop pl GA-3
East Highlands Ch—church AL-4
East Highlands Sch—school AL-4
East Highline Canal—canal CA-9
East Highline Eight Drain—canal CA-9
East Highline Fourteen Drain—canal CA-9
East Highline Lateral Eight—canal CA-9
East Highline Lateral Eleven—canal CA-9
East Highline Lateral Fifteen—canal CA-9
East Highline Lateral Five—canal CA-9
East Highline Lateral Fourteen—canal CA-9
East Highline Lateral One—canal CA-9
East Highline Lateral Six (lower)—canal CA-9
East Highline Lateral Sixteen—canal CA-9
East Highline Lateral Ten—canal CA-9
East Highline Lateral Thirteen—canal CA-9
East Highline Lateral Tweleve—canal CA-9
East Highline Seven Drain—canal CA-9
East Highline Side Main One—canal CA-9
East Highline Six Drain—canal CA-9
East Highline Ten Drain—canal CA-9
East Highline Thirteen Drain—canal CA-9
East Highline Vateral Seven—canal CA-9
East Highline 14 Drain—canal CA-9
East High Meadow—swamp NY-2
East High Peak—summit OK-5
East High Point Sch (abandoned)—school MO-7
*East High School* PA-2
East High State Sch—school PA-2
East High Street District—hist pl OH-6
*East High Street Elem Sch* PA-2
East High Street Hist Dist—hist pl OH-6
East High Street Sch—school PA-2
East Highway Ch—church TX-5
*East Hill* MA-1
East Hill—locale PA-2
**East Hill**—pop pl CT-1
**East Hill**—pop pl NY-2
**East Hill**—pop pl TN-4
East Hill—ridge NH-1
East Hill—summit (2) CT-1
East Hill—summit (5) MA-1
East Hill—summit MT-8
East Hill—summit (13) NY-2
East Hill—summit PA-2
East Hill—summit (4) VT-1
East Hill—summit WI-6
East Hill—uninc pl FL-3
East Hill Canyon—valley NM-5
East Hill Cem—cemetery IN-6
East Hill Cem—cemetery KS-7
East Hill Cem—cemetery MI-6
East Hill Cem—cemetery NH-1
East Hill Cem—cemetery (2) NY-2
East Hill Cem—cemetery OK-5
East Hill Cem—cemetery TX-5
East Hill Cem—cemetery (2) VT-1
East Hill Cem—cemetery (2) VA-3
East Hill Ch—church NY-2
East Hill Ch of Christ—church TN-4
East Hill Christian Sch—school FL-3
East Hill Coulee—valley MT-8
East Hill Elem Sch—school PA-2
East Hill Hist Dist—hist pl NY-2
East Hillister Oil Field—oilfield TX-5
East Hill Lake—lake NE-7
East Hill Park—park TX-5
**East Hills**—pop pl NY-2
**East Hills**—pop pl PA-2
East Hills—range ID-8
**East Hillsboro**—pop pl MS-4
East Hill Sch—school NH-1
East Hill Sch—school NY-2
East Hill Sch—school (2) VT-1
**East Hillsdale**—pop pl NY-2
East Hillside Cem—cemetery NY-2
East Hills JHS—school MI-6
East Hills MS—school PA-2
East Hills Park—park NJ-2
East Hills Park—park PA-2
**East Hills (subdivision)**—pop pl PA-2
East Hill Well—well NM-5
East Hilton—uninc pl VA-3
East Hinman—fmr MCD NE-7
East Hinson Indian Mounds—summit FL-3
East Hinson Island—island FL-3
East Hinson Marsh—swamp FL-3
East Hinson Strand—swamp FL-3
**East Hiram**—pop pl ME-1
East Hitchen Creek—stream KS-7
East Hobbs Oil Field—other NM-5
East Hobolochitto Creek—stream MS-4
East Hodgdon—locale ME-1
**East Hodge**—pop pl LA-4
East Hodges—locale TN-4
*East Hogback ridge* MT-8
East Hog Branch—stream LA-4
East Hogshead Rock—rock MA-1
*East Hogup Mountains* UT-8
East Holbrook Ch—church CO-8
East Holbrook Interchange—crossing AZ-5
East Holcomb Windmill—locale TX-5
**East Holden**—pop pl ME-1
*East Holden Station* ME-1
**East Holderness**—pop pl NH-1
East Hole—bay FL-3
East Hole Tank—reservoir TX-5
**East Holladay Condominium**—pop pl UT-8
**East Holladay Slopes Subdivision**—pop pl UT-8
East Holland Cem—cemetery MI-6
East Holland Creek—stream KS-7
**East Holliston**—pop pl MA-1
East Hollow—valley (3) MO-7
East Hollow—valley NY-2
East Hollow—valley TX-5
East Holloway Canal—canal FL-3
East Holloway Creek—stream TX-5
East Holly Springs Hist Dist—hist pl MS-4
East Hollywood Private Sch—school FL-3
East Holt Creek—stream NE-7
**East Homer**—pop pl NY-2
East Homer Sch—school NY-2
East Homerville Ch—church OH-6
East Hominy Oil Field—oilfield OK-5
**East Honaker**—pop pl VA-3
**East Honesdale**—pop pl PA-2
East Honey Creek—stream MO-7
East Honomaele—civil HI-9
East Hooks Sch—school TX-5
*East Hoosic* MA-1
*East Hoosic, Town of* MA-1
East Hoosick—locale NY-2
**East Hope**—pop pl ID-8
**East Hopewell**—pop pl SC-3
East Hopewell Ch—church IN-6
**East Hopewell (Township of)**—pop pl PA-2
East Hopkinton Cem—cemetery MA-1
*East Hopland* CA-9
**East Hopland**—pop pl CA-9
**East Hoquiam**—pop pl WA-9
*East Hoquiam River* WA-9
East Horn—summit WY-8
East Horne Brook—stream NH-1
East Horse Basin Rsvr—reservoir ID-8
East Horse Cove—valley NC-3
East Horse Creek—stream CO-8
East Horse Creek—stream SD-7
East Horse Flat—flat UT-8
East Horsehead Lake—lake WI-6
East Horsely Windmill—locale TX-5
*East Horse Neck Beach* MA-1
East Horseneck Beach—beach MA-1
*East Horseneck Shoal* FL-3
East Horse Pasture Windmill—locale TX-5
East Horseshoe Rsvr—reservoir WY-8
East Horse Windmill—locale NM-5
*East Houghton* MI-6
East Houma Sch—school LA-4
East Hounsfield—locale NY-2
**East Houston**—pop pl TX-5
East Houston Sch—school TX-5
East Howard County Oil Field—oilfield TX-5
*East Howards Creek* TX-5
East Howellsville (Township of)—fmr MCD NC-3
East HQ Pasture—flat KS-7
East HQ Well—well NM-5
East HQ Windmill—locale TX-5
East HS—hist pl NY-2
East HS—school AZ-5
East HS—school (2) CO-8
East HS—school IL-6
East HS—school (3) IA-7
East HS—school (2) KS-7
East HS—school (2) MI-6
East HS—school MN-6
East HS—school MS-4
East HS—school MO-7
East HS—school NE-7
East HS—school (4) NY-2
East HS—school (4) OH-6
East HS—school (4) TN-4
East HS—school UT-8
East HS—school WA-9
East HS—school WV-2
East HS—school (2) WI-6
East HS—school WY-8
*East Hubbardston* MA-1
**East Hubbardton**—pop pl VT-1
East Hubbardton Cem—cemetery VT-1
East Hudson Ch—church NC-3
East Hue and Cry—bar ME-1
*East Huffman Creek* TX-5
*East Humboldt Range* NV-8
East Humboldt Range—range NV-8
East Humbug Creek—stream (2) OR-9
East Hume Sch—school IL-6
East Hunter Canyon—valley TX-5
East Hunter Creek—stream CO-8
East Hunter Flat—flat UT-8
East Hunter Lake—lake MN-6
East Hunter Mesa Spring—spring WY-8
East Huntingdon HS—school PA-2
**East Huntingdon (Township of)**—pop pl PA-2
**East Huntington**—pop pl NY-2
East Huntington—uninc pl WV-2
East Huntsville Assembly of God Ch—church AL-4
East Huntsville Baptist Ch—church AL-4
East Huntsville Ch of Christ—church AL-4
East Huntsville Christian Ch (historical)—church AL-4
East Hurricane Creek—stream IL-6
East Hurricane Creek—stream MS-4
East Hutchinson—uninc pl KS-7
East Immanuel Cem—cemetery ND-7
East Imperial (CCD)—cens area CA-9
*Eastin* KS-7
Eastin-Arcola Union Sch—school CA-9
*Eastinaula Creek* TN-4
Eastin Cem—cemetery MO-7
*East Independence* MO-7
**East Independence**—pop pl MO-7
**East Independence (historical)**—pop pl OR-9
*East Index Mountain* WA-9
*East Indian Creek* CO-8
*East Indian Creek* ID-8
*East Indian Creek* WY-8
East Indian Creek—stream (2) IA-7
East Indian Creek—stream KS-7
East Indian Creek—stream MN-6
East Indian Creek—stream TX-5
East Indianola Elem Sch—school KS-7
East Indian Tank—reservoir AZ-5
East Indian Windmill—locale TX-5
*East India Pond* MA-1
East Indies Pond—lake MA-1
East Indies Rocks—island CT-1
East Inlet—bay NY-2
East Inlet—stream CO-8
East Inlet—stream ME-1
East Inlet—stream NH-1
East Inlet—stream (2) NY-2
East Inlet Bald Mountain Pond—stream ME-1
East Inlet Brook—stream NY-2
East Inlet Mtn—summit NY-2
East Inlet Trail—trail CO-8
East Interception Canal—canal CA-9
East Ionine Creek—stream OK-5
*East Iowa River* IA-7
East Iredell Sch—school NC-3
East Irish Creek—stream SD-7
East Iron Creek—stream WY-8
**East Irondale**—pop pl AL-4
**East Iron Hills**—pop pl IA-7
East Ironhills Ch—church IA-7
**East Irvine**—pop pl CA-9
**East Irvine (Valencia)**—pop pl CA-9
East Irving Mission—church MN-6
**East Irvington**—pop pl NY-2
East Irvington Sch—hist pl NY-2
East Island—island (2) AK-9
East Island—island MO-7
East Island—island (2) NY-2
East Island—island OR-9
East Island—island RI-1
East Island—island VA-3
East Island—island MH-9
East Island Lateral—canal WA-9
East Island Mesa Spring—spring CO-8
**East Islip**—pop pl NY-2
East Islip HS—school NY-2
East Islip JHS—school NY-2
East Italian Rsvr—reservoir CO-8
**East Ithaca**—pop pl NY-2
East Jack Creek—stream OK-5
East Jack Hollow Creek—stream OK-5
East Jacksboro Baptist Ch—church TN-4
East Jackson—unorg reg SD-7
East Jackson Baptist Ch—church TN-4
East Jackson (CCD)—cens area OK-5
East Jackson Cem—cemetery PA-2
East Jackson HS—school MI-6
East Jackson JHS—school MI-6
East Jackson Memorial Sch—school MI-6
East Jackson Sch—school OH-6
East Jack Tank—reservoir AZ-5
*East Jaffrey* NH-1
East Jakeman Creek—stream CO-8
**East Jamaica**—pop pl VT-1
**East Jamestown**—pop pl TN-4
East Jamestown Sch—school TN-4
East Janesville Ch—church IA-7
East Java—other NY-2
East Jefferson—locale NY-2
East Jefferson (CCD)—cens area TX-5
East Jefferson HS—school LA-4
East Jefferson Prairie Cem—cemetery WI-6
East Jellico Branch—stream KY-4
East Jellico Ch—church KY-4
**East Jenkins**—pop pl KY-4
**East Jermyn**—pop pl PA-2
East Jerome Butte—summit CA-9
East Jerusalem Baptist Ch—church (3) MS-4
East Jerusalem Ch—church LA-4
East Jerusalem Ch—church (2) MS-4
**East Jesse**—pop pl OK-5
**East Jessie**—pop pl OK-5
East Jetty—dam (4) LA-4
**East Jewett**—pop pl NY-2
East Jewett Range—summit NY-2
East JHS—school AR-4
East JHS—school CA-9
East JHS—school (2) CO-8
East JHS—school ID-8
East JHS—school IA-7
East JHS—school KS-7
East JHS—school (2) MA-1
East JHS—school (2) MI-6
East JHS—school MN-6
East JHS—school MS-4
East JHS—school (2) MO-7
East JHS—school MT-8
East JHS—school NM-5
East JHS—school NY-2
East JHS—school NC-3
East JHS—school ND-7
East JHS—school OH-6
East JHS—school SC-3
East JHS—school (2) TN-4
East JHS—school TX-5
East JHS—school WY-8
East Jim Ned Creek—stream TX-5
East Job Canyon—valley NV-8

East Joe Windmill—*locale* NM-5
**East Johnson**—*pop pl* VT-1
East Johnson Creek—*stream* IL-6
*East Johnson Fork Creek* TX-5
East Johnson Lake—*lake* LA-4
East Johnston (CCD)—*cens area* OK-5
*East Joliet* IL-6
**East Joliet**—*pop pl* IL-6
East Jones Chapel—*church* MS-4
East Jones Creek—*stream* MT-8
East Jones Creek—*stream* TX-5
**East Jordan**—*pop pl* MI-6
East Jordan Canal—*canal* UT-8
East Jordan Gulch—*valley* CO-8
East Jordan Tank—*reservoir* NM-5
East Joy Well—*well* AZ-5
East Juliand Hill—*summit* NY-2
**East Juliette**—*pop pl* GA-3
East Junction—*locale* OK-5
East Junction—*locale* TN-4
**East Junction**—*pop pl* IL-6
**East Junction**—*pop pl* MA-1
**East Junction (Gibson Junction)**—*pop pl* NC-3
East Juniata HS—*school* PA-2
**East Kamiah**—*pop pl* ID-8
East Kammerdiner Run—*stream* PA-2
**East Kane**—*pop pl* PA-2
**East Kansas**—*pop pl* VT-1
**East Kansas City**—*pop pl* MO-7
East Kansas City Airp—*airport* MO-7
*East Karankawa River* TX-5
East Kasson Cem—*cemetery* MI-6
East Kate Creek Spring—*spring* MT-8
East Kaupakulua—*civil* HI-9
**East Keansburg**—*pop pl* NJ-2
**East Keating (Township of)**—*pop pl* PA-2
East Keen Well—*well* NM-5
East Keggy Coulee—*valley* MT-8
East Kellehan Creek—*stream* WY-8
*East Kellerman* AL-4
East Kellerman Ch—*church* AL-4
East Kelly Field—*military* (2) TX-5
East Kemper Elem Sch—*school* MS-4
*East Kemper HS* MS-4
East Kendall Street Sch—*school* MA-1
East Kennebago Mtn—*summit* ME-1
East Kennedy Lake—*lake* CA-9
East Kent—*locale* CT-1
East Kent Creek—*stream* NY-2
East Kentucky Creek—*stream* KS-7
*East Keokuk* IL-6
East Keokuk Oil Field—*oilfield* OK-5
**East Kermit**—*pop pl* WV-2
East Kern (CCD)—*cens area* CA-9
East Kettle Creek—*stream* MS-4
East Key—*island* (2) FL-3
East Keyser Creek—*stream* MT-8
East Kickapoo Creek—*stream* (2) TX-5
East Kill—*stream* NY-2
*East Killbuck Creek* IL-6
East Kill Creek—*stream* KS-7
East Killdeer Creek—*stream* SD-7
**East Killen**—*pop pl* AL-4
**East Killingly**—*pop pl* CT-1
*East Kill Valley* NY-2
East Kill Valley Ch—*church* NY-2
East Kilns—*locale* NY-2
East Kimbark Canyon—*valley* CA-9
East Kingman Interchange—*crossing* AZ-5
East Kings Creek—*stream* TX-5
**East Kingsford**—*pop pl* MI-6
**East Kingsport**—*pop pl* TN-4
**East Kingston**—*pop pl* NH-1
**East Kingston**—*pop pl* NY-2
**East Kingston**—*pop pl* WV-2
East Kingston Cem—*cemetery* NH-1
**East Kingston (Town of)**—*pop pl* NH-1
East King Tank—*reservoir* NM-5
East Kiowa—*unorg reg* KS-7
East Kiowa Creek—*stream* KS-7
*East Kirkwood* MO-7
East Kiska Lake—*lake* AK-9
**East Kittanning (subdivision)**—*pop pl* PA-2
East Kittitas—*locale* WA-9
East Kittson (Unorganized Territory of)—*unorg* MN-6
East Knee—*summit* MT-8
East Knob—*summit* VA-3
East Knox—*locale* ME-1
East Knox County Elem Sch—*school* TN-4
East Knox Sch—*school* ME-1
East Knuckey Creek—*stream* MN-6
East Koochiching (Unorganized Territory of)—*unorg* MN-6
East Koogle Creek—*stream* TX-5
East K O Sch—*school* TX-5
East Koshkonkong Ch—*church* WI-6
**East Koy**—*pop pl* NY-2
East Koy Creek—*stream* NY-2
East Kremlin Gas Field—*oilfield* OK-5
**East Krok**—*pop pl* WI-6
East Krotz Springs—*locale* LA-4
East Krotz Springs—*uninc pl* LA-4
East Kuiaha Gulch—*valley* HI-9
*East Kuiaha Stream* HI-9
East Kurtz Spring—*spring* ID-8
East Labelle Canal—*canal* ID-8
East Laberdie Creek—*stream* KS-7
East Lacey Creek—*stream* AR-4
**East Lackawannock (Township of)**—*pop pl* PA-2
East Lacy Fork—*valley* AZ-5
East Ladoga Cem—*cemetery* WI-6
East Lafferty Creek—*stream* AR-4
East Lagoon—*bay* FM-9
East Lagoon—*lake* IL-6
East Lagoon—*lake* MP-9
East La Jolla Canyon—*valley* NM-5
*Eastlake* AL-4
*East Lake* CO-8
*East Lake* FL-3
*East Lake* IN-6
*East Lake* MA-1
*East Lake* (2) MI-6
*East Lake* MN-6
*East Lake* MT-8
*Eastlake* TN-4
*East Lake* TX-5
*East Lake* WI-6
East Lake—*lake* AZ-5
East Lake—*lake* AR-4
East Lake—*lake* (4) CA-9
East Lake—*lake* CO-8
East Lake—*lake* (5) FL-3
East Lake—*lake* ID-8
East Lake—*lake* IN-6
East Lake—*lake* IA-7
East Lake—*lake* KS-7
East Lake—*lake* (2) LA-4
East Lake—*lake* ME-1
East Lake—*lake* (12) MI-6
East Lake—*lake* (5) MN-6
East Lake—*lake* MS-4
East Lake—*lake* (2) MT-8
East Lake—*lake* NE-7
East Lake—*lake* NV-8
East Lake—*lake* (4) NM-5
East Lake—*lake* NY-2
East Lake—*lake* NC-3
East Lake—*lake* OR-9
East Lake—*lake* PA-2
East Lake—*lake* TX-5
East Lake—*lake* UT-8
East Lake—*lake* WA-9
East Lake—*lake* (4) WI-6
East Lake—*locale* GA-3
East Lake—*locale* NJ-2
East Lake—*locale* NC-3
**East Lake**—*pop pl* AL-4
**Eastlake**—*pop pl* CO-8
**East Lake**—*pop pl* MI-6
**East Lake**—*pop pl* MN-6
**Eastlake**—*pop pl* OH-6
**East Lake**—*pop pl* OR-9
**East Lake**—*pop pl* TN-4
East Lake—*reservoir* (2) AL-4
East Lake—*reservoir* IA-7
East Lake—*reservoir* (3) NJ-2
East Lake—*reservoir* NM-5
East Lake—*reservoir* PA-2
East Lake—*reservoir* UT-8
Eastlake—*uninc pl* CO-8
East Lake—*uninc pl* DE-2
East Lake, Lakes—*lake* OH-6
East Lake Abert Archeol District—*hist pl* OR-9
East Lake Andes Ch—*church* SD-7
East Lake Andes Lutheran Cem—*cemetery* SD-7
*East Lake Andes Lutheran Church* SD-7
East Lake Badus—*lake* SD-7
East Lake Baptist Ch—*church* TN-4
East Lake Branch Birmingham Public Library—*building* AL-4
East Lake Branch Carp River—*stream* MI-6
East Lake Brook—*stream* CT-1
East Lake Cem—*cemetery* AL-4
East Lake Cem—*cemetery* OH-6
East Lake (census name East Lake Park)—*uninc pl* FL-3
East Lake Ch—*church* NC-3
East Lake Ch of Christ—*church* AL-4
East Lake Ch of the Christian—*church* AL-4
East Lake Ch of the Nazarene—*church* TN-4
East Lake Christian Ch—*church* TN-4
East Lake Country Club—*other* GA-3
East Lake Creek—*stream* CO-8
East Lake Creek—*stream* MI-6
East Lake Creek—*stream* PA-2
East Lake Cumberland Presbyterian Ch—*church* AL-4
East Lake Cumberland Presbyterian Ch—*church* TN-4
East Lake Dam—*dam* AL-4
East Lake Dam—*dam* (3) NJ-2
East Lake Ditch—*canal* IN-6
East Lake Drive Interchange—*other* IL-6
East Lake Elem Sch—*school* TN-4
East Lake Ellis—*lake* FL-3
**East Lake Estates**—*pop pl* IN-6
**East Lake Estates**—*pop pl* TN-4
East Lakefield Cem—*cemetery* MI-6
*East Lake Fork* IL-6
East Lake Fork—*stream* IL-6
East Lake Fork—*stream* UT-8
*East Lake Fork Ditch* IL-6
**East Lake Francis Shores**—*pop pl* MN-6
**East Lake Gardens**—*pop pl* DE-2
East Lake JHS—*school* TN-4
East Lake Landing—*locale* NC-3
East Lake Lillian (Township of)—*civ div* MN-6
East Lake Methodist Ch—*church* AL-4
Eastlake Methodist Ch—*church* DE-2
East Lake-Orient Park—*CDP* FL-3
East Lake Palourde Oil and Gas Field—*oilfield* LA-4
East Lake Park—*park* AL-4
Eastlake Park—*park* AZ-5
East Lake Park—*park* GA-3
East Lake Park—*park* PA-2
East Lake Park—*park* TN-4
**East Lake Park (census name for East Lake)**—*pop pl* FL-3
East Lake Park Dam—*dam* AL-4
East Lake Ponca—*reservoir* OK-5
*Eastlake Post Office* TN-4
East Lake Post Office—*building* TN-4
*East Lake Reservoir* CO-8
East Lake Ripley—*lake* MN-6
**East Lake Ronkonkoma**—*pop pl* NY-2
*East Lake RR Dam* SD-7
**Eastlake (RR name East Lake)**—*pop pl* MI-6
East Lake (RR name for Eastlake Weir)—*other* FL-3
East Lake Rsvr—*reservoir* CO-8
East Lake Rsvr—*reservoir* CT-1
Eastlake Rsvr No 1—*reservoir* CO-8
Eastlake Rsvr No 2—*reservoir* CO-8
Eastlake Rsvr No 3—*reservoir* CO-8
East Lakes—*lake* MI-6
East Lakes—*lake* WA-9
East Lake Sand Oil and Gas Field—*oilfield* LA-4
East Lake Sch—*school* AL-4
East Lake Sch—*school* CA-9
East Lake Sch—*school* FL-3
East Lake Sch—*school* GA-3
East Lake Sch—*school* MO-7
East Lake Sch—*school* NY-2
East Lakes Dam—*dam* OR-9
Eastlake Square (Shop Ctr)—*locale* FL-3
East Lakes Rsvr—*reservoir* OR-9
**East Lake (subdivision)**—*pop pl* AL-4
East Lake Swamp—*swamp* MI-6
East Lake Tohopekaliga—*lake* FL-3
*East Lake Tohopekeliga* FL-3
East Lake (Township of)—*fmr MCD* NC-3
Eastlake (Township of)—*other* OH-6
East Lake United Methodist Ch—*church* TN-4
East Lake (Unorganized Territory of)—*unorg* MN-6
East Lake Verret Gas and Oil Field—*oilfield* LA-4
East Lakeview Sch—*school* CO-8
East Lakeville Cem—*cemetery* OH-6
**Eastlake Weir**—*pop pl* FL-3
**Eastlake Weir (RR name East Lake)**—*pop pl* FL-3
East Lake Windmill—*locale* TX-5
East Lake Woodlands Plaza (Shop Ctr)—*locale* FL-3
**East Lakewood (subdivision)**—*pop pl* MS-4
East Lamar HS—*school* TX-5
East La Mirada (census name for La Mirada East)—*CDP* CA-9
**East Lamoine**—*pop pl* ME-1
East Lamont Oil Field—*oilfield* OK-5
East Lampeter HS—*school* PA-2
East Lampeter Sch—*school* PA-2
East Lampeter Township Community Park—*park* PA-2
**East Lampeter (Township of)**—*pop pl* PA-2
**East Lancaster**—*pop pl* NY-2
East Lancaster Ave Hist Dist—*hist pl* PA-2
East Lancaster Township—*fmr MCD* IA-7
Eastland—*locale* PA-2
Eastland—*locale* TN-4
**Eastland**—*pop pl* KY-4
**Eastland**—*pop pl* MS-4
**Eastland**—*pop pl* TX-5
**Eastland**—*pop pl* UT-8
Eastland—*post sta* OH-6
Eastland—*uninc pl* KY-4
Eastland Baptist Ch—*church* FL-3
Eastland (CCD)—*cens area* TX-5
Eastland Cem—*cemetery* IL-6
Eastland Cem—*cemetery* TN-4
*Eastland Center* MI-6
Eastland Ch—*church* MO-7
Eastland Ch—*church* TN-4
Eastland Ch—*church* VA-3
Eastland Ch of Christ—*church* TN-4
Eastland Christian Sch—*school* FL-3
*Eastland Church* MS-4
**Eastland (County)**—*pop pl* TX-5
Eastland Creek—*stream* AK-9
Eastland Creek—*stream* (2) VA-3
Eastland Creek Landing—*locale* VA-3
East Landergin Well—*well* TX-5
*Eastland Gardens* IN-6
**Eastland Gardens**—*pop pl* IN-6
*Eastland Heights* NV-8
Eastland Heights—*locale* GA-3
**Eastland Heights**—*pop pl* MA-1
Eastland Heights Baptist Ch—*church* TN-4
**Eastland Hills**—*pop pl* (3) PA-2
Eastland JHS—*school* MI-6
Eastland Junior High Annex—*school* MI-6
Eastland Lake—*reservoir* TX-5
Eastland Mall—*locale* NC-3
Eastland Mall Shop Ctr—*locale* MI-6
Eastland Morris Oil Field—*oilfield* TX-5
**Eastland Park**—*pop pl* (2) KY-4
Eastland Parkway Ch—*church* KY-4
Eastland Post Office (historical)—*building* TN-4
Eastland Sch—*school* MI-6
Eastland Sch (historical)—*school* TN-4
Eastland Shop Ctr—*locale* MI-6
Eastland Shop Ctr—*locale* OH-6
Eastland Shop Ctr—*locale* OK-5
*Eastlands Old Stand* TN-4
Eastland Stand (historical)—*locale* TN-4
**Eastland Township**—*pop pl* UT-8
East Langsdale Oil Field—*oilfield* MS-4
**East Lansdowne**—*pop pl* PA-2
East Lansdowne Borough—*civil* PA-2
East Lansdowne Elem Sch—*school* PA-2
**East Lansing**—*pop pl* MI-6
**East Lansing**—*pop pl* NY-2
**East Laport**—*pop pl* NC-3
East Laporte Street Footbridge—*hist pl* IN-6
East Largoeta Well—*well* NM-5
East La Salle—*locale* CO-8
**East Las Vegas**—*pop pl* NV-8
East Las Vegas Park—*park* NV-8
East Las Virgenes Canyon—*valley* CA-9
East Lateral—*canal* (2) CO-8
East Lateral—*canal* ID-8
East Lateral—*canal* (2) OR-9
East Lateral—*canal* UT-8
East Lateral—*canal* WA-9
East Lateral Farmers Irrigation Company Ditch—*canal* CO-8
East Latigo Tank—*reservoir* NM-5
*East Laurel Baptist Church* TN-4
East Laurens HS—*school* GA-3
East Laurens Sch—*school* GA-3
**East Laurinburg**—*pop pl* NC-3
East Laurinburg Center for Exceptional Children—*school* NC-3
East La Vega Sch—*school* TX-5
East Lawn—*other* MI-6
**Eastlawn**—*pop pl* MI-6
**East Lawn**—*pop pl* OH-6
**East Lawn**—*pop pl* PA-2
Eastlawn—*uninc pl* MS-4
Eastlawn Baptist Ch—*church* MS-4
Eastlawn Burial Park—*cemetery* OH-6
East Lawn Cem—*cemetery* AR-4
East Lawn Cem—*cemetery* CA-9
East Lawn Cem—*cemetery* CT-1
East Lawn Cem—*cemetery* GA-3
Eastlawn Cem—*cemetery* GA-3
East Lawn Cem—*cemetery* (2) IL-6
Eastlawn Cem—*cemetery* IL-6
East Lawn Cem—*cemetery* (2) IA-7
East Lawn Cem—*cemetery* KY-4
Eastlawn Cem—*cemetery* MA-1
East Lawn Cem—*cemetery* MI-6
East Lawn Cem—*cemetery* MO-7
East Lawn Cem—*cemetery* (2) NE-7
East Lawn Cem—*cemetery* NY-2
Eastlawn Cem—*cemetery* (2) PA-2
Eastlawn Cem—*cemetery* TX-5
East Lawn Cem—*cemetery* TX-5
East Lawn Cem—*cemetery* (2) WI-6
*East Lawn Cemetery* UT-8
*Eastlawn Church* IN-6
*East Lawn Elementary School* MS-4
Eastlawn Elem Sch—*school* (2) IN-6
*Eastlawn Gardens* PA-2
Eastlawn Gardens—*CDP* PA-2
East Lawn Memorial Cem—*cemetery* MO-7
East Lawn Memorial Cem—*cemetery* OH-6
East Lawn Memorial Garden—*cemetery* IL-6
East Lawn Memorial Garden—*cemetery* IA-7
Eastlawn Memorial Gardens—*cemetery* CO-8
East Lawn Memorial Gardens—*cemetery* (2) MI-6
Eastlawn Memorial Gardens—*cemetery* VA-3
East Lawn Memorial Hills—*cemetery* UT-8
Eastlawn Memorial Park—*cemetery* TN-4
East Lawn Memorial Park Cem—*cemetery* TN-4
Eastlawn Park—*park* KS-7
East Lawn Park—*park* ND-7
Eastlawn Sch—*school* MI-6
East Lawn Sch—*school* MS-4
Eastlawn Sch—*school* NC-3
East Lawn Southgate Cem—*cemetery* CA-9
Eastlawn United Methodist Ch—*church* MS-4
Eastlawn Wesleyan Ch—*church* IN-6
East Lawrence—*locale* PA-2
East Lawrence Elem Sch—*school* PA-2
East Lawrence Sch—*school* AL-4
East Lawrence Sch—*school* PA-2
**East Lawrenceville**—*pop pl* PA-2
**East Layton**—*pop pl* UT-8
*East Layton Elementary School* UT-8
**East Layton Hills Subdivision**—*pop pl* UT-8
East Layton Sch—*school* UT-8
East Leach Park—*park* IA-7
East Lead—*bay* MI-6
East Leaf Lake—*lake* MN-6
East Leake—*locale* VA-3
East Leavenworth—*locale* MO-7
*East Lebanon* NH-1
**East Lebanon**—*pop pl* ME-1
**East Lebanon**—*pop pl* OR-9
East Leck Windmill—*locale* TX-5
**East Lee**—*pop pl* MA-1
East Lee Canyon—*valley* NV-8
East Lee County JHS—*school* NC-3
East Leesville Ch—*church* LA-4
East Lehman Windmill—*locale* TX-5
East Leidy—*summit* WY-8
East Leland Cem—*cemetery* MI-6
East Lelia Lake Creek—*stream* TX-5
East Lemke Creek—*stream* WI-6
East Lemolo Camp—*park* OR-9
**East Lemon**—*pop pl* PA-2
East Lemon Cem—*cemetery* PA-2
East Lemonweir Ch—*church* WI-6
**East Lempster**—*pop pl* NH-1
East Lenox—*locale* PA-2
East Lenox Cem—*cemetery* OH-6
**East Leon**—*pop pl* NY-2
*East Leonard Canyon* AZ-5
East Leonard Canyon—*valley* AZ-5
East Leonard Canyon Creek—*stream* AZ-5
East Leonard Sch—*school* MI-6
East Leon Creek—*stream* CO-8
East Leptondale Ch—*church* NY-2
East Leroux Creek—*stream* CO-8
**East Leroy**—*pop pl* MI-6
**East Letart**—*pop pl* OH-6
**East Leverett**—*pop pl* MA-1
**East Lewisburg**—*pop pl* PA-2
East Lewis (CCD)—*cens area* TN-4
East Lewis Creek—*stream* CO-8
East Lewis Division—*civil* TN-4
*East Lewiston* ID-8
**East Lewistown**—*pop pl* OH-6
**East Lexington**—*pop pl* MA-1
**East Lexington**—*pop pl* VA-3
East Leyden Sch—*school* IL-6
*East Liberty* PA-2
East Liberty—*locale* PA-2
East Liberty—*locale* TX-5
**East Liberty**—*pop pl* IN-6
**East Liberty**—*pop pl* (3) OH-6
**East Liberty**—*pop pl* PA-2
East Liberty (CCD)—*cens area* FL-3
East Liberty Cem—*cemetery* IA-7
East Liberty Cem—*cemetery* MO-7
East Liberty Cem—*cemetery* OH-6
East Liberty Cem—*cemetery* TX-5
East Liberty Ch—*church* IN-6
East Liberty Ch—*church* IA-7
East Liberty Ch—*church* MI-6
East Liberty Ch—*church* OH-6
East Liberty Ch—*church* TX-5
East Liberty Market—*hist pl* PA-2
East Liberty Sch—*school* (4) IL-6
East Liberty Sch—*school* TX-5
East Liberty Station—*building* PA-2
*East Lick Creek* IN-6
East Lick Creek—*stream* MO-7
East Lick Creek—*stream* NY-2
East Licking Creek—*stream* PA-2
East Light—*locale* OR-9
East Light Ch—*church* GA-3
*East Lightning Creek* MT-8
East Lime Creek—*stream* CO-8
East Lime Lake—*lake* AK-9
**East Limestone**—*pop pl* AL-4
East Limestone Sch—*school* AL-4
**East Limington**—*pop pl* ME-1
East Lincoln—*locale* MS-4
East Lincoln Baptist Ch—*church* MS-4
East Lincoln Ch—*church* WI-6
East Lincoln Consolidated Sch (historical)—*school* MS-4
*East Lincoln Elementary School* TN-4
East Lincoln HS—*school* NC-3
East Lincoln HS (abandoned)—*school* NC-3
East Lincoln JHS—*school* NC-3
East Lincoln Ridge—*ridge* AZ-5
East Lincoln Sch—*school* IA-7
East Lincoln Sch—*school* SD-7
East Lincoln Townhall—*building* IA-7
East Lincoln Township—*fmr MCD* IA-7
East Lincoln (Township of)—*civ div* IL-6
**East Lind**—*pop pl* WA-9
East Linden Sch—*school* OH-6
East Lindley—*locale* NY-2
**Eastline**—*pop pl* NV-8
**East Line**—*pop pl* NY-2
East Line Spring—*spring* ID-8
East Line Township—*inact MCD* NV-8
East Line Union Cem—*cemetery* NY-2
*Eastlings Lake* WI-6
East Linn (CCD)—*cens area* OR-9
East Linn Cem—*cemetery* IA-7
East Litchfield—*locale* CT-1
East Little Constance Bayou—*stream* LA-4
East Little Creek—*stream* IL-6
East Little Fork Ch—*church* MN-6
*East Little Owyhee River* ID-8
*East Little Owyhee River* NV-8
*East Little Pine Hollow* OR-9
*East Little Porcupine Creek* MT-8
East Little Post Oak Creek—*stream* TX-5
**East Little Rock**—*pop pl* AR-4
*East Little San Bernard Creek* TX-5
East Little Seneca Creek—*stream* VA-3
*East Little Sugar Creek* IN-6
East Little Sugar Creek—*stream* IN-6
**East Littleton**—*pop pl* MA-1
*East Littleton Station* MA-1
*East Little Walla Walla River* OR-9
East Little Walla Walla River—*stream* WA-9
East Livermore—*locale* ME-1
East Livermore Campgrounds—*locale* ME-1
East Livermore Ch—*church* ME-1
**East Liverpool**—*pop pl* OH-6
**East Liverpool North**—*pop pl* OH-6
East Liverpool Post Office—*hist pl* OH-6
East Liverpool Pottery—*hist pl* OH-6
East Liverpool (Township of)—*other* OH-6
*East Livingston Creek* AR-4
East Livingston Creek—*stream* AR-4
East Loch—*bay* HI-9
East Locust Creek—*stream* MO-7
East Logan—*unorg reg* ND-7
East Logan (CCD)—*cens area* OK-5
East Logan Draw—*valley* WY-8
East Lone Star Lateral—*canal* CO-8
East Long Beach—*uninc pl* CA-9
**East Long Branch**—*pop pl* NJ-2
East Long Branch Station—*locale* NJ-2
East Long Creek—*stream* IA-7
*East Longfellow School* IN-6
East Long Hollow—*valley* OR-9
East Long Lake—*lake* MI-6
*East Long Meadow* MA-1
**East Longmeadow**—*pop pl* MA-1
East Longmeadow Rod and Gun Club—*locale* MA-1
**East Longmeadow (Town of)**—*pop pl* MA-1
East Longnose Creek—*stream* SC-3
East Long Park Spring No 2—*spring* WY-8
East Long Pond—*lake* VT-1
East Longs Peak Trail—*trail* CO-8
East Longville Oil Field—*oilfield* LA-4
East Longwell Ridge—*ridge* NV-8
East Lookout Tower—*locale* GU-9
East Loon Bay—*bay* MN-6
East Looney Township—*civil* MO-7
East Loon Lake—*lake* IL-6
**East Loon Lake**—*pop pl* IL-6
**East Los Angeles**—*pop pl* CA-9
East Los Angeles Administration Center—*other* CA-9
East Los Angeles Junior Coll—*school* CA-9
East Lost Creek—*stream* CO-8
East Lost Creek—*stream* MO-7
East Lostine River—*stream* OR-9
East Lost Lake—*lake* CO-8
East Lost Lake—*lake* MN-6
East Lost Park—*flat* CO-8
**East Louisiana**—*pop pl* IL-6
East Louisiana State Hosp—*hospital* LA-4
East Louisiana State Hosp Colony Number 1—*hospital* LA-4
East Louisiana State Hosp Colony Number 2—*hospital* LA-4
East Louisiana State Hosp Colony Number 5—*hospital* LA-4
East Louisiana State Hosp Colony Number 6—*hospital* LA-4
East Louisville—*uninc pl* KY-4
*East Louisville Baptist Church* MS-4
East Louisville Ch—*church* MS-4
East Love (CCD)—*cens area* OK-5
East Lovell Oil Field—*oilfield* OK-5
East Love Tank—*reservoir* TX-5
East Lovington Oil Field—*other* NM-5
East Low Canal—*canal* WA-9
**East Lowell**—*pop pl* ME-1
East Lowell Sch—*school* WI-6
East Low Gap—*gap* CA-9
East Lucas Township—*fmr MCD* IA-7
**East Lumberton**—*pop pl* NC-3
Eastlund Lake—*lake* MN-6
East Lutheran Cem—*cemetery* IA-7
East Luxen Draw—*valley* CO-8
East Lycoming HS—*school* PA-2
*East Lyme* CT-1
**East Lyme**—*pop pl* CT-1
East Lyme HS—*school* CT-1
*East Lyme (sta.) (Niantic)* CT-1
**East Lyme (Town of)**—*pop pl* CT-1
*East Lyndon* ME-1
East Lyndon—*locale* ME-1
**East Lyndon**—*pop pl* VT-1
East Lynn—*locale* PA-2
**East Lynn**—*pop pl* IL-6
**East Lynn**—*pop pl* WV-2
East Lynn Cem—*cemetery* IL-6
East Lynn Ch—*church* WV-2
East Lynn Ditch—*canal* CO-8
**East Lynne**—*pop pl* MO-7
**East Lynne Addition (subdivision)**—*pop pl* UT-8
East Lynne Sch—*school* CA-9
East Lynn Grove Cem—*cemetery* MO-7
East Lynn Gulch—*valley* WA-9
East Lynn Lake—*reservoir* WV-2
*East Lynn Rsvr* WV-2
East Lynn Station (historical)—*locale* MA-1
**East Lynn (subdivision)**—*pop pl* MA-1
East Lynwood—*uninc pl* CA-9
**East Macedonia**—*pop pl* MS-4
*East Macedonia Church* MS-4
**East Machias**—*pop pl* ME-1
East Machias Hist Dist—*hist pl* ME-1
East Machias River—*stream* ME-1
**East Machias (Town of)**—*pop pl* ME-1
East Macon Ch (historical)—*church* TN-4
*East Macungie* PA-2
East Madalene Oil Field—*oilfield* OK-5
East Madden Lateral—*canal* ID-8
**East Madison**—*pop pl* ME-1
**East Madison**—*pop pl* NH-1
East Madison Cem—*cemetery* IA-7
East Madison Sch—*school* MO-7
East Madison Sch—*school* OH-6
East Madison Shop Ctr—*locale* AL-4
East Madison Township—*civil* MO-7
East Madrid—*locale* ME-1
East Madrid Sch—*school* ME-1
**East Magna**—*pop pl* UT-8
**East Magna Subdivision**—*pop pl* UT-8
East Magnolia Sewage Lagoon Dam—*dam* MS-4
**East Mahanoy Junction**—*pop pl* PA-2
*East Mahantango Creek* PA-2
East Maher Landing—*locale* AL-4
East Mahoning Ch—*church* PA-2
**East Mahoning (Township of)**—*pop pl* PA-2
East Maiden Ch—*church* NC-3
East Main Canal—*canal* AZ-5
East Main Canal—*canal* ID-8
East Main Ch of Christ—*church* MS-4
East Main Drain—*canal* ID-8
East Main Drain—*canal* TX-5
**East Maine**—*pop pl* NY-2
East Main Street Bridge—*hist pl* KY-4
East Main Street Cem—*cemetery* MA-1
East Main Street Commercial Hist Dist—*hist pl* NY-2
East Main Street-Glen Miller Park Hist Dist—*hist pl* IN-6
East Main Street Hist Dist—*hist pl* CT-1
East Main Street Hist Dist—*hist pl* KY-4
East Main Street Hist Dist—*hist pl* LA-4
East Main Street Hist Dist—*hist pl* NY-2
East Main Street Hist Dist—*hist pl* (2) OH-6
East Main Street Hist Dist—*hist pl* SC-3
East Main Street Hist Dist—*hist pl* (2) TN-4
East Main Street Residential District—*hist pl* GA-3
East Main Street Residential Hist Dist—*hist pl* GA-3
East Main Street Residential Hist Dist—*hist pl* TX-5
East Main Street Sch—*school* NY-2
East Major (CCD)—*cens area* OK-5
East Makaiwa—*civil* HI-9
East Malcom Sch—*school* AL-4
East Maljamar Oil Field—*other* NM-5
East Malone Lateral—*canal* OR-9
East Malpais Windmill—*locale* NM-5
*East Mam Creek* CO-8
East Mamm Creek—*stream* CO-8
*Eastman* VA-3
Eastman—*locale* MS-4
Eastman—*locale* OK-5
Eastman—*locale* WA-9
**Eastman**—*pop pl* GA-3
**Eastman**—*pop pl* NH-1
**Eastman**—*pop pl* SC-3
**Eastman**—*pop pl* WI-6
Eastman, George, House—*hist pl* NY-2
Eastman Ave Sch—*school* CA-9
Eastman Basin—*basin* CO-8
Eastman Brake—*swamp* AR-4
Eastman Branch—*stream* SC-3
Eastman Brook—*stream* (2) ME-1
Eastman Brook—*stream* (4) NH-1
Eastman Canyon—*valley* CA-9
Eastman (CCD)—*cens area* GA-3
Eastman Cem—*cemetery* ME-1
Eastman Cem—*cemetery* (2) NH-1
Eastman Cem—*cemetery* NY-2
Eastman Cem—*cemetery* ND-7
Eastman Cem—*cemetery* OH-6
Eastman Cem—*cemetery* SD-7
Eastman Cem—*cemetery* WI-6
**East Manchester (Township of)**—*pop pl* PA-2
Eastman Corners—*locale* (2) NY-2
**Eastman Corners**—*pop pl* NH-1
East Mancos River—*stream* CO-8
Eastman Cottage—*hist pl* NY-2
Eastman Creek—*stream* CA-9
Eastman Creek—*stream* CO-8
Eastman Creek—*stream* MT-8
Eastman Creek—*stream* (2) NC-3
Eastman Creek—*stream* OK-5
Eastman Creek—*stream* OR-9
**East Mandarin**—*pop pl* FL-3
Eastman Dental Dispensary—*hist pl* NY-2
Eastman Ditch—*canal* MT-8
Eastman Family Cem—*cemetery* UT-8
Eastman Gulch—*valley* CA-9
Eastman Gulch—*valley* OR-9
East Manhattan (Site)—*locale* NV-8
East Manhattan Spring—*spring* NV-8
East Manhattan Wash—*stream* NV-8
**Eastman Heights**—*pop pl* DE-2
Eastman Hill—*summit* (3) ME-1
Eastman Hill—*summit* (2) NH-1
Eastman Hill—*summit* NY-2
Eastman Hill—*summit* PA-2
Eastman Hill—*summit* WA-9
Eastman Hills—*range* OK-5
**Eastman (historical)**—*pop pl* TN-4
Eastman Hosp—*hospital* NH-1
*Eastman Lake* CA-9
Eastman Lake—*lake* CA-9
Eastman Lake—*lake* (2) NY-2
Eastman Lateral—*canal* CA-9
Eastman Ledges—*bench* NH-1
**Eastman Mills**—*pop pl* GA-3
Eastman Mine—*mine* CA-9
Eastman Mtn—*summit* GA-3
Eastman Mtn—*summit* NH-1

Eastman Oil Field—*oilfield* KS-7
**East Manor**—*pop pl* TN-4
**East Manor Estates (subdivision)**—*pop pl* MS-4
Eastman Park—*park* MN-6
Eastman Park—*park* NY-2
Eastman Place—*locale* CA-9
Eastman Place—*locale* WY-8
**Eastman Point**—*pop pl* NH-1
Eastman Pond—*lake* NH-1
Eastman Pond—*lake* VT-1
Eastman Pond—*lake* WA-9
Eastman Pond—*reservoir* CT-1
Eastman Post Office (historical)—*building* MS-4
Eastman Ranch—*locale* CA-9
Eastman Rec Area—*park* TN-4
*Eastmans Brake* AR-4
Eastmans Branch—*stream* MO-7
Eastmans Brook—*stream* MA-1
Eastmans Brook—*stream* NJ-2
Eastman Sch—*school* (2) NH-1
Eastman Sch—*school* NY-2
Eastman Sch—*school* NC-3
Eastman Sch (historical)—*school* PA-2
Eastman Sch Number 4 (historical)—*school* SD-7
Eastman Sch of Music—*school* NY-2
**East Mansfield**—*pop pl* MA-1
**East Mansfield**—*pop pl* OH-6
Eastman-Shaver House—*hist pl* OR-9
Eastmans Island—*island* MI-6
Eastman Slough—*gut* NH-1
Eastman Slough—*gut* SD-7
Eastman State Wildlife Mngmt Area—*park* SD-7
Eastman Terrace—*hist pl* NY-2
*East Mant Island* FM-9
**Eastman (Town of)**—*pop pl* WI-6
**Eastman Township**—*pop pl* ND-7
**Eastmanville**—*pop pl* MI-6
Eastman Windmill—*locale* CO-8
Eastman Windmill—*locale* TX-5
East Maple Lake Sch—*school* MN-6
East Maplewood Sch—*school* WI-6
Eastmar—*uninc pl* WI-6
East Marable Street Hist Dist—*hist pl* GA-3
East Marco Bay—*bay* FL-3
**East Marianna**—*pop pl* PA-2
**East Marietta**—*pop pl* GA-3
*East Marietta Baptist Church* MS-4
East Marietta Ch—*church* MS-4
East Marin Island—*island* CA-9
**East Marion**—*pop pl* MA-1
**East Marion**—*pop pl* NY-2
**East Marion**—*pop pl* NC-3
East Marion (CCD)—*cens area* FL-3
East Marion Cem—*cemetery* MI-6
East Marion (census name for Marion East)—*CDP* NC-3
East Marion Ch—*church* MI-6
East Marion Community Center—*locale* MS-4
East Marion (Election Precinct)—*fmr MCD* IL-6
*East Marion High School* MS-4
East Marion Sch—*school* FL-3
East Mark Island Ledge—*bar* ME-1
**East Marlborough (Township of)**—*pop pl* PA-2
East Maroon Creek—*stream* CO-8
East Maroon Pass—*gap* CO-8
East Marsh Creek—*stream* KS-7
*East Marshfield* MA-1
*East Marshfield* OR-9
East Marshfield Station (historical)—*locale* MA-1
East Marsh Island—*island* SC-3
East Marsh River Ch—*church* MN-6
East Martin Cem—*cemetery* MI-6
East Martinsburg—*locale* NY-2
East Martinsburg Hist Dist—*hist pl* WV-2
*East Martin School* KS-7
East Martin Windmill—*locale* TX-5
East Martis Creek—*stream* CA-9
East Marvine Creek—*stream* CO-8
East Mary Island—*island* NY-2
East Maryvile Cem—*cemetery* TN-4
*East Maryville Baptist Church* TN-4
East Maryville Ch—*church* TN-4
East Mason Creek—*stream* MS-4
East Mason Lake—*lake* MN-6
**East Masonville**—*pop pl* NY-2
East Masonville Creek—*stream* NY-2
East Massapequa—*CDP* NY-2
East Matagorda Bay—*bay* TX-5
**East Matunuck (Snug Harbor)**—*pop pl* RI-1
*East Mauch Chunk* PA-2
East Mauch Chunk (Wahnetah)—*uninc pl* PA-2
**East Maupin**—*pop pl* OR-9
East Maverick Canyon—*valley* CO-8
East Max Hoeck Creek—*gut* FL-3
East Mayes (CCD)—*cens area* OK-5
East Mayfield—*uninc pl* TX-5
East Maysville Oil Field—*oilfield* OK-5
East May Valley Ditch—*canal* CO-8
East Mc afee Canyon—*valley* NM-5
East McCarron Sch—*school* MI-6
East McClain (CCD)—*cens area* OK-5
East McComb Baptist Ch—*church* MS-4
East McDaniel School—*locale* IL-6
East McDonough—*locale* NY-2
**East McDowell**—*pop pl* KY-4
East McDowell Creek—*stream* KS-7
East Mcdowell JHS—*school* NC-3
East Mc Elmo Creek—*stream* CO-8
East McElmo Creek—*stream* UT-8
East McFarland Lake—*lake* OR-9
East Mchenry—*unorg reg* ND-7
East Mcintosh—*unorg reg* ND-7
East McKay Flat (historical)—*flat* UT-8
East McKee Draw—*valley* CO-8
East McKee Draw—*valley* UT-8
East McKee Rsvr—*reservoir* CO-8
**East McKeesport**—*pop pl* PA-2
East McKeesport Borough—*civil* PA-2
East Mckenzie—*unorg reg* ND-7
East Mcleon—*unorg reg* ND-7
East McNeil Oil And Gas Field—*oilfield* AR-4
East Meacham Creek—*stream* OR-9
East Meadow—*CDP* NY-2
East Meadow—*flat* NY-2
**East Meadow**—*pop pl* GA-3
**East Meadow**—*pop pl* MD-2
*East Meadowbrook* IL-6
**East Meadowbrook**—*pop pl* IL-6
East Meadow Brook—*stream* CT-1
East Meadow Brook—*stream* NY-2
East Meadow Creek—*stream* CO-8
East Meadow HS—*school* NY-2
East Meadow Pond—*lake* NY-2
East Meadow River—*stream* MA-1
East Meadow River—*stream* NH-1
**East Meadows**—*pop pl* NY-2
**East Meadows Subdivision**—*pop pl* UT-8
**East Meadow Subdivision**—*pop pl* UT-8
*East Meadowview* IL-6
**East Mead (Township of)**—*pop pl* PA-2
East Means Oil Field—*oilfield* TX-5
**East Mecca**—*pop pl* OH-6
East Mecca Cem—*cemetery* OH-6
East Mecklenburg HS—*school* NC-3
East Medicine Tank—*reservoir* AZ-5
*East Medolenihmw* FM-9
*East Medway* MA-1
*East Melvindale* MI-6
East Memorial Cem—*cemetery* TX-5
East Memphis—*uninc pl* TN-4
East Menard Creek—*stream* TX-5
**East Mercer**—*pop pl* ME-1
East Mercer—*unorg reg* ND-7
**East Meredith**—*pop pl* NY-2
East Merrimack—*CDP* NH-1
East Mesa—*bench* NM-5
**East Mesa**—*pop pl* AZ-5
East Mesa—*summit* (3) AZ-5
East Mesa—*summit* (3) CA-9
East Mesa—*summit* CO-8
East Mesa—*summit* NM-5
East Mesa—*summit* TX-5
East Mesa Ch—*church* NM-5
East Mesa Creek—*stream* CO-8
East Mesa Ditch—*canal* (2) CO-8
East Mesa Interchange—*locale* NV-8
East Mesa Mine—*mine* AZ-5
East Mesa Sch—*school* NM-5
East Mesa Trail—*trail* UT-8
East Metate Creek—*stream* TX-5
*East Mexico* MO-7
East Meyer (historical)—*locale* TN-4
East Meyer Mine—*mine* TN-4
East Michigan Ave Hist Dist—*hist pl* MI-6
**East Middleboro**—*pop pl* MA-1
*East Middle Borough* MA-1
East Middleborough Station (historical)—*locale* MA-1
**East Middlebury**—*pop pl* VT-1
East Middle Cedar Creek—*stream* KS-7
East Middle Creek—*stream* CO-8
East Middle Creek—*stream* NE-7
East Middle East Windmill—*locale* WY-8
East Middle Fork Falls—*falls* CO-8
East Middle Fork Parachute Creek—*stream* CO-8
East Middle Patent Sch—*school* NY-2
East Middle River—*stream* AK-9
East Middle River—*stream* LA-4
East Middlesex Canal Grant—*unorg* ME-1
*East Middletown* CT-1
**East Middletown**—*pop pl* NY-2
East Middletown (census name for Mechanicstown)—*CDP* NY-2
East Midvale Sch—*school* UT-8
East Midway Cem—*cemetery* IL-6
East Midway Lake—*reservoir* NE-7
East Mile Creek—*stream* MI-6
*East Milford* NE-7
**East Milford**—*pop pl* NH-1
East Mill—*locale* AL-4
East Mill Basin—*bay* NY-2
East Mill Brook—*stream* NY-2
East Millbrook Intermediate Sch—*school* NC-3
**East Millbury**—*pop pl* MA-1
*East Mill Creek* IA-7
*East Mill Creek* PA-2
*East Mill Creek* UT-8
**East Millcreek**—*pop pl* UT-8
East Mill Creek—*stream* IL-6
East Mill Creek—*stream* IA-7
East Mill Creek—*stream* MO-7
East Mill Creek—*stream* (2) TX-5
East Millcreek Sch—*school* UT-8
*East Mill Creek School* UT-8
East Miller Canyon—*valley* AZ-5
East Miller Creek—*stream* CO-8
**East Miller's Cove**—*pop pl* TN-4
**East Millersport**—*pop pl* OH-6
**East Millfield**—*pop pl* OH-6
East Mill Flow—*swamp* NY-2
East Mill Gulch—*valley* CO-8
East Mill (historical)—*locale* AL-4
*East Milligan Canyon* CO-8
East Millinocket Center—*other* ME-1
East Millinocket (East Millinocket Center)—*CDP* ME-1
**East Millinocket (Town of)**—*pop pl* ME-1
East Mill Lake—*lake* MI-6
East Millpond—*reservoir* NY-2
**East Mill Run (subdivision)**—*pop pl* DE-2
**East Millsboro**—*pop pl* PA-2
East Millsboro Elem Sch—*school* DE-2
**East Millstone**—*pop pl* NJ-2
East Millstone Hist Dist—*hist pl* NJ-2
**East Millville**—*pop pl* PA-2
East Mill Well—*well* AZ-5
East Milton—*locale* ME-1
**East Milton**—*pop pl* FL-3
East Milton Elem Sch—*school* FL-3
**East Milton (subdivision)**—*pop pl* MA-1
East Milwaukee Street Hist Dist—*hist pl* WI-6
**East Milwaukie**—*pop pl* OR-9
East Mims—*locale* FL-3
East Mine Canyon Spring—*spring* CA-9
East Mine Creek—*stream* OR-9
East Minehart Run—*stream* PA-2
East Mine Hole Run—*stream* PA-2
East Mineral Creek—*stream* CO-8
East Mineral Hill—*summit* MA-1
East Miner Creek—*stream* WY-8
**East Mines**—*pop pl* PA-2
*East Mingo Branch* NC-3
East Mingo Creek—*stream* NC-3
East Mini Well Park—*park* AZ-5
*East Minneapolis* MN-6
East Minnow Branch—*stream* FL-3
East Minor Brook—*stream* CT-1
**East Minquadale**—*pop pl* DE-2
Eastminster Ch—*church* OH-6
Eastminster Ch—*church* SC-3
Eastminster Ch—*church* TN-4
*Eastminster Church* IN-6
Eastminster United Presbyterian Ch—*church* IN-6
East Mission Ch—*church* LA-4
East Mission Creek—*stream* KS-7
East Mississippi Female Coll (historical)—*school* MS-4
*East Mississippi Insane Asylum* MS-4
East Mississippi Junior Coll—*school* MS-4
East Mississippi State Hosp—*hospital* MS-4
**East Missoula**—*pop pl* MT-8
East Mitchel Canyon—*valley* CA-9
East Mitchell Lake—*lake* WI-6
East Mitchell Street Hist Dist—*hist pl* MI-6
East Mitten Butte—*summit* AZ-5
East Moddersville Cem—*cemetery* MI-6
**East Modesto**—*pop pl* CA-9
East Moe Ch—*church* MN-6
**East Mojave**—*pop pl* CA-9
**East Moline**—*pop pl* IL-6
East Moline State Hosp—*hospital* IL-6
East Molokai (CCD)—*cens area* HI-9
**East Monbo**—*pop pl* NC-3
Eastmoney Cem—*cemetery* MS-4
East Money Ch—*church* MS-4
East Mongaup River—*stream* NY-2
**East Monkton**—*pop pl* VT-1
East Monkton Cem—*cemetery* VT-1
**East Monmouth**—*pop pl* ME-1
East Monmt—*pillar* CO-8
**East Monongahela**—*pop pl* PA-2
**East Monroe**—*pop pl* OH-6
East Monroe Creek—*stream* NE-7
East Monroe (Election Precinct)—*fmr MCD* IL-6
Eastmont—*locale* PA-2
**Eastmont**—*pop pl* MI-6
**Eastmont**—*pop pl* (2) PA-2
**Eastmont**—*pop pl* SC-3
**Eastmont**—*pop pl* WA-9
Eastmont—*uninc pl* CA-9
East Montcalm Cem—*cemetery* MI-6
*East Mont Elem Sch* PA-2
East Mont Elem Sch—*school* PA-2
East Montgomery Elem Sch—*school* TN-4
East Montgomery HS—*school* NC-3
**East Monticello**—*pop pl* IN-6
**East Monticello**—*pop pl* IA-7
Eastmont JHS—*school* CA-9
Eastmont MS—*school* UT-8
Eastmont Park Sch—*school* OH-6
**East Montpelier**—*pop pl* VT-1
**East Montpelier Center**—*pop pl* VT-1
**East Montpelier (Town of)**—*pop pl* VT-1
Eastmont Plaza Shop Ctr—*locale* AL-4
**Eastmont (subdivison)**—*pop pl* AL-4
East Monument Rsvr—*reservoir* ID-8
East Moody Canyon—*valley* UT-8
East Moody Island—*island* ME-1
*East Moon Lake* MN-6
East Moon Lake—*lake* AR-4
East Moore Sch (historical)—*school* TN-4
East Moorhead Elem Sch—*school* MS-4
Eastmoor HS—*school* OH-6
Eastmoor JHS—*school* OH-6
Eastmoor Park—*park* AZ-5
East Moose Head Spring—*spring* CO-8
**Eastmor**—*pop pl* NY-2
East Moran Bay—*bay* MI-6
**East Moravia**—*pop pl* PA-2
*East Moreland* OR-9
**Eastmoreland**—*pop pl* OR-9
**Eastmoreland**—*pop pl* VA-3
Eastmoreland Golf Course—*other* OR-9
*East Morgan Island* FL-3
East Morgan Key—*island* FL-3
East Morgan Spring—*spring* OR-9
East Morgantown Oil Field—*oilfield* MS-4
**East Moriches**—*pop pl* NY-2
East Morland Sch—*school* MO-7
East Mormon Mtns—*range* NV-8
East Morningside Creek—*stream* IA-7
East Morris—*locale* CT-1
**East Morris**—*pop pl* IL-6
East Morris Brook—*stream* CT-1
East Morton—*unorg reg* ND-7
East Morton Baptist Ch—*church* MS-4
East Morton Cem—*cemetery* MS-4
East Moscow Lookout—*locale* ID-8
East Moss Lake Oil and Gas Field—*oilfield* LA-4
**East Moss Point**—*pop pl* MS-4
East Moss Point Baptist Ch—*church* MS-4
Eastmost River—*stream* NC-3
Eastmost Swamp—*swamp* NC-3
East Mott Creek—*stream* OK-5
East Mott Windmill—*locale* TX-5
East Moultrie—*uninc pl* GA-3
East Mound—*summit* TX-5
East Mound Branch—*stream* (2) MO-7
*East Mound Branch - in part* MO-7
East Mound Cem—*cemetery* (2) TX-5
East Mound Cotton Gin—*locale* TX-5
East Mound Park—*park* IL-6
*East Mountain* CO-8
*East Mountain* CT-1
**East Mountain**—*pop pl* CT-1
**East Mountain**—*pop pl* TX-5
East Mountain—*ridge* MA-1
East Mountain Brook—*stream* (2) CT-1
East Mountain Cem—*cemetery* TX-5
East Mountain Country Club—*locale* MA-1
East Mountain Creek—*stream* TX-5
East Mountain Rsvr—*reservoir* CT-1
East Mountain Rsvr—*reservoir* ID-8
East Mountain Sch—*school* MA-1
East Mountain State Forest—*forest* MA-1
East Mountaintown Creek—*stream* GA-3
East Mountain Trail—*trail* OR-9
East Mountain View Ch—*church* TN-4
East Mountain Way—*trail* ID-8
**East Mount Carmel**—*pop pl* IN-6
East Mount Cem—*cemetery* TX-5
*East Mount Olive Baptist Ch* MS-4
*East Mount Olive Ch* MS-4
East Mount Olive Ch—*church* MS-4
East Mount Pleasant Cem—*cemetery* MS-4
East Mount Pleasant Cem—*cemetery* OK-5
East Mount Vernon—*other* ME-1
East Mount Zion Cem—*cemetery* KS-7
East Mount Zion Ch—*church* MS-4
*East Mouth* FL-3
East Mouth—*channel* LA-4
Eastmouth Bay—*bay* NC-3
East Moxie (Township of)—*unorg* ME-1
East MS—*school* SC-3
East MS—*school* TN-4
*East Mtn* AR-4
*East Mtn* MA-1
East Mtn—*summit* AK-9
East Mtn—*summit* AZ-5
East Mtn—*summit* AR-4
East Mtn—*summit* ID-8
East Mtn—*summit* (4) MA-1
East Mtn—*summit* (8) NY-2
East Mtn—*summit* OR-9
East Mtn—*summit* (3) PA-2
East Mtn—*summit* (2) TX-5
East Mtn—*summit* (2) UT-8
East Mtn—*summit* (6) VT-1
East Mud Cave—*cave* AL-4
East Mud Creek—*stream* CO-8
East Mud Creek—*stream* OK-5
East Muddy—*fmr MCD* (2) NE-7
East Muddy Cem—*cemetery* NE-7
*East Muddy Creek* MT-8
East Muddy Creek—*stream* CO-8
East Muddy Creek—*stream* (2) NE-7
East Muddy Creek—*stream* WY-8
East Mud Lake—*lake* NY-2
East Mud Spring—*spring* UT-8
**East Mulberry**—*pop pl* FL-3
East Mule Creek—*stream* WY-8
East Muley Creek—*stream* OR-9
**East Muncy**—*pop pl* PA-2
East Murray (CCD)—*cens area* OK-5
East Murrayville Cabin Area—*locale* TN-4
East Murray Windmill—*locale* TX-5
East Muskegon Ch—*church* MI-6
East Musquash Lake—*lake* ME-1
East Mustang Creek—*stream* TX-5
East Myers Tank—*reservoir* NM-5
East Mytle Windmill—*locale* NM-5
East Nagai Strait—*channel* AK-9
East Nancy Oil Field—*oilfield* MS-4
**East Nantmeal**—*pop pl* PA-2
East Nantmeal Ch—*church* PA-2
**East Nantmeal (Township of)**—*pop pl* PA-2
East Napa Rsvr—*reservoir* CA-9
**East Naples**—*pop pl* (2) FL-3
East Naples MS—*school* FL-3
East Naples United Methodist Ch—*church* FL-3
East Narrows Prairie Cem—*cemetery* WI-6
East Nashville Hist Dist—*hist pl* TN-4
**East Nassau**—*pop pl* NY-2
*East Natick* RI-1
**East Natick**—*pop pl* RI-1
**East Natick (subdivision)**—*pop pl* MA-1
East Naturita Creek—*valley* CO-8
East Navidad River—*stream* TX-5
East Nebo Oil Field—*oilfield* LA-4
East Neck—*cape* ME-1
East Neck—*cape* NY-2
**East Neck**—*pop pl* NY-2
East Neebish Channel—*channel* MI-6
East Nekoosa Ch—*church* WI-6
East Nelson Cem—*cemetery* MI-6
East Nelson Creek—*stream* CA-9
East Nelson Lake—*lake* MN-6
**East Nelson (Township of)**—*pop pl* IL-6
East Neshoba Sch—*school* MS-4
*East Neward* NJ-2
East Newark—*locale* NY-2
**East Newark**—*pop pl* (2) NJ-2
East Newbern—*locale* IL-6
**East New Castle**—*pop pl* PA-2
**East New Castle (Joyce)**—*pop pl* PA-2
East New Hope Ch—*church* TX-5
East New Hope Ch—*church* VA-3
*East New London* CT-1
**East New London**—*pop pl* CT-1
East Newman Hill—*summit* AZ-5
East Newman Park—*flat* AZ-5
**East Newman Township**—*pop pl* NE-7
*East Newmarket* MD-2
**East New Market**—*pop pl* MD-2
East New Market Cem—*cemetery* MD-2
East New Market Hist Dist—*hist pl* MD-2
**East Newnan**—*pop pl* GA-3
East Newnan Lake—*reservoir* GA-3
East Newport—*locale* ME-1
**East Newport**—*pop pl* PA-2
East Newport—*uninc pl* CA-9
East New Port Ch—*church* FL-3
East Newport Hist Dist—*hist pl* KY-4
**East New Portland**—*pop pl* ME-1
East Newton HS—*school* MO-7
East Newton Sch—*school* GA-3
East Newton Sch—*school* NC-3
East New Water Tank—*reservoir* AZ-5
**East New York**—*pop pl* NY-2
East Nichols—*locale* NY-2
**East Nicolaus**—*pop pl* CA-9
East Nidaros Ch—*church* SD-7
*East Nidaros Lutheran Church* SD-7
East Nimishillen Ch—*church* OH-6
East Ninemile Canyon—*valley* NE-7
East Ninemile Creek—*stream* NE-7
East Ninemile Well—*well* AZ-5
East Nine Section Windmill—*locale* TX-5
East Nine Windmill—*locale* TX-5
**East Ninnekah**—*pop pl* OK-5
East Niota Baptist Ch—*church* TN-4
*East Nishnabotna River* IA-7
East Nishnabotna River—*stream* IA-7
**East Nitro**—*pop pl* WV-2
East Noble (CCD)—*cens area* OK-5
East Noble HS—*school* IN-6
East Nodaway River—*stream* IA-7
East No Name Creek—*stream* CO-8
East Nonations—*bar* NY-2
East Nooksack Glacier—*glacier* WA-9
East Norden Ch—*church* SD-7
East Norman Oil Field—*oilfield* OK-5
*East Norris Creek* TN-4
East Norristown MS—*school* PA-2
East Norriton—*CDP* PA-2
**East Norriton (Township of)**—*pop pl* PA-2
**East Northfield**—*pop pl* MA-1
*East Northfield Station* MA-1
**East Northfield Station**—*pop pl* MA-1
East Northport—*locale* ME-1
**East Northport**—*pop pl* NY-2
East Northport Cem—*cemetery* ME-1
East Northport (Northport (sta.))—*CDP* NY-2
East Northumberland Canyon—*valley* NV-8
*East North Yarmouth* ME-1
**East Norton**—*pop pl* MA-1
East Norton—*uninc pl* VA-3
**East Norview**—*pop pl* VA-3
*East Norwalk* CT-1
**East Norwalk**—*pop pl* CT-1
**East Norwalk**—*pop pl* OH-6
*East Norway* KS-7
**East Norwegian (Township of)**—*pop pl* PA-2
**East Norwich**—*pop pl* NY-2
*East Norwood* OH-6
**East Norwood**—*pop pl* OH-6
East Notch—*gap* NY-2
East Notch Mtn—*summit* NY-2
East Nottingham Friends Meetinghouse—*hist pl* MD-2
**East Nottingham (Township of)**—*pop pl* PA-2
East Nubble—*summit* ME-1
*East Nueces River* TX-5
East Nugget Gulch—*valley* SD-7
East Numa Lateral—*canal* CO-8
East Nunatak Glacier—*glacier* AK-9
East Oak Canyon—*valley* NE-7
*East Oakchia Landing* AL-4
**East Oak Cliff**—*pop pl* TX-5
*East Oak Creek* KS-7
East Oak Creek—*stream* (2) KS-7
**East Oakfield**—*pop pl* NY-2
East Oak Grove Cem—*cemetery* WV-2
**East Oak Hill**—*pop pl* WV-2
East Oakie—*other* IL-6
East Oakland—*uninc pl* CA-9
East Oakland Branch—*stream* TX-5
East Oakland (Township of)—*civ div* IL-6
**East Oakmont**—*pop pl* PA-2
**East Oaks Subdivision**—*pop pl* UT-8
East Oakview Sch—*school* MI-6
East Oakwood Cem—*cemetery* MO-7
East Oberlin Community Ch—*church* OH-6
East Ocean—*post sta* FL-3
**East Ocean View**—*pop pl* VA-3
East Ocean View Sch—*school* VA-3
East Odom Windmill—*locale* TX-5
East Of The Navajo—*area* UT-8
East Ohia—*civil* HI-9
East Oil Field—*oilfield* TX-5
East Oio Gulch—*valley* HI-9
East Okemah Oil Field—*oilfield* OK-5
East Okoboji Beach—*beach* IA-7
East Okoboji Lake—*lake* IA-7
East Okoboji Lake State Game Mgt Area—*park* IA-7
East Okoboji Lake State Game Mngmt Area—*park* IA-7
Eastok Sch—*school* NC-3
East Oldenburg Oil Field—*oilfield* MS-4
East Oldtown Ch—*church* OH-6
**East Olean**—*pop pl* NY-2
East Oliver—*unorg reg* ND-7
East Olive Sch—*school* NE-7
East Olmos Creek—*stream* TX-5
East Olson Lake—*lake* MN-6
**East Olympia**—*pop pl* WA-9
**East Olympus Heights Subdivision**—*pop pl* UT-8
**East Omaha**—*pop pl* NE-7
*Easton* ME-1
*Easton* MA-1
*Easton* MT-8
*Easton* NC-3
Easton—*locale* AL-4
Easton—*locale* WV-2
**Easton**—*pop pl* CA-9
**Easton**—*pop pl* CT-1
**Easton**—*pop pl* IL-6
**Easton**—*pop pl* KS-7
**Easton**—*pop pl* KY-4
**Easton**—*pop pl* LA-4
**Easton**—*pop pl* ME-1
**Easton**—*pop pl* MD-2
**Easton**—*pop pl* MA-1
**Easton**—*pop pl* MI-6
**Easton**—*pop pl* MN-6
**Easton**—*pop pl* MO-7
**Easton**—*pop pl* NH-1
**Easton**—*pop pl* NY-2
**Easton**—*pop pl* (2) OH-6
**Easton**—*pop pl* (2) PA-2
**Easton**—*pop pl* TX-5
**Easton**—*pop pl* WA-9
**Easton**—*pop pl* WI-6
Easton, Lake—*reservoir* WA-9
Easton Airp—*airport* PA-2
**Easton Anglers**—*pop pl* PA-2
Easton Anglers Dam—*dam* PA-2
Easton Area MS—*school* PA-2
Easton Bay—*bay* RI-1
Easton Beach—*beach* RI-1
Easton Branch—*stream* KY-4
*Easton Branch Bushkill Creek* PA-2
Easton Canyon—*valley* OR-9
Easton Catholic Elem Sch—*school* PA-2
Easton Cem—*cemetery* AR-4
Easton Cem—*cemetery* IL-6
Easton Cem—*cemetery* MA-1
Easton Cem—*cemetery* MI-6
Easton Cem—*cemetery* PA-2
Easton Cem—*cemetery* TX-5
Easton Cem—*cemetery* WI-6
*Easton Center* CT-1
*Easton Center* NH-1
**Easton Center**—*pop pl* ME-1
**Easton Center**—*pop pl* MA-1
*Easton Centre* MA-1
Easton Ch—*church* AR-4
Easton Ch—*church* MI-6
Easton Childrens Home—*building* PA-2
Easton City—*civil* PA-2
*Easton Corners* ME-1
Easton Country Club—*locale* MA-1
Easton Cove—*bay* VA-3
Easton Creek—*stream* CA-9
**Eastondale**—*pop pl* MA-1
Eastondale (historical P.O.)—*locale* MA-1
Easton Dam—*dam* PA-2
**Easton (Easton Center)**—*pop pl* MA-1
*Easton Furnace* MA-1
*Easton Glacier* WA-9
Easton Glacier—*glacier* WA-9
**Easton Green**—*pop pl* MA-1
Easton Gulch—*valley* CO-8
Easton Heights Cem—*cemetery* PA-2
Easton Hill—*summit* OH-6
Easton Hist Dist—*hist pl* MD-2
Easton Hist Dist—*hist pl* PA-2
Easton House—*hist pl* PA-2
Easton HS—*school* LA-4
Easton HS—*school* PA-2
**Easton in Holladay Condominium**—*pop pl* UT-8
Easton JHS—*school* MA-1
*Easton Lake* WA-9
Easton Lake—*lake* WI-6
*Easton Landing* MS-4
Easton Mound—*summit* WI-6
**Easton Place**—*pop pl* IA-7
**Easton Place**—*pop pl* VA-3
Easton Plaza—*locale* PA-2
*Easton Point* ME-1
Easton Point—*cape* MD-2
Easton Point—*cape* RI-1
**Easton Point**—*pop pl* MD-2
*Easton Pond* RI-1
Easton Pond—*lake* RI-1
Easton Pond—*reservoir* RI-1
Easton Pond North Dam—*dam* RI-1
Easton Pond South Dam—*dam* RI-1
Easton Ridge—*ridge* WA-9
Easton Rod and Gun Club—*locale* MA-1
Easton Roller Mill—*hist pl* WV-2
Easton Rsvr—*reservoir* CT-1
*Eastons Bay* RI-1
*Eastons Beach* RI-1
Easton's Castle—*hist pl* SD-7
Easton Sch—*school* VT-1
Easton Sch—*school* WI-6
*Eastons Point* RI-1
*Eastons Pond* RI-1
Easton Spring—*spring* CA-9
Easton Spring—*spring* OR-9
**Easton (sta.)**—*pop pl* MA-1
Easton State Airp—*airport* WA-9
**Easton Station**—*pop pl* ME-1
**Easton Station**—*pop pl* MA-1
**Easton (subdivision)**—*pop pl* AL-4
East Ontario—*mine* UT-8
**Easton Terrace (subdivision)**—*pop pl* TN-4
Easton Townhall—*building* MA-1
**Easton (Town of)**—*pop pl* CT-1
**Easton (Town of)**—*pop pl* ME-1
**Easton (Town of)**—*pop pl* MA-1
**Easton (Town of)**—*pop pl* NH-1
**Easton (Town of)**—*pop pl* NY-2
**Easton (Town of)**—*pop pl* (2) WI-6
*Easton Township* PA-2
**Easton Township**—*pop pl* KS-7
**Easton Township**—*pop pl* ND-7
**Easton (Township of)**—*pop pl* MI-6
*Easton Tract, The* PA-2
**Easton View**—*pop pl* NC-3
*Easton Village* PA-2
*Eastonville* MS-4
Eastonville—*locale* CO-8
Eastonville Cem—*cemetery* CO-8
East Onward Landing (historical)—*locale* TN-4
**East Oolitic**—*pop pl* IN-6
*East Opal Creek* OR-9
East Opdal Cem—*cemetery* ND-7
East Opdal Cem (old)—*cemetery* ND-7
East Opolis Sch (abandoned)—*school* MO-7
**East Orange**—*pop pl* NJ-2
**East Orange**—*pop pl* VT-1
East Orange Branch—*stream* VT-1
East Orange (CCD)—*cens area* FL-3
East Orange Golf Course—*other* NJ-2
East Orange Sch—*school* SC-3
East Orange Station—*hist pl* NJ-2
East Orange Station—*locale* NJ-2
East Orange Township—*fmr MCD* IA-7
East Orchard Mesa—*summit* CO-8
East Orchard Mesa Community Hall—*locale* CO-8
East Ord Mtn—*summit* CA-9
East Ordway Lateral—*canal* CO-8
**East Oreland**—*pop pl* PA-2
East Oriental Covered Bridge—*hist pl* PA-2
East Orient Sch—*school* OR-9
**East Orland**—*pop pl* ME-1
East Orlando Baptist Ch—*church* FL-3
East Orlando Shop Ctr—*locale* FL-3
**East Orleans**—*pop pl* MA-1
East Oro Bay—*bay* WA-9
**East Orosi**—*pop pl* CA-9
**East Orrington**—*pop pl* ME-1
*East Orwell* OH-6
**East Orwell**—*pop pl* OH-6
East Osage City Oil Field—*oilfield* OK-5
East Otis—*fmr MCD* NE-7
**East Otis**—*pop pl* MA-1
**East Otisfield**—*pop pl* ME-1
East Otter Creek—*stream* (2) IA-7
East Otter Creek—*stream* (2) OK-5
East Otter Lake—*lake* MN-6
East Otterson Wash—*valley* WY-8
**East Otto**—*pop pl* NY-2
East Otto Creek—*stream* NY-2
**East Otto (Town of)**—*pop pl* NY-2
**East Ottumwa**—*pop pl* IA-7
East Oumalik Test Well—*well* AK-9
East Outer Channel—*channel* MI-6
East Outlet—*stream* (2) ME-1
East Oval Lake—*lake* WA-9
Eastover—*locale* VA-3
**Eastover**—*pop pl* MA-1
**Eastover**—*pop pl* NC-3

**Eastover**—pop pl SC-3
**Eastover**—pop pl TN-4
Eastover—uninc pl VA-3
East Over Bayou—stream LA-4
Eastover Brook—stream NY-2
Eastover (CCD)—cens area SC-3
Eastover/Central Elementary School NC-3
Eastover Ch—church SC-3
**Eastover Estates (subdivision)**—pop pl NC-3
**Eastover Farms**—pop pl MI-6
**Eastover Gardens**—pop pl VA-3
Eastover Hills—uninc pl DE-2
Eastover Hunting Club—other SC-3
**Eastover Junction**—pop pl SC-3
Eastover Lookout Tower—locale SC-3
Eastover Park—park TX-5
Eastover Sch—school MI-6
Eastover Sch—school NC-3
**Eastover (subdivision)**—pop pl AL-4
**Eastover (subdivision)**—pop pl MS-4
**Eastover (subdivision)**—pop pl (2) NC-3
Eastover (Township of)—fmr MCD NC-3
East Ovid Ch—church MI-6
East Owl Creek MT-8
**Eastowne (subdivision)**—pop pl NC-3
East Oxbow Brook MA-1
East Oxbow Brook—stream MA-1
East Oxford Cem—cemetery ME-1
East Oxford Ch—church MS-4
East Pace City Oil and Gas Field—oilfield AR-4
East Pacific Mine—mine MT-8
East Page Ditch—canal MI-6
East Pahranagat Range—range NV-8
East Paint Creek Ch—church IA-7
East Painter Creek—stream OH-6
East Painterhood Creek—stream KS-7
East Paint Lake—lake MI-6
**East Palatka**—pop pl FL-3
East Palatka (CCD)—cens area FL-3
East Palatka Mini-Mall—locale FL-3
East Palermo—locale ME-1
**East Palermo**—pop pl NY-2
**East Palestine**—pop pl OH-6
**East Palmyra**—pop pl NY-2
East Palmyra Cem—cemetery NY-2
**East Palo Alto**—pop pl CA-9
**East Palo Alto (Nairobi)**—pop pl CA-9
East Palo Alto (P.O.)—uninc pl CA-9
East Panguitch Canal—canal UT-8
East Panther Creek—stream CA-9
East Panther Creek—stream IL-6
East Panton Cem—cemetery VT-1
East Panton Sch—school VT-1
East Papoose Creek MT-8
East Paradise Sch—school IL-6
East Paradox Creek—stream CO-8
East Paraje Mesa—summit NM-5
East Paris MI-6
East Paris TN-4
**East Paris**—pop pl MI-6
**East Parish**—pop pl MA-1
East Parish Burying Ground—hist pl MA-1
East Paris Sch—school MI-6
East Park—park (2) AZ-5
East Park—park ID-8
East Park—park IA-7
East Park—park KS-7
East Park—park MO-7
East Park—park MT-8
East Park—park PA-2
East Park—park TN-4
East Park—park TX-5
East Park—park WI-6
**East Park**—pop pl IN-6
**East Park**—pop pl NY-2
**East Park Addition (subdivision)**—pop pl UT-8
East Park )AL-T70) AL-4
East Park Campground—locale UT-8
East Park Cem—cemetery GA-3
East Park Ch—church IL-6
East Park Creek—stream CO-8
East Park Dam—dam AZ-5
East Park Dam—dam UT-8
East Park Elementary School MS-4
East Park JHS—school IL-6
East Park Lakes—lake WY-8
**East Parkland**—pop pl NC-3
**East Parkrose**—pop pl OR-9
East Park Rsvr—reservoir CA-9
East Park Rsvr—reservoir PA-2
East Park Rsvr—reservoir UT-8
East Park Sch—school LA-4
East Park Sch—school MS-4
East Park Sch—school MO-7
East Park Sch—school (2) WV-2
East Park Shop Ctr—locale PA-2
East Park Speedway—other SC-3
**East Park (subdivision)**—pop pl AL-4
**East Park (subdivision)**—pop pl TN-4
East Park Towers—hist pl IL-6
**East Park (Township of)**—pop pl MN-6
East Park United Methodist Ch—church IN-6
East Parlin Spring—spring CO-8
East Parrish Ch—church MA-1
East Parrot Creek—stream MT-8
East Parsonfield ME-1
**East Parsonfield**—pop pl ME-1
**East Parsonsfield**—pop pl ME-1
East Parsons Tanks—reservoir CO-8
East Parsons Windmill—locale CO-8
East Part—locale NY-2
East Part Cem—cemetery MA-1
East Part Cem—cemetery NY-2
**East Pasadena**—pop pl CA-9
**East Pascagoula**—pop pl MS-4
East Pascagoula River - in part MS-4
**East Pasco**—pop pl WA-9
East Pasco Adventist Educational Center—school FL-3
East Pasco Med Ctr—hospital FL-3
East Pass—channel (5) FL-3
East Pass—channel (2) LA-4
East Pass—channel UT-8
East Pass—channel MP-9
East Pass—gap AZ-5
East Pass—gap NV-8
East Pass—gut LA-4
East Passage—channel FM-9
East Passage, Narragansett Bay—channel RI-1
East Passaic NJ-2
East Pass Calcasieu River—channel LA-4
East Pass Canyon—valley NV-8
East Pass Creek—stream CO-8
East Pass Creek—stream ID-8
East Pass Creek—stream MT-8
East Pass Creek—stream OR-9
East Pass Creek—stream SD-7
East Pass Creek—stream WY-8
East Pass Wash—stream NV-8
East Pasture—flat NV-8
East Pasture Corral—locale NV-8
East Pasture North Well—well NM-5
East Pasture South Well—well NM-5
East Pasture Tank—reservoir (2) AZ-5
East Pasture Tank—reservoir (2) NM-5
East Pasture Trail—trail NH-1
East Pasture Well—locale AZ-5
East Pasture Well—well MT-8
East Pasture Windmill—locale (2) CO-8
East Pasture Windmill—locale TX-5
**East Patchogue**—pop pl NY-2
East Patchogue Sch—school NY-2
East Paterson (2) NJ-2
East Patuk Creek—stream AK-9
East Pauls Valley Oil Field—oilfield OK-5
East Paw Paw Cem—cemetery IL-6
**East Peacham**—pop pl VT-1
East Peak CA-9
East Peak NV-8
East Peak—summit (3) AK-9
East Peak—summit AZ-5
East Peak—summit (2) CA-9
East Peak—summit CT-1
East Peak—summit ID-8
East Peak—summit ME-1
East Peak—summit (2) MT-8
East Peak—summit NV-8
East Peak—summit NH-1
East Peak—summit OR-9
East Peak—summit TX-5
East Peak—summit (2) WA-9
East Peak Lake—lake ID-8
**East Pea Ridge**—pop pl WV-2
East Pearl Baptist Church MS-4
East Pearl Ch—church MS-4
East Pearl Creek—stream SD-7
East Pearl River LA-4
East Peavine Creek—stream OK-5
East Pecatonica WI-6
**East Pecos**—pop pl NM-5
East Pecos JHS—school TX-5
East Pedarosa Windmill—locale TX-5
East Pelican Reef—bar FL-3
**East Pembroke**—pop pl MA-1
**East Pembroke**—pop pl NY-2
East Pembroke (historical P.O.)—locale MA-1
**East Penfield**—pop pl NY-2
East Penfield Ch—church NY-2
East Peninsula Peak UT-8
East Penn Airp—airport PA-2
East Penn Elem Sch PA-2
East Penn Elem Sch—school PA-2
**East Penn Junction**—pop pl PA-2
**East Pennsauken**—pop pl NJ-2
East Pennsboro Area MS—school PA-2
East Pennsboro Area Senior HS—school PA-2
**East Pennsboro (Township of)**—pop pl PA-2
East Penn Sch—school PA-2
East Pennsylvania Junction—locale PA-2
**East Penn (Township of)**—pop pl PA-2
East Penny Creek—stream KS-7
East Penny Creek—stream NE-7
East Penobscot Bay—bay ME-1
**East Pensacola Heights**—pop pl FL-3
**East Peoria**—pop pl IL-6
East Pepin Cem—cemetery WI-6
East Pepper Creek—stream FL-3
**East Pepperell**—pop pl MA-1
East Pepperell (RR name Pepperell (sta.))—CDP MA-1
East Perkins—unorg reg SD-7
East Perkins Oil and Gas Field—oilfield LA-4
East Perry High School AL-4
East Perry Sch—school AL-4
East Perryville Dewatering Area—basin TN-4
East Perryville Landing—locale TN-4
East Pershing Oil Field—oilfield OK-5
**East Pershing Plaza**—pop pl AZ-5
**East Peru**—pop pl ME-1
East Peru Cemeteries—cemetery ME-1
**East Peru (Peru PO)**—pop pl IA-7
**East Petersburg**—pop pl PA-2
East Petersburg Borough—civil PA-2
East Petersburg Civic Grounds—park PA-2
East Petersburg Elem Sch—school PA-2
East Peterson Creek—stream MT-8
**East Pharsalia**—pop pl NY-2
East Philadelphia Baptist Ch—church MS-4
East Phillips and Sons Pond MA-1
East Phillips Creek—stream OR-9
East Phillipston MA-1
East Phoenix AZ-5
East Pickerel Pond—lake WI-6
East Pierce Gulch—valley CO-8
East Pie Town Tank—reservoir NM-5
East Pigeon Creek—stream AR-4
East Pigeon Creek—stream MO-7
East Pike Elem Sch—school PA-2
East Pike Lake—lake MN-6
East Pikeland Elem Sch—school PA-2
**East Pikeland (Township of)**—pop pl PA-2
**East Pike Run (Township of)**—pop pl PA-2
East Pine Barren Creek—stream AL-4
East Pine Ch—church MS-4
East Pine Creek—stream CO-8
East Pine Creek—stream ID-8
East Pine Creek—stream IA-7
East Pine Creek—stream OR-9
East Pine Island Lake—lake TX-5
East Pine Knot Ch—church KY-4
East Pine Pond—lake (2) NY-2
East Pine River Cem—cemetery WI-6
East Pinery—woods CA-9
**East Pines**—pop pl MD-2
East Pine Sch (abandoned)—school MO-7
**East Pineville**—pop pl KY-4
East Pineville Ch—church LA-4
East Pine Wash—stream NV-8
East Piney Ch—church VA-3
East Piney Creek—stream TX-5
East Piney River—stream TN-4
East Pinkham Creek—stream MT-8
East Pinkstaff Ch—church IL-6
East Pinnacle—pillar KY-4
East Pinnacles Creek—stream CA-9
East Pin Oak Creek—stream MO-7
East Pinos Creek CO-8
East Pintlar Peak MT-8
East Pinto Creek—stream MT-8
East Pinto Creek—stream TX-5
East Pioche Mine—mine UT-8
East Pipe Creek KS-7
East Pipe Creek—stream KS-7
East Pipe Lake—lake MN-6
East Piquett Creek—stream MT-8
East Pitcairn—locale NY-2
East Pittman Creek—stream FL-3
**East Pittsburgh**—pop pl PA-2
East Pittsburgh Borough—civil PA-2
East Pittsburg (historical)—locale KS-7
**East Pittsford**—pop pl VT-1
**East Pittston**—pop pl ME-1
East Pittstown—locale NY-2
East Place MS-4
**East Plainfield**—pop pl NH-1
East Plains OH-6
**East Plains**—pop pl OH-6
East Plains Cem—cemetery MI-6
Eastplain Sch—school NY-2
East Plains Tank—reservoir NM-5
East Plainview Sch—school CO-8
East Plane—locale WY-8
East Planter Brook NY-2
**East Plantsite**—pop pl AZ-5
East Plantsite School AZ-5
East Platner Brook—stream NY-2
East Plattekill Cem—cemetery NY-2
East Platte River—stream IA-7
East Platte Sch—school MO-7
East Plattsmouth (historical)—locale IA-7
East Playground—park NY-2
East Plaza Shop Ctr—locale FL-3
East Plaza Shop Ctr—locale MS-4
East Pleasant Grove Baptist Church MS-4
East Pleasant Grove Cemetery MS-4
East Pleasant Grove Ch—church MS-4
East Pleasanton—locale CA-9
**East Pleasant Plain**—pop pl IA-7
East Pleasant Plains Sch—school MT-8
East Pleasant Ridge Sch—school WI-6
East Plowboy Mountain ID-8
East Plumbago Draw—valley WY-8
East Plum Creek—stream CO-8
East Plum Creek—stream KS-7
East Plum Creek—stream WY-8
East Plum River—stream IL-6
**East Plumville (subdivision)**—pop pl PA-2
East Plymouth OH-6
East Plymouth—locale CT-1
**East Plymouth**—pop pl CT-1
East Plymouth Hist Dist—hist pl CT-1
**East Pocahontas**—pop pl AR-4
East Pocket—basin AZ-5
East Pocket—bay TX-5
East Pocket Knob—summit AZ-5
East Pocket Lookout Tower—tower AZ-5
East Pocket Tank—reservoir AZ-5
**East Poestenkill**—pop pl NY-2
East Point AL-4
East Point FL-3
East Point ME-1
East Point MA-1
Eastpoint PA-2
East Point—bar ME-1
East Point—bend AK-9
East Point—cape (4) AK-9
East Point—cape AZ-5
East Point—cape CA-9
East Point—cape FL-3
East Point—cape ID-8
East Point—cape (5) ME-1
East Point—cape MD-2
East Point—cape MA-1
East Point—cape MS-4
East Point—cape NH-1
East Point—cape NJ-2
East Point—cape (3) NY-2
East Point—cape (2) NC-3
East Point—cape OR-9
East Point—cape UT-8
East Point—cape (2) VA-3
East Point—cape WA-9
East Point—cape WI-6
East Point—cape (2) MP-9
East Point—cape VI-3
East Point—locale TX-5
East Point—locale VA-3
**East Point**—pop pl AL-4
**Eastpoint**—pop pl FL-3
**East Point**—pop pl GA-3
**East Point**—pop pl KY-4
**East Point**—pop pl LA-4
**Eastpoint**—pop pl MD-2
**East Point**—pop pl PA-2
**Eastpoint**—pop pl PA-2
**East Point**—pop pl TN-4
**East Point**—pop pl VA-3
East Point—ridge MP-9
East Point—summit (2) CA-9
East Point—summit WA-9
East Point Assembly of God Ch—church FL-3
Eastpoint Bar—bar AL-4
Eastpoint (CCD)—cens area FL-3
East Point (CCD)—cens area GA-3
Eastpoint Cem—cemetery FL-3
East Point Cem—cemetery VA-3
East Point Ch—church AL-4
East Point Ch—church AR-4
East Point Channel NJ-2
East Point Channel—channel NJ-2
East Pointe Hosp—hospital FL-3
Eastpointe Sch—school MI-6
East Point Fire Tower (historical)—tower PA-2
East Point Industrial District—hist pl GA-3
East Point Marsh—swamp VA-3
East Point Mtn—summit AR-4
East Point Sch—school NE-7
East Point Sch (abandoned)—school MO-7
**Eastpoint Terminal**—pop pl IN-6
East Point Terrace IN-6
East Point Thorofare NJ-2
East Pokegama Creek—stream MN-6
**East Poland (Empire Road Station)**—pop pl ME-1
East Polecat Canyon—valley AZ-5
East Pole Creek—stream UT-8
East Pole Gulch—valley CO-8
East Pole Windmill—locale NV-8
East Ponchatoula Creek—stream LA-4
East Pond MA-1
East Pond—bar MA-1
East Pond—bay ME-1
East Pond—lake (2) ME-1
East Pond—lake MA-1
East Pond—lake NH-1
East Pond—lake (9) NY-2
East Pond—reservoir NY-2
East Pond Bog—swamp ME-1
East Pond Brook—stream NH-1
East Pond Creek—stream MI-6
East Pond Creek—stream OK-5
East Pond Mtn NY-2
East Pond Mtn—summit NY-2
East Pond Trail—trail NH-1
East Pontchatoula Creek LA-4
East Pontotoc Missionary Baptist Ch—church MS-4
East Pool—reservoir MN-6
East Poor Hollow—valley TX-5
East Pope Lake—lake MN-6
East Poplar Creek TN-4
East Poplar Oil Field—oilfield MT-8
East Porcupine Creek—stream MT-8
Eastport—locale AR-4
Eastport—locale CA-9
Eastport—locale FL-3
Eastport—locale IA-7
Eastport—locale OH-6
Eastport—locale OK-5
**Eastport**—pop pl ID-8
**Eastport**—pop pl ME-1
**Eastport**—pop pl MD-2
**Eastport**—pop pl MI-6
**Eastport**—pop pl MS-4
**Eastport**—pop pl NY-2
**Eastport**—pop pl (2) TN-4
East Portage Creek—stream AK-9
East Portal—dam CO-8
East Portal—locale CA-9
East Portal—locale CO-8
East Portal—locale MT-8
East Portal—locale UT-8
**East Portal**—pop pl CO-8
East Portal Adit—other CA-9
East Portal Duchesne Tunnel—tunnel UT-8
East Portal (inundated)—locale UT-8
East Portal Park—park CA-9
East Port Branch MS-4
Eastport Branch—stream MS-4
Eastport Cem—cemetery OK-5
Eastport Ch—church FL-3
East Port Chester CT-1
**East Port Chester**—pop pl CT-1
Eastport Creek—stream MI-6
East Port Dock TN-4
Eastport Dock—locale MS-4
Eastport Dock—locale TN-4
Eastport Elementary School TN-4
Eastport Elem Sch—school IN-6
East Porter Cow Camp—locale WY-8
East Porter Creek—stream CO-8
East Porter Creek—stream OR-9
East Porterville (Doyle Colony)—CDP CA-9
Eastport Female Acad (historical)—school MS-4
Eastport Ferry (historical)—locale TN-4
Eastport Hist Dist—hist pl ME-1
**East Port (historical)**—pop pl IA-7
**East Portland**—pop pl OR-9
East Portland Branch, Public Library of Multnomah County—hist pl OR-9
Eastport Landing AL-4
East Port Landing—locale AL-4
Eastport Landing (historical)—locale MS-4
Eastport Male Acad (historical)—school MS-4
East-Port Orange Congregations of Jehovahs Witnesses—church FL-3
**East Port Orchard**—pop pl WA-9
Eastport Saltpeter Cave—cave TN-4
Eastport Sch—school MS-4
Eastport Sch—school TN-4
East Portsmouth OH-6
East Poteau Mtn—summit AR-4
East Potholes—flat CA-9
East Potholes Meadow CA-9
East Potomac Park—park DC-2
East Potrillo Mountains—other NM-5
East Potter—locale NY-2
East Potter—unorg reg SD-7
East Potters Creek—stream TX-5
East Potts Flowage—reservoir WI-6
**East Poultney**—pop pl VT-1
East Poultney Hist Dist—hist pl VT-1
East Powder Coulee—valley MT-8
East Powder River—cens area MT-8
**East Prairie**—pop pl MO-7
East Prairie Branch—stream TX-5
East Prairie Ch—church TX-5
East Prairie Creek—stream KS-7
East Prairie Grove Sch (historical)—school MO-7
East Prairie Sch—school (2) IL-6
**East Prairieville**—pop pl MN-6
East Pratt Island CT-1
East Premont Oil Field—oilfield TX-5
**East Prentiss**—pop pl MS-4
East Prentiss Baptist Church MS-4
East Prentiss Cem—cemetery MS-4
East Prentiss Ch—church MS-4
East Prentiss Sch (historical)—school MS-4
East Presley Windmill—locale TX-5
East Pretty Creek—stream SD-7
East Pride Sch—school NE-7
East Primrose Cem—cemetery WI-6
**East Princeton**—pop pl MA-1
East Promontory—locale UT-8
East Prong FL-3
East Prong MD-2
East Prong TN-4
East Prong—summit WY-8
East Prong Abolochitto Creek MS-4
East Prong Abolochitto River MS-4
East Prong Alamocitos Creek—stream TX-5
East Prong Anderson Branch—stream KY-4
East Prong Bashi Creek AL-4
East Prong Bayou—stream LA-4
East Prong Bear Creek—stream FL-3
East Prong Beard Creek—stream NC-3
East Prong Beaverdam Creek—stream VA-3
East Prong Beechy Creek—stream KY-4
East Prong Big Brown Creek—stream MS-4
East Prong Big Creek—stream TX-5
East Prong Big Timber Creek—stream TX-5
East Prong Bird Creek—stream TN-4
East Prong Bogue Falaya—stream LA-4
East Prong Branch VA-3
East Prong Brice Creek—stream NC-3
East Prong Broad Creek—stream NC-3
East Prong Calf Creek—stream TX-5
East Prong Caney Creek AL-4
East Prong Catfish Creek—stream TX-5
East Prong Cathey's Creek—stream TN-4
East Prong Cedar Bluff Creek—stream MO-7
East Prong Chaparrosa Creek—stream TX-5
East Prong Chattooga River NC-3
East Prong Chattooga River SC-3
East Prong Clear Fork TN-4
East Prong Creek AL-4
East Prong Crooked Creek—stream KY-4
East Prong Crooked Creek—stream MO-7
East Prong Cypress Branch—stream NC-3
East Prong Cypress Creek FL-3
East Prong Deer Creek—stream WY-8
East Prong Difficult Creek—stream VA-3
East Prong Dismal Branch—stream AL-4
East Prong Doe Creek—stream TN-4
East Prong Dry Creek—stream OR-9
East Prong Fish River AL-4
East Prong Fleming Creek AR-4
East Prong Fort Ewell Creek—stream TX-5
East Prong Fox Creek—stream MO-7
East Prong Franks Drain—stream IN-6
East Prong Furnace Creek—stream VA-3
East Prong Gales Creek—stream NC-3
East Prong Goff Creek—stream MO-7
East Prong Green Canyon—valley WY-8
East Prong Green Creek—stream IN-6
East Prong Hakert Draw—valley WY-8
East Prong Hickey Fork—stream NC-3
East Prong Hill Creek—stream TN-4
East Prong Hunting Creek—stream NC-3
East Prong Indian Bayou—stream MS-4
East Prong Indian Camp Creek—stream KY-4
East Prong Indian Creek—stream (2) MO-7
East Prong Indian Hollow—valley TX-5
East Prong Jasons Branch—stream NC-3
East Prong Jennings Fork—stream TN-4
East Prong Juniper Creek—stream NC-3
East Prong Lake Bayou—gut LA-4
East Prong Little Creek—stream MO-7
East Prong Little Generostee Creek—stream SC-3
East Prong Little Klickitat River—stream WA-9
East Prong Little Walla Walla River WA-9
East Prong Little Walla Walla River—stream OR-9
East Prong Little Yadkin River—stream NC-3
East Prong Locust Creek—stream KY-4
East Prong Lower Little River—stream NC-3
East Prong McKim Creek—stream TX-5
East Prong Mill Creek—stream MS-4
East Prong Minnow Creek—stream AR-4
East Prong Moccasin Creek—stream TN-4
East Prong Moon Creek—stream NC-3
East Prong Mortons Mill Pond—stream NC-3
East Prong Nicks Creek—stream TN-4
East Prong Nueces River—stream TX-5
East Prong of Grand Bayou—stream LA-4
East Prong of Osgood Branch—stream NC-3
East Prong Old River—stream TX-5
East Prong Pollywog Creek—stream FL-3
East Prong Pursley Creek—stream AL-4
East Prong Quapaw Creek—stream OK-5
East Prong Reed Creek—stream MT-8
East Prong Ridge—ridge TN-4
East Prong Roaring River NC-3
East Prong Roaring River—stream NC-3
East Prong Rock Creek—stream AL-4
East Prong Rock Hole Creek—stream NC-3
East Prong Shetley Creek—stream MO-7
East Prong Silas Creek—stream AL-4
East Prong Silver Creek—stream MS-4
East Prong Simpson Canyon—valley TX-5
East Prong Sister Grove Creek—stream TX-5
East Prong Slocum Creek—stream NC-3
East Prong Spring—spring CO-8
East Prong Spring—spring OR-9
East Prong Spring Creek—stream IL-6
East Prong Steele Bayou—stream MS-4
East Prong Steep Creek AL-4
East Prong Steritt Swamp—stream SC-3
East Prong Town Branch—stream AR-4
East Prong Wells Creek—stream AR-4
East Prong White River—stream AR-4
East Prong Whites Creek—stream TX-5
East Prong Wildcat Creek—stream CO-8
East Prong Willow Bayou—gut LA-4
East Prong Windmill—locale TX-5
East Prong Wolf Creek*—stream NE-7
East Prong Wolf Creek—stream SD-7
East Prong Youngs Bayou—stream LA-4
**East Prospect**—pop pl PA-2
East Prospect Borough—civil PA-2
East Prospect Peak CA-9
East Prospect Rsvr—reservoir PA-2
East Protection Levee—levee LA-4
**East Providence**—pop pl RI-1
**East Providence Center**—pop pl RI-1
East Providence Reservoir MA-1
East Providence Sch—school MS-4
**East Providence (Township of)**—pop pl PA-2
East Providence Wharf RI-1
East Pryor Creek MT-8
East Pryor Creek—stream MT-8
East Pryor Mtn—summit MT-8
East Puerto De Luna Ditch—canal NM-5
East Pump Canal—canal UT-8
East Pump Canyon—valley CO-8
East Pump Lateral—canal CA-9
East Pump Rsvr—reservoir HI-9
East Punta de Agua Windmill—locale TX-5
East Purdum Sch—school NE-7
**East Purdy**—pop pl MO-7
East Purebred Windmill—locale TX-5
East Putnam—locale CT-1
**East Putney**—pop pl VT-1
East Putney Brook—stream VT-1
East Putney Brook Stone Arch Bridge—hist pl VT-1
East Putney Station—locale VT-1
East Pyramid Peak—summit AK-9
East Quartzsite Interchange—crossing AZ-5
**East Quilcene**—pop pl WA-9
**East Quincy**—pop pl CA-9
East Quinn Lake—lake OR-9
**East Quogue**—pop pl NY-2
East Rabbit Mtn—summit WY-8
East Rabbit Spring—spring UT-8
East Radford—uninc pl VA-3
East Ragged Brook—stream ME-1
East Ragsdale Creek—stream TX-5
East Rainbow Creek—stream KS-7
East Rainelle WV-2
East Rainelle—uninc pl WV-2
East Rainy Butte—summit ND-7
East Raisinville Ch—church MI-6
East Ramsey—summit TN-4
East Ranch—locale NE-7
East Ranch Branch—stream TX-5
**East Randolph**—pop pl NY-2
**East Randolph**—pop pl VT-1
East Randolph Cem—cemetery VT-1
East Range—range NV-8
East Rankin Acad—school MS-4
**East Rapids**—pop pl IA-7
East Rattlesnake Branch—stream MS-4
**East Raymond**—pop pl ME-1
**East Redbanks**—pop pl CA-9
East Red Canyon—valley NM-5
East Red Castle Lake—lake UT-8
East Redcliff Island—island AK-9
East Red Creek—stream CO-8
East Red Lodge Creek—stream MT-8
East Redmond—uninc pl WA-9
East Red Pasture—area NM-5
East Red Point Draw—valley CO-8
East Redrock Canyon—valley CO-8
East Red Wash—stream CO-8
East Redwater Creek—stream MT-8
East Red Windmill—locale TX-5
**East Redwood Subdivision**—pop pl UT-8
East Reedley Ditch—canal CA-9
East Reef—ridge UT-8
East Reid Creek WY-8
East Renton Highlands—CDP WA-9
East Republic Township—civil MO-7
East Rhudes Creek—stream KY-4
East Rhudes Creek Ch—church KY-4
East Richardson Ponds—lake ME-1
East Richey Square (Shop Ctr)—locale FL-3
East Richfield Channel—canal CA-9
East Richford—locale NY-2
**East Richford**—pop pl VT-1
East Richford (local name for Missisquoi)—other VT-1
**East Richland**—pop pl OH-6
East Richloam Lookout Tower—tower FL-3
**East Richmond**—pop pl CA-9
**East Richmond**—pop pl VA-3
**East Richmond Heights**—pop pl CA-9
**East Richwood**—pop pl AR-4
**East Richwoods**—pop pl AR-4
**East Rickardsville**—pop pl IA-7
East Rickardsville Sch—school IA-7
**Eastridge**—pop pl CO-8
**East Ridge**—pop pl (2) TN-4
East Ridge—ridge CA-9
East Ridge—ridge ME-1
East Ridge—ridge NV-8
East Ridge—ridge NC-3
East Ridge—ridge VA-3
East Ridge—ridge WV-2
East Ridge—ridge WI-6
East Ridge—ridge WY-8
East Ridge—uninc pl TX-5
Eastridge Arm—bay TN-4
East Ridge Arm Ditch TN-4
Eastridge Arm Ditch—canal TN-4
East Ridge Baptist Ch—church TN-4
Eastridge Bend—bend TN-4
East Ridge Branch—stream KY-4
East Ridge (CCD)—cens area TN-4
Eastridge Cem—cemetery KS-7
Eastridge Cem—cemetery KY-4
East Ridge Cem—cemetery ME-1
Eastridge Cem—cemetery NC-3
Eastridge Cem—cemetery VA-3
East Ridge Ch—church ME-1
East Ridge Ch—church PA-2
Eastridge Ch—church TX-5
East Ridge Ch of Christ—church TN-4
EAst Ridge Ch of God—church TN-4
Eastridge Ch of the Nazarene—church KS-7
East Ridge Christian Ch—church TN-4
East Ridge City Hall—building TN-4
East Ridge Community Hosp—hospital TN-4
East Ridge Division—civil TN-4
East Ridge Elem Sch—school TN-4
**Eastridge Estates Subdivision**—pop pl UT-8
East Ridge HS—school NY-2
East Ridge HS—school TN-4
East Ridge JHS—school CT-1
East Ridge JHS—school TN-4
**Eastridge Manor**—pop pl IN-6
East Ridge MS—school TN-4
East Ridge Post Office—building TN-4
Eastridge Post Office (historical)—building TN-4
East Ridge Presbyterian Ch—church TN-4
Eastridge Sch—school CO-8
East Ridge Sch—school (2) ME-1
Eastridge Sch—school NE-7
East Ridge Sch—school TX-5
East Ridge Shop Ctr—locale NC-3
East Ridge Shop Ctr—locale TN-4
Eastridge South CO-8
**Eastridge (subdivision)**—pop pl AL-4

**East Ridge (subdivision)**—*pop pl* ... TN-4
**Eastridge Subdivision**—*pop pl* (2) ... UT-8
**East Ridge Subdivision**—*pop pl* ... UT-8
East Ried Coulee—*valley* ... MT-8
East Rifle Creek—*stream* ... CO-8
East Rim—*cliff* ... CO-8
East Rim—*cliff* ... UT-8
East Rim—*cliff* ... WY-8
East Rimmy Tank—*reservoir* ... AZ-5
East Rim Tank—*reservoir* ... NM-5
East Rim Trail—*hist pl* ... UT-8
East Rim Trail—*trail* ... CO-8
East Rim Trail—*trail* ... UT-8
East Rim Viewpoint—*locale* ... AZ-5
**East Rindge**—*pop pl* ... NH-1
**East Ringgold**—*pop pl* ... OH-6
**East Rio**—*pop pl* ... WI-6
**Fast Ripley**—*pop pl* ... NY-2
*East Ripley Baptist Mission* ... MS-4
East Rita Blanca Creek—*stream* ... TX-5
East Rive Beach—*beach* ... CT-1
*East River* ... CO-8
*East river* ... CT-1
*East River* ... ID-8
*East River* ... WV-2
East River—*channel* ... MA-1
East River—*channel* ... NY-2
East River—*channel* ... NC-3
East River—*gut* ... FL-3
**East River**—*pop pl* ... CT-1
**East River**—*pop pl* ... IL-6
**East River**—*pop pl* ... NY-2
**East River**—*pop pl* (2) ... TX-5
East River—*stream* ... CO-8
East River—*stream* ... CT-1
East River—*stream* (5) ... FL-3
East River—*stream* ... GA-3
East River—*stream* ... ID-8
East River—*stream* ... IA-7
East River—*stream* (2) ... MN-6
East River—*stream* ... NY-2
East River—*stream* (2) ... VA-3
East River—*stream* ... WV-2
East River—*stream* (2) ... WI-6
**East River Beach**—*pop pl* ... CT-1
East River (CCD)—*cens area* ... GA-3
East River Ch—*church* ... MN-6
East River Ch—*church* ... TX-5
East River Cut Off—*channel* ... FL-3
East Riverdale—*CDP* ... MD-2
East River Front Park—*park* ... IA-7
East River Island—*island* ... FL-3
East River Island—*island* ... NC-3
East River Lookout—*locale* ... TX-5
East River Mountain—*ridge* ... WV-2
East River Mtn—*summit* ... VA-3
East River No 1 Ditch—*canal* ... CO-8
East River No 2 Dich—*canal* ... CO-8
East River Park—*park* ... IL-6
East River Park—*park* ... NY-2
East River Park—*park* ... WI-6
East River Pool—*reservoir* ... FL-3
East River Road Hist Dist—*hist pl* ... MI-6
East River Road Hist Dist I—*hist pl* ... OH-6
East River Road Hist Dist II—*hist pl* ... OH-6
East River Sch—*school* ... MI-6
East Riverside—*locale* ... PA-2
East Riverside Ch—*church* ... PA-2
East Riverside Slide—*valley* ... CO-8
**East Riverton**—*pop pl* ... NJ-2
East River Township—*fmr MCD* ... IA-7
East River Trail—*trail* ... NY-2
East River Valley Sch—*school* ... WI-6
East Rives Cem—*cemetery* ... MI-6
East Road—*locale* ... ME-1
East Road Cem—*cemetery* ... NY-2
East Road Cem—*cemetery* ... VT-1
East Road Gulch—*valley* ... CO-8
East Road Gulch—*valley* ... OR-9
East Road Gulch Spring—*spring* ... OR-9
East Road Springs—*spring* ... OR-9
East Roaring Creek—*stream* ... OK-5
East Roatcap Creek—*stream* ... CO-8
*East Roatcap Gulch* ... CO-8
East Robert Hall—*hist pl* ... NY-2
East Roberts Canyon—*valley* ... CO-8
East Robertson HS—*school* ... TN-4
*East Robertson Sch* ... TN-4
East Robert Toombs Hist Dist—*hist pl* ... GA-3
East Robeson Lookout Tower—*locale* ... NC-3
East Robeson Sch—*school* ... NC-3
East Robinson Lake Gas Field—*oilfield* ... TX-5
East Robinson Spring—*spring* ... NV-8
*East Rochester* ... NH-1
**East Rochester**—*pop pl* ... NH-1
**East Rochester**—*pop pl* ... NY-2
**East Rochester**—*pop pl* ... OH-6
**East Rochester**—*pop pl* ... PA-2
East Rochester Borough—*civil* ... PA-2
East Rochester Ch—*church* ... MA-1
East Rochester (Town of)—*civ div* ... NY-2
East Rock—*island* ... AK-9
East Rock—*summit* ... CT-1
East Rock—*summit* ... MA-1
East Rock—*summit* ... WA-9
**East Rockaway**—*pop pl* ... NY-2
East Rockaway Channel—*channel* ... NY-2
East Rockaway Inlet—*channel* ... NY-2
East Rock Bluffs—*fmr MCD* ... NE-7
*East Rock Creek* ... SC-3
East Rock Creek—*stream* ... OK-5
East Rock Creek—*stream* (2) ... OR-9
East Rock Creek—*stream* ... TN-4
East Rock Creek—*stream* ... TX-5
East Rock Creek Ch—*church* ... MN-6
*East Rockford* ... IL-6
East Rockford Hist Dist—*hist pl* ... IL-6
East Rockhill Chapel—*church* ... PA-2
East Rockhill Sch—*school* ... PA-2
**East Rockhill (Township of)**—*pop pl* ... PA-2
**East Rockingham**—*pop pl* ... NC-3
East Rockland Key—*island* ... FL-3
**East Rockland Key**—*pop pl* ... FL-3
East Rock Park—*park* ... CT-1
East Rock Spring Campground—*locale* ... NV-8
**East Rockwood**—*pop pl* ... MI-6
East Rockwood Sch—*school* ... OR-9
East Rocky Bayou—*stream* ... AR-4
East Rocky Branch—*stream* ... TX-5
East Rocky Creek—*stream* ... FL-3
East Rocky Creek—*stream* ... TX-5
East Rocky Gutter Brook—*stream* ... MA-1
East Rocky Mount—*uninc pl* ... NC-3
East Rodent Creek Trail—*trail* ... WY-8
**East Rodman**—*pop pl* ... NY-2
East Roger Mills (CCD)—*cens area* ... OK-5
East Rolette—*unorg reg* ... ND-7
East Rome Cem—*cemetery* ... MI-6
East Rome Hist Dist—*hist pl* ... GA-3
East Rome HS—*school* ... GA-3
East Romero Well—*well* ... NM-5
East Romero Windmill—*locale* ... TX-5
East Rondell Cem—*cemetery* ... SD-7
**East Rondell Township**—*pop pl* ... SD-7
East Roosevelt—*cens area* ... MT-8
**East Roscoe**—*pop pl* ... PA-2
East Rosebud Creek—*stream* ... MT-8
East Rosebud Lake—*lake* ... MT-8
East Rosebud Park—*park* ... MT-8
East Rosebud Plateau—*plain* ... MT-8
East Rosedale Oil Field—*oilfield* ... OK-5
East Rose Draw—*valley* ... TX-5
East Rosiclare (Election Precinct)—*fmr MCD* ... IL-6
East Round Hill Brook—*stream* ... CT-1
East Round Rock—*rock* ... MA-1
East Rowan HS—*school* ... NC-3
**East Roxbury**—*pop pl* ... VT-1
East Royce Mtn—*summit* ... ME-1
East Royce Trail—*trail* ... ME-1
**East Royles**—*pop pl* ... AL-4
East RR Canyon—*valley* ... NM-5
East RR Lateral—*canal* ... ID-8
East RR Well—*well* ... NV-8
East Rsvr—*reservoir* ... CA-9
East Rsvr—*reservoir* (2) ... CO-8
East Rsvr—*reservoir* ... OH-6
East Rsvr—*reservoir* ... TX-5
East Rsvr—*reservoir* ... WY-8
**East Rubens Subdivision**—*pop pl* ... UT-8
East Rumford Cem—*cemetery* ... ME-1
*East Run* ... MD-2
**Eastrun**—*pop pl* ... PA-2
**East Run**—*pop pl* ... PA-2
East Run—*stream* ... IL-6
East Run—*stream* ... PA-2
East Run—*stream* ... VA-3
East Run—*stream* (3) ... WV-2
East Run Ch—*church* ... WV-2
East Run Cracker Branch—*stream* ... FL-3
**East Rupert**—*pop pl* ... VT-1
East Rush—*locale* ... PA-2
*East Rush Cem* ... PA-2
East Rush Cem—*cemetery* ... PA-2
*East Rush Creek* ... CO-8
*East Rush Valley Pony Express and Stage Station* ... UT-8
East Russell Street Area Hist Dist—*hist pl* ... SC-3
**East Rutherford**—*pop pl* ... NJ-2
East Rutherford HS—*school* ... NC-3
**East Ryegate**—*pop pl* ... VT-1
East Saddle—*gap* ... ID-8
East Saddle—*gap* ... UT-8
East Sager Sch (abandoned)—*school* ... MO-7
*East Saginaw* ... MI-6
East Saginaw—*locale* ... AL-4
East Saginaw Historic Business District—*hist pl* ... MI-6
**East Saint Clair (Township of)**—*pop pl* ... PA-2
East Saint George Springs—*spring* ... UT-8
**East Saint Johns**—*pop pl* ... OR-9
**East Saint Johnsbury**—*pop pl* ... VT-1
East Saint Josephs Sch—*school* ... IA-7
**East Saint Louis**—*pop pl* ... IL-6
East Saint Louis Creek—*stream* ... CO-8
East Saint Louis Mine—*mine* ... CO-8
East Saint Louis (Township of)—*civ div* ... IL-6
East Saint Marys Peak—*summit* ... MT-8
East Saint Olaf Ch—*church* ... MN-6
*East Saint Paul* ... MN-6
East Salamanca—*uninc pl* ... NY-2
East Salem—*other* ... NY-2
**East Salem**—*pop pl* ... PA-2
**East Salem**—*pop pl* ... WV-2
East Salem Cem—*cemetery* ... MS-4
East Salem Cem—*cemetery* ... ND-7
East Salem Cem—*cemetery* ... PA-2
East Salem Ch—*church* ... AL-4
East Salem Ch—*church* ... MS-4
East Salem Sch—*school* ... IL-6
East Salem Sch—*school* ... VA-3
East Saline Creek—*stream* ... AR-4
**East Saline Township**—*pop pl* ... KS-7
*East Salisbury* ... MA-1
*East Salt Creek* ... TX-5
East Salt Creek—*stream* ... CO-8
East Salt Creek—*stream* ... KS-7
East Salt Creek—*stream* ... TX-5
East Salt Creek Oil Field—*oilfield* ... WY-8
East Salt Creek Sch—*school* ... OH-6
East Salt Shed Dam—*dam* ... AZ-5
East Salt Shed Tank—*reservoir* ... AZ-5
*East Salt Wells Creek* ... WY-8
East Salt Wells Creek—*stream* ... WY-8
East San Bruno—*uninc pl* ... CA-9
*East Sanches Creek* ... TX-5
East Sanchez Creek—*stream* ... TX-5
East Sand Butte—*summit* ... CA-9
East Sand Canyon—*valley* ... CO-8
East Sand Canyon Windmill—*locale* ... CO-8
*East Sand Creek* ... KS-7
East Sand Creek—*stream* ... CO-8
East Sand Creek Ch—*church* ... MS-4
East Sand Creek Spring—*spring* ... UT-8
East Sanders Windmill—*locale* ... TX-5
East Sand Hills—*range* ... CO-8
**East San Diego**—*pop pl* ... CA-9
*East Sand Lake* ... NY-2
East Sand Ridge Cem—*cemetery* ... IN-6
East Sand Slough—*stream* ... CA-9
East Sand Springs—*spring* ... NM-5
East Sand Springs Windmill—*locale* ... NM-5
East Sand Tank—*reservoir* ... NM-5
**East Sandwich**—*pop pl* ... MA-1
**East Sandwich**—*pop pl* ... NH-1
East Sandwich Beach—*beach* ... MA-1
East Sandwich Chapel—*church* ... NH-1
East Sandwich Station—*building* ... MA-1
East Sand Windmill—*locale* ... NM-5
East Sandy—*locale* ... PA-2
*East Sandy Creek* ... TX-5
East Sandy Creek—*stream* ... GA-3
East Sandy Creek—*stream* (2) ... OK-5
East Sandy Creek—*stream* ... PA-2
East Sandy Creek—*stream* (4) ... TX-5
East Sandy Sch—*school* ... PA-2
East Sandy Sch—*school* ... UT-8
East Sandy Wash—*stream* ... NV-8
East San Gabriel—*uninc pl* ... CA-9
East San Gabriel Valley (CCD)—*cens area* ... CA-9
East Sangerville—*locale* ... ME-1
*East San Jacinto River* ... TX-5
East San Jose Sch—*school* ... NM-5
East Sanko Creek—*stream* ... MT-8
East San Pedro—*uninc pl* ... CA-9
East San Simon Interchange—*crossing* ... AZ-5
East Santa Cruz—*uninc pl* ... CA-9
East Santa Fe Sch—*school* ... CA-9
East Sappony Creek—*stream* ... VA-3
**East Sarasota**—*pop pl* ... FL-3
East Sarnia Cem—*cemetery* ... ND-7
East Sattes Sch—*school* ... WV-2
**East Saugatuck**—*pop pl* ... MI-6
East Saugatuck Ch—*church* ... MI-6
East Saugus Station—*locale* ... MA-1
East Savannah—*uninc pl* ... GA-3
East Savannah Cem—*cemetery* ... GA-3
East Savanna River—*stream* ... MN-6
East Savoy Creek—*stream* ... MT-8
East Sawmill Canyon—*valley* ... AZ-5
**East Saxton**—*pop pl* ... PA-2
East Scalp Creek—*stream* ... TX-5
East Sch—*school* ... AZ-5
East Sch—*school* (2) ... AR-4
East Sch—*school* (3) ... CO-8
East Sch—*school* ... CT-1
East Sch—*school* (6) ... IL-6
East Sch—*school* ... IN-6
East Sch—*school* (4) ... IA-7
East Sch—*school* (2) ... KS-7
East Sch—*school* ... LA-4
East Sch—*school* ... ME-1
East Sch—*school* (5) ... MA-1
East Sch—*school* (5) ... MI-6
East Sch—*school* (2) ... MS-4
East Sch—*school* ... MO-7
East Sch—*school* ... NE-7
East Sch—*school* ... NH-1
East Sch—*school* ... NC-3
East Sch—*school* (11) ... OH-6
East Sch—*school* ... OK-5
East Sch—*school* ... OR-9
East Sch—*school* (3) ... TN-4
East Sch—*school* (4) ... TX-5
East Sch—*school* (2) ... UT-8
East Sch—*school* (3) ... WI-6
East Sch (abandoned)—*school* (2) ... PA-2
East Schaghticoke—*locale* ... NY-2
East Sch No 7—*school* ... NE-7
East Sch No 8—*school* ... NE-7
**East Schodack**—*pop pl* ... NY-2
East Schrader Creek—*stream* ... MI-6
**East Schuyler**—*pop pl* ... NY-2
East Schuyler Ch—*church* ... NY-2
East Science Sch—*school* ... IL-6
*East Scituate* ... MA-1
East Scott—*locale* ... NY-2
East Scotties Canyon—*valley* ... CA-9
East Scottville Cem—*cemetery* ... IL-6
East Scotty Creek—*stream* ... OR-9
East Seabolt Creek—*stream* ... GA-3
East Searsmont Cem—*cemetery* ... ME-1
East Seattle—*other* ... WA-9
East Seattle (CCD)—*cens area* ... WA-9
East Seattle Sch—*school* ... WA-9
**East Sebago**—*pop pl* ... ME-1
East Sebewa Cem—*cemetery* ... MI-6
**East Sebwa (Sebwa Corners)**—*pop pl* ... MI-6
East Second Street Commercial Hist Dist—*hist pl* ... MN-6
East Second Street District—*hist pl* (2) ... OH-6
East Second Street District(Boundary Increase)—*hist pl* ... OH-6
East Section Well—*well* ... NM-5
East Sedge—*island* ... NJ-2
East Seelye Bay—*bay* ... MN-6
East Seep Canyon—*valley* ... UT-8
East Sojita Oil Field—*oilfield* ... TX-5
East Selah—*locale* ... WA-9
*East Self Creek* ... AR-4
East Seljord Cem—*cemetery* ... MN-6
**East Seneca**—*pop pl* ... NY-2
East Senior HS—*school* ... PA-2
East Sentinel—*summit* ... WY-8
East Sentinel Island—*island* ... AK-9
East Sepulga River—*stream* ... AL-4
East Serviceberry Draw—*valley* ... CO-8
**East Setauket**—*pop pl* ... NY-2
East Setauket (RR name Setauket (sta.))—*uninc pl* ... NY-2
East Setting Spring—*spring* ... NV-8
East Sevenmile Creek—*stream* ... MT-8
East Seventeenth Ave Parkway—*hist pl* ... CO-8
East Seventh Ave Parkway—*hist pl* ... CO-8
East Shadley Creek—*stream* ... AR-4
East Shady Grove Ch—*church* ... MS-4
East Shady Grove Ch—*church* ... TX-5
East Shafter Lake Oil Field—*oilfield* ... TX-5
East Shag Rock—*rock* ... MA-1
East Shamburg—*locale* ... PA-2
East Shannon—*unorg reg* ... SD-7
East Sharon—*locale* ... PA-2
**East Sharon**—*pop pl* ... MA-1
East Sharon Sch—*school* ... MA-1
**East Sharpsburg**—*pop pl* ... PA-2
East Shasta (CCD)—*cens area* ... CA-9
East Shawnee Oil Field—*oilfield* ... OK-5
East Shed Lake—*lake* ... MI-6
East Sheep Creek—*stream* ... CO-8
East Sheep Creek—*stream* ... MO-7
East Sheep Creek—*stream* ... MT-8
East Sheep Creek—*stream* ... OR-9
East Sheep Island—*island* ... ME-1
East Sheep Mtn—*summit* ... CO-8
**East Sheffield**—*pop pl* ... AL-4
**East Sheffield**—*pop pl* ... MA-1
*East Sheffield Elementary School* ... AL-4
*East Shelburn* ... IN-6
**East Shelburn**—*pop pl* ... IN-6
**East Shelburne**—*pop pl* ... MA-1
**East Shelby**—*pop pl* ... NY-2
East Shelby Cem—*cemetery* ... NY-2
East Shelbyville District—*hist pl* ... KY-4
**East Sheldon**—*pop pl* ... IL-6
**East Sheldon**—*pop pl* ... VT-1
East Shell Creek—*stream* ... CO-8
East Shell Creek—*stream* ... WY-8
East Sheridan Creek Trail—*trail* ... ID-8
East Sherman Sch—*school* ... SD-7
East Shingle Creek Lake—*lake* ... UT-8
East Shirley Bog—*swamp* ... ME-1
*East Shoals* ... IN-6
East Shoo Fly Creek—*stream* ... KS-7
East Shore—*beach* ... TX-5
Eastshore—*locale* ... KS-7
**East Shoreham**—*pop pl* ... NY-2
East Shoreham Cem—*cemetery* ... VT-1
East Shoreham Covered RR Bridge—*hist pl* ... VT-1
**East Shoreham (Shoreham Station)**—*pop pl* ... VT-1
East Shore Loon Lake Recreation Site—*park* ... OR-9
East Shore Park—*park* ... CA-9
East Shore Park—*park* ... CT-1
Eastshore Picnic Area—*locale* ... CA-9
East Shore Rec Area—*park* ... SD-7
East Shore Road Hist Dist—*hist pl* ... NY-2
East Short Pine Hills—*range* ... SD-7
East Shotgun Creek—*stream* ... MT-8
East Shotgun Spring—*spring* ... OR-9
East Shreve Run—*stream* ... PA-2
East Shuler Oil And Gas Field—*oilfield* ... AR-4
*East Side* ... IL-6
*East Side* ... MI-6
*East Side* ... OH-6
*East Side* ... RI-1
*East Side* ... TN-4
East Side—*locale* ... CA-9
East Side—*locale* ... IL-6
East Side—*locale* ... MS-4
Eastside—*locale* ... OK-5
**Eastside**—*pop pl* ... MS-4
**Eastside**—*pop pl* ... NY-2
**East Side**—*pop pl* ... OH-6
**Eastside**—*pop pl* ... OR-9
**East Side**—*pop pl* ... PA-2
**East Side**—*pop pl* (2) ... TN-4
**East Side**—*pop pl* (2) ... TX-5
**East Side**—*pop pl* ... WV-2
Eastside—*post sta* ... ID-8
East Side—*post sta* ... LA-4
Eastside—*post sta* ... MN-6
Eastside—*post sta* ... OK-5
East Side—*uninc pl* ... AL-4
East Side—*uninc pl* ... GA-3
Eastside—*uninc pl* ... MS-4
East Side—*uninc pl* ... NJ-2
East Side—*uninc pl* ... NY-2
East Side—*uninc pl* ... OK-5
East Side—*uninc pl* ... PA-2
Eastside—*uninc pl* ... TN-4
Eastside—*uninc pl* ... WV-2
East Side—*uninc pl* ... WI-6
**Eastside Acres**—*pop pl* ... CA-9
East Side Assembly of God Ch—*church* ... FL-3
Eastside Assembly of God Ch—*church* ... MS-4
Eastside Baptist Ch—*church* (2) ... AL-4
Eastside Baptist Ch—*church* (2) ... FL-3
East Side Baptist Ch—*church* ... KS-7
East Side Baptist Ch—*church* ... MS-4
Eastside Baptist Ch—*church* ... MS-4
East Side Baptist Ch—*church* ... TN-4
Eastside Baptist Ch—*church* ... TN-4
Eastside Baptist Church—*hist pl* ... OK-5
**Eastside (Bluewing)**—*pop pl* ... TN-4
East Side Borough—*civil* ... PA-2
East Side Buck Creek Campground—*locale* ... WA-9
Eastside Bypass—*canal* ... CA-9
*Eastside Canal* ... OR-9
East Side Canal—*canal* (2) ... CA-9
Eastside Canal—*canal* ... CA-9
East Side Canal—*canal* (2) ... CA-9
East Side Canal—*canal* ... ID-8
East Side Canal—*canal* (3) ... NM-5
East Side Canal—*canal* ... OR-9
East Side Canal—*canal* ... WY-8
East Side Canal Ditch—*canal* ... ID-8
Eastside (CCD)—*cens area* ... OR-9
East Side Cem—*cemetery* ... AL-4
East Side Cem—*cemetery* ... AZ-5
Eastside Cem—*cemetery* ... CT-1
Eastside Cem—*cemetery* ... GA-3
East Side Cem—*cemetery* ... IA-7
Eastside Cem—*cemetery* ... KS-7
East Side Cem—*cemetery* ... MN-6
Eastside Cem—*cemetery* ... MN-6
Eastside Cem—*cemetery* ... MS-4
East Side Cem—*cemetery* ... MO-7
East Side Cem—*cemetery* ... NY-2
Eastside Cem—*cemetery* (2) ... NY-2
East Side Cem—*cemetery* (3) ... NC-3
Eastside Cem—*cemetery* ... ND-7
East Side Cem—*cemetery* ... TN-4
East Side Cem—*cemetery* ... UT-8
East Side Cem—*cemetery* (3) ... WI-6
Eastside Cem—*cemetery* (2) ... WI-6
East Side Cem—*cemetery* ... WI-6
Eastside Cem—*cemetery* ... WI-6
*Eastside Cemetery* ... UT-8
East Side Central Sch—*school* ... OH-6
Eastside Ch—*church* ... AL-4
East Side Ch—*church* ... AL-4
East Side Ch—*church* ... AR-4
Eastside Ch—*church* ... FL-3
East Side Ch—*church* ... FL-3
East Side Ch—*church* ... GA-3
Eastside Ch—*church* (4) ... GA-3
East Side Ch—*church* ... IN-6
Eastside Ch—*church* ... LA-4
Eastside Ch—*church* ... MD-2
Eastside Ch—*church* ... MS-4
East Side Ch—*church* (2) ... MS-4
East Side Ch—*church* ... NC-3
Eastside Ch—*church* (2) ... NC-3
East Side Ch—*church* ... NC-3
Eastside Ch—*church* (2) ... NC-3
East Side Ch—*church* ... SC-3
Eastside Ch—*church* ... SC-3
East Side Ch—*church* ... SC-3
Eastside Ch—*church* ... SC-3
East Side Ch—*church* ... SC-3
Eastside Ch—*church* ... TN-4
East Side Ch—*church* ... TX-5
*East Side Channel* ... VA-3
*East Side Ch of Christ* ... AL-4
East Side Ch of Christ—*church* ... AL-4
East Side Ch of God in Christ—*church* ... KS-7
**Eastside Columbia**—*pop pl* ... LA-4
East Side Commercial Block—*hist pl* ... OH-6
East Side Commercial Hist Dist—*hist pl* ... WI-6
East Side Consolidated Sch—*school* ... IN-6
East Side Day Sch—*school* ... ND-7
East Side Ditch—*canal* ... ID-8
East Side Ditch—*canal* ... MT-8
East Side Ditch—*canal* ... WY-8
East Side Drain—*canal* ... CA-9
*East Side Drainage Ditch* ... OK-5
Eastside Draw Windmill—*locale* ... TX-5
*Eastside Elem Sch* ... MS-4
*East Side Elem Sch* ... TN-4
Eastside Elem Sch—*school* ... FL-3
East Side Elem Sch—*school* (2) ... IN-6
Eastside Elem Sch—*school* ... KS-7
East Side Elem Sch—*school* (2) ... MS-4
East Side Elem Sch—*school* (3) ... TN-4
Eastside Elem Sch—*school* ... TN-4
Eastside Emmanuel Ch—*church* ... AL-4
East Side Fire Station—*hist pl* ... OH-6
Eastside Freewill Baptist Ch—*church* ... AL-4
East Side Hist Dist—*hist pl* (2) ... NY-2
East Side Hist Dist—*hist pl* ... TX-5
Eastside Historic Cemetery District—*hist pl* ... MI-6
Eastside HS—*school* ... FL-3
East Side HS—*school* ... MS-4
East Side HS—*school* ... NJ-2
East Side HS—*school* ... WV-2
East Side HS—*school* ... WI-6
East Side Irrigation Canal—*canal* ... CA-9
East Side JHS—*hist pl* ... TN-4
East Side JHS—*school* ... AR-4
East Side JHS—*school* ... GA-3
Eastside JHS—*school* ... SC-3
East Side JHS—*school* ... TN-4
Eastside Junior-Senior HS—*school* ... IN-6
East Side Lake—*lake* ... MN-6
East Side Launch Ramp—*locale* ... CA-9
*East Side Methodist Ch* ... AL-4
Eastside Mine—*mine* ... NV-8
Eastside Mine (underground)—*mine* ... AL-4
Eastside Missionary Baptist Ch—*church* ... AL-4
East Side Missionary Baptist Ch—*church* ... AL-4
East Side Nazarene Ch—*church* ... IN-6
East Side New Hope Baptist Ch—*church* ... IN-6
East Side No. 2 Ditch—*canal* ... CO-8
Eastside Park—*park* ... AL-4
Eastside Park—*park* ... AR-4
Eastside Park—*park* (2) ... CA-9
East Side Park—*park* (2) ... IN-6
Eastside Park—*park* ... MN-6
East Side Park—*park* (2) ... MN-6
East Side Park—*park* ... MS-4
Eastside Park—*park* ... MO-7
East Side Park—*park* ... NJ-2
East Side Park—*park* ... NM-5
East Side Park—*park* ... OH-6
Eastside Park—*park* ... OK-5
Eastside Park—*park* ... OR-9
Eastside Park—*park* ... SD-7
East Side Park—*park* ... TX-5
**East Side Park**—*pop pl* (2) ... NC-3
*Eastside Pelahatchie Baptist Church* ... MS-4
Eastside Plaza—*locale* ... SD-7
Eastside Presbyterian Ch—*church* ... AL-4
Eastside Ranch—*locale* ... CA-9
**Eastside Ranch**—*pop pl* ... CA-9
East Side Residential District—*hist pl* ... MT-8
East Side Rincon Site—*hist pl* ... NM-5
East Side Rsvr—*reservoir* (2) ... CA-9
East Side Rsvr—*reservoir* ... WY-8
East Side Salvage Drain—*canal* ... NM-5
*East Side Sch* ... TN-4
East Side Sch—*hist pl* ... GA-3
East Side Sch—*hist pl* ... WY-8
Eastside Sch—*school* ... AL-4
Eastside Sch—*school* (4) ... AR-4
Eastside Sch—*school* (2) ... CA-9
East Side Sch—*school* ... CT-1
Eastside Sch—*school* (2) ... FL-3
East Side Sch—*school* (2) ... GA-3
Eastside Sch—*school* ... GA-3
East Side Sch—*school* ... GA-3
Eastside Sch—*school* ... GA-3
East Side Sch—*school* (3) ... ID-8
East Side Sch—*school* (2) ... IL-6
East Side Sch—*school* ... IN-6
Eastside Sch—*school* ... KY-4
Eastside Sch—*school* ... ME-1
East Side Sch—*school* ... MI-6
East Side Sch—*school* ... MN-6
Eastside Sch—*school* (2) ... MS-4
East Side Sch—*school* ... MT-8
East Side Sch—*school* ... NE-7
East Side Sch—*school* ... NM-5
East Side Sch—*school* (2) ... NY-2
East Side Sch—*school* ... NC-3
East Side Sch—*school* (3) ... OH-6
Eastside Sch—*school* ... OK-5
East Side Sch—*school* ... OK-5
Eastside Sch—*school* ... OK-5
East Side Sch—*school* ... OK-5
Eastside Sch—*school* (2) ... OR-9
East Side Sch—*school* ... PA-2
East Side Sch—*school* ... TN-4
Eastside Sch—*school* ... TN-4
East Side Sch—*school* (4) ... TX-5
East Side Sch—*school* (2) ... WI-6
East Side Sch—*school* ... WY-8
East Side Sch (abandoned)—*school* ... PA-2
Eastside School (Abandoned)—*locale* ... ID-8
Eastside Seventh Day Adventist Ch—*church* ... IN-6
East Side Shop Ctr—*locale* ... AL-4
East Side Shop Ctr—*locale* ... AZ-5
East Side Shop Ctr—*locale* ... MS-4
Eastside Speedway—*other* ... VA-3
Eastside Spring—*spring* ... CO-8
**East Side (subdivision)**—*pop pl* ... MS-4
East Side Tank—*reservoir* (2) ... AZ-5
East Side Tank—*reservoir* ... NM-5
East Side Tank—*reservoir* ... TX-5
**East Side (Township of)**—*pop pl* ... MN-6
**East Side Village**—*pop pl* ... DE-2
Eastside Village (Shop Ctr)—*locale* ... FL-3
East Side Windmill—*locale* ... AZ-5
East Side Wood Gulch Spring—*spring* ... CO-8
East Side Youth Center—*park* ... WA-9
East Siding—*locale* ... TN-4
East Sidney—*locale* ... NY-2
East Sidney Cem—*cemetery* ... NY-2
East Sierra (CCD)—*cens area* ... CA-9
East Signal Peak—*summit* ... OK-5
East Signal Trail—*trail* ... OK-5
East Silent Lake—*lake* ... MN-6
East Silver Lake—*reservoir* ... WI-6
*East Silver Mesa* ... CO-8
East Silver Spring Sch—*school* ... MD-2
**East Silver Springs Shore (subdivision)**—*pop pl* ... FL-3
*East Simons Creek* ... IN-6
East Simpson Well—*well* ... CO-8
East Simpson Windmill—*locale* ... TX-5
East Sinai Cem—*cemetery* ... SD-7
**East Sioux Falls**—*pop pl* ... SD-7
East Sister—*bar* ... ME-1
East Sister—*summit* ... ID-8
East Sister—*summit* ... NV-8
East Sister Creek—*stream* ... TX-5
*East Sister Island* ... ME-1
East Sister Island—*island* ... ME-1
East Sister Peak—*summit* ... ID-8
East Sister Rock—*island* ... FL-3
*East Six Mile Bayou* ... MS-4
East Sixmile Bayou—*stream* ... MS-4
East Six Sch Number 3—*school* ... ND-7
East Sixteenth Street Christian Ch—*church* ... IN-6
East Sixth Ave Parkway—*hist pl* ... CO-8
East Skelly Gulch—*valley* ... MT-8
East Skinner Butte Hist Dist—*hist pl* ... OR-9
East Slab Trail—*trail* ... PA-2
East Slang Creek—*stream* ... VT-1
East Sleeping River—*stream* ... MI-6
East Slide Lake—*lake* ... UT-8
East Slope—*slope* ... CA-9
East Slope, The—*slope* ... UT-8
East Slope Cem—*cemetery* ... KS-7
East Slope Memorial Gardens—*cemetery* ... MO-7
East Slope Spring—*spring* ... UT-8
East Slough—*gut* ... AR-4
East Slough—*gut* (2) ... FL-3
East Slough—*lake* ... SD-7
East Slough—*stream* ... CA-9
**East Smethport**—*pop pl* ... PA-2
East Smith Canyon—*valley* ... NE-7
**East Smithfield**—*pop pl* ... PA-2
East Smith Lake—*lake* ... MN-6
East Snake Knob—*summit* ... AR-4
East Sneech Brook—*stream* ... RI-1
*East Sneech Pond Brook* ... RI-1
East Snow Draw—*valley* ... TX-5
East Snowflake Ditch—*canal* ... AZ-5
East Snowmass and Brush Creek Ditch—*canal* ... CO-8
East Snowmass Creek—*stream* ... CO-8
East Snow Windmill—*locale* ... TX-5
East Soap Creek—*stream* ... CO-8
East Soddy Ch—*church* ... TN-4
*East Sokehs Island* ... FM-9
East Soldier Ditch—*canal* ... IA-7
East Soldier Lake—*lake* ... MI-6
East Soldier River—*stream* ... IA-7
East Soldier Tank—*reservoir* ... AZ-5
East Somerset—*uninc pl* ... KY-4
East Somerset Ch—*church* ... KY-4
**East Somerville (subdivision)**—*pop pl* ... MA-1
East Sopris Creek—*stream* ... CO-8
*East Sound* ... WA-9
East Sound—*bay* ... WA-9
**Eastsound**—*pop pl* ... WA-9
East Sourdough Creek—*stream* ... OK-5
East South Salado Peak Tank—*reservoir* ... NM-5
East South Town Windmill—*locale* ... TX-5
East Spafford Branch—*stream* ... IL-6
East Spaniard Creek—*stream* ... OK-5
East Spanish Peak—*summit* ... CO-8
**East Sparta**—*pop pl* ... OH-6
East Sparta Acad (historical)—*school* ... TN-4
*East Sparta Elem Sch* ... TN-4
**East Spartanburg**—*pop pl* ... SC-3
East Spear Creek—*stream* ... AZ-5
East Spearfish Creek—*stream* ... SD-7
East Speer Canal—*canal* ... CO-8
**East Spencer**—*pop pl* ... NC-3
East Spider Tank—*reservoir* ... AZ-5
East Spiller Creek—*stream* ... AR-4
East Spirit Lake—*lake* ... MN-6
East Spit—*bar* ... AK-9
East Split Rock River—*stream* ... MN-6
**East Spokane**—*pop pl* ... WA-9
**East Spotswood**—*pop pl* ... NJ-2
**East Spotswood (sta.)**—*pop pl* ... NJ-2
East Spread Mtn—*summit* ... MT-8
East Spring—*spring* ... AZ-5
East Spring—*spring* (2) ... CO-8
East Spring—*spring* ... ID-8
East Spring—*spring* ... MT-8
East Spring—*spring* (3) ... NV-8
East Spring—*spring* (4) ... OR-9
East Spring—*spring* ... TX-5
East Spring—*spring* (2) ... UT-8
East Spring—*spring* ... WY-8
East Spring Branch—*stream* ... LA-4
*East Springbrook* ... ND-7
**East Springbrook**—*pop pl* ... MD-2
**East Springbrook**—*pop pl* ... TN-4
East Spring Brook—*stream* ... CT-1
East Spring Canyon—*valley* ... UT-8
East Spring Canyon Dam—*dam* ... AZ-5
East Spring Ch—*church* ... FL-3
East Spring Ch—*church* ... PA-2
East Spring Coulee—*valley* ... MT-8
*East Spring Creek* ... KS-7
East Spring Creek—*stream* ... CO-8
East Spring Creek—*stream* (4) ... KS-7
East Spring Creek—*stream* ... OK-5
East Spring Draw—*valley* (2) ... WY-8
East Springer Lateral—*canal* ... WY-8

East Springer Main Lateral—*canal* ... NE-7
East Springer Main Lateral—*canal* ... WY-8
East Springer Spring—*spring* ... OR-9
East Springfield—*locale* ... NH-1
**East Springfield**—*pop pl* ... NY-2
**East Springfield**—*pop pl* ... OH-6
**East Springfield**—*pop pl* ... PA-2
*East Springfield Brook* ... NY-2
East Springfield Ch—*church* ... IN-6
East Springfield Station—*locale* ... PA-2
**East Springfield (subdivision)**—*pop pl* ... MA-1
*East Spring Hill* ... PA-2
East Spring Run—*stream* ... PA-2
East Springs—*spring* ... ID-8
East Spring Street Sch—*school* ... IN-6
East Springwater Cem—*cemetery* ... NY-2
East Spring Windmill—*locale* ... TX-5
**East Spruce**—*pop pl* ... PA-2
East Spruce Brook—*stream* ... CT-1
East Spur—*ridge* ... CA-9
East Square Mountain Rsvr—*reservoir* ... OR-9
East Squaw Canyon—*valley* ... CO-8
East Squaw Canyon—*valley* ... UT-8
East Squaw Creek—*stream* ... NV-8
East Squaw Creek—*stream* ... SD-7
East Squirrel Creek—*stream* ... TX-5
*Easts Store* ... AL-4
East Stack Creek—*stream* ... OR-9
**East Stamford**—*pop pl* ... TX-5
East Stancel Corral—*locale* ... NM-5
East Standard—*mine* ... UT-8
*East Standing Stone Creek* ... PA-2
**East Stanwood**—*pop pl* ... WA-9
East Star Ch—*church* ... LA-4
East Star Ch—*church* ... MS-4
East Star Corral Oil Field—*oilfield* ... WY-8
East Stark—*unorg reg* ... ND-7
East Starkville Ch—*church* ... MS-4
East Star Sch—*school* ... NE-7
East Star Sch (historical)—*school* ... MO-7
**East Startex**—*pop pl* ... SC-3
*East Station* ... MS-4
East Steamburg—*locale* ... NY-2
East Steel Creek—*stream* ... ID-8
East Steele Windmill—*locale* ... NM-5
**East Steels Corners**—*pop pl* ... OH-6
East Steep Hill Valley—*valley* ... AZ-5
Eaststep Gap—*gap* ... TN-4
**East Sterling**—*pop pl* ... PA-2
East Steuben—*locale* ... NY-2
**East Steuben**—*pop pl* ... ME-1
East Steuben Creek—*stream* ... CO-8
**East Steubenville**—*pop pl* ... WV-2
East Stevens Creek—*stream* ... NM-5
East Stock Ditch—*canal* ... WY-8
East Stockton—*uninc pl* ... CA-9
East Stone Arabia—*locale* ... NY-2
East Stone Cabin Valley—*valley* ... NV-8
**East Stone Gap**—*pop pl* ... VA-3
**East Stone Gap (RR name Elverton)**—*pop pl* ... VA-3
**East Stoneham**—*pop pl* ... ME-1
East Stoneham Rsvr—*reservoir* ... CO-8
East Stone Hill Sch—*school* ... IA-7
East Stone House Creek—*stream* ... KS-7
East Stony Creek—*stream* ... NY-2
East Stony Point Sch (historical)—*school* ... TN-4
East Stooping Bush Island—*island* ... CT-1
East Stover Sch (historical)—*school* ... MS-4
**East Strang Junction**—*pop pl* ... NE-7
East Strawberry Sch (historical)—*school* ... MO-7
East Stream—*stream* ... ME-1
East Stream Sch—*school* ... ME-1
East Street—*locale* ... CT-1
East Street Bridge—*bridge* ... PA-2
East Street Cem—*cemetery* ... CT-1
East Street Cem—*cemetery* (2) ... MA-1
East Street Park—*park* ... NC-3
East Street Sch—*school* ... CO-8
East Street Sch—*school* ... CT-1
East Street Sch—*school* (3) ... MA-1
East Street Sch—*school* ... NY-2
East Stringtown Sch—*school* ... IL-6
East Strip East Fork Mujares Creek—*stream* ... TX-5
**East Stroudsburg**—*pop pl* ... PA-2
East Stroudsburg Borough—*civil* ... PA-2
East Stroudsburg Dam—*dam* ... PA-2
East Stroudsburg RR Station—*hist pl* ... PA-2
East Stroudsburg Rsvr—*reservoir* ... PA-2
East Stroudsburg Senior HS—*school* ... PA-2
East Stroudsburg Univ of Pennsylvania—*school* ... PA-2
East Stylus Lake—*lake* ... MI-6
*East Sudbury* ... MA-1
**East Sudbury**—*pop pl* ... MA-1
*East Sudbury, Town of* ... MA-1
**East Sudbury Station**—*pop pl* ... MA-1
East Suffolk Gardens—*uninc pl* ... VA-3
East Suffolk HS—*school* ... VA-3
*East Sugar Creek* ... AR-4
East Sugarloaf—*summit* ... CT-1
East Sugarloaf Creek—*stream* ... AR-4
East Sugarloaf Mtn—*summit* ... NM-5
*East Sugar Works Run* ... PA-2
**East Sullivan**—*pop pl* ... ME-1
**East Sullivan**—*pop pl* ... NH-1
East Sullivan County Volunteer Fire Department—*building* ... TN-4
East Sullivan (Township of)—*fmr MCD* ... AR-4
East Sully—*unorg reg* ... SD-7
East Sulphur Branch—*stream* ... TX-5
East Sulphur Creek—*stream* ... CA-9
East Sulphur Creek—*stream* ... MO-7
East Summit—*summit* ... CO-8
East Summit—*summit* ... UT-8
East Summit Sch—*school* ... UT-8
**East Sumner**—*pop pl* ... ME-1
*East Sump* ... NV-8
East Sumter—*CDP* ... SC-3
*East Sunbury* ... PA-2
East Sunbury—*other* ... PA-2
East Sunflower Sch—*school* ... MS-4
East Sunny Hill Ch—*church* ... MS-4
East Sunnyside Sch—*school* ... WA-9
East Sunnyview Ch—*church* ... TN-4
East Sunsbury Ch—*church* ... OH-6
East Sunset City Gulch—*valley* ... CO-8
East Sunset Mtn—*summit* ... AZ-5
East Sunshine Lake—*lake* ... AK-9
**East Surry**—*pop pl* ... ME-1
East Surry HS—*school* ... NC-3
**East Sutton**—*pop pl* ... MA-1
**East Sutton**—*pop pl* ... NH-1
East Sutton Ridge—*locale* ... VT-1
East Sveadahl Ch—*church* ... MN-6
East Swamp Brook—*stream* (2) ... CT-1
East Swamp Ch—*church* ... PA-2
East Swamp Creek—*stream* ... OR-9
*East Swamp Creek Swamp Creek* ... PA-2
East Swan Creek—*stream* ... NC-3
East Swan Lake State Games Mngmt Area—*park* ... IA-7
East Swan River—*stream* ... MN-6
**East Swansea**—*pop pl* ... MA-1
**East Swanton**—*pop pl* ... OH-6
**East Swanzey**—*pop pl* ... NH-1
East Sweden—*locale* ... ME-1
East Sweden—*locale* ... TX-5
East Sweden Cem—*cemetery* ... NY-2
East Sweetman Mtn—*summit* ... MA-1
**East Sweetwater**—*pop pl* ... TN-4
East Sweetwater Gulch—*valley* ... WY-8
**East Sweetwater (Pumpkin Center)**—*pop pl* ... TN-4
East Sweetwater River—*stream* ... WY-8
East Sweet Well—*well* ... NM-5
**East Swiftwater**—*pop pl* ... PA-2
East Sycamore Creek—*stream* ... TX-5
East Sylvian Oil Field—*oilfield* ... OK-5
**East Syracuse**—*pop pl* ... NY-2
East Syracuse Rsvr—*reservoir* ... NY-2
East Table—*summit* ... NE-7
East Table Creek—*stream* ... WY-8
East Table Creek Campground—*locale* ... WY-8
East Table Sch—*school* ... NE-7
**East Tabor**—*pop pl* ... NC-3
East Tagelib—*island* ... MP-9
*East Tagelib Island* ... MP-9
**East Taghkanic**—*pop pl* ... NY-2
*East Tallahala Creek* ... MS-4
East Tallahalla Creek Oil Field—*oilfield* ... MS-4
*East Tallahatchie High School* ... MS-4
East Tallahoma Ch—*church* ... MS-4
East Tallahone Windmill—*locale* ... TX-5
East Tallapoosa Med Ctr—*hospital* ... AL-4
East Tallassee—*uninc pl* ... AL-4
East Tallassee Baptist Ch—*church* ... AL-4
East Tallassee Grammar Sch (historical)—*school* ... AL-4
East Tallassee Methodist Episcopal Ch—*church* ... AL-4
**East Tampa**—*pop pl* ... FL-3
East Tampa (RR name for Gibsonton)—*other* ... FL-3
*East Tank* ... NM-5
East Tank—*reservoir* (17) ... AZ-5
East Tank—*reservoir* ... CO-8
East Tank—*reservoir* (24) ... NM-5
East Tank—*reservoir* (8) ... TX-5
East Tank Hollow Prospect—*mine* ... TN-4
East Tank No 3—*reservoir* ... NM-5
East Tannen Creek—*stream* ... OR-9
East Tannen Lake—*lake* ... OR-9
*East Tarkie Creek* ... IA-7
East Tarkio Creek—*stream* (2) ... IA-7
*East Tarkio River* ... IA-7
*East Tarkio River* ... MO-7
East Tarter Gulch—*valley* ... OR-9
East Tate Elem Sch—*school* ... MS-4
**East Taunton**—*pop pl* ... MA-1
East Taunton Fire Station—*hist pl* ... MA-1
East Tavaputs Plateau—*plain* ... UT-8
**East Tawakoni**—*pop pl* ... TX-5
**East Tawas**—*pop pl* ... MI-6
East Tawas-Tawas City (RR name for East Tawas)—*other* ... MI-6
East Taylor Canyon—*valley* ... NV-8
East Taylor Ditch—*canal* ... AZ-5
**East Taylor (Township of)**—*pop pl* ... PA-2
East T Bar Canyon—*valley* ... TX-5
East Teapot Creek—*stream* ... WY-8
East Teapot Dome Oil Field—*oilfield* ... WY-8
East Technical HS—*school* ... OH-6
East Tehama (CCD)—*cens area* ... CA-9
East Tehuacana Creek—*stream* ... TX-5
East Telephone Canyon—*valley* ... NM-5
**East Tempe**—*pop pl* ... TX-5
East Tempe Ch—*church* ... TX-5
East Tempe Creek—*stream* ... TX-5
East Temple, The—*summit* ... UT-8
East Temple Ch—*church* ... TX-5
*East Temple Creek* ... TX-5
East Temple Peak—*summit* ... WY-8
**East Templeton**—*pop pl* ... MA-1
*East Templeton Pond* ... MA-1
East Templeton Pond—*lake* ... MA-1
East Templin Cem—*cemetery* ... KS-7
*East Tencent Creek* ... OR-9
East Ten Cent Creek—*stream* ... OR-9
East Tenmile Creek—*stream* ... TX-5
East Tennessee Baptist Hosp—*hospital* ... TN-4
East Tennessee Chest Disease Hosp—*hospital* ... TN-4
East Tennessee Childrens Hosp—*hospital* ... TN-4
East Tennessee Creek—*stream* ... CO-8
*East Tennessee Hosp for the Insane* ... TN-4
East Tennessee Iron Manufacturing Company Blast Furnace—*hist pl* ... TN-4
East Tennessee Masonic Female Institute (historical)—*school* ... TN-4
*East Tennessee State Coll* ... TN-4
*East Tennessee State Normal Sch* ... TN-4
*East Tennessee State Teachers Coll* ... TN-4
East Tennessee State Univ—*school* ... TN-4
*East Tennessee Tuberculosis Hospital* ... TN-4
East Tensleep Creek—*stream* ... WY-8
East Tensleep Lake—*lake* ... WY-8
East Ten Tank—*reservoir* ... AZ-5
East Tenth Streeet Ch of God—*church* ... IN-6
East Tenth United Methodist Ch—*church* ... IN-6
East Terrapin Creek—*stream* ... OK-5
East Terrell (CCD)—*cens area* ... TX-5
East Terrell Creek—*stream* ... MT-8
**East Terrell Hills**—*pop pl* ... TX-5
**East Terrell Hills Heights**—*pop pl* ... TX-5
East Terrell Hills Sch—*school* ... TX-5
*East Terror Creek* ... CO-8
East Teton Canal—*canal* ... ID-8
**East Texas**—*pop pl* ... PA-2
East Texas Baptist Coll—*school* ... TX-5
East Texas Baptist Encampment—*locale* ... TX-5
East Texas (East Texas State Teachers College)—*uninc pl* ... TX-5
East Texas Fairground—*locale* ... TX-5
East Texas Guidance and Achievement Center—*other* ... TX-5
East Texas Oil Field—*oilfield* ... TX-5
East Texas State Coll—*school* ... TX-5
East Texas Tuberculosis Hosp—*hospital* ... TX-5
East Thalheim Lateral—*canal* ... CA-9
**East Thermopolis**—*pop pl* ... WY-8
**East Thetford**—*pop pl* ... MI-6
**East Thetford**—*pop pl* ... VT-1
East Third Ave Historic Residential District—*hist pl* ... CO-8
East Third Creek—*stream* ... TN-4
East Third Street Ch of Christ—*church* ... TN-4
*East Thirsty Canyon* ... NV-8
East Thirteen Ditch—*canal* ... NM-5
East Thirteen Oil Field—*oilfield* ... TX-5
**East Thomas**—*pop pl* ... AL-4
East Thomas Baptist Ch—*church* ... AL-4
**East Thomas Gardens**—*pop pl* ... AL-4
East Thomas Gardens Dam—*dam* ... AL-4
East Thomas Gardens Lake—*reservoir* ... AL-4
*East Thomas Gardens Lake Dam* ... AL-4
East Thomas Park—*park* ... AL-4
**East Thomaston**—*pop pl* ... GA-3
East Thomas Yards—*locale* ... AL-4
**East Thompson**—*pop pl* ... CT-1
East Thompson Creek—*stream* ... MT-8
East Thorndike—*locale* ... ME-1
East Thorndike Cem—*cemetery* ... ME-1
East Thorp Cem—*cemetery* ... WI-6
East Threemile Creek—*stream* ... ID-8
East Three Tank—*reservoir* ... AZ-5
East Thunder Creek—*stream* ... WI-6
East Thunder Hawk Creek—*stream* ... SD-7
East Thurmon Creek—*stream* ... ID-8
*East Tidwell Canyon* ... UT-8
East Tidwell Canyon—*valley* ... UT-8
East Tidwell Spring—*spring* ... UT-8
East Tiger Creek—*stream* ... MS-4
East Tillman (CCD)—*cens area* ... OK-5
**East Tilton**—*pop pl* ... NH-1
East Timbalier Island—*island* ... LA-4
East Timbalier Island Natl Wildlife Ref—*park* ... LA-4
East Timbalier Island Reservation—*park* ... LA-4
East Timber Canyon—*valley* ... CO-8
East Timber Creek—*stream* ... WY-8
East Timberlake Creek—*stream* ... CO-8
East Timothy Dam—*dam* ... UT-8
East Timothy Lake—*lake* ... UT-8
East Timothy Lake—*reservoir* ... UT-8
East Tintic Coalition—*mine* ... UT-8
East Tintic Mtns—*range* ... UT-8
East Tioga Oil and Gas Field—*oilfield* ... ND-7
*East Tipp High School* ... IN-6
East Tipp JHS—*school* ... IN-6
East Tippo Bayou—*gut* ... MS-4
East Tisdale Oil Field—*oilfield* ... WY-8
**East Titusville**—*pop pl* ... PA-2
East Todd—*unorg reg* ... SD-7
East Toe—*summit* ... CO-8
*East Toledo* ... OH-6
East Toll Gate Creek—*stream* ... CO-8
East Tom Green (CCD)—*cens area* ... TX-5
East Tom Patterson Canyon—*valley* ... UT-8
*East Toops Ditch* ... IN-6
East Topaz 2 Rsvr—*reservoir* ... UT-8
East Topeka Interchange—*locale* ... KS-7
East Topeka United Methodist Ch—*church*. KS-7
*East Topisaw Creek* ... MS-4
East Topisaw Creek—*stream* ... MS-4
**East Topsham**—*pop pl* ... VT-1
East Toqua Lake—*lake* ... MN-6
East Torch River—*stream* ... WI-6
East Torrey Creek—*stream* ... WY-8
East Towanda—*locale* ... PA-2
East Tower—*tower* ... FL-3
East Tower Camp—*locale* ... FL-3
*East Town* ... MA-1
East Town Corner Lake—*lake* ... MI-6
East Town Creek—*stream* ... TX-5
*East Towne Mall* ... PA-2
East Towne Mall—*post sta* ... PA-2
East Towne Mall Shop Ctr—*locale* ... TN-4
East Towne Market—*locale* ... NC-3
East Town Hollow—*valley* ... VA-3
East Town Mall—*locale* ... PA-2
East Town Park—*park* ... IA-7
East Town Plaza Shop Ctr—*locale* ... AL-4
**East Townsend**—*pop pl* ... OH-6
East Townsend Cem—*cemetery* ... OH-6
East Townsend Windmill—*locale* ... NM-5
East Township—*fmr MCD* ... IA-7
**East Township**—*pop pl* ... NY-2
**East (Township of)**—*pop pl* ... OH-6
East Town Street Hist Dist—*hist pl* ... OH-6
**Easttown (Township of)**—*pop pl* ... PA-2
**Easttown Woods**—*pop pl* ... PA-2
East Toxaway Creek—*stream* ... SC-3
East Trail Creek—*stream* ... MT-8
East Trap Tank—*reservoir* ... TX-5
**East Tremont**—*pop pl* ... NY-2
East Trent Creek—*stream* ... WY-8
**East Trenton**—*pop pl* ... NJ-2
**East Trenton Heights**—*pop pl* ... NJ-2
*East Trenton Lake* ... MO-7
East Trinity Ch—*church* ... NC-3
East Trinity Creek—*stream* ... OR-9
East Trion—*locale* ... GA-3
East Tritt Lake—*lake* ... WA-9
East Trough Spring—*spring* ... WY-8
East Trout Brook—*stream* ... NY-2
East Trout Creek—*stream* ... CO-8
East Trout Lake—*lake* ... MI-6
East Troy—*locale* ... ME-1
**East Troy**—*pop pl* ... PA-2
**East Troy**—*pop pl* ... WI-6
East Troy Cem—*cemetery* (2) ... PA-2
East Troy Ch—*church* ... PA-2
*East Troy Lake* ... WI-6
East Troy Oil Field—*oilfield* ... AR-4
**East Troy (Town of)**—*pop pl* ... WI-6
**East Trumbull**—*pop pl* ... OH-6
East Trumbull Cem—*cemetery* ... OH-6
East Tschuddi Gulch—*valley* ... CO-8
**East Tulare**—*pop pl* ... CA-9
East Tule Bench Rsvr—*reservoir* ... UT-8
East Tule Creek—*stream* ... CA-9
East Tule Well—*well* ... AZ-5
East Tuley Springs—*spring* ... CA-9
*East Tulip Creek* ... AR-4
**East Tulsa**—*pop pl* ... OK-5
East Tulsa Interchange—*other* ... OK-5
East Tunstill Oil Field—*oilfield* ... TX-5
East Tupelo—*uninc pl* ... MS-4
East Tupelo Ch of Christ—*church* ... MS-4
East Turbine Lateral—*canal* ... WA-9
East Turkey Canyon—*valley* ... CO-8
East Turkey Creek—*stream* ... AL-4
East Turkey Creek—*stream* ... AZ-5
East Turkey Creek—*stream* ... KS-7
East Turkey Creek—*stream* ... TX-5
East Turkey Tank—*reservoir* ... AZ-5
East Turner Mtn—*summit* ... ME-1
East Turtle Creek—*stream* (2) ... OH-6
East Turtle Shoal—*bar* ... FL-3
**East Tustin**—*pop pl* ... CA-9
East Twelfth Sch—*school* ... NE-7
East Twelve Ditch—*canal* ... NM-5
East Twentyninth Street Sch—*school* ... WV-2
East Twenty-third Street Baptist Ch—*church* ... TN-4
East Twin—*summit* ... ID-8
East Twin Bay—*bay* ... AK-9
East Twin Brook—*stream* ... ME-1
East Twin Butte—*summit* ... ND-7
East Twin Butte—*summit* ... WA-9
East Twin Creek—*stream* ... AR-4
East Twin Creek—*stream* (2) ... CA-9
East Twin Creek—*stream* (2) ... KS-7
East Twin Creek—*stream* (2) ... MT-8
East Twin Creek—*stream* ... UT-8
East Twin Creek—*stream* (2) ... WA-9
East Twin Creek—*stream* (2) ... WY-8
East Twin Glacier—*glacier* ... AK-9
East Twin Gulch—*valley* ... CO-8
*East Twin Lake* ... MI-6
East Twin Lake—*lake* (2) ... AK-9
East Twin Lake—*lake* ... IA-7
East Twin Lake—*lake* (2) ... MI-6
East Twin Lake—*lake* (5) ... MN-6
East Twin Lake—*lake* (2) ... NE-7
East Twin Lake—*lake* (2) ... WI-6
East Twin Lake State Game Mngmt Area—*park* ... IA-7
East Twin Peak—*summit* ... AK-9
*East Twin Pup Lake* ... MI-6
East Twin River—*stream* ... WA-9
East Twin River—*stream* ... WI-6
East Twin Wash—*stream* ... AZ-5
East Twin Wash—*stream* ... CO-8
East Twin Windmill—*locale* ... NM-5
East Two Creek—*stream* ... CO-8
East Two River—*stream* (2) ... MN-6
East Two Tank—*reservoir* ... AZ-5
East Tyronza Cem—*cemetery* ... AR-4
East Uall Creek—*stream* ... MT-8
East Uall Sch—*school* ... MT-8
East Ullensvang Cem—*cemetery* ... IA-7
East Union—*locale* ... KY-4
East Union—*locale* ... NY-2
**East Union**—*pop pl* ... IN-6
**East Union**—*pop pl* ... ME-1
**East Union**—*pop pl* ... MN-6
**East Union**—*pop pl* (2) ... OH-6
**East Union**—*pop pl* ... TN-4
East Union—*uninc pl* ... WA-9
*East Union Baptist Ch* ... MS-4
East Union Baptist Ch—*church* ... TN-4
East Union Bayou—*bay* ... TX-5
East Union Canyon—*valley* ... NV-8
East Union Cem—*cemetery* ... IL-6
East Union Cem—*cemetery* ... IN-6
East Union Cem—*cemetery* ... NE-7
East Union Cem—*cemetery* (3) ... OH-6
East Union Ch—*church* ... AR-4
East Union Ch—*church* ... IA-7
East Union Ch—*church* ... KY-4
East Union Ch—*church* ... MN-6
East Union Ch—*church* (2) ... OH-6
East Union Ch—*church* (2) ... PA-2
East Union Ch (historical)—*church* ... MS-4
East Union Community Hall—*locale* ... KS-7
East Union Creek—*stream* ... SD-7
East Union HS—*school* ... CA-9
**East Union (McCleary)**—*pop pl* ... OH-6
*East Union Middle School* ... NC-3
East Union Sch—*school* ... CA-9
East Union Sch—*school* ... IL-6
East Union Sch—*school* ... MS-4
East Union Sch—*school* ... NC-3
East Union Sch—*school* ... PA-2
East Union Sch (historical)—*school* ... MS-4
East Uniontown—*CDP* ... PA-2
**East Union (Township of)**—*pop pl* ... OH-6
**East Union (Township of)**—*pop pl* ... PA-2
**East Unity**—*pop pl* ... NH-1
East Unity Ch—*church* ... PA-2
East Unit 1 Highline Canal—*canal* ... WA-9
East Upper Big Creek—*stream* ... WI-6
East Upper Elem Sch—*school* ... KS-7
East Utah Shaft—*mine* ... UT-8
East Ute Creek—*stream* ... CO-8
East Ute Mesa—*summit* ... CO-8
East Valdor Gulch—*valley* ... CA-9
**Eastvale**—*pop pl* ... PA-2
**Eastvale**—*pop pl* ... TX-5
Eastvale Borough—*civil* ... PA-2
Eastvale Park—*park* ... TX-5
Eastvale Sch—*school* ... CA-9
East Vallejo—*uninc pl* ... CA-9
East Valley—*fmr MCD* ... NE-7
East Valley—*valley* (2) ... UT-8
East Valley Cem—*cemetery* ... NY-2
East Valley City Interchange—*crossing* ... ND-7
East Valley Creek—*stream* ... CA-9
East Valley Creek—*stream* ... NY-2
East Valley HS—*school* ... WA-9
East Valley JHS—*school* ... WA-9
East Valley Lake—*lake* ... NE-7
East Valley Mound Wasteway—*canal* ... ID-8
East Valley Sch—*school* ... CA-9
East Valley Sch—*school* ... KS-7
East Valley Sch—*school* ... MI-6
East Valley Sch (abandoned)—*school* ... MO-7
East Valley School (Abandoned)—*locale* ... NE-7
**East Valley (Township of)**—*pop pl* ... MN-6
**East Valley View Subdivision**—*pop pl* ... UT-8
East Vancorum—*locale* ... CO-8
East Van Creek—*stream* ... WA-9
**East Vandergrift**—*pop pl* ... PA-2
East Vandergrift Borough—*civil* ... PA-2
East Vang Ch—*church* ... ND-7
East Van Zandt Sch—*school* ... TX-5
**East Varick**—*pop pl* ... NY-2
**East Vassalboro**—*pop pl* ... ME-1
East Vassalboro Grist and Saw Mill—*hist pl* ... ME-1
East Vaughn—*uninc pl* ... NM-5
East Vealmoor Oil Field—*oilfield* ... TX-5
East Venice—*locale* ... NY-2
**East Venice**—*pop pl* ... FL-3
East Ventura—*uninc pl* ... CA-9
East Verde Creek—*stream* ... TX-5
East Verde River—*stream* ... AZ-5
*East Verdigris Creek* ... KS-7
East Vermillion Lake—*reservoir* ... SD-7
East Vermillion Lake Dam—*dam* ... SD-7
East Vernon Ch—*church* ... GA-3
**East Vernonia**—*pop pl* ... OR-9
**East Verona**—*pop pl* ... NY-2
**East Vestal**—*pop pl* ... NY-2
**East Victor**—*pop pl* ... NY-2
**East Vidalia**—*pop pl* ... GA-3
East Vidette—*summit* ... CA-9
East Vidler Creek—*stream* ... OR-9
East View—*locale* ... TN-4
**Eastview**—*pop pl* ... AR-4
**Eastview**—*pop pl* ... CA-9
**Eastview**—*pop pl* ... KY-4
**Eastview**—*pop pl* (2) ... MD-2
**Eastview**—*pop pl* ... MI-6
**Eastview**—*pop pl* ... MS-4
**Eastview**—*pop pl* ... NH-1
**East View**—*pop pl* ... NY-2
**Eastview**—*pop pl* ... OH-6
**East View**—*pop pl* ... PA-2
**East View**—*pop pl* ... SC-3
**Eastview**—*pop pl* (2) ... TN-4
**East View**—*pop pl* ... TN-4
**East View**—*pop pl* ... WV-2
East View—*uninc pl* ... GA-3
East View—*uninc pl* ... TX-5
**Eastview Acres**—*pop pl* ... CT-1
Eastview Ave Sch—*school* ... NY-2
*East View Baptist Ch* ... TN-4
Eastview Baptist Ch—*church* ... IN-6
Eastview Baptist Ch—*church* ... MS-4
East View Baptist Ch—*church* ... TN-4
Eastview Cem—*cemetery* ... AL-4
East View Cem—*cemetery* ... GA-3
Eastview Cem—*cemetery* ... GA-3
East View Cem—*cemetery* ... GA-3
Eastview Cem—*cemetery* ... GA-3
East View Cem—*cemetery* (2) ... GA-3
Eastview Cem—*cemetery* (3) ... GA-3
Eastview Cem—*cemetery* ... IN-6
Eastview Cem—*cemetery* (2) ... NC-3
East View Cem—*cemetery* ... NC-3
Eastview Cem—*cemetery* ... OH-6
East View Cem—*cemetery* ... PA-2
Eastview Cem—*cemetery* ... SC-3
East View Cem—*cemetery* ... SC-3
East View Cem—*cemetery* ... TN-4
Eastview Cem—*cemetery* (3) ... TN-4
East View Cem—*cemetery* ... TN-4
Eastview Cem—*cemetery* (2) ... TX-5
East View Cem—*cemetery* ... WV-2
Eastview Ch—*church* ... AL-4
East View Ch—*church* ... GA-3
Eastview Ch—*church* ... KY-4
Eastview Ch—*church* ... MS-4
East View Ch—*church* ... MO-7
Eastview Ch—*church* ... OH-6
East View Ch—*church* (2) ... TN-4
Eastview Ch—*church* ... TN-4
East View Ch—*church* (2) ... WV-2
East View Christian Sch—*school* ... MI-6
Eastview Elem Sch—*school* ... IN-6
Eastview Elem Sch—*school* (2) ... TN-4
**Eastview Estates (subdivision)**—*pop pl* ... UT-8
**Eastview Hills**—*pop pl* ... WA-9
Eastview JHS—*school* ... OH-6
Eastview Lake—*lake* ... OH-6
East View Park—*park* ... IL-6
East View Park—*park* ... OH-6
**Eastview Park (subdivision)**—*pop pl* ... MA-1
East View Playground—*park* ... MN-6
East View-Ramer (CCD)—*cens area* ... TN-4
East View-Ramer Division—*civil* ... TN-4
**Eastview (RR name East View)**—*pop pl* ... KY-4
East View (RR name for Eastview)—*other* ... KY-4
East View Sch—*school* ... GA-3
East View Sch—*school* ... IN-6
East View Sch—*school* ... MO-7
Eastview Sch—*school* ... SC-3
East View Sch—*school* ... SD-7
East View Sch—*school* ... TX-5
East View Sch—*school* ... WI-6
East View Sch (abandoned)—*school* ... SD-7
East View Sch (historical)—*school* ... TN-4
*Eastview School* ... TN-4
Eastview School (Abandoned)—*locale* ... NM-5
**Eastview Subdivision**—*pop pl* ... UT-8
**Eastview Subdivision 1-13**—*pop pl* ... UT-8
Eastview Terrace Park—*park* ... IL-6
*East Village* ... MA-1
**East Village**—*pop pl* (2) ... CT-1
**East Village**—*pop pl* (2) ... MA-1
**East Village**—*pop pl* ... TN-4
East Village Creek—*stream* ... SC-3
East Village Green—*park* ... NY-2
East Village Hist Dist—*hist pl* ... MA-1
East Village Meetinghouse—*hist pl* ... VT-1
East Village Mills Oil Field—*oilfield* ... TX-5
Eastville—*locale* ... GA-3
**Eastville**—*pop pl* (2) ... MA-1
**Eastville**—*pop pl* ... MO-7
**Eastville**—*pop pl* ... PA-2
**Eastville**—*pop pl* ... VA-3
Eastville (Magisterial District)—*fmr MCD* ... VA-3
Eastville P.O. (historical)—*locale* ... AL-4
Eastville Run—*stream* ... PA-2
**Eastville Station**—*pop pl* ... VA-3
East Vincent Ch—*church* ... PA-2
**East Vincent (Township of)**—*pop pl* ... PA-2
**East Vindex**—*pop pl* ... MD-2
**East Vineland**—*pop pl* ... NJ-2
East Vineland Sch—*school* ... NJ-2
East Vinton Sch—*school* ... VA-3
East Virgil—*locale* ... NY-2
*East Virgil Creek* ... NY-2
*East Vivian* ... WV-2
**East Vivian**—*pop pl* ... WV-2
East Vocational HS—*school* ... NY-2
**East Voth**—*pop pl* ... TX-5
**Eastvue**—*pop pl* ... PA-2
*East Wachusett Brook* ... MA-1
East Wachusett Brook—*stream* ... MA-1
**East Waco**—*pop pl* ... TX-5
East Waco JHS—*school* ... TX-5
East Waco Sch—*school* ... TX-5
*East Waddell Creek* ... CA-9
East Waddell Creek—*stream* ... CA-9
East Wadesboro—*other* ... NC-3
East Waikalua—*civil* ... HI-9
East Wailuaiki Stream—*stream* ... HI-9
East Wailuanui Stream—*stream* ... HI-9
East Wait Brook—*stream* ... MA-1
**East Wakefield**—*pop pl* ... NH-1
East Wakulla (CCD)—*cens area* ... FL-3
East Walbright Creek—*stream* ... WY-8
**East Walden**—*pop pl* ... NY-2
East Wales—*locale* ... ME-1
East Walker River—*stream* ... CA-9
East Walker River—*stream* ... NV-8
East Walker River Petroglyph Site—*hist pl* ... NV-8
*East Walker River Reservoir* ... CA-9
East Walker Sch (historical)—*school* ... NV-8
*East Walkers Reservoir* ... CT-1
*East Walker Well* ... NV-8
East Walle Evangelical Lutheran—*cemetery* ... ND-7
**East Wallingford**—*pop pl* ... CT-1
**East Wallingford**—*pop pl* ... VT-1
*East Wall Rock Spring* ... OR-9
East Walnut Baptist Ch—*church* ... AL-4
East Walnut Canyon—*valley* ... AZ-5
East Walnut Grove Sch—*school* ... IL-6
East Walnut Hills Firehouse—*hist pl* ... OH-6
East Walnut Sch—*school* ... OK-5
**East Walpole**—*pop pl* ... MA-1
East Walworth—*unorg reg* ... SD-7
*East Wapsipinicon River* ... IA-7
*East Ward* ... MA-1
Eastward—*hist pl* ... NJ-2
Eastward—*locale* ... WA-9
*East Ward Elem Sch* ... PA-2
East Ward Elem Sch—*school* ... MS-4
East Ward Elem Sch—*school* ... PA-2
Eastward Ho Country Club—*locale* ... MA-1
East Ward JHS—*school* ... TX-5
Eastward Point—*cape* ... MD-2
Eastward Point—*cape* ... MA-1
*East Ward Sch* ... IN-6
East Ward Sch—*hist pl* ... MI-6
East Ward Sch—*school* ... KY-4
East Ward Sch—*school* ... MI-6
East Ward Sch—*school* (2) ... NE-7
East Ward Sch—*school* ... PA-2
East Ward Sch—*school* (6) ... TX-5
**East Wareham**—*pop pl* ... MA-1
East Wareham (historical P.O.)—*locale* ... MA-1
**East Wareham (RR name Onset (sta.))**—*pop pl* ... MA-1
East Wareham Station (historical)—*locale* ... MA-1
East Warm Creek Ditch—*canal* ... UT-8
East Warm Springs Oil Field—*oilfield* ... WY-8
East Warren—*locale* ... VT-1
**East Warren**—*pop pl* ... ME-1
**East Warren**—*pop pl* ... PA-2
**East Warren**—*pop pl* ... RI-1
East Warren Creek—*stream* ... OK-5
East Warrenton—*locale* ... GA-3
**East Warrenton**—*pop pl* ... GA-3
East Warrior Peak—*summit* ... ID-8
East Washabaugh—*unorg reg* ... SD-7
*East Washacum Pond* ... MA-1
East Washboard Wash—*stream* ... AZ-5
East Washerwoman Shoal—*bar* ... FL-3
**East Washington**—*pop pl* ... NH-1
**East Washington**—*pop pl* ... PA-2
East Washington Borough—*civil* ... PA-2
East Washington Ch—*church* ... MI-6
**East Washington Heights (subdivision)**—*pop pl* ... DC-2
East Washington Hist Dist—*hist pl* ... PA-2
East Washington Oil Field—*oilfield* ... OK-5
East Washington Sch—*school* ... MO-7
**East Washington Township**—*pop pl* ... KS-7
**East Waterboro**—*pop pl* ... ME-1
*East Waterbury Island* ... CT-1
Eastwater Canyon—*valley* ... AZ-5
East Water Canyon—*valley* ... NM-5
East Waterford—*locale* ... ME-1
**East Waterford**—*pop pl* ... PA-2
East Waterford Cem—*cemetery* ... PA-2
East Waterford Narrows—*locale* ... PA-2
East Waterford Sch—*school* ... IL-6
*East Waterloo* ... IA-7
East Waterloo Township—*fmr MCD* ... IA-7
Eastwater Spring—*spring* ... AZ-5
**East Watertown**—*pop pl* ... NY-2
East Watertown Sch—*school* ... MI-6
**East Watertown (subdivision)**—*pop pl* ... MA-1
East Waupun—*locale* ... WI-6
*East Waushaccum Pond* ... MA-1
East Waushacum Pond—*lake* ... MA-1
**East Waverly**—*pop pl* ... NY-2
**East Wawarsing**—*pop pl* ... NY-2
Eastway—*post sta* ... NC-3
Eastway Ch—*church* ... NC-3
Eastway Community Center—*building* ... GA-3
**Eastway Heights (subdivision)**—*pop pl* ... NC-3
Eastway JHS—*school* ... NC-3
East Wayland Cem—*cemetery* ... NY-2
Eastway Mobile Home Park—*locale* ... AZ-5

Ebeling, Arthur, House—*hist pl* IA-7
Ebeling, Henry, House—*hist pl* IA-7
Ebeling Ditch—*canal* MN-6
Ebel Lake—*lake* ND-7
Ebell Cem—*cemetery* AL-4
Ebell Creek—*stream* OR-9
Ebell Creek Divide—*ridge* OR-9
Ebell Park—*park* CA-9
Ebell Picnic Area—*park* OR-9
*Eben* MI-6
Eben—*locale* NY-2
Eben Creek—*stream* ID-8
Ebenecook Harbor—*bay* ME-1
*Ebeneezer Baptist Church* AL-4
Ebeneezer Cem—*cemetery* AL-4
Ebeneezer Cem—*cemetery* TN-4
*Ebeneezer Ch* AL-4
Ebeneezer Ch—*church* AL-4
Ebeneezer Ch—*church* GA-3
Ebeneezer Ch (historical)—*church* MS-4
*Ebeneezer Church* MS-4
*Ebeneezer Methodist Church* TN-4
Ebeneezer Sch (historical)—*school* TN-4
Ebeneza Ch—*church* PA-2
Ebenezar Sch—*school* SC-3
Ebeneze Ch—*church* AR-4
*Ebenezer* AL-4
Ebenezer—*cemetery* AL-4
Ebenezer—*cemetery* LA-4
Ebenezer—*locale* AR-4
Ebenezer—*locale* GA-3
Ebenezer—*locale* NJ-2
Ebenezer—*locale* NC-3
Ebenezer—*locale* (2) TN-4
Ebenezer—*locale* (2) TX-5
Ebenezer—*locale* VA-3
Ebenezer—*locale* WI-6
**Ebenezer**—*pop pl* AL-4
**Ebenezer**—*pop pl* (2) FL-3
**Ebenezer**—*pop pl* (3) KY-4
**Ebenezer**—*pop pl* LA-4
**Ebenezer**—*pop pl* (4) MS-4
**Ebenezer**—*pop pl* MO-7
**Ebenezer**—*pop pl* NY-2
**Ebenezer**—*pop pl* (2) PA-2
**Ebenezer**—*pop pl* (3) SC-3
**Ebenezer**—*pop pl* (3) TN-4
Ebenezer Acad—*hist pl* SC-3
Ebenezer Academy, Bethany Presbyterian Church and Cemetery—*hist pl* NC-3
Ebenezer Alexis Cem—*cemetery* AL-4
Ebenezer AME Zion Ch—*church* AL-4
Ebenezer Associate Reformed Presbyterian Church—*hist pl* SC-3
Ebenezer Ballplay Ch—*church* TN-4
Ebenezer Baptist Cem—*cemetery* SD-7
*Ebenezer Baptist Ch* AL-4
*Ebenezer Baptist Ch* MS-4
*Ebenezer Baptist Ch* TN-4
Ebenezer Baptist Ch—*church* (2) AL-4
Ebenezer Baptist Ch—*church* DE-2
Ebenezer Baptist Ch—*church* FL-3
Ebenezer Baptist Ch—*church* IN-6
Ebenezer Baptist Ch—*church* (6) MS-4
Ebenezer Baptist Ch—*church* TN-4
Ebenezer Bar—*bar* ID-8
*Ebenezer Branch* MS-4
*Ebenezer Branch* MO-7
Ebenezer Branch—*stream* AR-4
Ebenezer Branch—*stream* DE-2
Ebenezer Branch—*stream* MS-4
Ebenezer Branch—*stream* TN-4
Ebenezer Brook—*stream* ME-1
Ebenezer Brook—*stream* NY-2
Ebenezer Campground—*hist pl* AR-4
Ebenezer Cave—*cave* TN-4
*Ebenezer Cem* MS-4
Ebenezer Cem—*cemetery* (13) AL-4
Ebenezer Cem—*cemetery* (9) AR-4
Ebenezer Cem—*cemetery* CO-8
Ebenezer Cem—*cemetery* (2) FL-3
Ebenezer Cem—*cemetery* (11) GA-3
Ebenezer Cem—*cemetery* (7) IL-6
Ebenezer Cem—*cemetery* (6) IN-6
Ebenezer Cem—*cemetery* (3) IA-7
Ebenezer Cem—*cemetery* (2) KS-7
Ebenezer Cem—*cemetery* KY-4
Ebenezer Cem—*cemetery* (3) LA-4
Ebenezer Cem—*cemetery* (2) MD-2
Ebenezer Cem—*cemetery* (8) MN-6
Ebenezer Cem—*cemetery* (16) MS-4
Ebenezer Cem—*cemetery* (6) MO-7
Ebenezer Cem—*cemetery* (2) NE-7
Ebenezer Cem—*cemetery* (2) NC-3
Ebenezer Cem—*cemetery* (2) ND-7
Ebenezer Cem—*cemetery* (6) OH-6
Ebenezer Cem—*cemetery* OK-5
Ebenezer Cem—*cemetery* PA-2
Ebenezer Cem—*cemetery* (3) SC-3
Ebenezer Cem—*cemetery* (4) SD-7
Ebenezer Cem—*cemetery* (5) TN-4
Ebenezer Cem—*cemetery* (7) TX-5
Ebenezer Cem—*cemetery* (2) VA-3
Ebenezer Cem—*cemetery* (3) WI-6
*Ebenezer Ch* AL-4
*Ebenezer Ch* DE-2
*Ebenezer Ch* MO-7
Ebenezer Ch—*church* (38) AL-4
Ebenezer Ch—*church* (12) AR-4
Ebenezer Ch—*church* (2) DE-2
Ebenezer Ch—*church* (10) FL-3
Ebenezer Ch—*church* (47) GA-3
Ebenezer Ch—*church* (14) IL-6
Ebenezer Ch—*church* (10) IN-6
Ebenezer Ch—*church* IA-7
Ebenezer Ch—*church* (5) KS-7
Ebenezer Ch—*church* (6) KY-4
Ebenezer Ch—*church* (10) LA-4
Ebenezer Ch—*church* (7) MD-2
Ebenezer Ch—*church* MI-6
Ebenezer Ch—*church* (5) MN-6
Ebenezer Ch—*church* (27) MS-4
Ebenezer Ch—*church* (7) MO-7
Ebenezer Ch—*church* (2) NE-7
Ebenezer Ch—*church* (2) NJ-2
Ebenezer Ch—*church* (36) NC-3
Ebenezer Ch—*church* (13) OH-6
Ebenezer Ch—*church* (2) OK-5
Ebenezer Ch—*church* (13) PA-2
Ebenezer Ch—*church* (36) SC-3
Ebenezer Ch—*church* (3) SD-7
Ebenezer Ch—*church* (23) TN-4
Ebenezer Ch—*church* (11) TX-5
Ebenezer Ch—*church* (40) VA-3
Ebenezer Ch—*church* (6) WV-2
Ebenezer Chapel—*hist pl* WV-2
Ebenezer Ch (historical)—*church* (3) AL-4
Ebenezer Ch (historical)—*church* MS-4
Ebenezer Ch (historical)—*church* (3) TN-4
Ebenezer Ch of God in Christ—*church* UT-8
Ebenezer Christian Ch—*church* FL-3
Ebenezer Church (historical)—*locale* MO-7
Ebenezer Community Center—*building* AL-4
Ebenezer County Line Ch—*church* IN-6
Ebenezer Covered Bridge—*hist pl* PA-2
*Ebenezer-Craig Cemetery* AL-4
*Ebenezer Creek* GA-3
Ebenezer Creek—*stream* GA-3
Ebenezer Creek—*stream* ID-8
Ebenezer Creek—*stream* IN-6
*Ebenezer Dam* PA-2
Ebenezer Day Care and Kindergarten—*school* FL-3
Ebenezer East Ch—*church* AL-4
Ebenezer Elem Sch—*school* PA-2
Ebenezer Fiske House Site—*locale* MA-1
*Ebenezer Freewill Baptist Ch* AL-4
Ebenezer (historical)—*locale* AL-4
Ebenezer (historical)—*locale* MS-4
Ebenezer (historical)—*locale* SD-7
Ebenezer Hollow—*valley* TN-4
Eben-Ezer Hosp—*hospital* CO-8
Ebenezer Independent Free Methodist Ch—*church* FL-3
**Ebenezer Junction**—*pop pl* NY-2
Ebenezer Lake—*lake* PA-2
Ebenezer Landing—*locale* GA-3
Ebenezer Latin-American AOG—*church* UT-8
Ebenezer Leon Baptist Ch—*church* FL-3
Ebenezer Lutheran Chapel—*hist pl* SC-3
Ebenezer Maxwell House—*building* PA-2
*Ebenezer Methodist Ch* MS-4
Ebenezer Methodist Ch—*church* DE-2
Ebenezer Methodist Ch—*church* (2) MS-4
Ebenezer Methodist Ch (historical)—*church* MS-4
Ebenezer Methodist Ch (historical)—*church* TN-4
*Ebenezer Methodist Church* AL-4
Ebenezer Methodist Church—*hist pl* NC-3
Ebenezer Methodist Episcopal Chapel and Cemetery—*hist pl* IL-6
Ebenezer Methodist Episcopal Ch (historical)—*church* AL-4
Ebenezer Mill—*hist pl* TN-4
Ebenezer Missionary Baptist Ch—*church* (2) AL-4
Ebenezer Missionary Baptist Ch (historical)—*church* AL-4
Ebenezer Missionary Baptist Church—*hist pl* AL-4
Ebenezer Mtn—*summit* NY-2
Ebenezer Post Office (historical)—*building* MS-4
Ebenezer Post Office (historical)—*building* TN-4
*Ebenezer Presbyterian Church* MS-4
*Ebenezer Presbyterian Church* TN-4
Ebenezer Presbyterian Church—*hist pl* KY-4
Ebenezer Primitive Baptist Ch (historical)—*church* MS-4
*Ebenezer Primitive Baptist Church* MS-4
Ebenezer Reese Claim—*civil* MS-4
*Ebenezer Reformed Cemetery* SD-7
Ebenezer Ridge—*ridge* IN-6
Ebenezer Run—*stream* WV-2
*Ebenezer Sch* MS-4
Ebenezer Sch—*hist pl* KY-4
Ebenezer Sch—*school* (2) AL-4
Ebenezer Sch—*school* AR-4
Ebenezer Sch—*school* GA-3
Ebenezer Sch—*school* (5) IL-6
Ebenezer Sch—*school* (2) KY-4
Ebenezer Sch—*school* LA-4
Ebenezer Sch—*school* MD-2
Ebenezer Sch—*school* MS-4
Ebenezer Sch—*school* (2) NC-3
Ebenezer Sch—*school* (7) SC-3
Ebenezer Sch—*school* TN-4
Ebenezer Sch—*school* WV-2
Ebenezer Sch (historical)—*school* (4) AL-4
Ebenezer Sch (historical)—*school* (3) MS-4
Ebenezer Sch (historical)—*school* (2) MO-7
Ebenezer Sch (historical)—*school* SD-7
Ebenezer Sch (historical)—*school* (2) TN-4
Ebenezer Spring—*spring* LA-4
Ebenezer Townsite and Jerusalem Lutheran Church—*hist pl* GA-3
*Ebenezer United Methodist Church* MS-4
*Ebenezer United Methodist Church* TN-4
Ebenfeld Cem—*cemetery* OK-5
Ebenfeld Sch—*school* KS-7
Ebenflure Ch—*church* KS-7
*Ebenicook Harbor* ME-1
Eben Island—*island* ME-1
**Eben Junction**—*pop pl* MI-6
Eben (LS&i RR name for Eben Junction)—*other* MI-6
Ebenmg—*island* MP-9
*Ebenmg Island* MP-9
*Ebenniyu To* MP-9
*Ebennyu-to* MP-9
**Ebensburg**—*pop pl* PA-2
Ebensburg Airp—*airport* PA-2
Ebensburg Borough—*civil* PA-2
Ebensburg Junction—*locale* PA-2
Ebensburg Rsvr—*reservoir* PA-2
Ebensburg State Sch—*school* PA-2
Ebensburg Storage Dam—*dam* PA-2
*Ebens Pond* MA-1
Ebens Spring—*spring* AZ-5
**Ebenville**—*pop pl* MA-1
Ebenzer Ch—*church* AL-4
Ebenzer Ch—*church* NC-3
Ebenzer Ch—*church* VA-3
Ebenzer Ch—*church* WV-2
Eber—*locale* OH-6
Eber Creek—*stream* OR-9
Eber Ditch—*canal* CO-8
Eber Ditch—*canal* OH-6
Eberhard Ch—*church* IN-6
Eberhard Island—*island* MN-6
Eberhard Lake—*lake* MI-6
Eberhard Ranch—*locale* WY-8
Eberhardt—*locale* NV-8
**Eberhardt**—*pop pl* (2) PA-2
Eberhardt and Ober Brewery—*hist pl* PA-2
Eberhardt Canyon—*valley* NV-8
Eberhardt Cem—*cemetery* MO-7
Eberhardt Ford—*locale* MO-7
Eberhardt Mansion—*hist pl* NY-2
Eberhardt Mine—*mine* NV-8
Eberhardt Ranch—*locale* AZ-5
Eberhardt Tunnel—*tunnel* NV-8
Eberhardt Vee—*cape* WY-8
Eberhart, Adolph O., House—*hist pl* MN-6
Eberhart Cem—*cemetery* IN-6
Eberhart Sch—*school* IL-6
Eberhart Sch (historical)—*school* MO-7
Eberia Well—*well* TX-5
Eberiru—*island* MP-9
*Eberiru Island* MP-9
*Eberiru-To* MP-9
Eberle—*locale* KY-4
**Eberle**—*pop pl* IL-6
Eberle Cem—*cemetery* OK-5
*Eberle Dam* PA-2
*Eberlein Mill Creek* AL-4
Eberle Knobs—*summit* KY-4
Eberle Mine—*mine* NM-5
Eberle Park—*park* TX-5
Eberle Sch—*school* IL-6
**Eberleys Mill**—*pop pl* PA-2
*Eberlien Mill Creek* AL-4
Eberlin Cem—*cemetery* MO-7
Eberline Mill Creek—*stream* AL-4
Eberling Tank—*reservoir* AZ-5
Eberl Ranch—*locale* MT-8
**Eberly**—*pop pl* CA-9
Eberly, Johannes, House—*hist pl* PA-2
Eberly, Mount—*summit* AK-9
Eberly Cem—*cemetery* IA-7
Eberly Cem—*cemetery* PA-2
Eberly Ditch—*canal* IN-6
Eberly Flat—*flat* CA-9
Eberly Glacier—*glacier* AK-9
Eberly Ridge—*ridge* CA-9
**Eberlys Mill**—*pop pl* PA-2
*Eberneber Church* AL-4
*Eberneezer Baptist Church* TN-4
Eberneezer Ch—*church* TN-4
*Eberneezer Methodist Church* MS-4
**Ebernezer**—*pop pl* GA-3
*Ebernezer Ch* TN-4
Ebers Camp—*locale* TX-5
Ebers Creek—*stream* MI-6
Ebersole Quarry Cave—*cave* PA-2
Ebersoll Dam—*dam* SD-7
Ebers Tank—*reservoir* TX-5
Ebert Creek—*stream* SD-7
Ebert Ditch—*canal* IN-6
Ebert-Dulany House—*hist pl* MO-7
Ebert Lake—*lake* WI-6
Ebert Mound Group (47Bt28)—*hist pl* WI-6
Ebert Mtn—*summit* AZ-5
**Eberton**—*pop pl* DE-2
Ebert Ranch—*hist pl* MT-8
Eberts Branch—*stream* MO-7
Eberts Cem—*cemetery* MO-7
Ebert Sch—*school* CO-8
Ebert Tank—*reservoir* AZ-5
*Eberty Branch* MO-7
**Ebervale**—*pop pl* PA-2
Eberwhite Sch—*school* MI-6
E Besler Ranch—*locale* SD-7
Ebey Canyon—*valley* CA-9
Ebeye—*island* MP-9
*Ebeye Island* MP-9
Ebey Hill—*summit* WA-9
Ebey Island—*island* WA-9
Ebey Lake—*lake* CA-9
Ebeys Landing—*locale* WA-9
Ebey Slough—*stream* WA-9
Ebeys Prairie—*flat* WA-9
EBF Bridge over Powder River—*hist pl* WY-8
Ebhorse Stream—*stream* ME-1
*Ebigie-To* MP-9
*Ebijie* MP-9
*Ebijierikku Island* MP-9
*Ebijie To* MP-9
Ebil—*channel* PW-9
*Ebilup* FM-9
Ebinger Sch—*school* IL-6
*Ebinifau* FM-9
*Ebioaji Island* MP-9
*Ebitar* FM-9
*Ebiup* FM-9
Ebjapik—*island* MP-9
*Ebjapik Island* MP-9
Eb Lake—*lake* OR-9
Eblen Cave—*cave* TN-4
Eblen Cem—*cemetery* TN-4
**Eblen Estates**—*pop pl* TN-4
Eblen Gap—*gap* TN-4
Eblen-Powell Number One Dam—*dam* TN-4
Eblen-Powell Number One Rsvr—*reservoir* TN-4
Eblen-Powell Number Two Dam—*dam* TN-4
Eblen-Powell Number Two Rsvr—*reservoir* TN-4
Eblen Spring—*spring* CA-9
Eblin Cem—*cemetery* OH-6
Ebling Cem—*cemetery* KY-4
Eblis—*uninc pl* CA-9
E. B. Lyons Prairie-Woodlawn Preserve—*park* IA-7
Ebner—*locale* IL-6
Ebner Coulee—*valley* WI-6
Ebner Falls—*falls* AK-9
Ebner-Free House—*hist pl* IN-6
Ebo Creek—*stream* MO-7
Ebo Landing—*locale* GA-3
*Ebon* MP-9
Ebon—*locale* KY-4
Ebon Atoll—*island* (2) MP-9
Ebon Channel—*channel* MP-9
Ebon (County-equivalent)—*civil* MP-9
Ebonese Ch—*church* NC-3
*Ebongruppe* MP-9
*Ebon Island* MP-9
Ebon Island—*island* MP-9
Ebonne (not verified)—*island* MP-9
Ebony—*locale* TX-5
Ebony—*locale* VA-3
**Ebony**—*pop pl* AR-4
Ebony Canal—*canal* CA-9
Ebony Cem—*cemetery* TX-5
Ebony cove—*bay* NV-8
Ebony Grove Cem—*cemetery* TX-5
Ebony Heights Sch—*school* TX-5
Ebony Hill—*summit* TX-5
Ebony Hills Country Club—*other* TX-5
Ebony Lake—*lake* MI-6
Ebony Lateral—*canal* ID-8
*Ebony Mine* AL-4
Ebony Sch—*school* AR-4
*Eboon* MP-9
Eborn Point—*cape* (2) NC-3
*Ebo School* MO-7
E Bradberry—*locale* TX-5
E-B Ranch—*locale* CO-8
E Brenna Ranch—*locale* ND-7
**Ebright**—*pop pl* DE-2
**Ebro**—*pop pl* FL-3
**Ebro**—*pop pl* MN-6
Ebro Cem—*cemetery* FL-3
E B Rogers Lake Dam—*dam* MS-4
Ebro Sch—*school* FL-3
Ebro Springs—*spring* WY-8
E Bruske Dam—*dam* SD-7
E B Spring—*spring* AZ-5
Ebster Park—*park* GA-3
*Ebta* MP-9
E B Tank—*reservoir* AZ-5
E Burns Ranch—*locale* ND-7
Ebwaj—*island* MP-9
*Ebwaj Island* MP-9
E B Wilson Dam—*dam* SD-7
Eby—*locale* KY-4
Eby—*locale* WV-2
**Eby**—*pop pl* IN-6
Eby, Tom, Storage Bldg—*hist pl* NM-5
Eby Cem—*cemetery* PA-2
Eby Creek—*stream* CO-8
Eby Creek—*stream* ID-8
Eby Drain—*stream* MI-6
Eby Hill—*summit* MO-7
Eby (historical P.O.)—*locale* IN-6
*Eby Lake* CA-9
Eby Point—*cliff* CO-8
Eby Ranch—*locale* NM-5
Eby Ridge—*ridge* PA-2
Eby Sch—*school* OR-9
Eby's Mill—*locale* IA-7
E Camp Windmill—*locale* TX-5
E Canal—*canal* CA-9
E Canal—*canal* MT-8
E Canal—*canal* OR-9
Ecard Ch—*church* WV-2
E Carr Ranch—*locale* NE-7
EC Bennett—*locale* TX-5
Eccher Gulch—*valley* CO-8
Eccles—*locale* ID-8
Eccles—*locale* MO-7
Eccles—*locale* NV-8
Eccles—*locale* WY-8
**Eccles**—*pop pl* WV-2
Eccles, David, House—*hist pl* UT-8
Eccles, Henry, House—*hist pl* NC-3
Eccles, Mount—*summit* AK-9
Eccles Ave Hist Dist—*hist pl* UT-8
Eccles Bldg—*hist pl* UT-8
Eccles Butte—*summit* ID-8
Eccles Canyon—*valley* UT-8
Eccles Ch—*church* SC-3
Eccles Creek—*stream* AK-9
Ecclesia Ch—*church* MO-7
**Eccles Junction**—*pop pl* WV-2
Eccles Lagoon—*bay* AK-9
**Eccles Park (subdivision)**—*pop pl* NC-3
Eccles Pass—*gap* CO-8
Eccles Peak—*summit* UT-8
Eccles Ranch—*locale* NV-8
Eccles Sch—*school* MI-6
Eccles Sch—*school* OR-9
**Eccles Subdivision**—*pop pl* UT-8
Eccleston—*locale* MD-2
Eccleston Brook—*stream* CT-1
Eccleston Elem Sch—*school* FL-3
Eccles Windmill—*locale* NM-5
**Ecco**—*pop pl* KY-4
**Ecco**—*pop pl* LA-4
E.C. COLLIER—*hist pl* MD-2
ECC Peak—*summit* AZ-5
*Ecell* KY-4
Echada Rsvr—*reservoir* NV-8
Echang—*locale* PW-9
**Echang**—*pop pl* PW-9
Echard Canyon—*valley* UT-8
Echard Creek—*stream* UT-8
Echart Creek—*stream* OR-9
*Echau Creek* SC-3
Echave Dam—*dam* OR-9
Echave Rsvr—*reservoir* OR-9
Echave Well—*well* OR-9
Echaw Creek—*stream* SC-3
*Echebucasassa Creek* FL-3
Echeconnee—*locale* GA-3
Echeconnee Creek—*stream* GA-3
*Echeepocrassa* FL-3
Echee Pond—*lake* SC-3
Echelberger Lake—*lake* MI-6
Echelberger Lateral—*canal* ID-8
**Echelon**—*pop pl* NJ-2
Echerd Airfield—*airport* OH-6
Echeta—*locale* WY-8
Echevarria, Pedro, House—*hist pl* ID-8
Echinique Draw—*valley* AZ-5
Echinique Place—*locale* AZ-5
Echinique Tank—*reservoir* AZ-5
Echinus Geyser—*geyser* WY-8
*Echler Mountain* WA-9
Echo—*locale* AR-4
Echo—*locale* CO-8
Echo—*locale* KY-4
Echo—*locale* PA-2
Echo—*locale* TX-5
Echo—*locale* WA-9
Echo—*locale* WV-2
**Echo**—*pop pl* AL-4
**Echo**—*pop pl* IA-7
**Echo**—*pop pl* LA-4
**Echo**—*pop pl* MN-6
**Echo**—*pop pl* NC-3
**Echo**—*pop pl* OH-6
**Echo**—*pop pl* OR-9
**Echo**—*pop pl* PA-2
**Echo**—*pop pl* TX-5
**Echo**—*pop pl* UT-8
Echo, Lake—*lake* FL-3
Echo, Lake—*lake* GA-3
Echo, Lake—*reservoir* TN-4
Echo, Mount—*summit* NH-1
**Echo Acres (subdivision)**—*pop pl* NC-3
Echo Amphitheater—*other* NM-5
Echo Basin—*basin* CO-8
Echo Bay—*bay* (2) ID-8
Echo Bay—*bay* IA-7
Echo Bay—*bay* (2) MN-6
Echo Bay—*bay* NV-8
Echo Bay—*bay* (4) NY-2
Echo Bay—*bay* OK-5
Echo Bay—*bay* WA-9
**Echo Bay**—*pop pl* NV-8
Echo Bay Airp—*airport* NV-8
**Echo Beach**—*pop pl* ID-8
**Echo Bluff Trailer Park**—*pop pl* NC-3
Echo Bridge—*bridge* MA-1
Echo Bridge—*hist pl* MA-1
Echo Brook—*stream* ME-1
Echo Butte—*summit* OR-9
Echo Camp—*hist pl* NY-2
Echo Camp—*locale* UT-8
Echo Campground—*locale* NM-5
Echo Campground—*locale* UT-8
Echo Campground—*park* OR-9
Echo Canyon—*valley* (5) AZ-5
Echo Canyon—*valley* (2) CA-9
Echo Canyon—*valley* (7) CO-8
Echo Canyon—*valley* ID-8
Echo Canyon—*valley* MT-8
Echo Canyon—*valley* (6) NV-8
Echo Canyon—*valley* OR-9
Echo Canyon—*valley* (3) TX-5
Echo Canyon—*valley* (2) UT-8
Echo Canyon—*valley* WY-8
Echo Canyon Bowl—*basin* AZ-5
Echo Canyon Breastworks—*hist pl* UT-8
*Echo Canyon Creek* UT-8
Echo Canyon Park—*park* AZ-5
Echo Canyon Reservoir State Rec Area—*park* NV-8
Echo Canyon Rsvr—*reservoir* (2) NV-8
Echo Canyon Trail—*trail* UT-8
Echo Cave Ruin—*locale* AZ-5
Echo (CCD)—*cens area* AL-4
Echo Cem—*cemetery* OR-9
Echo Cem—*cemetery* UT-8
Echo Ch—*church* WV-2
*Echo City* UT-8
Echo Cliff—*cliff* CO-8
Echo Cliff—*cliff* NV-8
Echo Cliff—*cliff* NY-2
Echo Cliffs—*cliff* AZ-5
Echo Cliffs—*cliff* WA-9
Echo Cove—*bay* (2) AK-9
Echo Cove—*bay* ME-1
Echo Crater—*crater* ID-8
Echo Creek—*stream* AK-9
Echo Creek—*stream* CA-9
Echo Creek—*stream* (4) CO-8
Echo Creek—*stream* (2) ID-8
Echo Creek—*stream* MN-6
Echo Creek—*stream* MT-8
Echo Creek—*stream* NV-8
Echo Creek—*stream* (3) OR-9
Echo Creek—*stream* TN-4
Echo Creek—*stream* UT-8
Echo Creek—*stream* (2) WA-9
Echo Creek Trail—*trail* OR-9
**Echo Crest**—*pop pl* IN-6
Echo Dam—*dam* UT-8
**Echo Dell**—*pop pl* OR-9
Echo Dell Ranch—*locale* CA-9
Echo Dell Sch (historical)—*school* MO-7
Echo Dell School—*locale* ID-8
Echo Ditch—*canal* CO-8
Echo Ditch—*canal* NM-5
Echo Division—*civil* AL-4
Echo Falls—*falls* OR-9
Echo Falls Canyon—*valley* CA-9
**Echo Farms (subdivision)**—*pop pl* NC-3
Echo Flat—*flat* CA-9
Echo Glacier—*glacier* AK-9
Echo Glen Sch—*school* WI-6
**Echo Glen (subdivision)**—*pop pl* TN-4
Echo Gulch—*valley* (2) MT-8
Echo Harbor—*bay* MI-6
**Echo Heights**—*pop pl* IN-6
**Echo Heights**—*pop pl* NC-3
Echo Hill—*summit* NH-1
Echo Hill Camp—*locale* NJ-2
Echo Hill Camp—*locale* OH-6
Echo Hill Golf Course—*other* OH-6
Echo Hill Ranch—*locale* TX-5
Echo Hills—*summit* NV-8
**Echo Hills (subdivision)**—*pop pl* AL-4
**Echo Hills (subdivision)**—*pop pl* NC-3
**Echo Hills (subdivision)**—*pop pl* TN-4
**Echo Hill (subdivision)**—*pop pl* AL-4
Echo (historical)—*locale* KS-7
Echo (historical)—*locale* MS-4
Echo (historical)—*locale* SD-7
Echo Hollow—*valley* ID-8
Echo Hollow—*valley* TN-4
Echo Hollow Park—*park* OR-9
Echo House—*locale* CO-8
Echoing Lake—*lake* AK-9
Echo Interchange—*crossing* OR-9
Echo Island—*island* AK-9
Echo Island—*island* ME-1
Echo Island—*island* MI-6
Echo Island—*island* MN-6
Echo Island—*island* NH-1
Echo Island—*island* NY-2
Echo Island—*island* OR-9
Echo Island (historical)—*island* SD-7
*Echo Islands* CT-1
Echo JHS—*school* AL-4
Echol—*bay* PW-9
**Echol**—*pop pl* PW-9
**Echola**—*pop pl* AL-4
*Echo Lake* CO-8
*Echo Lake* IN-6
*Echo Lake* MA-1
*Echo Lake* MI-6
*Echo Lake* MN-6
*Echo Lake* MS-4
*Echo Lake* NE-7
*Echo Lake* RI-1
Echo Lake—*lake* AL-4
Echo Lake—*lake* AK-9
Echo Lake—*lake* (9) CA-9
Echo Lake—*lake* CO-8
Echo Lake—*lake* CT-1
Echo Lake—*lake* (3) FL-3
Echo Lake—*lake* (2) ID-8
Echo Lake—*lake* IL-6
Echo Lake—*lake* (4) ME-1
Echo Lake—*lake* (2) MA-1
Echo Lake—*lake* (6) MI-6
Echo Lake—*lake* (9) MN-6
Echo Lake—*lake* (3) MT-8
Echo Lake—*lake* NV-8
Echo Lake—*lake* (2) NH-1
Echo Lake—*lake* NJ-2
Echo Lake—*lake* (11) NY-2
Echo Lake—*lake* OH-6
Echo Lake—*lake* (3) OR-9
Echo Lake—*lake* (3) PA-2
Echo Lake—*lake* UT-8
Echo Lake—*lake* (3) VT-1
Echo Lake—*lake* (5) WA-9
Echo Lake—*lake* (9) WI-6
Echo Lake—*lake* WY-8
Echo Lake—*locale* NJ-2
**Echo Lake**—*pop pl* CA-9
**Echo Lake**—*pop pl* CO-8
**Echo Lake**—*pop pl* IL-6
**Echo Lake**—*pop pl* PA-2
**Echo Lake**—*pop pl* RI-1
**Echo Lake**—*pop pl* WA-9
Echo Lake—*reservoir* (2) AL-4
Echo Lake—*reservoir* CO-8
Echo Lake—*reservoir* ID-8
Echo Lake—*reservoir* (3) IN-6
Echo Lake—*reservoir* (2) MA-1
Echo Lake—*reservoir* (2) NJ-2
Echo Lake—*reservoir* (2) NY-2
Echo Lake—*reservoir* (2) NC-3
Echo Lake—*reservoir* PA-2
Echo Lake—*reservoir* RI-1
Echo Lake—*reservoir* TN-4
Echo Lake—*reservoir* TX-5
Echo Lake—*reservoir* WI-6
Echo Lake Brook—*stream* CT-1
Echo Lake Ch—*church* (2) NJ-2
Echo Lake Channel—*stream* NJ-2
Echo Lake Creek—*stream* MI-6
Echo Lake Dam—*dam* (3) AL-4
Echo Lake Dam—*dam* (2) IN-6
Echo Lake Dam—*dam* MA-1
Echo Lake Dam—*dam* (2) NC-3
Echo Lake Dam—*dam* OR-9
Echo Lake Dam—*dam* PA-2
Echo Lake Dam—*dam* TN-4
**Echo Lake Glen**—*pop pl* OH-6
Echo Lake Golf Course—*other* NJ-2
Echo Lake Park—*park* CO-8
Echo Lake Park—*park* NJ-2
**Echo Lake Ranch**—*pop pl* MO-7
Echo Lakes—*lake* WY-8
Echo Lake Spillway Dam—*dam* NJ-2
**Echo Lakes (subdivision)**—*pop pl* NC-3
Echo Lake Trail—*trail* CA-9
Echo Lake Truck Trail—*trail* WA-9
Echo Lateral—*canal* ID-8
Echol Lake—*reservoir* CT-1
Echo Lode Mine—*mine* SD-7
*Echols* MS-4
Echols—*locale* KY-4
Echols—*locale* MN-6
Echols—*locale* TX-5
Echols, Brig. Gen. John, House—*hist pl* WV-2
Echols Cave—*cave* AL-4
*Echols Cem* TX-5
Echols Cem—*cemetery* (2) AL-4
Echols Cem—*cemetery* AR-4
Echols Cem—*cemetery* (2) GA-3
Echols Cem—*cemetery* MS-4
Echols Cem—*cemetery* TX-5
Echols Cem—*cemetery* WV-2
**Echols (County)**—*pop pl* GA-3
*Echols Creek* VA-3
Echols Creek—*stream* ID-8
Echols Creek—*stream* TX-5
Echols Crossroads—*locale* AL-4
**Echols Crossroads (Bluff City)**—*pop pl* AL-4
Echols Gravesite Cem—*cemetery* AL-4
**Echols Hill**—*pop pl* AL-4
Echols Hills—*uninc pl* AL-4
Echols Lake—*lake* TX-5
Echols Mtn—*summit* ID-8
Echols Sch—*school* AR-4
Echols Sch—*school* TX-5
Echols Spring—*spring* AZ-5
Echo Meadows—*flat* OR-9
Echo Mills—*locale* PA-2
Echo Mine—*mine* NV-8
Echo Mine—*mine* WA-9
Echo Mine (historical)—*mine* SD-7
*Echo Mtn* CA-9
Echo Mtn—*summit* (2) AK-9
Echo Mtn—*summit* (2) CA-9
Echo Mtn—*summit* CO-8
Echo Mtn—*summit* MT-8
Echo Mtn—*summit* (2) NY-2
Echo Mtn—*summit* OR-9
Echo Mtn—*summit* TX-5
Echo Mtn—*summit* WA-9
Echo Oil Field—*oilfield* TX-5
Echooka River—*stream* AK-9
Echo Park—*flat* AZ-5
Echo Park—*flat* (2) CO-8
Echo Park—*park* AZ-5
Echo Park—*park* CA-9
Echo Park—*park* MI-6
Echo Park—*park* (2) NY-2
Echo Park—*park* NC-3
Echo Park—*park* WI-6
**Echo Park**—*pop pl* NC-3
Echo Pass—*gap* AK-9

**Edgewood**—pop pl ... TN-4
**Edgewood**—pop pl ... TX-5
**Edgewood**—pop pl (3) ... VA-3
**Edgewood**—pop pl ... WA-9
**Edgewood**—pop pl (3) ... WV-2
**Edgewood**—pop pl ... WI-6
Edgewood—uninc pl ... KY-4
Edgewood—uninc pl ... PA-2
Edgewood—uninc pl ... SC-3
Edgewood—uninc pl ... TN-4
Edgewood—uninc pl ... TX-5
Edgewood, Lake—reservoir ... IN-6
Edgewood Acad—school ... AL-4
**Edgewood Acres**—pop pl ... TN-4
**Edgewood Acres**—pop pl ... WV-2
Edgewood Acres—uninc pl ... PA-2
**Edgewood Acres (subdivision)**—pop pl ... MS-4
Edgewood Arsenal (Army Chemical Center)—other ... MD-2
Edgewood Ave and Smyrna Street Shop Ctr—locale ... FL-3
Edgewood Ave Sch—school ... CT-1
Edgewood Baptist Ch—church ... AL-4
Edgewood Baptist Ch—church ... TN-4
Edgewood Borough—civil ... PA-2
Edgewood (CCD)—cens area ... TX-5
Edgewood Cem—cemetery ... AR-4
Edgewood Cem—cemetery ... CT-1
Edgewood Cem—cemetery (2) ... FL-3
Edgewood Cem—cemetery ... GA-3
Edgewood Cem—cemetery ... IL-6
Edgewood Cem—cemetery ... IA-7
Edgewood Cem—cemetery ... KY-4
Edgewood Cem—cemetery ... MI-6
Edgewood Cem—cemetery ... MO-7
Edgewood Cem—cemetery ... NH-1
Edgewood Cem—cemetery ... NY-2
Edgewood Cem—cemetery (2) ... NC-3
Edgewood Cem—cemetery ... OH-6
Edgewood Cem—cemetery (2) ... PA-2
Edgewood Cem—cemetery ... SC-3
Edgewood Cem—cemetery (2) ... TN-4
Edgewood Cem—cemetery (2) ... TX-5
Edgewood Cem—cemetery ... VA-3
Edgewood Cem—cemetery ... WI-6
Edgewood Ch—church (2) ... AL-4
Edgewood Ch—church ... FL-3
Edgewood Ch—church (6) ... NC-3
Edgewood Ch—church ... TN-4
Edgewood Ch—church ... TX-5
Edgewood Ch—church ... VA-3
Edgewood Chapel—church ... IL-6
Edgewood Chapel—church ... KY-4
Edgewood Chapel—church ... WV-2
Edgewood City Lake—reservoir ... TX-5
Edgewood Coll—school ... WI-6
Edgewood Community Park—park ... WA-9
Edgewood Congregational Methodist Ch—church ... AL-4
Edgewood Country Club—other ... CT-1
Edgewood Country Club—other ... IL-6
Edgewood Country Club—other ... IN-6
Edgewood Country Club—other ... MI-6
Edgewood Country Club—other ... PA-2
Edgewood Creek ... KS-7
Edgewood Creek—stream ... NV-8
Edgewood Creek—stream ... OR-9
Edgewood Crossroads—locale ... GA-3
Edgewood Drive Ch—church ... LA-4
Edgewood Elementary School ... AL-4
Edgewood Elem Sch—school ... GA-3
Edgewood Elem Sch—school (3) ... IN-6
Edgewood Elem Sch—school ... KS-7
Edgewood Elem Sch—school (2) ... PA-2
**Edgewood Estates Subdivision**—pop pl ... UT-8
Edgewood Farms ... OH-6
**Edgewood Forest (subdivision)**—pop pl ... AL-4
**Edgewood Garden**—pop pl ... NY-2
Edgewood Golf Club—other ... OH-6
Edgewood Golf Course—locale ... MA-1
Edgewood Grove ... IN-6
Edgewood Grove—uninc pl ... PA-2
Edgewood Grove Station—locale ... PA-2
Edgewood Gun Club (historical)—locale ... PA-2
**Edgewood Heights**—pop pl ... IL-6
**Edgewood Heights**—pop pl ... MD-2
**Edgewood Heights**—pop pl ... TN-4
**Edgewood Hills**—pop pl ... DE-2
**Edgewood Hills**—pop pl ... TN-4
**Edgewood Hills Addition (subdivision)**—pop pl ... UT-8
**Edgewood Hills (subdivision)**—pop pl ... PA-2
**Edgewood Hills Subdivision**—pop pl ... UT-8
Edgewood House—hist pl ... NY-2
Edgewood HS—school ... CA-9
Edgewood HS—school ... TX-5
Edgewood Industrial Park (subdivision)—locale ... UT-8
Edgewood JHS—school ... CA-9
Edgewood JHS—school ... FL-3
Edgewood JHS—school ... MN-6
Edgewood JHS—school ... TX-5
Edgewood Lake—lake ... FL-3
Edgewood Lake—lake ... NJ-2
Edgewood Lake—lake ... RI-1
**Edgewood Lake**—pop pl ... IN-6
Edgewood Lake—reservoir ... IN-6
Edgewood Lake Dam—dam ... IN-6
Edgewood Lakes—lake ... NY-2
**Edgewood Manor (subdivision)**—pop pl ... DE-2
**Edgewood Meadows**—pop pl ... MD-2
Edgewood Memorial Park (cemetery)—cemetery ... PA-2
Edgewood Missionary Baptist Church ... AL-4
Edgewood MS—school ... NC-3
Edgewood MS—school ... PA-2
Edgewood MS—school ... SC-3
Edgewood Mtn—summit ... OR-9
Edgewood Oil Field—oilfield ... MS-4
Edgewood Park—park ... CT-1
Edgewood Park—park ... FL-3
Edgewood Park—park ... IL-6
Edgewood Park—park (2) ... IA-7
Edgewood Park—park ... KS-7
Edgewood Park—park ... MS-4
Edgewood Park—park ... OH-6
Edgewood Park—park ... OR-9
Edgewood Park—park ... SC-3
Edgewood Park—park ... TX-5
**Edgewood Park**—pop pl ... MD-2
**Edgewood Park**—pop pl ... NJ-2
**Edgewood Park**—pop pl ... NY-2
**Edgewood Park**—pop pl (2) ... PA-2
Edgewood Park Hist Dist—hist pl ... CT-1
**Edgewood Park (subdivision)**—pop pl ... NC-3
**Edgewood Park (Trailer Court)**—pop pl ... IN-6
Edgewood Pines Golf Course—locale ... PA-2
Edgewood Plaza (Shop Ctr)—locale ... FL-3
Edgewood Pond ... RI-1
Edgewood Presbyterian Ch—church ... AL-4
Edgewood Proving Ground—other ... MD-2
Edgewood Ranch—locale ... OR-9
Edgewood Regional HS—school ... NJ-2
Edgewood Sch ... PA-2
Edgewood Sch—school (2) ... AL-4
Edgewood Sch—school ... AR-4
Edgewood Sch—school (3) ... FL-3
Edgewood Sch—school (3) ... IL-6
Edgewood Sch—school ... IN-6
Edgewood Sch—school (5) ... MI-6
Edgewood Sch—school (3) ... MN-6
Edgewood Sch—school ... MO-7
Edgewood Sch—school ... NM-5
Edgewood Sch—school ... NY-2
Edgewood Sch—school (2) ... NC-3
Edgewood Sch—school ... OH-6
Edgewood Sch—school ... OR-9
Edgewood Sch—school (4) ... PA-2
Edgewood Sch—school ... SC-3
Edgewood Sch—school ... TN-4
Edgewood Sch—school (2) ... TX-5
Edgewood Sch—school ... WV-2
Edgewood Sch—school ... WI-6
Edgewood Sch (historical)—school ... TN-4
Edgewood Sch of Domestic Arts—hist pl ... IA-7
Edgewood Shop Ctr—locale ... MA-1
Edgewood Shop Ctr—locale ... MO-7
Edgewood Shop Ctr—locale ... TX-5
Edgewood South Oil Field—oilfield ... OK-5
Edgewood Spring—spring ... OR-9
Edgewood Spring (historical)—spring ... NV-8
Edgewood Station ... VA-3
**Edgewood (subdivision)**—pop pl ... FL-3
**Edgewood (subdivision)**—pop pl (4) ... NC-3
**Edgewood (subdivision)**—pop pl ... TN-4
**Edgewood Subdivision**—pop pl ... UT-8
**Edgewood Terrace**—pop pl ... NC-3
Edgewood Trust Number 1 Upper Dam—dam ... MA-1
Edgewood Trust Number 3 Dam—dam ... MA-1
Edgewood United Methodist Church ... TN-4
Edgewood Valley Country Club—other ... IL-6
**Edgewood Village**—pop pl ... IN-6
**Edgewood (Wildwood Gardens)**—pop pl ... NJ-2
Edgeworth—locale ... TX-5
**Edgeworth**—pop pl ... PA-2
Edgeworth Baptist Church ... MS-4
Edgeworth Borough—civil ... PA-2
Edgeworth Cem—cemetery ... MS-4
Edgeworth Ch—church ... MS-4
Edgeworth Creek—stream ... ID-8
Edgeworth Elem Sch—school ... PA-2
**Edgeworth (historical)**—pop pl ... TN-4
**Edgeworth Place**—pop pl ... TX-5
Edgeworth Post Office (historical)—building ... TN-4
Edgeworth Sch—school ... NY-2
**Edgeworth (subdivision)**—pop pl ... MA-1
Edgey Store (historical)—locale ... TN-4
Edgigen—island ... MP-9
Edgigen Island ... MP-9
**Edgil**—pop pl ... AL-4
Edgil Branch—stream ... AL-4
Edgil Ch—church ... AL-4
Edgil Grove Cem—cemetery ... AL-4
Edgil Grove Church ... AL-4
Edgil Post Office (historical)—building ... AL-4
**Edgin**—pop pl ... TX-5
Edging Lake—lake ... MI-6
Edging Rock—ridge ... NC-3
Edgington—locale ... KY-4
**Edgington**—pop pl ... IL-6
Edgington Cem—cemetery ... IL-6
Edgington Center Sch—school ... IL-6
Edgington Island—island ... ID-8
Edgington Mound—hist pl ... OH-6
**Edgington (Township of)**—pop pl ... IL-6
Edgington Well—well ... NM-5
**Edginton**—pop pl ... IL-6
Edginton Hill—ridge ... OH-6
Edgison Lake—reservoir ... NC-3
Edgmand Cem—cemetery ... KS-7
Edgmon Cem—cemetery ... TN-4
Edgmont ... PA-2
**Edgmont (Township name for Edgemont)**—pop pl ... PA-2
**Edgmont (Township of)**—pop pl ... PA-2
Edgor ... FM-9
Edgoten—locale ... KY-4
Edgwater ... NY-2
Ed Harris Dam—dam ... NC-3
Ed Harris Dam Number One—dam ... NC-3
Ed Harris Dam Number Two—dam ... NC-3
Ed Henry Flat—flat ... WY-8
Ed Hollow—valley ... MO-7
Edholm—locale ... NE-7
**Edhube**—pop pl ... TX-5
Ediceton Bridge—hist pl ... MS-4
Edick Cem—cemetery ... NY-2
Edick Creek—stream ... NY-2
Edick Lake—lake ... IL-6
Edick Pond—lake ... NY-2
**Edicks**—pop pl ... NY-2
**Edie**—pop pl ... PA-2
Edie Creek—stream ... GA-3
Edie Creek—stream ... ID-8
Edie Creek Ch—church ... GA-3
Edienleng—summit ... FM-9
Edie Ranch—locale ... ID-8
Edies Creek—stream ... WI-6
Edies Siding—locale ... NY-2
Edificio Alcaldia—hist pl ... PR-3
Edificio Jose de Diego—hist pl ... PR-3
Edificio Oliver—hist pl ... PR-3
Ediger Rsvr—reservoir ... OR-9
Ediger State Public Shooting Area—park ... SD-7
Edil Mine—mine ... WA-9
Edilou—locale ... MT-8
**Edina**—pop pl ... MN-6
**Edina**—pop pl ... MO-7
Edina Country Club—other ... MN-6
Edina Golf Club—other ... MO-7
Edina Highlands Sch—school ... MN-6
Edina HS—school ... MN-6
Edina Rsvr—reservoir ... MO-7
**Edinboro**—pop pl ... PA-2
Edinboro Borough—civil ... PA-2
Edinboro Elem Sch—school ... PA-2
Edinboro (historical)—locale ... NC-3
Edinboro Lake—lake ... PA-2
Edinboro Lake Dam—dam ... PA-2
Edinboro State Coll—school ... PA-2
Edinborough Cem—cemetery ... KS-7
Edinburg ... IN-6
Edinburg—locale ... IA-7
**Edinburg**—pop pl ... IL-6
**Edinburg**—pop pl ... MS-4
**Edinburg**—pop pl ... MO-7
**Edinburg**—pop pl ... NJ-2
**Edinburg**—pop pl ... NY-2
**Edinburg**—pop pl ... ND-7
**Edinburg**—pop pl ... OH-6
**Edinburg**—pop pl ... PA-2
**Edinburg**—pop pl ... TX-5
**Edinburg**—pop pl ... VA-3
Edinburg, Lake—reservoir ... TX-5
Edinburg Academy ... MS-4
Edinburg Attendance Center—school ... MS-4
Edinburg (CCD)—cens area ... TX-5
Edinburg Cem—cemetery ... IA-7
Edinburg Cem—cemetery ... ME-1
Edinburg Cem—cemetery ... NY-2
Edinburg Ch—church ... MO-7
Edinburg Ch—church ... NY-2
Edinburg Church of God ... MS-4
Edinburg East Gas Field—oilfield ... TX-5
Edinburg East Main Canal—canal ... TX-5
Edinburg Gap—gap ... VA-3
Edinburg Gas Field—oilfield ... TX-5
Edinburgh ... ND-7
**Edinburgh**—pop pl ... IN-6
Edinburgh (historical)—locale ... ND-7
**Edinburgh of Holladay Condominium**—pop pl ... UT-8
**Edinburg Junction**—pop pl ... TX-5
Edinburg Main Canal—canal ... TX-5
Edinburg Mill—hist pl ... VA-3
Edinburg North Main Canal—canal ... TX-5
**Edinburg Park**—pop pl ... NJ-2
Edinburg Pump—other ... TX-5
Edinburg Rsvr—reservoir ... VA-3
Edinburg Run—stream ... VA-3
Edinburg Sch (historical)—school ... MS-4
Edinburg Settling Basin—reservoir ... TX-5
Edinburg Station—locale ... PA-2
**Edinburg (Town of)**—pop pl ... ME-1
**Edinburg (Town of)**—pop pl ... NY-2
**Edinburg (Township of)**—pop pl ... OH-6
Edinburg Yard—locale ... TX-5
Edinger, Edward, House—hist pl ... IA-7
Edinger Bridge—bridge ... CO-8
Edingers Sch—school ... PA-2
Edings Point ... SC-3
Edingsville Beach—beach ... SC-3
Edington Branch—stream ... KY-4
Edington Branch—stream ... VA-3
Edington Cem—cemetery ... MS-4
Edington Cem—cemetery ... TN-4
Edington Cove—valley ... VA-3
**Edington (historical)**—pop pl ... TN-4
Edington Hollow—valley ... KY-4
Edin Park—park ... IL-6
Edinsei—locale ... FM-9
Edisen Fishery—hist pl ... MI-6
Edison ... IA-7
Edison—locale ... FL-3
Edison—locale (2) ... NJ-2
Edison—locale ... PA-2
**Edison**—pop pl ... CA-9
**Edison**—pop pl ... CO-8
**Edison**—pop pl ... GA-3
**Edison**—pop pl ... KS-7
**Edison**—pop pl ... NE-7
**Edison**—pop pl ... OH-6
**Edison**—pop pl ... WA-9
**Edison**—pop pl ... WV-2
Edison, Mount—summit ... AK-9
Edison, Thomas A., Memorial Tower—hist pl ... NJ-2
Edison, Thomas Alva, Birthplace—hist pl ... OH-6
Edison Acres Park—park ... NJ-2
Edison and Ricks Canal—canal ... ID-8
Edison Bridge—bridge ... FL-3
Edison Bridge—bridge ... OH-6
Edison Butte—summit ... OR-9
Edison Cabin ... CA-9
Edison Camp Bend—bend ... LA-4
Edison Camp Bend (historical )—bend ... TX-5
Edison (CCD)—cens area ... GA-3
Edison Cem—cemetery ... GA-3
Edison Cem—cemetery ... KY-4
Edison Cem—cemetery ... MO-7
Edison Cem—cemetery ... NE-7
**Edison Center**—pop pl ... FL-3
Edison Chapel ... AL-4
Edison Club Golf Course—other (2) ... NY-2
Edison Community Coll—school ... FL-3
Edison Creek ... MT-8
Edison Creek ... SD-7
Edison Elem Sch ... PA-2
Edison Elem Sch—school ... PA-2
Edison Gulch—valley ... OR-9
Edison Hist Dist—hist pl ... CA-9
Edison Hollow—valley ... OH-6
Edison Hollow—valley ... WV-2
Edison HS—school (3) ... CA-9
Edison HS—school ... MN-6
Edison HS—school ... NY-2
Edison HS—school ... OK-5
Edison HS—school ... PA-2
Edison HS—school ... TX-5
Edison HS—school ... VA-3
Edison HS—school ... WA-9
Edison Ice Cave—cave ... OR-9
Edison Ice Cave Trail—trail ... OR-9
Edison Institute ... TN-4
Edison JHS ... PA-2
Edison JHS—school ... CA-9
Edison JHS—school (2) ... IL-6
Edison JHS—school ... MI-6
Edison JHS—school ... NJ-2
Edison JHS—school (2) ... OH-6
Edison JHS—school ... SD-7
Edison JHS—school ... TX-5
Edison JHS—school ... WV-2
Edison JHS—school (2) ... WI-6
Edison JHS (abandoned)—school ... PA-2
Edison Junction ... FL-3
Edison Junction—locale ... FL-3
Edison Learning Center—school ... FL-3
Edison Mall—locale ... FL-3
Edison Memorial Tower—locale ... NJ-2
Edison Mine—mine ... SD-7
Edison Natl Historic Site—park ... NJ-2
Edison Oil Field ... CA-9
Edison Park ... IL-6
Edison Park ... IN-6
Edison Park—park ... AZ-5
Edison Park—park ... IL-6
Edison Park—park (2) ... IN-6
Edison Park Sch—school (2) ... FL-3
Edison Pond—lake ... NJ-2
Edison Post Office (historical)—building ... PA-2
Edison Private Sch (1st Campus)—school ... FL-3
Edison Private Sch (2nd Campus)—school ... FL-3
Edison Products Company—airport ... NJ-2
Edison Russell Sch—school ... FL-3
**Edisons**—pop pl ... ND-7
Edison Sch ... PA-2
Edison Sch—hist pl ... CO-8
Edison Sch—school (2) ... AZ-5
Edison Sch—school (16) ... CA-9
Edison Sch—school (3) ... CO-8
Edison Sch—school ... CT-1
Edison Sch—school (2) ... FL-3
Edison Sch—school (8) ... IL-6
Edison Sch—school (2) ... IA-7
Edison Sch—school ... KS-7
Edison Sch—school ... ME-1
Edison Sch—school (8) ... MI-6
Edison Sch—school (2) ... MN-6
Edison Sch—school ... MO-7
Edison Sch—school ... NE-7
Edison Sch—school (2) ... NJ-2
Edison Sch—school ... NM-5
Edison Sch—school (5) ... NY-2
Edison Sch—school ... ND-7
Edison Sch—school (6) ... OH-6
Edison Sch—school (7) ... OK-5
Edison Sch—school ... OR-9
Edison Sch—school (3) ... PA-2
Edison Sch—school ... SD-7
Edison Sch—school ... TN-4
Edison Sch—school (2) ... TX-5
Edison Sch—school ... UT-8
Edison Sch—school (4) ... WA-9
Edison Sch—school (2) ... WI-6
Edison School ... IN-6
Edison School Number 47 ... IN-6
Edison Senior High School ... IN-6
Edison Slough—stream ... WA-9
Edison Spring—spring ... AR-4
Edison Square ... IL-6
Edison Square (Shop Ctr)—locale ... FL-3
Edison State Park—park ... NJ-2
Edison Station ... FL-3
**Edison Station**—pop pl ... WA-9
Edison Technical Sch—school ... WA-9
Edison Tech Sch—school ... NY-2
**Edison Township**—pop pl ... SD-7
**Edison (Township of)**—pop pl ... MN-6
**Edison (Township of)**—pop pl ... NJ-2
Edison Trails Park—park ... CA-9
**Edisonville**—pop pl (2) ... PA-2
Edison Vocational Sch—school ... NJ-2
Edison West Little River Neighborhood Center—locale ... FL-3
Edisto—CDP ... SC-3
Edisto Beach—beach ... SC-3
**Edisto Beach**—pop pl (2) ... SC-3
Edisto Beach State Park—park ... SC-3
Edisto Ch—church (4) ... SC-3
**Edisto Club**—pop pl ... SC-3
Edisto Experimental Station (Clemson University)—other ... SC-3
Edisto HS—school ... SC-3
Edisto Island—island ... SC-3
**Edisto Island**—pop pl ... SC-3
Edisto Island Baptist Church—hist pl ... SC-3
Edisto Island (CCD)—cens area ... SC-3
Edisto Island Ch—church ... SC-3
Edisto Island Library—building ... SC-3
Edisto Island Presbyterian Church—hist pl ... SC-3
Edisto MS—school ... SC-3
Edisto River—stream ... SC-3
Edisto Sch—school (2) ... SC-3
Edisto-Shaws (CCD)—cens area ... SC-3
Edisvold Ch—church ... MN-6
E Ditch—canal ... CA-9
E Ditch—canal ... MT-8
Edith—locale ... OK-5
Edith—locale ... TX-5
**Edith**—pop pl ... CO-8
**Edith**—pop pl ... GA-3
**Edith**—pop pl ... TN-4
**Edith**—pop pl ... WV-2
Edith, Lake—lake ... MN-6
Edith, Lake—reservoir ... CO-8
Edith, Lake—reservoir ... GA-3
Edith, Mount—summit ... MT-8
Edith Aspden Park—park ... UT-8
Edith Bowen Sch—school ... UT-8
Edith Chapel—church ... IL-6
Edith C Justice Dam ... PA-2
Edith Creek—stream ... MT-8
Edith Creek—stream ... WA-9
Edith Creek—stream ... WY-8
Edith Crossroads ... VA-3
Edith Ditch—canal ... CO-8
Edith Gap—gap ... VA-3
Edith Grove Ch—church ... NC-3
Edith Gulch—valley ... CO-8
Edith Hammock—island ... AL-4
Edith Island—island ... AK-9
Edith I Starke Elem Sch—school ... FL-3
Edith Lake ... CA-9
Edith Lake ... WI-6
Edith Lake—lake ... CA-9
Edith Lake—lake ... ID-8
Edith Lake—lake ... MN-6
Edith Lake—lake (2) ... MT-8
Edith Lake—lake (3) ... WI-6
Edith Mtn—summit ... CO-8
Edith Peak—summit ... MT-8
Edith Peak Lookout—locale ... MT-8
Edith Point—cape ... AK-9
Edith Point—cape ... WA-9
Edith Post Office (historical)—building ... AL-4
Edith Post Office (historical)—building ... TN-4
Edith Rsvr—reservoir ... MT-8
Edith Sch (historical)—school ... TN-4
Ediths Hammock ... AL-4
**Edithton Beach**—pop pl ... WI-6
Edith Valley—basin ... NE-7
Editj ... MP-9
**Editors Park**—pop pl ... MD-2
Ediza Lake—lake ... CA-9
Edizer Lake ... CA-9
Ediz Hook—cape ... WA-9
Edjaken—island ... MP-9
Edjell—island ... MP-9
Edjit ... MP-9
Ed Joe Draw—valley ... CO-8
Ed Joe Rsvr—reservoir ... CO-8
Ed Johnson Cave—cave ... AL-4
Ed Jones Pond—lake ... ME-1
Ed Keller Draw—valley ... TX-5
Ed Knob—summit ... NC-3
Ed Ladd Lake—reservoir ... NM-5
Ed Lamb Brook—stream ... CT-1
Ed Lamb Point—cape ... UT-8
Ed Lamb Point—cliff ... AZ-5
Ed Large Field Airp—airport ... WA-9
E. D. Latta Nurses' Residence—hist pl ... NC-3
Edleman Creek ... WY-8
**Edler**—pop pl ... CO-8
Edler Spring ... CA-9
Edler Spring—spring ... OR-9
Edley Cem—cemetery ... MO-7
Edlinburg Cem—cemetery ... OH-6
Edlin Cem—cemetery ... KY-4
Edlin Creek—stream ... KY-4
Edlin Ditch ... IN-6
Edlin Ditch—canal (2) ... IN-6
Edlin Ranch—locale ... TX-5
Ed Loy Tank—reservoir ... AZ-5
EDL Peloux Bridge—hist pl ... WY-8
Ed MacDowell Grove—cemetery ... NH-1
Edma Lake—lake ... MN-6
Edman—locale ... GA-3
Edmands Col—gap ... NH-1
Edmands Park—park ... MA-1
Edmands Path—trail ... NH-1
Ed Mayo School ... MS-4
EDMEE S. (log canoe)—hist pl ... MD-2
**Edmeston**—pop pl ... NY-2
**Edmeston (Town of)**—pop pl ... NY-2
E D Mine—mine ... CO-8
Edminston Spring ... WA-9
Edmisten Cem—cemetery (2) ... NC-3
Edmister Coulee—valley ... MT-8
Ediniston—locale ... CA-9
Edmiston, Bazle, House—hist pl ... KY-4
Edmiston, D. N., House—hist pl ... AR-4
Edmiston, John, House—hist pl ... AR-4
Edmiston, Zeb, House—hist pl ... AR-4
Edmiston Cem—cemetery ... AR-4
Edmiston Ch—church ... WV-2
Edmiston Creek—stream ... LA-4
Edmiston Spring—spring ... WA-9
Edmo Buttes—range ... WY-8
**Edmon**—pop pl ... PA-2
**Edmond**—pop pl ... AL-4
**Edmond**—pop pl ... KS-7
**Edmond**—pop pl ... OK-5
**Edmond**—pop pl ... WV-2
Edmond, Lake—reservoir ... AL-4
Edmond Branch—stream ... AL-4
Edmond Bridge—bridge ... VT-1
Edmond Brook—stream ... NY-2
Edmond Cem—cemetery ... IA-7
Edmond Cem—cemetery ... KS-7
Edmond Cem—cemetery ... TN-4
Edmond Ditch—canal ... IN-6
Edmond Doyles Grant—civil ... FL-3
Edmond Island—island ... MI-6
Edmond Lake—lake ... MN-6
Edmond Lake—lake ... WY-8
Edmond Marsh—swamp ... WA-9
Edmond Point ... WA-9
Edmond Post Office (historical)—building ... AL-4
Edmonds ... PA-2
Edmonds—locale ... ID-8
**Edmonds**—pop pl ... NC-3
**Edmonds**—pop pl ... WA-9
Edmonds Branch—stream ... GA-3
Edmonds Branch—stream ... TN-4
Edmonds Branch—stream ... WV-2
Edmonds Bridge—bridge ... MS-4
Edmonds (CCD)—cens area ... WA-9
Edmonds Cem—cemetery ... KY-4
Edmonds Ch—church ... GA-3
Edmonds Ch—church ... KS-7
Edmonds Corner—locale ... VA-3
Edmonds Creek ... AL-4
Edmonds Creek—stream ... AK-9
Edmonds Creek—stream ... LA-4
Edmonds Creek—stream ... OR-9
Edmond Sewage Disposal—other ... OK-5
Edmonds Glacier ... WA-9
Edmonds HS—school ... VT-1
Edmonds HS—school ... WA-9
Edmonds Lake ... NY-2
Edmonds Lake—lake ... AK-9
Edmonds Lake Dam—dam ... AL-4
Edmond Slough—gut ... OK-5
Edmonds Mine—mine ... OR-9
**Edmondson**—pop pl ... AR-4
**Edmondson**—pop pl ... NC-3
Edmondson—uninc pl ... MD-2
Edmondson Bend—bend ... TX-5
Edmondson Branch—stream ... GA-3
Edmondson Branch—stream ... TN-4
Edmondson Bridge—bridge ... TN-4
Edmondson Cem—cemetery ... AL-4
Edmondson Cem—cemetery ... AR-4
Edmondson Cemetery ... MS-4
Edmondson Creek ... TN-4
Edmondson Creek—stream ... LA-4
Edmondson Creek—stream ... MO-7
Edmondson Dam—dam ... VA-3
Edmondson Gap—gap ... GA-3
**Edmondson Heights**—pop pl ... MD-2
**Edmondson (historical)**—pop pl ... TN-4
Edmondson Hollow—valley ... MO-7
Edmondson Mtn—summit ... NC-3
Edmondson Pond—lake ... MO-7
**Edmondson Ridge**—pop pl ... MD-2
Edmondsons Ferry (historical)—crossing ... TN-4
Edmondson Slough—gut ... IL-6
Edmondson Spring—spring (2) ... CO-8
Edmondson-Woodward House—hist pl ... NC-3
Edmonds Pool—oilfield ... KS-7
Edmonds Sch—school ... NC-3
Edmonds Sch—school ... PA-2
Edmonds Sch—school ... WA-9
Edmonds Spring—spring ... TN-4
Edmonds Top—summit ... GA-3
Edmondson Hollow ... MO-7
Edmonson ... NC-3
Edmonson—locale ... AR-4
**Edmonson**—pop pl ... MO-7
**Edmonson**—pop pl ... TX-5
Edmonson Cem—cemetery (2) ... AL-4
Edmonson Cem—cemetery (2) ... MS-4
Edmonson Cem—cemetery ... TN-4
Edmonson Cem—cemetery ... TX-5
Edmonson Ch—church ... MO-7
**Edmonson (County)**—pop pl ... KY-4
Edmonson JHS—school ... MI-6
Edmonson Sch—school (2) ... MI-6
Edmonson Spring—spring ... OR-9
**Edmonston**—pop pl ... MD-2
Edmonston Cem—cemetery ... TN-4
Edmonston House—hist pl ... NY-2
Edmonston Sch—school ... MD-2
**Edmonton**—pop pl ... KY-4
Edmonton (CCD)—cens area ... KY-4
**Edmonton Heights**—pop pl ... AL-4
Edmoore Creek—stream ... TX-5
**Edmore**—pop pl ... IA-7
**Edmore**—pop pl ... MI-6
**Edmore**—pop pl ... ND-7
Edmore Cem—cemetery ... ND-7
Edmore Coulee—valley ... ND-7
Edmore Dam—dam ... ND-7
Edmore State Game Area—park ... MI-6
**Edmund**—pop pl ... SC-3
**Edmund**—pop pl ... WI-6
Edmund Bayou—stream ... LA-4
Edmund Branch—stream ... TN-4
Edmund Creek—stream ... MI-6
Edmund Hill—summit ... MA-1
Edmund Hooker Lake Dam—dam ... MS-4
Edmund Lake ... NY-2
Edmund-Lyon Park—park ... NY-2
Edmund Point—cape ... MD-2
Edmunds ... OH-6
Edmunds ... WA-9
Edmunds—other ... OH-6
**Edmunds**—pop pl ... ME-1
**Edmunds**—pop pl ... ND-7
Edmunds, Charles Penn, House—hist pl ... KY-4
Edmunds, Henry R., Sch—hist pl ... PA-2
Edmunds, John, Apartment House—hist pl ... FL-3
Edmunds Bog Brook—stream ... ME-1
Edmunds Brook—stream ... NY-2
Edmunds Cem—cemetery ... VT-1
Edmunds County—civil ... SD-7
Edmunds Cove—bay ... NH-1
Edmunds Glacier—glacier ... WA-9
Edmunds-Heptinstall House—hist pl ... NC-3
Edmunds Hill—summit ... ME-1
Edmunds (historical)—locale ... SD-7
Edmunds Hole—basin ... UT-8
Edmunds HS—school ... SC-3
Edmunds Lake ... ME-1
Edmundson ... NC-3
**Edmundson**—pop pl ... MO-7
**Edmundson Acres**—pop pl ... CA-9
Edmundson Ch—church ... MS-4
Edmundson Creek—stream ... TN-4
**Edmundson Crossroads**—pop pl ... NC-3
Edmundson Hollow—valley ... AL-4
Edmundson Hollow—valley ... TN-4
Edmundson Neck—cape ... MD-2
Edmundson Park—park ... IA-7
Edmundsons Mill ... AL-4
Edmunds Peak—summit ... VT-1
Edmunds Point ... WA-9
Edmunds Pond ... ME-1
Edmunds Pond—lake ... MA-1
Edmund Springs—spring ... WY-8
Edmunds Sch—school ... AR-4
Edmunds Sch—school ... PA-2
Edmunds Sch—school ... VA-3
Edmunds Slough (historical)—gut ... MS-4
**Edmunds Switch**—pop pl ... OH-6
**Edmunds Township**—pop pl ... ND-7
Edmunds (Township of)—unorg ... ME-1
Edmunson Branch—stream ... TN-4
Edmunson Creek—stream ... TX-5
Edmunson Pond—reservoir ... NC-3
Edmunson Pond Dam—dam ... NC-3
Edmunston Creek—stream ... GA-3
Edna ... KS-7
Edna ... MS-4
Edna ... MP-9
Edna—locale ... AL-4
Edna—locale ... AR-4
Edna—locale ... CA-9
Edna—locale ... GA-3
Edna—locale ... KY-4
Edna—locale ... OK-5
Edna—locale ... WA-9
**Edna**—pop pl ... IA-7
**Edna**—pop pl ... KS-7
**Edna**—pop pl ... LA-4
**Edna**—pop pl ... MS-4
**Edna**—pop pl ... TN-4
**Edna**—pop pl ... TX-5
**Edna**—pop pl ... WV-2
Edna, Lake—lake ... MN-6
Edna, Lake—lake ... OR-9

Edna, Lake—lake WA-9
Edna, Lake—reservoir AL-4
Edna, Lake—reservoir GA-3
Edna, Lake—reservoir TN-4
Edna, Mount—summit CA-9
Edna, Mount—summit NE-7
Edna Baptist Church MS-4
Edna Bay—bay AK-9
**Edna Bay**—pop pl AK-9
**Edna (Brady)**—pop pl WV-2
Edna Cem—cemetery KS-7
Edna Ch—church MS-4
Edna Chapel—church OH-6
Edna City Dam—dam KS-7
Edna-Cordele (CCD)—cens area TX-5
Edna Creek—stream AK-9
Edna Creek—stream (2) ID-8
Edna Creek—stream (2) MT-8
Edna Creek—stream WA-9
Edna Creek Campground—locale ID-8
Edna Creek Trail—trail MT-8
**Edna (Edna Mine No. 1)**—pop pl PA-2
EDNA E. LOCKWOOD (Chesapeake Bay bugeye)—hist pl MD-2
Edna Grey Spring—spring NV-8
EDNA G (tugboat)—hist pl MN-6
Edna Hazel Mine—mine SD-7
Edna Hill—locale TX-5
Edna Hill Ch—church AL-4
Edna Hill Sch—school CA-9
Edna (historical)—locale SD-7
Edna Lake CA-9
Edna Lake—lake CA-9
Edna Lake—lake ID-8
Edna Lake—lake MN-6
Edna Lake—lake OR-9
Edna Lake Reservoir CA-9
Edna Mae Mine—mine CO-8
Edna May Creek—stream ID-8
**Ednam Forest**—pop pl VA-3
Ednam House—hist pl VA-3
**Edna Mills**—pop pl IN-6
Edna Mine—mine CO-8
Edna Mine—mine OR-9
Edna Mine—mine WA-9
Edna Mine No. 2—other PA-2
Edna Mtn—summit MT-8
Edna Mtn—summit NV-8
Edna Municipal Airp—airport KS-7
**Edna Number One**—pop pl PA-2
**Edna Number Two**—pop pl PA-2
Edna Peak—summit UT-8
Edna Pond—swamp TX-5
Edna Post Office (historical)—building AL-4
Edna Post Office (historical)—building MS-4
Edna Sch—school SD-7
Edna Sch (historical)—school MS-4
Edna Sch (historical)—school PA-2
Ednas Creek—stream TX-5
Ednas Mill—locale VA-3
Ednas Point—cape OR-9
Edna Township—civil SD-7
Edna Township—fmr MCD IA-7
**Edna Township**—pop pl ND-7
**Edna (Township of)**—pop pl MN-6
Edna Wilslef Ditch—canal NV-8
Edney Branch—stream NC-3
Edney Cem—cemetery NC-3
Edney Chapel—church SC-3
**Edneyville**—pop pl NC-3
Edneyville—summit NC-3
Edneyville Cem—cemetery NC-3
Edneyville Ch—church NC-3
Edneyville (Township of)—fmr MCD NC-3
Edneyville 5—summit NC-3
**Ednor**—pop pl MD-2
**Ednor Acres**—pop pl MD-2
Edom—locale CA-9
Edom—locale VA-3
**Edom**—pop pl TX-5
Edom Church MS-4
Edom Hill—summit CA-9
**Edon**—pop pl OH-6
Edon Cem—cemetery MS-4
Edon Ch—church MS-4
Edospm JHS—school MA-1
Ed Overton Creek SD-7
Ed Parry Park—park CA-9
Ed Pit—uninc pl TX-5
Ed Point—cliff WY-8
Ed Pond—lake AL-4
Edquist Lake—lake MN-6
E Drain—canal CA-9
**Edray**—pop pl WV-2
Ed Ray Canyon—valley TX-5
Edray Ch—church WV-2
Edray (Magisterial District)—fmr MCD WV-2
Edri—locale PA-2
Ed Richie Creek—stream UT-8
Edrijok-en' MP-9
Edris Creek—stream OR-9
Edrizon Cem—cemetery MS-4
**Edroy**—pop pl TX-5
Edroy Cem—cemetery TX-5
Edsall, William S., House—hist pl IN-6
**Edsalla (historical)**—pop pl OR-9
**Edsall (Industrial Area)**—pop pl VA-3
**Edsall Park**—pop pl VA-3
Edsall Park Sch—school VA-3
Edsall Ranch—locale WY-8
Edsall Station—locale VA-3
Edsallville Post Office (historical)—building PA-2
Eds Camp—locale AZ-5
Eds Camp—locale MO-7
Ed Scott Bridge—bridge FL-3
Eds Creek—stream MT-8
Eds Creek—stream TX-5
Eds Defeat Rsvr—reservoir ID-8
Ed Seaton Fire Station—building TN-4
Edsel—locale KY-4
Edsel Adams Dam—dam AL-4
Edsel Ford HS—school MI-6
Edsel Hills—summit WY-8
Edsel Turner Pond Dam—dam MS-4
Edsfield AZ-5
Eds Field—airport AZ-5
Eds Fork—stream WV-2
Eds Fork Sch—school WV-2
Ed Shave Lake—lake MN-6
Eds Hill—summit NV-8
Eds Key—island FL-3
Eds Lake—lake OH-6
Eds Lake—lake WI-6
Eds Lake—lake WY-8
Eds Lick—stream KY-4
Eds Meadow—flat OR-9
Ed Snow Lake Dam—dam MS-4
Edson AL-4
Edson—locale NY-2
Edson—locale WY-8
**Edson**—pop pl KS-7
**Edson**—pop pl WI-6
Edson Arroyo—stream CO-8
Edson Arroyo—valley CO-8
Edson Brook—stream CT-1
Edson Brook—stream MA-1
Edson Butte—summit OR-9
Edson Cabin—locale CA-9
Edson Canyon—valley CA-9
Edson Cem—cemetery KS-7
Edson Cem—cemetery MA-1
Edson Center WI-6
Edson Center—other WI-6
Edson Ch—church ND-7
Edson Corners—locale NY-2
Edson County Park—park OR-9
Edson Creek ID-8
Edson Creek MT-8
Edson Creek—stream CA-9
Edson Creek—stream OH-6
Edson Creek—stream (2) OR-9
Edson Grove—woods CA-9
Edson (historical)—locale SD-7
Edson Lake—lake CA-9
Edson Millpond—lake NC-3
Edson Millpond (historical)—reservoir NC-3
Edson Pond—reservoir MA-1
Edson Ranch—locale (2) NM-5
Edson Ridge—ridge WY-8
**Edsons**—pop pl AL-4
Edson Sch—school ID-8
Edson Shop Ctr—locale NC-3
**Edson (Town of)**—pop pl WI-6
Eds Point—cliff AZ-5
Eds Point Tank—reservoir AZ-5
Eds Pond—lake AZ-5
Ed Spring—spring AZ-5
Eds Slough—lake ND-7
Eds Spring—spring AZ-5
Eds Spring—spring ID-8
Eds Tank—reservoir (3) AZ-5
Ed Stone Branch—stream WV-2
E D Strains Pond Dam—dam MS-4
Edstrom Rsvr—reservoir OR-9
**Edsville**—pop pl MS-4
Eds Well—well NV-8
Ed Taylor Hollow—valley AR-4
Ed Top—summit NC-3
Ed Turner Lake Dam—dam MS-4
Eduardo Tank—reservoir NM-5
Educational Alternative Program—school FL-3
Educational Foundation—school VA-3
Educational Testing—airport NJ-2
Education and Research Center—school MS-4
Educket Creek—stream WA-9
Edueket Creek WA-9
Ed Vela Draw—valley CO-8
Ed Vela Gas Field—oilfield TX-5
Ed Walker Tank—reservoir AZ-5
**Edwall**—pop pl WA-9
Edwall Cem—cemetery WA-9
**Edward**—pop pl KS-7
**Edward**—pop pl NC-3
**Edward**—pop pl OH-6
Edward, Lake—lake CO-8
Edward, Lake—lake FL-3
Edward, Lake—lake MN-6
Edward, Lake—reservoir IN-6
Edward, Mount—summit MI-6
Edward A Hauss Forest Nursery AL-4
Edward and Manuel Hobus Dam—dam SD-7
Edward A Palmer Elementary School AL-4
Edward Arthur Patterson Lake—reservoir ND-7
Edward Ball Wildlife Mngmt Area—park FL-3
Edward Bayou—stream MS-4
Edward Beecher Rec Area—locale MO-7
Edward Beecher Trail Campground MO-7
Edward Bell HS—school AL-4
Edward Best Elementary School NC-3
Edward Boone Grave—cemetery KY-4
Edward Branch—stream KY-4
Edward Branch—stream TN-4
Edward Brothers Pond Dam—dam MS-4
Edward Burton Rodgers Bridge—bridge SC-3
Edward Cem—cemetery AL-4
Edward Cem—cemetery IN-6
Edward Cem—cemetery NC-3
Edward Chapel—church AL-4
Edward Chapel Cem—cemetery IL-6
**Edward Cordrey Subdivision**—pop pl DE-2
Edward Cove—valley NC-3
Edward Creek—stream GA-3
Edward Creek—stream MT-8
Edward Creek—stream NJ-2
**Edward Daigle**—pop pl LA-4
Edward Dam—dam AL-4
Edward Devotion School MA-1
Edward Ditch—canal IN-6
Edward Draw—valley WY-8
Edward Eggleston Elem Sch—school IN-6
Edwardes River—stream AK-9
Edward Fontaine Sch (historical)—school MS-4
Edward G. Bevan Fish and Wildlife Mngmt Area—park NJ-2
Edward Grenfell County Park—park OR-9
Edward Grove—locale TN-4
Edward Grove Sch (historical)—school TN-4
Edward Hand Junior High School PA-2
Edward Hauss State Forest Nursery—park AL-4
Edward (historical)—locale AL-4
Edward Hollow—valley KY-4
Edward Hosp—hospital IL-6
Edward H White Memorial Hosp—hospital FL-3
Edward H White Sch—school TX-5
Edward H White Senior HS—school FL-3
**Edwardian Place (subdivision)**—pop pl AL-4
Edward Island—island MI-6
Edward Islands—island AK-9
Edward Lake—lake (2) MN-6
Edward Lewis Lake Dam—dam IN-6
Edward MacDowell Dam—dam NH-1
Edward MacDowell Reservoir NH-1
Edward Meyer Memorial Hosp—hospital NY-2
Edward Mtn—summit MT-8
Edward Myers Dam—dam AL-4
Edwardo Lake—lake NM-5
Edwardo Tank—reservoir NM-5
Edwardo Windmill—locale TX-5
Edward Passage—channel AK-9
Edward Payson Park—park ME-1
Edward Peak—summit WA-9
Edward Pond—lake TN-4
Edward R Murrow Park—park DC-2
Edwards AL-4
Edwards TN-4
Edwards—locale AL-4
Edwards—locale AR-4
Edwards—locale CO-8
Edwards—locale MN-6
Edwards—locale MT-8
Edwards—locale OR-9
Edwards—locale TX-5
Edwards—locale WA-9
**Edwards**—pop pl CA-9
**Edwards**—pop pl IL-6
**Edwards**—pop pl IA-7
**Edwards**—pop pl KY-4
**Edwards**—pop pl MI-6
**Edwards**—pop pl MS-4
**Edwards**—pop pl MO-7
**Edwards**—pop pl NY-2
**Edwards**—pop pl SC-3
**Edwards**—pop pl WI-6
Edwards, Broadus, House—hist pl SC-3
Edwards, David, House—hist pl KY-4
Edwards, Frank G., House—hist pl CA-9
Edwards, Jesse, House—hist pl OR-9
Edwards, Joel, House—hist pl WA-9
Edwards, John, House—hist pl OH-6
Edwards, John Stark, House—hist pl OH-6
Edwards, Lake—lake FL-3
Edwards, Lake—reservoir OH-6
Edwards, Mount—summit CO-8
Edwards, Thomas, House and Quarters—hist pl KY-4
Edwards, Thompsie, House—hist pl TN-4
Edwards, W. A., House—hist pl AR-4
**Edwards Acres (subdivision)**—pop pl NC-3
Edwards AFB—military CA-9
Edwards Airp—airport TN-4
Edwards Archeol Site—hist pl OK-5
Edwards Attendence Center—school MS-4
Edwards Bar—bar AL-4
Edwards Bay FL-3
Edwards Bayou—stream (2) LA-4
Edwards Bayou—stream MS-4
Edwards Bldg—hist pl NY-2
Edwards Bluff—cliff MO-7
Edwards Branch VA-3
Edwards Branch—stream AL-4
Edwards Branch—stream (3) KY-4
Edwards Branch—stream LA-4
Edwards Branch—stream (2) MO-7
Edwards Branch—stream (5) NC-3
Edwards Branch—stream SC-3
Edwards Branch—stream (5) TN-4
Edwards Branch—stream (3) TX-5
Edwards Branch—stream (2) VA-3
Edwards Bridge—bridge AL-4
Edwards Bridge—locale NC-3
Edwards Brook—stream ME-1
**Edwardsburg**—pop pl ID-8
**Edwardsburg**—pop pl MI-6
Edwards Butte—summit (2) OR-9
Edwards Cabin MO-7
Edwards Canyon—valley (2) CA-9
Edwards Canyon—valley OR-9
Edwards Canyon—valley UT-8
Edwards Cattle Company Number 1 Dam—dam SD-7
Edwards Cem AL-4
Edwards Cem—cemetery (2) AL-4
Edwards Cem—cemetery (4) AR-4
Edwards Cem—cemetery CT-1
Edwards Cem—cemetery FL-3
Edwards Cem—cemetery GA-3
Edwards Cem—cemetery (3) IL-6
Edwards Cem—cemetery IN-6
Edwards Cem—cemetery IA-7
Edwards Cem—cemetery KS-7
Edwards Cem—cemetery (5) KY-4
Edwards Cem—cemetery (4) LA-4
Edwards Cem—cemetery MI-6
Edwards Cem—cemetery (5) MS-4
Edwards Cem—cemetery (4) MO-7
Edwards Cem—cemetery (3) NY-2
Edwards Cem—cemetery (8) NC-3
Edwards Cem—cemetery OH-6
Edwards Cem—cemetery (2) OK-5
Edwards Cem—cemetery (12) TN-4
Edwards Cem—cemetery (6) TX-5
Edwards Cem—cemetery (4) VA-3
Edwards Cem—cemetery WV-2
Edwards Ch—church FL-3
Edwards Ch—church GA-3
Edwards Ch—church MI-6
Edward Sch—school OH-6
Edwards Chapel TN-4
Edwards Chapel—church AR-4
Edwards Chapel—church GA-3
Edwards Chapel—church KY-4
Edwards Chapel—church NY-2
Edwards Chapel—church PA-2
Edwards Chapel—church SC-3
Edwards Chapel—church (2) VA-3
Edwards Chapel—church WV-2
Edwards Chapel Cem—cemetery MS-4
Edwards Chapel (historical)—church MO-7
Edwards Corners—locale MI-6
Edwards County—civil KS-7
**Edwards (County)**—pop pl IL-6
**Edwards (County)**—pop pl TX-5
Edwards County Courthouse and Jail—hist pl TX-5
Edwards County Park—park IA-7
Edwards Cove—bay ME-1
Edwards Cove—valley GA-3
Edwards Creek—channel FL-3
Edwards Creek—church OK-5
Edwards Creek—stream AK-9
Edwards Creek—stream CA-9
Edwards Creek—stream GA-3
Edwards Creek—stream (2) ID-8
Edwards Creek—stream KS-7
Edwards Creek—stream LA-4
Edwards Creek—stream (2) MI-6
Edwards Creek—stream (3) MT-8
Edwards Creek—stream (2) NV-8
Edwards Creek—stream (2) NC-3
Edwards Creek—stream (2) OR-9
Edwards Creek—stream TN-4
Edwards Creek—stream (2) TX-5
Edwards Creek—stream (2) VA-3
Edwards Creek—stream WA-9
Edwards Creek—stream (2) WY-8
Edwards Creek Valley—basin (2) NV-8
Edwards Creek Well Number One—well NV-8
Edwards Crossing—locale CA-9
Edwards Crossing—locale MT-8
Edwards Crossing—locale PA-2
Edwards Crossroads—locale NC-3
**Edwards Crossroads**—pop pl (2) NC-3
Edwards Dam—dam AL-4
Edwards Dam—dam PA-2
Edwards Depot MS-4
Edwards Ditch—canal (3) IN-6
Edwards Drain—canal MI-6
Edwards Draw—valley CO-8
Edwards Draw—valley NM-5
Edwards Draw—valley (3) TX-5
**Edwards Estates**—pop pl CA-9
Edwards Falls—falls NY-2
Edwards Ferry (historical)—locale AL-4
Edwards Field—park ME-1
Edwards Flats—flat FL-3
Edwards Ford (historical)—locale MO-7
Edwards Fork—locale NC-3
Edwards Fork—stream KY-4
Edwards Fork—valley UT-8
Edwards-Fowler House—hist pl TN-4
Edwards Gap—gap NC-3
Edwards Grove TN-4
Edwards Grove Cem—cemetery OH-6
Edwards Grove Ch—church TN-4
Edwards Grove School TN-4
Edwards Gulch—valley ID-8
Edwards Gulch—valley MT-8
Edwards Gymnasium/Pfieffer Natatorium—hist pl OH-6
Edwards Hall—hist pl KY-4
Edwards Hill—locale NC-3
**Edwards Hill**—pop pl NY-2
Edwards Hill—summit (2) NY-2
Edwards Hill—summit OH-6
Edwards Hill—summit TN-4
Edwards Hill—summit VA-3
Edwards (historical)—locale AL-4
Edwards Hollow—valley (4) TN-4
Edwards Hosp—hospital FL-3
Edwards Hotel—hist pl MS-4
Edwards House—hist pl KY-4
Edwards HS—school IL-6
Edwards HS—school TX-5
Edwards Island MI-6
Edwards Island MT-8
Edwards Island—island AK-9
Edwards Island—island MI-6
Edwards Island—island WI-6
Edwards Islands—island FL-3
Edwards Islands, The FL-3
Edwards JHS—school NC-3
Edwards JHS—school SC-3
Edwards Junction—locale AR-4
Edwards Junction—uninc pl NC-3
Edwards Knob—summit TN-4
Edwards Knob—summit VA-3
Edwards Lake—lake FL-3
Edwards Lake—lake GA-3
Edwards Lake—lake ID-8
Edwards Lake—lake MI-6
Edwards Lake—lake (3) MN-6
Edwards Lake—lake NE-7
Edwards Lake—lake WY-8
Edwards Lake—reservoir (2) AL-4
Edwards Lake—reservoir (2) GA-3
Edwards Lake—reservoir (2) MS-4
Edwards Lake—reservoir NC-3
Edwards Lake—reservoir SC-3
Edwards Lake—reservoir TN-4
Edwards Lake Dam—dam (3) MS-4
Edwards Lake Dam—dam NC-3
Edwards Lake Dam—dam TN-4
Edwards Lake Dam—reservoir TN-4
Edwards Lakes—reservoir GA-3
Edwards Lake Spring—spring AL-4
Edwards Landing—locale AR-4
Edwards Landing—locale TN-4
Edwards Lateral—canal AZ-5
Edwards Lateral—canal CA-9
Edwards Lateral—canal ID-8
Edwards Lookout Tower—locale AZ-5
Edwards Mill AL-4
Edwards Mill Creek—stream LA-4
Edwards Mill (historical)—locale MS-4
Edwards Millpond—reservoir GA-3
Edwards Mill Road Sch—school NC-3
Edwards Mine—mine AZ-5
Edward Smith Cave—cave AL-4
Edwards Mtn—summit AL-4
Edwards Mtn—summit KY-4
Edwards Mtn—summit MT-8
Edwards Mtn—summit NC-3
Edwards Mtn—summit TX-5
Edwards Oil Field—oilfield TX-5
Edwardson Cem—cemetery WI-6
**Edwards Palisades**—pop pl CA-9
Edwards Park NC-3
Edwards Park—flat AZ-5
Edwards Park—locale NY-2
Edwards Park—park FL-3
Edwards Park—park OH-6
Edwards Park—park OK-5
Edwards Park—park TN-4
Edwards Park—uninc pl WI-6
Edwards Park (historical)—park FL-3
Edwards Pass—gap UT-8
Edwards Peak—summit AZ-5
Edwards Peninsula—cape MT-8
Edwards Place—hist pl IL-6
Edwards Place—locale TX-5
Edward's Plain-Dowse's Corner Hist Dist—hist pl MA-1
Edwards Plateau—plain TX-5
Edwards Pocosin—swamp NC-3
Edwards Point MT-8
Edward's Point TX-5
Edwards Point—cape MD-2
Edwards Point—cape TX-5
Edwards Point—cape WA-9
Edwards Point—cliff TN-4
Edwards Point—locale TN-4
Edwards Point Sch—school TN-4
Edwards Pond TN-4
Edwards Pond—lake (2) GA-3
Edwards Pond—lake MA-1
Edwards Pond—lake NY-2
Edwards Pond—lake RI-1
Edwards Pond—reservoir AL-4
Edwards Pond—reservoir PA-2
Edwards Pond Dam—dam AL-4
Edwards Ponds—lake AL-4
**Edwardsport**—pop pl IN-6
Edward Spring—spring UT-8
Edward Spring Branch—stream FL-3
Edward Springs Cem—cemetery MS-4
Edward Springs Ch—church MS-4
Edward Springs Sch (historical)—school MS-4
Edwards Ranch ID-8
Edwards Ranch—locale MT-8
Edwards Ranch—locale NE-7
Edwards Ranch—locale NM-5
Edwards Ranch—locale (2) TX-5
Edwards Ranch—locale (2) WY-8
Edwards Ranch (historical)—locale AZ-5
Edwards River—stream IL-6
Edwards Rock—rock MA-1
Edwards Run—stream NJ-2
Edwards Run—stream PA-2
Edwards Run—stream WV-2
Edwards Sch OR-9
Edwards Sch—school (2) CA-9
Edwards Sch—school IL-6
Edwards Sch—school IA-7
Edwards Sch—school LA-4
Edwards Sch—school (3) MA-1
Edwards Sch—school MS-4
Edwards Sch—school OK-5
Edwards Sch—school OR-9
Edwards Sch—school (2) SC-3
Edwards Sch—school SD-7
Edwards Sch—school TN-4
Edwards Sch—school (2) TX-5
Edwards Sch—school VT-1
Edwards Sch (historical)—school AL-4
Edwards Sch (historical)—school (2) MS-4
Edwards School—locale MI-6
Edwards Shaft Portal—mine PA-2
Edwards Shoal—bar MA-1
Edwards Shop—locale VA-3
Edwards Siding—locale CA-9
Edwards Siding—locale CO-8
Edwards Slough—stream WA-9
Edwards Spring AZ-5
Edwards Spring—spring AL-4
Edwards Spring—spring (2) AZ-5
Edwards Spring—spring CO-8
Edwards Spring—spring (2) NV-8
Edwards Spring—spring TN-4
Edwards Spur—locale ID-8
Edwards Station (historical)—locale AL-4
Edwards Store—hist pl OK-5
Edwards Store (historical)—locale MS-4
Edwards Street Sch—school CT-1
**Edwards Subdivision**—pop pl UT-8
Edwards Swamp VA-3
Edwards Swamp—stream VA-3
Edwards Swamp—swamp NY-2
Edwards-Swayze House—hist pl IA-7
Edwards Tank—reservoir AZ-5
Edwards Tank—reservoir NM-5
Edward Station Sch—school OH-6
Edwards Theatre—hist pl FL-3
Edward Store AL-4
**Edwards (Town of)**—pop pl NY-2
Edwards (Township of)—fmr MCD NC-3
**Edwards (Township of)**—pop pl MI-6
**Edwards (Township of)**—pop pl MN-6
Edwards Valley Sch—school IL-6
Edwardsville KS-7
Edwardsville—locale DE-2
Edwardsville—locale NY-2
Edwardsville—locale OH-6
**Edwardsville**—pop pl (2) AL-4
**Edwardsville**—pop pl IL-6
**Edwardsville**—pop pl IN-6
**Edwardsville**—pop pl KS-7
**Edwardsville**—pop pl PA-2
**Edwardsville**—pop pl VA-3
Edwardsville Acad (historical)—school AL-4
Edwardsville Borough—civil PA-2
Edwardsville Cem—cemetery KS-7
Edwardsville Cem—cemetery OK-5
Edwardsville Chapter House—hist pl IL-6
Edwardsville Junction IL-6
Edwardsville (Township of)—civ div IL-6
Edwards Waterhole—lake TX-5
Edwards Well—well NM-5
Edwards Well—well TX-5
Edwards Well—well WA-9
**Edwards (Wherry Housing)**—pop pl CA-9
Edward Township KS-7
Edward Tracy Elem Sch—school PA-2
Edward T Robbins Sch—school TX-5
Edward Turner Grant—civil FL-3
Edward Wageman Dam—dam OR-9
Edward Wageman Rsvr—reservoir OR-9
Edward White Sch—school LA-4
Ed White MS—school AL-4
**Edwight**—pop pl WV-2
Edwin KS-7
Edwin—locale CA-9
**Edwin**—pop pl AL-4
Edwina—locale OH-6
**Edwina**—pop pl TN-4
Edwin A. Link Field-Broome County Airp—airport NY-2
Edwina Post Office (historical)—building TN-4
Edwina Sch (historical)—school TN-4
Edwin Averett Dam—dam AL-4
Edwin Averett Lake—reservoir AL-4
Edwin Bridge UT-8
Edwin Brown Sch—school OR-9
Edwin Cem—cemetery AL-4
Edwin Ch—church AL-4
Edwin Ch—church SD-7
Edwin Forrest Home—building PA-2
Edwin (historical)—locale KS-7
Edwin Lake—lake MN-6
Edwin Post Office (historical)—building AL-4
Edwin Post Office (historical)—building SD-7
Edwin Pray Lake—reservoir IN-6
Edwin Pray Lake Dam—dam IN-6
Edwin Scott Pond Dam—dam MS-4
Edwins Sch—school FL-3
Edwinton ND-7
Edwin Warner Park—park TN-4
Edw J Gay Sch—school LA-4
Edwood Glen Country Club—other IN-6
Edworth Park—park OH-6
Edys Island—island MA-1
Edyth Lake—lake CA-9
EDZ Irigary Bridge—hist pl WY-8
E E Bass Junior High School MS-4
E E Canyon—valley NM-5
E E Corral—other NM-5
Eeds Cem—cemetery IL-6
E. E. Foust Regional Airport—airport WY-8
Eegonos—hist pl ME-1
Eehui Stream HI-9
**Eek**—pop pl AK-9
Eekayruk Creek—stream AK-9
Eekayruk Mtn—summit AK-9
Eek Channel—channel AK-9
Eek Inlet—bay AK-9
Eek Island—island AK-9
Eek Lake—lake (2) AK-9
Eek Mountains—other AK-9
Eek Point—cape (2) AK-9
Eek River—stream AK-9
E E Lane Airp—airport MS-4
Eelbank Point—cape VA-3
Eel Bay—bay NY-2
Eel Beach MH-9
Eelbeck—locale GA-3
Eel Branch—stream KY-4
Eel Branch—stream TN-4
Eel Branch Prospect—mine TN-4
Eel Cliffs MH-9
Eel Creek—stream ID-8
Eel Creek—stream IN-6
Eel Creek—stream MA-1
Eel Creek—stream OR-9
Eel Creek—stream VT-1
Eel Creek—stream VA-3
Eel Creek Campground—park OR-9
Eel Creek Forest Camp—locale OR-9
Eel Ditch—canal NH-1
Eel Glacier—glacier AK-9
Eel Glacier—glacier WA-9
Eel Grass Cove—cove MA-1
Eel Grasslands MH-9
Eel Gut—gut VA-3
Eel Hole—lake GA-3
Eel Hope Point—cape MD-2
Eel Lake—lake MI-6
Eel Lake—lake MN-6
Eel Lake—lake OR-9
Eells Park—park OH-6
Eells-Stow House—hist pl CT-1
Eel Point MH-9
Eel Point—cape CA-9
Eel Point—cape MA-1
Eel Point Marsh—swamp MA-1
Eel Pond RI-1
Eel Pond—bay (2) MA-1
Eel Pond—lake CT-1
Eel Pond—lake (4) MA-1
Eel Pond—lake NH-1
Eel Pond Marshes—swamp (2) MA-1
Eelpot Creek—stream NY-2
Eel River IN-6
Eel River—cove MA-1
**Eel River**—pop pl IN-6
Eel River—stream CA-9
Eel River—stream (2) IN-6
Eel River—stream (2) MA-1
Eel River Cem—cemetery IN-6
Eel River Ch—church (3) IN-6
Eel River Chapel Cem—cemetery IN-6
Eel River Conservation Camp—locale CA-9
Eel River Prairie—flat IN-6
Eel River Sch—school CA-9
Eel River Station—locale CA-9
**Eel River (Township of)**—pop pl (2) IN-6
Eel Rock—island CA-9
Eel Rock—locale CA-9
Eels Hill CT-1
Eels Hill—summit CT-1
Eels Park—park WA-9
Eels Ridge—ridge OR-9
Eels Run—stream OH-6
**Eel (Township of)**—pop pl IN-6
Eel Weir Bridge—bridge ME-1
Eel Weir Canal—canal ME-1
Eel Weir Hollow—valley NY-2
Eel Weir Picnic Area—locale NY-2
Eel Weir Power Station—other ME-1
Eely Pond—reservoir CT-1
Eely's Pond CT-1
E E Main Drain—canal ID-8
E E Moorehead Lake Dam—dam MS-4
Eena Creek—stream ID-8
Eena Lake OR-9
Eenayarak River—stream AK-9
Een Ridge—ridge ME-1
Een Sch—school MT-8
Eensenada Mesa NM-5
Een-to MP-9
E E Pettegrew Dam—dam SD-7
E E Pettegrew Dam Number 2—dam SD-7
Eerie Point—cape AK-9
Eerkes Spring—spring WA-9
Eerukku MP-9
Eerukku—island MP-9
Eerukku Island MP-9
Eerukku-To MP-9
E E Smith HS—school NC-3
E E Smith JHS NC-3

Eight Acre Bluff—*cliff* TN-4
Eight Acre Reservoir Dam—*dam* MA-1
*Eight Acre Rock* AL-4
Eight Acre Rsvr—*reservoir* MA-1
Eight A Lateral—*canal* CA-9
**Eight and One-half Mile Camp**—*pop pl* HI-9
Eight Ave Sch—*school* TX-5
Eight Camp—*locale* TX-5
Eight Canyon—*valley* NM-5
**Eight Corners**—*pop pl* ME-1
**Eight Corners**—*pop pl* WI-6
Eight Creek—*stream* WA-9
Eight Day Swamp—*swamp* NJ-2
Eight Dollar Mtn—*summit* OR-9
Eighteen, Lake—*lake* MI-6
Eighteen Bells Mobile Home Park—*locale* AZ-5
Eighteen Bog—*swamp* ME-1
Eighteen Creek—*stream* CA-9
Eighteen Creek—*stream* TX-5
Eighteen Creek—*stream* WA-9
Eighteen Creek Windmill—*locale* TX-5
Eighteen Eighty-One Moses Carver House—*building* MO-7
Eighteenfoot Falls—*falls* WI-6
Eighteen Gulch—*valley* AK-9
Eighteen Hollow—*valley* PA-2
Eighteen Hundred Block Park Road, NW.—*hist pl* DC-2
Eighteen-Inch Telescope—*other* CA-9
Eighteen Lake—*lake* (2) MN-6
Eighteenmile—*locale* ID-8
Eighteenmile Bend—*bend* NM-5
Eighteenmile Canyon—*valley* NV-8
Eighteenmile Canyon—*valley* WY-8
Eighteenmile Ch—*church* KY-4
*Eighteen Mile Creek* SC-3
Eighteenmile Creek—*stream* CA-9
Eighteenmile Creek—*stream* (2) ID-8
Eighteenmile Creek—*stream* KY-4
Eighteenmile Creek—*stream* MI-6
Eighteenmile Creek—*stream* MN-6
Eighteenmile Creek—*stream* (2) NY-2
Eighteenmile Creek—*stream* (2) SC-3
Eighteenmile Creek—*stream* TX-5
Eighteenmile Creek—*stream* (2) WV-2
Eighteenmile Creek—*stream* (2) WI-6
Eighteenmile Creek Springs—*spring* WI-6
Eighteenmile Draw—*valley* NM-5
Eighteenmile Hill—*summit* NM-5
Eighteen Mile House—*hist pl* OH-6
Eighteenmile House (Site)—*locale* NV-8
Eighteenmile Island—*island* KY-4
Eighteenmile Island—*island* OR-9
Eighteenmile Knoll—*summit* WY-8
Eighteenmile Mill—*locale* NM-5
Eighteenmile Peak—*summit* ID-8
Eighteenmile Peak—*summit* MT-8
Eighteenmile Ranch—*locale* NV-8
Eighteen Mile Ranch (historical)—*locale* SD-7
Eighteenmile Well—*well* TX-5
Eighteenmile Well—*well* WY-8
Eighteen Pond—*lake* ME-1
Eighteen Pond Brook—*stream* ME-1
Eighteen Q Camp—*locale* CA-9
Eighteen Quarry Pond—*lake* ME-1
Eighteen Ranch—*locale* TX-5
Eighteen Run—*stream* OH-6
Eighteen Tank—*reservoir* AZ-5
Eighteen Tank—*reservoir* TX-5
Eighteenth Ave Sch—*school* NJ-2
Eighteenth District Sch—*hist pl* OH-6
Eighteenth Infantry Bluff—*cliff* WA-9
Eighteenth Saint Ch—*church* KY-4
Eighteenth Street Bridge—*bridge* IN-6
Eight Fathom Bight—*bay* AK-9
Eightfoot Falls—*falls* WI-6
Eight-Foot High Speed Tunnel—*hist pl* VA-3
Eight Foot Lake—*lake* MI-6
Eight Foot Rapids—*rapids* UT-8
Eightfoot Windmill—*locale* TX-5
Eight Gulch—*valley* AK-9
Eighth and Center Streets Baptist Church—*hist pl* MO-7
Eighth Ave Baptist Ch—*church* MS-4
Eighth Ave Ch of God—*church* MS-4
Eighth Ave North Grotto—*cave* AL-4
Eighth Ave South Reservoir—*dam* TN-4
Eighth Ave South Reservoir—*hist pl* TN-4
Eighth Bayou—*stream* MS-4
Eighth Bottom Hollow—*valley* PA-2
Eighth Branch—*stream* KY-4
Eighth Creek—*stream* OR-9
Eighth Crow Wing Lake—*lake* MN-6
Eighth Debsconeag Pond—*lake* ME-1
*Eighth District Elem Sch* TN-4
Eighth District Sch—*school* TN-4
*Eighth Lake* MN-6
Eighth Lake—*lake* NY-2
Eighth & Master Streets Yard Airp—*airport* PA-2
*Eighth Mile Station* NV-8
Eighth Precinct Police Station—*hist pl* MI-6
Eighth Regiment Armory—*hist pl* IL-6
Eighth Regiment Armory—*hist pl* NY-2
Eighth Street Elem Sch—*school* FL-3
Eighth Street-Forrester District—*hist pl* NM-5
Eighth Street Hist Dist—*hist pl* WI-6
Eighth Street Park Hist Dist—*hist pl* DE-2
Eighth Street Park Hist Dist (Boundary Increase)—*hist pl* DE-2
Eighthundred Acre Windmill—*locale* TX-5
Eight Hundred Block of F St. NW—*hist pl* DC-2
Eight Hundred Foot Well—*well* NM-5
Eighth Ward Sch—*school* LA-4
Eighth Ward Sch—*school* PA-2
Eighth Ward Sch (abandoned)—*school* PA-2
*Eight Lake* MN-6
Eight Lake—*lake* NY-2
Eight Lakes Basin—*basin* OR-9
Eight Lakes Creek—*stream* OR-9
Eight Lazy Y Ranch—*locale* WY-8
*Eight Mile* MO-7
Eightmile—*locale* AK-9
Eightmile—*locale* NV-8
Eightmile—*locale* OR-9
Eight Mile—*other* WV-2
**Eight Mile**—*pop pl* AL-4
**Eight Mile**—*pop pl* TX-5
Eightmile Bench—*bench* MT-8
Eightmile Branch—*stream* AL-4
Eightmile Branch—*stream* IA-7
Eightmile Branch—*stream* NJ-2
Eightmile Branch—*stream* SC-3
Eightmile Bridge—*bridge* MT-8
Eightmile Bridge—*bridge* WY-8
Eightmile Brook—*stream* (2) CT-1
Eightmile Cabin—*locale* AK-9
**Eightmile Camp**—*pop pl* HI-9
Eightmile Campground—*locale* ID-8
Eightmile Campground—*locale* WA-9
*Eight Mile Canyon* ID-8
*Eightmile Canyon* NV-8
Eightmile Canyon—*valley* CO-8
Eightmile Canyon—*valley* (3) ID-8
Eightmile Canyon—*valley* NV-8
Eightmile Canyon—*valley* NM-5
Eightmile Canyon—*valley* OR-9
Eightmile Canyon—*valley* (2) UT-8
Eight Mile Canyon Prospect—*mine* AK-9
Eight Mile Cem—*cemetery* AR-4
Eightmile Cem—*cemetery* (2) OR-9
Eight Mile Ch—*church* AR-4
Eightmile Ch—*church* KS-7
Eightmile Corner—*locale* MI-6
Eightmile Coulee—*valley* (3) MT-8
Eightmile Cove—*bay* AK-9
*Eight Mile Creek* AL-4
*Eightmile Creek* ID-8
*Eight Mile Creek* IN-6
*Eight Mile Creek* KS-7
*Eight Mile Creek* MT-8
*Eight Mile Creek* NV-8
*Eightmile Creek* SD-7
*Eightmile Creek* TX-5
*Eight Mile Creek* UT-8
*Eight Mile Creek* WA-9
Eightmile Creek—*stream* (4) AL-4
Eightmile Creek—*stream* (3) AK-9
Eightmile Creek—*stream* AZ-5
Eight Mile Creek—*stream* (2) AR-4
Eightmile Creek—*stream* (3) CA-9
Eightmile Creek—*stream* (2) CO-8
Eightmile Creek—*stream* (3) FL-3
Eightmile Creek—*stream* (2) GA-3
Eightmile Creek—*stream* (5) ID-8
Eightmile Creek—*stream* (2) IN-6
Eightmile Creek—*stream* (2) KS-7
Eightmile Creek—*stream* LA-4
Eightmile Creek—*stream* (2) MN-6
Eightmile Creek—*stream* MO-7
Eightmile Creek—*stream* (5) MT-8
Eightmile Creek—*stream* NE-7
Eightmile Creek—*stream* (2) NV-8
Eightmile Creek—*stream* (2) NY-2
Eightmile Creek—*stream* ND-7
Eightmile Creek—*stream* (3) OH-6
Eightmile Creek—*stream* (2) OK-5
Eightmile Creek—*stream* (2) OR-9
Eightmile Creek—*stream* PA-2
Eightmile Creek—*stream* SD-7
Eightmile Creek—*stream* TX-5
Eightmile Creek—*stream* UT-8
Eightmile Creek—*stream* (6) WA-9
Eightmile Creek—*stream* WV-2
Eightmile Creek—*stream* WI-6
Eightmile Creek Ch—*church* AL-4
Eightmile Crossing Campground—*park* OR-9
Eightmile Dam Hollow—*valley* PA-2
*Eight Mile Ditch* AR-4
*Eightmile Ditch* WI-6
Eightmile Ditch—*canal* AR-4
Eightmile Ditch—*canal* CO-8
Eightmile Divide—*ridge* SD-7
Eightmile Draw—*valley* (3) NM-5
Eightmile Draw—*valley* (3) TX-5
Eightmile Draw—*valley* WY-8
*Eightmile Ferry* NJ-2
Eightmile Fishing Access Site—*locale* MT-8
Eightmile Flat—*flat* NV-8
Eightmile Flat—*flat* UT-8
Eightmile Gap—*gap* UT-8
Eightmile Gap—*valley* AZ-5
Eightmile Glade—*flat* CA-9
Eight Mile Grove—*fmr MCD* NE-7
Eightmile Guard Station—*locale* WA-9
Eightmile Harvey Ridge Trail—*trail* MT-8
*Eight Mile Hills* UT-8
Eightmile Hills—*summit* UT-8
Eightmile Hollow—*valley* WV-2
Eight-Mile House—*hist pl* KY-4
Eightmile House—*locale* KS-7
**Eight Mile House**—*pop pl* CA-9
Eightmile Island—*island* AK-9
Eightmile Island—*island* ID-8
Eightmile Island—*island* MN-6
Eightmile Island—*island* WV-2
Eightmile Lake—*lake* (2) AK-9
Eightmile Lake—*lake* WA-9
Eightmile Lake—*lake* (2) WY-8
Eightmile Lake Basin—*basin* WY-8
Eightmile Lateral—*canal* ID-8
Eightmile Lookout—*locale* CA-9
Eightmile Meadow—*flat* OR-9
Eightmile Mesa—*summit* CO-8
Eightmile Mtn—*summit* ID-8
Eightmile Mtn—*summit* NV-8
Eightmile Mtn—*summit* OK-5
Eightmile Mtn—*summit* WA-9
Eightmile Number Four Ditch—*canal* IN-6
Eightmile Number Three Ditch—*canal* IN-6
Eightmile Number Two Ditch—*canal* IN-6
Eightmile Park—*flat* CO-8
Eightmile Pass—*gap* UT-8
Eight Mile Pass—*gap* UT-8
Eightmile Pass—*gap* WA-9
Eightmile Peak—*summit* MT-8
Eightmile Peak—*summit* WA-9
Eightmile Point—*cape* NJ-2
Eightmile Point—*locale* UT-8
Eightmile Point—*summit* NV-8
Eightmile Point—*summit* OR-9
Eightmile Pond—*lake* FL-3
*Eightmile Pony Station* NV-8
Eightmile Post—*locale* GA-3
Eightmile Prairie—*flat* ID-8
Eightmile Prairie Mtn—*summit* OR-9
Eightmile Ranch—*locale* CA-9
Eightmile Ranger Station—*locale* ID-8
Eight Mile Reach—*stream* AR-4
Eightmile Ridge—*ridge* (2) CA-9
Eightmile Ridge—*ridge* WA-9
Eightmile Ridge—*ridge* WV-2
Eightmile Ridge Ch—*church* WV-2
Eightmile River—*stream* (2) CT-1
*Eight Mile River Cove* CT-1
Eightmile Rock—*pillar* UT-8
Eightmile Rsvr—*reservoir* OR-9
Eightmile Rsvr—*reservoir* UT-8
Eightmile Saddle—*gap* MT-8
Eight Mile Sch—*school* AL-4
Eightmile Sch—*school* ID-8
Eightmile Sch—*school* MO-7
Eightmile Sch—*school* WV-2
Eightmile School—*locale* CO-8
Eight Mile Shop Ctr—*locale* AL-4
Eightmile Slough—*stream* AK-9
Eightmile Slough—*stream* FL-3
*Eight Mile Spring* UT-8
Eightmile Spring—*spring* (3) NV-8
Eightmile Spring—*spring* (5) UT-8
Eightmile Springs—*reservoir* MT-8
Eightmile Springs—*spring* UT-8
**Eightmile Still**—*pop pl* GA-3
Eightmile Tank—*reservoir* CA-9
Eightmile Tank—*reservoir* (2) TX-5
Eightmile Valley—*stream* CA-9
Eightmile Valley—*valley* NV-8
Eightmile Wash—*valley* UT-8
Eightmile Wash—*valley* WY-8
Eightmile Waterhole—*lake* (3) TX-5
Eightmile Well—*well* AZ-5
Eightmile Well—*well* NV-8
Eightmile Well—*well* NM-5
Eightmile Wells—*other* NM-5
Eightmile Windmill—*locale* TX-5
Eight Oak Ridge—*ridge* TN-4
*Eight P.M. Island* FM-9
Eight Point Lake—*lake* MI-6
**Eight Point Lake**—*pop pl* MI-6
Eight Section Tank—*reservoir* AZ-5
Eight Spring—*spring* WY-8
Eight Square Cem—*cemetery* IN-6
Eight Square Cem—*cemetery* NY-2
Eight Square Cem—*cemetery* OH-6
Eight Square Chapel—*church* PA-2
Eight Square Leagues On Stanislaus River—*civil* CA-9
Eight Square Sch (abandoned)—*school* (2) PA-2
Eight Stream—*stream* WA-9
Eight Street Shop Ctr—*locale* KS-7
Eight Tank—*reservoir* AZ-5
Eighty, Tank—*reservoir* AZ-5
Eighty Acre Bay—*swamp* FL-3
Eighty Acre Creek—*stream* OR-9
Eighty Acre Lake—*lake* MN-6
Eighty Arpent Canal—*canal* (2) LA-4
Eighty Day Creek—*stream* ID-8
**Eighty Eight**—*pop pl* KY-4
Eightyeight Ch—*church* AR-4
Eighty-Eighth Street Sch—*school* WI-6
Eightyeight Mine—*mine* AZ-5
Eighty-Eight Ranch (site)—*locale* WY-8
Eightyeight Ridge—*ridge* ID-8
Eighty Eight Sch (abandoned)—*school* MO-7
Eighty-eight Shaft—*mine* UT-8
Eightyfifth Street Baptist Ch—*church* AL-4
Eightyfirst Street Sch—*school* LA-4
Eighty First Street Sch—*school* WI-6
Eightyfive Bar Spring—*spring* AZ-5
Eightyfive Creek—*stream* WY-8
Eightyfive Divide—*ridge* WY-8
Eightyfive Hill—*summit* NM-5
Eightyfive Mile Rapids—*rapids* AZ-5
Eightyfoot Ditch—*canal* CA-9
Eightyfoot Well—*well* NV-8
*Eighty-Four* PA-2
**Eighty Four**—*pop pl* PA-2
Eightyfour, Lake—*reservoir* PA-2
**Eighty Four (RR name Eighty-four)**—*pop pl* PA-2
Eighty-four (RR name for Eighty Four)—*other* PA-2
Eightymile Well—*well* NV-8
Eighty Mtn—*summit* NM-5
Eightynine A Tank—*reservoir* AZ-5
Eightynine Tank—*reservoir* AZ-5
Eighty Nineth Street—*post sta* OK-5
Eightyone, Point—*summit* ID-8
Eightyone Airp—*airport* KS-7
Eightyone Ch—*church* AR-4
Eightyone Mile Point—*cape* LA-4
Eightyone Pasture—*flat* KS-7
Eighty-o-one Manchester Center (Shop Ctr)—*locale* MO-7
Eighty Peak—*summit* ID-8
Eighty Peak—*summit* MT-8
Eighty Rod Ditch—*canal* UT-8
Eightysecond Street Park—*park* NJ-2
Eighty Second Street Sch—*school* WI-6
Eightyseven Mile Peak—*summit* ID-8
Eightyseven Mile Peak—*summit* MT-8
*Eighty-seventh Street* IL-6
Eighty-Seventh Street Sch—*school* CA-9
Eighty Six Ch—*church* AR-4
Eighty Spring—*spring* AZ-5
Eighty Tank—*reservoir* TX-5
Eighty Tank Draw—*valley* TX-5
*Eighty-third Street* IL-6
Eightythree Mile Rapids—*rapids* AZ-5
Eightytwo Plaza Shop Ctr—*locale* MS-4
Eiguren Rsvr—*reservoir* OR-9
Eiguren Rsvr Number One—*reservoir* OR-9
Eiguren Rsvr Number Two—*reservoir* OR-9
Eiguren Spring—*spring* OR-9
Eike Ranch—*locale* WY-8
Eikerman Cem—*cemetery* MO-7
Eiland Branch—*stream* AL-4
Eiland Cem—*cemetery* NM-5
Eiland Lake Dam—*dam* MS-4
Eilebrecht Ditch No 1—*canal* CO-8
Eileen—*locale* ID-8
**Eileen**—*pop pl* IL-6
Eileen, Lake—*lake* (2) CO-8
Eileen, Lake—*lake* GA-3
Eileen, Lake—*lake* NH-1
Eileen, Loch—*lake* WA-9
**Eileen Gardens**—*pop pl* OH-6
Eileen Lake—*lake* OR-9
Eileen Spring—*spring* AZ-5
**Eileen (Town of)**—*pop pl* WI-6
*Eilenbergers Island* PA-2
Eiler—*locale* AL-4
Eiler, Lake—*lake* CA-9
Eiler Butte—*summit* CA-9
Eiler Cem—*cemetery* IL-6
Eiler Creek—*stream* OR-9
Eiler Gulch—*valley* CA-9
Eiler Hall—*building* GA-3
Eilerman Ditch—*canal* OH-6
Eiler Mine—*mine* CA-9
**Eilers**—*pop pl* CO-8
Eilers Cem—*cemetery* TX-5
**Eilers Corner**—*pop pl* NJ-2
**Eilers Corners**—*pop pl* NJ-2
Eilers Lake—*lake* MN-6
Eilertsen Creek—*stream* OR-9
*Eilertsen Meadow* OR-9
Eilertson Lake—*lake* MN-6
Eilertson Meadow—*flat* OR-9
Eiley Lake—*lake* WA-9
Eil Hollow—*valley* UT-8
*Eilison Creek* NV-8
*Eil Malik* PW-9
*Eil Malk* PW-9
Eil Malk—*bay* PW-9
Eil Malk—*cave* PW-9
*Eil Malk Island* PW-9
*Eimelik* PW-9
Eimnlapp—*island* MP-9
*Eimonetto-to* MP-9
*Eineiere* MP-9
Einerson Sch—*school* WI-6
Einert Creek—*stream* WI-6
*Einfahrt* FM-9
*Einmlapp* MP-9
Eino Lake—*lake* MN-6
Einsel Oil and Gas Field—*oilfield* KS-7
Einstein—*post sta* NY-2
Einstein, Albert, House—*hist pl* NJ-2
Einstein, Mount—*summit* AK-9
Einstein Coll—*school* NY-2
Einstein House—*hist pl* CA-9
Einstein JHS—*school* CA-9
*Einstein Med Ctr Northern Division* PA-2
Einstein Mine—*mine* MO-7
Einstein Park—*park* CA-9
Einstein Sch—*school* IL-6
Einstein Sch—*school* (2) MI-6
Einstein Sch—*school* NY-2
Einstein Statue—*park* DC-2
*Eiol* FM-9
*Eiol Island* FM-9
Eiramataw—*tunnel* FM-9
*Eirech* FM-9
Eirek Island—*island* MP-9
*Eiri-to* MP-9
Eirke—*civil* FM-9
*Eisaman* PA-2
**Eisaman**—*pop pl* PA-2
Eisaman Corners—*locale* NY-2
Eisbermans Island Natl Wildlife Ref—*park* VA-3
Eisbuts Draw—*valley* WY-8
Eisele Cem—*cemetery* MI-6
Eisele Lake—*lake* MO-7
Eiseman Hollow—*valley* IN-6
Eisen, Mount—*summit* CA-9
Eisenbeis, John, House—*hist pl* SD-7
Eisenbraum Ditch—*canal* OH-6
*Eisen Brown Corners* PA-2
Eisenglass Mtn—*summit* NY-2
*Eisenhart* PA-2
Eisenhart Hill—*summit* NM-5
Eisenhauer Canyon—*valley* AZ-5
Eisenhauer JHS—*school* TX-5
Eisenhauer Spring—*spring* AZ-5
Eisenheimer Peak—*summit* CA-9
Eisenhour Cem—*cemetery* OH-6
Eisenhour Ch—*church* MO-7
Eisenhour Hollow—*valley* TN-4
Eisenhour Ridge—*ridge* ID-8
Eisenhower, Mount—*summit* NH-1
Eisenhower Army Med Ctr—*other* GA-3
Eisenhower Branch—*stream* TX-5
Eisenhower Center—*locale* KS-7
**Eisenhower College**—*pop pl* NY-2
*Eisenhower Dam* AZ-5
Eisenhower Divide—*ridge* ND-7
*Eisenhower Elem Sch* PA-2
Eisenhower Elem Sch—*school* AZ-5
Eisenhower Elem Sch—*school* FL-3
Eisenhower Elem Sch—*school* (3) KS-7
Eisenhower Elem Sch—*school* (2) PA-2
Eisenhower Home—*hist pl* KS-7
Eisenhower HS—*school* CA-9
Eisenhower HS—*school* (2) IL-6
Eisenhower HS—*school* MI-6
Eisenhower HS—*school* OK-5
Eisenhower HS—*school* (2) PA-2
Eisenhower HS—*school* WA-9
Eisenhower JHS—*school* FL-3
Eisenhower JHS—*school* KS-7
Eisenhower JHS—*school* OH-6
Eisenhower JHS—*school* (2) OK-5
Eisenhower JHS—*school* UT-8
Eisenhower Lake—*lake* RI-1
Eisenhower Lake—*reservoir* RI-1
Eisenhower Lake Dam—*dam* RI-1
Eisenhower Lock—*pillar* NY-2
Eisenhower Med Ctr—*hospital* CA-9
Eisenhower Memorial Park—*park* NY-2
Eisenhower Memorial Tunnel—*tunnel* CO-8
Eisenhower Mid Sch—*school* IL-6
*Eisenhower MS* PA-2
Eisenhower Natl Historic Site—*park* PA-2
Eisenhower Park—*park* TX-5
*Eisenhower Sch* PA-2
Eisenhower Sch—*school* (2) CA-9
Eisenhower Sch—*school* IL-6
Eisenhower Sch—*school* (2) IA-7
Eisenhower Sch—*school* (2) MI-6
Eisenhower Sch—*school* MN-6
Eisenhower Sch—*school* (2) OK-5
Eisenhower Sch—*school* (3) PA-2
Eisenhower Sch—*school* WI-6
Eisenhower State Park—*park* TX-5
Eisenhuth Dam—*dam* PA-2
Eisenhuth Rsvr—*reservoir* PA-2
*Eisenhuth Run Dam* PA-2
Eisenmenger Fork—*stream* AK-9
**Eisenstein (Town of)**—*pop pl* WI-6
Eiserman Street Park—*park* MO-7
Eishelman Run—*stream* VA-3
Eisinore Peak—*summit* CA-9
Eisler Spring—*spring* SD-7
Eisnaugle Hollow—*valley* OH-6
Eisner Park—*park* IL-6
Eison Branch—*stream* KY-4
Eison Branch—*stream* SC-3
**Eison Crossroads**—*pop pl* SC-3
Eissler Sch—*school* CA-9
Eister Creek—*stream* MI-6
*Eitelblong* PW-9
*Eitelblong Island* PW-9
Eitel Hosp—*hospital* MN-6
Eithtmile Mtn—*summit* AK-9
Eitsert Cem—*cemetery* WI-6
**Eitzen**—*pop pl* MN-6
Eitzen Stone Barn—*hist pl* MN-6
EJE Bridge over Shell Creek—*hist pl* WY-8
*Ejej* MP-9
*Ejel Island* MP-9
E J Hayes Sch—*school* NC-3
Ejimaan—*bar* MP-9
Ejinkoto Shoal—*bar* PW-9
Ejirien Island—*island* MP-9
*Ejiri-to* MP-9
Ejit—*island* MP-9
*Ejit Island* MP-9
*Ejitto-to* MP-9
*Ejjela Island* MP-9
E J Mooney Dam Number 1—*dam* SD-7
E J Moran Number One Dam—*dam* AL-4
E J Moran Number Two Dam—*dam* AL-4
Ejod Lake—*lake* UT-8
E Johnson Lake Dam—*dam* MS-4
Ejowa—*island* MP-9
*Ejowa-To* MP-9
EJP County Line Bridge—*hist pl* WY-8
E J Pearson Lake Dam—*dam* MS-4
EJ Smith County Park—*park* WI-6
E J Smith Tank—*reservoir* AZ-5
E Justice Lake Dam—*dam* MS-4
*Ejwa* MP-9
EJZ Bridge over Shoshone River—*hist pl* WY-8
Ekaafuto—*bar* FM-9
Ekaha—*bay* HI-9
Ekahanui—*summit* HI-9
Ekahanui Gulch—*valley* HI-9
Ekahi Rsvr—*reservoir* HI-9
*Ekaje* MP-9
Ekakevik Creek—*stream* AK-9
Ekakevik Mtn—*summit* AK-9
**Ekalaka**—*pop pl* MT-8
Ekalgruak Lake—*lake* AK-9
Ekaluakat River—*stream* AK-9
**Ekanachatte (historical)**—*pop pl* FL-3
Ekaneetlee Branch—*stream* TN-4
Ekaneetlee Creek—*stream* NC-3
Ekaneetlee Gap—*gap* NC-3
Ekaneetlee Gap—*gap* TN-4
*Ekanetelee* NC-3
*Ekanetelee Gap* TN-4
*Ekanfinaka* GA-3
Ekarotrosu—*bar* FM-9
Ekashluak Creek—*stream* AK-9
Ekasluktuli River—*stream* AK-9
**Ekastown**—*pop pl* PA-2
Ekaterina, Lake—*lake* AK-9
*E K Baker Elementary School* TN-4
E K Baker Sch—*school* TN-4
E-K Creek—*stream* WY-8
Ekdahl—*airport* NJ-2
Ekdahl-Goudreau Site—*hist pl* MI-6
Ekdall Ch—*church* WI-6
*Eke* HI-9
Eke—*summit* HI-9
Eke Crater—*crater* HI-9
*Eke Crater Peak* HI-9
Eke Drainage System Ditch—*canal* IN-6
E Keller Ranch—*locale* NE-7
Ekelund Ch—*church* MN-6
Ekelund Lake—*lake* MI-6
**Ekerts Corners**—*pop pl* OH-6
Ekey Cem—*cemetery* MO-7
Ekey Park—*park* KS-7
Ekichuk Lake—*lake* AK-9
Ekiek Creek—*stream* AK-9
Ekilukruak Entrance—*channel* AK-9
**Ekin**—*pop pl* IN-6
E Kincaid Lake—*lake* NE-7
E Kinney Lake—*lake* NE-7
Ekker Butte—*summit* UT-8
Ekker Ranch—*locale* UT-8
Ek (Leif) Lake—*lake* MN-6
*Ekler Canyon* KS-7
*Ekler Canyon* OK-5
**Eklo**—*pop pl* MD-2
Eklund Cem—*cemetery* MN-6
Eklund J 3 Ranch—*locale* WY-8
Eklund Lake—*lake* WY-8
Eklund Number 4 Dam—*dam* SD-7
Eklund Number 5 Dam—*dam* SD-7
**Eklutna**—*pop pl* AK-9
Eklutna, Mount—*summit* AK-9
Eklutna Flats—*flat* AK-9
Eklutna Glacier—*glacier* AK-9
Eklutna(Included In Anchorage) ANV778—*reserve* AK-9
Eklutna Lake—*reservoir* AK-9
Eklutna Powerhouse—*other* AK-9
Eklutna Power Plant—*hist pl* AK-9
Eklutna River—*stream* AK-9
E K Mines Branch—*stream* KY-4
E K Mtn—*summit* WY-8
E K Oil Field—*other* NM-5
Ekokpuk Creek—*stream* AK-9
Ekolina Creek—*stream* AK-9
**Ekom**—*pop pl* SC-3
Ekonk—*locale* CT-1
Ekonk Brook—*stream* CT-1
Ekonk Ch—*church* CT-1
**Ekonk Hill**—*pop pl* CT-1
Ekonk Hill—*summit* CT-1
**Ekre Spur**—*pop pl* ND-7
**Ekron**—*pop pl* KY-4
Eks Bay—*bay* MN-6
Ekstein JHS—*school* WA-9
Ekstrand Sch—*school* CA-9
E K Tank—*reservoir* AZ-5
E-k Trail—*trail* WY-8
Ekuk—*locale* AK-9
Ekuk ANV779—*reserve* AK-9
Ekuk Bluff—*cliff* AK-9
Ekuk Spit—*bar* AK-9
Ekund Drain—*canal* MI-6
*Ekuohapuaa* HI-9
Ekuokapuaa—*cape* HI-9
Ekwanok Country Club—*other* VT-1
**Ekwok**—*pop pl* AK-9
*Ekwortzel Draw* MT-8
Ekwortzel Draw—*valley* MT-8
**Ela**—*pop pl* NC-3
El Aceitero Trap—*summit* TX-5
El Aceitero Well Fiftyone (flowing)—*well* TX-5
El Adobe De Los Robles Historic Marker—*park* CA-9
El Aguila—*summit* NM-5
**Elaine**—*pop pl* AR-4
Elaine, Lake—*lake* MT-8
Elaine Castle—*summit* AZ-5
Elaine Draw—*valley* WY-8
Elaine Lake—*reservoir* AZ-5
Elaine Lake—*reservoir* TN-4
Elaine Lake Dam—*dam* TN-4
Elaine Mission—*church* AR-4
Elaine Oil Field—*oilfield* TX-5
Elaine Pond—*lake* ME-1
Elaines Detention Rsvr—*reservoir* WY-8
Elaine Township—*civil* SD-7
**Elajay (historical)**—*pop pl* TN-4
E-la-ka-wee Camp—*locale* WY-8
Elaktoveach Channel—*channel* AK-9
El Alamo Park—*park* TX-5
El Alazan Windmill—*locale* TX-5
El Alisal (Bernal)—*civil* CA-9
El Alisal (Hartnell)—*civil* CA-9
El Alto—*area* NM-5
**El Alto**—*pop pl* NM-5
**El Alto**—*pop pl* PR-3
El Alto—*ridge* PR-3
El Alto Windmill—*locale* (2) TX-5
Elam—*locale* VA-3
**Elam**—*pop pl* LA-4
**Elam**—*pop pl* PA-2
Elam—*uninc pl* TX-5
Elam, Mount—*summit* MA-1
Elam Baptist Ch (historical)—*church* AL-4
*Elam Baptist Church* MS-4
Elam Bend State Wildlife Area—*area* MO-7
Elam Bluff P.O. (historical)—*locale* AL-4
Elam Branch—*stream* (2) AL-4
Elam Branch—*stream* (4) KY-4
Elam Branch—*stream* LA-4
Elam Branch—*stream* TN-4
Elam Campground—*locale* CA-9
Elam-Camp House—*hist pl* GA-3
Elam Canyon—*valley* TX-5
Elam Cem—*cemetery* (3) AL-4
Elam Cem—*cemetery* AR-4
Elam Cem—*cemetery* (3) GA-3
Elam Cem—*cemetery* (2) KY-4
Elam Cem—*cemetery* (2) MS-4
Elam Cem—*cemetery* (2) TN-4
Elam Cem—*cemetery* (2) VA-3
*Elam Ch* AL-4
Elam Ch—*church* (9) AL-4
Elam Ch—*church* (6) GA-3
Elam Ch—*church* KY-4
Elam Ch—*church* MS-4
Elam Ch—*church* SC-3
Elam Ch—*church* TN-4
Elam Ch—*church* (2) VA-3
Elam Ch (historical)—*church* AL-4
Elam Creek—*stream* (3) AL-4
Elam Creek—*stream* (2) CA-9
Elam Creek—*stream* MS-4
Elam Creek—*stream* MO-7
Elam Creek—*stream* MT-8
Elam Creek—*stream* TN-4
Elam Creek—*stream* (2) TX-5
*Elam Creek Church* AL-4
Elam Dam—*dam* AL-4
Elam-Davidson Memorial Cem—*cemetery* AL-4
Elam Ditch—*canal* KY-4
Elam Grove Ch—*church* NC-3
Elam Grove Ch—*church* TX-5
Elam Hill—*summit* TN-4
Elam Hollow—*valley* AR-4
Elam Hollow—*valley* MO-7
Elam Homestead—*hist pl* TN-4
Elam Lake—*reservoir* AL-4
*Elam Methodist Church* AL-4
Elam Mound Archeol Site—*hist pl* KY-4
Elam Mtn—*summit* TX-5
Elam Ridge—*ridge* MS-4
Elam-Rodgers—*locale* AL-4
Elams—*locale* NC-3
Elam Sch—*school* AL-4
Elams Mill (historical)—*locale* TN-4
Elamsville—*locale* VA-3
Elamton—*locale* KY-4
Elamtown—*locale* VA-3
**Elamville**—*pop pl* AL-4
*Elamville Church* AL-4
Elana—*locale* WV-2
Elan Cem—*cemetery* IA-7
**El Ancon**—*pop pl* NM-5
Eland—*locale* ND-7
**Eland**—*pop pl* WI-6
Eland Cem—*cemetery* WI-6
Eland Lake Dam—*dam* MS-4
Eland Rough—*summit* TX-5
Elangelab—*island* FM-9
Elangkileku—*island* FM-9
Elan Hill—*summit* VT-1
Elan Memorial Cem—*cemetery* PA-2
Elanor—*locale* WA-9
*Elapaha River* FL-3
*Elapaha River* GA-3
Elarbee Cem—*cemetery* GA-3
El Arco—*ridge* CA-9
Ela River—*stream* NH-1
Elaroniluk Creek—*stream* AK-9
El Arroyo Zopilote—*valley* TX-5
*Elat Creek Church* AL-4
E Lateral—*canal* CA-9
Elaterite Basin—*basin* UT-8

Elkhorn River—stream NE-7
Elkhorn Rock—summit WV-2
Elkhorn Rsvr—reservoir UT-8
Elkhorn Run PA-2
Elkhorn Run—stream (2) PA-2
Elk Horn Run—stream VA-3
Elkhorn Run—stream (3) WV-2
Elkhorn Scarp—cliff CA-9
Elkhorn Sch—school CA-9
Elkhorn Sch—school CO-8
Elkhorn Sch—school IL-6
Elkhorn Sch—school (2) KY-4
Elkhorn Sch—school MI-6
Elkhorn Sch—school MO-7
Elkhorn Sch—school ND-7
Elkhorn Sch—school WY-8
Elkhorn Skyline Mine—mine MT-8
Elkhorn Slough CA-9
Elkhorn Slough—stream (2) CA-9
Elkhorn Spring—spring CO-8
Elk Horn Spring—spring CO-8
Elk Horn Spring—spring ID-8
Elkhorn Spring—spring MT-8
Elkhorn Spring—spring (3) OR-9
Elkhorn Springs MT-8
**Elkhorn Springs**—pop pl MT-8
Elkhorn Springs—spring AR-4
Elkhorn Springs—spring WY-8
Elkhorn Stage Station (ruins)—locale WY-8
Elkhorn Station—locale CA-9
Elkhorn Stock Driveway—trail CO-8
Elkhorn Stock Driveway—trail WY-8
Elkhorn Stomp Ditch—canal CO-8
Elkhorn Tank—reservoir (3) AZ-5
Elk Horn Tank—reservoir NM-5
Elkhorn Tavern—locale AR-4
Elkhorn Tower State Public Hunting Grounds—park MO-7
Elk Horn Township—civil MO-7
Elkhorn Township—fmr MCD (2) IA-7
**Elkhorn Township**—pop pl KS-7
**Elkhorn Township**—pop pl (2) NE-7
**Elkhorn Township**—pop pl ND-7
Elkhorn (Township of)—fmr MCD MO-7
**Elkhorn (Township of)**—pop pl IL-6
Elkhorn Trail—trail PA-2
Elkhorn Trail—trail WY-8
Elkhorn Trough—valley UT-8
Elkhorn Upper Camp—locale MT-8
Elkhorn Valley—valley OR-9
**Elkhorn Village**—pop pl CA-9
Elkhorn Village Sch—school CA-9
Elkhorn Warm Spring—spring ID-8
Elkhorn Woods Park—park OR-9
Elkhurst—locale MO-7
Elkhurst—locale WY-8
**Elkhurst**—pop pl WV-2
Elkin—locale KY-4
Elkin—locale PA-2
**Elkin**—pop pl NC-3
Elkin Airp—airport NC-3
Elkin City Park—park NC-3
Elkin Creek—stream NC-3
Elkin Creek Mill—hist pl NC-3
Elkin Elem Sch—school NC-3
Elkington Creek—stream AK-9
Elkin House—hist pl KY-4
Elkin HS—school NC-3
Elkin Municipal Airp—airport NC-3
Elkin Park—park TX-5
Elkin River NC-3
Elkin Rsvr—reservoir NC-3
Elkins—locale NM-5
Elkins—locale TN-4
**Elkins**—pop pl (2) AR-4
**Elkins**—pop pl NH-1
**Elkins**—pop pl TN-4
**Elkins**—pop pl VA-3
**Elkins**—pop pl WV-2
Elkins, Senator Stephen Benton, House—hist pl WV-2
Elkins Branch—stream GA-3
Elkins Branch—stream KY-4
Elkins Branch—stream TN-4
Elkins Branch—stream TX-5
Elkins Branch—stream (2) VA-3
Elkins Branch—stream (3) WV-2
Elkins Brook—stream ME-1
Elkins Brook—stream NY-2
Elkins Camp—locale NM-5
Elkins Cem—cemetery AL-4
Elkins Cem—cemetery (2) GA-3
Elkins Cem—cemetery KY-4
Elkins Cem—cemetery (4) TN-4
Elkins Cem—cemetery TX-5
Elkins Cem—cemetery VA-3
Elkins Cem—cemetery (3) WV-2
Elkins Ch—church TN-4
Elkins Ch of Christ TN-4
Elkins Coal and Coke Company Hist Dist—hist pl WV-2
Elkins Creek VA-3
Elkins Creek—stream CA-9
Elkins Creek—stream GA-3
Elkins Creek—stream MS-4
Elkins Creek—stream OH-6
Elkins Creek—stream SC-3
Elkins Draw—valley TX-5
Elkins Flat—flat CA-9
Elkins Fork—stream KY-4
Elkins Gap—gap WV-2
Elkins Hills—summit TX-5
**Elkins Hills (subdivision)**—pop pl NC-3
**Elkins (historical)**—pop pl TN-4
Elkins Hollow—valley AR-4
Elkins Hollow—valley MO-7
Elkins House—hist pl TX-5
Elkins Junction—locale WV-2
Elkins Lake—lake WI-6
Elkins Lake—reservoir TX-5
Elkins Landing—locale MO-7
Elkins Landing—locale TN-4
Elkins Marsh—swamp VA-3
Elkins Mill (historical)—locale TN-4
Elkins Mountains—range TX-5
**Elkins Park**—pop pl AR-4
**Elkins Park**—pop pl PA-2
Elkins Park Elementary School PA-2
**Elkins Park Gardens**—pop pl PA-2
Elkins Park JHS—school PA-2
Elkins Point—cape NH-1
Elkins Ranch—locale (2) NM-5
Elkins Round Barn—hist pl WV-2
Elkins Sch (historical)—school TN-4
Elkinss Landing MO-7
Elkins Speedway—other WV-2
Elkins Spring—spring NM-5
Elkins Star Lake Ranch—locale NM-5
Elkins Tank—reservoir NM-5
Elkins Tavern—hist pl VT-1
**Elkinsville**—pop pl IN-6
Elkinsville Cem—cemetery IN-6
Elkins Water Tank—reservoir NM-5
Elkins Well—well NM-5
Elkins Windmill—locale (2) TX-5
Elkinton Millpond—lake NJ-2
Elkin (Township of)—fmr MCD NC-3
**Elkin Valley**—pop pl NC-3
Elk Island SD-7
Elk Island—island MT-8
Elk Island—island VA-3
Elk Island—island WY-8
Elk Knob—summit CA-9
Elk Knob—summit (2) CO-8
Elk Knob—summit (2) NC-3
Elk Knob—summit PA-2
Elk Knob—summit SD-7
Elk Knob—summit (2) VA-3
Elk Knob—summit (2) WV-2
Elk Knob Ch—church NC-3
Elk Knob Ch—church WV-2
Elk Knob Trail—trail CA-9
Elk Knob Vista—locale PA-2
Elk Lake CA-9
Elk Lake MN-6
Elk Lake MS-4
Elk Lake ND-7
Elk Lake OR-9
Elk Lake—lake (3) CA-9
Elk Lake—lake (3) CO-8
Elk Lake—lake (4) ID-8
Elk Lake—lake IA-7
Elk Lake—lake (5) MI-6
Elk Lake—lake (7) MN-6
Elk Lake—lake (8) MT-8
Elk Lake—lake NY-2
Elk Lake—lake (2) OR-9
Elk Lake—lake PA-2
Elk Lake—lake (6) WA-9
Elk Lake—lake WI-6
Elk Lake—lake (4) WY-8
Elk Lake—locale PA-2
**Elk Lake**—pop pl OR-9
Elk Lake—reservoir NJ-2
Elk Lake—reservoir OH-6
Elk Lake—reservoir PA-2
Elk Lake—reservoir WY-8
Elk Lake Ch—church MI-6
Elk Lake Creek—stream (2) MI-6
Elk Lake Creek—stream OR-9
Elk Lake Dam—dam MS-4
Elk Lake Dam—dam NJ-2
Elk Lake Dam—dam PA-2
Elk Lake Marcy Trail—trail NY-2
Elk Lakes PA-2
Elk Lakes—lake CO-8
Elk Lakes—lake WY-8
Elk Lake Springs—spring OR-9
Elk Lake State Game Mgt Area—park IA-7
Elk Lake Stream—stream PA-2
**Elk Lake (Township of)**—pop pl MN-6
Elk Lake Trail—trail OR-9
Elkland—other NC-3
**Elkland**—pop pl MN-6
**Elkland**—pop pl MO-7
**Elkland**—pop pl PA-2
Elkland Borough—civil PA-2
Elkland Cem—cemetery MI-6
Elk Landing—hist pl MD-2
Elkland Meetinghouse—chu ch PA-2
Elkland Sch—school MO-7
Elkland Sch—school NC-3
Elkland Sch (abandoned)—school PA-2
**Elkland (Township of)**—pop pl MI-6
**Elkland (Township of)**—pop pl (2) PA-2
Elklick WV-2
Elk Lick—locale OH-6
Elk Lick—spring CA-9
Elk Lick—spring OR-9
Elk Lick—stream (3) KY-4
Elk Lick—stream OH-6
Elk Lick—stream (3) WV-2
Elk Lick, Mount—summit WA-9
Elk Lick Bluff—cliff PA-2
Elklick Branch WV-2
Elk Lick Branch—stream (2) KY-4
Elklick Branch—stream (2) WV-2
Elk Lick Ch—church (2) KY-4
Elk Lick Creek PA-2
Elk Lick Creek—stream (3) KY-4
Elklick Creek—stream PA-2
Elk Lick Creek—stream PA-2
Elk Lick Creek—stream WA-9
Elklick Creek—stream WV-2
Elklick Fork—stream KY-4
Elk Lick Fork—stream KY-4
Elk Lick Knob—summit PA-2
Elk Lick Post Office (historical)—building PA-2
Elk Lick Road Mound—hist pl OH-6
Elklick Run PA-2
Elklick Run—stream (2) MD-2
Elk Lick Run—stream MD-2
Elk Lick Run—stream (4) PA-2
Elklick Run—stream (2) PA-2
Elklick Run—stream VA-3
Elklick Run—stream (7) WV-2
Elk Lick Run—stream WV-2
Elklick Run—stream (3) WV-2
Elklick Sch (historical)—school PA-2
**Elk Lick (Township of)**—pop pl PA-2
Elk Lodge Mtn—summit NC-3
Elklore CAbin Site—locale TN-4
Elklore Camp TN-4
Elk Lovell Canal—canal WY-8
Elk (Magisterial District)—fmr MCD WV-2
Elk Meadow—flat CA-9
Elk Meadow—flat CO-8
Elk Meadow—flat (2) ID-8
Elk Meadow—flat WY-8
Elk Meadow—swamp MT-8
Elk Meadow Pit—basin WY-8
Elk Meadows UT-8
Elk Meadows—flat AZ-5
Elk Meadows—flat (3) ID-8
Elk Meadows—flat OR-9
Elk Meadows—swamp OR-9
Elk Meadows Trail—trail OR-9
Elk Mill MD-2
Elk Mills—locale TN-4
**Elk Mills**—pop pl MD-2
**Elk Mills**—pop pl PA-2
Elk Mills Baptist Ch—church TN-4
Elk Mills Post Office (historical)—building TN-4
Elk Mills Sch (historical)—school TN-4
**Elk Mill Village**—pop pl TN-4
Elk Mine—mine TN-4
**Elkmont**—pop pl AL-4
**Elkmont**—pop pl TN-4
Elkmont Baptist Church IN-4
Elkmont Ch—church AL-4
Elkmont Ch—church TN-4
Elkmont Helipad Airp—airport TN-4
Elkmont HS—school AL-4
Elkmont Post Office—building AL-4
Elkmont Ranger Station—locale TN-4
Elkmont Spring TN-4
Elkmont Spring Post Office TN-4
**Elkmont Springs**—pop pl TN-4
Elkmont Springs—spring TN-4
Elkmont Springs Post Office (historical)—building TN-4
**Elkmore**—pop pl MD-2
**Elk Mound**—pop pl WI-6
Elk Mound Marsh—swamp WI-6
Elk Mound Scenic County Park—park WI-6
**Elk Mound (Town of)**—pop pl WI-6
Elk Mountain CO-8
Elk Mountain MA-1
Elk Mountain PA-2
**Elk Mountain**—pop pl NC-3
**Elk Mountain**—pop pl WY-8
Elk Mountain Cem—cemetery CO-8
Elk Mountain Cem—cemetery WY-8
Elk Mountain Chapel—church WV-2
Elk Mountain (historical)—locale SD-7
Elk Mountain Hotel—hist pl WY-8
Elk Mountain Lodge—locale CO-8
Elk Mountain Mission Fort Site—hist pl UT-8
Elk Mountains—other NM-5
Elk Mountains—range NC-3
Elk Mountains—range SD-7
Elk Mountain Sch (abandoned)—school SD-7
Elk Mountain Ski Center—locale PA-2
Elk Mountains Lookout Tower—tower SD-7
Elk Mountain Station—locale CA-9
Elk Mountain Trail—trail CO-8
Elk Mountain Trail—trail MT-8
Elk Mountain Trail—trail OR-9
Elkmount Town Hall—building ND-7
**Elkmount Township**—pop pl ND-7
Elk Mtn OR-9
Elk Mtn—summit (2) CA-9
Elk Mtn—summit (7) CO-8
Elk Mtn—summit (6) ID-8
Elk Mtn—summit (11) MT-8
Elk Mtn—summit NV-8
Elk Mtn—summit (2) NM-5
Elk Mtn—summit OK-5
Elk Mtn—summit (11) OR-9
Elk Mtn—summit (2) SD-7
Elk Mtn—summit UT-8
Elk Mtn—summit VA-3
Elk Mtn—summit (3) WA-9
Elk Mtn—summit (4) WV-2
Elk Mtn—summit (8) WY-8
Elk Mtns—range CO-8
Elk Neck—cape MD-2
Elk Neck—locale MD-2
**Elkneck**—pop pl MD-2
Elk Neck State For—forest MD-2
Elk Neck State Park—park MD-2
Elko—locale AL-4
Elko—locale KY-4
Elko—locale MO-7
Elko—locale VA-3
**Elko**—pop pl GA-3
**Elko**—pop pl MN-6
**Elko**—pop pl NV-8
**Elko**—pop pl SC-3
Elko Camp—locale OR-9
Elko (CCD)—cens area GA-3
**Elko Colony Ind Res**—pop pl NV-8
Elko County—civil NV-8
Elko County Fish Hatchery NV-8
Elko Creek OR-9
Elko Creek—stream GA-3
Elko Creek—stream OR-9
Elko-Hamilton Stage Line Route NV-8
Elko Hamilton Stage Road NV-8
Elko Hamilton Stage Route—trail NV-8
Elko Hills—summit NV-8
Elko Ind Res—reserve NV-8
**Elkol**—pop pl WY-8
Elko Lake—lake CO-8
Elkol Strip Mine—mine WY-8
Elko Mountain NV-8
Elko Mountain Rsvr—reservoir NV-8
Elko Mountains NV-8
Elko Mtn—summit NV-8
Elko Mtns—summit NV-8
Elko Municipal Airport—airport NV-8
Elko Municipal - J C Harris Field (airport)—airport NV-8
Elko Park—flat CO-8
Elko Prince Mine—mine NV-8
Elko Range NV-8
Elko Summit—gap NV-8
Elko Summit Rsvr Number One—reservoir NV-8
Elko Summit Rsvr Number Two—reservoir NV-8
Elko (Town of)—other NY-2
Elko Township—inact MCD NV-8
Elk Park CO-8
Elk Park—flat (12) CO-8
Elk Park—flat (4) MT-8
Elk Park—flat UT-8
Elk Park—flat (2) WY-8
Elk Park—locale MT-8
Elk Park—park CA-9
Elk Park—park WY-8
**Elk Park**—pop pl CO-8
**Elk Park**—pop pl NC-3
**Elk Park**—pop pl PA-2
Elk Park Campground—locale MT-8
Elk Park Elem Sch—school NC-3
Elk Park Pass—gap MT-8
Elk Park Rsvr—reservoir CO-8
Elk Park Trail—trail CO-8
Elk Pass—gap (3) MT-8
Elk Pass—gap NY-2
Elk Pass—gap OK-5
Elk Pass—gap (2) WA-9
Elk Pass—gap WY-8
Elk Pass Trail (pack)—trail MT-8
Elk Pasture Gap—gap NC-3
Elk Patrol Lookout—locale ID-8
Elk Peak—summit CA-9
Elk Peak—summit ID-8
Elk Peak—summit (3) MT-8
Elk Peak—summit OR-9
Elk Peak—summit WA-9
Elk Peak—summit WY-8
Elk Plain—locale WA-9
Elk Plaza—flat WY-8
Elk Point WA-9
Elk Point—cape NV-8
Elk Point—cape OR-9
Elk Point—cape UT-8
Elk Point—cliff ID-8
Elk Point—cliff MT-8
Elk Point—cliff WY-8
**Elk Point**—pop pl NV-8
**Elk Point**—pop pl SD-7
Elk Point—ridge ID-8
Elk Point—summit (2) MT-8
Elk Point—summit OR-9
Elk Point—summit WA-9
**Elk Point Township**—pop pl SD-7
Elk Pond PA-2
Elk Pond—lake KY-4
Elk Pond—lake NY-2
Elk Pond Branch—stream VA-3
Elk Pond Creek—stream KY-4
Elk Pond Mtn—summit VA-3
Elk Pool—lake MN-6
**Elkport**—pop pl IA-7
Elk Prairie—area CA-9
Elk Prairie—flat CA-9
Elk Prairie—flat OR-9
Elk Prairie—flat (2) WA-9
Elk Prairie—locale ID-8
Elk Prairie—woods CA-9
Elk Prairie Ch—church IL-6
Elk Prairie Ch—church MO-7
Elk Prairie Sch—school MO-7
Elk Prairie Sch—school OR-9
**Elk Prairie (Township of)**—pop pl IL-6
Elk Prairie Trail—trail CA-9
Elk Ranch—locale AR-4
Elk Ranch—locale (2) CO-8
Elk Ranch Hollow—valley AR-4
**Elk Ranch Park**—pop pl MD-2
Elk Ranch Rsvr—reservoir WY-8
Elk Range CO-8
Elk Range—ridge CA-9
Elk Rapids KS-7
**Elk Rapids**—pop pl MI-6
Elk Rapids Township Hall—hist pl MI-6
**Elk Rapids (Township of)**—pop pl MI-6
Elk Ravine—valley CA-9
Elk Ridge UT-8
Elk Ridge WV-2
Elk Ridge—cliff AZ-5
**Elkridge**—pop pl MD-2
**Elk Ridge**—pop pl UT-8
**Elkridge**—pop pl (2) WV-2
Elk Ridge—ridge (3) CA-9
Elk Ridge—ridge (2) CO-8
Elk Ridge—ridge (3) ID-8
Elk Ridge—ridge KY-4
Elk Ridge—ridge MD-2
Elk Ridge—ridge (5) MT-8
Elk Ridge—ridge (4) NC-3
Elk Ridge—ridge OR-9
Elk Ridge—ridge TN-4
Elk Ridge—ridge UT-8
Elk Ridge—ridge VA-3
Elk Ridge—ridge WA-9
Elk Ridge—ridge (4) WY-8
Elk Ridge Cem—cemetery LA-4
Elkridge Cem—cemetery PA-2
Elk Ridge Cem—cemetery (2) TN-4
Elk Ridge Ch—church KY-4
**Elkridge (Elk Ridge)**—pop pl MD-2
Elkridge-Harford Hunt Club—other MD-2
Elkridge Hunt Club—other MD-2
**Elkridge Junction**—pop pl WV-2
Elk Ridge Presbyterian Ch (historical)—church TN-4
Elk Ridge Rsvr—reservoir MT-8
Elk Ridge Sch—school TN-4
Elk Ridge Sch (historical)—school TN-4
Elkridge Site—hist pl MD-2
Elk Ridge South (CCD)—cens area TN-4
Elk Ridge South Division—civil TN-4
Elk Ridge Spring—spring MT-8
Elk Ridge Villa IL-6
Elk Riffle—rapids KY-4
Elk River CO-8
Elk River IA-7
Elk River MI-6
Elk River MN-6
Elk River PA-2
Elk River—locale PA-2
**Elk River**—pop pl CA-9
**Elk River**—pop pl CO-8
**Elk River**—pop pl ID-8
**Elk River**—pop pl MN-6
Elk River—stream AL-4
Elk River—stream CA-9
Elk River—stream CO-8
Elk River—stream (2) KS-7
Elk River—stream MD-2
Elk River—stream MI-6
Elk River—stream MN-6
Elk River—stream MO-7
Elk River—stream MT-8
Elk River—stream NC-3
Elk River—stream OK-5
Elk River—stream OR-9
Elk River—stream (2) TN-4
Elk River—stream WA-9
Elk River—stream WV-2
Elk River—stream WI-6
Elk River Archeol District—hist pl KS-7
Elk River Baptist Church TN-4
Elk River Basin—basin MT-8
Elk River Ch—church (2) TN-4
Elk River Ch—church WV-2
Elk River Corners—locale CA-9
Elk River Country Club—other MN-6
Elk River Dam—dam TN-4
Elk River East Township—civil MO-7
Elk River Fish Hatchery—other AL-4
Elk River Junction—locale IA-7
Elk River Junction—locale WV-2
Elk River Lake TN-4
Elk River Lodge State Park—park AL-4
Elk River Lookout Tower—locale WI-6
Elk River Memorial Gardens—cemetery AL-4
Elk River Mills Bridge—bridge AL-4
Elk River Mills Post Office (historical)—building AL-4
Elk River Post Office (historical)—building TN-4
Elk River Public Hunting Area—park WV-2
Elk River Reservoir TN-4
Elk River Sch—school CA-9
Elk River Scout Camp—locale CA-9
Elk River Shaft Mine (underground)—mine AL-4
Elk River Shoals AL-4
Elk River Shoals Canal (historical)—canal AL-4
Elk River Shoals (inundated)—bar AL-4
Elk River Township—fmr MCD IA-7
Elk River (Township of)—fmr MCD MO-7
Elk River (Township of)—other MN-6
Elk River View—locale AL-4
Elk River West Township—civil MO-7
**Elk Rock**—pop pl OR-9
Elk Rock—summit PA-2
Elk Rock—summit WA-9
Elk Rock Island—island OR-9
Elk Rock Lookout—locale WA-9
Elk Rock Run—stream PA-2
Elk Rsvr—reservoir CO-8
Elk Rsvr—reservoir ID-8
Elk Run IA-7
Elk Run PA-2
Elk Run—locale VA-3
**Elkrun**—pop pl VA-3
Elk Run—stream (2) IN-6
Elk Run—stream (4) IA-7
Elk Run—stream NE-7
Elk Run—stream (9) OH-6
Elk Run—stream (7) PA-2
Elk Run—stream (6) VA-3
Elk Run—stream (6) WV-2
Elk Run—stream WI-6
Elkrun Cem—cemetery OH-6
Elk Run Cem—cemetery PA-2
Elk Run Cem—cemetery VA-3
Elk Run Ch—church PA-2
Elk Run Ch—church (2) VA-3
Elk Run Creek—stream WY-8
**Elk Run Heights**—pop pl IA-7
Elk Run Heights Park—park IA-7
Elk Run Junction PA-2
Elk Run Junction—locale PA-2
**Elk Run Junction**—pop pl WV-2
Elk Run Post Office (historical)—building PA-2
**Elkrun (Township of)**—pop pl OH-6
**Elks**—pop pl LA-4
Elks Athletic Club—hist pl KY-4
Elks Bay—bay MN-6
Elks Bldg—hist pl AZ-5
Elks Bldg—hist pl CA-9
Elks Bldg—hist pl (2) WA-9
Elks Bldg and Theater—hist pl AZ-5
Elks Branch—stream IL-6
Elks Camp—locale NY-2
Elk Sch—school KY-4
Elk Sch—school VA-3
Elk Sch (abandoned)—school PA-2
Elks Club—hist pl AR-4
Elks Club—hist pl OH-6
Elks Club—hist pl WV-2
Elks Club Camp—locale NC-3
Elks Club Lake—reservoir OK-5
Elks Club Lodge #501—hist pl MO-7
Elks Country Club—other IL-6
Elks Country Club—other (5) IN-6
Elks Country Club—other MI-6
Elks Country Club—other MT-8
Elks Country Club—other OK-5
Elks Country Club—other PA-2
Elks Country Club—other WI-6
Elks Golf and Country Club—other WA-9
Elks Golf Club—locale PA-2
Elk Shoal—locale NC-3
Elk Shoal Cem—cemetery NC-3
Elk Shoal Creek NC-3
Elk Shoal Creek—stream (2) NC-3
Elk Shoals Camp—locale NC-3
Elk Shoals Ch—church NC-3
Elk Shoals Creek—stream NC-3
**Elk Shores (subdivision)**—pop pl AL-4
Elks Hosp—hospital AZ-5
Elk- Silver—locale NM-5
Elk Sink Spring—spring UT-8
Elks Knoll—summit UT-8
Elks Lake—reservoir CA-9
Elks Lake—reservoir MS-4
Elks Lodge—hist pl OH-6
Elks Lodge Bldg—hist pl MI-6
Elks Lodge Bldg—hist pl NM-5
Elks Lodge Bldg—hist pl OK-5
Elk's Lodge BPOE No. 2—hist pl PA-2
Elk's Lodge No. 468—hist pl AZ-5
Elk Slough—stream CA-9
Elks Memorial Park—park NY-2
Elks Park—park AZ-5
Elks Park—park MI-6
Elks Park—park (2) ND-7
Elks Point NV-8
**Elks Point**—pop pl NV-8
Elk Spring UT-8
Elk Spring—spring (3) AZ-5
Elk Spring—spring CA-9
Elk Spring—spring (3) ID-8
Elk Spring—spring KY-4
Elk Spring—spring NV-8
Elk Spring—spring NM-5
Elk Spring—spring (6) OR-9
Elk Spring—spring (4) UT-8
Elk Spring—spring WA-9
Elk Spring—spring WY-8
Elk Spring Campground—locale ID-8
Elk Spring Cem—cemetery KY-4
Elk Spring Cienega—flat AZ-5
Elk Spring Creek—stream KY-4
Elk Springs ID-8
**Elk Springs**—pop pl CO-8
**Elk Springs**—pop pl MO-7
Elk Springs—spring CO-8
Elk Springs—spring MT-8
Elk Springs—spring NM-5
Elk Springs Creek—stream ID-8
Elk Springs Creek—stream WY-8
Elk Springs Draw—valley AZ-5
Elk Springs Draw—valley CO-8
Elk Springs Ridge—ridge CO-8
Elk Spring Valley—valley KY-4
Elk Spring Valley Ch—church KY-4
Elk Spur—ridge VA-3
Elk Spur Branch—stream VA-3
Elk Spur Ch—church NC-3
Elk Spur Ch—church VA-3
Elks Retreat—locale CA-9
Elks-Rogers Hotel—hist pl IA-7
Elks Run—stream WV-2
Elk State For—forest PA-2
Elk State Park—park PA-2
Elks Temple—hist pl ID-8
Elks Temple—hist pl OR-9
Elks Temple Bldg—hist pl MI-6
**Elks Terrace**—pop pl NJ-2
Elk Summit—gap ID-8
Elk Summit—locale ID-8
Elk Summit—summit ID-8
Elksville (historical)—locale MS-4
Elk Swamp Creek—stream MT-8
Elks Well—well AZ-5
Elk Tank—reservoir (11) AZ-5
Elk Terrace NJ-2
Elkton—locale CO-8
Elkton—locale NC-3
**Elkton**—pop pl CO-8
**Elkton**—pop pl FL-3
**Elkton**—pop pl IL-6
**Elkton**—pop pl IA-7
**Elkton**—pop pl KY-4
**Elkton**—pop pl MD-2
**Elkton**—pop pl MI-6
**Elkton**—pop pl MN-6
**Elkton**—pop pl MO-7
**Elkton**—pop pl OH-6
**Elkton**—pop pl OR-9
**Elkton**—pop pl SD-7
**Elkton**—pop pl TN-4
**Elkton**—pop pl VA-3
Elkton Airfield—airport OR-9
Elkton Armory—hist pl MD-2
Elkton Baptist Ch—church TN-4
Elkton (CCD)—cens area KY-4
Elkton (CCD)—cens area TN-4
Elkton Cem—cemetery KY-4
Elkton Cem—cemetery MN-6
Elkton Cem—cemetery OR-9
Elkton Cem—cemetery TN-4
Elkton Ch—church MI-6
Elkton Ch—church NC-3
Elkton City Hall—building TN-4
Elkton Cumberland Presbyterian Ch—church TN-4
Elkton Division—civil TN-4
Elkton Drain—canal MI-6
Elkton-Drain (CCD)—cens area OR-9
Elkton Elem Sch—school TN-4
Elkton Fair Drain—canal MI-6
Elk Tongue Creek—stream WY-8
**Elkton Heights**—pop pl MD-2
**Elktonia**—pop pl MD-2
Elkton Landing—locale MD-2
Elkton Marsh NC-3
Elkton Mine—mine CO-8
Elkton-Pigeon-Bay Port HS—school MI-6
Elkton Post Office—building TN-4
Elkton Road Baptist Church AL-4
Elkton Road Ch—church AL-4
Elkton Rsvr—reservoir MD-2
Elkton Sch—school MO-7
Elkton Spring—spring VA-3
Elkton Swamp—stream NC-3
**Elkton Township**—pop pl SD-7
**Elkton (Township of)**—pop pl MN-6
Elkton United Methodist Ch—church TN-4
Elk Tooth—pillar CO-8
**Elk (Town of)**—pop pl WI-6
Elk Township KS-7
Elk Township—civil KS-7
Elk Township—civil SD-7
Elk Township—fmr MCD (3) IA-7
**Elk Township**—pop pl (2) KS-7
**Elk Township**—pop pl MO-7
**Elk Township**—pop pl NE-7
**Elk Township**—pop pl ND-7
Elk (Township Name For Elk City)—other PA-2
Elk (Township of)—fmr MCD (3) NC-3
**Elk (Township of)**—pop pl IL-6
**Elk (Township of)**—pop pl (2) MI-6
**Elk (Township of)**—pop pl MN-6
**Elk (Township of)**—pop pl NJ-2
**Elk (Township of)**—pop pl (2) OH-6
**Elk (Township of)**—pop pl (4) PA-2
Elk Trace Branch—stream (2) WV-2
Elk Trace Cem—cemetery WV-2
Elk Track Lakes—lake ID-8
Elk Trail Sch—school OR-9
Elk Trick Tank—reservoir AZ-5
Elk Twomile Creek—stream WV-2
Elkugu Bay—bay AK-9
Elkugu Island—island AK-9
Elk Vale Cem—cemetery SD-7
Elk Valley—basin CA-9
Elk Valley—basin UT-8
**Elk Valley**—pop pl NC-3
**Elk Valley**—pop pl TN-4
Elk Valley—valley (4) CA-9
Elk Valley—valley MO-7

Elk Valley—valley OR-9
Elk Valley—valley TN-4
Elk Valley (CCD)—cens area TN-4
Elk Valley Ch (historical)—church (2) TN-4
Elk Valley Creek—stream OR-9
Elk Valley Ditch—canal CO-8
Elk Valley Division—civil TN-4
Elk Valley Elem Sch—school KS-7
Elk Valley Elem Sch—school TN-4
Elk Valley First Baptist Ch—church TN-4
Elk Valley Golf Course—locale PA-2
Elk Valley Guard Station—locale UT-8
Elk Valley HS—school KS-7
Elk Valley Post Office (historical)—building TN-4
Elk Valley Sch—school CA-9
Elkview—locale PA-2
**Elkview**—pop pl WV-2
Elkview Country Club—other PA-2
Elkview Sch—school PA-2
Elkville MS-4
**Elkville**—pop pl IL-6
**Elkville**—pop pl NC-3
Elkville Cem—cemetery IL-6
Elkville Rsvr—reservoir IL-6
Elk Wallow—basin OR-9
Elk Wallow Campground—locale CO-8
Elk Wallow Creek—stream NC-3
Elk Wallow Creek—stream OR-9
Elk Wallow Gap—gap NC-3
Elkwallow Gap—gap VA-3
Elk Wallow Knob—summit NC-3
Elkwallow Knob—summit NC-3
Elk Wallows—basin OR-9
Elkwallow Shelter—locale VA-3
Elk Wallow Spring—spring (4) OR-9
Elk Wallows Rsvr—reservoir CO-8
Elk Wallow Well—well ID-8
Elkwater—locale WV-2
Elkwater Ch—church WV-2
Elkwater Fork—stream WV-2
Elkwood—hist pl KY-4
**Elkwood**—pop pl AL-4
**Elkwood**—pop pl VA-3
Elkwood Cem—cemetery MN-6
Elkwood Cem—cemetery ND-7
Elkwood Ch—church (2) AL-4
**Elkwood Estates**—pop pl MD-2
Elkwood Post Office (historical)—building AL-4
Elkwood Sch (historical)—school AL-4
Ell, The—rapids TN-4
Ella—island FM-9
Ella—locale KY-4
Ella—locale OR-9
Ella—locale TX-5
**Ella**—pop pl PA-2
**Ella**—pop pl WV-2
**Ella**—pop pl WI-6
Ella, Bayou—stream LA-4
Ella, Lake—lake (3) FL-3
Ella, Lake—lake MI-6
Ella Bay—bay AK-9
Ella Beach Ditch—canal OH-6
**Ellabell**—pop pl GA-3
Ellabell Ch—church GA-3
Ellabelle (RR name for Ellabell)—other GA-3
**Ellabell (RR name Ellabelle)**—pop pl GA-3
**El Laberinto**—pop pl PR-3
Ella Brown Ditch—canal IN-6
Ella Butte—summit OR-9
Ella Creek OR-9
Ella Creek—stream (2) AK-9
Ella Creek—stream OR-9
Ella Darling School MS-4
Elladene Tank—reservoir NM-5
Ella Ditch—canal CO-8
Ella Fohs Camp Pond—reservoir CT-1
**Ella Gap**—pop pl GA-3
Ella Gardner Corners—locale PA-2
Ella G Clark Sch—school NJ-2
**El Lago**—pop pl TX-5
Ella Green Church MS-4
Ella Grove Ch—church GA-3
Ella Gulch—stream OR-9
El Lagunito Palo Quemador—summit NM-5
Ella Hall Lake—lake MN-6
Ella Island—island GA-3
Ella Lake—lake AK-9
Ella Lake—lake FL-3
Ella Lake—lake (2) MN-6
Ella Lee Lake—reservoir MI-6
Ella Mae Well—well AZ-5
**Ellamar**—pop pl AK-9
Ellamar Mtn—summit AK-9
Ella May Canyon—valley NV-8
Ella Mine—mine ID-8
Ella Mine Group—mine CA-9
**Ellamore**—pop pl (2) WV-2
Ella Mtn—summit NV-8
Ellandale Ch—church MS-4
Ella Park Cem—cemetery GA-3
Ella Park Ch—church GA-3
Ella Pasture—flat TX-5
Ella Point—cape AK-9
**Ellard**—pop pl MS-4
**Ellards**—pop pl AL-4
Ellard Sch (historical)—school AL-4
El Laredo Windmill—locale TX-5
Ella Rsvr—reservoir CO-8
Ella Sch—school CA-9
Ellas Draw—valley AZ-5
Ellas-McKay House—hist pl AR-4
Ella Smillie Sch—school GA-3
Ella Spring—spring NV-8
Elluville MS-4
Ellaville—locale (2) FL-3
Ellaville—locale OK-5
**Ellaville**—pop pl GA-3
**Ellaville**—pop pl MD-2
Ellaville North (CCD)—cens area GA-3
Ellaville South (CCD)—cens area GA-3
Ella Wash—stream CA-9
Ellawhite Cem—cemetery AL-4
Ellawhite Church AL-4
Ellawhite Elem Sch (historical)—school AL-4
Ellawhite Post Office (historical)—building AL-4
**Ellawhite (subdivision)**—pop pl AL-4
Ella Windmill—locale TX-5
Ell Branch—stream NC-3
Ell Chapel (historical)—church MS-4
Ell Cove—bay AK-9
Ell Creek—stream IN-6
Elle—island MP-9
Elleb MP-9
Elleber Knob—summit WV-2
Elleber Ridge—ridge WV-2
Elleber Run—stream WV-2
Elleb Island MP-9
Elleb Passage MP-9
Elledge Branch—stream AL-4
Elledge Cem—cemetery AL-4
Elledge Draw—valley CO-8
Elledge Holley Cem—cemetery IL-6
Elledge Hollow TN-4
Elledge Hollow Branch TN-4
Elledge Lake—reservoir AL-4
Elledge Lake Dam—dam AL-4
Elledge Mill Ditch—canal NM-5
Elledge Peak—summit CA-9
Elledge Sewage Treatment Plant—locale NC-3
Ellejoy—locale TN-4
Ellejoy Baptist Ch—church TN-4
Ellejoy Cem—cemetery TN-4
Ellejoy Church TN-4
Ellejoy Creek—stream TN-4
Ellejoy Post Office (historical)—building TN-4
Ellejoy Valley—valley TN-4
Ellemachun Mountain WA-9
Ellemeham Draw—valley WA-9
Ellemeham Mtn—summit WA-9
Ellen KS-7
Ellen—locale KY-4
Ellen—locale TX-5
Ellen, Lake—lake AK-9
Ellen, Lake—lake CA-9
Ellen, Lake—lake (4) FL-3
Ellen, Lake—lake MI-6
Ellen, Lake—lake MN-6
Ellen, Lake—lake WA-9
Ellen, Lake—lake WI-6
Ellen, Lake—reservoir TN-4
Ellen, Martha, Auditorium—hist pl NE-7
Ellen, Mount—summit CA-9
Ellen, Mount—summit UT-8
Ellen, Mount—summit VT-1
Ellenberger Park—park IN-6
Ellenberger Sch (historical)—school PA-2
**Ellenboro**—pop pl NC-3
**Ellenboro**—pop pl WV-2
**Ellenboro**—pop pl WI-6
Ellenboro Elem Sch—school NC-3
Ellenboro Hill—summit MD-2
Ellenboro Hill Run—stream MD-2
**Ellenboro (Town of)**—pop pl WI-6
Ellen Branch—stream MS-4
Ellen Brook—stream ME-1
**Ellenburg**—pop pl NY-2
Ellenburg Branch—stream SC-3
**Ellenburg Center**—pop pl NY-2
Ellenburg Creek—stream OR-9
**Ellenburg Depot**—pop pl NY-2
**Ellenburg Depot (Ellenburg)**—pop pl NY-2
Ellenburger Hills—summit TX-5
Ellenburger Oil Field—oilfield TX-5
Ellenburg Mtn—summit AL-4
Ellenburg Mtn—summit NY-2
**Ellenburg (Town of)**—pop pl NY-2
Ellen Cem—cemetery LA-4
Ellen Cem—cemetery NC-3
Ellen Chapel—church PA-2
Ellen Cockran Hollow—valley AR-4
Ellen Creek—stream OR-9
Ellen Creek—stream WA-9
Ellendale—locale VA-3
**Ellendale**—pop pl DE-2
**Ellendale**—pop pl LA-4
**Ellendale**—pop pl MN-6
**Ellendale**—pop pl MO-7
**Ellendale**—pop pl NC-3
**Ellendale**—pop pl ND-7
**Ellendale**—pop pl OR-9
**Ellendale**—pop pl TN-4
Ellendale Country Club—locale ND-7
Ellendale Creek—stream OR-9
Ellendale Elem Sch—school NC-3
Ellendale Ford—locale VA-3
Ellendale Forge—locale PA-2
Ellendale Forge Radio Tower—tower PA-2
Ellendale Municipal Airp—airport ND-7
Ellendale Park—park IN-6
Ellendale Sch—school ND-7
Ellendale State For—forest DE-2
Ellendale Swamp—swamp DE-2
**Ellendale Township**—pop pl ND-7
Ellendale Township Dam—dam ND-7
Ellendale (Township of)—fmr MCD NC-3
Ellendale Water Supply Dam—dam ND-7
Ellender Ferry—locale LA-4
Ellen Ditch—canal CO-8
Ellen D. Mtn—summit NV-8
Ellen Furnace Site (38CK68)—hist pl SC-3
Ellen Gowan—locale PA-2
Ellen Grove Ch—church NC-3
Ellen Island VA-3
Ellen Lake NY-2
Ellen Lake—lake (3) MN-6
Ellen Lake—lake WI-6
Ellen Meyers Elementary School TN-4
Ellenorah—locale MO-7
Ellen Peak, Mount—summit UT-8
Ellen Run—stream PA-2
ELLEN RUTH (launch)—hist pl MN-6
Ellen Sands WA-9
Ellen Sands—bar WA-9
**Ellensburg**—pop pl WA-9
Ellensburg (CCD)—cens area WA-9
Ellensburg Hist Dist—hist pl WA-9
Ellensburg Pass—gap WA-9
Ellensburg Power Canal—canal WA-9
Ellen Sch—school CA-9
Ellen's Isle WA-9
Ellensmere, Lake—lake OH-6
Ellen Spring—spring CA-9
Ellen Tadlock Pond Dam—dam MS-4
**Ellenton**—pop pl FL-3
**Ellenton**—pop pl GA-3
**Ellenton**—pop pl PA-2
Ellenton—uninc pl SC-3
**Ellenton Junction**—pop pl FL-3
**Ellenville**—pop pl NY-2
Ellenville Central Sch—school NY-2
Ellen Wilson, Lake—lake MT-8
**Ellenwood**—pop pl GA-3
Ellenwood Brook MA-1
Ellenwood Cem—cemetery KS-7
Ellenwood Hill—summit VT-1
Ellenwood House—hist pl OH-6
Ellen Wood Ridge—ridge ME-1
Ellenwood Sch—school OH-6
El-Leo Lake—reservoir TX-5
El Leon—summit CA-9
El Leoncito Tank—reservoir TX-5
Ellep MP-9
Ellep—island MP-9
Ellep Passage MP-9
Ellep Passage—channel MP-9
Eller NC-3
Eller—island MP-9
**Eller**—pop pl KY-4
Eller Apartments—hist pl NM-5
**Ellerbe**—pop pl NC-3
Ellerbe Bay—basin SC-3
Ellerbe Cem—cemetery NC-3
Ellerbe Ch—church LA-4
**Ellerbeck**—pop pl UT-8
Ellerbe Creek—stream NC-3
**Ellerbee**—pop pl FL-3
Ellerbe Elem Sch—school NC-3
Ellerbee No 1, Lake—reservoir GA-3
Ellerbee No 2, Lake—reservoir GA-3
**Ellerbees Mill**—pop pl SC-3
Ellerbeetown—locale GA-3
**Ellerbe Grove**—pop pl NC-3
Ellerbe JHS—school NC-3
Ellerbe's Mill—hist pl SC-3
Ellerbe Springs Hotel—hist pl NC-3
Ellerbracht Cem—cemetery TX-5
Eller Branch—stream IA-7
Eller Branch—stream NC-3
Eller Bridge—bridge IN-6
Eller Cem—cemetery NC-3
Eller Cove—valley (3) NC-3
Eller Ditch—canal IN-6
Eller Gap—gap GA-3
Eller Hollow—valley WV-2
Ellerhorst Sch—school CA-9
Eller-Hosford House—hist pl IN-6
Eller Island MP-9
Ellerman, Arthur C., House—hist pl SD-7
Ellermeyer Gulch—valley CO-8
**Eller (Midway)**—pop pl NC-3
Eller Mill Creek—stream NC-3
Eller Pass MP-9
Eller Passage—channel MP-9
Eller Place—locale NM-5
Ellerport Airp—airport WA-9
Eller Run—stream IN-6
Eller Sch—school NC-3
Ellers Chapel—church AL-4
Ellers Lake—reservoir GA-3
Ellerslie—hist pl MD-2
Ellerslie—hist pl NC-3
Ellerslie—hist pl VA-3
Ellerslie—locale FL-3
**Ellerslie**—pop pl GA-3
**Ellerslie**—pop pl LA-4
**Ellerslie**—pop pl MD-2
**Ellerslie**—pop pl PA-2
Ellerslie Plantation—locale LA-4
Eller Slough—stream CA-9
**Ellerson**—pop pl VA-3
Ellerson Mill—locale VA-3
Ellerson-Mortenson Cem—cemetery MN-6
Ellers Sch—school NY-2
Ellerth—locale MN-6
Ellerton—locale MD-2
**Ellerton**—pop pl OH-6
Ellerville—locale OK-5
Eller Well—locale NM-5
**Ellery**—pop pl IL-6
Ellery Brockel Dam—dam SD-7
**Ellery Center**—pop pl NY-2
Ellery Creek—stream CA-9
Ellery (Election Precinct)—fmr MCD IL-6
Ellery Lake—lake CA-9
Ellery Lake Campground—locale CA-9
**Ellery (Town of)**—pop pl NY-2
Ellesic Trail PA-2
**Elleslie**—pop pl MS-4
Ellet OH-6
**Ellet**—pop pl OH-6
Ellet Park—park OH-6
Ellets Crossing VA-3
Elletson Sch—school MN-6
Ellets Run WV-2
Ellett VA-3
Ellett—locale VA-3
**Ellett**—pop pl VA-3
Ellett Creek VA-3
Elletts Crossing—locale VA-3
Ellett Station VA-3
**Ellettsville**—pop pl IN-6
Ellettville IN-6
Ellevalas IN-6
Elley Villa—hist pl KY-4
Elli MP-9
Elliber Run—stream WV-2
**Elliber Spring**—pop pl WV-2
Elliber Spring—spring WV-2
Ellice, Point—cape WA-9
Ellick Creek—stream OR-9
Ellick Lake—lake MS-4
Ellick Slough WA-9
Elllcott MD-2
Ellicott NY-2
Ellicott—locale CA-9
**Ellicott**—pop pl CO-8
**Ellicott**—pop pl NY-2
Ellicott, Andrew, House—hist pl PA-2
Ellicott Bridge—bridge CA-9
Ellicott Circle—locale DC-2
**Ellicott City**—pop pl MD-2
Ellicott City Hist Dist—hist pl MD-2
Ellicott City JHS—school MD-2
Ellicott City Station—hist pl MD-2
Ellicott Consolidated Sch—school CO-8
Ellicott Creek—stream NY-2
Ellicott Creek Park—park NY-2
Ellicotte Creek NY-2
Ellicott Key FL-3
Ellicott Mtn—summit NC-3
Ellicott (P.O.)—uninc pl NY-2
Ellicott Rock—hist pl SC-3
Ellicott Rock—pillar GA-3
Ellicott Rock Trail—trail NC-3
Ellicott Run—stream PA-2
Ellicotts Mills MD-2
Ellicott's Mills Hist Dist—hist pl MD-2
Ellicotts Mound—summit GA-3
Ellicott Stone—hist pl AL-4
Ellicottsville NY-2
**Ellicott (Town of)**—pop pl NY-2
Ellicott Trail—trail CA-9
**Ellicottville**—pop pl NY-2
Ellicottville Town Hall—hist pl NY-2
**Ellicottville (Town of)**—pop pl NY-2
Ellidge Point—cape TN-4
Ellie Lake—lake ID-8
Ellies Canyon—valley UT-8
Ellie Spring—spring OR-9
**Elliff**—pop pl MO-7
**Elliger Park**—pop pl PA-2
Elligo, Lake—lake VT-1
Elligo Pond VT-1
Elligo-Sigo River VT-1
Ellijay—locale GA-3
**Ellijay**—pop pl GA-3
**Ellijay**—pop pl NC-3
Ellijay (CCD)—cens area GA-3
Ellijay Ch—church NC-3
Ellijay Creek—stream NC-3
Ellijay River—stream GA-3
**Ellijay (sta.)**—pop pl GA-3
Ellijay (Township of)—fmr MCD NC-3
Ellijoy Creek TN-4
Elliker Basin—basin UT-8
Ellin FM-9
**Ellinger**—pop pl TX-5
Ellinger Cove—bay VA-3
Ellingson Coulee—valley WI-6
Ellingson Farm—hist pl TX-5
Ellingson Farm District—hist pl ND-7
**Ellingson (historical)**—pop pl SD-7
Ellingson Lake—lake (2) MN-6
Ellingson Lumber Company Airstrip—airport OR-9
**Ellingson Mill**—pop pl OR-9
Ellingson Sch—school SD-7
Ellingson Spring (historical)—spring SD-7
Ellingson Valley WI-6
Ellingson Warehouse—hist pl AZ-5
Ellings Spring—spring CA-9
Ellingswood Corner ME-1
**Ellingswood Corner**—pop pl ME-1
Ellington MN-6
Ellington—locale KY-4
Ellington—locale LA-4
Ellington—locale MI-6
**Ellington**—pop pl CT-1
**Ellington**—pop pl MO-7
**Ellington**—pop pl NY-2
Ellington, Douglas, House—hist pl NC-3
Ellington, Edward Kennedy "Duke", House—hist pl NY-2
Ellington AFB—military TX-5
Ellington Agriculture Center—locale TN-4
Ellington Airp—airport CT-1
Ellington Airp—airport TN-4
Ellington Bear Creek—stream KY-4
Ellington Branch—stream GA-3
Ellington Branch—stream NC-3
Ellington Canal—canal LA-4
Ellington Cem—cemetery AR-4
Ellington Cem—cemetery GA-3
Ellington Cem—cemetery IA-7
Ellington Cem—cemetery (2) KY-4
Ellington Cem—cemetery MI-6
Ellington Cem—cemetery (2) MS-4
Ellington Cem—cemetery WI-6
Ellington Center CT-1
Ellington Ch—church IL-6
Ellington Creek—stream CO-8
Ellington Creek—stream MS-4
Ellington Creek—stream MO-7
Ellington Creek—stream TX-5
Ellington-Ellis Farm—hist pl NC-3
Ellington Gulch—valley CA-9
**Ellington Heights (subdivision)**—pop pl NC-3
Ellington (historical P.O.)—locale IA-7
Ellington Hollow—valley (2) MO-7
Ellington Memorial Cem—cemetery MO-7
Ellington Prairie Cem—cemetery IA-7
Ellington-Redus Cemetery MS-4
Ellington Rsvr—reservoir CO-8
Ellington Run—stream KY-4
Ellington Sch—school (2) CA-9
Ellington Sch—school IL-6
Ellingtons Creek NC-3
**Ellington (Town of)**—pop pl CT-1
**Ellington (Town of)**—pop pl NY-2
**Ellington (Town of)**—pop pl WI-6
Ellington Township—fmr MCD (2) IA-7
**Ellington (Township of)**—pop pl IL-6
**Ellington (Township of)**—pop pl MI-6
**Ellington (Township of)**—pop pl MN-6
**Elling Township**—pop pl ND-7
Ellingwood Corner—locale ME-1
Ellingwood Falls—falls NH-1
Ellingwood Mtn—summit ME-1
Ellingwood Peak CO-8
Ellingwood Point—summit CO-8
Ellingwood Ridge—ridge CO-8
Ellingwood Rock—Island ME-1
Ellingwoods Corner ME-1
Ellinor—locale KS-7
Ellinor, Mount—summit WA-9
**Ellinor Village**—pop pl FL-3
Ellinor Village Shop Ctr—locale FL-3
**Ellinwood**—pop pl KS-7
Ellinwood Airport KS-7
Ellinwood Brook—stream MA-1
Ellinwood Cem—cemetery MA-1
Ellinwood Cem—cemetery WI-6
Ellinwood Ch—church KS-7
Ellinwood Elem Sch—school KS-7
Ellinwood HS—school KS-7
Ellinwood JHS—school KS-7
Ellinwood Municipal Airp—airport KS-7
Ellinwood Ranch—locale AZ-5
Elliot MD-2
Elliot MS-4
Elliot OH-6
Elliot—locale WA-9
**Elliot**—pop pl IA-7
**Elliot**—pop pl OH-6
Elliot, Dr. F. C., House—hist pl WI-6
Elliot, Gen. Simon, House—hist pl MA-1
Elliota Cem—cemetery MN-6
**Elliot Acres (subdivision)**—pop pl NC-3
Elliot Bay—bay ID-8
Elliot-Bester House—hist pl MD-2
Elliot Branch OR-9
Elliot Branch—stream MI-6
Elliot Branch—stream (2) MO-7
Elliot Branch—stream (2) TN-4
Elliot Branch—stream (2) VA-3
Elliot Brook—stream ME-1
Elliot Canyon OR-9
Elliot Canyon—valley NM-5
Elliot Cem TN-4
Elliot Cem—cemetery GA-3
Elliot Cem—cemetery KY-4
Elliot Cem—cemetery ME-1
Elliot Cem—cemetery (2) MO-7
Elliot Cem—cemetery NY-2
Elliot Cem—cemetery NC-3
Elliot Cem—cemetery OH-6
Elliot Cem—cemetery SC-3
Elliot Cem—cemetery TN-4
Elliot Cem—cemetery TX-5
Elliot Cemeteries—cemetery TN-4
Elliot Ch—church MS-4
Elliot Cove—harbor CA-9
Elliot Creek CA-9
Elliot Creek IL-6
Elliot Creek IA-7
Elliot Creek SC-3
Elliot Creek TX-5
Elliot Creek—stream CA-9
Elliot Creek—stream CO-8
Elliot Creek—stream IN-6
Elliot Creek—stream MI-6
Elliot Creek—stream MT-8
Elliot Creek—stream NC-3
Elliot Creek—stream (3) OR-9
Elliot Creek—stream TX-5
Elliot Creek Ridge—ridge OR-9
Elliot Creek Sch (historical)—school AL-4
Elliot Ditch—canal OR-9
Elliot Draw—valley MT-8
Elliot Duncan Elem Sch—school NC-3
**Elliot Estates Subdivision**—pop pl UT-8
Elliot Ferry (historical)—crossing TN-4
Elliot Ford—locale MO-7
Elliot-Harris-Miner House—hist pl RI-1
Elliot Hill—summit CA-9
Elliot Hill—summit NY-2
Elliot Hollow—valley MO-7
Elliot Hosp—hospital NH-1
Elliot House—hist pl OH-6
Elliot Key FL-3
Elliot Lake—lake MS-4
Elliot Lake—lake TX-5
Elliot Landing TN-4
Elliot Landing—locale ME-1
Elliot Mansion—hist pl NH-1
Elliot Marsh—swamp WA-9
Elliot Mills PA-2
Elliot Mine—mine CA-9
Elliot Mine—mine OR-9
Elliot Mtn—summit NC-3
Elliot Park—park IL-6
Elliot Park—park MN-6
Elliot Point WA-9
Elliot Point—cape TN-4
Elliot Point—cape WA-9
Elliot Pond Dam—dam MS-4
Elliot Ranch NV-8
Elliot Ranch—locale CA-9
Elliot Ranch—locale SD-7
Elliot Ridge OR-9
Elliot Ridge—ridge SD-7
Elliot Run—stream OH-6
Elliot Run—stream PA-2
**Elliots Addition (subdivision)**—pop pl DE-2
Elliotsburg PA-2
Elliots Cabin—locale CA-9
Elliot Sch—school ME-1
Elliot Sch—school MN-6
Elliot Sch—school WA-9
Elliots Chapel—church TN-4
Elliot School (historical)—locale MO-7
Elliots Creek AL-4
Elliot's Creek VA-3
Elliots Creek—stream NJ-2
Elliots Creek Work Center—building AL-4
Elliots Hill Ch—church VA-3
Elliots Landing (historical)—locale TN-4
Elliot Slough—stream OR-9
Elliots Mill PA-2
Elliots Mine (underground)—mine AL-4
Elliots Pond—reservoir VA-3
Elliot Spring OR-9
Elliot Spring—spring CA-9
Elliot Spring—spring MT-8
Elliot Spring—spring (2) OR-9
Elliot Spring House—locale CA-9
Elliots Resort—locale MT-8
Elliots Sch (abandoned)—school PA-2
Elliots Shoals—bar TN-4
Elliot Street Shopping Plaza—locale MA-1
**Elliotsville**—pop pl AL-4
Ellforsville Cemetery AL-4
Elliott OH-6
Elliott—locale MS-4
Elliott—locale MO-7
Elliott—locale OK-5
**Elliott**—pop pl AR-4
**Elliott**—pop pl IL-6
**Elliott**—pop pl IN-6
**Elliott**—pop pl IA-7
**Elliott**—pop pl MD-2
**Elliott**—pop pl NC-3
**Elliott**—pop pl ND-7
**Elliott**—pop pl PA-2
**Elliott**—pop pl (2) SC-3
**Elliott**—pop pl (2) TX-5
Elliott, Charles D., House—hist pl MA-1
Elliott, Dr. Samuel MacKenzie, House—hist pl NY-2
Elliott, Edward C., House—hist pl WI-6
Elliott, John W., House—hist pl AL-4
Elliott, Lake—reservoir SC-3
Elliott, Luther, House—hist pl MA-1
Elliott, Mount—summit AZ-5
Elliott, Mount—summit UT-8
Elliott, S. B., State Park Day Use District—hist pl PA-2
Elliott, S. B., State Park Family Cabin District—hist pl PA-2
Elliott, S. T., House—hist pl AZ-5
Elliott And Stoddard Halls, Miami Univ—hist pl OH-6
**Elliott Ave**—pop pl WA-9
Elliott Baptist Ch—church MS-4
Elliott Bay—bay WA-9
Elliott Branch—stream AL-4
Elliott Branch—stream (3) KY-4
Elliott Branch—stream NC-3
Elliott Bridge (historical)—locale NC-3
Elliott Canyon—valley AZ-5
Elliott Canyon—valley OR-9
Elliott-Carnegie Library—hist pl NC-3
Elliott Cem—cemetery (4) AL-4
Elliott Cem—cemetery AR-4
Elliott Cem—cemetery CA-9
Elliott Cem—cemetery FL-3
Elliott Cem—cemetery GA-3
Elliott Cem—cemetery (2) IL-6
Elliott Cem—cemetery (3) IN-6
Elliott Cem—cemetery (2) KY-4
Elliott Cem—cemetery (4) MS-4
Elliott Cem—cemetery MO-7
Elliott Cem—cemetery NC-3
Elliott Cem—cemetery (3) OH-6
Elliott Cem—cemetery PA-2
Elliott Cem—cemetery (7) TN-4
Elliott Cem—cemetery (2) TX-5
Elliott Cem—cemetery VA-3
Elliott Cem—cemetery WY-8
Elliott Cemetery Run—stream IN-6
Elliott Ch—church NC-3
Elliott Ch of Christ—church MS-4
Elliott Community TX-5
Elliott Corner—locale CA-9
**Elliott (County)**—pop pl KY-4
Elliott Cove Branch—stream NC-3
Elliott Creek AL-4
Elliott Creek MI-6
Elliott Creek MT-8
Elliott Creek OR-9
Elliott Creek—stream (2) AK-9
Elliott Creek—stream (2) CA-9
Elliott Creek—stream (2) CO-8
Elliott Creek—stream ID-8
Elliott Creek—stream (2) IL-6
Elliott Creek—stream (2) IA-7
Elliott Creek—stream MD-2
Elliott Creek—stream MN-6
Elliott Creek—stream MS-4
Elliott Creek—stream (2) OR-9
Elliott Creek—stream (2) TX-5
Elliott Creek—stream VA-3
Elliott Creek—stream (2) WA-9
Elliott Creek Camp—locale WA-9
Elliott Creek Ridge OR-9
Elliott Creek Rsvr—reservoir TX-5
Elliott Crossroads—locale AL-4
Elliott Crossroads—locale OH-6
Elliott Cut—channel SC-3
Elliott Ditch—canal IN-6
Elliott-Donaldson House—hist pl MS-4
Elliott Drain—canal MI-6
Elliott Falls—flat ME-1
Elliott Grove Cem—cemetery MO-7
Elliott Gulch—valley CO-8
Elliott Gut—gut ME-1
Elliott Hall, Sturges Library, And Merrick Hall—hist pl OH-6
Elliott Heights—uninc pl DE-2
Elliott Heights—uninc pl PA-2
Elliott High Ranch—locale NV-8
Elliott Hill—summit CA-9
Elliott Hill—summit GA-3
Elliott Hill—summit (2) MA-1
Elliott (historical)—locale MS-4
Elliott Hollow—valley AL-4
Elliott Hollow—valley AR-4
Elliott Hollow—valley TN-4
Elliott House—hist pl AZ-5
Elliott House—hist pl (2) AR-4
Elliott House—hist pl OH-6
Elliott House—hist pl SC-3
Elliott Island—island AL-4
Elliott Island—island AK-9
Elliott Island—island MD-2
Elliott Island Marsh—swamp MD-2
Elliott Key—island FL-3
Elliott Key Harbor—harbor FL-3
Elliott Key Park Harbor Light 2—locale FL-3
Elliott Key Visitor Center—locale FL-3
Elliott Knob—summit KY-4
Elliott Knob—summit VA-3
Elliott Knob Trail—trail VA-3
Elliott Lake AL-4
Elliott Lake—lake MI-6
Elliott Lake—lake MN-6
Elliott Lake—reservoir AL-4
Elliott Lake—reservoir SC-3
Elliott Lake Dam—dam (2) AL-4
Elliott Lake Dam—dam MS-4
Elliott Lick Branch—stream KY-4
Elliott Littman Oil Field—oilfield TX-5
Elliott Littman Oil Field—other NM-5
Elliott-Meek House—hist pl AR-4
Elliott Mesa—summit UT-8
Elliott Millpond—reservoir SC-3
Elliott Mills PA-2
Elliott Mtn—summit CO-8
Elliott Mtn—summit ME-1
Elliott Park—park AZ-5
Elliott Park—park NY-2
Elliott Park—park OK-5
Elliott Park—park TX-5
Elliott Place—hist pl KY-4
Elliott Plot—cemetery TX-5
Elliott Point WA-9
Elliott Point—cape MN-6

Elliott Point—*cape* WA-9
Elliott Point—*summit* WY-8
Elliott Point Sch—*school* FL-3
Elliott Pond Branch—*stream* DE-2
Elliott Prairie—*flat* OR-9
**Elliott Prairie**—*pop pl* OR-9
Elliott Prairie Sch—*school* OR-9
Elliot Trail—*trail* WA-9
Elliott Ranch—*locale* (2) MT-8
Elliott Ranch—*locale* NV-8
Elliott Ranch—*locale* NM-5
Elliott Reservation—*park* AL-4
Elliott Ridge—*ridge* OR-9
Elliott Ridge—*ridge* WV-2
Elliott Rsvr—*reservoir* TX-5
Elliott Run—*stream* IN-6
Elliott Run—*stream* (2) OH-6
Elliott Run—*stream* PA-2
Elliott Run—*stream* WV-2
*Elliotts* MD-2
*Elliotts* MS-4
Elliotts—*locale* CT-1
Elliott's, Robert, Wholesale Grocery—*hist pl* MO-7
**Elliotts Bluff**—*pop pl* GA-3
Elliotts Brook—*stream* CT-1
**Elliottsburg**—*pop pl* PA-2
Elliott Sch—*school* CA-9
Elliott Sch—*school* KY-4
Elliott Sch—*school* (3) MI-6
Elliott Sch—*school* MN-6
Elliott Sch—*school* OK-5
Elliott Sch—*school* SD-7
Elliott Sch—*school* TN-4
Elliott Sch—*school* TX-5
Elliott Sch (historical)—*school* (2) MO-7
Elliott Sch (historical)—*school* PA-2
*Elliott School* IN-6
*Elliott's creek* VA-3
Elliotts Creek—*stream* AL-4
Elliotts Creek—*stream* VA-3
*Elliotts Crossing* AL-4
Elliott Seminary (historical)—*school* TN-4
Elliotts (historical)—*locale* AL-4
*Elliotts Island* MD-2
*Elliotts Key* FL-3
*Elliott's Knob* VA-3
Elliotts Lake—*reservoir* (2) AL-4
Elliotts Lake Dam—*dam* AL-4
Elliott Slough—*lake* AR-4
Elliott Slough—*stream* OR-9
Elliott Slough—*stream* WA-9
**Elliotts Mill**—*pop pl* PA-2
**Elliotts Mills**—*pop pl* PA-2
Elliotts Mills (historical)—*locale* MS-4
*Elliotts Mtn* ME-1
Elliotts Neck—*cape* VA-3
**Elliottson**—*pop pl* PA-2
Elliott Spring—*spring* AZ-5
Elliott Spring—*spring* OR-9
Elliott Spring—*spring* SD-7
Elliott Springs—*spring* OR-9
Elliott Springs Run—*stream* VA-3
Elliott Square Playground—*park* KY-4
Elliotts Quarters—*locale* AL-4
*Elliotts Run* PA-2
Elliotts Run—*stream* (2) PA-2
Elliotts Run—*stream* WV-2
Elliotts Sch—*school* CT-1
Elliotts Store (historical)—*locale* MS-4
Elliott State For—*forest* OR-9
*Elliott Station* MS-4
**Elliottstown**—*pop pl* IL-6
Elliott Street Hist Dist—*hist pl* IL-6
Elliott Street Sch—*school* NJ-2
**Elliottsville**—*pop pl* PA-2
Elliottsville Ch—*church* AL-4
Elliottsville (Plantation of)—*unorg* ME-1
Elliotts Vineyard (historical)—*locale* AL-4
*Elliotts Vineyard P.O.* AL-4
Elliott Tank—*reservoir* AZ-5
Elliott Tank—*reservoir* NM-5
Elliott (Town of)—*other* NY-2
**Elliott Township**—*pop pl* ND-7
**Elliott Township**—*pop pl* SD-7
Elliott Village Site—*hist pl* KS-7
**Elliottville**—*pop pl* KY-4
**Elliottville**—*pop pl* OH-6
Elliottville Lower Mill—*hist pl* CT-1
Elliott Well—*well* OR-9
Elliott Well—*well* TX-5
Elliott Windmill—*locale* NM-5
Elliott Yard—*locale* AL-4
*Elliottville* IN-6
*Elliot Well* OR-9
Ellipse, The—*park* DC-2
*Ellis* NJ-2
Ellis—*locale* AL-4
Ellis—*locale* CA-9
Ellis—*locale* (2) IL-6
Ellis—*locale* IA-7
Ellis—*locale* LA-4
Ellis—*locale* MN-6
Ellis—*locale* OH-6
Ellis—*locale* SD-7
Ellis—*locale* WV-2
**Ellis**—*pop pl* AR-4
**Ellis**—*pop pl* FL-3
**Ellis**—*pop pl* ID-8
**Ellis**—*pop pl* IL-6
**Ellis**—*pop pl* (3) IN-6
**Ellis**—*pop pl* KS-7
**Ellis**—*pop pl* ME-1
**Ellis**—*pop pl* MA-1
**Ellis**—*pop pl* (2) MO-7
**Ellis**—*pop pl* (2) NE-7
**Ellis**—*pop pl* NY-2
**Ellis**—*pop pl* WI-6
Ellis—*post sta* TX-5
Ellis, Asa, House—*hist pl* MA-1
Ellis, Dr. Billie V., House—*hist pl* TX-5
Ellis, Dr. J. W., House—*hist pl* ME-1
Ellis, E. G., House—*hist pl* MT-8
Ellis, Evan F., Farmhouse—*hist pl* IA-7
Ellis, Isaac Newton, House—*hist pl* MS-4
Ellis, James, Stone Tavern—*hist pl* KY-4
Ellis, Lake—*lake* MA-1
Ellis, Moses, House—*hist pl* MA-1
Ellis, Mount—*summit* (2) MT-8
Ellis, Samuel, House—*hist pl* KY-4
Ellis, William C., and Sons Ironworks and Machine Shop—*hist pl* TN-4
Ellis Apiary Campground—*locale* CA-9
Ellis Auditorium—*building* TN-4
Ellis Ave Hist Dist—*hist pl* SC-3
Ellis Ave Plaza Shop Ctr—*locale* MS-4
Ellis Bar—*bar* MS-4
Ellis Basin—*basin* MT-8
Ellis Bay—*bay* MD-2
Ellis Bay—*swamp* FL-3
Ellis Bend—*bend* TN-4
Ellis Bog—*swamp* ME-1
Ellis Bog—*swamp* MA-1
**Ellisboro**—*pop pl* NC-3
Ellisboro Ch—*church* NC-3
*Ellis Branch* SC-3
Ellis Branch—*stream* (2) AR-4
Ellis Branch—*stream* FL-3
Ellis Branch—*stream* (2) KY-4
Ellis Branch—*stream* MO-7
Ellis Branch—*stream* (5) TN-4
Ellis Branch—*stream* (3) TX-5
Ellis Branch—*stream* (2) WV-2
Ellis Branch—*stream* WI-6
Ellis Brett Pond—*lake* MA-1
Ellis Bridge (historical)—*bridge* TN-4
*Ellis Brook* MA-1
Ellis Brook—*stream* CT-1
Ellis Brook—*stream* ME-1
Ellis Brook—*stream* MA-1
Ellis Brook—*stream* (2) NY-2
Ellis Brook—*stream* (2) VT-1
*Ellisburg* NJ-2
Ellisburg—*locale* KY-4
**Ellisburg**—*pop pl* NJ-2
**Ellisburg**—*pop pl* NY-2
**Ellisburg**—*pop pl* PA-2
Ellisburg Creek—*stream* PA-2
**Ellisburg (Town of)**—*pop pl* NY-2
Ellis Butt—*summit* TN-4
Ellis Camp—*locale* TX-5
Ellis Camp Branch—*stream* WV-2
*Ellis Canyon* UT-8
Ellis Canyon—*valley* CA-9
Ellis Canyon—*valley* MT-8
Ellis Canyon—*valley* (2) NM-5
Ellis Canyon—*valley* OR-9
Ellis Canyon—*valley* UT-8
Ellis Cave—*cave* (2) AL-4
Ellis Cem—*cemetery* AL-4
Ellis Cem—*cemetery* AR-4
Ellis Cem—*cemetery* GA-3
Ellis Cem—*cemetery* IL-6
Ellis Cem—*cemetery* (2) IN-6
Ellis Cem—*cemetery* IA-7
Ellis Cem—*cemetery* (4) KY-4
Ellis Cem—*cemetery* LA-4
Ellis Cem—*cemetery* MI-6
Ellis Cem—*cemetery* (6) MO-7
Ellis Cem—*cemetery* (2) NE-7
Ellis Cem—*cemetery* (4) NY-2
Ellis Cem—*cemetery* (3) NC-3
Ellis Cem—*cemetery* (4) OH-6
Ellis Cem—*cemetery* OK-5
Ellis Cem—*cemetery* (5) TN-4
Ellis Cem—*cemetery* (4) TX-5
Ellis Cem—*cemetery* (3) WV-2
Ellis Ch—*church* IN-6
Ellis Ch—*church* IA-7
Ellis Ch—*church* NC-3
Ellis Chapel—*church* AR-4
Ellis Chapel—*church* (2) GA-3
Ellis Chapel—*church* (2) NC-3
Ellis Chapel—*church* OH-6
Ellis Chapel—*church* OK-5
**Ellis Chapel**—*pop pl* AR-4
Ellis Chapel Cem—*cemetery* GA-3
Ellis Chapel Cem—*cemetery* TX-5
Ellis Chapel Sch (historical)—*school* MS-4
**Ellis Church**—*pop pl* FL-3
Ellis Cliffs—*cliff* MS-4
Ellis Cliffs—*locale* MS-4
Ellis Cliffs Oil Field—*oilfield* MS-4
Ellis Corner—*locale* (2) ME-1
Ellis Corner—*locale* SD-7
Ellis Corners—*locale* MI-6
Ellis Corners—*locale* PA-2
Ellis Coulee—*valley* MT-8
Ellis County—*civil* KS-7
**Ellis (County)**—*pop pl* OK-5
**Ellis (County)**—*pop pl* TX-5
Ellis County Courthouse—*hist pl* OK-5
Ellis County Courthouse Hist Dist—*hist pl* TX-5
Ellis County State Wildlife Mngmt Area—*park* OK-5
Ellis Cove—*bay* NC-3
Ellis Cove—*bay* WA-9
*Ellis Creek* GA-3
*Ellis Creek* IN-6
*Ellis Creek* MI-6
*Ellis Creek* MT-8
Ellis Creek—*stream* (2) AL-4
Ellis Creek—*stream* AK-9
Ellis Creek—*stream* (2) CA-9
Ellis Creek—*stream* FL-3
Ellis Creek—*stream* GA-3
Ellis Creek—*stream* (3) ID-8
Ellis Creek—*stream* MI-6
Ellis Creek—*stream* (2) MS-4
Ellis Creek—*stream* (3) MT-8
Ellis Creek—*stream* NY-2
Ellis Creek—*stream* (2) NC-3
Ellis Creek—*stream* (2) OR-9
Ellis Creek—*stream* (2) PA-2
Ellis Creek—*stream* SC-3
Ellis Creek—*stream* (2) TN-4
Ellis Creek—*stream* (2) VA-3
Ellis Creek—*stream* (3) WA-9
Ellis Creek—*stream* (2) WV-2
Ellis Creek Ch—*church* NC-3
Ellis Creek Ch—*church* VA-3
Ellis Crossroads—*locale* AL-4
**Ellis Crossroads**—*pop pl* NC-3
**Ellisdale**—*pop pl* NJ-2
Ellis Dam—*dam* CT-1
Ellis Dam—*dam* OH-6
Ellis Ditch—*canal* IN-6
Ellis Ditch—*canal* OR-9
Ellis Drain—*canal* (2) MI-6
*Ellis Draw* TX-5
Ellis Draw—*valley* WY-8
*Ellise Canyon* UT-8
Ellis Elem Sch—*school* KS-7
Ellis Falls—*falls* ME-1
Ellis Ferry Access Point—*locale* AL-4
Ellis Ferry (historical)—*locale* AL-4
Ellis Ferry (historical)—*locale* NC-3
Ellis Ferry (historical)—*locale* TN-4
Ellis Fire Tank—*reservoir* CA-9
Ellis Flat—*flat* CA-9
Ellis Flats—*locale* RI-1
Ellis Fly-In—*airport* IN-6
*Ellisford* WA-9
**Ellisford (Ellisforde)**—*pop pl* WA-9
Ellis Ford (historical)—*locale* TN-4
Ellis Forest Service Station—*locale* OR-9
*Ellis Fork* VA-3
Ellis Fork—*locale* VA-3
Ellis Fork—*stream* KY-4
Ellis Fork—*stream* (2) WV-2
Ellis Gap—*gap* (2) TN-4
Ellis Gap Branch—*stream* TN-4
**Ellis Grove**—*pop pl* IL-6
Ellis Grove Cem—*cemetery* OH-6
Ellis Grove Ch—*church* TN-4
Ellis Grove Ch—*church* WV-2
*Ellisgrove (corporate name Ellis Grove)* IL-6
Ellis Grove (Election Precinct)—*fmr MCD* IL-6
Ellis Grove Sch—*school* TN-4
Ellis Gulch—*valley* ID-8
Ellis Gulch—*valley* MT-8
Ellis Gulf—*valley* AL-4
Ellis-Hampton House—*hist pl* OR-9
Ellis Hill—*summit* ME-1
Ellis (historical)—*locale* AL-4
**Ellis Hollow**—*pop pl* NY-2
Ellis Hollow—*valley* AR-4
Ellis Hollow—*valley* MO-7
Ellis Hollow—*valley* PA-2
Ellis Hollow—*valley* (6) TN-4
Ellis Hollow—*valley* WV-2
Ellis Hollow Cem—*cemetery* NY-2
Ellis Hosp—*hospital* NY-2
Ellis House—*building* MA-1
Ellis HS—*school* KS-7
Ellisic Trail—*trail* PA-2
Ellis II Site—*hist pl* TX-5
Ellis Indian Site (historical)—*locale* SD-7
*Ellis Island* AL-4
*Ellis Island* CT-1
Ellis Island—*island* MO-7
Ellis Island—*island* NJ-2
Ellis Isle Shop Ctr—*locale* MS-4
Ellis JHS—*school* IL-6
Ellis JHS—*school* OH-6
Ellis Kelley Lake—*reservoir* TX-5
Ellis Knob—*summit* GA-3
Ellis Knob—*summit* KY-4
Ellis Knob—*summit* WV-2
Ellis Knoll—*summit* NC-3
*Ellis Lake* FL-3
*Ellis Lake* MN-6
*Ellis Lake* NC-3
*Ellis Lake* WY-8
Ellis Lake—*lake* (2) CA-9
Ellis Lake—*lake* (2) FL-3
Ellis Lake—*lake* ID-8
Ellis Lake—*lake* (2) MI-6
Ellis Lake—*lake* MN-6
Ellis Lake—*lake* NY-2
Ellis Lake—*reservoir* AL-4
Ellis Lake—*reservoir* GA-3
Ellis Lake—*reservoir* OK-5
Ellis Lake Dam—*dam* AL-4
Ellis Lake Dam—*dam* IN-6
Ellis Lake Dam—*dam* (4) MS-4
Ellis Landing Field—*airport* KS-7
Ellis Landing (historical)—*locale* AL-4
Ellis Lateral—*canal* AZ-5
Ellis Lick—*stream* KY-4
Ellislie Plantation (historical)—*locale* MS-4
Ellis Lookout—*locale* WA-9
*Ellis Meadow* CA-9
Ellis Meadow—*flat* CA-9
Ellis Mill—*locale* TN-4
Ellis Mill Creek—*stream* AL-4
Ellis Mills—*locale* TN-4
Ellis Mills Cem—*cemetery* TN-4
Ellis Mills Ch—*church* TN-4
Ellis Mills (historical)—*locale* MA-1
Ellis Mills Post Office (historical)—*building* TN-4
*Ellis Mills Upper Reservoir* MA-1
Ellis Mine—*mine* KY-4
Ellis Mine Hollow—*valley* VT-1
Ellis Mounds—*hist pl* OH-6
Ellis Mountain—*ridge* AR-4
Ellis Mtn—*summit* CA-9
Ellis Mtn—*summit* (2) MT-8
Ellis Mtn—*summit* (3) NY-2
Ellis Mtn—*summit* NC-3
Ellis Mtn—*summit* TN-4
Ellis Mtn—*summit* WA-9
Ellis-Nance Cem—*cemetery* TX-5
Ellis Oil Field—*oilfield* TX-5
*Ellison* WV-2
Ellison—*locale* AR-4
Ellison—*locale* NV-8
Ellison—*locale* WV-2
**Ellison**—*pop pl* IN-6
Ellison, Mount—*summit* AK-9
**Ellison Acres**—*pop pl* FL-3
Ellison Airp—*airport* IN-6
Ellison Bar—*bar* IL-6
Ellison Bay—*bay* WI-6
**Ellison Bay**—*pop pl* WI-6
Ellison Bend—*bend* TN-4
Ellison Bluff—*cliff* WI-6
Ellison Bluff Park—*park* WI-6
*Ellison Branch* TX-5
Ellison Branch—*stream* (2) NC-3
Ellison Branch—*stream* (3) TX-5
Ellison Branch—*stream* WV-2
Ellison Brook—*stream* NH-1
Ellison Cabin Two hundred eighty three Trail—*trail* AZ-5
Ellison Cem—*cemetery* (2) AL-4
Ellison Cem—*cemetery* AR-4
Ellison Cem—*cemetery* GA-3
Ellison Cem—*cemetery* IA-7
Ellison Cem—*cemetery* KS-7
Ellison Cem—*cemetery* MS-4
Ellison Cem—*cemetery* (2) MO-7
Ellison Cem—*cemetery* NY-2
Ellison Cem—*cemetery* (5) TN-4
Ellison Cem—*cemetery* TX-5
Ellison Cem—*cemetery* (2) WV-2
Ellison Ch—*church* MS-4
Ellison Ch—*church* WV-2
*Ellison Creek* AZ-5
*Ellison Creek* GA-3
*Ellison Creek* ME-1
Ellison Creek—*stream* (2) AZ-5
Ellison Creek—*stream* CA-9
Ellison Creek—*stream* GA-3
Ellison Creek—*stream* ID-8
Ellison Creek—*stream* IL-6
Ellison Creek—*stream* KY-4
Ellison Creek—*stream* MS-4
Ellison Creek—*stream* NV-8
Ellison Creek—*stream* NC-3
Ellison Creek—*stream* ND-7
Ellison Creek—*stream* OH-6
Ellison Creek Diversion Ditch—*canal* IL-6
Ellison Creek Rsvr—*reservoir* TX-5
Ellison Creek Tank—*reservoir* AZ-5
Ellison Creek Watershed Structure 3 Dam—*dam* MS-4
Ellison Creek Watershed Structure 4 Dam—*dam* MS-4
Ellison Creek Watershed Structure 7 Dam—*dam* MS-4
Ellison Creek Watershed 1 Dam—*dam* MS-4
Ellison Crossroads—*locale* AL-4
Ellison Ditch—*canal* IN-6
Ellison Ditch—*canal* MT-8
Ellison Draw—*valley* WY-8
Ellison Gap—*gap* NC-3
Ellison Gulch—*valley* CO-8
Ellison Hill—*summit* AR-4
Ellison Hollow—*valley* (2) TN-4
Ellison Hollow—*valley* WV-2
Ellison HS—*school* MA-1
Ellison Knob—*summit* TN-4
Ellison Lake—*lake* AR-4
Ellison Lake—*lake* MI-6
Ellison Lake—*lake* MS-4
Ellison Lake—*lake* WI-6
Ellison Lake—*reservoir* GA-3
Ellison Mill (historical)—*locale* TN-4
Ellison Mine—*mine* AZ-5
Ellison Mtn—*summit* CO-8
Ellison Mtn—*summit* NC-3
Ellison No. 2 Site (34SQ85)—*hist pl* OK-5
Ellison Park—*park* NY-2
Ellison Park—*park* WI-6
Ellison Pass—*gap* WY-8
Ellison Place—*locale* AZ-5
**Ellison Place Subdivision**—*pop pl* UT-8
Ellison Ranch—*locale* AZ-5
Ellison Ranch—*locale* MT-8
Ellison Ranch—*locale* NV-8
Ellison Ranger Station—*locale* NV-8
Ellison Ridge—*locale* WV-2
**Ellison Ridge**—*pop pl* MS-4
Ellison Ridge—*ridge* KY-4
Ellison Ridge—*ridge* (2) WV-2
*Ellison Ridge Baptist Church* MS-4
Ellison Ridge Cem—*cemetery* MS-4
Ellison Ridge Ch—*church* MS-4
Ellison Rsvr—*reservoir* NV-8
Ellison Run—*stream* WV-2
Ellison Sch—*school* IL-6
Ellison Sch—*school* SC-3
Ellison Sch (abandoned)—*school* MO-7
*Ellison's Creek* ME-1
Ellisons Landing—*locale* GA-3
Ellison Slough—*stream* WA-9
Ellisons Mill (historical)—*locale* AL-4
Ellison Spring—*spring* (2) NV-8
Ellison Spring—*spring* TN-4
Ellison Spring—*spring* TX-5
Ellison Spring Branch—*stream* TX-5
Ellison Spring Cem—*cemetery* TX-5
Ellison Spring Number 2—*spring* NV-8
Ellisons Store—*locale* TN-4
**Ellison Subdivision**—*pop pl* UT-8
**Ellison (Township of)**—*pop pl* IL-6
**Ellisonville**—*pop pl* OH-6
Ellisonville Creek—*stream* OH-6
Ellison West Ditch—*canal* IN-6
**Ellison Woods Subdivision**—*pop pl* UT-8
Ellis Park—*park* FL-3
Ellis Park—*park* (2) IL-6
Ellis Park—*park* (2) IA-7
Ellis Park—*park* KY-4
Ellis Park—*park* NC-3
Ellis Park—*park* (2) OH-6
Ellis Park—*park* TN-4
**Ellis Park Subdivision**—*pop pl* UT-8
Ellis Peak—*summit* CA-9
Ellis Peak—*summit* MT-8
Ellis Pens—*locale* TX-5
Ellis Place—*locale* CA-9
**Ellis Plantation**—*pop pl* GA-3
Ellis Point—*cape* DE-2
Ellis Point—*cape* NJ-2
Ellis Point—*cape* NY-2
*Ellis Pond* MA-1
Ellis Pond—*lake* DE-2
Ellis Pond—*lake* (2) FL-3
Ellis Pond—*lake* (4) ME-1
Ellis Pond—*lake* (2) MA-1
Ellis Pond—*lake* NY-2
**Ellis Pond**—*pop pl* ME-1
Ellis Pond—*reservoir* (2) AL-4
Ellis Pond—*reservoir* GA-3
Ellis Pond—*reservoir* ME-1
Ellis Pond—*reservoir* MA-1
Ellis Pond—*reservoir* NC-3
Ellis Pond Dam—*dam* (2) MA-1
Ellis Pond Dam—*dam* NC-3
Ellis Ponds—*lake* MA-1
Ellis Pond Slough—*swamp* TX-5
**Ellisport**—*pop pl* WA-9
Ellisport Bay—*bay* ID-8
Ellis-Porter Park—*park* MO-7
Ellis Post Office (historical)—*building* TN-4
Ellis Prairie—*locale* MO-7
Ellis Prairie Cem—*cemetery* TX-5
Ellis Prairie Chapel—*church* MO-7
Ellis Prairie Sch (historical)—*school* MO-7
Ellis Push Mine (underground)—*mine* AL-4
Ellis Ranch—*locale* (2) AZ-5
Ellis Ranch—*locale* NM-5
Ellis Ranch—*locale* SD-7
Ellis Ranch—*locale* (3) TX-5
Ellis Ranch—*locale* (2) WY-8
*Ellis' Reef* CT-1
Ellis Reef—*bar* CT-1
Ellis Ridge—*ridge* AR-4
Ellis Ridge—*ridge* TN-4
Ellis Ridge Sch—*school* IL-6
*Ellis River* MA-1
Ellis River—*stream* ME-1
Ellis River—*stream* NH-1
Ellis Rsvr—*reservoir* NH-1
Ellis Run—*stream* (3) OH-6
Ellis Run—*stream* VA-3
Ellis Run—*stream* WV-2
Ellis Sch—*hist pl* WI-6
Ellis Sch—*school* (3) CA-9
Ellis Sch—*school* CO-8
Ellis Sch—*school* (2) GA-3
Ellis Sch—*school* (2) IL-6
Ellis Sch—*school* LA-4
Ellis Sch—*school* (2) MA-1
Ellis Sch—*school* (3) MI-6
Ellis Sch—*school* MS-4
Ellis Sch—*school* MO-7
Ellis Sch—*school* OH-6
Ellis Sch—*school* (2) PA-2
Ellis Sch—*school* TN-4
Ellis Sch—*school* TX-5
Ellis Sch—*school* UT-8
Ellis Sch—*school* VA-3
Ellis Sch—*school* WI-6
Ellis Sch for Girls (abandoned)—*school* PA-2
Ellis Sch (historical)—*school* (2) AL-4
Ellis Sch (historical)—*school* MO-7
Ellis Sch (historical)—*school* TN-4
Ellis School (Abandoned)—*locale* CA-9
Ellis School (historical)—*locale* MO-7
Ellis-Shackelford House—*hist pl* AZ-5
Ellis Simon Lake—*lake* NC-3
*Ellis Slough* CA-9
Ellis Slough—*gut* WA-9
Ellis-Smeathere Ferry—*locale* IN-6
Ellis Spring—*spring* AR-4
Ellis Spring—*spring* CA-9
Ellis Spring—*spring* GA-3
Ellis Spring—*spring* ID-8
Ellis Spring—*spring* SD-7
Ellis Spring—*spring* (2) TN-4
*Ellis Station* MA-1
Ellis Store—*locale* NC-3
**Ellis Subdivision**—*pop pl* MS-4
Ellis Tabernacle—*church* LA-4
Ellis Tank—*reservoir* NM-5
Elliston—*hist pl* CA-9
Elliston—*locale* KY-4
**Elliston**—*pop pl* IN-6
**Elliston**—*pop pl* KY-4
**Elliston**—*pop pl* MT-8
**Elliston**—*pop pl* OH-6
**Elliston**—*pop pl* VA-3
Elliston, Joseph, House—*hist pl* TN-4
Elliston Creek—*stream* IN-6
Elliston Creek—*stream* MT-8
Elliston-Lafayette—*CDP* VA-3
Elliston Lafayette Sch—*school* VA-3
Elliston Mine (underground)—*mine* TN-4
Elliston Sch—*school* MS-4
Elliston Sch—*school* MO-7
**Elliston Township**—*pop pl* SD-7
**Ellistown**—*pop pl* MS-4
**Ellistown**—*pop pl* NY-2
Ellistown Cem—*cemetery* MS-4
Ellistown Post Office (historical)—*building* MS-4
Ellis Township—*fmr MCD* IA-7
**Ellis Township**—*pop pl* KS-7
Ellis (Township of)—*fmr MCD* AR-4
**Ellis (Township of)**—*pop pl* MI-6
Ellis Trail—*trail* CO-8
Ellis Trail—*trail* VA-3
Ellisville—*locale* AL-4
Ellisville—*locale* FL-3
Ellisville—*locale* KY-4
Ellisville—*locale* NH-1
Ellisville—*locale* OH-6
Ellisville—*locale* WA-9
**Ellisville**—*pop pl* (2) AL-4
**Ellisville**—*pop pl* IL-6
**Ellisville**—*pop pl* IN-6
**Ellisville**—*pop pl* MA-1
**Ellisville**—*pop pl* MS-4
**Ellisville**—*pop pl* MO-7
**Ellisville**—*pop pl* WI-6
Ellisville Baptist Ch—*church* MS-4
Ellisville Cem—*cemetery* MS-4
Ellisville Ch—*church* AL-4
Ellisville Ch—*church* AR-4
Ellisville Ch—*church* VA-3
Ellisville Community Bldg—*building* ND-7
*Ellisville Depot* MS-4
Ellisville Elem Sch—*school* MS-4
Ellisville First United Methodist Ch—*church* MS-4
Ellisville Harbor—*cove* MA-1
Ellisville Junction—*locale* MS-4
Ellisville Junction Sch (historical)—*school* MS-4
Ellisville Lagoon Dam—*dam* MS-4
Ellisville Landing—*locale* MA-1
Ellisville Municipal Hosp—*hospital* MS-4
Ellisville Post Office (historical)—*building* SD-7
Ellisville State Sch—*school* MS-4
Ellisville State School Lake Dam—*dam* MS-4
Ellisville Station—*locale* IL-6
**Ellisville Township**—*pop pl* ND-7
**Ellisville Township**—*pop pl* SD-7
**Ellisville (Township of)**—*pop pl* IL-6
Ellis Well—*well* NM-5
Ellis Wharf—*locale* DE-2
Ellis Wiltbank Dam—*dam* AZ-5
Ellis Wiltbank Rsvr—*reservoir* AZ-5
Ellis Windmill—*locale* TX-5
Ellis Wise Dam—*dam* AL-4
Ellis Wise Lake—*reservoir* AL-4
Ellis Woods Cem—*cemetery* PA-2
Ellsworth Cem—*cemetery* MI-6
Ellis Wright Canyon—*valley* NM-5
**Ellithorpe**—*pop pl* CT-1
Ellithorpe Run—*stream* PA-2
Ellixson, William, House—*hist pl* NC-3
Elljean Ch—*church* SC-3
*Ell Lake* WI-6
Ell Lake—*lake* MI-6
Ell Lake—*lake* MN-6
Ell Lake—*lake* (2) NE-7
Ell Lake—*lake* WA-9
Ell Lake—*lake* WI-6
**El Llanito**—*pop pl* NM-5
El Llanito Blanco—*area* NM-5
**El Llano**—*pop pl* (2) NM-5
El Llano de Abeyta—*area* NM-5
El Llano Ditch—*canal* NM-5
El Llano Tank—*reservoir* TX-5
El Llano Windmill—*locale* TX-5
Ell Long Ranch—*locale* TX-5
**Ellmaker**—*pop pl* IA-7
Ellmaker State Park—*park* OR-9
Ellmitch—*locale* KY-4
Ellmore Canyon—*valley* CO-8
Ellmore Canyon—*valley* NM-5
Ellmore Sch—*school* TN-4
El Lobanillo Creek—*stream* TX-5
El Lobo—*summit* CA-9
Ellofson Lake—*lake* WI-6
*Ellomachan Mountain* WA-9
Ellon Ch—*church* TX-5
**Elloree**—*pop pl* SC-3
Elloree (CCD)—*cens area* SC-3
El Loro—*summit* CA-9
Ell Peak—*summit* CA-9
Ell Pond—*lake* MA-1
Ell Pond—*lake* RI-1
**Ellport**—*pop pl* PA-2
Ellport Borough—*civil* PA-2
Ellquist Lake—*lake* MN-6
Ell Ridge—*ridge* NC-3
Ellrod—*uninc pl* PA-2
**Ells**—*pop pl* IA-7
Ellsaesser Pond—*reservoir* KS-7
Ell-Saline Elem Sch—*school* KS-7
Ell-Saline HS—*school* KS-7
**Ellsberry**—*pop pl* ND-7
**Ellsberry**—*pop pl* OH-6
Ellsberry Lake—*lake* IL-6
Ellsborough Ch—*church* MN-6
**Ellsborough (Township of)**—*pop pl* MN-6
Ells Branch—*stream* KY-4
Ells Branch Ch—*church* KY-4
Ells Branch Sch—*school* KY-4
**Ellsburg (Township of)**—*pop pl* MN-6
*Ellsbury* OH-6
Ellsbury Divide—*ridge* WY-8
Ellsbury (historical)—*locale* ND-7
Ellsbury Ranch—*locale* WY-8
**Ellsbury Township**—*pop pl* ND-7
Ell Sch—*school* ME-1
Ells Creek—*stream* ID-8
Ells HS—*school* CA-9
**Ellsinore**—*pop pl* MO-7
Ellson—*locale* MN-6
Ell Springs—*spring* SD-7
Ells Sch—*school* MI-6
Ells Station—*locale* IA-7
**Ellston**—*pop pl* IA-7
**Ellston Township**—*pop pl* SD-7
Ellstrom Lake—*lake* MN-6
Ells Well—*well* NM-5
*Ellsworth* MA-1
Ellsworth—*locale* CT-1
Ellsworth—*locale* IA-7
Ellsworth—*locale* TX-5
**Ellsworth**—*pop pl* IL-6
**Ellsworth**—*pop pl* IN-6
**Ellsworth**—*pop pl* IA-7
**Ellsworth**—*pop pl* KS-7
**Ellsworth**—*pop pl* LA-4
**Ellsworth**—*pop pl* ME-1
**Ellsworth**—*pop pl* MI-6
**Ellsworth**—*pop pl* MN-6
**Ellsworth**—*pop pl* NE-7
**Ellsworth**—*pop pl* NH-1
**Ellsworth**—*pop pl* (2) OH-6
**Ellsworth**—*pop pl* PA-2
**Ellsworth**—*pop pl* WA-9
**Ellsworth**—*pop pl* WI-6
Ellsworth—*uninc pl* VA-3
Ellsworth, Benjamin, House—*hist pl* MN-6
Ellsworth, Col. Elmer E., Monmt and Grave—*hist pl* NY-2
Ellsworth, Horace H., House—*hist pl* CT-1
Ellsworth, Lake—*reservoir* OK-5
Ellsworth, Mount—*summit* MT-8
Ellsworth, Mount—*summit* UT-8
Ellsworth, Oliver, Homestead—*hist pl* CT-1
Ellsworth AFB—*military* SD-7
*Ellsworth Airport* KS-7
Ellsworth Barranca—*valley* CA-9
Ellsworth Borough—*civil* PA-2
Ellsworth Canyon—*valley* NV-8
Ellsworth Cem—*cemetery* AR-4
Ellsworth Cem—*cemetery* IL-6
Ellsworth Cem—*cemetery* IA-7
Ellsworth Cem—*cemetery* MI-6
Ellsworth Cem—*cemetery* OH-6
Ellsworth City Hall—*hist pl* ME-1
Ellsworth Clear Lake Cem—*cemetery* IA-7
Ellsworth College Park—*park* IA-7
Ellsworth Congregational Church—*hist pl* ME-1
Ellsworth Coulee—*valley* MT-8
Ellsworth County—*civil* KS-7
Ellsworth County Dam—*dam* KS-7
*Ellsworth Creek* IA-7
Ellsworth Creek—*stream* CO-8
Ellsworth Creek—*stream* IL-6
Ellsworth Creek—*stream* NC-3
Ellsworth Creek—*stream* (2) WA-9
Ellsworth Cut—*other* AK-9
Ellsworth Elem Sch—*school* KS-7
*Ellsworth Falls* ME-1
**Ellsworth Falls**—*pop pl* ME-1
Ellsworth Glacier—*glacier* AK-9
Ellsworth Hill—*ridge* NH-1
Ellsworth Hill—*summit* CT-1
Ellsworth Hill—*summit* PA-2
Ellsworth Hills—*summit* AZ-5

El Monte Windmill—locale (2) TX-5
Elmont Road Park—park NY-2
Elmont Road Sch—school NY-2
Elmont Sch—school VA-3
Elmont United Methodist Ch—church KS-7
E L Moore Bridge—bridge FL-3
Elmo Pond—lake UT-8
*Elmora* IN-6
*Elmora* PA-2
Elmora—locale PA-2
**Elmora**—pop pl NJ-2
**Elmora**—pop pl PA-2
**Elmora (Bakerton)**—pop pl PA-2
Elmora Ch—church NJ-2
Elmora Sch—school IA-7
Elmora Sch—school NJ-2
Elmora Station—locale NJ-2
*Elmore* OK-5
*Elmore* VT-1
*Elmore* MP-9
Elmore—locale ND-7
Elmore—locale (2) TN-4
Elmore—locale WV-2
**Elmore**—pop pl AL-4
**Elmore**—pop pl (2) IL-6
**Elmore**—pop pl ME-1
**Elmore**—pop pl MN-6
**Elmore**—pop pl NC-3
**Elmore**—pop pl OH-6
**Elmore**—pop pl SD-7
**Elmore**—pop pl WI-6
Elmore, Lake—lake ID-8
Elmore, Lake—lake VT-1
Elmore, Samuel, Cannery—hist pl OR-9
*Elmore and Center Church* AL-4
Elmore Arroyo—stream CO-8
Elmore Bay—bay CA-9
Elmore Bible Chapel—church AL-4
Elmore Branch—stream KY-4
Elmore Branch—stream NC-3
Elmore Branch—stream TN-4
Elmore Branch—stream VT-1
Elmore-Carter House—hist pl KY-4
Elmore (CCD)—cens area AL-4
Elmore Cem—cemetery AL-4
Elmore Cem—cemetery CA-9
Elmore Cem—cemetery KY-4
Elmore Cem—cemetery (2) MO-7
Elmore Cem—cemetery (4) TN-4
Elmore Cem—cemetery VA-3
Elmore Cem—cemetery WV-2
Elmore Cem—cemetery WI-6
Elmore Cem Number One—cemetery TN-4
*Elmore Cem Number Three* TN-4
*Elmore Cem Number Two* TN-4
Elmore Center—locale KS-7
Elmore Center Ch—church AL-4
Elmore Ch—church (2) AL-4
Elmore Ch—church AR-4
*Elmore Ch of Christ* AL-4
**Elmore City**—pop pl OK-5
Elmore City (CCD)—cens area OK-5
Elmore City Cem—cemetery OK-5
**Elmore County**—pop pl AL-4
*Elmore County Area Vocational School* AL-4
Elmore County Courthouse—hist pl ID-8
Elmore County Experimental
Farm—locale AL-4
Elmore County Hosp—hospital AL-4
Elmore County HS—school AL-4
Elmore County Landfill—locale AL-4
Elmore County Training Sch—school AL-4
Elmore County Vocational Sch—school AL-4
Elmore Creek—stream AL-4
Elmore Creek—stream (2) CA-9
Elmore Creek—stream TN-4
Elmore Dam—dam NC-3
**Elmore Desert Ranch**—pop pl CA-9
Elmore Division—civil AL-4
Elmore Hill—summit VT-1
Elmore Houses—hist pl CT-1
Elmore HS—school TX-5
Elmore Lake—reservoir AL-4
Elmore Lake—reservoir NC-3
Elmore Memorial Hosp—hospital ID-8
Elmore Mine—mine WY-8
Elmore Mtn—summit CA-9
Elmore Mtn—summit VT-1
Elmore Park—park KS-7
Elmore Park—park TX-5
**Elmore Park**—pop pl TN-4
Elmore Pond—swamp IN-6
Elmore Pond Brook—stream VT-1
Elmore Pond Dam—dam MS-4
Elmore Sch—school NC-3
Elmore Sch—school WI-6
Elmore Sch (historical)—school TN-4
**Elmores Crossroads**—pop pl NC-3
Elmore State Park—park VT-1
Elmore State Public Shooting Area—park SD-7
Elmore Tank—reservoir NM-5
Elmore Tank Number One—reservoir AZ-5
Elmore Tank Number Two—reservoir AZ-5
Elmore Temporary Sch—school CA-9
**Elmore (Town of)**—pop pl VT-1
**Elmore (Township of)**—pop pl IN-6
**Elmore (Township of)**—pop pl MN-6
Elmo Ridge—ridge MO-7
*El Morillo Banco Number One hundred Thirty-four* TX-5
El Morito Creek—stream TX-5
**El Moro**—pop pl CO-8
El Moro Creek—stream TX-5
Elmoro Sch (historical)—school TN-4
El Morrillo—summit PR-3
*El Morro* IL-6
El Morro—locale NM-5
**El Morro**—pop pl NM-5
*El Morro Bay* CA-9
El Morro Cem—cemetery NM-5
*El Morro Creek* CA-9
El Morro Island—island TX-5
El Morro Mesa—summit NM-5
El Morro Natl Monmt—hist pl NM-5
El Morro Natl Monmt—park NM-5
El Morro Ranch—locale NM-5
*El Morro Rock* CA-9
El Morro Sch—school CA-9
El Morro Theater—hist pl NM-5
Elmo Sch—school MO-7
Elmo Sch—school WI-6
Elmo State Wildlife Mngmt Area—park MN-6
Elmo Tank—reservoir NM-5
Elmot Bar—bar AR-4
Elmot Bar—bar TN-4
**Elmo (Township of)**—pop pl MN-6
Elmoville—locale IL-6
El Movo Crossing—locale TX-5
Elm Park—hist pl MA-1
Elm Park—locale AR-4
Elm Park—locale MN-6
Elm Park—park IL-6
Elm Park—park MA-1
Elm Park—park MI-6
**Elm Park**—pop pl LA-4
**Elm Park**—pop pl NY-2
Elm Park Cem—cemetery MN-6
Elm Park Cem—cemetery OK-5
Elm Park Ch—church (2) LA-4
Elm Park Methodist Ch—church PA-2
Elm Park Sch—school IA-7
Elm Park Sch—school MA-1
Elm Park Sch—school MO-7
Elm Pass—gap TX-5
Elm Place Sch—school IL-6
Elm Point—cape (2) MN-6
Elm Point—cape NY-2
Elm Point—cape OH-6
Elm Point—cape VT-1
**Elm Point**—pop pl MO-7
Elm Point Branch—stream IL-6
Elm Point Cem—cemetery IL-6
*Elm Point Place* (2) MO-7
Elm Point Rec Area—park OK-5
*Elm Pond* RI-1
Elm Pond—lake ME-1
Elm Pond—lake MO-7
Elm Pond—lake NY-2
*Elm Pond Church* MO-7
Elm Pond Mtn—summit ME-1
Elm Pool Creek—stream TX-5
Elm Post Office (historical)—building AL-4
Elm Post Office (historical)—building PA-2
Elm Prong Mill Bayou—stream AR-4
Elm Ranch—locale WY-8
Elm Ridge—ridge NH-1
Elm Ridge—ridge (2) NY-2
Elm Ridge—ridge TX-5
Elm Ridge Cem—cemetery CA-9
Elm Ridge Ch—church MO-7
Elm Ridge Ch—church (2) TX-5
Elm Ridge Memorial Park—cemetery IN-6
Elm Ridge Park—park CT-1
Elm Ridge Sch—school NH-1
Elm Ridge Sch—school TX-5
**Elm Ridge (subdivision)**—pop pl AL-4
*Elm River* IL-6
Elm River—stream IL-6
Elm River—stream MI-6
Elm River—stream (3) ND-7
Elm River—stream SD-7
Elm River Cem—cemetery ND-7
Elm River Ch—church IL-6
Elm River Dam—dam ND-7
Elm River Diversion Drain—canal ND-7
*Elm River Drainage Ditch* IL-6
Elm River Drainage Ditch—canal IL-6
Elm River Lookout Tower—locale MI-6
Elm River Number 1 Dam—dam ND-7
Elm River Number 2 Dam—dam ND-7
Elm River Number 3 Dam—dam ND-7
**Elm River (sta.)**—pop pl MI-6
Elm River Town Hall—building ND-7
**Elm River Township**—pop pl ND-7
**Elm River (Township of)**—pop pl IL-6
**Elm River (Township of)**—pop pl MI-6
Elm Road Elem Sch—school IN-6
Elm Road Sch—school OH-6
Elmrock—locale KY-4
Elm Root Hollow—valley VA-3
Elm Root Slough—stream AR-4
Elm Run—stream IN-6
Elm Run—stream (2) OH-6
Elm Run—stream WV-2
Elms—hist pl ME-1
**Elms**—pop pl ME-1
Elms, The—hist pl AR-4
Elms, The—hist pl MS-4
Elms, The—hist pl NE-7
Elms, The—hist pl RI-1
Elms, The—hist pl VA-3
**Elms, The**—pop pl NY-2
**Elms Acres**—pop pl OH-6
Elm Saint Sch—school VT-1
Elm Sch—school CA-9
Elm Sch—school (4) IL-6
Elm Sch—school MO-7
Elm Sch—school NE-7
Elm Sch—school NH-1
Elm Sch—school (2) OH-6
Elm Sch—school VA-3
Elm Sch—school WI-6
Elm Sch (abandoned)—school PA-2
Elms Coll—school MA-1
Elms Court—hist pl MS-4
Elms Court Plantation (historical)—locale MS-4
Elms Dam—dam OR-9
Elms Ditch—canal OR-9
**Elmsford**—pop pl NY-2
Elmsford Reformed Church and
Cemetery—hist pl NY-2
Elm Shoal Branch—stream KY-4
Elms Hotel—hist pl MO-7
Elms Lake—lake MN-6
Elm Slough—gut (2) LA-4
Elm Slough—stream AR-4
Elm Slough—stream (2) KS-7
Elm Slough—stream LA-4
Elm Slough—stream (5) TX-5
Elm Slue—stream TX-5
**Elmsmere**—pop pl NY-2
**Elm Spring**—pop pl IA-7
Elm Spring—spring (6) MO-7
Elm Spring—spring TX-5
Elm Spring Branch—stream AR-4
Elm Spring Branch—stream (2) MO-7
Elm Spring Cem—cemetery MO-7
Elm Spring Ch—church MO-7
Elm Spring Hollow—valley AR-4
Elm Spring Hollow—valley MO-7
Elm Springs—hist pl TN-4
Elm Springs—locale SD-7
**Elm Springs**—pop pl AR-4
**Elm Springs**—pop pl TN-4
Elm Springs—spring AR-4
Elm Springs—spring KS-7
Elm Springs Branch—stream MO-7
Elm Springs Branch—stream TN-4
Elm Springs Cem—cemetery AR-4
Elm Springs Ch—church KS-7
Elm Springs Ch—church SD-7
Elm Springs Ch—church TN-4
Elm Spring Sch—school MO-7
*Elm Springs Colony* SD-7
**Elm Springs Colony**—pop pl SD-7
Elm Springs Lake—lake MO-7
Elm Springs Sch (historical)—school TN-4
Elm Springs (Township of)—fmr MCD AR-4
*Elm Springs United Methodist Church* TN-4
**Elm Square**—pop pl MA-1
Elms Road Sch—school MI-6
Elms Rsvr—reservoir OR-9
Elms Run—stream KY-4
Elms Sch—school MI-6
Elms Shop Ctr—locale MO-7
**Elms (subdivision), The**—pop pl DE-2
Elm St. Hist Dist—hist pl NE-7
**Elm Store**—pop pl AR-4
Elm Store (Township of)—fmr MCD AR-4
**Elms Township**—pop pl ND-7
Elm Stream—stream ME-1
Elm Stream (Township of)—unorg ME-1
Elm Street Baptist Ch—church TN-4
Elm Street Cem—cemetery CT-1
Elm Street Ch—church NC-3
Elm Street Ch—church TX-5
Elm Street Fire Station—hist pl MA-1
Elm Street Hist Dist—hist pl CT-1
Elm Street Methodist Church—hist pl TN-4
Elm Street On Jones River
Reservoir—dam MA-1
Elm Street Park—park MN-6
Elm Street Park—park NC-3
Elm Street Sch—school AZ-5
Elm Street Sch—school CA-9
Elm Street Sch—school (3) GA-3
Elm Street Sch—school NJ-2
Elm Street Sch—school (2) NY-2
Elm Street Sch—school OH-6
Elm Street Sch—school PA-2
Elm Street Sch—school SC-3
Elm Street Station—locale PA-2
Elm Stump Ch—church NY-2
Elm Swamp—swamp NY-2
**Elm Terrace**—pop pl WV-2
Elmtown—locale TX-5
Elm Town Hall—building ND-7
*Elm Township* KS-7
Elm Township—civ div NE-7
**Elm Township**—pop pl KS-7
**Elm Township**—pop pl MO-7
**Elm Township**—pop pl (2) NE-7
**Elm Township**—pop pl (2) ND-7
Elm Tree—locale NY-2
Elm Tree Cem—cemetery NV-8
**Elm Tree Corners**—pop pl WI-6
Elm Tree Corners—uninc pl WI-6
Elm Tree Cove—bay ME-1
**Elm Tree Crossroads**—pop pl IN-6
Elm Tree Draw—valley SD-7
Elm Tree Island—island NY-2
*Elm Tree Point* ME-1
Elm Tree Point—cape MD-2
*Elm Tree Post Office* TN-4
Elmtree Post Office (historical)—building TN-4
Elm Tree Ridge—summit NY-2
Elm Tree Sch—school IL-6
Elm Tree Sch—school PA-2
Elm Tree Sch—school WI-6
Elm Tree Square—locale ND-7
**Elm Tree Township**—pop pl ND-7
El Muerto Peak—summit TX-5
El Muerto Spring (Dead Mans
Hole)—spring TX-5
Elmvale Cem—cemetery CT-1
**Elm Valley**—pop pl NY-2
Elm Valley—valley MI-6
Elm Valley—valley NY-2
Elm Valley—valley TX-5
Elmview—locale GA-3
**Elm View**—pop pl CA-9
**Elmview**—pop pl OH-6
**Elm View**—pop pl TX-5
Elm View Sch—school WI-6
**Elmville**—pop pl CT-1
**Elmville**—pop pl KY-4
**Elmville**—pop pl OH-6
Elm Waterhole—lake (2) TX-5
Elm Waterhole—spring TX-5
Elm Waterhole Creek—stream TX-5
Elm Waterhole Windmill—locale TX-5
*Elm West* AL-4
*Elmwood* IN-6
*Elmwood* MN-6
*Elmwood* MS-4
*Elmwood* PA-2
*Elmwood* RI-1
Elmwood—hist pl (2) KY-4
Elmwood—hist pl MA-1
Elmwood—hist pl MI-6
Elmwood—hist pl NY-2
Elmwood—hist pl (3) NC-3
Elmwood—hist pl ND-7
Elmwood—hist pl TN-4
Elmwood—hist pl (2) VA-3
Elmwood—hist pl (2) WV-2
Elmwood—locale (3) AR-4
Elmwood—locale KY-4
Elmwood—locale LA-4
Elmwood—locale (2) MI-6
Elmwood—locale MO-7
Elmwood—locale NY-2
Elmwood—locale OH-6
Elmwood—locale TX-5
Elmwood—locale WV-2
**Elmwood**—pop pl (2) CT-1
**Elmwood**—pop pl GA-3
**Elmwood**—pop pl IL-6
**Elmwood**—pop pl IN-6
**Elmwood**—pop pl ME-1
**Elmwood**—pop pl MD-2
**Elmwood**—pop pl MA-1
**Elmwood**—pop pl MO-7
**Elmwood**—pop pl NE-7
**Elmwood**—pop pl (2) NH-1
**Elmwood**—pop pl NY-2
**Elmwood**—pop pl (2) NC-3
**Elmwood**—pop pl OK-5
**Elmwood**—pop pl (2) PA-2
**Elmwood**—pop pl RI-1
**Elmwood**—pop pl TN-4
**Elmwood**—pop pl WV-2
**Elmwood**—pop pl WI-6
Elmwood—uninc pl CA-9
Elmwood Acres (subdivision)—locale SD-7
Elmwood Branch—stream MO-7
Elmwood Canal—canal LA-4
Elmwood Canyon—valley CA-9
Elmwood Cem—cemetery (2) AL-4
Elmwood Cem—cemetery (2) AR-4
Elmwood Cem—cemetery (2) CO-8
Elmwood Cem—cemetery (3) CT-1
Elmwood Cem—cemetery ID-8
Elmwood Cem—cemetery (11) IL-6
Elmwood Cem—cemetery (2) IN-6
Elmwood Cem—cemetery (8) IA-7
Elmwood Cem—cemetery (4) KS-7
Elmwood Cem—cemetery (2) KY-4
Elmwood Cem—cemetery (3) ME-1
Elmwood Cem—cemetery (5) MA-1
Elmwood Cem—cemetery (6) MI-6
Elmwood Cem—cemetery (2) MN-6
Elmwood Cem—cemetery (2) MS-4
Elmwood Cem—cemetery (5) MO-7
Elmwood Cem—cemetery NE-7
Elmwood Cem—cemetery (2) NH-1
Elmwood Cem—cemetery (2) NJ-2
Elmwood Cem—cemetery (12) NY-2
Elmwood Cem—cemetery (5) NC-3
Elmwood Cem—cemetery ND-7
Elmwood Cem—cemetery (2) OH-6
Elmwood Cem—cemetery (4) OK-5
Elmwood Cem—cemetery (2) SC-3
Elmwood Cem—cemetery (3) TN-4
Elmwood Cem—cemetery TX-5
Elmwood Cem—cemetery VT-1
Elmwood Cem—cemetery VA-3
Elmwood Cem—cemetery (2) WV-2
Elmwood Cem—cemetery (2) WI-6
Elmwood Cemetery—hist pl MO-7
Elmwood Cemetery Gates—hist pl IL-6
Elmwood Cemetery Office and Entrance
Bridge—hist pl TN-4
Elmwood Ch—church CO-8
Elmwood Ch—church IN-6
Elmwood Ch—church LA-4
Elmwood Ch—church MI-6
Elmwood Ch—church (2) MO-7
Elmwood Ch—church OK-5
Elmwood Ch—church TX-5
Elmwood Ch—church WV-2
**Elmwood Corners**—pop pl NH-1
Elmwood Country Club—other NY-2
Elmwood County Club—other IA-7
*Elm Wood Creek* VA-3
Elmwood Creek—stream VA-3
Elmwood Day Sch—school NY-2
Elmwood Elem Sch—school IN-6
**Elmwood Estates**—pop pl VA-3
**Elmwood Farm**—pop pl OH-6
Elmwood Franklin Sch—school NY-2
Elmwood Golf Course—locale (2) SD-7
Elmwood Hall—hist pl KY-4
**Elmwood Heights**—pop pl WV-2
Elmwood Hill—summit CT-1
Elmwood Hills Country Club—other MI-6
Elmwood Hist Dist—hist pl RI-1
**Elmwood (historical)**—pop pl MA-1
Elmwood (historical P.O.)—locale MA-1
Elmwood HS—school OH-6
Elmwood Island—island MN-6
Elmwood Island—island WI-6
Elmwood Landing—locale MS-4
Elmwood Memorial Cem—cemetery IL-6
Elmwood Memorial Estates—cemetery AL-4
Elmwood Memorial Park—cemetery TX-5
Elmwood Park—airport NJ-2
Elmwood Park—park MA-1
Elmwood Park—park NE-7
Elmwood Park—park NJ-2
Elmwood Park—park NY-2
Elmwood Park—park (2) OH-6
Elmwood Park—park (2) PA-2
Elmwood Park—park VA-3
**Elmwood Park**—pop pl IL-6
**Elmwood Park**—pop pl MO-7
**Elmwood Park**—pop pl NJ-2
**Elmwood Park**—pop pl SC-3
**Elmwood Park**—pop pl WI-6
**Elmwood Park (East
Paterson)**—pop pl NJ-2
Elmwood Park Hist Dist—hist pl PA-2
Elmwood Park HS—school IL-6
Elmwood Place—hist pl OH-6
**Elmwood Place**—pop pl OH-6
Elmwood Place (Township of)—other OH-6
Elmwood Plantation—hist pl NC-3
Elmwood Plantation—locale MS-4
Elmwood Playground—park OH-6
Elmwood Point—cape NY-2
Elmwood Post Office—building TN-4
Elmwood Rehabilitation Center—hospital CA-9
Elmwood Rsvr—reservoir CO-8
Elmwood Sanatorium—hospital TX-5
Elmwood Sch—school (2) CA-9
Elmwood Sch—school CO-8
Elmwood Sch—school (2) ID-8
Elmwood Sch—school (6) IL-6
Elmwood Sch—school IA-7
Elmwood Sch—school KS-7
Elmwood Sch—school ME-1
Elmwood Sch—school MA-1
Elmwood Sch—school (3) MI-6
Elmwood Sch—school NE-7
Elmwood Sch—school NH-1
Elmwood Sch—school NJ-2
Elmwood Sch—school NY-2
Elmwood Sch—school (3) OH-6
Elmwood Sch—school (2) SD-7
Elmwood Sch—school (4) WI-6
Elmwood Sch (historical)—school MO-7
Elmwood Sch (historical)—school (2) TN-4
*Elmwood School* KS-7
*Elmwood School Number 21* SD-7
Elmwood Shaft—mine PA-2
*Elmwood Siding* MI-6
**Elmwood Station**—pop pl MA-1
Elmwood Street Sch—school MA-1
**Elmwood (subdivision)**—pop pl DE-2
**Elmwood (subdivision)**—pop pl MA-1
**Elm Wood Subdivision**—pop pl UT-8
Elmwood Terrace—locale PA-2
Elmwood Township—civil MO-7
**Elmwood Township**—pop pl ND-7
**Elmwood (Township of)**—pop pl IL-6
**Elmwood (Township of)**—pop pl (2) MI-6
**Elmwood (Township of)**—pop pl MN-6
Elmwood Tract—civil CA-9
Elmwood Trailer Park—locale AZ-5
Elmwood United Methodist Ch—church TN-4
Elna—locale KY-4
Elna Lake—lake WI-6
**El Naranjito**—pop pl PR-3
El Naranjo Windmills—locale TX-5
El Negro—CDP PR-3
El Negro—summit PR-3
El Negro Ranch—locale (3) TX-5
El Negro Windmill—locale TX-5
El Neuvo Windmill—locale TX-5
**El Nido**—pop pl (3) CA-9
**El-Nido**—pop pl VA-3
**El Nido**—pop pl VA-3
El Nido Canal—canal CA-9
El Nido Dam—dam CA-9
El Nido Mine—mine AK-9
El Nido Peak—summit AK-9
El Nido Rsvr—reservoir CA-9
El Nido Windmill—locale TX-5
El Niguel Country Club—locale CA-9
Elni Lake—lake MI-6
El Nogal Campground—locale NM-5
Elnora—locale AR-4
**Elnora**—pop pl IN-6
**Elnora**—pop pl NY-2
Elnora Elem Sch—school IN-6
El Norte Tank—reservoir NM-5
El Norte Windmill—locale (5) TX-5
El Novillo Windmill—locale TX-5
El Nuevo Windmill—locale (3) TX-5
Elo—locale WI-6
**Elo**—pop pl MI-6
Elo Cem—cemetery MI-6
Elo Ch—church MI-6
**El Ocho**—pop pl PR-3
Elochoman Lake—lake WA-9
Elochoman Pass—gap WA-9
Elochoman River—stream WA-9
Elochoman Slough—stream WA-9
*Elochomin River* WA-9
*Elochomon River* WA-9
*Elochomon Slough* WA-9
El Ocho Windmill—locale TX-5
*Elockaman River* WA-9
Elodesachel—spring PW-9
Elohim Ch—church NY-2
*Eloi* AZ-5
Eloi, Bayou—gut LA-4
Eloi, Lake—lake LA-4
Eloi, Point—cape LA-4
Eloi Bay—bay LA-4
Eloika Lake—lake WA-9
Eloise—locale MI-6
Eloise—locale TX-5
**Eloise**—pop pl FL-3
**Eloise**—pop pl WV-2
Eloise, Lake—lake FL-3
Eloise Branch—stream KY-4
Eloise Cem—cemetery MI-6
Eloise Ch—church KY-4
Eloise Lake—lake OR-9
Eloise Lake—lake WI-6
Eloise Lake—lake WY-8
**Eloise Woods**—pop pl FL-3
El Ojito—locale NM-5
El Ojito—spring NM-5
El Ojo—CDP PR-3
El Ojo Escondido—spring NM-5
El Ojo Negro—spring NM-5
*Elok* MP-9
*Elokoman River* WA-9
*Elokomin Slough* WA-9
Elomont Creek—stream TX-5
Elon—locale AL-4
Elon—locale IA-7
**Elon**—pop pl IN-6
**Elon**—pop pl VA-3
Elon Cem—cemetery TN-4
Elon Ch—church AL-4
Elon Ch—church MS-4
Elon Ch—church TN-4
Elon Ch—church VA-3
**Elon College**—pop pl NC-3
Elon Douglas Dam—dam TN-4
Elon Douglas Lake—reservoir TN-4
Elon Elem Sch—school NC-3
Elongozhik Slough—gut AK-9
Elongozhik Slough—stream AK-9
**Elon (historical)**—pop pl MS-4
Elon (Magisterial District)—fmr MCD VA-3
Elon Maynard Ditch—canal IN-6
Elon Post Office (historical)—building AL-4
Elon Post Office (historical)—building TN-4
Elon (Township of)—fmr MCD AR-4
*Elora* AL-4
Elora—locale CA-9
**Elora**—pop pl PA-2
**Elora**—pop pl TN-4
*Elora Lake* MN-6
Elora Post Office—building TN-4
Elora Sch (historical)—school TN-4
**Elora Township**—pop pl ND-7
*Eloree* SC-3
Elore Mine—mine NM-5
*Eloria* TN-4
El Oro—locale NM-5
El Oro Cem—cemetery AZ-5
El Oro Mine—mine ID-8
El Oro Mountains—ridge NM-5
Elo Sch—hist pl ID-8
El Oso—locale TX-5
El Oso Mine—mine AZ-5
*El Oso Park* AZ-5
Eloso Park—park AZ-5
Elos Prairie—flat OR-9
Elota Lateral—canal NM-5
Elouise Mine—mine AZ-5
Elovoi Island—island AK-9
Elowah Falls—falls OR-9
Elowsky Dam—dam MI-6
**Eloy**—pop pl AZ-5
Eloy (CCD)—cens area AZ-5
*Eloye Lake Lake Elosia* NE-7
Eloy Farms—locale AZ-5
Eloy Intermediate Elem Sch—school AZ-5
Eloy JHS—school AZ-5
Eloy Memorial Park—cemetery AZ-5
Eloy Municipal Airp—airport AZ-5
Eloy RR Station—building AZ-5
El Pablito Indian Ruins—locale NM-5
El Padre Canyon—valley TX-5
El Padre Mine—mine NV-8
**El Padro**—pop pl NM-5
El Paisano Hotel—hist pl TX-5
El Pajaro—summit CA-9
**El Pajuil**—pop pl PR-3
El Palacio Ranch—locale NM-5
El Paraiso Ranch—locale TX-5
*Elpardo* TN-4
Elpardo Post Office (historical)—building TN-4
El Parr Windmill—locale TX-5
El Parterre-Ojo De Agua—hist pl PR-3
El Pasaje—hist pl FL-3
El Paseo and Casa de la Guerra—hist pl CA-9
El Paseo Cahuenga Park—park CA-9
**El Paseo (subdivision)**—pop pl (2) AZ-5
*El Paso* KS-7
*El Paso* NC-3
El Paso—gap CA-9
El Paso—locale NC-3
**El Paso**—pop pl AR-4
**El Paso**—pop pl IL-6
**El Paso**—pop pl TX-5
**El Paso**—pop pl WI-6
El Paso And Southwestern Railway Water
Supply System—hist pl NM-5
El Paso and Southwestern RR Passenger
Depot-Douglas—hist pl AZ-5
El Paso and Southwestern RR
YMCA—hist pl AZ-5
El Paso Canyon—valley AZ-5
El Paso Canyon—valley (2) NM-5
El Paso (CCD)—cens area TX-5
El Paso Ch—church TX-5
El Paso Country Club—other TX-5
**El Paso (County)**—pop pl TX-5
El Paso County Courthouse—hist pl CO-8
El Paso Creek—stream CA-9
El Paso Creek—stream (2) CO-8
*El Paso del Norte* TX-5
**El Paso de Robles (corporate name for
Paso Robles)**—pop pl CA-9
El Paso East (CCD)—cens area TX-5
El Paso Elem Sch—school KS-7
El Paso Gap—gap NM-5
El Paso Gap Ch—church NM-5
El Paso HS—hist pl TX-5
El Paso International Airp—airport TX-5
El Paso Iron Pit—mine NM-5
El Paso Mine—mine CO-8
El Paso Mine—mine NV-8
El Paso Mountains—range CA-9
El Paso Natural Gas Company Compressor
Station—other (3) AZ-5
El Paso North Central (CCD)—cens area TX-5
El Paso Northwest (CCD)—cens area TX-5
El Paso Peaks—summit CA-9
El Paso Ridge—ridge NM-5
El Paso Sch—school KS-7
E L Paso Tank—reservoir NM-5
**El Paso (Town of)**—pop pl WI-6
El Paso (Township of)—fmr MCD AR-4
**El Paso (Township of)**—pop pl IL-6
El Paso Union Passenger Station—hist pl TX-5
El Peco Ranch—locale CA-9
El Pedregoso Creek—stream CO-8
El Penon—summit PR-3
El Perdido Creek—stream CO-8
El Perdido Waterhole—lake TX-5
El Perdido Windmill—locale (2) TX-5
El Perdid Windmill—locale TX-5
El Perno—summit CA-9
El Perro—summit CA-9
El Perro Windmill—locale TX-5
El Pescadero (Grimes)—civil CA-9
El Pescadero Park—park CA-9
El Pescadero (Pico and Naglee)—civil CA-9
Elphee Creek—stream NY-2
El Pico—summit TX-5
El Pilar Tank—reservoir AZ-5
El Pinal—locale CA-9
Elpino—locale GA-3
El Piojo—civil CA-9
El Piojo Creek—stream CA-9
**Elpis**—pop pl NY-2
Elpis Ch—church VA-3
El Piso—summit CA-9
El Piton—summit CA-9
El Pleasant—locale TX-5
**El Polvorin**—pop pl (2) PR-3
**El Portal**—pop pl CA-9
**El Portal**—pop pl FL-3
El Portal Archeol District—hist pl CA-9
El Portal del Sol Sch—school CA-9
El Portal Municipal Bldg—building FL-3
El Portal Sch—school (3) CA-9
**El Portero**—pop pl NM-5
El Porticito—other NM-5
El Portillo—gap CA-9
**El Porto Beach**—pop pl CA-9
**El Porton**—pop pl (2) PR-3
El Porvenir—locale NM-5
El Porvenir Bridge—bridge TX-5
El Porvenir Campground—locale NM-5
El Porvenir Community Ditch—hist pl NM-5
El Poso—area NM-5
El Poso Arroyo—stream CO-8
El Poso Creek—stream NM-5
El Poso Ranch—locale NM-5
*El Potrero* AZ-5
El Potrero De San Carlos—civil CA-9

Ely—locale VT-1
**Ely**—pop pl IA-7
**Ely**—pop pl MN-6
**Ely**—pop pl NV-8
Ely, Hervey, House—hist pl NY-2
Ely, Homestead—hist pl IN-6
Ely, Joshua, House—hist pl PA-2
Ely, Mount—summit NV-8
Ely, Richard T., House—hist pl WI-6
Elya Creek—stream MT-8
Ely Airport—airport NV-8
Ely Airport/Yelland Field—airport NV-8
El Yano Windmill—locale TX-5
Ely Block—hist pl OH-6
Ely Branch—stream MO-7
Ely Branch—stream TX-5
Ely Bridge—bridge IN-6
Ely Canyon—valley OR-9
Ely Cem—cemetery CT-1
Ely Cem—cemetery IL-6
Ely Cem—cemetery MN-6
Ely Cem—cemetery NJ-2
Ely Cem—cemetery TN-4
Ely Cem—cemetery (4) VA-3
Ely-Centennial Tunnel—mine NV-8
Ely Ch—church MI-6
Ely Colony—reserve NV-8
**Ely Colony Ind Res**—pop pl NV-8
Ely Creek—stream CA-9
Ely Creek—stream ID-8
Ely Creek—stream MI-6
Ely Creek—stream MN-6
Ely Creek—stream MS-4
Ely Creek—stream MO-7
Ely Creek—stream NY-2
Ely Creek—stream OR-9
Ely Creek—stream UT-8
Ely Creek—stream (2) VA-3
Ely Creek—stream WY-8
Ely-Criglar House—hist pl FL-3
Elydale Sch—school VA-3
Ely Flat—flat CA-9
Ely Fork—stream WV-2
Ely Gap—gap VA-3
Ely Hill—summit CO-8
Ely Hollow—valley WV-2
Ely HS—school FL-3
*Ely Ind Res* NV-8
Ely Ind Res—reserve NV-8
Ely Island—island MN-6
Ely Island—island PA-2
Ely Lake—lake MI-6
Ely Lake—lake (2) MN-6
Ely Lake—lake PA-2
Ely Lake (Township of)—civ div MN-6
Ely Landing (historical)—locale AL-4
Ely Meadow—flat CA-9
Ely Memorial Ch—church VA-3
Ely Mine—mine VT-1
Ely Mound—hist pl VA-3
Ely Mound—summit CT-1
Ely Mtn—summit CA-9
Ely Mtn—summit NY-2
Ely Park—park (2) NY-2
Ely Park—park OH-6
Ely Park—park TX-5
Ely Pond—lake CT-1
*Ely Range* NV-8
Ely Range—range NV-8
Ely Ranger District—forest NV-8
*Ely Ranger District, subdivision of* NV-8
Ely Ray Mine—mine CA-9
**Elyria**—pop pl KS-7
**Elyria**—pop pl NE-7
**Elyria**—pop pl OH-6
Elyria Cem—cemetery NE-7
Elyria Cem—cemetery OH-6
Elyria Country Club—other OH-6
Elyria Elks Club—hist pl OH-6
Elyria Hosp—hospital OH-6
Elyria HS - Washington Bldg—hist pl OH-6
Elyria Oil Field—oilfield KS-7
Elyria Sch—school CO-8
Elyria Township—civ div NE-7
**Elyria (Township of)**—pop pl OH-6
Ely Ridge—ridge LA-4
Ely Run—stream IN-6
**Elys**—pop pl KY-4
Elys Branch—stream (2) KY-4
**Elysburg**—pop pl PA-2
Ely Sch—school CT-1
Ely Sch—school MI-6
Ely Sch—school MO-7
Ely Sch—school OH-6
Ely Sch—school VT-1
Ely Sch—school WV-2
Elys Corner—locale NJ-2
Elys Creek—stream IA-7
**Elysian**—pop pl MN-6
**Elysian, Lake**—pop pl MN-6
Elysian Burial Gardens—cemetery UT-8
Elysian Creek—stream CA-9
Elysian Fields—flat WA-9
**Elysian Fields**—pop pl TX-5
Elysian Fields Cem—cemetery TX-5
Elysian Fields Ch—church TX-5
Elysian Fields (historical)—locale MS-4
Elysian Fields Lookout Tower—locale TX-5
Elysian Fields Sch—school TX-5
Elysian Gas Field—oilfield TX-5
**Elysian Grove**—pop pl TN-4
Elysian Grove Sch (historical)—school TN-4
Elysian Heights Sch—school CA-9
Elysian Park—park CA-9
Elysian Park—park NJ-2
Elysian Public Sch—hist pl MN-6
**Elysian Township**—pop pl ND-7
**Elysian (Township of)**—pop pl MN-6
Elysian Valley—valley CA-9
Elysian View Cem—cemetery NE-7
Elysian Water Tower—hist pl MN-6
**Elysian Woods**—pop pl VA-3
*Elys Island* MN-6
Elysium Lake—lake MD-2
Elys Peak—summit MN-6
Ely Spring—spring WY-8
Ely Springs—spring NV-8
Ely Springs Canyon—valley NV-8
Ely Springs Ranch—locale NV-8
Ely Springs Range—summit NV-8
Ely's Stone Bridge—hist pl IA-7
Ely Stadium—other OH-6
Ely Tank—reservoir (2) AZ-5
**Elyton**—pop pl AL-4
Elyton Ch—church AL-4
*Elyton Methodist Ch* AL-4
Elyton Sch (historical)—school AL-4
*Elytown* NJ-2
Ely Township—inact MCD NV-8
Ely (Township of)—other OH-6
**Ely (Township of)**—pop pl MI-6
El Yunque—summit PR-3
Ely Valley Mines—mine NV-8
ELY Wind River Diversion Dam Bridge—hist pl WY-8
Elywood Park—park OH-6
*Elza* TN-4
**Elza**—pop pl GA-3
**Elza**—pop pl TN-4
Elza, Lake—lake FL-3
Elza Ch—church GA-3
Elza Ch (historical)—church TN-4
Elza Run—stream WV-2
Elza Seligman Camp—locale NM-5
Elza Trail—trail WV-2
Elze Ch—church SC-3
Elze Webber Ditch—canal CO-8
Elzey Chapel Cem—cemetery FL-3
Elzner, August, House—hist pl TX-5
Elzner, Prince, House—hist pl TX-5
Elzner House—hist pl TX-5
El Zurron Banco Number 26—levee TX-5
Elzy (historical)—locale MS-4
Elzy Sch—school MS-4
Emachaya Creek—stream OK-5
Emahnuhto Bluffs—cliff AK-9
Emaiksoun Lake—lake AK-9
E Main Saint Cem—cemetery NY-2
Emajagua—CDP PR-3
Emajagua (Barrio)—fmr MCD PR-3
Emajagual (Barrio)—fmr MCD PR-3
Emaline Stutts Cem—cemetery AL-4
*Eman* MP-9
Emancipation Ch—church SC-3
Emancipation Gardens—post sta VI-3
Emancipation Hill—summit CO-8
Emancipation Monmt—park DC-2
Emancipation Park—park TX-5
**Emandal (Hearst)**—pop pl CA-9
Emandal Resort—locale CA-9
**Emandell (historical)**—pop pl NC-3
Emanguk (Emmonak)—other AK-9
Emanuals Reformed Ch—church PA-2
*Emanuel* AR-4
Emanuel—locale KY-4
**Emanuel**—pop pl AR-4
Emanuel AME Ch—church (2) AL-4
Emanuel AME Church—hist pl AL-4
Emanuel Baptist Ch—church (2) AL-4
Emanuel Baptist Ch—church FL-3
Emanuel Bend—bend FL-3
Emanuel Bldg—hist pl AL-4
Emanuel Cem—cemetery AL-4
Emanuel Cem—cemetery CT-1
Emanuel Cem—cemetery IL-6
Emanuel Cem—cemetery KS-7
Emanuel Cem—cemetery (2) LA-4
Emanuel Cem—cemetery MD-2
Emanuel Cem—cemetery (2) MN-6
Emanuel Cem—cemetery ND-7
Emanuel Cem—cemetery OH-6
Emanuel Cem—cemetery OR-9
Emanuel Cem—cemetery PA-2
Emanuel Cem—cemetery SD-7
Emanuel Cem—cemetery TX-5
Emanuel Cem—cemetery VA-3
Emanuel Cem—cemetery (3) WI-6
Emanuel Ch—church FL-3
Emanuel Ch—church (7) GA-3
Emanuel Ch—church (3) IL-6
Emanuel Ch—church KS-7
Emanuel Ch—church KY-4
Emanuel Ch—church LA-4
Emanuel Ch—church MI-6
Emanuel Ch—church MO-7
Emanuel Ch—church NJ-2
Emanuel Ch—church NC-3
Emanuel Ch—church ND-7
Emanuel Ch—church (4) OH-6
Emanuel Ch—church (5) PA-2
Emanuel Ch—church (2) SC-3
Emanuel Ch—church (2) TN-4
Emanuel Ch—church WV-2
Emanuel Ch—church (3) WI-6
**Emanuel (County)**—pop pl GA-3
Emanuel Creek—stream SD-7
Emanuel Creek—stream WA-9
Emanuel Creek Rec Area—park SD-7
Emanuel Episcopal Ch—church AL-4
Emanuel Fairview Ch—church TN-4
Emanuel Hill—summit WV-2
**Emanuel (historical)**—pop pl NC-3
Emanuel Holiness Ch—church (3) AL-4
Emanuel Home—church MI-6
Emanuel Hosp—hospital CA-9
Emanuel Hosp—hospital OR-9
Emanuel Hospital Heliport—airport OR-9
Emanuel Landing—locale FL-3
Emanuel Lutheran Cem—cemetery SD-7
Emanuel Lutheran Ch—church PA-2
Emanuel Lutheran Ch (CLC)—church FL-3
*Emanuel Lutheran Church* SD-7
Emanuel Lutheran Church of Montra—hist pl OH-6
Emanuel Lutheran Sch—school IN-6
Emanuel Memorial Park—cemetery TX-5
*Emanuel Missionary Ch* MO-7
Emanuel Point—cape FL-3
Emanuel Reformed Ch—church PA-2
Emanuel Rock (historical)—pillar ND-7
Emanuels Cem—cemetery KS-7
*Emanuel Sch* IN-6
Emanuels Ch—church OH-6
Emanuels Ch—church PA-2
Emanuel Sch—school IN-6
Emanuel Sch—school MI-6
Emanuel Sch—school PA-2
Emanuel Sch—school SC-3
**Emanuelsville**—pop pl PA-2
Emanuel Township—civil SD-7
Emanuel United Church of Christ Cemetery—hist pl NC-3
Emanvicrok Channel—stream AK-9
**Emardville (Township of)**—pop pl MN-6
*Emassee Creek* AL-4
*Emasses* FL-3
**Emathla**—pop pl FL-3
**Emathla**—pop pl FL-3
Emauhee—locale AL-4
Emauhee Creek—stream AL-4
Emauhee Mine (historical)—mine AL-4
*Emaus* PA-2
Emaus—other PA-2
Emaus Ch—church GA-3
Emaus Ch—church WI-6
Embach Lake—lake MI-6
Embar—locale WY-8
*Embarass River* WI-6
*Embarcadero Cove* CA-9
Embarcadero De Santa Clara—civil CA-9
Embargo—locale CO-8
Embargo Creek—stream CO-8
**Embarkation**—pop pl NY-2
Embar Lake—lake TX-5
Embar Oil Field—oilfield TX-5
Embarque Well—well TX-5
Embarque Windmill—locale TX-5
Embar Ranch—locale TX-5
Embarras River—stream IL-6
Embarrass—locale IL-6
**Embarrass**—pop pl MN-6
**Embarrass**—pop pl WI-6
Embarrass Cem—cemetery MN-6
Embarrass Ch—church IL-6
Embarrass Lake—lake MN-6
Embarrass Mine—mine MN-6
Embarrass Mountains—range MN-6
*Embarrass River* IL-6
Embarrass River—stream MN-6
Embarrass River—stream WI-6
*Embarrass Slough* IL-6
**Embarrass (Township of)**—pop pl IL-6
**Embarrass (Township of)**—pop pl MN-6
Embassy Bldg No. 10—hist pl DC-2
**Embassy East (subdivision)**—pop pl NC-3
Embassy of the Union of Soviet Socialist Republics Bldg—building DC-2
Embassy Plaza (Shop Ctr)—locale FL-3
Embassy Theater and Indiana Hotel—hist pl IN-6
Embden—locale ME-1
**Embden**—pop pl ND-7
Embden Interchange—crossing ND-7
Embden Pond—lake ME-1
**Embden (Town of)**—pop pl ME-1
Embergo Ditch—canal NM-5
Emberhill Cem—cemetery MS-4
Emberhill Ch—church MS-4
Ember Lake—lake MN-6
Ember Lake—lake WI-6
Emberry Cem—cemetery IL-6
Emberry Ch—church (2) KY-4
**Emberson**—pop pl TX-5
Emberson Cem—cemetery MD-2
Emberson Hill—summit MD-2
Embert, John, Farm—hist pl MD-2
Emberton—locale KY-4
E M Billingslea Lake Dam—dam MS-4
Embla Lake—lake MN-6
Emblem—locale TX-5
Emblem—locale WY-8
**Emblem**—pop pl PA-2
Emblem Bench—bench (2) WY-8
Emblem Cem—cemetery WY-8
Emblem Ch—church TX-5
Emblem Draw—valley WY-8
Embleton Coulee—valley MT-8
Embleton Oil Field—oilfield TX-5
**Embody (historical)**—pop pl OR-9
Embody Mine—mine CA-9
**Embogcht**—pop pl NY-2
Em Branch—stream NC-3
Embre Cem—cemetery MS-4
Embree—locale SC-3
**Embree**—pop pl MO-7
Embree Cem—cemetery OR-9
Embree House—hist pl TN-4
Embree Number 13 Mine—mine TN-4
Embree Number 14 Mine—mine TN-4
Embree Number 15 Mine—mine TN-4
Embrees Dam (historical)—dam TN-4
Embree Slough—stream OR-9
Embreeville—locale PA-2
**Embreeville**—pop pl TN-4
Embreeville Cove Baptist Ch—church TN-4
Embreeville Dam—dam PA-2
Embreeville Hist Dist—hist pl PA-2
Embreeville Junction (census name Y Section)—other TN-4
Embreeville Mtn—summit TN-4
Embreeville Sch (historical)—school TN-4
Embreeville State Hosp—hospital PA-2
Embreeville United Methodist Ch—church TN-4
Embreville Post Office (historical)—building TN-4
Embrey Cem—cemetery IN-6
Embrey Ch—church VA-3
Embrey Hill—summit VA-3
Embrey Hill—summit WA-9
**Embro**—pop pl NC-3
Embro Lake—lake WA-9
*Embry* AL-4
Embry—locale MS-4
**Embry**—pop pl GA-3
Embry Bend—bend AL-4
**Embry Bend**—pop pl AL-4
Embry Cem—cemetery KY-4
Embry Cem—cemetery (2) MS-4
Embry Ch—church MS-4
Embry Chapel A M E Ch—church UT-8
Embry Chapel Church—hist pl KY-4
Embry Creek—stream MS-4
**Embry Crossroads**—pop pl TN-4
Embry-Decherd Cem—cemetery TN-4
Embry Draw—valley WY-8
**Embry Hills**—pop pl GA-3
Embry (historical)—locale KS-7
Embry Lake—lake MO-7
Embryo Lake—lake AK-9
Embryo Lake—lake CO-8
Embry Pike Ch—church TN-4
Embry Post Office (historical)—building MS-4
Embry-Riddle Aeronautical Univ—school FL-3
*Embrys Crossing* AL-4
*Embrys Ferry* AL-4
Embudito Canyon—valley NM-5
Embudo—locale NM-5
Embudo Canyon—valley NM-5
Embudo Cave—cave NM-5
Embudo Creek—stream NM-5
Embudo Hist Dist—hist pl NM-5
Embudo Post Office—locale NM-5
Embudo Presbyterian Hosp—hospital NM-5
Embudo Spring—spring NM-5
Embury Ch—church (2) IN-6
Embury Ch—church IA-7
Embury Ch—church TN-4
Embury Corners—locale NY-2
Emby King Sch—school KY-4
E M Carr Pond Dam—dam MS-4
E McMillen Ranch—locale NM-5
*Emco* MN-6
**Emco**—pop pl AL-4
Emco-Listerhill Junction—locale AL-4
*Emden* SD-7
Emden—locale LA-4
Emden—locale WA-9
**Emden**—pop pl IL-6
**Emden**—pop pl MO-7
Emden Cem—cemetery MN-6
Emden Garage Park—park MO-7
Emden (historical)—locale ND-7
Emden Lake—lake WI-6
Emden Sch—school LA-4
Emden Sch—school MO-7
E-M Drain—canal MI-6
E Meadows—locale TX-5
Emebonwon Dam—dam MI-6
Emeghee Point—cape AK-9
**Emeigh**—pop pl PA-2
Emeigh Run—stream PA-2
E Meike Ranch—locale WY-8
*Emej* MP-9
*Emejiwa* MP-9
*Emejiwan* MP-9
Emejiwan—island MP-9
*Emejiwan Island* MP-9
*Emejwa* MP-9
Emekyalok Point—cape AK-9
Emele Ditch—canal OR-9
*Emeleol* PW-9
Emelie—hist pl IN-6
**Emeline**—pop pl IA-7
Emeline, Lake (historical)—lake SD-7
Emeline Lake—lake MI-6
Emeline Pass—channel LA-4
Emelita Street Sch—school CA-9
**Emelle**—pop pl AL-4
Emelle Ch—church AL-4
Emelle Ditch—canal WY-8
*Emeormij Island* MP-9
**Emerado**—pop pl ND-7
Emerado Cem—cemetery ND-7
Emerald—locale MS-4
Emerald—locale WA-9
Emerald—mine UT-8
**Emerald**—pop pl MI-6
**Emerald**—pop pl NE-7
**Emerald**—pop pl OH-6
**Emerald**—pop pl (2) PA-2
**Emerald**—pop pl (2) WI-6
Emerald, Lake—lake (2) FL-3
Emerald, Lake—lake MN-6
Emeralda—locale FL-3
Emerald Acres Number Two Subdivision Water Retention Basin—reservoir AZ-5
**Emerald Acres (subdivision)**—pop pl TN-4
Emerald Acres Subdivision Number Two Mini Park—park AZ-5
Emeralda Island—island FL-3
Emeralda Marsh—swamp FL-3
Emerald Ave United Methodist Ch—church TN-4
Emerald Ball Park—park PA-2
Emerald Bay—bay (2) AK-9
Emerald Bay—bay (3) CA-9
**Emerald Bay**—pop pl (2) CA-9
Emerald Bay State Park—park CA-9
**Emerald Beach**—pop pl MO-7
Emerald Beach Dock—locale AL-4
*Emerald Beach Marina* AL-4
Emerald Butte—summit ID-8
Emerald Canyon—valley AZ-5
Emerald Canyon—valley CA-9
Emerald Cave—cave TX-5
Emerald Cem—cemetery MN-6
Emerald Cem—cemetery NE-7
Emerald Cove—bay AK-9
Emerald Cove—bay TX-5
*Emerald Creek* ID-8
Emerald Creek—locale ID-8
Emerald Creek—stream AK-9
Emerald Creek—stream ID-8
Emerald Creek—stream WY-8
Emerald Drive Playground—park MI-6
Emerald Garden Plantation (historical)—locale MS-4
**Emerald Gardens (subdivision)**—pop pl NC-3
*Emerald Green* IL-6
**Emerald Green**—pop pl NY-2
Emerald Green Golf Course—locale NV-8
**Emerald Grove**—pop pl WI-6
Emerald Gulch—valley AZ-5
*Emerald Heights* OR-9
Emerald Heights—uninc pl OR-9
Emerald Heights—uninc pl WV-2
Emerald Hill—hist pl TN-4
Emerald Hill Ch—church GA-3
Emerald Hills—uninc pl WA-9
**Emerald Hills Condominium**—pop pl UT-8
**Emerald Hills Estates (subdivision)**—pop pl NC-3
Emerald Hills Golf Course—other CA-9
Emerald Hills Memorial Park—park TX-5
**Emerald Hills Subdivision**—pop pl (2) UT-8
Emerald (historical)—locale KS-7
Emerald (historical)—locale MS-4
Emerald-Hodgson Hosp—hospital TN-4
Emerald Island—island (4) AK-9
Emerald Island—island (2) MN-6
Emerald Island—island NH-1
Emerald Island—island WA-9
**Emerald Isle**—pop pl NC-3
**Emerald Isle**—pop pl UT-8
Emerald Isle Mine—mine AZ-5
Emerald JHS—school CA-9
Emerald JHS—school SC-3
*Emerald Lake* CA-9
*Emerald Lake* MN-6
*Emerald Lake* WI-6
Emerald Lake—lake AK-9
Emerald Lake—lake (6) CA-9
Emerald Lake—lake (6) CO-8
Emerald Lake—lake FL-3
Emerald Lake—lake (4) ID-8
Emerald Lake—lake IN-6
Emerald Lake—lake (4) MI-6
Emerald Lake—lake MN-6
Emerald Lake—lake (6) MT-8
Emerald Lake—lake NV-8
Emerald Lake—lake NJ-2
Emerald Lake—lake NY-2
Emerald Lake—lake (2) OR-9
Emerald Lake—lake (3) UT-8
Emerald Lake—lake VT-1
Emerald Lake—lake (3) WA-9
Emerald Lake—lake (2) WI-6
Emerald Lake—lake (4) WY-8
**Emerald Lake**—pop pl CA-9
Emerald Lake—reservoir MO-7
Emerald Lake—reservoir NC-3
Emerald Lakes—lake CA-9
Emerald Lakes—lake UT-8
**Emerald Lakes**—pop pl PA-2
Emerald Lake Shelter—locale UT-8
Emerald Lake State For—forest VT-1
Emerald Lake State Park—park VT-1
Emerald Mine—mine PA-2
Emerald Mission—church OH-6
Emerald Mound—summit IL-6
Emerald Mound—summit MS-4
Emerald Mound and Village Site—hist pl IL-6
Emerald Mound Grange—locale IL-6
Emerald Mound Site (22AD504)—hist pl MS-4
Emerald Mtn—summit CA-9
Emerald Mtn—summit CO-8
*Emerald Park* IA-7
Emerald Park—locale WA-9
Emerald Park—park OR-9
**Emerald Park**—pop pl IL-6
Emerald Park Creek—stream WA-9
Emerald Park Mine—mine WY-8
*Emerald Peak* ID-8
Emerald Peak—summit CA-9
Emerald Peak—summit CO-8
Emerald Peak—summit WA-9
Emerald Point—cape CA-9
Emerald Point—cliff AZ-5
Emerald Pond—lake IL-6
Emerald Pool—lake CA-9
Emerald Pool—lake NH-1
Emerald Pool—spring WY-8
Emerald Pools—lake UT-8
Emerald Pools Trail—hist pl UT-8
Emerald Pools Trail—trail UT-8
Emerald Post Office (historical)—building MS-4
Emerald Ridge—ridge WA-9
Emerald Rock—bar NY-2
Emerald Sch—school CO-8
Emerald Sch (historical)—school MS-4
**Emerald Shores**—pop pl AL-4
Emerald Spring—spring AZ-5
Emerald Square—locale MA-1
Emerald State Wildlife Mngmt Area—park MN-6
Emerald Station—locale WI-6
**Emerald Terrace**—pop pl IL-6
**Emerald (Town of)**—pop pl WI-6
**Emerald (Township of)**—pop pl MN-6
**Emerald (Township of)**—pop pl OH-6
Emerald Valley Boys Camp—locale CO-8
Emerald Valley Ranch—locale CO-8
Emerald Valley Resort—locale AL-4
**Emerald Village**—pop pl NC-3
Emerald Woods Plaza (Shop Ctr)—locale FL-3
*Emeral Lake* MI-6
Emergency Hosp—hospital DC-2
Emergency Point—cliff OR-9
Emergency Spillway of Nockamixon Dam—canal PA-2
Emergency Spring—spring WA-9
Emergency Windmill—locale TX-5
Emeric Creek—stream CA-9
Emerich—locale GA-3
*Emerich Dam* ND-7
Emerick—locale NE-7
Emerick Branch—stream IN-6
Emerick Cem—cemetery IL-6
Emerick Ditch—canal IN-6
Emerick Sch—school VA-3
**Emerickville**—pop pl PA-2
Emeric Lake—lake CA-9
Emerine Gap—gap TN-4
Emerine Gulch—valley MT-8
Emerine Mount—summit MT-8
Emerine Spring—spring MT-8
Emer Island—island MP-9
**Emerling**—pop pl KY-4
*Emerling Station* KY-4
*Emerly Branch* GA-3
Emerson—locale GA-3
Emerson—locale KY-4
Emerson—locale MI-6
Emerson—locale NY-2
Emerson—locale NC-3
Emerson—locale ND-7
Emerson—locale OR-9
Emerson—locale TX-5
Emerson—locale VT-1
Emerson—locale WV-2
**Emerson**—pop pl AR-4
**Emerson**—pop pl GA-3
**Emerson**—pop pl IL-6
**Emerson**—pop pl IA-7
**Emerson**—pop pl KY-4
**Emerson**—pop pl MO-7
**Emerson**—pop pl (2) NE-7
**Emerson**—pop pl NJ-2
**Emerson**—pop pl NC-3
**Emerson**—pop pl OH-6
**Emerson**—pop pl PA-2
**Emerson**—pop pl VA-3
Emerson, Capt. Oliver, Homestead—hist pl MA-1
Emerson, Mount—summit AK-9
Emerson, Mount—summit CA-9
Emerson, Ralph Waldo, House—hist pl MA-1
**Emerson Addition (subdivision)**—pop pl UT-8
Emerson Airp—airport MO-7
Emerson Ave Baptist Ch—church IN-6
Emerson Ave Ch of Christ—church IN-6
Emerson Bayou—gut FL-3
Emerson Branch—stream AR-4
Emerson Branch—stream GA-3
Emerson Branch—stream NC-3
Emerson Branch—stream TN-4
Emerson Bridge—bridge GA-3
Emerson Bridge—bridge SC-3
Emerson Bromo-Seltzer Tower—hist pl MD-2
Emerson Brook—stream ME-1
Emerson Brook—stream MA-1
Emerson Brook—stream (3) NH-1
Emerson Brook Lake Street Dam—dam MA-1
Emerson Brook Rsvr—reservoir MA-1
Emerson Campground—locale CO-8
Emerson Canyon—valley NM-5
Emerson (CCD)—cens area GA-3
Emerson Cem—cemetery IL-6
Emerson Cem—cemetery IA-7
Emerson Cem—cemetery (2) ME-1
Emerson Cem—cemetery MO-7
Emerson Cem—cemetery OH-6
**Emerson Center**—pop pl OK-5
Emerson Ch—church AR-4
Emerson Ch—church MI-6
Emerson Ch—church OK-5
Emerson City—locale IL-6
Emerson Coll—school MA-1
Emerson Corner—locale ME-1
Emerson Coulee—valley MT-8
*Emerson Creek* OH-6
*Emerson Creek* WA-9
Emerson Creek—stream CA-9
Emerson Creek—stream (2) ID-8
Emerson Creek—stream MT-8
Emerson Creek—stream OH-6
Emerson Creek—stream OR-9
Emerson Creek—stream TX-5
Emerson Creek Trail—trail CA-9
Emerson Ditch—canal CA-9
Emerson Ditch—canal IN-6
Emerson Ditch Lateral No 2—canal AR-4
Emerson Draw—valley TX-5
Emerson Electric Company Bldg—hist pl MO-7
Emerson Electric Manufacturing Company—facility MO-7
*Emerson Elem Sch* MS-4
Emerson Elem Sch—school IN-6
Emerson Elem Sch—school KS-7
Emerson Elem Sch—school (2) PA-2
Emerson Gulch—valley CO-8
Emerson Gulf—valley NY-2
Emerson Hall—hist pl WI-6
*Emerson Highlands* MI-6
**Emerson Hill**—pop pl NY-2
Emerson Hill—summit MA-1
Emerson Hill—summit (2) NH-1
Emerson Hill—summit NY-2
Emerson (historical)—locale KS-7
Emerson Hollow—valley MO-7
Emerson-Holmes Bldg—hist pl GA-3
Emerson Hosp—hospital MA-1
Emerson Hough Sch—school IA-7
Emerson House—building MA-1
Emerson House—hist pl MA-1
Emerson HS—school NY-2
*Emerson Institute Colored Industrial School* AL-4
Emerson JHS—school (4) CA-9
Emerson JHS—school (2) MI-6
Emerson JHS—school OH-6
Emerson Junction—locale MT-8
*Emerson Lake* MN-6
*Emerson Lake* WI-6
Emerson Lake—flat CA-9
Emerson Lake—lake (2) CA-9
Emerson Lake—lake (3) MI-6
Emerson Lake—lake MN-6
Emerson Lake—lake (2) TX-5
Emerson Lake—lake WA-9
Emerson Lake—lake (2) WI-6
Emerson Lake—reservoir NC-3
Emerson Lake—reservoir TX-5
Emerson Lake—reservoir WI-6
Emerson Lake—swamp MN-6
Emerson Lake Dam—dam NC-3
Emerson Lake Golf Club—other CA-9
**Emerson Main Street Addition (subdivision)**—pop pl UT-8
Emerson Manor Sch—school CA-9
Emerson Mission—church OK-5
Emerson Mtn—summit CO-8
Emerson Nipple—locale WA-9
Emerson Open Alternative Elem Sch—school KS-7
Emerson Park—park CA-9
Emerson Park—park KS-7
Emerson Park—park MI-6
Emerson Park—park NY-2
**Emerson Park**—pop pl GA-3
Emerson Park Sch—school GA-3
Emerson Pass—gap NV-8
Emerson Peak—summit CA-9
Emerson Peak—summit (2) MT-8
**Emerson Place**—pop pl TX-5
Emerson Point—cape FL-3
Emerson Point—cape ME-1
Emerson Point—cape MA-1
Emerson Pond—lake NH-1
**Emerson (Portersville)**—pop pl NC-3
Emerson Ranch—locale CA-9
Emerson Ranch—locale NM-5
Emerson Ranch—locale OR-9
Emerson Ranch—locale TX-5
Emerson Ridge—ridge ME-1
Emerson Ridge—ridge OR-9
Emerson Rsvr—reservoir OR-9
Emerson Run—stream PA-2
Emerson Runaround—stream ME-1

Emersons Bay—*bay* IA-7
Emerson Sch—*hist pl* KY-4
Emerson Sch—*school* AL-4
Emerson Sch—*school* (3) AZ-5
Emerson Sch—*school* (10) CA-9
Emerson Sch—*school* (3) CO-8
Emerson Sch—*school* FL-3
Emerson Sch—*school* (3) ID-8
Emerson Sch—*school* (9) IL-6
Emerson Sch—*school* (3) IN-6
Emerson Sch—*school* (3) IA-7
Emerson Sch—*school* KY-4
Emerson Sch—*school* (3) ME-1
Emerson Sch—*school* (5) MA-1
Emerson Sch—*school* (7) MI-6
Emerson Sch—*school* (2) MN-6
Emerson Sch—*school* (3) MO-7
Emerson Sch—*school* (2) MT-8
Emerson Sch—*school* (2) NE-7
Emerson Sch—*school* NH-1
Emerson Sch—*school* (3) NJ-2
Emerson Sch—*school* NM-5
Emerson Sch—*school* NY-2
Emerson Sch—*school* (6) OH-6
Emerson Sch—*school* (9) OK-5
Emerson Sch—*school* SD-7
Emerson Sch—*school* (3) TX-5
Emerson Sch—*school* UT-8
Emerson Sch—*school* (4) WA-9
Emerson Sch—*school* WV-2
Emerson Sch—*school* (5) WI-6
Emerson Sch (abandoned)—*school* PA-2
Emerson Sch (historical)—*school* AL-4
*Emerson Sch Number 58* IN-6
*Emerson School* PA-2
Emersons Cliff—*summit* MA-1
Emerson Siding—*locale* ME-1
Emerson Site—*hist pl* TX-5
*Emersons Mill Pond* ME-1
*Emersons Point* MA-1
Emerson Spring—*spring* CA-9
Emerson Spring—*spring* ID-8
Emersons Rocks—*bar* MA-1
**Emerson Station**—*pop pl* MI-6
**Emerson Township**—*pop pl* (2) NE-7
**Emerson Township**—*pop pl* SD-7
Emerson (Township of)—*fmr MCD* AR-4
**Emerson (Township of)**—*pop pl* MI-6
Emerson-Williams Sch—*school* CT-1
Emert Bluff—*cliff* TN-4
Emert Branch—*stream* AR-4
**Emerts Cove**—*pop pl* TN-4
Emerts Cove—*valley* TN-4
Emerts Mill (historical)—*locale* TN-4
*Emery* TN-4
Emery—*locale* IL-6
Emery—*locale* OR-9
**Emery**—*pop pl* AZ-5
**Emery**—*pop pl* IA-7
**Emery**—*pop pl* MI-6
**Emery**—*pop pl* NC-3
**Emery**—*pop pl* (2) PA-2
**Emery**—*pop pl* SD-7
**Emery**—*pop pl* UT-8
Emery, Abram, House—*hist pl* OH-6
Emery, James, House—*hist pl* ME-1
Emery, Lake—*lake* WI-6
*Emery Branch* GA-3
Emery Branch—*stream* GA-3
*Emery Bridge* ME-1
Emery Brook—*stream* ME-1
Emery Brook—*stream* VT-1
Emery Butte—*summit* ID-8
Emery Canal—*canal* UT-8
Emery Canyon—*valley* ID-8
Emery Canyon—*valley* (2) OR-9
Emery Canyon Spring—*spring* ID-8
Emery Cem—*cemetery* FL-3
Emery Cem—*cemetery* (2) IL-6
Emery Cem—*cemetery* IN-6
Emery Cem—*cemetery* (2) ME-1
Emery Cem—*cemetery* (2) MS-4
Emery Cem—*cemetery* OH-6
Emery Cem—*cemetery* SD-7
Emery Cem—*cemetery* (2) TN-4
Emery Cem—*cemetery* UT-8
Emery Cem—*cemetery* WI-6
Emery Ch—*church* AL-4
Emery Ch—*church* (2) MS-4
Emery Ch—*church* OH-6
Emery Ch (abandoned)—*church* MO-7
Emery Chapel—*church* OH-6
**Emery Chapel**—*pop pl* OH-6
Emery Chapel Cem—*cemetery* OH-6
*Emery Clark Open Drain* IN-6
Emery Corners—*locale* MD-2
Emery County—*civil* UT-8
Emery County Home—*building* UT-8
Emery County HS—*school* UT-8
Emery Cove—*bay* ME-1
*Emery Creek* IL-6
Emery Creek—*stream* AL-4
Emery Creek—*stream* AK-9
Emery Creek—*stream* GA-3
Emery Creek—*stream* (4) ID-8
Emery Creek—*stream* IL-6
Emery Creek—*stream* IA-7
Emery Creek—*stream* MT-8
Emery Creek—*stream* WA-9
Emery Dam—*dam* UT-8
Emery Ditch—*canal* CA-9
*Emery Falls* AZ-5
Emery Farmstead—*hist pl* WA-9
Emery-Ferron—*cens area* UT-8
Emery Ferron Division—*civil* UT-8
Emery Field—*airport* PA-2
*Emery Gap* TN-4
Emery Gap—*gap* NM-5
Emery Green Sch—*school* IL-6
Emery Green Sch—*school* KS-7
Emery Hill—*summit* ME-1
Emery Hill—*summit* MI-6
Emery Hill—*summit* MT-8
Emery Hill—*summit* NH-1
Emery Hill Cem—*cemetery* ME-1
Emery Hollow—*valley* MO-7
Emery Homestead—*hist pl* ME-1
Emery House—*hist pl* ME-1
Emery HS—*school* CA-9
*Emery Island* PA-2
Emery Island—*island* ME-1
Emery Island—*island* NY-2
*Emery Lake* WI-6
Emery Lake—*lake* MI-6
Emery Lake—*lake* MN-6
Emery LDS Church—*hist pl* UT-8
Emery Ledge—*bar* ME-1
Emery Mill—*locale* TN-4
**Emery Mills**—*pop pl* ME-1
Emery Mine—*mine* MT-8
Emery Mines—*mine* NY-2
Emery Moore Dam—*dam* OR-9
Emery Moore Rsvr—*reservoir* OR-9
Emery O Muncie Elem Sch—*school* IN-6
Emery Park—*park* KS-7
Emery Park—*park* NY-2
**Emery Park**—*pop pl* AZ-5
Emery Park Post Office—*building* AZ-5
Emery Park Sch—*school* CA-9
Emery Peak—*summit* CO-8
Emery Peak—*summit* NM-5
Emery Pond—*lake* CT-1
Emery Pond—*lake* MA-1
Emery-Price Hist Dist—*hist pl* KY-4
Emery Ranch—*locale* ID-8
Emery Riddle University—*post sta* FL-3
Emery Ridge—*ridge* (2) MT-8
*Emery River* TN-4
Emery Row—*hist pl* KY-4
Emery Rsvr—*reservoir* CA-9
Emery Rsvr—*reservoir* UT-8
*Emery's Bridge* ME-1
**Emerys Bridge**—*pop pl* ME-1
*Emery Sch* IN-6
Emery Sch—*school* CA-9
Emery Sch—*school* DC-2
Emery Sch—*school* TN-4
Emery Sch (historical)—*school* PA-2
Emerys Corner—*locale* ME-1
*Emerys Mills* ME-1
Emerys Misery—*summit* ME-1
Emery Spring—*spring* (2) OR-9
Emery Street Bungalow District—*hist pl* WI-6
Emery Swamp—*swamp* ME-1
Emery Tobin, Lake—*lake* AK-9
Emery Towers (US-I001/1-90/Superintendent/ Bradford Sch Dist)—*school* PA-2
**Emery (Town of)**—*pop pl* WI-6
**Emery Township**—*pop pl* SD-7
*Emery Valley* UT-8
Emery Valley—*basin* UT-8
Emery Vega—*area* NM-5
Emeryville—*locale* NY-2
**Emeryville**—*pop pl* CA-9
Emery Well—*well* OR-9
Emerywood—*uninc pl* NC-3
Emerywood Country Club—*locale* NC-3
Emesiochel—*cape* PW-9
Emes Windmill—*locale* TX-5
**Emet**—*pop pl* OK-5
Emet Cem—*cemetery* OK-5
Emeth Sch—*school* FL-3
Emeunot Cem—*cemetery* WA-9
Emeus Cem—*cemetery* AL-4
*Emeus Church* AL-4
Emfinger Branch—*stream* AL-4
Emge Ditch—*canal* IN-6
Emgeten Island—*island* AK-9
Emghem Mtn—*summit* AK-9
Emhaw Gulch—*valley* CO-8
Em Hollow—*valley* TN-4
**Emhouse**—*pop pl* TX-5
*Emiangel* PW-9
**Emida**—*pop pl* ID-8
Emida Peak—*summit* ID-8
Emidio Pumping Station—*other* CA-9
Emidj Island—*island* MP-9
*Emieangl* PW-9
*Emiej* MP-9
*Emieji To* MP-9
Emigant West Rec Area—*locale* MT-8
Emigh Cem—*cemetery* PA-2
Emigh Lake—*reservoir* PA-2
Emigh Ranch—*locale* CO-8
Emigh Run—*stream* PA-2
Emigh Run—*uninc pl* PA-2
Emig Mansion—*hist pl* PA-2
**Emigrant**—*pop pl* MT-8
Emigrant Butte—*summit* (2) OR-9
*Emigrant Butte Pass* OR-9
Emigrant Buttes—*summit* OR-9
Emigrant Canyon—*valley* AZ-5
Emigrant Canyon—*valley* (2) CA-9
Emigrant Canyon—*valley* ID-8
Emigrant Canyon—*valley* (4) NV-8
Emigrant Canyon—*valley* OR-9
Emigrant Canyon Trail Two Hundred Fiftyfive—*trail* AZ-5
Emigrant Cem—*cemetery* MT-8
Emigrant Cove—*valley* ID-8
Emigrant Creek—*stream* (3) CA-9
Emigrant Creek—*stream* IA-7
Emigrant Creek—*stream* MT-8
Emigrant Creek—*stream* (4) OR-9
Emigrant Creek—*stream* (2) WY-8
*Emigrant Creek Rsvr* OR-9
Emigrant Crossing—*locale* (2) ID-8
Emigrant Crossing—*locale* OR-9
Emigrant Crossing (site)—*locale* OR-9
Emigrant Dam—*dam* OR-9
Emigrant Ditch—*canal* WY-8
Emigrant Ford Campground—*locale* CA-9
Emigrant Forest Camp—*locale* OR-9
Emigrant Gap—*gap* CA-9
Emigrant Gap—*gap* MT-8
Emigrant Gap—*gap* WY-8
**Emigrant Gap**—*pop pl* CA-9
Emigrant Gap Historical Marker—*locale* CA-9
Emigrant Gap Ridge—*ridge* WY-8
Emigrant Gulch—*valley* MT-8
Emigrant Hill—*locale* WY-8
Emigrant Hill—*summit* CA-9
Emigrant Hill—*summit* OR-9
Emigrant Hills—*summit* AZ-5
Emigrant Hill Viewpoint—*locale* OR-9
**Emigrant (historical)**—*pop pl* OR-9
Emigrant Lake—*lake* (3) CA-9
Emigrant Lake—*lake* OR-9
Emigrant Lake—*reservoir* OR-9
Emigrant Meadow—*flat* CA-9
Emigrant Meadow Lake—*lake* CA-9
Emigrant Pass—*gap* AZ-5
Emigrant Pass—*gap* (4) CA-9
Emigrant Pass—*gap* (4) NV-8
Emigrant Pass—*gap* OR-9
Emigrant Pass—*gap* (2) UT-8
Emigrant Pass Ridge—*ridge* NV-8
*Emigrant Peak* WY-8
Emigrant Peak—*summit* MT-8
Emigrant Peak—*summit* (2) NV-8
Emigrant Ranger Station—*locale* CA-9
*Emigrant Rsvr* OR-9
Emigrant Rsvr—*reservoir* OR-9
Emigrant Spring—*spring* (3) CA-9
Emigrant Spring—*spring* (6) NV-8
Emigrant Spring—*spring* UT-8
Emigrant Spring—*spring* (3) WY-8
*Emigrant Springs* UT-8
Emigrant Springs—*hist pl* WY-8
Emigrant Springs—*locale* OR-9
Emigrant Springs—*spring* AZ-5
Emigrant Springs—*spring* (2) NV-8
Emigrant Springs—*spring* OR-9
Emigrant Spring State Park—*park* OR-9
Emigrant Tank—*reservoir* AZ-5
Emigrant Trail—*trail* (2) CA-9
Emigrant Trail—*trail* NE-7
Emigrant Trail—*trail* NV-8
Emigrant Trail—*trail* (10) WY-8
Emigrant Trail (Lander Cutoff)—*trail* (2) WY-8
Emigrant Trail (Mormon Trail)—*trail* UT-8
Emigrant Trail (Pack)—*trail* CA-9
Emigrant Trail (Slate Creek Trail)—*trail* WY-8
Emigrant Trail (Sublette Cutoff)—*trail* WY-8
Emigrant Valley—*basin* NV-8
Emigrant Wash—*stream* CA-9
Emigration—*cens area* UT-8
Emigration Campground—*locale* ID-8
Emigration Canyon—*hist pl* UT-8
Emigration Canyon—*valley* ID-8
Emigration Canyon—*valley* UT-8
Emigration Creek—*stream* ID-8
Emigration Creek—*stream* UT-8
Emigration Division—*civil* UT-8
**Emigration Oaks Subdivision**—*pop pl* UT-8
**Emigration Passive Solar Home Condominium**—*pop pl* UT-8
Emigration Spring—*spring* ID-8
Emigration Tunnel Spring—*spring* UT-8
Emig Sch—*school* PA-2
**Emigsville**—*pop pl* PA-2
*Emijwa* MP-9
Emiko—*locale* AZ-5
**Emil**—*pop pl* VA-3
Emil Cave—*cave* AL-4
Emil Creek—*stream* OR-9
Emil Creek Rsvr—*reservoir* OR-9
Emile Coulee—*valley* MT-8
Emile Creek—*stream* AK-9
Emile Creek—*stream* (2) OR-9
Emile Creek Recreation Site—*park* OR-9
**Emilee**—*pop pl* TX-5
Emile Falls—*falls* OR-9
Emile Gebel Dam—*dam* NC-3
Emile Gebel Lake—*reservoir* NC-3
Emile Huntzeker Mine (underground)—*mine* TN-4
Emile Lake—*lake* AK-9
Emile Shelter—*locale* OR-9
Emile Trail—*trail* OR-9
Emil Fritz Spring—*spring* NM-5
Emilie—*locale* PA-2
*Emilie Island* SD-7
Emilie Methodist Ch—*church* PA-2
Emilie Post Office (historical)—*building* PA-2
Emiline Lake—*lake* LA-4
Emiline Ridge—*ridge* NC-3
Emilio Perona Dam—*dam* NJ-2
Emil Lake—*lake* AK-9
Emil Lake—*lake* MN-6
Emil Lake—*lake* WI-6
Emil Post Office (historical)—*building* TN-4
Emil Spring—*lake* WI-6
**Emily**—*pop pl* MN-6
Emily, Lake—*lake* FL-3
Emily, Lake—*lake* MI-6
Emily, Lake—*lake* (5) MN-6
Emily, Lake—*lake* (2) WI-6
Emily, Mount—*summit* CA-9
Emily, Mount—*summit* (2) OR-9
Emily Babcock Dam—*dam* NC-3
Emily Babcock Lake—*reservoir* NC-3
Emily Bill Playground—*locale* MA-1
Emily Brittain Elem Sch—*school* PA-2
Emily Cabin—*locale* OR-9
Emily Cem—*cemetery* MO-7
Emily Cem—*cemetery* TN-4
Emily Creek—*stream* KY-4
Emily Creek—*stream* MN-6
Emily Creek—*stream* OR-9
Emily Creek—*stream* WI-6
Emily Creek Way—*trail* OR-9
Emily Flynn Home—*building* IN-6
Emily Foster Lake—*reservoir* AL-4
Emily Foster Lake Dam—*dam* AL-4
Emily Gray JHS—*school* AZ-5
Emily Gut—*gut* DE-2
Emily Hollow—*valley* MO-7
Emily Island—*island* AK-9
Emily Lake—*lake* CA-9
Emily Lake—*lake* MI-6
Emily Lake—*lake* (2) WI-6
Emily Lookout Tower—*locale* MN-6
Emily Number 5 Mine (surface)—*mine* AL-4
Emily Park—*park* IL-6
Emily Pond—*reservoir* AZ-5
Emily Proctor Shelter—*locale* VT-1
Emily Proctor Trail—*trail* VT-1
Emily Run—*stream* KY-4
Emilys Chapel Cem—*cemetery* MO-7
Emily State For—*forest* MN-6
Emily Ticasua Ivanhoff Brown Elem Sch—*school* AK-9
Eminence—*locale* AR-4
Eminence—*locale* MS-4
**Eminence**—*pop pl* IN-6
**Eminence**—*pop pl* KY-4
**Eminence**—*pop pl* MO-7
**Eminence**—*pop pl* NY-2
**Eminence**—*pop pl* TX-5
Eminence, The—*hist pl* MA-1
Eminence Bayou—*stream* AR-4
Eminence Break—*cliff* AZ-5
Eminence (CCD)—*cens area* KY-4
Eminence Cem—*cemetery* (2) KS-7
Eminence Cem—*cemetery* MS-4
Eminence Cem—*cemetery* (2) TX-5
Eminence Ch—*church* IL-6
Eminence Ch—*church* MS-4
Eminence Ch—*church* TX-5
Eminence Consolidated Sch—*school* IN-6
Eminence (historical)—*locale* KS-7
Eminence Historic Commercial District—*hist pl* KY-4
Eminence Lake—*reservoir* KY-4
Eminence Landing Strip—*airport* MO-7
Eminence Lookout Tower—*locale* MO-7
Eminence Sch—*school* MO-7
Eminence Sch (abandoned)—*school* MO-7
Eminence Sch (historical)—*school* MS-4
Eminence Sch (historical)—*school* TN-4
Eminence Township—*civil* KS-7
Eminence Township—*civil* MO-7
**Eminence (Township of)**—*pop pl* IL-6
*Eminence United Methodist Church* MS-4
**Emington**—*pop pl* IL-6
*Emis* PW-9
**Emison**—*pop pl* IN-6
Emison, Ash, Quarters—*hist pl* KY-4
Emison Sch (historical)—*school* TN-4
**Emit**—*pop pl* GA-3
**Emit**—*pop pl* NC-3
*Emita* AZ-5
Emit Grove Ch—*church* GA-3
*Emius Church* AL-4
Emkay—*locale* UT-8
**Emkay**—*pop pl* WY-8
E M Kee Junior Lake Dam—*dam* MS-4
Emlen, Eleanor Cope, Sch of Practice—*hist pl* PA-2
Emlen Sch—*school* PA-2
**Emlenton**—*pop pl* PA-2
Emlenton Borough—*civil* (2) PA-2
Emlenton Elem Sch—*school* PA-2
Emlenton Municipal Airp—*airport* PA-2
Emlenton Spur (locale)—*locale* PA-2
**Emlenton (sta.)**—*pop pl* PA-2
Emley Lake—*lake* MI-6
Emleys Hill Ch—*church* NJ-2
E M Lode Mine—*mine* SD-7
E. M. Loews Center for the Performing Arts—*building* MA-1
**Emlyn**—*pop pl* KY-4
Emlyn Harrison Marsteller Sch—*school* VA-3
Emma—*locale* CO-8
Emma—*locale* GA-3
Emma—*locale* LA-4
Emma—*locale* WV-2
**Emma**—*pop pl* CO-8
**Emma**—*pop pl* IL-6
**Emma**—*pop pl* IN-6
**Emma**—*pop pl* KY-4
**Emma**—*pop pl* MO-7
**Emma**—*pop pl* NC-3
Emma, Lake—*lake* AK-9
Emma, Lake—*lake* (2) CO-8
Emma, Lake—*lake* (2) FL-3
Emma, Lake—*lake* (2) MI-6
Emma, Lake—*lake* (5) MN-6
Emma, Lake—*lake* NJ-2
Emma, Lake—*lake* SD-7
Emma, Mount—*summit* AK-9
Emma, Mount—*summit* AZ-5
Emma, Mount—*summit* CA-9
Emma, Mount—*summit* CO-8
Emma Blair Sch—*school* NC-3
*Emma Boyd School* MS-4
Emma B Trask Elem Sch—*school* NC-3
Emma Burr Mtn—*summit* CO-8
*Emma Burr Peak* CO-8
Emma Butte—*summit* MT-8
Emma Canal—*canal* ID-8
Emma Cem—*cemetery* LA-4
*Emma Chapel* PA-2
Emma Concord Ch—*church* IL-6
Emma Cook Hollow—*valley* KY-4
*Emma Creek* MT-8
Emma Creek—*stream* (4) AK-9
Emma Creek—*stream* (2) ID-8
Emma Creek—*stream* IN-6
Emma Creek—*stream* KS-7
Emma Creek—*stream* (2) MT-8
Emma Creek—*stream* PA-2
Emma Dome—*summit* AK-9
Emma Elem Sch—*school* NC-3
Emma Frey Sch—*school* TX-5
Emma Grove Cem—*cemetery* OH-6
Emma Gulch—*valley* ID-8
Emma Gulch—*valley* (2) MT-8
**Emma (historical)**—*pop pl* OR-9
Emma Jarnagin Cem—*cemetery* TN-4
Emma Kraft Springs—*spring* MT-8
*Emma Lake* CO-8
Emma Lake—*lake* AK-9
Emma Lake—*lake* CA-9
Emma Lake—*lake* IN-6
Emma Lake—*lake* MN-6
Emma Lake—*lake* OR-9
Emma Lake—*lake* WA-9
Emma Lake—*lake* WI-6
Emma Lake—*swamp* MN-6
**Emmalane**—*pop pl* GA-3
Emma Lee Pond—*reservoir* FL-3
Emmalena—*locale* KY-4
Emmalena (CCD)—*cens area* KY-4
Emmaline Branch—*stream* TN-4
Emmaline Gap—*gap* NC-3
Emmaline Lake—*lake* CO-8
Emma Love Hardee Elem Sch—*school* FL-3
Emma Matilda Lake—*lake* WY-8
Emma Matilda Lake Trail—*trail* WY-8
Emma Matilda Overlook—*locale* WY-8
*Emma Mercer Institute* MS-4
Emma Mine—*mine* (2) CA-9
Emma Mine—*mine* (2) CO-8
Emma Mine—*mine* MT-8
Emma Mine—*mine* OR-9
Emma Mine—*mine* (2) UT-8
Emma Mishler Ditch—*canal* IN-6
Emma Morgan Sch—*school* KY-4
Emma Nevada Shaft—*mine* NV-8
*Emmanual Ch* AL-4
Emmanual Ch—*church* AL-4
*Emmanual Mission* AZ-5
*Emmanuel* TN-4
Emmanuel—*airport* NJ-2
**Emmanuel**—*pop pl* MS-4
Emmanuel AME Church—*hist pl* NC-3
Emmanuel Assembly of God Ch—*church* (2) MS-4
Emmanuel Baptist—*hist pl* MA-1
*Emmanuel Baptist Ch* MS-4
Emmanuel Baptist Ch—*church* (5) AL-4
Emmanuel Baptist Ch—*church* (3) FL-3
Emmanuel Baptist Ch—*church* IN-6
Emmanuel Baptist Ch—*church* KS-7
Emmanuel Baptist Ch—*church* (6) MS-4
Emmanuel Baptist Ch—*church* (2) TN-4
Emmanuel Baptist Ch—*church* UT-8
Emmanuel Baptist Church—*hist pl* NY-2
Emmanuel Cem—*cemetery* CT-1
Emmanuel Cem—*cemetery* IN-6
Emmanuel Cem—*cemetery* (3) IA-7
Emmanuel Cem—*cemetery* (2) KS-7
Emmanuel Cem—*cemetery* (5) MN-6
Emmanuel Cem—*cemetery* MS-4
Emmanuel Cem—*cemetery* (2) MO-7
Emmanuel Cem—*cemetery* (2) NE-7
Emmanuel Cem—*cemetery* NC-3
Emmanuel Cem—*cemetery* (2) OK-5
Emmanuel Cem—*cemetery* PA-2
Emmanuel Cem—*cemetery* (3) SD-7
Emmanuel Cem—*cemetery* TX-5
Emmanuel Cem—*cemetery* (2) VA-3
Emmanuel Cem—*cemetery* (3) WI-6
*Emmanuel Ch* TN-4
Emmanuel Ch—*church* (7) AL-4
Emmanuel Ch—*church* (2) AR-4
Emmanuel Ch—*church* CO-8
Emmanuel Ch—*church* (2) CT-1
Emmanuel Ch—*church* (3) FL-3
Emmanuel Ch—*church* (3) GA-3
Emmanuel Ch—*church* IL-6
Emmanuel Ch—*church* (9) IN-6
Emmanuel Ch—*church* (4) KS-7
Emmanuel Ch—*church* (4) KY-4
Emmanuel Ch—*church* (3) LA-4
Emmanuel Ch—*church* (4) MD-2
Emmanuel Ch—*church* MA-1
Emmanuel Ch—*church* (4) MI-6
Emmanuel Ch—*church* (7) MN-6
Emmanuel Ch—*church* (2) MS-4
Emmanuel Ch—*church* (2) MO-7
Emmanuel Ch—*church* (5) NE-7
Emmanuel Ch—*church* (2) NY-2
Emmanuel Ch—*church* (14) NC-3
Emmanuel Ch—*church* (6) ND-7
Emmanuel Ch—*church* (4) OH-6
Emmanuel Ch—*church* (17) PA-2
Emmanuel Ch—*church* (10) SC-3
Emmanuel Ch—*church* (4) SD-7
Emmanuel Ch—*church* (6) TN-4
Emmanuel Ch—*church* (4) TX-5
Emmanuel Ch—*church* (22) VA-3
Emmanuel Ch—*church* WV-2
Emmanuel Ch—*church* (8) WI-6
Emmanuel Chapel—*church* MO-7
Emmanuel Ch (historical)—*church* AL-4
*Emmanuel Ch of Christ* AL-4
Emmanuel Ch of Christ—*church* TN-4
Emmanuel Ch of Christ Oneness Pentecostal—*church* FL-3
Emmanuel Ch of God in Christ—*church* KS-7
Emmanuel Ch of God in Christ—*church* MS-4
Emmanuel Ch of God in Christ—*church* UT-8
Emmanuel Ch of the Nazarene—*church* MS-4
Emmanuel Christian Fellowship—*church* FL-3
Emmanuel Christian Methodist Episcopal Ch—*church* IN-6
Emmanuel Christian Sch—*school* AL-4
Emmanuel Church—*hist pl* OH-6
Emmanuel Church—*hist pl* (2) VA-3
Emmanuel Coll—*school* GA-3
Emmanuel Episcopal Ch—*church* FL-3
Emmanuel Episcopal Church—*hist pl* ID-8
Emmanuel Episcopal Church—*hist pl* PA-2
Emmanuel Episcopal Church—*hist pl* SD-7
Emmanuel Episcopal Church—*hist pl* (2) TX-5
Emmanuel Holiness Campground—*locale* AL-4
Emmanuel Holiness Ch—*church* (2) AL-4
Emmanuel Knob—*summit* OH-6
Emmanuel Lutheran Cem—*cemetery* (3) SD-7
*Emmanuel Lutheran Cemetery* SD-7
Emmanuel Lutheran Ch—*church* AL-4
Emmanuel Lutheran Ch—*church* IN-6
Emmanuel Lutheran Ch (LCA)—*church* FL-3
*Emmanuel Lutheran Church* SD-7
Emmanuel Lutheran Church—*hist pl* NE-7
Emmanuel Lutheran Church and Cemetery—*hist pl* SD-7
Emmanuel Memorial Park—*cemetery* MA-1
Emmanuel Mennonite Ch—*church* FL-3
Emmanuel Mission—*church* AZ-5
**Emmanuel Mission**—*pop pl* AZ-5
Emmanuel Missionary Baptist Ch—*church* (2) FL-3
Emmanuel Missionary Ch—*church* MO-7
Emmanuel Mission Baptist Ch—*church* AL-4
Emmanuel Mission Ch—*church* WV-2
Emmanuel Pentecostal Ch—*church* MS-4
Emmanuel Pentecostal Temple—*church* KS-7
Emmanuel Presbyterian Church—*hist pl* CO-8
Emmanuel Reformed Ch—*church* IA-7
Emmanuel-Saint Michael Lutheran Sch—*school* IN-6
*Emmanuel Sch* IN-6
Emmanuel Sch—*school* AL-4
Emmanuel Sch—*school* CA-9
Emmanuel Sch—*school* IL-6
Emmanuel Sch—*school* IN-6
Emmanuel Sch—*school* (2) MN-6
Emmanuel Sch—*school* NE-7
Emmanuel Sch—*school* (2) SC-3
Emmanuel Sch—*school* VA-3
Emmanuel Sch—*school* WI-6
Emmanuel Sch of Religion—*school* TN-4
*Emmanuels Church* PA-2
Emmanuel Seventh Day Adventist Ch—*church* AL-4
Emmanuel Shearith Israel Chapel—*hist pl* CO-8
Emmanuel Tabernacle—*church* WV-2
Emmanuel Tabernacle Cem—*cemetery* TN-4
Emmanuel Temple Ch—*church* KS-7
Emmanuel Temple Gospel Assembly Pentecostal Ch—*church* KS-7
Emmanuel Temple Pentecostal Ch—*church* MS-4
Emmanuel United Methodist Ch—*church* FL-3
Emmanuel United Presbyterian Ch—*church* TN-4
Emma Oil Field—*oilfield* TX-5
*Emma Park* UT-8
Emma Park—*flat* UT-8
Emma Paul Canyon—*valley* CO-8
Emma Peak—*summit* MT-8
Emma Peak—*summit* NV-8
Emma Ranch—*locale* WY-8
Emmart—*locale* WV-2
Emma Sansom HS—*school* AL-4
Emma Sater Park—*park* IA-7
*Emmas Creek* PA-2
Emmas Grove Ch—*church* NC-3
Emma Shaft—*mine* NV-8
Emma Shaft—*mine* NM-5
*Emma's Park* UT-8
Emmaton—*locale* CA-9
**Emma Township**—*pop pl* KS-7
**Emma (Township of)**—*pop pl* IL-6
Emmatrade Lake—*reservoir* MO-7
Emma Tunnel—*mine* UT-8
Emmauel Camp—*park* FL-3
*Emmaus* TN-4
Emmaus—*locale* TX-5
Emmaus—*locale* VI-3
**Emmaus**—*pop pl* PA-2
*Emmaus Baptist Ch* TN-4
Emmaus Baptist Ch—*church* FL-3
Emmaus Borough—*civil* PA-2
Emmaus Cem—*cemetery* (2) AL-4
Emmaus Cem—*cemetery* FL-3
Emmaus Cem—*cemetery* KY-4
Emmaus Cem—*cemetery* MO-7
Emmaus Cem—*cemetery* ND-7
Emmaus Ch—*church* AL-4
Emmaus Ch—*church* AR-4
Emmaus Ch—*church* (3) GA-3
Emmaus Ch—*church* IL-6
Emmaus Ch—*church* KS-7
Emmaus Ch—*church* KY-4
Emmaus Ch—*church* ME-1
Emmaus Ch—*church* MS-4
Emmaus Ch—*church* (2) NC-3
Emmaus Ch—*church* TN-4
Emmaus Ch—*church* TX-5
Emmaus Ch—*church* (5) VA-3
Emmaus Ch—*church* WI-6
Emmaus Community Park—*park* PA-2
**Emmaus (Emaus)**—*pop pl* PA-2
Emmaus Free Ch—*church* NE-7
Emmaus Home—*other* MO-7
Emmaus HS—*school* PA-2
Emmaus JHS—*school* PA-2
**Emmaus Junction (subdivision)**—*pop pl* PA-2
Emmaus Lutheran Sch—*school* IN-6
Emmaus Moravian Church and Manse—*hist pl* VI-3
Emmaus Sanitarium—*other* MO-7
*Emmaus Sch* IN-6
Emmaus Sch—*school* CO-8
Emmaus Sch—*school* IN-6
*Emmaville* MS-4
Emmaville—*locale* MN-6
**Emmaville**—*pop pl* PA-2
Emmaville Mtn—*summit* PA-2
Emma Welch Ditch—*canal* OH-6
Emma White Boys Camp—*locale* MO-7
Emma Willard Coll—*school* NY-2
*Emmedale Ch* AL-4
*Emmeji-to* MP-9
Emmel Bldg—*hist pl* IL-6
Emmel Hollow—*valley* MO-7
*Emmels Creek* MT-8
Emmelsville—*locale* NJ-2
Emmens Station—*locale* NJ-2
Emmeram—*locale* KS-7
Emmeram Northeast Oil Field—*oilfield* KS-7
Emmeram Oil Field—*oilfield* KS-7
Emmerich, Mount—*summit* AK-9
*Emmerich HS* IN-6
Emmerich Manual HS—*school* IN-6
Emmerson Airp—*airport* KS-7
*Emmerson Cemetery* MS-4
Emmerson Lake—*lake* CO-8
Emmerson Park—*park* IL-6
**Emmert**—*pop pl* MN-6
*Emmert-Hawthorne Cemetery* TN-4
**Emmerton**—*pop pl* VA-3
Emmerts Ch—*church* MD-2
Emmert Sch—*school* IL-6
Emmerts Mill (historical)—*locale* TN-4
**Emmertsville**—*pop pl* MD-2
*Emmet* MI-6
Emmet—*locale* SD-7
**Emmet**—*pop pl* AR-4
**Emmet**—*pop pl* NE-7
**Emmet**—*pop pl* ND-7
**Emmet**—*pop pl* OH-6
Emmet Cem—*cemetery* WI-6
**Emmet (County)**—*pop pl* MI-6
Emmet County Airp—*airport* MI-6
Emmet County Home—*locale* IA-7
Emmet Gulch—*valley* NV-8
Emmet Hebron Sch—*school* MI-6
Emmet (historical P.O.)—*locale* IA-7
Emmet Island—*island* AK-9
**Emmetsburg**—*pop pl* IA-7
Emmetsburg City Hall—*building* IA-7
Emmetsburg Public Library—*hist pl* IA-7
Emmetsburg Township—*fmr MCD* IA-7
Emmet Sch—*school* IL-6
Emmetsville Ch—*church* IN-6
*Emmett* AR-4
*Emmett* NE-7
Emmett—*locale* LA-4
Emmett—*locale* OH-6
Emmett—*locale* TX-5
Emmett—*locale* WV-2

Emmett—pop pl....ID-8
Emmett—pop pl....KS-7
Emmett—pop pl....MI-6
Emmett—pop pl....TN-4
Emmett—pop pl....TX-5
Emmett Abramson Lake Dam—dam....AL-4
Emmett Bench—bench....ID-8
Emmett Bench—cens area....ID-8
Emmett Cem—cemetery....ID-8
Emmett Cottage—hist pl....MA-1
Emmett Creek—stream....MT-8
Emmett Ditch—canal....IN-6
Emmett Drain—stream....MI-6
Emmett Elem Sch—school....TN-4
Emmett Hill—summit....AZ-5
Emmett Hollow—valley....OH-6
Emmett Irrigation District North Side Main canal—canal....ID-8
Emmett Mtn—summit....ID-8
Emmet (Town of)—pop pl (2)....WI-6
Emmet Township—fmr MCD....IA-7
Emmet Township—pop pl....NE-7
Emmet Township—pop pl....SD-7
Emmet (Township of)—fmr MCD....AR-4
Emmet (Township of)—other....MI-6
Emmet (Township of)—pop pl....IL-6
Emmet (Township of)—pop pl....MN-6
Emmett Post Office (historical)—building....TN-4
Emmett Presbyterian Church—hist pl....ID-8
Emmett Sellers Dam—dam....AL-4
Emmett Sellers Lake—reservoir....AL-4
Emmett Spring—spring....AZ-5
Emmett Thomas Playground—park....MS-4
Emmett Township....KS-7
Emmett Township—pop pl....KS-7
Emmett (Township of)—pop pl (2)....MI-6
Emmett Valley—cens area....ID-8
Emmett Valley—valley....ID-8
Emmett Wash—stream....AZ-5
Emmil Branch—stream....KY-4
Emminger, Corson, Round Barn—hist pl....SD-7
Emmins Hill—summit....IN-6
Emmit Bell Ditch....OH-6
Emmit Chapel—church....OH-6
Emmit Mine—mine....CO-8
Emmitsburg—pop pl....MD-2
Emmitsburg Junction—locale....MD-2
Emmitsburg Rsvr—reservoir....MD-2
Emmit Wood Lake—reservoir....AL-4
Emmit Wood Lake Dam....AL-4
Emmius Sch (historical)—school....AL-4
Emmonak—pop pl....AK-9
Emmonak Slough—stream....AK-9
Emmons—locale....AR-4
Emmons—locale....KS-7
Emmons—locale....PA-2
Emmons—pop pl....IA-7
Emmons—pop pl....KY-4
Emmons—pop pl....MN-6
Emmons—pop pl....NY-2
Emmons—pop pl....WV-2
Emmons, G.B., House—hist pl....MA-1
Emmons, Mount—pop pl....UT-8
Emmons, Mount—summit....AK-9
Emmons, Mount—summit....CO-8
Emmons, Mount—summit....NY-2
Emmons, Mount—summit....UT-8
Emmons Bayou—bay....FL-3
Emmons Brook—stream....NY-2
Emmonsburg—pop pl....NY-2
Emmonsburg Post Office (historical)—building....ND-7
Emmons Cabin—locale....CA-9
Emmons Canyon—valley....CA-9
Emmons Cem—cemetery (2)....AL-4
Emmons Cem—cemetery....IL-6
Emmons Cem—cemetery....KS-7
Emmons Cem—cemetery....MS-4
Emmons Cem—cemetery....MO-7
Emmons Cem—cemetery....NY-2
Emmons Cem—cemetery....OK-5
Emmons Cliff—cliff....TX-5
Emmons Cone—summit....WY-8
Emmons Corners—locale....CT-1
Emmons County—civil....ND-7
Emmons County Courthouse—hist pl....ND-7
Emmons Creek—stream....IL-6
Emmons Creek—stream....KS-7
Emmons Creek—stream....MT-8
Emmons Creek—stream....WI-6
Emmons Drain—stream....MI-6
Emmons Elementary and JHS—school....IN-6
Emmons Glacier—glacier....WA-9
Emmons Hollow—valley....TN-4
Emmons House—hist pl....AK-9
Emmons Island—island....AK-9
Emmons Lake—lake....AK-9
Emmons Lake—lake....MI-6
Emmons Lake—lake....OH-6
Emmons Lake—lake....WI-6
Emmons Mesa—summit....WY-8
Emmons Overlook—locale....WA-9
Emmons Peak....UT-8
Emmons Point—cape....AK-9
Emmons Pond—lake (2)....CT-1
Emmons Pond—lake....NY-2
Emmons Ridge—ridge....IN-6
Emmons Ridge Cem—cemetery....IN-6
Emmons Sch—school....IL-6
Emmons Sch—school....MI-6
Emmons Sch—school....WV-2
Emmons Sch (historical)—school....MO-7
Emmons School....IN-6
Emmons Siding—locale....NY-2
Emmons (Township of)—fmr MCD....NC-3
Emmord Branch—stream....MD-2
Emmords Hole—basin....TX-5
Emmorton—pop pl....MD-2
Emmorton Sch—school....MD-2
Emmous Ch—church....GA-3
Emmus Ch—church....KY-4
Emnavak Ridge—ridge....AK-9
Emo Branch—stream....MO-7
Emon—locale....AR-4
Emon Ch—church....OH-6
Emond Ranch—locale....MT-8
Emons Creek....KS-7
E Mooney Dam—dam....SD-7
Emoqualosha Plantation (historical)—locale....MS-4
Emorai Ch—church....AL-4
Emoral Ch....AL-4
Emoritt Lake—lake....IL-6
Emorok—bar....FM-9
Emory....MD-2
Emory....TN-4
Emory—locale....AL-4
Emory—locale....MS-4
Emory—locale....SC-3
Emory—locale....UT-8
Emory—pop pl....TX-5
Emory—pop pl....VA-3
Emory, Lake—reservoir....NC-3
Emory and Henry Coll—school....VA-3
Emory Bend....AL-4
Emory Bend—bend....TN-4
Emory-Blakeman-Penick House—hist pl....KY-4
Emory Branch—stream....AR-4
Emory Branch—stream....GA-3
Emory Branch—stream (2)....KY-4
Emory Branch—stream....NC-3
Emory Branch—stream....TN-4
Emory Brook—stream (2)....NY-2
Emory Canyon—valley....NM-5
Emory (CCD)—cens area....TX-5
Emory Cem....MS-4
Emory Cem—cemetery....MS-4
Emory Cem—cemetery....UT-8
Emory Ch—church....MD-2
Emory Ch—church....MS-4
Emory Ch—church....OH-6
Emory Ch—church....TN-4
Emory Ch—church (2)....VA-3
Emory Channel—channel....CA-9
Emory Chapel—church....AL-4
Emory Chapel—church....GA-3
Emory Chapel—church....MD-2
Emory Chapel—church....NY-2
Emory Chapel Cem—cemetery....PA-2
Emory Church—locale....MD-2
Emory Church—pop pl....MD-2
Emory Corner—locale....ME-1
Emory Corral—locale....TX-5
Emory Cove....MD-2
Emory Creek—bay....MD-2
Emory Creek—stream....AK-9
Emory Creek—stream....MO-7
Emory Creek—stream....NY-2
Emory Creek—stream....SC-3
Emory Creek—stream....WV-2
Emory Dam....NC-3
Emory Drain—canal....MI-6
Emory Draw—valley (2)....TX-5
Emory Estates—pop pl....TN-4
Emorygap....TN-4
Emory Gap—gap....AL-4
Emory Gap—gap....SC-3
Emory Gap—gap (2)....TN-4
Emory Gap—pop pl....TN-4
Emory Gap Branch—stream....TN-4
Emory Gap Cem—cemetery....TN-4
Emorygap Post Office....TN-4
Emory Gap Post Office (historical)—building....TN-4
Emory Gap Station....TN-4
Emory Golf And Country Club—locale....TN-4
Emory Green Sch—school....PA-2
Emory Grove—locale....MD-2
Emory Grove—pop pl....MD-2
Emory Heights—pop pl (2)....TN-4
Emory Heights Ch—church....TN-4
Emory Heights Elem Sch—school....TN-4
Emory Hills (subdivision)—pop pl....TN-4
Emory (historical)—locale....AL-4
Emory (historical)—locale....KS-7
Emory (historical)—pop pl....TN-4
Emory Hollow—valley....MO-7
Emory Independent Methodist Ch....MS-4
Emory Island—island....CA-9
Emory Junior Coll—school....GA-3
Emory-Meadow View—CDP....VA-3
Emory Methodist Ch....MS-4
Emory Mill Mountain—ridge....AR-4
Emory Orr Spring—spring....CO-8
Emory Park—park....NY-2
Emory Pass—gap....NM-5
Emory Peak—summit....TX-5
Emory Pond—lake....NH-1
Emory Pond (historical)—lake....MS-4
Emory Post Office (historical)—building....MS-4
Emory Post Office (historical)—building....TN-4
Emory River—stream....TN-4
Emory River Ch (historical)—church....TN-4
Emorys Bridge....ME-1
Emory Sch—school....CA-9
Emorys Chapel—church....GA-3
Emory Sch (historical)—school....AL-4
Emory Sch (historical)—school....TN-4
Emorys Creek....MD-2
Emorys Mill (historical)—locale....TN-4
Emory Univ—school....GA-3
Emory Univ District—hist pl....GA-3
Emory Univ Sch Of Dentistry—school....GA-3
Emory Valley—pop pl....TN-4
Emory Valley—valley....TN-4
Emory Valley Ch—church....TN-4
Emory Valley Sch—school....TN-4
Emoryville—pop pl....WV-2
Emorywood Estates (subdivision)—pop pl....NC-3
Empedrada Lake....CO-8
Empedrado Lake—lake....CO-8
Empedrados Draw—valley....NM-5
Empedrados Tank—reservoir....NM-5
Empedrado Tank—reservoir....NM-5
Emperado Tank—reservoir....NM-5
Emperor—hist pl....MI-6
Emperor and Duchess Mine—mine....AZ-5
Emperor Creek—stream....MI-6
Emperor Creek—stream....MT-8
Emperor Island—island....AK-9
Emperor Landing—locale....NC-3
Emperor Peak—summit....AK-9
Emperor Sch—school....CA-9
Empey Mtn—summit....WA-9
Empey Pond—lake....AZ-5
Empeyville—pop pl....NY-2
Empi Creek—stream (2)....WA-9
Empie Park—park....NC-3
Empie-Van Dyke House—hist pl....AR-4
Empire....AL-4
Empire....KS-7
Empire....OH-6
Empire—locale....IL-6
Empire—locale....IA-7
Empire—locale....NV-8
Empire—pop pl....AL-4
Empire—pop pl....AR-4
Empire—pop pl....CA-9
Empire—pop pl....CO-8
Empire—pop pl....GA-3
Empire—pop pl....KY-4
Empire—pop pl....LA-4
Empire—pop pl....ME-1
Empire—pop pl....MI-6
Empire—pop pl....MN-6
Empire—pop pl....MS-4
Empire—pop pl....MO-7
Empire—pop pl....NV-8
Empire—pop pl....NC-3
Empire—pop pl....OH-6
Empire—pop pl....OR-9
Empire—pop pl....SD-7
Empire—pop pl....WV-2
Empire Addition (subdivision)—pop pl....UT-8
Empire Air Force Station—military....MI-6
Empire Airp—airport....NV-8
Empire Amphitheater—basin....CO-8
Empire Bldg—hist pl....AL-4
Empire Block—hist pl....OR-9
Empire Block—hist pl....WI-6
Empire Bluffs—cliff....MI-6
Empire Canal—canal....CA-9
Empire Canal—canal....CO-8
Empire Canal—canal....NE-7
Empire Canyon—valley....NV-8
Empire Canyon—valley....UT-8
Empire (CCD)—cens area....AL-4
Empire Cem—cemetery....CO-8
Empire Cem—cemetery....IL-6
Empire Cem—cemetery....KS-7
Empire Cem—cemetery....MO-7
Empire Cem—cemetery....WI-6
Empire Ch—church....AL-4
Empire Ch—church....FL-3
Empire Ch—church....GA-3
Empire Ch—church....SD-7
Empire City....MN-6
Empire City....OR-9
Empire City—other....MN-6
Empire City—pop pl....KS-7
Empire City—pop pl....OK-5
Empire City—uninc pl....KS-7
Empire City Race Track....NY-2
Empire Creek....WI-6
Empire Creek—stream (6)....CA-9
Empire Creek—stream....MT-8
Empire Creek—stream (2)....WA-9
Empire Creek—stream....WI-6
Empire Cut—gut....CA-9
Empire District Electric Company Dam....MO-7
Empire Ditch—canal....CA-9
Empire Division—civil....AL-4
Empire Drift Mine (underground)—mine....AL-4
Empire Drive Trail—trail....WA-9
Empire Flat—flat....AZ-5
Empire Gardens Sch—school....CA-9
Empire Grove Campground—locale....ME-1
Empire Guard Station—locale....CO-8
Empire Gulch—valley....AZ-5
Empire Gulch—valley (2)....CO-8
Empire Gulch—valley....OR-9
Empire Hill—summit....CO-8
Empire (historical P.O.)—locale....IA-7
Empire House—hist pl....OH-6
Empire Intake Canal—canal....CO-8
Empire JHS—school....AL-4
Empire JHS—school....OH-6
Empire Junction—uninc pl....KS-7
Empire Lake—lake....NY-2
Empire Lake—lake....WA-9
Empire Lakes—lake....OR-9
Empire Landing—beach....CA-9
Empire Landing—pop pl....AZ-5
Empire Lateral—canal....CO-8
Empire Lock—other....LA-4
Empire Mall*, The—locale....SD-7
Empire Meadows—flat....CA-9
Empire Mine—hist pl....CA-9
Empire Mine—locale....VA-3
Empire Mine—mine....AZ-5
Empire Mine—mine (5)....CA-9
Empire Mine—mine....ID-8
Empire Mine—mine....IL-6
Empire Mine—mine....MT-8
Empire Mine—mine (2)....NV-8
Empire Mine—mine....SD-7
Empire Mine—mine....TN-4
Empire Mine—pop pl....MI-6
Empire Mine (surface)—mine....AL-4
Empire Mine (underground)—mine....AL-4
Empire (Modesto-Empire Junction)—pop pl....CA-9
Empire Mountains—summit....AZ-5
Empire Mtn—summit....CA-9
Empire No 2 Shaft (Active)—mine....NM-5
Empire Number 2 Mine (surface)—mine....AL-4
Empire Oil Field—oilfield....LA-4
Empire Oil Field—oilfield....OK-5
Empire Oil Field—other....NM-5
Empire Pass—gap....CO-8
Empire Peak—summit....NM-5
Empire Point—cape....FL-3
Empire Point—uninc pl....FL-3
Empire Prairie—locale....MO-7
Empire Prairie Sch—school....WI-6
Empire Ranch—hist pl....AZ-5
Empire Ranch—locale....AZ-5
Empire Ranch—locale (2)....CA-9
Empire Ranch Airp—airport....AZ-5
Empire Range Channel—channel....OR-9
Empire Ravine—valley....CA-9
Empire Ridge—ridge (2)....CA-9
Empire Road (RR name for East Poland)—other....ME-1
Empire Roadside Rest—park....CA-9
Empire Rsvr—reservoir (2)....CO-8
Empire Sch—school....AZ-5
Empire Sch—school (3)....IL-6
Empire Sch—school....OH-6
Empire Sch—school....OK-5
Empire Sch—school....SD-7
Empire Sch—school....WY-8
Empire Smelter (Site)—locale....ID-8
Empire Spit—bar....WA-9
Empire State—uninc pl....NY-2
Empire State Bldg—building....NY-2
Empire State Bldg—hist pl....NY-2
Empire State Bldg—hist pl....WA-9
Empire State Country Club—other....NY-2
Empire State Plaza—post sta....NY-2
Empire Swamp—swamp....WI-6
Empire Town Creek Mine (surface)—mine....AL-4
Empire (Town of)—pop pl....WI-6
Empire Township....KS-7
Empire Township—civil....MO-7
Empire Township—pop pl (2)....KS-7
Empire Township—pop pl....ND-7
Empire (Township of)—pop pl....IL-6
Empire (Township of)—pop pl....MI-6
Empire (Township of)—pop pl....MN-6
Empire Tract—civil....CA-9
Empire Wash—stream....NV-8
Empire Weir Number One—other....CA-9
Empire Weir Number Two—dam....CA-9
Empire Well—well....AZ-5
Empire Westside Ditch—canal....CA-9
Empire Westside Main Canal—canal....CA-9
Empire Zinc Mine—mine....NM-5
Emplazado—pop pl....NM-5
Employee's Hotel and Garage—hist pl....MT-8
Employees' New Dormitory and Club—hist pl....NM-5
Emporia—pop pl....FL-3
Emporia—pop pl....IN-6
Emporia—pop pl....KS-7
Emporia—pop pl....VA-3
Emporia, Lake—lake....FL-3
Emporia Ave Ch of Christ—church....KS-7
Emporia (ind. city)—pop pl....VA-3
Emporia Junction—pop pl....KS-7
Emporia Municipal Airp—airport....KS-7
Emporia Sch—school....NE-7
Emporia Sch (historical)—school....MO-7
Emporia State Univ—school....KS-7
Emporia Township—pop pl....KS-7
Emporia West Plaza—locale....KS-7
Emporium—hist pl....CA-9
Emporium—hist pl....MI-6
Emporium—pop pl....PA-2
Emporium Borough—civil....PA-2
Emporium Cable TV Most—tower....PA-2
Emporium Junction—locale....PA-2
Emporium Reservoir Dam—dam....PA-2
Emporium Rsvr....PA-2
Emporium Rsvr—reservoir....PA-2
Emporium Shop Ctr—locale....UT-8
Emporium Water Company Number 3 Dam....PA-2
Empress—locale....GA-3
Empress (CCD)—cens area....GA-3
Empress Condominium—pop pl....UT-8
Empress Gulch—valley....SD-7
Empress Mine—mine....NV-8
Empress Mine (Inactive)—mine....CA-9
Empress Theatre—hist pl....UT-8
Empson Branch—stream....TN-4
Empson Bridge—bridge....TN-4
Empson Cannery—hist pl....CO-8
Empson Cem—cemetery....IN-6
Empson Ditch—canal....CO-8
Empson Hill—summit....TN-4
Empty Jug Cabin—locale....MT-8
Empty Lake Well—lake....OR-9
Empy—pop pl....OK-5
Empy Meadows—flat....NV-8
Empy Mtn—summit....NV-8
Empy Pass—gap....NV-8
Empy Wash—stream....NV-8
Emrich Rsvr—reservoir....CO-8
Emrick—pop pl....ND-7
Emrick Canyon—valley....NM-5
Emrick Hill—summit....MO-7
Emrick Lake—lake....WI-6
Emrick Sch (historical)—school....PA-2
Emrick Spring—spring....NM-5
Emrickville....PA-2
Emry Cem—cemetery....OH-6
Emsay Windmill—locale....NM-5
Emscn Mine—mine....AZ-5
Emsey—locale....OK-5
E M Simpson Dam—dam....NC-3
Emsley A Laney HS—school....NC-3
Emsley Cem—cemetery....SD-7
EMS Ranch—locale....WY-8
Emstar Church....AL-4
Emsworth—pop pl....PA-2
Emsworth Back Channel Dam—dam....PA-2
Emsworth Borough—civil....PA-2
Emsworth Dam—dam....PA-2
Emsworth Locks And Dams—dam....PA-2
Emsworth Pool—reservoir....PA-2
Emuckalusha....MS-4
Emuckfaw Battleground (historical)—locale....AL-4
Emuckfaw Creek—stream....AL-4
Emuckfaw (historical)—locale....AL-4
Emuru-to....MP-9
Emussa (historical)—locale....AL-4
E M Whitesides Sch—school....UT-8
Enajet—island....MP-9
Enajet Island....MP-9
Enalik Island—island....MP-9
Enalik Islet....MP-9
Enanon Cem—cemetery....MS-4
Enanon Ch—church....MS-4
Enarikku To....MP-9
Enas Pond—reservoir....TX-5
Enatalik Creek—stream....AK-9
Enaville—locale....ID-8
Enberg Ranch—locale....WY-8
Enbom Lake—reservoir....NM-5
Encalade—pop pl....LA-4
Encalmado Windmill—locale....TX-5
Encampment—pop pl....WY-8
Encampment Cem—cemetery....WY-8
Encampment Creek—stream....AK-9
Encampment Creek—stream....MT-8
Encampment Ditch—canal....WY-8
Encampment Island—island....MN-6
Encampment Meadows—flat....CO-8
Encampment Platte Valley Ditch—canal....WY-8
Encampment River—stream....CO-8
Encampment River—stream....MN-6
Encampment River—stream....WY-8
Encantada....TX-5
Encantada Peak—summit....TX-5
Encanto—pop pl....CA-9
Encanto Eighteen Hole Golf Course—other....AZ-5
Encanto Lagoon—lake....AZ-5
Encanto Nine Hole Golf Course—other....AZ-5
Encanto-Palmcroft Hist Dist—hist pl....AZ-5
Encanto Park—park....AZ-5
Encanto Park—park....CA-9
Encanto Sch—school....AZ-5
Encanto Sch—school....CA-9
Encapment Creek....CO-8
Encarnacion (Barrio)—fmr MCD....PR-3
Encarnacion Canyon—valley....CO-8
Encarnacion Canyon—valley....NM-5
Encas (Eastern North Carolina Sanatorium)—uninc pl....NC-3
Encenada Community Ditch—hist pl....NM-5
Enchabi-to....MP-9
Enchanted Acres (trailer park)—pop pl....DE-2
Enchanted Beach—beach....NV-8
Enchanted Canyon—valley....UT-8
Enchanted Cove—bay....CA-9
Enchanted Creek....VA-3
Enchanted Creek—stream....VA-3
Enchanted Forest—pop pl....IL-6
Enchanted Forest Park—park....FL-3
Enchanted Gorge—valley....CA-9
Enchanted Hills—locale....CA-9
Enchanted Hills—pop pl....AL-4
Enchanted Hills—pop pl....IN-6
Enchanted Hills—uninc pl....NM-5
Enchanted Hills Subdivision—pop pl....UT-8
Enchanted Homes Addition Subdivision—pop pl....UT-8
Enchanted Island—island....ME-1
Enchanted Island—island....MN-6
Enchanted Island—island....WA-9
Enchanted Lake—lake....FL-3
Enchanted Lake—lake....NM-5
Enchanted Oaks—pop pl....TX-5
Enchanted Park—pop pl....FL-3
Enchanted Pond—lake....ME-1
Enchanted Prairie—area....OR-9
Enchanted Rock—summit....TX-5
Enchanted Rock Archeol District—hist pl....TX-5
Enchanted Stream—stream....ME-1
Enchanted Valley—valley....WA-9
Enchanted Village Subdivision—pop pl....UT-8
Enchantment Basin—basin....WA-9
Enchantment Lake—lake....MI-6
Enchantment Lakes—lake....WA-9
Enchantment Pass—gap....WA-9
Enchantment Peaks—range....WA-9
Enchanto, Lake—reservoir....CA-9
Enciente, Bayou L'—stream....MS-4
Encierro Canyon—valley....NM-5
Encinada Mesa—summit (2)....NM-5
Encinado Creek—stream....NM-5
Encinado Ditch....NM-5
Encina HS—school....CA-9
Encinal—locale....CA-9
Encinal—pop pl....NM-5
Encinal—pop pl....TX-5
Encinal—uninc pl....CA-9
Encina Lake—lake....TX-5
Encinal Basin—harbor....CA-9
Encinal Canyon—valley....CA-9
Encinal Canyon—valley....NM-5
Encinal (CCD)—cens area....TX-5
Encinal Creek—stream (2)....NM-5
Encinal HS—school....CA-9
Encinal Peninsula—cape....TX-5
Encinal Sch—school (3)....CA-9
Encinal Windmill—locale....TX-5
Encinal Y Buena Esperanza—civil....CA-9
Encinas, Canada De Los —valley....CA-9
Encinas, Canyon De Los—valley....CA-9
Encina Sola Windmill—locale....TX-5
Encinas Spring....AZ-5
Encinas Tank—reservoir....AZ-5
Encinitas—pop pl....CA-9
Encinitas Beach County Park—park....CA-9
Encinita Sch—school....CA-9
Encinitas Creek—stream....CA-9
Encinitas Oil Field—oilfield....TX-5
Encinitas Union Sch—school....CA-9
Encinitas Windmill—locale....TX-5
Encino—pop pl....CA-9
Encino—pop pl....NM-5
Encino—pop pl....TX-5
Encino Canyon—valley....NM-5
Encino (CCD)—cens area....NM-5
Encino (CCD)—cens area....TX-5
Encino Creek—stream....CA-9
Encino Dam No 81—dam....NM-5
Encino Dam No 83—dam....NM-5
Encino Dam No 85—dam....NM-5
Encino Dam No 86—dam....NM-5
Encino de la Cruz Artesian Well—well....TX-5
Encino Draw—valley (2)....NM-5
Encino Lookout—locale....NM-5
Encino Medical Plaza—hospital....NM-5
Encino Mucho Windmill—locale....TX-5
Encino Municipal Golf Course—other....CA-9
Encino Oil And Gas Field—oilfield....TX-5
Encino Ranch—locale (2)....TX-5
Encino Rsvr—reservoir....CA-9
Encinosa Canyon—valley....NM-5
Encinosa Creek—stream....CA-9
Encinosa Creek—stream....NM-5
Encinosa Draw—valley....NM-5
Encinosa Mesa—summit....NM-5
Encino Siding—locale....CA-9
Encinoso—pop pl....NM-5
Encinoso Canyon—valley (3)....NM-5
Encinoso Cem—cemetery....NM-5
Encinoso Picnic Area—park....AZ-5
Encino Spring—spring....NM-5
Encinos Wash, Los—stream....AZ-5
Encinos Windmill—locale....TX-5
Encino Tank—reservoir....AZ-5
Encino Viejo Windmill—locale....TX-5
Encino Wash—stream....NM-5
Encino Well—well....TX-5
Encio Gulch—valley....AK-9
Enclosure Creek—stream....ID-8
Enclosure Hist Dist—hist pl....NJ-2
Encroaching Corners....NJ-2
End—pop pl....PA-2
End Bailys Run Branch Station—building....PA-2
End Butte—summit....ID-8
End Canyon—valley....AZ-5
End Creek—stream....OR-9
Endean Playground—park....MA-1
Endeavers Inner....MA-1
Endeavor—pop pl....PA-2
Endeavor—pop pl....WI-6
Endeavors—bar....MA-1
Endeavors Inner....MA-1
Endeavors Inner—bar....MA-1
Endeavors Outer....MA-1
Endeavors Outer—bar....MA-1
Endee—locale....KY-4
Endee—locale....NM-5
Endee Cem—cemetery....NM-5
Endee Hill—summit....NM-5
Ende Kil....DE-2
Ender Ditch—canal....IN-6
Enderis Playground—park....WI-6
Enderlin—pop pl....ND-7
Enderlin Park Dam—dam....ND-7
Enderly—hist pl....VA-3
Enderly Heights Sch—school....VA-3
Enderly Park—park....NC-3
Enderly Park Sch—school....NC-3
Enderly Park (subdivision)—pop pl....NC-3
Enders—locale....AR-4
Enders—pop pl....NE-7
Enders—pop pl....PA-2
Endersbees Corners—locale....NY-2
Enders Bldg—hist pl....OR-9
Endersby—locale....OR-9
Endersby Sch—school....OR-9
Enders Dam—dam....NE-7
Enders-Fisherville Sch—school....PA-2
Enders Hill—summit....MI-6
Enders Island—island....CT-1
Enders Island—pop pl....CT-1
Enders Lake—lake....NE-7
Enders Lateral—canal....ID-8
Enders Marsh—lake....NE-7
Enders Mine—mine....AZ-5
Enders Pond—lake....CT-1
Enders Ranch—locale....NE-7
Enders Reservoir Rec Area—park....NE-7
Enders Road Sch—school....NY-2
Enders Rsvr—reservoir....NE-7
Enders Sch—school....CA-9
Enders Sch—school....NE-7
Endert's Beach Archeol Sites—hist pl....CA-9
Endfield Tank—reservoir....AZ-5
Endicott—locale....KY-4
Endicott—locale....VA-3
Endicott—pop pl....MA-1
Endicott—pop pl....NE-7
Endicott—pop pl....NY-2
Endicott—pop pl....WA-9
Endicott—pop pl....WV-2
Endicott Airp—airport....WA-9
Endicott Arm—channel....AK-9
Endicott Cem—cemetery....OK-5
Endicott Ch—church....KY-4
Endicott Ch—church....VA-3
Endicott Community Coll—school....MA-1
Endicott Creek—stream....NC-3
Endicott Creek—stream (2)....OR-9
Endicott Ditch—canal....IN-6
Endicott Gap—gap....AK-9
Endicott Hotel—hist pl....NH-1
Endicott Lake—lake....AK-9
Endicott Lake—reservoir....MI-6
Endicott Mountains—range....AK-9
Endicott Plaza (Shop Ctr)—locale....MA-1
Endicott River—stream....AK-9
Endicott Rock—hist pl....NH-1
Endicott Sch—school....MA-1
Endicott Square (Shop Ctr)—locale....MA-1
Endion....MN-6
Endion Passenger Depot—hist pl....MN-6
Endion Sch—hist pl....MN-6
Endion Sch—school....MN-6
End Key—island....FL-3
Endlee Sch—school....SD-7
Endless Branch—stream....NJ-2
Endless Brook—stream....VT-1
Endless Caverns—locale....VA-3
Endless Chain Mine—mine....AZ-5
Endless Draw—arroyo....NV-8
Endless Lake—lake....FL-3
Endless Lake—reservoir....ME-1
Endless Mountain Camp—locale....PA-2
Endless Mountains Airp—airport....PA-2
Endlich Hill—summit....WY-8
Endlich Mesa—summit....CO-8
Endlick Mesa....CO-8
End Lookout—locale....MT-8
End Mtn—summit....WA-9
Endoah Creek—stream....ID-8
End of Island Slough—gut....NC-3
End of Lake Powell—other....UT-8
End of Line Tank—reservoir....AZ-5
End of Line Tank—reservoir....NM-5
End of the Line Trough—reservoir....NV-8
End of the Rainbow Cave—cave....PA-2
End of the Road....TN-4
End of the Track, The....ND-7
End of the Trail—hist pl....WI-6
End of the Trail Rsvr—reservoir....OR-9
End of the World—ridge....CA-9
Endomile Ditch—canal....CO-8
End O'Narrows Bridge—bridge....PA-2
Endora (historical)—locale....AL-4
Endor Creek—stream....MT-8
Endor Iron Furnace—hist pl....NC-3
Endot—locale....UT-8
Endot—uninc pl....TX-5
Endovalley Campground—locale....CO-8
Endowment Mine—mine....NV-8
End Park—park....WI-6
Endres Draw—valley....WY-8
Endresen Cem—cemetery....MN-6
Endreson, Lars and Guri, House—hist pl....MN-6

English Branch—stream VA-3
English Brook—stream NY-2
English Camp—locale CO-8
English Camp—mine AZ-5
English Camp Hollow—valley TN-4
English Campsite—locale WA-9
English Canyon—valley CA-9
English Canyon—valley NV-8
English Cave—cave TN-4
English Cem—cemetery AR-4
English Cem—cemetery (2) GA-3
English Cem—cemetery IL-6
English Cem—cemetery (2) MN-6
English Cem—cemetery MO-7
English Cem—cemetery ND-7
English Cem—cemetery (3) OH-6
English Cem—cemetery SC-3
English Cem—cemetery TX-5
English Cemetery NC-3
**English Center**—pop pl PA-2
English Center, The—school FL-3
English Center Suspension Bridge—hist pl PA-2
English Ch—church TX-5
English Chapel—church NC-3
English Chapel FWB Ch NC-3
English Chapel (historical)—church NC-3
English Church—hist pl NH-1
English Church and Schoolhouse—hist pl NY-2
English Church Sch—school NY-2
**English Consul**—pop pl MD-2
English Coulee—stream ND-7
English Cove—valley TN-4
English Creek IA-7
English Creek SC-3
English Creek TN-4
English Creek—locale NJ-2
**English Creek**—pop pl TN-4
English Creek—stream AL-4
English Creek—stream AR-4
English Creek—stream CA-9
English Creek—stream CO-8
English Creek—stream FL-3
English Creek—stream ID-8
English Creek—stream (2) IA-7
English Creek—stream KY-4
English Creek—stream NE-7
English Creek—stream NJ-2
English Creek—stream NY-2
English Creek—stream NC-3
English Creek—stream (2) TN-4
English Creek Baptist Ch—church TN-4
**English Creek Landing**—pop pl NJ-2
English Creek Pond—reservoir NJ-2
English Creek Pond Dam—dam NJ-2
English Creek Sch (historical)—school TN-4
English Crossing—locale TX-5
English Crossroads—locale SC-3
English Cut GA-3
English-Dansby House—hist pl TX-5
English Draft—valley PA-2
English Drain—stream (2) MI-6
English Eddy—locale GA-3
English Eddy Ch—church GA-3
English Estates Elem Sch—school FL-3
English Family Cem—cemetery MS-4
English Farms—locale TX-5
English Field—park VA-3
English George Creek—stream MT-8
English-German Sch—hist pl TX-5
English Grove Cem—cemetery MN-6
English Grove Ch—church MO-7
English Grove Lake—lake MN-6
English Gulch—valley CO-8
English Gulch—valley MT-8
English Hill—summit CA-9
English Hill—summit IN-6
English Hill—summit OH-6
English Hill—summit TN-4
English Hills—range CA-9
English Hills—summit TX-5
English Hills, The—locale VA-3
**English Hills (subdivision)**—pop pl NC-3
English Hills Tank—reservoir TX-5
**English (historical)**—pop pl OR-9
English Hollow—valley TN-4
English Hollow—valley TX-5
English HS MA-1
English HS—hist pl (2) MA-1
English HS—school MA-1
English Kills—harbor NY-2
English Knob—summit NC-3
English Lake—lake AR-4
English Lake—lake CA-9
English Lake—lake FL-3
English Lake—lake MN-6
English Lake—lake (2) WI-6
**English Lake**—pop pl IN-6
English Landing (historical)—locale AL-4
English Lateral—canal ID-8
English Lookout—locale LA-4
English Lutheran Ch—church WI-6
Englishman Bay—bay ME-1
Englishman Butte—summit SD-7
Englishman Hill—summit OR-9
Englishman Island—island MN-6
**English Manor**—pop pl MD-2
English Manor Sch—school MD-2
**English Manor (subdivision)**—pop pl PA-2
**English Manor Subdivision**—pop pl UT-8
Englishman River—stream ME-1
English Meadow—flat (2) CA-9
English Mill (historical)—locale AL-4
English Millpond—reservoir GA-3
**English Mills**—pop pl PA-2
**English Mills**—pop pl VT-1
**English Mountain Resort**—pop pl TN-4
English Mtn—summit CA-9
English Mtn—summit NV-8
English Mtn—summit OR-9
English Mtn—summit TN-4
English Navy Cove—bay FL-3
English Neighborhood Brook—stream CT-1
English Neighbourhood NJ-2
English Park—park FL-3
English Park—park KS-7
English Peak—summit CA-9
English Pit—basin WA-9
English Place—locale AR-4
English-Poindexter House—hist pl TX-5
English Point ID-8
English Point—cape ID-8
English Pond—lake AL-4
English Pond—lake SC-3
English Pond—reservoir (2) AL-4
English Pond—reservoir GA-3
English Post Office (historical)—building TN-4
English Prairie Ch—church IN-6
English Prairie Sch—school IL-6
English Prairie Sch—school WI-6
English Queen ND-7
English Ridge—ridge CA-9
English Ridge—ridge WI-6
English Ridge Sch—school WI-6
English River—stream IA-7
English River—stream NY-2
English River Township—fmr MCD (2) IA-7
English (RR name for Lakewood)—other WA-9
English Rsvr—reservoir IN-6
English Run—stream (4) PA-2
English Run—stream WI-6
English Sch—school FL-3
English Sch—school IN-6
English Sch—school MI-6
English Sch (abandoned)—school MO-7
English Settlement—locale IA-7
English Settlement Sch—school VT-1
English Settlement Sch—school WI-6
Englishshoe Bar—bar AK-9
Englishs Landing (historical)—locale AL-4
English Spring—spring NM-5
English Spring—spring (2) OR-9
English Spur—ridge KY-4
English Swamp—swamp PA-2
English Tank—reservoir TX-5
English Tanks—reservoir NM-5
**English Terrace (subdivision)**—pop pl AL-4
Englishton Park Home—building IN-6
English Town NJ-2
English Town—locale CA-9
**Englishtown**—pop pl NJ-2
Englishtown Lake Dam—dam NJ-2
English Township—fmr MCD (2) IA-7
**English (Township of)**—pop pl IL-6
**English Turn**—pop pl LA-4
English Turn Cem—cemetery LA-4
English Valley—valley CO-8
English Valley—valley PA-2
English Valley—valley WI-6
English Village—hist pl VA-3
**English Village**—pop pl (2) AL-4
**English Village**—pop pl DE-2
**English Village**—pop pl MD-2
English Village Sch—school NY-2
English Village Shop Ctr—locale (2) AL-4
English Village Shop Ctr—locale PA-2
**English Village (subdivision)**—pop pl AL-4
**Englishville**—pop pl MI-6
Englishville Cem—cemetery MI-6
Englishville Sch—school MI-6
English Water Supply Dam—reservoir IN-6
English Well—well (2) NM-5
English Wells—well AZ-5
English Woods OH-6
**English Woods**—pop pl OH-6
Englund—locale MN-6
Engman Lake—lake MI-6
Engralson Lake—lake MN-6
Engram Branch—stream GA-3
Engstrom Creek—stream ID-8
Engstrom Ranch—locale MT-8
Engvall Sch—school CA-9
**Enhaut**—pop pl PA-2
Eni MP-9
Eni, Dolen—summit FM-9
Eniaetok—island MP-9
Eniaetok Island MP-9
Eniaidok MP-9
Eniaidokku MP-9
Eniaidokku Island MP-9
Eniaidokku-to MP-9
Eniairik—island MP-9
Eniairikku—island MP-9
Eniairikku-to MP-9
Eniairo—island MP-9
Eniairo Island MP-9
Eniaitoku-to MP-9
Eniak MP-9
Eniak—island MP-9
Eniak Island MP-9
Enialo—island MP-9
Enialo Island MP-9
Eniamumessi MP-9
Eniarikku-to MP-9
Eniarmidj MP-9
Eniarmis MP-9
Eniaro Island MP-9
Eniaro-to MP-9
Eniarumichi Island MP-9
Eniarumichi Island—island MP-9
Eniarumichi-to MP-9
Eniaru-to MP-9
Eniaui Island MP-9
Eniaui Island—island MP-9
Enibarbar MP-9
Enibarubaru Passage MP-9
Enibarubaru Passage—channel MP-9
Enibarubaru-Suido MP-9
Enibarubaru-to MP-9
Enibigangaaru To MP-9
Enibigangaru-to MP-9
Enibiibukku-to MP-9
Enibiji MP-9
Enibiji Island MP-9
Enibiji Island—island MP-9
Enibij Island MP-9
Enibing Island MP-9
Enibin Island—island (2) MP-9
Enibin-to MP-9
Eniboru To MP-9
Enibuas Island—island MP-9
Enibubuen MP-9
Enibubu-To MP-9
Enibuin MP-9
Enibujii MP-9
Enibuk Island—island MP-9
Enibukku MP-9
Enibung MP-9
Enibuni MP-9
Enibuni-to MP-9
Enibun To MP-9
Eniburo-to MP-9
Enichaen-To MP-9
Enichean-suido MP-9
Enichean-to MP-9
Enicherudo Island MP-9
Enicherudo-to MP-9
Enichien To MP-9
Enichierudo To MP-9
Enid—locale AZ-5
Enid—locale MT-8
Enid—locale OR-9
**Enid**—pop pl MS-4
**Enid**—pop pl OK-5
**Enid**—pop pl PA-2
Enid Armory—hist pl OK-5
Enid (CCD)—cens area OK-5
Enid Dam—dam MS-4
Enid Gulch—valley ID-8
Enid (historical)—locale AL-4
Enid Interchange—other OK-5
Enidje MP-9
Enidjek MP-9
Enidjuon MP-9
Enid Lake—lake OR-9
Enid Lake—reservoir MS-4
Enidrik MP-9
Enid RR Station—building AZ-5
Enid Rsvr MS-4
Enid Sch (historical)—school PA-2
Enid State Sch—school OK-5
Enid Woodring Municipal Airp—airport OK-5
Eniebing MP-9
Eniej MP-9
Enierippu Island MP-9
Enierippu-To MP-9
Eniet MP-9
Enigain-to MP-9
Enigan Island MP-9
Enigan Island—island MP-9
Enigan Pass MP-9
Enigan Pass—channel MP-9
Enigan-to MP-9
Enigaran MP-9
Enigaranrikiraru-to MP-9
Enigaran-to MP-9
Enigarmek MP-9
Enighed—hist pl VI-3
Enighed—locale VI-3
**Enighed**—pop pl VI-3
Enigma—locale TN-4
**Enigma**—pop pl GA-3
Enigma (CCD)—cens area GA-3
Enigma Post Office (historical)—building TN-4
Enigma Ridge—ridge AK-9
Enigoen-to MP-9
Enigu—island MP-9
Enigu Island MP-9
Enigu-to MP-9
Eniiarumichi-To MP-9
Eniibin Island MP-9
Eniibin-To MP-9
Eniibuji-to MP-9
Eniibukku Island MP-9
Eniibukku Pass—channel MP-9
Eniibukku-Suido MP-9
Eniibun-to MP-9
Eniibuuji To MP-9
Eniiecchi Island—island MP-9
Eniien MP-9
Eniien—island MP-9
Eniierappukan MP-9
Eniierappukan-to MP-9
Eniijiette-To MP-9
Eniijietto-to MP-9
Eniijok MP-9
Eniikemu MP-9
Eniikemu Island—island MP-9
Eniikopure Island MP-9
Eniikopure Island—island MP-9
Eniiman Island MP-9
Eniiman Island—island MP-9
Eniiman (not verified)—island MP-9
Eniioru Island MP-9
Eniioru Island—island MP-9
Eniirikku MP-9
Eniirikku Pass MP-9
Eniirikku-suido MP-9
Eniirikku-to MP-9
Eniirin Island MP-9
Eniirin-To MP-9
Eniiro Island MP-9
Eniiuri MP-9
Eniiyakku MP-9
Eniiyakku—island MP-9
Eniiyakku Island MP-9
Eniiyakku-To MP-9
Enijabro Island—island MP-9
Enijabrok Island MP-9
Enijaburoo To MP-9
Enijaburo-to MP-9
Enijajdok MP-9
Enijaridoyu Island MP-9
Enijaridoyu Island—island MP-9
Enijaridoyu-To MP-9
Enije Channel—channel MP-9
Enije Island MP-9
Enije Island—island MP-9
Enije Pass MP-9
Enijibaaru-To MP-9
Enijibuaru Island MP-9
Enijin Durchfahrt MP-9
Enijin Eurkf MP-9
Enijiyo-to MP-9
Enijo To MP-9
Eniju MP-9
Enijun Channel—channel MP-9
Enijun Island MP-9
Enijun Island—island MP-9
Enijun Pass MP-9
Enijuri-to MP-9
Enijwa Island MP-9
Enikaieng MP-9
Enikannatto Island MP-9
Enikannatto Island—island MP-9
Enikannatto-To MP-9
Enikano Island MP-9
Enikano Island—island MP-9
Enikinmw—bar FM-9
Enikiyo MP-9
Enikiyo Island—island MP-9
Enikoion MP-9
Eniligere—island MP-9
Eniligere Island MP-9
Enilik MP-9
Enilikeri MP-9
Enilok—island MP-9
Enimagej MP-9
Enimagetto-to MP-9
Eniman MP-9
Enimanekku MP-9
Enimanekku-to MP-9
Enimanetsu Island MP-9
Enimanetsu Island—island MP-9
Enimman-to MP-9
Enimomu MP-9
Enimomu—island MP-9
Enimomu Island MP-9
Enimomu-To MP-9
Enimonetto MP-9
Enimonetto-To MP-9
Enimoni MP-9
Enimware—bar FM-9
Enin—civil FM-9
Enin, Unun En—cape FM-9
Eninaitok—island MP-9
Eninaitok Island MP-9
Enine MP-9
Ening—spring FM-9
Eningiar MP-9
Eninikugi MP-9
Eninikugi Island—island MP-9
Eninikugi-To MP-9
Eninlik MP-9
Eninman—island MP-9
Eninman Island MP-9
Eninon MP-9
Eninon—island MP-9
Eninrapugan Island—island MP-9
Eninrapugan-To MP-9
Enin Sch—school FM-9
Eninun MP-9
Enioa MP-9
Enion MP-9
Enion—locale IL-6
Eniong MP-9
Enioruuri Island MP-9
Enipeihn Pah—civil FM-9
Enipeihn Powe—civil FM-9
Enipein Pah, Dauen—gut FM-9
Enipin MP-9
Enipoas—civil FM-9
Enipoas, Dauen—gut FM-9
Enipoas, Pilen—stream FM-9
Eniqu Island MP-9
Eniramumesshi-to MP-9
Eniramumessi To MP-9
Eniramumetsushi To MP-9
Eniran—island MP-9
Eniran Island MP-9
Eniran Pass—channel MP-9
Enirebokut MP-9
Enirichikku Island MP-9
Enirichukku Island—island MP-9
Enirigerii To MP-9
Enirigirikku Island (not verified)—island MP-9
Enirigrukku (not verified)—bar MP-9
Enirigurii-to MP-9
Enirik MP-9
Enirik—island MP-9
Enirikku MP-9
Enirikku—island MP-9
Enirikku Island MP-9
Enirikku Pass MP-9
Enirikku-Suido MP-9
Enirikku To MP-9
Enirik Pass—channel MP-9
Enirin Island MP-9
Enirin Island—island MP-9
Eniriowganjirik MP-9
Enirolul MP-9
Eniroruuri—island MP-9
Eniroruuri Island MP-9
Eniroruuri-To MP-9
Enirorwiri Island MP-9
Enirukku-to MP-9
Enis Cem—cemetery AL-4
Enisetsu MP-9
Enisetsu Island MP-9
Enisetsu-To MP-9
Enitachopco Creek—stream AL-4
Enitachopco (historical)—locale AL-4
Eniue MP-9
Eniueraku To MP-9
Eniuetakku MP-9
Eniuetakku Island—island MP-9
Eniuetakku-To MP-9
Eniuetaku Suido MP-9
Eniumu MP-9
Eniumu Island MP-9
Eniumu Island—island MP-9
Eniwataku—island MP-9
Eniwataku—locale MP-9
Eniwataku-To MP-9
Eniwetak MP-9
Eniwetak—island MP-9
Eniwetak Channel MP-9
Eniwetak Island MP-9
Eniwetak Island—island MP-9
Eniwetakku Island MP-9
Eniwetakku-suido MP-9
Eniwetakku-to MP-9
Eniwetak Pass MP-9
Eniwetak Pass—channel MP-9
Eniwetak Passage MP-9
Eniwetak Passage—channel MP-9
Eniwetaku MP-9
Eniwetok—island MP-9
Eniwetok Atoll MP-9
Eniwetok Atoll—island MP-9
Eniwetok Group Eniwetok Gruppe MP-9
Eniwetok Island MP-9
Eniwetok Lagoon—lake MP-9
Eniwetok Passage MP-9
Eniyu-Suido MP-9
Eniyu-To MP-9
Enjar Lake—lake WA-9
Enjbei—island MP-9
Enjebi—island MP-9
En-Joie Park—park NY-2
**Enka**—pop pl NC-3
Enka Dam—dam TN-4
Enka HS—school NC-3
Enka Lake—reservoir NC-3
Enka Lake Dam—dam NC-3
Enkasar PW-9
Enkassar PW-9
Enkaumij—island MP-9
Enkaumij Island MP-9
**Enka Village**—pop pl NC-3
Enke Cem—cemetery MO-7
Enkor Island—island MP-9
Enkor Station MP-9
Enlaidokku Island MP-9
Enlarged Cherokee Ditch—canal WY-8
Enlarged Encampment Ditch—canal WY-8
Enlli Ch—church NY-2
Enlo ND-7
Enloe—locale ND-7
**Enloe**—pop pl TX-5
Enloe Cave—cave MO-7
Enloe Cem—cemetery (2) MO-7
Enloe Creek—stream NC-3
Enloe Dam—dam WA-9
Enloe Dam and Powerplant—hist pl WA-9
Enloe East HS—school NC-3
Enloe Hollow Branch—stream TN-4
Enloe Hosp—hospital CA-9
Enloe HS—school NC-3
Enloe Ridge—ridge NC-3
Enloe Slough—stream TX-5
**Enlow**—pop pl PA-2
Enlow Cem—cemetery IN-6
Enlow Cem—cemetery MS-4
Enlow Fork—stream PA-2
Enlow Fork—stream WV-2
Enman Field Ch—church AL-4
Enmat Island MP-9
En Medio—locale NM-5
Enmedio, Arroyo—valley TX-5
Enmedio Windmill—locale TX-5
Enmeeji To MP-9
Ennak MP-9
**Ennalls**—pop pl MD-2
Ennalls Wharf—locale MD-2
Ennanlik Channel—channel MP-9
Ennanlik Durchfahrt MP-9
Ennanlik Island—island MP-9
Ennanlik Pass MP-9
Ennejo MP-9
Ennerdale—locale NY-2
Enner Lake WI-6
Ennes Cem MO-7
Ennett Point—cape NC-3
Enni Camp CA-9
**Ennice**—pop pl NC-3
Enniefich—locale FM-9
Ennies Cem—cemetery KY-4
Enniibuji-to MP-9
Ennimenetto—island MP-9
Ennimenetto Island MP-9
Ennimenetto-To MP-9
Ennin FM-9
**Enning**—pop pl SD-7
Ennin Kumi FM-9
Ennin Village FM-9
Ennis AZ-5
Ennis—locale CA-9
Ennis—locale GA-3
Ennis—locale KY-4
Ennis—locale WA-9
**Ennis**—pop pl AZ-5
**Ennis**—pop pl MT-8
**Ennis**—pop pl TX-5
**Ennis**—pop pl WV-2
Ennis, Lake—lake FL-3
Ennis, Willis, House—hist pl KY-4
Ennis Archaeol Site (12 OW 229)—hist pl IN-6
Ennis Branch—stream GA-3
Ennis Branch—stream LA-4
Ennis Branch—stream TN-4
Ennis Butte—summit OR-9
Ennis Butte Spring—spring OR-9
Ennis Canal OR-9
Ennis Cave—cave AR-4
Ennis (CCD)—cens area TX-5
Ennis Cem—cemetery (2) GA-3
Ennis Cem—cemetery IL-6
Ennis Cem—cemetery KY-4
Ennis Cem—cemetery MO-7
Ennis Cem—cemetery MT-8
Ennis Cem—cemetery NY-2
Ennis Cem—cemetery NC-3
Ennis City KS-7
Ennis Commercial Hist Dist—hist pl TX-5
Enniscorthy—hist pl MD-2
Ennis Cotton Compress—hist pl TX-5
Ennis Creek—stream AR-4
Ennis Creek—stream IL-6
Ennis Creek—stream IN-6
Ennis Creek—stream MI-6
Ennis Creek—stream (3) OR-9
Ennis Creek—stream TX-5
Ennis Creek—stream (2) WA-9
Ennis Creek School (Abandoned)—locale TX-5
Ennis Cultural Station—locale MT-8
Ennis Ditch—canal CO-8
Ennis Draw—valley CO-8
Ennis Grade Sch—school MT-8
Ennis Gulch—valley ID-8
Ennis Hall—building PA-2
Ennis House—hist pl CA-9
Ennis HS—hist pl TX-5
Ennis Knob—summit OK-5
Ennis Lake WI-6
Ennis Lake—lake MT-8
Ennis Lake—lake WI-6
Ennis Lake Community Park—park MT-8
Ennis Lake Recreation Site—locale MT-8
Ennis Mtn—summit VA-3
Ennis Pond—reservoir NC-3
Ennis Pond—swamp VA-3
Ennis Ranch—locale CO-8
Ennis Recreation Site—locale MT-8
Ennis Ridge—ridge IN-6
Ennis Riffle—rapids OR-9
Ennis Rodeo Grounds—locale MT-8
Enniss MT-8
Ennis Sch—school MT-8
Ennis Sch—school TN-4
Ennis Station—locale AZ-5
Ennis Store (historical)—locale MS-4
Ennis Tartt Dam—dam AL-4
Ennis Tartt Pond—reservoir AL-4
**Ennisville**—pop pl PA-2
Ennix Cem—cemetery AL-4
Ennopu Island MP-9
Ennopu Island—island MP-9
Ennopu-To MP-9
Ennors Ranch—locale CA-9
Ennubirr—island MP-9
Ennubirr Island MP-9
Ennuebing—island MP-9
Ennuebing Island MP-9
Ennugarret—island MP-9
Ennugarret Island MP-9
Ennugenliggelap—island MP-9
Ennugenliggelap Island MP-9
Ennugenligglap MP-9
Ennumenetto MP-9
Ennumennent MP-9
Ennumennet—island MP-9
Ennumennet Island MP-9
Ennumet—island MP-9
Ennumet Island MP-9
Ennylabegan—island (2) MP-9
Ennylabegan Island MP-9
Eno PA-2
Eno—locale CO-8
Eno—locale OH-6
Eno—locale TN-4
**Eno**—pop pl NC-3
Eno, Amos, House—hist pl CT-1
Enoa Island MP-9
Enoa Island—island MP-9
Enob—island MP-9
Eno Cem—cemetery IA-7
Eno Ch—church NC-3
Enoch—locale KY-4
Enoch—locale PA-2
Enoch—locale TX-5
Enoch—locale WV-2
**Enoch**—pop pl UT-8
Enoch Branch—stream KY-4
Enoch Branch—stream (2) WV-2
Enoch Brook—stream ME-1
Enoch Brown Memorial Park—park PA-2
Enoch Brown Park and Memorial PA-2
Enoch Canyon—valley UT-8
Enoch Cem—cemetery TN-4
Enoch Cem—cemetery UT-8
Enoch Ch—church MO-7
Enoch City Cemetery UT-8
Enoch Creek AL-4
Enoch Creek—stream GA-3
Enoch Creek—stream OH-6
Enoch Crossroads SC-3
Enoch Divide—ridge UT-8
Enoch Fork—stream (2) KY-4
Enoch Fork—stream WV-2
Enoch Grove Cem—cemetery MS-4
Enoch Grove Ch—church MS-4
Enoch Gulch—valley CO-8
Enoch Hill—summit ME-1
Enoch Hollow—valley (3) TN-4
Enoch Knob—summit MO-7
Enoch Knob—summit VA-3
Enoch Lake—lake ME-1
Enoch Lee Ditch—canal IN-6
Enoch Mill Creek—stream NC-3
Enoch Point—cliff UT-8
Enoch Pond—lake GA-3
Enoch Post Office (historical)—building TN-4
Enoch Ridge—ridge UT-8
Enoch Run—stream WV-2
**Enochs**—pop pl TX-5
Enochs Branch—stream VA-3
**Enochsburg**—pop pl IN-6
Enochs Cem—cemetery TN-4
Enoch Sch—school MO-7
Enoch Sch—school UT-8
Enochs Creek—stream VA-3
Enochs Draw—valley WY-8
Enochs Grove Cem—cemetery MS-4
Enochs (historical)—locale MS-4
Enochs JHS—school MS-4
Enochs Lake—reservoir CO-8
Enochs Mill (historical)—locale MS-4
Enochs Pond—reservoir TX-5
Enoch Spring—spring UT-8
Enoch Stahl Sch—school PA-2
Enoch Stuart Park—park TX-5
Enochs-Weathersby Cem—cemetery MS-4
**Enoch (Township of)**—pop pl OH-6
Enoch Valley—valley ID-8
**Enochville**—pop pl NC-3
Enochville Elem Sch—school NC-3
Enock Landing GA-3
Enode Sch—school IL-6
Enoe—locale AL-4
Eno Hill—summit CT-1
Enok—locale MN-6
Enoka—locale LA-4
Enok Island—island MP-9
**Enola**—pop pl AR-4
**Enola**—pop pl LA-4
**Enola**—pop pl MS-4
**Enola**—pop pl NE-7
**Enola**—pop pl NC-3
**Enola**—pop pl PA-2
**Enola**—pop pl SC-3
Enola, Lake—lake FL-3
Enola, Lake—lake MI-6
Enola Hill—ridge OR-9
Enola Landing—locale MS-4
Enola Post Office (historical)—building MS-4
Enola (Township of)—fmr MCD AR-4
Enola Yards—locale PA-2
Enom Cem—cemetery WV-2
Enom Ch—church WV-2
Enon AL-4
Enon LA-4
Enon MA-1
Enon MS-4
Enon PA-2
Enon—locale (2) AL-4
Enon—locale AR-4
Enon—locale FL-3
Enon—locale KY-4
Enon—locale PA-2

Ephrata Post Office (historical)—building ... PA-2
Ephrata Sch—school ... PA-2
Ephrata-Soap Lake (CCD)—cens area ... WA-9
Ephrata Substation—other ... WA-9
**Ephrata (Township of)**—pop pl ... PA-2
Ephriah Canyon—valley ... AZ-5
Ephriam ... UT-8
Ephriam Branch—stream ... SC-3
Ephriam Brook—stream ... ME-1
Ephriam Ditch—canal ... CO-8
Eph Shoal—bar ... NJ-2
Eph Spring—spring ... AZ-5
Ephsum Spring—spring ... NV-8
Epichon—spring ... FM-9
Epichon—well ... FM-9
Epichun—bar ... FM-9
**Epico (historical)**—pop pl ... MS-4
Epidote Lake—lake ... MI-6
Epidote Mine—mine ... MI-6
Epidote Peak—summit ... CA-9
Epiineenouw ... FM-9
Epiitar ... FM-9
Epikepin—spring ... FM-9
Epil En Otta ... FM-9
**Epileptic Village (New Castle State Hospital)**—pop pl ... IN-6
Epin ... FM-9
**Epin**—pop pl ... FM-9
Epin, Oror En—locale ... FM-9
Epinenom—swamp ... FM-9
Epiner—bar ... FM-9
Epin Fenu ... FM-9
Epinfonu—bar ... FM-9
Epinifou—spring ... FM-9
Epinipat—spring ... FM-9
Epiniuit ... FM-9
Epiniwit ... FM-9
Epiniwit—well ... FM-9
Epinner ... FM-9
Epinnou—spring ... FM-9
Epino—spring ... FM-9
Epinom ... FM-9
Epinonak—bar ... FM-9
Epinosa—spring ... FM-9
Epinou—spring ... FM-9
Epinpat—tunnel ... FM-9
Epinua—locale ... FM-9
Epinun, Unun En—bar ... FM-9
**Epinup**—pop pl ... FM-9
Epinup, Oror En—locale ... FM-9
Epin Uratiw—channel ... FM-9
Epior—spring ... FM-9
**Epiphany**—pop pl ... SD-7
Epiphany Apostolic Coll—school ... NY-2
Epiphany Catholic Ch—church ... FL-3
Epiphany Cem—cemetery ... SD-7
Epiphany Ch—church ... FL-3
Epiphany Ch—church ... MI-6
Epiphany Ch—church (2) ... PA-2
Epiphany Ch—church ... SC-3
Epiphany Ch—church ... SD-7
Epiphany Ch—church ... VA-3
Epiphany Episcopal Ch—church ... FL-3
Epiphany Lutheran Ch—church ... FL-3
Epiphany Lutheran Sch—school ... FL-3
Epiphany of Our Lord Ch—church ... FL-3
Epiphany Sch—school ... AL-4
Epiphany Sch—school (2) ... CA-9
Epiphany Sch—school (3) ... FL-3
Epiphany Sch—school ... IL-6
Epiphany Sch—school ... IA-7
Epiphany Sch—school ... LA-4
Epiphany Sch—school ... MI-6
Epiphany Sch—school ... MN-6
Epiphany Sch—school ... OH-6
Epiphany Sch—school ... PA-2
Epirup ... FM-9
Epis ... FM-9
Episaton, Unun En—cape ... FM-9
Episcopal Acad—school ... PA-2
Episcopal Boys Sch (historical)—school ... SD-7
Episcopal Burying Ground and Chapel—hist pl ... KY-4
Episcopal Ch—church ... ND-7
Episcopal Ch—church ... SD-7
Episcopal Ch (historical)—church ... SD-7
Episcopal Ch Holy Comforter—church ... FL-3
Episcopal Ch of Saint John—church ... FL-3
Episcopal Ch of the Advent—church ... FL-3
Episcopal Ch of the Ascension—church ... AL-4
Episcopal Ch of the Ascension—church ... FL-3
Episcopal Ch of the Ascension—church ... MS-4
Episcopal Ch of the Creator—church ... MS-4
Episcopal Ch of the Good Shephard—church ... MS-4
Episcopal Ch of the Good Shepherd—church ... MS-4
Episcopal Ch of the Good Shepherd—church ... TN-4
Episcopal Ch of the Good Shepherd—church ... UT-8
Episcopal Ch of the Holy Comforter—church (2) ... AL-4
Episcopal Ch of the Holy Spirit—church ... FL-3
Episcopal Ch of the Holy Trinity—church ... MS-4
Episcopal Ch of the Incarnation—church ... MS-4
Episcopal Ch of the Mediator—church ... MS-4
Episcopal Ch of the Nativity—church ... IN-6
Episcopal Ch of the Reconciliation—church ... FL-3
Episcopal Ch of the Redeemer—church ... MS-4
Episcopal Ch of the Redeemer—church ... TN-4
Episcopal Ch of the Resurrection—church ... FL-3
Episcopal Ch of the Resurrection—church ... MS-4
Episcopal Church—hist pl ... NE-7
Episcopal Church Lake—reservoir ... NC-3
Episcopal Church Lake Dam—dam ... NC-3
Episcopal Church of All Angels—hist pl ... SD-7
Episcopal Church of Our Saviour—hist pl ... CA-9
Episcopal Church of the Advent—hist pl ... AL-4
Episcopal Church of the Ascension—hist pl ... CA-9
Episcopal Church of the Ascension and Manse—hist pl ... OH-6
Episcopal Church of the Epiphany—hist pl ... LA-4
Episcopal Church of the Good Shepherd—hist pl ... LA-4
Episcopal Church of the Incarnation—hist pl ... LA-4
Episcopal Church of the Nativity—hist pl ... AL-4
Episcopal Church of the Nativity—hist pl ... SC-3
Episcopal Church of the Redeemer ... AL-4
Episcopal Church of the Redeemer—hist pl ... ID-8
Episcopal Church of the Resurrection—hist pl ... OH-6
Episcopal Church of the Transfiguration—hist pl ... MN-6
Episcopal Day Sch—school ... TX-5
Episcopal Diocese of Southwest Florida—church ... FL-3
Episcopal Home for the Aged—building ... CA-9
Episcopal Hosp—hospital ... PA-2
Episcopal House of Prayer—church ... FL-3
Episcopal HS—school ... FL-3
Episcopal HS—school ... VA-3
Episcopal HS of Jacksonville—school ... FL-3
Episcopalian Cem—cemetery ... PA-2
Episcopalian Rectory—hist pl ... TX-5
Episcopal Indian Ch—church ... SD-7
Episcopal Trinity By-The-Cove Ch—church ... FL-3
Epison, Ununen—bar ... FM-9
Epison Branch—stream ... MS-4
Epison Hollow—valley ... TN-4
Episumur—bar ... FM-9
Epitar—bar ... FM-9
Epithany Sch—school ... NJ-2
Epizetka River—stream ... AK-9
E (Plantation of)—civ div ... ME-1
Epler Canyon—valley ... KS-7
Epler Church ... PA-2
Eplers Ch—church ... PA-2
Epler Sch (abandoned)—school ... PA-2
Epley*—locale ... IA-7
Epley—locale ... MS-4
Epley, Dr. Frank W., Office—hist pl ... WI-6
Epley Cem—cemetery ... IL-6
**Epleys**—pop pl ... KY-4
Epleys Cem—cemetery ... KY-4
Epling Cem—cemetery ... WV-2
Epling Chapel—church ... WV-2
Epling Draft ... VA-3
Epling Draft ... WV-2
Epling Run—stream ... WV-2
Epney—hist pl ... LA-4
Epon-suido ... MP-9
Epon-to ... MP-9
E Pool—reservoir ... MI-6
**Epoufette**—pop pl ... MI-6
Epoufette, Point—cape ... MI-6
Epoufette Bay—bay ... MI-6
Epoufette Cem—cemetery ... MI-6
Epoufette Island—island ... MI-6
Eppard Hosp—hospital ... MN-6
Eppards Point Ch—church ... IL-6
Eppards Point (Township of)—civ div ... IL-6
Epp Branch—stream ... MO-7
**Epperly**—pop pl ... WV-2
Epperly Heights Sch—school ... OK-5
Epperson—locale ... AL-4
Epperson—locale ... TN-4
**Epperson**—pop pl ... KY-4
Epperson, George, House—hist pl ... ID-8
Epperson Cem—cemetery (2) ... MO-7
Epperson Cem—cemetery (2) ... TN-4
Epperson Cem—cemetery ... VA-3
Epperson Ch—church ... KY-4
Epperson Creek—stream ... TN-4
Epperson Ditch—canal ... UT-8
Epperson Hollow ... TN-4
Epperson Hollow—valley ... KY-4
Epperson Hosp—hospital ... TN-4
Epperson Island—island (2) ... MO-7
Epperson Knob—summit ... AK-9
Epperson Knob—summit ... NC-3
Epperson-McNutt House—hist pl ... TX-5
Epperson Memorial United Methodist Ch—church ... FL-3
Epperson Post Office (historical)—building ... TN-4
Epperson Run—stream ... IL-6
Epperson Sch (historical)—school ... TN-4
Epperson Spring—spring ... UT-8
Eppert Hollow—valley ... VA-3
Eppes Creek—stream (2) ... VA-3
Eppes Fork—locale ... VA-3
Eppes Heights—uninc pl ... FL-3
Eppes Island—hist pl ... VA-3
Eppes Island—island ... VA-3
Epp Hosp—hospital ... OH-6
Eppich Apartments—hist pl ... CO-8
**Eppie Corners**—pop pl ... NY-2
**Epping**—pop pl ... ME-1
**Epping**—pop pl ... NH-1
**Epping**—pop pl ... ND-7
Epping Cem—cemetery ... ND-7
**Epping Compact (census name Epping)**—pop pl ... NH-1
Epping Creek—stream ... IA-7
Epping Dam—dam ... ND-7
Epping Dam—reservoir ... ND-7
Epping Forest—hist pl ... FL-3
**Epping Forest**—pop pl ... MD-2
Eppington—hist pl ... VA-3
**Epping (Town of)**—pop pl ... NH-1
Epple, Ludwig, House—hist pl ... IN-6
Eppley Airfield—airport ... NE-7
Eppley Camp—locale ... NE-7
Eppley Lake—reservoir ... KS-7
**Epplyanna**—pop pl ... IL-6
Epply Island—island ... PA-2
**Epps**—pop pl ... LA-4
**Epps**—pop pl ... MS-4
Epps, Edwin, House—hist pl ... LA-4
Epps Airpark—airport ... AL-4
Epps Branch—stream (2) ... MS-4
Epps Cem ... MS-4
Epps Cem—cemetery (2) ... MS-4
Epps Cem—cemetery ... MO-7
Epps Creek ... TX-5
Epps Creek—stream ... TX-5
Epps Ford—locale ... MS-4
Epps Gas Field—oilfield ... LA-4
Epps Hills—summit ... TN-4
Epps Hollow—valley (2) ... TN-4
Epps Island ... VA-3
Epps Lake ... AR-4
Epps Lake—reservoir ... MS-4
Epps Mtn—summit ... GA-3
Epps Park—park ... MO-7
Epps Post Office (historical)—building ... MS-4
Epps Ranch—locale ... TX-5
Epps Township—civil ... MO-7
E Prunty Ranch—locale ... NV-8
Epsaba Ch—church ... AR-4
Epsewasson ... VA-3
Epsey Bay—bay ... GA-3
Epsey Cave—cave ... TN-4
Epsey Mound—summit ... WI-6
Epsibeth Ch—church ... AL-4
Epsie—locale ... MT-8
Epsilon—locale ... MI-6
Epsilon II Archeol Site (12MO133)—hist pl ... IN-6
Epsilon Rock—island ... AK-9
**Epslion**—pop pl ... MI-6
Epsolon Mine—mine ... UT-8
Epsom—locale ... MN-6
**Epsom**—pop pl ... IN-6
**Epsom**—pop pl ... NH-1
**Epsom**—pop pl ... NC-3
Epsom Central Sch—school ... NH-1
Epsom Circle—locale ... NH-1
Epsom Downs—uninc pl ... TX-5
Epsom Elem Sch—school ... NC-3
Epsom Lateral—canal ... IN-6
Epsom Mtn—summit ... NH-1
Epsom Ridge—ridge ... IN-6
**Epsom (Town of)**—pop pl ... NH-1
Epson—locale ... KY-4
Epson Cem—cemetery ... MS-4
Epson Spring—spring ... TN-4
Epstein Canal—canal ... CA-9
Epstein Dam—dam ... MA-1
Epton Post Office (historical)—building ... PA-2
Epuk—bar ... FM-9
Epuk—summit ... FM-9
Epun—summit ... FM-9
Epwelkapw—summit ... FM-9
Epworth ... NC-3
Epworth—locale ... CA-9
Epworth—locale ... TN-4
Epworth—locale ... VA-3
**Epworth**—pop pl ... AL-4
**Epworth**—pop pl ... GA-3
**Epworth**—pop pl ... IL-6
**Epworth**—pop pl ... IA-7
**Epworth**—pop pl ... KY-4
**Epworth**—pop pl ... MO-7
**Epworth**—pop pl ... ND-7
**Epworth**—pop pl ... OH-6
**Epworth**—pop pl ... SC-3
Epworth, Mount—summit ... CO-8
Epworth AME Ch (historical)—church ... AL-4
Epworth-by-the-Sea Camp—locale ... GA-3
Epworth Camp—locale ... SC-3
Epworth Cem—cemetery ... IA-7
Epworth Cem—cemetery ... NE-7
Epworth Ch ... DE-2
Epworth Ch—church (2) ... AL-4
Epworth Ch—church ... DE-2
Epworth Ch—church ... GA-3
Epworth Ch—church (2) ... IN-6
Epworth Ch—church ... MD-2
Epworth Ch—church (2) ... MS-4
Epworth Ch—church (2) ... MO-7
Epworth Ch—church ... NY-2
Epworth Ch—church (3) ... NC-3
Epworth Ch—church ... OH-6
Epworth Ch—church (2) ... TN-4
Epworth Ch—church ... TX-5
Epworth Ch—church (5) ... VA-3
Epworth Chapel—church ... VA-3
Epworth Childrens Home—building ... SC-3
Epworth Fellowship Ch—church ... DE-2
**Epworth Forest**—pop pl ... IN-6
Epworth Hall—hist pl ... FL-3
Epworth Heights—other ... MI-6
**Epworth Heights**—pop pl ... OH-6
Epworth Lane Ch—church ... NC-3
Epworth Methodist Ch ... AL-4
Epworth Methodist Ch—church (2) ... AL-4
Epworth Methodist Evangelical Church—hist pl ... KY-4
Epworth Park—other ... IL-6
Epworth Park—park ... GA-3
Epworth United Methodist Ch ... AL-4
Epworth United Methodist Ch ... TN-4
Epworth United Methodist Ch—church ... DE-2
Epworth United Methodist Ch—church (2) ... MS-4
Epworth Woods Camp—locale ... PA-2
E Q Lunsford Pond Dam—dam ... MS-4
Equal Fork—stream (2) ... KY-4
**Equality**—pop pl (2) ... AL-4
**Equality**—pop pl ... IL-6
Equality Cem—cemetery ... AL-4
Equality Cem—cemetery ... OH-6
Equality Ch—church ... AL-4
Equality Ch—church ... KY-4
Equality JHS (historical)—school ... AL-4
**Equality (Kronos Station)**—pop pl ... KY-4
Equality Methodist Church ... AL-4
Equality Run—stream ... OH-6
Equality Township—civil ... MO-7
**Equality Township**—pop pl ... ND-7
**Equality (Township of)**—pop pl ... IL-6
**Equality (Township of)**—pop pl ... MN-6
Equalizer Lake—reservoir ... CO-8
Equalizing Reservoir ... WA-9
Equaloxic Creek—stream ... FL-3
Equal Rights Ch—church ... AR-4
EQUATOR (schooner)—hist pl ... WA-9
Equen Lake Dam—dam ... MS-4
**Equestrian Ranchettes Subdivision**—pop pl ... UT-8
**Equestrian Springs Subdivision**—pop pl ... UT-8
Equilibrium Rapids—rapids ... WA-9
Equinox House—hist pl ... VT-1
Equinox House Hist Dist—hist pl ... VT-1
Equinox Mill—CDP ... SC-3
Equinox Mtn—summit ... VT-1
Equinox Pond—lake ... VT-1
**Equinunk**—pop pl ... PA-2
Equinunk Creek—stream ... PA-2
Equipment Ford ... OR-9
Equirada Tank—reservoir ... TX-5
Equitable Bldg—hist pl ... CO-8
Equitable Bldg—hist pl ... NY-2
Equitable Bldg—hist pl ... OR-9
Equitable Trust Bldg—hist pl ... PA-2
Equity—locale ... OH-6
Equity Ditch—canal ... CO-8
Equity (historical)—locale ... KS-7
Equity Mine—mine (2) ... CO-8
Equity Park—park ... WI-6
Equivalent Lands ... MA-1
Equmen Lake—lake ... AK-9
Eqypt Baptist Ch—church ... MS-4
Era—locale ... ID-8
Era—locale ... KY-4
Era—locale ... VA-3
**Era**—pop pl ... OH-6
**Era**—pop pl ... TX-5
Erabais Creek ... CA-9
Erabin ... MP-9
Era Branch—stream ... TX-5
Erabuot ... MP-9
Era Cem—cemetery ... TX-5
Era Creek ... ID-8
Erady Branch—stream ... GA-3
Erakkueeru ... PW-9
Eram—locale ... OK-5
Eramosh Lake ... ND-7
E Ranch—locale ... CA-9
Eranistan—locale ... IA-7
Erappu Channel—channel ... MP-9
Erappu Pass ... MP-9
Erappu-suido ... MP-9
Erapuotsu Island—island ... MP-9
Erapuotsu-To ... MP-9
Erasmus—locale ... TN-4
Erasmus Hall Acad—hist pl ... NY-2
Erasmus Hall HS—school ... NY-2
Erasmus Post Office (historical)—building ... TN-4
Era Spring—spring ... MT-8
ERA Spring—spring ... OR-9
Erastra Spring—spring ... NV-8
Erastus—locale ... GA-3
Erastus—locale ... NC-3
**Erastus**—pop pl ... OH-6
Erastus Cem—cemetery ... NC-3
Erastus Ch—church ... GA-3
Erata Sch (historical)—school ... MS-4
Erath—locale ... TX-5
**Erath**—pop pl ... LA-4
**Erath (County)**—pop pl ... TX-5
Erath County Courthouse—hist pl ... TX-5
Erath Garden of Memory—cemetery ... TX-5
Erath Oil and Gas Field—oilfield ... LA-4
Eratt House—hist pl ... DE-2
Eratus—locale ... IA-7
Eravel ... KS-7
Eravel Trail—trail ... PA-2
**Eraw**—pop pl ... WV-2
Erb, Christopher, House—hist pl ... MD-2
**Erbacon**—pop pl ... WV-2
E R Baker Dam—dam ... OR-9
E R Baker Rsvr—reservoir ... OR-9
Erb Cem—cemetery ... IL-6
Erb Cem—cemetery ... OH-6
Erb Ditch ... IN-6
Erb Ditch—canal ... IN-6
Erb Drain—canal ... NV-8
Erbers Lake ... MI-6
Erbes Cem—cemetery ... IL-6
Erb Gap—gap ... PA-2
Erbie—locale ... AR-4
Erb Park—park ... WI-6
Erbs Ch—church ... PA-2
Erb's Covered Bridge—hist pl ... PA-2
Erbs Mill—locale ... PA-2
Erbs Mill Shelters—cave ... PA-2
Erby Cem—cemetery ... AR-4
Erchakrtuk Mtn—summit ... AK-9
Ercildoun—locale ... PA-2
Ercildoun Hist Dist—hist pl ... PA-2
Ercil Lake—reservoir ... CA-9
Erda—locale ... UT-8
Erdahi Cem—cemetery ... MN-6
**Erdahl**—pop pl ... MN-6
Erdahl Slough—lake ... ND-7
**Erdahl (Township of)**—pop pl ... MN-6
Erda Siding—locale ... UT-8
**Erdenheim**—pop pl ... PA-2
Erdenheim Elementary School ... PA-2
Erdenheim Sch—school ... PA-2
E R Dickson Elem Sch—school ... AL-4
Erdly Sch (abandoned)—school ... PA-2
**Erdman**—pop pl ... PA-2
**Erdman**—pop pl ... WI-6
Erdman, G. H., House—hist pl ... ID-8
Erdman Lake—lake ... WA-9
Erdman Mine—mine ... ID-8
Erdman Ranch—locale ... NE-7
Ere—island ... MP-9
Erebus Mtn—summit ... NY-2
Erect—locale ... NC-3
Ereeru To ... MP-9
Erefin—island ... FM-9
Eregub ... MP-9
Eregup ... MP-9
Ere Island ... MP-9
Erejeken ... MP-9
**Erekson Dairy Subdivision**—pop pl ... UT-8
Eremita Mesa—summit ... AZ-5
Eremita Tank—reservoir ... AZ-5
Erengel Reef ... PW-9
Erengoll—bar ... PW-9
Erenos Dam—dam ... OR-9
Erenos Rsvr—reservoir ... OR-9
Ereru-to ... MP-9
Eret—locale ... MS-4
Ere-to ... MP-9
Ereyan ... MP-9
Ereyan—island ... MP-9
Ereyan-To ... MP-9
Ergang Lake—lake ... MI-6
**Erhard**—pop pl ... MN-6
**Erhard**—pop pl ... PA-2
Erhard, A. A., House—hist pl ... TX-5
Erhard, Adolph A., House—hist pl ... TX-5
Erhard, E. C., House—hist pl ... TX-5
Erhard House—hist pl ... TX-5
Erhard-Maplewood Ch—church ... MN-6
Erhards Grove (Township of)—civ div ... MN-6
Erharkers—locale ... AL-4
**Erhart**—pop pl ... OH-6
Erhart Lake—lake ... OR-9
**Erial**—pop pl ... NJ-2
**Eric**—pop pl ... CA-9
Erica—locale ... VA-3
Eric Falls—falls ... PA-2
Erich Lake—lake ... AK-9
Erichleburg HS—school ... PA-2
Erick—locale ... GA-3
**Erick**—pop pl ... OK-5
Erick, Lake—lake ... MN-6
Erick (CCD)—cens area ... OK-5
Erick Cem—cemetery ... GA-3
Erick Creek—stream ... WA-9
Erick Hollow ... WV-2
Erick Hollow—valley ... PA-2
Ericksen Lake ... MN-6
Erickson—locale ... CA-9
Erickson, Edward, Farmstead—hist pl ... MN-6
Erickson, Even and Petrine, Farm—hist pl ... TX-5
Erickson, Johannes, House—hist pl ... MN-6
Erickson and Bohn Extension Ditch—canal ... CO-8
Erickson Animal Cem—cemetery ... KS-7
Erickson Basin—basin ... UT-8
Erickson Bluff—cliff ... WI-6
Erickson Camp—locale ... MI-6
Erickson Canyon ... UT-8
Erickson Canyon—valley ... NV-8
Erickson Canyon—valley ... WY-8
Erickson Cem—cemetery ... MT-8
Erickson Cem—cemetery ... SD-7
Erickson Corner—locale ... CT-1
Erickson Creek ... WI-6
Erickson Creek—stream (2) ... AK-9
Erickson Creek—stream ... CO-8
Erickson Creek—stream ... MI-6
Erickson Creek—stream ... MT-8
Erickson Creek—stream ... OR-9
Erickson Creek—stream ... UT-8
Erickson Creek—stream (3) ... WI-6
Erickson Ditch—canal ... OR-9
Erickson Drain—canal ... MI-6
Erickson Draw—valley ... WY-8
Erickson Elem Sch—school ... AZ-5
Erickson Field—airport (2) ... ND-7
Erickson Gulch—valley (2) ... AK-9
Erickson House—hist pl ... UT-8
Erickson Island—island ... WA-9
Erickson-Kent Ranch—locale ... WY-8
Erickson Knoll—summit ... UT-8
Erickson Lake—lake ... CO-8
Erickson Lake—lake (4) ... MI-6
Erickson Lake—lake (8) ... MN-6
Erickson Lake—lake ... ND-7
Erickson Lake—lake ... OR-9
Erickson Lake—lake (2) ... WA-9
Erickson Lake—lake ... WI-6
Erickson Lake Dam—dam ... MS-4
Erickson Lake Number 1 Dam—dam ... MS-4
Erickson Lake Number 2 Dam—dam ... MS-4
Erickson Lake Number 3 Dam—dam ... MS-4
Erickson Landing—locale ... MI-6
Erickson Landing Strip—airport ... ND-7
Erickson Meadow—flat ... ID-8
Erickson Mill—locale ... OR-9
Erickson Mine—mine ... CO-8
Erickson Park—park ... IA-7
Erickson Pass—gap ... UT-8
Erickson Peak—summit ... AZ-5
Erickson Play Field—park ... WA-9
Erickson Prospect—mine ... AK-9
Erickson Ranch—locale ... CO-8
Erickson Ranch—locale ... ID-8
Erickson Ranch—locale (2) ... MT-8
Erickson Ranch—locale (2) ... ND-7
Erickson Ranch—locale ... OR-9
Erickson Ranch—locale (2) ... SD-7
Erickson Ranch—locale ... WY-8
Erickson Ranch Airp—airport ... WA-9
Erickson Ridge—ridge ... AZ-5
Erickson Ridge—ridge ... CO-8
Erickson Rsvr—reservoir ... CO-8
Erickson Rsvr—reservoir ... MT-8
Erickson Sch—school ... IL-6
Erickson Sch—school ... MI-6
Erickson Sch—school ... MT-8
Erickson Sch (historical)—school ... PA-2
Erickson Slough—bay ... CA-9
Erickson Spring—spring ... MT-8
Erickson Spring—spring ... NV-8
Erickson Spring Branch—stream ... IA-7
Erickson Springs—spring ... CO-8
Ericksons Reef—bar ... MN-6
Ericksons Spring—spring ... CA-9
**Erickson Subdivision (subdivision)**—pop pl ... SD-7
Erickson Tank—locale ... AZ-5
**Ericksonville**—pop pl ... MN-6
Erickson Wash—valley ... UT-8
Eric Lake—lake ... ND-7
Eric Munz Ranch—locale ... CA-9
Eric Pit—cave ... AL-4
**Ericsburg**—pop pl ... MN-6
Ericson—locale ... IA-7
**Ericson**—pop pl ... NE-7
Ericson, Lake—lake ... MN-6
Ericson, Rudolf, House—hist pl ... MI-6
Ericson Coulee—valley ... ND-7
Ericson Crags—pillar ... CA-9
Ericson Creek—stream ... FL-3
Ericson Creek—stream ... ID-8
Ericson Creek—stream ... WI-6
**Ericson Lake**—pop pl ... NE-7
Ericson Lake—reservoir ... NE-7
Ericson Park—park ... MN-6
Ericson Public Library—hist pl ... IA-7
Ericson Ridge—ridge (2) ... CA-9
Ericson Ridge—ridge ... ID-8
Ericsons Bay—bay ... WA-9
Ericson Sch—school ... CA-9
**Ericson (Township of)**—pop pl ... MN-6
Eric Spring—spring ... CA-9
Ericsson, Mount—summit ... CA-9
Ericsson Memorial—park ... DC-2
Ericsson Sch—school (2) ... MN-6
Ericsson Sch—school ... WI-6
Eric Tank—reservoir ... NM-5
Eridj Island—island ... MP-9
**Eridu**—pop pl ... FL-3
Erie—locale ... KS-7
Erie—locale ... NV-8
Erie—locale ... OK-5
**Erie**—pop pl ... CO-8
**Erie**—pop pl ... FL-3
**Erie**—pop pl ... IL-6
**Erie**—pop pl (2) ... IN-6
**Erie**—pop pl ... KS-7
**Erie**—pop pl ... MI-6
**Erie**—pop pl ... MN-6
**Erie**—pop pl ... MO-7
**Erie**—pop pl ... ND-7
**Erie**—pop pl ... PA-2
**Erie**—pop pl ... TN-4
**Erie**—pop pl ... WV-2
Erie, Lake—lake ... CO-8
Erie, Lake—lake ... CT-1
Erie, Lake—lake ... FL-3
Erie, Lake—lake ... IL-6
Erie, Lake—lake ... MI-6
Erie, Lake—lake ... MN-6
Erie, Lake—lake ... NM-5
Erie, Lake—lake ... NY-2
Erie, Lake—lake ... OH-6
Erie, Lake—lake ... PA-2
Erie, Lake—lake ... WA-9
Erie, Lake—reservoir ... CO-8
Erie, Mount—summit ... WA-9
Erie Ave Bridge—bridge ... OH-6
Erie Barge Canal ... NY-2
Erie Basin—harbor (2) ... NY-2
Erie Bend—bend ... AL-4
Erie Bend Camp—locale ... AL-4
Erie Breaker—building ... PA-2
Erie Canal—canal ... NY-2
Erie Canal—canal (2) ... OH-6
Erie Canal—hist pl ... NY-2
Erie Canal: Second Genesee Aqueduct—hist pl ... NY-2
Erie Canal State Park—park ... NY-2
Erie Cem—cemetery ... AL-4
Erie Cem—cemetery ... ND-7
Erie Cem—cemetery ... OH-6
Erie Cem—cemetery ... PA-2
Erie Central Mall—locale ... PA-2
Erie Ch—church ... TN-4
Erie City ... KS-7
Erie City—civil ... PA-2
Erie Corfield Ranch—locale ... NE-7
**Erie (County)**—pop pl ... NY-2
**Erie (County)**—pop pl ... OH-6
**Erie County**—pop pl ... PA-2
Erie County Airp—airport ... PA-2
Erie County Fairgrounds—locale ... NY-2
Erie County Infirmary—hist pl ... OH-6
Erie County Jail—hist pl ... OH-6
Erie County Office Bldg—hist pl ... OH-6
Erie County Oil Products Co.—hist pl ... OH-6
Erie County Reforestation Area—forest (2) ... NY-2
Erie County Technical Institute—school ... NY-2
Erie Creek—stream ... AL-4
Erie Dam—dam ... ND-7
Erie Elem Sch—school ... AZ-5
Erie Elem Sch—school ... KS-7
Erie Extension Canal—canal ... PA-2
Erie Filtration Plant—building ... CO-8
Erie-Frederick—cens area ... CO-8
Erie Goodman Township—civil ... MO-7
Erie Harbor ... PA-2
Erie Harbor Entrance Channel—channel ... PA-2
**Erie Heights**—pop pl ... PA-2
Erie (historical)—locale ... AL-4
Erie (historical P.O.)—locale ... IA-7
Erie HS—school ... KS-7
Erie Industrial Park—facility ... OH-6
Erie International Airp—airport ... PA-2
Erie Island Sch—school ... OH-6
Erie Junction—locale ... ND-7
Erie Junction—locale ... PA-2
Erie-Lackawanna RR Terminal at Hoboken—hist pl ... NJ-2
Erie Lake ... MN-6
Erie Lake—lake ... FL-3
Erie Lake—lake ... MN-6
Erie Lake—reservoir ... CO-8
Erie Land Lighthouse—hist pl ... PA-2
Erie Lighthouse ... PA-2
Erie McNatt Township—civil ... MO-7
Erie Mine—mine ... CO-8
Erie Mine—mine ... MN-6
Erie Mine Number One Pit—basin ... MN-6
Erie Mine Number Two Pit—mine ... MN-6
Erie Municipal Golf Course—locale ... PA-2
Erie Natl Wildlife Ref—park ... PA-2
Erienna Sch—school ... IL-6
**Erienna (Township of)**—pop pl ... IL-6
Erie NWR Pool Number Nine—dam ... PA-2
Erie NWR Pool Number Seven—dam ... PA-2
Erie Ozark Mine—mine ... AR-4
Erie Point—cape ... CA-9
Erie Post Office (historical)—building ... TN-4
Erie RR Cleveland Powerhouse—hist pl ... OH-6
Erie RR Signal Tower, Waldwick Yard—hist pl ... NJ-2
Erie RR Station—hist pl ... NY-2
Erie RR Station—hist pl ... PA-2
Erieside Ch—church ... OH-6
Erie Siding ... OK-5
Erie Stadium—locale ... PA-2
Erie State Game Area—park ... MI-6
Erie Street Sch—school ... NY-2
Erie Terminal Building-Commerce Plaza Bldg—hist pl ... OH-6
**Erie Township**—pop pl (2) ... KS-7
**Erie Township**—pop pl ... ND-7
**Erie (Township of)**—pop pl ... IL-6
**Erie (Township of)**—pop pl ... IN-6
**Erie (Township of)**—pop pl ... MI-6
**Erie (Township of)**—pop pl ... MN-6
**Erie (Township of)**—pop pl ... OH-6
Erie Turning Basin—harbor ... PA-2
Erie Union Cem—cemetery ... MI-6
Erie United Ch—church ... MI-6
Erieview ... OH-6
Erie View Sch—school ... OH-6
**Erieville**—pop pl ... NY-2
Erie Yacht Club—locale ... PA-2
Eriirippu Island—island ... MP-9
Eriirippu-To ... MP-9
Eriji To ... MP-9

Eriki Ditch—*canal* CO-8
Erikson Dam—*dam* MA-1
*Erikson Kent Ranch* WY-8
*Erikson Springs* CO-8
Erikub—*island* MP-9
Erikub Atoll—*island* MP-9
Erikub (County-equivalent)—*civil* MP-9
*Erikub Inseln* MP-9
*Erikub Islan* MP-9
*Erikub Island* MP-9
Eriline—*locale* KY-4
*Erin* IN-6
Erin—*hist pl* VA-3
Erin—*locale* AL-4
Erin—*locale* TX-5
**Erin**—*pop pl* KY-4
**Erin**—*pop pl* NY-2
**Erin**—*pop pl* TN-4
**Erin**—*pop pl* WV-2
Erin, Lake—*lake* FL-3
Erin, Lake—*lake* MI-6
Erin, Lake—*lake* MN-6
Erin, Lake—*lake* NM-5
Erina—*fmr MCD* NE-7
Erina Ch—*church* NE-7
Erin Branch—*stream* TN-4
Erin (CCD)—*cens area* TN-4
Erin Cem—*cemetery* TN-4
*Erin Church* MS-4
Erin City Hall—*building* TN-4
Erin Corner—*locale* WI-6
Erin Creek—*stream* OR-9
Erin Cumberland Ch—*church* MS-4
Erin Division—*civil* TN-4
*Erin Elementary School* TN-4
**Erin (Erin Corner)**—*pop pl* WI-6
Erin Grove Cem—*cemetery* MI-6
Erin (historical)—*locale* MS-4
Erin Hollow—*valley* TN-4
Erin Lake—*lake* CA-9
Erin Meadow—*flat* OR-9
**Erin Meadows Subdivision**—*pop pl* UT-8
Erin Polytechnic Institute (historical)—*school* TN-4
Erin Post Office—*building* TN-4
Erin Post Office (historical)—*building* MS-4
**Erin Prairie (Town of)**—*pop pl* WI-6
Erin Sch—*school* TN-4
Erin Sch—*school* WI-6
Erin Sch (historical)—*school* MS-4
**Erin Springs**—*pop pl* OK-5
Erin Springs Mansion—*hist pl* OK-5
**Erin (Town of)**—*pop pl* NY-2
**Erin (Town of)**—*pop pl* WI-6
Erin Township—*fmr MCD* IA-7
**Erin (Township of)**—*pop pl* IL-6
**Erin (Township of)**—*pop pl* MN-6
Eripou—*bar* FM-9
*Erippu Island* MP-9
*Erippu-to* MP-9
**Eris**—*pop pl* OH-6
Erisman Cem—*cemetery* OH-6
Erismans Ch—*church* PA-2
*Eri-to* MP-9
**Eriton**—*pop pl* PA-2
E Rivers Sch—*school* GA-3
*Erjokah* MP-9
Erke Mine—*mine* ND-7
Erkenbeck Sch—*school* CO-8
Erkenbrack Hill—*summit* NY-2
Erkes Airp—*airport* PA-2
**Erlands Point**—*pop pl* WA-9
**Erlanger**—*pop pl* KY-4
**Erlanger**—*pop pl* NC-3
Erlanger—*post sta* TN-4
Erlanger, Joseph, House—*hist pl* MO-7
Erlanger Buildings—*hist pl* MD-2
Erlanger Hosp—*hospital* TN-4
*Erlanger Med Ctr* TN-4
**Erle**—*pop pl* CA-9
Erlebach Ranch—*locale* OR-9
**Erlen**—*pop pl* PA-2
Erler Cem—*cemetery* WI-6
Erler Lake—*lake* WI-6
*Erlers Lake* WI-6
Erle Siding—*'ɔcale* CA-9
Erlewine Sch—*school* CA-9
Erlich, F. W., House—*hist pl* OH-6
Erlie Island—*island* MP-9
**Erlin**—*pop pl* OH-6
Erling, Lake—*reservoir* AR-4
Erlmo—*locale* ID-8
**Erlton**—*pop pl* NJ-2
Erly—*locale* PA-2
**Erma**—*pop pl* NJ-2
**Erma Park**—*pop pl* NJ-2
Ermatinger, Francis, House—*hist pl* OR-9
Ermatinger Creek—*stream* MI-6
Ermen Lane Cem—*cemetery* AR-4
*Ermerick* NE-7
**Ermine**—*pop pl* KY-4
Ermine Brook—*stream* NY-2
Ermine Creek—*stream* (2) ID-8
Ermine Creek—*stream* MI-6
Ermine Creek—*stream* WA-9
Ermine Creek—*stream* WY-8
Ermine Glacier—*glacier* WA-9
Ermine Lake—*lake* AK-9
Ermine Lake—*lake* MI-6
Ermine Point—*cape* AK-9
Ermont Gulch—*valley* MT-8
Ermont Mill—*locale* MT-8
Ermont No 19 Mine—*mine* MT-8
Ermont No 2 Mine—*mine* MT-8
Erna—*locale* TX-5
Ernest—*locale* GA-3
Ernest—*locale* PA-2
**Ernest**—*pop pl* PA-2
Ernest A Love Field—*airport* AZ-5
Ernest Anderson Crossing—*crossing* TX-5
Ernest Blanco Spring—*spring* CA-9
Ernest Borough—*civil* PA-2
Ernest Bridge—*hist pl* OR-9
Ernest Canyon—*valley* CO-8
Ernest Chapel—*church* AL-4
Ernest Creek—*stream* MT-8
Ernest Creek—*stream* OR-9
Ernest Finley Pond Dam—*dam* MS-4
Ernest Fox Island (historical)—*island* TN-4
Ernest (historical)—*locale* KS-7
Ernest (historical)—*locale* ND-7
ERNESTINA (schooner)—*hist pl* MA-1
Ernestine, Lake—*lake* MI-6
Ernestine Creek—*stream* AK-9
Ernest Kolb Dam—*dam* (2) SD-7
Ernest Lake—*lake* MN-6
Ernest Lake—*lake* WY-8
Ernest L Dyess Dam—*dam* AL-4
Ernest L Dyess Pond—*reservoir* AL-4
Ernest L Ross Elem Sch—*school* TN-4
Ernest Lyons Bridge—*bridge* FL-3
Ernest Memorial Hosp—*hospital* GA-3
Ernest Miller Ridge—*ridge* MT-8
Ernest Montoya Ranch—*locale* NM-5
Erne Stnemec Number 1 Dam—*dam* SD-7
Ernesto Tank—*reservoir* TX-5
Ernest Point—*cape* AK-9
Ernest Rand Memorial State For—*forest* SC-3
Ernest R Elliott Elem Sch—*school* IN-6
Ernest Rightley Ditch—*canal* IN-6
Ernest Slough—*stream* LA-4
Ernest Sound—*bay* AK-9
Ernests Pond—*lake* OR-9
*Ernests Store* AL-4
Ernest Tank—*reservoir* AZ-5
Ernest Taylor Dam—*dam* TN-4
Ernest Taylor Lake—*reservoir* TN-4
**Ernest Township**—*pop pl* MO-7
Ernest Vickers Dam—*dam* TN-4
Ernest Vickers Lake—*reservoir* TN-4
Ernestville—*locale* TN-4
**Ernestville**—*pop pl* MO-7
Ernestville Post Office (historical)—*building* TN-4
**Erney**—*pop pl* PA-2
**Ern Hayes Subdivision**—*pop pl* UT-8
Ernie Canyon—*valley* UT-8
Ernie Creek—*stream* AK-9
Ernie Davis JHS—*school* NY-2
Ernie Howard Gulch—*valley* CO-8
Ernie King Hollow—*valley* TN-4
Ernie Lake—*lake* AK-9
Ernie Lake—*lake* OR-9
Ernie Pass—*gap* AK-9
Ernie Pyle Elem Sch—*school* (2) IN-6
Ernie Pyle Island—*island* IN-6
Ernie Pyle JHS—*school* NM-5
Ernie Pyle Rest Park—*park* IN-6
Ernie Pyle Sch—*school* CA-9
Ernie Pyle Sch—*school* IN-6
Ernies Country—*area* UT-8
**Ernies Grove**—*pop pl* WA-9
Ernie Spring—*spring* (2) OR-9
Ernies Tank—*reservoir* AZ-5
Ernie Tank—*reservoir* AZ-5
*Ernse Hollow* PA-2
Ernst—*locale* IL-6
Ernst Basin—*basin* TX-5
Ernst Cem—*cemetery* MO-7
Ernst Ditch—*canal* OH-6
Ernst Hollow—*valley* PA-2
**Ernston**—*pop pl* NJ-2
Ernst Pool—*reservoir* MN-6
Ernst Sch—*school* OH-6
Ernst Tank—*reservoir* TX-5
Ernst Tinaja—*reservoir* TX-5
*Ernst Valley* TX-5
Ernst Valley—*valley* TX-5
Ernstville—*locale* MD-2
**Ernul**—*pop pl* (2) NC-3
Erny Sch—*school* NE-7
*Erochi* MP-9
*Erochi-to* MP-9
Eroded Bowlder House (ruins)—*locale* UT-8
Eroded Mtn—*summit* AK-9
Eroh Cem—*cemetery* MI-6
*Ero Island* MP-9
Eroj—*island* MP-9
Eron Reach—*stream* AR-4
*Eroochi To* MP-9
**Eros**—*pop pl* AR-4
**Eros**—*pop pl* LA-4
EROS Data Center—*building* SD-7
Erose—*locale* KY-4
Erose Sch—*school* KY-4
Erosion Creek—*stream* MT-8
Erosion Tank—*reservoir* AZ-5
Erosion Wash—*valley* AZ-5
Eros Lake—*reservoir* IN-6
Erost Creek—*stream* MS-4
*Erotjeman Island* MP-9
Erotjeman Island—*island* MP-9
*Erpa* MP-9
Erpes Bloomary Forge (historical)—*locale* TN-4
Erpff, Philip, House—*hist pl* PA-2
Erquiaga Spring—*spring* NV-8
*Errakong* PW-9
Erramousbe Ranch—*locale* NM-5
Erramouspe Place—*locale* WY-8
Erramouspe Ranch—*locale* WY-8
Erramuzpe Trick Tank—*reservoir* AZ-5
Erranton Cem—*cemetery* TN-4
**Errata**—*pop pl* MS-4
Errata Lookout Tower—*locale* MS-4
Erratic Creek—*stream* AK-9
Erratic Rock Wayside—*locale* OR-9
Erratta—*locale* AL-4
Erratta Cem—*cemetery* MS-4
Erratta Ch—*church* MS-4
Erreca Ranch—*locale* CA-9
*Erreppu* MP-9
*Erreppu Passage* MP-9
*Erreppu-to* MP-9
Errett Cem—*cemetery* PA-2
Errick Road Sch—*school* NY-2
*Errigonabbu To* MP-9
*Errigorappu-to* MP-9
Errin Campground—*park* OR-9
*Errob Island* MP-9
*Errob Pass* MP-9
**Errol**—*pop pl* NH-1
**Errol**—*pop pl* OR-9
Errol Dam—*dam* NH-1
**Errol Estates**—*pop pl* FL-3
Errol Hassell Sch—*school* OR-9
**Errol Heights**—*pop pl* OR-9
Errol Hill—*summit* NH-1
*Errol Islands* LA-4
Errol Ridge—*ridge* OR-9
Errol Shoal—*bar* LA-4
Errolton—*building* MS-4
**Errol (Town of)**—*pop pl* NH-1
Erron Trail—*trail* PA-2
Error Island—*island* AK-9
Ershim Lake—*lake* CA-9
Erskine—*locale* OR-9
Erskine—*locale* SD-7
**Erskine**—*pop pl* MN-6
**Erskine**—*pop pl* NJ-2
Erskine, Lake—*lake* MN-6
Erskine, Lake—*reservoir* NJ-2
Erskine Acad—*school* ME-1
Erskine Bay—*bay* AK-9
Erskine Beal Spring—*spring* OR-9
Erskine Cave—*cave* SD-7
Erskine Cem—*cemetery* NJ-2
Erskine Cem—*cemetery* TX-5
Erskine Ch—*church* MI-6
Erskine Coll—*school* SC-3
Erskine College-Due West Hist Dist—*hist pl* SC-3
Erskine Covered Bridge—*hist pl* PA-2
*Erskine Creek* MS-4
Erskine Creek—*stream* CA-9
Erskine Creek—*stream* MI-6
Erskine Creek Cave—*cave* CA-9
Erskine Gulch—*valley* SD-7
Erskine House—*hist pl* AK-9
Erskine House No. 1—*hist pl* TX-5
*Erskine Lake* NJ-2
Erskine Lake—*lake* MN-6
**Erskine Lakes**—*pop pl* NJ-2
Erskine Log Pond—*reservoir* OR-9
Erskine Mine (underground)—*mine* AL-4
Erskine Mtn—*summit* AK-9
Erskine Playground—*park* MI-6
Erskine Point—*cape* AK-9
Erskine Rhodes—*locale* TX-5
Erskine Sch—*hist pl* SD-7
Erskine Sch—*school* IA-7
Erskine Sch—*school* SD-7
Erskine Sch—*school* TX-5
**Erskine Siding**—*pop pl* SC-3
Erskine State Wildlife Mngmt Area—*park* MN-6
**Erskine Station**—*pop pl* IN-6
Ersking—*summit* ME-1
Erskin Hollow—*valley* NY-2
*Erskin Lake* MN-6
ERT Bridge over Black's Fork—*hist pl* WY-8
Ertel Run—*stream* OH-6
**Ertong**—*pop pl* PW-9
Erts Brook—*stream* NY-2
Eru—*island* MP-9
*Erubaru* MP-9
*Eruchiekeen Island* MP-9
*Eruchiiken* MP-9
*Eruchoken Island* MP-9
Eruchoken Island—*island* MP-9
*Eruchoken-To* MP-9
*Eru-Insel* MP-9
*Eru Island* MP-9
*Erukku Island* MP-9
Erukku Island—*island* MP-9
*Erukku-to* MP-9
*Erukuppu-to* MP-9
*Erurukku-to* MP-9
*Erusumu Mountain* PW-9
*Eru-to* MP-9
Erva Township—*civil* SD-7
**Ervay**—*pop pl* WY-8
Ervay Basin—*basin* WY-8
Erve Adams Flat—*flat* AZ-5
*Ervin* TN-4
Ervin Branch—*stream* TN-4
Ervin Cem—*cemetery* IN-6
Ervin Cem—*cemetery* MO-7
Ervin Cem—*cemetery* TN-4
Ervin Cem—*cemetery* (2) VA-3
Ervin Chapel—*church* TN-4
Ervin Chapel—*church* VA-3
Ervin Creek—*stream* OR-9
Ervine Cem—*cemetery* TN-4
Ervine Creek—*stream* NE-7
Ervin Elem Sch—*school* IN-6
Ervine Sch—*school* NE-7
**Erving**—*pop pl* MA-1
Erving Ridge—*ridge* AR-4
Erving Sch—*school* MA-1
Ervings Chapel—*church* MD-2
Ervings Location—*fmr MCD* NH-1
Erving State For—*forest* MA-1
Ervington Sch—*school* VA-3
**Erving (Town of)**—*pop pl* MA-1
**Erving Township**—*pop pl* KS-7
Ervin JHS—*school* MO-7
Ervin Pond—*lake* ME-1
Ervin Ranch—*locale* NM-5
Ervin Ridge—*ridge* MT-8
Ervin Run—*stream* OH-6
*Ervins* TN-4
Ervin Scarberry Branch—*stream* KY-4
Ervin Sch—*school* OK-5
Ervinton (Magisterial District)—*fmr MCD* VA-3
**Ervintown**—*pop pl* NC-3
Ervin Town Hall—*building* ND-7
**Ervin Township**—*pop pl* ND-7
**Ervin (Township of)**—*pop pl* IN-6
Er-Wern Ridge—*ridge* CA-9
Erwin—*locale* IL-6
Erwin—*locale* TX-5
**Erwin**—*pop pl* (2) AR-4
**Erwin**—*pop pl* IN-6
**Erwin**—*pop pl* MS-4
**Erwin**—*pop pl* NC-3
**Erwin**—*pop pl* SC-3
**Erwin**—*pop pl* SD-7
**Erwin**—*pop pl* TN-4
**Erwin**—*pop pl* WV-2
Erwin, John, House—*hist pl* AL-4
Erwin, J. R., House—*hist pl* TX-5
Erwin Acad (historical)—*school* TN-4
Erwin Airp—*airport* NC-3
Erwin Area Vocational Technical Center—*school* FL-3
Erwin Bayou—*stream* LA-4
Erwin (CCD)—*cens area* TN-4
Erwin Cem—*cemetery* AL-4
Erwin Cem—*cemetery* IL-6
Erwin Cem—*cemetery* IN-6
Erwin Cem—*cemetery* NY-2
Erwin Cem—*cemetery* NC-3
Erwin Cem—*cemetery* SD-7
Erwin Cem—*cemetery* (4) TN-4
Erwin Cem—*cemetery* (2) TX-5
Erwin Chapel—*church* NC-3
Erwin Company Farm—*locale* MS-4
Erwin Cotton Mills Company Mill No. 1 HQ Bldg—*hist pl* NC-3
Erwin Cove—*bay* FL-3
Erwin Creek—*stream* MT-8
Erwin Creek—*stream* NY-2
Erwin Ditch—*canal* IN-6
Erwin Ditch—*canal* (2) OR-9
Erwin Division—*civil* TN-4
Erwin Draft—*valley* VA-3
Erwine Creek—*stream* ID-8
Erwine Creek—*stream* WY-8
Erwin Eisenbraun Dam—*dam* SD-7
Erwin Farm—*hist pl* TN-4
Erwin Hall, Marietta College—*hist pl* OH-6
**Erwin Heights**—*pop pl* NC-3
*Erwin High School* AL-4
Erwin Hill Ch—*church* GA-3
Erwin Hills Shop Ctr—*locale* NC-3
**Erwin (historical)**—*pop pl* OR-9
Erwin Hollow—*valley* AL-4
Erwin Hollow—*valley* KY-4
Erwin Hollow—*valley* NY-2
Erwin Hollow—*valley* (2) OH-6
Erwin House—*hist pl* FL-3
Erwin House—*hist pl* SC-3
Erwin JHS—*school* NC-3
Erwin JHS—*school* OH-6
**Erwin Junction**—*pop pl* NC-3
*Erwin Lake* WI-6
Erwin Lake—*flat* CA-9
Erwin Lake—*lake* MN-6
Erwin Lake—*lake* WI-6
Erwin Library and Pratt House—*hist pl* NY-2
Erwin Middle—*school* NC-3
**Erwinna**—*pop pl* PA-2
Erwinna Covered Bridge—*hist pl* PA-2
Erwinna Private Airp—*airport* PA-2
Erwinna Sch—*school* PA-2
Erwin Open Elem Sch—*school* NC-3
Erwin Park—*park* CA-9
Erwin Park—*park* NY-2
Erwin Park—*park* NC-3
Erwin Pond—*lake* NY-2
Erwin Post Office—*building* TN-4
Erwin Post Office (historical)—*building* AL-4
Erwin Rsvr—*reservoir* ID-8
**Erwins**—*pop pl* NY-2
*Erwins Brook* MA-1
Erwins Cem—*cemetery* NY-2
Erwin Sch—*school* CA-9
Erwin Sch—*school* NC-3
Erwin Sch—*school* OH-6
Erwin Sch—*school* VA-3
Erwin Slave Cem—*cemetery* TN-4
Erwin Spring—*spring* AL-4
Erwins Sch—*school* AL-4
Erwins Temple—*church* NC-3
Erwin Street Sch—*school* CA-9
*Erwinsville* NC-3
**Erwinsville (historical)**—*pop pl* NC-3
Erwinton Ch—*church* SC-3
**Erwin (Town of)**—*pop pl* NY-2
**Erwin (Township of)**—*pop pl* MI-6
Erwin Valley Sch—*school* NY-2
**Erwinville**—*pop pl* LA-4
Erwinville Post Office—*locale* LA-4
**Erwinville (P. O.)**—*pop pl* LA-4
**Erwinville (sta.)**—*pop pl* LA-4
Erychleb Cem—*cemetery* NE-7
Esadore Lake—*lake* WI-6
**Esadore Lake (Murat)**—*pop pl* WI-6
Esado Tank—*reservoir* TX-5
Esaps Lateral No 7—*canal* IA-7
*Esat Branch Held Creek* MI-6
Esau, Lake—*lake* MI-6
Esau Canyon—*valley* OR-9
Esau Junction—*locale* OK-5
Esau Spring—*spring* WY-8
Esau Street Ch of God in Christ—*church* AL-4
E Sawyer Ranch—*locale* TX-5
Esbenshade, Abraham H., House—*hist pl* WI-6
**Esbon**—*pop pl* KS-7
**Esbon**—*pop pl* TX-5
Esbon Cem—*cemetery* KS-7
Esbon Elem Sch—*school* KS-7
Esbon HS—*school* KS-7
**Esbon Township**—*pop pl* KS-7
**Esbrick**—*pop pl* SC-3
E S Brooks Dam—*dam* AL-4
**Escabosa**—*pop pl* NM-5
Escabrosa Ridge—*ridge* AZ-5
Escacado Canyon—*valley* AZ-5
*Escacholtz Island* MP-9
Escaladian Shaw Canal—*canal* CA-9
Escalanta Tank—*reservoir* AZ-5
*Esca Lante* UT-8
Escalante—*locale* CO-8
**Escalante**—*pop pl* UT-8
Escalante, Mount—*summit* UT-8
Escalante Breaks—*range* CO-8
Escalante Butte—*summit* AZ-5
Escalante Canon Bridge—*hist pl* CO-8
Escalante Canyon—*valley* (2) UT-8
Escalante Cem—*cemetery* UT-8
*Escalante Creek* UT-8
Escalante Creek—*stream* AZ-5
Escalante Creek—*stream* CO-8
Escalante Crossing—*crossing* UT-8
Escalante Crossing—*locale* AZ-5
Escalante Desert—*plain* UT-8
Escalante District Ranger Station—*locale* UT-8
Escalante Division—*civil* UT-8
Escalante Forks—*locale* CO-8
*Escalante Hills* CO-8
Escalante HS—*school* UT-8
Escalante Interpretive Site—*park* UT-8
*Escalante Lake* AZ-5
*Escalante Lake* UT-8
Escalante Mine—*mine* UT-8
Escalante Mine Canal—*canal* UT-8
*Escalante Mountain* UT-8
Escalante Mtns—*range* UT-8
Escalante Municipal Airp—*airport* UT-8
Escalante Natural Bridge—*other* UT-8
Escalante Overlook—*locale* CO-8
Escalante Park—*park* (2) AZ-5
Escalante Petrified Forest Campground—*locale* UT-8
Escalante Petrified Forest State Park—*park* UT-8
*Escalante Rim* UT-8
Escalante Rim—*cliff* CO-8
*Escalante River* UT-8
Escalante River—*stream* UT-8
Escalante Ruin—*hist pl* CO-8
Escalante Sch—*school* UT-8
Escalante Trail Historical Marker—*park* UT-8
Escalante Valley—*valley* UT-8
Escalante Valley Sch—*school* UT-8
Escalante Wash—*stream* AZ-5
Escalanti, Sierra—*range* UT-8
Escalle—*uninc pl* CA-9
**Escalon**—*pop pl* CA-9
Escalona Gulch—*valley* CA-9
Escalona Sch—*school* CA-9
Escalon (CCD)—*cens area* CA-9
Escambe—*hist pl* FL-3
**Escambia**—*pop pl* FL-3
**Escambia**—*pop pl* GA-3
Escambia Bay—*bay* FL-3
Escambia-Brewton Area Vocational Sch—*school* AL-4
Escambia Chapel—*church* FL-3
**Escambia County**—*pop pl* AL-4
**Escambia (County)**—*pop pl* FL-3
Escambia County Courthouse—*building* AL-4
*Escambia County Fire Control HQ* FL-3
Escambia County HS—*school* AL-4
Escambia County JHS—*school* AL-4
Escambia County Training Sch—*school* AL-4
*Escambia Creek* AL-4
*Escambia Creek* FL-3
Escambia Creek—*stream* AL-4
Escambia Farms—*locale* FL-3
**Escambia (historical)**—*pop pl* FL-3
Escambia HS—*school* FL-3
Escambia Juvenile Detention Sch—*school* FL-3
Escambia Natl Experimental For—*forest* AL-4
*Escambia River* AL-4
*Escambia River* FL-3
Escambia River—*stream* FL-3
Escambia RR Station—*locale* FL-3
Escambia Westgate Center—*school* FL-3
**Escanaba**—*pop pl* MI-6
Escanaba Lake—*lake* WI-6
*Escanaba River* MI-6
Escanaba River—*stream* MI-6
Escanaba River Lookout Tower—*locale* MI-6
Escanaba River State For—*forest* (3) MI-6
**Escanaba (Township of)**—*pop pl* MI-6
Escano Branch Number One Ditch—*canal* CA-9
Escano Ditch—*canal* CA-9
**Escape, The**—*pop pl* PA-2
Escape Cape—*cape* AK-9
Escape Point—*cape* AK-9
Escapule Mine—*mine* AZ-5
Escarpada, Mesa—*cliff* AZ-5
Escarpado Canyon—*valley* CA-9
**Escarpment**—*pop pl* NY-2
Escarpment Creek—*stream* WY-8
Escarpment Peak—*summit* CO-8
Escarrodio Canyon—*valley* NM-5
Escaso, Arroyo—*stream* CA-9
**Escatawpa**—*pop pl* AL-4
**Escatawpa**—*pop pl* MS-4
Escatawpa Assembly of God Ch—*church* MS-4
*Escatawpa Creek* AL-4
Escatawpa Elem Sch—*school* MS-4
Escatawpa River—*stream* AL-4
Escatawpa River—*stream* MS-4
Escatawpa United Methodist Ch—*church* MS-4
Escavada Wash—*stream* NM-5
**Escena**—*pop pl* MD-2
Eschbach—*locale* WA-9
Esch Creek—*stream* AK-9
Escheman Landing Strips—*airport* CO-8
Eschenbaugh Swamp—*swamp* PA-2
*Eschhotz Atoll* MP-9
Eschscholtz Bay—*bay* AK-9
*Eschscholtz Islands* MP-9
Esch's Spur Bridge—*hist pl* KS-7
*Eschweiler Lake* WI-6
*Es-cim-en zeen Spring* AZ-5
*Esco* TN-4
Esco—*locale* KY-4
Escobar Cem—*cemetery* OR-9
**Escobares**—*pop pl* TX-5
Escobar JHS—*school* TX-5
Escobas—*locale* TX-5
Escobas Creek—*stream* TX-5
Escobas Mesa—*summit* NM-5
Escobas Ranch—*locale* TX-5
Escobedo Park—*park* AZ-5
Escobedo Windmill—*locale* TX-5
Escoe Bldg—*hist pl* OK-5
Escoe Brook Ch—*church* VA-3
**Escoheag**—*pop pl* RI-1
Escoheag Hill—*summit* RI-1
*Escoheague Hill* RI-1
Escojeda Windmill—*locale* NM-5
*Esconaba River* MI-6
*Esconawba* MI-6
*Esconawba River* MI-6
*Esconawby River* MI-6
Escondia Gulch—*valley* OR-9
Escondida—*hist pl* KY-4
Escondida—*locale* KY-4
Escondida—*locale* NM-5
Escondida, Canada—*valley* NM-5
*Escondida Gulch* OR-9
Escondida Siding—*locale* NM-5
Escondida Tank—*reservoir* NM-5
Escondida Tank—*reservoir* TX-5
Escondida Windmill—*locale* TX-5
**Escondido**—*pop pl* CA-9
Escondido, Arroyo—*valley* TX-5
Escondido, Canon—*valley* CO-8
Escondido Artesian Well—*well* TX-5
Escondido Beach—*beach* CA-9
Escondido Camp Ground—*locale* CA-9
Escondido Canal—*canal* CA-9
Escondido Canyon—*valley* (3) CA-9
Escondido Canyon—*valley* CO-8
Escondido Canyon—*valley* (2) NM-5
Escondido Canyon—*valley* (2) TX-5
*Escondido Canyon Tank* NM-5
Escondido Cem—*cemetery* NM-5
Escondido Cem—*cemetery* TX-5
Escondido Creek—*stream* (2) CA-9
Escondido Creek—*stream* (3) NM-5
Escondido Creek—*stream* (3) TX-5
*Escondido Draw* TX-5
Escondido Draw—*valley* TX-5
Escondido HS—*school* CA-9
Escondido Junction—*locale* CA-9
*Escondido Lake* CO-8
Escondido Lake—*lake* WA-9
Escondido Lake—*reservoir* TX-5
Escondido Mtn—*summit* NM-5
Escondido Oil Field—*oilfield* TX-5
Escondido Park—*park* AZ-5
Escondido Ranch—*locale* (2) NM-5
Escondido Ranch—*locale* (2) TX-5
Escondido Ravine—*valley* CA-9
Escondido Rsvr—*reservoir* NM-5
Escondido Sch—*school* CA-9
Escondido Spring—*spring* (2) AZ-5
Escondido Springs—*spring* NM-5
Escondido Tank—*reservoir* AZ-5
Escondido Tank—*reservoir* (4) NM-5
Escondido Tank—*reservoir* (3) TX-5
Escondido Trail—*trail* WA-9
Escondido Wash—*arroyo* AZ-5
Escondido Wash—*stream* AZ-5
Escondido Water Hole—*lake* TX-5
Escondido Well—*well* (2) AZ-5
Escondido Well—*well* NM-5
Escondido Windmill—*locale* (3) TX-5
Esco Sch—*school* KY-4
Escott Brothers Dam—*dam* SD-7
Escott Drain—*canal* ID-8
Escribano Artesian Well—*well* TX-5
Escribano Point—*cape* FL-3
Escrito Canyon—*valley* NM-5
Escrito Oil Field—*other* NM-5
Escrito Spring—*spring* NM-5
Escrito Trading Post—*locale* NM-5
Escronges Lake—*lake* AR-4
Escudilla Mountains—*summit* AZ-5
Escudilla Mountain Tank—*reservoir* AZ-5
Escudilla Mtn—*summit* AZ-5
*Escudillo* AZ-5
Escue Cave—*cave* TN-4
Escuela Abraham Lincoln—*school* PR-3
Escuela Adrian Martinez Gandia—*school* PR-3
Escuela Adrian Medina—*school* PR-3
Escuela Aguas Blancas—*school* PR-3
Escuela Agua Tuna—*school* PR-3
Escuela Agustin Balseiro—*school* PR-3
Escuela Alberto Molina—*school* PR-3
Escuela Alberto Schweitzer—*school* PR-3
Escuela Alejandrina Benitez—*school* PR-3
Escuela Alerta—*school* PR-3
Escuela Algarrobos—*school* PR-3
Escuela Almacigo Alto Numero 1—*school* PR-3
Escuela Almirante Norte—*school* PR-3
Escuela Altamesa—*school* PR-3
Escuela Alto Dona Elena—*school* PR-3
Escuela Amalia Exposito—*school* PR-3
Escuela Amalia Marin—*school* PR-3
Escuela Andres Gonzalez—*school* PR-3
Escuela Anon—*school* PR-3
Escuela Anones Centro—*school* PR-3
Escuela Anones Diaz—*school* PR-3
Escuela Antonia Pagan—*school* PR-3
Escuela Antonio Longa—*school* PR-3
Escuela Antonio Sanchez de Padilla—*school* PR-3
Escuela Antonio S Pedreira—*school* PR-3
Escuela Arenas Abajo—*school* PR-3
Escuela Arturo Lluberas—*school* PR-3
Escuela Arturo Martinez—*school* PR-3
Escuela Asuncion Lopez—*school* PR-3
Escuela Atalaya—*school* PR-3
Escuela Atalaya Abajo—*school* PR-3
Escuela Atalaya Arriba—*school* PR-3
Escuela Atalaya Numero 3—*school* PR-3
Escuela Atravesada—*school* PR-3
Escuela Avelino Faner—*school* PR-3
Escuela Ayala—*school* PR-3
Escuela Baldorioty De Castro—*school* PR-3
Escuela Ballaja—*school* PR-3
Escuela Barahona—*school* PR-3
Escuela Barreal—*school* PR-3
Escuela Barrero—*school* PR-3
Escuela Bartolomei—*school* PR-3
Escuela Bartolome Las Casas—*school* PR-3
Escuela Basilio Charneco Caban—*school* PR-3
Escuela Beatriz—*school* PR-3
Escuela Beatriz Adventro—*school* PR-3
Escuela Benavente—*school* PR-3
Escuela Benita Gonzalez—*school* PR-3
Escuela Benito Medina—*school* PR-3
Escuela Betances—*school* PR-3
Escuela Booker T Washington—*school* PR-3
Escuela Braulio Dueno Colon—*school* PR-3
Escuela Buena Vista—*school* PR-3
Escuela Bunker—*school* PR-3
Escuela Caguabo—*school* PR-3
Escuela Caguitas Centro—*school* PR-3
Escuela Caimito—*school* PR-3
Escuela Caimito Adentro—*school* PR-3
Escuela Caimito Numero 1—*school* PR-3
Escuela Caimito Numero 2—*school* PR-3
Escuela Camarones—*school* PR-3
Escuela Camarones Centro—*school* PR-3
Escuela Cambalache—*school* PR-3
Escuela Cambrene—*school* PR-3
Escuela Candelaria Afuera—*school* PR-3
Escuela Canto Gallo—*school* PR-3
Escuela Caonillas Ceiba—*school* PR-3
Escuela Capaez—*school* PR-3
Escuela Capilla—*school* PR-3
Escuela Caracoles—*school* PR-3
Escuela Caracoles Arriba—*school* PR-3
Escuela Carite Chino—*school* PR-3
Escuela Carretera Ciales—*school* PR-3
Escuela Catala—*school* PR-3
Escuela Cayaguas—*school* PR-3
Escuela Ceiba Norte—*school* PR-3
Escuela Ceiba Sur—*school* PR-3
Escuela Cerrillos—*school* PR-3
Escuela Cerro Gordo—*school* PR-3

Escuela Certenejas—*school* PR-3
Escuela Cienaga Alta—*school* PR-3
Escuela Cienegueta—*school* PR-3
Escuela Ciriaco Gonzalez—*school* PR-3
Escuela Ciudad Nueva—*school* PR-3
Escuela Clavell—*school* PR-3
Escuela Collores—*school* PR-3
Escuela Collores Numero 1—*school* PR-3
Escuela Collores Numero 3—*school* PR-3
Escuela Collores Numero 4—*school* PR-3
Escuela Colon—*school* PR-3
Escuela Consejo Abajo—*school* PR-3
Escuela Consejo Arriba—*school* PR-3
Escuela Corral Falso—*school* PR-3
Escuela Cortes—*school* PR-3
Escuela C Ramirez Arrellano—*school* PR-3
Escuela Cruces Abajo—*school* PR-3
Escuela Cruces Arriba—*school* PR-3
Escuela Cruces Nuevas—*school* PR-3
Escuela Cruz Rosa Rivas—*school* PR-3
Escuela Cubuy—*school* PR-3
Escuela Cupey Alto—*school* PR-3
Escuela Cupey Marina—*school* PR-3
Escuela Dajaos Sexto—*school* PR-3
Escuela de Abajo—*school* NM-5
Escuela de Aldea—*school* PR-3
Escuela de Cadeca—*school* PR-3
Escuela de La Placita—*school* PR-3
Escuela de Rio Abajo—*school* PR-3
Escuela de San Patricio—*school* PR-3
Escuela Diego Hernandez—*school* PR-3
Escuela Doctor Gabriel Inguina—*school* PR-3
Escuela Doctor Gandara—*school* PR-3
Escuela Doctor Isidra Vidal—*school* PR-3
Escuela Doctor Martinez—*school* PR-3
Escuela Doctor Pedreira—*school* PR-3
Escuela Doctor Pita—*school* PR-3
Escuela Doctor Santiago Veve—*school* PR-3
Escuela Domingo Arana Marquez—*school* PR-3
Escuela Don Manolo—*school* PR-3
**Escuela Dr Liborio Cordova**—*pop pl* PR-3
Escuela Eduardo J Saldana—*school* PR-3
Escuela Eduardo Neumann Gandia—*school* PR-3
Escuela E M de Hostos—*school* PR-3
Escuela Emilio Alvarez Lopez—*school* PR-3
Escuela Emilio Castelar—*school* PR-3
Escuela Emilio Cuadra—*school* PR-3
Escuela Ensenada—*school* PR-3
Escuela Epifanio Estrada—*school* PR-3
Escuela Eugenio Maria de Hostos—*school* PR-3
Escuela Evaristo Camacho—*school* PR-3
Escuela Evaristo Izcoa Diaz—*school* PR-3
Escuela Extension El Comandante—*school* PR-3
Escuela Fabriciano Cuevas—*school* PR-3
Escuela Federico Degetau—*school* PR-3
Escuela Felipe Vargas Gonzalez—*school* PR-3
Escuela Fernandez Juncos—*school* PR-3
Escuela Florida Arriba—*school* PR-3
Escuela Frailes—*school* PR-3
Escuela Francisco Acevedo Nieves—*school* PR-3
Escuela Francisco Baco Soria—*school* PR-3
Escuela Francisco Oller—*school* PR-3
Escuela Francisco Ponce—*school* PR-3
Escuela Francisco Zenon Gely—*school* PR-3
Escuela Franklin Delano Roosevelt—*school* PR-3
Escuela Franquez—*school* PR-3
Escuela Fraternidad—*school* PR-3
Escuela Fraternidad Humana—*school* PR-3
Escuela Garcia—*school* PR-3
Escuela Garcia Cepeda—*school* PR-3
Escuela Garfield—*school* PR-3
Escuela Gaspar Vila Mayans—*school* PR-3
Escuela Gaya—*school* PR-3
Escuela Gerardo Selles—*school* PR-3
Escuela Gerardo Selles Sola—*school* PR-3
Escuela Gobeo—*school* PR-3
Escuela Gripinas—*school* PR-3
Escuela Guano—*school* PR-3
Escuela Guaraguao—*school* PR-3
Escuela Guaraguao Rincon—*school* PR-3
Escuela Guilarte—*school* PR-3
Escuela Guzman Arriba—*school* PR-3
Escuela Harris—*school* PR-3
Escuela Hato—*school* PR-3
Escuela Hato Nuevo—*school* PR-3
Escuela Herminio R Irizarry—*school* PR-3
Escuela Higuero—*school* PR-3
Escuela Hormigas—*school* PR-3
Escuela Huffman—*school* PR-3
Escuela Industrial de Ninas—*school* PR-3
Escuela Industrial Para Mujeres—*school* PR-3
Escuela Intermedia Luis Pales Matos—*school* PR-3
Escuela Intermedia Palvi—*school* PR-3
Escuela Jacana—*school* PR-3
Escuela Jacana Abajo—*school* PR-3
Escuela Jagual—*school* PR-3
Escuela Jagua Pasto Numero 1—*school* PR-3
Escuela Jaguas—*school* PR-3
Escuela Jaguey—*school* PR-3
Escuela Jagueyes Abajo—*school* PR-3
Escuela Jefferson—*school* PR-3
Escuela Joaquin Oronoz Rodon—*school* PR-3
Escuela Jose Antonio Davila—*school* PR-3
Escuela Jose Antonio Torres—*school* PR-3
Escuela Jose Barbosa—*school* PR-3
Escuela Jose C Barbosa—*school* PR-3
Escuela Jose Collazo—*school* PR-3
Escuela Jose Cordero—*school* PR-3
Escuela Jose de Diego—*school* PR-3
Escuela Jose D Zayas—*school* PR-3
Escuela Josefa Domingo—*school* PR-3
Escuela Josefa Miranda—*school* PR-3
Escuela Jose F Diaz—*school* PR-3
Escuela Jose Figueroa—*school* PR-3
Escuela Jose Gautier Benitez—*school* PR-3
Escuela Jose Hernandez—*school* PR-3
Escuela Jose J Acosta—*school* PR-3
Escuela Jose Maria del Valle—*school* PR-3
Escuela Jose M Cintron—*school* PR-3
Escuela Jose M Gallardo—*school* PR-3
Escuela Jose Noriega—*school* PR-3
Escuela Jose Rosario—*school* PR-3
Escuela Juan Asencio III—*school* PR-3
Escuela Juan Cuevas—*school* PR-3
Escuela Juan de Dios Lopez—*school* PR-3
Escuela Juan Gonzalez—*school* PR-3
Escuela Juan I Vega—*school* PR-3
Escuela Juan Maria Palmer—*school* PR-3
Escuela Juan Morell Campos—*school* PR-3
Escuela Juan Osuna—*school* PR-3
Escuela Juan Ramon Jimenez—*school* PR-3
Escuela Juan Resto—*school* PR-3
Escuela Juan Sanchez—*school* PR-3
Escuela Julia Hernandez—*school* PR-3
Escuela Julio Collazo Silva—*school* PR-3
Escuela Julio Gonzalez Quinones—*school* PR-3
Escuela Julio L Vizcarrondo—*school* PR-3
Escuela Julio Olivieri—*school* PR-3
Escuela Julio S Rivas—*school* PR-3
Escuela La Carmelita—*school* PR-3
Escuela Laguna—*school* PR-3
Escuela La Lima—*school* PR-3
Escuela La Mesa—*school* PR-3
Escuela La Mina—*school* PR-3
Escuela Las Rosas Numero 2—*school* PR-3
Escuela La Pista—*school* PR-3
**Escuela La Prieta**—*pop pl* PR-3
Escuela Las Americas—*school* PR-3
Escuela Las Flores—*school* PR-3
Escuela La Sierra—*school* PR-3
Escuela Las Parcelas—*school* PR-3
Escuela Las Salinas—*school* PR-3
Escuela Lebron Ramos—*school* PR-3
Escuela Liceo Ponceno—*school* PR-3
Escuela Lirios Dorado—*school* PR-3
Escuela Lizardi—*school* PR-3
Escuela Llano—*school* PR-3
Escuela Lola Rodriguez de Tio—*school* PR-3
Escuela Los Canos—*school* PR-3
Escuela Los Claudios—*school* PR-3
Escuela Los Cocos—*school* PR-3
Escuela Lucas Valdivieso—*school* PR-3
Escuela Luce—*school* PR-3
Escuela Luchetti—*school* PR-3
Escuela Luis Calderon—*school* PR-3
Escuela Luis Felipe P—*school* PR-3
Escuela Luis M Santiago—*school* PR-3
Escuela Luis Munoz Rivera—*school* PR-3
Escuela Luis Munoz Souffront—*school* PR-3
Escuela Luis Santaella—*school* PR-3
Escuela Luis T Balinas—*school* PR-3
Escuela Macana—*school* PR-3
Escuela Madre Cabrini—*school* PR-3
Escuela Maldonado—*school* PR-3
Escuela Mal Paso—*school* PR-3
Escuela Malpica—*school* PR-3
Escuela Mambiche Blanco—*school* PR-3
Escuela Mambiche Prieto—*school* PR-3
Escuela Mamey—*school* PR-3
Escuela Mamey Centro—*school* PR-3
Escuela Mamey Numero 1—*school* PR-3
Escuela Mancho Rojas—*school* PR-3
Escuela Mangual Lebron—*school* PR-3
Escuela Manuel A Rivera—*school* PR-3
Escuela Manuel Corchado—*school* PR-3
Escuela Manuel Negron Collazo—*school* PR-3
Escuela Manuel Surillo—*school* PR-3
Escuela Manuel Torres—*school* PR-3
Escuela Marcos Sanchez—*school* PR-3
Escuela Mariana Bracetti—*school* PR-3
Escuela Mariana Numero 1—*school* PR-3
Escuela Mariano Abril—*school* PR-3
Escuela Maria R C Claudio—*school* PR-3
Escuela Marias—*school* PR-3
Escuela Marias Numero 2—*school* PR-3
Escuela Marias Numero 3—*school* PR-3
Escuela Mario Mercado—*school* PR-3
Escuela Martin—*school* PR-3
Escuela Martin Gonzalez—*school* PR-3
Escuela M Cadilla—*school* PR-3
Escuela Medina—*school* PR-3
Escuela Miguel Cervantes Saavedra—*school* PR-3
Escuela Millones—*school* PR-3
Escuela Miradero—*school* PR-3
Escuela Mogote—*school* PR-3
Escuela Monte Llano—*school* PR-3
Escuela Morcelo—*school* PR-3
Escuela Morovis—*school* PR-3
Escuela Mulita Alvelo—*school* PR-3
Escuela Mulitas Dos—*school* PR-3
Escuela Munoz Rivera—*school* PR-3
Escuela Naranjo—*school* PR-3
Escuela Naranjo Abajo—*school* PR-3
Escuela Naranjo Arriba—*school* PR-3
**Escuela Negroni**—*pop pl* PR-3
Escuela Negroni—*school* PR-3
Escuela Notre Dame—*school* PR-3
Escuela Nuestra Senora de Belen—*school* PR-3
Escuela Nuestra Senora de la Piedad—*school* PR-3
Escuela Numero 1—*school* PR-3
Escuela Numero 2—*school* PR-3
Escuela Numero 3—*school* PR-3
Escuela Numero 4—*school* PR-3
Escuela Numero 5—*school* PR-3
Escuela Nusa—*school* PR-3
Escuela Osuna—*school* PR-3
Escuela Padre Rufo—*school* PR-3
Escuela Palma Escrita—*school* PR-3
Escuela Palmarito Centro—*school* PR-3
Escuela Palmazola—*school* PR-3
Escuela Parque—*school* PR-3
Escuela Pedro Acevedo—*school* PR-3
Escuela Pedro Arroyo—*school* PR-3
Escuela Pedro Carlos Timothee—*school* PR-3
Escuela Pellejas Hoyo—*school* PR-3
Escuela Pena Pobre Arriba—*school* PR-3
Escuela Peniel—*school* PR-3
Escuela Penon—*school* PR-3
Escuela Pepita Garriga—*school* PR-3
Escuela Piedra Azul—*school* PR-3
Escuela Piedras Blancas—*school* PR-3
Escuela Pimentel—*school* PR-3
Escuela Pinales Abajo—*school* PR-3
Escuela Pinales Arriba—*school* PR-3
Escuela Pinales Caracoles—*school* PR-3
Escuela Pollos—*school* PR-3
Escuela Portillo—*school* PR-3
Escuela Pozuelo—*school* PR-3
Escuela Puente Blanco—*school* PR-3
Escuela Puntas Nuevas—*school* PR-3
Escuela Quebrada—*school* PR-3
Escuela Quebrada Arenas—*school* (2) PR-3
Escuela Quebrada Grande—*school* PR-3
Escuela Quebrada Honda—*school* PR-3
Escuela Quebrada Larga—*school* PR-3
Escuela Quebrada Larga Abajo—*school* PR-3
Escuela Quebradas—*school* PR-3
Escuela Quebradas 1—*school* PR-3
Escuela Quebradas 2—*school* PR-3
Escuela Quebrado Cruz Cocos—*school* PR-3
Escuela Quemados—*school* PR-3
Escuela Rabanos—*school* PR-3
Escuela Rafael Colon Garcia—*school* PR-3
Escuela Rafael Cordero—*school* PR-3
Escuela Rafael Hernandez—*school* PR-3
Escuela Ramirez—*school* PR-3
Escuela Ramon Marin—*school* PR-3
Escuela Ramon Valle Seda—*school* PR-3
Escuela Ranchera—*school* PR-3
Escuela Regalada Rivera—*school* PR-3
Escuela Republica de Brasil—*school* PR-3
Escuela Republica de Colombia—*school* PR-3
Escuela Republica de San Salvador—*school* PR-3
Escuela Rexford G Tugwell—*school* PR-3
Escuela Rio—*school* PR-3
Escuela Rio Abajo—*school* PR-3
Escuela Rio Canas—*school* PR-3
Escuela Rio Canas Arriba—*school* PR-3
Escuela Rio Chiquito—*school* PR-3
Escuela Rio Grande—*school* PR-3
Escuela Rio Lajas—*school* PR-3
Escuela Rivera—*school* PR-3
Escuela Roig—*school* PR-3
Escuela Rojas—*school* PR-3
Escuela Roosevelt—*school* PR-3
Escuela Ruiz Belvis—*school* PR-3
Escuela Rural de Pugnado Afuera—*school* PR-3
Escuela Rural Emilio Pastor—*school* PR-3
Escuela Rural Lirios—*school* PR-3
Escuela Rural Maestra Gandro—*school* PR-3
Escuela Sabana Alta—*school* PR-3
Escuela Sabana Llana—*school* PR-3
Escuela Sabana Seca—*school* PR-3
Escuela Saco—*school* PR-3
Escuela Saliente Abajo—*school* PR-3
Escuela Saliente Arriba—*school* PR-3
Escuela Saltillo—*school* PR-3
Escuela Salto—*school* PR-3
Escuela Salvador Bousquets—*school* PR-3
Escuela Salvador Brau—*school* PR-3
Escuela Salvador Rodriguez—*school* PR-3
Escuela San Conrado—*school* PR-3
Escuela Sandalio Marcano—*school* PR-3
Escuela San Felipe—*school* PR-3
Escuela San Juan del Salvador—*school* PR-3
Escuela San Lorenzo—*school* PR-3
Escuela San Luis Rey—*school* PR-3
Escuela Santa Catalina—*school* PR-3
Escuela Santaella—*school* PR-3
Escuela Santa Olaya—*school* PR-3
Escuela Santa Rita—*school* PR-3
Escuela Santa Rosa—*school* PR-3
Escuela Santa Rosa Uno—*school* PR-3
Escuela Santas Pascuas—*school* PR-3
Escuela Santa Teresita—*school* PR-3
Escuela Santiago Medina—*school* PR-3
Escuela Santiago Veve Calzada—*school* PR-3
Escuela Sebastian Pabon Alyes—*school* PR-3
Escuela Secundino Diaz Morales—*school* PR-3
Escuela Segunda Unidad—*school* PR-3
Escuela Segunda Unidad Antonio A Caron Corre—*school* PR-3
Escuela Segunda Unidad Baldorioty de Castro—*school* PR-3
Escuela Segunda Unidad Bordaleza—*school* PR-3
Escuela Segunda Unidad Casiana Cepeda—*school* PR-3
Escuela Segunda Unidad de Anones—*school* PR-3
Escuela Segunda Unidad de Antonio Vasquez Ra—*school* PR-3
Escuela Segunda Unidad de Bajadero—*school* PR-3
Escuela Segunda Unidad de Barinas—*school* PR-3
Escuela Segunda Unidad de Bauta—*school* PR-3
Escuela Segunda Unidad de Bayamon—*school* PR-3
Escuela Segunda Unidad de Botijas No 1—*school* PR-3
Escuela Segunda Unidad de Botijas No 2—*school* PR-3
Escuela Segunda Unidad de Carlos Zayas—*school* PR-3
Escuela Segunda Unidad de Cupey Bajo—*school* PR-3
Escuela Segunda Unidad de Duey—*school* PR-3
Escuela Segunda Unidad de Eugenio M de Hosto—*school* PR-3
Escuela Segunda Unidad de Federico Degetau—*school* PR-3
Escuela Segunda Unidad de Francisco Valdes—*school* PR-3
Escuela Segunda Unidad de Frederico Degetau—*school* PR-3
Escuela Segunda Unidad de Fronton—*school* PR-3
Escuela Segunda Unidad de Hayales—*school* PR-3
Escuela Segunda Unidad de Isidro Vicens—*school* PR-3
Escuela Segunda Unidad de Jesus Maria Rod—*school* PR-3
Escuela Segunda Unidad de Jesus T Pinero—*school* PR-3
Escuela Segunda Unidad de Jose Barrenas Mart—*school* PR-3
Escuela Segunda Unidad de Jose Celso Barbo—*school* PR-3
Escuela Segunda Unidad de La America—*school* PR-3
Escuela Segunda Unidad de Magueyes—*school* PR-3
Escuela Segunda Unidad de Mameyes—*school* PR-3
Escuela Segunda Unidad de Mariana—*school* PR-3
Escuela Segunda Unidad de Maricao Afuera—*school* PR-3
Escuela Segunda Unidad de Mercedes Palma—*school* PR-3
Escuela Segunda Unidad de Palmarejo—*school* PR-3
Escuela Segunda Unidad de Paloma—*school* PR-3
Escuela Segunda Unidad de Pasto—*school* PR-3
Escuela Segunda Unidad de Pesas—*school* PR-3
Escuela Segunda Unidad de Rabanos—*school* PR-3
Escuela Segunda Unidad de Real—*school* PR-3
Escuela Segunda Unidad de Rio Hondo—*school* PR-3
Escuela Segunda Unidad de Santa Rosa—*school* PR-3
Escuela Segunda Unidad de Santiago Palmer—*school* PR-3
Escuela Segunda Unidad de Santo Domingo—*school* PR-3
Escuela Segunda Unidad de Tomas Berrios B—*school* PR-3
Escuela Segunda Unidad de Valenciano Abajo—*school* PR-3
Escuela Segunda Unidad de Vicenty—*school* PR-3
Escuela Segunda Unidad de Voladoras—*school* PR-3
Escuela Segunda Unidad Llanos Tuna—*school* PR-3
Escuela Segunda Unidad Luciano Rios—*school* PR-3
Escuela Segunda Unidad Rivera—*school* PR-3
Escuela Segunda Unidad Salto Arriba—*school* PR-3
Escuela Serra—*school* PR-3
Escuela Sierra Baja—*school* PR-3
Escuela Sinforoso Aponte—*school* PR-3
Escuela Sonadora—*school* PR-3
Escuela Sonadora Alta—*school* PR-3
Escuela Sonadora Llana—*school* PR-3
Escuela Superior—*school* PR-3
Escuela Superior Albert Einstein—*school* PR-3
Escuela Superior Central—*school* PR-3
Escuela Superior de Comerio—*school* PR-3
Escuela Superior Gabriela Mistral—*school* PR-3
Escuela Superior Guatier Benitez—*school* PR-3
Escuela Superior Trina Padilla de Sanz—*school* PR-3
Escuela Superior Vocacional—*school* PR-3
Escuela Superior Vocacional Tomas Ongay—*school* PR-3
Escuela Susua Alta—*school* PR-3
Escuela Tanama—*school* PR-3
Escuela Tejas Numero 1—*school* PR-3
Escuela Theodore Roosevelt—*school* PR-3
Escuela Thomas A Edison—*school* PR-3
Escuela Tijeras—*school* PR-3
Escuela Tomas Vera Ayala—*school* PR-3
Escuela Torrecillas—*school* PR-3
Escuela Tortugo—*school* PR-3
Escuela Vaello—*school* PR-3
Escuela Van Scoy—*school* PR-3
Escuela Vega Alegre—*school* PR-3
Escuela Vicente Usera—*school* PR-3
Escuela Victoriano Blanco—*school* PR-3
Escuela Villa San Jose—*school* PR-3
Escuela Virgilio Acevedo—*school* PR-3
Escuela Virgilio Morales—*school* PR-3
Escuela Vistamar—*school* PR-3
Escuela Vocacional Doctor Jose Padin—*school* PR-3
Escuela Vocacional Eugenio Maria de Hostos—*school* PR-3
Escuela Vocacional Miguel Such—*school* PR-3
Escuela W D Boyce—*school* PR-3
Escuela Yahueca Arriba—*school* PR-3
Escuela Yuca—*school* PR-3
Escuela Zamas—*school* PR-3
Escuela Zamora—*school* PR-3
Escuela Zoilo Gracia—*school* PR-3
Esculapia Hollow—*valley* AR-4
Esculapia (Township of)—*fmr MCD* AR-4
Escumbuit Island—*island* NH-1
Escures, Mount—*summit* AK-9
Escurial Island—*island* AK-9
*Escutarsis* ME-1
*Escutarsis Stream* ME-1
*Escutasis* ME-1
*Escutasis Stream* ME-1
*Escutassis Pond* ME-1
*Escutassis Stream Eskutarsis Stream* ME-1
**Esdaile**—*pop pl* WI-6
Esdaile Cem—*cemetery* WI-6
Esdon Brook—*stream* VT-1
Esdon Lake—*lake* MN-6
Esel Point—*cliff* WA-9
E Serrano Cabin—*locale* NM-5
**Eset (Pine Bluff)**—*pop pl* MS-4
Esetuk Creek—*stream* AK-9
Esetuk Glacier—*glacier* AK-9
**Esex**—*pop pl* CA-9
Esgate Cem—*cemetery* IA-7
Esha Canyon—*valley* CA-9
Esham Branch—*stream* KY-4
Esham Cem—*cemetery* KY-4
Eshamy Bay—*bay* AK-9
Eshamy Creek—*stream* AK-9
Eshamy Lagoon—*lake* AK-9
Eshamy Lake—*lake* AK-9
Eshamy Peak—*summit* AK-9
**Eshbach**—*pop pl* PA-2
**Eshcol**—*pop pl* PA-2
Eshcol Memorial Cem—*cemetery* PA-2
Eshcol Winery—*hist pl* CA-9
Eshelman, J., and Company Store—*hist pl* NY-2
Eshelman Ave Sch—*school* CA-9
Eshelman Rsvr—*reservoir* CO-8
Esherick, Wharton, Studio—*hist pl* PA-2
Eshleman Elem Sch—*school* PA-2
Eshleman Run—*stream* PA-2
Eshol Ch—*church* NC-3
Eshom Creek—*stream* CA-9
Eshom Point—*summit* CA-9
Eshom Sch—*school* IL-6
Eshom Valley—*valley* CA-9
*Eshquagama Lake* MN-6
Esiquio Windmill—*locale* TX-5
Esitty Valley—*valley* AZ-5
E-Six—*unorg reg* ND-7
E Six Butte—*summit* SD-7
**Eska**—*pop pl* AK-9
Eska Creek—*stream* AK-9
*Eskadere Mountains* AZ-5
Eska Lake—*lake* WI-6
Eskalapia Hollow—*valley* KY-4
Eskalapia Mtn—*summit* KY-4
Eska Mine—*mine* AK-9
Eska Mtn—*summit* AK-9
Eskar Pond—*lake* NY-2
**Eskay**—*pop pl* GA-3
**Eskay**—*pop pl* MT-8
**Eskdale**—*pop pl* UT-8
**Eskdale**—*pop pl* WV-2
Eskeline Creek—*stream* OR-9
Eskelton, Alvin, Barn—*hist pl* ID-8
Eskeridge Pettigrew Cem—*cemetery* AL-4
*Esker Island* AK-9
Esker Stream—*stream* AK-9
Eskew Branch—*stream* TX-5
Eskew No 2 Rsvr—*reservoir* WY-8
Eskimazene Ranch—*locale* AZ-5
*Eskimenzene Spring* AZ-5
*Eskimenzin Spring* AZ-5
Eskiminzin Fort Rock—*pillar* AZ-5
Eskiminzin Spring—*spring* AZ-5
Eskiminzin Wash—*stream* AZ-5
Eskimo Creek—*stream* (2) AK-9
Eskimo Creek—*stream* MT-8
Eskimo Creek—*stream* WY-8
Eskimo Hill—*summit* AK-9
Eskimo Hill—*summit* CA-9
Eskimo Islands—*area* AK-9
Eskimo Tank—*reservoir* AZ-5
Eskimo Tank—*reservoir* NM-5
Eskimo Well—*well* AZ-5
*Eskins Pond* NJ-2
Eskjo Ch—*church* MN-6
**Esko**—*pop pl* MN-6
Eskota—*locale* NC-3
Eskota—*locale* TX-5
*Eskquagama Lake* MN-6
**Eskridge**—*pop pl* KS-7
**Eskridge**—*pop pl* MS-4
Eskridge Cem—*cemetery* KS-7
Eskridge Cem—*cemetery* TN-4
Eskridge City Dam—*dam* KS-7
Eskridge Cove—*valley* NC-3
Eskridge Creek—*stream* MS-4
Eskridge Elem Sch—*school* KS-7
Eskridge Grove Ch—*church* NC-3
Eskridge Grove Sch—*school* NC-3
Eskridge Hotel—*hist pl* OK-5
Eskridge Lake—*reservoir* AL-4
Eskridge Lake Dam—*dam* AL-4
*Eskridges Gin* AL-4
**Eskridge (subdivision)**—*pop pl* MS-4
*Eskutarsis* ME-1
Eskutassis Pond—*lake* ME-1
Eskutassis Stream—*stream* ME-1
Eskwagama Lake—*lake* MN-6
Eslar Chapel—*church* WV-2
Eslava Branch—*stream* AL-4
Eslava Creek—*stream* (2) AL-4
E S Lee Lake Dam—*dam* MS-4
Esler Lake—*lake* MI-6
Esler Regional Airp—*airport* LA-4
Eslic Hollow—*valley* MO-7
Eslick Branch—*stream* TN-4
Eslick Canyon—*valley* WA-9
Eslick Creek—*stream* OR-9
Eslick Hollow—*valley* MO-7
Eslinger Cem—*cemetery* IA-7
Eslinger Cem—*cemetery* MO-7
Esling Hollow—*valley* MO-7
Esmay and Sandy Number 1 Dam—*dam* SD-7
Esmay and Sandy Number 2 Dam—*dam* SD-7
Esmay and Sandy Number 3 Dam—*dam* SD-7
Esmay Slough—*stream* IA-7
Esmen Center Sch—*school* IL-6
**Esmen (Township of)**—*pop pl* IL-6
**Esmeralda**—*pop pl* PR-3
Esmeralda County—*civil* NV-8
Esmeralda Creek—*stream* CA-9
Esmeralda Group—*mine* NV-8
Esmeralda Hill—*summit* MT-8
Esmeralda Mine—*mine* CA-9
Esmeralda Mine—*mine* CO-8
Esmeralda Mine—*mine* NV-8
Esmeralda Mine—*mine* OR-9
Esmeralda Mine (historical)—*mine* SD-7
Esmeralda Mtn—*summit* AK-9
Esmeralda Municipal Golf Course—*other* WA-9
Esmeralda Peaks—*summit* WA-9
Esmeralda Township—*inact MCD* NV-8
Esmeralda Well (Flowing)—*well* TX-5
*Esmereida Peaks* WA-9
Esmerelda Landing (historical)—*locale* MS-4
*Esmerelds Peaks* WA-9
E Smith—*locale* TX-5
Esmond—*locale* AZ-5
Esmond—*locale* GA-3
**Esmond**—*pop pl* IL-6
**Esmond**—*pop pl* ND-7
**Esmond**—*pop pl* RI-1
**Esmond**—*pop pl* SD-7
Esmond Cem—*cemetery* ND-7
Esmond Creamery (historical)—*locale* SD-7
Esmond Creek—*stream* OR-9
Esmond Creek—*stream* WY-8
Esmond Creek Rec Area—*park* OR-9
Esmond Forks—*stream* WY-8
Esmond Lake—*lake* MI-6
Esmond Lake—*lake* OR-9
Esmond Mtn—*summit* OR-9
Esmond Park—*flat* WY-8
Esmond Sch—*school* IL-6
**Esmond Township**—*pop pl* ND-7
**Esmond Township**—*pop pl* SD-7
Esmont—*hist pl* VA-3
**Esmont**—*pop pl* VA-3
Esmoris, Duran, Residencia—*hist pl* PR-3
Esnon—*locale* VA-3
**Esofea**—*pop pl* WI-6
Esofea Park—*park* WI-6
*Esom* GA-3
Esom Hill—*locale* GA-3
Esom Slough—*stream* AL-4
Esom Slough—*stream* GA-3
Eson Cem—*cemetery* KS-7
Esong—*slope* MH-9
Esook Trading Post (Abandoned)—*locale* AK-9
**Esopus**—*pop pl* NY-2
Esopus Creek—*stream* NY-2
Esopus Island—*island* NY-2
Esopus Lake—*lake* NY-2
*Esopus Lakes* NY-2
Esopus Meadows Lighthouse—*hist pl* NY-2
Esopus Meadows Lighthouse—*locale* NY-2
Esopus Meadows Point—*cape* NY-2
*Esopus Pond* NY-2
*Esopus Ponds* NY-2
**Esopus (Town of)**—*pop pl* NY-2
Esox Lake—*lake* WI-6
Espada, The—*flat* CA-9
Espada Aqueduct—*hist pl* TX-5
Espada Bluff—*cliff* CA-9
Espada Creek—*stream* CA-9
Espada Creek—*stream* TX-5
Espada Dam—*dam* TX-5
Espada Ditch—*canal* TX-5
Espada Park—*park* TX-5
Espada Ranch—*locale* TX-5
*Espado Creek* CA-9
*Espado Creek* TX-5
*Espanda Creek* TX-5
Espanola—*locale* WA-9
**Espanola**—*pop pl* FL-3
**Espanola**—*pop pl* NM-5
Espanola Cem—*cemetery* FL-3
Espanola Valley—*valley* NM-5
Espanol House—*locale* TX-5
Espanol Tank—*reservoir* TX-5
*Espanong* NJ-2
**Espanong (census name for Lake Hopatcong)**—*pop pl* NJ-2
Espanore Island—*island* MI-6
Espanore Lake—*lake* MI-6
**Espanta Sueno**—*pop pl* (2) PR-3
Espanto Mtn—*summit* AZ-5
Espantosa Lake—*reservoir* TX-5
Espantosa Slough—*stream* TX-5
Esparauza Tank—*reservoir* NM-5
**Esparto**—*pop pl* CA-9
Esparto (CCD)—*cens area* CA-9
Esp Ditch—*canal* MT-8
*Espe* SD-7
Espedeza Cem—*cemetery* MO-7
Espee Camp—*locale* AZ-5
Espe Elem Sch—*school* PA-2
Espee Mine—*mine* CA-9
Espee Ridge—*ridge* CA-9
*Espeil Coulee* MT-8
Espeil Coulee—*valley* MT-8
Espejo Butte—*summit* AZ-5
Espejo Creek—*stream* AZ-5
Espejo Ranch—*locale* TX-5
Espejo (Rosita) Creek—*stream* TX-5
Espejo Spring—*spring* AZ-5
Espe Lake—*lake* MN-6
Espeland-Ostrum-George Ditch—*canal* MT-8
Espelie—*locale* MN-6
Espelie State Wildlife Mngmt Area—*park* MN-6
**Espelie (Township of)**—*pop pl* MN-6
**Espenberg**—*pop pl* AK-9
Espenberg River—*stream* AK-9
Espendiza Windmill—*locale* TX-5
Espen Lakes—*lake* MN-6
Espenschied Chapel—*church* IL-6
**Esperance**—*pop pl* NY-2
Esperance—*uninc pl* WA-9
Esperance Landing—*locale* LA-4
Esperance Point—*cape* LA-4
Esperance Point Oil Field—*oilfield* LA-4
Esperance Sch—*school* WA-9
**Esperance (sta.)**—*pop pl* NY-2
**Esperance (Town of)**—*pop pl* NY-2
Esperanto Creek—*stream* AK-9
Esperanto Placer Mine—*mine* AK-9
Esperanza—*locale* CA-9
Esperanza—*locale* (2) TX-5
Esperanza—*locale* (2) PR-3
**Esperanza**—*pop pl* CA-9
**Esperanza**—*pop pl* MS-4
**Esperanza**—*pop pl* (8) PR-3
Esperanza, Rancho del—*locale* AZ-5
Esperanza Artesian Well—*well* TX-5
Esperanza (Barrio)—*fmr MCD* PR-3
Esperanza Canyon—*valley* CA-9
Esperanza Creek—*stream* AK-9
Esperanza Creek—*stream* CA-9
Esperanza Creek—*stream* TX-5
Esperanza Crossing—*locale* TX-5
Esperanza Drain—*canal* TX-5
Esperanza Draw—*valley* NM-5
Esperanza Fire Control Station—*locale* CA-9
Esperanza Mill—*mine* AZ-5
Esperanza Pit—*mine* AZ-5
Esperanza Pond—*lake* MD-2
Esperanza Post Office (historical)—*building* MS-4
Esperanza Ranch—*locale* (2) TX-5
Esperanza Spring—*spring* CA-9
Esperanza Tailings Dam—*dam* AZ-5
Esperanza Tank—*reservoir* AZ-5
Esperanza Valley—*valley* CA-9
Esperanza Wash—*stream* AZ-5
Esperanza Well—*well* AZ-5
Esperanza Well—*well* TX-5
Esperanza Windmill—*locale* (3) TX-5
**Esperenza**—*pop pl* FL-3
Esperero Canyon—*valley* AZ-5
Esperero Wash—*stream* AZ-5
*Espero* AZ-5
Esperson—*locale* TX-5
Esperson Dome Oil Field—*oilfield* TX-5
*Espe Sch* PA-2
Espey Boarding House—*hist pl* OR-9
Espil Ranch—*locale* AZ-5
Espina Hill—*summit* NV-8
Espinar (Barrio)—*fmr MCD* PR-3
Espinaso Ridge Pueblo—*hist pl* NM-5
*Espinazo Rojo* CO-8
**Espino**—*pop pl* PR-3
Espino (Barrio)—*fmr MCD* (4) PR-3
Espinosa—*locale* CO-8
**Espinosa**—*pop pl* PR-3

Espinosa (Barrio)—fmr MCD (2) ....PR-3
Espinosa Canyon—valley (2) .... CA-9
Espinosa Canyon—valley (2) .... NM-5
Espinosa Creek—stream .... CA-9
Espinosa Gulch—valley .... CO-8
Espinosa Lake—lake .... CA-9
Espinosa Lake—lake .... NM-5
Espinosa Ranch—locale .... NM-5
Espinosa Tank—reservoir .... AZ-5
Espinosa Well—well .... AZ-5
*Espinoso Canyon* .... CA-9
Espinoza Ditch—canal .... CO-8
Espio Creek—stream .... TX-5
Espirito Sch—school .... MA-1
Espiritu Canyon—valley .... AZ-5
Espiritu Santo Bay—bay .... TX-5
Espiritu Santo Ch—church .... FL-3
Espiritu Well—well .... AZ-5
Episcopal Ch of St. Francis—church .... UT-8
Espita Creek—stream .... TX-5
Espitallier Spring—spring .... WY-8
Espita Tank—reservoir .... TX-5
**Esplanada (subdivision)**—pop pl (2) .... AZ-5
Esplanade—uninc pl .... NY-2
Esplanade Apartments—hist pl .... IN-6
Esplanade Bench—bench .... AZ-5
Esplanade Ridge Hist Dist—hist pl .... LA-4
Esplanade Sch—school .... CA-9
Esplanade Worth Ave (Shop Ctr)—locale .... FL-3
**Esplen**—pop pl .... PA-2
Esplin Gulch—valley .... UT-8
Esplin Lake—lake .... MT-8
Esplin Rsvr—reservoir .... OR-9
Esplins Corral—locale .... AZ-5
Esplin Spring—spring .... UT-8
Esplin Tank—reservoir .... AZ-5
*Esplin Twin Tanks* .... AZ-5
Esplin Well—well .... NV-8
Espousal Retreat House—building .... MA-1
*Espuela* .... TX-5
**Espuela**—pop pl .... NM-5
Espuela Cem—cemetery .... TX-5
Espuela Tank—reservoir .... TX-5
Espuma, Monte de la—summit .... AZ-5
E Spurgeon Ranch—locale .... NM-5
**Espy**—pop pl .... PA-2
Espy, Lake—reservoir .... AL-4
Espy Branch—stream .... TX-5
Espy Cave—cave .... TN-4
Espy Cem—cemetery .... AL-4
Espy Cem—cemetery .... TN-4
Espy Creek—stream .... AL-4
Espy Gap—gap .... PA-2
Espy House—hist pl .... PA-2
Espy Pond—lake .... AL-4
Espy Ranch—locale (2) .... TX-5
Espy Run—stream .... PA-2
Espy Sch—school .... AL-4
Espy Sch—school .... OH-6
Espy Sch (historical)—school .... AL-4
Espy Slough—stream .... WA-9
Espy Springs—spring .... AL-4
Espy Springs Ch (historical)—church .... AL-4
**Espyville**—pop pl .... OH-6
**Espyville**—pop pl .... PA-2
Espyville (RR name for Espyville Station)—other .... PA-2
Espyville Station—locale .... PA-2
**Espyville Station (RR name Espyville)**—pop pl .... PA-2
Esquagama Club—building .... MN-6
*Esquagamah Lake* .... MN-6
Esquagamah Lake—reservoir .... MN-6
*Esquagama Lake* .... MN-6
Esquagama Lake—lake .... MN-6
*Esquagaman Creek* .... MN-6
Esquatzel Coulee—valley .... WA-9
Esquatzel Diversion Channel—canal .... WA-9
Esque Spring—spring .... NM-5
Esquibel Canyon—valley .... NM-5
Esquibel Island—island .... AK-9
Esquibel Tank—reservoir .... NM-5
Esquinado, Arroyo—stream .... CA-9
Esquina Llano Tank—reservoir .... TX-5
Esquina Well (Windmill)—locale .... TX-5
Esquipula Ch—church .... CO-8
**Esquire Acres Subdivision**—pop pl .... UT-8
**Esquire Acres Subdivision Five**—pop pl .... UT-8
**Esquire Estates Subdivision**—pop pl .... UT-8
Esquire Plaza—locale .... IN-6
**Esquire Subdivision**—pop pl .... UT-8
*Esquite Dry Lake* .... CA-9
Esquon—civil .... CA-9
**Esquon**—pop pl .... CA-9
E-S Ranch—locale .... TX-5
Esrey Park—park .... MI-6
Esrey Ranch—locale .... CA-9
**Essary Springs**—pop pl .... TN-4
Essary Springs Baptist Ch—church .... TN-4
Essary Springs Cem—cemetery .... TN-4
Essary Springs Post Office (historical)—building .... TN-4
Essau Ch—church .... KY-4
Essayons Lake—reservoir .... AL-4
Ess Creek—stream .... AZ-5
*Esse* .... TX-5
**Esselburn**—pop pl .... OH-6
Esselman Brothers General Store—hist pl .... MN-6
Esseltine Extension Drain—stream .... MI-6
Essen—locale .... NE-7
Essen—locale .... PA-2
**Essen**—pop pl .... LA-4
**Essen Heights**—pop pl .... LA-4
Essenmacher Drain—canal .... MI-6
Essenpries Mill (Site)—locale .... CA-9
**Esserville**—pop pl .... VA-3
Esseville—locale .... TX-5
Essex—locale .... CA-9
Essex—locale .... ND-7
Essex—locale .... WA-9
**Essex**—pop pl .... CA-9
**Essex**—pop pl .... CT-1
**Essex**—pop pl .... IL-6
**Essex**—pop pl .... IA-7
**Essex**—pop pl .... MD-2
**Essex**—pop pl .... MA-1
**Essex**—pop pl .... MS-4
**Essex**—pop pl .... MO-7
**Essex**—pop pl .... MT-8
**Essex**—pop pl .... NY-2
**Essex**—pop pl .... NC-3
**Essex**—pop pl .... OH-6
**Essex**—pop pl .... WV-2
Essex—uninc pl .... MA-1
Essex Ave Park—park .... NJ-2
Essex Bay—bay .... MA-1
Essex Bay Marshes—swamp .... MA-1
Essex Bayou—gut .... TX-5
Essex Bayou—stream .... AR-4
*Essex Branch* .... MA-1
Essex Branch—stream .... VA-3
Essex Cem—cemetery .... AR-4
Essex Cem—cemetery .... IA-7
Essex (census name for Essex Center)—CDP .... MA-1
**Essex Center**—pop pl .... VT-1
Essex Center (census name Essex)—other .... MA-1
**Essex Center (census name Essex)**—pop pl .... CT-1
Essex Chain Lakes—lake .... NY-2
Essex Company Machine Shop—hist pl .... MA-1
Essex Company Offices and Yard—hist pl .... MA-1
Essex County—airport .... NJ-2
**Essex County**—pop pl .... NJ-2
**Essex (County)**—pop pl .... NY-2
**Essex County**—pop pl .... VT-1
**Essex (County)**—pop pl .... VA-3
Essex County Agricultral and Technical Institution—school .... MA-1
Essex County Country Club—other .... NJ-2
Essex County Court Buildings—hist pl .... MA-1
Essex County Courthouse—hist pl .... NJ-2
Essex County Home and Farm—hist pl .... NY-2
**Essex County (in PMSA 1120,4160, 7090)**—pop pl .... MA-1
Essex County Jail—building .... MA-1
Essex County Park Commission Administration Bldg—hist pl .... NJ-2
Essex County Training Sch—school .... MA-1
**Essex Court Condo**—pop pl .... UT-8
Essex Creek—stream .... MT-8
Essex Ditch—canal .... WY-8
**Essex (Essex Center)**—pop pl .... VT-1
**Essex Falls**—pop pl .... MA-1
Essex Falls Station (historical)—locale .... MA-1
**Essex Fells**—pop pl .... NJ-2
Essex Fells Country Club—other .... NJ-2
Essex Fells Station—locale .... NJ-2
**Essex Fells (Township of)**—pop pl .... NJ-2
Essex Ferry—locale .... VT-1
Essex Ferry—trail .... NY-2
Essex Generating Station—airport .... NJ-2
Essex Group Plant—facility (2) .... IN-6
Essex Grove Sch—school .... IL-6
Essex Gulch—valley .... CA-9
Essex (historical)—locale .... KS-7
Essex HS—school .... VA-3
Essex Insitiute Hist Dist—hist pl .... MA-1
Essex Institute Museum Bldg—building .... MA-1
**Essex Junction**—pop pl .... VT-1
Essex Junction Village For—forest .... VT-1
**Essex Meadows**—pop pl .... VA-3
**Essex Mill**—pop pl .... VA-3
Essex Millpond—reservoir .... VA-3
Essex Mtn—summit .... MT-8
Essex Mtn—summit .... WY-8
Essex Park—park .... OR-9
Essex-Passaic Industrial Park—locale .... NJ-2
Essex Pond—lake .... CA-9
Essex Post Office—building .... MT-8
Essex River—stream .... MA-1
Essex River Causeway—bridge .... MA-1
Essex Rsvr—reservoir .... CA-9
Essex Sch—school .... AL-4
Essex Sch—school .... MD-2
Essex Sch—school .... MA-1
Essex Sch—school .... OH-6
Essex School—school .... MA-1
Essex Ship Bldg Museum—building .... MA-1
Essex Shoal—bar .... CT-1
Essex Shoal Channel—channel .... CT-1
Essex Spring—spring .... CA-9
Essex Springs—spring .... OR-9
Essex Station—locale .... NY-2
Essex Station (historical)—locale .... MA-1
**Essex (subdivision)**—pop pl .... NC-3
Essex Tank—reservoir .... CA-9
**Essex (Town of)**—pop pl .... CT-1
**Essex (Town of)**—pop pl .... MA-1
**Essex (Town of)**—pop pl .... NY-2
**Essex (Town of)**—pop pl .... VT-1
**Essex (Township of)**—pop pl (2) .... IL-6
**Essex (Township of)**—pop pl .... MI-6
Essex Village Hist Dist—hist pl .... NY-2
Essex Village Shop Ctr—locale .... FL-3
**Essexville**—pop pl .... MI-6
Essexville Oil Field—other .... MI-6
Essick Sch—school .... IL-6
Essie—locale .... KY-4
**Essie**—pop pl .... KY-4
Essie Creek—stream .... AK-9
*Essie R Grimsley HS* .... AL-4
Essie Sch—school .... KY-4
Essig—post sta (2) .... MN-6
Essigs Point—cape .... IL-6
**Essington**—pop pl .... PA-2
Essington-Lester (PC RR name for Essington)—other .... PA-2
**Essington (PC RR name Essington-Lester)**—pop pl .... PA-2
Ess Lake—lake .... AK-9
Ess Lake—lake .... MI-6
Ess Lake—lake .... WI-6
Essler Brook—stream .... ME-1
*Esslestrom Creek* .... OR-9
Essley Branch—stream .... MS-4
Esslinger Bldg—hist pl .... CA-9
Esslinger Cem—cemetery .... TN-4
Esslinger Cove—valley .... AL-4
Esslinger Cove Branch—stream .... AL-4
Esslinger Hollow—valley .... AL-4
Esslinger Island—island .... AL-4
Esslinger Spring—spring .... AL-4
Esslinger Spring Branch—stream .... AL-4
Essman Spring—spring .... MO-7
Essman Spring Hollow—valley .... MO-7
*Ess Mountain* .... WA-9
Essowah Harbor—bay .... AK-9
Essowah Lakes—area .... AK-9
Essowah Point—cape .... AK-9
*Essox Lake* .... WI-6
Ess Spring—spring .... AZ-5
E S Stewart Dam—dam .... AL-4
E S Stewart Pond—reservoir .... AL-4
Esswhtar Lake—lake .... MN-6
Estaban Tank—reservoir .... TX-5
Establishment Creek—stream .... MO-7
Establishment Island—island .... MO-7
*Estaboga* .... AL-4
*Estaboga Creek* .... AL-4
Estabrook—locale .... OR-9
**Estabrook**—pop pl .... CO-8
**Estabrook**—pop pl .... VA-3
Estabrook, Lake—lake .... OH-6
Estabrook, Rufus, House—hist pl .... MA-1
Estabrook Cem—cemetery .... ME-1
Estabrook Hill—summit .... ME-1
Estabrook Hist Dist—hist pl .... CO-8
Estabrook Octagon House—hist pl .... NY-2
Estabrook Park—park .... WI-6
**Estabrook Park**—pop pl .... VA-3
Estabrook Playground—park .... OH-6
Estabrook Sch—school .... MA-1
Estabrook Sch—school .... MI-6
Estabrook Sch—school .... ND-7
Estabrook Settlement—locale .... ME-1
**Estabrook Township**—pop pl .... ND-7
Esta Buena Mine—mine .... NV-8
*Estabutchie* .... MS-4
Estabutchie Sch (historical)—school .... MS-4
**Estaca**—pop pl .... NM-5
**Estacada**—pop pl .... OR-9
Estacada Airfield—airport .... OR-9
Estacada (CCD)—cens area .... OR-9
Estacada Lake—lake .... OR-9
Estacada MS—school .... OR-9
**Estacado**—pop pl (2) .... TX-5
Estacado Cem—cemetery .... TX-5
Estacado JHS—school .... TX-5
Estacas Lake—lake .... TX-5
Esta Ch—church .... WV-2
Estacion Botija—locale .... PR-3
**Estacion Botija**—pop pl .... PR-3
**Estacion Naguabo**—pop pl (2) .... PR-3
**Estacion Santa Isabel**—pop pl (2) .... PR-3
Estadio Municipal Hiram Bithorn—other .... PR-3
**Estados de La Mancha II (subdivision)**—pop pl (2) .... AZ-5
Estafeta Well—well .... NM-5
Estaline—locale .... VA-3
Estaline Canyon—valley .... NM-5
Estaline Furnace (Ruins)—locale .... VA-3
Estaline Schoolhouse—hist pl .... VA-3
Estaline Valley—valley .... VA-3
*Estamauler* .... TN-4
**Estanaula (historical)**—pop pl .... TN-4
**Estancia**—pop pl .... NM-5
Estancia (CCD)—cens area .... NM-5
Estancia Cem—cemetery .... NM-5
Estancita Spring—spring .... NM-5
Estanelle Sch—school .... TN-4
**Estanifanulga (historical)**—pop pl .... FL-3
E S Tank—reservoir .... AZ-5
*Estanolle Creek* .... GA-3
*Estapacha* .... MS-4
Estar—locale .... WV-2
Estate Beverhoudt—hist pl .... VI-3
Estate Botany Bay—hist pl .... VI-3
Estate Brewers Bay—hist pl .... VI-3
Estate Butler's Bay—hist pl .... VI-3
Estate Carolina Sugar Plantation—hist pl .... VI-3
*Estatee* .... NC-3
*Estatee Creek* .... NC-3
*Estatee Creek* .... SC-3
Estate Grove Place—hist pl .... VI-3
Estate Hafensight—hist pl .... VI-3
Estate Hogansborg—hist pl .... VI-3
Estate Judith's Fancy—hist pl .... VI-3
Estate Lake Dam—dam .... MS-4
*Estate Lane* .... IL-6
Estate La Reine—hist pl .... VI-3
Estate Little Princess—hist pl .... VI-3
**Estate Monterra (subdivision)**—pop pl (2) .... AZ-5
Estate Mount Victory—hist pl .... VI-3
Estate Neltjeberg—hist pl .... VI-3
Estate Niesky—hist pl .... VI-3
Estate Perseverance—hist pl .... VI-3
Estate Place—locale .... NV-8
Estate Prosperity—hist pl .... VI-3
Estate Saint George Hist Dist—hist pl .... VI-3
**Estates Hills (subdivision)**—pop pl .... NC-3
**Estates La Colina (subdivision)**—pop pl (2) .... AZ-5
Estate St. John—hist pl .... VI-3
Estate Tank—reservoir .... AZ-5
Estate Thomas—locale .... VI-3
Estate Windmill—locale .... TX-5
Estatoah Falls—falls .... GA-3
*Estatoe* .... NC-3
**Estatoe**—pop pl .... NC-3
Estatoe Ch—church .... NC-3
*Estatoe Creek* .... NC-3
*Estatoe Creek* .... SC-3
Estavanko Cem—cemetery .... GA-3
Estaville (historical)—locale .... AL-4
Estaville Post Office (historical)—building .... AL-4
*Estay Creek* .... IN-6
Estcourt—locale .... ME-1
Estcourt Station—locale .... ME-1
Estebania—locale .... PR-3
Esteban Park—park .... AZ-5
Esteban Windmill—locale .... TX-5
Este Cem—cemetery .... TX-5
Estees Brook—stream .... MA-1
*Estefanulga* .... FL-3
Estel Chapel—church .... OH-6
Estella—locale .... OK-5
**Estella**—pop pl .... PA-2
Estella Cem—cemetery .... WI-6
**Estella (Town of)**—pop pl .... WI-6
Estella Windmill—locale .... TX-5
Estell Creek—stream .... CA-9
Estelle—locale .... CA-9
Estelle—locale .... GA-3
Estelle—locale .... TX-5
**Estelle**—pop pl .... AL-4
**Estelle**—pop pl .... LA-4
**Estelle**—pop pl .... NC-3
Estelle, Lake—lake .... CA-9
Estelle, Lake—lake .... FL-3
Estelle, Lake—lake .... ID-8
Estelle, Mount—summit .... AK-9
Estelle Canal—canal .... LA-4
Estelle Ch—church .... AL-4
Estelle Ch—church .... OK-5
Estelle Creek—stream .... TX-5
*Estelle Manor* .... NJ-2
Estelle Mine—mine .... UT-8
Estelle Mtn—summit .... CA-9
Estelle Mtn—summit .... NY-2
Estelle Sch (historical)—school .... AL-4
Estelle Spring—spring .... GA-3
Estelle Tunnel—mine .... CA-9
Estell Falls—falls .... OR-9
*Estell Fork* .... AL-4
Estell Hollow—valley .... OH-6
**Estelline**—pop pl .... SD-7
**Estelline**—pop pl .... TX-5
Estelline (CCD)—cens area .... TX-5
Estelline Cem—cemetery .... TX-5
Estelline Spring—spring .... TX-5
**Estelline Township**—pop pl .... SD-7
Estelline Township (historical)—civil .... SD-7
**Estell Manor**—pop pl .... NJ-2
**Estell Manor (Risley)**—pop pl .... NJ-2
Estell Manor (Risley Station)—locale .... NJ-2
Estell Manor Sch—school .... NJ-2
*Estells Fork* .... AL-4
Estellville—locale .... NJ-2
*Estelville* .... NJ-2
Estelville—uninc pl .... NJ-2
*Estenaula Creek* .... TN-4
Esten Sch—school .... MA-1
Estep Branch—stream .... KY-4
Estep Branch—stream .... TN-4
Estep Cabin—locale .... ID-8
Estep Cem—cemetery (2) .... AR-4
Estep Cem—cemetery (2) .... MO-7
Estep Cem—cemetery (2) .... TN-4
Estep Cem—cemetery .... TX-5
Estep Cem—cemetery (2) .... VA-3
Estep Cem—cemetery (4) .... WV-2
Estep Creek—stream .... AR-4
Estep Creek—stream .... OR-9
Estep (historical)—locale .... AL-4
Estep Hollow—valley (2) .... TN-4
Estep Hollow—valley .... VA-3
Estep Physical Fitness Center—building .... TN-4
Estep Ridge—ridge .... WV-2
Esteps Branch—stream .... KY-4
Estep Sch—school .... WV-2
Estep (Site)—locale .... CA-9
Estep Tank—reservoir .... TX-5
Ester—CDP .... AK-9
**Ester**—pop pl .... AK-9
Ester Basin—basin .... AZ-5
**Esterbrook**—pop pl .... WY-8
Ester Brook—stream .... MN-6
Esterbrook Hill—summit .... WY-8
Ester Camp Hist Dist—hist pl .... AK-9
*Ester Church* .... TN-4
*Ester Creek* .... AR-4
Ester Creek—stream (2) .... AK-9
*Esterday* .... MN-6
Ester Dome—summit .... AK-9
Ester Dome Observatory—building .... AK-9
Esterdy—locale .... MN-6
Ester Hall (historical)—locale .... AL-4
Ester Hill—summit .... MI-6
Ester Island—island .... MN-6
Esterita Well—well .... TX-5
Esteritos Windmill—locale .... TX-5
Ester Lake—lake .... MN-6
Ester Lake—lake .... MT-8
Ester Lake—lake .... TX-5
Esterling and Burns Dam—dam .... AL-4
Esterlings Lake—reservoir .... AL-4
Esterly—uninc pl .... PA-2
Esterly Cem—cemetery .... SD-7
Esterly Lakes—lake .... OR-9
Esterly Mine—mine .... OR-9
Esterly Post Office—building .... PA-2
**Estero**—pop pl .... FL-3
Estero Americano—civil .... CA-9
*Estero Americano Creek* .... CA-9
Estero Bay—bay .... CA-9
Estero Bay—bay .... FL-3
Estero Bay Aquatic Preserve—park .... FL-3
Estero Country Day Sch—school .... FL-3
*Estero De Americano* .... CA-9
*Estero De San Antonio* .... CA-9
Estero Island—island .... FL-3
Estero Island (CCD)—cens area .... FL-3
Estero Lookout Tower—tower .... FL-3
*Estero Pass* .... FL-3
Estero Pass—channel .... FL-3
**Estero (P.O.)**—pop pl .... FL-3
*Estero River* .... CA-9
Estero River—stream .... FL-3
**Estero River Heights**—pop pl .... FL-3
Esteros, Los—swamp .... NM-5
*Esteros Bay* .... CA-9
Esteros Creek—stream .... NM-5
*Esteros Point* .... CA-9
**Estero (sta.)**—pop pl .... FL-3
Estero United Methodist Ch—church .... FL-3
Ester Pond—lake .... AZ-5
Ester Ridge—ridge .... IN-6
Ester Station—locale .... AK-9
*Esterwood* .... LA-4
Esterwood Ranch—locale .... TX-5
Estes—locale .... ID-8
Estes—locale .... MO-7
Estes—locale (2) .... TX-5
Estes—locale .... VA-3
Estes—locale .... WA-9
**Estes**—pop pl .... AR-4
**Estes**—pop pl .... MS-4
Estes, Lake—reservoir .... CO-8
**Estes Addition**—pop pl .... TX-5
Estes Arroyo—stream .... NM-5
Estes Bog—lake .... ME-1
Estes Branch—stream .... KY-4
Estes Branch—stream .... NC-3
Estes Branch—stream .... TN-4
*estes Brook* .... MA-1
**Estes Brook**—pop pl .... MN-6
Estes Brook—stream .... ME-1
Estes Brook—stream .... MN-6
Estes Brook Ch—church .... MN-6
Estesburg—locale .... KY-4
Estes Butte—summit .... WA-9
Estes Butte Lookout—locale .... WA-9
Estes Canyon—valley (2) .... AZ-5
Estes Canyon—valley .... NM-5
Estes Cem—cemetery .... GA-3
Estes Cem—cemetery .... IA-7
Estes Cem—cemetery .... KS-7
Estes Cem—cemetery (2) .... KY-4
Estes Cem—cemetery (3) .... MO-7
Estes Cem—cemetery .... NY-2
Estes Cem—cemetery (2) .... NC-3
Estes Cem—cemetery (6) .... TN-4
Estes Cem—cemetery .... TX-5
Estes Cem—cemetery .... VA-3
Estes Ch—church .... TN-4
*Estes Ch of Christ* .... TN-4
Estes City—locale .... NM-5
Estes Cone—summit .... CO-8
Estes Coulee—valley .... ND-7
Estes Cove—bay .... TX-5
Estes Creek—stream .... AL-4
Estes Creek—stream .... ID-8
Estes Creek—stream (2) .... OR-9
Estes Creek—stream .... SD-7
Estes Crossroads—locale .... AL-4
Estes Ditch—canal .... OR-9
Estes Drain—canal .... CA-9
Estes Draw—valley .... CO-8
Estes Draw—valley .... TX-5
Estes Flats—flat .... TX-5
Estes Gulch—valley .... CO-8
Estes Head—cliff .... ME-1
Estes Hill—locale .... ME-1
Estes Hills Sch—school .... NC-3
Estes (historical)—locale .... SD-7
**Estes (historical)**—pop pl .... OR-9
Estes Hollow—valley .... MO-7
Estes Hollow—valley .... PA-2
Estes Hollow—valley .... TN-4
Estes JHS—school .... NY-2
Estes Kefauver—uninc pl .... TN-4
Estes Kefauver Lake Dam—dam .... TN-4
*Estes Lake* .... CO-8
Estes Lake—lake .... MI-6
Estes Lake—lake .... MT-8
Estes Lake—reservoir .... ME-1
**Estes Lake (Trailer Park)**—pop pl .... ME-1
*Estes Mill* .... MS-4
**Estesmill**—pop pl .... MS-4
Estes Mill Creek—stream .... NC-3
Estes Mtn—summit .... ID-8
Estes Park—flat .... CO-8
**Estes Park**—pop pl .... CO-8
Estes Park Conference Camp—locale .... CO-8
Estes Park Filtration Plant—other .... CO-8
Estes Place—locale .... NM-5
Estes Pond—locale .... TN-4
Estes Ranch—locale .... AZ-5
Estes Ranch—locale .... NM-5
Estes Ranch—locale .... TX-5
Estes Resort—locale .... TN-4
Estes Sch—school .... KY-4
Estes Sch—school .... ND-7
Estes Sch—school .... OH-6
Estes Sch—school .... WI-6
Estes Sch (abandoned)—school .... MO-7
Estes Sch (historical)—school .... AL-4
Estes School (Abandoned)—locale .... IA-7
Estess Dam—dam .... AL-4
Estess Lake—reservoir .... AL-4
Estes Slough—stream .... OR-9
Estes Spring—spring .... ND-7
Estes Tank No 1—reservoir .... NM-5
Estes Well—well .... TX-5
Estes West Drain—canal .... CA-9
Estes Windmill—locale .... NM-5
*Estevan* .... AZ-5
Estevan Hall—hist pl .... AR-4
Esteven Park—park .... AZ-5
**Estey**—pop pl .... MI-6
*Estey Creek* .... IN-6
*Estey Glen* .... NY-2
Estey Hall—hist pl .... NC-3
Estey Hall—hist pl .... PA-2
Estey Hill—summit .... MA-1
Estey Mtn—summit .... ME-1
Estey Organ Company Factory—hist pl .... VT-1
**Esther**—pop pl .... LA-4
**Esther**—pop pl .... MO-7
Esther, Lake—lake .... CO-8
Esther, Mount—summit .... MA-1
Esther Bay—bay .... AK-9
Esther Branch—stream .... MO-7
Esther Brook—stream .... MA-1
Esther Ch—church .... AL-4
Esther Ch—church .... MN-6
Esther Ch—church .... PA-2
Esther Creek—stream .... OR-9
Estherdale (historical)—locale .... SD-7
Esther F Well—well .... AZ-5
**Esther (historical)**—pop pl .... PA-2
Esther Island—island (2) .... AK-9
Esther Island—island .... MA-1
Esther Island Light—other .... AK-9
Esther Lagoon—bay .... AK-9
Esther Lake—lake .... AK-9
Esther Lake—lake .... MN-6
Esther Lake—lake .... NE-7
Esther Landing Pad Airp—airport .... IN-6
Esther Mtn—summit .... NY-2
Esther Passage—channel .... AK-9
Esther Rock—island .... AK-9
Esther Run—stream .... PA-2
**Estherton**—pop pl .... PA-2
**Esther (Township of)**—pop pl .... MN-6
**Estherville**—pop pl .... IA-7
Estherville Beach—beach .... IA-7
Estherville JHS—school .... IA-7
Estherville Minim Creek Canal—canal .... SC-3
Estherville Plantation—locale .... SC-3
Estherville Township—fmr MCD .... IA-7
**Estherville Township**—pop pl .... ND-7
**Estherwood**—pop pl .... LA-4
Estherwood and Carriage House—hist pl .... NY-2
Estherwood Ferry—locale .... LA-4
Estic Canyon—valley .... CO-8
Estico—locale .... AR-4
Estiffanulga—locale .... FL-3
Estil Cem—cemetery .... IN-6
Estill—locale .... MO-7
**Estill**—pop pl .... KY-4
**Estill**—pop pl .... MS-4
**Estill**—pop pl .... SC-3
Estill, Wallace, Sr., House—hist pl .... WV-2
Estill Branch—stream .... AL-4
Estill (CCD)—cens area .... SC-3
**Estill (County)**—pop pl .... KY-4
*Estill Creek* .... TN-4
Estill Dudd Cave—cave .... AL-4
Estill-Fite House—hist pl .... TN-4
*Estill Fork* .... AL-4
Estillfork—locale .... AL-4
Estill Fork—stream .... AL-4
Estill Fork—stream .... TN-4
Estill Furnace Ruins—locale .... KY-4
Estill Post Office (historical)—building .... MS-4
*Estillsfork* .... AL-4
*Estills Fork* .... TN-4
**Estill Springs**—pop pl .... TN-4
Estill Springs Bridge—bridge .... TN-4
Estill Springs (CCD)—cens area .... TN-4
Estill Springs Cem—cemetery .... TN-4
Estill Springs City Hall—building .... TN-4
Estill Springs Division—civil .... TN-4
Estill Springs Park—park .... TN-4
Estill Springs Post Office—building .... TN-4
Estill Springs Sch—school .... TN-4
Estillville (Magisterial District)—fmr MCD .... VA-3
Estil Run—stream .... IN-6
Estis Mill Creek—stream .... AL-4
Estler Creek—stream .... MT-8
Estler Lake—reservoir .... MT-8
Estler Peak—summit .... AZ-5
Estling, Lake—reservoir .... NJ-2
**Estling Lake**—pop pl .... NJ-2
Estling Lake Dam—dam .... NJ-2
Esto—locale .... KY-4
Esto—locale .... LA-4
Esto—locale .... OH-6
**Esto**—pop pl .... FL-3
Estock Sch—school .... CA-9
*Estokish* .... MS-4
*Estokshish* .... MS-4
Estonian Cem—cemetery .... WI-6
Esto-Noma (CCD)—cens area .... FL-3
Estoos—locale .... OR-9
*Estopacha River* .... MS-4
*Estopinal* .... LA-4
Estopinal—other .... LA-4
**Estothel**—pop pl .... AL-4
Estouteville—hist pl .... VA-3
*Estport* .... AL-4
Est Post Office (historical)—building .... AL-4
Estracada House Well—well .... NM-5
Estracada Tank No 1—reservoir .... NM-5
Estracada Tank No 2—reservoir .... NM-5
Estracada Well—well .... NM-5
Estrada Cem—cemetery .... TX-5
Estrada Creek—locale .... TX-5
Estrada Creek—stream .... CA-9
Estrada de Aro Shop Ctr—locale .... AZ-5
Estrada Ranch—locale .... CA-9
**Estrado**—pop pl .... KY-4
**Estral Beach**—pop pl .... MI-6
Estray Creek—stream .... CA-9
Estrecho, Arroyo—stream .... CA-9
*Estrecho de La Florida* .... FL-3
Estrella—locale .... AZ-5
Estrella—locale .... CA-9
**Estrella**—pop pl .... CO-8
Estrella, Loma de la—summit .... TX-5
Estrella, Sierra—ridge .... AZ-5
Estrella Camp—locale .... AZ-5
*Estrella Creek* .... CA-9
Estrella Estates Family Park (trailer park)—locale .... AZ-5
**Estrella Estates Family Park (trailer park)**—pop pl .... AZ-5
Estrella JHS—school .... AZ-5
Estrella Mountain Regional Park—park .... AZ-5
*Estrella Mountains* .... AZ-5
Estrella River—stream .... CA-9
Estrella RR Station—building .... AZ-5
Estrella Sailport—airport .... AZ-5
Estrella Well (Windmill)—locale .... TX-5
Estrella Windmill—locale .... TX-5
Estrellita Ranch—locale .... AZ-5
Estritos Spring—spring .... NM-5
*Estros Bay* .... CA-9
*Estros Point* .... CA-9
**Estrup (historical)**—pop pl .... OR-9
Estudillo—uninc pl .... CA-9
Estudillo Canal—canal .... CA-9
Estudillo House—hist pl .... CA-9
Estudillo Park—park .... CA-9
Estufa—hist pl .... NM-5
Estufa Canyon—valley .... NM-5
Estufa Canyon—valley .... TX-5
Estufa Creek—stream .... NM-5
Estufa Ridge—ridge .... NM-5
Estufa Spring—spring .... TX-5
Estus Point—cape .... AK-9
Estus Post Office (historical)—building .... AL-4
Estworthy Ditch—canal .... OH-6
Esty—locale .... WV-2
Esty Glen—valley .... NY-2
Esty Point—cape .... NY-2
ES Volin Farmstead—hist pl .... SD-7
Eta Cave—cave .... AL-4
*Etach Creek* .... WA-9
*Etacrewac* .... NC-3
*Etagin* .... FM-9
*Etahoma Box* .... MS-4
*Etajce* .... FM-9
*Etajee* .... FM-9
Etal—island .... FM-9
Etal Atoll—island .... FM-9
Etam—locale .... WV-2
Etam Ch—church .... OH-6
E Tank—reservoir .... TX-5
*Etaosha Creek* .... MS-4
*Etawi River* .... GA-3
E. T. Barwick Plant and Warehouse—facility .... GA-3

Etbauer Dam—dam SD-7
E T Brown Pond Dam—dam MS-4
E T Canyon—valley NM-5
Etcharai Island MP-9
Etcharai-to MP-9
Etchardi Island MP-9
Etcharia—island MP-9
Etcharren Valley—valley CA-9
Etchart Canyon—valley NV-8
Etchart Cow Camp—locale MT-8
Etchart Springs—spring NV-8
Etchart Stone House—locale MT-8
Etchecopar Spring—spring CA-9
**Etchehoma (historical)**—pop pl MS-4
Etchepuk River—stream AK-9
Etcheron Valley CA-9
Etches Creek—stream AK-9
Etcheson Cem—cemetery IL-6
Etcheverria Well well NV 8
Etcheverry Ditch—canal ID-8
Etcheverry Ranch—locale NM-5
**Etchison**—pop pl MD-2
E T Conway Number 1 Dam—dam AL-4
ETD Bridge over Green River—hist pl WY-8
Etdot, Kannat I—stream MH-9
Etdot, Laderan I—cliff MH-9
Etdot, Sabanan—slope MH-9
Etegin FM-9
Etegin Insel FM-9
Etehoma MS-4
Etehoma Creek MS-4
Etehomo Creek—stream MS-4
Etekaek PW-9
Etekin FM-9
Etekkueiku Mountain PW-9
Etel FM-9
**Etelka (historical)**—pop pl OR-9
Etelka Sch—school OR-9
Etemuli Mtn—summit AS-9
Etemuli Stream—stream AS-9
**Etena**—pop pl AS-9
Eten Anchorage—harbor FM-9
Etengvo CA-9
Eten Island FM-9
Eternal Flat—flat UT-8
Eternal Glory Gardens Chapel—church GA-3
Eternal Hills Cem—cemetery OR-9
Eternal Hills Memorial Park (Cem)—cemetery CA-9
Eternal Light Mausoleums and Gardens—cemetery FL-3
Eternal Light Memorial Gardens—cemetery FL-3
Eternal Rest Cem—cemetery AR-4
Eternal Trinity Ch—church FL-3
Eternal Valley Memorial Park—cemetery AZ-5
Eternity Park (Cem)—cemetery TX-5
Etesich FM-9
Etet FM-9
Etet Island FM-9
Etha NE-7
Etha Ch—church AL-4
**Ethan**—pop pl SD-7
Ethanac (Romoland) CA-9
Ethanac Siding—locale CA-9
Ethan Allen Engine company No. 4—hist pl VT-1
Ethan Allen Park—park VT-1
Ethan Allen Sch—school CA-9
Ethan Allen Sch—school PA-2
Ethan Dam—dam SD-7
Ethania Falls—falls WA-9
Ethan Lake—reservoir SD-7
Ethan Mtn—summit NY-2
Ethan Pond—lake NH-1
Ethan Pond Trail—trail NH-1
Ethans Pond NH-1
Etha Post Office (historical)—building AL-4
Etheda Springs—locale CA-9
Ethel—locale FL-3
Ethel—locale OK-5
Ethel—locale VA-3
Ethel—locale (2) WA-9
**Ethel**—pop pl AL-4
**Ethel**—pop pl AR-4
**Ethel**—pop pl IN-6
**Ethel**—pop pl LA-4
**Ethel**—pop pl MS-4
**Ethel**—pop pl MO-7
**Ethel**—pop pl TX-5
**Ethel**—pop pl WV-2
Ethel, Lake—lake CA-9
Ethel, Lake—lake MN-6
Ethel, Lake—lake (2) WA-9
Ethel, Lake—lake WI-6
Ethel, Lake—lake WY-8
Ethel, Mount—summit (2) CO-8
Ethel, Mount—summit MA-1
**Ethel Acres**—pop pl CT-1
Ethel Apartment House—hist pl MA-1
Ethel Baptist Ch—church MS-4
Ethel (CCD)—cens area WA-9
Ethel Cem—cemetery TX-5
Ethel Creek—stream AK-9
Ethel Creek—stream (2) CO-8
Ethel Creek—stream (3) OR-9
Ethel Creek—stream WA-9
**Ethel Gardens Subdivision**—pop pl UT-8
Ethel Gulch—valley MT-8
**Ethel (historical)**—pop pl TN-4
Ethel Hollow—valley WV-2
Ethel HS—school MS-4
Ethel Intl Airp—airport WA-9
Ethel K Smith Library—building NC-3
Ethel Lake OR-9
Ethel Lake WI-6
Ethel Lake—lake CO-8
Ethel Lake—lake MN-6
Ethel Lake—lake WI-6
Ethel Lake—reservoir MO-7
Ethel Landing PA-2
Ethel Morrison Memorial Park—park AL-4
Ethel Mtn—summit OR-9
Ethel P. O. (historical)—locale AL-4
Ethel Pond—lake ME-1
Ethel Post Office (historical)—building TN-4
Ethel R Coop Sch—school TX-5
Ethel R Jones Elem Sch—school IN-6
Ethel Run—stream IN-6
Ethel Sch—school IL-6
Ethel Sch—school (2) KY-4
Ethels Creek—stream OR-9
Ethel Slope Mine (underground)—mine AL-4
Ethel Spring—spring WA-9
Ethel Springs Dam—dam PA-2
Ethel Springs Lake—reservoir PA-2
Ethel Springs Rsvr PA-2
**Ethelsville**—pop pl AL-4
Ethelsville Baptist Ch—church AL-4
Ethelsville (CCD)—cens area AL-4
Ethelsville Cem—cemetery AL-4
Ethelsville Church AL-4
**Ethelsville (corporate name for Ethelville)**—pop pl AL-4
Ethelsville Division—civil AL-4
Ethelsville United Methodist Ch—church AL-4
Ethelton—locale ID-8
Ethelville (corporate name Ethelsville) AL-4
Ethel Walker Sch school CT 1
Ethelwood—locale MI-6
**Ether**—pop pl NC-3
Ether Dome, Massachusetts General Hosp—hist pl MA-1
Etheredge Cem—cemetery GA-3
Etheredge Cem—cemetery SC-3
Etheredge House—hist pl FL-3
Etheredge Millpond—reservoir SC-3
Ether Hollow—valley UT-8
Etheridge Cem—cemetery TN-4
Etheridge Swamp—swamp NC-3
Etheridge Well—well NM-5
Etherington Pond—lake ME-1
Etherly Sch—school IL-6
Ether Peak—summit UT-8
Etherton—locale IL-6
Etherton Cem—cemetery IL-6
**Ethete**—pop pl WY-8
**Ethete Saint Michael Mission**—pop pl WY-8
Ethiopian Over Coming Church, The AL-4
Ethlen Wash—valley UT-8
**Ethlyn**—pop pl MO-7
Etholen—locale TX-5
Etholen Tank—reservoir TX-5
Ethol House—hist pl NY-2
Ethon Crossroads—locale SC-3
Ethridge—locale (2) GA-3
Ethridge—locale MT-8
**Ethridge**—pop pl KY-4
**Ethridge**—pop pl TN-4
Ethridge Baptist Ch—church TN-4
Ethridge Brake—swamp LA-4
Ethridge (CCD)—cens area TN-4
Ethridge Cem—cemetery IL-6
Ethridge Cem—cemetery NC-3
Ethridge Cem—cemetery TN-4
Ethridge Division—civil TN-4
Ethridge Elem Sch—school TN-4
Ethridge Gin Branch—stream AL-4
Ethridge Gulch—valley MT-8
Ethridge Hollow—valley TN-4
Ethridge Methodist Ch—church TN-4
Ethridge Point—cape NC-3
Ethridge Post Office—building TN-4
Ethridges Mill (historical)—locale AL-4
Ethyl Creek OR-9
Ethyl Draw—valley WY-8
Etichiech—summit PW-9
Eticuera Creek—stream CA-9
Eticura Creek CA-9
Eticurea Creek CA-9
Etiemar—locale FM-9
Etienne, Bayou—stream LA-4
Etienne Bay—bay AK-9
Etienne Head—cliff AK-9
Etienne Lake—lake AK-9
Etienne Pass—gap AK-9
Etier Cem—cemetery LA-4
Etiermar FM-9
Etigonik Mtn—summit AK-9
Etikamiut (Summer Camp)—locale AK-9
Etiruir—summit PW-9
Etivlik Lake—lake AK-9
Etivluk River—stream AK-9
**Etiwanda**—pop pl CA-9
Etiwanda (siding)—locale CA-9
**Etiwanda (sta.)**—pop pl CA-9
**Etlah**—pop pl MO-7
Etlah Knobs—other MO-7
Etlan—locale VA-3
Etna NJ-2
Etna ND-7
Etna—locale GA-3
Etna—locale KY-4
Etna—locale ME-1
Etna—locale MN-6
Etna—locale NE-7
Etna—locale NV-8
Etna—locale OH-6
Etna—locale OK-5
Etna—locale UT-8
Etna—locale WA-9
Etna—locale WI-6
**Etna**—pop pl AR-4
**Etna**—pop pl CA-9
**Etna**—pop pl IL-6
**Etna**—pop pl IN-6
**Etna**—pop pl MO-7
**Etna**—pop pl NH-1
**Etna**—pop pl NY-2
**Etna**—pop pl OH-6
**Etna**—pop pl PA-2
**Etna**—pop pl WY-8
Etna, Mount—summit AR-4
Etna, Mount—summit CA-9
Etna, Mount—summit MD-2
Etna, Mount—summit NV-8
Etna, Mount—summit NY-2
Etna Bog—swamp ME-1
Etna Borough—civil PA-2
Etna (CCD)—cens area CA-9
Etna Cem—cemetery ME-1
Etna Cem—cemetery MN-6
Etna Cem—cemetery MO-7
Etna Cem—cemetery OK-5
Etna Cem—cemetery OR-9
Etna Cem—cemetery WY-8
Etna Center—locale ME-1
Etna Ch—church OK-5
Etna Creek—stream CA-9
Etna Creek—stream MN-6
Etna Creek—stream UT-8
Etna Creek—stream WY-8
Etna Furnace NJ-2
Etna Furnace—hist pl PA-2
Etna Furnace—locale PA-2
**Etna Green**—pop pl IN-6
Etna Highlands—school NH-1
Etna (historical)—locale AL-4
**Etna (historical)**—pop pl OR-9
**Etna (historical)**—pop pl TN-4
Etna House—hist pl OH-6
Etna Lake—lake WI-6
Etna Mills CA-9
Etna Mills—locale VA-3
Etna Mine—mine CA-9
Etna Mine—mine UT-8
Etna Mission—church OH-6
Etna Mtn—summit CA-9
Etna Mtn summit CA 3
Etna Pond—lake ME-1
Etna (Post Office)—locale NC-3
**Etna (Post Office)**—pop pl NC-3
Etna Post Office (historical)—building TN-4
Etna Road Sch—school OH-6
Etna Rsvr—reservoir UT-8
Etna Spring—spring UT-8
Etna Summit—gap CA-9
**Etna (Town of)**—pop pl ME-1
Etna Township—fmr MCD IA-7
Etna Township Mounds I And II—hist pl OH-6
**Etna (Township of)**—pop pl IN-6
**Etna (Township of)**—pop pl OH-6
Etna-Troy Sch—school IN-6
**Etna-Troy (Township of)**—pop pl IN-6
E T Newell Pond Dam—dam MS-4
Etnire Sch—school IL-6
Etoi Ki—summit AZ-5
Etoile MP-9
Etoile—locale KY-4
**Etoile**—pop pl TX-5
Etoile Island—island MP-9
Etoile Lookout—locale TX-5
Etokek Slough—gut AK-9
Etokshish MS-4
**Etola**—pop pl TN-4
Eto Lake—reservoir CA-9
Etola Post Office (historical)—building TN-4
Etole Island MP-9
Etolin, Mount—summit AK-9
Etolin Island—island AK-9
Etolin Point—cape AK-9
Etolin Point Beacon—locale AK-9
Etolin Strait—channel AK-9
Etomba-igaby Creek AL-4
Eton—locale MO-7
**Eton**—pop pl GA-3
Eton Ave Sch—school CA-9
Eton Creek FL-3
Etonia Ch—church FL-3
Etonia Creek FL-3
Etonia Creek—stream FL-3
Etoniah Creek FL-3
Eton Park—park MI-6
Eton Sch—school MI-6
Eton Towers MO-7
**Etotulga (historical)**—pop pl FL-3
Etowah—locale WV-2
**Etowah**—pop pl AL-4
**Etowah**—pop pl AR-4
**Etowah**—pop pl NC-3
**Etowah**—pop pl OK-5
**Etowah**—pop pl TN-4
Etowah, Lake—lake FL-3
Etowah Ave Sch (historical)—school AL-4
Etowah (CCD)—cens area TN-4
Etowah Ch—church GA-3
Etowah Ch—church OK-5
Etowah City Hall—building TN-4
Etowah Conservation Dam—dam AL-4
Etowah Conservation Lake—reservoir AL-4
**Etowah County**—pop pl AL-4
Etowah County Courthouse—building AL-4
Etowah County HS—school AL-4
Etowah County Lake AL-4
Etowah County Vocational Sch—school AL-4
Etowah Cumberland Presbyterian Ch—church AL-4
Etowah Depot—hist pl TN-4
Etowah Division—civil TN-4
Etowah HS—school AL-4
Etowah Indian Mounds—locale GA-3
Etowah JHS—school TN-4
Etowah Male and Female Institute (historical)—school AL-4
Etowah Male and Female Seminary AL-4
Etowah Mounds—hist pl GA-3
Etowah MS AL-4
Etowah Post Office—building TN-4
Etowah River—stream GA-3
Etowah Shop Ctr—locale NC-3
Etowahton (historical)—locale AL-4
Etowahton P.O. AL-4
Etowah Valley Ch—church GA-3
Etowah Valley District—hist pl GA-3
Etowah Water Works—building TN-4
Etowah Yacht Club—other GA-3
Etowa River GA-3
**Etra**—pop pl NJ-2
Etra Lake—reservoir NJ-2
ETR Big Island Bridge—hist pl WY-8
Etress Fish Camp—locale AL-4
E.T. Rsvr—reservoir OR-9
Etsel Flat—flat CA-9
Etsel Ridge—ridge CA-9
Etsureppu MP-9
Etta CA-9
Etta—locale VA-3
**Etta**—pop pl MS-4
**Etta**—pop pl MO-7
**Etta**—pop pl OK-5
Etta, Lake—lake ND-7
Etta Bend Public Use Area—park OK-5
Etta Camp SD-7
Etta Ch—church OK-5
Etta Creek—stream AK-9
Ettadore Park CT-1
Etta Landing—locale AL-4
Ettal (Municipality)—civ div FM-9
Etta Mine (historical)—mine SD-7
E T Tank—reservoir NM-5
Etta Prairie—flat OR-9
Ettaton Sch—school TN-4
**Ettawa Springs**—pop pl CA-9
Etteca Sch—school AL-4
Ette Mokumok—island FM-9
Etten—island (2) FM-9
Etten Mokumok FM-9
Etten Mwekumwek FM-9
**Ettensan**—pop pl KS-7
Etten Sch—school FM-9
**Ettenson**—pop pl KS-7
**Etter**—pop pl MN-6
**Etter**—pop pl TN-4
**Etter**—pop pl TX-5
**Etter**—pop pl VA-3
Etter Baptist Ch—church TN-4
Etter Cave—cave TN-4
Etter Cem—cemetery IL-6
Etter Cem cemetery TN 4
Etter Creek—stream IA-7
Etter Ditch—canal IN-6
**Etter Junction**—pop pl TX-5
Etter Lake Cem—cemetery TX-5
Etters Bridge—hist pl PA-2
Ettersburg—locale CA-9
Etter Sch (historical)—school TN-4
Etters (corporate name Goldsboro) PA-2
**Etterville**—pop pl MO-7
Ettien Coulee—valley MT-8
Ettien Gulch—valley MT-8
Ettien Ridge—ridge MT-8
Ettien Spring—spring MT-8
Ettier Gulch MT-8
Ettinger Dam—dam OR-9
Ettinger Pond—lake OR-9
Ettinger Rsvr—reservoir OR-9
Etton—area GU-9
Ettrain Creek—stream AK-9
**Ettrick**—pop pl VA-3
**Ettrick**—pop pl WI-6
Ettrick Cem—cemetery VA-3
Ettrick Cem—cemetery WI-6
**Ettrick (Town of)**—pop pl WI-6
Etty—locale KY-4
Etun Enterence FM-9
Etun Entrance FM-9
E-Two Ditch—canal CA-9
Ety Enclosure—hist pl OH-6
Ety Habitation Site—hist pl OH-6
Etz Ahayem Congregation—church AL-4
Etz Chaim Sephardic Congregation—church IN-6
Etz Chayim Synagogue—church AL-4
Etzel, John L., House—hist pl IA-7
Etzkorn Dam—dam SD-7
Etzler Creek—stream CA-9
**Etzler Estates**—pop pl MD-2
**Euah Acres Subdivision**—pop pl UT-8
Euakor PW-9
Euans Cem—cemetery OH-6
EUB Acres—locale WV-2
**Eubank**—pop pl KY-4
Eubank, Achilles, House—hist pl KY-4
**Eubank Acres**—pop pl TX-5
Eubank Branch—stream TN-4
Eubank (CCD)—cens area KY-4
Eubank Cem—cemetery MO-7
Eubank Cem—cemetery TN-4
Eubank Corner—locale VA-3
Eubank Corral—other NM-5
Eubank Creek—stream CA-9
Eubank Creek—stream GA-3
Eubank Lake—reservoir GA-3
Eubank Oil Field—oilfield KS-7
Eubanks—locale NC-3
Eubanks—locale OK-5
Eubanks—locale VA-3
Eubanks Cem—cemetery KY-4
Eubanks Cem—cemetery (2) MS-4
Eubanks Cem—cemetery TN-4
Eubanks Ch—church OK-5
Eubank Sch—school KY-4
Eubank Sch—school NM-5
Eubanks Chapel Cem—cemetery TN-4
Eubank Sch (historical)—school AL-4
Eubanks Creek—stream MS-4
Eubanks Creek—stream TX-5
Eubanks Dam—dam TN-4
Eubanks-Dickerson Cem—cemetery MS-4
Eubanks Ford—locale KY-4
**Eubanks (historical)**—pop pl MS-4
Eubanks Lake—reservoir GA-3
Eubanks Lake—reservoir TN-4
Eubanks Lookout Tower—tower AL-4
Eubanks Mtn—summit AR-4
Eubanks Post Office (historical)—building MS-4
Eubanks-Tytus House—hist pl OH-6
Eubanks Windmill—locale NM-5
Eubanks Windmill—locale TX-5
Eubank Tank—reservoir AZ-5
Eubbiyae Island MP-9
Eub Cem—cemetery SD-7
Eubulus Ch—church WV-2
**Eubuna Gardens (subdivision)**—pop pl PA-2
Eucala Creek GA-3
Eucalyptus Canal—canal CA-9
Eucalyptus Five Drain—canal CA-9
Eucalyptus Grove—woods CA-9
**Eucalyptus Hills**—pop pl CA-9
Eucalyptus Island—island CA-9
Eucalyptus Lateral Eleven—canal CA-9
Eucalyptus Lateral Five—canal CA-9
Eucalyptus Lateral Four—canal CA-9
Eucalyptus Lateral Fourteen—canal CA-9
Eucalyptus Lateral Seventeen—canal CA-9
Eucalyptus Lateral Ten—mine CA-9
Eucalyptus Lateral Two—canal CA-9
Eucalyptus Lateral 10—canal CA-9
Eucalyptus Park—park (2) CA-9
Eucalyptus Sch—school (3) CA-9
Eucebia Branch TN-4
Eucebia Ch—church MO-7
Eucebia Creek TN-4
Eucha—locale OK-5
Eucha, Lake—reservoir OK-5
Eucha Cem—cemetery OK-5
Eucharist Cem—cemetery MD-2
Eucharistic Novitiate—church LA-4
Euchee—locale TN-4
Eucheeana FL-3
Eucheeanna—locale FL-3
Euchee Chapel—church TN-4
**Euchee Creek**—pop pl OK-5
Euchee Creek—stream (3) OK-5
Euchee Dock—locale TN-4
Euchee Dock Spring—spring TN-4
Euchee Old Fields (historical)—locale TN-4
Euchee Post Office (historical)—building TN-4
Euchee Sch (historical)—school (2) TN-4
Euchee Valley Ch—church FL-3
Euchella Branch—stream NC-3
Euchella Ch—church NC-3
Euchella Cove—valley NC-3
Euchre Bar—bar CA-9
Euchre Butte OR-9
Euchre Butte—summit OR-9
Euchre Creek—stream KS-7
Euchre Creek—stream (2) OR-9
Euchre Creek Pond lake OR 9
Euchre Falls—falls OR-9
Euchre Glade—flat CA-9
Euchre Mtn—summit AK-9
Euchre Mtn—summit OR-9
Euchuse Bay FL-3
Euchuze Bay FL-3
Euclautubba Baptist Church MS-4
Euclautubba Ch—church MS-4
Euclautubba Creek—stream MS-4
Euclid—locale AR-4
Euclid—locale IA-7
Euclid—locale WV-2
**Euclid**—pop pl CA-9
**Euclid**—pop pl MN-6
**Euclid**—pop pl NY-2
**Euclid**—pop pl OH-6
**Euclid**—pop pl PA-2
Euclid—uninc pl FL-3
Euclid—uninc pl VA-3
Euclid Acad (historical)—school MS-4
Euclid Ave Ch—church OH-6
Euclid Ave Presbyterian Church—hist pl OH-6
Euclid Ave Sch—hist pl NY-2
Euclid Ave Sch—school CA-9
Euclid Ave Sch—school FL-3
Euclid Ave Sch—school NY-2
Euclid Beach Park—flat OH-6
Euclid Cem—cemetery OH-6
**Euclid Center**—pop pl MI-6
Euclid Claussen Pond—reservoir GA-3
Euclid Court—hist pl CA-9
Euclid Creek—stream IA-7
Euclid Creek—stream OH-6
Euclid Creek Park—flat OH-6
Euclid Creek Reservation—park OH-6
**Euclid Estates**—pop pl AL-4
Euclid-Glenville Hosp—hospital OH-6
Euclid Gulch—valley (2) CO-8
Euclid Heights VA-3
**Euclid Heights**—pop pl AR-4
**Euclid (historical)**—pop pl OR-9
Euclid HS—school FL-3
Euclid JHS—school CO-8
Euclid Lake IL-6
Euclid Memorial Park Library—locale OH-6
Euclid Mine—mine CO-8
Euclid Park—flat OH-6
Euclid Park—locale PA-2
Euclid Park—park IL-6
Euclid Park—park WI-6
Euclid Park Sch—school OH-6
Euclid Place—uninc pl VA-3
Euclid Sch—school (2) CA-9
Euclid Sch—school FL-3
Euclid Sch—school IL-6
Euclid Sch—school NJ-2
Euclid Sch—school NY-2
Euclid Terrace—locale VA-3
**Euclid (Township of)**—pop pl MN-6
**Eucutta**—pop pl MS-4
Eucutta Creek—stream MS-4
Eucutta Methodist Ch—church MS-4
Eucutta Oil Field—oilfield MS-4
**Eudora**—pop pl AR-4
**Eudora**—pop pl GA-3
**Eudora**—pop pl KS-7
**Eudora**—pop pl MS-4
**Eudora**—pop pl MO-7
Eudora Baptist Ch—church MS-4
Eudora (CCD)—cens area GA-3
Eudora Cem—cemetery KS-7
Eudora Cem—cemetery MS-4
Eudora Cem—cemetery OK-5
Eudora Ch—church AR-4
Eudora Ch—church LA-4
Eudora Mtn—summit AK-9
Eudora Park—park VA-3
Eudora Plantation—hist pl GA-3
Eudora Post Office (historical)—building MS-4
Eudora Sch—school AR-4
Eudora Sch—school MO-7
Eudora Spring—spring MO-7
**Eudora Township**—pop pl KS-7
Eudowood—post sta MD-2
Eudowood Sanatorium—hospital MD-2
Eudy Cave—cave AL-4
Euell Cem—cemetery MO-7
Euer MP-9
Euers Valley CA-9
Euer Valley—valley CA-9
Eueu—spring FM-9
**Eufala (historical)**—pop pl FL-3
**Eufaula**—pop pl AL-4
**Eufaula**—pop pl OK-5
**Eufaula**—pop pl WA-9
Eufaula Baptist Church AL-4
Eufaula Business District—hist pl OK-5
Eufaula (CCD)—cens area AL-4
Eufaula (CCD)—cens area OK-5
Eufaula Cedar Creek Ch—church OK-5
Eufaula Country Club—other AL-4
Eufaula Creek AL-4
Eufaula Dam—dam OK-5
Eufaula District Acad (historical)—school AL-4
Eufaula Division—civil AL-4
Eufaula-hatchie Creek AL-4
Eufaula Heights—locale WA-9
Eufaula HS—school AL-4
Eufaula Methodist Church AL-4
Eufaula Natl Wildlife Ref—park AL-4
Eufaula Natl Wildlife Ref—park GA-3
Eufaula Post Office—building AL-4
Eufaula Presbyterian Church AL-4
Eufaula Rsvr OK-5
Eufaula Rsvr—reservoir OK-5
Eu-fau-lau-hatchie AL-4
Eufaulee Creek AL-4
Eufaulee Old Town AL-4
Eufoa NC-3
**Eufola**—pop pl NC-3
Eugene KS-7
Eugene—locale CA-9
Eugene—locale FL-3
Eugene—locale MI-6
**Eugene**—pop pl IN-6
**Eugene**—pop pl MO-7
**Eugene**—pop pl OR-9
Eugene, Bayou—stream LA-4
Eugene Bayou—gut AR-4
Eugene Bennett Pond Dam dam MS 4
Eugene Bible Sch—school OR-9
Eugene Blue Star Safety Rest Area—locale OR-9
Eugene Carlton Pond Dam—dam MS-4
Eugene Cem—cemetery IN-6
Eugene Country Club—other OR-9
Eugene Creek—stream OR-9
Eugene D Nims Lake MO-7
Eugene Field Elementary School KS-7
Eugene Field Elem Sch—school IN-6
Eugene Field Elem Sch—school (2) KS-7
Eugene Field Park—park IL-6
Eugene Field Sch—school CA-9
Eugene Field Sch—school (5) IL-6
Eugene Field Sch—school (8) MO-7
Eugene Field Sch—school (4) OK-5
Eugene Field Sch—school OR-9
Eugene Field Sch—school SD-7
Eugene Glacier—glacier OR-9
Eugene Gordy Tank—reservoir AZ-5
Eugene Gulch—valley AZ-5
Eugene Gulch—valley WA-9
Eugene (historical)—locale IA-7
Eugene (historical P.O.)—locale IA-7
Eugene Hosp—hospital OR-9
Eugene Hotel—hist pl OR-9
Eugene Island—island (2) LA-4
Eugene J Butler Seventh Grade Center—school FL-3
Eugene Junior Acad—school OR-9
Eugene Lake—lake MN-6
Eugene Lake—lake WI-6
Eugene Log Pond—reservoir OR-9
Eugene Miller Dam—dam SD-7
Eugene Mine—mine AZ-5
Eugene Mtns—range NV-8
Eugene O'Neil Natl Historic Site—park CA-9
Eugene Point—cape AL-4
Eugene Rankin Sch—school NC-3
Eugene Ridge—ridge AZ-5
Eugene R Majors Lake Dam—dam AL-4
Eugene Sch—school IL-6
Eugene Speedway—other OR-9
Eugene Spring—spring CA-9
Eugene-Springfield (CCD)—cens area OR-9
Eugene Station IN-6
Eugene Talmadge Memorial Bridge—bridge GA-3
**Eugene Township**—pop pl MO-7
**Eugene (Township of)**—pop pl IN-6
Eugene Ware Elem Sch—school KS-7
Eugene Water and Electric Board Canal—canal OR-9
Eugene Welder Dam—dam SD-7
Eugene Well—well CA-9
Eugene Yacht Club—other OR-9
Eugenia KS-7
**Eugenia**—pop pl PR-3
Eugenia, Point—cape AK-9
Eugenia Hosp—hospital PA-2
Eugenia Mine—mine CO-8
Eugenie, Lake—lake LA-4
Eugenie Lake LA-4
Eugenie Roy Mine (underground)—mine AL-4
Eugenie Stream—stream AZ-5
Eugenio Maria De Hostos Neighborhood Service Center—locale FL-3
Eugley Cem—cemetery ME-1
**Eugley Corner**—pop pl ME-1
Eugley Hill—summit ME-1
**Euharlee**—pop pl GA-3
Euharlee Ch—church GA-3
Euharlee Creek—stream GA-3
Euharlee Sch—school GA-3
Euharlee-Taylorsville (CCD)—cens area GA-3
Euharley GA-3
Euharley Creek GA-3
Euhaw Ch—church SC-3
Euhaw Creek—stream SC-3
Euidelchol—island PW-9
Eukelanaquaw Creek GA-3
Eukeway (historical)—locale KS-7
Eula KS-7
Eula—locale AR-4
**Eula**—pop pl KS-7
**Eula**—pop pl TX-5
Eula B Autrey Lake—reservoir AL-4
Eula B Autrey Lake Dam—dam AL-4
Eula Canyon—valley CA-9
Eula Canyon—valley NM-5
Eula Cem—cemetery TX-5
Eulachon Point—cape AK-9
Eulachon Slough—stream AK-9
Eula Dees Memorial Library—building MS-4
**Eulala**—pop pl SC-3
Eulalia FL-3
Eulalia, Lake—lake FL-3
Eulalia Cem—cemetery PA-2
**Eulalia (Township of)**—pop pl PA-2
**Eulalie (Bryce)**—pop pl TX-5
Eulalie (Site)—locale TX-5
Eulamo Drift Mine (underground)—mine AL-4
Eula Sch (historical)—school MS-4
**Eulaton**—pop pl AL-4
Eulaton Baptist Ch—church AL-4
Eulaton Elem Sch—school AL-4
Eulaton United Methodist Ch—church AL-4
Eulatubba Cem—cemetery MS-4
Eul Canyon—valley NM-5
Eulcid Church TN-4
Euler Branch—stream IN-6

Evans Cem—*cemetery* (3) GA-3
Evans Cem—*cemetery* IL-6
Evans Cem—*cemetery* (2) IN-6
Evans Cem—*cemetery* (3) IA-7
Evans Cem—*cemetery* KS-7
Evans Cem—*cemetery* (6) KY-4
Evans Cem—*cemetery* LA-4
Evans Cem—*cemetery* MI-6
Evans Cem—*cemetery* (3) MS-4
Evans Cem—*cemetery* (2) NH-1
Evans Cem—*cemetery* (2) NC-3
Evans Cem—*cemetery* (3) OH-6
Evans Cem—*cemetery* (3) PA-2
Evans Cem—*cemetery* (9) TN-4
Evans Cem—*cemetery* (2) TX-5
Evans Cem—*cemetery* (3) VA-3
Evans Cem—*cemetery* (4) WV-2
Evans Cem (historical)—*cemetery* MO-7
**Evans Center**—*pop pl* NY-2
Evans Center Sch—*school* IL-6
Evans Ch—*church* KY-4
Evans Ch—*church* LA-4
Evans Ch—*church* NC-3
Evans Ch—*church* SC-3
Evans Chambers Lake—*reservoir* OK-5
Evans Chapel—*church* (2) AL-4
Evans Chapel—*church* (2) GA-3
Evans Chapel—*church* KY-4
Evans Chapel—*church* NC-3
Evans Chapel—*church* (2) TN-4
Evans Chapel—*church* (3) TX-5
Evans Chapel Cem—*cemetery* AL-4
Evans Chapel Cem—*cemetery* TN-4
Evans Chapel (historical)—*church* MS-4
Evans Chapel (historical)—*church* TN-4
Evans Chapel Sch—*school* TN-4
*Evans Chapel United Methodist Church* AL-4
**Evans City**—*pop pl* AL-4
**Evans City**—*pop pl* PA-2
Evans City Borough—*civil* PA-2
Evans City Cem—*cemetery* PA-2
Evans City Elem Sch—*school* PA-2
Evans Coll—*school* NC-3
*Evans Corner* VA-3
Evans Corner—*locale* ME-1
Evans Corner—*locale* NJ-2
Evans Corner—*locale* NY-2
**Evans (County)**—*pop pl* GA-3
Evans County Courthouse—*hist pl* GA-3
Evans County Forestry Unit—*other* GA-3
Evans County HS—*school* GA-3
Evans County Park—*park* WI-6
Evans Cove—*bay* WA-9
*Evans Creek* CA-9
*Evans Creek* DE-2
*Evans Creek* IL-6
*Evans Creek* KY-4
*Evans Creek* WA-9
Evans Creek—*gut* (2) VA-3
Evans Creek—*stream* (2) AL-4
Evans Creek—*stream* (4) CA-9
Evans Creek—*stream* FL-3
Evans Creek—*stream* (5) ID-8
Evans Creek—*stream* IL-6
Evans Creek—*stream* IN-6
Evans Creek—*stream* KS-7
Evans Creek—*stream* LA-4
Evans Creek—*stream* (2) MI-6
Evans Creek—*stream* MN-6
Evans Creek—*stream* (2) MS-4
Evans Creek—*stream* MT-8
Evans Creek—*stream* (2) NV-8
Evans Creek—*stream* NY-2
Evans Creek—*stream* (2) NC-3
Evans Creek—*stream* OH-6
Evans Creek—*stream* (10) OR-9
Evans Creek—*stream* (2) TN-4
Evans Creek—*stream* (3) TX-5
Evans Creek—*stream* (2) VA-3
Evans Creek—*stream* (3) WA-9
Evans Creek—*stream* WV-2
Evans Creek—*stream* (3) WY-8
Evans Creek Campground—*locale* WY-8
Evans Creek Cem—*cemetery* LA-4
Evans Creek Ch—*church* LA-4
Evans Creek Ch—*church* OH-6
*Evans-Croom Cemetery* MS-4
**Evans Crossroad**—*pop pl* SC-3
Evansdale—*locale* NC-3
**Evansdale**—*pop pl* IA-7
**Evansdale**—*pop pl* WV-2
Evansdale Sch—*school* IA-7
**Evansdale (subdivision)**—*pop pl* FL-3
Evans Dam—*dam* AL-4
Evans Dam—*dam* OR-9
Evans Ditch—*canal* CA-9
Evans Ditch—*canal* OH-6
Evans Drain—*canal* (3) MI-6
Evans Draw—*valley* CO-8
Evans Draw—*valley* WY-8
Evans-Elbert Ranch—*hist pl* CO-8
Evans Elementary and JHS—*school* IN-6
Evans Elem Sch—*school* TN-4
**Evans (Evans Manor)**—*pop pl* PA-2
**Evans Falls**—*pop pl* PA-2
Evans Ferry Bridge—*bridge* TN-4
Evans Ferry (historical)—*crossing* TN-4
Evans Ferry (historical)—*locale* MS-4
Evans Field—*airport* PA-2
Evans Field—*flat* NV-8
Evans Field—*park* IL-6
Evans Flat—*flat* CA-9
Evans Flat—*flat* (2) NV-8
Evans Ford—*locale* KY-4
Evans Fork—*stream* (4) KY-4
Evans Fork—*stream* WV-2
Evans Gap—*gap* NC-3
Evans Glade—*flat* CA-9
Evans-Griffin—*locale* NM-5
Evans Grove—*woods* CA-9
Evans Gulch—*valley* (2) CO-8
Evans Gulch—*valley* MT-8
Evans Gulch—*valley* (2) OR-9
Evans Heliport—*airport* WA-9
Evans Hill—*summit* ME-1
Evans Hill—*summit* NH-1
Evans Hill—*summit* (2) PA-2
Evans Hill—*summit* WA-9
Evans Hill—*summit* WV-2
Evans Hill Ch—*church* TN-4
Evans Hollow—*valley* (3) AR-4
Evans Hollow—*valley* KY-4
Evans Hollow—*valley* (3) MO-7
Evans Hollow—*valley* OH-6
Evans Hollow—*valley* (2) PA-2
Evans Hollow—*valley* (2) TN-4
Evans Hollow—*valley* TX-5
Evans-Holton-Owens House—*hist pl* OH-6
Evans House—*hist pl* AZ-5
Evans House—*hist pl* KY-4
Evans House—*hist pl* OH-6
Evans House—*hist pl* VA-3
Evans HS—*school* FL-3
Evans HS—*school* TX-5
E Vansickel Dam—*dam* SD-7
Evans Industrial Bldg—*hist pl* TX-5
*Evans Island* TN-4
Evans Island—*area* MO-7
Evans Island—*island* AK-9
Evans Island—*island* MN-6
Evans Island—*island* NH-1
Evans Island—*island* (2) TN-4
Evans JHS—*school* DC-2
*Evans Junction* IA-7
Evans Knob—*summit* KY-4
Evans Knob—*summit* (2) NC-3
Evans Knob—*summit* OK-5
Evans Knob—*summit* TN-4
Evans Lake—*flat* NV-8
Evans Lake—*lake* (2) FL-3
Evans Lake—*lake* GA-3
Evans Lake—*lake* (6) MI-6
Evans Lake—*lake* (2) MN-6
Evans Lake—*lake* (2) MT-8
Evans Lake—*lake* NC-3
Evans Lake—*lake* TX-5
Evans Lake—*lake* (2) WA-9
Evans Lake—*lake* WI-6
**Evans Lake**—*pop pl* MI-6
Evans Lake—*reservoir* AL-4
Evans Lake—*reservoir* NC-3
Evans Lake—*reservoir* OH-6
Evans Lake—*reservoir* (3) TX-5
Evans Lake Dam—*dam* (2) MS-4
Evans Landing—*locale* GA-3
Evans Landing—*locale* ID-8
**Evans Landing**—*pop pl* IN-6
Evans Landing (historical)—*locale* AL-4
Evans Landing (historical)—*locale* TN-4
Evans Lateral—*canal* ID-8
Evans Lateral—*canal* SD-7
Evans Ledge—*summit* ME-1
Evans Lick Spring—*spring* ID-8
Evans Lodge—*locale* SC-3
Evans Lookout Tower—*locale* LA-4
Evans Lower Bar—*bar* AL-4
**Evans Manor**—*pop pl* PA-2
Evans McCrary Bridge—*bridge* FL-3
Evans Memorial Chapel—*hist pl* CO-8
Evans Memorial Library—*building* MS-4
Evans Memorial Park—*cemetery* IN-6
Evans Metropolitan AME Zion
Church—*hist pl* NC-3
Evans Mill—*locale* SC-3
Evans Mill Bridge—*other* IL-6
Evans Mill (historical)—*locale* MS-4
Evans Mill (historical)—*locale* (2) TN-4
**Evans Mills**—*pop pl* NY-2
Evans Mine—*mine* CO-8
Evans Mine—*mine* MO-7
Evans Mine—*mine* UT-8
Evans Mound (42IN40)—*hist pl* UT-8
Evans Mountain—*ridge* OR-9
Evans Mtn—*summit* AL-4
Evans Mtn—*summit* AZ-5
Evans Mtn—*summit* AR-4
Evans Mtn—*summit* MO-7
Evans Mtn—*summit* NH-1
Evans Mtn—*summit* (2) NC-3
Evans Mtn—*summit* SC-3
Evans Mtn—*summit* TN-4
Evans Notch—*gap* ME-1
Evans Notch Overlook—*locale* ME-1
Evans Number 1 Dam—*dam* SD-7
Evans Number 1 Sch—*school* NY-2
Evans Number 12 Sch—*school* NY-2
Evans Number 2 Dam—*dam* SD-7
Evans Old River—*lake* TX-5
Evans Park—*park* CA-9
Evans Park—*park* FL-3
Evans Park—*park* NV-8
Evans Park—*park* TX-5
Evans Park Sch—*school* NY-2
**Evans Park (subdivision)**—*pop pl* NC-3
**Evans Park (trailer park)**—*pop pl* DE-2
Evans Peak—*summit* (2) CA-9
Evans Peak—*summit* MT-8
**Evans Pines (subdivision)**—*pop pl* FL-3
Evans Place—*locale* CA-9
Evans Point—*cape* AK-9
Evans Point—*cape* TN-4
Evans Point—*cliff* AZ-5
Evans Point—*summit* CA-9
Evans Pond—*lake* CT-1
Evans Pond—*lake* FL-3
Evans Pond—*lake* ME-1
Evans Pond—*lake* MO-7
Evans Pond—*lake* WA-9
Evans Pond—*reservoir* AZ-5
Evans Pond—*reservoir* NJ-2
Evans Pond—*reservoir* NY-2
Evans Pond—*reservoir* NC-3
Evans Pond—*swamp* NY-2
Evans Pond Dam—*dam* NJ-2
Evans Pond Dam—*dam* NC-3
**Evansport**—*pop pl* (2) OH-6
Evansport Cem—*cemetery* OH-6
Evans Post Office (historical)—*building* MS-4
Evans Post Office (historical)—*building*
(2) TN-4
Evans Prairie—*lake* FL-3
Evans Prairie Cem—*cemetery* TX-5
Evan Spring—*spring* NV-8
Evans Quarry—*mine* (2) TN-4
Evans Ranch—*locale* NV-8
Evans Ranch—*locale* (4) NM-5
Evans Ranch—*locale* (2) WY-8
Evans Ranch HQ—*locale* CO-8
Evans Recreation Center—*building* TX-5
Evan S Recreation Pond Dam—*dam* MS-4
Evans Ridge—*ridge* AL-4
Evans Ridge—*ridge* CA-9
Evans Ridge—*ridge* NC-3
Evans Ridge—*ridge* UT-8
Evans Rock Slope Mine
(underground)—*mine* AL-4
Evans Rsvr—*reservoir* CO-8
Evans Rsvr—*reservoir* MT-8
Evans Rsvr—*reservoir* OR-9
Evans Rsvr—*reservoir* UT-8
Evans Run—*stream* (2) OH-6
Evans Run—*stream* (2) WV-2
*Evans Sch* IN-6
Evans Sch—*hist pl* CO-8
Evans Sch—*school* (2) AL-4
Evans Sch—*school* AZ-5
Evans Sch—*school* AR-4
Evans Sch—*school* CA-9
Evans Sch—*school* CO-8
Evans Sch—*school* FL-3
Evans Sch—*school* GA-3
Evans Sch—*school* IN-6
Evans Sch—*school* IA-7
Evans Sch—*school* (3) MI-6
Evans Sch—*school* MO-7
Evans Sch—*school* NE-7
Evans Sch—*school* NJ-2
Evans Sch—*school* NY-2
Evans Sch—*school* OK-5
Evans Sch—*school* PA-2
Evans Sch—*school* SD-7
Evans Sch—*school* TX-5
Evans Sch—*school* WI-6
Evans Sch (historical)—*school* MS-4
Evans Sch (historical)—*school* SD-7
*Evans Sch Number 11* IN-6
Evans Shoals—*bar* TN-4
Evans Signal Laboratory—*military* NJ-2
Evans Site—*hist pl* ND-7
Evans Slough—*gut* FL-3
Evans Slough—*stream* OR-9
Evans Spring—*spring* AZ-5
Evans Spring—*spring* CO-8
Evans Spring—*spring* MO-7
Evans Spring—*spring* TX-5
Evans Spring Branch—*stream* AL-4
*Evans Spring Church* AL-4
**Evans (sta.)**—*pop pl* IL-6
Evans Stadium—*other* OH-6
*Evans Station* KS-7
Evans Store (historical)—*locale* AL-4
Evans Store (historical)—*locale* MS-4
**Evans Subdivision**—*pop pl* FL-3
Evans Tabernacle—*church* MS-4
*Evans Tank* AZ-5
Evans Tank—*reservoir* (2) AZ-5
Evans Tank—*reservoir* NM-5
Evans Tank—*reservoir* TX-5
Evans-Tibbs House—*hist pl* DC-2
*Evanston* FL-3
*Evanston* OH-6
Evanston—*locale* KY-4
**Evanston**—*pop pl* CO-8
**Evanston**—*pop pl* IL-6
**Evanston**—*pop pl* IN-6
**Evanston**—*pop pl* IA-7
**Evanston**—*pop pl* MS-4
**Evanston**—*pop pl* (2) OH-6
**Evanston**—*pop pl* PA-2
**Evanston**—*pop pl* TN-4
**Evanston**—*pop pl* WY-8
Evanston Golf Club—*other* IL-6
**Evanston (historical)**—*pop pl* TN-4
Evanston Hosp—*hospital* IL-6
Evanston HS—*school* IL-6
Evanston Inn—*hist pl* CA-9
Evanston Lakeshore Hist Dist—*hist pl* IL-6
Evanston Post Office
(historical)—*building* MS-4
Evanston Post Office
(historical)—*building* TN-4
Evanston Pumping Station—*locale* WY-8
Evanston Ridge Hist Dist—*hist pl* IL-6
Evanston Towers—*hist pl* IL-6
**Evanston (Township of)**—*pop pl* IL-6
*Evanstor* IA-7
**Evanstown**—*pop pl* PA-2
Evanstown (historical)—*locale* AL-4
**Evans (Town of)**—*pop pl* NY-2
**Evans (Township of)**—*pop pl* IL-6
Evans Trail—*trail* OR-9
**Evans Trailer Park**—*pop pl* NC-3
Evans Upper Bar—*bar* AL-4
Evans Valley—*valley* OR-9
Evans Valley—*valley* TN-4
Evans Valley Sch—*school* (2) OR-9
Evansview Ch of Christ—*church* MO-7
*Evansville* AL-4
*Evansville* OH-6
*Evansville* TN-4
Evansville—*locale* CO-8
Evansville—*locale* GA-3
Evansville—*locale* (2) PA-2
**Evansville**—*pop pl* AL-4
**Evansville**—*pop pl* AK-9
**Evansville**—*pop pl* AR-4
**Evansville**—*pop pl* IL-6
**Evansville**—*pop pl* IN-6
**Evansville**—*pop pl* MN-6
**Evansville**—*pop pl* (2) MS-4
**Evansville**—*pop pl* (2) MO-7
**Evansville**—*pop pl* OH-6
**Evansville**—*pop pl* TN-4
**Evansville**—*pop pl* VT-1
**Evansville**—*pop pl* WA-9
**Evansville**—*pop pl* WV-2
**Evansville**—*pop pl* WI-6
**Evansville**—*pop pl* WY-8
Evansville ANV784—*reserve* AK-9
*Evansville Baptist Church* MS-4
Evansville Brewing Company—*hist pl* IN-6
Evansville Cem—*cemetery* OK-5
Evansville Ch—*church* MS-4
Evansville Ch—*church* WV-2
Evansville College—*hist pl* IN-6
Evansville Country Club—*other* IN-6
Evansville Creek—*stream* AR-4
Evansville Creek—*stream* OK-5
Evansville Dress Regional Airp—*airport* IN-6
Evansville (Election Precinct)—*fmr MCD* IL-6
Evansville Hist Dist—*hist pl* WI-6
Evansville (historical)—*locale* (2) KS-7
Evansville Journal News—*hist pl* IN-6
Evansville Mounds (22TU502)—*hist pl* MS-4
Evansville Municipal Market—*hist pl* IN-6
Evansville Post Office—*hist pl* IN-6
Evansville Post Office Site
(historical)—*locale* NC-3
Evansville State Hosp—*hospital* IN-6
Evansville Station (historical)—*locale* PA-2
**Evansville (Township of)**—*pop pl* MN-6
*Evansville University* IN-6
Evans Well—*well* AZ-5
Evans Well—*well* CO-8
Evans Well—*well* OR-9
Evans Wharf—*locale* VA-3
Evans Windmill—*locale* TX-5
**Evant**—*pop pl* TX-5
Evan Tank—*reservoir* TX-5
Evant (CCD)—*cens area* TX-5
**Evan Township**—*pop pl* KS-7
Evant Pumping Station—*other* TX-5
Eva Park—*park* TN-4
Eva Peak—*summit* AK-9
Eva Point—*cape* VI-3
Eva Post Office—*building* AL-4
Eva Post Office—*building* TN-4
Evaro—*locale* MT-8
Eva Road Lake—*reservoir* AL-4
Eva Road Lake Dam—*dam* AL-4
**Evart**—*pop pl* MI-6
Evart Cem—*cemetery* TX-5
*Evarts* KY-4
Evarts—*locale* IL-6
**Evarts**—*pop pl* KY-4
Evarts, Lake (historical)—*lake* SD-7
Evarts Cem—*cemetery* VT-1
Evarts Cem (historical)—*cemetery* SD-7
Evarts Creek—*stream* OR-9
Evarts (historical)—*locale* SD-7
**Evarts (historical)**—*pop pl* OR-9
Evarts Island—*island* NE-7
Evarts-McWilliams House—*hist pl* VT-1
*Evarts Mountain* WY-8
Evarts (RR name for North
Hartland)—*other* VT-1
**Evart (Township of)**—*pop pl* MI-6
*Evas Chapel Baptist Church* TN-4
Eva Sch (historical)—*school* TN-4
Evas Kill—*stream* NY-2
**Eva Subdivision**—*pop pl* TN-4
Eva Turnley Hollow—*valley* AR-4
E Vat Windmill—*locale* TX-5
Eva United Methodist Ch—*church* AL-4
Eva Woodframe Grain Elevator—*hist pl* OK-5
E V Cain Sch—*school* CA-9
Eve—*locale* KY-4
**Eve**—*pop pl* MO-7
Eve, Lake—*lake* (2) FL-3
Eve, Mount—*summit* CO-8
Eve, Mount—*summit* NY-2
Eve Branch—*stream* TX-5
Eve Gulch—*valley* ID-8
*Eve Island* PA-2
Eve Lake—*lake* CA-9
Eve Lake—*lake* IN-6
Eve Lake—*lake* MN-6
Eveland—*locale* IA-7
Eveland Bridge—*bridge* IA-7
Eveland Chapel—*church* AR-4
Eveland Grove (historical P.O.)—*locale* IA-7
Eveleigh—*locale* KY-4
Eveleigh Ch—*church* KY-4
Eveleigh Farms Airp—*airport* KS-7
Evelen Branch—*stream* IL-6
Evelen Charco Tank—*reservoir* AZ-5
**Eveleth**—*pop pl* MN-6
Eveleth Farm—*hist pl* NH-1
Eveleth Golf Course—*other* MN-6
Eveleth Hill—*summit* MA-1
Eveleth Manual Training Center—*hist pl* MN-6
Eveleth Nursery—*other* MN-6
Eveleth Recreation Bldg—*hist pl* MN-6
Eveleth Sch—*school* MA-1
Eveleth Sch—*school* MI-6
Eveleth Scout Camp—*locale* MN-6
Evelina Furnace (historical)—*locale* TN-4
*Eveline Mill Creek* AL-4
**Eveline (Township of)**—*pop pl* MI-6
Evelin Hill Creek—*stream* NY-2
Evelukpalik River—*stream* AK-9
Evelyn—*locale* CA-9
Evelyn—*locale* GA-3
Evelyn—*locale* KY-4
Evelyn—*locale* MI-6
Evelyn—*locale* TX-5
**Evelyn**—*pop pl* KY-4
**Evelyn**—*pop pl* LA-4
**Evelyn**—*pop pl* WV-2
Evelyn, Lake—*lake* CO-8
Evelyn, Lake—*lake* (2) WI-6
Evelyn, Mount—*summit* CO-8
Evelyn Ch—*church* GA-3
Evelyn Creek—*stream* CO-8
Evelyn Creek—*stream* WI-6
Evelyn Hamblen Elem Sch—*school* FL-3
*Evelyn Lake* WA-9
Evelyn Lake—*lake* (3) CA-9
Evelyn Lake—*lake* MN-6
Evelyn Lake—*lake* WI-6
Evelyn Mine—*mine* UT-8
Evelyn Site—*hist pl* IL-6
*Eve Mill* TN-4
Eve Mills—*locale* TN-4
Eve Mills Post Office
(historical)—*building* TN-4
**Evendale**—*pop pl* OH-6
**Evendale**—*pop pl* PA-2
Evendale Sch—*school* OH-6
Evendale (Township of)—*other* OH-6
Evening Branch—*stream* PA-2
Evening Chapel—*church* TX-5
Evening Creek—*stream* OR-9
Evening Ditch—*canal* ID-8
Evening Light Ch—*church* NC-3
Evening Light Ch—*church* SC-3
Evening Light Chapel—*church* NC-3
Evening Light Ch of God—*church* KS-7
Evening Lights Ch of God—*church* AL-4
Evening Primrose Spring—*spring* WY-8
**Evening Shade**—*pop pl* AR-4
**Evening Shade**—*pop pl* MO-7
*Evening Shade Baptist Ch* AL-4
Evening Shade Branch—*stream* MO-7
Evening Shade Cem—*cemetery* AR-4
Evening Shade Ch—*church* AL-4
Evening Shade Ch—*church* (2) AR-4
Evening Shade Ch—*church* (3) MO-7
Evening Shade Ch (historical)—*church* AL-4
*Evening Shade Sch* MO-7
Evening Shade Sch—*school* (2) AR-4
Evening Shade Sch—*school* MO-7
Evening Shade Sch (abandoned)—*school*
(2) MO-7
Evening Shade Sch (historical—*school* AL-4
Evening Shade (Township of)—*fmr MCD* AR-4
Evening Spring Ch—*church* AL-4
**Evening Star**—*pop pl* AR-4
Evening Star Cem—*cemetery* LA-4
Evening Star Cem—*cemetery* MS-4
*Evening Star Ch* AL-4
Evening Star Ch—*church* (4) AL-4
Evening Star Ch—*church* (2) AR-4
Evening Star Ch—*church* (2) LA-4
Evening Star Ch—*church* (4) MS-4
Evening Star Ch (historical)—*church* AL-4
Evening Star Ch (historical)—*church* MS-4
Evening Star Creek—*stream* AK-9
Evening Star Mine—*mine* (2) AZ-5
Evening Star Mine—*mine* (2) CA-9
Evening Star Mine—*mine* CO-8
Evening Star Mine—*mine* (2) NV-8
Evening Star Mine—*mine* WY-8
Evening Star Number 2 Ch—*church* LA-4
Evening Star Sch—*school* LA-4
Evening Star Sch—*school* MO-7
Evening Star Sch (historical)—*school* AL-4
Evening Star Sch (historical)—*school* TN-4
Evening Tech HS (historical)—*school* FL-3
Evening Time Ch—*church* AR-4
Evenmoe Lake—*lake* MN-6
*Evens* GA-3
Evens, Lake—*reservoir* NC-3
Evens Cem—*cemetery* TN-4
Evens Grove Ch—*church* NC-3
*Evens Lake* WA-9
Evens Lake—*lake* NY-2
Evens-McMullan House—*hist pl* AL-4
*Evens Mine* TN-4
Evens No. 2 Ditch—*canal* CO-8
Evenson Dam—*dam* SD-7
Evenson Irrigation Dam—*dam* SD-7
Evenson Lake—*lake* MN-6
Evenson North Irrigation Dam—*dam* SD-7
Evenson Sch—*school* MN-6
Evens Sch—*school* IN-6
Evens Town Ditch—*canal* CO-8
**Evensville**—*pop pl* TN-4
Evensville Elem Sch—*school* TN-4
Evensville Mine (underground)—*mine* TN-4
Evensville Peak—*summit* TX-5
Evensville Post Office—*building* TN-4
Evenswood Cem—*cemetery* WI-6
Eventide Cem—*cemetery* MO-7
Eventide Cem—*cemetery* SD-7
Eventide Cem—*cemetery* WV-2
*Eventide-Woonsocket Cemetery* SD-7
Evenwood—*locale* WV-2
Eve Point—*cape* AK-9
Ever—*locale* KY-4
*Everage Creek* TX-5
Everal, John W., Farm Buildings—*hist pl* OH-6
Everal Chapel—*church* OH-6
Everback Lake—*reservoir* KY-4
Everbreeze Island—*island* WI-6
**Everbreeze Plateau**—*pop pl* PA-2
Everdale Ch—*church* AL-4
Everdale Missionary Baptist Ch—*church* AL-4
**Everdell**—*pop pl* MN-6
Everest—*locale* ND-7
**Everest**—*pop pl* KS-7
Everest, D. C., House—*hist pl* WI-6
Everest Memorial Park
(Cemetery)—*cemetery* WA-9
Everest MS—*school* KS-7
Everest Sch—*school* WI-6
**Everest Township**—*pop pl* ND-7
Everets—*locale* VA-3
*Everett* GA-3
*Everett* KS-7
*Everett* VA-3
Everett—*locale* CO-8
Everett—*locale* GA-3
Everett—*locale* MS-4
Everett—*locale* TX-5
Everett—*locale* WV-2
**Everett**—*pop pl* GA-3
**Everett**—*pop pl* IL-6
**Everett**—*pop pl* (2) KY-4
**Everett**—*pop pl* MA-1
**Everett**—*pop pl* MO-7
**Everett**—*pop pl* NJ-2
**Everett**—*pop pl* OH-6
**Everett**—*pop pl* PA-2
**Everett**—*pop pl* WA-9
Everett, City of—*civil* MA-1
Everett, Lake—*lake* IN-6
Everett, Mount—*summit* MA-1
Everett Bay—*bay* NC-3
Everett Bldg—*hist pl* AL-4
Everett Bldg—*hist pl* TX-5
Everett Borough—*civil* PA-2
Everett Branch—*stream* (2) MS-4
Everett Branch—*stream* MO-7
Everett Branch—*stream* (2) TX-5
Everett Brook—*stream* ME-1
Everett Camp Lake—*lake* FL-3
*Everett Camp Pond* FL-3
Everett Canyon—*valley* TX-5
Everett Carnegie Library—*hist pl* WA-9
Everett (CCD)—*cens area* GA-3
Everett (CCD)—*cens area* WA-9
Everett Cem—*cemetery* AR-4
Everett Cem—*cemetery* FL-3
Everett Cem—*cemetery* KS-7
Everett Cem—*cemetery* KY-4
Everett Cem—*cemetery* (5) MS-4
Everett Cem—*cemetery* PA-2
Everett Ch—*church* MS-4
Everett Ch—*church* NC-3
Everett Ch—*church* TX-5
Everett Chapel—*church* NC-3
Everett Chapel—*church* TN-4
Everett Chapel Cem—*cemetery* TN-4
*Everett City* GA-3
Everett City Hall—*building* MA-1
Everett Cove—*cove* MA-1
Everett Cow Camp—*locale* CO-8
Everett Creek—*stream* AK-9
Everett Creek—*stream* MT-8
Everett Creek—*stream* (2) NC-3
Everett Creek—*stream* OR-9
Everett Creek—*stream* TX-5
Everett Creek—*stream* (3) WA-9
Everett Dam—*dam* NH-1
Everette Branch—*stream* LA-4
Everette-Gottig-Bilbo House—*hist pl* MS-4
Everett Flat—*flat* CA-9
Everett Football Field—*park* TN-4
Everett Ford—*locale* AL-4
Everett Golf And Country Club—*other* WA-9
**Everett Heights (subdivision)**—*pop pl* TN-4
*Everett High School* TN-4
Everett Hill—*summit* (3) MA-1
Everett Hills Baptist Ch—*church* TN-4
Everett Hollow—*valley* UT-8
Everett HS—*school* MA-1
Everett HS—*school* MI-6
Everett Island—*island* FL-3
Everett JHS—*school* NE-7
Everett JHS—*school* OH-6
Everett Junction—*uninc pl* MA-1
Everett Junior Coll—*school* WA-9
Everett Knoll Complex—*hist pl* OH-6
Everett Lake—*lake* CA-9
Everett Lake—*lake* (2) MN-6
Everett Lake—*lake* TN-4
Everett Lake—*lake* WA-9
Everett Lake—*lake* WI-6
Everett Lake—*reservoir* NC-3
Everett Lake Dam—*dam* NC-3
Everett Lookout Tower—*locale* NC-3
Everett Memorial Stadium—*locale* MA-1
*Everett Mill Pond* SC-3
Everett Mines—*mine* NV-8
Everett Mtn—*summit* GA-3
Everett Mtn—*summit* NC-3
Everett Park—*park* TN-4
Everett Peak—*summit* AK-9
Everett Peak—*summit* WA-9
Everett Pond—*lake* ME-1
Everett Ranch—*locale* (2) TX-5
Everett Reef—*bar* TX-5
Everett Ridge—*ridge* AR-4
Everett (RR name for Everetts)—*other* NC-3
**Everetts**—*pop pl* NC-3
Everetts Bay—*bay* MN-6
Everetts Branch—*stream* TN-4
Everett Sch—*school* (2) CA-9
Everett Sch—*school* (2) IL-6
Everett Sch—*school* IA-7
Everett Sch—*school* (3) MI-6
Everett Sch—*school* (2) MO-7
Everett Sch—*school* PA-2
Everett Sch—*school* SC-3
Everett Sch—*school* (2) TN-4
Everett Sch (abandoned)—*school* MO-7
Everett Sch (historical)—*school* MS-4
Everetts Corner—*locale* DE-2
**Everetts Crossroads**—*pop pl* NC-3
Everetts Lake—*reservoir* NC-3
Everett Slough—*gut* FL-3
Everetts Mill—*locale* NC-3
Everett-Southern HS—*school* PA-2
*Everett Special Education Center* TN-4
Everetts Point—*cape* MN-6
**Everett Springs**—*pop pl* GA-3
Everett Springs—*spring* GA-3
Everett Square—*locale* MA-1
**Everetts (RR name Everett)**—*pop pl* NC-3
Everetts Sch—*school* NC-3
Everetts Spring—*spring* AL-4
Everett-Stewart Airp—*airport* TN-4
Everett Swan Lake—*dam* MS-4
Everett Tank—*reservoir* AZ-5
Everett Township—*civil* KS-7
Everett Township—*civil* MO-7
**Everett Township**—*pop pl* (2) NE-7
**Everett (Township of)**—*pop pl* MI-6
**Everettville**—*pop pl* WV-2
Everett Windmill—*well* AZ-5
Everglade—*locale* AL-4
**Everglade**—*pop pl* CA-9
*Everglades* FL-3
Everglades—*other* FL-3
**Everglades**—*pop pl* FL-3
Everglades (CCD)—*cens area* (2) FL-3
Everglades Cem—*cemetery* NM-5
Everglades Channel—*channel* FL-3
**Everglades City**—*pop pl* FL-3
Everglades Experiment Station—*locale* FL-3
Everglades Island—*island* FL-3
Everglades JHS—*school* FL-3
Everglades Memorial Hosp—*hospital* FL-3
Everglades Natl Park—*park* FL-3
Everglades Sch—*school* (3) FL-3
Everglade State Wildlife Mngmt
Area—*park* MN-6
Everglades WMA Conservation Area Number
2A—*park* FL-3
Everglades WMA Conservation Area Number
2B—*park* FL-3
Everglades WMA Conservation Area Number
3—*park* FL-3
Everglades WMA Conservation Area Number
3A—*park* FL-3
Everglades WMA Conservation Area Number
3B—*park* FL-3
**Everglade (Township of)**—*pop pl* MN-6
*Evergreen* ME-1
Evergreen—*hist pl* MD-2
Evergreen—*hist pl* VA-3
Evergreen—*locale* AL-4
Evergreen—*locale* FL-3
Evergreen—*locale* ID-8
Evergreen—*locale* KY-4
Evergreen—*locale* MN-6
Evergreen—*locale* TN-4
Evergreen—*locale* TX-5
**Evergreen**—*pop pl* AL-4

**Evergreen**—*pop pl* CA-9
**Evergreen**—*pop pl* CO-8
**Evergreen**—*pop pl* GA-3
**Evergreen**—*pop pl* IA-7
**Evergreen**—*pop pl* (2) KY-4
**Evergreen**—*pop pl* LA-4
**Evergreen**—*pop pl* MD-2
**Evergreen**—*pop pl* (3) MS-4
**Evergreen**—*pop pl* MO-7
**Evergreen**—*pop pl* MT-8
**Evergreen**—*pop pl* (2) NC-3
**Evergreen**—*pop pl* (2) OH-6
**Evergreen**—*pop pl* (2) PA-2
**Evergreen**—*pop pl* SC-3
**Evergreen**—*pop pl* TX-5
**Evergreen**—*pop pl* VA-3
**Evergreen**—*pop pl* WA-9
**Evergreen**—*pop pl* WV-2
Evergreen—*post sta* WA-9
Evergreen—*uninc pl* MS-4
Evergreen—*uninc pl* NY-2
Evergreen, Lake—*lake* FL-3
Evergreen, Lake—*reservoir* OH-6
Evergreen, Mount—*summit* UT-8
Evergreen Acres—*hist pl* NY-2
Evergreen Acres—*locale* PA-2
**Evergreen Acres**—*pop pl* CA-9
**Evergreen Acres**—*pop pl* DE-2
**Evergreen Acres**—*pop pl* IN-6
**Evergreen Acres**—*pop pl* MI-6
Evergreen Acres Airp—*airport* DE-2
**Evergreen Acres (subdivision)**—*pop pl* DE-2
**Evergreen Acres Subdivision**—*pop pl* UT-8
Evergreen and Austin Drain—*canal* MI-6
Evergreen Baptist Ch—*church* MS-4
Evergreen Baptist Ch (historical)—*church* MS-4
*Evergreen Baptist Church* AL-4
**Evergreen Beach**—*pop pl* MI-6
Evergreen Bowl—*basin* AK-9
Evergreen Burial Park—*cemetery* (2) OH-6
Evergreen Cabins—*locale* MT-8
Evergreen Camp—*locale* WA-9
Evergreen Canal—*canal* (2) CA-9
Evergreen (CCD)—*cens area* AL-4
Evergreen Cem—*cemetery* (7) AL-4
Evergreen Cem—*cemetery* (2) AZ-5
Evergreen Cem—*cemetery* (3) AR-4
Evergreen Cem—*cemetery* (8) CA-9
Evergreen Cem—*cemetery* (5) CO-8
Evergreen Cem—*cemetery* (6) CT-1
Evergreen Cem—*cemetery* (13) FL-3
Evergreen Cem—*cemetery* (8) GA-3
Evergreen Cem—*cemetery* ID-8
Evergreen Cem—*cemetery* (10) IL-6
Evergreen Cem—*cemetery* IN-6
Evergreen Cem—*cemetery* (22) IA-7
Evergreen Cem—*cemetery* (7) KS-7
Evergreen Cem—*cemetery* (6) KY-4
Evergreen Cem—*cemetery* (3) LA-4
Evergreen Cem—*cemetery* (14) ME-1
Evergreen Cem—*cemetery* (2) MD-2
Evergreen Cem—*cemetery* (13) MA-1
Evergreen Cem—*cemetery* (15) MI-6
Evergreen Cem—*cemetery* (20) MN-6
Evergreen Cem—*cemetery* (3) MS-4
Ever Green Cem—*cemetery* MS-4
Evergreen Cem—*cemetery* (3) MS-4
Evergreen Cem—*cemetery* (6) MO-7
Evergreen Cem—*cemetery* (6) NE-7
Evergreen Cem—*cemetery* (2) NH-1
Evergreen Cem—*cemetery* (8) NJ-2
Evergreen Cem—*cemetery* (2) NM-5
Evergreen Cem—*cemetery* (26) NY-2
Evergreen Cem—*cemetery* (5) NC-3
Evergreen Cem—*cemetery* (14) OH-6
Evergreen Cem—*cemetery* (6) OK-5
Evergreen Cem—*cemetery* (2) OR-9
Evergreen Cem—*cemetery* (14) PA-2
Evergreen Cem—*cemetery* (5) SC-3
Evergreen Cem—*cemetery* (4) SD-7
Evergreen Cem—*cemetery* (7) TN-4
Evergreen Cem—*cemetery* (33) TX-5
Evergreen Cem—*cemetery* UT-8
Evergreen Cem—*cemetery* (4) VT-1
Evergreen Cem—*cemetery* (7) VA-3
Evergreen Cem—*cemetery* (4) WA-9
Evergreen Cem—*cemetery* (3) WV-2
Evergreen Cem—*cemetery* (28) WI-6
Evergreen Cemetery, The—*cemetery* FL-3
Evergreen Cemetry—*cemetery* MA-1
*Evergreen Ch* AL-4
Evergreen Ch—*church* (10) AL-4
Evergreen Ch—*church* (3) AR-4
Evergreen Ch—*church* (5) FL-3
Evergreen Ch—*church* (17) GA-3
Evergreen Ch—*church* IN-6
Evergreen Ch—*church* (13) LA-4
Evergreen Ch—*church* (2) MI-6
Evergreen Ch—*church* (7) MS-4
Evergreen Ch—*church* (2) MO-7
Evergreen Ch—*church* NE-7
Evergreen Ch—*church* NY-2
Evergreen Ch—*church* (3) NC-3
Evergreen Ch—*church* (2) OH-6
Evergreen Ch—*church* (3) SC-3
Evergreen Ch—*church* (4) TN-4
Evergreen Ch—*church* (6) TX-5
Evergreen Ch—*church* (9) VA-3
Evergreen Ch—*church* (4) WV-2
Evergreen Ch—*church* WI-6
Evergreen Chapel—*church* MI-6
Evergreen Ch (historical)—*church* MS-4
Evergreen Community Ch—*church* WA-9
Evergreen Conference District—*hist pl* CO-8
*Evergreen Creek* WI-6
Evergreen Creek—*stream* GA-3
Evergreen Creek—*stream* (2) MI-6
Evergreen Creek—*stream* NE-7
Evergreen Creek—*stream* (2) OR-9
Evergreen Creek—*stream* WA-9
Evergreen Creek—*stream* WI-6
Evergreen Division—*civil* AL-4
Evergreen Elem Sch—*school* AL-4
Evergreen Elem Sch—*school* NC-3
Evergreen Elem Sch—*school* PA-2
**Evergreen Estates (subdivision)**—*pop pl* AL-4
**Evergreen Estates (subdivision)**—*pop pl* NC-3
**Evergreen Estates (subdivision)**—*pop pl* TN-4
Evergreen Falls—*falls* WI-6
Evergreen Field Airp—*airport* WA-9
*Evergreen Fire Tower* AL-4
Evergreen Flat—*flat* NV-8
Evergreen Forest Campground—*park* OR-9
Evergreen General Hospital Heliport—*airport* WA-9
Evergreen Gillespie Cem—*cemetery* NC-3
Evergreen Glade Sch—*school* MI-6
Evergreen Golf Club—*locale* AL-4
Evergreen Golf Club—*other* IL-6
Evergreen Golf Course—*other* AZ-5
Evergreen Golf Course—*other* OR-9
Evergreen Grove Sch—*school* MN-6
Evergreen Hamlet—*hist pl* PA-2
**Evergreen Heights**—*pop pl* MD-2
Evergreen Hill—*summit* MA-1
Evergreen Hill Cem—*cemetery* IL-6
Evergreen Hill Cem—*cemetery* NY-2
Evergreen Hill Cem—*cemetery* WI-6
**Ever Green Hills**—*pop pl* CO-8
**Evergreen Hills**—*pop pl* SC-3
**Evergreen Hills**—*pop pl* VA-3
**Evergreen Hills**—*pop pl* WV-2
Evergreen Hill Sch—*school* WI-6
Evergreen Hist Dist—*hist pl* TN-4
Evergreen (historical)—*locale* IA-7
**Evergreen (historical)**—*pop pl* MS-4
Evergreen (historical P.O.)—*locale* IA-7
Evergreen Home Cem—*cemetery* NE-7
Evergreen Home for the Aged—*building* NJ-2
Evergreen Hosp—*hospital* AL-4
Evergreen Hotel—*hist pl* WA-9
Evergreen House—*hist pl* MD-2
Evergreen HS—*school* AL-4
Evergreen HS—*school* (2) WA-9
Evergreen Island—*island* NH-1
Evergreen Island—*island* NC-3
Evergreen JHS—*school* CO-8
Evergreen JHS—*school* LA-4
Evergreen JHS—*school* OR-9
Evergreen JHS—*school* UT-8
Evergreen JHS—*school* WA-9
Evergreen Knoll Cem—*cemetery* MN-6
Evergreen Lake—*lake* CA-9
Evergreen Lake—*lake* (2) MI-6
Evergreen Lake—*lake* MN-6
Evergreen Lake—*lake* (2) NY-2
Evergreen Lake—*lake* WA-9
Evergreen Lake—*lake* (4) WI-6
Evergreen Lake—*reservoir* CO-8
Evergreen Lake—*reservoir* IL-6
Evergreen Lake—*reservoir* PA-2
Evergreen Lakes—*lake* CO-8
Evergreen Lakes—*reservoir* MO-7
Evergreen Landing—*locale* ME-1
Evergreen Lands—*hist pl* NY-2
Evergreen Lateral Three—*canal* CA-9
Evergreen Lawn Cem—*cemetery* NY-2
Evergreen Lodge—*locale* CA-9
Evergreen Lodge—*locale* NM-5
Evergreen Lookout Tower—*locale* AL-4
**Evergreen (Lucille)**—*pop pl* SC-3
Evergreen Marsh—*swamp* TX-5
Evergreen Memorial Cem—*cemetery* NY-2
Evergreen Memorial Cem—*cemetery* NC-3
Evergreen Memorial Gardens—*cemetery* CO-8
Evergreen Memorial Gardens—*cemetery* (2) FL-3
Evergreen Memorial Gardens—*cemetery* GA-3
Evergreen Memorial Gardens—*cemetery* MN-6
Evergreen Memorial Gardens—*cemetery* MS-4
Evergreen Memorial Gardens—*cemetery* NC-3
Evergreen Memorial Gardens—*cemetery* (2) SC-3
Evergreen Memorial Gardens—*cemetery* WA-9
Evergreen Memorial Gardens Cem—*cemetery* FL-3
Evergreen Memorial Gardens Cem—*cemetery* MO-7
Evergreen Memorial Park—*cemetery* CO-8
Evergreen Memorial Park—*cemetery* FL-3
Evergreen Memorial Park—*cemetery* GA-3
Evergreen Memorial Park—*cemetery* IN-6
Evergreen Memorial Park—*cemetery* OR-9
Evergreen Memorial Park—*cemetery* PA-2
Evergreen Memorial Park—*cemetery* SC-3
Evergreen Memorial Park—*cemetery* VA-3
Evergreen Memorial Park—*park* MN-6
Evergreen Memorial Park—*park* TX-5
Evergreen Memorial Park Cem—*cemetery* NE-7
Evergreen Memorial Park Cem—*cemetery* OH-6
Evergreen Memorial Park (Cemetery)—*cemetery* WA-9
Evergreen Memory Gardens—*cemetery* IA-7
Evergreen Memory Gardens—*cemetery* NC-3
Evergreen Memory Gardens Cem—*cemetery* GA-3
Evergreen Mills—*locale* VA-3
Evergreen Mine—*mine* (2) CA-9
Evergreen Mine—*mine* ID-8
Evergreen Missionary Baptist Ch (historical)—*church* AL-4
Evergreen Mountain Lookout—*hist pl* WA-9
*Evergreen Mtn* MA-1
Evergreen Mtn—*summit* CO-8
Evergreen Mtn—*summit* ID-8
Evergreen Mtn—*summit* MT-8
Evergreen Mtn—*summit* NY-2
Evergreen Mtn—*summit* WA-9
Evergreen on the Falls—*hist pl* MD-2
Evergreen Orchards JHS—*school* WA-9
Evergreen Orchards Sch—*school* WA-9
*Evergreen Park* MI-6
Evergreen Park—*cemetery* OH-6
Evergreen Park—*park* AZ-5
Evergreen Park—*park* (3) IL-6
Evergreen Park—*park* IN-6
Evergreen Park—*park* IA-7
Evergreen Park—*park* MN-6
Evergreen Park—*park* NY-2
Evergreen Park—*park* PA-2
Evergreen Park—*park* UT-8
Evergreen Park—*park* (2) WA-9
Evergreen Park—*park* WI-6
**Evergreen Park**—*pop pl* IL-6
**Evergreen Park**—*pop pl* MD-2
**Evergreen Park**—*pop pl* PA-2
Evergreen Park—*uninc pl* WI-6
Evergreen Park Cem—*cemetery* IL-6
Evergreen Park Cem—*cemetery* WA-9
Evergreen Park Golf Course—*locale* PA-2
Evergreen Park Sch—*school* IL-6
**Evergreen Park (subdivision)**—*pop pl* NC-3
**Evergreen Park Subdivision**—*pop pl* UT-8
Evergreen Picnic Ground—*locale* UT-8
Evergreen Place—*hist pl* TN-4
Evergreen Plantation—*hist pl* MS-4
Evergreen Plantation—*locale* LA-4
**Evergreen Plantation**—*pop pl* LA-4
Evergreen Point—*cape* (2) TX-5
Evergreen Point—*cape* WA-9
Evergreen Point Bridge—*bridge* WA-9
Evergreen Post Office (historical)—*building* MS-4
Evergreen Presbyterian Ch—*church* AL-4
Evergreen Primitive Baptist Ch—*church* AL-4
Evergreen Pumping Plant—*other* WA-9
Evergreen Recreation Center—*park* CA-9
Evergreen Rest Cem—*cemetery* WI-6
Evergreen Ridge—*ridge* WA-9
*Evergreen River* WI-6
Evergreen River—*stream* WI-6
Evergreen River State Fishery Area—*park* WI-6
Evergreen Rsvr—*reservoir* WA-9
Evergreens, The—*hist pl* ME-1
Evergreens Cem—*cemetery* ME-1
*Evergreen Sch* PA-2
Evergreen Sch—*school* AZ-5
Evergreen Sch—*school* AR-4
Evergreen Sch—*school* (4) CA-9
Evergreen Sch—*school* ID-8
Evergreen Sch—*school* (6) IL-6
Evergreen Sch—*school* (2) IA-7
Evergreen Sch—*school* LA-4
Evergreen Sch—*school* (4) MI-6
Evergreen Sch—*school* MT-8
Evergreen Sch—*school* (3) NE-7
Evergreen Sch—*school* (3) NJ-2
Evergreen Sch—*school* OR-9
Evergreen Sch—*school* PA-2
Evergreen Sch—*school* (2) SC-3
Evergreen Sch—*school* (3) SD-7
Evergreen Sch—*school* VA-3
Evergreen Sch—*school* (3) WA-9
Evergreen Sch—*school* WV-2
Evergreen Sch—*school* WI-6
Evergreen Sch (abandoned)—*school* PA-2
Evergreen Sch (historical)—*school* (3) AL-4
Evergreen Sch (historical)—*school* MO-7
Evergreen Sch (historical)—*school* (2) TN-4
Evergreen School—*locale* TX-5
Evergreen Sewage Lagoon—*reservoir* AL-4
Evergreen Sewage Lagoon Dam—*dam* AL-4
Evergreens Golf Course—*other* PA-2
Evergreen Shopping Plaza—*locale* IL-6
**Evergreen Shores**—*pop pl* (2) MI-6
**Evergreen Shores**—*pop pl* NJ-2
**Evergreen Shores**—*pop pl* VA-3
Evergreen Sky Ranch Airp—*airport* WA-9
Evergreen Slough—*gut* NC-3
Evergreen Spring—*spring* OR-9
Evergreen State Fairgrounds—*locale* WA-9
Evergreen Station—*locale* AZ-5
**Evergreen (subdivision)**—*pop pl* MS-4
**Evergreen (subdivision)**—*pop pl* TN-4
**Evergreen Subdivision**—*pop pl* UT-8
Evergreen Substation—*locale* AZ-5
Evergreen (Town of)—*civ div* WI-6
**Evergreen (Town of)**—*pop pl* (2) WI-6
*Evergreen Township* KS-7
**Evergreen Township**—*pop pl* ND-7
**Evergreen (Township of)**—*pop pl* (2) MI-6
**Evergreen (Township of)**—*pop pl* MN-6
**Evergreen Trailer Park**—*pop pl* VA-3
Evergreen Union Ch—*church* NE-7
Evergreen United Methodist Ch—*church* AL-4
*Evergreen United Methodist Church* MS-4
**Evergreen Valley Estates**—*pop pl* MD-2
Evergreen Valley Ranch—*locale* NM-5
Evergreen Villa Mobile Home Park—*locale* AZ-5
Evergreen Wayside—*locale* OR-9
**Evergreen West**—*pop pl* CO-8
Everham Sch—*school* IA-7
Everhard and Baldwin Ditch—*canal* CO-8
Everhard Mission Ch—*church* TN-4
**Everhardt**—*pop pl* NC-3
Everhardt, W. H., House—*hist pl* KY-4
Everhardt Cem—*cemetery* IA-7
Everhardt Ranch—*hist pl* CO-8
Everhart, Hamilton, Farm—*hist pl* NC-3
Everhart, Riley, Farm and General Store—*hist pl* NC-3
Everhart, William, Buildings—*hist pl* PA-2
Everhart, William, House—*hist pl* PA-2
Everhart Cem—*cemetery* TN-4
Everhart Cem—*cemetery* TX-5
Everhart Hollow—*valley* MO-7
Everhart Lake—*lake* MN-6
Everhart Park—*park* PA-2
Everhart Ranch—*locale* AZ-5
**Everhartville**—*pop pl* PA-2
Everhart Well—*well* NM-5
Everidge Cabin and Cemetery—*hist pl* OK-5
Everidge Cem—*cemetery* OK-5
Everidge Lake Cut-off—*bend* TX-5
Everill Creek—*stream* CA-9
Everist, H. H., House—*hist pl* IA-7
Everist Cem—*cemetery* IA-7
**Everist Spur**—*pop pl* SD-7
Everit, John, House—*hist pl* NY-2
Everitt, Orson, House—*hist pl* MI-6
Everitt Cem—*cemetery* GA-3
Everitt Cem—*cemetery* IN-6
Everitt-Cox House—*hist pl* TX-5
*Everitt Creek* CA-9
Everitt Hill—*summit* CA-9
Everitt JHS—*school* CO-8
Everitt JHS—*school* FL-3
**Everitt (Magnolia)**—*pop pl* TX-5
**Everittstown**—*pop pl* NJ-2
Everittstown Hist Dist—*hist pl* NJ-2
Everlasting Branch—*stream* SC-3
Everlasting Bread of Life—*church* FL-3
*Everlasting Spring* TX-5
*Everleigh* KY-4
Everleigh Point—*cape* NY-2
Everlena Ch—*church* TX-5
Everley Cem—*cemetery* WV-2
**Everly**—*pop pl* IA-7
Everly, Mount—*summit* ID-8
Everly Branch—*stream* TN-4
Everly Cem—*cemetery* MO-7
Everly Cem—*cemetery* PA-2
Everly Cem—*cemetery* WV-2
*Everly Creek* WY-8
Everly Creek—*stream* WY-8
Everly Island—*island* TN-4
Everly Lake—*lake* ID-8
Everly Ranch—*locale* CA-9
Everly Rsvr—*reservoir* CA-9
Everly Sch (historical)—*school* MO-7
**Everman**—*pop pl* TX-5
Everman Cem—*cemetery* (3) KY-4
Everman Cem—*cemetery* TX-5
Everman Ch—*church* KY-4
Everman Creek—*stream* KY-4
*Everman Lake* UT-8
Evermann Creek—*stream* WY-8
Evermann Lake—*lake* UT-8
Evermay—*hist pl* DC-2
**Evermay**—*pop pl* GA-3
Evernade Point—*cape* ID-8
Everona—*locale* VA-3
Ever Pond—*swamp* FL-3
Ever Rest Cem—*cemetery* IL-6
Ever Rest Cem—*cemetery* WI-6
Ever Rest Memorial Gardens—*cemetery* IN-6
Everroad Lake—*reservoir* IN-6
**Everroad Park**—*pop pl* IN-6
*Everroad Park West* (2) IN-6
Evers—*locale* IL-6
Eversaw Tank—*reservoir* NM-5
Evers Bench—*bench* MT-8
Evers Cem—*cemetery* TX-5
Evers Coulee—*valley* MT-8
*Evers Creek* WI-6
Evers Creek—*stream* MT-8
Evers Ditch—*canal* IN-6
Evers Lake—*lake* OR-9
Eversole—*locale* KY-4
Eversole Basin—*basin* WY-8
Eversole Branch—*stream* KY-4
Eversole Cem—*cemetery* WY-8
Eversole Ch—*church* OH-6
Eversole Creek—*stream* IN-6
Eversole Creek—*stream* KY-4
Eversole Mine—*mine* MO-7
Eversole Ranch—*locale* (2) WY-8
Eversole Run—*stream* OH-6
Eversole Sch—*school* IL-6
Eversole Sch—*school* KY-4
*Eversoll Creek* IA-7
Eversoll Creek—*stream* IA-7
**Everson**—*pop pl* MT-8
**Everson**—*pop pl* PA-2
**Everson**—*pop pl* WA-9
**Everson**—*pop pl* WV-2
Everson Bench—*bench* MT-8
Everson Borough—*civil* PA-2
Everson Cabin—*locale* WY-8
Everson Cem—*cemetery* (2) MS-4
Everson Cem—*cemetery* MT-8
Everson Community Hall—*locale* MT-8
Everson Creek—*stream* ID-8
Everson Creek—*stream* MT-8
Everson Drain—*canal* MI-6
Everson Gulch—*valley* MT-8
Everson Lake—*lake* ID-8
Everson Lake—*lake* MN-6
Everson Sch—*school* SD-7
Everson Sch—*school* WI-6
**Eversonville**—*pop pl* MO-7
Evers Pond—*lake* CT-1
Evers Ranch—*locale* MT-8
Everstein Hollow—*valley* UT-8
Everstein Ridge—*ridge* UT-8
*Evers Valley* CA-9
Evert And Stewart Drain—*canal* MI-6
*Evert Canyon* TX-5
Evert House—*hist pl* IL-6
**Everton**—*pop pl* AR-4
**Everton**—*pop pl* IN-6
**Everton**—*pop pl* MO-7
**Everton**—*pop pl* NC-3
Everton Cem—*cemetery* IN-6
Everton Creek—*stream* MN-6
Everton Riffle—*rapids* OR-9
Everts, Caleb, House—*hist pl* MI-6
Everts, Mount—*summit* WY-8
Everts Ridge—*ridge* CA-9
**Everts (Township of)**—*pop pl* MN-6
Evertt Pond Dam—*dam* MS-4
Evertz Ranch—*locale* MT-8
Everwine Cem—*cemetery* MO-7
Everybodys Mission—*church* PA-2
Everybodys Tabernacle—*church* FL-3
Every Park—*park* IL-6
Everywhere Branch—*stream* MO-7
**Evesboro**—*pop pl* NJ-2
Eves Cave—*cave* TN-4
Eves Drain—*stream* MI-6
Eves Ferry (historical)—*locale* TN-4
**Eves Garden Subdivision**—*pop pl* (2) UT-8
Evesham Friends Meeting House—*hist pl* NJ-2
**Evesham (Township of)**—*pop pl* NJ-2
Eves Island—*island* PA-2
Eves Point—*cape* NY-2
Eve Station (historical)—*locale* TN-4
Evett Point—*cape* AL-4
*Evey* KY-4
Evey Canyon—*valley* CA-9
Evghinak Point—*cape* AK-9
E V Harrington Pond Dam—*dam* MS-4
Evic Hollow—*valley* WV-2
Evick Cem—*cemetery* OH-6
Evick Hollow—*valley* WV-2
Evick Knob—*summit* WV-2
Evick Spring—*spring* OR-9
Evies Pond—*lake* NY-2
Evil, Mount—*summit* TN-4
Eville—*locale* OK-5
Evilsizer Lake—*reservoir* CO-8
Evington—*locale* VA-3
Evins-Bivings House—*hist pl* SC-3
Evins Ferry (historical)—*locale* AL-4
**Evins Mill**—*pop pl* TN-4
Evins Mill Pond—*reservoir* TN-4
**Evinston**—*pop pl* FL-3
Evinton HS—*school* VA-3
Evitts—*locale* PA-2
**Evitts Creek**—*pop pl* MD-2
Evitts Creek—*stream* MD-2
Evitts Creek—*stream* PA-2
Evitts Hollow—*valley* TN-4
Evitts Mountain Trail—*trail* PA-2
Evitts Mtn—*range* PA-2
Evitts Mtn—*summit* MD-2
Evitts Run—*stream* WV-2
*Evitts Trail* PA-2
Evles Flat—*flat* NE-7
**Evna**—*pop pl* MD-2
**Evol**—*pop pl* VA-3
Evolution Amphitheater—*basin* AZ-5
Evolution Basin—*basin* CA-9
Evolution Creek—*stream* CA-9
Evolution Lake—*lake* CA-9
Evolution Meadow—*flat* CA-9
Evolution Trail—*trail* ID-8
Evolution Valley—*valley* CA-9
Evona—*locale* KY-4
**Evona**—*pop pl* MO-7
**Evona**—*pop pl* UT-8
**Evona Junction**—*pop pl* UT-8
Evoniuk Ranch—*locale* ND-7
E V Robbins Ditch—*canal* IN-6
Evrulivik Lake—*lake* AK-9
E V Spence Rsvr—*reservoir* TX-5
Evvitt Cem—*cemetery* NC-3
**Ewa**—*pop pl* HI-9
**Ewa Beach**—*pop pl* HI-9
Ewa Beach Park—*park* HI-9
Ewa Beach Sch—*school* HI-9
Ewa (CCD)—*cens area* HI-9
Ewa For Res—*forest* HI-9
Ewaklalik, Mount—*summit* AK-9
Ewal—*locale* AR-4
Ewald Lake—*lake* WI-6
Ewald Playground—*park* MI-6
Ewalt—*uninc pl* PA-2
Ewalt Creek—*stream* MT-8
Ewalt Crossroads—*locale* KY-4
Ewalt Draw—*valley* MT-8
*Ewa Mill* HI-9
Ewan—*locale* WA-9
**Ewan**—*pop pl* NJ-2
Ewan Bay—*bay* AK-9
Ewan Bldg—*hist pl* AR-4
Ewan Island—*island* AK-9
Ewan Lake—*lake* AK-9
Ewan Lake—*reservoir* NJ-2
Ewan Sch—*school* KY-4
Ewans Mill Dam—*dam* NJ-2
*Ewans Mills* NJ-2
**Ewansville**—*pop pl* NJ-2
E Ward Sch—*school* NE-7
*Ewards Creek* FL-3
**Ewart**—*pop pl* IA-7
**Ewart**—*pop pl* NC-3
Ewart Bldg—*hist pl* PA-2
Ewart Cem—*cemetery* IA-7
Ewart Creek—*stream* NY-2
Ewart Creek—*stream* WA-9
Ewart Doughty Dam—*dam* AL-4
Ewart Doughty Lake—*reservoir* AL-4
Ewartsville—*locale* WA-9
Ewa Sch—*school* HI-9
Ewa-Schofield Junction—*locale* HI-9
Ewatt Cem—*cemetery* OH-6
Ewatt Lake—*lake* MI-6
Ewauna, Lake—*lake* OR-9
Ewauna Camp—*locale* OR-9
Ewbank, Lancelot C., House—*hist pl* IN-6
Ewbanks—*locale* IL-6
E W Cotton Woods Memorial Airp—*airport* MO-7
Ewe Canyon—*valley* NV-8
Ewe Canyon—*valley* NM-5
Ewe Canyon Tank—*reservoir* NM-5
Ewe Creek—*stream* AK-9
Ewe Creek—*stream* OR-9
Ewe Creek Ranger Cabin No. 8—*hist pl* AK-9
Ewe Glacier—*glacier* AK-9
Ewe Island—*island* (2) ME-1
Ewelder—*locale* TX-5
Ewe Ledge—*cape* AK-9
*Ewell* GA-3
Ewell—*locale* KS-7
Ewell—*locale* TX-5
**Ewell**—*pop pl* AL-4
**Ewell**—*pop pl* FL-3
**Ewell**—*pop pl* MD-2
**Ewell**—*pop pl* VA-3
Ewell Bible Ch—*church* AL-4
*Ewell Canyon* CO-8
*Ewell Canyon* NM-5
Ewell C Forbes Dam—*dam* AL-4
Ewell Ch—*church* AL-4
Ewell Chapel—*church* TN-4
*Ewell County* AZ-5
Ewell Dam—*dam* UT-8
Ewell Farm—*hist pl* TN-4
Ewell Gulf—*valley* NY-2
Ewell Hollow—*valley* TX-5
Ewell Lake—*reservoir* TX-5
Ewell Methodist Ch—*church* AL-4
Ewell Pond—*lake* VT-1
Ewell Post Office (historical)—*building* UT-8
Ewell Regulating Rsvr—*reservoir* UT-8
Ewell Sch—*school* MI-6
Ewells Corner—*locale* NY-2
**Ewells Mills**—*pop pl* VT-1
Ewells Prong—*stream* VA-3
**Ewell Subdivision**—*pop pl* UT-8
Ewen—*locale* PA-2
**Ewen**—*pop pl* MI-6
Ewen Branch—*stream* KY-4
Ewen Cem—*cemetery* MI-6
Ewe Neck—*cape* WA-9
Ewenkep—*bay* FM-9
Ewen Park—*park* NY-2
Ewers Creek—*stream* OK-5
Ewers Hollow—*valley* WI-6
Ewers Lake—*lake* MI-6
Ewert, Ferdinand, Bldg—*hist pl* IA-7
*Ewes Creek* NC-3
E W F Stirrup Senior Elem Sch—*school* FL-3
E Wilson Dam—*dam* SD-7
Ewin Branch—*stream* TN-4
Ewin Breaker (historical)—*building* PA-2
*Ewing* KS-7
Ewing—*locale* AL-4
Ewing—*locale* CA-9
Ewing—*locale* LA-4
Ewing—*locale* NJ-2
Ewing—*locale* OH-6
Ewing—*locale* TX-5
**Ewing**—*pop pl* AL-4
**Ewing**—*pop pl* GA-3
**Ewing**—*pop pl* IL-6
**Ewing**—*pop pl* IN-6
**Ewing**—*pop pl* KY-4
**Ewing**—*pop pl* MO-7
**Ewing**—*pop pl* NE-7
**Ewing**—*pop pl* VA-3
Ewing—*uninc pl* FL-3
Ewing—*uninc pl* OK-5
Ewing, Alexander, House—*hist pl* TN-4
Ewing, D. H., & Sons Creamery—*hist pl* KY-4
Ewing, Frank, House—*hist pl* AZ-5
Ewing, James F., House—*hist pl* KY-4
Ewing, Ruth, House—*hist pl* AZ-5
*Ewing Acad* TN-4
*Ewing and Jefferson College* TN-4
Ewing Basin—*basin* WA-9
Ewing Bayou—*gut* AL-4
Ewing Branch—*stream* KY-4
Ewing (CCD)—*cens area* KY-4
Ewing Cem—*cemetery* (2) IN-6
Ewing Cem—*cemetery* LA-4
Ewing Cem—*cemetery* (2) MO-7
Ewing Cem—*cemetery* NE-7
Ewing Cem—*cemetery* NJ-2
Ewing Cem—*cemetery* (2) OH-6
Ewing Cem—*cemetery* (2) OK-5
Ewing Cem—*cemetery* (3) TN-4
Ewing Ch—*church* TN-4
Ewing Ch—*church* VA-3
Ewing Chapel—*church* OK-5
Ewing Chapel—*church* VA-3
Ewing Chapel Cem—*cemetery* OK-5
Ewing Complex—*airport* NJ-2
Ewing Corners—*locale* PA-2
Ewing County (historical)—*civil* SD-7
Ewing Cove—*bay* WA-9
*Ewing Creek* TN-4
Ewing Creek—*stream* IL-6
Ewing Creek—*stream* IN-6
Ewing Creek—*stream* KY-4
Ewing Creek—*stream* MI-6
Ewing Creek—*stream* OR-9
Ewing Creek—*stream* TN-4
Ewing Ditch—*canal* IN-6
Ewing Ditch—*canal* OR-9
Ewing Farm—*hist pl* TN-4
Ewing Farms—*locale* AL-4
*Ewing Ferry* AL-4
Ewing Ferry (historical)—*locale* AL-4
**Ewingford**—*pop pl* KY-4
Ewing Fork—*stream* WV-2
Ewing Gulch—*valley* CA-9
Ewing Gulch—*valley* CO-8
Ewing-Halsell HS—*school* OK-5
*Ewing Harbor* OR-9
Ewing Hill—*summit* AL-4
Ewing Hill—*summit* CA-9
Ewing (historical)—*locale* KS-7
**Ewing (historical)**—*pop pl* OR-9
**Ewing (historical)**—*pop pl* TN-4
Ewing Hollow—*valley* (2) TN-4
Ewing House—*hist pl* TN-4
Ewing HS—*school* NJ-2
Ewing Island—*island* (2) OH-6
Ewing Island—*island* WA-9
*Ewing Lake* MI-6
Ewing Lake—*lake* KY-4
Ewing Lake—*reservoir* NC-3
Ewing Lake Dam—*dam* NC-3
Ewing Lane Elem Sch—*school* IN-6
Ewing Memorial Hosp—*hospital* NY-2
Ewing Mine—*mine* TN-4
*Ewing Mtn* MA-1
Ewing Mtn—*summit* VA-3
Ewing Park—*locale* NJ-2
Ewing Park—*park* IA-7
Ewing Park JHS—*school* TN-4
Ewing Park Sch—*school* PA-2
Ewing Post Office (historical)—*building* TN-4
Ewing Ranch—*locale* AZ-5
Ewing Ranch—*locale* SD-7
Ewing Ranch—*locale* TX-5
Ewing Ridge—*ridge* KY-4
Ewing RR Station—*locale* FL-3
Ewing Run—*stream* (2) OH-6
*Ewings* AL-4
Ewings Branch—*stream* WV-2
*Ewing Sch* TN-4
Ewing Sch—*school* CA-9
Ewing Sch—*school* NM-5
Ewing Sch—*school* TN-4
Ewings Chapel—*church* GA-3
Ewings Landing—*locale* MS-4
Ewings Landing (historical)—*locale* MS-4
Ewings Mill—*locale* PA-2
Ewings Mill (historical)—*locale* AL-4
**Ewings Mill (Kellers Mill)**—*pop pl* PA-2
*Ewings Mtn* MA-1
*Ewings Neck* NJ-2
Ewing-Snell Ranch—*hist pl* MT-8
Ewings P.O. (historical)—*building* AL-4
*Ewingsport* KS-7
Ewing Spring—*spring* OR-9
Ewing Spur—*ridge* KY-4
Ewings Sch (historical)—*school* TN-4
**Ewing (subdivision)**—*pop pl* PA-2
**Ewingsville**—*pop pl* PA-2
**Ewingsville (Fort Pitt)**—*pop pl* PA-2
**Ewingsville (historical)**—*pop pl* TN-4
**Ewington**—*pop pl* IN-6
**Ewington**—*pop pl* KY-4
**Ewington**—*pop pl* OH-6
Ewington Acad—*hist pl* OH-6
Ewington Cem—*cemetery* IL-6
Ewington Sch—*school* IL-6
**Ewington (Township of)**—*pop pl* MN-6

*Ewingtown* ... MD-2
Ewing Township—*CDP* ... NJ-2
**Ewing Township**—*pop pl* ... NE-7
Ewing (Township of)—*fmr MCD* ... AR-4
**Ewing (Township of)**—*pop pl* ... IL-6
**Ewing (Township of)**—*pop pl* ... MI-6
**Ewing (Township of)**—*pop pl* ... NJ-2
Ewing Trail—*trail* ... PA-2
**Ewingville**—*pop pl* ... MD-2
**Ewingville**—*pop pl* ... NJ-2
**Ewingville**—*pop pl* ... TN-4
**Ewingville (Ewingtown)**—*pop pl* ... MD-2
Ewing Young Historical Marker—*other* ... OR-9
Ewing Young Park—*park* ... OR-9
Ewing Young Sch—*school* ... OR-9
Ewin Mine (underground)—*mine* ... AL-4
Ewin Narrows—*channel* ... ME-1
Ewin Run—*stream* ... VA-3
Ewin Run—*stream* ... WV-2
E. W. Norris Service Station—*hist pl* ... KS-7
*Ewo* ... MP-9
Ewoldt Sch—*school* ... NE-7
Ewoldt Township—*fmr MCD* ... IA-7
Ewoniuk Ranch—*locale* ... ND-7
Ewoz Creek—*stream* ... NV-8
E W Smith Lake Dam—*dam* ... MS-4
Ewtonville Ch—*church* ... TN-4
Ewy Lake—*lake* ... MN-6
EWZ Bridge over East Channel of Laramie River—*hist pl* ... WY-8
**Exall**—*pop pl* ... TX-5
Example (historical)—*locale* ... KS-7
Excalibur—*summit* ... AZ-5
Excavation Gulch—*valley* ... ID-8
**Excel**—*pop pl* ... AL-4
Excel Ch—*church* ... AL-4
*Excelcior* ... KS-7
Excel HS—*school* ... AL-4
Excel Industrial Park Subdivision—*locale* ... UT-8
Exceline Sch—*school* ... KS-7
*Excell* ... TX-5
Excell—*locale* ... TN-4
Excell Baptist Ch—*church* ... TN-4
Excell Corners—*locale* ... NY-2
Excello—*locale* ... OH-6
**Excello**—*pop pl* ... MO-7
Excell Post Office (historical)—*building* ... TN-4
Excell Sch (historical)—*school* ... MO-7
*Excelsior* ... PA-2
Excelsior—*cliff* ... CA-9
Excelsior—*lake* ... FL-3
Excelsior—*locale* ... AR-4
Excelsior—*locale* ... GA-3
Excelsior—*locale* ... PA-2
Excelsior—*locale* ... WV-2
**Excelsior**—*pop pl* ... GA-3
**Excelsior**—*pop pl* ... MN-6
**Excelsior**—*pop pl* ... MO-7
**Excelsior**—*pop pl* (2) ... WV-2
**Excelsior**—*pop pl* ... WI-6
Excelsior Acad (historical)—*school* ... TN-4
Excelsior Bar—*bar* ... NJ-2
Excelsior Bay—*bay* ... MN-6
**Excelsior Beach**—*pop pl* ... ID-8
**Excelsior Blvd**—*pop pl* ... MN-6
Excelsior Camp—*locale* ... WA-9
Excelsior Cem—*cemetery* (2) ... KS-7
Excelsior Ch—*church* (2) ... KS-7
Excelsior Ch—*church* ... MI-6
Excelsior Ch—*church* ... MO-7
Excelsior Ch—*church* ... PA-2
Excelsior Corner—*locale* ... PA-2
Excelsior Creek—*stream* (2) ... AK-9
Excelsior Creek—*stream* ... WA-9
Excelsior Ditch—*canal* ... CA-9
Excelsior Ditch—*canal* (2) ... CO-8
Excelsior Dock—*locale* ... NJ-2
Excelsior Evening HS—*school* ... CA-9
Excelsior Flour Mill—*hist pl* ... SD-7
Excelsior Fruit Growers Association Bldg—*hist pl* ... MN-6
Excelsior Geyser Crater—*lake* ... WY-8
Excelsior Glacier—*glacier* ... AK-9
Excelsior Glen—*valley* ... NY-2
Excelsior Group—*island* ... NY-2
Excelsior Gulch—*valley* ... CO-8
Excelsior Gulch—*valley* ... OR-9
Excelsior (historical)—*locale* ... KS-7
Excelsior Hotel—*hist pl* ... TX-5
Excelsior HS—*school* ... CA-9
Excelsior Institute—*school* ... MO-7
Excelsior Lake—*lake* ... AK-9
Excelsior Lake—*lake* ... LA-4
Excelsior Landing—*locale* ... MS-4
Excelsior Lode Mine—*mine* ... MT-8
Excelsior Lookout—*locale* ... WA-9
Excelsior Mine—*mine* ... AZ-5
Excelsior Mine—*mine* (3) ... CA-9
Excelsior Mine—*mine* ... SD-7
Excelsior Mine—*mine* ... WA-9
*Excelsior Mountain* ... NV-8
*Excelsior Mtn* ... WA-9
Excelsior Mtn—*summit* ... CA-9
Excelsior Mtn—*summit* ... NV-8
Excelsior Mtn—*summit* ... WA-9
Excelsior Mtns—*range* ... NV-8
Excelsior Pass—*gap* ... WA-9
Excelsior Peak—*summit* ... WA-9
Excelsior Playground—*park* ... CA-9
*Excelsior Point* ... WA-9
Excelsior Public Sch—*hist pl* ... MN-6
Excelsior Ravine—*valley* ... CA-9
Excelsior Ridge—*ridge* ... CO-8
Excelsior Sch—*school* (2) ... CA-9
Excelsior Sch—*school* ... CO-8
Excelsior Sch—*school* ... GA-3
Excelsior Sch—*school* (8) ... IL-6
Excelsior Sch—*school* (2) ... IA-7
Excelsior Sch—*school* (4) ... KS-7
Excelsior Sch—*school* ... MI-6
Excelsior Sch—*school* (3) ... MN-6
Excelsior Sch—*school* (2) ... MO-7
Excelsior Sch—*school* ... NE-7
Excelsior Sch—*school* ... SC-3
Excelsior Sch—*school* ... SD-7
Excelsior Sch—*school* (2) ... TX-5
Excelsior Sch—*school* (2) ... WI-6
Excelsior Sch (abandoned)—*school* (2) ... MO-7
Excelsior Sch (historical)—*school* ... MS-4
Excelsior Sch (historical)—*school* (5) ... MO-7
Excelsior School—*locale* ... MO-7
Excelsior School (historical)—*locale* ... MO-7
Excelsior Spring—*spring* ... NV-8
**Excelsior Springs**—*pop pl* ... MO-7
**Excelsior Springs**—*pop pl* ... NY-2
Excelsior Springs Junction—*locale* ... MO-7
Excelsior Springs Memorial Airp—*airport* ... MO-7
Excelsior Springs Waterworks—*other* ... MO-7
Excelsior Swamp—*swamp* ... MI-6
**Excelsior (Town of)**—*pop pl* ... WI-6
Excelsior Township—*fmr MCD* ... IA-7
**Excelsior Township**—*pop pl* ... ND-7
**Excelsior (Township of)**—*pop pl* ... MI-6
Excelsior Valley—*valley* ... CA-9
Excelsor Sch—*school* ... IL-6
Excelssior Ch—*church* ... IA-7
**Excel (Township of)**—*pop pl* ... MN-6
Exceptional Child Center—*school* ... FL-3
Exceptional Education Center—*school* (2) ... FL-3
Exceptional Education Contracted Services—*school* ... FL-3
Exceptional/Student-Off Campus—*school* ... FL-3
*Exchange* ... PA-2
Exchange—*locale* ... MO-7
Exchange—*locale* ... VA-3
Exchange—*locale* ... WV-2
**Exchange**—*pop pl* ... IN-6
**Exchange**—*pop pl* ... PA-2
**Exchange**—*pop pl* ... WA-9
Exchange, The—*hist pl* ... MD-2
Exchange and Provost—*hist pl* ... SC-3
Exchange Bank—*hist pl* ... AR-4
Exchange Bank—*hist pl* ... IL-6
Exchange Bank Bldg—*hist pl* ... AR-4
Exchange Bank Bldg—*hist pl* ... FL-3
Exchange Bank Bldg—*hist pl* ... MN-6
Exchange Bldg—*hist pl* ... DE-2
Exchange Bldg—*hist pl* ... VA-3
Exchange Bldg and Huber's Restaurant—*hist pl* ... OR-9
Exchange Club Park—*park* ... MI-6
Exchange Club Park—*park* ... NC-3
Exchange Club Playground—*park* ... MI-6
Exchange Cove—*bay* ... AK-9
Exchange Creek—*stream* ... AK-9
Exchange Hall—*hist pl* ... MA-1
Exchange Hotel—*hist pl* ... OH-6
Exchange Hotel—*hist pl* ... VA-3
Exchange Island—*island* ... AK-9
Exchange Lake—*lake* ... AK-9
Exchange Park—*park* ... AL-4
Exchange Park—*park* ... IA-7
Exchange Park—*park* ... MS-4
Exchange Park—*post sta* ... TX-5
Exchange Place Hist Dist—*hist pl* ... UT-8
Exchange Plantation—*locale* ... SC-3
Exchange Square Hist Dist—*hist pl* ... WI-6
Exchange State Bank—*hist pl* ... MN-6
Exchange Tank—*reservoir* ... AZ-5
Excheque Meadow—*flat* ... CA-9
Excheque Mine—*mine* ... CA-9
Exchequer Canyon—*valley* ... NV-8
Exchequer Creek—*stream* ... CA-9
Exchequer Dam—*dam* ... CA-9
Exchequer Mine—*mine* ... NV-8
*Exchequer Reservoir* ... CA-9
Exchequer Spring—*spring* ... NV-8
Exclusive Furniture Shop—*hist pl* ... AL-4
Excursion Inlet—*bay* ... AK-9
Excursion Inlet—*locale* ... AK-9
Excursion Mine—*mine* ... AZ-5
Excursion River—*stream* ... AK-9
Excuse Mine—*mine* ... OR-9
Execution Rocks Lighthouse—*locale* ... NY-2
Executive Club Dam—*dam* ... NC-3
Executive Club Lake—*reservoir* ... NC-3
Executive Golf Club—*other* ... TX-5
Executive Hills Polo Club Heliport—*airport* ... MO-7
**Executive House Condominiums**—*pop pl* ... UT-8
Executive Inn Airp—*airport* ... IN-6
*Executive-Johnson Company Airport* ... KS-7
Executive Mansion—*hist pl* ... IL-6
Executive Office Bldg—*hist pl* ... DC-2
**Executive Park**—*pop pl* ... GA-3
**Executive Park (subdivision)**—*pop pl* ... AL-4
Executive Park West—*locale* ... NC-3
Executive Plaza—*building* ... MA-1
Executive Plaza Research Center—*locale* ... AL-4
**Executive Suites of Fountain East Subdivision**—*pop pl* ... UT-8
Exeda Post Office (historical)—*building* ... TN-4
**Exeelsior**—*pop pl* ... IA-7
*Exel* ... TN-4
**Exeland**—*pop pl* ... WI-6
Exeland Cem—*cemetery* ... WI-6
Exeland Ch—*church* (2) ... WI-6
**Exell**—*pop pl* ... TX-5
*Exelsion* ... TX-5
*Exel Swamp* ... VA-3
*Exenia* ... OH-6
Exermont—*locale* ... IL-6
*Exeter* ... ME-1
*Exeter* ... RI-1
Exeter—*hist pl* ... MD-2
Exeter—*hist pl* ... VA-3
Exeter—*locale* ... CT-1
**Exeter**—*pop pl* ... CA-9
**Exeter**—*pop pl* ... IL-6
**Exeter**—*pop pl* ... MO-7
**Exeter**—*pop pl* ... NE-7
**Exeter**—*pop pl* ... NH-1
**Exeter**—*pop pl* ... PA-2
**Exeter**—*pop pl* ... RI-1
**Exeter**—*pop pl* ... VA-3
**Exeter**—*pop pl* ... WI-6
Exeter-Bluffs (Election Precinct)—*fmr MCD* ... IL-6
Exeter Borough—*civil* ... PA-2
Exeter Brook—*stream* ... CT-1
Exeter (CCD)—*cens area* ... CA-9
Exeter Cem—*cemetery* ... NE-7
Exeter Cem—*cemetery* ... NY-2
Exeter Cem—*cemetery* ... VA-3
Exeter Cem—*cemetery* ... WI-6
Exeter Center—*locale* ... ME-1
**Exeter Center**—*pop pl* ... NY-2
**Exeter Compact (census name Exeter)**—*pop pl* ... NH-1
**Exeter Corner**—*pop pl* ... ME-1
**Exeter Corner**—*pop pl* ... NY-2
**Exeter Corners**—*pop pl* ... ME-1
Exeter Creek—*stream* ... MT-8
*Exeter (Exeter Corners)* ... ME-1
Exeter Farms—*locale* ... CA-9
Exeter Farms Ch—*church* ... MN-6
Exeter Friends Meeting House—*building* ... PA-2
**Exeter Hampton Mobile Village**—*pop pl* ... NH-1
*Exeter Hill* ... RI-1
Exeter Hill—*summit* ... RI-1
Exeter (historical)—*locale* ... KS-7
**Exeter (historical)**—*pop pl* ... NC-3
*Exeter Hole* ... RI-1
*Exeter Hollow* ... RI-1
Exeter Mills—*locale* ... ME-1
Exeter Mine—*mine* ... VA-3
Exeter Public Golf Course—*locale* ... PA-2
*Exeter River* ... NH-1
Exeter River—*stream* ... NH-1
Exeter Rsvr—*reservoir* ... NH-1
Exeter Sch—*school* ... PA-2
Exeter Sch—*school* ... VA-3
Exeter Shaft (historical)—*mine* ... PA-2
Exeter Street Theatre—*building* ... MA-1
**Exeter (Town of)**—*pop pl* ... ME-1
**Exeter (Town of)**—*pop pl* ... NH-1
**Exeter (Town of)**—*pop pl* ... NY-2
**Exeter (Town of)**—*pop pl* ... RI-1
Exeter Township—*civil* ... MO-7
**Exeter Township**—*pop pl* ... KS-7
**Exeter Township**—*pop pl* ... NE-7
**Exeter (Township of)**—*pop pl* ... MI-6
**Exeter (Township of)**—*pop pl* (3) ... PA-2
Exeter Township Sch—*school* (2) ... PA-2
**Exeter Villa (Mobil Home Park)**—*pop pl* ... NH-1
Exeter Waterfront Commercial Hist Dist—*hist pl* ... NH-1
Exeter Waterfront Commercial Hist Dist (Boundary Increase)—*hist pl* ... NH-1
**Exeter West**—*pop pl* ... NH-1
Exhibition Mine—*mine* ... WV-2
Exhibition Pasture—*flat* ... OK-5
Exhibit Ridge—*ridge* ... TX-5
Exie—*locale* ... KY-4
Exie Ch—*church* ... AL-4
Exie Post Office (historical)—*building* ... AL-4
Exile—*locale* ... WI-6
Exile Cem—*cemetery* ... TX-5
**Exira**—*pop pl* ... IA-7
Exira HS—*school* ... IA-7
Exira Township—*fmr MCD* ... IA-7
Exit Glacier—*glacier* ... AK-9
Exley—*locale* ... GA-3
Exley (historical)—*locale* ... MS-4
Exline—*locale* ... MD-2
**Exline**—*pop pl* ... IL-6
**Exline**—*pop pl* ... IA-7
Exline Cem—*cemetery* ... OH-6
Exline Creek—*stream* ... FL-3
Exline Slough—*stream* ... IL-6
**Exline Township**—*pop pl* ... SD-7
Ex Mission De San Fernando—*civil* ... CA-9
Ex Mission San Buenaventura—*civil* ... CA-9
Ex Mission San Diego—*civil* ... CA-9
Ex Mission San Jose—*civil* ... CA-9
Ex Mission Soledad—*civil* ... CA-9
Exmoor—*locale* ... PA-2
**Exmoor**—*pop pl* ... AL-4
Exmoor Country Club—*other* ... IL-6
**Exmore**—*pop pl* ... VA-3
Exmore-Willis Wharf Sch—*school* ... VA-3
Exnell Lake—*lake* ... MN-6
Exner Airp—*airport* ... IN-6
Exodus Sch (historical)—*school* ... MO-7
Exol Cem—*cemetery* ... VA-3
Exol Swamp—*stream* ... VA-3
Expand Rsvr Number Thirty—*reservoir* ... OR-9
Expansion Bay—*bay* ... ND-7
Expectation Mine—*mine* ... CO-8
Expectation Mtn—*summit* ... CO-8
Expectation State Wildlife Mngmt Areas—*park* ... MN-6
*Expedit* ... PA-2
Expedition Harbor—*bay* ... AK-9
Expedition Island—*hist pl* ... WY-8
Expedition Lake—*lake* ... MT-8
Expedition Pass—*gap* ... MT-8
Expedition Point—*cape* ... AK-9
Expedit PO (historical)—*building* ... PA-2
Ex Pence Ditch—*canal* ... WY-8
Expensive Tank—*reservoir* ... NM-5
Experiment—*locale* ... AR-4
**Experiment**—*pop pl* ... GA-3
**Experiment**—*pop pl* ... PA-2
Experimental Breeder Reactor No. 1—*hist pl* ... ID-8
Experimental Draw—*valley* ... ID-8
Experimental Farm Number One—*locale* ... CA-9
Experimental Farm Number Two—*locale* ... CA-9
Experimental Forest HQ—*locale* ... OR-9
Experimental Gulch—*valley* ... CA-9
Experimental Mine—*mine* ... CA-9
Experimental Mine, U.S. Bureau Of Mines—*hist pl* ... PA-2
Experimental Pasture Rsvr—*reservoir* ... MT-8
Experiment Creek—*stream* ... OR-9
*Experiment Draw* ... ID-8
Experiment Lake—*lake* ... MN-6
Experiment School, The—*school* ... VT-1
Experiment Shoal—*bar* ... GA-3
*Experiment Station Lake* ... MS-4
**Experiment (U.S. Bureau of Mines)**—*pop pl* ... PA-2
Exploit Lake—*lake* ... MN-6
Exploration Peak—*summit* ... AK-9
Explorer Basin—*basin* ... AK-9
Explorer Bay—*bay* ... AK-9
Explorer Canyon—*valley* ... UT-8
Explorer Glacier—*glacier* ... AK-9
Explorer Island—*island* ... AK-9
*Explorer Lake* ... MN-6
Explorer Lake—*lake* ... MN-6
Explorer Mtn—*summit* ... AK-9
*Explorer Peak* ... UT-8
Explorer Peak—*summit* ... UT-8
Explorers Club—*other* ... ME-1
Explorers Falls—*falls* ... MI-6
Explorers Monument—*summit* ... AZ-5
Explorers Pass—*valley* ... CA-9
Explorers Peak—*summit* ... AK-9
*Explorers Rock* ... AZ-5
Explosion Lake—*lake* ... WI-6
*Expo* ... VA-3
Expo Park—*post sta* ... IL-6
**Export**—*pop pl* (2) ... PA-2
Export Borough—*civil* ... PA-2
Export Landing—*locale* ... AL-4
Export Mine (underground)—*mine* ... AL-4
Export Slope Mine (underground)—*mine* ... AL-4
**Expose**—*pop pl* ... MS-4
Expose Cem—*cemetery* ... MS-4
Exposed Reef Mine—*mine* ... AZ-5
Exposition Gardens—*other* ... IL-6
*Exposition Park* ... PA-2
Exposition Park—*park* ... CA-9
**Exposition View**—*pop pl* ... IL-6
*Exposure Creek* ... WA-9
Exposure Creek—*stream* (2) ... WA-9
*Express* ... OR-9
Express Bluff—*cliff* ... TN-4
Express Canyon—*valley* ... CA-9
Express Canyon—*valley* ... NV-8
Express Creek—*stream* ... CO-8
Express Creek—*stream* ... MT-8
Express Gulch—*valley* ... CO-8
Express Lateral—*canal* ... ID-8
Express Mine—*mine* ... CO-8
Express Rsvr—*reservoir* ... MT-8
Expressway Baptist Ch—*church* ... FL-3
Expressway Ch—*church* ... KY-4
Expressway Mall—*locale* ... FL-3
Expressway Sch—*school* ... LA-4
Exsho (historical)—*locale* ... AL-4
Extension—*locale* ... LA-4
Extension Chapel—*church* ... NE-7
**Extension Country Club**—*pop pl* ... PR-3
Extension Dickinson Ditch—*canal* ... WY-8
Extension Ditch—*canal* ... CA-9
*Extension Heights* ... IN-6
**Extension Heights**—*pop pl* ... IN-6
**Extension Mariani**—*pop pl* (2) ... PR-3
Exter Canyon—*valley* ... NM-5
Exter Spring—*spring* ... NM-5
Extine Hill—*ridge* ... OH-6
**Exton**—*pop pl* ... PA-2
Exton Airp—*airport* ... PA-2
Exton Hotel—*hist pl* ... PA-2
Exton Lake—*reservoir* ... PA-2
Exton Station—*locale* ... PA-2
**Extonville**—*pop pl* (2) ... NJ-2
Extortion Creek—*stream* ... MN-6
Extortion Lake—*lake* ... MN-6
Extra—*locale* ... WV-2
Extra Ch—*church* ... AR-4
Extract Brook—*stream* ... NY-2
Extra Dry Creek—*stream* ... AK-9
*Extra Post Office* ... MS-4
Extra (Township of)—*fmr MCD* ... AR-4
Extrom Lake—*lake* ... WI-6
Exum—*locale* ... NC-3
Exum—*locale* ... TX-5
**Exum**—*pop pl* ... AL-4
Exum Cem—*cemetery* ... MS-4
Exum Mill Branch—*stream* ... NC-3
Exum Post Office (historical)—*building* ... TN-4
**Exway**—*pop pl* ... NC-3
**Ex-Way**—*pop pl* ... NC-3
Eyak—*CDP* ... AK-9
Eyak, Mount—*summit* ... AK-9
Eyak Cannery—*other* ... AK-9
Eyak Lake—*lake* ... AK-9
Eyak River—*stream* ... AK-9
Eyak Trail—*trail* ... AK-9
*Eybbiyae* ... MP-9
Eybbiyae—*island* ... MP-9
Eychaner Coulee—*valley* ... MT-8
Eye And Ear Hosp—*hospital* ... PA-2
Eyebrow, The—*summit* ... MT-8
Eyechaner Draw—*valley* ... WY-8
*Eyecreek* ... AR-4
Eye Creek—*stream* ... AR-4
Eye Creek—*stream* ... CA-9
**Eyedylwild Beach**—*pop pl* ... MI-6
**Eyedywild Beach**—*pop pl* ... MI-6
Eye Fork—*stream* ... KY-4
Eyeful Vista Point—*locale* ... MT-8
Eye Hill—*summit* ... WV-2
Eyeler Valley—*valley* ... MD-2
Eyeler Valley Chapel—*church* ... MD-2
Eyelet Pond—*lake* ... ME-1
Eyelet Ridge—*ridge* ... NC-3
Eyeman-Bryant Cem—*cemetery* ... OH-6
Eye of Needle—*arch* ... UT-8
Eye of the Needle—*arch* ... WY-8
Eye of the Whale Arch—*arch* ... UT-8
Eye Opener Light, The—*locale* ... AK-9
Eyer—*locale* ... PA-2
Eyer Cem—*cemetery* ... OH-6
*Eyerhaven* ... NJ-2
Eyer JHS—*school* ... PA-2
Eyer Sch—*school* ... IL-6
**Eyers Grove**—*pop pl* ... PA-2
**Eyersgrove Junction**—*pop pl* ... PA-2
**Eyers Grove (RR name Eyersgrove)**—*pop pl* ... PA-2
Eyersgrove (RR name for Eyers Grove)—*other* ... PA-2
*Eyerton* ... KS-7
Eyes, Mount—*summit* ... OH-6
Eyese Bar—*bar* ... CA-9
*Eye Spring* ... TN-4
*Eyes Run* ... WV-2
Eyford Ch—*church* ... ND-7
Eyhott Island—*island* ... WA-9
Eylar—*locale* ... IL-6
Eylar, Mathew, Barn No. 1—*hist pl* ... KS-7
Eylar, Mathew, Barn No. 2—*hist pl* ... KS-7
Eylar Canyon—*valley* ... CA-9
Eylar Mtn—*summit* ... CA-9
Eylar Sch—*school* ... IL-6
**Eylau**—*pop pl* ... TX-5
Eylau Siding—*locale* ... TX-5
Eyler Sch—*school* ... MI-6
Eyman, Jessie-Judson, Wilma, House—*hist pl* ... HI-9
E Y Mangum Lake Dam—*dam* ... MS-4
Eymann Ranch—*locale* ... NE-7
Eyman Ranch—*locale* (2) ... MT-8
Eymard Seminary—*school* ... NY-2
**Eynon**—*pop pl* ... PA-2
Eynon Draw—*valley* ... WY-8
Eynon Shop Ctr—*locale* ... PA-2
**Eyota**—*pop pl* ... MN-6
Eyota Farmers Cooperative Creamery Association—*hist pl* ... MN-6
**Eyota (Township of)**—*pop pl* ... MN-6
Eyraud Lakes—*lake* (2) ... MT-8
Eyre, Wilson, House—*hist pl* ... PA-2
Eyre Basin—*basin* ... CO-8
Eyre Creek—*stream* ... CO-8
Eyre Hall—*hist pl* ... VA-3
*Eyre Hall Branch* ... VA-3
*Eyre Hall Creek* ... VA-3
Eyrehall Creek—*stream* ... VA-3
Eyrehall Neck—*cape* ... VA-3
Eyreville Creek—*stream* ... VA-3
Eyreville Neck—*cape* ... VA-3
Eyrie Canyon—*valley* ... ID-8
Eyrie Creek—*stream* ... WY-8
Eyrie Meadows, Mount—*flat* ... UT-8
**Eyrie Meadows Subdivision**—*pop pl* ... UT-8
*Eyrie Peak* ... UT-8
Eyrie Peak—*summit* ... ID-8
Eyrie Spring—*spring* ... ID-8
Eysnogel Hill—*summit* ... WI-6
Eyster Ranch—*locale* ... SD-7
Eytcheson Park—*park* ... WI-6
E-Z Acres Airp—*airport* ... IN-6
*Ezbon* ... KS-7
*Ezbon Township* ... KS-7
Ezcelsior Sch—*school* ... MO-7
E Z Creek—*stream* ... CO-8
*Ezekial B Hall Cemetery* ... MS-4
Ezekial Rsvr—*reservoir* ... MT-8
*Ezekials Pond* ... MA-1
Ezekiel Branch—*stream* ... AL-4
Ezekiel Branch—*stream* (2) ... WV-2
Ezekiel Ch—*church* (2) ... AL-4
Ezekiel Ch—*church* ... GA-3
Ezekiel Ch (historical)—*church* ... AL-4
Ezekiel Pond—*lake* ... MA-1
Ezekiel Pond—*lake* ... NH-1
*Ezekiels Pond* ... MA-1
*Ezel* ... AL-4
**Ezel**—*pop pl* ... KY-4
*Ezell* ... AL-4
*Ezell* ... KY-4
Ezell—*locale* ... VA-3
**Ezell**—*pop pl* ... AL-4
Ezell Branch—*stream* ... LA-4
Ezell Branch—*stream* ... SC-3
Ezell Branch—*stream* ... TN-4
Ezell Branch—*stream* ... TX-5
Ezell Branch—*stream* ... VA-3
Ezell Camp—*locale* ... AL-4
Ezell Camp—*locale* ... FL-3
Ezell Cave—*cave* ... AL-4
Ezell Cem—*cemetery* ... KY-4
Ezell Cem—*cemetery* ... MS-4
Ezell Cem—*cemetery* ... MO-7
Ezell Cem—*cemetery* (3) ... TN-4
*Ezell Creek* ... AL-4
Ezell Creek—*stream* ... MS-4
Ezelle Ch—*church* ... VA-3
Ezell Hollow—*valley* ... AR-4
Ezell Hollow—*valley* ... TN-4
*Ezel (Linwood)* ... AL-4
Ezell Jenkins Dam—*dam* ... AL-4
Ezell Jenkins Lake—*reservoir* ... AL-4
**Ezell Place (subdivisions)**—*pop pl* ... AL-4
*Ezell Pond* ... AL-4
Ezell Sch (historical)—*school* ... AL-4
Ezell Slough—*gut* ... TX-5
Eziah Ch—*church* ... MD-2
Ezion Ch—*church* ... AL-4
Ezion Fair Baptist Ch—*church* ... DE-2
Ezion Mount Carmel Methodist Ch—*church* ... DE-2
Ezi Slough—*lake* ... AK-9
Ez-Kim-In-Zin Picnic Area—*park* ... AZ-5
**Ezra**—*pop pl* ... AL-4
Ezra Bridge Park—*park* ... NC-3
**Ezra Clark Subdivision**—*pop pl* ... UT-8
Ezra Creek—*stream* ... ID-8
Ezra Fork—*stream* ... NC-3
Ezra Mc Bench—*bench* ... UT-8
**Ezra (Pershing)**—*pop pl* ... IL-6
Ezra Run—*stream* ... WV-2
Ezras Dedground—*flat* ... TX-5
Ezras Flat—*flat* ... UT-8
E-Z-Way Shop Ctr—*locale* ... MA-1
Ezwkial Number One Rsvr—*reservoir* ... MT-8
Ezzell—*locale* ... TX-5
Ezzell Branch—*stream* (2) ... AL-4
Ezzell Bridge (historical)—*bridge* ... AL-4
Ezzell Camp—*locale* ... TX-5
Ezzell Cem—*cemetery* ... AL-4
Ezzell Ford—*locale* ... AL-4
Ezzell House—*hist pl* ... TX-5
Ezzell Oil Field—*oilfield* ... TX-5
Ezzell River Oil Field—*oilfield* ... TX-5
Ezzelltown—*locale* ... NC-3
E-2 Creek—*stream* ... MT-8
E-4 Extension Canal—*canal* ... NV-8
E-7 Ranch—*locale* ... WY-8

# F

F.A.A. and U.S. Airforce Reservation—military ... FL-3
Fnnberg Cem—cemetery ... WI-6
**Faal**—pop pl ... FM-9
Faalaaga—locale ... AS-9
Faalagiumu Point—cape ... AS-9
Faalefu—locale ... AS-9
Faalefu Rock—island ... AS-9
Faalogologotala Rock (Lions Head)—cape ... AS-9
Faalogo Stream—stream ... AS-9
Faanbiywol—cape ... FM-9
F A Anderson Lake Dam—dam ... MS-4
Faanikep ... FM-9
Faanipw ... FM-9
Faan Kacaw ... FM-9
Faasamene Cove—bay ... AS-9
Faasouga Point—cape ... AS-9
Faata—area ... GU-9
Faataaga Point—cape ... AS-9
Faatafa Rocks—island ... AS-9
Faatafe Stream—stream ... AS-9
Faata Springs—spring ... GU-9
Faa Tracking Station—other ... GA-3
Faay—bay ... FM-9
Faaye ... FM-9
Fabac Ranch—locale ... MT-8
Faben Point—cape ... WA-9
**Fabens**—pop pl ... TX-5
Fabens Bldg—hist pl ... MA-1
Fabens Dam—dam ... TX-5
Fabens Desert Chapel—church ... TX-5
Fabens Drain—canal ... TX-5
Fabens Intercepting Drain—canal ... TX-5
Faben's Point ... WA-9
Fabens Waste Channel—canal ... TX-5
Faber—locale ... AR-4
Faber—locale ... KY-4
Faber—locale ... VA-3
Faber Canyon—valley ... AZ-5
Faber Cove—bay ... FL-3
Faber Ferry—locale ... WA-9
Faber Hollow—valley ... WV-2
Faber Park—park ... KS-7
Faber Point—cape ... FL-3
Faber Rsvr—reservoir ... CO-8
Faber Sch—school ... MT-8
Faber Spring—spring ... AZ-5
Fabian And Bell Canal—canal ... CA-9
Fabian And Tyler Ditch—canal ... WY-8
Fabian Ditch—canal ... WY-8
Fabians ... PA-2
Fabick Heliport—airport ... MO-7
Fabing, Frederick, House—hist pl ... OH-6
Fabius ... AL-4
Fabius—locale ... AL-4
Fabius—locale ... MI-6
Fabius—locale ... MO-7
**Fabius**—pop pl ... NY-2
Fabius Brook—stream ... NY-2
Fabius Cave—cave ... AL-4
Fabius Ch—church ... MO-7
Fabius Creek ... MO-7
Fabius Island—island ... MO-7
Fabius River ... MO-7
Fabius River—stream ... MO-7
Fabius San Hilo Point ... MH-9
**Fabius (Town of)**—pop pl ... NY-2
Fabius Township—civil (3) ... MO-7
Fabius Township—fmr MCD ... IA-7
**Fabius (Township of)**—pop pl ... MI-6
Fable Hollow—valley ... MO-7
Fable Lake—lake ... MN-6
Fable Spring—spring ... UT-8
Fable Valley—valley ... UT-8
**Fabyan**—pop pl ... CT-1
**Fabyan**—pop pl ... NH-1
Fabyan For Preserve—forest ... IL-6
Fabyan House (2) ... NH-1
Fabyan Point—cape ... NH-1
Fabyan Villa—hist pl ... IL-6
F A Canyon—valley ... TX-5
Face Camp Branch—stream ... TN-4
Face Canyon (inundated)—valley ... UT-8
Face Mtn ... AZ-5
Face Mtn—summit ... AK-9
Face Mtn—summit ... AZ-5
Facenelli Ranch (reduced usage)—locale ... WY-8
Facer Creek—stream ... UT-8
Facer Lateral—canal ... ID-8
Face Rock—island ... OR-9
Face Rock—pillar ... AZ-5
Face Rock—pillar ... WI-6
Face Rock—summit ... NC-3
Face Rock—summit ... PA-2
Face Rock Overlook—locale ... PA-2
Facer's Store—hist pl ... OH-6
Face Run—stream ... PA-2
**Faceville**—pop pl ... GA-3
Faceville (CCD)—cens area ... GA-3
Faceville Landing—locale ... GA-3
Faceville Sch—school ... GA-3
Facey Gulch—valley ... CA-9
Facey Mine—mine ... CA-9
Facham, Unun En—bar ... FM-9
Facher Butte—summit ... WA-9
Fac Hill—summit ... NV-8
Fachno' ... FM-9
Fachnoog—summit ... FM-9
Fachounon—summit ... FM-9
Facht Homestead—locale ... CA-9
Facht Place—locale ... CA-9
Facich Bayou ... LA-4
Facieo Cem—cemetery ... TX-5
Facil—locale ... FL-3
Facilo, Point—cape ... MS-4
Facing Gut—stream ... NC-3
Facing Hills ... MA-1
Facing Hills—summit ... MA-1
Facing-hills Rock ... MA-1
Facing Point—cape ... NC-3
Facing Red Points—cape ... AZ-5
Facing Rock—summit ... MA-1
**Fackler**—pop pl ... AL-4
Fackler Pass—gap ... WY-8
Fackler Ranch—locale ... NE-7
**Fackrell Subdivision**—pop pl ... UT-8
Facpi—area ... GU-9
Facpi Island—island ... GU-9
Facpi Point—cape ... GU-9
Fact—locale ... KS-7
Fact Canyon Creek ... UT-8
**Factor**—pop pl ... PR-3
Factor (Barrio)—fmr MCD ... PR-3
Factor Butte ... UT-8
Factoria—post sta ... WA-9
Factors Row and Thiberge Buildings—hist pl ... LA-4
Factor State Wildlife Mngmt Area—park ... MN-6
Factory—locale ... TN-4
**Factory**—pop pl ... WV-2
Factory Bay—bay ... FL-3
Factory Bayou—stream ... TX-5
Factory Bench—bench ... UT-8
Factory Branch—stream ... NJ-2
Factory Branch—stream (2) ... NC-3
Factory Branch—stream ... OH-6
Factory Branch—stream (2) ... TN-4
Factory Bridge—hist pl ... PA-2
Factory Brook—stream ... CT-1
Factory Brook—stream (5) ... ME-1
Factory Brook—stream ... MA-1
Factory Brook—stream (2) ... NY-2
Factory Brook—stream ... RI-1
Factory Butte—summit (2) ... UT-8
Factory Butte Coal Mine—mine ... UT-8
Factory Cem—cemetery ... AL-4
Factory Cem—cemetery ... SC-3
Factory Cem—cemetery (2) ... TN-4
Factory Ch (historical)—church ... MS-4
Factory Creek—channel ... SC-3
Factory Creek—stream (2) ... AL-4
Factory Creek—stream (3) ... GA-3
Factory Creek—stream ... MO-7
Factory Creek—stream ... OH-6
Factory Creek—stream ... OK-5
Factory Creek—stream ... PA-2
Factory Creek—stream (2) ... TN-4
Factory Falls—falls ... PA-2
Factory Hill—locale ... VA-3
**Factory Hill**—pop pl ... PA-2
Factory Hill—summit ... WY-8
Factory Hill-Frog Bottom-Burns Bottom Hist Dist—hist pl ... MS-4
Factory Hollow—locale ... NY-2
**Factory Hollow**—pop pl ... MA-1
Factory Hollow—uninc pl ... MA-1
Factory Hollow—valley ... MO-7
Factory Hollow—valley ... TN-4
Factory Hollow Pond—reservoir ... MA-1
Factory Island—island ... ME-1
Factory Lake—reservoir ... MT-8
Factory Landing—locale ... NC-3
Factory Merchant Outlet Stores ... MO-7
Factory Outlet Mall - Orlando—locale ... FL-3
Factory Point—cape ... VA-3
Factory Point Cem—cemetery ... VT-1
Factory Pond ... CT-1
Factory Pond ... MA-1
Factory Pond—lake ... CT-1
Factory Pond—lake ... MA-1
Factory Pond—lake ... MO-7
Factory Pond—lake ... OH-6
Factory Pond—lake ... RI-1
Factory Pond—reservoir (2) ... MA-1
Factory Pond Dam—dam ... MA-1
Factory Post Office (historical)—building ... TN-4
Factory Sch—school ... NH-1
Factory Sch—school ... PA-2
Factory Sch (abandoned)—school ... PA-2
Factory Sch (historical)—school ... TN-4
Factory Shoals—bar ... GA-3
Factory Site—hist pl ... OH-6
Factory Spring—spring ... TN-4
Factory Street Dam ... RI-1
Factory Village ... MA-1
Factory Village ... NH-1
**Factory Village**—pop pl ... NY-2
**Factory Village (historical)**—pop pl ... MA-1
Factory Village Pond—reservoir ... MA-1
Factory Village Pond Dam—dam ... MA-1
Factoryville—locale ... PA-2
**Factoryville**—pop pl ... MI-6
**Factoryville**—pop pl ... NY-2
**Factoryville**—pop pl ... PA-2
Factoryville Borough—civil ... PA-2
Factoryville Sch—school ... MI-6
Factoryville Station—locale ... PA-2
Faculty Club—hist pl ... CA-9
Faculty Springs—spring ... AZ-5
Facus Springs—spring ... NE-7
Fada—locale ... TX-5
Fadang, I—bench ... MH-9
Fad Creek ... OR-9
Faddlen Lake—swamp ... MN-6
Fade Away Ridge—ridge ... NM-5
Fadeaway Spring—spring ... OR-9
Faden Slough—gut ... IL-6
Fader Draw—valley ... CO-8
Fader Rsvr—reservoir ... CO-8
Fader Spring—spring ... CO-8
Fades—locale ... PA-2
Fades Creek—stream ... PA-2
**Fadette**—pop pl ... AL-4
Fadette Church ... AL-4
Fadette Sch—school ... AL-4
Fadian—area ... GU-9
Fadian Point—summit ... GU-9
Fadler Airp—airport ... PA-2
Fadner Point—cape ... MI-6
Fadness Sch—school ... WI-6
Fad Shaft—mine ... NV-8
Faegre Prairie—area ... IA-7
Faehn State Public Shooting Area—park ... SD-7
Fafaga Point—cape ... AS-9
Fafai Beach—beach ... GU-9
Fafai Beach Site—hist pl ... GU-9
Fafalog—ridge ... GU-9
Fafiga Peak—summit ... AS-9
Fafnir, Mount—summit ... AK-9
Faga—locale ... AS-9
**Fagaalu**—pop pl ... AS-9
**Faga'alu**—pop pl ... AS-9
Fagaalu Stream—stream ... AS-9
Faga Cove—bay ... AS-9
Fagafue Bay—bay ... AS-9
Fagailiili Point—cape ... AS-9
**Fagaitua**—pop pl ... AS-9
Fagaitua Bay—bay ... AS-9
**Fagalea**—pop pl ... AS-9
Fagalea Point—cape ... AS-9
Fagalele Boys Sch—hist pl ... AS-9
Fagalele JHS—school ... AS-9
Fagaleoo Point—cape ... AS-9
**Fagalii**—pop pl ... AS-9
**Fagali'i**—pop pl ... AS-9
Fagall Branch—stream ... TN-4
Fagalua Cove—bay ... AS-9
**Fagamalo**—pop pl ... AS-9
Fagamalo Cove—bay ... AS-9
Fagamow—bay ... FM-9
Fagamutu—locale ... AS-9
Fagan ... KS-7
Fagan—locale ... CA-9
Fagan—locale ... GA-3
Fagan—locale ... KY-4
**Fagan**—pop pl ... NC-3
Fagan, Mount—summit ... AZ-5
Fagan Branch—stream ... KY-4
Fagan Canyon—valley ... CA-9
Fagan Cem—cemetery ... KS-7
Fagan Cem—cemetery (2) ... TN-4
Fagan Cem—cemetery ... TX-5
Fagan Creek—stream ... AL-4
Fagan Creek—stream ... AR-4
Fagan Creek—stream ... CA-9
Fagan Creek—stream ... ID-8
Fagan Creek—stream ... MO-7
Fagan Creek—stream ... OK-5
Fagan Creek—stream ... OR-9
**Faganeanea**—pop pl ... AS-9
Fagan Hollow—valley ... AL-4
Fagan Lake—lake (2) ... MI-6
Fagan Lake—lake ... TX-5
Fagan Lake—lake ... WA-9
Fagan Mill Creek—stream ... TN-4
Fagan Oil Field—oilfield ... TX-5
Fagan Reef—bar ... MI-6
Fagan Sch—school ... MO-7
Fagan Sch (historical)—school ... TN-4
Fagan Slough—stream ... CA-9
Fagan Spring—spring ... AL-4
Fagan Spring Cave—cave ... AL-4
Fagaone Point—cape ... AS-9
Fagaoo Point—cape ... AS-9
Faga Point—cape ... AS-9
Fagar Sch—school ... IL-6
**Fagasa**—pop pl ... AS-9
Fagasa Bay—bay ... AS-9
Fagasa Point—cape ... AS-9
**Fagatele**—pop pl ... AS-9
Fagatele Bay—bay ... AS-9
Fagatele Cove—bay ... AS-9
Fagatele Crater—crater ... AS-9
Fagatele Point—cape ... AS-9
Fagatiale Point—cape ... AS-9
**Fagatogo**—pop pl ... AS-9
Fagatuitui Cove—bay ... AS-9
Fagen Cem—cemetery ... MO-7
Fagen Lake—lake ... MN-6
Fagens Chapel—church ... TN-4
**Fagen Springs Estates (subdivision)**—pop pl ... AL-4
Fagerhaug Sch—school ... SD-7
Fagerland Private Airp—airport ... ND-7
Fagernes Ch—church ... WI-6
Fagerness Point—cape ... MN-6
Fages-De Anza Trail-Southern Emigrant Road—hist pl ... CA-9
Fages-Zalvidea Trails Marker—other ... CA-9
Fagg—locale ... VA-3
Faggart—locale ... NC-3
Faggarts ... NC-3
**Faggarts Crossroads**—pop pl ... NC-3
Faggerts ... NC-3
Fagg Hollow—valley ... VA-3
Fagg Lake ... WI-6
Faggot Hill—summit ... MA-1
Faggs Ranch—locale ... CA-9
Faggs Rsvr—reservoir ... CA-9
Fagilee Lake ... TX-5
Fagin—locale ... TN-4
Fagin Mtn—summit ... NV-8
Fagin Run—stream ... OH-6
Fagins Mills (historical)—locale ... AL-4
Fagin Spring—spring ... NV-8
Fagin Station ... TN-4
Fag Lake—lake ... MN-6
Faglea—lake ... TX-5
Fagley House—hist pl ... PA-2
Fagley Junior High School ... IN-6
Fagley Run—stream ... PA-2
Fagleysville—locale ... PA-2
Faglie Lake ... TX-5
Fagmow ... FM-9
**Fagot**—pop pl ... PR-3
Fagueyao—area ... GU-9
Fagundus—locale ... PA-2
Fagundus Corners ... PA-2
Fagundus Run—stream ... PA-2
**Fagus**—pop pl ... MO-7
Faha, John, House—hist pl ... KY-4
Fahan ... MH-9
Fahang Beach ... MH-9
Fahe Cabin—locale ... CA-9
Faherty Bridge—bridge ... MN-6
Faherty Lake—lake ... MN-6
Fahey Meadow—flat ... CA-9
Fahey Ranch—locale ... CA-9
Fahi Brook—stream ... ME-1
F A Hill Ranch—locale ... TX-5
Fahi Pond—lake ... ME-1
Fahkahatchee Bay ... FL-3
Fah-Kah-Hatchee River ... FL-3
Fahkahnatcheea River ... FL-3
Fahka Union Bay ... FL-3
Fahl Ditch—canal ... IN-6
Fahlgren Coulee—valley ... MT-8
Fahlgren Gulch—valley ... MT-8
Fahlun Cem—cemetery ... MN-6
Fahlun Ch—church ... MN-6
**Fahlun (Township of)**—pop pl ... MN-6
Fahnestock Corners—locale ... NY-2
Fahnestock Hill—summit ... PA-2
Fahnestock Run—stream ... PA-2
Fahnestock Ski Slope—other ... NY-2
Fa-Ho-Lo Park—park ... MI-6
Fahra Union Bay ... FL-3
Fahrbach Lake Dam—dam ... MS-4
Fahrens Creek—stream ... CA-9
Fahrman ... KS-7
Fahrney Branch—stream ... MD-2
Fahrney Keedy Mem. Home—post sta ... MD-2
Fahrney Point—cape ... WI-6
Fahul Lake—lake ... MN-6
Fahys Creek—stream ... OR-9
Fahys Lake—lake ... OR-9
Faia, Unun En—bar ... FM-9
Faiaiulu Point—cape ... AS-9
Faiava—locale ... AS-9
Faibus Point ... MH-9
Faibus-san-hilo ... MH-9
Faibus San Hilo Point ... MH-9
Faibus Sanpapa ... MH-9
Faibus San Papa Point ... MH-9
Faibusu San Hiro Saki ... MH-9
Faicho—spring ... FM-9
Faichopuech—locale ... FM-9
Faichu—well ... FM-9
Faichuk—island ... FM-9
Faichuk JHS—school ... FM-9
Faiferlick State Public Shooting Area—park ... SD-7
Faiga Ridge—ridge ... AS-9
Faigatoa Stream—stream ... AS-9
Faile Creek ... CO-8
Failer Cem—cemetery ... MO-7
Failer Creek—stream ... WY-8
Failes Creek—stream ... CO-8
Failetown—locale ... AL-4
Fail (historical)—locale ... AL-4
Failing Creek—stream ... MI-6
Failing Hill—summit ... NY-2
Failing Lake—lake ... IN-6
Faille Lake—lake ... MN-6
**Failolo**—pop pl ... AS-9
Failor Creek—stream ... OR-9
Fail Ranch—locale ... MT-8
Fails Lookout Tower—locale ... TX-5
Failure Canyon—valley ... UT-8
Faiman Spring—spring ... OR-9
Faimulivai Marsh—swamp ... AS-9
Fain—locale ... GA-3
Fain Branch—stream ... TN-4
Fain Branch—stream ... TX-5
Fain Cabin—locale ... NC-3
Fain Cem—cemetery (2) ... GA-3
Fain Cem—cemetery (3) ... TN-4
Fain Compressor Station—other ... TX-5
Fain Cove—valley ... NC-3
Fain Cove—valley ... TN-4
Fain Creek—stream ... GA-3
Fain Ford—locale ... NC-3
Fain Hill—summit ... TN-4
Fain Hollow—valley ... TN-4
Fain House—hist pl ... TX-5
Fain Lake—lake ... NM-5
Fain Mtn—summit ... AZ-5
Fain Mtn—summit ... CA-3
Fain Mtn—summit ... NC-3
Fain Plantation—hist pl ... TN-4
Fain Ranch—locale ... TX-5
Fains Branch ... AL-4
Fain Sch—school ... GA-3
Fain Sch—school ... TX-5
Fains Creek Forge ... AL-4
Fains Island ... TN-4
Fains Post Office (historical)—building ... TN-4
Fain Spring—spring ... AZ-5
Fain Spring Creek—stream ... TN-4
Fains Shoals—bar ... TN-4
Fain Tank—reservoir (2) ... AZ-5
Faint Hope Cem—cemetery ... TN-4
Fainu—bar ... FM-9
**Fair**—pop pl ... NC-3
Fair Acres ... IN-6
Fairacres ... TN-4
**Fair Acres**—pop pl ... IN-6
**Fairacres**—pop pl ... NM-5
**Fair Acres**—pop pl (2) ... PA-2
**Fair Acres**—pop pl ... TN-4
Fair Acres—uninc pl ... TN-4
Fair Acres Branch—stream ... TX-5
Fairacres (CCD)—cens area ... NM-5
Fair Acres Geriatric Center—building ... PA-2
Fairacres Golf Club—other ... OH-6
**Fair Acres (subdivision)**—pop pl ... TN-4
Fairall Ch—church ... PA-2
Fairangel Creek—stream ... AK-9
Fair Ave Sch—school ... CA-9
Fairbank ... IN-6
**Fairbank**—pop pl ... AZ-5
**Fairbank**—pop pl ... IA-7
**Fairbank**—pop pl ... MD-2
**Fairbank**—pop pl ... PA-2
Fairbank (historical)—locale ... SD-7
Fairbank Island—island ... MI-6
Fairbank Point—cape ... CA-9
Fairbank Point—cape ... MI-6
Fairbank Post Office (historical)—building ... SD-7
Fairbank RR Station—building ... AZ-5
Fairbank Run—stream ... PA-2
Fairbanks ... PA-2
Fairbanks—locale ... AR-4
Fairbanks—locale ... CA-9
Fairbanks—locale ... IL-6
Fairbanks—locale (2) ... KY-4
Fairbanks—locale ... NM-5
Fairbanks—locale ... OR-9
Fairbanks—locale ... WA-9
Fairbanks—locale ... WV-2
**Fairbanks**—pop pl ... AK-9
**Fairbanks**—pop pl ... FL-3
**Fairbanks**—pop pl ... GA-3
**Fairbanks**—pop pl ... IN-6
**Fairbanks**—pop pl ... LA-4
**Fairbanks**—pop pl ... ME-1
**Fairbanks**—pop pl ... MN-6
**Fairbanks**—pop pl ... PA-2
**Fairbanks**—pop pl ... TX-5
Fairbanks, Franklin, House—hist pl ... VT-1
Fairbanks, J. Leo, House—hist pl ... OR-9
Fairbanks, J. Leo, House—hist pl ... UT-8
Fairbanks, Morse and Company Bldg—hist pl ... IL-6
Fairbanks Airp—airport ... MO-7
Fairbanks Ave Sch—school ... CA-9
Fairbanks Canyon ... NV-8
Fairbanks Canyon—valley (2) ... NV-8
Fairbanks Cem—cemetery ... KS-7
Fairbank Sch—school ... MA-1
Fairbanks Child Care Center—school ... FL-3
Fairbanks Corner—locale ... RI-1
Fairbanks Corners—locale ... NY-2
Fairbanks Corners—locale ... PA-2
Fairbanks Country Club—locale ... AK-9
Fairbanks Creek—stream (2) ... AK-9
Fairbanks Creek—stream (2) ... NV-8
Fairbanks Creek—stream ... SD-7
Fairbanks Creek—stream ... WI-6
Fairbanks Creek Camp—locale ... AK-9
Fairbanks Crossing—locale ... UT-8
Fairbanks Draw—valley ... WY-8
Fairbanks Elem Sch—school (2) ... IN-6
Fairbanks Flats—hist pl ... WI-6
Fairbanks Gap—gap ... OR-9
Fairbanks Hill—summit ... MA-1
Fairbanks House—hist pl ... FL-3
Fairbanks House—hist pl ... MA-1
Fairbanks International Airp—airport ... AK-9
Fairbanks Lake—lake ... MI-6
Fairbanks Lake—lake (3) ... MN-6
Fairbanks Lateral—canal (2) ... CA-9
Fairbanks Lookout Tower—locale ... LA-4
Fairbanks Mills—locale ... VT-1
Fairbanks Mound—summit ... IN-6
**Fairbanks North Star (Borough)**—pop pl ... AK-9
Fairbanks-North Star (Census Subarea)—cens area ... AK-9
Fairbanks Oil Field—oilfield ... TX-5
Fairbanks Park—park ... AZ-5
Fairbanks Point—cape ... NY-2
Fairbanks Pond—lake ... ME-1
Fairbanks Pumping Station—other ... IL-6
Fairbanks Ranch—flat ... IL-6
Fairbanks Rsvr—reservoir ... NV-8
Fairbanks Sch—school ... MI-6
Fairbanks Sch—school (2) ... MO-7
Fairbanks School Number 105 ... IN-6
Fairbanks Shop Ctr—locale ... TN-4
Fairbanks Spring—spring (2) ... NV-8
Fairbanks Spring—spring ... OH-6
Fairbanks Springs ... NV-8
**Fairbanks (Town of)**—pop pl ... WI-6
**Fairbanks Township**—pop pl ... ND-7
**Fairbanks (Township of)**—pop pl ... IN-6
**Fairbanks (Township of)**—pop pl ... MI-6
**Fairbanks (Township of)**—pop pl ... MN-6
Fairbanks-Williams House—hist pl ... MA-1
Fairbank Township—civil ... SD-7
Fairbank Township—fmr MCD ... IA-7
Fairbault ... MN-6
Fairberry Windmill—locale ... TX-5
**Fair Bluff**—pop pl ... NC-3
Fair Bluff Elem Sch—school ... NC-3
Fair Bluff (Township of)—fmr MCD ... NC-3
**Fairborn**—pop pl ... OH-6
Fairborn Ch—church ... OH-6
Fairborn Plaza Shop Ctr—locale ... OH-6
Fair Branch Ch—church ... SC-3
Fairbrook—locale ... PA-2
**Fairbrook**—pop pl ... NC-3
**Fairbrook**—pop pl ... PA-2
Fair Brook—stream (2) ... IN-6
Fair Brook—stream ... VT-1
**Fairbrook Condominium**—pop pl ... UT-8
Fairbrook Country Club—locale ... MA-1
Fairbrook Sch—school ... OH-6
Fairbrother Bog—swamp ... ME-1
**Fairburn**—pop pl ... GA-3
**Fairburn**—pop pl ... SD-7
**Fairburn**—pop pl ... WI-6
Fairburn Ave Sch—school ... CA-9
Fairburn Cem—cemetery ... LA-4
Fairburn Cem—cemetery ... SD-7
Fairburn Cem—cemetery ... WI-6
Fairburn Commercial Hist Dist—hist pl ... GA-3
Fairburn Industrial Park—facility ... GA-3
Fairburn Mtn—summit ... CO-8
Fairburn-Union City (CCD)—cens area ... GA-3
**Fairbury**—pop pl ... IL-6
**Fairbury**—pop pl ... NE-7
Fairbury Cem—cemetery ... NE-7
Fairbury Public-Carnegie Library—hist pl ... NE-7
Fair Cem—cemetery ... AL-4
Fair Cem—cemetery ... IN-6
Fair Ch—church ... OK-5
**Fairchance**—pop pl (2) ... PA-2
Fairchance Borough—civil ... PA-2
Fairchance Furnace (40HS168)—hist pl ... TN-4
Fairchance-Georges HS—school ... PA-2
Fairchance-Georges Sch—school ... PA-2
Fairchance Iron Works ... PA-2
Fairchance Reservoir—dam ... PA-2
Fairchance Rsvr—reservoir ... PA-2
**Fairchester**—pop pl ... VA-3
Fairchild—locale ... GA-3
Fairchild—locale ... WA-9
Fairchild—other ... CA-9
**Fairchild**—pop pl ... WI-6
Fairchild, Mount—summit ... WA-9
Fairchild Afb Airp—airport ... WA-9
Fairchild Air Force Base—military ... WA-9
Fairchild Basin ... NY-2
Fairchild Branch—stream (2) ... KY-4
Fairchild Cem—cemetery (2) ... GA-3
Fairchild Cem—cemetery ... IL-6
Fairchild Cem—cemetery (2) ... MS-4
Fairchild Cem—cemetery ... NY-2
Fairchild Ch—church ... OH-6
Fairchild Chapel—church ... MI-6
Fairchild Creek—stream ... ID-8
Fairchild Creek—stream ... MI-6
Fairchild Creek—stream ... MS-4
Fairchild Creek—stream ... OR-9
Fairchild Creek—stream (3) ... WA-9
Fairchild Ditch—canal ... MT-8
Fairchild Draw—valley ... AZ-5
Fairchild Glacier—glacier ... WA-9
Fairchild Gulch—valley ... CA-9
Fairchild Gulch—valley ... ID-8
**Fairchild Heights Subdivision**—pop pl ... NC-3
Fairchild Lake—lake ... MI-6
Fairchild Mansion—hist pl ... NY-2
Fairchild Memorial Park—cemetery ... CT-1
Fairchild Mill ... MS-4
Fairchild Mill Pond (historical)—reservoir ... MS-4
Fairchild Mtn—summit ... CO-8
Fairchild Park—park ... NC-3
Fairchild Park—park ... TX-5
Fairchild Point—summit ... OR-9
Fairchild Pond—reservoir ... PA-2
Fairchild Pond—reservoir ... WI-6
Fairchild Ranch—locale ... AZ-5
Fairchild Ranch—locale ... NE-7
Fairchild Ranch—locale ... NM-5
Fairchilds—locale ... TX-5
Fairchilds Bend—bend ... MS-4
Fairchild Sch—school ... CA-9
Fairchild Sch—school ... FL-3
Fairchild Sch—school ... GA-3
Fairchild Sch—school ... IL-6
Fairchild Sch—school ... TX-5
Fairchilds Corners—locale ... NY-2
Fairchilds Creek—stream (2) ... MS-4
Fairchilds Creek—stream ... TX-5

Fairchilds Creek Oil Field—oilfield MS-4
Fairchilds Crossroads—locale MS-4
Fairchilds Dam PA-2
Fairchilds Island Number 114—island MS-4
Fairchilds Mill (historical)—locale MS-4
Fairchild Spring—spring (2) OR-9
Fairchild Springs—spring MS-4
Fairchild State For—forest TX-5
Fairchild Swamp—swamp CA-9
**Fairchild (Town of)**—pop pl WI-6
Fairchild Tropical Garden—park FL-3
Fairchild Well—well AZ-5
Fairchild-Wheeler Park—park CT-1
Fairchild Winery—hist pl OK-5
Faircloth—locale LA-4
Faircloth Cem—cemetery AL-4
Faircloth Lake—reservoir NC-3
Faircloth Lake Dam—dam NC-3
Faircloth Lakes—reservoir FL-3
Faircloth Plantation—locale SC-3
Faircloth Ranch—locale NM-5
Faircloth Well—locale NM-5
Fairclough Cem—cemetery MO-7
Fairclough Industrial Park (subdivision)—locale UT-8
Faircourt Shop Ctr—locale AL-4
Fair Creek—stream IN-6
Fair Creek—stream MS-4
Faircrest Park—park OH-6
Fairdale—locale OR-9
Fairdale—locale TX-5
**Fairdale**—pop pl AL-4
**Fairdale**—pop pl IL-6
**Fairdale**—pop pl IN-6
**Fairdale**—pop pl KY-4
**Fairdale**—pop pl NY-2
**Fairdale**—pop pl ND-7
**Fairdale**—pop pl OH-6
**Fairdale**—pop pl (2) PA-2
**Fairdale**—pop pl WV-2
Fairdale Cem—cemetery IN-6
Fairdale Cem—cemetery NE-7
Fairdale Ch—church NE-7
Fairdale Hill—summit ME-1
Fairdale HS—school KY-4
Fairdale-Logan—fmr MCD NE-7
Fairdale Mineral Spring—spring OR-9
Fairdale Sch—school NE-7
Fairdale Sch—school WY-8
Fairdale Slough—lake ND-7
Fairdale Slough Natl Waterfowl Production Area—park ND-7
Fairdealing—locale KY-4
**Fairdealing**—pop pl MO-7
Fairdealing (CCD)—cens area KY-4
Fair Elementary School MS-4
Fairelond—hist pl KY-4
Faires, F. C., House—hist pl TX-5
Faires-Bell House—hist pl TX-5
**Fairey**—pop pl SC-3
Fairfax (2) IN-6
Fairfax—hist pl TN-4
Fairfax—locale NC-3
Fairfax—locale WA-9
Fairfax—locale WV-2
**Fairfax**—pop pl CA-9
**Fairfax**—pop pl DE-2
**Fairfax**—pop pl GA-3
**Fairfax**—pop pl (3) IN-6
**Fairfax**—pop pl IA-7
**Fairfax**—pop pl KS-7
**Fairfax**—pop pl LA-4
**Fairfax**—pop pl MI-6
**Fairfax**—pop pl MN-6
**Fairfax**—pop pl MO-7
**Fairfax**—pop pl (2) OH-6
**Fairfax**—pop pl OK-5
**Fairfax**—pop pl SC-3
**Fairfax**—pop pl SD-7
**Fairfax**—pop pl VT-1
Fairfax—post sta CA-9
Fairfax—uninc pl KS-7
Fairfax, Lake—reservoir VA-3
**Fairfax Acres**—pop pl VA-3
Fairfax Arms—hist pl VA-3
Fairfax Bridge—hist pl WA-9
Fairfax Bridge (Toll)—other MO-7
Fairfax (CCD)—cens area OK-5
Fairfax (CCD)—cens area SC-3
Fairfax Cem—cemetery AL-4
Fairfax Cem—cemetery IA-7
Fairfax Cem—cemetery OK-5
Fairfax Ch—church IN-6
Fairfax Circle—locale VA-3
Fairfax City Lake—reservoir OK-5
**Fairfax Civil Township**—pop pl SD-7
**Fairfax (County)**—pop pl VA-3
Fairfax County Courthouse—building VA-3
Fairfax County Courthouse—hist pl VA-3
Fairfax County Courthouse and Jail (Boundary Increase)—hist pl VA-3
Fairfax Covered Bridge—hist pl VT-1
Fairfax Creek—stream CA-9
Fairfax Elem Sch—school KS-7
**Fairfax Falls**—pop pl VT-1
Fairfax Farm—locale TN-4
**Fairfax Farms**—pop pl VA-3
**Fairfax Farms (subdivision)**—pop pl DE-2
**Fairfax Forest**—pop pl VA-3
Fairfax Gin—other CA-9
Fairfax Hall—hist pl VA-3
Fairfax Hall Sch—school VA-3
**Fairfax Heights**—pop pl TN-4
**Fairfax Heights**—pop pl VA-3
**Fairfax Heights (subdivision)**—pop pl NC-3
**Fairfax Hills**—pop pl VA-3
**Fairfax Hills (subdivision)**—pop pl NC-3
Fairfax (historical)—locale KS-7
Fairfax Hollow—valley WV-2
Fairfax Hosp—hospital VA-3
Fairfax HS—school CA-9
**Fairfax (ind. city)**—pop pl VA-3
Fairfax Industrial District KS-7
Fairfax Lake—lake SD-7
Fairfax Lake Dam—dam SD-7
Fairfax (Magisterial District)—fmr MCD WV-2
Fairfax Memory Garden—cemetery VA-3
Fairfax Municipal Airp—airport KS-7
Fairfax Park—park TX-5
**Fairfax Park**—pop pl VA-3
Fairfax Pond—reservoir WV-2
Fairfax Sanitarium—hospital WA-9
Fairfax Sch—school (2) CA-9
Fairfax Sch—school NE-7
Fairfax Sch—school OH-6
Fairfax Shop Ctr—locale DE-2
Fairfax State Rec Area—park IN-6
**Fairfax Station (RR name for Fairfax Station)**—pop pl VA-3
Fairfax Stone—locale WV-2
Fairfax Stone Site—hist pl WV-2
**Fairfax (subdivision)**—pop pl AL-4
**Fairfax (Town of)**—pop pl VT-1
Fairfax Township—civil SD-7
Fairfax Township—fmr MCD IA-7
**Fairfax Township**—pop pl KS-7
Fairfax Township (historical)—civil SD-7
**Fairfax (Township of)**—pop pl MN-6
**Fairfax Villa**—pop pl VA-3
**Fairfax Village**—pop pl DC-2
Fairfax Villa Sch—school VA-3
**Fairfax Woods**—pop pl VA-3
**Fairfax Woods (subdivision)**—pop pl NC-3
Fairfield (3) IN-6
Fairfield MA-1
Fairfield NJ-2
Fairfield OH-6
Fairfield WV-2
Fairfield—CDP NJ-2
Fairfield—fmr MCD NE-7
Fairfield—hist pl VA-3
Fairfield—locale AR-4
Fairfield—locale IL-6
Fairfield—locale KY-4
Fairfield—locale MN-6
Fairfield—locale NY-2
Fairfield—locale OR-9
Fairfield—locale TN-4
Fairfield—other OH-6
Fairfield—other PA-2
**Fairfield**—pop pl (4) AL-4
**Fair Field**—pop pl AR-4
**Fairfield**—pop pl AR-4
**Fairfield**—pop pl CA-9
**Fairfield**—pop pl (2) CT-1
**Fairfield**—pop pl DE-2
**Fairfield**—pop pl FL-3
**Fairfield**—pop pl GA-3
**Fairfield**—pop pl ID-8
**Fairfield**—pop pl IL-6
**Fairfield**—pop pl IN-6
**Fairfield**—pop pl IA-7
**Fairfield**—pop pl KY-4
**Fairfield**—pop pl ME-1
**Fairfield**—pop pl (3) MD-2
**Fairfield**—pop pl MI-6
**Fairfield**—pop pl MS-4
**Fairfield**—pop pl MT-8
**Fairfield**—pop pl NE-7
**Fairfield**—pop pl NJ-2
**Fairfield**—pop pl NY-2
**Fairfield**—pop pl (4) NC-3
**Fairfield**—pop pl ND-7
**Fairfield**—pop pl (2) OH-6
**Fairfield**—pop pl OR-9
**Fairfield**—pop pl (3) PA-2
**Fairfield**—pop pl (4) TN-4
**Fairfield**—pop pl (2) TX-5
**Fairfield**—pop pl UT-8
**Fairfield**—pop pl (2) VT-1
**Fairfield**—pop pl (2) VA-3
**Fairfield**—pop pl WA-9
**Fairfield**—pop pl WI-6
Fairfield—uninc pl FL-3
Fairfield—uninc pl SC-3
Fairfield, Mount—summit AK-9
**Fairfield Acres**—pop pl TN-4
**Fairfield Acres Subdivision**—pop pl UT-8
Fairfield Addition MI-6
Fairfield Airp—airport MS-4
Fairfield Ave Hist Dist—hist pl KY-4
Fairfield Baptist Ch TN-4
Fairfield Baptist Ch—church TN-4
Fairfield Bar CT-1
Fairfield Bar—bar OR-9
Fairfield Bay—bay AR-4
**Fairfield Bay**—pop pl AR-4
Fairfield Beach—beach (2) CT-1
**Fairfield Beach**—pop pl OH-6
Fairfield Bldg—hist pl OH-6
Fairfield Borough—civil PA-2
Fairfield Brook—stream MA-1
Fairfield Canal—canal CA-9
Fairfield Canal—canal NC-3
Fairfield Causeway—other IN-6
Fairfield (CCD)—cens area TX-5
Fairfield Cem—cemetery AR-4
Fairfield Cem—cemetery GA-3
Fairfield Cem—cemetery IL-6
Fairfield Cem—cemetery IN-6
Fairfield Cem—cemetery (4) IA-7
Fairfield Cem—cemetery KS-7
Fairfield Cem—cemetery KY-4
Fairfield Cem—cemetery ME-1
Fairfield Cem—cemetery MI-6
Fairfield Cem—cemetery (3) MS-4
Fairfield Cem—cemetery (2) NE-7
Fairfield Cem—cemetery NY-2
Fairfield Cem—cemetery (2) OH-6
Fairfield Cem—cemetery UT-8
Fairfield Cem—cemetery WA-9
Fairfield Cem—cemetery WI-6
Fairfield Center—locale PA-2
**Fairfield Center**—pop pl IN-6
**Fairfield Center**—pop pl ME-1
Fairfield Center Sch—school WI-6
Fairfield Ch AL-4
Fairfield Ch—church (3) AL-4
Fairfield Ch—church (8) GA-3
Fairfield Ch—church (5) IL-6
Fairfield Ch—church IN-6
Fairfield Ch—church KY-4
Fairfield Ch—church LA-4
Fairfield Ch—church (2) MS-4
Fairfield Ch—church MO-7
Fairfield Ch—church (3) NC-3
Fairfield Ch—church OH-6
Fairfield Ch—church OK-5
Fairfield Ch—church (2) PA-2
Fairfield Ch—church (4) SC-3
Fairfield Ch—church (2) TN-4
Fairfield Ch—church WV-2
Fairfield Ch (historical)—church AL-4
Fairfield Ch (historical)—church TN-4
Fairfield Ch of Christ AL-4
Fairfield Christian Union Ch—church AR-4
Fairfield City Hall—building AL-4
Fairfield City Hall—building IA-7
Fairfield CME Church AL-4
**Fairfield Commons (subdivision)**—pop pl MS-4
Fairfield Compact (census name Fairfield)—other ME-1
**Fairfield Condominium**—pop pl UT-8
Fairfield Country Day Sch—school CT-1
**Fairfield (County)**—pop pl OH-6
**Fairfield (County)**—pop pl SC-3
Fairfield County Courthouse—hist pl CT-1
**Fairfield County (in PMSA 1160,1930, 5760,8040)**—pop pl CT-1
Fairfield County Jail—hist pl CT-1
Fairfield Court Sch—school VA-3
Fairfield Creek MN-6
Fairfield Creek—stream MN-6
Fairfield Creek—stream NE-7
Fairfield Creek—stream WY-8
**Fairfield Crest**—pop pl DE-2
Fairfield District Sch—hist pl UT-8
Fairfield Ditch—canal IN-6
Fairfield Ditch No 1—canal IL-6
Fairfield Drive Ch—church FL-3
Fairfield Dutch Reformed Church—hist pl NJ-2
Fairfield Elem Sch—school KS-7
**Fairfield Estates Subdivision**—pop pl UT-8
Fairfield Falls—falls NC-3
**Fairfield Farm Estates Subdivision**—pop pl UT-8
**Fairfield Farms**—pop pl DE-2
**Fairfield Farms**—pop pl NY-2
Fairfield First Baptist Ch—church AL-4
Fairfield First United Methodist Ch—church AL-4
**Fairfield Gardens**—pop pl NY-2
Fairfield Glade—locale TN-4
Fairfield Glade Post Office—building TN-4
Fairfield Grange—locale OR-9
Fairfield Grange Hall—building KS-7
Fairfield Greenville Cem—cemetery IL-6
Fairfield Gulch—valley CO-8
**Fairfield Harbor**—pop pl NC-3
**Fairfield Heights**—pop pl PA-2
**Fairfield Highlands**—pop pl AL-4
Fairfield Highlands Baptist Ch—church AL-4
Fairfield Highlands Ch of Christ—church AL-4
Fairfield Highlands Presbyterian Ch—church AL-4
Fairfield Hill—summit ME-1
Fairfield Hill—summit (2) WY-8
Fairfield Hist Dist—hist pl CT-1
Fairfield Hist Dist—hist pl LA-4
Fairfield Hist Dist—hist pl NC-3
Fairfield (historical)—locale (2) AL-4
Fairfield (historical)—locale KS-7
Fairfield (historical)—locale MS-4
**Fairfield (historical)**—pop pl MO-7
Fairfield HS—school AL-4
Fairfield HS—school CA-9
Fairfield HS—school IA-7
Fairfield HS—school KS-7
Fairfield Inn—hist pl NC-3
Fairfield Inn—hist pl PA-2
Fairfield JHS—school IN-6
Fairfield JHS—school IA-7
Fairfield JHS—school VA-3
Fairfield Junior-Senior HS—school IN-6
**Fairfield Knolls**—pop pl MD-2
Fairfield Lake—reservoir (3) NC-3
Fairfield Lake Dam—dam (2) NC-3
Fairfield Landing—locale VA-3
Fairfield (Magisterial District)—fmr MCD (2) VA-3
Fairfield Mall—locale MA-1
Fairfield Manor—hist pl IN-6
Fairfield Memorial Hosp—hospital SC-3
Fairfield Memorial Park—cemetery CT-1
Fairfield Mine—mine CO-8
Fairfield Missionary Baptist Ch—church MS-4
Fairfield North Sch—school OH-6
Fairfield Oil Field—oilfield TX-5
**Fairfield Park (subdivision)**—pop pl NC-3
Fairfield Peak—summit CA-9
Fairfield Plantation—hist pl SC-3
**Fairfield Plantation (subdivision)**—pop pl NC-3
Fairfield Plaza (Shop Ctr)—locale FL-3
Fairfield P.O. (historical)—locale MS-4
Fairfield Point—cape GA-3
Fairfield Pond—lake MA-1
Fairfield Pond—lake NY-2
Fairfield Pond—lake VT-1
Fairfield Post Office (historical)—building TN-4
Fairfield Presbyterian Ch—church AL-4
Fairfield Public Library—hist pl IA-7
Fairfield Public Use Area—locale MO-7
Fairfield Rice Mill Chimney—hist pl SC-3
Fairfield Ridge—ridge NC-3
Fairfield River—stream VT-1
Fairfield Saint Sch—school VT-1
Fairfields Cem—cemetery VA-3
Fairfields Ch—church VA-3
Fairfield Sch—school (2) CA-9
Fairfield Sch—school FL-3
Fairfield Sch—school IL-6
Fairfield Sch—school LA-4
Fairfield Sch—school ME-1
Fairfield Sch—school MO-7
Fairfield Sch—school NY-2
Fairfield Sch—school ND-7
Fairfield Sch—school (2) OR-9
Fairfield Sch—school (2) PA-2
Fairfield Sch—school WV-2
Fairfield Sch—school WI-6
Fairfield Sch (historical)—school (2) AL-4
Fairfield Sch (historical)—school MS-4
Fairfield Sch (historical)—school (2) TN-4
Fairfield School TN-4
Fairfield Seep—stream NE-7
Fairfield Shopping Mall—locale MA-1
Fairfield Site—hist pl VA-3
Fairfields Sch—school VA-3
Fairfield Stadium—other WV-2
Fairfield State For—forest NY-2
Fairfield State Hosp—hospital CT-1
Fairfield Station—locale PA-2
Fairfield Station—locale VT-1
Fairfield Station (historical)—building UT-8
**Fairfield (subdivision)**—pop pl NC-3
**Fairfield (subdivision)**—pop pl TN-4
**Fairfield Subdivision**—pop pl UT-8
Fairfield-Suisun (CCD)—cens area CA-9
Fairfield Town Hall—building ND-7
**Fairfield (Town of)**—pop pl ME-1
**Fairfield (Town of)**—pop pl NY-2
**Fairfield (Town of)**—pop pl VT-1
**Fairfield (Town of)**—pop pl WI-6
Fairfield Township ND-7
Fairfield Township—civil PA-2
Fairfield Township—fmr MCD (6) IA-7
**Fairfield Township**—pop pl KS-7
**Fairfield Township**—pop pl MO-7
**Fairfield Township**—pop pl (2) NE-7
**Fairfield Township**—pop pl ND-7
**Fairfield Township**—pop pl SD-7
Fairfield Township Cem—cemetery (2) IA-7
Fairfield (Township of)—fmr MCD NC-3
**Fairfield (Township of)**—pop pl IL-6
**Fairfield (Township of)**—pop pl (3) IN-6
**Fairfield (Township of)**—pop pl (2) MI-6
**Fairfield (Township of)**—pop pl (2) MN-6
**Fairfield (Township of)**—pop pl (2) NJ-2
**Fairfield (Township of)**—pop pl (7) OH-6
**Fairfield (Township of)**—pop pl (3) PA-2
Fairfield Township Works I—hist pl OH-6
Fairfield Union Special Ditch—canal IL-6
Fairfield Univ—school CT-1
**Fairfield Village**—pop pl AL-4
Fairfield Village (Shop Ctr)—locale FL-3
Fairfield Waterworks—other IL-6
Fairfield West Sch—school OH-6
Fairfield Woods Sch—school CT-1
Fair Fight IN-6
**Fairfiled (Greene Po)**—pop pl (2) PA-2
**Fairfiled Terrace**—pop pl SC-3
**Fairford**—pop pl AL-4
Fairford Fire Tower—locale AL-4
Fairford Landing AL-4
Fairford Sch—school AL-4
Fairford Sch—school CA-9
Fairfords Landing AL-4
**Fairforest**—pop pl SC-3
Fair Forest Camp—locale KY-4
Fairforest Cem—cemetery SC-3
Fair Forest Ch—church SC-3
Fairforest Creek—stream SC-3
Fair Forest (Fairforest) SC-3
**Fairforest (Fair Forest)**—pop pl SC-3
**Fairforest Finishing Plant**—pop pl SC-3
Fair Forest Hotel—hist pl SC-3
Fair Garden—locale TN-4
Fair Garden Cem—cemetery TN-4
Fair Garden Elementary School TN-4
Fair Garden Sch—school TN-4
**Fair Gate**—pop pl FL-3
Fair Glacier—glacier CO-8
Fairglade Sch—school FL-3
Fairglen Elem Sch—school FL-3
**Fairgo**—pop pl MD-2
**Fairgrange**—pop pl IL-6
**Fair Grange (Fairgrange)**—pop pl IL-6
**Fairgreen Acres**—pop pl MD-2
Fairground CT-1
Fair Ground—locale IA-7
Fairground—locale IA-7
Fairground—other NM-5
**Fairground**—pop pl MS-4
**Fairground**—pop pl VT-1
Fairground Cem—cemetery GA-3
Fairground Ch—church GA-3
Fairground Hill—summit PA-2
Fairground Park—park (2) MO-7
Fairground Pond—lake TN-4
Fairground Post Office (historical)—building MS-4
Fairgrounds ID-8
Fair Grounds IN-6
Fair Grounds ME-1
Fair Grounds MO-7
**Fairgrounds**—pop pl FL-3
**Fair Grounds**—pop pl NY-2
**Fair Grounds**—pop pl OR-9
**Fair Grounds**—pop pl PA-2
Fair Grounds—uninc pl KY-4
Fair Grounds—uninc pl LA-4
Fairgrounds—uninc pl TN-4
Fairgrounds—uninc pl UT-8
Fairgrounds Cem—cemetery TX-5
Fairground Sch—school IL-6
Fairground Sch—school KS-7
Fairground Sch—school WI-6
Fair Ground Sch (historical)—school TN-4
Fairgrounds Creek—stream AR-4
Fairgrounds Elem Sch—school IA-7
Fairgrounds Park—park IL-6
Fairgrounds Park—park TN-4
Fairgrounds Sch—school PA-2
Fairgrounds Station Post Office—building UT-8
Fairgrounds Substation—other CA-9
Fairground Street Bridge—hist pl MS-4
**Fairground Subdivision**—pop pl MS-4
Fairgrove MO-7
**Fairgrove**—pop pl MI-6
**Fair Grove**—pop pl MO-7
**Fair Grove**—pop pl NC-3
**Fairgrove**—pop pl NC-3
Fairgrove Airp—airport NC-3
Fairgrove Ave Hist Dist—hist pl MI-6
Fairgrove Branch—stream MO-7
Fairgrove Ch—church MI-6
Fairgrove Ch—church NC-3
Fair Grove Ch—church NC-3
Fair Grove Methodist Church Cemetery—hist pl NC-3
Fair Grove Mound—summit MO-7
Fairgrove Sch NC-3
Fairgrove Sch—school CA-9
Fairgrove Sch—school NC-3
Fair Grove Sch—school NC-3
Fair Grove Sch (historical)—school MO-7
**Fairgrove (Township of)**—pop pl MI-6
Fair Harbor—locale WA-9
**Fair Harbor**—pop pl NY-2
Fair Haven CT-1
Fair Haven IL-6
Fair Haven MD-2
Fairhaven MO-7
Fairhaven NJ-2
Fair Haven—CDP VT-1
Fair Haven—other NY-2
**Fairhaven**—pop pl AK-9
**Fairhaven**—pop pl CA-9
**Fair Haven**—pop pl CT-1
**Fairhaven**—pop pl IL-6
**Fairhaven**—pop pl MD-2
**Fair Haven**—pop pl MD-2
**Fairhaven**—pop pl MA-1
**Fair Haven**—pop pl MI-6
**Fairhaven**—pop pl MN-6
**Fairhaven**—pop pl MS-4
**Fair Haven**—pop pl MO-7
**Fair Haven**—pop pl NJ-2
**Fair Haven**—pop pl (2) NY-2
**Fairhaven**—pop pl OH-6
**Fair Haven**—pop pl VT-1
**Fair Haven**—pop pl VA-3
**Fairhaven**—pop pl VA-3
Fairhaven—post sta WA-9
Fair Haven—uninc pl PA-2
Fairhaven Baptist Ch—church MS-4
Fairhaven Bay NY-2
Fairhaven Bay—lake MA-1
Fair Haven Beach State Park—park NY-2
Fairhaven Brook MA-1
Fair Haven Camp—locale MI-6
Fair Haven Campsite—locale AL-4
Fair Haven Cem—cemetery AR-4
Fairhaven Cem—cemetery MO-7
Fairhaven Cem—cemetery TX-5
**Fair Haven Center**—pop pl VT-1
Fair Haven Center Sch—school IL-6
Fair Haven Ch—church (2) AL-4
Fair Haven Ch—church GA-3
Fair-Haven Ch—church GA-3
Fairhaven Ch—church IN-6
Fair Haven Ch—church (2) IN-6
Fairhaven Ch—church MD-2
Fairhaven Ch—church MI-6
Fairhaven Ch—church MS-4
Fairhaven Ch—church NE-7
Fair Haven Ch—church (2) NC-3
Fairhaven Ch—church OH-6
Fair Haven Ch—church SC-3
Fair Haven Ch—church WV-2
Fair Haven Childrens Home—building SC-3
Fairhaven Cliffs—cliff MD-2
Fairhaven Creek—stream AK-9
Fairhaven Ditch—canal AK-9
Fairhaven Ditch—hist pl AK-9
Fair Haven East CT-1
**Fair Haven East**—pop pl CT-1
Fair Haven Flour Mill—hist pl MN-6
Fair Haven Green Hist Dist—hist pl VT-1
**Fairhaven Heights**—pop pl PA-2
Fair Haven Hill MA-1
Fairhaven Hill—summit MA-1
Fairhaven Hist Dist—hist pl WA-9
Fairhaven (historical)—locale KS-7
Fair Haven Home—building MI-6
Fairhaven Home for Girls—building CA-9
Fairhaven HS—hist pl MA-1
Fairhaven HS—school MA-1
Fairhaven Library—hist pl WA-9
Fairhaven Memorial Park (Cemetery)—cemetery CA-9
Fairhaven Mission—church IN-6
Fairhaven MS—school WA-9
**Fairhaven-on-the-Bay**—pop pl MD-2
Fairhaven Park—park WA-9
Fairhaven Plantation House—hist pl LA-4
Fairhaven Plaza (Shop Ctr)—locale MA-1
Fairhaven Pond MA-1
Fair Haven Reach—channel NJ-2
Fair Haven Rest Home—building MI-6
**Fairhaven (Rolph)**—pop pl CA-9
Fair Havens Ch—church TN-4
Fairhaven Sch—school (2) CA-9
Fairhaven Sch—school IL-6
Fair Haven Sch—school MI-6
Fair Haven Sch—school NJ-2
Fairhaven Sch—school OR-9
Fairhaven Sch—school PA-2
Fairhaven Townhall—building MA-1
Fairhaven Town Hall—hist pl MA-1
**Fairhaven (Town of)**—pop pl MA-1
Fair Haven Township NJ-2
**Fairhaven (Township of)**—pop pl IL-6
**Fairhaven (Township of)**—pop pl MI-6
**Fair Haven (Township of)**—pop pl MN-6
Fairhead Ranch—locale NE-7
Fairhill PA-2
Fairhill—locale MS-4
Fair Hill—locale VA-3
**Fair Hill**—pop pl MD-2
**Fairhill**—pop pl PA-2
**Fair Hill**—pop pl PA-2
**Fair Hill**—pop pl VA-3
Fairhill—uninc pl PA-2
Fair Hill Cem—cemetery MS-4
Fairhill Cem—cemetery PA-2
Fair Hill Cem—cemetery PA-2
Fair Hill Ch—church MS-4
Fair Hill Ch—church OK-5
Fairhill Junction—uninc pl PA-2
**Fairhill Manor**—pop pl NH-1
Fair Hill Plantation (historical)—locale AL-4
Fair Hill Race Track—other MD-2
**Fair Hills**—pop pl PA-2
Fairhill Sch—school PA-2
Fair Hill Sch (historical)—school PA-2
Fairhill Square—park PA-2
**Fairhills (subdivision)**—pop pl TN-4
Fairhill Swamp—swamp NH-1
Fairholm—locale WA-9
Fairhome Sch—school OH-6
Fairhope—locale AL-4
Fairhope—locale GA-3
**Fairhope**—pop pl AL-4
**Fairhope**—pop pl OH-6
**Fairhope**—pop pl (2) PA-2
Fairhope-Arnold City—CDP PA-2
Fairhope Ave Baptist Church AL-4
Fairhope Baptist Church AL-4
Fairhope Bayfront District—hist pl AL-4
Fairhope Bluff—cliff MS-4
Fairhope (CCD)—cens area AL-4
Fairhope Cem—cemetery KS-7
Fairhope Ch—church AL-4
Fairhope Ch—church MS-4
Fair Hope Ch—church SC-3
Fairhope Christian Ch—church AL-4
Fairhope Colony Cem—cemetery AL-4
Fairhope Division—civil AL-4
Fairhope Elementary and Junior High School AL-4
Fairhope Elem Sch—school AL-4
Fairhope HS—school AL-4
Fairhope Memorial Gardens—cemetery AL-4
Fairhope MS—school AL-4
Fairhope Municipal Airp—airport AL-4
Fairhope Municipal Park—park AL-4
Fairhope Plantation (historical)—locale AL-4
Fairhope Public Library—building AL-4
Fair Hope School (Abandoned)—locale NE-7
**Fairhope (Township of)**—pop pl PA-2
Fairhope Yacht Club—other AL-4
Fairhurst Chapel—church OH-6
**Fairidge**—pop pl MD-2
**Fairindale**—pop pl AR-4
Fairington Cem—cemetery AL-4
Fairington Cem—cemetery VT-1
Fair Island—island AK-9
Fair Island—island MD-2
Fair Island Canal—canal MD-2
Fair Isle FL-3
**Fairknoll**—pop pl MD-2
Fair Lake—lake (2) MI-6
Fair Lake—lake SC-3
Fairland KS-7
Fairland WI-6
Fairland—locale MD-2
Fairland—locale MI-6
Fairland—locale MN-6
Fairland—locale PA-2
Fairland—locale TX-5
**Fairland**—pop pl IL-6
**Fairland**—pop pl IN-6
**Fairland**—pop pl KY-4
**Fairland**—pop pl LA-4
**Fairland**—pop pl OK-5
**Fairland**—pop pl VA-3
**Fairland Acres**—pop pl MD-2
Fairland Cem—cemetery IL-6
Fairland Cem—cemetery KY-4
Fairland Cem—cemetery MO-7
Fairland Cem—cemetery OK-5
Fairland Cem—cemetery PA-2
Fairland Ch—church AR-4
Fairland Ch—church NY-2
Fairland East Sch—school OH-6
Fairland Elementary School PA-2
**Fairland Heights**—pop pl MD-2
Fairland HS—school OH-6
Fair Landing—locale AR-4
Fairland Sch—school GA-3
Fairland Sch—school KY-4
Fairland Sch—school LA-4
Fairland Sch—school MI-6
Fairland Sch—school PA-2
Fairland Sch No 2—school OH-6
Fairland Sch No 3—school OH-6
Fairland Sch No 4—school OH-6
**Fairland Township**—pop pl SD-7
Fair Lane—hist pl MI-6
**Fairlane**—pop pl LA-4
**Fairlane**—pop pl MN-6
**Fairlane**—pop pl OH-6
**Fairlane**—pop pl TN-4
Fairlane—post sta MS-4
Fairlane Cem—cemetery LA-4
Fairlane Ch—church LA-4
Fairlane Ch—church MI-6
Fairlane Elementary School TN-4
**Fairlane Estates**—pop pl FL-3
**Fairlane Estates**—pop pl TN-4
**Fairlane Heights Subdivision**—pop pl UT-8
Fairlane Park—park AL-4
Fairlane Sch—school (2) MI-6
Fairlane Sch—school TN-4
Fairlane Shop Ctr—locale MS-4
**Fairlane (subdivision)**—pop pl AL-4
**Fairlane (subdivision)**—pop pl NC-3
Fair Lanes Village Center—locale AZ-5
Fairlane Village Mall—locale PA-2
Fair Lawn CT-1
Fairlawn IN-6
Fairlawn OH-6
Fairlawn RI-1
Fairlawn—hist pl KY-4
Fairlawn—hist pl MA-1
Fair Lawn—hist pl NY-2
**Fair Lawn**—pop pl CT-1
**Fairlawn**—pop pl FL-3
**Fairlawn**—pop pl MA-1
**Fair Lawn**—pop pl NJ-2
**Fairlawn**—pop pl (2) OH-6
**Fairlawn**—pop pl PA-2
**Fairlawn**—pop pl RI-1
**Fairlawn**—pop pl (2) VA-3
**Fairlawn Acres**—pop pl GA-3
Fairlawn Baptist Ch—church FL-3
Fairlawn Cem—cemetery GA-3
Fairlawn Cem—cemetery (2) IL-6
Fairlawn Cem—cemetery IN-6
Fairlawn Cem—cemetery KS-7
Fairlawn Cem—cemetery NJ-2
Fairlawn Cem—cemetery (2) NY-2
Fairlawn Cem—cemetery (5) OK-5
Fair Lawn Cem—cemetery OK-5
Fairlawn Cem—cemetery SD-7
Fairlawn Cem—cemetery TX-5
Fairlawn Cem—cemetery VA-3
Fairlawn Cemeteries—cemetery OK-5
**Fairlawn Center**—pop pl IN-6
Fairlawn Ch—church OH-6
Fairlawn Ch—church TN-4
Fairlawn Ch—church VA-3
Fairlawn Ch of the Nazarene—church KS-7
Fairlawn Community Center—locale SC-3
Fairlawn Elementary and JHS—school IN-6
Fairlawn Elem Sch—school FL-3
**Fairlawn Estates**—pop pl NY-2

**Fairlawn Estates**—pop pl ... VA-3
Fairlawn Golf Club—other ... IL-6
Fairlawn Heights Wesleyan Ch—church ... KS-7
Fairlawn Hosp—hospital ... MA-1
Fairlawn HS—school ... OH-6
Fairlawn Mennonite Brethren—church ... KS-7
Fairlawn Plaza ... OH-6
Fairlawn Sch ... IN-6
Fairlawn Sch—school ... CA-9
Fairlawn Sch—school ... FL-3
Fairlawn Sch—school ... IN-6
Fairlawn Sch—school (2) ... OH-6
Fairlawn Schools—school ... OH-6
Fairlawn Shop Ctr—locale ... MA-1
Fairlawn (sta.) ... OH-6
**Fairlawn (subdivision)**—pop pl ... AL-4
**Fairlawn (subdivision)**—pop pl ... NC-3
**Fairlawn (subdivision)**—pop pl ... TN-4
**Fairlea**—pop pl ... WV-2
**Fairlee**—pop pl ... MD-2
**Fairlee**—pop pl ... VT-1
**Fairlee**—pop pl ... VA-3
Fairlee, Lake—lake ... VT-1
Fairlee Creek—stream ... MD-2
Fairlee Lake—reservoir ... MD-2
Fairlee Manor Camp House—hist pl ... MD-2
Fairlee Neck—cape ... MD-2
**Fairlee (Town of)**—pop pl ... VT-1
Fairleigh ... MO-7
Fairleigh Dickinson Univ—school ... NJ-2
Fairleigh Street Baptist Ch—church ... TN-4
**Fairless**—pop pl ... PA-2
**Fairless Hills**—pop pl ... PA-2
Fairless Hills Shop Ctr—locale ... PA-2
Fairless Junction—locale ... PA-2
Fairless View Sch—school ... PA-2
Fairley Bridge Landing—locale ... MS-4
Fairley Bridge Landing Rec Area—park ... MS-4
Fairley Cem—cemetery (5) ... MS-4
Fairley Ferry (historical)—locale ... MS-4
Fairley HS—school ... TN-4
Fairley Lake Dam—dam (2) ... MS-4
Fairley Post Office (historical)—building ... MS-4
Fairlie ... KY-4
**Fairlie**—pop pl ... TX-5
Fairlie-Poplar Hist Dist—hist pl ... GA-3
**Fairlington**—pop pl ... VA-3
Fairlington Sch—school ... VA-3
Fairly Windmill—locale ... NM-5
Fairman—locale ... AR-4
Fairman—locale ... IL-6
Fairman Bldg—hist pl ... MI-6
Fairman Coulee—valley ... OR-9
Fairman Lake—reservoir ... KS-7
Fairman Oil Field—other ... IL-6
Fairmaont ... KY-4
**Fairmead**—pop pl ... CA-9
**Fairmeade**—pop pl ... KY-4
Fair Meadows—hist pl ... MD-2
**Fair Meadows**—pop pl ... TX-5
**Fair Meadows**—pop pl ... VA-3
Fair Meadows—uninc pl ... AL-4
**Fairmeadows Condo**—pop pl ... UT-8
Fair Meadows Estates—uninc pl ... VA-3
**Fairmeadows (subdivision)**—pop pl ... NC-3
Fairmede Sch—school ... CA-9
Fairmon Cem—cemetery ... MO-7
Fairmont ... DE-2
Fairmont ... IN-6
Fairmont ... TN-4
Fairmont ... TX-5
Fairmont—hist pl ... TN-4
Fairmont—locale ... CA-9
Fairmont—locale ... IL-6
Fairmont—locale (2) ... IA-7
Fairmont—locale ... KY-4
Fairmont—locale ... PA-2
Fairmont—locale ... TX-5
Fairmont—other ... TN-4
**Fairmont**—pop pl ... AL-4
**Fairmont**—pop pl ... IL-6
**Fairmont**—pop pl ... KS-7
**Fairmont**—pop pl ... KY-4
**Fairmont**—pop pl ... LA-4
**Fairmont**—pop pl ... MD-2
**Fairmont**—pop pl ... MN-6
**Fairmont**—pop pl ... MO-7
**Fairmont**—pop pl ... NE-7
**Fairmont**—pop pl ... NC-3
**Fairmont**—pop pl ... OK-5
**Fairmont**—pop pl ... PA-2
**Fairmont**—pop pl ... SC-3
**Fairmont**—pop pl ... UT-8
**Fairmont**—pop pl (2) ... WA-9
**Fairmont**—pop pl ... WV-2
Fairmont—uninc pl ... FL-3
Fairmont—uninc pl ... TN-4
**Fairmont Addition**—pop pl ... KS-7
Fairmont Ave Hist Dist—hist pl ... OH-6
Fairmont Ave Sch—school ... NJ-2
Fairmont Bay—bay ... AK-9
Fairmont Butte—summit ... CA-9
Fairmont Cem—cemetery ... KS-7
Fairmont Cem—cemetery (3) ... KY-4
Fairmont Cem—cemetery ... MD-2
Fairmont Cem—cemetery ... NE-7
Fairmont Cem—cemetery ... NM-5
Fairmont Cem—cemetery ... NY-2
Fairmont Cem—cemetery ... OH-6
Fairmont Cem—cemetery ... TX-5
Fairmont Cem—cemetery ... WV-2
Fairmont Ch—church ... NC-3
Fairmont Ch—church ... PA-2
Fairmont Ch—church ... SD-7
Fairmont Ch—church ... VA-3
Fairmont Ch—church ... WV-2
**Fairmont City**—pop pl ... IL-6
**Fairmont City**—pop pl ... PA-2
Fairmont Creamery Company—hist pl ... MN-6
Fairmont Creamery Company Bldg—hist pl ... NE-7
Fairmont Elementary School ... TN-4
Fairmont Elem Sch—school ... IN-6
Fairmont Field Club—other ... WV-2
Fairmont Heights ... MD-2
Fairmont Hill ... MA-1
Fairmont Hollow—valley ... KY-4
Fairmont Hosp—hospital ... CA-9
Fairmont Hosp—hospital ... NJ-2
Fairmont HS—school ... NC-3
Fairmont HS—school ... OH-6
Fairmont-Intercity—CDP ... WA-9
Fairmont Island—island ... AK-9
Fairmont (Magisterial District)—fmr MCD ... WV-2
Fairmont Manor—uninc pl ... VA-3
Fairmont Mills—locale ... SC-3
Fairmont Mills (CCD)—cens area ... SC-3
Fairmont Mines—mine ... KY-4
Fairmont Missionary Baptist Church ... AL-4
Fairmont MS—school ... NC-3
Fairmont Municipal Airp—airport ... MN-6
Fairmont Opera House—hist pl ... MN-6
Fairmont Park—park ... CO-8
Fairmont Park—park ... CT-1
Fairmont Park—park ... ME-1
Fairmont Park—uninc pl ... VA-3
Fairmont Park Elem Sch—school ... FL-3
Fairmont Park Golf Course—other ... CA-9
Fairmont Park Rsvr—reservoir ... CO-8
Fairmont Point—cape ... AK-9
Fairmont Presbyterian Ch—church ... TN-4
Fairmont Ranch—locale ... TX-5
Fairmont Rsvr—reservoir ... CA-9
Fairmont Run—stream ... WV-2
Fairmont Sch ... IN-6
Fairmont Sch—school ... AL-4
Fairmont Sch—school (4) ... CA-9
Fairmont Sch—school ... CO-8
Fairmont Sch—school ... GA-3
Fairmont Sch—school ... IL-6
Fairmont Sch—school ... ME-1
Fairmont Sch—school ... MO-7
Fairmont Sch—school ... OH-6
Fairmont Sch—school ... TN-4
Fairmont Sch—school ... WI-6
Fairmont Sch (historical)—school ... MO-7
Fairmont Sch (historical)—school (2) ... PA-2
Fairmont Sch (historical)—school ... TN-4
Fairmont School—locale ... AR-4
Fairmont School Cave—cave ... TN-4
Fairmont Station—locale ... PA-2
**Fairmont (subdivision)**—pop pl ... NC-3
**Fairmont Terrace**—pop pl ... CA-9
Fairmont Terrace Park—park ... CA-9
Fairmont Terrace Park—park ... ME-1
Fairmont Terrace Sch—school ... CA-9
**Fairmont Township**—pop pl ... NE-7
Fairmont (Township of)—fmr MCD ... NC-3
**Fairmont (Township of)**—pop pl ... MN-6
Fairmoor Sch—school ... OH-6
**Fairmor**—pop pl ... WV-2
Fairmound Cem—cemetery ... OH-6
Fairmount ... CT-1
Fairmount ... DE-2
Fair Mount ... MA-1
Fairmount ... MO-7
Fairmount ... OH-6
Fairmount ... PA-2
Fairmount ... RI-1
Fair Mount ... TN-4
Fairmount—CDP ... NY-2
Fairmount—locale ... DE-2
Fairmount—locale ... MD-2
Fairmount—locale ... NJ-2
Fairmount—locale (3) ... PA-2
Fairmount—locale ... TX-5
**Fairmount**—pop pl ... AL-4
**Fairmount**—pop pl ... AR-4
**Fairmount**—pop pl ... CT-1
**Fairmount**—pop pl ... GA-3
**Fairmount**—pop pl (3) ... IL-6
**Fairmount**—pop pl ... IN-6
**Fairmount**—pop pl ... KS-7
**Fairmount**—pop pl ... KY-4
**Fairmount**—pop pl ... ME-1
**Fairmount**—pop pl ... MO-7
**Fairmount**—pop pl ... NJ-2
**Fairmount**—pop pl ... NY-2
**Fairmount**—pop pl ... ND-7
**Fairmount**—pop pl ... OH-6
**Fairmount**—pop pl (2) ... PA-2
**Fairmount**—pop pl (2) ... TN-4
Fairmount—uninc pl ... PA-2
Fairmount Ave Elem Sch—school ... PA-2
Fairmount Ave (Fairmount)—other ... CA-9
Fairmount Blvd District—hist pl ... OH-6
Fairmount Branch—stream ... TN-4
Fairmount (CCD)—cens area ... GA-3
Fairmount Cem—cemetery (2) ... AR-4
Fairmount Cem—cemetery (2) ... CO-8
Fairmount Cem—cemetery ... IL-6
Fairmount Cem—cemetery (3) ... IN-6
Fairmount Cem—cemetery ... IA-7
Fairmount Cem—cemetery (2) ... KS-7
Fairmount Cem—cemetery ... KY-4
Fairmount Cem—cemetery ... MD-2
Fairmount Cem—cemetery ... MA-1
Fairmount Cem—cemetery ... MO-7
Fairmount Cem—cemetery (2) ... NJ-2
Fairmount Cem—cemetery ... NM-5
Fairmount Cem—cemetery ... NY-2
Fairmount Cem—cemetery ... ND-7
Fairmount Cem—cemetery (3) ... OH-6
Fairmount Cem—cemetery ... OK-5
Fairmount Cem—cemetery ... PA-2
Fairmount Cem—cemetery (2) ... TX-5
Fairmount Cem—cemetery ... VT-1
Fairmount Cem—cemetery ... VA-3
Fair Mount Ch ... MS-4
Fairmount Ch—church ... AL-4
Fairmount Ch—church ... GA-3
Fairmount Ch—church ... KS-7
Fairmount Ch—church (2) ... KY-4
Fairmount Ch—church ... MD-2
Fairmount Ch—church ... MS-4
Fairmount Ch—church (2) ... MO-7
Fairmount Ch—church (2) ... NC-3
Fairmount Ch—church (2) ... OH-6
Fairmount Ch—church (3) ... PA-2
Fairmount Ch—church (3) ... VA-3
Fairmount Childrens Home—building ... OH-6
Fairmount City ... IL-6
Fairmount City ... PA-2
**Fairmount City**—pop pl ... PA-2
Fairmount Community Hall—locale ... AR-4
Fairmount Cottage—hist pl ... KS-7
Fairmount Dam—dam ... PA-2
Fairmount Elem Sch ... PA-2
Fairmount Elem Sch—school ... PA-2
Fairmount Elem Sch—school ... TN-4
Fairmount (Fairmount Avenue)—uninc pl ... CA-9
**Fairmount Heights**—pop pl ... MD-2
Fairmount Heights HS—school ... MD-2
Fairmount Heights Sch—school ... MD-2
Fairmount Hill—summit ... MA-1
Fairmount (historical)—locale ... AL-4
Fairmount (historical)—locale ... MS-4
Fairmount Hosp—hospital ... MI-6
Fairmount Hosp—hospital ... MO-7
Fairmount Hotel, The—hist pl ... TX-5
Fairmount Jockey Club—other ... IL-6
Fairmount Memorial Cem—cemetery ... OH-6
Fairmount Memorial Park (Cemetery)—cemetery ... WA-9
Fairmount MS ... PA-2
Fairmount MS—school ... IN-6
Fairmount Neck—cape ... MD-2
Fairmount Park—hist pl ... PA-2
Fairmount Park—park ... CA-9
Fairmount Park—park (2) ... IA-7
Fairmount Park—park ... KS-7
Fairmount Park—park ... MN-6
Fairmount Park—park (2) ... OR-9
Fairmount Park—park (2) ... PA-2
Fairmount Park—park ... UT-8
**Fairmount Park**—pop pl ... VA-3
**Fairmount Park Annex Subdivision**—pop pl (2) ... UT-8
Fairmount Park Sch—school ... WA-9
**Fairmount Park Subdivision**—pop pl ... UT-8
Fair Mount Post Office (historical)—building ... AL-4
Fairmount Post Office (historical)—building ... TN-4
Fairmount Rsvr—reservoir ... OH-6
Fairmount Sch—school ... AL-4
Fairmount Sch—school ... CO-8
Fairmount Sch—school ... GA-3
Fairmount Sch—school (2) ... IL-6
Fairmount Sch—school (2) ... KS-7
Fairmount Sch—school ... KY-4
Fairmount Sch—school ... MA-1
Fairmount Sch—school ... MN-6
Fairmount Sch—school (2) ... MO-7
Fairmount Sch—school (2) ... NJ-2
Fairmount Sch—school (2) ... NY-2
Fairmount Sch—school ... OR-9
Fairmount Sch—school ... WA-9
Fairmount Sch (abandoned)—school ... MO-7
Fairmount Sch (historical)—school ... TN-4
Fairmount School ... TN-4
Fairmount Springs—locale ... PA-2
**Fairmount Springs**—pop pl ... PA-2
Fairmount State Wildlife Mngmt Area—park ... MD-2
**Fairmount (subdivision)**—pop pl ... MA-1
**Fairmount Subdivision**—pop pl ... UT-8
Fairmount Temple Sch—school ... OH-6
**Fairmount Township**—pop pl (2) ... KS-7
**Fairmount Township**—pop pl ... ND-7
**Fairmount (Township of)**—pop pl ... IL-6
**Fairmount (Township of)**—pop pl ... IN-6
**Fairmount (Township of)**—pop pl ... PA-2
Fairmount Union Sch—school ... CA-9
Fairmount Waterworks—building ... PA-2
Fairmount Water Works—hist pl ... PA-2
Fair Mtn—summit ... NC-3
**Fairnelson**—pop pl ... AL-4
Fairntosh—locale ... NC-3
Fairntosh Plantation—hist pl ... NC-3
Fairo—spring ... FM-9
Fairoak Beach—beach ... IA-7
Fair Oak Ch—church ... MO-7
Fair Oak Ch—church ... OK-5
Fairoaks ... AL-4
Fair Oaks ... IL-6
Fairoaks ... NY-2
Fairoaks ... OR-9
Fair Oaks—hist pl ... MS-4
Fair Oaks—locale ... AL-4
Fair Oaks—locale ... AZ-5
Fair Oaks—locale ... NY-2
Fair Oaks—locale ... OR-9
**Fairoaks**—pop pl ... AL-4
**Fair Oaks**—pop pl ... AR-4
**Fair Oaks**—pop pl (2) ... CA-9
**Fair Oaks**—pop pl ... GA-3
**Fair Oaks**—pop pl ... IL-6
**Fair Oaks**—pop pl ... IN-6
**Fair Oaks**—pop pl (3) ... OH-6
**Fair Oaks**—pop pl ... OK-5
**Fair Oaks**—pop pl ... OR-9
**Fairoaks**—pop pl ... OR-9
**Fairoaks**—pop pl (2) ... PA-2
**Fair Oaks**—pop pl ... TN-4
**Fairoaks**—pop pl ... TX-5
**Fair Oaks**—pop pl (2) ... VA-3
Fair Oaks—uninc pl ... CA-9
Fair Oaks (CCD)—cens area ... GA-3
Fair Oaks Cem—cemetery ... GA-3
Fair Oaks Cem—cemetery ... IA-7
Fair Oaks Cem—cemetery ... OR-9
Fair Oaks Cem—cemetery ... PA-2
Fair Oaks Ch—church ... MN-6
Fairoaks Ch—church ... PA-2
Fair Oak Sch—school ... MO-7
Fair Oak Sch (abandoned)—school ... PA-2
Fairoak Sch (abandoned)—school ... PA-2
Fair Oaks County Park—park ... OR-9
**Fairoaks (Fair Oaks) (Township name Leet)**—pop pl ... PA-2
Fair Oaks Hill ... MA-1
Fair Oaks Hosp at Boca/Delray—hospital ... FL-3
Fair Oaks Mall—post sta ... VA-3
Fair Oaks Mine—mine ... CA-9
Fairoaks Park—park ... CA-9
Fair Oak Springs—locale ... MS-4
Fair Oak Springs Consolidated Sch (historical)—school ... MS-4
**Fair Oaks Ranch**—pop pl ... TX-5
Fair Oaks Sch—school (3) ... CA-9
Fairoaks Sch—school (2) ... CA-9
Fair Oaks Sch—school ... CA-9
Fair Oaks Sch—school ... CT-1
Fair Oaks Sch—school ... MN-6
Fair Oaks Shop Ctr—locale ... TX-5
**Fair Oaks Springs**—pop pl ... MS-4
**Fairoaks Subdivision**—pop pl ... UT-8
Fair Oaks (Township of)—fmr MCD ... AR-4
Fair Oil Field—oilfield ... TX-5
Fair Park—park (4) ... TX-5
**Fair Park**—pop pl ... AL-4
Fair Park Baptist Church ... AL-4
Fair Park Ch—church ... AL-4
Fair Park Ch—church ... LA-4
Fair Park HS—school ... LA-4
Fair Park Racetrack—other ... TX-5
Fair Park Sch—school ... AR-4
Fair Park Sch—school ... TX-5
Fair Park Sch—school ... WI-6
**Fair Plain**—pop pl ... MI-6
**Fair Plain**—pop pl ... PA-2
**Fairplain**—pop pl ... PA-2
**Fairplain**—pop pl ... WV-2
Fair Plain Archeol District—hist pl ... VI-3
Fairplain Ch—church ... SC-3
Fair Plain Ch (historical)—church ... AL-4
Fair Plain Grange Hall—building ... KS-7
Fairplain Historic and Archeol District—hist pl ... VI-3
Fairplain Plaza—post sta ... MI-6
**Fairplains**—pop pl ... NC-3
Fair Plains Cem—cemetery ... MI-6
Fairplains Cem—cemetery ... MI-6
Fairplains Ch—church ... MI-6
Fairplains Sch—school ... NE-7
Fairplains Sch—school ... NC-3
Fairplains Sch—school ... WV-2
**Fairplain (Township of)**—pop pl ... MI-6
Fairplay ... MO-7
Fairplay ... OH-6
Fair Play ... PA-2
Fairplay ... SC-3
Fairplay—locale ... GA-3
Fairplay—locale ... KY-4
Fairplay—locale ... MD-2
Fair Play—locale ... NJ-2
Fair Play—locale ... TX-5
Fairplay—locale ... VA-3
**Fair Play**—pop pl ... CA-9
**Fairplay**—pop pl ... CO-8
**Fairplay**—pop pl ... GA-3
**Fair Play**—pop pl ... MD-2
**Fairplay**—pop pl ... MD-2
**Fair Play**—pop pl ... MO-7
**Fairplay**—pop pl (2) ... OH-6
**Fairplay**—pop pl ... PA-2
**Fair Play**—pop pl ... SC-3
**Fair Play**—pop pl ... WI-6
Fairplay, Mount—summit ... AK-9
Fairplay (CCD)—cens area ... GA-3
Fairplay Cem—cemetery ... CO-8
Fairplay Ch—church ... AR-4
Fairplay Ch—church (2) ... GA-3
Fairplay Ch—church ... KS-7
Fair Play Ch—church ... OH-6
Fairplay Community Building—locale ... CO-8
Fair Play Creek—stream ... SC-3
Fair Play Creek—stream ... WI-6
Fair Play (historical P.O.)—locale ... IN-6
Fair Play Mine—mine ... NV-8
Fairplay Mining Ditch—canal ... CO-8
Fairplay Mound—summit ... IN-6
Fair Play-Oakway Sch—school ... SC-3
Fair Play P.O. (historical)—locale ... AL-4
Fair Play Sch—school ... CA-9
Fairplay Sch—school ... GA-3
Fairplay Sch—school ... IL-6
Fair Play Sch—school ... IL-6
Fairplay Sch—school ... IL-6
Fairplay Sch—school ... KS-7
Fairplay Sch—school ... NE-7
Fairplay Sch—school ... OR-9
**Fairplay Township**—pop pl ... KS-7
Fairplay (Township of)—fmr MCD ... AR-4
**Fairplay (Township of)**—pop pl ... IN-6
Fair Plaza, The—locale ... MA-1
Fair Point ... KS-7
Fair Point—cape ... FL-3
Fairpoint—locale ... SD-7
**Fairpoint**—pop pl ... OH-6
Fairpoint Cem—cemetery ... MN-6
Fairpoint Cem—cemetery ... SD-7
Fairpoint Ch—church ... PA-2
Fairport ... OH-6
Fairport—locale ... NC-3
Fairport—other ... OH-6
**Fairport**—pop pl ... IA-7
**Fairport**—pop pl ... KS-7
**Fairport**—pop pl ... MI-6
**Fairport**—pop pl ... MO-7
**Fairport**—pop pl ... NY-2
**Fair Port**—pop pl ... VA-3
**Fairport**—pop pl ... VA-3
Fairport Cem—cemetery ... IA-7
Fairport Cem—cemetery ... KS-7
Fairport Harbor—bay ... OH-6
**Fairport Harbor (Fairport)**—pop pl ... OH-6
**Fairport (historical)**—pop pl ... MS-4
Fairport HS—school ... NY-2
Fairport Marine Museum—hist pl ... OH-6
Fairport Oil Field—oilfield ... KS-7
Fairport Post Office (historical)—building ... MS-4
Fairport Reservoirs—reservoir ... NY-2
Fairport Sch—school ... OH-6
Fair Post Office (historical)—building ... TN-4
Fair Prairie Sch—school ... IL-6
Fair Promise Ch—church ... NC-3
Fair Promise Stock Farm—locale ... MD-2
Fair Prospect Cem—cemetery ... AL-4
Fair Ridge Cem—cemetery ... NY-2
Fair Ridge Ch—church ... MS-4
Fair Ridge Ch—church ... PA-2
Fair Ridge Missionary Baptist Ch ... MS-4
Fair River—locale ... MS-4
Fair River—stream ... MS-4
Fair River Baptist Church ... MS-4
Fair River Ch—church ... MS-4
Fair River Hall Sch (historical)—school ... MS-4
Fair River Post Office (historical)—building ... MS-4
Fair River Store (historical)—locale ... MS-4
Fair Run—stream ... PA-2
Fair-Rutherford and Rutherford Houses—hist pl ... SC-3
Fair Sch—school ... CA-9
Fair Sch—school ... IL-6
Fair Sch—school ... MS-4
Fair Sch—school ... OH-6
Fair Sch (abandoned)—school ... PA-2
Fair Sch (historical)—school ... MS-4
Fairs Creek ... MS-4
Fairs Crossroads—locale ... SC-3
Fairs Hill Ch—church ... MS-4
Fair Shoals (historical)—bar ... AL-4
Fair Shop Ctr, The—locale (2) ... MA-1
Fair Shopping Plaza—locale ... MA-1
Fairside Sch—school ... AR-4
Fairsite Sch—school ... CA-9
Fairs Lake—reservoir ... NC-3
Fairs Lake Dam—dam ... NC-3
Fairsmith Station—locale ... OH-6
Fair Spring—spring ... MO-7
Fair Street Cem—cemetery ... OH-6
Fair Street Sch—school ... GA-3
Fairs Valley—basin ... PA-2
**Fairthorne (subdivision)**—pop pl ... DE-2
**Fairton**—pop pl ... NJ-2
Fairtown ... MD-2
**Fairtown**—pop pl ... MD-2
Fair Town Heights Wesleyan Ch—church ... KS-7
Fair Township—civil ... MO-7
**Fair Township**—pop pl ... SD-7
Fairvalley—locale ... OK-5
**Fair Valley**—pop pl ... OK-5
Fair Valley—valley ... WI-6
Fairvalley Cem—cemetery ... OK-5
Fair Valley Community Hall—locale ... OK-5
Fairvalley Sch—school ... CA-9
**Fair Vernon**—pop pl ... VA-3
Fairview ... AZ-5
Fairview (2) ... IL-6
Fairview ... LA-4
Fairview ... NJ-2
Fairview ... ND-7
Fairview (2) ... OH-6
Fairview ... PA-2
Fairview ... SD-7
Fair View ... UT-8
Fairview ... VA-3
Fairview ... WV-2
Fairview—fmr MCD (4) ... NE-7
Fairview—hist pl ... DE-2
Fairview—hist pl ... KY-4
Fairview—hist pl ... NE-7
Fairview—locale (8) ... AL-4
Fairview—locale (2) ... AR-4
Fairview—locale ... CA-9
Fairview—locale (2) ... CO-8
Fairview—locale ... FL-3
Fairview—locale (3) ... GA-3
Fairview—locale (2) ... ID-8
Fairview—locale (2) ... KY-4
Fairview—locale ... LA-4
Fairview—locale (3) ... MD-2
Fairview—locale ... MS-4
Fairview—locale ... MO-7
Fairview—locale ... NH-1
Fairview—locale ... NY-2
Fairview—locale (3) ... OH-6
Fairview—locale (2) ... OR-9
Fairview—locale (2) ... PA-2
Fairview—locale ... SC-3
Fairview—locale (4) ... TN-4
Fair View—locale ... TN-4
Fairview—locale (5) ... TN-4
Fairview—locale (9) ... TX-5
Fairview—locale (6) ... VA-3
Fairview—locale ... WA-9
Fairview—locale (3) ... WV-2
Fairview—locale ... WY-8
Fairview—other ... OH-6
Fairview—other ... PA-2
**Fair View**—pop pl ... AL-4
**Fairview**—pop pl (10) ... AL-4
**Fairview**—pop pl (7) ... AR-4
**Fairview**—pop pl (4) ... CA-9
**Fairview**—pop pl (2) ... CO-8
**Fairview**—pop pl ... DE-2
**Fairview**—pop pl ... FL-3
**Fairview**—pop pl ... GA-3
**Fairview**—pop pl ... ID-8
**Fairview**—pop pl (2) ... IL-6
**Fairview**—pop pl (5) ... IN-6
**Fairview**—pop pl (2) ... IA-7
**Fairview**—pop pl ... KS-7
**Fairview**—pop pl (6) ... KY-4
**Fairview**—pop pl ... MD-2
**Fairview**—pop pl ... MI-6
**Fairview**—pop pl (3) ... MS-4
**Fairview**—pop pl (2) ... MO-7
**Fairview**—pop pl ... MT-8
**Fairview**—pop pl (10) ... NJ-2
**Fairview**—pop pl ... NM-5
**Fairview**—pop pl (3) ... NY-2
**Fairview**—pop pl (7) ... NC-3
**Fairview**—pop pl (5) ... OH-6
**Fairview**—pop pl ... OK-5
**Fairview**—pop pl (4) ... OR-9
**Fairview**—pop pl (13) ... PA-2
**Fairview**—pop pl (4) ... SC-3
**Fairview**—pop pl ... SD-7
**Fairview**—pop pl (20) ... TN-4
**Fairview**—pop pl (5) ... TX-5
**Fairview**—pop pl ... UT-8
**Fairview**—pop pl (4) ... VA-3
**Fairview**—pop pl (2) ... WA-9
**Fairview**—pop pl (5) ... WV-2
**Fairview**—pop pl (2) ... WI-6
**Fairview**—pop pl ... WY-8
**Fairview**—pop pl ... PR-3
Fairview—summit ... MD-2
Fairview—uninc pl ... AL-4
Fairview—uninc pl ... AK-9
Fairview—uninc pl ... CA-9
Fairview—uninc pl ... TX-5
Fairview—uninc pl ... WI-6
Fairview—unorg reg ... SD-7
Fairview, Lake—lake ... FL-3
Fairview, Mount—summit ... CO-8
Fairview Acres ... MO-7
**Fairview Acres**—pop pl ... MO-7
**Fairview Acres**—pop pl ... TN-4
**Fairview Acres (subdivision)**—pop pl ... NC-3
**Fairview Addition**—pop pl ... IL-6
Fairview Alpha—locale ... LA-4
Fairview Apartments—hist pl ... UT-8
Fairview Baptist Ch ... AL-4
Fairview Baptist Ch ... MS-4
Fairview Baptist Ch ... TN-4
Fairview Baptist Ch—church (4) ... AL-4
Fairview Baptist Ch—church (2) ... MS-4
Fairview Baptist Ch—church (5) ... TN-4
Fairview Bar—bar ... OR-9
**Fairview Beach**—pop pl ... VA-3
**Fairview Beach**—pop pl ... WI-6
Fairview Bethel Cem—cemetery ... PA-2
Fairview Bethel Cem—cemetery ... WV-2
Fairview Bethel Ch—church ... PA-2
Fairview Bethel Ch—church ... WV-2
Fairview Bible Baptist Ch—church ... TN-4
Fairview Borough—civil (2) ... PA-2
Fairview Branch—stream ... MS-4
Fairview Branch—stream ... MO-7
Fairview Bridge—bridge ... OR-9
Fairview Cabin Site Area ... TN-4
Fairview Camp—locale ... OR-9
Fairview Camp—park ... OR-9
Fairview Canal—canal ... LA-4
Fairview Canal—canal (2) ... WY-8
Fairview Canyon—valley ... CA-9
Fairview Canyon—valley ... UT-8
Fairview Canyon—valley ... WA-9
Fairview Catholic Cemetery ... SD-7
Fairview (CCD)—cens area ... OK-5
Fairview (CCD)—cens area (2) ... TN-4
Fairview Cem ... AL-4
Fairview Cem ... PA-2
Fairview Cem—cemetery (15) ... AL-4
Fairview Cem—cemetery (5) ... AR-4
Fairview Cem—cemetery ... CA-9
Fairview Cem—cemetery (9) ... CO-8
Fairview Cem—cemetery (2) ... CT-1
Fairview Cem—cemetery ... GA-3
Fairview Cem—cemetery (3) ... ID-8
Fairview Cem—cemetery (3) ... IL-6
Fairview Cem—cemetery (13) ... IN-6
Fair View Cem—cemetery ... IN-6
Fairview Cem—cemetery (6) ... IN-6
Fairview Cem—cemetery (25) ... IA-7
Fairview Cem—cemetery (42) ... KS-7
Fairview Cem—cemetery (10) ... KY-4
Fairview Cem—cemetery (2) ... LA-4
Fairview Cem—cemetery (10) ... ME-1
Fairview Cem—cemetery (2) ... MD-2
Fairview Cem—cemetery (6) ... MA-1
Fairview Cem—cemetery (13) ... MI-6
Fairview Cem—cemetery (16) ... MN-6
Fairview Cem—cemetery (6) ... MS-4
Fairview Cem—cemetery ... MO-7
Fair View Cem—cemetery ... MO-7
Fairview Cem—cemetery (23) ... MO-7
Fairview Cem—cemetery (4) ... MT-8
Fairview Cem—cemetery (16) ... NE-7
Fairview Cem—cemetery ... NH-1
Fairview Cem—cemetery (6) ... NJ-2
Fairview Cem—cemetery (2) ... NM-5
Fairview Cem—cemetery (27) ... NY-2
Fairview Cem—cemetery ... NC-3
Fair View Cem—cemetery ... NC-3
Fairview Cem—cemetery (6) ... NC-3
Fairview Cem—cemetery (8) ... ND-7
Fairview Cem—cemetery (9) ... OH-6
Fair View Cem—cemetery ... OH-6
Fairview Cem—cemetery (11) ... OH-6
Fair View Cem—cemetery ... OK-5
Fairview Cem—cemetery (17) ... OK-5
Fair View Cem—cemetery ... OK-5
Fairview Cem—cemetery (2) ... OK-5
Fairview Cem—cemetery (4) ... OR-9
Fairview Cem—cemetery (38) ... PA-2
Fairview Cem—cemetery ... SC-3
Fairview Cem—cemetery ... SD-7
Fair View Cem—cemetery ... SD-7
Fairview Cem—cemetery (6) ... SD-7
Fairview Cem—cemetery (9) ... TN-4
Fairview Cem—cemetery (28) ... TX-5
Fairview Cem—cemetery (2) ... UT-8
Fairview Cem—cemetery (3) ... VT-1
Fair View Cem—cemetery ... VT-1
Fairview Cem—cemetery ... VT-1
Fairview Cem—cemetery (7) ... VA-3
Fairview Cem—cemetery (2) ... WA-9
Fairview Cem—cemetery (5) ... WV-2
Fair View Cem—cemetery ... WV-2
Fairview Cem—cemetery ... WV-2
Fairview Cem—cemetery (4) ... WI-6
Fairview Cem—cemetery ... WY-8
Fairview Cemetery ... KS-7
Fairview Cemetery ... SD-7
Fairview Center Sch—school ... SD-7
Fairview Ch ... AL-4
Fair View Ch ... TN-4
Fairview Ch—church (32) ... AL-4
Fairview Ch—church (4) ... AR-4
Fair View Ch—church ... AR-4
Fairview Ch—church (2) ... AR-4
Fair View Ch—church ... AR-4
Fairview Ch—church (3) ... AR-4
Fairview Ch—church ... CA-9
Fairview Ch—church ... CO-8
Fairview Ch—church ... FL-3
Fairview Ch—church (14) ... GA-3
Fairview Ch—church ... ID-8
Fairview Ch—church (10) ... IL-6
Fairview Ch—church (19) ... IN-6
Fairview Ch—church ... IA-7
Fair View Ch—church ... IA-7
Fairview Ch—church (7) ... IA-7
Fairview Ch—church (4) ... KS-7
Fairview Ch—church (10) ... KY-4
Fair View Ch—church ... KY-4
Fairview Ch—church (2) ... KY-4
Fair View Ch—church ... KY-4
Fairview Ch—church (12) ... KY-4
Fairview Ch—church (5) ... LA-4
Fairview Ch—church (4) ... MD-2
Fairview Ch—church (2) ... MI-6
Fair View Ch—church ... MS-4
Fairview Ch—church (5) ... MS-4
Fair View Ch—church ... MS-4
Fairview Ch—church (10) ... MS-4
Fairview Ch—church (33) ... MO-7
Fairview Ch—church ... MT-8
Fairview Ch—church (4) ... NE-7
Fairview Ch—church ... NJ-2
Fairview Ch—church ... NM-5
Fairview Ch—church (27) ... NC-3
Fairview Ch—church (2) ... ND-7
Fairview Ch—church (26) ... OH-6

Fairview Ch—*church* (11) OK-5
Fairview Ch—*church* (24) PA-2
Fairview Ch—*church* (16) SC-3
Fairview Ch—*church* TN-4
Fair View Ch—*church* TN-4
Fairview Ch—*church* (38) TN-4
Fairview Ch—*church* (22) TX-5
Fairview Ch—*church* (21) VA-3
Fairview Ch—*church* (33) WV-2
Fairview Ch—*church* WI-6
Fairview Ch (abandoned)—*church* MO-7
Fairview Channel—*canal* CA-9
Fairview Chapel—*church* KS-7
Fairview Chapel—*church* KY-4
Fairview Chapel—*church* OH-6
Fairview Chapel—*church* VA-3
Fairview Ch (historical)—*church* (5) AL-4
Fairview Ch (historical)—*church* MS-4
Fairview Ch (historical)—*church* (2) MO-7
Fairview Ch (historical)—*church* (2) TN-4
Fairview Ch Number 2—*church* AL-4
*Fairview Ch of Christ* TN-4
Fairview Ch of Christ—*church* AL-4
Fairview Ch of Christ—*church* TN-4
*Fairview Ch of God* TN-4
*Fairview Ch of God in Prophecy* MS-4
Fairview Ch of the Nazarene—*church* AL-4
Fairview Christian Ch—*church* KS-7
*Fairview Church* NC-3
Fairview Church—*locale* PA-2
**Fairview Church**—*pop pl* NC-3
Fairview Church Cem—*cemetery* AL-4
Fairview Church Cem—*cemetery* AR-4
Fairview Church Cem—*cemetery* PA-2
Fairview Church (historical)—*locale* (2) MO-7
*Fairview Churh of Christ* TN-4
*Fairview City Cemetery* UT-8
Fairview City Hall—*hist pl* UT-8
Fairview City Wells—*well* OK-5
Fairview Coll (historical)—*school* MS-4
Fairview Community Center—*building* AL-4
Fairview Community Center—*locale* IL-6
Fairview Community Center—*locale* TX-5
*Fairview Congregational Church* AL-4
Fairview Corners—*locale* NY-2
**Fairview Corners**—*pop pl* OH-6
Fairview Country Club—*other* NY-2
Fairview Cove—*bay* MI-6
Fairview Creek—*stream* AK-9
Fairview Creek—*stream* AR-4
Fairview Creek—*stream* ID-8
Fairview Creek—*stream* IN-6
Fairview Creek—*stream* MT-8
Fairview Creek—*stream* (4) OR-9
Fairview Creek—*stream* WA-9
*Fairview Crossroads* NC-3
**Fairview Cross Roads**—*pop pl* NC-3
**Fairview Crossroads**—*pop pl* SC-3
Fairview Cumberland Cem—*cemetery* MS-4
Fairview Cumberland Ch—*church* TX-5
*Fairview Cumberland Methodist Church* AL-4
Fairview Cumberland Presbyterian Ch (historical)—*church* AL-4
Fairview/Devils Step Campground—*locale* TN-4
Fairview District—*hist pl* NJ-2
Fairview Ditch—*canal* CA-9
Fairview Ditch—*canal* CO-8
Fairview Ditch—*canal* IL-6
Fairview Division—*civil* (2) TN-4
Fairview Dome—*summit* CA-9
Fairview Drain—*stream* IL-6
**Fairview Drive**—*pop pl* PA-2
*Fairview Elementary School* MS-4
*Fairview Elem Sch* PA-2
*Fairview Elem Sch* TN-4
Fairview Elem Sch—*school* DE-2
Fairview Elem Sch—*school* FL-3
Fairview Elem Sch—*school* (2) IN-6
Fairview Elem Sch—*school* KS-7
Fairview Elem Sch*—*school* KS-7
Fairview Elem Sch—*school* (7) KS-7
Fairview Elem Sch—*school* NC-3
Fairview Elem Sch—*school* PA-2
Fairview Elem Sch—*school* (2) TN-4
**Fairview Estates**—*pop pl* MD-2
**Fairview Estates**—*pop pl* NJ-2
**Fairview Estates**—*pop pl* TN-4
Fairview Evergreen Airp—*airport* PA-2
Fairview Extension Ditch—*canal* WY-8
Fairview Farm—*hist pl* VA-3
**Fairview Farms**—*pop pl* VA-3
Fairview-Ferndale—*CDP* PA-2
Fairview Field Airp—*airport* MO-7
Fairview Fire Tower—*locale* AR-4
Fairview First Congregational Methodist Ch—*church* TN-4
Fairview Forest Camp—*locale* OR-9
*Fairview Freewill Baptist Ch* AL-4
*Fairview Freewill Baptist Ch* TN-4
Fairview Freewill Baptist Ch—*church* AL-4
Fairview Gap—*gap* NC-3
*Fairview Gardens* IL-6
**Fairview Gardens Subdivision**—*pop pl* UT-8
Fairview Golf Course—*locale* PA-2
Fairview Goodwill Ch—*church* VA-3
Fairview Guard Station—*locale* ID-8
Fairview Guard Station—*locale* MT-8
Fairview Gulch—*valley* CO-8
Fairview Gullies—*basin* TN-4
Fairview Hall—*locale* (2) WA-9
Fairview Hall Sch—*school* PA-2
Fairview Hall Sch (abandoned)—*school* PA-2
Fairview Harbor—*harbor* TN-4
*Fairview Heights* OH-6
*Fairview Heights* PA-2
Fairview Heights—*locale* TN-4
**Fairview Heights**—*pop pl* IL-6
**Fairview Heights**—*pop pl* OH-6
**Fairview Heights**—*pop pl* (4) PA-2
**Fairview Heights**—*pop pl* SC-3
**Fairview Heights**—*pop pl* (2) TN-4
**Fairview Heights**—*pop pl* (2) VA-3
Fairview Heights—*uninc pl* KY-4
Fairview Heights—*uninc pl* (2) VA-3
Fairview Heights Baptist Ch—*church* AL-4
Fairview Heights Sch—*school* OH-6
**Fairview Heights (subdivision)**—*pop pl* AL-4
**Fairview Heights (subdivision)**—*pop pl* SD-7
**Fairview Heights (subdivision)**—*pop pl* TN-4
**Fairview Hill**—*pop pl* KY-4
Fairview Hill—*summit* CO-8
Fairview Hill—*summit* (2) ME-1
Fairview Hill—*summit* (2) MA-1
**Fairview Hills**—*pop pl* PA-2
Fairview Hills Golf Course—*other* MI-6
**Fairview Hills (subdivision)**—*pop pl* NC-3
Fairview Hist Dist—*hist pl* GA-3
Fairview (historical)—*locale* IA-7
Fairview (historical)—*locale* SD-7
**Fairview (historical)**—*pop pl* MS-4
**Fairview (historical)**—*pop pl* (2) SD-7
**Fairview (historical)**—*pop pl* TN-4
Fairview Hollow—*valley* OK-5
Fairview Home—*building* OR-9
Fairview Home Prigg Cottage—*building* OR-9
*Fairview Homes* NC-3
Fairview Hosp—*hospital* AL-4
Fairview Hosp—*hospital* MN-6
Fairview HS—*school* AL-4
Fairview HS—*school* CO-8
Fairview HS—*school* KY-4
Fairview HS—*school* OH-6
Fairview HS—*school* TN-4
Fairview HS—*school* (2) TX-5
Fairview Independent Sch—*school* IA-7
Fairview Indian Site—*hist pl* CA-9
Fairview Industrial Park—*locale* PA-2
Fairview Inn—*hist pl* AK-9
Fairview Interchange—*crossing* SD-7
Fairview JHS—*school* MN-6
Fairview JHS—*school* MS-4
*Fairview Junction* OR-9
Fairview Junction—*locale* ND-7
Fairview Knob—*summit* ID-8
**Fairview Knolls**—*pop pl* NJ-2
**Fairview Knolls**—*pop pl* PA-2
*Fairview Lake* UT-8
Fairview Lake—*lake* (2) CO-8
Fairview Lake—*lake* FL-3
Fairview Lake—*lake* NJ-2
Fairview Lake—*lake* OR-9
Fairview Lake—*lake* WA-9
Fairview Lake—*reservoir* PA-2
Fairview Lake—*reservoir* SC-3
*Fairview Lake Dam* UT-8
Fairview Lake Dam—*dam* PA-2
Fairview Lakes—*reservoir* UT-8
Fairview Lakes Dam—*dam* UT-8
Fairview Lakeside Country Club—*other* OK-5
Fairview Landing—*locale* MS-4
Fairview Landing (historical)—*locale* MS-4
Fairview Landing (22Yz561)—*hist pl* MS-4
Fairview Lanes—*CDP* OH-6
Fairview-Lester Cem—*cemetery* IA-7
Fairview Lode Mine—*mine* NM-5
Fairview Lookout Tower—*locale* MS-4
Fairview Lookout Tower—*locale* MO-7
Fairview Lookout Tower—*locale* OH-6
Fairview Main Street Branch—*other* FL-3
Fairview Male and Female Acad (historical)—*school* MS-4
Fairview Manor—*uninc pl* VA-3
*Fairview Marguerite Elementary School* TN-4
Fairview Marguerite Sch—*school* TN-4
Fairview Meadow—*flat* OR-9
Fairview Memorial Cem—*cemetery* AR-4
Fairview Memorial Cem—*cemetery* NJ-2
Fairview Memorial Estate—*cemetery* PA-2
Fairview Memorial Park—*cemetery* NC-3
Fairview Memorial Park—*cemetery* OH-6
Fairview Memorial Park Cem—*cemetery* MN-6
Fairview Memorial Sch—*school* MA-1
*Fairview Methodist Ch* AL-4
Fairview Methodist Ch—*church* AL-4
Fairview Methodist Ch (historical)—*church* MS-4
*Fairview Methodist Church* TN-4
Fairview Methodist Church—*hist pl* KY-4
Fairview Methodist Episcopal Ch South (historical)—*church* AL-4
Fairview Mill—*locale* MD-2
Fairview Mine—*mine* CA-9
Fairview Mine—*mine* (3) CO-8
Fairview Mine—*mine* (2) MT-8
Fairview Mine—*mine* NV-8
Fairview Mine (underground)—*mine* AL-4
Fairview Mission—*church* OH-6
*Fairview Missionary Baptist Church* AL-4
*Fairview Mountain* CO-8
*Fairview Mountain* NV-8
Fairview Mtn—*summit* AL-4
Fairview Mtn—*summit* AK-9
Fairview Mtn—*summit* CA-9
Fairview Mtn—*summit* MD-2
Fairview Mtn—*summit* MT-8
Fairview Mtn—*summit* (3) OR-9
Fairview Mtn—*summit* WV-2
Fairview Neck—*cape* VA-3
Fairview North Sch—*school* IL-6
Fairview Number One Mine—*mine* CA-9
Fairview Number Two Mine—*mine* CA-9
Fairview Nursing Home—*building* MN-6
Fairview Oil Field—*oilfield* LA-4
Fairview Outlet—*stream* PA-2
Fairview Park—*park* (3) AL-4
Fairview Park—*park* (2) ID-8
Fairview Park—*park* (4) IL-6
Fairview Park—*park* (2) IN-6
Fairview Park—*park* IA-7
Fairview Park—*park* MN-6
Fairview Park—*park* (4) OH-6
Fairview Park—*park* PA-2
Fairview Park—*park* (2) TN-4
**Fairview Park**—*pop pl* IN-6
**Fairview Park**—*pop pl* NC-3
**Fairview Park**—*pop pl* OH-6
**Fairview Park**—*pop pl* (4) PA-2
Fairview Park Cem—*cemetery* OH-6
Fairview Park Sch—*school* IN-6
**Fairview Park (subdivision)**—*pop pl* NC-3
**Fairview Park Subdivision**—*pop pl* UT-8
Fairview Peak—*summit* (2) CO-8
Fairview Peak—*summit* MT-8
Fairview Peak—*summit* (3) NV-8
Fairview Peak—*summit* OR-9
Fairview Plantation—*locale* LA-4
Fairview Plantation (historical)—*locale* (2) MS-4
Fairview Plateau—*plain* MT-8
Fairview Playground—*park* WI-6
Fairview Plaza—*locale* MA-1
Fairview Plaza Shop Ctr—*locale* AL-4
Fairview P.O. (historical)—*building* MS-4
*Fairview Point* FL-3
Fairview Point—*cape* LA-4
Fairview Point—*cape* (2) MD-2
Fairview Point—*summit* OR-9
Fairview Post Office—*building* TN-4
Fairview Post Office—*building* UT-8
Fairview Post Office (historical)—*building* AL-4
Fairview Post Office (historical)—*building* (2) TN-4
Fairview Presbyterian Ch—*church* IN-6
Fairview Presbyterian Ch (historical)—*church* AL-4
Fairview Presbyterian Church—*hist pl* SC-3
Fairview Ranch—*locale* AZ-5
Fairview Ranch—*locale* UT-8
Fairview Range—*range* NV-8
*Fairview Reservoir* UT-8
Fairview Resort—*locale* MI-6
Fairview Ridge—*ridge* AR-4
Fairview Ridge—*ridge* IN-6
Fairview Ridge—*ridge* (2) KY-4
Fairview Ridge—*ridge* (2) OH-6
Fairview Ridge—*ridge* WA-9
Fairview Ridge—*ridge* WV-2
Fairview Ridge—*ridge* (2) WI-6
Fairview Riverside State Park—*park* LA-4
Fairview Rsvr—*reservoir* CO-8
Fairview Rsvr—*reservoir* CT-1
Fairview Rsvr—*reservoir* OK-5
*Fairview Sch* PA-2
*Fairview Sch* TN-4
Fairview Sch—*hist pl* TN-4
Fairview Sch—*school* (4) AL-4
Fairview Sch—*school* (6) AR-4
Fairview Sch—*school* (8) CA-9
Fairview Sch—*school* (6) CO-8
Fairview Sch—*school* FL-3
Fairview Sch—*school* (4) GA-3
Fairview Sch—*school* ID-8
Fairview Sch—*school* (31) IL-6
Fairview Sch—*school* (2) IN-6
Fairview Sch—*school* (11) IA-7
Fairview Sch—*school* (2) KS-7
Fairview Sch—*school* (5) KY-4
Fairview Sch—*school* LA-4
Fairview Sch—*school* ME-1
Fairview Sch—*school* (9) MI-6
Fair View Sch—*school* MN-6
Fairview Sch—*school* MS-4
Fairview Sch—*school* (25) MO-7
Fairview Sch—*school* (6) MT-8
Fairview Sch—*school* (23) NE-7
Fairview Sch—*school* (3) NJ-2
Fairview Sch—*school* (6) NC-3
Fairview Sch—*school* (4) OH-6
Fairview Sch—*school* (4) OK-5
Fairview Sch—*school* (2) OR-9
Fairview Sch—*school* (15) PA-2
Fairview Sch—*school* SC-3
Fairview Sch—*school* (13) SD-7
Fairview Sch—*school* (14) TN-4
Fairview Sch—*school* (4) TX-5
Fairview Sch—*school* UT-8
Fairview Sch—*school* (5) VA-3
Fairview Sch—*school* (3) WA-9
Fairview Sch—*school* (9) WV-2
Fairview Sch—*school* (6) WI-6
Fairview Sch—*school* WY-8
Fairview Sch (abandoned)—*school* (7) MO-7
Fairview Sch (abandoned)—*school* (8) PA-2
Fairview Sch (abandoned)—*school* SD-7
Fairview Sch (historical)—*school* (6) AL-4
Fairview Sch (historical)—*school* IA-7
Fairview Sch (historical)—*school* (4) MS-4
Fairview Sch (historical)—*school* (10) MO-7
Fairview Sch (historical)—*school* (2) PA-2
Fairview Sch (historical)—*school* SD-7
Fairview Sch (historical)—*school* (19) TN-4
Fair View Sch (historical)—*school* TN-4
Fairview Sch (historical)—*school* (8) TN-4
Fair View Sch (historical)—*school* TN-4
Fairview Sch (historical)—*school* TN-4
Fair View Sch (historical)—*school* TN-4
Fairview Sch (historical)—*school* (2) TN-4
Fairview Sch Number 1—*school* (2) ND-7
Fairview Sch Number 3—*school* ND-7
Fairview School (abandoned)—*locale* CA-9
Fairview School (abandoned)—*locale* MO-7
Fairview School (historical)—*locale* (2) MO-7
Fairview Schoolhouse—*hist pl* NJ-2
*Fairview School Number 6* SD-7
Fairview School Oil Field—*oilfield* KS-7
Fairview Shop Ctr—*locale* MA-1
Fairview Shop Ctr—*locale* NC-3
Fairview Shopping Plaza—*locale* MA-1
**Fairview Shores**—*pop pl* FL-3
Fairview Shores Baptist Ch—*church* FL-3
Fairview (Site)—*locale* ID-8
Fairview (Site)—*locale* NV-8
Fairview-Southdale Hosp—*hospital* MN-6
Fairview South Sch—*school* IL-6
*Fairview Spring* UT-8
Fairview Spring—*spring* OR-9
Fairview Spring—*spring* (2) WA-9
**Fairview (sta.)**—*pop pl* NC-3
Fairview State Hosp—*hospital* CA-9
Fairview State Hosp—*hospital* PA-2
**Fairview Station**—*pop pl* IN-6
*Fair View Store* AL-4
*Fairview Store* TN-4
**Fairview (subdivision)**—*pop pl* (2) AL-4
**Fairview (subdivision)**—*pop pl* MA-1
**Fairview (subdivision)**—*pop pl* (2) NC-3
**Fairview (subdivision)**—*pop pl* TN-4
Fairview Substation—*locale* AZ-5
Fairview-Sumach—*CDP* WA-9
Fairview Tabernacle—*church* NC-3
Fairview Tabernacle—*church* TN-4
Fairview Tithing Office/Bishop's Storehouse—*hist pl* UT-8
*Fairview Township* KS-7
Fairview Township—*civil* (2) KS-7
Fairview Township—*civil* PA-2
Fairview Township—*civil* (5) SD-7
Fairview Township—*fmr MCD* (6) IA-7
**Fairview Township**—*pop pl* (8) KS-7
**Fairview Township**—*pop pl* (3) MO-7
**Fairview Township**—*pop pl* NE-7
**Fairview Township**—*pop pl* (2) ND-7
**Fairview Township**—*pop pl* (6) SD-7
Fairview Township Cem—*cemetery* IA-7
Fairview Township (historical)—*civil* ND-7
Fairview (Township of)—*fmr MCD* AR-4
Fairview (Township of)—*fmr MCD* NC-3
**Fairview (Township of)**—*pop pl* IL-6
**Fairview (Township of)**—*pop pl* IN-6
**Fairview (Township of)**—*pop pl* (2) MN-6
**Fairview (Township of)**—*pop pl* (5) PA-2
Fairview Trail—*trail* MT-8
Fair View Trail—*trail* PA-2
*Fairview (Trailer Park)* IL-6
**Fairview (Trailer Park)**—*pop pl* MD-2
*Fairview United Methodist Ch* TN-4
*Fairview United Methodist Church* AL-4
*Fairview United Methodist Church* MS-4
*Fairview Valley* NV-8
Fairview Valley—*basin* CA-9
Fairview Valley—*basin* NV-8
Fairview Valley Sch—*school* CO-8
**Fairview Village**—*pop pl* PA-2
Fairview Wash—*stream* NV-8
*Fairview Wesleyan Church* AL-4
Fairview West—*locale* AL-4
Fairview West Ch—*church* AL-4
*Fairview West Missionary Baptist Ch* AL-4
Fairview West Shop Ctr—*locale* AL-4
Fairview Wildlife—*reservoir* NC-3
Fairview Wildlife Club Dam—*dam* NC-3
Fairview Windmill—*locale* NM-5
Fairview Work Center—*building* AL-4
Fairview Youth Camp—*locale* VA-3
**Fairvilla**—*pop pl* FL-3
Fairvilla Shopping Center—*locale* FL-3
Fairville—*locale* CA-9
Fairville—*locale* MO-7
**Fairville**—*pop pl* IA-7
**Fairville**—*pop pl* NY-2
**Fairville**—*pop pl* (2) PA-2
Fairville Post Office (historical)—*building* PA-2
Fairville Station—*locale* NY-2
**Fairville Township**—*pop pl* ND-7
Fairvue—*hist pl* (2) TN-4
**Fairwater**—*pop pl* WI-6
Fairwater Cem—*cemetery* MN-6
*Fair Water (corporate and RR name Fairwater)* WI-6
Fair Watershed Y-24-1 Dam—*dam* MS-4
**Fairway**—*pop pl* KS-7
**Fairway**—*pop pl* KY-4
**Fairway**—*pop pl* (2) MD-2
**Fairway**—*pop pl* PA-2
**Fairway Acres**—*pop pl* NC-3
Fairway Center (Shop Ctr)—*locale* FL-3
Fairway Creek—*stream* MT-8
**Fairway Drive (subdivision)**—*pop pl* AL-4
Fairway Elem Sch—*school* FL-3
*Fairway Estates* (2) IL-6
**Fairway Estates**—*pop pl* CO-8
**Fairway Estates**—*pop pl* TN-4
**Fairway Estates Condominium**—*pop pl* UT-8
**Fairway Estates Subdivision**—*pop pl* UT-8
**Fairway Falls**—*pop pl* DE-2
**Fairway Fields Subdivision**—*pop pl* UT-8
**Fairway Forest (subdivision)**—*pop pl* NC-3
**Fairway Heights (subdivision)**—*pop pl* NC-3
**Fairway Hills**—*pop pl* MD-2
**Fairway Hills**—*pop pl* NC-3
Fairway Hunt Club—*other* TX-5
Fairway Island—*island* (2) AK-9
Fairway Lake—*lake* FL-3
Fairway Market Shop Ctr—*locale* FL-3
**Fairway Oaks**—*pop pl* GA-3
*Fairway of Country Lakes, The* IL-6
*Fairway Park* CA-9
Fairway Park—*park* FL-3
Fairway Park—*uninc pl* CA-9
**Fairway Park Subdivision**—*pop pl* UT-8
Fairway Reef—*bar* AK-9
Fairway Rock—*island* AK-9
Fairways Airfield—*airport* OR-9
Fairway Sch—*school* FL-3
Fairway Shop Ctr—*locale* FL-3
Fairway Shops—*locale* KS-7
**Fairway Trace**—*pop pl* IL-6
**Fairway View Estates**—*pop pl* OH-6
**Fairway Villas (subdivision)**—*pop pl* DE-2
*Fair Weather* IL-6
Fairweather—*other* IL-6
Fairweather, James F.-Lamb, Jacob C., House—*hist pl* MI-6
Fairweather, Mount—*summit* AK-9
Fairweather Bay—*bay* WA-9
**Fairweather Corners**—*pop pl* NY-2
Fairweather Glacier—*glacier* AK-9
Fairweather Ground—*bar* AK-9
Fairweather Hill—*summit* MA-1
*Fairweather Island* CT-1
*Fairweather Point* WA-9
Fairweather Range—*range* AK-9
Fairween Spring—*spring* NV-8
*Fairwind Acres* OH-6
**Fairwind Acres**—*pop pl* OH-6
**Fairwinds**—*pop pl* DE-2
Fairwinds Baptist Ch—*church* DE-2
Fairwinds Baptist Church Sch—*school* DE-2
Fairwinds Independent Bible Ch—*church* DE-2
**Fairwinds Mobile Home Park**—*pop pl* DE-2
**Fairwold**—*pop pl* SC-3
Fairwold JHS—*school* SC-3
Fairwood—*CDP* WA-9
Fairwood—*locale* VA-3
Fairwood Acres—*locale* VA-3
Fairwood Cem—*cemetery* VA-3
Fairwood Ch—*church* VA-3
Fairwood Drain—*stream* IN-6
*Fairwood Hills* IN-6
**Fairwood Hills**—*pop pl* IN-6
Fairwood Park—*park* FL-3
Fairwood Park—*park* MN-6
Fairwood Park—*park* OH-6
**Fairwood Park Subdivision**—*pop pl* UT-8
**Fairwoods**—*pop pl* NJ-2
Fairwood Sch—*school* CA-9
Fairwood Sch—*school* IL-6
Fairwood Sch—*school* (2) OH-6
**Fairwood VIII (subdivision)**—*pop pl* (2) AZ-5
Fairy—*locale* GA-3
**Fairy**—*pop pl* TX-5
Fairy, Lake—*lake* FL-3
Fairy Bluff—*cliff* WI-6
Fairy Castle—*pillar* UT-8
*Fairy Cave* MO-7
Fairy Cem—*cemetery* TX-5
*Fairy Creek* OR-9
Fairy Creek—*stream* MT-8
Fairy Creek—*stream* OR-9
Fairy Creek—*stream* WY-8
Fairy Creek Trail—*trail* WY-8
Fairy Dell—*flat* NV-8
Fairy Fair—*stream* NC-3
Fairy Falls—*falls* WA-9
Fairy Falls—*falls* WY-8
Fairy Flat—*flat* OR-9
Fairy Head—*cliff* ME-1
Fairy Hills—*summit* CO-8
Fairy Hill Sch (historical)—*school* MS-4
Fairy Ladder Falls—*falls* NY-2
*Fairy Lake* LA-4
*Fairy Lake* TX-5
Fairy Lake—*lake* CT-1
Fairy Lake—*lake* (2) FL-3
Fairy Lake—*lake* (3) MN-6
Fairy Lake—*lake* MT-8
**Fairy Lake**—*pop pl* CT-1
*Fairy Lake Brook* CT-1
Fairy Lake Campground—*locale* MT-8
Fairyland—*area* UT-8
Fairyland—*other* GA-3
**Fairyland**—*pop pl* FL-3
**Fairyland**—*pop pl* TN-4
*Fairyland Acres* TN-4
Fairyland Canyon—*valley* UT-8
Fairyland Caverns—*cave* AL-4
Fairyland (CCD)—*cens area* GA-3
*Fairyland Crescent Castle* UT-8
Fairyland Island—*island* NY-2
*Fairyland Loop Trail* UT-8
Fairyland Park—*park* MO-7
Fairyland Point—*cliff* UT-8
Fairyland Pond—*lake* MA-1
Fairyland Trail—*trail* UT-8
Fairylawn—*locale* ID-8
Fairy Rock—*summit* MN-6
Fairy Shelter—*locale* OR-9
Fairy Springs—*spring* WY-8
Fairystone Ch—*church* VA-3
Fairy Stone Lake—*reservoir* VA-3
Fairy Stone State Park—*park* VA-3
*Fairy Temple* UT-8
Fairy Valley—*valley* GA-3
Fairyview Sch—*school* IA-7
Fairyview Sch—*school* SD-7
Fairywood—*uninc pl* PA-2
Fairywood Sch—*school* PA-2
Fais—*island* FM-9
**Fais, Oror En**—*pop pl* FM-9
Faisawan—*well* FM-9
Faisefin, Ununen—*bar* FM-9
FAI Seventeen Interchange—*crossing* AZ-5
Faisewan—*well* FM-9
Fais (Municipality)—*civ div* FM-9
**Faison**—*pop pl* NC-3
Faison—*stream* FM-9
Faison—*well* FM-9
Faison, Oror En—*locale* FM-9
Faison Cem—*cemetery* NC-3
Faison Hill—*summit* AL-4
**Faisonia**—*pop pl* MS-4
Faisonia P.O. (historical)—*building* MS-4
*Faisonia School* MS-4
**Faisons**—*pop pl* NC-3
Faisons Chapel—*church* NC-3
*Faisons Old Tavern* NC-3
Faison (Township of)—*fmr MCD* NC-3
Faisst Cem—*cemetery* AR-4
Faith—*locale* AR-4
Faith—*locale* MO-7
Faith—*other* KY-4
**Faith**—*pop pl* MN-6
**Faith**—*pop pl* NC-3
**Faith**—*pop pl* SD-7
Faith, Hope and Charity Pentecostal Ch—*church* MS-4
Faith, Lake—*lake* FL-3
Faith Alliance Ch—*church* NC-3
Faith Apostolic Mission—*church* IN-6
Faith Apostolic Pentecostal Ch—*church* IN-6
Faith Assembly Ch—*church* AR-4
Faith Assembly of God—*church* KS-7
Faith Assembly of God Ch—*church* FL-3
Faith Assembly of God Ch—*church* IN-6
Faith Assembly of God Ch—*church* (3) MS-4
Faith Assembly of God Ch—*church* MO-7
*Faith Baptist Ch* AL-4
*Faith Baptist Ch* TN-4
Faith Baptist Ch—*church* (5) AL-4
Faith Baptist Ch—*church* DE-2
Faith Baptist Ch—*church* (8) FL-3
Faith Baptist Ch—*church* IN-6
Faith Baptist Ch—*church* KS-7
Faith Baptist Ch—*church* (3) MS-4
Faith Baptist Ch—*church* (2) TN-4
Faith Baptist Ch (Bountiful)—*church* UT-8
Faith Baptist Ch (Layton)—*church* UT-8
Faith Baptist Ch of Margate—*church* FL-3
Faith Baptist Ch of Starkville—*church* MS-4
Faith Baptist Ch of the Deaf—*church* AL-4
Faith Baptist Ch (Salina)—*church* UT-8
Faith Baptist Ch (Springville)—*church* UT-8
Faith Baptist Church Sch—*school* FL-3
Faith Baptist Sch—*school* MS-4
Faith Baptist Temple—*church* FL-3
Faith Bible Ch—*church* AL-4
Faith Bible Ch—*church* IL-6
Faith Bible Ch—*church* (3) MI-6
Faith Bible Ch—*church* MS-4
Faith Bible Ch—*church* TN-4
Faith Bible Ch—*church* VA-3
Faith Bible Chapel—*church* PA-2
Faith Blvd Ch—*church* AL-4
Faith Cem—*cemetery* AL-4
Faith Cem—*cemetery* IA-7
Faith Cem—*cemetery* MI-6
Faith Cem—*cemetery* (5) MN-6
Faith Cem—*cemetery* ND-7
Faith Cem—*cemetery* SD-7
*Faith Ch* AL-4
*Faith Ch* DE-2
*Faith Ch* IN-6
Faith Ch—*church* (17) AL-4
Faith Ch—*church* (3) AR-4
Faith Ch—*church* CT-1
Faith Ch—*church* DE-2
Faith Ch—*church* (7) FL-3
Faith Ch—*church* (9) GA-3
Faith Ch—*church* (6) IL-6
Faith Ch—*church* (3) IN-6
Faith Ch—*church* (2) KY-4
Faith Ch—*church* (2) LA-4
Faith Ch—*church* (3) MD-2
Faith Ch—*church* (12) MI-6
Faith Ch—*church* (9) MN-6
Faith Ch—*church* (3) MS-4
Faith Ch—*church* (3) MO-7
Faith Ch—*church* (3) NJ-2
Faith Ch—*church* (4) NY-2
Faith Ch—*church* (22) NC-3
Faith Ch—*church* (2) ND-7
Faith Ch—*church* (6) OH-6
Faith Ch—*church* OK-5
Faith Ch—*church* (9) PA-2
Faith Ch—*church* (10) SC-3
Faith Ch—*church* (3) TN-4
Faith Ch—*church* (4) TX-5
Faith Ch—*church* (11) VA-3
Faith Ch—*church* WV-2
Faith Ch—*church* (6) WI-6
Faith Chapel—*church* (5) AL-4
Faith Chapel—*church* (2) FL-3
Faith Chapel—*church* KY-4
Faith Chapel—*church* MI-6
Faith Chapel—*church* MN-6
Faith Chapel—*church* (2) MS-4
Faith Chapel—*church* MO-7
Faith Chapel—*church* NM-5
Faith Chapel—*church* NY-2
Faith Chapel—*church* (2) OK-5
Faith Chapel—*church* (2) PA-2
Faith Chapel—*church* TN-4
Faith Chapel—*church* (2) TX-5
Faith Chapel—*church* VA-3
Faith Chapel—*hist pl* GA-3
Faith Chapel Assembly of God Ch—*church* FL-3
*Faith Chapel Baptist Ch* AL-4
*Faith Chapel Ch* AL-4
Faith Chapel Ch—*church* (2) AL-4
Faith Chapel Ch—*church* AR-4
Faith Chapel Foursquare Gospel Ch—*church* UT-8
Faith Chapel Full Gospel Ch—*church* KS-7
Faith Chapel Pentecostal Holiness Ch—*church* AL-4
Faith Child Development Center—*school* FL-3
Faith Childrens Home Mission—*church* AL-4
Faith Ch of God in Christ—*church* IN-6
*Faith Ch of the Nazarene* AL-4
Faith Christian Acad—*school* FL-3
Faith Christian Acad—*school* PA-2
Faith Christian Acad—*school* TN-4
Faith Christian Center—*church* MS-4
Faith Christian Ch—*church* IA-7
Faith Christian Ch—*church* KS-7
Faith Christian Day Sch—*school* NC-3
Faith Christian Fellowship Ch—*church* FL-3
Faith Christian Sch—*school* (2) FL-3
Faith Church Cem—*cemetery* GA-3
Faith City Ch—*church* FL-3
Faith City Christian Sch—*school* DE-2
Faith Congregational Methodist Ch—*church* TN-4
Faith Covenant Ch—*church* FL-3
Faith Creation Fellowship—*church* FL-3
Faith Creek—*stream* (2) AK-9
Faith Day Sch—*school* CA-9
Faith Deliverance Ch—*church* GA-3
Faith Deliverance Ch of God in Christ—*church* KS-7
Faith Elem Sch—*school* NC-3
Faith Evangelical Ch—*church* IA-7
Faith Fellowship Foursquare Gospel Ch—*church* UT-8
Faith Freewill Baptist Ch—*church* AL-4
Faith Freewill Baptist Ch—*church* MS-4
Faith Freewill Baptist Ch—*church* TN-4
Faithful Band Ch—*church* NC-3
Faithful Ch—*church* GA-3
Faithful Ch—*church* LA-4
Faithful Christian Ch—*church* GA-3
Faithful Green Lake—*reservoir* PA-2
Faithful Missionary Baptist Ch—*church* DE-2
Faith Gulch—*valley* MT-8
*Faith Hill Ch* AL-4
Faith Hill Ch—*church* AL-4
Faith Hill Ch—*church* KY-4
Faith Home For Children—*building* VA-3
Faith Home Teen Ranch—*locale* CA-9
Faith Hope Ch—*church* VA-3
Faith Hosp—*hospital* MO-7
Faith Independent Baptist Ch—*church* UT-8
*Faith Lake* MN-6
Faith Lake—*lake* MN-6
Faith Lake—*lake* MT-8
Faith Lighthouse Ch—*church* NC-3
Faith Lighthouse Tabernacle—*church* NC-3
Faith Lutheran Ch—*church* AL-4
Faith Lutheran Ch—*church* (2) FL-3
Faith Lutheran Ch—*church* IN-6
Faith Lutheran Ch—*church* KS-7
Faith Lutheran Ch—*church* MI-6
Faith Lutheran Ch—*church* MS-4
Faith Lutheran Ch—*church* MO-7
Faith Lutheran Ch—*church* TN-4
Faith Lutheran Ch—*church* UT-8
Faith Lutheran Ch (LCA)—*church* FL-3
Faith Lutheran Ch (LCMS)—*church* FL-3
Faith Lutheran Christian Day Sch—*school* FL-3
Faith Lutheran Preschool and Kindergarten—*school* FL-3
Faith Lutheran Sch—*school* CA-9
Faith Lutheran Sch—*school* (4) FL-3

Faith Manna Bible Mission—*church* ... OK-5
Faith Manor (historical)—*locale* ... AL-4
Faith Memorial Cem—*cemetery* ... AL-4
Faith Memorial Ch—*church* ... AR-4
Faith Memorial Chapel—*church* ... NC-3
Faith Mennonite HS—*school* ... PA-2
Faith Milling Company—*hist pl* ... MN-6
Faith Mission—*church* ... TN-4
Faith Mission—*hist pl* ... CA-9
Faith Missionary Baptist Ch—*church* ... IN-6
Faith Missionary Ch—*church* ... LA-4
Faith Missionary Ch—*church* ... NC-3
Faith Mission Ch—*church* ... VA-3
Faith Mission Ch of God—*church* ... AL-4
Faith Mission Ch of God in Christ—*church*. KS-7
Faith Mission Covenant Ch—*church* ... AL-4
Faith Mount Ch—*church* ... KY-4
Faith Municipal Airp—*airport* ... SD-7
Faith Nursing Home—*hospital* ... IA-7
Faith Olive Ch—*church* ... NC-3
Faithorn—*locale* ... IL-6
**Faithorn**—*pop pl* ... MI-6
Faithorn Creek—*stream* ... MI-6
**Faithorn (Township of)**—*pop pl* ... MI-6
Faith Pentecostal Ch of God—*church* ... MS-4
*Faith Presbyterian Ch* ... AL-4
Faith Presbyterian Ch—*church* ... DE-2
Faith Presbyterian Ch—*church* ... FL-3
Faith Presbyterian Ch—*church* ... IN-6
Faith Presbyterian Ch—*church* (4) ... MS-4
Faith Preschool—*school* ... FL-3
Faith Reform Presbyterian Ch—*church* ... PA-2
Faith Rescue Mission—*church* ... AL-4
Faith Rescue Mission Farm—*locale* ... AL-4
Faith Revival Center—*church* ... MS-4
Faith Revival Center—*church* ... MO-7
Faith Sch—*school* ... AL-4
Faith Sch—*school* ... CO-8
Faith Sch—*school* (2) ... GA-3
Faith Sch—*school* ... LA-4
Faith Sch—*school* ... MI-6
Faith Sch—*school* ... MN-6
Faith Sch—*school* ... MO-7
Faith Sch—*school* ... SD-7
Faith Southern Methodist Ch—*church* ... TN-4
Faith Spring—*spring* ... OR-9
Faith Spring Forest Camp—*locale* ... OR-9
Faith State Wildlife Mngmt Area—*park* ... MN-6
Faith Swedish Cem—*cemetery* ... MN-6
Faith Tabernacle—*church* (2) ... AL-4
Faith Tabernacle—*church* ... AR-4
Faith Tabernacle—*church* (3) ... FL-3
Faith Tabernacle—*church* (3) ... GA-3
Faith Tabernacle—*church* ... MS-4
Faith Tabernacle—*church* (2) ... MO-7
Faith Tabernacle—*church* (6) ... NC-3
Faith Tabernacle—*church* (2) ... OK-5
Faith Tabernacle—*church* ... SC-3
Faith Tabernacle—*church* (2) ... TN-4
Faith Tabernacle—*church* (2) ... TX-5
Faith Tabernacle—*church* (2) ... VA-3
Faith Tabernacle—*church* ... WV-2
Faith Tabernacle Ch—*church* (2) ... AL-4
Faith Tabernacle Ch—*church* (2) ... MS-4
Faith Tabernacle Ch—*church* ... NC-3
Faith Tabernacle Ch of God—*church* ... AL-4
Faith Tabernacle of Tampa—*church* ... FL-3
Faith Tabernacle United Holiness Ch—*church* ... DE-2
Faith Temple—*church* (2) ... AL-4
Faith Temple—*church* (2) ... FL-3
Faith Temple—*church* (2) ... GA-3
Faith Temple—*church* ... NC-3
Faith Temple—*church* ... PA-2
Faith Temple—*church* (2) ... SC-3
Faith Temple—*church* ... TX-5
Faith Temple—*church* (2) ... VA-3
Faith Temple Assembly of God—*church* ... FL-3
Faith Temple Ch—*church* ... AL-4
Faith Temple Ch—*church* ... KY-4
Faith Temple Ch—*church* ... MI-6
Faith Temple Ch—*church* ... NC-3
Faith Temple Ch—*church* (4) ... TX-5
Faith Temple Ch of God—*church* ... AL-4
Faith Temple Ch of God—*church* ... FL-3
Faith Temple Ch of God in Christ—*church* ... MS-4
Faith Temple Ch of God in Christ—*church* (2) ... TN-4
Faith Temple Holiness Ch—*church* ... AL-4
Faith Temple Number 2—*church* ... AL-4
Faith Temple Pentecostal Ch—*church* ... UT-8
Faith Theological Seminary—*school* ... PA-2
Faith United Ch—*church* ... FL-3
Faith United Ch—*church* ... KS-7
Faith United Ch—*church* ... PA-2
Faith United Ch of Christ—*church* ... FL-3
Faith United Methodist Ch—*church* (2) ... IN-6
Faith Valley—*flat* ... CA-9
Faith Valley Ch—*church* ... GA-3
Faith Valley Christian Sch—*school* ... PA-2
Faith View Ch—*church* ... AL-4
Faithway Baptist Ch—*church* ... MS-4
Faithway Ch—*church* ... AL-4
Faithway Landmark Ch—*church* ... MS-4
Faith Wesleyan Ch—*church* ... FL-3
Faith Wesleyn Ch—*church* ... FL-3
Faith World—*church* ... FL-3
Faith-7 Sch—*school* ... OK-5
Faiti, Unun En—*bar* ... FM-9
*Faitruk-Berg* ... FM-9
*Faituk* ... FM-9
Faiumuolegau Rocks—*island* ... AS-9
Faiver Drain—*canal* ... MI-6
Faiview Cem—*cemetery* ... NY-2
Faix—*locale* ... TN-4
Faja—*ridge* ... GU-9
Fajada Butte—*summit* ... NM-5
Fajada Wash—*stream* ... NM-5
**Fajardo**—*pop pl* (2) ... PR-3
Fajardo, Rada—*other* ... PR-3
Fajardo (Municipio)—*civil* ... PR-3
Fajardo (Pueblo)—*fmr MCD* ... PR-3
Fakahatchee—*locale* ... FL-3
Fakahatchee Bay—*bay* ... FL-3
Fakahatchee Pass—*channel* ... FL-3
Fakahatchee River—*stream* ... FL-3
Fakahatchee Strand—*swamp* ... FL-3
Fakahatchee Strand State Preserve—*park* .. FL-3
*Fakanachia River* ... FL-3
Fakasur—*spring* ... FM-9
Faka Union Bay—*bay* ... FL-3
Faka Union Canal—*canal* ... FL-3
Faka Union River—*stream* ... FL-3
Fake Creek—*stream* ... OR-9
Fake Creek Trail—*trail* ... OR-9
Fake Pass—*channel* ... AK-9
Faker—*locale* ... TX-5
Fakes Cem—*cemetery* ... AR-4
Fakes Cem—*cemetery* ... KY-4
Fakes Chapel—*church* ... AR-4
*Fakha Union Bay* ... FL-3
*Fakitchipunta Creek* ... AL-4
*Fakit Lapali Creek* ... MS-4
**Fakowon, Oror En**—*pop pl* ... FM-9
Fakuruwon—*summit* ... FM-9
*Fal* ... DE-2
*Fal* ... FM-9
Fal—*locale* ... LA-4
Fala Ane Point—*cape* ... AS-9
*Falabanges* ... FM-9
*Fala-Beguets Island* ... FM-9
Fala-Beguets (Municipality)—*civ div* ... FM-9
*Falabenas* ... FM-9
*Falafa* ... FM-9
Falagon—*slope* ... MH-9
*Falai Island* ... FM-9
*Falaik* ... FM-9
Falais Siding—*locale* ... NV-8
Falaite Island—*island* ... FM-9
**Falakto**—*pop pl* ... AL-4
Falalis—*island* ... FM-9
Falalop—*CDP* ... FM-9
Falalop—*island* ... FM-9
*Falalu Island* ... FM-9
*Falam* ... FM-9
Falamalok—*island* ... FM-9
*Falami* ... FM-9
*Falamu* ... FM-9
Falana Island—*island* ... FL-3
*Falanan* ... FM-9
*Falang* ... FM-9
*Falanu* ... FM-9
*Falape* ... FM-9
*Falapi* ... FM-9
*Falas* ... FM-9
Falaseeitoafa Point—*cape* ... AS-9
*Falas Islands* ... FM-9
*Falasit* ... FM-9
*Falasit Island* ... FM-9
*Falasit Riff* ... FM-9
*Falat* ... FM-9
*Falau* ... FM-9
*Falauenival* ... FM-9
*Falauw* ... FM-9
Falaya, Bogue—*stream* ... LA-4
Falba Cem—*cemetery* (2) ... TX-5
Falbo Park—*park* ... OH-6
**Falco**—*pop pl* ... AL-4
Falco Bay—*swamp* ... AL-4
Falco (CCD)—*cens area* ... AL-4
Falco Ch—*church* ... AL-4
Falco Division—*civil* ... AL-4
Falcomer Cem—*cemetery* ... MS-4
Falcon—*locale* ... AR-4
Falcon—*locale* ... ID-8
Falcon—*locale* ... KY-4
**Falcon**—*pop pl* ... CO-8
**Falcon**—*pop pl* ... MS-4
**Falcon**—*pop pl* ... MO-7
**Falcon**—*pop pl* ... NC-3
**Falcon**—*pop pl* ... TN-4
**Falcon**—*pop pl* ... TX-5
Falcon, Bayou—*stream* ... LA-4
Falcon, Cape—*cape* ... OR-9
Falcon, Mount—*summit* ... CO-8
Falcona Beach—*beach* ... GU-9
Falcon Arm—*bay* ... AK-9
*Falcon Baptist Church* ... TN-4
Falcon Bayou—*stream* ... LA-4
Falconberry Guard Station—*locale* ... ID-8
Falconberry Lake—*lake* ... ID-8
Falconberry Peak—*summit* ... ID-8
Falconberry Ranch—*locale* ... ID-8
**Falcon Bridge (subdivision)**—*pop pl* ... NC-3
Falconbury Cem—*cemetery* ... KY-4
Falcon Butte—*summit* ... OR-9
Falcon Camp—*locale* ... NJ-2
Falcon Camp—*locale* ... PA-2
Falcon Canyon—*valley* ... NV-8
Falcon Castle Ruins—*locale* ... CO-8
Falcon Cem—*cemetery* ... AR-4
Falcon Cem—*cemetery* ... TN-4
Falcon Ch—*church* ... MO-7
Falcon Ch—*church* ... TN-4
Falcon Chiquita Dam—*dam* ... TX-5
**Falcon Courts North**—*pop pl* ... NJ-2
Falcon Creek—*stream* ... IN-6
Falcon Creek—*stream* ... OR-9
Falcon Creek—*stream* ... WY-8
**Falconcrest**—*pop pl* ... PA-2
**Falconcrest Subdivision**—*pop pl* ... UT-8
Falcon Dam—*dam* ... TX-5
Falcon Dam Station—*locale* ... TX-5
Falcon Divide—*ridge* ... AZ-5
**Falconer**—*pop pl* ... NY-2
**Falconer Junction**—*pop pl* ... NY-2
Falconer Park—*park* ... NY-2
Falconer Sch—*school* ... IL-6
Falconer Town Hall—*building* ... ND-7
**Falconer Township**—*pop pl* ... ND-7
**Falconerville**—*pop pl* ... VA-3
**Falcon Estates**—*pop pl* ... AZ-5
**Falcon Estates**—*pop pl* ... CO-8
Falcon Field Airp—*airport* ... AZ-5
Falcon Field (airport)—*airport* ... MS-4
**Falconhead**—*pop pl* ... OK-5
**Falconhead (subdivision)**—*pop pl* ... AL-4
**Falcon Heights**—*pop pl* ... MN-6
**Falcon Heights**—*pop pl* ... OR-9
**Falcon Heights**—*pop pl* ... TX-5
Falcon Heights Sch—*school* ... MN-6
Falcon Helipad Heliport—*airport* ... MO-7
Falcon Hill—*summit* ... NV-8
Falconhurst—*hist pl* ... TN-4
**Falconhurst Subdivision**—*pop pl* ... UT-8
Falcon Lake—*lake* ... AK-9
Falcon Lake—*lake* ... CO-8
Falcon Lake—*lake* ... WA-9
**Falcon Lake**—*pop pl* ... TX-5
Falcon Manor—*locale* ... NY-2
**Falcon Mesa**—*pop pl* ... TX-5
Falcon Mine—*mine* ... CA-9
Falcon Mines—*mine* ... NV-8
Falcon Oil And Gas Field—*oilfield* ... AR-4
Falcon Park—*park* ... AZ-5
Falcon Park—*park* ... OR-9
Falcon Park—*park* ... TX-5
Falcon Park—*park* ... WI-6
*Falcon Point* ... MD-2
Falcon Point—*cape* ... NC-3
**Falcon Point (subdivision)**—*pop pl* ... NC-3
Falcon Post Office (historical)—*building* ... TN-4
Falcon Rock—*island* ... OR-9
Falcon Rsvr—*reservoir* ... TX-5
Falcon Sch—*school* ... MS-4
Falcon Sch—*school* ... OK-5
**Falcon Shores**—*pop pl* ... TX-5
Falcon Springs Wildlife Area—*park* ... IA-7
Falcon Stadium—*other* ... CO-8
Falcon State Park—*park* ... TX-5
Falcon Substation—*locale* ... AZ-5
Falcon Tabernacle—*hist pl* ... NC-3
Falcon Valley—*valley* ... AZ-5
Falcon Valley Ranch—*locale* ... AZ-5
**Falcon Village**—*pop pl* ... TX-5
Falcon Windmill—*locale* ... TX-5
**Falconwood**—*pop pl* ... NY-2
*Faldot* ... ND-7
*Falealei Durchfahrt* ... FM-9
*Falealej Durchfahrt* ... FM-9
*Faleallej Pass* ... FM-9
*Faleannej Pass* ... FM-9
Faleapoi Point—*cape* ... AS-9
**Faleasao**—*pop pl* ... AS-9
Faleasao (County of)—*civ div* ... AS-9
*Faleasicz* ... FM-9
*Faleasioz Reef* ... FM-9
*Faleasits* ... FM-9
*Faleasits Reef* ... FM-9
*Faleat* ... FM-9
*Faleat Island* ... FM-9
Faleau, Bayou—*gut* ... LA-4
*Falebenges* ... FM-9
Faleiulu Stream—*stream* ... AS-9
Falema Creek, Bogue—*stream* ... MS-4
**Faleniu**—*pop pl* ... AS-9
*Faleosicz Island* ... FM-9
Faleoteine Point—*cape* ... AS-9
Faler Creek—*stream* ... WY-8
Faler Lake—*lake* ... WY-8
Fales, David G., House—*hist pl* ... RI-1
Fales Basin—*basin* ... CA-9
Fales Ch—*church* ... GA-3
Fales Creek—*stream* ... CA-9
Fales Creek—*stream* ... WY-8
Faleselau Ridge—*ridge* ... AS-9
Fales Flat—*flat* ... MT-8
Fales Hill—*summit* ... ME-1
*Fales Hot Spring* ... CA-9
**Fales Hot Springs**—*pop pl* ... CA-9
Fales Rocks—*summit* ... WY-8
Fales Sch—*school* ... MA-1
*Faleu Island* ... FM-9
*Faleu Islet* ... FM-9
Falewaidid—*island* ... FM-9
Falfa—*locale* ... AZ-5
Falfa—*locale* ... CO-8
**Falfa**—*pop pl* ... OK-5
Falfa Ch—*church* ... OK-5
**Falfurrias**—*pop pl* ... TX-5
Falfurrias (CCD)—*cens area* ... TX-5
Falfurrias Oil Field—*oilfield* ... TX-5
Fal'gaeg—*summit* ... FM-9
**Falgoust**—*pop pl* ... LA-4
Falgout Canal—*canal* ... LA-4
Falgout Canal Bayou—*gut* ... LA-4
*Falia* ... MS-4
Falia, Bogue—*stream* ... MS-4
Faliah, Bogue—*stream* ... MS-4
Falice Creek—*stream* ... OR-9
Falifi—*island* ... FM-9
Falili—*locale* ... AS-9
Falin Branch—*stream* ... VA-3
Falingun Hanom, Liyang—*cave* ... MH-9
*Falingun Hanum* ... MH-9
*Falipe* ... MH-9
Falipe, As—*slope* ... MH-9
Falipe, Kannat—*stream* ... MH-9
*Falipe Place* ... MH-9
*Falipe Ravine* ... MH-9
*Falipe Valley* ... MH-9
Falipi Island—*island* ... FM-9
*Falipu Island* ... FM-9
Falk Bridge—*bridge* ... ID-8
Falk Cem—*cemetery* ... ID-8
*Falk Cemetery* ... AL-4
Falk Creek—*stream* ... WA-9
Falke And Tillman Ditch—*canal* ... CA-9
Falke and Tillman Ditch—*canal* ... NV-8
Falkenberg Ranch—*locale* ... UT-8
Falkenham Camp—*locale* ... NH-1
Falkenrath Cem—*cemetery* ... MO-7
Falkenstein, Lewis, House—*hist pl* ... CA-9
Falker Swamp Cem—*cemetery* ... PA-2
Falk Hill—*summit* ... MI-6
*Falkingham's Cove* ... ME-1
**Falkirk**—*pop pl* ... ND-7
*Falk Island* ... OR-9
Falk Lake—*lake* ... MN-6
Falk Lake—*lake* ... WI-6
*Falkland* ... AL-4
Falkland—*hist pl* ... VA-3
**Falkland**—*pop pl* ... NC-3
**Falkland Apartments**—*pop pl* ... MD-2
Falkland (Township of)—*fmr MCD* ... NC-3
Falk Mill Hollow—*valley* ... MO-7
**Falkner**—*pop pl* ... AL-4
**Falkner**—*pop pl* ... MS-4
Falkner Baptist Ch—*church* ... MS-4
*Falkner Cem* ... MS-4
Falkner Cem—*cemetery* ... MS-4
Falkner Elem Sch—*school* ... MS-4
Falkner HS—*school* ... MS-4
Falkner Methodist Ch—*church* ... MS-4
Falkner Park—*park* ... NY-2
Falkner Presbyterian Ch—*church* ... MS-4
Falkner Sch (historical)—*school* ... AL-4
Falkner Spring—*spring* ... OR-9
Falkner Windmill—*locale* ... TX-5
*Falko* ... AL-4
Falk (Ruins)—*locale* ... CA-9
Falk Run—*stream* ... PA-2
Falk Sch—*school* ... TX-5
Falk Sch—*school* ... WI-6
Falks Lake—*lake* ... AK-9
Falks Lake—*reservoir* ... CA-9
**Falk (Township of)**—*pop pl* ... MN-6
**Falkville**—*pop pl* ... AL-4
Falkville (CCD)—*cens area* ... AL-4
Falkville Division—*civil* ... AL-4
Falkville HS—*school* ... AL-4
Fall—*locale* ... VA-3
Fall, The—*falls* ... OR-9
Fallager Creek—*stream* ... CA-9
Fallah, Bogue—*stream* ... MS-4
*Fallasberg* ... MI-6
*Fallasburg* ... MI-6
Fallasburg Covered Bridge—*hist pl* ... MI-6
Fallas Draw—*valley* ... WY-8
Fallas Mesa—*summit* ... CO-8
**Fallassburg**—*pop pl* ... MI-6
Fallassburg County Park—*park* ... MI-6
Fallass Cem—*cemetery* ... MI-6
Fallas Spring—*spring* ... CO-8
Fallback Plantation (historical)—*locale* ... MS-4
Fall Bluff—*cliff* ... AL-4
*Fall Branch* ... AL-4
*Fallbranch* ... TN-4
**Fall Branch**—*pop pl* ... TN-4
Fall Branch—*stream* (4) ... AL-4
Fall Branch—*stream* ... AR-4
Fall Branch—*stream* (4) ... GA-3
Fall Branch—*stream* (2) ... IN-6
Fall Branch—*stream* (3) ... KY-4
Fall Branch—*stream* (14) ... NC-3
Fall Branch—*stream* ... OK-5
Fall Branch—*stream* ... SC-3
Fall Branch—*stream* (20) ... TN-4
Fall Branch—*stream* (3) ... TX-5
Fall Branch—*stream* (3) ... VA-3
Fall Branch—*stream* ... WV-2
Fall Branch Cem—*cemetery* (2) ... TN-4
Fall Branch Ch—*church* ... NC-3
*Fall Branch Elementary School* ... TN-4
Fall Branch First Baptist Ch—*church* ... TN-4
Fall Branch Knob—*summit* ... GA-3
*Fallbranch Post Office* ... TN-4
Fall Branch Post Office—*building* ... TN-4
Fall Branch Scenic Area—*park* ... TN-4
Fall Branch Sch—*school* ... TN-4
Fall Branch Spring—*spring* ... TN-4
Fall Branch United Methodist Ch—*church* .. TN-4
*Fallbrook* ... PA-2
Fall Brook—*locale* ... PA-2
**Fallbrook**—*pop pl* ... CA-9
Fall Brook—*stream* (2) ... CT-1
Fall Brook—*stream* (3) ... ME-1
Fall Brook—*stream* (5) ... MA-1
Fall Brook—*stream* (9) ... NY-2
Fall Brook—*stream* (4) ... PA-2
Fall Brook—*stream* (3) ... VT-1
Fallbrook (CCD)—*cens area* ... CA-9
Fallbrook Country Club—*other* ... CA-9
Fall Brook Falls—*falls* ... NY-2
Fallbrook Falls—*falls* ... PA-2
**Fallbrook Junction**—*pop pl* ... CA-9
Fall Brook Lake—*reservoir* ... PA-2
Fall Brook Mines—*mine* ... PA-2
Fallbrook Point—*cape* ... NY-2
Fall Brook Reservoir Dam—*dam* ... MA-1
Fall Brook Rsvr—*reservoir* ... MA-1
Fall Brook Sch—*school* ... MA-1
Fallbrook Union HS—*school* ... CA-9
Fallbush Mtn—*summit* ... VA-3
Fallbush Mtn—*summit* ... WV-2
Fall Cabin Camp—*locale* ... CO-8
Fall Camp Lake—*lake* ... AK-9
Fall Camp Spring—*spring* ... CO-8
*Fall Canyon* ... WY-8
Fall Canyon—*valley* (3) ... AZ-5
Fall Canyon—*valley* (4) ... CA-9
Fall Canyon—*valley* (2) ... NM-5
Fall Canyon—*valley* ... OR-9
Fall Canyon—*valley* ... UT-8
Fall Cem—*cemetery* ... MS-4
Fall City—*locale* ... WA-9
**Fall City**—*pop pl* ... TN-4
**Fall City**—*pop pl* ... WA-9
**Fall City**—*pop pl* ... WI-6
*Fall City Baptist Church* ... TN-4
Fall City Cem—*cemetery* ... WA-9
Fall City Ch—*church* ... TN-4
*Fall City Church* ... AL-4
**Fallcliff**—*pop pl* ... NC-3
Fall Clove—*valley* ... NY-2
Fall Coulee—*valley* ... WI-6
*Fall Creek* ... ID-8
*Fall Creek* ... IN-6
*Fall Creek* ... MT-8
*Fall Creek* ... OR-9
*Fallcreek* ... TN-4
*Fall Creek* ... TX-5
*Fall Creek* ... WA-9
*Fall Creek* ... WY-8
Fall Creek—*locale* ... IL-6
Fall Creek—*locale* ... TN-4
Fall Creek—*locale* ... TX-5
**Fall Creek**—*pop pl* ... CO-8
**Fall Creek**—*pop pl* ... ID-8
**Fall Creek**—*pop pl* ... NC-3
**Fall Creek**—*pop pl* ... OR-9
**Fall Creek**—*pop pl* ... TN-4
**Fall Creek**—*pop pl* ... WI-6
Fall Creek—*stream* (4) ... AL-4
Fall Creek—*stream* (6) ... AK-9
Fall Creek—*stream* (2) ... AZ-5
Fall Creek—*stream* (3) ... AR-4
Fall Creek—*stream* (16) ... CA-9
Fall Creek—*stream* (12) ... CO-8
Fall Creek—*stream* (28) ... ID-8
Fall Creek—*stream* (2) ... IL-6
Fall Creek—*stream* (6) ... IN-6
Fall Creek—*stream* (2) ... KS-7
Fall Creek—*stream* (2) ... KY-4
Fall Creek—*stream* (2) ... MI-6
Fall Creek—*stream* ... MO-7
Fall Creek—*stream* (2) ... MT-8
Fall Creek—*stream* (3) ... NV-8
Fall Creek—*stream* (3) ... NY-2
Fall Creek—*stream* (8) ... NC-3
Fall Creek—*stream* ... OH-6
Fall Creek—*stream* ... OK-5
Fall Creek—*stream* (59) ... OR-9
Fall Creek—*stream* (3) ... PA-2
Fall Creek—*stream* (3) ... SC-3
Fall Creek—*stream* (11) ... TN-4
Fall Creek—*stream* (6) ... TX-5
Fall Creek—*stream* ... UT-8
Fall Creek—*stream* (5) ... VA-3
Fall Creek—*stream* (11) ... WA-9
Fall Creek—*stream* (2) ... WI-6
Fall Creek—*stream* (8) ... WY-8
Fall Creek Baptist Ch—*church* ... IN-6
*Fall Creek Baptist Church* ... TN-4
Fall Creek Bar—*bar* ... ID-8
Fall Creek Basin—*basin* ... ID-8
Fall Creek Cabin—*locale* ... OR-9
Fall Creek Campground—*locale* ... TN-4
Fall Creek Campground—*park* ... OR-9
Fall Creek Cave—*cave* ... TN-4
Fall Creek Cem—*cemetery* ... IL-6
Fall Creek Cem—*cemetery* ... IN-6
Fall Creek Cem—*cemetery* ... KS-7
Fall Creek Cem—*cemetery* ... TN-4
Fall Creek Cem—*cemetery* ... TX-5
Fall Creek Ch—*church* ... IL-6
Fall Creek Ch—*church* ... KY-4
Fall Creek Ch—*church* (3) ... NC-3
Fall Creek Ch—*church* ... OH-6
Fall Creek Ch—*church* ... SC-3
Fall Creek Ch—*church* (4) ... TN-4
Fall Creek Ch—*church* ... VA-3
Fall Creek Copper Mine—*mine* ... OR-9
Fall Creek Dam—*dam* ... OR-9
Fall Creek Elem Sch—*school* ... IN-6
Fall Creek Falls—*falls* ... ID-8
Fall Creek Falls—*falls* (3) ... OR-9
Fall Creek Falls—*falls* ... TN-4
*Fall Creek Falls State Park* ... TN-4
Fall Creek Guard Station—*locale* ... OR-9
Fall Creek Heights Sch—*school* ... IN-6
**Fall Creek Highland**—*pop pl* ... IN-6
*Fall Creek Highlands* (2) ... IN-6
**Fall Creek Junction**—*pop pl* ... OR-9
Fall Creek Lake—*reservoir* ... OR-9
Fall Creek Meetinghouse—*building* ... IN-6
Fall Creek Mtn—*summit* ... CA-9
Fall Creek Oil Field—*oilfield* ... KS-7
Fall Creek Pass—*gap* ... CO-8
Fall Creek Point—*summit* ... ID-8
Fall Creek Pond—*reservoir* ... WI-6
*Fall Creek Post Office* ... TN-4
Fall Creek Post Office (historical)—*building* ... AL-4
Fallcreek Post Office (historical)—*building*. TN-4
Fall Creek Ranger Station—*locale* ... ID-8
Fall Creek Rec Area—*park* ... KY-4
*Fall Creek Rsvr* ... OR-9
Fall Creek Saddle—*gap* ... ID-8
Fall Creek Sch—*school* ... CA-9
Fall Creek Sch—*school* ... NY-2
Fall Creek Sch—*school* ... NC-3
Fall Creek Settling Basin—*basin* ... IL-6
**Fall Creek (sta)**—*pop pl* ... OR-9
Fall Creek Station—*locale* ... OR-9
Fall Creek (Township of)—*other* ... NC-3
**Fall Creek (Township of)**—*pop pl* ... IL-6
**Fall Creek (Township of)**—*pop pl* (3) ... IN-6
Fall Creek Trail—*trail* (2) ... CO-8
Fall Creek Trail—*trail* ... ID-8
Fall Creek Trail (historical)—*trail* ... OR-9
**Fallcrest (subdivision)**—*pop pl* ... NC-3
Fall Draw—*valley* ... SD-7
Fallen Arch Lake—*lake* ... MN-6
Fallen Ash Creek—*stream* (2) ... AR-4
*Fallen Branch* ... FL-3
Fallen Branch—*stream* ... FL-3
Fallen City—*summit* ... WY-8
Fallen Creek—*stream* ... AR-4
Fallen Creek—*stream* ... MS-4
*Fallen Creek Baptist Church* ... MS-4
Fallen Creek Ch—*church* ... MS-4
Fallen Field—*park* ... OR-9
Fallen Fork—*stream* ... WV-2
Fallen Goliath—*other* ... CA-9
Fallen HS—*school* ... NY-2
Fallen-In Cave—*cave* ... NV-8
**Fallen Leaf**—*pop pl* ... CA-9
Fallen Leaf Campground—*locale* ... CA-9
Fallen Leaf Lake—*reservoir* ... CA-9
Fallen Leaf Spring—*spring* ... CA-9
*Fallen Rock Arch* ... UT-8
Fallenrock Branch—*stream* ... KY-4
Fallen Rock Hollow—*valley* ... IN-6
Fallen Rock Overlook—*locale* ... CO-8
Fallen Rock Sch—*school* ... KY-4
Fallen Rock Shelter—*cave* ... PA-2
Fallen Timber—*locale* ... WV-2
**Fallentimber**—*pop pl* ... PA-2
Fallen Timber Branch—*stream* (2) ... KY-4
Fallentimber Branch—*stream* ... WV-2
Fallen Timber Ch—*church* ... OH-6
Fallen Timber Creek—*stream* ... KY-4
Fallen Timber Creek—*stream* (2) ... OH-6
Fallen Timber Golf Course—*locale* ... PA-2
Fallen Timber Ridge—*ridge* ... NM-5
Fallen Timber Ridge—*ridge* ... WV-2
Fallen Timber Run—*stream* ... PA-2
Fallentimber Run—*stream* ... PA-2
Fallen Timber Run—*stream* ... PA-2
Fallen Timber Run—*stream* ... WV-2
Fallentimber Run—*stream* ... WV-2
Fallen Timber Run—*stream* (4) ... WV-2
*Fallen Timbers* ... PA-2
**Fallen Timbers**—*pop pl* ... PA-2
Fallen Timbers Battlefield—*hist pl* ... OH-6
Fallen Timbers Ch—*church* ... PA-2
Fallen Timbers JHS—*school* ... OH-6
Fallen Timbers State Memorial—*park* ... OH-6
Fallen Timber Trail—*trail* ... PA-2
Fallentree Kill—*stream* ... NY-2
Fallen Water Creek—*stream* ... KY-4
Fallen Water Creek—*stream* ... TN-4
*Fallert* ... ID-8
Fallert Cave—*cave* ... MO-7
Fallert Springs—*spring* ... ID-8
Fallet Branch—*stream* ... IL-6
Falley Home—*hist pl* ... IN-6
Fall Fork—*stream* ... IN-6
*Fall Fork Clifty Creek* ... IN-6
Fall Gap—*gap* ... PA-2
Fall Gap Ch—*church* ... TN-4
Fall Gulch—*valley* ... CO-8
Fall Gulch—*valley* ... OR-9
**Fall Hall Glen**—*pop pl* ... WI-6
Fall Hill—*hist pl* ... VA-3
Fall Hill—*summit* ... AR-4
Fall Hill—*summit* ... CT-1
Fall Hill—*summit* (2) ... MA-1
Fall Hill—*summit* ... TX-5
Fall Hill—*summit* ... VA-3
Fall Hill Brook—*stream* ... MA-1
Fall Hill Meadow—*swamp* ... MA-1
Fall Hills—*ridge* ... WV-2
Fall Hollow—*valley* ... AL-4
Fall Hollow—*valley* (3) ... TN-4
Fall Hollow—*valley* ... VA-3
*Fall Hollow Branch* ... VA-3
Falling Branch—*locale* ... KY-4
Falling Branch—*stream* ... FL-3
Falling Branch—*stream* ... KY-4
Falling Branch—*stream* ... MD-2
Falling Branch—*stream* ... OH-6
Falling Branch—*stream* ... PA-2
Falling Branch—*stream* ... VA-3
Falling Branch Ch—*church* ... VA-3
Falling Cave—*cave* ... AL-4
Falling Cliff—*cliff* ... TN-4
Falling Cove—*bay* ... MD-2
*Falling Creek* ... NC-3
**Falling Creek**—*pop pl* ... NC-3
**Falling Creek**—*pop pl* ... VA-3
Falling Creek—*stream* ... AL-4
Falling Creek—*stream* ... FL-3
Falling Creek—*stream* (4) ... GA-3
Falling Creek—*stream* (5) ... NC-3
Falling Creek—*stream* ... OR-9
Falling Creek—*stream* (6) ... VA-3
Falling Creek—*swamp* ... FL-3
Falling Creek Ch—*church* ... FL-3
Falling Creek Ch—*church* ... GA-3
Falling Creek Ch—*church* ... NC-3
**Falling Creek Farms**—*pop pl* ... VA-3
Falling Creek Rsvr—*reservoir* ... VA-3
Falling Creek Sch—*school* ... GA-3
Falling Creek Sch—*school* ... VA-3
Falling Creek Sch (historical)—*school* ... MS-4
Falling Creek Station—*locale* ... NC-3
Falling Creek (Township of)—*fmr MCD* ... NC-3
Falling Falls Creek—*stream* ... FL-3
Falling Glacier—*glacier* ... AK-9
Falling Ice Glacier—*glacier* ... WY-8
Falling Iron Cliff—*cliff* ... NM-5
Falling Iron Cliffs—*cliff* ... AZ-5
Falling Iron Cliffs—*cliff* ... NM-5
Falling Leaf Lake—*lake* ... MT-8
*Falling Mill Brook* ... CT-1
Falling Mtn—*summit* ... AK-9
Falling Over Branch—*stream* ... TN-4
Falling Point—*cape* ... DE-2
*Falling River* ... VA-3
Falling River—*stream* ... VA-3
Falling River Ch—*church* ... VA-3
Falling River Country Club—*other* ... VA-3
Falling River Sch—*school* ... VA-3
**Falling Rock**—*pop pl* ... WV-2
Falling Rock—*rock* ... AL-4
Falling Rock Branch—*stream* (2) ... KY-4
Falling Rock Branch—*stream* ... MO-7
Falling Rock Camp—*locale* ... OH-6
Falling Rock Canyon—*valley* ... CA-9
Falling Rock Creek—*stream* ... NC-3
Falling Rock Creek—*stream* (3) ... VA-3
Falling Rock Creek—*stream* ... WV-2
Falling Rock Falls—*falls* ... VA-3
Falling Rock Fork—*stream* ... WV-2
Falling Rock Gulch—*valley* ... CO-8
Falling Rock Hollow—*valley* ... AR-4
Falling Rocks—*locale* ... GA-3
Falling Rock Spring—*spring* ... CO-8
*Falling Run* ... IN-6
*Falling Run* ... NC-3
Falling Run—*stream* ... IN-6
Falling Run—*stream* (3) ... VA-3
Falling Run—*stream* (2) ... WV-2
Falling Run Cem—*cemetery* ... VA-3
Falling Run Ch—*church* ... NC-3
Falling Run Park—*park* ... IN-6
Falling Spring—*locale* ... PA-2
**Falling Spring**—*pop pl* ... IL-6
**Falling Spring**—*pop pl* ... PA-2
**Falling Spring**—*pop pl* ... VA-3
**Falling Spring**—*pop pl* ... WV-2
Falling Spring—*spring* (2) ... MO-7
Falling Spring—*spring* ... PA-2
Falling Spring Branch—*stream* ... MS-4
Falling Spring Branch—*stream* ... PA-2
Falling Spring Cave—*cave* ... AL-4
Falling Spring Cem—*cemetery* ... MO-7
Falling Spring Ch—*church* ... VA-3
**Falling Spring (corporate name for Renick)**—*pop pl* ... WV-2
Falling Spring Creek—*stream* ... VA-3
Falling Spring Elem Sch—*school* ... PA-2
Falling Spring Falls—*summit* ... VA-3
Falling Spring Hollow—*valley* ... VA-3
Falling Spring (Magisterial District)—*fmr MCD* ... VA-3
Falling Spring (Magisterial District)—*fmr MCD* ... WV-2
Falling Spring Mtn—*summit* ... WV-2
Falling Spring Run—*stream* ... PA-2
Falling Spring Run—*stream* (2) ... VA-3
Falling Spring Run—*stream* (2) ... WV-2
*Falling Springs* ... PA-2
*Falling Springs* ... WV-2
**Falling Springs**—*pop pl* ... CA-9
**Falling Springs**—*pop pl* ... IL-6
Falling Springs—*spring* ... IA-7
Falling Springs—*spring* (2) ... KY-4
Falling Springs—*spring* ... WA-9
*Falling Springs Baptist Church* ... TN-4
Falling Springs Cave—*cave* ... TN-4
Falling Springs Cem—*cemetery* ... TN-4
Falling Springs Ch—*church* ... KY-4
Falling Springs Ch—*church* ... TN-4
Falling Springs Dam—*dam* ... PA-2
Falling Springs Gap—*gap* ... WV-2
Falling Springs Hollow—*valley* ... PA-2

Falling Springs Rsvr—reservoir PA-2
Falling Springs Run—stream PA-2
Falling Spring Township—civil MO-7
Falling Spring Valley—valley VA-3
Falling Timber Branch—stream IN-6
Falling Timber Branch—stream (3) KY-4
Falling Timber Creek—stream IN-6
Falling Timber Creek—stream KY-4
Falling Timber Run—stream PA-2
Fallingtimber Run—stream WV-2
Falling Timber Sch—school KY-4
Falling Water—falls FL-3
Fallingwater—hist pl PA-2
**Falling Water**—pop pl TN-4
Falling Water Baptist Ch—church TN-4
Falling Water Branch—stream GA-3
Falling Water Branch—stream NC-3
Falling Water Branch—stream TN-4
Falling Water Cem—cemetery TN-4
Falling Water Ch—church (2) TN-4
Falling Water Ch—church VA-3
Falling Water Ch—church WV-2
Falling Water Cove—valley TN-4
Falling Water Creek—stream AK-9
Falling Water Creek—stream AR-4
Fallingwater Creek—stream KY-4
Falling Water Creek—stream TN-4
Fallingwater Creek—stream VA-3
Falling Water Elem Sch—school TN-4
Falling Water Falls—falls TN-4
Falling Water Gap—gap KY-4
Falling Water Gap—gap VA-3
Falling Water Hill—summit FL-3
Fallingwater Overlook—locale VA-3
Falling Water Post Office (historical)—building TN-4
Falling Water River—stream TN-4
**Falling Waters**—pop pl WV-2
Falling Waters Ch—church VA-3
Falling Water Sch—school AR-4
Falling Water Sch (historical)—school TN-4
Falling Waters Creek TN-4
Falling Waters Hollow—valley TN-4
Falling Waters (Magisterial District)—fmr MCD WV-2
Falling Waters (museum)—building PA-2
Falling Waters State Rec Area—park FL-3
Falling Water Trail—trail NH-1
Fallin Hollow—valley VA-3
Fallini Spring—spring ID-8
Fallini Well—well NV-8
Fall-in-lake WI-6
Fallins Millpond—reservoir VA-3
Fallis—locale KY-4
**Fallis**—pop pl OK-5
Fall Island—island PA-2
Fallison Lake—lake WI-6
Fallis Run—stream KY-4
Fallis Sch—school CO-8
Fallis Sch—school IL-6
Falliston—locale AL-4
Falliston Mine (underground)—mine AL-4
Fall Kill—stream (2) NY-2
Fall Lake WA-9
Fall Lake—lake AK-9
Fall Lake—lake MN-6
Fall Lake—lake NY-2
Fall Lakes—lake UT-8
**Fall Lake (Township of)**—pop pl MN-6
**Fall Leaf**—pop pl (2) KS-7
Fall Lick—stream KY-4
Fall Lick Creek—stream TN-4
Fall Line Hills—range AL-4
Fall-Meyer Sch—school OH-6
Fall Mills TN-4
Fall Mills Post Office (historical)—building TN-4
Fall Mountain CT-1
Fall Mountain Lake—lake CT-1
**Fall Mountain Lake**—pop pl CT-1
Fall Mountain Spring—spring OR-9
Fall Mtn—summit AR-4
Fall Mtn—summit CO-8
Fall Mtn—summit CT-1
Fall Mtn—summit NH-1
Fall Mtn—summit NC-3
Fall Mtn—summit (2) OR-9
Fall Mtn—summit WA-9
Fall Off, The—falls AL-4
Falloff Branch—stream AR-4
Fall-Off Hollow—valley AR-4
Fallon—locale (2) CA-9
Fallon—locale OK-5
Fallon—locale TX-5
Fallon—locale WA-9
**Fallon**—pop pl MT-8
**Fallon**—pop pl NV-8
**Fallon**—pop pl ND-7
Fallon Cem—cemetery MT-8
Fallon Cem—cemetery NV-8
Fallon Colony—reserve NV-8
Fallon Creek MT-8
Fallon Creek—stream UT-8
Fallon Eagle Mine—mine NV-8
Fallon Flat—flat MT-8
Fallon Indian Sub-Agency—building NV-8
**Fallon Ind Res**—pop pl NV-8
Fallon Lake—lake MN-6
Fallon Municipal Airp—airport NV-8
Fallon Natl Wildlife Ref—park NV-8
Fallon Naval Air Station—military NV-8
Fallon Park—park VA-3
Fallon Radio Range Station—locale NV-8
Fallon Ranch—locale NM-5
Fallon Sch—school CA-9
Fallon Spring—spring MT-8
Fallon Spring—spring UT-8
Fallout Hills—summit NV-8
Fallout Tank—reservoir TX-5
Fallover Bend—bend KY-4
**Fallow**—pop pl IA-7
Fallowfield Cem—cemetery PA-2
Fallowfield Ch—church PA-2
Fallowfield Elem Sch—school PA-2
**Fallowfield (Township of)**—pop pl PA-2
Fallowfield Township School PA-2
Fallow Hollow—valley PA-2
Fallow Marsh—swamp IA-7
Fallow Marsh State Game Mngmt Area—park IA-7
Fall Point—summit ID-8
Fall Quarry Run—stream VA-3
Fall Ridge—ridge TN-4
Fall Ridge—ridge VA-3
Fall River CA-9
Fall River CO-8
Fall River CT-1
Fall River ID-8
Fall River MA-1
Fall River RI-1
Fallriver TN-4
Fall River WY-8
**Fall River**—pop pl KS-7
**Fall River**—pop pl MA-1
**Fall River**—pop pl TN-4
**Fallriver**—pop pl TN-4
**Fall River**—pop pl WI-6
Fall River—stream (2) CA-9
Fall River—stream (2) CO-8
Fall River—stream KS-7
Fall River—stream (2) MA-1
Fall River—stream MN-6
Fall River—stream OR-9
Fall River—stream SD-7
Fall River—stream VT-1
Fall River—stream WA-9
Fall River, City of—civil MA-1
Fall River Bleachery—hist pl MA-1
Fall River Campground—locale CA-9
Fall River Campground—park OR-9
Fall River Canal—canal ID-8
Fall River Cem—cemetery TN-4
Fall River Cem—cemetery WI-6
Fall River Center—locale MA-1
Fall River County—civil SD-7
Fall River Creek—stream IL-6
Fall River Dam—dam KS-7
Fall River Entrance—locale CO-8
Fall River Entrance Hist Dist—hist pl CO-8
Fall River Falls—falls OR-9
Fall River Fish Hatchery—other OR-9
Fall River Guard Station—locale OR-9
Fall River HS—school MA-1
Fall River Joint HS—school CA-9
Fall River Lake—reservoir KS-7
Fall River Lodge—locale OR-9
Fall River Mill Pond WI-6
**Fall River Mills**—pop pl CA-9
Fall River Pass—gap CO-8
Fall River Pass Ranger Station—hist pl CO-8
Fall River Post Office TN-4
Fallriver Post Office (historical)—building TN-4
Fall River Public Library—building MA-1
Fall River Reservoir KS-7
Fall River Road—hist pl CO-8
Fall River Rod and Gun Club—locale MA-1
Fall River Rsvr—reservoir MA-1
Fall River Sch (historical)—school TN-4
Fall River Spring—spring TN-4
Fall River State Park—park KS-7
**Fall River Station (subdivision)**—pop pl MA-1
Fall River Stream MA-1
**Fall River Township**—pop pl (2) KS-7
**Fall River (Township of)**—pop pl IL-6
Fall River Valley—valley CA-9
Fall River Village MA-1
Fall River Waterworks—hist pl MA-1
Fall River Wildlife Area—park KS-7
Fall Rock—locale KY-4
Fall Rock Branch—stream KY-4
Fall Rock Branch—stream TN-4
Fallrock Branch—stream (2) WV-2
Fallrock Hollow—valley WV-2
Fallrock Junction—locale CA-9
Fall Run IN-6
Fall Run PA-2
Fall Run VA-3
Fall Run WV-2
Fall Run—stream IN-6
Fall Run—stream (2) OH-6
Fall Run—stream (4) PA-2
Fall Run—stream VA-3
Fall Run—stream (11) WV-2
Fall Run Cem—cemetery WV-2
Falls UT-8
Falls—locale VA-3
Falls—locale WV-2
**Falls**—pop pl AK-9
**Falls**—pop pl NC-3
**Falls**—pop pl PA-2
Falls—post sta MA-1
Falls—uninc pl NY-2
Falls, Lake—reservoir NC-3
Falls, Lake of the—lake WI-6
Falls, The CT-1
Falls, The (2) ME-1
Falls, The NJ-2
Falls, The SD-7
Falls, The—falls AL-4
Falls, The—falls (2) AK-9
Falls, The—falls AZ-5
Falls, The—falls (2) CA-9
Falls, The—falls ID-8
Falls, The—falls (2) ME-1
Falls, The—falls MO-7
Falls, The—falls NM-5
Falls, The—falls NY-2
Falls, The—falls SC-3
Falls, The—falls TN-4
Falls, The—falls (2) TX-5
Falls, The—falls UT-8
Falls, The—falls VA-3
Falls, The—locale CA-9
Falls, The—locale VA-3
Falls, The (Shop Ctr)—locale FL-3
Falls at Lake—lake MT-8
Falls Ave Sch—school CT-1
Falls Bay—bay AK-9
Falls Branch NC-3
Falls Branch TN-4
Falls Branch VA-3
Falls Branch—stream (2) AL-4
Falls Branch—stream AR-4
Falls Branch—stream (3) GA-3
Falls Branch—stream IN-6
Falls Branch—stream (3) KY-4
Falls Branch—stream LA-4
Falls Branch—stream MO-7
Falls Branch—stream NE-7
Falls Branch—stream (6) NC-3
Falls Branch—stream OK-5
Falls Branch—stream (2) SC-3
Falls Branch—stream (4) TN-4
Falls Branch—stream (2) TX-5
Falls Branch—stream (2) VA-3
Falls Branch—stream (4) WV-2
Falls Branch Mine—mine TN-4
Falls Branch Post Office TN-4
Falls Branch Trail—trail TN-4
Falls Bridge—bridge NE-7
Falls Bridge—bridge PA-2
Falls Brook—stream (3) CT-1
Falls Brook—stream (4) ME-1
Falls Brook—stream (2) MA-1
Falls Brook—stream (2) NH-1
Falls Brook—stream (4) NY-2
Falls Brook—stream (2) VT-1
Falls Brook Lake—lake ME-1
**Fallsburg**—pop pl KY-4
**Fallsburg**—pop pl NY-2
**Fallsburg**—pop pl OH-6
Fallsburg Creek—stream NY-2
Fallsburg Creek—stream VA-3
Fallsburgh—other NY-2
**Fallsburg (Town of)**—pop pl NY-2
**Fallsbury (Township of)**—pop pl OH-6
Falls Camp—locale (2) ME-1
Falls Campground—locale ID-8
Falls Campground—locale WY-8
Falls Campground, The—locale CO-8
Falls Canyon NV-8
Falls Canyon—valley (5) CA-9
Falls Canyon—valley NV-8
Falls Canyon—valley (2) NM-5
Falls Canyon—valley SD-7
Falls Canyon—valley (2) TX-5
Falls Canyon Trail—trail MT-8
Falls Cem—cemetery MS-4
Falls Cem—cemetery OK-5
Falls Ch—church MN-6
Falls Ch—church NE-7
Fall Sch—hist pl TN-4
Fall Sch—school TN-4
Falls Chapel—locale AR-4
Falls Ch of Christ—church AL-4
Falls Church—hist pl VA-3
Falls Church, The—church VA-3
Falls Church HS—school VA-3
**Falls Church (ind. city)**—pop pl VA-3
Falls Church Park—park VA-3
**Falls Church (subdivision)**—pop pl NC-3
Falls City PA-2
**Falls City**—pop pl AL-4
**Falls City**—pop pl ID-8
**Falls City**—pop pl NE-7
**Falls City**—pop pl OR-9
**Falls City**—pop pl TX-5
**Falls City**—pop pl WI-6
Falls City (CCD)—cens area OR-9
Falls City (CCD)—cens area TX-5
Falls City Cem—cemetery NE-7
Falls City Cem—cemetery OR-9
Falls City Cem—cemetery TX-5
Falls City Cem—cemetery WI-6
Falls City Country Club—other NE-7
Falls City Jeans and Woolen Mills—hist pl KY-4
Falls City Oil Field—oilfield NE-7
Falls City Oil Field—oilfield TX-5
Falls City Rsvr—reservoir OR-9
Falls City Sch House—hist pl ID-8
Falls Coulee—valley MT-8
**Falls (County)**—pop pl TX-5
Falls County Cem—cemetery TX-5
Falls County Missionary—church TX-5
Falls Creek ID-8
Falls Creek OR-9
Falls Creek TN-4
Falls Creek WA-9
Falls Creek WV-2
**Falls Creek**—pop pl PA-2
Falls Creek—stream (2) AL-4
Falls Creek—stream (14) AK-9
Falls Creek—stream AR-4
Falls Creek—stream (7) CA-9
Falls Creek—stream (4) CO-8
Falls Creek—stream (14) ID-8
Falls Creek—stream MD-2
Falls Creek—stream (2) MN-6
Falls Creek—stream (19) MT-8
Falls Creek—stream (2) NM-5
Falls Creek—stream NY-2
Falls Creek—stream (2) NC-3
Falls Creek—stream OH-6
Falls Creek—stream OK-5
Falls Creek—stream (6) OR-9
Falls Creek—stream (6) PA-2
Falls Creek—stream SC-3
Falls Creek—stream (2) TN-4
Falls Creek—stream (4) TX-5
Falls Creek—stream VA-3
Falls Creek—stream (25) WA-9
Falls Creek—stream (3) WV-2
Falls Creek—stream (6) WY-8
**Falls Creek Assembly**—pop pl OK-5
Falls Creek Borough—civil (2) PA-2
Falls Creek Campground—locale WA-9
Falls Creek Falls OR-9
Falls Creek Falls TN-4
Falls Creek Falls Lake—reservoir TN-4
Falls Creek Falls Lake Dam—dam TN-4
Falls Creek Falls Scout Camp—locale TN-4
Falls Creek Falls State Park—park TN-4
Falls Creek Falls State Park and Forest TN-4
Falls Creek Forest Camp—locale OR-9
Falls Creek Forest Camp—locale WA-9
Falls Creek Lake MT-8
Falls Creek Lake—lake GA-3
Falls Creek Mine—mine AK-9
Falls Creek Mine—mine ID-8
Falls Creek Ridge—ridge MT-8
Falls Creek Sch—school MT-8
Falls Creek Sch—school NC-3
**Falls Creek (subdivision)**—pop pl NC-3
Falls Creek Trail—trail (2) WA-9
Falls Creek Trail (Pack)—trail CA-9
Falls Cut Tunnel—tunnel PA-2
Fallsdale—locale PA-2
Fallsdale Pond—reservoir PA-2
Falls Dam NC-3
Falls Dam—dam NC-3
Falls Eagle—stream AK-9
Falls Factory Sch (abandoned)—school PA-2
Falls Fashion Center, The (Shop Ctr)—locale FL-3
Falls Ferry (historical)—locale NC-3
Falls Fork Rock Creek—stream MT-8
Falls Gap—gap WV-2
Falls Gulch—valley (2) CA-9
Falls Gulch—valley (3) CO-8
Falls Gulch—valley (2) MT-8
Falls Gulch—valley NM-5
Falls Gulch Mtn—summit CO-8
**Falls Hill**—pop pl VA-3
Falls Hill Ch—church VA-3
Falls Hill Creek—stream VA-3
Falls (historical)—locale AL-4
Falls-Hobbs House—hist pl NC-3
Falls Hollow—valley AL-4
Falls Hollow—valley (3) AR-4
Falls Hollow—valley (2) MO-7
Falls Hollow—valley NC-3
Falls Hollow—valley (6) TN-4
Falls Hollow—valley (5) VA-3
**Fallsington**—pop pl PA-2
Fallsington Hist Dist—hist pl PA-2
Fallsington Post Office (historical)—building PA-2
Falls International Airp—airport MN-6
Falls Island MD-2
Falls Island—island ME-1
Falls JHS—school OH-6
Falls Junction—locale MN-6
**Falls Junction**—pop pl AL-4
**Falls Junction**—pop pl NY-2
**Falls Junction**—pop pl OH-6
Falls Junction—uninc pl MD-2
Falls Lake WA-9
Falls Lake—lake (3) AK-9
Falls Lake—lake NY-2
Falls Lake—lake WA-9
Falls Lake—reservoir NC-3
Falls Lake—reservoir NC-3
Falls Lakes—lake MN-6
Falls Location Hist Dist—hist pl MI-6
Fallsmill WV-2
Falls Mill—hist pl TN-4
Falls Mill—locale TN-4
Falls Mill—locale WV-2
Falls Mill Creek—stream SC-3
Falls Mills—locale NY-2
**Falls Mills**—pop pl VA-3
**Falls Mills**—pop pl WV-2
Falls Mills Dam—dam VA-3
Falls Mills Hist Dist—hist pl TN-4
Falls Mtn—summit CT-1
Falls Mtn—summit (2) GA-3
FALLS OF CLYDE—hist pl HI-9
Falls of Gouges Creek—falls NC-3
Falls of Hills Creek—falls WV-2
Falls of Neuse Road Ch—church NC-3
**Falls of New Hope (subdivision)**—pop pl NC-3
Falls Of Passaic NJ-2
Falls of Rough—locale KY-4
**Falls of Rough**—pop pl KY-4
Falls of Rough Hist Dist—hist pl KY-4
Falls Of Saint Anthony MN-6
Falls of Schuylkill—falls PA-2
Falls Of Seneca—falls WV-2
Falls of the Cahawba AL-4
Falls of the Neuse Dam—dam NC-3
Falls of the Neuse Manufacturing Company—hist pl NC-3
Falls of Wahconah Brook MA-1
**Falls Orchard**—pop pl MD-2
Falls-Overfield Sch—school PA-2
Falls Park—park IN-6
Falls Park—park SD-7
**Falls Park**—pop pl VA-3
Falls Point ME-1
Falls Point—cape AK-9
Falls Point—cape ME-1
Falls Point—cliff ID-8
Falls Point—cliff MT-8
Falls Point—summit MT-8
Falls Pond ME-1
Falls Pond MA-1
Falls Pond—lake CT-1
Falls Pond—lake NH-1
Falls Pond—lake NY-2
Falls Pond Dam—dam MA-1
Falls Pond Outlet—stream NY-2
Falls Poplar Cove—valley NC-3
Fall Spring—spring (2) AZ-5
Fall Spring—spring (2) NM-5
Falls Prong—stream TX-5
Falls Prong Spring—spring TX-5
Falls Prong Windmill—locale TX-5
Falls Ranch—locale NM-5
Falls Ranger Station—locale ID-8
Falls Ridge—ridge CA-9
Falls Ridge—ridge VA-3
Falls River CT-1
Falls River MA-1
Falls River OR-9
Falls River VT-1
Falls River—stream CT-1
Falls River—stream ID-8
Falls River—stream MI-6
Falls River—stream WY-8
Falls River Basin—basin WY-8
Falls River - in part CT-1
Falls River - in part RI-1
Falls River Pond—reservoir CT-1
Falls River Ridge—area ID-8
Falls Rsvr—reservoir NC-3
Falls Run PA-2
Falls Run—stream MD-2
Falls Run—stream (3) PA-2
Falls Run—stream (2) VA-3
Falls Run—stream (6) WV-2
Falls Run Ch—church WV-2
Falls Run Trail—trail PA-2
Falls Sch—school CT-1
Falls Sch—school OK-5
Falls Sch—school (2) SD-7
Falls Site (22LF507)—hist pl MS-4
Falls Spring—spring AZ-5
Falls Spring—spring NV-8
Falls Spring—spring TX-5
Falls Springs Wash—stream AZ-5
Falls Switch CT-1
Fallstad Lake—lake MN-6
**Fallstaff**—pop pl MD-2
Falls The AL-4
Fallston NC-3
**Fallston**—pop pl MD-2
**Fallston**—pop pl NC-3
**Fallston**—pop pl PA-2
Fallston Borough—civil PA-2
Fallston Ch—church MD-2
Fallston Elem Sch—school NC-3
Falls Township—CDP PA-2
Falls Township—fmr MCD IA-7
**Falls Township**—pop pl (2) KS-7
**Falls (Township of)**—pop pl (2) OH-6
**Falls (Township of)**—pop pl (2) PA-2
Fallstown (Township of)—fmr MCD NC-3
Falls Trail—trail NV-8
Falls Trail—trail NH-1
Falls Trail—trail VA-3
Fall Stream—stream NY-2
Fall Street-Trinity Lane Hist Dist—hist pl NY-2
Fallsvale CA-9
**Fallsvale**—pop pl CA-9
Fallsvale Sch—school CA-9
**Fallsview**—pop pl OR-9
**Fallsview**—pop pl WV-2
**Falls View**—pop pl WV-2
Falls View Cem—cemetery ID-8
Falls Village MA-1
**Falls Village**—pop pl CT-1
Falls Village District—hist pl CT-1
Fallsville CA-9
Fallsville—locale AR-4
Fallsville State Wildlife Area—park OH-6
Fall Swamp—stream NC-3
Fall Swamp Islands—island NC-3
**Falls Yard**—pop pl MT-8
Fall Tank—reservoir AZ-5
Falltown Plantation MA-1
Fallulah Brook MA-1
Fallulah Reservoir MA-1
Fall Valley—valley OR-9
**Fallville**—pop pl VA-3
Fallwell Creek—stream TX-5
Fally Cem—cemetery IL-6
Falma HS—school CA-9
Falmers PA-2
Falmouth—locale FL-3
**Falmouth**—pop pl IL-6
**Falmouth**—pop pl IN-6
**Falmouth**—pop pl KY-4
**Falmouth**—pop pl ME-1
**Falmouth**—pop pl MA-1
**Falmouth**—pop pl MI-6
**Falmouth**—pop pl PA-2
**Falmouth**—pop pl VA-3
Falmouth, Lake—reservoir NC-3
Falmouth Beach—beach MA-1
Falmouth (CCD)—cens area KY-4
Falmouth (census name for Falmouth Center)—CDP MA-1
Falmouth Center (census name Falmouth)—other MA-1
Falmouth Chapel—church IL-6
Falmouth Cliffs—cliff MA-1
**Falmouth Foreside**—pop pl ME-1
Falmouth Harbor—bay AK-9
Falmouth Harbor—harbor MA-1
Falmouth-Hartwood (Magisterial District)—fmr MCD VA-3
Falmouth Heights—cliff MA-1
**Falmouth Heights**—pop pl MA-1
Falmouth Hill MA-1
Falmouth Hist Dist—hist pl VA-3
Falmouth Historical Society—building MA-1
Falmouth House—hist pl ME-1
Falmouth HS—school ME-1
Falmouth HS—school MA-1
Falmouth Inner Harbor—bay MA-1
Falmouth Inner Harbor Light—locale MA-1
Falmouth Intermediate Sch—school MA-1
Falmouth Lookout Tower—tower FL-3
Falmouth Mall (Shop Ctr)—locale MA-1
Falmouth Plaza (Shop Ctr)—locale MA-1
Falmouth Post Office (historical)—building PA-2
Falmouth Spring—spring FL-3
Falmouth Townhall—building MA-1
**Falmouth (Town of)**—pop pl ME-1
**Falmouth (Town of)**—pop pl MA-1
Falnes Ch—church SD-7
Falo FM-9
Falo Island FM-9
Faloma FM-9
**Faloma**—pop pl OR-9
Faloon AR-4
Falope FM-9
Falos—spring FM-9
Faloupet FM-9
Falow—cape FM-9
False DE-2
False Alarm Cave—cave AL-4
False Arden—cape AK-9
False Bay CA-9
False Bay—bay (2) AK-9
False Bay—bay WA-9
False Bayou LA-4
False Bayou—stream LA-4
False Berm—levee LA-4
False Bottom Creek—stream SD-7
False Branch Bayou—canal LA-4
False Cape—cape CA-9
False Cape—cape FL-3
False Cape—locale VA-3
False Cape Landing—locale VA-3
False Cape Rock—island CA-9
False Channel NY-2
False Channel—channel NY-2
False Channel—channel NC-3
False Channel—gut FL-3
False Channel Creek NY-2
False Channel Meadow—swamp NY-2
False Cove—bay AK-9
False Creek—stream (2) ID-8
False Detour Channel—channel MI-6
False Egg Island Point—cape NJ-2
False Face Mtn—summit OR-9
False-Front Commercial Bldg—hist pl ID-8
False Gap—gap CA-9
False Gap—gap NC-3
False Gap—gap TN-4
False Gap—gap WV-2
False Gap Prong—stream TN-4
False Halibut Rock—bar ME-1
False Hook—bar NJ-2
False Hook Channel—channel NJ-2
False Island—island AK-9
False Island Point—cape AK-9
False Klamath Cove—bay CA-9
False Klamath Rock—island CA-9
False Lindenberg Head—cape AK-9
False Live Oak Point—cape TX-5
False Marias Pass MT-8
False Mouth Bay—bay LA-4
False Mouth Bayou—stream LA-4
**Falsen Township**—pop pl ND-7
False Pass—locale AK-9
False Pass ANV786—reserve AK-9
False Point—cape AK-9
False Point—cape CA-9
False Point—cape NY-2
False Point Pybus—cape AK-9
False Point Retreat—cape AK-9
False Point Spur CA-9
False Presque Isle—island MI-6
False Presque Isle Harbor—bar MI-6
False River—gut CA-9
False River—gut LA-4
False River—lake LA-4
False River—stream MS-4
False River Cem—cemetery LA-4
False River Ch—church LA-4
False River Cutoff—bend LA-4
False River (historical)—stream MS-4
False Spit—bar MA-1
False Summit—locale MT-8
False Summit—summit (2) WA-9
False Sur—summit CA-9
False Trail Canyon—valley UT-8
False Whitehead Harbor—bay ME-1
Falsey Draw—valley NM-5
Falson ND-7
Falsoola Mtn—summit AK-9
Falter Place—locale NE-7
Faluamot FM-9
Faluaw FM-9
Faluelegalao—island FM-9
Faluelemariete—island FM-9
Faluelepalape—island FM-9
Falulah Brook—stream MA-1
Falulah Rsvr MA-1
Falulah Rsvr—reservoir MA-1
Falula Spring—spring UT-8
**Falun**—pop pl KS-7
**Falun**—pop pl WI-6
Falun Cem—cemetery KS-7
Falun Cem—cemetery MN-6
**Falun-Summit Township**—pop pl KS-7
**Falun (Township of)**—pop pl MN-6
Falvey Lake—lake CA-9
Falvey Lake—lake TX-5
Falvey Memorial Ch—church TX-5
Falvy Sch—school IA-7
Falwe—locale FM-9
Falwe, Infal—stream FM-9
Falwell—uninc pl VA-3
Falwell Cem—cemetery VA-3
Falxa Camp—locale WY-8
Famalaoan, Chalan—slope MH-9
Famalao'an, Sabanetan—slope MH-9
Fambro Chapel—church GA-3
Fambro Creek—stream GA-3
Fambrough Cem—cemetery GA-3
Fambroughs Landing—locale TN-4
Fame—locale OK-5
Fame—locale WV-2
**Fame**—pop pl MS-4
Fame Branch—stream OK-5
Fame Branch—stream TX-5
Fame Cem—cemetery OK-5
Fame Ch—church IL-6
Fame Ch—church MS-4
Fame Ch of God MS-4
Famechon Ridge—ridge WI-6
Fame (historical)—locale KS-7
Fameichon—spring FM-9
**Famersburg**—pop pl IA-7
Fame Sch (historical)—school MS-4
Fameys Branch DE-2
Familton KS-7
Family Baptist Ch—church MS-4
Family Butte—summit UT-8
Family Camp—locale WA-9
Family Cem—cemetery AR-4
Family Center, The (Shop Ctr)—locale (2) UT-8
Family Center at Midvalley, The (Shop Ctr)—locale UT-8
Family Church, The—church FL-3
Family Club—other CA-9
Family Draw—valley TX-5
**Family Estates (subdivision)**—pop pl UT-8
Family of God Ch—church NC-3
Family Park—park KS-7
Family Peak—summit MT-8
Family Post Office (historical)—building TN-4
Family Worship Center—church FL-3
Famine Lake—lake MN-6
Famine Lake—lake OR-9
Famja—area GU-9
Fammatre Sch—school CA-9
Famolsa Landing (historical)—locale MS-4
Famosla—locale MS-4
Famosla Cut-Off—bend MS-4
**Famoso**—pop pl CA-9
Famous Mine—mine CO-8
Famuliner—locale TX-5
Famuliner Farms Airp—airport MO-7
Famys Branch DE-2
Fan, Lake—lake FL-3
Fan, The AZ-5
Fan, The—flat AZ-5
Fana—island PW-9
Fanaagich—summit FM-9
Fanaan FM-9
Fanaanu FM-9
Fanaapiin FM-9
Fanaasic FM-9

Fanaat ... FM-9
Fanabachal ... FM-9
Fanabchagil—bar ... FM-9
Fanabchal ... FM-9
Fanabter ... FM-9
Fanabyuwol ... FM-9
Fanacharong—well ... FM-9
Fanachau—spring ... FM-9
Fanachaw—mine ... FM-9
Fanachik—bar ... FM-9
Fanadik—island ... FM-9
Fanafo ... FM-9
Fanagahnam ... MH-9
Fanaganam ... MH-9
Fana Ganan ... MH-9
Fanaganan Kattan, Kannat—stream ... MH-9
Fanaganan Lichan, Kannat—stream ... MH-9
Fanaguro' ... FM-9
Fanaguroq—summit ... FM-9
Fanaik—island ... FM-9
Fanakuk ... FM-9
Fanal ... FM-9
Fanalang ... FM-9
Fanalili ... FM-9
Fanaliliy ... FM-9
Fanalon ... FM-9
Fanama ... FM-9
Fanamar ... FM-9
Fanamar Island ... FM-9
Fanamau—island ... FM-9
Fanamo—spring ... FM-9
Fanamter—bay ... FM-9
Fanamu ... FM-9
Fanamu Island ... FM-9
Fanamu Islet ... FM-9
Fanan—bar ... FM-9
Fanan—island ... FM-9
Fananaaney ... FM-9
Fanananei—bar ... FM-9
Fanananei, Mochun—channel ... FM-9
Fananan Island ... FM-9
Fananas ... FM-9
Fananawen—spring ... FM-9
Fananeen ... FM-9
Fanang, Unun En—bar ... FM-9
Fananganan—slope ... MH-9
Fanangat—island ... FM-9
Fanani Meadow—flat ... CA-9
Fanan Island ... FM-9
Fanannang—bar ... FM-9
Fanannon—island ... FM-9
Fanano ... FM-9
Fanano—bar ... FM-9
Fanano Island—island ... FM-9
**Fananowas, Oror En**—pop pl ... FM-9
Fananu—bar ... FM-9
Fananu Island—island ... FM-9
Fananuk ... FM-9
Fananu (Municipality)—civ div ... FM-9
Fanapanges—island ... FM-9
Fanapeges ... FM-9
Fanapi Bank—bar ... FM-9
Fanapin ... FM-9
Fanaran ... FM-9
Fan Area Hist Dist—hist pl ... VA-3
Fan Area Hist Dist (Boundary Increase)—hist pl ... VA-3
Fanasas ... FM-9
Fanasich—island ... FM-9
Fanasich, Ununen—cape ... FM-9
Fanasito—locale ... FM-9
Fanat—island ... FM-9
Fanatchie Creek ... AL-4
Fanato—summit ... FM-9
Fanatu Island ... FM-9
Fanau ... FM-9
Fanauamu ... FM-9
Fanaw ... FM-9
Fanaw—well ... FM-9
Fanayik ... FM-9
Fanayulay—stream ... FM-9
Fanbacheal—summit ... FM-9
Fanbatear ... FM-9
Fanbiywol—summit ... FM-9
Fan Branch—stream ... DE-2
Fan Branch—stream ... NC-3
Fan Camajan—area ... GU-9
Fan Canyon—valley ... CA-9
Fan Canyon—valley (2) ... UT-8
**Fancher**—pop pl ... CA-9
**Fancher**—pop pl ... IL-6
**Fancher**—pop pl ... NY-2
**Fancher**—pop pl ... WI-6
Fancher Branch—stream ... KY-4
Fancher Branch—stream ... TN-4
Fancher Cabin—locale ... NV-8
Fancher Cave—cave ... TN-4
Fancher Cem—cemetery ... AR-4
Fancher Cem—cemetery ... OH-6
Fancher Creek—stream ... CA-9
Fancher Creek—stream ... CO-8
Fancher Creek—stream ... IL-6
Fancher Creek Canal—canal ... CA-9
Fancher Field Airp—airport ... WA-9
Fancher Hill Baptist Church ... MS-4
Fancher Hill Ch—church ... MS-4
Fancher Hill Sch (historical)—school ... MS-4
Fancher Lake ... NY-2
Fancher Memorial Airway Beacon—other ... WA-9
Fancher Post Office (historical)—building ... MS-4
Fancher Sch—school ... MI-6
Fancher Sch—school ... WI-6
Fanchers Dam—dam ... WA-9
Fanchers Mills—locale ... TN-4
Fanchers Mills Post Office (historical)—building ... TN-4
Fanchers Willow Branch Campground—locale ... TN-4
Fanchertown (historical)—locale ... MS-4
**Fancher Township**—pop pl ... ND-7
Fanchon—locale ... MO-7
Fanchon Lake ... MN-6
Fanchor Lake ... MN-6
**Fanco**—pop pl ... WV-2
Fan Creek ... WY-8
Fan Creek—stream ... AK-9
Fan Creek—stream (4) ... ID-8
Fan Creek—stream (3) ... MT-8
Fan Creek—stream (3) ... OR-9
Fan Creek—stream ... WY-8
Fan Creek Campground—park ... OR-9
Fan Creek Recreation Site—park ... OR-9
Fan Creek Saddle—gap ... ID-8
**Fancy**—pop pl ... TN-4
**Fancy Bluff**—pop pl ... GA-3
Fancy Bluff Creek—channel ... GA-3
Fancy Canyon—valley ... KS-7
Fancy Community Hall—building ... KS-7
Fancy Creek ... KS-7
Fancy Creek—stream ... CO-8
Fancy Creek—stream (2) ... IL-6
Fancy Creek—stream (3) ... KS-7
Fancy Creek—stream ... WI-6
Fancy Creek Cem—cemetery ... IL-6
Fancy Creek Cem—cemetery ... KS-7
Fancy Creek Ch—church ... KS-7
Fancy Creek Ch—church ... WI-6
Fancy Creek (historical)—locale ... KS-7
Fancy Creek Randolph Cem—cemetery ... KS-7
Fancy Creek State Park ... KS-7
Fancy Creek State Park—park ... KS-7
**Fancy Creek Township**—pop pl ... KS-7
**Fancy Creek (Township of)**—pop pl ... IL-6
Fancy Farm—hist pl ... VA-3
**Fancy Farm**—pop pl ... KY-4
Fancy Farm (CCD)—cens area ... KY-4
**Fancy Gap**—pop pl ... VA-3
Fancy Gap Ch—church ... VA-3
Fancy Gap (Magisterial District)—fmr MCD ... VA-3
Fancy Gap Sch—school ... VA-3
Fancy Gulch—valley ... ID-8
Fancy Hall—locale ... GA-3
Fancy Hall Creek—stream ... GA-3
Fancy Hill ... AR-4
Fancy Hill ... NC-3
Fancy Hill—locale ... AR-4
Fancy Hill—locale ... VA-3
**Fancy Hill**—pop pl ... VA-3
Fancy Hill—summit ... GA-3
Fancy Hill—summit ... NH-1
Fancy Hill—summit ... PA-2
Fancy Hill Ch—church ... NC-3
Fancy Hill Mtn—summit ... AR-4
**Fancy (historical)**—pop pl ... NC-3
Fancy Lake—lake ... CO-8
Fancy Oil Field—oilfield ... KS-7
Fancy Pass—gap ... CO-8
Fancy Point Chute—stream ... LA-4
Fancy Point Towhead—island ... LA-4
Fancy Post Office (historical)—building ... TN-4
**Fancy Prairie**—pop pl ... IL-6
Fancy Prairie (Election Precinct)—fmr MCD ... IL-6
Fancy Sch (historical)—school ... TN-4
Fancy Tract—locale ... NY-2
Fandangle Canyon—valley ... UT-8
Fandangle Well—well ... UT-8
Fandango Canyon—valley ... NV-8
Fandango Canyon—valley ... OR-9
Fandango Creek—stream ... TX-5
Fandango Hill—summit ... NV-8
Fandango Pass—gap ... CA-9
Fandango Peak—summit ... CA-9
Fandango Valley—valley ... CA-9
F And H Oil Field—oilfield ... TX-5
F and M Athletic Field ... PA-2
**Fandon**—pop pl ... IL-6
Fandora Mine—mine ... OR-9
Fandry Park—park ... WI-6
Fands ... FM-9
Fane—area ... GU-9
Fane—locale ... CA-9
Faneakaan—locale ... FM-9
Faneakaan—summit ... FM-9
Faneakargoy—summit ... FM-9
Fanebiyuwol ... FM-9
Fane Creek—stream ... AR-4
Faneene ... FM-9
Faneher Lake—lake ... IN-6
Faneich—spring ... FM-9
Fanek ... FM-9
Fanekan ... FM-9
Fanekorgoy ... FM-9
Fanels Branch—stream ... MD-2
Fanemoch—island ... FM-9
Fanemwoc ... FM-9
Fanen ... FM-9
Fanengyll ... FM-9
Fanengiy—bar ... FM-9
Faneno—island ... FM-9
Faneout—bar ... FM-9
Fanepiraw—well ... FM-9
Faner ... FM-9
Fanesich—island ... FM-9
**Fanetta Gardens**—pop pl ... TN-4
Faneu ... FM-9
Faneuil Hall—building ... MA-1
Faneuil Hall—hist pl ... MA-1
Faneuil Park—park ... NY-2
Faneuil Station (historical)—locale ... MA-1
**Faneuil (subdivision)**—pop pl ... MA-1
Faneu Island ... FM-9
Fanew—island ... FM-9
Fanew, Mochun—channel ... FM-9
Fan Falls—falls ... CO-8
Fang, The—bay ... NH-1
Fang, The—island ... ME-1
Fangel ... FM-9
Fanger Drain—stream ... MI-6
Fangio Mesa—summit ... NM-5
Fan Glacier—glacier ... AK-9
Fangle Retreat Landing (historical)—locale ... MS-4
Fanglewood Camp—locale ... GA-3
Fangmann's Siding (Croxton Yards)—uninc pl ... NJ-2
Fang Mtn—summit ... AK-9
Fangoch—summit ... FM-9
Fangollano (ruins)—locale ... OR-9
Fangon Sch—school ... SD-7
Fangoro' ... FM-9
Fang Point—cape ... AK-9
Fang Ridge—ridge ... NV-8
Fang Spring—spring ... OR-9
Fangsrud Lake Bed—flat ... ND-7
Fan Gulch—valley ... CA-9
Fan Gulch—valley ... CO-8
Fan Gulch—valley ... ID-8
Fanhang, Unai—beach ... MH-9
Fanhang Kattan, Kannat—stream ... MH-9
Fanhang Lichan, Kannat—stream ... MH-9
Fan Hill—summit ... CA-9
Fan Hill—summit ... NY-2
Fan Hill—summit ... VT-1
Fan Hill Canyon—valley ... CA-9
Fanhl Lake ... MN-6
Fani, Puntan As—cape ... MH-9
Fanichuluyan ... MH-9
Fanif—civil ... FM-9
Fanif (Municipality)—civ div ... FM-9
Fanif Sch—school ... FM-9
Fanihe Point ... MH-9
Fanika—tunnel ... FM-9
Fanikep, Ununen—cape ... FM-9
Fanikep Point ... FM-9
Fanikop ... FM-9
Fanildo—island ... FM-9
Faninon—spring ... FM-9
Fanip—civil ... FM-9
**Fanip**—pop pl ... FM-9
Fanip, Oror En—locale ... FM-9
Fanipat—well ... FM-9
Fanip Kumi ... FM-9
Fan Island—island ... ME-1
Fan Island—summit ... AZ-5
Faniti, Nomun—bay ... FM-9
**Fankachau**—pop pl ... FM-9
Fankboner Lake—reservoir ... IN-6
Fankboner Lake Dam—dam ... IN-6
Fankhauser Sch (abandoned)—school ... MO-7
Fankuda Islet—island ... AK-9
Fankun—well ... FM-9
Fankuruwon ... FM-9
Fanlagon—slope ... MH-9
Fan Lake—lake ... MN-6
Fan Lake—lake (2) ... WA-9
Fanlew—locale ... FL-3
Fan Lily Lakes—lake ... MN-6
Fan Megit ... FM-9
Fanmeion—spring ... FM-9
Fanmeiot—spring ... FM-9
Fanmeiror—spring ... FM-9
Fanmenew—spring ... FM-9
Fanmengit—summit ... FM-9
Fanmenig ... FM-9
Fan Meseirong—bar ... FM-9
Fan Metirar—spring ... FM-9
Fanmono, Unun En—bar ... FM-9
Fan Mountains—summit ... VA-3
Fan Mtn—summit ... AK-9
Fan Mtn—summit ... MT-8
Fannaanwin—bar ... FM-9
Fannaapiin—cape ... FM-9
Fannan Creek—stream ... KY-4
Fanncomb Hollow—valley ... MO-7
Fannegusha Creek—stream (2) ... MS-4
Fannegusha Creek - in part ... MS-4
Fannegusha Ditch—canal ... MS-4
Fannelle ... AL-4
Fannen—spring ... FM-9
Fannen Cem—cemetery ... MO-7
Fanneranu ... FM-9
**Fannett**—pop pl ... TX-5
Fannette Island—island ... CA-9
Fannett-Metal HS—school ... PA-2
Fannett Oil Field—oilfield ... TX-5
**Fannettsburg**—pop pl ... PA-2
Fannett Sch—school ... TX-5
**Fannett (Township of)**—pop pl ... PA-2
Fanneys Gut—gut ... MD-2
Fanneys Point—cape ... VA-3
Fannie ... VA-3
**Fannie**—pop pl ... AL-4
**Fannie**—pop pl ... AR-4
Fannie, Lake—lake ... FL-3
Fannie, Lake—lake ... MN-6
Fannie Bald Hollow ... AL-4
Fannie Branch—stream ... TN-4
Fannie Branch—stream ... TX-5
Fannie Cem—cemetery ... SC-3
Fannie Church ... AL-4
Fannie Creek—stream ... CA-9
Fannie Creek—stream ... NC-3
Fannie Field Cem—cemetery ... TN-4
Fannie Hill—summit ... NM-5
Fannie Hollow ... VA-3
Fannie Hollow—valley ... AL-4
Fannie Island—island ... AK-9
FANNIE L. DAUGHERTY—hist pl ... MD-2
**Fannie May**—pop pl ... MS-4
Fannie Meadows—flat ... OR-9
Fannie Mine—mine ... CO-8
Fannie Mine—mine ... NM-5
Fannie Mine (historical)—mine ... SD-7
Fannie Mullins Elementary School ... MS-4
Fannie Ridge—ridge ... NC-3
Fannie Woodward Ranch—locale ... TX-5
Fannin—locale ... KY-4
**Fannin**—pop pl ... MS-4
**Fannin**—pop pl ... TX-5
Fannin, Lake—reservoir ... TX-5
Fannin, Oliver P., House—hist pl ... GA-3
Fannin Baptist Ch—church ... MS-4
Fannin Bayou—bay ... FL-3
Fannin Branch—stream ... AL-4
Fannin Branch—stream (3) ... KY-4
Fannin Branch—stream ... TX-5
Fannin Cem—cemetery ... AL-4
Fannin Cem—cemetery ... GA-3
Fannin Cem—cemetery (2) ... KY-4
Fannin Cem—cemetery ... MS-4
Fannin Cem—cemetery ... TX-5
Fannin Cem—cemetery (2) ... VA-3
Fannin Ch—church ... KY-4
**Fannin (County)**—pop pl ... GA-3
**Fannin (County)**—pop pl ... TX-5
Fannin County Regional Hosp—hospital ... GA-3
Fannin Creek—stream (2) ... TX-5
Fannin Dam—dam ... AL-4
Fannin East Oil Field—oilfield ... TX-5
Fanning—fmr MCD ... NE-7
**Fanning**—pop pl ... KS-7
**Fanning**—pop pl ... MS-4
**Fanning**—pop pl ... MO-7
Fanning Archeol Site—hist pl ... KS-7
Fanning Bayou ... FL-3
Fanning Bend—bend ... KY-4
Fanning Bend—bend ... TN-4
Fanning Branch—stream ... AL-4
Fanning Branch—stream ... FL-3
Fanning Bridge—bridge ... NC-3
Fanning Cem—cemetery ... AL-4
Fanning Cem—cemetery ... CT-1
Fanning Cem—cemetery ... KS-7
Fanning Cem—cemetery ... MO-7
Fanning Cem—cemetery (2) ... TN-4
Fanning Ch—church ... AR-4
Fanning Chapel—church ... NC-3
Fanning Cove—valley ... AL-4
Fanning Creek—stream ... SC-3
Fanning Ditch—canal ... CA-9
Fanning Draw—valley ... NM-5
Fanning Field—airport ... ID-8
Fanning Heights Ch of Christ—church ... AL-4
Fanning Hollow—valley ... AL-4
Fanning Hollow—valley ... TN-4
Fanning Island—island ... FL-3
Fanning Low Gap—gap ... AL-4
Fanning Point—cape ... NY-2
Fanning Ranch—locale ... NM-5
Fanning Ranch—locale ... WY-8
Fanning Sch—school (2) ... MO-7
Fannings Crossing—locale ... AL-4
Fanning's Point ... NY-2
**Fanning Springs**—pop pl ... FL-3
Fanning Springs—spring ... FL-3
Fanning Springs Bridge—bridge ... FL-3
Fanning Well—well ... NM-5
Fannin Hill—summit ... AL-4
Fannin Hollow—valley ... KY-4
Fannin Methodist Ch—church ... MS-4
Fannin Mill Creek—stream ... AL-4
Fannin Post Office (historical)—building ... MS-4
Fannins Branch—stream ... KY-4
Fannin Sch—school (11) ... TX-5
Fannins Fork—stream ... KY-4
Fannin Springs ... FL-3
Fannin State Park—park ... TX-5
Fannin Station—locale ... MS-4
Fannin Tank—reservoir ... AZ-5
Fanno—locale ... OR-9
Fanno, Augustus, Farmhouse—hist pl ... OR-9
Fanno Creek—stream (2) ... OR-9
Fannog ... PW-9
Fanno Peak—summit ... OR-9
Fannora Creek—stream ... MT-8
Fanno Ridge—ridge ... OR-9
Fannuk—island ... FM-9
Fanny ... MN-6
**Fanny**—pop pl ... WV-2
Fanny, Lake—lake (2) ... FL-3
Fanny, Mount—summit ... OR-9
Fanny Allen Hosp—hospital ... VT-1
Fanny Arnold Park—park ... MS-4
Fanny Bass Pond—swamp ... FL-3
Fanny Bay—swamp ... FL-3
Fanny Branch—stream ... IL-6
Fanny Branch—stream (2) ... TN-4
Fanny Ch—church ... AL-4
Fanny Cook Bay—stream ... LA-4
Fanny Creek—stream ... CA-9
Fanny Creek—stream ... IN-6
Fanny Creek—stream ... OK-5
Fanny Fern Cem—cemetery ... IA-7
Fanny Fern Mine—mine ... CO-8
Fanny Gap—gap ... GA-3
Fanny Harrington Chapel—church ... TX-5
Fanny Hollow—valley ... KY-4
Fanny Hollow—valley ... VA-3
Fanny Hooe, Lake—lake ... MI-6
Fanny Keys—island ... FL-3
Fanny Knob—summit ... KY-4
Fanny Knob—summit ... TN-4
Fanny Lake ... MN-6
Fanny Lake—lake ... FL-3
Fanny Lake—lake (2) ... MN-6
Fanny Lake—lake ... WI-6
Fanny Mtn—summit ... AK-9
Fanny Peak—summit ... WY-8
Fannys Branch—stream ... AL-4
Fannys Creek—stream ... KY-4
Fannys Fancy—locale ... VI-3
Fannys Hole—locale ... ID-8
Fannys Marsh—swamp ... MI-6
Fanny Spring—spring ... NM-5
**Fanny (Township of)**—pop pl ... MN-6
Fanny Wynn Branch—stream ... KY-4
Fano—island ... FM-9
Fanochoetiw—bar ... FM-9
Fanochopenges—bar ... FM-9
Fanochuluyan—slope ... MH-9
Fanochuluyan, Kannat—stream ... MH-9
Fanochuluyan, Unai—beach ... MH-9
Fanodiy ... FM-9
Fanofa Island—island ... FM-9
**Fanomo**—pop pl ... FM-9
**Fanomo, Oror En**—pop pl ... FM-9
Fanonchuluyan, Bahia—bay ... MH-9
Fanonchuluyan, Puntan—cape ... MH-9
Fanonimea—bar ... FM-9
Fanoodiy—summit ... FM-9
Fanope ... FM-9
Fanope Island ... FM-9
Fanos—island ... FM-9
Fan Palm Hammock—island ... FL-3
Fanpinonow—summit ... FM-9
Fan Pisinakich—bar ... FM-9
Fan Point—cape ... AK-9
Fanpuanu—tunnel ... FM-9
Fanpuechepuech—bar ... FM-9
Fanpukuan—spring ... FM-9
Fanqaliiliy—locale ... FM-9
Fanqamat—island ... FM-9
**Fanrock**—pop pl ... WV-2
Fanru Pung—spring ... FM-9
**Fansafak, Oror En**—pop pl ... FM-9
Fans Branch School ... TN-4
Fanshaw, Mount—summit ... AK-9
Fanshaw Bay—bay ... AK-9
**Fanshawe**—pop pl ... OK-5
Fanshaw Range—other ... AK-9
Fan Shell Beach—locale ... CA-9
Fansinifo—stream ... FM-9
Fanska Oil Field—oilfield ... KS-7
Fanska South Oil Field—oilfield ... KS-7
Fansler ... IA-7
**Fanslers**—pop pl ... IA-7
**Fansler Spur**—pop pl ... ID-8
Fan Spring—spring ... OR-9
Fans Run—stream ... PA-2
Fanstinas ... AL-4
**Fantail**—pop pl ... SD-7
Fantail Branch—stream ... TN-4
Fantail Creek—stream ... ND-7
Fantail Creek—stream ... OR-9
Fantail Creek—stream ... SD-7
Fantail Junction (historical)—locale ... SD-7
Fantail Lake—lake ... MN-6
Fantail Spring—spring ... OR-9
Fantan Lake—lake ... WY-8
Fantastic Caverns—cave (2) ... MO-7
Fantastic Lava Beds—lava ... CA-9
Fantasy Canyon—valley ... UT-8
Fantasy Hills—locale ... GA-3
Fantasy Park—park ... NV-8
Fant Cem—cemetery ... MS-4
Fant Ch—church ... MS-4
Fant Creek—stream ... CA-9
Fantine Cem—cemetery ... NY-2
Fantine Kill ... NY-2
**Fantinekill**—pop pl ... NY-2
Fantine Kill—stream ... NY-2
Fantle Memorial Park—park ... SD-7
Fantom Lake ... SD-7
Fantom Lake—lake ... SD-7
Fanton Hill—summit ... CT-1
Fanton Hollow—valley ... PA-2
Fanton Plaza Trail—trail ... OR-9
Fan Top Tree—pillar ... CO-8
Fant Pasture—flat ... TX-5
Fant-Rozell Cemetery ... MS-4
Fant Sch (historical)—school ... MS-4
Fants Grove Ch—church ... SC-3
Fant Windmill—locale ... TX-5
Fantz Ranch—locale ... OR-9
Fanuamos Durchfahrt ... FM-9
Fanuamot ... FM-9
Fanuamot Durchfahrt ... FM-9
Fanuanbuin Island ... FM-9
Fanuanpue—island ... FM-9
Fanueissane—island ... FM-9
Fanuela ... FM-9
Fanuela Island ... FM-9
Fanueranu ... FM-9
Fanueranu Island ... FM-9
Fanuet Island ... FM-9
Fanufan Reef ... FM-9
Fanufan Riff ... FM-9
Fanufon—bar ... FM-9
Fanu Island ... FM-9
Fanumo—island ... FM-9
Fanunchuluyan ... MH-9
Fanunchuluyan Bay ... MH-9
Fanunchuluyan Beach ... MH-9
Fanunchuluyan Point ... MH-9
Fanunchuluyan Valley ... MH-9
Fanurmot—island ... FM-9
Fanurmot Island ... FM-9
Fanusamos ... FM-9
Fanusamoz Pass—channel ... FM-9
Fanweg—bar ... FM-9
Fanwon—summit ... FM-9
**Fanwood**—pop pl ... NJ-2
Fanwood Park—park ... NJ-2
Fanwood Station—locale ... NJ-2
Fanwwon ... FM-9
Fanybugol ... FM-9
Fanyoruw ... FM-9
Fanyuubogol—summit ... FM-9
Fao—bar ... FM-9
Faounaoupei ... FM-9
Fapiano Creek ... OR-9
Faqua Pond ... MA-1
Far—locale ... WV-2
Fara' ... FM-9
**Farabee**—pop pl ... IN-6
Farabee Creek—stream ... NC-3
Farabees Station ... IN-6
Faraby Island—island ... NC-3
Faraday—locale ... OR-9
Faraday—locale ... WV-2
Faraday Dam—dam ... OR-9
Faraday Forebay—reservoir ... OR-9
Faraday Forebay Dam—dam ... OR-9
Faraday Gulch—valley ... AK-9
Faraday Hollow—valley ... UT-8
Faraday Lake—reservoir ... OR-9
**Faraday Park**—pop pl ... PA-2
Farad Powerhouse—other ... CA-9
Farafor—island ... FM-9
Faragon ... MH-9
Farahns Creek ... CA-9
Farailes—island ... FM-9
Farallon (Barrio)—fmr MCD ... PR-3
Farallon Bay—bay ... AK-9
Farallon de Medinilla—island ... MH-9
Farallon de Pajajos ... MH-9
Farallon de Pajaros—island ... MH-9
Farallone Islands—hist pl ... CA-9
Farallones, Gulf of the—bay ... CA-9
Farallone View Sch—school ... CA-9
Farallon (historical)—locale ... AZ-5
Farallon Islands—area ... CA-9
Farallon Islands—island ... CA-9
Farallon Natl Wildlife Ref—park (2) ... CA-9
Farallon Paxaros ... MH-9
Faran ... FM-9
Faranuf Ranch—locale ... MT-8
Faraq—locale ... FM-9
Fararan ... FM-9
Fararu ... FM-9
Faras Run—stream ... AR-4
Faras Run Creek ... AR-4
Faraulep Island—island ... FM-9
Faraulep (Municipality)—civ div ... FM-9
Faraw ... FM-9
Faraway Branch—stream ... NJ-2
Faraway Farm—hist pl ... WV-2
Faraway Ranch—locale ... AZ-5
Faraway Ranch—locale ... CA-9
Faraway Ranch Hist Dist—hist pl ... AZ-5
Faraway Rock—summit ... WA-9
Faraway Tank—reservoir ... AZ-5
Faraway Wash—stream ... AZ-5
Far Bald Spring Branch—stream ... NC-3
**Farber**—pop pl ... MO-7
Farber Cem—cemetery ... AR-4
Farber Cem—cemetery ... MO-7
Farber Cem—cemetery ... OH-6
Farber Creek—stream ... TX-5
Farber-Knotts Cem—cemetery ... OH-6
Farber Lake—lake ... MN-6
Farber Point—summit ... ID-8
Farbique Sch—school ... KS-7
Far Branch—stream ... NC-3
Far Brook Sch—school ... NJ-2
Farce ... MS-4
Farce Creek—stream ... MI-6
Farchimoon ... FM-9
Farchumoqon—summit ... FM-9
Far Clifty Creek—stream ... KY-4
Far Creek—stream ... NC-3
Far Crooked Creek—stream ... AL-4
Fardale ... NE-7
**Fardale**—pop pl ... NJ-2
**Farden (Township of)**—pop pl ... MN-6
Fardick Creek—stream ... SC-3
**Fardown Estates Subdivision**—pop pl ... UT-8
Far Draw—valley ... CO-8
Far Draw Spring—spring ... CO-8
Fareham—locale ... VI-3
Fareham Bay—bay ... VI-3
Fareham Hill—summit ... VT-1
Fareham Point—cape ... VI-3
Farekich—locale ... FM-9
Farelly Lake—locale ... AR-4
Far End Canyon—valley ... AZ-5
Farewell—locale ... AR-4
Farewell—locale ... MO-7
**Farewell**—pop pl ... AK-9
Farewell Bend—bend ... OR-9
Farewell Bend Forest Camp—locale ... OR-9
**Farewell Bend (historical)**—pop pl ... OR-9
Farewell Bend State Park—park ... OR-9
Farewell Canyon—valley ... CA-9
Farewell Corner—locale ... SC-3
Farewell Creek—stream ... MT-8
Farewell Creek—stream (2) ... WA-9
Farewell Gap—gap ... CA-9
Farewell Gulch—valley ... CO-8
Farewell Hole—cave ... TN-4
Farewell Lake—lake ... AK-9
Farewell Lake—lake ... MI-6
Farewell Lake Lodge—locale ... AK-9
Farewell Landing—locale ... AK-9
Farewell Mtn—summit ... AK-9
Farewell Peak—summit ... WA-9
**Farewells (historical)**—pop pl ... MS-4
Farewell Spring—spring ... OR-9
Far Field Hollow—valley ... TN-4
Far Fork Sandsuck Creek—stream ... KY-4
Far Gap ... PA-2
Fargason Cem—cemetery ... AL-4
Fargason-Wyatt Cem ... AL-4
Fargher Airfield—airport ... OR-9
**Fargher (historical)**—pop pl ... OR-9
**Fargher Lake**—pop pl ... WA-9
Fargher Spring—spring ... OR-9
Fargo—locale ... IL-6
Fargo—locale (2) ... NY-2
Fargo—locale ... OH-6
Fargo—locale ... OR-9
Fargo—locale ... WI-6
**Fargo**—pop pl ... AR-4
**Fargo**—pop pl ... GA-3
**Fargo**—pop pl (2) ... IN-6
**Fargo**—pop pl ... MI-6
**Fargo**—pop pl ... ND-7
**Fargo**—pop pl ... OK-5
**Fargo**—pop pl ... TX-5
Fargo, Enoch J., House—hist pl ... WI-6
Fargo, Lake (historical)—lake ... SD-7
Fargo, L. D., Public Library—hist pl ... WI-6
Fargo Canyon—valley ... CA-9
Fargo (CCD)—cens area ... GA-3
Fargo Cem—cemetery ... ID-8
Fargo Cem—cemetery ... OK-5
Fargo Ch—church ... TX-5
Fargo City Detention Hosp—hist pl ... ND-7
Fargo Coulee—valley ... MT-8
Fargo Creek—stream ... PA-2
Fargo Dam Number 3—dam ... ND-7
Fargo Dam Number 4 ... ND-7
Fargo Dam 2—dam ... ND-7
Fargo Gulch—valley ... CO-8
Fargo High Line Canal—canal ... ID-8
Fargo (historical)—locale ... KS-7
Fargo Low Line Canal—canal ... ID-8
Fargo-Odell (CCD)—cens area ... TX-5
Fargo Oil Field—oilfield ... TX-5
Fargo Run—stream ... IL-6
Fargo Sch—school ... MO-7
Fargo Sch—school ... NE-7
Fargo's Furniture Store—hist pl ... WI-6
Fargo South Residential District—hist pl ... ND-7
Fargo Springs (historical)—locale ... KS-7
Fargo Theatre Bldg—hist pl ... ND-7
Fargo Township—civ div ... ND-7
**Fargo Township**—pop pl ... KS-7
Fargo Wasteway—canal ... ID-8
Fargo 12th Ave Dam—dam ... ND-7
Fargo 4th Street South Dam—dam ... ND-7
Farham ... KS-7
Far Hills ... OH-6
**Far Hills**—pop pl ... NJ-2
Far Hills Day Sch—school ... NJ-2
Far Hills Station—hist pl ... NJ-2
Far Hills Station—locale ... NJ-2
Farhman—locale ... KS-7
Far Horizons—hist pl ... NH-1
**Faria**—pop pl (2) ... PR-3
Faria Sch—school ... CA-9
Farias Park—park ... TX-5
Farias Sch—school ... TX-5
Farias Wheel Airp—airport ... NV-8
**Faribault**—pop pl ... MN-6
Faribault, Alexander, House—hist pl ... MN-6
Faribault City Hall—hist pl ... MN-6
**Faribault (County)**—pop pl ... MN-6
Faribault County Courthouse—hist pl ... MN-6
Faribault Historic Commercial District—hist pl ... MN-6
Faribault Park—park ... MN-6
Faribault Water Works—hist pl ... MN-6
Farick Ranch—locale ... MT-8
Farid Creek ... OR-9
Faries Park—park ... IL-6
**Faries Trailer Park**—pop pl ... NC-3
**Farifield Park Subdivision**—pop pl ... UT-8
**Farill**—pop pl ... AL-4

Fassbinder Gulch—*valley* CO-8
Fassett—*locale* PA-2
Fassett Brook—*stream* NH-1
Fassett Cem—*cemetery* WI-6
*Fassett Creek* GA-3
Fassett Glacier—*glacier* AK-9
Fassett Island—*island* AK-9
Fassett JHS—*school* OH-6
Fassett Point—*cape* AK-9
Fassett Point—*cape* MD-2
Fassett Sch—*school* MI-6
Fassett Sch—*school* NY-2
*Fassetts Point* MD-2
Fassnight Creek—*stream* MO-7
Fassnight Park—*park* MO-7
Fast Bay Oil Field—*oilfield* LA-4
*Fast Branch* AL-4
Fast Cem—*cemetery* OH-6
Fast Cem—*cemetery* OR-9
Fast Creek—*stream* CA-9
Fast Creek—*stream* MT-8
Fast Horse Creek—*stream* SD-7
Fast Lake—*lake* MN-6
*Fast Landing* DE-2
Fastrill Bridge—*bridge* TX-5
Fast Sch—*school* MI-6
Fasulo Park—*park* FL-3
Fatal Hollow—*valley* WY-8
Fatal Rock—*rock* MA-1
**Fatama**—*pop pl* AL-4
Fatamaday—*cape* FM-9
Fatap—*well* FM-9
Fatatele Point—*cape* AS-9
Fat Boy Tank—*reservoir* AZ-5
Fat Buck Ridge—*ridge* CA-9
Fatch Chapel—*church* IN-6
Fat Cow Meadow—*flat* CA-9
Fat Creek—*stream* WV-2
Fat Deer Key—*island* FL-3
Fat Doe Gulch—*valley* CA-9
**Fate**—*pop pl* TX-5
Fate Cove—*bay* NC-3
Fate Creek—*stream* OR-9
Fate Dam—*dam* SD-7
Fate Dam—*reservoir* SD-7
Fate Dam State Public Shooting
Area—*park* SD-7
Fate Irvin Knob—*summit* TN-4
Fate Lee Mtn—*summit* KY-4
Fat Elk Creek—*stream* OR-9
Fate Osteen Cove—*valley* NC-3
Fate Puett Cove—*valley* NC-3
Fath Ch—*church* SC-3
Father And Son—*bar* WA-9
Father And Son Mine—*mine* CA-9
Father and Sons Campground—*locale* ID-8
*Father Cassidys Boys Ranch* ND-7
Father DeSmet Historical Monmt—*park* WY-8
Father DeSmet's Prairie Mass
Site—*hist pl* WY-8
Father Dickson Cem—*cemetery* MO-7
Father Diego Luis de Sanvitores
Monument—*other* GU-9
Father Duenas Sch—*school* GU-9
Father Dunn Camp—*locale* MO-7
Father Dyer Peak—*summit* CO-8
Father Flanagan's Boys' Home—*hist pl* NE-7
Father Flanagan's House—*hist pl* NE-7
Father Garces Monument—*other* CA-9
Father Hennepin State Park—*park* MN-6
Father Judge HS—*school* PA-2
Father Judge Mission Seminary—*school* VA-3
*Fatherland Ch* MS-4
Fatherland Ch—*church* MS-4
Fatherland Mounds—*summit* MS-4
Fatherland Sch (historical)—*school* MS-4
Father Lobell House—*hist pl* ID-8
Father Mtn—*summit* OR-9
Fatherree Cem—*cemetery* MS-4
Father Ryan Sch—*school* TN-4
Fathers, Crossing of the
(historical)—*crossing* UT-8
Father Time Jewel Box—*cave* UT-8
Father Timothy Benavides Park—*park* TX-5
Father White Sch—*school* MD-2
Fat Hog Spring—*spring* TX-5
Fathometer Reef—*bar* AK-9
Fat Horse Hollow—*valley* OK-5
Fatifati Mtn—*summit* AS-9
Fatigue Bay—*bay* AK-9
Fatikat—*island* FM-9
Fatima Ch—*church* NY-2
Fatima HS—*school* MO-7
Fatima Sch—*school* MI-6
Fatima Sch—*school* NM-5
Fatina Cem—*cemetery* TX-5
Fatio—*locale* FL-3
Fat Jack Mine—*mine* AZ-5
Fat John Slough—*gut* AK-9
Fat Klamath Meadows—*flat* OR-9
Fat Lake—*lake* MN-6
Fat Lake—*lake* WI-6
Fatler Ridge—*ridge* OH-6
Fatma, Bayou—*gut* LA-4
Fatman Mtn—*summit* MT-8
Fat Mtn—*summit* VA-3
Fat Oxen—*hist pl* MD-2
Fats Draw—*valley* WY-8
Fattebort Hill—*summit* CA-9
Fattic Cem—*cemetery* IN-6
Fattig Creek—*stream* MT-8
Fatty Bread Branch—*stream* TN-4
Fattybread Branch—*stream* TN-4
Fatty Canyon—*valley* CO-8
Fatty Canyon—*valley* UT-8
Fatty Creek—*stream* AL-4
Fatty Creek—*stream* MT-8
Fatty Lake—*lake* MT-8
Fatty Martin Lake—*lake* NV-8
Fatty Tank—*reservoir* AZ-5
Fatuaga Point—*cape* AS-9
Fatuana Point—*cape* AS-9
Fatuapule Point—*cape* AS-9
Fatuasina Point—*cape* AS-9
Fatuelo Point—*cape* AS-9
Fatugau Rock—*island* AS-9
*Fatula Spring* UT-8
**Fatumafuti**—*pop pl* AS-9
Fatumaga Rocks—*island* AS-9
Fatu Rock (Tower Rock)—*island* AS-9
Fatutea Ridge—*ridge* AS-9
Fatutea Spring—*spring* AS-9
Fatutoaga Rock—*island* AS-9
Fatuuli Rock—*island* AS-9
Fat Woman Canyon—*valley* NV-8
Fat Woman Canyon—*valley* UT-8
*Fauba* FM-9
Fauba Archaelogical Site—*hist pl* FM-9
Fauber Cem—*cemetery* WV-2
Fauber Ranch—*locale* WY-8
**Faubion**—*pop pl* OR-9
Faubion Cem—*cemetery* TN-4
Faubion Crossing—*locale* TX-5
Faubion Sch—*school* MO-7
Faubion Sch—*school* OR-9
Faubion Spring—*spring* TN-4
**Faubourg**—*pop pl* LA-4
Faubourg Marigny—*hist pl* LA-4
Faubus Cem—*cemetery* AR-4
**Faubush**—*pop pl* KY-4
Faubush Creek—*stream* KY-4
Faucet Canyon—*valley* NM-5
Faucet Lake—*lake* TX-5
**Faucett**—*pop pl* MO-7
Faucett, Peter S., House—*hist pl* DE-2
Faucett Canyon—*valley* UT-8
Faucett Cem—*cemetery* IN-6
Faucett Cem—*cemetery* KY-4
*Faucett Creek* GA-3
Faucett Creek—*stream* KY-4
Faucett Creek—*stream* UT-8
*Faucette* TN-4
Faucette, James Peter, House—*hist pl* AR-4
Faucette Bldg—*hist pl* AR-4
Faucette Cem—*cemetery* MS-4
Faucette Hollow—*valley* TN-4
Faucett Mill and House—*hist pl* NC-3
Faucett Sch (historical)—*school* MO-7
*Faucetts Lake* GA-3
Faucett (Township of)—*fmr MCD* NC-3
Faucha—*locale* FM-9
Faucherie Lake—*lake* CA-9
Fauck Ferry—*locale* FL-3
Faudie Grange—*locale* PA-2
Faudie Sch (abandoned)—*school* PA-2
Faught—*locale* TX-5
Faught Canyon—*valley* AZ-5
Faught Creek—*stream* OR-9
Faught Ridge—*ridge* AZ-5
Faught Ridge Lookout—*locale* AZ-5
*Faukelau* FM-9
Faulconer—*locale* KY-4
Faulconer Cem—*cemetery* VA-3
**Faulconerville**—*pop pl* VA-3
Fauline Ch—*church* AR-4
Faulk and Gauntt Bldg—*hist pl* TX-5
Faulk Bridge—*bridge* AL-4
Faulk Bridge—*bridge* LA-4
Faulk Canal—*canal* FL-3
Faulk Canal—*canal* LA-4
Faulk Cem—*cemetery* GA-3
Faulk Cem—*cemetery* IL-6
Faulk Cem—*cemetery* (2) NC-3
Faulk Ch—*church* AL-4
Faulk County—*civil* SD-7
Faulk Ditch—*stream* MS-4
Faulkenberry Cem—*cemetery* TX-5
*Faulkenberry Creek* TX-5
Faulkenberry Creek—*stream* TX-5
Faulkenbury Cem—*cemetery* TX-5
*Faulker Creek* NV-8
Faulkey Gully—*valley* TX-5
Faulk Lake—*lake* MS-4
Faulk Lake Dam—*dam* IN-6
**Faulkland**—*pop pl* DE-2
**Faulkland Heights**—*pop pl* DE-2
**Faulkland Woods**—*pop pl* DE-2
Faulk Mill Creek—*stream* AL-4
Faulk Millpond—*lake* AL-4
*Faulkner* KY-4
*Faulkner* TN-4
Faulkner—*locale* KS-7
Faulkner—*locale* TX-5
**Faulkner**—*pop pl* GA-3
**Faulkner**—*pop pl* IA-7
**Faulkner**—*pop pl* MD-2
**Faulkner**—*pop pl* WV-2
Faulkner, Judge Franklin, House—*hist pl* OK-5
Faulkner, William, House—*hist pl* MS-4
Faulkner Branch—*stream* AL-4
Faulkner Branch—*stream* AR-4
Faulkner Branch—*stream* MD-2
Faulkner Brook—*stream* PA-2
Faulkner Canyon—*valley* NM-5
Faulkner Cave—*cave* AL-4
Faulkner Cem—*cemetery* AL-4
Faulkner Cem—*cemetery* AR-4
Faulkner Cem—*cemetery* FL-3
Faulkner Cem—*cemetery* (2) KY-4
Faulkner Cem—*cemetery* MS-4
Faulkner Cem—*cemetery* NY-2
Faulkner Cem—*cemetery* (2) OK-5
Faulkner Cem—*cemetery* TN-4
Faulkner Cem—*cemetery* VA-3
Faulkner Ch—*church* AL-4
Faulkner Ch—*church* TX-5
**Faulkner (County)**—*pop pl* AR-4
Faulkner County Jail—*hist pl* AR-4
Faulkner County Park—*park* CA-9
Faulkner Creek—*stream* MT-8
Faulkner Creek—*stream* NV-8
Faulkner Creek—*stream* NC-3
Faulkner Creek—*stream* SD-7
**Faulkner Crossroads**—*pop pl* NC-3
Faulkner Dam—*dam* AL-4
Faulkner Draw—*valley* CO-8
Faulkner Draw—*valley* WY-8
Faulkner Ford—*locale* AL-4
Faulkner Gap—*gap* AR-4
Faulkner Gap Ch—*church* AR-4
Faulkner Gulch—*valley* OR-9
Faulkner Hill—*summit* MA-1
Faulkner Hollow—*valley* AL-4
Faulkner Homestead—*hist pl* MA-1
Faulkner Hosp—*hospital* MA-1
Faulkner House—*hist pl* VA-3
Faulkner HS—*school* MA-1
Faulkner Lake—*lake* LA-4
Faulkner Lake—*lake* ME-1
Faulkner Lake—*lake* WI-6
Faulkner Lake—*reservoir* (2) AL-4
Faulkner Lake—*reservoir* GA-3
Faulkner Lake—*swamp* AR-4
Faulkner Lake Dam—*dam* AL-4
Faulkner Lake Dam—*dam* MS-4
Faulkner Lateral—*canal* AZ-5
Faulkner Mound—*summit* FL-3
Faulkner Mountain Lookout Tower—*locale* SC-3
Faulkner Mtn—*summit* AR-4
Faulkner Ponds—*lake* NY-2
Faulkner Ranch—*locale* ID-8
**Faulkner Ridge**—*pop pl* MD-2
Faulkner Run—*stream* VA-3
Faulkner Sch—*school* IL-6
Faulkners Coulee—*valley* MT-8
Faulkner Spring—*spring* MO-7
Faulkner Spring—*spring* NM-5
**Faulkner Springs**—*pop pl* TN-4
Faulkner State Junior Coll—*school* AL-4
Faulkner Station (historical)—*locale* MA-1
Faulkner Street Elem Sch—*school* FL-3
**Faulkner (subdivision)**—*pop pl* MA-1
Faulkner Sulphur Spring—*spring* KY-4
Faulkner (Township of)—*fmr MCD* AR-4
**Faulknerville**—*pop pl* AR-4
Faulknet Park—*park* VT-1
Faulks Cem—*cemetery* LA-4
Faulks Ch—*church* NC-3
Faulks Chapel—*church* GA-3
Faulks Ferry Landing—*locale* FL-3
Faulks Landing (historical)—*locale* TN-4
Faulkstein Camp—*spring* CA-9
**Faulkton**—*pop pl* SD-7
Faulkton, Lake—*reservoir* SD-7
Faulkton Cem—*cemetery* SD-7
Faulkton Dam—*dam* SD-7
Faulkton Municipal Airp—*airport* SD-7
Faulkton Township (historical)—*civil* SD-7
Faulkville Ch—*church* AL-4
**Faulkwoods**—*pop pl* DE-2
Faull Branch—*stream* TN-4
Faull Slough—*stream* CA-9
Faulman Drain—*stream* MI-6
Faul-Mathison Dam—*dam* ND-7
Fault Cave—*cave* MO-7
Fault Creek—*stream* (3) AK-9
Fault Creek—*stream* MT-8
Fault Draw—*valley* TX-5
Fault Lake—*lake* ID-8
Fault Lake—*lake* MN-6
Fault Lake—*lake* MT-8
Faultline Tank—*reservoir* TX-5
Fault Peak—*summit* MT-8
Fault Point—*cape* AK-9
Fault Point—*cape* UT-8
Fault Scarp of 1954—*ridge* NV-8
Fault Tunnel—*tunnel* HI-9
Fault Wash—*stream* CA-9
Fauna—*locale* TX-5
Fauna Creek—*stream* AK-9
**Fauna (historical)**—*pop pl* NC-3
*Faunamot Durchfahrt* FM-9
Faunce—*locale* MN-6
**Faunce**—*pop pl* PA-2
Faunce Cem—*cemetery* IL-6
Faunce Ch—*church* MA-1
**Faunce Corner**—*pop pl* MA-1
Faunce Hill—*summit* ME-1
Faunce Lake—*lake* MN-6
*Faunce Slough* MN-6
Faunces Mtn—*summit* MA-1
Fauncetown—*locale* PA-2
Faun Creek—*stream* OR-9
Faun Hollow—*valley* UT-8
*Faun Lake* MA-1
Faun Lake—*lake* NY-2
*Faunsamoz Pass* FM-9
**Faunsdale**—*pop pl* AL-4
Faunsdale (CCD)—*cens area* AL-4
*Faunsdale Cemetery* AL-4
Faunsdale Division—*civil* AL-4
Faunsdale JHS—*school* AL-4
**Fauntleroy**—*pop pl* WA-9
Fauntleroy Canyon—*valley* CA-9
Fauntleroy Cem—*cemetery* LA-4
Fauntleroy Cove—*bay* WA-9
Fauntleroy Point—*cape* WA-9
Fauntleroy Rock—*island* CA-9
Fauntleroy Rock—*summit* CA-9
Fauntleroy Sch—*school* WA-9
Faun Trail—*trail* NV-8
*Faunupei* FM-9
Faunus—*locale* MI-6
*Faup* FM-9
Faup—*CDP* FM-9
Faupel Lake—*lake* MN-6
Faupell Lake—*lake* MI-6
*Faupo* FM-9
Fauquier Ch—*church* VA-3
**Fauquier (County)**—*pop pl* VA-3
Fauquier Hosp—*hospital* VA-3
Fauquier HS—*school* VA-3
**Fauquier Springs**—*pop pl* VA-3
Fauquier Springs Country Club—*other* VA-3
Fauquier White Sulphur Springs—*locale* VA-3
*Faurell Lake* MI-6
Faure Well—*well* WY-8
Fauries Cove—*bay* TX-5
Fauries Peak—*summit* CA-9
Faurot Park—*park* OH-6
Faurot Sch—*school* OH-6
*Faurup* FM-9
Faus, Dr. Robert, House—*hist pl* HI-9
Fausan, Lake—*lake* LA-4
*Fauscett Creek* GA-3
Fausett Creek—*stream* GA-3
*Fausette Hollow* TN-4
Fausett Lake—*reservoir* GA-3
*Fausetts Lake* GA-3
Fausey Sch—*school* MA-1
Fausse, Bayou—*stream* LA-4
*Fausse Lake* LA-4
Fausse Pointe—*cape* LA-4
Fausse Pointe, Lake—*lake* LA-4
Fausse Pointe Oil Field—*oilfield* LA-4
*Fausse River* LA-4
*Fausse River Cutoff* LA-4
Fausset Cem—*cemetery* IN-6
Fauss Ford—*locale* AL-4
Faust—*locale* UT-8
**Faust**—*pop pl* NC-3
Faust Branch—*stream* LA-4
Faust Cabin—*locale* CA-9
Faust Cem—*cemetery* MS-4
Faust Creek—*stream* UT-8
*Faust Elementary School* PA-2
Faust Flat—*flat* PA-2
Faust Houses and Outbuildings—*hist pl* GA-3
Faustina Cem—*cemetery* AR-4
Faustina Ch—*church* (2) AR-4
**Faustinas**—*pop pl* AL-4
*Faustinas Beach* AL-4
Faustino Windmill—*locale* TX-5
Faust Island—*island* AK-9
Faust Island—*island* WI-6
Faust Lake—*lake* WI-6
Faust Meadows—*flat* ID-8
Faust Mill (Ruins)—*locale* CA-9
Fauston Post Office (historical)—*building* SD-7
Faust Park—*park* ND-7
*Faust Pony Express Interpretive Site* UT-8
Faust Rock—*other* AK-9
*Faust Station* UT-8
Faust Temple Ch of God in Christ—*church* FL-3
Faust Valley—*basin* UT-8
Faust Valley—*valley* PA-2
Faus Well—*well* NM-5
*Faut* FM-9
*Fautt Branch* TN-4
Fautt Branch—*stream* TN-4
*Fauup* FM-9
Fauver Cem—*cemetery* TN-4
Fauver Hill Sch—*school* WI-6
Faux, Jabez, House and Barn—*hist pl* UT-8
Faver Cem—*cemetery* GA-3
*Faver Dykes State Park* FL-3
Faver Sch—*school* OK-5
Faver Tank—*reservoir* AZ-5
Favil Lake—*lake* WI-6
Faville Grove Sch—*school* WI-6
Favinger Place—*locale* CA-9
**Favonia**—*pop pl* VA-3
Favoni-Harris, Dr. Charles and William
Shakespeare House—*hist pl* NC-3
Favonius Lake—*lake* MT-8
Favor Cem—*cemetery* OK-5
Favor Dykes State Park—*park* FL-3
**Favoretta (Favorita Station)**—*pop pl*
(2) FL-3
*Favorita* FL-3
**Favorita**—*pop pl* FL-3
Favorita Island—*island* AK-9
Favorite, Mount—*summit* AK-9
Favorite Anchorage—*bay* AK-9
Favorite Bay—*bay* AK-9
Favorite Channel—*channel* AK-9
Favorite Creek—*stream* AL-4
Favorite Creek—*stream* AK-9
Favorite Creek—*stream* OR-9
Favorite Gulch—*valley* (2) MT-8
Favorite Hills—*summit* UT-8
Favorite Hill Sch—*school* OH-6
Favorite Reef—*bay* AK-9
Favorite Sch—*school* MI-6
Favorite Slough—*stream* OR-9
Favor Peak—*summit* AK-9
Favot Coulee—*valley* MT-8
Favour Tank—*reservoir* AZ-5
Favreau Brook—*stream* NH-1
Favre Lake—*lake* NV-8
Favret Canyon—*valley* NV-8
Fawcett—*locale* OH-6
Fawcett, Mount—*summit* AK-9
Fawcett, Wilford H., House—*hist pl* MN-6
Fawcett Ch—*church* PA-2
*Fawcett Creek* GA-3
Fawcett Creek—*stream* OR-9
Fawcett Draw—*valley* WY-8
Fawcette Sch—*school* PA-2
Fawcett Gap—*gap* VA-3
**Fawcett Gap**—*pop pl* VA-3
Fawcett Lake—*lake* MN-6
Fawcett Memorial Hosp—*hospital* FL-3
Fawcett Ranch—*locale* (2) TX-5
Fawcett Run—*stream* VA-3
*Fawcetts* IN-6
Fawcett Sch—*school* WA-9
Fawcetts Pond—*lake* MA-1
Fawcett Stadium—*other* OH-6
**Fawcett Subdivision**—*pop pl* UT-8
Fawil—*locale* TX-5
F A Windmill—*locale* TX-5
*Fawkes Run* PA-2
Fawks Cem—*cemetery* MO-7
Fawlers Prairie—*lake* FL-3
Fawley Hollow—*valley* VA-3
*Fawn* KS-7
Fawn—*locale* OR-9
**Fawn**—*pop pl* OR-9
Fawn Basin—*basin* NV-8
Fawn Bayou—*gut* LA-4
Fawn Branch—*stream* NC-3
Fawn Branch—*stream* SC-3
Fawn Branch—*stream* VA-3
Fawn Brook—*stream* CT-1
Fawn Butte—*summit* CA-9
Fawn Butte—*summit* OR-9
Fawn Camp—*locale* OR-9
Fawn Camp Trail—*trail* OR-9
*Fawn Creek* CO-8
*Fawn Creek* ID-8
*Fawn Creek* KS-7
*Fawn Creek* MT-8
*Fawn Creek* UT-8
Fawn Creek—*stream* AK-9
Fawn Creek—*stream* (2) CA-9
Fawn Creek—*stream* (4) CO-8
Fawn Creek—*stream* (9) ID-8
Fawn Creek—*stream* IA-7
Fawn Creek—*stream* (2) KS-7
Fawn Creek—*stream* MN-6
Fawn Creek—*stream* (6) MT-8
Fawn Creek—*stream* (3) NV-8
Fawn Creek—*stream* NJ-2
Fawn Creek—*stream* OK-5
Fawn Creek—*stream* (12) OR-9
Fawn Creek—*stream* (2) WA-9
Fawn Creek—*stream* (4) WY-8
Fawn Creek Bar—*bar* ID-8
Fawn Creek Cem—*cemetery* KS-7
Fawn Creek Sch—*school* IL-6
**Fawn Creek Township**—*pop pl* KS-7
Fawn Draw—*valley* WY-8
Fawn Elem Sch—*school* PA-2
Fawn Ford—*crossing* FL-3
**Fawn Ford**—*pop pl* FL-3
**Fawn Gardens Subdivision**—*pop pl* UT-8
**Fawn Grove**—*pop pl* PA-2
Fawn Grove Borough—*civil* PA-2
Fawn Grove Ch—*church* MS-4
*Fawn Grove Freewill Baptist Ch* MS-4
Fawn Gulch—*valley* CO-8
Fawn Gulch—*valley* NV-8
Fawn Gulch—*valley* OR-9
**Fawn Haven Number One**—*pop pl* PA-2
**Fawn Haven Number Two**—*pop pl* PA-2
Fawn Hill Brook—*stream* CT-1
Fawn Hollow—*valley* CO-8
Fawn Hollow—*valley* WV-2
Fawn Island—*island* (2) AK-9
Fawn Island—*island* OH-6
Fawn Island—*island* OR-9
Fawn Island—*island* WA-9
*Fawn Lake* MI-6
Fawn Lake—*lake* (2) AK-9
Fawn Lake—*lake* (4) CA-9
Fawn Lake—*lake* (4) ID-8
Fawn Lake—*lake* (2) MA-1
Fawn Lake—*lake* MI-6
Fawn Lake—*lake* (10) MN-6
Fawn Lake—*lake* (2) MT-8
Fawn Lake—*lake* NE-7
Fawn Lake—*lake* (3) NY-2
Fawn Lake—*lake* (2) OR-9
Fawn Lake—*lake* (2) WA-9
Fawn Lake—*lake* (10) WI-6
Fawn Lake—*reservoir* AL-4
Fawn Lake—*reservoir* NJ-2
Fawn Lake—*reservoir* (2) PA-2
Fawn Lake—*reservoir* WI-6
Fawn Lake Creek—*stream* ID-8
Fawn Lake Dam—*dam* AL-4
Fawn Lake Dam—*dam* PA-2
**Fawn Lake Forest**—*pop pl* PA-2
Fawn Lake Mtn—*summit* NY-2
Fawn Lakes—*lake* NM-5
Fawn Lakes Campground—*locale* NM-5
**Fawn Lake (Township of)**—*pop pl* MN-6
Fawn Lake Trail—*trail* OR-9
Fawn Lake Trail—*trail* WA-9
Fawn Lake Vly—*swamp* NY-2
Fawn Lake Way—*trail* OR-9
Fawn Lodge—*locale* CA-9
Fawn Meadow—*flat* CA-9
Fawn Meadow—*flat* ID-8
Fawn Meadow—*flat* OR-9
**Fawn Meadows**—*pop pl* MS-4
Fawn Mtn—*summit* AK-9
Fawn Mtn—*summit* NC-3
Fawn Pass—*gap* WY-8
Fawn Pass Trail—*trail* MT-8
Fawn Pass Trail—*trail* WY-8
Fawn Peak—*summit* MT-8
Fawn Peak—*summit* OR-9
Fawn Peak—*summit* WA-9
Fawn Point—*cape* AK-9
*Fawn Pond* MA-1
Fawn Pond—*lake* ME-1
Fawn Pond—*lake* MA-1
Fawn Prairie—*area* CA-9
**Fawn Ridge**—*pop pl* NY-2
Fawn Ridge—*ridge* CA-9
Fawn Ridge—*ridge* ID-8
Fawn Ridge—*ridge* PA-2
Fawn Ridge—*ridge* WA-9
*Fawn River* IN-6
**Fawn River**—*pop pl* MI-6
Fawn River—*stream* IN-6
Fawn River—*stream* MI-6
Fawn River Drain—*canal* MI-6
Fawn River Fish Hatchery—*other* IN-6
Fawn River Sch—*school* MI-6
**Fawn River (Township of)**—*pop pl* MI-6
Fawn Rock—*pillar* OR-9
Fawn Rsvr—*reservoir* ID-8
Fawn Rsvr—*reservoir* OR-9
Fawn Run—*stream* IN-6
Fawn Run—*stream* PA-2
Fawn Sch (historical)—*school* MS-4
**Fawnskin**—*pop pl* CA-9
Fawnskin Valley—*basin* CA-9
Fawns Mill Trail—*trail* WA-9
Fawn Spring—*spring* AZ-5
Fawn Spring—*spring* (2) CA-9
Fawn Spring—*spring* ID-8
Fawn Spring—*spring* (5) OR-9
Fawn Spring—*spring* UT-8
Fawn Spring—*spring* WY-8
Fawn Springs—*spring* CO-8
Fawn Springs Bench—*bench* CO-8
Fawn Springs No 5 Mine—*mine* CO-8
Fawn Springs No 9 Mine—*mine* CO-8
Fawn Spring Trail—*trail* OR-9
Fawn Tank—*reservoir* NM-5
**Fawn (Township of)**—*pop pl* (2) PA-2
Fawn Valley—*valley* NM-5
Fawn Valley Mobile Home Park—*locale* PA-2
**Fawsett Farms**—*pop pl* MD-2
Fawver Creek—*stream* TN-4
Faw Wells—*well* CO-8
*Fax Branch* NC-3
Fax Brown Lake—*reservoir* NC-3
Fax Brown Lake Dam—*dam* NC-3
Fax Creek—*stream* NC-3
*Fax Gap* NC-3
Faxon—*locale* KY-4
**Faxon**—*pop pl* OK-5
**Faxon**—*pop pl* (2) PA-2
**Faxon**—*pop pl* TN-4
Faxon Cem—*cemetery* OK-5
Faxon Ch—*church* TN-4
*Faxon Hills* OH-6
**Faxon Hills**—*pop pl* OH-6
Faxon Lake—*lake* UT-8
Faxon Park—*park* MA-1
Faxon Post Office (historical)—*building* TN-4
Faxon Sch—*school* IL-6
Faxon Sch—*school* KY-4
Faxon Sch—*school* MO-7
Faxon Sch (historical)—*school* TN-4
Faxons Pond—*lake* NY-2
Faxon-Thomas Mansion—*hist pl* TN-4
**Faxon (Township of)**—*pop pl* MN-6
*Fax Pond* FL-3
Faxton Hosp—*hospital* NY-2
*Fay* FM-9
Fay—*locale* NV-8
Fay—*locale* NY-2
Fay—*locale* OH-6
**Fay**—*pop pl* IL-6
**Fay**—*pop pl* OK-5
Fay, Charles, House—*hist pl* OH-6
Fay, Cyrus, House—*hist pl* OH-6
Fay, Issac, House—*hist pl* MA-1
Fay, Mount—*summit* NY-2
*Fayal* MN-6
Fayal Number Two Pit—*mine* MN-6
Fayal Pit—*mine* MN-6
Fayal Pond—*lake* MN-6
Fayal Sch—*school* MN-6
**Fayal (Township of)**—*pop pl* MN-6
Fayal Township State Game Ref—*park* MN-6
Fay-Bainbridge State Park—*park* WA-9
Fayblock—*uninc pl* NC-3
Fay Branch—*stream* AL-4
Fay Brook—*stream* NY-2
Fay Brook—*stream* VT-1
Fayburg—*locale* TX-5
Fay Canyon—*valley* (2) AZ-5
Fay Canyon—*valley* CA-9
Fay Canyon—*valley* NV-8
Fay Canyon—*valley* OR-9
Fay Canyon Arch—*arch* AZ-5
Fay Canyon Dam—*dam* OR-9
Fay Canyon Rsvr—*reservoir* OR-9
Fay Cem—*cemetery* MA-1
Fay Cem—*cemetery* MO-7
Fay Cem—*cemetery* NV-8
Fay Cem—*cemetery* VA-3
Fay Club—*hist pl* MA-1
Fay Creek—*stream* (2) AK-9
Fay Creek—*stream* (2) CA-9
Fay Creek—*stream* TN-4
Fay Dam—*dam* OH-6
Fay De Berard Ranch—*locale* CO-8
Fay Dennis Draw—*valley* WY-8
Faye—*locale* KY-4
Faye Park—*park* HI-9
Fayerweather, George, Blacksmith
Shop—*hist pl* RI-1
Fayerweather Cem—*cemetery* NY-2
Fayerweather Island—*island* CT-1
Fayes Gulch—*valley* OR-9
Fayette—*hist pl* MI-6
Fayette—*locale* CA-9
Fayette—*locale* CO-8
Fayette—*locale* MI-6
Fayette—*locale* ND-7
Fayette—*locale* WV-2
**Fayette**—*pop pl* AL-4
**Fayette**—*pop pl* IL-6
**Fayette**—*pop pl* IN-6
**Fayette**—*pop pl* IA-7
**Fayette**—*pop pl* ME-1
**Fayette**—*pop pl* MS-4
**Fayette**—*pop pl* MO-7
**Fayette**—*pop pl* NY-2
**Fayette**—*pop pl* OH-6
**Fayette**—*pop pl* (2) PA-2
**Fayette**—*pop pl* UT-8
**Fayette**—*pop pl* WI-6
Fayette, Lake—*reservoir* GA-3
Fayette Acad—*school* AL-4
Fayette Baptist Ch—*church* MS-4
*Fayette Baptist Church* AL-4
Fayette Branch—*stream* AL-4
Fayette (CCD)—*cens area* AL-4
Fayette (CCD)—*cens area* KY-4
Fayette Cem—*cemetery* UT-8
Fayette Cem—*cemetery* WI-6
Fayette Central Elem Sch—*school* IN-6
Fayette Chapel—*locale* PA-2
Fayette Ch of Christ—*church* AL-4
**Fayette City**—*pop pl* PA-2
Fayette City Borough—*civil* PA-2
Fayette City Cem—*cemetery* AL-4
Fayette Civic Center—*building* AL-4
*Fayette Corner* TN-4
Fayette Corner—*locale* ME-1
*Fayette Corner Post Office* TN-4
**Fayette Corners**—*pop pl* TN-4
Fayette Corners (CCD)—*cens area* TN-4
Fayette Corners Division—*civil* TN-4
Fayette Corners Post Office
(historical)—*building* TN-4
Fayette Country Club—*locale* AL-4
*Fayette (County)* KY-4
**Fayette County**—*pop pl* AL-4
**Fayette (County)**—*pop pl* GA-3
**Fayette (County)**—*pop pl* IL-6
**Fayette County**—*pop pl* IN-6
**Fayette (County)**—*pop pl* OH-6
**Fayette County**—*pop pl* PA-2
**Fayette County**—*pop pl* TN-4
**Fayette (County)**—*pop pl* TX-5
**Fayette (County)**—*pop pl* WV-2
Fayette County Airp—*airport* TN-4
Fayette County Courthouse—*building* AL-4
Fayette County Courthouse—*building* TN-4
Fayette County Courthouse—*hist pl* GA-3
Fayette County Courthouse—*hist pl* IA-7
Fayette County Courthouse—*hist pl* OH-6
Fayette County Courthouse—*hist pl* WV-2
Fayette County Courthouse and
Jail—*hist pl* TX-5
Fayette County Courthouse
District—*hist pl* AL-4
Fayette County Farm (historical)—*locale* TN-4
Fayette County Home—*building* IA-7
Fayette County Home—*hospital* PA-2
Fayette County Hosp—*hospital* AL-4
Fayette County HS—*school* AL-4
Fayette County Lake—*reservoir* AL-4
*Fayette County Public Lake* AL-4
Fayette County Public Lake Dam—*dam* AL-4
Fayette County Training Sch
(historical)—*school* TN-4
*Fayette County Vocational Center* AL-4
Fayette County Vocational Center—*school* TN-4
*Fayette Depot Town* AL-4

Fayette Ditch—canal WY-8
Fayette Division—civil AL-4
Fayette Drain—stream IL-6
Fayette Elem Sch—school AL-4
Fayette Flying Field—airport MO-7
Fayette Grammar Sch AL-4
**Fayette Heights**—pop pl WV-2
Fayette Hill ME-1
**Fayettehill**—pop pl MS-4
Fayette Junction—locale AR-4
Fayette Lake—lake WY-8
Fayette Lake—reservoir MO-7
Fayette-Lexington Health Center—hospital KY-4
Fayette Male and Female Institute (historical)—school AL-4
Fayette Mall—locale KY-4
**Fayette Manor**—pop pl NY-2
Fayette Methodist Episcopal Church AL-4
Fayette Natl Bank Bldg—hist pl KY-4
Fayette Oil And Gas Field—oilfield MS-4
**Fayette Park**—pop pl VA-3
Fayette Post Office—locale MI-6
Fayette Ridge—summit ME-1
Fayette Safety Vault and Trust Company Bldg—hist pl KY-4
Fayette Saint Sch—school WV-2
Fayette Sch—hist pl PA-2
Fayette Sch—school SD-7
Fayette Sch (abandoned)—school PA-2
Fayette Sch (historical)—school MS-4
Fayettes Corner—locale MI-6
Fayette Spring—spring UT-8
**Fayette Springs**—pop pl PA-2
Fayette Square Shop Ctr—locale AL-4
Fayette State Experiment For—forest AL-4
**Fayette (sta.) (Wabash River Power Station)**—pop pl IN-6
**Fayette (Town of)**—pop pl ME-1
**Fayette (Town of)**—pop pl NY-2
**Fayette (Town of)**—pop pl WI-6
Fayette Township—civil SD-7
Fayette Township—fmr MCD (2) IA-7
Fayette Township (historical)—civil SD-7
Fayette (Township of)—fmr MCD AR-4
**Fayette (Township of)**—pop pl IL-6
**Fayette (Township of)**—pop pl IN-6
**Fayette (Township of)**—pop pl MI-6
**Fayette (Township of)**—pop pl OH-6
**Fayette (Township of)**—pop pl PA-2
Fayetteville IN-6
Fayetteville PA-2
Fayetteville—locale OR-9
**Fayetteville**—pop pl AL-4
**Fayetteville**—pop pl AR-4
**Fayetteville**—pop pl GA-3
**Fayetteville**—pop pl IL-6
**Fayetteville**—pop pl (2) IN-6
**Fayetteville**—pop pl MO-7
**Fayetteville**—pop pl NY-2
**Fayetteville**—pop pl NC-3
**Fayetteville**—pop pl OH-6
**Fayetteville**—pop pl (2) PA-2
**Fayetteville**—pop pl TN-4
**Fayetteville**—pop pl TX-5
**Fayetteville**—pop pl WV-2
Fayetteville, Lake—reservoir AR-4
Fayetteville Acad—school NC-3
Fayetteville Baptist Ch—church AL-4
Fayetteville (CCD)—cens area GA-3
Fayetteville (CCD)—cens area TN-4
Fayetteville (CCD)—cens area TX-5
Fayetteville Ch—church AL-4
Fayetteville City Hall—building TN-4
Fayetteville Country Club—other AR-4
Fayetteville Division—civil TN-4
Fayetteville Elem Sch—school PA-2
Fayetteville First Baptist Ch—church TN-4
Fayetteville Golf And Country Club—locale TN-4
Fayetteville HS—school AL-4
Fayetteville Ice and Manufacturing Company:Plant and Engineer's House—hist pl NC-3
Fayetteville JHS—school TN-4
Fayetteville Mall—locale NC-3
Fayetteville-Manlius HS—school NY-2
Fayetteville Municipal Airp—airport NC-3
Fayetteville Municipal Airp—airport TN-4
Fayetteville Municipal Airp (Grannis Field)—airport NC-3
Fayetteville Mutual Insurance Company Bldg—hist pl NC-3
Fayetteville North—uninc pl NC-3
Fayetteville Post Office—building TN-4
Fayetteville Pumping Station—building TN-4
Fayetteville Pumping Station—locale TN-4
Fayetteville State Univ—school NC-3
Fayetteville Station—locale PA-2
Fayetteville Street Elem Sch—school NC-3
Fayetteville (Township of)—civ div IL-6
Fayetteville VAH Airp—airport NC-3
Fayetteville Women's Club and Oval Ballroom—hist pl NC-3
Fayette Ware HS—school TN-4
Fayette Wash—valley UT-8
Fayettville PA-2
Fay Falls—falls NH-1
**Fayfield**—pop pl PA-2
Fay Fuller Camp—locale VT-1
Fay Hill—summit MA-1
Fay Hill—summit TN-4
Fay (historical)—locale KS-7
Fay Hollow—valley NY-2
Fay Hollow—valley PA-2
Fay Hollow—valley VA-3
Fayhs Lake OR-9
Fay Island—island CA-9
Fay Lake MI-6
Fay Lake—lake FL-3
Fay Lake—lake MI-6
Fay Lake—lake MN-6
Fay Lake—lake OR-9
Fay Lake—lake WI-6
Fay Lake Outlet—stream WI-6
Fay Lakes—lake CO-8
Faylane Sch—school CA-9
Fayler Cem—cemetery OH-6
Fay Mine—mine NV-8
Faymont Ch—church NC-3
Fay Mtn—summit MA-1
Fayne Creek—stream AL-4
Faynefngin FM-9
Faynes Branch AL-4
**Fayne Siding**—pop pl IN-6
Fayo—island FM-9
Fay Peak—summit WA-9
Fay Post Office (historical)—building MS-4
Fay Ranch—locale SD-7
**Fays**—pop pl AL-4
Fays Bridge—bridge MA-1
Fay Sch—school MA-1
Fay School Number 21 IN-6
Fays Corner—locale TX-5
**Fays Corner**—pop pl VT-1
Fay Scott Bog—swamp ME-1
Fays Hill MA-1
Fays Hill—summit MA-1
Fay's Lake MT-8
Fay Slough—gut CA-9
Fays Mtn MA-1
Fayson Lakes—lake NJ-2
**Fayson Lakes**—pop pl NJ-2
Fayson Lakes Lower Dam—dam NJ-2
Fay Station AL-4
Fayston Sch—school VT-1
**Fayston (Town of)**—pop pl VT-1
**Fays Trailer Park**—pop pl UT-8
**Faysville**—pop pl TX-5
**Fay Terrace**—pop pl PA-2
**Fay Township**—pop pl ND-7
Fay-Usborne Mill—hist pl NY-2
Fayville MA-1
Fayville—locale IL-6
Fayville—locale VT-1
**Fayville**—pop pl MA-1
**Fayville**—pop pl NY-2
Fayville Branch—stream VT-1
Fayville Creek—stream NY-2
Fayville Post Office (historical)—building TN-4
Fayville Trail—trail CO-8
Fay Wayside—park NH-1
Faywood NM-5
Faywood—locale KY-4
**Faywood (Dwyer)**—pop pl NM-5
Faywood Hot Springs—locale NM-5
**Faywood Hot Springs**—pop pl NM-5
Faywood Station—locale NM-5
Fayy Station IL-6
**Fazendeville**—pop pl LA-4
Fazon, Lake—lake WA-9
F Bagleys Heirs Grant—civil FL-3
F Baker Ranch—locale NV-8
F B Ashe—locale TX-5
F Bethune Grant—civil FL-3
F B Hayes Lake Dam—dam MS-4
F B I Academy—post sta VA-3
F B P O—post sta VA-3
F Bridge—bridge MT-8
F B Woodley Elementary School MS-4
F Canal—canal CA-9
F Canal—canal ID-8
F Canal—canal OR-9
F Canal—canal UT-8
F C Havens Sch—school CA-9
F Churchill—locale TX-5
F. C. LEWIS, JR—hist pl MD-2
F C Ranch—locale TX-5
F Curtis Dam—dam SD-7
F Ditch—canal MT-8
F D Lateral—canal CO-8
F Dolch—locale TX-5
F Drain—canal (2) CA-9
F D Roosevelt Golf Course—locale PA-2
F D Roosevelt Home Natl Historic Site—park NY-2
F D Roosevelt JHS—school PA-2
F D R Sch—school GA-3
FD Tank—reservoir NM-5
**Fe**—pop pl PR-3
Fead, John L., House—hist pl MI-6
Feadamach—bay FM-9
Feagans Cem—cemetery VA-3
Feagans Island—island VA-3
**Feagaville**—pop pl MD-2
Feagin Cem—cemetery AL-4
Feagin Cem—cemetery GA-3
Feagin Cem—cemetery TX-5
Feagin Creek—stream (2) AL-4
Feagin Hill Creek—stream GA-3
Feagin Negro Cemetery AL-4
Feagin Ranch—locale OR-9
Feagins Creek—stream AL-4
Feagins Gap—gap TN-4
Feagins Store AL-4
Feagles Creek—stream OR-9
Feagles Lake—reservoir NY-2
Feake, Mount—summit MA-1
Feak Hollow—valley NY-2
Fealeasicz Reef FM-9
Feamster Ch—church WV-2
Feanifengin—summit FM-9
Feanimeen—summit FM-9
Fear, Cape—cape NC-3
Fear Creek—stream CO-8
Fear Ditch Rsvr—reservoir WY-8
Fearing Hill—summit MA-1
Fearing Pond—lake MA-1
Fearings Hill MA-1
Fearings Pond MA-1
Fearing Tavern—building MA-1
**Fearing (Township of)**—pop pl OH-6
Fearis Cem—cemetery KY-4
Fearisville—locale KY-4
Fearman, Bayou—stream LA-4
Fearman Lake—lake LA-4
Fearn Branch—stream AL-4
Fearn Cem—cemetery AL-4
Fearn Creek—stream ID-8
Fearn Creek Trail—trail ID-8
F Earnests Shoals—bar TN-4
Fearnot—locale PA-2
Fearnow Lake—reservoir IN-6
Fearnow Lake Dam—dam IN-6
**Fearnowville**—pop pl CO-8
Fearnside Lake—lake GA-3
Fearn Springs MS-4
**Fearns Springs**—pop pl MS-4
Fearns Springs Post Office (historical)—building MS-4
Fears Bluff—cliff MO-7
Fears Corner—locale VA-3
Fears Lake—swamp AR-4
Fear Spring—spring MT-8
Fears Site (34SQ76)—hist pl OK-5
**Fearsville**—pop pl KY-4
Feary Creek—stream ID-8
Feaselburg Cem—cemetery OH-6
Feaser Sch—school PA-2
Feaster—locale AZ-5
Feaster Branch—stream MO-7
Feaster Cem—cemetery MO-7
Feaster Cem—cemetery PA-2
Feaster Cem—cemetery SC-3
Feaster Lake—reservoir OK-5
**Feaster Park**—pop pl NJ-2
Feaster Sch—school CA-9
Feaster Sch—school MO-7
Feasters Rocks—cliff OR-9
Feasterville—locale SC-3
**Feasterville**—pop pl PA-2
**Feasterville Gardens**—pop pl PA-2
**Feasterville Heights**—pop pl PA-2
Feasterville Post Office (historical)—building PA-2
**Feasterville-Trevose**—pop pl PA-2
Featherbed Bank—bar FL-3
Featherbed Bay—bay FL-3
Featherbed Bay—swamp GA-3
Featherbed Branch—stream NJ-2
Featherbed Branch—stream NC-3
Featherbed Camp—locale WA-9
Featherbed Creek—stream MT-8
Featherbed Creek—stream WA-9
Featherbed Hill—summit IN-6
Feather Bed Hollow—valley KY-4
Featherbed Lake—lake MN-6
Feather Bed Lake—lake OR-9
Feather Bed Lake Waterhole—reservoir OR-9
Featherbed Marsh—swamp MI-6
Featherbed Swamp—swamp MA-1
Feather Branch—stream WI-6
Feathercamp Branch—stream VA-3
Feather Camp Lookout Tower—locale VA-3
Feathercamp Ridge—ridge VA-3
Feather Cave—hist pl NM-5
Feather Cem—cemetery KY-4
Feather Creek ID-8
Feather Creek WY-8
Feather Creek—stream ID-8
Feather Creek—stream IL-6
Feather Creek—stream IN-6
Feather Creek—stream MT-8
Feather Creek—stream OK-5
Feather Falls—falls CA-9
**Feather Falls**—pop pl CA-9
Feather Falls (CCD)—cens area CA-9
Featherfoot Cave—cave TN-4
Feather Fork—stream IN-6
Feather Fork Mine (Inactive)—mine CA-9
Feather Gulch—valley MT-8
Featherhoff Sch—school SD-7
Feather Island—island WI-6
Feather Lake CA-9
Feather Lake—lake (3) CA-9
Feather Lake—lake MI-6
Feather Lake—lake MN-6
Feather Lakes—lake ID-8
Featherly Branch—stream MO-7
Featherly Creek—stream AK-9
Featherly Pass—gap AK-9
Feather On Head Lake—lake SD-7
Feather Plume Falls—falls MT-8
Feather Ridge—ridge TN-4
Feather River—stream AK-9
Feather River—stream CA-9
Feather River—stream ID-8
Feather River Experimental For—forest CA-9
Feather River Fish Hatchery—other CA-9
Feather River Homesite—locale CA-9
**Feather River Inn**—pop pl CA-9
Feather River Meadows—flat CA-9
**Feather River Park**—pop pl CA-9
Feather River Prep Sch—school CA-9
Feather River Rod And Gun Club—other CA-9
Feather River Sch—school CA-9
Feather Rock—other AK-9
Feather Rock—summit NM-5
Feather Run—stream IN-6
Feathersburg—locale KY-4
Feathers Chapel—church TN-4
**Feathers Chapel**—pop pl TN-4
Feathers Chapel Baptist Church TN-4
Feathers Creek—stream NY-2
Feathers Hollow—valley TN-4
Feathers Hollow—valley VA-3
Featherson Cem—cemetery TN-4
Feather Sound Square (Shop Ctr)—locale FL-3
Feathers Sch (historical)—school TN-4
Featherston—locale OK-5
Featherston, Edmonson and Clark Houses—hist pl KY-4
Featherston Cem—cemetery OK-5
Featherston Cem—cemetery TN-4
Featherston Creek—stream OK-5
**Featherstone**—pop pl VA-3
Featherstone Canyon—valley CA-9
Featherstone Chapel TN-4
Featherstone Creek—stream NC-3
Featherstone Fork—locale VA-3
Featherstone Ranch—locale CA-9
Featherstone Sch—school VA-3
**Featherstone Shores**—pop pl VA-3
**Featherstone Subdivision**—pop pl UT-8
**Featherstone Terrace**—pop pl VA-3
Featherstone (Township of)—civ div MN-6
Featherstonhaugh Lake—lake NY-2
Featherville—locale ID-8
Feather Woman Falls—falls MT-8
Feather Woman Lake—lake MT-8
Feather Woman Mtn—summit MT-8
**Featherwood Village Subdivision**—pop pl UT-8
Feathery Bay—swamp SC-3
Feathery Hill—summit NM-5
Feattop AL-4
Feazel Cem—cemetery LA-4
Febbas, Mount—summit WY-8
Febco Tunnel No 1—mine NM-5
Feb Fork—stream KY-4
Febice Cave—cave AL-4
Febletown—locale NJ-2
Febley Run PA-2
**February**—pop pl TN-4
February, Bayou—gut LA-4
February Mine—mine SD-7
February Post Office (historical)—building TN-4
Febuary TN-4
Febure River IL-6
Febvre River WI-6
Fechin, Nicholai, House—hist pl NM-5
Feching—cape FM-9
**Fechtig**—pop pl SC-3
Fectley Rsvr—reservoir OR-9
Fecto Point MN-6
Fectos Point—cape MN-6
Fed KY-4
Fedamacg FM-9
Fe Damach FM-9
Fedaor FM-9
Fedar Creek—stream ID-8
**Fedco**—pop pl TN-4
Fedco Siding—locale TN-4
Fed Cove—valley (2) NC-3
Fed Cove Overlook—locale NC-3
**Feddisburg**—pop pl AL-4
Fedeor FM-9
Federal IN-6
Federal NV-8
Federal—locale KY-4
Federal—locale OH-6
Federal—locale WY-8
**Federal**—pop pl AK-9
**Federal**—pop pl IL-6
**Federal**—pop pl MS-4
**Federal**—pop pl (2) MO-7
**Federal**—pop pl OR-9
**Federal**—pop pl PA-2
**Federal**—pop pl WV-2
Federal—post sta CA-9
Federal—post sta CT-1
Federal—post sta MA-1
Federal—post sta MI-6
Federal—post sta SC-3
Federal—uninc pl (2) CA-9
Federal—uninc pl DE-2
Federal—uninc pl GA-3
Federal—uninc pl NY-2
Federal—uninc pl SC-3
Federal—uninc pl WA-9
Federal—uninc pl WV-2
**Federal Annex**—pop pl GA-3
Federal Aviation Administration Bldg—building DC-2
Federal Aviation Administration Communication Center—other CA-9
Federal Aviation Administration Records Center—hist pl WV-2
Federal Aviation Agency HQ—building GU-9
Federal Barn—hist pl PA-2
Federal Bldg—building UT-8
Federal Bldg—hist pl AK-9
Federal Bldg—hist pl LA-4
Federal Bldg—hist pl (3) MI-6
Federal Bldg—hist pl MO-7
Federal Bldg—hist pl (2) NM-5
Federal Bldg—hist pl NY-2
Federal Bldg—hist pl (2) NC-3
Federal Bldg—hist pl OH-6
Federal Bldg—hist pl RI-1
Federal Bldg—hist pl WI-6
Federal Bldg and Courthouse—hist pl GA-3
Federal Bldg and Courthouse—hist pl NC-3
Federal Bldg and Post Office—hist pl NY-2
Federal Bldg and U.S. Courthouse—hist pl AL-4
Federal Bldg and U.S. Courthouse—hist pl GA-3
Federal Bldg and U.S. Courthouse—hist pl SD-7
Federal Bogs—swamp MA-1
Federal Building—uninc pl (2) CA-9
Federal Building—uninc pl NC-3
Federal Building, U.S. Courthouse, Downtown Postal Station—hist pl FL-3
Federal Building-Courthouse—hist pl KY-4
Federal Building-U.S. Courthouse—hist pl AK-9
Federal Building-US Post Office—hist pl KS-7
Federal Bureau of Investigation Bldg DC-2
Federal Butte—summit ID-8
Federal Center—building MI-6
Federal Center—hist pl MI-6
Federal Center SW Metro Station—locale DC-2
Federal Corner—locale NH-1
Federal Corners—locale NY-2
Federal Correctional Institution—other MI-6
Federal Correctional Institution—other TX-5
Federal Correctional Institution (Oxford)—other WI-6
Federal Courthouse—building MA-1
Federal Courthouse and Post Office—hist pl (2) MN-6
Federal Creek OH-6
Federal Creek—stream (2) OH-6
**Federal Dam**—pop pl MN-6
Federal Fibre Mills Bldg—hist pl LA-4
Federal Flat Cem—cemetery NY-2
Federal Fortifications Along Bear Creek—hist pl MS-4
Federal Furnace Pond MA-1
Federal Gulch—valley ID-8
Federal Gulch Campground—locale ID-8
Federal Hall Natl Memorial—hist pl NY-2
Federal Hall Natl Memorial—park NY-2
Federal Harbor—bay ME-1
**Federal Heights**—pop pl CO-8
**Federal-Heights Subdivision**—pop pl UT-8
Federal Hill IN-6
Federal Hill RI-1
Federal Hill—hist pl (2) VA-3
**Federal Hill**—pop pl IN-6
**Federal Hill**—pop pl MD-2
Federal Hill—summit CT-1
Federal Hill—summit MD-2
Federal Hill—summit (2) MA-1
Federal Hill—summit NH-1
Federal Hill—summit NJ-2
Federal Hill—summit (2) NY-2
Federal Hill Cem—cemetery FL-3
Federal Hill Cem—cemetery NY-2
Federal Hill Hist Dist—hist pl CT-1
Federal Hill Hist Dist—hist pl MD-2
Federal Hill Hist Dist—hist pl VA-3
Federal Hill Park—park MD-2
Federal Hill Sch—school NY-2
Federal (historical)—locale KS-7
Federal House—hist pl KY-4
Federal House on Hickman Creek—hist pl KY-4
**Federal Junction**—pop pl WV-2
Federal Lake—reservoir TX-5
Federal Land Office—hist pl OH-6
Federal Law Enforcement Training Center—school GA-3
Federal Mall—locale FL-3
Federal Mine—mine AZ-5
Federal Mine—uninc pl WV-2
Federal Office Bldg—hist pl NY-2
Federal Office Bldg—hist pl TN-4
Federal Office Bldg—hist pl WA-9
Federal Penitentiary Farm—locale MO-7
Federal Plaza—locale MA-1
Federal Point—cape FL-3
Federal Point—cape NC-3
**Federal Point**—pop pl FL-3
Federal Point Cem—cemetery NC-3
Federal Point (Township of)—fmr MCD NC-3
Federal Pond—reservoir MA-1
Federal Pond Dam—dam MA-1
Federal Post Office—hist pl CA-9
Federal Prison Camp—other AZ-5
Federal Quarry—mine CO-8
Federal Realty Bldg—hist pl CA-9
Federal Reformatory For Women—building WV-2
Federal Reservation (CCD)—cens area WA-9
Federal Reserve MO-7
Federal Reserve (2) OH-6
Federal Reserve—uninc pl GA-3
Federal Reserve—uninc pl NY-2
Federal Reserve—uninc pl (2) PA-2
Federal Reserve—uninc pl TN-4
Federal Reserve—uninc pl VA-3
Federal Reserve Bank Airp—airport PA-2
Federal Reserve Bank Bldg—hist pl AR-4
Federal Reserve Bank of Atlanta—hist pl TN-4
Federal Reserve Bank Of Cleveland—hist pl OH-6
Federal Reserve Bank of New York—hist pl NY-2
Federal Reserve Bank of Richmond, Baltimore Branch—hist pl MD-2
Federal Reserve Bank of San Francisco—hist pl CA-9
Federal Reserve Board Bldg—building DC-2
Federal Ridge—ridge WV-2
Federal Row—hist pl PA-2
Federal Rsvr—reservoir CO-8
Federal Run PA-2
Federal Run—stream PA-2
Federal S—locale MA-1
Federalsburg—locale DE-2
**Federalsburg**—pop pl MD-2
Federal Sch—hist pl PA-2
Federal Sch—school MI-6
Federal Siege Trench—hist pl MS-4
Federal Spring—spring OR-9
Federal Spring Branch—stream MD-2
Federal Spring Recreation Center—park MD-2
Federal Springs—spring NJ-2
Federal Square—park MA-1
Federal Square—uninc pl PA-2
Federal Station MI-6
Federal Station—post sta GA-3
Federal Street District—hist pl MA-1
Federal Street Hist Dist—hist pl ME-1
Federal Street Sch—hist pl PA-2
Federal Street Sch—school MA-1
Federal Terrace—uninc pl CA-9
Federal Terrace Sch—school CA-9
Federalton—hist pl OH-6
Federal Trade Commission—building DC-2
Federal Trade Commission Bldg—building DC-2
Federal Triangle Metro Station—locale DC-2
Federal Valley Ch—church OH-6
Federal Warehouse—building DC-2
**Federal Way**—pop pl WA-9
Federal Well—well MT-8
Federal Works Agency Bldg DC-2
Federated Ch—church ME-1
Federated Ch—church MA-1
Federated Sportsmans Field—park CA-9
Federation Forest State Park—park WA-9
Federation of Womens Clubs State For—forest MA-1
Federer Draw—valley WY-8
Federick Cem—cemetery AL-4
**Federman**—pop pl MI-6
Federman Valley—valley WI-6
Federson Hollow—valley TN-4
Federwitz Branch—stream SC-3
Fed Fork—stream TN-4
Fed Gap—gap NC-3
Fedge, Lake—lake ND-7
**Fedhaven**—pop pl FL-3
Fed Hollow—valley VA-3
Fedibchig—bar FM-9
Fedja Lake MN-6
Fedje Lake—lake MN-6
Fedji Lake MN-6
Fedoor FM-9
Fed'or FM-9
Fedor—locale TX-5
**Fedora**—pop pl SD-7
Fedora Cem—cemetery SD-7
Fedora (historical)—locale AL-4
Fedora (historical)—locale MS-4
Fedora Methodist Ch (historical)—church MS-4
Fedora Point—cape MA-1
Fedora Post Office (historical)—building TN-4
Fedor Ch—church TX-5
Feds Branch—stream NC-3
Feds Camp Branch—stream VA-3
**Fedscreek**—pop pl KY-4
Feds Creek—stream (2) KY-4
Feds Creek—stream NC-3
Fedscreek (CCD)—cens area KY-4
Feds Hollow—valley KY-4
Feds Mtn—summit NC-3
Fee—locale MT-8
Fee, John Gregg, House—hist pl KY-4
Feeback Draw—valley MT-8
Fee Cem—cemetery KY-4
Fee Cem—cemetery OH-6
Fee Cem—cemetery VA-3
Fee Chapel Cem—cemetery IA-7
Feed Box Spring—spring AZ-5
Feed Canal—canal (2) OR-9
Feeder Basin—basin IL-6
Feeder Canal VA-3
Feeder Canal—canal ID-8
Feeder Canal—canal OH-6
Feeder Creek—stream MT-8
Feederdam Bridge—bridge IN-6
Feeder Ditch—canal VA-3
Feeder Ditch No 2—canal WY-8
Feeder Drain Number Five—canal AZ-5
Feeder Drain Number Four—canal AZ-5
Feeder Lake—lake (2) MI-6
Feeder Mtn—summit MT-8
Feeder Mtn—summit NY-2
Feeder Pond—lake NY-2
Feeder Race River—stream OH-6
Feeder Wash UT-8
Feeding Ground Creek—stream MI-6
Feeding Ground Lake MI-6
Feeding Ground Lake—lake MI-6
Feeding Hill MA-1
**Feeding Hills**—pop pl MA-1
Feeding Ridge—ridge NC-3
Feedings Hills MA-1
Feedline Canal—canal CO-8
Feedlot Windmill—locale TX-5
Feed Pasture Tank—reservoir NM-5
Feed Spring OH-6
Feed Springs—locale OH-6
Feedstone Mtn—summit VA-3
Feed Trough AZ-5
Feedtrough Run—stream WV-2
Feed Trough Tank—reservoir AZ-5
**Feeduqor**—pop pl FM-9
Feefan FM-9
Fee Fee Cem—cemetery MO-7
Fee Fee Creek—stream MO-7
Fee Fee Point—cape VT-1
Feehan, John C., House—hist pl ID-8
Feehanville IL-6
Feehanville Ditch—canal IL-6
Feehanville Sch—school IL-6
Fee Hollow—valley AR-4
**Fee (Insull)**—pop pl KY-4
Fee Lake—lake IN-6
Fee Lake—lake MN-6
Feeler Cem—cemetery MO-7
Feeler Sch (abandoned)—school MO-7
Feeley Cem—cemetery MN-6
Feeley Ditch—canal MT-8
Feeley Hill—summit MT-8
Feeley Lake WI-6
Feeley Lake—lake CA-9
**Feeley (Township of)**—pop pl MN-6
Feely—locale MT-8
Feelyater School (abandoned)—locale WI-6
Feely Lake WI-6
Feely Lake—lake WI-6
Feely Sch—school MT-8
**Feely Spur**—pop pl ID-8
Feeman Dry Camp—locale OR-9
Feemster Cave—cave AL-4
Feemster Gap—gap AL-4
Feeney Ditch—canal IN-6
Feeney Draw—valley SD-7
Feeny Creek CA-9
Feeny Gulch—valley CA-9
Feeny Park—park NY-2
Feeny Ridge—ridge CA-9
Feeny Run—stream WV-2
Feenyville—locale AR-4
Feeny Wells—well ID-8
Feereel—summit FM-9
Fee Rsvr—reservoir CA-9
Fee Run—stream PA-2
Fees Branch—stream NC-3
Fees Branch—stream VA-3
Fees Branch—stream WV-2
**Feesburg**—pop pl OH-6
Fees Cem—cemetery MO-7
Feese Creek—stream CA-9
**Feesersburg**—pop pl MD-2
Fees JHS—school AZ-5
Fees Ridge—ridge VA-3
Fees Ridge Cem—cemetery VA-3
Feesterman Valley—basin NE-7
Fee Windmill—locale CO-8
Feeyoer—bay FM-9
Feezell Barn—hist pl TN-4
Feezell Branch—stream TN-4
**Feezor**—pop pl NC-3
Feezor Cem—cemetery KY-4
Fefan—island FM-9
Fefan (Municipality)—civ div FM-9
Fefen FM-9
Fegley—locale MO-7
Fegley Cem—cemetery IN-6
Fegley Hollow—valley PA-2
Fegua Cem—cemetery TX-5
Fehd Ditch—canal IN-6
F E Henderson—locale NM-5
Fehl Cem—cemetery OH-6
Fehley Gulch—valley OR-9
Fehley Run—stream PA-2
Fehling Ranch—locale CO-8
Fehlings Cow Camp—locale CO-8
Fehlings REservoir CO-8
Fehl Sch—school TX-5
Fehr, Charles, Round Barn—hist pl IL-6
Fehrenbacher Dam—dam OR-9
Fehrenbacker Rsvr—reservoir OR-9
Fehrer Lake—lake IL-6
Fehringer Bar—bar TN-4
Fehringer No 1 Ditch—canal CO-8
Fehringer No 2 Ditch—canal CO-8
Fehr Lake—lake UT-8
Fehr Sch—school TN-4
Feia Point—cape AS-9
Feiblecorn Drain—stream MI-6
Feibus San Papa Point MH-9
Feicht Sch—school NE-7
Feifarek Sch—school WI-6
Feigel Hill—summit VT-1
Feigel Point—summit OK-5

Feigenspan Mansion—hist pl NJ-2
Feigh Mine—mine MN-6
Feighner Cem—cemetery IN-6
Feightner Cem—cemetery PA-2
**Feigler Ferry**—pop pl MO-7
Feigles Pond—reservoir SC-3
Feiker Sch—school MA-1
Feik Hill WV-2
Feik Rsvrs—reservoir OR-9
Feik Run PA-2
Feilbach Sch—school OH-6
Feilif FM-9
Feimster House—hist pl NC-3
Fein FM-9
Fein, Mochun—channel FM-9
Fein, Oror En—locale FM-9
Feinberg Sch—school FL-3
Feinburg Park—park NY-2
Fein Durchfahrt FM-9
**Feini**—pop pl FM-9
Feinif FM-9
Feinif—swamp FM-9
Feinif—well FM-9
Feinit—island FM-9
Fein Pass FM-9
Feinsinger Lake—lake FL-3
Feinstein Lake—lake SD-7
Feiro—bar FM-9
Feist Branch—stream TN-4
Feist Creek—stream ID-8
Feisterville PA-2
Feistner Cem—cemetery SD-7
Feitabul—island FM-9
Feitshams Ditch—canal OH-6
Feitshans Sch—school IL-6
Fejervary Home—locale IA-7
Fejervary Park—park IA-7
Fejt Ranch—locale NE-7
Felammie Creek MS-4
Felan Gulch—valley MT-8
Felat FM-9
Felber Park—park NE-7
Felbert Creek—stream LA-4
**Felce**—pop pl AR-4
**Felch**—pop pl MI-6
Felchak Branch—stream TX-5
**Felch Corner**—pop pl ME-1
Felch Creek—stream CO-8
**Felch Mountain**—pop pl MI-6
Felchner Brook—stream VT-1
**Felch (Township of)**—pop pl MI-6
**Felchville**—pop pl VT-1
**Felchville (subdivision)**—pop pl MA-1
**Feld**—pop pl TX-5
Felda—locale FL-3
Felda Ch—church FL-3
Felda (Station)—locale FL-3
Feldcher Creek—stream WI-6
**Felder**—pop pl KY-4
**Felder**—pop pl SC-3
Felder, E. King, House—hist pl TX-5
Felder Bayou—stream LA-4
Felder Branch—stream SC-3
Felder Cem—cemetery LA-4
Felder Cem—cemetery (3) MS-4
Felder Chapel—church SC-3
Felder Creek—stream CA-9
Felder Creek—stream ID-8
Felder Creek—stream MS-4
Felder (historical)—locale MS-4
Felder Lake Dam—dam MS-4
Felder-Richmond House—hist pl MS-4
Felders Campground—locale MS-4
Felder School ( Abandoned)—locale MO-7
Felders Mill (historical)—locale MS-4
**Felderville**—pop pl SC-3
Felderville Sch—school SC-3
Felder-Williams Cem—cemetery MS-4
Feldges Lake—lake MN-6
Feldhauser Sch—school MI-6
Feldheimer Ferry (site)—locale OR-9
Feld House—hist pl MS-4
Feldhut Cem—cemetery KS-7
Feldman Oil and Gas Field—oilfield TX-5
Feldman Rsvr—reservoir OR-9
Feldner Coulee ND-7
Feldners Creek—stream WI-6
Feldspar Brook—stream NY-2
Feldtman Lake MI-6
Feldtmann Lake—lake MI-6
Feldtmann Ridge—ridge MI-6
Feldtmann Ridge Trail—trail MI-6
Feldy Mtn—summit VA-3
Felesit FM-9
F-Eleven Tailings Pond—reservoir TN-4
F-Eleven Tailings Pond Dam—dam TN-4
Felgag FM-9
Felgates Creek—stream VA-3
Felgates Crossing—locale VA-3
Felger Ditch—canal IN-6
Felica FL-3
**Felica**—pop pl FL-3
Felice Bayou—channel LA-4
Felice Bayou—gut LA-4
Felice Strait—channel AK-9
Felicia—locale FL-3
Felicia—locale TX-5
**Felicia**—pop pl PR-3
Felicia Creek—stream TX-5
Feliciana—locale KY-4
Feliciana Creek—stream CA-9
Feliciana Mine—mine CA-9
Feliciana Mtn—summit CA-9
Feliciana Plantation—locale LA-4
**Feliciano**—pop pl PR-3
Felician Sisters Acad—school PA-2
Felician Sisters Cem—cemetery PA-2
Felicia Sch—school SD-7
Felicia 1 (Barrio)—fmr MCD PR-3
Felicia 2 (Barrio)—fmr MCD PR-3
**Felicita**—pop pl PR-3
Felicita Sch—school CA-9
**Felicity**—pop pl OH-6
Felicity Bay—lake LA-4
Felicity Bayou—gut LA-4
**Felicity Cove**—pop pl MD-2
Felicity Cove Marsh—swamp MD-2
Felicity Island—swamp LA-4
**Felida**—pop pl WA-9
Felida Sch—school WA-9
Feline Creek—stream MT-8
Felins Branch—stream KY-4
Felip FM-9
Felipe Chavez Canyon—valley NM-5
Felipe Gutierres or Bernalillo Grant—civil NM-5
Felipe Pass—gap AZ-5
Felipe Tafoya—civil NM-5
Felipito Canyon—valley NM-5
Felix AL-4
Felix TN-4
Felix—locale CA-9
**Felix**—pop pl WY-8
Felix, Bayou—stream LA-4
Felix, N. J., House—hist pl NY-2
Felix Allen Cemetery MS-4
Felix Basin—basin MT-8
Felix Basin Trail—trail MT-8
Felix-Block Bldg—hist pl LA-4
Felix Canyon—valley MT-8
Felix Canyon—valley NV-8
Felix Canyon—valley NM-5
Felix Cem—cemetery OK-5
Felix Creek—stream ID-8
Felix Creek—stream (2) MT-8
Felix Creek—stream NE-7
Felix Creek—stream SD-7
Felix Creek—stream WA-9
Felix Creek—stream WY-8
Felix Dam—reservoir PA-2
Felix Dee Tank—reservoir NM-5
Felix Draw—valley WY-8
Felix Edwards Cem—cemetery AL-4
Felix Gulch—valley OR-9
Felix Hollow—valley GA-3
Felix Ladner Cem—cemetery MS-4
Felix Lake—lake LA-4
Felix Lake—lake MN-6
Felix Ledge—bar MA-1
Felix Mine—mine MT-8
Felix Neck—cape MA-1
Felix Pass—gap UT-8
Felix Peak—summit MT-8
Felix Pond—lake AR-4
Felix Post Office AL-4
Felix Post Office TN-4
Felix Post Office (historical)—building PA-2
Felix Run—stream PA-2
Felix School AL-4
Felix Spring—spring NM-5
Felix Township—fmr MCD IA-7
**Felix (Township of)**—pop pl IL-6
**Felixville**—pop pl LA-4
Felixville (Post Office)—locale LA-4
Felix Well—locale NM-5
Felix Windmill—locale NM-5
Feliz—civil CA-9
Feliz Canyon—valley CA-9
Feliz Creek—stream CA-9
Feliz Ranch—locale NM-5
Felkel—locale FL-3
Felkel Sch—school IL-6
Felker IL-6
Felker—locale OK-5
Felker—locale TN-4
Felker Cem—cemetery KY-4
Felker Field—park MI-6
Felker Hill—summit KY-4
Felker Lake—lake MN-6
Felker Pond—lake ME-1
Felker Post Office (historical)—building TN-4
Felkers Island—island GA-3
Felker Town AR-4
Felker (Township of)—fmr MCD AR-4
Felkins Creek—stream AR-4
Felkins Post Office (historical)—building AL-4
Felk Lateral—canal NM-5
Felkner-Anderson House—hist pl OH-6
Felkner Cem—cemetery IA-7
Felkner Hill—summit CA-9
Felkner Ridge—ridge CA-9
Felknor Hollow—valley IN-6
Felky Slough—stream IL-6
Fell, D. Newlin, Sch—hist pl PA-2
Fell Arm—canal IN-6
Fell Branch—stream SC-3
Fell Cem—cemetery AL-4
Fell Cem—cemetery IA-7
Fell Cem—cemetery PA-2
Fell Creek—stream ID-8
Fell Cut—gut LA-4
Fell Ditch IN-6
Fell Ditch—canal IN-6
Felldown Hollow—valley TN-4
Feller Cem—cemetery OH-6
**Feller Drive Subdivision**—pop pl UT-8
Feller Pond—lake OR-9
Feller Reservoir CO-8
Feller Rsvr—reservoir IN-6
Fellers—locale OR-9
Fellews Drain—canal MI-6
Fellger Playlot—park IL-6
Fellhauer Ranch—locale WY-8
Fell Hill—summit WA-9
Fell Hist Dist—hist pl DE-2
Fell Lake—lake OH-6
Fellowbed Branch—stream VA-3
Fellow Brook—stream IN-6
Fellow Creek UT-8
Fellow Flat Sch (historical)—school AL-4
Fellow Island ME-1
**Fellows**—pop pl CA-9
**Fellows**—pop pl WI-6
Fellows, James C., House—hist pl IA-7
Fellows, Mount—summit AK-9
Fellows Branch—stream GA-3
Fellows Branch—stream NC-3
Fellows Cem—cemetery IL-6
Fellows Cem—cemetery IA-7
Fellows Cem—cemetery (2) NY-2
Fellows Cem—cemetery OR-9
Fellows Cem—cemetery VT-1
Fellows Creek—stream MI-6
Fellows Creek—stream PA-2
Fellows Creek Golf Course—other MI-6
Fellows Falls—falls NY-2
Fellows Hill—summit NH-1
Fellows Hill—summit NY-2
Fellowship—locale FL-3
Fellowship—locale (2) TX-5
**Fellowship**—pop pl LA-4
**Fellowship**—pop pl MS-4
**Fellowship**—pop pl NJ-2
Fellowship And Union Cemeteries—cemetery PA-2
Fellowship Baptist Ch AL-4
Fellowship Baptist Ch MS-4
Fellowship Baptist Ch TN-4
Fellowship Baptist Ch—church AL-4
Fellowship Baptist Ch—church (6) FL-3
Fellowship Baptist Ch—church IN-6
Fellowship Baptist Ch—church MS-4
Fellowship Baptist Ch—church (3) TN-4
Fellowship Baptist Ch (historical)—church TN-4
Fellowship Baptist Sch—school FL-3
Fellowship Bible Ch—church FL-3
Fellowship Branch—stream SC-3
Fellowship Camp Grove—locale PA-2
Fellowship (CCD)—cens area FL-3
Fellowship Cem—cemetery (5) AL-4
Fellowship Cem—cemetery (2) GA-3
Fellowship Cem—cemetery (2) LA-4
Fellowship Cem—cemetery MD-2
Fellowship Cem—cemetery (8) MS-4
Fellowship Cem—cemetery SC-3
Fellowship Cem—cemetery (3) TN-4
Fellowship Cem—cemetery TX-5
Fellowship Ch AL-4
Fellowship Ch MS-4
Fellowship Ch—church (15) AL-4
Fellowship Ch—church (2) AR-4
Fellowship Ch—church (4) FL-3
Fellowship Ch—church (13) GA-3
Fellowship Ch—church IL-6
Fellowship Ch—church (2) IN-6
Fellowship Ch—church IA-7
Fellowship Ch—church KY-4
Fellowship Ch—church (9) LA-4
Fellowship Ch—church MD-2
Fellowship Ch—church (4) MI-6
Fellowship Ch—church MN-6
Fellowship Ch—church (14) MS-4
Fellowship Ch—church (5) MO-7
Fellowship Ch—church (2) NY-2
Fellowship Ch—church (18) NC-3
Fellowship Ch—church (2) OH-6
Fellowship Ch—church (2) SC-3
Fellowship Ch—church (7) TN-4
Fellowship Ch—church (3) TX-5
Fellowship Ch—church (8) VA-3
Fellowship Chapel—church KY-4
Fellowship Ch (historical)—church AL-4
Fellowship Creek—stream LA-4
Fellowship Deaconry—church NJ-2
**Fellowship Forest**—pop pl MD-2
Fellowship Free Church ND-7
Fellowship Freewill Baptist Ch—church MS-4
Fellowship Holiness Ch—church VA-3
Fellowship Knob—summit KY-4
Fellowship Lake—lake GA-3
Fellowship Lake—reservoir NC-3
Fellowship Lake Dam—dam NC-3
Fellowship Lutheran Ch—church FL-3
Fellowship Meeting House TN-4
Fellowship Missionary Baptist Ch MS-4
Fellowship Missionary Baptist Ch—church KS-7
Fellowship Missionary Baptist Ch—church TN-4
Fellowship of Southern Churchmen Camp—locale NC-3
**Fellowship Park**—pop pl FL-3
Fellowship Presbyterian Ch AL-4
Fellowship Presbyterian Ch—church FL-3
Fellowship Sanatorium—hospital NC-3
Fellowship Sch—school (4) LA-4
Fellowship Tabernacle—church AL-4
Fellowship Tabernacle—church GA-3
Fellowship Tabernacle—church VA-3
Fellowship Temple—church AL-4
Fellowship United Baptist Ch TN-4
Fellowship with Christ—church FL-3
Fellows Island—island ME-1
Fellows Lake—reservoir MO-7
Fellows Pond—lake ME-1
Fellows Sch—school IA-7
Fellows Spring—spring CA-9
**Fellowsville**—pop pl WV-2
Fellowview Cem—cemetery TX-5
Fell Park—park MI-6
Fellrath JHS—school MI-6
**Fells**—pop pl MA-1
**Fellsburg**—pop pl KS-7
**Fellsburg**—pop pl PA-2
Fellsburg Cem—cemetery KS-7
Fells Ch—church PA-2
Fell Sch—school MD-2
Fell Sch—school PA-2
**Fells Corners**—pop pl PA-2
Fells Cove—bay FL-3
Fells Creek—stream CA-9
Fells Creek—stream PA-2
Fells Flat—flat CA-9
Fells Lake—lake AL-4
**Fellsmere**—pop pl FL-3
Fellsmere (CCD)—cens area FL-3
Fellsmere Elem Sch—school FL-3
Fellsmere Park—park MA-1
Fellsmere Pond—lake MA-1
Fells Point—cape MD-2
Fells Point Hist Dist—hist pl MD-2
Fells Point Hist Dist (Boundary Increase)—hist pl MD-2
Fells Reservoir Middle Dike—dam MA-1
Fells Res North Dike—dam MA-1
Fells Rsvr—reservoir MA-1
Fells Sch (abandoned)—school PA-2
Fells Spring—spring OR-9
Fellsway—uninc pl MA-1
Fellsway Fashion Center (Shop Ctr)—locale MA-1
Fellsway Plaza (Shop Ctr)—locale MA-1
**Fell (Township of)**—pop pl PA-2
Fellure Cem—cemetery OH-6
**Fellwick (Camp Hill)**—pop pl PA-2
Fellwick Station—locale PA-2
Fellwock Garage—hist pl IN-6
Felly Tree Acres—locale PA-2
Felmont Oil Company Dam—dam IN-6
Felmont Oil Company Rsvr—reservoir IN-6
Felps—locale LA-4
Felps Cem—cemetery TX-5
Felps Chapel—church MO-7
Fels Cem—cemetery OH-6
Felsengarten—hist pl NH-1
**Felsenthal**—pop pl AR-4
Felson Town Hall—building ND-7
**Felson Township**—pop pl ND-7
Fels Planetarium—building PA-2
Fels Sch—school PA-2
Felstein Lake Dam—dam IN-6
**Felt**—pop pl ID-8
**Felt**—pop pl OK-5
Felt, Cyrus, House—hist pl IL-6
Felta Creek—stream CA-9
Felta Sch—school CA-9
Felt Canyon—valley NV-8
Felt Cem—cemetery ID-8
Felt Cem—cemetery MI-6
Felt Cem—cemetery TN-4
Felt Dam—dam ID-8
Felt Electric—hist pl UT-8
Feltenberger Airp—airport PA-2
Felten MS—school KS-7
Felter, Lake—lake FL-3
Felter Branch—stream OK-5
Felter Creek—stream WY-8
Felter Gulch—valley CA-9
Felter Park—park OH-6
**Felters Corners**—pop pl NY-2
Feltham—locale ID-8
Feltham Creek—stream ID-8
Feltham Creek Point—cliff ID-8
Felt Hill—summit NH-1
Felthouse Ranch—locale TX-5
Felt Knob—summit VA-3
Felt Lake—reservoir CA-9
Feltman Dam SD-7
Feltman Dam—dam SD-7
Feltman Dam 1—dam SD-7
Feltner Ch—church AR-4
Feltner Creek WY-8
Felton PA-2
Felton SD-7
Felton—locale GA-3
**Felton**—pop pl AR-4
**Felton**—pop pl CA-9
**Felton**—pop pl DE-2
**Felton**—pop pl MN-6
**Felton**—pop pl PA-2
Felton, Nathaniel, Houses—hist pl MA-1
Felton, Rebecca Latimer, House—hist pl GA-3
Felton, William Hamilton, House—hist pl GA-3
Felton Ave Sch—school CA-9
Felton Borough—civil PA-2
Felton Bridge—bridge NY-2
Felton Brook—stream NY-2
Felton Camp—locale NH-1
Felton Cave—cave TX-5
Felton (CCD)—cens area DE-2
Felton Cem—cemetery GA-3
Felton Cem—cemetery IN-6
Felton Cem—cemetery MN-6
Felton Cem—cemetery MS-4
Felton Cem—cemetery TX-5
Felton Cem—cemetery WI-6
Felton Chapel—church GA-3
Felton Covered Bridge—hist pl CA-9
Felton Creek—stream AK-9
Felton Creek—stream ID-8
Felton Creek—stream IN-6
Felton Creek—stream MN-6
Felton Creek—stream OR-9
Felton Field—locale MA-1
**Felton Grove**—pop pl CA-9
Felton Grove—woods CA-9
Felton Grove Ch—church NC-3
Felton Guard State—locale CA-9
**Felton Heights**—pop pl DE-2
Felton Hill—summit VT-1
Felton Hist Dist—hist pl DE-2
Felton HS—school NY-2
Felton Lake—lake FL-3
Felton Lake—reservoir MA-1
Felton Lake Brook—stream MA-1
**Felton Manor**—pop pl DE-2
Felton Mills—locale PA-2
Felton Mtn—summit AZ-5
Felton Park Road Plaza (Shop Ctr)—locale FL-3
Felton Presbyterian Church—hist pl CA-9
Felton RR Station—hist pl DE-2
Felton Sch—hist pl OH-6
Felton Sch—school MA-1
Felton Sch—school OH-6
Felton Sch—school SC-3
Felton Sch—school VT-1
Feltons Creek—stream NC-3
Feltons Mill Covered Bridge—hist pl PA-2
Felton Spring—spring (2) AZ-5
Felton State Wildlife Mngmt Area—park MN-6
**Felton Station**—pop pl DE-2
Felton Street Sch—hist pl MA-1
Felton Street Sch—school MA-1
Felton Tank—reservoir AZ-5
**Felton (Township of)**—pop pl MN-6
Felton United Methodist Ch—church DE-2
Feltonville MA-1
**Feltonville**—pop pl NC-3
**Feltonville**—pop pl (2) PA-2
Feltonville Sch—school PA-2
Feltonville Sch No. 2—hist pl PA-2
Felt Plains Cem—cemetery MI-6
Felt Plains Ch—church MI-6
Felt Ranch—locale CA-9
Felt Robison Canyon—valley NV-8
Felt Robison Mine—mine NV-8
Felts Branch—stream VA-3
Felts Brook—stream ME-1
Felts Cem—cemetery IL-6
Felts Cem—cemetery KY-4
Felts Cem—cemetery TN-4
Felts Ch—church KY-4
Felt's Farm—hist pl IN-6
Felts Field Airp—airport WA-9
Felts JHS—school VA-3
Felts Lake—lake AK-9
Felts Memorial Cem—cemetery VA-3
**Felts Mills**—pop pl NY-2
Felts Mills Creek—stream NY-2
Felt Spring—spring NV-8
Felt Springs—spring CA-9
Felts Sch—school KY-4
Feltsvillle—locale PA-2
Feltville Hist Dist—hist pl NJ-2
Felt Wash—stream NV-8
Felty—locale KY-4
Felty, Nando, Saloon—hist pl KY-4
Felty Cem—cemetery IL-6
Felty Cem—cemetery KY-4
Felty Gap—gap KY-4
Felty Sch—school PA-2
Felty Stewart Run—stream PA-2
Feltz Ridge—ridge VA-3
Female Acad at Decatur (historical)—school AL-4
Female Canyon—valley AZ-5
Female Mtn—summit ME-1
Female Point—ridge AZ-5
Female Pond—lake ME-1
Female Rock—pillar AZ-5
Femco Farm No. 2—hist pl MN-6
Femling Lake—lake MN-6
**Femme Osage**—pop pl MO-7
Femme Osage Creek—stream MO-7
Femmons—locale CA-9
Fems Park—park NJ-2
Fena—area GU-9
Fena—spring FM-9
Fenacha Creek AL-4
Fenache Creek—stream AL-4
Fenaik FM-9
Fenanche Creek AL-4
Fenat FM-9
Fena Valley Rsvr—reservoir GU-9
Fena Water Treatment Plant—other GU-9
Fenawaw FM-9
Fenby—locale MD-2
**Fence**—pop pl GA-3
**Fence**—pop pl WI-6
Fence Camp Flat—flat CA-9
Fence Camp Spring—spring CA-9
Fence Canyon UT-8
Fence Canyon—valley (2) AZ-5
Fence Canyon—valley CO-8
Fence Canyon—valley (4) NM-5
Fence Canyon—valley UT-8
Fence Canyon Gas Field—oilfield UT-8
Fence Canyon Well—well NM-5
Fence Corner Spring—spring MT-8
Fence Creek WA-9
Fence Creek—stream CA-9
Fence Creek—stream CO-8
Fence Creek—stream CT-1
Fence Creek—stream ID-8
Fence Creek—stream NJ-2
Fence Creek—stream OR-9
Fence Creek—stream WA-9
Fence Creek—stream (2) WY-8
Fence Creek Oil Field—oilfield WY-8
Fenced Tank—reservoir TX-5
Fenced-Up Horse Valley—valley NM-5
Fence Forest Creek—stream OR-9
Fence Gulch—valley (2) CO-8
Fence Gulch—valley OR-9
Fence Lake—lake (2) MI-6
Fence Lake—lake MN-6
Fence Lake—lake MS-4
Fence Lake—lake NM-5
Fence Lake—lake TX-5
Fence Lake—lake (2) WI-6
**Fence Lake**—pop pl NM-5
Fence Lake—reservoir NM-5
Fence Lake (CCD)—cens area NM-5
Fence Line Rsvr—reservoir OR-9
Fenceline Spring—spring OR-9
Fence Line Spring—spring TX-5
Fenceline Tank—reservoir AZ-5
Fence Line Tank—reservoir (2) AZ-5
Fence Line Tank—reservoir (2) NM-5
Fenceline Tank—reservoir NM-5
Fence Line Well—well TX-5
Fenceline Windmill—locale NM-5
Fence Line Windmill—locale NM-5
Fence Line Windmill—locale (3) TX-5
Fencemaker—ridge NV-8
Fencemaker Camp—locale NV-8
Fencemaker Canyon—valley NV-8
Fencemaker Pass—gap NV-8
Fence Martin Trap Windmill—locale TX-5
Fence Meadow—flat CA-9
Fence Meadow Lookout—locale CA-9
Fence Mtn—summit TX-5
Fence Point—cliff AZ-5
Fence Pond—lake AZ-5
Fencepost Draw—valley TX-5
Fence Ridge—ridge AZ-5
Fence River—stream MI-6
Fence Rsvr—reservoir UT-8
Fence Run—stream IN-6
Fence Spring—spring NV-8
Fence Spring—spring OR-9
Fence Spring—spring UT-8
Fence Tank—reservoir (6) AZ-5
Fence Tank—reservoir (4) NM-5
Fence Tank—reservoir TX-5
**Fence (Town of)**—pop pl WI-6
Fence V A B M—locale WY-8
Fence Well—well NM-5
Fence Windmill—locale TX-5
Fenchel Creek—stream IA-7
Fench Lake NV-8
Fench Wash AZ-5
**Fencroft**—pop pl KY-4
Fendall—locale SC-3
Fendall Creek—stream OR-9
Fendall Hall—building AL-4
Fendall Hall—hist pl AL-4
Fendall School (abandoned)—locale OR-9
Fender CO-8
Fender GA-3
**Fender**—pop pl AR-4
**Fender**—pop pl GA-3
Fender Brook—stream NY-2
Fender Cem—cemetery AR-4
Fender Cem—cemetery IL-6
Fender Cem—cemetery IN-6
Fender Cem—cemetery NC-3
Fender Ch—church GA-3
Fender Creek WY-8
Fender Creek—stream SC-3
Fender Creek—stream WY-8
Fender Flat—flat CA-9
Fender Flat Spring—spring CA-9
Fender J H Airp—airport MO-7
Fender Knob NC-3
Fender Knob—summit NC-3
Fender Lake—lake NE-7
Fender Mtn—summit NC-3
Fender Point—cape FL-3
**Fender (RR name Eldorado)**—pop pl GA-3
**Fenders**—pop pl CO-8
Fenders Cem—cemetery LA-4
Fenders Ch—church TN-4
Fenders Chapel TN-4
Fender School (Abandoned)—locale IL-6
Fenders Flat—flat CA-9
Fenderson Brook—stream ME-1
Fenders United MethodistChurch TN-4
Fendig—locale GA-3
Fendlason Cem—cemetery LA-4
Fendley—locale AR-4
Fendley Branch—stream GA-3
Fendley Creek IN-6
Fenealiliy FM-9
Fenecu FM-9
Feneich—bar FM-9
Feneis Drain—canal MI-6
Fenekan FM-9
Fenekkuk FM-9
Fenekorugoy FM-9
Fenelon—locale NV-8
Fenelon Place Elevator—hist pl IA-7
**Fenelton**—pop pl PA-2
Fenemwu FM-9
Feneney Gulch CA-9
Fenenga Ranch—locale SD-7
Fenenuuk FM-9
Fenepi FM-9
Feneppi—island FM-9
Fenesit FM-9
Fenessic FM-9
Fenessich FM-9
Fenew—island FM-9
Fenewech—bar FM-9
Feney Ravine—valley CA-9
Fengatau FM-9
Fenger Brook—stream CT-1
Fen Hollow—valley OH-6
**Fenholloway**—pop pl FL-3
Fenholloway River—stream FL-3
Fenholloway River Approach Light FR—locale FL-3
Fenholloway Station—building FL-3
Feniak Lake—lake AK-9
Fenimen FM-9
**Fenimore**—pop pl NY-2
Fenimore Landing DE-2
Fenimore Pass—channel AK-9
Fenimore Rock—island AK-9
Fenimore Rsvr OR-9
**Fenix**—pop pl NC-3
Fenkell MI-6
Fenkofuru, Mount—summit FM-9
Fen Lake—lake AZ-5
Fenlason Playground—park MN-6
Fenley Commercial Bldg—hist pl TX-5
Fenley Creek IN-6
Fenlon Bend—bend AZ-5
Fenlon Creek—stream MI-6
Fenlons Cem—cemetery MI-6
Fenmeias FM-9
Fenmore—locale MI-6
Fenmore—locale PA-2
Fenmore Dam—dam OR-9
**Fenn**—pop pl AR-4
**Fenn**—pop pl ID-8
Fenn, Henry, House—hist pl NJ-2
Fenn Brook—stream (2) CT-1
Fenn Cabin Spring—spring ID-8
Fenn Cem—cemetery MS-4
Fenn Coll—school OH-6
Fenn Creek—stream WY-8
Fennel Creek—stream WA-9
Fennel Island (historical)—island AL-4
Fennell Cem—cemetery AL-4
Fennell Cem—cemetery NC-3
Fennell Hill—hist pl SC-3
Fennell Hill Landing—locale SC-3
Fennell Hollow VT-1
Fennell Lake—lake IN-6
Fennell Lake—lake OR-9
Fennell Memory Garden—cemetery TX-5
Fennell Point—cape MD-2
Fennell/Robertson Genealogy Society Library—building TX-5
Fennelltown Ch—church PA-2
Fennel Memorial Ch—church AL-4
Fennel Memorial United Methodist Ch AL-4
Fennels Cove—bay NC-3
Fennel Slough—gut FL-3
Fennels Store TN-4
Fennel Store (historical)—locale TN-4
Fennels Turnout AL-4
Fennemore—locale AZ-5
Fennemore, Dr. George, House—hist pl UT-8
Fennemore, James, House—hist pl UT-8
Fennemore RR Station—building AZ-5
Fenner—locale AZ-5
Fenner—locale CA-9
Fenner—locale NY-2
**Fenner**—pop pl NY-2
Fenner Branch—stream TN-4
Fenner Canyon—valley CA-9
Fenner Cem—cemetery OH-6
Fenner Creek—stream AK-9
Fenner Creek—stream MI-6
Fenner Hill—summit RI-1
Fenner Hills—summit CA-9
Fenner Lake—lake AK-9
Fenner Lake—lake MI-6
Fenner Lake—lake WI-6
Fenner Lakes—lake NE-7
Fenner Meadow Brook—stream NY-2
Fenner Meadows—flat NY-2
Fenner Mill Run—stream PA-2
Fennern, Henry P., House—hist pl IA-7
Fenner No 1 Cem—cemetery OH-6
Fenner No 2 Cem—cemetery OH-6
Fenner No 3 Cem—cemetery OH-6
Fenner Pond—lake RI-1
Fenner RR Station—building AZ-5

Fenner Run—stream PA-2
Fenners Lake WI-6
Fenner-Snyder Mill—hist pl PA-2
Fenners Pond RI-1
Fenners Pond—reservoir NC-3
Fenners Pond Dam—dam NC-3
Fenner Spring—spring CA-9
Fennersville PA-2
**Fenner (Town of)**—pop pl NY-2
Fenner Valley—valley CA-9
**Fennerville**—pop pl MA-1
Fennessey Flat—flat TX-5
Fennessy Lake—lake MI-6
Fennewald Cem—cemetery MO-7
Fenn Gin (historical)—locale AL-4
**Fenn Haven**—pop pl IN-6
Fenn Haven Lake—reservoir IN-6
Fenn Hill—summit CT-1
Fon Nif Ngain FM 9
**Fennimore**—pop pl WI-6
Fennimore Bridge—bridge DE-2
Fennimore Community Sch—school WI-6
Fennimore Creek WI-6
Fennimore Fork—stream WI-6
Fennimore Landing—locale DE-2
Fennimore Store—hist pl DE-2
**Fennimore (Town of)**—pop pl WI-6
Fenning Cemetery TN-4
Fenn Mountain Trail—trail MT-8
Fenn Mtn—summit ID-8
Fenn Mtn—summit MT-8
Fenno, John A., House—hist pl MA-1
Fenno Creek—stream AK-9
Fennon Slough—gut MT-8
Fenno Sch (abandoned)—school PA-2
Fennos Hill—summit MA-1
Fenn Pond—lake CT-1
Fenn Ranger Station—locale ID-8
**Fenns**—pop pl IN-6
Fenn Sch—school MA-1
Fenns (historical P.O.)—locale IN-6
Fenns Peak ID-8
Fennu FM-9
**Fennville**—pop pl MI-6
Fenny Creek—stream MS-4
Fenrich Springs—spring WI-6
Fenrick Canyon—valley OR-9
Fen Ridge—ridge OH-6
Fens—locale MN-6
Fenske Lake—lake MN-6
Fenske Lake—lake WI-6
Fenske Lake Campground—locale MN-6
Fensol River—stream GU-9
Fenstad Lake MN-6
Fensted Lake MN-6
Fenster Creek—stream ID-8
Fenstermachers (historical)—locale PA-2
Fenstermaker Grave—cemetery NV-8
Fenstermaker Point—cape ID-8
Fenstermaker Ranch—locale ID-8
Fenstermaker Wash—stream NV-8
Fensterman Slough—lake SD-7
Fenster Sch—school AZ-5
Fenster School Airp—airport AZ-5
Fensterwald, Lake—reservoir TX-5
Fente Lake—lake MN-6
Fenter—locale AR-4
Fenters Ditch—canal IN-6
Fenter (Township of)—fmr MCD (2) AR-4
Fenton—locale KY-4
Fenton—locale MS-4
Fenton—locale WY-8
**Fenton**—pop pl AL-4
**Fenton**—pop pl IL-6
**Fenton**—pop pl IA-7
**Fenton**—pop pl LA-4
**Fenton**—pop pl MI-6
**Fenton**—pop pl MO-7
Fenton, Enoch Madison, House—hist pl MO-7
Fenton, Frank W., House—hist pl OR-9
Fenton, Gov. Reuben, Mansion—hist pl NY-2
Fenton, Lake—lake MI-6
Fenton, William D., House—hist pl OR-9
Fenton Ave Sch—school CA-9
Fenton Ave School—spring CA-9
Fenton Brook CT-1
Fenton Brook—stream MA-1
Fenton Canyon—valley CA-9
Fenton Cem—cemetery IL-6
Fenton Cem—cemetery IA-7
Fenton Cem—cemetery OH-6
Fenton Cem—cemetery TX-5
Fenton Creek—stream ID-8
Fenton Creek—stream MI-6
Fenton Creek—stream (2) MO-7
Fenton Creek—stream NY-2
Fenton Draw—valley NM-5
Fenton Draw—valley (2) WY-8
Fenton Flat—flat OR-9
Fenton Flat Rsvr—reservoir OR-9
Fenton (historical)—locale KS-7
Fenton HS—school IL-6
Fenton Island—island NJ-2
Fenton Knob—summit PA-2
Fenton Lake—lake (2) WI-6
Fenton Lake—reservoir NM-5
Fenton Lake—reservoir OK-5
Fenton Lateral—canal ID-8
Fenton Lawn Sch—school MI-6
Fenton Little Park—park AL-4
Fenton Mtn—summit MA-1
Fenton Park—park IL-6
Fenton Park—park NY-2
Fenton Park Mall—locale MO-7
Fenton Park Mall (Shop Ctr)—locale MO-7
Fenton Pass—gap WY-8
Fenton Plaza—locale MO-7
Fenton P.O. AL-4
Fenton Post Office (historical)—building MS-4
Fenton Ranch—locale (2) CA-9
Fenton Ranch—locale (2) NM-5
Fenton Ranch—locale ND-7
Fenton Ravine—valley CA-9
Fenton Ridge—ridge CA-9
Fenton River—stream CT-1
Fenton Road Chapel—church MI-6
Fenton RR Depot—hist pl MI-6
Fenton Rsvr—reservoir OR-9
Fenton Run—stream PA-2
Fenton School—locale WY-8
Fentons Corner PA-2
Fenton Seminary—hist pl MI-6
Fenton Spring—spring OR-9
Fenton Springs Branch—stream TX-5
**Fenton (Town of)**—pop pl NY-2
Fenton Township—fmr MCD IA-7
Fenton Township Cem—cemetery IA-7
**Fenton (Township of)**—pop pl IL-6
**Fenton (Township of)**—pop pl MI-6
**Fenton (Township of)**—pop pl MN-6
**Fentonville**—pop pl MA-1
**Fentonville**—pop pl NY-2
Fentrees Lookout—locale KY-4
Fentrees McMahan—locale KY-4
**Fentress**—pop pl MS-4
**Fentress**—pop pl SC-3
**Fentress**—pop pl TX-5
**Fentress**—pop pl (2) VA-3
Fontross Com comotory MS 4
**Fentress County**—pop pl TN-4
Fentress County Courthouse—building TN-4
Fentress County General Hosp—hospital TN-4
**Fentress McMahon**—pop pl KY-4
Fentress (Township of)—fmr MCD NC-3
Fent Wiley Hollow—valley VA-3
Fenuoruw FM-9
Fenuwamwu FM-9
Fenuwepwin FM-9
Fenuwomwoc FM-9
**Fenway**—pop pl MO-7
Fenway-Boylston Street District—hist pl MA-1
Fenway Golf Club—other NY-2
Fenway Studios Bldg—hist pl MA-1
Fenwick—locale KY-4
Fenwick—locale MO-7
Fenwick—locale SC-3
**Fenwick**—pop pl CT-1
**Fenwick**—pop pl MD-2
**Fenwick**—pop pl MI-6
**Fenwick**—pop pl MS-4
**Fenwick**—pop pl NJ-2
**Fenwick**—pop pl WV-2
Fenwick—uninc pl KY-4
Fenwick, Lake—lake WA-9
Fenwick Branch—stream DC-2
Fenwick Branch—stream MD-2
Fenwick Bridge—bridge NJ-2
Fenwick Club Annex—hist pl OH-6
Fenwick Creek MD-2
Fenwick Creek—stream NJ-2
**Fenwick Crossroads**—pop pl SC-3
Fenwick Cut—channel SC-3
**Fenwick Development (subdivision)**—pop pl DE-2
Fenwicke Monument NJ-2
**Fenwick Estates (subdivision)**—pop pl DE-2
Fenwick Hall—hist pl SC-3
**Fenwick Hills**—pop pl SC-3
Fenwick HS—school IL-6
Fenwick HS—school MA-1
Fenwick HS—school OH-6
Fenwick Island—island DE-2
Fenwick Island—island MD-2
Fenwick Island—island SC-3
**Fenwick Island**—pop pl DE-2
Fenwick Island Lighthouse—locale DE-2
Fenwick Island Lighthouse Station—hist pl DE-2
Fenwick Island Shoal DE-2
Fenwick Island State Park—park DE-2
**Fenwick Landing (subdivision)**—pop pl DE-2
Fenwick Mines Campground—locale VA-3
Fenwick Monmt—park NJ-2
Fenwick Nature Trail—trail VA-3
Fenwick Oil Field—oilfield MS-4
Fenwick Park—park OH-6
**Fenwick Park**—pop pl VA-3
Fenwick Rsvr OR-9
Fenwicks SC-3
Fenwick Sch—school MD-2
Fenwick Sch—school TX-5
Fenwick Shoal—bar DE-2
Fenwicks Island DE-2
Fenwick Spring—spring ID-8
**Fenwick West (subdivision)**—pop pl DE-2
Fenwiks Creek MD-2
**Fenwood**—pop pl WI-6
Fenwood Creek—stream WI-6
Fenyes Estate—hist pl CA-9
Fenyoeruw—cape FM-9
Feoupech, Unun En—bar FM-9
Fer, Point Au—cape NY-2
Fer, Pount au—cape LA-4
Fera Canyon—valley UT-8
Fera Drain—canal NM-5
Feralla Draw—valley WY-8
Fera No 38 Well—well UT-8
Ferara Island FM-9
Feraud General Merchandise Store—hist pl CA-9
Feraud Park—park CA-9
Fera Well—well (3) NV-8
Fera Well Number 80—well UT-8
Ferber—locale IL-6
Ferber Flat—flat NV-8
Ferber Hills—summit NV-8
Ferber Hills—summit UT-8
Ferber Mining District—civil NV-8
Ferber Peak—summit NV-8
Ferber Rsvr Number One—reservoir NV-8
Ferber Wash—stream NV-8
Ferber Wash—valley (2) UT-8
Ferblanc, Bayou—gut LA-4
Ferchig Cem—cemetery FM-9
Ferda—locale AR-4
Ferda Ch—church AR-4
Ferdaline Spring—spring NV-8
Ferd Creek—stream MS-4
Ferdelford Creek—stream NV-8
Ferdelman, Lake—lake MI-6
Ferdig—locale MT-8
Ferdig Number 1 Dam—dam SD-7
**Ferdinand**—pop pl ID-8
**Ferdinand**—pop pl IN-6
Ferdinand, Bayou a—stream LA-4
Ferdinand Bog—swamp VT-1
Ferdinand Consolidated Sch—school IN-6
Ferdinand Forest Dam—dam IN-6
Ferdinand Gulch—valley MT-8
Ferdinand Hotz Park—park WI-6
Ferdinand Mine—mine MT-8
Ferdinand Old Lake—reservoir IN-6
Ferdinand Old Lake Dam—dam IN-6
Ferdinand Plaza—park FL-3
Ferdinand Run—stream IN-6
Ferdinands Mills—locale NJ-2
Ferdinand State For—forest IN-6
Ferdinand State Forest Lake—reservoir IN-6
Ferdinand Station IN-6
Ferdinand (Town of)—fmr MCD VT-1
**Ferdinand (Township of)**—pop pl IN-6
Ferdinand Water Supply Reservoir Dam—dam IN-6
Ferdinand Water Supply Rsvr—reservoir IN-6
Ferdon Creek—stream MI-6
Ferdon House—hist pl NJ-2
Ferdun Creek MI-6
**Foroboo** pop pl NC 3
Ferebee Glacier—glacier AK-9
Ferebee Landing Strip—airport NC-3
Ferebee River—stream AK-9
Feree PA-2
Ferel FM-9
Ferello Lake MN-6
**Ferenbaugh**—pop pl NY-2
Ferenz Ch—church LA-4
Ferganchick Orchard Rock Art Site—hist pl CO-8
Fergason Cem—cemetery AL-4
Ferger Place Hist Dist—hist pl TN-4
Fergerson Branch—stream NC-3
Fergerson Cem—cemetery AL-4
Fergerson Cem—cemetery LA-4
Fergerson Lake Dam—dam AL-4
Fergerson Ridge Pentecostal Church TN-4
Fergerson Sch (historical)—school TN-4
Fergersons Creek SC-3
Ferges Cem—cemetery IL-6
**Fergestown**—pop pl IL-6
Ferg Pond—reservoir AZ-5
Fergus—locale CA-9
Fergus—locale MI-6
**Fergus**—pop pl MT-8
**Fergus**—pop pl TX-5
Fergus County HS—hist pl MT-8
Fergus County Improvement Corporation Dormitory—hist pl MT-8
Fergus Dam ND-7
Fergusen Lake WA-9
**Fergus Falls**—pop pl MN-6
Fergus Falls City Hall—hist pl MN-6
Fergus Falls State Hosp—hospital MN-6
Fergus Falls State Hosp Complex—hist pl MN-6
Fergus Falls State Junior Coll—school MN-6
Fergus Falls State Wildlife Mngmt Area—park MN-6
Fergus Falls (Township of)—civ div MN-6
Ferguson KS-7
Ferguson—locale ID-8
Ferguson—locale KY-4
Ferguson—locale LA-4
Ferguson—locale (2) MS-4
Ferguson—locale TX-5
**Ferguson**—pop pl AL-4
**Ferguson**—pop pl AR-4
**Ferguson**—pop pl IN-6
**Ferguson**—pop pl IA-7
**Ferguson**—pop pl KY-4
**Ferguson**—pop pl MO-7
**Ferguson**—pop pl NC-3
**Ferguson**—pop pl OH-6
**Ferguson**—pop pl (2) PA-2
**Ferguson**—pop pl (2) WV-2
Ferguson, Albert W., House—hist pl OR-9
Ferguson, Andrew, House—hist pl OH-6
Ferguson, Benjamin, House—hist pl IN-6
Ferguson, Charles W., House—hist pl MO-7
Ferguson, Dr. James, Office—hist pl NY-2
Ferguson, Gar, Site—hist pl KY-4
Ferguson, John H., House—hist pl TX-5
Ferguson, John W., House—hist pl NJ-2
Ferguson, Joseph C., Sch—hist pl PA-2
Ferguson, J. T., Store—hist pl NC-3
Ferguson, Lake—lake AR-4
Ferguson, Lake—lake MS-4
Ferguson, Mount—summit NV-8
Ferguson, Robert, House—hist pl DE-2
Ferguson, Thompson Benton, House—hist pl OK-5
Ferguson, William, Farm—hist pl PA-2
Ferguson, William H., House—hist pl NE-7
Ferguson Bay—bay FL-3
Ferguson Bayou—gut MI-6
Ferguson-Becker Sch—school NE-7
Ferguson Box (historical)—locale MS-4
Ferguson Branch—stream IN-6
Ferguson Branch—stream (3) KY-4
Ferguson Branch—stream MO-7
Ferguson Branch—stream (2) NC-3
Ferguson Branch—stream (7) TN-4
Ferguson Branch—stream TX-5
Ferguson Branch—stream VA-3
Ferguson Branch—stream WV-2
Ferguson Bridge—bridge NC-3
Ferguson Bridge—bridge OR-9
Ferguson Brook—stream (3) ME-1
Ferguson Brook—stream (2) NH-1
Ferguson Brook—stream NY-2
Ferguson Buttes—range SD-7
Ferguson-Calderara House—hist pl AR-4
Ferguson Canyon—valley NM-5
Ferguson Canyon—valley UT-8
Ferguson Canyon—valley WY-8
Ferguson Cem—cemetery AR-4
Ferguson Cem—cemetery (3) GA-3
Ferguson Cem—cemetery (2) IN-6
Ferguson Cem—cemetery IA-7
Ferguson Cem—cemetery KS-7
Ferguson Cem—cemetery (5) KY-4
Ferguson Cem—cemetery MI-6
Ferguson Cem—cemetery MN-6
Ferguson Cem—cemetery (4) MS-4
Ferguson Cem—cemetery (2) MO-7
Ferguson Cem—cemetery NY-2
Ferguson Cem—cemetery (2) NC-3
Ferguson Cem—cemetery (2) OH-6
Ferguson Cem—cemetery PA-2
Ferguson Cem—cemetery SC-3
Ferguson Cem—cemetery (4) TN-4
Ferguson Cem—cemetery (4) TX-5
Ferguson Cem—cemetery (4) VA-3
Ferguson Cem—cemetery (3) WV-2
Ferguson Ch—church OK-5
Ferguson Ch—church TX-5
Ferguson Chapel Sch—school TN-4
Ferguson CME Chapel—church AL-4
**Ferguson Corner**—pop pl WY-8
Ferguson Corners—locale MI-6
Ferguson Corners—locale NY-2
Ferguson Cove—valley NC-3
Ferguson Creek SC-3
Ferguson Creek WA-9
Ferguson Creek WV-2
Ferguson Creek—stream AR-4
Ferguson Creek—stream CA-9
Ferguson Creek—stream CO-8
Forguson Crook stroam (2) ID 8
Ferguson Creek—stream IL-6
Ferguson Creek—stream KS-7
Ferguson Creek—stream (2) KY-4
Ferguson Creek—stream MI-6
Ferguson Creek—stream (2) NV-8
Ferguson Creek—stream NY-2
Ferguson Creek—stream (4) OR-9
Ferguson Creek—stream SC-3
Ferguson Creek—stream TN-4
Ferguson Creek—stream UT-8
Ferguson Creek—stream WA-9
Ferguson Creek—uninc pl KY-4
Ferguson Creek Drain—canal IL-6
Ferguson Crossing—locale TX-5
Ferguson Crossroad—locale AL-4
**Ferguson Crossroads**—pop pl AR-4
Ferguson Desert—plain UT-8
Ferguson Desert Reservoir UT-8
Ferguson Ditch—canal CO-8
Ferguson Ditch—canal (2) IN-6
Ferguson Ditch—canal OH-6
Ferguson Ditch No 2—canal CO-8
Ferguson Draw—valley AK-9
Ferguson Draw—valley SD-7
Ferguson Dump—other CA-9
Ferguson Elem Sch—school NC-3
Ferguson Elem Sch—school PA-2
Ferguson Farm Complex—hist pl NY-2
Ferguson Farms Airp—airport MO-7
Ferguson Field Municipal—airport NC-3
Ferguson-Fields Park—park IA-7
Ferguson Flat—flat CA-9
Ferguson Flat—flat ID-8
Ferguson Flat—flat NV-8
Ferguson Ford—locale IL-6
Ferguson Glacier—glacier AK-9
Ferguson Grove—woods SD-7
Ferguson Grove Ch—church VA-3
Ferguson Gulch—valley CA-9
Ferguson Gulch—valley WY-8
**Ferguson Hill**—pop pl IN-6
Ferguson Hill—summit NV-8
Ferguson Hill—summit NC-3
Ferguson Hill—summit VT-1
Ferguson Hollow—valley AR-4
Ferguson Hollow—valley (2) KY-4
Ferguson Hollow—valley (2) MO-7
Ferguson Hollow—valley PA-2
Ferguson Hollow—valley TN-4
Ferguson House—hist pl (2) AR-4
Ferguson House—hist pl IN-6
Ferguson House—hist pl OK-5
Ferguson House—hist pl TX-5
Ferguson HS—school VA-3
Ferguson Lake—lake CA-9
Ferguson Lake—lake FL-3
Ferguson Lake—lake ME-1
Ferguson Lake—lake (2) MI-6
Ferguson Lake—lake MS-4
Ferguson Lake—lake MT-8
Ferguson Lake—lake SC-3
Ferguson Lake—lake TX-5
Ferguson Lake—lake WA-9
Ferguson Lake—lake WI-6
Ferguson Lake—reservoir AR-4
Ferguson Lake—reservoir NM-5
Ferguson Lake Dam—dam MS-4
Ferguson Landing—locale AR-4
Ferguson Landing—locale SC-3
Ferguson Maintenance Station NV-8
Ferguson Meadow—flat CA-9
Ferguson Mine—mine SD-7
Ferguson Mtn—summit ME-1
Ferguson Mtn—summit NV-8
Ferguson Mtn—summit NM-5
Ferguson Mtn—summit (2) NY-2
Ferguson Mtn—summit OR-9
Ferguson Park—park (2) TX-5
Ferguson Park—park WA-9
Ferguson Peak—summit AK-9
Ferguson Peak—summit NC-3
Ferguson Place Windmill—locale AZ-5
Ferguson Point MN-6
Ferguson Point—cape MN-6
Ferguson Pond—lake FL-3
Ferguson Pond—lake ME-1
Ferguson Pond—lake WI-6
Ferguson Pond—reservoir GA-3
Ferguson Ranch—locale KS-7
Ferguson Ranch—locale NE-7
Ferguson Ranch—locale NV-8
Ferguson Ranch—locale (2) WY-8
Ferguson Ridge—ridge AZ-5
Ferguson Ridge—ridge CA-9
Ferguson Ridge—ridge KY-4
Ferguson Ridge—ridge OR-9
Ferguson Ridge—ridge WV-2
Ferguson River—stream FL-3
Ferguson Rsvr—reservoir OH-6
Ferguson Run—stream (2) OH-6
Ferguson Run—stream (2) PA-2
Fergusons Bridge (historical)—bridge MS-4
Ferguson Sch—school (2) IL-6
Ferguson Sch—school KY-4
Ferguson Sch—school MI-6
Ferguson Sch—school NE-7
Ferguson Sch—school OR-9
Ferguson Sch—school PA-2
Ferguson Sch—school SD-7
Ferguson Sch (abandoned)—school PA-2
Ferguson Sch Central School—hist pl MO-7
Ferguson Sch (historical)—school TN-4
Ferguson School TN-4
Fergusons Corners—locale NY-2
**Fergusons Corners**—pop pl NY-2
Fergusons Crossroads AL-4
**Fergusons Cross Roads**—pop pl AL-4
Fergusons Flying Circus Airp—airport TN-4
Fergusons Lake—reservoir NY-2
Fergusons Mill (historical)—locale AL-4
Ferguson Spring NV-8
Ferguson Spring—locale KY-4
Ferguson Spring—spring AL-4
Ferguson Spring—spring (2) OR-9
Ferguson Spring—spring UT-8
Ferguson Spring—spring WY-8
Ferguson Spring Ch—church KY-4
Ferguson Springs—spring NV-8
Ferguson Springs Maintenence Station locale NV 8
Ferguson State Prison Farm—other TX-5
Ferguson Stream—stream ME-1
Fergusons Valley PA-2
Fergusons Wharf VA-3
Ferguson Tank—reservoir AZ-5
Ferguson Township—civil MO-7
Ferguson (Township of)—fmr MCD AR-4
**Ferguson (Township of)**—pop pl (2) PA-2
Ferguson Trail—trail OK-5
Ferguson Trail—trail UT-8
Ferguson Valley—basin PA-2
Ferguson Valley—valley AZ-5
Ferguson Valley—valley AR-4
Ferguson Valley—valley MN-6
Fergusonville—locale VA-3
**Fergusonville**—pop pl NY-2
**Fergusonville**—pop pl PA-2
Ferguson Wash—stream CA-9
Ferguson Windmill—locale NM-5
Fergusson Desert Reservoir UT-8
Fergusson Hollow—valley KY-4
Fergussons Wharf VA-3
Fergy Gulch—valley AK-9
Ferichs Well—well AZ-5
Feridell Ranch—locale CA-9
Feris creek NV-8
Ferit—island FM-9
**Feriton**—pop pl WA-9
Ferkens Creek NJ-2
Ferkingstad Cem—cemetery SD-7
Ferkingstad Ch—church SD-7
**Fermanagh (Township of)**—pop pl PA-2
Ferman Artesian Well—well TX-5
Fermandez Spring—spring CA-9
Ferman Lake—lake MN-6
Ferme, Lake—lake LA-4
**Fermina**—pop pl PR-3
Fermin Des Loge Hosp—hospital MO-7
Fermine De Viller Grant—civil FL-3
Fermi Nuclear Plant—facility MI-6
Fermi Sch—school IL-6
Fermory (Unorganized Territory of) MN-6
**Fermoy**—pop pl PA-2
Fermoy Sch—school PA-2
Fern—locale AR-4
Fern—locale CA-9
Fern—locale KS-7
Fern—locale LA-4
Fern—locale MI-6
Fern—locale PA-2
Fern—locale WI-6
**Fern**—pop pl IN-6
**Fern**—pop pl IA-7
**Fern**—pop pl OK-5
**Fern**—pop pl OR-9
**Fern**—pop pl PA-2
**Fern**—pop pl TX-5
Fern, Lake—lake FL-3
Ferna MN-6
Fernades Windmill—locale TX-5
Fernald—locale OH-6
**Fernald**—pop pl IA-7
**Fernald**—pop pl NH-1
Fernald, George P., House—hist pl MA-1
Fernald Brook—stream ME-1
Fernald Brook—stream NH-1
Fernald Hill—summit NH-1
Fernald Point—cape CA-9
Fernald Point—cape ME-1
Fernald Point Prehistoric Site—hist pl ME-1
Fernald Pond—lake (2) ME-1
**Fernald Shore**—pop pl ME-1
Fernalds Neck—cape ME-1
Fernald State Sch—school (2) MA-1
Fernan Creek—stream (2) ID-8
Fernandes Ranch—locale TX-5
Fernandes Randolph Shoppers Plaza—locale MA-1
Fernandes Raynham Shop Ctr—locale MA-1
Fernandex, Canon—valley CO-8
Fernandez—civil CA-9
Fernandez, Bernardo, House—hist pl CA-9
Fernandez Camp—locale NM-5
Fernandez Canal—canal LA-4
Fernandez Canyon—valley NM-5
Fernandez Creek—stream (2) CA-9
Fernandez Juncos—post sta PR-3
Fernandez Lakes—lake CA-9
Fernandez Pass—gap CA-9
Fernandez Ranch—locale (3) NM-5
**Fernandez Rosal**—pop pl PR-3
Fernandez Tank—reservoir NM-5
Fernandez Trail (Pack)—trail CA-9
**Fernandez Village**—pop pl HI-9
Fernandina FL-3
Fernandina KS-7
**Fernandina Beach**—pop pl FL-3
Fernandina Beach (CCD)—cens area FL-3
Fernandina Beach Hist Dist—hist pl FL-3
Fernandina Beach Hist Dist (Boundary Increase)—hist pl FL-3
Fernandina Beach HS—school FL-3
Fernandina Beach JHS—school FL-3
Fernandina Beach Municipal Airp—airport FL-3
Fernandina Entrance FL-3
**Fernando**—pop pl MN-6
Fernando Creek CA-9
Fernando De Taos—civil NM-5
Fernando Ditch—canal CO-8
Fernando Mountains—ridge NM-5
Fernando Tank—reservoir TX-5
Fernangeles Recreation Center—park CA-9
Fernangeles Sch—school CA-9
Fernan Lake—lake ID-8
**Fernan Lake**—pop pl ID-8
**Fern Ann Falls**—pop pl CA-9
Fernash Creek TX-5
Fernback OH-6
Fernbank OH-6
**Fernbank**—pop pl AL-4
**Fernbank**—pop pl OH-6
Fernbank Baptist Ch—church AL-4
Fern Bank (Fernbank) AL-4
**Fernbank (Fern Bank)**—pop pl AL-4
Fernbank Forest and Recreational Center—park GA-3
Fernbank HS (historical)—school AL-4
Fernbank Post Office (historical)—building AL-4
Fern Basin Camp—locale CA-9
Fernbell Park—park AL-4
Fernberg Lookout Tower—locale MN-6
Fern Bluff—cliff TX-5
Fern Branch—stream KY-4
Fern Branch—stream (2) TN-4
Fernbridge—hist pl CA-9
Fernbridge—locale CA-9
**Fernbrook**—pop pl CA-9
**Fern Brook**—pop pl PA-2
Fern Brook—stream NJ-2
Fern Brook Cem—cemetery PA-2
Fern Camp Cave—cave TN-4
Fern Camp Creek—stream TN-4
Fern Campground—locale CA-9
Fern Canal—canal CA-9
Fern Canyon AZ-5
Fern Canyon—valley (10) CA-9
Fern Canyon—valley (2) CO-8
Fern Cascades—falls WY-8
Fern Cave—cave AL-4
Fern Cave—cave CA-9
Fern Cave—cave MO-7
Fern Cave Archeol Site—hist pl CA-9
Fern Cave Natl Wildlife Ref—park AL-4
Fern Cem—cemetery IL-6
Fern Cem—cemetery OK-5
Fern Chamber—other CA-9
Fern Chapel—church MO-7
Fern Church AL-4
Fern Cliff—cliff IN-6
Ferncliff—locale MD-2
Ferncliff—locale VA-3
**Ferncliff**—pop pl CO-8
**Ferncliff**—pop pl WA-9
Ferncliff Camp—locale AR-4
Ferncliff Cem—cemetery NY-2
Ferncliff Cem—cemetery OH-6
Fern Cliff Cem—cemetery OK-5
**Ferncliffe**—pop pl CO-8
Ferncliff Gap—gap AL-4
Ferncliff (historical)—locale AL-4
Fern Cliff Prospect Mine—mine SD-7
Fern Cliff Sch—school NY-2
Ferncliff Sch—school VA-3
Fern Corner—locale OR-9
Fern Cottage—locale CA-9
Fern Cottage Hist Dist—hist pl CA-9
Fern Cove—bay WA-9
Fern Creek CA-9
Fern Creek MT-8
**Fern Creek**—pop pl KY-4
Fern Creek—stream (5) CA-9
Fern Creek—stream (4) CO-8
Fern Creek—stream FL-3
Fern Creek—stream (10) ID-8
Fern Creek—stream IA-7
Fern Creek—stream KY-4
Fern Creek—stream MI-6
Fern Creek—stream (3) MT-8
Fern Creek—stream (5) OR-9
Fern Creek—stream (2) WA-9
Fern Creek—stream WV-2
Fern Creek Sch—school FL-3
Fern Creek Stock Driveway—trail CO-8
Ferncrest Sch—school LA-4
**Fern Crest Village**—pop pl FL-3
**Ferncroft**—pop pl MA-1
**Ferncroft**—pop pl NH-1
Ferncroft Hill—summit MA-1
Ferncroft Station MA-1
Ferndale MI-6
Ferndale PA-2
Ferndale—locale PA-2
**Ferndale**—pop pl AR-4
**Ferndale**—pop pl CA-9
**Ferndale**—pop pl CO-8
**Ferndale**—pop pl FL-3
**Ferndale**—pop pl IL-6
**Ferndale**—pop pl IN-6
**Ferndale**—pop pl KY-4
**Ferndale**—pop pl MD-2
**Ferndale**—pop pl MI-6
**Ferndale**—pop pl MT-8
**Ferndale**—pop pl NY-2
**Ferndale**—pop pl OR-9
**Ferndale**—pop pl (3) PA-2
**Ferndale**—pop pl WA-9
Ferndale—uninc pl SC-3
Ferndale Borough—civil PA-2
Ferndale Branch—stream GA-3
Ferndale (CCD)—cens area CA-9
Ferndale (CCD)—cens area WA-9
Fern-Dale Cem—cemetery ME-1
Ferndale Cem—cemetery MI-6
Ferndale Cem—cemetery NY-2
Ferndale Ch—church MD-2
Ferndale Ch—church OH-6
Ferndale Country Club—other MN-6
Ferndale Creek—stream AR-4
Ferndale Creek—stream MN-6
**Ferndale Gardens**—pop pl VA-3
Ferndale Lake—reservoir TX-5
Ferndale Lake Club—other TX-5
Ferndale Lower Range Channel—channel OR-9
Ferndale MS—school NC-3
Ferndale Park—park MI-6
Ferndale Park—park OH-6
**Ferndale Park**—pop pl VA-3
Ferndale Picnic Area—locale CO-8
Ferndale Post Office (historical)—building PA-2
Ferndale Ranch—locale CA-9

Ferndale (RR name for Garrison)—*other* WV-2
Ferndale Sch—*school* KY-4
Ferndale Sch—*school* OR-9
Ferndale Sch—*school* WV-2
Ferndale Sch (historical)—*school* TN-4
Ferndale School (Abandoned)—*locale* WA-9
Ferndale Seminary—*school* CT-1
Ferndale Upper Range Channel—*channel* OR-9
Fern Dell Sch—*school* WI-6
Ferndell Spring—*spring* AZ-5
Fern Drive Sch—*school* CA-9
Ferne Clyffe State Park—*park* IL-6
Ferne Creek—*stream* MN-6
Ferne Lake—*lake* MN-6
**Fernell Heights**—*pop pl* OH-6
Ferner, Matthais, Bldg—*hist pl* IA-7
Fernette Mtn—*summit* NY-2
Ferney—*locale* PA-2
**Ferney**—*pop pl* SD-7
Ferney, John, House—*hist pl* OH-6
Ferney Gulch—*valley* WY-8
Ferney Run—*stream* PA-2
Ferney Run Trail—*trail* PA-2
Ferneys Branch—*stream* WV-2
*Fern Falls* WY-8
Fern Falls—*falls* CO-8
Fern Falls—*falls* ID-8
Fern Feather Tank—*reservoir* AZ-5
Fern Feather Wash—*stream* AZ-5
Fern Flat—*flat* CA-9
Fern Flat—*flat* UT-8
Fern Gap—*gap* WA-9
Fern Gap Guard Station—*locale* WA-9
Fern Glade—*flat* CA-9
Fern Glen—*locale* PA-2
Fernglen—*locale* PA-2
**Fern Glen**—*pop pl* MO-7
Fern Glen Canyon—*valley* AZ-5
**Fernglen Manor**—*pop pl* MD-2
Fern Glen Rapids—*rapids* AZ-5
Fern-Greenwood Sch—*school* CA-9
Fern Grotto—*cave* HI-9
Fern Gulch—*valley* CA-9
Fern Gulch—*valley* ID-8
Fern Hammock Springs—*spring* FL-3
Fern Harbor—*bay* AK-9
Fern Heath—*locale* WA-9
*Fern Hill* CA-9
*Fernhill* PA-2
**Fern Hill**—*pop pl* (2) OR-9
**Fern Hill**—*pop pl* PA-2
**Fern Hill**—*pop pl* WA-9
Fern Hill—*summit* NH-1
Fern Hill—*summit* OR-9
Fern Hill Cem—*cemetery* FL-3
Fern Hill Cem—*cemetery* KY-4
Fern Hill Cem—*cemetery* MA-1
Fern Hill Cem—*cemetery* OR-9
Fern Hill Cem—*cemetery* (5) WA-9
Fern Hill Ch—*church* NC-3
Fernhill Lake—*reservoir* PA-2
Fern Hill Park—*park* MN-6
Fernhill Park—*park* OR-9
Fernhill Park—*park* PA-2
Fern Hill Sch—*school* MN-6
Fern Hill Sch—*school* WA-9
Fernhill School (abandoned)—*locale* OR-9
Fern Hollow—*valley* KY-4
Fern Hollow—*valley* OR-9
Fern Hollow—*valley* PA-2
Fern Hollow—*valley* TX-5
**Fern Hook**—*pop pl* DE-2
Fern Hook Marsh—*swamp* DE-2
Fernia Creek—*stream* MI-6
Fern Island—*island* CA-9
Fern Island—*island* (2) NY-2
Fern Isle Park—*park* FL-3
Fern Knob—*summit* NC-3
Fern Knoll Cem—*cemetery* PA-2
Fern Lake—*lake* AK-9
Fern Lake—*lake* (4) CA-9
Fern Lake—*lake* CO-8
Fern Lake—*lake* FL-3
Fern Lake—*lake* (2) MI-6
Fern Lake—*lake* (3) MN-6
Fern Lake—*lake* NY-2
Fern Lake—*lake* UT-8
Fern Lake—*lake* VT-1
Fern Lake—*lake* (2) WA-9
Fern Lake—*lake* WY-8
Fern Lake—*reservoir* CA-9
Fern Lake—*reservoir* KY-4
Fern Lake—*reservoir* (2) TN-4
Fern Lake—*reservoir* (2) TX-5
Fern Lake Dam—*dam* TN-4
Fern Lake Mtn—*summit* NY-2
Fern Lake Patrol Cabin—*hist pl* CO-8
Fern Lake Patrol Cabin—*locale* WY-8
**Fernland**—*pop pl* AL-4
Fern Lateral Eight—*canal* CA-9
Fern Lateral Four—*canal* CA-9
Fern Lateral Nine—*canal* CA-9
Fern Lateral Three—*canal* CA-9
Fernleaf—*locale* KY-4
*Fernleaf Gulch* CO-8
Fernleaf Gulch—*valley* CO-8
**Fernley**—*pop pl* NV-8
Fernley, Edward, House—*hist pl* UT-8
Fernley, William, House—*hist pl* UT-8
Fernley Drain—*canal* NV-8
Fernley State Wildlife Mngmt Area—*park* NV-8
Fern Loop Nature Trail—*trail* TN-4
Fern-Marylyn Apartments—*hist pl* UT-8
Fern Mine—*mine* AK-9
Fern Mine—*mine* ID-8
Fern Mountain Ranch—*hist pl* AZ-5
Fern Mountain Tank—*reservoir* AZ-5
Fern Mtn—*summit* AZ-5
Fern Mtn—*summit* AR-4
Fern Mtn—*summit* CA-9
Fern Mtn—*summit* NC-3
Fern Mtn—*summit* (2) OK-5
Fern Oak Cem—*cemetery* IN-6
Fernold, Lake—*lake* MN-6
Ferno Mesa—*summit* AZ-5
Ferno Trick Tank—*reservoir* AZ-5
Fernow, Mount—*summit* (2) WA-9
*Fernow Canyon* UT-8
Fernow Hall—*hist pl* NY-2
Fernow Mtn—*summit* NY-2
Fernow Tank—*reservoir* AZ-5
Fern Park—*park* VA-3
**Fern Park**—*pop pl* FL-3
Fern Park Cem—*cemetery* LA-4
Fern Park Ch of the Nazarene—*church* FL-3
Fern Park Shop Ctr—*locale* FL-3
Fern Patch—*area* CA-9
Fern Peak—*summit* CA-9
Fern Place Sch—*school* NY-2
Fern Point—*cape* AK-9
Fern Point—*cape* CA-9
Fern Point—*cape* WA-9
Fern Point—*summit* NV-8
Fern Point Bridge—*bridge* CA-9
Fern Point Spring—*spring* NV-8
Fern Pond—*swamp* FL-3
Fern Pond—*swamp* GA-3
Fern Prairie—*area* (2) CA-9
**Fern Prairie**—*pop pl* WA-9
Fern Prairie Cem—*cemetery* WA-9
Fern Reef—*bar* AK-9
**Fernridge**—*pop pl* MO-7
**Fern Ridge**—*pop pl* OR-9
**Fernridge**—*pop pl* PA-2
Fern Ridge—*ridge* CA-9
Fern Ridge—*ridge* ID-8
Fern Ridge—*ridge* (3) OR-9
Fern Ridge Cem—*cemetery* OR-9
Fern Ridge Dam—*dam* OR-9
Fern Ridge Day Sch—*school* FL-3
Fern Ridge Lake—*reservoir* OR-9
*Fern Ridge Rsvr* OR-9
Fernridge Sch—*school* MO-7
**Fernridge (subdivision)**—*pop pl* AL-4
Fern River Park—*park* NJ-2
**Fern Rock**—*pop pl* PA-2
Fern Rock Creek—*stream* OR-9
Fern Rock Rest Area—*locale* OR-9
Fern Run—*stream* WV-2
Fern Sch—*hist pl* WI-6
Fern Sch—*school* CA-9
Fern Sch—*school* HI-9
Fern Sch—*school* MO-7
**Ferns (historical)**—*pop pl* OR-9
Fernside—*locale* NC-3
Fern Sidemain—*canal* CA-9
Fernsides Cove—*valley* AR-4
Ferns Nipple—*summit* UT-8
Fern Spring—*spring* AR-4
Fern Spring—*spring* (5) CA-9
Fern Spring—*spring* ME-1
Fern Spring—*spring* NV-8
Fern Spring—*spring* (3) OR-9
Fern Spring—*spring* UT-8
Fern Spring Canyon—*valley* CA-9
*Fern Spring Mountain* AR-4
Fern Springs—*spring* (2) CA-9
Fern Springs Branch—*stream* TN-4
Fern Springs Ch—*church* AL-4
Fern Springs Picnic Area—*locale* GA-3
Ferns Quarter (historical)—*locale* AL-4
Ferns Tank—*reservoir* AZ-5
*Fernster Creek* ID-8
Fernstrom Tank—*reservoir* AZ-5
Fern Tank—*reservoir* (2) AZ-5
Fern Top—*summit* OR-9
**Fern (Town of)**—*pop pl* WI-6
**Fern (Township of)**—*pop pl* MN-6
Fernvale—*locale* OR-9
Fernvale—*locale* TN-4
Fernvale Ch of Christ—*church* TN-4
Fernvale Dam—*dam* TN-4
Fernvale (historical)—*locale* AL-4
Fernvale Lake—*reservoir* TN-4
Fernvale Post Office (historical)—*building* TN-4
Fernvale Sch—*school* TN-4
*Fernvale Spring* TN-4
**Fernvale Springs (historical)**—*pop pl* TN-4
Fernvale Springs Post Office (historical)—*building* TN-4
**Fern Valley**—*pop pl* CA-9
Fern Valley—*valley* OR-9
Fern Valley (historical P.O.)—*locale* IA-7
Fern Valley Township—*fmr MCD* IA-7
**Fern View**—*pop pl* KY-4
**Fernview Estates**—*pop pl* MO-7
Fernview Forest Camp—*locale* OR-9
**Fern Village**—*pop pl* PA-2
**Fernville**—*pop pl* PA-2
**Fernville**—*pop pl* VT-1
*Fernway* IL-6
Fernway—*CDP* PA-2
**Fernway**—*pop pl* IL-6
**Fernway Park**—*pop pl* IL-6
Fernway Sch—*school* IL-6
Fernway Sch—*school* OH-6
Fernwood—*hist pl* MA-1
Fernwood—*locale* CA-9
Fernwood—*locale* NY-2
Fernwood—*locale* OH-6
Fernwood—*locale* OR-9
Fernwood—*locale* WA-9
**Fernwood**—*pop pl* CA-9
**Fernwood**—*pop pl* CT-1
**Fernwood**—*pop pl* DE-2
**Fernwood**—*pop pl* GA-3
**Fernwood**—*pop pl* ID-8
**Fernwood**—*pop pl* MD-2
**Fernwood**—*pop pl* MS-4
**Fernwood**—*pop pl* NH-1
**Fernwood**—*pop pl* NJ-2
**Fernwood**—*pop pl* (2) NY-2
**Fernwood**—*pop pl* (2) PA-2
**Fernwood**—*pop pl* TN-4
Fernwood Archeol Site, RI-702—*hist pl* RI-1
Fernwood Baptist Ch—*church* MS-4
*Fernwood Baptist Church* TN-4
*Fernwood Campground* UT-8
Fernwood Canal—*canal* LA-4
Fernwood Cem—*cemetery* AR-4
Fernwood Cem—*cemetery* CA-9
Fernwood Cem—*cemetery* KY-4
Fernwood Cem—*cemetery* MI-6
Fernwood Cem—*cemetery* MS-4
Fernwood Cem—*cemetery* (2) NJ-2
Fernwood Cem—*cemetery* OH-6
Fernwood Cem—*cemetery* (2) PA-2
Fernwood Ch—*church* TN-4
Fernwood Country Club—*other* MS-4
**Fernwood Estates**—*pop pl* AL-4
Fernwood Golf Course—*locale* PA-2
Fernwood Grange Hall—*locale* OR-9
**Fernwood Heights**—*pop pl* TN-4
**Fernwood Hollow Subdivision**—*pop pl* UT-8
Fernwood Hosp—*hospital* CT-1
*Fernwood Junior High School* MS-4
Fernwood Lake—*reservoir* MA-1
Fernwood Lake Dam—*dam* MA-1
Fernwood Lake East Dam—*dam* MA-1
Fernwood Lake West Dam—*dam* MA-1
Fernwood MS—*school* MS-4
Fernwood Park—*park* IL-6
Fernwood Recreation Site—*park* UT-8
Fernwood Rsvr—*reservoir* MA-1
Fernwood Sch—*school* IL-6
Fernwood Sch—*school* MD-2
Fernwood Sch—*school* (2) OR-9
Fernwood Sch—*school* WI-6
Fernwood Sewage Lagoon Dam—*dam* MS-4
Fernwood (ski area)—*locale* PA-2
Fernwood Station—*building* PA-2
**Fernwood (subdivision)**—*pop pl* AL-4
**Fernwood (subdivision)**—*pop pl* (2) NC-3
**Fernwood Terrace**—*pop pl* NJ-2
**Fernwood-Yeadon**—*pop pl* PA-2
Ferny Branch—*stream* TN-4
**Fero**—*pop pl* NC-3
Fero Draw—*valley* WY-8
Ferosa Canyon—*valley* AZ-5
Feroy Well—*well* NV-8
Feroz Terrace—*bench* AZ-5
*Ferrago* NJ-2
Ferra Gulch—*valley* AZ-5
Ferrall Point—*cape* VI-3
Ferrand Bay—*bay* LA-4
Ferrand Bayou—*gut* LA-4
Ferrand Lake—*lake* LA-4
Ferrand Memorial Park—*cemetery* MI-6
Ferran Park—*park* FL-3
*Ferra Peak* AZ-5
Ferra Peak—*summit* AZ-5
Ferrara Sch—*school* CT-1
Ferraro Ranch—*locale* NV-8
Ferrarre Ditch—*canal* OH-6
Ferre Canal—*canal* LA-4
Ferree Covered Bridge—*hist pl* IN-6
Ferree Gilead Ch—*church* OH-6
Ferreira Cem—*cemetery* FL-3
Ferreira Field—*airport* PA-2
Ferreira Point—*cape* FL-3
Ferrel—*locale* IL-6
**Ferrel**—*pop pl* NC-3
**Ferreland Acres Subdivision**—*pop pl* UT-8
Ferrel Cem—*cemetery* TN-4
Ferrel Creek—*stream* AR-4
Ferrel Creek—*stream* MT-8
Ferrel Fork—*stream* KY-4
*Ferrell* MS-4
**Ferrell**—*pop pl* NJ-2
**Ferrell**—*pop pl* VA-3
**Ferrell**—*pop pl* WV-2
Ferrell, Silas, House—*hist pl* OH-6
*Ferrell Branch* TX-5
Ferrell Branch—*stream* AL-4
Ferrell Branch—*stream* FL-3
Ferrell Branch—*stream* TN-4
Ferrell Branch—*stream* WV-2
Ferrell Branch Spring—*spring* TX-5
Ferrell Cem—*cemetery* MO-7
Ferrell Cem—*cemetery* OK-5
Ferrell Cem—*cemetery* (2) TN-4
Ferrell Cem—*cemetery* TX-5
Ferrell Cem—*cemetery* VA-3
Ferrell Cem—*cemetery* (7) WV-2
Ferrell Ch—*church* IL-6
Ferrell Cliff—*cliff* KY-4
*Ferrell Creek* MS-4
*Ferrell Creek* NC-3
Ferrell Creek—*stream* KY-4
Ferrell Creek—*stream* MT-8
Ferrell Creek Ch—*church* KY-4
Ferrell Crossroads—*locale* GA-3
Ferrell Dead River—*lake* MS-4
Ferrell Field Airp—*airport* WA-9
Ferrell-Holder House—*hist pl* GA-3
Ferrell Hollow—*valley* TN-4
Ferrell Hollow—*valley* WV-2
Ferrell-Holt House—*hist pl* WV-2
*Ferrell-Judkins Cemetery* TN-4
Ferrell Lake—*lake* MN-6
Ferrell Lake—*lake* MT-8
Ferrell Landing (historical)—*locale* AL-4
Ferrell Oil Field—*oilfield* KS-7
Ferrell Ridge—*ridge* WV-2
Ferrells Bridge Dam—*dam* TX-5
*Ferrells Bridge Reservoir* TX-5
**Ferrellsburg**—*pop pl* WV-2
*Ferrells Creek* NC-3
**Ferrells Creek**—*pop pl* KY-4
Ferrell Shingle Mill (historical)—*locale* TX-5
Ferrell South Oil Field—*oilfield* KS-7
Ferrells (Township of)—*fmr MCD* NC-3
**Ferrellton**—*pop pl* PA-2
Ferrelltown Creek—*stream* NC-3
Ferrelltown Lake—*reservoir* NC-3
Ferrell Women Graves—*cemetery* TX-5
Ferrelo, Cape—*cape* OR-9
**Ferrelton**—*pop pl* PA-2
**Ferrelview**—*pop pl* MO-7
**Ferremont Junction**—*pop pl* NJ-2
Ferret Creek—*stream* MT-8
Ferret Lake—*lake* MN-6
Ferrey, Aaron, House—*hist pl* OH-6
Ferric Creek—*stream* AK-9
**Ferriday**—*pop pl* LA-4
Ferrier Creek—*stream* WA-9
Ferrier Peak—*summit* WA-9
Ferrier Ridge—*ridge* CO-8
Ferrier Run—*stream* PA-2
Ferriers Gulch—*valley* OR-9
Ferrill Branch—*stream* TX-5
Ferrill Cem—*cemetery* MS-4
Ferrill Cem—*cemetery* TN-4
Ferrill Cem—*cemetery* TX-5
Ferrill Rsvr—*reservoir* KY-4
Ferrill Spring—*spring* MO-7
*Ferrils Gulch* CA-9
**Ferrin**—*pop pl* IL-6
Ferrin Brook—*stream* NH-1
Ferrin Knob—*summit* NC-3
Ferrin Knob Tunnel No 1—*tunnel* NC-3
Ferrin Knob Tunnel No 2—*tunnel* NC-3
Ferrin Knob Tunnel No 3—*tunnel* NC-3
Ferrin Run—*stream* PA-2
Ferrin Sch—*school* IL-6
Ferris—*locale* PA-2
Ferris—*locale* WY-8
**Ferris**—*pop pl* IL-6
**Ferris**—*pop pl* TX-5
Ferris, Eliphalet, House—*hist pl* OH-6
Ferris, George, Mansion—*hist pl* WY-8
Ferris, G. W. G., House—*hist pl* NV-8
Ferris, Joseph, House—*hist pl* OH-6
Ferris, Zachariah, House—*hist pl* DE-2
**Ferrisburg**—*pop pl* VT-1
**Ferrisburg (Town of)**—*pop pl* VT-1
Ferris Canyon—*valley* (2) CA-9
Ferris Canyon—*valley* CO-8
Ferris Canyon—*valley* NV-8
Ferris (CCD)—*cens area* TX-5
*Ferris Cem* TN-4
Ferris Cem—*cemetery* LA-4
Ferris Cem—*cemetery* (3) NY-2
Ferris Ch—*church* MI-6
**Ferris Corners**—*pop pl* PA-2
Ferris Creek—*harbor* NY-2
Ferris Creek—*stream* CA-9
Ferris Creek—*stream* NV-8
Ferris Creek—*stream* (2) OR-9
Ferris Creek—*stream* WY-8
Ferris Ditch—*canal* IN-6
**Ferris Estates**—*pop pl* CT-1
Ferris Flat—*flat* CA-9
Ferris Fork—*stream* WY-8
Ferris Fork Creek—*stream* KY-4
Ferris Gulch—*valley* OR-9
Ferris-Haggarty Mine—*mine* WY-8
Ferris Hill—*summit* CT-1
Ferris Hill—*summit* NY-2
Ferris Hollow—*valley* VA-3
Ferris House—*hist pl* NY-2
Ferris HS—*school* WA-9
Ferris Industrial Sch—*school* DE-2
Ferris Institute—*school* MI-6
*Ferris Lake* NY-2
Ferris Lake—*lake* NY-2
Ferris Lake—*lake* WY-8
Ferris Mine—*mine* CA-9
Ferris Mountain Ranch—*locale* WY-8
Ferris Mtns—*range* WY-8
Ferris Park—*park* MI-6
Ferris Park Cem—*cemetery* TX-5
Ferris Pit—*cave* TN-4
Ferris Pond—*lake* CT-1
Ferris Ridge—*ridge* IN-6
Ferris Ridge—*ridge* WY-8
Ferris Rock—*island* NY-2
Ferris Rsvr—*reservoir* CO-8
Ferris Run—*stream* OH-6
Ferris Sch—*school* IL-6
Ferris Sch—*school* (2) MI-6
Ferris Sch—*school* SC-3
Ferris Site—*hist pl* OH-6
*Ferris Slough* MS-4
Ferris Slough—*stream* ID-8
Ferris Spring—*spring* AL-4
Ferris Spring—*spring* CO-8
**Ferristown**—*pop pl* OH-6
**Ferris (Township of)**—*pop pl* MI-6
Ferrisville Cem—*cemetery* IN-6
*Ferrit* FM-9
Ferrol—*locale* VA-3
*Ferro Mont* NJ-2
**Ferron**—*pop pl* UT-8
Ferron, John, House—*hist pl* PA-2
Ferron Box Pictographs and Petroglyphs—*hist pl* UT-8
Ferron Canyon—*valley* UT-8
Ferron Canyon Campground—*locale* UT-8
Ferron City Cem—*cemetery* UT-8
Ferron Creek—*stream* UT-8
Ferron Dam—*dam* UT-8
Ferron Debris Basin Number Five Dam—*dam* UT-8
Ferron Debris Basin Number Four Dam—*dam* UT-8
Ferron Debris Basin Number One Dam—*dam* UT-8
Ferron Debris Basin Number Three Dam—*dam* UT-8
Ferron Debris Basin Number Two Dam—*dam* UT-8
Ferron District Ranger Station—*locale* UT-8
Ferron Mill—*locale* UT-8
Ferron Mtn—*summit* UT-8
Ferron Park—*park* NV-8
**Ferron Park**—*pop pl* WI-6
Ferron Point—*cape* MI-6
Ferron Presbyterian Church and Cottage—*hist pl* UT-8
Ferron Reservoir Campground—*park* UT-8
Ferron Rsvr—*reservoir* UT-8
*Ferron School* UT-8
*Ferrons City* UT-8
Ferro Post Office (historical)—*building* TN-4
Ferros Ranch Airp—*airport* MO-7
Ferrous Creek—*stream* WA-9
Ferrum—*locale* CA-9
**Ferrum**—*pop pl* VA-3
Ferrum Creek—*stream* AK-9
Ferrum Junior Coll—*school* VA-3
Ferrut Pond—*lake* NH-1
*Ferry* NE-7
Ferry—*locale* WA-9
**Ferry**—*pop pl* AK-9
**Ferry**—*pop pl* MI-6
**Ferry**—*pop pl* (2) OH-6
Ferry, Edward P., House—*hist pl* MI-6
Ferry, Mount—*summit* WA-9
Ferry, Pierre P., House—*hist pl* WA-9
Ferryall Reef—*bar* NY-2
Ferry Ave Sch—*school* NY-2
Ferry Ave Station—*locale* NJ-2
Ferry Bar—*cape* MD-2
Ferry Bar Channel (east Section)—*channel* MD-2
Ferry Bar Channel (West Section)—*channel* MD-2
Ferry Basin—*basin* MT-8
Ferry Bayou—*gut* LA-4
Ferry Bayou—*stream* AR-4
*Ferry Beach* ME-1
Ferry Beach—*beach* NY-2
**Ferry Beach**—*pop pl* ME-1
*Ferry Beach Ponds* ME-1
Ferry Bend—*bend* MS-4
Ferry Bldg—*building* CA-9
Ferry Bluff—*cliff* WI-6
Ferry Boat Island—*island* MA-1
Ferry Branch—*stream* GA-3
Ferry Branch—*stream* (2) MD-2
Ferry Branch—*stream* SC-3
Ferry Branch—*stream* TX-5
Ferry Branch—*stream* WV-2
Ferry Bridge—*bridge* ME-1
Ferry Bridge (historical)—*bridge* MS-4
Ferry Brook—*stream* NH-1
Ferry Butte—*summit* ID-8
Ferry Canyon—*valley* (3) OR-9
Ferry Cem—*cemetery* MI-6
Ferry Cem—*cemetery* NY-2
Ferry Cliff—*cliff* RI-1
**Ferry County**—*pop pl* WA-9
Ferry County Airp—*airport* WA-9
Ferry Cove—*bay* DE-2
Ferry Cove—*bay* MD-2
*Ferry Creek* MD-2
*Ferry Creek* OR-9
Ferry Creek—*stream* CT-1
Ferry Creek—*stream* ID-8
Ferry Creek—*stream* MT-8
Ferry Creek—*stream* (3) OR-9
Ferry Creek—*stream* (2) VA-3
Ferry Creek—*stream* WV-2
Ferry Creek Dam—*dam* OR-9
Ferry Creek Rsvr—*reservoir* OR-9
*Ferry Cross Creek* TN-4
Ferry Cutoff—*bay* FL-3
Ferrydale Cem—*cemetery* OR-9
Ferry Ditch—*canal* IN-6
**Ferry Farm**—*pop pl* VA-3
**Ferry Farms**—*pop pl* MD-2
**Ferry Farms**—*pop pl* VA-3
Ferry Farm Site—*hist pl* VA-3
Ferry Field—*park* MI-6
Ferry Grade—*locale* OR-9
Ferry Gulch—*valley* (2) CA-9
Ferry Hall Sch—*school* IL-6
**Ferry Hill**—*pop pl* MA-1
Ferry Hill—*summit* CT-1
Ferry Hill—*summit* (2) MA-1
Ferry Hill—*summit* RI-1
Ferry Hill—*summit* VT-1
Ferry Hill Hollow—*valley* TN-4
Ferry Hills—*summit* TN-4
Ferry (historical P.O.)—*locale* IA-7
Ferry Hole Bar—*bar* OR-9
Ferry Hollow—*valley* ID-8
Ferry Island—*island* WY-8
Ferry JHS—*school* MI-6
*Ferry Lake* LA-4
*Ferry Lake* TX-5
Ferry Lake—*lake* GA-3
Ferry Lake—*lake* IL-6
Ferry Lake—*lake* LA-4
Ferry Lake—*lake* WA-9
Ferry Lake—*lake* (3) WI-6
Ferry Lake—*lake* WY-8
Ferry Lake—*locale* GA-3
**Ferry Lake**—*pop pl* LA-4
Ferry Lake Trail—*trail* WA-9
Ferry Landing—*locale* DE-2
Ferry Landing—*locale* GA-3
Ferry Landing—*locale* (2) NC-3
Ferry Lookout Tower—*locale* MI-6
Ferry Neck—*cape* MD-2
Ferry Neck Ch—*church* MD-2
Ferry Newlight Landing—*locale* LA-4
Ferry Office—*locale* NC-3
Ferry Park—*park* OR-9
**Ferry Pass**—*pop pl* FL-3
Ferry Pass Baptist Ch—*church* FL-3
Ferry Pass Bayou—*stream* FL-3
Ferry Pass Elem Sch—*school* FL-3
Ferry Pass MS—*school* FL-3
Ferry Pass Plaza (Shop Ctr)—*locale* FL-3
Ferry Peak—*summit* WA-9
Ferry Place—*hist pl* LA-4
*Ferry Point* CA-9
*Ferry Point* RI-1
Ferry Point—*cape* CA-9
Ferry Point—*cape* CT-1
Ferry Point—*cape* FL-3
Ferry Point—*cape* ME-1
Ferry Point—*cape* (6) MD-2
Ferry Point—*cape* MA-1
Ferry Point—*cape* MO-7
Ferry Point—*cape* NJ-2
Ferry Point—*cape* (2) NC-3
Ferry Point—*cape* SC-3
Ferry Point—*cape* (6) VA-3
Ferry Point—*cliff* CA-9
Ferry Point—*point* MA-1
**Ferry Point**—*pop pl* CT-1
Ferry Point Park—*park* NY-2
**Ferry Road**—*pop pl* MD-2
**Ferry Road Manor**—*pop pl* NJ-2
Ferry Road Park—*park* OR-9
Ferry Rock—*cape* ME-1
Ferry Run—*stream* WV-2
**Ferrysburg**—*pop pl* MI-6
Ferrys Canyon—*valley* NV-8
Ferry Sch—*school* CT-1
Ferry Sch—*school* ME-1
Ferry Sch—*school* (2) MI-6
**Ferry Shores**—*pop pl* AL-4
Ferry Slough—*channel* IA-7
Ferry Spring—*spring* UT-8
Ferry Springs—*spring* OR-9
Ferry Springs—*spring* WI-6
Ferry Springs Canyon—*valley* OR-9
Ferry Station Post Office Bldg—*hist pl* CA-9
Ferry Street Bridge—*bridge* OR-9
*Ferry Swale* AZ-5
Ferry Swale—*valley* AZ-5
Ferry Swale Canyon—*valley* AZ-5
**Ferry Township**—*pop pl* ND-7
**Ferry (Township of)**—*pop pl* MI-6
**Ferry View Heights**—*pop pl* CT-1
**Ferry Village**—*pop pl* NY-2
**Ferryville**—*pop pl* WI-6
Fersenden School, The—*school* MA-1
**Fersners**—*pop pl* SC-3
Ferson Creek—*stream* IL-6
Ferster Gap—*gap* PA-2
Ferteg Creek—*stream* WA-9
Fertig Cem—*cemetery* IN-6
Fertig Cem—*cemetery* KS-7
Fertig Draw—*valley* WY-8
**Fertigs**—*pop pl* PA-2
Fertigs Gospel Tabernacle—*church* PA-2
Fertigs Post Office (historical)—*building* PA-2
**Fertile**—*pop pl* IA-7
**Fertile**—*pop pl* MN-6
**Fertile**—*pop pl* MO-7
Fertile Township—*fmr MCD* IA-7
**Fertile Township**—*pop pl* (2) ND-7
Fertile Valley—*valley* WA-9
Fertile Valley Creek—*stream* OR-9
Fertile Valley Dam—*dam* ND-7
**Fertile Valley Township**—*pop pl* ND-7
**Fertility**—*pop pl* PA-2
Fertility Post Office (historical)—*building* PA-2
Fertilla (Ruins)—*locale* CA-9
Fertitta Lake—*reservoir* TX-5
Fescue Creek—*stream* WY-8
Fescue Ridge—*ridge* MT-8
*Fesefang* FM-9
Fesenmaier, Bernard, House—*hist pl* MN-6
**Fessenden**—*pop pl* FL-3
**Fessenden**—*pop pl* ND-7
Fessenden, Reginald A., House—*hist pl* MA-1
Fessenden Branch—*stream* TX-5
Fessenden Cem—*cemetery* ME-1
Fessenden Dam—*dam* ND-7
Fessenden Hill—*summit* ME-1
Fessenden HS—*school* FL-3
Fessenden Ledge—*bar* ME-1
*Fessenden Shoals* ME-1
Fesser Cem—*cemetery* OK-5
Fessey Hollow—*valley* TN-4
Fess Hotel—*hist pl* WI-6
Fessland Lake—*lake* MN-6
Fessler Cem—*cemetery* IN-6
Fessler Cem—*cemetery* IA-7
Fessler Creek—*stream* MT-8
Fessler Spring—*spring* MT-8
Fessler Springs—*spring* MT-8
Fester Hollow—*valley* PA-2
Festerling Mine—*mine* AZ-5
**Festina**—*pop pl* IA-7
Festival, The (Shop Ctr)—*locale* FL-3
Festo Lake—*lake* WY-8
Festoon Post Office (historical)—*building* TN-4
Festuca Creek—*stream* MI-6
Festus—*locale* FL-3
Festus—*locale* WV-2
**Festus**—*pop pl* MO-7
Festus (historical)—*locale* AL-4
Festus Jackson Dam—*dam* TN-4
Festus Jackson Lake—*reservoir* TN-4
Festus Memorial Airp—*airport* MO-7
Fetch Ditch—*canal* IN-6
*Fetegaan* FM-9
Feterita—*locale* KS-7
**Fetherolfsville**—*pop pl* PA-2
Fetherolfsville Bridge—*bridge* PA-2
Fetid Creek—*stream* IN-6
Fetke Lake—*lake* WI-6
**Fetner**—*pop pl* NC-3
Feton Park—*park* ND-7
Fetrow Cem—*cemetery* PA-2
Fetser Cem—*cemetery* AR-4
*Fetteman Creek* WY-8
Fetterhoff Ch—*church* PA-2
Fetterling Cem—*cemetery* OH-6
Fetterman—*locale* WY-8
**Fetterman**—*pop pl* WV-2
Fetterman Creek—*stream* WY-8
Fetterman Monmt—*park* WY-8
*Fettermans Creek* PA-2
Fetter Pond—*lake* PA-2
Fetter Ranch—*locale* MT-8
*Fetters* IN-6
Fetter Sch—*school* PA-2
Fetters Construction Airp—*airport* PA-2
**Fetters Hot Springs**—*pop pl* CA-9
Fetters Hot Springs-Agua Caliente—*CDP* CA-9
Fetters Lake—*lake* MN-6
Fetters Martin Ditch—*canal* IN-6
Fetters Run—*stream* OH-6
Fetters Trail—*trail* MT-8
**Fetterville**—*pop pl* PA-2
Fetty Sch—*school* WV-2
Fetus Creek—*stream* WA-9
*Fetzer* IL-6
Fetzer—*locale* TX-5
Fetzer Branch—*stream* TN-4
Fetzer Gap—*gap* VA-3
Fetzer Gap Trail—*trail* VA-3
Fetzer Hollow—*valley* PA-2
Fetzer Hollow Camp—*locale* PA-2
**Fetzerton (historical)**—*pop pl* TN-4
Fetzerton Post Office (historical)—*building* TN-4
**Fetzertown**—*pop pl* PA-2
Feucht Lake—*lake* MN-6
Feuchtwanger Stable—*hist pl* NY-2
Feullard Lake—*lake* NY-2
Feullard Mtn—*summit* NY-2
Feullard Vly—*swamp* NY-2
Feuquay Cem—*cemetery* MO-7
Feuquay Elevator—*hist pl* OK-5
**Feura Bush**—*pop pl* NY-2
Feuri Spruyt—*stream* NY-2
Feurt Cem—*cemetery* OH-6
Feurt Hill—*summit* OH-6
Feurt Mounds And Village Site—*hist pl* OH-6
Feurt Mounds and Village Site (Boundary Increase)—*hist pl* OH-6
Feurt Sch (abandoned)—*school* MO-7
Feusier Octagon House—*hist pl* CA-9
Feustal Lake—*lake* WA-9
Feustel, Robert M., House—*hist pl* IN-6
Feutral Cem—*cemetery* AR-4
Feutz Ridge—*ridge* IN-6
Feuz Knob—*summit* KY-4
*Fever Branch* KY-4
*Fever Brook* MA-1
Fever Brook—*stream* MA-1

Fever Hammock—*island* ... FL-3
*Fever River* ... IL-6
*Fever River* ... WI-6
*Fevre River* ... IL-6
*Fevre River* ... WI-6
**Few**—*pop pl* ... NC-3
Few, George, House—*hist pl* ... SD-7
Few Acres Ranch—*locale* ... WY-8
*F.e. Warren Air Force Base* ... WY-8
Few Branch—*stream* ... AR-4
Few Ch—*church* ... AR-4
Few Chapel—*church* ... TN-4
**Few Chapel**—*pop pl* ... TN-4
Few Chapel Cem—*cemetery* ... TN-4
Fewel Cem—*cemetery* (2) ... MO-7
Fewell—*locale* ... OK-5
**Fewell**—*pop pl* ... MS-4
Fewell Cem—*cemetery* ... OK-5
Fewell Island—*island* ... SC-3
Fewell-Reynolds House—*hist pl* ... NC-3
**Fewell Rhoades**—*pop pl* ... IN-6
Fewell Sch—*hist pl* ... OK-5
*Fewemaaraw* ... FM-9
Few Hollow—*valley* ... TN-4
*Fewkes Canyon* ... UT-8
Fewkes Canyon—*valley* ... CO-8
Fewkes Canyon—*valley* ... UT-8
Fewkes Group Archeol Site—*hist pl* ... TN-4
Few Lake—*reservoir* ... NC-3
Few Lake Dam—*dam* ... NC-3
Fewlass Lake—*lake* ... MI-6
Fewless Creek—*stream* ... OH-6
Fews Chapel—*church* ... SC-3
Fews Chapel Sch (historical)—*school* ... TN-4
Fewsmith Memorial Ch—*church* ... NJ-2
Fews Sch—*school* ... AL-4
*Fewukanaw* ... FM-9
*Fewurupw* ... FM-9
*Fewuwar* ... FM-9
*Fewy Rop* ... TX-5
Fey Coulee—*valley* ... MT-8
Feye Archeol Site—*hist pl* ... NE-7
Feyer County Park—*park* ... OR-9
*Feyin* ... FM-9
*Feyinif* ... FM-9
Fey Lakes—*lake* ... MT-8
**Feylers Corner**—*pop pl* ... ME-1
Fey Mill—*locale* ... NY-2
*Feyor* ... FM-9
Fey Ranch, A—*locale* ... MT-8
Fey Sch—*school* ... IL-6
Feys Grove—*locale* ... PA-2
Fez Creek—*stream* ... WV-2
Fezip Creek—*stream* ... ID-8
Fez Sch—*school* ... WV-2
FFA Youth Center Dam Number 1—*dam* ... IN-6
FFA Youth Lake—*reservoir* ... IN-6
F F Creek—*stream* ... WY-8
F Four Ditch—*canal* ... MT-8
F G B Lateral—*canal* ... CO-8
F Genzler Dam—*dam* ... SD-7
F Gibson Ranch—*locale* ... NE-7
F Gillick—*locale* ... TX-5
F G Lateral—*canal* ... CO-8
F Goicoechea Ranch—*locale* ... NV-8
F Hanna Ranch—*locale* ... NE-7
F Haugen Ranch—*locale* ... ND-7
F Henderson Ranch—*locale* ... NE-7
F Hinton Ranch—*locale* ... NE-7
F H Morgan Lake—*reservoir* ... AL-4
F H Morgan Lake Dam—*dam* ... AL-4
F Houston Mcilvain Dam—*dam* ... PA-2
F H Tank—*reservoir* ... AZ-5
FH-three Tank—*reservoir* ... AZ-5
Fiander Lake—*lake* ... WA-9
Fiasco Lake—*lake* ... AK-9
Fiat—*locale* ... KS-7
Fiat—*locale* ... OH-6
**Fiat**—*pop pl* ... IN-6
Fiat Branch—*stream* ... GA-3
*Fiatt* ... IN-6
**Fiatt**—*pop pl* ... IL-6
Fiatt Cem—*cemetery* ... IL-6
Fiberboard Lake—*reservoir* ... TX-5
Fiber Industies Water Supply Dam—*dam* ... NC-3
Fiber Industies Water Supply Lake—*reservoir* ... NC-3
Fiber King Mine—*mine* ... AZ-5
Fiber Lake—*reservoir* ... NC-3
Fiber Lake Dam—*dam* ... NC-3
**Fiberloid (subdivision)**—*pop pl* ... MA-1
*Fiberoid* ... MA-1
**Fiberton**—*pop pl* ... NC-3
Fiberville—*uninc pl* ... NC-3
Fibles Run—*stream* ... KY-4
Fiborn Pond—*lake* ... MI-6
Fibre—*locale* ... MI-6
Fibre Creek—*stream* ... OR-9
Fibre Rock—*summit* ... OR-9
**Fibreville**—*pop pl* ... NC-3
Fical Cem—*cemetery* ... NY-2
Fical Corners—*locale* ... NY-2
*Ficay Creek* ... CA-9
Fice Cem—*cemetery* ... AL-4
Fice Creek—*stream* ... MS-4
*Fichbine* ... ND-7
Ficher Ditch—*canal* ... IN-6
Ficht Cem—*cemetery* ... IL-6
Fichter Canyon—*valley* ... OR-9
*Ficht Pond* ... PA-2
Fickas Cem—*cemetery* ... MO-7
Fick Cove—*bay* ... AK-9
Fick Creek—*stream* ... OR-9
Ficke Block—*hist pl* ... IA-7
Fickels Hill—*summit* ... PA-2
Ficken's Warehouse—*hist pl* ... NJ-2
Fickes Field—*park* ... PA-2
Fickes Sch—*school* ... PA-2
Fickett Creek—*stream* ... AK-9
Fickett Glacier—*glacier* ... AK-9
Fickett Point—*cape* ... ME-1
Fickey Run—*stream* ... WV-2
**Fickle**—*pop pl* ... IN-6
Fickle Cem—*cemetery* ... VA-3
Fickle Hill—*summit* (2) ... CA-9
Fickle Lake—*lake* ... WI-6
Ficklen, E. B., House—*hist pl* ... NC-3
Ficklen Ch—*church* ... GA-3
Fickler Creek—*stream* ... MT-8
Fickler Ranch—*locale* ... MT-8
Fickles Corner—*locale* ... NY-2
Fickles Island (historical)—*island* ... TN-4
Ficklin—*locale* ... GA-3
**Ficklin**—*pop pl* ... IL-6
Ficklin-Crawford Cottage—*hist pl* ... VA-3
Ficklin Fork—*stream* ... KY-4
*Fickling* ... GA-3
Fickling Branch—*stream* ... AL-4
*Fickling Creek* ... AL-4
Fickling Creek—*stream* ... SC-3
Fickling Mill—*locale* ... GA-3
*Ficklings Mill* ... GA-3
**Ficklings Mill**—*pop pl* ... GA-3
Ficklings Sch—*school* ... TX-5
Ficklin Island—*island* ... LA-4
Ficklin Knob—*summit* ... KY-4
Ficklin Lake—*lake* ... LA-4
Ficklin Sch—*school* ... VA-3
*Ficklins Mill* ... GA-3
Fick Point—*cape* ... ID-8
*Fiction Creek* ... MT-8
Fiction Creek—*stream* ... MT-8
**Fidalgo**—*pop pl* ... WA-9
Fidalgo Bay—*bay* ... WA-9
Fidalgo Head—*cliff* ... WA-9
Fidalgo Island—*island* ... WA-9
Fidalgo Sch—*school* ... WA-9
**Fiday View**—*pop pl* ... IL-6
*Fidbury Branch* ... DE-2
Fiddleback Ranch—*locale* ... WY-8
Fiddleback Rsvr—*reservoir* ... WY-8
Fiddle Bow—*locale* ... KY-4
Fiddle Box Spring—*spring* ... WA-9
*Fiddle Branch* ... DE-2
*Fiddle Creek* ... AL-4
Fiddle Creek—*stream* ... CA-9
Fiddle Creek—*stream* (2) ... ID-8
Fiddle Creek—*stream* ... IA-7
Fiddle Creek—*stream* ... MN-6
Fiddle Creek—*stream* ... MO-7
Fiddle Creek—*stream* ... MT-8
Fiddle Creek—*stream* ... OR-9
Fiddle Creek—*stream* ... SD-7
Fiddle Creek—*stream* ... WA-9
Fiddle Creek Camp—*locale* ... MO-7
Fiddle Creek Camp Ground—*locale* ... CA-9
Fiddle Creek Dam—*dam* ... SD-7
Fiddle Creek Rapids—*rapids* ... ID-8
Fiddle Creek Ridge—*ridge* ... CA-9
Fiddle Creek Rsvr—*reservoir* ... SD-7
Fiddle Head—*island* ... ME-1
Fiddlehead Island—*island* ... ME-1
Fiddle Head Rock—*rock* ... MA-1
Fiddle Lake—*lake* ... ID-8
Fiddle Lake—*lake* ... MI-6
Fiddle Lake—*lake* ... MN-6
Fiddle Lake—*lake* ... PA-2
Fiddle Lake—*lake* ... WI-6
Fiddle Lake Creek—*stream* ... PA-2
Fiddle Pond—*lake* ... SC-3
Fiddle Pond Creek—*stream* ... SC-3
Fiddle Prairie—*flat* ... CA-9
Fiddler Bridge—*other* ... IL-6
Fiddler Butte—*summit* ... UT-8
Fiddler Camp Spring—*spring* ... AZ-5
*Fiddler Canyon* ... UT-8
Fiddler Cove—*basin* ... UT-8
Fiddler Cove Canyon—*valley* ... UT-8
*Fiddler Creek* ... CA-9
*Fiddler Creek* ... ID-8
Fiddler Creek—*stream* ... CO-8
Fiddler Creek—*stream* ... LA-4
Fiddler Creek—*stream* ... MT-8
Fiddler Creek—*stream* ... VA-3
Fiddler Creek—*stream* ... WY-8
Fiddler Creek Oil Field—*oilfield* ... WY-8
Fiddler Ditch—*canal* ... IN-6
*Fiddler Elbow* ... NY-2
**Fiddlergreen**—*pop pl* ... PA-2
Fiddler Green Canal—*canal* ... CA-9
Fiddler Gulch—*valley* ... CA-9
Fiddler Gulch—*valley* ... MT-8
Fiddler Gulch—*valley* ... OR-9
Fiddler Hollow—*valley* ... TX-5
Fiddler Island—*island* ... ME-1
Fiddler Ledge—*bar* ... ME-1
Fiddler Mtn—*summit* ... OR-9
Fiddler Peak—*summit* ... CO-8
Fiddler Point—*cape* ... LA-4
Fiddler Reach—*channel* ... ME-1
Fiddler Ridge—*ridge* ... CO-8
Fiddlers Bluff—*cliff* ... WA-9
Fiddlers Branch—*stream* ... TN-4
Fiddlers Bridge—*bridge* ... DE-2
Fiddlers Bridge—*bridge* ... VA-3
**Fiddlersburg**—*pop pl* ... MD-2
Fiddlers Canyon—*valley* ... UT-8
Fiddlers Canyon Sch—*school* ... UT-8
Fiddlers Cove—*cove* ... MA-1
*Fiddlers Creek* ... CA-9
*Fiddlers Creek* ... SC-3
Fiddlers Creek—*stream* ... AR-4
Fiddlers Creek—*stream* ... KY-4
Fiddlers Creek—*stream* ... MS-4
Fiddlers Creek—*stream* ... NE-7
Fiddlers Creek—*stream* ... NJ-2
Fiddlers Creek—*stream* ... NC-3
Fiddlers Creek—*stream* ... OK-5
Fiddlers Creek—*stream* ... SC-3
Fiddlers Creek—*stream* ... WY-8
Fiddlers Draw—*valley* ... NM-5
Fiddlers Elbow—*cape* ... NY-2
Fiddlers Elbow Country Club—*airport* ... NJ-2
Fiddlers Ford—*locale* ... MO-7
Fiddlers Green—*basin* ... UT-8
Fiddlers Green—*flat* ... CA-9
Fiddlers Green—*flat* ... UT-8
Fiddlers Green—*locale* ... CA-9
Fiddlers Green—*locale* ... PA-2
**Fiddlers Green**—*pop pl* ... PA-2
Fiddlers Green Dam—*dam* ... MA-1
Fiddlers Green Rsvr—*reservoir* ... WY-8
Fiddlers Green Sch—*school* ... WI-6
Fiddlers Hell—*valley* ... OR-9
Fiddlers Hollow—*valley* ... TN-4
Fiddlers Hollow—*valley* ... UT-8
Fiddlers Island—*island* ... GA-3
*Fiddlers Lake* ... NY-2
Fiddlers Lake—*lake* ... LA-4
Fiddlers Lake—*lake* ... WY-8
Fiddlers Lake Campground—*locale* ... WY-8
Fiddlers Lake Gas Field—*oilfield* ... LA-4
*Fiddler South Fork* ... NC-3
Fiddlers Point—*cape* (2) ... FL-3
Fiddler Spring—*spring* ... MO-7
Fiddler Springs—*spring* ... NM-5
Fiddlers Run—*stream* ... NC-3
Fiddlers Run—*stream* (2) ... PA-2
Fiddlers Sail—*lake* ... MS-4
*Fiddlers South Fork* ... NC-3
Fiddlers Spring—*spring* ... CA-9
Fiddlertown Sch—*school* ... NY-2
**Fiddlesburg**—*pop pl* ... MD-2
Fiddle Springs—*spring* ... MO-7
Fiddle Springs Hollow—*valley* ... MO-7
Fiddlestring Bay—*swamp* ... FL-3
Fiddletown—*hist pl* ... CA-9
Fiddletown—*locale* ... PA-2
**Fiddletown**—*pop pl* ... CA-9
Fiddock Sch—*school* ... VT-1
Fiddyment Creek—*stream* ... IL-6
Fidel Brothers Irrigation Rsvr—*reservoir* ... OR-9
Fidel Brothers Irrigation Rsvr Dike—*dam* ... OR-9
**Fidele**—*pop pl* ... GA-3
Fidelio—*locale* ... KY-4
Fidelis—*locale* ... FL-3
Fidelis Cem—*cemetery* ... FL-3
Fidelis Ch—*church* ... FL-3
*Fidelity* ... IN-6
Fidelity—*locale* ... KY-4
Fidelity—*other* ... OH-6
**Fidelity**—*pop pl* ... IL-6
**Fidelity**—*pop pl* (2) ... KS-7
**Fidelity**—*pop pl* ... MO-7
Fidelity—*uninc pl* ... PA-2
Fidelity Branch—*stream* ... MO-7
Fidelity Cem—*cemetery* ... MO-7
Fidelity Ch—*church* ... NC-3
Fidelity Ch (historical)—*church* ... AL-4
Fidelity Gulch—*valley* ... ID-8
Fidelity Island—*island* ... TX-5
Fidelity Manor Sch—*school* ... TX-5
Fidelity Mine—*mine* ... CO-8
Fidelity Mine (underground)—*mine* ... AL-4
Fidelity Mutual Life Insurance Company Bldg—*hist pl* ... PA-2
Fidelity-Philadelphia Trust Company Bldg—*hist pl* ... PA-2
**Fidelity (Township of)**—*pop pl* ... IL-6
Fidelity Trust Bldg—*hist pl* ... IN-6
Fidelle—*locale* ... GA-3
Fidel Rsvr—*reservoir* ... OR-9
Fidel Windmill—*locale* ... AZ-5
Fidilly Top—*summit* ... NC-3
*Fidler Creek* ... WY-8
Fidler Creek—*stream* ... CA-9
Fidler Creek—*stream* ... OR-9
*Fidler Run* ... PA-2
Fidlers Bend—*bend* ... OK-5
*Fidlers Creek* ... PA-2
Fidler Springs—*spring* ... OR-9
Fidlers Run—*stream* ... PA-2
Fiducia Ch—*church* ... TN-4
Fiebelman Cem—*cemetery* ... MO-7
Fiebing, J. H., House—*hist pl* ... WI-6
Fiebing, Otto F., House—*hist pl* ... WI-6
Fiechter, John, House—*hist pl* ... OR-9
Fie Creek—*stream* ... NC-3
**Fiedler**—*pop pl* ... PA-2
Fiedler, Henry, House—*hist pl* ... WI-6
Fiedler Cem—*cemetery* ... IA-7
Fiedler Creek—*stream* ... CA-9
Fiedler Sch—*school* ... IA-7
Fiedler Sch—*school* ... MI-6
Fiegel Point—*cape* ... NY-2
Fiegel Sch—*school* ... MI-6
Fiege Rsvr—*reservoir* ... CA-9
Fiehler Sch—*school* ... MO-7
*Field* ... MO-7
Field—*locale* ... CA-9
Field—*locale* ... NM-5
Field, Albert, Tack Company—*hist pl* ... MA-1
Field, Eugene, House—*hist pl* ... CO-8
Field, Eugene, House—*hist pl* ... MO-7
Field, John, House—*hist pl* ... KY-4
Field, Marshall, III, Estate—*hist pl* ... NY-2
Field, Mount—*summit* ... MT-8
Field, Thomas M., House—*hist pl* ... CO-8
Field, Walter, House—*hist pl* ... OH-6
**Fieldale**—*pop pl* ... VA-3
Fieldale-Collinsville HS—*school* ... VA-3
Field and Tule Club—*locale* ... CA-9
*Field Bay* ... VT-1
Field Bay—*swamp* ... FL-3
Field Bayou—*stream* ... AR-4
Field Bayou Ditch—*canal* ... AR-4
Field Branch—*stream* (3) ... KY-4
Field Branch—*stream* ... LA-4
Field Branch—*stream* (2) ... NC-3
Field Branch—*stream* ... TX-5
Field Branch—*stream* ... WV-2
Field Branch Cem—*cemetery* ... KY-4
*Field Brook* ... MA-1
**Fieldbrook**—*pop pl* ... CA-9
Field Brook—*stream* ... PA-2
Fieldbrook Sch—*school* ... CA-9
Field Campsite—*locale* ... ME-1
*Field Canyon* ... AZ-5
Field Canyon Spring—*spring* ... AZ-5
Field Cem—*cemetery* ... IN-6
Field Cem—*cemetery* ... IA-7
Field Cem—*cemetery* (3) ... KY-4
Field Cem—*cemetery* ... ME-1
Field Cem—*cemetery* ... MA-1
Field Cem—*cemetery* ... MO-7
Field Cem—*cemetery* ... NJ-2
Field Cem—*cemetery* ... NM-5
Field Cem—*cemetery* ... NC-3
Field Cem—*cemetery* ... SC-3
Field Cem—*cemetery* ... TN-4
Field Cem—*cemetery* ... TX-5
Field Circle Interchange—*locale* ... TX-5
Field Club Sch—*school* ... NE-7
**Field Corners**—*pop pl* ... NY-2
Field Coulee—*valley* ... MT-8
*Field Creek* ... OR-9
*Field Creek* ... TX-5
*Field Creek* ... VA-3
Field Creek—*locale* ... TX-5
Field Creek—*stream* ... AR-4
Field Creek—*stream* ... CO-8
Field Creek—*stream* (2) ... ID-8
Field Creek—*stream* ... IN-6
Field Creek—*stream* ... MS-4
Field Creek—*stream* ... MT-8
Field Creek—*stream* (2) ... OR-9
Field Creek—*stream* ... TN-4
Field Creek—*stream* ... TX-5
Field Creek—*stream* ... WA-9
Field Creek Cem—*cemetery* ... AR-4
Field Creek Ch—*church* ... AR-4
Field Creek Rsvr—*reservoir* ... OR-9
*Fieldcrest* ... IL-6
*Field Crest* ... WV-2
**Fieldcrest**—*pop pl* ... IN-6
**Field Crest**—*pop pl* ... TN-4
**Fieldcrest**—*pop pl* ... WV-2
Fieldcrest Ch—*church* ... NC-3
**Field Crest Estates**—*pop pl* ... CT-1
Field (Crockett)—*locale* ... KY-4
**Field Crossing**—*pop pl* ... NY-2
Field Dam—*reservoir* ... AZ-5
Field Doughery Ditch—*canal* ... MT-8
Field Drain—*canal* ... CA-9
Field Draw—*valley* ... TX-5
Field Draw—*valley* ... WY-8
Field Elem Sch—*school* ... AZ-5
Field Elem Sch—*school* ... KS-7
Fielden—*locale* ... KY-4
Fielden Cem—*cemetery* ... TN-4
Fielden Sch (historical)—*school* ... TN-4
Fielden Store—*locale* ... TN-4
Fielder Bottom (historical)—*bend* ... SD-7
Fielder Branch—*stream* ... TN-4
Fielder Cem—*cemetery* (2) ... TN-4
Fielder Cem—*cemetery* ... TX-5
Fielder Chapel—*church* ... TX-5
Fielder Creek—*stream* ... OR-9
Fielder Creek—*stream* ... SD-7
*Fielder Ferry* ... AL-4
Fielder Hollow—*valley* ... OH-6
Fielder Hollow—*valley* (2) ... TN-4
Fielder House—*hist pl* ... AR-4
Fielder Lake—*reservoir* ... GA-3
*Fielder Mountain* ... AL-4
Fielder Mtn—*summit* ... OR-9
Fielder Park—*park* (2) ... TX-5
Fielder Post Office (historical)—*building* ... SD-7
Fielder Ridge—*ridge* ... AL-4
Fielder Road Ch—*church* ... TX-5
Fielders Branch—*stream* ... TN-4
Fielders Cem—*cemetery* ... KY-4
Fielder Spring—*spring* (2) ... TN-4
Field Estate—*hist pl* ... FL-3
Field Fifteen Well (windmill)—*locale* ... TX-5
*Field Fork* ... WV-2
Field Fourteen Well (windmill)—*locale* ... TX-5
Field Hill—*summit* ... MA-1
Field Hill—*summit* ... RI-1
Field Hollow—*valley* (2) ... MO-7
Field Hollow—*valley* ... NY-2
Field Hollow—*valley* ... OK-5
Field Hollow—*valley* ... TN-4
Field Hollow—*valley* ... VA-3
Field Hollow—*valley* ... WV-2
Fieldhouse Cut—*gap* ... WY-8
Fielding—*locale* ... IA-7
**Fielding**—*pop pl* ... UT-8
Fielding Airp—*airport* ... WA-9
Fielding Cem—*cemetery* ... AL-4
Fielding City Cem—*cemetery* ... UT-8
Fielding Coal Creek Fire Trail—*trail* ... MT-8
Fielding Coal Creek Trail—*trail* ... MT-8
Fielding Coulee—*valley* ... MT-8
Fielding Garr Ranch—*hist pl* ... UT-8
Fielding Guard Station—*locale* ... MT-8
Fielding Lake—*lake* ... AK-9
Fielding Mtn—*summit* ... VA-3
Fielding Patrol Cabin—*locale* ... MT-8
Fielding Sch—*school* ... NJ-2
Fielding Sch—*school* ... UT-8
*Fielding School* ... TN-4
*Fieldings Corners* ... PA-2
Fieldings Grove Ch—*church* ... GA-3
Fielding Siding—*locale* ... UT-8
Fielding Snowshoe Patrol Cabin—*hist pl* ... MT-8
Fielding Springs Ch—*church* ... GA-3
**Fielding Station**—*pop pl* ... UT-8
Fielding Windmill—*locale* ... TX-5
Field Island—*island* ... TN-4
Field Kindley Memorial HS—*school* ... KS-7
Field Lake—*lake* ... AR-4
Field Lake—*lake* ... MN-6
Field Lake—*lake* ... TX-5
Field Lake—*swamp* ... LA-4
Field Lark Branch—*stream* ... VA-3
Field Memorial Community Hosp—*hospital* ... MS-4
**Fieldmore Springs**—*pop pl* ... PA-2
Field Mtn—*summit* ... AR-4
Field Museum of Natural History—*hist pl* ... IL-6
**Fieldon**—*pop pl* ... IL-6
Fieldon Hollow—*valley* ... IL-6
**Fieldon (Township of)**—*pop pl* ... MN-6
Field Park—*park* ... TX-5
Field Park—*park* ... WI-6
Field Park Sch—*school* ... IL-6
Field Pasture Windmill—*locale* ... TX-5
Field Plantation (historical)—*locale* ... MS-4
*Field Point* ... NC-3
*Field Point* ... RI-1
Field Point—*cape* ... CT-1
Field Point—*cape* ... ME-1
Field Point—*cape* ... MI-6
Field Pond—*lake* ... AZ-5
Field Pond—*reservoir* ... MA-1
Field Pond Branch—*stream* ... TN-4
Field Pond Dam—*dam* ... MA-1
Field Ranch—*locale* ... CO-8
Field Ranch—*locale* (3) ... NM-5
Field Ranch—*locale* ... TX-5
Field Ranch—*locale* ... WY-8
Field Rocks—*bar* ... MA-1
**Field (RR name Crockett)**—*pop pl* ... KY-4
*Fields* ... OH-6
Fields—*locale* ... NC-3
Fields—*locale* ... OR-9
**Fields**—*pop pl* ... GA-3
**Fields**—*pop pl* ... IN-6
**Fields**—*pop pl* ... LA-4
**Fields**—*pop pl* ... MT-8
**Fields**—*pop pl* ... OH-6
**Fields**—*pop pl* ... OR-9
Fields, Lake—*lake* ... LA-4
Fields, Timothy, House—*hist pl* ... KY-4
Fields, William, House—*hist pl* ... NC-3
Fields Barn—*hist pl* ... IA-7
Fields Basin—*basin* ... OR-9
Fields Basin Seep Rsvr—*reservoir* ... OR-9
Fields Bay—*bay* ... VT-1
Fields Bayou—*stream* ... TX-5
Fieldsboro—*locale* ... DE-2
**Fieldsboro**—*pop pl* ... NJ-2
**Fieldsboro**—*pop pl* ... NC-3
*Fieldsborough* ... DE-2
*Fieldsborough* ... NJ-2
Fields Branch—*stream* ... FL-3
Fields Branch—*stream* ... GA-3
Fields Branch—*stream* (2) ... KY-4
Fields Bridge—*bridge* ... NH-1
Fields Bridge—*bridge* ... OR-9
*Fields Brook* ... PA-2
Fields Brook—*stream* ... ME-1
Fields Brook—*stream* ... NY-2
Fields Brook—*stream* ... OH-6
Fields Brook—*stream* ... WV-2
Fields Campsite—*locale* ... ME-1
Fields Canyon—*valley* ... TX-5
Fields Cem—*cemetery* ... AR-4
Fields Cem—*cemetery* (2) ... IL-6
Fields Cem—*cemetery* ... LA-4
Fields Cem—*cemetery* ... MO-7
Fields Cem—*cemetery* ... NC-3
Fields Cem—*cemetery* ... OH-6
Fields Cem—*cemetery* (3) ... OK-5
Fields Cem—*cemetery* ... SC-3
Fields Cem—*cemetery* (2) ... TN-4
Fields Cem—*cemetery* (2) ... TX-5
Fields Cem—*cemetery* (4) ... VA-3
Fields Cem—*cemetery* (2) ... WV-2
Fields Cemeteries—*cemetery* ... TN-4
*Field Sch* ... IN-6
Fields Ch—*church* ... IL-6
Fields Ch—*church* ... VA-3
Field Sch—*school* (3) ... CA-9
Field Sch—*school* ... CO-8
Field Sch—*school* (3) ... IL-6
Field Sch—*school* ... IN-6
Field Sch—*school* (2) ... KS-7
Field Sch—*school* ... KY-4
Field Sch—*school* (2) ... MI-6
Field Sch—*school* (2) ... MN-6
Field Sch—*school* (2) ... MO-7
Field Sch—*school* ... NE-7
Field Sch—*school* ... NJ-2
Field Sch—*school* ... OH-6
Field Sch—*school* ... SD-7
Field Sch—*school* (3) ... TX-5
Field Sch—*school* ... WA-9
Fields Chapel—*church* ... GA-3
Fields Chapel—*church* ... OK-5
Fields Chapel—*church* ... TX-5
Field Sch (historical)—*school* ... MS-4
*Field School* ... KS-7
*Field School* ... MS-4
Fields Corner Municipal Bldg—*hist pl* ... MA-1
**Fields Corner (subdivision)**—*pop pl* ... MA-1
*Fields Creek* ... UT-8
Fields Creek—*stream* ... MO-7
Fields Creek—*stream* (3) ... OR-9
Fields Creek—*stream* ... TX-5
Fields Creek—*stream* (2) ... WV-2
Fields Creek Cem—*cemetery* ... MO-7
Fields Creek Sch—*school* ... MO-7
Fields Creek Township—*civil* ... MO-7
Fields Crossroads—*locale* ... GA-3
Fields Crossroads—*locale* ... VA-3
Fields Cut—*channel* ... SC-3
Fields Draw—*valley* (2) ... WY-8
Fields Family Cem—*cemetery* ... MS-4
Fields Ferry (historical)—*locale* ... MS-4
Fields Fork—*stream* ... KY-4
Fields Gap—*gap* ... GA-3
Fields Gap—*gap* ... VA-3
Fields Gulch—*valley* (2) ... MT-8
Fields Gulch—*valley* ... WA-9
Fields Heirs—*hist pl* ... DE-2
*Fields Hill* ... MA-1
*Fields Hill* ... RI-1
Fields Hill—*summit* ... ME-1
Fields Hill Cem—*cemetery* ... ME-1
Fields (historical)—*locale* ... AL-4
Fields Hollow—*valley* ... MO-7
Fields Hollow—*valley* ... TN-4
Fieldside Sch—*school* ... NE-7
Fields Island—*island* ... WI-6
Fields Lake—*lake* ... FL-3
Fields Lake—*lake* ... MN-6
Fields Lake—*lake* ... MS-4
Fields Lake—*lake* ... TX-5
Fields Lake—*lake* ... WA-9
Fields Lake—*reservoir* ... AL-4
Fields Lake—*reservoir* ... TX-5
Fields Landing—*locale* ... GA-3
**Fields Landing**—*pop pl* ... CA-9
*Fields Landing Channel* ... CA-9
**Fields Landing (South Bay)**—*pop pl* ... CA-9
Fields Lookout Tower—*locale* ... LA-4
**Fields of the Wood**—*pop pl* ... NC-3
Fields Oil Field—*oilfield* ... LA-4
Fields Oil Field—*oilfield* ... TX-5
**Fieldson Crossroad**—*pop pl* ... PA-2
**Fieldsons Crossroads**—*pop pl* ... PA-2
Fields Peak—*summit* ... OR-9
Fields Place-Vickery House—*hist pl* ... GA-3
Fields Playground—*park* ... MI-6
Fields Point—*cape* ... ME-1
Fields Point—*cape* ... RI-1
Fields Point—*cape* ... SC-3
*Fields Pond* ... PA-2
Fields Pond—*lake* ... ME-1
Field Spring—*spring* ... OR-9
Fields Prospect—*mine* ... UT-8
Fields Ranch—*locale* ... TX-5
Fields Ridge—*ridge* ... CA-9
Fields Rsvr—*reservoir* ... MT-8
Fields Rsvrs—*reservoir* ... OR-9
Fields Run—*stream* ... PA-2
Fields Run—*stream* ... VA-3
Fields Run Trail—*trail* ... PA-2
Fields Sch—*school* ... AL-4
Fields Sch—*school* ... AR-4
Fields Sch—*school* ... TN-4
Fields Settlement—*locale* ... NY-2
Fields Settlement Cem—*cemetery* ... NY-2
Fields Spring—*spring* ... AZ-5
Fields Spring—*spring* ... WA-9
Fields Spring State Park—*park* ... WA-9
Fields Station—*locale* ... PA-2
**Fields Station**—*pop pl* ... IN-6
Fields Tank—*reservoir* ... AZ-5
Field Station Lake—*reservoir* ... OK-5
**Fields Terrace**—*pop pl* ... OH-6
**Fieldston**—*pop pl* ... MA-1
Fieldston—*uninc pl* ... NY-2
*Fieldstone* ... MA-1
**Fieldstone**—*pop pl* ... NJ-2
Fieldstone Ch—*church* ... MO-7
Fieldstone Lake—*lake* ... FL-3
Fieldston Lake—*lake* ... NY-2
Fieldston Sch—*school* ... NY-2
Fieldstown—*locale* ... VA-3
**Fieldstown**—*pop pl* ... AL-4
Fieldstown Ch—*church* ... AL-4
**Fieldstream (subdivision)**—*pop pl* ... NC-3
Fieldsville—*locale* ... VT-1
Field Tank—*reservoir* ... AZ-5
Field Tank—*reservoir* ... TX-5
**Fieldton**—*pop pl* ... TX-5
**Field Township**—*pop pl* ... ND-7
**Field (Township of)**—*pop pl* ... IL-6
**Field (Township of)**—*pop pl* ... MN-6
Field Tract Campground—*locale* ... NM-5
Field Twelve Windmill—*locale* ... TX-5
Field Twentyfive Windmill—*locale* ... TX-5
**Fieldview**—*pop pl* ... TN-4
**Fieldville**—*pop pl* ... NJ-2
Field Well—*locale* ... NM-5
Field Well—*well* ... NM-5
Field Well—*well* ... TX-5
Field Windmill—*locale* ... NM-5
Field Windmill—*locale* (5) ... TX-5
**Fieldwood Addition (subdivision)**—*pop pl* ... DE-2
*Fieler School* ... IN-6
Fierce (historical)—*locale* ... IA-7
Fierek Lake—*lake* ... WI-6
Fiero, Conro, House—*hist pl* ... OR-9
Fieroe Mill Sch—*school* ... VT-1
Fiero Pond—*lake* ... NY-2
Fiero Truck Trail—*trail* ... MN-6
**Fierro**—*pop pl* ... NM-5
Fierro Cem—*cemetery* ... NM-5
Fierro Hill—*summit* ... NM-5
Fiery Fork—*stream* ... MO-7
Fiery Fork State For—*forest* ... MO-7
Fiery Furnace—*rock* ... UT-8
Fiery Furnace Viewpoint—*locale* ... UT-8
*Fiery Gizzard Creek* ... TN-4
Fiery Gizzard Furnace (historical)—*locale* ... TN-4
Fiery Mtn—*summit* ... ME-1
Fiery Run—*stream* ... VA-3
Fiery Siding—*locale* ... MD-2
**Fies**—*pop pl* ... KY-4
Fieselmann Lateral—*canal* ... ID-8
Fiesta Bay—*bay* ... CA-9
Fiesta Branch—*stream* ... TN-4
Fiesta Gardens—*park* ... TX-5
Fiesta Gardens Sch—*school* ... CA-9
Fiesta Grounds (County Fairgrounds)—*park* ... CA-9
Fiesta Island—*island* ... CA-9
Fiesta Key—*island* ... FL-3
Fiesta Lakes Golf Course—*other* ... AZ-5
Fiesta Mall—*locale* ... AZ-5
Fiesta Park (trailer park)—*locale* ... AZ-5
**Fiesta Park (Trailer Park)**—*pop pl* ... AZ-5
Fiesta Plaza (Shop Ctr)—*locale* ... FL-3
*Fiesta Travel Trailer Park* ... AZ-5
Fiesta Village—*locale* ... FL-3
Fiesta Village at Willow Creek (Shop Ctr)—*locale* ... UT-8
Fiesta Village Shop Ctr—*locale* ... AZ-5
Fiestel Lake—*lake* ... ND-7
Fie Top—*summit* ... NC-3
Fife—*locale* ... ND-7
Fife—*locale* ... TX-5
Fife—*locale* ... VA-3
**Fife**—*pop pl* ... GA-3
**Fife**—*pop pl* ... MT-8
**Fife**—*pop pl* ... WA-9
Fife, Harry E., House—*hist pl* ... OH-6
Fife Bottom—*bend* ... MO-7
Fife Brook—*stream* ... MA-1
*Fife Brook Dam Site* ... MA-1
Fife Canyon—*valley* ... AZ-5
Fife Canyon—*valley* ... NV-8
Fife Canyon—*valley* ... TX-5
Fife Canyon Trail Two Hundred Fiftyeight—*trail* ... AZ-5
Fife Cem—*cemetery* ... AL-4
Fife Cem—*cemetery* ... LA-4
Fife Cem—*cemetery* ... TN-4
Fife Cem—*cemetery* ... TX-5
Fife Cem—*cemetery* ... VA-3
Fife Creek—*stream* ... CA-9
Fife Creek—*stream* (2) ... OK-5
Fife Creek—*stream* ... UT-8
Fife Flat—*flat* ... NV-8
Fife Flat Rsvr—*reservoir* ... NV-8
Fife Fork—*stream* ... KY-4
*Fife-Givens Cem* ... TN-4
**Fife Heights**—*pop pl* ... WA-9
Fife Hill—*summit* ... AR-4
Fife Lake—*lake* ... MI-6
**Fife Lake**—*pop pl* ... MI-6
Fife Lake Lookout Tower—*locale* ... MI-6
Fife Lake Outlet—*stream* ... MI-6
Fife Lake State For—*forest* ... MI-6
**Fife Lake (Township of)**—*pop pl* ... MI-6
Fife Lake-Union District No. 1 Schoolhouse—*hist pl* ... MI-6
Fife Mtn—*summit* ... NV-8
Fife Peak—*summit* ... AZ-5
Fife Ranch—*locale* (2) ... NM-5
Fifer-Cummock Ditch—*canal* ... MT-8
Fifer Gulch—*valley* ... MT-8
*Fife Run* ... PA-2
*Fife's* ... VA-3
Fife Saddle—*gap* ... AZ-5

Fife Sch—*school* MO-7
Fifes Creek—*stream* WA-9
Fife Slough—*stream* AR-4
Fifes Peaks—*summit* WA-9
Fife Spring—*spring* NV-8
Fifes Ridge—*ridge* WA-9
Fifes Ridge Trail—*trail* WA-9
Fifes Shop (historical)—*locale* AL-4
Fife Windmill—*locale* NM-5
Fiffeen Gulch—*valley* AK-9
**Fifficktown**—*pop pl* PA-2
Fifi, Bayou—*channel* LA-4
Fifi Bayou—*stream* LA-4
**Fifield**—*pop pl* WI-6
Fifield Brook—*stream* NH-1
Fifield Cem—*cemetery* MI-6
Fifield Cem—*cemetery* VT-1
Fifield Creek—*stream* MI-6
Fifield Creek—*stream* WI-6
Fifield Hill—*ridge* NH-1
Fifield Hill—*summit* NH-1
Fifield Lookout Tower—*locale* WI-6
Fifield Point—*cape* ME-1
Fifield Pond—*lake* VT-1
Fifield Ranch—*locale* CA-9
Fifield Ridge—*ridge* CA-9
Fifield Town Hall—*hist pl* WI-6
**Fifield (Town of)**—*pop pl* WI-6
Fifi Island—*island* LA-4
Fifteen—*locale* OH-6
Fifteen, Lake—*lake* (4) MI-6
Fifteen, Lake—*lake* MN-6
Fifteen, Lake—*lake* WA-9
Fifteen, Pool—*reservoir* WI-6
Fifteen Ave Sch—*school* NJ-2
Fifteen Creek—*stream* MI-6
Fifteen Creek—*stream* OK-5
Fifteen Creek—*stream* SD-7
Fifteen Creek, Lake—*stream* MI-6
Fifteen Gulch—*valley* AK-9
*Fifteen Lake* WA-9
Fifteen Lake—*lake* WI-6
Fifteenmile Arroyo—*valley* NM-5
*Fifteen Mile Bay* SC-3
Fifteenmile Bay—*swamp* SC-3
Fifteen Mile Bayou—*gut* MS-4
Fifteen Mile Bayou—*stream* AR-4
Fifteen Mile Campground—*park* OR-9
Fifteenmile Canyon—*valley* AZ-5
*Fifteenmile Coleto Creek* TX-5
Fifteenmile Coleto Creek—*stream* TX-5
Fifteenmile Corral—*locale* AZ-5
Fifteenmile Coulee—*valley* MT-8
*Fifteen Mile Creek* PA-2
*Fifteen Mile Creek* TX-5
*Fifteenmile Creek* UT-8
*Fifteen Mile Creek* WY-8
Fifteenmile Creek—*stream* AK-9
Fifteenmile Creek—*stream* GA-3
Fifteenmile Creek—*stream* ID-8
Fifteenmile Creek—*stream* KY-4
Fifteenmile Creek—*stream* MD-2
Fifteenmile Creek—*stream* MS-4
Fifteenmile Creek—*stream* (3) MT-8
Fifteenmile Creek—*stream* OH-6
Fifteenmile Creek—*stream* (3) OR-9
Fifteenmile Creek—*stream* PA-2
Fifteenmile Creek—*stream* SC-3
Fifteenmile Creek—*stream* TX-5
Fifteenmile Creek—*stream* UT-8
Fifteenmile Creek—*stream* VA-3
Fifteenmile Creek—*stream* (2) WA-9
Fifteenmile Creek—*stream* WV-2
Fifteenmile Creek—*stream* WY-8
Fifteenmile Creek Trail—*trail* OR-9
Fifteenmile Draw—*valley* WY-8
Fifteenmile Fork—*stream* WV-2
Fifteen Mile (historical)—*locale* IA-7
Fifteenmile Island—*island* AK-9
Fifteen Mile Island—*island* MS-4
Fifteenmile Knoll—*summit* WY-8
Fifteenmile Knoll Rsvr—*reservoir* WY-8
*Fifteenmile Picnic Ground* OR-9
Fifteenmile Point—*cape* CA-9
Fifteenmile Point—*cliff* UT-8
Fifteenmile Post—*locale* GA-3
Fifteenmile Rsvr Number One—*reservoir* MT-8
Fifteenmile Rsvr Number Two—*reservoir* MT-8
Fifteenmile Shelter—*locale* WA-9
Fifteenmile Siphon—*other* WY-8
Fifteenmile Spring—*spring* MT-8
Fifteenmile Spring—*spring* NV-8
Fifteenmile Spring—*spring* WY-8
Fifteenmile Stream—*stream* ME-1
Fifteenmile Valley—*basin* CA-9
Fifteenmile Well—*well* NV-8
Fifteenmile Well—*well* NM-5
Fifteenmile Windmill—*locale* NM-5
Fifteen Pup—*stream* AK-9
Fifteen Slough—*stream* AR-4
Fifteen Springs—*spring* NM-5
Fifteen Tank—*reservoir* AZ-5
Fifteenth and Allen Streets Shop Ctr—*locale* PA-2
Fifteenth Ave—*post sta* IN-6
Fifteenth Ave Baptist Ch—*church* MS-4
Fifteenth Stream—*stream* ME-1
Fifteenth Street Bridge—*bridge* PA-2
Fifteenth Street Ch of Christ—*church* FL-3
Fifteenth Street Park—*park* AZ-5
Fifteenth Street Sch—*school* AZ-5
Fifteenth Street Sch—*school* CA-9
Fifteenth Street Spring—*spring* PA-2
Fifteen Tree Hill—*summit* MA-1
Fifteen Windmill—*locale* TX-5
Fifth and Lawrence Streets Residential District—*hist pl* OH-6
Fifth and Main Plaza—*locale* KS-7
Fifth Ave Baptist Ch—*church* AL-4
Fifth Ave Baptist Ch—*church* FL-3
Fifth Ave Baptist Ch—*church* TN-4
Fifth Ave Bridge—*bridge* PA-2
Fifth Ave Commercial Buildings—*hist pl* MN-6
Fifth Ave Hist Dist—*hist pl* TN-4
Fifth Ave HS—*hist pl* PA-2
Fifth Ave Methodist Episcopal Ch (historical)—*church* AL-4
Fifth Ave Missionary Baptist Ch—*church* MS-4
Fifth Avenue-Fulton Street Hist Dist—*hist pl* NY-2
Fifth Ave Park—*park* AL-4
Fifth Ave Sch—*school* GA-3
Fifth Ave Sch—*school* KS-7
Fifth Ave Sch—*school* (2) NY-2
Fifth Ave Sch—*school* OH-6
Fifth Ave Shoppes—*locale* FL-3
Fifth Bayou—*gut* MS-4
Fifth Bottom Hollow—*valley* PA-2
Fifth Branch—*stream* SC-3
Fifth Coulee—*valley* MT-8
Fifth Creek—*stream* KS-7
Fifth Creek—*stream* NY-2
Fifth Creek—*stream* NC-3
Fifth Creek—*stream* OR-9
Fifth Creek—*stream* TX-5
Fifth Creek—*stream* WA-9
Fifth Creek—*stream* WY-8
Fifth Creek Ch—*church* NC-3
Fifth Creek Pass—*gap* WA-9
Fifth Creek Pond—*lake* NY-2
Fifth Crow Wing Lake—*lake* MN-6
Fifth Currier Brook—*stream* ME-1
Fifth Currier Pond—*lake* ME-1
Fifth Debsconeag Lake—*lake* ME-1
Fifth District Sch—*school* KY-4
*Fifth District Special Consolidated School* MS-4
Fifth Fork Rock Creek—*stream* ID-8
*Fifth Lake* WI-6
Fifth Lake—*lake* CA-9
Fifth Lake—*lake* CO-8
Fifth Lake—*lake* MI-6
Fifth Lake—*lake* (3) MN-6
Fifth Lake—*lake* (3) NY-2
Fifth Lake—*lake* WI-6
*Fifth Lake Brook* ME-1
Fifth Lake Mtn—*summit* ME-1
Fifth Lake Stream—*stream* ME-1
Fifth Machias Lake—*lake* ME-1
Fifth Maine Regiment Community Center—*hist pl* ME-1
*Fifth Mountain* PA-2
Fifth Musquacook Lake—*lake* ME-1
*Fifth Negro Brook Lake* ME-1
*Fifth Nigger Brook Lake* ME-1
Fifth of July Creek—*stream* AK-9
Fifth of July Mtn—*summit* WA-9
Fifth Peak—*summit* NY-2
Fifth Pelletier Brook—*stream* ME-1
Fifth Pelletier Brook Lake—*lake* ME-1
Fifth Plain Creek—*stream* WA-9
Fifth Pond—*lake* NY-2
Fifth Regiment Armory—*hist pl* MD-2
Fifth Regular Armory—*other* MD-2
Fifth Ridge—*ridge* MT-8
*Fifth Rock* ME-1
Fifth Saint Ch—*church* NC-3
Fifth Saint John Pond—*reservoir* ME-1
*Fifth Siding* ND-7
*Fifth Siding, The* ND-7
Fifth Street Baptist Ch—*church* FL-3
Fifth Street Baptist Ch—*church* (2) MS-4
*Fifth Street Baptist Church* AL-4
Fifth Street Bridge—*hist pl* CO-8
Fifth Street JHS—*school* ME-1
Fifth Street JHS—*school* MS-4
Fifth Street Park—*park* AZ-5
Fifth Street Sch—*school* MO-7
Fifth Street Sch—*school* PA-2
Fifth Street Sch—*school* WI-6
Fifth Street Sch (abandoned)—*school* PA-2
Fifth Street United Methodist Ch—*church* MS-4
**Fifth Ward**—*pop pl* LA-4
Fifth Ward Baptist Ch—*church* TN-4
Fifth Ward Meetinghouse—*hist pl* UT-8
*Fifth Ward Sch* PA-2
Fifth Ward Sch—*hist pl* KY-4
Fifth Ward Sch—*school* LA-4
Fifth Ward Sch—*school* NY-2
Fifth Ward Sch—*school* (3) PA-2
Fifth Ward Sch—*school* WV-2
Fifth Ward Sch (historical)—*school* PA-2
Fifth Ward Wardroom—*hist pl* RI-1
Fifth Water—*summit* UT-8
Fifth Water Creek—*stream* UT-8
Fifth Water Ridge—*ridge* UT-8
Fifthytwo-Inch Telescope—*other* CA-9
Fiftieth Street Baptist Ch—*church* AL-4
**Fiftone**—*pop pl* (2) FL-3
Fifty-cent Branch—*gut* SC-3
Fifty Dollar Bay—*bay* GA-3
Fifty Dollar Spring—*spring* AZ-5
Fiftyeight Branch—*stream* KY-4
Fiftyeight Tank—*reservoir* AZ-5
*Fifty-fifth Street* IL-6
Fifty-fifty Hill—*summit* NM-5
Fifty-five Ranch—*locale* WY-8
Fiftyfive Street Sch—*school* WI-6
Fiftyfive Tank—*reservoir* AZ-5
Fiftyfive Well—*well* TX-5
Fiftyfoot Falls—*falls* AZ-5
*Fiftyfour* TN-4
Fifty-four Cem—*cemetery* IN-6
Fifty-Four Cem—*cemetery* MD-2
Fiftyfour Creek—*stream* MT-8
Fiftyfour Pond—*lake* MI-6
Fifty-Fourth Ave Sch—*school* FL-3
Fiftyfourth Street Ch of God—*church* AL-4
Fifty-Fourth Street Sch—*school* CA-9
Fifty-Fourth Street Sch—*school* NJ-2
**Fifty Lakes**—*pop pl* MN-6
Fifty Lakes Post Office—*building* MN-6
Fiftymile Bench—*bench* UT-8
Fiftymile Bend—*locale* FL-3
Fiftymile Creek—*stream* UT-8
Fiftymile Flat—*flat* WY-8
*Fifty Mile Mountain* UT-8
Fiftymile Mountain—*ridge* UT-8
*Fifty Mile Point* LA-4
Fiftymile Point—*cape* LA-4
Fiftymile Point—*cape* UT-8
Fiftymile Spring—*spring* UT-8
Fifty Mountain Shelter Cabin—*locale* MT-8
Fiftynine Mile Creek—*stream* AK-9
Fiftynine Tank—*reservoir* AZ-5
*Fifty-ninth Street* IL-6
Fiftyninth Street Interchange—*other* IL-6
Fifty-Ninth Street Sch—*school* CA-9
Fifty-second Street—*uninc pl* PA-2
Fifty-Second Street Sch—*school* CA-9
**Fifty Seven Mile Siding**—*pop pl* VA-3
Fiftyseven Tank—*reservoir* AZ-5
**Fifty Seventh Ave**—*pop pl* FL-3
*Fifty-seventh Street* IL-6
**Fiftysix**—*pop pl* AR-4
Fifty Six Cem—*cemetery* NY-2
Fifty Six Ch—*church* NY-2
*Fiftysix (corporate name Fifty-Six)* AR-4
**Fifty-Six (corporate name for Fiftysix)**—*pop pl* AR-4
Fiftysix Mile Cabin—*locale* AK-9
Fiftysix Mine—*mine* NV-8
Fiftysix Rapids—*falls* MN-6
Fiftysix Tank—*reservoir* AZ-5
Fifty Third Street Sch—*school* WI-6
Fiftythree Bay—*swamp* GA-3
Fiftythree Hollow—*valley* NY-2
Fiftythree Windmill—*locale* TX-5
Fiftytwo Creek—*stream* OK-5
Fifty Well—*well* NM-5
**Fig**—*pop pl* NC-3
**Figarden**—*pop pl* CA-9
Figarden Sch—*school* CA-9
Figarden Shop Ctr—*locale* CA-9
**Figarden (sta.)**—*pop pl* CA-9
Figart—*locale* PA-2
*Figart Run* PA-2
Fig Canal—*canal* CA-9
Fig Drain—*canal* CA-9
Fig Drain One—*canal* CA-9
Figenscaus Harbor—*bay* WI-6
Figert Lake—*lake* NY-2
Figett Bend—*bend* KY-4
**Figg**—*pop pl* KY-4
Figg, Bushrod, House—*hist pl* KY-4
**Fig Garden**—*pop pl* CA-9
Fig Garden Golf Course—*other* CA-9
Fig Garden Village—*post sta* CA-9
Figg Drain—*stream* MI-6
Figge Hoblyn Mine—*mine* NV-8
Figge Lake—*reservoir* KS-7
Figgins Branch—*stream* TN-4
Figgins Cem—*cemetery* LA-4
Figgins Point—*cape* AK-9
Figgs—*locale* KY-4
*Figgs Branch* TN-4
Figgs Ditch—*canal* DE-2
Figgs Ditch—*canal* MD-2
Figgs Landing—*locale* MD-2
Fig Hill Ch—*church* MS-4
Fight and Holler Creek—*stream* TX-5
Fight Brook—*stream* ME-1
Fighting Bayou—*stream* MS-4
Fighting Butte—*summit* MT-8
Fighting Butte Creek—*stream* MT-8
Fighting Creek—*stream* ID-8
Fighting Creek—*stream* KY-4
Fighting Creek—*stream* TN-4
Fighting Creek—*stream* VA-3
Fighting Creek Gap—*gap* TN-4
Fighting Flat—*flat* TX-5
Fighting Fork—*stream* KY-4
Fighting Island—*island* NY-2
Fighting Island Channel—*channel* MI-6
Fighting John Peak—*summit* AK-9
**Fighting Pine**—*pop pl* GA-3
**Fighting Rock Corner**—*pop pl* MA-1
Fighting Spring—*spring* MT-8
Fighting Spring—*spring* UT-8
Fighting Spring Coulee—*valley* MT-8
Fightingtown Creek—*stream* GA-3
Fightingtown Creek—*stream* TN-4
Fight in Hollow Draw—*valley* NM-5
Fig Island—*island* GA-3
Fig Island—*island* SC-3
Fig Island Site—*hist pl* SC-3
Fig Lake—*lake* MN-6
Fig Lake—*lake* OR-9
Fig Lateral—*canal* CA-9
Fig Lateral Four—*canal* CA-9
Figley Branch—*stream* IL-6
Figley Cem—*cemetery* OH-6
Figley Coulee—*valley* ND-7
Fig Mtn—*summit* MT-8
*Fig Orchard* MS-4
Fig Orchard—*locale* CA-9
**Figridge**—*pop pl* (2) TX-5
Figsboro—*locale* VA-3
Fig Spring—*spring* (4) AZ-5
Fig Spring—*spring* CA-9
*Figtown* PA-2
Fig Tree—*valley* CA-9
*Figtree Ch* AL-4
Fig Tree Ch—*church* AL-4
Fig Tree Island—*island* AL-4
Fig Tree Landing—*locale* FL-3
Fig Tree Spring—*spring* (2) AZ-5
Fig Tree Spring—*spring* (2) CA-9
Fig Tree Valley—*valley* CA-9
Figueredo Wash—*stream* NM-5
**Figueroa**—*pop pl* PR-3
Figueroa—*uninc pl* CA-9
Figueroa Camp—*locale* CA-9
Figueroa Creek—*stream* CA-9
Figueroa Mtn—*summit* CA-9
Figueroa Ranch—*locale* AZ-5
Figueroa Station—*locale* CA-9
Figueroa Street Sch—*school* CA-9
Figueroa Tank—*reservoir* AZ-5
*Figuero Creek* CA-9
Figure Creek—*stream* AK-9
Figured Beech Cem—*cemetery* KY-4
Figuredo Wash—*stream* NM-5
Figure Eight Branch—*stream* KY-4
Figure Eight Creek—*stream* AK-9
Figure Eight Creek—*stream* MT-8
Figure Eight Creek—*stream* OK-5
Figure Eight Island—*island* NC-3
Figure Eight Lake—*lake* (3) AK-9
Figure Eight Lake—*lake* MN-6
Figure Eight Lake—*lake* NM-5
Figure Eight Mtn—*summit* NY-2
Figure Eight Pond—*lake* NY-2
**Figure Five**—*pop pl* AR-4
Figure Four Canyon—*valley* AZ-5
Figure Four Canyon—*valley* WY-8
Figure Four Creek—*stream* ID-8
Figure Four Lake—*lake* TX-5
Figure Four Mtn—*summit* AK-9
Figure Four Ranch—*locale* ND-7
Figure Four Spring—*spring* CO-8
Figurehead Mtn—*summit* CA-9
Figure Seven Ranch—*locale* TX-5
Figure Three Ranch—*locale* (2) TX-5
Figure Two Ranch—*locale* TX-5
Figure 8 Draw—*valley* WY-8
Figure 8 Rsvr—*reservoir* WY-8
Fiiang, Sabanan—*slope* MH-9
Fike and Inman Cem—*cemetery* AL-4
*Fike Brook* NJ-2
Fike Cem—*cemetery* MO-7
Fike Hill—*summit* WV-2
Fike Park—*park* KS-7
Fike Run—*stream* PA-2
Fike Run—*stream* WV-2
Fikes Hill—*summit* IL-6
**Fikes Mill**—*pop pl* TN-4
Fikes Run—*stream* MD-2
**Fikestown**—*pop pl* MS-4
**Fiketon**—*pop pl* TN-4
Fiketon Post Office (historical)—*building* TN-4
**Fiketown**—*pop pl* PA-2
Filadel Fia Christian Sch—*school* FL-3
Filardi House—*hist pl* PR-3
Filarea Tank—*reservoir* (2) AZ-5
Filaree Flat—*flat* (3) CA-9
Filaria Spring—*spring* AZ-5
F-l Lateral—*canal* CA-9
**Filbert**—*pop pl* PA-2
**Filbert**—*pop pl* SC-3
**Filbert**—*pop pl* WV-2
Filbert Pond—*lake* MD-2
Filbert Street Sch—*school* PA-2
Filbin Creek—*stream* SC-3
**Filburns Island**—*pop pl* OH-6
File—*locale* VA-3
File Butte—*summit* OR-9
File Cem—*cemetery* IL-6
*File Creek* KS-7
Fil'eenguuy—*channel* FM-9
File Factory Hollow—*valley* NY-2
Filene Center—*locale* VA-3
Filene's Department Store—*hist pl* MA-1
*Filenguy* FM-9
File Point—*cape* AK-9
File Post Office (historical)—*building* AL-4
**Filer**—*pop pl* ID-8
**Filer City**—*pop pl* MI-6
Filer Corners—*locale* NY-2
**Filer Corners**—*pop pl* PA-2
Filer Creek—*stream* ID-8
Filer Creek—*stream* (2) MI-6
Filer Hill—*summit* NY-2
Filer Sch—*school* FL-3
*Filers Corners* PA-2
Filers Lake—*lake* NY-2
**Filer (Township of)**—*pop pl* MI-6
Files Branch—*stream* AL-4
Files Brook—*stream* ME-1
Files Cem—*cemetery* AL-4
Files Cem—*cemetery* AR-4
Files Cem—*cemetery* MS-4
Files Cem—*cemetery* TX-5
Files Chapel—*church* VA-3
Files Creek—*stream* WV-2
**Files Crossroad**—*pop pl* WV-2
*Files Ferry* AL-4
Files Hill—*summit* ME-1
Files Hollow—*valley* AR-4
Files Pond (historical)—*lake* MS-4
*Files Run* WV-2
Files Run—*stream* WV-2
Files Valley—*locale* TX-5
**Filetown**—*pop pl* PA-2
Fileys Ch—*church* PA-2
Filgo Branch—*stream* TN-4
Filiae Mtn—*summit* AS-9
*Filibuster* AZ-5
Filibuster Creek—*stream* TX-5
Filibusters Camp—*locale* AZ-5
Filimaoi Ridge—*ridge* AS-9
Filing Shed Lake—*lake* WI-6
**Filion**—*pop pl* MI-6
Filion Drain—*canal* MI-6
**Filipino Camp**—*pop pl* HI-9
Filipino Patriot Monument—*other* GU-9
*Filipino Village* HI-9
Filippini Pond—*lake* NY-2
Filippini Well—*well* NV-8
*Filirea Flat* CA-9
Filivili Stream—*stream* AS-9
Filkin Hill—*summit* NY-2
Fill, The—*locale* WY-8
Fillaree Canal—*canal* CA-9
Fillaree Drain—*canal* CA-9
Fillaree Drain Four—*canal* CA-9
Fillaree Drain Three—*canal* CA-9
Fillaree Lateral One—*canal* CA-9
Fillauer Branch—*stream* TN-4
Fillauer Lake—*lake* TN-4
*Fillbate Creek* VA-3
*Fillbates Creek* VA-3
*Fill Branch* KY-4
Fillchew Hollow—*valley* MO-7
Fill Creek—*stream* OR-9
Filleman Tank—*reservoir* AZ-5
Filler—*locale* KS-7
Filler Creek—*stream* OR-9
Filler Ditch—*canal* AZ-5
**Filley**—*pop pl* MO-7
**Filley**—*pop pl* NE-7
Filley, Elijah, Stone Barn—*hist pl* NE-7
Filley Cem—*cemetery* NE-7
Filley Mtn—*summit* MA-1
Filley Park—*park* MI-6
**Filley Township**—*pop pl* NE-7
Fill Gulch—*valley* CO-8
Fill Hollow—*valley* WV-2
Fillibrown Brook—*stream* ME-1
*Fillibuster Camp* AZ-5
*Fillicum Creek* WA-9
Filligrum Bend—*bend* AR-4
Fillingame Cem—*cemetery* MS-4
*Fillingame Purvis Park Cem* MS-4
Fillinger Cem—*cemetery* WV-2
Fillippello Playground—*locale* MA-1
Fillippi Creek—*stream* CA-9
*Fillis Run* PA-2
Fillius Park—*park* CO-8
Fillman Bayou—*gut* FL-3
Fillman Hill Bay—*bay* FL-3
*Fillmans Bayou* FL-3
Fillmans Creek—*gut* FL-3
*Fillmore* KS-7
*Fillmore* OR-9
*Fillmore* TN-4
Fillmore—*locale* (2) KY-4
Fillmore—*locale* NC-3
Fillmore—*locale* OH-6
**Fillmore**—*pop pl* CA-9
**Fillmore**—*pop pl* IL-6
**Fillmore**—*pop pl* IN-6
**Fillmore**—*pop pl* IA-7
**Fillmore**—*pop pl* LA-4
**Fillmore**—*pop pl* MI-6
**Fillmore**—*pop pl* MN-6
**Fillmore**—*pop pl* MO-7
**Fillmore**—*pop pl* NY-2
**Fillmore**—*pop pl* ND-7
**Fillmore**—*pop pl* OK-5
**Fillmore**—*pop pl* (2) PA-2
**Fillmore**—*pop pl* UT-8
**Fillmore**—*pop pl* WI-6
Fillmore—*school* UT-8
Fillmore, Millard, House—*hist pl* NY-2
Fillmore, Mount—*summit* CA-9
Fillmore Airp—*airport* UT-8
Fillmore Arroyo—*valley* NM-5
Fillmore Bridge—*other* MO-7
Fillmore Canyon—*valley* NM-5
Fillmore Cem—*cemetery* IN-6
Fillmore Cem—*cemetery* LA-4
Fillmore Cem—*cemetery* OK-5
Fillmore Cem—*cemetery* UT-8
Fillmore Ch—*church* LA-4
Fillmore Ch—*church* ND-7
Fillmore Community Med Ctr—*hospital* UT-8
Fillmore Community Med Ctr Heliport—*airport* UT-8
Fillmore Corner—*locale* NY-2
**Fillmore (County)**—*pop pl* MN-6
Fillmore County Courthouse—*hist pl* NE-7
Fillmore County Jail and Carriage House—*hist pl* MN-6
Fillmore Creek—*stream* WY-8
Fillmore Ditch—*canal* CO-8
Fillmore Division—*civil* UT-8
Fillmore Elem Sch—*school* IN-6
Fillmore Glen State Park—*park* NY-2
Fillmore Hill—*summit* CA-9
Fillmore Inlet—*canal* AK-9
Fillmore Island—*island* AK-9
Fillmore JHS—*school* NY-2
Fillmore Lake—*reservoir* IL-6
Fillmore Mine—*mine* NV-8
Fillmore MS—*school* UT-8
Fillmore Park—*park* MN-6
Fillmore Peak—*summit* AK-9
Fillmore-Pine Bldg—*hist pl* CA-9
Fillmore-Piru (CCD)—*cens area* CA-9
Fillmore Post Office—*building* UT-8
Fillmore Post Office (historical)—*building* TN-4
Fillmore Ranch—*locale* WY-8
Fillmore Rec Area—*park* IA-7
Fillmore Rock—*other* AK-9
Fillmore Sch—*school* CA-9
Fillmore Sch—*school* DC-2
Fillmore Sch—*school* IL-6
Fillmore Sch—*school* MI-6
Fillmore Sch—*school* OK-5
Fillmore Sch—*school* VA-3
Fillmore Schools—*school* IA-7
Fillmore Spring—*spring* NM-5
Fillmore Street Presbyterian Ch (historical)—*church* MS-4
Fillmore Tank—*reservoir* AZ-5
Fillmore Township—*civil* MO-7
Fillmore Township—*fmr MCD* IA-7
**Fillmore Township**—*pop pl* ND-7
**Fillmore (Township of)**—*pop pl* IL-6
**Fillmore (Township of)**—*pop pl* MI-6
**Fillmore (Township of)**—*pop pl* MN-6
Fillmore Wash—*valley* UT-8
Fillmore Wash Rsvr—*reservoir* UT-8
Fill Run—*stream* WV-2
Fill Trestle Trail—*trail* PA-2
Fill Wash—*stream* WY-8
Filly Bayou—*stream* LA-4
Filly Branch—*stream* SC-3
Filly Creek—*stream* ID-8
Filly Lake—*lake* CA-9
*Fillylu Creek* MT-8
Film Center Bldg—*hist pl* NY-2
*Filmore* ND-7
Filmore Canyon—*valley* UT-8
Filmore Chapel—*church* NY-2
Filmore (historical)—*locale* KS-7
Filmore Hollow—*valley* PA-2
Filmore Jackson Ditch—*canal* OH-6
Filmore Park—*park* NE-7
Filmore Parrish Hollow—*valley* AR-4
Filmore Sch—*school* OH-6
Filmore Sch—*school* OR-9
Filmore Street Sch—*school* CA-9
Filmore Tower Sch—*school* IA-7
Filmore Township—*civil* SD-7
*Filpot River* DE-2
**Filson**—*pop pl* IL-6
Filson Creek—*stream* MN-6
Filson Park—*park* OH-6
Filson Sch—*school* IL-6
Filson Sch—*school* KY-4
Filson Spring—*spring* CA-9
**Filter**—*pop pl* CO-8
Filtrol Corporation Pond Dam—*dam* MS-4
Filtro Tank—*reservoir* AZ-5
Filtsix Well—*well* NM-5
*Filtz Pond* ME-1
Filucy Bay—*bay* WA-9
Fimian Creek—*stream* WI-6
*Fin* UT-8
Fina'atkos—*bay* MH-9
Fina'atkos, Puntan—*cape* MH-9
*Finadepo* MH-9
Finados Windmill—*locale* TX-5
Finado Windmill—*locale* TX-5
Finagtan—*slope* MH-9
*Finagukutan* MH-9
Final, Cape—*cliff* AZ-5
Finalay Field—*airport* OR-9
Final Bay—*bay* AK-9
Final Falls—*falls* OR-9
Final Mill Effluent Treatment Pon—*reservoir* AL-4
Final Point—*cliff* AZ-5
Fin and Feather Club—*other* NM-5
Fin and Feather Club Lake—*lake* TX-5
Fin and Feather Club Lake—*reservoir* TX-5
Fin And Feather Lake—*lake* OK-5
Fin and Feather Lake—*reservoir* AL-4
Fin and Feather Lake—*reservoir* KS-7
Fin And Feathers Club Lake—*reservoir* TX-5
Finansanta, Mount—*summit* GU-9
*Fina-sisu* MH-9
Fina' Sisu—*slope* MH-9
*Finasisu As Teo* MH-9
*Finast* RI-1
*Finasusu* MH-9
Finata—*slope* MH-9
**Finaunpes**—*pop pl* FM-9
Finaunpes, Foko—*reef* FM-9
Finberg Field—*park* MA-1
Finberg Lake—*lake* MN-6
Finberg State Wildlife Mngmt Area—*park* MN-6
Finca Juanita—*locale* PR-3
**Finca La Corza**—*pop pl* PR-3
**Finca Marini**—*pop pl* PR-3
Fin Canyon—*valley* UT-8
**Finca Pinones**—*pop pl* (2) PR-3
Finca San Miguel—*locale* PR-3
Fincastle—*locale* KY-4
Fincastle—*locale* OH-6
Fincastle—*locale* TX-5
**Fincastle**—*pop pl* IN-6
**Fincastle**—*pop pl* KY-4
**Fincastle**—*pop pl* TN-4
**Fincastle**—*pop pl* VA-3
Fincastle (CCD)—*cens area* TN-4
Fincastle Cem—*cemetery* OH-6
Fincastle Cem—*cemetery* TN-4
Fincastle Ch—*church* KY-4
Fincastle Ch—*church* VA-3
Fincastle Country Club—*other* VA-3
Fincastle Division—*civil* TN-4
Fincastle Hist Dist—*hist pl* VA-3
Fincastle Lake—*reservoir* TX-5
Fincastle (Magisterial District)—*fmr MCD* VA-3
Fincastle Methodist Ch—*church* TN-4
Fincastle Post Office (historical)—*building* TN-4
*Finch* NC-3
Finch—*locale* MT-8
**Finch**—*pop pl* AR-4
**Finch**—*pop pl* WV-2
Finch, Fred, House—*hist pl* IA-7
Finch, James W., House—*hist pl* CA-9
Finch, John A., Caretaker's House—*hist pl* ID-8
Finch, Vanslyck and McConville Dry Goods Company Bldg—*hist pl* MN-6
Finch Arboretum—*park* WA-9
Finch Bayou—*stream* LA-4
Finch Bldg—*hist pl* PA-2
Finch Bldg—*hist pl* WA-9
Finch Branch—*stream* AL-4
Finch Branch—*stream* IN-6
Finch Branch—*stream* TN-4
Finch Brook—*stream* CT-1
Finch Brook—*stream* NJ-2
Finchburg—*locale* AL-4
Finchburg Landing—*locale* AL-4
Finch Canyon—*valley* CO-8
Finch Cave—*cave* TN-4
Finch Cem—*cemetery* (2) AR-4
Finch Cem—*cemetery* (2) GA-3
Finch Cem—*cemetery* IL-6
Finch Cem—*cemetery* KY-4
Finch Cem—*cemetery* (2) MS-4
Finch Cem—*cemetery* OH-6
Finch Cem—*cemetery* (2) TN-4
Finch Cove—*bay* AK-9
Finch Cove—*valley* NC-3
Finch Cow Camp—*locale* WY-8
Finch Creek—*stream* (2) CA-9
Finch Creek—*stream* MI-6
Finch Creek—*stream* WA-9
Finch Draw—*valley* UT-8
*Finch Elementary School* MS-4
Fincher—*locale* FL-3
Fincher Bluff—*cliff* GA-3
Fincher Branch—*stream* TX-5
Fincher Cave—*cave* AR-4
Fincher Cem—*cemetery* GA-3
Fincher Ch—*church* GA-3
Fincher Chapel—*church* NC-3
Fincher Mtn—*summit* NC-3
Fincher Pond—*reservoir* AL-4
Fincher Sch—*school* WY-8
Fincher Sch (abandoned)—*school* MO-7
Fincherville—*locale* GA-3
Finches Ferry—*locale* AL-4
Finches Ferry Bar (historical)—*bar* AL-4
Finches Ferry Landing (historical)—*locale* AL-4
*Finches Ferry Park* AL-4
Finches Ferry Public Use Area—*park* AL-4
Finches Point—*cape* AL-4
Finches Pond—*reservoir* NY-2
Finch Field—*park* NC-3
**Finchford**—*pop pl* IA-7
Finch Gulch—*valley* MT-8
**Finch Hill**—*pop pl* PA-2
Finch Hill—*summit* PA-2
Finch Hill Ch—*church* PA-2
Finch (historical)—*locale* NC-3
**Finch (historical)**—*pop pl* AL-4
Finch Hollow—*valley* AR-4
Finch Hollow—*valley* (2) NY-2
Finch Hollow—*valley* PA-2
Finch Hollow—*valley* TN-4
Finch House—*hist pl* WA-9
Finch Island—*island* TN-4
Finch Lake—*lake* CA-9
Finch Lake—*lake* CO-8
Finch Lake—*lake* GA-3
Finch Lake—*lake* IL-6
Finch Lake—*lake* LA-4
Finch Lake—*lake* MI-6
Finch Lake—*lake* OR-9
Finch Lake-Pear Reservoir Trail—*trail* CO-8
Finchley—*locale* VA-3
Finch Marsh—*swamp* NY-2
**Finch Mill**—*pop pl* NC-3

Finch Mtn—*summit* ... AR-4
Finch Mtn—*summit* ... NY-2
Finch Park—*park* ... MO-7
Finch Park—*park* ... NJ-2
Finch Park—*park* ... NC-3
Finch Park—*park* ... TX-5
Finch Point—*cape* ... AK-9
Finch Quarry—*mine* ... WA-9
Finch Ranch—*locale* ... CO-8
Finch Ranch—*locale* ... MT-8
Finch Ranch—*locale* ... WY-8
Finchs Branch—*stream* ... VA-3
Finch Sch—*school* ... IL-6
Finch Sch—*school* ... MS-4
Finch Sch—*school* ... TX-5
Finch Sch—*school* ... WA-9
Finchs Corners—*locale* ... PA-2
Finchs Hill—*summit* ... VA-3
*Finch's Island* ... CT-1
Finchs Millpond—*reservoir* ... NC-3
Finchs Millpond Dam—*dam* ... NC-3
Finch Spring—*spring* ... AZ-5
Finchs Run—*stream* ... WV-2
Finchs Store—*locale* ... GA-3
Finch Tank—*reservoir* ... NM-5
Finchum Cem—*cemetery* (2) ... TN-4
Finchum Hollow—*valley* ... TN-4
Finchum Store (historical)—*locale* ... TN-4
Finchville—*locale* ... MD-2
Finchville—*locale* ... NE-7
Finchville—*locale* ... NY-2
Finchville—*other* ... VA-3
**Finchville**—*pop pl* ... KY-4
Finch Wash—*stream* ... AZ-5
Finch Well—*well* (2) ... NM-5
Finch Windmill—*locale* ... AZ-5
Fincke Cem—*cemetery* ... PA-2
Fin Cove—*bay* ... AK-9
Fin Creek—*stream* ... AK-9
Fin Creek—*stream* ... MD-2
Fin Creek Ridge—*ridge* ... MD-2
Find Cem—*cemetery* ... OK-5
Findell Creek—*stream* ... MT-8
Fin Del Mundo Canyon—*valley* ... TX-5
*Findern* ... NJ-2
**Finderne**—*pop pl* ... NJ-2
Finderne Station—*locale* ... NJ-2
Finders Cem—*cemetery* ... MO-7
*Findland* ... MN-6
**Findlay**—*pop pl* ... GA-3
**Findlay**—*pop pl* ... IL-6
**Findlay**—*pop pl* ... OH-6
**Findlay**—*pop pl* ... TN-4
Findlay, Robert, House—*hist pl* ... GA-3
Findlay Branch—*stream* ... KY-4
Findlay Cem—*cemetery* ... MI-6
*Findlay City* ... KS-7
Findlay Coll—*school* ... OH-6
Findlay Downtown Hist Dist—*hist pl* ... OH-6
*Findlay Elementary School* ... TN-4
Findlay Farm—*hist pl* ... PA-2
Findlay Hollow—*valley* ... AR-4
Findlay Hollow—*valley* ... ID-8
Findlay Knolls—*summit* ... AZ-5
Findlay Lake—*reservoir* ... WY-8
Findlay Market Bldg—*hist pl* ... OH-6
Findlay Mtn—*summit* ... VA-3
Findlay Playground—*park* ... OH-6
Findlay Ranch—*locale* ... UT-8
Findlay Rsvr—*reservoir* ... OH-6
Findlay Rsvr—*reservoir* ... WY-8
Findlay Run—*stream* ... PA-2
Findlay Sch—*school* ... TN-4
*Findlays Gap* ... TN-4
Findlay Springs—*spring* ... WY-8
Findlay Tank—*reservoir* ... AZ-5
Findlay (Township of)—*other* ... OH-6
**Findlay (Township of)**—*pop pl* ... PA-2
**Findlen**—*pop pl* ... MA-1
Findler Lake—*lake* ... WI-6
**Findley**—*pop pl* ... IA-7
**Findley**—*pop pl* ... MI-6
Findley, William, House—*hist pl* ... IA-7
Findley Bay—*swamp* ... SC-3
Findley Branch—*stream* ... SC-3
Findley Buttes—*summit* ... OR-9
Findley Cem—*cemetery* (3) ... GA-3
Findley Cem—*cemetery* ... IA-7
Findley Cem—*cemetery* ... KS-7
Findley Cem—*cemetery* ... MO-7
Findley Cem—*cemetery* ... OH-6
Findley Cem—*cemetery* ... PA-2
Findley Ch of Christ—*church* ... TN-4
*Findley Creek* ... CO-8
*Findley Creek* ... IN-6
Findley Creek—*stream* ... WA-9
Findley Field Airp—*airport* ... MO-7
**Findley Gardens**—*pop pl* ... OH-6
Findley Gulch—*valley* ... CO-8
Findley Lake—*lake* ... NY-2
Findley Lake—*lake* (2) ... WA-9
**Findley Lake**—*pop pl* ... NY-2
Findley Lake—*reservoir* ... OH-6
Findley Lateral—*canal* ... IN-6
Findley Methodist Ch—*church* ... TN-4
*Findley Mill* ... IN-6
*Findley Mountain* ... CA-9
Findley Peak—*summit* ... CA-9
Findley Rsvr—*reservoir* ... OR-9
Findley Run—*stream* ... PA-2
Findley Run Dam—*dam* ... PA-2
Findley Run Rsvr—*reservoir* ... PA-2
Findley Sch—*school* ... OH-6
*Findleys Mill* ... AL-4
Findleys Mill (historical)—*locale* (2) ... AL-4
Findley Spring—*spring* ... CO-8
Findley Spring—*spring* ... OR-9
Findley Spring—*spring* ... PA-2
Findley Spring Cave—*cave* ... AL-4
Findley State Park—*park* ... OH-6
Findley Tank—*reservoir* ... AZ-5
Findley Township—*civil* ... MO-7
**Findley (Township of)**—*pop pl* ... PA-2
Findman Spring—*spring* ... NV-8
Fin Dome—*summit* ... CA-9
**Findon**—*pop pl* ... MT-8
Find Reservoir, Lake—*reservoir* ... CO-8
**Fine**—*pop pl* ... NY-2
Fine, Judge John, House—*hist pl* ... NY-2
Fine Arts Bldg—*hist pl* ... MI-6
Fine Arts Bldg—*hist pl* ... OH-6
Fine Arts Center—*building* ... VA-3
Fine Branch—*stream* ... TN-4
Fineburg Lake—*reservoir* ... IN-6
Fineburg Lake Dam—*dam* ... IN-6
Fine Cem—*cemetery* ... TN-4
Fine Comb Branch—*stream* ... NC-3
Fine Creek—*stream* ... VA-3
Fine Creek Ch—*church* ... VA-3
**Fine Creek Mills**—*pop pl* ... VA-3
Finegan Artesian Well—*well* ... TX-5
Finegan Ford—*locale* ... WV-2
Finegayan—*other* ... GU-9
Finegayan Station—*CDP* ... GU-9
Fine Gold Cem—*cemetery* ... CA-9
Fine Gold Creek—*stream* ... CA-9
Fine Gold Gulch—*valley* ... CA-9
Fine Gold Mine—*mine* ... CA-9
Fine Lake—*lake* ... MI-6
Fine Lakes Cem—*cemetery* ... MN-6
**Fine Lakes (Township of)**—*pop pl* ... MN-6
Finelawn Memorial Park—*cemetery* ... WI-6
Finel Hollow—*valley* ... VT-1
Finel Hollow Brook—*stream* ... VT-1
Finell Cem—*cemetery* ... AR-4
Finely Chapel—*church* ... MS-4
Finely Sch (historical)—*school* ... MS-4
Finenga—*area* ... GU-9
Fine Park—*park* ... MI-6
Fineran Sch (historical)—*school* ... SD-7
Fine Ridge—*ridge* ... MT-8
Fine Ridge Spring No.1—*spring* ... MT-8
Fine Ridge Spring No.2—*spring* ... MT-8
Finerty Pond—*reservoir* ... MA-1
Finerty Pond Dam—*dam* ... MA-1
Fine Sch—*school* ... NJ-2
Fines Corner—*locale* ... VA-3
*Fines Creek* ... TN-4
**Fines Creek**—*pop pl* ... NC-3
Fines Creek—*stream* ... NC-3
Fines Creek Ch—*church* ... NC-3
Fines Creek Gap—*gap* ... NC-3
Fines Creek (Township of)—*fmr MCD* ... NC-3
Fines Ferry (historical)—*locale* ... TN-4
Fines Key—*island* ... FL-3
Fine Spring—*spring* (2) ... CA-9
Fine Spring—*spring* ... OR-9
Fines Sch—*school* ... NJ-2
**Finesville**—*pop pl* (2) ... NJ-2
Finesville Dam—*dam* ... NJ-2
**Fine (Town of)**—*pop pl* ... NY-2
Fine Trail Branch—*stream* ... TN-4
**Fineview**—*pop pl* ... NY-2
Fineview Cem—*cemetery* ... NY-2
Fine Wash—*stream* ... AZ-5
Fine Weather Draw—*valley* ... SD-7
Finey—*locale* ... MO-7
Finey Ch—*church* ... MO-7
Finey Creek—*stream* ... MI-6
Fin Feather Lake—*lake* ... TX-5
**Finfoko**—*pop pl* ... FM-9
**Finfokoa**—*pop pl* ... FM-9
**Finfukul**—*pop pl* ... FM-9
Fingal—*locale* ... ID-8
**Fingal**—*pop pl* ... CA-9
**Fingal**—*pop pl* ... ND-7
Fingal Ranch—*locale* ... CA-9
Fingalson Creek—*stream* ... WA-9
**Finger**—*pop pl* (2) ... NC-3
**Finger**—*pop pl* ... TN-4
*Finger, The* ... UT-8
Finger, The—*pillar* ... CO-8
Finger Bay—*bay* ... AK-9
Finger Bay—*bay* ... MN-6
Finger Board—*summit* ... CA-9
Fingerboard Corner—*locale* ... MI-6
*Finger Board Corner, The* ... MI-6
**Finger Board Corner, The**—*pop pl* ... MI-6
Fingerboard Gulch—*valley* ... OR-9
Finger Board Hollow—*valley* ... KY-4
Fingerboard Mtn—*summit* ... NY-2
Fingerboard Prairie—*flat* ... OR-9
Finger Board Ridge—*ridge* ... TN-4
Fingerboard Saddle—*gap* ... OR-9
Fingerboard Slough Creek—*stream* ... OR-9
Finger Board Trail—*trail* ... CA-9
Fingerbowl Lake—*lake* ... CA-9
Finger Butte—*summit* ... AZ-5
Finger Butte—*summit* ... SD-7
Finger Canyon—*valley* ... CA-9
Finger Canyon—*valley* ... UT-8
Finger (CCD)—*cens area* ... TN-4
Finger Cem—*cemetery* ... TN-4
Finger Chapel Cem—*cemetery* ... TN-4
Finger Cove—*bay* ... NV-8
Finger Creek—*stream* ... LA-4
Finger Creek—*stream* ... MN-6
Finger Creek—*stream* ... MT-8
Finger Creek—*stream* ... OR-9
Finger Creek—*stream* ... TN-4
Finger Creek—*stream* ... WY-8
Finger Division—*civil* ... TN-4
Finger Glacier—*glacier* (2) ... AK-9
*Finger Gulch* ... OR-9
*Finger Island* ... TX-5
*Finger Islands* ... AK-9
*Finger Islets* ... AK-9
*Finger Lake* ... MI-6
Finger Lake—*lake* ... AL-4
Finger Lake—*lake* (3) ... AK-9
Finger Lake—*lake* (2) ... CA-9
Finger Lake—*lake* ... CO-8
Finger Lake—*lake* ... GA-3
Finger Lake—*lake* ... IN-6
Finger Lake—*lake* ... MI-6
Finger Lake—*lake* (2) ... MN-6
Finger Lake—*lake* (2) ... MT-8
Finger Lake—*lake* ... TX-5
Finger Lake—*lake* (3) ... WI-6
Finger Lake—*reservoir* ... AL-4
Finger Lake—*reservoir* ... NM-5
Finger Lake Dam—*dam* ... AL-4
Finger Lakes—*lake* ... ID-8
Finger Lakes—*lake* ... NY-2
Finger Lakes Manor—*uninc pl* ... NY-2
Finger Lakes State Park—*park* ... MO-7
Fingerle Hollow—*valley* ... WY-8
Finger Mesa—*summit* ... CO-8
Finger Mtn—*summit* ... AK-9
Finger Mtn—*summit* ... MT-8
Fingernail Pit—*cave* ... AL-4
Finger Of Fate—*pillar* ... ID-8
Finger Park—*park* ... IL-6
Finger Peak—*summit* ... CA-9
Finger Peaks—*summit* ... CA-9
Finger Point—*cape* (3) ... AK-9
Finger Point—*cape* ... TX-5
Fingerpoint, The—*cape* ... UT-8
Finger Point Rock—*summit* ... AZ-5
Finger Pond—*lake* ... FL-3
Finger Post Office—*building* ... TN-4
Finger Ridge—*ridge* ... TN-4
Finger Ridge—*ridge* ... UT-8
Finger-Ring Draw—*valley* ... NM-5
Finger Road Sch—*school* ... WI-6
Finger Rock—*cliff* ... CO-8
Finger Rock—*island* ... OR-9
Finger Rock—*pillar* (2) ... AZ-5
Finger Rock—*pillar* (2) ... CA-9
Finger Rock—*pillar* ... CO-8
Finger Rock—*pillar* ... ID-8
Finger Rock—*pillar* ... WY-8
Finger Rock—*summit* (2) ... OR-9
Finger Rock Canyon—*valley* ... AZ-5
*Finger Rock Creek* ... CO-8
Finger Rock Fish Hatchery—*other* ... CO-8
Finger Rock Spring—*spring* ... AZ-5
Finger Rock Wash—*stream* ... NV-8
*Fingers* ... UT-8
*Fingers, The* ... UT-8
Fingers, The—*summit* ... CA-9
Fingers Bay—*bay* ... AK-9
Fingers Butte—*summit* ... ID-8
Fingers Butte Reservoir—*lake* ... ID-8
Fingers Butte Well—*well* ... ID-8
Fingers Canyon—*valley* ... OR-9
Fingers Chapel Sch (historical)—*school* ... TN-4
Finger Sch (historical)—*school* ... TN-4
*Fingers Cross Roads* ... MS-4
Finger Shoal—*bar* ... AK-9
**Fingerville**—*pop pl* ... SC-3
Fingerville (CCD)—*cens area* ... SC-3
*Finger Wash* ... UT-8
Finger Well—*well* ... TX-5
*Finholloway Creek* ... GA-3
*Finholoway River* ... GA-3
Finigan Creek—*stream* ... MT-8
Finigan Ditch—*canal* ... IN-6
Finigan Mtn—*summit* ... MT-8
Finikochika Creek—*stream* ... AL-4
Finile—*area* ... GU-9
Finile Creek—*stream* ... GU-9
Finis Branch—*stream* ... DE-2
*Finis Ewing Sch* ... TN-4
Finish, Mount—*summit* ... NH-1
**Finis Hook (historical)**—*pop pl* ... MS-4
Fin Island—*island* ... MN-6
Finisterre—*cape* ... NH-1
Finite Cave—*cave* ... AL-4
Finito, Arroyo—*stream* ... CA-9
Fink—*locale* ... CO-8
Fink—*locale* ... TX-5
Fink—*locale* ... WV-2
**Fink Basin**—*pop pl* ... NY-2
**Fink Bine (historical)**—*pop pl* ... MS-4
Fink Bridge—*locale* ... PA-2
Fink Cem—*cemetery* ... IN-6
Fink Cem—*cemetery* ... TN-4
Fink Cem—*cemetery* ... WV-2
**Fink Creek**—*pop pl* ... AK-9
Fink Creek—*stream* ... AK-9
Fink Creek—*stream* ... WA-9
Fink Creek—*stream* ... WV-2
Fink Creek—*stream* ... WI-6
Fink Creek-Utica—*other* ... AK-9
Fink Ditch—*canal* ... CA-9
Fink Drain—*canal* ... MI-6
Finke Ch—*church* ... IN-6
Finke Draw—*valley* ... OR-9
Finke Ranch—*locale* ... OR-9
Finke Spring—*spring* ... OR-9
Fink Hollow—*locale* ... NY-2
Finki Rsvr—*reservoir* ... CO-8
Fink Lake—*lake* ... MI-6
Fink Lake—*lake* ... MN-6
Finkle—*locale* ... MN-6
**Finklea**—*pop pl* ... SC-3
Finklea HS—*school* ... SC-3
Finkleas Lake—*reservoir* ... AL-4
Finkle Brook—*stream* ... NY-2
Finkol, Finol—*summit* ... FM-9
Finkol, Infal—*stream* ... FM-9
**Finkol Te**—*pop pl* ... FM-9
Finkol Wan—*locale* ... FM-9
Fink Park—*park* ... OK-5
Fink Prong—*stream* ... WY-8
Fink Ranch—*locale* ... WY-8
Fink Ridge—*ridge* ... PA-2
Fink Ridge Ch—*church* ... PA-2
Fink Ridge Sch—*school* ... PA-2
Fink Run—*stream* ... PA-2
Fink Run—*stream* (2) ... WV-2
Finks and Gokey Block—*hist pl* ... ND-7
**Finksburg**—*pop pl* ... MD-2
Finks Canyon—*valley* ... NV-8
Finks Cem—*cemetery* ... MO-7
Finks Dam—*dam* ... AL-4
Finks-Harvey Plantation—*hist pl* ... MO-7
Finks Lake—*reservoir* ... AL-4
Finks Millpond—*reservoir* ... AL-4
Finkton Ch—*church* ... MI-6
Fink-Type Truss Bridge—*hist pl* ... NJ-2
Fink-Van Valkenburg Cem—*cemetery* ... NY-2
Finland—*locale* ... PA-2
Finland—*locale* ... SC-3
**Finland**—*pop pl* ... MN-6
Finland Air Force Station—*military* ... MN-6
Finland Cave—*cave* ... PA-2
Finland Cem—*cemetery* ... MN-6
Finland Cem—*cemetery* ... OR-9
Finland Creek—*stream* ... AK-9
Finlander Bay—*bay* ... MI-6
Finlander Bay—*bay* ... MN-6
Finlander Island—*island* ... MN-6
Finlander Reef—*bar* ... MI-6
Finlander Spring—*spring* ... SD-7
**Finlandia Subdivision**—*pop pl* ... UT-8
Finland JHS—*school* ... OH-6
Finland Lookout Tower—*locale* ... MN-6
Finland Sch—*school* ... OH-6
Finland State For—*forest* ... MN-6
Finlay—*locale* ... TX-5
**Finlay Brook (subdivision)**—*pop pl* ... NC-3
Finlay Coll—*school* ... MO-7
Finlay House—*hist pl* ... MS-4
Finlay Mountains—*range* ... TX-5
Finlay Mountain Tank—*reservoir* ... TX-5
Finlay Plaza Shop Ctr—*locale* ... AL-4
Finlay Sch—*school* ... MI-6
Finlay (site)—*locale* ... NV-8
**Finlayson**—*pop pl* ... MN-6
Finlayson Mount—*summit* ... WA-9
Finlayson Mtn—*summit* ... NC-3
Finlayson Ranch—*locale* ... ID-8
**Finlayson (Township of)**—*pop pl* ... MN-6
Finlay Tank—*reservoir* ... TX-5
Finlay Township (historical)—*civil* ... SD-7
Finlen—*locale* ... MT-8
Finletter, Thomas K., Sch—*hist pl* ... PA-2
Finletter Sch—*school* ... PA-2
*Finley* ... IN-6
Finley—*locale* ... AL-4
Finley—*locale* ... NJ-2
Finley—*locale* ... NC-3
Finley—*locale* ... TX-5
**Finley**—*pop pl* ... CA-9
**Finley**—*pop pl* (2) ... KY-4
**Finley**—*pop pl* ... ND-7
**Finley**—*pop pl* ... OK-5
**Finley**—*pop pl* ... TN-4
**Finley**—*pop pl* ... WA-9
**Finley**—*pop pl* ... WI-6
Finley, Ebenezer, House—*hist pl* ... OH-6
Finley, James, House—*hist pl* ... AZ-5
Finley, James, House—*hist pl* ... PA-2
Finley, Thomas B., Law Office—*hist pl* ... NC-3
**Finley Addition**—*pop pl* ... KY-4
Finley Air Force Station—*obs name* ... ND-7
Finley Airp—*airport* ... ND-7
Finley and Adams Canyon—*valley* ... AZ-5
Finley Ave Ch of Christ—*church* ... AL-4
Finley Ave Sch—*school* ... AL-4
**Finley (Ballard Station)**—*pop pl* ... WV-2
Finley Baptist Ch—*church* ... TN-4
Finley Bar—*bar* ... AR-4
Finley Basin—*basin* ... MT-8
Finley Bend—*bend* ... OR-9
Finley Bluff—*cliff* ... MO-7
Finley Bogan—*swamp* ... ME-1
*Finley Branch* ... AL-4
Finley Branch—*stream* ... AL-4
Finley Branch—*stream* ... MS-4
Finley Branch—*stream* ... MO-7
Finley Branch—*stream* ... TN-4
Finley Branch—*stream* (3) ... TX-5
Finley Branch—*stream* ... VA-3
Finley Bridge—*bridge* ... PA-2
Finley Butte—*summit* ... CA-9
Finley Butte—*summit* ... MT-8
Finley Butte—*summit* ... NV-8
Finley Butte—*summit* ... OR-9
Finley Buttes—*summit* ... OR-9
Finley Camp (Site)—*locale* ... CA-9
Finley Canyon—*valley* ... CO-8
Finley Canyon—*valley* ... NM-5
Finley Canyon—*valley* ... WA-9
Finley Cave—*cave* ... AL-4
Finley Cem—*cemetery* (2) ... AL-4
Finley Cem—*cemetery* (2) ... IN-6
Finley Cem—*cemetery* (3) ... MS-4
Finley Cem—*cemetery* (3) ... MO-7
Finley Cem—*cemetery* ... NY-2
Finley Cem—*cemetery* ... NC-3
Finley Cem—*cemetery* ... OH-6
Finley Cem—*cemetery* ... OK-5
Finley Cem—*cemetery* (2) ... TN-4
Finley Cem—*cemetery* ... WV-2
Finley Ch—*church* (2) ... OH-6
Finley Chapel—*church* (2) ... GA-3
Finley Chapel AME Ch—*church* ... AL-4
Finley Chapel Cem—*cemetery* ... IN-6
Finley Corrals—*locale* ... OR-9
Finley Cove—*valley* ... AL-4
Finley Cove—*valley* ... TN-4
Finley Creek—*stream* (3) ... AL-4
Finley Creek—*stream* (2) ... AR-4
Finley Creek—*stream* ... CA-9
Finley Creek—*stream* ... IL-6
Finley Creek—*stream* ... IN-6
Finley Creek—*stream* (2) ... MO-7
Finley Creek—*stream* (3) ... MT-8
Finley Creek—*stream* ... NC-3
Finley Creek—*stream* ... OR-9
Finley Creek—*stream* ... TX-5
Finley Creek—*stream* ... VA-3
Finley Creek—*stream* ... WA-9
Finley Creek Ch—*church* ... AR-4
Finley Creek Cow Camp—*locale* ... OR-9
Finley Crossing—*locale* ... AL-4
Finley Crossing Cem—*cemetery* ... AL-4
*Finley Crossroads* ... AL-4
Finley Draw—*valley* ... WY-8
Finley Elem Sch—*school* ... TN-4
Finley Falls—*locale* ... MO-7
Finley Flats—*flat* ... MT-8
Finley Gap—*gap* ... TN-4
Finley Gulch—*valley* (2) ... CA-9
Finley Gulch—*valley* ... ID-8
Finley Gulch—*valley* ... WA-9
Finley Hill—*summit* ... KY-4
Finley Hill—*summit* ... NY-2
Finley Hollow—*valley* ... MO-7
Finley Hollow—*valley* ... PA-2
Finley Hollow—*valley* ... TN-4
Finley Hosp—*hospital* ... IA-7
Finley Island—*island* ... AL-4
Finley Island Cabin Site Area—*locale* ... AL-4
Finley JHS—*school* ... NY-2
Finley Lake—*lake* ... CA-9
Finley Lake—*lake* ... MI-6
Finley Lake—*lake* ... MN-6
Finley Lake—*lake* ... OR-9
Finley Lake—*lake* (2) ... WI-6
Finley Lakes—*lake* ... MT-8
Finley Memorial Ch—*church* ... VA-3
**Finley Mills**—*pop pl* ... PA-2
Finley Mine—*mine* ... CA-9
Finley Mtn—*summit* ... MO-7
Finley Mtn—*summit* ... WA-9
Finley Natl Wildlife Ref—*park* ... OR-9
**Finley Park (subdivision)**—*pop pl* ... NC-3
Finley Peak—*summit* ... WA-9
Finley Place—*locale* ... CA-9
Finley Point—*cape* ... MT-8
Finley Post Office—*building* ... TN-4
Finley Ranch—*locale* ... CA-9
Finley Ranch—*locale* (2) ... WY-8
Finley-Rattan (CCD)—*cens area* ... OK-5
Finley Ridge—*ridge* ... CA-9
Finley Ridge—*ridge* ... OR-9
Finley Ridge—*ridge* ... WY-8
*Finley River* ... MO-7
Finley Rsvr—*reservoir* ... WY-8
Finley Run—*stream* ... NJ-2
Finley Run—*stream* ... PA-2
Finley Run—*stream* ... WV-2
Finley Sch—*school* ... CA-9
Finley Sch—*school* ... FL-3
Finley Sch—*school* ... IL-6
Finley Sch—*school* ... IN-6
Finley Sch—*school* ... OK-5
Finley Sch—*school* ... SC-3
Finley Sch—*school* ... TN-4
Finley Sch (abandoned)—*school* ... MO-7
*Finleys Cross Roads* ... IN-6
Finleys (historical)—*locale* ... AZ-5
Finleys Lake—*reservoir* ... SC-3
Finley Slough—*stream* ... MS-4
**Finleyson**—*pop pl* ... GA-3
Finleyson (CCD)—*cens area* ... GA-3
Finley Spring—*spring* ... AZ-5
Finley Spring—*spring* ... CO-8
Finley Spring—*spring* ... MT-8
Finley Spring—*spring* ... WY-8
*Finley Station* ... NJ-2
Finley Store (historical)—*locale* ... TN-4
Finley Tank—*reservoir* ... AZ-5
Finley Tank—*reservoir* ... TX-5
**Finley (Town of)**—*pop pl* ... WI-6
Finley Township—*civil* (2) ... MO-7
**Finley Township**—*pop pl* ... KS-7
**Finley Township**—*pop pl* ... ND-7
**Finley (Township of)**—*pop pl* ... IN-6
**Finleyville**—*pop pl* (2) ... PA-2
Finleyville Airp—*airport* ... PA-2
Finleyville Borough—*civil* ... PA-2
Finleyville Cem—*cemetery* ... PA-2
Finley Well—*locale* ... NM-5
Finley Windmill—*locale* ... TX-5
Fin Little Point—*cape* ... UT-8
Fin Little Wash—*valley* ... UT-8
*Finlkochika Creek* ... AL-4
*Finlow* ... WV-2
*Finly* ... IN-6
**Finly (Carrollton) (Reedville)**—*pop pl* ... IN-6
**Finlyville**—*pop pl* ... PA-2
Finn—*locale* ... MT-8
Finn—*locale* ... OR-9
**Finn**—*pop pl* ... OK-5
Finn, The—*cape* ... AK-9
Finnak Brook—*stream* ... CT-1
Finnan Coulee—*valley* ... MT-8
Finnback Knob—*summit* ... CO-8
Finn Basin—*basin* ... VT-1
Finn Bay—*bay* ... MN-6
Finn Bayou—*stream* ... AR-4
Finnbear Lake—*lake* ... AK-9
Finn Branch—*stream* ... MO-7
Finn Brook—*stream* (2) ... ME-1
Finn Brook—*stream* ... NY-2
Finn Cabins—*locale* ... MT-8
Finn Canyon—*valley* ... UT-8
Finn Cem—*cemetery* ... CO-8
Finn Cem—*cemetery* ... ID-8
*Finn Creek* ... MT-8
Finn Creek—*stream* (3) ... ID-8
Finn Creek—*stream* ... MI-6
Finn Creek—*stream* (2) ... MN-6
Finn Creek—*stream* (3) ... MT-8
Finn Creek—*stream* ... OK-5
Finn Creek—*stream* ... OR-9
Finn Creek—*stream* ... TX-5
Finn Creek—*stream* ... WA-9
Finn Creek—*stream* ... WY-8
Finn Ditch—*canal* ... IN-6
Finn Ditch—*canal* (2) ... MT-8
Finn Draw—*valley* ... WY-8
Finnegan Brook—*stream* ... ME-1
Finnegan Brook—*stream* (2) ... NY-2
Finnegan Canyon—*valley* ... OR-9
Finnegan Corners—*locale* ... PA-2
*Finnegan Creek* ... OR-9
Finnegan Creek—*stream* ... MI-6
Finnegan Creek—*stream* ... OR-9
Finnegan Cut—*channel* ... CA-9
Finnegan Ditch—*canal* ... OH-6
Finnegan Hill—*summit* ... NY-2
*Finnegan Hollow* ... OR-9
Finnegan Lake—*lake* ... MI-6
Finnegan Lake—*lake* ... NE-7
Finnegan Lake—*lake* (2) ... WI-6
Finnegan Park—*park* ... NE-7
Finnegan Park—*park* ... TX-5
Finnegan Ridge—*ridge* ... MT-8
**Finnegans Corners**—*pop pl* ... NY-2
Finnegans Point—*locale* ... AK-9
*Finnel Lake* ... WA-9
Finnell Cem—*cemetery* ... AL-4
Finnell Cem—*cemetery* ... MO-7
Finnell Lake—*lake* ... WA-9
Finnel Spring—*spring* ... TN-4
Finnely, Lake—*lake* ... FL-3
Finneman Private Field—*airport* ... ND-7
Finnemore Camp—*locale* ... ME-1
Finneran Park—*park* ... IL-6
Finner Creek—*stream* ... WA-9
Finner Creek Campground—*locale* ... WA-9
Finnerd Brook—*stream* ... ME-1
Finnerty Lake—*lake* ... WI-6
*Finnerty Pond* ... MA-1
Finnertys Tunnel—*tunnel* ... PA-2
Finnerty Well—*well* ... WY-8
*Finnetytown* ... OH-6
*Finney* ... VA-3
Finney—*locale* ... OH-6
Finney—*locale* ... PA-2
Finney—*locale* (2) ... TX-5
**Finney**—*pop pl* ... IL-6
**Finney**—*pop pl* ... KY-4
Finney, Dr. Frank, House—*hist pl* ... CO-8
Finney and Egan Lake—*lake* ... OR-9
Finney Branch—*stream* ... AL-4
Finney Branch—*stream* ... VA-3
Finney Branch—*stream* ... WV-2
Finney Cem—*cemetery* (2) ... AL-4
Finney Cem—*cemetery* ... KY-4
Finney Cem—*cemetery* (2) ... MO-7
Finney Cem—*cemetery* (2) ... TN-4
Finney Cem—*cemetery* ... VA-3
Finney Community Center—*locale* ... TX-5
Finney Company Feedyard Incorporated Airp—*airport* ... KS-7
Finney County—*civil* ... KS-7
Finney County Game Ref—*park* ... KS-7
*Finney County State Game Refuge* ... KS-7
Finney Couty State Lake Dam—*dam* ... KS-7
*Finney Creek* ... VA-3
Finney Creek—*stream* ... CA-9
Finney Creek—*stream* ... GA-3
Finney Creek—*stream* ... KS-7
Finney Creek—*stream* ... LA-4
Finney Creek—*stream* (2) ... MO-7
Finney Creek—*stream* ... OR-9
Finney Creek—*stream* ... VA-3
Finney Creek—*stream* ... WA-9
Finney Creek Shelter—*locale* ... WA-9
Finney Creek Trail—*trail* ... WA-9
Finney Cuts—*stream* ... CO-8
Finney-Darrah House—*hist pl* ... OH-6
Finney Flat—*flat* ... WA-9
Finney Fork—*stream* ... KY-4
**Finney Heights**—*pop pl* ... IL-6
Finney (historical)—*locale* ... KS-7
Finney Hollow—*valley* ... VA-3
Finney HS—*school* ... MI-6
Finney Lake—*lake* ... CA-9
Finney Lake—*reservoir* ... KS-7
Finney Patch—*locale* ... TN-4
Finney Peak—*pillar* ... WA-9
Finney Peak—*summit* ... WA-9
Finney Peak Trail—*trail* ... WA-9
Finney Ridge—*ridge* ... WA-9
Finney (RR name for Coulwood)—*other* ... VA-3
Finney Rsvr—*reservoir* ... CO-8
Finneys Bay—*bay* ... AK-9
Finney Sch—*school* ... CA-9
Finneys Creek—*stream* ... VA-3
Finneys Island—*island* ... AK-9
Finneys Island—*island* ... VA-3
*Finney Slough* ... IL-6
Finneys Neck—*cape* ... VA-3
Finney Spring Branch—*stream* ... VA-3
Finney State Fishing Lake And Wildlife Area—*park* ... KS-7
Finney State Fishing Lake and Wildlife Area—*school* ... KS-7
*Finney State Game Mngmt Area* ... KS-7
Finneys Wharf—*locale* ... VA-3
Finney Tank—*reservoir* ... TX-5
**Finneytown**—*pop pl* ... OH-6
Finneytown HS—*school* ... OH-6
Finney Tunnel—*tunnel* ... PA-2
Finney Valley—*basin* ... CA-9
Finneyville—*locale* ... IL-6
Finneywood—*locale* ... VA-3
Finneywood Ch—*church* ... VA-3
Finneywood Creek—*stream* ... VA-3
Finn Farm Creek—*stream* ... MI-6
Finn Gap—*gap* ... TN-4
Finn Gulch—*valley* (2) ... MT-8
Finn Hall—*locale* ... ME-1
Finn Hall—*locale* (2) ... WA-9
Finn Harbor—*bay* ... WA-9
Finn Hill—*summit* (2) ... NY-2
Finn Hill—*summit* ... PA-2
Finn Hill—*summit* ... WA-9
Finn Hill Cem—*cemetery* ... WA-9
Finn Hollow—*valley* ... PA-2
Finnie Creek—*stream* ... SD-7
*Finnigan Creek Canyon* ... OR-9
Finnish and Swedish Mercantile Association Bldg—*hist pl* ... MI-6
Finnish Apostolic Lutheran Church—*hist pl* ... SD-7
Finnish Cem—*cemetery* (2) ... MI-6
Finnish Cem—*cemetery* (3) ... MN-6
Finnish Cem—*cemetery* (3) ... ND-7
Finnish Cem—*cemetery* ... WA-9
Finnish Cem—*cemetery* ... WI-6
Finnish Ch—*church* (3) ... MI-6
Finnish Ch—*church* (5) ... MN-6
Finnish Ch—*church* (3) ... ND-7
Finnish Ch—*church* ... SD-7
Finnish Ch—*church* (3) ... WI-6
Finnish Hall—*locale* ... MT-8
Finnish Hall—*locale* ... WA-9
Finnish Legation Bldg—*building* ... DC-2
Finnish Lutheran Cem—*cemetery* ... MN-6
Finnish Lutheran Ch—*church* ... MI-6
*Finnish Magnolia Cemetery* ... MS-4
Finnish Sauna—*hist pl* ... MN-6
*Finn Lake* ... MN-6
Finn Lake—*lake* (3) ... MI-6
Finn Lake—*lake* (4) ... MN-6
*Finnlands Creek* ... MI-6
Finn Lateral—*canal* ... SD-7
Finn Mtn—*summit* ... AK-9
Finn Oil Field—*oilfield* ... WY-8
Finnon Rsvr—*reservoir* ... CA-9
Finn Point—*cape* ... MI-6
*Finn Pond* ... PA-2
Finn Pond—*lake* ... MI-6
Finn Pond—*lake* ... MN-6
Finn Pond—*lake* ... PA-2
**Finn Rock**—*pop pl* ... OR-9
Finn Rock Safety Rest Area—*locale* ... OR-9
Finn Rsvr—*reservoir* ... MT-8
Finn Run—*stream* ... PA-2
Finns Cabin—*locale* ... ID-8
Finn Sch—*school* ... KS-7
Finn Sch—*school* ... MA-1
Finn Sch—*school* ... NY-2
Finns Corner—*locale* ... OR-9
Finns Creek—*stream* ... MI-6
Finns Hill—*summit* ... MA-1
Finns Island—*island* ... NC-3
*Finns Lake* ... MI-6
Finns Ledge—*rock* ... MA-1
Finns Point—*cape* ... DE-2
Finns Point—*cape* ... NJ-2

Finns Point Natl Cem—cemetery NJ-2
Finn's Point Rear Range Light—hist pl NJ-2
Finn Springs—spring MT-8
Finns River—stream KY-4
Finn Swamp—swamp PA-2
Finnswitch—locale AR-4
Finntown MT-8
Finn Township—pop pl ND-7
Finnup Park—park KS-7
Finnville—pop pl MA-1
Finn Well—well NM-5
Finn Windmill—locale CO-8
Finny Beach—beach AK-9
Finny Lake—lake GA-3
Fino Airp—airport PA-2
Finogchaan Toro—area GU-9
Finolof—pop pl FM-9
Fino Mine—mine CA-9
Finoodiy FM-9
Fin Point—cape AK-9
Finpukal—pop pl FM-9
Fin Roberts Creek—stream OR-9
Fin Rock—summit ID-8
Fins, The—rock UT-8
Finski Bay—bay AK-9
Finski Point—cape AK-9
Fins Point DE-2
Finsrem—locale FM-9
Finstad, Ole and Elizabeth, Homesite—hist pl TX-5
Finstad Creek—stream MN-6
Finstad Lake—lake MN-6
Finsted's Auto Marine Shop—hist pl MN-6
Finster—locale WV-2
Finster Canyon—valley OR-9
Finster Chapel—church WV-2
Finster Lakes—lake IN-6
Finsterwald Cem—cemetery OH-6
Fintasa River—stream GU-9
Fintcher Creek—stream OR-9
Fintches Corners—pop pl NY-2
Finted Lake MN-6
Finton AL-4
Finton—pop pl PA-2
Finton Creek AZ-5
Fintville Ch—church KY-4
Finucane Spring—spring OR-9
Finucan Valley—valley WI-6
Finyakwateen ID-8
Finzel—pop pl MD-2
Finzer, Nicholas, House—hist pl KY-4
Fio Forge Sch—school PA-2
Fio Forge Sch (historical)—school PA-2
Fiori Playground—park MI-6
Fipaco—uninc pl KY-4
Fip Island—island FL-3
Fipps Crossing—locale NC-3
Fir—locale CO-8
Fir—locale OR-9
Firbie Chapel—church VA-3
Fir Bluff—cliff ID-8
Firbox Meadows—flat ID-8
Fir Brook—stream NY-2
Fir Butte—summit OR-9
Fir Campground—locale NM-5
Fir Camp Saddle—gap CA-9
Fir Canyon—valley AZ-5
Fir Canyon—valley (2) CA-9
Fir Canyon—valley NM-5
Fir Cap—summit CA-9
Fircloff NY-2
Fir Coulee—valley MT-8
Fir Cove Campground—locale CA-9
Fir Crags—pillar CA-9
Fir Creek ID-8
Fir Creek—stream (2) CO-8
Fir Creek—stream GA-3
Fir Creek—stream (9) ID-8
Fir Creek—stream (3) MT-8
Fir Creek—stream (5) OR-9
Fir Creek—stream (5) WA-9
Fir Creek Campground—locale ID-8
Fir Creek Reload—locale WA-9
Fircrest—pop pl WA-9
Fir Crest Cem OR-9
Fircrest Cem—cemetery OR-9
Fircrest Golf Course—other WA-9
Fircrest Park—park OR-9
Fircrest Picnic Ground—locale UT-8
Fir Crest Recreation Site UT-8
Firdale—locale WA-9
Fir Draw—valley CA-9
Fir Draw—valley ID-8
Fire, Valley of—valley NV-8
Fire Alarm Station—hist pl WA-9
Fire Alcove—basin NV-8
Fire and Police Department—building NC-3
Fireball Ridge—ridge NV-8
Fire Baptizes Believers Church, The—church AL-4
Fire Barn—hist pl MA-1
Firebaugh—pop pl CA-9
Firebaugh (CCD)—cens area CA-9
Firebaugh Hollow—valley MO-7
Firebaugh Wasteway—canal CA-9
Fire Bay—bay NV-8
Firebird Camp—locale OH-6
Firebird Lake—lake AZ-5
Firebird Mine—mine CO-8
FIREBOAT NO.1—hist pl WA-9
Fireboat Station—hist pl WA-9
Fire Bowl—basin NV-8
Fire Bowl Cove—bay NV-8
Firebox Canyon—valley AZ-5
Firebox Canyon—valley NM-5
Firebox Creek—stream AZ-5
Firebox Creek—stream CO-8
Firebox Creek—stream ID-8
Fire Box Creek—stream WY-8
Firebox Lake—lake AZ-5
Firebox Meadows—flat ID-8
Firebox Park—flat CO-8
Fire Box Rsvr—reservoir CO-8
Firebox Spring—spring AZ-5
Firebox Summit—summit ID-8
Firebox Tank—reservoir AZ-5
Fire Branch—stream MO-7
Fire Branch—stream OK-5
Fire Branch—stream TN-4
Firebrand Pass—gap MT-8
Firebrand Pass Trail—trail MT-8
Firebrand Ranch (subdivision)—pop pl (2) AZ-5
Firebrick—locale CA-9
Firebrick—locale OH-6
Firebrick—pop pl KY-4
Fire Brick (Firebrick)—pop pl OH-6
Firebrick (RR name Fire Brick)—pop pl KY-4
Fire Brick (RR name for Firebrick)—other KY-4
Fire Brook—stream VT-1
Fire Butte—summit OR-9
Firecamp Lakes—lake OR-9
Fire Camp Saddle—gap ID-8
Fire Canyon—valley (2) NM-5
Fire Canyon—valley OK-5
Fire Canyon—valley UT-8
Fire Canyon—valley WY-8
Fire Canyon Wash—arroyo NV-8
Fire Cherry Branch—stream TN-4
Fireclay CO-8
Fire Clay—locale CO-8
Fire Clay—pop pl UT-8
Fire Clay Hill—summit AZ-5
Fireclay Plaza Condo—pop pl UT-8
Fire Clay Tank—reservoir AZ-5
Fireco—pop pl WV-2
Fire Cove—bay (2) AK-9
Firecracker Mine—mine CA-9
Fire Creek ID-8
Fire Creek MT-8
Fire Creek—stream (3) AK-9
Fire Creek—stream (4) ID-8
Fire Creek—stream (7) MT-8
Fire Creek—stream NV-8
Fire Creek—stream (2) OR-9
Fire Creek—stream (3) WA-9
Fire Creek—stream WV-2
Fire Creek—stream WY-8
Fire Creek Pass—gap WA-9
Fire Creek Point—cliff ID-8
Fire Creek Trail—trail WA-9
Fire Creek Way—trail WA-9
Fire Department and Town Hall—building NC-3
Fire Department Headquarters; Fire station #2—hist pl MO-7
Fire Department HQ—hist pl KY-4
Fire Draw—valley ID-8
Fire Engine House No. 9—hist pl TX-5
Firees Ranch (reduced usage)—locale CO-8
Firefighter Lookout Tower—locale MT-8
Firefighter Monument—locale WY-8
Firefighter Mtn—summit MT-8
Fire Fighters Memorial Campground UT-8
Fireflex Mine—mine CA-9
Firefly Country Club—locale MA-1
Firefly Island FM-9
Firefly Lake—lake WI-6
Firefly Mine—mine UT-8
Fire Gap Ridge—ridge NC-3
Fireguard Creek—stream NE-7
Fire Gulch ID-8
Fire Gulch—valley ID-8
Fire Gulch—valley (2) MT-8
Fire Hall—hist pl MT-8
Fireheart Creek—stream ND-7
Fire Hill—summit CA-9
Fire Hill—summit CT-1
Fire Hill Sch—school SC-3
Fire Hole, Lakes—lake WY-8
Firehole Basin—basin WY-8
Firehole Canyon—locale WY-8
Fire Hole Canyon—valley MT-8
Firehole Canyon—valley (2) WY-8
Firehole Falls—falls WY-8
Firehole Lake—lake WY-8
Firehole Lakes—lake WY-8
Firehole River—stream WY-8
Fire Hook DE-2
Firehouse, Engine Company 31—hist pl NY-2
Firehouse, Engine Company 33—hist pl NY-2
Fire House No. 1—hist pl MN-6
Firehouse No. 13—hist pl KY-4
Fire House No. 2—hist pl MT-8
Fire Hydrant Spring—spring MO-7
Fire Island NY-2
Fire Island—cape ME-1
Fire Island—island (3) AK-9
Fire Island—island LA-4
Fire Island—island (2) MI-6
Fire Island—island MT-8
Fire Island—island NY-2
Fire Island Beach NY-2
Fire Island Inlet—channel NY-2
Fire Island Light—other AK-9
Fire Island Light Station—hist pl NY-2
Fire Island Moose Range—park AK-9
Fire Island Natl Seashore—park NY-2
Fire Island Pines—pop pl NY-2
Fire Island Pines Ferry—trail NY-2
Fire Island Rapids ME-1
Fire Islands—island NY-2
Fire Island Sch—school NY-2
Fire Island Shoal—bar AK-9
Fire King—pop pl KY-4
Fire King Coal Mine (Abandoned)—locale WA-9
Fire Lake MI-6
Fire Lake MN-6
Fire Lake MT-8
Fire Lake—lake AK-9
Fire Lake—lake ID-8
Fire Lake—lake (2) MI-6
Fire Lake—lake MN-6
Fire Lake—lake MT-8
Fire Lake—lake UT-8
Fire Lake—lake WI-6
Fire Lake—uninc pl AK-9
Fire Lake Creek—stream MI-6
Fire Lake Dam—dam UT-8
Fire Lake (North Fork Number Five)—reservoir UT-8
Fire Lakes—lake MT-8
Firelander Meadows—flat WA-9
Firelands Community Park—park OH-6
Firelands HS—school OH-6
Firelands JHS—school OH-6
Firelands Reservation—park OH-6
Firelands Sch—school OH-6
Firelighters Cave—cave AL-4
Fireline Creek—stream (2) OR-9
Fireline Creek—stream PA-2
Fireline Creek—stream WA-9
Fire Line Sch (historical)—school PA-2
Fire Line Tank—reservoir AZ-5
Fireline Trail—trail CO-8
Fireline Trail—trail WY-8
Fireman Cem—cemetery NV-8
Fireman Lake AR-4
Fireman Park—park NY-2
Fireman Park—park (2) WI-6
Fireman Recreation Hall—building PA-2
Fireman's Drinking Fountain—hist pl PA-2
Fireman's Hall—hist pl NY-2
Firemans Hall Museum—building PA-2
Fireman's Hill TX-5
Firemans Leap—cliff OR-9
Firemans Park—park MS-4
Firemans Park—park PA-2
Firemans Park—park WI-6
Firemans Park—pop pl OH-6
Firemans Point—cape TX-5
Firemans Point—cliff MT-8
Fire Memorial Trail—trail WY-8
Firemen Lake—reservoir AL-4
Firemen Park—park WI-6
Firemen's Hall—hist pl MN-6
Firemens Home—hospital NY-2
Firemens Memorial Field—park NY-2
Firemens Memorial Park—park NY-2
Firemen's Monmt—hist pl NJ-2
Firemens Park—park TX-5
Fire Mountain KS-7
Fire Mountain—locale CA-9
Fire Mountain Canal—canal CO-8
Fire Mountains AZ-5
Fire Mtn—summit AZ-5
Fire Mtn—summit CA-9
Fire Mtn—summit CO-8
Fire Mtn—summit ID-8
Fire Mtn—summit (2) WA-9
Fire Pan Sog—swamp FL-3
Fire Park—flat CO-8
Fire Park Draw—valley CO-8
Fire Pine Creek—gut VA-3
Firepit Knoll—summit UT-8
Fireplace—pop pl NY-2
Fireplace Bluffs—cliff CA-9
Fireplace Creek—stream CA-9
Fireplace Lodge Girls Camp—pop pl NY-2
Fireplace Neck—cape NY-2
Fireplace Spring—spring AZ-5
Fire Point—cape AK-9
Fire Point—cape TX-5
Fire Point—cliff AZ-5
Fire Pond—lake WA-9
Fire Prairie—swamp FL-3
Fire Prairie Creek—stream MO-7
Fireproof Bldg—hist pl SC-3
Fire Ridge—ridge AZ-5
Fire Ridge—ridge CO-8
Fire Ridge—ridge MT-8
Fire Rock Island—island NY-2
Fire Rock Well—well NM-5
Fire Run—stream IN-6
Fire Run—stream OH-6
Firescald Branch—stream GA-3
Firescald Branch—stream KY-4
Firescald Branch—stream NC-3
Firescald Branch—stream (2) TN-4
Firescald Creek—stream NC-3
Firescald Creek—stream TN-4
Firescald Creek Stone Arch Bridge—hist pl TN-4
Firescald Gap—gap NC-3
Firescald Knob—summit TN-4
Firescald Mtn—summit (2) NC-3
Firescald Ridge NC-3
Firescald Ridge—ridge (2) NC-3
Fire Scald Ridge—ridge NC-3
Firescald Ridge—ridge (3) NC-3
Fire Scale Mtn—summit NC-3
Fires Creek—locale NC-3
Fires Creek—stream NC-3
Fires Creek Cem—cemetery NC-3
Fires Creek Wildlife Mngmt Area—park NC-3
Fireside—pop pl OH-6
Fireside Lakes—lake WI-6
Fireside Mine—mine UT-8
Fireside Park—pop pl DE-2
Fireside Park—pop pl PA-2
Fireside Terrace—pop pl PA-2
Fire Spring—spring (3) OR-9
Fire Springs OR-9
Fire Springs Trail—trail (2) OR-9
Fire Station and City Hall—hist pl TX-5
Fire Station No. 1—hist pl CO-8
Fire Station No. 1—hist pl VA-3
Fire Station No. 1—hist pl WA-9
Fire Station No. 10—hist pl WA-9
Fire Station No. 11—hist pl GA-3
Fire Station No. 14—hist pl WA-9
Fire Station No. 15—hist pl WA-9
Fire Station No. 18—hist pl WA-9
Fire Station No. 19—hist pl MN-6
Fire Station No. 2—hist pl IA-7
Fire Station No. 2—hist pl NC-3
Fire Station No. 2—hist pl WA-9
Fire Station No. 23—hist pl CA-9
Fire Station No. 23—hist pl WA-9
Fire Station No. 25—hist pl WA-9
Fire Station No. 4—hist pl FL-3
Fire Station No. 4—hist pl IA-7
Fire Station No. 4—hist pl MA-1
Fire Station No. 4—hist pl NY-2
Fire Station No. 4—hist pl RI-1
Fire Station No. 4—hist pl WI-6
Fire Station No. 5—hist pl AL-4
Fire Station No. 5—hist pl TN-4
Fire Station No. 5—hist pl WA-9
Fire Station No. 7—hist pl MA-1
Firestation No. 8—hist pl UT-8
Fire Station No. 9—hist pl IN-6
Fire Station No. 9—hist pl KS-7
Fire Station Number 1—building AL-4
Fire Station Number 1—building MI-6
Fire Station Number 1—building TN-4
Fire Station Number 2—building AL-4
Fire Station Number 2—building MI-6
Fire Station Number 2—building (2) TN-4
Fire Station Number 20—building TN-4
Fire Station Number 21—building TN-4
Fire Station Number 25—building TN-4
Fire Station Number 26—building TN-4
Fire Station Number 28—building TN-4
Fire Station Number 3—building AL-4
Fire Station Number 3—building MI-6
Fire Station Number 3—building TN-4
Fire Station Number 4—building MI-6
Fire Station Number 4—building TN-4
Fire Station Number 5—building MI-6
Firesteel—pop pl MI-6
Firesteel—pop pl SD-7
Firesteel Creek—stream (2) SD-7
Firesteel River—stream MI-6
Firesteel State Public Shooting Area—park SD-7
Firesteel Township—civil SD-7
Firesteel Township—pop pl SD-7
Firestone AL-4
Firestone—hist pl AZ-5
Firestone—locale VA-3
Firestone—pop pl CO-8
Firestone—pop pl GA-3
Firestone—pop pl NE-7
Firestone—pop pl NC-3
Firestone—uninc pl CA-9
Firestone Bldg—hist pl MO-7
Firestone Branch—stream AL-4
Firestone Butte—summit OR-9
Firestone Cem—cemetery NC-3
Firestone Country Club—other OH-6
Firestone Creek—stream AK-9
Firestone Field—park NC-3
Firestone HS—school OH-6
Firestone Lake—reservoir CO-8
Firestone Memorial Cem—cemetery NC-3
Firestone Metropolitan Park—park OH-6
Firestone Park OH-6
Firestone Park—park OH-6
Firestone Park—park TN-4
Firestone Park—pop pl CA-9
Firestone Park—pop pl OH-6
Firestone Park Sch—school OH-6
Firestone Pond—lake MA-1
Firestone Post Office (historical)—building AL-4
Firestone Ridge—ridge PA-2
Firestone Road and 103rd Street Shop Ctr—locale FL-3
Firestone Scout Reservation (Headquarters)—locale CA-9
Firestone (subdivision)—pop pl NC-3
Firestone Synthetic & Textile Company—facility KY-4
Firestone Tire and Rubber Store—hist pl IN-6
Firestone Valley PA-2
Firetag Lake—lake WI-6
Fire Tank—reservoir (2) AZ-5
Fire Tank—reservoir NM-5
Fire Temple—locale CO-8
Fire Tower Ch—church TX-5
Fire Tower Hill—summit MN-6
Fire Tower Hill—summit OK-5
Fire Tower Trail—trail PA-2
Firetown—pop pl CT-1
Fire Trail—trail VA-3
Fire Trail Creek—stream WY-8
Fire Warden Camp—locale ME-1
Fire Wardens Camp—locale ME-1
Fire Warden Trail—trail ME-1
Firewater Canyon—valley UT-8
Firewater Canyon—valley WA-9
Firewater Creek—stream MT-8
Firewater Point—cape UT-8
Firewater Rapids—rapids UT-8
Fireweed Camp—locale WA-9
Fireweed Creek—stream AK-9
Fireweed Mtn—summit AK-9
Fire Windmill—locale NM-5
Fireworks—pop pl MA-1
Firey Hill—summit NY-2
Fir Glade—flat CA-9
Fir Glade Swamp CA-9
Firgrove—pop pl OR-9
Fir Grove—pop pl OR-9
Firgrove—pop pl WA-9
Fir Grove Cem—cemetery (2) OR-9
Fir Grove Mtn—summit ID-8
Fir Grove Ranch—locale ID-8
Fir Grove Sch—school (3) OR-9
Firgrove Sch—school WA-9
Fir Grove School—locale OR-9
Fir Gulch—valley CA-9
Fir Gulch—valley (3) ID-8
Fir Gulch—valley OR-9
Fir Hill—summit CA-9
Fir (historical)—pop pl OR-9
Fir Hollow—valley OR-9
Fir Island NY-2
Fir Island—island ID-8
Fir Island—island NY-2
Fir Island—island WA-9
Firkin Sch—school KY-4
Firkins Creek NJ-2
Fir Lake UT-8
Fir Lake—lake (2) OR-9
Fir Lake—lake UT-8
Fir Lake—lake WA-9
Fir Lawn Cem—cemetery OR-9
Firlick Creek—stream IN-6
Firloch—pop pl WA-9
Firlock—locale OR-9
Firma—locale MO-7
Firman Canyon—valley NM-5
Firman Island—island NJ-2
Firman Spring—spring NM-5
Firmantown—pop pl KY-4
Firmenich Incorporated Property—airport NJ-2
Firmin CA-9
Firmin Desloge Hospital Heliport—airport MO-7
Firmin Sch—school OH-6
Firmis (historical)—locale KS-7
Fir Mtn—summit NY-2
Fir Mtn—summit OR-9
Fir Mtn—summit WA-9
Firnell Island—island FL-3
Firo—pop pl OR-9
Fir Point—cape ME-1
Fir Point—cape OR-9
Fir Point—summit AZ-5
Fir Ridge—pop pl OR-9
Fir Rock—other AK-9
Fir Root Spring—spring (2) CA-9
Fir (RR name for Conway)—other WA-9
Firs, The—locale UT-8
Firs Campground—locale CA-9
Firsco TX-5
Fir Spring WA-9
Fir Spring—spring (3) AZ-5
Fir Spring—spring (2) OR-9
First Advent Ch—church FL-3
First Advent Christian Ch—church AL-4
First African Baptist Ch—church (3) AL-4
First African Baptist Church—hist pl AL-4
First African Baptist Church—hist pl GA-3
First African Baptist Church—hist pl KY-4
First African Baptist Church—hist pl VA-3
First African Baptist Church and Parsonage—hist pl KY-4
First African Baptist Church Parsonage—hist pl GA-3
First African Ch—church (4) GA-3
First African Ch—church (2) SC-3
First African Methodist Episcopal Church—hist pl GA-3
First African Methodist Episcopal Zion Ch—church TN-4
Firstair Field Airp—airport WA-9
First Alkali Creek—stream CO-8
First Alliance Ch—church AL-4
First Alliance Ch—church (5) FL-3
First Alliance Ch—church KY-4
First AME Ch AL-4
First and Central Presbyterian Ch—church DE-2
First and F Street Bldg—hist pl CA-9
First Anvil Creek—stream CO-8
First Apache Canyon—valley NM-5
First Apache Canyon Well—well NM-5
First Apostolic Ch—church MI-6
First Apostolic Ch—church MS-4
First Apostolic Ch—church (2) TN-4
First Apostolic Ch of Forest City—church FL-3
First Apostolic (Pentecostal Holiness) Ch—church UT-8
First Arm—bay TN-4
First Assembly God Ch of Tampa—church FL-3
First Assembly of God—church DE-2
First Assembly of God—church (4) FL-3
First Assembly of God—church KS-7
First Assembly of God Ch—church (22) AL-4
First Assembly of God Ch—church (9) FL-3
First Assembly Of God Ch—church GA-3
First Assembly of God Ch—church KS-7
First Assembly of God Ch—church (23) MS-4
First Assembly of God Ch—church (5) TN-4
First Assembly of God Ch Bonita Springs—church FL-3
First Assembly of God Ch (Layton)—church UT-8
First Assembly of God Ch (Moab)—church UT-8
First Assembly of God Ch of Dover—church FL-3
First Assembly of God Ch of Seffner—church FL-3
First Assembly of God Ch of Winter Garden—church FL-3
First Assembly of God Ch (Tooele)—church UT-8
First Assembly of God of Bradenton—church FL-3
First Assembly of God of Lynn Haven—church FL-3
Fir Station—locale WA-9
First Ave Elem Sch—school AZ-5
First Ave Holiness Ch—church AL-4
First Ave JHS—school CA-9
First Ave Sch—school CT-1
First Ave Sch—school NJ-2
First Ave Sch—school OH-6
First Bald Hills—summit MA-1
First Bank of Joseph—hist pl OR-9
First Bank of the United States—building PA-2
First Bank of the United States—hist pl PA-2
First Bannon Slough—gut CA-9
First Baptist Ch of North Lauderdale—church FL-3
First Baptist Altamonte—church FL-3
First Baptist Cem—cemetery MS-4
First Baptist Central Church—hist pl OK-5
First Baptist Ch MS-4
First Baptist Ch—church (83) AL-4
First Baptist Ch—church (2) AR-4
First Baptist Ch—church (2) DE-2
First Baptist Ch—church (21) FL-3
First Baptist Ch—church (2) GA-3
First Baptist Ch—church IL-6
First Baptist Ch—church (4) IN-6
First Baptist Ch—church IA-7
First Baptist Ch—church (2) KS-7
First Baptist Ch—church LA-4
First Baptist Ch—church (2) MA-1
First Baptist Ch—church (4) MI-6
First Baptist Ch—church (92) MS-4
First Baptist Ch—church MO-7
First Baptist Ch—church (2) MT-8
First Baptist Ch—church (4) NC-3
First Baptist Ch—church (3) PA-2
First Baptist Ch—church SC-3
First Baptist Ch—church (27) TN-4
First Baptist Ch—church (3) UT-8
First Baptist Ch—church (2) VA-3
First Baptist Ch—church WI-6
First Baptist Chapel of Gasselberry—church FL-3
First Baptist Chapel (Payson)—church UT-8
First Baptist Ch at Union Park—church FL-3
First Baptist Ch (Blanding)—church UT-8
First Baptist Ch (Bountiful)—church UT-8
First Baptist Ch (Cedar City)—church UT-8
First Baptist Ch (Duchesne)—church UT-8
First Baptist Ch (Escalante)—church UT-8
First Baptist Ch (Ferron)—church UT-8
First Baptist Ch (Granger)—church UT-8
First Baptist Ch (Grantsville)—church UT-8
First Baptist Ch (Green River)—church UT-8
First Baptist Ch (Heber City)—church UT-8
First Baptist Ch (historical)—church AL-4
First Baptist Ch in Holly Hill—church FL-3
First Baptist Ch in Ocala—church FL-3
First Baptist Ch (Kanab)—church UT-8
First Baptist Ch (Kearns)—church UT-8
First Baptist Ch (Logan)—church UT-8
First Baptist Ch Markham Woods—church FL-3
First Baptist Ch of Alabama City—church AL-4
First Baptist Ch of Alcoa—church TN-4
First Baptist Ch of Apopka—church FL-3
First Baptist Ch of Attalla—church AL-4
First Baptist Ch of Bayou George—church FL-3
First Baptist Ch of Belleview—church FL-3
First Baptist Ch of Bemis—church TN-4
First Baptist Ch of Bonita Springs—church FL-3
First Baptist Ch of Bradenton—church FL-3
First Baptist Ch of Bridgeport—church AL-4
First Baptist Ch of Brooklyn—church MS-4
First Baptist Ch of Brozentown—church TN-4
First Baptist Ch of Bucksville—church AL-4
First Baptist Ch of Bunnell—church FL-3
First Baptist Ch of Cape Coral—church FL-3
First Baptist Ch of Carriere—church MS-4
First Baptist Ch of Citrus Park—church FL-3
First Baptist Ch of Clara—church MS-4
First Baptist Ch of Coffee Springs—church AL-4
First Baptist Ch of Coldwater—church MS-4
First Baptist Ch of Collinsville—church MS-4
First Baptist Ch of Coral Springs—church FL-3
First Baptist Ch of Cropwell—church AL-4
First Baptist Ch of Daisy—church TN-4
First Baptist Ch of Dandridge—church TN-4
First Baptist Ch of Dania—church FL-3
First Baptist Ch of Daytona Beach—church FL-3
First Baptist Ch of Dechard—church TN-4
First Baptist Ch of DeLand—church FL-3
First Baptist Ch of De Leon Springs—church FL-3
First Baptist Ch of Deltona—church FL-3
First Baptist Ch of D'Iberville—church MS-4
First Baptist Ch of Dyer—church TN-4
First Baptist Ch of Eaton Park—church FL-3
First Baptist Ch of Escatawpa—church MS-4
First Baptist Ch of Everglades City—church FL-3
First Baptist Ch of Fairfield—church AL-4
First Baptist Ch of Fairview—church AL-4
First Baptist Ch of Fifth Ave—church TN-4
First Baptist Ch of Fort Lauderdale—church FL-3
First Baptist Ch of Fort McCoy—church FL-3
First Baptist Ch of Fort Myers—church FL-3
First Baptist Ch of Fountain City—church TN-4
First Baptist Ch of Fultondale—church AL-4
First Baptist Ch of Gautier—church MS-4
First Baptist Ch of Geneva—church FL-3
First Baptist Ch of Glendale—church MS-4
First Baptist Ch of Gordo—church AL-4
First Baptist Ch of Hallandale—church FL-3
First Baptist Ch of Hamilton—church AL-4
First Baptist Ch of Harrogate—church TN-4
First Baptist Ch of Hartselle—church AL-4
First Baptist Ch of Helena—church MS-4
First Baptist Ch of Henleyfield—church MS-4
First Baptist Ch of Hixson TN-4
First Baptist Ch of Hollywood—church FL-3
First Baptist Ch of Hoover—church AL-4
First Baptist Ch of Hueytown—church AL-4
First Baptist Ch of Indian River City—church FL-3
First Baptist Ch of Irondale—church AL-4
First Baptist Ch of Kenton—church TN-4
First Baptist Ch of Kingston—church AL-4
First Baptist Ch of Kissimmee—church FL-3
First Baptist Ch of Knoxville—church TN-4
First Baptist Ch of Lake Park—church FL-3
First Baptist Ch of Lambert—church MS-4
First Baptist Ch of Lauderdale MS-4
First Baptist Ch of Laurel—church MS-4
First Baptist Ch of Lenoir Ave—church TN-4
First Baptist Ch of Longview—church MS-4
First Baptist Ch of Longwood—church FL-3
First Baptist Ch of Lookout Mountain—church TN-4
First Baptist Ch of Lugoff—church SC-3
First Baptist Ch of Maitland—church FL-3
First Baptist Ch of Marion—church MS-4
First Baptist Ch of Marks—church MS-4
First Baptist Ch of McLain—church MS-4
First Baptist Ch of Midfield—church AL-4
First Baptist Ch of Mims—church FL-3
First Baptist Ch of Miramar—church FL-3
First Baptist Ch of Naples—church FL-3
First Baptist Ch of Nesbit—church MS-4
First Baptist Ch of New Castle—church DE-2
First Baptist Ch of New Decatur AL-4
First Baptist Ch of Niota—church TN-4
First Baptist Ch of North Fort Myers—church FL-3
First Baptist Ch of Oak Grove AL-4
First Baptist Ch of Oakland—church (2) FL-3
First Baptist Ch of Ocoee—church FL-3
First Baptist Ch of Ojos—church FL-3
First Baptist Ch of Oneco—church FL-3
First Baptist Ch of Opa-Locka—church FL-3
First Baptist Ch of Orlando—church FL-3
First Baptist Ch of Osteen—church FL-3
First Baptist Ch of Oxford—church AL-4
First Baptist Ch of Ozona—church MS-4
First Baptist Ch of Panacea—church FL-3
First Baptist Ch of Panama City—church FL-3
First Baptist Ch of Parker—church FL-3
First Baptist Ch of Pearl—church MS-4
First Baptist Ch of Pensacola—church FL-3
First Baptist Ch of Perrine—church FL-3
First Baptist Ch of Petal—church MS-4
First Baptist Ch of Picayune—church MS-4
First Baptist Ch of Pierson—church FL-3
First Baptist Ch of Plantation—church FL-3
First Baptist Ch of Pompano—church FL-3
First Baptist Ch of Port Gibson—church MS-4
First Baptist Ch of Port Orange—church FL-3
First Baptist Ch of Powell—church TN-4
First Baptist Ch of Richland MS-4
First Baptist Ch of Ridgeland—church MS-4
First Baptist Ch of Rock Springs—church FL-3
First Baptist Ch of Roseberry City—church TN-4
First Baptist Ch of Saint Cloud—church FL-3

First Meridian Heights Presbyterian Ch—*church* .... IN-6
First Merritt Center (Shop Ctr)—*locale* .... FL-3
First Mesa—*summit* .... AZ-5
First Mesa Ditch—*canal* .... WY-8
*First Mesa Wash* .... AZ-5
First Methodist Ch—*church* (32) .... AL-4
First Methodist Ch—*church* (2) .... MS-4
First Methodist Ch—*church* .... PA-2
First Methodist Ch—*church* .... TN-4
First Methodist Ch of Dadeville—*church* .... AL-4
First Methodist Ch of Dyer—*church* .... TN-4
First Methodist Church—*hist pl* .... AR-4
First Methodist Church—*hist pl* .... ID-8
First Methodist Church—*hist pl* .... IA-7
First Methodist Church—*hist pl* .... LA-4
First Methodist Church—*hist pl* .... TN-4
First Methodist Church—*hist pl* (3) .... TX-5
First Methodist Church—*hist pl* (2) .... WI-6
First Methodist Church Bldg—*hist pl* .... OK-5
First Methodist Church of Batavia—*hist pl* .... IL-6
First Methodist Church of Burlington—*hist pl* .... VT-1
First Methodist Church of Clovis—*hist pl* .... NM-5
First Methodist Church of Greenwood—*hist pl* .... MS-4
*First Methodist Episcopal Ch* .... AL-4
First Methodist Episcopal Ch—*church* (9) .... AL-4
First Methodist Episcopal Ch (historical)—*church* .... AL-4
First Methodist Episcopal Church—*hist pl* .... CO-8
First Methodist Episcopal Church—*hist pl* .... IA-7
First Methodist Episcopal Church—*hist pl* .... MI-6
First Methodist Episcopal Church—*hist pl* .... NJ-2
First Methodist Episcopal Church—*hist pl* .... NM-5
First Methodist Episcopal Church—*hist pl* .... OH-6
First Methodist Episcopal Church and Parsonage—*hist pl* .... AZ-5
First Methodist Episcopal Church and Parsonage—*hist pl* .... MT-8
First Methodist Episcopal Church of Alliance, Ohio—*hist pl* .... OH-6
First Methodist Episcopal Church of Salem—*hist pl* .... OR-9
First Methodist Protestant Ch—*church* .... AL-4
First Mine Branch—*stream* .... MD-2
First Minister's House—*hist pl* .... MA-1
First Missionary Baptist Ch—*church* (5) .... AL-4
First Missionary Baptist Ch—*church* (2) .... FL-3
First Missionary Baptist Ch—*church* (3) .... MS-4
First Missionary Baptist Ch (ABA)—*church* .... FL-3
First Missionary Baptist Ch of Bithlo—*church* .... FL-3
First Missionary Baptist Church—*hist pl* .... AR-4
First Missionary Ch—*church* .... FL-3
First Missionary Ch—*church* .... IN-6
First Missionary Ch—*church* .... LA-4
First Mission Ch—*church* .... GA-3
First Missouri State Capitol Buildings—*hist pl* .... MO-7
First Morning Star Ch—*church* .... VA-3
First Mortage Company Bldg—*hist pl* .... TX-5
First Mound—*summit* .... UT-8
*First Mountain* .... NJ-2
First Mount Airy Ch—*church* .... VA-3
First Mount Calvary Ch—*church* .... GA-3
First Mount Moriah Ch—*church* .... SC-3
First Mount Zion Ch—*church* .... VA-3
First Mtn—*summit* .... NH-1
First Mtn—*summit* .... OK-5
First Mtn—*summit* .... PA-2
First Mtn—*summit* (3) .... VA-3
First Musquacook Lake—*reservoir* .... ME-1
First Musquash Pond—*lake* .... ME-1
First Narrows—*channel* .... AK-9
First Narrows—*channel* .... ME-1
First Narrows—*gap* .... PA-2
First Narrows—*gap* .... UT-8
First National, The—*bay* .... FL-3
First National-John A. Hand Bldg—*hist pl* .... AL-4
First Natl Bank—*bar* .... FL-3
First Natl Bank—*hist pl* (2) .... AL-4
First Natl Bank—*hist pl* .... AR-4
First Natl Bank—*hist pl* .... GA-3
First Natl Bank—*hist pl* .... IA-7
First Natl Bank—*hist pl* .... KS-7
First Natl Bank—*hist pl* .... KY-4
First Natl Bank—*hist pl* .... ME-1
First Natl Bank—*hist pl* (5) .... MN-6
First Natl Bank—*hist pl* (2) .... ND-7
First Natl Bank—*hist pl* .... OK-5
First Natl Bank—*hist pl* .... OR-9
First Natl Bank—*hist pl* .... SC-3
First Natl Bank—*hist pl* .... SD-7
First Natl Bank—*hist pl* .... UT-8
First Natl Bank—*hist pl* .... VA-3
First Natl Bank—*hist pl* .... WI-6
First Natl Bank—*post sta* .... OK-5
First Natl Bank, Vaupel Store and Oregon Hotel Buildings—*hist pl* .... OR-9
First Natl Bank and Masonic Lodge—*hist pl* .... OK-5
First Natl Bank and Trust Bldg—*hist pl* .... OH-6
First Natl Bank and Trust Bldg—*hist pl* .... TX-5
First Natl Bank and Trust Company Bldg—*hist pl* .... OK-5
First Natl Bank Bldg—*hist pl* .... AL-4
First Natl Bank Bldg—*hist pl* .... CT-1
First Natl Bank Bldg—*hist pl* .... IA-7
First Natl Bank Bldg—*hist pl* (2) .... MI-6
First Natl Bank Bldg—*hist pl* .... NE-7
First Natl Bank Bldg—*hist pl* .... NM-5
First Natl Bank Bldg—*hist pl* (2) .... NC-3
First Natl Bank Bldg—*hist pl* (3) .... OH-6
First Natl Bank Bldg—*hist pl* .... SD-7
First Natl Bank Bldg—*hist pl* (3) .... TX-5
First Natl Bank Bldg—*hist pl* .... VA-3
First Natl Bank Bldg—*hist pl* .... WY-8
First Natl Bank Bldg of Vermillion—*hist pl* .... SD-7
First Natl Bank-Kentucky Title Company Bldg—*hist pl* .... KY-4
First Natl Bank of Adams—*hist pl* .... MN-6
First Natl Bank of Beaver Creek—*hist pl* .... MN-6
First Natl Bank of Brewster—*hist pl* .... NY-2
First Natl Bank of Bristol—*hist pl* .... TN-4
First Natl Bank of Custer City—*hist pl* .... OK-5
First Natl Bank of Dickson—*hist pl* .... TN-4
First Natl Bank of Eddy—*hist pl* .... NM-5
First Natl Bank of Glendale Bldg—*hist pl* .... AZ-5
First Natl Bank of Greenville—*hist pl* .... MS-4
First Natl Bank of Haxtun—*hist pl* .... CO-8
First Natl Bank of Houlton—*hist pl* .... ME-1
First Natl Bank of Huntsville—*hist pl* .... TN-4
First Natl Bank of Lacona—*hist pl* .... NY-2
First Natl Bank of Mankato—*hist pl* .... MN-6
First Natl Bank of Milbank—*hist pl* .... SD-7
First Natl Bank of Morrilton—*hist pl* .... AR-4
First Natl Bank of Morrisville—*hist pl* .... NY-2
First Natl Bank of Rochester-Old Monroe County Savings Bank Bldg—*hist pl* .... NY-2
First Natl Bank of Rock River—*hist pl* .... WY-8
First Natl Bank of San Antonio—*hist pl* .... TX-5
First Natl Bank of Seaford—*hist pl* .... DE-2
First Natl Bank of Wagoner—*hist pl* .... OK-5
First Natl Bank of White Bear—*hist pl* .... MN-6
First Natl City Bank—*hist pl* .... NY-2
First Natl State Bank Bldg—*hist pl* .... NJ-2
First Natl Well—*well* .... AZ-5
First Nazarene Ch—*church* .... IL-6
*First Negro Baptist Church* .... MS-4
*First Negro Brook Lake* .... ME-1
First Neshanic River—*stream* .... NJ-2
First New Hope Ch—*church* .... MS-4
First New Hope Missionary Baptist Ch—*church* .... MS-4
*First Nicolson Creek* .... MO-7
First Night Hollow—*valley* .... KY-4
First Nottoway Ch—*church* .... VA-3
*First of Speedway Assembly of God Ch* .... IN-6
First of Speedway Ch—*church* .... IN-6
First Oil Well in Oklahoma—*hist pl* .... OK-5
First Old River—*lake* .... AR-4
First Old River Lake—*lake* .... AR-4
First Open Bible Ch—*church* .... AL-4
First Pacific Coast Salmon Cannery Site—*hist pl* .... CA-9
First Parish Burying Ground—*cemetery* .... MA-1
First Parish Cem—*cemetery* (2) .... ME-1
First Parish Cem—*cemetery* .... MA-1
First Parish Ch—*church* .... MA-1
First Parish Church—*hist pl* .... ME-1
First Parish Church—*hist pl* .... MA-1
First Parish Church—*hist pl* .... NH-1
First Parish Church Parsonage—*hist pl* .... MA-1
First Parish Church Site-Dover Point—*hist pl* .... NH-1
First Parish Meetinghouse—*hist pl* (2) .... ME-1
First Parish Unitarian Church—*hist pl* .... MA-1
First Park—*flat* .... CO-8
First (Park) Congregational Church—*hist pl* .... MI-6
First Parsonage for Second East Parish Church—*hist pl* .... MA-1
First Pawling Ch—*church* .... NY-2
First Peak—*summit* .... NY-2
First Peak—*summit* .... OR-9
First Peak—*summit* .... VA-3
First Pecan Bayou—*stream* .... TX-5
First Pelletier Brook Lake—*lake* .... ME-1
First Pentacostal Holiness Ch—*church* .... NC-3
First Pentecostal Ch—*church* (5) .... AL-4
First Pentecostal Ch—*church* (2) .... FL-3
First Pentecostal Ch—*church* .... KS-7
First Pentecostal Ch—*church* .... LA-4
First Pentecostal Ch—*church* (6) .... MS-4
First Pentecostal Ch—*church* .... TN-4
First Pentecostal Holiness Ch—*church* .... AL-4
First Pentecostal Holiness Ch—*church* .... FL-3
First Pentecostal Holiness Ch—*church* .... KS-7
First Pentecostal Holiness Ch of Christ—*church* .... AL-4
First Pentecostal Lighthouse Ch—*church* .... MS-4
First Pentecostal United Ch—*church* .... KS-7
First Perch Lake—*lake* .... MN-6
*First Periwinkle Creek* .... OR-9
First Pilgrim Ch—*church* .... IA-7
First Pilgrim Ch—*church* (2) .... PA-2
First Pilgrim Rest Ch—*church* .... MS-4
First Pines Hollow—*basin* .... OR-9
First Plymouth Ch—*church* .... IA-7
First Pocket—*bay* .... TN-4
*First Point* .... MA-1
*First Point* .... RI-1
First Point—*cape* .... FL-3
First Point—*cape* .... MA-1
First Point—*cliff* .... VA-3
First Point Spring—*spring* .... UT-8
First Police Precinct Station House—*hist pl* .... NY-2
**First Pommier**—*pop pl* .... IL-6
*First Pond* .... MA-1
*First Pond* .... NY-2
*First Pond* .... PA-2
First Pond—*lake* .... ME-1
First Pond—*lake* (3) .... NY-2
First Pond—*lake* .... PA-2
First Pond—*swamp* .... TX-5
First Porcupine Rapids—*rapids* .... WI-6
*First Potts Creek* .... NC-3
First Prairie Mtn—*summit* .... OR-9
First Presbyteran Ch—*church* .... TN-4
First Presbyterian Ch—*church* (42) .... AL-4
First Presbyterian Ch—*church* (3) .... DE-2
First Presbyterian Ch—*church* (5) .... FL-3
First Presbyterian Ch—*church* (5) .... IA-7
First Presbyterian Ch—*church* .... KS-7
First Presbyterian Ch—*church* (34) .... MS-4
First Presbyterian Ch—*church* .... MO-7
First Presbyterian Ch—*church* (2) .... MT-8
First Presbyterian Ch—*church* (2) .... NC-3
First Presbyterian Ch—*church* .... PA-2
First Presbyterian Ch—*church* (2) .... SD-7
First Presbyterian Ch—*church* (19) .... TN-4
First Presbyterian Ch (Logan)—*church* .... UT-8
First Presbyterian Ch of Apopka—*church* .... FL-3
First Presbyterian Ch of Coral Springs—*church* .... FL-3
First Presbyterian Ch of Dyer—*church* .... TN-4
First Presbyterian Ch of Ellisville—*church* .... MS-4
First Presbyterian Ch of Fruitland—*church* .... TN-4
First Presbyterian Ch of Homestead—*church* .... FL-3
First Presbyterian Ch of Laurel—*church* .... MS-4
First Presbyterian Ch of Maitland—*church* .... FL-3
First Presbyterian Ch of Naples—*church* .... FL-3
First Presbyterian Ch of Palm Beach—*church* .... FL-3
First Presbyterian Ch of Trussville—*church* .... AL-4
First Presbyterian Ch (Ogden)—*church* .... UT-8
First Presbyterian Ch (Salt Lake City)—*church* .... UT-8
*First Presbyterian Church* .... AL-4
First Presbyterian Church—*hist pl* (5) .... AL-4
First Presbyterian Church—*hist pl* (6) .... AR-4
First Presbyterian Church—*hist pl* .... CA-9
First Presbyterian Church—*hist pl* .... CO-8
First Presbyterian Church—*hist pl* .... FL-3
First Presbyterian Church—*hist pl* (3) .... GA-3
First Presbyterian Church—*hist pl* (3) .... ID-8
First Presbyterian Church—*hist pl* .... IL-6
First Presbyterian Church—*hist pl* .... IN-6
First Presbyterian Church—*hist pl* (2) .... IA-7
First Presbyterian Church—*hist pl* .... KS-7
First Presbyterian Church—*hist pl* (6) .... KY-4
First Presbyterian Church—*hist pl* .... LA-4
First Presbyterian Church—*hist pl* (2) .... MI-6
First Presbyterian Church—*hist pl* .... MN-6
First Presbyterian Church—*hist pl* (2) .... MO-7
First Presbyterian Church—*hist pl* (2) .... MT-8
First Presbyterian Church—*hist pl* (7) .... NY-2
First Presbyterian Church—*hist pl* (4) .... NC-3
First Presbyterian Church—*hist pl* (2) .... OH-6
First Presbyterian Church—*hist pl* .... OK-5
First Presbyterian Church—*hist pl* .... OR-9
First Presbyterian Church—*hist pl* .... SC-3
First Presbyterian Church—*hist pl* (4) .... TN-4
First Presbyterian Church—*hist pl* (5) .... TX-5
First Presbyterian Church—*hist pl* (2) .... WI-6
First Presbyterian Church and Churchyard—*hist pl* .... NC-3
First Presbyterian Church and Manse—*hist pl* .... MD-2
First Presbyterian Church and Pintard, Lewis, House—*hist pl* .... NY-2
First Presbyterian Church/Calvary Temple Evangelical Church—*hist pl* .... WV-2
First Presbyterian Church of Blissfield—*hist pl* .... MI-6
First Presbyterian Church of Chandler—*hist pl* .... OK-5
First Presbyterian Church of Clifton—*hist pl* .... TN-4
First Presbyterian Church of Elizabeth—*hist pl* .... NJ-2
First Presbyterian Church of Hanover—*hist pl* .... NJ-2
First Presbyterian Church of Highland Falls—*hist pl* .... NY-2
First Presbyterian Church of Lawton—*hist pl* .... OK-5
First Presbyterian Church Of Maumee Chapel—*hist pl* .... OH-6
First Presbyterian Church of Meridian—*hist pl* .... MS-4
First Presbyterian Church of Natchez—*hist pl* .... MS-4
First Presbyterian Church of Oyster Bay—*hist pl* .... NY-2
First Presbyterian Church of Portland—*hist pl* .... OR-9
First Presbyterian Church of Pulaski—*hist pl* .... TN-4
First Presbyterian Church of Ramah—*hist pl* .... CO-8
First Presbyterian Church of Wantage—*hist pl* .... NJ-2
First Presbyterian Church of Wapakoneta—*hist pl* .... OH-6
First Presbyterian Church of West Chester—*hist pl* .... PA-2
First Presbyterian Church Of Wetumpka—*hist pl* .... AL-4
First Presbyterian Church Rectory—*hist pl* .... NY-2
First Presbyterian Church Sanctuary Bldg—*hist pl* .... CA-9
First Presbyterian Congregation of Connecticut Farms—*hist pl* .... NJ-2
First Presbyterian Day Sch—*school* .... FL-3
First Presbyterian Preschool—*school* .... FL-3
First Price Pond—*lake* .... OH-6
First Prong—*stream* .... GA-3
First Prong—*stream* .... TN-4
First Protestant Church—*hist pl* .... TX-5
*First Public School Marker* .... MA-1
First Puncheon Branch—*stream* .... FL-3
First Pup—*stream* .... AK-9
First Quarters (historical)—*locale* .... AL-4
First Ranch Creek—*stream* .... WY-8
First Rapids—*rapids* .... AK-9
First Rapids—*rapids* .... WI-6
First Recess—*valley* .... CA-9
First Recess Lakes—*lake* .... CA-9
First Red Knoll—*summit* .... UT-8
*First Redtown* .... IL-6
First Reformed and First Lutheran Churches—*hist pl* .... OH-6
First Reformed Ch—*church* .... IA-7
First Reformed Ch—*church* .... WA-9
First Reformed Church—*hist pl* (2) .... NY-2
First Reformed Dutch Church of Bergen Neck—*hist pl* .... NJ-2
First Reformed Presbyterian Ch—*church* .... KS-7
First Regional Library—*building* .... MS-4
First Religious Society Church and Parish Hall—*hist pl* .... MA-1
First Ridge—*ridge* .... ME-1
First Ridge—*ridge* .... UT-8
First Right Fork Rock Canyon—*valley* .... UT-8
First River—*stream* .... MN-6
First Roach Pond—*reservoir* .... ME-1
First Rock Lake—*lake* .... MT-8
First Rocky Tunnel—*tunnel* .... NC-3
First RR Addition Hist Dist—*hist pl* .... WA-9
First Rsvr—*reservoir* .... AZ-5
First Rsvr—*reservoir* .... CO-8
First Rsvr—*reservoir* .... NY-2
*Firstrum Tank* .... AZ-5
First Run—*stream* .... WV-2
First Run Ditch—*canal* .... CO-8
First Saint Cem—*cemetery* .... WV-2
First Saint Pauls Ch—*church* .... GA-3
First Saint Pauls Ch—*church* .... VA-3
First Saint Sch—*school* .... CA-9
First Salem Ch—*church* .... GA-3
First Salem Ch—*church* .... IN-6
First Salt Creek—*stream* .... IL-6
First Salt Creek—*stream* .... UT-8
First Sand Creek—*stream* .... WY-8
First Sawmill Spring—*spring* .... NV-8
First Sch—*school* .... MI-6
First Self-Sustaining Nuclear Reaction, Site of—*hist pl* .... IL-6
*First Seventh Day Adventist Ch* .... AL-4
First Seventh Day Adventist Ch—*church* .... AL-4
First Seventh Day Adventist Ch—*church* (3) .... MS-4
First Seventh Day Adventist Ch—*church* .... TN-4
First Shearith Israel Graveyard—*hist pl* .... NY-2
First Sheep Camp Spring—*spring* .... OR-9
Firstside Hist Dist—*hist pl* .... PA-2
First Silver Lake—*lake* .... MN-6
First Silver Run—*stream* .... NC-3
First Sister Creek—*stream* .... SC-3
First Sister Lake—*lake* .... MI-6
First Slough—*gut* .... CA-9
First Slough—*gut* .... FL-3
First Society of Friends Ch—*church* .... IN-6
First Soil Conservation District Dedication Site—*hist pl* .... OK-5
First South Branch Oconto River—*stream* .... WI-6
First South Branch Russell Pond—*lake* .... ME-1
*First Southern Baptist Ch* .... AL-4
First Southern Baptist Ch—*church* .... IN-6
First Southern Baptist Ch—*church* (2) .... KS-7
First Southern Baptist Ch—*church* .... MS-4
First Southern Baptist Ch (Bountiful)—*church* .... UT-8
First Southern Baptist Ch (Clearfield)—*church* .... UT-8
First Southern Baptist Ch (Hurricane)—*church* .... UT-8
First Southern Baptist Ch (Monticello)—*church* .... UT-8
First Southern Baptist Ch (Mount Pleasant)—*church* .... UT-8
First Southern Baptist Ch (Salt Lake City)—*church* .... UT-8
First Southern Baptist Ch (St. George)—*church* .... UT-8
First Southern Ch—*church* .... FL-3
First Southern Methodist Ch—*church* (2) .... AL-4
First Southern Methodist Ch—*church* .... MS-4
First South Fork East Fork Clear Creek—*stream* .... CA-9
First Spanish Christian Ch—*church* .... FL-3
First Spring—*spring* .... CA-9
First Spring—*spring* .... CO-8
First Spring—*spring* .... MT-8
First Spring—*spring* (3) .... UT-8
First Spring—*spring* .... WY-8
First Spring Creek—*stream* .... ID-8
First Spring Creek—*stream* .... UT-8
First Spring Hollow—*valley* .... UT-8
First State Bank—*hist pl* .... KS-7
First State Bank—*hist pl* .... MN-6
First State Bank—*hist pl* .... OK-5
First State Bank and Trust Bldg—*hist pl* .... TX-5
First State Bank Bldg—*hist pl* .... SD-7
First State Bank of Baggs—*hist pl* .... WY-8
First State Bank of Bethany—*hist pl* .... NE-7
First State Bank of Buxton—*hist pl* .... ND-7
First State Bank of Indiahoma—*hist pl* .... OK-5
First State Bank of LeRoy—*hist pl* .... MN-6
First State Bank of Manlius—*hist pl* .... IL-6
First Stillwater—*lake* .... NY-2
First Stillwater—*reservoir* .... NY-2
*First Street* .... IA-7
First Street—*uninc pl* .... CA-9
First Street—*uninc pl* .... VA-3
First Street Ch of Christ—*church* .... TN-4
First Street District—*hist pl* .... KY-4
First Street Hist Dist—*hist pl* .... MI-6
First Street Sch—*school* .... FL-3
First Street Sch—*school* .... NY-2
First Street Sch—*school* .... OH-6
First Street Sch—*school* .... PA-2
First Sugarloaf—*summit* .... CA-9
First Swale Creek—*stream* .... OR-9
First Swamp—*stream* .... NC-3
First Swamp Ch—*church* .... NC-3
First Switchback Trail—*trail* .... PA-2
*First Tabernacle* .... IN-6
First Tabernacle Baptist Ch—*church* .... AL-4
First Tank—*reservoir* (3) .... AZ-5
First Tank—*reservoir* (2) .... TX-5
First Territorial Capitol—*hist pl* .... KS-7
First Thessalonia Bible Ch—*church* .... KS-7
*First-Third School* .... IN-6
First Thonotosassa Baptist Ch—*church* .... FL-3
First Thought Lake—*lake* .... WA-9
First Thought Mine—*mine* .... WA-9
First Thought Mtn—*summit* .... WA-9
First Timothy Baptist Ch—*church* .... FL-3
First Top—*summit* .... WA-9
First Trail Canyon—*valley* .... AZ-5
First Trail Canyon—*valley* .... CO-8
First Trestle Lake—*lake* .... MN-6
First Trinity Ch—*church* .... NC-3
First Trinity Evangelical Lutheran Ch—*church* .... IN-6
First Trinity Wesleyan Ch—*church* .... TN-4
First Trust Bldg and Garage—*hist pl* .... CA-9
First Trust Company Bldg—*hist pl* .... NY-2
First Union—*post sta* .... NC-3
First Union Baptist Ch—*church* .... MS-4
First Union Ch—*church* .... AR-4
First Union Ch—*church* .... KY-4
First Union Ch—*church* .... LA-4
First Union Ch—*church* .... NJ-2
First Union Ch—*church* (4) .... VA-3
First Unitarian Ch—*church* .... MA-1
First Unitarian Ch of Orlando—*church* .... FL-3
First Unitarian Church—*hist pl* .... CA-9
First Unitarian Church—*hist pl* .... MD-2
First Unitarian Church—*hist pl* .... MA-1
First Unitarian Church—*hist pl* .... PA-2
First Unitarian Church—*hist pl* .... WI-6
First Unitarian Church of Detroit—*hist pl* .... MI-6
First Unitarian Church Of Marietta—*hist pl* .... OH-6
First Unitarian Church of Oakland—*hist pl* .... CA-9
First Unitarian Church of Omaha—*hist pl* .... NE-7
First Unitarian Church of Portland—*hist pl* .... OR-9
First Unitarian Society Meetinghouse—*hist pl* .... WI-6
First Unitarian Universalist Church—*hist pl* .... CA-9
First United Babtist Ch—*church* .... MA-1
First United Cem—*cemetery* .... MN-6
First United Ch—*church* .... AL-4
First United Ch—*church* (2) .... IA-7
First United Ch—*church* .... KS-7
First United Ch—*church* (2) .... MS-4
First United Ch—*church* .... MO-7
First United Ch—*church* (2) .... TX-5
First United Ch of Christ—*church* .... TN-4
*First United Methodist Ch* .... TN-4
First United Methodist Ch—*church* (26) .... AL-4
First United Methodist Ch—*church* (13) .... FL-3
First United Methodist Ch—*church* .... KS-7
First United Methodist Ch—*church* (36) .... MS-4
First United Methodist Ch—*church* (19) .... TN-4
First United Methodist Ch of Alcoa—*church* .... TN-4
First United Methodist Ch of Apopka—*church* .... FL-3
First United Methodist Ch of Attalla—*church* .... AL-4
First United Methodist Ch of Brandon—*church* .... MS-4
First United Methodist Ch of Coral Springs—*church* .... FL-3
First United Methodist Ch of Decaturville—*church* .... TN-4
First United Methodist Ch of Flowood—*church* .... MS-4
First United Methodist Ch of Gadsden—*church* .... AL-4
First United Methodist Ch of Gordo—*church* .... AL-4
First United methodist Ch of Gulfport—*church* .... FL-3
First United Methodist Ch of Hueytown—*church* .... AL-4
First United Methodist Ch of Laurel—*church* .... MS-4
First United Methodist Ch of Magee—*church* .... MS-4
First United Methodist Ch of Oviedo—*church* .... FL-3
First United Methodist Ch of Pine Hills—*church* .... FL-3
First United Methodist Ch of Saks—*church* .... AL-4
First United Methodist Ch of Stevenson—*church* .... AL-4
First United Methodist Ch of Uniontown—*church* .... AL-4
First United Methodist Ch of Winter Garden—*church* .... FL-3
First United Methodist Ch of Winter Park—*church* .... FL-3
First United Methodist Ch (Ogden)—*church* .... UT-8
First United Methodist Christian Day Sch—*school* .... FL-3
First United Methodist Ch Saint Cloud—*church* .... FL-3
First United Methodist Ch (Salt Lake City)—*church* .... UT-8
First United Methodist Church—*hist pl* (3) .... AL-4
First United Methodist Church—*hist pl* (2) .... AR-4
First United Methodist Church—*hist pl* .... ID-8
First United Methodist Church—*hist pl* (2) .... KY-4
First United Methodist Church—*hist pl* (2) .... LA-4
First United Methodist Church—*hist pl* .... MI-6
First United Methodist Church—*hist pl* .... NV-8
First United Methodist Church—*hist pl* .... OH-6
First United Methodist Church—*hist pl* .... OK-5
First United Methodist Church—*hist pl* .... SD-7
First United Methodist Church—*hist pl* (2) .... TX-5
First United Methodist Church—*hist pl* .... WY-8
First United Methodist Church of Columbia—*hist pl* .... TN-4
First United Methodist Church of Drumright—*hist pl* .... OK-5
First United Methodist Church Preschool—*school* .... FL-3
First United Methodist Day Sch—*school* .... FL-3
First United Methodist Preschool—*school* .... FL-3
First United Methodist Sch—*school* .... FL-3
*First United Pentecostal Ch* .... MS-4
First United Pentecostal Ch—*church* (9) .... AL-4
First United Pentecostal Ch—*church* .... FL-3
First United Pentecostal Ch—*church* (8) .... MS-4
First United Pentecostal Ch—*church* (2) .... TN-4
First United Pentecostal Ch of Longwood—*church* .... FL-3
First United Pentecostal Ch Revival Center—*church* .... MS-4
First United Presbyterian Ch—*church* .... SD-7
First United Presbyterian Ch—*church* .... TN-4
First United Presbyterian Ch of Allegheny County—*church* .... PA-2
First United Presbyterian Church—*hist pl* .... CO-8
First United Presbyterian Church—*hist pl* .... MI-6
First United Presbyterian Church of Auburn—*hist pl* .... NE-7
First Unity Ch—*church* .... FL-3
First Universalist Ch—*church* (2) .... AL-4
First Universalist Chruch—*hist pl* .... MA-1
First Universalist Church—*hist pl* .... IL-6
First Universalist Church—*hist pl* .... ME-1
First Universalist Church—*hist pl* .... MA-1
First Universalist Church—*hist pl* .... NH-1
First Universalist Church—*hist pl* .... NY-2
First Universalist Church—*hist pl* .... OH-6
First Universalist Church—*hist pl* .... RI-1
First Universalist Church—*hist pl* .... WI-6
First Universalist Church of Cedar Rapids—*hist pl* .... IA-7
First Universalist Church of Olmsted—*hist pl* .... OH-6
First Valley—*valley* .... NM-5
**First View**—*pop pl* .... CO-8
First View—*summit* .... AZ-5
First Wannigan Rapids—*rapids* .... WI-6
First Ward Elem Sch—*school* .... PA-2
*First Ward Sch* .... PA-2
First Ward Sch—*school* .... AR-4
First Ward Sch—*school* .... LA-4
First Ward Sch—*school* .... NC-3
First Ward Sch—*school* (7) .... PA-2
First Ward Sch—*school* .... TX-5
First Ward Sch—*school* .... WV-2
First Ward Sch—*school* .... WI-6
First Ward Sch (abandoned)—*school* .... PA-2
First Ward Triangle Hist Dist—*hist pl* .... WI-6
First Ward Wardroom—*hist pl* .... RI-1
First Wasco County Courthouse—*hist pl* .... OR-9
First Washburn Tunnel—*tunnel* .... NC-3
First Watchung Mtn—*summit* .... NJ-2
First Water—*lake* .... UT-8
First Water Cabin—*locale* .... UT-8
First Water Canyon—*valley* .... AZ-5
First Water Canyon—*valley* .... UT-8
First Water Creek—*stream* .... AZ-5
Firstwater Creek—*stream* .... CA-9
Firstwater Creek—*stream* .... ID-8
First Water Creek—*stream* .... UT-8
First Water Creek—*stream* .... WY-8
First Water Draw—*valley* .... WY-8
First Waterfall Creek—*stream* .... AK-9
First Waterfall Hollow—*valley* .... UT-8
First Water Gulch—*valley* .... CO-8
First Water Gulch—*valley* (2) .... OR-9
First Water Ranch—*locale* .... AZ-5
First Water Ridge—*ridge* .... UT-8
First Water Spring—*spring* .... CO-8
First Water Spring—*spring* .... UT-8
First Water Trough Creek—*stream* .... CA-9
First Weches Sch (historical)—*school* .... TX-5
First Well ( Artesian)—*well* .... WY-8
First Welsh Congregational Church—*hist pl* .... IA-7
First Wesleyan Acad—*school* .... AL-4
First Wesleyan Ch—*church* .... AL-4
First Wesleyan Ch—*church* .... KS-7
First Wesleyan Ch—*church* .... NC-3
First Wesleyan Ch—*church* .... TN-4
First Wesleyan Methodist Ch—*church* .... AL-4
First West Branch Pond—*lake* .... ME-1
First West Prong Windmill—*locale* .... TX-5
First West Well—*locale* .... NM-5
First White House of the Confederacy—*building* .... AL-4
First White House of the Confederacy—*hist pl* .... AL-4
First Wolverine Creek—*stream* .... MT-8
*First Yegua Creek* .... TX-5
First Yellow Mule Creek—*stream* .... MT-8
First Zion Ch—*church* .... AL-4
First Zion Ch—*church* .... MS-4
First Zion Ch—*church* .... SC-3
Firt Baptist Ch—*church* .... TN-4
Firt Cumberland Presbyterian Ch—*church* .... TN-4
**Firth**—*pop pl* .... ID-8
**Firth**—*pop pl* .... NE-7
Firth Cem—*cemetery* .... NE-7
**Firthcliffe**—*pop pl* .... NY-2
Firthcliffe (census name for Cornwall)—*CDP* .... NY-2
**Firthcliffe Heights**—*pop pl* .... NY-2
Firth Lake—*lake* .... WI-6
Firth Lake Trail—*trail* .... WI-6
Firth River—*stream* .... AK-9
Firthtown—*uninc pl* .... NJ-2
Firth Youth Center—*building* .... NJ-2
Fir Timber Butte—*summit* .... OR-9
Firtop—*summit* .... CA-9
Fir Tree—*locale* .... WA-9
Fir Tree Alcove—*cave* .... AZ-5
Fir Tree Canyon—*valley* .... AZ-5
Fir Tree Canyon—*valley* (2) .... OR-9
Fir Tree Creek—*stream* (2) .... OR-9
Fir Tree Forest Camp—*locale* .... OR-9
Fir Tree Gulch—*valley* .... ID-8
Fir Tree Point—*cape* .... NY-2
Fir Tree Spring—*spring* (4) .... OR-9
**Fir Villa**—*pop pl* .... OR-9
**Firwood**—*pop pl* .... OR-9
**Firwood**—*pop pl* .... WA-9
Firwood Cem—*cemetery* .... NY-2
Firwood Creek—*stream* .... OR-9
**Firwood (historical)**—*pop pl* .... OR-9
Firwood Sch—*school* (2) .... WA-9
Firwood Veneer Corporation Dam—*dam* .... OR-9
Firwood Veneer Corporation Rsvr—*reservoir* .... OR-9
Fiscal—*locale* .... PA-2
**Fischbein Township**—*pop pl* .... ND-7
Fischer—*locale* .... ID-8
**Fischer**—*pop pl* .... TX-5
Fischer, Carl, Meats—*hist pl* .... OR-9
Fischer, Joseph, House—*hist pl* .... CA-9
Fischer Creek—*stream* .... OR-9
Fischer Creek—*stream* .... WI-6
Fischer Draw—*valley* .... CO-8
Fischer Draw—*valley* .... WY-8
Fischer Hollow—*valley* .... MO-7
Fischer House—*hist pl* .... LA-4
Fischer House—*hist pl* .... TX-5
Fischer Island—*island* .... OR-9
*Fischer Lake* .... WI-6
Fischer Lake—*lake* .... CO-8
Fischer Lake—*lake* .... FL-3
Fischer Lake—*lake* .... ME-1
Fischer Lake—*lake* .... MN-6
Fischer Lake—*lake* .... ND-7
Fischer Lake—*lake* (2) .... WI-6
Fischer Park—*park* .... WI-6
Fischer Private Airstrip—*airport* .... ND-7
Fischer Ranch—*locale* .... AZ-5
Fischer Ranch—*locale* .... CO-8
Fischer Rsvr—*reservoir* .... WY-8
Fischer Sch—*school* (2) .... MI-6
Fischer Sch—*school* (2) .... NE-7
**Fischers Mill**—*pop pl* .... OR-9
Fischer Spring—*spring* .... NM-5
**Fischner Phillips Condominium**—*pop pl* .... UT-8
Fischtner Covered Bridge—*hist pl* .... PA-2
**Fiscus**—*pop pl* (2) .... IA-7
Fiscus And Vanoni Ditch—*canal* .... WY-8
Fiscus Cem—*cemetery* .... IN-6
*Fiscus Church* .... PA-2
Fiscus Gulch—*valley* .... WY-8
*Fish* .... WA-9
Fish—*locale* .... GA-3
Fish, Abel H., House—*hist pl* .... CT-1
Fish, Hamilton, House—*hist pl* .... NY-2
Fish Acad—*school* .... TN-4
Fish and Fur Club—*hist pl* .... NY-2

Fish and Game Club—*other* TX-5
Fish and Game Experimental Station—*locale* CA-9
Fish And Game Farm Lake—*reservoir* KY-4
Fish and Hunter Camp (historical)—*locale* SD-7
Fish and Hunter Siding (historical)—*locale* SD-7
Fish and Wildlife Service Upper Station—*locale* AK-9
*Fishawk Lake* MI-6
**Fishback**—*pop pl* OH-6
Fishback, Jesse, House—*hist pl* KY-4
Fishback Butte—*summit* MT-8
Fishback Cem—*cemetery* KY-4
Fishback Creek—*stream* IN-6
Fishback Hill—*summit* OR-9
Fishback House (Boundary Increase)—*hist pl* SD-7
Fishback Sch—*school* AR-4
Fishback Tank—*reservoir* NM-5
Fish Barrier Dam—*dam* CA-9
Fish Basket Hollow—*valley* PA-2
Fishbaugh Lateral—*canal* AZ-5
*Fish Bay* AL-4
Fish Bay—*bay* (2) AK-9
Fish Bay—*bay* CO-8
Fish Bay—*bay* TX-5
Fish Bay—*bay* VI-3
Fish Bay—*locale* VI-3
Fish Bay Creek—*stream* AK-9
Fish Bay Gut—*stream* VI-3
Fish Bayou—*gut* (2) AR-4
Fish Bayou—*gut* (2) LA-4
Fish Bayou—*stream* (4) LA-4
Fish Bayou—*stream* (2) MS-4
Fish Bayou Ch—*church* LA-4
Fish Bayou Lake—*lake* LA-4
*Fishbeck Lake Dam* IN-6
Fishbench Tank—*reservoir* AZ-5
Fishberry Creek—*stream* NE-7
Fishbird Lake Rsvr—*reservoir* OR-9
Fish Bladder Island—*island* VT-1
Fishbone Beach—*locale* FL-3
*Fishbone Creek* AZ-5
Fishbone Creek—*stream* FL-3
Fishbone Island—*island* VA-3
Fish Bowl Spring—*spring* WY-8
Fish Box Gully—*gut* TX-5
Fishbox Island—*island* MN-6
**Fish Branch**—*pop pl* TX-5
Fish Branch—*stream* AL-4
Fish Branch—*stream* (3) FL-3
Fish Branch—*stream* GA-3
Fish Branch—*stream* KY-4
Fish Branch—*stream* (2) MO-7
Fish Branch—*stream* TN-4
Fish Branch—*stream* TX-5
Fish Branch Island—*island* FL-3
*Fish Brook* MA-1
Fish Brook—*stream* (5) ME-1
Fish Brook—*stream* (4) MA-1
Fish Brook—*stream* NY-2
Fish Brook Dam—*dam* MA-1
Fishbrook Pond—*lake* NY-2
Fish Brook Rsvr—*reservoir* MA-1
*Fishburn* AZ-5
Fishburn Ave Sch—*school* CA-9
Fishburn Cem—*cemetery* TN-4
Fishburn Drain—*canal* MI-6
Fishburne Creek—*stream* SC-3
Fishburne Military Sch—*hist pl* VA-3
Fishburne Sch—*school* SC-3
Fishburn Hollow—*valley* TN-4
*Fishburn Landing* SC-3
Fishburn Park—*park* VA-3
Fishburn Park Sch—*school* VA-3
Fishburn Run—*stream* PA-2
Fishburns Ch—*church* PA-2
Fishburn Sch—*school* IL-6
*Fish Butte* MT-8
Fish Butte—*summit* ID-8
Fish Butte Saddle—*gap* ID-8
Fish Cabin—*locale* CA-9
Fish Cabin Creek—*stream* NY-2
Fish Cabin Ridge—*ridge* PA-2
Fish Camp—*locale* AK-9
Fish Camp—*locale* CA-9
Fish Camp—*locale* MT-8
**Fish Camp**—*pop pl* CA-9
Fish Camp Flat—*flat* CA-9
Fish Camp Lake—*lake* AK-9
Fish Camp Pond—*lake* MI-6
Fish Camp Prong—*stream* TN-4
Fish Camp Slough—*stream* TX-5
Fish Canyon—*valley* AZ-5
Fish Canyon—*valley* (3) CA-9
Fish Canyon—*valley* CO-8
Fish Canyon—*valley* NE-7
Fish Canyon—*valley* (2) WY-8
Fish Canyon Ridge—*ridge* CO-8
Fish Canyon Spring—*spring* WY-8
Fish Canyon Trail—*trail* CA-9
Fish Cave—*cave* AL-4
Fish Cave—*cave* IL-6
Fish Cave—*cave* NV-8
Fish Cay—*island* VI-3
Fish Cem—*cemetery* CT-1
Fish Cem—*cemetery* IN-6
Fish Cem—*cemetery* ME-1
Fish Cem—*cemetery* MO-7
Fish Cem—*cemetery* (2) OH-6
Fish Cem—*cemetery* TN-4
Fish Cem—*cemetery* VT-1
Fish Cem—*cemetery* WI-6
Fish Commission Bldg (historical)—*building* DC-2
Fish Corners—*locale* PA-2
Fish Coulee—*lake* LA-4
*Fish Cove* RI-1
Fish Cove—*bay* MI-6
Fish Cove—*bay* NH-1
Fish Cove—*bay* NY-2
*Fish Cove Pond* RI-1
*Fish Creek* AL-4
*Fish Creek* AK-9
*Fish Creek* AZ-5
*Fish Creek* CA-9
*Fish Creek* CO-8
*Fish Creek* FL-3
*Fish Creek* IN-6
*Fish Creek* MI-6
*Fish Creek* MT-8
*Fish Creek* NY-2
*Fish Creek* ND-7
*Fish Creek* OK-5
*Fish Creek* OR-9
*Fish Creek* PA-2
*Fish Creek* SC-3
*Fish Creek* TX-5
*Fish Creek* UT-8
*Fish Creek* WV-2
*Fish Creek* WY-8
Fish Creek—*channel* FL-3
Fish Creek—*gut* (2) FL-3
Fish Creek—*gut* IL-6
Fish Creek—*gut* NY-2
Fish Creek—*locale* FL-3
Fish Creek—*locale* NY-2
**Fish Creek**—*pop pl* GA-3
**Fish Creek**—*pop pl* NY-2
**Fish Creek**—*pop pl* WI-6
Fish Creek—*stream* (12) AK-9
Fish Creek—*stream* (2) AZ-5
Fish Creek—*stream* AR-4
Fish Creek—*stream* (24) CA-9
Fish Creek—*stream* (9) CO-8
Fish Creek—*stream* (3) FL-3
Fish Creek—*stream* GA-3
Fish Creek—*stream* (16) ID-8
Fish Creek—*stream* (5) IN-6
Fish Creek—*stream* (2) IA-7
Fish Creek—*stream* (5) KS-7
Fish Creek—*stream* KY-4
Fish Creek—*stream* (2) LA-4
Fish Creek—*stream* ME-1
Fish Creek—*stream* (5) MI-6
Fish Creek—*stream* (6) MN-6
Fish Creek—*stream* MO-7
Fish Creek—*stream* (12) MT-8
Fish Creek—*stream* (2) NE-7
Fish Creek—*stream* (4) NV-8
Fish Creek—*stream* (2) NJ-2
Fish Creek—*stream* NM-5
Fish Creek—*stream* (14) NY-2
Fish Creek—*stream* NC-3
Fish Creek—*stream* (2) ND-7
Fish Creek—*stream* (4) OH-6
Fish Creek—*stream* (10) OK-5
Fish Creek—*stream* (19) OR-9
Fish Creek—*stream* PA-2
Fish Creek—*stream* SC-3
Fish Creek—*stream* (9) TX-5
Fish Creek—*stream* (12) UT-8
Fish Creek—*stream* (10) WA-9
Fish Creek—*stream* WV-2
Fish Creek—*stream* (6) WI-6
Fish Creek—*stream* (14) WY-8
Fish Creek Basin—*basin* ID-8
Fish Creek Basin—*basin* NV-8
*Fish Creek Bay* WI-6
Fish Creek Bay—*bay* FL-3
Fish Creek Bay—*bay* NY-2
Fish Creek Bridge—*hist pl* AZ-5
Fish Creek Campground—*locale* (2) CA-9
Fish Creek Campground—*locale* CO-8
Fish Creek Campground—*locale* UT-8
Fish Creek Campground—*park* OR-9
Fish Creek Canyon—*valley* CO-8
Fish Creek Cem—*cemetery* IN-6
Fish Creek Cem—*cemetery* MT-8
Fish Creek Ch—*church* KY-4
Fish Creek Ch—*church* MO-7
Fish Creek Ch—*church* OK-5
Fish Creek Ch—*church* TX-5
Fish Creek Corral—*locale* AZ-5
Fish Creek Cove—*valley* UT-8
Fish Creek Covered Bridge—*hist pl* WV-2
Fish Creek Dam—*dam* ND-7
Fish Creek Dam—*dam* OR-9
Fish Creek Dam—*dam* TX-5
Fish Creek Dam—*dam* UT-8
Fish Creek Dam—*hist pl* ID-8
Fish Creek Desert—*plain* OR-9
Fish Creek Ditch—*canal* NE-7
Fish Creek Divide—*ridge* OR-9
Fish Creek Falls—*falls* CO-8
Fish Creek Falls Trail—*trail* CO-8
Fish Creek Forebay—*reservoir* OR-9
Fish Creek Forest Camp—*locale* OR-9
Fish Creek Harbor—*bay* WI-6
*Fish Creek Hill* AZ-5
Fish Creek (historical)—*stream* SD-7
**Fish Creek (historical town)**—*pop pl* (2) AZ-5
*Fish Creek Hot Springs* CA-9
Fish Creek Island—*island* AK-9
Fish Creek Island—*island* WV-2
*Fish Creek Lake* MI-6
Fish Creek Lake—*lake* (2) AK-9
Fish Creek Lake—*lake* MT-8
Fish Creek Lake—*reservoir* UT-8
**Fish Creek Landing**—*pop pl* NY-2
Fish Creek Lookout Tower—*locale* ID-8
*Fish Creek Meadow* CA-9
Fish Creek Meadow Campground—*locale* ID-8
Fish Creek Meadows—*flat* UT-8
Fish Creek Meadows—*swamp* CA-9
*Fish Creek Mountains* NV-8
Fish Creek Mountains—*range* CA-9
*Fish Creek Mtn* CA-9
Fish Creek Mtn—*summit* AZ-5
Fish Creek Mtn—*summit* CA-9
Fish Creek Mtn—*summit* (2) NV-8
Fish Creek Mtn—*summit* OR-9
Fish Creek Mtn—*summit* WY-8
Fish Creek Mtns—*range* NV-8
Fish Creek Park—*flat* (2) WY-8
Fish Creek Park—*park* WY-8
Fish Creek Pass—*gap* WA-9
Fish Creek Pass—*gut* FL-3
Fish Creek Peak—*summit* AZ-5
*Fish Creek Pennsylvania Fork* WV-2
Fish Creek Point—*cliff* UT-8
Fish Creek Point—*summit* ID-8
Fish Creek Ponds—*lake* NY-2
Fish Creek Ranch—*locale* (2) NV-8
Fish Creek Range—*range* ID-8
Fish Creek Range—*range* NV-8
Fish Creek Ranger Station—*locale* MT-8
Fish Creek Rec Area—*park* ID-8
*Fish Creek Reservoir* UT-8
Fish Creek Ridge—*ridge* UT-8
Fish Creek Ridge—*ridge* WI-6
Fish Creek Ridge Ch—*church* WI-6
Fish Creek Rock—*pillar* CO-8
Fish Creek Rsvr—*reservoir* CO-8
Fish Creek Rsvr—*reservoir* ID-8
Fish Creek Rsvr—*reservoir* OR-9
Fish Creek Rsvr No 1—*reservoir* CO-8
Fish Creek Rsvr No 2—*reservoir* CO-8
Fish Creek Sch—*school* KS-7
Fish Creek Sch—*school* KY-4
Fish Creek Sch—*school* OH-6
Fish Creek Sch—*school* WI-6
Fish Creek Sch—*school* WY-8
Fish Creek Shelter—*locale* OR-9
*Fish Creek Slough* TX-5
Fish Creek Spring—*spring* ID-8
Fish Creek Springs—*spring* NV-8
**Fish Creek Spur**—*pop pl* MT-8
**Fish Creek Station**—*pop pl* NY-2
Fish Creek Table—*flat* NV-8
Fish Creek Test Well No 1 (Site)—*well* AK-9
Fish Creek Trail—*trail* CO-8
Fish Creek Trail (Pack)—*trail* CA-9
*Fish Creek Valley* NV-8
Fish Creek Valley—*basin* NV-8
Fish Creek Valley—*valley* OR-9
Fish Creek Wash—*stream* CA-9
Fish Creek Waterhole Number Forty—*reservoir* OR-9
Fish Creek Waterhole Number Forty-four—*reservoir* OR-9
Fish Creek Waterhole Number Forty-seven—*reservoir* OR-9
*Fish Creek Well* NV-8
Fish Creek Well—*well* NV-8
Fish Cut—*locale* WY-8
Fish Dam Cem—*cemetery* SC-3
Fish Dam Creek—*stream* NC-3
Fishdam Creek—*stream* TN-4
Fishdam Ford—*hist pl* SC-3
**Fishdam (historical)**—*pop pl* TN-4
Fishdam Park—*park* MI-6
Fishdam River—*stream* MI-6
Fish Dam Run—*stream* PA-2
Fish Dam Spring—*spring* ID-8
Fish Dam Trail—*trail* PA-2
Fishdance Lake—*lake* MN-6
Fishdom Post Office (historical)—*building* TN-4
Fish Draw—*valley* SD-7
Fish Draw—*valley* WY-8
Fish Draw Sch—*school* SD-7
Fisheating Bay—*bay* FL-3
Fisheating Creek—*stream* FL-3
Fisheating Creek Bridge—*bridge* FL-3
Fisheating Creek Wildlife Mngmt Area—*park* FL-3
Fisheating Creek Wildlife Ref—*park* FL-3
Fish Eddy—*rapids* OR-9
*Fisheeton* AL-4
Fish Egg Island—*island* AK-9
Fish Egg Reef—*bar* AK-9
Fishel—*locale* CA-9
Fishel Creek—*stream* MT-8
Fishel Creek—*stream* PA-2
Fishell Drain—*canal* MI-6
Fishel Ranch—*hist pl* SD-7
Fishel Ranch—*locale* SD-7
*Fisher* (2) MI-6
Fisher—*locale* CA-9
Fisher—*locale* KY-4
Fisher—*locale* OH-6
Fisher—*locale* OK-5
Fisher—*locale* OR-9
Fisher—*locale* TX-5
Fisher—*locale* WV-2
Fisher—*locale* WY-8
**Fisher**—*pop pl* (2) AR-4
**Fisher**—*pop pl* CA-9
**Fisher**—*pop pl* IL-6
**Fisher**—*pop pl* IN-6
**Fisher**—*pop pl* LA-4
**Fisher**—*pop pl* MI-6
**Fisher**—*pop pl* MN-6
**Fisher**—*pop pl* MS-4
**Fisher**—*pop pl* (3) PA-2
**Fisher**—*pop pl* WA-9
Fisher, Andrew, House—*hist pl* DE-2
Fisher, Bayou—*stream* (2) LA-4
Fisher, Burr, House—*hist pl* MT-8
Fisher, David, House—*hist pl* UT-8
Fisher, Ferdinand, House—*hist pl* OR-9
Fisher, Henry, House—*hist pl* PA-2
Fisher, James M., House—*hist pl* ID-8
Fisher, Lake—*reservoir* IA-7
Fisher, Lake—*reservoir* NC-3
Fisher, Lewis M., House—*hist pl* IA-7
Fisher, Maj. Jared B., House—*hist pl* PA-2
Fisher, Nathan, House—*hist pl* MA-1
Fisher, Nelson E., House-High Banks—*hist pl* MI-6
Fisher, O. C., Federal Bldg—*hist pl* TX-5
Fisher, William G., House—*hist pl* CO-8
Fisher Airp—*airport* PA-2
Fisher and Fry Lake—*lake* AZ-5
Fisher and New Center Buildings—*hist pl* MI-6
Fisher Basin—*basin* AZ-5
Fisher Basin Spring—*spring* AZ-5
Fisher Basin Trail Sixty four—*trail* AZ-5
Fisher Bay—*bay* MI-6
Fisher Bay—*bay* NY-2
Fisher Bayou—*stream* LA-4
Fisher Bend—*bend* KY-4
Fisher Bend—*bend* TX-5
Fisher Bldg—*hist pl* IL-6
Fisher Body Company—*facility* IL-6
Fisher Body Division, General Motors Corporation—*facility* (2) MI-6
Fisher Body Division (General Motors Corporation)—*facility* OH-6
Fisher Bog Dam—*dam* MA-1
Fisher Bog Rsvr—*reservoir* MA-1
Fisher Bottom—*bend* ID-8
Fisher Bottom—*bend* OK-5
Fisher Bowen Branch—*stream* WV-2
*Fisher Branch* DE-2
*Fisher Branch* VA-3
Fisher Branch—*stream* FL-3
Fisher Branch—*stream* IL-6
Fisher Branch—*stream* IN-6
Fisher Branch—*stream* KY-4
Fisher Branch—*stream* MS-4
Fisher Branch—*stream* MO-7
Fisher Branch—*stream* (2) NC-3
Fisher Branch—*stream* OK-5
Fisher Branch—*stream* (2) TN-4
Fisher Branch—*stream* TX-5
Fisher Branch—*stream* WV-2
Fisher Bridge—*bridge* AR-4
Fisher Bridge—*bridge* WA-9
*Fisher Brook* ME-1
Fisher Brook—*stream* IN-6
Fisher Brook—*stream* ME-1
Fisher Brook—*stream* MA-1
Fisher Brook—*stream* NH-1
Fisher Brook—*stream* VT-1
*Fisher Building* MI-6
Fisher Butte—*summit* MT-8
Fisher Butte—*summit* OR-9
Fisher Caldera—*basin* AK-9
Fisher Camp—*locale* AZ-5
Fisher Camp—*locale* CO-8
Fisher Canyon—*valley* AZ-5
Fisher Canyon—*valley* CA-9
Fisher Canyon—*valley* (3) ID-8
Fisher Canyon—*valley* (2) NV-8
Fisher Canyon—*valley* NM-5
Fisher Canyon—*valley* OK-5
Fisher Canyon—*valley* OR-9
Fisher Canyon—*valley* UT-8
Fisher Canyon—*valley* WY-8
Fishercap Lake—*lake* MT-8
Fisher Cave—*cave* (3) MO-7
Fisher Cave—*cave* TN-4
Fisher Cem—*cemetery* (2) AL-4
Fisher Cem—*cemetery* CO-8
Fisher Cem—*cemetery* FL-3
Fisher Cem—*cemetery* IL-6
Fisher Cem—*cemetery* (2) IA-7
Fisher Cem—*cemetery* KS-7
Fisher Cem—*cemetery* (4) KY-4
Fisher Cem—*cemetery* (2) LA-4
Fisher Cem—*cemetery* ME-1
Fisher Cem—*cemetery* MS-4
Fisher Cem—*cemetery* (2) MO-7
Fisher Cem—*cemetery* MT-8
Fisher Cem—*cemetery* NY-2
Fisher Cem—*cemetery* (2) NC-3
Fisher Cem—*cemetery* ND-7
Fisher Cem—*cemetery* (3) OH-6
Fisher Cem—*cemetery* OK-5
Fisher Cem—*cemetery* (2) PA-2
Fisher Cem—*cemetery* (8) TN-4
Fisher Cem—*cemetery* (3) TX-5
Fisher Cem—*cemetery* VA-3
Fisher Cem—*cemetery* (6) WV-2
Fisher Ch—*church* NY-2
Fisher Ch—*church* OK-5
*Fisher Channel* WA-9
Fisher Channel—*channel* NJ-2
Fisher Channel—*channel* OR-9
Fisher Chapel—*church* WV-2
Fisher Chimney—*pillar* WA-9
Fisher Corner—*locale* FL-3
**Fisher Corners**—*pop pl* PA-2
Fisher Coulee—*valley* (2) MT-8
Fisher Coulee—*valley* WI-6
**Fisher (County)**—*pop pl* TX-5
Fisher Cove—*bay* CA-9
Fisher Cove—*bay* VA-3
Fisher Cove—*valley* NC-3
Fisher Covered RR Bridge—*hist pl* VT-1
*Fisher Creek* MI-6
*Fisher Creek* MT-8
*Fisher Creek* TX-5
*Fisher Creek* WY-8
**Fisher Creek**—*pop pl* NC-3
**Fisher Creek**—*pop pl* TN-4
Fisher Creek—*stream* (3) AL-4
Fisher Creek—*stream* (3) AK-9
Fisher Creek—*stream* AR-4
Fisher Creek—*stream* (2) CA-9
Fisher Creek—*stream* (5) CO-8
Fisher Creek—*stream* DE-2
Fisher Creek—*stream* FL-3
Fisher Creek—*stream* (2) GA-3
Fisher Creek—*stream* (8) ID-8
Fisher Creek—*stream* IL-6
Fisher Creek—*stream* IA-7
Fisher Creek—*stream* (2) KS-7
Fisher Creek—*stream* (2) KY-4
Fisher Creek—*stream* (3) MI-6
Fisher Creek—*stream* (2) MS-4
Fisher Creek—*stream* (2) MO-7
Fisher Creek—*stream* (4) MT-8
Fisher Creek—*stream* NE-7
Fisher Creek*—*stream* NE-7
Fisher Creek—*stream* NM-5
Fisher Creek—*stream* (2) NC-3
Fisher Creek—*stream* (2) OK-5
Fisher Creek—*stream* (10) OR-9
Fisher Creek—*stream* (2) SD-7
Fisher Creek—*stream* TN-4
Fisher Creek—*stream* UT-8
Fisher Creek—*stream* (7) WA-9
Fisher Creek—*stream* WV-2
Fisher Creek—*stream* (6) WI-6
Fisher Creek—*stream* (2) WY-8
Fisher Creek Basin—*basin* WA-9
Fisher Creek Canyon—*valley* UT-8
Fisher Creek Ch—*church* TN-4
Fisher Creek Ridge—*ridge* TN-4
Fisher Creek Saddle—*gap* ID-8
Fisher Creek Sch—*school* TN-4
Fisher Crossroads—*locale* AL-4
**Fisherdale**—*pop pl* PA-2
Fisher Dam—*dam* AL-4
Fisher Dam—*dam* OR-9
Fisher Dam—*dam* TN-4
*Fisher Ditch* IN-6
Fisher Ditch—*canal* CO-8
Fisher Ditch—*canal* (4) IN-6
Fisher Ditch—*canal* WY-8
Fisher Dome—*summit* AK-9
Fisher Drain—*canal* (2) MI-6
Fisher Draw—*valley* WY-8
Fisher Eddy—*bay* ME-1
Fisher-Eldora—*CDP* PA-2
Fisher Elementary and Adult Education Center—*school* FL-3
**Fisher Estates (subdivision)**—*pop pl* SD-7
Fisher Farm Airp—*airport* IN-6
Fisher Farm Site—*hist pl* PA-2
Fisher Field—*airport* NC-3
Fisher Field—*airport* ND-7
Fisher Field—*park* TN-4
Fisher Field No 1 Ditch—*canal* WY-8
*Fisher Flat* CA-9
Fisher Flat—*flat* CA-9
Fisher Flat—*flat* OR-9
Fisher Flat—*flat* WA-9
Fisher Flats—*flat* OK-5
Fisher Flats Ch—*church* OK-5
Fisher Flowage—*reservoir* WI-6
Fisher Fork—*stream* KY-4
Fisher-Gabbert Archeol Site—*hist pl* MO-7
Fisher Gap—*gap* AR-4
Fisher/Goldwater House—*hist pl* AZ-5
Fisher-Gordon Ditch—*canal* IN-6
Fisher Grove—*area* SD-7
Fisher Gulch—*valley* CA-9
Fisher Gulch—*valley* (3) CO-8
Fisher Gulch—*valley* ID-8
Fisher Gulch—*valley* MT-8
Fisher Gulch—*valley* (2) OR-9
Fisher Gulch—*valley* WA-9
Fisher Gully—*valley* NY-2
Fisher Hall—*hist pl* TX-5
**Fisher Heights**—*pop pl* (2) PA-2
*Fisher Hill* RI-1
**Fisher Hill**—*pop pl* SC-3
Fisher Hill—*summit* (4) MA-1
Fisher Hill—*summit* MN-6
Fisher Hill—*summit* NM-5
Fisher Hill—*summit* TX-5
Fisher Hill—*summit* VT-1
Fisher Hill—*summit* WA-9
Fisher Hill Camp—*locale* PA-2
Fisher Hill Hist Dist—*hist pl* MA-1
*Fisher Hill Reservoir* MA-1
Fisher Hills—*summit* AZ-5
Fisher Hist Dist—*hist pl* LA-4
Fisher Hollow—*valley* AR-4
Fisher Hollow—*valley* ID-8
Fisher Hollow—*valley* KY-4
Fisher Hollow—*valley* NY-2
Fisher Hollow—*valley* OH-6
Fisher Hollow—*valley* (3) PA-2
Fisher Hollow—*valley* (4) TN-4
Fisher Hollow—*valley* (2) TX-5
Fisher Hollow—*valley* VA-3
Fisher Hollow—*valley* WV-2
Fisher Hollow—*valley* WI-6
Fisher Home—*building* MI-6
Fisher Homestead—*hist pl* DE-2
Fisher Homestead—*hist pl* KY-4
Fisher Homestead—*locale* MT-8
Fisher Hot Springs—*spring* OR-9
Fisher House—*hist pl* GA-3
Fisher House—*hist pl* KY-4
*Fisher Island* DE-2
Fisher Island—*bay* MI-6
Fisher Island—*island* AL-4
Fisher Island—*island* FL-3
Fisher Island—*island* IL-6
Fisher Island—*island* LA-4
Fisher Island—*island* MN-6
Fisher Island—*island* MT-8
Fisher Island—*island* WA-9
Fisher Island—*uninc pl* FL-3
*Fisher Island Channel* WA-9
Fisher Island Channel—*channel* OR-9
Fisher Island Channel—*channel* WA-9
*Fisher Island North Channel* WA-9
Fisher Island Pond—*lake* OR-9
Fisher Island Slough—*stream* WA-9
*Fisher Island Sound* CT-1
*Fisher Island Sound* NY-2
Fisher Knob—*summit* GA-3
Fisher Knob—*summit* SC-3
Fisher Knob—*summit* TN-4
Fisher Knob—*summit* (3) WV-2
Fisher Knobs—*summit* IN-6
*Fisher Lake* FL-3
*Fisher Lake* ND-7
*Fisher Lake* WI-6
Fisher Lake—*lake* AL-4
Fisher Lake—*lake* CA-9
Fisher Lake—*lake* FL-3
Fisher Lake—*lake* IA-7
Fisher Lake—*lake* ME-1
Fisher Lake—*lake* (9) MI-6
Fisher Lake—*lake* (3) MN-6
Fisher Lake—*lake* MT-8
Fisher Lake—*lake* ND-7
Fisher Lake—*lake* OR-9
Fisher Lake—*lake* UT-8
Fisher Lake—*lake* WA-9
Fisher Lake—*lake* (2) WI-6
Fisher Lake—*reservoir* AL-4
Fisher Lake—*reservoir* NC-3
Fisher Lake—*reservoir* TN-4
Fisher Lake—*reservoir* TX-5
Fisher Lake—*swamp* IA-7
Fisher Lakes—*lake* CA-9
Fisher Lakes—*lake* WA-9
*Fisher Landing* MN-6
*Fisher Landing* NY-2
*Fisher Landing* TN-4
Fisher Landing—*locale* DE-2
Fisher Landing Point—*cape* NC-3
Fisher Landing Recreation Site—*park* NC-3
Fisher Lateral—*canal* CA-9
Fisher Lateral—*canal* ID-8
Fisher Lookout Tower—*locale* LA-4
*Fisherman* VA-3
Fisherman Bay—*bay* CA-9
Fisherman Bay—*bay* MI-6
Fisherman Bay—*bay* NC-3
Fisherman Bay—*bay* WA-9
*Fisherman Beach* MA-1
Fisherman Beach—*beach* NY-2
Fisherman Camp—*locale* OR-9
Fisherman Chuck—*gut* AK-9
Fisherman Cove—*bay* (2) AK-9
Fisherman Cove—*bay* WA-9
Fisherman Creek—*stream* MD-2
Fisherman Creek—*stream* SC-3
Fisherman Creek—*stream* WY-8
Fisherman Creek Lake—*lake* WY-8
Fisherman Dan Coulee—*valley* MT-8
Fisherman Dan Rsvr—*reservoir* MT-8
*Fisherman Hame Cove* MI-6
Fisherman Harbor—*bay* WA-9
*Fisherman Inlet* VA-3
*Fisherman Island* VA-3
Fisherman Island—*island* FL-3
Fisherman Island—*island* ID-8
Fisherman Island—*island* (3) ME-1
Fisherman Island—*island* MI-6
Fisherman Island Passage—*channel* (2) ME-1
Fisherman Key—*island* FL-3
Fisherman Point—*cape* CA-9
Fisherman Point—*cape* FL-3
Fisherman Run—*stream* PA-2
Fishermans Bay—*bay* LA-4
Fishermans Bay—*bay* MI-6
Fishermans Bay—*bay* TX-5
Fishermans Beach—*beach* MA-1
Fishermans Bench Recreation Site—*park* UT-8
Fishermans Brook—*stream* MN-6
Fishermans Camp—*locale* CA-9
Fishermans Campground—*locale* CA-9
*Fishermans Channel* CA-9
Fishermans Channel—*channel* FL-3
Fisherman's Cottage—*hist pl* MS-4
Fishermans Cove—*bay* CA-9
Fishermans Cove—*bay* ME-1
Fishermans Cove—*bay* VA-3
*Fishermans Creek* WY-8
Fishermans Cut—*canal* CA-9
Fishermans Cut—*channel* CA-9
Fishermans Cut—*gut* TX-5
Fishermans Harbor—*bay* AK-9
Fisherman Shoal—*bar* WI-6
*Fishermans Home* MI-6
Fishermans Home Cove—*bay* MI-6
Fishermans Hosp—*hospital* FL-3
*Fisherman's Inlet* VA-3
Fishermans Inlet—*bay* VA-3
*Fisherman's Island* ME-1
*Fishermans Island* MA-1
*Fisherman's Island* VA-3
Fishermans Island—*island* VA-3
Fishermans Island (historical)—*island* SD-7
Fishermans Lake—*reservoir* CA-9
Fishermans Lake—*reservoir* (2) MO-7
Fishermans Landing—*locale* WI-6
**Fishermans Landing**—*pop pl* MA-1
Fishermans Paradise—*locale* PA-2
Fishermans Paradise—*locale* TX-5
Fishermans Park—*park* WI-6
**Fishermans Park (trailer park)**—*pop pl* DE-2
*Fishermans Peak* CA-9
*Fishermans Point* FL-3
*Fishermans Point* MD-2
Fishermans Point—*cape* AK-9
Fishermans Point—*cape* FL-3
Fishermans Point—*cape* WA-9
Fishermans Point—*cape* WI-6
Fishermans Point—*summit* PA-2
**Fishermans Resort**—*pop pl* AL-4
Fishermans Rest—*cape* FL-3
*Fisherman's Shoal* WI-6
Fishermans Slough—*gut* CA-9
Fishermans Trail—*trail* TN-4
Fishermans Village (Shop Ctr)—*locale* FL-3
Fishermans Wharf—*locale* CA-9
Fishermans Wharf Marina—*locale* AL-4
Fishermans Wharf Park—*park* IL-6
Fishermare Branch—*stream* NC-3
Fishermare Ridge—*ridge* NC-3
Fisher Marsh—*swamp* TX-5
Fisher Meadow—*swamp* MA-1
Fisher Memorial Chapel—*church* NY-2
Fisher Memorial Home—*hist pl* AZ-5
Fisher Memorial Park—*park* OR-9
Fishermens Monmt—*park* MA-1
Fisher Mesa—*summit* AZ-5
Fisher Mesa—*summit* UT-8
Fisher Mill (historical)—*locale* AL-4
**Fisher Mill Park (subdivision)**—*pop pl* DE-2
Fisher Mine—*mine* ID-8
Fisher Mine Station—*locale* PA-2
Fisher Mountain Trail—*trail* MT-8
Fisher Mtn—*summit* AR-4
Fisher Mtn—*summit* CO-8
Fisher Mtn—*summit* (2) MT-8
Fisher Mtn—*summit* NH-1
Fisher Mtn—*summit* (2) WV-2
Fisher Mtn—*summit* WY-8
Fisher Park—*park* CA-9
Fisher Park—*park* FL-3
Fisher Park—*park* IL-6
Fisher Park—*park* NM-5
Fisher Park—*park* NC-3
Fisher Park—*park* PA-2
**Fisher Park**—*pop pl* NC-3
Fisher Pass—*gap* WA-9
*Fisher Peak* MT-8
Fisher Peak—*summit* ID-8
Fisher Peak—*summit* MT-8
Fisher Peak—*summit* NV-8
Fisher Peak—*summit* NC-3
Fisher Peak—*summit* VA-3
Fisher Peak—*summit* WA-9
*Fisher Peak Mtn* NC-3
Fisher Pit—*reservoir* CO-8
Fisher Place—*locale* CA-9
**Fisher Place Subdivision**—*pop pl* UT-8
Fisher Point—*cape* CA-9
Fisher Point—*cape* NJ-2
Fisher Point—*cape* OR-9
Fisher Point—*cape* VA-3
Fisher Point—*cliff* AZ-5
Fisher Point—*cliff* PA-2
Fisher Point—*summit* AR-4
Fisher Point—*summit* MT-8
Fisher Point—*summit* PA-2
Fisher Point Range—*channel* NJ-2
Fisher Point Range—*channel* PA-2
Fisher Pond—*lake* CT-1
Fisher Pond—*lake* IN-6
Fisher Pond—*reservoir* MA-1
Fisher Pond—*reservoir* MO-7
Fisher Pond Dam—*dam* MA-1
Fisher Ponds—*lake* ME-1

Fisher Quarry—mine WA-9
Fisher Ranch—locale (2) MT-8
Fisher Ranch—locale NE-7
Fisher Ranch—locale NM-5
Fisher Ranch—locale SD-7
Fisher Ranch—locale TX-5
Fisher Ranch—locale UT-8
Fisher Ranch—locale WY-8
Fisher Ranch Airp—airport WA-9
Fisher Rapids—rapids WA-9
Fisher Ridge—ridge (3) CA-9
Fisher Ridge—ridge (2) KY-4
Fisher Ridge—ridge PA-2
Fisher Ridge—ridge (3) WV-2
**Fisher River**—pop pl MT-8
Fisher River—stream MT-8
Fisher River—stream NC-3
Fisher River—stream WI-6
Fisher River Siding—locale MT-8
Fisher Rsvr OR-9
Fisher Rsvr—reservoir (2) CO-8
Fisher Rsvr—reservoir MA-1
Fisher Rsvr—reservoir MT-8
Fisher Rsvr—reservoir OR-9
Fisher Run—stream ND-7
Fisher Run—stream OH-6
Fisher Run—stream PA-2
Fisher Run—stream (6) WV-2
Fishers WA-9
**Fishers**—pop pl IN-6
**Fishers**—pop pl ME-1
**Fishers**—pop pl NY-2
Fishers Bar—bar OR-9
Fishers Bay—bay NH-1
Fishers Branch—stream NC-3
Fishers Bridge—bridge MS-4
Fishers Brook—stream CT-1
**Fishersburg**—pop pl IN-6
Fishers Canyon—valley CO-8
Fishers Ch—church WV-2
Fisher Sch—school AL-4
Fisher Sch—school CA-9
Fisher Sch—school (2) IL-6
Fisher Sch—school (2) IA-7
Fisher Sch—school LA-4
Fisher Sch—school ME-1
Fisher Sch—school MA-1
Fisher Sch—school (6) MI-6
Fisher Sch—school NY-2
Fisher Sch—school SD-7
Fisher Sch—school (3) TX-5
Fisher Sch—school VT-1
Fisher Sch—school WA-9
Fisher Sch—school WV-2
Fisher Sch—school (3) WI-6
Fisher Sch (abandoned)—school PA-2
Fishers Channel WA-9
Fishers Chapel—church GA-3
Fisher Sch Bridge—hist pl OR-9
Fisher Sch (historical)—school MO-7
Fisher Sch Number 3—school ND-7
Fisher School Number 1 IN-6
Fishers Corner PA-2
**Fishers Corner**—pop pl OR-9
**Fishers Corner**—pop pl PA-2
Fishers Creek AL-4
Fishers Creek IN-6
Fishers Creek NC-3
Fishers Creek TN-4
Fishers Creek—gut LA-4
Fishers Creek—stream AL-4
Fishers Creek—stream IN-6
Fishers Creek—stream VA-3
Fishers Creek—stream WI-6
Fishers Creek Baptist Church TN-4
Fishers Creek Post Office
(historical)—building TN-4
Fishers Creek School TN-4
Fishers Crossing—locale CO-8
Fishers Crossing—locale WV-2
Fishers Dam—dam VA-3
Fishers Elem Sch—school IN-6
**Fishers Ferry**—pop pl PA-2
Fishers Ferry Bridge MS-4
Fishers Fork—stream IN-6
Fishers Gap AL-4
Fishers Gap—gap VA-3
Fishers Gap Ch—church NC-3
Fishers Grove SD-7
Fisher's Hill MA-1
Fishers Hill—locale VA-3
Fishers Hill—summit MA-1
Fishers Hill—summit VA-3
Fisher Shoals—bar TX-5
Fishers Hollow—valley AL-4
Fishers Hornpipe Creek—stream WA-9
Fishers Island DE-2
Fishers Island NH-1
Fishers Island WA-9
Fishers Island—island (2) FL-3
Fishers Island—island LA-4
Fishers Island—island NY-2
Fishers Island—island PA-2
Fishers Island—island WI-6
**Fishers Island**—pop pl NY-2
Fishers Island Ferry—locale CT-1
Fishers Island Ferry—trail NY-2
Fishers Island Sound—bay CT-1
Fishers Island Sound—bay NY-2
Fisher Site (36GR21)—hist pl PA-2
Fishers Lake—lake AR-4
Fishers Lake—lake MI-6
Fishers Lake—lake WI-6
**Fishers Lake**—pop pl MI-6
Fishers Lake—reservoir AL-4
Fishers Lake—reservoir NC-3
Fishers Landing WA-9
Fishers Landing—locale MA-1
Fishers Landing—locale NY-2
Fishers Landing—locale TN-4
**Fishers Landing**—pop pl AZ-5
**Fishers Landing**—pop pl MA-1
Fishers Landing Airp—airport AZ-5
Fishers Landing Post Office
(historical)—building TN-4
Fisher's Lane—hist pl PA-2
Fisher Slough—stream OR-9
Fishers Mill Bridge—bridge DE-2
Fishers of Men Lutheran Ch—church FL-3
Fisher's Paradise—hist pl DE-2
Fishers Peak—summit CO-8
Fishers Peak Historical Site—park NC-3
Fishers Peak Mesa—summit CO-8
Fishers Point DE-2
Fishers Point NJ-2
Fishers Point—cape SD-7
Fisher's Pond CT-1
Fisher Spring AZ-5
Fisher Spring—spring (2) AZ-5
Fisher Spring—spring CA-9
Fisher Spring—spring (2) ID-8
Fisher Spring—spring MT-8
Fisher Spring—spring OR-9
Fisher Spring—spring TN-4
Fisher Spring—spring UT-8
Fisher Spring—spring WA-9
Fisher Spring Run—stream WV-2
Fishers Reef Oil Field—oilfield TX-5
Fishers Ridge PA-2
Fishers Ridge—ridge KY-4
Fishers Rock TX-5
Fishers Run PA-2
Fishers Run—stream (2) PA-2
Fishers Siding—locale PA-2
Fishers Spring—spring AZ-5
Fishers Spring—spring UT-8
Fishers Spring—spring WY-8
Fishers Station IN-6
Fishers Station (corporate name Fishers) IN-6
**Fishers (subdivision)**—pop pl PA-2
Fishers Switch IN-6
Fisher Stream—stream ME-1
Fisher Street Sch—school NC-3
Fisher Summit—summit WV-2
Fishers View Mtn—summit VA-3
**Fishersville**—pop pl VA-3
Fisher Swamp—stream NC-3
Fishers Wash—valley UT-8
Fishers Wharf WA-9
**Fisher's Woodland**—pop pl IN-6
Fisher Tabernacle—church KY-4
Fisher Tank—reservoir (3) AZ-5
Fisher Tank Number One—reservoir AZ-5
Fisher Tank Number Two—reservoir AZ-5
Fisher Tanks—reservoir NM-5
Fisher Tie Camp—locale WY-8
Fisher Towers—pillar UT-8
Fisher Towers Campground UT-8
Fisher Towers Picnic Area—park UT-8
Fishertown MO-7
**Fisher Town**—pop pl NC-3
**Fishertown**—pop pl (2) PA-2
Fishertown Branch—stream KY-4
Fisher Township—fmr MCD IA-7
**Fisher Township**—pop pl ND-7
**Fisher (Township of)**—pop pl MN-6
Fishertown Station—locale PA-2
Fisher Trail—trail MA-1
Fisher Trail—trail (2) PA-2
Fisher Valley—valley TN-4
Fisher Valley—valley UT-8
Fisher Valley—valley VA-3
Fisher Valley—valley WI-6
Fisherville NC-3
Fisherville—locale LA-4
Fisherville—locale WI-6
**Fisherville**—pop pl IN-6
**Fisherville**—pop pl KY-4
**Fisherville**—pop pl MA-1
**Fisherville**—pop pl MI-6
**Fisherville**—pop pl NY-2
**Fisherville**—pop pl (2) PA-2
**Fisherville**—pop pl RI-1
**Fisherville**—pop pl TN-4
Fisherville Brook—stream RI-1
Fisherville (CCD)—cens area KY-4
Fisherville (CCD)—cens area TN-4
Fisherville Division—civil TN-4
Fisherville Historic and Archeol
District—hist pl RI-1
Fisherville Lake TN-4
Fisherville Pond—reservoir MA-1
Fisherville Pond Dam—dam MA-1
Fisherville Sch—school MA-1
Fisher Vly Lake—lake NY-2
Fisher Well—well NM-5
Fisher Windmill—locale NM-5
Fisher Woods—woods IL-6
Fishery—locale TN-4
Fishery Creek—stream AK-9
Fishery Island Point—cape MI-6
Fishery Point—cape (2) AK-9
Fishery Point—cape FL-3
Fishery Point—cape MI-6
Fishery Point—cape OR-9
Fishery Point—cape WA-9
Fishery Point—cliff PA-2
Fishery Post Office (historical)—building TN-4
Fishery Sch (abandoned)—school PA-2
Fishery Sch (historical)—school TN-4
Fisher-Zugelder House and Smith
Cottage—hist pl CO-8
Fisheye Arch—arch UT-8
Fish Farm Mound Group—hist pl IA-7
Fish Farms Mounds Wildlife Area—park IA-7
Fishfin Ridge—ridge ID-8
Fish Fin Rim—cliff OR-9
Fish Flake Hill Hist Dist—hist pl MA-1
Fish Flake Hill Hist Dist (Boundary
Increase)—hist pl MA-1
Fish Flats—flat PA-2
Fish Flats—flat WA-9
Fish Fork—stream CA-9
Fish Fork Camp—locale CA-9
Fish Fossil Rocks—cliff UT-8
Fish Fossil Rsvr—reservoir MT-8
Fish Fry Creek—stream OK-5
Fishfry Lake—lake MN-6
Fish Gap—gap GA-3
Fishgap Hill—summit TN-4
Fishgig Lake—lake MN-6
Fish Gulch—valley (3) CA-9
Fish Gut Branch—stream KY-4
Fishgut Creek—stream SD-7
Fishgut Lakes—lake CA-9
Fish Harbor—harbor CA-9
**Fish Hatchery**—pop pl WY-8
Fish Hatchery Cove—bay MO-7
Fish Hatchery Gulch—valley CO-8
Fish Hatchery Gulch—valley SD-7
Fish Hatchery Lake—lake UT-8
Fish Hatchery Lake—reservoir IN-6
Fish Hatchery Lake Dam—dam IN-6
Fish Hatchery Run—stream WV-2
Fish Hatchery Spring—spring PA-2
Fish Haul Archaeol Site
(38BU805)—hist pl SC-3
**Fish Haven**—pop pl ID-8
Fish Haven Canyon—valley ID-8
Fish Haven Creek—stream ID-8
Fishhawk Cem—cemetery OR-9
Fish Hawk Cliffs—cliff NY-2
Fish Hawk Creek—gut FL-3
Fishhawk Creek—stream FL-3
Fishhawk Creek—stream (2) OR-9
Fishhawk Creek—stream WY-8
Fishhawk Dam—dam OR-9
Fishhawk Falls—falls OR-9
Fishhawk Glacier—glacier WY-8
**Fishhawk (historical)**—pop pl OR-9
Fish Hawk Island—island ME-1
Fishhawk Islet ME-1
Fish Hawk Key—island FL-3
Fish Hawk Lake MI-6
Fish Hawk Lake—lake CO-8
Fishhawk Lake—lake MI-6
Fishhawk Lake—reservoir OR-9
Fishhawk Meadows—flat WY-8
Fishhawk Mtn—summit NC-3
Fish Hawk Point—cape FL-3
Fish Hawk Point—cape NC-3
Fish Head—cape ME-1
**Fishhead**—pop pl AL-4
Fish Head Hill—summit CA-9
Fish Head Rocks—summit CA-9
Fishhead Valley—valley AL-4
Fish Hill MS-4
Fish Hill—summit (2) ME-1
Fish Hill—summit MA-1
Fish Hill—summit (2) NY-2
Fish Hill—summit PA-2
Fish Hill—summit (2) VT-1
Fish Hill—swamp RI-1
Fish Hill Brook RI-1
Fish Hog Gut—gut VA-3
Fish Hole—gut LA-4
Fishhole Creek—stream OR-9
Fishhole Creek—stream TX-5
Fishhole Guard Station—locale OR-9
Fish Hole Landing—locale VA-3
Fishhole Mtn—summit OR-9
Fishhole Pond—lake NY-2
Fish Hole Run—stream WV-2
Fishhole Swamp—swamp GA-3
Fish Hollow PA-2
Fish Hollow—valley MO-7
Fish Hollow—valley NY-2
Fish Hollow—valley UT-8
Fish Hollow—valley VA-3
Fish Hollow Bluff—cliff MO-7
Fish Hollow Run—stream PA-2
**Fishhook**—pop pl IL-6
Fishhook Bay—bay AK-9
Fishhook Bend—bend (2) AK-9
Fishhook Branch—stream MS-4
Fish Hook Camp (historical)—locale OR-9
Fishhook (Chalkyitsik)—other AK-9
Fish Hook Creek WY-8
Fishhook Creek—stream (2) AK-9
Fishhook Creek—stream AZ-5
Fishhook Creek—stream CO-8
Fishhook Creek—stream (2) ID-8
Fishhook Creek—stream IL-6
Fishhook Creek—stream OK-5
Fish Hook Creek—stream OR-9
Fishhook Flats—flat WA-9
Fishhook Flats Trail—trail WA-9
Fishhook Fork—stream WV-2
Fishhook Hollow—valley MO-7
Fishhook Island—island AK-9
Fishhook Island—island CO-8
Fishhook Island—island MN-6
Fishhook Lake—lake CO-8
Fishhook Lake—lake MI-6
Fishhook Lake—lake (4) MN-6
Fishhook Lake—lake MS-4
Fishhook Lake—lake TX-5
Fish Hook Lake—reservoir VA-3
**Fish Hook Mobile Home Court (trailer
park)**—pop pl DE-2
Fishhook Park—park WA-9
Fishhook Peak—summit ID-8
Fish Hook Peak—summit OR-9
Fishhook Ridge—ridge AK-9
Fishhook Ridge—ridge NV-8
Fishhook River—stream MN-6
Fishhook Springs—spring AZ-5
Fishhook Well—well AZ-5
Fish House NJ-2
**Fish House**—pop pl NJ-2
**Fish House**—pop pl NY-2
Fishhouse Bay—bay MN-6
Fish House Cove—bay FL-3
Fish House Cove—bay ME-1
Fish House Island—island VA-3
**Fish House Junction**—pop pl NJ-2
Fishin Brook—stream MA-1
Fishin Brook—stream NH-1
Fishing Bay—bay MD-2
Fishing Bay—bay NC-3
Fishing Bay—bay VA-3
Fishing Bay—bay WA-9
Fishing Bayou—stream (2) MS-4
Fishing Bayou—swamp AR-4
Fishing Bayou Waterhole—lake AR-4
Fishing Bend—bay FL-3
Fishing Branch SC-3
Fishing Branch—stream DE-2
Fishing Branch—stream MO-7
Fishing Branch—stream NC-3
**Fishing Bridge**—pop pl WY-8
Fishing Brook MA-1
Fishing Brook—stream CT-1
Fishing Brook—stream ME-1
Fishing Brook—stream NY-2
Fishing Brook Mtn—summit NY-2
Fishing Brook Range—ridge NY-2
Fishing Camp—locale AK-9
Fishing Camp—locale WV-2
Fishing Cove—bay RI-1
Fishing Creek AL-4
Fishing Creek DE-2
Fishing Creek PA-2
Fishing Creek—bay (4) MD-2
Fishing Creek—channel MD-2
Fishing Creek—gut MD-2
Fishing Creek—gut NC-3
Fishing Creek—other PA-2
**Fishing Creek**—pop pl MD-2
**Fishing Creek**—pop pl NJ-2
Fishing Creek—stream AL-4
Fishing Creek—stream DE-2
Fishing Creek—stream FL-3
Fishing Creek—stream (5) GA-3
Fishing Creek—stream IN-6
Fishing Creek—stream (3) KY-4
Fishing Creek—stream (4) MD-2
Fishing Creek—stream MO-7
Fishing Creek—stream (5) NJ-2
Fishing Creek—stream (7) NC-3
Fishing Creek—stream OH-6
Fishing Creek—stream (10) PA-2
Fishing Creek—stream (3) SC-3
Fishing Creek—stream UT-8
Fishing Creek—stream (4) VA-3
Fishing Creek—stream WV-2
Fishing Creek Arbor Ch—church NC-3
Fishing Creek Bridge—bridge KY-4
Fishing Creek Cem—cemetery SC-3
Fishing Creek Ch—church (2) GA-3
Fishing Creek Ch—church KY-4
Fishing Creek Ch—church NJ-2
Fishing Creek Ch—church (2) NC-3
Fishing Creek Ch—church PA-2
Fishing Creek Ch—church (2) SC-3
Fishing Creek Chapel—church IN-6
Fishing Creek Gorge—valley PA-2
Fishing Creek - in part PA-2
Fishing Creek Marsh—swamp VA-3
Fishing Creek Methodist Ch
(historical)—church AL-4
Fishing Creek Millpond—reservoir NC-3
Fishing Creek Millpond Dam—dam NC-3
Fishing Creek Pond—lake KY-4
Fishing Creek Rsvr—reservoir MD-2
Fishing Creek Rsvr—reservoir SC-3
Fishing Creek Sch—school GA-3
Fishing Creek Sch—school NJ-2
Fishing Creek Sch—school (3) PA-2
Fishing Creek Sch—school SC-3
Fishing Creek Sch (abandoned)—school
(3) PA-2
Fishing Creek Schoolhouse—hist pl NJ-2
Fishing Creek Shoal—bar NJ-2
Fishing Creek (Township of)—fmr MCD
(2) NC-3
**Fishing Creek (Township of)**—pop pl PA-2
Fishing Ditch—bay MD-2
Fishinger Bridge—bridge OH-6
Fishinger Sch—school OH-6
Fishing Fork—stream VA-3
Fishing Gut—gut VA-3
Fishing Gut Creek—stream OH-6
Fishing Hammock—island GA-3
Fishinghawk Creek WV-2
Fishing Hawk Creek—stream WV-2
Fishing Hole Picnic Area—park NM-5
Fishing Island—island ME-1
Fishing Island—island MD-2
Fishing Island—island PA-2
Fishing Lake WI-6
Fishing Lake—lake (2) AL-4
Fishing Lake—lake (2) AR-4
Fishing Lake—lake GA-3
Fishing Lakes—lake MN-6
Fishing Ledge—rock MA-1
Fishing Place Cove RI-1
Fishing Point MA-1
Fishing Point—cape DE-2
Fishing Point—cape LA-4
Fishing Point—cape (8) MD-2
Fishing Point—cape NC-3
Fishing Point—cape (3) VA-3
Fishing Rip—bar SC-3
Fishing River MA-1
Fishing River—stream MO-7
Fishing River Township—civil (2) MO-7
Fishing Rock—bar ME-1
Fishing Rock—bar NY-2
Fishing Rock—cape OR-9
Fishing Rock—pillar NY-2
Fishing Rock—rock MA-1
Fishing Rocks Point CT-1
Fishing Run PA-2
Fishing Run—stream IN-6
Fishing Run—stream (2) PA-2
Fishing Run—stream VA-3
Fishing Shrine—church HI-9
Fishing Smack Bay—bay LA-4
Fishing Spring—spring MO-7
Fishing Springs—spring TX-5
Fishing Trough Hollow—valley WV-2
Fishin Jimmy Trail—trail NH-1
Fish Island NY-2
Fish Island—island AK-9
Fish Island—island LA-4
Fish Island—island (2) ME-1
Fish Island—island MD-2
Fish Island—island (3) MA-1
Fish Island—island NV-8
Fish Island—island NH-1
Fish Island—island NJ-2
Fish Island—island NY-2
Fish Island—island WI-6
Fish Island (historical)—island PA-2
Fish Island Ledge—bar ME-1
Fish Islands—area AK-9
Fish Islands—island CT-1
Fish Island Site—hist pl FL-3
**Fishkill**—pop pl NY-2
Fish Kill—stream NY-2
Fishkill Cem—cemetery NY-2
Fishkill Creek—stream NY-2
Fishkill Hassocks—island NY-2
**Fishkill Plains**—pop pl NY-2
Fishkill Supply Depot Site—hist pl NY-2
**Fishkill (Town of)**—pop pl NY-2
Fishkill Village District—hist pl NY-2
Fish Knob—summit GA-3
Fishko Dam—dam SD-7
Fishko Dam Number 2—dam SD-7
Fishko Dam Number 3—dam SD-7
Fish Ladder—falls AK-9
Fish Ladder Falls—falls WA-9
Fish Lake ID-8
Fish Lake IN-6
Fish Lake MI-6
Fish Lake MN-6
Fish Lake MS-4
Fish Lake NV-8
Fish Lake ND-7
Fish Lake OR-9
Fish Lake TX-5
Fish Lake WA-9
Fish Lake WI-6
Fish Lake WY-8
Fish Lake—bay WI-6
Fish Lake—gut AR-4
Fish Lake—lake (7) AK-9
Fish Lake—lake (7) AR-4
Fish Lake—lake (2) CA-9
Fish Lake—lake CO-8
Fish Lake—lake (5) FL-3
Fish Lake—lake (8) ID-8
Fish Lake—lake (6) IL-6
Fish Lake—lake (5) IN-6
Fish Lake—lake IA-7
Fish Lake—lake (2) KY-4
Fish Lake—lake (4) LA-4
Fish Lake—lake (17) MI-6
Fish Lake—lake (28) MN-6
Fish Lake—lake (14) MS-4
Fish Lake—lake (5) MO-7
Fish Lake—lake (10) MT-8
Fish Lake—lake (4) NE-7
Fish Lake—lake NV-8
Fish Lake—lake (3) ND-7
Fish Lake—lake (9) OR-9
Fish Lake—lake (2) SD-7
Fish Lake—lake (4) TX-5
Fish Lake—lake (3) UT-8
Fish Lake—lake (10) WA-9
Fish Lake—lake (11) WI-6
Fish Lake—lake (3) WY-8
Fish Lake—locale AK-9
**Fish Lake**—pop pl (2) IN-6
**Fish Lake**—pop pl MI-6
**Fish Lake**—pop pl UT-8
Fish Lake—reservoir AR-4
Fish Lake—reservoir IL-6
Fish Lake—reservoir LA-4
Fish Lake—reservoir MN-6
Fish Lake—reservoir MO-7
Fish Lake—reservoir OR-9
Fish Lake—reservoir (2) UT-8
Fish Lake—stream IA-7
Fish Lake—swamp AR-4
Fish Lake—swamp MN-6
Fish Lake—swamp MS-4
Fish Lake Bayou—gut MS-4
Fish Lake Brook—stream OR-9
Fish Lake Campground—park (3) OR-9
**Fish Lake (Carolina)**—pop pl FL-3
Fish Lake Cem—cemetery MS-4
Fish Lake Cem—cemetery WI-6
Fish Lake Ch—church MI-6
Fish Lake Ch—church (3) MN-6
Fish Lake Ch—church MS-4
Fish Lake County Park—park WI-6
Fish Lake Creek ID-8
Fish Lake Creek IA-7
Fish Lake Creek—stream AK-9
Fish Lake Creek—stream CA-9
Fish Lake Creek—stream ID-8
Fish Lake Creek—stream (2) OR-9
Fish Lake Creek—stream WY-8
Fish Lake Dam—dam MN-6
Fish Lake Dam—dam (2) OR-9
Fish Lake Dam—dam UT-8
Fish Lake Ditch IA-7
Fish Lake Ditch—canal IL-6
Fish Lake Ditch—canal MO-7
Fish Lake Drain—canal MI-6
Fish Lake Forest Camp—locale (2) OR-9
Fish Lake Guard Station—locale OR-9
Fish Lake Guard Station—locale WA-9
Fish Lake Hightop Plateau—plateau UT-8
Fishlake Mountain OR-9
Fish Lake Mountains UT-8
Fish Lake Mtn—summit WY-8
Fishlake Natl For—forest UT-8
Fishlake Plateau UT-8
Fishlake Ranger Station UT-8
Fish Lake Ranger Station—locale UT-8
Fish Lake Resort—locale OR-9
**Fishlake Resort**—pop pl UT-8
Fish Lake Rsvr—reservoir MN-6
Fish Lake Rsvr—reservoir UT-8
Fish Lake Run—stream WA-9
Fish Lakes UT-8
Fish Lakes—area AK-9
Fish Lakes—lake AK-9
Fish Lakes—lake MT-8
Fish Lakes—reservoir OK-5
Fish Lake Saddle—gap ID-8
Fish Lake Sch—school (2) MI-6
Fish Lake Sch—school MT-8
Fish Lake Slough TX-5
Fish Lake Slough—gut AR-4
Fish Lake Slough—stream TX-5
Fish Lake State Public Shooting
Area—park SD-7
Fish Lake Stream—stream WA-9
**Fish Lake (Township of)**—pop pl MN-6
Fish Lake Trail—trail CO-8
Fish Lake Trail—trail (2) OR-9
Fish Lake Trail—trail WY-8
Fish Lake Valley—basin NV-8
Fish Lake Valley—valley CA-9
Fish Lake Valley Community Hall—locale NV-8
Fish Lake Valley Wash—stream CA-9
Fish Lake Valley Wash—stream NV-8
Fish Lake Visitor Center—building UT-8
Fish Lateral—canal WY-8
Fishless Creek—stream AK-9
Fish Market—locale NH-1
Fish Meadow Brook—stream ME-1
Fish Memorial Hosp—hospital FL-3
Fish Memorial Hosp at DeLand—hospital FL-3
Fish Mountain Cem—cemetery NY-2
Fishmouth Lake—lake MN-6
Fish Mtn—summit AK-9
Fish Mtn—summit CA-9
Fish Mtn—summit NY-2
Fish Mtn—summit OR-9
Fish Mtn—summit WY-8
Fish Neck—cape VA-3
Fishner Lake—lake LA-4
Fish Net Bay MH-9
Fish Net Beach MH-9
Fish Net Gap—gut TX-5
Fishnet Lake—lake AK-9
Fish Net Point MH-9
Fish Net Ravine MH-9
Fishook Creek—stream WY-8
Fishook Junction—locale AK-9
Fishot Pass NV-8
Fish Park—flat CO-8
Fish Pass CO-8
Fish Pass—channel TX-5
Fish Peak—summit MT-8
Fishpen Gut—gut VA-3
Fish Point—cape (2) AK-9
Fish Point—cape (6) ME-1
Fish Point—cape (2) MI-6
Fish Point—cape NY-2
Fish Point—cape (2) WA-9
Fish Point Wildlife Area—park MI-6
Fishpole Lake—lake WI-6
Fishpole Lake—reservoir ID-8
Fishpole Outlet—stream NY-2
Fishpole Pond—lake (2) NY-2
Fishpond CA-9
Fish Pond ME-1
Fish Pond MA-1
Fish Pond—lake AL-4
Fish Pond—lake AR-4
Fish Pond—lake (5) FL-3
Fish Pond—lake (2) GA-3
Fishpond—lake HI-9
Fish Pond—lake KY-4
Fish Pond—lake (5) ME-1
Fish Pond—lake MA-1
Fish Pond—lake NH-1
Fish Pond—lake (3) NY-2
Fish Pond—lake SC-3
Fish Pond—lake TX-5
Fish Pond—lake VA-3
Fishpond—locale (2) AL-4
**Fish Pond**—pop pl AL-4
Fishpond—reservoir HI-9
Fish Pond—reservoir ID-8
Fish Pond—reservoir ME-1
Fish Pond—reservoir (2) MA-1
Fish Pond—reservoir NM-5
Fishpond—reservoir VA-3
Fish Pond—swamp OK-5
Fish Pond, The—lake VT-1
Fishpond, The—reservoir WV-2
Fish Pond Bay—swamp GA-3
Fish Pond Branch—stream AL-4
Fish Pond Branch—stream FL-3
Fishpond Branch—stream FL-3
Fishpond Branch—stream GA-3
Fishpond Branch—stream KY-4
Fishpond Branch—stream MO-7
Fishpond Branch—stream NC-3
Fish Pond Brook—stream ME-1
Fish Pond Campground—locale WA-9
Fish Pond Canyon—valley CO-8
Fishpond Cem—cemetery AL-4
Fish Pond Ch AL-4
Fishpond Ch—church AL-4
Fish Pond Ch—church SC-3
Fishpond Creek—stream AL-4
Fishpond Creek—stream KS-7
Fishpond Creek—stream VA-3
Fish Pond Dam—dam PA-2
Fish Pond Dam—reservoir PA-2
Fish Pond Dam C—dam MA-1
Fishpond Drain—stream GA-3
Fish Pond Hollow—valley TN-4
Fishpond Lake UT-8
Fish Pond Lake—lake CO-8
Fish Pond Lake—reservoir AZ-5
Fishpond Primitive Baptist Church AL-4
Fish Pond Rsvr—reservoir WY-8
Fish Ponds—lake MO-7
Fish Ponds—lake NY-2
Fish Ponds—lake OR-9
Fishponds, The—lake NC-3
Fishpond Sch—school KY-4
Fish Pond Spring—spring (2) NV-8
Fish Pond Springs—spring NV-8
Fishpond Swamp—lake IL-6
Fishpond Swamp—swamp NC-3
Fishpond Tank—locale NM-5
Fish Pond Tank—reservoir NM-5
Fish Pond Windmill—locale NM-5
Fishpool Creek—stream KY-4
Fishpool Plantation—hist pl KY-4
Fishpot Creek—stream MO-7
Fishpot Run—stream (2) PA-2
Fishpot Run—stream (4) WV-2
Fish Prairie—flat (3) FL-3
Fishprong Branch—stream NC-3
Fishrack Bay—bay AK-9
Fish Ranch—locale CA-9
Fish Ranch—locale NM-5
Fish Ranch—locale WY-8
Fish Ranch Bay—bay AK-9
Fish Research Station—locale PA-2
Fish Reservoirs—reservoir CO-8
Fish Ridge—ridge CA-9
Fish Ridge—ridge NC-3
Fish Ridge—ridge WV-2
Fish River WA-9
Fish River—stream AL-4
Fish River—stream (3) AK-9
Fish River—stream ME-1
Fish River Bridge (historical)—bridge AL-4
Fish River Ch—church AL-4
Fish River Falls—falls (2) ME-1
Fish River Island—island ME-1
Fish River Lake—lake ME-1
Fish River Point—cape AL-4
**Fish Rock**—pop pl CA-9
Fish Rock Beach—beach CA-9
Fish Rock Gulch—valley CA-9
Fish Rocks—island CA-9

Five Corners—*locale* DE-2
Five Corners—*locale* ID-8
Five Corners—*locale* ME-1
Five Corners—*locale* MI-6
Five Corners—*locale* NH-1
Five Corners—*locale* (8) NY-2
Five Corners—*locale* (2) VT-1
Five Corners—*locale* (2) WA-9
Five Corners—*locale* (2) WI-6
**Five Corners**—*pop pl* CA-9
**Five Corners**—*pop pl* ME-1
**Five Corners**—*pop pl* (4) MA-1
**Five Corners**—*pop pl* MN-6
**Five Corners**—*pop pl* NH-1
**Five Corners**—*pop pl* (7) NY-2
**Five Corners**—*pop pl* OH-6
**Five Corners**—*pop pl* OR-9
**Five Corners**—*pop pl* PA-2
**Five Corners**—*pop pl* WA-9
**Five Corners**—*pop pl* (2) WI-6
Five Corners—*uninc pl* NJ-2
**Five Corners, The**—*pop pl* NH-1
Five Corners Cem—*cemetery* IN-6
Five Corners Cem—*cemetery* OH-6
Five Corners (historical)—*locale* (2) MA-1
Five Counties Sportsmans Lake Dam—*dam* MS-4
Five County Sportsman Lake—*lake* MS-4
Five Coves Dam—*dam* TN-4
Five Coves Lake—*reservoir* TN-4
Five Creek—*stream* CA-9
Five Creek—*stream* KS-7
*Five Creeks Township* KS-7
**Five Creeks Township**—*pop pl* KS-7
Five Creek Township—*civil* KS-7
Five Daughters Run—*stream* MD-2
Five Day Slough—*gut* AK-9
Five Docks Canal—*canal* GA-3
Five Dog Creek—*stream* CA-9
Five Dollar Camp (Site)—*locale* CA-9
Five Dollar Canyon—*valley* NM-5
Five Dollar Spring—*spring* OR-9
Five Dot Ranch—*locale* CA-9
Five Falls Rsvr—*reservoir* NY-2
Five Farms Golf Course—*other* MD-2
Five Fathom Creek—*gut* SC-3
*Five Fathoms Bank* NC-3
Five Fine Rapids—*rapids* OR-9
Five Finger Bay—*bay* MI-6
Five Finger Brook—*stream* ME-1
Five Finger Camp—*locale* ME-1
Five Finger Cove—*bay* AR-4
Five Fingered Point—*cape* MA-1
Five Finger Gulch—*valley* OR-9
Five Finger Lighthouse—*locale* AK-9
*Five Finger Point* MA-1
Five Finger Point—*cape* NH-1
Five Fingers—*summit* CA-9
Five Fingers—*summit* NV-8
Five Fingers—*summit* TX-5
Five Fingers, The—*area* AK-9
Five Fingers Butte—*summit* WY-8
Five Five Sch—*school* IL-6
Five Flags Theater—*building* IA-7
Fivefoot Prong—*stream* DE-2
Five Foot Reef—*bar* MI-6
Five Foot Rock—*island* OR-9
*Five Fork* TN-4
Five Fork—*stream* AR-4
Fivefork Branch—*stream* WV-2
Five Fork Cem—*cemetery* SC-3
*Five Forks* VA-3
Five Forks—*locale* AL-4
Five Forks—*locale* (3) GA-3
Five Forks—*locale* KY-4
Five Forks—*locale* LA-4
Five Forks—*locale* (2) MD-2
Five Forks—*locale* OH-6
Five Forks—*locale* PA-2
Five Forks—*locale* (2) SC-3
Five Forks—*locale* (2) TN-4
Five Forks—*locale* (11) VA-3
Five Forks—*locale* (3) WV-2
**Five Forks**—*pop pl* GA-3
**Five Forks**—*pop pl* (4) NC-3
**Five Forks**—*pop pl* (2) OH-6
**Five Forks**—*pop pl* (2) PA-2
**Five Forks**—*pop pl* (3) SC-3
**Five Forks**—*pop pl* (4) VA-3
**Five Forks**—*pop pl* WV-2
Five Forks Battlefield—*hist pl* VA-3
Five Forks Bayou—*stream* AR-4
Five Forks Ch—*church* (2) NC-3
Five Forks Ch—*church* VA-3
**Five Forks (Five Points)**—*pop pl* GA-3
Five Forks Lake—*lake* AR-4
**Fiveforks (RR name Five Forks)**—*pop pl* PA-2
Five Forks (RR name for Fiveforks)—*other* PA-2
Five Hawks Sch—*school* MN-6
Five Houses—*locale* AZ-5
*Five Houses Butte* AZ-5
Five Houses Butte—*ridge* AZ-5
Five Hundred Flat—*flat* OR-9
Five Hundred Four Trick Tank—*reservoir* AZ-5
Five Hundred Pasture Tank—*reservoir* TX-5
*Five Island* OR-9
Five Island—*island* ME-1
Five Island—*locale* ID-8
Five Island Creek—*stream* WI-6
Five Island Lake—*lake* IA-7
Five Island Lake—*lake* MN-6
Five Island Lake—*lake* WI-6
*Five Island Lake Public Hunting Area* IA-7
Five Island Lake State Game Mngmt Area—*area* IA-7
Five Island Rapids—*rapids* ME-1
Five Islands—*island* (2) ME-1
Five Islands—*island* OR-9
Five Islands—*island* WI-6
**Five Islands**—*pop pl* ME-1
Five Islands Bar—*bar* OR-9
Five Islands Cove—*bay* ME-1
**Five Islands Park**—*pop pl* IL-6
Five Kezar Ponds—*lake* ME-1
*Five Lake* WI-6
Five Lake—*lake* MI-6
Five Lake—*lake* (2) MN-6
*Five Lakes* MI-6
Five Lakes—*lake* CA-9
Five Lakes—*lake* LA-4
Five Lakes—*lake* (3) MI-6
Five Lakes—*lake* MT-8
Five Lakes—*lake* UT-8
Five Lakes—*lake* WA-9
Five Lakes—*locale* MI-6
Five Lakes Airp—*airport* PA-2
Five Lakes Basin—*basin* CA-9
Five Lakes Butte—*summit* ID-8
Five Lakes Canyon—*valley* NM-5
Five Lakes Club—*other* AR-4
Five Lakes Creek—*stream* CA-9
Five Lakes Creek—*stream* MI-6
Five Lakes Drain—*canal* MI-6
Five Lakes Sch—*school* MI-6
Five Lick Creek—*stream* KY-4
Five Lick Creek—*stream* WV-2
Five Lick Ridge—*ridge* WV-2
Five Lick Run—*stream* WV-2
Five Line Tank—*reservoir* TX-5
Five Lock Combine and Locks 37 and 38, Black River Canal—*hist pl* NY-2
Five Locks—*locale* PA-2
Five Lower Branch, Canal (historical)—*canal* AZ-5
*Five Mile* NM-5
Fivemile—*locale* AR-4
Fivemile—*locale* KY-4
Five Mile—*locale* OK-5
Fivemile—*locale* TX-5
Fivemile—*locale* WV-2
**Five Mile**—*pop pl* KY-4
**Fivemile**—*pop pl* OH-6
**Five Mile**—*pop pl* OH-6
**Fivemile**—*pop pl* WV-2
Five Mile Arm—*bay* OR-9
Fivemile Bar—*bar* ID-8
Fivemile Bay—*swamp* FL-3
Fivemile Bay—*swamp* NC-3
*Fivemile Bayou* FL-3
Five Mile Beach—*beach* NJ-2
Fivemile Bluff—*cliff* WI-6
*Five Mile Branch* NC-3
*Fivemile Branch* TN-4
*Fivemile Branch* TX-5
Fivemile Branch—*stream* AL-4
Fivemile Branch—*stream* GA-3
Fivemile Branch—*stream* IL-6
Fivemile Branch—*stream* KY-4
Fivemile Branch—*stream* MD-2
Fivemile Branch—*stream* (2) MS-4
Fivemile Branch—*stream* (3) NC-3
Five Mile Branch—*stream* TN-4
Fivemile Branch—*stream* (4) TX-5
*Five Mile Branch Ditch* IL-6
Five Mile Branch Ditch—*canal* IL-6
Fivemile Bridge—*bridge* CA-9
Fivemile Bridge—*bridge* CO-8
Fivemile Bridge—*bridge* WY-8
Fivemile Brook—*stream* (2) CT-1
Fivemile Brook—*stream* (2) ME-1
Fivemile Butte—*summit* (2) OR-9
Fivemile Camp—*locale* WA-9
Fivemile Canyon—*valley* CA-9
Fivemile Canyon—*valley* CO-8
Fivemile Canyon—*valley* NV-8
Fivemile Canyon—*valley* (2) UT-8
Fivemile Cem—*cemetery* IL-6
Fivemile Cem—*cemetery* NY-2
Fivemile Cem—*cemetery* OK-5
Fivemile Cem—*cemetery* TX-5
*Five Mile Ch* AL-4
Fivemile Ch—*church* (2) AL-4
Fivemile Ch—*church* KY-4
Fivemile Ch—*church* OH-6
Fivemile Chapel—*church* OH-6
Five Mile Ch (historical)—*church* AL-4
*Five Mile Coleto Creek* TX-5
Fivemile Community Ch—*church* ID-8
Fivemile Corner—*locale* OK-5
**Fivemile Corner**—*pop pl* MI-6
Five Mile Corners—*locale* ME-1
Fivemile Coulee—*valley* (3) MT-8
Five Mile Cove Branch—*stream* GA-3
Fivemile Cow Camp—*locale* OR-9
*Five Mile Creek* AL-4
*Five Mile Creek* AR-4
*Five Mile Creek* GA-3
*Fivemile Creek* KS-7
*Five Mile Creek* MS-4
*Five Mile Creek* MT-8
*Fivemile Creek* NY-2
*Five Mile Creek* NC-3
*Five Mile Creek* TX-5
*Fivemile Creek* WA-9
*Fivemile Creek* WV-2
*Five-Mile Creek* WY-8
Fivemile Creek—*gut* FL-3
Fivemile Creek—*stream* (3) AL-4
Fivemile Creek—*stream* (2) AK-9
Fivemile Creek—*stream* AZ-5
Fivemile Creek—*stream* (4) AR-4
Fivemile Creek—*stream* (4) CA-9
Fivemile Creek—*stream* (3) CO-8
Fivemile Creek—*stream* (3) FL-3
Fivemile Creek—*stream* (3) GA-3
Fivemile Creek—*stream* (10) ID-8
Fivemile Creek—*stream* (2) IL-6
Fivemile Creek—*stream* IA-7
Fivemile Creek—*stream* (2) KS-7
Fivemile Creek—*stream* KY-4
Fivemile Creek—*stream* LA-4
Fivemile Creek—*stream* (3) MI-6
Fivemile Creek—*stream* MN-6
Fivemile Creek—*stream* (3) MS-4
Fivemile Creek—*stream* (2) MO-7
Fivemile Creek—*stream* (7) MT-8
Five Mile Creek—*stream* MT-8
Fivemile Creek—*stream* (2) MT-8
Fivemile Creek—*stream* NV-8
Fivemile Creek—*stream* NM-5
Fivemile Creek—*stream* (4) NY-2
Fivemile Creek—*stream* ND-7
Fivemile Creek—*stream* (5) OH-6
Fivemile Creek—*stream* (4) OK-5
Fivemile Creek—*stream* (7) OR-9
Fivemile Creek—*stream* PA-2
Fivemile Creek—*stream* SC-3
Fivemile Creek—*stream* (2) SD-7
Fivemile Creek—*stream* (2) TN-4
Fivemile Creek—*stream* (4) TX-5
Five Mile Creek—*stream* TX-5
Fivemile Creek—*stream* TX-5
Fivemile Creek—*stream* UT-8
Fivemile Creek—*stream* (2) WA-9
Fivemile Creek—*stream* (3) WV-2
Fivemile Creek—*stream* (5) WI-6
Fivemile Creek—*stream* (8) WY-8
Five Mile Creek Bridge—*hist pl* AL-4
Fivemile Creek Cem—*cemetery* OK-5
*Fivemile Creek Hollow* OH-6
*Five Mile Crossing* MS-4
Fivemile Crossing—*locale* NM-5
Fivemile Crossing—*locale* TX-5
Five Mile Crossing (historical)—*crossing* SD-7
Fivemile Cut—*gut* TX-5
Five Mile Cut—*stream* GA-3
Fivemile Dam—*dam* NY-2
Fivemile Dam—*dam* OR-9
Fivemile Ditch—*canal* VA-3
Fivemile Ditch—*canal* WY-8
Fivemile Ditch—*stream* WY-8
*Fivemile Draw* WY-8
Fivemile Draw—*bend* WY-8
Fivemile Draw—*valley* AZ-5
Fivemile Draw—*valley* NV-8
Fivemile Draw—*valley* NM-5
Fivemile Draw—*valley* SD-7
Fivemile Draw—*valley* (3) TX-5
Fivemile Draw—*valley* (2) WY-8
Fivemile Draw Well—*well* NV-8
Five Mile Drive-Sutter Creek Bridge—*hist pl* CA-9
Fivemile Flat—*flat* (2) NV-8
**Five Mile Fork**—*pop pl* VA-3
Fivemile Fork—*stream* (4) WV-2
*Fivemile Gulch* WY-8
Fivemile Gulch—*valley* AK-9
Fivemile Gulch—*valley* CA-9
Fivemile Gulch—*valley* NV-8
Fivemile Gully—*stream* FL-3
Fivemile Hill—*summit* AZ-5
Fivemile Hill—*summit* CT-1
Fivemile Hill—*summit* (2) MT-8
Fivemile Hill—*summit* (3) TX-5
Fivemile Hole—*bend* WY-8
*Fivemile Hollow* PA-2
Fivemile Hollow—*valley* (2) OK-5
Fivemile Hollow—*valley* PA-2
Fivemile Hollow—*valley* TX-5
Fivemile Hollow—*valley* UT-8
Fivemile Hollow—*valley* (2) WV-2
Five Mile House—*hist pl* OH-6
Fivemile House—*locale* CA-9
Fivemile Island—*island* AK-9
Fivemile Island—*island* NH-1
Fivemile Lake—*flat* OR-9
Fivemile Lake—*lake* AK-9
Fivemile Lake—*lake* (2) AZ-5
Fivemile Lake—*lake* CO-8
Fivemile Lake—*lake* FL-3
Fivemile Lake—*lake* MN-6
Fivemile Lake—*lake* MS-4
Five Mile Lake—*lake* (3) MS-4
Fivemile Lake—*lake* TX-5
Fivemile Lake—*lake* WA-9
Fivemile Lake—*lake* WY-8
Fivemile Lake—*reservoir* IL-6
Fivemile Landing—*locale* AZ-5
Fivemile Lane—*canal* MO-7
Fivemile Lateral—*canal* WY-8
Fivemile Lock Light—*locale* OR-9
Fivemile Lookout Tower—*locale* WI-6
Fivemile Main Lateral—*canal* WY-8
Fivemile Meadow—*area* PA-2
Fivemile Meadows—*flat* ID-8
Fivemile Mesa—*summit* TX-5
Fivemile Mtn—*summit* NY-2
Fivemile Mtn—*summit* UT-8
Fivemile Mtn—*summit* VA-3
Fivemile Oaks—*locale* LA-4
Fivemile Park—*flat* CO-8
Fivemile Pass—*gap* AZ-5
Fivemile Pass—*gap* TX-5
Fivemile Pass—*gap* UT-8
Fivemile Pass Tank—*reservoir* AZ-5
Fivemile Pass Tank Number One—*reservoir* AZ-5
Fivemile Pass Tank Number Two—*reservoir* AZ-5
*Five Mile Peak* AZ-5
Fivemile Peak—*summit* AZ-5
*Fivemile Point* NY-2
Fivemile Point—*cape* AK-9
Fivemile Point—*cape* GA-3
Five Mile Point—*cape* MI-6
Fivemile Point—*cape* MI-6
Fivemile Point—*cape* MN-6
Fivemile Point—*cape* (2) NY-2
Fivemile Point—*cape* OR-9
Fivemile Point—*cape* PA-2
Fivemile Point—*cape* VT-1
Fivemile Point—*cape* WY-8
Five Mile Point—*locale* PA-2
**Fivemile Point**—*pop pl* NY-2
Five Mile Point—*summit* AZ-5
Fivemile Point—*summit* TX-5
*Five Mile Pond* MA-1
*Five Mile Pond* PA-2
Fivemile Pond—*lake* (3) FL-3
Fivemile Pond—*lake* (2) MA-1
Fivemile Pond—*reservoir* CT-1
Fivemile Pond—*swamp* FL-3
Fivemile Ponds—*lake* MA-1
Fivemile Prairie—*flat* WA-9
Fivemile Ranch—*locale* NV-8
Fivemile Ranch—*locale* NM-5
Five Mile Ranch—*locale* WY-8
Fivemile Rapids—*rapids* ID-8
Fivemile Rapids Light—*locale* WA-9
Fivemile Rapids Site (35 WS 4)—*hist pl* OR-9
Fivemile Ridge—*ridge* WY-8
Fivemile Ridge—*summit* UT-8
*Five Mile River* MA-1
Fivemile River—*stream* (2) CT-1
Fivemile River—*stream* MA-1
Five Mile Rock—*bar* AL-4
Fivemile Rock—*pillar* CO-8
Five Mile Rsvr—*reservoir* AZ-5
Fivemile Rsvr—*reservoir* CO-8
Fivemile Rsvr—*reservoir* OR-9
Fivemile Rsvr—*reservoir* WY-8
*Five-Mile Run* OH-6
*Five Mile Run* PA-2
Fivemile Run—*stream* (2) OH-6
Fivemile Run—*stream* (3) PA-2
Fivemile Run—*stream* (2) WV-2
Five Mile Run—*stream* WV-2
Fivemile Run—*stream* WV-2
*Five Miles Beach* NJ-2
Fivemile Sch—*school* MI-6
Fivemile Sch—*school* WA-9
Fivemile Shelter—*locale* OR-9
Fivemile Slough—*gut* CA-9
Five Mile Slough—*stream* LA-4
Fivemile Spring—*spring* AR-4
Fivemile Spring—*spring* CA-9
Fivemile Spring—*spring* CO-8
Fivemile Spring—*spring* (3) NV-8
Fivemile Spring—*spring* OR-9
Fivemile Spring—*spring* (2) UT-8
Five Mile Spring—*spring* UT-8
Fivemile Springs—*spring* NV-8
*Five Mile Station* NV-8
**Fivemile Still**—*pop pl* GA-3
Fivemile Still Cem—*cemetery* LA-4
Fivemile Swamp—*swamp* FL-3
Fivemile Swamp—*swamp* SC-3
Fivemile Tank—*reservoir* NM-5
Fivemile Tank—*reservoir* (2) TX-5
**Five Mile Terrace**—*pop pl* CA-9
Five Mile Township—*civil* MO-7
Fivemile Valley—*valley* UT-8
Fivemile Viaduct—*canal* SC-3
*Five Mile Wash* UT-8
Fivemile Wash—*stream* (4) AZ-5
Fivemile Wash—*valley* (3) UT-8
Five Mile Wash Dam—*dam* AZ-5
Fivemile Waterhole—*lake* TX-5
Fivemile Well—*well* NV-8
Fivemile Well—*well* OR-9
Fivemile Well—*well* TX-5
Fivemile Windmill—*locale* TX-5
Fivemile 52 Drain—*canal* WY-8
Five Mine—*mine* MT-8
Five Minute Draw—*valley* OR-9
Five Monument Butte—*summit* WY-8
Five Mounds—*summit* KS-7
*Five Needles* HI-9
Five N Trail—*trail* OK-5
Five-O, Lake—*lake* FL-3
Five Oaks—*hist pl* OH-6
Five Oaks—*locale* VA-3
Five Oaks Ch—*church* AR-4
Five Oaks JHS—*school* OR-9
*Five O'clock Wash* AZ-5
Five Palms Spring—*spring* CA-9
Five Pine Canyon—*valley* CO-8
Five Pine Mesa—*summit* CO-8
Five Pine Mesa Creek—*stream* CO-8
Five Pine Mesa Ditch—*canal* CO-8
Five Pine Rapids—*rapids* ID-8
Five Pine Rsvr—*reservoir* CO-8
Five Pines Canyon—*valley* UT-8
Five Pines Island—*island* NC-3
Five Pockets—*basin* WY-8
*Five Point* MA-1
*Five Point* NC-3
*Five Point* TN-4
Five Point—*cape* LA-4
Five Point—*locale* IL-6
Five Point—*uninc pl* NC-3
*Five Point Baptist Church* TN-4
Five Point Butte—*summit* ND-7
Five Point Canyon—*valley* OR-9
Five Point Ch—*church* OH-6
Five Point Ch—*church* (2) TN-4
Five Point Ch—*church* TX-5
*Five Point Creek* OR-9
Five Point Forest Service Station—*locale* UT-8
Five Point Gulch—*valley* CO-8
Fivepoint Hill—*summit* OR-9
*Five Point Lake* MN-6
Five Point Lake—*lake* LA-4
Five Point Lake—*reservoir* UT-8
Five Point Lake Dam—*dam* UT-8
Five Point Mtn—*summit* AZ-5
Five Point Post Office—*building* TN-4
Five Point Rsvr—*reservoir* MT-8
*Fivepoints* AL-4
*Five Points* DE-2
*Five Points* GA-3
*Five Points* IL-6
*Five Points* (2) IN-6
*Five Points* ME-1
*Five Points* NJ-2
*Fivepoints* OH-6
*Five Points* OH-6
*Five Points* PA-2
Five Points—*cape* IN-6
Five Points—*cape* PA-2
Five Points—*locale* (3) AL-4
Five Points—*locale* (3) CA-9
Five Points—*locale* DE-2
Five Points—*locale* FL-3
Five Points—*locale* (15) GA-3
Five Points—*locale* ID-8
Five Points—*locale* IL-6
Five Points—*locale* IA-7
Five Points—*locale* KS-7
Five Points—*locale* MD-2
Five Points—*locale* MI-6
Five Points—*locale* MN-6
Five Points—*locale* NE-7
Five Points—*locale* (5) NY-2
Five Points—*locale* (2) NC-3
Five Points—*locale* (4) OH-6
Five Points—*locale* (21) PA-2
Five Points—*locale* SD-7
Five Points—*locale* (2) TN-4
Five Points—*locale* TX-5
Five Points—*locale* UT-8
Five Points—*locale* WA-9
Five Points—*locale* (3) WI-6
Five Points—*other* GA-3
**Five Points**—*pop pl* (13) AL-4
**Five Points**—*pop pl* (3) CA-9
**Five Points**—*pop pl* (2) CT-1
**Five Points**—*pop pl* FL-3
**Five Points**—*pop pl* (4) GA-3
**Five Points**—*pop pl* (10) IN-6
**Five Points**—*pop pl* KY-4
**Five Points**—*pop pl* ME-1
**Five Points**—*pop pl* (2) MI-6
**Five Points**—*pop pl* (4) NJ-2
**Five Points**—*pop pl* NM-5
**Five Points**—*pop pl* (8) NC-3
**Five Points**—*pop pl* (7) OH-6
**Five Points**—*pop pl* (14) PA-2
**Five Points**—*pop pl* (2) SC-3
**Five Points**—*pop pl* (2) TN-4
**Five Points**—*pop pl* TX-5
**Five Points**—*pop pl* UT-8
**Fivepoints**—*pop pl* WI-6
Five Points—*post sta* TX-5
Five Points—*uninc pl* FL-3
Five Points—*uninc pl* SC-3
*Five Points Baptist Ch* AL-4
Five Points Baptist Ch—*church* (2) AL-4
Five Points Baptist Ch—*church* TN-4
Five Points Campground—*locale* ID-8
Five Points (CCD)—*cens area* AL-4
Five Points (CCD)—*cens area* TN-4
Five Points Cem—*cemetery* OH-6
Five Points Cem—*cemetery* TN-4
Five Points Ch—*church* (3) AL-4
Five Points Ch—*church* GA-3
Five Points Ch—*church* IL-6
Five Points Ch—*church* MI-6
Five Point Sch—*school* NE-7
Five Point Sch—*school* WI-6
Five Point Sch (abandoned)—*school* PA-2
Five Points Ch of Christ—*church* TN-4
*Five Points Church* TN-4
Five Points Corner—*locale* MI-6
**Five Points Corner**—*pop pl* IN-6
*Fivepoints Creek* OR-9
Five Points Creek—*stream* ID-8
Five Points Creek—*stream* (2) OR-9
Five Points Ditch—*stream* AL-4
Five Points Division—*civil* AL-4
Five Points Division—*civil* TN-4
**Five Points East**—*pop pl* AL-4
Five Points East Shop Ctr—*locale* AL-4
*Five Points Elem Sch* AL-4
Five Points Elem Sch—*school* AL-4
Five Points Elem Sch—*school* PA-2
Five Points Helistop—*airport* PA-2
Five Points HS—*school* AL-4
*Five Points Junction* UT-8
Five Points Lake—*reservoir* GA-3
Five Points Lookout Tower—*locale* GA-3
Five Points Mine—*mine* ID-8
*Five Points Mtn* AZ-5
**Five Points North**—*pop pl* MI-6
Five Points Park—*park* AZ-5
Five Points Sch—*school* (2) AL-4
Five Points Sch—*school* FL-3
Five Points Sch—*school* MI-6
Five Points Sch—*school* NM-5
Five Points Sch—*school* (2) PA-2
Five Points Sch (historical)—*school* AL-4
Five Points Sch (historical)—*school* (2) TN-4
Five Points Shop Ctr—*locale* (2) AL-4
Five Points Shop Ctr—*locale* (2) FL-3
Five Points Shop Ctr—*locale* UT-8
**Five Points (Shopping Center)**—*pop pl* GA-3
**Five Points South**—*pop pl* AL-4
Five Points South Hist Dist—*hist pl* AL-4
Five Points South Hist Dist (Boundary Increase)—*hist pl* AL-4
**Five Points (subdivision)**—*pop pl* AL-4
**Five Points (subdivision)**—*pop pl* NC-3
Five Points Trail—*trail* OR-9
*Five Points West* MI-6
Five Points West—*uninc pl* AL-4
Five Points West Shop Ctr—*locale* AL-4
Five Point Tank—*reservoir* TX-5
Fivepointville—*locale* PA-2
Five Ponds—*lake* NY-2
Five Ponds—*swamp* SD-7
Five Poplar Branch—*stream* TN-4
**Five Pound Island**—*pop pl* MA-1
Five Rapids (historical)—*rapids* AZ-5
Five Rivers—*stream* OR-9
Five Rivers County Park—*park* OR-9
Five Rivers Farm—*locale* MD-2
Five Rivers Look Out—*locale* OR-9
Fiver Lake—*lake* MN-6
Five Runs Cem—*cemetery* AL-4
Five Runs Ch (historical)—*church* AL-4
Five Runs Creek—*stream* AL-4
Fives Creek—*stream* OR-9
Five Sections Windmill—*locale* TX-5
Five Section Tank—*reservoir* (2) TX-5
Five Section Windmill—*locale* (4) TX-5
Five Sheep Creek—*stream* AK-9
Five Sisters—*ridge* WA-9
Five Sisters, The—*island* MA-1
Five Sisters Islands—*island* MN-6
Five Sisters Springs—*spring* WY-8
Five Spring—*spring* CO-8
Five Spring—*spring* ID-8
Five Spring—*spring* NM-5
Five Spring Canyon—*valley* UT-8
*Five Spring Creek* UT-8
Five Spring Creek—*stream* CA-9
Five Spring Ridge—*ridge* CA-9
Five Springs—*locale* GA-3
Five Springs—*spring* (2) CA-9
Five Springs—*spring* (2) NV-8
Five Springs Basin—*basin* WY-8
Five Springs Campground—*locale* WY-8
Five Springs Canyon—*valley* NV-8
Five Springs Canyon—*valley* NM-5
Five Springs Ch—*church* KY-4
Five Springs Creek—*stream* WY-8
Five Springs Draw—*valley* CO-8
Five Springs Mtn—*summit* CA-9
Five Springs Point—*cape* WY-8
Five Star Mine—*mine* CA-9
Five Sticks Camp—*locale* OR-9
*Five Stream* WA-9
Five Stream—*stream* WA-9
Five Streams—*stream* NY-2
Five Thousand Thirty Trail—*trail* WA-9
Five Town Plaza—*locale* MA-1
Five T Ranch—*locale* FL-3
Five Troughs—*spring* CA-9
Five Trough Spring—*spring* MT-8
Five Troughs Springs—*spring* NV-8
Five Troughs Well—*well* NM-5
Five Tub Windmill—*locale* TX-5
Five Tunnels Mine—*mine* CA-9
Five Waters Corners—*locale* NY-2
Five Wells—*well* AZ-5
Five Wells Ranch—*locale* TX-5
Five Willow Spring—*spring* CA-9
Five Wounds Sch—*school* CA-9
Fix Cem—*cemetery* KS-7
Fix Creek—*stream* ID-8
Fix Creek—*stream* MT-8
Fixer—*locale* KY-4
Fixico Cem—*cemetery* OK-5
Fixico Creek—*stream* AL-4
Fixit Pass—*gap* UT-8
Fix Pond—*lake* MO-7
Fix Ridge—*ridge* ID-8
Fix Ridge Cem—*cemetery* ID-8
Fix Tank—*reservoir* AZ-5
*Fiyarumas* MH-9
*Fizzel Creek* OR-9
Fizzell Branch—*stream* OK-5
Fizzle Flat—*flat* TX-5
Fizzle Lake—*lake* MT-8
Fizzleout Creek—*stream* OR-9
Fizzle Ridge Airp—*airport* MO-7
Fizzle Spring—*spring* MT-8
Fizz Spring—*spring* OR-9
F J Advice Grant—*civil* FL-3
Fjalla Ch—*church* ND-7
F James Ranch—*locale* ND-7
F J Betts Pond—*lake* FL-3
Fjelberg Cem—*cemetery* IA-7
Fjestad Lake—*lake* MN-6
F J I Development Corporation Dam—*dam* NC-3
F J I Development Corporation Lake—*reservoir* NC-3
F J Lateral—*canal* CO-8
F Joens Dam—*dam* SD-7
F K Lateral—*canal* CO-8
**Flaat**—*pop pl* ND-7
Flaceys Lake—*lake* MO-7
**Flack**—*pop pl* AL-4
Flack Cem—*cemetery* OH-6
Flackey Branch—*stream* KY-4
Flackey Sch—*school* KY-4
*Flackler* AL-4
Flacks Lakes—*lake* MI-6
Flacks Pond—*lake* OH-6
Flack Spring—*spring* AL-4
*Flackville* IN-6
**Flackville**—*pop pl* IN-6
**Flackville**—*pop pl* NY-2
Flackville Cem—*cemetery* NY-2
Flackville Sch Number 100—*school* IN-6
Flack Well—*well* NM-5
Flactor Ch—*church* LA-4
*Flactor Creek* LA-4
Fladberg Bench—*bench* MT-8
Flader Cem—*cemetery* WI-6
Fladmark Lake—*lake* MN-6
*Flag* TN-4
Flag—*locale* AR-4
Flag—*locale* OH-6
Flag, Rio de—*stream* AZ-5
**Flagami**—*pop pl* FL-3
Flagami Elem Sch—*school* FL-3
Flagami Park—*park* FL-3
Flag Athletic Field—*locale* NM-5
Flag Bay—*bay* TX-5
Flag Branch—*locale* TN-4
Flag Branch—*stream* AL-4
Flag Branch—*stream* AR-4
Flag Branch—*stream* (2) KY-4
Flag Branch—*stream* LA-4
Flag Branch—*stream* (2) MO-7
Flag Branch—*stream* (4) NC-3
Flag Branch—*stream* OK-5
Flag Branch—*stream* (2) TN-4
Flag Branch—*stream* (6) TX-5
Flag Branch Lake—*reservoir* TX-5
Flag Branch Sch (historical)—*school* TN-4
Flag Brook—*stream* MA-1
Flag Brook—*stream* NY-2
Flag Butte—*summit* MT-8
Flag Butte—*summit* NE-7
Flag Butte—*summit* UT-8
Flag Butte—*summit* WY-8
Flag Butte Creek—*stream* WY-8
Flag Butte Sch—*school* NE-7
Flag Cadet Acad—*school* FL-3
Flag Canyon—*valley* CA-9
Flag Canyon—*valley* NV-8
Flag Cem—*cemetery* VA-3
**Flag Center**—*pop pl* IL-6
Flag Ch—*church* NC-3
Flag Chapel—*church* MS-4
*Flag Chapel Baptist Ch* MS-4
Flag Cove—*bay* MD-2
*Flag Creek* TX-5
Flag Creek—*stream* AK-9
Flag Creek—*stream* (2) CO-8
Flag Creek—*stream* FL-3
Flag Creek—*stream* ID-8
Flag Creek—*stream* IL-6
Flag Creek—*stream* MT-8
Flag Creek—*stream* NE-7
Flag Creek—*stream* NY-2
Flag Creek—*stream* NC-3
Flag Creek—*stream* OR-9
Flag Creek—*stream* SC-3
Flag Creek—*stream* (3) TX-5
Flagdale Cem—*cemetery* OH-6
Flagel Sch—*school* SD-7
Flager And Wadsworth Drain—*canal* MI-6
Flaget HS—*school* KY-4
Flag Flat—*flat* OR-9
Flag Ford—*locale* FL-3
Flag Fork—*locale* KY-4
**Flagfork**—*pop pl* KY-4
Flagg—*locale* OR-9
Flagg—*locale* TX-5
**Flagg**—*pop pl* IL-6
Flagg, Amos, House—*hist pl* MA-1
Flagg, Benjamin, House—*hist pl* MA-1

Flagg, James Montgomery,
House—*hist pl* ME-1
Flagg Branch—*stream* MO-7
Flagg Brook—*stream* MA-1
Flagg Brook—*stream* VT-1
Flagg Cem—*cemetery* TX-5
Flagg Center Cem—*cemetery* IL-6
Flagg-Coburn House—*hist pl* MA-1
Flagg Cove—*cove* MA-1
*Flagg Creek* SC-3
Flagg Dam—*dam* ME-1
Flagg Hill—*summit* CT-1
Flagg Hill—*summit* (2) MA-1
Flagg Island—*island* SC-3
Flagg Knob—*summit* VA-3
Flagg Lake—*lake* AR-4
Flagg Lake—*lake* OK-5
Flaggler Terrace Park—*park* FL-3
Flagg Lick—*stream* LA-4
*Flagg Meadow Brook* MA-1
*Flagg Mtn* AL-4
Flagg Mtn—*summit* AL-4
Flagg Mtn—*summit* WA-9
Flagg Pond—*lake* MD-2
Flagg Pond—*lake* SC-3
Flagg Pond—*lake* VT-1
Flagg Ranch—*locale* TX-5
Flagg Ranch—*locale* (2) WY-8
Flag Grove Sch—*school* TN-4
*Flaggs Hill* MA-1
Flaggs Manor—*locale* PA-2
Flaggs Mtn—*summit* WA-9
Flagg Spring—*locale* KY-4
Flagg Spring Creek—*stream* KY-4
Flagg Springs—*spring* OK-5
Flagg Springs Creek—*stream* OK-5
Flagg Street Sch—*school* MA-1
Flagg Swamp—*swamp* MA-1
*Flaggtown* NJ-2
**Flagg (Township of)**—*pop pl* IL-6
Flagg Township Public Library—*hist pl* IL-6
Flaggy Meadow—*locale* WV-2
Flaggy Meadow—*swamp* MA-1
Flaggy Meadow (local name for Natl
(sta.))—*other* WV-2
Flaggy Meadow Mtn—*summit* NY-2
Flaggy Meadow Playground—*park* MA-1
Flaggy Meadow Run—*stream* (2) WV-2
*Flag Hill* MA-1
Flag Hill—*summit* (2) AK-9
Flag Hill—*summit* ME-1
Flag Hill—*summit* MA-1
Flag Hill—*summit* TN-4
Flag Hill—*summit* (2) TX-5
Flag Hill—*summit* VI-3
Flag Hill Mine—*mine* WA-9
Flag Hollow—*valley* AR-4
Flag Hollow—*valley* MO-7
Flag House—*hist pl* MD-2
Flag Island—*island* (2) ME-1
Flag Island—*island* MI-6
Flag Island—*island* MN-6
Flag Island—*island* OR-9
Flag Island Ledge—*bar* ME-1
Flag Knob—*summit* (2) KY-4
Flag Knob—*summit* (3) WV-2
Flag Knoll—*summit* ID-8
*Flag Lake* WI-6
Flag Lake—*lake* AL-4
Flag Lake—*lake* (2) AR-4
Flag Lake—*lake* GA-3
Flag Lake—*lake* (2) LA-4
Flag Lake—*lake* (3) MS-4
Flag Lake—*lake* NM-5
Flag Lake—*lake* OK-5
Flag Lake—*lake* (6) TX-5
Flag Lake—*lake* WI-6
Flag Lake—*reservoir* LA-4
Flag Lake—*reservoir* (2) OK-5
Flag Lake—*swamp* MS-4
*Flaglake Canyon* UT-8
Flag Lake Canyon—*valley* UT-8
Flag Lake Ch—*church* TX-5
Flag Lake Crossing—*locale* AR-4
Flag Lake Drainage Canal—*canal* TX-5
Flag Lake Oil Field—*oilfield* TX-5
Flag Lake Sch (historical)—*school* MO-7
**Flagler**—*pop pl* CO-8
**Flagler**—*pop pl* IA-7
Flagler—*uninc pl* (2) FL-3
Flagler, Henry Morrison, House—*hist pl* FL-3
Flagler Airp—*airport* CO-8
**Flagler Beach**—*pop pl* FL-3
Flagler Beach (CCD)—*cens area* FL-3
Flagler Beach State Park—*park* FL-3
Flagler Branch—*stream* MS-4
Flagler Cem—*cemetery* CO-8
Flagler Cem—*cemetery* NY-2
Flagler Coll—*school* FL-3
Flagler College, Louise Wise
Library—*building* FL-3
**Flagler Corners**—*pop pl* NY-2
**Flagler County**—*pop pl* FL-3
Flagler County Adult Sch—*school* FL-3
Flagler Creek—*stream* OR-9
Flagler Dog Track—*locale* FL-3
Flagler Fork—*stream* CO-8
Flagler Hosp—*hospital* FL-3
Flagler Lookout Tower—*tower* FL-3
Flagler Memorial Bridge—*bridge* FL-3
Flagler Memorial Hosp—*hospital* FL-3
Flagler Memorial Library—*building* FL-3
Flagler Memorial Monmt—*park* FL-3
Flagler Memorial Park—*cemetery* FL-3
Flagler-Palm Coast HS—*school* FL-3
Flagler Rec Area—*park* CO-8
Flagler Rsvr—*reservoir* CO-8
Flagler Rsvr—*reservoir* PA-2
Flagler Run—*stream* PA-2
*Flagler Run Dam* PA-2
*Flagler's* IA-7
Flagler Sch—*school* FL-3
Flag Lick Creek—*stream* KY-4
Flag Marsh—*swamp* PA-2
Flag Marsh Run—*stream* NY-2
Flag Marsh Run—*stream* PA-2
Flag Mine—*mine* AZ-5
Flagmire Hollow—*valley* MO-7
Flag Mound—*summit* TX-5
Flag Mountain Trail—*trail* OR-9
Flag Mtn—*summit* AL-4
Flag Mtn—*summit* CO-8
Flag Mtn—*summit* MA-1
Flag Mtn—*summit* NM-5
Flag Mtn—*summit* OR-9
Flag Mtn—*summit* (3) SD-7
Flag Mtn—*summit* (4) TX-5
Flag Mtn—*summit* WA-9
Flagon Bayou—*stream* LA-4
Flagon Creek—*stream* LA-4
Flag Patch Cem—*cemetery* SC-3
Flag Patch Ch—*church* SC-3
*Flag Peak* WA-9
Flag Peak—*summit* (2) CA-9
Flag Peak—*summit* WY-8
Flag Plaza—*park* PA-2
Flag Point—*cape* (3) AK-9
Flag Point—*cape* MI-6
Flag Point—*cape* NJ-2
Flag Point—*cape* NC-3
Flag Point—*cape* OR-9
Flag Point—*cape* UT-8
Flag Point Channel—*channel* AK-9
Flag Point Lake—*lake* TX-5
Flag Point Trail—*trail* OR-9
Flag Pole, The—*summit* TN-4
Flagpole Bayou—*gut* LA-4
Flagpole Gulch—*valley* WA-9
Flagpole Hill—*summit* CO-8
Flagpole Hill—*summit* NY-2
Flagpole Hill—*summit* (2) TN-4
Flagpole Knob—*summit* TN-4
Flagpole Knob—*summit* VA-3
Flagpole Lookout Tower—*locale* OK-5
*Flag Pole Mtn* AL-4
Flagpole Mtn—*summit* (2) AL-4
Flagpole Mtn—*summit* CO-8
Flagpole Mtn—*summit* NM-5
Flagpole Mtn—*summit* (2) OK-5
Flagpole Mtn—*summit* SD-7
Flagpole Peak—*summit* CA-9
Flagpole Point—*cliff* TN-4
Flagpole Point—*summit* CA-9
Flagpole Ridge—*ridge* OR-9
*Flagpond* TN-4
Flag Pond—*lake* (4) FL-3
Flag Pond—*lake* (3) GA-3
Flag Pond—*lake* MD-2
Flag Pond—*lake* MA-1
Flag Pond—*lake* MO-7
Flag Pond—*lake* NH-1
Flag Pond—*lake* TN-4
Flag Pond—*lake* (5) TX-5
Flag Pond—*lake* (2) VA-3
**Flag Pond**—*pop pl* TN-4
**Flagpond**—*pop pl* VA-3
Flag Pond—*reservoir* (2) TX-5
Flag Pond—*swamp* (2) AR-4
Flag Pond—*swamp* IL-6
Flag Pond—*swamp* (2) TX-5
Flag Pond Baptist Ch—*church* TN-4
Flag Pond Branch—*stream* NC-3
Flag Pond Branch—*stream* SC-3
Flag Pond Branch—*stream* VA-3
Flag Pond (CCD)—*cens area* TN-4
Flag Pond Cem—*cemetery* VA-3
Flag Pond Creek—*stream* MD-2
Flag Pond Creek—*stream* TX-5
Flag Pond Division—*civil* TN-4
Flag Pond Elem Sch—*school* TN-4
Flag Pond Landing—*locale* VA-3
*Flagpond Post Office* TN-4
Flag Pond Post Office—*building* TN-4
Flag Ponds—*lake* MD-2
Flag Pond Sch—*school* MO-7
Flag Pond School (abandoned)—*spring* MO-7
Flag Prairie—*flat* OR-9
Flag Ranch—*locale* WY-8
Flag Ranch Well—*well* NM-5
Flagreed Creek—*stream* SC-3
Flag Ridge—*ridge* KY-4
Flag River—*stream* WI-6
Flag Rock—*pillar* SD-7
Flag Rock—*pillar* WI-6
Flag Rock—*summit* MA-1
*Flag Run* OH-6
Flag Run—*stream* IN-6
Flag Run—*stream* KY-4
Flag Run—*stream* (4) OH-6
Flag Run—*stream* PA-2
Flag Run—*stream* (2) VA-3
Flag Run—*stream* (3) WV-2
Flag Run Ch—*church* WV-2
Flag Run Gut—*stream* NC-3
Flag Run Landing—*locale* NC-3
Flag Sch—*school* (3) NE-7
Flag Slough Ditch—*canal* AR-4
*Flag Spring* KY-4
**Flag Spring**—*pop pl* KY-4
**Flag Spring**—*pop pl* MO-7
Flag Spring—*spring* AL-4
Flag Spring—*spring* AZ-5
Flag Spring—*spring* ID-8
Flag Spring—*spring* NM-5
Flag Spring—*spring* TX-5
Flag Spring Cem—*cemetery* OH-6
Flag Spring Ch—*church* (2) MO-7
Flag Spring Ch—*church* OH-6
Flag Springs—*locale* TX-5
**Flag Springs**—*pop pl* (2) MO-7
Flag Springs—*spring* NV-8
Flag Springs Ch—*church* NC-3
Flag Springs Creek—*stream* TX-5
Flag Springs Sch (historical)—*school* MO-7
Flag Springs Sch (historical)—*school* TN-4
Flagstaff—*hist pl* LA-4
**Flagstaff**—*pop pl* AZ-5
**Flagstaff Addition
Subdivision**—*pop pl* UT-8
Flagstaff Armory—*hist pl* AZ-5
Flagstaff Butte—*summit* ID-8
Flagstaff Butte—*summit* (2) OR-9
Flagstaff Canyon—*valley* NV-8
Flagstaff Cem—*cemetery* ME-1
Flagstaff City Park—*park* AZ-5
Flagstaff City Reservoirs—*reservoir* AZ-5
Flagstaff City Well Five—*well* AZ-5
Flagstaff City Well Four—*well* AZ-5
Flagstaff City Well One—*well* AZ-5
Flagstaff City Well Three—*well* AZ-5
Flagstaff City Well Two—*well* AZ-5
Flagstaff Community Hosp—*hospital* AZ-5
Flagstaff Compressor Station—*locale* AZ-5
Flagstaff Country Club—*other* AZ-5
Flagstaff Creek—*stream* AK-9
Flagstaff Creek—*stream* CO-8
Flagstaff Creek—*stream* MO-7
Flagstaff Creek—*stream* MT-8
Flagstaff Creek—*stream* WY-8
Flagstaff Department of Public Safety
Heliport—*airport* AZ-5
Flagstaff Dormitory—*other* AZ-5
Flagstaff Enclosure—*locale* MT-8
**Flagstaff Farming
Subdivision**—*pop pl* UT-8
Flagstaff Fire Station Number
One—*building* AZ-5
Flagstaff Fire Station Number
Two—*building* AZ-5
Flagstaff Gulch—*valley* OR-9
Flagstaff Hill—*summit* AK-9
Flagstaff Hill—*summit* CA-9
Flagstaff Hill—*summit* (3) MA-1
Flagstaff Hill—*summit* MT-8
Flagstaff Hill—*summit* ND-7
Flagstaff Hill—*summit* OR-9
Flagstaff HS—*school* AZ-5
Flagstaff JHS—*school* AZ-5
Flagstaff Lake—*lake* OR-9
Flagstaff Lake—*reservoir* ME-1
Flagstaff Mall Heliport—*airport* AZ-5
Flagstaff Memorial—*pillar* CO-8
Flagstaff Memorial Ch—*church* ME-1
Flagstaff Mine—*mine* AK-9
Flagstaff Mine—*mine* OR-9
Flagstaff Mine—*mine* (2) UT-8
*Flagstaff Mountain* UT-8
Flagstaff Mountain Overlook—*locale* PA-2
Flagstaff Mountain Park—*park* PA-2
Flagstaff Mtn—*summit* (2) CO-8
Flagstaff Mtn—*summit* (2) ME-1
Flagstaff Mtn—*summit* MT-8
Flagstaff Mtn—*summit* NV-8
Flagstaff Mtn—*summit* NY-2
Flagstaff Mtn—*summit* SD-7
Flagstaff Mtn—*summit* (2) UT-8
Flagstaff Mtn—*summit* WA-9
Flagstaff Peak—*summit* UT-8
Flagstaff Plaza Shop Ctr—*locale* AZ-5
Flagstaff Point—*cape* WA-9
Flagstaff Point—*cliff* OR-9
*Flagstaff Pond* ME-1
Flagstaff RR Station—*building* AZ-5
Flagstaff Rsvr—*reservoir* MT-8
Flagstaff Sch—*school* ME-1
Flagstaff Spring—*spring* AZ-5
Flagstaff (Township of)—*unorg* ME-1
Flagstaff Townsite Historic Residential
District—*hist pl* AZ-5
Flagstok Hill—*summit* VI-3
Flagstone Cem—*cemetery* OH-6
Flagstone Creek—*stream* OR-9
Flagstone Mtn—*summit* NM-5
Flagstone Park—*flat* CO-8
Flagstone Peak—*summit* OR-9
Flagstone Peak—*summit* WY-8
*Flag Stone Ridge* PA-2
*Flagstone Rock* OR-9
Flagstone Rsvr—*reservoir* WY-8
Flagstone Tank—*reservoir* AZ-5
Flag Swamp—*swamp* MA-1
Flag Swamp—*swamp* NY-2
Flagtail Cow Camp—*locale* OR-9
Flagtail Creek—*stream* OR-9
Flagtail Creek—*stream* TX-5
Flagtail Mtn—*summit* OR-9
*Flag Tail Spring* AZ-5
Flagtail Spring—*spring* AZ-5
Flag Tank—*reservoir* (2) AZ-5
Flag Top—*summit* KY-4
*Flagtown* NJ-2
**Flagtown**—*pop pl* NJ-2
Flagtown Cem—*cemetery* NJ-2
**Flagtown (Read Valley)**—*pop pl* NJ-2
Flag (Township of)—*fmr MCD* AR-4
*Flag Wash* AZ-5
Flag Wash—*stream* AZ-5
Flag Windmill—*locale* TX-5
Flahart Lake—*lake* AK-9
**Flaherty**—*pop pl* KY-4
Flaherty, Lake—*lake* MN-6
Flaherty (CCD)—*cens area* KY-4
Flaherty Coulee—*valley* MT-8
Flaherty Flat—*flat* MT-8
Flaherty Sch—*school* KY-4
Flahertys Pond—*lake* WA-9
Flaig—*locale* WA-9
Flake—*locale* TX-5
Flake, James M., House—*hist pl* AZ-5
*Flake Bar* ME-1
Flake Cem—*cemetery* IL-6
Flake Cem—*cemetery* IN-6
Flake Cem—*cemetery* MI-6
Flake Cem—*cemetery* TN-4
Flake Creek—*stream* AL-4
*Flakefjord Lake* WI-6
Flakefjord Lake—*lake* WI-6
Flake Island—*island* ME-1
Flake Lateral—*canal* ID-8
Flake Mills—*facility* GA-3
Flakemoore Canyon—*valley* TX-5
Flakemoore Windmill—*locale* TX-5
Flake Mtn—*summit* UT-8
Flake Point Bar—*bar* ME-1
Flake Ranch—*locale* AZ-5
Flake Swale—*valley* UT-8
Flake Tank—*reservoir* AZ-5
Flake Windmill—*locale* AZ-5
*Flakey Bottom* UT-8
Flalap—*island* FM-9
Flamang Lake—*lake* WI-6
**Flambeau**—*pop pl* WI-6
Flambeau Falls Rapids—*rapids* WI-6
*Flambeau Flowage* WI-6
Flambeau Lake—*lake* WI-6
Flambeau Lookout Tower—*locale* (2) WI-6
Flambeau Mission Church—*hist pl* WI-6
Flambeau Paper Company Office
Bldg—*hist pl* WI-6
*Flambeau Reservoir* WI-6
Flambeau Ridge—*ridge* WI-6
Flambeau River—*stream* AK-9
Flambeau River—*stream* WI-6
Flambeau River State For—*forest* WI-6
Flambeau (Town of)—*other* WI-6
**Flambeau (Town of)**—*pop pl* (2) WI-6
**Flamboyant Gardens**—*pop pl* PR-3
Flame Creek—*stream* ID-8
Flame Lake—*lake* MN-6
Flamenco, Bahia—*bay* PR-3
Flamenco (Barrio)—*fmr MCD* PR-3
Flame Peak—*summit* MT-8
Flaming—*locale* MN-6
Flaming Arrow Ranch—*locale* MT-8
Flaming Geyser Park—*park* WA-9
*Flaming Gorge, The* UT-8
Flaming Gorge Dam—*dam* UT-8
Flaming Gorge Dam Bureau of Reclamation
HQ—*locale* UT-8
Flaming Gorge Dam Visitor
Center—*locale* UT-8
Flaming Gorge (inundated)—*valley* UT-8
**Flaming Gorge Lodge**—*pop pl* UT-8
Flaming Gorge Natl Rec Area—*park* UT-8
Flaming Gorge Natl Rec Area—*park* (2) WY-8
Flaming Gorge Natl Rec AreaHQ—*locale* UT-8
Flaming Gorge Rsvr—*reservoir* UT-8
Flaming Gorge Rsvr—*reservoir* WY-8
Flaming Gorge Sch—*school* UT-8
**Flaming Gorge Summer Home
Area**—*pop pl* UT-8
Flaming Gorge Valley—*valley* UT-8
Flamingo—*locale* FL-3
**Flamingo**—*pop pl* FL-3
Flamingo, Lake—*lake* FL-3
Flamingo Bay—*bay* VI-3
Flamingo Bay—*locale* FL-3
Flamingo Bay—*swamp* FL-3
Flamingo Bay—*uninc pl* TX-5
*Flamingo Bayou* FL-3
Flamingo Campground—*locale* FL-3
Flamingo Canal—*canal* FL-3
*Flamingo-Coot Bay Canal* FL-3
Flamingo Cove—*bay* NV-8
Flamingo Elem Sch—*school* FL-3
**Flamingo Garden**—*pop pl* PR-3
**Flamingo Heights**—*pop pl* CA-9
**Flamingo Hills Subdivision**—*pop pl* UT-8
Flamingo Lakes—*reservoir* MO-7
Flamingo Mobile Home Resort—*locale* AZ-5
Flamingo Motel Heliport—*airport* OR-9
Flamingo-On-The-Lake
Apartments—*hist pl* IL-6
Flamingo Park—*park* AL-4
Flamingo Park—*park* (3) FL-3
Flamingo Plaza (Shop Ctr)—*locale* (2) FL-3
Flamingo Point—*cape* VI-3
Flamingo Reef—*bar* AZ-5
Flamingo Road Baptist Ch—*church* FL-3
Flamingo Sch—*school* FL-3
**Flamingo Village**—*pop pl* FL-3
Flamingo Wash—*stream* NV-8
*Flamingo Waterway* FL-3
Flamingo Waterway—*gut* FL-3
**Flamm City**—*pop pl* MO-7
Flamme Sch—*school* MN-6
*Flamstard Hill Swamp* VA-3
Flamstead, Mount—*summit* VT-1
Flamstead Hill Swamp—*stream* VA-3
Flanagan—*locale* KY-4
**Flanagan**—*pop pl* IL-6
**Flanagan**—*pop pl* TX-5
Flanagan, Dr. William H., House—*hist pl* OR-9
Flanagan, Judge, Residence—*hist pl* IL-6
Flanagan Bayou—*stream* LA-4
Flanagan Bluff—*cliff* MO-7
Flanagan Cem—*cemetery* AL-4
Flanagan Cem—*cemetery* LA-4
Flanagan Ch—*church* IL-6
Flanagan Creek—*stream* MT-8
Flanagan Harris Oil Field—*oilfield* TX-5
Flanagan Island—*island* VI-3
Flanagan Lake—*lake* TX-5
Flanagan Lake—*lake* WI-6
Flanagan Memorial Cem—*cemetery* WV-2
*Flanagan Mills* VA-3
Flanagan Mine—*mine* OR-9
Flanagan Mtn—*summit* OK-5
Flanagan Passage—*channel* VI-3
Flanagan Run—*stream* TX-5
Flanagan Sch—*school* WI-6
Flanagan School—*locale* IA-7
Flanagan (site)—*locale* OR-9
Flanagan Site (35 LA 218)—*hist pl* OR-9
Flanagan Slough—*lake* OR-9
*Flanagans Mill* VA-3
Flanagans Millpond—*reservoir* VA-3
*Flanagans Mills* VA-3
*Flanagans Pond* MA-1
Flanagin Law Office—*hist pl* AR-4
**Flanary**—*pop pl* KY-4
Flanary Archeol Site (44SC13)—*hist pl* VA-3
Flanary Branch—*stream* KY-4
Flanary Branch—*stream* VA-3
Flanary Bridge—*bridge* VA-3
Flanary Cem—*cemetery* KY-4
Flanary Cem—*cemetery* TX-5
Flanary Cem—*cemetery* VA-3
Flander Hollow—*valley* AR-4
Flanders—*locale* AL-4
Flanders—*locale* CT-1
Flanders—*locale* MI-6
**Flanders**—*pop pl* CT-1
**Flanders**—*pop pl* NJ-2
**Flanders**—*pop pl* NY-2
*Flanders Bay* NY-2
Flanders Bay—*bay* ME-1
Flanders Bay—*bay* NY-2
Flanders' Block—*hist pl* MN-6
Flanders Brook—*stream* ME-1
Flanders Brook—*stream* NH-1
Flanders Cave—*cave* MO-7
Flanders Cem—*cemetery* NY-2
Flanders Cem—*cemetery* OH-6
Flanders Corner—*locale* ME-1
*Flanders Creek* OK-5
Flanders Creek—*stream* IL-6
Flanders Creek—*stream* MT-8
Flanders Gap—*gap* AL-4
Flanders Hill—*summit* ME-1
Flanders Hill—*summit* NY-2
Flanders Hill—*summit* VT-1
Flanders Hist Dist—*hist pl* CT-1
Flanders Hole—*lake* SC-3
Flanders Lake—*lake* (2) MI-6
Flanders Lake—*lake* MN-6
Flanders Lake—*lake* MT-8
Flanders-Lee House and Carriage
House—*hist pl* KS-7
Flanders Mtn—*summit* CT-1
Flanders Mtn—*summit* MT-8
Flanders Pond—*reservoir* ME-1
Flanders Ranch—*locale* AZ-5
Flanders Sch—*school* (2) CT-1
Flanders Sch—*school* MI-6
Flanders Sch—*school* NY-2
Flanders Sch—*school* TX-5
Flanders Shady Bluff—*cliff* GA-3
Flanders Stream—*stream* ME-1
Flanders Valley—*airport* NJ-2
*Flanders Village* CT-1
Flandrau State Park—*park* MN-6
**Flandreau**—*pop pl* SD-7
Flandreau Creek—*stream* MN-6
Flandreau Creek—*stream* SD-7
Flandreau Indian Sch—*school* SD-7
Flandreau Ind Res—*reserve* SD-7
Flandreau Municipal Airp—*airport* SD-7
Flandreau Park—*park* SD-7
**Flandreau Township**—*pop pl* SD-7
F Lane Ranch—*locale* NE-7
Flanery Cem—*cemetery* AR-4
Fla-Net—*airport* NJ-2
**Flangas Subdivision**—*pop pl* UT-8
**Flanigan**—*pop pl* NV-8
Flanigan Arch—*arch* UT-8
Flanigan Branch—*stream* TX-5
Flanigan Branch—*stream* VA-3
Flanigan Creek—*stream* CA-9
Flanigan Creek—*stream* MI-6
Flanigan Creek—*stream* WI-6
Flanigan Hill—*summit* TN-4
*Flanigan Natural Arch* UT-8
Flanigan Sch (abandoned)—*school* PA-2
Flanigan Slough—*gut* MI-6
Flanigans Pond—*reservoir* GA-3
Flanigans River—*stream* PA-2
Flanigan Tank—*reservoir* AZ-5
Flanigan Well—*well* NV-8
Flank Creek—*stream* IA-7
Flankinstein Cem—*cemetery* OH-6
Flank Oil Field—*oilfield* CO-8
Flanly Peak—*summit* CA-9
Flannagan Creek Cave—*cave* AL-4
Flannagan Lake—*lake* WI-6
Flannagan Lookout Tower—*locale* WI-6
Flannagan Pond—*lake* MA-1
*Flannagan Reservoir* VA-3
Flannagan Ridge—*ridge* WI-6
*Flannagans Landing* IN-6
Flannagin Creek—*stream* AL-4
Flannegan Point—*cape* VA-3
Flanner Beach—*locale* NC-3
Flanner Sch—*school* CA-9
Flanners Creek—*stream* WI-6
Flannery Branch—*stream* MO-7
Flannery Cem—*cemetery* MO-7
Flannery Coulee—*valley* MT-8
Flannery County (historical)—*civil* ND-7
Flannery Creek—*stream* ID-8
Flannery Drain—*stream* MI-6
Flannery Fork—*stream* NC-3
Flannery Gulch—*valley* OR-9
Flannery Lake—*lake* WI-6
Flannery Mill—*other* PA-2
Flannery Ridge—*ridge* VA-3
Flannery Windmill—*locale* CO-8
Flannigan Branch—*stream* VA-3
Flannigan Butte—*summit* NE-7
Flannigan Cabin—*locale* SD-7
*Flannigan Creek* AL-4
*Flannigan Creek* ID-8
Flannigan Creek—*stream* ID-8
Flannigan Creek—*stream* OR-9
Flannigan Drain—*canal* MI-6
Flannigan Gut—*stream* NC-3
Flannigan Island—*island* IL-6
Flannigan Prairie—*flat* OR-9
Flannigan Rapids—*rapids* MI-6
Flannigan Run—*stream* WV-2
Flannigan Sch—*school* IL-6
**Flannigan (Township of)**—*pop pl* IL-6
Flansburg Drain—*canal* MI-6
Flansburg Sch—*school* MI-6
Flap Creek—*stream* MN-6
Flapjack Bar—*bar* CA-9
Flapjack Island—*island* AK-9
Flapjack Lakes—*lake* WA-9
Flapjack Point—*cape* WA-9
Flapjack Point—*cliff* WA-9
Flapjack Shelter—*locale* WA-9
Flap Lake—*lake* MN-6
Flapper Lake—*lake* MN-6
Flapper Springs—*spring* OR-9
Flapper Springs Guard Station—*locale* OR-9
Flare Hill—*summit* NM-5
Flarity Cem—*cemetery* TN-4
Flash Creek—*stream* AZ-5
Flash Creek—*stream* NE-7
**Flasher**—*pop pl* ND-7
Flasher Dam—*dam* ND-7
Flash Island—*island* ME-1
Flash Lake—*lake* MN-6
Flashman Cem—*cemetery* WV-2
Flashman Lookout Tower—*locale* OK-5
Flashman Trail—*trail* OK-5
Flash Peak—*summit* ID-8
Flash Point—*cape* AL-4
Flashy Pond—*lake* MA-1
Flask Canyon—*valley* NV-8
Flask Pond—*lake* MA-1
Flask Spring—*spring* NV-8
F Lassey Ranch—*locale* ND-7
Flasted Creek—*stream* MT-8
Flasted Hill—*summit* MT-8
*Flat* MS-4
Flat—*locale* AR-4
Flat—*locale* CO-8
Flat—*locale* KY-4
**Flat**—*pop pl* AK-9
**Flat**—*pop pl* MO-7
**Flat**—*pop pl* TX-5
Flat, Tank in—*reservoir* AZ-5
*Flat, The* AZ-5
Flat, The—*flat* NC-3
Flat, The—*flat* OR-9
Flat, The—*lake* FL-3
Flat, The—*swamp* GA-3
Flatau Cem—*cemetery* MN-6
Flat Bald Branch—*stream* NC-3
Flat Bank Creek—*stream* TX-5
*Flat Bay* NJ-2
Flat Bay—*bay* AK-9
Flat Bay—*bay* LA-4
Flat Bay—*bay* ME-1
Flat Bay—*bay* NC-3
Flat Bay—*bay* TX-5
Flat Bay—*swamp* (3) NC-3
Flat Bay—*swamp* (3) SC-3
Flat Bay (Carolina Bay)—*swamp* NC-3
Flat Bay Cem—*cemetery* ME-1
Flat Bayou—*gut* (6) LA-4
Flat Bayou—*gut* MS-4
Flat Bayou—*gut* (2) TX-5
Flat Bayou—*stream* AR-4
Flat Bayou—*stream* (4) LA-4
*Flat Bay Sound* NJ-2
Flatbench Point—*ridge* TN-4
Flat Bight—*bay* AK-9
Flat Black Rock—*island* OR-9
Flat Bluff—*cliff* TN-4
Flatboat Creek—*gut* FL-3
Flatboat Inside Pond—*bay* LA-4
Flatboat Outside Pond—*bay* LA-4
Flatboat Pass—*gut* LA-4
Flatboat Pond—*gut* LA-4
Flat Bois d'Arc Creek—*stream* AR-4
*Flat Bottom* PA-2
Flat Bottom—*valley* NE-7
Flat Bottom Canyon—*valley* UT-8
Flat Bottom Coulee—*valley* MT-8
Flatbottom Creek—*stream* WA-9
Flat Bottom Draw—*valley* MT-8
Flat Bottom Draw—*valley* WY-8
Flat Bottom Hill—*summit* UT-8
Flatbottom Pond—*lake* AZ-5
Flat Bottom Pond—*lake* MA-1
Flat Bottom Rsvr—*reservoir* WY-8
Flat Bottom Sch—*school* NE-7
*Flat Branch* AR-4
*Flat Branch* MS-4
Flat Branch—*gut* AL-4
Flat Branch—*locale* GA-3
Flat Branch—*locale* TN-4
**Flat Branch**—*pop pl* (2) NC-3
Flat Branch—*stream* (13) AL-4
Flat Branch—*stream* (3) AR-4
Flat Branch—*stream* FL-3
Flat Branch—*stream* (6) GA-3
Flat Branch—*stream* (6) IL-6
Flat Branch—*stream* IN-6
Flat Branch—*stream* (8) KY-4
Flat Branch—*stream* (3) LA-4
Flat Branch—*stream* (11) MS-4
Flat Branch—*stream* MO-7
Flat Branch—*stream* (14) NC-3
Flat Branch—*stream* (4) OH-6
Flat Branch—*stream* (3) SC-3
Flat Branch—*stream* (10) TN-4
Flat Branch—*stream* (7) TX-5
Flat Branch—*stream* (6) VA-3
Flat Branch—*stream* (5) WV-2
*Flat Branch Assembly of God Church* AL-4
Flat Branch Ch—*church* AL-4
Flat Branch Ch—*church* WV-2
Flat Branch Gap—*gap* NC-3
**Flat Branch Junction**—*pop pl* TN-4
Flat Branch Sch—*school* IL-6
Flat Branch Sch (historical)—*school* AL-4
Flat Branch Sch (historical)—*school* TN-4
**Flat Branch (Township of)**—*pop pl* IL-6
Flat Bridge—*bridge* AL-4
Flat Bridge—*bridge* (2) GA-3
**Flatbrook**—*pop pl* NY-2
Flat Brook—*stream* (4) CT-1
Flat Brook—*stream* (2) MA-1
Flat Brook—*stream* NJ-2
Flat Brook—*stream* (4) NY-2
Flatbrook Fish and Wildlife Mngmt
Area—*park* NJ-2
Flatbrookville—*locale* NJ-2
Flatbrush Run—*stream* WV-2
**Flatbush**—*pop pl* (2) NY-2
Flatbush Ave Terminal—*locale* NY-2
Flatbush Cem—*cemetery* MI-6
Flatbush Ch—*church* NY-2
Flatbush Dutch Reformed Church
Complex—*hist pl* NY-2
Flatbush Fork—*stream* WV-2
Flatbush Town Hall—*hist pl* NY-2
Flat Butte—*summit* AZ-5
Flat Butte Creek—*stream* MT-8
Flat Butte No. 12 Township—*civ div* SD-7
Flat Butte Township—*civil* SD-7
Flat Butte Township (historical)—*civil* SD-7
Flat Campground—*locale* WA-9
*Flat Canyon* UT-8
Flat Canyon—*valley* CO-8
Flat Canyon—*valley* (2) ID-8
Flat Canyon—*valley* (2) NV-8
Flat Canyon—*valley* NM-5
Flat Canyon—*valley* (2) TX-5
Flat Canyon—*valley* (11) UT-8
Flat Canyon Archeol District—*hist pl* UT-8
Flat Canyon Campground—*locale* UT-8
Flat Canyon Creek—*stream* ID-8
Flat Canyon Rapids—*rapids* UT-8
Flat Canyon Spring—*spring* NV-8
Flatcap Basin—*bay* MD-2
Flatcap Point—*cape* MD-2
Flat Car No. 473567—*hist pl* PA-2
Flat Cave—*cave* TN-4
Flat Cays—*island* VI-3
Flat (CCD)—*cens area* TX-5
Flat Cem—*cemetery* ME-1
Flat Church Bridge—*bridge* AL-4
Flat Cliff Hollow—*valley* TN-4
Flat Collins Filtration Plant—*other* CO-8
Flat Collins Irrigation Ditch—*canal* CO-8
Flat Cone Spring—*spring* WY-8

*Flat Coulee* .... MT-8
Flat Coulee—*valley* (6) .... MT-8
Flat Coulee Oil and Gas Field—*area* .... MT-8
Flat Cove—*bay* .... AK-9
Flat Cove—*bay* .... NC-3
*Flat Creek* .... ID-8
*Flat Creek* .... IN-6
*Flat Creek* .... KY-4
*Flat Creek* .... MS-4
*Flat Creek* .... MO-7
*Flat Creek* .... MT-8
*Flatcreek* .... TN-4
*Flat Creek* .... WY-8
Flat Creek—*channel* .... NY-2
Flat Creek—*gut* .... NJ-2
Flat Creek—*locale* .... ID-8
Flat Creek—*locale* .... LA-4
Flat Creek—*locale* .... NY-2
**Flat Creek**—*pop pl* .... AL-4
**Flat Creek**—*pop pl* .... MO-7
**Flat Creek**—*pop pl* .... NY-2
**Flat Creek**—*pop pl* .... NC-3
**Flat Creek**—*pop pl* (2) .... TN-4
Flat Creek—*stream* (13) .... AL-4
Flat Creek—*stream* (7) .... AK-9
Flat Creek—*stream* (15) .... AR-4
Flat Creek—*stream* (4) .... CA-9
Flat Creek—*stream* (3) .... FL-3
Flat Creek—*stream* (22) .... GA-3
Flat Creek—*stream* (16) .... ID-8
Flat Creek—*stream* (2) .... IL-6
Flat Creek—*stream* (7) .... IN-6
Flat Creek—*stream* (7) .... KY-4
Flat Creek—*stream* (7) .... LA-4
Flat Creek—*stream* .... MD-2
Flat Creek—*stream* (2) .... MI-6
Flat Creek—*stream* (4) .... MS-4
Flat Creek—*stream* (9) .... MO-7
Flat Creek—*stream* (17) .... MT-8
Flat Creek—*stream* (2) .... NE-7
Flat Creek—*stream* (3) .... NV-8
Flat Creek—*stream* (5) .... NJ-2
Flat Creek—*stream* (2) .... NY-2
Flat Creek—*stream* (11) .... NC-3
Flat Creek—*stream* .... ND-7
Flat Creek—*stream* (3) .... OK-5
Flat Creek—*stream* (12) .... OR-9
Flat Creek—*stream* (2) .... SC-3
Flat Creek—*stream* (2) .... SD-7
Flat Creek—*stream* (13) .... TN-4
Flat Creek—*stream* (20) .... TX-5
Flat Creek—*stream* (5) .... VA-3
Flat Creek—*stream* (5) .... WA-9
Flat Creek—*stream* .... WV-2
Flat Creek—*stream* .... WI-6
Flat Creek—*stream* (4) .... WY-8
Flat Creek A Township—*civil* .... MO-7
Flat Creek Bald—*summit* .... NC-3
Flat Creek Bridge—*bridge* .... TX-5
Flat Creek B Township—*civil* .... MO-7
Flat Creek Campsite—*locale* .... NC-3
Flat Creek Cem—*cemetery* .... AL-4
Flat Creek Cem—*cemetery* .... AR-4
Flat Creek Cem—*cemetery* .... IN-6
Flat Creek Cem—*cemetery* .... KY-4
Flat Creek Cem—*cemetery* .... NC-3
Flat Creek Cem—*cemetery* .... TN-4
Flat Creek Cem—*cemetery* .... TX-5
Flat Creek Ch—*church* (3) .... AL-4
Flat Creek Ch—*church* (2) .... FL-3
Flat Creek Ch—*church* (6) .... GA-3
Flat Creek Ch—*church* (2) .... KY-4
Flat Creek Ch—*church* .... MO-7
Flat Creek Ch—*church* .... MT-8
Flat Creek Ch—*church* (3) .... NC-3
Flat Creek Ch—*church* (2) .... SC-3
Flat Creek Ch—*church* .... TN-4
Flat Creek Ch—*church* .... TX-5
Flat Creek Ch—*church* .... VA-3
Flat Creek Elem Sch—*school* .... NC-3
Flat Creek Falls—*falls* .... NC-3
Flat Creek Flats—*flat* .... AK-9
Flat Creek Guard Station—*locale* .... OR-9
*Flat Creek Island* .... TN-4
Flat Creek Lake—*lake* .... AK-9
Flat Creek Lake—*reservoir* .... AL-4
Flat Creek Lake—*reservoir* .... SD-7
Flat Creek Lake Dam—*dam* .... AL-4
Flat Creek Lake Dam—*dam* .... SD-7
Flat Creek Landing (historical)—*locale* .... AL-4
Flat Creek (Magisterial District)—*fmr MCD* .... VA-3
Flat Creek Marsh—*swamp* .... MD-2
Flat Creek Memorial Ch—*church* .... IN-6
Flat Creek Mill (historical)—*locale* .... TN-4
Flat Creek Mine (underground)—*mine* .... AL-4
Flat Creek Mission Ch—*church* .... KY-4
Flat Creek Mtn—*summit* .... GA-3
Flat Creek-Normandy (CCD)—*cens area* .... TN-4
Flat Creek-Normandy Division—*civil* .... TN-4
Flat Creek Pass—*gap* .... MT-8
Flat Creek Pass Coulee—*valley* .... MT-8
*Flat Creek Post Office* .... TN-4
Flat Creek Post Office (historical)—*building* .... AL-4
Flatcreek Post Office (historical)—*building* .... TN-4
Flat Creek Ranch—*locale* .... NV-8
Flat Creek Ranch—*locale* .... WY-8
Flat Creek Sch—*school* .... MT-8
Flat Creek Sch (historical)—*school* .... TN-4
Flat Creek School—*locale* .... TN-4
Flat Creek Schools—*school* .... SC-3
Flat Creek Sewage Disposal—*other* .... GA-3
Flat Creek Shoals—*bar* .... TN-4
Flat Creek Spring—*spring* .... NV-8
Flat Creek Spring—*spring* .... OR-9
Flat Creek State Wildlife Mngmt Area—*park* .... WI-6
Flat Creek Township—*civil* (2) .... MO-7
**Flat Creek Township**—*pop pl* .... SD-7
Flat Creek (Township of)—*fmr MCD* .... AR-4
Flat Creek (Township of)—*fmr MCD* .... NC-3
Flat Creek Trail—*trail* .... OR-9
Flat Creek Valley—*valley* .... TN-4
Flat Creek-Wegra (CCD)—*cens area* .... AL-4
Flat Creek-Wegra Division—*civil* .... AL-4
Flat Cypress Creek—*stream* .... AR-4
Flat Cypress Creek—*stream* .... LA-4
Flat Cypress Creek—*stream* .... TX-5
Flat Dam—*dam* .... AZ-5
Flat Ditch—*canal* .... WY-8
Flat Draw—*valley* (3) .... WY-8
Flat Draw Rsvr—*reservoir* (2) .... WY-8
Flat Draw Tank—*reservoir* .... AZ-5
Flat Dutch Point—*cape* .... SC-3
Flately Brook—*stream* .... NY-2
Flaten Coulee—*valley* .... ND-7
Flaten Sch—*school* .... MN-6
F Lateral—*canal* .... CA-9
Flater Cem—*cemetery* .... IN-6
Flater Lake—*lake* .... TX-5
Flatfield Ridge—*ridge* .... NC-3
Flat Fields—*flat* .... NC-3
Flatfish Pond—*lake* .... NY-2
Flatfoot Cave—*cave* .... PA-2
Flatfoot Creek—*stream* .... WV-2
Flatfoot Lake—*lake* .... IL-6
Flat Ford—*locale* (2) .... GA-3
Flatford Cem—*cemetery* .... GA-3
Flat Ford Hollow—*valley* .... TN-4
Flat Fork—*locale* .... KY-4
Flat Fork—*locale* .... TX-5
Flat Fork—*stream* (5) .... KY-4
Flat Fork—*stream* .... NC-3
Flat Fork—*stream* (2) .... OH-6
Flat Fork—*stream* .... TN-4
Flat Fork—*stream* (3) .... WV-2
Flat Fork Ch—*church* .... KY-4
Flat Fork Ch—*church* (2) .... WV-2
*Flat Fork Creek* .... IN-6
*Flat Fork Creek* .... TN-4
*Flat Fork Creek* .... TX-5
Flat Fork Creek—*stream* .... AR-4
Flatfork Creek—*stream* .... IN-6
Flat Fork Creek—*stream* .... TX-5
*Flat Fork Little River* .... AR-4
*Flat Fork Of Tenaha Bayou* .... TX-5
Flatfork Post Office (historical)—*building* .... TN-4
Flat Fork Sch—*school* .... WV-2
Flat Fork Sch (historical)—*school* .... TN-4
*Flatgap* .... TN-4
Flat Gap—*gap* (2) .... GA-3
Flat Gap—*gap* (2) .... KY-4
Flat Gap—*gap* (2) .... NC-3
Flat Gap—*gap* (5) .... TN-4
Flat Gap—*gap* (3) .... VA-3
Flat Gap—*locale* .... TN-4
**Flatgap**—*pop pl* .... KY-4
**Flat Gap**—*pop pl* .... NC-3
**Flat Gap**—*pop pl* .... TN-4
**Flatgap**—*pop pl* .... TN-4
**Flat Gap**—*pop pl* .... VA-3
*Flat Gap Baptist Church* .... TN-4
Flat Gap Branch—*stream* .... VA-3
Flatgap (CCD)—*cens area* .... KY-4
Flat Gap Cem—*cemetery* .... TN-4
Flat Gap Ch—*church* .... KY-4
Flat Gap Ch—*church* .... TN-4
Flat Gap Ch—*church* .... VA-3
Flat Gap Creek—*stream* (2) .... TN-4
Flat Gap Elem Sch—*school* .... TN-4
*Flat Gap Post Office* .... TN-4
Flatgap Post Office (historical)—*building* .... TN-4
Flat Gap Ridge—*ridge* .... GA-3
Flat Gap Sch—*school* .... VA-3
Flat Gap Sch (historical)—*school* .... TN-4
Flat Ground—*bar* .... MA-1
Flat Grove Cem—*cemetery* .... MO-7
*Flat Gulch* .... MT-8
Flat Gulch—*valley* (2) .... MT-8
Flat Gut—*gut* .... DE-2
Flat Gut—*gut* .... VA-3
Flatgut Run—*stream* .... VA-3
Flat Hammock—*island* .... NY-2
F Latham Ranch—*locale* .... NM-5
Flathands—*uninc pl* .... NY-2
Flathead—*cens area* .... MT-8
Flat Head—*valley* .... FL-3
Flathead Alps—*spring* .... MT-8
Flathead Canyon—*valley* .... CO-8
Flathead Canyon—*valley* .... NM-5
Flathead Community Center—*locale* .... MT-8
Flathead County HS—*school* .... MT-8
Flathead Creek—*stream* .... MT-8
Flathead Flats—*flat* .... CA-9
Flathead Indian Trail—*trail* .... MT-8
Flathead Ind Res—*reserve* (4) .... MT-8
Flathead Lake—*lake* .... MT-8
Flathead Lake State Park—*park* .... MT-8
Flathead Mine—*mine* .... MT-8
Flathead Mtn—*summit* .... ME-1
Flathead Natl For—*forest* .... MT-8
*Flathead Pass* .... MT-8
Flathead Pass—*gap* .... MT-8
Flathead Picnic Area—*park* .... MT-8
Flathead Point—*summit* .... TX-5
Flathead Range—*range* .... MT-8
Flathead Ranger Station—*locale* .... MT-8
*Flathead River* .... MT-8
Flathead River—*stream* .... MT-8
Flathead River Ranger Station—*locale* .... MT-8
Flathead Rocks—*island* .... CT-1
Flathead Sunset Quarry—*mine* .... MT-8
Flathead Valley—*flat* .... MT-8
Flat Hill—*summit* .... CT-1
Flat Hill—*summit* .... ME-1
Flat Hill—*summit* (3) .... MA-1
Flat Hill—*summit* (2) .... NY-2
Flat Hill—*summit* .... VT-1
Flat Hills—*summit* .... MA-1
**Flat Hollow**—*pop pl* .... TN-4
Flat Hollow—*valley* (3) .... AR-4
Flat Hollow—*valley* .... ID-8
Flat Hollow—*valley* (3) .... KY-4
Flat Hollow—*valley* .... MO-7
Flat Hollow—*valley* (3) .... TN-4
Flat Hollow—*valley* .... VA-3
Flat Hollow—*valley* .... WV-2
Flat Hollow Boat Dock—*locale* .... TN-4
Flat Hollow Branch—*stream* .... AR-4
Flat Hollow Cem—*cemetery* .... TN-4
Flat Hollow Ch—*church* (2) .... TN-4
*Flat Hollow Ch of God* .... TN-4
Flat Hollow Sch—*school* .... TN-4
*Flat Hollow United Methodist Church* .... TN-4
Flat Horn Lake—*lake* .... AK-9
Flat Horn Lake—*lake* .... MN-6
Flat House Hollow—*valley* .... TN-4
Flat Huckleberry Island—*island* .... NY-2
*Flat Hummock* .... NY-2
*Flatiron* .... DE-2
*Flat Iron* .... OR-9
Flatiron—*flat* .... CA-9
Flat Iron—*flat* .... WY-8
Flat Iron—*locale* .... VA-3
Flatiron—*other* .... AK-9
**Flat Iron**—*pop pl* .... IN-6
**Flat Iron**—*pop pl* .... OH-6
**Flatiron**—*pop pl* .... OH-6
Flatiron—*summit* .... CA-9
Flat Iron—*summit* .... CO-8
Flatiron—*summit* .... CO-8
Flatiron—*summit* (2) .... ID-8
Flatiron—*summit* .... NM-5
Flatiron—*summit* .... OR-9
Flatiron—*summit* .... WA-9
Flatiron, The—*flat* .... ID-8
Flatiron, The—*ridge* .... OR-9
Flatiron, The—*summit* .... AZ-5
Flatiron, The—*summit* .... CO-8
Flatiron Arch—*arch* .... UT-8
Flatiron Bldg—*hist pl* .... NY-2
Flatiron Bldg—*hist pl* .... ND-7
Flatiron Bldg—*hist pl* .... TX-5
Flatiron Bldg—*hist pl* .... WA-9
Flatiron Bluff—*cliff* .... AR-4
Flatiron Brook—*stream* .... ME-1
Flatiron Brook—*stream* .... NY-2
Flatiron Butte—*summit* .... AZ-5
Flatiron Butte—*summit* .... CA-9
Flatiron Butte—*summit* (2) .... ID-8
Flatiron Butte—*summit* .... WY-8
Flatiron Canyon—*valley* .... NM-5
Flatiron Creek—*stream* .... ID-8
Flatiron Creek—*stream* .... MT-8
Flatiron Hill—*summit* .... ID-8
Flatiron Hill—*summit* .... UT-8
Flatiron Hollow—*valley* .... ID-8
Flatiron Hotel—*hist pl* .... NE-7
**Flatiron I (historical)**—*pop pl* .... SD-7
*Flat Iron Island* .... NY-2
Flatiron Island—*island* .... NY-2
Flatiron Knobs—*summit* .... ID-8
Flat Iron Lake—*lake* .... MI-6
Flat Iron Lake—*lake* .... WA-9
Flatiron Lake—*lake* .... WY-8
Flatiron Lakes—*reservoir* .... UT-8
Flatiron Mesa—*summit* .... AZ-5
Flatiron Mesa—*summit* (2) .... CO-8
Flatiron Mesa—*summit* .... NM-5
Flat Iron Mesa—*summit* (2) .... UT-8
Flatiron Mesa—*summit* .... UT-8
**Flat Iron Mesa Subdivision**—*pop pl* .... UT-8
Flatiron Mtn—*summit* .... AZ-5
Flatiron Mtn—*summit* .... CA-9
Flatiron Mtn—*summit* (3) .... CO-8
Flatiron Mtn—*summit* (3) .... ID-8
Flatiron Mtn—*summit* (4) .... MT-8
Flat Iron Mtn—*summit* .... OR-9
Flatiron Penstocks—*canal* .... CO-8
Flatiron Point—*cape* .... NY-2
Flatiron Point—*cape* .... PA-2
Flatiron Point—*cliff* .... OR-9
Flat Iron Point—*cliff* .... UT-8
Flatiron Pond—*lake* (3) .... ME-1
Flatiron Powerplant—*other* .... CO-8
Flatiron Ridge—*ridge* (2) .... CA-9
Flatiron Ridge—*ridge* (2) .... ID-8
Flatiron Ridge—*ridge* .... MT-8
Flatiron Ridge Recreation Site—*locale* .... MT-8
Flatiron Rock—*island* .... CA-9
Flatiron Rock—*summit* .... NY-2
Flatiron Rsvr—*reservoir* (2) .... CO-8
Flatirons, The—*summit* .... CO-8
Flatirons, The—*summit* .... OR-9
Flatiron Spring—*spring* .... CO-8
Flatiron Spring—*spring* .... ID-8
Flatiron Spring—*spring* .... OR-9
Flatirons Sch—*school* .... CO-8
Flat Iron Tree—*locale* .... CA-9
Flatiron Well—*well* .... AZ-5
*Flat Island* .... NY-2
Flat Island—*island* (7) .... AK-9
Flat Island—*island* .... FL-3
Flat Island—*island* (3) .... ME-1
Flat Island—*island* .... MD-2
Flat Island—*island* .... NJ-2
Flat Island—*island* .... WI-6
Flat Island Ledges—*bar* .... ME-1
Flat Islands—*island* .... AK-9
Flat Knob—*summit* .... KY-4
Flat Knob—*summit* .... NC-3
*Flat Lake* .... MI-6
*Flat Lake* .... MS-4
Flat Lake—*lake* .... AL-4
Flat Lake—*lake* (3) .... AK-9
Flat Lake—*lake* (3) .... AR-4
Flat Lake—*lake* .... CA-9
Flat Lake—*lake* .... CO-8
Flat Lake—*lake* .... FL-3
Flat Lake—*lake* (2) .... GA-3
Flat Lake—*lake* .... IL-6
Flat Lake—*lake* (2) .... IN-6
Flat Lake—*lake* .... IA-7
Flat Lake—*lake* .... KY-4
Flat Lake—*lake* (7) .... LA-4
Flat Lake—*lake* (2) .... MN-6
Flat Lake—*lake* (3) .... MS-4
Flat Lake—*lake* .... MT-8
Flat Lake—*lake* (2) .... NM-5
Flat Lake—*lake* .... ND-7
FLat Lake—*lake* .... OR-9
Flat Lake—*lake* (3) .... SC-3
Flat Lake—*lake* (2) .... SD-7
Flat Lake—*lake* (2) .... TX-5
Flat Lake—*lake* .... UT-8
Flat Lake—*lake* (2) .... WA-9
Flat Lake—*lake* .... WI-6
Flat Lake—*lake* .... WY-8
Flat Lake—*swamp* .... LA-4
Flat Lake Creek—*stream* .... AR-4
Flat Lake Lookout Tower—*locale* .... MN-6
Flat Lake Lookout Tower—*locale* .... OR-9
Flat Lake Oil Field—*oilfield* .... MS-4
Flat Lake Pass—*channel* .... LA-4
Flat Lake Ranch—*locale* .... NM-5
Flat Lake ( Salt)—*lake* .... NM-5
*Flatland* .... KS-7
*Flatland* .... PA-2
Flat Land Branch—*stream* .... NC-3
Flatland Cove—*bay* .... MD-2
Flat Landing—*locale* .... FL-3
Flat Landing—*locale* .... ME-1
Flat Landing (historical)—*locale* .... AL-4
Flatland Lake—*lake* .... MS-4
Flatland Marsh—*swamp* .... MD-2
Flatland Reach—*channel* .... DE-2
Flatlands—*locale* .... GA-3
**Flatlands**—*pop pl* .... NY-2
Flatlands Dutch Reformed Church—*hist pl* .... NY-2
Flat Laurel Creek—*stream* .... NC-3
Flat Laurel Gap—*gap* .... NC-3
Flat Ledge—*bar* .... ME-1
Flatley Ranch—*locale* .... NM-5
**Flat Lick**—*pop pl* .... KY-4
Flat Lick—*stream* .... KY-4
Flat Lick Bayou—*stream* .... LA-4
Flat Lick Branch—*stream* .... IL-6
Flat Lick Branch—*stream* .... NC-3
Flatlick Branch—*stream* .... VA-3
Flat Lick Ch—*church* (3) .... KY-4
Flat Lick Creek—*stream* (3) .... KY-4
Flatlick Creek—*stream* .... KY-4
Flat Lick Knob—*summit* .... KY-4
Flatlick Run—*stream* .... OH-6
Flat Meadow, Lake—*lake* .... UT-8
Flat Meadow Brook—*stream* .... NH-1
Flat Meadow Cove—*bay* .... RI-1
Flat Meadow Sch—*school* .... WI-6
*Flat Mesa* .... AZ-5
Flat Mesa—*summit* (4) .... AZ-5
Flat Mesa—*summit* .... NM-5
Flat Mesa—*summit* .... TX-5
Flat Mesa—*summit* .... UT-8
Flat Mingo Creek—*stream* .... MO-7
Flat Mountain—*ridge* .... NH-1
Flat Mountain Arm—*bay* .... WY-8
Flat Mountain Ch—*church* .... TN-4
Flat Mountain Ch—*church* .... WV-2
Flat Mountain Ponds—*lake* .... NH-1
Flat Mountain Pond Trail—*trail* .... NH-1
Flat Mtn—*summit* .... AL-4
Flat Mtn—*summit* (2) .... AK-9
Flat Mtn—*summit* .... AR-4
Flat Mtn—*summit* .... ID-8
Flat Mtn—*summit* .... MT-8
Flat Mtn—*summit* .... NH-1
Flat Mtn—*summit* (2) .... NY-2
Flat Mtn—*summit* (2) .... NC-3
Flat Mtn—*summit* .... OR-9
Flat Mtn—*summit* .... PA-2
Flat Mtn—*summit* (4) .... TN-4
Flat Mtn—*summit* .... WY-8
Flat Neck Point—*cape* .... CT-1
Flat Nose George Canyon—*valley* .... UT-8
Flatnose Ranch—*locale* .... NV-8
Flatnose Wash—*stream* .... NV-8
Flat Note Lake—*lake* .... CA-9
**Flatonia**—*pop pl* .... TX-5
Flatonia (CCD)—*cens area* .... TX-5
Flato Park—*park* .... TX-5
Flat Paint Creek—*stream* .... TX-5
Flat Point—*cape* .... AL-4
Flat Point—*cape* (3) .... AK-9
Flat Point—*cape* .... FL-3
Flat Point—*cape* .... ME-1
Flat Point—*cape* .... MD-2
Flat Point—*cape* (3) .... MA-1
Flat Point—*cape* .... RI-1
Flat Point—*cape* .... WA-9
*Flat Pond* .... MA-1
Flat Pond—*lake* .... AZ-5
Flat Pond—*lake* .... CA-9
Flat Pond—*lake* .... FL-3
Flat Pond—*lake* .... IL-6
Flat Pond—*lake* .... KY-4
Flat Pond—*lake* (2) .... MA-1
Flat Pond—*lake* (3) .... MO-7
Flat Pond—*lake* .... TX-5
Flat Pond—*swamp* .... NC-3
Flat Pond Marshes—*swamp* .... MA-1
Flat Prairie—*flat* .... IL-6
Flat Prairie—*locale* .... TX-5
Flat Prairie Baptist Ch—*church* .... TX-5
Flat Prairie Cem—*cemetery* .... TX-5
*Flat Prairie Ch* .... TX-5
Flat Prairie Ch—*church* .... TX-5
Flat Prairie Island—*island* .... LA-4
Flat Ravine—*valley* .... CA-9
*Flat Ridge* .... UT-8
Flat Ridge—*locale* .... OH-6
Flat Ridge—*locale* .... VA-3
**Flatridge**—*pop pl* .... VA-3
Flat Ridge—*ridge* .... AL-4
Flat Ridge—*ridge* .... CA-9
Flat Ridge—*ridge* .... ID-8
Flat Ridge—*ridge* .... LA-4
Flat Ridge—*ridge* .... MO-7
Flat Ridge—*ridge* .... NC-3
Flat Ridge—*ridge* .... PA-2
Flat Ridge—*ridge* (3) .... TN-4
Flat Ridge—*ridge* .... UT-8
Flat Ridge—*ridge* (2) .... VA-3
Flat Ridge—*ridge* (2) .... WV-2
Flat Ridge Canyon—*valley* .... UT-8
Flat Ridge Ch—*church* .... OH-6
Flat Ridge Ch—*church* .... VA-3
Flat Ridge Creek—*stream* .... CA-9
Flat Ridge Sch—*school* .... OH-6
Flat Ridge Spring—*spring* .... UT-8
Flat Ridge Trail—*trail* (2) .... PA-2
*Flat River* .... MI-6
*Flat River* .... RI-1
Flat River—*gut* .... LA-4
**Flat River**—*pop pl* .... MO-7
Flat River—*stream* (2) .... LA-4
Flat River—*stream* .... MI-6
Flat River—*stream* .... MO-7
Flat River—*stream* .... NC-3
Flat River—*stream* (2) .... RI-1
Flat River Ch—*church* .... NC-3
Flat River Ditch—*canal* .... LA-4
Flat River Drainage Canal—*canal* .... LA-4
Flat River Park—*park* .... MI-6
Flat River Reservoir Dam—*dam* .... RI-1
Flat River Rsvr—*reservoir* .... RI-1
Flat River State Game Area—*park* .... MI-6
Flat River (Township of)—*fmr MCD* .... NC-3
*Flatrock* .... AL-4
*Flat Rock* .... TN-4
Flat Rock—*bar* .... CA-9
Flat Rock—*bar* .... PA-2
Flat Rock—*cape* (2) .... NY-2
Flat Rock—*flat* .... NY-2
Flat Rock—*hist pl* .... VA-3
Flat Rock—*island* (2) .... CA-9
Flat Rock—*island* .... CT-1
Flat Rock—*island* .... OR-9
Flat Rock—*island* .... WA-9
Flat Rock—*locale* .... AR-4
Flat Rock—*locale* (2) .... GA-3
Flat Rock—*locale* (3) .... KY-4
Flat Rock—*locale* .... MS-4
Flat Rock—*locale* .... NC-3
Flat Rock—*locale* .... PA-2
Flatrock—*locale* .... TN-4
Flat Rock—*locale* .... TX-5
Flat Rock—*locale* .... VA-3
Flat Rock—*pillar* .... AZ-5
Flat Rock—*pillar* .... OR-9
Flat Rock—*pillar* .... RI-1
Flat Rock—*pillar* .... TN-4
Flat Rock—*pillar* .... UT-8
Flat Rock—*pillar* .... VT-1
**Flat Rock**—*pop pl* (3) .... AL-4
**Flat Rock**—*pop pl* .... AZ-5
**Flat Rock**—*pop pl* .... CT-1
**Flat Rock**—*pop pl* .... IL-6
**Flat Rock**—*pop pl* .... IN-6
**Flat Rock**—*pop pl* (2) .... KY-4
**Flat Rock**—*pop pl* (2) .... MI-6
**Flat Rock**—*pop pl* .... MS-4
**Flat Rock**—*pop pl* (3) .... NC-3
**Flat Rock**—*pop pl* .... OH-6
**Flat Rock**—*pop pl* .... PA-2
**Flat Rock**—*pop pl* (2) .... SC-3
**Flat Rock**—*pop pl* (3) .... TN-4
**Flat Rock**—*pop pl* .... VA-3
**Flatrock**—*pop pl* .... WV-2
**Flat Rock**—*pop pl* .... WV-2
Flat Rock—*rock* .... MA-1
Flat Rock—*summit* (2) .... AL-4
Flat Rock—*summit* .... CT-1
Flat Rock—*summit* .... NC-3
Flat Rock—*summit* .... OK-5
Flat Rock—*summit* (2) .... PA-2
Flat Rock—*summit* .... TX-5
Flat Rock—*summit* .... VT-1
Flat Rock—*uninc pl* .... AL-4
Flat Rock Airp—*airport* .... PA-2
Flat Rock Baptist Ch (historical)—*church* .... TN-4
*Flat Rock Baptist Church* .... MS-4
Flat Rock Bay—*bay* .... OK-5
*Flat Rock Branch* .... OR-9
*Flat Rock Branch* .... TN-4
Flatrock Branch—*stream* (2) .... AL-4
Flat Rock Branch—*stream* .... AL-4
Flat Rock Branch—*stream* .... AR-4
Flat Rock Branch—*stream* .... GA-3
Flatrock Branch—*stream* (2) .... GA-3
Flat Rock Branch—*stream* .... GA-3
Flat Rock Branch—*stream* (4) .... KY-4
Flat Rock Branch—*stream* (3) .... NC-3
Flat Rock Branch—*stream* .... OR-9
Flat Rock Branch—*stream* (3) .... SC-3
Flatrock Branch—*stream* (6) .... TN-4
Flat Rock Branch—*stream* .... TN-4
Flatrock Branch—*stream* (2) .... TN-4
Flat Rock Branch—*stream* .... TN-4
Flatrock Branch—*stream* (2) .... TN-4
Flat Rock Branch—*stream* .... TX-5
Flatrock Branch—*stream* (3) .... TX-5
Flat Rock Branch—*stream* .... VA-3
Flatrock Branch—*stream* .... VA-3
Flatrock Bridge—*bridge* .... ME-1
Flatrock Bridge—*bridge* .... NH-1
Flatrock Brook—*stream* .... NH-1
Flat Rock Brook—*stream* .... NJ-2
Flat Rock Brook—*stream* .... NY-2
Flat Rock Butte—*summit* .... ND-7
Flatrock Camp—*locale* .... MO-7
Flat Rock Campground—*locale* .... GA-3
Flat Rock Campground—*locale* .... ID-8
Flat Rock Canyon—*valley* .... TX-5
Flat Rock Cave—*cave* .... AL-4
Flat Rock Cem—*cemetery* (3) .... GA-3
Flat Rock Cem—*cemetery* .... IN-6
Flatrock Cem—*cemetery* .... KY-4
Flat Rock Cem—*cemetery* (2) .... KY-4
Flat Rock Cem—*cemetery* .... MS-4
Flat Rock Cem—*cemetery* .... OH-6
Flat Rock Cem—*cemetery* (4) .... SC-3
Flat Rock Cem—*cemetery* (2) .... TX-5
Flat Rock Ch—*church* (8) .... AL-4
Flat Rock Ch—*church* (2) .... AR-4
Flat Rock Ch—*church* (2) .... GA-3
Flatrock Ch—*church* .... GA-3
Flat Rock Ch—*church* (7) .... GA-3
Flatrock Ch—*church* (2) .... GA-3
Flat Rock Ch—*church* (2) .... KY-4
Flat Rock Ch—*church* .... MS-4
Flat Rock Ch—*church* .... MO-7
Flat Rock Ch—*church* (7) .... NC-3
Flat Rock Ch—*church* .... OH-6
Flat Rock Ch—*church* (5) .... SC-3
Flat Rock Ch—*church* (2) .... TN-4
Flat Rock Ch—*church* .... TX-5
Flat Rock Ch—*church* .... VA-3
Flatrock Ch—*church* .... VA-3
Flat Rock Ch—*church* (2) .... VA-3
Flat Rock Ch—*church* .... WV-2
*Flat Rock Ch of Christ* .... TN-4
Flat Rock Ch of Christ—*church* .... TN-4
Flat Rock Community Center—*building* .... AL-4
Flatrock Community Center—*locale* .... TX-5
*Flatrock Creek* .... IN-6
*Flat Rock Creek* .... NC-3
*Flat Rock Creek* .... OH-6
*Flat Rock Creek* .... SC-3
Flat Rock Creek—*stream* (2) .... AL-4
Flatrock Creek—*stream* .... AK-9
Flat Rock Creek—*stream* .... AR-4
Flatrock Creek—*stream* .... AR-4
Flat Rock Creek—*stream* (7) .... AR-4
Flat Rock Creek—*stream* .... CA-9
Flatrock Creek—*stream* (2) .... GA-3
Flatrock Creek—*stream* (2) .... IN-6
Flatrock Creek—*stream* .... IA-7
Flat Rock Creek—*stream* .... KS-7
Flat Rock Creek—*stream* .... KY-4
Flat Rock Creek—*stream* .... MI-6
Flatrock Creek—*stream* (2) .... MO-7
Flat Rock Creek—*stream* .... MO-7
Flatrock Creek—*stream* .... MO-7
Flat Rock Creek—*stream* (2) .... MT-8
Flatrock Creek—*stream* .... NC-3
Flatrock Creek—*stream* .... OH-6
Flat Rock Creek—*stream* (5) .... OK-5
Flatrock Creek—*stream* .... SC-3
Flat Rock Creek—*stream* (2) .... SC-3
Flatrock Creek—*stream* .... TN-4
Flat Rock Creek—*stream* .... TX-5
Flatrock Creek—*stream* .... TX-5
Flat Rock Creek—*stream* (3) .... TX-5
Flatrock Creek—*stream* .... TX-5
Flat Rock Creek—*stream* .... TX-5
Flatrock Creek—*stream* .... TX-5
Flat Rock Creek—*stream* .... TX-5
Flatrock Creek—*stream* .... TX-5
Flat Rock Creek—*stream* (2) .... TX-5
Flat Rock Creek—*stream* .... VA-3
Flatrock Creek—*stream* .... VA-3
Flat Rock Creek—*stream* .... WI-6
*Flat Rock Creek - in part* .... TN-4
Flat Rock Creek Public Use Area—*park* .... OK-5
Flatrock Crossing (Ford)—*locale* .... TX-5
Flat Rock Dam—*dam* .... PA-2
Flat Rock Dam—*dam* .... TX-5
Flat Rock Draw—*valley* (2) .... TX-5
Flat Rock Elementary—*school* .... NC-3
Flat Rock Falls—*falls* .... NY-2
Flat Rock Ford—*locale* .... AL-4
Flat Rock Ford—*locale* .... TN-4
Flatrock Ford—*locale* .... TX-5
**Flat Rock Forest**—*pop pl* .... NC-3
Flat Rock Forest Camp—*locale* .... OR-9
Flatrock Gap—*gap* .... GA-3
Flat Rock Guard Station—*locale* .... ID-8
*Flat-rock Hill* .... MA-1
Flat Rock Hill—*ridge* .... MS-4
Flat Rock Hill—*summit* .... CT-1
Flat Rock Hill—*summit* .... MA-1
Flatrock Hill—*summit* (2) .... MA-1
Flatrock Hill—*summit* .... NH-1
Flat Rock Hist Dist—*hist pl* .... NC-3
**Flat Rock (historical)**—*pop pl* .... TN-4
Flat Rock Hollow—*valley* (3) .... AR-4
Flatrock Hollow—*valley* .... IL-6
Flatrock Hollow—*valley* (3) .... MO-7
Flat Rock Hollow—*valley* (2) .... MO-7
Flatrock Hollow—*valley* .... OK-5
Flatrock Hollow—*valley* .... TX-5
Flat Rock Hollow—*valley* .... VA-3
Flat Rockhouse Branch—*stream* .... KY-4
Flat Rock JHS—*school* .... NC-3
Flat Rock Knob—*summit* .... NC-3
Flat Rock Lake—*lake* .... MT-8
Flat Rock Lookout Station—*locale* .... MT-8
Flat Rock Mesa—*summit* .... UT-8
Flat Rock Mtn—*summit* .... AR-4
Flatrock Mtn—*summit* .... NY-2
Flatrock Mtn—*summit* .... SC-3
Flat Rock Oil Field—*oilfield* .... MS-4
Flat Rock Oil Field—*oilfield* .... TX-5
Flat Rock Oil Field—*oilfield* .... UT-8
Flat Rock Park—*park* .... TX-5
**Flat Rock Park**—*pop pl* .... IN-6
Flatrock Park Lake—*reservoir* .... GA-3
*Flat Rock Park North* (2) .... IN-6
Flatrock Plains—*flat* .... WV-2
**Flat Rock Playhouse**—*pop pl* .... NC-3
Flat Rock P.O. (historical)—*locale* .... AL-4
Flat Rock Point—*cape* .... CA-9
Flat Rock Point—*cape* .... MI-6
Flatrock Point—*cliff* .... GA-3
Flat Rock Point Reef—*bar* .... MI-6
Flat Rock Pond—*reservoir* .... SC-3
Flat Rock Post Office (historical)—*building* .... TN-4
Flat Rock Powerplant—*other* .... NY-2
*Flat Rock Quarry Hill* .... MA-1
Flat Rock Ranch—*locale* .... TX-5
Flat Rock Reef—*bar* .... OH-6
Flat Rock Ridge—*ridge* .... NC-3
Flat Rock Ridge—*ridge* .... TN-4
*Flat Rock River* .... IN-6
*Flat Rock River* .... MI-6
Flatrock River—*stream* .... IN-6
Flat Rock Rsvr—*reservoir* .... AZ-5
Flat Rock Run—*stream* .... PA-2
Flatrock Run—*stream* .... WV-2
Flat Rock Run—*stream* .... WV-2
Flat Rock Sch—*school* .... AL-4
Flat Rock Sch—*school* (2) .... KY-4
Flatrock Sch—*school* .... MO-7
Flat Rock Sch—*school* (2) .... MO-7
Flat Rock Sch—*school* .... NC-3
Flat Rock Sch—*school* (2) .... SC-3
Flat Rock Sch—*school* (2) .... TN-4
Flat Rock Sch—*school* .... WI-6
Flat Rock Sch (abandoned)—*school* .... MO-7
Flat Rock Sch (abandoned)—*school* .... PA-2
Flat Rock Sch (historical)—*school* (6) .... AL-4
Flatrock Sch (historical)—*school* .... MO-7
Flat Rock Sch (historical)—*school* .... TN-4
Flatrock Sch (historical)—*school* .... TN-4
Flat Rock Siding—*locale* .... TN-4
Flat Rock Spring—*spring* (2) .... AZ-5
Flat Rock Spring—*spring* .... OK-5
Flat Rock Spring—*spring* .... OR-9
Flatrock Spring—*spring* (2) .... TX-5
Flat Rock Spring—*spring* (2) .... TX-5
Flat Rock Spring—*spring* (2) .... UT-8
Flat Rock State Wildlife Area—*park* .... MO-7
**Flat Rock (Township of)**—*pop pl* .... IN-6
**Flatrock (Township of)**—*pop pl* .... OH-6
Flat Rock Trail—*trail* .... PA-2
Flat Rock Trail—*trail* .... WV-2
Flat Rock Tunnel—*tunnel* .... PA-2
*Flat Rock United Methodist Church* .... AL-4
Flat Rock Windmill—*locale* (3) .... TX-5
Flat Rock Windmill—*well* .... AZ-5
Flat Rock Yard—*locale* .... MI-6
Flat Rough Ch—*church* .... SC-3
Flat Rsvr—*reservoir* .... NM-5
Flat Rsvr—*reservoir* .... OR-9
*Flat Run* .... WV-2
Flat Run—*locale* .... VA-3
Flat Run—*stream* (2) .... IN-6

Fleming Hill Sch (abandoned)—*school* PA-2
Fleming (historical)—*locale* AL-4
Fleming Hollow—*valley* TN-4
Fleming House—*building* NC-3
Fleming House—*hist pl* DE-2
Fleming Island—*island* AK-9
Fleming Island—*island* FL-3
Fleming JHS—*school* CA-9
Fleming Key—*island* FL-3
Fleming Key Cut—*channel* FL-3
Fleming Lake—*lake* CA-9
Fleming Lake—*lake* MI-6
Fleming Lake—*lake* MN-6
Fleming Lake—*reservoir* IN-6
Fleming Lake Dam—*dam* IN-6
Fleming Lateral—*canal* CA-9
Fleming Meadow—*flat* CA-9
**Fleming Meadows**—*pop pl* AL-4
Fleming Memorial Ch—*church* WV-2
Fleming Millpond—*reservoir* VA-3
Fleming Mtn—*summit* CA-9
Fleming Mtn—*summit* CO-8
Fleming Mtn—*summit* NY-2
Fleming Mtn—*summit* VA-3
**Fleming-Neon**—*pop pl* KY-4
Fleming Park—*park* CA-9
Fleming Park—*park* MI-6
Fleming Park—*park* MO-7
Fleming Park—*park* NY-2
Fleming Point—*cape* CA-9
Fleming Point—*cliff* CO-8
Fleming Point—*summit* ID-8
Fleming Ranch—*locale* (2) CA-9
Fleming Ranch—*locale* NM-5
Fleming Ranch—*locale* WY-8
Fleming Ridge—*ridge* CA-9
Fleming Ridge—*ridge* IL-6
Fleming Run—*stream* PA-2
Fleming Run—*stream* WV-2
*Flemings* NJ-2
**Flemingsburg**—*pop pl* KY-4
Flemingsburg (CCD)—*cens area* KY-4
Flemingsburg Hist Dist—*hist pl* KY-4
Flemingsburg Junction—*locale* KY-4
**Flemingsburg Junction (Johnson Junction)**—*pop pl* KY-4
Fleming Sch—*school* GA-3
Fleming Sch—*school* IL-6
Fleming Sch—*school* MI-6
Fleming Sch—*school* MS-4
Fleming Sch—*school* SC-3
Fleming Sch—*school* WV-2
Fleming Sch (abandoned)—*school* MO-7
Fleming Sch (historical)—*school* MS-4
*Flemings Corner* DE-2
**Flemings Corner**—*pop pl* DE-2
Flemings Creek—*stream* VA-3
Fleming Sheep Camp—*locale* CA-9
Flemings Lake—*lake* MI-6
Flemings Landing—*locale* DE-2
Flemings Landing (historical)—*locale* AL-4
**Flemings Landings**—*pop pl* DE-2
Fleming Slough—*stream* WY-8
Fleming Spit—*bar* AK-9
Flemings Pond—*lake* NY-2
Fleming Spring—*spring* (2) CA-9
Fleming Spring—*spring* OR-9
Fleming Spring—*spring* TN-4
Flemings Sch—*school* MA-1
Fleming Stadium—*locale* NC-3
Fleming Summit—*locale* PA-2
*Flemingsville* NY-2
**Flemington**—*pop pl* FL-3
**Flemington**—*pop pl* GA-3
**Flemington**—*pop pl* MO-7
**Flemington**—*pop pl* NJ-2
**Flemington**—*pop pl* PA-2
**Flemington**—*pop pl* VA-3
**Flemington**—*pop pl* WV-2
Flemington Borough—*civil* PA-2
Flemington Cem—*cemetery* GA-3
Flemington Cem—*cemetery* MO-7
Flemington Ch—*church* GA-3
Flemington Creek—*stream* IL-6
**Flemington Heights**—*pop pl* AL-4
Flemington Hist Dist—*hist pl* NJ-2
Flemington Junction—*locale* NJ-2
Flemington Presbyterian Church—*hist pl* GA-3
Flemington Township—*civil* MO-7
*Flemingtown* NJ-2
Flemingtown—*locale* VA-3
**Fleming (Town of)**—*pop pl* NY-2
**Fleming (Township of)**—*pop pl* (2) MN-6
Fleming Valley Sch—*school* NE-7
**Flemingville**—*pop pl* NY-2
Flemingville (historical P.O.)—*locale* IA-7
Fleming-Welder House—*hist pl* TX-5
Fleming Well—*well* CA-9
Fleming Well—*well* NM-5
Fleming Windmill—*locale* NM-5
Flemmer River—*stream* AK-9
*Flemming Branch* VA-3
Flemming Branch—*stream* MO-7
Flemming Brook—*stream* ME-1
Flemming Cem—*cemetery* VA-3
Flemming Ch—*church* VA-3
Flemming Creek—*stream* ID-8
Flemming Ditch—*canal* IN-6
*Flemming Drain* MI-6
*Flemming Draw* TX-5
Flemming Island—*island* AK-9
Flemming Lake—*lake* TX-5
Flemming Point—*summit* ID-8
Flemmings Creek—*stream* TN-4
*Flemmings Landing* DE-2
Flemming Slough—*bay* TX-5
Flemming Spring—*spring* AZ-5
Flemming Spring—*spring* TX-5
Flemming Springs—*spring* TX-5
Flemming Springs Branch—*stream* TX-5
Flemmings Rapids—*rapids* WI-6
Flemming Tank—*reservoir* TX-5
Flemming Wash—*stream* AZ-5
Flemon Cem—*cemetery* TN-4
Flemons Shoal (historical)—*bar* AL-4
Flems Fork—*stream* CA-9
*Flench Lake* OK-5
*Flenders Creek* OK-5
Flener—*locale* KY-4
Flener Chapel—*church* KY-4
*Flening* KS-7
Flenner Lake—*lake* MN-6
Flenniken Branch—*stream* TN-4
Flenniken Cem—*cemetery* TN-4
Flenniken Elem Sch—*school* TN-4
Flenniken Post Office (historical)—*building* TN-4
**Flensburg**—*pop pl* MN-6
Flensburg Post Office (historical)—*building* SD-7
Flentje, Ernst, House—*hist pl* MA-1
Flent Point—*cape* AK-9
Flerchinger Ridge—*ridge* WA-9
Flerchinger Spring—*spring* WA-9
*Flescher Run* WV-2
*Fleschman Bayou* AR-4
Fleschmans Bayou—*stream* AR-4
Flesher Cem—*cemetery* IL-6
Flesher Cem—*cemetery* IN-6
Flesher Lakes—*lake* MT-8
Flesher Oil Field—*oilfield* OK-5
Flesher Pass—*gap* MT-8
Flesher Pass Trail—*trail* MT-8
Flesher Run—*stream* (3) WV-2
Flesher Slough—*stream* OR-9
*Fleshersville* WV-2
*Flesherville* WV-2
Fleshlanana Creek—*stream* AK-9
Fleshman Creek—*stream* MT-8
*Flessner Creek* NE-7
Fleta—*locale* CA-9
**Fleta**—*pop pl* AL-4
Fletchall Ch—*church* MO-7
Fletchall Creek—*stream* IA-7
Fletchall Creek—*stream* MO-7
Fletchall Sch—*school* MO-7
Fletchall Township—*civil* MO-7
*Fletcher* ND-7
*Fletcher* TX-5
Fletcher—*locale* CA-9
Fletcher—*locale* FL-3
Fletcher—*locale* ID-8
Fletcher—*locale* IA-7
Fletcher—*locale* KY-4
Fletcher—*locale* MI-6
Fletcher—*locale* NV-8
Fletcher—*locale* SC-3
Fletcher—*locale* VA-3
Fletcher—*locale* WV-2
Fletcher—*locale* WY-8
**Fletcher**—*pop pl* FL-3
**Fletcher**—*pop pl* IL-6
**Fletcher**—*pop pl* IN-6
**Fletcher**—*pop pl* MN-6
**Fletcher**—*pop pl* MO-7
**Fletcher**—*pop pl* NC-3
**Fletcher**—*pop pl* OH-6
**Fletcher**—*pop pl* OK-5
**Fletcher**—*pop pl* TX-5
**Fletcher**—*pop pl* VT-1
Fletcher, Alfred P., Farmhouse—*hist pl* OR-9
Fletcher, Calvin I., House—*hist pl* IN-6
Fletcher, Francis, House—*hist pl* OR-9
Fletcher, John T., House—*hist pl* GA-3
Fletcher, Jonathan, House—*hist pl* MA-1
Fletcher, K. B., Mill—*hist pl* MD-2
Fletcher, Thomas C., House—*hist pl* MO-7
Fletcher Acad—*school* NC-3
Fletcher Airp—*airport* PA-2
*Fletcher Backwater* MI-6
Fletcher Bay—*bay* WA-9
**Fletcher Bay**—*pop pl* WA-9
Fletcher Bayou—*gut* MS-4
Fletcher Bayou—*stream* AR-4
Fletcher Bend Public Use Area—*park* AR-4
Fletcher Bluff—*cliff* ME-1
Fletcher Brake—*swamp* AR-4
Fletcher Branch—*stream* AL-4
Fletcher Branch—*stream* (2) AR-4
Fletcher Branch—*stream* GA-3
Fletcher Branch—*stream* (2) KY-4
Fletcher Branch—*stream* MS-4
Fletcher Branch—*stream* (2) MO-7
Fletcher Branch—*stream* (2) TN-4
Fletcher Branch—*stream* TX-5
Fletcher Branch—*stream* VA-3
Fletcher Branch Lookout Tower—*locale* GA-3
Fletcher Bridge—*bridge* AL-4
Fletcher Brook—*stream* (2) ME-1
Fletcher Brook—*stream* VT-1
Fletcher Butte—*summit* ID-8
Fletcher Cabin—*locale* CO-8
Fletcher Canyon—*valley* CA-9
Fletcher Canyon—*valley* NV-8
Fletcher Canyon—*valley* WA-9
Fletcher Canyon—*valley* WY-8
Fletcher Cascades—*falls* NH-1
Fletcher Cave—*cave* KY-4
Fletcher Cem—*cemetery* (2) AL-4
Fletcher Cem—*cemetery* GA-3
Fletcher Cem—*cemetery* ID-8
Fletcher Cem—*cemetery* IL-6
Fletcher Cem—*cemetery* (2) IN-6
Fletcher Cem—*cemetery* KY-4
Fletcher Cem—*cemetery* ME-1
Fletcher Cem—*cemetery* MS-4
Fletcher Cem—*cemetery* NC-3
Fletcher Cem—*cemetery* (2) OH-6
Fletcher Cem—*cemetery* OK-5
Fletcher Cem—*cemetery* OR-9
Fletcher Cem—*cemetery* PA-2
Fletcher Cem—*cemetery* (6) TN-4
Fletcher Cem—*cemetery* (6) VA-3
Fletcher Cem—*cemetery* WA-9
Fletcher Cem—*cemetery* WV-2
Fletcher Ch—*church* IL-6
Fletcher Ch—*church* IN-6
Fletcher Ch—*church* NC-3
Fletcher Ch—*church* (2) OH-6
Fletcher Ch—*church* PA-2
Fletcher Ch—*church* VA-3
Fletcher Channel—*stream* MT-8
Fletcher Chapel—*church* AL-4
Fletcher Chapel—*church* (2) IN-6
Fletcher Chapel—*church* (2) NC-3
Fletcher Chapel—*church* OH-6
Fletcher Chapel—*church* (2) VA-3
Fletcher Chapel—*church* WV-2
Fletcher Ch (historical)—*church* TN-4
Fletcher Cliff—*cliff* VA-3
Fletcher Corners—*locale* NY-2
Fletcher Covered Bridge—*hist pl* WV-2
*Fletcher Creek* AL-4
*Fletcher Creek* MI-6
Fletcher Creek—*stream* AL-4
Fletcher Creek—*stream* (2) AR-4
Fletcher Creek—*stream* (2) CA-9
Fletcher Creek—*stream* FL-3
Fletcher Creek—*stream* ID-8
Fletcher Creek—*stream* (2) MI-6
Fletcher Creek—*stream* (2) MN-6
Fletcher Creek—*stream* MO-7
Fletcher Creek—*stream* (4) MT-8
Fletcher Creek—*stream* (2) NC-3
Fletcher Creek—*stream* TN-4
Fletcher Creek—*stream* WA-9
*Fletcher Dam* AL-4
Fletcher Ditch—*canal* IA-7
Fletcher Drain—*canal* MI-6
Fletcher Drive Sch—*school* CA-9
Fletcher Estate Lake—*reservoir* AL-4
Fletcher Farm—*locale* WA-9
Fletcher Field—*locale* ME-1
Fletcher Field (airport)—*airport* MS-4
Fletcher Flat—*flat* WA-9
Fletcher Ford—*locale* VA-3
*Fletcher Fork* TN-4
Fletcher Fork—*stream* KY-4
*Fletcher Gap* KY-4
Fletcher Gilbert Dam—*dam* AL-4
Fletcher Gilberts Lake—*reservoir* AL-4
Fletcher Grove Ch—*church* SC-3
Fletcher Gulch—*valley* CA-9
Fletcher Gulch—*valley* CO-8
Fletcher Gulch—*valley* MT-8
Fletcher Gulch—*valley* OR-9
Fletcher Hill—*summit* CO-8
Fletcher Hill—*summit* (2) ME-1
Fletcher Hill—*summit* MA-1
Fletcher Hill—*summit* (2) NH-1
Fletcher Hill—*summit* PA-2
Fletcher Hill—*summit* VT-1
Fletcher Hills—*range* CA-9
Fletcher Hills Golf Course—*other* CA-9
Fletcher Hills Sch—*school* CA-9
**Fletcher (historical)**—*pop pl* NC-3
Fletcher Hollow—*valley* AL-4
Fletcher Hollow—*valley* KY-4
Fletcher Hollow—*valley* MO-7
Fletcher Hollow—*valley* NC-3
Fletcher Hollow—*valley* WV-2
Fletcher House—*hist pl* AR-4
Fletcher HS—*school* FL-3
Fletcher Island—*island* NH-1
Fletcher JHS—*school* FL-3
Fletcher Knob—*summit* KY-4
Fletcher Knob—*summit* NC-3
Fletcher Knob—*summit* VA-3
Fletcher Knob—*summit* WV-2
*Fletcher Lake* IN-6
*Fletcher Lake* LA-4
*Fletcher Lake* OR-9
Fletcher Lake—*lake* AR-4
Fletcher Lake—*lake* IN-6
Fletcher Lake—*lake* (2) MS-4
Fletcher Lake—*lake* NJ-2
Fletcher Lake—*lake* TN-4
**Fletcher Lake**—*pop pl* IN-6
Fletcher Lake Dam—*dam* MS-4
Fletcher Landing—*locale* FL-3
Fletcher Memorial Sch—*school* SC-3
Fletcher Mill—*locale* VA-3
Fletcher Miller Sch—*school* CO-8
Fletcher Mine—*mine* MO-7
*Fletcher Mine and Mill* MO-7
Fletcher Mountain—*ridge* NH-1
Fletcher Mtn—*summit* AR-4
Fletcher Mtn—*summit* CO-8
Fletcher Mtn—*summit* ME-1
Fletcher Mtn—*summit* OK-5
Fletcher Mtn—*summit* VT-1
Fletcher Mtn—*summit* VA-3
Fletcher Neck—*cape* ME-1
Fletcher Oil Company Bldg—*hist pl* ID-8
Fletcher Park—*locale* WY-8
Fletcher Park—*park* MI-6
Fletcher Park—*park* WY-8
Fletcher Park Monmt—*park* FL-3
Fletcher Peak—*summit* CA-9
Fletcher Peak—*summit* ME-1
Fletcher Peak—*summit* NV-8
Fletcher Peak—*summit* WY-8
Fletcher Place—*locale* CA-9
Fletcher Place Hist Dist—*hist pl* IN-6
Fletcher Playground—*park* MI-6
Fletcher Plaza (Shop Ctr)—*locale* FL-3
Fletcher Plaza (Shop Ctr)—*locale* NC-3
Fletcher Point—*cape* FL-3
Fletcher Point—*cape* NY-2
Fletcher Point—*cape* TN-4
*Fletcher Pond* MA-1
*Fletcher Pond* NJ-2
Fletcher Pond—*lake* FL-3
Fletcher Pond—*lake* MI-6
Fletcher Pond—*lake* NH-1
Fletcher Ponds—*lake* ME-1
Fletcher Properties Lake Dam—*dam* AL-4
Fletcher Ranch—*locale* CO-8
Fletcher Ranch—*locale* WY-8
Fletcher Retarding Basin—*reservoir* CA-9
Fletcher Ridge—*ridge* KY-4
Fletcher Ridge—*ridge* (2) VA-3
Fletcher Ridge—*ridge* WV-2
Fletcher Ridge Sch—*school* VA-3
Fletcher Rsvr—*reservoir* MT-8
Fletcher Rsvr—*reservoir* WY-8
Fletcher Run—*stream* PA-2
Fletchers—*locale* IL-6
Fletchers Branch—*stream* AR-4
Fletchers Bridge (historical)—*bridge* MS-4
Fletcher Sch—*school* CA-9
Fletcher Sch—*school* IL-6
Fletcher Sch—*school* (4) MI-6
Fletcher Sch—*school* NE-7
Fletcher Sch—*school* (2) NY-2
Fletcher Sch—*school* NC-3
Fletcher Sch—*school* OH-6
Fletcher Sch—*school* SD-7
Fletcher Sch—*school* TX-5
Fletcher Sch—*school* WI-6
Fletcher Sch (abandoned)—*school* PA-2
*Fletchers Chapel* AL-4
Fletchers Chapel—*church* MS-4
Fletchers Chapel—*church* NC-3
Fletchers Chapel—*church* OH-6
Fletchers Chapel—*church* SC-3
Fletchers Chapel—*church* (2) VA-3
*Fletchers Chapel Church* AL-4
*Fletchers Chapel United Methodist Ch* MS-4
Fletcher Sch (historical)—*school* MO-7
Fletcher Sch Number 8—*school* IN-6
Fletchers Coulee—*valley* MT-8
Fletchers Field—*park* MD-2
Fletchers Fork—*stream* TN-4
Fletchers Gap—*gap* TX-5
Fletcher Site—*hist pl* MI-6
*Fletchers Lake* IN-6
Fletchers Lake—*lake* (2) LA-4
Fletchers Lake—*reservoir* GA-3
**Fletchers Landing**—*pop pl* ME-1
Fletcher Slough—*stream* AR-4
*Fletcher's Neck* ME-1
Fletcher's Neck Lifesaving Station—*hist pl* ME-1
Fletchers Point—*summit* TX-5
Fletchers Pond—*reservoir* (2) MA-1
Fletchers Pond Dam—*dam* MA-1
Fletcher Spring—*spring* FL-3
Fletcher Spring—*spring* MT-8
Fletcher Spring—*spring* NV-8
Fletcher Spring—*spring* OR-9
Fletcher Spring—*spring* TN-4
Fletcher Spring Branch—*stream* TN-4
Fletchers Shop (historical)—*locale* MS-4
**Fletcher's Spur**—*pop pl* MI-6
Fletcher-Stretch House—*hist pl* OR-9
Fletcher Tank—*reservoir* AZ-5
Fletcher Towhead—*island* AR-4
**Fletcher (Town of)**—*pop pl* VT-1
Fletcher (Township of)—*fmr MCD* (2) AR-4
Fletcher Union Church—*hist pl* VT-1
Fletcher View Campground—*locale* NV-8
*Fletcherville* WV-2
**Fletcherville**—*pop pl* VA-3
Fletcherville Hist Dist—*hist pl* GA-3
Fletcher-Walker Sch—*school* CA-9
Fletcher Windmill—*locale* NM-5
Fletchum Hollow—*valley* KY-4
*Fleton Station* DE-2
Flett Cem—*cemetery* OR-9
Flett Creek—*stream* WA-9
Flett Glacier—*glacier* WA-9
**Fletts (historical)**—*pop pl* OR-9
Fleugel Ditch—*canal* IN-6
Fleur, Bayou de—*gut* LA-4
*Fleur de Hundred Creek* VA-3
Fleur de Lis (historical)—*locale* SD-7
Fleur Pond—*bay* LA-4
Fleur Pond—*lake* LA-4
Fleurs, Lac des—*lake* WI-6
Fleury Bay—*bay* VT-1
Fleury Lake—*lake* MI-6
Fleury Mtn—*summit* NY-2
Flewelen Branch—*stream* TX-5
Flewellen Cem—*cemetery* TX-5
Flewellen Creek—*stream* TX-5
*Flewellenes Crossroads* MS-4
**Flewellyn**—*pop pl* TN-4
Flewellyn Baptist Ch—*church* TN-4
Flewellyn Sch (historical)—*school* TN-4
Flewsie Creek—*stream* ID-8
Flexer Spring—*spring* OR-9
**Flick**—*pop pl* SC-3
Flick Branch—*stream* IL-6
Flick Cem—*cemetery* OH-6
Flick Creek—*stream* WA-9
Flick Creek Campground—*locale* WA-9
Flickenstein Gulch—*valley* CO-8
Flicker Creek—*stream* AK-9
Flicker Creek—*stream* ID-8
Flicker Lake—*lake* MI-6
Flicker Lake—*lake* MN-6
Flicker Spring—*spring* AZ-5
**Flickersville**—*pop pl* MD-2
Flickertail Dam—*dam* ND-7
Flickertail Lake—*reservoir* ND-7
**Flickerville**—*pop pl* IL-6
**Flickerville**—*pop pl* PA-2
*Flick Gulch* CO-8
Flick Gulch—*valley* CO-8
Flick Homestead—*locale* CO-8
Flickinger Cem—*cemetery* OH-6
Flickinger Rsvr—*reservoir* OR-9
Flickinger Sch (abandoned)—*school* PA-2
*Flickins Mill* GA-3
Flick Lake—*reservoir* MT-8
Flick Park—*park* IL-6
Flick Point—*cape* CA-9
Flicks Cave—*cave* MO-7
Flick Sch—*school* IN-6
**Flicks Corners**—*pop pl* OH-6
Flicks Run—*stream* PA-2
**Flicksville**—*pop pl* PA-2
Flight Acres—*flat* TX-5
Flight Lake—*lake* SD-7
Flight Run—*stream* IN-6
Flimflam Creek—*stream* OR-9
Flinch Post Office (historical)—*building* TN-4
**Flinderation**—*pop pl* WV-2
Flinders Ditch—*canal* UT-8
Fling Brook—*stream* ME-1
Flinger Branch—*stream* MO-7
Fling Island—*island* ME-1
Fling Pond—*lake* TX-5
Flingsville—*locale* KY-4
Fliniau Homestead—*locale* CO-8
Fliniau Ranch—*locale* CO-8
Flink Creek—*stream* MI-6
Flinks Slough—*gut* MN-6
Flinks State Wildlife Mngmt Area—*park* MN-6
*Flinn* MO-7
Flinn—*locale* WV-2
**Flinn**—*pop pl* MS-4
**Flinn**—*pop pl* MO-7
Flinn Block—*hist pl* OR-9
Flinn Cem—*cemetery* MO-7
Flinn Cem—*cemetery* TX-5
Flinn Cem—*cemetery* VA-3
Flinn Cem—*cemetery* WV-2
Flinner Lake—*reservoir* KS-7
Flinn Hollow—*valley* (2) WV-2
Flinn Pond—*lake* ME-1
Flinn Pond Brook—*stream* ME-1
Flinn Ranch—*locale* CA-9
**Flinns Crossroads**—*pop pl* SC-3
**Flinn Springs**—*pop pl* CA-9
Flinn Springs County Park—*park* CA-9
Flinn Springs Fire Control Station—*locale* CA-9
Flinsch Peak—*summit* MT-8
*Flint* AL-4
*Flint* MA-1
Flint—*locale* GA-3
Flint—*locale* ID-8
Flint—*locale* IL-6
Flint—*locale* KY-4
Flint—*locale* MD-2
Flint—*locale* NY-2
Flint—*locale* OK-5
Flint—*locale* WA-9
Flint—*locale* WV-2
**Flint**—*pop pl* CA-9
**Flint**—*pop pl* IN-6
**Flint**—*pop pl* MI-6
**Flint**—*pop pl* NY-2
**Flint**—*pop pl* OH-6
**Flint**—*pop pl* TX-5
**Flint**—*pop pl* WV-2
Flint, Lake—*reservoir* CA-9
Flint Beach—*beach* WA-9
Flint Bend—*bend* TX-5
Flint Bottom Creek—*stream* MO-7
Flint Branch—*stream* AL-4
Flint Branch—*stream* KY-4
Flint Branch—*stream* MO-7
Flint Branch—*stream* OK-5
Flint Branch—*stream* (3) TN-4
Flint Branch Ch—*church* GA-3
Flint Brewing Company—*hist pl* MI-6
Flint Bridge—*bridge* AL-4
Flint Brook—*stream* ME-1
Flint Brook—*stream* NY-2
Flint Brook—*stream* (2) VT-1
Flint Burying Ground—*cemetery* MA-1
Flint Butte—*summit* SD-7
Flint Canyon—*valley* ID-8
Flint Canyon—*valley* TX-5
Flint Cave—*cave* AL-4
Flint Cem—*cemetery* AL-4
Flint Cem—*cemetery* AR-4
Flint Cem—*cemetery* IL-6
Flint Cem—*cemetery* IN-6
Flint Cem—*cemetery* IA-7
Flint Cem—*cemetery* ME-1
Flint Cem—*cemetery* MA-1
Flint Cem—*cemetery* MI-6
Flint Cem—*cemetery* NY-2
Flint Cem—*cemetery* NC-3
Flint Cem—*cemetery* OH-6
Flint Cem—*cemetery* TX-5
Flint Cem—*cemetery* WI-6
Flint Ch—*church* (2) AL-4
Flint Ch—*church* KY-4
Flint Chaffee Cem—*cemetery* NY-2
**Flint City**—*pop pl* AL-4
**Flint City (Flint)**—*pop pl* AL-4
Flint Coll Univ of Michigan—*school* MI-6
Flint Cove—*valley* UT-8
Flint Covered Bridge—*hist pl* VT-1
*Flint Creek* AL-4
*Flint Creek* MT-8
*Flint Creek* TN-4
**Flint Creek**—*pop pl* AR-4
**Flint Creek**—*pop pl* TX-5
Flint Creek—*stream* AL-4
Flint Creek—*stream* AK-9
Flint Creek—*stream* AZ-5
Flint Creek—*stream* AR-4
Flint Creek—*stream* CA-9
Flint Creek—*stream* CO-8
Flint Creek—*stream* FL-3
Flint Creek—*stream* (3) ID-8
Flint Creek—*stream* (2) IL-6
Flint Creek—*stream* (2) IN-6
Flint Creek—*stream* IA-7
Flint Creek—*stream* KY-4
Flint Creek—*stream* MN-6
Flint Creek—*stream* MS-4
Flint Creek—*stream* MO-7
Flint Creek—*stream* (2) MT-8
Flint Creek—*stream* NY-2
Flint Creek—*stream* OK-5
Flint Creek—*stream* (2) OR-9
Flint Creek—*stream* SC-3
Flint Creek—*stream* SD-7
Flint Creek—*stream* (2) TN-4
Flint Creek—*stream* (2) TX-5
Flint Creek—*stream* WI-6
Flint Creek—*stream* WY-8
Flint Creek Campground—*locale* MT-8
Flint Creek Canal—*canal* MT-8
Flint Creek Cem—*cemetery* AR-4
*Flint Creek Ch* AL-4
Flint Creek Ch—*church* AL-4
Flint Creek Dam—*dam* MT-8
Flint Creek Island—*island* AL-4
Flint Creek Mission—*church* TX-5
*Flint Creek Missionary Baptist Church* AL-4
Flint Creek Range—*range* MT-8
Flint Creek Reservoir Dam—*dam* MS-4
Flint Creek Rsvr—*reservoir* MS-4
Flint Creek Water Park—*park* MS-4
Flint Elem Sch—*school* AL-4
Flint Estate, The—*hist pl* NH-1
Flint Factory Post Office (historical)—*building* AL-4
Flint Farm—*hist pl* MA-1
Flintfield Branch—*stream* KY-4
Flint Flat—*flat* UT-8
*Flint Fork* CO-8
Flint Fork—*stream* KY-4
Flint Fork—*stream* TN-4
Flint Gap—*gap* (2) GA-3
Flint Gap—*gap* (2) NC-3
Flint Gap—*gap* (5) TN-4
Flint Gap—*gap* (2) VA-3
Flint Gap Ch—*church* TN-4
Flint Gap Trail Shelter—*locale* NC-3
Flint Grove Sch—*school* GA-3
Flint Groves Sch—*school* NC-3
Flint Hall—*hist pl* FL-3
Flintham Ditch—*canal* CO-8
Flintham Memorial Forest Plantation—*other* CA-9
Flinthead Island—*island* FL-3
Flinthead Lake—*lake* FL-3
Flintheart Draw—*valley* MT-8
Flint Hill—*locale* GA-3
Flint Hill—*locale* KY-4
Flint Hill—*locale* MO-7
Flint Hill—*locale* NC-3
Flint Hill—*locale* (2) VA-3
**Flint Hill**—*pop pl* (2) AL-4
**Flint Hill**—*pop pl* GA-3
**Flint Hill**—*pop pl* MD-2
**Flint Hill**—*pop pl* MS-4
**Flint Hill**—*pop pl* MO-7
**Flint Hill**—*pop pl* (2) NC-3
**Flint Hill**—*pop pl* SC-3
**Flint Hill**—*pop pl* (2) VA-3
Flint Hill—*summit* AL-4
Flint Hill—*summit* GA-3
Flint Hill—*summit* IN-6
Flint Hill—*summit* MO-7
Flint Hill—*summit* (2) NH-1
Flint Hill—*summit* NC-3
Flint Hill—*summit* (2) PA-2
Flint Hill—*summit* SD-7
Flint Hill—*summit* VA-3
Flint Hill Aboriginal Quartzite Quarry—*hist pl* SD-7
Flint Hill Branch—*stream* MO-7
Flint Hill Cem—*cemetery* (2) AL-4
Flint Hill Cem—*cemetery* GA-3
Flint Hill Cem—*cemetery* MO-7
Flint Hill Cem—*cemetery* VA-3
*Flint Hill Ch* AL-4
Flint Hill Ch—*church* (5) AL-4
Flint Hill Ch—*church* AR-4
Flint Hill Ch—*church* (6) GA-3
Flint Hill Ch—*church* (2) MS-4
Flint Hill Ch—*church* MO-7
Flint Hill Ch—*church* (5) NC-3
Flint Hill Ch—*church* PA-2
Flint Hill Ch—*church* (5) SC-3
Flint Hill Ch—*church* TX-5
Flint Hill Ch—*church* VA-3
Flint Hill Ch (historical)—*church* AL-4
Flint Hill Ch (historical)—*church* MO-7
Flint Hill Dam—*dam* AL-4
Flint Hill (historical)—*locale* NC-3
Flint Hill Lake—*reservoir* AL-4
Flint Hill Methodist Ch—*church* AL-4
Flint Hills—*other* CA-9
Flint Hills—*range* KS-7
Flint Hills—*range* SD-7
Flint Hills—*summit* NM-5
Flint Hills—*summit* OR-9
*Flinthill Salt River* MO-7
Flint Hill Sch—*school* AR-4
Flint Hill Sch—*school* MS-4
Flint Hill Sch—*school* TX-5
Flint Hill Sch—*school* (2) VA-3
Flint Hill Sch (abandoned)—*school* MO-7
Flint Hill Sch (historical)—*school* AL-4
Flinthills HS—*school* KS-7
Flinthills Mall—*locale* KS-7
Flint Hills Natl Wildlife Ref—*park* KS-7
Flint Hills Park—*park* IA-7
Flint Hills Sch—*school* IA-7
Flint Hills Village—*locale* KS-7
Flint (historical P.O.)—*locale* IA-7
Flint Hollow—*valley* NY-2
Flint Hollow—*valley* PA-2
Flint Hollow—*valley* (2) WV-2
Flint Hollow Sch—*school* MO-7
Flint Island—*island* KY-4
Flint Island—*island* ME-1
Flint Island Narrows—*channel* ME-1
Flint Junction—*uninc pl* IA-7
Flint Knob—*summit* AR-4
Flint Knob—*summit* GA-3
Flint Knob—*summit* KY-4
Flint Knob—*summit* (2) NC-3
Flint Knob—*summit* WV-2
Flint Knob Mine—*mine* TN-4
Flint Knoll—*summit* AZ-5
Flintkote Company (Orangeburg Division)—*facility* OH-6
Flint Lake—*lake* IN-6
Flint Lake—*lake* (2) MN-6
Flint Lake Elem Sch—*school* IN-6
Flint Lakes—*lake* CO-8
Flint Lateral—*canal* AZ-5
Flint Level Branch—*stream* NC-3
Flintlock Field Airp—*airport* MO-7
**Flintlock Ridge (subdivision)**—*pop pl* PA-2
Flint Memorial Park—*cemetery* MI-6
Flint Mesa—*summit* ID-8
Flint Mill Gap—*gap* TN-4
Flint Mills—*hist pl* MA-1
Flint Mill Trail—*trail* (2) TN-4
Flint Mine Hill—*summit* NY-2
Flint Mine Hill Archeol District—*hist pl* NY-2
Flint Mtn—*summit* MT-8
Flint Mtn—*summit* NC-3
Flint Mtn—*summit* TN-4
Flint Mtn—*summit* VA-3
Flintner, Frank, House—*hist pl* WA-9
**Flinton**—*pop pl* IL-6
**Flinton**—*pop pl* PA-2
Flinton Creek—*stream* MI-6
Flinton Lake—*lake* MI-6
Flintoy Creek—*stream* VA-3
Flint Park—*park* NY-2
Flint Park Lake—*lake* MI-6
Flint Pass—*gap* CO-8
Flint Peak—*summit* CA-9
Flint Peak—*summit* NM-5
Flint Point—*cape* FL-3
Flint Point—*cape* RI-1
Flint Pond—*lake* MA-1
Flint Pond—*reservoir* MA-1
Flint Post Office (historical)—*building* AL-4
Flint Ranch—*locale* MT-8
*Flintridge* CA-9
*Flintridge* KS-7
*Flint Ridge* PA-2
*Flint Ridge* TN-4
Flint Ridge—*locale* MO-7
Flint Ridge—*ridge* (3) AL-4

Flint Ridge—*ridge* CA-9
Flint Ridge—*ridge* KY-4
Flint Ridge—*ridge* NC-3
Flint Ridge—*ridge* OH-6
Flint Ridge—*ridge* OK-5
Flint Ridge—*ridge* OR-9
Flint Ridge—*ridge* PA-2
Flint Ridge—*ridge* (4) TN-4
Flint Ridge—*ridge* (3) VA-3
Flintridge—*uninc pl* CA-9
Flintridge Acad of the Sacred Heart—*school* CA-9
Flint Ridge Ch—*church* (2) GA-3
Flint Ridge Ch—*church* (2) NC-3
Flint Ridge Ch—*church* SC-3
Flint Ridge Chapel—*church* SC-3
Flint Ridge (historical)—*locale* KS-7
Flint Ridge Park—*park* OH-6
Flint Ridge Ranger Station—*locale* KY-4
Flint Ridge Sch—*school* MO-7
Flintridge Sch for Boys—*school* CA-9
Flint Ridge Sch (historical)—*school* AL-4
Flint Ridge State Memorial—*hist pl* OH-6
*Flint River* IA-7
Flint River—*stream* AL-4
Flint River—*stream* GA-3
Flint River—*stream* MI-6
Flint River—*stream* TN-4
Flint River Acad—*school* GA-3
*Flint River Baptist Church* AL-4
Flint River Cem—*cemetery* AL-4
Flint River Cem—*cemetery* MI-6
*Flint River Ch* AL-4
Flint River Ch—*church* (2) AL-4
Flint River Ch—*church* GA-3
Flint River Place—*hist pl* AL-4
Flint River Post Office (historical)—*building* AL-4
Flint River Towhead (historical)—*island* AL-4
Flint River Township—*fmr MCD* IA-7
Flint Rock—*pillar* TN-4
Flintrock Branch—*stream* TN-4
Flint Rock Branch—*stream* TN-4
Flint Rock Cove—*valley* NC-3
Flint Rock Creek—*stream* SD-7
*Flint Rock Gap* TN-4
Flint Rock Gap—*gap* NC-3
Flint Rock Head—*summit* CA-9
Flint Rock Hill—*summit* TX-5
Flint Rock Hill (historical)—*summit* SD-7
Flintrock Park—*park* GA-3
Flint Rock Point—*cliff* CO-8
Flintrock Pond—*lake* MA-1
Flint Rock Township—*obs name* SD-7
Flint (RR name Flint Village)—*uninc pl* MA-1
Flint Run—*stream* IN-6
Flint Run—*stream* KY-4
Flint Run—*stream* (3) OH-6
Flint Run—*stream* VA-3
Flint Run—*stream* (3) WV-2
Flint Run Archeol District—*hist pl* VA-3
Flint Run Sch—*school* WV-2
Flints Brook—*stream* ME-1
Flints Brook—*stream* NH-1
*Flints Camp* ME-1
Flint Sch—*school* KS-7
Flint Sch—*school* MO-7
Flint Sch (historical)—*school* MS-4
Flint Sch (historical)—*school* MO-7
**Flints Corner**—*pop pl* MA-1
Flint Seep—*spring* UT-8
Flint Sewage Disp—*other* MI-6
Flints Hill—*summit* NH-1
**Flintside**—*pop pl* GA-3
*Flint Siding* WV-2
*Flints Mill* OH-6
Flints Mtn—*summit* (3) ME-1
Flints Point—*cape* AK-9
*Flints Pond* MA-1
Flints Pond—*lake* NH-1
Flints Pond—*reservoir* MA-1
*Flint Spring* UT-8
Flint Spring—*spring* AR-4
Flint Spring—*spring* NV-8
Flint Spring—*spring* (2) UT-8
Flintspring Branch—*stream* NC-3
Flint Spring Canyon—*valley* NV-8
Flint Spring Ch—*church* AR-4
Flint Spring Creek—*stream* NC-3
Flint Spring Gap—*gap* (2) NC-3
*Flint Springs* KY-4
Flint Springs—*locale* KY-4
Flint Springs—*locale* TN-4
Flint Springs Acad (historical)—*school* TN-4
Flint Springs Cem—*cemetery* TN-4
Flint Springs Male and Female Acad (historical)—*school* TN-4
Flint Springs Presbyterian Ch—*church* TN-4
Flint Springs Sch (historical)—*school* TN-4
Flintsteel River—*stream* MI-6
**Flintstone**—*pop pl* GA-3
**Flintstone**—*pop pl* MD-2
*Flintstone Brook* MA-1
*Flint Stone Creek* PA-2
Flintstone Creek—*stream* MD-2
Flintstone Creek—*stream* PA-2
Flintstone Creek—*stream* VA-3
Flintstone Creek Sch—*school* PA-2
Flint Stone Mtn—*summit* VA-3
*Flint Stone Ridge* PA-2
Flintstone Sch—*school* MD-2
Flint Store—*locale* AR-4
Flint Street Ch—*church* TN-4
*Flintsville* MS-4
Flint Tank—*reservoir* TX-5
Flint Town—*locale* NY-2
Flint Town—*locale* WV-2
**Flint Township**—*pop pl* ND-7
Flint (Township of)—*fmr MCD* AR-4
**Flint (Township of)**—*pop pl* IL-6
**Flint (Township of)**—*pop pl* MI-6
Flint Trail—*trail* UT-8
Flint Trail Overlook—*locale* UT-8
*Flint Valley* PA-2
Flint Valley—*basin* CA-9
Flint Valley—*valley* PA-2
Flint Valley Ch—*church* TN-4
Flint Village HS—*school* MA-1
Flint Village (RR name for Flint)—*other* MA-1
**Flint Village (subdivision)**—*pop pl* MA-1

Flintville—*locale* KY-4
**Flintville**—*pop pl* PA-2
**Flintville**—*pop pl* TN-4
**Flintville**—*pop pl* WI-6
Flintville (CCD)—*cens area* TN-4
Flintville Division—*civil* TN-4
Flintville Elem Sch—*school* TN-4
Flintville First Baptist Ch—*church* TN-4
Flintville JHS—*school* TN-4
Flintville Post Office—*building* TN-4
*Flintwood* IN-6
**Flintwood Hills**—*pop pl* CO-8
Flintwood Park—*park* MN-6
Flinty Gap—*gap* NC-3
Flinty Knoll Ch—*church* NC-3
Flip-O-Way Trail—*trail* WA-9
**Flippen**—*pop pl* GA-3
Flippen Creek—*stream* TN-4
Flippen Creek—*stream* (2) VA-3
Flippen Millpond—*reservoir* VA-3
Flippen Sch (historical)—*school* TN-4
Flippen Windmill—*locale* TX-5
Flipper Bend—*bend* TN-4
Flipper Creek—*stream* AL-4
Flipper Creek—*stream* ME-1
Flipper Park—*park* TX-5
Flipper Point—*RIDGE* MP-9
**Flippin**—*pop pl* AR-4
**Flippin**—*pop pl* KY-4
**Flippin**—*pop pl* TN-4
Flippin, Thomas J., House—*hist pl* OR-9
Flippin Cem—*cemetery* NC-3
Flippin Cem—*cemetery* TX-5
Flippin Ch—*church* NC-3
*Flippin Creek* AL-4
Flippin Creek—*stream* KY-4
Flippin Creek—*stream* TX-5
**Flipping**—*pop pl* WV-2
*Flipping Creek* KY-4
Flipping Creek—*stream* WV-2
**Flipping Creek Junction**—*pop pl* WV-2
Flippin Post Office (historical)—*building* TN-4
*Flippins* TN-4
Flippin Sch—*school* KY-4
*Flippin School* TN-4
Flippins Creek—*stream* VA-3
Flippins Ridge—*ridge* WV-2
Flippins Run—*stream* KY-4
Flippo Branch—*stream* TN-4
Flippo Chapel—*church* AR-4
Flippo Ford—*locale* AL-4
Flippo Grave—*cemetery* TN-4
Flippo Hill—*summit* KY-4
Flippo Hollow—*valley* AL-4
Flippo Spring—*spring* TN-4
Flip Rock—*rock* MA-1
Flirtation Island—*island* NY-2
Flirtation Peak—*summit* CO-8
Flirt Hill—*summit* CT-1
Flis Pond—*reservoir* MA-1
Flis Pond Dam—*dam* MA-1
Flitner Rsvr—*reservoir* WY-8
Flitners Corner—*locale* WY-8
F L Lateral—*canal* CO-8
Fllinger Branch—*stream* TX-5
Flo—*locale* TX-5
*Floa Island* NY-2
Float Bayou—*gut* LA-4
Float Bayou—*stream* MS-4
Float Bridge—*bridge* VT-1
Float Camp Rec Area—*park* (2) MO-7
Float Canal—*canal* LA-4
Float Creek—*stream* AR-4
Float Creek—*stream* (2) ID-8
Floate Draw—*valley* WY-8
Floaters Haven Park—*park* WI-6
Floater Waterhole—*lake* OR-9
Floathaven Airstrip Airp—*airport* WA-9
Floathaven Seaplane Base—*airport* WA-9
Floating Battery Island—*island* NY-2
Floating Bog Bay—*bay* MN-6
Floating Bridge Pond—*lake* MA-1
Floating Glade—*swamp* TX-5
Floating House Ruins—*locale* AZ-5
Floating Island—*island* NJ-2
Floating Island—*summit* UT-8
Floating Island—*swamp* MA-1
Floating Island Lake—*lake* CA-9
Floating Island Lake—*lake* UT-8
Floating Island Lake—*lake* WY-8
Floating Island Lava Flow—*lava* WA-9
Floating Lake—*lake* CO-8
Floating Lake—*lake* (2) LA-4
Floating Mill Hollow—*valley* KY-4
Floating Mill Island—*island* KY-4
Floating Mill Island (historical)—*island* TN-4
Floating Mill Park—*park* TN-4
*Floating Mill Rec Area* TN-4
Floating Moss Lake—*lake* MN-6
Floating Prairie—*flat* OR-9
Floating Turf Bayou—*stream* LA-4
*Floating Turtle Creek* AL-4
Floating W Ranch—*locale* CO-8
Float Road Bayou—*stream* MS-4
Float Road Ditch—*canal* AR-4
Float Sch—*school* KS-7
Flobec Heliport—*airport* MO-7
Floberg Home for Children—*building* IL-6
Flock Canyon—*valley* ID-8
Flock Cem—*cemetery* IN-6
Flock Mtn—*summit* OR-9
Flock Rock—*other* AK-9
*Flocks Run* PA-2
Flocktown Schoolhouse—*hist pl* NJ-2
Floctaw Creek—*stream* LA-4
Flodelle Creek—*stream* WA-9
Flodin Lake—*lake* MN-6
Floe—*locale* WV-2
Floe, The—*lake* NY-2
Floed, Creed, House—*hist pl* OR-9
Floe Gulch—*valley* MT-8
*Floersch* KS-7
Floe Tank—*reservoir* AZ-5
Floeter Pond—*reservoir* OR-9
Floglesong Cem—*cemetery* VA-3
Flogus Pond—*lake* CO-8
Flohr Creek—*stream* WY-8
**Flohrville**—*pop pl* MD-2
Floka—*locale* NV-8
*Floka Siding* NV-8

**Flom**—*pop pl* MN-6
**Flomaton**—*pop pl* AL-4
Flomaton Airp—*airport* AL-4
Flomaton (CCD)—*cens area* AL-4
Flomaton Division—*civil* AL-4
Flomaton Elem Sch—*school* AL-4
Flomaton HS—*school* AL-4
**Flomot**—*pop pl* TX-5
**Flom (Township of)**—*pop pl* MN-6
Flonellis—*locale* CA-9
Flood—*locale* (2) VA-3
Flood, James C., Mansion—*hist pl* CA-9
Flood Bay—*bay* MN-6
Flood Branch—*stream* MS-4
Flood Branch—*stream* MO-7
Flood Brook—*stream* ME-1
Flood Brook—*stream* VT-1
Flood Canyon—*valley* (3) UT-8
Flood Catcher Hollow—*valley* KY-4
Flood Cem—*cemetery* MO-7
Flood Control Dam No 20—*dam* NC-3
Flood Coulee—*valley* WI-6
Flood Cove—*bay* ME-1
Flood Creek—*stream* (3) AK-9
Flood Creek—*stream* CA-9
Flood Creek—*stream* IA-7
Flood Creek—*stream* MD-2
Flood Creek—*stream* (4) MT-8
Flood Creek—*stream* NE-7
Flood Creek—*stream* (2) OR-9
Flood Creek—*stream* (2) WI-6
Flood Creek Cem—*cemetery* IA-7
*Flood Dam* PA-2
Flood Dam Tank—*reservoir* AZ-5
Flood Dam 482—*dam* PA-2
Flood Dam 483—*dam* PA-2
Flood Dam 485—*dam* PA-2
Flooded Lake—*lake* AK-9
Floodgate Bay—*swamp* NC-3
Floodgate Creek—*stream* CA-9
Flood Gulch—*valley* UT-8
Flood Hollow—*valley* WV-2
Flood Homestead—*locale* NM-5
Flood Island—*island* GA-3
Flood JHS—*school* CO-8
Flood Lake—*lake* ME-1
Flood Marker of 1771—*hist pl* VA-3
Flood Meadow—*flat* OR-9
Flood Mtn—*summit* AR-4
Flood Mtn—*summit* KY-4
Flood Park—*park* CA-9
Flood Point—*cape* (2) VA-3
Flood Pond—*lake* ME-1
**Flood (Poverty)**—*pop pl* VA-3
Flood Prevention Dam Number 7—*dam* TX-5
Flood Run—*stream* IN-6
Flood Sch—*school* CA-9
Floods Chapel—*church* NC-3
**Floods Chapel**—*pop pl* NC-3
Floods Hole—*bay* VA-3
Flood Slough—*gut* CA-9
Flood Slough—*swamp* MN-6
Floods Pond—*lake* ME-1
Flood Spring—*spring* WI-6
Flood Stream—*stream* ME-1
Flood Tank—*reservoir* NM-5
Flood Victims Memorial—*other* IN-6
Floodwater Flats—*flat* OR-9
Flood Water Retarding Dam Number One—*dam* TN-4
**Floodway**—*pop pl* AR-4
Floodway, The—*area* MO-7
Floodwood—*locale* MI-6
Floodwood—*locale* NY-2
**Floodwood**—*pop pl* MN-6
**Floodwood**—*pop pl* OH-6
Floodwood Cem—*cemetery* MN-6
Floodwood Creek—*stream* ID-8
Floodwood Creek—*stream* (2) MI-6
Floodwood Creek—*stream* PA-2
Floodwood Lake—*lake* MN-6
Floodwood Lakes—*lake* MI-6
Floodwood Memorial For—*forest* MN-6
Floodwood Mtn—*summit* (2) NY-2
Floodwood Pond—*lake* (2) NY-2
Floodwood River—*stream* MI-6
Floodwood River—*stream* MN-6
Floodwood Swamp—*swamp* MI-6
Floodwood Swamp Rsvr—*reservoir* MI-6
**Floodwood (Township of)**—*pop pl* MN-6
*Floody Branch* TN-4
Flook Lake—*lake* OR-9
Flook Ranch—*locale* OR-9
Floore House—*hist pl* KY-4
Floor Island Number Thirty-three—*island* TN-4
Flopbuck Creek—*stream* FL-3
Flopper Creek—*stream* MI-6
Floprock Peak—*summit* AK-9
*Flora* AL-4
*Flora* WI-6
Flora—*locale* OK-5
Flora—*locale* PA-2
Flora—*locale* TX-5
**Flora**—*pop pl* FL-3
**Flora**—*pop pl* IL-6
**Flora**—*pop pl* (2) IN-6
**Flora**—*pop pl* KY-4
**Flora**—*pop pl* LA-4
**Flora**—*pop pl* MS-4
**Flora**—*pop pl* ND-7
**Flora**—*pop pl* OH-6
**Flora**—*pop pl* OR-9
Flora, Lake—*lake* WA-9
Flora, Mount—*summit* CO-8
Flora Baptist Ch—*church* MS-4
Flora Branch—*stream* FL-3
Flora Branch—*stream* TN-4
Flora Branch Sch—*school* SC-3
Flora (CCD)—*cens area* OR-9
Flora Cem—*cemetery* AL-4
Flora Cem—*cemetery* AR-4
Flora Cem—*cemetery* KY-4
Flora Cem—*cemetery* ND-7
Flora Cem—*cemetery* TN-4
Flora Ch—*church* AR-4
Flora Ch—*church* IL-6
Flora Creek—*stream* AK-9
Flora Creek—*stream* CO-8
Flora Creek—*stream* MO-7
Floradale—*locale* PA-2

Flora Dell Creek—*stream* OR-9
Flora Dell Lake—*reservoir* WI-6
*Floradora* AL-4
Flora Elem Sch—*school* MS-4
Flora Ferry (historical)—*locale* TN-4
Flora Fountain—*locale* WI-6
Flora Glen—*valley* MA-1
Flora Glen Brook—*stream* MA-1
Flora Gulch—*valley* ID-8
Flora Hammock—*island* GA-3
**Flora Heights (subdivision)**—*pop pl* FL-3
Flora Hills Cem—*cemetery* MS-4
Flora Holliday Branch—*stream* KY-4
**Florahome**—*pop pl* FL-3
Flora House—*hist pl* MS-4
Flora HS—*school* SC-3
*Flora island* NY-2
Flora Island—*island* AK-9
*Floral* CO-8
Floral—*locale* KS-7
Floral—*locale* KY-4
**Floral**—*pop pl* AR-4
**Florala**—*pop pl* AL-4
Florala (CCD)—*cens area* AL-4
Florala Ch—*church* AL-4
Florala City Sch—*school* AL-4
Florala Division—*civil* AL-4
Florala HS—*school* AL-4
Flora Lake—*lake* AK-9
Flora Lake—*lake* (2) CA-9
Flora Lake—*lake* FL-3
Flora Lake—*lake* (2) MN-6
Flora Lake—*lake* (2) WI-6
Flora Lake—*lake* WY-8
Florala Memorial Hosp—*hospital* AL-4
Florala Municipal Airp—*airport* AL-4
Florala State Park—*park* AL-4
Floral Ave Elem Sch—*school* FL-3
*Floral Beach* SC-3
**Floral Bluff**—*pop pl* FL-3
Floral Cem—*cemetery* WI-6
*Floral Church* AL-4
**Floral City**—*pop pl* FL-3
Floral City Elem Sch—*school* FL-3
**Floral College**—*pop pl* NC-3
**Floral Crest**—*pop pl* AL-4
Floral Garden Cem—*cemetery* MI-6
Floral Garden Cem—*cemetery* NC-3
Floral Gardens (Shop Ctr)—*locale* NC-3
Floral Grove Cem—*cemetery* (2) OH-6
**Floral Grove Estates Subdivision**—*pop pl* UT-8
Floral Hall—*hist pl* IN-6
Floral Hall—*hist pl* (2) IA-7
Floral Hall—*hist pl* KY-4
Floral Hall—*hist pl* (2) OH-6
Floral Haven Memorial Gardens—*cemetery* OK-5
Floral Heights Sch—*school* FL-3
Floral Hill—*locale* GA-3
**Floralhill**—*pop pl* GA-3
**Floral Hill**—*pop pl* NJ-2
Floral Hill Cem—*cemetery* IL-6
Floral Hill Ch—*church* VA-3
Floral Hill Memorial Garden—*cemetery* VA-3
Floral Hills—*other* AK-9
Floral Hills Cem—*cemetery* MS-4
Floral Hills Cem—*cemetery* MO-7
Floral Hills Cem—*cemetery* OH-6
Floral Hills Memorial Gardens—*cemetery* KY-4
Floral Hills Memorial Gardens—*cemetery* TN-4
Floral Hills Memorial Gardens Cem—*cemetery* IA-7
Floral Hills Memorial Gardens (Cemetery)—*cemetery* WV-2
*Floral Hills Memory Gardens* MS-4
Floral Hills Memory Gardens—*cemetery* OH-6
Floral Hills Memory Gardens Cem—*cemetery* OH-6
Floral Lawn Memorial Gardens (cemetery)—*cemetery* MI-6
Floral Lawns Memorial Gardens—*cemetery* IL-6
Floral Lawns Memorial Gardens—*cemetery* NE-7
Floral Memorial Cem—*cemetery* CA-9
Floral Memory Gardens—*cemetery* FL-3
Floral Mound—*summit* TX-5
Flora Lode Mine—*mine* SD-7
Floral Park—*basin* MT-8
Floral Park—*park* LA-4
Floral Park—*park* MN-6
**Floral Park**—*pop pl* CT-1
**Floral Park**—*pop pl* FL-3
**Floral Park**—*pop pl* MT-8
**Floral Park**—*pop pl* NJ-2
**Floral Park**—*pop pl* NY-2
**Floral Park**—*pop pl* PR-3
Floral Park—*uninc pl* NY-2
Floral Park Baptist Ch—*church* MT-8
Floral Park Campground—*locale* CO-8
Floral Park Cem—*cemetery* IN-6
Floral Park Cem—*cemetery* NH-1
Floral Park Cem—*cemetery* NY-2
Floral Park Playground—*park* NY-2
Floral Pass—*gap* AK-9
Floral Sch—*school* CA-9
Floral Sch—*school* KS-7
Floral Sch (historical)—*school* AL-4
Floral Spring—*spring* NV-8
Floral View Memorial Gardens—*cemetery* MI-6
Flor-a-mar—*other* FL-3
*Flor-A-mar Gulf Harbor* FL-3
Flora Miller Hill—*summit* ID-8
Flora Mtn—*summit* WA-9
Flora Municipal Airp—*airport* IN-6
Floranada Sch—*school* FL-3
**Florance Township**—*pop pl* ND-7
Flora Oregon State Highway Division Maintenance Station—*locale* OR-9
Flora P.O. (historical)—*locale* AL-4
Flora Post Office—*building* MS-4
Flora Post Office (historical)—*building* SD-7
Flora Public Library—*building* MS-4
Flora RR Station—*locale* FL-3
Flora Sch (historical)—*school* MO-7
Floras Creek—*stream* (2) OR-9
Floras Lake—*lake* OR-9
Floras Lake State Park—*park* OR-9
Flora Thew Sch—*school* AZ-5
**Floraton**—*pop pl* TN-4

Flora Township—*civil* SD-7
**Flora Township**—*pop pl* KS-7
**Flora (Township of)**—*pop pl* IL-6
**Flora (Township of)**—*pop pl* MN-6
Flora United Methodist Ch—*church* MS-4
Flora View Sch—*school* AZ-5
**Floraville**—*pop pl* IL-6
Floraville Hist Dist—*hist pl* OH-6
**Flora Vista**—*pop pl* NM-5
Flora Vista Arroyo—*stream* NM-5
Flora Vista Cem—*cemetery* NM-5
Flora Vista Park—*park* CA-9
Flora Vista Sch—*school* NM-5
Flora Vista Tank—*reservoir* NM-5
**Flora (Weaver)**—*pop pl* LA-4
*Flora Weaver Station* LA-4
**Flora Weaver Station**—*pop pl* LA-4
Flordale—*uninc pl* FL-3
**Flor de Alba**—*pop pl* PR-3
*Flor de Hundred Creek* VA-3
**Flordell Hills**—*pop pl* MO-7
Flor de Mayo Tank—*reservoir* TX-5
Flordillo Canyon—*valley* NM-5
**Flordon**—*pop pl* VA-3
Flore,lake—*lake* WA-9
Florea Sch—*school* NE-7
**Florece Subdivision**—*pop pl* UT-8
Floree, Lake—*reservoir* GA-3
**Floreffe**—*pop pl* PA-2
Floreffe Post Office—*building* PA-2
Floren, Lake—*reservoir* CT-1
*Florence* AL-4
*Florence* IN-6
*Florence* KS-7
*Florence* MO-7
*Florence* PA-2
Florence—*fmr MCD* NE-7
Florence—*locale* AR-4
Florence—*locale* DE-2
Florence—*locale* FL-3
Florence—*locale* GA-3
Florence—*locale* ID-8
Florence—*locale* IL-6
Florence—*locale* IA-7
Florence—*locale* NJ-2
Florence—*locale* OH-6
Florence—*locale* TN-4
Florence—*other* KY-4
**Florence**—*pop pl* AL-4
**Florence**—*pop pl* AZ-5
**Florence**—*pop pl* CA-9
**Florence**—*pop pl* CO-8
**Florence**—*pop pl* (2) IL-6
**Florence**—*pop pl* IN-6
**Florence**—*pop pl* KS-7
**Florence**—*pop pl* KY-4
**Florence**—*pop pl* LA-4
**Florence**—*pop pl* MD-2
**Florence**—*pop pl* MA-1
**Florence**—*pop pl* MN-6
**Florence**—*pop pl* MS-4
**Florence**—*pop pl* MO-7
**Florence**—*pop pl* MT-8
**Florence**—*pop pl* NJ-2
**Florence**—*pop pl* NY-2
**Florence**—*pop pl* (2) NC-3
**Florence**—*pop pl* (4) OH-6
**Florence**—*pop pl* OR-9
**Florence**—*pop pl* PA-2
**Florence**—*pop pl* SC-3
**Florence**—*pop pl* SD-7
**Florence**—*pop pl* TX-5
**Florence**—*pop pl* VT-1
**Florence**—*pop pl* WA-9
**Florence**—*pop pl* WI-6
Florence—*uninc pl* PA-2
Florence, Fred, Hall—*hist pl* TX-5
Florence, Lake—*lake* AK-9
Florence, Lake—*lake* (6) FL-3
Florence, Lake—*lake* GA-3
Florence, Lake—*lake* MN-6
Florence, Lake—*lake* MT-8
Florence, Lake—*lake* (2) NY-2
Florence, Lake—*lake* SC-3
Florence, Lake—*lake* SD-7
Florence, Lake—*reservoir* AR-4
Florence, Lake—*reservoir* UT-8
Florence, Mount—*summit* CA-9
Florence, Point—*cape* NY-2
Florence Apartments—*hist pl* PA-2
Florence Ave Ch—*church* NC-3
Florence Ave Sch—*school* CA-9
Florence Ave Sch—*school* NJ-2
*Florence Baptist Church* AL-4
Florence Basin—*basin* ID-8
Florence Basin—*basin* NV-8
Florence Bay—*bay* AK-9
Florence Bay—*bay* MI-6
Florence Bend—*bend* IA-7
Florence Bend—*bend* NE-7
Florence Bend—*channel* NJ-2
Florence Bend—*channel* PA-2
*Florence Bethel Presbyterian Church* AL-4
Florence Black Sch—*school* TX-5
Florence Blvd Ch of Christ—*church* AL-4
*Florence Blvd Interchange* AZ-5
Florence Blvd Missionary Baptist Ch—*church* AL-4
*Florence Bowser Primary School* VA-3
Florence Branch—*stream* GA-3
Florence Bridge—*other* MI-6
Florence Bridge (historical)—*bridge* AL-4
Florence Cabin—*locale* OR-9
Florence Cabiniss Lake—*reservoir* AL-4
Florence Cabiniss Lake Dam—*dam* AL-4
Florence Canal—*canal* AL-4
Florence Canal—*canal* AZ-5
Florence Canal—*canal* LA-4
Florence Canal—*canal* MT-8
Florence Canyon—*valley* NV-8
Florence Canyon—*valley* WY-8
Florence-Carlton Cem—*cemetery* MT-8
Florence-Carlton Sch—*school* MT-8
Florence Casa Grande Canal—*canal* AZ-5
Florence Casa Grande Canal Extension—*canal* AZ-5
Florence (CCD)—*cens area* AL-4
Florence (CCD)—*cens area* AZ-5
Florence (CCD)—*cens area* KY-4
Florence (CCD)—*cens area* SC-3

Florence (CCD)—*cens area* TX-5
*Florence Cem* AL-4
Florence Cem—*cemetery* (2) AL-4
Florence Cem—*cemetery* AZ-5
Florence Cem—*cemetery* GA-3
Florence Cem—*cemetery* (2) MS-4
Florence Cem—*cemetery* (2) OH-6
Florence Cem—*cemetery* OK-5
Florence Ch—*church* AL-4
Florence Ch—*church* MI-6
Florence Ch—*church* MS-4
Florence Ch—*church* SC-3
Florence Ch—*church* TX-5
*Florence Chapel* TN-4
Florence Ch of Christ—*church* MS-4
Florence Christian Acad—*school* AL-4
Florence City-County Airp—*airport* SC-3
Florence City Hall—*building* AL-4
Florence City Water Reservoirs—*reservoir* CO-8
Florence Coffee House—*hist pl* LA-4
Florence Corners Sch—*hist pl* OH-6
Florence-Council On The Iowa Site—*hist pl* IA-7
**Florence (County)**—*pop pl* SC-3
**Florence (County)**—*pop pl* WI-6
Florence County Courthouse and Jail—*hist pl* WI-6
Florence Creek—*stream* (2) AK-9
Florence Creek—*stream* CA-9
Florence Creek—*stream* GA-3
Florence Creek—*stream* NY-2
Florence Creek—*stream* (3) OR-9
Florence Creek—*stream* (2) UT-8
Florence Creek—*stream* WA-9
Florence Creek Lake—*lake* AK-9
Florence Crittenden Home—*park* AZ-5
Florence Crittenton Home—*hist pl* AR-4
Florence Diversion Dam—*dam* AZ-5
Florence Division—*civil* AL-4
Florence Elem Sch—*school* AZ-5
Florence Elem Sch—*school* KS-7
Florence Elem Sch—*school* MS-4
Florence Elem Sch—*school* NC-3
Florence Falls—*falls* MT-8
Florence Fay Elem Sch—*school* IN-6
Florence Ferry (historical)—*locale* AL-4
Florence Golf and Country Club—*other* AL-4
Florence-Graham—*CDP* CA-9
Florence Gulch—*valley* AK-9
Florence Hill—*locale* NY-2
Florence Hill—*locale* TX-5
**Florence Hill**—*pop pl* NV-8
Florence Hill—*summit* NV-8
Florence (historical)—*locale* SD-7
**Florence (historical)**—*pop pl* (2) SD-7
Florence Hollow—*valley* TN-4
**Florence Hollow Subdivision**—*pop pl* UT-8
Florence HS—*school* MS-4
Florence HS (historical)—*school* AL-4
*Florence Island* AL-4
Florence Island—*island* AK-9
Florence Island—*island* MI-6
Florence Island—*island* NY-2
Florence Islands—*island* AK-9
Florence JHS—*school* AL-4
Florence Junction—*locale* AZ-5
**Florence Junction**—*pop pl* VT-1
Florence Junction Airp—*airport* AZ-5
Florence Lake—*lake* AK-9
Florence Lake—*lake* (2) CA-9
Florence Lake—*lake* CO-8
Florence Lake—*lake* FL-3
Florence Lake—*lake* ID-8
Florence Lake—*lake* (2) MI-6
Florence Lake—*lake* (2) MN-6
Florence Lake—*lake* MT-8
Florence Lake—*lake* ND-7
Florence Lake—*lake* (2) WA-9
Florence Lake—*lake* WI-6
Florence Lake—*lake* (2) WY-8
Florence Lake—*reservoir* CA-9
Florence Lake—*reservoir* PA-2
Florence Lake Natl Wildlife Ref—*park* ND-7
**Florence Lake Township**—*pop pl* ND-7
*Florence Landing* DE-2
Florence Landing—*locale* LA-4
Florence Landing (historical)—*locale* AL-4
Florence Landing Rec Area—*park* GA-3
Florence Lauderdale Industrial Park—*locale* AL-4
Florence Lookout Tower—*locale* WI-6
Florence Mack Mine—*mine* CA-9
Florence Memorial Ch—*church* WV-2
*Florence Methodist Church* MS-4
Florence Milit Reservation—*military* AZ-5
Florence Mill—*hist pl* CT-1
Florence Mill Hollow—*valley* AL-4
*Florence Mine* NV-8
Florence Mine—*mine* CA-9
Florence Mine—*mine* MT-8
Florence Mine—*mine* (2) NV-8
Florence Mine—*mine* SD-7
Florence Mine Number 1—*mine* NV-8
Florence Municipal Airp—*airport* OR-9
Florence Municipal Park—*park* AL-4
Florence Nellie Mine—*mine* CO-8
Florence Park—*park* IA-7
Florence Park—*park* NE-7
**Florence Park Addition (subdivision)**—*pop pl* UT-8
Florence Pass—*gap* WY-8
*Florence Peak* CO-8
Florence Peak—*summit* CA-9
Florence Peak—*summit* WA-9
Florence Picnic Area—*locale* CO-8
Florence Plaza—*locale* MA-1
Florence Plaza Shop Ctr—*locale* AL-4
Florence Pond—*lake* MA-1
Florence Pond—*lake* MI-6
Florence Pond—*lake* NY-2
Florence Post Office—*building* MS-4
Florence Post Office (historical)—*building* MS-4
Florence Public Library—*building* MS-4
Florence Range—*channel* NJ-2
Florence Range—*channel* PA-2
*Florence Retarding Dam* AZ-5
Florence-Roebling—*CDP* NJ-2
Florence Sch—*school* CA-9
Florence Sch—*school* MI-6
Florence Sch—*school* NE-7

Fog Creek—*stream* ... SD-7
Fogel—*locale* ... AR-4
Fogel—*locale* ... OK-5
Fogelberg Lake—*lake* ... MN-6
Fogelin Hill—*summit* ... ME-1
Fogelin Pond—*lake* ... ME-1
Fogelman Cem—*cemetery* ... TX-5
Fogelman Dam—*dam* ... TN-4
Fogelman Lake—*reservoir* ... TN-4
**Fogelmarks Corners**—*pop pl* ... CT-1
Fogelpole Cave—*cave* ... IL-6
**Fogelsville**—*pop pl* ... PA-2
Fogelsville Elem Sch—*school* ... PA-2
Fogelsville Pond—*lake* ... PA-2
*Fogen* ... FM-9
Fogenberg Pass—*gap* ... AK-9
*Foger Lake* ... MN-6
Fogertown—*locale* ... KY-4
Fogertown Sch—*school* ... KY-4
Fogerty Park—*park* ... MO-7
Fogey Cave—*cave* ... MO-7
Fogey Cave Hollow—*valley* ... MO-7
*Fogey Creek* ... MT-8
Fogg Art Museum—*building* ... MA-1
Fogg Art Museum—*hist pl* ... MA-1
Fogg Bldg—*hist pl* ... MA-1
Fogg Brook—*stream* (3) ... ME-1
Fogg Brook—*stream* (2) ... NH-1
Fogg Butte—*summit* ... ID-8
Fogg Butte Well—*well* ... ID-8
Fogg Cabin—*locale* ... AZ-5
Fogg Cem—*cemetery* (2) ... ME-1
Fogg Cem—*cemetery* (2) ... TN-4
**Fogg Corner**—*pop pl* ... NH-1
**Fogg Corners**—*pop pl* ... NH-1
Fogg Cove—*bay* ... ME-1
Fogg Farm—*locale* ... ME-1
Fogg Gulch—*valley* ... CA-9
*Fogg Hill* ... NH-1
Fogg Hill—*summit* ... ID-8
Fogg Hill—*summit* ... ME-1
Fogg Hill—*summit* (2) ... NH-1
**Fogg (historical)**—*pop pl* ... TN-4
Fogg Hollow—*valley* (2) ... TN-4
Fogg Hollow Mines (surface)—*mine* ... TN-4
Fog Glacier—*glacier* ... AK-9
Fogg Lake—*lake* ... ID-8
Fogg Lake—*lake* ... MI-6
Fogg Library—*building* ... MA-1
Fogg Library—*hist pl* ... MA-1
Fogg Millsite Well—*well* ... ID-8
Fogg Mtn—*summit* ... ME-1
Fogg Mtn—*summit* ... VA-3
Fogg Point—*cape* ... ME-1
Fogg Pond—*lake* (2) ... ME-1
Fogg Post Office (historical)—*building* ... TN-4
Foggs Corner—*locale* (2) ... ME-1
Foggs Hill—*summit* ... ME-1
Foggs Ridge—*ridge* ... NH-1
Fog Gulch—*valley* ... WY-8
Foggy Bay—*bay* ... AK-9
Foggy Bottom - GWU Metro Station—*locale* ... DC-2
Foggy Bottom Hist Dist—*hist pl* ... DC-2
Foggy Bottoms—*bend* ... MD-2
Foggy Bottoms Gut—*gut* ... MD-2
Foggy Cape—*cape* ... AK-9
Foggy Creek—*stream* ... OR-9
Foggy Creek Camp—*locale* ... OR-9
Foggy Dew Campground—*locale* ... WA-9
Foggy Dew Creek—*stream* ... WA-9
Foggy Dew Falls—*falls* ... WA-9
Foggy Dew Ridge—*ridge* ... WA-9
Foggy Flat—*flat* ... WA-9
Foggy Island—*island* ... AK-9
Foggy Island Bay—*bay* ... AK-9
Foggy Lake—*lake* ... MI-6
Foggy Lake—*lake* ... WA-9
Foggy Park—*flat* ... CO-8
Foggy Pass—*gap* ... AK-9
Foggy Pass—*gap* (2) ... WA-9
Foggy Peak—*summit* ... WA-9
Foggy Point—*cape* ... AK-9
Foggytop Mtn—*summit* ... AK-9
Fog Hill—*summit* ... NY-2
Fog Island—*island* (2) ... ME-1
Fog Lake—*lake* ... AK-9
Fog Lake—*lake* (2) ... MN-6
Fog Lakes—*lake* ... AK-9
*Fogland* ... RI-1
Fogland Point—*cape* ... RI-1
**Fogland Point**—*pop pl* ... RI-1
Fogleman Branch—*stream* ... VA-3
Fogleman Cem—*cemetery* ... MO-7
Fogleman Cem—*cemetery* ... VA-3
Foglemans Lake—*reservoir* ... NC-3
Foglemans Lake Dam—*dam* ... NC-3
Fogleman (Township of)—*fmr MCD* ... AR-4
*Fogles* ... PA-2
Foglesong Park—*park* ... CA-9
Foglesong Valley—*valley* ... VA-3
*Foglesville* ... PA-2
Fogle Tank—*reservoir* ... AZ-5
Fog Mountain Saddle—*gap* ... ID-8
Fog Mtn—*summit* ... ID-8
Fogol—*summit* ... FM-9
Fogon Windmill—*locale* ... NM-5
Fog Point—*cape* ... GA-3
Fog Point—*cape* ... MD-2
Fog Point Cove—*bay* ... MD-2
Fog River—*stream* ... AK-9
*Fogs Land* ... RI-1
Fogtown—*locale* ... PA-2
**Fog Town**—*pop pl* ... TX-5
*Fogus Creek* ... ID-8
Fogwell Cem—*cemetery* ... IN-6
Fohl Creek—*stream* ... ID-8
Fohlin Creek—*stream* ... AK-9
Fohl Picnic Area—*locale* ... ID-8
Fohn Hill—*summit* ... TX-5
Fohs Canal—*canal* ... LA-4
Fohs Hall—*hist pl* ... KY-4
Foidel Canyon Sch—*hist pl* ... CO-8
Foidel Creek—*stream* ... CO-8
Foidel Sch—*school* ... CO-8
**Foil**—*pop pl* ... MO-7
Foilage Park—*park* ... LA-4
Foil Cem—*cemetery* ... MS-4
*Foilliet Mountain* ... OK-5
Foim—*tunnel* ... FM-9
Foin Gulch—*valley* ... CO-8
Foir—*bar* ... FM-9
**Fola**—*pop pl* ... WV-2
Foland Creek—*stream* ... OR-9
Folau Point—*cape* ... AS-9
**Folcroft**—*pop pl* ... PA-2
Folcroft Borough—*civil* ... PA-2
Foldager Slough—*lake* ... SD-7
**Foldahl (Township of)**—*pop pl* ... MN-6
Folded Hills Ranch—*locale* ... CA-9
Folden Cem—*cemetery* ... OH-6
Folden Ch—*church* (2) ... MN-6
**Folden (Township of)**—*pop pl* ... MN-6
Folden Woods State Wildlife Mngmt Area—*park* ... MN-6
Fold of Christ Apostolic Ch—*church* ... IN-6
Folette Spring—*spring* ... AZ-5
*Foley* ... WV-2
Foley—*locale* ... OK-5
Foley—*locale* ... PA-2
Foley—*locale* ... SD-7
Foley—*other* ... WV-2
**Foley**—*pop pl* ... AL-4
**Foley**—*pop pl* ... FL-3
**Foley**—*pop pl* ... IN-6
**Foley**—*pop pl* (2) ... LA-4
**Foley**—*pop pl* ... MN-6
**Foley**—*pop pl* ... MO-7
**Foley**—*pop pl* ... SD-7
Foley, James W., House—*hist pl* ... ND-7
Foley, Jennie, Bldg—*hist pl* ... IL-6
Foley, John, House—*hist pl* ... IA-7
Foley, Michael, Cottage—*hist pl* ... MA-1
Foley, Richard T., Site (36GR52)—*hist pl* ... PA-2
Foley, Stephan A., House—*hist pl* ... IL-6
Foley, W. L., Bldg—*hist pl* ... TX-5
Foley Bldg—*hist pl* ... OR-9
Foley Branch—*stream* ... PA-2
Foley Branch—*stream* ... TN-4
Foley Branch—*stream* ... TX-5
Foley Branch—*stream* ... VA-3
Foley Branch—*stream* ... WI-6
Foley Brook—*stream* ... MN-6
Foley-Brower-Bohmer House—*hist pl* ... MN-6
Foley Butte—*summit* ... OR-9
Foley Canyon—*valley* ... CA-9
Foley (CCD)—*cens area* ... AL-4
Foley Cem—*cemetery* ... AL-4
Foley Cem—*cemetery* ... OH-6
Foley Cem—*cemetery* (2) ... WV-2
Foley Corner—*locale* ... PA-2
Foley Creek—*stream* ... AK-9
Foley Creek—*stream* ... CA-9
Foley Creek—*stream* (2) ... MI-6
Foley Creek—*stream* ... MS-4
Foley Creek—*stream* (3) ... OR-9
Foley Creek Campground—*locale* ... MI-6
Foley Dam—*dam* ... AZ-5
Foley Division—*civil* ... AL-4
Foley Draft—*valley* ... PA-2
Foley Drain—*canal* ... MI-6
Foley Gap—*gap* ... VA-3
Foley Gulch—*valley* ... OR-9
Foley Hall—*hist pl* ... IN-6
Foley Hill—*summit* ... VA-3
**Foley (historical)**—*pop pl* ... OR-9
Foley Hollow—*valley* (2) ... KY-4
Foley Hot Springs—*spring* ... OR-9
Foley HS—*school* ... AL-4
Foley Junction—*building* ... FL-3
Foley Lake—*lake* ... OR-9
Foley Lakes Rsvr—*reservoir* ... OR-9
Foley Lookout Tower—*tower* ... FL-3
Foley Machinery—*airport* ... NJ-2
Foley Mound—*summit* ... MN-6
Foley Mound Group—*hist pl* ... WI-6
Foley MS—*school* ... AL-4
Foley Mtn—*summit* ... SD-7
Foley Municipal Airp—*airport* ... AL-4
Foley Outlet—*stream* ... ME-1
Foley Peak—*summit* ... OR-9
Foley Pond—*lake* ... ME-1
Foley Pond—*lake* ... MA-1
Foley Public Access—*locale* ... MO-7
Foley Ridge—*ridge* ... KY-4
Foley Ridge—*ridge* (2) ... OR-9
Foley Ridge Trail—*trail* ... OR-9
Foley Sch—*school* ... AL-4
Foley Sch—*school* (2) ... MI-6
Foley Sch—*school* ... MN-6
Foley Sch (historical)—*school* ... MO-7
Foleys Dam—*dam* ... PA-2
Foleys Island—*island* ... MI-6
Foley Slough—*stream* ... OR-9
Foley Spring—*spring* (2) ... OR-9
Foley Springs—*locale* ... OR-9
Foleys Siding—*locale* ... PA-2
Foley State Wildlife Mngmt Area—*park* ... MN-6
Foley Station—*building* ... FL-3
Foley Station (historical)—*building* ... PA-2
*Folger* ... MA-1
Folger—*locale* ... AK-9
Folger Cem—*cemetery* ... SC-3
Folger Creek—*stream* ... AK-9
Folger Ditch—*canal* ... IN-6
Folger Gulch—*valley* ... CO-8
Folger Hill—*summit* ... MA-1
**Folger (historical)**—*pop pl* ... TN-4
Folger Mine—*mine* ... SD-7
Folger Park—*park* ... DC-2
Folger Peak—*summit* ... CA-9
Folger Point—*cape* ... MA-1
Folger Post Office (historical)—*building* ... TN-4
Folger Shakespeare Library—*hist pl* ... DC-2
*Folgers Hill* ... MA-1
Folger Slough—*stream* ... AK-9
Folgers Marsh—*swamp* ... MA-1
Foliart Mtn—*summit* ... OK-5
**Folk**—*pop pl* ... MO-7
Folk Chapel—*church* ... AR-4
Folk Creek—*stream* ... OR-9
**Folkenberg**—*pop pl* ... OR-9
Folker Township—*civil* ... MO-7
Folkes Cem—*cemetery* (2) ... MS-4
*Folkes Cemetery* ... AL-4
Folkes Creek—*stream* ... MS-4
Folkingham Cove—*bay* ... ME-1
Folkner Branch—*stream* ... NC-3
Folk Pond—*lake* ... MO-7
Folk Pond—*lake* ... SC-3
*Folk Run* ... IN-6
*Folk Run* ... PA-2
Folks Cem—*cemetery* ... MS-4
Folk Sch—*school* ... SC-3
Folks Creek—*stream* ... FL-3
Folks Creek—*stream* ... IL-6
Folks Park—*park* ... GA-3
Folks Siding—*locale* ... OH-6
**Folkston**—*pop pl* ... GA-3
Folkston (CCD)—*cens area* ... GA-3
Folkstone—*locale* ... NC-3
**Follansbee**—*pop pl* ... WV-2
Follansbee House—*hist pl* ... MA-1
Follansbee (Magisterial District)—*fmr MCD* ... WV-2
Follen Community Church—*hist pl* ... MA-1
**Follen Heights**—*pop pl* ... MA-1
Follensby Clear Pond—*lake* ... NY-2
Follensby Junior Pond—*lake* ... NY-2
Follensby Pond—*lake* ... NY-2
*Follens Pond* ... MA-1
Follen Street Hist Dist—*hist pl* ... MA-1
Follet Creek—*stream* ... ID-8
Follet Lake—*lake* ... TX-5
Follets Island—*island* ... TX-5
**Follett**—*pop pl* ... TX-5
Follett (CCD)—*cens area* ... TX-5
Follett Cem—*cemetery* ... MI-6
Follett Creek—*stream* ... AL-4
Follette Creek—*stream* ... IN-6
Follette Sch—*school* ... SD-7
Follett House—*hist pl* ... VT-1
Follett-Moss-Moss Residences—*hist pl* ... OH-6
**Folletts**—*pop pl* (2) ... IA-7
Folletts Brook—*stream* ... NH-1
Follett Slough—*gut* ... MN-6
Follett Stone Arch Bridge Hist Dist—*hist pl* ... VT-1
Folley—*locale* ... TX-5
Folley Branch—*stream* ... NC-3
Folley Branch—*stream* ... TX-5
Folley Canyon—*valley* ... TX-5
Folley Canyon—*valley* ... UT-8
Folley Creek—*stream* ... AL-4
Folley Creek—*stream* ... MS-4
Folley Park—*flat* ... TX-5
Folley Park—*park* ... AZ-5
Folley Ridge—*ridge* ... UT-8
Folley Spring—*spring* ... UT-8
Follies State Wildlife Mngmt Area—*park* ... MN-6
*Folliet Mtn* ... OK-5
Follins Pond—*lake* ... MA-1
Follis Cem—*cemetery* ... IL-6
Follis Chapel—*church* ... TN-4
*Follis Chapel Methodist Ch* ... TN-4
Foll Lake—*lake* ... FL-3
Follmer, Clogg and Company Umbrella Factory—*hist pl* ... PA-2
Follmer Ch—*church* ... PA-2
Follmer Sch (abandoned)—*school* ... PA-2
Followell Creek—*stream* ... KY-4
Followers Church, The—*church* ... OK-5
Followfield Grange—*locale* ... PA-2
Follows Camp—*locale* ... CA-9
*Foll Pond* ... FL-3
*Follstown* ... PA-2
Folly—*hist pl* ... VA-3
Folly—*locale* ... VA-3
**Folly**—*pop pl* ... NC-3
Folly, Mount—*summit* ... VA-3
Folly, The—*area* ... SC-3
Folly, The—*island* ... ME-1
Folly Beach—*beach* ... SC-3
**Folly Beach**—*pop pl* ... SC-3
Folly Branch—*stream* ... MD-2
Folly Bridge—*bridge* ... NC-3
Folly Brook—*stream* (2) ... CT-1
Folly Castle Hist Dist—*hist pl* ... VA-3
Folly Cem—*cemetery* ... LA-4
*Folly Cove* ... MA-1
Folly Cove—*cove* ... MA-1
*Folly Cove Village* ... MA-1
Folly Creek—*stream* ... MN-6
Folly Creek—*stream* ... NC-3
Folly Creek—*stream* (2) ... SC-3
Folly Creek—*stream* ... VA-3
Folly Creek Landing—*locale* ... VA-3
Folly Ditch—*canal* ... NC-3
*Follyfarm* ... OR-9
Folly Farm Flat—*flat* ... OR-9
Folly Farm (site)—*locale* ... OR-9
**Folly Field**—*pop pl* ... SC-3
*Folly Field Beach* ... SC-3
**Folly Fork**—*pop pl* ... NC-3
Folly Gap—*gap* ... NC-3
Folly Gap—*gap* ... SC-3
Folly Grove Sch—*school* ... IL-6
Folly Hill—*summit* ... MA-1
Folly Hill Rsvr—*reservoir* ... MA-1
Folly House—*hist pl* ... NJ-2
*Folly Island* ... SC-3
Folly Island—*island* (2) ... ME-1
Folly Island—*island* ... SC-3
Folly Island Channel—*channel* ... SC-3
Folly Lake—*lake* ... MN-6
Folly Landing—*locale* ... RI-1
Folly Ledge—*bar* ... ME-1
Folly Lick Branch—*stream* ... VA-3
*Folly Mill Creek* ... VA-3
Folly Mills—*locale* ... VA-3
Folly Mills Creek—*stream* ... VA-3
Folly Peak—*summit* ... CA-9
*Folly Point* ... MA-1
Folly Point—*cape* ... MA-1
Folly Point—*cape* ... NJ-2
Folly Pond—*lake* ... CT-1
Folly Pond—*lake* ... ME-1
Folly Pond—*lake* ... MA-1
Folly Pond—*reservoir* ... ME-1
Folly Ranch—*locale* ... WY-8
Folly River—*gut* ... GA-3
Folly River—*stream* ... SC-3
Folly Run—*stream* ... MD-2
Folly Run—*stream* ... WV-2
Folly Swamp—*stream* ... NC-3
Folly Swamp—*swamp* ... SC-3
Folly Works Brook—*stream* ... CT-1
Folmar Dam—*dam* ... AL-4
Folmars Pond—*reservoir* (2) ... AL-4
Folmer Ponds—*reservoir* ... AL-4
*Fololuk* ... FM-9
Folse, Bayou—*stream* ... LA-4
*Folsom* ... KS-7
Folsom—*airport* ... NJ-2
Folsom—*locale* ... AL-4
Folsom—*locale* ... IA-7
Folsom—*locale* ... OK-5
Folsom—*locale* ... SD-7
Folsom—*locale* (2) ... TX-5
Folsom—*locale* ... VT-1
Folsom—*locale* ... WI-6
**Folsom**—*pop pl* ... AL-4
**Folsom**—*pop pl* ... CA-9
**Folsom**—*pop pl* ... GA-3
**Folsom**—*pop pl* ... KY-4
**Folsom**—*pop pl* ... LA-4
**Folsom**—*pop pl* ... NJ-2
**Folsom**—*pop pl* ... NM-5
**Folsom**—*pop pl* ... OH-6
**Folsom**—*pop pl* ... PA-2
**Folsom**—*pop pl* ... WV-2
Folsom, W.H.C., House—*hist pl* ... WI-6
Folsom Bluff—*cliff* ... MO-7
Folsom Branch—*stream* ... GA-3
Folsom Bridge—*bridge* (2) ... AL-4
Folsom Brook—*stream* ... ME-1
Folsom Brook—*stream* ... NH-1
Folsom Brook—*stream* ... VT-1
Folsom (CCD)—*cens area* ... AL-4
Folsom (CCD)—*cens area* ... CA-9
Folsom Cem—*cemetery* ... FL-3
Folsom Cem—*cemetery* ... GA-3
Folsom Cem—*cemetery* ... MS-4
Folsom Cem—*cemetery* ... NM-5
Folsom Ch—*church* ... LA-4
Folsom Coulee—*valley* ... MT-8
Folsom Creek—*stream* ... GA-3
Folsom Creek—*stream* ... KS-7
Folsom Creek—*stream* ... NY-2
Folsom Creek—*stream* ... TX-5
**Folsomdale**—*pop pl* ... KY-4
**Folsomdale**—*pop pl* ... NY-2
Folsomdale Cem—*cemetery* ... NY-2
*Folsom Dam* ... CA-9
Folsom Dam—*dam* ... CA-9
Folsom Depot—*hist pl* ... CA-9
Folsom Division—*civil* ... AL-4
Folsome (historical)—*locale* ... SD-7
*Folsom Elementary School* ... AL-4
Folsome Mill Creek—*stream* ... AL-4
Folsom Falls—*falls* ... NM-5
Folsom Farm—*locale* ... ME-1
Folsom Field—*park* ... CO-8
Folsom Field (airport)—*airport* ... AL-4
Folsom Highway Ch—*church* ... OK-5
Folsom Hill—*summit* ... WA-9
Folsom Hills—*summit* ... TX-5
Folsom Hotel—*hist pl* ... NM-5
Folsom Island—*island* ... MN-6
Folsom Junction—*locale* ... CA-9
Folsom Lake—*lake* ... IA-7
Folsom Lake—*lake* ... WA-9
Folsom Lake—*lake* ... WI-6
Folsom Lake—*reservoir* ... CA-9
Folsom Lake State Rec Area—*park* ... CA-9
Folsom Lateral—*canal* ... ID-8
Folsom Mission Sch—*school* ... LA-4
Folsom Park—*park* ... MN-6
Folsom Peak—*summit* ... WY-8
Folsom Point Diggings—*locale* ... CO-8
Folsom Pond—*lake* (2) ... ME-1
Folsom Pond—*lake* ... MA-1
Folsom Post Office (historical)—*building* ... AL-4
Folsom Powerhouse—*hist pl* ... CA-9
*Folsom Reservoir* ... CA-9
Folsom Ridge—*ridge* ... CA-9
Folsom Ridge—*ridge* ... ID-8
Folsom Ridge—*ridge* ... ME-1
Folsom Rosenwald Sch—*school* ... LA-4
Folsom Sch—*school* ... AL-4
Folsom Sch—*school* ... MI-6
Folsom Sch—*school* ... VT-1
Folsoms Creek—*stream* ... AL-4
*Folsom Siding* ... IA-7
Folsom Site—*hist pl* ... NM-5
Folsom Spring—*spring* ... NV-8
Folsoms Spring—*spring* ... OR-9
Folsom State Monmt—*park* ... NM-5
*Folsom State Prison* ... CA-9
Folsom State Prison (Represa PO)—*building* ... CA-9
**Folsom (Township of)**—*pop pl* ... MN-6
**Folsomville**—*pop pl* ... IN-6
Folsom Wildlife Public Hunting Area—*area* ... IA-7
Folson Island—*island* ... WI-6
*Folson Pond* ... MA-1
**Folsons Addition (subdivision)**—*pop pl* ... UT-8
Folston Lake—*lake* ... MN-6
**Folstown**—*pop pl* ... PA-2
Folsum Branch—*stream* ... AL-4
*Folsum Creek* ... GA-3
*Foltz* ... IN-6
*Foltz* ... PA-2
Foltz—*other* ... PA-2
**Foltz**—*pop pl* ... MS-4
Foltz Creek—*stream* (2) ... VA-3
Foltz Sch—*school* ... IL-6
Foltz Sch—*school* ... IN-6
Foltz Sch—*school* ... PA-2
Folwell—*locale* ... NJ-2
Folwell JHS—*school* ... MN-6
Folwell Park—*park* ... MN-6
Folwell Sch—*school* ... MN-6
*Folwix Brook* ... CT-1
Folwix Brook—*stream* ... CT-1
**Fombell**—*pop pl* ... PA-2
**Fomby**—*pop pl* ... AR-4
Fombys Ferry (historical)—*locale* ... AL-4
**Fomer**—*pop pl* ... MA-1
**Fomseng**—*pop pl* ... FM-9
Fonce Flat—*flat* ... CO-8
Fonce Lake—*lake* ... CO-8
Fonce Wash—*valley* ... CO-8
**Foncine**—*pop pl* ... TX-5
Fonda—*locale* ... WY-8
**Fonda**—*pop pl* ... IA-7
**Fonda**—*pop pl* ... NY-2
**Fonda**—*pop pl* ... ND-7
**Fonda**—*pop pl* ... VT-1
Fonda—*uninc pl* ... WI-6
Fonda (historical)—*locale* ... KS-7
Fonda Junction—*other* ... VT-1
Fonda Lake—*lake* ... MI-6
**Fondale**—*pop pl* ... LA-4
Fonda Point—*cape* ... WY-8
Fonda Rsvr—*reservoir* ... NY-2
Fond Branch—*stream* ... TN-4
*Fond Du Lac* ... MN-6
**Fond du Lac**—*pop pl* ... MN-6
**Fond du Lac**—*pop pl* ... WI-6
**Fond du Lac (County)**—*pop pl* ... WI-6
Fond du Lac Hosp—*hospital* ... MN-6
Fond Du Lac Ind Res—*reserve* ... MN-6
Fond Du Lac Park—*park* ... MN-6
Fond du Lac River—*stream* ... WI-6
Fond Du Lac State For—*forest* ... MN-6
**Fond du Lac (Town of)**—*pop pl* ... WI-6
**Fonde**—*pop pl* ... KY-4
Fonde Park—*park* ... TX-5
Fonder Cem—*cemetery* ... CO-8
Fondillos Draw—*valley* ... CO-8
Fondis—*locale* ... CO-8
Fondo—*locale* ... CA-9
Fondren—*uninc pl* ... MS-4
Fondren—*uninc pl* ... TX-5
Fondren Cem—*cemetery* ... MS-4
Fondren Cem—*cemetery* ... TX-5
Fondren Ch—*church* ... AR-4
Fondren Presbyterian Ch—*church* ... MS-4
Fondren Sch—*school* ... TX-5
Fondren Temple—*church* ... TN-4
**Fon-Du-Lac**—*pop pl* ... IL-6
Fondulac Cem—*cemetery* ... IL-6
*Fondulac Dam* ... IL-6
Fondulac Dam—*dam* ... IL-6
Fondulac Golf Course—*other* ... IL-6
Fondulac Park—*park* ... IL-6
**Fondulac (Township of)**—*pop pl* ... IL-6
F One Ditch—*canal* ... MT-8
Fones Canyon—*valley* ... OR-9
Fones Cliffs—*cliff* ... VA-3
Fones House—*hist pl* ... AR-4
Fones Pond—*lake* ... RI-1
Foneswood—*locale* ... VA-3
*Foney Bush Creek* ... MS-4
Fongen—*locale* ... FM-9
Fon Gera, Bayou—*gut* ... LA-4
Fong Wah Bar—*bar* ... CA-9
Fong Wah Gulch—*valley* ... CA-9
Fonner Run—*stream* ... PA-2
*Fono* ... FM-9
Fonokuk—*island* ... FM-9
*Fonomo* ... FM-9
*Fonomu* ... FM-9
Fono Mu—*island* ... FM-9
Fononang—*island* ... FM-9
Fononuk—*island* ... FM-9
*Fono Penges* ... FM-9
Fonotok—*gut* ... FM-9
*Fonou* ... FM-9
Fonouk—*island* ... FM-9
Fons Butte—*summit* ... CA-9
Fonso Branch—*stream* ... MO-7
Fonsylvania—*hist pl* ... MS-4
Font—*locale* ... PA-2
Fontail Creek—*stream* ... ID-8
*Fontainbleau* ... MS-4
*Fontaine* ... MS-4
Fontaine—*locale* ... PA-2
**Fontaine**—*pop pl* ... AR-4
**Fontaine**—*pop pl* ... VA-3
Fontaine, Lake—*lake* ... FL-3
Fontaine Bldg—*hist pl* ... GA-3
*Fontainebleau* ... MS-4
**Fontainebleau**—*pop pl* ... MS-4
Fontainebleau Post Office (historical)—*building* ... MS-4
Fontainebleau State Park—*park* ... LA-4
**Fontaine Bleu Subdivision**—*pop pl* ... UT-8
Fontaine Ch—*church* ... VA-3
**Fontaine Claire Subdivision**—*pop pl* ... UT-8
*Fontaine Creek* ... NC-3
*Fontaine Creek* ... VA-3
Fontaine Creek Ch—*church* ... VA-3
Fontaine Ferry Park—*park* ... KY-4
Fontaine Island—*island* ... AK-9
Fontaine Park—*park* ... AL-4
**Fontaine Village (subdivision)**—*pop pl* ... AL-4
Fontal, Lake—*lake* ... WA-9
*Fontana* ... NC-3
**Fontana**—*pop pl* ... CA-9
**Fontana**—*pop pl* ... KS-7
**Fontana**—*pop pl* ... PA-2
**Fontana**—*pop pl* ... WI-6
Fontana Bird Park—*park* ... CA-9
Fontana Cem—*cemetery* ... IA-7
Fontana Ch—*church* ... PA-2
Fontana Christian Sch—*school* ... CA-9
Fontana Copper Mine—*mine* ... NC-3
*Fontana (corporate name Fontana on Geneva Lake)* ... WI-6
*Fontana Creek* ... AZ-5
Fontana Dam—*dam* (2) ... NC-3
**Fontana Dam**—*pop pl* ... NC-3
Fontana Dock—*locale* ... NC-3
Fontana Elem Sch—*school* ... KS-7
Fontana Farms Company Ranch House, Camp No. 1—*hist pl* ... CA-9
Fontana HS—*school* ... CA-9
Fontana JHS—*school* ... CA-9
Fontana Lake—*lake* ... IA-7
Fontana Lake—*reservoir* (2) ... NC-3
Fontanalis, Lake—*lake* ... WY-8
*Fontana Milldam* ... IA-7
**Fontana-On-Geneva-Lake (corporate name for Fontana)**—*pop pl* ... WI-6
Fontana Park—*park* ... IA-7
Fontana Pit and Groove Petroglyph Site—*hist pl* ... CA-9
Fontana Plaza (Shop Ctr)—*locale* ... FL-3
*Fontana Rsvr* ... NC-3
**Fontana Village**—*pop pl* ... NC-3
**Fontanelle**—*pop pl* ... IA-7
**Fontanelle**—*pop pl* ... NE-7
Fontanelle, Bayou—*gut* ... LA-4
Fontanelle Bank—*hist pl* ... NE-7
Fontanelle Bayou—*gut* ... LA-4
Fontanelle Cem—*cemetery* ... IA-7
Fontanelle Township Hall—*hist pl* ... NE-7
**Fontanet**—*pop pl* ... IN-6
*Fontania* ... KS-7
Fontania Ch—*church* ... LA-4
*Fontanilis Lake* ... CA-9
Fontanillis Lake—*lake* ... CA-9
Fontbonne Coll—*school* ... MO-7
Fontbonne Hall Sch—*school* ... NY-2
Fontbonne Hall Sch—*school* ... PA-2
Fonte—*area* ... GU-9
Fontella Post Office (historical)—*building* ... AL-4
**Fontenelle**—*pop pl* ... WY-8
Fontenelle Apartments—*hist pl* ... UT-8
Fontenelle Basin—*basin* ... WY-8
Fontenelle Creek—*stream* ... WY-8
Fontenelle Dam—*dam* ... WY-8
Fontenelle Forest Hist Dist—*hist pl* ... NE-7
Fontenelle Gap—*gap* ... WY-8
Fontenelle Hogbacks—*ridge* ... WY-8
Fontenelle Lakes—*lake* ... WY-8
Fontenelle Park—*park* ... NE-7
Fontenelle Plaza (Shop Ctr)—*locale* ... FL-3
Fontenelle Rec Area—*park* ... WY-8
Fontenelle Rsvr—*reservoir* ... WY-8
Fontenelle Sch—*school* ... NE-7
Fontenette-Durand Maison Dimanche—*hist pl* ... LA-4
**Fontenot**—*pop pl* ... LA-4
Fontenot, Alexandre, fils, House—*hist pl* ... LA-4
Fontenot Cem—*cemetery* (3) ... LA-4
**Fontenoy**—*pop pl* ... WI-6
Fonte River—*stream* ... GU-9
Fontez Creek—*stream* ... ID-8
Fonthill—*hist pl* ... PA-2
Fonthill—*locale* ... KY-4
**Font Hill**—*pop pl* ... MD-2
Fonthill, Mercer Museum and Moravian Pottery and Tile Works—*hist pl* ... PA-2
Fonthill Castle and the Administration Bldg of the College of Mount St. Vincent—*hist pl* ... NY-2
**Font Hill Manor**—*pop pl* ... MD-2
Fonti Flora Plantation—*hist pl* ... SC-3
Fontinalis Club—*other* ... MI-6
*Fontinalis Creek* ... MI-6
Font Lake—*lake* ... MI-6
Fonts Point—*cape* ... CA-9
Fonts Point Wash—*stream* ... CA-9
Font-Ubides House—*hist pl* ... PR-3
Fonuamock—*bar* ... FM-9
Fonuchu—*island* ... FM-9
Fonuenipim—*island* ... FM-9
*Fonuenipin* ... FM-9
Fonuenrenong—*bar* ... FM-9
Fonuenrue—*bar* ... FM-9
Fonum, Unun En—*bar* ... FM-9
Fonuou—*island* ... FM-9
**Fonville**—*pop pl* (2) ... NC-3
Fonville Cem—*cemetery* ... AR-4
Fonville JHS—*school* ... TX-5
Fon Wells—*well* ... TX-5
Fonwood Sch—*school* ... TX-5
Fonzo—*locale* ... WV-2
Food and Drug Administration Bldg—*building* ... DC-2
Foodco RR Station—*locale* ... FL-3
Food World Shop Ctr—*locale* ... NC-3
*Foogman Dam* ... ND-7
Fooks Cem—*cemetery* ... KY-4
*Fooks Pond* ... MD-2
*Foo'l* ... FM-9
Foo Lake—*lake* ... WI-6
*Fool Bay* ... LA-4
Fool Bear Creek—*stream* ... ND-7
Fool Brook—*stream* ... ME-1
*Fool Creek* ... PA-2
Fool Creek—*locale* ... UT-8
Fool Creek—*stream* ... AR-4
Fool Creek—*stream* ... CO-8
Fool Creek—*stream* ... ID-8
Fool Creek—*stream* ... MT-8
Fool Creek—*stream* ... OK-5
Fool Creek—*stream* ... TX-5
Fool Creek—*stream* ... UT-8
Fool Creek—*stream* ... WY-8
Fool Creek Basin—*basin* ... WY-8
Fool Creek Flat—*flat* ... UT-8
Fool Creek Number One Dam—*dam* ... UT-8
Fool Creek Number Two Dam—*dam* ... UT-8
Fool Creek Number Two Rsvr—*reservoir* ... UT-8
*Fool Creek Pass* ... UT-8
Fool Creek Peak—*summit* ... UT-8
Fool Creek Point—*ridge* ... UT-8
Fool Creek Rsvr No 1—*reservoir* ... UT-8
Fool Creek Trail—*trail* ... ID-8
Fool Gap—*gap* ... TX-5
Fool Gulch—*valley* ... CA-9
Fool Gulch Camp—*locale* ... CA-9
Foolhen Creek—*stream* (2) ... ID-8
Fool Hen Creek—*stream* ... MN-6
Foolhen Creek—*stream* ... MT-8
Fool Hen Creek—*stream* ... MT-8
Foolhen Creek—*stream* (2) ... MT-8
Foolhen Creek—*stream* ... WA-9
Fool Hen Creek—*stream* ... WA-9
Foolhen Creek Trail—*trail* ... MT-8
Fool Hen Hill—*locale* ... MT-8
*Foolhen Lake* ... MT-8
Fool Hen Lake—*lake* ... MN-6
Fool Hen Lake—*lake* ... MT-8
Foolhen Lake—*lake* ... MT-8
Fool Hen Lake—*lake* ... WA-9
Foolhen Meadows—*flat* ... ID-8
Foolhen Mountain Trail—*trail* ... MT-8
Foolhen Mtn—*summit* ... ID-8
Foolhen Mtn—*summit* (2) ... MT-8
Foolhen Ranger Cabin—*locale* ... MT-8
Foolhen Ridge—*ridge* ... MT-8
Foolhen Ridge Fire Trail (historical)—*trail* ... ID-8
Fool Hen Spring—*spring* ... OR-9
Foolhen Way—*trail* ... ID-8
*Fool Hollow* ... AZ-5
Fool Hollow—*valley* ... KY-4
Fool Hollow Dam—*dam* ... AZ-5
*Fool Hollow Draw* ... AZ-5
Fool Inlet—*bay* ... AK-9
Foolish Hill—*summit* ... MA-1
Foolish Lake—*lake* ... CA-9
Fool Island—*island* ... AK-9
Fool Killer, The—*summit* ... NH-1
Fool Lake—*lake* ... LA-4

Fords—*locale* LA-4
Fords—*locale* OK-5
**Fords**—*pop pl* NJ-2
Fords Arm—*bay* FL-3
Fords Bar—*locale* CA-9
Fords Bay—*bay* KY-4
**Fords Branch**—*pop pl* KY-4
Fords Branch—*stream* AR-4
Fords Branch—*stream* KY-4
Fords Branch—*stream* MO-7
**Fordsbush**—*pop pl* NY-2
Fords Cem—*cemetery* AL-4
Fords Cem—*cemetery* MS-4
Ford Sch—*school* CA-9
Ford Sch—*school* FL-3
Ford Sch—*school* ID-8
Ford Sch—*school* (2) IL-6
Ford Sch—*school* (3) MI-6
Ford Sch—*school* MS-4
Ford Sch—*school* NE-7
Ford Sch—*school* SC-3
Ford Sch—*school* SD-7
Ford Sch—*school* TX-5
Ford Sch—*school* WA-9
Ford Sch—*school* WV-2
Fords Chapel Cem—*cemetery* AL-4
*Fords Chapel Methodist Church* TN-4
Ford Sch (historical)—*school* AL-4
Ford Sch (historical)—*school* MS-4
Ford Sch (historical)—*school* (2) MO-7
Fords Corner—*locale* DE-2
Fords Corner—*locale* TX-5
Fords Cove—*bay* MD-2
Fords Cove—*bay* MI-6
*Fords Creek* KY-4
*Fords Creek* TN-4
**Fords Creek**—*pop pl* MS-4
Fords Creek—*stream* AR-4
Fords Creek—*stream* (2) GA-3
Fords Creek—*stream* KY-4
Fords Creek—*stream* LA-4
Fords Creek—*stream* (3) MS-4
Fords Creek—*stream* (2) MT-8
Fords Creek Ch—*church* MS-4
Fords Creek Sch—*school* MS-4
Fords Crossing—*locale* NH-1
*Fords Depot* VA-3
Fords Dry Lake—*lake* CA-9
Fords Dry Lake—*lake* WA-9
Ford's Farm—*locale* MD-2
*Ford's Ferry* KY-4
Fords Ferry—*locale* KY-4
Fords Fort (historical)—*military* MS-4
Fords Hill—*summit* (2) NY-2
*Fords Island* HI-9
Fords Lake—*reservoir* (2) PA-2
Fords Lake Dam—*dam* PA-2
Ford Slough—*gut* AR-4
Ford Slough—*lake* ND-7
Fords Mill—*locale* NH-1
Fords Mill—*locale* OR-9
Fords Mill Ch—*church* AL-4
*Fords Mill Missionary Baptist Ch* AL-4
Fords Mountaindale Ranch—*locale* CO-8
*Fordson* MN-6
**Fordson**—*pop pl* MI-6
Fordson HS—*school* MI-6
Fordson Island—*island* MI-6
Fords Park—*park* NJ-2
*Fords Point* MD-2
Fords Pond—*lake* OR-9
Fords Prairie—*locale* TX-5
**Fords Prairie**—*pop pl* WA-9
Ford Spring—*spring* (2) AR-4
Ford Spring—*spring* (2) CA-9
Ford Spring—*spring* CO-8
Ford Spring—*spring* KY-4
Ford Spring—*spring* OR-9
Ford Spring—*spring* UT-8
Ford Spring—*spring* WA-9
Fords Ranch—*locale* TX-5
Fords Run—*stream* WV-2
Fords Run Ch—*church* WV-2
Fords Run Sch—*school* WV-2
Fords Sch (historical)—*school* MS-4
*Fords Spur* MS-4
*Ford's Store* MD-2
Fords Terror—*bay* AK-9
Fords Theatre Natl Historic Site—*park* DC-2
Ford Stone House—*hist pl* KY-4
Ford Street Creek—*stream* PA-2
Fords Valley—*valley* AL-4
*Fords Valley Church* AL-4
Fordsville—*locale* VA-3
**Fordsville**—*pop pl* KY-4
Fordsville (CCD)—*cens area* KY-4
**Fordsville (historical)**—*pop pl* MS-4
Fordsville Post Office (historical)—*building* (2) MS-4
Ford Swamp—*swamp* GA-3
Ford Swamp—*swamp* SC-3
Fords Well Ch—*church* MS-4
Fords Well (historical)—*locale* MS-4
Ford Tank—*reservoir* NM-5
**Fordtown**—*pop pl* (2) TN-4
Fordtown Baptist Ch—*church* TN-4
Fordtown Bridge—*bridge* TN-4
Fordtown Ch—*church* TN-4
**Ford (Town of)**—*pop pl* WI-6
Fordtown Post Office (historical)—*building* TN-4
**Ford Township**—*pop pl* KS-7
**Ford (Township of)**—*pop pl* MN-6
**Fordtran**—*pop pl* TX-5
Fordtran Cem—*cemetery* TX-5
Ford Valley—*valley* VA-3
Ford Valley Ch—*church* AL-4
**Ford View**—*pop pl* PA-2
**Fordview**—*pop pl* PA-2
*Fordville* VA-3
Fordville—*hist pl* NJ-2
Fordville—*locale* AZ-5
**Fordville**—*pop pl* FL-3
**Fordville**—*pop pl* NJ-2
**Fordville**—*pop pl* ND-7
**Fordville**—*pop pl* PA-2
Fordville Airp—*airport* ND-7
**Fordville (historical)**—*pop pl* TN-4
Fordville Post Office (historical)—*building* TN-4
Fordway Brook—*stream* NH-1
Fordway Mtn—*summit* NY-2
Ford Well—*well* CA-9
Ford Well—*well* NV-8
*Ford Wells* NV-8
Fordwick—*locale* VA-3
Ford-Williams House—*hist pl* MS-4
Ford Willow Creek Trail—*trail* MT-8
Ford Windmill—*locale* NM-5
Ford Windmill—*locale* TX-5
Ford Woods—*cemetery* IL-6
Ford Woods Park—*park* MI-6
Fordyce—*locale* AL-4
**Fordyce**—*pop pl* AR-4
**Fordyce**—*pop pl* NE-7
**Fordyce**—*pop pl* PA-2
Fordyce Brook—*stream* IN-6
Fordyce Cem—*cemetery* PA-2
Fordyce Channel—*channel* MP-9
Fordyce Country Club—*other* AR-4
Fordyce Creek—*stream* CA-9
Fordyce Home Accident Ins. Co.—*hist pl* AR-4
Fordyce House—*hist pl* (2) AR-4
Fordyce Lake—*reservoir* CA-9
*Fordyce Run* PA-2
Fordyce Summit—*summit* CA-9
Fordyce (Township of)—*fmr MCD* AR-4
*Fordye Channel* MP-9
Fordyke—*locale* MS-4
*fore* ME-1
*Foreacher* OH-6
Foreaker Bridge—*hist pl* OH-6
Fore and Atkinson Levee—*levee* IN-6
Forebay—*locale* CA-9
Forebay—*locale* ID-8
Forebay, The—*lake* UT-8
Forebay, The—*reservoir* AZ-5
Fore Bay Golf Club—*other* CA-9
Forebay Lookout—*locale* CA-9
*Forebay Reservoir* CA-9
Fore Cem—*cemetery* AR-4
Fore Cem—*cemetery* (2) MO-7
Fore Cem—*cemetery* NC-3
Fore Cem—*cemetery* SC-3
Fore Cem—*cemetery* TX-5
*Fore Creek* MD-2
Fore Creek—*stream* MD-2
Foredyce Spring—*spring* WA-9
Foree Branch—*stream* MO-7
*Foree Clinic* TN-4
Foree Ditch—*canal* NE-7
Foree Hosp—*hospital* TN-4
Foreen, Lake—*reservoir* AL-4
Forehand, Clarence, Round Barn—*hist pl* IL-6
Forehand Branch—*stream* TX-5
Forehand Cem—*cemetery* FL-3
Forehand Cem—*cemetery* GA-3
Forehand Cem—*cemetery* OK-5
Forehand Ch—*church* AL-4
Forehand Hollow—*valley* TN-4
Forehand Pond—*lake* FL-3
Forehand Ranch—*locale* NM-5
Forehand West Well—*well* NM-5
Forehead, The—*summit* VT-1
Fore (historical P.O.)—*locale* AL-4
Fore Knobs—*ridge* WV-2
Fore Knobs—*summit* WV-2
Fore Lake—*lake* FL-3
Fore Lake—*reservoir* TN-4
Fore Lake Dam—*dam* TN-4
Fore Lake Rec Area—*park* FL-3
Fore Landing Creek—*stream* VA-3
Foreland Lake—*lake* AK-9
**Forelle**—*pop pl* WY-8
Forellen Peak—*summit* WY-8
Foreman—*locale* OK-5
**Foreman**—*pop pl* LA-4
**Foreman**—*pop pl* PA-2
Foreman, Grant, House—*hist pl* OK-5
Foreman Bay—*swamp* GA-3
*Foreman Branch* MO-7
Foreman Branch—*stream* AL-4
Foreman Branch—*stream* IN-6
Foreman Branch—*stream* MD-2
Foreman Butte—*summit* ND-7
Foreman Cem—*cemetery* GA-3
Foreman Cem—*cemetery* IL-6
Foreman Cem—*cemetery* LA-4
Foreman Cem—*cemetery* MS-4
Foreman Cem—*cemetery* MO-7
Foreman Cem—*cemetery* (3) OK-5
Foreman Chapel—*church* TX-5
**Foreman (corporate name for New Rocky Comfort)**—*pop pl* AR-4
Foreman Coulee—*valley* ND-7
*Foreman Creek* AL-4
*Foreman Creek* MO-7
*Foreman Creek* WI-6
Foreman Creek—*stream* (4) CA-9
Foreman Creek—*stream* KY-4
Foreman Creek—*stream* MD-2
Foreman Creek—*stream* NV-8
Foreman Creek—*stream* NM-5
Foreman Creek—*stream* NC-3
Foreman Creek—*stream* OK-5
Foreman Elem Sch—*school* IN-6
Foreman Field—*other* VA-3
Foreman Glade—*flat* CA-9
Foreman Hollow—*valley* NY-2
Foreman Hollow—*valley* UT-8
Foreman Hollow—*valley* WI-6
Foreman HS—*school* IL-6
Foreman Lake—*lake* MI-6
Foreman Lake—*reservoir* AR-4
Foreman Lakes—*lake* MI-6
Foreman Mill Branch—*stream* GA-3
**Foreman (New Rocky Comfort)**—*pop pl* AR-4
Foreman Point—*summit* OR-9
*Foremans Branch* IN-6
Foremans Cem—*cemetery* GA-3
Foreman Sch—*school* OK-5
**Foremans Corner**—*pop pl* MD-2
Foremans Hall—*locale* LA-4
*Foremans Mill* AL-4
Foremans Mine (underground)—*mine* AL-4
*Foremans Point* OR-9
Foreman Spring—*spring* CA-9
Foreman Spring—*spring* UT-8
Foremans Rsvr—*reservoir* ID-8
*Foreman Wash* AZ-5
Foreman Well—*locale* NM-5
Foreman Well—*well* AZ-5
Foremaster Tank—*reservoir* AZ-5
Fore Memorial Ch—*church* AL-4
Foremost Mtn—*summit* WV-2
Foremost Rock—*island* AK-9
Foremost Run—*stream* VA-3
Fore Mtn—*summit* VA-3
Forepaugh—*locale* AZ-5
Forepaugh Airp—*airport* AZ-5
Forepaugh Peak—*summit* AZ-5
Forepaugh RR Station—*building* AZ-5
Forepaugh Tank—*reservoir* (2) AZ-5
*Forepaw* AZ-5
Fore Point—*cape* NH-1
*Fore River* NH-1
Fore River—*stream* ME-1
Fore River—*uninc pl* MA-1
Fore River Field—*locale* MA-1
Fore Sch—*school* MO-7
Foresee Cem—*cemetery* AR-4
Foreside Church, The—*church* ME-1
Foresight Creek—*stream* ID-8
**Foresman**—*pop pl* (2) IN-6
**Foresmans Switch**—*pop pl* IN-6
*Forest* AL-4
*Forest* MS-4
Forest—*locale* DE-2
Forest—*locale* PA-2
Forest—*locale* TX-5
Forest—*locale* WA-9
**Forest**—*pop pl* AL-4
**Forest**—*pop pl* CA-9
**Forest**—*pop pl* ID-8
**Forest**—*pop pl* IN-6
**Forest**—*pop pl* LA-4
**Forest**—*pop pl* ME-1
**Forest**—*pop pl* MS-4
**Forest**—*pop pl* NY-2
**Forest**—*pop pl* NC-3
**Forest**—*pop pl* OH-6
**Forest**—*pop pl* PA-2
**Forest**—*pop pl* SC-3
**Forest**—*pop pl* VA-3
**Forest**—*pop pl* WV-2
**Forest**—*pop pl* WI-6
Forest, Lake—*lake* MI-6
Forest, Lake—*lake* NY-2
Forest, Lake—*lake* (2) OH-6
Forest, Lake—*reservoir* (2) AL-4
Forest, Lake—*reservoir* CT-1
Forest, Lake—*reservoir* IN-6
Forest, Lake—*reservoir* OH-6
Forest, Lake—*reservoir* TX-5
Forest, Lake of the—*reservoir* KS-7
Forest, Mount—*summit* NH-1
Forest, Mount—*summit* WA-9
Forest, The, and Annex—*hist pl* IL-6
**Foresta**—*pop pl* CA-9
Foresta, Mount—*summit* AK-9
Forest Academy Ch—*church* TX-5
**Forest Acres**—*pop pl* AL-4
**Forest Acres**—*pop pl* IL-6
**Forest Acres**—*pop pl* NJ-2
**Forest Acres**—*pop pl* SC-3
Forest Acres—*uninc pl* SC-3
**Forest Acres (subdivision)**—*pop pl* NC-3
**Forest Acres (subdivision)**—*pop pl* TN-4
Foresta Falls—*falls* CA-9
Forest Aid Ch—*church* MS-4
Forest and Stout Mine—*mine* CA-9
Forest Area Sch—*school* PA-2
**Forestasia (subdivision)**—*pop pl* AL-4
Forest Assembly Ground—*locale* WI-6
Forest Assembly of God Ch—*church* FL-3
Forest Ave Ch—*church* NY-2
Forest Ave Elem Sch—*school* AL-4
Forest Ave Hist Dist—*hist pl* SD-7
Forest Ave Methodist Ch—*church* AL-4
Forest Ave Sch—*hist pl* MA-1
Forest Ave Sch—*school* AL-4
Forest Ave Sch—*school* MA-1
Forest Ave Sch—*school* (2) NJ-2
Forest Ave Sch—*school* NY-2
Forest Ave Viaduct—*bridge* TX-5
Forest Baptist Ch—*church* MS-4
*Forest Baptist Church* AL-4
Forest Bay—*bay* MI-6
Forest Bay—*bay* NY-2
Forest Bay Cem—*cemetery* MI-6
Forest Beach—*beach* MA-1
**Forest Beach**—*pop pl* MI-6
**Forest Beach**—*pop pl* NY-2
**Forest Beach**—*pop pl* SC-3
**Forest Beach**—*pop pl* (2) WA-9
Forest Bluff Sch—*school* KS-7
Forest Boundry Tank—*reservoir* AZ-5
Forest Branch—*stream* MS-4
Forestbrook—*CDP* SC-3
**Forest Brook Estates**—*pop pl* AL-4
**Forest Brook Glen**—*pop pl* DE-2
Forest Brook Sch—*school* NY-2
**Forest Brook (subdivision)**—*pop pl* NC-3
Forestburg—*locale* NC-3
**Forestburg**—*pop pl* NY-2
**Forestburg**—*pop pl* SD-7
**Forestburg**—*pop pl* TX-5
Forestburg Cem—*cemetery* NY-2
Forestburg Cem—*cemetery* TX-5
Forestburg (historical)—*locale* SD-7
**Forestburgh (Town of)**—*pop pl* NY-2
Forestburg Junction (historical)—*locale* SD-7
Forestburg Lutheran Ch—*church* SD-7
Forestburg Pond—*lake* NY-2
*Forestburg Township* SD-7
Forest-Burr Cem—*cemetery* WI-6
Forest Cabins—*locale* MI-6
*Forest Camp* OR-9
Forest Camp—*locale* ID-8
Forest Camp—*locale* OR-9
Forest Camp—*locale* UT-8
Forest Canal—*canal* ID-8
Forest Canyon—*valley* CO-8
Forest Canyon Overlook—*locale* CO-8
Forest Canyon Pass—*gap* CO-8
Forest Capital Center State Park—*park* FL-3
Forest Castle—*uninc pl* PA-2
Forest Castle Station—*locale* PA-2
Forest (CCD)—*cens area* SC-3
Forest Cem—*cemetery* DE-2
Forest Cem—*cemetery* IA-7
Forest Cem—*cemetery* KS-7
Forest Cem—*cemetery* LA-4
Forest Cem—*cemetery* ME-1
Forest Cem—*cemetery* MA-1
Forest Cem—*cemetery* (2) MN-6
Forest Cem—*cemetery* MS-4
Forest Cem—*cemetery* NY-2
Forest Cem—*cemetery* NC-3
Forest Cem—*cemetery* (3) OH-6
Forest Cem—*cemetery* (2) OK-5
Forest Cem—*cemetery* PA-2
Forest Cem—*cemetery* WA-9
Forest Cem—*cemetery* (3) WI-6
Forest Center—*locale* WA-9
**Forest Center**—*pop pl* MN-6
Forest Center Ch—*church* WI-6
Forest Ch—*church* (2) AL-4
Forest Ch—*church* IL-6
Forest Ch—*church* MD-2
Forest Ch—*church* OK-5
Forest Ch—*church* TX-5
Forest Ch—*church* (3) VA-3
Forest Chapel—*church* AL-4
Forest Chapel—*church* AR-4
Forest Chapel—*church* GA-3
Forest Chapel—*church* IA-7
Forest Chapel—*church* NC-3
Forest Chapel—*church* TN-4
Forest Chapel—*church* VA-3
**Forest Chapel**—*pop pl* PA-2
**Forest Chapel**—*pop pl* TN-4
**Forest Chapel**—*pop pl* TX-5
Forest Chapel Cem—*cemetery* PA-2
Forest Chapel Ch—*church* TX-5
Forest Chapel (historical)—*church* PA-2
*Forest Chapel Methodist Episcopal Ch* AL-4
Forest Church Cem—*cemetery* (2) AL-4
Forest City—*locale* FL-3
Forest City—*locale* KS-7
Forest City—*locale* ME-1
Forest City—*locale* NY-2
**Forest City**—*pop pl* IL-6
**Forest City**—*pop pl* IN-6
**Forest City**—*pop pl* IA-7
**Forest City**—*pop pl* MN-6
**Forest City**—*pop pl* MO-7
**Forest City**—*pop pl* NC-3
**Forest City**—*pop pl* PA-2
**Forest City**—*pop pl* SD-7
Forest City—*uninc pl* WA-9
Forest City Borough—*civil* PA-2
Forest City Breaker—*building* PA-2
Forest City Brewery—*hist pl* OH-6
Forest City Cem—*cemetery* ME-1
Forest City Cem—*cemetery* MO-7
Forest City Elem Sch—*school* FL-3
Forest City Flat—*flat* CA-9
Forest City Hall—*building* MS-4
Forest City (historical)—*locale* SD-7
Forest City Hosp—*hospital* OH-6
Forest City Lake—*lake* WV-2
*Forest City Landing* ME-1
Forest City Landing—*locale* ME-1
Forest City Municipal Golf Course—*locale* NC-3
Forest City No. 1—*fmr MCD* NE-7
Forest City Park—*park* NY-2
Forest City Public Library—*hist pl* IA-7
Forest City Rec Area—*park* SD-7
Forest City Sch—*school* SD-7
Forest City Sch—*school* WI-6
Forest City South (historical)—*locale* SD-7
**Forest City Station**—*pop pl* PA-2
Forest City Stream—*gut* ME-1
Forest City Township—*civil* SD-7
Forest City Township—*fmr MCD* IA-7
Forest City Township (historical)—*civil* SD-7
**Forest City (Township of)**—*pop pl* IL-6
**Forest City (Township of)**—*pop pl* MN-6
Forest City (Township of)—*unorg* ME-1
Forest Community Ch—*church* FL-3
Forest Community Ch of Lake George—*church* FL-3
Forest Cottage—*locale* KY-4
Forest Country Club Lake Dam—*dam* MS-4
**Forest County**—*pop pl* PA-2
**Forest (County)**—*pop pl* WI-6
Forest Cove—*bay* MD-2
**Forest Cove**—*pop pl* TX-5
*Forest Creek* OR-9
*Forest Creek* PA-2
Forest Creek—*stream* AK-9
Forest Creek—*stream* AR-4
Forest Creek—*stream* (2) CA-9
Forest Creek—*stream* MI-6
Forest Creek—*stream* (5) MT-8
Forest Creek—*stream* (4) OR-9
Forest Creek—*stream* TX-5
Forest Creek—*stream* UT-8
Forest Creek—*stream* VA-3
Forest Creek—*stream* WA-9
Forest Creek—*stream* (2) WY-8
**Forest Creek Cove PUD Subdivision**—*pop pl* UT-8
Forest Creek Forest Camp—*locale* OR-9
Forest Creek Trail—*trail* OR-9
Forest Crest Cem—*cemetery* AL-4
Forest Crossing—*locale* OR-9
*Forestdale* VT-1
Forestdale—*locale* MS-4
Forestdale—*locale* NY-2
**Forestdale**—*pop pl* AL-4
**Forestdale**—*pop pl* MA-1
**Forestdale**—*pop pl* OH-6
**Forestdale**—*pop pl* RI-1
**Forest Dale**—*pop pl* UT-8
**Forest Dale**—*pop pl* VT-1
**Forestdale Addition (subdivision)**—*pop pl* UT-8
**Forestdale by the Brook (subdivision)**—*pop pl* AL-4
Forestdale Canyon—*valley* AZ-5
Forestdale Canyon Tank—*reservoir* AZ-5
Forestdale Cem—*cemetery* MA-1
Forest Dale Cem—*cemetery* MA-1
Forestdale Cem—*cemetery* MS-4
Forestdale Cem—*cemetery* NY-2
Forestdale Ch—*church* MS-4
Forest Dale Ch—*church* OH-6
*Forestdale Creek* AZ-5
Forestdale Creek—*stream* AZ-5
Forestdale Creek—*stream* CA-9
Forestdale Divide—*ridge* CA-9
**Forestdale Estates**—*pop pl* MA-1
Forest Dale Golf Course—*other* UT-8
Forestdale (historical)—*locale* AL-4
Forestdale Iron Furnace—*hist pl* VT-1
Forestdale Mill Village Hist Dist—*hist pl* RI-1
Forestdale Plantation—*hist pl* MS-4
Forestdale Pond—*reservoir* RI-1
Forestdale Pond Dam—*dam* RI-1
Forestdale Sch—*school* KY-4
Forest Dale Sch—*school* ME-1
Forestdale Sch—*school* MA-1
Forest Dale Sch—*school* OR-9
Forestdale Sch (historical)—*school* MS-4
Forestdale Spring—*spring* AZ-5
Forestdale Square Shop Ctr—*locale* AL-4
**Forestdale (subdivision)**—*pop pl* AL-4
**Forestdale (subdivision)**—*pop pl* NC-3
**Forestdale (subdivision)**—*pop pl* TN-4
Forestdale Tank—*reservoir* AZ-5
Forestdale Trading Post—*locale* AZ-5
Forest Dell—*basin* WY-8
Forest Dell Ch—*church* MO-7
Forest Dell Sch (abandoned)—*school* MO-7
Forest Divide—*ridge* WA-9
Forest Drain—*stream* MI-6
Forest Drive Ch—*church* SC-3
Forest Edge Sch—*school* VA-3
Forest Elem Sch—*school* MS-4
*Forester* OK-5
**Forester**—*pop pl* AL-4
**Forester**—*pop pl* MI-6
Forester Cem—*cemetery* AL-4
Forester Cem—*cemetery* OR-9
**Forester Chapel**—*pop pl* AL-4
Forester Chapel Ch—*church* AL-4
Forester Creek—*stream* CA-9
Forester Creek—*stream* MI-6
Forester Gulch—*valley* GA-3
Forester Lake—*lake* CA-9
Forester Lake—*lake* NE-7
Forester Pass—*gap* CA-9
Forester Pond—*lake* VT-1
Foresters Creek—*stream* KY-4
Forester's Hall—*hist pl* PA-2
Foresters Leap Canyon—*valley* CA-9
Forester Spring—*spring* GA-3
Foresters Spur—*ridge* KY-4
**Forester (Township of)**—*pop pl* MI-6
**Forest Estates**—*pop pl* IL-6
**Forest Estates**—*pop pl* MD-2
**Forest Falls**—*pop pl* CA-9
Forest Field Sch—*school* (2) WI-6
Forest Flower Sch—*school* IL-6
Forest Flower School (Abandoned)—*lake* MO-7
*Forest Garden* IL-6
**Forest Gardens**—*pop pl* IL-6
Forest Gem School (historical)—*locale* MO-7
Forest G Hay Elem Sch—*school* IN-6
Forest Glade—*locale* WA-9
**Forest Glade**—*pop pl* TX-5
Forest Glade Cem—*cemetery* MA-1
Forest Glade Cem—*cemetery* NH-1
Forest Glade Cem—*cemetery* TX-5
*Forest Glen* IL-6
*Forest Glen* LA-4
Forest Glen—*locale* NY-2
**Forest Glen**—*pop pl* CA-9
**Forest Glen**—*pop pl* CT-1
**Forest Glen**—*pop pl* GA-3
**Forest Glen**—*pop pl* IN-6
**Forest Glen**—*pop pl* LA-4
**Forest Glen**—*pop pl* MD-2
**Forest Glen**—*pop pl* NY-2
**Forest Glen**—*pop pl* PA-2
**Forest Glen**—*pop pl* TN-4
**Forest Glen**—*pop pl* UT-8
Forest Glen Annex-Walter Reed Army Med Ctr—*military* MD-2
**Forest Glen Beach**—*pop pl* WI-6
Forest Glen Campground—*locale* CA-9
Forest Glen Cem—*cemetery* MA-1
Forest Glen Ch—*church* OH-6
Forest Glen Ch—*church* WV-2
Forest Glen Lake—*lake* NY-2
Forest Glen Landing—*locale* OR-9
**Forest Glen Park**—*pop pl* MD-2
Forest Glen Sch—*school* IL-6
Forest Glen Sch—*school* PA-2
Forest Glen Woods—*woods* IL-6
**Forest Green**—*pop pl* MO-7
**Forest Green**—*pop pl* MT-8
Forest Green Cem—*cemetery* MN-6
**Forest Green Estates**—*pop pl* MI-6
**Forest Green Estates Subdivision**—*pop pl* UT-8
*Forest Green Resort* MT-8
**Forest Greens**—*pop pl* MD-2
Forest Greens Country Club—*other* MD-2
**Forest Green (subdivision)**—*pop pl* MS-4
*Forest Grove* (2) MT-8
Forest Grove—*locale* AR-4
Forest Grove—*locale* FL-3
Forest Grove—*locale* MD-2
Forest Grove—*locale* MN-6
Forest Grove—*locale* (2) NJ-2
Forest Grove—*locale* (2) TX-5
**Forest Grove**—*pop pl* AR-4
**Forest Grove**—*pop pl* KY-4
**Forest Grove**—*pop pl* MD-2
**Forest Grove**—*pop pl* MI-6
**Forest Grove**—*pop pl* MS-4
**Forestgrove**—*pop pl* MT-8
**Forest Grove**—*pop pl* NC-3
**Forest Grove**—*pop pl* OR-9
**Forest Grove**—*pop pl* (2) PA-2
**Forest Grove**—*pop pl* (2) TN-4
**Forest Grove**—*pop pl* TX-5
Forest Grove Bend—*bend* TN-4
Forest Grove Branch—*stream* MD-2
Forest Grove Bridge—*bridge* TN-4
Forest Grove Cem—*cemetery* AR-4
Forest Grove Cem—*cemetery* FL-3
Forest Grove Cem—*cemetery* GA-3
Forest Grove Cem—*cemetery* IN-6
Forest Grove Cem—*cemetery* IA-7
Forest Grove Cem—*cemetery* (2) KS-7
Forest Grove Cem—*cemetery* ME-1
Forest Grove Cem—*cemetery* MI-6
Forest Grove Cem—*cemetery* (2) MS-4
Forest Grove Cem—*cemetery* (4) MO-7
Forest Grove Cem—*cemetery* OH-6
Forest Grove Cem—*cemetery* TN-4
Forest Grove Cem—*cemetery* (2) TX-5
Forest Grove Cem—*cemetery* WI-6
Forest Grove Ch—*church* AR-4
Forest Grove Ch—*church* DE-2
Forest Grove Ch—*church* FL-3
Forest Grove Ch—*church* GA-3
Forest Grove Ch—*church* KY-4
Forest Grove Ch—*church* MD-2
Forest Grove Ch—*church* (5) MS-4
Forest Grove Ch—*church* (3) MO-7
Forest Grove Ch—*church* (2) OH-6
Forest Grove Ch—*church* TN-4
Forest Grove Ch—*church* (2) TX-5
Forest Grove Ch—*church* (5) VA-3
Forest Grove Chapel—*church* NC-3
*Forest Grove Christian Church* MS-4
Forest Grove Community Hosp—*hospital* OR-9
Forest Grove-Cornelius (CCD)—*cens area* OR-9
Forest Grove Creek—*stream* NC-3
*Forest Grove Freewill Baptist Ch* TN-4
Forest Grove Hist Dist—*hist pl* PA-2
Forest Grove JHS—*school* MA-1
Forest Grove Junction—*locale* OR-9
Forest Grove Park—*park* MO-7
Forest Grove Plantation—*locale* LA-4
*Forest Grove Presbyterian Ch* MS-4
Forest Grove Sch—*school* CA-9
Forest Grove Sch—*school* IA-7
Forest Grove Sch—*school* KY-4
Forest Grove Sch—*school* LA-4
Forest Grove Sch—*school* MD-2
Forest Grove Sch—*school* MS-4
Forest Grove Sch—*school* (4) MO-7
Forest Grove Sch—*school* OK-5
Forest Grove Sch—*school* PA-2
Forest Grove Sch (historical)—*school* (2) MS-4
Forest Grove Sch (historical)—*school* TN-4
Forest Grove School (abandoned)—*spring* MO-7
Forest Grove School (historical)—*locale* MO-7
**Forest Grove Station**—*pop pl* MI-6
**Forest Grove (subdivision)**—*pop pl* NC-3
Forest Grove Tower—*tower* FL-3
Forest Gulch—*valley* ID-8
**Foresthaven**—*pop pl* IL-6
*Forest Heights* CT-1
*Forest Heights* IL-6
Forest Heights—*locale* MT-8
Forest Heights—*locale* TN-4
**Forest Heights**—*pop pl* CT-1
**Forest Heights**—*pop pl* MD-2
**Forest Heights**—*pop pl* TX-5
Forest Heights—*uninc pl* FL-3
Forest Heights—*uninc pl* NM-5
Forest Heights Baptist Ch—*church* FL-3
Forest Heights Ch—*church* FL-3
Forest Heights Ch—*church* NM-5
Forest Heights Country Club—*other* GA-3
Forest Heights Elem Sch—*school* NC-3
Forest Heights JHS—*school* AR-4
Forest Heights Park—*park* MN-6
Forest Heights Sch—*school* AR-4
Forest Heights Sch—*school* MD-2
Forest Heights Shop Ctr—*locale* NC-3
Forest Helton Lake Dam—*dam* IN-6
Forest Highlands—*locale* FL-3
**Forest Highlands**—*pop pl* TN-4
**Forest Highlands (subdivision)**—*pop pl* AL-4
*Forest Hill* IL-6
*Forest Hill* MA-1
*Forest Hill* OH-6
*Forest Hill* TN-4
Forest Hill—*locale* TX-5
Forest Hill—*locale* WV-2
**Forest Hill**—*pop pl* AL-4
**Foresthill**—*pop pl* CA-9
**Forest Hill**—*pop pl* (2) IN-6
**Forest Hill**—*pop pl* KY-4
**Forest Hill**—*pop pl* LA-4
**Forest Hill**—*pop pl* MD-2
**Forest Hill**—*pop pl* MI-6
**Forest Hill**—*pop pl* MS-4
**Forest Hill**—*pop pl* (2) NJ-2
**Forest Hill**—*pop pl* NY-2
**Forest Hill**—*pop pl* NC-3
**Forest Hill**—*pop pl* OH-6
**Forest Hill**—*pop pl* OK-5
**Foresthill**—*pop pl* PA-2
**Forest Hill**—*pop pl* PA-2
**Forest Hill**—*pop pl* (4) TN-4
**Forest Hill**—*pop pl* (2) TX-5
**Forest Hill**—*pop pl* VA-3
Forest Hill—*summit* AZ-5
Forest Hill—*summit* CO-8
Forest Hill—*summit* MA-1
Forest Hill—*summit* MT-8
Forest Hill—*summit* NY-2
Forest Hill—*uninc pl* NJ-2
Forest Hill—*uninc pl* TX-5
Forest Hill—*uninc pl* VA-3
*Forest Hill Academy* AL-4
Forest Hill Acad (historical)—*school* TN-4
Forest Hill Assembly of God Ch—*church* MS-4
Foresthill-Back Country (CCD)—*cens area* CA-9
*Forest Hill Baptist Ch* TN-4
Forest Hill Baptist Ch—*church* MS-4
Forest Hill Baptist Ch—*church* TN-4
Forest Hill Cem—*cemetery* (2) AL-4
Forest Hill Cem—*cemetery* (3) FL-3
Forest Hill Cem—*cemetery* (2) IL-6
Forest Hill Cem—*cemetery* (3) IN-6
Forest Hill Cem—*cemetery* IA-7
Forest Hill Cem—*cemetery* KS-7
Forest Hill Cem—*cemetery* (4) ME-1
Forest Hill Cem—*cemetery* (2) MA-1
Forest Hill Cem—*cemetery* (6) MI-6
Forest Hill Cem—*cemetery* (9) MN-6
Forest Hill Cem—*cemetery* (2) MS-4
Forest Hill Cem—*cemetery* MO-7
Forest Hill Cem—*cemetery* NH-1
Forest Hill Cem—*cemetery* NM-5
Forest Hill Cem—*cemetery* (3) NY-2
Forest Hill Cem—*cemetery* NC-3
Forest Hill Cem—*cemetery* (3) OH-6

Forest Hill Cem—*cemetery* OK-5
Forest Hill Cem—*cemetery* OR-9
Forest Hill Cem—*cemetery* (2) PA-2
Forest Hill Cem—*cemetery* SD-7
Forest Hill Cem—*cemetery* (5) TN-4
Forest Hill Cem—*cemetery* TX-5
Forest Hill Cem—*cemetery* VA-3
Forest Hill Cem—*cemetery* (7) WI-6
Forest Hill Cemetery Mound Group—*hist pl* WI-6
Forest Hill Ch—*church* (2) AL-4
Forest Hill Ch—*church* (2) AR-4
Forest Hill Ch—*church* (3) GA-3
Forest Hill Ch—*church* KY-4
Forest Hill Ch—*church* MI-6
Forest Hill Ch—*church* OK-5
Forest Hill Ch—*church* (2) TN-4
Forest Hill Ch—*church* (3) TX-5
Forest Hill Ch—*church* (2) VA-3
Forest Hill Chapel—*church* SC-3
Forest Hill Chapel (historical)—*church* AL-4
Forest Hill Ch (historical)—*church* MS-4
Forest Hill Ch (historical)—*church* TN-4
Forest Hill Ch of God—*church* AL-4
Forest Hill Community Center—*building* KY-4
Forest Hill Cottage—*hist pl* MA-1
Forest Hill Country Club—*other* MO-7
Forest Hill Divide—*ridge* CA-9
Forest Hill Drag Strip—*other* TX-5
Forest Hill Elem Sch—*school* IN-6
Forest Hill Elem Sch—*school* NC-3
Forest Hill Elem Sch—*school* TN-4
Forest Hill Field Club—*other* NJ-2
Forest Hill Hist Dist—*hist pl* OH-6
Forest Hill (historical)—*locale* KS-7
**Forest Hill (historical)**—*pop pl* (2) TN-4
Forest Hill HS—*school* FL-3
Forest Hill HS—*school* MS-4
Forest Hill Lake—*reservoir* NJ-2
Forest Hill Lake—*reservoir* OH-6
Forest Hill Memorial Park—*park* WI-6
Forest Hill Methodist Ch—*church* AL-4
Forest Hill Mine—*mine* CO-8
Forest Hill Park—*park* NC-3
Forest Hill Park—*park* OH-6
Forest Hill Park—*park* TX-5
Forest Hill Park—*park* VA-3
**Forest Hill Park**—*pop pl* VA-3
Forest Hill Parkway—*park* OH-6
Forest Hill Plantation (historical)—*locale* AL-4
Forest Hill Presbyterian Ch (historical)—*church* TN-4
*Forest Hills* IL-6
*Forest Hills* (3) IN-6
*Forest Hills* OH-6
Forest Hills—*locale* OH-6
**Forest Hills**—*pop pl* (3) AL-4
**Forest Hills**—*pop pl* CA-9
**Forest Hills**—*pop pl* CO-8
**Forest Hills**—*pop pl* (2) FL-3
**Forest Hills**—*pop pl* (2) GA-3
**Forest Hills**—*pop pl* IN-6
**Forest Hills**—*pop pl* KS-7
**Forest Hills**—*pop pl* (2) KY-4
**Forest Hills**—*pop pl* MA-1
**Forest Hills**—*pop pl* (2) MI-6
**Forest Hills**—*pop pl* (4) NC-3
**Forest Hills**—*pop pl* OH-6
**Forest Hills**—*pop pl* (3) PA-2
**Forest Hills**—*pop pl* (4) TN-4
**Forest Hills**—*pop pl* TX-5
**Forest Hills**—*pop pl* VA-3
**Forest Hills**—*pop pl* (2) WV-2
**Forest Hills**—*pop pl* PR-3
Forest Hills—*post sta* KY-4
Forest Hills—*uninc pl* FL-3
Forest Hills—*uninc pl* KS-7
Forest Hills—*uninc pl* NY-2
Forest Hills—*uninc pl* NC-3
Forest Hills—*uninc pl* PA-2
Forest Hills—*uninc pl* TX-5
**Forest Hills Addition**—*pop pl* WA-9
Forest Hills Baptist Ch—*church* AL-4
Forest Hills Baptist Ch—*church* FL-3
Forest Hills Borough—*civil* PA-2
Forest Hills Cem—*cemetery* (3) NY-2
Forest Hills Cem—*cemetery* NC-3
Forest Hills Cem—*cemetery* OH-6
Forest Hills Cem—*cemetery* PA-2
Forest Hills Cem—*cemetery* TN-4
Forest Hills Ch—*church* KY-4
Forest Hills Ch—*church* NC-3
Forest Hills Ch—*church* TN-4
Forest Hill Sch—*school* AL-4
Forest Hill Sch—*school* CA-9
Forest Hill Sch—*school* FL-3
Forest Hill Sch—*school* IL-6
Forest Hill Sch—*school* NC-3
Forest Hill Sch—*school* (2) OK-5
Forest Hill Sch—*school* (3) TN-4
Forest Hill Sch—*school* (2) TX-5
Forest Hill Sch (abandoned)—*school* (2) MO-7
Forest Hill Sch (historical)—*school* MS-4
Forest Hill Sch (historical)—*school* MO-7
Forest Hill Sch (historical)—*school* (2) TN-4
Forest Hills Country Club—*other* IL-6
Forest Hills Country Club—*other* MI-6
Forest Hills Country Club—*other* MO-7
Forest Hills Elem Sch—*school* AL-4
Forest Hills Elem Sch—*school* (3) FL-3
**Forest Hills Estates**—*pop pl* OH-6
**Forest Hills Estates (subdivision)**—*pop pl* NC-3
Forest Hills Golf Course—*other* IN-6
Forest Hills Golf Course—*other* OR-9
Forest Hills Hist Dist—*hist pl* IN-6
Forest Hill Shop Ctr—*locale* AL-4
Forest Hills HS—*school* MI-6
Forest Hills HS—*school* NY-2
Forest Hills HS—*school* NC-3
Forest Hills JHS—*school* AL-4
**Forest Hills Manor**—*pop pl* PA-2
*Forest Hills Memorial Cemetery* NC-3
Forest Hills Memorial Park—*cemetery* AR-4
Forest Hills Memorial Park—*cemetery* FL-3
Forest Hills Memorial Park—*cemetery* GA-3
Forest Hills MS—*school* PA-2
Forest Hills North Sch—*school* MO-7
Forest Hills Park—*park* NC-3
Forest Hills Park—*park* PA-2
**Forest Hills Park**—*pop pl* DE-2
Forest Hill Speedway—*other* LA-4
Forest Hills Presbyterian Ch—*church* AL-4
**Forest Hills (Road Fork)**—*pop pl* KY-4
Forest Hills Run—*stream* PA-2
Forest Hills Sch—*hist pl* TN-4
Forest Hills Sch—*school* FL-3
Forest Hills Sch—*school* IL-6
Forest Hills Sch—*school* MI-6
Forest Hills Sch—*school* NC-3
Forest Hills Sch—*school* OR-9
Forest Hills Sch—*school* VA-3
Forest Hills Shop Ctr—*locale* AL-4
Forest Hills Shop Ctr—*locale* NC-3
Forest Hills Stadium—*other* NY-2
Forest Hills Station—*locale* MA-1
**Forest Hills (subdivision)**—*pop pl* (5) AL-4
**Forest Hills (subdivision)**—*pop pl* MA-1
**Forest Hills (subdivision)**—*pop pl* MS-4
**Forest Hills (subdivision)**—*pop pl* (10) NC-3
**Forest Hills (subdivision)**—*pop pl* PA-2
**Forest Hills (subdivision)**—*pop pl* (6) TN-4
Forest Hill Station—*locale* NJ-2
**Forest Hills (Trailer Park)**—*pop pl* CT-1
**Forest Hill (subdivision)**—*pop pl* NC-3
Forest Hill United Methodist Ch—*church* MS-4
Forest (historical)—*locale* AL-4
**Forest (historical)**—*pop pl* OR-9
*Forest Home* CA-9
*Forest Home* KS-7
Forest Home—*hist pl* AL-4
Forest Home—*locale* CA-9
Forest Home—*locale* IA-7
Forest Home—*locale* LA-4
Forest Home—*locale* NV-8
**Forest Home**—*pop pl* AL-4
**Forest Home**—*pop pl* (2) CA-9
**Forest Home**—*pop pl* NY-2
**Forest Home**—*pop pl* TN-4
Forest Home Ave Sch—*school* WI-6
Forest Home (CCD)—*cens area* AL-4
Forest Home Cem—*cemetery* AL-4
Forest Home Cem—*cemetery* IL-6
Forest Home Cem—*cemetery* (2) IA-7
Forest Home Cem—*cemetery* KY-4
Forest Home Cem—*cemetery* ME-1
Forest Home Cem—*cemetery* (3) MI-6
Forest Home Cem—*cemetery* MN-6
Forest Home Cem—*cemetery* NY-2
Forest Home Cem—*cemetery* OH-6
Forest Home Cem—*cemetery* OK-5
Forest Home Cem—*cemetery* TX-5
Forest Home Cem—*cemetery* WA-9
Forest Home Cem—*cemetery* (10) WI-6
Forest Home Cemetery and Chapel—*hist pl* WI-6
*Forest Home Ch* AL-4
Forest Home Ch—*church* (2) AL-4
Forest Home Ch—*church* AR-4
Forest Home Ch—*church* MO-7
Forest Home Ch—*church* NC-3
Forest Home Ch—*church* (2) TX-5
Forest Home Chute—*gut* MS-4
Forest Home Community Ch—*church* WI-6
Forest Home Corners—*locale* PA-2
Forest Home Creek—*stream* NV-8
Forest Home Division—*civil* AL-4
**Forest Home Farms**—*pop pl* TN-4
Forest Home Grange Hall—*building* KS-7
Forest Home Landing (historical)—*locale* MS-4
Forest Home Oil Field—*oilfield* MS-4
Forest Home Park—*locale* WA-9
Forest Home Plantation—*hist pl* MS-4
Forest Home Plantation (historical)—*locale* MS-4
Forest Home Post Office (historical)—*building* TN-4
**Forest Homes**—*pop pl* IL-6
Forest Home Sch (historical)—*school* AL-4
Forest Home Sch (historical)—*school* TN-4
**Forest Homes (subdivision)**—*pop pl* NC-3
**Forest Home Subdivision**—*pop pl* UT-8
Forest Home Towhead—*area* MS-4
**Forest Home (Township of)**—*pop pl* MI-6
Forest Hosp—*hospital* IL-6
*Forest House* PA-2
Forest House—*locale* CA-9
Forest House—*locale* NY-2
Forest HS—*school* (2) FL-3
Forest HS—*school* MS-4
Forest HS—*school* TX-5
Forestiere Underground Gardens—*hist pl* CA-9
Forest Ingram Lake—*reservoir* (2) AL-4
Forest Ingram Lake Dam—*dam* AL-4
Forest Inn—*locale* PA-2
**Forest Junction**—*pop pl* WI-6
Forest King Gulch—*valley* ID-8
Forest King Mine—*mine* ID-8
Forest King Mtn—*summit* CO-8
**Forest Knolls**—*pop pl* CA-9
**Forest Knolls**—*pop pl* (2) MD-2
**Forest Knolls**—*pop pl* NY-2
**Forest Knolls**—*pop pl* PA-2
Forest Knolls Sch—*school* MD-2
*Forest Lake* KS-7
*Forest Lake* MA-1
*Forest Lake* MI-6
*Forest Lake* NC-3
*Forest Lake* PA-2
Forest Lake—*lake* AK-9
Forest Lake—*lake* (3) CA-9
Forest Lake—*lake* CO-8
Forest Lake—*lake* (2) FL-3
Forest Lake—*lake* IL-6
Forest Lake—*lake* LA-4
Forest Lake—*lake* ME-1
Forest Lake—*lake* MA-1
Forest Lake—*lake* (3) MI-6
Forest Lake—*lake* (4) MN-6
Forest Lake—*lake* (2) MT-8
Forest Lake—*lake* (2) NH-1
Forest Lake—*lake* (4) NY-2
Forest Lake—*lake* NC-3
Forest Lake—*lake* PA-2
Forest Lake—*lake* (2) VT-1
Forest Lake—*lake* (3) WA-9
Forest Lake—*lake* (4) WI-6
Forest Lake—*lake* WY-8
**Forest Lake**—*pop pl* (2) CA-9
**Forest Lake**—*pop pl* IL-6
**Forest Lake**—*pop pl* IN-6
**Forest Lake**—*pop pl* MD-2
**Forest Lake**—*pop pl* MA-1
**Forest Lake**—*pop pl* MI-6
**Forest Lake**—*pop pl* MN-6
**Forest Lake**—*pop pl* NH-1
**Forest Lake**—*pop pl* PA-2
**Forest Lake**—*pop pl* (2) SC-3
Forest Lake—*reservoir* (3) GA-3
Forest Lake—*reservoir* IN-6
Forest Lake—*reservoir* MA-1
Forest Lake—*reservoir* MI-6
Forest Lake—*reservoir* (3) MO-7
Forest Lake—*reservoir* NJ-2
Forest Lake—*reservoir* (2) NY-2
Forest Lake—*reservoir* (4) NC-3
Forest Lake—*reservoir* (2) PA-2
Forest Lake—*reservoir* (2) SC-3
Forest Lake—*reservoir* UT-8
Forest Lake—*uninc pl* GA-3
Forest Lake Acad—*school* FL-3
Forest Lake Baptist Ch—*church* AL-4
Forest Lake Camp—*locale* IA-7
Forest Lake Cem—*cemetery* ME-1
Forest Lake Chapter House—*building* AZ-5
Forest Lake Country Club—*other* SC-3
Forest Lake Creek—*stream* PA-2
Forest Lake Dam—*dam* AL-4
Forest Lake Dam—*dam* (2) IN-6
Forest Lake Dam—*dam* MA-1
Forest Lake Dam—*dam* NJ-2
Forest Lake Dam—*dam* (4) NC-3
Forest Lake Dam—*dam* (2) PA-2
Forest Lake Golf Course—*other* MI-6
Forest Lake Guard Station—*locale* MT-8
**Forest Lake Hills**—*pop pl* VA-3
Forest Lake HS—*school* MN-6
Forest Lake Lookout Tower—*locale* MI-6
Forest Lake Park—*park* OH-6
Forest Lake Park—*park* PA-2
Forest Lake RR Station—*locale* FL-3
Forest Lakes—*lake* CO-8
Forest Lakes—*post sta* AZ-5
Forest Lakes—*post sta* FL-3
Forest Lake Sch—*school* MN-6
Forest Lake Sch—*school* NY-2
Forest Lake Sch—*school* SC-3
**Forest Lakes Estates**—*pop pl* AZ-5
Forest Lake Seventh-Day Adventist Ch—*church* FL-3
**Forest Lakes Park (subdivision)**—*pop pl* FL-3
Forest Lakes Plaza (Shop Ctr)—*locale* FL-3
**Forest Lake (subdivision)**—*pop pl* AL-4
**Forest Lake (Township of)**—*pop pl* MN-6
**Forest Lake (Township of)**—*pop pl* PA-2
Forest Lake United Methodist Ch—*church* AL-4
Forest Lake Wash—*valley* AZ-5
Forest Lake Well—*well* AZ-5
Forest Landing—*locale* DE-2
**Forest Landing (subdivision)**—*pop pl* NC-3
Forestland Sch—*school* MN-6
*Forest Lawn* MI-6
**Forest Lawn**—*pop pl* NY-2
Forest Lawn Cem—*cemetery* AL-4
Forest Lawn Cem—*cemetery* FL-3
Forest Lawn Cem—*cemetery* ID-8
Forest Lawn Cem—*cemetery* IL-6
Forest Lawn Cem—*cemetery* IN-6
Forest Lawn Cem—*cemetery* KY-4
Forest Lawn Cem—*cemetery* LA-4
Forest Lawn Cem—*cemetery* (3) MI-6
Forest Lawn Cem—*cemetery* MN-6
Forest Lawn Cem—*cemetery* (2) NE-7
Forest Lawn Cem—*cemetery* NM-5
Forest Lawn Cem—*cemetery* (2) NY-2
Forest Lawn Cem—*cemetery* (5) NC-3
Forest Lawn Cem—*cemetery* OH-6
Forest Lawn Cem—*cemetery* PA-2
Forest Lawn Cem—*cemetery* SC-3
Forest Lawn Cem—*cemetery* (2) TX-5
Forest Lawn Cem—*cemetery* (2) VA-3
Forest Lawn Cem—*cemetery* (2) WA-9
Forest Lawn Cem—*cemetery* WV-2
Forest Lawn Ch—*church* NC-3
Forest-Lawn Ch—*church* VA-3
Forest Lawn Garden—*cemetery* MS-4
Forest Lawn Gardens—*cemetery* PA-2
Forestlawn Gardens Cem—*cemetery* AL-4
Forest Lawn Golf Course—*other* GA-3
Forest Lawn Memorial Cem—*cemetery* SC-3
Forest Lawn Memorial Ch—*church* TN-4
Forest Lawn Memorial Garden—*cemetery* IA-7
Forest Lawn Memorial Gardens—*cemetery* CA-9
Forest Lawn Memorial Gardens—*cemetery* (2) FL-3
Forest Lawn Memorial Gardens—*cemetery* IL-6
Forest Lawn Memorial Gardens—*cemetery* WV-2
Forest Lawn Memorial Gardens Cem—*cemetery* FL-3
Forest Lawn Memorial Park—*cemetery* (2) CA-9
Forest Lawn Memorial Park—*cemetery* GA-3
Forest Lawn Memorial Park—*cemetery* IL-6
Forest Lawn Memorial Park—*cemetery* LA-4
Forest Lawn Memorial Park—*cemetery* OR-9
Forest Lawn Memorial Park—*cemetery* PA-2
Forest Lawn Memorial Park—*cemetery* (3) TX-5
Forest Lawn Memorial Park (Cemetery)—*cemetery* (2) CA-9
Forest Lawn Memorial Park (Cemetery)—*cemetery* NY-2
Forest Lawn Memorial Park (Cemetery)—*cemetery* OH-6
Forest Lawn Memorial Park of Broward County—*cemetery* FL-3
Forest Lawn Memory Gardens—*cemetery* FL-3
Forest Lawn of Santa Rosa—*cemetery* FL-3
Forest Lawn Sch—*school* ID-8
Forestlawn Sch—*school* OH-6
Forest Level Ch—*church* VA-3
Forest Line Ditch—*canal* NC-3
Forest Lodge—*locale* NY-2
**Forest Lodge Acres**—*pop pl* VA-3
*Forest Manor* IN-6
**Forest Manor**—*pop pl* IL-6
**Forest Manor**—*pop pl* MD-2
*Forest Manor Church* IN-6
**Forest Manor (subdivision)**—*pop pl* AL-4
Forest Manor United Methodist Ch—*church* IN-6
**Forest Meade (subdivision)**—*pop pl* TN-4
Forest Meadows Memorial Park—*cemetery* FL-3
Forest Memorial Park—*cemetery* (2) MS-4
Forest Memorial Park (Cemetery)—*cemetery* WV-2
Forestmere Lakes—*lake* NY-2
Forest Methodist Ch—*church* MS-4
*Forest Methodist Church* AL-4
**Forest Mill**—*pop pl* TN-4
Forest Mill Ch—*church* TN-4
*Forest Mills* PA-2
*Forest Mills* TN-4
Forest Mills—*locale* MN-6
**Forest Mills**—*pop pl* MO-7
**Forest Mills**—*pop pl* TN-4
Forest Mill Sch—*school* MO-7
Forest Mill Sch (historical)—*school* TN-4
**Forest Mills (historical)**—*pop pl* TN-4
Forest Mills Post Office (historical)—*building* TN-4
Forest Mine—*mine* MN-6
Forest Moon Ranch—*locale* NV-8
Forest Mountain Spring No 1—*spring* WA-9
Forest Mountain Spring No 2—*spring* WA-9
Forest Mountain Spring No 3—*spring* WA-9
Forest Mtn—*summit* (2) WA-9
Forest Municipal Airp—*airport* MS-4
Forest Murphy Pond Dam—*dam* MS-4
Forest-Norman Hist Dist—*hist pl* NY-2
Forest Oak Ch—*church* VA-3
Forest Oak Elem Sch—*school* DE-2
**Forest Oaks**—*pop pl* LA-4
Forest Oak Sch—*school* KY-4
Forest Oaks Lake—*reservoir* NC-3
Forest Oaks Lake Dam—*dam* NC-3
Forest Oaks Memorial Park—*cemetery* TX-5
**Forest Oaks (subdivision)**—*pop pl* NC-3
**Forest of Brentwood**—*pop pl* TN-4
Foreston—*locale* IA-7
Foreston—*locale* MD-2
**Foreston**—*pop pl* MN-6
**Foreston**—*pop pl* SC-3
Foreston Cem—*cemetery* IA-7
Foreston Lookout Tower—*locale* SC-3
*Forest Park* IL-6
*Forest Park* IN-6
*Forest Park* MO-7
Forest Park—*hist pl* AL-4
Forest Park—*park* (3) IL-6
Forest Park—*park* IN-6
Forest Park—*park* (3) KS-7
Forest Park—*park* LA-4
Forest Park—*park* MA-1
Forest Park—*park* MI-6
Forest Park—*park* MO-7
Forest Park—*park* NM-5
Forest Park—*park* NY-2
Forest Park—*park* NC-3
Forest Park—*park* OR-9
Forest Park—*park* PA-2
Forest Park—*park* TN-4
Forest Park—*park* (2) TX-5
Forest Park—*park* WA-9
Forest Park—*park* WI-6
**Forest Park**—*pop pl* (2) AL-4
**Forest Park**—*pop pl* (2) CA-9
**Forest Park**—*pop pl* CT-1
**Forest Park**—*pop pl* DE-2
**Forest Park**—*pop pl* (2) GA-3
**Forest Park**—*pop pl* (2) IL-6
**Forest Park**—*pop pl* (2) IN-6
**Forest Park**—*pop pl* LA-4
**Forest Park**—*pop pl* (2) MD-2
**Forest Park**—*pop pl* MA-1
**Forest Park**—*pop pl* MT-8
**Forest Park**—*pop pl* NM-5
**Forest Park**—*pop pl* NY-2
**Forest Park**—*pop pl* (3) OH-6
**Forest Park**—*pop pl* OK-5
**Forest Park**—*pop pl* (2) PA-2
**Forest Park**—*pop pl* TN-4
Forest Park—*uninc pl* AR-4
Forest Park—*uninc pl* MA-1
Forest Park—*uninc pl* (2) VA-3
Forest Park—*uninc pl* WA-9
Forest Park Baptist Ch—*church* AL-4
Forest Park Baptist Ch—*church* FL-3
**Forest Park Beach**—*pop pl* IN-6
Forest Park Bible Ch—*church* AL-4
Forest Park Campground—*locale* WY-8
Forest Park Cem—*cemetery* (2) AR-4
Forest Park Cem—*cemetery* IL-6
Forest Park Cem—*cemetery* KS-7
Forest Park Cem—*cemetery* (2) LA-4
Forest Park Cem—*cemetery* MO-7
Forest Park Cem—*cemetery* NY-2
Forest Park Cem—*cemetery* (3) TX-5
Forest Park Ch—*church* KY-4
Forest Park Ch—*church* (2) NC-3
Forest Park Ch—*church* TX-5
Forest Park Club Lake Dam—*dam* MS-4
Forest Park Country Club—*other* VA-3
*Forest Park Elementary School* NC-3
Forest Park Elem Sch—*school* FL-3
Forest Park Elem Sch—*school* (2) IN-6
**Forest Park Estates (subdivision)**—*pop pl* MS-4
**Forest Park Heights**—*pop pl* IN-6
Forest Park Heights Hist Dist—*hist pl* MA-1
Forest Park Hotel—*hist pl* MO-7
Forest Park HQ Bldg—*hist pl* MO-7
Forest Park HS—*school* IN-6
Forest Park JHS—*school* MA-1
Forest Park JHS—*school* TX-5
**Forest Park Mobile Home Court**—*pop pl* IA-7
Forest Park-Morrow (CCD)—*cens area* GA-3
*Forest Park North* IN-6
Forest Park Plaza Shop Ctr—*locale* OH-6
Forest Park Sch—*school* AR-4
Forest Park Sch—*school* FL-3
Forest Park Sch—*school* MD-2
Forest Park Sch—*school* MI-6
Forest Park Sch—*school* MO-7
Forest Park Sch—*school* MT-8
Forest Park Sch—*school* NY-2
Forest Park Sch—*school* NC-3
Forest Park Sch—*school* OH-6
Forest Park Sch—*school* OK-5
Forest Park Sch—*school* VA-3
Forest Park Sch—*school* WI-6
**Forest Park (subdivision)**—*pop pl* (2) AL-4
**Forest Park (subdivision)**—*pop pl* MA-1
**Forest Park (subdivision)**—*pop pl* NC-3
**Forest Park Subdivision**—*pop pl* UT-8
Forest Park Swimming Pool—*reservoir* IN-6
Forest Park Swimming Pool Dam—*dam* IN-6
Forest Park (Township of)—*other* OH-6
**Forest Park (trailer park)**—*pop pl* DE-2
Forest Park Upper Dam—*dam* MA-1
Forest Park West Cem—*cemetery* LA-4
**Forest Pawtuckett (subdivision)**—*pop pl* NC-3
Forest Peak—*summit* OR-9
Forest Pine Ch—*church* SC-3
Forest Pipeline—*other* ID-8
*Forest Point* TN-4
Forest Point—*cape* MD-2
**Forest Point (subdivision)**—*pop pl* MS-4
*Forest Pond* MA-1
Forest Pond—*lake* GA-3
Forest Pond—*lake* (2) ME-1
Forest Pond—*lake* (2) NH-1
Forest Pond—*lake* (2) NY-2
**Forest Pond**—*pop pl* GA-3
Forest Pond Brook—*stream* NH-1
**Forestport**—*pop pl* NY-2
Forestport Rsvr—*reservoir* NY-2
Forestport Station—*locale* NY-2
**Forestport (Town of)**—*pop pl* NY-2
Forest Post Office—*building* MS-4
Forest Prairie Creek—*stream* MN-6
Forest Prairie (Township of)—*civ div* MN-6
Forest Presbyterian Ch—*church* MS-4
Forest Queen Mine—*mine* (2) CO-8
Forest Queen (site)—*locale* OR-9
Forest Ranch—*locale* NM-5
Forest Ranch—*locale* TX-5
**Forest Ranch**—*pop pl* CA-9
Forest Ranch Fire Control Station—*locale* CA-9
Forest Ranch Windmill—*locale* AZ-5
**Forest Rawtucket (subdivision)**—*pop pl* NC-3
Forest Retreat Farm and Tavern—*hist pl* KY-4
*Forest Ridge* NH-1
**Forest Ridge**—*pop pl* (2) IN-6
Forest Ridge—*ridge* OH-6
Forest Ridge—*uninc pl* FL-3
Forest Ridge Ch—*church* IL-6
**Forest Ridge Estates**—*pop pl* IN-6
Forest Ridge Park—*park* WA-9
Forest Ridge Sch—*school* IL-6
Forest Ridge Sch—*school* WI-6
Forest Ridge Union Ch—*church* TN-4
**Forest River**—*pop pl* IL-6
**Forest River**—*pop pl* ND-7
Forest River—*stream* GA-3
Forest River—*stream* MA-1
Forest River—*stream* ND-7
Forest River—*uninc pl* MA-1
**Forest River Colony**—*pop pl* ND-7
Forest River Colony Cem—*cemetery* ND-7
**Forest River Farms**—*pop pl* GA-3
Forest River (historical)—*locale* ND-7
Forest River Marshes—*swamp* MA-1
Forest River Park—*park* MA-1
**Forest River Township**—*pop pl* ND-7
Forest Road Lake—*lake* NY-2
Forest Road Sch—*school* IL-6
Forest Road Sch—*school* MI-6
Forest Road Sch—*school* NY-2
Forest Rose Cem—*cemetery* OH-6
Forest Rose Mine—*mine* MT-8
Forest Rose Sch—*school* KY-4
Forest Rsvr—*reservoir* OR-9
Forest Run—*stream* IN-6
Forest Run—*stream* OH-6
Forest Run—*stream* WV-2
Forest Run Ch—*church* OH-6
Forest Run Ch—*church* WV-2
Forestry Camp Number Four—*locale* CA-9
*Forestry House* PA-2
Forest Sch—*school* (2) IL-6
Forest Sch—*school* MA-1
Forest Sch—*school* MI-6
Forest Sch—*school* (2) MN-6
Forest Sch—*school* MS-4
Forest Sch—*school* (2) MO-7
Forest Sch—*school* NY-2
Forest Sch—*school* OH-6
Forest Sch—*school* (3) PA-2
Forest Sch—*school* UT-8
Forest Sch—*school* WI-6
Forest Sch—*school* WY-8
Forest Sch (historical)—*school* (2) MS-4
Forest Sch (historical)—*school* PA-2
Forest Sch No 2—*school* MI-6
*Forest School* TN-4
*Forest Separate Sch* MS-4
*Forest Service Range Rider Camp* NM-5
Forest Service Station—*locale* ID-8
Forest Service Tank—*reservoir* AZ-5
Forest Service Warehouse—*other* NM-5
Forest Service Winter Range—*locale* MT-8
Forest Sewage Lagoon Dam—*dam* MS-4
Forest Shores—*locale* WA-9
Forest Siding—*locale* ID-8
*Forest Spring* MO-7
Forest Spring—*spring* (2) NV-8
Forest Spring—*spring* (2) OR-9
**Forest Spring Park**—*pop pl* MD-2
Forest Springs—*locale* KY-4
Forest Springs—*locale* MO-7
**Forest Springs**—*pop pl* (2) CA-9
Forest Springs—*spring* WY-8
Forest Springs Lateral—*canal* CA-9
Forest Springs Sch—*school* CA-9
Forest Street Parkway—*hist pl* CO-8
Forest Street Sch—*school* MA-1
Forest Street Sch—*school* NJ-2
Forest Street United Methodist Ch—*church* TN-4
Forest Strip Airp—*airport* TN-4
Forest Tank—*reservoir* (3) AZ-5
Forest Tank—*reservoir* (2) NM-5
Forest Tower Ch—*church* AR-4
**Forest (Town of)**—*pop pl* (4) WI-6
Forest Township—*civil* MO-7
Forest Township—*fmr MCD* IA-7
**Forest (Township of)**—*pop pl* IN-6
**Forest (Township of)**—*pop pl* (3) MI-6
**Forest (Township of)**—*pop pl* (2) MN-6
Forest (Township of)—*unorg* ME-1
Forestuale Cem—*cemetery* MA-1
Forest United Presbyterian Ch—*church* DE-2
Forest Vale Cem—*cemetery* MT-8
Forestvale Cem—*cemetery* OR-9
*Forest Valley* NY-2
**Forest Valley Mobile Home Subdivision**—*pop pl* NC-3
Forest Valley Sch—*school* IL-6
**Forest Valley (subdivision)**—*pop pl* NC-3
**Forestview**—*pop pl* GA-3
**Forest View**—*pop pl* IL-6
**Forest View**—*pop pl* OH-6
**Forest View**—*pop pl* SC-3
Forest View—*uninc pl* VA-3
Forest View Cem—*cemetery* CT-1
Forestview Cem—*cemetery* IL-6
Forest View Cem—*cemetery* OR-9
Forest View Cem—*cemetery* (3) WI-6
Forest View Ch—*church* GA-3
Forest View Ch—*church* (2) TN-4
Forest View Ch—*church* WI-6
*Forest View Hills* IL-6
Forest View HS—*school* IL-6
Forest View Sch—*school* (2) IL-6
Forest View Sch—*school* (2) MI-6
Forest View Sch—*school* MN-6
Forest View Sch—*school* OH-6
Forest View Sch—*school* VA-3
Forest View Sch (historical)—*school* MO-7
**Forest View (subdivision)**—*pop pl* TN-4
**Forest Villa**—*pop pl* MD-2
**Forest Village**—*pop pl* CT-1
*Forestville* CT-1
Forestville—*locale* IA-7
Forestville—*locale* KY-4
Forestville—*locale* MN-6
Forestville—*locale* PA-2
**Forestville**—*pop pl* CA-9
**Forestville**—*pop pl* (2) CT-1
**Forestville**—*pop pl* MD-2
**Forestville**—*pop pl* MI-6
**Forestville**—*pop pl* NY-2
**Forestville**—*pop pl* NC-3
**Forestville**—*pop pl* OH-6
**Forestville**—*pop pl* (3) PA-2
**Forestville**—*pop pl* (2) VA-3
**Forestville**—*pop pl* WI-6
Forestville Baptist Church—*hist pl* NC-3
Forestville Cem—*cemetery* CT-1
Forestville Cem—*cemetery* IA-7
Forestville Cem—*cemetery* MN-6
Forestville Cem—*cemetery* WI-6
Forestville Ch—*church* NC-3
Forestville Ch—*church* SC-3
Forestville Ch—*church* VA-3
Forestville Ch—*church* WI-6
Forestville Commonwealth—*hist pl* NY-2
Forestville Creek—*stream* MN-6
**Forestville Estates**—*pop pl* MD-2
Forestville Flowage—*reservoir* WI-6
Forest Ville (historical)—*locale* KS-7
Forestville (historical)—*locale* SD-7
Forestville North Sch—*school* IL-6
Forestville Passenger Station—*hist pl* CT-1
**Forestville Phelps Addition**—*pop pl* MD-2
**Forestville (RR name Harrisville (sta.))**—*pop pl* PA-2
Forestville Sch—*school* MD-2
**Forestville (Town of)**—*pop pl* WI-6
**Forestville (Township of)**—*pop pl* MN-6
Forestville Townsite-Meighan Store—*hist pl* MN-6
Forestville Zion Ch—*church* NC-3
Forest Wayside State Park—*park* OR-9
*Forest Well* NM-5
Forest Well—*well* (3) NM-5
Forest Well Tank—*reservoir* NM-5
Forest West—*uninc pl* TX-5
Forest West Park—*park* TX-5
Forest Windmill—*locale* AZ-5
Forest Windmill—*locale* TX-5
**Forestwood**—*pop pl* TN-4
Forestwood Park—*park* NY-2
Foreverglades Mausoleum Gardens—*cemetery* FL-3
Forfar—*locale* ND-7
**Forfar**—*pop pl* OR-9
**Forgan**—*pop pl* OK-5
Forgan Cem—*cemetery* OK-5
*Forgarty* ND-7
Forgay Point—*cape* CA-9
*Forge* MA-1
**Forge**—*pop pl* PA-2
**Forge, The**—*pop pl* NY-2
**Forge Acres**—*pop pl* MD-2
Forge Branch—*stream* MD-2
*Forge Brook* CT-1
*Forge Creek* PA-2
Forge Creek—*stream* ID-8
Forge Creek—*stream* KY-4
Forge Creek—*stream* MT-8
Forge Creek—*stream* PA-2
Forge Creek—*stream* (2) TN-4
Forge Farm—*hist pl* RI-1
**Forge Heights**—*pop pl* MD-2
*Forge Hill* CT-1
Forge Hill—*hist pl* PA-2
**Forge Hill**—*pop pl* WV-2
Forge Hill—*summit* (2) MA-1
Forge Hill—*summit* (2) PA-2
Forge Hill—*summit* RI-1
**Forge Hollow**—*pop pl* NY-2
Forge Knob—*summit* NC-3
Forge Knob—*summit* TN-4
Forge Knob Branch—*stream* TN-4
Forge Lake—*lake* MN-6
Forge Mill—*locale* GA-3
Forge Mine—*mine* NV-8
Forge Mountain Grist Mill Dam—*dam* NC-3
Forge Mountain Grist Mill Lake—*reservoir* NC-3
Forge Mountain Mine—*mine* TN-4

Forge Mtn—*summit* ... CT-1
Forge Mtn—*summit* ... NY-2
Forge Mtn—*summit* ... NC-3
Forge Mtn—*summit* ... TN-4
Forge Mtn—*summit* ... VA-3
Forgen Slough—*gut* ... WY-8
Forge Park—*park* ... TX-5
Forge Point—*cape* ... NY-2
*Forge Pond* ... CT-1
Forge Pond—*lake* (2) ... MA-1
Forge Pond—*lake* (2) ... NJ-2
Forge Pond—*reservoir* (7) ... MA-1
Forge Pond Dam—*dam* (4) ... MA-1
Forge Pond Dike—*dam* ... MA-1
Forge Post Office (historical)—*building* ... TN-4
**Forge Ridge**—*pop pl* ... TN-4
Forge Ridge—*ridge* (2) ... TN-4
Forge Ridge Baptist Ch—*church* ... TN-4
Forge Ridge Cem—*cemetery* ... TN-4
Forge Ridge HS (historical)—*school* ... TN-4
*Forge Ridge Sch* ... TN-4
Forge River—*stream* ... MA-1
Forge River—*stream* ... NY-2
Forge River Rsvr—*reservoir* ... MA-1
*Forge Road Elementary School* ... PA-2
Forge Road Hist Dist—*hist pl* ... RI-1
*Forge Run* ... PA-2
Forge Run—*stream* ... WV-2
Forgery Ranch—*locale* ... WY-8
Forgery Sch—*school* ... LA-4
Forge Sch—*school* ... TN-4
*Forges Pond* ... MA-1
Forge Stack Bridge—*bridge* ... TN-4
Forge Street Sch—*school* ... PA-2
Forget-me-not Brook—*stream* ... MA-1
Forget-Me-Not Canal—*canal* ... CA-9
Forget-Me-Not Drain—*canal* ... CA-9
Forget-me-not Lake—*lake* ... MN-6
Forget-me-not Lakes—*lake* ... WY-8
Forget-Me-Not Lateral One—*canal* ... CA-9
Forget-Me-Not Lateral Two—*canal* ... CA-9
Forget Road Dam—*dam* ... MA-1
Forge Union Ch—*church* ... PA-2
Forge Valley Ch—*church* ... NC-3
**Forge Village**—*pop pl* ... MA-1
Forgey Cem—*cemetery* ... IN-6
Forgey Cem—*cemetery* ... OH-6
Forgey Creek—*stream* ... MT-8
Forgey Creek—*stream* ... TN-4
Forgey Ditch—*canal* ... IN-6
*Forgey Island* ... TN-4
Forgey Knob—*summit* ... MO-7
Forgey Pond—*lake* ... MO-7
Forgotten, Mount—*summit* ... WA-9
Forgotten Canyon—*valley* ... CA-9
Forgotten Canyon—*valley* ... UT-8
*Forgotten Crater* ... OR-9
Forgotten Creek—*stream* ... AK-9
Forgotten Springs—*spring* ... WA-9
Forgotten Valley—*valley* ... CA-9
Forgotten Valley—*valley* ... CO-8
**Forgy**—*pop pl* ... OH-6
Forgys Branch—*stream* ... KY-4
Forgys Mill—*locale* ... KY-4
Forhand Hollow—*valley* ... TN-4
Forhan Pond—*lake* ... FL-3
Foringer, Alonzo, House and
  Studio—*hist pl* ... NJ-2
Forinier Institute—*school* ... IL-6
**Foristall Corners**—*pop pl* ... ME-1
**Foristell**—*pop pl* ... MO-7
Forjer Lake—*lake* ... MN-6
*Fork* ... MS-4
*Fork* ... NC-3
*Fork* ... UT-8
Fork—*locale* ... AR-4
**Fork**—*pop pl* ... MD-2
**Fork**—*pop pl* ... NC-3
**Fork**—*pop pl* ... SC-3
Fork—*stream* ... MO-7
Fork, Point of—*cape* ... VA-3
*Fork, The* ... AL-4
Fork, The—*cape* ... TN-4
Fork, The—*plain* ... AL-4
*Fork Bad River* ... MI-6
Fork Bend—*bend* ... TN-4
Fork Bottom Bend—*bend* ... SC-3
*Fork Branch* ... DE-2
*Fork Branch* ... TN-4
Fork Branch—*stream* ... DE-2
Fork Branch—*stream* (2) ... NC-3
*Fork Branch School* ... DE-2
Fork Bridge Creek—*stream* ... VA-3
Fork Brook—*stream* ... ME-1
Fork Camp—*locale* ... CA-9
Fork Camp—*locale* ... WY-8
*Fork Canyon* ... AZ-5
Fork (CCD)—*cens area* ... SC-3
Fork Cem—*cemetery* ... MI-6
Fork Ch—*church* ... MD-2
Fork Ch—*church* ... MI-6
Fork Ch—*church* ... NC-3
Fork Ch—*church* ... SC-3
Fork Ch—*church* (2) ... VA-3
Fork Chapel—*church* ... GA-3
Fork Chapel—*church* ... NC-3
*Fork Church* ... MS-4
Fork Church—*hist pl* ... VA-3
*Fork Courthouse* ... GA-3
*Fork Creek* ... NC-3
*Fork Creek* ... OR-9
Fork Creek—*stream* ... AK-9
Fork Creek—*stream* (2) ... GA-3
Fork Creek—*stream* ... IL-6
Fork Creek—*stream* (2) ... IN-6
Fork Creek—*stream* ... IA-7
Fork Creek—*stream* ... KY-4
Fork Creek—*stream* ... MI-6
Fork Creek—*stream* ... MO-7
Fork Creek—*stream* (6) ... NC-3
Fork Creek—*stream* ... OH-6
Fork Creek—*stream* ... SC-3
Fork Creek—*stream* (2) ... TN-4
Fork Creek—*stream* ... VA-3
Fork Creek—*stream* ... WA-9
Fork Creek—*stream* ... WV-2
*Fork Creek Canyon* ... UT-8
Fork Creek Cem—*cemetery* ... SC-3
Fork Creek Ch—*church* (2) ... GA-3
Fork Creek Ch—*church* ... NC-3
Fork Creek Ch—*church* ... SC-3
Fork Creek Ch—*church* ... TN-4
Fork Creek State Public Hunting
  Area—*park* ... WV-2
Fork Dam—*dam* ... CO-8
Forked Branch—*stream* ... GA-3
Forked Branch—*stream* ... IN-6
Forked Brook—*stream* (2) ... NJ-2
Forked Butte—*summit* ... OR-9
Forked Canyon—*valley* ... OR-9
*Forked Creek* ... NJ-2
Forked Creek—*lake* ... MD-2
Forked Creek—*stream* ... CA-9
Forked Creek—*stream* ... FL-3
Forked Creek—*stream* ... IL-6
Forked Creek—*stream* ... MD-2
Forked Creek—*stream* ... ND-7
Forked Creek—*stream* ... TN-4
Forked Creek—*stream* ... WY-8
**Forked Deer**—*pop pl* ... TN-4
Forked Deer Cave—*cave* ... TN-4
Forked Deer Creek—*stream* ... TN-4
Forked Deer Dikes—*levee* ... TN-4
Forked Deer Hollow—*valley* ... TN-4
Forked Deer Island—*island* ... TN-4
*Forked Deer Island Number Twentysix and*
  *Twentyseven* ... TN-4
Forked Deer Post Office
  (historical)—*building* ... TN-4
*Forked Deer River* ... TN-4
Forked Deer River—*stream* ... TN-4
Forked Deer Sch—*school* ... TN-4
Forked Draw—*valley* ... TX-5
Forked Field Slough—*stream* ... TN-4
Forked Flat—*flat* ... UT-8
Forked Gulch—*valley* (2) ... CO-8
Forked Hollow Cove—*bay* ... MO-7
Forked Horn Butte—*summit* (2) ... OR-9
Forked Horn Springs—*spring* ... OR-9
Forked Island—*island* ... LA-4
**Forked Island**—*pop pl* ... LA-4
Forked Lake—*lake* ... AR-4
Forked Lake—*lake* ... GA-3
Forked Lake—*lake* ... KY-4
Forked Lake—*lake* (2) ... MS-4
Forked Lake—*lake* ... OK-5
Forked Lake—*lake* (2) ... TN-4
Forked Lake—*reservoir* ... NY-2
Forked Lake—*swamp* ... MI-6
Forked Lake Campsite—*locale* ... NY-2
Forked Lightning Ranch—*locale* ... NM-5
Forked Meadow—*flat* ... CA-9
Forked Meadow Creek—*stream* ... CA-9
Forked Mountain Cem—*cemetery* ... AR-4
Forked Mouth Creek—*stream* ... KY-4
Forked Mtn—*summit* ... AR-4
Forked Mtn—*summit* ... NC-3
Forked Oak Cem—*cemetery* ... MS-4
Forked Oak Ch—*church* ... MS-4
*Forked Oak Missionary Baptist Ch* ... MS-4
Forked Pine Branch—*stream* ... LA-4
Forked Pine Campground—*park* ... AZ-5
Forked Pine Nature Trail—*trail* ... TN-4
Forked Pine Picnic Area—*park* ... AZ-5
*Forked Pond* ... MA-1
*Forked Pond* ... SC-3
Forked Pond—*bay* ... TN-4
Forked Pond Ditch—*canal* ... IN-6
*Forked Ponds* ... MA-1
Forked Pond Valley—*valley* ... MA-1
Forked Post Pond—*lake* ... UT-8
Forked Ridge—*ridge* (3) ... NC-3
Forked Ripple (historical)—*rapids* ... AL-4
**Forked River**—*pop pl* ... NJ-2
Forked River—*stream* ... NJ-2
**Forked River Beach**—*pop pl* ... NJ-2
Forked River Game Farm—*park* ... NJ-2
Forked River Mtn—*summit* ... NJ-2
**Forked River Point**—*pop pl* ... NJ-2
*Forked Run* ... NJ-2
Forked Run—*stream* ... OH-6
Forked Run—*stream* ... WV-2
Forked Run Lake—*reservoir* ... OH-6
Forked Run State Park—*park* ... OH-6
Forked Spring—*spring* ... PA-2
Forked Spring—*spring* ... UT-8
*Forked Tongue Creek* ... CO-8
Fork Ellis Creek—*stream* ... WV-2
Forkenbrock Funeral Home—*hist pl* ... MT-8
**Forker**—*pop pl* ... MO-7
**Forker Boomer Post Office**—*pop pl* ... MO-7
Forker Creek—*stream* ... IN-6
Forker Creek—*stream* ... LA-4
Fork Ferry Bridge—*bridge* ... GA-3
Fork Handle Hollow—*valley* ... OK-5
Fork Hill—*summit* ... ME-1
Fork Hill—*summit* (4) ... PA-2
Fork Hill Ch—*church* ... SC-3
**Fork Hill Crossroads**—*pop pl* ... SC-3
Fork Hill Trail—*trail* (4) ... PA-2
Fork Hollow—*valley* (2) ... VA-3
Fork Island—*island* ... NY-2
Fork Island—*island* ... TN-4
**Fork Junction**—*pop pl* ... WV-2
Fork Knob—*summit* ... NC-3
Fork Lake—*lake* (2) ... MI-6
Fork Lake—*lake* ... OR-9
Forkland—*locale* ... KY-4
Forkland—*locale* ... MS-4
**Forkland**—*pop pl* ... AL-4
Forkland Bar—*bar* ... AL-4
Forkland Cem—*cemetery* ... MS-4
Forkland Ch—*church* ... MS-4
Fork Landing—*locale* ... NJ-2
Fork Landing—*locale* ... NC-3
Fork Landing Bridge—*bridge* ... DE-2
*Forkland Landing* ... AL-4
Forkland-Tishabee (CCD)—*cens area* ... AL-4
Forkland-Tishabee Division—*civil* ... AL-4
Fork Lane Sch—*school* ... NY-2
*Fork Lick* ... WV-2
Fork Lick Creek—*stream* ... KY-4
Fork Lick Hollow—*valley* ... VA-3
Fork Lick (Magisterial District)—*fmr MCD* . WV-2
Fork (Magisterial District)—*fmr MCD* ... VA-3
Fork McKeen Historic Site—*park* ... ND-7
Fork Meadow—*flat* ... ID-8
**Fork Mountain**—*pop pl* ... TN-4
Fork Mountain—*ridge* ... AR-4
Fork Mountain Cave—*cave* ... TN-4
Fork Mountain Cem—*cemetery* ... NC-3
Fork Mountain Ch—*church* ... NC-3
Fork Mountain Ch—*church* ... VA-3
Fork Mountain Mine
  (underground)—*mine* ... AL-4
Fork Mountain Overlook—*locale* ... VA-3
Fork Mountain-Peewee Mountain Mine
  (surface)—*mine* ... TN-4
Fork Mountain Pond—*lake* ... PA-2
Fork Mountain Prospect—*mine* ... TN-4
Fork Mountain Sch (historical)—*school* ... TN-4
Fork Mountain (Township of)—*fmr MCD* ... NC-3
Fork Mountain Trail—*trail* ... WV-2
Fork Mountain Tunnel—*tunnel* ... NC-3
*Fork Mtn* ... AR-4
*Fork Mtn* ... TN-4
Fork Mtn—*summit* ... AL-4
Fork Mtn—*summit* (2) ... AR-4
Fork Mtn—*summit* ... NY-2
Fork Mtn—*summit* (17) ... NC-3
Fork Mtn—*summit* ... SC-3
Fork Mtn—*summit* (4) ... TN-4
Fork Mtn—*summit* (8) ... VA-3
Fork Mtn—*summit* (6) ... WV-2
Fork Nacimiento River—*stream* ... CA-9
Fork Neck—*cape* ... MD-2
Forkner Alluvial Canal—*canal* ... CA-9
Forkner Canal—*canal* ... CA-9
Forkner Chapel—*church* ... TN-4
Forkner Ditch—*canal* ... IN-6
Forkners Chapel Cem—*cemetery* ... TN-4
*Forkners Chapel Methodist Episcopal Church*
  *South* ... TN-4
**Forkners Hill**—*pop pl* ... MO-7
Fork Number One Pepper Creek—*stream* .. DE-2
Fork of Bane Creek—*stream* ... PA-2
*Fork of Hound Creek* ... MT-8
*Fork Of Middle Oconee River* ... GA-3
Fork Of North Canal—*canal* ... WY-8
**Fork Of Pike**—*pop pl* ... TN-4
Fork Of Pup Creek—*stream* ... KY-4
*Fork of River* ... TN-4
*Fork of Rock Creek* ... NV-8
Fork of the Creeks Sch—*school* ... FL-3
*Fork Of White Creek* ... IN-6
Fork of Willis Ch—*church* ... VA-3
Forkosh Hosp—*hospital* ... IL-6
*Fork Pass Creek* ... MT-8
Fork Peak—*summit* ... AK-9
Fork Point—*cape* ... FL-3
Fork Point—*cape* ... MD-2
Fork Point—*cape* (3) ... NC-3
Fork Point—*summit* ... PA-2
Fork Point Island—*island* ... NC-3
Fork Pond—*lake* ... ME-1
*Fork Ridge* ... NC-3
*Fork Ridge* ... TN-4
*Fork Ridge* ... WV-2
Fork Ridge—*locale* ... VA-3
**Fork Ridge**—*pop pl* ... TN-4
Fork Ridge—*ridge* (2) ... GA-3
Fork Ridge—*ridge* ... IN-6
Fork Ridge—*ridge* (2) ... KY-4
Fork Ridge—*ridge* ... NY-2
Fork Ridge—*ridge* (18) ... NC-3
Fork Ridge—*ridge* (10) ... TN-4
Fork Ridge—*ridge* (7) ... VA-3
Fork Ridge—*ridge* (8) ... WV-2
Fork Ridge Ch—*church* (2) ... WV-2
Fork Ridge Community Bldg—*building* ... WV-2
Fork Ridge Mine (underground)—*mine* ... TN-4
Fork Ridge Post Office
  (historical)—*building* ... TN-4
Fork Ridge Sch—*school* ... TN-4
Fork Ridge Trail—*trail* ... TN-4
*Fork Rips* ... ME-1
Fork River Bald—*summit* ... NC-3
Fork River Ridge—*ridge* ... NC-3
Fork Rock Creek—*stream* ... AZ-5
Fork Rocklick Branch—*stream* ... KY-4
Fork Rock Mesa—*summit* ... NM-5
Fork Rsvr—*reservoir* ... MT-8
*Fork Run* ... PA-2
Fork Run—*stream* ... IN-6
Fork Run—*stream* ... MD-2
Fork Run—*stream* (2) ... NC-3
Fork Run—*stream* (3) ... PA-2
*Forks* ... CO-8
Forks—*locale* ... MT-8
Forks—*locale* ... PA-2
**Forks**—*pop pl* ... NY-2
**Forks**—*pop pl* ... WA-9
*Forks, The* ... CO-8
*Forks, The* ... ND-7
*Forks, The* ... PA-2
Forks, The—*area* ... KY-4
Forks, The—*cape* ... SC-3
Forks, The—*harbor* ... IN-6
Forks, The—*locale* ... CA-9
Forks, The—*locale* ... MT-8
Forks, The—*locale* (2) ... NY-2
Forks, The—*locale* ... SC-3
Forks, The—*locale* ... TX-5
Forks, The—*locale* ... UT-8
Forks, The—*locale* ... WY-8
Forks, The—*other* ... AK-9
**Forks, The**—*pop pl* ... CA-9
**Forks, The**—*pop pl* ... ME-1
**Forks, The**—*pop pl* ... NY-2
Forks, The—*stream* ... AK-9
Forks Airp—*airport* ... WA-9
*Fork San Ygnacio Creek* ... TX-5
Forks Brook—*stream* ... NY-2
**Forksburg**—*pop pl* ... WV-2
Forksburg Sch—*school* ... WV-2
Forks Butte—*summit* ... AZ-5
Forks Campground—*locale* ... CA-9
Forks Campground—*locale* ... SC-3
Forks Campground—*locale* ... WY-8
Forks Campground, The—*locale* ... CO-8
Forks (CCD)—*cens area* ... WA-9
Forks Ch—*church* ... MD-2
Fork Sch—*school* ... SC-3
Forks Chapel—*church* ... SC-3
**Forks Church**—*pop pl* ... PA-2
Forks Cow Camp, The—*locale* ... MT-8
*Forks Creek* ... WA-9
Forks Creek—*stream* ... AK-9
Forks Creek—*stream* ... CA-9
Forks Creek—*stream* ... ID-8
Forks Creek—*stream* ... NY-2
Forks Creek—*stream* (2) ... OR-9
Forks Creek—*stream* ... WA-9
Forks Creek Ch—*church* ... TN-4
*Forks Creek School* ... TN-4
Forks Dix River Ch—*church* ... KY-4
Fork Section—*ridge* ... NC-3
Forks Flat—*flat* ... CA-9
Forks Forest Camp—*locale* ... OR-9
Forks Grove Ch—*church* ... TN-4
Forks Guard Station—*locale* ... OR-9
**Fork Shoals**—*pop pl* ... SC-3
Fork Shoals Lookout Tower—*locale* ... SC-3
Fork Shop—*locale* ... VA-3
Forks House (Site)—*locale* ... CA-9
Forks House Trail—*trail* ... CA-9
Forks La Grue Ch—*church* ... AR-4
Forks Lake—*lake* ... SC-3
Forks Lookout—*summit* ... MT-8
Forks Mtn—*summit* (3) ... NY-2
*Forks North* ... PA-2
Forks Number Two—*locale* ... NY-2
*Forks of Big Pine Creek Campground* ... ID-8
Forks Of Big Pine Creek
  Campground—*locale* ... ID-8
Forks of Brushy Sch—*school* (2) ... KY-4
Forks of Buffalo—*locale* ... VA-3
Forks of Butte—*locale* ... CA-9
*Forks-of-Cacapon* ... WV-2
Forks of Cacapon—*locale* ... WV-2
*Forks of Capon* ... WV-2
Forks of Cheat Ch—*church* ... WV-2
**Forks of Coal**—*pop pl* ... WV-2
Forks of Coal Memorial Park—*cemetery* ... WV-2
Forks of Cranberry Trail—*trail* ... WV-2
Forks of Creek Sch (historical)—*school* ... TN-4
*Forks of Cypress Plantation* ... AL-4
**Forks Of Elkhorn**—*pop pl* ... KY-4
Forks Of Elkhorr Ch—*church* ... KY-4
Forks of Hullem Tank—*reservoir* ... TX-5
Forks of Huntington Campground—*park* ... UT-8
Forks of Hurricane—*locale* ... WV-2
**Forks of Ivy**—*pop pl* ... NC-3
Forks of Little River Ch—*church* ... NC-3
Forks of Machias—*locale* ... ME-1
Forks of Pike Post Office
  (historical)—*building* ... TN-4
*Forks of River* ... TN-4
**Forks of River**—*pop pl* ... TN-4
Forks of Salmon—*locale* ... CA-9
*Forks of Tar River* ... NC-3
Forks of the Creek—*locale* ... FL-3
Forks of the Creek—*locale* ... NY-2
Forks of the Ohio—*hist pl* ... PA-2
**Forks of the River**—*pop pl* (2) ... TN-4
Forks of the River (CCD)—*cens area* ... TN-4
Forks of the River Division—*civil* ... TN-4
Forks of the River Industrial Park—*locale* .. TN-4
Forks of Trace Sch—*school* ... KY-4
*Forks Of Water* ... VA-3
Forks Of Waters—*locale* ... VA-3
Fork Special Ditch, Lake—*canal* ... IL-6
Forks Plantation (historical), The—*locale* ... AL-4
Forks (Plantation of), The—*civ div* ... ME-1
Forks Prairie—*flat* ... WA-9
*Forks Prairie Creek* ... WA-9
Fork Spring—*spring* (2) ... AZ-5
Fork Spring—*spring* ... CA-9
Fork Spring—*spring* ... KY-4
Forks Ranch—*locale* ... MT-8
Forks Ranch—*locale* ... NV-8
*Forks Recreation Site* ... UT-8
Forks Ridge—*ridge* ... CA-9
Forks Ridge—*ridge* ... OR-9
Forks Ridge—*ridge* ... PA-2
*Forks River Elementary School* ... TN-4
Forks River Sch—*school* ... TN-4
Forks Rsvr—*reservoir* ... CA-9
Forks Rsvr—*reservoir* ... MT-8
Forks Rsvr—*reservoir* ... OR-9
Forks Sch—*school* ... OR-9
Forks Sch (historical)—*school* ... PA-2
Forks Spring—*spring* ... MT-8
Forks Springs—*spring* ... CA-9
Forks Tank—*reservoir* ... AZ-5
Forks Tank—*reservoir* ... OR-9
**Forkston**—*pop pl* ... PA-2
Forkston Mtn—*summit* ... PA-2
**Forkston (Township of)**—*pop pl* ... PA-2
Forks Township Elem Sch—*school* ... PA-2
**Forks (Township of)**—*pop pl* (2) ... PA-2
Forkstown (T3R2) (Township of)—*unorg* ... ME-1
Forks Trail—*trail* ... PA-2
Forks Trail—*trail* ... WV-2
Forks Valley—*valley* ... UT-8
Forksville—*cemetery* ... PA-2
Forksville—*locale* ... VA-3
**Forksville**—*pop pl* ... LA-4
**Forksville**—*pop pl* ... PA-2
Forksville Borough—*civil* ... PA-2
Forksville Ch—*church* ... SC-3
Forksville Covered Bridge—*hist pl* ... PA-2
**Forksville (RR name Skelton)**—*pop pl* .. VA-3
Fork Swamp—*stream* (3) ... NC-3
Fork Swamp—*swamp* ... NC-3
Fork Swamp—*swamp* ... SC-3
Fork Swamp—*swamp* ... VA-3
Fork Swamp Hunting Club—*other* ... SC-3
Forks Windmill—*locale* ... NM-5
Forks Windmill—*locale* (2) ... TX-5
Fork Tank—*reservoir* (5) ... AZ-5
Fork Tank—*reservoir* (2) ... NM-5
Forkton—*locale* ... KY-4
**Forktown**—*pop pl* ... TN-4
Fork (Township of)—*fmr MCD* (2) ... NC-3
**Fork (Township of)**—*pop pl* ... MI-6
**Fork (Township of)**—*pop pl* ... MN-6
Forkum Post Office (historical)—*building* ... TN-4
**Fork Union**—*pop pl* ... VA-3
Fork Union Ch—*church* ... VA-3
Fork Union (Magisterial
  District)—*fmr MCD* ... VA-3
Fork Union Military Acad—*school* ... VA-3
Fork Union Sch—*school* ... VA-3
**Forkvale (historical)**—*pop pl* ... TN-4
Forkvale Post Office (historical)—*building* . TN-4
**Forkville**—*pop pl* ... AL-4
**Forkville**—*pop pl* ... MS-4
Forkville Ch—*church* ... SC-3
Forkville Lookout Tower—*locale* ... MS-4
Forky Creek—*stream* ... AK-9
Forky Creek—*stream* ... GA-3
Forky Deer Creek—*stream* ... AR-4
*Forley's* ... MD-2
*Forley's Creek* ... MD-2
Forlies Rocks—*bar* ... NY-2
*Forlorn* ... MS-4
Forlorn Hope Mine—*mine* ... NV-8
Forlorn Hope Spring—*spring* ... NV-8
Forlorn Lakes—*lake* ... WA-9
Forman—*locale* ... IL-6
Forman—*locale* ... WV-2
**Forman**—*pop pl* ... IL-6
**Forman**—*pop pl* ... ND-7
**Forman**—*pop pl* ... OK-5
Forman, Tom, House—*hist pl* ... KY-4
*Forman Branch* ... GA-3
Forman Branch—*stream* ... TX-5
Forman Canyon—*valley* ... OR-9
Forman Cem—*cemetery* (2) ... AL-4
Forman Cem—*cemetery* ... MS-4
Forman Creek—*stream* ... IL-6
Formander Ridge—*ridge* ... OR-9
Forman Ditch—*canal* ... IN-6
Forman Gate Sch—*school* ... WV-2
Forman Hollow—*valley* ... IN-6
Forman HS—*school* ... IL-6
*Forman Lake* ... WI-6
Forman Lake—*lake* ... TX-5
Forman Ranch—*locale* ... AZ-5
Forman Ravine—*valley* ... CA-9
Forman Sch—*school* ... FL-3
Forman Sch (historical)—*school* ... PA-2
Forman School, The—*school* ... CT-1
Forman Shaft—*mine* ... NV-8
**Forman Township**—*pop pl* ... ND-7
Forman Wash—*stream* ... AZ-5
For-mar Nature Preserve—*park* ... MI-6
Formaster Tank—*reservoir* ... AZ-5
Formaster Well—*well* ... AZ-5
Formation Canyon—*valley* ... ID-8
Formation Cave—*cave* ... ID-8
Formation Pit—*cave* ... AL-4
*Former* ... NC-3
Former Bay Mine—*mine* ... CO-8
Former Emigrant Industrial Savings
  Bank—*hist pl* ... NY-2
Former Fire Station—*hist pl* ... CT-1
Former First Presbyterian Church—*hist pl* ... IN-6
Former Immaculate Conception
  Church—*hist pl* ... RI-1
Former McLean County
  Courthouse—*hist pl* ... ND-7
Former Montana Executive
  Mansion—*hist pl* ... MT-8
Former New York Life Insurance Company
  Bldg—*hist pl* ... NY-2
Former North Dakota Executive
  Mansion—*hist pl* ... ND-7
Former Police HQ Bldg—*hist pl* ... NY-2
Former Sioux County Courthouse—*hist pl* . ND-7
Former Vanderburgh County Sheriff's
  Residence—*hist pl* ... IN-6
Formica—*airport* ... NJ-2
Formidable, Mount—*summit* ... WA-9
Formo Lake—*lake* ... MN-6
Formosa—*locale* ... AR-4
Formosa—*locale* ... VA-3
Formosa—*uninc pl* ... FL-3
Formosa, Lake—*lake* ... FL-3
Formosa, Lake—*lake* ... LA-4
Formosa Junction—*locale* ... IL-6
Formosa Mine—*mine* ... SD-7
**Formoso**—*pop pl* ... KS-7
Form Point—*cape* ... AK-9
Formwalt Sch—*school* ... GA-3
Formwalt Windmill—*locale* ... TX-5
Fornachon Sch—*school* ... NJ-2
Fornance—*uninc pl* ... SC-3
Fornation Islands—*island* ... LA-4
Forndale Ch—*church* ... PA-2
Fornea Cem—*cemetery* ... LA-4
Fornear Lake—*lake* ... MS-4
Forness Park—*park* ... NY-2
Forney—*locale* ... ID-8
Forney—*locale* ... KS-7
Forney—*locale* ... OK-5
Forney—*locale* ... SC-3
**Forney**—*pop pl* ... AL-4
**Forney**—*pop pl* ... TX-5
Forney, Jacob, Jr., House—*hist pl* ... NC-3
Forney, James M., House—*hist pl* ... IA-7
Forney AAF Airp—*airport* ... MO-7
Forney Army Air Field—*airport* ... MO-7
Forney Ave Ch—*church* ... TX-5
Forney Branch—*stream* (2) ... AL-4
Forney Branch—*stream* ... SC-3
Forney (CCD)—*cens area* ... TX-5
Forney Cem—*cemetery* ... NC-3
Forney Cem—*cemetery* ... OH-6
Forney Cem—*cemetery* ... OK-5
Forney Cove—*bay* ... CA-9
Forney Creek—*stream* (2) ... NC-3
Forney Ditch—*canal* ... WY-8
Forney Draw—*valley* ... WY-8
Forney Post Office (historical)—*building* ... AL-4
Forney Ridge—*ridge* ... NC-3
Forney Ridge Parking Area—*locale* ... NC-3
Forneys Creek (Township of)—*fmr MCD* ... NC-3
Forneys Lake—*lake* ... IA-7
Forneys Lake State Game Mngmt
  Area—*park* ... IA-7
Forney Springs—*spring* ... WY-8
Forney Township (historical)—*civil* ... SD-7
*Fornfelt* ... MO-7
Fornham Creek—*stream* ... ID-8
Forni Creek—*stream* ... CA-9
Forni Lake—*lake* (2) ... CA-9
Fornis—*locale* ... CA-9
Fornof Sch—*school* ... OH-6
Forrer Number One, Lake—*reservoir* ... AL-4
Forrer Number Two, Lake—*reservoir* ... AL-4
Forrer Number 1 Dam—*dam* ... AL-4
Forrer Number 2 Dam—*dam* ... AL-4
*Forrest* ... IN-6
Forrest—*locale* ... AZ-5
**Forrest**—*pop pl* ... IL-6
**Forrest**—*pop pl* ... NM-5
Forrest, Edwin, House—*hist pl* ... PA-2
Forrest, Edwin, Sch—*hist pl* ... PA-2
Forrest, Lake—*lake* ... NM-5
Forrest, Nathan Bedford, Boyhood
  Home—*hist pl* ... TN-4
Forrest, W. B., House—*hist pl* ... TX-5
Forrest Aid Ch—*church* ... AR-4
Forrest Airp—*airport* ... AZ-5
Forrestal—*airport* ... NJ-2
Forrestal Bldg—*building* ... DC-2
Forrestal Sch—*school* ... NY-2
**Forrestal Village**—*pop pl* ... IL-6
Forrest Ave Baptist Ch—*church* ... AL-4
Forrest Ave Baptist Ch—*church* ... MS-4
Forrest Beach—*other* ... FL-3
Forrest Block—*hist pl* ... IA-7
Forrest Bonner—*locale* ... AR-4
Forrest Brook—*stream* ... NH-1
Forrest Cem—*cemetery* ... AL-4
Forrest Cem—*cemetery* ... IA-7
Forrest Cem—*cemetery* ... OK-5
Forrest Cem—*cemetery* ... TN-4
**Forrest City**—*pop pl* ... AR-4
**Forrest City (historical)**—*pop pl* ... MS-4
Forrest City Mine—*mine* ... SD-7
**Forrest County**—*pop pl* ... MS-4
*Forrest County Agricultural High School* ... MS-4
Forrest County Agricultural Sch—*school* ... MS-4
Forrest County Courthouse—*building* ... MS-4
Forrest County General Hosp—*hospital* ... MS-4
Forrest County Home—*locale* ... MS-4
Forrest Creek—*stream* ... NC-3
*Forrest Crossing* ... OR-9
**Forrestdale**—*pop pl* ... KY-4
Forrest Ditch—*canal* ... CO-8
Forrester—*locale* ... GA-3
Forrester—*locale* ... OK-5
Forrester—*other* ... TX-5
Forrester—*park* ... MA-1
Forrester, John T., House—*hist pl* ... AR-4
Forrester Branch—*stream* ... AR-4
Forrester Brown Ditch—*canal* ... CO-8
Forrester Cem—*cemetery* ... CO-8
Forrester Cem—*cemetery* ... GA-3
Forrester Cem—*cemetery* ... KY-4
Forrester Cem—*cemetery* ... MO-7
Forrester Cem—*cemetery* ... TN-4
Forrester Ch—*church* ... GA-3
Forrester Creek—*stream* (2) ... CO-8
Forrester Creek—*stream* ... KS-7
Forrester Ditch No. 1—*canal* ... CO-8
Forrester (historical)—*locale* ... KS-7
Forrester House—*hist pl* ... KY-4
Forrester Island—*island* ... AK-9
Forrester Island Bird Ref—*park* ... AK-9
Forrester Point—*cape* ... FL-3
Forrester Ranch—*locale* ... TX-5
Forrester Ridge—*ridge* ... NC-3
*Forresters Landing Strip* ... PA-2
*Forresters Point* ... FL-3
**Forrester Township**—*pop pl* ... KS-7
Forrester Warehouse (historical)—*locale* ... MA-1
*Forrest Grove* ... PA-2
*Forrest Grove* ... TX-5
**Forrest Grove Village (trailer**
  **park)**—*pop pl* ... DE-2
Forrest Hall—*locale* ... MD-2
Forrest Hall Branch—*stream* ... MD-2
Forrest Helton Lake—*reservoir* ... IN-6
*Forrest Hill* ... PA-2
Forrest Hill Cem—*cemetery* ... ME-1
Forrest Hill Ch—*church* ... TN-4
Forrest Hill Ch—*church* (2) ... VA-3
**Forrest Hills**—*pop pl* ... FL-3
**Forrest Hills**—*pop pl* ... GA-3
**Forrest Hills**—*pop pl* ... IN-6
**Forrest Hills**—*pop pl* ... SC-3
**Forrest Hills**—*pop pl* ... TN-4
Forrest Hills Cem—*cemetery* ... MO-7
**Forrest Hills (subdivision)**—*pop pl* ... MS-4
**Forrest Hills (subdivision)**—*pop pl* (2) .. TN-4
**Forrest (historical)**—*pop pl* ... MS-4
Forrest Home Ch—*church* ... AL-4
*Forrest Home Oil Field* ... MS-4
Forrest Ingram Dam—*dam* (2) ... AL-4
Forrest Lake—*reservoir* (2) ... NC-3
Forrest Lake Dam—*dam* (2) ... NC-3
**Forrest Lake Estates**—*pop pl* ... NJ-2
Forrest Lake (historical)—*reservoir* ... TN-4
Forrest Landing—*locale* ... VA-3
Forrest Landing Cove—*bay* ... MD-2
Forrest Lawn Cem—*cemetery* ... TX-5
Forrest Lowe Tank—*reservoir* ... TX-5
Forrest-Marbury House—*hist pl* ... DC-2
Forrest Maxie Sch—*school* ... MS-4
Forrest Memorial—*other* ... AL-4
Forrest Memorial Ch—*church* ... VA-3
Forrest Memorial Gardens—*cemetery* ... MS-4
Forrest Memorial Park—*cemetery* ... MS-4
**Forrest Mill**—*pop pl* ... MO-7
Forrest Milling Company Oatmeal
  Mill—*hist pl* ... IA-7
Forrest Mill Methodist Ch—*church* ... TN-4
*Forrest Mills Baptist Ch* ... TN-4
Forrest Oil Field—*other* ... NM-5
**Forreston**—*pop pl* ... IL-6
**Forreston**—*pop pl* ... MS-4
**Forreston**—*pop pl* ... TX-5
Forreston Cem—*cemetery* ... TX-5
**Forreston (Township of)**—*pop pl* ... IL-6
Forrest Park—*park* ... AL-4
Forrest Park—*park* ... TN-4
**Forrest Park**—*pop pl* ... CA-9
**Forrest Park**—*pop pl* ... KY-4
**Forrest Park**—*pop pl* ... TN-4
Forrest Park Cem—*cemetery* ... AR-4
Forrest Park Sch—*school* ... AR-4
Forrest Point—*cape* ... TN-4
*Forrest Port* ... NY-2
Forrest Ranch—*locale* ... AZ-5
*Forrest River* ... GA-3
**Forrest Road Homes**
  **(subdivision)**—*pop pl* ... NC-3
Forrest Road Sch—*school* ... GA-3
Forrest Rsvr—*reservoir* ... MT-8
Forrest Sch—*school* ... OH-6
Forrest Sch—*school* ... PA-2
Forrest Sch—*school* ... TN-4
Forrest Sch (historical)—*school* ... MS-4
Forrest Sch (historical)—*school* ... MO-7
*Forrest Springs* ... MO-7
*Forrests Ranch* ... AZ-5

Fort Early Ch—*church* ... GA-3
Fort Easley (historical)—*military* ... AL-4
Fort Ebey Military Reservation—*other* ... WA-9
Fort Eddy—*lake* ... NH-1
Fort Edgecomb—*hist pl* ... ME-1
**Fort Edgecomb**—*pop pl* ... ME-1
**Fort Edward**—*pop pl* ... NY-2
**Fort Edward (Town of)**—*pop pl* ... NY-2
Fort Egypt—*hist pl* ... VA-3
**Fort Elfsborg**—*pop pl* ... NJ-2
Fort Elliott (Historical Site)—*locale* ... TX-5
Fort Ellis Farm Bureau Community Bldg—*building* ... MT-8
Fort Ellis Historical Marker—*park* ... MT-8
*Fort Ellsworth* ... KS-7
Fort Ellsworth—*locale* ... VA-3
*Fort Elsenburgh* ... NJ-2
Fort Emory—*locale* ... VA-3
Fortenberry—*locale* ... MS-4
Fortenberry Cem—*cemetery* (4) ... MS-4
Fortenberry Creek—*stream* ... GA-3
Fortenberry Lake Dam—*dam* ... MS-4
Fortenberry Pond Dam—*dam* ... MS-4
Fortenberry West Oil Field—*oilfield* ... TX-5
**Fortener Addition**—*pop pl* ... VA-3
**Fortenia**—*pop pl* ... PA-2
*Forten Island* ... NC-3
*Forter Island* ... NC-3
**Fortescue**—*pop pl* ... MO-7
**Fortescue**—*pop pl* ... NJ-2
Fortescue Beach—*beach* ... NJ-2
*Fortescue Creek* ... NC-3
Fortescue Creek—*gut* ... NJ-2
Fortescue Creek—*stream* ... NC-3
Fortescue Fish and Wildlife Mngmt Area—*park* ... NJ-2
Fortescue Hill—*summit* ... TN-4
Fortescue Island (historical)—*island* ... NJ-2
Fortescue Neck—*cape* ... NJ-2
*Fortesque* ... NJ-2
*Fortesque Beach* ... NJ-2
*Fortesque Creek* ... NJ-2
*Fortesque Neck* ... NJ-2
**Fort Estill**—*pop pl* ... KY-4
Fort Ethan Allen—*locale* ... VA-3
Fort Ethan Allen Milit Reservation—*military* ... VT-1
Fort Eugene Hall Armory—*military* ... AL-4
Fort Eustis Milit Reservation—*military* ... VA-3
Fort Eustis (U.S. Army)—*military* ... VA-3
Fort Ewell Creek—*stream* ... TX-5
Fort Ewell Historical Monmt—*park* ... TX-5
**Fort Fairfield**—*pop pl* ... ME-1
**Fort Fairfield (Town of)**—*pop pl* ... ME-1
Fort Falls—*falls* ... NE-7
Fort Fanning (historical)—*locale* ... FL-3
Fort Farm Island—*island* ... NE-7
Fort Farnsworth—*locale* ... VA-3
**Fort Fetter**—*pop pl* ... PA-2
Fort Fetterman—*hist pl* ... WY-8
Fort Fetterman Cem—*cemetery* ... WY-8
Fort Fillmore—*hist pl* ... NM-5
Fort Fillmore (Ruins)—*locale* ... NM-5
*Fort Fin* ... TX-5
Fort Fisher—*hist pl* ... NC-3
Fort Fisher—*locale* ... VA-3
Fort Fisher Air Force Station—*military* ... NC-3
Fort Fisher Country Club—*locale* ... NC-3
Fort Fisher State Historic Site—*park* ... NC-3
Fort Fitzhugh (site)—*locale* ... TX-5
Fort Fizzle—*locale* ... OH-6
Fort Fizzle Site—*hist pl* ... MT-8
Fort Flagler—*hist pl* ... WA-9
Fort Flagler State Park—*park* ... WA-9
Fort Flat—*flat* ... MA-1
Fort Flatmouth Mounds—*hist pl* ... MN-6
*Fort Fletcher* ... KS-7
**Fort Florida**—*pop pl* ... FL-3
Fort Florida Point—*cape* ... FL-3
**Fort Flournoy (historical)**—*pop pl* ... OR-9
*Fort Floyd* ... ND-7
Fort Floyd (historical)—*locale* ... FL-3
*Fort Foote* ... MD-2
Fort Foote—*locale* ... MD-2
**Fort Foote Estates**—*pop pl* ... MD-2
Fort Foote Park—*park* ... MD-2
Fort Foote Sch—*school* ... MD-2
**Fort Foote Village**—*pop pl* ... MD-2
Fort Foster—*hist pl* ... FL-3
Fort Foster (historical)—*locale* ... FL-3
Fort Francis E Warren Target And Maneuver Reservation—*other* ... WY-8
Fort Frederica Natl Monmt—*hist pl* ... GA-3
Fort Frederica Natl Monmt—*park* ... GA-3
Fort Frederick—*hist pl* ... SC-3
Fort Frederick—*locale* ... VI-3
Fort Frederick State Park—*hist pl* ... MD-2
Fort Frederick State Park—*park* ... MD-2
*Fort Fred Steele* ... WY-8
Fort Fred Steele—*locale* ... WY-8
**Fort Fremont**—*pop pl* ... SC-3
Fort Frye Sch—*school* ... OH-6
Fort Funston Milit Reservation—*military* ... CA-9
Fort Gadsden—*locale* ... FL-3
Fort Gadsden Bridge—*bridge* ... FL-3
Fort Gadsden Creek—*stream* ... FL-3
Fort Gadsden Historic Memorial—*hist pl* ... FL-3
Fort Gadsden State Historic Site—*park* ... FL-3
*Fort Gadsden State Park* ... FL-3
Fort Gage—*locale* ... IL-6
Fort Gaines—*hist pl* ... AL-4
Fort Gaines—*locale* ... AL-4
**Fort Gaines**—*pop pl* ... GA-3
Fort Gaines (CCD)—*cens area* ... GA-3
Fort Gaines Cemetery Site—*hist pl* ... GA-3
Fort Gaines Hist Dist—*hist pl* ... GA-3
Fort Gaines (historical)—*locale* ... DC-2
*Fort Gaines Lake* ... AL-4
*Fort Gaines Lock and Dam* ... AL-4
Fort Galpin (historical)—*locale* ... SD-7
Fort Gap—*gap* ... NC-3
Fort Gardner (historical)—*locale* ... FL-3
Fort Garland—*hist pl* ... CO-8
**Fort Garland**—*pop pl* ... CO-8
Fort Garland Cem—*cemetery* ... CO-8
Fort Garrett Point—*cliff* ... AZ-5
Fort Garrett (ruin)—*locale* ... AZ-5
Fort Garrison—*hist pl* ... MD-2
Fort Garrott (historical)—*locale* ... MS-4
**Fort Gates**—*pop pl* ... FL-3
**Fort Gates**—*pop pl* ... TX-5
Fort Gatlin Alliance Ch—*church* ... FL-3
**Fort Gay**—*pop pl* ... WV-2
**Fort Gay (Cassville)**—*pop pl* ... WV-2
Fort Gay Hill—*summit* ... MT-8
*Fort George* (2) ... FL-3
*Fort George* ... OR-9
*Fort George* ... VA-3
Fort George—*hist pl* ... ME-1
Fort George—*locale* ... ME-1
Fort George—*uninc pl* ... NY-2
Fort George Butte—*summit* ... SD-7
*Fort George Buttes* ... SD-7
Fort George Creek—*stream* ... SD-7
Fort George Creek Archeol District—*hist pl* ... SD-7
**Fort George G Meade**—*pop pl* ... MD-2
**Fort George G. Meade (Fort Meade) (U.S. Army)**—*pop pl* ... MD-2
Fort George G Mead Junction—*locale* ... MD-2
Fort George (historical)—*locale* ... SD-7
Fort George Inlet—*gut* ... FL-3
Fort George Island—*island* ... FL-3
Fort George Island—*locale* ... FL-3
Fort George Island (Fort George)—*uninc pl* ... FL-3
Fort George Island (historical)—*island* ... SD-7
Fort George River—*gut* ... FL-3
Fort George Site—*hist pl* ... FL-3
Fort George Wright Hist Dist—*hist pl* ... WA-9
*Fort Gibson* ... MS-4
Fort Gibson—*hist pl* ... OK-5
**Fort Gibson**—*pop pl* ... OK-5
Fort Gibson Cem—*cemetery* ... OK-5
Fort Gibson Dam—*dam* ... OK-5
**Fort Gibson (historical)**—*pop pl* ... IN-6
Fort Gibson Lake—*reservoir* ... OK-5
Fort Gibson Natl Cem—*cemetery* ... OK-5
*Fort Gibson Reservoir* ... OK-5
Fort Gibson Stockade—*locale* ... OK-5
Fort Gillem (U S Army)—*military* ... GA-3
Fort Gilmer—*locale* ... VA-3
Fort Glenn—*locale* ... AK-9
Fort Goff—*locale* ... CA-9
Fort Goff Creek—*stream* ... CA-9
Fort Goicoechea Ranch—*locale* ... NV-8
Fort Golgotha and the Old Burial Hill Cemetery—*hist pl* ... NY-2
*Fort Goodwin* ... AZ-5
Fort Gordon—*locale* ... GA-3
Fort Gordon (CCD)—*cens area* ... GA-3
Fort Gordon Rec Area—*park* ... GA-3
Fort Gordon (U.S. Army)—*military* ... GA-3
Fort Gorges—*hist pl* ... ME-1
Fort Gorges—*locale* ... ME-1
Fort Graham Cem—*cemetery* ... TX-5
**Fort Grand**—*pop pl* ... WV-2
**Fort Grande**—*pop pl* ... WV-2
Fort Granger—*hist pl* ... TN-4
Fort Grant (historical)—*locale* ... AZ-5
*Fort Grant Military Reservation* ... AZ-5
Fort Grant Road Interchange—*crossing* ... AZ-5
Fort Grant (State Industrial School)—*school* ... AZ-5
Fort Grant Training Center—*other* ... AZ-5
Fort Grant Vista Point—*locale* ... AZ-5
Fort Gratiot—*hist pl* ... MI-6
Fort Gratiot Lighthouse—*hist pl* ... MI-6
Fort Gratiot (Township of)—*civ div* ... MI-6
Fort Greble—*locale* ... DC-2
Fort Greely—*locale* ... AK-9
Fort Greely (U.S. Army)—*military* ... AK-9
Fort Green—*locale* ... FL-3
**Fort Greene**—*pop pl* ... NY-2
Fort Greene Hist Dist—*hist pl* ... NY-2
Fort Greene Hist Dist (Boundary Increase)—*hist pl* ... NY-2
Fort Greene Park—*park* ... NY-2
Fort Green Post Office—*building* ... FL-3
**Fort Green Springs**—*pop pl* ... FL-3
Fort Gregg—*locale* ... VA-3
Fort Griffin—*hist pl* ... TX-5
Fort Griffin—*locale* ... TX-5
Fort Griffin Brazos River Bridge—*hist pl* ... TX-5
Fort Griffin Cem—*cemetery* ... TX-5
Fort Griffin (Historical Site)—*locale* ... TX-5
Fort Griffin State Park—*park* ... TX-5
**Fort Griffin (State Park)**—*pop pl* ... TX-5
Fort Griswold—*hist pl* ... CT-1
Fort Griswold State Park—*park* ... CT-1
Fort Grizzly Site—*locale* ... CA-9
*Fort Growl* ... MS-4
Fort Haldimand Site—*hist pl* ... NY-2
Fort Hale (historical)—*locale* ... SD-7
Fort Halifax—*hist pl* ... ME-1
Fort Hall—*cens area* (3) ... ID-8
Fort Hall—*hist pl* ... ID-8
**Fort Hall**—*pop pl* ... ID-8
Fort Hall Bottoms—*flat* ... ID-8
Fort Hall Canyon—*valley* ... ID-8
Fort Halleck—*hist pl* ... WY-8
Fort Halleck Cem—*cemetery* ... NV-8
Fort Halleck Historical Marker—*park* ... NV-8
*Fort Halleck Historic Site* ... NV-8
Fort Halleck Memorial—*locale* ... WY-8
Fort Hall Hill—*summit* ... ID-8
Fort Hall Historic Monmt—*park* ... ID-8
Fort Hall Indian Agency—*locale* ... ID-8
**Fort Hall Ind Res**—*pop pl* ... ID-8
Fort Hall Main Canal—*canal* ... ID-8
Fort Hall Mine—*mine* ... ID-8
Fort Hall No 2 Historic Site—*locale* ... ID-8
Fort Hall Site—*hist pl* ... ID-8
Fort Hall Spring—*spring* ... ID-8
*Fort Hamblin* ... UT-8
Fort Hamer—*locale* ... FL-3
*Fort Hamilton* ... UT-8
Fort Hamilton—*locale* ... NY-2
**Fort Hamilton**—*pop pl* ... NY-2
Fort Hamilton Cem—*cemetery* ... IN-6
Fort Hamilton HS—*school* ... NY-2
Fort Hamilton Monmt—*pillar* ... OH-6
Fort Hamilton Park—*park* ... NY-2
Fort Hamilton (U.S. Army)—*military* ... NY-2
Fort Hamlin Hills—*other* ... AK-9
Fort Hamlin (Site)—*locale* ... AK-9
Fort Hammock—*island* ... GA-3
*Fort Hampton* ... AL-4
Fort Hampton (historical)—*military* ... AL-4
*Fort Hampton Post Office* ... AL-4
*Fort Hampton Road Dam* ... AL-4
Fort Hancock—*military* ... NJ-2
**Fort Hancock**—*pop pl* ... TX-5
Fort Hancock, U.S. Life Saving Station—*hist pl* ... NJ-2
Fort Hancock and the Sandy Hook Proving Ground Hist Dist—*hist pl* ... NJ-2
Fort Hancock (CCD)—*cens area* ... TX-5
Fort Hancock (U.S. Army)—*other* ... NJ-2
*Fort Handcock* ... TX-5
Fort Hand Historical Marker—*other* ... PA-2
*Fort Harker* ... KS-7
Fort Harker—*hist pl* ... AL-4
Fort Harker Guardhouse—*hist pl* ... KS-7
Fort Harker (historical)—*locale* ... KS-7
Fort Harker Officers' Quarters—*hist pl* ... KS-7
Fort Harkness (Site)—*locale* ... ID-8
Fort Harmony Monmt—*park* ... UT-8
Fort Harmony Site—*hist pl* ... UT-8
Fort Harney (site)—*locale* ... OR-9
Fort Harold Calhoun Natl Guard Armory—*military* ... AL-4
Fort Harrison—*locale* ... VA-3
**Fort Harrison**—*pop pl* ... MT-8
Fort Harrison Country Club—*other* ... IN-6
Fort Harrison (historical)—*locale* ... FL-3
**Fort Harrison (historical)**—*pop pl* ... IN-6
Fort Harrison Terminal Station—*hist pl* ... IN-6
Fort Harry—*locale* ... TN-4
Fort Hartsuff—*hist pl* ... NE-7
Fort Hartsuff Sch—*school* ... NE-7
Fort Hartsuff (site)—*locale* ... NE-7
Fort Hase Cove—*bay* ... HI-9
Fort Hatch (Ruins)—*locale* ... NM-5
Fort Hatteras—*locale* ... NC-3
Fort Hawkins Archeol Site—*hist pl* ... GA-3
Fort Hawkins Cem—*cemetery* ... GA-3
Fort Hawkins Sch—*school* ... GA-3
Fort Hayes—*hist pl* ... OH-6
Fort Hayes Milit Reservation—*military* ... OH-6
Fort Hays—*hist pl* ... KS-7
Fort Hays (historical)—*locale* ... KS-7
Fort Hays Memorial Gardens—*cemetery* ... KS-7
*Fort Hays State College* ... KS-7
Fort Hays State Univ—*school* ... KS-7
Fort Hazel Sch—*school* ... NE-7
Forth Cem—*cemetery* ... IL-6
**Fort Heath**—*pop pl* ... MA-1
Fort Heilman (historical)—*locale* ... FL-3
Fort Heiman—*locale* ... KY-4
Fort Heiman Site—*hist pl* ... KY-4
**Fort Henrietta (historical)**—*pop pl* ... OR-9
Fort Henry—*locale* ... MO-7
**Fort Henry**—*pop pl* ... TN-4
Fort Henry Branch—*stream* ... TN-4
Fort Henry Bridge—*other* ... WV-2
Fort Henry Historic Monmt—*park* ... ID-8
Fort Henry Landing (historical)—*locale* ... TN-4
Fort Henry Mall Shop Ctr—*locale* ... TN-4
Fort Henry Post Office (historical)—*building* ... TN-4
Fort Henry Sch—*school* ... IL-6
Fort Henry Site—*hist pl* ... TN-4
**Fort Herkimer**—*pop pl* ... NY-2
Fort Herkimer Church—*hist pl* ... NY-2
Fort Herriman Historical Marker—*park* ... UT-8
*Fort Hill* ... ME-1
*Fort Hill* ... OH-6
Fort Hill—*hist pl* ... OH-6
Fort Hill—*hist pl* ... SC-3
Fort Hill—*locale* ... CT-1
Fort Hill—*locale* (3) ... NY-2
**Fort Hill**—*pop pl* ... CT-1
**Fort Hill**—*pop pl* ... MA-1
**Fort Hill**—*pop pl* ... NY-2
**Fort Hill**—*pop pl* ... OR-9
**Fort Hill**—*pop pl* (2) ... PA-2
**Fort Hill**—*pop pl* (2) ... VA-3
**Fort Hill**—*pop pl* ... WV-2
Fort Hill—*summit* (5) ... CT-1
Fort Hill—*summit* ... GA-3
Fort Hill—*summit* ... KY-4
Fort Hill—*summit* (3) ... ME-1
Fort Hill—*summit* (2) ... MD-2
Fort Hill—*summit* (3) ... MA-1
Fort Hill—*summit* ... MS-4
Fort Hill—*summit* ... NH-1
Fort Hill—*summit* (3) ... NY-2
Fort Hill—*summit* ... NC-3
Fort Hill—*summit* ... OH-6
Fort Hill—*summit* ... OK-5
Fort Hill—*summit* ... OR-9
Fort Hill—*summit* (4) ... PA-2
Fort Hill—*summit* (2) ... RI-1
Fort Hill—*summit* ... SC-3
Fort Hill—*summit* (2) ... TN-4
Fort Hill—*summit* (2) ... WV-2
Fort Hill—*summit* ... WY-8
Fort Hill Brook—*stream* ... CT-1
Fort Hill Brook—*stream* ... ME-1
Fort Hill Cem—*cemetery* ... IL-6
Fort Hill Cem—*cemetery* ... KY-4
Fort Hill Cem—*cemetery* ... ME-1
Fort Hill Cem—*cemetery* ... MA-1
Fort Hill Cem—*cemetery* ... NY-2
Fort Hill Cem—*cemetery* ... TN-4
Fort Hill Ch—*church* ... IN-6
Fort Hill Ch—*church* ... PA-2
Fort Hill Estate—*hist pl* ... NY-2
Fort Hill HS—*school* ... MD-2
Fort Hill Memorial Park Cem—*cemetery* ... VA-3
Fort Hill Park—*park* ... CT-1
Fort Hill Park—*park* ... MA-1
Fort Hill Park—*park* ... NY-2
*Fort Hills* ... PA-2
Fort Hill Sch—*school* ... GA-3
Fort Hill Sch (abandoned)—*school* ... PA-2
Fort Hill State Park—*hist pl* ... OH-6
Fort Hill (U.S. Army)—*military* ... VA-3
Fort Hill Village Shop Ctr—*locale* ... VA-3
Fort Hill Youth Camp—*locale* ... OH-6
Forth Island—*island* ... FL-3
Fort Hoke—*locale* ... VA-3
Fort Holabird—*locale* ... MD-2
**Fort Holabird**—*pop pl* ... MD-2
Fort Hollow—*valley* ... AL-4
Fort Hollow—*valley* ... TX-5
Fort Holmes—*locale* ... MI-6
*Fort Honk* ... NY-2
Fort Hood—*military* ... TX-5
Fort Hood (CCD)—*cens area* (2) ... TX-5
Fort Hood Rec Area—*park* ... TX-5
Fort Hood (U.S. Army)—*military* ... TX-5
Fort Horn Monmt—*park* ... AZ-5
*Fort Hoskins* ... OR-9
Fort Hoskins Site—*hist pl* ... OR-9
Fort House—*hist pl* ... TX-5
Fort Houston Cem—*cemetery* (2) ... TX-5
**Fort Howard**—*pop pl* ... MD-2
Fort Howard Cem—*cemetery* ... WI-6
Fort Howard Hosp—*hist pl* ... WI-6
Fort Howard Officers' Quarters—*hist pl* ... WI-6
Fort Howard Park—*park* ... WI-6
Fort Howard Sch—*school* ... WI-6
Fort Howard Veterans Hosp—*hospital* ... MD-2
Fort Howard (Veterans Hospital)—*hospital* ... MD-2
Fort Howard Ward Bldg—*hist pl* ... WI-6
Fort Howes (Historical Site)—*locale* ... MT-8
Fort Howes Ranger Station—*locale* ... MT-8
Fort Huachuca—*hist pl* ... AZ-5
Fort Huachuca—*military* ... AZ-5
*Fort Huachuca Milit Reservation* ... AZ-5
Fort Hudson Ch—*church* ... TN-4
Fort Hudson Sch (historical)—*school* ... TN-4
*Fort Huger* ... AL-4
*Fort Hull Cemetery* ... AL-4
Fort Hull Ch—*church* ... AL-4
Fort Hull Sch (historical)—*school* ... AL-4
Fort Humboldt State Historical Monmt—*park* ... CA-9
*Fort Humphreys* ... VA-3
Fort Hunt—*CDP* ... VA-3
Fort Hunt—*hist pl* ... VA-3
**Fort Hunter**—*pop pl* (2) ... NY-2
**Fort Hunter**—*pop pl* ... PA-2
Fort Hunter Hist Dist—*hist pl* ... PA-2
Fort Hunter Liggett—*military* ... CA-9
Fort Hunter Museum—*building* ... PA-2
Fort Hunt HS—*school* ... VA-3
Fort Hunt Natl Park—*park* ... VA-3
**Forthun Township**—*pop pl* ... ND-7
Fortier, Bayou—*stream* ... LA-4
Fortier Cem—*cemetery* ... MN-6
Fortier Creek—*stream* ... ID-8
Fortier Field—*park* ... OR-9
**Fortier Heights**—*pop pl* ... LA-4
Fortier HS—*school* ... LA-4
Fortier Pond—*lake* ... VT-1
**Fortier (Township of)**—*pop pl* ... MN-6
**Fortieth Street**—*pop pl* ... PA-2
Fortieth Street Boca Raton Bridge—*bridge* ... FL-3
Fortieth Street Bridge—*hist pl* ... PA-2
Fortieth Street Sch—*school* ... AZ-5
Fortification—*locale* ... CO-8
Fortification Bluff—*cliff* ... AK-9
Fortification Creek—*stream* ... CO-8
Fortification Creek—*stream* ... WY-8
*Fortification Hall* ... CO-8
Fortification Hill—*summit* ... AZ-5
*Fortification Island* ... NV-8
*Fortification Mtn* ... AZ-5
Fortification Mtn—*summit* ... WY-8
Fortification Range—*range* ... NV-8
Fortification Ridge—*ridge* ... AZ-5
*Fortification Rock* ... NV-8
Fortification Rocks—*pillar* ... CO-8
Fortification Spring—*spring* ... NV-8
Fortification Well—*well* ... NV-8
Fortified Hill Works—*hist pl* ... OH-6
Fortified Peak—*summit* ... AZ-5
Fortin Bay—*bay* ... NC-3
Fortin de la Cienega—*hist pl* ... TX-5
Fort Independence—*hist pl* ... MA-1
Fort Independence—*locale* ... MA-1
**Fort Independence Ind Res**—*pop pl* ... CA-9
Fort Independence Park—*park* ... NY-2
Fortin de San Geronimo de Boqueron—*hist pl* ... PR-3
Fort Indiantown Gap—*locale* ... PA-2
Fort Indiantown Gap—*military* ... PA-2
Fortin Draw—*valley* ... WY-8
Fort Industry Square—*hist pl* ... OH-6
**Fortine**—*pop pl* ... MT-8
Fortine Creek—*stream* ... MT-8
Fort Inge—*locale* ... TX-5
Fort Inge Archeol Site—*hist pl* ... TX-5
Fortin Island—*island* ... NC-3
Fortin Site—*hist pl* ... NY-2
*Fort Irwin* ... CA-9
Fort Irwin (U.S. Army)—*military* ... CA-9
*Fort Island* ... AK-9
*Fort Island* ... ME-1
Fort Island—*island* ... FL-3
Fort Island—*island* (2) ... ME-1
Fort Island—*island* ... NC-3
Fort Island—*island* ... RI-1
*Fort Island Key* ... FL-3
Fort Island Sch—*school* ... OH-6
Fort Island Works—*hist pl* ... OH-6
Fort Islet—*island* ... AK-9
Fort Jackson—*hist pl* ... GA-3
Fort Jackson—*hist pl* ... LA-4
Fort Jackson—*locale* ... LA-4
Fort Jackson—*military* ... SC-3
Fort Jackson—*other* ... GA-3
**Fort Jackson**—*pop pl* ... NY-2
Fort Jackson (historical)—*military* ... AL-4
Fort Jackson Hopkinton Cem—*cemetery* ... NY-2
Fort James H Wright, Jr Armory—*military* ... AL-4
Fort James (39HS48)—*hist pl* ... SD-7
Fort Jay—*hist pl* ... NY-2
Fort Jay—*locale* ... NY-2
Fort Jeb Stuart (historical)—*locale* ... AL-4
Fort Jefferson—*locale* ... FL-3
**Fort Jefferson**—*pop pl* ... OH-6
Fort Jefferson Natl Monmt—*hist pl* ... FL-3
Fort Jefferson Natl Monmt—*park* ... FL-3
Fort Jefferson Site—*hist pl* ... OH-6
Fort Jefferson State Memorial—*park* ... OH-6
**Fort Jennings**—*pop pl* ... OH-6
*Fort Jessup* ... LA-4
Fort Jessup State Commemorative Area—*park* ... LA-4
Fort Jesup—*hist pl* ... LA-4
Fort Jesup—*locale* ... LA-4
*Fort Jewell* ... KS-7
Fort Jewell (historical)—*locale* ... KS-7
*Fort Jim* ... CA-9
Fort Johnson—*hist pl* ... NY-2
Fort Johnson—*locale* ... UT-8
Fort Johnson—*locale* ... VA-3
**Fort Johnson**—*pop pl* ... NY-2
Fort Johnson Creek—*stream* ... SC-3
Fort Johnson Marine Biological Station—*locale* ... SC-3
Fort Johnson/Powder Magazine—*hist pl* ... SC-3
*Fort Johnston* ... NC-3
Fort Johnston—*hist pl* ... NC-3
**Fort Jones**—*pop pl* ... CA-9
Fort Jones (CCD)—*cens area* ... CA-9
Fort Jones Historic Marker—*locale* ... CA-9
Fort Jones House—*hist pl* ... CA-9
Fort Julesburg—*locale* ... CO-8
Fort Junction—*locale* ... NC-3
Fort Kamehameha Milit Reservation—*military* ... HI-9
*Fort Kasimier* ... DE-2
Fort Kaskaskia State Park—*park* ... IL-6
Fort Kearney—*hist pl* ... NE-7
Fort Kearney State Park—*park* ... NE-7
Fort Kent—*hist pl* ... ME-1
**Fort Kent**—*pop pl* ... ME-1
Fort Kent Center (census name Fort Kent)—*other* ... ME-1
**Fort Kent Mills**—*pop pl* ... ME-1
Fort Kent Pit—*locale* ... ME-1
**Fort Kent (Town of)**—*pop pl* ... ME-1
**Fort Kent Village**—*pop pl* ... ME-1
Fort Keogh—*hist pl* ... MT-8
**Fort Keogh**—*pop pl* ... MT-8
**Fort King Acres**—*pop pl* ... FL-3
Fort King Baptist Ch—*church* ... FL-3
Fort King Burial Grounds—*cemetery* ... FL-3
Fort King George—*hist pl* ... GA-3
Fort King (historical)—*locale* ... FL-3
Fort King JHS—*school* ... FL-3
Fort Kipp—*locale* ... MT-8
Fort Kirkland Branch—*stream* ... FL-3
Fort Kissimmee—*locale* ... FL-3
Fort Kissimmee Cem—*cemetery* ... FL-3
**Fort Klamath**—*pop pl* ... OR-9
Fort Klamath Cem—*cemetery* ... OR-9
Fort Klamath Elem Sch—*school* ... OR-9
Fort Klamath Junction—*locale* ... OR-9
Fort Klamath Park—*park* ... OR-9
Fort Klamath Site—*hist pl* ... OR-9
Fort Klock—*hist pl* ... NY-2
Fort Knob—*summit* ... WV-2
*Fortknocker* ... UT-8
Fortknocker Canyon—*valley* ... UT-8
Fort Knox (CCD)—*cens area* ... KY-4
**Fort Knox (historical)**—*pop pl* ... IN-6
Fort Knox II Site—*hist pl* ... IN-6
Fort Knox State Park—*hist pl* ... ME-1
Fortknox State Park—*park* ... ME-1
Fort Knox (U.S. Army)—*military* ... KY-4
Fort LaClede—*locale* ... WY-8
Fort LaFramboise Number One (historical)—*locale* ... SD-7
Fort LaFramboise Number Two (historical)—*locale* ... SD-7
Fort Lake—*lake* ... TX-5
Fort Lake—*lake* ... WY-8
Fort Lamar—*locale* ... GA-3
Fort Lancaster—*hist pl* ... TX-5
Fort Lancaster—*locale* ... TX-5
Fort Landing—*locale* ... NC-3
Fort Lane (historical)—*locale* ... FL-3
Fort Lane Military Post Site—*hist pl* ... OR-9
**Fort Lane Plaza Condominium**—*pop pl* ... UT-8
Fort Lane Shop Ctr—*locale* ... UT-8
Fort Lane (site)—*locale* ... OR-9
**Fort Lane Subdivision**—*pop pl* ... UT-8
**Fort Laramie**—*pop pl* ... WY-8
Fort Laramie Canal—*canal* ... NE-7
Fort Laramie Canal—*canal* ... WY-8
Fort Laramie Ditch—*canal* ... WY-8
Fort Laramie Natl Historical Site—*park* ... WY-8
Fort Laramie Natl Monmt—*park* ... WY-8
Fort Laramie Three-Mile Hog Ranch—*hist pl* ... WY-8
Fort Laramie To Fort Robinson Trail—*trail* ... NE-7
Fort Larned Natl Historic Site—*hist pl* ... KS-7
Fort Larned Natl Historic Site—*park* ... KS-7
*Fort Larned Natl Landmark* ... KS-7
*Fort Lashley* ... AL-4
*Fort Lasslie* ... AL-4
**Fort Lauderdale**—*pop pl* ... FL-3
Fort Lauderdale Beach—*beach* ... FL-3
**Fort Lauderdale Beach**—*pop pl* ... FL-3
Fort Lauderdale (CCD)—*cens area* ... FL-3
Fort Lauderdale Christian Reford Ch—*church* ... FL-3
Fort Lauderdale Christian Sch—*school* ... FL-3
Fort Lauderdale Coll—*school* ... FL-3
Fort Lauderdale-Hollywood International Airp—*airport* ... FL-3
Fort Lauderdale Hosp—*hospital* ... FL-3
Fort Lauderdale HS—*school* ... FL-3
Fort Lauderdale Stadium—*locale* ... FL-3
Fort Lauderdale Strip Shop Ctr—*locale* ... FL-3
Fort Laurens Cem—*cemetery* ... OH-6
Fort Laurens Site—*hist pl* ... OH-6
Fort Laurens State Memorial—*park* ... OH-6
**Fort Lawn**—*pop pl* ... SC-3
Fort Lawton—*hist pl* ... WA-9
Fort Lawton Army Heliport—*airport* ... WA-9
Fort Lawton Military Reservation—*other* ... WA-9
Fort Lawton (U.S. Army)—*military* ... WA-9
Fort Leaton—*hist pl* ... TX-5
Fort Leaton State Historic Site—*park* ... TX-5
*Fort Leavenworth* ... KS-7
Fort Leavenworth—*hist pl* ... KS-7
Fort Leavenworth—*military* ... KS-7
Fort Leavenworth Milit Reservation—*military* ... KS-7
Fort LeBoeuf Senior HS—*school* ... PA-2
Fort Lee—*locale* (2) ... VA-3
**Fort Lee**—*pop pl* ... NJ-2
Fort Lee Air Force Station—*military* ... VA-3
Fort Lee Milit Reservation—*military* ... VA-3
Fort Lee Rec Area—*park* ... VA-3
Fort Lee (U.S. Army)—*military* ... VA-3
Fort Leflore—*hist pl* ... MS-4
Fort Leflore (historical)—*locale* ... MS-4
Fort Lemhi—*hist pl* ... ID-8
Fort Lemhi Monmt—*park* ... ID-8
Fort Leonard Wood—*other* ... MO-7
Fort Leonard Wood Milit Reservation—*military* ... MO-7
Fort Leonard Wood Rec Area—*park* ... MO-7
Fort Leonard Wood State Wildlife Mngmt Area—*park* ... MO-7
Fort Leslie (historical)—*locale* ... AL-4
Fort Levett—*locale* ... ME-1
Fort Lewis—*locale* ... VA-3
Fort Lewis—*other* ... WA-9
Fort Lewis Cem—*cemetery* ... WA-9
Fort Lewis Ch—*church* ... VA-3
Fort Lewis Coll—*school* ... CO-8
Fort Lewis-Dupont (CCD)—*cens area* ... WA-9
Fort Lewis Mesa Sch—*school* ... CO-8
Fort Lewis Mtn—*summit* ... VA-3
Fort Lewis North Post—*other* ... WA-9
Fort Lewis Sch—*school* ... VA-3
Fort Lewis Terrace—*uninc pl* ... VA-3
Fort Lewis Trail—*trail* ... VA-3
Fort Lewis (U.S. Army)—*military* ... WA-9
Fortlick Run—*stream* ... WV-2
Fort Ligonier—*locale* ... PA-2
Fort Ligonier Site—*hist pl* ... PA-2
Fort Lincoln—*military* ... DC-2
**Fort Lincoln**—*pop pl* ... ND-7
Fort Lincoln Cem—*cemetery* ... MD-2
Fort Lincoln Cem—*cemetery* ... ND-7
**Fort Lincoln Estates**—*pop pl* ... ND-7
Fort Lincoln Historic Site—*park* ... ND-7
Fort Lincoln New Town—*locale* ... DC-2
Fort Lincoln State Park—*park* ... ND-7
Fort Lipantitlan—*locale* ... TX-5
Fort Liscum (Site)—*locale* ... AK-9
**Fort Littleton**—*pop pl* ... PA-2
Fort Littleton Cem—*cemetery* ... PA-2
*Fort Littleton Interchange* ... PA-2
Fort Livingston—*hist pl* ... LA-4
Fort Livingston Ruins—*locale* ... LA-4
*Fort Logan* ... CO-8
Fort Logan—*locale* ... MT-8
Fort Logan and Blockhouse—*hist pl* ... MT-8
Fort Logan H. Roots Military Post—*hist pl* ... AR-4
*Fort Logan Mental Health Center* ... CO-8
Fort Logan Mental Health Center—*other* ... CO-8
Fort Logan Natl Cem—*cemetery* ... CO-8
Fort Logan Sch—*school* ... CO-8
**Fort Lonely**—*pop pl* ... FL-3
Fort Lonesome—*locale* ... FL-3
*Fort Lookout* ... SD-7
Fort Lookout (historical)—*locale* (2) ... SD-7
Fort Lookout Sch (historical)—*school* ... PA-2
Fort Lookout Tower—*locale* ... MN-6
**Fort Loramie**—*pop pl* ... OH-6
**Fort Loring**—*pop pl* ... MS-4
Fort Loring Landing—*locale* ... MS-4
Fort Louden Historical Property—*locale* ... PA-2
Fort Loudon—*locale* ... TN-4
**Fort Loudon**—*pop pl* ... PA-2
Fort Loudon Dam—*dam* ... TN-4
**Fort Loudon Estates**—*pop pl* ... TN-4
Fort Loudon Lake—*reservoir* ... TN-4
*Fort Loudon Rsvr* ... TN-4
*Fort Loudoun* ... TN-4
Fort Loudoun—*hist pl* ... TN-4
Fort Loudoun Boat Launching Ramp—*locale* ... TN-4
Fort Loudoun Dam—*dam* ... TN-4
*Fort Loudoun Dam Marina* ... TN-4
Fort Loudoun Lake—*reservoir* ... TN-4
Fort Loudoun MS—*school* ... TN-4
*Fort Loudoun Reservoir* ... TN-4
Fort Loudoun State Historic Area—*park* ... TN-4
*Fort Loudoun State Park* ... TN-4
Fort Loudoun Yacht Club Dock—*locale* ... TN-4
Fort Louis De La Louisiane—*hist pl* ... AL-4
Fort Louise Augusta Light—*locale* ... VI-3
Fort Louis Historical Marker—*park* ... AL-4
Fort Lowell (historical site)—*locale* ... AZ-5
Fort Lowell Park—*hist pl* ... AZ-5
Fort Lowell Sch—*school* ... AZ-5
Fort Lowell Shop Ctr—*locale* ... AZ-5
Fort Lucas—*locale* ... MA-1
**Fort Lupton**—*pop pl* ... CO-8
Fort Lurleen B Wallace—*military* ... AL-4
**Fort Lynn**—*pop pl* ... AR-4
Fort Lyon—*locale* ... CO-8
Fort Lyon—*locale* ... ME-1
Fort Lyon—*locale* ... VA-3
Fort Lyon Canal—*canal* ... CO-8
Fort Lyon Cem—*cemetery* ... CO-8
Fort Lyon Diversion Dam—*dam* ... CO-8
**Fort Lyons Heights**—*pop pl* ... VA-3
Fort Lyon Storage Canal—*canal* ... CO-8
Fort Lyon Veterans Hosp—*hospital* ... CO-8
Fort Lytle—*hist pl* ... KY-4
Fort Lyttelton Site—*hist pl* ... SC-3
Fort MacArthur Lower Reservation—*military* ... CA-9
Fort MacArthur Milit Reservation—*military* ... CA-9
Fort MacArthur Upper Reservation—*military* ... CA-9
Fort Macarthur (U.S. Army)—*uninc pl* ... CA-9
Fort MacKenzie—*hist pl* ... WY-8
Fort Mackenzie—*hospital* ... WY-8
Fort Mackinac—*hist pl* ... MI-6
Fort Mackinac—*locale* ... MI-6
Fort Macomb—*hist pl* ... LA-4
**Fort Macomb**—*pop pl* ... LA-4
Fort Macon—*hist pl* ... NC-3
Fort Macon—*locale* ... NC-3
Fort Macon Coast Guard Base—*military* ... NC-3
Fort Macon Creek—*bay* ... NC-3
Fort Macon State Park—*park* ... NC-3
Fort Macon Village—*uninc pl* ... NC-3
*Fort Madison* ... AL-4
**Fort Madison**—*pop pl* ... IA-7
Fort Madison Ch—*church* ... MO-7
Fort Madison City Cem—*cemetery* ... IA-7
Fort Madison City Hall—*building* ... IA-7
Fort Madison Industrial Park—*facility* ... IA-7
Fort Maginnis Cem—*cemetery* ... MT-8
Fort Maginnis Sch—*school* ... MT-8
Fort Mahan (historical)—*military* ... DC-2
Fort Mahan Park—*park* ... DC-2
Fort Malone Historical Marker—*park* ... WA-9
Fort Mandan Historic Site—*park* ... ND-7
Fort Maneury Bend (historical)—*bend* ... ND-7

Fort Maneury (historical)—*locale* ND-7
Fortmann Basin—*harbor* CA-9
Fort Mann (historical)—*locale* KS-7
Fort Mansker (historical)—*military* TN-4
Fort Manuel—*hist pl* SD-7
Fort Manuel (historical)—*locale* SD-7
Fort Marcy—*locale* VA-3
Fort Marcy Officer's Residence—*hist pl* NM-5
Fort Marcy Park—*park* NM-5
Fort Marcy Ruins—*hist pl* NM-5
**Fort Martin**—*pop pl* WV-2
Fort Martin Ch—*church* WV-2
Fort Martin Sch—*school* WV-2
Fort Martin Scott—*hist pl* TX-5
Fort Mason—*locale* FL-3
Fort Mason—*uninc pl* CA-9
Fort Mason Hist Dist—*hist pl* CA-9
Fort Mason Hist Dist (Boundary Increase)—*hist pl* CA-9
Fort Mason (historical)—*locale* AZ-5
Fort Mason Milit Rsvr—*reservoir* CA-9
*Fort Massachusets* MA-1
Fort Massachusetts—*hist pl* MS-4
Fort Massachusetts (historical)—*locale* MA-1
Fort Massac Site—*hist pl* IL-6
Fort Massac State Park—*park* IL-6
Fort Matanzas—*locale* FL-3
Fort Matanzas Natl Monmt—*hist pl* FL-3
Fort Matanzas Natl Monmt—*park* FL-3
Fort Maurepas (historical)—*locale* MS-4
Fort Maurepas State park—*park* MS-4
Fort McAllister—*hist pl* GA-3
**Fort McAllister**—*pop pl* GA-3
Fort McClary—*hist pl* ME-1
Fort McClary State Park—*park* ME-1
Fort McClellan (U.S. Army)—*military* AL-4
*Fort McComb* LA-4
**Fort McCoy**—*pop pl* FL-3
**Fort McCoy**—*pop pl* WI-6
Fort McCoy-Anthony (CCD)—*cens area* FL-3
Fort McCoy Elem Sch—*school* FL-3
Fort McCoy Lookout Tower—*tower* FL-3
Fort McCoy Wildlife Mngmt Area—*park* FL-3
Fort McCulloch—*hist pl* OK-5
**Fort McDermitt Ind Res**—*pop pl* NV-8
Fort McDermitt Ind Res (also NV)—*reserve* OR-9
Fort McDermitt Ind Res (Also NV)—*reserve* OR-9
Fort McDermitt Ranch HQ—*locale* NV-8
Fort McDermott—*locale* AL-4
Fort McDonald—*locale* AZ-5
Fort McDowell—*locale* CA-9
**Fort McDowell**—*pop pl* AZ-5
**Fort McDowell Ind Res**—*pop pl* AZ-5
*Fort McDowell Reservation* AZ-5
Fort McGraw (Historical Marker)—*park* WY-8
*Fort McHenry* MS-4
Fort McHenry—*locale* MD-2
Fort McHenry Channel—*channel* MD-2
Fort McHenry Natl Monmt—*park* MD-2
Fort McHenry Natl Monmt and Historic Shrine—*park* MD-2
Fort McIntosh—*hist pl* TX-5
Fort McIntosh—*locale* TX-5
Fort McIntosh JHS—*school* PA-2
Fort McIntosh Site—*hist pl* PA-2
**Fort McKavett**—*pop pl* TX-5
Fort McKavett Hist Dist—*hist pl* TX-5
*Fort McKeen* ND-7
**Fort McKinley**—*pop pl* OH-6
Fort McKinley Hist Dist—*hist pl* ME-1
Fort McKinney—*hist pl* WY-8
Fort McLean—*locale* VA-3
Fort McNair (U.S. Army)—*military* DC-2
Fort McPherson—*locale* GA-3
Fort McPherson Natl Cem—*cemetery* NE-7
Fort McPherson (site)—*locale* NE-7
Fort McPherson (U.S. Army)—*military* GA-3
*Fort Mcrae* FL-3
Fort McRae (Historical Site)—*locale* NM-5
Fort McRee—*locale* FL-3
Fort McRee Leading Light—*locale* FL-3
*Fort McTeer* TN-4
**Fort Meade**—*pop pl* FL-3
**Fort Meade**—*pop pl* SD-7
Fort Meade Cem—*cemetery* FL-3
Fort Meade Cem—*cemetery* SD-7
Fort Meade District—*hist pl* SD-7
Fort Meade Junction (Annapolis Junction)—*other* MD-2
Fort Meade Junior-Senior HS—*school* FL-3
Fort Meade MS—*school* FL-3
Fort Meade (U.S. Army)—*military* MD-2
Fort Meade Veterans Hosp—*hospital* SD-7
*Fort Meadow Brook* MA-1
Fort Meadow Brook—*stream* MA-1
Fort Meadow Rsvr—*reservoir* MA-1
Fort Meadow Sch—*school* MA-1
Fort Meigs—*hist pl* OH-6
Fort Meigs Cem—*cemetery* OH-6
**Fort Meigs Place**—*pop pl* OH-6
Fort Meigs State Memorial—*park* OH-6
Fort Meigs (Township of)—*other* OH-6
*Fort Mellon* FL-3
Fort Mellon Park—*park* FL-3
Fort Mercer—*uninc pl* NJ-2
Fort Merrill (Site)—*locale* TX-5
Fortmeyer Airp—*airport* KS-7
Fort Meyer (Historical)—*locale* TX-5
*Fort Miami* IN-6
*Fort Miami Addition* OH-6
Fort Miami Sch—*school* OH-6
Fort Miamis Site—*hist pl* OH-6
Fort Michilimackinac—*hist pl* MI-6
Fort Michilimackinac State Park—*park* MI-6
Fort Miffin—*locale* PA-2
Fort Mifflin—*hist pl* PA-2
Fort Mifflin—*uninc pl* PA-2
Fort Mifflin Disposal Area—*reservoir* PA-2
Fort Mifflin Hosp—*hist pl* PA-2
Fort Milam (Site)—*locale* TX-5
*Fort Miley* CA-9
Fort Miley Military Reservation—*hist pl* CA-9
Fort Miley Military Rsvr—*reservoir* CA-9
Fort Miley (Veterans Administration Hospital)—*hospital* CA-9
**Fort Mill**—*pop pl* SC-3
Fort Mill (CCD)—*cens area* SC-3
**Fort Miller**—*pop pl* NY-2
Fort Miller JHS—*school* CA-9
Fort Milroy—*locale* VA-3
Fort Milroy Cem—*cemetery* WV-2
Fort Mimms Ch—*church* AL-4
Fort Mimms (historical)—*locale* AL-4
Fort Mimms Lookout Tower—*tower* AL-4
Fort Mims Site—*hist pl* AL-4
**Fort Miner (historical)**—*pop pl* OR-9
Fort Misery—*locale* AZ-5
Fort Missoula—*locale* MT-8
Fort Missoula Hist Dist—*hist pl* MT-8
Fort Mitchell—*locale* VA-3
**Fort Mitchell**—*pop pl* AL-4
**Fort Mitchell**—*pop pl* KY-4
Fort Mitchell Country Club—*other* KY-4
Fort Mitchell Sch—*school* AL-4
Fort Mitchell Site—*hist pl* AL-4
Fort Mitchell Site—*hist pl* NE-7
Fort Mitchell Site—*locale* SC-3
Fort Mohave—*post sta* AZ-5
*Fort Mohave Reservation* AZ-5
Fort Mojave Ind Res—*reserve* NV-8
Fort Mojave Ind Res—*127 (1980)* CA-9
**Fort Mojave Ind Res (Also CA)**—*pop pl* AZ-5
Fort Mojave Ind Res (Also NV)—*reserve* CA-9
Fort Monmouth—*military* NJ-2
Fort Monmouth (U.S. Army)—*military* NJ-2
Fort Monroe—*hist pl* VA-3
Fort Monroe—*locale* VA-3
Fort Monroe Milit Reservation—*military* VA-3
Fort Monroe (U.S. Army)—*military* VA-3
Fort Montgomery—*hist pl* NY-2
Fort Montgomery—*locale* NY-2
**Fort Montgomery**—*pop pl* NY-2
Fort Montgomery (historical)—*locale* AL-4
Fort Montgomery Ruins—*locale* NY-2
Fort Montgomery Site—*hist pl* NY-2
*Fort Monument* KS-7
Fort Moore (historical)—*locale* MS-4
Fort Moore-Savano Town Site—*hist pl* SC-3
Fort Moosa (historical)—*locale* FL-3
Fort Morgan—*hist pl* AL-4
Fort Morgan—*locale* AL-4
**Fort Morgan**—*pop pl* CO-8
Fort Morgan Airp—*airport* CO-8
Fort Morgan Canal—*canal* CO-8
Fort Morgan Canal Headgate—*dam* CO-8
Fort Morgan Country Club—*other* CO-8
Fort Morgan Museum—*building* AL-4
Fort Morgan Oil Field—*oilfield* CO-8
Fort Mornson—*locale* MA-1
*Fort Moroni* AZ-5
Fort Morris—*hist pl* GA-3
Fort Morris—*locale* MA-1
Fort Morris (Site)—*locale* GA-3
Fort Mossity—*locale* MS-4
**Fort Mott**—*pop pl* NJ-2
Fort Mott and Finns Point Natl Cemetery District—*hist pl* NJ-2
**Fort Motte**—*pop pl* SC-3
Fort Motte Battle Site—*hist pl* SC-3
Fort Motte Bridge—*bridge* SC-3
Fort Motte-Lone Star (CCD)—*cens area* SC-3
Fort Mott State Park—*park* NJ-2
Fort Moultrie—*locale* SC-3
Fort Moultrie (historical)—*locale* FL-3
*Fort Mountain* VA-3
Fort Mountain—*hist pl* GA-3
Fort Mountain Lake—*lake* GA-3
Fort Mountain State Park—*park* GA-3
Fort Mouton (historical)—*locale* AL-4
Fort Mtn—*summit* (2) AR-4
Fort Mtn—*summit* (2) CA-9
Fort Mtn—*summit* CT-1
Fort Mtn—*summit* (2) GA-3
Fort Mtn—*summit* ME-1
Fort Mtn—*summit* NH-1
Fort Mudge—*locale* GA-3
**Fort Myer Heights**—*pop pl* VA-3
Fort Myer Hist Dist—*hist pl* VA-3
Fort Myer (North Area)—*military* VA-3
**Fort Myers**—*pop pl* FL-3
**Fort Myers Beach**—*pop pl* FL-3
Fort Myers Beach Elem Sch—*school* FL-3
Fort Myers (CCD)—*cens area* FL-3
Fort Myers Cem—*cemetery* FL-3
Fort Myers Christian Sch—*school* FL-3
Fort Myers Community Hosp—*hospital* FL-3
Fort Myers HS—*school* FL-3
Fort Myers Junior Acad—*school* FL-3
Fort Myers-Lee County Library—*building* FL-3
Fort Myers Memorial Gardens—*cemetery* FL-3
Fort Myers MS—*school* FL-3
Fort Myer (South Area)—*military* VA-3
Fort Myers Shop Ctr—*locale* FL-3
**Fort Myers Shores**—*pop pl* FL-3
Fort Myers Shores (CCD)—*cens area* FL-3
**Fort Myers Southeast**—*pop pl* FL-3
**Fort Myers Southwest**—*pop pl* FL-3
**Fort Myers Villas**—*pop pl* FL-3
Fort Myer (U.S. Army)—*military* VA-3
*Fort Nantusiunk Island* RI-1
Fortnas Dam—*dam* PA-2
Fort Nashborough—*locale* TN-4
Fort Nash (historical)—*locale* TN-4
Fort Nassau Industrial Park—*locale* NJ-2
Fort Nathan Hale—*hist pl* CT-1
Fort Neal—*uninc pl* WV-2
**Fort Necessity**—*pop pl* LA-4
Fort Necessity Natl Battlefield—*hist pl* PA-2
Fort Necessity Sch—*school* LA-4
Fort Necessity State Park—*park* PA-2
Fort Neck—*cape* NY-2
*Fort Neck Pond* RI-1
Fort Ned Pond—*lake* CT-1
Fort Negley—*hist pl* TN-4
Fort Negly Park—*park* TN-4
*Fort Nelson Point* VA-3
**Fortner**—*pop pl* SC-3
*Fortner Branch* KY-4
Fortner Branch—*stream* KY-4
Fortner Branch—*stream* (2) TN-4
Fortner Branch Prospect—*mine* TN-4
Fortner Cem—*cemetery* AL-4
Fortner Cem—*cemetery* FL-3
Fortner Cem—*cemetery* GA-3
Fortner Cem—*cemetery* NC-3
Fortner Cem—*cemetery* (2) TN-4
Fortner Cem—*cemetery* WV-2
Fortner Ch—*church* WV-2
Fortnerfield Branch—*stream* VA-3
Fortner Hollow—*valley* (2) AR-4
Fortner Hollow—*valley* (2) TN-4
Fortner Mounds I, II—*hist pl* OH-6
Fortner Pond—*reservoir* GA-3
Fortners Camp—*locale* FL-3
Fortner Sch (historical)—*school* AL-4
Fortners Ferry (historical)—*locale* MS-4
**Fortney**—*pop pl* PA-2
Fortney Branch—*stream* KY-4
Fortney Branch—*stream* VA-3
Fortney Cem—*cemetery* IL-6
Fortney Cem—*cemetery* KY-4
Fortney Cem—*cemetery* MO-7
Fortney Ch—*church* IL-6
Fortney P O (historical)—*building* PA-2
Fortney Ridge—*ridge* WI-6
Fortneys Forge—*locale* NC-3
**Fort Niagara Beach**—*pop pl* NY-2
Fort Niagara Light—*hist pl* NY-2
Fort Niagara State Park—*park* NY-2
Fort Ninigret—*hist pl* RI-1
Fort Ninigret—*locale* RI-1
Fort Niobrara Natl Wildlife Ref—*park* NE-7
Fort Nisqually—*locale* WA-9
Fort Nisqually Granary and Factor's House—*hist pl* WA-9
Fort Nisqually Site—*hist pl* WA-9
Fort Noble Mtn—*summit* NY-2
*Fort Nogales* MS-4
Fort Nonsense—*hist pl* MD-2
Fort Nonsense—*locale* VA-3
Fort Nonsense Historical Natl Park—*park* NJ-2
Fort Norfolk—*hist pl* VA-3
Fort Norfolk—*locale* VA-3
Fort Northkill—*locale* PA-2
Fort Nottoway—*locale* VA-3
Fort No. 5—*hist pl* AL-4
Fort Nuestra Senora de la Soledad—*hist pl* GU-9
Fort O'Brien—*hist pl* ME-1
Fort O'Brien Point—*cape* ME-1
**Fort Ogden**—*pop pl* FL-3
Fort Ogden Cem—*cemetery* FL-3
**Fort Oglethorpe**—*pop pl* GA-3
Fort Oglethorpe Hist Dist—*hist pl* GA-3
Fort Oglethorpe-Lakeview (CCD)—*cens area* GA-3
Fort Okanogan, Sites of—*hist pl* WA-9
*Fort Okanogan Lake* WA-9
Fort Okanogan (Site)—*locale* WA-9
Fort Okanogan (Site 2)—*locale* WA-9
*Fort Omaha* NE-7
Fort Omaha Hist Dist—*hist pl* NE-7
Fort Ontario—*hist pl* NY-2
Fort Ontario—*locale* NY-2
*Fort Oplandt* DE-2
Fort Ord Golf Course—*other* CA-9
Fort Ord Milit Reservation—*military* CA-9
Fort Ord (Ord) (U.S. Army)—*military* CA-9
Fort Ord Village—*uninc pl* CA-9
Fort Orford—*locale* CA-9
Fort Osage—*hist pl* MO-7
Fort Osage—*other* MO-7
Fort Osage Archeol District—*hist pl* MO-7
Fort Osage (historical)—*locale* MO-7
Fort Osage HS—*school* MO-7
Fort Osage Township—*civil* MO-7
*Fort Ouiatenon* IN-6
Fort Ouiatenon—*hist pl* IN-6
Fort Owen—*hist pl* MT-8
Fort Owen (Historical Site)—*locale* MT-8
Fort Palmer Ch—*church* PA-2
Fort Palmetto—*hist pl* SC-3
*Fort Panmure* MS-4
Fort Parker—*locale* TX-5
Fort Parker Branch—*stream* KY-4
Fort Parker Memorial Cem—*cemetery* TX-5
Fort Parker State Park—*park* TX-5
Fort Patrick Henry Dam—*dam* (2) TN-4
Fort Patrick Henry Lake—*reservoir* (2) TN-4
**Fort Payne**—*pop pl* AL-4
Fort Payne Acad (historical)—*school* AL-4
Fort Payne Boating Club—*locale* AL-4
*Fort Payne Cave* AL-4
Fort Payne (CCD)—*cens area* AL-4
Fort Payne City Auditorium—*building* AL-4
Fort Payne City Lake—*reservoir* AL-4
Fort Payne Dam—*dam* AL-4
Fort Payne Division—*civil* AL-4
Fort Payne Gap—*gap* AL-4
Fort Payne HS—*school* AL-4
Fort Payne Opera House—*hist pl* AL-4
Fort Payne Recreation Center—*building* AL-4
Fort Payne Residential Hist Dist—*hist pl* AL-4
Fort Payne Water Works—*other* AL-4
Fort Peace (historical)—*locale* MS-4
Fort Pearce—*hist pl* UT-8
Fort Pearce (Ruins)—*locale* UT-8
Fort Pearce Wash—*stream* AZ-5
Fort Pearce Wash—*valley* UT-8
Fort Pease (site)—*locale* MT-8
**Fort Peck**—*pop pl* MT-8
Fort Peck Agency—*hist pl* MT-8
Fort Peck Dam—*dam* MT-8
Fort Peck Dam—*hist pl* MT-8
**Fort Peck Ind Res**—*pop pl* MT-8
Fort Peck Lake—*reservoir* MT-8
Fort Peck Original Houses Hist Dist—*hist pl* MT-8
Fort Peck Reservation—*cens area* (4) MT-8
*Fort Peck Reservoir* MT-8
Fort Peck Theatre—*hist pl* MT-8
Fort Peck Trout Pond—*reservoir* MT-8
Fort Pelham (historical)—*locale* MA-1
Fort Pemberton (historical)—*locale* MS-4
Fort Pemberton Landing (historical)—*locale* MS-4
Fort Pemberton Site—*hist pl* MS-4
Fort Pemberton Site—*hist pl* SC-3
Fort Pendleton—*locale* MD-2
Fort Perry—*hist pl* GA-3
Fort Perry Creek—*stream* GA-3
Fort Perry Station—*building* PA-2
**Fort Peyton**—*pop pl* FL-3
Fort Peyton (historical)—*locale* FL-3
Fort Phantom Hill—*hist pl* TX-5
Fort Phantom Hill—*locale* TX-5
Fort Phantom Hill, Lake—*reservoir* TX-5
Fort Phantom Hill Cem—*cemetery* TX-5
*Fort Phantom Hill Reservoir* TX-5
Fort Philip (historical)—*military* AL-4
Fort Philip Long—*hist pl* VA-3
Fort Phil Kearny and Associated Sites—*hist pl* WY-8
Fort Phil Kearny ( Historical Site)—*locale* WY-8
Fort Phoenix—*hist pl* MA-1
Fort Phoenix—*park* MA-1
Fort Phoenix Beach State Reservation—*park* MA-1
Fort Pickens—*hist pl* FL-3
**Fort Pickens**—*pop pl* FL-3
Fort Pickens Monument—*other* WV-2
Fort Pickens Ruins—*locale* FL-3
Fort Pickens State Park—*park* FL-3
Fort Pickens State Park Aquatic Preserve—*park* FL-3
Fort Pickering—*hist pl* MA-1
Fort Pickering—*locale* MA-1
Fort Pickett—*military* VA-3
Fort Picolata (historical)—*locale* FL-3
Fort Piegan—*locale* MT-8
**Fort Pierce**—*pop pl* FL-3
Fort Pierce Beach—*uninc pl* FL-3
Fort Pierce (CCD)—*cens area* FL-3
Fort Pierce Cem—*cemetery* FL-3
Fort Pierce Central HS—*school* FL-3
Fort Pierce Cut—*channel* FL-3
*Fort Pierce Dry Wash* AZ-5
*Fort Pierce Dry Wash* UT-8
Fort Pierce Elem Sch—*school* FL-3
Fort Pierce Inlet—*gut* FL-3
Fort Pierce Inlet Center Range Front Light—*locale* FL-3
Fort Pierce Inlet State Rec Area—*park* FL-3
Fort Pierce Northwest—*CDP* FL-3
Fort Pierce Shop Ctr—*locale* FL-3
**Fort Pierce Shores (subdivision)**—*pop pl* FL-3
Fort Pierce Site—*hist pl* FL-3
Fort Pierce South—*CDP* FL-3
*Fort Pierce Wash* AZ-5
*Fort Pierce Wash* UT-8
Fort Pierce Westwood HS—*school* FL-3
**Fort Pierre**—*pop pl* SD-7
Fort Pierre Chouteau Site—*hist pl* SD-7
Fort Pierre Number One (historical)—*locale* SD-7
Fort Pierre Number Two (historical)—*locale* SD-7
Fort Pike—*hist pl* LA-4
Fort Pike Bridge—*bridge* LA-4
Fort Pike Chapel—*church* LA-4
Fort Pike State Monmt—*park* LA-4
Fort Pillow—*hist pl* TN-4
**Fort Pillow**—*pop pl* TN-4
Fort Pillow (Fort Pillow Prison Farm)—*building* TN-4
Fort Pillow (historical)—*locale* TN-4
Fort Pillow Landing—*locale* TN-4
Fort Pillow Post Office (historical)—*building* TN-4
Fort Pillow Sch (historical)—*school* TN-4
Fort Pillow State Farm—*locale* TN-4
Fort Pillow State Historic Area—*park* TN-4
Fort Pillow State Park—*park* TN-4
*Fort Pillow State Prison Farm* TN-4
Fort Pillow Street Park Lake—*reservoir* TN-4
Fort Pillow Street Park Lake Dam—*dam* TN-4
Fort Piqua Hotel—*hist pl* OH-6
Fort Pitt—*locale* PA-2
Fort Pitt Block House—*building* PA-2
Fort Pitt Bridge—*bridge* PA-2
Fort Pitt Elem Sch—*hist pl* PA-2
Fort Pitt Elem Sch—*school* (2) PA-2
Fort Pitt Museum—*building* PA-2
*Fort Pittsburgh* PA-2
**Fort Pittsburgh**—*pop pl* PA-2
*Fort Pittsburgh Bridge* PA-2
*Fort Pittsburgh Tunnel* PA-2
*Fort Pitt School* PA-2
Fort Pitt Tunnel—*tunnel* PA-2
Fort Piute—*locale* CA-9
Fort Place Landing (historical)—*locale* MS-4
**Fort Plain**—*pop pl* NY-2
Fort Plain Conservation Area—*hist pl* NY-2
Fort Plain (historical)—*locale* IA-7
**Fort Plain (RR name South Fort Plain)**—*pop pl* NY-2
Fort Plain Rsvr—*reservoir* NY-2
**Fort Plains**—*pop pl* NJ-2
Fort Plains Rsvr—*reservoir* NY-2
Fort Plain (sta.) (RR name for Nelliston)—*other* NY-2
Fort Plank Sch—*school* NY-2
Fort Pleasant—*hist pl* WV-2
Fort Point—*cape* (2) AK-9
Fort Point—*cape* CA-9
Fort Point—*cape* CT-1
Fort Point—*cape* GA-3
Fort Point—*cape* LA-4
Fort Point—*cape* (6) ME-1
Fort Point—*cape* (2) MD-2
Fort Point—*cape* (2) MA-1
Fort Point—*cape* MS-4
Fort Point—*cape* NH-1
Fort Point—*cape* NJ-2
Fort Point—*cape* (2) NC-3
Fort Point—*cape* OR-9
Fort Point—*cape* TX-5
*Fort-point Channel* MA-1
Fort Point Channel—*channel* MA-1
Fort Point Cove—*bay* ME-1
Fort Point Ledge—*bar* ME-1
Fort Point Light Station—*hist pl* ME-1
Fort Point Natl Historic Site—*park* CA-9
Fort Point Rock—*island* CA-9
Fort Point State Park—*park* ME-1
Fort Polk—*military* LA-4
Fort Polk North—*CDP* LA-4
Fort Polk South—*CDP* LA-4
Fort Polk (U.S. Army)—*military* LA-4
Fort Pomme de Terre Site—*hist pl* MN-6
Fort Pond—*lake* MA-1
Fort Pond—*lake* NY-2
Fort Pond—*reservoir* MA-1
Fort Pond—*reservoir* SC-3
Fort Pond Bay—*bay* NY-2
Fort Pond Brook—*stream* MA-1
Fort Pond Brook Rsvr—*reservoir* MA-1
Fort Pond Dam—*dam* MA-1
Fort Popham—*locale* ME-1
Fort Popham Memorial—*hist pl* ME-1
Fort Powell (historical)—*locale* AL-4
Fort Powhatan—*locale* VA-3
Fort Pownall Memorial—*hist pl* ME-1
Fort Preble—*locale* ME-1
Fort Primeau (historical)—*locale* SD-7
Fort Pringle—*hist pl* SC-3
Fort Proctor—*hist pl* LA-4
Fort Pulaski Natl Monmt—*hist pl* GA-3
Fort Pulaski Natl Monmt—*park* GA-3
Fort Pupo (historical)—*locale* FL-3
Fort Putnam—*locale* NY-2
*Fort Pyramid* KS-7
Fort Quitman—*locale* TX-5
Fort Quitman Lake—*reservoir* TX-5
**Fort Rains**—*pop pl* WA-9
**Fort Raleigh City**—*pop pl* NC-3
Fort Raleigh Natl Historical Site—*park* NC-3
*Fort Raleigh Natl Park* NC-3
Fort Ramirez Ruins—*locale* TX-5
Fort Ranch—*locale* (2) NM-5
Fort Ranch—*locale* WY-8
Fort Randall—*hist pl* SD-7
**Fort Randall**—*pop pl* SD-7
Fort Randall Dam—*dam* SD-7
Fort Randall Eagle Roost—*locale* SD-7
Fort Randall Historic Site—*locale* SD-7
Fort Randolph—*hist pl* LA-4
Fort Randolph—*locale* LA-4
Fort Randolph (historical)—*locale* TN-4
**Fort Ransom**—*pop pl* ND-7
Fort Ransom Dam—*dam* ND-7
**Fort Ransom Township**—*pop pl* ND-7
Fort Ransom Township (historical)—*civil* ND-7
*Fort Rascal* AL-4
Fort Reading Historical Marker—*military* CA-9
Fort Reading Ranch—*locale* CA-9
**Fort Recovery**—*pop pl* OH-6
Fort Recovery (historical)—*locale* SD-7
Fort Recovery Site—*hist pl* OH-6
*Fort Red* IN-6
Fort Redoubt—*locale* FL-3
**Fort Reed**—*pop pl* FL-3
Fort Reed RR Station—*locale* FL-3
*Fort Reno* OK-5
Fort Reno—*hist pl* OK-5
Fort Reno—*hist pl* WY-8
Fort Reno—*locale* WY-8
Fort Reno—*uninc pl* OK-5
Fort Reno Draw—*valley* WY-8
Fort Reno Park—*park* DC-2
Fort Reno Post Cem—*cemetery* OK-5
*Fortress* VA-3
Fortress, The—*summit* WY-8
Fortress Arch—*arch* UT-8
Fortress Canyon—*valley* UT-8
Fortress Cliff—*cliff* TX-5
Fortress Creek—*stream* (2) AK-9
*Fortress Hill* AZ-5
Fortress Hill—*summit* WY-8
Fortress Island—*island* WA-9
Fortress Lakes—*lake* WY-8
Fortress Mtn—*summit* AK-9
Fortress Mtn—*summit* MT-8
Fortress Mtn—*summit* WA-9
Fortress Mtn—*summit* WY-8
Fortress Point—*cape* AK-9
Fortress Ridge—*ridge* AK-9
Fortress Rock—*summit* MT-8
Fortress Rosecrans Site—*hist pl* TN-4
**Fort Revere (subdivision)**—*pop pl* MA-1
**Fort Reynolds**—*pop pl* CO-8
**Fort Rice**—*pop pl* ND-7
Fort Rice Cem—*cemetery* ND-7
Fort Rice Historical Site—*park* ND-7
Fort Rice Landing (historical)—*locale* ND-7
Fort Rice Military Cem—*cemetery* ND-7
Fort Rice Rec Area—*park* ND-7
**Fort Richardson**—*pop pl* AK-9
Fort Richardson (Historical)—*locale* TX-5
Fort Richardson Military Reservation—*military* AK-9
Fort Richardson (U.S. Army)—*military* AK-9
Fort Ridge—*ridge* ME-1
Fort Ridge—*summit* WY-8
Fort Ridge (historical)—*locale* TN-4
Fort Ridgely—*hist pl* MN-6
Fort Ridgely and Dale Ch—*church* MN-6
Fort Ridgely Creek—*stream* MN-6
Fort Ridgely State Park—*park* MN-6
Fort Riel Natl Guard Armory—*military* AL-4
*Fort Riley* KS-7
Fort Riley—*military* (2) KS-7
Fort Riley-Camp Whiteside—*CDP* KS-7
Fort Riley Milit Reservation—*military* KS-7
Fort Riley North—*CDP* (2) KS-7
**Fort Ringgold**—*pop pl* TX-5
Fort Ripley—*hist pl* MN-6
**Fort Ripley**—*pop pl* MN-6
Fort Ripley Cem—*cemetery* MN-6
**Fort Ripley (Township of)**—*pop pl* MN-6
Fort Ritchie Military Reservation—*other* MD-2
*Fort Ritchie (sta.) (Cascade)* MD-2
Fort Ritchie (U.S. Army)—*military* MD-2
**Fort Ritner**—*pop pl* IN-6
*Fort River* MA-1
Fort River—*stream* MA-1
**Fort River Caves (subdivision)**—*pop pl* (2) AZ-5
Fort Roberdeau—*hist pl* PA-2
**Fort Roberston**—*pop pl* PA-2
Fort Robertson—*locale* PA-2
Fort Robidoux Historical Monmt—*park* UT-8
*Fort Robidoux Monument* UT-8
*Fort Robinett* MS-4
Fort Robinette—*hist pl* MS-4
*Fort Robinson* PA-2
**Fort Robinson**—*pop pl* NE-7
**Fort Robinson**—*pop pl* TN-4
Fort Robinson and Red Cloud Agency—*hist pl* NE-7
Fort Robinson Sch—*school* PA-2
*Fort Robinson School* TN-4
Fort Robinson State Park—*park* (2) NE-7
Fort Robinson State Park Museum—*park* NE-7
Fort Robinson Trail—*trail* NE-7
Fort Robinson Wildlife Area—*park* NE-7
*Fort Rock* AZ-5
Fort Rock—*locale* OR-9
Fort Rock—*rock* NH-1
Fort Rock—*summit* OR-9
Fort Rock Cave—*cave* OR-9
Fort Rock Cave—*hist pl* OR-9
*Fort Rock Creek* AZ-5
Fort Rock Elemetary Sch—*school* OR-9
Fort Rock Ranch—*locale* AZ-5
Fort Rock State Park—*park* OR-9
Fort Rock Valley—*basin* OR-9
Fort Rodes—*hist pl* VA-3
**Fort Romie**—*pop pl* CA-9
Fort Roots Veterans Administration Hosp—*hospital* AR-4
*Fort Rosalie* MS-4
**Fort Rosecrans**—*pop pl* CA-9
Fort Rosecrans Natl Cem—*cemetery* CA-9
Fort Rosecrans (U.S. Army)—*other* CA-9
Fort Ross—*hist pl* CA-9
Fort Ross—*locale* CA-9
Fort Ross Commander's House—*hist pl* CA-9
Fort Ross Cove—*bay* CA-9
Fort Ross Creek—*stream* CA-9
Fort Ross Reef—*bar* CA-9
Fort Ross Sch—*school* CA-9
Fort Ross State Historic Park—*park* CA-9
Fort Ruby—*hist pl* NV-8
Fort Ruby Ranch—*locale* NV-8
Fort Ruby Ranch Airstrip Airp—*airport* NV-8
Fort Ruby Spring—*spring* NV-8
Fort Rucker (CCD)—*cens area* AL-4
Fort Rucker Dam—*dam* AL-4
Fort Rucker Division—*civil* AL-4
Fort Rucker Rec Area—*park* FL-3
Fort Rucker (U.S. Army)—*military* AL-4
Fort Ruger—*military* HI-9
Fort Ruger (Air Natl Guard)—*other* HI-9
Fort Ruger Hist Dist—*hist pl* HI-9
Fort Ruin—*locale* UT-8
**Fort Run**—*pop pl* WV-2
Fort Run—*stream* NC-3
Fort Run—*stream* PA-2
Fort Run—*stream* VA-3
Fort Run—*stream* WV-2
Fort Russell Neighborhood Hist Dist—*hist pl* ID-8
Fort Russell (Township of)—*civ div* IL-6
Fort Sage Mountains—*range* CA-9
Fort Sage Mtns—*summit* NV-8
*Fort Saginaw* MI-6
Fort Saint Charles—*locale* MN-6
Fort Saint Clair State Park—*park* OH-6
Fort Saint Frederic Ruins—*locale* NY-2
Fort Saint Joseph Park—*park* MI-6
**Fort Saint Leon**—*pop pl* LA-4
Fort Saint Peter (site)—*locale* MS-4
*Fort Saint Philip* AL-4
Fort Saint Phillip—*locale* LA-4
Fort Saint Vrain—*locale* CO-8
Fort Salonga—*hist pl* NY-2
**Fort Salonga**—*pop pl* NY-2
Fort Sam Houston—*hist pl* TX-5
Fort Sam Houston—*military* TX-5
Fort Sam Houston Sch—*school* TX-5
Fort Sam Houston (U.S. Army)—*military* TX-5
Fort San Carlos—*locale* FL-3
Fort Sanders—*locale* WY-8
Fort Sanders Baptist Ch—*church* TN-4
Fort Sanders Guardhouse—*hist pl* WY-8
Fort Sanders Hist Dist—*hist pl* TN-4
Fort Sanders Hosp—*hospital* TN-4
*Fort Sanders Regional Med Ctr* TN-4
Fort San Jose—*hist pl* GU-9
Fort San Jose (Ruins)—*locale* GU-9
Fort San Marcos de Apalache—*hist pl* FL-3
Fort San Marcos De Apalache State Park and Monmt—*park* FL-3
Fort San Miguel (ruins)—*locale* NM-5
Fort Santa Agueda—*hist pl* GU-9
Fort Santa Agueda (Site)—*locale* GU-9
Fort Santa Cruz (Site)—*locale* GU-9
Fort Santiago (Site)—*locale* GU-9
Fort Santo Angel—*hist pl* GU-9
Fort Santo Angel (Ruins)—*locale* GU-9
Fort Saratoga (historical)—*locale* DC-2
Fort Saulsbury—*locale* DE-2
Forts Baker, Barry, and Cronkhite—*hist pl* CA-9
Forts Bear Hole—*basin* FL-3
Fortsberg—*hist pl* VI-3
Fortsberg—*summit* VI-3
Fort Scammel—*locale* ME-1
Fort Scammel Point—*cape* ME-1
Fort Scammon—*hist pl* WV-2
Fort Sch (abandoned)—*school* PA-2
*Fort Schellbourne* NV-8
Fort Schellbourne—*hist pl* NV-8
Fort Schellbourne (Boundary Increase)—*hist pl* NV-8
*Forts Church* MS-4
Fort Schuyler—*building* NY-2
Fort Schuyler—*hist pl* NY-2
Fort Schuyler Park—*park* NY-2
*Fort Scott* CA-9
**Fort Scott**—*pop pl* CA-9
**Fort Scott**—*pop pl* KS-7
**Fort Scott Camps**—*pop pl* OH-6
Fort Scott Community Coll—*school* KS-7
Fort Scott Country Club—*other* KS-7
Fort Scott Gulch—*valley* CO-8
Fort Scott-Gunn Park Dam—*dam* KS-7
Fort Scott HS—*school* KS-7
Fort Scott JHS—*school* KS-7
*Fort Scott Junior College* KS-7
Fort Scott Municipal Airp—*airport* KS-7
Fort Scott Municipal Dam—*dam* KS-7
Fort Scott Natl Historic Site—*hist pl* KS-7
Fort Scott Natl Historic Site—*park* KS-7
Fort Scott Park—*park* VA-3
Fort Scott Public Carnegie Library—*hist pl* KS-7
Fort Screven—*locale* GA-3
Fort Screven Hist Dist—*hist pl* GA-3
Fort Sedgwick—*locale* CO-8
Fort Sedgwick Military Cem—*cemetery* CO-8
Fort Selden—*hist pl* NM-5
**Fort Selden**—*pop pl* NM-5
Fort Selden State Monument—*other* NM-5
**Fort Seneca**—*pop pl* OH-6

Fortsens Mill AL-4
Fort Serra Croos—pillar CA-9
Fort Sewall—hist pl MA-1
Fort Sewall—locale MA-1
Fort Seward ND-7
**Fort Seward**—pop pl CA-9
Fort Seward Historic Site—park ND-7
Fort Seybert—locale WV-2
Forts Ferry Sch—school NY-2
Forts Grove Ch—church GA-3
Fort Shafter—military HI-9
Fort Shafter Milit Reservation—military HI-9
Fort Shafter (U.S. Army)—military HI-9
Fort Shantok—hist pl CT-1
Fort Shantok State Park—park CT-1
**Fort Shaw**—pop pl MT-8
Fort Shaw Canal (reduced usage)—canal MT-8
Fort Shaw Hist Dist and Cemetery—hist pl MT-8
**Fort Shawnee**—pop pl OH-6
Fort Shelby MI-6
Fort Shelby Hotel—hist pl MI-6
Fort Sheridan—other IL-6
Fort Sheridan Cem—cemetery IL-6
Fort Sheridan Hist Dist—hist pl IL-6
Fort Sherman Buildings—hist pl ID-8
Fort Shirley (historical)—locale MA-1
**Forts (historical)**—pop pl TN-4
Fort Sidney Hist Dist—hist pl NE-7
Fort Sidney Johnston (historical)—locale AL-4
Fort Sill—hist pl OK-5
Fort Sill—other OK-5
**Fort Sill Indian School Reservation**—pop pl OK-5
Fort Sill (U.S. Army)—military OK-5
Fort Simcoe State Park—hist pl WA-9
Fort Simmons Branch—stream FL-3
Fort Simons Ridge—ridge ID-8
Fort Sinquefield—hist pl AL-4
Fort Sinquefield (historical)—military AL-4
Fort Sisseton—hist pl SD-7
Fort Sisseton State Park—park SD-7
Forts Lake Cem—cemetery MS-4
Forts Lake Ch—church MS-4
Fort Slemmer—locale DC-2
Fort Slocum (historical)—locale DC-2
Fort Slocum Milit Reservation—military NY-2
Fort Slocum Park—park DC-2
Fort Smallwood Park—park MD-2
Fort Smallwood Sch—school MD-2
Fort Smith—locale GA-3
**Fort Smith**—pop pl AR-4
**Fort Smith**—pop pl MT-8
Fort Smith, Lake—reservoir AR-4
Fort Smith Community Center—building AR-4
Fort Smith Courthouse—building AR-4
Fort Smith Filtration Plant—other AR-4
Fort Smith Junior Coll—school AR-4
Fort Smith Library—building AR-4
Fort Smith Municipal Airp—airport AR-4
Fort Smith Municipal Auditorium—building AR-4
Fort Smith Natl Cem—cemetery AR-4
Fort Smith Natl Historical Site—building AR-4
Fort Smith Natl Historic Site (Also AR)—park OK-5
Fort Smith Natl Historic Site (Also OK)—park AR-4
Fort Smith Public Use Area—park AR-4
Fort Smith Ruins—locale MT-8
Fort Smith's Belle Grove Hist Dist—hist pl AR-4
Fort Smith Village MT-8
Fort Snelling—hist pl MN-6
Fort Snelling-Mendota Bridge—hist pl MN-6
Fort Snelling Military Reservation—other MN-6
Fort Snelling Natl Cem—cemetery MN-6
Fort Snelling (Unorganized Territory of)—unorg MN-6
Fort Sod KS-7
Fort Soda CA-9
Fort Soledad (Ruins)—locale GU-9
Fortson—locale GA-3
Fortson—locale WA-9
Fortson, H. E., House—hist pl GA-3
Fortson Cem—cemetery TX-5
Fortson Ch—church GA-3
Fortson (Florida Rock)—uninc pl GA-3
Fortsonia—locale GA-3
Fortson Lake—lake MS-4
Fortson Ponds—lake WA-9
Fortsons Mills (historical)—locale AL-4
Fort South West Point TN-4
Fort Southwest Point (historical)—locale TN-4
Fort Spokane—locale WA-9
Fort Spokane Historic Site—locale WA-9
Fort Spokane Military Reserve—hist pl WA-9
**Fort Spring**—pop pl KY-4
**Fort Spring**—pop pl WV-2
Fort Spring—spring OR-9
Fort Spring (Magisterial District)—fmr MCD WV-2
Fort Spring Tunnel—tunnel WV-2
Fort Spunky—locale TX-5
Fort Spunky Cem—cemetery TX-5
Fort Stambaugh Historical—locale WY-8
Fort Stamford Site—hist pl CT-1
Fort Standish—military MA-1
**Fort Standish**—pop pl MA-1
Fort Stanton—hist pl NM-5
Fort Stanton—locale DC-2
**Fort Stanton**—pop pl NM-5
Fort Stanton Mesa—summit NM-5
Fort Stanton Park—park DC-2
Fort Stanwix Natl Monmt—hist pl NY-2
Fort Stanwix Natl Monmt—park NY-2
Fort Stanwix Sch—school NY-2
Fort St. Charles Archeol Site—hist pl MN-6
Fort St. Clair Site—hist pl OH-6
Fort Steele—hist pl WY-8
Fort Steele—locale WY-8
Fort Steele Breaks—range WY-8
Fort Steele Trail—trail MT-8
Fort Steilacoom—hist pl WA-9
**Fort Steilacoom (Western State Hospital)**—pop pl WA-9
Fort Ste Marie De Gannentaha—locale NY-2
Fort Stephens (historical)—military MS-4
Fort Steuben Bridge—other WV-2
Fort Steuben Burial Estates—cemetery OH-6
Fort Steuben (Township of)—other OH-6
Fort Stevens—hist pl OR-9
Fort Stevens—locale DC-2
**Fort Stevens**—pop pl OR-9
Fort Stevens Natl Military Cem—cemetery OR-9
Fort Stevenson Public Use Area—park ND-7
Fort Stevens Park—park DC-2
Fort Stevens State Park—park OR-9
Fort Stewart—other GA-3
**Fort Stewart**—pop pl GA-3
Fort Stewart (CCD)—cens area GA-3
Fort Stewart (U.S. Army)—military GA-3
Fort St. Frederic—hist pl NY-2
Fort St. John—hist pl LA-4
Fort St. Joseph Site—hist pl MI-6
Fort St. Louis Site—hist pl TX-5
Fort St. Michael—hist pl AK-9
**Fort Stockton**—pop pl TX-5
Fort Stockton (CCD)—cens area TX-5
Fort Stockton Hist Dist—hist pl TX-5
Fort Stockton Oil And Gas Field—oilfield TX-5
**Fort Stoddard**—pop pl AL-4
Fort Stodderd AL-4
Fort Story Milit Reservation—military VA-3
Fort Story (U.S. Army)—military VA-3
Fort St. Philip—hist pl LA-4
Fort Street Hist Dist—hist pl ID-8
Fort Street Presbyterian Church—hist pl MI-6
Fort Street Presbyterian Church—hist pl TX-5
Fort Strong—locale VA-3
Fort Strong—military MA-1
Fort Strother (historical)—locale AL-4
Fort Strother Site—hist pl AL-4
Fort Sullivan—hist pl ME-1
Fort Sully (historical)—locale (2) SD-7
Fort Sumner KS-7
**Fort Sumner**—pop pl MD-2
**Fort Sumner**—pop pl NM-5
Fort Sumner Cem—cemetery NM-5
Fort Sumner Diversion Dam—dam NM-5
Fort Sumner Fort Stanton Trail—trail NM-5
Fort Sumner Main Canal—canal NM-5
Fort Sumner RR Bridge—hist pl NM-5
Fort Sumner Ruins—hist pl NM-5
Fort Sumner Valley—valley NM-5
**Fort Sumpter (historical)**—pop pl OR-9
Fort Sumter Natl Monmt—hist pl SC-3
Fort Sumter Natl Monmt—park SC-3
Fort Sumter Rock—summit IA-7
Fort Sumter Sch (historical)—school TN-4
**Fort Supply**—pop pl OK-5
Fort Supply Hist Dist—hist pl OK-5
Fort Supply Lake—reservoir OK-5
Fort Supply Rsvr OK-5
**Fort Supply (Supply)**—pop pl OK-5
Fort Sutter—uninc pl CA-9
Fortsville—hist pl VA-3
**Fortsville**—pop pl NY-2
Fort Sweeney Site—hist pl MN-6
Fort Taber District—hist pl MA-1
Fort Taylor TX-5
Fort Taylor—locale FL-3
Fort Taylor Hardin—military AL-4
Fort Taylor (historical)—locale FL-3
Fort Tecumseh (historical)—locale SD-7
Fort Tejon—hist pl CA-9
Fort Tejon Sch—school CA-9
Fort Tejon Siphon—canal CA-9
Fort Tejon State Historical Park—park CA-9
Fort Tenoxtitlan (Site)—locale TX-5
Fort Terrett Peak—summit TX-5
Fort Terrett Ranch (Historical Site)—locale TX-5
Fort Terror (historical)—military MS-4
Fort Teton (historical)—locale SD-7
Fort Texas (historical)—locale MS-4
Fort Thayer—military DC-2
**Fort Thomas**—pop pl AZ-5
**Fort Thomas**—pop pl KY-4
Fort Thomas Canal—canal AZ-5
Fort Thomas Elem Sch—school AZ-5
Fort Thomas H. Moorer—military AL-4
Fort Thomas HS—school AZ-5
Fort Thomas Military Reservation District—hist pl KY-4
Fort Thomas Post Office—building AZ-5
Fort Thomas R Boroughs—military AL-4
Fort Thomas Union High School AZ-5
Fort Thomas Ward Cem—cemetery AZ-5
**Fort Thompson**—pop pl SD-7
Fort Thompson Archeol District—hist pl SD-7
Fort Thompson (historical)—locale FL-3
Fort Thompson Mounds—hist pl SD-7
Fort Thompson Rec Area—park SD-7
Fort Ticonderoga—hist pl NY-2
Fort Ticonderoga—locale NY-2
Fort Ticonderoga Post Office—locale NY-2
Fort Ticonderoga Station—locale NY-2
Fort Tilden—locale NY-2
Fort Tilden Hist Dist—hist pl NY-2
Fort Tilden (U.S. Army)—uninc pl NY-2
Fort Tilton Historical Marker—park WA-9
Fort Tombecbee—hist pl AL-4
Fort Tombecbe (historical)—locale AL-4
Fort Tombeckbe AL-4
Fort Tombeckbee AL-4
Fort Tombekbi AL-4
Fort Tombikbee AL-4
Fort Tompkins Quadrangle—hist pl NY-2
Fort Totten ND-7
Fort Totten—hist pl ND-7
**Fort Totten**—pop pl (2) ND-7
Fort Totten (historical)—locale DC-2
Fort Totten (historical)—locale NC-3
Fort Totten Indian Agency—locale ND-7
Fort Totten Ind Res—reserve ND-7
Fort Totten Milit Reservation—military NY-2
Fort Totten Officers' Club—hist pl NY-2
Fort Totten Park—park DC-2
Fort Totten Station—locale ND-7
Fort Totten (U.S. Army) (inactive)—uninc pl NY-2
Fort Toulouse—hist pl AL-4
Fort Toulouse Natl Historic Park—park AL-4
Fort Town MS-4
**Fort Township**—pop pl SD-7
Fort Towson—hist pl OK-5
**Fort Towson**—pop pl OK-5
Fort Towson (CCD)—cens area OK-5
Fort Towson Cem—cemetery OK-5
Fort Tracy (historical)—locale AL-4
Fort Trail—trail OH-6
Fort Travis—locale TX-5
Fort Trefalldigheet DE-2
Fort Trenholm—hist pl SC-3
Fort Trial Ch—church VA-3
Fort Trinity DE-2
Fort Trumbull—hist pl CT-1
Fort Trumbull—locale CT-1
**Fort Trumbull**—pop pl CT-1
Fort Trumbull Beach CT-1
Fort Trumbull Beach—beach CT-1
Fort Tryon Park—park NY-2
Fort Tryon Park and the Cloisters—hist pl NY-2
Fort Tule—locale AZ-5
**Fort Tuthill**—pop pl AZ-5
Fort Tuthill County Park—park AZ-5
Fort Tyson AZ-5
Fort Umpqua (historical)—military OR-9
Fort Umqua OR-9
Fortuna—locale AZ-5
Fortuna—locale PA-2
Fortuna—locale PR-3
**Fortuna**—pop pl CA-9
**Fortuna**—pop pl MO-7
**Fortuna**—pop pl ND-7
**Fortuna**—pop pl (4) PR-3
Fortuna, Point—cape LA-4
Fortuna Air Force Station—military ND-7
Fortuna Bay—bay VI-3
Fortuna Canyon—valley UT-8
Fortuna (CCD)—cens area CA-9
Fortuna Hill—summit VI-3
Fortuna Interchange—crossing AZ-5
**Fortuna Ledge (native name: Marshall)**—pop pl AK-9
Fortuna Mine—mine (3) AZ-5
Fortuna Mine—mine NV-8
Fortuna Mtn—summit CA-9
Fortuna Nursery Sch—school CA-9
Fortuna Peak—summit AZ-5
Fortuna Point—cape AK-9
Fortuna Reefs—bar AK-9
Fortuna Station AZ-5
Fortuna Strait—channel AK-9
Fortuna Wash—stream (2) AZ-5
**Fortune**—pop pl TX-5
Fortune, T. Thomas, House—hist pl NJ-2
Fortune Bar—bar AR-4
Fortune Bend—bend TX-5
**Fortune Branch**—pop pl OR-9
Fortune Branch—stream MO-7
Fortune Branch—stream OR-9
Fortune Branch—stream TN-4
Fortune Cem—cemetery KY-4
Fortune Cem—cemetery NC-3
Fortune Ch—church AR-4
Fortune Cove—valley NC-3
Fortune Creek—stream AK-9
Fortune Creek—stream ID-8
Fortune Creek—stream WA-9
Fortune Ditch—canal IN-6
Fortune Ditch—canal OH-6
Fortune Ferry (historical)—locale AL-4
Fortune Field—basin NC-3
**Fortune Fork**—pop pl LA-4
Fortune Hollow—valley MO-7
Fortune Lake—lake FL-3
**Fortune Lake**—pop pl MI-6
Fortune Lake Creek—stream MI-6
Fortune Lakes—lake MI-6
Fortune Meadows—flat ID-8
Fortune Mine—mine CO-8
Fortune Mine—mine UT-8
Fortune Mtn—summit AR-4
Fortune Mtn—summit WA-9
Fortune Placer Mine—mine CO-8
Fortune Point—cliff AR-4
Fortune Point—summit ID-8
Fortune Pond FL-3
Fortune Ponds—lake WA-9
Fortune Ranch—locale AZ-5
Fortunes Cove—valley VA-3
Fortunes Fork NC-3
Fortune Slough—stream AR-4
Fortune Spring—spring MT-8
Fortunes Rocks ME-1
**Fortunes Rocks**—pop pl ME-1
Fortunes Rocks Beach—beach ME-1
Fortunes Rocks Cove—bay ME-1
Fortune Teller Creek—stream PA-2
Fort Union—locale FL-3
Fort Union Cem—cemetery NM-5
Fort Union Corral—locale NM-5
**Fort Union Cove Condo**—pop pl UT-8
Fort Union Natl Monmt—hist pl NM-5
Fort Union Natl Monmt—park NM-5
Fort Union Ranch—locale NM-5
Fort Union Road—trail NM-5
Fort Union Trading Post Nat. Historic Site—park MT-8
Fort Union Trading Post Nat. Hist. Site—park ND-7
Fort Union Trading Post Natl Historic Site—hist pl MT-8
Fort Union Trading Post Natl Historic Site—hist pl ND-7
Fort Union Trading Post Natl Historic Site—park MT-8
Fort Union Trading Post Natl Historic Site—park ND-7
Fort Urmston—locale VA-3
**Fort Valley**—pop pl GA-3
Fort Valley—valley AZ-5
Fort Valley—valley VA-3
Fort Valley (CCD)—cens area GA-3
Fort Valley Ch—church VA-3
Fort Valley Experimental For—forest AZ-5
Fort Valley Experimental Forest Station—locale AZ-5
Fort Valley Overlook—locale (2) VA-3
Fort Valley Sch—school VA-3
Fort Valley State Coll—school GA-3
Fort Vancouver WA-9
Fort Vancouver HS—school WA-9
Fort Vancouver Natl Historic Site—park WA-9
Fort Vannoy Sch—school OR-9
Fort Vasquez Site—hist pl CO-8
Fort Verde AZ-5
Fort Verde District—hist pl AZ-5
Fort Verde District (Boundary Increase)—hist pl AZ-5
**Fort Verde Estates (subdivision)**—pop pl (2) AZ-5
Fortville—locale GA-3
**Fortville**—pop pl IN-6
Fortville Cem—cemetery GA-3
Fortville Park—park IN-6
Fort Wacahoota (historical)—locale FL-3
Fort Waccasassa Site—locale FL-3
Fort Wadsworth—locale VA-3
**Fort Wadsworth**—pop pl NY-2
Fort Wadsworth Agency and Scout HQ Bldg—hist pl MN-6
Fort Wadsworth (U.S. Army)—military NY-2
Fort Wagner Monument—locale SC-3
Fort Wainwright—other AK-9
Fort Wainwright (U.S. Army)—military AK-9
Fort Wales Rock—pillar WI-6
Fort Wallace Post Cemetery and Museum—park KS-7
Fort Wallace (Site)—locale KS-7
Fort Walla Walla Hist Dist—hist pl WA-9
Fort Walla Walla Historical Monmt—park WA-9
Fort Walla Walla Park—park WA-9
Fort Wallen AZ-5
**Fort Walton Beach**—pop pl FL-3
Fort Walton Beach (CCD)—cens area FL-3
Fort Walton Beach Hosp Extended Care—hospital FL-3
Fort Walton Beach HS—school FL-3
Fort Walton Beach Park—park FL-3
Fort Walton Beach Public Library—building FL-3
Fort Walton Mound—hist pl FL-3
Fort Walton Square (Shop Ctr)—locale FL-3
Fort Ward—hist pl VA-3
**Fort Ward Heights**—pop pl VA-3
Fort Ward Hist Dist—hist pl WA-9
Fort Ward Park—park VA-3
Fort Ward State Park—park WA-9
Fort Warner—locale OR-9
Fort Warren—hist pl MA-1
Fort Warren—military MA-1
**Fort Warren**—pop pl MA-1
**Fort Washakie**—pop pl WY-8
Fort Washakie Hist Dist—hist pl WY-8
Fort Washakie Underground Rsvr—reservoir WY-8
Fort Washington—hist pl MD-2
Fort Washington—hist pl MA-1
**Fort Washington**—pop pl PA-2
Fort Washington—post sta MD-2
Fort Washington—uninc pl NY-2
Fort Washington Ch—church MD-2
Fort Washington Country Club—other CA-9
**Fort Washington Estates**—pop pl MD-2
Fort Washington For—forest MD-2
Fort Washington Interchange PA-2
Fort Washington Lincoln Sch—school CA-9
Fort Washington Marina—other MD-2
Fort Washington Natl Park—park MD-2
Fort Washington Park—park MD-2
Fort Washington Park—park NY-2
Fort Washington Point—cape NY-2
Fort Washington Sch—school CA-9
Fort Washington Site—hist pl NY-2
Fort Washington State Park—park (2) PA-2
Fort Washita—hist pl OK-5
Fort Washita—locale OK-5
Fort Watauga (historical)—military TN-4
Fort Wayne—hist pl MI-6
Fort Wayne—locale MI-6
**Fort Wayne**—pop pl IN-6
Fort Wayne Bible Coll—school IN-6
Fort Wayne City Hall—hist pl IN-6
Fort Wayne Country Club—other IN-6
Fort Wayne Junction MI-6
Fort Wayne Municipal Airp—airport IN-6
Fort Wayne Printing Company Bldg—hist pl IN-6
Fort Wayne State Hosp and Training Center—hospital IN-6
Fort Webb—hist pl KY-4
Fort Welch—locale VA-3
Fort West Ditch—canal NM-5
Fort Western—hist pl ME-1
Fort West Hill—summit NM-5
Fort Wetherill—summit RI-1
Fort Wheaton—locale VA-3
Fort Whipple AZ-5
Fort Whipple—locale AZ-5
**Fort White**—pop pl FL-3
Fort White Adult Education Sch—school FL-3
Fort White-Bethlehem Sch—school FL-3
Fort White (CCD)—cens area FL-3
Fort White (historical)—locale FL-3
Fort Whiting Natl Guard Armory—military AL-4
Fort Wilkins—hist pl MI-6
Fort Wilkinson Historical Site—locale GA-3
Fort Wilkins State Park—park MI-6
Fort Willard—locale VA-3
Fort William Bend—bend OR-9
Fort William Everette Armory—military AL-4
Fort William Henry—hist pl ME-1
Fort William Henry—locale NY-2
Fort William Henry Harrison—military MT-8
Fort William H. Seward—hist pl AK-9
Fort Williams—hist pl KY-4
**Fort Williams**—pop pl ME-1
Fort Williams Bend OR-9
Fort Williams Cem—cemetery AL-4
Fort Williams Ch—church IN-6
Fort Williams Ferry (historical)—locale AL-4
Fort Williams (historical)—locale AL-4
Fort William Shop Ctr—locale AL-4
Fort Williams Indian War Cemetery AL-4
Fort Williams Shoals (historical)—bar AL-4
Fort Wilson—locale ID-8
Fort-Wimberly Cem—cemetery TN-4
Fort Winder Ch—church FL-3
Fort Winfield Scott—locale CA-9
**Fort Wingate**—pop pl NM-5
Fort Wingate Archeol Site—hist pl NM-5
Fort Wingate Army Depot (Inactive)—military NM-5
Fort Wingate Hist Dist—hist pl NM-5
Fort Winnebago Site—hist pl WI-6
Fort Winnebago Surgeon's Quarters—hist pl WI-6
**Fort Winnebago (Town of)**—pop pl WI-6
**Fort Winthrop**—pop pl MA-1
Fort Wolters—military TX-5
Fort Wood LA-4
Fort Wood Hist Dist—hist pl TN-4
Fort Wood Lookout Tower—locale MO-7
Fort Wool—hist pl VA-3
Fort Wool—locale VA-3
Fort Wool Light—locale VA-3
Fort Wooster Park—park CT-1
Fort Worden—hist pl WA-9
**Fort Worden (Fort Worden School)**—pop pl WA-9
Fort Worden Military Reservation—other WA-9
Fort Worth—locale VA-3
**Fort Worth**—pop pl TX-5
Fort Worth and Dallas Freight Depot—locale TX-5
Fort Worth Bible Ch—church TX-5
Fort Worth (CCD)—cens area TX-5
Fort Worth Elks Lodge 124—hist pl TX-5
Fort Worth General Depot—locale TX-5
Fort Worthington Sch—school MD-2
Fort Worth Public Market—hist pl TX-5
Fort Worth Stockyards Hist Dist—hist pl TX-5
Fort Worth Village Creek Sewage Disposal—other TX-5
**Fort Wright**—pop pl KY-4
Fort Wright Coll—school WA-9
Fort Wright College of Holy Names—other WA-9
Fort Wright (Fort Wright College of Holy Names)—uninc pl WA-9
Fort W W Brandon—military AL-4
Fort Wyman Heights MO-7
Forty Acre Bay—bay FL-3
Forty Acre Bayou—gut LA-4
Forty Acre Hill—summit ME-1
Forty Acre Hollow—valley TX-5
Forty Acre Island AL-4
Forty Acre Island—island GA-3
Forty Acre Knob—summit KY-4
Fortyacre Lake—bay WI-6
Forty Acre Lake—reservoir CO-8
Forty Acre Meadow—flat CO-8
Forty-Acre Opening—flat CA-9
Forty Acre Pond—lake FL-3
Forty Acre Pond—reservoir OH-6
Forty Acre Pond—swamp FL-3
Forty Acre Reef—bar TX-5
Forty Acre Sinkhole—basin MO-7
Forty Acres Island (historical)—island AL-4
Forty Acre Well—well (2) NM-5
Forty Acre Woods—woods IL-6
Fort Yamhill Site—hist pl OR-9
Forty and Eight Lake*—reservoir KS-7
Forty and One-half Mile Creek—stream AK-9
Fort Yankton Historic Site—locale SD-7
Fort Yargo State Park—park GA-3
Forty Arpent Canal—canal (3) LA-4
**Fort Yates**—pop pl ND-7
Fort Yates Rec Area—park ND-7
Forty Bar Ranch—locale MT-8
Forty Brook—stream NY-2
Forty Caves Canyon—valley AZ-5
Forty Creek—stream (2) MT-8
Forty Day Creek—stream OR-9
Fortyday Creek—stream WA-9
Forty East Shop Ctr—locale FL-3
Forty-eight, Lake—reservoir KS-7
Fortyeight Cem—cemetery TN-4
Fortyeight Creek—stream TN-4
Fortyeight Creek Bridge—locale TN-4
Fortyeight Creek Bridge Sch (historical)—school TN-4
Fortyeight Creek Sch (historical)—school TN-4
Fortyeight Forge Cem—cemetery TN-4
Fortyeight Forge (historical)—locale TN-4
Forty-eight Forge (40WY63)—hist pl TN-4
Fortyeight Freewill Baptist Ch—church TN-4
Fortyeight Mile Creek—stream MT-8
Fortyeight Mile Creek—stream SD-7
Fortyeight Mile Point—cape LA-4
Forty Eight Post Office (historical)—building TN-4
**Forty-eight Street**—pop pl NJ-2
Fortyeight Tank—reservoir TX-5
Fortyeight Ten Cave—cave AL-4
Fortyfifth Street Baptist Ch—church AL-4
FortyFifth Street Sch—school GA-3
Forty Five—locale TN-4
Forty Five Baptist Ch—church TN-4
Forty-Five Canal—canal CA-9
Forty-Five Ch TN-4
Forty-five Creek—stream ID-8
Forty Five Creek—stream MI-6
Forty-five Creek—stream MT-8
Forty-Five Lode Mine—mine SD-7
Fortyfive Mile Campground—locale CA-9
Forty-five Ninety Mine—mine CO-8
Fortyfive Pup—stream AK-9
Forty Five Sch (historical)—school TN-4
Forty Five Siding TN-4
Forty-five Spring—spring OR-9
Fortyfive Windmill—locale TX-5
Forty Foot Hole—lake OK-5
Fortyfoot Windmill—locale TX-5
Forty Forks—locale TN-4
Forty Forks Baptist Ch—church TN-4
**Forty Fort**—pop pl PA-2
Forty Fort Borough—civil PA-2
Forty Fort Meetinghouse—hist pl PA-2
Forty Four—locale AR-4
Forty Four Canyon AZ-5
Fortyfour Canyon—valley AZ-5
Fortyfour Canyon—valley CO-8
Fortyfour Cem—cemetery OK-5
Fortyfour Coulee—valley MT-8
Fortyfour Creek—stream CA-9
Forty-four Creek—stream ID-8
Forty-four Creek—stream MT-8
Fortyfour Creek—stream MT-8
Fortyfour Lake—lake OR-9
Fortyfour Spring—spring AZ-5
Fortyfour Store—locale NM-5
Fortyfour Tank—reservoir AZ-5
Forty-fourth Street Pier—locale NJ-2
Forty-Four Trail—trail ID-8
Fortyfour Windmill—locale TX-5
**Forty (historical)**—pop pl MS-4
Forty Island Creek—stream AR-4
Forty Islands—island NH-1
Fortymile Bend—locale FL-3
Fortymile Canal—canal MT-8
Fortymile Canyon—valley NV-8
Fortymile Canyon—valley WA-9
Fortymile Cave—cave OR-9
Forty Mile Creek WY-8
Fortymile Creek—stream AK-9
Fortymile Creek—stream MT-8
Fortymile Creek—stream UT-8
Fortymile Creek—stream WA-9
Fortymile Creek—stream WY-8
Fortymile Desert—plain NV-8
Fortymile Desert Tank—reservoir AZ-5
Fortymile Dome—summit AK-9
Fortymile Flat—flat WY-8
Fortymile Gulch—valley UT-8
Fortymile Knoll—summit NV-8
Fortymile Lake—lake AK-9
Fortymile Peak—summit WY-8
Forty Mile Point—cape MI-6
Forty Mile Point Light Station—hist pl MI-6
Fortymile Ridge—ridge UT-8
Fortymile River—stream AK-9
Fortymile (Site)—locale AK-9
Fortymile Slide—slope UT-8
Fortymile Slough—stream AK-9
Fortymile Spring—spring UT-8
Fortymile Spring—spring WY-8
Forty Mile Springs Creek WY-8
Fortymile Wash—stream NV-8
Forty Mountain Trail—trail NY-2
Forty Mourners Ch—church PA-2
Forty Mtn—summit NY-2
Forty-nine Butte MT-8
Fortynine Camp—locale NV-8
Forty-Nine Country Club—other AZ-5
Fortynine Creek—stream CA-9
Fortynine Creek—stream NV-8
Fortynine Gap—gap CA-9
Fortynine Gulch—valley ID-8
Fortynine Hill—summit AZ-5
Fortynine Lake—lake NV-8
Fortynine Meadows—flat ID-8
Fortynine Mtn—summit NV-8
Fortynine Palms Canyon—valley CA-9
Fortynine Palms Oasis—spring CA-9
Forty Nine Pond—lake MI-6
Forty-Niner Ridge—ridge NM-5
Forty-nine Slough—stream ID-8
Fortynine Spring—spring OR-9
Fortynine Wash—stream AZ-5
Fortynine Well—well TX-5
Forty Ninth Street—uninc pl FL-3
Forty-ninth Street—uninc pl PA-2
Fortyninth Street Baptist Ch—church AL-4
Forty-Ninth Street Sch—school CA-9
Fortyone Creek—stream WI-6
Fortyone Creek Spring—spring WI-6
Forty-one Cut-off Lake—lake OK-5
Fortyone Draw—valley (3) TX-5
Fortyone Island—island MN-6
Fortyone Mile Creek—stream MT-8
Forty-one Ranch—locale OR-9
Fortyone Tank—reservoir TX-5
Fortyone Windmill—locale (2) TX-5
Fort York AL-4
Forty Point—cape NH-1
Forty Point Lake—swamp AR-4
Forty Pond—lake MI-6
Forty Pond—lake OR-9
Forty Rod Creek—stream WY-8
Forty Rod Flat—flat WY-8
Forty Rod Flat Well—well WY-8
Forty Rod Rsvr—reservoir WY-8
Forty Sch—school KS-7
Fortysecond Street Sch—school CA-9
Fortysecond Street Swamp—swamp GA-3
Fortyseven and Meadow Trail—trail CO-8
Fortyseven Cow Camp—locale CO-8
Fortyseven Creek—stream AK-9
Forty-seven Creek—stream CO-8
Forty-seven Gulch—valley AK-9
Fortyseven Mile Creek—stream MI-6
Fortyseven Pup—stream AK-9
Fortyseven Ranch—locale AZ-5
Forty Seventh Street Ch of Christ—church KS-7
Forty-seventh Street (Kenwood) IL-6
Fortyseven Trail—trail CO-8
Forty Six Corners—locale NY-2
Fortysix Creek—stream (2) MT-8
Fortysix Creek—stream TX-5
Fortysix Mile Cabin—locale AK-9
Fortysixth Street Baptist Ch—church AL-4
Forty Springs Valley—stream CA-9
Forty Steps—cliff MA-1
Forty Steps—cliff RI-1
Forty Steuben Camp—locale OH-6
Forty Thicket Sch—school TN-4
Forty-third Street—uninc pl NJ-2
Forty Three—locale WV-2
Fortythree Creek—stream MN-6
Fortythree Pup—stream AK-9
Fortythree Tank—reservoir TX-5
Fortytwo Gulch—valley AK-9
Fortytwo Mile Campground—locale CA-9
Fortytwo Mile Creek—stream AK-9
Forty Tyler Cem—cemetery GA-3
**Fort Yukon**—pop pl AK-9
Fort Yukon (Air Force) Station—military AK-9
Fort Yukon Christian Sled Trail—trail AK-9
**Fort Yuma (Indian Hill)**—pop pl CA-9
Fort Yuma Ind Res—1105 (1980) CA-9
Fort Yuma Ind Res (Also AZ)—reserve CA-9
**Fort Yuma Ind Res (Also CA)**—pop pl AZ-5
Fort Yuma Reservation AZ-5
Fort Yuma Reservation CA-9
Forty Wink Creek—stream IN-6
Fort Zachary Taylor—hist pl FL-3
Fort Zarah (historical)—locale KS-7
Fort Zarah Park—park KS-7
**Fort Zumwalt**—pop pl MO-7
Fort Zumwalt Sch—school MO-7
Fort Zumwalt State Park—park MO-7
**Forum**—pop pl AR-4
Forum Center—locale MO-7
Forum Center (Shop Ctr)—locale MO-7
Forum Lookout Tower—locale AR-4
Forum of Civics—hist pl TX-5

Forum of Many Truths—church (2) FL-3
Forum Pond NH-1
Forum Shop Ctr—locale MO-7
Forward—locale PA-2
Forward—locale WI-6
Forward Mill—locale CA-9
Forward Park—park CA-9
Forward Sch—school CA-9
Forward Sch—school WI-6
Forward Spring—spring OR-9
**Forwardstown**—pop pl PA-2
Forwardtown PA-2
**Forward Township**—pop pl ND-7
**Forward (Township of)**—pop pl (2) PA-2
Forwe Hollow—valley IL-6
Forwood Elem Sch—school DE-2
Forwood JHS—school DE-2
Forwood Sch DE-2
**Forwood (subdivision)**—pop pl DE-2
Forzano Park—park FL-3
Fosback Marsh—swamp OR-9
Fosburg Run—stream PA-2
**Foscoe**—pop pl NC-3
Fosco Playground—park IL-6
Foscue Creek—stream AL-4
Foscue Creek Area—park AL-4
Foscue Plantation House—hist pl NC-3
Foscue-Whitfield House—hist pl AL-4
Fosdick, Point—cape WA-9
Fosdick Lake—lake MN-6
Fosdick-Masten Park HS—hist pl NY-2
Fosdick-Masten Park HS—school NY-2
Fosdic Lake—reservoir TX-5
Fosgan—area GU-9
Fosgate Brook—stream MA-1
Foshalee Lake—lake FL-3
Foshalee Slough—gut FL-3
Foshay JHS—school CA-9
Foshay Pass—gap CA-9
Foshay Spring—spring CA-9
Foshay Tower—hist pl MN-6
Foshea Branch—stream MS-4
Foshee—locale AL-4
Foshee Cem—cemetery (3) AL-4
Foshee Cem—cemetery LA-4
Foshee Ch TN-4
Foshee Chapel—church TN-4
Foshee Eddy—rapids MS-4
Foshee Islands—island AL-4
Foshee Lake—lake AL-4
Foshee Pass Rec Area—park TN-4
**Fosheeton**—pop pl AL-4
Fosilen Lake—lake MN-6
Fosil Ridge MT-8
Foskett Island—island CT-1
Foskett Mill Stream—stream MA-1
Foskett Spring—spring OR-9
Fosmire Sch—school IL-6
Foso de Arcilla—mine PR-3
Foso de Prestamo—mine PR-3
Foso Jacinto—other PR-3
Foss MI-6
**Foss**—pop pl OK-5
**Foss**—pop pl OR-9
Foss, Horatio G., House—hist pl ME-1
Foss, Levi, House—hist pl ME-1
Foss, Oscar, Memorial Library—hist pl NH-1
Foss Acres IL-6
Foss and Knowlton Brook—stream ME-1
Foss and Knowlton Pond—lake ME-1
Foss and Wells House—hist pl MN-6
Fossan Lake—lake MN-6
Fossati, E. J., House—hist pl TX-5
Fossback Marsh OR-9
Foss Beach—beach NH-1
Foss Brook—stream ME-1
Foss Brook—stream NH-1
Foss Camp—locale CA-9
Foss Cem—cemetery ME-1
Foss Coulee—valley MT-8
Foss Cove ME-1
Foss Creek—stream WA-9
Foss Ditch—canal IN-6
Fosset Gulch—valley CO-8
Fossett Cem—cemetery GA-3
Fossett Cove ME-1
Fossetts Cove ME-1
Fossetts Cove—bay ME-1
Fossett Spring—spring CA-9
Fosseum Mtn—summit MT-8
Foss Harbor NH-1
Foss Hill—summit (2) ME-1
Foss Hill—summit WA-9
Foss Hill Cem—cemetery ME-1
Foss House—hist pl MN-6
Fossicks Rock Quarry AL-4
Fossil—locale WY-8
**Fossil**—pop pl OR-9
Fossil Basin—basin MT-8
Fossil Bay—basin AZ-5
Fossil Bay—bay WA-9
Fossil Bluffs—cliff AK-9
Fossil Bone Exhibit—locale TX-5
Fossil Butte—summit ID-8
Fossil Butte—summit WY-8
Fossil Butte Natl Monument—park WY-8
Fossil Canyon—valley AZ-5
Fossil Canyon—valley (3) CA-9
Fossil Canyon—valley ID-8
Fossil Canyon—valley OR-9
Fossil Cave—cave CA-9
Fossil (CCD)—cens area OR-9
Fossil Creek TX-5
Fossil Creek WA-9
Fossil Creek—stream (3) AK-9
Fossil Creek—stream AZ-5
Fossil Creek—stream CA-9
Fossil Creek—stream CO-8
Fossil Creek—stream ID-8
Fossil Creek—stream KS-7
Fossil Creek—stream MT-8
Fossil Creek—stream OR-9
Fossil Creek—stream (4) WA-9
Fossil Creek Bridge—hist pl AZ-5
Fossil Creek Cave—cave TN-4
Fossil Creek Reservoir Inlet—canal CO-8
Fossil Creek Reservoir Outlet—canal CO-8
Fossil Creek Rsvr—reservoir CO-8
Fossil Creek Sch—school CO-8
Fossil Creek Sch—school KS-7
Fossil Cycad Natl Monmt—park SD-7
Fossil Falls Archeol District—hist pl CA-9
Fossil Fish Quarries—other WY-8
Fossil Forest MT-8
Fossil Forest—locale WY-8
Fossil Gulch—valley ID-8
Fossil Hill—summit (2) NV-8
Fossil Hill—summit WY-8
Fossil Knobs—summit TX-5
Fossil Lake—lake AK-9
Fossil Lake—lake MT-8
Fossil Lake—lake OR-9
Fossil Lake—reservoir KS-7
Fossil Mtn—summit AK-9
Fossil Mtn—summit AZ-5
Fossil Mtn—summit CO-8
Fossil Mtn—summit MT-8
Fossil Mtn—summit UT-8
Fossil Mtn—summit WY-8
Fossil Park—park OR-9
Fossil Peak—summit AK-9
Fossil Peak—summit MT-8
Fossil Peak—summit NV-8
Fossil Pocket—basin AZ-5
Fossil Point—cape AK-9
Fossil Point—cape CA-9
Fossil Point—cape OR-9
Fossil Rapids—rapids AZ-5
Fossil Ravine—basin MD-2
Fossil Ridge—ridge CA-9
Fossil Ridge—ridge CO-8
Fossil Ridge—ridge MT-8
Fossil Ridge—ridge NV-8
Fossil Ridge—ridge UT-8
Fossil Ridge—ridge WY-8
Fossil Ridge—summit SD-7
Fossil Ridge Trail—trail CO-8
Fossil River—stream AK-9
Fossil Rock OR-9
Fossil Rock—summit WA-9
Fossil Rsvr—reservoir CO-8
Fossil Sand Dunes—summit GA-3
Fossil Spring—spring MT-8
Fossil Springs—spring AZ-5
Fossil Station KS-7
Fossil Station WY-8
**Fossilville**—pop pl PA-2
Foss Lake WI-6
Foss Lake—lake (2) MN-6
Foss Lake—lake WA-9
Foss Lake—reservoir WI-6
**Fossland**—pop pl IL-6
Foss Mountain—ridge NH-1
Foss Mtn—summit ID-8
Foss Mtn—summit (2) ME-1
Fossom Creek—stream MI-6
Foss Park—park IL-6
Foss Park—park MA-1
Foss Playground—park PA-2
Foss Point—cape ME-1
Foss Pond—lake ME-1
Foss Pond—lake PA-2
Foss Ponds—lake ME-1
Foss Ranch—locale CA-9
Foss Ranch—locale WY-8
Foss Reservoir Dam—dam MA-1
Foss River—stream WA-9
Foss River Camp—locale WA-9
Foss River Campground—locale WA-9
Foss Rsvr—reservoir MA-1
Foss Rsvr—reservoir OK-5
Foss Sch—school CA-9
Foss Sch—school MA-1
Foss Sch—school NH-1
Foss Spring—spring MT-8
Foss Spring—spring (2) OR-9
Fosston—locale CO-8
**Fosston**—pop pl MN-6
**Fossum**—pop pl MN-6
Fossum Cem—cemetery WI-6
**Fossum (Township of)**—pop pl MN-6
Foss Valley—valley CA-9
Fostaire Heliport—airport MO-7
Foster PA-2
Foster—locale (2) CA-9
Foster—locale MS-4
Foster—locale MT-8
Foster—locale OH-6
Foster—locale PA-2
Foster—locale RI-1
Foster—locale (2) TX-5
Foster—locale VA-3
Foster—locale WY-8
**Foster**—pop pl GA-3
**Foster**—pop pl IN-6
**Foster**—pop pl IA-7
**Foster**—pop pl KY-4
**Foster**—pop pl LA-4
**Foster**—pop pl ME-1
**Foster**—pop pl MI-6
**Foster**—pop pl MN-6
**Foster**—pop pl MO-7
**Foster**—pop pl NE-7
**Foster**—pop pl NY-2
**Foster**—pop pl NC-3
**Foster**—pop pl OK-5
**Foster**—pop pl OR-9
**Foster**—pop pl PA-2
**Foster**—pop pl WA-9
**Foster**—pop pl WV-2
**Foster**—pop pl WI-6
Foster, A. C., Bldg—hist pl CO-8
Foster, Dr. Charles A., House—hist pl NY-2
Foster, Ernest LeNeve, House—hist pl CO-8
Foster, Gen. Gideon, House—hist pl MA-1
Foster, Josiah, Bldg—hist pl AR-4
Foster, Mount—summit (2) AK-9
Foster, Philip, Farm—hist pl OR-9
Foster, Reuben, House and Cleaves, Perley, House—hist pl NH-1
Foster, Walter, K., House—hist pl MA-1
Foster Arbor Ch—church LA-4
Foster-Armstrong House—hist pl NJ-2
Foster Ave Sch—school MI-6
Foster Bar—bar OR-9
Foster Bay—bay FL-3
Foster Bayou—gut FL-3
Foster Bayou—gut LA-4
Foster/Bell House—hist pl IA-7
Foster Bend—bend GA-3
Foster Botanic Garden—other HI-9
Foster Branch—stream (2) AR-4
Foster Branch—stream GA-3
Foster Branch—stream (2) IN-6
Foster Branch—stream KY-4
Foster Branch—stream LA-4
Foster Branch—stream MD-2
Foster Branch—stream MO-7
Foster Branch—stream PA-2
Foster Branch—stream SC-3
Foster Branch—stream (4) TN-4
Foster Branch—stream (3) TX-5
Foster Branch—stream VA-3
Foster Branch—stream WV-2
Foster Bridge—bridge AL-4
Foster Bridge—bridge TN-4
Foster Brook PA-2
**Foster Brook**—pop pl PA-2
Foster Brook—stream (2) ME-1
Foster Brook—stream MA-1
Foster Brook—stream (2) NY-2
Foster Brook—stream PA-2
**Fosterburg**—pop pl IL-6
Fosterburg Cem—cemetery IL-6
Foster Burgess Pond—lake FL-3
Foster Butte—summit (2) OR-9
Foster Buttes—summit WY-8
Foster Camp—locale ME-1
Foster Canal—canal LA-4
Foster Canyon—valley AZ-5
Foster Canyon—valley CA-9
Foster Canyon—valley (3) NM-5
Foster Canyon—valley WA-9
Foster (CCD)—cens area KY-4
Foster Cem—cemetery (3) AL-4
Foster Cem—cemetery (5) AR-4
Foster Cem—cemetery (3) GA-3
Foster Cem—cemetery IL-6
Foster Cem—cemetery (3) IN-6
Foster Cem—cemetery IA-7
Foster Cem—cemetery (2) KS-7
Foster Cem—cemetery (2) KY-4
Foster Cem—cemetery LA-4
Foster Cem—cemetery ME-1
Foster Cem—cemetery MA-1
Foster Cem—cemetery MN-6
Foster Cem—cemetery (2) MS-4
Foster Cem—cemetery (5) MO-7
Foster Cem—cemetery OH-6
Foster Cem—cemetery OK-5
Foster Cem—cemetery OR-9
Foster Cem—cemetery (2) PA-2
Foster Cem—cemetery SC-3
Foster Cem—cemetery (7) TN-4
Foster Cem—cemetery (8) TX-5
Foster Cem—cemetery (2) WV-2
Foster Center—locale RI-1
Foster Center Hist Dist—hist pl RI-1
Foster Channel NC-3
Foster Channel—channel ME-1
Foster Chapel—church AL-4
Foster Chapel—church AR-4
Foster Chapel—church IN-6
Foster Chapel—church MS-4
Foster Chapel—church WV-2
Foster Chapel Baptist Ch—church TN-4
Foster Chapel Cem—cemetery OH-6
**Foster City**—pop pl CA-9
**Foster City**—pop pl MI-6
Foster City Sch—school CA-9
Foster Coll Sch—school MO-7
Foster Corner—locale PA-2
Foster Corner—locale SC-3
**Foster Corners**—pop pl NH-1
Foster Coulee—valley WA-9
Foster County—civil ND-7
Foster County Courthouse—hist pl ND-7
Foster Cove ME-1
Foster Cove—basin NC-3
Foster Cove—bay (2) RI-1
Foster Cove Archeol Site—hist pl RI-1
Foster Creek AR-4
Foster Creek—locale NC-3
Foster Creek—stream (2) AL-4
Foster Creek—stream (2) AK-9
Foster Creek—stream (2) AR-4
Foster Creek—stream (3) CA-9
Foster Creek—stream ID-8
Foster Creek—stream KS-7
Foster Creek—stream (3) LA-4
Foster Creek—stream MI-6
Foster Creek—stream MN-6
Foster Creek—stream (5) MS-4
Foster Creek—stream MO-7
Foster Creek—stream (5) MT-8
Foster Creek—stream NE-7
Foster Creek—stream (2) NC-3
Foster Creek—stream (6) OR-9
Foster Creek—stream PA-2
Foster Creek—stream (3) SC-3
Foster Creek—stream (2) SD-7
Foster Creek—stream (2) TX-5
Foster Creek—stream (4) WA-9
Foster Creek—stream WI-6
Foster Creek Forest Camp—locale OR-9
Foster Creek Sch—school MT-8
**Foster Crossroad**—pop pl AL-4
Foster Crossroads SC-3
Foster Cross Roads TN-4
Foster Crossroads—locale AL-4
Foster Crossroads—locale TN-4
Foster Cross Roads Sch (historical)—school TN-4
Foster Creek—stream OR-9
**Fosterdale**—pop pl NY-2
Foster Dam—dam NC-3
Foster Dam—dam OR-9
Foster Dam—dam UT-8
Foster-Davis Cem—cemetery AL-4
Foster Ditch—canal IN-6
Foster Ditch—canal OH-6
Foster Drain—canal (2) MI-6
Foster Drain—canal WA-9
Foster Draw—valley CA-9
Foster Draw—valley MT-8
Foster Draw—valley NV-8
Foster Draw—valley (3) NM-5
Foster Draw—valley (3) WY-8
Foster Drive Ch—church FL-3
Foster Elem Sch—school PA-2
Foster Falls—falls TN-4
Foster Falls (RR name for Fosters Falls)—other VA-3
Foster Falls Sch—school TN-4
Foster Ferry Bridge—bridge AL-4
Foster Field—flat ME-1
Foster Field—park OR-9
Foster Field Cem—cemetery KY-4
Foster Flat—flat OR-9
Foster Flat Meadow—flat OR-9
Foster Ford (historical)—locale AL-4
Foster Fork—locale VA-3
**Foster (Forrester)**—pop pl TX-5
Foster Glades—flat CA-9
Foster Glades—flat OR-9
Foster Golf Course—other WA-9
**Foster-Grant Subdivision**—pop pl UT-8
Foster Grove Ch—church AL-4
Foster Grove Sch—school SC-3
Foster Gulch—valley (3) CO-8
Foster Gulch—valley (4) MT-8
Foster Gulch—valley OR-9
Foster Gulch—valley SD-7
Foster Gulch—valley WY-8
Foster Hall—hist pl TX-5
Foster Heliport—airport WA-9
Foster Hill—locale AR-4
Foster Hill—ridge NH-1
Foster Hill—summit (3) ME-1
Foster Hill—summit (2) MA-1
Foster Hill—summit (2) NH-1
Foster Hill—summit NY-2
Foster Hill—summit (2) PA-2
Foster Hill—summit VT-1
Foster Hill—summit WA-9
Foster Hill Cem—cemetery NY-2
Foster Hills—locale GA-3
Foster Hill Sch (historical)—school PA-2
Foster-Hixson Cem—cemetery TN-4
Foster Hole—bay CT-1
Foster Hollow—valley AR-4
Foster Hollow—valley GA-3
Foster Hollow—valley (2) KY-4
Foster Hollow—valley PA-2
Foster Hollow—valley (2) TN-4
Foster Hollow—valley TX-5
Foster Hollow—valley WV-2
Foster Hollow Prospect—mine TN-4
Foster Home/Sylvan Plantation—hist pl AL-4
Foster Hotel—hist pl NM-5
Foster House—hist pl AR-4
Foster House—hist pl TX-5
Foster HS—school VA-3
Foster HS—school WA-9
Foster Island PA-2
Foster Island—island CA-9
Foster Island—island (4) ME-1
Foster Island—island MI-6
Foster Island—island WA-9
Foster JHS—school OK-5
Foster Joseph Sayers Dam—dam PA-2
Foster Joseph Sayers Lake—reservoir PA-2
Foster Joseph Sayers Rsvr PA-2
Foster Junction—locale WI-6
Foster Key—island FL-3
Foster Knob—summit NC-3
Foster Knob—summit (2) VA-3
Foster Lake CO-8
Foster Lake CT-1
Foster Lake WI-6
Foster Lake—lake (2) CA-9
Foster Lake—lake IL-6
Foster Lake—lake ME-1
Foster Lake—lake (4) MI-6
Foster Lake—lake MN-6
Foster Lake—lake MS-4
Foster Lake—lake NE-7
Foster Lake—lake NM-5
Foster Lake—lake (2) OR-9
Foster Lake—lake (3) WI-6
Foster Lake—reservoir NY-2
Foster Lake—reservoir (2) NC-3
Foster Lake—reservoir OR-9
Foster Lake—reservoir TX-5
Foster Lake Dam—dam (2) MS-4
Foster Lake Dam—dam NC-3
Foster Landing—locale (2) AL-4
Foster Ledge—bench RI-1
Foster Ledges—bar ME-1
Foster Meadow—swamp CA-9
Foster Meadows—flat WY-8
Foster Memorial A.M.E. Zion Church—hist pl NY-2
Foster Memorial Ch—church NC-3
Foster Memorial Hosp—hospital CA-9
Foster Mill—locale SC-3
Foster Mill (historical)—locale AL-4
Foster Mills—locale GA-3
Foster Mine—mine MT-8
Foster Mine (underground)—mine AL-4
Foster Mound Cem—cemetery MS-4
Foster Mounds—summit MS-4
Foster Mtn—summit AL-4
Foster Mtn—summit (2) CA-9
Foster Mtn—summit KY-4
Foster Mtn—summit NC-3
Foster Notch—gap VT-1
Foster Number 1 Dam—dam SD-7
Foster Number 2 Dam—dam SD-7
Foster Number 3 Dam—dam SD-7
Foster Number 4 Dam—dam SD-7
Foster Oil Company—hist pl OR-9
Foster Oil Field—oilfield TX-5
Foster Park—park CA-9
Foster Park—park FL-3
Foster Park—park IL-6
Foster Park—park (3) IN-6
Foster Park—park IA-7
Foster Park—park KS-7
Foster Park—park NM-5
Foster Park—park TX-5
Foster Park Canyon—valley NM-5
Foster Park Sch—school IL-6
Foster Park Sch—school SC-3
Foster-Payne House—hist pl RI-1
Foster Pit—cave AL-4
**Foster Place**—pop pl TX-5
Foster Point—cape FL-3
Foster Point—cape (3) ME-1
Foster Point—cape MN-6
Foster Point—cape NY-2
Foster Point—cape TX-5
Foster Point—cape WA-9
Foster Point Cem—cemetery IL-6
Foster Pond NH-1
Foster Pond—lake CT-1
Foster Pond—lake IL-6
Foster Pond—lake (2) ME-1
Foster Pond—lake MA-1
Foster Pond—lake NH-1
Foster Pond—lake NY-2
Foster Pond—lake OH-6
Foster Pond—lake OR-9
**Foster Pond**—pop pl IL-6
Foster Pond—reservoir CT-1
Foster Pond—reservoir KY-4
Foster Pond—reservoir NC-3
Foster Pond Dam—dam NC-3
Foster Ranch—locale AZ-5
Foster Ranch—locale CA-9
Foster Ranch—locale (3) MT-8
Foster Ranch—locale (2) NM-5
Foster Ranch—locale OR-9
Foster Ranch—locale (5) TX-5
Foster Ranch—locale (3) WY-8
Foster Ranch House—hist pl SD-7
Foster Ranch HQ—locale NM-5
Foster Ranch Tanks—reservoir NM-5
Foster Rand Brook—stream ME-1
Foster Rapids AZ-5
Foster Rapids—rapids OR-9
Foster Reregulating Rsvr OR-9
Foster Ridge—ridge CA-9
Foster Ridge—ridge LA-4
Foster Ridge—ridge ME-1
Foster Ridge—ridge NC-3
Foster Ridge—ridge TN-4
Foster Ridge—ridge WV-2
Foster Road Sch—school CA-9
Foster (RR name for Hop Bottom)—other PA-2
Foster Rsvr OR-9
Foster Rsvr—reservoir (2) CO-8
Foster Rsvr—reservoir ID-8
Foster Rsvr—reservoir OR-9
Foster Rsvr—reservoir UT-8
Foster Rsvr—reservoir WY-8
Foster Rsvrs—reservoir OR-9
Foster Run—stream NJ-2
Foster Run—stream (3) PA-2
Foster Run—stream WV-2
Foster's KY-4
Fosters—locale AL-4
Fosters—locale LA-4
**Fosters**—pop pl ME-1
**Fosters**—pop pl MI-6
**Fosters**—pop pl SC-3
Fosters Bar—bar AL-4
Fosters Bay—swamp SC-3
Fosters Branch IN-6
Fosters Branch—stream SC-3
Fosters Brook—stream ME-1
Fosters Cabin—locale (2) CA-9
**Fosters Canal**—pop pl LA-4
Foster's Castle—hist pl VA-3
Fosters (CCD)—cens area AL-4
Foster Sch PA-2
Foster Sch—hist pl PA-2
Foster Sch—school (4) CA-9
Foster Sch—school CO-8
Foster Sch—school (2) FL-3
Foster Sch—school (5) IL-6
Foster Sch—school (2) KY-4
Foster Sch—school (3) MA-1
Foster Sch—school (2) MI-6
Foster Sch—school (2) MO-7
Foster Sch—school MT-8
Foster Sch—school OH-6
Foster Sch—school SC-3
Foster Sch—school (2) SD-7
Foster Sch—school (3) TX-5
Foster Sch—school WI-6
Fosters Channel—channel NC-3
Fosters Chapel—church KY-4
Fosters Chapel—church (2) SC-3
Fosters Chapel—church TN-4
Fosters Chapel Church AL-4
Fosters Chapel Methodist Church MS-4
Foster Sch (historical)—school MS-4
Foster Sch Number 32—school IN-6
Foster Sch Number 67 IN-6
Foster School IN-6
Foster School—locale (2) TX-5
**Fosters Corner**—pop pl (2) ME-1
**Fosters Corner**—pop pl PA-2
**Fosters Corners**—pop pl ME-1
Foster's Creek ME-1
Fosters Creek MS-4
Fosters Creek—stream NY-2
Fosters Creek—stream VA-3
Fosters Creek Ch—church VA-3
**Fosters Crossroads**—pop pl SC-3
Fosters Cross Roads Post Office (historical)—building TN-4
Fosters Division—civil AL-4
**Fosters Falls**—pop pl VA-3
Fosters Falls Cem—cemetery VA-3
Fosters Falls Mtn—summit VA-3
**Fosters Falls (RR name Foster Falls)**—pop pl VA-3
Foster's Ferry WI-6
Fosters Ferry Bridge AL-4
Fosters Ferry (historical)—locale AL-4
**Fosters (Foster)**—pop pl OH-6
Foster's Hill MA-1
Fosters (historical)—locale MS-4
Foster's Island ME-1
Fosters Landing—locale VA-3
Fosters Landing (historical)—locale AL-4
Foster Slough—stream ID-8
Fosters Mill—locale AL-4
Fosters Mill Bridge AL-4
Fosters Mill (historical)—locale (2) AL-4
Fosters Mill (historical)—locale TN-4
Fosters Millpond—lake VA-3
Fosters Mills—locale PA-2
**Fosters Mills**—pop pl GA-3
Foster's Mound—hist pl MS-4
Foster Spinning Co.—hist pl MA-1
Fosters Point AL-4
Fosters Point ME-1
Fosters Point—cape MA-1
Fosters Pond CT-1
Foster's Pond MA-1
Fosters Pond—lake CT-1
Fosters Pond—lake VT-1
Fosters Pond—reservoir MA-1
Fosters Pond Dam—dam MA-1
Foster Spring—spring AL-4
Foster Spring—spring AZ-5
Foster Spring—spring CA-9
Foster Spring—spring MT-8
Foster Spring—spring (4) OR-9
Foster Spring—spring WA-9
Foster Springs Branch—stream NC-3
**Fosters Ridge**—pop pl IN-6
Fosters Ridge Ch—church IN-6
Foster's River ME-1
Fosters Sch—school SC-3
Fosters Settlement AL-4
Fosters Shop Ctr—locale AL-4
Fosters Site (20SA74)—hist pl MI-6
Fosters Spring AL-4
Fosters Store—locale TX-5
Fosters Store (historical)—locale AL-4
**Fosters (Sylvan)**—pop pl AL-4
Foster Station—building PA-2
Foster Station—locale NJ-2
Foster's Tavern—hist pl SC-3
Fosters Temple—locale OR-9
**Foster Store**—pop pl TX-5
Foster Swamp—swamp NH-1
Fosters Wharf—locale MA-1
Foster Tank—reservoir AZ-5
Foster Tank—reservoir (4) NM-5
Fostertown—locale NJ-2
**Fostertown**—pop pl NY-2
**Foster (Town of)**—pop pl RI-1
**Foster (Town of)**—pop pl WI-6
**Foster Township**—pop pl PA-2
**Foster Township**—pop pl (3) SD-7
Foster Township Municipal Bldg—building PA-2
Foster (Township of)—fmr MCD AR-4
**Foster (Township of)**—pop pl (2) IL-6
**Foster (Township of)**—pop pl MI-6
**Foster (Township of)**—pop pl (2) MN-6
**Foster (Township of)**—pop pl (2) PA-2
Foster Truck Trail (Boulder Ooks Spur)—trail CA-9
Foster Valley Creek—stream TX-5
**Foster Village**—pop pl HI-9
Foster Village—uninc pl NJ-2
Fosterville OH-6
Fosterville PA-2
Fosterville—locale OH-6
Fosterville—locale TX-5
Fosterville—other PA-2
**Fosterville**—pop pl NY-2
**Fosterville**—pop pl OH-6
**Fosterville**—pop pl TN-4
**Fosterville**—pop pl WV-2
Foster Vly—swamp NY-2
Foster Well—locale NM-5
Foster Well—well AZ-5
Foster Well—well NM-5
Foster-Wheeler Junction—uninc pl NY-2
Foster Windmill—locale (2) TX-5
Foster Woods Park—park IA-7
Fostner Cem—cemetery TN-4
Foston Chapel—church KY-4
Fostoria MS-4
Fostoria—locale TX-5
**Fostoria**—pop pl AL-4
**Fostoria**—pop pl IA-7
**Fostoria**—pop pl KS-7
**Fostoria**—pop pl MI-6
**Fostoria**—pop pl OH-6
**Fostoria**—pop pl PA-2
Fostoria Drain—canal MI-6
Fostoria Mausoleum—hist pl OH-6
Fostoria Rsvr—reservoir OH-6
Fostoria Sch—school KS-7
**Fostoria (Township of)**—pop pl OH-6
Fost Sch—school OK-5
Fotch Island—island FL-3
Foth, Christian, House—hist pl WI-6
Fotheringay—hist pl VA-3
Fotheringham, Caroline, House—hist pl UT-8
Fotheringham, William, House—hist pl UT-8
Fothills—locale WA-9
Fotterall Square—park PA-2
Fottler Mine—mine NV-8
Fouborge LA-4
**Fouborge**—pop pl LA-4
**Fouch**—pop pl MI-6
Foucha FM-9
Foucha, Unun En—cape FM-9
Fouch Camp CA-9
Fouch Cem—cemetery MI-6
Fouch Ditch—canal IN-6
Fouche—locale GA-3
Fouche Gap—gap GA-3
Fouche Lake Dam—dam (2) MS-4
Foucher Coulee—valley MT-8
Fouches Creek MS-4
Fouch Hill—summit MI-6
Fouchichi, Ununen—bar FM-9
Fouchim—bar FM-9
Fouchmiah Creek—stream LA-4
Fouchong—island FM-9
Foudy Ranch—locale AZ-5
Fouetin—bar FM-9
Fou Feining—bar FM-9
Fougharty Cem—cemetery WV-2
Fought Cem—cemetery OH-6
Fouha Bay—bay GU-9
Fouha Bay—hist pl GU-9
Fouha Point—summit GU-9
Fouichen—bar FM-9
Fouichen, Mochun—channel FM-9
Foukachen FM-9
Fou Kachen—summit FM-9
Fouke—locale MS-4
Fouke—locale TX-5
**Fouke**—pop pl AR-4
Fouke Cem—cemetery AR-4
Fouke Cem—cemetery TX-5
Fouke-Hawkins HS—school TX-5
Foukenau—summit FM-9
Fouke Oil Field—oilfield AR-4
Foukomus—bar FM-9

Foul Bay—*bay* (3) ... AK-9
Foulds Creek—*stream* ... WI-6
Foulds Springs—*spring* ... WI-6
Foulertons Brook—*stream* ... NJ-2
Foules—*locale* ... LA-4
*Foulgers Hill* ... MA-1
Foul Ground Creek—*stream* ... VA-3
*Fouling Gut* ... VA-3
Foulk Cem—*cemetery* ... SC-3
Foulke, Claude, House—*hist pl* ... AR-4
Foulk Road Sch—*school* ... DE-2
Foulk Run—*stream* ... PA-2
Foulks Cem—*cemetery* ... IL-6
Foulks Ditch—*canal* ... OH-6
**Foulk Woods**—*pop pl* ... DE-2
Foul Pass—*channel* ... AK-9
Foul Pond—*lake* ... GA-3
Foul Rift—*channel* ... PA-2
**Foul Rift**—*pop pl* ... NJ-2
*Foul Rift, The* ... NJ-2
Foul Rift Falls—*falls* ... NJ-2
Foul Rift Ferry—*locale* ... PA-2
*Foul Rift Island* ... PA-2
Foul Rift Islands—*island* ... NJ-2
Foul Rift Islands—*island* ... PA-2
Foulweather, Cape—*cape* ... OR-9
Foulweather Bluff—*cliff* ... WA-9
Foumarau—*bar* ... FM-9
*Foumaraw* ... FM-9
Foumat—*bar* ... FM-9
Foumew—*cape* ... FM-9
Foumew—*island* ... FM-9
*Foumouma* ... FM-9
*Foumouna* ... FM-9
Foumuna—*summit* ... FM-9
Foumuna—*tunnel* ... FM-9
Foumwa—*bar* ... FM-9
Founakar—*swamp* ... FM-9
*Foundary Canyon* ... NV-8
Foundary Hill Sch (historical)—*school* ... TN-4
Foundation Ch—*church* ... KY-4
Foundation Ch—*church* ... SC-3
*Foundation Creek* ... WA-9
Foundation Creek—*stream* ... ID-8
Foundation Creek—*stream* ... MT-8
Foundation Creek—*stream* ... OR-9
Foundation Creek—*stream* ... WA-9
Foundation Fork—*stream* ... WV-2
Foundation Gap—*gap* ... KY-4
Foundation Island—*island* ... WA-9
**Foundation Park**—*pop pl* ... VA-3
Foundation Park—*uninc pl* ... VA-3
Foundation Ridge—*ridge* ... WA-9
Foundation Spring—*spring* ... NM-5
Foundation Spring—*spring* (2) ... OR-9
Foundaway Canyon—*valley* ... NV-8
Found Creek—*stream* (2) ... OR-9
Found Creek—*stream* ... WA-9
Found Creek—*stream* ... WI-6
Founder Creek—*stream* ... WI-6
Founder Lake—*lake* ... WI-6
Founders Bridge—*bridge* ... CT-1
Founders Brook—*stream* ... RI-1
Founders Cem—*cemetery* ... MS-4
Founders Grove—*woods* ... CA-9
Founders Hall—*building* ... PA-2
Founders Hall—*hist pl* ... ME-1
Founder's Hall—*hist pl* ... MA-1
Founder's Hall, Girard College—*hist pl* ... PA-2
Founders Hall, Heidelberg College—*hist pl* ... OH-6
Founder's Hall, The Rockefeller Univ—*hist pl* ... NY-2
*Founders Hall-Milton Hershey Sch* ... PA-2
Founders Landing Park—*park* ... NY-2
Founders' Rock—*hist pl* ... CA-9
Founders Tree—*locale* ... CA-9
Found Fish Lake—*lake* ... AK-9
Found Girl Creek—*stream* ... ID-8
Found Island—*island* ... AK-9
Found Lake—*lake* ... CA-9
Found Lake—*lake* ... MN-6
Found Lake—*lake* ... OR-9
Found Lake—*lake* ... WA-9
Found Lake—*lake* ... WI-6
Found Lakes—*lake* ... WA-9
Found Mesa—*summit* ... UT-8
*Foundry* ... IN-6
*Foundry* ... NH-1
**Foundry**—*pop pl* ... NH-1
Foundry Branch—*stream* ... DC-2
Foundry Branch—*stream* ... TX-5
Foundry Brook—*stream* ... MA-1
Foundry Brook—*stream* ... NY-2
Foundry Ch—*church* ... VA-3
*Foundry Church* ... TN-4
Foundry Cove—*bay* ... NY-2
**Foundry Hill**—*pop pl* ... TN-4
Foundry Lake—*reservoir* ... MA-1
Foundry Pond—*lake* ... MA-1
Foundry Pond—*reservoir* (2) ... MA-1
Foundry Pond Dam—*dam* ... MA-1
Foundry Run—*stream* (2) ... PA-2
Foundry Siding—*uninc pl* ... MD-2
**Foundry Village**—*pop pl* ... MA-1
**Foundryville**—*pop pl* ... PA-2
**Foundryville (historical)**—*pop pl* ... PA-2
Foun Nikichmacho—*bar* ... FM-9
Fount—*locale* ... KY-4
*Fountain* ... IN-6
Fountain—*locale* ... PA-2
Fountain—*locale* ... TX-5
Fountain—*locale* ... VI-3
**Fountain**—*pop pl* ... AL-4
**Fountain**—*pop pl* ... CO-8
**Fountain**—*pop pl* (2) ... FL-3
**Fountain**—*pop pl* ... IL-6
**Fountain**—*pop pl* ... IN-6
**Fountain**—*pop pl* ... MI-6
**Fountain**—*pop pl* ... MN-6
**Fountain**—*pop pl* (2) ... NC-3
**Fountain**—*pop pl* ... PA-2
Fountain, Bayou—*stream* ... LA-4
Fountain, William, House—*hist pl* ... IN-6
Fountain Airp—*airport* ... NC-3
Fountain-Bessac House—*hist pl* ... MI-6
Fountainbleau Creek—*stream* ... MS-4
Fountainbleau Sch—*school* ... MS-4
**Fountainbleau (subdivision)**—*pop pl* ... TN-4
Fountain Blue Sch (historical)—*school* ... MO-7
Fountain Bluff—*cliff* ... IL-6
Fountain Bluff Lookout Tower—*locale* ... IL-6
Fountain Bluff Station—*locale* ... IL-6
Fountain Bluff (Township of)—*civ div* ... IL-6
Fountain Branch—*stream* ... GA-3
Fountain Branch—*stream* ... NC-3
Fountain Branch—*stream* ... SC-3
Fountain Bridge—*bridge* ... GA-3
Fountain Campground—*locale* ... GA-3
Fountain Cem—*cemetery* ... IA-7
Fountain Cem—*cemetery* ... LA-4
Fountain Cem—*cemetery* ... MN-6
Fountain Cem—*cemetery* ... MO-7
Fountain Cem—*cemetery* ... NY-2
Fountain Cem—*cemetery* ... OH-6
Fountain Cem—*cemetery* ... OK-5
Fountain Cem—*cemetery* ... SD-7
Fountain Ch—*church* ... IL-6
Fountain Ch—*church* ... IN-6
Fountain Ch—*church* ... MD-2
Fountain Ch—*church* ... OH-6
Fountain Ch—*church* ... OK-5
Fountain Ch—*church* ... WI-6
Fountain Chapel—*church* ... MS-4
Fountain Chapel Cem—*cemetery* ... OH-6
*Fountain City* ... SD-7
**Fountain City**—*pop pl* ... IN-6
**Fountain City**—*pop pl* ... TN-4
**Fountain City**—*pop pl* ... WI-6
*Fountain City, The* ... ND-7
Fountain City Baptist Ch—*church* ... AL-4
Fountain City Bay—*channel* ... WI-6
Fountain City Cem—*cemetery* ... WI-6
Fountain City Elem Sch—*school* ... TN-4
Fountain City Park—*park* ... TN-4
Fountain City Post Office—*building* ... TN-4
Fountain City Presbyterian Ch—*church* ... TN-4
Fountain City Ridge—*ridge* ... WI-6
Fountain City Shop Ctr—*locale* ... TN-4
Fountain City Sportsmens Club—*locale* ... TN-4
Fountain City United Methodist Ch—*church* ... TN-4
**Fountain County**—*pop pl* ... IN-6
Fountain Cove—*bay* ... VA-3
*Fountain Creek* ... WI-6
Fountain Creek—*locale* ... IL-6
Fountain Creek—*other* ... TN-4
Fountain Creek—*stream* ... AR-4
Fountain Creek—*stream* ... CO-8
Fountain Creek—*stream* ... ID-8
Fountain Creek—*stream* (2) ... IL-6
Fountain Creek—*stream* (2) ... IN-6
Fountain Creek—*stream* ... MI-6
Fountain Creek—*stream* ... NE-7
Fountain Creek—*stream* ... TN-4
Fountain Creek—*stream* (2) ... TX-5
Fountain Creek—*stream* (2) ... WI-6
Fountain Creek Bridge—*hist pl* ... IL-6
Fountain Creek Ch—*church* ... TN-4
Fountain Creek (Township of)—*civ div* ... IL-6
**Fountaincrest**—*pop pl* ... TN-4
*Fountaindale* ... PA-2
**Fountaindale**—*pop pl* ... MD-2
**Fountain Dale**—*pop pl* ... PA-2
Fountaindale Sch—*school* ... MD-2
Fountaindale Spring—*spring* ... PA-2
Fountain Ditch—*canal* ... CO-8
*Fountain East Mobile Home Park, The* ... AZ-5
Fountain East (trailer park)—*locale* ... AZ-5
**Fountain East (Trailer Park)**—*pop pl* ... AZ-5
**Fountainebleau**—*pop pl* ... MS-4
Fountainebleau Golf Course—*locale* ... FL-3
Fountainebleau Park—*park* ... FL-3
Fountain Elms—*hist pl* ... NY-2
Fountain Farm—*locale* ... MO-7
Fountain Farm Branch—*stream* ... MO-7
Fountain Farm Ch—*church* ... MO-7
Fountain Flats—*flat* ... WY-8
**Fountain Fork**—*pop pl* ... NC-3
Fountain Fork Creek—*stream* ... NC-3
**Fountain Gap**—*pop pl* ... IL-6
Fountain Gate—*locale* ... VA-3
**Fountain Green**—*pop pl* ... IL-6
**Fountain Green**—*pop pl* ... MD-2
**Fountain Green**—*pop pl* ... UT-8
Fountain Green Cem—*cemetery* ... IL-6
Fountain Green Cem—*cemetery* ... UT-8
Fountain Green Fish Hatchery—*locale* ... UT-8
**Fountain Green Heights**—*pop pl* ... MD-2
Fountain Green Pole Canyon—*valley* ... UT-8
Fountain Green Post Office—*building* ... UT-8
Fountain Green Sch—*school* ... UT-8
Fountain Green (Township of)—*civ div* ... IL-6
Fountain Group—*spring* ... WY-8
**Fountain Grove**—*pop pl* ... MO-7
**Fountain Grove**—*pop pl* ... TN-4
Fountain Grove Cem—*cemetery* ... NJ-2
Fountain Grove Ch—*church* ... GA-3
Fountain Grove Ch—*church* ... TN-4
Fountain Grove Ch—*church* ... VA-3
*Fountain Grove Methodist Ch* ... TN-4
Fountain Grove Wildlife Mngmt Area—*park* ... MO-7
Fountain Gulch—*valley* ... CO-8
*Fountain Head* ... AL-4
Fountain Head—*CDP* ... MD-2
Fountainhead—*hist pl* ... MS-4
**Fountain Head**—*pop pl* ... TN-4
*Fountain Head Brook* ... MA-1
Fountainhead Brook—*stream* ... MA-1
Fountain Head Cem—*cemetery* ... MS-4
Fountainhead Ch—*church* ... KY-4
Fountain Head Ch—*church* ... MS-4
Fountain Head Country Club—*other* ... MD-2
*Fountain Head Hills* ... NV-8
Fountainhead Lake—*reservoir* ... AL-4
Fountain Head Lake—*reservoir* ... AR-4
Fountainhead Memorial Park—*cemetery* ... FL-3
Fountain Head Post Office (historical)—*building* ... TN-4
*Fountain Head Sch* ... TN-4
Fountain Head Sch—*school* ... TN-4
Fountainhead Spring—*spring* ... CA-9
**Fountainhead (subdivision)**—*pop pl* ... TN-4
**Fountain Heights**—*pop pl* ... AL-4
**Fountain Heights**—*pop pl* ... FL-3
**Fountain Heights**—*pop pl* ... TN-4
Fountain Heights (CCD)—*cens area* ... TN-4
Fountain Heights Division—*civil* ... TN-4
Fountain Heights Methodist Ch—*church* ... AL-4
Fountain Heights Park—*park* ... AL-4
**Fountain Hill**—*pop pl* ... AR-4
**Fountain Hill**—*pop pl* (2) ... NC-3
**Fountain Hill**—*pop pl* ... PA-2
Fountain Hill—*summit* ... AL-4
Fountain Hill Acad (historical)—*school* ... TN-4
Fountain Hill Borough—*civil* ... PA-2
Fountain Hill Cem—*cemetery* ... CT-1
Fountain Hill Cem—*cemetery* ... OH-6
Fountain Hill Elem Sch—*school* ... PA-2
Fountain Hill Hist Dist—*hist pl* ... PA-2
**Fountain Hills**—*pop pl* ... AZ-5
Fountain Hills Airp—*airport* ... AZ-5
Fountain Hills Dam—*dam* ... AZ-5
Fountain Hills Dam Number Eleven—*dam* ... AZ-5
Fountain Hills Dam Number Four—*dam* ... AZ-5
Fountain Hills Dam Number Nineteen—*dam* ... AZ-5
Fountain Hills Dam Number Seven—*dam* ... AZ-5
Fountain Hills Dam Number Six—*dam* ... AZ-5
Fountain Hills Dam Number Thirty Six—*dam* ... AZ-5
Fountain Hills Elementary and JHS—*school* ... AZ-5
Fountain Hills Golf Course—*other* ... AZ-5
Fountain (historical)—*locale* ... SD-7
Fountain Hole—*lake* ... GA-3
Fountain House—*hist pl* ... PA-2
**Fountain House**—*pop pl* ... PA-2
**Fountain House Corners**—*pop pl* ... PA-2
Fountain House Hill—*summit* ... CA-9
**Fountain Inn**—*pop pl* ... SC-3
Fountain Inn (CCD)—*cens area* ... SC-3
*Fountain Lake* ... AL-4
Fountain Lake—*lake* ... FL-3
Fountain Lake—*lake* (2) ... MN-6
Fountain Lake—*lake* ... WA-9
Fountain Lake—*lake* ... WI-6
**Fountain Lake**—*pop pl* (2) ... AR-4
Fountain Lake—*reservoir* ... PA-2
Fountain Lake Rsvr—*reservoir* ... CT-1
Fountain Lawn Memorial Park Cem—*cemetery* ... NJ-2
Fountain Millpond—*reservoir* ... GA-3
Fountain Mills—*locale* ... MD-2
Fountain Mill Spring—*spring* ... IA-7
Fountain Nook Sch—*school* ... OH-6
Fountain of Life Assembly of God—*church* ... FL-3
Fountain of Life Ch—*church* ... NC-3
Fountain of Life Tabernacle Ch—*church* ... MS-4
Fountain of the Sun Golf Course—*other* ... AZ-5
Fountain of the Sun Shop Ctr—*locale* ... AZ-5
**Fountain of the Sun (subdivision)**—*pop pl* ... AZ-5
**Fountain of the Sun (Trailer Park)**—*pop pl* ... AZ-5
Fountain Of Youth Camp—*locale* ... CA-9
Fountain of Youth Coulee—*valley* ... MT-8
Fountain of Youth Park—*park* ... FL-3
Fountain of Youth Spring—*spring* ... CA-9
Fountain of Youth Spring—*spring* ... NV-8
Fountain Paint Pot—*spring* ... WY-8
Fountain Park—*park* ... MA-1
Fountain Park—*park* ... MN-6
Fountain Park—*park* ... MO-7
Fountain Park—*park* ... NV-8
Fountain Park—*park* ... OH-6
Fountain Park—*park* ... PA-2
Fountain Park—*park* ... WI-6
**Fountain Park**—*pop pl* (2) ... IN-6
**Fountain Park**—*pop pl* ... MI-6
**Fountain Park**—*pop pl* ... OH-6
**Fountain Park**—*pop pl* ... TX-5
Fountain Park Cem—*cemetery* ... IN-6
Fountain Park Sch—*school* ... WI-6
Fountain Patrol Cabin—*locale* ... WY-8
Fountain Peak—*summit* ... CA-9
Fountain Pit—*cave* ... AL-4
Fountain Place—*locale* ... CA-9
**Fountain Place**—*pop pl* ... LA-4
**Fountain Place Subdivision**—*pop pl* ... UT-8
Fountain Plaza Apartments—*hist pl* ... IL-6
Fountain Plaza Shop Ctr—*locale* ... AL-4
Fountain Plaza (Shop Ctr)—*locale* ... FL-3
**Fountain Point**—*pop pl* ... MI-6
Fountain Pond—*lake* ... GA-3
Fountain Pond—*lake* ... MA-1
Fountain Pond—*lake* ... TX-5
Fountain Pond—*reservoir* ... MA-1
Fountain Pond Dam—*dam* ... MA-1
Fountain Post Office—*locale* ... NC-3
**Fountain Prairie**—*pop pl* ... AR-4
Fountain Prairie Cem—*cemetery* ... WI-6
**Fountain Prairie (Town of)**—*pop pl* ... WI-6
Fountain Prairie (Township of)—*civ div* ... MN-6
Fountain Ridge Sch—*school* ... KS-7
Fountain River—*stream* ... AK-9
Fountain Road Interchange—*other* ... OK-5
Fountain Rock—*bar* ... AK-9
Fountain Rock—*island* ... OR-9
Fountain Rock—*locale* ... MD-2
Fountain Rsvr—*reservoir* ... CO-8
**Fountain Run**—*pop pl* ... KY-4
Fountain Run (CCD)—*cens area* ... KY-4
Fountain Run Cem—*cemetery* ... KY-4
Fountain Run Sch—*school* ... KY-4
Fountains, The (Shop Ctr)—*locale* ... FL-3
Fountain Sch—*school* ... GA-3
Fountain Sch—*school* (2) ... MI-6
Fountain Sch—*school* ... MO-7
Fountain Sch—*school* ... NC-3
Fountain Sch—*school* ... SD-7
Fountain Sch—*school* ... WV-2
Fountains Creek—*stream* ... VA-3
*Fountains East Mobile Home Park* ... AZ-5
Fountains Memorial Park, The—*cemetery* ... FL-3
Fountain Spring—*locale* ... RI-1
Fountain Spring Cem—*cemetery* ... TN-4
Fountain Spring Lake—*reservoir* ... NJ-2
*Fountain Spring Pond* ... RI-1
Fountain Springs—*locale* ... CA-9
**Fountain Springs**—*pop pl* ... PA-2
Fountain Springs—*spring* ... WA-9
Fountain Springs Ch—*church* ... GA-3
Fountain Springs Creek—*stream* ... IA-7
Fountain Springs Gulch—*valley* ... CA-9
*Fountain Square* ... IN-6
*Fountain Square* ... OH-6
Fountain Square—*hist pl* ... TN-4
Fountain Square—*locale* ... TN-4
Fountain Square—*park* ... NE-7
**Fountain Square**—*pop pl* ... OH-6
Fountain Square (Shop Ctr)—*locale* ... FL-3
*Fountain Station* ... IN-6
Fountain Stream—*stream* ... AK-9
Fountain-Tallman Soda Works—*hist pl* ... CA-9
**Fountaintown**—*pop pl* ... IN-6
**Fountain (Town of)**—*pop pl* ... WI-6
**Fountain Township**—*pop pl* ... KS-7
**Fountain Township**—*pop pl* ... SD-7
Fountain (Township of)—*fmr MCD* ... NC-3
**Fountain (Township of)**—*pop pl* ... MN-6
**Fountain Valley**—*pop pl* ... CA-9
**Fountain Valley**—*pop pl* ... MD-2
**Fountain Valley**—*pop pl* ... WI-6
Fountain Valley Channel—*canal* ... CA-9
Fountain Valley Sch—*school* ... CA-9
Fountain Valley Sch—*school* ... CO-8
**Fountain Valley School**—*pop pl* ... CO-8
**Fountain Valley (Talbert)**—*pop pl* ... CA-9
**Fountain View (subdivision)**—*pop pl* (2) ... AZ-5
Fountain Village Shop Ctr—*locale* ... TN-4
**Fountain Village (subdivision)**—*pop pl*. TN-4
Fountainville—*locale* ... GA-3
Fountainville—*locale* ... PA-2
Fountainville Hills—*locale* ... PA-2
Fountain Well—*well* ... CO-8
Fountain Woods—*woods* ... NJ-2
**Fountian Springs**—*pop pl* ... PA-2
**Foup**—*pop pl* ... FM-9
Fouper—*bar* ... FM-9
**Foupo**—*pop pl* ... FM-9
Foupo—*summit* ... FM-9
*Foupo Mtn* ... FM-9
*Foupo Village* ... FM-9
Four, Canal (historical)—*canal* ... AZ-5
Four, Canyon—*valley* ... CA-9
Four, Lake—*lake* ... AK-9
Four, Lake—*lake* (2) ... MI-6
Four, Lake—*lake* (3) ... MN-6
Four, Lake—*lake* ... WI-6
Four, Tank—*reservoir* ... AZ-5
Four Ace Mine—*mine* ... NV-8
Four Aces Creek—*stream* ... ID-8
*Four Aces Mine* ... NV-8
Four Aces Mine—*mine* ... UT-8
Four Acre Creek—*stream* ... GA-3
Four Acre Hollow—*valley* ... OH-6
Four Acre Island—*island* ... MA-1
Four Acre Island—*island* ... MO-7
Four Acre Lake—*lake* ... MN-6
Four Acres—*hist pl* ... VA-3
Four Acres Sanitarium—*other* ... CA-9
Four Acre Tank—*reservoir* ... TX-5
*Four A.M. Island* ... FM-9
Four A Mtn—*summit* ... NM-5
Four Bac Windmill—*locale* ... NM-5
*Four Bar Four Mesa* ... AZ-5
Four Bar Mesa—*summit* ... AZ-5
Four Bar Mesa Tanks—*reservoir* ... AZ-5
Four Bar Spring—*spring* ... OR-9
Four Bars Ranch—*locale* ... AZ-5
Four Bar Tank—*reservoir* ... AZ-5
Four Base Lake—*reservoir* ... CO-8
Four Bayou—*gut* ... LA-4
Four B Creek—*stream* ... MT-8
Four Bear Coulee—*valley* ... MT-8
Four Bear Creek—*stream* ... AK-9
Four Bear Creek—*stream* ... WY-8
Four Bear Oil Field—*oilfield* ... WY-8
Four Bear Ranch—*locale* ... WY-8
Four Bears Bay—*bay* ... ND-7
Four Bear Sch (historical)—*school* ... SD-7
**Four Bears Health Center**—*pop pl* ... ND-7
Four Bears Memorial Bridge—*bridge* ... ND-7
Four Bears State Park—*park* ... ND-7
Four Bit Creek—*stream* ... ID-8
Four Bit Creek—*stream* ... OR-9
Fourbit Creek—*stream* ... OR-9
Four-bit Flat—*swamp* ... OR-9
Fourbit Ford—*locale* ... OR-9
*Fourbit Guard Station* ... OR-9
*Fourbit Gulch* ... OR-9
Fourbit Gulch—*valley* ... CA-9
Four Bit Gulch—*valley* ... CA-9
Four Bit Gulch—*valley* ... OR-9
Four Bits Creek—*stream* ... CA-9
Four Bits Pond—*lake* ... AZ-5
Four Bit Spur—*ridge* ... ID-8
Four Bit Summit—*summit* ... ID-8
Fourblock Island—*island* ... MN-6
**Fourborge**—*pop pl* ... LA-4
Four Bridges—*locale* ... NJ-2
Four Bridges Ch—*church* ... SC-3
Four Brooks Ch—*church* ... PA-2
Four Brothers—*summit* ... CA-9
Four Brothers—*summit* ... WA-9
Four Brothers, The—*island* ... NY-2
Four Brothers Key—*island* ... FL-3
Four Brothers Knobs—*summit* ... NC-3
Four Buttes—*locale* ... MT-8
Four Buttes—*spring* ... MT-8
Four by Four Cave—*cave* ... MT-8
Four Cabin Corner—*locale* ... OR-9
Four Canyons—*flat* ... CA-9
*Four Canyons Meadow* ... CA-9
**Fourche**—*pop pl* ... AR-4
Fourche, Bayou—*stream* ... LA-4
Fourche, Bayou la—*gut* ... AL-4
*Fourche a du Clos Creek* ... MO-7
*Fourche a Loup Creek* ... AR-4
*Fourche a'loupe* ... AR-4
Fourche a Loupe Ch—*church* ... AR-4
*Fourche A'loupe Creek* ... AR-4
Fourche a Loupe Creek—*stream* ... AR-4
*Fourche a Polite* ... MO-7
Fourche a Renault—*stream* ... MO-7
Fourche a Renault Cem—*cemetery* ... MO-7
Fourche a Renault Ch (abandoned)—*church* ... MO-7
Fourche Bayou—*gut* ... AR-4
*Fourche Creek* ... AR-4
*Fourche Creek* ... MO-7
*Fourche Creek* ... WI-6
Fourche Creek—*stream* ... AR-4
Fourche Creek—*stream* ... MO-7
Fourche Creek—*stream* ... WI-6
Fourche Creek State For—*forest* ... MO-7
*Fourche de Republicaine* ... KS-7
Fourche Island—*island* ... AR-4
Fourche Junction—*locale* ... AR-4
Fourche Lafave River—*stream* ... AR-4
Fourche Lafave (Township of)—*fmr MCD* ... AR-4
Fourche Lake—*lake* ... MO-7
Fourche Lake Boat Access—*locale* ... MO-7
*Fourche Malene* ... OK-5
Fourche Maline—*stream* ... OK-5
Fourche Maline Arm—*bay* ... OK-5
Fourche Maline Creek—*stream* ... OK-5
*Fourche Maline River* ... OK-5
*Fourche Mountain* ... AR-4
Fourche Mountain—*ridge* (3) ... AR-4
*Fourche Mountains* ... AR-4
Fourche Pinnacle—*summit* ... AR-4
Fourche River—*stream* ... AR-4
Fourche River—*stream* ... MO-7
**Fourchette**—*pop pl* ... MT-8
Fourchette Creek—*stream* ... MT-8
Fourche Valley Sch—*school* ... AR-4
Fourchon, Pass—*channel* ... LA-4
*Fourchon City* ... LA-4
Four Colonies Shop Ctr—*locale* ... KS-7
Four Corner Bridge—*bridge* ... SD-7
Four Cornered Peak—*summit* ... CA-9
*Four Corners* ... CA-9
*Four Corners* ... CT-1
*Four Corners* ... ME-1
*Four Corners* ... MA-1
*Four Corners* ... NY-2
*Four Corners* ... OH-6
*Four Corners* ... TX-5
Four Corners—*locale* (2) ... AK-9
Four Corners—*locale* (15) ... CA-9
Four Corners—*locale* (2) ... CO-8
Four Corners—*locale* ... CT-1
Four Corners—*locale* (2) ... ID-8
Four Corners—*locale* ... IA-7
Four Corners—*locale* ... KS-7
Four Corners—*locale* (2) ... KY-4
Four Corners—*locale* (2) ... MD-2
Four Corners—*locale* ... MI-6
Four Corners—*locale* ... MS-4
Four Corners—*locale* (6) ... MT-8
Four Corners—*locale* ... NH-1
Four Corners—*locale* (3) ... NY-2
Four Corners—*locale* ... OH-6
Four Corners—*locale* (4) ... OK-5
Four Corners—*locale* (7) ... OR-9
Four Corners—*locale* ... TN-4
Four Corners—*locale* (4) ... TX-5
Four Corners—*locale* ... UT-8
Four Corners—*locale* ... VT-1
Four Corners—*locale* ... VA-3
Four Corners—*locale* (3) ... WA-9
Four Corners—*locale* (4) ... WY-8
Four Corners—*other* ... TX-5
Four Corners—*park* ... AZ-5
**Four Corners**—*pop pl* (2) ... CA-9
**Four Corners**—*pop pl* ... CT-1
**Four Corners**—*pop pl* ... FL-3
**Four Corners**—*pop pl* ... IL-6
**Four Corners**—*pop pl* ... IN-6
**Four Corners**—*pop pl* ... LA-4
**Four Corners**—*pop pl* (2) ... ME-1
**Four Corners**—*pop pl* ... MD-2
**Four Corners**—*pop pl* (2) ... MA-1
**Four Corners**—*pop pl* ... MN-6
**Four Corners**—*pop pl* ... MS-4
**Four Corners**—*pop pl* ... NH-1
**Four Corners**—*pop pl* ... NJ-2
**Four Corners**—*pop pl* (3) ... OR-9
**Four Corners**—*pop pl* ... PA-2
**Four Corners**—*pop pl* ... TX-5
**Four Corners**—*pop pl* (2) ... WA-9
**Four Corners**—*pop pl* (4) ... WI-6
Four Corners, The—*locale* ... CA-9
**Four Corners, The**—*pop pl* ... VT-1
**Four Corners (Beechers Corner)**—*pop pl* ... CA-9
*Four Corners Butte* ... NV-8
Four Corners Campground—*park* ... OR-9
Four Corners Cem—*cemetery* ... KS-7
Four Corners Cem—*cemetery* ... MA-1
Four Corners Cem—*cemetery* ... NY-2
Four Corners Cem—*cemetery* ... OH-6
Four Corners Ch—*church* ... NY-2
Four Corners Ch—*church* (2) ... OK-5
Four Corners Community Hall—*locale* ... MO-7
Four Corners Cow Camp—*locale* ... NM-5
Four Corners Cow Camp—*locale* ... TX-5
Four Corners Crossing—*locale* ... CO-8
Four Corners Dam—*dam* ... ID-8
Four Corners Hist Dist—*hist pl* ... MS-4
Four Corners (historical P.O.)—*locale* ... IA-7
Four Corners (historical P.O.)—*locale* ... MA-1
*Four Corners Monmt* ... AZ-5
Four Corners Monument—*other* ... NM-5
Four Corners Pen—*locale* ... NM-5
Four Corners Powerplant—*other* ... NM-5
*Four Corners Region* ... AZ-5
Four Corners Rock—*pillar* ... CA-9
Four Corners Rsvr—*reservoir* ... ID-8
Four Corners Sch—*school* (2) ... IL-6
Four Corners Sch—*school* ... IN-6
Four Corners Sch—*school* (2) ... KS-7
Four Corners Sch—*school* ... MD-2
Four Corners Sch—*school* ... MA-1
Four Corners Sch—*school* ... MO-7
Four Corners Sch—*school* (2) ... NE-7
Four Corners Sch—*school* ... OR-9
Four Corners Sch—*school* ... SD-7
Four Corners Sch—*school* (3) ... VT-1
Four Corners Sch—*school* ... WI-6
Four Corners School (Abandoned)—*locale* ... IA-7
**Four Corners Subdivision**—*pop pl* ... UT-8
Four Corners Tank—*reservoir* ... AZ-5
*Four Corners Wash* ... NV-8
Four Corners Windmill—*locale* ... NM-5
Four Corners Windmill—*locale* (2) ... TX-5
Four Corner Well—*well* ... TX-5
Four Corner Windmill—*locale* (2) ... TX-5
Four County Drain—*stream* ... MI-6
Four County Plaza—*locale* ... MO-7
Four County State Fish Hatchery—*other* ... SC-3
*Four Creek* ... AR-4
Four Creek—*stream* ... SD-7
Four-D Creek—*stream* ... OK-5
Four D Ditch—*canal* ... MT-8
Four Diamond Ridge—*ridge* ... NC-3
Four Diamond Tank—*reservoir* ... AZ-5
Four Dollar Bayou—*gut* ... MS-4
Four Drag Ranch—*locale* ... AZ-5
Four D Ranch—*locale* ... MT-8
Four Draw—*valley* ... WY-8
Four Ducks Lake—*lake* ... WI-6
Four Eared Bat Cave—*cave* ... MT-8
Four Echoes Camp—*locale* ... ID-8
Four Elk Creek—*stream* ... CO-8
Fouress Mine—*mine* ... WA-9
Four-eyed Nicks Springs—*spring* ... NV-8
Four Eyes Canyon—*valley* ... MT-8
Four Falls Lake—*lake* ... AK-9
*Four-feet Rock* ... ME-1
Four Foot Rapids—*rapids* ... UT-8
Fourfoot Rock—*bar* ... ME-1
Four Foot Shoal—*bar* ... WI-6
*Four Fork Creek* ... MS-4
Fourfork Creek—*stream* ... CA-9
*Four Forks* ... TX-5
Four Forks—*locale* ... AR-4
Four Forks—*locale* ... MS-4
Four Forks—*locale* ... NM-5
Four Forks—*locale* ... NC-3
Four Forks—*locale* ... VA-3
**Four Forks**—*pop pl* ... AR-4
**Four Forks**—*pop pl* ... LA-4
Four Forks Creek—*stream* ... CA-9
Four Forks Creek—*stream* ... MS-4
Four Forks Inn—*locale* ... VA-3
Four Forks Lookout Tower—*locale* ... LA-4
Four Gables—*summit* ... CA-9
Four Gulch—*valley* ... AK-9
Four Gums—*locale* ... AR-4
Four-H Camp—*locale* ... CA-9
Four H Camp—*locale* ... MN-6
Four H Camp—*locale* ... NM-5
Four H Camp*—*locale* ... ND-7
Four H Camp—*locale* ... OH-6
Four H Camp—*locale* ... VA-3
Four-H Camp—*locale* ... VA-3
FourH Club—*other* ... VA-3
Four H Club Camp—*locale* ... CA-9
Four-H Club Camp—*locale* ... CT-1
Four-H Club Camp—*locale* ... TN-4
Four H Club Camp (University of Nevada)—*locale* ... NV-8
Four-H Club Fairgrounds—*park* ... IN-6
Four H Draw—*valley* ... WY-8
Four Hills—*summit* ... AZ-5
Four Hills, The—*summit* ... NH-1
Four Hills Mine—*mine* ... CA-9
Four Hills Ranch—*locale* ... NM-5
Four-H Lake—*lake* ... TX-5
Four-H Lake—*reservoir* ... IL-6
Four Holes—*locale* ... SC-3
Four Hole Sch—*school* ... SC-3
Four Hole Swamp—*stream* ... SC-3
Four Horn Cem—*cemetery* ... IA-7
Four Horns Cem—*cemetery* ... MT-8
Four Horns Feeder Canal—*canal* ... MT-8
Four Horns Lake—*lake* ... MT-8
Four Horns Outlet Canal—*canal* ... MT-8
*Four Horse Creek* ... WY-8
Four Horse Creek—*stream* ... WY-8
Four Horse Smith Spring—*spring* ... OR-9
Four-H Park—*park* ... IN-6
Four H Park—*park* ... WI-6
Four Hundred Acre Spring—*spring* ... WY-8
Four-Hundred Acre Windmill—*locale* ... TX-5
Four Hundred and Five Creek—*stream* ... MI-6
Four Hundred and Seventy—*locale* ... NM-5
Four Hundred Cotton Gin—*locale* ... TX-5
Four Hundred Dollar Bayou—*stream* ... LA-4
Four Hundred Eighteen, Lake—*lake* ... MN-6
Four Hundred Tank—*reservoir* ... AZ-5
Four Hundred Well—*well* ... AZ-5
Four In One Cone—*summit* ... OR-9
Four Island Bayou—*gut* ... LA-4
Four Island Lake—*lake* ... MI-6
Four Islands—*island* ... FL-3
Four Isle Bay Oil and Gas Field—*oilfield* ... LA-4
Four J Basin—*basin* ... WY-8
Four J Rim—*cliff* ... WY-8
Fourkiller Cem—*cemetery* ... OK-5
Four K Ranch—*locale* ... NM-5
Four Lakes—*lake* ... CA-9
Four Lakes—*lake* ... IL-6
Four Lakes—*lake* ... MI-6
Four Lakes—*lake* ... UT-8
**Four Lakes**—*pop pl* ... IL-6
**Four Lakes**—*pop pl* ... WA-9
Four Lakes Area—*area* ... NM-5
Four Lakes Basin—*basin* ... ID-8
Four Lakes Basin—*basin* ... UT-8
Four Lakes Communications Station—*other* ... WA-9
Four Lakes Creek—*stream* ... MT-8
Four Lakes Forest Preserve—*park* ... IL-6
Four Lakes Interchange—*locale* ... WA-9
**Four Lakes (Meadon Lake)**—*pop pl* ... WA-9
Four Lakes Ranch—*locale* ... NM-5
*Four Lanes Ends* ... PA-2
Four Lane Shop Ctr—*locale* ... AL-4
Four Lantern Flat—*flat* ... CA-9
Four L Bar Ranch—*locale* ... NM-5
*Four League Bay* ... LA-4
Fourleague Bay—*bay* ... LA-4
Fourleague Bay Gas Field—*oilfield* ... LA-4
*Four Legged Lake* ... MN-6
Four Locks—*locale* ... MD-2
Four Locusts Lake—*reservoir* ... VA-3
Fourlog Park—*locale* ... WY-8
**Fourmans Corners**—*pop pl* ... OH-6
Four Metal Mine—*mine* ... UT-8
Four Metals Mine—*mine* ... AZ-5
Four Metals Mine—*mine* ... WA-9
*Four Mile* ... FL-3
*Four Mile* ... KS-7
*Fourmile* ... NY-2
*Fourmile* ... WV-2
Four Mile—*fmr MCD* ... NE-7
Fourmile—*locale* ... AL-4
Four Mile—*locale* ... NY-2
Fourmile—*locale* ... OR-9
Fourmile—*locale* ... SD-7
**Four Mile**—*pop pl* ... AL-4
**Fourmile**—*pop pl* ... KY-4
**Four Mile**—*pop pl* ... MS-4

**Four Mile**—*pop pl* ... NJ-2
**Four Mile**—*pop pl* ... NC-3
**Four Mile**—*pop pl* ... SC-3
**Four Mile**—*pop pl* ... WV-2
*Fourmile Baptist Church* ... AL-4
*Four Mile Baptist Church* ... TN-4
Four Mile Bar—*bar* ... AL-4
Fourmile Basin—*basin* ... MT-8
Fourmile Basin—*basin* ... NV-8
Fourmile Basin Lakes—*lake* ... MT-8
Fourmile Bay—*bay* ... MN-6
*Four Mile Bayou* ... FL-3
*Four Mile Bayou* ... MS-4
Fourmile Bayou—*gut* ... LA-4
Fourmile Bayou—*stream* (5) ... LA-4
Fourmile Bayou—*stream* (3) ... MS-4
*Fourmile Bench* ... UT-8
Four Mile Bench—*bench* ... UT-8
Fourmile Bench—*bench* (2) ... UT-8
Fourmile Bend—*bend* ... CA-9
Fourmile Board Hill—*summit* ... TN-4
Fourmile Bottom—*bend* ... UT-8
*Four Mile Branch* ... AL-4
*Four Mile Branch* ... MS-4
*Four Mile Branch* ... SC-3
Fourmile Branch—*stream* (2) ... AL-4
Four Mile Branch—*stream* ... FL-3
Fourmile Branch—*stream* ... GA-3
Fourmile Branch—*stream* (4) ... KY-4
Fourmile Branch—*stream* ... LA-4
Fourmile Branch—*stream* (3) ... MS-4
Fourmile Branch—*stream* ... MO-7
Fourmile Branch—*stream* (2) ... NJ-2
Fourmile Branch—*stream* (2) ... NC-3
Fourmile Branch—*stream* ... OK-5
Fourmile Branch—*stream* (2) ... SC-3
Fourmile Branch—*stream* ... TN-4
Fourmile Branch—*stream* (3) ... TX-5
Fourmile Branch—*stream* ... WV-2
Fourmile Branch Ch—*church* ... OK-5
Four Mile Branch Post Office (historical)—*building* ... TN-4
Fourmile Bridge—*bridge* (2) ... WY-8
Four Mile Bridge—*hist pl* ... CO-8
**Fourmile Bridge (historical)**—*pop pl* ... TN-4
*Four Mile Brook* ... ME-1
*Four Mile Brook* ... MA-1
Fourmile Brook—*stream* (2) ... CT-1
Fourmile Brook—*stream* (9) ... ME-1
Fourmile Brook—*stream* (3) ... MA-1
Fourmile Brook—*stream* ... NH-1
Fourmile Brook—*stream* ... NY-2
Fourmile Burnout—*area* ... TX-5
Fourmile Butte—*summit* ... CA-9
Fourmile Butte—*summit* (2) ... NV-8
Fourmile Butte—*summit* ... OR-9
Fourmile Butte—*summit* ... SD-7
Fourmile Camp—*locale* ... AK-9
Fourmile Camp—*locale* ... ME-1
Fourmile Camp—*locale* ... WA-9
Fourmile Camp—*park* ... OR-9
Fourmile Campground—*locale* (2) ... ID-8
*Four Mile Canyon* ... CO-8
*Four Mile Canyon* ... NV-8
*Four Mile Canyon* ... UT-8
Fourmile Canyon—*valley* (3) ... AZ-5
Four Mile Canyon—*valley* ... CA-9
Fourmile Canyon—*valley* (2) ... CO-8
Fourmile Canyon—*valley* ... ID-8
Fourmile Canyon—*valley* (6) ... NV-8
Fourmile Canyon—*valley* (3) ... NM-5
Fourmile Canyon—*valley* (3) ... OR-9
Fourmile Canyon—*valley* (6) ... UT-8
Fourmile Canyon—*valley* ... WA-9
Fourmile Canyon Creek—*stream* ... CO-8
Fourmile Cem—*cemetery* (2) ... AL-4
Fourmile Cem—*cemetery* ... CO-8
Fourmile Cem—*cemetery* ... KS-7
Four Mile Cem—*cemetery* ... MS-4
Fourmile Cem—*cemetery* ... MS-4
Fourmile Cem—*cemetery* ... MO-7
Four Mile Cem—*cemetery* ... MO-7
Fourmile Cem—*cemetery* ... MT-8
Fourmile Cem—*cemetery* ... OH-6
Four Mile Cem—*cemetery* ... TN-4
Fourmile Cem—*cemetery* ... TX-5
*Fourmile Ch* ... TN-4
Fourmile Ch—*church* (2) ... AL-4
Fourmile Ch—*church* (2) ... GA-3
Fourmile Ch—*church* ... IN-6
Fourmile Ch—*church* ... NE-7
Fourmile Ch—*church* (2) ... OH-6
Fourmile Ch—*church* ... PA-2
Fourmile Ch—*church* ... SC-3
Fourmile Ch—*church* ... TN-4
Fourmile Ch—*church* ... TX-5
Fourmile Ch—*church* ... WV-2
Fourmile Chute—*channel* ... IL-6
**Four Mile Circle**—*pop pl* ... NJ-2
Four Mile Consolidated Sch (historical)—*school* ... MS-4
Fourmile Corner—*locale* ... AR-4
**Four Mile Corner**—*pop pl* ... AR-4
**Fourmile Corner**—*pop pl* ... MI-6
**Four Mile Corner**—*pop pl* ... MI-6
**Fourmile Corner**—*pop pl* ... MO-7
Fourmile Corners—*locale* ... KS-7
Fourmile Coulee—*valley* (4) ... MT-8
Fourmile Cove—*bay* ... FL-3
*Four Mile Creek* ... AL-4
*Four Mile Creek* ... CO-8
*Fourmile Creek* ... IL-6
*Fourmile Creek* ... IN-6
*Four Mile Creek* ... KS-7
*Four Mile Creek* ... MN-6
*Four Mile Creek* ... MS-4
*Four Mile Creek* ... NV-8
*Four Mile Creek* ... NY-2
*Fourmile Creek* ... NC-3
*Fourmile Creek* ... OH-6
*Four Mile Creek* ... PA-2
*Fourmile Creek* ... SC-3
*Four Mile Creek* ... TN-4
*Four Mile Creek* ... TX-5
*Fourmile Creek* ... UT-8
*Four Mile Creek* ... VA-3
*Four Mile Creek* ... WI-6
*Four Mile Creek* ... WY-8
Fourmile Creek—*gut* ... FL-3
Fourmile Creek—*gut* ... MS-4
Fourmile Creek—*stream* (2) ... AL-4
Four Mile Creek—*stream* ... AL-4
Fourmile Creek—*stream* (5) ... AL-4
Fourmile Creek—*stream* (3) ... AK-9
Fourmile Creek—*stream* ... AZ-5
Fourmile Creek—*stream* (5) ... AR-4
Fourmile Creek—*stream* (7) ... CA-9
Fourmile Creek—*stream* (12) ... CO-8
Fourmile Creek—*stream* ... FL-3
Four Mile Creek—*stream* ... FL-3
Fourmile Creek—*stream* (2) ... FL-3
Fourmile Creek—*stream* (3) ... GA-3
Fourmile Creek—*stream* (9) ... ID-8
Fourmile Creek—*stream* (2) ... IL-6
Fourmile Creek—*stream* (2) ... IN-6
Fourmile Creek—*stream* (8) ... IA-7
Fourmile Creek—*stream* (10) ... KS-7
Fourmile Creek—*stream* (6) ... KY-4
Fourmile Creek—*stream* (2) ... LA-4
Fourmile Creek—*stream* (2) ... MI-6
Fourmile Creek—*stream* (3) ... MN-6
Fourmile Creek—*stream* (2) ... MS-4
Four Mile Creek—*stream* ... MS-4
Fourmile Creek—*stream* ... MS-4
Four Mile Creek—*stream* ... MS-4
Fourmile Creek—*stream* ... MO-7
Fourmile Creek—*stream* (9) ... MT-8
Fourmile Creek—*stream* ... NE-7
Four Mile Creek*—*stream* ... NE-7
Fourmile Creek—*stream* (2) ... NE-7
Fourmile Creek—*stream* (2) ... NV-8
Fourmile Creek—*stream* (3) ... NY-2
Fourmile Creek—*stream* ... NC-3
Fourmile Creek—*stream* (2) ... ND-7
Fourmile Creek—*stream* (4) ... OH-6
Four Mile Creek—*stream* ... OH-6
Fourmile Creek—*stream* (3) ... OH-6
Fourmile Creek—*stream* (8) ... OK-5
Fourmile Creek—*stream* (6) ... OR-9
Fourmile Creek—*stream* ... PA-2
Fourmile Creek—*stream* (2) ... SC-3
Fourmile Creek—*stream* (4) ... SD-7
Fourmile Creek—*stream* (2) ... TN-4
Four Mile Creek—*stream* ... TN-4
Fourmile Creek—*stream* (2) ... TN-4
Fourmile Creek—*stream* (6) ... TX-5
Fourmile Creek—*stream* (3) ... UT-8
Fourmile Creek—*stream* (2) ... VA-3
Fourmile Creek—*stream* (4) ... WA-9
Fourmile Creek—*stream* ... WV-2
Fourmile Creek—*stream* (7) ... WI-6
Fourmile Creek—*stream* (8) ... WY-8
Four Mile Creek Baptist Ch—*church* ... MS-4
Fourmile Creek Bridge—*bridge* ... GA-3
Fourmile Creek Canal—*canal* ... SC-3
Fourmile Creek Ch—*church* ... VA-3
Four Mile Creek Shoals—*bar* ... TN-4
Fourmile Creek State Park—*park* ... NY-2
Four Mile Crossing—*locale* ... OK-5
Fourmile Crossing—*locale* (2) ... TX-5
Four Mile Cutoff—*channel* ... LA-4
*Four Mile Dam* ... PA-2
Fourmile Dam—*dam* ... MI-6
*Four Mile Ditch* ... IN-6
Fourmile Ditch—*canal* (2) ... CO-8
Fourmile Ditch—*canal* ... IN-6
*Fourmile Draw* ... TX-5
Fourmile Draw—*valley* ... AZ-5
Fourmile Draw—*valley* (4) ... NM-5
Fourmile Draw—*valley* ... SD-7
Fourmile Draw—*valley* (5) ... TX-5
Fourmile Draw—*valley* (2) ... WY-8
Fourmile Flat—*flat* ... CA-9
Fourmile Flat—*flat* ... NV-8
Fourmile Flats—*flat* ... NV-8
Fourmile Fork—*locale* ... VA-3
**Four Mile Fork**—*pop pl* ... VA-3
Fourmile Fork—*stream* ... KY-4
Fourmile Fork—*stream* (4) ... WV-2
**Four Mile (Fourmile)**—*pop pl* ... AL-4
Fourmile Gaging Station—*locale* ... CO-8
Fourmile Gap—*gap* (2) ... OR-9
Fourmile Glade—*flat* ... CA-9
Fourmile Grove Cem—*cemetery* ... IL-6
Four Mile Grove Cem—*cemetery* ... IA-7
Fourmile Grove Creek—*stream* ... IL-6
Fourmile Guard Station—*locale* ... MT-8
Fourmile Gulch—*valley* (4) ... CO-8
Fourmile Gulch—*valley* ... MT-8
Fourmile Gulch—*valley* ... WY-8
*Fourmile Hill* ... AR-4
**Fourmile Hill**—*pop pl* ... AR-4
Fourmile Hill—*ridge* ... NV-8
Fourmile Hill—*summit* ... AK-9
Fourmile Hill—*summit* ... AR-4
Fourmile Hill—*summit* ... CA-9
Fourmile Hill—*summit* ... MT-8
Fourmile Hill—*summit* ... NM-5
Fourmile Hill—*summit* ... TN-4
Fourmile Hill—*summit* (3) ... TX-5
Fourmile Hill—*summit* ... UT-8
Fourmile Hill—*summit* ... WY-8
Fourmile Hill Ch—*church* ... OH-6
Fourmile Hill Creek—*stream* ... NV-8
Four Mile (historical)—*locale* ... MS-4
Fourmile Hole—*lake* ... TX-5
Fourmile Hollow—*valley* (2) ... PA-2
Fourmile Hollow—*valley* ... TN-4
Fourmile Hollow—*valley* ... TX-5
Fourmile Hollow—*valley* ... UT-8
Fourmile Hollow—*valley* ... WV-2
Four-Mile House—*hist pl* ... CO-8
Fourmile House Cem—*cemetery* ... OH-6
**Fourmile House Corner**—*pop pl* ... OH-6
Fourmile Island—*island* (2) ... FL-3
Fourmile Island—*island* ... GA-3
Fourmile Island—*island* ... ID-8
Fourmile Island—*island* ... IL-6
Fourmile Island—*island* ... WI-6
Fourmile Knoll—*summit* ... AZ-5
Fourmile Knoll—*summit* ... UT-8
Fourmile Knoll—*summit* ... WY-8
*Four Mile Lake* ... MS-4
*Fourmile Lake* ... WI-6
Fourmile Lake—*lake* ... AK-9
Fourmile Lake—*lake* ... CO-8
Fourmile Lake—*lake* ... FL-3
Fourmile Lake—*lake* ... MI-6
Fourmile Lake—*lake* (3) ... MN-6
Fourmile Lake—*lake* ... MS-4
Fourmile Lake—*lake* ... OR-9
Fourmile Lake—*lake* ... SD-7
Fourmile Lake—*lake* (2) ... TX-5
Fourmile Lake—*lake* ... WA-9
Fourmile Lake—*lake* ... WI-6
Fourmile Lake—*locale* ... MI-6
**Four Mile Lake**—*pop pl* ... MI-6
Fourmile Lake—*reservoir* ... IA-7
Fourmile Lake Campground—*park* ... OR-9
Fourmile Lake Dam—*dam* ... OR-9
*Four Mile Lake School* ... MS-4
Fourmile Lock—*other* ... OH-6
Four Mile Meadow—*flat* ... NY-2
Fourmile Meadow—*flat* ... WY-8
Fourmile Meadow Picnic Area—*locale* ... WY-8
Fourmile Mesa—*summit* ... NM-5
Fourmile Mesa Tank—*reservoir* ... AZ-5
Fourmile Mill Branch—*stream* ... AL-4
Fourmile Mine—*mine* ... ID-8
Fourmile Mtn—*summit* ... AR-4
Fourmile No. 9 Ditch—*canal* ... CO-8
Fourmile Park—*flat* ... CO-8
*Four Mile Peak* ... AZ-5
Fourmile Peak—*summit* ... AZ-5
Fourmile Point—*cape* ... AK-9
Fourmile Point—*cape* (3) ... FL-3
Fourmile Point—*cape* ... GA-3
Fourmile Point—*cape* ... NY-2
Fourmile Point—*cliff* ... WY-8
*Four Mile Point Bar* ... FL-3
*Four Mile Point Lump* ... FL-3
Fourmile Point Well—*well* ... NV-8
*Four Mile Pond* ... MA-1
Fourmile Pond—*gut* ... MO-7
Fourmile Pond—*lake* ... FL-3
Fourmile Pond—*lake* ... GA-3
Fourmile Pond—*lake* ... PA-2
Fourmile Pond—*reservoir* ... MA-1
Fourmile Pond—*reservoir* ... MI-6
Fourmile Pond Dam—*dam* ... MA-1
Fourmile Ranch—*locale* ... AZ-5
Fourmile Ranch—*locale* ... CO-8
Fourmile Ranch—*locale* ... UT-8
Fourmile Ranch—*locale* ... WY-8
Fourmile Ridge—*ridge* ... CA-9
Fourmile Ridge—*ridge* ... MD-2
Fourmile Ridge—*ridge* ... UT-8
Fourmile Ridge—*ridge* ... WA-9
Fourmile Ridge—*ridge* ... WY-8
Fourmile River—*stream* ... CT-1
Fourmile Rock—*locale* ... WA-9
Four Mile (RR name for Fourmile)—*other* ... KY-4
**Fourmile (RR name Four Mile)**—*pop pl* ... KY-4
Fourmile Rsvr—*reservoir* ... CA-9
Fourmile Rsvr—*reservoir* ... NM-5
Fourmile Rsvr—*reservoir* ... WY-8
*Four Mile Run* ... OH-6
*Fourmile Run* ... PA-2
*Fourmile Run* ... SC-3
*Fourmile Run* ... VA-3
Fourmile Run—*stream* ... KY-4
Fourmile Run—*stream* (4) ... OH-6
Fourmile Run—*stream* (9) ... PA-2
Four Mile Run—*stream* ... VA-3
Fourmile Run—*stream* (5) ... WV-2
Fourmile Run Ch—*church* ... OH-6
Four Mile Run Dam—*dam* ... PA-2
Fourmile Run Dam—*dam* ... PA-2
Fourmile Sch—*school* ... CO-8
Four Mile Sch—*school* ... IL-6
Fourmile Sch—*school* ... IL-6
Fourmile Sch—*school* ... KS-7
Four Mile Sch—*school* ... KY-4
Fourmile Sch—*school* ... KY-4
Fourmile Sch—*school* ... OK-5
Fourmile Sch—*school* ... PA-2
Fourmile Sch—*school* (2) ... SD-7
Four Mile Sch (abandoned)—*school* ... MO-7
Four Mile Sch (historical)—*school* ... AL-4
Fourmile Sch (historical)—*school* ... AL-4
Four Mile Sch (historical)—*school* ... AL-4
Fourmile Sch (historical)—*school* ... MO-7
Four Mile Sch (historical)—*school* ... TN-4
Fourmile Slough—*gut* ... TX-5
Fourmile Slough—*stream* ... OR-9
Fourmile Slough—*stream* ... TN-4
*Four Mile Spring* ... AZ-5
Fourmile Spring—*spring* ... AL-4
Fourmile Spring—*spring* (2) ... AZ-5
Fourmile Spring—*spring* ... CO-8
Fourmile Spring—*spring* ... ID-8
Fourmile Spring—*spring* (2) ... MT-8
Fourmile Spring—*spring* (3) ... NV-8
Fourmile Spring—*spring* (3) ... OR-9
Fourmile Spring—*spring* ... TX-5
Fourmile Spring—*spring* (3) ... UT-8
*Four Mile Spring Run - in part* ... PA-2
Fourmile Springs—*spring* ... AZ-5
Fourmile Springs—*spring* ... MT-8
Fourmile Springs—*spring* ... OR-9
Fourmile Stock Trail—*trail* ... CO-8
Fourmile Swamp—*stream* ... SC-3
Fourmile Swamp—*swamp* (2) ... FL-3
Fourmile Swamp—*swamp* ... SC-3
Fourmile Tank—*reservoir* (2) ... AZ-5
Fourmile Tank—*reservoir* ... NM-5
Fourmile Tank—*reservoir* (4) ... TX-5
Four Mile Tank Dam—*dam* ... AZ-5
Four Mile Township—*fmr MCD* ... IA-7
**Four Mile (Township of)**—*pop pl* ... IL-6
Four Mile Tree—*hist pl* ... VA-3
Four Mile Tree—*locale* ... VA-3
*Fourmile United Methodist Church* ... AL-4
Fourmile Valley—*valley* ... CA-9
Four Mile Village—*locale* ... FL-3
*Fourmile Wash* ... UT-8
Fourmile Wash—*stream* ... AZ-5
Fourmile Wash—*stream* ... NM-5
Fourmile Wash—*valley* (2) ... UT-8
Fourmile Water—*spring* ... UT-8
Fourmile Waterhole—*lake* ... TX-5
Four Mile Well—*well* ... NV-8
Fourmile Well—*well* (2) ... NV-8
Fourmile Wells—*other* ... NM-5
Fourmile Windmill—*locale* ... TX-5
Four Mills—*locale* ... TX-5
Four Mound Fire Station—*locale* ... WA-9
Four Mound Prairie—*flat* ... WA-9
Four Mouths, The—*bay* ... VA-3
Fourness Canal—*canal* ... AZ-5
*Fournie Creek* ... MT-8
Fournie Park—*park* ... MI-6
**Fournier**—*pop pl* ... ME-1
Fournier Creek—*stream* ... MT-8
Fournier Ranch—*locale* ... CA-9
Four Notch Lookout—*locale* ... TX-5
Four Oaks—*locale* ... KY-4
**Four Oaks**—*pop pl* ... NC-3
Four Oaks Camp—*locale* ... KY-4
Four Oaks Elem Sch—*school* ... NC-3
Four Oaks Ranch—*locale* ... TX-5
Four Oaks Sch (historical)—*school* ... AL-4
Four Oaks Shop Ctr—*locale* ... TN-4
Four O'Clock Lake—*lake* ... OR-9
Four O'Clock Rsvr—*reservoir* ... MT-8
Four One Half Mile Bridge—*bridge* ... OR-9
Four Outlet, Lake—*stream* ... MI-6
Four Palms Canyon—*valley* ... AZ-5
Four Palms Spring—*spring* ... CA-9
Fourpeaked Glacier—*glacier* ... AK-9
Fourpeaked Mtn—*summit* ... AK-9
Four Peaks—*summit* (2) ... AZ-5
Four Peaks Dam—*dam* ... AZ-5
Four Peaks Elem Sch—*school* ... AZ-5
*Four Peaks Mountain* ... AZ-5
*Four Peaks of McDowell* ... AZ-5
Four Peaks Spring Number One—*spring* ... AZ-5
Four Peaks Spring Number Two—*spring* ... AZ-5
Four Peaks Trail—*trail* ... AZ-5
Four Pines—*locale* ... CA-9
Four Pines Island—*island* ... FL-3
Four Pine Spring—*spring* ... CA-9
Four Pines Sch—*school* ... SC-3
Four Pines Sch—*school* ... TX-5
*Four P.M. Island* ... FM-9
**Four Point**—*pop pl* ... AL-4
**Four Point**—*pop pl* ... TN-4
*Four Point Baptist Church* ... TN-4
Four Point Bayou—*gut* ... LA-4
Four Point Camp—*locale* ... WA-9
Fourpoint Canyon—*valley* ... CA-9
Four Point Cem—*cemetery* ... AL-4
Four Point Ch—*church* ... AL-4
Four Point Creek—*stream* ... WA-9
Four Point Lake—*lake* ... MN-6
Four Point Lake—*lake* ... WA-9
Four Point Marsh—*swamp* ... VA-3
Four Point Ridge—*ridge* ... OR-9
*Four Points* ... AL-4
Four Points—*locale* ... GA-3
Fourpoints—*locale* ... MD-2
Four Points—*locale* ... MS-4
Four Points—*locale* ... MO-7
Four Points—*locale* ... PA-2
Four Points—*locale* ... TN-4
**Four Points**—*pop pl* ... CA-9
**Four Points**—*pop pl* (2) ... FL-3
**Four Points**—*pop pl* (2) ... GA-3
**Four Points**—*pop pl* ... NM-5
**Four Points**—*pop pl* (2) ... TN-4
**Four Points**—*pop pl* ... TX-5
Four Points—*summit* ... WY-8
*Four Points Baptist Ch* ... AL-4
Four Points Baptist Ch—*church* ... AL-4
Fourpoints Bridge—*hist pl* ... MD-2
Four Points Ch—*church* ... TN-4
Four Points Rsvr—*reservoir* ... OR-9
Four Point Well—*well* ... NM-5
Fourpole Creek—*stream* (2) ... WV-2
Four Ponds—*lake* ... MA-1
Four Ponds—*swamp* ... TX-5
Four Ponds Brook—*stream* ... ME-1
Four Ponds Mtn—*summit* ... ME-1
Four Pools Spring—*spring* ... UT-8
**Four Presidents Corners**—*pop pl* ... IN-6
Four Prong Lake—*lake* ... FL-3
Four-Q Lakes—*lake* ... CA-9
Fourqurean House—*hist pl* ... VA-3
Four Ranch (historical)—*locale* ... SD-7
Four Range—*locale* ... MT-8
Fourr Canyon—*valley* ... AZ-5
Fourr Cem—*cemetery* ... AZ-5
Four Ridge Knob—*summit* ... WV-2
Four Ridge Trail—*trail* ... PA-2
Four Rivers—*gut* ... LA-4
Four Rivers Boy Scout Reservation—*park* ... KY-4
Four Roads—*locale* ... AL-4
Four-Room House—*hist pl* ... ID-8
Fourseam—*locale* ... KY-4
Four Season Mall—*locale* ... NC-3
**Four Seasons**—*pop pl* ... DE-2
Four Seasons—*post sta* ... NC-3
*Four Seasons, Islands Of The* ... FM-9
*Four Seasons Golf Course* ... PA-2
Four Seasons Marina—*locale* ... TN-4
**Four Seasons Park**—*pop pl* ... DE-2
Four Seasons Shop Ctr—*locale* ... MO-7
**Four Seasons (subdivision)**—*pop pl* ... FL-3
**Four Seasons (subdivision)**—*pop pl* (2) ... NC-3
**Four Seasons Village Condominium**—*pop pl* ... UT-8
Four Section Tank—*reservoir* (2) ... AZ-5
Four Section Tank—*reservoir* ... TX-5
Four Section Well—*well* (2) ... NM-5
Four Section Well—*well* ... TX-5
Four Section Windmill—*locale* ... AZ-5
Four Section Windmill—*locale* (3) ... TX-5
Four Seven Ridge—*ridge* ... OR-9
Four Sisters Mine—*mine* ... NV-8
Foursome, Lake—*reservoir* ... LA-4
Foursome Country Club—*other* ... IA-7
Four Spot Ch—*church* ... AL-4
Four Spring Hollow—*valley* ... MO-7
Four Springs—*spring* ... AZ-5
Four Springs—*spring* ... NV-8
Four Springs Gulch—*valley* ... CA-9
Four Springs Hollow—*valley* ... WI-6
Four Square—*hist pl* ... VA-3
Foursquare—*locale* ... VA-3
Four Square Ch—*church* ... AL-4
Foursquare Ch—*church* ... FL-3
Foursquare Ch—*church* ... GA-3
Four Square Ch—*church* ... KS-7
Four Square Ch—*church* ... KY-4
Foursquare Ch—*church* (2) ... MS-4
Four Square Ch—*church* ... MS-4
Four Square Ch—*church* ... NC-3
Foursquare Ch—*church* (2) ... NC-3
Four Square Ch—*church* ... NC-3
Four Square Ch—*church* ... OH-6
Foursquare Ch—*church* ... OH-6
Foursquare Ch—*church* ... PA-2
Four Square Ch—*church* ... PA-2
Foursquare Ch—*church* ... PA-2
Four Square Ch—*church* ... TN-4
Four Square Ch of God in Christ Tabernacle—*church* ... IN-6
Four Square Crusador Camp—*locale* ... NC-3
Foursquare Gospel Ch—*church* ... AL-4
Foursquare Gospel Ch—*church* ... FL-3
Foursquare Gospel Ch—*church* ... KS-7
Foursquare Gospel Ch—*church* ... NY-2
Foursquare Gospel Ch—*church* ... OK-5
Four-S Ranch—*locale* ... CA-9
Four S Ranch—*locale* ... CA-9
Four-S Ranch—*locale* ... CA-9
Four Stake Prairie—*flat* ... FL-3
**Four States**—*pop pl* ... WV-2
*Four Stream* ... WA-9
Four Stream—*stream* ... WA-9
Four Tanks Canyon—*valley* ... AZ-5
Four Tanks Spring—*spring* ... NV-8
Fourteen, Canal (historical)—*canal* ... AZ-5
Fourteen, Lake—*lake* (2) ... MI-6
Fourteen, Lake—*lake* (2) ... MN-6
Fourteen Acre Pond—*lake* ... CT-1
Fourteen Creek—*stream* ... AK-9
Fourteen Creek—*stream* ... MT-8
Fourteen Creek—*stream* ... TN-4
Fourteen Inch Tank—*reservoir* ... AZ-5
*Fourteen Islands* ... MP-9
Fourteenmile Bridge—*other* ... MI-6
Fourteenmile Cabin—*locale* (2) ... AK-9
Fourteenmile Coulee—*valley* ... MT-8
*Fourteen Mile Creek* ... IN-6
*Fourteen Mile Creek* ... MT-8
*Fourteen Mile Creek* ... TX-5
Fourteenmile Creek—*stream* ... AK-9
Fourteenmile Creek—*stream* ... AR-4
Fourteenmile Creek—*stream* ... CO-8
Fourteenmile Creek—*stream* ... IN-6
Fourteenmile Creek—*stream* ... MS-4
Fourteenmile Creek—*stream* ... MT-8
Fourteenmile Creek—*stream* ... OK-5
Fourteenmile Creek—*stream* ... SC-3
Fourteenmile Creek—*stream* (2) ... WA-9
Fourteenmile Creek—*stream* ... WV-2
Fourteenmile Creek—*stream* ... WI-6
Fourteenmile Creek—*stream* ... WY-8
Fourteenmile Hammock—*island* ... FL-3
Fourteen Mile Hills—*other* ... OK-5
Fourteenmile House—*locale* (2) ... CA-9
Fourteenmile Island—*island* ... NY-2
*Fourteen Mile Lake* ... MI-6
Fourteenmile Lake—*lake* ... AK-9
*Fourteen Mile Narrows* ... PA-2
Fourteenmile Narrows—*gap* ... PA-2
Fourteenmile Park—*park* ... TX-5
Fourteen Mile Point—*cape* ... MI-6
Fourteenmile Ranch—*locale* ... WY-8
Fourteenmile Ridge—*ridge* ... CO-8
*Fourteen Mile Run* ... PA-2
Fourteenmile Slough—*gut* ... CA-9
Fourteen Mile Tree Campsite—*locale* ... ID-8
Fourteen Rsvr—*reservoir* ... MT-8
Fourteen Section Tank—*reservoir* ... TX-5
Fourteen Slough—*stream* ... AR-4
Fourteen Tank—*reservoir* (2) ... AZ-5
Fourteenth—*park* ... CA-9
Fourteenth District Sch—*school* ... KY-4
*Fourteenth Siding* ... ND-7
Fourteenth Street Park—*park* ... NC-3
Fourteenth Street Pier—*locale* ... NJ-2
Fourteenth Street Pompano Bridge—*bridge* ... FL-3
Fourteenth Street Sch—*school* ... ME-1
Fourteenth Street Sch—*school* ... NE-7
Fourteenth Street Sch—*school* ... NC-3
Fourteenth Ward Industrial Sch—*hist pl* ... NY-2
Fourteen Vega—*area* ... NM-5
Fourth and Dauphin Park—*park* ... PA-2
Fourth and Gill Hist Dist—*hist pl* ... TN-4
Fourth Ave—*uninc pl* ... PA-2
Fourth Ave Ch of God—*church* ... TN-4
Fourth Ave Hist Dist—*hist pl* ... AL-4
Fourth Ave Hist Dist—*hist pl* ... PA-2
Fourth Ave JHS—*hist pl* ... AZ-5
Fourth Ave JHS—*school* ... AZ-5
Fourth Ave Methodist Episcopal Church—*hist pl* ... KY-4
Fourth Ave Public Library—*building* ... GA-3
Fourth Ave Theatre (AHRS Site No. ANC-284)—*hist pl* ... AK-9
Fourth Ave Underpass—*hist pl* ... AZ-5
Fourth Baptist Church—*hist pl* ... VA-3
*Fourth Bass Lake* ... WI-6
Fourth Bayou—*gut* ... MS-4
Fourth Bottom Hollow—*valley* ... PA-2
Fourth Boulder Creek—*stream* ... NV-8
Fourth Branch—*stream* ... GA-3
Fourth Butte—*summit* ... CA-9
Fourth Chain Lake—*lake* ... UT-8
Fourth Ch of Christian Scientist—*church* ... IN-6
Fourth Cliff—*cliff* ... MA-1
**Fourth Cliff**—*pop pl* ... MA-1
Fourth Cliff U. S. Life Saving Station (historical)—*locale* ... MA-1
Fourth Congregational Church—*hist pl* ... CT-1
Fourth Connecticut Lake—*lake* ... NH-1
Fourth Creek—*stream* ... AL-4
Fourth Creek—*stream* (2) ... ID-8
Fourth Creek—*stream* (2) ... KS-7
Fourth Creek—*stream* ... MI-6
Fourth Creek—*stream* ... MS-4
Fourth Creek—*stream* (2) ... MT-8
Fourth Creek—*stream* ... NJ-2
Fourth Creek—*stream* (2) ... NY-2
Fourth Creek—*stream* ... NC-3
Fourth Creek—*stream* (3) ... OR-9
Fourth Creek—*stream* ... SC-3
Fourth Creek—*stream* ... TN-4
Fourth Creek—*stream* ... TX-5
Fourth Creek—*stream* (3) ... WA-9
Fourth Creek—*stream* (4) ... WY-8
Fourth Creek Ch—*church* ... AL-4
Fourth Creek Rsvr—*reservoir* ... OR-9
Fourth Creek Rsvr—*reservoir* ... WY-8
Fourth Creek Sch (historical)—*school* ... AL-4
Fourth Creek Trail Spring—*spring* ... OR-9
Fourth Crossing—*locale* ... CA-9
Fourth Crossing—*locale* ... TX-5
Fourth Crow Wing Lake—*lake* ... MN-6
Fourth Currier Pond—*lake* ... ME-1
Fourth Davis Pond—*lake* ... ME-1
Fourth Debsconeag Lake—*lake* ... ME-1
Fourth District Sch—*hist pl* ... CT-1
Fourth District Sch—*school* ... WI-6
Fourth District Sch (historical)—*school* ... TN-4
Fourth Fork Rock Creek—*stream* ... ID-8
Fourth Gap—*gap* ... PA-2
Fourth Gap Trail—*trail* ... PA-2
Fourth Glacier—*glacier* ... AK-9
Fourth Gulch—*valley* ... ID-8
*Fourth Hanson Lake* ... MN-6
Fourth Hole—*basin* ... UT-8
Fourth Hollow—*valley* ... AZ-5
Fourth Hollow—*valley* ... ID-8
Fourth Hollow—*valley* ... NY-2
Fourth Infantry Bluff—*cliff* ... WA-9
*Fourth Kokadjo Lake* ... ME-1
*Fourth Lake* ... ME-1
*Fourth Lake* ... NH-1
*Fourth Lake* ... WI-6
Fourth Lake—*lake* ... CA-9
Fourth Lake—*lake* ... CO-8
Fourth Lake—*lake* ... IL-6
Fourth Lake—*lake* (2) ... ME-1
Fourth Lake—*lake* (6) ... MI-6
Fourth Lake—*lake* (4) ... MN-6
Fourth Lake—*lake* (6) ... NY-2
Fourth Lake—*lake* ... OR-9
Fourth Lake—*lake* ... WI-6
**Fourth Lake**—*pop pl* ... NY-2
Fourth Lake Stream—*stream* ... ME-1
Fourth Machias Lake—*lake* ... ME-1
Fourth Mine Branch—*stream* ... MD-2
Fourth Model Community Center (historical)—*locale* ... TN-4
Fourth Model Sch (historical)—*school* ... TN-4
Fourth Mount Zion Ch—*church* ... VA-3
Fourth Mtn—*summit* ... ME-1
Fourth Mtn—*summit* ... VA-3
Fourth Musquacook Lake—*lake* ... ME-1
*Fourth Negro Brook Lake* ... ME-1
Fourth Newlin Creek—*stream* ... CO-8
*Fourth Nigger brook Lake* ... ME-1
Fourth North Shop Ctr—*locale* ... UT-8
Fourth of July—*valley* ... CA-9
Fourth Of July Basin—*basin* ... WA-9
Fourth of July Branch—*stream* ... SC-3
Fourth of July Butte—*summit* ... AZ-5
Fourth of July Camp—*locale* ... CA-9
Fourth of July Campground—*locale* ... CO-8
Fourth of July Canyon—*valley* ... CA-9
Fourth Of July Canyon—*valley* ... ID-8
Fourth of July Canyon—*valley* ... NM-5
Fourth of July Cave—*cave* ... AL-4
Fourth of July Cove—*bay* ... CA-9
*Fourth of July Creek* ... WA-9
Fourth of July Creek—*stream* (6) ... AK-9
Fourth of July Creek—*stream* ... CO-8
Fourth of July Creek—*stream* ... ID-8
Fourth Of July Creek—*stream* ... ID-8
Fourth of July Creek—*stream* (4) ... ID-8
Fourth Of July Creek—*stream* (3) ... ID-8
Fourth of July Creek—*stream* (5) ... MT-8
Fourth of July Creek—*stream* (3) ... OR-9
Fourth of July Creek—*stream* ... WA-9
Fourth Of July Creek—*stream* (2) ... WA-9
Fourth of July Flat—*flat* ... CA-9
Fourth of July Flat—*flat* ... NV-8
Fourth of July Gulch—*valley* ... CA-9
Fourth of July Gulch—*valley* (3) ... MT-8
Fourth of July Hill—*summit* ... AK-9
Fourth of July Lake—*lake* ... CA-9
Fourth Of July Lake—*lake* ... ID-8
Fourth of July Lake—*lake* ... WA-9
Fourth Of July Lake—*lake* ... WA-9
Fourth of July Mine—*mine* ... CA-9
Fourth of July Mine—*mine* ... CO-8
Fourth of July Mtn—*summit* ... CO-8
Fourth of July Mtn—*summit* ... NV-8
Fourth of July Mtn—*summit* ... WA-9
Fourth Of July Mtn—*summit* ... WA-9
Fourth of July Pass—*gap* ... WA-9
Fourth of July Peak—*summit* ... ID-8
Fourth Of July Peak—*summit* ... WA-9
Fourth Of July Ridge—*ridge* ... ID-8
Fourth of July Ridge—*ridge* ... MT-8
Fourth of July Ridge—*ridge* ... WA-9
Fourth of July Spring—*spring* (2) ... CA-9
Fourth of July Spring—*spring* (2) ... ID-8
Fourth of July Spring—*spring* ... NM-5
Fourth of July Spring—*spring* (2) ... OR-9
Fourth Of July Spring—*spring* ... WA-9
Fourth Of July Summit—*summit* ... ID-8
Fourth of July Wash—*stream* ... AZ-5
Fourth of July Wash—*valley* ... WY-8
Fourth of July Windmill—*locale* ... TX-5
Fourth Pelletier Brook Lake—*lake* ... ME-1
Fourth Plain—*uninc pl* ... WA-9
Fourth Plains—*flat* ... WA-9
Fourth Point—*cape* ... MD-2
*Fourth Pond* ... NY-2
Fourth Pond—*lake* ... ME-1
Fourth Pond Bog—*swamp* ... ME-1
Fourth Presbyterian Church of Chicago—*hist pl* ... IL-6
Fourth Pumping Station County Park*—*park* ... IA-7
Fourth Recess—*valley* ... CA-9
Fourth Recess Lake—*lake* ... CA-9
Fourth Ridge—*ridge* ... MT-8
Fourth Roach Pond—*lake* ... ME-1
Fourth Run—*stream* ... PA-2
Fourth Saint Ch—*church* ... AR-4
Fourth Saint John Pond—*lake* ... ME-1
Fourth Saint Sch—*school* ... CA-9
Fourth Saint Sch—*school* ... PA-2
Fourth Sawmill Spring—*spring* ... NV-8
*Fourth Siding* ... ND-7
Fourth Slough—*stream* ... IL-6
Fourth Spring Creek—*stream* ... ID-8
Fourth Street Bridge—*hist pl* ... CO-8
Fourth Street Center (Shop Ctr)—*locale* ... FL-3
Fourth Street Elem Sch—*school* ... NC-3
Fourth Street Hist Dist—*hist pl* ... OH-6

Fourth Street Missionary Baptist Ch—*church* ... MS-4
Fourth Street Park—*park* ... UT-8
Fourth Street Sch—*hist pl* ... WI-6
Fourth Street Sch—*school* ... GA-3
Fourth Street Sch—*school* ... IL-6
Fourth Street Sch—*school* ... KY-4
Fourth Street Sch—*school* ... MI-6
Fourth Street Sch—*school* ... OH-6
Fourth Street Sch—*school* (2) ... WI-6
Fourth Street Shop Ctr—*locale* ... KS-7
Fourth Street Underpass—*crossing* ... AZ-5
Fourth Sucker Lake—*lake* ... MN-6
Fourthteenth Ave Sch—*school* ... NJ-2
Fourth Terrace Baptist Ch—*church* ... AL-4
Fourth United Presbyterian Ch—*church* ... TN-4
*Fourth Upper Saint John Pond* ... ME-1
*Fourth Ward Brook* ... NJ-2
Fourth Ward District—*hist pl* ... NM-5
Fourth Ward Park—*park* ... NJ-2
Fourth Ward Park—*park* ... WI-6
Fourth Ward Polling Place—*hist pl* ... MI-6
Fourth Ward Sch—*hist pl* ... NY-2
Fourth Ward Sch—*hist pl* ... TX-5
Fourth Ward Sch—*school* ... GA-3
Fourth Ward Sch—*school* (3) ... LA-4
Fourth Ward Sch—*school* ... NV-8
Fourth Ward Sch—*school* (4) ... PA-2
Fourth Ward Sch—*school* ... TX-5
**Fourth Ward (subdivision)**—*pop pl* ... NC-3
Fourth Water Creek—*stream* ... CA-9
Fourth Water Creek—*stream* ... UT-8
Fourth Water Ridge—*ridge* ... UT-8
Fourth Water Spring—*spring* ... CO-8
Fourth West Branch Pond—*lake* ... ME-1
Four Town—*locale* ... MN-6
**Four Town**—*pop pl* ... MN-6
Four Town Chapel—*church* ... MN-6
Four Town Corners—*locale* ... NY-2
Four Townes Shop Ctr—*locale* ... FL-3
Four Town Lake—*lake* ... MN-6
Fourtown Lake—*lake* ... MN-6
**Four Towns**—*pop pl* ... MI-6
Four Towns Grange Hall—*locale* ... MI-6
Fourtowns Sch—*school* ... MI-6
Four-T Ranch—*locale* ... CA-9
Four Tree Cut Off—*channel* ... FL-3
Four Tree Island—*island* ... NH-1
Four Trees—*locale* ... CA-9
Four Trees Sch—*school* ... CA-9
Four Troughs Spring—*spring* ... NM-5
Four Troughs Well—*well* ... TX-5
Fourts Horn—*summit* ... WY-8
Fourty Acre Rock—*summit* ... SC-3
*Fourty Eight Mile Creek* ... TN-4
*Fourty Eight Mile Furnace* ... TN-4
*Fourup* ... FM-9
Fourup—*island* ... FM-9
*Fourup Island* ... FM-9
Fouruu—*bar* ... FM-9
Fouruw—*bar* ... FM-9
Four V Canyon—*valley* ... NM-5
Fourvert Tank—*reservoir* ... AZ-5
**Fourville**—*pop pl* ... TN-4
Four V Ranch—*locale* ... NM-5
Four Wall Tank—*reservoir* ... AZ-5
Four Way—*locale* ... TX-5
Fourway—*locale* ... VA-3
**Fourway**—*pop pl* ... NC-3
**Four Way**—*pop pl* ... TN-4
Fourway Booster Station—*other* ... TX-5
**Fourway (Burkes Garden Siding)**—*pop pl* ... VA-3
Four- Way Channel—*channel* ... FL-3
Four Way Divide—*summit* ... KS-7
Fourway Farm—*locale* ... TX-5
Fourway Junction—*locale* ... ID-8
Fourway Number 2 Mine (underground)—*mine* ... AL-4
*Fourways* ... TX-5
Four-Way Sch—*school* ... CO-8
Four Way Well—*well* ... TX-5
Four Way Windmill—*locale* (2) ... TX-5
Four Weirs—*dam* ... CA-9
Four Wells—*locale* ... NM-5
Four Wells—*well* ... TX-5
Four Wells Cave—*cave* ... AL-4
**Four Winds**—*pop pl* ... MD-2
Four Winds, Lake—*reservoir* ... MO-7
Four Winds Corners—*locale* ... NY-2
Four Winds Country Club—*other* ... NE-7
Four Winds Farm Airp—*airport* ... NC-3
Four Winds Lake—*lake* ... OH-6
Four Winds Mine—*mine* ... AZ-5
Four Winds Mtn—*summit* ... AK-9
**Four Winds (subdivision)**—*pop pl* ... AL-4
Four Wing Lake—*lake* ... AL-4
Four Wing Lake Dam—*dam* ... AL-4
Four Wire Lake—*stream* ... TX-5
Four X Draw—*valley* ... WY-8
Four-4 Line Camp Rsvr—*reservoir* ... WY-8
Fouse Bayou—*stream* ... LA-4
Fouses Airp—*airport* ... PA-2
**Fousetown**—*pop pl* ... PA-2
**Foushee**—*pop pl* ... NC-3
Foushee Island—*island* ... AR-4
Foushee Slough—*stream* ... AR-4
**Foust**—*pop pl* ... TN-4
Foust, Julius I., Bldg—*hist pl* ... NC-3
Foust Branch—*stream* ... TN-4
Foust Cem—*cemetery* ... OH-6
Foust Cem—*cemetery* (3) ... TN-4
Foust Creek—*stream* ... AR-4
Foust Creek—*stream* ... PA-2
Foust Elem Sch—*school* ... NC-3
Foust Ford—*locale* ... VA-3
Foust-Hilburn Ranch—*locale* ... NM-5
Foust Hollow—*valley* ... AL-4
Foust Hollow—*valley* (2) ... TN-4
Foust JHS—*school* ... KY-4
**Foustown**—*pop pl* ... PA-2
Foust Pond (historical)—*lake* ... TN-4
Fousts Ferry (historical)—*locale* ... PA-2
*Fousts Shop* ... MS-4
*Foust Valley* ... PA-2
**Foustwell**—*pop pl* ... PA-2
Fout—*bar* ... FM-9
Fout Cem—*cemetery* ... NC-3
*Foutch Camp* ... CA-9
Foutch Cem—*cemetery* ... IL-6
Foutch Cem—*cemetery* ... TN-4
Foutch Sch—*school* (2) ... IL-6
Foute Island—*island* ... TN-4
Foutes Mill (historical)—*locale* ... TN-4
*Fouts* ... TX-5
Fouts Branch—*stream* ... MO-7
Fouts Camp—*locale* ... CA-9
Fouts Cem—*cemetery* ... KS-7
Fouts Cem—*cemetery* ... SC-3
Fouts Ch—*church* ... IL-6
Fouts Ditch—*canal* ... IN-6
Fouts Field—*park* ... TX-5
*Fouts Island* ... TN-4
Fouts Knob—*summit* ... WV-2
Fouts Mill—*locale* ... GA-3
Fouts Sch—*school* ... MI-6
**Fouts Springs**—*pop pl* ... CA-9
Fouty Creek—*stream* ... MI-6
Fouty Hollow—*valley* ... WV-2
Foutz Cem—*cemetery* ... OH-6
Foutz Cem—*cemetery* ... VA-3
Fouwar—*summit* ... FM-9
*Fouwar, Mount* ... FM-9
**Fowblesburg**—*pop pl* ... MD-2
**Fowers Subdivision**—*pop pl* ... UT-8
Fowkes—*locale* ... MO-7
Fowkes Canyon Creek—*stream* ... WY-8
Fowl Canyon—*valley* ... NM-5
Fowl Craw Lake—*lake* ... SC-3
Fowl Craw Point—*cape* ... GA-3
Fowle, Edmund, House—*hist pl* ... MA-1
Fowle Brook—*stream* ... MA-1
Fowle Cove—*bay* ... ME-1
Fowle Point—*cape* ... ME-1
*Fowler* ... PA-2
Fowler—*locale* (2) ... AL-4
Fowler—*locale* ... AR-4
Fowler—*locale* ... MT-8
Fowler—*locale* ... OK-5
**Fowler**—*pop pl* ... AZ-5
**Fowler**—*pop pl* ... CA-9
**Fowler**—*pop pl* ... CO-8
**Fowler**—*pop pl* ... IL-6
**Fowler**—*pop pl* ... IN-6
**Fowler**—*pop pl* ... KS-7
**Fowler**—*pop pl* ... LA-4
**Fowler**—*pop pl* ... MI-6
**Fowler**—*pop pl* ... MO-7
**Fowler**—*pop pl* ... NY-2
**Fowler**—*pop pl* ... OH-6
**Fowler**—*pop pl* ... SC-3
Fowler, Absalom, House—*hist pl* ... AR-4
Fowler, Benjamin Piatt, House—*hist pl* ... KY-4
Fowler, Capt. Enoch S., House—*hist pl* ... WA-9
Fowler, Charles N., House—*hist pl* ... NJ-2
Fowler, D. D., House—*hist pl* ... TX-5
Fowler, Henry T., House—*hist pl* ... MO-7
Fowler, Jeremiah, House—*hist pl* ... ME-1
Fowler, Moses, House—*hist pl* ... IN-6
Fowler, William J., Mill and House—*hist pl* ... TN-4
Fowler Airfield—*airport* ... CO-8
Fowler Airp—*airport* ... KS-7
Fowler Ave Baptist Ch—*church* ... FL-3
Fowler Beach—*beach* ... DE-2
Fowler Bend—*bend* ... NC-3
*Fowler Bluff* ... FL-3
**Fowler Bluff**—*pop pl* ... FL-3
Fowler Bog—*swamp* ... ME-1
*Fowler Branch* ... TN-4
Fowler Branch—*stream* (3) ... AL-4
Fowler Branch—*stream* ... FL-3
Fowler Branch—*stream* (2) ... GA-3
Fowler Branch—*stream* ... IL-6
Fowler Branch—*stream* ... IN-6
Fowler Branch—*stream* ... MS-4
Fowler Branch—*stream* ... MO-7
Fowler Branch—*stream* ... NC-3
Fowler Branch—*stream* ... SC-3
Fowler Branch—*stream* (3) ... TN-4
Fowler Branch—*stream* ... WV-2
*Fowler Brook* ... CT-1
Fowler Brook—*stream* (4) ... ME-1
Fowler Brook—*stream* (2) ... NH-1
Fowler Brook—*stream* ... PA-2
Fowler Brook—*stream* ... VT-1
Fowler Brook Ch (historical)—*church* ... PA-2
Fowler Camp—*locale* ... CA-9
Fowler Canyon—*valley* (2) ... NM-5
Fowler (CCD)—*cens area* ... CA-9
Fowler Cem—*cemetery* (5) ... AL-4
Fowler Cem—*cemetery* (2) ... AR-4
Fowler Cem—*cemetery* ... CA-9
Fowler Cem—*cemetery* (4) ... GA-3
Fowler Cem—*cemetery* ... IN-6
Fowler Cem—*cemetery* (5) ... KS-7
Fowler Cem—*cemetery* (2) ... ME-1
Fowler Cem—*cemetery* (2) ... MI-6
Fowler Cem—*cemetery* ... NC-3
Fowler Cem—*cemetery* (2) ... OH-6
Fowler Cem—*cemetery* (2) ... SC-3
Fowler Cem—*cemetery* (3) ... TN-4
Fowler Cem—*cemetery* (2) ... TX-5
Fowler Cem—*cemetery* (2) ... WV-2
Fowler Center Hist Dist—*hist pl* ... OH-6
Fowler Ch—*church* ... MD-2
Fowler Ch—*church* ... MO-7
*Fowler City* ... KS-7
Fowler Coulee—*valley* (2) ... MT-8
Fowler Cove—*valley* (2) ... AL-4
Fowler Cove—*valley* ... NC-3
*Fowler Creek* ... KS-7
Fowler Creek—*stream* ... AL-4
Fowler Creek—*stream* ... AK-9
Fowler Creek—*stream* (4) ... CA-9
Fowler Creek—*stream* ... CO-8
Fowler Creek—*stream* ... KY-4
Fowler Creek—*stream* (2) ... MI-6
Fowler Creek—*stream* ... MS-4
Fowler Creek—*stream* ... MO-7
Fowler Creek—*stream* ... MT-8
Fowler Creek—*stream* ... NC-3
Fowler Creek—*stream* (2) ... OR-9
Fowler Creek—*stream* ... TN-4
**Fowler Crossroads**—*pop pl* ... NC-3
Fowler Ditch—*canal* ... IN-6
Fowler Drain—*canal* (2) ... MI-6
Fowler Drain—*stream* ... MI-6
Fowler Draw—*valley* (2) ... WY-8
Fowle-Reed-Wyman House—*hist pl* ... MA-1
Fowler Elem Sch—*school* ... AL-4
Fowler Elem Sch—*school* ... AZ-5
Fowler Elem Sch—*school* ... KS-7
Fowler Ferry (historical)—*locale* ... AL-4
Fowler Fork—*stream* ... WV-2
Fowler Golf Course—*other* ... CO-8
Fowler Green—*locale* ... ME-1
Fowler Grove—*locale* ... TN-4
Fowler Grove Cem—*cemetery* ... IL-6
Fowler Grove Creek—*stream* ... TN-4
Fowler Grove Sch (historical)—*school* ... TN-4
Fowler Gulch—*valley* ... CA-9
Fowler Gulch—*valley* ... ID-8
**Fowler Heights**—*pop pl* ... PA-2
Fowler Hill—*summit* ... KS-7
Fowler Hill—*summit* ... PA-2
Fowler Hill—*summit* ... TX-5
Fowler Hill Cem—*cemetery* ... PA-2
Fowler (historical)—*locale* ... AL-4
Fowler Hollow—*valley* ... PA-2
Fowler Hollow—*valley* (3) ... TN-4
*Fowler Hollow Picnic Area* ... PA-2
Fowler Hollow Run—*stream* ... PA-2
Fowler Hollow State Park—*park* ... PA-2
Fowler House—*hist pl* ... MA-1
Fowler House—*hist pl* (2) ... TX-5
Fowler HS—*school* ... KS-7
Fowler Island—*island* ... AK-9
Fowler Island—*island* ... CT-1
Fowler Island—*island* ... NJ-2
Fowler-Jenkins House—*hist pl* ... TX-5
Fowler JHS—*school* ... OR-9
Fowler Knob—*summit* ... WV-2
Fowler Knob Ch—*church* ... WV-2
*Fowler Lake* ... WA-9
Fowler Lake—*lake* ... AL-4
Fowler Lake—*lake* ... CA-9
Fowler Lake—*lake* ... IL-6
Fowler Lake—*lake* ... MI-6
Fowler Lake—*reservoir* ... IN-6
Fowler Lake—*reservoir* ... WI-6
Fowler Lake Dam—*dam* ... AL-4
Fowler Lake Dam—*dam* ... IN-6
Fowler Lake Number One—*reservoir* ... NC-3
Fowler Lake Number One Dam—*dam* ... NC-3
Fowler Lake Number Two—*reservoir* ... NC-3
Fowler Lake Number Two Dam—*dam* ... NC-3
Fowler Landing—*locale* ... ME-1
Fowler Landing—*locale* ... NC-3
Fowler Lateral—*canal* ... ID-8
Fowler Lookout—*locale* ... CA-9
*Fowler Mesa* ... CO-8
Fowler Mesa—*summit* ... NM-5
Fowler Methodist Episcopal Church—*hist pl* ... MN-6
*Fowler Mills* ... OH-6
Fowler Mine—*mine* ... TN-4
Fowler Mtn—*summit* ... AL-4
Fowler Mtn—*summit* ... CA-9
Fowler Mtn—*summit* ... CT-1
Fowler Mtn—*summit* ... GA-3
Fowler Mtn—*summit* ... NC-3
Fowler Mtn—*summit* ... TX-5
Fowler Narrows—*gap* ... AL-4
Fowler Old River—*lake* ... TX-5
Fowler Park Dam—*dam* ... IN-6
Fowler Park Lake—*reservoir* ... IN-6
Fowler Pass—*gap* ... NM-5
Fowler Peak—*summit* ... CA-9
Fowler Peak—*summit* ... CO-8
Fowler Peak Trail—*trail* ... CA-9
Fowler Point—*cape* ... ME-1
Fowler Point—*cape* ... NC-3
Fowler Point—*cliff* ... AR-4
Fowler Pond—*lake* ... ME-1
Fowler Pond—*lake* ... WA-9
Fowler Pond—*reservoir* ... GA-3
Fowler Ranch—*locale* (2) ... NE-7
Fowler Ranch—*locale* ... TX-5
Fowler Ranch—*locale* ... WY-8
Fowler Ridge—*ridge* ... KY-4
Fowler Ridge—*ridge* ... OH-6
Fowler Ridge—*ridge* ... TN-4
Fowler River—*stream* ... NH-1
Fowler Rock—*pillar* ... RI-1
Fowler Rocks—*pillar* ... RI-1
Fowler RR Station—*building* ... AZ-5
Fowler Rsvr—*reservoir* (2) ... MT-8
Fowler Rsvr—*reservoir* ... OR-9
*Fowler Run* ... PA-2
Fowler Run—*stream* (3) ... PA-2
Fowler Run—*stream* ... WV-2
Fowlers—*other* ... PA-2
**Fowlers**—*pop pl* ... TN-4
Fowlers Bluff—*locale* ... FL-3
Fowlers Branch—*stream* ... VA-3
Fowlers Cave—*cave* ... AL-4
Fowler Sch—*school* ... CA-9
Fowler Sch—*school* ... CT-1
Fowler Sch—*school* ... IL-6
Fowler Sch—*school* ... KS-7
Fowler Sch—*school* ... MA-1
Fowler Sch—*school* ... MT-8
Fowler Sch—*school* ... NY-2
Fowler Sch—*school* ... SC-3
Fowler Sch—*school* ... TX-5
Fowler Sch (abandoned)—*school* ... MO-7
Fowler Sch (abandoned)—*school* ... PA-2
Fowler Sch (historical)—*school* ... TN-4
*Fowlers Cove* ... AL-4
Fowlers Cove Cave—*cave* ... AL-4
*Fowlers Creek* ... MO-7
**Fowlers Crossroads**—*pop pl* ... AL-4
**Fowlers Crossroads**—*pop pl* ... NC-3
Fowlers Fork—*stream* ... KY-4
*Fowlers Grove* ... TN-4
Fowlers Grove Ch—*church* ... TN-4
*Fowlers Grove Creek* ... TN-4
*Fowlers Grove School* ... TN-4
*Fowlers Grove United Methodist Ch* ... TN-4
Fowler-Sherman Cem—*cemetery* ... WI-6
Fowlers Hill—*summit* ... MA-1
Fowlers Island—*island* ... MA-1
Fowlers Lake—*lake* ... FL-3
Fowlers Landing Post Office (historical)—*building* ... TN-4
**Fowlers Mill**—*pop pl* ... OH-6
Fowlers Mill Branch—*stream* ... MD-2
Fowlers Mill Creek—*stream* ... NC-3
Fowlers Mill (historical)—*locale* ... AL-4
Fowlers Nw 40 Airp—*airport* ... WA-9
Fowlers Pit Number One—*cave* ... AL-4
Fowlers Pit Number Three—*cave* ... AL-4
Fowlers Pit Number Two—*cave* ... AL-4
Fowlers Pond—*lake* ... NJ-2
Fowlers Pond—*lake* ... NY-2
Fowlers Pond—*reservoir* ... AL-4
Fowlers Prairie—*flat* ... FL-3
**Fowler Spring**—*pop pl* ... AL-4
Fowler Spring—*spring* ... AL-4
Fowler Spring—*spring* ... CA-9
Fowler Spring—*spring* ... NV-8
Fowler Spring—*spring* ... OR-9
Fowler Spring—*spring* (2) ... TN-4
Fowler Spring—*spring* ... VA-3
Fowler Spring Branch—*stream* ... TN-4
Fowler Springs—*spring* ... ID-8
Fowler Springs Cem—*cemetery* ... AL-4
Fowler Springs Ch—*church* ... AL-4
Fowler Square (Shop Ctr)—*locale* ... FL-3
*Fowlers Rocks* ... RI-1
Fowlers Sch (historical)—*school* ... AL-4
Fowlers Spring Cave—*cave* ... AL-4
*Fowlers Store* ... TN-4
Fowlers Store (historical)—*locale* ... AL-4
Fowler-Steele House—*hist pl* ... VT-1
**Fowlerston**—*pop pl* ... WV-2
Fowler Street Sch—*school* ... GA-3
Fowler Street Shop Ctr—*locale* ... FL-3
Fowler Substation—*locale* ... AZ-5
*Fowlersville* ... NY-2
*Fowlersville* ... WV-2
Fowlersville—*locale* ... NY-2
Fowlersville—*locale* ... PA-2
Fowlersville Covered Bridge—*hist pl* ... PA-2
Fowler Switch Canal—*canal* ... CA-9
Fowler Tank—*reservoir* ... TX-5
**Fowlerton**—*pop pl* ... IN-6
**Fowlerton**—*pop pl* ... TX-5
Fowlerton Cemeteries—*cemetery* ... TX-5
Fowlerton Drain—*stream* ... IN-6
**Fowlertown**—*pop pl* ... GA-3
**Fowler (Town of)**—*pop pl* ... NY-2
**Fowler Township**—*pop pl* ... KS-7
**Fowler (Township of)**—*pop pl* ... OH-6
Fowler (Township of)—*unorg* ... ME-1
*Fowlerville* ... OK-5
*Fowlerville* ... PA-2
Fowlerville—*locale* ... NY-2
**Fowlerville**—*pop pl* ... MI-6
**Fowlerville**—*pop pl* (2) ... NY-2
Fowlerville Sch—*school* ... MI-6
Fowler Well—*well* ... NM-5
Fowley Brook—*stream* ... CT-1
Fowley Drain—*stream* ... MI-6
Fowl Hill—*summit* ... PA-2
Fowlie Creek—*stream* ... OR-9
Fowling Creek—*stream* ... MD-2
Fowling Gut—*gut* ... VA-3
Fowling Point—*cape* ... VA-3
Fowling Point Gut—*gut* ... VA-3
Fowlkes—*locale* ... TX-5
**Fowlkes**—*pop pl* ... TN-4
Fowlkes Baptist Ch—*church* ... TN-4
Fowlkes-Boyle House—*hist pl* ... TN-4
Fowlkes Branch—*stream* ... TN-4
Fowlkes (CCD)—*cens area* ... TN-4
Fowlkes Cem—*cemetery* ... AL-4
Fowlkes Cem—*cemetery* (4) ... TN-4
Fowlkes Division—*civil* ... TN-4
Fowlkes Hill—*summit* ... TN-4
Fowlkes Run—*stream* ... WV-2
Fowlks Post Office—*building* ... TN-4
Fowl Lake Site—*hist pl* ... MN-6
*Fowl Meadow* ... MA-1
Fowl Meadows—*swamp* ... MA-1
*Fowl Point* ... GA-3
Fowl Pond—*lake* ... GA-3
*Fowl River* ... AL-4
**Fowl River**—*pop pl* ... AL-4
Fowl River—*stream* ... AL-4
Fowl River Bay—*bay* ... AL-4
Fowl River Ch—*church* ... AL-4
Fowl River Point—*cape* ... AL-4
*Fowl River Station* ... AL-4
Fowl Roost Island—*island* ... GA-3
**Fowlstown**—*pop pl* ... GA-3
**Fowlstown (RR name Fowltown)**—*pop pl* ... GA-3
Fowlstown Swamp—*swamp* ... GA-3
*Fowlton* ... GA-3
*Fowltown* ... GA-3
Fowltown Creek—*stream* ... GA-3
Fowltown (RR name for Fowlstown)—*other* ... GA-3
*Fowl Towns* ... FL-3
Fowlwood Brook—*stream* ... NY-2
*Fox* ... AL-4
*Fox* ... ND-7
*Fox* ... TX-5
Fox—*locale* ... AZ-5
Fox—*locale* ... KY-4
Fox—*locale* ... MI-6
Fox—*locale* ... MO-7
Fox—*locale* ... MT-8
Fox—*locale* ... NY-2
Fox—*locale* ... TX-5
Fox—*locale* ... VA-3
**Fox**—*pop pl* ... AK-9
**Fox**—*pop pl* ... AR-4
**Fox**—*pop pl* ... IL-6
**Fox**—*pop pl* ... IN-6
**Fox**—*pop pl* ... MI-6
**Fox**—*pop pl* ... MN-6
**Fox**—*pop pl* ... MS-4
**Fox**—*pop pl* ... OH-6
**Fox**—*pop pl* ... OK-5
**Fox**—*pop pl* ... OR-9
**Fox**—*pop pl* ... TX-5
**Fox**—*pop pl* ... UT-8
Fox—*uninc pl* ... TX-5
Fox, Herbert M., House—*hist pl* ... MN-6
Fox, Jacob, House—*hist pl* ... TX-5
Fox, J. C., Bldg—*hist pl* ... ID-8
Fox, John, Jr., House—*hist pl* ... VA-3
Fox, Lake—*lake* ... FL-3
Fox, Lake—*reservoir* ... AL-4
Fox, Mount—*summit* ... MT-8
Fox, S. H., House—*hist pl* ... TX-5
Fox, William, House—*hist pl* ... KY-4
**Fox Acres**—*pop pl* ... OH-6
Fox and Fur Lodge—*locale* ... NM-5
Fox Area—*locale* ... UT-8
Fox Ave Park—*park* ... NC-3
Fox Bark—*summit* ... NC-3
Fox Barranca—*valley* ... CA-9
Fox Bay—*bay* (3) ... AK-9
Fox Bay—*bay* ... LA-4
Fox Bay—*bay* ... NV-8
Fox Bay—*swamp* (2) ... NC-3
Fox Bay—*swamp* (2) ... SC-3
Fox Bayou—*gut* ... NE-7
Fox Bayou—*stream* ... MS-4
Fox Beach—*beach* ... AK-9
Fox Beach—*beach* ... NV-8
Fox Bend Sch—*school* ... IL-6
Foxbird Island—*island* ... ME-1
Fox Bldg—*hist pl* ... AL-4
Fox Bluff—*cliff* (2) ... WI-6
Fox Bluff—*locale* ... TN-4
Fox Bluff Post Office (historical)—*building* ... TN-4
**Foxboro**—*pop pl* ... KY-4
**Foxboro**—*pop pl* ... MA-1
**Foxboro**—*pop pl* ... WI-6
Foxboro Grange Hall—*hist pl* ... MA-1
Foxboro Hollow—*valley* ... WI-6
Foxboro Lake—*reservoir* ... AZ-5
Foxboro Lake Dam—*dam* ... AZ-5
Foxboro Point—*cape* ... CT-1
Foxboro Point—*cape* ... NJ-2
Foxboro Ranch—*locale* ... AZ-5
Foxboro Sch—*school* ... WI-6
Foxboro Shop Ctr—*locale* ... MA-1
**Foxboro (subdivision)**—*pop pl* ... AZ-5
*Foxborough* ... CO-8
*Foxborough* ... MA-1
Foxborough—*CDP* ... MA-1
*Foxborough Centre* ... MA-1
Foxborough HS—*school* (2) ... MA-1
Foxborough State For—*forest* ... MA-1
**Foxborough (Town of)**—*pop pl* ... MA-1
Fox Bottom—*bend* ... OH-6
Fox Bottom—*valley* ... MA-1
Foxbouough Country Club—*locale* ... MA-1
*Fox Branch* ... TX-5
**Foxbranch**—*pop pl* ... TN-4
**Fox Branch**—*pop pl* ... TN-4
Fox Branch—*stream* (3) ... AL-4
Fox Branch—*stream* ... AR-4
Fox Branch—*stream* (3) ... FL-3
Fox Branch—*stream* (2) ... GA-3
Fox Branch—*stream* ... IL-6
Fox Branch—*stream* ... IN-6
Fox Branch—*stream* (2) ... KY-4
Fox Branch—*stream* (4) ... LA-4
Fox Branch—*stream* (2) ... MS-4
Fox Branch—*stream* (3) ... MO-7
Fox Branch—*stream* (2) ... NC-3
Fox Branch—*stream* ... OH-6
Fox Branch—*stream* (2) ... OK-5
Fox Branch—*stream* (2) ... SC-3
Fox Branch—*stream* (5) ... TN-4
Fox Branch—*stream* (6) ... VA-3
Fox Branch Ch—*church* ... TN-4
Fox Branch Sch—*school* ... TN-4
Fox Bridge—*bridge* ... OR-9
Fox Bridge—*bridge* ... VA-3
Fox Bridge Cem—*cemetery* ... OR-9
Fox Brook—*stream* (4) ... CT-1
Fox Brook—*stream* (3) ... ME-1
Fox Brook—*stream* (3) ... MA-1
Fox Brook—*stream* (3) ... NH-1
Fox Brook—*stream* ... NJ-2
Fox Brook—*stream* (2) ... NY-2
Fox Brook Rapids—*rapids* ... ME-1
Fox Brook Trail—*trail* ... ME-1
*Foxburg* ... PA-2
**Foxburg**—*pop pl* (3) ... PA-2
Foxburg Borough—*civil* ... PA-2
Foxburg Corners—*locale* ... PA-2
Foxburg Golf Course—*locale* ... PA-2
Fox-Bush Oil Field—*oilfield* ... KS-7
Fox Butte—*summit* ... ID-8
Fox Butte—*summit* ... OR-9
Fox Cabin—*locale* ... TN-4
Fox Cabin Spring—*spring* ... NV-8
Fox Cabin Spring—*spring* ... WY-8
Fox California Theater—*hist pl* ... CA-9
Fox Camp Creek—*stream* ... CA-9
Fox Camp Spring—*spring* ... CA-9
Fox Camp Spring—*spring* ... TN-4
Fox Canal—*canal* ... FL-3
*Fox Canyon* ... NV-8
Fox Canyon—*valley* (3) ... AZ-5
Fox Canyon—*valley* (7) ... CA-9
Fox Canyon—*valley* (2) ... CO-8
Fox Canyon—*valley* (2) ... ID-8
Fox Canyon—*valley* ... KS-7
Fox Canyon—*valley* ... NV-8
Fox Canyon—*valley* (2) ... NM-5
Fox Canyon—*valley* ... OR-9
Fox Canyon—*valley* (2) ... TX-5
Fox Canyon Creek—*stream* ... CO-8
Fox Canyon Creek—*stream* ... OR-9
Fox Canyon Spring—*spring* ... NV-8
Fox Canyon Tank—*reservoir* ... AZ-5
Fox Canyon Tank Number One—*reservoir* ... AZ-5
Fox Canyon Tank Number Two—*reservoir* ... AZ-5
Fox Canyon Wash—*stream* ... AZ-5
Fox Cape—*cape* ... AK-9
Fox Castle—*cliff* ... AK-9
Foxcatcher Airp—*airport* ... PA-2
*Foxcatcher Heliport* ... PA-2
Fox Cave—*cave* ... NM-5
Fox Cave—*cave* ... TN-4
Fox Cem—*cemetery* ... CT-1
Fox Cem—*cemetery* (2) ... IL-6
Fox Cem—*cemetery* (6) ... KY-4
Fox Cem—*cemetery* ... ME-1
Fox Cem—*cemetery* ... MA-1
Fox Cem—*cemetery* (2) ... MS-4
Fox Cem—*cemetery* (2) ... MO-7
Fox Cem—*cemetery* ... NY-2
Fox Cem—*cemetery* ... NC-3
Fox Cem—*cemetery* ... OH-6
Fox Cem—*cemetery* ... OK-5
Fox Cem—*cemetery* (7) ... TN-4
Fox Cem—*cemetery* (3) ... TX-5
Fox Cem—*cemetery* (3) ... WV-2
*Fox Centre* ... PA-2
Fox Ch—*church* ... TN-4
**Fox Chapel**—*pop pl* ... MD-2
**Fox Chapel**—*pop pl* ... PA-2
Fox Chapel Country Club—*other* ... PA-2
Fox Chapel Golf Course—*other* ... PA-2
Fox Chapel HS—*school* ... PA-2
**Fox Chapel North**—*pop pl* ... MD-2
Fox Chapel Sch—*school* ... PA-2
Fox Chase—*locale* ... PA-2
**Fox Chase**—*pop pl* ... KY-4
**Fox Chase**—*pop pl* ... NJ-2
**Fox Chase**—*pop pl* ... OH-6
**Fox Chase**—*pop pl* ... PA-2
Fox Chase Inn—*hist pl* ... PA-2
**Fox Chase Manor**—*pop pl* ... PA-2
**Fox Chase Park**—*pop pl* ... DE-2
Fox Chase Sch—*school* ... PA-2
**Foxchase (subdivision)**—*pop pl* ... AL-4
**Fox Chase (subdivision)**—*pop pl* ... PA-2
Fox Cliff—*cliff* ... IN-6
Foxcliff Lake—*reservoir* ... IN-6
Foxcliff Lake Dam—*dam* ... IN-6
Fox Cobble, The—*summit* ... VT-1
Fox Coll—*school* ... OR-9
Fox Coll (historical)—*school* ... MS-4
Fox-Cook Farm—*hist pl* ... VT-1
Fox Corner—*locale* ... VA-3
Fox Corners—*locale* ... NY-2
Fox Corral—*locale* ... OR-9
Fox Coulee—*valley* (2) ... MT-8
Fox Coulee—*valley* (2) ... WI-6
Fox Court—*hist pl* ... CA-9
Fox Cove—*bay* ... WA-9
*Fox Creek* ... MT-8
*Fox Creek* ... NJ-2
*Fox Creek* ... NC-3
*Fox Creek* ... OR-9
*Fox Creek* ... SD-7
Fox Creek—*bay* (2) ... MD-2
Fox Creek—*gut* ... NC-3
Fox Creek—*locale* ... ID-8
Fox Creek—*locale* ... WI-6
**Fox Creek**—*pop pl* ... CO-8
**Fox Creek**—*pop pl* ... KY-4
**Fox Creek**—*pop pl* ... MO-7
**Foxcreek**—*pop pl* ... MO-7
Fox Creek—*post sta* ... MI-6
Fox Creek—*stream* (6) ... AL-4
Fox Creek—*stream* (10) ... AK-9
Fox Creek—*stream* ... AR-4
Fox Creek—*stream* (7) ... CA-9
Fox Creek—*stream* (5) ... CO-8
Fox Creek—*stream* (3) ... FL-3
Fox Creek—*stream* (2) ... GA-3
Fox Creek—*stream* (13) ... ID-8
Fox Creek—*stream* (3) ... IL-6
Fox Creek—*stream* (2) ... IA-7
Fox Creek—*stream* (2) ... KS-7
Fox Creek—*stream* (2) ... KY-4
Fox Creek—*stream* ... MA-1
Fox Creek—*stream* (2) ... MI-6
Fox Creek—*stream* (3) ... MN-6
Fox Creek—*stream* (2) ... MS-4
Fox Creek—*stream* (7) ... MO-7
Fox Creek—*stream* (11) ... MT-8
Fox Creek—*stream* (2) ... NE-7
Fox Creek—*stream* ... NV-8
Fox Creek—*stream* ... NJ-2
Fox Creek—*stream* (4) ... NY-2
Fox Creek—*stream* (3) ... NC-3
Fox Creek—*stream* (2) ... OH-6
Fox Creek—*stream* (16) ... OR-9
Fox Creek—*stream* (2) ... SC-3
Fox Creek—*stream* ... SD-7
Fox Creek—*stream* (2) ... TN-4
Fox Creek—*stream* ... TX-5
Fox Creek—*stream* (3) ... VA-3
Fox Creek—*stream* (4) ... WA-9
Fox Creek—*stream* ... WI-6
Fox Creek—*stream* (6) ... WY-8
Fox Creek Campground—*locale* ... WA-9
Fox Creek Campground—*locale* ... WY-8
Fox Creek Cem—*cemetery* ... CO-8
Fox Creek Cem—*cemetery* ... IL-6
Fox Creek Cem—*cemetery* ... NY-2
Fox Creek Ditch—*canal* ... WY-8
Fox Creek Gap—*gap* ... WY-8
Fox Creek Lake—*lake* ... CA-9
Fox Creek Lake—*reservoir* (2) ... TN-4
Fox Creek Lake Dam—*dam* ... TN-4
Fox Creek Marsh—*swamp* ... MD-2
Fox Creek Marshes—*swamp* ... MA-1
*Fox Creek Pass* ... WY-8
Fox Creek Pass—*gap* ... WY-8
Fox Creek Patrol Cabin—*locale* ... WY-8
Fox Creek Peak—*summit* ... NV-8
Fox Creek Ridge—*ridge* ... OR-9
Fox Creek Sch—*school* ... NE-7
**Fox Creek Township**—*pop pl* ... MO-7
Fox Creek Trail—*trail* ... OR-9
Fox Creek Watershed Dam Number 2—*dam* ... AL-4
**Foxcroff (subdivision)**—*pop pl* ... NC-3
*Fox Croft* ... PA-2
Foxcroft—*locale* ... PA-2
**Foxcroft**—*pop pl* ... IL-6
Foxcroft—*post sta* ... PA-2
Foxcroft Center Sch—*school* ... ME-1
Foxcroft Country Club—*other* ... PA-2
Foxcroft Elem Sch—*school* ... PA-2
Foxcroft Lake—*reservoir* ... NC-3
Foxcroft Lake Dam—*dam* ... NC-3
*Foxcroft Sch* ... PA-2
Foxcroft Sch—*school* ... VA-3
**Foxcroft (subdivision)**—*pop pl* (2) ... NC-3
**Foxcroft West**—*pop pl* ... PA-2
Fox Crossing—*locale* ... MT-8
Fox Crossing Sch (abandoned)—*school* ... MO-7
*Fox Crossroads* ... SC-3
Fox Cut—*channel* ... FL-3
Foxdale—*uninc pl* ... PA-2
Fox Dam—*dam* ... AZ-5
Fox Dam—*dam* ... NC-3
Fox Dam—*dam* ... OR-9
**Fox Den**—*pop pl* ... CT-1
**Fox Den**—*pop pl* ... TN-4
Fox Den Branch—*stream* ... GA-3
Fox Den Cave—*cave* ... AL-4
Foxden Cave—*cave* ... AL-4

Fox Den Creek—stream CO-8
Fox Den Hill—summit KY-4
Fox Den Hollow—valley KY-4
Fox Den Hollow—valley MO-7
Fox Den Knob—summit OH-6
Fox Den Rsvr—reservoir CO-8
Fox Den Sch—school IL-6
Fox Den Spring—spring AR-4
**Fox Den (subdivision)**—pop pl TN-4
Fox Ditch—canal CO-8
Fox Ditch—canal NV-8
Fox Ditch—canal OH-6
Fox Ditch—canal UT-8
Fox Ditch—canal WY-8
Fox Drain—canal MI-6
Fox Draw—valley CA-9
Fox Ears—bar ME-1
Fox Elem Sch—school GA-3
Foxen Adobe (site)—locale CA-9
Foxen Canyon—valley CA-9
Foxen Canyon Cem—cemetery CA-9
Foxes Bend—bend TX-5
Foxes Creek NY-2
Foxes Creek—stream NY-2
Foxes Creek—stream VA-3
Foxesee Creek CA-9
Foxes Lost Cave—cave AL-4
Foxes Run—stream PA-2
Foxes Store (historical)—locale TN-4
Foxey Creek—stream MT-8
Fox Farm—CDP WY-8
Fox Farm—hist pl KY-4
Fox Farm—locale AZ-5
Fox Farm Campground—locale CA-9
Fox Farm Creek—stream MI-6
Fox Farm Lake—lake MI-6
Fox Farm Lake—lake MN-6
Fox Farm Site—hist pl VA-3
Fox Ferry Point—cape MD-2
**Foxfield**—pop pl DE-2
Foxfield Plaza—locale MA-1
**Foxfire**—pop pl DE-2
**Foxfire**—pop pl NC-3
**Foxfire**—pop pl (2) TN-4
**Fox Fire**—pop pl (2) TN-4
Foxfire Campground—locale AL-4
Foxfire Country Club Airpark—airport NC-3
Foxfire Lake—reservoir AL-4
Foxfire Lake Dam—dam AL-4
**Foxfire Meadow (subdivision)**—pop pl DE-2
**Foxfire (subdivision)**—pop pl (2) NC-3
**Fox Fire Subdivision**—pop pl UT-8
Fox Fire Trail—trail PA-2
Fox Flat—flat (2) CA-9
Fox Flat—flat ID-8
Fox Flats—flat AK-9
Fox Forest Rec Area—park IA-7
Fox Gap—gap MD-2
Fox Gap—gap (2) NC-3
Fox Gap—gap (2) PA-2
Fox Gap—gap VA-3
**Foxglen**—pop pl IN-6
Fox Glen—valley WI-6
**Fox Glen (subdivision)**—pop pl (2) AZ-5
**Foxglen Subdivision**—pop pl UT-8
Foxglove Canal—canal CA-9
Foxglove Lateral Seven—canal CA-9
Foxglove Pond—lake NH-1
Foxgrape Run—stream WV-2
Fox Grove Park—park CA-9
Fox Gulch—valley (4) AK-9
Fox Gulch—valley AZ-5
Fox Gulch—valley (4) CA-9
Fox Gulch—valley ID-8
Fox Gulch—valley (2) MT-8
Fox Gulch Spring—spring AZ-5
Fox Gulch Sycamore Creek—stream AZ-5
Fox Gully Branch—stream SC-3
Fox Hall—hist pl VT-1
Fox Hall—hist pl WI-6
**Fox Hall**—pop pl DE-2
**Foxhall**—pop pl MD-2
Foxhall—uninc pl VA-3
Fox Hall Ch—church VA-3
**Foxhall Courtside**—pop pl DE-2
Foxhall Draw—valley WY-8
**Fox Hall (historical)**—pop pl VA-3
**Fox Hall Park**—pop pl VA-3
Fox Hall Shop Ctr—locale VA-3
**Fox Hall (subdivision)**—pop pl NC-3
Fox Hall Swamp—stream VA-3
**Foxhall Village**—pop pl DC-2
Fox Harbor—bay MD-2
Fox Haven Plantation—hist pl NC-3
**Fox Haven (subdivision)**—pop pl AL-4
Fox Head—swamp GA-3
Fox Head Branch—stream FL-3
Foxhead Branch—stream GA-3
Foxhead Branch—stream MS-4
Fox Head Point NH-1
Fox Hill PA-2
Fox Hill—island MA-1
Fox Hill—locale NJ-2
Fox Hill—locale PA-2
**Fox Hill**—pop pl AR-4
**Fox Hill**—pop pl IN-6
**Fox Hill**—pop pl NY-2
**Fox Hill**—pop pl (2) PA-2
**Fox Hill**—pop pl VA-3
Fox Hill—summit AK-9
Fox Hill—summit (2) CT-1
Fox Hill—summit FL-3
Fox Hill—summit GA-3
Fox Hill—summit IL-6
Fox Hill—summit KY-4
Fox Hill—summit ME-1
Fox Hill—summit MD-2
Fox Hill—summit (9) MA-1
Fox Hill—summit NJ-2
Fox Hill—summit (9) NY-2
Fox Hill—summit NC-3
Fox Hill—summit OR-9
Fox Hill—summit (2) PA-2
Fox Hill—summit (3) RI-1
Fox Hill—summit (3) VT-1
Fox Hill—summit WI-6
Fox Hill Cem—cemetery MA-1
Fox Hill Country Club—other PA-2
Fox Hill Country Club—other WV-2
Fox Hill Cove RI-1
Fox Hill Cove—cove MA-1
Fox Hill - in part PA-2
Fox Hill Lake—lake CT-1
Fox Hill Level—locale MD-2
Fox Hill Plantation—hist pl VA-3
Fox Hill Point—cape MD-2
Fox Hill Point—cape NH-1
Fox Hill Pond—lake RI-1
Fox Hill Range—range NJ-2
Foxhill Recreation Center MD-2
Fox Hill Recreation Center—locale MD-2
**Fox Hills**—pop pl MD-2
**Fox Hills**—pop pl NY-2
**Fox Hills**—pop pl TN-4
Fox Hills—range ID-8
Fox Hills—summit AK-9
Fox Hills—uninc pl NJ-2
Fox Hill Sch—hist pl MA-1
Fox Hill Sch—school KY-4
Foxhill Sch—school MD-2
Fox Hill Sch—school MA-1
Fox Hill Sch—school PA-2
Fox Hill Sch (abandoned)—school PA-2
Fox Hills Country Club—other CA-9
Fox Hills Country Club—other MI-6
Fox Hills Country Club—other WI-6
Fox Hills Sch—school UT-8
**Fox Hills Subdivision**—pop pl UT-8
**Fox Hill (Tartown)**—pop pl PA-2
Fox (historical)—locale AL-4
Fox (historical)—locale MS-4
Fox Hole—bay AK-9
Fox Hole Branch—stream TN-4
Foxhole Creek MD-2
Fox Hole Creek—bay MD-2
Foxhole Landing MD-2
Fox Hole Landing—locale MD-2
Fox Hole Log MD-2
Fox Hollow—bay TX-5
**Fox Hollow**—pop pl NC-3
**Foxhollow**—pop pl WI-6
Fox Hollow—valley (2) AR-4
Fox Hollow—valley ID-8
Fox Hollow—valley IL-6
Fox Hollow—valley IN-6
Fox Hollow—valley (4) KY-4
Fox Hollow—valley (6) MO-7
Fox Hollow—valley (3) NY-2
Fox Hollow—valley (2) OH-6
Fox Hollow—valley OR-9
Fox Hollow—valley (2) PA-2
Fox Hollow—valley (10) TN-4
Fox Hollow—valley (4) TX-5
Fox Hollow—valley (3) UT-8
Fox Hollow—valley (4) VA-3
Fox Hollow—valley WV-2
Fox Hollow—valley (2) WI-6
Fox Hollow Branch—stream MO-7
Fox Hollow Branch—stream (3) TN-4
Fox Hollow Cave—cave TN-4
Fox Hollow Ch—church (2) PA-2
Fox Hollow Ch—church WI-6
Fox Hollow Creek—stream TX-5
Fox Hollow Dam—dam NJ-2
Fox Hollow Golf Course PA-2
**Fox Hollow (historical)**—pop pl OR-9
Fox Hollow Lake—reservoir NJ-2
Fox Hollow Sch—school MA-1
Fox Hollow Sch—school WI-6
Fox Hollow Spring—spring UT-8
Fox Hollow Spur—trail PA-2
**Fox Hollow (subdivision)**—pop pl NC-3
**Fox Hollow Subdivision**—pop pl UT-8
**Fox Hollow Woods**—pop pl NJ-2
**Foxholm**—pop pl ND-7
**Foxholm Township**—pop pl ND-7
**Foxhome**—pop pl MN-6
Foxhome Cem—cemetery MN-6
Fox Homestead—locale MT-8
**Foxhome (Township of)**—pop pl MN-6
**Foxhorn Village (subdivision)**—pop pl NC-3
Fox Hosp—hospital NY-2
Fox Hotel—hist pl OK-5
Fox House—hist pl AR-4
Fox House—hist pl MS-4
Fox House—hist pl SC-3
**Foxhunter Lane**—pop pl OH-6
Fox Hunters Hill—summit TX-5
Fox Hunters Lake—reservoir MS-4
Fox Hunters Paradise Cave MO-7
Fox Hunt Hollow—valley IL-6
Fox Irrigation Dam—dam SD-7
Fox Island RI-1
Fox Island TN-4
Fox Island VA-3
Fox Island—island (7) AK-9
Fox Island—island CT-1
Fox Island—island IL-6
Fox Island—island (4) ME-1
Fox Island—island (2) MI-6
Fox Island—island (2) MN-6
Fox Island—island MS-4
Fox Island—island MO-7
Fox Island—island NJ-2
Fox Island—island NY-2
Fox Island—island OH-6
Fox Island—island RI-1
Fox Island—island VT-1
Fox Island—island (2) WA-9
Fox Island—island WI-6
Fox Island—locale WA-9
**Fox Island**—pop pl MS-4
Fox Island Anchorage—bay AK-9
Fox Island Bend—bend MS-4
Fox Island Cem—cemetery WA-9
Fox Island Creek—stream MA-1
Fox Island (historical)—island SD-7
Fox Island (historical)—island TN-4
Fox Islands—island AK-9
Fox Islands—island ME-1
Fox Islands—island VA-3
Fox Island Sch—hist pl WA-9
Fox Island State Park—park OH-6
Fox Islands Thorofare—channel ME-1
Fox JHS—school MD-2
**Fox Junction**—pop pl CO-8
Fox Knob NC-3
Fox Knob—summit KY-4
Fox Knob—summit (2) NC-3
Fox Knob—summit TN-4
Fox Knob—summit VA-3
Fox Knob—summit WV-2
Fox Knoll Lake—lake MI-6
**Foxlair (subdivision)**—pop pl NC-3
Fox Lake MI-6
Fox Lake MN-6
Fox Lake WI-6
Fox Lake—lake (3) AK-9
Fox Lake—lake CA-9
Fox Lake—lake (5) FL-3
Fox Lake—lake (3) IL-6
Fox Lake—lake (2) IN-6
Fox Lake—lake LA-4
Fox Lake—lake (9) MI-6
Fox Lake—lake (10) MN-6
Fox Lake—lake (2) MT-8
Fox Lake—lake NE-7
Fox Lake—lake NY-2
Fox Lake—lake (3) ND-7
Fox Lake—lake OR-9
Fox Lake—lake (2) SD-7
Fox Lake—lake UT-8
Fox Lake—lake (8) WI-6
**Fox Lake**—pop pl IL-6
**Fox Lake**—pop pl IN-6
**Fox Lake**—pop pl MN-6
**Fox Lake**—pop pl WI-6
Fox Lake—reservoir CO-8
Fox Lake—reservoir FL-3
Fox Lake—reservoir KS-7
Fox Lake—reservoir (3) NC-3
Fox Lake—reservoir (2) OH-6
Fox Lake—reservoir PA-2
Fox Lake—reservoir TN-4
Fox Lake—reservoir UT-8
Fox Lake—reservoir VA-3
Fox Lake—reservoir WI-6
Fox Lake—swamp AR-4
Fox Lake—swamp MN-6
Fox Lakebed—flat MN-6
Fox Lake Cem—cemetery IL-6
Fox Lake Cem—cemetery ND-7
Fox Lake Ch—church IL-6
Fox Lake Dam—dam MS-4
Fox Lake Dam—dam (2) NC-3
Fox Lake Dam—dam PA-2
Fox Lake Dam—dam UT-8
**Fox Lake Hills**—pop pl IL-6
Fox Lake Junction—locale WI-6
Fox Lake Park (county park)—park FL-3
Fox Lake RR Depot—hist pl WI-6
Fox Lakes—lake FL-3
Fox Lakes—lake WA-9
Fox Lake State Wildlife Mngmt Area—park SD-7
**Fox Lake (Town of)**—pop pl WI-6
**Fox Lake (Township of)**—pop pl MN-6
**Fox Lake Vista**—pop pl IL-6
**Foxland Hall (subdivision)**—pop pl TN-4
Fox Landing Strip—airport KS-7
**Fox Lawn**—pop pl IL-6
Fox Ledge—summit MA-1
**Foxlee**—pop pl VA-3
Foxleigh—locale FL-3
Foxley NE-7
**Foxley Manor**—pop pl MD-2
Fox Maple Branch—stream NC-3
Fox Marsh—swamp MD-2
Fox Marsh—swamp NY-2
Fox Meadow—flat CA-9
Fox Meadow—flat WA-9
**Fox Meadow**—pop pl NY-2
**Fox Meadow Farm**—pop pl DE-2
Fox Meadow Lake—lake MN-6
Fox Meadows—uninc pl NY-2
Fox Meadow Sch—school NY-2
Fox Meadows Country Club—locale TN-4
Fox Meadows Country Club—other KS-7
Fox Meadows Sch—school TN-4
**Fox Meadows (suvdivision)**—pop pl NC-3
Fox Memorial Ch—church VA-3
Fox Memorial Park—park NM-5
Fox Mill NJ-2
Fox Mill—locale OR-9
**Fox Mill Estates**—pop pl VA-3
Fox Mill (historical)—locale TN-4
Fox Mill Run—stream VA-3
Fox Mill Woods Park—park VA-3
Fox Mine—mine CO-8
Fox Mine—mine NV-8
Fox Mine Hollow—valley MO-7
Foxmoor Shop Ctr—locale FL-3
**Foxmoor (subdivision)**—pop pl MS-4
**Foxmoor (subdivision)**—pop pl TN-4
**Foxmoor Subdivision**—pop pl UT-8
**Foxmoor Subdivision #2**—pop pl UT-8
Fox Mountain—ridge GA-3
Fox Mountain Burn—area CA-9
Fox Mountain Cem—cemetery TX-5
Fox Mountain Fire Tower—tower PA-2
Fox Mountain Lake—reservoir NC-3
Fox Mountain Lake Dam—dam NC-3
Fox Mountain Spring—spring CA-9
Foxmount Preparatory Sch—school FL-3
Fox Mtn—summit AL-4
Fox Mtn—summit AZ-5
Fox Mtn—summit (4) CA-9
Fox Mtn—summit (2) CO-8
Fox Mtn—summit GA-3
Fox Mtn—summit (2) MT-8
Fox Mtn—summit (2) NV-8
Fox Mtn—summit NM-5
Fox Mtn—summit NY-2
Fox Mtn—summit (3) NC-3
Fox Mtn—summit PA-2
Fox Mtn—summit (2) TX-5
Fox Mtn—summit (3) VA-3
Fox Mtn—summit WA-9
Fox Mtn—summit WY-8
Fox-Oakland Theater—hist pl CA-9
Fox Oil Field—oilfield TX-5
**Foxon**—pop pl CT-1
Foxon Pond—lake CT-1
Fox Park WY-8
Fox Park—flat CO-8
Fox Park—flat ID-8
Fox Park—flat MT-8
Fox Park—park IL-6
Fox Park—park MI-6
**Foxpark**—pop pl WY-8
Fox Park Flat—flat WY-8
Fox Park Patrol Cabin—locale WY-8
Fox Passage—channel ME-1
Foxpaw Lake—lake MI-6
Fox Peak—summit (2) ID-8
Fox Peak—summit MT-8
Fox Peak—summit WA-9
Fox Pictograph—hist pl AR-4
**Fox Place Minor Subdivision**—pop pl UT-8
Fox Point IL-6
Fox Point RI-1
Fox Point—cape (3) AK-9
Fox Point—cape LA-4
Fox Point—cape ME-1
Fox Point—cape (3) MD-2
Fox Point—cape (2) MA-1
Fox Point—cape MI-6
Fox Point—cape (2) NH-1
Fox Point—cape (2) NY-2
Fox Point—cape RI-1
Fox Point—cape UT-8
Fox Point—cape VA-3
Fox Point—cape WA-9
Fox Point—cape (3) WI-6
Fox Point—cliff OR-9
**Fox Point**—pop pl WI-6
Fox Point—summit AK-9
Fox Point—summit OH-6
Fox Point Branch DE-2
Fox Point Island—island AK-9
Fox Point Marsh—swamp MD-2
Fox Point Sch—school WI-6
Fox Pond GA-3
Fox Pond PA-2
Fox Pond—lake (2) FL-3
Fox Pond—lake GA-3
Fox Pond—lake IN-6
Fox Pond—lake (6) ME-1
Fox Pond—lake (2) NY-2
Fox Pond—lake TN-4
Fox Pond—reservoir MO-7
Fox Pond—reservoir NC-3
Fox Pond—swamp FL-3
Fox Pond—swamp SC-3
Fox Pond Bay—swamp NC-3
Fox Pond Dam—dam (2) NC-3
**Foxport**—pop pl KY-4
Foxport Cem—cemetery KY-4
Fox Prairie—area IN-6
Fox Queant Pass—gap UT-8
Fox Ranch—locale (2) AZ-5
Fox Ranch—locale ID-8
Fox Ranch—locale NM-5
Fox Ranch—locale SD-7
Fox Ranch (reduced use)—locale UT-8
Fox Range—range NV-8
Fox Ravine (historical)—valley AZ-5
Fox Research For (State Forest)—forest NH-1
**Fox Rest Woods**—pop pl MD-2
Fox Ridge—locale NY-2
**Fox Ridge**—pop pl IN-6
**Fox Ridge**—pop pl PA-2
**Fox Ridge**—pop pl SD-7
Fox Ridge—ridge CA-9
Fox Ridge—ridge IL-6
Fox Ridge—ridge IN-6
Fox Ridge—ridge KY-4
Fox Ridge—ridge SD-7
Fox Ridge—ridge TN-4
Fox Ridge—ridge (2) VA-3
Fox Ridge—ridge WI-6
Fox Ridge Cem—cemetery IN-6
**Fox Ridge Court (subdivision)**—pop pl PA-2
Foxridge Sch—school CA-9
Fox Ridge Sch—school IL-6
Fox Ridge Sch—school MO-7
Fox Ridge Sch—school SD-7
**Fox Ridge (subdivision)**—pop pl NC-3
Fox River NJ-2
**Fox River**—pop pl IL-6
**Fox River**—pop pl WI-6
Fox River—stream (3) AK-9
Fox River—stream (4) IL-6
Fox River*—stream IA-7
Fox River—stream MI-6
Fox River—stream MO-7
Fox River—stream (2) WI-6
Fox River Campground—locale MI-6
Fox River Cem—cemetery IL-6
**Fox River Estates**—pop pl IL-6
**Fox River Grove**—pop pl IL-6
**Fox River Heights**—pop pl IL-6
Fox River House—hist pl IL-6
Fox River Park—park WI-6
Fox River Public Access—locale MI-6
Fox River State Park—park IL-6
Fox River Township—fmr MCD IA-7
Fox River Valley WI-6
**Fox River Valley Gardens**—pop pl IL-6
Fox Road Dock—locale TN-4
Fox Rock—island AK-9
Fox Rock—island OR-9
Foxrock Hollow—valley KY-4
Fox Rocks—island ME-1
Fox RR Station—building AZ-5
Fox Rsvr NC-3
Fox Rsvr—reservoir MT-8
Fox Rsvr—reservoir NC-3
Fox Rsvr—reservoir (2) OR-9
**Fox Run**—pop pl NC-3
**Fox Run**—pop pl PA-2
Fox Run—stream (2) IN-6
Fox Run—stream IA-7
Fox Run—stream (2) KY-4
Fox Run—stream MD-2
Fox Run—stream (4) OH-6
Fox Run—stream (9) PA-2
Fox Run—stream (4) WV-2
**Fox Run Colony (subdivision)**—pop pl MS-4
Fox Run Golf Course—locale PA-2
Fox Run Industrial Park—locale AL-4
Fox Run Sch—school CT-1
Fox Run Sch (historical)—school PA-2
**Fox Run (subdivision)**—pop pl (2) AL-4
**Fox Run (subdivision)**—pop pl MS-4
**Fox Run (subdivision)**—pop pl (6) NC-3
**Fox Run (subdivision)**—pop pl TN-4
**Fox Run (trailer park)**—pop pl DE-2
Fox's Brewery-Diamond Wine Co.—hist pl OH-6
Foxs Brook—stream NJ-2
Foxs Camp—locale ME-1
Fox Sch—school IL-6
Fox Sch—school IA-7
Fox Sch—school MA-1
Fox Sch—school (3) MI-6
Fox Sch—school MO-7
Fox Sch—school MT-8
Fox Sch—school PA-2
Fox Sch—school VA-3
Fox Sch—school WA-9
Fox Sch—school WV-2
Fox Sch (abandoned)—school (2) MO-7
Fox Sch (abandoned)—school PA-2
Fox Sch (historical)—school MO-7
**Foxs Corner**—pop pl FL-3
Foxs Creek AL-4
Fox's Ferry MD-2
Foxs Ferry Point MD-2
Fox's Gap MD-2
**Fox Shadow Subdivision**—pop pl UT-8
Foxshire Plaza—locale PA-2
Fox's Hole Creek MD-2
Foxs Island TN-4
Fox's Kill NY-2
Foxskin Bayou—stream LA-4
Foxs Lake Dam—dam NJ-2
Foxs Landing (historical)—locale MS-4
Fox Slip—gut FL-3
Foxs Mill MS-4
Foxs Mill—locale NJ-2
Foxs Mill Pond NJ-2
Foxs Path—trail PA-2
Fox Spit WA-9
Foxs Pond—bay LA-4
Foxs Pond—lake NJ-2
Fox Spring NV-8
Fox Spring TN-4
Fox Spring—spring AK-9
Fox Spring—spring AZ-5
Fox Spring—spring (5) CA-9
Fox Spring—spring ID-8
Fox Spring—spring NV-8
Fox Spring—spring (3) OR-9
Fox Spring—spring TN-4
Fox Spring Canyon—valley NM-5
Fox Spring Post Office TN-4
Foxspring Post Office (historical)—building TN-4
**Fox Springs**—pop pl MO-7
Fox Springs—spring KY-4
Fox Springs Ch of Christ (historical)—church TN-4
Fox Spring School TN-4
**Fox Springs (historical)**—pop pl TN-4
Fox Springs Ranch—locale NV-8
Fox Springs Sch (historical)—school TN-4
Fox Square—park PA-2
Fox Squirrel Branch—stream NC-3
Fox Squirrel Point—summit AL-4
Fox Squirrel Ridge—ridge SC-3
**Foxs Subdivision**—pop pl UT-8
Fox Station IN-6
**Fox Station**—pop pl MI-6
Fox Swamp VA-3
Fox Swamp Canal—canal SC-3
Fox Tail Bay—bay WI-6
Fox Tail Camp NV-8
Foxtail Camp—locale NV-8
Foxtail Canyon UT-8
Foxtail Canyon—valley NV-8
Foxtail Creek—stream NM-5
Foxtail Flats—flat NM-5
Foxtail Hollow—valley VA-3
Foxtail Lake—reservoir NV-8
Fox Tail Point—cape WI-6
Foxtail Ridge UT-8
Fox Tail Snow Play and Picnic Area—locale NV-8
Fox Tank—reservoir (2) AZ-5
Fox Tank—reservoir NM-5
Fox Tank (Water)—other NM-5
Fox Tech HS—school TX-5
Fox Terminal—locale IL-6
Fox Theater—hist pl MO-7
Fox Theater—hist pl WI-6
Fox Theater Bldg—hist pl MI-6
Fox Theater Ch—church MO-7
Fox Theatre—hist pl GA-3
Fox Theatre—hist pl NE-7
Fox Theatre Hist Dist—hist pl GA-3
Fox Thicket Creek—stream TN-4
**Foxton**—pop pl CO-8
**Foxton**—pop pl PA-2
Foxton Lake—reservoir PA-2
Foxton Lake Dam—dam PA-2
Foxton State Public Shooting Area—park SD-7
**Foxton Township**—pop pl SD-7
Foxtown FL-3
Foxtown KS-7
Foxtown—locale KY-4
Foxtown—locale MD-2
Foxtown—locale OH-6
Foxtown—locale SC-3
**Foxtown**—pop pl CT-1
**Fox Town**—pop pl FL-3
**Fox Town**—pop pl KS-7
**Foxtown**—pop pl PA-2
Foxtown Cem—cemetery CT-1
Foxtown Gap—gap PA-2
Fox Townhall—building IA-7
**Foxtown Hill**—pop pl PA-2
Foxtown Hill—summit PA-2
Foxtown Mtn—summit NC-3
Foxtown Ridge—ridge NC-3
Fox Township—civil MO-7
Fox Township—fmr MCD IA-7
**Fox (Township of)**—pop pl (2) IL-6
**Fox (Township of)**—pop pl OH-6
**Fox (Township of)**—pop pl (2) PA-2
Foxtown Union Sch—school KS-7
Fox Trail—trail PA-2
**Fox Trailer Village**—pop pl MD-2
Fox Trail Lake—reservoir NJ-2
Fox Trail Lake Dam—dam NJ-2
Fox Trap Branch—stream TN-4
Foxtrap Ch—church AL-4
Foxtrap Ch of Christ AL-4
Foxtrap Creek—stream AL-4
**Foxtrap (historical)**—pop pl MS-4
Foxtrap Post Office (historical)—building MS-4
Foxtrap Prairie—area MS-4
Foxtree Run—stream WV-2
Foxtrott MS-4
**Foxvale**—pop pl MA-1
Foxvale Park—park VA-3
Fox Valley—locale OR-9
**Fox Valley**—pop pl OR-9
Fox Valley—valley AR-4
Fox Valley—valley OH-6
Fox Valley—valley OR-9
Fox Valley—valley WI-6
Fox Valley Cem—cemetery (2) OR-9
Fox Valley Country Club—other IL-6
Fox Valley East IL-6
Fox Valley Golf Course—other WI-6
**Fox Village**—pop pl CT-1
Foxville—locale SC-3
**Foxville**—pop pl MD-2
**Foxville**—pop pl VT-1
Foxville Lookout Tower—locale MD-2
Foxville Sch—school MD-2
Fox Vly NY-2
Fox Wash—stream AZ-5
Fox-Watson Theater Bldg—hist pl KS-7
Fox Well—well (2) NM-5
Fox Well—well SD-7
Foxwell Brook—stream ME-1
**Foxwells**—pop pl VA-3
**Foxwells (Westland)**—pop pl VA-3
Fox-Wheatley Cemetery TN-4
Fox Windmill—locale CO-8
Fox Windmill—locale NM-5
Fox Windmill—locale TX-5
Fox-Wisconsin Portage Site—hist pl WI-6
**Foxwood Estates (subdivision)**—pop pl TN-4
Foxwood Golf Course—locale NC-3
**Foxwood Heights (subdivision)**—pop pl TN-4
**Foxwood Park**—pop pl PA-2
**Fox Woods (subdivision)**—pop pl DE-2
**Foxwood (subdivision)**—pop pl AL-4
**Foxwood (subdivision)**—pop pl NC-3
**Foxwood Trace (subdivision)**—pop pl AL-4
**Foxworth**—pop pl MS-4
Foxworth Cem—cemetery MS-4
Foxworth Elementary School MS-4
Foxworth First Baptist Ch—church MS-4
Foxworth Mill Creek—stream FL-3
**Foxworth (West Columbia)**—pop pl MS-4
Foxworthy Draw—valley WY-8
Foxworthy School (Abandoned)—locale IA-7
**Foxxborough (subdivision)**—pop pl TN-4
Foxx Sch—school IL-6
Foxy Grandpa Tank—reservoir NM-5
Foxy Hollow—valley PA-2
**Foy**—pop pl WA-9
Foy—uninc pl CA-9
Foy Bench—bench UT-8
Foy Cem—cemetery KY-4
Foy Cem—cemetery MN-6
Foy Corners Sch (abandoned)—school PA-2
Foy Dam UT-8
Foye Creek—stream WA-9
Foye Rental Houses—hist pl MT-8
**Foyes Corner**—pop pl NH-1
**Foyil**—pop pl OK-5
Foy Ingram Dam—dam AL-4
Foy Ingram Pond—reservoir AL-4
Foy Lake—lake LA-4
Foy Lake—lake MT-8
Foy Lake Sch—school MT-8
Foyle Creek—stream TX-5
Foyll OK-5
Foy Reservoir UT-8
Foy Run—stream PA-2
**Foys**—pop pl NC-3
Foys Bend—bend MT-8
Foys Ch—church NC-3
Foys Hill—summit MD-2
Foys Landing—locale NC-3
Foys Pond—reservoir AL-4
Foys Pond Dam—dam AL-4
Foys Store (historical)—locale TN-4
Foyster Creek—stream SC-3
Foy Tabernacle—church MN-6
Fozzard Creek—gut FL-3
F P Fatio Grant—civil FL-3
F Phillips Ranch—locale NE-7
F P Murphy Ranch—locale CO-8
F P Number One Dam—dam OR-9
F P Number One Rsvr—reservoir OR-9
F Pool—reservoir MI-6
F Portal—mine PA-2
FPP Cooling Pond TX-5
F-P Rsvr—reservoir OR-9
F P Sanchez Grant—civil (2) FL-3
FP Tank No 4—reservoir NM-5
F Quarter Circle Ranch—locale CO-8
Fra FM-9
Fracas Canyon—valley AZ-5
Fracas Canyon Tank—reservoir AZ-5
Fracas Lake—lake AZ-5
Frackles Canyon UT-8
**Frackville**—pop pl PA-2
Frackville Area Elem Sch—school PA-2
Frackville Borough—civil PA-2
Frackville City PA-2
**Frackville Junction**—pop pl PA-2
Fra Cristobal Mtn—summit NM-5
Fra Cristobal Range—range NM-5
Fraction Extension—mine NV-8
Fraction Mine—mine CO-8
Fraction Point Sch (abandoned)—school MO-7
Fraction Run—stream IL-6
**Fractionville**—pop pl VA-3
Fracture Creek—stream AK-9
Fracture Creek—stream OR-9
Fradd Cem—cemetery OH-6
Fradean Oil Field—oilfield TX-5
Frady Branch—stream GA-3
Frady Cem—cemetery GA-3
Frady Cove Dam—dam NC-3
Frady Cove Lake—reservoir NC-3
Frady Creek—stream GA-3
Frady Creek—stream NC-3
Frady Gulf—valley GA-3
Frady Lake—reservoir NC-3
Frady Mtn—summit GA-3

Frady Mtn—*summit* NC-3
Fradys Rough—*summit* NC-3
Fraesfield Mtn—*summit* AZ-5
Fragaria—*locale* WA-9
Fragaria Creek—*stream* WA-9
*Fragile* MP-9
*Fragita Mtn* AZ-5
*Fragita Peak* AZ-5
*Fragley Junior High School* IN-6
Fragoso Canyon—*valley* NM-5
Fragoso Ridge—*ridge* NM-5
Fragrance Lake—*lake* WA-9
Fragrant—*locale* KY-4
**Fragrant Hill Township**—*pop pl* KS-7
Fragrant Island—*island* AK-9
*Fraguita Mtn* AZ-5
Fraguita Peak—*summit* AZ-5
Fraguita Spring—*spring* AZ-5
Fraguita Wash—*stream* AZ-5
Fraguita Wash—*valley* AZ-5
*Frahling Falls* MI-6
Frahm JHS—*school* ID-8
Frahm Lake—*lake* WI-6
Frahm Spring—*spring* ID-8
Fraigeson Creek—*stream* LA-4
Frailan, Kannat As—*stream* MH-9
*Frailan Ravine* MH-9
Fraile (Barrio)—*fmr MCD* PR-3
Frailes (Barrio)—*fmr MCD* (2) PR-3
Frailey Mountain Truck Trail—*trail* WA-9
Frailey Mtn—*summit* WA-9
Frailey Point—*summit* OR-9
Frailey Point Trail—*trail* OR-9
**Frailey (Township of)**—*pop pl* PA-2
**Frailie**—*pop pl* MO-7
Frailie Sch (abandoned)—*school* MO-7
Frailing, Henry H., House—*hist pl* MI-6
Frail Knob—*summit* WV-2
Frailon, Okso—*summit* MH-9
Frain Lake—*lake* MI-6
**Frain Lake**—*pop pl* MI-6
Fraiser Cem—*cemetery* GA-3
Fraizer, Joel, House—*hist pl* KY-4
Fraizer Farms—*locale* CO-8
**Fraizer Forest (subdivision)**—*pop pl* NC-3
Fraker Cem—*cemetery* MO-7
Fraker Creek—*stream* WA-9
Fraker Mtn—*summit* AR-4
Fraker Mtn—*summit* NY-2
Fraker Mtn—*summit* WY-8
Fraker Pass—*gap* WY-8
Frakes—*locale* KY-4
Frakes Cabin—*locale* OR-9
Frakes Cem—*cemetery* (2) IN-6
Frakes Cem—*cemetery* MO-7
Fraland Beach—*beach* DE-2
Fraland Cove—*bay* DE-2
Fraleighs—*locale* NY-2
Fraley Branch—*stream* (3) KY-4
Fraley Branch—*stream* VA-3
Fraley Cem—*cemetery* IL-6
Fraley Cem—*cemetery* MO-7
Fraley Cem—*cemetery* (2) VA-3
Fraley Chapel—*church* KY-4
Fraley Chapel—*church* MS-4
Fraley Chapel Branch—*stream* KY-4
Fraley Cove—*valley* TN-4
Fraley Creek—*stream* KY-4
Fraley Flat—*flat* KY-4
Fraley Fork—*stream* WV-2
Fraley Gap—*gap* TN-4
Fraley Gap Mine (underground)—*mine* TN-4
Fraley Hollow—*valley* MO-7
Fraley Hollow—*valley* VA-3
Fraley Park—*park* OK-5
Fraley Park—*park* TX-5
Fraley Pond—*lake* KY-4
Fraley Ridge—*ridge* KY-4
*Fraleys Chapel Ch of Christ* MS-4
*Fraleys Mill Hollow* TN-4
Fraleytown—*locale* VA-3
Fralick Cem—*cemetery* KY-4
Fralick Hollow—*valley* KY-4
Fralick South Oil Field—*oilfield* KS-7
Fralick West Oil Field—*oilfield* KS-7
Fralin Bridge—*bridge* VA-3
Fralise Pond—*lake* TX-5
Frame—*locale* TX-5
**Frame**—*pop pl* WV-2
Frame, Andrew, House—*hist pl* WI-6
Frame Cabin Run—*stream* PA-2
Frame Cem—*cemetery* IN-6
Frame Cem—*cemetery* (2) OH-6
Frame Cem—*cemetery* TN-4
Frame Cem—*cemetery* (2) WV-2
Frame Ch—*church* PA-2
Frame Chapel—*church* WV-2
Frame Cottage—*hist pl* NV-8
Frame Creek—*stream* WA-9
*Framed Arch* UT-8
Frame Field—*airport* PA-2
Frame Fork—*stream* WV-2
Frame Knob—*summit* WV-2
Frame Park—*park* WI-6
Frame Point—*cape* NH-1
Frame Ranch—*locale* MT-8
Frame Run—*stream* (2) WV-2
Frames Branch—*stream* KY-4
Frame Sch (abandoned)—*school* PA-2
**Frames Corner**—*pop pl* NJ-2
Frames Cove—*bay* DE-2
Frames Creek—*stream* WI-6
Frames Draft—*valley* VA-3
*Frames Island* TN-4
Frames Landing Campground—*locale* MN-6
Frames Peak—*summit* CA-9
Frames Point—*cape* DE-2
Frames Run—*stream* PA-2
Frame Switch—*locale* TX-5
**Frametown**—*pop pl* WV-2
Fram Field—*airport* AZ-5
Framingham—*locale* MA-1
**Framingham**—*pop pl* MA-1
**Framingham Center (RR name Framingham Centre)**—*pop pl* MA-1
**Framingham Center (subdivision)**—*pop pl* MA-1
*Framingham Centre* MA-1
Framingham Centre (RR name for Framingham)—*other* MA-1
Framingham Memorial Sch—*school* MA-1
Framingham North HS—*school* MA-1
Framingham Plaza—*locale* MA-1
*Framingham Pond* MA-1
Framingham RR Station—*hist pl* MA-1
Framingham Rsvr Number One—*reservoir* MA-1
Framingham Rsvr Number Three—*reservoir* MA-1
Framingham Rsvr Number Two—*reservoir* MA-1
Framingham South HS—*school* MA-1
Framingham State Coll—*school* MA-1
**Framingham (Town of)**—*pop pl* MA-1
**Framnas (Township of)**—*pop pl* MN-6
Frampton—*locale* OH-6
Frampton Inlet—*gut* SC-3
Frampton Post Office (historical)—*building* PA-2
*Framptons Inlet* SC-3
Frampton Well—*well* NM-5
**Fram Township**—*pop pl* ND-7
Fran Brook—*stream* ME-1
Francais, Bayou—*gut* LA-4
France—*locale* ID-8
France Brook—*stream* NY-2
France Canyon—*valley* UT-8
France Cem—*cemetery* CO-8
France Cem—*cemetery* IN-6
France Cem—*cemetery* KY-4
France Cem—*cemetery* MO-7
France Cem—*cemetery* (4) TN-4
France Cem—*cemetery* VA-3
France Creek—*stream* VA-3
France Hall—*hist pl* OH-6
*France Hollow* TN-4
France Hotel—*hist pl* IL-6
France Memorial United Presbyterian Church—*hist pl* WY-8
France Mountain Pit—*cave* TN-4
France Mtn—*summit* (2) TN-4
France Park—*park* MO-7
France Park—*park* OH-6
France Post Office (historical)—*building* TN-4
*Frances* KS-7
Frances—*locale* CA-9
**Frances**—*pop pl* IN-6
**Frances**—*pop pl* KY-4
**Frances**—*pop pl* WA-9
Frances, Lake—*lake* CA-9
Frances, Lake—*lake* (3) FL-3
Frances, Lake—*lake* (2) MT-8
Frances, Lake—*lake* NY-2
Frances, Lake—*lake* OR-9
Frances, Lake—*reservoir* AR-4
Frances, Lake—*reservoir* (2) GA-3
Frances, Lake—*reservoir* NC-3
Frances, Lake—*reservoir* OK-5
Frances, Lake—*reservoir* SC-3
Frances Apartment Bldg—*hist pl* OH-6
Frances Bay—*bay* MN-6
Frances Boley Sch—*school* LA-4
*Frances Branch* WV-2
Frances Branch—*stream* KY-4
Frances Branch—*stream* MS-4
Frances Canyon Ruin—*hist pl* NM-5
Frances Canyon Ruin (LA 2135) (Boundary Increase)—*hist pl* NM-5
Frances-Carlton Apartments—*hist pl* FL-3
Frances Cem—*cemetery* TN-4
Frances Cem—*cemetery* TX-5
Frances Chapel—*church* GA-3
Frances Chapel—*church* SC-3
Franceschi Park—*park* CA-9
Frances Creek—*stream* AK-9
Frances Creek—*stream* IN-6
Frances Creek—*stream* NV-8
Frances Creek—*stream* NM-5
Frances Creek—*stream* TX-5
Frances Creek—*stream* WV-2
Frances Creek Sch—*school* WV-2
Frances Ditch—*canal* WY-8
Frances E Willard Sch—*school* WI-6
*Frances Ferry* AL-4
Frances Gut—*gut* MD-2
Frances Heights—*bench* MT-8
**Frances Heights**—*pop pl* AL-4
Frances Heights Sch—*school* MT-8
Frances Hill—*summit* MA-1
Frances House—*hist pl* AK-9
Frances K Caine Dam—*dam* AL-4
Frances K Caine Lake—*reservoir* AL-4
*Frances Lake* OR-9
Frances Lake—*lake* GA-3
Frances Lake—*lake* TX-5
Frances Lake—*reservoir* TN-4
Frances Lake Ch—*church* GA-3
Frances Lake Dam—*dam* TN-4
Frances Mesa—*summit* NM-5
Frances Packing House—*hist pl* CA-9
Frances Park—*park* MI-6
**Frances Place**—*pop pl* LA-4
Frances Pond—*lake* NY-2
Frances Sch (abandoned)—*school* PA-2
Frances Slocum Dam—*dam* PA-2
Frances Slocum Elem Sch—*school* IN-6
Frances Slocum Lake—*reservoir* PA-2
Frances Slocum State For—*forest* IN-6
Frances Slocum State Park—*park* PA-2
Frances Slocum State Rec Area—*park* IN-6
Frances S Tucker Elem Sch—*school* FL-3
**Francestown**—*pop pl* NH-1
**Francestown (Town of)**—*pop pl* NH-1
France Street Dam—*dam* MA-1
*France Street Reservoir* MA-1
**Francesville**—*pop pl* IN-6
Frances Wakeland Elem Sch—*school* FL-3
France Swamp—*stream* VA-3
Frances Willard Elem Sch—*school* KS-7
Frances W Parker Elem Sch—*school* IN-6
Franceville Mine—*mine* CO-8
*Francham Mountain* MT-8
Francham Mtn—*summit* MT-8
Franchian, Lake—*lake* WI-6
Franchies Ch—*church* AL-4
Franchini Creek—*stream* CA-9
Franch Lake—*lake* WI-6
Franchot Field—*park* NY-2
Franch Tableland Cem—*cemetery* NE-7
Francie Creek—*stream* AK-9
*Francie Lake* UT-8
*Francis* AR-4
Francis—*locale* AL-4
Francis—*locale* IL-6
Francis—*locale* MT-8
Francis—*locale* TX-5
**Francis**—*pop pl* AR-4
**Francis**—*pop pl* FL-3
**Francis**—*pop pl* MS-4
**Francis**—*pop pl* MO-7
**Francis**—*pop pl* OK-5
**Francis**—*pop pl* PA-2
**Francis**—*pop pl* UT-8
**Francis**—*pop pl* WV-2
Francis—*uninc pl* WV-2
Francis, Cape—*cape* FL-3
Francis, D. M., House—*hist pl* AZ-5
Francis, Dr. J. C., Office—*hist pl* AL-4
Francis, Dr. Tappan Eustis, House—*hist pl* MA-1
Francis, Frederick, Woodland Palace—*hist pl* IL-6
Francis, James H., House—*hist pl* CA-9
FRANCIS, JOSEPH, IRON SURF BOAT—*hist pl* OH-6
Francis, Lake—*lake* (5) FL-3
Francis, Lake—*lake* (3) MN-6
Francis, Lake—*lake* NY-2
Francis, Lake—*lake* ND-7
Francis, Lake—*lake* OR-9
Francis, Lake—*lake* SD-7
Francis, Lake—*reservoir* CA-9
Francis, Lake—*reservoir* NH-1
Francis, Lake—*reservoir* PA-2
Francis, Lake—*reservoir* SC-3
Francis, Mount—*summit* (2) AK-9
Francis, Mount—*summit* AZ-5
Francis, Point—*cape* ME-1
Francis, Point—*cape* WA-9
Francis Anchorage—*bay* AK-9
Francis Asbury Ch—*church* VA-3
Francis Asbury Statue—*park* DC-2
Francis Ashbury Ch—*church* NC-3
Francis Bagley Grant—*civil* FL-3
Francis Barbee Grant—*civil* FL-3
Francis Bay—*bay* VI-3
Francis Beach—*beach* CA-9
Francis Bellamy Elem Sch—*school* IN-6
Francis Bend—*bend* AR-4
Francis Branch—*stream* AL-4
Francis Branch—*stream* (2) KY-4
Francis Branch—*stream* PA-2
Francis Brothers Ranch—*locale* MT-8
Francis Cabin—*locale* CA-9
Francis Cabin—*locale* NV-8
*Francis Cahoons Pond* MA-1
Franciscan Convent—*church* NJ-2
Franciscan Convent—*school* IL-6
Franciscan Creek—*stream* CA-9
Franciscan Fathers Novitiate—*church* MD-2
Franciscan Lake—*lake* NM-5
Franciscan Monastery—*church* CT-1
Franciscan Monastery—*church* DC-2
Franciscan Monastery—*church* WI-6
Franciscan Park—*uninc pl* CA-9
Franciscan Retreat Center—*church* MN-6
Franciscan Windmill—*locale* NM-5
Francis Canyon—*valley* (2) UT-8
Francis Canyon—*valley* WA-9
Francis Case, Lake—*reservoir* SD-7
*Francis Case Memorial Bridge* DC-2
Francis Cave—*cave* AL-4
Francis Cem—*cemetery* AL-4
Francis Cem—*cemetery* IL-6
Francis Cem—*cemetery* IN-6
Francis Cem—*cemetery* (2) KY-4
Francis Cem—*cemetery* MA-1
Francis Cem—*cemetery* MS-4
Francis Cem—*cemetery* (2) MO-7
Francis Cem—*cemetery* NC-3
Francis Cem—*cemetery* OK-5
Francis Cem—*cemetery* PA-2
Francis Cem—*cemetery* (3) TN-4
Francis Cem—*cemetery* UT-8
Francis Chaffee Dam Number 1—*dam* SD-7
Francis Chapel (historical)—*church* MS-4
Francisco—*locale* AL-4
**Francisco**—*pop pl* IN-6
**Francisco**—*pop pl* MI-6
**Francisco**—*pop pl* NC-3
Francisco, Mount—*summit* NY-2
Francisco, Peter, House—*hist pl* VA-3
Francisco Baldor Sch—*school* (2) FL-3
Francisco Barrios Grant—*civil* FL-3
Francisco Cem—*cemetery* IA-7
Francisco Cem—*cemetery* (2) TN-4
Francisco Cem—*cemetery* VA-3
Francisco Collin Grant—*civil* FL-3
Francisco Cordova Homestead (Ruins)—*locale* NM-5
Francisco Creek—*stream* AK-9
Francisco Elem Sch—*school* IN-6
Francisco Elem Sch—*school* NC-3
Francisco Elias Esquer Park—*park* AZ-5
Francisco Grande—*park* AZ-5
Francisco JHS—*school* CA-9
Francisco Lake—*reservoir* AZ-5
Francisco (Magisterial District)—*fmr MCD* VA-3
Francisco Montes Vigil—*civil* NM-5
Francisco Park—*park* NJ-2
Francisco Plaza—*hist pl* CO-8
Francisco Rascon Place—*locale* NM-5
**Francis Corners**—*pop pl* NY-2
Francisco Sch—*school* MI-6
Francisco Sepulveda JHS—*school* CA-9
Francis Cove—*bay* AK-9
Francis Cove—*valley* NC-3
Francis Cove Ch—*church* NC-3
Francisco Vidall Grant—*civil* FL-3
Francis Cow Camp—*locale* CA-9
Francisco Well—*well* NM-5
Francis Crater—*crater* AZ-5
*Francis Creek* WY-8
**Francis Creek**—*pop pl* WI-6
Francis Creek—*stream* (3) AK-9
Francis Creek—*stream* AZ-5
Francis Creek—*stream* AR-4
Francis Creek—*stream* CA-9
Francis Creek—*stream* CO-8
Francis Creek—*stream* ID-8
Francis Creek—*stream* IL-6
Francis Creek—*stream* LA-4
Francis Creek—*stream* MT-8
Francis Creek—*stream* (3) OR-9
Francis Creek—*stream* UT-8
Francis Creek—*stream* WI-6
Francis Creek Camp—*locale* AZ-5
Francis Creek Natl Cem—*cemetery* WI-6
Francis Creek Oil Field—*oilfield* MS-4
Francis Creek Shelter—*locale* WA-9
Francis Ditch—*canal* WY-8
Francis Drain—*canal* (2) MI-6
Francis D Raub MS—*school* PA-2
Francis Draw—*valley* WY-8
Francis E Walter Dam—*dam* PA-2
Francis E Walter Rsvr—*reservoir* PA-2
Francis E. Warren AFB—*military* WY-8
Francis E Warren Air Force Base—*other* WY-8
*Francis E Willard Public and Boarding School* AL-4
Francis Family Cem—*cemetery* MS-4
Francis Farm Petroglyphs Site (36FA35)—*hist pl* PA-2
Francis Ferry—*locale* AL-4
Francis Flat—*flat* CA-9
*Francis Folly* MA-1
Francis Galloway Lake Dam—*dam* MS-4
*Francis Gate* MA-1
Francis Gate—*dam* MA-1
Francis Godfroy Cem—*cemetery* IN-6
Francis Goodwin Grant—*civil* FL-3
**Francis Grove**—*pop pl* MI-6
*Francis Hill* MA-1
Francis Hill—*summit* NY-2
Francis (historical)—*locale* KS-7
Francis Hollow—*valley* MO-7
Francis Hollow—*valley* TN-4
Francis Howell HS—*school* MO-7
Francis Howell JHS—*school* MO-7
Francis HS—*school* CA-9
Francis H Sheckler Elem Sch—*school* PA-2
Francis Island—*island* (2) AK-9
Francis Island—*island* MN-6
Francis JHS—*school* DC-2
Francis Joseph Reitz HS—*school* IN-6
Francis Judkins Sch—*school* CA-9
Francis Kay Mine—*mine* NM-5
Francis-King-Lucas Cem—*cemetery* AL-4
Francis Lake—*lake* (2) CA-9
Francis Lake—*lake* FL-3
Francis Lake—*lake* MI-6
Francis Lake—*lake* MN-6
Francis Lake—*lake* MO-7
Francis Lake—*lake* NJ-2
Francis Lake—*lake* NY-2
Francis Lake—*lake* (2) OR-9
Francis Lake—*lake* UT-8
Francis Lake—*lake* (2) WA-9
Francis Lake—*lake* WY-8
Francis Lake Dam—*dam* MS-4
Francis Lewis HS—*school* NY-2
Francis Lewis Park—*park* NY-2
Francis Lowery Lake Dam—*dam* MS-4
Francis Marin Grant—*civil* FL-3
Francis Marion Bridge—*bridge* SC-3
**Francis Marion College**—*pop pl* SC-3
Francis Marion HS—*school* AL-4
Francis Martin Bayou—*gut* LA-4
*Francis McKee Draw* UT-8
Francis Mill—*locale* AL-4
Francis Mill—*locale* NC-3
Francis Mill Creek—*stream* VA-3
**Francis Mills**—*pop pl* NJ-2
Francis Mine—*locale* PA-2
Francis Mine—*mine* CA-9
Francis Mine—*mine* MI-6
*Francis Mountain* OR-9
Francis M Price Elem Sch—*school* IN-6
Franciso Windmill—*locale* TX-5
Francis Park—*park* IL-6
Francis Park—*park* MO-7
Francis Peak—*summit* UT-8
Francis Peak Heliport—*airport* UT-8
Francis Peak Overlook—*locale* UT-8
Francis Peak Pumping Station—*building* UT-8
Francis P Fatio Grant—*civil* FL-3
Francis Pine Chapel—*church* VA-3
**Francis Place**—*pop pl* LA-4
Francis Plantation—*hist pl* GA-3
Francis Point—*cape* MI-6
Francis Point—*cape* TN-4
Francis Polytechnic HS—*school* CA-9
Francis Pond—*lake* NY-2
Francis P Sanchez Grant—*civil* FL-3
Francis Quadrangle Hist Dist—*hist pl* MO-7
Francis Radar Station—*tower* UT-8
Francis Ranch—*locale* (2) MT-8
Francis Richard Grant—*civil* (4) FL-3
Francis R Sanchez Grant—*civil* (2) FL-3
*Francis Run* PA-2
Francis Sch—*school* IA-7
Francis Sch—*school* MT-8
Francis Sch—*school* TX-5
Francis Sch—*school* VA-3
Francis Scott Key Annex—*building* CA-9
Francis Scott Key Elem Sch—*school* IN-6
Francis Scott Key JHS—*school* MD-2
Francis Scott Key Sch—*school* CA-9
*Francis Slocum State Forest* IN-6
Francis Spring—*spring* CA-9
Francis Spring—*spring* TN-4
*Francis Springs* AL-4
Francis Spring Sch (historical)—*school* TN-4
Francis S Stevens Sch—*school* CA-9
Francis S Taylor Wildlife Mngmt Area—*park* FL-3
**Francis Subdivision**—*pop pl* MS-4
Francis Tank—*reservoir* AZ-5
Francis T Nicholls State Coll—*school* LA-4
Francis Township—*civ div* ND-7
**Francis Township**—*pop pl* NE-7
Francis (Township of)—*fmr MCD* AR-4
Francis Vigo Elem Sch—*school* IN-6
*Francisville* IN-6
Francisville—*locale* KY-4
**Francisville (historical)**—*pop pl* OR-9
Francisville Playground—*park* PA-2
Francis Walbert Ditch—*canal* MT-8
Francis Way—*trail* OR-9
Francis Willard Sch—*school* IL-6
Francis William Park—*park* MA-1
Francis Xavier Ch—*church* CO-8
**Francitas**—*pop pl* TX-5
Francitas Cem—*cemetery* TX-5
Francitas Oil Field—*oilfield* TX-5
Francks Camp—*locale* ME-1
**Francktown**—*pop pl* NC-3
Franco American Sch—*school* MA-1
Francoeur, Lake—*lake* MI-6
Francois, Bayou—*stream* LA-4
Francois, Lac —*lake* LA-4
Francois Bay—*bay* LA-4
Francois Bend—*bay* LA-4
Francois Ch—*church* AR-4
Francois Coulee—*stream* LA-4
Francois Creek—*stream* AR-4
Francois Creek—*stream* MT-8
Francois Matthes Point—*cliff* AZ-5
Franconia—*locale* AZ-5
Franconia—*locale* PA-2
**Franconia**—*pop pl* MN-6
**Franconia**—*pop pl* NH-1
**Franconia**—*pop pl* VA-3
Franconia Branch—*stream* NH-1
Franconia Brook Trail—*trail* NH-1
Franconia Cem—*cemetery* AL-4
Franconia Cem—*cemetery* MN-6
Franconia Cem—*cemetery* OH-6
Franconia Coll—*school* NH-1
**Franconia Commons**—*pop pl* VA-3
Franconia Falls—*falls* NH-1
Franconia Golf Course—*locale* MA-1
Franconia Hills—*locale* VA-3
Franconia Hist Dist—*hist pl* MN-6
Franconia (historical)—*locale* AL-4
Franconia Mountain Range—*ridge* NH-1
Franconia Notch—*gap* NH-1
Franconia Notch State Park—*park* NH-1
**Franconia (P.O.)**—*pop pl* VA-3
Franconia Ridge—*ridge* NH-1
Franconia Ridge Trail—*trail* NH-1
Franconia Sch—*school* PA-2
Franconia Sch—*school* VA-3
Franconia Shelter—*locale* NH-1
**Franconia (Town of)**—*pop pl* NH-1
**Franconia (Township of)**—*pop pl* MN-6
**Franconia (Township of)**—*pop pl* PA-2
*Franconiaville* PA-2
Franconia Wash—*stream* AZ-5
Franco Ranch—*locale* AZ-5
Franco Rsvr—*reservoir* NV-8
Francovich House—*hist pl* NV-8
Francs Fork—*stream* WY-8
Francs Peak—*summit* WY-8
Francure (Township of)—*fmr MCD* AR-4
**Francway**—*pop pl* AR-4
Fran Day Spring—*spring* AZ-5
*Frandor* MI-6
Frandsen Ranch—*locale* MT-8
Franer Canal—*canal* ID-8
Franer Gulch—*valley* ID-8
*Franesille* IN-6
Franey Creek—*stream* MN-6
Franey Rock—*summit* WY-8
**Franjo**—*pop pl* FL-3
Franjo Park—*park* FL-3
*Frank* PA-2
Frank—*locale* NC-3
**Frank**—*pop pl* OH-6
**Frank**—*pop pl* (2) PA-2
**Frank**—*pop pl* WV-2
Frank, Charles, House And Store—*hist pl* OH-6
Frank, George W., House—*hist pl* NE-7
Frank, Henry, House—*hist pl* KY-4
Frank, Henry S., Memorial Synagogue—*hist pl* PA-2
Frank, Joseph M., House—*hist pl* AR-4
Frank, Lake—*lake* AK-9
Frank, Lake—*lake* MN-6
Frank, Lake—*reservoir* GA-3
Frank, M. Lloyd, Estate—*hist pl* OR-9
Frank A Burtsfield Elem Sch—*school* IN-6
Frank Alexander Lake—*reservoir* IN-6
Frank Alexander Lake Dam—*dam* IN-6
Frank and Bess Smithe Redwood Grove—*woods* CA-9
Frank Anderson Dam—*dam* SD-7
Frank And Poet Drain—*stream* MI-6
Frank A Wacha Bridge, The—*bridge* FL-3
Frank Baker Creek—*stream* TX-5
Frank Ball Homestead—*locale* CO-8
Frank Barney Spring—*spring* UT-8
Frank Bay—*bay* MN-6
Frank Bay—*bay* VI-3
*Frank B Butler State Park* FL-3
Frank Berry Cem—*cemetery* TN-4
Frank Blair Ranch—*locale* CO-8
Frank Borman JHS—*school* AZ-5
Frank Born Creek—*stream* WA-9
Frank Branch—*stream* SC-3
Frank Branch—*stream* TN-4
Frank Branch—*stream* WV-2
*Frank Brice Creek* OR-9
Frank Britt Pond—*reservoir* AL-4
Frank Britt Pond Dam—*dam* AL-4
Frank Brothers—*hist pl* GA-3
Frank Brown Creek—*stream* ID-8
Frank Butler Civitan Park—*park* AL-4
Frank Camp Ridge—*ridge* TX-5
Frank Canyon—*valley* CA-9
Frank Canyon—*valley* CO-8
Frank Canyon Spring—*spring* CA-9
Frank Cauthen Lake Dam—*dam* MS-4
Frank Cem—*cemetery* GA-3
Frank Cem—*cemetery* KY-4
Frank Cem—*cemetery* PA-2
Frank Center Ford—*locale* TN-4
Frank Ch—*church* GA-3
Frank Ch—*church* NC-3
Frank Church River of No Return Wilderness—*park* ID-8
**Frankclay**—*pop pl* MO-7
Frank C Martin Elem Sch—*school* FL-3
Frank Coe Hollow—*valley* VA-3
Frank Coker Mine—*mine* TN-4
Frank Cothran Dam—*dam* AL-4
Frank Cothran Lake—*reservoir* AL-4
Frank Coulee—*valley* MT-8
*Frank Creek* OR-9
Frank Creek—*stream* AK-9
Frank Creek—*stream* GA-3
Frank Creek—*stream* (2) MT-8
Frank Creek—*stream* NM-5
Frank Creek—*stream* NC-3
Frank Creek—*stream* ND-7
Frank Creek—*stream* (2) OR-9
Frank Creek—*stream* TN-4
Frankcrest Pond—*lake* NY-2
Frank Crockett Ranch HQ—*locale* NM-5
Frank Dam—*dam* TN-4
Frank Davis Dam—*dam* (2) AL-4
Frank Davis Lake—*reservoir* (2) AL-4
Frank Davis Ranch—*locale* AZ-5
Frank Day Hollow—*valley* TN-4
Frank D Comerford Hydro-Electric Plant—*other* VT-1
Frank Denman Dam—*dam* AL-4
Frank Dobson Bridge—*bridge* AL-4
Frank Draw—*valley* (2) WY-8
Franke, C. F., House—*hist pl* IA-7
Frankeberger Cem—*cemetery* IL-6
Frankeburger Cem—*cemetery* IL-6
Frank E Heller Dam—*dam* PA-2
Franke Lake—*reservoir* IN-6
Franke Lake Dam—*dam* IN-6
Frankel City—*locale* TX-5
Frankel Hill—*summit* CT-1
Frankell—*locale* TX-5
Frankel Ridge—*ridge* IA-7
Frank E Masland Natural Area—*area* PA-2
Frankenberg House—*hist pl* AZ-5
Frankenburg Creek—*stream* OH-6
Frankenfield Covered Bridge—*hist pl* PA-2
*Frankenfield Sch* PA-2
Frankenfield Sch—*school* IL-6
**Frankenlust (Township of)**—*pop pl* MI-6
**Frankenmuth**—*pop pl* MI-6
**Frankenmuth (Township of)**—*pop pl* MI-6
**Frankenstein**—*pop pl* MO-7
Frankenstein Cliff—*cliff* NH-1
**Frankentrost**—*pop pl* MI-6
Franke Park—*park* IN-6
Franke Park Elem Sch—*school* IN-6
Frankes Lake—*lake* MI-6
**Frankewing**—*pop pl* TN-4
Frankewing Cem—*cemetery* TN-4
Frankewing Post Office—*building* TN-4
Frankewing Presbyterian Ch—*church* TN-4
Frankewing United Methodist Ch—*church* TN-4
Frank Ferry (historical)—*crossing* TN-4
**Frankford**—*pop pl* DE-2
**Frankford**—*pop pl* MO-7
**Frankford**—*pop pl* PA-2
**Frankford**—*pop pl* WV-2
Frankford Airp—*airport* PA-2
Frankford Arsenal—*hist pl* PA-2
Frankford Arsenal—*military* PA-2
Frankford Ave Bridge—*hist pl* PA-2
Frankford Cem—*cemetery* MN-6
Frankford Channel—*channel* NJ-2
Frankford Channel—*channel* PA-2
Frankford Creek—*stream* PA-2
Frankford Elem Sch—*school* DE-2
Frankford Ementary Sch—*school* PA-2
Frankford HS—*school* PA-2
Frankford Junction—*uninc pl* PA-2
Frankford (Magisterial District)—*fmr MCD* WV-2
Frankford Plains Ch—*church* NJ-2
Frankford Sch No 1—*school* KY-4
**Frankford (Township of)**—*pop pl* MN-6
**Frankford (Township of)**—*pop pl* NJ-2
Frankford United Methodist Ch—*church* DE-2
*Frankfort* DE-2
*Frankfort* IN-6
*Frankfort* NE-7
*Frankfort* OR-9
*Frankfort* PA-2
*Frankfort* WV-2
Frankfort—*locale* OK-5
Frankfort—*locale* TN-4
Frankfort—*locale* WA-9
**Frankfort**—*pop pl* AL-4
**Frankfort**—*pop pl* IL-6
**Frankfort**—*pop pl* IN-6
**Frankfort**—*pop pl* KS-7
**Frankfort**—*pop pl* KY-4
**Frankfort**—*pop pl* ME-1
**Frankfort**—*pop pl* MI-6
**Frankfort**—*pop pl* NJ-2
**Frankfort**—*pop pl* NY-2
**Frankfort**—*pop pl* (2) OH-6
**Frankfort**—*pop pl* SD-7
Frankfort Bank—*bar* FL-3
Frankfort Barracks District—*hist pl* KY-4
Frankfort (CCD)—*cens area* KY-4
Frankfort Cem—*cemetery* AL-4
Frankfort Cem—*cemetery* IL-6
Frankfort Cem—*cemetery* IA-7
Frankfort Cem—*cemetery* KS-7
Frankfort Cem—*cemetery* NE-7
Frankfort Cem—*cemetery* WV-2
Frankfort Cemetery and Chapel—*hist pl* KY-4
**Frankfort Center**—*pop pl* NY-2
Frankfort Center Sch—*school* NY-2
Frankfort Commercial Hist Dist—*hist pl* KY-4
Frankfort Community Park—*locale* IL-6
Frankfort Country Club—*other* KY-4
Frankfort Ditch—*canal* OH-6
Frankfort Gorge—*valley* NY-2
*Frankfort Heights* IL-6
Frankfort Hill—*locale* NY-2
Frankfort Hill Cem—*cemetery* NY-2
**Frankfort (historical)**—*pop pl* IA-7
Frankfort Island—*island* ME-1
Frankfort JHS—*school* AL-4
Frankfort JHS—*school* IN-6
Frankfort (Magisterial District)—*fmr MCD* WV-2
Frankfort Municipal Airp—*airport* IN-6
Frankfort Oil Field—*oilfield* OK-5
Frankfort Post Office (historical)—*building* TN-4
Frankfort Road Ch—*church* AL-4
Frankfort Sch—*hist pl* KS-7
Frankfort Sch—*school* MI-6
Frankfort Sch—*school* NE-7
Frankfort Sch—*school* TN-4
Frankfort School Spring—*spring* AL-4
Frankfort Senior HS—*school* IN-6
**Frankfort Springs**—*pop pl* PA-2

Frankfort Springs—spring PA-2
Frankfort Springs Borough—civil PA-2
Frankfort Springs Grange—locale PA-2
Frankfort Springs (historical)—locale PA-2
Frankfort State Hosp—hospital KY-4
Frankfort State Sch—school KY-4
**Frankfort (Town of)**—pop pl ME-1
**Frankfort (Town of)**—pop pl NY-2
**Frankfort (Town of)**—pop pl (2) WI-6
Frankfort Township—fmr MCD IA-7
**Frankfort Township**—pop pl NE-7
**Frankfort Township**—pop pl SD-7
Frankfort Township (historical)—civil SD-7
**Frankfort (Township of)**—pop pl (2) IL-6
**Frankfort (Township of)**—pop pl MN-6
Frankfort Works Mound—hist pl OH-6
Frank Free Canyon—valley NV-8
Frank Fulton Canyon OR-9
Frank Fulton Canyon valley OR 9
Frank Gap—gap NC-3
Frank Garrett Hollow—valley IN-6
Frank G Clement Bridge—bridge TN-4
Frank Gebracht Dam—dam SD-7
Frank Geroge Hollow—valley AR-4
Frank Gilbert Coulee—valley MT-8
Frank Gotch State Park—park IA-7
Frank Grubb Ridge—ridge IN-6
Frank Hall Creek—stream ID-8
Frank Hall Park—park MN-6
Frank Harris Bend—bend TX-5
Frank Harris Point—summit CA-9
Frank Hartman Lake Dam—dam MS-4
Frankhauser Lake—lake ND-7
Frank Hayes Dam—dam SD-7
Frank Helen Canyon—valley NV-8
Frank Henry Creek—stream OK-5
Frank Hill Cem—cemetery MN-6
Frank Hollow—valley KY-4
Frank Hollow—valley UT-8
Frank Horan Slough—gut CA-9
Frank House—hist pl MO-7
Frank H Trotter Sch—school TN-4
Frank Hughes Sch—school TN-4
Frank H Wheeler Elem Sch—school IN-6
Frankie, Lake—reservoir AL-4
Frankie and Johnny Spring—spring OR-9
Frankie Creek—stream AK-9
Frankie Hollow—valley UT-8
Frankie Mine—mine CO-8
Frankie Point—cape MD-2
Frankin County Courthouse—building MS-4
**Frank (Industry)**—pop pl PA-2
Frankin Elem Sch—school MS-4
Frankin Sch—school ID-8
Frankirk Oil Field—oilfield TX-5
Frank Isaac Spring—spring AZ-5
Frankish Bldg—hist pl CA-9
Frankish Canyon—valley CA-9
Frankish Peak—summit CA-9
Frank Island—island MN-6
Frank Island—island WY-8
Frank Jones Brook—stream NY-2
Frank Jones Ranch—locale NM-5
Frank Junkin Lake Dam—dam MS-4
Frank Key—island FL-3
Frank Lake—lake MI-6
Frank Lake—lake MN-6
Frank Lake—lake MT-8
Frank Lake—lake TX-5
Frank Lake—lake WI-6
Frank Lake—reservoir TN-4
Frank Lake Ch—church MN-6
Frankland Cem—cemetery TX-5
Frankland Pass—gap TX-5
Frankland Point—cape TX-5
Frank Lapere Creek—stream AR-4
Frank Lapere Creek—stream LA-4
Frank Lawler Private Airp—airport ND-7
Frank Ledge—bar CT-1
Franklee Correctional Youth
Center—building AL-4
Frank Lee Youth Center AL-4
Franklin AL-4
Franklin ID-8
Franklin IN-6
Franklin IA-7
Franklin MI-6
Franklin MS-4
Franklin NJ-2
Franklin OH-6
Franklin PA-2
Franklin SD-7
Franklin TX-5
Franklin—fmr MCD NE-7
Franklin—locale AK-9
Franklin—locale CT-1
Franklin—locale FL-3
Franklin—locale (2) IA-7
Franklin—locale MS-4
Franklin—locale MT-8
Franklin—locale NV-8
Franklin—locale (3) NJ-2
Franklin—locale OK-5
Franklin—locale PA-2
Franklin—locale SD-7
Franklin—locale WV-2
**Franklin**—pop pl (2) AL-4
**Franklin**—pop pl AZ-5
**Franklin**—pop pl AR-4
**Franklin**—pop pl (3) CA-9
**Franklin**—pop pl CT-1
**Franklin**—pop pl GA-3
**Franklin**—pop pl ID-8
**Franklin**—pop pl IL-6
**Franklin**—pop pl (2) IN-6
**Franklin**—pop pl IA-7
**Franklin**—pop pl KS-7
**Franklin**—pop pl KY-4
**Franklin**—pop pl LA-4
**Franklin**—pop pl ME-1
**Franklin**—pop pl MD-2
**Franklin**—pop pl MA-1
**Franklin**—pop pl MI-6
**Franklin**—pop pl (2) MN-6
**Franklin**—pop pl MS-4
**Franklin**—pop pl MO-7
**Franklin**—pop pl NE-7
**Franklin**—pop pl NH-1
**Franklin**—pop pl NJ-2
**Franklin**—pop pl NY-2
**Franklin**—pop pl (2) NC-3
**Franklin**—pop pl (2) OH-6
**Franklin**—pop pl OR-9
**Franklin**—pop pl (3) PA-2
**Franklin**—pop pl TN-4
**Franklin**—pop pl (2) TX-5
**Franklin**—pop pl VT-1
**Franklin**—pop pl (2) WV-2
**Franklin**—pop pl (3) WI-6
Franklin—uninc pl MD-2
Franklin, Benjamin, Sch—hist pl PA-2
Franklin, Bernard, House—hist pl NC-3
Franklin, Lake—lake FL-3
Franklin, Lake—lake MN-6
Franklin, Lake—reservoir GA-3
Franklin, Lake—reservoir TX-5
Franklin, Lawson D., House—hist pl TN-4
Franklin, Mount—summit (2) MI-6
Franklin, Mount—summit NH-1
Franklin, Mount summit TX 5
Franklin, Thomas H., House—hist pl TX-5
Franklin Acad—school MS-4
Franklin Acad—school NY-2
Franklin Acad—school NC-3
Franklin Academy AL-4
Franklin Acad (historical)—school AL-4
Franklin Acad (historical)—school TN-4
Franklin Acres—uninc pl KY-4
Franklin Airp—airport IN-6
Franklin Airp—airport PA-2
Franklin and Armfield Office—hist pl VA-3
Franklin and Marshall Athletic
Field—park PA-2
Franklin and Marshall Coll—school PA-2
Franklin and Marshall Coll Baker
Campus—school PA-2
Franklin and Marshall Coll North
Campus—school PA-2
Franklin and Sims Ditch IN-6
Franklin Area HS—school PA-2
Franklin Area MS—school PA-2
Franklin Avenue MN-6
Franklin Ave Presbyterian Church—hist pl MI-6
Franklin Ave Sch—school CA-9
Franklin Ave Sch—school MA-1
Franklin Ave Sch—school NY-2
Franklin Ave Station—locale NJ-2
Franklin Basin—basin ID-8
Franklin Battlefield—hist pl TN-4
Franklin Bay ME-1
Franklin Bayou—stream AL-4
Franklin Bend—bend AL-4
Franklin Bend—bend TX-5
Franklin Bend Mine (underground)—mine AL-4
Franklin Block—hist pl NH-1
Franklin Bluffs—cliff AK-9
Franklin Blvd Chapel—church NC-3
Franklin Blvd Hist Dist—hist pl MI-6
Franklin Borough—civil PA-2
Franklin Branch—stream IL-6
Franklin Branch—stream (3) KY-4
Franklin Branch—stream (2) LA-4
Franklin Branch—stream (2) MD-2
Franklin Branch—stream MI-6
Franklin Branch—stream NC-3
Franklin Branch—stream OH-6
Franklin Branch—stream SC-3
Franklin Branch—stream TN-4
Franklin Branch—stream (3) TX-5
Franklin Branch—stream VA-3
Franklin Bridge PA-2
Franklin Bridge—bridge NJ-2
Franklin Brook—stream NH-1
Franklin Butte—summit OR-9
Franklin Butte—summit UT-8
Franklin Butte Cem—cemetery OR-9
Franklin Cabin—locale CA-9
Franklin Canal—canal LA-4
Franklin Canal—canal NE-7
Franklin Canal—canal TX-5
Franklin Canyon OR-9
Franklin Canyon—valley (5) CA-9
Franklin Canyon—valley ID-8
Franklin Canyon—valley NM-5
Franklin Canyon—valley UT-8
Franklin Canyon Rsvr—reservoir CA-9
Franklin (CCD)—cens area GA-3
Franklin (CCD)—cens area KY-4
Franklin (CCD)—cens area TN-4
Franklin (CCD)—cens area TX-5
Franklin Cem—cemetery (2) AL-4
Franklin Cem—cemetery GA-3
Franklin Cem—cemetery ID-8
Franklin Cem—cemetery (5) IL-6
Franklin Cem—cemetery (5) IN-6
Franklin Cem—cemetery (4) IA-7
Franklin Cem—cemetery (3) KS-7
Franklin Cem—cemetery (5) KY-4
Franklin Cem—cemetery LA-4
Franklin Cem—cemetery ME-1
Franklin Cem—cemetery MD-2
Franklin Cem—cemetery MN-6
Franklin Cem—cemetery (2) MS-4
Franklin Cem—cemetery (2) MO-7
Franklin Cem—cemetery (3) NE-7
Franklin Cem—cemetery (5) NC-3
Franklin Cem—cemetery (4) OH-6
Franklin Cem—cemetery OK-5
Franklin Cem—cemetery (4) PA-2
Franklin Cem—cemetery SC-3
Franklin Cem—cemetery SD-7
Franklin Cem—cemetery (6) TN-4
Franklin Cem—cemetery (4) TX-5
Franklin Cem—cemetery VT-1
Franklin Cem—cemetery VA-3
Franklin Cem—cemetery WV-2
Franklin Cem—cemetery (2) WI-6
Franklin Center—building PA-2
Franklin Center—locale PA-2
**Franklin Center**—pop pl MA-1
**Franklin Center**—pop pl PA-2
**Franklin Center**—pop pl TX-5
Franklin Center Airp—airport PA-2
Franklin Center Sch—school IN-6
Franklin Center Sch—school MI-6
Franklin Central Christian Ch—church IN-6
Franklin Central HS—school IN-6
Franklin Centre IA-7
Franklin Centre MA-1
Franklin Ch—church (2) GA-3
Franklin Ch—church IN-6
Franklin Ch—church (3) IA-7
Franklin Ch—church MD-2
Franklin Ch—church MI-6
Franklin Ch—church (3) MS-4
Franklin Ch—church NJ-2
Franklin Ch—church (3) OH-6
Franklin Ch—church (3) PA-2
Franklin Ch—church TN-4
Franklin Ch—church VA-3
Franklin Chapel—church OH-6
Franklin Chapel—church TN-4
Franklin Chapel Cem—cemetery MS-4
Franklin Ch (historical)—church TX-5
Franklin Church AL-4
Franklin Church MO-7
Franklin City—civil PA-2
Franklin City—locale VA-3
Franklin City PO MA-1
Franklin Cliffs cliff VA 3
Franklin Cliffs Overlook—locale VA-3
Franklin College IN-6
Franklin College Bldg No. 5—hist pl OH-6
Franklin College Library (Shirk
Hall)—hist pl IN-6
Franklin College-Old Main—hist pl IN-6
Franklin Coll of Indiana—school IN-6
**Franklin Colony (subdivision)**—pop pl NC-3
Franklin Corner—locale NJ-2
**Franklin Corner**—pop pl IL-6
Franklin Corners PA-2
Franklin Corners—locale PA-2
**Franklin Corners**—pop pl IL-6
**Franklin Corners**—pop pl PA-2
Franklin Corners Hist Dist—hist pl NJ-2
Franklin County—civil KS-7
**Franklin County**—pop pl AL-4
**Franklin (County)**—pop pl AR-4
**Franklin County**—pop pl FL-3
**Franklin (County)**—pop pl GA-3
**Franklin (County)**—pop pl IL-6
**Franklin County**—pop pl IN-6
**Franklin (County)**—pop pl KY-4
**Franklin (County)**—pop pl ME-1
**Franklin County**—pop pl MA-1
**Franklin County**—pop pl MS-4
**Franklin County**—pop pl MO-7
**Franklin (County)**—pop pl NY-2
**Franklin County**—pop pl NC-3
**Franklin (County)**—pop pl OH-6
**Franklin County**—pop pl PA-2
**Franklin County**—pop pl TN-4
**Franklin (County)**—pop pl TX-5
**Franklin (County)**—pop pl VT-1
**Franklin (County)**—pop pl VA-3
**Franklin County**—pop pl WA-9
Franklin County Adult Sch—school FL-3
Franklin County Airp—airport NC-3
Franklin County Airp—airport TN-4
Franklin County Baptist Assoc Dam AL-4
Franklin County Country Club—other MO-7
Franklin County Courthouse—building AL-4
Franklin County Courthouse—building TN-4
Franklin County Courthouse—hist pl GA-3
Franklin County Courthouse—hist pl ID-8
Franklin County Courthouse—hist pl IA-7
Franklin County Courthouse—hist pl KS-7
Franklin County Courthouse—hist pl ME-1
Franklin County Courthouse—hist pl MS-4
Franklin County Courthouse—hist pl PA-2
Franklin County Courthouse—hist pl WA-9
Franklin County Courthouse, Southern
District—hist pl AR-4
Franklin County Farm (historical)—locale AL-4
Franklin County Golf And Country
Club—locale TN-4
Franklin County Hosp—hospital MA-1
Franklin County Hosp—hospital TN-4
Franklin County HS—school TN-4
Franklin County Irrigation Canal—canal WA-9
Franklin County Jail—building MA-1
Franklin County Jail—hist pl AR-4
Franklin County Jail—hist pl PA-2
Franklin County Jail—hist pl TN-4
Franklin County Lake Dam—dam MS-4
Franklin County Memorial
Hosp—hospital MS-4
Franklin County Park—park TN-4
Franklin County Seminary—hist pl IN-6
Franklin County Special Education Center PA-2
Franklin County Special Education
Center—school PA-2
Franklin County Vocational Technical
Sch—school PA-2
Franklin Court—building PA-2
Franklin Covenant Ch—church GA-3
Franklin Creek IN-6
Franklin Creek SD-7
Franklin Creek VA-3
Franklin Creek—stream AL-4
Franklin Creek—stream (2) AK-9
Franklin Creek—stream AR-4
Franklin Creek—stream (5) CA-9
Franklin Creek—stream GA-3
Franklin Creek—stream ID-8
Franklin Creek—stream IL-6
Franklin Creek—stream IN-6
Franklin Creek—stream KS-7
Franklin Creek—stream KY-4
Franklin Creek—stream (2) MS-4
Franklin Creek—stream MO-7
Franklin Creek—stream OR-9
Franklin Creek—stream SD-7
Franklin Creek—stream TN-4
Franklin Creek—stream VA-3
Franklin Creek—stream WA-9
Franklin Creek Baptist Church MS-4
Franklin Creek Ch—church MS-4
**Franklin Cross Roads**—pop pl KY-4
**Franklindale**—pop pl PA-2
Franklin Dam NC-3
Franklin Delano Roosevelt HS—school NY-2
**Franklin Depot**—pop pl NY-2
Franklin Division—civil TN-4
Franklin Downtown Commercial
District—hist pl KY-4
Franklin Downtown Commercial District
(Boundary Increase)—hist pl KY-4
Franklin Drain—canal (2) MI-6
Franklin Drain—canal TX-5
Franklin Draw—valley TX-5
Franklin D. Roosevelt—post sta NY-2
Franklin D Roosevelt Canal FL-3
Franklin D Roosevelt Elementary School PA-2
Franklin D Roosevelt House—building DC-2
Franklin D Roosevelt JHS—school (2) CA-9
Franklin D Roosevelt Lake—lake WA-9
Franklin D Roosevelt Lake—reservoir WA-9
Franklin D Roosevelt Memorial—park DC-2
Franklin D Roosevelt Memorial
Bridge—bridge GA-3
Franklin D Roosevelt Sch—school WV-2
Franklin D Roosevelt State Park—park GA-3
Franklin D Roosevelt Veterans
Administration—hospital NY-2
Franklin (Election Precinct)—fmr MCD (2) IL-6
Franklin Elementary School NC-3
Franklin Elem Sch PA-2
Franklin Elem Sch—school (2) IN-6
Franklin Elem Sch school (4) KS 7
Franklin Elem Sch—school (4) PA-2
Franklin Elem Sch—school TN-4
Franklin Elem Sch (abandoned)—school PA-2
Franklin Falls NH-1
Franklin Falls—falls WA-9
Franklin Falls—locale NY-2
Franklin Falls Dam—dam NH-1
Franklin Falls Hist Dist—hist pl NH-1
Franklin Falls Pond—reservoir NY-2
**Franklin Farms**—pop pl PA-2
Franklin Feeder—canal TX-5
Franklin Feed Mill—hist pl WI-6
Franklin Ferry Bridge—bridge AL-4
Franklin Ferry (historical)—locale AL-4
Franklin Ferry (historical)—locale TN-4
Franklin Field—other WI-6
Franklin Field—park CA-9
Franklin Field—park PA-2
Franklin Field (airport)—airport AL-4
Franklin Field (historical)—park TN-4
Franklin Ford—locale AL-4
**Franklin Forest**—pop pl VA-3
**Franklin Forge**—pop pl PA-2
**Franklin Forks**—pop pl PA-2
Franklin Furnace NJ-2
Franklin Furnace—locale PA-2
**Franklin Furnace**—pop pl OH-6
**Franklin Furnace**—pop pl PA-2
Franklin Gap—gap NC-3
**Franklin Gardens**—pop pl AL-4
Franklin General Hosp—hospital NY-2
Franklin Gin (historical)—locale AL-4
Franklin Grange Cem—cemetery OR-9
Franklin Grove—locale IA-7
Franklin Grove—locale NJ-2
**Franklin Grove**—pop pl IL-6
**Franklin Grove**—pop pl NC-3
Franklin Grove Cem—cemetery MO-7
Franklin Grove Ch—church MO-7
Franklin Grove Ch—church VA-3
Franklin Gulch—valley (3) CA-9
Franklin Gulch—valley MT-8
Franklin Gulf—valley NY-2
Franklin Hall Sch (abandoned)—school PA-2
**Franklin Heights**—pop pl VA-3
Franklin Heights—uninc pl KY-4
Franklin Heights Ch—church FL-3
Franklin Heights Ch—church VA-3
Franklin Heights HS—school OH-6
Franklin Heights Sch—school PA-2
**Franklin Hill**—pop pl TN-4
Franklin Hill—summit AR-4
Franklin Hill—summit CA-9
Franklin Hill—summit IL-6
Franklin Hill—summit KY-4
Franklin Hill—summit (2) MD-2
Franklin Hill—summit MA-1
Franklin Hill—summit MT-8
Franklin Hill—summit OR-9
Franklin Hill—summit UT-8
Franklin Hill Cem—cemetery PA-2
Franklin Hill Ch—church PA-2
Franklin Hill Country Club—other MI-6
**Franklin Hills**—pop pl IN-6
Franklin Hill Sch (abandoned)—school (3) PA-2
Franklin Hills Memory Garden—cemetery OH-6
**Franklin Hill (Upsonville)**—pop pl PA-2
Franklin Hist Dist—hist pl LA-4
Franklin Hist Dist—hist pl MI-6
Franklin Hist Dist—hist pl PA-2
Franklin Hist Dist—hist pl TN-4
Franklin Hist Dist—hist pl VA-3
Franklin Hist Dist—hist pl WV-2
Franklin Hist Dist (Boundary
Increase)—hist pl TN-4
Franklin (historical)—locale (2) AL-4
Franklin (historical)—locale KS-7
Franklin (historical P.O.)—locale IA-7
Franklin Hollow RI-1
Franklin Hollow—valley KY-4
Franklin Hollow—valley OH-6
Franklin Hollow—valley (4) TN-4
Franklin Hollow—valley TX-5
Franklin Hollow—valley WV-2
Franklin Home Site Ch—church CA-9
Franklin Hose Company No. 28—hist pl PA-2
Franklin Hosp—hospital IL-6
Franklin Hospital Airp—airport PA-2
Franklin Hotel—hist pl OR-9
Franklin Hotel—hist pl SC-3
Franklin House—hist pl GA-3
Franklin HS IN-6
Franklin HS—school (2) CA-9
Franklin HS—school MD-2
Franklin HS—school MA-1
Franklin HS—school MI-6
Franklin HS—school MS-4
Franklin HS—school NY-2
Franklin HS—school OR-9
Franklin HS—school PA-2
Franklin HS—school TN-4
Franklin HS—school WA-9
**Franklin (ind. city)**—pop pl VA-3
Franklin Institute—hist pl PA-2
Franklin Institute—hospital PA-2
Franklin Institute Research Lab—building PA-2
Franklin Institute Science
Museum—hist pl PA-2
Franklin Island—island ME-1
Franklin Island—island MO-7
Franklin JHS—school (4) CA-9
Franklin JHS—school CT-1
Franklin JHS—school FL-3
Franklin JHS—school ID-8
Franklin JHS—school (4) IL-6
Franklin JHS—school (2) IA-7
Franklin JHS—school ME-1
Franklin JHS—school MI-6
Franklin JHS—school (2) MN-6
Franklin JHS—school NJ-2
Franklin JHS—school (2) OH-6
Franklin JHS—school TN-4
Franklin JHS—school TX-5
Franklin JHS—school WA-9
Franklin JHS—school WV-2
Franklin JHS—school (3) WI-6
Franklin Journal Plant—facility IN-6
Franklin Junction—locale OH-6
Franklin Junction—locale PA-2
Franklin Junction locale VA 3
Franklin Junior High School IN-6
Franklin Junior High School PA-2
Franklin Juniper Swamp—swamp FL-3
**Franklin Knolls**—pop pl MD-2
**Franklin Knolls**—pop pl MI-6
Franklin Labor Camp—locale ID-8
Franklin Lake—lake CA-9
Franklin Lake—lake (2) MN-6
Franklin Lake—lake NV-8
Franklin Lake—lake TX-5
Franklin Lake—lake (2) WI-6
Franklin Lake—reservoir AL-4
Franklin Lake—reservoir CO-8
Franklin Lake—reservoir (2) NJ-2
Franklin Lake—reservoir PA-2
Franklin Lake Campground—hist pl WI-6
Franklin Lake Campground—locale WI-6
Franklin Lake Dam—dam NJ-2
Franklin Lakes—lake CA-9
**Franklin Lakes**—pop pl NJ-2
Franklin Lakes—reservoir MO-7
Franklin Lakes—reservoir TX-5
**Franklin Lakes (Campgan)**—pop pl NJ-2
Franklin Lane HS—school NY-2
Franklin Lateral—canal AZ-5
Franklin Light and Power Company Steam
Generating Station—hist pl GA-3
Franklin Local Sch—school OH-6
Franklin Lookout Tower—locale MS-4
Franklin Lookout Tower—tower MS-4
Franklin (Magisterial District)—fmr MCD VA-3
Franklin (Magisterial District)—fmr MCD WV-2
Franklin Mall—locale PA-2
**Franklin Manor (Franklin Manor on-the-
Bay)**—pop pl MD-2
**Franklin Manor-on-the-Bay**—pop pl MD-2
Franklin-Marion State For—forest TN-4
Franklin Memorial Ch—church MD-2
Franklin Memorial Garden—cemetery SC-3
Franklin Memorial Park—cemetery NJ-2
Franklin Memorial Park—cemetery VA-3
Franklin Memory Gardens—cemetery AL-4
Franklin Mesa—summit CO-8
Franklin Mid Sch—school IL-6
Franklin Mill Creek—stream AL-4
Franklin Mill (historical)—locale TN-4
Franklin Mills Sch—school IA-7
Franklin Mine—mine CA-9
Franklin Mine—mine CO-8
Franklin Mine—mine (2) ID-8
Franklin Mine—mine MT-8
Franklin Mine—mine VA-3
Franklin Mine—mine WY-8
**Franklin Mine**—pop pl MI-6
Franklin Mines—mine KY-4
**Franklin Mines**—pop pl KY-4
Franklin Mine (underground)—mine (2) AL-4
Franklin Mint Heliport—airport PA-2
Franklin Mission—church NC-3
Franklin Mountains—other AK-9
Franklin Mountains—range NM-5
Franklin Mountains—range TX-5
Franklin MS—school TN-4
Franklin Mtn—summit NH-1
Franklin Mtn—summit NY-2
Franklin Mtn—summit (3) NC-3
Franklin Mtn—summit OR-9
Franklin Mtn—summit TX-5
Franklin Nichols Pond Dam—dam MS-4
Franklin Number One Township—civil MO-7
Franklin Number Two Township—civil MO-7
Franklin Oil Field—oilfield LA-4
**Franklin Parish**—pop pl LA-4
Franklin Parish Training Sch—school LA-4
Franklin Park ID-8
Franklin Park—CDP FL-3
Franklin Park—locale (2) KS-7
Franklin Park—park CA-9
Franklin Park—park DC-2
Franklin Park—park (2) IL-6
Franklin Park—park (3) IN-6
Franklin Park—park (2) IA-7
Franklin Park—park MI-6
Franklin Park—park MN-6
Franklin Park—park MT-8
Franklin Park—park (2) OH-6
Franklin Park—park OR-9
Franklin Park—park PA-2
Franklin Park—park TN-4
Franklin Park—park (3) WA-9
Franklin Park—park WI-6
**Franklin Park**—pop pl IL-6
**Franklin Park**—pop pl MD-2
**Franklin Park**—pop pl NJ-2
**Franklin Park**—pop pl NY-2
**Franklin Park**—pop pl PA-2
**Franklin Park**—pop pl VA-3
Franklin Park—post sta OH-6
Franklin Park Conservatory—hist pl OH-6
Franklin Park Golf Course—locale PA-2
Franklin Park (historical P.O.)—locale MA-1
Franklin Park Kindergarten/Day Care
Center—school FL-3
Franklin Park Sch—school FL-3
Franklin Park Sch—school IL-6
Franklin Park Station (historical)—locale MA-1
**Franklin Park (subdivision)**—pop pl MA-1
**Franklin Park (subdivision)**—pop pl NC-3
Franklin Pass—gap CA-9
Franklin Peaks—summit AK-9
**Franklin Pierce College**—pop pl NH-1
Franklin Pierce Lake—reservoir NH-1
**Franklin Pike Corners**—pop pl PA-2
Franklin Pit—mine CA-9
**Franklin Place Addition
(subdivision)**—pop pl UT-8
Franklin Plaza—locale MA-1
Franklin Plaza (Shop Ctr)—locale NC-3
Franklin Plaza Shop Ctr—locale PA-2
Franklin P.O. (historical)—locale AL-4
Franklin Point—cape AR-4
Franklin Point—cape CA-9
Franklin Point—cape MD-2
Franklin Point—cape NY-2
Franklin Point—summit CA-9
Franklin Pond VT-1
Franklin Pond—lake FL-3
Franklin Pond—reservoir AL-4
Franklin Pond—reservoir GA-3
Franklin Pond reservoir NJ 2
Franklin Pond Creek—stream NJ-2
Franklin Pond Dam—dam NJ-2
Franklin Post Office—building PA-2
Franklin Post Office (historical)—building MS-4
Franklin Presbyterian Church—hist pl NC-3
Franklin Printing House—hist pl IA-7
Franklin Print Shop—building PA-2
Franklin Quarry—mine KY-4
Franklin Ranch—locale NM-5
Franklin Ranch—locale (2) TX-5
Franklin Range TX-5
Franklin Regional Med Ctr Airport PA-2
Franklin Regional Senior HS—school PA-2
Franklin Reservoir NC-3
Franklin Reservoirs—reservoir MA-1
Franklin Ridge—ridge CA-9
Franklin River—stream NV-8
**Franklin Road**—pop pl ME-1
Franklin Road Baptist Ch—church IN-6
Franklin Road Ch—church GA-3
Franklin Road Ch—church TN-4
Franklin Roosevelt Sch—school TX-5
Franklin Rsvr—reservoir CO-8
Franklin Run PA-2
Franklin Run—stream IN-6
Franklin Saint Sch—school NC-3
Franklins Bluff—cliff GA-3
Franklin Sch IN-6
Franklin Sch PA-2
Franklin Sch—hist pl DC-2
Franklin Sch—hist pl ID-8
Franklin Sch—hist pl NY-2
Franklin Sch—school (2) AZ-5
Franklin Sch—school (2) AR-4
Franklin Sch—school (25) CA-9
Franklin Sch—school (4) CO-8
Franklin Sch—school (4) CT-1
Franklin Sch—school ID-8
Franklin Sch—school (30) IL-6
Franklin Sch—school (7) IN-6
Franklin Sch—school (10) IA-7
Franklin Sch—school KS-7
Franklin Sch—school (2) KY-4
Franklin Sch—school (3) ME-1
Franklin Sch—school (6) MA-1
Franklin Sch—school (9) MI-6
Franklin Sch—school (5) MN-6
Franklin Sch—school (2) MS-4
Franklin Sch—school (11) MO-7
Franklin Sch—school (3) MT-8
Franklin Sch—school (3) NE-7
Franklin Sch—school (2) NH-1
Franklin Sch—school (14) NJ-2
Franklin Sch—school (9) NY-2
Franklin Sch—school (3) NC-3
Franklin Sch—school ND-7
Franklin Sch—school (15) OH-6
Franklin Sch—school (7) OK-5
Franklin Sch—school OR-9
Franklin Sch—school (14) PA-2
Franklin Sch—school (3) SD-7
Franklin Sch—school TN-4
Franklin Sch—school (6) TX-5
Franklin Sch—school (2) UT-8
Franklin Sch—school VA-3
Franklin Sch—school (5) WA-9
Franklin Sch—school (14) WI-6
Franklin Sch (abandoned)—school (3) MO-7
Franklin Sch (abandoned)—school (6) PA-2
Franklin Sch (historical)—school (2) AL-4
Franklin Sch (historical)—school IA-7
Franklin Sch (historical)—school MO-7
Franklin Sch (historical)—school (2) TN-4
Franklin Sch (historical)—school TX-5
Franklin Sch (Medford)—school MA-1
Franklin Sch (Melrose Highlands)—school MA-1
Franklin Sch No 2—school KY-4
Franklin Sch Number 36—school IN-6
Franklin School (Abandoned)—locale WI-6
Franklin Sch (Wakefield)—school MA-1
Franklin Seminary of Literature and Science
(historical)—school TN-4
Franklins Ferry AL-4
Franklins Grove—cemetery PA-2
Franklin Sherman Sch—school VA-3
Franklins Hole AZ-5
Franklin Shop Ctr—locale AL-4
Franklin Shop Ctr—locale NC-3
Franklin-Simpson HS—school KY-4
Franklins Landing (historical)—locale AL-4
Franklin Slough NV-8
Franklin-Smithfield OR-9
**Franklin (Smithfield)**—pop pl OR-9
Franklin South Side Pump Canal—canal NE-7
Franklins Pond—reservoir GA-3
Franklin Spring AL-4
Franklin Spring—spring CO-8
Franklin Spring—spring TX-5
Franklin Spring—spring WI-6
Franklin Spring Branch—stream TN-4
**Franklin Springs**—pop pl GA-3
**Franklin Springs**—pop pl NY-2
Franklin Square CT-1
Franklin Square—building MS-4
Franklin Square—hist pl IL-6
Franklin Square—hist pl PA-2
Franklin Square—park MD-2
Franklin Square—park MA-1
Franklin Square—park PA-2
**Franklin Square**—pop pl IL-6
**Franklin Square**—pop pl NY-2

Fraziers Landing—locale CA-9
Fraziers Pass—locale PA-2
Fraziers Point SC-3
Fraziers Pond—reservoir NC-3
Fraziers Pond Dam—dam NC-3
Frazier Spring—spring CA-9
Frazier Spring—spring (3) OR-9
Frazier Spring—spring TN-4
Frazier Spring—spring UT-8
Fraziers Well AZ-5
Fraziers Well—well NV-8
Frazier Tank—reservoir AZ-5
**Fraziertown**—pop pl KY-4
**Frazier Township**—pop pl ND-7
Frazier Trailer Park—park UT-8
Frazier Upland—plain OR-9
Frazier Valley—valley CA-9
Frazier Well AZ-5
Frazier Well—well NM-5
**Frazier Wells**—pop pl AZ-5
Frazier Wells—well AZ-5
Frazlers Creek NV-8
Frazor Windmill—locale NM-5
Fr Co-op Ditch—canal MT-8
Freak Mtns—range WY-8
Freak Well Tank—reservoir TX-5
Freaner Butte CA-9
Freaner Peak—summit CA-9
Frear Lake—lake MN-6
**Frear Park**—pop pl NY-2
Frear Park Golf Course—other NY-2
Freasburg NJ-2
Freathy Creek CA-9
Frecanian Ch—church FL-3
Frechette Creek—stream MI-6
Frechette Lake—lake WI-6
Frechette Point—cape MI-6
Freck—locale AR-4
Freckle Branch—stream MO-7
Freckles Canyon—valley UT-8
Freckles Meadow—flat CA-9
Freckles Tank—reservoir AZ-5
Freckleton Park—park ID-8
Freck Lookout Tower—locale AR-4
Fred MP-9
**Fred**—pop pl LA-4
**Fred**—pop pl TX-5
Freda—locale CA-9
**Freda**—pop pl MI-6
**Freda**—pop pl ND-7
Fred A Anderson Elem Sch—school NC-3
Freda Creek—stream MT-8
Freda Creek—stream WY-8
**Fredalba**—pop pl CA-9
Fredalba Creek—stream CA-9
Fredalba Spur—trail CA-9
Fredalba Trail—trail CA-9
Fred Anderson Cem—cemetery MS-4
Fred Anderson Dam—dam MS-4
Fred and George Creek—stream MT-8
Fred and George Creek Oil and Gas Field—oilfield MT-8
Fred and Mary Draw—arroyo ID-8
**Freda Township**—pop pl ND-7
Fred A Vaught Memorial Library—building TN-4
Fred Bahnson Number One Dam—dam NC-3
Fred Bahnson Number One Lake—reservoir NC-3
Fred Bahnson Number Two Dam—dam NC-3
Fred Bahnson Number Two Lake—reservoir NC-3
Fred Bayou—gut FL-3
Fred Bayou—gut LA-4
Fred Beers Brook—stream CT-1
Fred Bliss Rocks—bar MA-1
Fred Branch—stream LA-4
Fred Bryant Ditch—canal MT-8
Fred Burr Creek—stream (3) MT-8
Fred Burr Lake—lake (2) MT-8
Fred Burr Pass—gap MT-8
Fred Burr Rsvr—reservoir MT-8
Fred B Utter Ranch—locale MT-8
Fred Canyon—valley CA-9
Fred Canyon—valley NM-5
Fred Cook Tank—reservoir AZ-5
Fred C Owen Lodge Lake Dam—dam IN-6
Fred Creek—stream (2) AK-9
Fred Creek—stream OK-5
Fred Creek—stream OR-9
Fred Creek Lake—lake OR-9
Fred Damrow Ranch—locale WY-8
Freddeke Creek—stream IA-7
Fred Denman Lake—reservoir AL-4
Fredd Gulch—valley CO-8
Freddie Creek—stream MT-8
Freddies Cistern—valley UT-8
Fred Dorr Brook—stream ME-1
Fred Draw—valley WY-8
Freddy Camp—locale OR-9
Freddy Rsvr—reservoir CO-8
Freddy Well—well WY-8
Fredella, Joseph J., House and Garage—hist pl NY-2
Fredella Ave Hist Dist—hist pl NY-2
Fredell Post Office (historical)—building PA-2
**Fredenberg**—pop pl MN-6
Fredenberg Creek—stream MN-6
Fredenberg Lake—lake MN-6
**Fredenberg (Township of)**—pop pl MN-6
Fredenborg Lake—lake WI-6
Fredenburg, Andrew J., House—hist pl OR-9
Fredenburg Butte—summit OR-9
Fredenburg House—hist pl NY-2
Fredenburg Ranch OR-9
Fredenburg Spring—spring OR-9
Fredenbury Spring—spring OR-9
Frendendall Block—hist pl WI-6
Fred Enke Golf Course—other AZ-5
**Fredensborg**—pop pl VI-3
Fredensburg PA-2
Fredens Cem—cemetery IL-6
**Fredensdal**—pop pl VI-3
Frederic—locale IA-7
**Frederic**—pop pl MI-6
**Frederic**—pop pl WI-6
Frederica IA-7
**Frederica**—pop pl DE-2
Frederica Acad—school GA-3
Frederica Hist Dist—hist pl DE-2
Frederica Landing DE-2
Frederica Mtn—summit NY-2
Frederica River—gut GA-3
Frederic Cem—cemetery ME-1
Frederic Creek TX-5
Frederic Island ME-1
Frederick WI-6
**Frederick**—pop pl CO-8
**Frederick**—pop pl FL-3
**Frederick**—pop pl IL-6
**Frederick**—pop pl KS-7
**Frederick**—pop pl MD-2
**Frederick**—pop pl (2) OH-6
**Frederick**—pop pl OK-5
**Frederick**—pop pl PA-2
**Frederick**—pop pl SD-7
Frederick, Lake—lake NY-2
Frederick, Mount—summit NY-2
**Frederick Acres (subdivision)**—pop pl DE-2
Frederick Armory—hist pl MD-2
Frederick Bayou—gut LA-4
Frederick Butte—summit OR-9
Frederick (CCD)—cens area OK-5
Frederick Cem—cemetery AL-4
Frederick Cem—cemetery IN-6
Frederick Cem—cemetery OH-6
Frederick Cem—cemetery OK-5
Frederick Cem—cemetery SD-7
Frederick Cem—cemetery WV-2
Frederick Ch—church OH-6
Frederick Coll—school VA-3
Frederick Corner NY-2
**Frederick Corner**—pop pl MA-1
Frederick Corners—locale NY-2
**Frederick (County)**—pop pl MD-2
**Frederick (County)**—pop pl VA-3
Frederick Cove—bay AK-9
Frederick Creek—stream MN-6
Frederick Creek—stream MO-7
Frederick Creek—stream NY-2
Frederick Creek—stream OH-6
Frederick Creek—stream OK-5
Frederick Creek—stream TN-4
Frederick Creek—stream TX-5
Frederick Creek—stream WI-6
Frederick Dam—dam ND-7
Frederick Dam—dam SD-7
Frederick Douglas—unin pl NY-2
Frederick Douglass Elem Sch—school (2) IN-6
Frederick Douglass Home—locale DC-2
Frederick Douglass Intermediate Sch—school DE-2
Frederick Douglass Sch DE-2
Frederick Douglass Stubbs Sch—school DE-2
Frederick Filtration Plant—other MD-2
Frederick Flowage—lake WI-6
Frederick Gap—gap PA-2
**Frederick Hall**—pop pl VA-3
Frederick Hartley Grant—civil FL-3
**Frederick Heights**—pop pl VA-3
Frederick Hill—summit AL-4
Frederick Hist Dist—hist pl MD-2
Frederick Hist Dist (Boundary Increase)—hist pl MD-2
Frederick Hollow—valley UT-8
Frederick House—hist pl LA-4
Frederick Island—island NY-2
Frederick JHS—school LA-4
Frederick Junction—locale MD-2
Frederick Lake—lake (2) MN-6
Frederick Lake—reservoir SD-7
Frederick Lake—swamp MN-6
Frederick Law Olmstead Natl Historic Site—park MA-1
Frederick Memorial Gardens—cemetery SC-3
Frederick Military Acad—school VA-3
Frederick Mine—mine CA-9
Frederick Mine—mine CO-8
Frederick Mound—summit TX-5
Frederick Oil Field—oilfield KS-7
Frederick Peak—summit NE-7
Frederick Peak—summit WY-8
Frederick Point—cape AK-9
Frederick Ranch—locale (2) WY-8
Frederick Ridge—ridge TN-4
Frederick Road—unin pl MD-2
**Fredericks Addition (subdivision)**—pop pl DE-2
Frederick Sasscer HS—school MD-2
Fredericksburg AL-4
Fredericksburg PA-2
Fredericksburg—locale VA-3
**Fredericksburg**—pop pl CA-9
**Fredericksburg**—pop pl IN-6
**Fredericksburg**—pop pl IA-7
**Fredericksburg**—pop pl MO-7
**Fredericksburg**—pop pl OH-6
**Fredericksburg**—pop pl (4) PA-2
**Fredericksburg**—pop pl TX-5
Fredericksburg and Spotsylvania County Battlefield Memorial National Military Park—hist pl VA-3
Fredericksburg Battlefield—locale VA-3
Fredericksburg Canyon—valley CA-9
Fredericksburg (CCD)—cens area TX-5
Fredericksburg Ch—church MO-7
**Fredericksburg (Clovercreek)**—pop pl PA-2
Fredericksburg Country Club—other VA-3
Fredericksburg Ditch—canal NV-8
Fredericksburg East (CCD)—cens area TX-5
Fredericksburg Elem Sch—school PA-2
Fredericksburg Gun Manufactory Site—hist pl VA-3
Fredericksburgh IN-6
Fredericksburg Hist Dist—hist pl TX-5
Fredericksburg Hist Dist—hist pl VA-3
**Fredericksburg (ind. city)**—pop pl VA-3
Fredericksburg Memorial Library—hist pl TX-5
Fredericksburg-Spotsylvania Natl Military Park—park VA-3
Fredericksburg Township—fmr MCD IA-7
Fredericks Cem—cemetery NJ-2
Fredericks Cem—cemetery ND-7
Frederick Sch—school SC-3
**Fredericksdale**—pop pl (2) OH-6
Fredericks Dam—dam OR-9
Fredericks Ditch—canal IN-6
Fredericksen Sch—school IA-7
Fredericks Ferry AL-4
Fredericks Grove Church MS-4
Fredericks Hall—locale VA-3
Fredericks House—hist pl AZ-5
Fredericks House—hist pl NJ-2
Fredericks Mill (historical)—locale AL-4
Frederickson—locale WA-9
Frederickson Cem—cemetery WI-6
Frederickson Hill—summit WA-9
Frederickson Mine—mine NV-8
Frederickson Slough—lake MN-6
Frederick Sound—bay AK-9
Fredericks Park—park MA-1
Fredericks Ranch (historical)—locale NV-8
Fredericks Rsvr—reservoir OR-9
Fredericks Spring—spring CA-9
Frederick Stock Sch—school IL-6
Frederickstown PA-2
Frederick Street Park—park MS-4
Fredericksville—locale PA-2
Fredericksville Chapel—church PA-2
Fredericktown KS-7
Frederick Town MD-2
**Fredericktown**—pop pl KY-4
**Fredericktown**—pop pl MD-2
**Fredericktown**—pop pl MO-7
**Fredericktown**—pop pl (2) OH-6
**Fredericktown**—pop pl PA-2
Fredericktown Country Club—locale MO-7
**Fredericktown Hill**—pop pl PA-2
Fredericktown Municipal Airp—airport MO-7
Fredericktown Presbyterian Church—hist pl OH-6
**Frederick Township**—pop pl ND-7
**Frederick Township**—pop pl SD-7
Frederick Township Hall—building SD-7
Frederick Township (historical)—civil SD-7
**Frederick (Township of)**—pop pl IL-6
Frederick Trail—trail PA-2
Frederickville IN-6
**Frederic (Township of)**—pop pl MI-6
**Frederika**—pop pl IA-7
Frederika Creek—stream AK-9
Frederika Glacier—glacier AK-9
Frederika Mtn—summit AK-9
Frederika Township—fmr MCD IA-7
Frederika Township Cem—cemetery IA-7
Fredriksberg Point—cape VI-3
Frederiks Haab—locale VI-3
Frederiksted—1054 (1980) VI-3
Frederiksted (Census Subdistrict)—cens area VI-3
Frederiksted Hist Dist—hist pl VI-3
Frederiksted JHS—school VI-3
Frederiksted Southeast—CDP VI-3
Fredervek Landing (historical)—locale AL-4
Fred Gaddis Lake—dam MS-4
Fred Gaddis Lake Dam—dam MS-4
Fred Gaddis Pond Dam—dam MS-4
Fred G Bond Metro Park—park NC-3
Fred Hall Homestead—locale ID-8
Fred Hartley Grant—civil FL-3
Fred Haught Canyon—valley AZ-5
Fred Haught Ridge—ridge AZ-5
Fred Haught Spring—spring AZ-5
Fred Hertel Dam—dam SD-7
Fred Hildesheim Dam—dam AL-4
Fred Hollow—valley (2) KY-4
Fred Hollow—valley MS-4
Fred Hollow Trail—trail PA-2
Fred Jackson Spring—spring AZ-5
Fred Joens Dam—dam SD-7
Fred John—unin pl WI-6
Fred J Page HS—school TN-4
Fred Kerner Number 1 Dam—dam SD-7
Fred Key—island FL-3
Fred L Aiken Elem Sch—school PA-2
Fred Lateral—canal ID-8
Fredley Apartments—hist pl AZ-5
Fredley House—hist pl AZ-5
Fred Low Hill—summit ME-1
Fredlund Sch—school SD-7
**Fredlund Township**—pop pl SD-7
Fred McNeil Campground—park OR-9
Fred N Cooper Elem Sch—school IA-7
Fredom Cem—cemetery TX-5
Fredon—locale NJ-2
Fredona Church TN-4
Fredonger Butte—summit CA-9
Fredonia DE-2
Fredonia MS-4
Fredonia—locale SC-3
Fredonia—locale (2) TN-4
Fredonia—locale TX-5
Fredonia—locale WA-9
**Fredonia**—pop pl AL-4
**Fredonia**—pop pl (2) AZ-5
**Fredonia**—pop pl IN-6
**Fredonia**—pop pl IA-7
**Fredonia**—pop pl KS-7
**Fredonia**—pop pl KY-4
**Fredonia**—pop pl NY-2
**Fredonia**—pop pl ND-7
**Fredonia**—pop pl OH-6
**Fredonia**—pop pl PA-2
**Fredonia**—pop pl (2) TN-4
**Fredonia**—pop pl TX-5
**Fredonia**—pop pl WI-6
Fredonia Airp—airport KS-7
Fredonia Baptist Church MS-4
Fredonia Baptist Church TN-4
Fredonia Borough—civil PA-2
Fredonia (CCD)—cens area KY-4
Fredonia Cem—cemetery AR-4
Fredonia Cem—cemetery IA-7
Fredonia Cem—cemetery (4) MS-4
Fredonia Cem—cemetery OH-6
Fredonia Cem—cemetery (3) TN-4
Fredonia Ch—church AL-4
Fredonia Ch—church (2) GA-3
Fredonia Ch—church IN-6
Fredonia Ch—church (4) MS-4
Fredonia Ch—church MO-7
Fredonia Ch—church (5) TN-4
Fredonia Ch—church TX-5
Fredonia Ch—church WV-2
Fredonia Church—hist pl MS-4
Fredonia Commons Hist Dist—hist pl NY-2
**Fredonia (corporate name for Biscoe)**—pop pl AR-4
Fredonia Country Club—other KS-7
Fredonia Cumberland Presbyterian Church—hist pl KY-4
Fredonia Dam—dam AZ-5
Fredonia Elem Sch—school AZ-5
Fredonia Female Acad (historical)—school AL-4
Fredonia Fire Tower—tower AL-4
Fredonia Gulch—valley CO-8
Fredonia Hill—summit AR-4
Fredonia Hill (reduced usage)—cemetery TX-5
**Fredonia Hill (reduced usage)**—pop pl TX-5
Fredonia (historical)—locale KS-7
Fredonia HS—school AZ-5
Fredonia HS—school KS-7
Fredonia JHS—school KS-7
Fredonia Male Acad (historical)—school AL-4
Fredonia Methodist Ch—church TN-4
Fredonia Methodist Church MS-4
Fredonia Pass CA-9
Fredonia Pit—cave TN-4
Fredonia Post Office (historical)—building TN-4
Fredonia Rsvr—reservoir NY-2
Fredonia Sch—school IL-6
Fredonia Sch—school (2) MS-4
Fredonia Sch—school TN-4
Fredonia Sch (historical)—school (4) TN-4
**Fredonia (Town of)**—pop pl WI-6
Fredonia Township—fmr MCD IA-7
**Fredonia (Township of)**—pop pl MI-6
Fredonia Valley—basin KY-4
Fredonia Valley Quarry—mine KY-4
**Fredon (Township of)**—pop pl NJ-2
Fredonyer Campground—locale CA-9
Fredonyer Pass—gap CA-9
Fredonyer Peak—summit (2) CA-9
Fredonyer Rsvr—reservoir CA-9
Fred Pond—lake OR-9
Fred Pranty Cabin—locale AZ-5
Fredrica, Lake—lake FL-3
Fredrick—locale PA-2
Fredrick, Bayou—gut LA-4
Fredrick Cem—cemetery KY-4
Fredrick Draw—valley WY-8
Fredrick Ferry (historical)—locale AL-4
Fredrick Lateral—canal OR-9
**Fredrick Lodge Mobile Home Park**—pop pl DE-2
Fredrick Ranch—locale TX-5
Fredricksburg PA-2
Fredricksburg VA-3
Fredricksburg—locale OH-6
Fredricksburg Ch—church NE-7
Fredricks Chapel—church KY-4
Fredricks Ditch—canal (2) IN-6
Fredricks Ditch—canal KY-4
Fredrickson, Lake—reservoir MN-6
Fredrickson Draw—valley WY-8
Fredrickson No. 2 (22-Pa-821)—hist pl MS-4
Fredrickson Sch—school MI-6
Fredrickson Slough—stream WA-9
Fredricks Trail—trail PA-2
Fredrick Tunnel—mine UT-8
Fred Riddles Dam—dam OR-9
Fred Riddles Rsvr—reservoir OR-9
Fredriksdal—locale VI-3
Fred Rohr Gulch—valley CO-8
Freds Camp—locale CO-8
Fred Sch—school IL-6
Freds Creek—stream AK-9
Freds Creek—stream CA-9
Freds Creek—stream IL-6
Freds Draw—valley UT-8
Freds Draw—valley WY-8
Fred Seifer Ranch—locale NE-7
Freds Field—flat NV-8
Freds Flat—flat UT-8
Freds Hollow—valley UT-8
Freds Islands—island ME-1
Freds Lake—lake FL-3
Freds Lake—lake WA-9
Freds Mound—summit ID-8
Freds Mountain Lake—lake WA-9
Freds Mtn—summit NV-8
Freds Mtn—summit VA-3
Freds Mtn—summit WA-9
Freds Mtn—summit WY-8
Freds Ridge—ridge UT-8
Freds Run—stream WV-2
Freds Spring—spring ID-8
Freds Spring—spring (2) UT-8
Freds Tank—reservoir (2) AZ-5
**Fredsville**—pop pl IA-7
Freds Well—well NV-8
Fred Tank—reservoir AZ-5
Fred Tank—reservoir NM-5
Fred Taylor Ranch—locale WY-8
Fred T. Colter Dam AZ-5
Fred True Well—well NV-8
Fred T Stimpson State Game Sanctuary—park AL-4
Fredville—locale KY-4
**Fredville**—pop pl MO-7
Fred Vines Camp—locale AL-4
Fred Wall Place—locale CO-8
Fred Wild Elem Sch—school FL-3
Fred Williams Trail—trail CA-9
Fred Wygal Sch—school VA-3
**Free**—pop pl IN-6
Free Acad—school CT-1
Free Acad—school NY-2
**Free Acres**—pop pl NJ-2
Free Alliance MS-4
Free America Mine—mine CO-8
Free and Easy Creek—stream OR-9
Free and Easy Pass—gap OR-9
Freebairns Ranch (historical)—locale UT-8
Free Baptist Ch—church MN-6
Free Bend—bend GA-3
Freebe Rsvr—reservoir CA-9
Freebody Hill—summit RI-1
Freebody Point RI-1
Freebodys Hill RI-1
**Freeborn**—pop pl MN-6
Freeborn Cem—cemetery MN-6
Freeborn Ch—church WA-9
**Freeborn (County)**—pop pl MN-6
Freeborn Lake—lake MN-6
Freeborn Lake—reservoir MN-6
Freeborn Mtn—summit CA-9
Freeborn Ranch—locale TX-5
**Freeborn Township**—pop pl MO-7
**Freeborn Township**—pop pl ND-7
**Freeborn (Township of)**—pop pl MN-6
Free Branch—stream AL-4
Free Branch—stream KY-4
Free Branch Ch—church MS-4
Free Branches Ch MS-4
Free Branch Sch—school GA-3
Free Bridge—bridge NY-2
Free Bridge—bridge NC-3
Freebridge—locale OR-9
Free Bridge Corners—locale NY-2
Free Bridge (historical)—bridge AL-4
Free Bridge Historical Site—locale OR-9
**Freeburg**—pop pl IL-6
**Freeburg**—pop pl MN-6
**Freeburg**—pop pl MO-7
**Freeburg**—pop pl OH-6
**Freeburg**—pop pl PA-2
Freeburg Borough—civil PA-2
Freeburg Cove—cave PA-2
Freeburg Creek PA-2
Freeburg Lookout Tower—tower MO-7
Freeburg Station—locale OH-6
**Freeburg (Township of)**—pop pl IL-6
Freeburg Washington Elem Sch—school PA-2
Freeburg Windmill—locale NM-5
Free Burial Ground—cemetery OH-6
**Freeburn**—pop pl KY-4
Freeburn Mtn—summit AK-9
Freeburrow Lake—lake CO-8
Freecastle Swamp—swamp GA-3
Free Cem—cemetery IN-6
Free Ch—church IL-6
Free Ch—church MD-2
Free Ch—church (4) MI-6
Free Ch—church MS-4
Free Ch—church OH-6
Free Ch—church OK-5
Free Ch—church (5) PA-2
Free Ch—church WV-2
Free Chapel—church MA-1
Free Chapel—church NC-3
Free Ch of God—church IN-6
Free Church—hist pl IN-6
Free Church (Abandoned)—locale MN-6
Free Church Cem—cemetery MI-6
Free Church Cem—cemetery (3) MN-6
Free Church Cem—cemetery NE-7
Free Church Cem—cemetery ND-7
Free Church Parsonage—hist pl NY-2
Free Coinage Mine—mine MT-8
**Free Communion**—pop pl TN-4
Free Communion Ch—church TN-4
Free Coulee—valley MN-6
**Free Country Estates (subdivision)**—pop pl UT-8
Free Creek—stream MT-8
Freed—locale WV-2
Freed Canyon—valley CO-8
Freed Cem—cemetery IN-6
Freed Hardeman Coll—school TN-4
**Freedhem**—pop pl MN-6
Freed JHS—school CO-8
**Freedleyville**—pop pl VT-1
**Freedman**—pop pl SC-3
Freedman Cem—cemetery GA-3
Freedman Hill Ch—church MS-4
Freedman Home—building NY-2
Freedman-Raulerson House—hist pl FL-3
Freedmans SC-3
Freedmans Bureau Landing (historical)—locale MS-4
Freedman Sch—school SC-3
Freedmans Institute (historical)—school TN-4
Freedmen's Town Hist Dist—hist pl TX-5
Freedom IN-6
Freedom PA-2
Freedom—fmr MCD NE-7
Freedom—locale KY-4
Freedom—locale MI-6
Freedom—locale NE-7
Freedom—locale PA-2
Freedom—locale WA-9
Freedom—other PA-2
**Freedom**—pop pl CA-9
**Freedom**—pop pl ID-8
**Freedom**—pop pl IN-6
**Freedom**—pop pl KY-4
**Freedom**—pop pl ME-1
**Freedom**—pop pl MD-2
**Freedom**—pop pl (2) MO-7
**Freedom**—pop pl NH-1
**Freedom**—pop pl NY-2
**Freedom**—pop pl OH-6
**Freedom**—pop pl OK-5
**Freedom**—pop pl PA-2
**Freedom**—pop pl UT-8
**Freedom**—pop pl WI-6
**Freedom**—pop pl WY-8
Freedom—post sta NC-3
Freedom—post sta TX-5
Freedom—unin pl TX-5
Freedom Acad—school ME-1
**Freedom Acres Subdivision**—pop pl UT-8
Freedom Assembly of God—church FL-3
Freedom Baptist Ch—church (2) FL-3
Freedom Borough—civil PA-2
Freedom Branch—stream KY-4
Freedom Bridge—bridge AL-4
Freedom Bridge—bridge FL-3
Freedom Cem—cemetery FL-3
Freedom Cem—cemetery ID-8
Freedom Cem—cemetery IL-6
Freedom Cem—cemetery (2) IN-6
Freedom Cem—cemetery IA-7
Freedom Cem—cemetery KS-7
Freedom Cem—cemetery KY-4
Freedom Cem—cemetery MI-6
Freedom Cem—cemetery MN-6
Freedom Cem—cemetery (2) MO-7
Freedom Cem—cemetery OK-5
Freedom Cem—cemetery SC-3
Freedom Cem—cemetery UT-8
Freedom Cem—cemetery WV-2
Freedom Cem—cemetery WI-6
Freedom Ch—church (4) AR-4
Freedom Ch—church FL-3
Freedom Ch—church (2) GA-3
Freedom Ch—church (2) IL-6
Freedom Ch—church (3) IN-6
Freedom Ch—church IA-7
Freedom Ch—church (8) KY-4
Freedom Ch—church LA-4
Freedom Ch—church MD-2
Freedom Ch—church MS-4
Freedom Ch—church (4) MO-7
Freedom Ch—church (3) NC-3
Freedom Ch—church OK-5
Freedom Ch—church SC-3
Freedom Ch—church (3) TN-4
Freedom Ch—church TX-5
Freedom Ch—church WI-6
Freedom Chapel—church KY-4
Freedom Ch (historical)—church MO-7
Freedom Christian Acad—school FL-3
Freedom Christian Academy—church FL-3
Freedom Church—chruch IN-6
Freedom Community Center—locale MO-7
Freedom Congregational Church—hist pl OH-6
Freedom Corners—locale WI-6
Freedom Creek ID-8
Freedom Creek—stream (2) AR-4
Freedom Creek—stream WA-9
Freedom Creek Cem—cemetery AR-4
Freedom Field—park MS-4
Freedom Hall Civic Center—building TN-4
Freedom Hill NC-3
Freedom Hill—summit VA-3
Freedom Hill Ch—church TN-4
Freedom Hills—range AL-4
Freedom Hills—summit MS-4
Freedom Hills Ch—church AL-4
Freedom Hill Sch—school VA-3
Freedom HS—school NC-3
Freedom HS—school PA-2
Freedom Island—island MN-6
Freedom JHS—school CA-9
Freedom Lake MI-6
Freedom Mall—locale NC-3
Freedom Missionary Ch—church LA-4
Freedom Mtn—summit AR-4
Freedom Park—park AZ-5
Freedom Park—park NV-8
Freedom Park—park (2) NC-3
**Freedom Plains**—pop pl NY-2
Freedom Rest Ch—church LA-4
Freedom Ridge—ridge KY-4
Freedom Sch—school CA-9
Freedom Sch—school (2) IL-6
Freedom Sch—school IN-6
Freedom Sch—school (2) IA-7
Freedom Sch—school (5) KY-4
Freedom Sch—school (3) MO-7
Freedom Sch—school MT-8
Freedom Sch—school NC-3
Freedom Sch—school OH-6
Freedom Sch—school PA-2
Freedom Sch—school WI-6
Freedom Sch (historical)—school MO-7
Freedom Sch (historical)—school TN-4
Freedom Separater Ch—church KY-4
**Freedom (sta.)**—pop pl OH-6
**Freedom Station**—pop pl OH-6
Freedom Street Dam MA-1
Freedom Strip Airp—airport MS-4
Freedom Tower—hist pl FL-3
**Freedom (Town of)**—pop pl ME-1
**Freedom (Town of)**—pop pl NH-1
**Freedom (Town of)**—pop pl NY-2
**Freedom (Town of)**—pop pl (3) WI-6
Freedom Township—civil KS-7
Freedom Township—civil MO-7
Freedom Township—fmr MCD (2) IA-7
**Freedom Township**—pop pl (3) KS-7
**Freedom Township**—pop pl ND-7
**Freedom Township**—pop pl SD-7
Freedom (Township of)—fmr MCD AR-4
**Freedom (Township of)**—pop pl (2) IL-6
**Freedom (Township of)**—pop pl MI-6
**Freedom (Township of)**—pop pl MN-6
**Freedom (Township of)**—pop pl (3) OH-6
**Freedom (Township of)**—pop pl (2) PA-2
Freedom Village—locale NC-3
Freedom West Cem—cemetery OH-6
Freedona AL-4
Freedonia OH-6
Freedonia Ch—church (2) AR-4
Freedonia Ch—church GA-3
Freedonia Ch—church IN-6
Freedonia Ch—church TX-5
Freed Park—park TX-5
Freed Pen Well—well NM-5
Freed Sch—school IL-6
Freed State Wildlife Mngmt Area—park MN-6
Freed Tank—reservoir TX-5
Freedwell Branch—stream IL-6
Free Enterprise Mine—mine MT-8
Free Evangelical Lutheran Church-Bethania Scandinavian Evangelical Lutheran Congregation—hist pl WI-6
Free Ferry SC-3
Freefield Cem—cemetery MS-4
Free Gift Ch—church AL-4
Free Gift Ch—church (2) GA-3
Free Gold Creek—stream ID-8
Free Gospel Ch—church PA-2
Free Gospel Tabernacle—church VA-3
Free Grace Cem—cemetery OH-6
Free Grace Ch—church (2) MS-4
Free Grace Ch—church NC-3
Free Grace Ch—church PA-2
Free Grove Cem—cemetery NY-2
Free Haven NJ-2
**Free Hill**—pop pl TN-4
Free Hill—ridge TN-4
Free Hill Cem—cemetery TN-4
Free Hill Cem—cemetery VA-3
Freehill Ch—church (2) AL-4
Free Hill Ch—church (2) AR-4
Free Hill Ch—church (2) VA-3
Free Hill Ch (historical)—church TN-4
Freehill Creek—stream NV-8
Free Hill Post Office (historical)—building TN-4
Free Hills TN-4
**Free Hills**—pop pl TN-4
Free Hills—range TN-4
Freehill Sch—school IL-6
Free Hills Ch of Christ—church TN-4
Free Hills Community Center—building TN-4
Free Hills Sch (historical)—school TN-4

Freezeout Creek—*stream* AZ-5
Freezeout Creek—*stream* CA-9
Freezeout Creek—*stream* CO-8
Freezeout Creek—*stream* (2) ID-8
Freezeout Creek—*stream* (5) MT-8
Freezeout Creek—*stream* OK-5
Freezeout Creek—*stream* (4) OR-9
Freezeout Creek—*stream* WA-9
Freezeout Dam—*dam* AZ-5
Freezeout Flat—*flat* CA-9
Freezeout Flat—*flat* MT-8
Freezeout Gulch—*stream* OR-9
Freezeout Gulch—*valley* (2) MT-8
Freeze Out Gulch—*valley* OR-9
Freezeout Gulch—*valley* OR-9
*Freeze-Out Hills* WY-8
Freezeout Island—*island* WY-8
Freezeout Lake—*lake* MT-8
Freezeout Lake—*lake* OR-9
Freezeout Lake—*lake* WA-9
Freezeout Lakes—*lake* MT-8
Freezeout Lookout Tower—*locale* ID-8
Freezeout Meadow—*flat* CA-9
*Freezeout Mountain* ID-8
*Freezeout Mountains* WY-8
Freezeout Mtn—*summit* AZ-5
Freezeout Mtn—*summit* ID-8
Freezeout Mtn—*summit* MT-8
Freezeout Mtn—*summit* OR-9
Freezeout Mtn—*summit* WA-9
Freezeout Mtns—*range* WY-8
Freezeout Pass—*gap* MT-8
*Freezeout Peak* WY-8
*Freezeout Point* WY-8
Freeze Out Point—*summit* WY-8
*Freezeout Ridge* OR-9
Freezeout Ridge—*ridge* ID-8
Freezeout Ridge—*ridge* OR-9
Freezeout Ridge—*ridge* WA-9
Freezeout Road—*trail* ME-1
Freezeout Rsvr—*reservoir* OR-9
Freezeout Saddle—*gap* ID-8
Freezeout Saddle—*gap* OR-9
Freezeout Sch—*school* OR-9
Freezeout Spring—*spring* AZ-5
Freezeout Spring—*spring* CA-9
Freeze-Out Spring—*spring* CA-9
Freezeout Spring—*spring* (2) ID-8
Freezeout Spring—*spring* (2) OR-9
Freezeout Summit Rsvr—*reservoir* OR-9
Freezeout Tank—*reservoir* AZ-5
Freezeout Tank—*reservoir* NM-5
Freezeout Trail—*trail* ID-8
Freezeout Trail—*trail* OR-9
Freezeout Trail (jeep)—*trail* OR-9
Freezeout Trail Lookout—*locale* ID-8
Freezeout Well—*well* AZ-5
Freeze Out Windmill—*locale* TX-5
Free Zion Ch—*church* KY-4
Free Zion Ch—*church* VA-3
Freezland Flat—*flat* VA-3
Freezland Hollow—*valley* VA-3
*Freezor* NC-3
Freezout Lake Game Mngmt Area—*park* MT-8
*Freezout Ridge* OR-9
*Freezout Spring* ID-8
*Freezout Springs* ID-8
Frego Creek—*stream* MN-6
Frehner Canyon—*valley* AZ-5
*Frehold* NJ-2
Freiberg Ranch—*locale* SD-7
Freiberg Spring—*spring* SD-7
**Freiburgers**—*pop pl* MI-6
Freiburg Mine—*mine* CO-8
Freiburg Mine—*mine* NV-8
**Freidberger**—*pop pl* MI-6
Freidell, William, House—*hist pl* NE-7
Freidel Prong—*stream* DE-2
Freidenfeld Cem—*cemetery* ND-7
Freidens Cem—*cemetery* MT-8
Freidens Cem—*cemetery* ND-7
Freidens Cem—*cemetery* SD-7
Freidens Ch—*church* MT-8
Freidens Ch—*church* OH-6
Freidensthal Cem—*cemetery* SD-7
Freidlein Prairie—*flat* AZ-5
Freidline Cem—*cemetery* IN-6
Freighter Gap—*gap* WY-8
Freighters Defeat—*stream* NV-8
Freighters Gulch—*valley* MT-8
Freighter Spring—*spring* ID-8
Freighter Spring—*spring* WY-8
Freighters Well—*well* UT-8
Freight House—*hist pl* WI-6
Freight Locomotive No. 5741—*hist pl* PA-2
Freight Station—*locale* CA-9
Freight Trail Tank—*reservoir* AZ-5
Freight Yard Hist Dist—*hist pl* MA-1
**Freiheit**—*pop pl* TX-5
Freiheit Spring—*locale* MN-6
Freilburg—*locale* AL-4
Freiling Ranch—*locale* MT-8
Freindship Cem—*cemetery* KY-4
Freisner Cem—*cemetery* OH-6
**Freistadt**—*pop pl* WI-6
Freistadt—*uninc pl* WI-6
**Freistatt**—*pop pl* MO-7
Freistatt Township—*civil* MO-7
Freitag Pond—*reservoir* MA-1
Freitag's Pure Oil Service
Station—*hist pl* WI-6
Freitas Spring—*spring* CA-9
Freize Knoll—*summit* ID-8
Frelick Homestead—*locale* MT-8
Frelinghuysen, Gen. John, House—*hist pl* NJ-2
**Frelinghuysen (Township of)**—*pop pl* NJ-2
Frellsen—*locale* LA-4
Frellsen Lake—*lake* MN-6
**Frelsburg**—*pop pl* TX-5
Frelsburg Oil Field—*oilfield* TX-5
Frels Lake—*lake* WI-6
Fremac—*uninc pl* VA-3
Fremad Association Bldg—*hist pl* MN-6
Fremington Cem—*cemetery* IL-6
*Fremont* KS-7
*Fremont* KY-4
*Fremont* NY-2
*Fremont* PA-2
Fremont—*locale* (2) CA-9
Fremont—*locale* VA-3
Fremont—*other* PA-2
**Fremont**—*pop pl* AL-4
**Fremont**—*pop pl* IN-6
**Fremont**—*pop pl* IA-7
**Fremont**—*pop pl* KY-4
**Fremont**—*pop pl* MI-6
**Fremont**—*pop pl* MN-6
**Fremont**—*pop pl* MO-7
**Fremont**—*pop pl* NE-7
**Fremont**—*pop pl* NH-1
**Fremont**—*pop pl* NY-2
**Fremont**—*pop pl* NC-3
**Fremont**—*pop pl* OH-6
**Fremont**—*pop pl* TN-4
**Fremont**—*pop pl* UT-8
**Fremont**—*pop pl* WA-9
**Fremont**—*pop pl* WI-6
Fremont—*uninc pl* NY-2
Fremont, Elkhorn and Missouri Valley RR
Depot—*hist pl* NE-7
Fremont, John C., Branch—*hist pl* CA-9
Fremont, Lake—*lake* MN-6
Fremont, Mount—*summit* WA-9
Fremont, Mount Morse—*summit* AK-9
Fremont Bench—*bench* UT-8
Fremont Branch—*stream* IN-6
Fremont Bridge—*bridge* OR-9
Fremont Bridge—*bridge* WA-9
Fremont Bridge—*hist pl* WA-9
Fremont Butte—*summit* CO-8
Fremont Butte—*summit* WY-8
*Fremont Buttes* CO-8
Fremont Butte Well—*well* WY-8
Fremont Campground—*locale* CA-9
Fremont Canal—*canal* CA-9
*Fremont Canyon* UT-8
Fremont Canyon—*valley* CA-9
Fremont Canyon—*valley* OR-9
Fremont Canyon—*valley* (2) UT-8
Fremont Canyon—*valley* WY-8
Fremont (CCD)—*cens area* CA-9
Fremont Cem—*cemetery* (3) IA-7
Fremont Cem—*cemetery* (4) MI-6
Fremont Cem—*cemetery* UT-8
*Fremont Center* NY-2
Fremont Center—*locale* IL-6
**Fremont Center**—*pop pl* NY-2
**Fremont Center (Fremont)**—*pop pl* NY-2
Fremont Center (Shop Ctr)—*locale* MO-7
**Fremont (Centerville)**—*pop pl* CA-9
**Fremont (Centerville District)**—*pop pl* CA-9
Fremont Central Park—*park* CA-9
Fremont Ch—*church* (3) IA-7
Fremont Ch—*church* (2) VA-3
Fremont County Airp—*airport* CO-8
Fremont County Cem—*cemetery* IA-7
Fremont County Courthouse—*hist pl* ID-8
Fremont County Courthouse—*hist pl* IA-7
Fremont County Golf Course—*locale* IA-7
Fremont County Youth Camp—*locale* WY-8
*Fremont Creek* CO-8
*Fremont Creek* WY-8
Fremont Creek—*stream* AK-9
Fremont Creek—*stream* WY-8
Fremont Crossing—*locale* WY-8
Fremont Cutoff Ditch—*canal* NE-7
Fremont Ditch—*canal* (2) CO-8
Fremont Ditch—*canal* WY-8
Fremont Drain—*canal* MI-6
Fremont Elem Sch—*school* IN-6
Fremont Elem Sch—*school* NC-3
Fremont Falls—*falls* IN-6
Fremont Ford—*locale* CA-9
Fremont Ford State Park—*park* CA-9
Fremont Fort—*summit* CO-8
Fremont-Foxen Monument—*other* CA-9
Fremont Foxon Historical Marker—*park* CA-9
Fremont Gap—*gap* AL-4
Fremont Glacier—*glacier* WA-9
Fremont Glaciers—*glacier* WY-8
**Fremont Hills**—*pop pl* NY-2
Fremont Hills Sch—*school* CA-9
Fremont (historical)—*locale* OR-9
Fremont House—*hist pl* AZ-5
Fremont HS—*school* (3) CA-9
Fremont Indian State Park—*park* UT-8
Fremont Island—*island* UT-8
Fremont Island Bar—*bar* UT-8
Fremont JHS—*school* AZ-5
Fremont JHS—*school* (6) CA-9
Fremont JHS—*school* NV-8
*Fremont Junction* IL-6
Fremont Junction—*locale* UT-8
Fremont Junior High—*school* OR-9
Fremont Junior-Senior HS—*school* IN-6
Fremont Knoll—*summit* CO-8
Fremont Lake—*lake* CA-9
Fremont Lake—*lake* MI-6
Fremont Lake—*lake* MN-6
Fremont Lake—*lake* NE-7
Fremont Lake—*reservoir* WY-8
Fremont Landing (Site)—*locale* CA-9
Fremont Lateral—*canal* ID-8
Fremont Loa Ditch—*canal* UT-8
Fremont Lookout Fortification
Site—*hist pl* CO-8
Fremont Lookout Tower—*locale* MO-7
Fremont Meadow—*flat* OR-9
Fremont Memorial Park—*park* CA-9
Fremont Memory Gardens—*cemetery* CO-8
Fremont Mine—*mine* CA-9
Fremont Park—*park* (3) CA-9
Fremont Park—*park* KS-7
Fremont Park—*park* MN-6
Fremont Pass—*gap* CA-9
Fremont Pass—*gap* CO-8
Fremont Pass—*gap* UT-8
Fremont Peak—*summit* AZ-5
Fremont Peak—*summit* (3) CA-9
Fremont Peak—*summit* CO-8
Fremont Peak—*summit* ME-1
Fremont Peak—*summit* WY-8
*Fremont Peak Range* CA-9
Fremont Peak State Park—*park* CA-9
Fremont Point—*locale* KS-7
Fremont Point—*summit* OR-9
Fremont Post Office (historical)—*building* TN-4
Fremont Powerhouse—*building* OR-9
Fremont Powerhouse—*hist pl* OR-9
Fremont Raceways—*other* CA-9
*Fremont Reservoir* UT-8
Fremont Ridge—*ridge* WY-8
*Fremont River* UT-8
Fremont River—*stream* UT-8
Fremont Route (1845)—*trail* NV-8
Fremont Saddle—*gap* (2) AZ-5
*Fremonts Butte* CO-8
Fremont Sch—*school* (23) CA-9
Fremont Sch—*school* IL-6
Fremont Sch—*school* (2) MI-6
Fremont Sch—*school* MO-7
Fremont Sch—*school* NV-8
Fremont Sch—*school* NY-2
Fremont Sch—*school* (2) OR-9
Fremont Sch—*school* (2) UT-8
Fremont Sch—*school* WI-6
Fremont Sch No 1—*school* CO-8
Fremont School—*locale* CO-8
Fremont Slough—*gut* NE-7
Fremont Slough—*stream* NE-7
*Fremont's Pass* CO-8
Fremont Spring—*spring* CA-9
Fremont Spring—*spring* UT-8
*Fremonts Pyramid* NV-8
Fremont Square—*park* CA-9
Fremont (Station)—*locale* WI-6
**Fremont Station**—*pop pl* NH-1
*Fremonts Wash* UT-8
Fremont Tower Picnic Area—*locale* MO-7
**Fremont (Town of)**—*pop pl* NH-1
**Fremont (Town of)**—*pop pl* (2) NY-2
**Fremont (Town of)**—*pop pl* (2) WI-6
Fremont Township—*civil* SD-7
Fremont Township—*fmr MCD* (11) IA-7
**Fremont Township**—*pop pl* KS-7
**Fremont Township**—*pop pl* ND-7
**Fremont Township**—*pop pl* SD-7
Fremont Township Cem—*cemetery* IA-7
Fremont (Township of)—*other* OH-6
**Fremont (Township of)**—*pop pl* IL-6
**Fremont (Township of)**—*pop pl* IN-6
**Fremont (Township of)**—*pop pl* (4) MI-6
**Fremont (Township of)**—*pop pl* MN-6
Fremont Trail—*trail* WY-8
Fremont Valley—*valley* CA-9
Fremont Wash—*stream* CA-9
Fremont Wash—*valley* UT-8
Fremont Weir—*levee* CA-9
Fremont Well—*well* CA-9
Fremont Wildlife Mngmt Area—*park* MN-6
*Fremount* IN-6
Fremstadt Lake—*lake* WI-6
*French* IN-6
*French* TN-4
*French* WV-2
French—*locale* AR-4
French—*locale* MN-6
French—*locale* NM-5
**French**—*pop pl* IN-6
**French**—*pop pl* WV-2
French, Alice, House—*hist pl* AR-4
French, Alice, House—*hist pl* IA-7
French, Col. William Henderson,
House—*hist pl* WV-2
French, Lake—*lake* FL-3
French, Pete, Round Barn—*hist pl* OR-9
French, Simon, House—*hist pl* KY-4
French, Teter Myers, House—*hist pl* WV-2
French, Thomas, Jr., House—*hist pl* NJ-2
French Annie Creek—*stream* MI-6
French Asylum Ch—*church* PA-2
French Azilum—*locale* PA-2
French Azilum Overlook—*locale* PA-2
French Bar—*bar* (3) CA-9
French Bar—*bar* MT-8
French Bar—*locale* CA-9
French Bar Mtn—*summit* MT-8
French Basin—*basin* MT-8
*French Bay* NY-2
French Bay—*bay* MI-6
French Bayou—*gut* MS-4
French Bayou—*stream* TX-5
Frenchboro—*civ div* ME-1
**Frenchboro**—*pop pl* ME-1
French Bottom—*bend* MO-7
French Boy Canyon—*valley* NV-8
*French Boys Canyon* NV-8
*French Branch* OR-9
French Branch—*stream* AR-4
French Branch—*stream* LA-4
French Branch—*stream* MS-4
French Branch—*stream* NC-3
*Frenchbroad* TN-4
French Broad—*locale* (2) TN-4
*French Broad Baptist Church* TN-4
French Broad Ch—*church* (3) NC-3
French Broad Ch—*church* (2) TN-4
French Broad Post Office
(historical)—*building* TN-4
Frenchbroad Post Office
(historical)—*building* TN-4
French Broad Ranger Station—*locale* NC-3
French Broad River—*stream* NC-3
French Broad River—*stream* TN-4
French Broad Sch—*school* NC-3
French Broad Shoals—*rapids* TN-4
French Broad (Township of)—*fmr MCD* NC-3
French Broad Valley Ch—*church* TN-4
French Broad Work Center—*locale* NC-3
French Brook—*stream* CT-1
French Brook—*stream* ME-1
French Brook—*stream* (2) MA-1
French Brook—*stream* NJ-2
French Brook—*stream* NY-2
French Brook—*stream* VT-1
**Frenchburg**—*pop pl* KY-4
**Frenchburg**—*pop pl* WV-2
Frenchburg (CCD)—*cens area* KY-4
Frenchburg Job Corps Conservation
Center—*other* KY-4
Frenchburg Sch Campus—*hist pl* KY-4
French Burial Ground—*locale* NJ-2
French Butte—*summit* AZ-5
French Butte—*summit* WA-9
French Cabin—*locale* OR-9
French Cabin Basin—*basin* WA-9
French Cabin Creek—*stream* WA-9
French Cable Hut—*hist pl* MA-1
French Cable Station—*hist pl* MA-1
French Cable Station Museum—*building* MA-1
French Camp—*locale* (3) CA-9
**French Camp**—*pop pl* CA-9
**French Camp**—*pop pl* MS-4
French Camp Acad (historical)—*school* MS-4
French Camp Cem—*cemetery* MS-4
French Camp Elem Sch—*school* MS-4
French Camp Ridge—*ridge* CA-9
*French Camps* MS-4
French Camp (Site)—*locale* CA-9
French Camp Slough—*stream* CA-9
French Canal—*canal* NV-8
French Canyon—*valley* (3) CA-9
French Canyon—*valley* IL-6
French Canyon—*valley* NM-5
French Canyon—*valley* OR-9
French Canyon—*valley* WA-9
French Cave—*cave* MA-1
French Cem—*cemetery* AR-4
French Cem—*cemetery* IL-6
French Cem—*cemetery* (2) IN-6
French Cem—*cemetery* IA-7
French Cem—*cemetery* (2) KY-4
French Cem—*cemetery* LA-4
French Cem—*cemetery* ME-1
French Cem—*cemetery* MS-4
French Cem—*cemetery* MO-7
French Cem—*cemetery* (3) NY-2
French Cem—*cemetery* OH-6
French Cem—*cemetery* OK-5
French Cem—*cemetery* (5) TN-4
French Cem—*cemetery* (2) VA-3
French Cem—*cemetery* WV-2
French Cem—*cemetery* WI-6
French Ch—*church* AR-4
French Ch—*church* IL-6
French Ch—*church* IA-7
French Ch—*church* NC-3
French Chapel—*church* VA-3
French Charlie Canyon—*valley* OR-9
French Colonial Hist Dist—*hist pl* IL-6
French Congregational Church—*hist pl* MA-1
French Corner—*locale* ID-8
French Corner Ch—*church* LA-4
*French Corners* PA-2
French Corners—*locale* NM-5
French Corral—*locale* WA-9
**French Corral**—*pop pl* CA-9
French Corral Creek—*stream* CA-9
French Corral Meadow—*flat* OR-9
French Corral Spring—*spring* OR-9
**French Cort Village
Condominium**—*pop pl* UT-8
French Coulee—*valley* MT-8
French Cove—*valley* (2) CA-9
*French Creek* AL-4
*French Creek* CA-9
*French Creek* CO-8
*French Creek* ID-8
*French Creek* MT-8
*French Creek* NC-3
*French Creek* VA-3
*French Creek* WY-8
French Creek—*locale* ID-8
**French Creek**—*pop pl* NY-2
**French Creek**—*pop pl* WV-2
French Creek—*stream* AL-4
French Creek—*stream* (3) AK-9
French Creek—*stream* (2) AZ-5
French Creek—*stream* (3) AR-4
French Creek—*stream* (16) CA-9
French Creek—*stream* (6) CO-8
French Creek—*stream* (10) ID-8
French Creek—*stream* (3) IL-6
French Creek—*stream* IN-6
French Creek—*stream* (2) IA-7
French Creek—*stream* (4) KS-7
French Creek—*stream* KY-4
French Creek—*stream* LA-4
French Creek—*stream* MI-6
French Creek—*stream* (2) MN-6
French Creek—*stream* (7) MT-8
French Creek—*stream* NE-7
French Creek—*stream* (2) NY-2
French Creek—*stream* ND-7
French Creek—*stream* OH-6
French Creek—*stream* (8) OR-9
French Creek—*stream* (3) PA-2
French Creek—*stream* SD-7
French Creek—*stream* (5) TX-5
French Creek—*stream* UT-8
French Creek—*stream* VA-3
French Creek—*stream* (5) WA-9
French Creek—*stream* (2) WV-2
French Creek—*stream* (6) WI-6
French Creek—*stream* (3) WY-8
*French Creek Bar* CA-9
French Creek Bay—*bay* NY-2
French Creek Campground—*locale* WA-9
French Creek Cem—*cemetery* KS-7
French Creek Cem—*cemetery* WI-6
French Creek Ch—*church* WV-2
French Creek Ch—*church* WI-6
French Creek Cove Public Use Area—*park* KS-7
French Creek Cow Camp—*locale* WY-8
*French Creek Dam* PA-2
French Creek (Election Precinct)—*fmr MCD* IL-6
French Creek Falls—*other* PA-2
French Creek Farm—*hist pl* PA-2
French Creek Flats—*flat* PA-2
French Creek Forest Camp—*locale* WA-9
French Creek Game Farm—*park* WV-2
French Creek (historical P.O.)—*locale* IA-7
French Creek Lakes—*lake* ID-8
French Creek Picnic Ground—*locale* WY-8
French Creek Presbyterian
Church—*hist pl* WV-2
French Creek Public Use Area—*park* AL-4
French Creek Ranch—*locale* (2) WY-8
French Creek Ridge—*ridge* OR-9
French Creek Sch—*school* CA-9
French Creek Sch—*school* SD-7
French Creek Sch (abandoned)—*school* SD-7
French Creek State Park—*park* PA-2
French Creek State Park: Organized Group
Camp 4 District—*hist pl* PA-2
French Creek State Park Six Penny Day Use
District—*hist pl* PA-2
**French Creek (Town of)**—*pop pl* NY-2
French Creek Township—*fmr MCD* IA-7
**Frenchcreek (Township of)**—*pop pl* PA-2
**French Creek (Township of)**—*pop pl* PA-2
French Creek Trail—*trail* OR-9
French Creek Valley Elem Sch—*school* PA-2
French Diggings—*area* OR-9
French Ditch—*canal* (2) IN-6
French Drain—*canal* MI-6
French Draw—*valley* OK-5
*French Elementary School* MS-4
French Embassy Bldg—*building* DC-2
French-England House—*hist pl* AR-4
Frenches Bayou—*gut* LA-4
*Frenches Creek* NC-3
Frenches Draw—*valley* NM-5
Frenches Knob—*summit* NC-3
Frenches Peak—*summit* UT-8
Frenches Pond—*reservoir* NJ-2
Frenches Pond Dam—*dam* NJ-2
French Family Farm—*hist pl* NY-2
French Farm—*hist pl* CT-1
French Farm Creek—*stream* MI-6
French Farm Lake—*lake* MI-6
French Field—*park* MI-6
*French Flat* CA-9
French Flat—*flat* (3) CA-9
French Flat—*flat* OR-9
French Forest Camp—*locale* OR-9
French Fork—*gut* LA-4
French Fork Little River—*stream* LA-4
French Fork Oil Field—*oilfield* LA-4
French Frigate Shoals—*bar* HI-9
French Gap—*gap* AZ-5
French Gap Spring—*spring* AZ-5
French George Crossing—*locale* WY-8
**Frenchglen**—*pop pl* OR-9
Frenchglen Hotel—*hist pl* OR-9
French Grove Ch—*church* AR-4
French Grove County Wildlife Area—*park* IA-7
*French Gulch* CA-9
**French Gulch**—*pop pl* CA-9
French Gulch—*stream* OR-9
French Gulch—*valley* (2) AK-9
French Gulch—*valley* AZ-5
French Gulch—*valley* (13) CA-9
French Gulch—*valley* (2) CO-8
French Gulch—*valley* (6) ID-8
French Gulch—*valley* (7) MT-8
French Gulch—*valley* (7) OR-9
French Gulch County Park—*park* CA-9
French Gulch Divide—*ridge* OR-9
French Gulch Hist Dist—*hist pl* CA-9
French Gulch Lake Patrol Station—*locale* CA-9
French Hall Branch—*stream* KY-4
French Harbor—*bay* AK-9
**French Hay**—*pop pl* VA-3
French Henry Creek—*stream* OK-5
French-Henry Mine—*mine* NM-5
French Hill—*summit* AL-4
French Hill—*summit* (4) CA-9
French Hill—*summit* (3) ME-1
French Hill—*summit* (2) MA-1
French Hill—*summit* NH-1
French Hill—*summit* (3) NY-2
French Hill—*summit* TN-4
French Hill—*summit* (2) VT-1
French Hill Brook—*stream* VT-1
French Hill Mine—*mine* CA-9
**French Hill (subdivision)**—*pop pl* AL-4
*French Hollow* IL-6
French Hollow—*locale* VT-1
French Hollow—*valley* ID-8
French Hollow—*valley* IN-6
French Hollow—*valley* IA-7
French Hollow—*valley* KY-4
French Hollow—*valley* (2) TN-4
French Hollow—*valley* UT-8
French Hollow—*valley* VT-1
French Home Trading Post—*hist pl* TX-5
French Hosp—*hospital* (2) CA-9
French Hotel Creek—*stream* CA-9
French House, The—*hist pl* LA-4
French House Island—*island* ME-1
French House (Site)—*locale* CA-9
French HS—*school* TX-5
Frenchie Creek—*stream* NV-8
Frenchie Creek—*stream* OR-9
Frenchie Creek—*stream* WY-8
Frenchie Draw—*valley* WY-8
Frenchie Flat—*flat* NV-8
Frenchie Place—*locale* MT-8
Frenchie Ranch—*locale* NV-8
Frenchie Rsvr—*reservoir* WY-8
Frenchies Cabin—*locale* NM-5
Frenchies Gulch—*valley* MT-8
*French Island* IN-6
French Island—*CDP* WI-6
French Island—*island* CA-9
French Island—*island* IA-7
French Island—*island* (3) ME-1
French Island—*island* PA-2
French Island—*island* TX-5
French Island—*island* WI-6
*French Island City* IN-6
French Island No 1—*island* KY-4
French Island No 2—*island* KY-4
French JHS—*school* KS-7
French JHS—*school* MI-6
French Joe Camp—*locale* AZ-5
French Joe Canyon—*valley* AZ-5
*French Joe Creek* WY-8
French Joe Creek—*stream* WY-8
French Joe Meadow—*flat* CA-9
French Joe Mtn—*summit* AK-9
French Joe Peak—*summit* AZ-5
French Joe Spring—*spring* AZ-5
French Joe Tank—*reservoir* AZ-5
French John Creek—*stream* TX-5
French John Hill—*summit* ID-8
French Johns Lake—*lake* WA-9
*French Kakigo Lake* MN-6
French King Bridge—*bridge* MA-1
French King Rock—*rock* MA-1
*French Lake* LA-4
*French Lake* MI-6
French Lake—*lake* CA-9
French Lake—*lake* IN-6
French Lake—*lake* LA-4
French Lake—*lake* (7) MN-6
French Lake—*lake* MT-8
French Lake—*lake* NV-8
French Lake—*lake* NJ-2
French Lake—*lake* NM-5
French Lake—*lake* (2) NY-2
French Lake—*lake* OK-5
French Lake—*lake* (3) WI-6
**French Lake**—*pop pl* IN-6
**French Lake**—*pop pl* MN-6
French Lake—*reservoir* CA-9
French Lake—*reservoir* CO-8
French Lake—*reservoir* OK-5
French Lake Ch—*church* (2) MN-6
French Lake Dam—*dam* NJ-2
French Lake Dam—*dam* OK-5
**French Lake (Township of)**—*pop pl* MN-6
*French Landing* MI-6
French Landing—*locale* MI-6
**French Lane (historical)**—*pop pl* OR-9
French Laundry—*hist pl* CA-9
French Legation—*hist pl* TX-5
**French Lick**—*pop pl* IN-6
French Lick Creek—*stream* IN-6
French Lick Dam Number F-2—*dam* IN-6
French Lick Municipal Airp—*airport* IN-6
French Lick Run—*stream* PA-2
*French Lick Springs* IN-6
**French Lick (Township of)**—*pop pl* IN-6
French Lilly Mine—*mine* AZ-5
French Lode Mine—*mine* MT-8
French Madam Spring—*spring* CA-9
**Frenchman**—*pop pl* NV-8
Frenchman Bay—*bay* ME-1
Frenchman Bay—*bay* VI-3
Frenchman Bayou—*gut* (2) AR-4
Frenchman Branch—*stream* TX-5
Frenchman Brook—*stream* NH-1
Frenchman Butte—*summit* ID-8
Frenchman Campground—*locale* CA-9
Frenchman Camp Trail—*trail* OR-9
Frenchman Coulee—*valley* MT-8
Frenchman Coulee—*valley* WA-9
Frenchman Cove—*bay* ME-1
Frenchman Cove—*valley* CA-9
Frenchman Creek—*stream* AK-9
Frenchman Creek—*stream* (2) CA-9
Frenchman Creek—*stream* (3) CO-8
Frenchman Creek—*stream* FL-3
Frenchman Creek—*stream* (2) ID-8
Frenchman Creek—*stream* (2) MI-6
Frenchman Creek—*stream* MO-7
Frenchman Creek—*stream* (2) MT-8
Frenchman Creek—*stream* NE-7
Frenchman Creek—*stream* (2) NV-8
Frenchman Creek—*stream* NY-2
Frenchman Creek—*stream* SC-3
Frenchman Dam—*dam* CA-9
Frenchman Draw—*valley* WY-8
Frenchman Flat—*flat* NV-8
Frenchman Gulch—*valley* CA-9
Frenchman Gulch—*valley* CO-8
Frenchman Hill—*summit* CA-9
Frenchman Hill—*summit* MO-7
Frenchman Hill—*summit* VI-3
Frenchman Hills—*range* WA-9
Frenchman Hills—*summit* TX-5
Frenchman Hills Lake—*lake* WA-9
Frenchman Hills Pumping Plant—*other* WA-9
Frenchman Hills Wasteway—*canal* WA-9
Frenchman Hills Wasteway—*stream* WA-9
Frenchman Hollow—*valley* PA-2
Frenchman Island—*island* NY-2
Frenchman Knob—*summit* KY-4
Frenchman Knob Ch—*church* KY-4
Frenchman Lake—*lake* AK-9
Frenchman Lake—*lake* MI-6
Frenchman Lake—*lake* NV-8
Frenchman Lake—*lake* NM-5
Frenchman Lake—*reservoir* CA-9
Frenchman Ledge—*bar* ME-1
Frenchman Mine—*mine* AZ-5
Frenchman Mine—*mine* NV-8
*Frenchman Mountain* AZ-5
Frenchman Mtn—*summit* NV-8
Frenchman Mtn—*summit* WA-9
*Frenchman Peak* NV-8
Frenchman Ravine—*valley* CA-9
*Frenchman Reservoir* CA-9
*Frenchman River* CO-8
*Frenchman River* NE-7
Frenchmans, The—*locale* UT-8
*Frenchmans Bayou* AR-4
**Frenchmans Bayou**—*pop pl* AR-4
Frenchmans Bayou—*stream* AR-4
Frenchmans Bluff—*cliff* MO-7
Frenchmans Bluff—*summit* MN-6
Frenchmans Branch—*stream* PA-2
Frenchmans Butte—*summit* CO-8
Frenchmans Cabin—*locale* ID-8
Frenchmans Canyon—*valley* CA-9
Frenchmans Canyon—*valley* TX-5
*Frenchman's Cove* IL-6
Frenchmans Cove—*bay* WA-9
*Frenchmans Creek* CO-8
*Frenchmans Creek* NE-7
*Frenchmans Creek* NV-8
Frenchmans Creek—*stream* CA-9
Frenchmans Creek—*stream* FL-3
Frenchmans Creek Mall—*locale* (2) NC-3
Frenchmans Flat—*flat* CA-9
Frenchmans Flat Campground—*locale* CA-9
*Frenchman's Fork* NE-7
Frenchmans Lake—*lake* MI-6
Frenchman's Mountain Methodist Episcopal
Church And Cemetery—*hist pl* AR-4
Frenchmans Pit—*cave* AL-4
Frenchmans Point—*cape* NC-3
Frenchmans Point—*cape* WA-9
Frenchman Spring—*spring* ID-8
Frenchman Spring—*spring* NV-8
Frenchman Spring—*spring* WA-9
*Frenchman Springs Coulee* WA-9
Frenchman Springs Pumping
Plant—*other* WA-9
Frenchmans Ridge—*ridge* MT-8
*Frenchmans River* NE-7
Frenchmans Slough—*stream* IN-6
Frenchmans Spring—*spring* ID-8
*Frenchmans Station* NV-8
*Frenchman Station* NV-8
Frenchmans Well—*well* NM-5
Frenchmans Well—*well* TX-5
Frenchman Tank—*reservoir* (2) AZ-5

Frenchman Tank—reservoir NM-5
Frenchman Trail—trail PA-2
Frenchman Well—well NV-8
Frenchman Windmill, The—locale CO-8
French Market—post sta OK-5
French Market-Old Vegetable Market—hist pl LA-4
French Meadow CA-9
French Meadow—flat (2) CA-9
French Meadow Gulch CA-9
French Meadows—flat (2) CA-9
French Meadows Rsvr—reservoir CA-9
French Memorial Park—park IL-6
Frenchmen River CO-8
Frenchmen River NE-7
Frenchmens River CO-8
Frenchmens River NE-7
French Mesa—summit NM-5
French Mill—locale AL-4
French Mill—locale ME-1
French Mill—locale TN-4
French Mill Creek—stream AL-4
French Mills PA-2
French Mills—locale MO-7
French Mills Brook—stream ME-1
French Mine—mine CA-9
**French Mountain**—pop pl NY-2
French Mtn OR-9
French Mtn—summit CA-9
French Mtn—summit CO-8
French Mtn—summit CT-1
French Mtn—summit ID-8
French Mtn—summit ME-1
French Mtn—summit NY-2
French Mtn—summit NC-3
French Mtn—summit OR-9
French Mtn—summit VT-1
French Park—park OH-6
French-Parks House—hist pl OK-5
French Pass CA-9
French Pass—gap CO-8
French Pass—gap OR-9
French Peak CO-8
French Peak—summit (2) NV-8
French Peak—summit OR-9
French Peak—summit WA-9
French Pete Creek—stream OR-9
French Pete Forest Camp—locale OR-9
French Pit—basin CA-9
French Placer Canal—canal CA-9
French Point—cape KY-4
French Point—cape ME-1
French Point—cape NY-2
French Point—cape (2) WA-9
French Point Mtn—summit NY-2
French Point Rocks—island WA-9
French Pond CT-1
French Pond ME-1
French Pond—lake (2) NH-1
French Pond—lake NY-2
French Pond—reservoir ME-1
French Pond—reservoir MA-1
French Pond Dam—dam MA-1
**Frenchport**—pop pl AR-4
French Portage Road Hist Dist—hist pl NY-2
Frenchport Ch—church AR-4
Frenchport Landing—locale AR-4
French Post Office (historical)—building TN-4
French Potholes—lake WA-9
French Prairie—flat OR-9
French Prairie Cem—cemetery AR-4
French Quarter—other LA-4
French Quarter Creek—stream SC-3
French Ranch—locale (4) CA-9
French Ranch—locale MT-8
French Ranch—locale SD-7
French Ranch Gulch—valley CA-9
French Ravine—valley (5) CA-9
French Reef—bar FL-3
French Ridge—ridge (3) CA-9
French Ridge—ridge IN-6
French Ridge—ridge ME-1
French Ridge—ridge OH-6
French Ridge—ridge (2) WA-9
**French River**—pop pl MN-6
French River—stream CT-1
French River—stream MA-1
French River—stream MN-6
French River Rsvr—reservoir MA-1
French Road Ch—church NY-2
French Road Sch—school NY-2
French Rocks—pillar WY-8
French Rsvr—reservoir CA-9
French Run—stream (2) IN-6
French Run—stream (2) PA-2
French Run—stream WV-2
French Run Sch—school OH-6
French Saddle—gap ID-8
Frenchs Brook—stream NH-1
Frenchs Brook—stream NY-2
Frenchs Cemetery TN-4
French Sch—school (2) IL-6
French Sch—school (2) MI-6
French Sch—school MS-4
French Sch—school NY-2
French Sch—school SD-7
French Sch—school TX-5
French Sch (abandoned)—school MO-7
Frenchs Chapel (historical)—church AL-4
French's Chapel Sch—school IL-6
Frenchs Commons—park MA-1
Frenchs Corner PA-2
Frenchs Corner—locale ME-1
**Frenchs Corners**—pop pl PA-2
Frenchs Creek NC-3
Frenchs Creek—stream (2) NC-3
Frenchs Creek Swamp—swamp NC-3
Frenchs Creek (Township of)—fmr MCD NC-3
French Settlement—locale PA-2
**French Settlement**—pop pl LA-4
**French Settlement**—pop pl ME-1
Frenchs Flat—flat CA-9
Frenchs Hill MA-1
Frenchside Fishing Village—hist pl WI-6
French Site (22HO565)—hist pl MS-4
Frenchs Landing (historical)—locale AL-4
Frenchs Ledge—bench NH-1
French Slough—gut WI-6
Frenchs Mill AL-4
Frenchs Mill TN-4
Frenchs Mill (historical)—locale TN-4
**Frenchs Mobile Homes**—pop pl DE-2
Frenchs Pass—gap CA-9
French Speaking Baptist Ch—church FL-3
French's Point KY-4
French Spring—spring CA-9
French Spring—spring ID-8
French Spring—spring NM-5
French Spring—spring (2) OR-9
French Spring—spring UT-8
French Spring Fork—valley UT-8
Frenchs Store—locale MS-4
French'S Stream MA-1
French Stream—stream ME-1
French Stream—stream MA-1
Frenchs Vly—swamp NY-2
French Tableland—summit NE-7
**Frenchton**—pop pl WV-2
Frenchtown IN-6
Frenchtown WV-2
Frenchtown—locale (2) CA-9
Frenchtown—locale MD-2
French Town—locale MT-8
Frenchtown—locale PA-2
**Frenchtown**—pop pl IN-6
**Frenchtown**—pop pl MD-2
**Frenchtown**—pop pl MI-6
**French Town**—pop pl MI-6
**Frenchtown**—pop pl MT-8
**Frenchtown**—pop pl NJ-2
**Frenchtown**—pop pl (2) OH-6
**Frenchtown**—pop pl (3) PA-2
**Frenchtown**—pop pl RI-1
**Frenchtown**—pop pl VI-3
Frenchtown Brook—stream RI-1
Frenchtown Cem—cemetery MT-8
Frenchtown Ch—church MI-6
Frenchtown-Evaro—cens area MT-8
**Frenchtown (historical)**—pop pl SD-7
Frenchtown Irrigation District Ditch—canal MT-8
Frenchtown Lake—lake IA-7
Frenchtown Monmt—park WA-9
Frenchtown Sch—school PA-2
Frenchtown Sch—school WI-6
French (Township of)—fmr MCD AR-4
**French (Township of)**—pop pl IN-6
**French (Township of)**—pop pl MN-6
**Frenchtown Township**—pop pl NE-7
**Frenchtown (Township of)**—pop pl MI-6
Frenchtown (Township of)—unorg ME-1
French Trail—trail PA-2
French Tunnel—mine CO-8
French Turn Ch—church LA-4
French Valley—basin NE-7
French Valley—valley CA-9
French Valley—valley WI-6
French Valley Ch—church KY-4
French Vee—locale WY-8
French Village IL-6
**French Village**—pop pl IL-6
**French Village**—pop pl MO-7
French Village Lookout Tower—locale MO-7
**Frenchville**—pop pl (3) ME-1
**Frenchville**—pop pl NY-2
**Frenchville**—pop pl PA-2
**Frenchville**—pop pl WI-6
Frenchville Cem—cemetery NY-2
Frenchville Station—locale PA-2
Frenchville Station (historical)—locale PA-2
**Frenchville (Town of)**—pop pl ME-1
French Wash AZ-5
French Watering Place—cove MA-1
French Watering Place Cove MA-1
Frenchwoman Creek—stream CO-8
French Woods—locale NY-2
Frenchy Basin—basin WY-8
Frenchy Butte—summit OR-9
Frenchy Canyon—valley AZ-5
Frenchy Creek—stream AK-9
Frenchy Creek—stream ID-8
Frenchy Creek—stream (2) MT-8
Frenchy Creek Mine—mine AK-9
Frenchy Draw—valley (2) WY-8
Frenchy Hill—summit AZ-5
Frenchy Lake—lake MI-6
Frenchy Lake—reservoir NV-8
Frenchy Meadows—flat NV-8
Frenchy Point—cape CA-9
Frenchy Rapids—rapids ID-8
Frenchy Rapids—rapids OR-9
Frenchy Spring—spring OR-9
Frenchy Springs—spring (2) WY-8
Frenchy Spring Tank—reservoir AZ-5
Frenchy Well—well NV-8
Frendenburg Butte OR-9
Frendenburg Ranch—locale OR-9
Frendship Ch—church GA-3
**Freneau**—pop pl NJ-2
Frene Creek—stream MO-7
Frenepiquant, Bayou—gut LA-4
Frenes, Point aux—cape MI-6
Frenge Branch—stream SC-3
Frenger Park—park NM-5
Frenier—locale LA-4
Frenier Beach—locale LA-4
Fren Oil Field—other NM-5
Frenstat—locale TX-5
Frentress Lake—lake IL-6
Frenyea Mtn—summit NY-2
Frenzel Creek—stream CA-9
Frenzel Sch—school MI-6
Frequency Changing Station—hist pl WA-9
Frer Creek CA-9
Frerichs Well—well AZ-5
Freschette Lake—lake MI-6
**Fresco**—pop pl AL-4
Fresenius—locale TX-5
Frese Pond—lake TN-4
Fresh Air Camp—locale CT-1
Fresh Air Camp—locale MI-6
Fresh Air Camp—locale MN-6
Fresh Air Camp—locale OH-6
Fresh Air Home—building PA-2
**Fresh Brook**—pop pl MA-1
Fresh Brook—stream MA-1
Fresh Brook Village MA-1
Fresh Creek MD-2
Fresh Creek—stream NH-1
Fresh Creek—stream (2) NJ-2
Fresh Creek—stream NY-2
Fresh Creek Basin NY-2
Freshet Draw—valley CO-8
Freshing Lead—stream SC-3
**Fresh Kills**—pop pl NY-2
Fresh Kills—stream NY-2
Fresh Kills Reach—channel NJ-2
Fresh Kills Reach—channel NY-2
Fresh Lake—lake ND-7
Freshley Branch—stream MS-4
Freshley Branch—stream SC-3
Freshley Shoals—bar SC-3
Fresh Marsh—swamp MD-2
Fresh Meadow—swamp ME-1
Fresh Meadow Country Club—other NY-2
Fresh Meadow Pond—reservoir MA-1
Fresh Meadow Pond Number 1 Dam—dam MA-1
**Fresh Meadows**—pop pl KY-4
**Fresh Meadows**—pop pl NY-2
Fresh Meadows—swamp CT-1
Freshour Branch—stream TN-4
Freshour Creek—stream NY-2
Freshour Hollow—valley TN-4
Fresh Pond CT-1
Fresh Pond MD-2
Fresh Pond MA-1
Fresh Pond RI-1
Fresh Pond VA-3
Fresh Pond—lake DE-2
Fresh Pond—lake (3) ME-1
Fresh Pond—lake (3) MD-2
Fresh Pond—lake (7) MA-1
Fresh Pond—lake (6) NY-2
Fresh Pond—lake (2) RI-1
Fresh Pond—locale CA-9
**Fresh Pond**—pop pl NY-2
Fresh Pond—post sta NY-2
Fresh Pond—reservoir MA-1
Fresh Pond—reservoir NJ-2
Fresh Pond—uninc pl MA-1
Fresh Pond Dam—dam MA-1
Fresh Pond Hill Coast Guard Station—military NC-3
Fresh Pond (historical)—lake SD-7
Fresh Pond Hotel—hist pl MA-1
Fresh Pond Junction—locale NY-2
Fresh Pond Landing—locale (2) NY-2
Fresh Pond Neck—cape MD-2
Fresh Pond Ravine—valley CA-9
**Fresh Ponds**—pop pl NJ-2
Fresh Pond Shop Ctr—locale MA-1
Fresh Pond-Traffic Hist Dist—hist pl NY-2
Fresh Ridge—ridge WI-6
Fresh River MA-1
Fresh River—stream MA-1
Fresh River—stream NH-1
Fresh Swamp—swamp RI-1
Freshwater CT-1
**Freshwater**—pop pl CA-9
**Freshwater**—pop pl CO-8
Freshwater Bay—bay AK-9
Freshwater Bay—bay WA-9
Freshwater Bayou LA-4
Freshwater Bayou—bay FL-3
Freshwater Bayou—bay TX-5
Fresh Water Bayou—gut (2) LA-4
Freshwater Bayou—stream LA-4
Freshwater Bayou Canal—canal LA-4
Freshwater Bayou Channel LA-4
Freshwater Bayou Channel—channel LA-4
Freshwater Bayou Gas Field—oilfield LA-4
Freshwater Branch—stream CA-9
Fresh Water Brook CT-1
Freshwater Brook—stream CT-1
Freshwater Brooks CT-1
freshwater Canal LA-4
**Freshwater Corners**—pop pl CA-9
Fresh Water Coulee—stream ND-7
Fresh Water Cove MA-1
Freshwater Cove—cove MA-1
Freshwater Cove—uninc pl MA-1
Freshwater Cove—valley VA-3
Fresh Water Cove Village MA-1
**Freshwater Cove Village**—pop pl MA-1
Freshwater Creek—stream AK-9
Freshwater Creek—stream (3) CA-9
Freshwater Creek—stream CO-8
Freshwater Creek—stream VA-3
Freshwater Creek—stream (2) WA-9
Freshwater Draw—valley ID-8
Fresh Water Draw—valley MT-8
Freshwater Gulch CA-9
Freshwater Gulch—valley CA-9
Fresh Water Hollow—valley MO-7
Freshwater Lagoon—lake CA-9
Fresh Water Lake—lake AK-9
Freshwater Lake—lake FL-3
Fresh Water Lake—lake LA-4
Fresh Water Lake—lake ND-7
Fresh Water Lake—lake (2) TX-5
Freshwater Lake—lake TX-5
Fresh Water Lake—lake TX-5
Freshwater Lake—lake WA-9
Freshwater Park—park CA-9
Fresh Water Pond MA-1
Freshwater Pond—lake CT-1
Fresh Water Pond—lake MA-1
Freshwater Slough—stream CA-9
Freshwater Slough—stream WA-9
Freshwater Spring—spring UT-8
Fresh Water Supply Pond—reservoir PA-2
Fresh Water Thayer Trail—trail AK-9
**Freshwater Township**—pop pl ND-7
Fresh Water Village MA-1
Freska Lake—lake MI-6
Fresnal AZ-5
**Fresnal**—pop pl TX-5
Fresnal, Cerro del—summit AZ-5
**Fresnal Canyon**—pop pl AZ-5
Fresnal Canyon—valley (3) AZ-5
Fresnal Canyon—valley NM-5
Fresnal Creek AZ-5
Fresnal Dam—dam AZ-5
Fresnal Hill—summit AZ-5
Fresnal Mtn AZ-5
Fresnal Ranger Station—locale NM-5
Fresnal Village AZ-5
Fresnal Wash—stream (4) AZ-5
Fresnal Well AZ-5
Fresno—locale AR-4
Fresno—locale MT-8
**Fresno**—pop pl CA-9
**Fresno**—pop pl OH-6
**Fresno**—pop pl TX-5
Fresno Air Natl Guard Base—building CA-9
Fresno Air Terminal (Airport)—airport CA-9
Fresno Airways Golf Course—other CA-9
Fresno Banner Mine—mine CA-9
Fresno Bee Bldg—hist pl CA-9
Fresno Brewing Company Office and Warehouse—hist pl CA-9
Fresno Camp—locale OR-9
Fresno Canal—canal CA-9
Fresno Canyon—valley (3) AZ-5
Fresno Canyon—valley (2) CA-9
Fresno Canyon—valley NM-5
Fresno Canyon—valley TX-5
Fresno (CCD)—cens area CA-9
Fresno City CA-9
Fresno City Coll—school CA-9
Fresno Colony Canal—canal CA-9
Fresno Colony Sch Number Two—school CA-9
Fresno Coulee—valley MT-8
**Fresno (County)**—pop pl CA-9
Fresno Creek—stream AK-9
Fresno Creek—stream OR-9
Fresno Creek—stream (3) TX-5
Fresno Crossing—locale CA-9
Fresno Dam—dam MT-8
Fresno Dome—summit CA-9
Fresno Dome Campground—locale CA-9
Fresno Flats—flat CA-9
Fresno Grove of Big Trees CA-9
Fresno Gulch—valley MT-8
Fresno Hosp—hospital CA-9
Fresno Hot Springs CA-9
Fresno HS—school CA-9
Fresno Memorial Gardens (Cemetery)—cemetery CA-9
Fresno Mine—mine TX-5
Fresno Mines—mine AK-9
Fresno Museum of Natural History—building CA-9
Fresno Peak—summit TX-5
Fresno Ranch—locale TX-5
Fresno Recreation Center—park CA-9
Fresno Republican Printery Bldg—hist pl CA-9
Fresno River—stream CA-9
Fresno Rsvr—reservoir MT-8
Fresno Slough CA-9
Fresno Slough—gut CA-9
Fresno Slough—stream CA-9
Fresno Slough Bypass CA-9
Fresno Spring—spring (4) AZ-5
Fresno Tank—reservoir AZ-5
Fresno Tank—reservoir TX-5
Fresno Union Acad—school CA-9
Fresno Wash—stream AZ-5
Fresno Waste Disposal Area—area CA-9
Fresno Well—well AZ-5
Fresno Well—well TX-5
Fresno Yard—locale CA-9
Frest Pond NJ-2
Fret Branch—stream MS-4
Fret Creek—stream OR-9
Frethem Lake—lake MN-6
Frethey Gulch CA-9
Frethy Gulch CA-9
Fretoso Ranch—locale NM-5
Fretter Island—island IA-7
**Frettim Township**—pop pl ND-7
Frettim Township State Mngmt Area—park ND-7
**Frettin**—pop pl TN-4
Fretts Brook—stream NH-1
Fretwell Rsvr—reservoir OR-9
Fretz Farm—hist pl PA-2
Fretz JHS—school PA-2
Fretz Sch—school PA-2
Freund Chapel—church IL-6
Freund Creek—stream WA-9
Freund Oil Field—oilfield TX-5
Freund Store—hist pl MN-6
Frevels Lake—lake MN-6
Frew—locale KY-4
Frew—locale WV-2
Frewen—locale WY-8
Frewen, Moreton, House—hist pl WY-8
Frewen Lake—lake WY-8
Frewens Castle—summit WY-8
Frewens Draw—valley WY-8
**Frew Estates Subdivision**—pop pl UT-8
Frewill Baptist Church TN-4
**Frewsburg**—pop pl NY-2
Frew Sch—school IL-6
Frews Run—stream NY-2
Frey—locale LA-4
Frey—locale OK-5
Frey, Lake—reservoir CA-9
Freya Castle—summit AZ-5
Freya Cem—cemetery WI-6
Freya (historical)—locale SD-7
Frey Branch—stream (2) TN-4
Freyburg—locale TX-5
Freyburg Community Hall—building TX-5
Frey Canyon UT-8
Frey Canyon—valley CA-9
Frey Cem—cemetery LA-4
Frey Cem—cemetery OH-6
Frey Cem—cemetery TX-5
Frey Ch (historical)—church PA-2
Freyco—locale VA-3
Frey Creek—stream (2) CA-9
Frey Creek—stream KY-4
Frey Creek—stream OR-9
Frey Creek—stream SC-3
Frey Creek Ch—church KY-4
Frey Creek Sch—school KY-4
Freyden Cave—cave AL-4
Frey Draw—valley WY-8
Freyee Islands—island ME-1
Freye Lake—lake OR-9
Freyer Ditch—canal IN-6
Freyer Island ME-1
Frey Ford—locale MO-7
Frey Gulch—valley CO-8
Frey-Haverstick Site (36LA6)—hist pl PA-2
Frey Hollow—valley WV-2
Frey Lake—lake MI-6
Frey Lake—reservoir MO-7
Frey Pond—reservoir PA-2
Frey Ranch—locale NV-8
**Freysbush**—pop pl NY-2
Frey Sch—school MI-6
Frey Sch—school OH-6
Freys Grove—locale PA-2
**Freys Hill**—pop pl KY-4
Freys Pond—lake NY-2
Freys Run PA-2
**Freysville**—pop pl PA-2
Freys Well—well NV-8
Freytown—locale PA-2
Freytown Cem—cemetery PA-2
Frezkat Creek—stream ID-8
F R Fackelman Dam—dam SD-7
Friable, Mount—summit AK-9
**Friant**—pop pl CA-9
Friant Dam—dam CA-9
Friant-Kern Canal—canal CA-9
Friar RI-1
**Friar**—pop pl TX-5
Friar, Alfred, House—hist pl TX-5
Friar, The—summit VA-3
Friar Branch—stream TN-4
Friar Head NY-2
Friar Point MS-4
Friar Roads—bay ME-1
Friars Bay—flat GA-3
Friars Bayou MS-4
Friars Cove—bay FL-3
Friar's Head NY-2
Friars Head—summit NY-2
Friars Hill—locale WV-2
Friars Hole—basin WV-2
Friars Island (historical)—island TN-4
Friars Landing—locale NJ-2
**Friars Point**—pop pl MS-4
Friars Point Elem Sch—school MS-4
Friar Swamp—swamp NC-3
Friason Swamp—stream SC-3
Friberg Cooper Ch—church TX-5
Friberger Park—park NJ-2
Friberg Lake WA-9
**Friberg (Township of)**—pop pl MN-6
Fribley Creek—stream MI-6
Friborg Ch—church MN-6
Fricaba, Mount—summit WA-9
FRI Camp—locale AK-9
Frick—locale CO-8
Frick, Henry Clay, Training Sch for Teachers—hist pl PA-2
Frick, William, House—hist pl OK-5
Frick Bldg and Annex—hist pl PA-2
Frick Cem—cemetery KS-7
Frick Collection—building NY-2
Frick Creek—stream GA-3
Frick Ditch—canal IN-6
Fricke Cem—cemetery (2) NE-7
Fricke Creek—stream ID-8
Fricker Draw—valley MT-8
Frickes Branch—stream IL-6
Frickey Canyon—valley OR-9
Frick JHS—school CA-9
Frick Lake—lake CA-9
Frick Lake—lake (2) WI-6
Frickland Coulee—valley WI-6
Frick MS—school PA-2
Frick Park—park MO-7
Frick Park—park PA-2
Frick Pond—lake NY-2
Frick Run TX-5
Fricks—locale PA-2
Fricks Cove—basin AL-4
Fricks Crossing—locale MD-2
**Fricks (Leidytown)**—pop pl PA-2
Fricks Lock—locale PA-2
Fricks Pond—reservoir CT-1
Frick's Tavern—hist pl IA-7
Fricot Bayou—channel LA-4
Fricot Ditch—canal CA-9
Fricot Ranch Sch—school CA-9
Friday—locale TX-5
Friday Adit—mine NM-5
Friday Bay—bay MN-6
Friday Branch—stream IN-6
Friday Branch—stream KY-4
Friday Butte—summit ID-8
Friday Camp—locale CA-9
Fridaycap Creek—stream GA-3
Friday Cem—cemetery AL-4
Friday Cem—cemetery OK-5
Friday Cem—cemetery TN-4
Friday Cem—cemetery WY-8
Friday Creek—stream (2) AK-9
Friday Creek—stream GA-3
Friday Creek—stream LA-4
Friday Creek—stream MD-2
Friday Creek—stream MS-4
Friday Creek—stream OH-6
Friday Creek—stream (3) OR-9
Friday Creek—stream (4) WA-9
Friday Creek—stream WI-6
Friday Draw—valley WY-8
Friday Family Cem—cemetery IA-7
Friday Gulch—valley MT-8
Friday Gulch—valley SD-7
Friday Harbor—bay WA-9
**Friday Harbor**—pop pl WA-9
Friday Harbor Airp—airport WA-9
Friday Harbor Seaplane Base—airport WA-9
Friday Hill—summit MT-8
Friday Hollow—valley IA-7
Friday Hollow—valley (2) TX-5
Friday Island FM-9
Friday Lake—lake AL-4
Friday Lake Dam—dam AL-4
Friday Lake Dam—dam MS-4
Friday Lode Mine—mine SD-7
Friday-Louden Mine—mine CA-9
Friday Meadow—flat OR-9
Friday Mine—mine AK-9
Friday Mine—mine CA-9
Friday Mine—mine OR-9
Friday Morning Club—hist pl CA-9
Friday Mtn—summit NY-2
Friday Mtn—summit TX-5
Friday Pass—gap ID-8
Friday Ridge—ridge CA-9
Friday Ridge—ridge ID-8
Fridays Chapel—church AL-4
**Fridays Crossing**—pop pl AL-4
Fridays Dream Point—cape GA-3
Fridays Hill—summit PA-2
Friday Spring—spring NM-5
Friday Spring—spring OR-9
Friday's Station—hist pl NV-8
Friday West Airp—airport WA-9
Friddle Branch—stream IL-6
Friddle Cave—cave TN-4
Friddle Creek—stream NC-3
Friddle Hollow—valley PA-2
Friddle Lake—reservoir SC-3
Fridel Cem—cemetery TX-5
Fridge Lake Dam—dam MS-4
Fridhem Cem—cemetery (3) MN-6
Fridhem Cem—cemetery (2) NE-7
Fridhem (historical)—locale SD-7
Fridhem Swedish Lutheran Ch (historical)—church SD-7
**Fridley**—pop pl MN-6
Fridley Branch—stream VA-3
Fridley Canyon—valley CA-9
Fridley Cove—valley VA-3
Fridley Creek—stream (2) MT-8
Fridley Ditch OH-6
Fridley Gap—gap VA-3
Fridley HS—school MN-6
Fridley JHS—school MN-6
Fridley Lakes—lake MT-8
Fridley-Oman Farm—hist pl OH-6
Fridley Peak—summit MT-8
Fridley Run—stream VA-3
Fridleys Branch VA-3
Fridleys Branch—stream VA-3
Fridsborg Cem—cemetery MN-6
Frieborn Canyon—valley NM-5
Friebus Post Office (historical)—building AL-4
**Fried**—pop pl ND-7
Fried, Samson, Estate—hist pl NY-2
Frieda Lake—lake WI-6
Friedaland—other KY-4
Friedbauer Lake—lake WI-6
Friedburg Ch—church NC-3
**Friedburg (subdivision)**—pop pl NC-3
**Friedel Property (subdivision)**—pop pl DE-2
Friedenberg Cem—cemetery MO-7
Friedenberg Mennonite Cem—cemetery SD-7
Friedenberg Mennonite Church SD-7
Friedenburg—locale MO-7
Frieden Cem—cemetery (2) MO-7
Frieden Cem—cemetery ND-7
Frieden Cem—cemetery TX-5
Frieden Cem—cemetery WI-6
Frieden Ch—church (2) MN-6
Frieden Ch—church TX-5
Frieden Ch (historical)—church PA-2
Frieden Ditch—canal IL-6
Friedenfeld Cem—cemetery ND-7
Friedenfeld Cem—cemetery SD-7
Frieden Park—park IA-7
Frieden Run—stream OH-6
**Friedens**—pop pl (2) PA-2
Friedensaals Ch—church PA-2
Friedensburg PA-2
**Friedensburg**—pop pl PA-2
Friedens Cem—cemetery IL-6
Friedens Cem—cemetery (2) MO-7
Friedens Cem—cemetery NY-2
Friedens Cem—cemetery ND-7
Friedens Cem—cemetery (2) SD-7
Friedens Cem—cemetery (2) TX-5
Friedens Cem—cemetery WI-6
Friedens Ch—church (2) IL-6
Friedens Ch—church KS-7
Friedens Ch—church MO-7
Friedens Ch—church NC-3
Friedens Ch—church (4) PA-2
Friedens Ch—church TX-5
Friedens Ch—church VA-3
Friedens Ch—church WI-6
Friedens Church IN-6
Friedens Elem Sch—school PA-2
**Friedensfeld**—pop pl VI-3
Friedensfeld Midlands Moravian Church and Manse—hist pl VI-3
Friedens Sch—school WI-6
Friedenstahl Cem—cemetery SD-7
Friedenstal Cem—cemetery KS-7
Friedenstal Ch—church KS-7
Friedensthal PA-2
Friedensthal Mission—hist pl VI-3
Friedens Township—civil MO-7
Friedens Union Ch—church PA-2
Friedens United Ch of Christ—church IN-6
Friedensville PA-2
**Friedensville**—pop pl PA-2
Friedensville Sch (abandoned)—school PA-2
**Friedenthal**—pop pl PA-2
Friederich Farmstead Hist Dist—hist pl WI-6
**Friedheim**—pop pl MO-7
Friedheim Station—locale MO-7
Friedhof Cem—cemetery IL-6
Friedhof Cem—cemetery SD-7
Friedland Ch—church NC-3
Friedlander, Abraham J., House—hist pl OH-6
Friedlander, Leo, Studio—hist pl NY-2
Friedlander Meadows—flat WA-9
Friedlein Cem—cemetery IA-7
Friedline Apartments—hist pl ID-8
Fried Liver Wash—stream CA-9
Friedman Chapel—church MI-6
Friedman Creek—stream ID-8
Friedman Library (historical)—building AL-4
Friedorf Gulch—valley ID-8
Friedrich Airp—airport IN-6
Friedrich Cem—cemetery TX-5
Friedrich Park—park TX-5
Friedrich Point—cape MN-6
Friedrick Sch (abandoned)—school SD-7
Frieds Bay—locale SC-3
**Fried Township**—pop pl ND-7
Frie Flow—stream NY-2
Frieler Creek—stream MT-8
Frieling Cem—cemetery SD-7
Frielings—locale IL-6
Friel Run—stream WV-2
Friel Street Sch—school MI-6
Frielund Lake—lake MN-6
Friend SC-3

Friend—*locale* NY-2
Friend—*locale* OR-9
**Friend**—*pop pl* KS-7
**Friend**—*pop pl* NE-7
Friend, Nathaniel, House—*hist pl* VA-3
Friend Branch—*stream* AL-4
Friend Branch—*stream* KY-4
Friend Bridge—*other* MO-7
Friend Brook—*stream* MI-6
Friend Cem—*cemetery* ME-1
Friend Cem—*cemetery* (4) MO-7
Friend Cem—*cemetery* OH-6
Friend Cem—*cemetery* OR-9
Friend Ch—*church* AL-4
Friend Ch—*church* KY-4
Friend Ch—*church* MO-7
Friend Creek—*stream* WY-8
Friend Draw—*valley* CO-8
Friend Elem Sch*—*school* KS-7
Friendfield—*locale* (2) SC-3
Friend Field Plantation—*locale* SC-3
*Friend Grove* IL-6
Friend Key—*island* FL-3
Friend Key Bank—*bar* FL-3
Friend Lake—*lake* CA-9
Friend Lake—*lake* IL-6
**Friendly**—*pop pl* MD-2
**Friendly**—*pop pl* WV-2
Friendly—*post sta* NC-3
**Friendly Acres**—*pop pl* PA-2
Friendly Acres Park—*park* AR-4
**Friendly Acres (subdivision)**—*pop pl* NC-3
Friendly Baptist Ch—*church* AL-4
Friendly Cem—*cemetery* WV-2
Friendly Ch—*church* (2) AL-4
Friendly Ch—*church* (4) NC-3
Friendly Ch—*church* OK-5
Friendly Ch—*church* TN-4
Friendly Ch—*church* VA-3
Friendly Ch—*church* WV-2
Friendly Chapel—*church* (2) NC-3
Friendly Chapel—*church* TN-4
Friendly Chapel (historical)—*church* TN-4
Friendly Community Ch—*church* NC-3
Friendly Corner—*locale* TX-5
**Friendly Corner**—*pop pl* IN-6
**Friendly Corners**—*pop pl* AZ-5
Friendly Creek—*stream* AK-9
**Friendly Farms**—*pop pl* MD-2
Friendly Grove—*hist pl* OH-6
Friendly Grove Ch—*church* (2) IN-6
Friendly Grove Ch—*church* KY-4
Friendly Grove Ch—*church* (2) NC-3
**Friendly Hills**—*pop pl* (2) CA-9
**Friendly Hills**—*pop pl* KY-4
**Friendly Homes (subdivision)**—*pop pl* NC-3
Friendly Hope Ch—*church* AR-4
Friendly Island—*island* NY-2
Friendly Lake—*reservoir* NC-3
Friendly Lake Dam—*dam* NC-3
Friendly Missionary Baptist Ch—*church* (2) FL-3
Friendly Park—*park* OR-9
Friendly Pines Camp—*locale* AZ-5
Friendly Reach—*channel* OR-9
Friendly Reach—*channel* WA-9
Friendly Riverside Ch—*church* NC-3
Friendly Sch—*school* IL-6
Friendly Sch—*school* TX-5
Friendly Tabernacle—*church* (2) NC-3
Friendly United Ch—*church* WV-2
**Friendly Valley**—*pop pl* MO-7
Friendly Valley Ch—*church* TN-4
**Friendly View**—*pop pl* WV-2
Friend Mine—*mine* AZ-5
Friend Mountain Tank—*reservoir* TX-5
Friend Mtn—*summit* CA-9
Friend Mtn—*summit* TX-5
Friend Park—*park* (2) WY-8
Friend Place—*locale* CA-9
Friend Ranch—*locale* TX-5
Friend Run—*stream* IN-6
*Friends* TN-4
Friends Acad—*school* MA-1
Friends Acad—*school* NY-2
Friends Bar—*bar* AL-4
Friends Branch—*stream* KY-4
Friends Burial Ground—*cemetery* OH-6
Friends Burial Lot—*cemetery* MA-1
Friends Cem—*cemetery* AL-4
Friends Cem—*cemetery* IL-6
Friends Cem—*cemetery* (4) IN-6
Friends Cem—*cemetery* (6) IA-7
Friends Cem—*cemetery* (4) KS-7
Friends Cem—*cemetery* (2) ME-1
Friends Cem—*cemetery* MD-2
Friends Cem—*cemetery* (4) MA-1
Friends Cem—*cemetery* (2) MO-7
Friends Cem—*cemetery* NE-7
Friends Cem—*cemetery* NH-1
Friends Cem—*cemetery* NJ-2
Friends Cem—*cemetery* (2) NY-2
Friends Cem—*cemetery* (6) OH-6
Friends Cem—*cemetery* OK-5
Friends Cem—*cemetery* OR-9
Friends Cem—*cemetery* (4) PA-2
Friends Cem—*cemetery* TN-4
Friends Cem—*cemetery* VT-1
Friends Central Cem—*cemetery* NJ-2
Friends Central Sch—*school* PA-2
Friends Ch—*church* AL-4
Friends Ch—*church* (2) IN-6
Friends Ch—*church* (2) IA-7
Friends Ch—*church* (3) KS-7
Friends Ch—*church* (3) ME-1
Friends Ch—*church* MA-1
Friends Ch—*church* MI-6
Friends Ch—*church* NE-7
Friends Ch—*church* NH-1
Friends Ch—*church* NY-2
Friends Ch—*church* (2) NC-3
Friends Ch—*church* (4) OH-6
Friends Ch—*church* (2) TN-4
Friends Ch—*church* VT-1
Friends Ch—*church* VA-3
Friend Sch—*school* OK-5
Friend Sch—*school* VA-3
Friends Chapel—*church* OH-6
Friends Chapel—*church* OK-5
Friends Chapels—*church* KS-7
Friends Church—*locale* OH-6
Friends Church (historical)—*locale* SD-7
Friends Community of West Wichita—*church* KS-7
Friends Cove—*valley* PA-2
Friends Cove Ch—*church* PA-2
*Friends Creek* IN-6
Friends Creek—*locale* MD-2
Friends Creek—*stream* CO-8
Friends Creek—*stream* IL-6
Friends Creek—*stream* (2) IN-6
Friends Creek—*stream* MD-2
Friends Creek—*stream* OH-6
Friends Creek—*stream* PA-2
Friends Creek Cem—*cemetery* IL-6
Friends Creek County Park—*park* IL-6
Friends Creek Ditch—*canal* IL-6
Friends Creek (Township of)—*civ div* IL-6
Friends Gap—*gap* WV-2
*Friends Grove* IL-6
Friends Grove Sch (abandoned)—*school* PA-2
*Friendship* AL-4
*Friendship* MS-4
*Friendship* NC-3
*Friendship* TN-4
Friendship—*locale* (3) AL-4
Friendship—*locale* (2) AR-4
Friendship—*locale* (5) GA-3
Friendship—*locale* KY-4
Friendship—*locale* (3) NJ-2
Friendship—*locale* NC-3
Friendship—*locale* SC-3
Friendship—*locale* (3) TN-4
Friendship—*locale* (10) TX-5
Friendship—*locale* VA-3
**Friendship**—*pop pl* (4) AL-4
**Friendship**—*pop pl* (2) AR-4
**Friendship**—*pop pl* IN-6
**Friendship**—*pop pl* LA-4
**Friendship**—*pop pl* ME-1
**Friendship**—*pop pl* (4) MD-2
**Friendship**—*pop pl* (3) MS-4
**Friendship**—*pop pl* NJ-2
**Friendship**—*pop pl* NY-2
**Friendship**—*pop pl* (4) NC-3
**Friendship**—*pop pl* OH-6
**Friendship**—*pop pl* OK-5
**Friendship**—*pop pl* (4) SC-3
**Friendship**—*pop pl* (3) TN-4
**Friendship**—*pop pl* TX-5
**Friendship**—*pop pl* WI-6
Friendship—*post sta* DC-2
Friendship Advent Christian Ch—*church* FL-3
Friendship African Methodist Episcopal Ch—*church* MS-4
*Friendship Airport* MD-2
*Friendship Assembly of God Ch* MS-4
*Friendship Baptist Cemetery* TN-4
*Friendship Baptist Ch* AL-4
*Friendship Baptist Ch* MS-4
*Friendship Baptist Ch* TN-4
Friendship Baptist Ch—*church* (8) AL-4
Friendship Baptist Ch—*church* AR-4
Friendship Baptist Ch—*church* DE-2
Friendship Baptist Ch—*church* FL-3
Friendship Baptist Ch—*church* (5) MS-4
Friendship Baptist Ch—*church* (5) TN-4
Friendship Baptist Ch (historical)—*church* AL-4
Friendship Baptist Ch (historical)—*church* TN-4
Friendship Baptist Church—*hist pl* CA-9
Friendship Bible Ch—*church* AL-4
Friendship Boat Dock—*locale* TN-4
*Friendship Branch* GA-3
Friendship Branch—*stream* TX-5
Friendship Campground—*locale* UT-8
Friendship (CCD)—*cens area* TN-4
*Friendship Cem* FL-3
*Friendship Cem* TN-4
Friendship Cem—*cemetery* (16) AL-4
Friendship Cem—*cemetery* (8) AR-4
Friendship Cem—*cemetery* (3) FL-3
Friendship Cem—*cemetery* (6) GA-3
Friendship Cem—*cemetery* (4) IN-6
Friendship Cem—*cemetery* KS-7
Friendship Cem—*cemetery* KY-4
Friendship Cem—*cemetery* (4) LA-4
Friendship Cem—*cemetery* ME-1
Friendship Cem—*cemetery* MD-2
Friendship Cem—*cemetery* MN-6
Friendship Cem—*cemetery* (16) MS-4
Friendship Cem—*cemetery* (5) MO-7
Friendship Cem—*cemetery* NC-3
Friendship Cem—*cemetery* (3) OH-6
Friendship Cem—*cemetery* OK-5
Friendship Cem—*cemetery* OR-9
Friendship Cem—*cemetery* PA-2
Friendship Cem—*cemetery* (2) SC-3
Friendship Cem—*cemetery* (6) TN-4
Friendship Cem—*cemetery* (7) TX-5
Friendship Cem—*cemetery* (2) WV-2
Friendship Cem—*cemetery* (2) WI-6
Friendship Cemetery—*hist pl* MS-4
*Friendship Ch* AL-4
*Friendship Ch* DE-2
*Friendship Ch* MS-4
*Friendship Ch* TN-4
Friendship Ch—*church* (97) AL-4
Friendship Ch—*church* (25) AR-4
Friendship Ch—*church* (20) FL-3
Friendship Ch—*church* (93) GA-3
Friendship Ch—*church* (4) IL-6
Friendship Ch—*church* (10) IN-6
Friendship Ch—*church* KS-7
Friendship Ch—*church* (21) KY-4
Friendship Ch—*church* (20) LA-4
Friendship Ch—*church* (6) MD-2
Friendship Ch—*church* MI-6
Friendship Ch—*church* (39) MS-4
Friendship Ch—*church* (18) MO-7
Friendship Ch—*church* (5) NJ-2
Friendship Ch—*church* (40) NC-3
Friendship Ch—*church* (4) OH-6
Friendship Ch—*church* (7) OK-5
Friendship Ch—*church* (2) PA-2
Friendship Ch—*church* (24) SC-3
Friendship Ch—*church* (26) TN-4
Friendship Ch—*church* (39) TX-5
Friendship Ch—*church* (8) VA-3
Friendship Ch—*church* (3) WV-2
*Friendship Chapel* AL-4
Friendship Chapel—*church* AL-4
Friendship Chapel—*church* GA-3
Friendship Chapel—*church* NC-3
Friendship Ch (historical)—*church* (2) AL-4
Friendship Ch (historical)—*church* MS-4
Friendship Ch (historical)—*church* MO-7
Friendship Ch (historical)—*church* (5) TN-4
*Friendship Ch Number Two* AL-4
Friendship Ch Number 2—*church* AL-4
*Friendship Ch of Christ* TN-4
Friendship Ch of the Living Word—*church* AL-4
Friendship Church (historical)—*locale* MO-7
Friendship Community Hall—*locale* MO-7
Friendship Congregational Methodist Ch—*church* AL-4
Friendship Country Home—*building* PA-2
Friendship Cove—*bay* UT-8
Friendship Cove Pictograph—*hist pl* UT-8
Friendship Cranberry Bogs—*swamp* NJ-2
Friendship Creek—*stream* AR-4
Friendship Creek—*stream* KY-4
Friendship Creek—*stream* NJ-2
Friendship Creek—*stream* OK-5
Friendship Creek Branch—*stream* NJ-2
Friendship Day Sch—*school* FL-3
Friendship Division—*civil* TN-4
*Friendship-Doolin Cemetery* AL-4
*Friendship Elementary School* AL-4
Friendship Elem Sch—*school* PA-2
Friendship Elem Sch—*school* TN-4
Friendship Freewill Baptist Ch—*church* (2) AL-4
**Friendship (Friendship Station)**—*pop pl* NJ-2
Friendship Gas Field—*oilfield* KS-7
Friendship Grange Hall—*locale* OH-6
Friendship Hall—*hist pl* MD-2
Friendship Harbor—*bay* ME-1
**Friendship Heights**—*pop pl* MD-2
**Friendship Heights**—*pop pl* PA-2
Friendship Hill—*summit* (2) PA-2
Friendship Hill Elem Sch—*school* PA-2
Friendship Hill Natl Historic Site—*park* PA-2
*Friendship Hill School* PA-2
Friendship (historical)—*locale* AL-4
**Friendship (historical)**—*pop pl* MS-4
Friendship Hollow—*valley* TN-4
Friendship House—*hist pl* DC-2
Friendship House—*hist pl* WI-6
*Friendship Interdominational Church* MS-4
*Friendship Island* ME-1
Friendship Knob—*summit* KY-4
Friendship Lake—*lake* WI-6
Friendship Lake—*reservoir* WI-6
Friendship Long Island—*island* ME-1
Friendship Memorial Cem—*cemetery* GA-3
Friendship Memorial Gardens—*cemetery* GA-3
Friendship Methodist Ch (historical)—*church* MS-4
*Friendship Methodist Church* MS-4
*Friendship Missionary Baptist Ch* AL-4
*Friendship Missionary Baptist Ch* MS-4
Friendship Missionary Baptist Ch—*church* AL-4
Friendship Missionary Baptist Ch—*church* (2) FL-3
Friendship Missionary Baptist Ch—*church* (3) MS-4
Friendship Missionary Baptist Ch—*church* TN-4
Friendship Mound—*summit* WI-6
Friendship Mtn—*summit* AL-4
*Friendship North Baptist Church* AL-4
Friendship North Cem—*cemetery* AL-4
Friendship North Ch—*church* AL-4
Friendship Oil Field—*oilfield* TX-5
Friendship Park—*park* AZ-5
Friendship Park—*park* MS-4
Friendship Park—*park* (2) TX-5
**Friendship Park**—*pop pl* MD-2
Friendship Park Cem—*cemetery* IN-6
Friendship Park Community Center—*building* MS-4
Friendship Pentecostal Ch (historical)—*church* MS-4
Friendship Post Office—*building* TN-4
Friendship Post Office (historical)—*building* MS-4
*Friendship Presbyterian Church* MS-4
Friendship Primitive Baptist Ch—*church* AL-4
Friendship Primitive Baptist Ch—*church* FL-3
*Friendship Primitive Baptist Church* TN-4
*Friendship Private School* AL-4
Friendship Public Sch (historical)—*school* MS-4
**Friendship Ranch**—*pop pl* CO-8
**Friendship Ranch Estates**—*pop pl* CO-8
Friendship Ridge—*ridge* WV-2
Friendship Run—*stream* IN-6
Friendship Sanctified Ch—*church* MS-4
*Friendship Sch* PA-2
*Friendship Sch* TN-4
Friendship Sch—*school* (5) AL-4
Friendship Sch—*school* (2) AR-4
Friendship Sch—*school* DE-2
Friendship Sch—*school* FL-3
Friendship Sch—*school* (2) GA-3
Friendship Sch—*school* IL-6
Friendship Sch—*school* LA-4
Friendship Sch—*school* MA-1
Friendship Sch—*school* (4) MO-7
Friendship Sch—*school* PA-2
Friendship Sch—*school* (5) SC-3
Friendship Sch—*school* TN-4
Friendship Sch—*school* (4) TX-5
Friendship Sch—*school* WV-2
Friendship Sch—*school* WI-6
Friendship Sch (historical)—*school* (6) AL-4
Friendship Sch (historical)—*school* (10) MS-4
Friendship Sch (historical)—*school* (7) TN-4
Friendship School (abandoned)—*locale* MO-7
Friendship Settlement House—*building* DC-2
Friendship State Line Ch—*church* TN-4
*Friendship Tabernacle* AL-4
Friendship Tabernacle—*church* GA-3
Friendship Temple—*church* TN-4
Friendship Temple Ch—*church* MS-4
**Friendship (Town of)**—*pop pl* ME-1
**Friendship (Town of)**—*pop pl* NY-2
**Friendship (Town of)**—*pop pl* WI-6
Friendship (Township of)—*fmr MCD* AR-4
Friendship (Township of)—*fmr MCD* NC-3
**Friendship (Township of)**—*pop pl* MI-6
**Friendship (Township of)**—*pop pl* MN-6
Friendship Tunnel—*tunnel* PA-2
Friendship United Methodist Ch—*church* (2) DE-2
Friendship United Methodist Ch—*church* MS-4
*Friendship United Methodist Church* AL-4
Friendship Valley Farm—*hist pl* MD-2
Friendship Valley Sch—*school* KS-7
**Friendship Village**—*pop pl* PA-2
Friendship West Ch—*church* MS-4
**Friendship (Work)**—*pop pl* TN-4
Friends Home Cem—*cemetery* KS-7
Friends Home Ch—*church* KS-7
Friends Home Ch—*church* OH-6
Friends Hosp—*hospital* PA-2
Friend Siding—*locale* MT-8
Friends Lake—*lake* NY-2
Friends Landing (historical)—*locale* AL-4
Friends Meeting Cem—*cemetery* NJ-2
*Friends Meeting House* PA-2
Friends Meetinghouse—*church* AL-4
Friends Meetinghouse—*church* DE-2
Friends Meeting House—*church* FL-3
Friends Meetinghouse—*church* (2) IN-6
Friends Meetinghouse—*church* NH-1
Friends Meetinghouse—*hist pl* DE-2
Friends Meetinghouse—*hist pl* ME-1
Friends Meetinghouse—*hist pl* MA-1
Friends Meetinghouse—*hist pl* NJ-2
Friends Meetinghouse—*hist pl* OH-6
Friends Meetinghouse—*hist pl* RI-1
Friends Meetinghouse and Sch—*hist pl* NY-2
Friends Meetinghouse Burial Grounds—*cemetery* NY-2
Friends Meetinghouse Cem—*cemetery* DE-2
Friends Mission (historical)—*locale* KS-7
*Friends Neck* SC-3
Friends Neck—*cape* SC-3
Friends Park—*park* CA-9
Friends Park—*park* KS-7
Friends Peak—*summit* OR-9
Friends Point—*cape* NY-2
**Friends Point**—*pop pl* NY-2
Friend Spring—*spring* AL-4
Friend Spring—*spring* MT-8
Friends Run—*stream* WV-2
Friends Run Ch—*church* WV-2
Friends Salt Petre Cave—*cave* MD-2
Friends Sch—*school* MD-2
Friends Sch—*school* OH-6
Friends Sch—*school* (4) PA-2
Friends Sch—*school* (2) VA-3
*Friends School* DE-2
Friends School—*building* RI-1
Friends Spring Meeting House—*hist pl* NC-3
**Friends Station**—*pop pl* TN-4
Friends Station Post Office (historical)—*building* TN-4
Friends Union Cem—*cemetery* NC-3
Friends Union Ch—*church* IN-6
Friends Union Ch—*church* NC-3
Friends Univ—*school* KS-7
Friendsview Baptist Ch—*church* TN-4
**Friendsville**—*pop pl* IL-6
**Friendsville**—*pop pl* MD-2
**Friendsville**—*pop pl* MI-6
**Friendsville**—*pop pl* OH-6
**Friendsville**—*pop pl* PA-2
**Friendsville**—*pop pl* TN-4
Friendsville Acad—*school* TN-4
Friendsville Borough—*civil* PA-2
Friendsville (CCD)—*cens area* TN-4
Friendsville Cem—*cemetery* OH-6
Friendsville Cem—*cemetery* TN-4
Friendsville Ch—*church* TN-4
Friendsville Division—*civil* TN-4
Friendsville (Election Precinct)—*fmr MCD* IL-6
Friendsville Elem Sch—*school* TN-4
Friendsville HS (historical)—*school* TN-4
*Friendsville Institute* TN-4
Friendsville Mill (historical)—*locale* TN-4
Friendsville Post Office—*building* TN-4
**Friendswood**—*pop pl* IN-6
**Friendswood**—*pop pl* TX-5
Friendswood Baptist Ch—*church* IN-6
Friendswood Cem—*cemetery* WI-6
Friendswood Oil Field—*oilfield* TX-5
**Friendswood (subdivision)**—*pop pl* NC-3
Friendy Ch—*church* VA-3
Frier Lake—*lake* MI-6
Frier Ranch—*locale* NM-5
**Frierson**—*pop pl* LA-4
Frierson—*uninc pl* LA-4
Frierson, Lucius, House—*hist pl* TN-4
Frierson Branch—*stream* LA-4
Frierson Ch—*church* MS-4
Frierson Chapel—*church* MS-4
Frierson Chapel—*church* TN-4
*Frierson Chapel United Methodist Ch* TN-4
Frierson-Coble House—*hist pl* TN-4
Frierson (historical)—*locale* AL-4
Frierson House—*hist pl* AR-4
Frierson Lake—*reservoir* AL-4
Frierson Lakes—*lake* FL-3
Frierson Mine (underground)—*mine* AL-4
Frierson Pond—*reservoir* SC-3
Friersons Branch—*stream* AL-4
*Friersons Chapel* MS-4
Friersons Shaft Mine (underground)—*mine* AL-4
Friersons Store—*locale* SC-3
Frierson Town—*locale* TN-4
Frier Spring—*spring* OR-9
**Fries**—*pop pl* VA-3
Fries Ave Sch—*school* CA-9
Friesburg—*locale* NJ-2
Fries Cem—*cemetery* IL-6
Fries Cem—*cemetery* PA-2
Fries Ch—*church* VA-3
*Fries Cove* RI-1
*Fries Creek* NC-3
Fries Creek—*stream* NC-3
Friese Creek—*stream* OR-9
Frieseke, Frederick, Birthplace and Boyhood Home—*hist pl* MI-6
Friesen Cem—*cemetery* NE-7
Friesenhahn Park—*park* TX-5
Friesen Rsvr—*reservoir* OR-9
Fries Junction—*locale* VA-3
Fries Knob—*summit* VA-3
*Fries Lake* WI-6
**Friesland**—*pop pl* MN-6
**Friesland**—*pop pl* WI-6
Friesland (historical)—*locale* SD-7
**Fries Mill**—*pop pl* NJ-2
Fries Mill Dam—*dam* NJ-2
*Fries Mills* NJ-2
**Fries Mills**—*pop pl* NJ-2
Fries Miners' Cabins—*hist pl* AK-9
Fries Park—*park* MI-6
Fries Place—*locale* MT-8
*Fries Pond* RI-1
Friess Lake—*lake* WI-6
Friess Lake Sch—*school* WI-6
Friess Ranch—*locale* TX-5
Fries Tabernacle—*church* VA-3
**Friesville**—*pop pl* PA-2
*Fries Wash* AZ-5
Frietas Gulch—*valley* CA-9
Frietsche Cem—*cemetery* AR-4
Frieze, Henry S., House—*hist pl* MI-6
Frieze Branch—*stream* IL-6
Frieze Lake—*lake* MN-6
Friezeland Creek—*stream* NC-3
**Frige Settlement**—*pop pl* TX-5
Fright Creek—*stream* MT-8
Frigid Air Pass—*gap* CO-8
Frigid Crags—*summit* AK-9
Frigid Creek—*stream* WA-9
Frigid Lake—*lake* CO-8
Frigid Spring—*spring* OR-9
Frigmire Cem—*cemetery* MI-6
Friis Bay—*bay* VI-3
Friis Campground—*locale* CA-9
Frijole Creek—*stream* CO-8
Frijole Draw—*valley* TX-5
Frijole Hill—*summit* CO-8
Frijole Ranch—*locale* TX-5
Frijoles, Arroyo De Los—*stream* CA-9
Frijoles Canyon—*valley* CO-8
Frijoles Canyon—*valley* (2) NM-5
Frijoles Creek—*stream* NM-5
Frijoles Mesa—*summit* NM-5
**Frijoles (Monument Headquarters)**—*pop pl* (2) NM-5
Frijoles Peak—*summit* NM-5
Frijoles Spring—*locale* NM-5
Frijoles Stone Lions Trail—*trail* NM-5
Frijole Tank—*reservoir* NM-5
Frijole Tank—*reservoir* TX-5
Frijole Windmill—*locale* (2) TX-5
Frijolito Ruins—*locale* NM-5
Frijollio Windmill—*locale* TX-5
Frijol Morro—*area* NM-5
Frijol Tank—*reservoir* TX-5
Frijol Windmill—*locale* TX-5
Frijon Windmill—*locale* TX-5
Friley—*locale* AR-4
*Friley Creek* AL-4
Friley Creek—*stream* AR-4
*Frileys Creek* AR-4
Frileys Creek—*stream* AL-4
Frilio Sch—*school* MA-1
Frilloby Creek—*stream* MS-4
Frills Corners—*locale* PA-2
Frills Run—*stream* PA-2
Frincher Creek—*stream* LA-4
**Fringer (Spec)**—*pop pl* VA-3
Frink—*locale* CA-9
Frink—*locale* FL-3
Frink—*locale* OK-5
*Frink Bay* NY-2
Frink Brook—*stream* CT-1
Frink Brook—*stream* NY-2
Frink Canyon—*valley* CA-9
Frink Cem—*cemetery* NY-2
Frink Ch—*church* FL-3
Frink-Chambers Sch—*school* OK-5
Frink Corner—*locale* NY-2
Frink Creek—*stream* IA-7
Frink Crossing—*locale* NC-3
Frink Draw—*valley* SD-7
*Frink Hill* ME-1
Frink Island—*island* ME-1
Frink Park—*park* WA-9
Frink Rsvr—*reservoir* OR-9
Frink Run—*stream* OH-6
Frinks—*locale* PA-2
Frink Sch—*school* MI-6
Frink Sch—*school* NC-3
Frinks Corner—*locale* NY-2
Frink Spring—*spring* CA-9
Frink Trail—*trail* CO-8
Frio Canyon—*valley* (2) CO-8
**Frio (County)**—*pop pl* TX-5
Frio Draw—*valley* NM-5
Frio Draw—*valley* (3) TX-5
**Friona**—*pop pl* TX-5
Friona (CCD)—*cens area* TX-5
Frio Ranch—*locale* TX-5
*Frio River* TX-5
Frio River—*stream* TX-5
Frio Spring—*spring* AZ-5
Frio Tank—*reservoir* NM-5
Frio Town—*locale* TX-5
Frio Town Cem—*cemetery* TX-5
Frio Waterhole—*lake* TX-5
Frio Waterhole Draw—*valley* TX-5
Frio Windmill—*locale* TX-5
Fripo Island—*island* AK-9
Fripp, Edgar, Mausoleum, St. Helena Island Parish Church—*hist pl* SC-3
Fripp, Isaac, House Ruins—*hist pl* SC-3
Fripp Cem—*cemetery* SC-3
Fripp Inlet—*gut* SC-3
Fripp Island—*island* (2) SC-3
**Fripp Island**—*pop pl* SC-3
**Fripp Landing**—*pop pl* SC-3
Fripp Point—*cape* SC-3
Fripp Point Cem—*cemetery* SC-3
*Fripps Inlet* SC-3
*Fripps Island* SC-3
Fripps Point—*cape* SC-3
*Frisbee* PA-2
**Frisbee**—*pop pl* MO-7
Frisbee, Judge Gideon, House—*hist pl* NY-2
Frisbee Branch—*stream* NC-3
Frisbee Creek—*stream* NY-2
Frisbee Hill—*summit* NY-2
Frisbee Lake—*lake* AK-9
Frisbee Park—*park* MS-4
Frisbee Sch—*school* ME-1
Frisbee Wharf—*locale* ME-1
Frisbie—*locale* KS-7
Frisbie—*locale* PA-2
Frisbie, Edward, Homestead—*hist pl* CT-1
Frisbie, Edward, House—*hist pl* CT-1
Frisbie Ditch—*canal* WY-8
Frisbie Island—*island* CT-1
Frisbie Island—*island* NY-2
Frisbie JHS—*school* CA-9
Frisbie Landing Strip—*airport* KS-7
Frisbie Park—*park* CA-9
Frisbie Sch—*school* CT-1
Frisbie Sch (abandoned)—*school* PA-2
Frisbies Point—*cape* NY-2
Frisby—*locale* KY-4
Frisby, Joseph H., House—*hist pl* UT-8
Frisby, Leander F., House—*hist pl* WI-6
Frisby Branch—*stream* KY-4
Frisby Branch—*stream* (2) NC-3
Frisby Branch—*stream* VA-3
Frisby Cem—*cemetery* TX-5
**Frisby (historical)**—*pop pl* SD-7
Frisby Knob—*summit* VA-3
Frisby Lake—*lake* MN-6
Frisch Cem—*cemetery* MO-7
Frisch Gulch—*valley* ID-8
Frischknecht—*locale* WA-9
**Frischnecht**—*pop pl* WA-9
Frisch Valley—*valley* MN-6
*Frisco* NM-5
Frisco—*locale* AL-4
Frisco—*locale* AR-4
Frisco—*locale* ID-8
Frisco—*locale* OK-5
Frisco—*locale* UT-8
Frisco—*locale* VA-3
**Frisco**—*pop pl* CO-8
**Frisco**—*pop pl* IL-6
**Frisco**—*pop pl* LA-4
**Frisco**—*pop pl* MO-7
**Frisco**—*pop pl* NC-3
**Frisco**—*pop pl* PA-2
**Frisco**—*pop pl* TN-4
**Frisco**—*pop pl* TX-5
Frisco Bay—*bay* CO-8
Frisco Bldg—*hist pl* MO-7
Frisco Branch—*stream* SC-3
Frisco Bridge—*bridge* AR-4
Frisco Bridge—*bridge* TN-4
Frisco Canyon—*valley* AZ-5
Frisco Canyon—*valley* CO-8
Frisco Canyon—*valley* OR-9
Frisco Cem—*cemetery* MS-4
Frisco Cem—*cemetery* (2) OK-5
Frisco Charcoal Kilns—*hist pl* UT-8
**Frisco City**—*pop pl* AL-4
Frisco City (CCD)—*cens area* AL-4
Frisco City Division—*civil* AL-4
Frisco Contact Mine—*mine* UT-8
Frisco Creek—*stream* AK-9
Frisco Creek—*stream* (2) OK-5
Frisco Creek—*stream* TX-5
Frisco Creek—*stream* WA-9
Frisco Dam—*dam* KS-7
*Frisco Depot* AL-4
Frisco Depot—*hist pl* AR-4
Frisco Depot—*locale* OK-5
Frisco Ditch—*canal* AR-4
Frisco Gulch—*valley* ID-8
Frisco Hill—*summit* MO-7
Frisco (historical)—*locale* KS-7
Frisco (historical)—*locale* UT-8
Frisco Hot Spring—*spring* NM-5
**Frisco Junction**—*pop pl* AR-4
Frisco Lake—*lake* CO-8
Frisco Lake—*lake* MO-7
Frisco Lake—*reservoir* KS-7
Frisco Lake Park Dam—*dam* KS-7
Frisco Marina—*locale* CO-8
Frisco Mine—*mine* ID-8
*Frisco Mount* UT-8
*Frisco Mountain* UT-8
Frisco Mtn—*summit* (2) WA-9
Frisco Oil Field—*oilfield* LA-4
Frisco Park—*park* MS-4
Frisco Park—*park* MO-7
Frisco Park—*park* TX-5
Frisco Peak—*summit* ID-8
Frisco Peak—*summit* UT-8
Frisco Plaza Tank No 1—*reservoir* NM-5
Frisco Plaza Tank No 2—*reservoir* NM-5
**Frisco Quarters**—*pop pl* AL-4
Frisco Ridge—*ridge* OK-5
*Frisco River* AZ-5
Frisco Rsvr—*reservoir* MO-7
Frisco Sch—*school* AL-4
Frisco Sch—*school* TX-5
Frisco School (abandoned)—*locale* MO-7
Frisco School (historical)—*locale* MO-7
Frisco Schoolhouse—*hist pl* CO-8
Frisco Springs—*spring* AR-4
Frisco Springs Cem—*cemetery* AR-4
Frisco Station—*hist pl* OK-5
Frisco Summit—*gap* UT-8
Frisco Tank—*reservoir* OK-5
Frisco Wash—*valley* UT-8
Frisell Brook—*stream* MA-1
Frish Ranch—*locale* ID-8
*Frishton* IN-6
Frisinger Cem—*cemetery* OH-6
Frisinger Ditch—*stream* OH-6
Frisinger Park—*park* MI-6
Frisken Wye—*locale* WA-9
Frisk Lake—*lake* (3) MN-6
Friskney Ditch—*canal* IN-6
Frisky Creek—*stream* AK-9
Frisky Creek—*stream* UT-8
*Frisky Flat Creek* UT-8
*Frison Chapel Church* AL-4
Frison Ch (historical)—*church* MS-4
Frissel Crossing Forest Camp—*locale* OR-9
Frissell, Mount—*summit* MA-1
Frissell Creek—*stream* OR-9
Frissell Point—*cape* OR-9
Frissell Point Trail—*trail* OR-9
Fristad Cem—*cemetery* WI-6
**Fristoe**—*pop pl* MO-7
Fristoe Branch—*stream* MO-7

Fristoe Township—*civil* ... MO-7
**Frit**—*pop pl* ... AL-4
**Fritch**—*pop pl* ... TX-5
Fritch Canyon—*valley* ... TX-5
Fritch Creek—*stream* ... CA-9
F Ritche—*locale* ... TX-5
Fritchen Sch—*school* ... WI-6
Fritche Tank—*reservoir* ... AZ-5
Fritch Fortress Picnic Area—*locale* ... TX-5
Fritchie Marsh—*swamp* ... LA-4
Fritch Island—*island* ... GA-3
*Fritch Lake* ... OH-6
*Fritch Lake Outlet* ... OH-6
**Fritchleys Corners**—*pop pl* ... OH-6
Fritchman, H. K., House—*hist pl* ... ID-8
Fritch Ranch—*locale* ... CA-9
**Fritchton**—*pop pl* ... IN-6
Fritchton Cem—*cemetery* ... IN-6
Frith Branch—*stream* ... AL-4
Frith Branch—*stream* ... LA-4
Frith Cem—*cemetery* ... MS-4
Frith Hill Ch—*church* ... AL-4
Frithland—*hist pl* ... LA-4
Frith-Plunkett House—*hist pl* ... AR-4
Frith Spring Branch—*stream* ... TN-4
**Frith Spur**—*pop pl* ... IA-7
Fritsch—*fmr MCD* ... NE-7
Fritsch, J. A., Block—*hist pl* ... UT-8
**Fritsch and Zulchs Addition**
**(subdivision)**—*pop pl* ... UT-8
Fritsche Cabin—*locale* ... OR-9
Fritsche Cem—*cemetery* ... TX-5
Fritsche Creek—*stream* ... MN-6
Fritsche Ranch—*locale* ... CA-9
Fritsche Tank—*reservoir* ... AZ-5
Fritsche Well—*well* ... AZ-5
Fritschle Cem—*cemetery* ... IL-6
Fritsch Sch—*school* ... NV-8
Fritser Creek—*stream* ... ID-8
Fritser Ford—*locale* ... ID-8
Fritter Cove—*bay* ... AK-9
Fritters Corner—*locale* ... VA-3
Fritts Cem—*cemetery* ... AR-4
Fritts Cem—*cemetery* ... IL-6
Fritts Creek—*stream* ... AR-4
Fritts Spring—*spring* ... OR-9
*Fritz* ... AR-4
Fritz—*locale* ... KY-4
**Fritz**—*pop pl* ... AR-4
Fritz, Mount—*summit* ... AK-9
Fritz Bluff—*cliff* ... WI-6
Fritz Branch—*stream* ... MO-7
**Fritzburg**—*pop pl* ... MI-6
Fritz Butte—*summit* ... ND-7
Fritz Camp—*locale* ... PA-2
Fritz Canal—*canal* ... WY-8
Fritz Canyon—*valley* ... AZ-5
Fritz Cem—*cemetery* ... MI-6
Fritz Cem—*cemetery* ... NM-5
Fritz Cem—*cemetery* ... OH-6
**Fritz Corner**—*pop pl* ... IN-6
Fritz Cove—*bay* ... AK-9
Fritz Cove—*uninc pl* ... AK-9
*Fritz Creek* ... ID-8
Fritz Creek—*CDP* ... AK-9
Fritz Creek—*stream* ... AK-9
Fritz Creek—*stream* ... AR-4
Fritz Creek—*stream* (2) ... ID-8
Fritz Creek—*stream* ... MI-6
Fritz Creek—*stream* ... MS-4
Fritz Creek—*stream* ... MO-7
Fritz Creek—*stream* (2) ... OR-9
Fritz Creek—*stream* ... WA-9
Fritz Creek Dam—*dam* ... OR-9
Fritz Ditch—*canal* ... CO-8
Fritz Ditch—*canal* ... IN-6
*Fritzer Creek* ... ID-8
Fritzer Flat—*flat* ... ID-8
Fritzer Gulch—*valley* ... ID-8
Fritz Hammock—*island* ... FL-3
**Fritz (historical)**—*pop pl* ... PA-2
Fritz Island—*island* ... AK-9
Fritz Island—*island* ... FL-3
Fritz Island—*island* ... LA-4
Fritz Island—*island* (2) ... PA-2
Fritz Landing—*locale* ... TN-4
Fritzler Coulee—*valley* ... MT-8
Fritzler Fair Haven Ranch—*locale* ... NE-7
Fritz Mtn—*summit* ... MT-8
Fritzner Coulee—*valley* ... MT-8
Fritz Oil Well Windmill—*locale* ... NM-5
Fritz Park—*park* ... MI-6
Fritzpatrick Gas Field—*oilfield* ... KS-7
*Fritz Patrick Gulch* ... CO-8
*Fritzpatrick Lake* ... MT-8
Fritz Peak—*summit* ... ID-8
Fritz Pond—*lake* ... NY-2
Fritz Ranch—*locale* ... AZ-5
Fritz Ranch—*locale* ... ND-7
Fritz Revetment—*levee* ... TN-4
Fritz Run—*stream* ... PA-2
Fritz Sch—*school* ... MI-6
Fritzsche Creek—*stream* ... TN-4
Fritz Sch (historical)—*school* ... TN-4
Fritz Spring—*spring* ... CO-8
Fritz Spring—*spring* ... PA-2
*Fritz Springs* ... AZ-5
Fritz Tank—*reservoir* ... AZ-5
**Fritztown**—*pop pl* ... PA-2
Fritz Windmill—*locale* ... NM-5
*Frizelburg* ... PA-2
Frizell—*locale* ... KS-7
Frizelle Branch—*stream* ... TX-5
Frize Sch (historical)—*school* ... IA-7
*Frizleburg* ... PA-2
*Frizzelburg* ... MD-2
*Frizzel Hill* ... MA-1
**Frizzell**—*pop pl* ... LA-4
Frizzell, Andrew P., House and Farm
Complex—*hist pl* ... MD-2
**Frizzellburg**—*pop pl* ... MD-2
Frizzell Cem—*cemetery* ... KY-4
Frizzell Cem—*cemetery* ... TN-4
Frizzell Creek—*stream* ... OR-9
Frizzell Hill—*summit* ... MA-1
*Frizzell Lookout Tower* ... FL-3
Frizzell Tower—*tower* ... FL-3
Frizzel Mtn—*summit* ... OR-9
**Frizzleburg**—*pop pl* ... PA-2
*Frizzle Creek* ... OR-9

Frkovich, Mike, House—*hist pl* ... UT-8
Frnka Cem—*cemetery* ... TX-5
Frnka Oil Field—*oilfield* ... TX-5
Frnklin Cem—*cemetery* ... MS-4
Froberg Sch—*school* ... IL-6
Frobese, William, Sr., House—*hist pl* ... TX-5
Fro Creek—*stream* ... ID-8
Froebel Howard Sch—*school* ... MI-6
Froebel Sch—*school* ... IL-6
Froebel Sch—*school* ... IN-6
Froebel Sch—*school* ... MO-7
F Roedeske Ranch—*locale* ... ND-7
Froehel Sch—*school* ... MI-6
**Froehlich Addition**—*pop pl* ... SD-7
Froehlich Butte—*summit* ... MT-8
Froehlich Coulee—*valley* ... MT-8
Froe Hollow—*valley* ... MO-7
**Froelich**—*pop pl* ... IA-7
Froelich, John, House—*hist pl* ... OH-6
**Froelich Addition**
**(subdivision)**—*pop pl* ... SD-7
Froelich Dam—*dam* ... ND-7
Froelich Dam State Game Mngmt
Area—*park* ... ND-7
Froelich Ranch—*locale* ... AZ-5
Froen Ch—*church* ... MN-6
Froens Cem—*cemetery* ... WI-6
**Froerer Plaza (subdivision)**—*pop pl* ... UT-8
*Froest Creek* ... UT-8
Frog—*locale* ... TX-5
Frog, The—*cape* ... ME-1
Frog, The—*ridge* ... OR-9
Frog, The—*summit* ... WY-8
Frog Ague Creek—*stream* ... AL-4
Frog Alley—*locale* ... TN-4
Frog Alley Sch—*school* ... IL-6
Frog Bay—*bay* ... WI-6
Frog Bayou—*stream* ... AR-4
*Frog Bayou Creek* ... AR-4
Frog Bottom—*bend* ... TX-5
Frog Bottom Creek—*stream* ... GA-3
Frog Bottom (historical)—*basin* ... AL-4
*Frog Branch* ... TN-4
*Frog Branch* ... TX-5
Frog Branch—*stream* (3) ... KY-4
Frog Branch—*stream* ... MS-4
Frog Branch—*stream* (3) ... TN-4
Frog Branch—*stream* ... TX-5
Frog Branch—*stream* ... VA-3
*Frog Brook* ... CT-1
Frog Camp—*locale* ... OR-9
Frog Camp Creek—*stream* ... OR-9
Frog Camp Hollow—*valley* ... PA-2
Frog Canyon—*valley* ... CA-9
Frog Cem—*cemetery* ... KS-7
Frog Chapel (historical)—*church* ... TN-4
Frog City—*locale* ... FL-3
**Frog City**—*pop pl* ... IL-6
Frog City Sch—*school* ... NY-2
Frog Coulee—*valley* ... MT-8
*Frog Creek* ... MI-6
*Frog Creek* ... OR-9
Frog Creek—*stream* ... AL-4
Frog Creek—*stream* (3) ... CA-9
Frog Creek—*stream* ... FL-3
Frog Creek—*stream* (2) ... ID-8
Frog Creek—*stream* ... IN-6
Frog Creek—*stream* ... IA-7
Frog Creek—*stream* (3) ... KS-7
Frog Creek—*stream* (2) ... MT-8
Frog Creek—*stream* ... NV-8
Frog Creek—*stream* ... NJ-2
Frog Creek—*stream* ... NC-3
Frog Creek—*stream* (4) ... OR-9
Frog Creek—*stream* (3) ... SD-7
Frog Creek—*stream* (3) ... TX-5
Frog Creek—*stream* (2) ... WA-9
Frog Creek—*stream* ... WV-2
Frog Creek—*stream* (2) ... WI-6
Frog Creek—*stream* ... WY-8
Frog Creek Ditch—*canal* ... OR-9
Frog Creek Oil Field—*oilfield* ... WY-8
Frog Creek Sch (historical)—*school* ... SD-7
**Frog Creek (Town of)**—*pop pl* ... WI-6
Frog Creek Trail—*trail* ... OR-9
Frog Eye—*locale* ... AL-4
Frogeye—*locale* ... MD-2
*Frog Foot Brook* ... MA-1
Frogfoot Brook—*stream* ... MA-1
Frogfoot Brook Rsvr—*reservoir* ... MA-1
Frogfoot Reservoir Dam—*dam* ... MA-1
*Frog Foot River* ... MA-1
*Frog Foot Rsvr* ... MA-1
Frogge Cem—*cemetery* ... MO-7
Frogge Chapel—*locale* ... TN-4
Frogge Chapel Cem—*cemetery* ... TN-4
*Frogge Chapel Methodist Church* ... TN-4
Frogge Mtn—*summit* ... TN-4
Frogge Sch (abandoned)—*school* ... MO-7
Froggs Fault Cave—*cave* ... MT-8
Frog Gulch—*valley* ... OR-9
*Froggy Bottom* ... AL-4
Froggy Bottom Pond—*reservoir* ... AL-4
Froggy Branch—*stream* ... MO-7
*Frog Hall Branch* ... VA-3
*Frog Hall Creek* ... VA-3
Frog Heaven—*lake* ... WA-9
Frog Heaven Meadow—*flat* ... OR-9
Frog Hill—*summit* ... NY-2
Frog Hole—*bend* ... MA-1
Frog Hole Swamp—*swamp* ... NY-2
Frog Hollow—*hist pl* ... CT-1
**Frog Hollow**—*pop pl* ... CT-1
Frog Hollow—*valley* ... ID-8
Frog Hollow—*valley* ... IA-7
Frog Hollow—*valley* (2) ... KY-4
Frog Hollow—*valley* (3) ... MD-2
Frog Hollow—*valley* ... MO-7
Frog Hollow—*valley* ... NH-1
Frog Hollow—*valley* (3) ... NY-2
Frog Hollow—*valley* ... OH-6
Frog Hollow—*valley* ... OR-9
Frog Hollow—*valley* ... PA-2
Frog Hollow—*valley* (2) ... TN-4
Frog Hollow—*valley* ... TX-5
Frog Hollow—*valley* ... UT-8
Frog Hollow—*valley* (2) ... VA-3
Frog Hollow—*valley* (2) ... WV-2
Frog Hollow—*valley* ... WI-6
Frog Hollow Branch—*stream* ... TN-4

Frog Hollow Brook—*stream* ... NY-2
Frog Hollow Cove—*bay* ... MD-2
*Frog Hollow Creek* ... TX-5
Frog Hollow Debris Basin Dam—*dam* ... UT-8
Frog Hollow Debris Basin Rsvr—*reservoir* ... UT-8
Frog Hollow Hist Dist (Boundary
Increase)—*hist pl* ... CT-1
Frog Hollow Oil Field—*oilfield* ... KS-7
Frog Hop—*locale* ... TX-5
*Frogie Bottom Lake* ... AL-4
Frog Island—*island* ... LA-4
Frog Island—*island* ... ME-1
Frog Island—*island* ... WI-6
**Frog Island**—*pop pl* ... MS-4
**Frog Island**—*pop pl* ... NC-3
Frog Island Fishing Club—*locale* ... NC-3
Frog Island Slough—*gut* ... LA-4
**Frog Jump**—*pop pl* (2) ... TN-4
**Frog Jump (Gilliland)**—*pop pl* ... TN-4
Frog Knob Cem—*cemetery* ... MO-7
*Frog Lake* ... CA-9
*Frog Lake* ... MI-6
*Frog Lake* ... MN-6
Frog Lake—*lake* ... AK-9
Frog Lake—*lake* ... AZ-5
Frog Lake—*lake* (8) ... CA-9
Frog Lake—*lake* ... FL-3
Frog Lake—*lake* (6) ... ID-8
Frog Lake—*lake* ... LA-4
Frog Lake—*lake* ... MI-6
Frog Lake—*lake* (2) ... MN-6
Frog Lake—*lake* ... MT-8
Frog Lake—*lake* (4) ... OR-9
Frog Lake—*lake* ... UT-8
Frog Lake—*lake* (5) ... WA-9
Frog Lake—*lake* (5) ... WI-6
Frog Lake—*reservoir* ... CA-9
Frog Lake—*reservoir* ... OR-9
*Frog Lake Butte* ... OR-9
Frog Lake Buttes—*summit* ... OR-9
Frog Lake Cliff—*cliff* ... CA-9
Frog Lake Dam—*dam* ... OR-9
Frog Lakes—*lake* (2) ... CA-9
Frog Lakes—*lake* ... ID-8
Frog Lakes—*lake* ... MI-6
Frog Lakes—*lake* ... MT-8
Frog Lake Tank—*reservoir* ... NM-5
*Frog Level* ... AL-4
*Frog Level* ... SC-3
Frog Level—*flat* ... TN-4
Frog Level—*flat* ... VA-3
Frog Level—*hist pl* ... AR-4
Frog Level—*locale* ... NC-3
Frog Level—*locale* ... TN-4
**Frog Level**—*pop pl* ... VA-3
Frog Level Branch—*stream* ... AL-4
Frog Level Branch—*stream* ... TN-4
**Frog Level (Oakland)**—*pop pl* ... NC-3
Frog Level Plantation—*locale* ... AR-4
Frog Level Ridge—*ridge* ... KY-4
Frog Level Swamp—*swamp* ... NC-3
Frog Marsh—*swamp* (2) ... MI-6
Frog Marshes—*swamp* ... MD-2
Frog Meadow—*flat* ... CA-9
Frog Meadow Guard Station—*locale* ... CA-9
Frog Meadows—*flat* ... ID-8
Frog Mesa—*ridge* ... NM-5
Frog Mine—*mine* ... TN-4
**Frogmoor**—*pop pl* ... TN-4
Frogmoor Yards—*locale* ... TN-4
Frogmore—*hist pl* ... LA-4
Frogmore—*hist pl* ... SC-3
**Frogmore**—*pop pl* (2) ... LA-4
**Frogmore**—*pop pl* ... SC-3
Frogmore Cem—*cemetery* ... SC-3
Frog Mortar Creek—*stream* ... MD-2
*Frog Mountain* ... TN-4
Frog Mountain—*locale* ... AL-4
Frog Mountains—*other* ... AK-9
Frog Mtn—*summit* ... AL-4
Frog Mtn—*summit* ... NC-3
Frog Mtn—*summit* ... TX-5
Frog Mtn—*summit* (2) ... WA-9
Frogneck Sch (historical)—*school* ... MO-7
Frogner—*locale* ... MN-6
Frognot—*locale* ... TX-5
Frogonery Branch—*stream* ... KY-4
Frog Paradise Drain—*stream* ... MI-6
Frog Peak—*summit* ... ID-8
Frog Point—*cape* ... MD-2
*Frog Pond* (2) ... AL-4
Frog Pond—*lake* ... CA-9
Frog Pond—*lake* (2) ... CT-1
Frog Pond—*lake* ... ID-8
Frog Pond—*lake* ... IN-6
Frog Pond—*lake* (3) ... ME-1
Frog Pond—*lake* (4) ... MA-1
Frog Pond—*lake* ... MI-6
Frog Pond—*lake* ... MT-8
Frog Pond—*lake* ... NH-1
Frog Pond—*lake* ... NY-2
Frog Pond—*lake* (2) ... OR-9
Frog Pond—*lake* ... WY-8
Frog Pond—*other* ... NC-3
**Frog Pond**—*pop pl* ... NC-3
**Frog Pond**—*pop pl* (2) ... TN-4
Frog Pond—*reservoir* (2) ... AZ-5
Frog Pond—*reservoir* ... PA-2
Frog Pond—*reservoir* ... WV-2
Frog Pond—*swamp* ... TX-5
Frog Pond, The—*flat* ... CA-9
Frogpond Basin—*basin* ... MT-8
Frog Pond Butte—*summit* ... OR-9
Frog Pond Cem—*cemetery* ... TN-4
*Frog Pond Cemetery* ... AL-4
Frog Pond Ch—*church* ... TN-4
*Frog Pond Church* ... AL-4
*Frog Pond Church* ... MS-4
Frog Pond Creek—*stream* ... TX-5
Frog Pond Gulch—*valley* ... CA-9
Frogpond Hollow—*valley* ... KY-4
Frog Pond Hollow—*valley* ... KY-4
Frog Pond Hollow—*valley* ... TN-4
Frogpond Hollow—*valley* ... TN-4
Frog Pond Lake—*lake* ... MT-8
Frog Pond Mine—*mine* ... OR-9
Frog Pond Mtn—*summit* ... CA-9
Frog Pond Ridge—*ridge* ... IN-6
Frogpond Ridge—*ridge* ... VA-3
Frog Ponds—*lake* ... OR-9

Frogpond Sch—*school* ... IL-6
Frog Pond Sch—*school* (2) ... IL-6
Frog Pond Sch—*school* ... IA-7
Frog Pond Sch—*school* ... MO-7
Frog Pond Sch (abandoned)—*school* ... MO-7
Frog Pond Sch (historical)—*school* ... AL-4
Frog Pond Sch (historical)—*school* (2) ... TN-4
*Frog Pond School* ... AL-4
Frog Pond Valley—*valley* ... TN-4
Frog Pool—*reservoir* (2) ... AZ-5
Frog Ridge Ch—*church* ... AL-4
Frog Rock—*island* ... CA-9
Frog Rock—*other* ... AK-9
Frog Rock—*pillar* ... NM-5
Frog Rock—*pillar* ... OR-9
Frog Rsvr—*reservoir* ... OR-9
Frog Run—*stream* (2) ... OH-6
Frog Run—*stream* (3) ... WV-2
Frogsboro—*locale* ... NC-3
Frogs Flat—*flat* ... UT-8
Frog Slough—*stream* ... IL-6
*Frog's Neck* ... NY-2
Frog Spring—*spring* (4) ... AZ-5
Frog Spring—*spring* ... CA-9
Frog Spring—*spring* ... ID-8
Frog Spring—*spring* ... NV-8
Frog Spring—*spring* (2) ... OR-9
Frog Spring (historical)—*spring* ... ID-8
Frog Springs Canyon—*valley* ... OR-9
Frog Springs Draw—*valley* ... TX-5
Frog Station—*locale* ... WI-6
Frogstool—*locale* ... VA-3
Frogstool Branch—*stream* ... VA-3
*Frogsville* ... TN-4
Frog Tank—*lake* ... NM-5
Frog Tank—*reservoir* (3) ... AZ-5
Frog Tank—*reservoir* (2) ... NM-5
Frog Tank—*reservoir* (2) ... TX-5
*Frog Tanks* ... AZ-5
*Frog Tanks Dam* ... AZ-5
*Frogtown* ... AR-4
*Frog Town* ... MS-4
*Frogtown* ... PA-2
Frogtown—*locale* (2) ... IL-6
Frogtown—*locale* ... KY-4
Frogtown—*locale* ... PA-2
Frogtown—*locale* ... VA-3
**Frog Town**—*pop pl* ... AR-4
**Frogtown**—*pop pl* ... KY-4
**Frogtown**—*pop pl* ... MD-2
**Frogtown**—*pop pl* ... MS-4
**Frogtown**—*pop pl* (5) ... PA-2
**Frogtown**—*pop pl* ... WV-2
Frogtown Cove—*valley* ... GA-3
Frogtown Creek—*stream* ... GA-3
Frogtown (Fairgrounds)—*locale* ... CA-9
*Frogtown Gap* ... GA-3
Frogtown Lake—*swamp* ... IL-6
Frogtown North Oil Field—*other* ... IL-6
Frogtown Sch (historical)—*school* ... PA-2
Frogtown (Site)—*locale* ... ID-8
Frogue—*locale* ... KY-4
Frog Valley—*valley* ... AL-4
Frog Valley—*valley* ... UT-8
Frogville—*locale* ... OK-5
Frogville Cem—*cemetery* ... OK-5
Frog Waterhole—*lake* ... CA-9
Frog Well—*well* ... AZ-5
Frohawk Creek—*stream* ... SC-3
*Froher Bay* ... NY-2
*Frohley Lake* ... IN-6
Frohman Wasteway—*canal* ... ID-8
**Frohna**—*pop pl* ... MO-7
Frohner Meadows—*flat* ... MT-8
Frohner Mine—*mine* ... MT-8
**Frohn (Township of)**—*pop pl* ... MN-6
Frohock Brook—*stream* ... ME-1
Frohock Brook—*stream* ... NH-1
**Frohock Mill (historical)**—*pop pl* ... NC-3
Frohock Mtn—*summit* ... ME-1
Frohock Valley—*valley* ... WI-6
**Froid**—*pop pl* ... MT-8
Froid, Point De—*cape* ... WI-6
*Froilam* ... MH-9
*Froilan* ... MH-9
*Froilllam* ... MH-9
*Froilma* ... MH-9
Frolic Creek—*stream* ... NM-5
Frolic Lake—*lake* ... MN-6
Frolictown Creek—*stream* ... NC-3
Froling Falls—*falls* ... MI-6
Frolke Branch—*stream* ... MO-7
Frolona—*locale* ... GA-3
**Froman**—*pop pl* ... PA-2
Froman Cem—*cemetery* (2) ... KY-4
Froman Creek—*stream* ... KY-4
**Froman (historical)**—*pop pl* ... OR-9
Froman Hollow—*valley* (2) ... KY-4
Froman Lake—*lake* ... KY-4
Froman Run—*stream* ... PA-2
Froman Run—*stream* ... VA-3
**Fromberg**—*pop pl* ... MT-8
Fromberg-Bridger—*cens area* ... MT-8
Fromby Creek—*stream* ... GA-3
Fromholtz Creek—*stream* ... AK-9
Fromm, Walter and Mabel,
House—*hist pl* ... WI-6
Fromm Cem—*cemetery* ... WI-6
**Fromme**—*pop pl* ... TX-5
Fromme, Mount—*summit* ... WA-9
Fromme-Birney Round Barn—*hist pl* ... KS-7
Fromme Oil Field—*oilfield* ... TX-5
Fromm Lookout Tower—*locale* ... WI-6
Fromm Site Sch—*school* ... MI-6
Froms Lake—*lake* ... WY-8
Fronabarger Ranch—*locale* ... NM-5
*Frona County Park* ... OR-9
Frona Park—*park* ... OR-9
Fron Bridge—*bridge* ... DC-2
Fron Cem—*cemetery* ... MN-6
Fron Ch—*church* ... ND-7
Fron Ch—*church* ... SD-7
Frondelius Corners—*locale* ... PA-2
Frond Lake—*lake* ... MN-6
Frone Corner—*locale* ... NY-2
Fronia Creek—*stream* ... WA-9
**Front**—*pop pl* ... TX-5
Frontagie Park—*park* ... IL-6
Front Bay—*bay* ... NH-1
Front Beach—*beach* ... MA-1

Front Cave—*cave* ... TN-4
Front Circle, Tift College—*hist pl* ... GA-3
Front Cove—*bay* ... VA-3
Front Creek—*stream* ... MD-2
Front Ditch—*canal* ... ID-8
*Frontenac* ... MN-6
Frontenac—*hist pl* ... WI-6
Frontenac—*locale* ... IL-6
**Frontenac**—*pop pl* ... FL-3
**Frontenac**—*pop pl* ... KS-7
**Frontenac**—*pop pl* ... MN-6
**Frontenac**—*pop pl* ... MO-7
**Frontenac**—*pop pl* ... NY-2
Frontenac, Plaza (Shop Ctr)—*locale* ... MO-7
Frontenac Cem—*cemetery* ... KS-7
Frontenac Creek—*stream* ... MN-6
Frontenac HS—*school* ... KS-7
Frontenac Island—*island* ... NY-2
Frontenac Lake—*lake* ... MN-6
**Frontenac Place**—*pop pl* ... IL-6
Frontenac Point—*cape* ... NY-2
Frontenac Springs—*spring* ... NY-2
Frontenac State Park—*park* ... MN-6
*Frontenac Station* ... MN-6
Frontenac Station—*other* ... MN-6
**Frontera (California Institution for**
**Women)**—*pop pl* ... CA-9
Frontera Park—*park* ... NY-2
Fronterhouse Creek—*stream* ... OK-5
Fronterhouse Lake—*lake* ... OK-5
Front Hill Canyon—*valley* ... CA-9
Front Hollow—*valley* ... TN-4
Front Hollow Spring—*spring* ... UT-8
Frontier—*locale* ... MN-6
Frontier—*locale* ... NV-8
Frontier—*locale* ... WA-9
**Frontier**—*pop pl* ... KS-7
**Frontier**—*pop pl* ... MI-6
**Frontier**—*pop pl* ... ND-7
**Frontier**—*pop pl* ... WY-8
Frontier—*post sta* ... FL-3
Frontier Cem—*cemetery* ... KS-7
Frontier Cem—*cemetery* ... MI-6
Frontier Ch—*church* ... NM-5
Frontier Christian Acad—*school* ... FL-3
Frontier Creek—*stream* ... WY-8
Frontier Creek Trail—*trail* ... WY-8
Frontier Ditch—*canal* ... KS-7
Frontier Elem Sch—*school* ... IN-6
Frontier Field—*park* ... ID-8
Frontier Hills—*other* ... NM-5
Frontier Historical Park—*park* ... KS-7
Frontier House—*hist pl* ... NY-2
Frontier HS—*school* ... IN-6
Frontier HS—*school* ... NY-2
Frontierland—*park* ... NC-3
Frontier MS—*school* ... IN-6
Frontier No 1 Mine—*mine* ... WY-8
Frontier No 3 Mine—*mine* ... WY-8
Frontier Park—*locale* ... OH-6
Frontier Park—*park* ... CA-9
Frontier Park—*park* ... PA-2
Frontier Park—*park* ... WY-8
Frontier Post—*locale* ... NM-5
Frontier Sch—*school* ... CA-9
Frontier Sch—*school* ... MA-1
Frontier Sch—*school* ... MT-8
Frontiers Repose Cem—*cemetery* ... OH-6
Frontier Town—*locale* ... MT-8
**Frontier Town**—*pop pl* ... OH-6
Frontiertown Plaza Shop Ctr—*locale* ... AZ-5
Frontier Village—*locale* ... ND-7
**Frontier Village**—*pop pl* ... TX-5
Frontier Village Shop Ctr—*locale* ... AZ-5
Frontier Village Shop Ctr—*other* ... WA-9
**Frontis**—*pop pl* ... NC-3
*Front Island* ... FM-9
Front Lake—*reservoir* ... NC-3
Front Lake Dam—*dam* ... NC-3
*Front Mtn* ... PA-2
Front Mtn—*summit* ... AK-9
Front Mtn—*summit* (3) ... PA-2
**Fronton**—*pop pl* ... TX-5
Fronton (Barrio)—*fmr MCD* ... PR-3
Fronton de La Brea—*other* ... PR-3
Fronton Island—*island* ... TX-5
Front Park—*park* ... NY-2
Front Park Ch—*church* ... NY-2
Front Point—*cape* ... AK-9
Front Range—*range* ... CO-8
Front Range Light—*locale* ... AL-4
Front Range Light—*locale* ... OR-9
Front Ridge—*ridge* ... LA-4
Front Ridge—*ridge* ... PA-2
Front Ridge—*ridge* ... TX-5
Front Ridge Cem—*cemetery* ... ME-1
Front River—*stream* (2) ... GA-3
**Front Royal**—*pop pl* ... VA-3
Front Royal Country Club—*other* ... VA-3
Front Royal Junction—*locale* ... VA-3
Front Run—*stream* ... PA-2
Front Saint Ch—*church* ... NC-3
Front Sch—*school* ... OH-6
**Front Street**—*pop pl* ... NY-2
Front Street—*uninc pl* ... TN-4
Front Street Block—*hist pl* ... MA-1
Front Street Ch—*church* ... NC-3
Front Street District—*hist pl* ... KY-4
Front Street Hist Dist—*hist pl* ... MS-4
Front Street Hist Dist—*hist pl* ... NH-1
Front Street-Parade Hill-Lower Warren Street
Hist Dist—*hist pl* ... NY-2
Front Street (River Park Drive) Hist
Dist—*hist pl* ... IA-7
*Front Wye River* ... MD-2
Frontz Hollow—*valley* ... WV-2
Froom Creek—*stream* ... CA-9
**Frosa**—*pop pl* ... TX-5
Frosa Chapel—*church* ... TX-5
Frosberg Park—*park* ... CO-8
Froschs Swamp—*swamp* ... NY-2
*Frosh Dam* ... SD-7
*Frost* ... PA-2
*Frost* ... TN-4
Frost—*locale* ... CA-9
Frost—*locale* ... CO-8
Frost—*locale* ... KY-4
Frost—*locale* ... MI-6
Frost—*locale* ... OH-6
Frost—*locale* ... OK-5

Frost—*locale* ... SC-3
Frost—*locale* ... TN-4
**Frost**—*pop pl* ... LA-4
**Frost**—*pop pl* ... MI-6
**Frost**—*pop pl* ... MN-6
**Frost**—*pop pl* ... TX-5
**Frost**—*pop pl* ... WV-2
Frost, David, House—*hist pl* ... MA-1
Frost, Elizabeth, Tenanthouse—*hist pl* ... MA-1
Frost, John, House—*hist pl* ... TN-4
Frost, Levi B., House—*hist pl* ... CT-1
Frost, Robert, Farm—*hist pl* (2) ... VT-1
Frost, Robert, Homestead—*hist pl* ... NH-1
Frost, Robert, House—*hist pl* ... MA-1
Frost, Walter, House—*hist pl* ... MA-1
Frost and Adams Ridge—*ridge* ... ME-1
Frost Arroyo—*stream* ... NM-5
Frostbite Peak—*summit* ... AK-9
*Frostbite Sch* ... TN-4
Frost Bit Sch (historical)—*school* ... TN-4
Frost Bldg—*hist pl* ... TN-4
**Frost Bottom**—*pop pl* ... TN-4
Frost Bottom Baptist Ch—*church* ... TN-4
**Frost Bottom (Frost)**—*pop pl* ... TN-4
Frost Bottom Sch (historical)—*school* ... TN-4
Frost Branch—*stream* (2) ... TN-4
Frost Branch—*stream* ... TX-5
Frost Branch Cem—*cemetery* ... SC-3
Frost Branch Ch—*church* ... SC-3
*Frostbridge* ... MS-4
Frost Bridge—*bridge* ... CT-1
Frost Bridge—*bridge* ... MS-4
**Frostbridge**—*pop pl* ... MS-4
Frost Bridge Camp—*locale* ... MS-4
*Frost Brook* ... ME-1
Frost Brook—*stream* (2) ... ME-1
Frost Brook—*stream* (3) ... NH-1
**Frostburg**—*pop pl* ... MD-2
**Frostburg**—*pop pl* (2) ... PA-2
Frostburg Hist Dist—*hist pl* ... MD-2
Frostburg Pumping Station—*other* ... MD-2
Frostburg Rsvr—*reservoir* ... MD-2
Frostburg State Teachers Coll—*school* ... MD-2
Frost Canyon—*valley* ... UT-8
Frost Cave—*cave* ... WY-8
Frost Cem—*cemetery* (2) ... AL-4
Frost Cem—*cemetery* ... KS-7
Frost Cem—*cemetery* ... KY-4
Frost Cem—*cemetery* ... ME-1
Frost Cem—*cemetery* ... OH-6
Frost Cem—*cemetery* ... TN-4
Frost Cem—*cemetery* ... TX-5
Frost Ch—*church* ... MI-6
Frost Chapel Ch—*church* ... AL-4
**Frost Corners**—*pop pl* ... MI-6
Frost Coulee—*valley* ... MT-8
Frost Cove—*bay* ... ME-1
*Frost Creek* ... WA-9
Frost Creek—*stream* (2) ... AL-4
Frost Creek—*stream* ... AK-9
Frost Creek—*stream* (2) ... CA-9
Frost Creek—*stream* ... CO-8
Frost Creek—*stream* (2) ... ID-8
Frost Creek—*stream* ... IA-7
Frost Creek—*stream* ... MI-6
Frost Creek—*stream* ... MT-8
Frost Creek—*stream* (2) ... NV-8
Frost Creek—*stream* ... NM-5
Frost Creek—*stream* ... NY-2
Frost Creek—*stream* (2) ... TX-5
Frost Creek—*stream* (3) ... WA-9
Frost Creek—*stream* ... WY-8
Frost Dam—*dam* ... AL-4
Frost Drain—*canal* (5) ... MI-6
Frost Draw—*valley* ... WY-8
Frost Drift Mine (underground)—*mine* ... AL-4
Frost Farm—*hist pl* ... NH-1
*Frost-fish Brook* ... MA-1
Frost Fish Brook—*stream* ... MA-1
*Frostfish Cove* ... MA-1
Frostfish Cove—*cove* ... MA-1
Frost Fish Creek—*stream* ... MA-1
Frost Ford—*locale* ... TN-4
Frost Garrison and House—*hist pl* ... ME-1
Frost Gulch—*valley* ... CA-9
Frost Gulch—*valley* ... OR-9
Frost Gulf—*valley* ... AL-4
Frost Gully Brook—*stream* ... ME-1
Frost Head—*cliff* ... ME-1
Frost Hill—*summit* ... AL-4
Frost Hill—*summit* ... CA-9
Frost Hill—*summit* (2) ... ME-1
Frost Hill—*summit* (2) ... NH-1
Frost Hill—*summit* ... NY-2
Frost Hollow—*locale* ... NY-2
Frost Hollow—*valley* ... KY-4
Frost Hollow—*valley* ... NY-2
Frost Hollow—*valley* (2) ... PA-2
Frost Hollow—*valley* (2) ... VT-1
Frost Intermediate Sch—*school* ... VA-3
Frost Island—*island* ... ME-1
Frost Island—*island* ... WA-9
Frost Jackson Swamp—*swamp* ... LA-4
Frost JHS—*school* ... KY-4
Frost JHS—*school* (3) ... MI-6
Frost Lake—*lake* (3) ... MI-6
Frost Lake—*lake* (2) ... MN-6
Frost Lake—*lake* (2) ... TX-5
Frost Lake—*lake* ... WI-6
Frost Lake—*lake* ... WY-8
Frost Lake—*reservoir* ... AL-4
Frost Lake Sch—*school* ... MN-6
Frost Lake Trail—*trail* ... WY-8
Frost Ledge—*bar* ... ME-1
Frost Meadows—*flat* ... WA-9
Frost Mill—*locale* ... OR-9
Frost Mill Creek—*stream* ... NC-3
Frost Mine—*mine* ... AZ-5
Frost Mountain Lookout Trail—*trail* ... WA-9
*Frost Mtn* ... AL-4
Frost Mtn—*summit* ... AL-4
Frost Mtn—*summit* ... ME-1
Frost Mtn—*summit* ... VT-1
Frost Mtn—*summit* ... WA-9
Frostown—*locale* ... MD-2
Frostown Branch—*stream* ... MD-2
Frost Park—*park* ... FL-3
Frost Park—*park* ... VT-1
Frost Park—*park* ... WI-6
Frost Peak—*summit* ... ID-8

Frost Place—hist pl ... NH-1
Frost Place—locale ... ID-8
Frost Point—cape ... AR-4
Frost Point—cape ... CT-1
Frost Point—cape ... NH-1
Frost Pond—lake (4) ... ME-1
Frost Pond—lake ... NH-1
Frost Pond—reservoir ... AL-4
Frost Pond—reservoir ... LA-4
Frost Pond Brook—stream ... ME-1
Frost Pond Flowage—channel ... ME-1
Frost Post Office (historical)—building ... TN-4
Frost Prairie—flat ... WA-9
Frost Proof ... FL-3
**Frostproof**—pop pl ... FL-3
Frostproof (CCD)—cens area ... FL-3
Frostproof Elem Sch—school ... FL-3
Frostproof Junior-Senior HS—school ... FL-3
Frostproof Tower (fire tower)—tower ... FL-3
Frost Ranch—locale (2) ... NM-5
Frost Ranch—locale ... TX-5
Frost River—stream ... MN-6
Frost Road Pond—lake ... CT-1
Frost Run—stream ... OH-6
Frost Run—stream ... WV-2
Frosts ... PA-2
**Frosts**—pop pl ... PA-2
Frost Sch—school ... CA-9
Frost Sch—school ... CO-8
Frost Sch—school ... LA-4
Frost Sch—school (3) ... MI-6
Frost Sch—school ... NY-2
Frost Sch—school ... SD-7
Frost Sch—school ... TX-5
Frost Sch—school ... WA-9
Frost Sch (historical)—school ... MO-7
Frost Sch (historical)—school ... PA-2
Frost Sch Number 106 ... IN-6
Frost Settlement Cem—cemetery ... PA-2
Frosts Hill ... ME-1
Frosts Landing—locale ... AL-4
Frost Slough—gut ... CA-9
Frosts Mills ... NY-2
Frosts Point ... NH-1
Frost Spring—spring ... TN-4
Frost Spring Hollow—valley ... TN-4
**Frost Subdivision**—pop pl ... UT-8
Frost Tank—reservoir (2) ... AZ-5
**Frost Town**—pop pl ... LA-4
**Frost (Township of)**—pop pl ... MI-6
**Frost Valley**—pop pl ... NY-2
Frost Valley Sch—school ... NE-7
**Frost (Vick)**—pop pl ... AL-4
Frostville—locale ... WI-6
Frostwood Sch—school ... TX-5
Frosty Bay—bay ... AK-9
Frosty Canyon—valley ... OR-9
Frosty Creek—stream ... AK-9
Frosty Creek—stream ... MT-8
Frosty Creek—stream (3) ... WA-9
Frosty Gap—gap ... WV-2
Frosty Gap Trail—trail ... WV-2
Frosty Gulch—valley ... OR-9
Frosty Hollow—basin ... CA-9
Frosty Hollow Park ... PA-2
Frosty Jack Creek—stream ... MT-8
Frosty Knob—summit ... NC-3
Frosty Lake—lake ... MT-8
Frosty Lake—lake ... WA-9
Frosty Meadow—flat ... WA-9
Frosty Meadows—flat ... ID-8
Frosty Mtn—summit ... GA-3
Frosty Pass—gap (2) ... WA-9
Frosty Peak—summit ... AK-9
Frosty Reef—bar ... AK-9
Frosty Run—stream ... PA-2
Frosty Run Shaft—locale ... PA-2
Frosty Tank—reservoir ... TX-5
Frosty Valley—valley ... PA-2
Frosty Valley Country Club—other ... PA-2
Froth Hole—bend ... NY-2
Frothing Falls ... MI-6
Frothingham Lake—lake ... NY-2
Froud Hill—summit ... OR-9
Froula Park—park ... WA-9
Frovold Lake—lake ... MN-6
Frowland Creek ... NC-3
Frowlands Creek ... NC-3
Frowning Ridge—ridge ... CA-9
Frowning Rock Prong—stream ... NC-3
Frozard—locale ... LA-4
Frozard Plantation House—hist pl ... LA-4
Froze Creek—stream ... CO-8
Froze Creek Spring—spring ... CO-8
Frozen Bluff—cliff ... FL-3
Frozen Branch—stream ... GA-3
Frozen Branch—stream ... TN-4
Frozen Branch—stream ... WV-2
Frozen Calf Mtn—summit ... AK-9
Frozencamp—locale ... WV-2
Frozen Camp Creek—stream ... KY-4
Frozencamp Creek—stream ... WV-2
**Frozen Camp (Frozencamp)**—pop pl ... WV-2
Frozen Camp Run—stream ... MD-2
Frozen Chapel—church ... WV-2
Frozen Creek—locale ... KY-4
Frozen Creek—stream (3) ... KY-4
Frozen Creek—stream (2) ... NC-3
Frozen Creek—stream ... OR-9
Frozen Creek Ch—church ... KY-4
Frozen Dog Coulee—valley ... MT-8
Frozen Feet Windmill—well ... AZ-5
Frozenfoot Creek—stream ... AK-9
Frozen Fork—stream ... KY-4
Frozen Gap—gap (2) ... GA-3
Frozen Head—summit ... TN-4
Frozen Head Mine (underground)—mine ... TN-4
Frozen Head Mtn—summit ... TN-4
Frozenhead Ridge—ridge ... NC-3
Frozen Head State Environmental Education Area—park ... TN-4
Frozen Head State Park ... TN-4
Frozen Hollow—valley ... AL-4
Frozen Hollow—valley ... WV-2
Frozen Horse Creek—stream ... MT-8
Frozen Horse Creek—stream ... SD-7
Frozen Knob ... TN-4
Frozen Knob—summit (2) ... GA-3
Frozen Knob—summit ... KY-4
Frozen Knob—summit (2) ... NC-3
Frozen Knob—summit ... TN-4
Frozen Knob—summit ... VA-3
Frozen Lake—lake (2) ... CO-8
Frozen Lake—lake ... MT-8
Frozen Lake—lake (2) ... WA-9
Frozen Lake—lake (2) ... WY-8
Frozen Lake—reservoir ... NC-3
Frozen Lake Creek—stream ... WY-8
Frozen Lake Dam—dam ... NC-3
Frozen Lakes—lake ... WY-8
Frozen Leg Canyon—valley ... MT-8
Frozen Lick—stream ... WV-2
Frozen Lookout Tower—locale ... KY-4
Frozen Man Creek—stream ... SD-7
Frozen Mtn—summit ... NC-3
Frozen Mtn—summit ... WA-9
Frozen Niagara Entrance—cave ... KY-4
Frozen Oak ... TN-4
Frozen Ocean—lake ... ME-1
Frozen Point ... RI-1
Frozen Point—cape ... TX-5
Frozen River Cave—cave ... CA-9
Frozen Rock—island ... AK-9
Frozen Rock Cem—cemetery ... OK-5
Frozen Run—stream (2) ... PA-2
Frozen Run—stream ... WV-2
Frozen to Death Creek—stream ... MT-8
Frozen-to-Death Creek—stream ... MT-8
Frozentop—summit ... GA-3
Froze to Death Creek—stream ... MT-8
Froze-to-Death Lake—lake ... MT-8
Froze-to-Death Mtn—summit ... MT-8
F Rsvr—reservoir ... OR-9
Fruchthendler School ... AZ-5
Fruedenberg Creek—stream ... TN-4
Fruedenberg Ridge—ridge ... TN-4
Frueh Private Field—airport ... ND-7
Frugality—locale ... PA-2
Fruhstucks Island ... MP-9
Fruin Corners—locale ... MI-6
Fruin Sch—school ... IL-6
Fruin Spring—spring ... MT-8
Fruit—locale ... IL-6
**Fruita**—pop pl ... CO-8
**Fruita**—pop pl ... FL-3
**Fruita**—pop pl ... OR-9
**Fruita**—pop pl ... UT-8
Fruita Aqueduct—canal ... CO-8
Fruita Bridge—hist pl ... CO-8
Fruita Campground—park ... UT-8
Fruita Canyon—valley ... CO-8
Fruita Canyon View—locale ... CO-8
Fruit and Flower Mission—hist pl ... OR-9
Fruita Picnic Area—locale ... CO-8
Fruita Rsvr—reservoir ... CO-8
Fruita Rsvr No 1—reservoir ... CO-8
Fruita Rsvr No 2—reservoir ... CO-8
Fruita Rsvr No 3—reservoir ... CO-8
Fruita Schoolhouse—hist pl ... UT-8
Fruit Branch—stream ... IN-6
Fruit Ch—church ... KY-4
Fruit City Hollow—valley ... MO-7
Fruit Cove—locale ... FL-3
Fruit Cove (CCD)—cens area ... FL-3
Fruit Cove-Switzerland—CDP ... FL-3
Fruit Creek—stream ... OR-9
Fruitdale—locale ... OH-6
**Fruitdale**—pop pl ... AL-4
**Fruitdale**—pop pl ... IN-6
**Fruitdale**—pop pl ... OR-9
**Fruitdale**—pop pl ... SD-7
**Fruitdale**—pop pl ... TX-5
Fruitdale Bridge—hist pl ... SD-7
Fruitdale (CCD)—cens area ... AL-4
Fruitdale Cem—cemetery ... AL-4
Fruitdale Creek—stream ... OR-9
Fruitdale Division—civil ... AL-4
Fruitdale HS—school ... AL-4
Fruitdale Sch—hist pl ... SD-7
Fruitdale Sch—school ... CO-8
Fruitdale Sch—school ... OR-9
Fruitdale Seminary (historical)—school ... AL-4
Fruitdale Store—hist pl ... SD-7
Fruit Fly Camp—locale ... FL-3
Fruit Growers Rsvr—reservoir ... CO-8
**Fruit Heights**—pop pl ... UT-8
Fruit Hill—hist pl ... WV-2
Fruit Hill—locale ... KY-4
**Fruithill**—pop pl ... KY-4
**Fruit Hill**—pop pl ... OH-6
**Fruit Hill**—pop pl ... RI-1
**Fruit Hill**—pop pl ... SC-3
Fruit Hill—summit ... RI-1
Fruit Hill Ch—church ... PA-2
Fruit Hill Community Center—locale ... SC-3
Fruit Hill Sch—school ... IL-6
Fruit Hill Sch—school ... MO-7
**Fruithurst**—pop pl ... AL-4
Fruithurst (CCD)—cens area ... AL-4
Fruithurst Division—civil ... AL-4
Fruithurst Elem Sch—school ... AL-4
Fruit Island—island ... CA-9
Fruit Island—island ... ID-8
Fruit Lake—lake ... CA-9
Fruitland—locale ... CA-9
Fruitland—locale ... GA-3
Fruitland—locale ... NC-3
Fruitland—locale ... UT-8
Fruitland—locale ... WA-9
**Fruitland**—pop pl ... CA-9
**Fruitland**—pop pl ... FL-3
**Fruitland**—pop pl ... ID-8
**Fruitland**—pop pl ... IL-6
**Fruitland**—pop pl ... IA-7
**Fruitland**—pop pl ... KS-7
**Fruitland**—pop pl ... MD-2
**Fruitland**—pop pl (2) ... MO-7
**Fruitland**—pop pl ... NM-5
**Fruitland**—pop pl ... NY-2
**Fruitland**—pop pl ... NC-3
**Fruitland**—pop pl ... OR-9
**Fruitland**—pop pl ... TN-4
**Fruitland**—pop pl ... TX-5
Fruitland Bible Institute—school ... NC-3
Fruitland Cem—cemetery ... AZ-5
Fruitland Cem—cemetery ... KS-7
Fruitland Cem—cemetery ... MI-6
Fruitland Cem—cemetery ... NC-3
Fruitland Cem—cemetery ... UT-8
Fruitland Ch—church ... MI-6
Fruitland Ch (abandoned)—church ... MO-7
Fruitland Cove—bay ... FL-3
Fruitland Creek—stream ... OR-9
Fruitland Ditch—canal ... CO-8
Fruitland Irrigation Canal—canal ... NM-5
Fruitland Landing—locale ... IL-6
Fruitland Mesa—summit ... CO-8
Fruitland Mesa Ditch—canal ... CO-8
Fruitland Park—park ... WA-9
**Fruitland Park**—pop pl ... FL-3
**Fruitland Park**—pop pl ... MS-4
Fruitland Park Elem Sch—school ... FL-3
Fruitland Park-Lady Lake (CCD)—cens area ... FL-3
Fruitlands—hist pl ... GA-3
Fruitlands—hist pl ... MA-1
Fruitland Sch—school ... FL-3
Fruitland Sch—school ... OH-6
Fruitland Sch—school ... WA-9
Fruitland Township—fmr MCD ... IA-7
**Fruitland (Township of)**—pop pl ... MI-6
Fruitland Union School—locale ... CA-9
Fruit Mtn—summit ... CA-9
Fruit Of The Loom Dam—dam ... RI-1
Fruit Oil and Gas Field—oilfield ... KS-7
Fruit Plain—locale ... VA-3
**Fruitport**—pop pl ... MI-6
Fruitport Country Club—other ... MI-6
**Fruitport (Township of)**—pop pl ... MI-6
Fruit Ranch—locale ... CA-9
Fruit Research Labratory of Penn State—building ... PA-2
**Fruitridge**—pop pl ... CA-9
Fruit Ridge—ridge ... CA-9
Fruit Ridge—ridge ... OH-6
**Fruit Ridge Center**—pop pl ... MI-6
**Fruitridge Manor**—pop pl ... CA-9
Fruit Ridge Manor—uninc pl ... CA-9
Fruit Ridge Sch—school ... CA-9
Fruits Cem—cemetery ... IN-6
Fruit Sch—school ... PA-2
Fruits Island Ford—crossing ... TN-4
Fruit Spring—spring ... OR-9
Fruit Springs—spring ... OR-9
Fruit Street Sch—school ... ME-1
Fruit Street Sch—school ... MA-1
**Fruittown**—pop pl ... PA-2
Fruitvale—locale ... OR-9
**Fruitvale**—pop pl ... CA-9
**Fruitvale**—pop pl ... CO-8
**Fruitvale**—pop pl ... ID-8
**Fruitvale**—pop pl ... TN-4
**Fruitvale**—pop pl ... TX-5
**Fruitvale**—pop pl ... WA-9
Fruitvale—uninc pl ... CA-9
Fruitvale Mine—mine ... CA-9
Fruitvale Oil Field ... CA-9
Fruitvale Oil Field—oilfield ... TX-5
Fruitvale Post Office—building ... TN-4
Fruitvale Sch—school (4) ... CA-9
Fruitvale Sch—school ... CO-8
Fruitvale Sch—school ... OR-9
Fruitvale Station—locale ... CA-9
Fruit Valley—basin ... TN-4
**Fruit Valley**—pop pl ... NY-2
**Fruit Valley**—pop pl ... TN-4
Fruit Valley Sch—school ... WA-9
Fruitville—locale ... MN-6
Fruitville—locale (2) ... PA-2
**Fruitville**—pop pl ... FL-3
**Fruitville**—pop pl ... PA-2
Fruitville Elem Sch—school ... FL-3
Fruitville Junction—locale ... FL-3
Fruitville Quarry—mine ... PA-2
Fruitville Sch (abandoned)—school ... MO-7
Fruitville (Township of)—fmr MCD ... NC-3
**Frumet**—pop pl ... MO-7
Frusha Cem—cemetery ... LA-4
**Frush Valley**—pop pl ... PA-2
Frustee Bend Cutoff—channel ... AR-4
Frustration Cave—cave ... AL-4
Frustration Creek—stream ... CA-9
Frustration Falls—falls ... OR-9
**Frutcheys**—pop pl ... PA-2
Fruth Sch—school ... WV-2
Fruto—locale ... CA-9
Frutosa Lake—lake ... NM-5
Fry ... WV-2
Fry—locale ... GA-3
Fry—locale ... KY-4
Fry—locale ... OR-9
Fry—locale ... WV-2
Fry—locale ... WY-8
**Fry**—pop pl ... AZ-5
**Fry**—pop pl ... TN-4
**Fry**—pop pl ... WA-9
Fry, Froman, Farm—hist pl ... KY-4
Fry, L. C., Farm—hist pl ... KY-4
Fry, Merrit, Farm—hist pl ... ID-8
Fry, P. A., House—hist pl ... TX-5
Fryar Branch ... TN-4
Fryar Branch—stream ... MS-4
Fryar Cem—cemetery ... NC-3
Fryar Cem—cemetery (3) ... TN-4
Fryar Graveyard ... MS-4
Fryar Lake—reservoir ... NC-3
Fryar Lake Dam—dam ... NC-3
Fryar Stadium—park ... TN-4
Frya Run—stream ... PA-2
Fryatt—locale ... AR-4
Fryatt Cem—cemetery ... AR-4
Fryback Cem—cemetery ... OH-6
Fry-Barry House—hist pl ... TX-5
Fryberg Lake—lake ... WA-9
Fry Bluff—cliff ... MO-7
Fry Brake—swamp ... MS-4
Fry Branch—stream ... GA-3
Fry Branch—stream ... KY-4
Fry Branch—stream ... MO-7
Fry Branch—stream (2) ... TN-4
Fry Branch—stream ... TX-5
Fry Branch Ch—church ... TN-4
Fry Brook—stream ... RI-1
Fry Building-Baxter Block—hist pl ... AZ-5
Fryburg ... PA-2
Fryburg—locale ... OH-6
**Fryburg**—pop pl ... ND-7
**Fryburg**—pop pl ... OH-6
**Fryburg**—pop pl ... PA-2
Fryburgh ... PA-2
Fryburg Oil Field—oilfield ... ND-7
**Fry Canyon**—pop pl ... UT-8
Fry Canyon—valley (2) ... AZ-5
Fry Canyon—valley ... NV-8
Fry Canyon—valley ... UT-8
Fry Canyon Store and RV Park—park ... UT-8
Fry Cave—cave ... TN-4
Fry Cem—cemetery ... OH-6
Fry Cem—cemetery (3) ... TN-4
Fry Cem—cemetery ... TX-5
Fry Cem—cemetery (2) ... WV-2
Fry Ch—church ... TN-4
Fry Creek ... ID-8
Fry Creek—stream ... AK-9
Fry Creek—stream (2) ... CA-9
Fry Creek—stream (3) ... ID-8
Fry Creek—stream (2) ... MN-6
Fry Creek—stream ... MO-7
Fry Creek—stream ... NY-2
Fry Creek—stream (3) ... OR-9
Fry Creek—stream (2) ... WA-9
**Frydek**—pop pl ... TX-5
Frydek Cem—cemetery ... TX-5
Frydek Sch—school ... TX-5
**Frydendal**—pop pl ... VI-3
Fry Ditch—canal ... AR-4
Fry Ditch—canal ... IN-6
Fry Drain—stream ... MI-6
Frydrych, John, Farmstead—hist pl ... SD-7
Frye—locale ... ME-1
**Frye**—pop pl ... PA-2
Frye, C. E., Farm—hist pl ... KY-4
Frye, J. O., House—hist pl ... OR-9
Frye, Nathan, House—hist pl ... MA-1
Frye, Sen. William P., House—hist pl ... ME-1
Frye Branch—stream ... TN-4
Frye Bridge—bridge ... NY-2
Frye Brook—stream ... ME-1
**Fryeburg**—pop pl ... LA-4
**Fryeburg**—pop pl ... ME-1
Fryeburg Acad—school ... ME-1
**Fryeburg Center**—pop pl ... ME-1
Fryeburg Compact (census name Fryeburg)—other ... ME-1
Fryeburg Harbor—bay ... ME-1
**Fryeburg Harbor**—pop pl ... ME-1
Fryeburgh (historical P.O.)—locale ... IA-7
Fryeburg Registry of Deeds—hist pl ... ME-1
**Fryeburg (Town of)**—pop pl ... ME-1
Frye Camp (historical)—locale ... ME-1
Frye Canal—canal ... FL-3
Frye Canyon ... AZ-5
Frye Canyon—valley ... AZ-5
Frye Cem—cemetery ... AR-4
Frye Cem—cemetery ... IN-6
Frye Cem—cemetery ... MI-6
Frye Cem—cemetery ... MS-4
Frye Cem—cemetery (2) ... NC-3
Frye Cem—cemetery (2) ... PA-2
Frye Cem—cemetery (3) ... WV-2
Frye Cove—bay ... WA-9
Frye Creek—stream ... AZ-5
Frye Creek—stream ... CA-9
Frye Creek—stream ... NC-3
Frye Creek Dam ... AZ-5
Frye Creek Retarding Dam—dam ... AZ-5
Frye Hill—summit ... MA-1
Frye (historical)—locale ... AZ-5
Frye Hollow—valley ... WI-6
Frye Island—island ... ME-1
Frye Knob—summit ... WV-2
Frye Lake—lake (4) ... NE-7
Frye Lake—lake ... WA-9
Frye Lake—reservoir ... IL-6
Frye Lake—reservoir ... WY-8
Frye Lakes—reservoir ... TX-5
Fryelands—locale ... WA-9
Frye Mesa—summit ... AZ-5
Frye Mesa Reservoir Dam—dam ... AZ-5
Frye Mesa Rsvr—reservoir ... AZ-5
Frye Mountain ... NC-3
Frye Mountain State Game Mngmt Area—park ... ME-1
Frye Mtn—summit ... ME-1
Frye Point—cape ... AK-9
Frye Point—ridge ... ID-8
Frye Pond—lake (2) ... MA-1
Fryer—locale ... KY-4
Fryer, Lake—reservoir ... TX-5
Fryer Acad—school ... CA-9
Frye-Randolph House and Fryemont Inn—hist pl ... NC-3
Fryer Branch—stream ... KY-4
Fryer Brook—stream ... NY-2
Fryer Canyon—valley ... CA-9
Fryer Cem—cemetery ... MS-4
Fryer Cem—cemetery ... OH-6
Fryer Cem—cemetery ... TX-5
Fryer Creek—stream ... MT-8
Fryer Hill—summit ... CO-8
Fryer Hotel—hist pl ... UT-8
Fryer House—hist pl ... KY-4
Fryers Branch P.O. (historical)—locale ... AL-4
Fryers Creek—stream ... TX-5
Fryer Spring—spring ... UT-8
Fryer Swamp ... NC-3
Fryer Tank—reservoir ... AZ-5
Fryes Canyon ... AZ-5
Fryes Ch—church ... KY-4
Frye Sch—school ... IL-6
Frye Sch—school ... ME-1
Fryes Creek ... AZ-5
Fryes Creek—stream ... MS-4
Fryes Creek—stream ... NC-3
Fryes Dam ... PA-2
Fryes Feeder—stream ... WI-6
Fryes Lake—reservoir ... NC-3
Fryes Leap—cliff ... ME-1
Fryes Point Cemetery ... TN-4
Fryes Pond ... RI-1
Fryes Run ... WV-2
Frye Teen Center—building ... AZ-5
Frye Trail Twelve—trail ... AZ-5
Frye Village ... MA-1
Fryeville ... MA-1
**Fryeville**—pop pl ... MA-1
Fry Fields—flat ... TN-4
Fry Fork—stream ... PA-2
Fry Gap—gap ... AL-4
Fry Gulch—valley ... CO-8
Fry Gulch—valley (2) ... OR-9
Fry Hill—summit ... CO-8
Fry Hill—summit ... VA-3
Fry Hollow—valley ... PA-2
Fry Hollow—valley ... TN-4
Frying Pan ... MD-2
Frying Pan ... VA-3
Frying Pan—bay ... AK-9
Frying Pan—flat ... TN-4
Frying Pan—locale ... CA-9
Frying Pan—locale ... NC-3
Frying Pan, The—bay (2) ... NC-3
Frying Pan, The—flat ... UT-8
Fryingpan, The—flat ... VA-3
Frying Pan, The—summit ... UT-8
Fryingpan-Arkansaw North Side Collection System—other ... CO-8
Fryingpan-Arkansaw South Side Collection System—other ... CO-8
Fryingpan Basin—basin ... CO-8
Frying Pan Basin—basin ... ID-8
Frying Pan Basin—basin ... MT-8
Frying Pan Bend—bend ... NC-3
Frying Pan Branch—stream ... VA-3
Fryingpan Brook—stream ... VT-1
Frying Pan Campground—locale ... UT-8
Fryingpan Canyon—valley ... CA-9
Fryingpan Canyon—valley ... NM-5
Frying Pan Canyon—valley ... NM-5
Frying Pan Catchment—basin ... UT-8
Frying Pan Ch—church ... VA-3
Frying Pan City ... CO-8
Fryingpan Cove—bay ... MD-2
Fryingpan Creek ... CO-8
Frying Pan Creek ... MT-8
Frying Pan Creek—stream ... AK-9
Fryingpan Creek—stream (2) ... CA-9
Frying Pan Creek—stream ... CO-8
Fryingpan Creek—stream ... ID-8
Frying Pan Creek—stream ... MT-8
Frying Pan Creek—stream ... NC-3
Fryingpan Creek—stream (2) ... OR-9
Fryingpan Creek—stream (2) ... VA-3
Fryingpan Creek—stream ... WA-9
Frying Pan Flat—flat (2) ... UT-8
Fryingpan Gap—gap ... GA-3
Fryingpan Gap—gap ... NC-3
Fryingpan Gap—gap ... PA-2
Frying Pan Gap Trail—trail ... PA-2
Fryingpan Glacier—glacier ... WA-9
Frying Pan Gulch—valley ... MT-8
Frying Pan Hill—summit ... NH-1
Frying Pan Hollow—valley ... PA-2
Frying Pan Island ... NC-3
Frying Pan Island—island ... AK-9
Frying Pan Island—island ... MI-6
Frying Pan Island—island ... SD-7
Frying Pan Lake—lake (2) ... CA-9
Frying Pan Lake—lake ... MI-6
Frying Pan Lake—lake ... MN-6
Frying Pan Lake—lake ... ND-7
Frying Pan Lake—lake ... OR-9
Fryingpan Lake—lake ... WA-9
Fryingpan Lake—lake ... WI-6
Frying Pan Lake—lake ... WY-8
Fryingpan Lakes—lake ... CO-8
Frying Pan Landing—locale ... GA-3
Frying Pan Landing—locale ... NC-3
Fryingpan Mountain Lookout—locale ... NC-3
Fryingpan Mtn—summit ... NC-3
Fryingpan Mtn—summit ... WA-9
Frying Pan Point—cape ... MD-2
Frying Pan Point—cape ... SC-3
Frying Pan Pond—lake ... RI-1
Frying Pan Ranch—locale ... OR-9
Fryingpan Ranch—locale ... TX-5
Fryingpan Ridge—ridge ... CA-9
Frying Pan River ... CO-8
Fryingpan River—stream ... CO-8
Frying Pan Run—stream ... PA-2
Fryingpan Shoal ... WI-6
Frying Pan Shoal—bar ... MI-6
Frying Pan Shoal—bar ... WI-6
Frying Pan Shoals—bar ... NC-3
Frying Pan Spring—spring ... CO-8
Frying Pan Spring—spring (2) ... ID-8
Frying Pan Spring—spring ... MT-8
Frying Pan Spring—spring ... NV-8
Fryingpan Spring—spring ... NM-5
Frying Pan Spring—spring ... OR-9
Frying Pan Spring—spring ... WA-9
Frying Pan Spring—spring ... WY-8
Fryingpan Springs—spring ... CA-9
Frying Pan Tank—reservoir ... NM-5
Fryingpan Trail—trail ... CO-8
Frying Pan Well—well ... NM-5
Fryingpan Well—well ... TX-5
Fry Island—island ... AK-9
Fry Island—island ... OR-9
Fryk, E. J., Barn—hist pl ... MN-6
Frykesende Cem—cemetery ... MN-6
Fry Lake—lake ... AZ-5
Fry Lake—lake ... MN-6
Fry Lake—lake ... NM-5
Fry Lake—reservoir ... OK-5
Fry Landing—locale ... OR-9
Fryley Fork ... WV-2
Fryleys Branch—stream ... KY-4
Fryman, Meyer, House—hist pl ... MI-6
Fryman Canyon—valley ... CA-9
Fry Meadow—flat ... OR-9
Fry Meadow Creek—stream ... OR-9
Fry Meadow Guard Station—locale ... OR-9
Fry Mesa—area ... UT-8
Fry Mesa—summit ... CO-8
Frymier Field—flat ... ID-8
Fry Mine—mine ... AZ-5
Frymire—locale ... KY-4
Frymire Sch—school ... IL-6
Frymire Sch—school ... KY-4
Fry Mountains—range ... CA-9
Frymoyer Airp—airport ... PA-2
Frymoyer Ridge—ridge ... PA-2
Fry Mtn—summit ... GA-3
Fry Mtn—summit ... NC-3
Fryor Run—stream ... PA-2
Fry Pan Creek—stream (2) ... ID-8
Frypan Meadow—flat ... CA-9
Frypan Pond—lake ... ME-1
Frypan Valley—basin ... TX-5
Fry Park—flat ... AZ-5
Fry Place—locale ... OR-9
Fry Point—cape ... NC-3
Fry Pond—lake ... RI-1
Fry Post Office (historical)—building ... TN-4
Fryrear Butte—summit ... OR-9
Fry Ridge—ridge ... MO-7
Fry Rsvr—reservoir ... OR-9
Frysburg ... PA-2
Frys Camp Spring—spring ... OR-9
Fry Sch—school ... IL-6
Fry Sch—school ... IA-7
Fry Sch—school ... MO-7
Frys Chapel—church ... NC-3
Fry School (historical)—locale ... MO-7
Frys Corner—locale ... RI-1
**Frys Corners**—pop pl ... OH-6
Frys Creek—stream ... OH-6
Frys Gap—locale ... TX-5
Frys Gap Station ... TX-5
Frys Gulch—valley ... ID-8
Fry's Hamlet Hist Dist—hist pl ... RI-1
Frys Harbor—bay ... CA-9
Fry Slough—gut ... MN-6
**Frys Mill**—pop pl ... AR-4
Frys Point—summit ... CA-9
Frys Point Cem—cemetery ... TN-4
Frys Point Ch—church ... TN-4
Frys Pond—lake ... RI-1
Fry Spring—spring ... NV-8
Fry Spring—spring ... OR-9
Fry Spring—spring ... UT-8
Frys River ... RI-1
Frys Run ... PA-2
Frys Run—stream ... PA-2
**Frystown**—pop pl ... PA-2
Fry's Trading Post—hist pl ... ID-8
Frys Valley Ch—church ... OH-6
Frysville—locale ... PA-2
**Fry's Wheatland View**—pop pl ... IL-6
Frytown ... IA-7
Frytown—locale ... PA-2
Frytown—locale ... VA-3
**Frytown**—pop pl ... OH-6
Fry Trail—trail ... PA-2
Fry Valley—basin ... CA-9
Fry Village ... MA-1
Fryville ... MA-1
**Fryville**—pop pl ... MA-1
Fry Windmill—locale ... NM-5
F S Blanchards Dam Number Three—dam ... NC-3
F Shively Ranch—locale ... NV-8
F S Scout Ranch Lake ... MO-7
F S Spring—spring ... ID-8
F S Spring Creek—stream ... ID-8
F S Tank—reservoir ... AZ-5
F Street—post sta ... DC-2
F Street Bridge—hist pl ... CO-8
F Street Bridge—hist pl ... WA-9
FT Ch—church ... LA-4
F Thurman Ranch—locale ... NM-5
Ft. Pierre II (39ST217)—hist pl ... SD-7
**F T Sanfords Subdivision**—pop pl ... UT-8
Fuaau Ridge—ridge ... AS-9
Fuafua Stream—stream ... AS-9
Fuaibusu-san-hiro-saki ... MH-9
Fuaibusu San Papa ... MH-9
Fuaibusu San Papa Saki ... MH-9
Fualbusu San Papa Saki ... MH-9
Fuaragon ... MH-9
Fuaru ... FM-9
Fuasubukoru—island ... FM-9
Fuausan Island—island ... FM-9
Fuban Peak ... ID-8
Fubar Peak—summit ... ID-8
Fubuuy—summit ... FM-9
Fubuy ... FM-9
Fuca Pillar—bar ... WA-9
Fucas Straits ... WA-9
Fucat Lake—lake ... MN-6
Fuch Ditch—canal ... IN-6
Fuches Creek ... MS-4
Fuches Gulch—valley ... CO-8
Fuchs Ditch—canal ... CO-8
Fuchs Lake—lake ... MN-6
Fuchs Park—park ... FL-3
Fuchs Rsvr—reservoir (2) ... CO-8
Fucht Hill ... PA-2
Fucich Bayou—gut ... LA-4
Fucson ... AZ-5
Fuda Creek—stream ... NC-3
**Fudgearound**—pop pl ... TN-4
Fudge Branch—stream ... WV-2
Fudge Cem—cemetery ... KY-4
Fudge Chapel—church ... TN-4
Fudge Creek—stream ... ID-8
Fudge Creek—stream ... IN-6
Fudge Creek—stream ... IA-7
Fudge Farm—hist pl ... TN-4
Fudge Hill—summit ... MA-1
Fudge Hill—summit ... NM-5
Fudge Hollow—valley ... KY-4
Fudge Hollow—valley ... MO-7
Fudge Hollow—valley ... TN-4
Fudge Point—cape ... WA-9
Fudge Quarry—mine ... TN-4
Fudger Creek ... WV-2
Fudger Lake—lake ... OH-6
**Fudges**—pop pl ... SC-3
Fudges Chapel United Methodist Church ... TN-4
Fudges Creek ... AL-4
Fudges Creek—stream ... WV-2
Fudgetown Cemetery ... MS-4
Fuegan Brothers Dam—dam ... SD-7
Fuego—locale ... OR-9
Fuego Mtn—summit ... OR-9
Fuelhart Run ... PA-2
Fuellhart Island—island ... PA-2
Fuellhart Run—stream ... PA-2
Fuel Tank—reservoir ... AZ-5
Fuenle Park—park ... AZ-5
Fuente Canyon—valley ... NM-5
Fuente Piscina—spring ... PR-3
Fuentes, Ramirez, Residencia—hist pl ... PR-3
Fuentes Ranch—locale ... NM-5
Fuentes Well—well ... NM-5
Fuerbringer Sch—school ... MI-6
Fuerste House—hist pl ... IA-7
Fuersville—locale ... MO-7
Fuersville Cem—cemetery ... MO-7

Fuersville Ch (historical)—church ... MO-7
Fuertecitos Ditch—canal ... CO-8
Fuerte de la Conception—hist pl ... PR-3
Fuerte de Vieques—hist pl ... PR-3
Fuerte San Cristobal—locale ... PR-3
**Fuerte San Cristobal**—pop pl ... PR-3
Fuerte San Geronimo—locale ... PR-3
**Fuerte San Geronimo**—pop pl ... PR-3
Fuerte Sch—school ... CA-9
Fuertes Spring—spring (2) ... NM-5
Fues Hill—summit ... AZ-5
Fueslein Drain—canal ... MI-6
Fues Spring—spring ... AZ-5
Fues Tank—reservoir ... AZ-5
Fugal Dugout House—hist pl ... UT-8
Fugalei Ridge—ridge ... AS-9
Fugal Spring—spring ... UT-8
Fuga Post Office (historical)—building ... TN-4
Fuga Sch (historical)—school ... TN-4
*Fugate* ... TN-4
Fugate—locale ... OK-5
**Fugate**—pop pl ... MS-4
Fugate Branch—stream (2) ... KY-4
Fugate Cem—cemetery ... KY-4
Fugate Cem—cemetery ... MO-7
Fugate Cem—cemetery ... TN-4
Fugate Cem—cemetery (2) ... VA-3
Fugate Ditch—canal ... UT-8
Fugate Ford—locale ... TN-4
Fugate Fork—stream (2) ... KY-4
Fugate Fork Sch—school ... KY-4
Fugate Gap—gap ... TN-4
Fugate Gap—gap ... VA-3
*Fugate Hill* ... VA-3
**Fugate Hill**—pop pl ... VA-3
Fugate Sch—school ... IL-6
Fugate Sch—school ... KY-4
Fugate Sch—school ... TN-4
Fugate Sch (historical)—school ... MO-7
*Fugate's Hill* ... VA-3
Fugates Hill—locale ... VA-3
Fugate Siding (historical)—locale ... TN-4
*Fugatt Cemetery* ... AL-4
Fugels Mill Historical Site—locale ... MN-6
Fugere Ranch—locale ... ND-7
Fuger Lateral—canal ... ID-8
Fuget—locale ... KY-4
Fuget Branch—stream ... KY-4
Fugett Cem—cemetery ... KY-4
Fuggett Branch—stream ... GA-3
Fugina House—hist pl ... WI-6
Fugitive Creek—stream ... AK-9
Fugit Springs—spring ... AR-4
Fugitt Cem—cemetery ... TX-5
Fugitt Creek—stream ... KY-4
**Fugit (Township of)**—pop pl ... IN-6
Fugleberg Farm Airp—airport ... ND-7
Fugowee Creek—stream ... OR-9
*Fugower Creek* ... OR-9
*Fugua Creek* ... OR-9
**Fugua Farms**—pop pl ... VA-3
Fugua Ridge—ridge ... CA-9
Fuguitt Sch—school ... FL-3
*Fuhi Shima* ... FM-9
Fuhr Gulch—valley ... CO-8
*Fuhrmam Alke* ... WI-6
Fuhrmam Lake—lake ... WI-6
Fuhrman Community Center—locale ... MT-8
Fuhrman Lake—lake ... WA-9
Fuhrman Mascho Oil Field—oilfield ... TX-5
Fuhrmann JHS—school ... MI-6
Fuhrmans Mill—locale ... PA-2
Fuhrmans Sch (abandoned)—school ... PA-2
**Fuig**—pop pl ... PR-3
*Fuinagute* ... MH-9
**Fuit Subdivision**—pop pl ... UT-8
Fuji Creek—stream ... OR-9
Fuji Meadow—flat ... OR-9
Fuji Mountain Trail—trail ... OR-9
Fuji Mtn—summit ... OR-9
Fuji Park—park ... NV-8
*Fuji-Shima* ... FM-9
Fukiru Point—cape ... FM-9
Fukunsral, Foko—reef ... FM-9
**Fulbright**—pop pl ... TX-5
Fulbright Cem—cemetery (3) ... MO-7
Fulbright Cem—cemetery ... NC-3
Fulbright Cove—valley ... NC-3
Fulbright Hill—summit ... AR-4
Fulbright Pond—reservoir ... GA-3
Fulbright Sch (abandoned)—school ... MO-7
Fulbright Spring Park—park ... MO-7
Fulbright Windmill—locale ... TX-5
**Fulcher**—pop pl ... MS-4
Fulcher Branch—stream ... NC-3
Fulcher Cem—cemetery (2) ... GA-3
Fulcher Cem—cemetery ... TN-4
Fulcher Cem—cemetery ... VA-3
Fulcher Creek—bay ... NC-3
Fulcher Creek—stream ... TX-5
Fulcher Gulch—valley ... CO-8
Fulcher Hollow—valley ... MO-7
**Fulcher Landing**—pop pl ... NC-3
Fulcher Millpond—reservoir ... VA-3
Fulcher Mtn—summit ... NC-3
Fulcher Pipe—other ... CA-9
Fulcher Post Office (historical)—building ... MS-4
Fulcher Ranch—locale ... AZ-5
Fulchers Creek—stream ... NC-3
**Fulchers Landing**—pop pl ... NC-3
Fulchertown—locale ... NC-3
**Fulco**—pop pl ... GA-3
**Fulco Junction**—pop pl ... GA-3
Fulcrod Lake—lake ... TX-5
*Fulda* ... KS-7
Fulda—locale ... TX-5
**Fulda**—pop pl ... IN-6
**Fulda**—pop pl ... MN-6
**Fulda**—pop pl (2) ... OH-6
Fulda Creek—stream ... CA-9
Fulda First Lake—lake ... MN-6
*Fuldah* ... IN-6
Fulda Second Lake—lake ... MN-6
Fulda State Wildlife Mngmt Area—park ... MN-6
Fuld Hall—locale ... NJ-2
*Fulemmys Town* ... FL-3
Fulfer Branch—stream ... IL-6
Fulfer Creek—stream ... IL-6
*Fulford* ... MD-2
Fulford—locale ... NC-3
**Fulford**—pop pl ... CO-8
Fulford Cave—cave ... CO-8
Fulford Cave Campground—locale ... CO-8
Fulford Cave Spring—spring ... CO-8
Fulford Cem—cemetery ... IL-6
Fulford Cem—cemetery ... NC-3
Fulford Christian Day Care Center—school ... FL-3
Fulford Point—cape (2) ... NC-3
Fulford Sch—school ... FL-3
*Fulfords Crossroads* ... AL-4
Fulger Point—cape ... CA-9
**Fulgham**—pop pl ... KY-4
Fulgham Bridge—bridge ... VA-3
Fulghum Hollow—valley ... TX-5
Fulghum Tank—reservoir ... AZ-5
Fulgum Cem—cemetery ... FL-3
Fulgum Cem—cemetery ... TN-4
*Fulgurite Peak* ... MT-8
Fulham Cem—cemetery ... MS-4
Fulingenton Cem—cemetery ... MO-7
Fulingim Ranch—locale ... NM-5
Fulk Bldg—hist pl ... AR-4
Fulk Cabin—locale ... OR-9
Fulk Cem—cemetery ... IN-6
Fulk Ch—church ... NC-3
*Fulk Creek* ... IN-6
*Fulker Island* ... NC-3
*Fulker Islands* ... NC-3
Fulkers Island (historical)—island ... NC-3
Fulkerson—locale ... VA-3
Fulkerson, J. W., House—hist pl ... OK-5
Fulkerson Branch—stream ... KY-4
Fulkerson Cem—cemetery ... IL-6
Fulkerson Cem—cemetery ... MO-7
Fulkerson Cem—cemetery (2) ... TN-4
Fulkerson Ditch—canal ... IN-6
Fulkerson Ditch—canal ... KY-4
Fulkerson Landing—locale ... IL-6
Fulkerson (Magisterial District)—fmr MCD ... VA-3
Fulkerson Sch—school ... PA-2
Fulk Hollow—valley ... AR-4
Fulk Lake—lake ... IN-6
Fulk Mountains—summit ... AR-4
Fulk Mtn—summit ... VA-3
Fulkner Cave—cave ... OK-5
*Fulkners Island* ... NC-3
Fulks Cem—cemetery ... IL-6
Fulks Cem—cemetery ... WV-2
Fulks Dugout—stream ... TX-5
Fulks Point—cape ... AL-4
Fulks Run—locale ... VA-3
Fulks Run Ch—church ... VA-3
**Full**—pop pl ... IL-6
Fullalove Cem—cemetery ... LA-4
Fullam Brook—stream ... VT-1
Fullam Hill—summit ... MA-1
Fullam Hill—summit ... NH-1
Fullam Pond—lake ... NH-1
Fullard Creek—stream ... NC-3
Full Armor Bible Center—church ... UT-8
*Full Armor Christian Center* ... UT-8
Full Blood Windmill—locale ... TX-5
Fullbright Windmill—locale ... AZ-5
Fullbrook Shop Ctr—locale ... AL-4
Full Creek—stream ... OR-9
Fullen Branch—stream ... VA-3
Fullen Cem—cemetery (2) ... VA-3
Fullens—other ... TN-4
*Fullens Post Office* ... TN-4
Fullenwider House—hist pl ... KY-4
Fullenwielder, Peter, House—hist pl ... KY-4
*Fuller* ... MI-6
*Fuller* ... MS-4
Fuller—locale ... CA-9
Fuller—locale ... ID-8
Fuller—locale ... IL-6
Fuller—locale ... KS-7
Fuller—locale ... MI-6
Fuller—locale ... MT-8
Fuller—locale (2) ... PA-2
Fuller—locale ... TN-4
Fuller—locale ... TX-5
Fuller—locale ... WA-9
**Fuller**—pop pl ... AL-4
**Fuller**—pop pl ... MD-2
Fuller—uninc pl ... OK-5
Fuller, Amos, House—hist pl ... MA-1
Fuller, Capt. Edward, Farm—hist pl ... MA-1
Fuller, Enoch, House—hist pl ... MA-1
Fuller, Frances Ensign, House—hist pl ... OH-6
Fuller, John, House—hist pl ... CT-1
Fuller, Lake—lake ... FL-3
Fuller, Margaret, House—hist pl ... MA-1
Fuller, Montezuma, House—hist pl ... CO-8
Fuller, Mount—summit ... MI-6
Fuller, Mount—summit ... VT-1
Fuller, Peter, Bldg—hist pl ... MA-1
Fuller, Robert, House—hist pl ... MA-1
Fuller, Royal K., House—hist pl ... NY-2
Fuller, William Griffin, House—hist pl ... MA-1
Fuller, W. Joseph, House—hist pl ... IA-7
**Fuller Acres**—pop pl ... CA-9
Fuller Arm—canal ... IN-6
Fuller-Baker Log House—hist pl ... MD-2
Fuller Basin—basin ... AZ-5
Fuller Bay—bay ... NY-2
Fuller Bay—swamp ... SC-3
Fuller Block—hist pl ... MA-1
Fuller Bottom—flat ... UT-8
Fuller Bottom Draw—valley ... UT-8
Fuller Branch—stream (2) ... AL-4
Fuller Branch—stream ... AR-4
Fuller Branch—stream ... GA-3
Fuller Branch—stream ... KY-4
Fuller Branch—stream (2) ... TN-4
Fuller Branch—stream (2) ... VA-3
Fuller Bridge—bridge ... CO-8
Fuller Bridge—bridge ... OR-9
*Fuller Brook* ... MA-1
Fuller Brook—stream ... CT-1
Fuller Brook—stream (4) ... ME-1
Fuller Brook—stream (5) ... MA-1
Fuller Brook—stream ... NY-2
Fuller Brook—stream ... PA-2
Fuller Brook—stream ... VT-1
Fuller Brothers L P Ranch—locale ... TX-5
Fuller Buttes—summit ... CA-9
Fuller Canal—canal ... LA-4
*Fuller Canyon* ... AZ-5
Fuller Canyon—valley ... AZ-5
Fuller Canyon—valley ... CA-9
Fuller Canyon—valley ... NM-5
Fuller Canyon—valley ... OR-9
Fuller Canyon—valley ... SD-7
Fuller Cem—cemetery (5) ... AL-4
Fuller Cem—cemetery ... AR-4
Fuller Cem—cemetery (3) ... IL-6
Fuller Cem—cemetery (2) ... IN-6
Fuller Cem—cemetery ... KS-7
Fuller Cem—cemetery ... KY-4
Fuller Cem—cemetery ... LA-4
Fuller Cem—cemetery ... ME-1
Fuller Cem—cemetery (2) ... MI-6
Fuller Cem—cemetery ... NE-7
Fuller Cem—cemetery (2) ... NY-2
Fuller Cem—cemetery ... OH-6
Fuller Cem—cemetery ... SC-3
Fuller Cem—cemetery ... TN-4
Fuller Cem—cemetery (3) ... TX-5
Fuller Cem—cemetery (3) ... VA-3
Fuller Cem—cemetery ... WI-6
Fuller Chapel—church ... NC-3
Fuller Chapel—church ... TN-4
Fuller Chapel—church ... VA-3
Fuller Chapel Cem—cemetery ... TN-4
*Fuller Chapel Methodist Church* ... TN-4
Fuller Corner Cem—cemetery ... ME-1
Fuller Coulee—valley ... ND-7
Fuller Coulee—valley ... WI-6
Fuller Cove—bay ... UT-8
Fuller Covered Bridge—hist pl ... VT-1
*Fuller Creek* ... AZ-5
*Fuller Creek* ... CA-9
Fuller Creek—stream (4) ... AL-4
Fuller Creek—stream ... AK-9
Fuller Creek—stream ... AZ-5
Fuller Creek—stream (3) ... CA-9
Fuller Creek—stream ... FL-3
Fuller Creek—stream ... KY-4
Fuller Creek—stream ... MI-6
Fuller Creek—stream (2) ... MS-4
Fuller Creek—stream ... OH-6
Fuller Creek—stream (3) ... OR-9
Fuller Creek—stream ... UT-8
Fuller Creek—stream ... WA-9
Fuller Creek—stream ... WI-6
Fuller Crossroad—locale ... AL-4
*Fuller Crossroads* ... AL-4
**Fullerdale (subdivision)**—pop pl ... NC-3
Fuller-Dauphin Estate—hist pl ... MA-1
Fuller Ditch—canal (2) ... IN-6
Fuller Ditch No 2—canal ... CO-8
Fuller Drain—stream ... MI-6
Fuller Draw—valley ... MT-8
Fuller Drift Mine (underground)—mine ... AL-4
**Fuller Estates (subdivision)**—pop pl ... TN-4
Fuller Field—airport ... IN-6
Fuller Field—park (2) ... MA-1
Fuller Flat—flat ... CA-9
Fuller Gap—gap ... GA-3
Fuller Gap—gap ... VA-3
**Fuller Gardens Subdivision**—pop pl ... UT-8
Fuller Gulch—valley ... ID-8
Fuller Gulch—valley (2) ... MT-8
Fuller Gulch—valley ... WY-8
Fuller Gulf Creek—stream ... NY-2
**Fuller Heights**—pop pl ... FL-3
*Fuller Hill* ... VT-1
Fuller Hill—locale ... CO-8
Fuller Hill—summit ... CT-1
Fuller Hill—summit ... ME-1
Fuller Hill—summit ... NY-2
Fuller Hill—summit (2) ... VT-1
**Fuller (historical P.O.)**—pop pl ... IA-7
Fuller Hollow—valley ... AL-4
Fuller Hollow—valley ... AR-4
Fuller Hollow—valley ... GA-3
Fuller Hollow—valley ... KY-4
Fuller Hollow—valley (2) ... NY-2
Fuller Hollow—valley ... PA-2
Fuller Hollow—valley ... TN-4
Fuller Hollow Creek—stream ... NY-2
Fuller House—hist pl ... DC-2
Fuller House—hist pl ... MA-1
Fuller House—hist pl ... NC-3
Fuller Houses—hist pl ... RI-1
Fuller Island—island ... ID-8
Fuller Lake—lake (2) ... AK-9
Fuller Lake—lake ... CO-8
Fuller Lake—lake ... FL-3
Fuller Lake—lake ... IL-6
Fuller Lake—lake (5) ... MI-6
Fuller Lake—lake (2) ... MN-6
Fuller Lake—lake ... NV-8
Fuller Lake—lake ... OR-9
Fuller Lake—lake ... PA-2
Fuller Lake—lake (2) ... WI-6
Fuller Lake—reservoir ... CA-9
Fuller Lake—reservoir ... SD-7
Fuller Lake State Fish And Waterfowl Mngmt Area—park ... IL-6
Fuller Lake Trail—trail ... AK-9
Fuller Lateral—canal ... AZ-5
Fuller Meadow—flat ... CA-9
Fuller Meadow Sch—school ... MA-1
Fuller Memorial Sanitarium—hospital ... MA-1
Fuller Mesa—summit ... AZ-5
Fuller Mesa Tank—reservoir ... AZ-5
Fuller Mesa Tank Number Two—reservoir ... AZ-5
Fuller Mill—locale ... NC-3
Fuller Mill Creek—stream ... CA-9
Fuller Mill Creek Camp—locale ... CA-9
Fuller Mine—mine ... OR-9
Fullermore Swamp—stream ... NC-3
Fuller Mtn—summit ... AK-9
Fuller Mtn—summit (2) ... CA-9
Fuller Mtn—summit ... CT-1
Fuller Mtn—summit ... GA-3
Fuller Mtn—summit ... ME-1
Fuller Mtn—summit ... SC-3
Fuller Mtn—summit ... VA-3
Fuller Mtn—summit ... WA-9
Fuller Oil Field—oilfield ... TX-5
Fuller Park—park ... CA-9
Fuller Park—park ... CO-8
Fuller Park—park ... IL-6
Fuller Park—park ... OH-6
Fuller Park—uninc pl ... CA-9
Fuller Pass—gap ... SD-7
Fuller Pasture—flat ... ID-8
Fuller Peak—summit ... CO-8
Fuller Peak—summit ... ID-8
Fuller Peak—summit ... WY-8
Fuller Point—cape ... MA-1
Fuller Point Sch—school ... IL-6
Fuller Pond—lake ... CT-1
Fuller Pond—lake (3) ... MA-1
Fuller Pond—lake (2) ... NY-2
Fuller Pond—reservoir ... NC-3
Fuller Pond Dam—dam ... NC-3
Fuller Ranch—locale ... CO-8
Fuller Ranch—locale (3) ... NM-5
Fuller Ranch—locale ... SD-7
Fuller Ranch—locale (2) ... TX-5
Fuller Ranch—locale (4) ... WY-8
**Fuller Ranch (subdivision)**—pop pl (2) ... AZ-5
*Fuller Reservation Dam* ... MA-1
Fuller Ridge—ridge ... CA-9
Fuller Ridge—ridge ... TN-4
Fuller Rock—island ... ME-1
Fuller Rsvr—reservoir ... CO-8
Fuller Rsvr—reservoir ... ID-8
Fuller Rsvr—reservoir ... WY-8
Fuller Run—stream ... PA-2
Fullers—locale ... FL-3
Fullers—locale ... KY-4
Fullers—locale ... NY-2
**Fullers**—pop pl ... NY-2
**Fullers**—pop pl ... NC-3
Fullers Bay—bay ... ID-8
Fullersberg Cem—cemetery ... IL-6
Fullersberg Park—park ... IL-6
Fullers Branch—stream ... AL-4
Fullers Branch—stream (2) ... KY-4
Fullers Brook—stream ... MA-1
Fuller Sch—school ... AZ-5
Fuller Sch—school ... AR-4
Fuller Sch—school (2) ... CA-9
Fuller Sch—school ... IL-6
Fuller Sch—school ... IA-7
Fuller Sch—school ... MA-1
Fuller Sch—school ... MN-6
Fuller Sch—school ... MO-7
Fuller Sch—school (2) ... NC-3
Fuller Sch—school ... SC-3
Fuller Sch—school ... SD-7
Fullers Chapel—church ... GA-3
Fullers Chapel—church ... TN-4
Fullers Chapel Sch (historical)—school ... TN-4
*Fullers Chapel United Methodist Church* ... TN-4
Fuller Sch (historical)—school ... AL-4
Fullers Creek—stream ... MN-6
Fullers Creek—stream ... MS-4
**Fullers Crossroads**—pop pl ... AL-4
Fullers Ditch—gut ... NC-3
Fullers Earth Creek—stream ... SC-3
**Fullers Earth (subdivision)**—pop pl ... FL-3
*Fuller Seep* ... AZ-5
Fuller Seep—spring ... AZ-5
Fullers Hill—summit ... MA-1
**Fuller Shores**—pop pl ... MA-1
Fullers Lake—lake ... GA-3
Fullers Lake—reservoir ... PA-2
Fullers Lake—swamp ... ND-7
Fullers Lakes—reservoir ... AL-4
Fuller Slough—gut ... TN-4
Fullers Marsh—swamp ... MA-1
Fullers Mill (historical)—locale ... IA-7
*Fullers Mills* ... PA-2
*Fuller Spirng* ... AZ-5
Fullers Point—cliff ... MA-1
Fullers Pond—reservoir ... AL-4
Fuller Spring—spring ... AZ-5
Fuller Spring—spring ... SD-7
Fuller Spring—spring ... UT-8
**Fuller Springs**—pop pl ... TX-5
Fuller Springs Sch—school ... TX-5
Fullers Ranch (historical)—locale ... AZ-5
**Fuller's Siding**—pop pl ... SC-3
Fullers Spring—spring ... AZ-5
Fuller State Park—park ... TN-4
Fuller's Tavern—hist pl ... NY-2
Fuller Store (historical)—locale ... AL-4
Fuller Street Baptist Ch—church ... TN-4
Fuller Street Bog Rsvr—reservoir ... MA-1
Fuller Street Dam—dam ... MA-1
Fuller Summer Camp—locale ... WY-8
Fuller Swamp—stream ... SC-3
Fuller Swamp—swamp ... MA-1
Fuller Swamp—swamp ... NY-2
Fuller Swamp Brook—stream ... MA-1
Fuller Tank—reservoir (4) ... AZ-5
Fuller Tank—reservoir ... NM-5
Fuller Theological Seminary—school ... CA-9
*Fullerton* ... IN-6
Fullerton—locale ... IL-6
**Fullerton**—pop pl ... AL-4
**Fullerton**—pop pl ... AR-4
**Fullerton**—pop pl ... CA-9
**Fullerton**—pop pl ... KY-4
**Fullerton**—pop pl ... LA-4
**Fullerton**—pop pl (2) ... MD-2
**Fullerton**—pop pl ... NE-7
**Fullerton**—pop pl ... ND-7
**Fullerton**—pop pl (2) ... PA-2
**Fullerton**—pop pl ... TX-5
Fullerton—uninc pl ... FL-3
Fullerton Archeol Site—hist pl ... NE-7
Fullerton Bend—bend ... TN-4
Fullerton Bluff—cliff ... TN-4
Fullerton (CCD)—cens area ... KY-4
Fullerton Cem—cemetery ... AL-4
Fullerton Cem—cemetery ... IL-6
Fullerton Cem—cemetery ... MO-7
Fullerton (census name for Whitehall)—CDP ... PA-2
Fullerton Ch—church ... IL-6
Fullerton Ch—church ... LA-4
Fullerton Coulee—valley ... MT-8
Fullerton Creek—stream ... CA-9
Fullerton Dam—dam ... CA-9
Fullerton Dam—hist pl ... OK-5
Fullerton East Oil Field—oilfield ... TX-5
Fullerton Golf Club—other ... CA-9
Fullerton Gulch—valley ... MT-8
Fullerton HS—school ... CA-9
Fullerton Inn—hist pl ... PA-2
Fullerton Junior Coll—school ... CA-9
Fullerton Lake—reservoir ... LA-4
Fullerton Memorial Ch (historical)—church ... OH-6
Fullerton Mill and Town—hist pl ... LA-4
Fullerton Oil Field—oilfield ... TX-5
Fullerton Park—flat ... CO-8
Fullerton Park—park ... IA-7
Fullerton Pavilion—building ... IL-6
**Fullerton (P.O.)**—pop pl ... PA-2
Fullerton Post Office (historical)—building ... AL-4
Fullerton Sch—school ... CA-9
Fullerton Sch—school ... IL-6
Fullerton Sch—school ... KY-4
Fullerton Sch—school ... MD-2
Fullerton Sch—school ... OH-6
Fullerton's Westminster Place—hist pl ... MO-7
**Fullerton Township**—pop pl ... NE-7
Fullerton Union Pacific Depot—hist pl ... CA-9
Fullerton Water Plant—other ... CA-9
Fullerton Well—well ... NM-5
Fullerton Woods East—woods ... IL-6
Fullerton Woods West—woods ... IL-6
**Fullertown**—pop pl ... OH-6
**Fuller Township**—pop pl ... SD-7
Fullerville—locale ... FL-3
Fullerville—locale ... TX-5
**Fullerville**—pop pl ... NY-2
Fullerville—uninc pl ... GA-3
Fullerville Ch—church ... NY-2
**Fullerville (historical)**—pop pl ... MA-1
Fullerville Sands—summit ... NY-2
Fuller Warren Bridge—bridge ... FL-3
Fuller-Weston House—hist pl ... ME-1
Fullerwood Elem Sch—school ... FL-3
Fulles Lake Dam—dam ... PA-2
Full Gospel Assembly—church ... FL-3
Full Gospel Assembly Ch—church ... UT-8
Full Gospel Assembly of God Ch—church ... AL-4
*Full Gospel Ch* ... PA-2
Full Gospel Ch—church ... AL-4
Full Gospel Ch—church (2) ... AR-4
Full Gospel Ch—church ... GA-3
Full Gospel Ch—church ... IL-6
Full Gospel Ch—church ... LA-4
Full Gospel Ch—church ... MD-2
Full Gospel Ch—church (2) ... MI-6
Full Gospel Ch—church (6) ... MO-7
Full Gospel Ch—church ... NH-1
Full Gospel Ch—church (6) ... NC-3
Full Gospel Ch—church (2) ... OK-5
Full Gospel Ch—church ... PA-2
Full Gospel Ch—church ... TN-4
Full Gospel Ch—church (2) ... VA-3
Full Gospel Ch—church ... WV-2
Full Gospel Ch—church ... WY-8
Full Gospel Chapel—church ... KS-7
Full Gospel Chapel—church ... MO-7
Full Gospel Ch of God—church ... AL-4
Full Gospel Ch of Orlando—church ... FL-3
Full Gospel Ch of the Living God—church ... FL-3
Full Gospel Church—hist pl ... WA-9
Full Gospel Church, The—church ... PA-2
Full Gospel Deliverance Ch—church ... IN-6
Full Gospel Fellowship Ch—church ... AL-4
Full Gospel Lighthouse—church ... AR-4
Full Gospel Lighthouse—church ... FL-3
Full Gospel Lighthouse—church ... IA-7
Full Gospel Mission—church ... GA-3
Full Gospel Mission—church ... MO-7
Full Gospel Mission—church (2) ... NY-2
Full Gospel Mission—church ... TN-4
Full Gospel Mission—church ... TX-5
Full Gospel Mission—church ... WI-6
Full Gospel Mission Ch—church ... MS-4
Full Gospel Mission Ch—church ... MO-7
Full Gospel Pentecostal Ch—church ... MS-4
*Full Gospel Tabernacle* ... SD-7
Full Gospel Tabernacle—church (3) ... AL-4
Full Gospel Tabernacle—church ... AR-4
Full Gospel Tabernacle—church (2) ... GA-3
Full Gospel Tabernacle—church ... KS-7
Full Gospel Tabernacle—church (2) ... KY-4
Full Gospel Tabernacle—church (2) ... NC-3
Full Gospel Tabernacle—church ... VA-3
Full Gospel Tabernacle—church ... WI-6
Full Gospel Tabernacle Ch—church ... AL-4
Full Gospel Temple—church ... AR-4
Full Gospel Temple—church ... MS-4
Fullhart Knob—summit ... VA-3
Full Hollow—valley ... KY-4
Fullilove Cem—cemetery ... MS-4
Fullilove Cem—cemetery ... TX-5
Fullilove -Jackson Cem—cemetery ... GA-3
Fullilove Lake—lake ... MS-4
Fulling Brook—stream ... VT-1
Fullingim Draw—valley ... NM-5
*Fulling Mill Branch* ... MD-2
Fulling Mill Brook—stream ... CT-1
Fulling Mill Brook—stream (2) ... MA-1
Fulling Mill Creek—stream ... MA-1
Fulling Mill Mtn—summit ... ME-1
*Fulling Millpond* ... MA-1
Fulling Mill Pond—reservoir ... MA-1
Fulling Millpond Dam—dam ... MA-1
Fulling Mill Stream—stream ... NJ-2
Fullington Creek—stream ... IA-7
*Fullingwilder* ... NC-3
Fullmer—locale ... ID-8
Fullmer Canal—canal ... UT-8
Fullmer Cem—cemetery ... SC-3
*Fullmer Dam* ... AL-4
Fullmer Drain—canal ... MI-6
Fullmer Hollow—valley ... UT-8
*Fullmer Lake* ... AL-4
Fullmers Cabins—locale ... UT-8
Fullmer Spring—spring ... UT-8
*Full Mill Branch* ... MD-2
Full Mill Branch—stream ... MD-2
Full Mill Hill—summit ... PA-2
Full Mission—church ... PA-2
Full Moon Creek—stream ... ID-8
Full Moon Gulch—valley ... CO-8
Full Moon Lake—lake ... WY-8
*Full Moon Shoal* ... NC-3
Full of Fish, Lake—lake ... MN-6
Fullon Brook—stream ... VT-1
Fullove Hill—summit ... KY-4
Fulls—locale ... IL-6
Full Scale Tunnel—hist pl ... VA-3
Full Service Sch—school ... FL-3
Fulls Fork—stream ... WV-2
Fullturn Creek—stream ... WY-8
Fullview Ch—church ... TN-4
*Fullwood Branch* ... TN-4
*Fullwood Ch* ... TN-4
Fullwood Chapel—church ... TN-4
*Fullwood Creek* ... TN-4
Fullwood Creek—stream ... GA-3
Fullwood Plaza Shop Ctr—locale ... NC-3
Fullwood Springs—locale ... GA-3
Fulman Canyon—valley ... NV-8
Fulmer Cem—cemetery ... MS-4
Fulmer Cem—cemetery ... NY-2
*Fulmer Creek* ... TX-5
Fulmer Creek—stream ... NY-2
Fulmer Ditch—canal (2) ... IN-6
Fulmer Falls—falls ... PA-2
Fulmer JHS—school ... SC-3
Fulmer Lake—lake (2) ... MI-6
Fulmer Mine (underground)—mine ... AL-4
Fulmer Ranch—locale ... AZ-5
*Fulmers Lake* ... MI-6
Fulmer Valley—locale ... NY-2
Fulmer Valley—valley ... NY-2
**Fulmor**—pop pl ... PA-2
Fulmor, Lake—reservoir ... CA-9
Fulmore JHS—school (2) ... TX-5
*Fulmor Heights* ... PA-2
**Fulmor Heights**—pop pl ... PA-2
Fulmor Ranch—locale ... CA-9
Fulmor Station—locale ... PA-2
**Fulp**—pop pl ... NC-3
Fulp Ch—church ... NC-3
Fulp Memorial Ch—church ... NC-3
*Fulsaws Branch* ... AL-4
**Fulshear**—pop pl ... TX-5
Fulshear Lake—lake ... TX-5
Fulshear Oil Field—oilfield ... TX-5
Fulshear-Simonton (CCD)—cens area ... TX-5
Fulsher Sch—school ... WI-6
Fulsom Cem—cemetery ... OK-5
Fulsome Creek—stream ... GA-3
Fulsom Ranch—locale ... KS-7
Fulsos Ranch—locale ... CO-8
Fulstone Number One Spring—spring ... NV-8
Fulstone Number Three Spring—spring ... NV-8
Fulstone Number Two Spring—spring ... NV-8
Fulstone Spring—spring ... CA-9
*Fulton* ... KS-7
*Fulton* ... NC-3
Fulton—locale ... OR-9
**Fulton**—pop pl ... AL-4
**Fulton**—pop pl ... AR-4
**Fulton**—pop pl ... CA-9
**Fulton**—pop pl ... IL-6
**Fulton**—pop pl ... IN-6
**Fulton**—pop pl ... IA-7
**Fulton**—pop pl ... KS-7
**Fulton**—pop pl ... KY-4
**Fulton**—pop pl ... LA-4
**Fulton**—pop pl ... MD-2
**Fulton**—pop pl (2) ... MI-6
**Fulton**—pop pl ... MS-4
**Fulton**—pop pl ... MO-7
**Fulton**—pop pl ... NY-2
**Fulton**—pop pl ... OH-6
**Fulton**—pop pl ... OR-9
**Fulton**—pop pl ... PA-2
**Fulton**—pop pl ... SC-3
**Fulton**—pop pl ... SD-7
**Fulton**—pop pl ... TN-4
**Fulton**—pop pl ... TX-5
**Fulton**—pop pl ... WV-2
**Fulton**—pop pl ... WI-6
Fulton—uninc pl ... MD-2
Fulton—uninc pl ... VA-3
Fulton, George W., Mansion—hist pl ... TX-5
Fulton, Lake—reservoir ... SD-7
Fulton, Robert, Birthplace—hist pl ... PA-2
Fulton, Robert, Sch—hist pl ... PA-2
Fulton Acad (historical)—school ... TN-4
Fulton Airp—airport ... KS-7
Fulton Baptist Ch—church ... TN-4
**Fulton Beach**—pop pl ... TX-5
Fulton Beach Gas And Oil Field—oilfield ... TX-5
Fulton Branch—stream ... AL-4
Fulton Branch—stream ... AR-4
Fulton Branch—stream ... IL-6
**Fulton Bridge**—pop pl ... AL-4
Fulton Bridge Cem—cemetery ... AL-4
Fulton Bridge Ch—church ... AL-4
Fulton Bridge (historical)—bridge ... ME-1
*Fulton Bridge Missionary Baptist Ch* ... AL-4
Fulton Canal—canal ... MS-4
*Fulton Canyon* ... OR-9
Fulton Canyon—reservoir ... AZ-5
Fulton Canyon—valley ... AZ-5
Fulton Canyon—valley ... OR-9
Fulton Canyon Tank—reservoir ... AZ-5
Fulton (CCD)—cens area ... AL-4
Fulton (CCD)—cens area ... KY-4
Fulton (CCD)—cens area ... TX-5
Fulton Cem—cemetery ... AL-4
Fulton Cem—cemetery ... AR-4
Fulton Cem—cemetery ... IN-6
Fulton Cem—cemetery ... IA-7
Fulton Cem—cemetery ... KY-4
Fulton Cem—cemetery (3) ... MS-4
Fulton Cem—cemetery (3) ... MO-7
Fulton Cem—cemetery (2) ... NY-2
Fulton Cem—cemetery (3) ... OH-6
Fulton Cem—cemetery ... PA-2
Fulton Cem—cemetery ... TX-5
Fulton Cem—cemetery ... WV-2
Fulton Cem—cemetery ... WI-6
*Fulton Center* ... WI-6
**Fulton Center**—pop pl ... MI-6
Fulton Center Ch—church ... MI-6
Fulton Ch—church ... MI-6
Fulton Ch—church ... MS-4
Fulton Ch—church ... NC-3
Fulton Ch—church ... SC-3
Fulton Ch—church ... VA-3
*Fulton Chain* ... NY-2
Fulton Chain Lakes—lake ... NY-2
Fulton Chapel—church ... MS-4
Fulton Ch of Christ—church ... MS-4
Fulton-Commercial Streets District—hist pl ... MA-1
Fulton Congregational Church—hist pl ... WI-6
**Fulton (County)**—pop pl ... AR-4

**Fulton (County)**—*pop pl* GA-3
**Fulton (County)**—*pop pl* IL-6
**Fulton County**—*pop pl* IN-6
**Fulton (County)**—*pop pl* KY-4
**Fulton (County)**—*pop pl* NY-2
**Fulton (County)**—*pop pl* OH-6
**Fulton County**—*pop pl* PA-2
Fulton County Airp—*airport* IN-6
Fulton County Courthouse—*hist pl* GA-3
Fulton County Courthouse—*hist pl* KY-4
Fulton County Courthouse—*hist pl* NY-2
Fulton County Courthouse—*hist pl* OH-6
Fulton County HS—*school* KY-4
Fulton County Jail—*hist pl* NY-2
*Fulton Creek* MT-8
*Fulton Creek* TX-5
Fulton Creek—*bay* KY-4
Fulton Creek—*stream* AL-4
Fulton Creek—*stream* AK-9
Fulton Creek—*stream* CA-9
Fulton Creek—*stream* GA-3
Fulton Creek—*stream* ID-8
Fulton Creek—*stream* IL-6
Fulton Creek—*stream* MI-6
Fulton Creek—*stream* MS-4
Fulton Creek—*stream* MT-8
Fulton Creek—*stream* NC-3
Fulton Creek—*stream* OH-6
Fulton Creek—*stream* OK-5
Fulton Creek—*stream* OR-9
Fulton Creek—*stream* TN-4
Fulton Creek—*stream* WA-9
Fulton Creek—*stream* WV-2
Fulton Crossroads—*locale* SC-3
**Fultondale**—*pop pl* AL-4
Fultondale Elem Sch—*school* AL-4
Fultondale HS—*school* AL-4
Fulton Dam—*dam* SD-7
*Fulton-Dame Point Cutoff Range* FL-3
Fulton Ditch—*canal* CO-8
Fulton Division—*civil* AL-4
Fulton Draw—*valley* SD-7
*Fulton Elementry Sch* PA-2
*Fulton Elem Sch* PA-2
Fulton Elem Sch—*hist pl* PA-2
Fulton Elem Sch—*school* AL-4
Fulton Elem Sch—*school* MS-4
Fulton Elem Sch—*school* PA-2
Fulton Extension Ditch—*canal* CO-8
Fulton Farm—*hist pl* OH-6
Fulton Ferry District—*hist pl* NY-2
Fulton Field—*airport* IN-6
Fulton Fork—*stream* KY-4
*Fulton Freewill Baptist Church* MS-4
Fulton Gap—*gap* AL-4
Fulton Gap—*gap* PA-2
Fulton Gap—*gap* TN-4
Fulton Gulch—*valley* CA-9
**Fultonham**—*pop pl* NY-2
**Fultonham**—*pop pl* OH-6
Fultonham Cem—*cemetery* OH-6
*Fultonham Station* OH-6
Fulton Heights—*uninc pl* CO-8
Fulton Heights Methodist Ch—*church* AL-4
Fulton Heights Sch—*school* CO-8
**Fulton Heights (subdivision)**—*pop pl* NC-3
Fulton Hill—*summit* (2) NY-2
Fulton Hill Cem—*cemetery* NY-2
**Fulton (historical)**—*pop pl* NC-3
Fulton Hollow—*valley* AR-4
Fulton Hosp—*hospital* KY-4
Fulton House—*hist pl* PA-2
Fulton House—*locale* PA-2
Fulton House Post Office (historical)—*building* PA-2
Fulton HS—*school* GA-3
Fulton HS—*school* MI-6
Fulton HS—*school* TN-4
Fulton Islands—*island* IN-6
Fulton-Itawamba County Airp—*airport* MS-4
Fulton JHS—*school* CA-9
Fulton JHS—*school* IN-6
Fulton JHS—*school* MS-4
Fulton JHS—*school* TX-5
Fulton Junction—*uninc pl* MD-2
Fulton Knob—*summit* PA-2
Fulton Lake—*lake* ME-1
Fulton Lake—*lake* MN-6
Fulton Lake—*reservoir* SD-7
Fulton Lake Dam—*dam* AL-4
*Fulton Lakes* CO-8
Fulton Lateral Ditch—*canal* CO-8
Fulton Log House—*hist pl* PA-2
Fulton Mall—*park* CA-9
Fulton Municipal Airp—*airport* MO-7
Fulton Normal Institute (historical)—*school* MS-4
Fulton Opera House—*building* PA-2
Fulton Opera House—*hist pl* PA-2
Fulton Park—*park* CT-1
Fulton Park—*park* NY-2
Fulton Park—*park* OR-9
Fulton Peak—*summit* AK-9
Fulton Peak—*summit* CA-9
Fulton Playground—*park* CA-9
Fulton Pond—*lake* NH-1
Fulton Pond—*lake* OH-6
Fulton Pond—*lake* WI-6
Fulton Pond—*reservoir* MA-1
Fulton Pond Dam—*dam* MS-4
Fulton Post Office (historical)—*building* TN-4
Fulton-Presbyterian Cemetery—*hist pl* OH-6
Fulton Ranch—*locale* AZ-5
Fulton Ranch—*locale* (2) TX-5
Fulton Rec Area—*park* MS-4
Fulton Ridge—*ridge* GA-3
Fulton Ridge—*ridge* OR-9
Fulton Ridge Park—*park* AL-4
Fulton Road—*uninc pl* AL-4
Fulton Road Baptist Ch—*church* AL-4
**Fulton Run**—*pop pl* PA-2
Fulton Run—*stream* (2) PA-2
**Fulton Run Junction**—*pop pl* PA-2
*Fulton Sch* PA-2
Fulton Sch—*school* (2) CA-9
Fulton Sch—*school* CO-8
Fulton Sch—*school* (2) IL-6
Fulton Sch—*school* IN-6
Fulton Sch—*school* (2) IA-7
Fulton Sch—*school* (2) MA-1
Fulton Sch—*school* MN-6
Fulton Sch—*school* NJ-2
Fulton Sch—*school* (4) NY-2
Fulton Sch—*school* (4) OH-6
Fulton Sch—*school* OK-5
Fulton Sch—*school* (2) PA-2
Fulton Sch—*school* SC-3
Fulton Sch—*school* TX-5
Fulton Sch—*school* VA-3
Fulton Sch (abandoned)—*school* PA-2
Fulton Sch (historical)—*school* TN-4
Fultons Creek—*stream* IA-7
*Fultons Gap* AL-4
Fultons (historical P.O.)—*locale* AL-4
Fultons Lake—*reservoir* AL-4
Fulton Spring—*spring* AZ-5
Fulton Spring—*spring* MO-7
Fulton Spring—*spring* MT-8
**Fulton Springs**—*pop pl* AL-4
Fultons Reef—*bar* NV-8
*Fultons Run* PA-2
Fulton Station—*locale* CA-9
Fulton Street Cem—*cemetery* MI-6
Fulton Street Cem—*cemetery* NY-2
**Fulton (subdivision)**—*pop pl* FL-3
Fulton Tank—*reservoir* AZ-5
Fulton Terminal—*uninc pl* NY-2
**Fulton (Town of)**—*pop pl* NY-2
**Fulton (Town of)**—*pop pl* WI-6
Fulton Township—*fmr MCD* (2) IA-7
Fulton (Township of)—*fmr MCD* (2) AR-4
Fulton (Township of)—*fmr MCD* NC-3
**Fulton (Township of)**—*pop pl* IL-6
**Fulton (Township of)**—*pop pl* IN-6
**Fulton (Township of)**—*pop pl* MI-6
**Fulton (Township of)**—*pop pl* OH-6
**Fulton (Township of)**—*pop pl* PA-2
Fulton Township Sch—*school* PA-2
Fulton Union Ch—*church* OH-6
Fulton United Methodist Church—*hist pl* NC-3
*Fultonville* OR-9
**Fultonville**—*pop pl* NY-2
Fulton West (CCD)—*cens area* KY-4
Fulton 4 H Club Camp—*locale* GA-3
**Fults**—*pop pl* IL-6
Fults Cem—*cemetery* KY-4
Fults Cem—*cemetery* (2) TN-4
*Fults Cove* TN-4
Fults Creek—*stream* IL-6
Fults Creek—*stream* TN-4
Fults Creek Ditch—*canal* IL-6
Fults Hill—*summit* TN-4
Fults Hollow—*valley* TN-4
*Fults Number 1 Cemetery* TN-4
*Fults Number 2 Cemetery* TN-4
Fultz—*locale* KY-4
Fultz Cem—*cemetery* (2) TN-4
Fultz Cove—*valley* TN-4
Fultz Creek—*stream* TN-4
Fultz Mtn—*summit* AR-4
Fultz Rsvr—*reservoir* CO-8
Fultz Run—*stream* VA-3
Fultz Saltpeter Cave—*cave* TN-4
Fulveg Mine—*mine* ND-7
Fulweiter Creek—*stream* CA-9
Fulwider Gulch—*valley* ID-8
Fulwiler Hill—*summit* TN-4
Fulwiler Sch—*school* MS-4
Fulwood Branch—*stream* (2) TN-4
Fulwood Park—*park* GA-3
*Fum* FM-9
Fumarole Butte—*summit* UT-8
Fumarole Cove—*bay* AK-9
Fumatahachi Island—*island* FM-9
Fume Creek—*stream* ID-8
Fumee Creek—*stream* MI-6
Fumee Lake—*lake* MI-6
*Fumor Heights* PA-2
*Funacha Creek* AL-4
Funchion Creek—*stream* AK-9
Funck, Josiah, Mansion—*hist pl* PA-2
Fun Creek—*stream* IN-6
Fundamental Baptist Ch—*church* FL-3
Fundamental Ch of God—*church* KS-7
Fundamental Gospel Ch—*church* IA-7
Fundamental Methodist Ch—*church* AL-4
Fundarosa Airp—*airport* MS-4
*Fundee* AL-4
Funderbunk Cem—*cemetery* IL-6
Funderburg Cem—*cemetery* OH-6
Funderburg Cem—*cemetery* TN-4
Funderburg Draw—*valley* NM-5
Funderburg Spring—*spring* NM-5
Funderburg Tank—*reservoir* NM-5
Funderburk Creek—*stream* GA-3
Funderburk Mtn—*summit* AR-4
Funderburks Lake—*reservoir* NC-3
Fund Pond—*lake* MA-1
*Funds Branch* TN-4
*Funds Branch School* TN-4
Fundy Bayou—*stream* FL-3
Fundy Channel—*channel* NY-2
Fundy Cove—*bay* NH-1
Funeral Mountains—*range* CA-9
Funeral Peak—*summit* CA-9
Funfar Sch—*school* MN-6
Fun Forest Park—*park* TX-5
Fungi Passage—*channel* VI-3
Fungo Hollow—*valley* AL-4
**Fungo Hollow (subdivision)**—*pop pl* AL-4
Fungo Valley—*valley* AL-4
Fungus Lake—*lake* (2) MN-6
*Funiya Point* MH-9
*Funiya-Saki* MH-9
**Funk**—*pop pl* NE-7
**Funk**—*pop pl* OH-6
Funk, Harriet, House—*hist pl* KY-4
Funk, James H., House—*hist pl* KY-4
Funk, Joseph, House—*hist pl* VA-3
Funk Branch—*stream* MO-7
Funk Branch (wilderness camping)—*locale* MO-7
Funk Canyon—*valley* UT-8
Funk Cem—*cemetery* IL-6
Funk Cem—*cemetery* (3) IN-6
Funk Cem—*cemetery* MO-7
Funk Cem—*cemetery* (2) OH-6
Funk Cem—*cemetery* VA-3
Funk Ditch—*canal* IN-6
Funke Bridge—*bridge* OR-9
Funk Hill—*summit* CA-9
Funk Hollow—*valley* IN-6
Funk House—*hist pl* WA-9
Funkhouse Quarry—*mine* PA-2
**Funkhouser**—*pop pl* GA-3
**Funkhouser**—*pop pl* IL-6
Funkhouser Branch—*stream* AR-4
Funkhouser Cem—*cemetery* IL-6
Funkhouser Creek—*stream* MO-7
Funkhouser Knob—*summit* VA-3
Funkhouser Mill (historical)—*locale* PA-2
Funkhouser Sch—*school* IL-6
*Funk Lake* MN-6
*Funk Lake* WI-6
Funk Lake—*lake* MN-6
Funk Lake—*lake* WI-6
**Funkley**—*pop pl* MN-6
Funkley Lake—*lake* MN-6
Funk Mountain Trail—*trail* WA-9
Funk Mtn—*summit* WA-9
Funk Oil Field—*oilfield* TX-5
Funk Quarry—*mine* TN-4
Funk Rsvr—*reservoir* CO-8
Funk Run—*stream* PA-2
Funks Bayou—*stream* LA-4
Funks Branch—*stream* IL-6
Funks Canyon—*valley* UT-8
Funks Cave—*cave* PA-2
Funk Sch—*school* IL-6
Funks Creek—*stream* CA-9
Funks Creek—*stream* FL-3
Funks Creek—*stream* MI-6
Funks Grove—*locale* IL-6
Funks Grove Ch—*church* IL-6
**Funks Grove (Township of)**—*pop pl* IL-6
*Funks Lake* UT-8
*Funks Lake* WI-6
Funks Meadow—*flat* CA-9
Funks Run—*stream* IL-6
Funks Run—*stream* KY-4
Funks Sch—*school* PA-2
*Funks Station* IN-6
**Funkstown**—*pop pl* MD-2
*Funks Valley* UT-8
Funk Windmill No 2—*locale* CO-8
Fun Lake—*lake* MN-6
Funland Park—*park* AL-4
Funmaker Flowage—*reservoir* WI-6
*Funn Branch* TN-4
*Funnegusha Creek* MS-4
Funnel, The—*basin* AL-4
Funnel Branch—*stream* TN-4
Funnel Canyon—*valley* OR-9
Funnel Creek—*stream* (2) AK-9
Funnel Draw—*valley* MT-8
Funnel Falls—*falls* UT-8
Funnel Lake—*lake* CA-9
Funnel Lake—*lake* WY-8
Funnel Rock—*pillar* TN-4
Funnel Top—*summit* NC-3
Funneltop Mtn—*summit* NC-3
*Funnigusha Creek* MS-4
Funns Branch—*stream* TN-4
Funns Branch Sch (historical)—*school* TN-4
Funny Bug Basin Spring—*spring* OR-9
Funny Bug Mine—*mine* CA-9
Funny Butte—*summit* OR-9
Funny Creek—*stream* MS-4
Funny Louis, Bayou—*stream* LA-4
Funny River—*stream* AK-9
Funny Rock ( Rock Formation)—*summit* WY-8
Funny Yockana Creek—*stream* MS-4
Funring Cem—*cemetery* MO-7
Funrue Dam—*dam* OR-9
Funrue Rsvr—*reservoir* OR-9
Funseth, Carlott, Round Barn—*hist pl* ND-7
Funshoot Mtn—*summit* AK-9
Funsten, Bishop, House—*hist pl* ID-8
Funston—*fmr MCD* NE-7
Funston—*locale* AR-4
Funston—*locale* CO-8
Funston—*locale* KY-4
Funston—*locale* NC-3
Funston—*locale* ND-7
Funston—*locale* TX-5
**Funston**—*pop pl* GA-3
**Funston**—*pop pl* KS-7
**Funston**—*pop pl* LA-4
Funston (CCD)—*cens area* GA-3
Funston Creek—*stream* CA-9
Funston Elem Sch—*school* KS-7
*Funston Hollow* PA-2
Funston Home—*hist pl* KS-7
Funston Lake—*lake* CA-9
Funston Meadow—*flat* CA-9
Funston Monmt—*pillar* KS-7
Funston Playground—*park* CA-9
Funston Run—*stream* PA-2
Funston Sch—*school* IL-6
*Funstons Pool* CO-8
Funta, As—*slope* MH-9
*Funtanasupanie Point* MH-9
*Funtanasupanie-Saki* MH-9
Funter—*locale* AK-9
Funter Bay—*bay* AK-9
**Funter (Variant: Funter Bay)**—*pop pl* AK-9
Fun Valley—*valley* CA-9
Fuoss Sch—*school* IL-6
*Fuoukanan, Mount* FM-9
Fuqua—*locale* TX-5
Fuqua, Lake—*reservoir* OK-5
Fuqua A Bar Ranch—*locale* TX-5
Fuqua Cem—*cemetery* (2) AL-4
Fuqua Cem—*cemetery* VA-3
Fuqua Creek—*stream* (2) OR-9
*Fuqua Draw* TX-5
Fuqua Draw—*valley* TX-5
Fuqua Gin (historical)—*locale* AL-4
Fuqua Hollow—*valley* (2) TN-4
Fuqual Cem—*cemetery* AL-4
Fuqua Pond—*reservoir* AL-4
Fuqua Pond—*reservoir* GA-3
Fuqua Ranch—*locale* CO-8
Fuqua Spring—*spring* AL-4
Fuqua Spring Cave—*cave* AL-4
Fuquay-Angier Field—*airport* NC-3
Fuquay Cem—*cemetery* KY-4
Fuquay Cem—*cemetery* TX-5
Fuquay Creek—*stream* WV-2
Fuquay Mineral Spring—*hist pl* NC-3
Fuquay MS—*school* NC-3
Fuquay Sch—*school* NC-3
Fuquay Senior HS—*school* NC-3
*Fuquay Springs* NC-3
Fuquay Springs Ch—*church* NC-3
Fuquay Springs (RR name for Fuquay-Varina)—*other* NC-3
**Fuquay-Varina**—*pop pl* NC-3
**Fuquay-Varina (RR name Fuquay Springs)**—*pop pl* NC-3
*Furabush* NY-2
Furaganger Bay—*bay* MN-6
Furance Corners—*locale* PA-2
*Furarappu* FM-9
*Furarisu* FM-9
*Furariyosu* FM-9
*Fura Udden* DE-2
Furay—*locale* IA-7
Furazuo—*island* FM-9
Furbay Cem—*cemetery* OH-6
Furbee Cem—*cemetery* WV-2
Furbee Ridge—*ridge* WV-2
Furbee Run—*stream* WV-2
Furber, John P., House—*hist pl* MN-6
Furber Hill—*summit* NH-1
Furber (historical)—*locale* NV-8
Furber Marsh—*swamp* OR-9
*Furber's Strait* NH-1
Furber Strait—*channel* NH-1
Furbush Branch—*stream* KY-4
Furbush Cem—*cemetery* ME-1
Furbush Creek—*stream* WI-6
Furbush Hill—*summit* ME-1
Furbush Lake—*lake* WI-6
Furcher Branch—*stream* MS-4
Furches—*locale* NC-3
Fur Creek—*stream* NC-3
Fure's Cabin—*hist pl* AK-9
Fur Farm Lake—*lake* MI-6
Fur Farm Lake—*lake* WI-6
Fur Farm Pond—*lake* MI-6
Furgerson Cem—*cemetery* KY-4
Furgerson Cem—*cemetery* (2) TN-4
Furgerson Chapel—*church* TN-4
Furgerson JHS—*school* OH-6
Furgerson Ridge—*ridge* TN-4
*Furgerson Ridge Church* TN-4
Furgersons Cave—*cave* AL-4
*Furgerson School* TN-4
Furgersons Pit—*cave* AL-4
Furgeson Lake—*lake* MI-6
Furgeson Ranch—*locale* MT-8
Furgeson Ranch—*locale* WY-8
Furguson—*locale* TX-5
*Furguson Creek* NV-8
*Furgusons Spring* NV-8
Furguson Tank—*reservoir* AZ-5
**Fur Hollow Subdivision**—*pop pl* UT-8
Furious Creek—*stream* MT-8
Fur Lake—*lake* MN-6
Furland Creek—*stream* WA-9
**Furley**—*pop pl* KS-7
Furley Oil Field—*oilfield* KS-7
Furlick Branch—*stream* SC-3
Furlong—*locale* PA-2
Furlong, Mount—*summit* MT-8
*Furlong Creek* CA-9
Furlong Creek—*stream* AL-4
Furlong Creek—*stream* MI-6
Furlong Creek—*stream* SD-7
Furlong Field—*park* CA-9
Furlong Gulch—*valley* CA-9
*Furlong Mtn* ME-1
Furlong Pond—*lake* ME-1
Furlong Pond—*lake* MI-6
Furlong Post Office (historical)—*building* PA-2
Furlough Creek—*stream* WA-9
Furlough Lake—*reservoir* NY-2
**Furlow**—*pop pl* AR-4
Furlow Cem—*cemetery* LA-4
Furlow (Township of)—*fmr MCD* AR-4
**Furman**—*pop pl* AL-4
**Furman**—*pop pl* IL-6
**Furman**—*pop pl* SC-3
Furman Bridge—*bridge* NE-7
Furman Cem—*cemetery* NY-2
Furman Cem—*cemetery* PA-2
Furman Chapel—*church* KY-4
Furman Creek—*stream* MT-8
Furman Drain—*stream* MI-6
*Furman Hollow* NY-2
Furman Institution Academic Bldg—*hist pl* SC-3
Furman Institution Faculty Residence—*hist pl* SC-3
Furman Park—*park* CA-9
Furman Ranch—*locale* CO-8
Furman Sch—*school* TX-5
Furmans Corner—*locale* NJ-2
Furman-Scotia (CCD)—*cens area* SC-3
Furman Shoals—*bar* GA-3
Furman Univ—*school* (2) SC-3
Furman Univ Womens Coll—*school* SC-3
Fur Mtn—*summit* OR-9
*Furnace* MA-1
Furnace—*locale* CA-9
Furnace—*locale* KY-4
Furnace—*locale* (2) MD-2
Furnace—*locale* VA-3
**Furnace**—*pop pl* IN-6
**Furnace**—*pop pl* MA-1
**Furnace**—*pop pl* (2) TN-4
Furnace, Bay—*bay* MI-6
Furnace Bay—*bay* MD-2
**Furnace Branch**—*pop pl* MD-2
Furnace Branch—*stream* AL-4
Furnace Branch—*stream* (3) KY-4
Furnace Branch—*stream* (2) MD-2
Furnace Branch—*stream* (3) TN-4
Furnace Branch—*stream* VA-3
Furnace Branch—*stream* WI-6
*Furnace Brook* MA-1
*Furnace Brook* VT-1
**Furnace Brook**—*pop pl* NY-2
Furnace Brook—*stream* (2) CT-1
Furnace Brook—*stream* (4) MA-1
Furnace Brook—*stream* NH-1
Furnace Brook—*stream* (3) NY-2
Furnace Brook—*stream* (2) VT-1
*Furnace Brook Lake* NY-2
Furnace Canyon—*valley* CA-9
Furnace Cem—*cemetery* TN-4
Furnace Cem—*cemetery* VA-3
Furnace Chapel—*church* PA-2
Furnace Covered Bridge No. 11—*hist pl* PA-2
*Furnace Creek* GA-3
Furnace Creek—*stream* CA-9
Furnace Creek—*stream* (2) GA-3
Furnace Creek—*stream* ID-8
Furnace Creek—*stream* IL-6
Furnace Creek—*stream* MD-2
Furnace Creek—*stream* (2) MO-7
Furnace Creek—*stream* NY-2
Furnace Creek—*stream* (4) PA-2
Furnace Creek—*stream* SC-3
Furnace Creek—*stream* (2) TN-4
Furnace Creek—*stream* (2) VA-3
Furnace Creek—*stream* (2) WI-6
Furnace Creek Ch—*church* VA-3
Furnace Creek Dam—*dam* PA-2
Furnace Creek Inn—*locale* CA-9
Furnace Creek Ranch—*locale* CA-9
Furnace Creek Wash—*stream* CA-9
Furnace Dam—*dam* PA-2
Furnace Ditch—*canal* UT-8
Furnace Flat—*flat* CA-9
Furnace Ford—*locale* MD-2
Furnace Fork—*stream* KY-4
**Furnace Hill**—*pop pl* (2) PA-2
**Furnace Hill**—*pop pl* VA-3
Furnace Hill—*summit* (4) PA-2
Furnace Hill Brook—*stream* RI-1
Furnace Hill Brook Historic and Archeol District—*hist pl* RI-1
Furnace Hill Ch—*church* AL-4
Furnace Hill (historical)—*locale* AL-4
Furnace Hills—*range* PA-2
Furnace Hills Camp—*locale* PA-2
**Furnace Hollow**—*pop pl* CT-1
Furnace Hollow—*valley* IA-7
Furnace Hollow—*valley* MO-7
Furnace Hollow—*valley* OH-6
Furnace Hollow—*valley* PA-2
Furnace Hollow—*valley* (3) TN-4
**Furnace Junction**—*pop pl* AL-4
Furnace Knob—*summit* VA-3
*Furnace Lake* CT-1
*Furnace Lake* MA-1
*Furnace Lake* MI-6
Furnace Lake—*lake* MI-6
Furnace Lake Dam—*dam* MA-1
Furnace Landing—*locale* TN-4
Furnace Mine (underground)—*mine* AL-4
Furnace Mountain—*locale* VA-3
Furnace Mountain Trail—*trail* VA-3
Furnace Mtn—*summit* KY-4
Furnace Mtn—*summit* (2) NY-2
Furnace Mtn—*summit* (3) VA-3
Furnace Point—*cape* NY-2
*Furnace Pond* MA-1
Furnace Pond—*lake* (4) MA-1
Furnace Pond—*reservoir* NY-2
**Furnace Pond Colony**—*pop pl* MA-1
*Furnace Pond Furnace Village Pond* MA-1
Furnace Post Office (historical)—*building* TN-4
Furnace Ridge—*ridge* OH-6
*Furnace River* RI-1
Furnace Road Dam—*dam* NJ-2
*Furnace Run* PA-2
*Furnace Run* VA-3
**Furnace Run**—*pop pl* PA-2
Furnace Run—*stream* OH-6
Furnace Run—*stream* (13) PA-2
Furnace Run—*stream* VA-3
Furnace Run—*stream* WV-2
Furnace Run Aqueduct—*hist pl* OH-6
Furnace Run Reservation—*park* (2) OH-6
Furnace Sch—*school* (3) PA-2
Furnace Sch—*school* VT-1
Furnace Sch (historical)—*school* PA-2
Furnace Spring—*spring* CA-9
Furnace Spring—*spring* VA-3
Furnace Spring Lodge—*locale* PA-2
Furnace Stack Hollow—*valley* (2) TN-4
Furnace Station (historical)—*locale* AL-4
Furnace Street Flume A Dam—*dam* MA-1
Furnace Street Flume B Dam—*dam* MA-1
Furnace Trail—*trail* PA-2
Furnace Valley—*basin* GA-3
*Furnace Village* MA-1
**Furnace Village**—*pop pl* MA-1
**Furnace Village**—*pop pl* NY-2
Furnace Village Hist Dist—*hist pl* MA-1
Furnace Village Sch—*school* MA-1
**Furnaceville**—*pop pl* (2) NY-2
Furnaceville Cem—*cemetery* NY-2
**Furnace Woods**—*pop pl* NY-2
Furnal Windmill—*locale* NE-7
Furnance Brook—*stream* MA-1
Furnas Cem—*cemetery* OH-6
Furnas Ditch—*canal* OH-6
Furneaux Creek—*stream* TX-5
Furnell Ranch—*locale* MT-8
**Furner**—*pop pl* MO-7
Furner Canyon—*valley* UT-8
Furner Creek—*stream* UT-8
Furner Pass—*gap* UT-8
Furner Ridge—*ridge* UT-8
Furner Valley—*valley* UT-8
Furness, Horace, JHS—*hist pl* PA-2
Furness Arroyo—*stream* CO-8
Furness Branch—*stream* TN-4
*Furness Hollow* TN-4
Furness JHS—*school* PA-2
Furness Library—*hist pl* PA-2
*Furness Senior HS* PA-2
**Furnessville**—*pop pl* IN-6
Furnett Creek—*stream* WV-2
**Furney Richardson**—*pop pl* TX-5
Furney-Richardson Sch—*school* TX-5
*Furneys Run* PA-2
Furnias (Barrio)—*fmr MCD* PR-3
*Furnish Canal* OR-9
Furnish Canal—*canal* OR-9
Furnish Canyon—*valley* CO-8
Furnish Creek—*stream* OR-9
Furnish Ditch—*canal* OR-9
Furniss—*locale* NY-2
Furniss—*locale* PA-2
Furniture—*locale* GA-3
**Furniture City**—*pop pl* GA-3
Furniture Draw—*valley* UT-8
Furnitureland—*post sta* NC-3
Furnondaga—*other* PA-2
*Furodàisu-suido* MP-9
Furport—*locale* WA-9
Furport Hill—*summit* WA-9
*Furquar Lake* MN-6
Furr Branch—*stream* MS-4
Furr Cem—*cemetery* AR-4
*Furr Creek* AR-4
Furrer Ditch—*canal* IL-6
*Furr Grave* AZ-5
Furr HS—*school* TX-5
*Furrier Coulee* WA-9
Furr Lake—*reservoir* NC-3
Furr Lake Dam—*dam* NC-3
Furr-Lambert House—*hist pl* GA-3
Furrow Cem—*cemetery* VA-3
Furrow Creek—*stream* AK-9
Furrow Ranch—*locale* NE-7
Furr Ranch—*locale* TX-5
**Furrs**—*pop pl* MS-4
Furrs Baptist Ch—*church* MS-4
**Furrs (historical)**—*pop pl* NC-3
Furrs Landing (historical)—*locale* TN-4
Furrs Post Office (historical)—*building* MS-4
Furrs Run—*stream* VA-3
Furr (Township of)—*fmr MCD* NC-3
Furry—*locale* AR-4
Furry—*locale* MS-4
Furry, Frederic E., House—*hist pl* OR-9
Furry Bend—*bend* TN-4
Furry Community Ch—*church* AR-4
Furry Sch—*school* OH-6
Fur Seal Rookeries—*hist pl* AK-9
Furse Cem—*cemetery* SC-3
*Furse Creek* IN-6
Furse Creek—*stream* SC-3
Furse Pond—*reservoir* SC-3
Fursman Spring—*spring* MO-7
Furst Landing Strip—*airport* MO-7
Furst Park—*park* IN-6
**Fursville**—*pop pl* OH-6
Furtado Creek—*stream* OR-9
**Further Creek**—*pop pl* MA-1
Further Creek (historical)—*bay* MA-1
Further Water—*lake* UT-8
Furuhelm, Mount—*summit* AK-9
Fury, Mount—*summit* WA-9
Fury Ditch—*canal* ID-8
Fury Island Park—*park* MN-6
Fury Knob—*summit* WV-2
Fury Lake—*lake* WA-9
Fury Lake—*swamp* MN-6
Fury State Wildlife Mngmt Area—*park* MN-6
Fuse Creek—*stream* ID-8
Fuse Creek—*stream* MT-8
Fuse Hill—*summit* MO-7
Fuse Lake—*lake* MT-8
Fush Creek—*stream* TX-5
Fusi—*locale* AS-9
**Fusi**—*pop pl* AS-9
Fusier Canyon—*valley* CA-9
Fusil, Bayou—*stream* LA-4
Fusilier, Bayou—*stream* (2) LA-4
Fusilier Of The Swamps, Bayou—*stream* LA-4
Fusillade Mtn—*summit* MT-8
Fusiloa Stream—*stream* AS-9
Fusi Ridge—*ridge* AS-9
Fusky (historical)—*locale* MS-4
Fuson—*locale* MO-7
Fuson Branch—*stream* (2) KY-4
Fuson Canyon—*valley* SD-7
Fuson Cem—*cemetery* KY-4
Fuson Ch—*church* KY-4
Fuson Chapel—*church* KY-4
Fuson Gap—*gap* KY-4
Fusonia—*locale* KY-4
**Fussel**—*pop pl* TX-5
Fussel Cem—*cemetery* LA-4
**Fussell**—*pop pl* LA-4
Fussell Cem—*cemetery* GA-3
Fussell Cem—*cemetery* LA-4
Fusselle Cem—*cemetery* GA-3
Fussell Mill Branch—*stream* NC-3
**Fussells Corner**—*pop pl* FL-3
Fusselman Canyon—*valley* TX-5
Fusselman Canyon Rock Art District—*hist pl* TX-5
**Fussels Corner**—*pop pl* FL-3
Fussel Slough—*gut* FL-3
Fuss Hollow—*valley* TN-4
Fussman Cem—*cemetery* KS-7
Fussville—*locale* WI-6
Fussville—*uninc pl* WI-6
Fussy Branch—*stream* AR-4
Fussy Creek—*stream* WV-2
Fustero Point—*summit* CA-9
Fuste Windmill—*locale* TX-5
Fuston Camp Windmill—*locale* TX-5
Fuston Cem—*cemetery* MS-4
Fuston Cem—*cemetery* (2) TN-4
Fuston Hollow—*valley* TN-4
Fusulina Peak—*summit* NV-8
*Futako Jima* FM-9
*Futako Shima* FM-9
F U Tank—*reservoir* AZ-5
Futch Beach—*beach* SC-3
Futch Branch—*stream* AR-4
Futch Branch—*stream* (2) GA-3
Futch Cem—*cemetery* TX-5
Futch Cove—*bay* FL-3
*Futch Creek* MS-4
Futch Creek—*stream* NC-3
*Futches Pond* GA-3
Futch Point—*cape* FL-3
Futch Run—*stream* FL-3
Futchs Bridge—*bridge* GA-3
Futchs Cem—*cemetery* MS-4
Futchs Creek—*stream* MS-4
*Futch's Pond* GA-3
Futchs Pond—*reservoir* GA-3
**Futheyville**—*pop pl* MS-4
**Futiga**—*pop pl* AS-9
Futi Rock—*island* AS-9
Futral Creek—*stream* AL-4
Futrell—*locale* KY-4
Futrell Store (historical)—*locale* TN-4
*Futtegalga Creek* AL-4

# G

G, Lateral—*canal* ... MT-8
G, Tank—*reservoir* ... AZ-5
G, Well—*well* ... NV-8
Gaakaan—*cape* ... FM-9
*Gaakeyoguru Reef* ... PW-9
Gaalegos Rsvr—*reservoir* ... CO-8
Gaamaak Cove—*bay* ... AK-9
*Gaanaak Cove* ... AK-9
Gaanaak Cove—*bay* ... AK-9
*Gaanaun* ... FM-9
Gaan Be Ti Ye Mesa—*summit* ... AZ-5
*Gaanelay* ... FM-9
*Gaanilay'* ... FM-9
*Gaani M'uth* ... FM-9
*Gaanipan* ... FM-9
Gaan Point—*cape* ... GU-9
Gaan River—*stream* ... GU-9
Gaar, Abram, House and Farm—*hist pl* ... IN-6
Gaar Corner—*locale* ... OK-5
Gaarde Cem—*cemetery* ... MN-6
Gaards Lake—*lake* ... MN-6
Gaar-Fenton House—*hist pl* ... KY-4
*Gaarii* ... MP-9
*Gaarii To* ... MP-9
Gaar Mtn—*summit* ... VA-3
Gaar Place—*locale* ... NV-8
**Gaars Mill**—*pop pl* ... LA-4
Gaars Mill Sch—*school* ... LA-4
*Gaarukadakku* ... PW-9
*Gaarukadokku* ... PW-9
*Gaarukadokku-San* ... PW-9
*Gaarukagakku Mountain* ... PW-9
**Gaastra**—*pop pl* ... MI-6
Gaatmaqon—*locale* ... FM-9
Gaboch—*channel* ... FM-9
*Gabadaguru Point* ... PW-9
Gabaladon Rsvr—*reservoir* ... NM-5
Gabaldon—*locale* ... NM-5
Gabaldon Drain—*canal* ... NM-5
Gabaldon Lateral—*canal* ... NM-5
Gabaldon Mine—*mine* ... NM-5
**Gabaldon (Ojitos Frios)**—*pop pl* ... NM-5
Gabaret Island—*island* ... IL-6
Gabaret Slough—*channel* ... IL-6
Gabarino Hill—*summit* ... AZ-5
*Gabaru Reef* ... PW-9
*Gabaru Sho* ... PW-9
*Gabatouru River* ... PW-9
Gabb, Mount—*summit* ... CA-9
Gabbard Branch—*stream* (2) ... KY-4
Gabbard Cem—*cemetery* ... KY-4
Gabbard Cem—*cemetery* ... TN-4
Gabbard Flat Cem—*cemetery* ... KY-4
Gabbard Hills—*summit* ... NV-8
*Gabbard Hollow* ... AR-4
Gabbard Hollow—*valley* ... AR-4
Gabbard Sch—*school* ... KY-4
**Gabbard (Sebastion)**—*pop pl* ... KY-4
Gabbatha Post Office (historical)—*building* (2) ... TN-4
Gabbert, William, House—*hist pl* ... IA-7
Gabbert Cem—*cemetery* (2) ... TN-4
Gabbert Mtn—*summit* ... AR-4
*Gabbett Church* ... AL-4
Gabbett (historical)—*locale* ... AL-4
Gabbett Post Office (historical)—*building* ... AL-4
Gabbettville—*locale* ... GA-3
Gabbit Lake—*lake* ... MI-6
*Gabbot Meadow* ... CA-9
Gabbot Meadow—*flat* ... CA-9
**Gabbotts Addition (subdivision)**—*pop pl* ... UT-8
Gabbro Falls—*falls* ... MI-6
Gabbro Lake—*lake* ... MN-6
Gabbro Pass—*gap* ... UT-8
Gabbro Peak—*summit* ... CA-9
**Gabbs**—*pop pl* ... NV-8
Gabbs Airp—*airport* ... NV-8
*Gabbs Township* ... NV-8
Gabbs Valley—*basin* ... NV-8
Gabbs Valley Range—*range* ... NV-8
Gabbs Wash—*stream* ... NV-8
Gabby Branch—*stream* ... NC-3
**Gabby Heights**—*pop pl* ... PA-2
Gabby Reed Brake—*stream* ... MS-4
Gab Creek—*stream* ... GA-3
Gabe—*locale* ... KY-4
**Gabe**—*pop pl* ... VA-3
Gabe—*uninc pl* ... OK-5
Gabe Branch—*stream* ... KY-4
Gabe Branch—*stream* ... NC-3
Gabe Branch—*stream* ... VA-3
Gabe Canyon—*valley* ... NM-5
Gabe Creek—*stream* ... ID-8
Gabe Creek—*stream* ... MT-8
Gabe Creek—*stream* ... OR-9
Gabe Fork—*stream* ... WV-2
**Gabe (historical)**—*pop pl* ... TN-4
Gabe Hollow Trail—*trail* ... VA-3
Gabel, Daniel, House—*hist pl* ... OH-6
Gabel, George, House—*hist pl* ... WI-6
Gabe Lake—*reservoir* ... TX-5
Gabel Canyon—*valley* ... NV-8
Gabel Creek—*stream* ... WA-9
Gabel Draw—*valley* ... WY-8
Gabel Hill—*summit* ... PA-2
Gabel Knob—*summit* ... WV-2
*Gabelle* ... MP-9
Gabelle Island—*island* ... MP-9
**Gabels Corner**—*pop pl* ... OH-6
*Gabelson Lake* ... WI-6
Gabelsville—*locale* ... PA-2
Gabe Meyer Sch—*school* ... AR-4
*Gabenur* ... MP-9
*Gabere-To* ... MP-9
Gabe Ridge—*ridge* ... ID-8
Gabe Rock—*pillar* ... NE-7
Gaberonne—*locale* ... FL-3
Gabert Island—*island* ... FM-9
Gabe Run—*stream* ... OH-6
Gabes Bathtub—*lake* ... ID-8
Gabes Branch—*stream* ... KY-4
Gabes Creek—*stream* ... KY-4
Gabes Creek—*stream* ... TN-4
Gabes Creek—*stream* ... WV-2
Gabes Knob—*summit* ... VA-3
Gabes Mtn—*summit* ... NC-3
Gabes Mtn—*summit* ... TN-4
Gabes Peak—*summit* ... ID-8
Gabes Spring—*spring* (2) ... OR-9
*Gabes Rock* ... NE-7
Gabes Rock—*summit* ... CA-9
Gabe Tank—*reservoir* ... NM-5
Gabettas Rsvr—*reservoir* ... ID-8
Gabgab Beach—*beach* ... GU-9
Gabica Butte—*summit* ... NV-8
Gabica Fork Willow Creek—*stream* ... NV-8
Gabica Ranch—*locale* ... ID-8
Gabica Well—*well* ... NV-8
Gabilan—*uninc pl* ... CA-9
**Gabilan Acres**—*pop pl* ... CA-9
Gabilan Creek—*stream* (2) ... CA-9
Gabilan Lodge No. 372-Independent Order of Odd Fellows—*hist pl* ... CA-9
*Gabilan Peak* ... CA-9
Gabilan Range—*range* (2) ... CA-9
Gabimichigami Lake—*lake* ... MN-6
*Gabin* ... MP-9
Gabino Canyon—*valley* ... CA-9
*Gabisch Bulch* ... MT-8
Gabish Gulch—*valley* ... MT-8
**Gable**—*pop pl* ... SC-3
Gable, The—*cliff* ... CO-8
*Gable Bay* ... MI-6
Gable Branch—*stream* ... FL-3
Gable Branch—*stream* ... GA-3
Gable Branch—*stream* ... TN-4
Gable Branch—*stream* ... VA-3
Gable Butte—*summit* ... MT-8
Gable Canyon—*valley* ... AZ-5
Gable Cave—*cave* ... PA-2
Gable Cem—*cemetery* ... IN-6
Gable Cem—*cemetery* ... OK-5
Gable Creek—*bay* ... NC-3
Gable Creek—*stream* ... CA-9
Gable Creek—*stream* ... ID-8
Gable Creek—*stream* ... OR-9
Gable Creek Sch—*school* ... OR-9
Gable Creek Trail—*trail* ... ID-8
Gable Ditch—*canal* ... IN-6
Gable Ditch—*canal* ... OH-6
Gable Hollow—*valley* ... KY-4
Gable Hollow—*valley* ... TN-4
Gable Lake—*lake* ... MN-6
Gable Lakes—*lake* ... CA-9
Gable Mtn—*summit* ... AK-9
Gable Mtn—*summit* ... MT-8
Gable Mtn—*summit* ... WA-9
Gable Pass—*gap* ... MT-8
Gable Pass Trail—*trail* ... MT-8
Gable Peaks—*summit* ... MT-8
Gable Ranch—*locale* ... CA-9
Gable Run—*stream* ... IN-6
Gables—*locale* ... NE-7
Gables, The—*hist pl* ... CA-9
Gables Acad of Miami—*school* ... FL-3
Gables Branch Cem—*cemetery* ... KY-4
**Gables Condo**—*pop pl* ... UT-8
*Gables Creek* ... AL-4
**Gables Estates**—*pop pl* ... FL-3
Gables Lake—*lake* ... MN-6
Gable Spring—*spring* ... AZ-5
Gables Ridge—*ridge* ... MO-7
Gables Run—*stream* ... PA-2
*Gables Wash* ... CA-9
Gabletop Mtn—*summit* ... CO-8
Gable Well—*well* ... NM-5
Gable Well Number One—*well* ... AZ-5
Gable Well Number Two—*well* ... AZ-5
*Gabodel* ... PW-9
*Gabodel Island* ... PW-9
*Gaboderu* ... PW-9
*Gaboderu Island* ... PW-9
*Gabokkudo* ... PW-9
**Gabriel**—*pop pl* ... KY-4
Gabriel, George, House—*hist pl* ... MA-1
Gabriel, Loc—*lake* ... LA-4
Gabriel, Rees, House—*hist pl* ... IA-7
Gabriel Bay—*swamp* ... NC-3
Gabriel Branch—*stream* ... KY-4
Gabriel Cem—*cemetery* ... OR-9
Gabriel Cem—*cemetery* ... TX-5
Gabriel Corners—*locale* ... OH-6
Gabriel Creek—*stream* ... AL-4
Gabriel Creek—*stream* ... MO-7
Gabriel Creek—*stream* ... NC-3
Gabriel Creek—*stream* ... OR-9
Gabriel Creek—*stream* ... WA-9
Gabriel Creek Ch—*church* ... NC-3
Gabriel-Filer House—*hist pl* ... OR-9
Gabriel Fork—*stream* ... KY-4
Gabriel Heights Memorial Gardens—*cemetery* ... AR-4
Gabriel Icefall—*falls* ... AK-9
Gabriel Knob—*summit* ... PA-2
**Gabriella**—*pop pl* ... FL-3
Gabriel Lake—*lake* ... NY-2
Gabriel Lake—*lake* ... WI-6
Gabriel Lake—*reservoir* ... CO-8
Gabriel Long Branch—*stream* ... TX-5
Gabriel Mills—*locale* ... TX-5
Gabriel Mills Cem—*cemetery* ... TX-5
Gabriel Mine—*mine* ... MO-7
Gabriel Park—*park* ... OR-9
Gabriel Peak—*summit* ... WA-9
Gabriel Ranch—*locale* ... SD-7
Gabriel Richard Park—*park* ... MI-6
**Gabriels**—*pop pl* ... NY-2
*Gabriels Creek* ... AL-4
Gabriels Creek—*stream* ... NC-3
Gabriels HS—*school* ... MI-6
Gabriels Junction—*locale* ... NY-2
**Gabriels Mills**—*pop pl* ... MO-7
Gabrielson Cem—*cemetery* ... SD-7
Gabrielson Island—*island* ... TX-5
Gabrielson Lake—*lake* ... MN-6
Gabrielson Lake—*lake* ... WI-6
Gabrielson Pool—*lake* ... IA-7
Gabriel Spring—*spring* ... OR-9
Gabriel Tank—*reservoir* ... AZ-5
Gabriel Tank—*reservoir* ... TX-5
Gabriel Trail—*trail* ... PA-2
Gabriel-Will House—*hist pl* ... OR-9
Gabril Creek—*stream* ... WA-9
*Gabro Lake* ... MN-6
Gabryck Park—*park* ... MN-6
**Gabtown**—*pop pl* ... TN-4
*Gabulko* ... PW-9
**Gaby Hills**—*pop pl* ... TN-4
Gace Ch—*church* ... ME-1
Gacey Spring—*spring* (2) ... OR-9
Gachaam—*summit* ... FM-9
Gachado Well—*well* ... AZ-5
Gachado Well and Line Camp—*hist pl* ... AZ-5
Gachalaaw—*bar* ... FM-9
**Gachalaaw**—*pop pl* ... FM-9
*Gachalau* ... FM-9
*Gachalau* ... FM-9
*Gachalaw* ... FM-9
*Gacham* ... FM-9
*Gachapar* ... FM-9
*Gachepar* ... FM-9
Gaches, George H., Cellar and Ice House—*hist pl* ... ID-8
*Gachlaw* ... FM-9
Gacho Tank—*reservoir* ... NM-5
Gacho Windmill—*locale* ... NM-5
**Gachpar**—*pop pl* ... FM-9
*Gachug* ... FM-9
Gachupin Canyon—*valley* ... NM-5
Gachupines, Loma de las—*summit* ... TX-5
Gachuug—*gut* ... FM-9
Gack Creek—*stream* ... AR-4
Gackenbachs Sch (abandoned)—*school* ... PA-2
**Gackle**—*pop pl* ... ND-7
Gackle Municipal Airp—*airport* ... ND-7
*Gacuug* ... FM-9
*Gad* ... AL-4
Gadao's Cave—*hist pl* ... GU-9
Gadara Baptist Ch—*church* ... FL-3
*Gadaraku Reef* ... PW-9
*Gadaraku-Sho* ... PW-9
Gadaus Lake—*lake* ... FL-3
Gadberry—*locale* ... KY-4
Gadbolt Lake—*lake* ... MN-6
Gadd Cabin—*locale* ... CO-8
Gadd Cem—*cemetery* ... AL-4
Gadd Creek—*stream* ... NC-3
Gaddes Canyon—*valley* ... AZ-5
Gaddes Canyon Trail—*trail* ... AZ-5
Gaddes Creek—*stream* ... VA-3
*Gaddes Run* ... PA-2
Gaddes Spring—*spring* ... AZ-5
Gaddies Chapel—*church* ... AL-4
Gaddies Chapel Cem—*cemetery* ... AL-4
Gaddis, Thomas, Homestead—*hist pl* ... PA-2
Gaddis Bluff—*cliff* ... TX-5
Gaddis Branch—*stream* ... NC-3
Gaddis Canyon—*valley* ... AZ-5
Gaddis Canyon Spring—*spring* ... AZ-5
Gaddis Cem—*cemetery* ... OH-6
Gaddis Chapel—*church* ... MS-4
Gaddis Creek—*stream* ... CA-9
Gaddis Creek—*stream* ... OK-5
Gaddis Creek—*stream* ... WA-9
Gaddis Farms Lake Dam—*dam* ... MS-4
Gaddis Mtn—*summit* ... GA-3
Gaddis Ridge—*ridge* ... KY-4
Gaddis Ridge Cem—*cemetery* ... KY-4
Gaddis School (abandoned)—*locale* ... MO-7
Gaddis Spring—*spring* ... AZ-5
Gaddis Spring—*spring* ... CA-9
Gaddistown—*locale* ... GA-3
Gaddis Wash—*stream* ... AZ-5
Gaddle Cem—*cemetery* ... KY-4
Gadd Ridge—*ridge* ... TN-4
**Gaddy**—*pop pl* ... OK-5
Gaddy Branch—*stream* ... NC-3
Gaddy Cem—*cemetery* (2) ... AL-4
Gaddy Cem—*cemetery* ... NC-3
Gaddy Mill Pond—*reservoir* ... SC-3
Gaddy Prospect—*mine* ... TN-4
Gaddy School (abandoned)—*locale* ... MO-7
Gaddys Crossroads—*locale* ... SC-3
Gaddys Goose Pond—*reservoir* ... NC-3
Gaddys Goose Pond Dam—*dam* ... NC-3
Gaddys Goose Ponds—*lake* ... NC-3
Gaddys Millpond—*reservoir* ... SC-3
Gaddys Mtn—*summit* ... NC-3
Gaddys Pond—*reservoir* ... NC-3
Gaddys Pond Dam—*dam* ... NC-3
**Gaddysville**—*pop pl* ... NC-3
Gaddy (Township of)—*fmr MCD* ... NC-3
Gaddy Well—*well* ... NM-5
*Gadeaus Bend* ... AL-4
*Gadeaux Bend* ... AL-4
*Gaden River* ... PW-9
Gadeous Bend—*bend* ... AL-4
Gadii Ahi Tank—*reservoir* ... AZ-5
Gadis Sch—*school* ... IL-6
*Gadjebar* ... FM-9
*Gadkip* ... PW-9
Gadny Bay—*swamp* ... GA-3
*Gadowa Spring* ... OR-9
Gadow's Mill—*hist pl* ... WI-6
Gadsby—*locale* ... UT-8
Gadsby, Lake—*lake* ... WY-8
Gadsby Cem—*cemetery* ... PA-2
Gadsby Hollow—*valley* ... NY-2
Gadsby's Tavern—*hist pl* ... VA-3
Gad Sch—*school* ... WI-6
Gads Cove—*valley* ... NC-3
**Gadsden**—*pop pl* ... AL-4
**Gadsden**—*pop pl* ... AZ-5
**Gadsden**—*pop pl* ... IN-6
**Gadsden**—*pop pl* ... SC-3
**Gadsden**—*pop pl* (2) ... TN-4
Gadsden Acad (historical)—*school* ... AL-4
Gadsden Adult Education Center—*school* ... FL-3
Gadsden Air Force Depot—*military* ... AL-4
Gadsden Alliance Ch—*church* ... AL-4
Gadsden Baptist Temple—*church* ... AL-4
Gadsden Bible Missionary Ch—*church* ... AL-4
Gadsden (CCD)—*cens area* ... AL-4
Gadsden (CCD)—*cens area* ... TN-4
Gadsden Center Univ of Alabama—*school* ... AL-4
Gadsden Christian Acad—*school* ... FL-3
Gadsden Country Club—*locale* ... AL-4
**Gadsden County**—*pop pl* ... FL-3
Gadsden Division—*civil* ... AL-4
Gadsden Division—*civil* ... TN-4
Gadsden Elem Sch—*school* ... AZ-5
Gadsden Elem Sch—*school* ... TN-4
Gadsden First Baptist Ch—*church* ... TN-4
Gadsden Hotel—*hist pl* ... AZ-5
Gadsden HS—*school* ... AL-4
Gadsden Junior and Senior HS—*school* ... NM-5
Gadsden Kiwanis Park—*park* ... AL-4
Gadsden Mall Shop Ctr—*locale* ... AL-4
Gadsden Memorial Hosp—*hospital* ... FL-3
Gadsden Moragne Park—*park* ... AL-4
Gadsden Municipal Airp—*airport* ... AL-4
Gadsden Ordnance Plant (historical)—*military* ... AL-4
Gadsden Park—*park* ... AZ-5
Gadsden Park Community Hosp—*hospital* ... MS-4
Gadsden Peak—*summit* ... AZ-5
Gadsden Point—*cape* ... FL-3
Gadsden Post Office—*building* ... AZ-5
Gadsden Post Office—*building* ... TN-4
Gadsden Purchase—*area* ... AZ-5
Gadsden Raceway—*locale* ... AL-4
Gadsden Sch—*school* ... SC-3
Gadsden Sch (historical)—*school* ... TN-4
Gadsden Shaft—*mine* ... AZ-5
*Gadsden State Community College* ... AL-4
Gadsden State Junior Coll—*school* ... AL-4
Gadsden State Technical Institute—*school* ... AL-4
Gadsden Times-News Bldg—*hist pl* ... AL-4
Gadsden Village—*uninc pl* ... SC-3
*Gadsen* ... ND-7
Gadsen Spring—*spring* ... FL-3
Gads Hill—*locale* ... MO-7
Gadson Cem—*cemetery* ... SC-3
**Gadston**—*pop pl* ... TX-5
Gad Valley—*basin* ... UT-8
Gad Valley Gulch—*valley* ... UT-8
Gadwah Notch—*gap* ... NH-1
Gadwall Canal—*canal* ... CA-9
Gadwall Lake—*lake* ... MI-6
**Gadwall Lake**—*lake* ... MN-6
Gadwall Pool—*reservoir* ... UT-8
Gadwall State Wildlife Mngmt Area—*park* ... MN-6
Gadwell Canyon—*valley* ... AZ-5
Gadwell Tank—*reservoir* ... AZ-5
*Gae* ... MP-9
Gaebe Hill—*summit* ... ND-7
Gaebler Tanks—*reservoir* ... TX-5
Gaedecker Cem—*cemetery* ... TX-5
*Gael* ... AZ-5
Gael—*bay* ... FM-9
**Gael'**—*pop pl* ... FM-9
**Gaeland Township**—*pop pl* ... KS-7
Gaensien Sch—*school* ... WI-6
Gaenssien, Phillip, House—*hist pl* ... OH-6
Gaenssien Ranch—*locale* ... WY-8
Gaer Ballard Cem—*cemetery* ... IA-7
*Gaeregei* ... FM-9
Gaerky Creek—*stream* ... OR-9
Gaerte Cem—*cemetery* ... IN-6
Gaerte Lake—*lake* ... IN-6
*Gae-to* ... MP-9
Gaferut (Island)—*civ div* ... FM-9
Gaff Creek—*stream* ... WY-8
*Gaff Ditch* ... IN-6
Gaff Ditch—*canal* ... IN-6
Gaffeney Pass—*gap* ... MT-8
Gaffers Creek—*stream* ... PA-2
Gaffey Creek—*stream* ... CA-9
**Gaffey Heights**—*pop pl* ... KY-4
Gaffey Landing—*locale* ... NC-3
Gaffield Cem—*cemetery* ... IL-6
Gaffield Cem—*cemetery* ... OH-6
Gaffield Creek—*stream* ... IL-6
Gaffield Park—*park* ... MA-1
Gaffield Sch—*school* ... WI-6
Gaff Lake—*lake* ... NE-7
Gaffnee Post Office (historical)—*building* ... PA-2
Gaffney—*locale* ... PA-2
**Gaffney**—*pop pl* ... SC-3
Gaffney Branch—*stream* ... AL-4
Gaffney (CCD)—*cens area* ... SC-3
Gaffney Chapel—*church* ... SC-3
*Gaffney City* ... SC-3
Gaffney Commercial Hist Dist—*hist pl* ... SC-3
Gaffney Country Club—*other* ... SC-3
Gaffney Creek—*stream* ... MI-6
Gaffney Day Sch—*school* ... SC-3
Gaffney Gulch—*valley* ... NV-8
Gaffney Hill—*summit* ... PA-2
Gaffney House—*hist pl* ... KY-4
Gaffney Lake—*lake* ... WI-6
Gaffney Lane Sch—*school* ... OR-9
Gaffney Memorial Park—*cemetery* ... SC-3
Gaffney Oil Field—*oilfield* ... KS-7
Gaffney Oil Field—*oilfield* ... TX-5
Gaffney Point—*cape* ... CA-9
Gaffney Point—*cape* ... MI-6
Gaffney Residential Hist Dist—*hist pl* ... SC-3
Gaffney Sch—*school* ... CT-1
Gaffney Sch—*school* ... SD-7
Gaffney Sch—*school* ... WI-6
Gaffneys Landing—*locale* ... GA-3
Gafford Branch—*stream* ... AR-4
Gafford Chapel—*locale* ... TX-5
*Gafford Creek* ... AR-4
Gafford Creek—*stream* ... AL-4
Gafford Creek—*stream* ... AR-4
Gafford Ranch—*locale* ... WY-8
*Gaffords Creek* ... AR-4
*Gaffrey Lake* ... WI-6
Gafield Hollow—*valley* ... AR-4
Gafney Point Sch—*school* ... SC-3
Gafvert Lake—*lake* ... MN-6
Gafvery Creek—*stream* ... WA-9
Gag, Wanda, Childhood Home—*hist pl* ... MN-6
Gagamoe Stream—*stream* ... AS-9
Gagan—*island* ... MP-9
Gaganen Hulo'—*slope* ... MH-9
Gagani—*slope* ... MH-9
*Gagan Island* ... MP-9
*Gagans Pond* ... MA-1
*Gagaraku Reef* ... PW-9
Gagara Lake—*lake* ... AK-9
Gagarin Island—*island* ... AK-9
Gagaryah River—*stream* ... AK-9
Gagas—*area* ... GU-9
**Gag Corner**—*pop pl* ... ME-1
*Gage* ... KS-7
*Gage* ... NE-7
Gage—*locale* ... NM-5
Gage—*locale* ... OH-6
Gage—*locale* ... WV-2
Gage—*other* ... NY-2
**Gage**—*pop pl* ... AL-4
**Gage**—*pop pl* ... KY-4
**Gage**—*pop pl* ... MT-8
**Gage**—*pop pl* ... OK-5
**Gage**—*pop pl* ... TX-5
**Gage**—*pop pl* ... WV-2
Gage, Lake—*lake* ... IN-6
Gage Airp—*airport* ... IN-6
Gage and Tollner Restaurant—*hist pl* ... NY-2
Gage Bald—*summit* ... NC-3
*Gagebrough, Town of* ... MA-1
Gageby—*locale* ... TX-5
Gageby Ch—*church* ... TX-5
Gageby Creek—*stream* ... CO-8
Gageby Creek—*stream* ... TX-5
Gage Canal—*canal* ... CA-9
Gage Canyon—*valley* ... NM-5
Gage Cem—*cemetery* (2) ... MI-6
Gage Cem—*cemetery* ... NY-2
Gage Cem—*cemetery* ... OK-5
Gage Cem—*cemetery* ... TN-4
Gage Cem—*cemetery* ... TX-5
Gage Cem—*cemetery* ... VT-1
Gage Cem—*cemetery* ... WI-6
Gage Center—*post sta* ... KS-7
Gage Chapel—*church* ... NY-2
*Gage Community* ... MT-8
Gage Corner Windmill—*locale* ... TX-5
Gage Creek—*stream* ... MI-6
Gage Creek—*stream* ... NC-3
Gage Creek—*stream* ... OR-9
Gage Creek—*stream* ... TX-5
Gage Elem Sch—*school* ... KS-7
Gage Farm Airp—*airport* ... KS-7
Gage Flying Farmer Landing Strip—*airport* ... ND-7
Gage Gap—*gap* ... NC-3
Gage Group-Ascher, Keith, and Gage Buildings—*hist pl* ... IL-6
Gage Gulf—*valley* ... NY-2
Gage Gully—*valley* ... NY-2
Gage Hill—*summit* ... CO-8
Gage Hill—*summit* (2) ... NH-1
Gage Hill—*summit* ... TN-4
Gage Indian Creek Ranch—*locale* ... TX-5
Gage Island—*island* ... AK-9
Gage JHS—*school* (2) ... CA-9
Gage Lake—*lake* ... MN-6
Gage Mtn—*summit* ... AR-4
Gage Mtn—*summit* ... NY-2
Gage/Murphy House—*hist pl* ... AZ-5
Gagen—*locale* ... WI-6
Gagena Rsvr—*reservoir* ... MT-8
Gagen-Sherlock House—*hist pl* ... WA-9
Gage Park—*park* ... IL-6
Gage Park—*park* ... KS-7
Gage Park—*park* ... MA-1
Gage Park Baptist Ch—*church* ... KS-7
Gage Park HS—*school* ... IL-6
Gage Park Sch—*school* ... IL-6
*Gage Park School* ... KS-7
Gage Park Wesleyan Ch—*church* ... KS-7
Gage Pioneer Memorial—*other* ... MT-8
Gage Point—*cape* ... AK-9
Gage Post Office (historical)—*building* ... TN-4
Gage Ranch—*locale* ... NM-5
Gage Ranch—*locale* ... TX-5
Gage Ridge—*ridge* ... NC-3
*Gager's Pond* ... CT-1
Gagers Pond—*lake* ... CT-1
Gage Rsvr—*reservoir* ... OR-9
Gages Brook—*stream* ... CT-1
Gage Sch—*school* ... CA-9
Gage Sch—*school* ... DC-2
Gage Sch—*school* ... MI-6
Gage Sch—*school* ... MN-6
Gage Sch—*school* ... VT-1
Gage Sch (historical)—*school* ... TN-4
*Gages Creek* ... TX-5
Gages Creek—*stream* ... MI-6
Gage Shop Ctr—*locale* ... KS-7
Gages Lake—*CDP* ... IL-6
Gages Lake—*lake* ... IL-6
Gages Lake—*lake* ... MI-6
Gages Lake—*lake* ... WA-9
Gages Lightning Ranch—*locale* ... TX-5
Gages Slough—*stream* ... WA-9
Gages Springs Cem—*cemetery* ... MS-4
Gages Springs Ch—*church* ... MS-4
Gage State Wildlife Mngmt Area—*park* ... MN-6
**Gagetown**—*pop pl* ... MI-6
Gage Valley—*fmr MCD* ... NE-7
*Gageville* ... VT-1
Gageville—*locale* ... OH-6
**Gageville**—*pop pl* ... VT-1
Gageville Cem—*cemetery* ... MO-7
Gageville Sch (historical)—*school* ... MO-7
Gage Windmill—*locale* ... NM-5
Gaggs Camp—*locale* ... CA-9
*Gagil* ... FM-9
*Gagil District* ... FM-9
*Gagil* ... FM-9
*Gagil Municipality* ... FM-9
Gagil (Municipality)—*civ div* ... FM-9
Gagil Sch—*school* ... FM-9
Gagil Tamil—*island* ... FM-9
*Gagil-Tomil* ... FM-9
*Gagil-Tomil Island* ... FM-9
Gaging Station Lock No 6—*dam* ... KY-4
*Gagiru* ... FM-9
*Gagiru-Tomiru To* ... FM-9
Gag Mesa—*summit* ... NM-5
Gagnon Creek—*stream* ... AK-9
Gagnon Brook—*stream* ... ME-1
Gagnon Creek—*stream* ... AK-9
Gagnon Dam—*dam* ... MI-6
Gagnon Flat—*flat* ... ME-1
Gagnon Hill—*summit* ... ME-1
Gagnon Island—*island* ... MN-6
Gagnon Ridge—*ridge* ... NY-2
Gagnon Rsvr—*reservoir* ... MT-8
Gagnon Sugar Camp—*locale* ... ME-1
Gag Spring—*spring* ... NM-5
*Gaguan* ... MH-9
Ga-Gwa-Dosh Creek—*stream* ... MN-6
Gahagan—*locale* ... LA-4
Gahagan Cem—*cemetery* ... NC-3
**Gahagen**—*pop pl* ... PA-2
**Gahanna**—*pop pl* ... OH-6
*Gahara River* ... WI-6
Gah Chidi—*summit* ... AZ-5
Gahew Spring—*spring* ... UT-8
*Gahl* ... FM-9
Gahlman Sch—*school* ... WI-6
Gahl Ranch—*locale* ... SD-7
**Gahn**—*pop pl* ... LA-4
Gahona Roadhouse—*hist pl* ... AK-9
Gahr HS—*school* ... CA-9
*Gaiangas Island* ... PW-9
*Gaianges* ... PW-9
*Gaiangsu* ... PW-9
**Gaibleton**—*pop pl* ... PA-2
**Gaiblton**—*pop pl* ... PA-2
Gaier Ditch—*canal* ... OH-6
Gaiety Hill-Bush's Pasture Park Hist Dist—*hist pl* ... OR-9
Gaige Homestead—*hist pl* ... NY-2
Gaikema Creek—*stream* ... AK-9

**Gail**—*pop pl* TX-5
Gail, James P., Farmhouse—*hist pl* MN-6
**Gai Land Estates (subdivision)**—*pop pl* UT-8
Gail Ballard Municipal Airp—*airport* KS-7
Gail Canyon—*valley* CA-9
Gail Creek—*stream* TX-5
*Gailee Baptist Ch* MS-4
*Gailett Creek* GA-3
Gailey Branch—*stream* MO-7
Gailey Cem—*cemetery* MO-7
Gailey Creek—*stream* AK-9
*Gailey Hill* NY-2
Gailey Hollow Farmstead—*hist pl* AR-4
Gailey Lake—*lake* AK-9
Gailey Park—*park* UT-8
Gailey Pond—*reservoir* GA-3
Gaileys Island—*island* WA-9
**Gailey Subdivision**—*pop pl* UT-8
**Gail (historical)**—*pop pl* TN-4
*Gail Lake* MN-6
Gail Lake—*lake* WI-6
**Gail Lake (Township of)**—*pop pl* MN-6
Gaillard—*locale* GA-3
Gaillard, Lake—*reservoir* CT-1
Gaillard Crossroads—*locale* SC-3
Gaillard Island—*island* AL-4
Gaillard Island—*island* SC-3
Gaillard Sch—*school* SC-3
*Gaillards Island* SC-3
Gaillards Lake—*lake* MS-4
Gailliard Cem—*cemetery* LA-4
Gail Mtn—*summit* TX-5
Gail North (CCD)—*cens area* TX-5
**Gailor**—*pop pl* TN-4
Gailord Gulch—*valley* OR-9
Gailor HS—*school* TN-4
Gails Coulee—*valley* MT-8
Gail South (CCD)—*cens area* TX-5
Gail Spring—*spring* CA-9
Gail Swamp—*swamp* NY-2
Gail Tank—*reservoir* (2) NM-5
Gail Vrooman Dam—*dam* SD-7
Gaily Creek—*stream* OR-9
*Gaina* MS-4
Gain Branch—*stream* KY-4
*Gainer Bay* FL-3
Gainer Bayou—*bay* FL-3
Gainer Cem—*cemetery* FL-3
**Gainer (Ganer)**—*pop pl* AL-4
Gainer Lake—*swamp* FL-3
Gainer Memorial Dam—*dam* RI-1
*Gainer Pond* FL-3
Gainer Ranch—*locale* NM-5
*Gainers Bayou* FL-3
*Gainers Store* AL-4
Gainers Store P.O. (historical)—*locale* AL-4
*Gaines* ID-8
*Gaines* SC-3
Gaines—*locale* MO-7
**Gaines**—*pop pl* MI-6
**Gaines**—*pop pl* MS-4
**Gaines**—*pop pl* NY-2
**Gaines**—*pop pl* PA-2
**Gaines**—*pop pl* SC-3
**Gaines**—*pop pl* WV-2
Gaines, Col. Abner, House—*hist pl* KY-4
Gaines, James, House—*hist pl* KY-4
Gaines, Ralph, House—*hist pl* GA-3
*Gaines Bar* AL-4
Gaines Bar—*bar* ID-8
**Gaines Basin**—*pop pl* NY-2
Gaines Bend—*bend* TX-5
**Gainesboro**—*pop pl* AR-4
**Gainesboro**—*pop pl* TN-4
**Gainesboro**—*pop pl* VA-3
Gainesboro Bridge—*bridge* TN-4
Gainesboro (CCD)—*cens area* TN-4
Gainesboro Division—*civil* TN-4
Gainesboro Elem Sch—*school* TN-4
Gainesboro Ferry (historical)—*crossing* TN-4
Gainesboro First Baptist Ch—*church* TN-4
Gainesboro Landing—*locale* TN-4
Gainesboro (Magisterial District)—*fmr MCD* VA-3
Gainesboro Post Office—*building* TN-4
Gainesboro Sch—*school* VA-3
*Gainesborough* TN-4
*Gainesborough Post Office* TN-4
Gaines Branch—*stream* AR-4
Gaines Branch—*stream* IL-6
Gaines Branch—*stream* TN-4
Gaines Canyon—*valley* CO-8
Gaines Cem—*cemetery* GA-3
Gaines Cem—*cemetery* (2) IL-6
Gaines Cem—*cemetery* ND-7
Gaines Cem—*cemetery* OR-9
Gaines Cem—*cemetery* SC-3
Gaines Cem—*cemetery* (2) TN-4
*Gaines Cemetery* AL-4
Gaines Ch—*church* AR-4
Gaines Ch—*church* MD-2
Gaines Ch—*church* MI-6
*Gaines Chapel* MS-4
Gaines Chapel—*church* AL-4
Gaines Chapel—*church* (2) GA-3
Gaines Chapel—*church* LA-4
Gaines Chapel—*church* MS-4
Gaines Chapel—*church* VA-3
Gaines Chapel African Methodist Episcopal Ch—*church* AL-4
*Gaines Chapel AME Ch* AL-4
Gaines Chapel Methodist Ch (historical)—*church* AL-4
Gaines Chapel United Methodist Ch—*church* MS-4
Gaines Community—*uninc pl* GA-3
**Gaines (County)**—*pop pl* TX-5
Gaines Cove—*valley* TN-4
Gaines Cove Branch—*stream* TN-4
*Gaines Creek* MD-2
Gaines Creek—*stream* AL-4
Gaines Creek—*stream* AR-4
Gaines Creek—*stream* (2) MS-4
Gaines Creek—*stream* OK-5
Gaines Creek Rec Area—*park* OK-5
Gaines Crossroads—*locale* SC-3
Gaines Ferry—*locale* MO-7
Gaines Ford Branch—*stream* MO-7
Gaines Ford (historical)—*locale* MO-7

Gaines Grove Ch—*church* NC-3
Gaines Gulch—*valley* CO-8
Gaines Hill—*summit* AL-4
Gaines Hill Sch—*school* KY-4
Gaines (historical)—*locale* PA-2
**Gaines (historical)**—*pop pl* OR-9
Gaines Hollow—*valley* TX-5
Gaines Island—*island* FL-3
Gaines Junction—*locale* PA-2
Gaines Lake—*reservoir* GA-3
*Gaines Landing* AL-4
Gaines Landing—*locale* AR-4
Gaines Landing (historical)—*locale* MS-4
Gaines Mill—*locale* VA-3
**Gaines Mill Estates**—*pop pl* VA-3
Gainesmore—*locale* TX-5
Gaines Mtn—*summit* VA-3
Gaines Point—*cape* MT-8
Gaines Point—*cape* VA-3
Gaines Pond—*reservoir* CT-1
Gaines Run—*stream* PA-2
Gaines Run—*stream* VA-3
Gaines Sch—*school* CA-9
Gaines Sch—*school* GA-3
Gaines Sch—*school* IL-6
Gaines Sch—*school* LA-4
Gaines Sch—*school* MI-6
Gaines Sch (historical)—*school* TN-4
Gaines Slough—*gut* FL-3
Gaines Slough—*stream* AR-4
Gaines Slough—*stream* MO-7
*Gaines Station* MI-6
Gaines Street Baptist Ch—*church* AL-4
Gainestown—*locale* AL-4
Gainestown Ch—*church* AL-4
Gainestown Ferry (historical)—*locale* AL-4
Gainestown Landing—*locale* AL-4
**Gaines (Town of)**—*pop pl* NY-2
Gainestown Public Sch (historical)—*school* AL-4
*Gainestown River Landing* AL-4
**Gaines (Township of)**—*pop pl* (2) MI-6
**Gaines (Township of)**—*pop pl* PA-2
*Gaines Village* MI-6
Gainesville—*locale* (2) TX-5
**Gainesville**—*pop pl* AL-4
**Gainesville**—*pop pl* AR-4
**Gainesville**—*pop pl* FL-3
**Gainesville**—*pop pl* GA-3
**Gainesville**—*pop pl* KY-4
**Gainesville**—*pop pl* MS-4
**Gainesville**—*pop pl* MO-7
**Gainesville**—*pop pl* NY-2
**Gainesville**—*pop pl* TN-4
**Gainesville**—*pop pl* TX-5
**Gainesville**—*pop pl* VA-3
Gainesville Acad—*school* AL-4
Gainesville Access Area—*park* AL-4
Gainesville Baptist Ch—*church* AL-4
Gainesville Bar—*bar* AL-4
Gainesville (CCD)—*cens area* AL-4
Gainesville (CCD)—*cens area* FL-3
Gainesville (CCD)—*cens area* GA-3
Gainesville (CCD)—*cens area* TX-5
Gainesville Cem—*cemetery* AR-4
Gainesville Cem—*cemetery* MO-7
Gainesville Cem—*cemetery* TX-5
Gainesville Center—*locale* WV-2
Gainesville Ch—*church* TX-5
Gainesville Community Ch—*church* MS-4
**Gainesville Cotton Mills**—*pop pl* GA-3
Gainesville Country Club—*locale* FL-3
Gainesville Country Day Sch—*school* FL-3
Gainesville District Sch—*school* VA-3
Gainesville Division—*civil* AL-4
**Gainesville East**—*pop pl* FL-3
*Gainesville Female Academy* AL-4
Gainesville Ferry (historical)—*locale* AL-4
Gainesville Fire Control HQ—*tower* FL-3
Gainesville Headstart Sch—*school* AL-4
Gainesville Hist Dist—*hist pl* AL-4
Gainesville HS—*school* FL-3
Gainesville HS—*school* MO-7
*Gainesville Junction* MS-4
*Gainesville Junction P.O.* MS-4
Gainesville Lake—*reservoir* AL-4
Gainesville (Magisterial District)—*fmr MCD* VA-3
Gainesville Mall—*locale* FL-3
Gainesville Marina—*other* GA-3
Gainesville Memorial Airp—*airport* MO-7
Gainesville Mill Cem—*cemetery* GA-3
Gainesville Mill Sch—*school* GA-3
Gainesville North—*uninc pl* FL-3
Gainesville Point—*cape* AL-4
Gainesville Post Office (historical)—*building* MS-4
Gainesville Regional Airp—*airport* FL-3
Gainesville RR Station—*locale* FL-3
Gainesville Sch (historical)—*school* TN-4
Gainesville Shop Ctr—*locale* FL-3
Gainesville Southeast (CCD)—*cens area* TX-5
Gainesville Speedway—*locale* FL-3
Gainesville State Sch For Girls—*school* TX-5
*Gainesville Station* MS-4
*Gainesville Station P.O.* MS-4
**Gainesville (Town of)**—*pop pl* NY-2
Gainesville Waterworks—*other* GA-3
**Gainesville West**—*pop pl* FL-3
Gainesway—*uninc pl* KY-4
Gaines Well—*well* (3) NM-5
Gaineswood—*hist pl* AL-4
Gainey Cem—*cemetery* GA-3
Gainey Island—*island* GA-3
Gainey Millpond—*reservoir* NC-3
Gainey Park—*park* MN-6
**Gainey Ranch**—*pop pl* AZ-5
Gaineys Place—*locale* NE-7
Gain Island—*island* AK-9
Gaino—*locale* AL-4
Gainor Mtn—*summit* TX-5
Gainor Peak—*summit* CA-9
*Gainsboro* TN-4
Gainsboro—*locale* AR-4
Gainsboro (Township of)—*fmr MCD* AR-4
Gains Creek—*stream* IL-6
Gains Cem—*cemetery* TN-4
Gains Chapel—*church* LA-4
*Gainsforth Lake* NE-7
*Gainstown* AL-4
*Gainsville* TN-4

**Gainsville**—*pop pl* TN-4
Gainsville Ch—*church* NC-3
Gainsville Ch—*church* TX-5
Gainsville Highland Sch—*school* KY-4
Gainwell Cem—*cemetery* GA-3
Gair Cem—*cemetery* CO-8
**Gaird**—*pop pl* AL-4
Gair Township (historical)—*civil* SD-7
Gaiser Park—*park* IN-6
Gaisman Park—*park* TN-4
**Gait**—*pop pl* IA-7
Gaiter Lake—*lake* FL-3
Gaiter Lake—*swamp* MN-6
Gaites Cem—*cemetery* WV-2
Gaither—*locale* AR-4
**Gaither**—*pop pl* MD-2
Gaither, Dr. Nathan, House—*hist pl* KY-4
Gaither Canyon—*valley* CA-9
Gaither Cem—*cemetery* AR-4
Gaither Cem—*cemetery* TN-4
Gaither Cove—*valley* AR-4
Gaither Dam—*dam* NC-3
Gaither Hollow—*valley* TN-4
Gaither House—*hist pl* (2) NC-3
Gaither HS—*school* FL-3
Gaither Lake—*reservoir* NC-3
Gaither Mtn—*summit* AR-4
Gaither Pond—*lake* TN-4
Gaithers—*locale* KY-4
Gaithers Branch—*stream* GA-3
**Gaithersburg**—*pop pl* MD-2
Gaithersburg B & O RR Station and Freight Shed—*hist pl* MD-2
Gaithersburg Latitude Observatory—*hist pl* MD-2
Gaithers Ch—*church* GA-3
Gaither Sch (historical)—*school* (2) TN-4
Gaither (Township of)—*fmr MCD* AR-4
**Gaitherville**—*pop pl* TN-4
Gaithes Point—*cape* LA-4
Gaiths Hollow—*valley* KY-4
Gaitskill Mound Archeol Site—*hist pl* KY-4
*Gajaugan* MH-9
**Gajan**—*pop pl* LA-4
*Gajangeru To* PW-9
Gajewski Field (airport)—*airport* ND-7
*Gakan* FM-9
*Gakee Creek* MI-6
Gakey, J. H., House—*hist pl* ID-8
*Gakip* PW-9
*Gakkibu* PW-9
Gakolik Mountains—*summit* AZ-5
**Gakona**—*pop pl* AK-9
Gakona, Mount—*summit* AK-9
Gakona ANV789—*reserve* AK-9
Gakona Glacier—*glacier* AK-9
**Gakona Junction**—*pop pl* AK-9
Gakona River—*stream* AK-9
*Gal* FM-9
**Gala**—*pop pl* VA-3
**Galader Station**—*pop pl* IN-6
*Galadolman* PW-9
*Galael Head* PW-9
Galagher Canyon—*valley* OR-9
Galagher Ridge—*ridge* OR-9
Galahad Point—*cliff* AZ-5
Galahoe Cem—*cemetery* WV-2
Galaide, Chalan—*hist pl* MH-9
Galainena Ranch—*locale* CA-9
Gala Lake—*reservoir* VA-3
*Galalee* RI-1
Galalee Ch (historical)—*church* MS-4
*Galalen* MP-9
Galaltin Post Office—*building* TN-4
*Galalud* PW-9
*Galamadei* PW-9
Galamore Branch—*stream* NC-3
Galanis Park—*park* CA-9
Galankin Island—*island* AK-9
*Galap* PW-9
*Galapao* PW-9
*Galapao Head* PW-9
*Galaperai* MH-9
*Galap Point* PW-9
*Galasmoo Point* PW-9
Galas Point—*cape* AK-9
**Galata**—*pop pl* MT-8
Galata Cem—*cemetery* MT-8
Galata Ravine—*valley* MT-8
Galatas Cem—*cemetery* LA-4
Galatea—*locale* CO-8
**Galatea**—*pop pl* OH-6
Galatea Creek—*stream* AK-9
Galateo—*CDP* PR-3
Galateo Alto (Barrio)—*fmr MCD* PR-3
**Galateo Bajo**—*pop pl* (2) PR-3
Galateo Bajo (Barrio)—*fmr MCD* PR-3
Galateo (Barrio)—*fmr MCD* PR-3
Galatia—*locale* NY-2
**Galatia**—*pop pl* IL-6
**Galatia**—*pop pl* KS-7
**Galatia**—*pop pl* NC-3
Galatia Ch—*church* AR-4
Galatia Ch—*church* NC-3
Galatia Ch—*church* VA-3
*Galatia Creek* NY-2
Galatia Ditch—*canal* IN-6
Galatian Baptist Ch—*church* FL-3
**Galatia (Township of)**—*pop pl* IL-6
Galatin Country Club—*locale* TN-4
*Galauekkel* PW-9
*Galaus* PW-9
*Galavan Creek* TX-5
Galaville Post Office (historical)—*building* TN-4
Galavon—*locale* SC-3
Galaway Creek*—*stream* NE-7
Galaway Creek—*stream* NE-7
Galax Cem—*cemetery* VA-3
Galax Ch—*church* VA-3
Galaxie Park—*park* MN-6
Galaxie View Park—*park* CA-9
**Galax (ind. city)**—*pop pl* VA-3
**Galaxy**—*pop pl* SC-3
**Galaxy Acres**—*pop pl* OH-6
Galaxy Elem Sch—*school* FL-3
Galaxy Grade Sch—*school* FL-3
**Galaxy Heights**—*pop pl* TN-4
Galaxy of Coral Gables (Shop Ctr)—*locale* FL-3
Galaxy Sch—*school* FL-3

Galband du Fort, Jean Philippe, House—*hist pl* NY-2
Galberry Island—*island* GA-3
Galbeth Creek—*stream* CO-8
Galboway Cem—*cemetery* KY-4
Galbraith—*locale* IA-7
Galbraith—*locale* MT-8
**Galbraith**—*pop pl* LA-4
**Galbraith**—*pop pl* TN-4
Galbraith, John, House—*hist pl* WA-9
Galbraith Airp—*airport* UT-8
Galbraith Branch—*stream* TN-4
Galbraith Cem—*cemetery* IN-6
Galbraith Cem—*cemetery* MO-7
Galbraith Cem—*cemetery* NC-3
Galbraith Ch—*church* TN-4
Galbraith Creek—*stream* NC-3
Galbraith Creek—*stream* WA-9
Galbraith Drain—*canal* (2) MI-6
Galbraith Gap—*gap* PA-2
Galbraith Gap Run—*stream* PA-2
Galbraith Lake—*lake* AK-9
Galbraith Lake Camp—*locale* AK-9
Galbraith Mill Creek—*stream* AL-4
Galbraith Sch—*school* TN-4
Galbraith Sch (historical)—*school* TN-4
Galbraith Springs—*locale* TN-4
Galbraith Springs Post Office (historical)—*building* TN-4
*Galbraiths Springs* TN-4
*Galbraiths Springs Post Office* TN-4
Galbraith Station—*locale* LA-4
Gal Branch—*stream* MO-7
Gal Branch—*stream* SC-3
*Galbreath* MT-8
Galbreath, John, Mound—*hist pl* OH-6
Galbreath Cem—*cemetery* AL-4
Galbreath Cem—*cemetery* GA-3
Galbreath Creek—*stream* MO-7
Galbreath Ditch—*canal* IN-6
Galbreath Ditch—*canal* OH-6
Galbreath Hollow—*valley* TN-4
Galbreath Ranch—*locale* TX-5
*Galbreath Run* PA-2
Galbreath Sch Number 2—*school* PA-2
*Galbreaths Creek* MO-7
Galbreth Branch—*stream* TN-4
Galbreth Ridge—*ridge* TN-4
Galbriath Cem—*cemetery* MN-6
*Galbuis Head* PW-9
*Galbuis Point* PW-9
*Galbuko* PW-9
Galcatcher Hollow—*valley* OK-5
**Galchutt**—*pop pl* ND-7
*Galcier Lake* WY-8
Gal Creek—*stream* TX-5
Galde Dam—*dam* ND-7
Galdia—*locale* KY-4
Galdin Key—*island* FL-3
Galdon Lake—*lake* NE-7
Gale—*locale* CA-9
Gale—*locale* IA-7
Gale—*locale* NY-2
Gale—*locale* WV-2
**Gale**—*pop pl* ID-8
**Gale**—*pop pl* IL-6
**Gale**—*pop pl* IN-6
**Gale**—*pop pl* PA-2
Gale, George, House—*hist pl* (2) MA-1
Gale, Henry C., House—*hist pl* UT-8
Gale, Judge Jacob, House—*hist pl* IL-6
Gale, Levi H., House—*hist pl* RI-1
Gale, Mrs. Thomas H., House—*hist pl* IL-6
Gale, Walter, House—*hist pl* IL-6
Gale, Zona, House—*hist pl* WI-6
Galea, Lake—*lake* AK-9
Gale-Bancroft House—*hist pl* VT-1
Gale Brook—*stream* MN-6
Gale-Brooks Sch—*school* MA-1
Gale Cem—*cemetery* MI-6
Gale Cem—*cemetery* SD-7
*Gale Creek* WA-9
Gale Creek—*stream* AL-4
Gale Creek—*stream* CA-9
Gale Creek—*stream* IL-6
Gale Creek—*stream* NC-3
Gale Creek—*stream* (2) OR-9
Gale Creek—*stream* (3) WA-9
Gale Creek Point—*cape* NC-3
*Galeds* PW-9
Galeed Ch—*church* NC-3
Gale Grazing Association Number 1 Dam—*dam* SD-7
Gale Grazing Association Number 2 Dam—*dam* SD-7
*Galegui* PW-9
Galehead Hut—*locale* NH-1
Gale Hill—*summit* MA-1
Gale Hill—*summit* NY-2
Gale Hill—*summit* OR-9
Gale Hills—*range* NV-8
Gale (historical)—*locale* MS-4
*Gale Island* NY-2
Gale Island—*island* MI-6
Gale Island—*island* MS-4
*Galekui* PW-9
Gale Lake—*lake* CA-9
Gale Lake—*lake* (2) MI-6
Gale Lake—*lake* MN-6
*Gale Ledge* MA-1
Gale Memorial Library—*hist pl* NH-1
Gale-Merwin Dam—*dam* OR-9
Gale Morgan Ranch—*locale* NE-7
**Galen**—*pop pl* MT-8
**Galen**—*pop pl* TN-4
Galen, Mount—*summit* AK-9
*Galena* NV-8
Galena—*locale* AR-4
Galena—*locale* CO-8
Galena—*locale* ID-8
Galena—*locale* MS-4
Galena—*locale* OR-9
Galena—*locale* SD-7
Galena—*mine* AZ-5
**Galena**—*pop pl* AK-9
**Galena**—*pop pl* AZ-5
**Galena**—*pop pl* IL-6
**Galena**—*pop pl* IN-6
**Galena**—*pop pl* KS-7
**Galena**—*pop pl* MD-2

**Galena**—*pop pl* MO-7
**Galena**—*pop pl* NV-8
**Galena**—*pop pl* NY-2
**Galena**—*pop pl* OH-6
**Galena**—*pop pl* VA-3
Galena Air Force Base—*military* AK-9
Galena Airport—*mil airp* AK-9
Galena Basin—*basin* WY-8
Galena Bay—*bay* AK-9
Galena Bay—*locale* AK-9
Galena Camp—*locale* WA-9
Galena Canal—*canal* UT-8
Galena Canyon—*valley* CA-9
Galena Canyon—*valley* NV-8
Galena Cem—*cemetery* MS-4
Galena Cem—*cemetery* OK-5
Galena Cem—*cemetery* OR-9
Galena Cem—*cemetery* TX-5
Galena Ch—*church* TX-5
Galena Chain Lakes—*lake* WA-9
Galena Creek—*stream* AK-9
Galena Creek—*stream* CA-9
Galena Creek—*stream* (2) CO-8
Galena Creek—*stream* (2) ID-8
Galena Creek—*stream* (2) MT-8
Galena Creek—*stream* NV-8
Galena Creek—*stream* OR-9
Galena Creek—*stream* SD-7
Galena Creek—*stream* VA-3
Galena Creek—*stream* (3) WA-9
Galena Creek—*stream* (2) WY-8
Galena Creek Picnic Area—*park* NV-8
Galena Elem Sch—*school* (2) IN-6
Galena Farm Mine—*mine* WA-9
Galena Flats—*flat* NV-8
Galena Gulch—*valley* AZ-5
Galena Gulch—*valley* (2) CO-8
Galena Gulch—*valley* ID-8
Galena Gulch—*valley* MT-8
Galena Hill—*locale* PA-2
Galena Hill—*summit* CA-9
Galena Hill Mine—*mine* NV-8
Galena Hist Dist—*hist pl* IL-6
Galena Hollow—*valley* MO-7
Galena HS—*school* KS-7
Galena Junction—*locale* IL-6
Galena Junction (historical)—*locale* SD-7
Galena Kindergarten—*school* KS-7
Galena Knob Mine—*mine* WA-9
Galena Lake—*lake* (2) CO-8
Galena Lion Gulch—*valley* CO-8
Galena Mine—*mine* ID-8
Galena Mine—*mine* (2) MT-8
Galena Mine—*mine* (2) UT-8
Galena Mtn—*summit* (3) CO-8
Galena Mtn—*summit* OR-9
Galena Overlook—*locale* ID-8
**Galena Park**—*pop pl* TX-5
Galena Peak—*summit* CA-9
Galena Peak—*summit* CO-8
Galena Peak—*summit* ID-8
Galena Peak—*summit* NV-8
Galena Pioneer Cem—*cemetery* ID-8
Galena Point—*cape* MO-7
Galena Point—*cliff* WA-9
*Galena Rarden Post Office* OH-6
Galena Ridge—*ridge* WY-8
Galena River—*stream* IL-6
Galena River—*stream* IN-6
Galena River—*stream* MI-6
Galena River—*stream* WI-6
Galena Saddle—*gap* NV-8
Galena Sch—*school* MS-4
Galena ( Site)—*locale* WA-9
**Galena ( Site)**—*pop pl* WA-9
Galena Spring—*spring* MO-7
Galena Summit—*gap* NV-8
Galena Summit—*summit* ID-8
Galena Township—*civil* MO-7
**Galena Township**—*pop pl* NE-7
**Galena (Township of)**—*pop pl* IN-6
**Galena (Township of)**—*pop pl* MN-6
Galen Creek—*stream* CA-9
Galen Hall—*locale* PA-2
Galen Hall Golf Course—*locale* PA-2
**Galen (historical)**—*pop pl* MS-4
Galen Post Office (historical)—*building* TN-4
Galen Ridge—*ridge* CA-9
Galen Sch (historical)—*school* TN-4
Galen Spur—*locale* MT-8
**Galen (Town of)**—*pop pl* NY-2
*Galeos* PW-9
Gale Peak—*summit* AK-9
Gale Peak—*summit* CA-9
*Gale Point* MA-1
Gale Pond—*lake* CT-1
Gale Post Office (historical)—*building* SD-7
Galeppi Cattle Trail—*trail* CA-9
Galeppi Creek—*stream* CA-9
Galer Branch—*stream* TN-4
Gale Ridge Sch—*school* SD-7
Gale River—*stream* NH-1
Gale River Trail—*trail* (2) NH-1
Galeros Butte—*summit* AZ-5
Gale Run—*stream* OH-6
**Gales Addition**—*pop pl* WA-9
Gales Branch—*stream* MS-4
*Gales Brook* MA-1
Gales Brook—*stream* ME-1
Gales Brook—*stream* MA-1
Galesburg—*other* WI-6
**Galesburg**—*pop pl* IL-6
**Galesburg**—*pop pl* IA-7
**Galesburg**—*pop pl* KS-7
**Galesburg**—*pop pl* MI-6
**Galesburg**—*pop pl* MO-7
**Galesburg**—*pop pl* ND-7
Galesburg City (Township of)—*civ div* IL-6
Galesburg Elem Sch—*school* KS-7
*Galesburgh* KS-7
Galesburg Hist Dist—*hist pl* IL-6
Galesburg (historical)—*locale* KS-7
**Galesburg Township**—*pop pl* KS-7
**Galesburg Township**—*pop pl* ND-7
**Galesburg (Township of)**—*pop pl* IL-6
Gales Cem—*cemetery* MN-6
Gale Sch—*school* AZ-5
Gale Sch—*school* IL-6
Gale Sch—*school* ME-1
Gale Sch—*school* (2) MI-6

*Gales Creek* MD-2
**Gales Creek**—*pop pl* OR-9
Gales Creek—*stream* LA-4
Gales Creek—*stream* (2) MD-2
Gales Creek—*stream* MS-4
Gales Creek—*stream* NC-3
Gales Creek—*stream* (2) OR-9
Gales Creek Cem—*cemetery* OR-9
Gales Creek Childrens Camp—*locale* OR-9
Gales Creek Forest Park—*park* OR-9
**Gales Ferry**—*pop pl* CT-1
Gales Lake—*lake* MN-6
Gales Landing—*locale* MS-4
Gales Landing—*locale* OR-9
Gales Ledge—*bar* MA-1
Gales Orchard—*locale* CA-9
Gales Peak—*summit* OR-9
Gales Point—*cape* MA-1
Gales Pond—*lake* MI-6
Gales Pond—*lake* NY-2
Gales Pond—*reservoir* MA-1
Gales Pond Dam—*dam* MA-1
Gale Spring—*spring* CA-9
Gale Spring—*spring* NV-8
Gales Ridge—*ridge* CA-9
Gales State Wildlife Mngmt Area—*park* MN-6
Galestina Canyon—*valley* NM-5
**Galestown**—*pop pl* MD-2
**Gales Township**—*pop pl* SD-7
**Gales (Township of)**—*pop pl* MN-6
**Gale Subdivision**—*pop pl* UT-8
Galesvale Sch—*school* OR-9
*Galesville* AL-4
Galesville—*locale* OR-9
**Galesville**—*pop pl* IL-6
**Galesville**—*pop pl* MD-2
**Galesville**—*pop pl* WI-6
**Galet**—*pop pl* AR-4
Gale Tank—*reservoir* AZ-5
**Galeton**—*pop pl* CO-8
**Galeton**—*pop pl* PA-2
Galeton Borough—*civil* PA-2
Galeton Dam—*dam* PA-2
Galeton Lake—*reservoir* PA-2
Galetown—*locale* OH-6
**Gale (Town of)**—*pop pl* WI-6
**Gale Township**—*pop pl* KS-7
Galets, Ile aux—*island* MI-6
Galeville—*locale* NY-2
**Galeville**—*pop pl* NY-2
*Galewood* IL-6
*Galewood* MI-6
*Galewood* TN-4
**Galewood**—*pop pl* TN-4
Galewood Playground—*park* IL-6
**Galewood (subdivision)**—*pop pl* DE-2
*Galey* ND-7
Galey Cem—*cemetery* IN-6
Galey Ch—*church* OK-5
Galey Creek—*stream* GA-3
Galey Hollow—*valley* AR-4
Galeyville—*locale* AZ-5
Galford Gap—*gap* VA-3
Galford Gap—*gap* WV-2
Galford Run—*stream* WV-2
Galfred Ridge—*ridge* WV-2
*Galfred Run* WV-2
Galhand Ridge—*ridge* MT-8
Gal Hill—*summit* UT-8
Galian—*bar* FM-9
*Galiano* LA-4
Galiano Glacier—*glacier* AK-9
**Galice**—*pop pl* OR-9
Galice Creek—*stream* OR-9
*Galice Ranger Station* OR-9
Galice Riffle—*rapids* OR-9
Galichia Airp—*airport* KS-7
**Galicias**—*pop pl* PR-3
Galickson Creek—*stream* AK-9
Galien—*locale* CO-8
**Galien**—*pop pl* MI-6
Galien River—*stream* MI-6
**Galien (Township of)**—*pop pl* MI-6
Galiger's Ranch—*locale* MT-8
Galigher, James, House—*hist pl* OH-6
Galigo Table—*summit* SD-7
Galilea Baptist Ch—*church* AL-4
Galilean Acad—*school* FL-3
Galilean Baptist Ch—*church* FL-3
Galilean Baptist Ch—*church* MS-4
Galilean Ch—*church* MI-6
Galilean Ch—*church* WV-2
Galilean Childrens Home—*building* KY-4
*Galilee* MS-4
Galilee—*locale* AR-4
Galilee—*locale* NY-2
Galilee—*locale* (2) TX-5
**Galilee**—*pop pl* MS-4
**Galilee**—*pop pl* NJ-2
**Galilee**—*pop pl* PA-2
**Galilee**—*pop pl* RI-1
Galilee, Lake—*lake* FL-3
Galilee, Lake—*lake* WI-6
Galilee, Lake—*reservoir* TN-4
Galilee Baptist Ch—*church* FL-3
Galilee Baptist Ch—*church* IN-6
Galilee Baptist Ch (historical)—*church* MS-4
*Galilee Baptist Church* MS-4
*Galilee Baptist Church* TN-4
Galilee Baptist Temple of Bellview—*church* FL-3
Galilee Cem—*cemetery* FL-3
Galilee Cem—*cemetery* LA-4
Galilee Cem—*cemetery* (3) MS-4
Galilee Cem—*cemetery* TN-4
Galilee Cem—*cemetery* TX-5
*Galilee Ch* MS-4
Galilee Ch—*church* (11) AL-4
Galilee Ch—*church* (5) AR-4
Galilee Ch—*church* (7) FL-3
Galilee Ch—*church* (6) GA-3
Galilee Ch—*church* IL-6
Galilee Ch—*church* KY-4
Galilee Ch—*church* (9) LA-4
Galilee Ch—*church* MD-2
Galilee Ch—*church* MN-6
Galilee Ch—*church* (16) MS-4
Galilee Ch—*church* (7) NC-3
Galilee Ch—*church* (2) OK-5
Galilee Ch—*church* (7) SC-3

Galusha Hill—*summit* ... VT-1
Galusha House—*hist pl* ... VT-1
Galusha Island—*island* ... NY-2
Galusha Ranch—*locale* ... NE-7
**Galva**—*pop pl* ... IL-6
**Galva**—*pop pl* ... IA-7
**Galva**—*pop pl* ... KS-7
**Galva**—*pop pl* ... LA-4
Galva Canal—*canal* ... LA-4
Galva Cem—*cemetery* ... IL-6
Galva Grange Hall—*locale* ... IL-6
Galvan Creek—*stream* ... TX-5
Galvaneno Creek —*stream* ... TX-5
Galvan Ranch—*locale* (2) ... TX-5
Galvan South River Tank—*reservoir* ... TX-5
Galva Opera House—*hist pl* ... IL-6
Galva Township—*fmr MCD* ... IA-7
Galva Township Cem—*cemetery* ... IA-7
**Galva (Township of)**—*pop pl* ... IL-6
Galverth Lake Dam—*dam* ... MS-4
Galveston—*locale* ... VA-3
**Galveston**—*pop pl* ... IN-6
**Galveston**—*pop pl* ... KY-4
**Galveston**—*pop pl* ... TX-5
Galveston Airp—*airport* ... IN-6
Galveston Bay—*bay* ... TX-5
*Galveston Bay Channel* ... TX-5
Galveston Causeway—*hist pl* ... TX-5
Galveston (CCD)—*cens area* ... TX-5
Galveston Channel—*channel* ... TX-5
Galveston Coast Guard Base—*military* ... TX-5
**Galveston (County)**—*pop pl* ... TX-5
Galveston County Industrial Water Rsvr—*reservoir* ... TX-5
Galveston County Memorial Hosp—*hospital* ... TX-5
Galveston County Park—*park* ... TX-5
Galveston County Water Company Canal—*canal* ... TX-5
Galveston Elem Sch—*school* ... AZ-5
Galveston Island—*island* ... TX-5
Galveston Jetty Light—*locale* ... TX-5
Galveston Memorial Cem—*cemetery* ... TX-5
Galveston Orphans Home—*hist pl* ... TX-5
**Galveston PO**—*pop pl* ... KY-4
Galveston Ranch—*locale* ... TX-5
Galveston Seawall—*hist pl* ... TX-5
*Galveston West Bay* ... TX-5
**Galvez**—*pop pl* ... LA-4
Galvez Ch—*church* ... LA-4
Galvez Hotel—*hist pl* ... TX-5
Galvez Sch—*school* ... LA-4
**Galvez Town**—*pop pl* ... LA-4
**Galvin**—*pop pl* ... WA-9
Galvin Cem—*cemetery* ... VT-1
*Galvin Chapel* ... MS-4
Galvin Creek—*stream* ... AK-9
Galvin Memorial Park—*park* ... IA-7
Galvin Park—*park* ... CA-9
Galvin Pond—*reservoir* ... PA-2
Galvin Pond Dam—*dam* ... PA-2
*Galway* ... TN-4
**Galway**—*pop pl* ... NY-2
Galway Country Club—*other* ... NY-2
Galway Lake—*flat* ... CA-9
**Galway Lake**—*pop pl* ... NY-2
Galway Lake—*reservoir* ... NY-2
*Galway Post Office* ... TN-4
**Galway (Town of)**—*pop pl* ... NY-2
Galyan Springs—*lake* ... WI-6
Galyon Cem—*cemetery* ... TN-4
Galyon Gap—*gap* ... TN-4
Galyon Ridge—*ridge* ... TN-4
Galyon Spring—*spring* ... TN-4
**Gama**—*pop pl* ... MS-4
Gamache Creek—*stream* ... CA-9
Gamache Creek—*stream* ... ND-7
Gamache Pond—*lake* ... MA-1
Gamage Creek—*stream* ... WA-9
*Gamalie* ... KY-4
**Gamaliel**—*pop pl* ... AR-4
**Gamaliel**—*pop pl* ... KY-4
Gamaliel Landing—*locale* ... AR-4
Gamape Hill—*summit* ... ME-1
Gama Post Office (historical)—*building* ... MS-4
Gamash Brook—*stream* ... ME-1
*Gamasiogel Cave* ... PW-9
*Gambel Islands* ... ID-8
**Gambell**—*pop pl* ... AK-9
Gambell Cem—*cemetery* ... TN-4
Gambell Sites—*hist pl* ... AK-9
*Gambels* ... PA-2
**Gamber**—*pop pl* ... MD-2
Gamber Brinker Ditch—*canal* ... CO-8
Gamber Spring—*spring* ... OR-9
**Gambier**—*pop pl* ... OH-6
Gambier Bay—*bay* ... AK-9
Gambier Bay Entrance Light—*locale* ... AK-9
Gambier Island—*island* ... AK-9
**Gambill**—*pop pl* ... IN-6
Gambill, J. C., Site—*hist pl* ... NC-3
Gambill Branch—*stream* ... KY-4
Gambill Cem—*cemetery* ... MO-7
Gambill Creek—*stream* ... NC-3
Gambill Hollow—*valley* ... AL-4
Gambil Tank—*reservoir* ... NM-5
**Gamble**—*pop pl* ... AL-4
Gamble, James, House—*hist pl* ... IA-7
Gamble, Port—*bay* ... WA-9
Gamble, Robert, House—*hist pl* ... FL-3
Gamble Basin—*basin* ... NV-8
Gamble Branch—*stream* ... AL-4
Gamble Branch—*stream* ... GA-3
Gamble Branch—*stream* ... IL-6
Gamble Branch—*stream* (2) ... TN-4
Gamble Canyon—*valley* ... NV-8
Gamble Cave—*cave* ... AL-4
Gamble Cave—*cave* ... TN-4
Gamble Cem—*cemetery* ... AL-4
Gamble Cem—*cemetery* (2) ... AR-4
Gamble Cem—*cemetery* ... GA-3
Gamble Cem—*cemetery* ... IN-6
Gamble Cem—*cemetery* ... LA-4
Gamble Cem—*cemetery* ... MO-7
Gamble Cem—*cemetery* (3) ... TN-4
Gamble Chapel—*church* ... SC-3
Gamble Coulee—*valley* ... MT-8
*Gamble Creek* ... TN-4
Gamble Creek—*stream* (2) ... AR-4
Gamble Creek—*stream* ... FL-3
Gamble Creek—*stream* ... MI-6
Gamble Creek—*stream* ... NV-8
Gamble Drain—*stream* ... MI-6
Gamble Draw—*valley* ... NV-8
Gamble Gulch—*valley* ... CO-8
Gamble Gulch—*valley* ... ID-8
Gamble Gully—*valley* ... TX-5
Gamble Hill—*summit* ... NC-3
Gamble Hill Ch—*church* ... NC-3
Gamble (historical)—*locale* ... SD-7
Gamble Hollow—*valley* ... MO-7
Gamble House—*hist pl* ... CA-9
Gamble House—*hist pl* ... SC-3
Gamble Island—*island* ... ID-8
Gamble JHS—*school* ... OH-6
Gamble Lake—*lake* ... AR-4
Gamble Lake—*lake* ... ID-8
Gamble Lake—*lake* ... MI-6
Gamble Lake—*lake* ... MS-4
Gamble Lake—*lake* ... MO-7
Gamble Mill—*hist pl* ... PA-2
Gamble Mill—*locale* ... NY-2
Gamble Mill Pond—*reservoir* ... GA-3
Gamble Mines Post Office (historical)—*building* ... AL-4
Gamble Mines (underground)—*mine* ... AL-4
Gamble Point—*cape* ... FL-3
Gamble Pond—*lake* ... FL-3
Gamble Pond—*reservoir* ... AL-4
Gamble Post Office (historical)—*building* ... AL-4
Gamble Ranch—*locale* ... NV-8
Gambler Corral Wash—*valley* ... AZ-5
Gambler Creek—*stream* ... CA-9
Gambler Creek—*stream* ... MT-8
Gambler Lake—*lake* ... AZ-5
Gambler Lake Wash—*valley* ... AZ-5
Gamble Road Ch—*church* ... TN-4
Gamble Roof Hill—*summit* ... NY-2
Gamblers Bayou—*gut* ... LA-4
Gamblers Bend—*bay* ... LA-4
*Gamblers Gap* ... TN-4
Gamblers Rsvr—*reservoir* ... WY-8
Gamble Rsvr—*reservoir* ... OR-9
Gamble Run—*stream* (2) ... PA-2
Gamble Run—*stream* ... WV-2
Gamble Run Trail—*trail* ... PA-2
**Gambles**—*pop pl* ... PA-2
Gamble Sch—*school* ... KS-7
Gamble Sch—*school* ... PA-2
Gamble Sch (abandoned)—*school* (2) ... PA-2
Gambles Creek—*stream* ... MI-6
Gambles Creek—*stream* ... NC-3
Gambles Fort (historical)—*locale* ... TN-4
Gambles Gap—*gap* ... TN-4
Gambles Gut—*gut* ... DE-2
Gambles Hole—*well* ... NV-8
Gamble Slough—*gut* ... AK-9
Gambles Mill (Site)—*locale* ... WA-9
Gamble Spring—*spring* ... GA-3
Gamble Spring—*spring* ... NV-8
Gamble Spring—*spring* ... TN-4
Gamble Spring Canyon—*valley* ... CA-9
*Gambles Run* ... PA-2
*Gambles Run* ... WV-2
Gambles Run (PA-T131/1880)—*stream* ... PA-2
*Gambles Station* ... TN-4
Gambles Store Post Office (historical)—*building* (2) ... TN-4
Gamble Station—*locale* ... AL-4
*Gamble Store* ... TN-4
**Gamble (Township of)**—*pop pl* ... PA-2
Gamble Trail—*trail* ... PA-2
Gamble Valley—*valley* ... TN-4
Gamble Well—*well* ... NV-8
Gamblin—*locale* ... TX-5
Gamblin Branch—*stream* ... KY-4
Gamblin Cem—*cemetery* ... KY-4
Gamblin Cem—*cemetery* ... TX-5
Gambling Hollow—*valley* ... MO-7
Gamblin Hollow—*valley* ... TN-4
*Gamblin Lake* ... ID-8
Gamblin Spring—*spring* ... MO-7
Gamboa Point—*cape* ... CA-9
Gamboa Trail—*trail* ... CA-9
Gambo Creek—*stream* ... VA-3
*Gambol Lake* ... MI-6
*Gambol Run* ... WV-2
Gambrel Cem—*cemetery* ... KY-4
Gambrel Hollow—*valley* ... KY-4
**Gambrell**—*pop pl* ... MS-4
Gambrell Ch—*church* ... LA-4
*Gambrell Crossing* ... MS-4
Gambrell Mines (underground)—*mine* ... AL-4
Gambrell Street Ch—*church* ... TX-5
Gambrel Prospect—*mine* ... TN-4
Gambrill—*locale* ... IA-7
Gambrill House—*hist pl* ... MD-2
**Gambrills**—*pop pl* ... MD-2
Gambrill State Park—*park* ... MD-2
Gambrill Storage Bldg—*hist pl* ... SD-7
**Gambrinus**—*pop pl* ... OH-6
Gambrinus Gulch—*valley* ... ID-8
Gambrinus Mine—*mine* ... ID-8
Gambrinus Surprise Mine—*mine* ... ID-8
Gambs Lake—*lake* ... MI-6
Gamburg—*locale* ... MO-7
Gambusi Lake—*reservoir* ... AZ-5
Gamco Mine—*mine* ... NM-5
*Game* ... MO-7
Game—*locale* ... PA-2
Game—*other* ... KY-4
Game Bird Park—*park* ... OR-9
Game Branch—*stream* ... NJ-2
Game Branch—*stream* ... NC-3
Game Cem—*cemetery* ... LA-4
Gamecock Canyon—*valley* ... CA-9
Game Cock Island—*island* ... CT-1
Gamecock Lake—*lake* ... GA-3
Gamecock Raceway—*other* ... SC-3
Gamecock Reach—*channel* ... GA-3
Game Coulee—*valley* ... MT-8
Game Cove—*bay* ... AK-9
Game Creek—*stream* (2) ... AK-9
Game Creek—*stream* ... CO-8
Game Creek—*stream* ... FL-3
Game Creek—*stream* ... GA-3
Game Creek—*stream* (4) ... ID-8
Game Creek—*stream* (2) ... KS-7
Game Creek—*stream* ... MT-8
Game Creek—*stream* ... NJ-2
Game Creek—*stream* (3) ... WY-8
Game Creek Bay—*bay* ... FL-3
Game Creek Bowl—*basin* ... CO-8
Game Creek Trail—*trail* ... WY-8
Game Dike Mine—*mine* ... CA-9
Game Farm Pond—*lake* ... CT-1
Game Farm Pond—*lake* ... GA-3
Game Fork—*stream* ... KS-7
Game Gulch—*valley* ... CO-8
Game Hill—*summit* ... WY-8
Game Lake—*lake* ... OR-9
Game Lake—*lake* ... WI-6
Game Lake Lookout (historical)—*locale* ... OR-9
Game Ledge—*bench* ... CT-1
Gamel Hexadecagon Barn—*hist pl* ... NY-2
Gamenthaler Creek—*stream* ... TX-5
Game Pass—*gap* ... MT-8
Game Point—*cape* ... AK-9
**Gamerco**—*pop pl* ... NM-5
Gamerco Wash—*stream* ... NM-5
Game Refuge Trail—*trail* (2) ... PA-2
Game Reserve Windmill—*locale* ... NM-5
Game Ridge—*ridge* ... CO-8
Game Ridge—*ridge* ... MT-8
Game Rsvr—*reservoir* ... MT-8
Game Rsvr—*reservoir* ... OR-9
*Gamesiogle Cave* ... PW-9
Games Lake—*lake* ... MN-6
Game Spring—*spring* ... OR-9
Games Ridge—*ridge* ... WV-2
Games Rsvr—*reservoir* ... OR-9
**Game (Stubtown)**—*pop pl* ... MO-7
Gamesway—*locale* ... KY-4
Game Tank—*reservoir* ... AZ-5
*Game Trail - in part* ... PA-2
Game Trail Lake—*lake* ... AK-9
Game Warden Camp—*locale* ... ME-1
Game Warden Creek—*stream* ... WY-8
Game Warden Saddle—*gap* ... ID-8
Game Warden Windmill—*locale* ... TX-5
**Gamewell**—*pop pl* ... NC-3
Game Well—*well* ... NM-5
Gamewell Elem Sch—*school* ... NC-3
Gamewell MS—*school* ... NC-3
Gam Hollow—*valley* ... TN-4
*Gamirisshu* ... PW-9
*Gamirisshu Shoto* ... PW-9
*Gamirisshu To* ... PW-9
*Gamliangel* ... PW-9
*Gamliangel Bay* ... PW-9
Gamlin Cabin—*hist pl* ... CA-9
*Gamlin Lake* ... ID-8
**Gamma**—*pop pl* ... MO-7
Gamma Cave—*cave* ... AL-4
Gamma Creek—*stream* ... WA-9
**Gammage**—*pop pl* ... GA-3
Gammage Creek—*stream* ... MS-4
*Gammage Crossroads* ... AL-4
*Gammage Island* ... ME-1
Gamma Gulch—*valley* ... CA-9
Gamma Hot Springs—*spring* ... WA-9
Gammans Park—*park* ... OR-9
Gamma Peak—*summit* ... WA-9
Gamma Ridge—*ridge* ... WA-9
Gamma Slope Mine (underground)—*mine* ... AL-4
Gammay Cem—*cemetery* ... ME-1
*Gammay Island* ... ME-1
Gamm Creek—*stream* ... WA-9
Gamm Creek Camp—*locale* ... WA-9
*Gammell Slough* ... TN-4
Gammel Run—*stream* ... WV-2
Gammerdinger Valley—*valley* ... WI-6
Gammett Creek—*stream* ... UT-8
Gammey Creek—*stream* ... MI-6
Gammill, Orvall, Barn—*hist pl* ... AR-4
Gammill Cem—*cemetery* ... IA-7
Gammill Cem—*cemetery* ... TN-4
Gammill Ranch—*locale* ... NM-5
Gammill Slough—*stream* ... TN-4
Gammil Well—*well* ... NM-5
**Gammon**—*pop pl* ... AR-4
Gammon, Point—*cape* ... MA-1
Gammon Brook—*stream* ... ME-1
*Gammon Creek* ... WY-8
Gammon Creek—*stream* ... TN-4
Gammon Creek—*stream* ... WY-8
Gammon Draw—*valley* ... WY-8
Gammon Hill—*summit* ... ME-1
Gammon Mtn—*summit* ... ME-1
Gammon Pond—*lake* ... ME-1
*Gammon Prong* ... WY-8
Gammon Prong—*stream* ... WY-8
Gammon Ridge—*ridge* ... ME-1
Gammons Branch—*stream* ... TN-4
Gammon Sch—*school* ... WI-6
Gammons Creek—*stream* ... VA-3
Gammons Pond—*reservoir* ... NC-3
Gammons Pond Dam—*dam* ... NC-3
Gammons Store—*locale* ... VA-3
Gammon Theological Seminary—*school* ... GA-3
Gamoca—*locale* ... WV-2
*Gamolei* ... PW-9
*Gamolei Island* ... PW-9
*Gamorei Point* ... PW-9
*Gampaga* ... MH-9
Gampapa'—*basin* ... MH-9
Gamphor Branch—*stream* ... KY-4
Gampost Mine—*mine* ... MT-8
**Gams Crest**—*pop pl* ... DE-2
**Gams Crest (subdivision)**—*pop pl* ... DE-2
Gamsjager-Wysong Farm—*hist pl* ... WV-2
*Gamudok Island* ... PW-9
*Gamudoko Island* ... PW-9
*Gamudoko To* ... PW-9
Gamuw—*summit* ... FM-9
Gamwell House—*hist pl* ... WA-9
**Ganado**—*pop pl* ... AZ-5
**Ganado**—*pop pl* ... TX-5
Ganado Airp—*airport* ... AZ-5
Ganado (CCD)—*cens area* ... TX-5
Ganado Cem—*cemetery* ... TX-5
Ganado Community Cem—*cemetery* ... AZ-5
Ganado Dam—*dam* ... AZ-5
Ganado Elem Sch—*school* ... AZ-5
Ganado HS—*school* ... AZ-5
Ganado JHS—*school* ... AZ-5
Ganado Lake—*reservoir* ... AZ-5
Ganado Lake Campground—*park* ... AZ-5
Ganado Lake Well—*well* ... AZ-5
Ganado Mesa—*summit* ... AZ-5
Ganado Mission Cem—*cemetery* ... AZ-5
Ganado Oil Field—*oilfield* ... TX-5
Ganado Post Office—*building* ... AZ-5
Ganado Trading Post—*locale* ... AZ-5
*Ganado Wash* ... AZ-5
Ganado West Oil Field—*oilfield* ... TX-5
Ganafif—*bay* ... FM-9
Ganaga Falls—*falls* ... PA-2
Ganagiil'—*summit* ... FM-9
**Ganahgote**—*pop pl* ... NY-2
Ganahgote Sch—*school* ... NY-2
Ganamush Lake—*lake* ... MI-6
Ganargua Creek—*stream* ... NY-2
*Ganargwa Creek* ... NY-2
*Ga'naun* ... FM-9
Ganaway Creek—*stream* ... AR-4
Ganaway Creek—*stream* ... MO-7
Ganaway Gin (historical)—*locale* ... AL-4
*Gance* ... AL-4
Gance Creek—*stream* ... NV-8
**Gandara**—*pop pl* (2) ... PR-3
G and D Heinrich Ranch—*locale* ... ND-7
Gandee Cem—*cemetery* (3) ... WV-2
Gandee Chapel—*church* ... WV-2
Gandee Run—*stream* ... WV-2
Gandees Run—*stream* ... WV-2
**Gandeeville**—*pop pl* ... WV-2
Gandeeville Cem—*cemetery* ... WV-2
*Gander* ... KY-4
Gander Bay—*bay* ... VT-1
Ganderbill Branch—*stream* ... KY-4
Gander Branch—*stream* (2) ... KY-4
Gander Branch—*stream* ... TN-4
Gander Brook—*stream* ... ME-1
Gander Brook—*stream* ... NJ-2
Gander Creek—*stream* ... AK-9
Gander Creek—*stream* ... FL-3
Gander Creek—*stream* ... IN-6
Gander Creek—*stream* ... OR-9
**Gander Hill (subdivision)**—*pop pl* ... DE-2
Gander Hollow—*valley* ... TN-4
Ganderhook Creek—*stream* ... OH-6
Gander Island—*island* ... ME-1
Gander Lake—*gut* ... AL-4
Gander Lake—*lake* ... MN-6
Gander Lake—*lake* ... OR-9
Gander Lake—*lake* ... WI-6
Gander Mtn—*summit* ... IL-6
Gander Pond—*lake* ... CO-8
Gander Pond—*lake* ... ME-1
Gander Pond—*swamp* ... AL-4
Gander Run—*stream* ... IN-6
Gander Run—*stream* (?) ... OH-6
Gander Run—*stream* ... PA-2
Ganders Canyon—*valley* ... NV-8
Ganders Cem—*cemetery* ... MO-7
Ganderslaugh Landing—*locale* ... MS-4
Ganders Peak—*summit* ... AR-4
Ganderstep Knob—*summit* ... PA-2
Gandertown—*locale* ... KY-4
Ganderville Cem—*cemetery* ... AR-4
Gandia Branch—*stream* ... TX-5
Gandia Slough—*gut* ... TX-5
Gandil Mtn—*summit* ... AK-9
G and J Heck Number 1 Dam—*dam* ... SD-7
G and J Heck Number 2 Dam—*dam* ... SD-7
G And L Mine—*mine* ... IL-6
Gandma Davis Draw—*valley* ... NE-7
Gandolfo Canyon—*valley* ... NV-8
Gandolfo Ranch—*locale* ... CA-9
Gandolfo Ranch (historical)—*locale* ... NV-8
Gandolfo Theater—*hist pl* ... AZ-5
*Gando Trading Post* ... AZ-5
Gandrud Lake—*lake* ... MN-6
Gand Saddle—*gap* ... OR-9
Gandsi—*locale* ... MS-4
Gandsi Cem—*cemetery* ... MS-4
Gandsi Ch—*church* ... MS-4
Gandsi Post Office (historical)—*building* ... MS-4
*Gandy* ... KS-7
Gandy—*locale* ... NE-7
Gandy—*locale* ... SC-3
Gandy—*locale* ... TX-5
Gandy—*locale* ... WV-2
**Gandy**—*pop pl* ... LA-4
**Gandy**—*pop pl* ... NE-7
**Gandy**—*pop pl* ... TN-4
**Gandy**—*pop pl* ... UT-8
Gandy, Lake—*lake* ... FL-3
Gandy Bayou—*stream* ... LA-4
Gandy Belting Company Bldg—*hist pl* ... MD-2
Gandy Bend—*bend* ... TX-5
Gandy Bridge—*bridge* (2) ... FL-3
Gandy Cem—*cemetery* ... FL-3
Gandy Cem—*cemetery* ... GA-3
Gandy Cem—*cemetery* (2) ... MS-4
Gandy Cem—*cemetery* ... SC-3
Gandy Cem—*cemetery* ... TN-4
Gandy Cem—*cemetery* ... TX-5
Gandy Ch—*church* ... LA-4
Gandy Cove—*locale* ... AL-4
Gandy Cove—*valley* ... AL-4
Gandy Cove Ch—*church* ... AL-4
Gandy Creek—*stream* ... AL-4
Gandy Creek—*stream* ... WV-2
Gandy Ditch—*canal* ... IN-6
Gandy Farms—*locale* ... TX-5
*Gandy Fork* ... AL-4
Gandy Gulch—*valley* ... CO-8
Gandy Hollow—*valley* ... AL-4
Gandy HS—*school* ... VA-3
Gandy Lake—*lake* ... MS-4
Gandy Lake Dam—*dam* ... MS-4
*Gandy Mill Creek* ... MS-4
Gandy Mine (underground)—*mine* ... AL-4
Gandy Plaza (Shop Ctr)—*locale* ... FL-3
Gandy Run—*stream* ... WV-2
**Gandys Beach**—*pop pl* ... NJ-2
Gandys Bridge—*bridge* ... AL-4
*Gandys Cove* ... AL-4
**Gandys Cove**—*pop pl* ... AL-4
Gandys Cove Post Office (historical)—*building* ... AL-4
**Gandy Spur**—*pop pl* ... LA-4
Gandyville—*locale* ... FL-3
Gane, Henry, House—*hist pl* ... MA-1
**Ganeer (Township of)**—*pop pl* ... IL-6
**Ganer**—*pop pl* ... AL-4
*Ganer Canyon* ... UT-8
Ganer Sch (historical)—*school* ... AL-4
Ganes Creek—*locale* ... AK-9
Ganes Creek—*stream* ... AK-9
Ganesha—*uninc pl* ... CA-9
Ganesha HS—*school* ... CA-9
Ganesha Park—*park* ... CA-9
*Ganey* ... MD-2
Ganey Cem—*cemetery* ... AL-4
Ganeyville—*locale* ... LA-4
Ganey Wharf—*locale* ... MD-2
*Ganfif* ... FM-9
*Ganfiif* ... FM-9
*Ganger Ditch* ... IN-6
**Ganges**—*pop pl* ... MI-6
**Ganges**—*pop pl* ... OH-6
**Ganges (Township of)**—*pop pl* ... MI-6
*Gangil* ... FM-9
*Gang Lakes* ... MI-6
Gangloff Park—*park* ... OR-9
**Gang Mills**—*pop pl* ... NY-2
Gangney Sch (historical)—*school* ... PA-2
Gang of Lakes—*lake* ... MI-6
Gang Pirogue Trail—*canal* ... LA-4
Gangs Bayou—*gut* ... TX-5
Gangway—*bar* ... ME-1
Gangway, The—*channel* ... MA-1
Gangway Ledge—*bar* (3) ... ME-1
*Gangway Passage* ... MA-1
Gangway Rock—*rock* ... MA-1
Gangwer Ditch—*canal* (3) ... IN-6
Gan Hollow—*valley* ... OK-5
Ganiard Sch—*school* ... MI-6
Ganies Cem—*cemetery* ... IL-6
*Ganiir* ... FM-9
Ganiir Bridge—*bridge* ... FM-9
*Ganimuth* ... FM-9
*Ganir* ... FM-9
**Ganister**—*pop pl* ... PA-2
Ganister Blue Hole—*lake* ... PA-2
Ganley Mtn—*summit* ... CO-8
*Ganmurchg* ... FM-9
Ganmurchig—*summit* ... FM-9
*Gann* ... CO-8
*Gann* ... OK-5
**Gann**—*pop pl* ... TN-4
Gannaway Creek—*stream* ... VA-3
Gann Bldg—*hist pl* ... AR-4
Gann Bluff—*cliff* ... TN-4
Gann Branch—*stream* (2) ... AL-4
Gann Branch—*stream* ... TN-4
Gann Branch—*stream* ... TX-5
Gann Cem—*cemetery* ... AL-4
Gann Cem—*cemetery* ... AR-4
Gann Cem—*cemetery* ... GA-3
Gann Cem—*cemetery* ... LA-4
Gann Cem—*cemetery* ... TN-4
Gann Cem—*cemetery* (2) ... TX-5
Gann Chapel—*church* ... AR-4
**Gann (corporate name for Brinkhaven)**—*pop pl* ... OH-6
**Gann Crossroad**—*pop pl* ... AL-4
*Gann Crossroads* ... AL-4
Gann Ditch—*canal* ... IL-6
Gannet Cove—*bay* ... AK-9
Gannet Island—*island* ... AK-9
Gannet Lake—*lake* ... GA-3
Gannet Ledge—*bar* ... MA-1
Gannet Pond—*lake* ... FL-3
*Gannet Rock* ... MA-1
Gannet Rocks—*bar* ... MA-1
Gannet Rocks—*island* ... AK-9
*Gannets, The* ... MA-1
Gannet Slough—*gut* ... FL-3
Gannet Strand—*swamp* ... FL-3
**Gannett**—*pop pl* (2) ... ID-8
**Gannett**—*pop pl* ... NE-7
Gannett, Guy P., House—*hist pl* ... ME-1
Gannett, Mount—*summit* ... AK-9
Gannett Bldg—*hist pl* ... NY-2
Gannett Brook—*stream* ... ME-1
Gannett Camp—*locale* ... ME-1
**Gannett Corners**—*pop pl* ... MA-1
*Gannett Cove* ... TN-4
Gannett Creek—*stream* ... WY-8
Gannett Glacier—*glacier* ... AK-9
Gannett Glacier—*glacier* ... WY-8
Gannett Hill—*summit* ... NY-2
Gannett Hills—*range* ... ID-8
Gannett Hills—*range* ... WY-8
*Gannett Lake* ... GA-3
Gannett Peak—*summit* ... WY-8
*Gannetts Corners* ... MA-1
Gannevait, Bayou—*stream* ... LA-4
Gann Hill—*summit* ... AR-4
Gann Hollow—*valley* ... AR-4
Gann Hollow—*valley* (2) ... TN-4
Gann House—*hist pl* ... AR-4
Gannon—*locale* ... MD-2
Gannon—*locale* ... TX-5
Gannon, M. V., House—*hist pl* ... IA-7
Gannon Branch—*stream* ... KY-4
Gannon Canal—*canal* ... LA-4
Gannon Coll—*school* ... PA-2
*Gannon Creek* ... MN-6
Gannon Creek—*stream* ... CA-9
Gannon Creek—*stream* ... KS-7
Gannon Creek—*stream* ... MN-6
Gannon Creek—*stream* ... TX-5
Gannondale Acad—*school* ... PA-2
Gannon Draw—*valley* ... WY-8
**Gannon (Franklin)**—*pop pl* ... MD-2
Gannon Lake—*lake* ... IN-6
Gannon Lake—*lake* ... MN-6
Gannon Ridge—*ridge* ... AR-4
Gannon Ridge—*ridge* ... MT-8
Gannon Sch (historical)—*school* ... MO-7
Gannon Slough—*stream* ... CA-9
Gannoway Lake—*lake* ... TX-5
Gann Post Office (historical)—*building* ... AL-4
Gann Post Office (historical)—*building* ... TN-4
Gann Ranch—*locale* ... CA-9
Gann Ridge—*ridge* ... AR-4
Gann Run—*stream* ... PA-2
**Ganns**—*pop pl* ... CA-9
Gann Sch—*school* ... CO-8
Gann Sch (historical)—*school* ... MO-7
Gann Sch (historical)—*school* ... TN-4
Ganns Creek—*stream* ... CA-9
Gannsey Mine (underground)—*mine* ... AL-4
Ganns-Middle Valley Elem Sch—*school* ... TN-4
Gann's Pharmacy—*hist pl* ... GA-3
Gann Spring—*spring* ... NV-8
Gann Tank—*reservoir* ... AZ-5
Gann Tank—*reservoir* ... NM-5
**Ganntown**—*pop pl* ... IL-6
Gannts Bay—*swamp* ... SC-3
*Gann Valley* ... SD-7
**Gannvalley**—*pop pl* ... SD-7
Gann Windmill—*locale* ... NM-5
Gano—*locale* ... KS-7
Gano—*locale* ... OK-5
**Gano**—*pop pl* ... OH-6
**Gano**—*pop pl* ... TX-5
Gano, Peter, House—*hist pl* ... CA-9
Ganoe Cem—*cemetery* ... PA-2
Ganoe Hill—*summit* ... WI-6
Ganoga Glen—*valley* ... PA-2
Ganoga Lake—*lake* ... PA-2
Gano Island—*island* ... AR-4
**Gano (Lejunior Post Office)**—*pop pl* (2) ... KY-4
Ganong Cem—*cemetery* ... MI-6
**Ganor**—*pop pl* ... GA-3
*Ganoree* ... SC-3
Gano Spring—*spring* ... TX-5
**Ganotown**—*pop pl* ... WV-2
Ganoung Sch—*school* ... AZ-5
*Ganower Creek* ... IN-6
**Gans**—*pop pl* ... OK-5
**Gans**—*pop pl* ... PA-2
Gans, Solomon, House—*hist pl* ... AR-4
Gansberger Sch—*school* ... CA-9
Gans Branch—*stream* ... TN-4
Gans Cem—*cemetery* ... OK-5
Gans Creek—*stream* ... MO-7
Gansel—*locale* ... OK-5
**Ganser Bar**—*pop pl* ... CA-9
Ganser Ranch—*locale* ... NE-7
Gansett Point—*cape* ... MA-1
**Gansevoort**—*pop pl* ... NY-2
Gansevoort-Bellamy Hist Dist—*hist pl* ... NY-2
Gansevoort/East Steuben Streets Hist Dist—*hist pl* ... NY-2
Gansevoort Mansion—*hist pl* ... NY-2
Gansey Lake—*lake* ... MN-6
Gans Hill Sch—*school* ... PA-2
Gans Hole Spring—*spring* ... AZ-5
Gans Klein Ditch—*canal* ... MT-8
Gansley Drain—*canal* ... MI-6
Gansman Coulee—*valley* ... MT-8
Gansner Bar Campground—*locale* ... CA-9
Gansner Creek—*stream* ... CA-9
Ganson Hill—*summit* ... VT-1
Gans Prairie—*area* ... CA-9
**Gansville**—*pop pl* ... LA-4
Gansy Island—*island* ... NH-1
**Gant**—*pop pl* ... TN-4
Gant Arroyo—*stream* ... CO-8
Gant Branch—*stream* ... VA-3
Gant Cem—*cemetery* ... AL-4
Gant Cem—*cemetery* ... KY-4
Gant Cem—*cemetery* ... TN-4
Gant Cem—*cemetery* ... WV-2
Gant Creek—*stream* ... ID-8
Gante Cem—*cemetery* ... IA-7
Gantenbein Lake—*reservoir* ... WI-6
Ganter Ave Sch—*school* ... NJ-2
*Ganters Creek* ... AL-4
Ganter State Public Hunting Area—*park* ... MO-7
Gant Gulch—*valley* ... CA-9
Gant Gulch—*valley* ... CO-8
Gant Hills—*summit* ... TX-5
Gant Hollow—*valley* ... TN-4
*Gant Inlet* ... NC-3
Gant Lake—*lake* ... FL-3
Gant Lake—*reservoir* ... NC-3
Gant Lake Canal—*canal* ... FL-3
Gant Mtn—*summit* ... ID-8
Gantners Landing—*locale* ... ME-1
Gant Pond—*lake* ... TN-4
Gant Ridge—*ridge* ... ID-8
Gant Ridge—*ridge* ... TN-4
Gant Ridge Trail—*trail* ... ID-8
Gantry Creek—*stream* ... GA-3
Gants Bluff—*cliff* ... MS-4
Gant Sch—*school* ... CA-9
Gants Mill Branch—*stream* ... SC-3
Gant Spring—*spring* ... OR-9
Gantt—*CDP* ... SC-3
Gantt—*other* ... TX-5
**Gantt**—*pop pl* ... AL-4
**Gantt**—*pop pl* ... SC-3
Gantt Cem—*cemetery* ... AL-4
Gantt Dam—*dam* ... AL-4
Gantt Hill—*summit* ... VA-3
Gantt-Jones House—*hist pl* ... TX-5
Gantt Lake—*reservoir* ... AL-4
Gantt Lake—*reservoir* ... NC-3
Gantt Lake Dam—*dam* ... NC-3
*Gantt Mill Pond* ... AL-4
Gantt Millpond—*reservoir* ... AL-4
*Gantt Rsvr* ... AL-4
Gantts Grove Ch—*church* ... NC-3
Gantts Junction—*locale* ... AL-4
Gantts Mill Creek—*stream* ... SC-3
Gantts Pond—*lake* ... SC-3
**Gantts Quarry**—*pop pl* ... AL-4
*Gantz Creek* ... NV-8
Gantz Creek—*stream* ... OH-6
Gantz Homestead—*hist pl* ... OH-6
Gantz Knob—*summit* ... OH-6
Gantz Ranch—*locale* ... WY-8
Gantzs Ch—*church* ... PA-2
Gantz Sch—*school* ... SC-3
Ganungs Hill—*summit* ... NY-2
Ganus Mill (historical)—*locale* ... AL-4
Ganus Sch—*school* ... LA-4
Ganus Sch (historical)—*school* ... AL-4
Ganyard Cem—*cemetery* ... OH-6
*Ganz Creek* ... NV-8
Ganzer Cem—*cemetery* ... MO-7
*Ganzer Creek* ... OR-9
Ganzer Lake—*lake* ... MN-6
Ganzert Lake—*reservoir* ... TX-5
Ganz Lake—*lake* ... MN-6
Gaoa Stream—*stream* ... AS-9
*Gaonan* ... MH-9
Gap—*locale* ... NC-3
Gap—*locale* ... OK-5
Gap—*other* ... KY-4
**Gap**—*pop pl* ... OR-9

**Gap**—pop pl ... PA-2
Gap, The—gap ... AK-9
Gap, The—gap (2) ... AZ-5
Gap, The—gap ... CA-9
Gap, The—gap (2) ... CO-8
Gap, The—gap ... MS-4
Gap, The—gap ... MT-8
Gap, The—gap ... NV-8
Gap, The—gap (2) ... OR-9
Gap, The—gap ... TN-4
Gap, The—gap (2) ... TX-5
Gap, The—gap (5) ... UT-8
Gap, The—gap ... VA-3
Gap, The—gap (2) ... WY-8
Gap, The—locale ... AZ-5
Gap, The—locale ... UT-8
Gapac (railroad station)—locale ... FL-3
GAPA Launch Site and
Blockhouse—hist pl ... UT-8
G. A. Parker Dam—dam ... OR-9
G. A. Parker Rsvr—reservoir ... OR-9
Gap Bay—swamp (2) ... NC-3
Gap Branch—stream ... FL-3
Gap Branch—stream (3) ... KY-4
Gap Branch—stream (2) ... NC-3
Gap Branch—stream (2) ... TN-4
Gap Branch—stream ... WV-2
Gap Cem—cemetery ... KY-4
Gap Ch—church (2) ... TN-4
Gap Ch—church ... WI-6
Gap Civil (Township of)—fmr MCD ... NC-3
Gap Cove—cove ... MA-1
Gap Creek ... GA-3
Gap Creek ... KY-4
Gap Creek ... MT-8
Gap Creek ... TN-4
Gapcreek—locale ... KY-4
Gap Creek—locale ... SC-3
Gap Creek—locale ... TN-4
**Gapcreek**—pop pl ... KY-4
**Gapcreek**—pop pl ... TN-4
Gap Creek—stream ... AZ-5
Gap Creek—stream (9) ... AR-4
Gap Creek—stream ... CA-9
Gap Creek—stream (2) ... FL-3
Gap Creek—stream ... GA-3
Gap Creek—stream ... ID-8
Gap Creek—stream ... KY-4
Gap Creek—stream ... MT-8
Gap Creek—stream (2) ... NC-3
Gap Creek—stream ... OK-5
Gap Creek—stream ... SC-3
Gap Creek—stream ... SD-7
Gap Creek—stream (5) ... TN-4
Gap Creek—stream (2) ... TX-5
Gap Creek—stream (2) ... VA-3
Gap Creek—stream ... WA-9
Gap Creek—stream ... WY-8
Gap Creek Ch—church ... NC-3
Gap Creek Ch—church ... SC-3
Gap Creek Ch—church (3) ... TN-4
Gap Creek Christian Church ... TN-4
Gap Creek Elementary School ... TN-4
**Gapcreek (historical)**—pop pl ... TN-4
Gap Creek Missionary Baptist Church ... TN-4
Gap Creek Mountain ... TN-4
Gap Creek Post Office ... TN-4
Gapcreek Post Office
(historical)—building ... TN-4
Gap Creek Prospect—mine ... TN-4
Gap Creek Sch—school (2) ... TN-4
Gap Creek Trail—trail ... VA-3
Gap Draw—valley (2) ... NM-5
Gap Falls—falls ... MD-2
Gap Field Ridge—ridge ... TN-4
Gap Fork—stream (2) ... KY-4
Gap Head—cape ... MA-1
Gap Hill—summit ... KY-4
Gap Hill—summit ... MD-2
Gap Hill—summit ... NM-5
Gap Hill—summit (2) ... PA-2
Gap Hill—summit ... WI-6
Gap Hill Ch—church ... SC-3
Gap Hollow—valley ... AR-4
Gap Hollow—valley ... IN-6
Gap Hollow—valley (2) ... KY-4
Gap Hollow—valley ... TN-4
Gap Hollow Cem—cemetery ... WV-2
Gap Hollow Ch—church ... IN-6
Gap in Knob—locale ... KY-4
Gap Inlet—cape ... NC-3
Gap Island ... PA-2
Gap Lake—lake ... FL-3
Gap Lake—lake ... WY-8
Gap Lakes ... WY-8
Gap Lake Swamp—swamp ... FL-3
**Gapland**—pop pl ... MD-2
Gap Landing—locale ... NC-3
Gap Lode Mine—mine ... SD-7
**Gap Mills**—pop pl ... WV-2
Gap Mountain—ridge ... WV-2
Gap Mountain Trail—trail ... AR-4
Gap Mtn—summit (2) ... AK-9
Gap Mtn—summit ... AR-4
Gap Mtn—summit ... NV-8
Gap Mtn—summit ... NH-1
Gap Mtn—summit (2) ... TX-5
Gap Mtn—summit ... VA-3
Gap Mtn—summit ... WV-2
Gap Of Sandy—gap ... VA-3
Gap Of Smith Mountain—gap ... VA-3
Gap of the Knobs—gap ... TN-4
Gap of the Mountain—gap ... TN-4
**Gap of the Mountain**—pop pl ... AL-4
Gap-of-the-Mountain Ch—church ... NC-3
Gap Of The Ridge—gap ... KY-4
**Gap of the Ridge**—pop pl ... TN-4
Gap of the Ridge Baptist Church ... TN-4
Gap of the Ridge Church ... TN-4
**Gap of the Ridge (Stony
Gap)**—pop pl ... WV-2
Gap on the Blue Mtn ... PA-2
Gappa ... MN-6
Gappas Landing Campground—locale ... MN-6
Gap Point—cape ... AK-9
Gap Point—cape ... FL-3
Gap Point—cape ... MD-2
Gap Point—cape ... NC-3
Gap Pond ... FL-3
Gap Pond Ch—church ... FL-3
Gap Pond Swamp ... FL-3
Gap Post Office (historical)—building ... AL-4
Gap Prairie—flat ... OK-5
Gapps Slough—stream ... TX-5
Gap Rock—summit ... VA-3
Gap Run ... PA-2
**Gap Run**—pop pl ... TN-4
Gap Run—stream ... MD-2
Gap Run—stream ... PA-2
Gap Run—stream ... TN-4
Gap Run—stream (4) ... VA-3
Gap Run—stream (2) ... WV-2
Gap Run Post Office (historical)—building ... TN-4
Gap Run Trail—trail ... VA-3
Gap Sch—school ... PA-2
Gap Sch (abandoned)—school ... PA-2
Gap Sch (historical)—school ... TN-4
Gaps of the Bays Cem—cemetery ... GA-3
Gap Spring—locale ... TN-4
Gap Spring—spring ... NV-8
Gap Spring—spring (2) ... OR-9
Gap Spring—spring ... WY-8
Gap Spring, The—spring ... UT-8
Gap Spring Ridge—ridge ... GA-3
Gap Spring Ridge—ridge ... TN-4
Gap Springs ... TN-4
Gap Springs (Township of)—fmr MCD ... AR-4
**Gapstore**—pop pl ... VA-3
**Gapsville**—pop pl ... PA-2
Gap Swamp—swamp ... GA-3
Gap Tank—reservoir (5) ... AZ-5
Gap Tank—reservoir ... NM-5
Gap Tank—reservoir ... TX-5
Gap Tank, The—reservoir ... NM-5
Gapton ... PA-2
Gap (Township of)—fmr MCD ... AR-4
**Gap (Trading Post), The**—pop pl ... AZ-5
Gap View Airp—airport ... PA-2
Gapville—locale ... KY-4
Gapville Sch—school ... KY-4
Gap Wash—arroyo ... NV-8
Gap Wash—stream ... NV-8
Gapway—locale ... SC-3
Gapway Baptist Ch—church ... FL-3
Gapway Bay—swamp ... SC-3
Gapway Cem—cemetery ... FL-3
Gapway Cem—cemetery ... NC-3
Gapway Ch—church ... FL-3
Gapway Creek—stream ... NC-3
Gapway Ridge—ridge ... NC-3
Gapway Sch—school ... SC-3
Gapway Swamp ... SC-3
Gapway Swamp—stream (2) ... NC-3
Gapway Swamp—swamp ... NC-3
Gapway Swamp—swamp ... SC-3
Gap Well—locale ... NM-5
Gap Well—well ... TX-5
Gap Windmill—locale ... AZ-5
Gap Windmill—locale ... TX-5
Gaqaneelaey'—summit ... FM-9
Gaqnaqun—locale ... FM-9
Gaqnim'uuth—cape ... FM-9
Gaqnipaan—locale ... FM-9
Gara ... MO-7
**Gara**—pop pl ... MO-7
Garaa To ... MP-9
Garabarasu To ... PW-9
Garabini Ravine—valley ... CA-9
Garadai ... PW-9
Garage and Fire Station—hist pl ... MT-8
Garage Creek—stream ... OR-9
Garage Tank—reservoir ... AZ-5
Garagon To ... PW-9
Garahy Cem—cemetery ... LA-4
Garairu ... PW-9
Garakakurao To ... PW-9
Garakasan ... PW-9
Garakayo ... PW-9
Garakayo Island ... PW-9
Garakayo To ... PW-9
Garakirimu To ... PW-9
Garakoru Island ... PW-9
Garambolo Tank—reservoir ... AZ-5
Garambulla Well—well ... NM-5
Garambuyo Gulch—valley ... CO-8
Garamedeiu-Hana ... PW-9
Garamediu-Hana ... PW-9
Garamejo ... PW-9
Garamendi Mine—mine ... NV-8
Garameyaosu Island ... PW-9
Garameyaosu To ... PW-9
**Garanbuio**—pop pl ... NM-5
Garanbuio Dam—dam ... NM-5
Garand Creek—stream ... ID-8
Garangaoi Cove—bay ... PW-9
Garangoru To ... PW-9
Garant Bayou—stream ... AR-4
**Garapan**—pop pl ... MH-9
Garapan, Lagunan—bay ... MH-9
Garapan Anchorage ... MH-9
Garapao ... PW-9
Garapao Hana ... PW-9
Garapao To ... PW-9
Garaparasu To ... PW-9
Garapau Hana ... PW-9
Garapito Creek—stream ... CA-9
Garardsfort ... PA-2
**Garards Fort**—pop pl ... PA-2
Garards Fort Shaft—locale ... PA-2
Garard Trail—trail ... PA-2
Gararudo ... PW-9
Garaseg ... PW-9
Garashiyoo ... PW-9
Garashiyoo Hill ... PW-9
Garasho ... PW-9
Garasho Mountain ... PW-9
Garasumao ... PW-9
Garasuun ... PW-9
Gara-to ... MP-9
**Garau**—pop pl ... PR-3
Garayama Island ... PW-9
Garayamu ... PW-9
Garbacon Creek—stream ... NC-3
Garbage Cave—cave ... AL-4
Garbage Island ... NY-2
Garbage Stink Cave—cave ... AL-4
Garbancillo Tank—reservoir ... TX-5
Garbareno Rsvr—reservoir (2) ... CO-8
Garbarero Spring—spring ... CO-8
Gar Bayou—gut ... LA-4
Garber—locale ... AR-4
Garber—locale ... IL-6
Garber—locale ... MO-7
Garber—locale ... TN-4
**Garber**—pop pl ... IA-7
**Garber**—pop pl ... OK-5
Garber Branch ... KY-4
Garber Cave—cave ... PA-2
Garber Cem—cemetery ... OH-6
Garber Chapel—church ... VA-3
Garber Creek ... CO-8
Garber Creek—stream ... CO-8
Garber Draw—valley ... WY-8
Garber Grove—hist pl ... NE-7
Garber House—hist pl ... NH-1
Garber HS—school ... MI-6
Garber Memorial Cem—cemetery ... MO-7
Garber Park—park ... CA-9
Garber Rsvr—reservoir ... OR-9
Garber Run—stream ... OH-6
Garbers ... TN-4
Garbers Ch—church ... VA-3
Garber Sch (historical)—school ... MO-7
Garbers Coulee—valley ... WI-6
Garbers Mills ... TN-4
Garbers Mills Post Office ... TN-4
Garbers Post Office (historical)—building ... TN-4
Garbers Station (historical)—locale ... TN-4
**Garberville**—pop pl ... CA-9
Garberville (CCD)—cens area ... CA-9
Garbett Gulch—valley ... UT-8
Garbin Cem—cemetery ... SC-3
GAR Bldg—hist pl ... MI-6
GAR Bldg—hist pl ... PA-2
**Garborg Township**—pop pl ... ND-7
Garbose Bldg—hist pl ... MA-1
Garbrick Airp—airport ... PA-2
Garbry Creek—stream ... OH-6
**Garbutt**—pop pl ... NY-2
Garbutt House—hist pl ... CA-9
Garbutt Island—island ... WI-6
Garbutts Cem—cemetery ... GA-3
Garbutt Wash—valley ... ID-8
Garby Cem Number 1—cemetery ... OH-6
Garby Cem Number 2—cemetery ... OH-6
Garceau Gulch—valley ... MT-8
Garcelon, A. A., House—hist pl ... ME-1
Garcelon Bog—swamp ... ME-1
Garcelon Cem—cemetery ... ME-1
GAR Cem—cemetery ... AR-4
Gar Cem—cemetery ... KS-7
G A R Cem—cemetery ... MN-6
G A R Cem—cemetery ... ND-7
Gar Cem—cemetery ... OR-9
G A R Cem—cemetery ... OR-9
G A R Cem—cemetery ... SD-7
Gar Cem—cemetery (2) ... WA-9
**Garceno**—pop pl ... TX-5
Garceno, Arroyo —stream ... TX-5
Garceno Bend —bend ... TX-5
Garces Circle—other ... CA-9
Garces HS—school ... CA-9
Garces Mesas—summit ... AZ-5
Garces Terrace—bench ... AZ-5
Garcetas River ... TX-5
Garci, Bayou—gut ... LA-4
Garcia—locale ... NM-5
Garcia—locale ... WA-9
**Garcia**—pop pl ... CO-8
**Garcia**—pop pl (2) ... PR-3
Garcia, Canada —valley ... CA-9
Garcia, Juan, House—hist pl ... NM-5
Garcia, Juan Antonio, House—hist pl ... NM-5
Garcia Bend—bend ... CA-9
Garcia Canyon—valley (3) ... CA-9
Garcia Canyon—valley ... CO-8
Garcia Canyon—valley (7) ... NM-5
Garcia Canyon Pueblito (LA
36608)—hist pl ... NM-5
Garcia Cem—cemetery ... CO-8
Garcia Cem—cemetery ... NM-5
Garcia Cem—cemetery (8) ... TX-5
Garcia Cove—bay ... AK-9
Garcia Cow Camp—locale ... NM-5
Garcia Creek—stream (2) ... CA-9
Garcia Creek—stream (4) ... NM-5
Garcia Creek—stream ... TX-5
Garcia Ditch—canal (2) ... CO-8
Garcia Ditch—canal ... NM-5
Garcia Falls—falls ... NM-5
Garcia Falls Canyon—valley ... NM-5
Garcia Flat—flat ... NV-8
Garcia Flat—flat ... NM-5
Garcia-Garza House—hist pl ... TX-5
Garcia Gulch—valley ... CO-8
Garcia Hollow—valley ... TX-5
Garcia JHS—school ... TX-5
Garcia Lake—lake ... NM-5
Garcia Lake—lake ... TX-5
Garcia Lake—reservoir ... CO-8
Garcia Lateral No 1—canal ... NM-5
Garcia Mountain—ridge ... CA-9
Garcia Oil Field—oilfield (2) ... TX-5
Garcia Opera House—hist pl ... NM-5
Garcia Park—flat ... NM-5
Garcia Park—park ... NM-5
Garcia Pasture Site—hist pl ... TX-5
Garcia Peak—summit ... NM-5
Garcia Peaks—other ... NM-5
Garcia Place—locale (2) ... NM-5
Garcia Plaza Cem—cemetery ... NM-5
Garcia Ranch—locale (3) ... AZ-5
Garcia Ranch—locale (6) ... NM-5
Garcia Ranch—locale (2) ... TX-5
Garcia Rancho—locale ... CA-9
Garcia River—stream ... CA-9
Garcia Sch—hist pl ... AZ-5
Garcia Sch—school ... AZ-5
Garcias Creek—stream ... TX-5
Garcia Spring—spring ... CO-8
Garcia Spring—spring (2) ... NM-5
Garcia Station ... WA-9
**Garciasville**—pop pl ... TX-5
Garcias Well—well ... NM-5
Garcias Windmill—locale (2) ... TX-5
Garcia Tank—reservoir ... AZ-5
Garcia Tank—reservoir ... CO-8
Garcia Tank—reservoir (4) ... NM-5
Garcia Tank—reservoir ... TX-5
Garcia Well—well ... AZ-5
Garcia Well—well ... NV-8
Garcia Well—well (2) ... NM-5
Garcia Well (dry)—well ... AZ-5
Garcia Windmill—locale (2) ... NM-5
Garcie Lake ... TX-5
Garcitas Cove—bay ... TX-5
Garcitas Creek—stream ... TX-5
Garcitas River ... TX-5
Garcock Hill—summit ... ME-1
Garcock Pond—lake ... ME-1
Garcon Point—cape ... FL-3
Garcon Swamp—swamp ... FL-3
Gar Creek ... AR-4
Gar Creek ... KS-7
Gar Creek ... OK-5
**Gar Creek**—pop pl ... IN-6
Gar Creek—stream ... AR-4
Gar Creek—stream ... IL-6
Gar Creek—stream ... IN-6
Gar Creek—stream ... KS-7
Gar Creek—stream ... KY-4
Gar Creek—stream ... NJ-2
Gar Creek—stream ... NC-3
Gar Creek—stream (5) ... OK-5
Gar Creek—stream ... SC-3
Gar Creek Cem—cemetery ... OK-5
Gar Creek Ch—church ... AR-4
Gar Creek Ditch—canal ... IL-6
Gard—locale ... IL-6
Garda, Lake—lake ... CT-1
Garda Falls—falls ... WA-9
**Gardar**—pop pl ... ND-7
**Gardar Township**—pop pl ... ND-7
Gard Cem—cemetery ... IL-6
Gard Cem—cemetery ... KS-7
Gard Cem—cemetery ... OH-6
Gard Creek—stream ... IA-7
**Gardeau**—pop pl ... PA-2
Gardeau Overlook—park ... NY-2
Gardella Canyon—valley ... NV-8
Gardeman Sch—school ... SD-7
Garden ... IN-6
Garden ... NC-3
Garden—locale ... AL-4
Garden—locale ... OH-6
**Garden**—pop pl ... MI-6
**Garden**—pop pl ... OH-6
Garden, The—locale ... ID-8
Gardena ... IL-6
Gardena—locale ... ID-8
Gardena—locale ... WA-9
**Gardena**—pop pl ... CA-9
**Gardena**—pop pl ... FL-3
**Gardena**—pop pl ... IL-6
**Gardena**—pop pl ... ND-7
Gardena Creek ... OR-9
Gardena Creek ... WA-9
Gardena Creek—stream ... WA-9
Garden Acres ... OH-6
Garden Acres—CDP ... CA-9
**Garden Acres**—pop pl (2) ... IN-6
**Garden Acres**—pop pl (2) ... OH-6
**Garden Acres**—pop pl ... TX-5
Garden Acres Park—park ... CA-9
**Garden Acres Subdivision**—pop pl (2) ... UT-8
Gardena Ditch—canal ... WA-9
Gardena HS—school ... CA-9
Garden Air Golf Course—other ... CA-9
Gardena Playground—park ... IN-6
Gardena RR Station—locale ... FL-3
Gardenas Butte ... AZ-5
Gardena Sch—school ... CA-9
Gardena Sch—school ... MN-6
Garden Ave Sch—school ... CA-9
**Gardena Village**—pop pl ... CA-9
Garden Baptist Church ... AL-4
Garden Bar—locale ... CA-9
Garden Basin—basin ... CO-8
Garden Basin—basin (2) ... UT-8
Garden Bay—bay ... LA-4
Garden Bay—bay ... MI-6
Garden Bayou—bay ... TX-5
Garden Bluff—cliff ... MI-6
Garden Bluff Cem—cemetery ... WI-6
Garden Branch—stream ... AR-4
Garden Branch—stream (3) ... KY-4
Garden Brook—stream ... MI-6
Garden Canon ... AZ-5
Garden Canon (Sierra Vista) ... AZ-5
Garden Canyon ... AZ-5
Garden Canyon ... NV-8
Garden Canyon—valley ... AZ-5
Garden Canyon—valley ... CA-9
Garden Canyon—valley (2) ... NV-8
Garden Canyon—valley ... WY-8
Garden Canyon Archeol Site—hist pl ... AZ-5
Garden Canyon Petroglyphs—hist pl ... AZ-5
Garden Cem ... AL-4
Garden Cem—cemetery ... AL-4
Garden Cem—cemetery ... FL-3
Garden Cem—cemetery ... MA-1
Garden Cem—cemetery ... TX-5
Garden Center Cem—cemetery ... CT-1
Garden Center Conservatory—locale ... FL-3
Garden Ch—church (2) ... AL-4
Garden Ch—church ... ND-7
Garden Chapel—locale ... MS-4
Garden Chute ... LA-4
Garden City ... RI-1
Garden City ... SD-7
Garden City—locale ... FL-3
Garden City—locale ... NJ-2
**Garden City**—pop pl ... AL-4
**Garden City**—pop pl ... CO-8
**Garden City**—pop pl ... CT-1
**Garden City**—pop pl ... FL-3
**Garden City**—pop pl ... GA-3
**Garden City**—pop pl ... ID-8
**Garden City**—pop pl (2) ... IN-6
**Garden City**—pop pl ... IA-7
**Garden City**—pop pl ... KS-7
**Garden City**—pop pl ... LA-4
**Garden City**—pop pl ... MI-6
**Garden City**—pop pl ... MN-6
**Garden City**—pop pl ... MS-4
**Garden City**—pop pl ... MO-7
**Garden City**—pop pl ... NJ-2
**Garden City**—pop pl ... NY-2
**Garden City**—pop pl ... NC-3
**Garden City**—pop pl ... OH-6
**Garden City**—pop pl ... OK-5
**Garden City**—pop pl (2) ... PA-2
**Garden City**—pop pl ... RI-1
**Garden City**—pop pl ... SD-7
**Garden City**—pop pl ... TX-5
**Garden City**—pop pl ... UT-8
**Garden City**—pop pl (2) ... VA-3
**Garden City**—pop pl ... WA-9
Garden City—uninc pl ... TX-5
Garden City—uninc pl ... VA-3
**Garden City Addition
(subdivision)**—pop pl ... UT-8
**Garden City Beach**—pop pl ... SC-3
Garden City Canyon—valley ... UT-8
Garden City Cem—cemetery ... MO-7
Garden City Cem—cemetery ... SD-7
Garden City Cem—cemetery ... TX-5
Garden City Cem—cemetery ... UT-8
Garden City Ch of Christ—church ... AL-4
Garden City Ch of Christ—church ... FL-3
Garden City Christian Ch—church ... IN-6
Garden City Community Coll—school ... KS-7
Garden City Country Club—other ... NY-2
Garden City Creek—stream ... MI-6
Garden City Ditch—canal ... WA-9
Garden City Elem Sch—school ... FL-3
Garden City Elem Sch—school ... IN-6
Garden City Experiment Station
Airp—airport ... KS-7
Garden City Gas and Oil Field—oilfield ... LA-4
Garden City HS—school ... AL-4
Garden City HS—school ... KS-7
Garden City HS—school ... MI-6
Garden City-Laketown—cens area ... UT-8
Garden City-Laketown Division—civil ... UT-8
Garden City Mtn—summit ... AL-4
Garden City Municipal Airp—airport ... KS-7
Garden City North ... MI-6
Garden City North (CCD)—cens area ... TX-5
Garden City Opera House—hist pl ... SD-7
Garden City Park—park ... MN-6
**Garden City Park**—pop pl ... NY-2
Garden City Post Office—building ... AL-4
Garden City Post Office
(historical)—building ... MS-4
Garden City Pumping Station—other ... TX-5
Garden City Sch—school ... FL-3
Garden City Sch—school ... MN-6
Garden City Sch—school ... NE-7
Garden City Sch—school ... TX-5
**Garden City South**—pop pl ... NY-2
Garden City South (CCD)—cens area ... TX-5
Garden City Station—locale ... CA-9
**Garden City Township**—pop pl ... KS-7
**Garden City (Township of)**—pop pl ... MN-6
Garden Club Of America Grove—woods ... CA-9
Garden Club of Georgia Museum-Headquarters
House,Founder's Memorial—hist pl ... GA-3
**Garden Corners**—pop pl ... MI-6
Garden Coulee—valley (2) ... MT-8
Garden Coulee—valley ... ND-7
Garden Coulee Creek ... MT-8
Gardencourt—hist pl ... RI-1
Garden Court Apartments—hist pl ... MI-6
Gardencourt Hist Dist—hist pl ... KY-4
Garden Court Hist Dist—hist pl ... PA-2
Garden Court Hist Dist (Boundary
Increase)—hist pl ... PA-2
Garden Cove—bay (2) ... AK-9
Garden Cove—bay ... FL-3
Garden Cove—locale ... FL-3
Garden Creek ... ID-8
Garden Creek ... TX-5
Garden Creek ... VA-3
Garden Creek—bay ... NC-3
Garden Creek—gut ... FL-3
**Garden Creek**—pop pl ... NC-3
Garden Creek—stream ... AK-9
Garden Creek—stream (2) ... AZ-5
Garden Creek—stream ... CA-9
Garden Creek—stream ... CO-8
Garden Creek—stream ... FL-3
Garden Creek—stream (11) ... ID-8
Garden Creek—stream ... LA-4
Garden Creek—stream ... MI-6
Garden Creek—stream (5) ... MT-8
Garden Creek—stream ... NE-7
Garden Creek—stream (2) ... NV-8
Garden Creek—stream (2) ... NC-3
Garden Creek—stream ... OH-6
Garden Creek—stream (2) ... OR-9
Garden Creek—stream ... SD-7
Garden Creek—stream ... TX-5
Garden Creek—stream (2) ... UT-8
Garden Creek—stream (2) ... VA-3
Garden Creek—stream (5) ... WY-8
Garden Creek Ch—church ... NC-3
Garden Creek Ch—church ... VA-3
Garden Creek Gap—gap ... ID-8
Garden Creek Trail—trail ... ID-8
Garden Creek Waterfall—falls ... WY-8
Gardendale—locale ... TX-5
**Gardendale**—pop pl ... AL-4
**Gardendale**—pop pl ... MI-6
**Gardendale**—pop pl ... PA-2
**Gardendale**—pop pl (2) ... TX-5
Gardendale (CCD)—cens area ... AL-4
Gardendale Commercial Sch—school ... AL-4
Gardendale Division—civil ... AL-4
Gardendale Elem Sch—school ... AL-4
Gardendale Elem Sch—school ... FL-3
Gardendale HS—school ... AL-4
Gardendale Sch—school ... OH-6
Gardendale Sch—school ... TX-5
**Gardendale (subdivision)**—pop pl ... AL-4
Garden Dam—dam ... AZ-5
Garden District—hist pl ... AL-4
Garden District—hist pl ... LA-4
Garden District Cem—cemetery ... LA-4
Garden Ditch—canal ... CA-9
Garden Ditch—canal ... CO-8
Garden Ditch—canal ... WY-8
Garden Draw—valley ... MT-8
Garden Draw—valley ... TX-5
Garden Draw—valley ... WY-8
Gardene, Bay—bay ... LA-4
Garden Eden Brook—stream ... ME-1
Garden Elem Sch—school ... FL-3
Gardener Bayou—stream ... LA-4
Gardener Butte—summit ... OR-9
Gardener Cem—cemetery ... AR-4
Gardener Dam—dam ... OR-9
Gardener Draw—valley (2) ... TX-5
Gardener Grade Sch—school ... KS-7
Gardener Hollow—valley ... MO-7
Gardener Rsvr—reservoir ... OR-9
Gardener Sch—school ... MA-1
Gardener Sch—school ... NE-7
Gardeners Creek ... AL-4
Gardeners Creek—stream ... MI-6
Gardeners Pond ... RI-1
Gardener Wash—stream ... AZ-5
Gardener Well—well ... AZ-5
Gardener Windmill—locale ... TX-5
**Garden Farms**—pop pl ... CA-9
**Garden Farms**—pop pl ... TN-4
Garden Gap Branch—stream ... WV-2
Garden Gate HS—school ... CA-9
Garden Gate Pass—gap ... NV-8
Garden Gate Sch—school ... CA-9
**Garden Gate Village**—pop pl ... CA-9
**Garden Ground**—pop pl ... WV-2
Garden Ground Mtn—summit ... WV-2
Garden Grove—locale ... OK-5
**Garden Grove**—pop pl ... CA-9
**Garden Grove**—pop pl ... FL-3
**Garden Grove**—pop pl (2) ... IA-7
Garden Grove Ave Sch—school ... CA-9
Garden Grove Church And Sch—school ... GA-3
Garden Grove Day Sch—school ... CA-9
Garden Grove Elem Sch—school ... FL-3
**Garden Grove (Garden Grove
Estates)**—pop pl ... FL-3
Garden Grove HS—school ... CA-9
Garden Grove Municipal Golf
Course—other ... CA-9
Garden Grove Park—park ... CA-9
**Garden Grove Subdivision**—pop pl ... UT-8
Garden Grove Township—fmr MCD ... IA-7
Garden Gulch ... AZ-5
Garden Gulch ... CA-9
Garden Gulch ... ID-8
Garden Gulch—valley (8) ... CA-9
Garden Gulch—valley ... CO-8
Garden Gulch—valley (6) ... ID-8
Garden Gulch—valley (3) ... MT-8
Garden Gulch—valley (2) ... OR-9
Garden Gulch—valley ... WA-9
Garden Gulch—valley ... WY-8
Garden Gulch Trail—trail ... CA-9
Garden Heights ... TN-4
**Garden Heights**—pop pl ... IL-6
Garden Heights—uninc pl ... PA-2
**Garden Highlands**—pop pl ... AL-4
Garden Hill—summit ... VT-1
Garden Hill Cem—cemetery ... AL-4
Garden Hill Creek—stream ... MI-6
**Garden Hills**—pop pl ... PA-2
**Garden Hills**—pop pl ... PR-3
Gardenhill Sch—school ... CA-9
Garden Hills Hist Dist—hist pl ... GA-3
Garden Hills Sch—school ... IL-6
**Garden Hill (Township of)**—pop pl ... IL-6
Gardenhire Cem—cemetery ... TN-4
Gardenhire Drain—canal ... AZ-5
Gardenhire Gulch—valley ... CO-8
Gardenhires Ferry (historical)—locale ... TN-4
Garden Hole—bay ... VA-3
Garden Hollow—valley (2) ... KY-4
Garden Hollow—valley ... UT-8
Garden Hollow—valley (2) ... WV-2
**Garden Home**—pop pl ... OR-9
**Garden Homes**—pop pl ... IL-6
Garden Home Sch—school ... OR-9
Garden Home Sch—school ... WI-6
**Garden Homes (subdivision)**—pop pl ... NC-3
Garden Home-Whitford—CDP ... OR-9
Garden HS—school ... VA-3
Gardenia ... MP-9
Gardenia Gardens—uninc pl ... FL-3
Gardenia Lake—lake ... NM-5
Garden Island ... HI-9
Garden Island—island (3) ... AK-9
Garden Island—island (3) ... FL-3
Garden Island—island ... ME-1
Garden Island—island (2) ... MI-6
Garden Island—island ... MN-6
Garden Island—island (2) ... NY-2
Garden Island—island ... VT-1
Garden Island—island ... WA-9
Garden Island—uninc pl ... AK-9
Garden Island Bay—bay ... LA-4
Garden Island Bay Oil and Gas
Field—oilfield ... LA-4
Garden Island Harbor—bay ... MI-6
Garden Island Indian Cemetery—hist pl ... MI-6
Garden Island Ledge—bar ... ME-1
Garden Island Ledge—bar ... NY-2
Garden Island Pass—channel ... LA-4
Garden Islands—island ... ME-1
Garden Island Shoal—bar ... MI-6
Garden Island South Ledge—bar ... ME-1
Garden Isle—locale ... OH-6
**Garden Isles**—pop pl ... FL-3
Garden Isles Shop Ctr—locale ... FL-3
Garden Key—island ... FL-3
Garden Lake—lake (3) ... FL-3
Garden Lake—lake (2) ... MN-6
Garden Lake—lake ... NV-8
Garden Lake—lake ... WI-6
Garden Lake—reservoir (2) ... TX-5
Garden Lake—uninc pl ... NJ-2
Garden Lakes ... WY-8
Garden Lakes—CDP ... GA-3
**Gardenland**—pop pl ... CA-9
**Garden Lot Addition**—pop pl ... UT-8
Garden (Magisterial District)—fmr MCD ... VA-3
**Garden Mart**—pop pl ... PA-2
Garden Memorial Cem—cemetery ... AR-4
Garden Memorial Park
(cemetery)—cemetery ... MS-4
Garden Mine—mine ... CO-8
Garden Mission Ch—church ... VA-3
Garden Mountain—ridge ... VA-3
Garden Mountain Lookout Tower—locale ... TN-4
Garden Mtn—summit ... NV-8
Garden Mtn—summit ... VA-3
Garden Oaks—uninc pl ... TX-5
Garden Oaks Sch—school ... CA-9
Garden Oaks Sch—school ... OK-5

Garden Oaks Sch—*school* TX-5
*Garden of Allah* AZ-5
*Garden of Eden* UT-8
Garden of Eden—*area* UT-8
Garden Of Eden—*flat* WA-9
Garden of Eden—*hist pl* KS-7
**Garden of Eden**—*pop pl* IL-6
Garden of Eden Sch—*school* MI-6
Garden of Everlasting Life—*cemetery* TN-4
Garden of Gethsemane Park—*park* AZ-5
Garden of Heavenly Rest—*cemetery* FL-3
Garden of Hope Cem—*cemetery* WI-6
Garden of Memories—*cemetery* FL-3
Garden of Memories—*cemetery* IL-6
Garden Of Memories—*cemetery* IA-7
Garden Of Memories—*cemetery* LA-4
Garden of Memories—*cemetery* MN-6
Garden of Memories—*cemetery* NJ-2
Garden of Memories—*cemetery* SC-3
Garden of Memories—*cemetery* (2) TX-5
Garden of Memories Cem—*cemetery* (3) AL-4
Garden of Memories Cem—*cemetery* FL-3
Garden of Memories Cem—*cemetery* IL-6
Garden of Memories Cem—*cemetery* KS-7
Garden of Memories Cem—*cemetery* (2) LA-4
Garden Of Memories Cem—*cemetery* MO-7
Garden of Memories Cem—*cemetery* NC-3
Garden of Memories Cem—*cemetery* (2) OK-5
Garden of Memories Cem—*cemetery* PA-2
Garden of Memories Cem—*cemetery* SD-7
Garden of Memories Cem—*cemetery* (3) TX-5
Garden Of memories Cem—*cemetery* TX-5
Garden of Memories (Cemetery)—*cemetery* (2) TX-5
Garden of Memory Cem—*cemetery* MS-4
Garden of Memory Cem—*cemetery* OK-5
Garden of Memory Cem—*cemetery* WI-6
Garden of Peace Cem—*cemetery* (2) FL-3
Garden of Peace Ch—*church* FL-3
Garden Of Prayer Cem—*cemetery* GA-3
Garden of the Cross Cem—*cemetery* TX-5
*Garden of The Gods* UT-8
Garden Of The Gods—*basin* WY-8
Garden of the Gods—*park* CO-8
Garden of the Gods—*summit* CA-9
Garden Park—*flat* CO-8
Garden Park—*park* IN-6
Garden Park—*park* MN-6
Garden Park—*park* WV-2
Garden Park Cem—*cemetery* TX-5
Garden Park Corral—*locale* CO-8
Garden Park Dinosaur Monmt—*pillar* CO-8
**Garden Park Estates**—*pop pl* NY-2
Garden Park Memorial Hosp—*hospital* CA-9
Garden Park Sch—*school* AZ-5
Garden Park Sch—*school* CA-9
Garden Park Sch—*school* CO-8
**Garden Park (subdivision)**—*pop pl* MS-4
**Garden Park (subdivision)**—*pop pl* NC-3
*Garden Pass* WA-9
Garden Pass—*gap* NV-8
Garden Pass Creek—*stream* NV-8
Garden Peak—*summit* ID-8
Garden Peninsula—*cape* MI-6
Garden Pier—*locale* NJ-2
Garden Place Sch—*school* CO-8
*Gardenplain* KS-7
Gardenplain—*other* IL-6
**Garden Plain**—*pop pl* IL-6
**Garden Plain**—*pop pl* KS-7
Garden Plain Cem—*cemetery* NE-7
Garden Plain Elem Sch—*school* KS-7
Garden Plain HS—*school* KS-7
**Garden Plain Township**—*pop pl* KS-7
Garden Plain (Township of)—*civ div* IL-6
Garden Plaza—*locale* MA-1
Garden Point—*cape* ME-1
Garden Point—*cape* NC-3
Garden Point—*cliff* MT-8
Garden Pond—*lake* FL-3
Garden Pond—*lake* NJ-2
Garden Pond—*lake* RI-1
Garden Prairie—*locale* IA-7
**Garden Prairie**—*pop pl* IL-6
Garden Prairie Cem—*cemetery* IL-6
Garden Prairie Cem—*cemetery* IA-7
Garden Prairie Ch—*church* (2) IA-7
Garden Prairie Ch—*church* NE-7
Garden Prairie Sch (abandoned)—*school* (2) MO-7
**Garden Prairie Township**—*pop pl* SD-7
Garden Prairie Township (historical)—*civil*. SD-7
*Garden Quarter* IL-6
Garden Ranch—*locale* ID-8
Garden-Reynolds-Shaffer Oil Field—*oilfield* KS-7
**Garden Ridge**—*pop pl* (2) TX-5
Garden Ridge—*ridge* AZ-5
Garden Ridge—*ridge* CA-9
Garden Ridge—*summit* MT-8
Garden Ridge Ch—*church* MO-7
Garden Road Sch—*school* CA-9
Garden Run—*stream* (2) IN-6
Gardens—*uninc pl* NJ-2
Gardens, The—*flat* CA-9
Gardens, The—*locale* FL-3
Garden Sanctuary, The—*cemetery* FL-3
Garden Sch—*school* (2) CA-9
Garden Sch—*school* CT-1
Gardens Ch of Christ—*church* FL-3
**Gardens Corner**—*pop pl* SC-3
Gardens East Shop Ctr—*locale* FL-3
Garden Shores—*uninc pl* VA-3
**Gardenside**—*pop pl* KY-4
Garden Slough—*stream* (2) MN-6
Garden Slough—*stream* WA-9
**Gardens Of Eden (subdivision)**—*pop pl* UT-8
Gardens of Faith—*cemetery* NC-3
**Gardens of Gulf Cove**—*pop pl* FL-3
Gardens of Memory—*cemetery* IN-6
Gardens of Memory Cem—*cemetery* AL-4
Gardens of Memory Cem—*cemetery* IN-6
Gardens of Rest—*cemetery* AL-4
Gardens Oil Field—*oilfield* MS-4
Gardens Park—*park* TX-5
Gardens Park Plaza (Shop Ctr)—*locale* FL-3
Garden Spot—*gap* NC-3
*Garden Spot, The* AL-4
Garden Spot, The—*summit* TN-4
Garden Spot (historical)—*locale* AL-4
Garden Spot Junior Senior HS—*school* PA-2
**Gardenspot Subdivision**—*pop pl* MS-4
*Garden Spring* CA-9
Garden Spring—*spring* (3) AZ-5
Garden Spring—*spring* ID-8
Garden Spring—*spring* (6) NV-8
Garden Spring—*spring* OR-9
Garden Spring—*spring* TX-5
Garden Spring—*spring* UT-8
Garden Spring Canyon—*valley* AZ-5
**Garden Springs**—*pop pl* KY-4
Garden Springs—*spring* NV-8
Garden Springs—*spring* (2) TX-5
Garden Springs Ch—*church* AR-4
Garden Springs Creek—*stream* WA-9
Garden Springs Lake—*reservoir* GA-3
Garden Springs Sch—*school* KY-4
Garden Springs Sch—*school* WA-9
*Garden Springs Wash* NV-8
Garden Square Shop Ctr—*locale* CA-9
**Garden Square (subdivision)**—*pop pl* AL-4
Gardens Sch—*school* TX-5
Garden State—*post sta* NJ-2
Garden State Park—*park* NJ-2
Garden State Plaza—*locale* NJ-2
Garden Street Mall—*locale* FL-3
**Garden (subdivision)**—*pop pl* PA-2
Garden Tank—*reservoir* (2) AZ-5
Garden Tank—*reservoir* CA-9
Garden Tank—*reservoir* NM-5
Garden Tank—*reservoir* TX-5
*Garden Terrace* OH-6
**Garden Terrace**—*pop pl* NY-2
Garden Theater Block—*hist pl* MA-1
**Garden Towers Condominium**—*pop pl* UT-8
*Garden Township* KS-7
Garden Township—*fmr MCD* IA-7
**Garden Township**—*pop pl* (2) KS-7
Garden (Township of)—*fmr MCD* AR-4
**Garden (Township of)**—*pop pl* MI-6
**Garden (Township of)**—*pop pl* MN-6
Garden Valley—*basin* NV-8
Garden Valley—*flat* AZ-5
Garden Valley—*locale* CA-9
Garden Valley—*locale* GA-3
Garden Valley—*locale* TX-5
**Garden Valley**—*pop pl* ID-8
**Garden Valley**—*pop pl* TX-5
Garden Valley—*valley* ID-8
Garden Valley—*valley* NV-8
Garden Valley—*valley* OR-9
Garden Valley—*valley* WI-6
Garden Valley Cem—*cemetery* ND-7
Garden Valley Ch—*church* TX-5
Garden Valley Ditch—*canal* SD-7
Garden Valley Elem Sch—*school* ID-8
Garden Valley HS—*school* ID-8
Garden Valley Pioneer Cem—*cemetery* ID-8
Garden Valley Ranger Station—*locale* ID-8
Garden Valley Sch—*school* (2) CA-9
Garden Valley Sch—*school* KS-7
Garden Valley Sch—*school* OR-9
Garden Valley Sch—*school* TX-5
Garden Valley Sch (historical)—*school* SD-7
**Garden Valley (Town of)**—*pop pl* WI-6
Garden Valley Trail—*trail* AZ-5
*Garden View* PA-2
**Gardenview**—*pop pl* MO-7
**Gardenview**—*pop pl* PA-2
**Garden View**—*pop pl* (2) PA-2
**Garden Village**—*pop pl* IN-6
**Garden Village**—*pop pl* KY-4
**Garden Village**—*pop pl* WV-2
**Garden Village**—*pop pl* WI-6
Garden Village—*uninc pl* CA-9
Garden Village Sch—*school* CA-9
Garden Village Sch—*school* MI-6
**Garden Villas**—*pop pl* (2) TX-5
Garden Villas Park—*park* TX-5
Garden Villas Sch—*school* TX-5
**Gardenville**—*pop pl* FL-3
**Gardenville**—*pop pl* MD-2
**Gardenville**—*pop pl* MI-6
**Gardenville**—*pop pl* NJ-2
**Gardenville**—*pop pl* NY-2
**Gardenville**—*pop pl* PA-2
Gardenville—*uninc pl* WA-9
Gardenville Beach—*beach* FL-3
**Gardenville Center**—*pop pl* NJ-2
Gardenville Sch—*school* MD-2
Gardenville Sch—*school* MI-6
Gardenville Sch—*school* PA-2
**Gardenville (sta.)**—*pop pl* NY-2
Garden Wall, The—*cliff* MT-8
Garden Wall, The—*ridge* AK-9
Garden Wall, The—*ridge* MT-8
Garden Wash—*stream* (2) NV-8
Garden Wash—*valley* AZ-5
Garden Wash—*valley* UT-8
Garden Well—*well* NM-5
Garden Wells—*well* TX-5
Garden Windmill—*locale* (2) NM-5
Garden Windmill—*locale* (3) TX-5
Garden Windmill, The—*locale* TX-5
**Garden Wood Park**—*pop pl* VA-3
Gardenwood Park—*uninc pl* VA-3
Garden Yards—*locale* NJ-2
Garder Canyon—*valley* UT-8
Garder Cem—*cemetery* CO-8
Garder Cem—*cemetery* WV-2
Gardere—*locale* LA-4
Gardere Canal—*canal* LA-4
Gard Fork—*stream* KY-4
**Gardi**—*pop pl* GA-3
Gardi Creek—*stream* GA-3
Gardine Butte—*summit* OR-9
*Gardineer Corners* PA-2
Gardiner—*locale* NM-5
**Gardiner**—*pop pl* IA-7
**Gardiner**—*pop pl* ME-1
**Gardiner**—*pop pl* MT-8
**Gardiner**—*pop pl* NE-7
**Gardiner**—*pop pl* NY-2
**Gardiner**—*pop pl* OR-9
**Gardiner**—*pop pl* WA-9
Gardiner, Capt. Oliver, House—*hist pl* RI-1
Gardiner, Dr. Thomas, House—*hist pl* KY-4
Gardiner, Mount—*summit* CA-9
Gardiner Basin—*basin* CA-9
Gardiner Brook—*stream* NH-1
*Gardiner Canyon* MT-8
*Gardiner Canyon* WY-8
Gardiner Canyon—*valley* NM-5
Gardiner Cem—*cemetery* IL-6
Gardiner Center Shop Ctr—*locale* MS-4
Gardiner Chapel—*church* NC-3
Gardiner-Cooke—*cens area* MT-8
Gardiner Creek—*stream* AK-9
Gardiner Creek—*stream* CA-9
Gardiner Creek—*stream* CO-8
Gardiner Creek—*stream* ID-8
Gardiner Creek—*stream* WA-9
Gardiner Ditch—*canal* MT-8
Gardiner Elem Sch—*school* KS-7
**Gardiner Estates Subdivision**—*pop pl* UT-8
Gardiner Fork—*stream* ID-8
Gardiner Fork—*stream* KY-4
Gardiner Gulch—*valley* CO-8
Gardiner Hist Dist—*hist pl* ME-1
Gardiner HS—*school* MS-4
Gardiner Island—*island* AL-4
Gardiner Island—*island* VT-1
*Gardiner JHS* MS-4
*Gardiner Junction* OR-9
**Gardiner Junction**—*pop pl* OR-9
Gardiner Lakes—*lake* CA-9
Gardiner Landing—*locale* OR-9
Gardiner Manor Sch—*school* NY-2
Gardiner Mtn—*summit* NH-1
Gardiner Park—*park* MS-4
Gardiner Pass—*gap* CA-9
Gardiner Peak—*summit* ID-8
Gardiner-Pingree House—*hist pl* MA-1
Gardiner Place Hist Dist—*hist pl* NY-2
Gardiner Pond—*lake* ME-1
Gardiner Pond—*lake* RI-1
Gardiner Pond—*reservoir* RI-1
Gardiner Pond Dam—*dam* RI-1
Gardiner Pond Shell Midden—*hist pl* RI-1
Gardiner Ridge—*ridge* ME-1
*Gardiner River* MT-8
*Gardiner River* WY-8
Gardiner RR Station—*hist pl* ME-1
Gardiner Rsvr—*reservoir* OR-9
Gardiners Ave Sch—*school* NY-2
Gardiners Bay—*bay* NY-2
**Gardiners Bay Estates**—*pop pl* NY-2
Gardiner Sch—*school* OH-6
Gardiner Sch—*school* OR-9
*Gardiners Creek* PA-2
Gardiners Creek—*gut* NY-2
**Gardiners Gin**—*pop pl* AL-4
*Gardiners Island* AL-4
Gardiners Island—*island* NY-2
**Gardiners Island**—*pop pl* NY-2
Gardiners Island Two Lookout Tower—*locale* NY-2
Gardiners Island Windmill—*hist pl* NY-2
*Gardiner's Lake* ME-1
*Gardiners Lake* MI-6
Gardiners Landing—*locale* NJ-2
Gardiner Slip—*channel* LA-4
*Gardiner'S Neck* MA-1
Gardiners Point—*island* NY-2
*Gardiners Pond* RI-1
*Gardiners Rock* MA-1
Gardiners Rock—*bar* MA-1
**Gardiner (Town of)**—*pop pl* NY-2
Gardiner-Tyler House—*hist pl* NY-2
Gardinier Corners—*locale* PA-2
Gardipee Bottoms—*bend* MT-8
Gardisky Lake—*lake* CA-9
Gard Island—*island* MI-6
Gardison Ridge—*ridge* UT-8
Gardi Swamp—*swamp* GA-3
Gardling Hollow—*valley* TN-4
Gardner—*locale* AR-4
Gardner—*locale* (2) FL-3
Gardner—*locale* KY-4
Gardner—*locale* MI-6
Gardner—*locale* MO-7
Gardner—*locale* PA-2
Gardner—*locale* (2) WV-2
**Gardner**—*pop pl* CO-8
**Gardner**—*pop pl* GA-3
**Gardner**—*pop pl* IL-6
**Gardner**—*pop pl* IA-7
**Gardner**—*pop pl* KS-7
**Gardner**—*pop pl* LA-4
**Gardner**—*pop pl* MA-1
**Gardner**—*pop pl* MO-7
**Gardner**—*pop pl* ND-7
**Gardner**—*pop pl* OH-6
**Gardner**—*pop pl* PA-2
**Gardner**—*pop pl* TN-4
**Gardner**—*pop pl* VA-3
Gardner, City of—*civil* MA-1
Gardner, Ezekial, House—*hist pl* RI-1
Gardner, Ira W., House—*hist pl* UT-8
Gardner, Isabella Stewart, Museum—*hist pl* MA-1
Gardner, James, House—*hist pl* UT-8
Gardner, James I., Store—*hist pl* AZ-5
Gardner, Jefferson, House—*hist pl* OK-5
Gardner, Judge D. W., House—*hist pl* KY-4
Gardner, Lake—*lake* NH-1
Gardner, Lake—*reservoir* MA-1
Gardner, Lake—*reservoir* SD-7
Gardner, Mount—*summit* WA-9
Gardner, Port—*bay* WA-9
Gardner, Robert W., House—*hist pl* IL-6
Gardner, Silas, House—*hist pl* NY-2
Gardner-Bailey House—*hist pl* PA-2
Gardner Bar—*bar* OR-9
Gardner Bay—*bay* AK-9
Gardner Bay—*bay* NH-1
Gardner Bluehill Mine—*mine* CA-9
*Gardner Branch* TN-4
Gardner Branch—*stream* KY-4
Gardner Branch—*stream* SC-3
Gardner Branch—*stream* TN-4
Gardner Branch—*stream* WV-2
Gardner Brook—*stream* (3) CT-1
Gardner Brook—*stream* (7) ME-1
Gardner Brook—*stream* MA-1
Gardner Brook—*stream* MN-6
*Gardner Butte* OR-9
Gardner Butte—*summit* CO-8
Gardner Butte—*summit* MT-8
*Gardner Cabin* IA-7
Gardner Camp—*locale* TX-5
Gardner Canal—*canal* ID-8
Gardner Canal—*canal* UT-8
Gardner Canyon—*valley* (5) AZ-5
Gardner Canyon—*valley* ID-8
Gardner Canyon—*valley* MT-8
Gardner Canyon—*valley* NM-5
Gardner Canyon—*valley* (2) UT-8
Gardner Canyon—*valley* WY-8
Gardner Canyon Sixty seven Trail—*trail* AZ-5
Gardner Cave—*cave* WA-9
Gardner Cem—*cemetery* AL-4
Gardner Cem—*cemetery* (3) AR-4
Gardner Cem—*cemetery* CO-8
Gardner Cem—*cemetery* CT-1
Gardner Cem—*cemetery* (2) IL-6
Gardner Cem—*cemetery* (2) IN-6
Gardner Cem—*cemetery* KY-4
Gardner Cem—*cemetery* MD-2
Gardner Cem—*cemetery* (2) MA-1
Gardner Cem—*cemetery* (3) MI-6
Gardner Cem—*cemetery* (2) MS-4
Gardner Cem—*cemetery* (3) MO-7
Gardner Cem—*cemetery* (5) NY-2
Gardner Cem—*cemetery* NC-3
Gardner Cem—*cemetery* (2) OH-6
Gardner Cem—*cemetery* OK-5
Gardner Cem—*cemetery* (3) TN-4
Gardner Cem—*cemetery* (2) TX-5
Gardner Cem—*cemetery* VT-1
Gardner Cem—*cemetery* (4) VA-3
*Gardner Centre* MA-1
Gardner Ch—*church* VA-3
Gardner Chapel—*church* AL-4
Gardner Chapel—*church* VA-3
Gardner City Dam—*dam* KS-7
Gardner City Hall—*building* MA-1
*Gardner Creek* NV-8
*Gardner Creek* OR-9
*Gardner Creek* WY-8
Gardner Creek—*stream* AZ-5
Gardner Creek—*stream* CO-8
Gardner Creek—*stream* FL-3
Gardner Creek—*stream* ID-8
Gardner Creek—*stream* KY-4
Gardner Creek—*stream* MS-4
Gardner Creek—*stream* (3) NV-8
Gardner Creek—*stream* NY-2
Gardner Creek—*stream* NC-3
Gardner Creek—*stream* OK-5
Gardner Creek—*stream* (2) OR-9
Gardner Creek—*stream* (2) PA-2
Gardner Creek—*stream* (2) TN-4
Gardner Creek—*stream* TX-5
Gardner Creek—*stream* UT-8
Gardner Creek—*stream* VA-3
Gardner Creek—*stream* WA-9
Gardner Creek—*stream* (3) WI-6
Gardner Creek—*stream* (2) WY-8
Gardner Creek Dam—*dam* PA-2
Gardner Creek Rsvr—*reservoir* PA-2
Gardner Crossroads—*locale* SC-3
Gardner Dam Camp—*locale* WI-6
*Gardner Ditch* OR-9
Gardner Draw—*valley* KS-7
Gardner Draw—*valley* NM-5
Gardner Draw—*valley* TX-5
Gardner Draw—*valley* UT-8
Gardner Falls Main Dam—*dam* MA-1
*Gardner Falls Station Canal* MA-1
Gardner Falls Station Canal Dam—*dam* MA-1
Gardner Falls Station Canal Rsvr—*reservoir* MA-1
*Gardner Falls Station Rsvr* MA-1
Gardner Farms Lake—*reservoir* MO-7
Gardner Fire Station—*building* NC-3
Gardner Gap—*gap* TN-4
**Gardner Gardens Subdivision**—*pop pl* UT-8
Gardner Grove Ch—*church* GA-3
Gardner Gulch—*valley* (2) CA-9
Gardner Gulch—*valley* (2) CO-8
Gardner Gulch—*valley* (2) ID-8
Gardner Gulch—*valley* WY-8
Gardner Gulch Corral—*locale* ID-8
Gardner Hiar Drain—*canal* MI-6
Gardner Hill—*locale* PA-2
Gardner Hill—*summit* AL-4
Gardner Hill—*summit* (2) NY-2
Gardner Hill Sch—*school* PA-2
Gardner (historical)—*locale* AL-4
Gardner Hollow—*valley* AL-4
Gardner Hollow—*valley* AR-4
Gardner Hollow—*valley* MA-1
Gardner Hollow—*valley* MO-7
Gardner Hollow—*valley* (3) UT-8
Gardner Hollow Brook—*stream* NY-2
Gardner Hollow Reservoirs—*reservoir* UT-8
Gardner House—*hist pl* MI-6
Gardner House—*hist pl* MO-7
Gardner House—*hist pl* NY-2
Gardner House—*hist pl* NC-3
Gardner House—*hist pl* OH-6
Gardner HS—*school* KS-7
Gardner HS—*school* MA-1
*Gardner Island* AL-4
Gardner Island—*area* MO-7
Gardner Island—*island* LA-4
Gardner Island—*island* ME-1
Gardner Island—*island* RI-1
Gardner Island—*island* WI-6
Gardner JHS—*school* MA-1
Gardner Junction—*locale* WV-2
Gardner Knob—*summit* KY-4
*Gardner Lake* MA-1
*Gardner Lake* SD-7
Gardner Lake—*lake* CO-8
Gardner Lake—*lake* CT-1
Gardner Lake—*lake* FL-3
Gardner Lake—*lake* GA-3
Gardner Lake—*lake* ME-1
Gardner Lake—*lake* MI-6
Gardner Lake—*lake* (3) MN-6
Gardner Lake—*lake* (2) WI-6
Gardner Lake—*lake* WY-8
**Gardner Lake**—*pop pl* KS-7
Gardner Lake—*reservoir* ID-8
Gardner Lake—*reservoir* KS-7
Gardner Lake Dam—*dam* SD-7
Gardner Lake Sch—*school* ME-1
Gardner Landing—*locale* FL-3
*Gardner Landing Field* KS-7
Gardner Lateral—*canal* NM-5
Gardner Lookout Tower—*locale* LA-4
Gardner Lookout Tower—*locale* MI-6
Gardner-Mays Cottage—*hist pl* VA-3
Gardner-McKnight Cem—*cemetery* MS-4
Gardner Meadow—*flat* CA-9
Gardner Meadows—*flat* WA-9
Gardner Mill—*hist pl* UT-8
Gardner Mill Race Ditch—*canal* OR-9
Gardner Mills—*locale* VA-3
Gardner Mine—*mine* MI-6
Gardner Mine—*mine* OR-9
Gardner Mine RR Station—*locale* FL-3
Gardner Mine (underground)—*mine* AL-4
Gardner Mountain—*ridge* AR-4
Gardner Mountain—*ridge* (2) NH-1
Gardner Mountain Trail—*trail* WA-9
Gardner Mtn—*summit* AZ-5
Gardner Mtn—*summit* CA-9
Gardner Mtn—*summit* ME-1
Gardner Mtn—*summit* WA-9
Gardner Mtn—*summit* WY-8
Gardner Municipal Airp—*airport* KS-7
Gardner News Bldg—*hist pl* MA-1
Gardner-O'Brien Cem—*cemetery* MS-4
Gardner Park—*flat* CO-8
Gardner Park—*park* IA-7
Gardner Park—*park* NE-7
Gardner Park—*park* OH-6
**Gardner Park**—*pop pl* NC-3
Gardner Park Elem Sch—*school* NC-3
Gardner Park Rsvr—*reservoir* CO-8
Gardner Peak—*summit* CO-8
Gardner Peak—*summit* NM-5
Gardner Peak—*summit* OR-9
Gardner Peak—*summit* UT-8
Gardner-Pingree House—*building* MA-1
Gardner Pinnacles—*island* HI-9
Gardner Point—*summit* MT-8
*Gardner Pond* RI-1
Gardner Pond—*lake* (2) ME-1
Gardner Pond—*lake* (2) NY-2
Gardner Pond—*reservoir* SC-3
Gardner Post Office (historical)—*building* TN-4
Gardner Powell Ditch—*canal* IN-6
Gardner Prospect—*mine* TN-4
*Gardner Ranch* TX-5
Gardner Ranch—*locale* AZ-5
Gardner Ranch—*locale* CA-9
Gardner Ranch—*locale* NE-7
Gardner Ranch—*locale* (2) NV-8
Gardner Ranch—*locale* OR-9
Gardner Ranch—*locale* TX-5
Gardner Ranch—*locale* UT-8
Gardner Ranch—*locale* WY-8
Gardner Ridge—*ridge* CO-8
Gardner Ridge—*ridge* OR-9
Gardner Rips—*rapids* ME-1
Gardner River—*stream* MT-8
Gardner River—*stream* WY-8
Gardner Road Sch—*school* NY-2
*Gardner Rsvr* AZ-5
Gardner Rsvr—*reservoir* AZ-5
Gardner Rsvr—*reservoir* CO-8
Gardner Run—*stream* FL-3
Gardner Run—*stream* OH-6
Gardner Run—*stream* PA-2
**Gardners**—*pop pl* PA-2
Gardners Basin—*harbor* NJ-2
*Gardner's Bay* NY-2
Gardners Bluff—*cliff* AL-4
Gardners Branch—*stream* KS-7
Gardners Branch—*stream* NC-3
Gardners Cabin—*locale* CO-8
Gardners Ch—*church* NC-3
Gardners Ch—*church* PA-2
Gardner Sch—*school* AR-4
Gardner Sch—*school* CA-9
Gardner Sch—*school* (3) IL-6
Gardner Sch—*school* IN-6
Gardner Sch—*school* ME-1
Gardner Sch—*school* MA-1
Gardner Sch—*school* (2) MI-6
Gardner Sch—*school* NY-2
Gardner Sch—*school* PA-2
Gardner Sch—*school* SC-3
Gardner Sch—*school* WI-6
Gardner Sch (abandoned)—*school* PA-2
Gardners Chapel—*church* NC-3
*Gardners Chapel Church* AL-4
Gardner Sch (historical)—*school* MO-7
Gardner Sch (historical)—*school* PA-2
Gardner Sch (historical)—*school* TN-4
Gardners Corners—*locale* (2) NY-2
**Gardners Corners**—*pop pl* MI-6
*Gardners Creek* NY-2
*Gardners Creek* PA-2
*Gardners Creek Reservoir* PA-2
Gardners Crossroads—*locale* VA-3
**Gardners Cross Roads**—*pop pl* VA-3
Gardners Ford (historical)—*locale* NC-3
Gardners Fork—*stream* (2) UT-8
**Gardners Grove**—*pop pl* NH-1
Gardners Hole—*basin* WY-8
*Gardner's Lake* ME-1
Gardners Landing (historical)—*locale* AL-4
Gardner Slough—*stream* TX-5
Gardners Neck—*cape* MA-1
*Gardner's Point* NY-2
Gardners Point—*cape* CA-9
Gardners Pond—*lake* PA-2
Gardners Pond—*reservoir* NJ-2
Gardners Pond Dam—*dam* NJ-2
Gardners Prairie—*flat* FL-3
Gardner Spring—*spring* ID-8
Gardner Spring—*spring* (2) NV-8
Gardner Spring—*spring* NM-5
Gardner Spring—*spring* UT-8
Gardners Rocks—*summit* PA-2
Gardners Sch—*school* NC-3
*Gardners Station* TN-4
*Gardners Station Post Office* TN-4
Gardners Store (historical)—*locale* MS-4
Gardner Stadium—*park* MS-4
Gardner State Hosp—*hospital* MA-1
Gardner State Park—*park* MA-1
*Gardner Station* TN-4
Gardner Street Sch—*school* CA-9
*Gardnersville* TN-4
Gardnersville—*locale* KY-4
**Gardnersville**—*pop pl* NY-2
*Gardnersville Post Office* TN-4
Gardner Swamp—*swamp* WI-6
Gardner Tank—*reservoir* AZ-5
Gardnertown—*CDP* NY-2
**Gardnertown**—*pop pl* NY-2
**Gardner (Town of)**—*pop pl* WI-6
**Gardner Township**—*pop pl* KS-7
**Gardner Township**—*pop pl* NE-7
**Gardner Township**—*pop pl* ND-7
Gardner (Township of)—*fmr MCD* NC-3
**Gardner (Township of)**—*pop pl* IL-6
Gardner Trail—*trail* PA-2
**Gardnerville**—*pop pl* MO-7
**Gardnerville**—*pop pl* NV-8
**Gardnerville**—*pop pl* NY-2
**Gardnerville**—*pop pl* NC-3
Gardnerville Cem—*cemetery* NV-8
Gardnerville-Minden—*CDP* NV-8
**Gardnerville Ranchos**—*pop pl* NV-8
Gardner Webb Coll—*school* NC-3
Gardner Webb Ditch—*canal* IN-6
Gardner Windmill—*locale* AZ-5
Gardner Windmill—*locale* NM-5
Gardner Windmill—*locale* TX-5
Gardner Winter Ranch—*locale* WY-8
**Gardner Wood (subdivision)**—*pop pl* NC-3
Gard Sch—*school* MI-6
Gards Corher Sch—*school* WI-6
Gards Point—*locale* IL-6
**Gardspoint**—*pop pl* IL-6
Gardwell Cem—*cemetery* KY-4
Gardy Millpond—*reservoir* VA-3
Gardys Landing (historical)—*locale* AL-4
Gardys Millpond—*reservoir* VA-3
*Gareek, The* LA-4
*Garegei* FM-9
Garelle, Bayou—*gut* LA-4
Garell Peak—*summit* CO-8
Gareloi, Mount—*summit* AK-9
Gareloi Island—*island* AK-9
Garenflo Gap—*gap* NC-3
Garesalem Cem—*cemetery* WI-6
*Garetta* GA-3
Garett Park—*park* AL-4
**Garey**—*pop pl* CA-9
Garey HS—*school* CA-9
Garey Lake—*lake* MI-6
*Garey Millpond Branch* DE-2
*Garey Millpond Branch* MD-2
Garey Mill Pond Branch—*stream* DE-2
Garey Mill Pond Branch—*stream* MD-2
Garey Mtn—*summit* ME-1
*Garey Springs* AL-4
Garface Cem—*cemetery* OH-6
*Garfias Creek* AZ-5
Garfias Mtn—*summit* AZ-5
Garfias Wash—*stream* AZ-5
*Garfield* IN-6
Garfield—*civ div* MI-6
Garfield—*fmr MCD* (6) NE-7
Garfield—*locale* IA-7
Garfield—*locale* MD-2
Garfield—*locale* MI-6
Garfield—*locale* MO-7
Garfield—*locale* PA-2
Garfield—*locale* TX-5
Garfield—*locale* UT-8
Garfield—*locale* WV-2
Garfield—*locale* WI-6
**Garfield**—*pop pl* AR-4
**Garfield**—*pop pl* CA-9
**Garfield**—*pop pl* CO-8
**Garfield**—*pop pl* GA-3
**Garfield**—*pop pl* (2) ID-8
**Garfield**—*pop pl* IL-6
**Garfield**—*pop pl* IN-6
**Garfield**—*pop pl* KS-7
**Garfield**—*pop pl* KY-4
**Garfield**—*pop pl* MN-6
**Garfield**—*pop pl* NJ-2
**Garfield**—*pop pl* NM-5
**Garfield**—*pop pl* NY-2
**Garfield**—*pop pl* (2) OH-6
**Garfield**—*pop pl* OR-9
**Garfield**—*pop pl* TX-5
**Garfield**—*pop pl* VT-1
**Garfield**—*pop pl* WA-9
Garfield, Halsey, House—*hist pl* OH-6
Garfield, James A., Sch—*hist pl* MI-6
Garfield, Lake—*lake* FL-3
Garfield, Lake—*reservoir* MA-1
Garfield, Milton, House—*hist pl* OH-6
Garfield, Mount—*summit* (3) CO-8
Garfield, Mount—*summit* NH-1
**Garfield Addition (subdivision)**—*pop pl* UT-8
Garfield Ave Sch—*school* WI-6
Garfield Basin—*basin* UT-8
Garfield Bay—*bay* ID-8
Garfield Bay Recreation Site—*locale* ID-8
Garfield Bight—*bay* FL-3
Garfield Bldg—*hist pl* CA-9
Garfield Bridge—*bridge* OH-6
Garfield-Broad Apartments—*hist pl* OH-6
Garfield Brook—*stream* NY-2
Garfield Canal—*canal* NM-5
Garfield Canyon—*valley* ID-8
Garfield Canyon—*valley* MT-8
Garfield Canyon—*valley* NM-5
Garfield Cem—*cemetery* IA-7
Garfield Cem—*cemetery* (3) KS-7
Garfield Cem—*cemetery* MI-6
Garfield Cem—*cemetery* (2) NE-7
Garfield Cem—*cemetery* (2) NY-2
Garfield Cem—*cemetery* (2) SD-7
Garfield Cem—*cemetery* TX-5
Garfield Cem—*cemetery* WA-9
Garfield Center—*locale* KS-7
Garfield Center Sch—*school* MI-6
Garfield Center Sch—*school* NE-7
Garfield Ch—*church* MI-6
Garfield Ch—*church* MN-6
Garfield Ch—*church* ND-7
Garfield Ch—*church* OH-6
Garfield Ch—*church* SD-7
Garfield Chapel—*church* OH-6
Garfield County—*civil* UT-8

Gar Pond—*lake* (2) FL-3
Gar Pond—*lake* LA-4
Gar Pond—*lake* MS-4
Garpond Cem—*cemetery* KY-4
Garra—*island* (2) MP-9
Garrabrant Pond—*lake* NY-2
Garradella Gulch—*valley* OR-9
*Garra Island* MP-9
Gar Ranch—*locale* MT-8
Garrapata Canyon—*valley* NM-5
*Garrapata Creek* CA-9
Garrapata Creek—*stream* (2) CA-9
Garrapata Ridge—*ridge* NM-5
Garrard—*locale* KY-4
Garrard, James, House—*hist pl* KY-4
Garrard Bluff—*cliff* MN-6
Garrard Branch—*locale* ID-8
Garrard Branch—*stream* KY-4
Garrard Cave Spring—*spring* TN-4
Garrard Ch—*church* IN-6
Garrard Ch—*church* KY-4
**Garrard (County)**—*pop pl* KY-4
Garrard County Jail—*hist pl* KY-4
Garrard Creek—*stream* WA-9
Garrard Ditch—*canal* IN-6
Garrard Ditch—*canal* WY-8
Garrard Ford—*locale* TN-4
Garrard Lake—*lake* MT-8
Garrard Landing—*locale* TN-4
Garrard Mills—*hist pl* KY-4
**Garrards Crossroads**—*pop pl* AL-4
**Garratt**—*pop pl* NE-7
**Garrattsville**—*pop pl* NY-2
Garraway Cem—*cemetery* MS-4
Garraway Creek—*stream* MS-4
Garr Canyon—*valley* MT-8
Garr Cem—*cemetery* AL-4
*Garr Creek* KS-7
Garr Creek—*stream* NE-7
Garr Creek—*stream* NC-3
Garr Dam—*dam* SD-7
Garred House, Chapel, and Burial Vault—*hist pl* KY-4
*Garrel* LA-4
Garren Branch—*stream* NC-3
Garren Cove—*bay* GA-3
Garren Creek—*stream* NC-3
Garren Grove Ch—*church* NC-3
**Garren Hill**—*pop pl* NC-3
Garren Lake—*reservoir* SC-3
Garren Mtn—*summit* (2) NC-3
Garren Ranch—*locale* TX-5
*Garrentons Island* NC-3
Garreru—*island* PW-9
*Garrerui* PW-9
*Garreru Island* PW-9
*Garreru To* PW-9
Garret Bay—*bay* WI-6
Garret Branch—*stream* TX-5
*Garret Butte* NV-8
Garret Cem—*cemetery* SC-3
Garret Creek—*stream* OR-9
Garret Creek—*stream* WA-9
Garret Dam—*dam* MA-1
Garret Flat—*flat* CA-9
Garret Fork—*stream* UT-8
*Garret Grove* AR-4
**Garret Grove**—*pop pl* AR-4
Garret Grove Ch—*church* TX-5
*Garret Hill* NJ-2
Garret Hill—*summit* NH-1
Garret Island—*island* TX-5
Garret Knob—*summit* PA-2
Garret Lake—*lake* TX-5
Garret Lake Number 2—*reservoir* AL-4
Garret Ranch—*locale* WY-8
Garret Ridge—*ridge* UT-8
Garret Ridge Lateral—*canal* CO-8
*Garrets Bluff* OK-5
Garrets Lake—*reservoir* AL-4
**Garretson**—*pop pl* SD-7
Garretson, Peter, House—*hist pl* NJ-2
Garretson Ditch—*canal* IA-7
Garretson Heights Sch—*school* CA-9
Garretson Hollow—*valley* PA-2
Garretson Outlet Ditch—*canal* IA-7
Garretson Ranch—*locale* WY-8
Garretson Sch—*school* CA-9
Garrets Point—*cape* SC-3
Garret Spring—*spring* NV-8
Garret Spring—*spring* UT-8
*Garrett* TN-4
Garrett—*locale* AR-4
Garrett—*locale* TN-4
Garrett—*locale* WY-8
**Garrett**—*pop pl* IL-6
**Garrett**—*pop pl* IN-6
**Garrett**—*pop pl* (2) KY-4
**Garrett**—*pop pl* PA-2
**Garrett**—*pop pl* TX-5
**Garrett**—*pop pl* WA-9
Garrett, Bayou—*stream* LA-4
Garrett, Isaiah, Law Office—*hist pl* LA-4
Garrett, Lake—*lake* WA-9
Garrett, Patrick Floyd, House—*hist pl* NM-5
Garrett, William, House—*hist pl* KY-4
Garrett, William, Plantation House—*hist pl* TX-5
Garretta—*locale* GA-3
Garrett Acad—*school* FL-3
Garrett Airp—*airport* PA-2
Garrett Baptist Ch—*church* TN-4
Garrett Basin Spring—*spring* OR-9
Garrett Bldg—*hist pl* MD-2
Garrett Borough—*civil* PA-2
Garrett Branch—*stream* AL-4
Garrett Branch—*stream* FL-3
Garrett Branch—*stream* (2) GA-3
Garrett Branch—*stream* (3) KY-4
Garrett Branch—*stream* NC-3
Garrett Branch—*stream* TN-4
Garrett Branch—*stream* TX-5
Garrett Branch—*stream* VA-3
Garrett Bridge—*bridge* AL-4
**Garrett Bridge**—*pop pl* AR-4
Garrett Brown Park—*park* TX-5
Garrett-Bullock House—*hist pl* GA-3
Garrett Butte—*summit* NV-8
Garrett Canyon—*valley* NV-8
Garrett Canyon—*valley* WA-9
Garrett Cem—*cemetery* (4) AL-4
Garrett Cem—*cemetery* (3) AR-4
Garrett Cem—*cemetery* (4) GA-3
Garrett Cem—*cemetery* IN-6
Garrett Cem—*cemetery* IA-7
Garrett Cem—*cemetery* KS-7
Garrett Cem—*cemetery* (2) KY-4
Garrett Cem—*cemetery* (2) MS-4
Garrett Cem—*cemetery* (2) MO-7
Garrett Cem—*cemetery* (2) NC-3
Garrett Cem—*cemetery* (2) OH-6
Garrett Cem—*cemetery* OK-5
Garrett Cem—*cemetery* PA-2
Garrett Cem—*cemetery* SC-3
Garrett Cem—*cemetery* (15) TN-4
Garrett Cem—*cemetery* (3) TX-5
Garrett Cem—*cemetery* (3) VA-3
Garrett Cem—*cemetery* (3) WV-2
Garrett Ch—*church* GA-3
Garrett Ch—*church* WV-2
Garrett Chapel—*church* KY-4
Garrett Chapel—*church* WV-2
Garrett City Ditch—*canal* IN-6
Garrett Coliseum—*building* AL-4
**Garrett (County)**—*pop pl* MD-2
Garrett County Courthouse—*hist pl* MD-2
*Garrett Cove* TN-4
Garrett Cow Camp—*locale* WY-8
*Garrett Creek* TX-5
Garrett Creek—*stream* AK-9
Garrett Creek—*stream* CA-9
Garrett Creek—*stream* (2) GA-3
Garrett Creek—*stream* ID-8
Garrett Creek—*stream* IN-6
Garrett Creek—*stream* (3) KY-4
Garrett Creek—*stream* LA-4
Garrett Creek—*stream* (2) MS-4
Garrett Creek—*stream* (2) NC-3
Garrett Creek—*stream* OH-6
Garrett Creek—*stream* OK-5
Garrett Creek—*stream* TN-4
Garrett Creek—*stream* (2) TX-5
Garrett Creek—*stream* VA-3
Garrett Creek—*stream* WA-9
Garrett Creek—*stream* WV-2
Garrett Creek—*stream* WY-8
Garrett Creek Cem—*cemetery* AR-4
Garrett Creek Ch—*church* TN-4
Garrett Creek Sch—*school* WV-2
Garrett Ditch—*canal* CO-8
Garrett Ditch—*canal* IN-6
Garrett Draw—*valley* TX-5
*Garrett Ferry Bridge* AL-4
Garrett Ferry (historical)—*locale* AL-4
Garrettford—*locale* PA-2
**Garrettford**—*pop pl* PA-2
Garrettford Elem Sch—*school* PA-2
**Garrett Forest**—*pop pl* MD-2
Garrett Fork—*stream* WV-2
Garrett Fork Ch—*church* WV-2
Garrett Grove—*locale* AR-4
Garrett Grove Ch—*church* NC-3
Garrett Grove Sch—*school* PA-2
Garrett Gut—*stream* NC-3
*Garrett Hall Elementary School* MS-4
Garrett Heights Sch—*school* MD-2
**Garrett Heights (subdivision)**—*pop pl* AL-4
**Garrett Hill**—*pop pl* PA-2
Garrett Hill—*summit* MD-2
Garrett Hill—*summit* MT-8
Garrett Hill—*summit* NJ-2
Garrett Hill—*summit* PA-2
Garrett Hist Dist—*hist pl* IN-6
Garrett Hollow—*valley* AR-4
Garrett Hollow—*valley* KY-4
Garrett Hollow—*valley* (3) TN-4
Garrett Hollow—*valley* VA-3
Garrett HS—*school* IN-6
Garrett Island—*island* MD-2
Garrett Knob—*summit* TN-4
*Garrett Lake* LA-4
Garrett Lake—*lake* SC-3
Garrett Lake—*reservoir* GA-3
Garrett Lake—*reservoir* TN-4
*Garrett Lake Dam* TN-4
Garrett Lake Number 1—*reservoir* AL-4
Garrett Lakes—*lake* TX-5
Garrett Lead—*channel* NY-2
Garrett Marsh—*swamp* NY-2
Garrett Memorial Chapel—*church* NY-2
Garrett Mill Ch (historical)—*church* AL-4
Garrett Mine—*mine* NV-8
Garrett Mountain Reservation—*park* NJ-2
*Garrett Mountain Reservoir Dam* NJ-2
Garrett Mtn—*summit* AR-4
Garrett Mtn—*summit* CA-9
Garrett Mtn—*summit* CT-1
Garrett Mtn—*summit* TX-5
Garrett Oil Field—*oilfield* OK-5
**Garrett Park**—*pop pl* MD-2
**Garrett Park Estates**—*pop pl* MD-2
Garrett Park Hist Dist—*hist pl* MD-2
Garrett Park Sch—*school* MD-2
Garrett Peak—*summit* AK-9
Garrett Place—*locale* OR-9
Garrett Pond—*reservoir* VA-3
Garrett Ranch—*locale* AZ-5
Garrett Ranch—*locale* NM-5
Garrett Ranch—*locale* (2) WY-8
*Garrett Reservoir* PA-2
Garrett Ridge—*ridge* AR-4
Garrett Ridge—*ridge* OR-9
Garrett Ridge—*ridge* WA-9
**Garrett Road**—*pop pl* PA-2
Garrett Rock—*pillar* ID-8
*Garrett Run* PA-2
**Garretts**—*pop pl* TN-4
**Garretts Bend**—*pop pl* WV-2
Garretts Bluff—*cliff* OK-5
**Garretts Bluff**—*pop pl* TX-5
Garretts Branch—*stream* IA-7
Garretts Bridge—*bridge* GA-3
Garrettsburg—*locale* KY-4
Garrettsburg—*locale* MO-7
Garrettsburg—*locale* TN-4
Garrett Sch—*school* GA-3
Garrett Sch—*school* KY-4
Garrett Sch—*school* MI-6
Garrett Sch—*school* OK-5
Garretts Chapel—*church* GA-3
Garrett Sch (historical)—*school* (2) TN-4
Garrett Schoolhouse (historical)—*school* AL-4
*Garretts Creek* LA-4
*Garretts Creek* TX-5
Garretts Creek—*stream* TX-5
*Garretts Creek Church* TN-4
Garretts Crossroads—*locale* AL-4
Garretts Gap—*gap* NC-3
*Garretts Hill* NJ-2
Garretts Hollow—*valley* UT-8
*Garretts Landing* TN-4
Garretts Landing (historical)—*locale* AL-4
**Garrett Slope**—*pop pl* PA-2
Garrett Slope Station—*locale* PA-2
Garretts Mill—*locale* MD-2
Garretts Mill—*locale* TN-4
*Garretts Mill Landing* AL-4
Garrett Snuff Mill—*hist pl* DE-2
Garrett Snuff Mills Hist Dist—*hist pl* DE-2
Garretts Pond—*lake* GA-3
Garretts Pond—*lake* MA-1
Garrett Spring—*spring* KY-4
Garrett Spring—*spring* NV-8
Garrett Spring—*spring* NM-5
Garretts Reach—*channel* NJ-2
**Garretts Run**—*pop pl* PA-2
Garretts Run—*stream* PA-2
*Garretts Shop* AL-4
Garretts Store—*locale* VA-3
Garretts Store (historical)—*locale* MS-4
**Garrettsville**—*pop pl* OH-6
Garrettsville-Hiram (RR name for Garrettsville)—*other* OH-6
Garrettsville (Township of)—*other* OH-6
*Garrettsville Village* OH-6
Garrett Tank—*reservoir* AZ-5
Garrett Thorofare—*channel* NJ-2
**Garrett (Township of)**—*pop pl* IL-6
*Garrettville* PA-2
Garrettville Ch—*church* MO-7
Garrett (Walla Walla West)—*CDP* WA-9
Garrett Well—*well* NM-5
Garrett West Oil And Gas Field—*oilfield* OK-5
Garrett-White House—*hist pl* NC-3
Garrett Windmill—*locale* NM-5
Garrett Windmill—*locale* (2) TX-5
**Garretville**—*pop pl* IA-7
Garr Hill—*summit* IN-6
Garr House—*hist pl* KY-4
*Garrick Creek* CA-9
Garriety Hill—*summit* WI-6
Garrigan HS—*school* IA-7
Garrigus Creek—*stream* OR-9
Garrigus Ditch—*canal* MT-8
Garringer Branch—*stream* NC-3
Garrington Sch—*school* CT-1
Garrington Spring Mine (underground)—*mine* AL-4
*Garriott Branch* KY-4
Garris Chapel—*church* NC-3
Garris Grove Ch—*church* NC-3
*Garrish Cove* ME-1
Garrish Draw—*valley* WY-8
Garrish Farm Airp—*airport* NC-3
Garrish Valley—*basin* OR-9
Garris Knoll—*summit* AZ-5
*Garr Island* UT-8
*Garrison* ND-7
Garrison—*locale* IL-6
Garrison—*locale* NM-5
**Garrison**—*pop pl* IA-7
**Garrison**—*pop pl* KY-4
**Garrison**—*pop pl* MD-2
**Garrison**—*pop pl* MN-6
**Garrison**—*pop pl* MO-7
**Garrison**—*pop pl* MT-8
**Garrison**—*pop pl* NE-7
**Garrison**—*pop pl* NY-2
**Garrison**—*pop pl* ND-7
**Garrison**—*pop pl* PA-2
**Garrison**—*pop pl* TX-5
**Garrison**—*pop pl* UT-8
**Garrison**—*pop pl* WV-2
Garrison, Augustus M. House—*hist pl* AR-4
Garrison, Garret, House—*hist pl* NJ-2
Garrison, William Lloyd, House—*hist pl* MA-1
Garrison, William Lloyd, Sch—*hist pl* MA-1
*Garrison Agency* TN-4
Garrison Airp—*airport* UT-8
Garrison Apartments—*hist pl* GA-3
*Garrison Baptist Church* TN-4
Garrison Bay—*bay* MN-6
Garrison Bay—*bay* ND-7
Garrison Bay—*bay* WA-9
Garrison Bight—*bay* FL-3
Garrison Bight Channel—*channel* FL-3
Garrison Bluff—*cliff* TN-4
Garrison Branch—*stream* (2) MO-7
Garrison Branch—*stream* (3) NC-3
Garrison Branch—*stream* (2) TN-4
Garrison Bridge—*other* IL-6
Garrison Butte—*summit* OR-9
Garrison Cabin—*locale* MT-8
Garrison Canyon—*valley* CA-9
Garrison Canyon—*valley* CO-8
Garrison Cave—*cave* MO-7
Garrison (CCD)—*cens area* KY-4
Garrison (CCD)—*cens area* TX-5
Garrison Cem—*cemetery* (2) AR-4
Garrison Cem—*cemetery* (2) IL-6
Garrison Cem—*cemetery* (2) IN-6
Garrison Cem—*cemetery* IA-7
Garrison Cem—*cemetery* (2) KS-7
Garrison Cem—*cemetery* KY-4
Garrison Cem—*cemetery* (3) MO-7
Garrison Cem—*cemetery* NY-2
Garrison Cem—*cemetery* (2) NC-3
Garrison Cem—*cemetery* OH-6
Garrison Cem—*cemetery* (2) PA-2
Garrison Cem—*cemetery* (5) TN-4
Garrison Cem—*cemetery* VA-3
Garrison Ch—*church* (2) TN-4
Garrison Channel—*channel* FL-3
Garrison Chapel—*church* (2) IN-6
**Garrison Corner**—*pop pl* NJ-2
*Garrison Creek* IN-6
Garrison Creek—*stream* GA-3
Garrison Creek—*stream* IN-6
Garrison Creek—*stream* (2) KY-4
Garrison Creek—*stream* LA-4
Garrison Creek—*stream* MN-6
Garrison Creek—*stream* MO-7
Garrison Creek—*stream* NC-3
Garrison Creek—*stream* ND-7
Garrison Creek—*stream* (2) OK-5
Garrison Creek—*stream* SC-3
Garrison Creek—*stream* TN-4
Garrison Creek—*stream* TX-5
Garrison Creek—*stream* WA-9
Garrison Creek—*stream* WI-6
Garrison Creek Ch—*church* IN-6
Garrison Dam—*dam* ND-7
*Garrison Dam Lake* ND-7
Garrison Dam Natl Fish Hatchery—*locale* ND-7
*Garrison Dam Reservoir* ND-7
Garrison Ditch—*canal* KY-4
Garrison-Dolphus Mine (underground)—*mine* AL-4
Garrison Drain—*stream* MI-6
Garrison Draw—*valley* TX-5
Garrison Draw—*valley* WY-8
Garrison Elem Sch—*school* KS-7
Garrison Ferry (historical)—*locale* TN-4
Garrison Fire Tower—*locale* AL-4
Garrison Flat—*flat* ID-8
Garrison Flat—*flat* WA-9
Garrison Forest Sch For Girls—*school* MD-2
Garrison Fork—*stream* KY-4
Garrison Fork—*stream* PA-2
Garrison Fork—*stream* (2) TN-4
Garrison Fork—*stream* WV-2
*Garrison Fork Baptist Church* TN-4
Garrison Fork Cave—*cave* TN-4
Garrison Fork Ch—*church* TN-4
Garrison Four Corners—*locale* NY-2
Garrison Glacier—*glacier* AK-9
Garrison Grove Cem—*cemetery* WI-6
Garrison Hammock—*summit* FL-3
Garrison Hill—*summit* NH-1
Garrison Hill Park and Tower—*hist pl* NH-1
Garrison (historical)—*locale* KS-7
Garrison Hollow—*valley* IL-6
Garrison Hollow—*valley* MO-7
Garrison Hollow—*valley* VA-3
Garrison Island—*island* ME-1
Garrison Island—*island* WI-6
Garrison JHS—*school* WA-9
*Garrison Lagoon* OR-9
*Garrison Lake* ND-7
Garrison Lake—*lake* NJ-2
Garrison Lake—*lake* (2) OR-9
Garrison Lake—*reservoir* KS-7
Garrison Landing Hist Dist—*hist pl* NY-2
**Garrison Manor**—*pop pl* NY-2
Garrison Mine—*mine* MT-8
Garrison Mine—*mine* TN-4
Garrison Mines—*mine* UT-8
Garrison Monster (Site)—*locale* UT-8
Garrison Municipal Airp—*airport* ND-7
*Garrison-on-Hudson* NY-2
Garrison Park—*park* AZ-5
Garrison-Pilcher Sch—*school* GA-3
Garrison Place—*hist pl* AR-4
Garrison Point—*cape* NC-3
Garrison Point Post Office (historical)—*building* AL-4
Garrison Pond—*lake* NY-2
Garrison Pond—*reservoir* GA-3
Garrison Pond—*reservoir* NJ-2
Garrison Post Office—*building* UT-8
Garrison Rec Area—*park* KS-7
*Garrison Reservoir* ND-7
Garrison Ridge—*ridge* LA-4
Garrison Ridge—*ridge* MO-7
Garrison Ridge—*ridge* NC-3
**Garrison (RR name Ferndale)**—*pop pl* WV-2
Garrison Rsvr—*reservoir* OR-9
Garrison Rsvr—*reservoir* WY-8
Garrison Run—*stream* WV-2
*Garrison's* NY-2
Garrisons Cem—*cemetery* NC-3
Garrison Sch—*school* CA-9
Garrison Sch—*school* DC-2
Garrison Sch—*school* (4) IL-6
Garrison Sch—*school* MD-2
Garrison Sch—*school* (2) MO-7
Garrison Sch—*school* NH-1
Garrison Sch—*school* NY-2
Garrison Sch—*school* UT-8
Garrison Sch—*school* WI-6
Garrison Sch (historical)—*school* TN-4
*Garrisons Creek* IN-6
Garrison-Sevier Lake—*cens area* UT-8
Garrison-Sevier Lake Division—*civil* UT-8
*Garrisons Fork* TN-4
Garrison Shoals—*beach* GA-3
Garrisons Knob—*summit* VA-3
Garrisons Lake—*reservoir* AL-4
Garrisons Lake—*reservoir* DE-2
Garrisons Lake Dam—*dam* DE-2
*Garrison's Landing* NY-2
Garrison Slough—*stream* AK-9
*Garrisons Pond* DE-2
*Garrisons Pond* NJ-2
Garrison Spring—*spring* MT-8
Garrison Spring—*spring* WA-9
Garrison Spring Branch—*stream* TN-4
Garrison Square—*locale* MO-7
Garrison Tank—*reservoir* NM-5
Garrison Temple—*church* IL-6
Garrison Township—*civil* MO-7
**Garrison (Township of)**—*pop pl* MN-6
Garrison Union Free Sch—*hist pl* NY-2
*Garrison United Methodist Church* TN-4
**Garrisonville**—*pop pl* VA-3
**Garrisonville Estates**—*pop pl* VA-3
Garrison Well—*locale* NM-5
Garris Pond—*reservoir* NC-3
Garrissere Canyon—*valley* CA-9
Garrit Schoolhouse Coulee—*valley* MT-8
Garrity Cave—*cave* MT-8
Garrity Creek—*stream* CA-9
Garrity Mtn—*summit* MT-8
Garrity Peak—*summit* CA-9
Garrity Ridge—*ridge* CA-9
Garr Knolls—*summit* UT-8
**Garrochales**—*pop pl* (2) PR-3
Garrochales (Barrio)—*fmr MCD* (2) PR-3
Garrod Dam—*dam* NM-5
*Garrott* TN-4
Garrott Cem—*cemetery* KY-4
Garrotte Creek—*stream* CA-9
Garrott House—*hist pl* AR-4
Garrott Post Office (historical)—*building* TN-4
*Garrotts School* TN-4
Garrow Ranch—*locale* MT-8
Garrows Bend—*bend* AL-4
Garrows Bend Channel—*channel* AL-4
Garr Rsvr—*reservoir* MT-8
Garr Spring—*spring* MT-8
Garr Spring Number Three—*spring* MT-8
Garr Spring Number Two—*spring* MT-8
*Garruck Mountain* CT-1
Gar Run—*stream* PA-2
Garry Creek—*stream* AK-9
Garry JHS—*school* WA-9
Garry Lake Waterhole—*lake* OR-9
Garry Lookout Tower—*locale* MT-8
Garry Owen—*locale* IA-7
Garryowen—*locale* MT-8
Garryowen Creek—*stream* AK-9
*Garsey Creek* CA-9
Garsia Bayou—*gut* LA-4
*Garside* NV-8
Garside JHS—*school* NV-8
Garside-McMullin House—*hist pl* UT-8
*Garside Reservoir* MA-1
Garska Meadow—*flat* NE-7
Garska Ranch—*locale* (2) NE-7
**Garske**—*pop pl* ND-7
Garski Flowage—*channel* WI-6
Gar Slough—*gut* (3) AR-4
**Garson**—*pop pl* AR-4
Garson Cem—*cemetery* KY-4
Garst, John, House—*hist pl* OH-6
Garst Airp—*airport* MO-7
Garst Canyon—*valley* NM-5
Garst House—*hist pl* OH-6
Garst Playground—*park* MI-6
Gartell Spring—*spring* UT-8
**Garten**—*pop pl* WV-2
Garten Creek—*stream* ID-8
Garten Verein Pavilion—*hist pl* TX-5
Gartersnake Windmill—*locale* NM-5
Garth—*other* KY-4
**Garth**—*pop pl* AL-4
**Garth**—*pop pl* MI-6
**Garth**—*pop pl* TX-5
Garth, John, House—*hist pl* MO-7
Garth, John M., House—*hist pl* KY-4
Garth Cem—*cemetery* AL-4
Garth Ch—*church* AL-4
Garth Lake—*lake* WI-6
Garth Mtn—*summit* AL-4
Garth Point—*cape* MI-6
Garthright House—*building* VA-3
Garth Run—*stream* VA-3
Garth Sch—*hist pl* KY-4
Garth Sch—*school* KY-4
Garth Slough—*bay* AL-4
Garth Spring Run—*stream* VA-3
**Garth Warner Subdivision**—*pop pl* UT-8
Gartiez Spring—*spring* NV-8
Gartina Creek—*stream* AK-9
Gartin Branch—*stream* KY-4
Gartin Fork—*stream* WV-2
Gartin Rsvr—*reservoir* OR-9
Gartin Sch—*school* MO-7
Gartly-Ramsay Hosp—*hist pl* TN-4
Gartman Cem—*cemetery* MO-7
Gartman Creek—*stream* WY-8
Gartman View—*locale* TX-5
Gartner, Carl Friedrick, Homestead—*hist pl* SD-7
Gartney Mtn—*summit* UT-8
Garton—*locale* NJ-2
Garton Cem—*cemetery* TN-4
**Garton Development**—*pop pl* DE-2
*Garton Fork* WV-2
Gartrell Lake—*reservoir* GA-3
**Gartside**—*pop pl* IL-6
Gartside Rsvr—*reservoir* MT-8
Gartung Cem—*cemetery* MO-7
Gartz Court—*hist pl* CA-9
*Garuanguru Suido* PW-9
*Garuanguru To* PW-9
*Garubaeru* PW-9
*Garubaeru Mountain* PW-9
*Garubaeru San* PW-9
*Garubuisu Island* PW-9
*Garubuisu Point* PW-9
*Garudokku* PW-9
*Garudoman Wan* PW-9
*Garudomau Wan* PW-9
*Garudoriruko* PW-9
*Garudoruko* PW-9
*Garudowaishi Point* PW-9
*Garudowaishi Saki* PW-9
*Garuguuei* FM-9
*Garuguwei* FM-9
*Garu Island*—*island* MP-9
*Garukatan River* PW-9
*Garukoru* PW-9
*Garukoru Island* PW-9
*Garukoru To* PW-9
*Garumetai To* PW-9
*Garumishukan Swamp* PW-9
*Garumisukan* PW-9
*Garumisukan Colony* PW-9
*Garumisukan River* PW-9
*Garumisukan Swamp* PW-9
*Garumokudo-To* PW-9
*Garumureaka* PW-9
*Garurudo* PW-9
*Garuruon* PW-9
*Garusaru* PW-9
*Garutoeru Reef* PW-9
**Garvanza**—*pop pl* CA-9
Garvanza Sch—*school* CA-9
Garven Ch—*church* IL-6
Garven Lateral—*canal* AZ-5
Garven Store—*locale* TX-5
Garver Barn—*hist pl* OH-6
Garver Brothers Store—*hist pl* OH-6
Garver Chapel Sch (historical)—*school* TN-4
Garver Creek—*stream* MT-8
Garver Hill—*summit* NY-2
Garver Hollow—*valley* AR-4
Garverich Ranch—*locale* MT-8
Garverich Spring—*spring* MT-8
Garverick Cem—*cemetery* OH-6
Garver Lake—*lake* MI-6
Garver Mtn—*summit* MT-8
Garver Park—*park* OH-6
Garver Sch—*school* MI-6
**Garvers Ferry**—*pop pl* PA-2
Garveson Creek—*stream* ID-8
Garvey Bar—*bar* CA-9
Garvey Branch—*stream* CO-8
Garvey Canyon—*valley* CO-8
Garvey Creek—*stream* KS-7
Garvey Drain—*canal* (2) MI-6
Garvey Glade—*flat* CA-9
Garvey Gulch—*valley* CA-9
Garvey Gulch—*valley* CO-8
Garvey Hill—*summit* NY-2
Garvey Knob—*summit* TN-4
**Garvey Melton**—*pop pl* PA-2
Garvey Pond—*lake* IL-6
Garvey Ponds—*lake* MI-6
Garvey Ranch Park—*park* CA-9
Garvey Rsvr—*reservoir* CA-9
Garvey Sch—*school* IL-6
Garvey Sch—*school* IA-7
Garvies Point Preserve—*park* NY-2
Garvin—*locale* KS-7
**Garvin**—*pop pl* MN-6
**Garvin**—*pop pl* OK-5
**Garvin**—*pop pl* TX-5
Garvin Basin—*basin* MT-8
Garvin Branch—*stream* KY-4
Garvin Branch—*stream* OK-5
Garvin Bridge—*bridge* AL-4
*Garvin Brook* MN-6
Garvin Brook—*stream* MN-6
Garvin Brook—*stream* NH-1
Garvin Canyon—*valley* KS-7
Garvin Cem—*cemetery* KY-4
Garvin Cem—*cemetery* OH-6
Garvin Cem—*cemetery* OK-5
Garvin Ch—*church* TX-5
**Garvin (County)**—*pop pl* OK-5
Garvin County Courthouse—*hist pl* OK-5
Garvin Creek—*stream* OK-5
Garvin Gulch—*valley* OR-9
Garvin Heights City Park—*park* MN-6
Garvin Hill—*summit* NH-1
Garvin Hill—*summit* VT-1
Garvin Lake—*lake* WI-6
Garvin Mesa—*summit* CO-8
Garvin Park—*hist pl* IN-6
Garvin Park—*park* IN-6
Garvin Park—*park* KS-7
Garvin Park—*park* MO-7
Garvin Ridge—*locale* KY-4
Garvin Rock Church—*hist pl* OK-5
*Garvins* MS-4
Garvins Airfield—*airport* OR-9
Garvin Sch—*school* (2) OK-5
Garvins Falls Dam—*dam* NH-1
Garvins Ferry (historical)—*locale* MS-4
Garvins Ferry Post Office (historical)—*building* MS-4
Garvins Ferry Sch (historical)—*school* MS-4
Garvins Millpond—*reservoir* SC-3
Garvins Pond—*reservoir* SC-3
Garvin Spring—*spring* AL-4
Garvin State Wildlife Mngmt Area—*park* MN-6
Garvin Tank—*reservoir* NM-5
Garvy Ledges—*bench* RI-1
Garway—*locale* PA-2
**Garwin**—*pop pl* IA-7
Garwin Cem—*cemetery* AL-4
Garwin Union Cem—*cemetery* IA-7
*Garwood* PA-2
Garwood—*locale* ID-8
**Garwood**—*pop pl* MO-7
**Garwood**—*pop pl* NJ-2
**Garwood**—*pop pl* SC-3
**Garwood**—*pop pl* TX-5
**Garwood**—*pop pl* WV-2
Garwood, Bayou—*stream* LA-4
Garwood Bridge—*bridge* CA-9
Garwood Butte—*summit* OR-9
Garwood (CCD)—*cens area* TX-5
Garwood Cem—*cemetery* OH-6
Garwood Cem—*cemetery* TX-5
Garwood Creek—*stream* OR-9
**Garwood Estates (subdivision)**—*pop pl* DE-2
Garwood Lake—*lake* MI-6
Garwood Lake—*lake* TX-5
Garwood Lookout Tower—*locale* MO-7
Garwood Memorial Airp—*airport* IN-6
Garwood Methodist Cem—*cemetery* TX-5
Garwood Ranch—*locale* TX-5
Garwood RR Station—*locale* FL-3
Garwood Run—*stream* OH-6
**Garwoods**—*pop pl* NY-2
GAR Woods—*woods* IL-6
**Garwoods (Whitney Crossings)**—*pop pl* NY-2
*Gary* CA-9
*Gary* FL-3
*Gary* MN-6
Gary—*locale* CO-8
Gary—*locale* GA-3
Gary—*locale* MD-2
Gary—*locale* NM-5
Gary—*locale* TX-5
Gary—*locale* VA-3
**Gary**—*pop pl* FL-3
**Gary**—*pop pl* IN-6
**Gary**—*pop pl* (2) MN-6
**Gary**—*pop pl* SC-3
**Gary**—*pop pl* SD-7
**Gary**—*pop pl* TX-5
**Gary**—*pop pl* WV-2
Gary, John C., House—*hist pl* KY-4
Gary, Lake—*lake* (2) FL-3
Gary, Lake—*reservoir* AL-4
Gary Allen Quarry—*mine* NV-8
Gary and Joyce Holt Reservoir Dam—*dam* UT-8
Gary and Joyce Holt Rsvr—*reservoir* UT-8
Gary Braggs Camp—*locale* NC-3
Gary Bridge—*bridge* OK-5
Gary Cem—*cemetery* KY-4
Gary Cem—*cemetery* MN-6
**Gary City**—*pop pl* TX-5

Gary City (CCD)—*cens area* .......... TX-5
Gary Corner—*locale* .......... NJ-2
Gary Country Club—*other* .......... IN-6
*Gary Creek* .......... MT-8
Gary Creek—*bay* .......... MD-2
Gary Creek—*stream* .......... CA-9
Gary Creek—*stream* .......... ID-8
Gary Creek—*stream* .......... KY-4
Gary Creek—*stream* .......... TX-5
Gary David Tank—*reservoir* .......... AZ-5
Gary Draw—*valley* .......... TX-5
*Gary-Ensley Elementary School* .......... AL-4
Gary-Ensley Sch—*school* .......... AL-4
**Gary Estates (subdivision)**—*pop pl* .......... MS-4
**Gary Gardens**—*pop pl* .......... IL-6
Gary Harbor—*bay* .......... IN-6
Gary Harbor Breakwater Light—*locale* .......... IN-6
Gary Harbor Bulkhead Light—*locale* .......... IN-6
Gary Harbor East Pierhead Light—*locale* .......... IN-6
Gary Harbor West Pierhead Light—*locale* .......... IN-6
Gary Hill—*summit* .......... TX-5
Gary (historical)—*locale* .......... AL-4
Gary Island—*island* .......... MN-6
Gary Island—*island* .......... OR-9
Gary Island Range Channel—*channel* .......... OR-9
*Gary Lake* .......... WI-6
Gary Lake—*lake* .......... TN-4
Gary Lake—*lake* .......... WI-6
Gary Land Company Bldg—*hist pl* .......... IN-6
Gary Larson Dam—*dam* .......... SD-7
Gary Memorial Hosp—*hospital* .......... LA-4
Gary Mtn—*summit* .......... TX-5
Gary Municipal Airp—*airport* .......... IN-6
*Garyo* .......... PW-9
*Garyo Island* .......... PW-9
*Garyo To* .......... PW-9
Gary Owen Mine—*mine* .......... CO-8
Gary Park—*park* .......... MI-6
Gary Playground—*park* .......... FL-3
Gary Playground—*park* .......... OK-5
Gary Ridge—*ridge* (2) .......... KY-4
Gary Rsvr—*reservoir* .......... OR-9
Gary Rsvr—*reservoir* .......... WY-8
Garys Airp—*airport* .......... MO-7
**Garysburg**—*pop pl* .......... NC-3
Garysburg Elem Sch—*school* .......... NC-3
*Garysburgh* .......... NC-3
Garysburg United Methodist Church and Cemetery—*hist pl* .......... NC-3
Garys Ch—*church* .......... VA-3
Gary Sch—*school* .......... FL-3
Gary Sch—*school* (2) .......... IL-6
Gary Sch—*school* .......... IN-6
Gary Sch—*school* .......... KY-4
Gary Sch—*school* .......... PA-2
Gary Sch—*school* .......... TX-5
Garys Chapel—*church* .......... NC-3
Gary Sch (historical)—*school* .......... AL-4
*Garys Creek* .......... MD-2
Garys Drop Cave—*cave* .......... AL-4
Gary Self Cave—*cave* .......... AL-4
Garys Pit—*cave* .......... AL-4
**Gary Springs**—*pop pl* .......... AL-4
Garys Run—*stream* .......... PA-2
Garys Tank—*reservoir* .......... TX-5
Gary Stotts Drain—*stream* .......... IN-6
Garysville—*locale* .......... VA-3
Gary-Taylor Cem—*cemetery* .......... TX-5
Gary Technical Vocational Sch—*school* .......... IN-6
**Garyton**—*pop pl* .......... IN-6
*Garytown* .......... FL-3
**Garyville**—*pop pl* .......... LA-4
Gary Wash—*stream* .......... CA-9
Gary Well—*well* .......... AZ-5
**Garywood**—*pop pl* .......... AL-4
Garza Canyon—*valley* .......... NM-5
**Garza (County)**—*pop pl* .......... TX-5
Garza Creek—*stream* .......... CA-9
Garza Crossing—*locale* .......... TX-5
*Garza Dam* .......... TX-5
*Garza-Little Dam* .......... TX-5
*Garza-Little Elm Lake* .......... TX-5
Garza-Little Elm Rsvr—*reservoir* .......... TX-5
Garza Memorial Hosp—*hospital* .......... TX-5
Garza Oil Field—*oilfield* .......... TX-5
Garza Park—*park* (2) .......... TX-5
Garza Peak—*summit* .......... CA-9
*Garza Ranch* .......... TX-5
Garza Ranch—*locale* .......... TX-5
Garzas, Isletas de—*island* .......... PR-3
Garzas (Barrio)—*fmr MCD* .......... PR-3
*Garzas Creek* .......... CA-9
Garzas Creek—*stream* .......... CA-9
Garza Spring—*spring* .......... WY-8
Garza Windmill—*locale* .......... TX-5
**Gas**—*pop pl* .......... KS-7
*Gasakan* .......... PW-9
*Gasarao* .......... PW-9
Gasaway Bench—*bench* .......... CO-8
Gas Belt Township—*civil* .......... SD-7
Gas Branch—*stream* .......... AL-4
Gasburg—*locale* .......... VA-3
**Gasburg**—*pop pl* .......... IN-6
Gasburg Creek—*stream* .......... CA-9
*Gasburgh* .......... IN-6
**Gas Camp 01**—*pop pl* .......... WY-8
Gas Canyon—*valley* (2) .......... CA-9
Gas Center—*locale* .......... PA-2
Gascha, Lake—*lake* .......... LA-4
*Gas City* .......... KS-7
Gas City—*locale* .......... OK-5
**Gas City**—*pop pl* .......... IN-6
Gas City Oil Field—*oilfield* .......... MT-8
Gasco—*locale* .......... OR-9
Gasco—*uninc pl* .......... GA-3
Gasco—*uninc pl* .......... TX-5
Gascoigne Bluff—*cliff* .......... GA-3
**Gascola**—*pop pl* .......... PA-2
Gascon—*locale* .......... KY-4
Gascon—*locale* .......... NM-5
**Gasconade**—*pop pl* .......... MO-7
Gasconade Church Cem—*cemetery* .......... MO-7
*Gasconade City* .......... MO-7
**Gasconade County**—*pop pl* .......... MO-7
Gasconade River—*stream* .......... MO-7
*Gasconades Creek* .......... TX-5
Gasconades Creek—*stream* .......... TX-5
Gasconades Tank—*reservoir* .......... TX-5
Gasconade Township—*civil* .......... MO-7
**Gasconade Township**—*pop pl* .......... MO-7
Gascon Creek—*stream* .......... NC-3
**Gascondy**—*pop pl* .......... MO-7
Gascon Point—*cape* .......... NM-5
Gascon Trail (Pack)—*trail* .......... NM-5
Gascot—*locale* .......... AL-4
**Gascoyne**—*pop pl* .......... ND-7
Gascoyne Dam—*dam* .......... ND-7
Gascoyne Lake—*reservoir* .......... ND-7
Gascoyne Lake Dam—*dam* .......... ND-7
**Gascoyne Township**—*pop pl* .......... ND-7
Gascozark Hills Resort—*locale* .......... MO-7
Gas Creek—*stream* .......... AK-9
Gas Creek—*stream* .......... CA-9
Gas Creek—*stream* (2) .......... CO-8
Gas Creek—*stream* .......... TX-5
Gas Creek—*stream* .......... WY-8
Gas Creek Sch (reduced usage)—*school* .......... CO-8
Gas Draw—*valley* .......... WY-8
Gas Draw Oil Field—*oilfield* .......... WY-8
Gas Drum Flat—*flat* .......... CA-9
*Gaseburu* .......... PW-9
*Gaseburu Island* .......... PW-9
*Gaseway Creek* .......... TN-4
Gash, The—*valley* .......... CO-8
Gash Branch—*stream* .......... IN-6
Gash Canyon—*valley* .......... UT-8
Gash Cem—*cemetery* .......... IL-6
Gash Creek—*stream* .......... MT-8
Gash Creek—*stream* (2) .......... NC-3
Gashell Run—*stream* .......... WV-2
Gasher Brook—*stream* .......... NY-2
**Gashes Creek**—*pop pl* .......... NC-3
Gashes Creek—*stream* .......... NC-3
Gasheys Creek—*stream* .......... MD-2
Gash Flat—*flat* .......... AZ-5
Gas Hill Mine—*mine* .......... CA-9
**Gas Hills**—*pop pl* .......... WY-8
Gas Hills—*range* .......... WY-8
*Gashkosu To* .......... PW-9
*Gashland* .......... MO-7
**Gashland**—*pop pl* .......... MO-7
Gashland Ch—*church* .......... MO-7
Gash Mtn—*summit* .......... AZ-5
*Gashokosu* .......... PW-9
*Gashokuso To* .......... PW-9
Gas Hollow—*valley* .......... OH-6
Gas Hollow—*valley* .......... PA-2
Gashouse Cove—*bay* .......... CA-9
Gash Point—*summit* .......... MT-8
Gash Tank—*reservoir* .......... AZ-5
*Gaskan* .......... PW-9
Gaske Hill—*summit* .......... IL-6
Gaskell—*locale* .......... NV-8
*Gaskell Siding* .......... NV-8
Gaskell Slough—*stream* .......... WA-9
Gasket Cem—*cemetery* .......... KS-7
Gasket Lake—*lake* .......... MN-6
Gaskil—*locale* .......... CO-8
Gaskil Ch—*church* .......... IL-6
**Gaskill**—*pop pl* .......... KY-4
**Gaskill**—*pop pl* .......... NY-2
Gaskill Branch—*stream* .......... TN-4
Gaskill Bridge—*bridge* .......... IN-6
Gaskill Cem—*cemetery* .......... OH-6
Gaskill Cem—*cemetery* .......... TN-4
Gaskill Creek—*stream* (2) .......... MT-8
Gaskill (historical)—*locale* .......... KS-7
Gaskill House—*hist pl* .......... TN-4
Gaskill HS—*school* .......... NY-2
Gaskill Landing—*locale* .......... NC-3
Gaskill Peak—*summit* .......... CA-9
Gaskill Point—*cape* .......... NC-3
Gaskill Rsvr—*reservoir* .......... MT-8
**Gaskill (Township of)**—*pop pl* .......... PA-2
**Gaskin**—*pop pl* .......... FL-3
Gaskin Bay—*bay* .......... FL-3
Gaskin Branch—*stream* .......... FL-3
Gaskin Branch—*stream* .......... NJ-2
Gaskin Chapel—*church* .......... VA-3
Gaskin Field—*park* .......... MA-1
Gaskin Lake—*lake* .......... IL-6
Gaskin Lake—*lake* .......... MN-6
Gaskin Pond—*lake* .......... VA-3
**Gaskins**—*pop pl* .......... FL-3
Gaskins Branch—*stream* .......... LA-4
Gaskins Branch—*stream* .......... SC-3
Gaskins Camp—*locale* .......... KY-4
Gaskins Cem—*cemetery* .......... GA-3
Gaskins Cem—*cemetery* .......... NC-3
Gaskins Landing (historical)—*locale* .......... MS-4
Gaskins-Malany House—*hist pl* .......... OH-6
Gaskins Point—*cape* .......... VA-3
Gaskins Pond—*lake* .......... GA-3
Gaskin Springs Camp—*locale* .......... GA-3
Gaskins Run—*stream* .......... PA-2
Gaskins Sch—*school* .......... SC-3
**Gaskins Still**—*pop pl* .......... FL-3
Gaskins Switch Cem—*cemetery* .......... AR-4
Gaskin Still—*locale* .......... FL-3
Gaskin Wildlife Mngmt Area—*park* .......... FL-3
*Gas Lake* .......... WA-9
Gas Lake—*lake* .......... AK-9
Gas Lake—*reservoir* .......... KS-7
Gaslamp Quarter Hist Dist—*hist pl* .......... CA-9
Gasley Lake—*lake* .......... MI-6
Gaslight Mine (underground)—*mine* .......... AL-4
Gaslight Square—*locale* .......... MO-7
Gaslight Square Shop Ctr—*locale* .......... AZ-5
**Gas Light Village**—*pop pl* .......... IL-6
Gaslin—*fmr MCD* .......... NE-7
Gaslin Cem—*cemetery* .......... NE-7
Gas Line Tank—*reservoir* (2) .......... AZ-5
Gas Line Tank—*reservoir* .......... NM-5
Gas Line Trail—*trail* .......... PA-2
**Gaslyn**—*pop pl* .......... WI-6
Gaslyn Creek Sch—*school* .......... WI-6
Gaslyn Lake—*lake* .......... WI-6
**Gasman Township**—*pop pl* .......... ND-7
Gas Mine Ridge—*ridge* .......... CA-9
*Gasna Gora Sch* .......... MA-1
Gasna Gora Sch—*school* .......... MA-1
Gasner Hollow—*valley* .......... WI-6
Gasoline—*locale* .......... TX-5
Gasoline Alley—*locale* .......... CA-9
*Gasoline Curve* .......... CA-9
Gasoline Lake—*lake* .......... AK-9
Gasow Cem—*cemetery* .......... MN-6
Gaspar Bayou—*gut* .......... LA-4
Gaspard, D. Julius, House—*hist pl* .......... IA-7
Gaspard, Leon, House—*hist pl* .......... NM-5
Gaspard Creek—*stream* .......... VA-3
Gaspardo Creek—*stream* .......... WI-6
Gasparilla—*locale* .......... FL-3
Gasparilla Island—*island* .......... FL-3
Gasparilla Pass—*channel* .......... FL-3
Gasparilla Sound—*bay* .......... FL-3
Gaspar Inside Pond—*lake* .......... LA-4
Gaspar Island—*island* .......... LA-4
Gaspar Outside Pond—*gut* .......... LA-4
*Gaspar Rico* .......... MP-9
*Gaspar Rico Islands* .......... MP-9
Gaspars Dairy—*locale* .......... HI-9
*Gaspe* .......... AZ-5
*Gaspee Point* .......... RI-1
Gaspee Point—*cape* .......... RI-1
Gaspee Point—*hist pl* .......... RI-1
**Gasper**—*pop pl* .......... KY-4
Gasper Bay—*bay* .......... LA-4
Gasper Creek—*stream* .......... CA-9
Gasper Creek—*stream* .......... ID-8
Gasper Meadow—*flat* .......... CA-9
Gasper River—*stream* .......... KY-4
Gasper River (CCD)—*cens area* .......... KY-4
Gasper River Cem—*cemetery* .......... KY-4
Gaspers Creek—*stream* .......... LA-4
**Gasper (Township of)**—*pop pl* .......... OH-6
Gaspipe Spring—*spring* .......... CA-9
Gas Plant Camp—*locale* .......... WY-8
Gas Plant Lake—*lake* .......... AR-4
Gas Point—*locale* .......... CA-9
**Gasport**—*pop pl* .......... NY-2
Gas Post Office (historical)—*building* .......... TN-4
*Gasqua Chapel* .......... MS-4
Gasque—*locale* .......... AL-4
Gasque Chapel—*church* .......... MS-4
**Gasquet**—*pop pl* .......... CA-9
Gasquet Gulch—*valley* .......... CA-9
Gasquet Mtn—*summit* .......... CA-9
Gas Ridge Oil Field—*oilfield* .......... TX-5
Gas Rock—*island* .......... AK-9
Gas Rocks, The—*other* .......... AK-9
Gass—*locale* .......... GA-3
Gass, Lake—*lake* .......... FL-3
Gassabias Lake—*lake* .......... ME-1
Gassabias Stream—*stream* .......... ME-1
*Gassa Lake* .......... MN-6
**Gassaway**—*pop pl* .......... KY-4
**Gassaway**—*pop pl* .......... TN-4
**Gassaway**—*pop pl* .......... WV-2
Gassaway Branch—*stream* .......... IL-6
Gassaway Cem—*cemetery* .......... SC-3
Gassaway Ch—*church* .......... SC-3
Gassaway Ch of Christ—*church* .......... TN-4
Gassaway Creek—*stream* .......... TN-4
Gassaway Ferry (historical)—*locale* .......... MS-4
*Gassaway High School* .......... TN-4
*Gassaway Island* .......... MD-2
Gassaway Landing—*locale* .......... MS-4
Gassaway Post Office (historical)—*building* .......... TN-4
Gassaway Rsvr—*reservoir* .......... CA-9
Gassaway Sch—*school* .......... TN-4
*Gassaways Island* .......... MD-2
Gass Bridge Sch (historical)—*school* .......... TN-4
Gass Cem—*cemetery* .......... AR-4
Gass Cem—*cemetery* .......... GA-3
Gass Cem—*cemetery* .......... TN-4
Gass Creek—*stream* .......... ID-8
Gass Creek—*stream* .......... TN-4
Gassel Lake—*lake* .......... MI-6
Gassel Lodge—*locale* .......... MI-6
Gassel Oil Field—*oilfield* .......... KS-7
Gassenberg Spring—*spring* .......... CA-9
Gasser Park—*park* .......... MN-6
Gasser Point—*cape* .......... ID-8
Gasset Bluff—*cliff* .......... OR-9
**Gassett**—*pop pl* .......... AR-4
Gassett Cem—*cemetery* .......... AR-4
**Gassetts**—*pop pl* .......... VT-1
Gass Flat—*flat* .......... MT-8
Gass Gulch—*valley* .......... AK-9
Gass House—*hist pl* .......... PA-2
Gassick Cem—*cemetery* .......... GA-3
Gass Lake—*lake* .......... WI-6
Gassman Coulee—*valley* .......... ND-7
Gassman Creek—*stream* .......... AK-9
Gassmann Park—*park* .......... IL-6
Gassman Sch—*school* .......... SD-7
Gassman Township—*civil* .......... SD-7
Gass Memorial Ch—*church* .......... TN-4
Gassoway—*locale* .......... LA-4
Gassoway Branch—*stream* .......... AL-4
Gassoway Lake—*lake* .......... LA-4
Gass Peak—*summit* .......... NV-8
Gas Spring—*locale* .......... NY-2
Gas Spring—*spring* .......... CA-9
Gas Spur—*locale* .......... LA-4
Gass Spring—*spring* .......... NV-8
**Gassville**—*pop pl* .......... AR-4
Gassy Creek—*stream* .......... OR-9
Gast, Matthias, House and General Store—*hist pl* .......... OH-6
Gas Tank—*reservoir* .......... AZ-5
Gas Tank Wash—*stream* .......... NM-5
Gast Corner—*locale* .......... OH-6
Gast Ditch—*canal* (2) .......... IN-6
Gasten Beattie Well—*well* .......... ID-8
Gastens Branch—*stream* .......... TN-4
Gaster Hill—*summit* .......... AR-4
Gasters Creek—*stream* .......... NC-3
Gasteyer Sch—*school* .......... IL-6
Gastineau Channel—*channel* .......... AK-9
Gastineau Peak—*summit* .......... AK-9
Gastinel Canal—*canal* .......... LA-4
Gastis Creek—*stream* .......... LA-4
Gast Lake—*reservoir* .......... KS-7
Gast Mansion—*hist pl* .......... CO-8
Gaston—*locale* .......... AL-4
Gaston—*locale* .......... CA-9
**Gaston**—*pop pl* .......... AR-4
**Gaston**—*pop pl* .......... IN-6
**Gaston**—*pop pl* .......... MS-4
**Gaston**—*pop pl* .......... NC-3
**Gaston**—*pop pl* .......... OR-9
**Gaston**—*pop pl* .......... SC-3
**Gaston**—*pop pl* .......... WV-2
Gaston, Lake—*reservoir* .......... NC-3
Gaston, Lake—*reservoir* .......... VA-3
*Gaston Baptist Church* .......... MS-4
Gaston Bar—*bar* .......... AL-4
Gaston Bldg—*hist pl* .......... AL-4
Gaston Branch—*stream* .......... AL-4
Gaston Branch—*stream* .......... TX-5
**Gastonburg**—*pop pl* .......... AL-4
Gastonburg Cem—*cemetery* .......... AL-4
Gastonburg Ch—*church* .......... AL-4
Gaston Cave—*cave* .......... AL-4
Gaston Cave Spring—*spring* .......... AL-4
Gaston Cem—*cemetery* .......... AL-4
Gaston Cem—*cemetery* (2) .......... AR-4
Gaston Cem—*cemetery* .......... IL-6
Gaston Cem—*cemetery* (2) .......... MS-4
*Gaston Ch* .......... AL-4
Gaston Ch—*church* .......... AL-4
Gaston Ch—*church* .......... MS-4
Gaston Ch—*church* .......... NC-3
Gaston Chapel—*hist pl* .......... NC-3
*Gaston Chapel Church* .......... AL-4
Gaston Chapel Primitive Baptist Ch—*church* .......... AL-4
Gaston Coll—*school* .......... NC-3
Gaston Country Club Lake—*reservoir* .......... NC-3
Gaston Country Club Lake Dam—*dam* .......... NC-3
**Gaston County**—*pop pl* .......... NC-3
Gaston County Courthouse—*hist pl* .......... NC-3
Gaston County Farm Lake—*reservoir* .......... NC-3
Gaston County Farm Lake Dam—*dam* .......... NC-3
Gaston Creek—*stream* .......... TX-5
Gaston Dam—*dam* .......... NC-3
Gaston Day Sch—*school* .......... NC-3
Gaston Elem Sch—*school* .......... IN-6
Gaston Gulley—*arroyo* .......... AL-4
Gaston Hewes Recreation Center—*park* .......... MS-4
Gaston Hill—*summit* .......... IN-6
Gaston Hill Ch—*church* .......... AL-4
Gaston Hollow—*valley* .......... AL-4
Gaston Hosp—*hospital* .......... TX-5
Gaston HS—*school* .......... AL-4
Gastonia—*locale* .......... TX-5
**Gastonia**—*pop pl* .......... NC-3
*Gastonia Central Elementary School* .......... NC-3
Gastonia Country Club—*locale* .......... NC-3
**Gastonia East**—*pop pl* .......... NC-3
Gastonia HS—*hist pl* .......... NC-3
Gastonia Municipal Airp—*airport* .......... NC-3
Gastonia Municipal Golf Course—*locale* .......... NC-3
Gastonia Natl Golf Course—*locale* .......... NC-3
**Gastonia North**—*pop pl* .......... NC-3
Gastonia South (census name South Gastonia)—*other* .......... NC-3
Gastonia (Township of)—*fmr MCD* .......... NC-3
Gaston JHS—*school* .......... NC-3
Gaston JHS—*school* .......... TX-5
Gaston Junction—*locale* .......... WV-2
Gaston Lake—*reservoir* .......... AL-4
Gaston Lake Two—*reservoir* .......... AL-4
Gaston Landfill—*locale* .......... NC-3
Gaston Lookout Tower—*locale* .......... AR-4
Gaston Mall—*locale* .......... NC-3
Gaston Memorial Cem—*cemetery* .......... NC-3
Gaston Memorial Hosp—*hospital* .......... NC-3
**Gaston Mill**—*pop pl* .......... SC-3
Gaston Mine (Inactive)—*mine* .......... CA-9
Gaston Mountain—*ridge* .......... AR-4
Gaston Park—*park* .......... NC-3
Gaston Park—*park* .......... PA-2
Gaston Park—*park* .......... TN-4
Gaston-Perdue House—*hist pl* .......... AL-4
Gaston Point—*cape* .......... MS-4
Gaston Point Elem Sch—*school* .......... MS-4
*Gaston Pond* .......... TX-5
Gaston Pond—*reservoir* .......... MA-1
Gaston Pond Dam—*dam* .......... MA-1
Gaston Ridge—*ridge* .......... CA-9
Gaston Rsvr—*reservoir* .......... OR-9
Gaston Sch—*school* .......... NC-3
Gaston Sch—*school* .......... TX-5
Gaston Sch—*school* .......... WI-6
Gaston Sch (abandoned)—*school* .......... PA-2
Gaston Sch (historical)—*school* .......... MS-4
Gaston Sch (historical)—*school* .......... PA-2
Gaston Shoals—*rapids* .......... SC-3
Gaston's Mill-Lock No. 36, Sandy And Beaver Canal District—*hist pl* .......... OH-6
Gaston Spring—*spring* .......... CA-9
Gaston Springs Cem—*cemetery* .......... MS-4
Gaston Springs Ch—*church* .......... MS-4
Gaston Square Shop Ctr—*locale* .......... NC-3
Gaston Swamp—*swamp* .......... NC-3
Gaston (Township of)—*fmr MCD* .......... NC-3
Gaston Valley—*locale* .......... AL-4
Gaston Valley Ch—*church* .......... AL-4
**Gastonville**—*pop pl* .......... PA-2
Gastonville Elem Sch—*school* .......... PA-2
**Gastow**—*pop pl* .......... PA-2
**Gastown**—*pop pl* .......... PA-2
*Gasupan* .......... PW-9
*Gasville* .......... MS-4
Gasville—*locale* .......... OH-6
Gasville Sch—*school* .......... IL-6
Gas Well Hollow—*valley* .......... KY-4
Gas Well Hollow—*valley* (4) .......... PA-2
Gas Well Lilly Windmill—*locale* .......... TX-5
Gas Well No 12—*well* .......... AK-9
Gas Well No 14—*well* .......... AK-9
Gas Well No 3—*locale* .......... AK-9
Gas Well No 4—*well* .......... AK-9
Gaswell Trail—*trail* .......... PA-2
**Gas Works**—*pop pl* .......... OR-9
*Gata Creek* .......... CO-8
Gatagama Point—*cliff* .......... AZ-5
Gatagama Terrace—*bench* .......... AZ-5
Gata No 2 Rsvr—*reservoir* .......... WY-8
**Gatbraith**—*pop pl* .......... LA-4
*Gatchaparu* .......... FM-9
**Gatchel**—*pop pl* .......... IN-6
Gatchell, Kenneth, House—*hist pl* .......... MS-4
Gatchell Cem—*cemetery* .......... ME-1
*Gatchell Lake* .......... MN-6
Gatchellville—*locale* .......... PA-2
Gatchel Pond—*lake* .......... IN-6
Gatchen Creek—*stream* .......... CT-1
*Gatch Falls* .......... OR-9
Gatch Falls—*falls* .......... OR-9
*Gatchiyapuru* .......... FM-9
*Gatchrll* .......... IN-6
Gatch Site—*hist pl* .......... OH-6
*Gate* .......... AL-4
Gate—*locale* .......... WA-9
Gate—*locale* .......... WY-8
**Gate**—*pop pl* .......... OK-5
*Gate, The* .......... ME-1
Gate, The—*channel* .......... AK-9
Gate, The—*gap* .......... CA-9
Gate, The—*gap* (2) .......... CO-8
Gate, The—*locale* .......... AZ-5
Gate Bay—*bay* .......... FL-3
Gate Branch—*stream* .......... TN-4
*Gate Brook* .......... MA-1
Gate Camp—*locale* .......... LA-4
Gate Canyon—*valley* .......... NM-5
Gate Canyon—*valley* .......... UT-8
Gate Cem—*cemetery* .......... MA-1
Gate Cem—*cemetery* .......... OK-5
Gate Ch (historical)—*church* .......... AL-4
**Gate City**—*pop pl* .......... AL-4
**Gate City**—*pop pl* .......... VA-3
Gate City—*uninc pl* .......... GA-3
Gate City Cave—*cave* .......... AL-4
Gate City Natl Bank—*hist pl* .......... MO-7
Gate City Sch—*school* .......... AL-4
Gatecliff—*ridge* .......... NV-8
Gatecliff Rockshelter—*hist pl* .......... NV-8
*Gate Creek* .......... CO-8
Gate Creek—*stream* .......... AK-9
Gate Creek—*stream* .......... ID-8
Gate Creek—*stream* (2) .......... MT-8
Gate Creek—*stream* .......... NM-5
Gate Creek—*stream* (5) .......... OR-9
Gate Creek—*stream* (2) .......... WA-9
Gate Creek Campground—*locale* .......... WA-9
Gate Creek Forest Camp—*locale* .......... OR-9
Gate Creek Park—*park* .......... OR-9
Gate Creek Spring—*spring* .......... MT-8
Gate Creek Spring Number One—*spring* .......... MT-8
Gate Creek Spring Number Two—*spring* .......... MT-8
Gate Fork—*stream* .......... WV-2
Gate Gap—*gap* .......... TN-4
Gate Hill Brook—*stream* .......... MA-1
Gate Hollow—*valley* .......... KY-4
Gate Hollow—*valley* .......... TX-5
Gate Hollow—*valley* .......... WV-2
Gatehook Spring—*spring* .......... CO-8
Gatehouse at Colestown Cemetery—*hist pl* .......... NJ-2
Gatehouse on Deerhill Road—*hist pl* .......... NY-2
Gatehouse Pond—*lake* .......... NY-2
*Gate Island* .......... LA-4
Gate Island—*island* .......... AK-9
Gate Island—*island* .......... MA-1
Gate Lake—*lake* .......... CA-9
Gate Lake—*lake* .......... MT-8
Gate Lake—*reservoir* .......... OK-5
Gateley—*locale* .......... CA-9
Gatelot Ave Sch—*school* .......... NY-2
Gately Hill—*summit* .......... MA-1
Gately Stadium Park—*park* .......... IL-6
Gateman Ch—*church* .......... SC-3
Gate Mtn—*summit* .......... VA-3
Gate No 1—*other* .......... KY-4
Gate No 2—*other* .......... KY-4
Gate No 4—*other* .......... KY-4
Gate No 5—*other* .......... KY-4
Gate No 6—*other* .......... KY-4
Gate Number Eleven—*locale* .......... TN-4
Gate Number One—*locale* .......... TN-4
Gate Number Ten—*locale* .......... TN-4
Gate Number Three—*locale* .......... TN-4
Gate Number Two—*locale* .......... TN-4
Gate of Heaven Cem—*cemetery* .......... MD-2
Gate of Heaven Cem—*cemetery* .......... MI-6
Gate of Heaven Cem—*cemetery* (2) .......... NJ-2
Gate Of Heaven Cem—*cemetery* .......... NY-2
Gate of Heaven Cem—*cemetery* .......... NY-2
Gate Of heaven Cem—*cemetery* .......... NY-2
Gate Of Heaven Cem—*cemetery* .......... OH-6
Gate of Heaven Cem—*cemetery* .......... SC-3
*Gate of the Mountains* .......... MT-8
Gate Place (Site)—*locale* .......... CA-9
Gate Pond—*swamp* .......... AL-4
Gate Post Hill—*summit* .......... KY-4
Gate Post Hollow—*valley* .......... MO-7
Gater Cem—*cemetery* .......... IN-6
Gate Ridge—*ridge* (2) .......... VA-3
Gater Lake—*lake* .......... MS-4
*Gate Rock* .......... NE-7
Gate Rock—*pillar* .......... CO-8
*Gaters Church* .......... MS-4
Garers Sch (historical)—*school* .......... MS-4
Gate Run—*stream* .......... VA-3
*Gates* .......... MS-4
*Gates* .......... ND-7
Gates—*locale* .......... CA-9
Gates—*locale* .......... CO-8
Gates—*locale* .......... NE-7
Gates—*locale* .......... WV-2
**Gates**—*pop pl* .......... CA-9
**Gates**—*pop pl* .......... KY-4
**Gates**—*pop pl* .......... NY-2
**Gates**—*pop pl* .......... NC-3
**Gates**—*pop pl* .......... OR-9
**Gates**—*pop pl* .......... PA-2
**Gates**—*pop pl* .......... TN-4
Gates—*uninc pl* .......... NY-2
Gates—*uninc pl* .......... TX-5
Gates, Gen. Horatio, House, and Golden Plough Tavern—*hist pl* .......... PA-2
Gates, Holsey, House—*hist pl* .......... OH-6
Gates, J. M., House—*hist pl* .......... AZ-5
Gates, Judge Louis, House—*hist pl* .......... KS-7
Gates, Neil H., House—*hist pl* .......... AZ-5
Gates, The—*gap* .......... AK-9
Gates, The—*gap* .......... UT-8
Gates, The—*locale* .......... UT-8
Gates and Mullen Spring—*spring* .......... AZ-5
Gates Bay—*bay* .......... VA-3
Gates Branch—*stream* .......... GA-3
Gates Branch—*stream* .......... NJ-2
Gates Branch—*stream* (2) .......... TX-5
Gates Brook—*stream* (2) .......... MA-1
Gates Brook—*stream* .......... NH-1
**Gatesburg**—*pop pl* .......... PA-2
*Gatesburgh* .......... PA-2
Gatesburg Ridge—*ridge* .......... PA-2
Gates Butte—*summit* .......... WY-8
Gates Cabin—*locale* .......... CA-9
Gates Cabin Tank—*reservoir* .......... AZ-5
Gates Camp—*locale* .......... CO-8
Gates Canal—*canal* .......... CA-9
Gates Canyon—*valley* (3) .......... CA-9
Gates Canyon—*valley* .......... UT-8
Gates (CCD)—*cens area* .......... TN-4
Gates Cem—*cemetery* .......... AL-4
Gates Cem—*cemetery* .......... CT-1
Gates Cem—*cemetery* .......... MS-4
Gates Cem—*cemetery* .......... NE-7
Gates Cem—*cemetery* .......... OH-6
Gates Cem—*cemetery* .......... OR-9
Gates Cem—*cemetery* (2) .......... TN-4
Gates Cem—*cemetery* .......... TX-5
Gates Cem—*cemetery* (2) .......... VT-1
**Gates Center**—*pop pl* .......... NY-2
Gates Ch—*church* .......... NC-3
Gates Channel—*channel* .......... VA-3
Gates Chapel—*church* .......... GA-3
Gates Chapel Sch (historical)—*school* .......... MS-4
Gates-Chili HS—*school* .......... NY-2
Gates-Chili JHS—*school* .......... NY-2
Gates Circle—*locale* .......... NY-2
Gates Coll—*school* .......... IA-7
Gates College Gymnasium—*hist pl* .......... NE-7
*Gates Corner* .......... NH-1
Gates Corner—*locale* (2) .......... MN-6
**Gates Corner**—*pop pl* (2) .......... IN-6
**Gates Corner**—*pop pl* .......... NH-1
Gates Corners—*locale* (2) .......... NY-2
**Gates County**—*pop pl* .......... NC-3
Gates County Courthouse—*hist pl* .......... NC-3
Gates Cove—*cove* .......... MA-1
*Gates Creek* .......... NY-2
Gates Creek—*stream* (3) .......... CA-9
Gates Creek—*stream* .......... FL-3
Gates Creek—*stream* .......... ID-8
Gates Creek—*stream* .......... MI-6
Gates Creek—*stream* .......... MT-8
Gates Creek—*stream* .......... NY-2
Gates Creek—*stream* .......... OK-5
Gates Creek—*stream* .......... OR-9
Gates Creek—*stream* .......... TN-4
Gates Creek—*stream* .......... UT-8
Gates Creek—*stream* .......... WY-8
**Gates Crossing**—*pop pl* .......... MA-1
Gates-Daves House—*hist pl* .......... AL-4
Gates Ditch—*canal* (2) .......... IN-6
Gates Division—*civil* .......... TN-4
*Gates Drain* .......... MI-6
Gates Drain—*canal* .......... MI-6
Gates Draw—*valley* .......... UT-8
Gates Draw—*valley* .......... WY-8
Gates Extension Drain—*stream* .......... MI-6
Gates Farm Covered Bridge—*hist pl* .......... VT-1
Gates Ford—*locale* .......... TN-4
Gates Ford Branch—*stream* .......... SC-3
Gates-Fourth Ch—*church* .......... OH-6
Gates Glacier—*glacier* .......... AK-9
Gates Guard Station—*locale* .......... OR-9
Gates Gulch—*valley* .......... WA-9
Gates Hill—*summit* .......... CT-1
Gates Hill—*summit* .......... ME-1
Gates Hill—*summit* .......... MA-1
Gates Hill—*summit* (2) .......... NY-2
Gates Hill—*summit* .......... PA-2
Gates Hill—*summit* .......... VT-1
Gates Hill—*summit* .......... WI-6
Gates Hill Ch—*church* .......... NY-2
Gates Hollow—*valley* .......... OH-6
Gates Hollow—*valley* .......... PA-2
Gates Hollow—*valley* .......... VA-3
Gates Hosp—*hospital* .......... OH-6
Gates House—*hist pl* .......... ME-1
Gates Island—*island* .......... AR-4
Gates Island—*island* .......... CT-1
Gates Island—*island* .......... ME-1
Gates-Jones Canal—*canal* .......... CA-9
Gates Lake—*lake* .......... MT-8
Gates Lake—*lake* (3) .......... WI-6
Gates Lake—*reservoir* .......... UT-8
Gates Lane Sch—*school* .......... MA-1
Gates Meadow—*flat* .......... PA-2
Gates Memorial Library—*hist pl* .......... TX-5
Gates Mill (historical)—*locale* .......... AL-4
*Gates Mills* .......... PA-2
**Gates Mills**—*pop pl* .......... OH-6
Gates Mills Methodist Episcopal Church—*hist pl* .......... OH-6
Gates Mtn—*summit* .......... NH-1
Gates-North-Gates—*CDP* .......... NY-2
Gates of Heaven Cem—*cemetery* .......... AL-4
Gates of Heaven Congregation Synagogue (historical)—*church* .......... AL-4
Gates of Heaven Memorial Cem—*cemetery* .......... TX-5
Gates of Heaven Memorial Park—*cemetery* .......... NJ-2
Gates of Lodore—*gap* .......... CO-8
Gates of Peace Cem—*cemetery* .......... MO-7
Gates of the Antipodes—*other* .......... CA-9
Gates of the Arctic—*other* .......... AK-9
Gates of the Artic Natl Park—*park* .......... AK-9
*Gates of the Mountains* .......... MT-8
Gates of the Mountains Interchange—*other* .......... MT-8
Gates of the Rocky Mountains—*gap* .......... MT-8
Gates Park—*flat* .......... MT-8
Gates Park—*park* .......... IA-7
Gates Park—*park* .......... PA-2
Gates Park—*park* .......... TX-5
Gates Park Guard Station—*locale* .......... MT-8
Gates Pass—*gap* .......... AZ-5
*Gates Pond* .......... MA-1
Gates Pond—*lake* .......... CT-1
Gates Pond—*lake* .......... VT-1
Gates Pond—*reservoir* .......... MA-1
Gates Pond—*reservoir* .......... OR-9
Gates Pond Brook—*stream* .......... MA-1
Gates Post Office—*building* .......... TN-4
Gate Spring—*spring* .......... AZ-5
Gate Spring—*spring* .......... OR-9
Gate Spring Canyon—*valley* .......... OR-9
Gates Ridge—*ridge* .......... WV-2
Gates Ridge Ch—*church* .......... WV-2
Gates Road Ch—*church* .......... MS-4
Gates Run—*stream* .......... PA-2
Gates Saint Sch—*school* .......... CA-9
Gates Sch—*school* .......... CA-9
Gates Sch—*school* .......... ME-1
Gates Sch—*school* .......... MI-6
Gates Sch—*school* .......... MS-4
Gates Sch—*school* .......... OH-6
Gates Sch—*school* .......... TX-5

Gates Sch—*school* ... WI-6
Gates Sch (historical)—*school* ... MO-7
Gates Sch (historical)—*school* ... TN-4
Gates Spring—*spring* ... AZ-5
Gates Spring—*spring* (2) ... UT-8
Gates Spring—*spring* ... WA-9
Gates Substation—*other* ... CA-9
Gates Tank—*reservoir* ... AZ-5
Gates Tank—*reservoir* ... UT-8
**Gates (Town of)**—*pop pl* ... NY-2
**Gates Township**—*pop pl* ... ND-7
Gatesville—*locale* ... KY-4
Gatesville—*locale* ... MS-4
**Gatesville**—*pop pl* ... IN-6
**Gatesville**—*pop pl* ... IA-7
**Gatesville**—*pop pl* ... NC-3
**Gatesville**—*pop pl* ... TX-5
Gatesville Bridge—*bridge* ... MS-4
Gatesville Bridge—*hist pl* ... MS-4
Gatesville (CCD)—*cens area* ... TX-5
Gatesville Elem Sch—*school* ... NC-3
Gatesville (historical)—*locale* ... AL-4
Gatesville (historical)—*locale* ... KS-7
Gatesville State Sch for Boys—*school* ... TX-5
Gatesville (Township of)—*fmr MCD* ... NC-3
Gate Swamp—*swamp* ... NH-1
Gates Williams Windmill—*locale* ... TX-5
Gateswood—*locale* ... AL-4
Gate Tank—*reservoir* ... NM-5
Gate Tank—*reservoir* ... TX-5
**Gate Township**—*pop pl* ... ND-7
Gate Valley—*basin* ... NE-7
Gateview—*locale* ... CO-8
Gateway—*locale* ... CO-8
Gateway—*locale* ... MO-7
Gateway—*locale* ... MT-8
Gateway—*locale* ... NC-3
Gateway—*locale* ... ND-7
Gateway—*locale* ... UT-8
**Gateway**—*pop pl* ... AR-4
**Gateway**—*pop pl* ... CA-9
**Gateway**—*pop pl* ... OR-9
Gateway—*post sta* ... CO-8
Gateway—*post sta* ... GA-3
Gateway—*post sta* ... MO-7
Gateway—*post sta* ... OH-6
Gateway—*uninc pl* ... CA-9
Gateway, The—*gap* ... AK-9
Gateway, The—*gap* ... CA-9
Gateway Arch—*hist pl* ... MO-7
Gateway Arch—*other* ... MO-7
Gateway Army Ammun Plant—*military* ... MO-7
Gateway Baptist Ch—*church* (2) ... FL-3
Gateway Baptist Ch—*church* ... MS-4
Gateway Bridge—*bridge* ... TX-5
Gateway Cabin—*locale* ... MT-8
Gateway Canal—*canal* ... UT-8
*Gateway Canyon* ... AZ-5
Gateway Canyon—*valley* ... CO-8
Gateway Center—*building* ... PA-2
Gateway Center Station—*building* ... PA-2
Gateway Ch—*church* ... FL-3
Gateway Ch—*church* ... GA-3
Gateway Ch—*church* ... IN-6
Gateway Ch—*church* ... MO-7
Gateway Ch—*church* (2) ... TN-4
Gateway Ch—*church* ... TX-5
Gateway Christian Elem Sch—*school* ... FL-3
Gateway Clipper Fleet Dock—*locale* ... PA-2
**Gateway Condominium**—*pop pl* ... UT-8
Gateway Cove—*bay* ... AZ-5
Gateway Creek—*stream* ... MT-8
*Gateway Drive* ... MO-7
**Gateway Drive**—*pop pl* ... MO-7
Gateway Elem Sch—*school* ... FL-3
**Gateway Farms**—*pop pl* ... DE-2
**Gateway (Gateway Park)**—*pop pl* ... CA-9
Gateway Gorge—*gap* ... MT-8
Gateway Greens—*locale* ... PA-2
Gateway HS—*school* ... FL-3
Gateway HS—*school* ... PA-2
*Gateway Interchange* ... PA-2
Gateway JHS—*school* ... PA-2
Gateway Junior Acad—*school* ... FL-3
Gateway Knob—*island* ... AK-9
Gateway Lake—*reservoir* ... AL-4
Gateway Lake Dam—*dam* ... AL-4
Gateway Lodge—*locale* ... AK-9
Gateway Mall—*post sta* ... FL-3
Gateway Mall (Shop Ctr)—*locale* ... ND-7
Gateway Natl Rec Area—*park* ... NJ-2
Gateway Natl Rec Area—*park* ... NY-2
Gateway Natl Rec Area(Also NJ)—*park* ... NY-2
Gateway Natl Rec Area(Also NY)—*park* ... NJ-2
**Gateway North (subdivision)**—*pop pl* ... MS-4
Gateway Park—*park* ... CA-9
Gateway Park—*park* ... FL-3
Gateway Park—*park* ... IA-7
Gateway Park—*park* ... MI-6
Gateway Park—*park* ... OR-9
*Gateway Pass* ... MT-8
Gateway Pass—*gap* ... MT-8
Gateway Peak—*summit* ... ID-8
Gateway Plaza—*locale* ... PA-2
Gateway Plaza (Shop Ctr)—*locale* ... FL-3
Gateway Plaze Hosp—*hospital* ... FL-3
*Gateway Point* ... MT-8
Gateway Points—*summit* ... MT-8
Gateway Rapids—*rapids* ... AZ-5
Gateway Regional HS—*school* ... MA-1
Gateway Regional HS—*school* ... NJ-2
Gateway Sch—*school* ... CA-9
Gateway Sch—*school* ... TN-4
Gateway Sch—*school* ... TX-5
Gateway Shop Ctr—*locale* ... AL-4
Gateway Shop Ctr—*locale* (3) ... FL-3
Gateway Shop Ctr—*locale* ... MA-1
Gateway Shop Ctr—*locale* ... MS-4
Gateway Shop Ctr—*locale* (2) ... NC-3
Gateway Shop Ctr—*locale* ... PA-2
Gateway Shopping Plaza—*locale* ... MA-1
*Gateway Spring* ... WA-9
Gateway Tabernacle—*church* ... NC-3
**Gateway Terrace**—*pop pl* ... TX-5
Gateway to the Narrows Trail—*hist pl* ... UT-8
Gateway to the Narrows Trail—*trail* ... UT-8
Gateway Trailer Park—*park* ... UT-8
Gateway Tunnel—*tunnel* ... UT-8
Gateway Upper Elem Sch—*school* ... PA-2
Gateway Vocational-Technical Sch—*school* ... AR-4
*Gatewood* ... IN-6
Gatewood—*hist pl* ... OH-6
Gatewood—*locale* ... GA-3
Gatewood—*locale* ... KY-4
Gatewood—*locale* ... MS-4
Gatewood—*locale* ... VA-3
**Gatewood**—*pop pl* ... MO-7
**Gatewood**—*pop pl* ... NC-3
**Gatewood**—*pop pl* ... TN-4
**Gatewood**—*pop pl* ... TX-5
**Gatewood**—*pop pl* ... WV-2
Gatewood Acad—*school* ... GA-3
*Gatewood Branch* ... WV-2
Gatewood Bridge—*bridge* ... TN-4
Gatewood Canyon—*valley* ... AZ-5
Gatewood Cem—*cemetery* (2) ... MS-4
Gatewood Cem—*cemetery* ... VA-3
Gatewood Ch—*church* (2) ... MS-4
*Gatewood Ch of God* ... MS-4
**Gatewood Condo**—*pop pl* ... UT-8
Gatewood Family Cem—*cemetery* ... MS-4
Gatewood (historical)—*locale* ... MS-4
*Gatewood Hollow* ... VA-3
Gatewood House—*hist pl* ... GA-3
**Gatewood Housing**—*pop pl* ... AZ-5
Gatewood Lookout Tower—*locale* ... WV-2
Gatewood Oil Field—*oilfield* ... TX-5
**Gatewood Park**—*pop pl* ... VA-3
Gatewood Rsvr—*reservoir* ... VA-3
Gatewood Sch—*school* ... OK-5
Gatewood Sch—*school* ... TN-4
Gatewood Sch—*school* ... VA-3
Gatewood Sch—*school* ... WA-9
Gatewood Station Ch—*church* ... NC-3
**Gatewood (subdivision)**—*pop pl* ... NC-3
Gatewood Township—*civil* ... MO-7
**Gatex**—*pop pl* ... UT-8
*Gatgug Entrance* ... FM-9
Gath—*locale* ... TN-4
**Gath**—*pop pl* ... OH-6
Gatham Bend—*bend* ... TN-4
Gath Baptist Ch—*church* ... TN-4
Gath Branch—*stream* ... TN-4
Gathel Spring—*spring* ... TN-4
Gatherer Rock—*bar* ... AK-9
**Gather (historical)**—*pop pl* ... NC-3
Gather Hollow—*valley* ... AR-4
Gathers Run—*stream* ... PA-2
Gath Post Office (historical)—*building* ... TN-4
Gathright Branch—*stream* ... KY-4
Gathright Hill—*summit* ... KY-4
Gathwright Institute (historical)—*school* ... MS-4
Gatia Point—*cape* ... AS-9
Gatiffi State Fish Hatchery—*other* ... KY-4
Gatignole, Eugenio, House—*hist pl* ... NM-5
*Gatimoon* ... FM-9
Gatin Hollow—*valley* ... TN-4
*Gatjalau* ... FM-9
*Gatjapar* ... FM-9
*Gatjug Entrance* ... FM-9
Gatlena Gap—*gap* ... AK-9
Gatlen Cem—*cemetery* ... AR-4
Gatley Cem—*cemetery* ... TN-4
**Gatliff**—*pop pl* ... KY-4
**Gatliff**—*pop pl* ... WI-6
Gatliff, Dr. Ancil, House—*hist pl* ... KY-4
Gatliff, J. B., House—*hist pl* ... KY-4
Gatliff Cem—*cemetery* ... IA-7
Gatliff Lookout Tower—*locale* ... KY-4
*Gatliff Post Office* ... TN-4
*Gatlin* ... MS-4
Gatlin, Lake—*lake* ... FL-3
Gatlin Beach—*beach* ... NC-3
Gatlin Branch—*stream* ... TN-4
Gatlin Branch—*stream* ... TX-5
**Gatlinburg**—*pop pl* ... TN-4
Gatlinburg (CCD)—*cens area* ... TN-4
Gatlinburg City Dump—*locale* ... TN-4
Gatlinburg Division—*civil* ... TN-4
Gatlinburg Golf Course—*locale* ... TN-4
*Gatlinburgh* ... TN-4
Gatlinburg-Pittman HS—*school* ... TN-4
Gatlin Canyon—*valley* ... NM-5
Gatlin Cem—*cemetery* ... AL-4
Gatlin Cem—*cemetery* ... AZ-5
Gatlin Cem—*cemetery* ... AR-4
Gatlin Cem—*cemetery* ... GA-3
Gatlin Cem—*cemetery* (2) ... LA-4
Gatlin Cem—*cemetery* ... MS-4
Gatlin Cem—*cemetery* (3) ... TN-4
Gatlin Cem—*cemetery* ... TX-5
Gatlin Creek—*stream* ... NC-3
Gatlin Creek—*stream* ... TX-5
Gatlin Creek Sch—*school* ... NC-3
*Gatlin Crossing* ... MS-4
Gatlin Gabel HS—*school* ... OR-9
Gatling Branch—*stream* ... GA-3
Gatling Branch—*stream* ... IL-6
Gatling Creek—*stream* ... MS-4
Gatling Point—*cape* ... VA-3
*Gatling Spring* ... TN-4
Gatlington Landing—*locale* ... NC-3
Gatlin Gulch—*valley* ... MT-8
Gatlin Island—*island* ... TX-5
Gatlin Lake—*reservoir* ... NM-5
Gatlin Mine—*mine* ... MT-8
Gatlin Point Lake Access—*park* ... TN-4
Gatlin Ranch—*locale* ... AZ-5
Gatlin Ranch (reduced usage)—*locale* ... TX-5
Gatlin Sch—*school* ... OK-5
Gatlin Sch (historical)—*school* ... MS-4
Gatlin Site—*hist pl* ... AZ-5
Gatlin Waterhole—*spring* ... CO-8
Gatman Lake—*lake* ... UT-8
Gatman (RR name for Gattman)—*other* ... MS-4
*Gatmon* ... FM-9
*Gatmoon* ... FM-9
*Gato* ... CO-8
Gato—*locale* ... CA-9
**Gato**—*pop pl* ... CO-8
Gato, Arroyo del—*valley* ... TX-5
Gato, Canada Del —*valley* ... CA-9
Gato, Eduardo H., House—*hist pl* ... FL-3
Gato, Loma del—*summit* ... TX-5
Gato, Ojo—*spring* ... AZ-5
Gato, Rito—*stream* ... CO-8
Gato Arroyo—*valley* ... TX-5
Gato (Barrio)—*fmr MCD* ... PR-3
Gato Canyon—*valley* ... CA-9
Gato Canyon—*valley* (2) ... NM-5
*Gato Creek* ... CO-8
*Gato Creek* ... TX-5
Gato Creek—*stream* (3) ... TX-5
Gato Lake—*lake* ... WI-6
*Gatomel* ... PW-9
Gato-Montes, Canyon Del—*valley* ... CA-9
Gato Point—*summit* ... NM-5
Gato Quarry—*mine* ... TX-5
Gator Bay—*cove* ... FL-3
Gator Bay Branch—*gut* ... FL-3
Gator Bay Canal—*canal* ... FL-3
Gator Bay Prairie—*flat* ... FL-3
Gator Bowl—*locale* ... FL-3
*Gator Branch* ... NC-3
Gator Branch—*gut* ... FL-3
Gator Branch—*stream* ... FL-3
Gator Branch—*stream* ... GA-3
Gator Branch—*stream* (2) ... MS-4
Gator Creek—*gut* ... FL-3
Gator Creek—*stream* (4) ... FL-3
Gator Creek—*stream* ... GA-3
Gator Gap—*gap* ... FL-3
Gator Head—*swamp* ... FL-3
Gator Head—*swamp* ... GA-3
Gator Head Pond—*lake* ... GA-3
Gator Hole—*basin* ... FL-3
Gator Hole—*bay* (2) ... FL-3
Gator Hole—*gut* ... LA-4
Gator Hole—*swamp* ... FL-3
Gator Hole Pond—*reservoir* ... MS-4
Gator Holes—*lake* ... SC-3
Gator Hole Slough—*swamp* ... FL-3
Gator Hook Strand—*swamp* ... FL-3
Gator Hook Swamp—*swamp* ... FL-3
Gato Ridge—*ridge* ... CA-9
*Gato Ridge Oil Field* ... CA-9
Gator Island—*island* ... FL-3
Gator Lake—*lake* ... AL-4
Gator Lake—*lake* (5) ... FL-3
Gator Lake—*lake* (2) ... GA-3
Gator Lake—*lake* ... MS-4
Gator Lake—*lake* ... SC-3
Gator Plaza (Shop Ctr)—*locale* ... FL-3
Gator Point—*cape* ... FL-3
Gator Point Campground—*locale* ... TN-4
*Gator Pond* ... FL-3
Gator Pond—*lake* (3) ... FL-3
Gator Pond—*lake* ... SC-3
Gator Pond—*lake* ... TX-5
Gator Pond—*swamp* ... FL-3
Gator Slide—*swamp* ... GA-3
Gator Slough—*gut* ... FL-3
Gator Slough—*gut* ... GA-3
Gator Slough—*stream* ... FL-3
Gator Slough—*swamp* ... FL-3
Gator Slough Canal—*canal* ... FL-3
Gator Wallow—*swamp* ... GA-3
Gato Tank—*reservoir* ... AZ-5
Gato Tank—*reservoir* ... TX-5
Gato Trail—*trail* ... CA-9
Gato Windmill—*locale* (2) ... TX-5
*Gatschapa* ... FM-9
*Gatschapar* ... FM-9
Gatson Bay—*swamp* ... SC-3
*Gatsuereru To* ... PW-9
*Gatsugu-Ko* ... FM-9
*Gatsugu-Kuchi* ... FM-9
*Gatsumeru* ... PW-9
*Gatsumudokku* ... PW-9
*Gatsureru To* ... PW-9
Gatte Cem—*cemetery* ... LA-4
Gatten Lake—*lake* ... ND-7
Gattin Ranch—*locale* ... ID-8
Gattis Cem—*cemetery* ... TN-4
Gattis Creek—*stream* ... AR-4
Gattis Creek—*stream* ... TN-4
Gattistown—*locale* ... TN-4
Gattistown Branch—*stream* ... TN-4
Gattling Creek—*stream* ... TX-5
**Gattman**—*pop pl* ... MS-4
Gattman Baptist Ch—*church* ... MS-4
*Gattman Holiness Ch* ... MS-4
**Gattman (RR name Gatman)**—*pop pl* ... MS-4
Gattman United Methodist Ch—*church* ... MS-4
Gatton—*other* ... KY-4
Gatton Creek—*stream* ... WA-9
Gatton Rock—*locale* ... OH-6
Gattons Park—*flat* ... NM-5
Gatts Corner—*locale* ... MD-2
Gatts Ridge—*ridge* ... WV-2
**Gatun**—*pop pl* ... KY-4
Gatuna Canyon—*valley* ... NM-5
Gatuna Wash—*stream* ... CA-9
Gatun Pond—*reservoir* ... NJ-2
**Gatzke**—*pop pl* ... MN-6
*Gatzki* ... MN-6
Gatzmer—*locale* ... WV-2
Gaubert Cem—*cemetery* ... ME-1
Gauble Sch—*school* ... IL-6
Gauche, Bayou—*channel* ... LA-4
Gauco Pond—*reservoir* ... MA-1
Gauco Pond Dam—*dam* ... MA-1
Gaudette Brook—*stream* ... VT-1
Gaudette Tote Road—*trail* ... VT-1
*Gaudichand Island* ... FM-9
Gaudin, Bayou—*gut* ... LA-4
Gaudineer Knob—*summit* ... WV-2
Gaudineer Scenic Area—*park* ... WV-2
Gaudineer Sch—*school* ... NJ-2
Gaudin Lateral—*canal* ... NM-5
Gaud School Playground—*park* ... SC-3
Gauer Sch—*school* ... CA-9
**Gauff Hill**—*pop pl* ... PA-2
Gauff-Roth House—*hist pl* ... PA-2
*Gaugan* ... MH-9
Gauge Island—*island* ... AK-9
Gaughan Spring—*spring* ... OR-9
Gaugh Cem—*cemetery* ... KY-4
Gaughen Township (historical)—*civil* ... SD-7
Gaughf Sch (historical)—*school* ... MS-4
*Gauilan Wash* ... CA-9
*Gauke Hammock Island* ... GA-3
Gaukler Point—*cape* ... MI-6
Gaul, The—*stream* ... SC-3
Gaulden Branch—*stream* ... TN-4
Gaulden Cem—*cemetery* ... MS-4
Gauldin Cem—*cemetery* ... TN-4
Gaulding Cem—*cemetery* ... MO-7
Gauldin Sch—*school* ... CA-9
**Gauldinville**—*pop pl* ... AL-4
Gauldy, Mount—*summit* ... OR-9
Gauldy Ridge—*ridge* ... OR-9
*Gaule Mountain* ... WV-2
Gauler, John, Houses—*hist pl* ... IL-6
Gaulett—*locale* ... AR-4
Gauley—*locale* ... WV-2
Gauley Branch—*stream* (2) ... KY-4
**Gauley Bridge**—*pop pl* ... WV-2
Gauley Bridge RR Station—*hist pl* ... WV-2
Gauley Cem—*cemetery* ... MS-4
Gauley Divide—*ridge* ... WV-2
Gauley Mill (RR name for Gauley Mills)—*other* ... WV-2
**Gauley Mills**—*pop pl* ... WV-2
**Gauley Mills (RR name Gauley Mill)**—*pop pl* ... WV-2
Gauley Mountain—*ridge* ... WV-2
Gauley Mountain Lookout Tower—*locale* ... WV-2
Gauley Mountain Trail—*trail* ... WV-2
Gauley Mtn—*summit* ... WV-2
Gauley Ranger Station—*locale* ... WV-2
Gauley Ridge—*ridge* (2) ... VA-3
Gauley River—*stream* ... WV-2
Gaulin, Alphonse, Jr., House—*hist pl* ... RI-1
Gault—*other* ... MS-4
**Gault**—*pop pl* ... KY-4
Gault Branch—*stream* ... AR-4
Gault Branch—*stream* ... MS-4
Gault Creek—*stream* ... OH-6
Gault Creek—*stream* ... SC-3
*Gault Dam* ... AL-4
*Gault Ditch* ... IN-6
Gault Ditch—*canal* ... IN-6
Gault Hill—*summit* ... PA-2
Gault Hollow—*valley* (2) ... WI-6
Gault Lake—*reservoir* ... AL-4
Gault Lake Dam—*dam* ... AL-4
Gault Sch—*school* ... CA-9
Gault Sch (abandoned)—*school* ... PA-2
Gault Sch (historical)—*school* ... PA-2
Gault Street Sch—*school* ... CA-9
Gault Tank—*reservoir* ... TX-5
Gaum Canyon—*valley* ... CO-8
Gaume Windmill—*locale* ... NM-5
*Gaunce Creek* ... NV-8
*Gauney Cem* ... TN-4
Gaunt, Thomas, House—*hist pl* ... MO-7
Gaunt Cem—*cemetery* ... TN-4
Gaunt Creek—*stream* ... MN-6
Gaunt Ford (historical)—*locale* ... MO-7
Gaunt Hill—*summit* ... TN-4
Gaunt Lake—*lake* ... NE-7
Gauntlet Brook—*stream* ... ME-1
Gauntlet Falls—*falls* ... ME-1
Gauntlet Island—*island* ... AK-9
Gauntlet Pond—*lake* ... ME-1
Gaunt Park—*park* ... OH-6
Gaunt Point—*cape* ... NJ-2
Gaunts Brook—*stream* ... NJ-2
Gauntts Mill (historical)—*locale* ... AL-4
*Gauose Mountain* ... WA-9
Gaus Cem—*cemetery* ... MO-7
Gausdal Ch—*church* ... MN-6
Gausdale—*locale* ... KY-4
Gause—*locale* ... TN-4
**Gause**—*pop pl* ... TX-5
*Gause Beach* ... NC-3
Gause Cem—*cemetery* ... FL-3
Gause Cem—*cemetery* (2) ... SC-3
*Gause Island* ... FL-3
Gause Landing—*locale* ... NC-3
Gause-Milano (CCD)—*cens area* ... TX-5
Gause Sch (historical)—*school* ... TN-4
*Gaussburg* ... TN-4
Gauss Cem—*cemetery* ... LA-4
Gaussion Canyon—*valley* ... CO-8
Gautali River—*stream* ... GU-9
*Gautam the Buddha Creek* ... OR-9
Gautche Point—*cape* ... CA-9
Gautche Springs—*spring* ... CA-9
*Gaut Creek* ... OR-9
Gauthier Creek—*stream* ... MI-6
Gauthier Creek—*stream* ... MN-6
Gauthier Hill—*summit* ... ME-1
Gauthier Pond—*bay* ... LA-4
**Gautier**—*pop pl* ... MS-4
Gautier Bridge—*bridge* ... CA-9
Gautier Ch of Christ—*church* ... MS-4
Gautier Christian Sch—*school* ... MS-4
Gautier Elem Sch—*school* ... MS-4
Gautier JHS—*school* ... MS-4
Gautier Plaza Shop Ctr—*locale* ... MS-4
Gautier Public Library—*building* ... MS-4
Gautier United Methodist Ch—*church* ... MS-4
Gauzley Bayou—*stream* ... AR-4
Gavan Hill—*summit* ... AK-9
*Gavens Point Dam* ... NE-7
*Gavens Point Dam* ... SD-7
Gavers—*locale* ... OH-6
**Gave Spring**—*pop pl* ... AL-4
Gavett Creek—*stream* ... TX-5
Gavettes Brook—*stream* ... NY-2
Gavettes Mtn—*summit* ... NY-2
*Gavetts Branch* ... NY-2
Gavia Lake—*lake* ... AK-9
*Gavica Fork Willow Creek* ... NV-8
Gavilan—*locale* ... NM-5
Gavilan, Mesa del—*summit* ... TX-5
Gavilan Arroyo—*stream* ... NM-5
Gavilan Canyon—*valley* ... AZ-5
Gavilan Canyon—*valley* (3) ... NM-5
Gavilan Creek—*stream* (2) ... NM-5
Gavilan Ditch—*canal* ... NM-5
Gavilan Junior Coll—*school* ... CA-9
Gavilan Lake—*reservoir* ... NM-5
Gavilan Mesa—*summit* ... NM-5
Gavilan Mine—*mine* ... CA-9
Gavilan Mine—*mine* ... NM-5
Gavilan Mtn—*summit* ... CA-9
*Gavilan Peak* ... CA-9
Gavilan Peak—*summit* (2) ... AZ-5
Gavilan Peak—*summit* ... CA-9
Gavilan Plateau—*plain* ... CA-9
*Gavilan Range* ... CA-9
Gavilan Ridge—*ridge* ... CA-9
Gavilan Ridge—*ridge* (2) ... NM-5
Gavilan Rock—*pillar* ... CA-9
Gavilan Springs Ranch—*locale* ... CA-9
Gavilan Tank—*reservoir* ... NM-5
Gavilan (Tapicitoes Post Office)—*locale* ... NM-5
Gavilan Wash—*stream* ... CA-9
Gavilan Well—*well* ... TX-5
Gavilan Windmill—*locale* ... TX-5
Gavin—*locale* ... AR-4
Gavina Ridge—*ridge* ... TX-5
Gavin Canyon—*valley* ... CA-9
Gavin Coulee—*valley* ... WI-6
Gavin Gulch—*valley* ... CO-8
Gavin Lake—*lake* ... MI-6
Gavin Lake—*lake* ... MS-4
Gavin Ranch—*locale* ... UT-8
Gavin Siding—*locale* ... NE-7
Gavins Point—*cape* ... SD-7
Gavins Point Dam—*dam* ... NE-7
Gavins Point Dam—*dam* ... SD-7
*Gavins Point Damsite* ... SD-7
Gavins Point Natl Fish Hatchery—*locale* ... SD-7
Gavins Point Rec Area—*park* ... SD-7
*Gavins Point Reservoir* ... NE-7
*Gavins Point Reservoir* ... SD-7
Gavins Pond—*lake* ... MA-1
Gavin Watson Site—*hist pl* ... ME-1
Gaviota—*locale* ... CA-9
Gaviota, Canada De La —*valley* ... CA-9
Gaviota Beach State Park—*park* ... CA-9
Gaviota Bend—*bend* ... WA-9
*Gaviota Canyon* ... CA-9
*Gaviota Gorge* ... CA-9
Gaviota Islets—*area* ... AK-9
Gaviota Omni Radio Range Station—*other* ... CA-9
Gaviota Pass—*gap* ... CA-9
Gaviota Peak—*summit* ... CA-9
Gaviotito Creek—*stream* ... CA-9
Gaviso Arroyo—*stream* ... NM-5
Gavi Tank—*reservoir* ... NM-5
*Gavit School* ... IN-6
Gavitt Cem—*cemetery* ... OH-6
Gawain Abyss—*valley* ... AZ-5
Gaw Branch—*stream* ... TN-4
Gawdy Lake—*lake* ... MI-6
Gawley Creek—*stream* ... OR-9
Gawley Meadow—*flat* ... OR-9
**Gawthrop**—*pop pl* ... WV-2
Gay—*locale* ... ID-8
**Gay**—*pop pl* ... FL-3
**Gay**—*pop pl* ... GA-3
**Gay**—*pop pl* ... MI-6
**Gay**—*pop pl* ... NC-3
**Gay**—*pop pl* ... OK-5
**Gay**—*pop pl* ... WV-2
Gay, Alpheus, House—*hist pl* ... NH-1
Gay, Andrew H., House—*hist pl* ... LA-4
Gay, Charles, House—*hist pl* ... HI-9
Gay, Daniel, House—*hist pl* ... VT-1
Gay, Ebenezer, House—*hist pl* ... CT-1
Gay, Lake—*lake* ... NY-2
Gay, Mary, House—*hist pl* ... GA-3
Gay, Thomas Haskins, House—*hist pl* ... SD-7
Gayan, Laderan—*cliff* ... MH-9
Gay Archeol Site—*hist pl* ... MO-7
Gayarre Sch—*school* ... LA-4
*Gayaugan* ... MH-9
Gayaugan—*slope* ... MH-9
Gay Ave Sch—*school* ... TX-5
**Gaybourn**—*pop pl* ... KY-4
Gay Branch—*stream* ... AL-4
Gay Branch—*stream* ... KY-4
Gay Branch—*stream* ... TN-4
Gay Branch—*stream* ... VA-3
Gay Bridge—*bridge* ... AL-4
Gay Brook—*stream* ... ME-1
Gay Brook—*stream* ... NH-1
Gay Brook—*stream* ... NY-2
Gay Cave—*cave* ... TN-4
Gay (CCD)—*cens area* ... GA-3
Gay Cem—*cemetery* (2) ... AL-4
Gay Cem—*cemetery* (2) ... CT-1
Gay Cem—*cemetery* ... GA-3
Gay Cem—*cemetery* (2) ... NC-3
Gay City State Park—*park* ... CT-1
*Gay Cove* ... MA-1
Gay Cove—*bay* ... ME-1
Gay Creek—*stream* ... AL-4
Gay Creek—*stream* (2) ... AK-9
Gay Creek—*stream* ... CA-9
Gay Creek—*stream* ... GA-3
Gay Creek—*stream* ... IL-6
Gay Creek—*stream* ... MT-8
Gay Creek—*stream* ... NY-2
Gay Creek—*stream* ... WY-8
*Gayden* ... MS-4
Gayden Brake—*swamp* ... MS-4
**Gaydens**—*pop pl* ... SC-3
Gaydens Creek—*stream* ... SC-3
Gay El Rancho Lodge—*locale* ... MI-6
Gayer, Jacob, House—*hist pl* ... OH-6
Gayer, Jacob M., House—*hist pl* ... OH-6
Gay Farm—*hist pl* ... MA-1
**Gayfields**—*pop pl* ... MD-2
Gay Ford—*locale* ... MS-4
Gay Gulch—*valley* ... AK-9
*Gayhead* ... MA-1
Gay Head—*cape* ... MA-1
**Gay Head**—*pop pl* ... MA-1
**Gayhead**—*pop pl* (2) ... NY-2
Gayhead Cem—*cemetery* ... MA-1
Gay Head Cliffs—*cliff* ... MA-1
Gay Head Coast Guard Station—*building* ... MA-1
Gay Head Indian Burying Ground—*cemetery* ... MA-1
Gay Head Light—*hist pl* ... MA-1
Gay Head Light—*locale* ... MA-1
Gay Head Lighthouse—*locale* ... MA-1
Gayhead Pond—*lake* ... NY-2
**Gay Head (Town of)**—*pop pl* ... MA-1
Gayhead Vly—*swamp* ... NY-2
Gayheart Branch—*stream* ... KY-4
Gayheart Slough—*stream* ... OR-9
Gay Hill—*locale* ... TX-5
**Gay Hill**—*pop pl* ... TX-5
Gay Hill—*summit* ... ME-1
Gay Hill—*summit* ... MA-1
Gay Hill Cem—*cemetery* ... TX-5
Gay Hill-Independence (CCD)—*cens area* ... TX-5
Gay Hill Sch—*school* ... TX-5
Gay Hills Country Club—*other* ... VA-3
Gay (historical)—*locale* ... AL-4
Gay Hollow—*valley* ... NY-2
Gay Hollow—*valley* (2) ... TX-5
Gay Hosp—*hospital* ... IA-7
Gay House—*hist pl* ... AL-4
**Gayinero**—*pop pl* ... GU-9
Gay Island—*island* ... ME-1
Gayitt Point—*cape* ... CT-1
Gay JHS—*school* ... TX-5
Gay Knob—*summit* ... WV-2
Gay Lake—*lake* ... GA-3
Gay Lake—*lake* ... ID-8
Gay Lake—*lake* ... NE-7
**Gaylan Heights**—*pop pl* ... TN-4
Gaylanta Lake—*lake* ... MI-6
**Gayle**—*pop pl* ... SC-3
Gayle, Lake—*reservoir* ... VA-3
Gayle Evans Lake Dam—*dam* ... MS-4
Gayle JHS—*school* ... VA-3
Gayle Mill—*other* ... SC-3
Gay Lemon Park—*park* ... MS-4
**Gayler**—*pop pl* ... AR-4
Gayler Cem—*cemetery* ... AR-4
*Gaylers Creek* ... TN-4
**Gayles**—*pop pl* ... LA-4
Gayle Sch—*school* ... SC-3
Gayles Store (historical)—*locale* ... AL-4
**Gaylesville**—*pop pl* ... AL-4
Gaylesville Gap—*gap* ... AL-4
Gaylesville HS—*school* ... AL-4
Gaylesville Post Office—*building* ... AL-4
Gayle Tank—*reservoir* ... AZ-5
Gayley, Mount—*summit* ... CA-9
*Gay-Lindsey Cemetery* ... AL-4
*Gaylon Heights* ... TN-4
Gaylon Heights—*uninc pl* ... TN-4
Gaylon Lake Dam—*dam* ... MS-4
Gaylon Spring—*spring* ... TN-4
Gaylon Williams Lake Dam—*dam* ... MS-4
*Gaylor* ... AR-4
Gaylor And Warnock Ditch—*canal* ... WY-8
Gaylor Cem—*cemetery* ... TN-4
Gaylor Cove—*bay* ... NC-3
Gaylor Creek—*stream* ... GA-3
Gaylor Creek—*stream* ... TN-4
Gaylor Creek—*stream* ... TX-5
Gaylord—*locale* ... OR-9
Gaylord—*locale* ... TX-5
Gaylord—*locale* ... VA-3
**Gaylord**—*pop pl* ... KS-7
**Gaylord**—*pop pl* ... MI-6
**Gaylord**—*pop pl* ... MN-6
**Gaylord**—*pop pl* (2) ... NC-3
**Gaylord**—*pop pl* ... ND-7
Gaylord Bay—*bay* ... NC-3
Gaylord Canyon—*valley* ... NM-5
Gaylord Cem—*cemetery* ... KS-7
Gaylord Cem—*cemetery* ... MI-6
Gaylord Creek—*stream* ... ID-8
Gaylord Creek—*stream* ... MI-6
Gaylord Creek—*stream* ... PA-2
Gaylord Creek—*stream* ... WY-8
Gaylord Crossing Pond—*reservoir* ... SC-3
Gaylord Elem Sch—*school* ... KS-7
Gaylord Farms Sanatorium—*hospital* ... CT-1
Gaylord Gulch—*valley* ... MT-8
Gaylord Lake—*lake* ... MI-6
Gaylord Lake—*lake* ... WY-8
Gaylord-Levy House—*hist pl* ... TX-5
Gaylord Norman Number 1 Dam—*dam* ... SD-7
Gaylord Norman Number 2 Dam—*dam* ... SD-7
Gaylord Peak—*summit* ... NM-5
Gaylord Point—*cape* ... MN-6
Gaylord Pond—*lake* ... CT-1
Gaylord Rsvr—*reservoir* ... WY-8
Gay Lord Sauceman Dam—*dam* ... SD-7
**Gaylords Crossroads**—*pop pl* ... SC-3
Gaylord Siding—*locale* ... OR-9
Gaylord Siding (historical)—*locale* ... UT-8
Gaylords Island—*island* ... NC-3
Gaylord Stark Lake—*reservoir* ... IN-6
Gaylord Stark Lake Dam—*dam* ... IN-6
**Gaylordsville**—*pop pl* ... CT-1
Gaylordsville Cem—*cemetery* ... CT-1
Gaylordsville Sch—*school* ... CT-1
Gaylordsville Station—*locale* ... CT-1
Gaylor Gap—*gap* ... KY-4
**Gaylor (Gayler)**—*pop pl* ... AR-4
Gaylor Hole—*lake* ... NY-2
Gaylor Hollow—*valley* ... TN-4
Gaylor Homestead—*locale* ... MT-8
Gaylor Lake—*lake* ... TX-5
*Gaylor Lakes* ... CA-9
Gaylor Lakes—*lake* ... CA-9
Gaylor Mtn—*summit* ... AR-4
Gaylor Peak—*summit* ... CA-9
*Gaylor Ridge* ... AL-4
Gaylors Branch—*stream* ... NC-3
*Gaylors Creek* ... TX-5
Gayloup Cove—*bay* ... GU-9
Gayloup Point—*cape* ... GU-9
Gayly—*locale* ... PA-2
**Gayly (Union Church)**—*pop pl* ... PA-2
Gay Meadows Ch of Christ—*church* ... AL-4
Gay Meadows Shop Ctr—*locale* ... AL-4
**Gay Meadows (subdivision)**\—*pop pl* ... AL-4
Gay Mont—*hist pl* ... VA-3
Gaymont—*locale* ... WV-2
Gay Mtn—*summit* ... CA-9
Gay Mtn—*summit* ... NC-3
Gay Mtn—*summit* ... VA-3
Gaynor—*locale* ... MO-7
**Gaynor**—*pop pl* ... KY-4
**Gaynor Heights**—*pop pl* ... VA-3
Gaynor Hollow—*valley* ... MO-7
Gaynor Lake—*lake* ... CO-8
*Gaynor Peak* ... CA-9
Gaynor Pond—*lake* ... FL-3
Gaynor Ridge—*ridge* ... IN-6
**Gaynorsville**—*pop pl* ... IN-6
Gayon—*area* ... GU-9
*Gayosa* ... AL-4
Gayosa—*locale* ... AL-4
Gayosa Mine (underground)—*mine* ... AL-4
Gayosa Mtn—*summit* ... AL-4
Gayosa Post Office (historical)—*building* ... AL-4
*Gayoso* ... AL-4
Gayoso-Peabody Hist Dist—*hist pl* ... TN-4
Gay Playground—*park* ... NY-2
*Gay Pond* ... CT-1
Gay Pond—*lake* ... NY-2
Gay Ridge—*ridge* ... AR-4
**Gay Ridge Estates**—*pop pl* ... NY-2

Gay (RR name for Mount Gay)—other ... WV-2
Gay Run—stream ... OH-6
**Gays**—pop pl ... IL-6
*Gaysan* ... PW-9
Gays Branch—stream ... MS-4
Gays Branch—stream ... WV-2
Gay Sch—school ... MI-6
Gay Sch—school (2) ... OK-5
Gay Sch (abandoned)—school ... PA-2
Gays Chapel—church (2) ... NC-3
Gays Creek—locale ... KY-4
Gays Creek—stream ... KY-4
Gays Ferry (historical)—locale ... AL-4
**Gay Sha Lor Subdivision**—pop pl ... UT-8
*Gay-she-say-ing* ... MI-6
Gays Hill—summit ... MA-1
Gays Hill Ch—church ... GA-3
*Gays Landing* ... AL-4
**Gays Mills**—pop pl ... WI-6
Gays Mills Cem—cemetery ... WI-6
Gays Mills Ridge—ridge ... WI-6
Gays Mills Sch—school ... WI-6
Gays Pass—gap ... CA-9
Gays Point—cape ... NY-2
**Gaysport**—pop pl ... PA-2
**Gaysport (Blue Rock Post Office)**—pop pl ... OH-6
Gaysport Cem—cemetery ... OH-6
Gay Spring—spring ... OR-9
Gay Spring—spring ... TN-4
Gays Slough—stream ... LA-4
Gay Street—post sta ... PA-2
Gay Street Bridge—bridge ... TN-4
Gay Street Commercial Hist Dist—hist pl ... TN-4
Gay Street Sch—hist pl ... PA-2
Gay Street Sch—school (2) ... PA-2
Gay Street Sch—school ... TX-5
**Gaysville**—pop pl ... VT-1
Gaytine—locale ... LA-4
Gayton—locale ... VA-3
Gayton Cem—cemetery ... ND-7
Gayton Gulf—valley ... GA-3
Gayton Post Office (historical)—building ... ND-7
Gay Township—fmr MCD ... IA-7
Gayuse Spring—spring ... MT-8
Gay Valley Camp—locale ... NC-3
**Gayville**—pop pl ... NY-2
**Gayville**—pop pl (2) ... SD-7
Gayville Cem—cemetery ... SD-7
**Gayville Township**—pop pl ... SD-7
Gaywas Peak—summit ... OR-9
Gay Water Tank—reservoir ... NM-5
Gayway Corner—locale ... ID-8
Gay Windmill—locale ... TX-5
**Gaywood**—pop pl ... MD-2
Gay Wood—uninc pl ... TX-5
Gaywood Sch—school ... MD-2
**Gaza**—pop pl ... IA-7
**Gaza**—pop pl ... NH-1
Gazebo, The (Shop Ctr)—locale ... FL-3
**Gazelle**—pop pl ... CA-9
Gazelle Creek—stream ... MT-8
Gazelle Creek Pack Trail—trail ... MT-8
Gazelle Mine—mine ... AZ-5
Gazelle Mtn—summit ... CA-9
Gazelle Rock—bar ... MA-1
**Gazette**—pop pl ... MO-7
Gazette Bldg—hist pl ... AR-4
Gazlay Cem—cemetery ... NY-2
*Gazlay Lake* ... MI-6
**Gazley**—pop pl ... OR-9
Gazley Creek—stream ... TX-5
Gazos Creek—stream ... CA-9
*Gazza* ... RI-1
Gazza Hill—summit ... RI-1
Gazzam—locale ... PA-2
Gazzam Creek—stream ... AK-9
Gazzam Lake—lake ... WA-9
Gazzam Run—stream ... PA-2
Gazzaville—locale ... RI-1
*Gazzem Run* ... PA-2
Gazzola and Vaccaro Bldg—hist pl ... AR-4
*Gazzoway* ... AZ-5
*Gazzoway Canyon* ... AZ-5
G Ballard Ranch—locale ... MT-8
G Bar Ranch—locale ... AZ-5
G B Blankenship Dam—dam ... AL-4
G B Chaneys Landing—locale ... AL-4
*G B Cheneys Landing* ... AL-4
*G B Chenney Landing* ... AL-4
G B Mathison Dam—dam ... AL-4
G B Mortarman Pond Dam—dam ... MS-4
G Boke Number 1 Dam—dam ... SD-7
G Boke Number 2 Dam—dam ... SD-7
G Boldt Dam—dam ... SD-7
G Boyd—locale ... TX-5
G B Shaffner Ranch—locale ... MT-8
G B Smith—locale ... TX-5
G Canal—canal ... CA-9
G Canal—canal ... ID-8
G Canal—canal ... MT-8
G Canal—canal ... OR-9
G Castro (historical)—locale ... AZ-5
G Coupland Ranch—locale ... NM-5
G C Outlaw Dam—dam ... AL-4
G Creek—stream ... FL-3
G Creek—stream ... NV-8
G Daly Ranch—locale ... NE-7
G Ditch—canal ... MT-8
G D Neely Lake Dam—dam ... MS-4
G Drain—canal ... CA-9
Gea—island ... MP-9
Geahlin Ditch—canal ... OH-6
Gean Cem—cemetery ... TN-4
Gean Hollow—valley ... TN-4
Geanquakin Creek—stream ... MD-2
Gean Well—well ... NM-5
Gea Pass—channel ... MP-9
*Gea Passage* ... MP-9
Gear—locale ... IA-7
Gear, Lake—lake ... FL-3
Gear Drain—canal ... MI-6
**Gearhart**—pop pl ... OR-9
Gearhart Cem—cemetery ... VA-3
Gearhart Creek—stream ... OR-9
Gearhart Ditch—canal ... IN-6
Gearhart Fork—stream ... KY-4
Gearhart Golf Course—other ... OR-9
Gearhart Grade Sch—school ... OR-9
Gearhart Marsh—swamp ... OR-9
Gearhart Mine—mine ... CO-8
Gearhart Mountain Wilderness—park ... OR-9
Gearhart Mtn—summit ... OR-9
Gearhart Ranch—locale ... TX-5
Gearhart Ranch—locale ... WY-8
Gearhart Ridge—ridge ... PA-2
Gearhart Sch—school ... KY-4
Gearhart Sch—school ... SD-7
Gearhart (Township of)—uninc pl ... PA-2
Gearhart Trail (pack)—trail ... OR-9
**Gearhartville**—pop pl ... PA-2
Gearheart—other ... KY-4
Gearheart Branch—stream ... KY-4
Gearheart Private Airp—airport ... WA-9
Gearing—locale ... MT-8
*Gearing Creek* ... AL-4
Gearin Hollow—valley ... TN-4
Gearins Chapel—church ... TN-4
*Gearins Chapel Baptist Ch* ... TN-4
*Gearins Ferry* ... OR-9
Gear Lake—lake ... MI-6
Gearns Ferry (site)—locale ... OR-9
**Gears Ferry**—pop pl ... IL-6
Gears Gulf—valley ... NY-2
Gears Ranch—locale ... AZ-5
Gears Ranch (historical)—locale ... SD-7
Gear Workings—mine ... TN-4
**Geary**—pop pl ... OK-5
Geary—uninc pl ... CA-9
Geary, Mathew, House—hist pl ... MI-6
Geary (CCD)—cens area ... OK-5
*Geary City* ... KS-7
Geary County—civil ... KS-7
Geary County State Lake—reservoir ... KS-7
Geary County State Lake Dam—dam ... KS-7
Geary County State Park—park ... KS-7
*Geary Creek* ... CO-8
Geary Creek—stream (2) ... CO-8
Geary Creek—stream ... OR-9
Geary Creek—stream ... WY-8
Geary Gulch—valley ... MT-8
Geary (historical)—locale ... KS-7
Geary Hollow—valley ... UT-8
Geary (Magisterial District)—fmr MCD ... WV-2
Geary Meadow—flat ... OR-9
Geary Ranch—locale ... ND-7
Geary Sch—school ... CA-9
Geary Sch—school ... KS-7
Geary Spring—spring ... AZ-5
Geary State Fishing Lake And Wildlife Area—park ... KS-7
Geary Theatre—hist pl ... CA-9
*Gearyville* ... PA-2
Geasland Cem—cemetery ... TN-4
Geauga Community Hosp—hospital ... OH-6
**Geauga (County)**—pop pl ... OH-6
*Geauga Lake* ... OH-6
Geauga Lake—lake ... OH-6
**Geauga Lake**—pop pl ... OH-6
Geban Creek—stream ... CO-8
Gebauer Lake—lake ... NE-7
Gebbie Corner—locale ... VT-1
*Gebeig* ... ME-1
*Ge-be-on-a-quet Lake* ... MN-6
*Ge-be-on-e-quat Creek* ... MN-6
*Ge-be-on-equat Lake* ... MN-6
Ge-be-on-e-quet Creek—stream ... MN-6
Ge-be-on-e-quet Lake—lake ... MN-6
Geber Branch—stream ... GA-3
Gebert Drain—canal ... ID-8
Gebhard Run—stream ... PA-2
*Gebhards Run* ... PA-2
Gebhard State Park—park ... IL-6
Gebhardt Bakery—hist pl ... TX-5
Gebhardt Hollow—valley ... AR-4
*Gebhardt Lake* ... CA-9
*Gebhardt Well* ... OR-9
Gebhard Well—well ... OR-9
Gebhart—locale ... PA-2
Gebhart, S. P., House—hist pl ... KS-7
Gebhart Church Cem—cemetery ... OH-6
*Gebhartsburg* ... PA-2
*Gebharts Run* ... PA-2
**Gebo**—pop pl ... WY-8
Gebo, Henry, House—hist pl ... MT-8
Gebo Lake—lake ... MN-6
*Ge-B-On-P-Que Lake* ... MN-6
Gechiak Creek—stream ... AK-9
Gechiak Lake—lake ... AK-9
Gechiak Mountains—other ... AK-9
**Gecko**—pop pl ... LA-4
Ged—locale ... LA-4
Geddes—hist pl ... VA-3
Geddes—locale ... KY-4
**Geddes**—pop pl ... MI-6
**Geddes**—pop pl ... SD-7
Geddes, James, Engine Company No. 6—hist pl ... TN-4
Geddes, Lake—reservoir ... SD-7
Geddes-Bertrand Mine—mine ... NV-8
Geddes Brook—stream ... NY-2
*Geddesburg* ... KS-7
Geddes Creek—stream ... MT-8
Geddes Dam—dam ... SD-7
Geddes Hist Dist—hist pl ... SD-7
Geddes Lake—lake ... WY-8
Geddes Mtn—summit ... VA-3
*Geddes Run* ... PA-2
Geddes Run—stream ... PA-2
Geddes Sch—school ... CA-9
Geddes Tank—reservoir ... AZ-5
**Geddes (Town of)**—pop pl ... NY-2
**Geddie**—pop pl ... LA-4
Geddis Canyon—valley ... TX-5
Geddis Canyon Rock Art Site—hist pl ... TX-5
Geden Branch—stream ... AL-4
**Gederos Estates (subdivision)**—pop pl ... SD-7
Ged Lake—lake ... LA-4
Gedney—uninc pl ... NY-2
Gedney and Cox Houses—hist pl ... MA-1
Gedney Brook—stream ... NY-2
Gedney Butte—summit ... ID-8
Gedney Cem—cemetery ... NY-2
Gedney Channel—channel ... AK-9
*Gedney Creek* ... NV-8
Gedney Creek—stream ... ID-8
Gedney Creek—stream ... OR-9
Gedney Creek Camp—locale ... OR-9
Gedney Field—park ... NY-2
Gedney Harbor—bay ... AK-9
Gedney Island—island ... AK-9
Gedney Island—island ... WA-9
Gedney Mtn—summit ... ID-8
Gedney Pass—channel ... AK-9
Gedney Pond—reservoir ... NY-2
Gedney Spring—spring ... NV-8
Gedney Swamp—swamp ... NY-2
Ged Post Office (historical)—building ... TN-4
*Gedry Cemetery* ... TX-5
Gedstad Sch—school ... SD-7
Geduhn, Mount—summit ... MT-8
Gee—locale ... KY-4
Gee Branch—stream ... AL-4
Gee Branch—stream ... AR-4
Gee Branch—stream ... KY-4
Gee Branch—stream (2) ... MS-4
Gee Branch—stream ... TN-4
*Gee Brook* ... NY-2
Gee Brook—locale ... NY-2
Gee Brook—stream ... NH-1
Gee Brook—stream (4) ... NY-2
**Geeburg**—pop pl ... OH-6
Gee Cave—cave ... TN-4
Gee Cem—cemetery ... KY-4
Gee Cem—cemetery ... LA-4
Gee Cem—cemetery ... OH-6
Gee Cem—cemetery (2) ... TN-4
*Gee Creek* ... OR-9
Gee Creek—stream ... AR-4
Gee Creek—stream ... FL-3
Gee Creek—stream (2) ... LA-4
Gee Creek—stream ... OR-9
Gee Creek—stream ... TN-4
Gee Creek—stream (2) ... WA-9
Gee Creek Swamp—swamp ... OR-9
Gee Creek Trail—trail ... TN-4
Gee Dee Hills—summit ... MS-4
Gee Ditch—canal ... NV-8
**Geedville**—pop pl ... TN-4
*Geedville School* ... TN-4
Gee Ford Bridge—bridge ... TN-4
Gee Hammock—swamp ... FL-3
Gee Hill—summit ... TN-4
Gee Hollow—valley ... OH-6
Gee Hollow—valley (2) ... PA-2
Gee HS—school ... TX-5
Gee Knob—summit ... TN-4
Gee Lake—lake ... MI-6
Gee Lake—lake ... SD-7
Gee Lake—reservoir ... MS-4
Geelick Ch—church ... WV-2
Geelick Run—stream ... WV-2
Geels—locale ... MI-6
Gee Mill—locale ... NH-1
Gee Mtn—summit ... GA-3
Gee Point—summit ... WA-9
Gee Point Trail—trail ... WA-9
Gee Pond—lake ... GA-3
Geer—locale ... OR-9
Geer—locale ... VA-3
Geer, R. C., Farmhouse—hist pl ... OR-9
Geer Brook—stream ... MA-1
Geer Cove—valley ... TN-4
Geer Gulch—valley ... CO-8
Geer Hill—summit ... CT-1
*Geer Hill Brook* ... CT-1
Geer Lake—lake ... MI-6
Geer Lake Dam—dam ... MS-4
Geer Mountain Camp—locale ... CT-1
Geer Mtn—summit ... CT-1
Geer North Ranch—locale ... CO-8
Geer Park—park ... MI-6
Geer Pond—lake ... GA-3
Geer Ranch—locale (2) ... CO-8
Geersbeck Island—island ... NY-2
Geer Sch—school ... SC-3
**Geers Corners**—pop pl ... NY-2
Geers Ferry (historical)—locale ... PA-2
Geers Gulch—valley ... CA-9
Geers Point—summit ... WY-8
Geer Substation—other ... CA-9
Geertsen Canyon—valley ... UT-8
Geertson, Lars, House—hist pl ... ID-8
Geertson Creek—stream ... ID-8
Geertson Creek Sch (historical)—school ... ID-8
Geer Williams Drain—canal ... MI-6
Geesaman Mine Group—mine ... AZ-5
Geesaman Spring—spring ... AZ-5
Geesaman Wash—stream ... AZ-5
*Gees Bend* ... AL-4
Gees Bend—bend ... AL-4
Gees Bend Access Point—locale ... AL-4
Gees Bridge—bridge ... VA-3
Gees Corner—locale ... NY-2
*Gees Creek* ... OR-9
Gees Creek—stream ... MS-4
Gees Creek—stream ... MO-7
Geese Channel—channel ... AK-9
Geese Drain—stream ... MI-6
Geese Islands—island ... AK-9
Geese Lake—lake ... AK-9
Geese Lakes—lake ... AK-9
Geesey Drain—canal ... MI-6
Geesey Park—park ... PA-2
**Geeseytown**—pop pl ... PA-2
Gees Gin (historical)—locale ... AL-4
Gees Grove Ch—church ... NC-3
**Geeslin Corner**—pop pl ... MS-4
Gees Memorial Ch—church ... TX-5
Gees Point—cape ... NY-2
Gees Sch (abandoned)—school ... MO-7
Gee's Slough Mound Group—hist pl ... WI-6
Geeter Sch—school ... TN-4
Geeting Covered Bridge—hist pl ... OH-6
Geeting Farm—hist pl ... MD-2
Geetings Ditch—canal ... IN-6
**Geetingsville**—pop pl ... IN-6
**Geeville**—pop pl ... MS-4
Geeville Mtn—summit ... MS-4
Geeville Sch (historical)—school ... MS-4
Geffas Apartments—hist pl ... UT-8
**Geff (Jeffersonville)**—pop pl ... IL-6
*Gefle* ... KS-7
Gefo Lake—lake ... CA-9
Geghus Ridge—ridge ... CA-9
Gegibu—island ... MP-9
*Gegibu Island* ... MP-9
Gegoka, Lake—lake ... MN-6
*Gegol* ... PW-9
Gehering Point—cape ... MN-6
Gehh—island ... MP-9
*Gehh Island* ... MP-9
Gehlen House and Barn—hist pl ... IA-7
Gehling's Theatre—hist pl ... NE-7
Gehman Cave—cave ... PA-2
Gehmans Ch—church ... PA-2
Gehmans Sch—school ... PA-2
Geho Run—stream ... WV-2
*Gehou River* ... SD-7
Gehring And Gumz Ditch—canal ... IN-6
**Gehring and Gumz Ditch**—pop pl ... IN-6
*Gehring And Gumz Lateral* ... IN-6
Gehring Clinic—hist pl ... ME-1
Gehring Ditch—canal ... IN-6
Gehringer Ch—church ... KY-4
Gehringer Sch—school ... CA-9
*Gehring-gumz Ditch* ... IN-6
Gehris Airp—airport ... PA-2
Gehrke Lake—lake ... WA-9
Gehrke Private Strip—airport ... ND-7
Gehrke Wildlife Area—park ... IA-7
Gehrman Creek—stream ... WI-6
Gehrmann Park—park ... IL-6
Gehrton Sch (historical)—school ... PA-2
Geib—locale ... WA-9
Geibel HS—school ... PA-2
Geibler Creek—stream ... MT-8
Geibler Lake—lake ... OR-9
*Geifer Creek* ... MT-8
*Geifer Lake* ... MT-8
Geiga—island ... MP-9
*Geiga Island* ... MP-9
**Geiger**—pop pl ... AL-4
**Geiger**—pop pl ... PA-2
Geiger, Dr. Jacob, House-Maud Wyeth Painter House—hist pl ... MO-7
Geiger, Fred, and Sons Natl Biscuit Company—hist pl ... IN-6
Geiger Archeol Site—hist pl ... MO-7
Geiger Branch—stream ... WV-2
Geiger Building-Old Polk County Courthouse—hist pl ... WI-6
Geiger Canal—canal ... CA-9
Geiger Cave—cave ... AL-4
Geiger Cem—cemetery (2) ... FL-3
Geiger Cem—cemetery (2) ... MS-4
Geiger Cem—cemetery ... TX-5
Geiger Covered Bridge—bridge ... PA-2
Geiger Covered Bridge—hist pl ... PA-2
Geiger Creek—stream ... FL-3
Geiger Creek—stream ... OR-9
Geiger Creek Rsvr—reservoir ... OR-9
Geiger Drain—canal (2) ... MI-6
Geiger Field (RR name for Spokane Int. Airport)—airport ... WA-9
Geiger Gap—gap ... NV-8
Geiger Gulch—valley ... WA-9
**Geiger Heights**—pop pl ... WA-9
**Geiger Heights (Military Housing)**—pop pl ... WA-9
Geiger Hollow—valley ... NY-2
Geiger Island—island ... TN-4
Geiger Key—island ... FL-3
*Geiger Lake* ... IN-6
Geiger Lake—lake ... FL-3
Geiger Lake—lake ... KY-4
Geiger Lake—reservoir ... MS-4
Geiger Lakes—lake ... MT-8
Geiger Memorial Park—park ... NY-2
Geiger Pond—lake ... SC-3
Geiger Ridge Pond—lake ... IN-6
Geiger Sch—school ... SC-3
Geiger Sch—school ... WA-9
Geiger Sch (abandoned)—school ... PA-2
**Geigers Landing**—pop pl ... FL-3
Geigers Point—cape ... FL-3
Geigers Pond—reservoir ... SC-3
Geiger Station—locale ... PA-2
Geiger Summit—gap ... NV-8
**Geigertown**—pop pl ... PA-2
Geigertown Station (historical)—locale ... PA-2
Geigle Dam—dam ... SD-7
*Geigsby* ... TX-5
*Geike Monument* ... AZ-5
Geikie, Mount—summit ... WY-8
Geikie Glacier—glacier ... AK-9
Geikie Inlet—bay ... AK-9
Geikie Peak—summit ... AZ-5
Geikie Rock—island ... AK-9
Geiles Sch—school ... MO-7
Geiles Spring—spring ... PA-2
Geis Creek—stream ... MT-8
Geis Ditch—canal ... CA-9
Geise Cem—cemetery ... WI-6
Geise Creek—stream ... TN-4
Geise Hollow—valley ... AL-4
Geisel Monmt State Park—park ... OR-9
*Geisel Monmt Wayside* ... OR-9
Geiser Bar—bar ... TN-4
Geiser Creek—stream ... OR-9
Geiser (site)—locale ... OR-9
Geiserts Strip—airport ... NJ-2
Geising Cem—cemetery ... IN-6
Geisinger Hollow—valley ... PA-2
Geisinger Hosp—hospital ... PA-2
Geisinger Ranch—locale ... WY-8
Geis Lake—lake ... MN-6
Geisler Creek—stream ... WA-9
Geisler Hollow—valley ... AR-4
Geisler Run—stream ... PA-2
Geisler Swamp—swamp ... MA-1
**Geismar**—pop pl ... LA-4
Geissler Mtn—summit ... CO-8
Geissler Spring—spring ... TN-4
Geis Spring—spring ... WY-8
Geist, John, and Sons, Blacksmith Shop and House—hist pl ... TN-4
Geist, Mount—summit ... AK-9
Geist Ch—church ... MD-2
**Geistown**—pop pl ... PA-2
Geistown Borough—civil ... PA-2
Geis Trail—trail ... WY-8
*Geist Reservoir* ... PA-2
Geist Reservoir Dam—dam ... IN-6
Geist Rsvr—reservoir ... IN-6
Geist Storage Dam—dam ... PA-2
Geitner, Clement, House—hist pl ... NC-3
Geitner Branch—stream ... NC-3
*Geiugel* ... PW-9
Gejen Island—island ... MP-9
*Gejiboi-to* ... MP-9
**Gekay**—pop pl ... KY-4
*Gekelemukpechunk* ... OH-6
Gekeler Ditch—canal ... OR-9
Gekeler Drain—canal ... MI-6
Gekeler Slough—stream ... OR-9
*G E Kimbrough* ... AL-4
G E Kimbrough Dam—dam ... AL-4
Gela—locale ... NC-3
*Gelaspas Point* ... ME-1
*Gelaspus Point* ... ME-1
**Gelatt**—pop pl ... PA-2
Gelatt Lake—lake ... WY-8
Gelbert Mtn—summit ... WA-9
Geldner Sawmill—hist pl ... MN-6
Geldrich Ditch—canal ... MT-8
Gelhar Siding—locale ... WI-6
Gelhorn Creek—stream ... TX-5
*Geligal Marsh* ... PW-9
Gelina Basin—basin ... NY-2
Gellatly Cem—cemetery ... TX-5
Gellatly Creek—stream ... OR-9
Geller Ditch—canal ... IN-6
Gellerman Canal—canal ... OR-9
*Gellerman-Froman Canal* ... OR-9
Gellermann Ranch—locale ... TX-5
Gellett, Capt. Charles, House—hist pl ... MN-6
Gellinam—island ... MP-9
*Gellinam Island* ... MP-9
*Gellison Cape* ... ME-1
**Gelnett**—pop pl ... PA-2
Gelnett Sch (abandoned)—school ... PA-2
Gelot Hill—summit ... ME-1
Gelot Pond—lake ... ME-1
**Gelowe**—pop pl ... AL-4
*Gelsum* ... PW-9
*Gelsum Mountain* ... PW-9
Gelvin Creek—stream ... LA-4
Gelvin Sch (abandoned)—school ... PA-2
Gem—locale ... ID-8
Gem—locale ... OH-6
Gem—locale ... OR-9
Gem—locale ... TX-5
**Gem**—pop pl ... IN-6
**Gem**—pop pl ... KS-7
Gem, Lake—lake (5) ... FL-3
Gem Acres Interchange—crossing ... AZ-5
G E Mason Catfish Pond Dam—dam ... MS-4
G E Mason Catfish Ponds Dam—dam ... MS-4
Gem Bay—bay ... FL-3
**Gem Beach**—pop pl ... OH-6
Gem Cem—cemetery ... MO-7
Gem Cem—cemetery ... ND-7
Gem City Mine—mine ... NC-3
Gem City Park—park ... IN-6
Gemco—locale ... CA-9
Gemco Lake—reservoir ... IN-6
Gemco Lake Dam—dam ... IN-6
Gem County Courthouse—hist pl ... ID-8
Gem County Drainage—canal ... ID-8
Gem County Stock Trail—trail ... ID-8
Gem Cove—bay ... AK-9
Gemcraft-Wittmer Bldg—hist pl ... IN-6
Gem Creek—stream (2) ... ID-8
Gem Creek—stream ... IN-6
Gem Creek—stream ... MT-8
Gem Creek—stream ... NC-3
Gem District D Canal—canal ... ID-8
Gemein Haus—building ... NC-3
Gemeinhaus-Lewis David De Schweinitz Residence—hist pl ... PA-2
Gemelo Mesa—summit ... TX-5
Gemelo Tank—reservoir ... AZ-5
Gemfield—locale ... NV-8
Gem Glacier—glacier ... MT-8
Gem Gulch—valley ... ID-8
Gem Hill—summit (2) ... CA-9
Gem (historical)—locale ... AL-4
Gem (historical)—locale ... SD-7
**Gem (historical)**—pop pl ... OR-9
Gem (historical P.O.)—locale ... IA-7
Geminde Cem—cemetery ... ND-7
Gemini—mine ... UT-8
Gemini—summit ... CA-9
Gemini Arch—arch ... UT-8
Gemini Elem Sch—school ... FL-3
Gemini Lakes—lake ... MI-6
Gemini Peak—summit ... CO-8
Gemini Trail—trail ... NH-1
Gem Island—island ... IN-6
Gem Island—island ... ME-1
Gem Island—island ... MI-6
*Gem Lake* ... WA-9
Gem Lake—lake (4) ... CA-9
Gem Lake—lake (2) ... CO-8
Gem Lake—lake ... FL-3
Gem Lake—lake (3) ... ID-8
Gem Lake—lake (2) ... MN-6
Gem Lake—lake (2) ... MT-8
Gem Lake—lake ... NE-7
Gem Lake—lake (2) ... NY-2
Gem Lake—lake ... UT-8
Gem Lake—lake ... WA-9
Gem Lake—lake (2) ... WI-6
Gem Lake—lake ... WY-8
**Gem Lake**—pop pl ... MN-6
Gem Lake—reservoir ... CO-8
Gem Lake Golf Course—other ... MN-6
Gem Lakes—lake ... CA-9
Gem Lake Trail—trail (2) ... CO-8
Gem Mary, Lake—lake ... FL-3
Gem Meadows—flat ... OR-9
*Gemmel Creek* ... MT-8
**Gemmell**—pop pl ... MN-6
Gemmell Creek—stream ... MT-8
Gemmill Gulch—valley ... CA-9
*Gemmills* ... MD-2
Gem Mine—mine ... CA-9
Gem Mine—mine ... CO-8
Gem Mine—mine ... NV-8
Gem Mine—mine ... OR-9
Gem Mine (historical)—mine ... OR-9
Gem Mtn—summit ... CO-8
Gemodedon Island—island ... AK-9
*Gemogi* ... MP-9
Gem Oil Field—other ... NM-5
G E Morgan Lake Dam—dam (2) ... MS-4
Gem Pass—gap ... CA-9
Gem Peak—summit ... MT-8
Gempeler Round Barn—hist pl ... WI-6
Gem Point—cape ... AK-9
Gem Pond—reservoir ... OR-9
Gem Quartz Mine—mine ... OR-9
**Gem (RR name Coger)**—pop pl ... WV-2
Gem Saloon—hist pl ... MT-8
Gem Sch—school ... MO-7
Gem Shaft—mine ... AZ-5
Gem State Mine—mine ... ID-8
*Gem Station* ... IN-6
**Gem Township**—pop pl ... ND-7
**Gem Township**—pop pl ... SD-7
Gem Township Hall—building ... SD-7
Gemuk Creek—stream ... AK-9
Gemuk Mtn—summit ... AK-9
Gemuk River—stream ... AK-9
Gem Valley—basin ... NE-7
Gem Valley—valley ... ID-8
**Gem Village**—pop pl ... CO-8
*Gena* ... MI-6
Genaders Pond—lake ... NJ-2
*Genalga* ... AL-4
**Genasco**—pop pl ... NJ-2
Gender Creek—stream ... OR-9
Gendron, Peter, House—hist pl ... OH-6
Gendron Ranch—locale ... NV-8
**Gene**—pop pl ... CA-9
**Gene**—pop pl ... TX-5
Gene Armstrong Landing Strip—airport ... SD-7
*Gene Autry* ... OK-5
**Gene Autry**—pop pl ... OK-5
Gene Brown Hollow—valley ... PA-2
Geneceda Creek—stream ... PA-2
Gene Creek—stream ... KS-7
Gene Creek—stream ... MT-8
Gene Creek—stream ... OR-9
Gene Creek—stream ... WA-9
Gene Creek Rsvr—reservoir ... MT-8
Gene Creek Spring—spring ... MT-8
Gene Draw—valley ... WY-8
Gene Edwards Mtn—summit ... NY-2
*Genega de los Pimas* ... AZ-5
**Genegantslet**—pop pl ... NY-2
Genegantslet Cem—cemetery ... NY-2
Genegantslet Creek—stream ... NY-2
Genegantslet Lake—lake ... NY-2
Gene Howe Park—park ... TX-5
Gene Howe Wildlife Mngmt Area—park ... TX-5
Geneill—locale ... MS-4
*Gene Lake* ... MI-6
Gene Lake—lake (2) ... AK-9
Gene Lake—lake ... WI-6
Genele, Lake—reservoir ... NC-3
Genella, Mary Louise Kennedy, House—hist pl ... LA-4
Gene Nunnery Dam—dam ... MS-4
Gene Pond—lake ... MI-6
Gene Pumping Station—other ... CA-9
Generac Corporation—facility ... WI-6
General, Mount—summit ... CA-9
General, The—hist pl ... GA-3
General Accounting Office—building ... DC-2
General Allen Branch—stream ... KY-4
General Assembly Ch—church ... KY-4
General Assembly Ch—church ... OK-5
General Assembly of the Lord Ch—church ... WV-2
General Beadle State Coll—school ... SD-7
*General Bidwell Lake* ... CA-9
General (Billy) Mitchell Field—mil airp ... WI-6
General Bldg—hist pl ... TN-4
General Brees Field—airport ... WY-8
*General Brooks Island* ... SD-7
General Brown HS—school ... NY-2
General Burnside Island State Park—park ... KY-4
General Butler State Park—park ... KY-4
*General Canyon* ... CA-9
General Canyon—valley ... CA-9
*General Carl A Spaatz Field* ... PA-2
General C C Andrews State For—forest ... MN-6
General Cem—cemetery ... NY-2
General Ch—church ... KY-4
*General Church* ... MO-7
General Creek—stream ... CA-9
General Custer Monmt—pillar ... OH-6
General Davidson Memorial Historic Site—park ... NC-3
General Dean Suspension Bridge—hist pl ... IL-6
General Developers Lake—lake ... FL-3
General Dewitt Spain Airp—airport ... TN-4
General Edgar Jadwin Dam—dam ... PA-2
General Edwards Bridge—bridge ... MA-1
General Electric (Battery Business Section Plant)—facility ... FL-3
General Electric Bldg—hist pl ... CO-8
General Electric Company—facility ... IN-6
General Electric Company—facility ... KY-4
General Electric Lake Number Two—reservoir ... NC-3
General Electric Number Two Dam—dam ... NC-3
General Electric (Plant)—facility ... OH-6
General Electric Realty Plot—hist pl ... NY-2
General Electric Research Laboratory—hist pl ... NY-2
General Electric Space Center—locale ... PA-2
General Electric Switchgear Plant—hist pl ... PA-2
General Engineering Company Bldg—hist pl ... UT-8
General Forrest JHS—school ... AL-4
*General Forrest MS* ... AL-4
General German Orphan Home—hospital ... MD-2
General German Protestant Orphans Home—hist pl ... IN-6
General Grant Grove—woods ... CA-9
General Grant Grove Section Kings Canyon Natl Park—park ... CA-9
General Grant Mine—mine ... AZ-5
General Grant Natl Memorial—hist pl ... NY-2
General Grant Natl Memorial—park ... NY-2
General Grant Shop Ctr—locale ... MO-7
*General Green, The* ... PA-2
General Hancock Statue—park ... DC-2
*General Harney Mine* ... SD-7
General Henry H. Arnold Elem Sch—school ... DE-2
General Hitchcock Picnic Area—park ... AZ-5
General Hosp—hospital (2) ... CA-9
General Hosp—hospital ... DE-2
General Hosp—hospital ... KY-4
General Hosp—hospital ... LA-4
General Hosp—hospital ... MO-7

General Hosp—*hospital* MT-8
General Hosp—*hospital* (2) NJ-2
General Hosp—*hospital* (2) NY-2
General Hosp—*hospital* (2) OH-6
General Hospial—*hospital* NE-7
General Hospital Of Everett Heliport—*airport* WA-9
General Industries—*facility* OH-6
General J B Robertson Home—*building* TX-5
General John J Pershing Memorial Airp—*airport* MO-7
General John J Pershing Memorial Hospital Heliport—*airport* MO-7
General Lafayette—*uninc pl* NJ-2
General Laundry Bldg—*hist pl* LA-4
General Lee Marina—*locale* AL-4
General Leonard Wood Homestead—*building* MA-1
General Leslie R Groves Park—*park* WA-9
General Logan Mine—*mine* UT-8
General Lyman Field (Airport)—*airport* HI-9
*General Lyman Island* CT-1
General MacArthur HS—*school* NY-2
**General Mail Center**—*pop pl* FL-3
General McLane HS—*school* PA-2
General Meade Statue—*park* DC-2
General Mine—*mine* ID-8
General Morgan Bridge—*bridge* VA-3
General Motors Bldg—*hist pl* MI-6
*General Motors Desert Proving Grounds* AZ-5
General Motors Institute—*school* MI-6
General Motors (Lansing)—*facility* MI-6
General Motors (Parts Division)—*facility* (2) MI-6
*General Motors Proving Ground* AZ-5
General Motors Proving Grounds—*facility* MI-6
General Motors (Ypsilanti)—*facility* MI-6
General Myers Sch—*school* AZ-5
General Officers Quarters—*hist pl* OK-5
General Patch Bridge—*bridge* OR-9
General Pershing Statue—*park* DC-2
General Petroleum Oil Field—*oilfield* WY-8
General Pickens Monument—*other* SC-3
General Post Office—*hist pl* DC-2
General Post Office—*post sta* MI-6
General Printing Ink—*facility* IN-6
General Pumice Mine—*mine* NM-5
General Roca Park—*park* CA-9
General Rock—*pillar* RI-1
General Rsvr—*reservoir* OR-9
General Sam Houston Home—*building* TX-5
Generals Cut—*gut* GA-3
General Service Administration Bldg—*building* DC-2
**Generals Greene**—*pop pl* DE-2
General Shafter Mine—*mine* MT-8
General Shanks Elem Sch—*school* IN-6
General Sherman JHS—*school* OH-6
General Sherman Statue—*park* DC-2
General Sherman Tree—*locale* CA-9
Generals' Highway Stone Bridges—*hist pl* CA-9
General Shoe Tank—*other* AL-4
General Sibley Park Area—*park* ND-7
*Generals Island* GA-3
General Springs—*spring* AZ-5
General Springs Cabin—*building* AZ-5
General Springs Canyon—*valley* AZ-5
General Springs Ranger Station—*locale* AZ-5
General Squier Community Club—*locale* MI-6
General Sullivan Bridge—*bridge* NH-1
General Sumters Tomb—*cemetery* SC-3
General Superintendent's House—*hist pl* MN-6
General Teller Mine—*mine* CO-8
General Theological Seminary—*church* NY-2
General Thomas Hills—*summit* NV-8
General Thomas Mine—*mine* NV-8
General Thomas Monmt—*pillar* VT-1
General Tire & Rubber Company—*facility* IL-6
General Tire & Rubber Company—*facility* KY-4
General Turner Hill—*summit* ME-1
General Vaughan Bridge—*bridge* VA-3
**General Warren Village**—*pop pl* PA-2
*General Washington Golf Course* PA-2
General Washington Inn—*hist pl* PA-2
*General Washington Recreation Center* PA-2
**General Wayne**—*pop pl* PA-2
General Wayne Blockhouse—*locale* PA-2
General Wayne Inn—*hist pl* PA-2
General Wayne JHS—*school* PA-2
General Wayne Statue—*other* PA-2
Genero, Lake—*reservoir* PA-2
Gene Rock Dam—*dam* SD-7
Gene Rogers Dam—*dam* TN-4
Gene Rogers Lake—*reservoir* TN-4
Generostee Ch—*church* (2) SC-3
*Generostee Creek* SC-3
**Genery**—*pop pl* AL-4
Genesar—*hist pl* MD-2
Genesareth, Lake—*reservoir* MI-6
Genes Creek—*stream* UT-8
Genesee—*locale* CA-9
**Genesee**—*pop pl* CO-8
**Genesee**—*pop pl* ID-8
**Genesee**—*pop pl* MI-6
**Genesee**—*pop pl* PA-2
**Genesee**—*pop pl* WI-6
**Genesee And Wyoming Junction**—*pop pl* NY-2
Genesee Avenue-Walker Street Hist Dist—*hist pl* MI-6
Genesee Brook—*stream* RI-1
Genesee Camp—*locale* CO-8
**Genesee (County)**—*pop pl* MI-6
**Genesee (County)**—*pop pl* NY-2
Genesee County Courthouse—*hist pl* NY-2
Genesee County Courthouse Hist Dist—*hist pl* NY-2
Genesee Creek—*stream* WI-6
**Genesee Depot**—*pop pl* WI-6
Genesee Dock—*locale* NY-2
Genesee Exchange Bank—*hist pl* ID-8
**Genesee Falls (Town of)**—*pop pl* NY-2
*Genesee Fork - in part* PA-2
*Genesee Forks* PA-2
Genesee Forks—*stream* PA-2
Genesee Grove Ch—*church* IL-6
Genesee Hill Sch—*school* WA-9
Genesee Hills Golf Course—*other* MI-6
Genesee Hosp—*hospital* MI-6
Genesee Hosp—*hospital* NY-2
Genesee Junction—*locale* NY-2
Genesee Lighthouse—*hist pl* NY-2
Genesee Memorial Hosp—*hospital* NY-2
Genesee Mtn—*summit* CO-8
Genesee Park—*park* CO-8
Genesee Prairie Cem—*cemetery* MI-6
Genesee Rec Area—*park* MI-6
Genesee River—*stream* NY-2
Genesee River—*stream* PA-2
*Genesee Run* RI-1
Genesee (sta.) (RR name for Genesee Depot)—*other* WI-6
Genesee Street Hill-Limestone Plaza Hist Dist—*hist pl* NY-2
Genesee Street Sch—*school* MI-6
Genesee Swamp—*swamp* RI-1
Genesee Town Hall—*hist pl* WI-6
**Genesee (Town of)**—*pop pl* NY-2
**Genesee (Town of)**—*pop pl* WI-6
**Genesee (Township of)**—*pop pl* IL-6
**Genesee (Township of)**—*pop pl* MI-6
**Genesee (Township of)**—*pop pl* PA-2
Genesee Tunnel—*tunnel* CT-1
Genesee Valley—*valley* CA-9
Genesee Valley Canal—*canal* NY-2
Genesee Valley Ch—*church* NY-2
Genesee Valley Park—*park* NY-2
Genesee Wesleyan Seminary and Genesee College Hall—*hist pl* NY-2
**Geneseo**—*pop pl* IL-6
**Geneseo**—*pop pl* KS-7
**Geneseo**—*pop pl* NY-2
**Geneseo**—*pop pl* ND-7
Geneseo Cem—*cemetery* KS-7
Geneseo Ch—*church* IA-7
Geneseo Creek—*stream* IL-6
Geneseo-Edwards Oil Field—*oilfield* KS-7
Geneseo Elem Sch—*school* KS-7
Geneseo Sch—*school* CA-9
**Geneseo (Town of)**—*pop pl* NY-2
Geneseo Township—*fmr MCD* (2) IA-7
**Geneseo Township**—*pop pl* SD-7
Geneseo Township Hall—*building* SD-7
**Geneseo (Township of)**—*pop pl* IL-6
Geneserath, Lake—*lake* MI-6
*Genese River* PA-2
Genesis—*locale* TN-4
Genesis Bay—*bay* NJ-2
Genesis Methodist Ch (historical)—*church* TN-4
Genesis P.O (historical)—*building* TN-4
Genesis Sch (historical)—*school* TN-4
**Genessee**—*pop pl* LA-4
*Genessee Brook* RI-1
Genessee Mine—*mine* CO-8
*Genessee River* PA-2
Genessee Sch—*school* WI-6
Genesse Humboldt JHS—*school* NY-2
Genes Spray Strip (airport)—*airport* SD-7
Gene Stratton Porter State Memorial—*park* IN-6
Genetta Ditch—*canal* AL-4
*Geneva* IL-6
*Geneva* UT-8
Geneva—*hist pl* LA-4
Geneva—*locale* AR-4
Geneva—*locale* OR-9
Geneva—*locale* TN-4
**Geneva**—*pop pl* AL-4
**Geneva**—*pop pl* FL-3
**Geneva**—*pop pl* GA-3
**Geneva**—*pop pl* ID-8
**Geneva**—*pop pl* IL-6
**Geneva**—*pop pl* (2) IN-6
**Geneva**—*pop pl* (2) IA-7
**Geneva**—*pop pl* KS-7
**Geneva**—*pop pl* (2) KY-4
**Geneva**—*pop pl* MI-6
**Geneva**—*pop pl* MN-6
**Geneva**—*pop pl* MO-7
**Geneva**—*pop pl* NE-7
**Geneva**—*pop pl* NY-2
**Geneva**—*pop pl* (2) OH-6
**Geneva**—*pop pl* PA-2
**Geneva**—*pop pl* RI-1
**Geneva**—*pop pl* TX-5
**Geneva**—*pop pl* UT-8
**Geneva**—*pop pl* WA-9
Geneva, Lake—*lake* AL-4
Geneva, Lake—*lake* (7) FL-3
Geneva, Lake—*lake* (2) MI-6
Geneva, Lake—*lake* MN-6
Geneva, Lake—*lake* (2) MT-8
Geneva, Lake—*lake* NY-2
Geneva, Lake—*lake* WA-9
Geneva, Lake—*lake* WY-8
**Geneva, Lake**—*pop pl* WI-6
Geneva, Lake—*reservoir* GA-3
Geneva, Lake—*reservoir* IN-6
Geneva, Lake—*reservoir* WI-6
Geneva, Lake—*swamp* ND-7
**Geneva Addition (subdivision)**—*pop pl* UT-8
Geneva Bar—*bar* OR-9
Geneva Basin Ski Area—*other* CO-8
Geneva Bog Brook—*stream* ME-1
Geneva Branch—*stream* AL-4
Geneva Bridge—*bridge* FL-3
*Geneva Bridge Dam* PA-2
Geneva (CCD)—*cens area* AL-4
Geneva Cem—*cemetery* FL-3
Geneva Cem—*cemetery* GA-3
Geneva Cem—*cemetery* ID-8
Geneva Cem—*cemetery* KS-7
Geneva Cem—*cemetery* MI-6
Geneva Cem—*cemetery* MN-6
Geneva Cemetery—*cememtery* OR-9
Geneva Center Sch—*school* MI-6
Geneva Ch—*church* AL-4
Geneva Ch—*church* AR-4
Geneva Ch—*church* KY-4
Geneva Ch—*church* (2) NC-3
Geneva Coal Mine—*mine* UT-8
Geneva Coll—*school* PA-2
Geneva Country Club—*other* IA-7
Geneva Country Club—*other* NY-2
**Geneva County**—*pop pl* AL-4
Geneva County Courthouse—*building* AL-4
Geneva County Grammar Sch—*school* AL-4
Geneva County Hosp—*hospital* AL-4
Geneva County HS—*school* AL-4
Geneva County Lake—*reservoir* AL-4
Geneva County Lake Number One Dam—*dam* AL-4
Geneva County Number 2 Dam—*dam* AL-4
*Geneva County Public Lake* AL-4
Geneva Creek—*stream* CO-8
Geneva Creek—*stream* TX-5
Geneva Ditch—*canal* ID-8
Geneva Division—*civil* AL-4
Geneva Elem Sch—*school* FL-3
Geneva Elem Sch—*school* IN-6
Geneva Fork—*stream* TX-5
*Geneva Gulch* CO-8
Geneva Hall and Trinity Hall, Hobart & William Smith College—*hist pl* NY-2
*Geneva Hill* PA-2
**Geneva Hill**—*pop pl* PA-2
Geneva (historical)—*locale* SD-7
Geneva Hope Ch—*church* MI-6
Geneva HS—*school* AL-4
Geneva Island—*island* IA-7
Geneva Junction—*locale* WA-9
*Geneva Lake* WI-6
Geneva Lake—*lake* (2) CO-8
Geneva Lake—*lake* (2) MI-6
Geneva Lake—*reservoir* MN-6
Geneva Mine—*mine* MI-6
Geneva Mine—*mine* NV-8
Geneva Mine—*obs name* UT-8
Geneva Mtn—*summit* CO-8
Geneva Municipal Airp—*airport* AL-4
**Geneva-on-the-Lake**—*pop pl* OH-6
Geneva Park—*flat* CO-8
Geneva Park—*park* AR-4
**Geneva Park**—*pop pl* VA-3
Geneva Pass—*gap* WY-8
Geneva Peak—*summit* CO-8
Geneva Point—*cape* NH-1
Geneva Presbyterian Ch—*church* MS-4
**Geneva Road**—*pop pl* IL-6
**Geneva Road**—*pop pl* WI-6
Geneva Rsvr—*reservoir* AZ-5
Geneva Rsvr—*reservoir* OH-6
Geneva Sch—*school* GA-3
Geneva Sch—*school* IA-7
Geneva Sch—*school* MI-6
Geneva Sch—*school* UT-8
Geneva Siding—*locale* PA-2
Geneva State For—*forest* AL-4
Geneva Steel Plant—*other* UT-8
Geneva Street Hist Dist—*hist pl* AL-4
Geneva Summit—*summit* ID-8
Geneva Tank—*reservoir* TX-5
**Geneva (Town of)**—*pop pl* NY-2
**Geneva (Town of)**—*pop pl* WI-6
Geneva Township—*fmr MCD* IA-7
**Geneva Township**—*pop pl* KS-7
**Geneva Township**—*pop pl* NE-7
**Geneva (Township of)**—*pop pl* IL-6
**Geneva (Township of)**—*pop pl* IN-6
**Geneva (Township of)**—*pop pl* (2) MI-6
**Geneva (Township of)**—*pop pl* MN-6
**Geneva (Township of)**—*pop pl* OH-6
Geneveive Lake—*lake* WI-6
Gene Verell Lake Dam—*dam* MS-4
**Genevesta**—*pop pl* WI-6
*Genevia* AR-4
**Genevia (College Station)**—*pop pl* AR-4
Genevieve—*locale* MT-8
Genevieve, Lake—*lake* (2) CA-9
Genevieve, Lake—*lake* NJ-2
Genevieve, Lake—*reservoir* KY-4
Genevieve Ch—*church* MO-7
Genevra—*locale* CA-9
Genevra, Mount—*summit* CA-9
Gene Wallace Ranch—*locale* TX-5
Gene Wash—*valley* CA-9
Gene Wash Rsvr—*reservoir* CA-9
Gene Williams Windmill—*locale* TX-5
Genie, Lake—*lake* FL-3
Genie Drew Village Shop Ctr—*locale* AL-4
Genil Mine—*mine* CA-9
*Genini Bridges* UT-8
Genito—*locale* VA-3
Genito Creek—*stream* (2) VA-3
Genivieve Lake—*lake* AK-9
Genlee—*locale* NC-3
Gen Martin HS—*school* NY-2
**Gennessee (Township of)**—*pop pl* MN-6
*Gennett* TN-4
**Gennett**—*pop pl* GA-3
Gennett, Henry and Alice, House—*hist pl* IN-6
**Gennett Camp**—*pop pl* TN-4
Gennette Creek—*stream* NV-8
Gennett Post Office (historical)—*building* TN-4
**Gennetts**—*pop pl* OH-6
Gennian Gulch—*valley* MT-8
Gennie Branch—*stream* AL-4
Gennings Creek—*stream* CO-8
Genntown—*locale* OH-6
Genoa—*hist pl* KY-4
Genoa—*locale* FL-3
Genoa—*locale* IA-7
Genoa—*locale* ND-7
Genoa—*locale* SC-3
Genoa—*locale* VA-3
**Genoa**—*pop pl* AR-4
**Genoa**—*pop pl* CO-8
**Genoa**—*pop pl* IL-6
**Genoa**—*pop pl* (2) MN-6
**Genoa**—*pop pl* NE-7
**Genoa**—*pop pl* NV-8
**Genoa**—*pop pl* NJ-2
**Genoa**—*pop pl* NY-2
**Genoa**—*pop pl* NC-3
**Genoa**—*pop pl* (2) OH-6
**Genoa**—*pop pl* TX-5
**Genoa**—*pop pl* WV-2
**Genoa**—*pop pl* WI-6
Genoa Area HS—*school* OH-6
Genoa Bluff—*locale* IA-7
Genoa Canyon—*valley* NV-8
Genoa Cem—*cemetery* IA-7
Genoa Cem—*cemetery* NV-8
Genoa Cem—*cemetery* NY-2
Genoa Cem—*cemetery* TX-5
**Genoa City**—*pop pl* WI-6
Genoa Community Cem—*cemetery* CO-8
*Genoa Creek* NV-8
Genoa Gulch—*valley* MT-8
*Genoah* WV-2
Genoa Hist Dist—*hist pl* NV-8
Genoa (historical P.O.)—*locale* IA-7
Genoa Mine—*mine* MN-6
Genoa Peak—*summit* NV-8
Genoa Ridge—*ridge* WI-6
Genoa Sch—*school* OH-6
Genoa Sch—*school* WV-2
Genoa Site—*hist pl* NE-7
Genoa Town Hall—*hist pl* OH-6
**Genoa (Town of)**—*pop pl* NY-2
**Genoa (Town of)**—*pop pl* WI-6
**Genoa Township**—*pop pl* NE-7
**Genoa (Township of)**—*pop pl* IL-6
**Genoa (Township of)**—*pop pl* MI-6
**Genoa (Township of)**—*pop pl* OH-6
Genoes Point—*cape* NC-3
**Genola**—*pop pl* MN-6
**Genola**—*pop pl* UT-8
Genola Cem—*cemetery* NY-2
*Genora* ND-7
Genou Sch—*school* MT-8
Genovar Park—*park* FL-3
Genow Creek Highway—*channel* MI-6
Genral Motors Corporation—*facility* OH-6
*Genright Creek* CO-8
Gensemer Run—*stream* PA-2
Gensey Branch—*stream* OK-5
Gensimore Run—*stream* PA-2
Gensrich Landing Strip—*airport* ND-7
Gent—*other* KY-4
Gent Branch—*stream* VA-3
**Gent City**—*pop pl* IL-6
Genter Hill Sch—*school* IL-6
Genter Mine—*mine* CO-8
**Genterville**—*pop pl* OH-6
Gentey Cem—*cemetery* KY-4
Genther Station—*locale* TX-5
Gentian—*locale* MI-6
**Gentian**—*pop pl* GA-3
Gentian Creek—*stream* AK-9
Gentian Creek—*stream* WY-8
*Gentian Hollow* VA-3
Gentian Lake—*lake* (2) ID-8
Gentian Pond—*lake* NH-1
Gentian Road Sch—*school* GA-3
Gentian Shelter—*locale* NH-1
Genti Bay—*bay* VI-3
*Gentil Annies Gulch* ID-8
Gentile, Lake—*lake* FL-3
Gentile A F Depot—*military* OH-6
Gentile Ch—*church* NC-3
**Gentiles**—*pop pl* FL-3
Gentile Valley—*valley* ID-8
Gentile Valley Canal—*canal* ID-8
Gentile Wash—*valley* UT-8
**Gentilly**—*pop pl* MN-6
Gentilly—*uninc pl* LA-4
Gentilly, Bayou—*gut* (2) LA-4
Gentilly Branch First Baptist Ch—*church* AL-4
Gentilly Forest—*uninc pl* AL-4
Gentilly River—*stream* MN-6
Gentilly Sch—*school* LA-4
Gentilly Terrace—*uninc pl* LA-4
Gentilly Terrace Sch—*school* LA-4
**Gentilly (Township of)**—*pop pl* MN-6
Gentilly Woods—*uninc pl* LA-4
**Gentily Forest (subdivision)**—*pop pl* AL-4
Gentle Annie Gulch—*valley* ID-8
Gentle Annie Mine (historical)—*mine* SD-7
Gentle Annies Spring—*spring* WY-8
Gentle Band Ridge—*ridge* UT-8
Gentle Band Spring—*spring* UT-8
Gentle Cem—*cemetery* AL-4
Gentle Creek—*stream* TX-5
Gentle Horse Lake—*lake* ID-8
Gentle Lake—*lake* ME-1
Gentle Ranch—*locale* NE-7
Gentle Sch—*school* MI-6
Gentle Sch (abandoned)—*school* MO-7
Gentles Cove—*valley* AL-4
Gentle Site—*hist pl* VA-3
Gentles Lake—*lake* GA-3
Gentle Woods Park—*park* OR-9
Gentner Cove—*bay* ME-1
Gentner Drain—*canal* MI-6
Gentral Ch—*church* MO-7
*Gentry* WV-2
Gentry—*locale* ID-8
Gentry—*locale* TN-4
Gentry—*locale* TX-5
**Gentry**—*pop pl* AR-4
**Gentry**—*pop pl* KY-4
**Gentry**—*pop pl* MO-7
Gentry, Lake—*lake* FL-3
Gentry, William T., House—*hist pl* GA-3
*Gentry Branch* MO-7
*Gentry Branch* TN-4
Gentry Branch—*stream* MO-7
Gentry Branch—*stream* (2) NC-3
Gentry Branch—*stream* (2) TN-4
Gentry Branch—*stream* TX-5
Gentry Campground—*park* AZ-5
Gentry Canyon—*valley* (3) AZ-5
Gentry Canyon Spring—*spring* AZ-5
Gentry Cave—*cave* MO-7
Gentry Cave—*cave* TN-4
Gentry Cem—*cemetery* AL-4
Gentry Cem—*cemetery* (3) AR-4
Gentry Cem—*cemetery* IL-6
Gentry Cem—*cemetery* KY-4
Gentry Cem—*cemetery* (5) MO-7
Gentry Cem—*cemetery* NC-3
Gentry Cem—*cemetery* (9) TN-4
Gentry Cem—*cemetery* TX-5
Gentry Ch—*church* VA-3
Gentry Ch—*church* WV-2
Gentry Chapel—*church* TN-4
Gentry Ch (historical)—*church* TN-4
*Gentry City* AR-4
Gentry Corner—*locale* AR-4
**Gentry County**—*pop pl* MO-7
Gentry County Courthouse—*hist pl* MO-7
*Gentry Creek* TX-5
Gentry Creek—*stream* AL-4
Gentry Creek—*stream* AZ-5
Gentry Creek—*stream* AR-4
Gentry Creek—*stream* IL-6
Gentry Creek—*stream* OK-5
Gentry Creek—*stream* OR-9
Gentry Creek—*stream* (2) TN-4
Gentry Creek—*stream* (2) TX-5
Gentry Creek Cem—*cemetery* TX-5
Gentry Creek Falls—*falls* TN-4
Gentry Creek Public Use Area—*park* OK-5
Gentry Crossing—*locale* TX-5
Gentry Ford Bridge—*bridge* MS-4
Gentry Gap—*gap* GA-3
Gentry Gap—*gap* NC-3
Gentry Gap—*gap* TN-4
**Gentry (Gentry City)**—*pop pl* AR-4
Gentry Gulch—*valley* CA-9
Gentry Hill—*summit* AR-4
Gentry Hill—*summit* KY-4
Gentry Hill—*summit* LA-4
Gentry Hollow—*valley* (2) TN-4
Gentry Hollow—*valley* UT-8
Gentry HS—*school* MS-4
*Gentry Lake* TX-5
Gentry Lake—*lake* TX-5
Gentry Lake—*reservoir* TN-4
Gentry Lake Dam—*dam* MS-4
Gentry Lake Dam—*dam* TN-4
Gentry Lookout Tower—*building* AZ-5
Gentry Mesa Tank—*reservoir* AZ-5
Gentry Mine—*mine* TN-4
Gentry MS—*school* NC-3
Gentry Mtn—*summit* AZ-5
Gentry Mtn—*summit* TN-4
Gentry Mtn—*summit* UT-8
Gentry Park—*park* TN-4
Gentry Post Office (historical)—*building* AL-4
Gentry Post Office (historical)—*building* (2) TN-4
Gentry Ranch—*locale* TX-5
Gentry Recreation Site—*park* AZ-5
Gentry Ridge—*ridge* AZ-5
Gentry Ridge—*ridge* UT-8
Gentry Sch—*school* IL-6
Gentry Sch—*school* (2) MO-7
Gentry Sch—*school* NC-3
Gentry Sch (abandoned)—*school* MO-7
Gentrys Chapel—*church* TN-4
Gentry Sch (historical)—*school* (2) TN-4
Gentrys Mill—*locale* KY-4
Gentrys Mill—*locale* TX-5
Gentrys Mill Ch—*church* TX-5
Gentry Spring—*spring* AZ-5
Gentry Spring—*spring* MT-8
Gentry Spring—*spring* TN-4
Gentry Springs—*spring* AL-4
*Gentrys School* TN-4
*Gentrys Store* NC-3
**Gentry Store**—*pop pl* NC-3
Gentry Store (historical)—*locale* AL-4
Gentry Tank—*locale* AZ-5
Gentry Tank—*reservoir* AZ-5
Gentry (Township of)—*fmr MCD* AR-4
Gentry Trail Tank—*reservoir* AZ-5
**Gentryville**—*pop pl* IN-6
**Gentryville**—*pop pl* (2) MO-7
Gentry Well—*well* MT-8
Gents Creek—*stream* MI-6
Gents Mtn—*summit* AL-4
Gentsville—*locale* MD-2
Genty Cem—*cemetery* KY-4
Gentzel Sch (abandoned)—*school* PA-2
Gentzel Sch (historical)—*school* PA-2
**Genung Corners**—*pop pl* OH-6
Genung Mtn—*summit* AZ-5
Genung Spring—*spring* AZ-5
Genzer Creek—*stream* OR-9
Geode Beds—*flat* CA-9
Geode Beds—*flat* UT-8
*Geode Creek* WY-8
Geode Creek—*stream* WY-8
Geode Pit—*cave* AL-4
Geode State Park—*park* IA-7
Geodetic Center of the United States—*hist pl* KS-7
Geodetic Hill—*summit* WA-9
Geoduck Creek—*stream* WA-9
Geoffrey, Lake—*lake* FL-3
Geoghegan, Charles, House—*hist pl* NY-2
Geoghegan Canal—*canal* LA-4
Geoghegan Cem—*cemetery* KY-4
Geographical Center of North America Monmt—*park* ND-7
Geographic Center Of Alaska—*other* AK-9
Geographic Center of the Conterminous United States—*locale* KS-7
Geographic Harbor—*bay* AK-9
**Geography Hall**—*pop pl* OH-6
Geohenda Creek—*stream* AK-9
*Geo Island* MP-9
Geology Vista—*locale* AZ-5
Geo Mee Tank—*reservoir* NM-5
Geo Mee Windmill—*locale* NM-5
Geophysics Well—*well* CA-9
*George* CA-9
*George* DE-2
*George* VA-3
George—*locale* AR-4
George—*locale* TX-5
**George**—*pop pl* IA-7
**George**—*pop pl* MS-4
**George**—*pop pl* NC-3
**George**—*pop pl* OR-9
**George**—*pop pl* PA-2
**George**—*pop pl* WA-9
George, Alexander, House—*hist pl* AR-4
George, Bayou—*stream* (2) FL-3
George, Bayou—*stream* LA-4
George, Cape—*cape* WA-9
George, Charles Noden, House—*hist pl* NC-3
George, Henry, Birthplace—*hist pl* PA-2
George, James Z., Law Office—*hist pl* MS-4
George, Lake—*lake* AK-9
George, Lake—*lake* CA-9
George, Lake—*lake* CT-1
George, Lake—*lake* (4) FL-3
George, Lake—*lake* IL-6
George, Lake—*lake* (2) IN-6
George, Lake—*lake* IA-7
George, Lake—*lake* ME-1
George, Lake—*lake* (7) MI-6
George, Lake—*lake* (6) MN-6
George, Lake—*lake* MS-4
George, Lake—*lake* (2) NE-7
George, Lake—*lake* NJ-2
George, Lake—*lake* (3) ND-7
George, Lake—*lake* (2) OH-6
George, Lake—*lake* SD-7
George, Lake—*lake* WA-9
George, Lake—*lake* WI-6
George, Lake—*lake* WY-8
George, Lake—*reservoir* AL-4
George, Lake—*reservoir* AR-4
George, Lake—*reservoir* CO-8
George, Lake—*reservoir* IN-6
George, Lake—*reservoir* MA-1
George, Lake—*reservoir* MO-7
George, Lake—*reservoir* NJ-2
George, Lake—*reservoir* NY-2
George, Lake—*reservoir* ND-7
George, Lake—*reservoir* OK-5
George, Lake—*reservoir* WI-6
George, Lake—*reservoir* WY-8
George, Lake—*swamp* SD-7
George, Mount—*summit* (2) AK-9
George, Mount—*summit* CA-9
George, Mount—*summit* CO-8
George, Mount—*summit* ID-8
George, Point—*cape* WA-9
George, Ron, Round Barn—*hist pl* IL-6
George, Saint—*cape* AK-9
George, Samuel, House—*hist pl* TN-4
George, Warren B., House—*hist pl* WI-6
George AFB—*military* CA-9
George Aiken Sch—*school* OR-9
*George Alexander* SD-7
George Allard Ranch—*locale* CO-8
George Allen Branch—*stream* WV-2
George Allen Gulch—*valley* CA-9
George Allen Oil Field—*oilfield* TX-5
George A. Mears House—*hist pl* NC-3
George and Charlie Mine—*mine* NV-8
George Anderson Grant—*civil* FL-3
George And Rand Airp—*airport* PA-2
George Ann Lake—*lake* FL-3
*George Arnold Pond* RI-1
George Atkinson Grant—*civil* (2) FL-3
George Baine Meadows—*flat* NV-8
George Bain Slough—*gut* IL-6
George Bath Elem Sch—*school* PA-2
George Beard, Lake—*lake* UT-8
George Birner Ranch—*locale* NM-5
George Black Gulch—*valley* OR-9
George B Loomis Elem Sch—*school* IN-6
George Bluff—*cliff* IL-6
George Bowser Ditch—*canal* IN-6
George Branch—*stream* (2) AL-4
George Branch—*stream* (5) KY-4
George Branch—*stream* MS-4
George Branch—*stream* MO-7
George Branch—*stream* NC-3
George Branch—*stream* SC-3
George Branch—*stream* (2) TN-4
George Branch—*stream* (3) WV-2
George Brook—*stream* ME-1
George Brook—*stream* VT-1
George Brook Flowage—*lake* ME-1
George Brown Branch—*stream* NC-3
George Brown Bridge—*bridge* NY-2
George Bruce Hollow—*valley* KY-4
George B Stevenson Dam—*dam* (2) PA-2
George Buck JHS—*school* IN-6
George Bud Church Memorial Hospital Heliport—*airport* MO-7
George Camp—*locale* NV-8
George Camp—*locale* TX-5
*George Campbell Trail* PA-2
George Canal—*canal* FL-3
George Canyon—*valley* AZ-5
George Canyon—*valley* CA-9
George Canyon—*valley* CO-8
George Canyon—*valley* (2) NM-5
George Canyon—*valley* OR-9
George Canyon—*valley* TX-5
George Canyon Windmill—*locale* CO-8
George Carter Island Bay—*swamp* GA-3
George (CCD)—*cens area* WA-9
George Cem—*cemetery* (2) AL-4
George Cem—*cemetery* AR-4
George Cem—*cemetery* GA-3
George Cem—*cemetery* IA-7
George Cem—*cemetery* LA-4
George Cem—*cemetery* MA-1
George Cem—*cemetery* (4) MO-7
George Cem—*cemetery* (2) NC-3
George Cem—*cemetery* OH-6
George Cem—*cemetery* OR-9
George Cem—*cemetery* (8) TN-4
George Cem—*cemetery* (3) TX-5
George Chapel—*church* MS-4
George Chapel—*church* TN-4
George Clark Dam—*dam* SD-7
George Clark Ranch—*locale* OR-9
George Clark Tank—*reservoir* NM-5
George Claussen Pond—*reservoir* GA-3
George Clem Sch—*school* TN-4
George C Marshall HS—*school* VA-3
George C Miller, Jr MS—*school* FL-3
**George County**—*pop pl* MS-4
George County Courthouse—*building* MS-4
George County Hosp—*hospital* MS-4
George County HS—*school* MS-4
*George Creek* AR-4
*George Creek* CO-8
*George Creek* ID-8
*George Creek* MD-2
*George Creek* PA-2
*George Creek* SC-3
*George Creek* TX-5
George Creek—*stream* AL-4
George Creek—*stream* (4) AK-9
George Creek—*stream* (2) AR-4
George Creek—*stream* CA-9
George Creek—*stream* (3) CO-8
George Creek—*stream* (4) ID-8
George Creek—*stream* IN-6
George Creek—*stream* (3) MT-8
George Creek—*stream* (2) OH-6
George Creek—*stream* OK-5
George Creek—*stream* (8) OR-9
George Creek—*stream* PA-2
George Creek—*stream* (2) TN-4
George Creek—*stream* TX-5
George Creek—*stream* UT-8

Georgia, Strait of—*channel* WA-9
Georgia Acad For The Blind—*school* GA-3
Georgia Avenue-Butler Ave Hist Dist—*hist pl* SC-3
Georgia Ave Sch—*school* GA-3
Georgia Ave Sch—*school* TN-4
Georgia Bend—*bend* AL-4
Georgia Bend Cem—*cemetery* MS-4
*Georgia Boys Estate* GA-3
Georgia Branch—*stream* (2) NC-3
Georgia Branch—*stream* (2) TN-4
Georgia Branch—*stream* TX-5
Georgia Branch—*stream* (2) VA-3
Georgia Camp Ch—*church* TX-5
Georgia Camp Creek—*stream* TX-5
*Georgia Camp Hollow* VA-3
Georgia Camp Hollow—*valley* VA-3
Georgia Cem—*cemetery* AR-4
Georgia Cem—*cemetery* MI-6
**Georgia Center**—*pop pl* VT-1
Georgia Ch—*church* IL-6
Georgia City Cem—*cemetery* MO-7
Georgia Coastal Plain Experimental Station—*other* GA-3
Georgia Coll—*school* GA-3
Georgia Conference Center—*building* GA-3
Georgia Cottage—*hist pl* AL-4
Georgia Creek—*stream* AL-4
Georgia Creek—*stream* MT-8
Georgia Creek—*stream* NY-2
Georgia Creek—*stream* OR-9
Georgia Crossing—*locale* TN-4
Georgia Cumberland Acad—*school* GA-3
**Georgia Diagnostic and Classification Center**—*pop pl* GA-3
Georgia Ditch—*canal* CO-8
Georgia Fruit Farm Creek—*stream* FL-3
Georgia Grove Ch—*church* GA-3
Georgia Gulch—*valley* CA-9
Georgia Gulch—*valley* (4) CO-8
*Georgia Heights* IN-6
Georgia Industrial Home—*building* GA-3
Georgia Infirmary—*hospital* GA-3
Georgia Institute of Technology—*school* GA-3
Georgia Institute of Technology Hist Dist—*hist pl* GA-3
*Georgia Lake* OR-9
Georgia Lake—*lake* AR-4
Georgia Lake—*lake* OR-9
Georgia Matthews Elem Sch—*school* KS-7
Georgia Mesa—*summit* CO-8
Georgia Mesa School—*locale* CO-8
Georgia Military Acad—*school* GA-3
Georgia Military Coll—*school* GA-3
Georgia Mountain Experiment Station—*other* GA-3
Georgia Mtn—*summit* (2) AL-4
Georgia Mtn—*summit* NY-2
Georgia Mtn—*summit* VT-1
**Georgiana**—*pop pl* AL-4
**Georgiana**—*pop pl* FL-3
Georgiana, Cape—*cape* AK-9
Georgiana, Mount—*summit* AK-9
Georgiana Acad (historical)—*school* AL-4
Georgiana Canyon—*valley* UT-8
Georgiana Falls—*falls* NH-1
Georgiana HS—*school* AL-4
Georgiana-McKenzie (CCD)—*cens area* AL-4
Georgiana-McKenzie Division—*civil* AL-4
Georgiana Slough—*stream* CA-9
Georgian Court—*hist pl* NJ-2
Georgian Court Coll—*school* NJ-2
**Georgian Forest**—*pop pl* MD-2
Georgian Forest Sch—*school* MD-2
Georgian Heights Sch—*school* OH-6
Georgian Hills Ch—*church* TN-4
Georgian Hills JHS—*school* TN-4
Georgian Hills Park—*park* TN-4
Georgian Hills Sch—*school* TN-4
**Georgian North Hills (subdivision)**—*pop pl* DE-2
Georgian Swamp—*lake* RI-1
Georgia O'Keeffe Natl Historic Site—*park* NM-5
Georgia Pacific, Lake—*lake* AR-4
Georgia Pacific Lake Dam—*dam* MS-4
Georgia Pacific Wildlife Mngmt Area—*park* FL-3
Georgia Pass—*gap* CO-8
**Georgia Plain**—*pop pl* VT-1
**Georgia Plains**—*pop pl* VT-1
Georgia Power Company (Atkinson Plant)—*facility* GA-3
Georgia Power Company (Hammond Plant)—*facility* GA-3
Georgia Power Company (Wansley Unit No. 1)—*facility* GA-3
Georgia Power Company (Yates Plant)—*facility* GA-3
Georgia Ridge—*ridge* (2) AR-4
*Georgia Road Church* AL-4
Georgia Row House—*hist pl* NE-7
Georgia Rug Mill Warehouse—*facility* GA-3
Georgia Sch for the Deaf Hist Dist—*hist pl* GA-3
*Georgias Creek* AL-4
Georgia Sink—*basin* GA-3
Georgia Site No. 9 CG 43—*hist pl* GA-3
Georgia Slide—*locale* CA-9
**Georgia Southern**—*pop pl* GA-3
Georgia Southern Coll—*school* GA-3
Georgia Southern (Collegeboro)—*uninc pl* GA-3
Georgia Southwestern Coll—*school* GA-3
**Georgia (sta.) (East Georgia)**—*pop pl* VT-1
Georgia State Capitol—*hist pl* GA-3
Georgia State Prison—*building* GA-3
*Georgia Strait* WA-9
Georgia Street Hist Dist—*hist pl* MO-7
**Georgia Terrace (subdivision)**—*pop pl* TN-4
**Georgia (Town of)**—*pop pl* VT-1
**Georgia Township**—*pop pl* SD-7
Georgia (Township of)—*fmr MCD* AR-4
Georgia University—*uninc pl* GA-3
Georgia Veterans Memorial State Park—*park* GA-3
**Georgiaville**—*pop pl* AL-4
**Georgiaville**—*pop pl* RI-1
Georgiaville Hist Dist—*hist pl* RI-1
Georgiaville Pond—*reservoir* RI-1
Georgiaville Pond Dam—*dam* RI-1
*Georgiaville Reservoir* RI-1
Georgiaville Sch (historical)—*school* AL-4
Georgia Washington Sch—*school* AL-4
**Georgica**—*pop pl* NY-2
Georgica Cove—*bay* NY-2
Georgica Pond—*lake* NY-2
*Georgie Creek* OR-9
Georgie Creek—*stream* (2) AK-9
Georgie Hollow—*valley* UT-8
Georgie Pond—*reservoir* SC-3
Georgies Chapel—*church* MS-4
Georgies Windmill—*locale* TX-5
**Georgieville**—*pop pl* SC-3
Georgina, Lake—*lake* NY-2
Georgine Mine—*mine* NV-8
Georgs Hole—*lake* TX-5
**Georgtown Station**—*pop pl* NY-2
Georigia Bay—*bay* NC-3
Georob Oil Field—*oilfield* KS-7
Geory Spring—*spring* MI-6
Geotz Ditch—*canal* KY-4
Geo Washington HS—*school* NY-2
*Geowic* AZ-5
Geo Winkler Ranch—*locale* NM-5
Gepford—*locale* CA-9
**Gephart**—*pop pl* OH-6
Gephart JHS—*school* CA-9
Gephart-Mageet Ditch—*canal* IN-6
*Gephart's* OH-6
**Gepharts**—*pop pl* OH-6
Gephart Sch—*school* MD-2
Gepp—*locale* AR-4
Geppert Butte—*summit* OR-9
Geppert Creek—*stream* (2) OR-9
Gepperts Lake—*reservoir* IL-6
Gera—*locale* VA-3
**Gera**—*pop pl* MI-6
Gerald—*locale* AL-4
Gerald—*locale* IL-6
Gerald—*locale* NV-8
**Gerald**—*pop pl* IL-6
**Gerald**—*pop pl* IN-6
**Gerald**—*pop pl* MO-7
**Gerald**—*pop pl* OH-6
**Gerald**—*pop pl* TX-5
Gerald, Amos, House—*hist pl* ME-1
Gerald, Lake—*lake* MI-6
Gerald, Lake—*reservoir* AL-4
Gerald Adams Elem Sch—*school* FL-3
Gerald Brook—*stream* ME-1
Gerald Cem—*cemetery* (2) LA-4
Gerald Cem—*cemetery* MS-4
Gerald Cem—*cemetery* SC-3
Gerald Cem—*cemetery* TX-5
Gerald Ch—*church* TX-5
*Gerald Cove* WA-9
Gerald Crowley Lake And Dam—*dam* AL-4
Gerald-Dowdell House—*hist pl* AL-4
Gerald Gut—*gut* SC-3
Gerald Hills—*summit* AZ-5
Gerald Hills Tank—*reservoir* AZ-5
**Gerald (historical)**—*pop pl* MS-4
**Geraldine**—*pop pl* AL-4
**Geraldine**—*pop pl* MT-8
Geraldine (CCD)—*cens area* AL-4
Geraldine Division—*civil* AL-4
Geraldine Lake—*lake* MN-6
Geraldine Lakes—*lake* CA-9
Geraldine Mine—*mine* CA-9
Geraldine Sch—*school* AL-4
Gerald Lake—*lake* SC-3
Gerald Lake Dam—*dam* AL-4
Gerald Martian Dam—*dam* SD-7
Gerald Oldland Ranch—*locale* CO-8
Gerald Post Office (historical)—*building* MS-4
Gerald Sch—*school* TX-5
Gerald Spring—*spring* AZ-5
Gerald Wallace Lake Number One—*reservoir* AL-4
Gerald Wallace Lake Number Two—*reservoir* AL-4
Gerald Wallace Number 1 Dam—*dam* AL-4
Gerald Wallace Number 2 Dam—*dam* AL-4
Gerald Wash—*stream* AZ-5
Gerald Well—*well* AZ-5
Gerance, Bayou—*stream* LA-4
Geranen, Paul and Fredriika, Farm—*hist pl* SD-7
Geranium Ch—*church* NE-7
Geranium Park—*flat* SD-7
Geranium Sch—*school* NE-7
**Geranium Township**—*pop pl* NE-7
Gerar, Lake—*lake* DE-2
Gerard, Lake—*lake* NJ-2
Gerard Creek—*stream* MT-8
Gerard Gulch—*valley* CO-8
Gerard Homestead—*locale* MT-8
Gerard HS—*school* AZ-5
Gerard Landing—*locale* NC-3
Gerardo's Bldg—*hist pl* AZ-5
**Gerard Park**—*pop pl* NY-2
Gerard Point—*cape* AK-9
Gerard Pond—*lake* ME-1
Gerard Ranch—*locale* MT-8
Gerards Chapel—*church* NC-3
Gerbaz Dale—*obs name* CO-8
**Gerber**—*pop pl* CA-9
**Gerber**—*pop pl* MT-8
Gerber, J. W., House—*hist pl* MN-6
Gerber Butte—*summit* ID-8
Gerber Cem—*cemetery* (2) IN-6
Gerber Cem—*cemetery* MO-7
Gerber Childrens Center—*school* FL-3
*Gerber Creek* MT-8
Gerber Dam—*dam* OR-9
Gerber Ditch—*canal* IN-6
Gerber Hosp and Garage—*hist pl* MN-6
Gerber Joint Ditch—*canal* IN-6
Gerber Lake—*lake* WI-6
Gerber Lateral—*canal* IL-6
Gerber Lower Division Rsvr—*reservoir* OR-9
Gerber Pond—*lake* IN-6
Gerber Ranch—*locale* OR-9
Gerber Rim—*cliff* OR-9
Gerber Rsvr—*reservoir* OR-9
Gerber Rsvr Recreation Site—*park* OR-9
Gerbers Ch—*church* PA-2
Gerber Sch—*school* IL-6
Gerber Spring—*spring* OR-9
Gerber Spring—*spring* UT-8
**Gerber Township**—*pop pl* ND-7
Gerbes Center (Shop Ctr)—*locale* MO-7
Gerbick Lake—*lake* WI-6
Gerbracht Camp—*locale* CA-9
Gerdel Ditch—*canal* WY-8
Gerdes Cem—*cemetery* IL-6
Gerdes Ditch—*canal* OH-6
Gerdes Woods—*woods* IL-6
Gerdine, Mount—*summit* AK-9
Gerdine Lake—*lake* OR-9
Gerdin Lake—*lake* MN-6
Gerdins Cem—*cemetery* MN-6
Gere Bank Bldg—*hist pl* NY-2
Gere Creek—*stream* IA-7
*Geregorie* FM-9
Gere Hill—*summit* MA-1
Gere (historical)—*locale* KS-7
*Geren* MS-4
Geren—*other* MS-4
Geren Creek—*stream* CO-8
*Gerengol Reef* PW-9
Geren Island—*island* OR-9
*Gereniyan-to* MP-9
Geren Rsvr—*reservoir* CO-8
*Gerens Crossroads* MS-4
*Gerenton* MS-4
Gerfers Cem—*cemetery* TX-5
Gergen Creek—*stream* MT-8
Gerhard Hollow—*valley* TX-5
Gerhard Miller Ranch—*locale* NV-8
**Gerhards**—*pop pl* PA-2
Gerhardt Cem—*cemetery* NM-5
Gerhardt Cem—*cemetery* TX-5
Gerhardt Creek—*stream* IL-6
Gerhardt Lake—*lake* MN-6
Gerhardt Octagonal Pig House—*hist pl* ND-7
Gerhardt Valley—*valley* NM-5
Gerhart Ranch—*locale* TX-5
Gerhart-Rust Residence—*hist pl* OH-6
Gerholdt Cem—*cemetery* IA-7
Gerholt Cem—*cemetery* IN-6
Gerholz Park—*park* MI-6
**Geridge**—*pop pl* AR-4
Geridge Cem—*cemetery* AR-4
Gerig Camp—*locale* CA-9
Gerig Dam—*dam* CA-9
Gerig Spring—*spring* CA-9
*Gerikuregeru Reef* PW-9
Gerimond, Bayou—*stream* LA-4
**Gering**—*pop pl* NE-7
Gering And Fort Laramie Irrigation Tunnel—*tunnel* NE-7
*Gering Canal* NE-7
Gering Canal—*canal* NE-7
Gering Lateral—*canal* NE-7
Gering-Mitchell Canal—*canal* WY-8
Gering Valley—*valley* NE-7
Gering Valley Sch—*school* NE-7
Gerisch Sch—*school* MI-6
Gerity Rsvr—*reservoir* ID-8
Gerizim Ch—*church* SC-3
Gerke Ditch—*canal* IN-6
Gerken Coulee—*valley* MN-6
*Gerkerville* DE-2
Gerke Sch—*school* OH-6
Gerking Canyon—*valley* OR-9
Gerking Creek—*stream* OR-9
Gerking Flat—*flat* OR-9
Gerking Spring—*spring* OR-9
Gerkin Lake—*reservoir* SD-7
Gerkin Refuge Number 1 Dam—*dam* SD-7
Gerkin Refuge Number 2 Dam—*dam* SD-7
Gerkin Refuge Number 3 Dam—*dam* SD-7
Gerkin Rsvr—*reservoir* WY-8
*Gerkins Canyon* OR-9
Gerkin State Wildlife Ref—*park* SD-7
Gerkman Creek—*stream* WA-9
Gerlach—*locale* OK-5
**Gerlach**—*pop pl* NV-8
Gerlach Cem—*cemetery* OH-6
Gerlach Mill—*locale* MS-4
Gerlach Sch (historical)—*school* SD-7
Gerlach Spring—*spring* CA-9
Gerlach Township—*inact MCD* NV-8
Gerlach Water Tower—*hist pl* NV-8
Gerlane—*locale* KS-7
**Gerlaw**—*pop pl* IL-6
Gerle Creek—*stream* CA-9
Gerled—*locale* IA-7
Gerle Meadow—*flat* CA-9
Gerler Lake—*reservoir* MO-7
Gerlinger—*locale* OR-9
Gerlinger County Park—*park* OR-9
Gerlock Hollow—*valley* MD-2
Gerloff Hollow—*valley* MO-7
Germahville Cem—*cemetery* IL-6
Germaine, Lake—*lake* IL-6
Germaine Coulee—*valley* MT-8
Germaine Creek—*stream* MI-6
Germaine Spring—*spring* MI-6
Germain Lake—*lake* ME-1
Germain Lake—*lake* MI-6
*German* NY-2
*German* OH-6
German—*civil* CA-9
German—*fmr MCD* NE-7
**German**—*pop pl* NY-2
**German**—*pop pl* OH-6
German-American Bank Bldg—*hist pl* MO-7
German American Cem—*cemetery* MN-6
German Bank—*hist pl* IN-6
German Bank—*hist pl* IA-7
German Bank Bldg—*hist pl* KY-4
German Baptist Cem—*cemetery* (2) ND-7
German Baptist Ch—*church* OH-6
German Baptist Ch—*church* (2) SD-7
German Baptist Ch (historical)—*church* (2) SD-7
German Bar Mine—*mine* CA-9
German Branch—*stream* KY-4
German Branch—*stream* MD-2
German Branch—*stream* MO-7
German Brethen Ch—*church* MD-2
German Builder's House—*hist pl* AR-4
German Canal—*canal* ID-8
German Canyon—*valley* NV-8
German Catholic Ch (historical)—*church* SD-7
German Cem—*cemetery* AL-4
German Cem—*cemetery* (2) IL-6
German Cem—*cemetery* (4) IN-6
German Cem—*cemetery* IA-7
German Cem—*cemetery* LA-4
German Cem—*cemetery* (3) MI-6
German Cem—*cemetery* (3) MN-6
German Cem—*cemetery* (5) MO-7
German Cem—*cemetery* (3) NE-7
German Cem—*cemetery* NY-2
German Cem—*cemetery* (2) ND-7
German Cem—*cemetery* (10) OH-6
German Cem—*cemetery* (2) OK-5
German Cem—*cemetery* (2) OR-9
German Cem—*cemetery* (2) PA-2
German Cem—*cemetery* (2) SD-7
German Cem—*cemetery* (2) TX-5
German Cem—*cemetery* (3) WI-6
German Cemetery—*hist pl* FM-9
German Central Elem Sch—*school* PA-2
German Ch—*church* FL-3
German Ch—*church* IN-6
German Ch—*church* MI-6
German Ch—*church* MO-7
German Ch—*church* NY-2
German Ch—*church* (3) OH-6
German Ch—*church* OK-5
German Chapel—*church* NC-3
German Chapel Cem—*cemetery* OH-6
German Ch (historical)—*church* MO-7
German Church and Cemetery—*hist pl* ME-1
German City Ch—*church* IA-7
German Community Hall—*building* MO-7
German Congregational Ch—*church* SD-7
German Corner—*locale* IL-6
German Corners—*locale* WI-6
**German Corners**—*pop pl* PA-2
German Coulee—*stream* WI-6
German Coulee—*valley* (2) WI-6
*German Creek* AL-4
*German Creek* IA-7
*German Creek* WA-9
German Creek—*stream* CA-9
German Creek—*stream* CO-8
German Creek—*stream* ID-8
German Creek—*stream* IA-7
German Creek—*stream* NE-7
German Creek—*stream* TN-4
German Creek—*stream* WI-6
German Creek Cabin Area—*locale* TN-4
German Creek Dock—*locale* TN-4
German Creek Springs—*spring* CO-8
German Crossing—*locale* AL-4
German Diggins Wash—*stream* CA-9
German Ditch—*canal* CO-8
German Ditch—*canal* WY-8
German Drain—*stream* MI-6
German Embassy Bldg—*building* DC-2
German-English Acad—*hist pl* WI-6
German Evangelical Cem—*cemetery* NE-7
German Evangelical Church of Christ Complex—*hist pl* KY-4
German Evangelical Pastors' Home Hist Dist—*hist pl* MO-7
German Evangelical Reformed Church—*hist pl* IA-7
German Evangelical Salem Church—*hist pl* MN-6
German Evangelical Zion Lutheran Church—*hist pl* PA-2
German Evangelist Ch (historical)—*church* SD-7
German Five Corners—*locale* NY-2
German Flat—*flat* UT-8
German Flats—*flat* NE-7
German Flats—*flat* VT-1
**German Flatts (Town of)**—*pop pl* NY-2
German Ford—*locale* AL-4
**German Four Corners**—*pop pl* NY-2
German Gap—*gap* CA-9
German Gulch—*valley* ID-8
German Gulch—*valley* MT-8
German hill—*summit* MA-1
German Hill—*summit* (2) PA-2
German Hill Cem—*cemetery* PA-2
*German Hill Church* PA-2
German Hollow—*valley* IA-7
German Hollow—*valley* (2) NY-2
German Hollow—*valley* (2) OH-6
German Hollow—*valley* TX-5
*Germania* PA-2
Germania—*locale* NJ-2
Germania—*locale* PA-2
Germania—*locale* TX-5
Germania—*locale* WI-6
**Germania**—*pop pl* AL-4
**Germania**—*pop pl* MS-4
**Germania**—*pop pl* MO-7
**Germania**—*pop pl* WI-6
Germania Bank Bldg—*hist pl* MN-6
Germania Basin—*basin* ID-8
Germania Bldg—*hist pl* WI-6
Germania Bldg Complex—*hist pl* MI-6
Germania Branch—*stream* PA-2
Germania Bridge Trail—*trail* PA-2
Germania Cem—*cemetery* MI-6
Germania Cem—*cemetery* (2) MO-7
Germania Cem—*cemetery* NJ-2
Germania Cem—*cemetery* (2) TX-5
Germania Cem—*cemetery* WI-6
Germania Club—*hist pl* IL-6
Germania Consolidated Mine—*mine* WA-9
Germania Creek—*stream* ID-8
Germania Creek—*stream* IN-6
**Germania Gardens**—*pop pl* NJ-2
**Germania Gardens Subdivision**—*pop pl* UT-8
Germania Hall—*building* TX-5
Germania Hill—*summit* PA-2
Germania (historical)—*locale* KS-7
Germania (historical)—*locale* SD-7
Germania Marsh Wildlife Area—*park* WI-6
Germania-Miller/Standard Hotel—*hist pl* IA-7
Germania Mine—*mine* WA-9
Germanian Cem—*cemetery* WI-6
Germania Oil Field—*oilfield* TX-5
Germania Post Office (historical)—*building* PA-2
Germania Sch—*school* MO-7
Germania Sch (historical)—*school* MS-4
Germania Spring—*spring* AL-4
Germania Springs (historical)—*locale* AL-4
Germania Station—*locale* PA-2
**Germania (Town of)**—*pop pl* WI-6
**Germania Township**—*pop pl* ND-7
**Germania (Township of)**—*pop pl* MN-6
Germania Turnverein Bldg—*hist pl* PA-2
German Insurance Bank—*hist pl* KY-4
German Island—*island* GA-3
German Lake—*lake* ID-8
German Lake—*lake* (3) MN-6
German Lake State Game Ref—*park* MN-6
German Lane Cem—*cemetery* MS-4
German Lutheran Cem—*cemetery* IA-7
German Lutheran Cem—*cemetery* MN-6
German Lutheran Ch—*church* AL-4
German Lutheran Ch (historical)—*church* (2) SD-7
*German Lutheran Church* SD-7
German Lutheran Sch (historical)—*school* AL-4
German Methodist Ch—*church* IL-6
German Methodist Ch (historical)—*church* SD-7
German Methodist Episcopal Church—*hist pl* IA-7
German Mine—*mine* NM-5
German Mtn—*summit* GA-3
Germann—*locale* AZ-5
Germanna Bridge—*bridge* VA-3
Germanna Site—*hist pl* VA-3
**Germano**—*pop pl* OH-6
German Opening—*flat* CA-9
*German Plains Cemetery* KS-7
German Pond—*lake* FL-3
German Prairie—*flat* WA-9
German Presbyterian Cem—*cemetery* OR-9
German Reform Cem—*cemetery* OH-6
German Reformed Ch—*church* IL-6
German Reformed Ch—*church* MO-7
German Reformed Church—*hist pl* IN-6
German Reformed Sanctity Church Parsonage—*hist pl* NY-2
German Ridge—*ridge* (2) CA-9
German Ridge—*ridge* (2) IN-6
German Ridge—*ridge* (2) MN-6
German Ridge—*ridge* VA-3
German Ridge Cem—*cemetery* (2) IN-6
German Ridge Cem—*cemetery* OH-6
German Ridge Lookout Tower—*tower* IN-6
German River—*stream* VA-3
German Rsvr No 1—*reservoir* CO-8
German Rsvr No 2—*reservoir* CO-8
German Run—*stream* (2) PA-2
Germans—*locale* PA-2
German Sch—*school* (2) IL-6
German Sch—*school* KS-7
German Sch—*school* MI-6
German Sch—*school* ND-7
German Sch—*school* TX-5
German Sch (abandoned)—*school* MO-7
German Sch (historical)—*school* (2) PA-2
German Sch Number 2—*school* ND-7
German Sch Number 3—*school* ND-7
German Sch Number 4—*school* ND-7
*Germans Corner* PA-2
Germans Corner—*locale* VA-3
Germans Corners—*locale* PA-2
German Settlement—*locale* ID-8
German Settlement—*locale* PA-2
German Settlement Cem—*cemetery* IN-6
German Settlement Cem—*cemetery* NY-2
German Settlement Cem—*cemetery* WI-6
German Settlement Ch—*church* WI-6
German Settlement Sch (historical)—*school* PA-2
*Germans Hill* MA-1
German Shoals—*bar* TN-4
*Germans Mill* PA-2
German Spring—*spring* NV-8
**Germansville**—*pop pl* PA-2
German Swamp—*stream* VA-3
German Tank—*reservoir* TX-5
German Temple—*church* KS-7
*Germanton* NC-3
**Germanton**—*pop pl* NC-3
*Germantown* CT-1
*Germantown* IN-6
*Germantown* KS-7
*German Town* MA-1
*Germantown* NJ-2
*Germantown* NC-3
Germantown—*hist pl* LA-4
Germantown—*locale* NY-2
Germantown—*locale* NC-3
Germantown—*locale* PA-2
Germantown—*locale* TN-4
Germantown—*locale* VA-3
**Germantown**—*pop pl* CT-1
**Germantown**—*pop pl* (2) IL-6
**Germantown**—*pop pl* (3) IN-6
**Germantown**—*pop pl* IA-7
**German Town**—*pop pl* KY-4
**Germantown**—*pop pl* KY-4
**Germantown**—*pop pl* (4) MD-2
**Germantown**—*pop pl* (2) NY-2
**Germantown**—*pop pl* (2) OH-6
**Germantown**—*pop pl* (4) PA-2
**Germantown**—*pop pl* SC-3
**Germantown**—*pop pl* (2) TN-4
**Germantown**—*pop pl* (2) WI-6
Germantown Acad—*school* (2) PA-2
Germantown Archeol Sites—*hist pl* VA-3
Germantown Baptist Church—*hist pl* TN-4
Germantown Bay—*bay* NC-3
Germantown Cem—*cemetery* IN-6
Germantown Cem—*cemetery* KS-7
Germantown Cem—*cemetery* LA-4
Germantown Cem—*cemetery* MN-6
Germantown Cem—*cemetery* NE-7
Germantown Cem—*cemetery* OH-6
Germantown Ch—*church* LA-4
Germantown Ch—*church* MD-2
Germantown Ch—*church* MN-6
Germantown Ch—*church* SD-7
*Germantown Church* PA-2
*Germantown Creek* IN-6
Germantown Cricket Club—*hist pl* PA-2
Germantown Cricket Club—*other* PA-2
Germantown Dam—*dam* OH-6
Germantown East Oil Field—*other* IL-6
Germantown Elem Sch—*school* NC-3
**Germantown Estates**—*pop pl* MD-2
Germantown Grammar Sch—*hist pl* PA-2
**Germantown Hills**—*pop pl* IL-6
Germantown Hills Ch—*church* IL-6
Germantown Hist Dist—*hist pl* TN-4
Germantown (historical)—*locale* KS-7
**Germantown (historical)**—*pop pl* MO-7
Germantown Hosp—*hospital* PA-2
Germantown HS—*school* PA-2
Germantown Junction—*locale* PA-2
**Germantown (Noah)**—*pop pl* MO-7
**German (Town of)**—*pop pl* NY-2
*Germantown (Pershing)* IN-6
Germantown Point—*cape* MA-1
Germantown Reformed Cem—*cemetery* NY-2
Germantown Road—*uninc pl* PA-2
Germantown Rsvr—*reservoir* OH-6
Germantown Sch—*school* MD-2
Germantown Sch—*school* SD-7
Germantown Sch Number 2—*school* ND-7
German Township—*fmr MCD* (2) IA-7
**German Township**—*pop pl* KS-7
**German Township**—*pop pl* ND-7
**German Township**—*pop pl* SD-7
German Township HS—*school* PA-2
**German (Township of)**—*pop pl* IL-6
**German (Township of)**—*pop pl* (4) IN-6
**German (Township of)**—*pop pl* (5) OH-6
**German (Township of)**—*pop pl* PA-2
Germantown State Bank Bldg—*hist pl* NE-7
**Germantown (subdivision)**—*pop pl* (2) MA-1
**Germantown (subdivision)**—*pop pl* PA-2
**Germantown (Town of)**—*pop pl* NY-2
**Germantown (Town of)**—*pop pl* (2) WI-6
**Germantown Township**—*pop pl* ND-7
**Germantown Township**—*pop pl* (2) SD-7
**Germantown (Township of)**—*pop pl* IL-6
**Germantown (Township of)**—*pop pl* MN-6
*German Valley* NJ-2
German Valley—*basin* NE-7
**German Valley**—*pop pl* IL-6
**German Valley**—*pop pl* IA-7
German Valley—*valley* NJ-2
German Valley—*valley* TX-5
German Valley—*valley* UT-8
German Valley—*valley* (4) WI-6
German Valley Cem—*cemetery* NE-7
German Valley Cem—*cemetery* TX-5
German Valley Cem—*cemetery* (2) WI-6
German Valley Hist Dist—*hist pl* NJ-2
German Valley Sch—*school* WI-6
German Valley Sch (historical)—*school* PA-2
German Village—*hist pl* OH-6
**German Village**—*pop pl* GA-3
**German Village**—*pop pl* NY-2
German Village (Boundary Increase)—*hist pl* OH-6
Germanville—*fmr MCD* NE-7
Germanville—*locale* IA-7
Germanville Catholic Cem—*cemetery* IA-7
Germanville (historical P.O.)—*locale* IA-7
**Germanville (Township of)**—*pop pl* IL-6
*Germany* AL-4
*Germany* PA-2
Germany—*locale* GA-3
**Germany**—*pop pl* IN-6
**Germany**—*pop pl* PA-2
**Germany**—*pop pl* TX-5
Germany Branch—*stream* MS-4
Germany Branch—*stream* (2) TN-4
Germany Brook—*stream* MA-1
Germany Cem—*cemetery* AL-4
Germany Cem—*cemetery* GA-3
Germany Ch—*church* PA-2
Germany Cove—*valley* NC-3
Germany Creek—*stream* AR-4
Germany Creek—*stream* GA-3
Germany Creek—*stream* LA-4
Germany Creek—*stream* TX-5
Germany Creek—*stream* WA-9
Germany Family Cem—*cemetery* AL-4
Germany Ferry (historical)—*locale* AL-4
Germany Flats—*flat* NJ-2
Germany Hill—*locale* NY-2
Germany Hollow—*valley* (2) OH-6
Germany Hollow Ch—*church* OH-6
Germany Knob—*summit* WV-2
*Germany Mountains - in part* AL-4
Germany Ridge—*ridge* PA-2
Germany Sch—*school* IL-6
*Germany Settlement* WV-2
Germanys Ferry Bridge—*bridge* AL-4
Germany Springs Park—*park* AL-4
*Germany Springs Rec Area* AL-4
**Germany (Township of)**—*pop pl* PA-2
Germany Valley—*valley* PA-2
Germany Valley—*valley* WV-2
Germany Valley Cem—*cemetery* PA-2
Germany Wells—*well* TX-5
Germatown Sch—*school* MD-2
Germeny Lake Dam—*dam* MS-4
Germer Basin—*basin* ID-8
Germer Park—*summit* ID-8
**Germfask**—*pop pl* MI-6
Germfask Cem—*cemetery* MI-6
Germfask Ch—*church* MI-6
**Germfask (Township of)**—*pop pl* MI-6
Germo Coulee—*valley* MT-8
Germond Hill—*summit* NY-2
**Germonds**—*pop pl* NY-2
Germ Tank—*reservoir* AZ-5
Germy Creek—*stream* VA-3
**Gernada Chapel**—*pop pl* AR-4
*Gernant Church* PA-2
Gernt—*locale* TN-4
Gernt, Bruno, House—*hist pl* TN-4
Gernt Post Office (historical)—*building* TN-4
Gero, Lake—*lake* LA-4
Geroe Creek—*stream* AK-9
Gerogetown HS—*school* NC-3
Geroge Watch Lake—*lake* MN-6
Gero Island—*island* ME-1
Gerome Spring—*spring* AZ-5
Geronimo—*locale* AZ-5
**Geronimo**—*pop pl* OK-5
**Geronimo**—*pop pl* TX-5
Geronimo, Mount—*summit* AZ-5
Geronimo Alvarez Grant—*civil* FL-3
Geronimo Canyon—*valley* NM-5
Geronimo Cave—*cave* AZ-5
Geronimo Creek—*stream* CO-8
Geronimo Creek—*stream* (2) TX-5

Geronimo Dam—dam AZ-5
Geronimo Draw—valley NM-5
Geronimo Head—summit AZ-5
Geronimo Hill—summit OK-5
Geronimo Lake—reservoir TN-4
Geronimo Meadow—flat AZ-5
Geronimo Mtn—summit TX-5
Geronimo Number Two Tank—reservoir AZ-5
Geronimo Post Office—building AZ-5
Geronimo Ranch—locale NM-5
Geronimo Ridge—ridge OK-5
Geronimo Spring—spring (2) AZ-5
Geronimo Spring—spring NM-5
Geronimo Surrender Monmt—park AZ-5
Geronimo Surrender Site—locale AZ-5
Geronimo Tank—reservoir (2) AZ-5
Geronimo Tank—reservoir NM-5
Geronimo Trail—trail AZ-5
Geronimo Trap—cliff AZ-5
Geronimo Windmills—locale TX-5
Gero Pond—lake NY-2
Gero Tunnel—mine CO-8
Gerould Cem—cemetery NY-2
Gerow Brook—stream CT-1
Gerow Butte—summit OR-9
Gerow Millpond—lake CT-1
Gerow Spring—spring OR-9
Gerrard—locale CO-8
Gerrard—locale ID-8
Gerrard, Stephen A., Mansion—hist pl OH-6
Gerrard Drain—canal CA-9
Gerrard Gulch—valley CO-8
Gerrards Lake—reservoir NC-3
Gerrards Lake Dam—dam NC-3
**Gerrardstown**—pop pl WV-2
Gerrardstown (Magisterial District)—fmr MCD WV-2
**Gerrard Township**—pop pl ND-7
Gerrell Mtn—summit GA-3
Gerrell Windmill—locale NM-5
Gerren Creek—stream NC-3
**Gerren Heights**—pop pl TN-4
Gerring Cem—cemetery TN-4
Gerringer-Goodman Dam—dam NC-3
Gerringer-Goodman Pond—reservoir NC-3
Gerrish—locale NH-1
Gerrish Ave Sch—school CT-1
Gerrish Bridge—other IL-6
Gerrish Brook—stream ME-1
Gerrish Brook—stream NH-1
Gerrish Cem—cemetery (2) ME-1
Gerrish Ch—church MI-6
Gerrish Chapel—church NH-1
Gerrish Corner—locale ME-1
Gerrish Corner—locale NH-1
Gerrish Cove—bay ME-1
Gerrish Higgins Sch—school MI-6
Gerrish Hill—summit ME-1
Gerrish Island—island ME-1
Gerrish Isle—island NH-1
Gerrish Mtn—summit ME-1
Gerrish Ranch—locale CA-9
**Gerrish (Township of)**—pop pl MI-6
**Gerrishville**—pop pl ME-1
Gerrish Warehouse—hist pl ME-1
Gerrit—locale ID-8
**Gerritsen**—pop pl NY-2
Gerritsen Creek—stream NY-2
*Gerritsen Inlet* NY-2
Gerritsen Inlet—channel NY-2
Gerritsen Inlet—gut NY-2
Gerritts JHS—school WI-6
Gerro Gordo (historical)—locale KS-7
Gerry—locale ME-1
**Gerry**—pop pl NY-2
Gerry, Elbridge, House—hist pl MA-1
Gerry, Lake—lake NY-2
*Gerry, Town of* MA-1
Gerry Branch—stream TN-4
Gerry Cem—cemetery MO-7
Gerry Cem—cemetery NH-1
Gerry Cove—bay ME-1
Gerry Curtis Park—park FL-3
Gerry Gulch—valley ID-8
Gerry Hill—summit MA-1
Gerry Hill Cem—cemetery NY-2
Gerry Island—island MA-1
*Gerry Lake* MI-6
Gerry Mtn—summit OR-9
Gerry Sch—school MA-1
Gerry Sch (historical)—school PA-2
*Gerrys Hill* MA-1
*Gerrys Island* MA-1
Gerry Smith Ranch—locale NM-5
**Gerry (Town of)**—pop pl NY-2
Gersdorf Creek—stream TX-5
**Gershorm**—pop pl MS-4
Gershorm Baptist Ch—church MS-4
Gershorm Post Office (historical)—building MS-4
Gershorm Sch (historical)—school MS-4
Gerstacker Bridge—bridge TX-5
Gerstell—locale WV-2
Gerstell Hollow—valley WV-2
Gerstenberger Drain—canal MI-6
**Gerster**—pop pl MO-7
Gerster Gulch—valley UT-8
Gerstle Cove—bay CA-9
Gerstle Glacier—glacier AK-9
Gerstle Park—park CA-9
Gerstle River—stream AK-9
Gerstley Mine—mine CA-9
Gert Buttes—ridge ND-7
Gert Canyon—valley OR-9
Gertch Canyon—valley ID-8
Gertenslager Carriage and Wagon Company—hist pl OH-6
Gerth Cem—cemetery MO-7
Gertie—uninc pl VA-3
Gertie, Lake—lake FL-3
Gertie Butte—summit ID-8
Gertie Gulch—valley ID-8
Gertie Mine—mine SD-7
Gertie Sch—school VA-3
Gertison Dam—dam MT-8
**Gerton**—pop pl NC-3
Gerton Spring—spring WY-8
Gertrude—locale AR-4
Gertrude—locale GA-3
Gertrude—locale KY-4
Gertrude, Lake—lake AK-9
Gertrude, Lake—lake FL-3
Gertrude, Lake—lake MT-8
Gertrude Bell JHS—school CO-8
Gertrude Cove—bay AK-9
Gertrude Creek—stream (2) AK-9
Gertrude Creek—stream CA-9
Gertrude Herbert Art Institute—hist pl GA-3
Gertrude Island—island WA-9
Gertrude Lake—lake (2) CA-9
Gertrude Lake—lake (2) MN-6
Gertrude Lake—lake OR-9
Gertrude Lake—lake WA-9
Gertrude Lake—lake WI-6
Gertrude Lateral—canal CA-9
Gertrude Mine—mine CO-8
Gertrude Run—stream WV-2
Gertrude Sch (historical)—school TN-4
Gertrudes Meadow—flat ID-8
*Gertsen Canyon* UT-8
Gertsen Creek—stream UT-8
Gertson Slough—lake SD-7
Gertson Slough State Public Shooting Area—park SD-7
Gertulla Creek—stream OR-9
Gert Wash—stream CA-9
**Gerty**—pop pl OK-5
Gerty Cem—cemetery OK-5
*Geruhengeru* PW-9
*Geruheruguiru Pass* PW-9
Gerundegut Bay—bay MI-6
Gerund Lake—lake MN-6
*Geru Suido* PW-9
**Gervais**—pop pl OR-9
Gervais Grade Sch—school OR-9
Gervais Lake—lake MN-6
Gervais Run—stream OH-6
Gervais Street Bridge—hist pl SC-3
**Gervais (Township of)**—pop pl MN-6
Gerver—fmr MCD NE-7
Gerwick Ditch—canal OR-9
Gerwyne Creek—stream IL-6
Geryville—locale PA-2
Gerzium Cem—cemetery MS-4
*Gesegosu* PW-9
Gesend Pond—lake MN-6
*Geseru* PW-9
*Geseru To* PW-9
*Geshbokul* PW-9
*Geshibokuru* PW-9
*Geshibokuru* PW-9
*Geshibokuru Island* PW-9
*Geshibokuru To* PW-9
Geshi Canyon—valley AZ-5
Geskakmina Lake—lake AK-9
Geskey Creek—stream WI-6
Gesler, Edward R., House—hist pl NM-5
Gesler Lake—lake MI-6
Gesling—locale KY-4
**Gesner (historical)**—pop pl OR-9
Gessford—locale IA-7
**Gessie**—pop pl IN-6
Gest—locale KY-4
Gestner Branch—stream MI-6
Gestner Lake—lake MI-6
Gesu Church—hist pl FL-3
Gesu Church—hist pl WI-6
Gesu Sch—school MI-6
Gesu Sch—school (2) OH-6
Gesu Sch (historical)—school FL-3
**Getaway**—pop pl OH-6
Get Away Canyon—valley NM-5
Getaway Canyon—valley (2) TX-5
Getaway Coulee—valley MT-8
Getaway Creek—stream WA-9
Getaway Gap—gap TX-5
Getaway Mtn—summit ID-8
Getaway Pass—gap MT-8
Getaway Pens—locale TX-5
Getaway Point—cape WA-9
Getaway Point—summit ID-8
Getaway Spring—spring WA-9
Getaway Tank—reservoir TX-5
*Getchel Gulch* CA-9
Getchel Hill—summit CO-8
**Getchell**—pop pl WA-9
Getchell, O. W., House—hist pl CA-9
Getchell Lakes—lake ME-1
Getchell Brook—stream (2) ME-1
Getchell Cem—cemetery ME-1
Getchell Cem—cemetery MN-6
Getchell Ch—church ND-7
Getchell Corner—locale ME-1
Getchell Coulee—valley MT-8
Getchell Creek—stream MN-6
Getchell Gulch—valley CA-9
Getchell Lake—lake MN-6
Getchell Mine—mine NV-8
Getchell Mtn—summit ME-1
Getchell Riffles—rapids ME-1
Getchell Town Hall—building ND-7
**Getchell Township**—pop pl ND-7
Getchell Whitcher Sch—school ND-7
Getchel Mtn—summit ME-1
Getchel Ridge—ridge OR-9
Getchel Spring—spring NV-8
Geter Cem—cemetery GA-3
Geter Cem—cemetery MS-4
Geter Creek—stream TX-5
Gether—locale VA-3
Gething Lakes—reservoir TX-5
Gethman Cem—cemetery IA-7
Gethsemane—locale KY-4
Gethsemane—locale NC-3
**Gethsemane**—pop pl AR-4
**Gethsemane**—pop pl TX-5
Gethsemane Baptist Ch—church FL-3
Gethsemane Cem—cemetery CT-1
Gethsemane Cem—cemetery (2) GA-3
Gethsemane Cem—cemetery (2) MI-6
Gethsemane Cem—cemetery (3) MN-6
Gethsemane Cem—cemetery NY-2
Gethsemane Cem—cemetery (2) OH-6
Gethsemane Cem—cemetery PA-2
Gethsemane Cem—cemetery SD-7
Gethsemane Cem—cemetery (2) TX-5
Gethsemane Ch—church (3) AL-4
Gethsemane Ch—church (2) AR-4
Gethsemane Ch—church (3) GA-3
Gethsemane Ch—church IN-6
Gethsemane Ch—church KS-7
Gethsemane Ch—church KY-4
Gethsemane Ch—church MD-2
Gethsemane Ch—church MI-6
Gethsemane Ch—church (2) MN-6
Gethsemane Ch—church (6) NC-3
Gethsemane Ch—church (2) ND-7
Gethsemane Ch—church (11) SC-3
Gethsemane Ch—church (3) TN-4
Gethsemane Ch—church TX-5
Gethsemane Ch—church (4) VA-3
Gethsemane Chapel—church IA-7
Gethsemane Ch (historical)—church TN-4
Gethsemane Episcopal Cathedral—hist pl ND-7
Gethsemane Episcopal Church—hist pl MN-6
Gethsemane Evangelical Lutheran Church—hist pl MI-6
**Gethsemane (historical)**—pop pl TN-4
Gethsemane Lutheran Ch—church IN-6
Gethsemane Lutheran Church—hist pl TX-5
Gethsemane Missionary Baptist Ch—church TN-4
Gethsemane Sch—school IN-6
Gethsemane Sch—school MI-6
Gethsemane Sch—school MN-6
Gethsemane Sch—school NC-3
Gethsemane Sch (historical)—school TN-4
Gethsemani Cem—cemetery OR-9
Gethsemans Cem—cemetery IA-7
Getman Cem—cemetery (2) NY-2
**Getman Corners**—pop pl NY-2
Getman Hill—summit NY-2
Getman Memorial Ch—church FL-3
Getmore Number 2 Mine (surface)—mine AL-4
Getmuna Creek—stream AK-9
Getner Creek—stream MT-8
Get Out Creek—stream FL-3
Getout Run—stream WV-2
Getsey Lake—lake WI-6
*Getsuyo To* FM-9
Getta Creek—stream ID-8
Gettamy Sch—school PA-2
Gettel Drain—canal MI-6
Gettel School—locale MT-8
Gettem Canyon—valley NM-5
Gettem Spring—spring NM-5
Getters Island—island PA-2
Gettinger Ditch—canal IN-6
Gettinger Sch—school IA-7
*Gettings Creek* OR-9
Gettings Creek—stream OR-9
Gettins Bridge—other IL-6
Gettis Cem—cemetery KS-7
Gettis Ridge—ridge PA-2
Gettman Hollow—valley MO-7
**Getty Heights**—pop pl PA-2
*Getty Ridge* PA-2
Getty Run—stream PA-2
Gettys, James R., House—hist pl TN-4
Gettys, James R., Mill—hist pl TN-4
*Gettysburg* SD-7
**Gettysburg**—pop pl (2) OH-6
**Gettysburg**—pop pl PA-2
**Gettysburg**—pop pl SD-7
Gettysburg Area Senior HS—school PA-2
Gettysburg Battlefield Hist Dist—hist pl PA-2
Gettysburg Borough—civil PA-2
Gettysburg Cem—cemetery OH-6
Gettysburg Cem—cemetery SD-7
Gettysburg Coll—school PA-2
*Gettysburgh* OH-6
*Gettysburgh* PA-2
Gettysburg Heliport—airport PA-2
Gettysburg (historical)—locale KS-7
Gettysburg JHS—school PA-2
Gettysburg Junction—uninc pl PA-2
Gettysburg Mine—mine CO-8
Gettysburg Municipal Airp—airport SD-7
*Gettysburg Natl Historical Park* PA-2
Gettysburg Natl Historical Park—park PA-2
Gettysburg Natl Military Park—hist pl PA-2
Gettysburg Natl Military Park—park PA-2
Gettysburg Park—locale PA-2
Gettysburg Peak—summit TX-5
*Gettysburg Pike Interchange* PA-2
Gettysburg Radar Station—locale SD-7
Gettysburg Ranch—locale WA-9
Gettysburg Sch—school CA-9
Gettysburg Sch—school OH-6
Gettysburg Shaft—mine NM-5
Gettysburg Shop Ctr—locale PA-2
Gettysburg Township—civil SD-7
**Gettysburg Township**—pop pl KS-7
Gettys Butte—summit WA-9
Gettys Canyon—valley SD-7
Gettys Chapel (historical)—church TN-4
Gettys Creek—stream OR-9
Gettys Siding—locale CA-9
Gettys Mill (historical)—locale (2) TN-4
*Gettys Mill Post Office* TN-4
Gettys Park—park MN-6
Gettys Ridge—ridge TN-4
**Gettysville**—pop pl SC-3
Getty Tomb—hist pl IL-6
**Getty (Township of)**—pop pl MN-6
Getukti Cliff—cliff AK-9
Get Up and Get Creek—stream CA-9
Getup Post Office (historical)—building AL-4
*Getuyo To* FM-9
Getwell Ch—church TN-4
Getwell Sch—school TN-4
Getz—locale AZ-5
**Getz**—pop pl VA-3
Getz Corner—locale VA-3
Getz Ditch—canal CO-8
Getzendaner Memorial Park—park TX-5
Getzen Memorial Ch—church GA-3
Getz Mtn—summit WV-2
Getz Ranch—locale AZ-5
Getz RR Station—building AZ-5
Getz Sch—school AZ-5
**Getzville**—pop pl NY-2
Getz Well—well AZ-5
*Geuda* KS-7
**Geuda Springs**—pop pl KS-7
Geuda Springs Cem—cemetery KS-7
Geuda Springs Oil Field—oilfield KS-7
Geugao—area GU-9
*Geugel-Makaep Passage* PW-9
Geum Creek—stream ID-8
Geurin Cemetery—cemetery AR-4
*Geurin Creek* OR-9
**Geurts Subdivision**—pop pl UT-8
Geus River—stream GU-9
Geus Valley—valley GU-9
Gevedon Branch—stream KY-4
Gew, Wong K., Mansion—hist pl CA-9
**Geyer**—pop pl OH-6
Geyer Cem—cemetery OH-6
Geyer Ditch—canal (2) IN-6
*Geyer Junior High School* IN-6
Geyer Lake—lake FL-3
**Geyer Springs**—pop pl AR-4
Geyer Springs Sch—school AR-4
Geyers United Methodist Ch—church PA-2
*Geyes Ch* PA-2
Geyler Tank—reservoir AZ-5
*Geyson* PW-9
Geyselman Lake—lake ID-8
**Geyser**—pop pl MT-8
Geyser, The—geyser NV-8
*Geyser Basin* WA-9
Geyser Bight—bay AK-9
Geyser Brook—stream NY-2
Geyser Canyon—valley CA-9
Geyser Cem—cemetery MT-8
*Geyser Creek* MT-8
Geyser Creek—stream CO-8
Geyser Creek—stream (2) MT-8
Geyser Creek—stream (2) NV-8
Geyser Creek—stream UT-8
Geyser Creek—stream (2) WY-8
Geyser Creek Park—flat WY-8
Geyser Creek Trail—trail WY-8
Geyser Dam—dam AZ-5
Geyser Hollow—valley PA-2
*Geyser Hunters Hot Spring* OR-9
Geyser Lake—lake WI-6
Geyser Maintenance Station—locale NV-8
Geyser-Marion Mine—mine UT-8
Geyser Park—flat CO-8
Geyser Pass—gap UT-8
Geyser Peak—summit CA-9
Geyser Peak—summit UT-8
Geyser Ranch—locale NV-8
Geyser Ranch Airp—airport NV-8
**Geyser Resort**—pop pl CA-9
Geyser Rock—pillar CA-9
Geyser Rsvr—reservoir CO-8
**Geysers, The**—pop pl CA-9
Geysers, The—spring CA-9
Geysers, The—spring NV-8
Geyser Spring—spring MT-8
Geyser Spring—spring NV-8
Geyser Spring—spring OR-9
Geyser Spring Coulee—valley MT-8
Geyser Springs—spring WY-8
*Geyser Springs Group* WY-8
Geysers Resort—locale CA-9
Geysers (Steam Wells), The—geyser CA-9
Geyser Valley—valley WA-9
**Geyserville**—pop pl CA-9
Geyserville Union Sch—hist pl CA-9
*Gey's Gap* VA-3
Geyso, Mrs. Frank, Houses—hist pl IL-6
Gezel Creek—stream ID-8
G-five Farm Spring—spring AZ-5
G-five Farm Tank—reservoir AZ-5
G-five Tank—reservoir AZ-5
G F Lateral—canal CO-8
G Flats—flat CO-8
G Flier Dam—dam SD-7
G French Homestead Dam—dam SD-7
G Gap—gap CO-8
*Ggathla* AZ-5
Ghaaghaztail—flat AZ-5
G Hand Dam—dam SD-7
Gharky, George H., House—hist pl OH-6
G H B Lateral—canal CO-8
G H C Lateral—canal CO-8
G H Curtis Lake Dam—dam MS-4
G H D Lateral—canal CO-8
*Ghedsy Creek* MS-4
Ghee Bridge—bridge OH-6
**Gheen**—pop pl MN-6
Gheena Point—cape AK-9
**Gheen Corner**—pop pl MN-6
**Gheens**—pop pl LA-4
Gheens Ch—church LA-4
Gheen Spring—spring NV-8
Gheen (Unorganized Territory of)—unorg MN-6
Gheils Cem—cemetery OH-6
**Ghennes Heights**—pop pl PA-2
Ghent—locale ME-1
Ghent—locale PA-2
**Ghent**—pop pl KY-4
**Ghent**—pop pl MN-6
**Ghent**—pop pl NY-2
**Ghent**—pop pl OH-6
**Ghent**—pop pl VA-3
**Ghent**—pop pl WV-2
Ghent Cem—cemetery PA-2
Ghent Ch—church OH-6
Ghent Creek—stream NC-3
Ghent Hist Dist—hist pl KY-4
Ghent Hist Dist—hist pl NC-3
Ghent Hist Dist—hist pl VA-3
Ghent Homestead—locale WY-8
Ghent Mtn—summit TX-5
Ghent Park—park VA-3
Ghent Parks—flat WY-8
Ghents Branch—stream SC-3
Ghents Branch Ch—church SC-3
*Ghents Creek* NC-3
Ghents Hollow—valley TN-4
Ghent Slope—flat WY-8
Ghent Substation—other PA-2
**Ghent (Town of)**—pop pl NY-2
*Gherkin Canyon* OR-9
Ghesquiere Park—park MI-6
G H Hall Ranch—locale ID-8
Ghico Creek—stream WA-9
Ghilds Pond—reservoir CT-1
**Ghio**—pop pl NC-3
**Ghio Scholl Station**—pop pl NC-3
Gholar Cem—cemetery MS-4
Gholdston Slough—gut TN-4
G Holloway Dam—dam SD-7
**Gholson**—pop pl MS-4
**Gholson**—pop pl TX-5
Gholson Bar—bar AL-4
Gholson Bridge—bridge VA-3
Gholson Bridge—hist pl VA-3
Gholson Cem—cemetery IL-6
Gholson Cem—cemetery MS-4
Gholson Cem—cemetery TX-5
Gholson Cem—cemetery VA-3
Gholson Creek—stream (2) TX-5
Gholson Gap—gap TX-5
Gholson Grove Ch—church IL-6
Gholson Mine (underground)—mine AL-4
Gholson Mtn—summit MS-4
Gholson Post Office (historical)—building MS-4
Gholson Post Office (historical)—building TN-4
Gholson Sch—school TX-5
Gholsonville—locale VA-3
Gholston Ch—church GA-3
Gholston Stand Crossroads—locale GA-3
*Ghookville* GA-3
Ghormley Cem—cemetery OK-5
Ghormley Mtn—summit NC-3
G Horner Ranch—locale NE-7
Ghoshen Center Sch—school MA-1
Ghost, The—summit AZ-5
Ghost Bayou—gut TX-5
Ghost Branch—stream TX-5
Ghost Brook—stream NY-2
Ghost Camp—locale CA-9
Ghost Camp—locale OR-9
Ghost Coulee—stream MT-8
Ghost Cove—bay FL-3
Ghost Creek—stream FL-3
Ghost Creek—stream MI-6
Ghost Creek—stream OR-9
Ghost Creek—stream SD-7
Ghost Creek—stream TX-5
Ghost Creek—stream WI-6
Ghost Creek—stream (3) WY-8
Ghost Creek Cave—cave AL-4
Ghost Dance Ridge—ridge NV-8
Ghost Hawk Lake—reservoir SD-7
Ghost Hawk Park—locale SD-7
Ghost Head Swamp—swamp AL-4
Ghost Hill—summit MA-1
Ghost Hill—summit MN-6
Ghost Hill—summit OH-6
Ghost Hill—summit TX-5
Ghost Hollow—valley IL-6
Ghost Hollow—valley IA-7
Ghost Hollow—valley KY-4
Ghost Hollow—valley (2) OH-6
Ghost Hollow—valley (3) OK-5
Ghost Hollow—valley WV-2
Ghost Hollow Creek—stream IN-6
Ghost Knob—summit VA-3
Ghost Lake—lake CO-8
Ghost Lake—lake MI-6
Ghost Lake—lake MN-6
Ghost Lake—lake (2) WA-9
Ghost Lake—lake (3) WI-6
Ghost Landing Bar—bar ME-1
Ghost Mine—mine CA-9
Ghost Mine—mine CO-8
Ghost Mound—summit OK-5
Ghost Mtn—summit CA-9
Ghost Mtn—summit ID-8
Ghost Point—cape FL-3
Ghost Point—cliff WA-9
Ghost Ranch—locale ID-8
Ghost Ranch—locale NM-5
Ghost Ridge—ridge OR-9
Ghost Ridge—ridge UT-8
Ghost Rock—pillar UT-8
Ghost Rocks—island AK-9
Ghost Sch—school TX-5
Ghost Tank—reservoir AZ-5
*Ghost Town Capitol of Roberts County, The* SD-7
Ghost Town in the Glen—locale PA-2
Ghoul Basin—basin ID-8
*Ghoul Branch* TN-4
Ghoul Creek—stream WA-9
Ghouls Fork—stream NC-3
**Ghylin Township**—pop pl ND-7
Ghylin Union Cem—cemetery ND-7
Giacoma Camp—locale AZ-5
Giacometto Ranch—locale NV-8
Giacometto Spring—spring NV-8
Giacomini Prairie—flat CA-9
Gialla Tank—reservoir TX-5
Gianella Bridge—hist pl CA-9
Gianelli Cabin—locale CA-9
Gianero Ranch—locale NM-5
Giannini Hall—hist pl CA-9
Giannonatti Creek—stream SD-7
Giannonatti Ranch—hist pl SD-7
Giano Sch—school CA-9
Gianotti JHS—school CT-1
Giant—locale CA-9
**Giant**—pop pl SC-3
Giant Bar Marsh—swamp NY-2
Giant Braid—locale CA-9
*Giant Butte* AZ-5
Giant Canyon—valley AZ-5
Giant Castle Mtn—summit WY-8
*Giant Chair* AZ-5
Giant City State Park—park IL-6
Giant City State Park Lodge and Cabins—hist pl IL-6
Giant Crater—crater CA-9
Giant Cricket Cave—cave AL-4
Giant Falls—falls NH-1
Giant Falls—falls WA-9
Giant Footprint Ruins—locale NM-5
Giant For—forest CA-9
**Giant Forest (Giant Forest Lodge)**—pop pl CA-9
Giant Forest Lodge Hist Dist—hist pl CA-9
Giant Forest Village-Camp Kaweah Hist Dist—hist pl CA-9
Giant Gap—gap CA-9
Giant Gap Gulch—valley CA-9
Giant Gap Ridge—ridge CA-9
Giant Gulch—valley CO-8
Giant Hill—summit MT-8
Giant Hill—summit NE-7
Giant Indian Intaglios—other CA-9
Giant King Mine—mine CA-9
Giant Ledge—cliff NY-2
Giant Ledge Mine—mine CA-9
Giant Logs—area AZ-5
Giant Mine—mine AK-9
Giant Mine—mine AZ-5
Giant Mine—mine CA-9
Giant Mine—mine MT-8
Giant Mine—mine NV-8
*Giant Neck* CT-1
Giant Pine Campground—locale MN-6
Giant Point—cape AK-9
Giant Powder Creek—stream MT-8
Giant Rock—pillar CA-9
*Giants at Rest* AL-4
Giants Chair—pillar AZ-5
Giants Coffins Butte—summit NE-7
Giants Grave—summit NV-8
Giants Grave—summit VA-3
Giants Grave Spring—spring NV-8
Giants Graveyard—island WA-9
Giants Head—cape AK-9
*Giants Head Point* AK-9
Giant Shop Ctr—locale NC-3
Giants Neck—cape CT-1
**Giants Neck**—pop pl CT-1
**Giants Neck Heights**—pop pl CT-1
Giants Nose—summit ID-8
Giant Spring—spring MT-8
Giant Springs—spring MT-8
*Giants Rest* AL-4
Giant Staircase—slope UT-8
Giant Stairs—slope NH-1
Giants Thumb—pillar WY-8
Giant Sunrise Mine—mine MT-8
*Giant Track* CO-8
Gianttrack Mtn—summit CO-8
Giant Tree—locale CA-9
Giant-Volney Mine—mine SD-7
Giant Washbowl—lake NY-2
**Giard**—pop pl IA-7
Giard Cem—cemetery IA-7
Giards Bay—bay VT-1
**Giard Station (historical)**—pop pl IA-7
Giard Townhall—building IA-7
Giard Township—fmr MCD IA-7
*Giareau Trading Post* KS-7
Giatana Cem—cemetery MS-4
**Giatto**—pop pl WV-2
**Giauque Beach**—pop pl MI-6
Gibbard Drain—canal MI-6
Gib Bay—swamp MS-4
Gibbe Flat—flat CA-9
Gibbens Creek—stream TX-5
*Gibbens Spring* UT-8
Gibbes, Carter W., House—hist pl AZ-5
Gibbes, William, House—hist pl SC-3
Gibbes JHS—school SC-3
Gibbet Hill—summit MA-1
*Gibbett Hill* MA-1
*Gibbeys Creek* UT-8
*Gibbins Branch* TX-5
Gibbins Cem—cemetery TN-4
Gibbins Hollow—valley AR-4
*Gibbler* ID-8
*Gibbler Canyon* CO-8
Gibbler Gulch—valley CO-8
Gibbler Mtn—summit CO-8
*Gibbon* MS-4
Gibbon—locale OK-5
Gibbon—locale WA-9
**Gibbon**—pop pl MN-6
**Gibbon**—pop pl NE-7
**Gibbon**—pop pl OR-9
Gibbon Anchorage—bay AK-9
Gibbon Canyon—valley CA-9
Gibbon Canyon—valley WY-8
Gibbon Cem—cemetery MN-6
Gibbon Cem—cemetery OK-5
Gibbon Creek—stream CA-9
Gibbon Draw—valley WY-8
Gibbon Falls—falls WY-8
Gibbon Geyser Basin—basin WY-8
**Gibbon Glade**—pop pl PA-2
*Gibbon Hill* ME-1
Gibbon Hill—summit WY-8
Gibbon Hill Geyser—geyser WY-8
Gibbon Meadows—flat WY-8
Gibbon Mtn—summit AZ-5
Gibbon Peak—summit AK-9
Gibbon Peak—summit CA-9
Gibbon Ridge—ridge OR-9
Gibbon River—stream WY-8
Gibbon River Rapids—rapids WY-8
**Gibbons**—pop pl AR-4
**Gibbons**—pop pl MS-4
**Gibbons**—pop pl MO-7
Gibbons, John Chisum, House—hist pl TX-5
Gibbons, Lake—reservoir TX-5
Gibbons Air Park—airport MO-7
*Gibbons Branch* TX-5
Gibbons Branch—stream AL-4
Gibbons Branch—stream TX-5
Gibbons Brook—stream NY-2
Gibbons Canyon—valley ID-8
Gibbons Cem—cemetery AR-4
Gibbons Cem—cemetery TX-5
Gibbons Ch—church MD-2
Gibbons Corners—locale NY-2
Gibbons Creek—stream IL-6
Gibbons Creek—stream MT-8
Gibbons Creek—stream (2) TX-5
Gibbons Creek—stream (2) WA-9
Gibbons Drain—canal MI-6
Gibbons Drain—stream MI-6
Gibbons Draw—valley WY-8
*Gibbons Fork* WY-8
*Gibbons Glade Run* PA-2
*Gibbons Glade Run* WV-2
Gibbons HS—school NC-3
Gibbons Landing (historical)—locale AL-4
Gibbons Mansion—hist pl NJ-2
Gibbons Mill Canyon—valley OR-9
Gibbons Pass—gap MT-8
*Gibbons Peak* WA-9
*Gibbons Point* WA-9
Gibbon Springs—spring AZ-5
Gibbons Ranch—locale (2) NM-5
*Gibbons Run* PA-2
Gibbons Run—stream WV-2
Gibbons Sch—school IL-6
Gibbons Sch—school MA-1
Gibbons Sch—school MT-8
Gibbons Sch—school OH-6
Gibbons Spring—spring AZ-5

Gibbons Springs—*spring* (2) UT-8
Gibbons Street Elem Sch—*school* FL-3
Gibbons Trail—*trail* PA-2
**Gibbonsville**—*pop pl* ID-8
**Gibbon Township**—*pop pl* NE-7
Gibbon Village Hall—*hist pl* MN-6
*Gibb Point* WA-9
Gibb Point—*cape* NC-3
Gibbs—*locale* ID-8
Gibbs—*locale* KS-7
Gibbs—*locale* KY-4
**Gibbs**—*pop pl* AR-4
**Gibbs**—*pop pl* CT-1
**Gibbs**—*pop pl* LA-4
**Gibbs**—*pop pl* (2) MO-7
**Gibbs**—*pop pl* TN-4
Gibbs, Heman, Farmstead—*hist pl* MN-6
Gibbs, John, House—*hist pl* KY-4
Gibbs, John, House—*hist pl* MI-6
Gibbs, Lester, House—*hist pl* KY-4
Gibbs, Mount—*summit* CA-9
Gibbs, Nicholas, House—*hist pl* TN-4
Gibbs, Paul, House—*hist pl* MA-1
Gibbs Bog—*swamp* MA-1
**Gibbsboro**—*pop pl* NJ-2
Gibbsboro Air Force Station—*military* NJ-2
*Gibbsborough* NJ-2
Gibbs Box (historical)—*locale* MS-4
Gibbs Branch—*stream* AL-4
Gibbs Branch—*stream* MS-4
Gibbs Branch—*stream* (2) NC-3
*Gibbs Brook* MA-1
Gibbs Brook—*stream* (3) MA-1
Gibbs Brook—*stream* NH-1
Gibbs Butte—*summit* WY-8
Gibbs Cabin—*locale* WY-8
Gibbs Canyon—*valley* CA-9
Gibbs (CCD)—*cens area* TN-4
Gibbs Cem—*cemetery* (2) AL-4
Gibbs Cem—*cemetery* AR-4
Gibbs Cem—*cemetery* (4) GA-3
Gibbs Cem—*cemetery* ME-1
Gibbs Cem—*cemetery* MA-1
Gibbs Cem—*cemetery* MS-4
Gibbs Cem—*cemetery* (3) MO-7
Gibbs Cem—*cemetery* (2) NC-3
Gibbs Cem—*cemetery* OR-9
Gibbs Cem—*cemetery* (5) TN-4
Gibbs Chapel—*church* AL-4
Gibbs Chapel—*church* DE-2
Gibbs Chapel—*church* NC-3
Gibbs Chapel Cem—*cemetery* AL-4
*Gibbs Chapel Church* AL-4
Gibbs Chute—*gut* WI-6
**Gibbs City**—*pop pl* MI-6
**Gibbs Corners**—*pop pl* MI-6
Gibbs Coulee—*valley* MT-8
*Gibbs Creek* OR-9
*Gibbs Creek* WI-6
Gibbs Creek—*bay* NC-3
Gibbs Creek—*stream* AR-4
Gibbs Creek—*stream* CO-8
Gibbs Creek—*stream* IL-6
Gibbs Creek—*stream* (2) MS-4
Gibbs Creek—*stream* (2) MT-8
Gibbs Creek—*stream* NE-7
Gibbs Creek—*stream* (2) NC-3
Gibbs Creek—*stream* OK-5
Gibbs Creek—*stream* OR-9
Gibbs Creek—*stream* TX-5
Gibbs Creek—*stream* WI-6
Gibbs Creek—*stream* WY-8
**Gibbs Crossing**—*pop pl* MA-1
*Gibbs Cross Roads* TN-4
Gibbs Crossroads—*locale* SC-3
Gibbs Crossroads—*locale* TN-4
*Gibbs Cross Roads Post Office* TN-4
Gibbs Crossroads Post Office (historical)—*building* TN-4
Gibbs Ditch—*canal* CO-8
Gibbs Division—*civil* TN-4
Gibbs Draw—*valley* WY-8
Gibbs Elem Sch—*school* TN-4
Gibbs Falls—*falls* VA-3
Gibbs Ferry Park—*park* TN-4
Gibbs-Flournoy House—*hist pl* TX-5
Gibbs Gap—*gap* NC-3
**Gibbs Grove**—*pop pl* MA-1
Gibbs Gulch—*valley* CO-8
Gibbs Hill—*locale* PA-2
Gibbs Hollow—*valley* TX-5
Gibbs House—*hist pl* AL-4
Gibbs House—*hist pl* NC-3
Gibbs HS—*school* FL-3
Gibbs HS—*school* TN-4
Gibbs Island—*island* FL-3
Gibbs Island—*island* ME-1
Gibbs Island—*island* SC-3
Gibbs Knob—*summit* TN-4
*Gibbs Lake* NV-8
Gibbs Lake—*lake* CA-9
Gibbs Lake—*lake* MS-4
Gibbs Lake—*lake* NY-2
Gibbs Lake—*lake* (2) WA-9
Gibbs Lake—*lake* (2) WI-6
Gibbs Lookout Tower—*locale* MI-6
Gibbs Meadow—*flat* OR-9
Gibbs Memorial Ch—*church* GA-3
Gibbs MS—*school* TN-4
Gibbs Mtn—*summit* GA-3
Gibbs Mtn—*summit* MA-1
Gibbs Mtn—*summit* (2) NC-3
Gibbs Narrows—*gut* MA-1
Gibbs Number 2 Dam—*dam* MA-1
Gibbs Number 3 Dam—*dam* MA-1
Gibbs Peak—*summit* CO-8
Gibbs Place—*locale* NM-5
Gibbs Place—*locale* WY-8
*Gibbs Point* TN-4
*Gibbs Point* WA-9
Gibbs Point—*cape* FL-3
Gibbs Point—*cape* NY-2
Gibbs Point—*cape* (4) NC-3
*Gibbs Pond* MA-1
Gibbs Pond—*lake* AL-4
Gibbs Pond—*lake* FL-3
Gibbs Pond—*lake* MD-2
Gibbs Pond—*lake* (2) MA-1
Gibbs Pond—*lake* NY-2
Gibbs Pond—*lake* WY-8
Gibbs Pond (historical)—*lake* MA-1
Gibb Spring—*spring* KY-4
Gibbs Ranch—*locale* NV-8
Gibbs Ranch—*locale* TX-5
Gibbs Ranch—*locale* (2) WY-8
Gibbs Rock—*bar* MA-1
Gibbs Rock—*island* AK-9
Gibbs Sch—*school* AR-4
Gibbs Sch—*school* GA-3
Gibbs Sch—*school* (2) IL-6
Gibbs Sch—*school* LA-4
Gibbs Sch—*school* MA-1
Gibbs Sch—*school* (2) MS-4
Gibbs Sch—*school* (3) NJ-2
Gibbs Sch—*school* OH-6
Gibbs Sch—*school* TN-4
Gibbs Sch (abandoned)—*school* MO-7
Gibbs School (historical)—*locale* MO-7
Gibbs Shoal—*bar* NC-3
Gibbs Siphon—*canal* CA-9
Gibbs Site—*hist pl* MO-7
Gibbs Slough—*gut* LA-4
Gibbs Spring—*spring* (2) CA-9
Gibbs Spring—*spring* ID-8
Gibbs Spring—*spring* MO-7
Gibbs Spring—*spring* UT-8
Gibbs Store (historical)—*locale* AL-4
Gibbs Swamp—*swamp* MA-1
Gibbs Tank—*reservoir* AZ-5
Gibbs-Thomas House—*hist pl* UT-8
**Gibbstown**—*pop pl* LA-4
**Gibbstown**—*pop pl* NJ-2
**Gibbs Township**—*pop pl* ND-7
**Gibbstown (Township name Greenwich)**—*pop pl* NJ-2
Gibbs Trail—*trail* PA-2
Gibbs Union Cem—*cemetery* MO-7
**Gibbs Village (subdivision)**—*pop pl* AL-4
Gibbsville—*locale* IA-7
**Gibbsville**—*pop pl* WI-6
Gibbsville Cem—*cemetery* WI-6
Gibbs-Von Seutter House—*hist pl* MS-4
Gibbs Woods—*woods* NC-3
**Gibbton**—*pop pl* NC-3
**Gibbtown**—*pop pl* MT-8
Gibb Wash—*stream* AZ-5
*Gibby Branch* NC-3
Gibby Branch—*stream* (3) NC-3
Gibby Island—*island* NC-3
Gibby Point—*cape* FL-3
Gibby Rock—*other* AK-9
Gib Creek—*stream* WA-9
Gibeaut Lake—*reservoir* AL-4
Gibeon—*locale* VA-3
Giberson, Capt. George W., House—*hist pl* NJ-2
Giberson Bay—*bay* CO-8
**Giberson (Eureka)**—*pop pl* IN-6
Gibert Brook—*stream* ME-1
Gibert Mtn—*summit* WA-9
Gibex Point—*ridge* UT-8
*Gibeys* UT-8
Gibhard Playground—*park* IN-6
*Gibibwishe Lake* MN-6
Gibibwisher Lake—*lake* MN-6
*Gibidwense Lake* MN-6
Gibinrii Island—*island* MP-9
*Gibinrii-to* MP-9
**Gibisonville**—*pop pl* OH-6
Gibler—*locale* ID-8
Gibler Cem—*cemetery* (2) OH-6
*Gibler Creek* MO-7
Gibler Ditch—*canal* CO-8
Gibler Gulch—*valley* CO-8
Giblin Gulch—*valley* WY-8
Giblo Spring—*spring* MT-8
Giblyn Sch—*school* NY-2
Giboa Ch—*church* VA-3
Giboney—*locale* MO-7
Giboney Island—*island* IL-6
Giboney Lake—*reservoir* IN-6
Giboney Lake Dam—*dam* IN-6
Gibonney Canyon—*valley* CA-9
Gibon Sch—*school* PA-2
**Gibos Corners**—*pop pl* MI-6
*Gibraltar* WA-9
Gibraltar—*locale* WA-9
**Gibraltar**—*pop pl* MI-6
**Gibraltar**—*pop pl* PA-2
Gibraltar—*summit* CA-9
Gibraltar, Lake—*lake* CO-8
Gibraltar Bay—*bay* MI-6
Gibraltar Cave—*cave* TN-4
Gibraltar Cem—*cemetery* MI-6
Gibraltar Creek—*stream* OR-9
Gibraltar Dam—*dam* CA-9
Gibraltar District Sch No. 2—*hist pl* WI-6
Gibraltar Hill—*summit* AK-9
Gibraltar Hill—*summit* PA-2
Gibraltar Lake—*lake* AK-9
Gibraltar Mine—*mine* (3) CA-9
Gibraltar Mine—*mine* NV-8
Gibraltar Mtn—*summit* AZ-5
Gibraltar Mtn—*summit* OR-9
Gibraltar Mtn—*summit* WA-9
Gibraltar Rock—*pillar* WA-9
Gibraltar Rock—*pillar* WI-6
Gibraltar Rock—*summit* (2) WA-9
Gibraltar Rock County Park—*park* WI-6
Gibraltar Rsvr—*reservoir* CA-9
**Gibraltar (Town of)**—*pop pl* WI-6
*Gibralter* MI-6
*Gibralter* WA-9
Gibralter—*summit* KY-4
Gibralter, Mount—*summit* MT-8
Gibralter Coal Company—*facility* KY-4
Gibralter Ditch—*canal* CO-8
Gibralter Ledge—*bench* ME-1
Gibralter Point—*summit* AK-9
Gibralter Ridge—*ridge* MT-8
**Gibsland**—*pop pl* LA-4
*Gibson* AL-4
*Gibson* (2) IN-6
*Gibson* MS-4
*Gibson* NE-7
*Gibson* ND-7
Gibson—*fmr MCD* NE-7
Gibson—*locale* AL-4
Gibson—*locale* CA-9
Gibson—*locale* ID-8
Gibson—*locale* NM-5
Gibson—*locale* OH-6
Gibson—*locale* WY-8
Gibson—*other* KY-4
**Gibson**—*pop pl* AZ-5
**Gibson**—*pop pl* (2) AR-4
**Gibson**—*pop pl* FL-3
**Gibson**—*pop pl* GA-3
**Gibson**—*pop pl* IL-6
**Gibson**—*pop pl* IN-6
**Gibson**—*pop pl* IA-7
**Gibson**—*pop pl* LA-4
**Gibson**—*pop pl* MD-2
**Gibson**—*pop pl* MS-4
**Gibson**—*pop pl* (2) MO-7
**Gibson**—*pop pl* NY-2
**Gibson**—*pop pl* NC-3
**Gibson**—*pop pl* OK-5
**Gibson**—*pop pl* (2) PA-2
**Gibson**—*pop pl* SC-3
**Gibson**—*pop pl* TN-4
Gibson—*uninc pl* NY-2
Gibson—*uninc pl* WI-6
Gibson, A. J., House—*hist pl* MT-8
Gibson, E. R., House—*hist pl* IA-7
Gibson, John S., Farmhouse—*hist pl* GA-3
Gibson, John W., House—*hist pl* OK-5
Gibson, J. W., House—*hist pl* MO-7
Gibson, Lake—*lake* (2) FL-3
Gibson, Lake—*reservoir* IN-6
Gibson, Mount—*summit* CA-9
Gibson, William B., House—*hist pl* CA-9
Gibson Airp—*airport* IN-6
*Gibson and Henry Island* MT-8
Gibson Arroyo—*valley* AZ-5
Gibson Assembly Camp—*locale* OK-5
Gibson Ave Ch—*church* TN-4
Gibson Baptist Ch—*church* TN-4
Gibson Basin—*basin* ID-8
Gibson Bay—*swamp* SC-3
Gibson Bayou—*stream* AR-4
Gibson Bayou—*stream* MS-4
Gibson Bayou Ch—*church* AR-4
Gibson Bend—*bend* IA-7
Gibson Bend—*bend* NE-7
Gibson Blair Ditch—*canal* CO-8
Gibson-Blair Ditch—*canal* WY-8
Gibson Blair Ditch—*canal* WY-8
*Gibson Brake* AR-4
Gibson Brake—*gut* AR-4
Gibson Brake—*swamp* AR-4
*Gibson Branch* TN-4
Gibson Branch—*stream* GA-3
Gibson Branch—*stream* (5) KY-4
Gibson Branch—*stream* MS-4
Gibson Branch—*stream* (2) NC-3
Gibson Branch—*stream* (2) SC-3
Gibson Branch—*stream* (3) TX-5
Gibson Branch—*stream* VA-3
Gibson Branch—*stream* WV-2
Gibson Branch Ch—*church* GA-3
Gibson Bridge—*bridge* AL-4
Gibson Bridge—*bridge* NC-3
Gibson Bridge—*bridge* TN-4
**Gibsonburg**—*pop pl* OH-6
Gibson Canal—*canal* ID-8
Gibson Canyon—*valley* (2) NM-5
Gibson Canyon—*valley* (2) OR-9
Gibson Canyon—*valley* UT-8
Gibson Canyon Creek—*stream* CA-9
Gibson Canyon - Deadman Hiline Trail—*trail* AZ-5
Gibson (CCD)—*cens area* GA-3
Gibson (CCD)—*cens area* TN-4
*Gibson Cem* TN-4
Gibson Cem—*cemetery* (6) AL-4
Gibson Cem—*cemetery* (4) AR-4
Gibson Cem—*cemetery* ID-8
Gibson Cem—*cemetery* (2) IL-6
Gibson Cem—*cemetery* IA-7
Gibson Cem—*cemetery* (4) KY-4
Gibson Cem—*cemetery* (4) MS-4
Gibson Cem—*cemetery* (5) MO-7
Gibson Cem—*cemetery* NH-1
Gibson Cem—*cemetery* (3) NC-3
Gibson Cem—*cemetery* OH-6
Gibson Cem—*cemetery* OK-5
Gibson Cem—*cemetery* PA-2
Gibson Cem—*cemetery* SC-3
Gibson Cem—*cemetery* SD-7
Gibson Cem—*cemetery* (8) TN-4
Gibson Cem—*cemetery* TX-5
Gibson Cem—*cemetery* (7) VA-3
Gibson Cem—*cemetery* (3) WV-2
Gibson Ch—*church* AL-4
Gibson Ch—*church* LA-4
Gibson Chapel—*church* LA-4
Gibson Chapel—*church* OH-6
Gibson Chapel—*church* TX-5
Gibson Chapel—*church* (2) VA-3
Gibson Chapel (historical)—*church* TN-4
*Gibson City* ID-8
Gibson City—*post sta* IL-6
**Gibson Corners**—*pop pl* NY-2
Gibson Coulee—*valley* (2) MT-8
**Gibson County**—*pop pl* IN-6
**Gibson County**—*pop pl* TN-4
Gibson County Airp—*airport* TN-4
Gibson County Courthouse—*hist pl* IN-6
Gibson County Courthouse—*hist pl* TN-4
Gibson County HS—*school* TN-4
Gibson County Memorial Library—*building* TN-4
Gibson County Park—*park* FL-3
Gibson Cove—*bay* AK-9
Gibson Cove—*valley* (2) AL-4
Gibson Cove—*valley* (2) NC-3
Gibson Cove Branch—*stream* NC-3
*Gibson Creek* PA-2
Gibson Creek—*channel* GA-3
**Gibson Creek**—*pop pl* WA-9
Gibson Creek—*stream* (2) AZ-5
Gibson Creek—*stream* AR-4
Gibson Creek—*stream* (6) CA-9
Gibson Creek—*stream* (2) CO-8
Gibson Creek—*stream* GA-3
Gibson Creek—*stream* (2) ID-8
Gibson Creek—*stream* KS-7
Gibson Creek—*stream* (3) KY-4
Gibson Creek—*stream* MO-7
Gibson Creek—*stream* MT-8
Gibson Creek—*stream* NJ-2
Gibson Creek—*stream* OH-6
Gibson Creek—*stream* OK-5
Gibson Creek—*stream* (3) OR-9
Gibson Creek—*stream* SC-3
Gibson Creek—*stream* TN-4
Gibson Creek—*stream* (2) TX-5
Gibson Creek—*stream* UT-8
Gibson Creek—*stream* VA-3
Gibson Creek—*stream* (3) WA-9
**Gibson Crossroads**—*pop pl* AL-4
**Gibsondale**—*pop pl* PA-2
Gibson Dam—*dam* AL-4
Gibson Ditch—*canal* CO-8
Gibson Ditch—*canal* (2) IN-6
Gibson Ditch—*stream* LA-4
Gibson Ditch—*stream* MT-8
Gibson Division—*civil* TN-4
Gibson Drain—*canal* (2) MI-6
Gibson Drain—*canal* OR-9
Gibson Drain—*stream* ID-8
Gibson Drain—*stream* MI-6
Gibson Draw—*valley* WA-9
Gibson Draw—*valley* WY-8
Gibson Falls—*falls* WA-9
**Gibson Farm Subdivision**—*pop pl* TN-4
Gibson Flat—*flat* CA-9
Gibson Flats—*flat* MT-8
**Gibson Flats**—*pop pl* MT-8
Gibson Fork—*locale* NC-3
**Gibson Four Corners**—*pop pl* NH-1
Gibson Gap—*gap* (3) AL-4
Gibson Gap—*gap* GA-3
Gibson Gap—*gap* TN-4
Gibson Grove Ch—*church* MD-2
Gibson Gulch—*valley* CA-9
Gibson Gulch—*valley* (4) CO-8
Gibson Gulch—*valley* MT-8
Gibson Gulch—*valley* (3) OR-9
**Gibson Hall**—*pop pl* TN-4
Gibson Hall Sch (historical)—*school* TN-4
Gibson Hill—*summit* AL-4
Gibson Hill—*summit* CA-9
Gibson Hill—*summit* CO-8
Gibson Hill—*summit* CT-1
Gibson Hill—*summit* MO-7
Gibson Hill—*summit* NY-2
Gibson Hill—*summit* OR-9
Gibson Hill—*summit* PA-2
Gibson Hill—*summit* VA-3
Gibson Hill Cem—*cemetery* AL-4
Gibson Hill Ch—*church* AL-4
Gibson Hill Mine (surface)—*mine* AL-4
**Gibson Hill (subdivision)**—*pop pl* AL-4
Gibson (historical)—*locale* KS-7
Gibson Hollow—*valley* IN-6
Gibson Hollow—*valley* (4) KY-4
Gibson Hollow—*valley* MO-7
Gibson Hollow—*valley* OK-5
Gibson Hollow—*valley* PA-2
Gibson Hollow—*valley* (2) TN-4
Gibson Hollow—*valley* (3) VA-3
Gibson Hollow—*valley* WV-2
Gibson Hollow Spring—*spring* PA-2
Gibson Homestead—*locale* CO-8
Gibson Hosp—*hospital* AL-4
Gibson Hot Spring—*spring* OR-9
Gibson House—*hist pl* NE-7
Gibson House—*hist pl* OH-6
Gibson House—*hist pl* PA-2
Gibson House Museum—*building* MA-1
Gibson House Site—*locale* MO-7
Gibson HS—*school* MS-4
Gibson HS—*school* TN-4
**Gibsonia**—*pop pl* FL-3
**Gibsonia**—*pop pl* IL-6
**Gibsonia**—*pop pl* PA-2
Gibsonia Baptist Ch—*church* FL-3
Gibson Inn—*locale* TN-4
Gibson Island—*island* AK-9
Gibson Island—*island* (2) GA-3
Gibson Island—*island* MD-2
Gibson Island—*island* OH-6
Gibson Island—*island* OR-9
**Gibson Island**—*pop pl* MD-2
Gibson Island Beach—*beach* MD-2
Gibson Jack Creek—*stream* ID-8
Gibson JHS—*school* NV-8
Gibson Junction—*other* NC-3
Gibson Knob—*summit* (2) KY-4
Gibson Knob—*summit* (2) NC-3
Gibson Knob—*summit* TN-4
Gibson Knob—*summit* VA-3
Gibson Knob—*summit* WV-2
*Gibson Lake* MT-8
Gibson Lake—*lake* AL-4
Gibson Lake—*lake* AR-4
Gibson Lake—*lake* CO-8
Gibson Lake—*lake* (2) MI-6
Gibson Lake—*lake* (2) MN-6
Gibson Lake—*lake* MS-4
Gibson Lake—*lake* NM-5
Gibson Lake—*lake* (2) OR-9
Gibson Lake—*lake* TX-5
Gibson Lake—*lake* (2) WI-6
Gibson Lake—*locale* MI-6
Gibson Lake—*reservoir* GA-3
Gibson Lake—*reservoir* MS-4
Gibson Lake—*swamp* LA-4
Gibson Lake Dam—*dam* MS-4
Gibson Lakes—*lake* ID-8
Gibson Landing—*locale* LA-4
Gibson Landing—*locale* MS-4
Gibson Landing—*locale* NJ-2
Gibson Landing—*locale* NC-3
**Gibson Landing**—*pop pl* NY-2
Gibson Lateral—*canal* AZ-5
Gibson Levee—*locale* AR-4
Gibson Lookout Tower—*tower* FL-3
**Gibson Manor (Gibson)**—*pop pl* MD-2
Gibson Meadow—*flat* CA-9
Gibson Meadows—*flat* WY-8
Gibson Memorial Ch—*church* VA-3
Gibson Methodist Ch—*church* TN-4
Gibson Methodist Episcopal Church—*hist pl* LA-4
Gibson Mill—*locale* NC-3
Gibson Mill—*locale* VA-3
Gibson Mill Branch—*stream* AL-4
Gibson Mill (historical)—*locale* AL-4
Gibson Mill Site—*locale* MO-7
Gibson Mine—*mine* NM-5
Gibson Mine—*mine* UT-8
Gibson Mine (underground)—*mine* AL-4
Gibson Mtn—*summit* ID-8
Gibson Mtn—*summit* NH-1
Gibson Mtn—*summit* TX-5
Gibson Mtn—*summit* (3) VA-3
Gibson Neighborhood Park—*park* AZ-5
Gibson Oatfield—*locale* MO-7
Gibson Oil and Gas Field—*oilfield* KS-7
Gibson Oil Field—*oilfield* LA-4
Gibson Oil Field—*oilfield* TX-5
Gibson Park—*park* FL-3
Gibson Park—*park* MT-8
Gibson Park—*park* PA-2
*GIBSON PEAK* ID-8
Gibson Peak—*summit* AZ-5
Gibson Peak—*summit* CO-8
Gibson Peak—*summit* MT-8
Gibson Peak—*summit* WA-9
Gibson Pen Windmill—*locale* TX-5
Gibson Pinnacle—*pillar* NY-2
Gibson Place—*locale* NM-5
Gibson Plantation—*locale* LA-4
*Gibson Point* GA-3
Gibson Point—*cape* MN-6
Gibson Point—*cape* MO-7
Gibson Point—*cape* PA-2
Gibson Point—*cape* WA-9
Gibson Point—*summit* ID-8
Gibson Pond—*lake* AL-4
Gibson Pond—*lake* NH-1
Gibson Pond—*lake* VA-3
Gibson Pond—*reservoir* NC-3
Gibson Pond—*reservoir* SC-3
Gibson Pond—*reservoir* TN-4
Gibson-Porter Cem—*cemetery* MO-7
Gibson Post Office—*building* TN-4
Gibson Prairie—*flat* OR-9
Gibson Public Service Generation Plant Dam—*dam* IN-6
Gibson Pumping Station—*other* PA-2
Gibson Ranch—*locale* (2) AZ-5
Gibson Ranch—*locale* (2) MT-8
Gibson Ranch—*locale* NE-7
Gibson Ranch County Park—*park* CA-9
Gibson Rennig Ditch—*canal* MT-8
Gibson Ridge—*ridge* AR-4
Gibson Ridge—*ridge* (3) CA-9
Gibson Ridge—*ridge* CO-8
Gibson Ridge—*ridge* (2) NC-3
Gibson Ridge—*ridge* TN-4
Gibson Ridge—*ridge* VA-3
Gibson Rock Hollow—*valley* TN-4
Gibson Rosewald Sch—*school* TN-4
Gibson Rsvr—*reservoir* MT-8
Gibson Rsvr—*reservoir* OR-9
Gibson Run—*stream* (3) WV-2
Gibsons Beach—*beach* NY-2
Gibson Sch—*school* AL-4
Gibson Sch—*school* (2) CA-9
Gibson Sch—*school* FL-3
Gibson Sch—*school* MI-6
Gibson Sch—*school* MO-7
Gibson Sch—*school* PA-2
Gibson Sch—*school* SD-7
Gibson Sch—*school* TN-4
Gibson Sch—*school* (2) VA-3
Gibson Sch (abandoned)—*school* MO-7
Gibson Sch (abandoned)—*school* PA-2
Gibson Sch (historical)—*school* MS-4
Gibson's Covered Bridge—*hist pl* PA-2
Gibsons Creek—*stream* NC-3
Gibsons Gap—*gap* KY-4
Gibsons Gap—*gap* VA-3
Gibson Shop Ctr—*locale* (2) KS-7
*Gibsons Landing* LA-4
*Gibsons Landing* MS-4
*Gibsons Landing Post Office* TN-4
Gibsons Millpond—*reservoir* NC-3
Gibsons Neck—*cape* SC-3
*Gibsons Pass* MT-8
Gibson Spit—*bar* WA-9
*Gibsons Point* GA-3
Gibsons Point—*uninc pl* PA-2
*Gibsons Pond* SC-3
Gibsons Pond—*lake* SD-7
Gibsons Pond—*reservoir* SC-3
*Gibsons Port* MS-4
Gibson Spring—*spring* AZ-5
Gibson Spring—*spring* CO-8
Gibson Spring—*spring* MT-8
Gibson Spring—*spring* OR-9
Gibson Spring—*spring* TN-4
Gibson Spring—*spring* UT-8
Gibson Spring—*spring* WY-8
Gibsons Roost Well—*well* AZ-5
Gibsons Ruby Mine—*mine* NC-3
Gibsons Sch (historical)—*school* TN-4
*Gibsons Spring* TN-4
*Gibson Stand* TN-4
*Gibson Station* IN-6
*Gibson Station* TN-4
**Gibson Station**—*pop pl* VA-3
Gibson Station Acad (historical)—*school* TN-4
Gibson Station (Post Office)—*locale* VA-3
**Gibson (subdivision)**—*pop pl* MS-4
**Gibson Subdivision**—*pop pl* TN-4
*Gibsons Well* TN-4
*Gibsons Wells Post Office* TN-4
Gibson Tank—*lake* NM-5
Gibson Tank—*reservoir* (2) AZ-5
Gibson Tank—*reservoir* (2) NM-5
Gibson-Todd House—*hist pl* WV-2
**Gibsonton**—*pop pl* FL-3
**Gibsonton**—*pop pl* PA-2
Gibsonton (CCD)—*cens area* FL-3
Gibsonton Elem Sch—*school* FL-3
**Gibsonton (RR name East Tampa)**—*pop pl* FL-3
Gibson Towhead (inundated)—*island* AL-4
**Gibsontown**—*pop pl* NC-3
**Gibsontown**—*pop pl* TN-4
**Gibson (Town of)**—*pop pl* WI-6
**Gibson (Township of)**—*pop pl* IN-6
**Gibson (Township of)**—*pop pl* MI-6
**Gibson (Township of)**—*pop pl* OH-6
**Gibson (Township of)**—*pop pl* (2) PA-2
Gibsonville—*locale* AL-4
**Gibsonville**—*pop pl* CA-9
**Gibsonville**—*pop pl* NC-3
Gibsonville Elem Sch—*school* NC-3
Gibsonville (historical)—*locale* MS-4
Gibsonville Post Office (historical)—*building* TN-4
Gibsonville Ridge—*ridge* (2) CA-9
Gibson Well—*well* (2) NM-5
Gibson Wells—*locale* TN-4
Gibson Wells Methodist Ch—*church* TN-4
Gibson Wells Post Office (historical)—*building* TN-4
Gibson Wells Sch (historical)—*school* TN-4
Gibson Windmill—*locale* NV-8
Gibson Windmill—*locale* NM-5
Gibson Windmill—*locale* TX-5
Gib Spring—*spring* OR-9
Gibtown—*locale* TX-5
*Gicht Hanne* PA-2
Gid—*locale* AR-4
Gidd Branch—*stream* WV-2
*Gidden Pass* ID-8
Giddens, James, House—*hist pl* TN-4
Giddens, L. D., and Son Jewelry Store—*hist pl* NC-3
Giddens Ch—*church* AL-4
Giddens Chapel Cem—*cemetery* AL-4
*Giddens Chapel Church* AL-4
Giddens Gift Ch—*church* GA-3
Giddens Hill—*summit* LA-4
Giddens Mill Creek—*stream* GA-3
Giddens Pond—*lake* GA-3
**Giddensville**—*pop pl* NC-3
*Giddenville* NC-3
Giddeonson Hollow—*valley* IL-6
**Gidding**—*pop pl* MI-6
*Gidding Brook* CT-1
Gidding Lake—*lake* MI-6
Gidding Rsvr—*reservoir* OR-9
*Giddings* OH-6
Giddings—*locale* CO-8
Giddings—*locale* MI-6
**Giddings**—*pop pl* OH-6
**Giddings**—*pop pl* TX-5
Giddings, Joshua Reed, Law Office—*hist pl* OH-6
Giddings, Mount—*summit* AK-9
Giddings Ave Sch—*school* OH-6
Giddings Bldg—*hist pl* CO-8
Giddings Brook—*stream* (2) VT-1
Giddings (CCD)—*cens area* TX-5
Giddings Cem—*cemetery* OH-6
*Giddings Creek* OR-9
Giddings Flat—*flat* SD-7
Giddings Grave—*cemetery* AZ-5
Giddings Hall, Georgetown College—*hist pl* KY-4
Giddings Hill—*summit* VT-1
*Giddings Lake* MI-6
Giddings Lake—*lake* FL-3
Giddings Post Office (historical)—*building* SD-7
Giddings-Stone Mansion—*hist pl* TX-5
Giddingsville—*locale* NY-2
Giddingsville Cem—*cemetery* NY-2
Giddings-Wilkin House—*hist pl* TX-5
Giddis Brook—*stream* NH-1
Giddon Lake—*lake* FL-3
Giddy Swamp Creek—*stream* SC-3
Gideon—*locale* OK-5
Gideon—*locale* PA-2
**Gideon**—*pop pl* MO-7
Gideon, Peter, Farmhouse—*hist pl* MN-6
Gideon Baptist Ch—*church* KS-7
Gideon Bay—*bay* MN-6
Gideon Cave—*cave* MO-7
Gideon Cem—*cemetery* TN-4
Gideon Cem—*cemetery* TX-5
Gideon Ch—*church* NC-3
Gideon Ch—*church* TN-4
Gideon Ch—*church* TX-5
Gideon Ch (historical)—*church* TN-4
Gideon Creek—*stream* NC-3
Gideon Creek—*stream* OR-9
Gideon Creek—*stream* TX-5
Gideon Ditch—*canal* OH-6
Gideon (historical)—*locale* KS-7
Gideon (Magisterial District)—*fmr MCD* WV-2
Gideon Memorial Airp—*airport* MO-7
Gideon Pond Sch—*school* MN-6
Gideon Ranch—*locale* MT-8
Gideon Sch—*school* NE-7
Gideon Swamp—*stream* NC-3
Gid Hollow—*valley* (2) TN-4
Gid Lake—*lake* NY-2
Gidley Sch—*school* CA-9
Gidley Sch—*school* MA-1
Gidley Sch—*school* MI-6
**Gidleys Corner**—*pop pl* MA-1
*Gidney Creek* NV-8
Gidney Creek—*stream* CA-9
Gidneytown Creek—*stream* NY-2
Gid Sch—*school* AR-4
Gidsville—*locale* VA-3
Gid (Township of)—*fmr MCD* AR-4
*Gidweon Methodist Church* TN-4
Gidwitz Sch (historical)—*school* MS-4
*Gieb* WA-9
Giebeler Lake—*lake* OR-9
Giebner Sch (historical)—*school* PA-2
Gieck Ranch—*locale* CO-8
Giedd Sch—*school* SD-7
*Gie djiedj* MP-9
Giefer Creek—*stream* MT-8
Giefer Lake—*lake* MT-8
Giefer Twentyfive Mile Creek Trail—*trail* MT-8
Gieger Ditch—*canal* IN-6
*Giegg Canyon* NV-8
Gielap—*island* FM-9
Gienger Cem—*cemetery* SD-7
Gierau Ranch—*locale* NE-7
Gierin Creek—*stream* WA-9
**Gieringer**—*pop pl* OH-6
Gierin Hill—*summit* WA-9
Gierke Creek—*stream* MI-6
Gier Park Sch—*school* MI-6
Giers Basin—*basin* AZ-5
Giers Branch—*stream* AL-4
Giers Cave—*cave* AL-4
Gierse Draw—*valley* WY-8

Giers Mtn—*summit* AZ-5
Giers Wash—*stream* AZ-5
Giesboro Point—*cape* DC-2
**Giese**—*pop pl* MN-6
**Gieseck**—*pop pl* AR-4
Gieseke Bay—*bay* MN-6
Giese Lake—*lake* WI-6
Giesel Hollow—*valley* MO-7
Gieselmann Lake—*lake* CA-9
Giesen-Hauser House—*hist pl* MN-6
Giese Truck Trail—*trail* MN-6
Gieske, William F., House—*hist pl* MN-6
Giesky Creek—*stream* GA-3
Giesky Creek—*stream* NC-3
Giesley Mill—*locale* VA-3
Giesy Mineral Spring—*spring* OR-9
G I F Clarke or Cocifacio Grant—*civil* FL-3
**Gifco**—*pop pl* TX-5
Giffels Lake—*lake* MI-6
Giffen—*locale* MT-8
**Giffen Cantua Ranch**—*pop pl* CA-9
Giffen Cem—*cemetery* OH-6
Giffen Coulee—*valley* MT-8
Giffey Sch—*school* ND-7
**Giffhill**—*pop pl* SC-3
Giffin Airp—*airport* PA-2
Giffin Canal—*canal* TX-5
*Giffin Elementary School* TN-4
Giffin Glacier—*glacier* AK-9
Giffin House—*hist pl* NH-1
Giffin Lake—*lake* WA-9
Giffin Sch—*school* TN-4
Giffins Corners Sch—*school* NY-2
Giffin Springs—*spring* TX-5
Giffon Windmill—*locale* TX-5
Gifford—*locale* KY-4
Gifford—*locale* TX-5
Gifford—*locale* WA-9
**Gifford**—*pop pl* AR-4
**Gifford**—*pop pl* FL-3
**Gifford**—*pop pl* ID-8
**Gifford**—*pop pl* (2) IL-6
**Gifford**—*pop pl* IN-6
**Gifford**—*pop pl* IA-7
**Gifford**—*pop pl* LA-4
**Gifford**—*pop pl* NY-2
**Gifford**—*pop pl* PA-2
**Gifford**—*pop pl* SC-3
Gifford, Dr. William, House—*hist pl* OH-6
Gifford, Lake—*lake* FL-3
Gifford Arboretum—*park* FL-3
Gifford Brook—*stream* ME-1
Gifford Canyon—*valley* UT-8
Gifford Cem—*cemetery* AR-4
Gifford Cem—*cemetery* IL-6
Gifford Cem—*cemetery* IA-7
Gifford Cem—*cemetery* NY-2
Gifford Covered Bridge—*hist pl* VT-1
Gifford Creek—*stream* (2) NY-2
Gifford Cut—*channel* FL-3
Gifford Dam—*dam* PA-2
Gifford-Davidson House—*hist pl* IL-6
**Gifford (Davis)**—*pop pl* PA-2
*Gifford Ditch* IN-6
Gifford Ditch—*canal* (2) IN-6
Gifford Drain—*canal* MI-6
*Gifford Dredge Ditch* IN-6
Gifford Farm—*hist pl* MA-1
Gifford Grange Hall—*hist pl* NY-2
Gifford Hill—*summit* (4) NY-2
Gifford Hill Gravel Pit—*mine* AR-4
Gifford Hill Sch—*school* NY-2
Gifford Hollow—*valley* (2) AL-4
Gifford Hollow—*valley* (2) PA-2
Gifford Hollow—*valley* TN-4
Gifford House—*hist pl* MT-8
Gifford House—*hist pl* WI-6
Gifford Island—*island* FL-3
Gifford Knoll—*summit* CO-8
*Gifford Lake* OR-9
Gifford Lake—*lake* (2) MI-6
Gifford Lake—*lake* MN-6
Gifford Lake—*lake* NY-2
Gifford Lakes—*lake* OR-9
Gifford Lakes—*lake* WA-9
Gifford Ledge—*rock* MA-1
Gifford Number 1 Dam—*dam* SD-7
Gifford Park—*park* NE-7
Gifford Peak—*summit* WA-9
Gifford Pinchot (CCD)—*cens area* WA-9
Gifford Pinchot Natl For—*forest* WA-9
Gifford Pinchot State Park—*park* PA-2
Gifford Point—*cape* FL-3
Gifford Point—*cape* NY-2
Gifford Ranch—*locale* CA-9
Gifford Run—*stream* PA-2
Giffords Branch—*stream* NC-3
Giffords Brook—*stream* CT-1
Gifford Sch—*school* AR-4
Gifford Sch—*school* IL-6
**Giffords Corner**—*pop pl* MA-1
Giffords Mill Branch—*stream* NJ-2
**Gifford (South Gifford)**—*pop pl* MO-7
Giffords Pond—*lake* MA-1
Gifford Spring—*spring* CA-9
Gifford Spring—*spring* ID-8
Giffords Woods State Forest Park—*park* VT-1
**Giffordtown**—*pop pl* NJ-2
Gifford (Township of)—*fmr MCD* AR-4
Gifford Valley—*valley* NY-2
Gifford Valley Cem—*cemetery* NY-2
Gifford-Walker Farm—*hist pl* NY-2
Gift—*locale* MS-4
**Gift**—*pop pl* TN-4
Gift Butte—*summit* OR-9
Gift Creek—*stream* CO-8
Gift Hill—*summit* VI-3
Gift Lake—*lake* MN-6
Gift Sch—*school* MS-4
Gift Sch (historical)—*school* MS-4
Gigandet Gulch—*valley* CO-8
Gigantes Buttes, Los—*summit* AZ-5
Gigantic City—*locale* NJ-2
Giger Ch (historical)—*church* MS-4
Giger Creek—*stream* FL-3
*Giges* MH-9
Giggey Hill—*summit* ME-1
Giggey Lake—*lake* CO-8
Giggle Hollow—*valley* NY-2
Gig Harbor—*bay* WA-9
**Gig Harbor**—*pop pl* WA-9
Gig Harbor Cem—*cemetery* WA-9
Gig Harbor Peninsula (CCD)—*cens area* WA-9
Gig Harbor Seaplane Base—*airport* WA-9
Gig Harbor Sportsmens Club—*other* WA-9
Gigling Siding—*locale* CA-9
Gig Pass—*channel* AK-9
*Gig River* ME-1
Gig Rock—*bar* ME-1
*Gihmel River* PW-9
Gihon Ch—*church* WV-2
Gihon River—*stream* VT-1
Gihon Sch—*school* WV-2
*Giiko* MP-9
*Giikoo To* MP-9
*Giiko-to* MP-9
*Giisen* MP-9
Giisen—*island* MP-9
*Gijibai Island* MP-9
Gijibai Island—*island* MP-9
*Gijibai-to* MP-9
Gijik Creek—*stream* MI-6
Gijikiki Lake—*lake* MN-6
*Gijik Lake* MN-6
Gijik Lake—*lake* MN-6
Gijosa—*civil* NM-5
*Giko To* MP-9
Gil, Jose Mario, Adobe—*hist pl* CA-9
**Gila**—*pop pl* IL-6
**Gila**—*pop pl* NM-5
**Gila Bend**—*pop pl* AZ-5
Gila Bend Air Force Auxiliary Field—*military* AZ-5
Gila Bend Canal—*canal* AZ-5
Gila Bend (CCD)—*cens area* AZ-5
Gila Bend Elem Sch—*school* AZ-5
**Gila Bend (Gila)**—*pop pl* AZ-5
Gila Bend HS—*school* AZ-5
Gila Bend Ind Res—*reserve* AZ-5
Gila Bend Mountains—*range* AZ-5
Gila Bend Municipal Airp—*airport* AZ-5
Gila Bend Overpass—*hist pl* AZ-5
Gila Bend Post Office—*building* AZ-5
Gila Bend RR Station—*building* AZ-5
*Gila Bend Station* AZ-5
Gila Bend Substation—*locale* AZ-5
Gila Bend Town Hall—*building* AZ-5
*Gila Bonita Creek* AZ-5
Gila Box—*valley* AZ-5
Gila Butte—*summit* AZ-5
Gila Center—*locale* AZ-5
*Gila City* AZ-5
*Gila City Mountains* AZ-5
Gila Cliff Dwellings Natl Monument—*hist pl* NM-5
Gila Compressor Station—*locale* AZ-5
Gila Compressor Station Airstrip—*airport* AZ-5
**Gila County**—*pop pl* AZ-5
Gila County Courthouse—*hist pl* AZ-5
Gila County Fair Ground and Race Track—*locale* AZ-5
Gila County Hosp—*hospital* AZ-5
**Gila Crossing**—*pop pl* AZ-5
Gila Crossing Day Sch—*school* AZ-5
*Giladon Creek* TX-5
Giladon Creek—*stream* TX-5
*Gilaew* FM-9
Gilaew Spring—*spring* FM-9
Gila Farm Ditch—*canal* NM-5
Gila Flat—*flat* NM-5
Gila Flat Tank—*reservoir* NM-5
*Gila (Gila Bend)* AZ-5
Gilahina Butte—*summit* AK-9
Gilahina River—*stream* AK-9
**Gila Hot Springs**—*pop pl* NM-5
*G. I. Lake* MN-6
Gila Lower Box—*valley* NM-5
Gila Main Canal—*canal* AZ-5
Gilam Draw—*valley* SD-7
Gila Middle Box—*valley* NM-5
Gila Mine—*mine* NV-8
Gila Monster Canyon—*valley* AZ-5
Gila Monster (historical)—*ridge* AZ-5
Gila Monster Mine—*mine* AZ-5
Gila Mountains—*range* (2) AZ-5
Gila Natl For—*forest* NM-5
Gilanta Rocks—*area* AK-9
Gila Peak—*summit* AZ-5
Gila Port Airp—*airport* AZ-5
Gila Pueblo—*hist pl* AZ-5
Gila Pueblo Campus Community Coll Extension—*school* AZ-5
*Gila Ranch* AZ-5
*Gila Range* AZ-5
Gila Range—*range* AZ-5
Gila Reservation Career Center—*building* AZ-5
Gila River—*stream* AZ-5
Gila River—*stream* NM-5
Gila River Bridge—*hist pl* AZ-5
Gila River Canyon—*valley* AZ-5
Gila River (CCD)—*cens area* AZ-5
**Gila River Ind Res**—*pop pl* AZ-5
Gila River Ranch—*locale* AZ-5
*Gila River Reservation* AZ-5
**Gilark**—*pop pl* LA-4
Gila Scout Camp—*locale* NM-5
Gilas Lake—*lake* WI-6
*Gila Station* AZ-5
Gila Substation—*locale* AZ-5
Gila Tank—*reservoir* AZ-5
G-I Lateral—*canal* CA-9
*Gilaux* PA-2
Gila Valley—*valley* AZ-5
Gila Valley Bank and Trust Bldg—*hist pl* AZ-5
Gila Valley Lookout—*locale* AZ-5
Gila Vista JHS—*school* AZ-5
Gila Vistors Center—*building* NM-5
*Gilaw* FM-9
Gila Well—*well* AZ-5
Gilbanes Pond—*lake* RI-1
Gilbane's Service Center Bldg—*hist pl* RI-1
Gilbault Sch—*school* IN-6
Gilbeaugh Creek—*stream* OR-9
*Gilbersons Mill* NJ-2
*Gilbersonville* NJ-2
*Gilbert* KS-7
*Gilbert* ND-7
Gilbert—*locale* AL-4
Gilbert—*locale* KS-7
Gilbert—*locale* KY-4
Gilbert—*locale* MI-6
Gilbert—*locale* NV-8
Gilbert—*locale* NY-2
Gilbert—*locale* OH-6
Gilbert—*locale* OK-5
Gilbert—*locale* PA-2
Gilbert—*locale* VA-3
Gilbert—*locale* WA-9
**Gilbert**—*pop pl* AZ-5
**Gilbert**—*pop pl* AR-4
**Gilbert**—*pop pl* IA-7
**Gilbert**—*pop pl* LA-4
**Gilbert**—*pop pl* MN-6
**Gilbert**—*pop pl* MO-7
**Gilbert**—*pop pl* OR-9
**Gilbert**—*pop pl* PA-2
**Gilbert**—*pop pl* SC-3
**Gilbert**—*pop pl* TX-5
**Gilbert**—*pop pl* WV-2
Gilbert, Andrew T., House—*hist pl* OR-9
Gilbert, Elisha, House—*hist pl* NY-2
Gilbert, F.A., House—*hist pl* OH-6
Gilbert, Giles, House—*hist pl* MI-6
Gilbert, Goldsmith C., Hist Dist—*hist pl* IN-6
Gilbert, Henry, House—*hist pl* MI-6
Gilbert, H. M., House—*hist pl* WA-9
Gilbert, Horace/Morgan and Enos Miller House—*hist pl* MI-6
Gilbert, Jane, House—*hist pl* OH-6
Gilbert, Jeremiah S., House—*hist pl* GA-3
Gilbert, Lake—*lake* FL-3
Gilbert, Mount—*summit* (2) AK-9
Gilbert, Mount—*summit* CA-9
Gilbert, Mount—*summit* NV-8
Gilbert, Mount Lewis—*summit* AK-9
Gilbert, Newington, House—*hist pl* MN-6
Gilbert, Philip E., Houses—*hist pl* OH-6
Gilbert, Samuel and Julia, House—*hist pl* TX-5
Gilbert Airp—*airport* PA-2
Gilbert-Alexander House—*hist pl* GA-3
Gilbert Ave Sch—*school* NJ-2
Gilbert Baker Special Use Area—*park* NE-7
Gilbert-Baker Wildlife Area—*park* NE-7
Gilbert Bay—*bay* AK-9
Gilbert Bay—*bay* UT-8
Gilbert Bay—*bay* WI-6
Gilbert Bennett Brook—*stream* CT-1
Gilbert Bldg—*hist pl* OR-9
Gilbert Bldg—*hist pl* PA-2
Gilbert Branch—*stream* (2) AL-4
Gilbert Branch—*stream* AR-4
Gilbert Branch—*stream* IN-6
Gilbert Branch—*stream* LA-4
Gilbert Branch—*stream* MI-6
Gilbert Branch—*stream* (2) NC-3
Gilbert Branch—*stream* (6) TN-4
Gilbert Bridge—*bridge* AL-4
Gilbert Brook—*stream* CT-1
Gilbert Brook—*stream* (2) ME-1
Gilbert Brook—*stream* VT-1
Gilbert Butte—*summit* WA-9
Gilbert Campground—*locale* CA-9
Gilbert Canyon—*valley* AZ-5
Gilbert Canyon—*valley* NV-8
Gilbert (CCD)—*cens area* SC-3
Gilbert Cem—*cemetery* AL-4
Gilbert Cem—*cemetery* AR-4
Gilbert Cem—*cemetery* (3) GA-3
Gilbert Cem—*cemetery* IL-6
Gilbert Cem—*cemetery* KS-7
Gilbert Cem—*cemetery* KY-4
Gilbert Cem—*cemetery* MN-6
Gilbert Cem—*cemetery* (3) MO-7
Gilbert Cem—*cemetery* (2) NY-2
Gilbert Cem—*cemetery* (2) OH-6
Gilbert Cem—*cemetery* TN-4
Gilbert Cem—*cemetery* TX-5
Gilbert Cem—*cemetery* (2) VA-3
Gilbert Ch—*church* ID-8
Gilbert Chapel—*church* KY-4
Gilbert Chapel—*church* (2) TX-5
Gilbert Chute—*stream* MO-7
Gilbert Clock Factory—*hist pl* CT-1
Gilbert Corners—*locale* PA-2
**Gilbert Corners**—*pop pl* CT-1
**Gilbert Corners**—*pop pl* (3) NY-2
*Gilbert Creek* KY-4
*Gilbert Creek* WV-2
Gilbert Creek—*stream* (2) AK-9
Gilbert Creek—*stream* (2) CA-9
Gilbert Creek—*stream* GA-3
Gilbert Creek—*stream* ID-8
Gilbert Creek—*stream* IN-6
Gilbert Creek—*stream* (2) KY-4
Gilbert Creek—*stream* MD-2
Gilbert Creek—*stream* (2) MI-6
Gilbert Creek—*stream* MN-6
Gilbert Creek—*stream* (3) MT-8
Gilbert Creek—*stream* (2) NV-8
Gilbert Creek—*stream* NY-2
Gilbert Creek—*stream* OK-5
Gilbert Creek—*stream* (4) OR-9
Gilbert Creek—*stream* TX-5
Gilbert Creek—*stream* (2) UT-8
Gilbert Creek—*stream* (2) WA-9
Gilbert Creek—*stream* WV-2
Gilbert Creek—*stream* (2) WI-6
Gilbert Creek—*stream* (2) WY-8
Gilbert Creek Basin—*basin* UT-8
Gilbert Creek Sch—*school* KY-4
Gilbert Crossroads—*locale* AL-4
**Gilbert Crossroads**—*pop pl* SC-3
Gilbert Dam—*dam* AL-4
Gilbert Development Corp Heliport—*airport* NV-8
Gilbert Ditch—*canal* ID-8
Gilbert Ditch—*canal* IN-6
Gilbert Ditch—*canal* MT-8
Gilbert Ditch—*canal* WY-8
Gilbert Drain—*canal* MI-6
Gilbert Drain—*stream* MI-6
Gilbert Draw—*valley* SD-7
Gilbert Draw—*valley* WY-8
Gilbert Elem Sch—*hist pl* AZ-5
Gilbert Estates Phase Two Mini Park—*park* AZ-5
Gilbert Estates Phase Two Water Retention Basin—*reservoir* AZ-5
Gilbert Farmhouse—*hist pl* NY-2
Gilbert Fire Tower—*locale* SC-3
Gilbert Fork—*stream* KY-4
Gilbert Fork—*stream* VA-3
**Gilbert Gardens**—*pop pl* VA-3
Gilbert Gulch—*valley* MT-8
Gilbert Head—*cape* ME-1
Gilbert Heights Sch—*school* OR-9
Gilbert Henry Ch—*church* KY-4
Gilbert Hill—*summit* CT-1
Gilbert Hill—*summit* NY-2
Gilbert Hill—*summit* VT-1
Gilbert Hill—*summit* WY-8
*Gilbert Hills* IL-6
Gilbert (historical)—*locale* SD-7
Gilbert Hollow—*valley* AR-4
Gilbert Hollow—*valley* PA-2
Gilbert Hollow—*valley* TN-4
Gilbert Homestead—*locale* MT-8
Gilbert HS—*school* AZ-5
Gilbert Inlet—*bay* AK-9
Gilbert Island—*island* (2) MO-7
Gilbert JHS—*school* AZ-5
Gilbert JHS—*school* FL-3
**Gilbert Junction**—*pop pl* MN-6
*Gilbert Lake* MI-6
Gilbert Lake—*lake* AL-4
Gilbert Lake—*lake* (2) AK-9
Gilbert Lake—*lake* CA-9
Gilbert Lake—*lake* GA-3
Gilbert Lake—*lake* IL-6
Gilbert Lake—*lake* IN-6
Gilbert Lake—*lake* (4) MI-6
Gilbert Lake—*lake* (2) MN-6
Gilbert Lake—*lake* MT-8
Gilbert Lake—*lake* NY-2
Gilbert Lake—*lake* UT-8
Gilbert Lake—*lake* WA-9
Gilbert Lake—*lake* (6) WI-6
Gilbert Lake—*lake* WY-8
Gilbert Lake—*reservoir* GA-3
Gilbert Lake—*reservoir* IN-6
Gilbert Lake—*reservoir* SC-3
Gilbert Lake Dam—*dam* AL-4
Gilbert Lake Oil Field—*other* MI-6
Gilbert Lakes—*reservoir* MO-7
Gilbert Lake State Park—*park* NY-2
Gilbert Landing—*locale* GA-3
Gilbert Landing—*locale* MO-7
Gilbert Landing—*locale* TX-5
Gilbert Lateral—*canal* AZ-5
Gilbert Mansion—*hist pl* TN-4
Gilbert Meadow—*flat* UT-8
*Gilbert Meadows* UT-8
Gilbert Memorial Cem—*cemetery* LA-4
Gilbert Memorial Ch—*church* VA-3
Gilbert Mill—*locale* VA-3
**Gilbert Mills**—*pop pl* NY-2
Gilbert Mine—*mine* MN-6
Gilbert MS—*school* OR-9
Gilbert Number One Rsvr—*reservoir* SD-7
Gilbert Number Two Rsvr—*reservoir* SD-7
Gilbert Number 1 Dam—*dam* SD-7
Gilbert Number 2 Dam—*dam* SD-7
Gilbert Number 3 Dam—*dam* SD-7
**Gilberton**—*pop pl* PA-2
**Gilberton**—*pop pl* WA-9
Gilberton Borough—*civil* PA-2
Gilberton Coal Company Site Three Wmf Dam—*dam* PA-2
Gilberton Plant Station—*locale* PA-2
**Gilbertown**—*pop pl* AL-4
Gilbertown Cem—*cemetery* CT-1
Gilbertown Ch—*church* AL-4
*Gilbertown Ch of God* AL-4
Gilbertown Dock—*locale* AL-4
Gilbertown JHS—*school* AL-4
Gilbertown Oil Field—*oilfield* AL-4
Gilbertown-Toxey (CCD)—*cens area* AL-4
Gilbertown-Toxey Division—*civil* AL-4
Gilbert Park—*park* AZ-5
Gilbert Park—*park* CA-9
Gilbert Park—*park* FL-3
Gilbert Park—*park* IL-6
Gilbert Park—*park* TX-5
Gilbert Park—*park* WA-9
Gilbert Park Sch—*school* OR-9
Gilbert Peak—*summit* UT-8
Gilbert Peak—*summit* WA-9
Gilbert Peninsula—*cape* AK-9
Gilbert Plaza Shop Ctr—*locale* AZ-5
Gilbert Point—*cape* NH-1
Gilbert Point—*summit* AK-9
Gilbert Pond—*lake* GA-3
Gilbert Pond—*lake* ME-1
Gilbert Pond—*reservoir* FL-3
Gilbert Ponds—*lake* ME-1
Gilbert Post Office—*building* AZ-5
Gilbert Ranch—*locale* CA-9
Gilbert Ranch—*locale* MT-8
Gilbert Ranches Pond Number 1 Dam—*dam* SD-7
Gilbert Ranch Oil Field—*oilfield* TX-5
Gilbert Retarding Basin—*reservoir* CA-9
Gilbert Ridge—*ridge* AK-9
Gilbert Ridge—*ridge* AR-4
Gilbert Ridge—*ridge* OR-9
Gilbert Ridge—*ridge* TN-4
Gilbert Ridge—*ridge* WV-2
Gilbert Ridge Spring—*spring* OR-9
Gilbert River—*stream* OR-9
Gilbert Row—*hist pl* OH-6
Gilbert Run—*stream* OH-6
Gilbert Run—*stream* (2) PA-2
*Gilberts* PA-2
Gilberts—*locale* CA-9
**Gilberts**—*pop pl* IL-6
Gilberts Angels Nursery Day Care Center—*school* FL-3
Gilberts Big Creek—*stream* KY-4
**Gilbertsboro**—*pop pl* AL-4
Gilbertsboro P. O. (historical)—*locale* AL-4
Gilbertsboro Sch (historical)—*school* AL-4
Gilberts Branch—*stream* GA-3
Gilbert Sch—*school* AL-4
Gilbert Sch—*school* AZ-5
Gilbert Sch—*school* (2) CA-9
Gilbert Sch—*school* MI-6
Gilbert Sch—*school* NV-8
Gilbert Sch—*school* OH-6
Gilbert Sch—*school* WA-9
Gilbert Sch—*school* WI-6
Gilbert Sch (abandoned)—*school* PA-2
Gilberts Corner—*locale* VA-3
**Gilberts Corner**—*pop pl* NY-2
*Gilberts Corners* NY-2
Gilberts Cove—*cove* MA-1
*Gilberts Creek* NV-8
Gilberts Creek—*stream* KY-4
Gilberts Creek—*stream* NC-3
Gilberts Creek Ch—*church* KY-4
Gilberts Ferry (historical)—*locale* AL-4
Gilbert Shoal—*bar* FL-3
Gilberts Hole—*bay* MI-6
Gilbert-Sinton Hist Dist—*hist pl* OH-6
*Gilberts Island* MO-7
Gilbert Site—*hist pl* TX-5
Gilberts Lake—*reservoir* (2) AL-4
Gilberts Lake—*reservoir* MS-4
*Gilberts Lake Dam* AL-4
Gilberts Little Creek—*stream* KY-4
Gilberts Mill—*locale* FL-3
Gilberts Mill Creek—*stream* FL-3
Gilberts Mill (historical)—*locale* AL-4
Gilberts Mine—*mine* NV-8
Gilbertson Cem—*cemetery* ND-7
Gilbertson Field—*airport* ND-7
Gilbertson Ford (historical)—*locale* MO-7
Gilbertson Lake—*lake* (2) MN-6
Gilbertson Sch—*school* WI-6
Gilbertson Slough—*stream* WA-9
Gilbertsons Slough—*gut* MN-6
Gilbert Spit—*bar* AK-9
Gilbert Spring—*spring* NV-8
Gilberts (RR name for Burkettsville)—*other* OH-6
**Gilberts Tannery**—*pop pl* VT-1
Gilbert State Public Shooting Area—*park* SD-7
**Gilbert Station**—*pop pl* OR-9
*Gilbert Stuart Pond* RI-1
*Gilbert Stuart Pond Dam* RI-1
Gilbert Substation—*locale* AZ-5
*Gilbertsville* IA-7
*Gilbertsville* KY-4
**Gilbertsville**—*pop pl* KY-4
**Gilbertsville**—*pop pl* NY-2
**Gilbertsville**—*pop pl* PA-2
Gilbertsville Golf Course—*locale* PA-2
Gilbertsville Hist Dist—*hist pl* NY-2
Gilbertsville Hist Dist (Boundary Increase)—*hist pl* NY-2
**Gilbertsville (P.O.) (KY Dam Village State Park)**—*pop pl* KY-4
Gilbertsville Sch—*school* KY-4
Gilbert Swamp Run—*stream* MD-2
Gilberts Wells—*well* NM-5
Gilbert Thomas Lake—*reservoir* AL-4
*Gilbert Tommie Lake* AL-4
Gilbert Tommie Lake Dam—*dam* AL-4
Gilbert Tommie Number 2 Dam—*dam* AL-4
*Gilbert Township* ND-7
**Gilbert Township**—*pop pl* SD-7
Gilbert Trail—*trail* MT-8
Gilbert Trivitts Ditch—*stream* DE-2
Gilbert Valley—*bend* TX-5
Gilbert Valley—*valley* MN-6
**Gilbertville**—*pop pl* IA-7
**Gilbertville**—*pop pl* ME-1
**Gilbertville**—*pop pl* MA-1
Gilbert Warren Ditch—*canal* WY-8
Gilbert Well—*well* AZ-5
**Gilbert Yard**—*pop pl* WV-2
Gilbertz Ranch—*locale* WY-8
Gilbirds—*locale* IL-6
**Gilboa**—*pop pl* NH-1
**Gilboa**—*pop pl* NY-2
**Gilboa**—*pop pl* OH-6
**Gilboa**—*pop pl* WV-2
Gilboa, Mount—*summit* IN-6
Gilboa, Mount—*summit* ME-1
Gilboa, Mount—*summit* (2) MA-1
Gilboa, Mount—*summit* MN-6
Gilboa, Mount—*summit* NJ-2
Gilboa Brook—*stream* MA-1
Gilboa Cem—*cemetery* IN-6
Gilboa Cem—*cemetery* (2) OH-6
Gilboa Cem—*cemetery* PA-2
Gilboa Ch—*church* (3) NC-3
Gilboa Dam—*dam* NY-2
*Gilboa Hill* ME-1
Gilboa Hill—*summit* NH-1
*Gilboa Lake* NY-2
Gilboa Main Street Hist Dist—*hist pl* OH-6
Gilboa Methodist Church—*hist pl* NC-3
Gilboa Mtn—*summit* NH-1
Gilboa Pond—*reservoir* MA-1
Gilboa Pond Dam—*dam* MA-1
*Gilboa Reservoir* NY-2
Gilboa Sch (abandoned)—*school* PA-2
**Gilboa (Town of)**—*pop pl* NY-2
**Gilboa (Township of)**—*pop pl* IN-6
*Gilbod Pond* MA-1
Gilbor Cem—*cemetery* WV-2
Gilbor Ch—*church* WV-2
Gilbo Tank—*reservoir* TX-5
Gilbraltar Island—*island* OH-6
*Gilbralter Ledge* ME-1
Gilbralter Rocks—*pillar* CT-1
**Gilbreath**—*pop pl* TN-4
*Gilbreath Cem* AL-4
Gilbreath Cem—*cemetery* AL-4
Gilbreath Cem—*cemetery* IN-6
Gilbreath Cem—*cemetery* TN-4
Gilbreath Chapel—*church* AL-4
Gilbreath Creek—*stream* OR-9
Gilbreath Creek—*stream* TN-4
Gilbreath-McLorn House—*hist pl* MO-7
Gilbreath Mtn—*summit* AR-4
Gilbreath Ridge—*ridge* TN-4
Gilbreath Sch (historical)—*school* TN-4
Gilbreath Spring—*spring* WA-9
Gilbreth—*locale* TX-5
Gilbreth Gap—*gap* AL-4
**Gilbur**—*pop pl* IA-7
**Gilburg**—*pop pl* TX-5
**Gilby**—*pop pl* ND-7
Gilby (historical)—*locale* ND-7
**Gilby Township**—*pop pl* ND-7
Gilchrest—*hist pl* NH-1
Gilchrest Cave Number One—*cave* AL-4
Gilchrest Cave Number Two—*cave* AL-4
Gilchrist—*fmr MCD* NE-7
Gilchrist—*locale* FL-3
Gilchrist—*locale* IL-6
**Gilchrist**—*pop pl* IL-6
**Gilchrist**—*pop pl* (2) MI-6
**Gilchrist**—*pop pl* OR-9
**Gilchrist**—*pop pl* TN-4
**Gilchrist**—*pop pl* (2) TX-5
Gilchrist Adult Education—*school* FL-3
Gilchrist Bar (historical)—*bar* AL-4
Gilchrist Bend—*bend* KY-4
*Gilchrist Branch* TN-4
Gilchrist Branch—*stream* TN-4
Gilchrist Butte—*summit* (2) OR-9
Gilchrist Cem—*cemetery* (2) AL-4
Gilchrist Cem—*cemetery* NC-3
Gilchrist Cem—*cemetery* TN-4
**Gilchrist County**—*pop pl* FL-3
Gilchrist County Lookout Tower (fire tower)—*tower* FL-3
Gilchrist Creek—*stream* MI-6
Gilchrist Creek—*stream* MS-4
Gilchrist Ditch No 4—*canal* WY-8
Gilchrist Ditch No 9—*canal* WY-8
Gilchrist Elem Sch—*school* FL-3
**Gilchrist (Hillcrest)**—*pop pl* AR-4
Gilchrist House—*hist pl* AL-4
Gilchrist Island—*island* AL-4
Gilchrist Island—*island* FL-3
Gilchrist Island (historical)—*island* AL-4
Gilchrist Junction—*locale* OR-9
Gilchrist Lake—*lake* (2) MN-6
Gilchrist Lateral—*canal* WY-8
Gilchrist Mine (Abandoned)—*mine* IL-6
Gilchrist Park—*park* FL-3
Gilchrist Park Sch—*school* GA-3
Gilchrist Rock—*island* ME-1
Gilchrist Rsvr—*reservoir* OR-9
Gilchrist Rsvr—*reservoir* WY-8
Gilchrist Sch—*school* IL-6
Gilchrist Sch—*school* WY-8
Gilchrist Sch (historical)—*school* (2) TN-4
Gilchrist Spring—*spring* OR-9
**Gilchrist (Township of)**—*pop pl* MN-6
Gilchrist Tunnel—*tunnel* NM-5
Gilcrease—*post sta* OK-5
Gilcrease JHS—*school* OK-5
**Gilcrest**—*pop pl* CO-8
Gilcrest Log Pond—*reservoir* OR-9
Gilcrest Peak—*summit* CA-9
Gilcrest Shop Ctr—*locale* AL-4
Gilcrist Bridge—*bridge* FL-3
Gilcrist House—*hist pl* OH-6
Gildan Spring—*spring* AL-4
Gildart Creek—*stream* MT-8
Gildart Lakes—*lake* MT-8
Gildart Peak—*summit* MT-8
Gildart Sch—*school* MI-6
Gilda Spring—*spring* AZ-5
Gilday Drain—*canal* MI-6
Gilded Age Number 1 Mine—*mine* NV-8
Gilded Age Number 2 Mine—*mine* NV-8
*Gildehaus* MO-7
Gildehaus Sch—*school* MO-7
**Gildehouse**—*pop pl* MO-7
*Gilden* VA-3
*Gilden Canyon* TX-5
Gilden Creek—*stream* TX-5
Gilden Hollow—*valley* WV-2
Gilder Cem—*cemetery* AL-4
Gilder Creek—*stream* AL-4
Gilder Creek—*stream* SC-3
*Gilderoy* IN-6
Gilder Pond—*reservoir* MA-1
Gilder Pond Dam—*dam* MA-1
Gilder Ridge—*ridge* CA-9
Gilders Creek—*stream* SC-3
**Gildersleeve**—*pop pl* CT-1
Gildersleeve, Andrew, Octagonal Bldg—*hist pl* NY-2
**Gildersleeve Float**—*pop pl* AK-9
Gildersleeve House—*hist pl* IL-6
Gildersleeve Island—*island* CT-1
Gildersleeve Mine—*mine* MT-8
Gildersleeve Sch—*school* OH-6
Gildfield Ch—*church* TN-4
**Gildford**—*pop pl* MT-8
Gildford Hill County Cem—*cemetery* MT-8
Gildridge Branch—*stream* TN-4
*Gildridge Creek* TN-4
Gile—*locale* NY-2
**Gile**—*pop pl* WI-6
Gile—*uninc pl* WI-6
Gile, Ephraim C., House—*hist pl* MN-6
Gilead—*locale* CT-1
Gilead—*locale* LA-4
Gilead—*locale* NC-3
**Gilead**—*pop pl* IL-6
**Gilead**—*pop pl* IN-6
**Gilead**—*pop pl* IA-7
**Gilead**—*pop pl* ME-1
**Gilead**—*pop pl* MI-6
**Gilead**—*pop pl* NE-7
Gilead, Lake—*lake* NY-2
Gilead, Mount—*summit* MA-1
Gilead, Mount—*summit* VT-1
Gilead, Mount—*summit* VA-3
Gilead Baptist Ch—*church* UT-8
*Gilead Baptist Church* TN-4
Gilead Branch—*stream* KY-4
Gilead Brook—*stream* VT-1
Gilead Cem—*cemetery* CT-1
Gilead Cem—*cemetery* (2) IL-6
Gilead Cem—*cemetery* KY-4
Gilead Cem—*cemetery* LA-4
Gilead Cem—*cemetery* MI-6
Gilead Cem—*cemetery* NY-2
Gilead Cem—*cemetery* NC-3
Gilead Cemetery—*hist pl* NY-2
Gilead Ch—*church* AR-4
Gilead Ch—*church* CT-1
Gilead Ch—*church* (3) IL-6
Gilead Ch—*church* (2) IN-6
Gilead Ch—*church* (4) KY-4
Gilead Ch—*church* (2) MO-7
Gilead Ch—*church* NC-3
Gilead Ch—*church* SC-3
Gilead Ch—*church* TN-4
*Gilead Church* AL-4
Gilead Creek—*stream* AK-9
Gilead (Election Precinct)—*fmr MCD* IL-6

Gilead Hills Ch—church ... MO-7
Gilead Lake—lake ... MI-6
Gilead Landing—locale ... IL-6
Gilead Ridge—ridge ... NC-3
Gilead Slough—gut ... IL-6
**Gilead (Town of)**—pop pl ... ME-1
**Gilead (Township of)**—pop pl ... MI-6
**Gilead (Township of)**—pop pl ... OH-6
Gile Brook—stream ... NH-1
Gile Creek—stream ... AL-4
Gile Creek—stream ... WI-6
Gilefid ... FM-9
Gilefio ... FM-9
Gilefis ... FM-9
Gile Flowage—channel ... WI-6
Gile Lake—lake ... WA-9
Gile Logan—lake ... ME-1
Gile Mtn—summit ... ME-1
Gile Mtn—summit ... VT-1
**Gilene Subdivision**—pop pl ... UT-8
Gileon Lake—lake ... TX-5
Gile Pond—lake ... NH-1
Gile Ranch—locale ... WA-9
Giles ... AR-4
Giles ... NV-8
Giles—locale ... MS-4
Giles—locale ... TX-5
**Giles**—pop pl ... AL-4
**Giles**—pop pl ... IA-7
**Giles**—pop pl ... WV-2
Giles, Gen. James, House—hist pl ... NJ-2
Giles, Lake—lake ... FL-3
Giles, Lake—reservoir ... PA-2
Giles, Mount—summit ... ME-1
Giles Airp—airport ... MS-4
Giles Bay—bay ... AK-9
Giles Bay—swamp ... SC-3
Giles Bend—bend ... MS-4
Giles Bend Oil Field—oilfield ... MS-4
Giles Branch—stream ... TN-4
Giles Branch—stream ... TX-5
Giles Bridge—bridge ... VA-3
Giles Brook—stream ... MA-1
Giles Brook—stream (2) ... NH-1
Giles Canyon ... WA-9
Giles Canyon—valley ... NM-5
Giles Cem ... TN-4
Giles Cem—cemetery ... AR-4
Giles Cem—cemetery ... IL-6
Giles Cem—cemetery ... MS-4
Giles Cem—cemetery ... NE-7
Giles Cem—cemetery ... NY-2
Giles Cem—cemetery ... OK-5
Giles Cem—cemetery (5) ... TN-4
Giles Cem—cemetery ... TX-5
Giles Cem—cemetery (2) ... VA-3
Giles Ch—church ... MO-7
Giles Chapel—church (2) ... NC-3
Giles City ... KS-7
Giles Coll (historical)—school ... TN-4
**Giles County**—pop pl ... TN-4
**Giles (County)**—pop pl ... VA-3
Giles County Courthouse—building ... TN-4
Giles County Courthouse—hist pl ... VA-3
Giles County Hosp—hospital ... TN-4
Giles County HS—school ... TN-4
Giles Creek—cove ... MA-1
Giles Creek—stream ... MI-6
Giles Creek—stream ... NE-7
Giles Creek—stream (2) ... NC-3
Giles Creek—stream ... OR-9
Giles Creek—stream ... SD-7
Giles Cutoff—channel ... MS-4
Giles Flat—flat ... UT-8
Giles Flowage ... WI-6
Giles Hill—summit ... NH-1
Giles Hill—summit ... TN-4
Giles Hollow—valley (2) ... TN-4
Giles Hollow—valley ... UT-8
Giles HS—school ... IL-6
Giles HS—school ... VA-3
Giles Island—island ... AR-4
Giles Lake—lake ... AL-4
Giles Lake—lake ... AK-9
Giles Lake—lake ... MN-6
Giles Lake—lake ... SC-3
Giles Landing—locale ... MS-4
Giles Lee Ranch—locale ... NM-5
Giles (Magisterial District)—fmr MCD ... VA-3
Giles Memorial Gardens—cemetery ... TN-4
Giles Memorial Hosp—hospital ... VA-3
Giles Millpond—reservoir ... GA-3
Gilespie Place—locale ... WY-8
Giles Place—locale ... NV-8
Giles Plantation Landing ... MS-4
Giles Pond—lake ... CA-9
Giles Pond—lake ... ME-1
Giles Pond—lake ... NH-1
Giles Pond Brook—stream ... ME-1
Giles Post Office (historical)—building ... AL-4
Giles Post Office (historical)—building ... MS-4
Giles Ranch—locale ... NE-7
Giles & Ransome Airp—airport ... PA-2
Giles Run—stream ... VA-3
Giles Sch—school ... IL-6
Giles Sch—school ... MI-6
Giles Sch—school ... NE-7
Giles Sch—school ... TX-5
Giles & Sikorsky Airp—airport ... PA-2
Giles (Site)—locale ... UT-8
Giles Slough—stream ... WA-9
Giles Spur—locale ... AR-4
Giles Store—locale ... VA-3
Giles Tank—reservoir ... TX-5
**Gileston (historical)**—pop pl ... TN-4
**Giles Town**—pop pl ... TN-4
Giles (Township of)—fmr MCD ... AR-4
Giles Turkey Ridge ... AR-4
Giles Turney Ridge—ridge ... AR-4
Giles Well—well ... NM-5
Giles Williams Cem—cemetery ... AL-4
Gilette ... NJ-2
Gilette Sch—school ... TX-5
Gilex—area ... UT-8
Gilfield Branch—stream ... AL-4
Gilfield Ch ... AL-4
Gilfield Ch—church ... AL-4
Gilfield Ch—church ... LA-4
Gilfield Ch—church ... VA-3
Gilfield Missionary Baptist Ch ... AL-4
Gilfield Missionary Ch—church ... AL-4
Gilfillan—hist pl ... MN-6
Gilfillan—locale ... MN-6
Gilfillan Creek—stream ... IL-6
Gilfillan Farm—hist pl ... PA-2
Gilfillan (historical)—locale ... KS-7
Gilfillan House—hist pl ... TX-5
Gilfillan Lake—lake (2) ... MN-6
Gilfillan Sch—school ... MN-6
Gilfillian Creek—stream ... ID-8
Gilfillin Lake—lake ... MN-6
Gilfis ... FM-9
**Gilfith**—pop pl ... FM-9
Gilford—locale ... ME-1
**Gilford**—pop pl ... MI-6
**Gilford**—pop pl ... NH-1
Gilford Bowl—other ... NH-1
Gilford Creek—stream ... NV-8
Gilford Lake—swamp ... OK-5
Gilford Meadows—flat ... NV-8
Gilfordo Store (historical)—locale ... AL-4
Gilford Park—park ... MI-6
**Gilford Park**—pop pl ... NJ-2
**Gilford (Town of)**—pop pl ... NH-1
**Gilford (Township of)**—pop pl ... MI-6
**Gilfoyl**—pop pl ... PA-2
Gilfoyle—locale ... PA-2
Gilfoyle Run—stream ... PA-2
Gilfoyle Station—locale ... PA-2
Gilgal Baptist Ch—church ... FL-3
Gilgal Baptist Church ... AL-4
Gilgal Branch—stream ... KY-4
Gilgal Bridge—bridge ... SC-3
Gilgal Cem—cemetery ... AL-4
Gilgal Cem—cemetery ... IL-6
Gilgal Ch—church (2) ... AL-4
Gil Gal Ch—church ... IN-6
Gilgal Ch—church ... LA-4
Gilgal Ch—church ... MN-6
Gilgal Ch—church ... PA-2
Gilgal Ch—church (2) ... SC-3
Gilgal Ch—church ... WV-2
Gilgal Church Battle Site—hist pl ... GA-3
Gilg Canyon—valley ... WA-9
Gilger Ranch—locale ... SD-7
Gilgers Hill ... PA-2
Gilgers Ridge—ridge ... PA-2
Gilgo Beach—beach ... NY-2
**Gilgo Beach**—pop pl ... NY-2
Gilgo Cem—cemetery ... NC-3
Gilgo Coast ... NY-2
Gilgo Heading ... NY-2
Gilgo Heading—bay ... NY-2
Gilgo Island—island ... NY-2
Gilgo State Park—park ... NY-2
Gilham Branch—stream ... KY-4
Gilham Butte—summit ... CA-9
Gilham Cem—cemetery ... OH-6
Gilham Creek ... AL-4
Gilham Creek—stream ... CA-9
Gilham Creek—stream ... IL-6
Gilham Sch—school ... OR-9
Gilhams Lake—reservoir ... GA-3
Gil Harbor—bay ... AK-9
Gilhooley Slough—stream ... CA-9
Gilhula Creek—stream ... TX-5
Gilifith ... FM-9
Gilifiz ... FM-9
Gililland Intermediate School ... AZ-5
Gililland JHS—school ... AZ-5
Gilimaan' ... FM-9
Giliman ... FM-9
Giliotti Well—well ... NV-8
Gilita Creek—stream ... NM-5
Gilita Ridge—ridge ... NM-5
Giliy ... FM-9
Gilkerson—locale ... WV-2
**Gilkerson**—pop pl ... AR-4
Gilkerson Branch—stream (2) ... WV-2
Gilkerson Cem—cemetery ... TX-5
Gilkerson Dam—dam ... PA-2
Gilkerson Rsvr—reservoir ... PA-2
Gilkerson (Township of)—fmr MCD ... AR-4
Gilkes Cem—cemetery ... MI-6
Gilkeson—locale ... PA-2
Gilkeson Field—park ... GU-9
**Gilkey**—pop pl ... AR-4
**Gilkey**—pop pl ... NC-3
Gilkey Brook—stream ... ME-1
Gilkey Cemeteries—cemetery ... NH-1
Gilkey Coulee—valley ... MT-8
Gilkey Creek—stream ... AR-4
Gilkey Creek—stream ... MI-6
Gilkey Creek—stream ... OR-9
Gilkey Creek—stream ... SC-3
Gilkey Drain—canal ... MI-6
Gilkey Elem Sch—school ... NC-3
Gilkey Glacier—glacier ... AK-9
Gilkey Harbor—bay ... ME-1
Gilkey Lake—lake ... MI-6
Gilkey Lake—lake (2) ... WI-6
Gilkey Lake—reservoir ... KS-7
Gilkey River—stream ... AK-9
Gilkey Run—stream ... KY-4
Gilkey's Harbor ... ME-1
Gilkey (Township of)—fmr MCD ... AR-4
Gilkey (Township of)—fmr MCD ... NC-3
Gilkie Ranch—locale ... WY-8
Gill—locale ... MS-4
Gill—locale ... NC-3
Gill—locale ... TX-5
Gill—locale ... WV-2
**Gill**—pop pl ... AR-4
**Gill**—pop pl ... CO-8
**Gill**—pop pl ... GA-3
**Gill**—pop pl ... MA-1
**Gill**—pop pl ... MS-4
**Gill**—pop pl ... MO-7
Gill, Charles, House—hist pl ... MA-1
Gill, H., House—hist pl ... OH-6
Gill, J. K., Bldg—hist pl ... OR-9
Gill, Sherman, House—hist pl ... MT-8
Gill, Thomas J., House—hist pl ... NC-3
Gill Airp—airport ... KS-7
Gillam Branch—stream ... GA-3
Gillam Branch—stream ... KY-4
Gillam Cave—cave ... MO-7
Gillam Cem—cemetery ... AL-4
Gillam Coulee—valley ... MT-8
Gillam Creek—stream ... AR-4
Gillam Ditch—canal ... IN-6
Gillam Draw—valley ... CO-8
Gillam Draw—valley ... WY-8
Gillam Gap—gap ... NC-3
Gillam Glacier—glacier ... AK-9
Gillam Hill—summit ... KY-4
Gillam Knob—summit ... KY-4
Gillam Lake—lake ... AK-9
Gillam Park—park ... AR-4
**Gillam Park**—pop pl ... AR-4
Gillam Run—stream ... VA-3
Gillam Run Trail—trail ... VA-3
Gillam Sch—school ... AR-4
Gillam School ... TN-4
Gillam Spring—spring ... CA-9
Gillam Spring—spring ... NV-8
Gillam Springs—spring ... GA-3
**Gillam (Township of)**—pop pl ... IN-6
Gillan—fmr MCD ... NE-7
Gillan Creek—stream ... ID-8
Gilland—locale ... OK-5
Gilland Cem—cemetery ... AL-4
Gilland Gap—gap ... AL-4
Gilland Hollow—valley ... TX-5
Gilland Lake—reservoir ... AL-4
Gilland Rsvr—reservoir ... WY-8
Gillan Lake—lake ... MI-6
Gillans Run—stream ... PA-2
Gillard Creek ... SC-3
Gillard Hollow—valley ... MO-7
Gillard Hot Springs—spring ... AZ-5
Gillaspie ... VA-3
Gillaspie—fmr MCD ... NE-7
Gillaspies Creek ... TN-4
Gillaspies Ferry (historical)—locale ... TN-4
Gillaspies Island ... TN-4
Gillaspies Run ... WV-2
Gillaspy Ranch—locale ... CA-9
Gillaspy Sch (historical)—school ... MO-7
Gill Bay—swamp ... GA-3
Gill Bayou—stream ... LA-4
Gill Bog—swamp ... ME-1
Gill Branch ... AL-4
Gill Branch ... LA-4
Gill Branch—stream ... DE-2
Gill Branch—stream ... KY-4
Gill Branch—stream ... MO-7
Gill Branch—stream ... NC-3
Gill Brook—stream ... NY-2
**Gillburg**—pop pl ... NC-3
Gill Cem ... TN-4
Gill Cem—cemetery (2) ... AR-4
Gill Cem—cemetery (2) ... IL-6
Gill Cem—cemetery ... IN-6
Gill Cem—cemetery (2) ... LA-4
Gill Cem—cemetery ... MO-7
Gill Cem—cemetery (5) ... TN-4
Gill Cem—cemetery ... VT-1
Gill Cem—cemetery ... WV-2
Gill Center Cem—cemetery ... MA-1
Gill Chapel Cem—cemetery ... TN-4
Gill Chapel (historical)—church ... TN-4
Gill Coulee—valley ... WI-6
Gill Creek ... SC-3
Gill Creek—stream ... AL-4
Gill Creek—stream (2) ... CA-9
Gill Creek—stream ... CO-8
Gill Creek—stream ... LA-4
Gill Creek—stream ... MN-6
Gill Creek—stream (2) ... MT-8
Gill Creek—stream (2) ... NY-2
Gill Creek—stream ... OR-9
Gill Creek—stream ... SC-3
Gill Creek—stream ... UT-8
Gill Creek—stream ... WA-9
Gill Creek—stream (2) ... WI-6
Gill Creek Divide—ridge ... CO-8
Gill Creek Park—park ... NY-2
Gill Creek Trail—trail ... CO-8
Gilleland Creek—stream ... TX-5
Gillem Bluff—cliff ... CA-9
**Gillem Branch**—pop pl ... KY-4
Gillem Cem—cemetery ... KY-4
Gillem Hollow—valley ... KY-4
Gillem Lakes—lake ... CA-9
Gillem Lateral—canal ... NM-5
Gillems Camp—locale ... CA-9
Gillen Allen Cem—cemetery ... FL-3
Gillen Bayou—stream ... TX-5
Gillen Ditch—canal ... IN-6
Gillen Springs—spring ... MI-6
**Gillentine (historical)**—pop pl ... TN-4
Gillentine Post Office (historical)—building ... TN-4
Gillenwater Branch—stream ... VA-3
Gillenwater Cem—cemetery ... TN-4
Gillenwater Cem—cemetery ... VA-3
Gillenwater Chapel—church ... VA-3
**Gillenwater (historical)**—pop pl ... TN-4
Gillenwater Post Office (historical)—building ... TN-4
Gilleran Pond—reservoir ... RI-1
Gilles Branch—stream ... WV-2
Gilles Creek—stream ... AK-9
Gilles Ditch—canal ... KY-4
Gilles Ditch—canal ... SC-3
Gilles Hollow ... UT-8
Gillespi Branch—stream ... KY-4
Gillespie—locale ... AZ-5
Gillespie—locale ... NJ-2
Gillespie—locale (2) ... VA-3
Gillespie—locale ... WV-2
**Gillespie**—pop pl ... IL-6
**Gillespie**—pop pl ... PA-2
**Gillespie**—pop pl ... SC-3
Gillespie, Col. George, House—hist pl ... TN-4
Gillespie Ave Baptist Ch—church ... TN-4
Gillespie Bayou—stream ... LA-4
Gillespie Bend—bend (2) ... TN-4
Gillespie Brake—swamp ... LA-4
Gillespie Branch—stream ... GA-3
Gillespie Bridge—bridge ... MN-6
Gillespie Brook—stream ... MN-6
Gillespie Butte—summit ... OR-9
Gillespie Cem—cemetery (2) ... IL-6
Gillespie Cem—cemetery ... KY-4
Gillespie Cem—cemetery ... LA-4
Gillespie Cem—cemetery ... MS-4
Gillespie Cem—cemetery ... MO-7
Gillespie Cem—cemetery ... NC-3
Gillespie Cem—cemetery ... OH-6
Gillespie Cem—cemetery ... OR-9
Gillespie Cem—cemetery (2) ... TN-4
Gillespie Cem—cemetery (2) ... VA-3
Gillespie Ch—church (3) ... NC-3
Gillespie Ch—church ... TX-5
Gillespie Corners—locale ... OR-9
Gillespie Country Club—other ... IL-6
**Gillespie (County)**—pop pl ... TX-5
Gillespie Creek ... MT-8
Gillespie Creek—stream ... AL-4
Gillespie Creek—stream ... AK-9
Gillespie Creek—stream ... MT-8
Gillespie Creek—stream ... NM-5
Gillespie Cueto Tank—reservoir ... AZ-5
Gillespie Dam—dam ... AZ-5
Gillespie Dam—mine ... CA-9
Gillespie Dam Highway Bridge—hist pl ... AZ-5
Gillespie Ditch—canal ... AR-4
Gillespie Ditch—canal ... IN-6
Gillespie Draw—valley ... NM-5
Gillespie Flat—flat ... AZ-5
Gillespie Gap—gap ... NC-3
Gillespie Gulch—valley ... CO-8
Gillespie Gulch—valley ... ID-8
Gillespie Hill—summit ... NJ-2
Gillespie (historical)—locale ... AZ-5
Gillespie Hollow—valley ... GA-3
Gillespie House—hist pl ... NY-2
Gillespie Ironworks (historical)—locale ... TN-4
Gillespie-Jackson House—hist pl ... MS-4
Gillespie Lake ... IL-6
Gillespie Lake—lake ... MS-4
Gillespie Lake—reservoir ... SC-3
Gillespie Mine—mine ... NM-5
Gillespie Mtn—summit ... AZ-5
Gillespie Mtn—summit ... NM-5
Gillespie Mtn—summit ... VT-1
Gillespie Park—park ... FL-3
Gillespie Park Golf Course—locale ... NC-3
Gillespie Park Sch—school ... NC-3
Gillespie Pass—gap ... UT-8
Gillespie Peak—summit ... VT-1
Gillespie Point—cape ... CA-9
Gillespie Pond—lake ... NY-2
Gillespie Prospect—mine ... TN-4
Gillespie Ranch—locale ... AZ-5
Gillespie Ranch—locale ... MT-8
Gillespie Ranch—locale ... NM-5
Gillespie Reservoir ... IL-6
Gillespie Ridge—ridge ... GA-3
Gillespie Rsvr—reservoir ... MT-8
Gillespie Rsvr—reservoir ... WY-8
Gillespie Run—stream (2) ... PA-2
Gillespie Run—stream (3) ... WV-2
Gillespies, The—summit ... UT-8
Gillespie Sch—school ... IL-6
Gillespie Sch—school ... MI-6
Gillespie Sch—school ... PA-2
Gillespie Sch—school ... WV-2
Gillespie Sch (historical)—school ... MS-4
Gillespies Ditch ... AR-4
Gillespie Site (15MS50)—hist pl ... KY-4
Gillespies Landing (historical)—locale ... TN-4
Gillespies Pond—lake ... PA-2
Gillespie Spring—spring ... NM-5
Gillespie Spring—spring ... OR-9
Gillespies Shoals—bar ... TN-4
Gillespie Tank—reservoir ... TX-5
**Gillespie (Township of)**—pop pl ... IL-6
Gillespie Wash ... AZ-5
Gillespie Wash—stream ... AZ-5
Gillespie Well—well ... AZ-5
Gillespie-Wyen Oil Field—other ... IL-6
Gillespi Hill ... NJ-2
Gillespy Mineral Springs ... TN-4
Gillespys Fort (historical)—locale ... TN-4
Gilles-Sweet Sch—school ... OH-6
Gillet ... AL-4
Gillet ... AR-4
Gillet—locale ... CO-8
Gillete—locale ... CA-9
Gillet Gulch—valley ... OR-9
Gillet Lake—lake ... NE-7
Gillet Landing—locale ... MI-6
Gillets Creek—stream ... NC-3
Gillets Landing ... MI-6
**Gillett**—pop pl ... AR-4
**Gillett**—pop pl ... PA-2
**Gillett**—pop pl ... TX-5
**Gillett**—pop pl ... WI-6
Gillett, Asa, House—hist pl ... CT-1
Gillett, William J., House—hist pl ... NY-2
Gillett (CCD)—cens area ... TX-5
Gillett Cem—cemetery ... CT-1
Gillett Cem—cemetery ... NY-2
Gillett Cem—cemetery ... VT-1
Gillett Ch—church ... TX-5
Gillett Ch—church ... WI-6
**Gillett Corner**—pop pl ... MA-1
Gillett Creek—stream ... NY-2
Gillett Drain—stream ... MI-6
Gillette—locale ... AZ-5
Gillette—locale ... FL-3
Gillette—locale ... PA-2
**Gillette**—pop pl ... NJ-2
**Gillette**—pop pl ... WY-8
Gillette, Francis, House—hist pl ... CT-1
Gillette Brook ... CT-1
Gillette Brook—stream ... CT-1
Gillette Canyon—valley ... SD-7
Gillette Canyon—valley ... WY-8
Gillette Castle State Park—park ... CT-1
Gillette Cem—cemetery ... NY-2
Gillette Cem—cemetery ... TN-4
Gillette Ch—church (2) ... SC-3
Gillette Country Club—other ... WY-8
Gillette Creek—stream ... AK-9
Gillette Creek—stream ... MT-8
Gillette Creek—stream (2) ... NY-2
Gillette Creek—stream (2) ... WA-9
Gillette Ditch—canal ... MT-8
Gillette Ditch No. 1—canal ... CO-8
Gillette Ditch No. 2—canal ... CO-8
Gillette Ditch No. 3—canal ... CO-8
Gillette Fishing Lake—lake ... WY-8
Gillette Hill—summit ... VT-1
Gillette Hist Dist—hist pl ... OK-5
Gillette Hollow—valley ... MO-7
Gillette House—hist pl ... TX-5
Gillette Island—island ... MN-6
Gillette Lake—lake ... WA-9
Gillette Lake—lake ... WI-6
Gillette Lateral—canal ... SD-7
Gillette Mine—mine ... CA-9
Gillette Mine Trail—trail ... CA-9
Gillette Mountains ... WA-9
Gillette Mtn—summit ... WA-9
Gillette North—cens area ... WY-8
Gillette No. 26 Lateral—canal ... CO-8
Gillette Prairie—flat ... SD-7
Gillette Road Sch—school ... NY-2
Gillettes Brook—stream ... CT-1
Gillette Sch—school (2) ... NY-2
Gillette's Grist Mill—hist pl ... CT-1
Gillette South—cens area ... WY-8
Gillette Spring—spring ... OR-9
Gillettes Ranch ... SD-7
Gillettes Ranch (historical)—locale ... SD-7
Gillette State Hosp—hospital ... MN-6
Gillette Station RR Station—locale ... FL-3
Gillette Tanks—reservoir ... NM-5
Gillette-Tyrell Bldg—hist pl ... OK-5
Gillette Well—well ... NM-5
Gillette Well—well ... SD-7
Gillett Gap—gap ... NC-3
**Gillett (Gillette)**—pop pl ... FL-3
**Gillett Grove**—pop pl ... IA-7
Gillett Grove Township—fmr MCD ... IA-7
Gillett (historical)—locale ... AL-4
Gillett Island ... MN-6
Gillett Lake ... MI-6
Gillett Lake—lake ... MN-6
Gillett Lake—lake ... WI-6
Gillett Lake—reservoir ... TX-5
Gillett Mtn—summit ... CA-9
Gillett Pass—gap ... AK-9
Gillett Pond—lake ... VT-1
Gillett's ... IA-7
**Gilletts**—pop pl ... IL-6
Gilletts Brook—stream ... CT-1
Gillett Sch—school ... TX-5
Gillett-Shoemaker-Welsh House—hist pl ... OH-6
Gilletts Lake—lake ... MI-6
Gilletts Station ... PA-2
**Gillett (Town of)**—pop pl ... WI-6
Gilley—locale ... KY-4
Gilley—locale ... VA-3
Gilley Branch—stream ... KY-4
Gilley Cem—cemetery ... AL-4
Gilley Cem—cemetery ... NC-3
Gilley Cem—cemetery ... TN-4
Gilley Cem—cemetery ... VA-3
Gilley Creek—stream ... FL-3
Gilley Creek—stream ... GA-3
Gilley Creek—stream ... TX-5
Gilley Gully—stream ... LA-4
Gilley Hill Cem—cemetery ... TN-4
Gilley Hill Ch—church ... TN-4
Gilley Hill Methodist Ch ... TN-4
Gilley Hill Sch (historical)—school ... TN-4
Gilley Lake—reservoir ... CO-8
Gilley Ledge—bar ... ME-1
Gilleylen Cem—cemetery ... MS-4
Gilley Memorial Cem—cemetery ... AL-4
Gilley Mill Creek—stream ... AL-4
Gilleys Creek ... VA-3
Gilleys Grove—woods ... SD-7
Gilley-tofsland Octagonal Barn—hist pl ... WI-6
**Gilleyville**—pop pl ... LA-4
Gilleyville Ch—church ... KY-4
Gill Field—park ... IN-6
Gillfield Ch—church ... MS-4
Gillfield Ch—church ... VA-3
**Gillford (Township of)**—pop pl ... MN-6
Gillgal Ch—church ... FL-3
Gillgal Ch—church ... TX-5
Gill Grove Ch—church ... VA-3
Gill Gulch—valley ... ID-8
Gill Gully—valley ... NY-2
Gill Gum Hollow—valley ... VA-3
**Gill Hall**—pop pl ... PA-2
Gill Hall Elem Sch—school ... PA-2
Gill Hall Sch ... PA-2
**Gillham**—pop pl ... AR-4
Gillham Dam—dam ... AR-4
**Gillham (historical)**—pop pl ... OR-9
Gillham Hollow—valley ... TN-4
Gillham Lake—reservoir ... AR-4
Gillham Rsvr ... AR-4
Gillham Springs—spring ... AR-4
Gill Harbor—bay ... NY-2
Gill Hill ... NY-2
Gill Hill—summit ... NY-2
Gill Hill Ch—church ... VA-3
Gill (historical)—locale ... SD-7
Gill Hollow—valley ... TN-4
Gill Hollow—valley ... VA-3
Gill Hollow—valley ... WV-2
Gillhouser Run—stream ... PA-2
**Gillia**—pop pl ... OH-6
Gilliam ... MS-4
**Gilliam**—pop pl ... LA-4
**Gilliam**—pop pl ... MO-7
**Gilliam**—pop pl ... WA-9
**Gilliam**—pop pl ... WV-2
Gilliam Branch—stream ... KY-4
Gilliam Branch—stream ... VA-3
Gilliam Canyon—valley ... OR-9
Gilliam Cem—cemetery ... AL-4
Gilliam Cem—cemetery ... AR-4
Gilliam Cem—cemetery (2) ... KY-4
Gilliam Cem—cemetery ... MO-7
Gilliam Cem—cemetery ... NC-3
Gilliam Cem—cemetery (5) ... TN-4
Gilliam Cem—cemetery (4) ... VA-3
Gilliam Cemetery ... MS-4
Gilliam Ch—church ... NC-3
Gilliam Ch—church ... TX-5
Gilliam Chute—gut ... MS-4
**Gilliam County**—pop pl ... OR-9
Gilliam Cove—valley (2) ... TN-4
Gilliam Creek—stream ... AL-4
Gilliam Creek—stream ... CA-9
Gilliam Creek—stream (2) ... TN-4
Gilliam Draw—valley ... TX-5
Gilliam Gap—gap ... AL-4
Gilliam Hill ... AR-4
Gilliam Hollow—valley (2) ... TN-4
Gilliam Lake—reservoir ... NC-3
Gilliam Lake Dam—dam ... NC-3
Gilliam Landing—locale ... MS-4
Gilliam Ranch—locale ... TX-5
Gilliam Ridge—ridge ... CA-9
Gilliam Rock—summit ... CA-9
**Gilliams**—pop pl ... OR-9
Gilliams Branch—stream ... NC-3
Gilliams Branch—stream ... VA-3
Gilliams Ch—church ... SC-3
Gilliam Sch—school (2) ... VA-3
Gilliams Cove ... TN-4
Gilliams Island—island ... VA-3
Gilliams Landing ... MS-4
Gilliam Slough—gut ... AR-4
Gilliam Slough—stream ... LA-4
Gilliam Spring—spring ... AL-4
Gilliam Spring—spring ... TN-4
**Gilliam Springs**—pop pl ... AL-4
Gilliam Springs—spring ... TN-4
Gilliam Springs Baptist Church ... AL-4
Gilliam Springs Ch—church ... AL-4
Gilliamsville—locale ... VA-3
Gilliam Swale—valley ... OR-9
Gillian—locale ... WA-9
Gillian Chapel Cem—cemetery ... TN-4
Gilliand Cem—cemetery ... IN-6
Gilliand Cem—cemetery ... KY-4
Gilliand Cem—cemetery ... PA-2
Gilliand Gap ... AZ-5
Gilliand Pond—lake ... AL-4
Gilliand Spring ... AZ-5
Gillian Hollow—valley ... MO-7
Gillian Ridge—ridge ... AR-4
Gillian Sch—school ... AR-4
Gillian Settlement—locale ... AR-4
Gillians Knob—summit ... MD-2
**Gilliard**—pop pl ... SC-3
Gilliard Crossing—bridge ... SC-3
Gilliard Lake Oil Field—oilfield ... MS-4
Gillia Sch—school ... OH-6
Gilliatt—locale ... IA-7
Gillibrand Canyon—valley ... CA-9
Gillick Corner—locale ... VA-3
Gillie Cem—cemetery ... LA-4
Gillie Cem—cemetery ... TX-5
Gillie Creek—stream ... VA-3
Gillies Bridge—bridge ... MT-8
Gillies Creek—stream ... SC-3
Gillies Draw—valley ... WY-8
Gillies Hill—summit ... UT-8
Gillies Ranch—locale ... UT-8
Gillifits ... FM-9
Gillifitz ... FM-9
Gilligal Cem—cemetery ... TX-5
Gilligan, Mount—summit ... NY-2
Gilligan and Stevens Block—hist pl ... NY-2
Gilligan Butte—summit ... OR-9
Gilligan Creek ... VA-3
Gilligan Creek—stream ... OR-9
Gilligan Creek—stream ... VA-3
Gilligan Creek—stream ... WA-9
Gilligan Lake—lake (2) ... MI-6
Gilligans Bay—bay ... NY-2
Gilligan Shaft—mine ... NV-8
Gillikin Creek—stream ... NC-3
Gillilahd Canyon ... TX-5
Gillilan Cem—cemetery ... IA-7
Gilliland ... TN-4
Gilliland—other ... TN-4
**Gilliland**—pop pl ... TX-5
Gilliland, James, House—hist pl ... TN-4
Gilliland, William S., Log Cabin and Cemetery—hist pl ... WV-2
Gilliland Bridge (historical)—bridge ... AL-4
Gilliland Canyon—valley ... TX-5
Gilliland Cem—cemetery ... MS-4
Gilliland Cem—cemetery ... NY-2
Gilliland Cem—cemetery ... TN-4
Gilliland Cemetery ... AL-4
Gilliland Ch—church ... KY-4
Gilliland Creek ... TX-5
Gilliland Creek—stream ... AK-9
Gilliland Creek—stream ... NC-3
Gilliland Creek—stream ... TX-5
Gilliland Fork—stream ... TN-4
Gilliland Gap ... AL-4
Gilliland Gap—gap ... AZ-5
Gilliland Hill—summit ... KY-4
Gilliland House—hist pl ... KY-4
Gilliland North Well—well ... NM-5
Gilliland Oil Field—oilfield ... OK-5
Gilliland Ranch—locale ... MT-8
Gilliland Ridge—ridge ... TN-4
Gilliland Roy Number 1 Dam—dam ... SD-7
Gilliland Sch—school ... TN-4
Gilliland School—locale ... CO-8
Gillilands Farm Airp—airport ... KS-7
Gilliland Spring—spring ... AZ-5
Gilliland Tank—reservoir ... TX-5
Gillilandtown—locale ... NJ-2
Gilliman ... FM-9
Gillim House—hist pl ... KY-4
Gillingham—locale ... WI-6
**Gillingham**—pop pl ... PA-2
Gillingham Knoll—summit ... NY-2
Gillingham Pond—lake ... NH-1
Gillingham Sch—school ... WI-6
Gillin Ranch—locale ... MT-8
**Gillintown**—pop pl ... PA-2
Gillintown Mines Station—locale ... PA-2
Gillion Canyon ... TX-5
Gillion Creek ... KS-7
Gillionville—locale ... GA-3
Gillis—locale (2) ... CA-9
Gillis—locale ... TX-5
**Gillis**—pop pl ... LA-4
Gillis Bay—swamp ... FL-3
Gillis Bliss Run—stream ... PA-2
Gillis Bluff—cliff ... MO-7
Gillis Bluff Township—civil ... MO-7
Gillis Branch—stream ... AR-4
Gillis Branch—stream ... KY-4
Gillis Branch—stream ... NC-3
Gillis Brook—stream ... NY-2
Gillisburg ... MS-4
Gillis Camp—locale ... NV-8
Gillis Canyon ... NV-8
Gillis Canyon—valley ... CA-9
Gillis Canyon—valley ... NV-8
Gillis Cem—cemetery ... MS-4

Ginger Bay—bay TN-4
Ginger Bay Lake Access Area—park TN-4
Gingerberry—flat NC-3
**Ginger Blue**—pop pl MO-7
Gingerbread Ch—church MI-6
Gingerbread Corners—locale NY-2
Gingerbread Creek—stream TN-4
Gingerbread House—building MA-1
Gingerbread House Day Nursery—school FL-3
Gingerbread Islands RI-1
Gingerbread Sch Northeast—school FL-3
Gingerbread Wellington Sch—school FL-3
**Gingerbrook Estates Subdivision**—pop pl UT-8
Ginger Cake Creek—stream GA-3
Gingercake Creek—stream NC-3
Gingercake Mtn—summit NC-3
Gingercake Ridge—ridge KY-4
Ginger Creek ID-8
Ginger Creek IL-6
Ginger Creek—stream AK-9
Ginger Creek—stream CT-1
Ginger Creek—stream ID-8
Ginger Creek—stream IA-7
Ginger Creek—stream MA-1
Ginger Creek—stream NC-3
Ginger Creek—stream (3) OR-9
Ginger Creek—stream TN-4
Ginger Creek Cabin Area TN-4
Ginger Gulch—valley MT-8
Ginger Hill IL-6
Ginger Hill—locale OH-6
**Ginger Hill**—pop pl IL-6
**Ginger Hill**—pop pl PA-2
Ginger Hill—summit TN-4
Ginger Hill—summit UT-8
Ginger Hill—summit VA-3
Ginger Hill Sch—school IL-6
Ginger Hollow—valley VA-3
Gingerich Cem—cemetery (2) IA-7
Gingerich Gap—gap PA-2
Gingerich Lake Dam—dam IN-6
Ginger Peak—summit OR-9
Ginger Pond—lake NY-2
Ginger Ridge—ridge OH-6
Ginger Ridge Back Country Camp—locale TN-4
**Gingerville**—pop pl MD-2
Gingerville Creek—stream MD-2
**Gingerville-Wilenor Estates**—pop pl MD-2
Gingham Branch—stream TX-5
**Ginghamsburg**—pop pl OH-6
Ging Hollow—valley MO-7
Ging Lake—reservoir IL-6
Gingle Corners—locale IL-6
Gingle Mtn—summit OK-5
Gingles Cem—cemetery OR-9
Gingles Hollow—valley IA-7
Gingles Lake Dam—dam MS-4
Gingles Sch—school NC-3
**Gingles (Town of)**—pop pl WI-6
Gingleville MI-6
Gingoteague Creek—stream VA-3
Gingras Creek—stream MO-7
Gingras House and Trading Post—hist pl ND-7
Gingrass Draw—valley SD-7
Gingrass Lake—lake MI-6
**Gingrich**—pop pl IN-6
**Gingrich Addition**—pop pl IN-6
Gingrich Airp—airport PA-2
Gingrich Ch—church PA-2
Gingrich Run—stream PA-2
**Gings**—pop pl IN-6
Gings Station IN-6
Gin Gulch—valley MT-8
**Gin (historical)**—pop pl MS-4
Gin Hole—cave AL-4
Gin Hole Landing—locale FL-3
Gin Hollow—valley AL-4
Gin Hollow—valley AR-4
Gin Hollow—valley KY-4
Gin Hollow—valley (4) TN-4
Gin Hollow—valley WV-2
Gin Hollow Cave—cave AL-4
Gin Hollow Spring—spring AL-4
Ginholt Pond—reservoir CT-1
Gin House Bluff—cliff MS-4
Ginhouse Branch—stream (2) AL-4
Gin House Branch—stream AL-4
Ginhouse Branch—stream AL-4
Ginhouse Branch—stream FL-3
Gin House Branch—stream GA-3
Gin House Creek—stream AL-4
Ginhouse Creek—stream FL-3
Ginhouse Creek—stream GA-3
Ginhouse Hollow AL-4
Ginhouse Hollow—valley AL-4
Gin House Hollow—valley AL-4
Ginhouse Hollow Ch (historical)—church AL-4
Ginhouse Island—island AL-4
Ginhouse Lake—lake AL-4
Ginhouse Lake—lake AR-4
**Gin House Lake**—pop pl TN-4
Ginhouse Lake—reservoir GA-3
Gin House Lake—reservoir TN-4
Gin House Lake Dam—dam TN-4
Ginhouse Pond—lake (2) FL-3
Gin House Pond—lake FL-3
Ginhouse Pond—lake GA-3
Gin House Slough—stream AR-4
Ginkgo Creek—stream OR-9
Ginkgo State Park—park WA-9
Ginkgo Trail—trail OR-9
Ginko Creek OR-9
Gin Lake—lake FL-3
Gin Lake—lake (5) LA-4
Gin Lake—lake (2) MS-4
Gin Lake—lake TX-5
Gin Lake—swamp LA-4
Gin Landing—locale TN-4
**Ginlet**—pop pl MO-7
Gin Mtn—summit AL-4
Gin Mtn—summit AR-4
**Ginn**—pop pl NE-7
Ginn Brook—stream ME-1
Ginn Cem—cemetery MS-4
Ginn Cem—cemetery TN-4
Ginn Creek Baptist Church AL-4
Ginnette Lake—lake WA-9
Ginnett Hill—summit WA-9
Ginnevan Cem—cemetery WV-2
Ginney Branch—stream LA-4
Ginney Point—cape VA-3
Ginn Hollow—valley KY-4
Ginnie Spring—spring FL-3
Ginn Point—cape ME-1
Ginn Point—summit AL-4
Ginns Airp—airport PA-2
Ginns Corner—locale MD-2
**Ginns Corner**—pop pl DE-2
Ginns Corners—locale DE-2
Ginn's Furniture Store—hist pl KY-4
Ginns Lake—reservoir GA-3
Ginns Old Lake—reservoir GA-3
Ginn Spring—spring AZ-5
Ginny 'B' Airp—airport TN-4
Ginny Beach—beach VA-3
Ginny Creek—stream AK-9
Ginny Creek—stream MT-8
Ginny Lake—lake NV-8
Ginocchio Hist Dist—hist pl TX-5
Gin Oil Field—oilfield TX-5
Gin Pole Draw—valley WY-8
Ginpole Lake—lake MI-6
Gin Pond FL-3
Gin Pond—lake GA-3
Gin Pond Branch—stream TN-4
Gin Pond Creek—stream AL-4
Gin Pond (historical)—lake TN-4
Gin Post Office (historical)—building MS-4
Gin Raw Lake—lake GA-3
Ginrich Meeting House PA-2
Gin Ridge—ridge IL-6
Ginright Creek—stream CO-8
Gin Run—stream IN-6
Gin Run—stream WV-2
Ginsbach Sch—school SD-7
Ginsberg Point—summit OR-9
Ginsel Lake—lake MI-6
Ginseng—locale KY-4
Ginseng Branch—stream KY-4
Ginseng Creek—stream IL-6
Ginseng Creek—stream KY-4
Ginseng Hill—summit MD-2
Ginseng Hill—summit VT-1
Ginseng Hollow—valley PA-2
Ginseng Hollow—valley VA-3
Ginseng Hollow Trail—trail PA-2
Ginseng Mtn—summit NY-2
Ginseng Mtn—summit VA-3
Ginseng Run—stream MD-2
Gin Shop Hill—summit AL-4
Ginsite—locale TX-5
Gin Slough—gut (2) LA-4
Gin Slough—gut MS-4
Gin Slough—stream (2) LA-4
Gin Spring—spring OR-9
**Ginter**—pop pl PA-2
Ginter Cem—cemetery KY-4
Ginter Cem—cemetery WI-6
**Ginter Park**—pop pl VA-3
Ginter Park Hist Dist—hist pl VA-3
Ginter Park Sch—school VA-3
**Ginther**—pop pl PA-2
Ginther Sch—school NY-2
Gintown AL-4
**Ginty Corner**—pop pl MA-1
Ginty Lake—lake WI-6
Gin Windmill—locale TX-5
Gio MP-9
Gio Island MP-9
Giovannini Dam—dam PA-2
Gip AR-4
Gip—locale WV-2
Gip Creek—stream TX-5
Gipes Sch—school PA-2
Gipey—bay FM-9
Gipfel, The—summit NY-2
G I Pit TN-4
Gi Post Office (historical)—building AL-4
Gipp Creek—stream NC-3
Gippe, Henry, Farmstead—hist pl MN-6
Gipsey AL-4
Gipsey Cem—cemetery AL-4
Gipson—locale AR-4
Gipson Branch—stream TN-4
Gipson Cem—cemetery IN-6
Gipson Cem—cemetery MS-4
Gipson Cem—cemetery OK-5
Gipson Cem—cemetery (3) TN-4
Gipson Ch—church GA-3
Gipson Hollow—valley TN-4
Gipson Mtn—summit TN-4
Gipson Ranch—locale NM-5
Gipsonville Cem—cemetery TN-4
**Gipsy**—pop pl AL-4
**Gipsy**—pop pl MO-7
**Gipsy**—pop pl PA-2
Gipsy Creek—stream MI-6
Gipsy Creek—stream MT-8
Gipsy Lake—reservoir MT-8
Gipsy Post Office (historical)—building AL-4
Gipsy Spring—spring AL-4
Gipsy Trail Club—other NY-2
Gira and Ainsleys Dike Mine—mine SD-7
Girad CA-9
Giraffe Cave—cave AL-4
Giraffe Creek ID-8
Giraffe Creek WY-8
Giraffe Creek—stream ID-8
Giraffe Creek—stream WY-8
Giragoen Island—island MP-9
Giragoen-To MP-9
G I Ranch—locale OR-9
Girard Homestead—locale OR-9
Girands Creek TX-5
Girard—locale MN-6
Girard—locale MT-8
Girard—locale WV-2
**Girard**—pop pl AL-4
**Girard**—pop pl GA-3
**Girard**—pop pl IL-6
**Girard**—pop pl KS-7
**Girard**—pop pl LA-4
**Girard**—pop pl MI-6
**Girard**—pop pl OH-6
**Girard**—pop pl PA-2
**Girard**—pop pl TX-5
Girard, Lake—lake MN-6
Girard, Lake—reservoir OH-6
Girard Assembly of God Ch—church AL-4
Girard Ave—uninc pl PA-2
Girard Ave Elementary School AL-4
Girard Ave Hist Dist—hist pl PA-2
Girard Ave Junior High School AL-4
Girard Baptist Ch—church AL-4
Girard Boro PA-2
Girard Borough—civil PA-2
Girard Branch—stream MO-7
Girard Bridge—bridge PA-2
Girard Carnegie Library—hist pl KS-7
Girard (CCD)—cens area GA-3
Girard Cem—cemetery KS-7
Girard Cem—cemetery MN-6
Girard Ch—church NM-5
Girard Ch—church PA-2
Girard Chapel AME Ch—church AL-4
Girard Coll—school PA-2
Girard College Complex—hist pl PA-2
Girard Colored Mission—hist pl GA-3
Girard Creek—stream CA-9
Girard Creek—stream CO-8
Girarde—locale NY-2
Girardeau, Lake—reservoir MO-7
Girard Elem Sch PA-2
Girard Elem Sch—school KS-7
Girard Elem Sch—school PA-2
Girard Group—hist pl PA-2
Girard Gulch—valley MT-8
Girard Helistop—airport PA-2
Girard Hist Dist—hist pl AL-4
Girard HS—hist pl AL-4
Girard HS—school KS-7
Girard JHS—school AL-4
Girard JHS—school GA-3
Girard Junction—locale PA-2
Girard Junction Lookout Tower—locale WI-6
Girard Lake—lake MI-6
Girard Lake—lake ND-7
Girard Lake Rsvr OH-6
Girard Liberty Union Cem—cemetery OH-6
**Girard Manor**—pop pl PA-2
Girard Mill Site—locale CA-9
Girard Park—park LA-4
Girard Park—park PA-2
Girard P.O. (historical)—building AL-4
Girard Point—cape PA-2
Girard Point—uninc pl PA-2
Girard Pond—lake MA-1
Girard Ridge—ridge CA-9
Girard Rsvr—reservoir CA-9
Girard Sch—school AL-4
Girard Sch—school PA-2
Girard Sch Number 2—school ND-7
Girard Sch Number 3—school ND-7
**Girard (Township of)**—pop pl IL-6
**Girard (Township of)**—pop pl MI-6
**Girard (Township of)**—pop pl MN-6
**Girard (Township of)**—pop pl (2) PA-2
Girard Trail—trail CA-9
**Girardville**—pop pl PA-2
Girardville Borough—civil PA-2
Girardville Elem Sch—school PA-2
Girard Windmill—locale CO-8
Giras Claim Mine—mine SD-7
Giraud, Joseph, House—hist pl NV-8
Giraud Peak—summit CA-9
Gird Cem—cemetery NY-2
Gird Creek MT-8
Gird Creek—stream CA-9
Gird Creek—stream (2) MT-8
Girdland—locale PA-2
Girdle, The—range CA-9
Girdled Glacier—glacier AK-9
**Girdler**—pop pl KY-4
Girdler (CCD)—cens area KY-4
Girdle Road Sch—school MI-6
**Girdletree**—pop pl MD-2
Girdletree Landing MD-2
Girdley MS-4
Girdner—locale MO-7
Girdner Bend—bend CA-9
Girdner Cem—cemetery MO-7
Girdner Sch (abandoned)—school MO-7
Girdner Tank—reservoir (2) AZ-5
Gird Point—locale MT-8
Gird Pumping Station—other CA-9
Gird Sch—school CA-9
Girds Creek—stream OR-9
**Girdwood**—pop pl AK-9
Gireaus Claim SD-7
Gireniyan MP-9
Gireniyan-to MP-9
Girft Dam—dam ND-7
Girgir—bay FM-9
Girifitsu FM-9
Girifitzu FM-9
Girifuitsu FM-9
Girinien Island MP-9
Girinien-to MP-9
Girkin—locale KY-4
Girkin Canyon OR-9
Girking Canyon OR-9
Girkling Canyon OR-9
Girland PA-2
Girl Brook—stream NH-1
Girl Creek—stream AK-9
Girl Creek—stream OK-5
Girl Hollow—valley UT-8
Girl Lake—lake MN-6
Girl Lake—lake ND-7
Girls Club—hist pl CA-9
Girls Collegiate Sch—school CA-9
Girl Scout Camp—locale AZ-5
Girl Scout Camp—locale MA-1
Girl Scout Camp—locale NY-2
Girl Scout Camp—locale OH-6
Girl Scout Camp—locale PA-2
Girl Scout Camp—locale VA-3
Girl Scout Camp Lake Dam—dam MS-4
Girl Scout Camp Recreation Site NV-8
Girl Scout Dam—dam NC-3
Girl Scout Lake—reservoir NC-3
Girl Scout Lake Dam—dam AL-4
Girl Scout Park—park FL-3
Girl Scout Spring—spring AZ-5
Girls HS—school NY-2
Girls M I A Camp—locale UT-8
Girls Mtn—summit AK-9
Girls' Parental Sch—hist pl WA-9
Girls Polytechnic HS—school OR-9
Girls Town Of America—locale OH-6
Girls Town (State School)—school OK-5
Girls Town USA—locale TX-5
**Girlton (historical)**—pop pl TN-4
Girlton Post Office (historical)—building TN-4
**Giro**—pop pl IN-6
Giro Ch—church IN-6
Girod, Nicholas, House—hist pl LA-4
Giror FM-9
Girot Ranch—locale CA-9
Giroux Ridge—ridge CA-9
Giroux Bluff—cliff AK-9
Giroux Mine—mine NV-8
Giroux Springs—spring NV-8
Giroux Wash—stream NV-8
Girta—locale WV-2
Girt Creek—stream OR-9
Girten Hollow—valley MO-7
**Girton**—pop pl OH-6
Girton Cem—cemetery IN-6
Girton Ditch—canal IN-6
Girton Run—stream IN-6
**Girty**—pop pl PA-2
Girty Cem—cemetery (2) OK-5
Girty Island—island OH-6
Girty Run—stream WV-2
Girtys Notch—pillar PA-2
Girtys Run—stream PA-2
Girvan—locale CA-9
Girvin—locale TX-5
Girvin Butte—summit TX-5
Girvin Cem—cemetery MO-7
Girvin Cem—cemetery TX-5
Girwood (Aban'd)—locale AK-9
Girzzly Creek Dam No. 2—dam OR-9
Gisasa River—stream AK-9
Gisborn—locale UT-8
Gisborne Mtn—summit ID-8
Gise—locale NM-5
**Gisela**—pop pl AZ-5
Gisela Mtn—summit AZ-5
Gisela Tank—reservoir AZ-5
Gisel Peak—summit AK-9
**Gish**—pop pl TX-5
Gish Bay—bay AK-9
Gish Branch—stream VA-3
Gish Cem—cemetery KY-4
Gish Mine—mine MT-8
Gishna Creek—stream AK-9
Gish Sch—school KS-7
Gishton—locale KY-4
Gishville Cem—cemetery MN-6
Gisiss Lake MN-6
Gislason Lake—lake MN-6
Gismo Butte—summit UT-8
Gismo Creek—stream CO-8
Gismo Mine—mine UT-8
Gismonda—locale TN-4
Gissendanner Bridge—bridge SC-3
Giss-I-Was Creek—stream MI-6
Gist NC-3
Gist—locale GA-3
Gist—locale TX-5
**Gist**—pop pl MD-2
Gist, David, House—hist pl KY-4
Gist Cave—cave AL-4
Gist Cem—cemetery MD-2
Gist Cem—cemetery OR-9
Gist Creek—stream CA-9
Gist Lake—lake TX-5
Gist Ranch—locale MT-8
Gist Ridge—ridge MO-7
Gist Run—stream PA-2
Gist Sch—school AR-4
Gists Creek—stream TN-4
Gists Creek Cem—cemetery TN-4
Gists Creek Ch—church TN-4
Gist Settlement—locale OH-6
Gist Tanks—reservoir NM-5
Gisttown (historical)—locale AL-4
Gitaem—locale FM-9
Gitam FM-9
Gitano—locale MS-4
Gitano Oil And Gas Field—oilfield MS-4
Gitano Sch (historical)—school MS-4
Gitchegumee, Lake—reservoir MI-6
Gitchel—locale MI-6
Gitchell Creek—stream CA-9
Gitchie Manitou State Preserve—forest IA-7
Git'Em Creek—stream OR-9
Githens Cem—cemetery KY-4
Githens Jordan Junior-Senior HS—school NC-3
Githens Mtn—summit OR-9
Githgidunka Creek—stream AK-9
Gitmore Mines (underground)—mine AL-4
Gittin Down Mtn—summit OK-5
Gittings—locale MD-2
Gittings Cem—cemetery IL-6
Gittings Creek OR-9
Gittings Mound—summit IL-6
Gittins Spring—spring UT-8
**Gitts Run**—pop pl PA-2
Gitts Run—stream PA-2
Giusti Spring—spring ID-8
Givan Creek—stream NY-2
Givans Cem—cemetery KY-4
Givan Sch—school MO-7
Give A Dam Jones Ditch—canal CO-8
Give-A-Damn Canyon—valley NM-5
Give-A-Damn Well—well NM-5
Given—locale VA-3
**Given**—pop pl WV-2
Given Branch AL-4
Given Branch—stream VA-3
Given Cave—cave AL-4
Given Cem—cemetery WV-2
Given Creek TX-5
Given Creek—stream IA-7
Given Fork—stream WV-2
Given Mine (underground)—mine AL-4
Given Ranch NV-8
Given Run—stream WV-2
Givens—locale KY-4
Givens—locale OH-6
**Givens**—pop pl TX-5
Givens, Mount—summit CA-9
Givens Branch—stream (2) AL-4
Givens Branch—stream MD-2
Givens Bridge—locale AL-4
Givens Cem—cemetery AR-4
Givens Cem—cemetery KY-4
Givens Cem—cemetery MS-4
Givens Cem—cemetery MO-7
Givens Cem—cemetery TN-4
Givens Cem—cemetery VA-3
Givens Chapel—church IL-6
Givens Corner—locale WA-9
Givens Creek AL-4
Givens Creek—stream CA-9
Givens Creek—stream KY-4
Givens Creek—stream TX-5
Givens Fork—stream WV-2
Givens Gap—gap TN-4
Givens Headley and Co. Tobacco Warehouse—hist pl KY-4
Givens Hill—summit ME-1
Givens Hollow—valley OH-6
Givens Hollow—valley (2) TN-4
Givens Hollow—valley WV-2
Givens Homestead (abandoned)—locale WY-8
Givens Hot Springs—locale ID-8
Givens Lake—lake CA-9
Givens Lateral—canal CA-9
Givens-McGuire Cem—cemetery LA-4
Givens Meadow—flat CA-9
Givens Park—park TX-5
Givens Pond—lake ME-1
Givens Post Office (historical)—building TN-4
Given Spring—spring MO-7
Givens Ranch—locale NV-8
Givens Run—stream VA-3
Givens Sch—school CA-9
Givens Sch—school VA-3
Givens Sch—school WA-9
Givens Slough—stream OR-9
Givens Springs ID-8
Givens Swamp—swamp MD-2
Given Station—locale IA-7
Givens warm Springs ID-8
Giveout—locale ID-8
Giveout Creek—stream WA-9
Give Out Morgan Creek—stream MT-8
Giveout Mountain—ridge OR-9
**Givhans**—pop pl SC-3
Givhans Ferry State Park—park SC-3
Givhans Sch—school SC-3
Givies Creek—stream VA-3
Givin—locale IA-7
Givins IL-6
Givins Bayou—stream LA-4
Givins Branch—stream AR-4
Givins Branch—stream MO-7
Givins Cem—cemetery TN-4
Givins Grove Ch—church GA-3
Givins Gulch—valley CA-9
Givins Pond—swamp TX-5
Givler Sch—school PA-2
Givney Key—island FL-3
Givry FM-9
Givry Island FM-9
Gizella, Lake—lake AL-4
Gizoquit Brook—stream ME-1
Gizzard Branch—stream (2) GA-3
Gizzard Cove—valley TN-4
Gizzard Cove Cave—cave TN-4
Gizzard Creek TN-4
Gizzard Creek—stream IA-7
Gizzard Creek—stream (2) MO-7
Gizzard Lake—lake FL-3
Gizzard Point—cape AL-4
G Jacobsen Ranch—locale ND-7
Gjerde Ranch—locale MT-8
Gjerpen Cem—cemetery WI-6
G J Filleman Ranch—locale AZ-5
G K B Lateral—canal CO-8
G Kelly Creek OR-9
G K Fountain Correctional Farm AL-4
G K Lateral—canal CO-8
Gknowood Township—civil SD-7
Glabe Sch—school IL-6
Glable Branch—stream KY-4
Glace—locale WV-2
Glacia Ch—church AR-4
Glacial Boulder—locale WY-8
Glacial Boulder Trail—trail WY-8
Glacial Fan Creek—stream AK-9
Glacial Grooves State Memorial—park OH-6
Glacial Lake MN-6
Glacial Lake—lake AK-9
Glacial Lakes State Park—park MN-6
Glacial River—stream AK-9
Glacial Spring—spring WI-6
Glaciate Butte—summit WA-9
Glacier—locale (2) AK-9
Glacier—locale WA-9
**Glacier**—pop pl WA-9
Glacier, Lake—lake OH-6
Glacier Basin—basin AK-9
Glacier Basin—basin CO-8
Glacier Basin—basin MT-8
Glacier Basin—basin (2) WA-9
Glacier Basin—basin WY-8
Glacier Basin Campground Ranger Station—hist pl CO-8
Glacier Bay—bay AK-9
Glacier Bay Lodge—locale AK-9
Glacier Bay Natl Park—park AK-9
Glacier Bible Camp—locale MT-8
Glacier Brook CA-9
Glacier Camp—locale (2) CA-9
Glacier Campground—locale MT-8
Glacier Canyon—valley CA-9
Glacier Canyon Creek—stream AK-9
**Glacier Colony**—pop pl MT-8
Glacier Creek AK-9
Glacier Creek WA-9
Glacier Creek WY-8
Glacier Creek—stream (15) AK-9
Glacier Creek—stream (2) CA-9
Glacier Creek—stream (2) CO-8
Glacier Creek—stream ID-8
Glacier Creek—stream (2) MT-8
Glacier Creek—stream OR-9
Glacier Creek—stream (8) WA-9
Glacier Creek—stream (2) WY-8
Glacier Creek Glacier WA-9
Glacier Creek Trail—trail CO-8
Glacier Ditch—canal OR-9
Glacier Divide—ridge CA-9
Glacier Falls—falls CO-8
Glacier Falls—falls WY-8
Glacier Fork Knik River—stream AK-9
Glacier Fork Tlikakila River—stream AK-9
Glacier Gap Lake—lake AK-9
Glacier Gorge—valley CO-8
Glacier Gorge Junction—locale CO-8
Glacier Gulch—valley (2) AK-9
Glacier Gulch—valley ID-8
Glacier Gulch—valley WY-8
Glacier Gulch Turnout—locale WY-8
**Glacier Hills**—pop pl NJ-2
Glacier HS—school WA-9
Glacier Island—island AK-9
Glacier Island—island WA-9
Glacier King—summit AK-9
Glacier Knobs—summit CO-8
Glacier Lake CA-9
Glacier Lake MI-6
Glacier Lake MT-8
Glacier Lake WA-9
Glacier Lake—lake (3) AK-9
Glacier Lake—lake (3) CA-9
Glacier Lake—lake (3) ID-8
Glacier Lake—lake MN-6
Glacier Lake—lake (5) MT-8
Glacier Lake—lake OR-9
Glacier Lake—lake (3) WA-9
Glacier Lake—lake (2) WY-8
Glacier Lake—reservoir CO-8
Glacier Lakes—lake CA-9
Glacier Lakes—lake CO-8
Glacier Lakes—lake NM-5
Glacier Lakes—lake WY-8
Glacier Lake Trail—trail WA-9
Glacier Lodge—locale CA-9
Glacier Meadows—flat WA-9
Glacier Memorial Gardens—cemetery MT-8
**Glacier Mesa Subdivision**—pop pl UT-8
Glacier Mines—mine CA-9
Glacier Monument—summit CA-9
Glacier Mountain CO-8
Glacier Mtn—summit AK-9
Glacier Mtn—summit CO-8
Glacier Mtn—summit (2) OR-9
Glacier Natl Park—park (2) MT-8
Glacier Natl Park HQ—locale MT-8
Glacier Park (2) MT-8
Glacier Park Autumn Creek Trail—trail MT-8
Glacier Park International Airport—airport MT-8
Glacier Pass CA-9
Glacier Pass—gap (2) AK-9
Glacier Pass—gap OR-9
Glacier Pass—gap (2) WA-9
Glacier Pass—gap WY-8
Glacier Pass—trail CA-9
Glacier Peak OR-9
Glacier Peak WA-9
Glacier Peak—summit AK-9
Glacier Peak—summit CO-8
Glacier Peak—summit MT-8
Glacier Peak—summit WA-9
Glacier Peak Mines—mine WA-9
Glacier Peaks—summit MT-8
Glacier Peak Shelter—locale WA-9
Glacier Point—cape (3) AK-9
Glacier Point—cliff CA-9
Glacier Point—summit CO-8
Glacier Point Trailside Museum—hist pl CA-9
Glacier Pond—lake MN-6
Glacier Pup—stream AK-9
Glacier Ranger Station—hist pl WA-9
Glacier Ridge—ridge CA-9
Glacier Ridge—ridge CO-8
Glacier Ridge Trail—trail WA-9
Glacier River—stream (4) AK-9
Glacier Rock—summit CT-1
Glacier Sloughs—swamp MT-8
Glacier Spit—bar AK-9
Glacier Spring—spring AK-9
Glacier Spring Campground—locale CO-8
Glacier Springs—reservoir CO-8
**Glacier Township**—pop pl ND-7
Glacier Trail—trail (2) WY-8
Glacier Uplands—plain KS-7
Glacier Valley—valley CA-9
Glacier View—locale WA-9
Glacier View Camp—locale CO-8
Glacier View Campground—locale WA-9
Glacier View Mtn—summit MT-8
Glacierview Ranch—locale CA-9
Glacier View Turnout—locale WY-8
Glacier Wall—cliff MT-8
Glacier Way—trail OR-9
Glacio Park—park UT-8
**Glacio Park Subdivision**—pop pl UT-8
Glacken Hill—summit CO-8
Glad, Bayou—stream LA-4
Glad Acre Ch—church AR-4
**Gladbrook**—pop pl IA-7
Gladco Lake PA-2
Glad Creek—stream ID-8
Gladden—locale AZ-5
Gladden—locale PA-2
**Gladden**—pop pl AZ-5
**Gladden**—pop pl AR-4
**Gladden**—pop pl MO-7
Gladden, Joseph, House—hist pl PA-2
Gladden Bottom—bend KS-7
Gladden Branch—stream AL-4
Gladden Branch—stream LA-4
Gladden Branch—stream MD-2
Gladden Branch—stream MO-7
Gladden Branch—stream TN-4
Gladden Cem—cemetery AL-4
Gladden Cem—cemetery GA-3
Gladden Ch—church AR-4
Gladden Creek—stream MO-7
Gladden Elem Sch—school MO-7
Gladden Grove Ch—church SC-3
**Gladden Heights**—pop pl PA-2
Gladden Hollow—valley TN-4
Gladden Ravine—valley KS-7
Gladden Ridge—ridge NC-3
Gladden Sch—school KS-7
Gladden Sch—school NY-2
Gladden Sch (abandoned)—school MO-7
Gladden Sch (historical)—school AL-4
Gladdens Creek—stream NC-3
Gladdens Lake—reservoir NC-3

Glass Mine Top—*summit* GA-3
*Glass Mountain* OK-5
Glass Mountain Ridge—*ridge* CA-9
Glass Mountains—*range* OK-5
Glass Mountains—*range* TX-5
Glass Mountain Spring—*spring* OR-9
Glass Mtn—*summit* (3) CA-9
Glass Mtn—*summit* OR-9
Glass Mtns—*range* UT-8
Glass Number 1 Drift Mine (underground)—*mine* AL-4
Glassock Branch—*stream* KY-4
Glasson Cem—*cemetery* IN-6
Glass Park—*park* AK-9
Glass Peninsula—*cape* AK-9
Glass Playfield—*park* WA-9
Glass Point—*cape* AK-9
Glass Pond—*lake* GA-3
Glass Pond—*lake* KY-4
Glass Pond—*swamp* FL-3
Glass Pond—*swamp* NC-3
Glass Pond Dam Number One—*dam* PA-2
Glass Pond Dam Number Three—*dam* PA-2
Glass Pond Number One—*reservoir* PA-2
Glass Pond Number Three—*reservoir* PA-2
Glass Pond Number Two—*reservoir* PA-2
Glass Pond Number Two Dam—*dam* PA-2
**Glassport**—*pop pl* PA-2
Glassport Borough—*civil* PA-2
Glassport Central Elem Sch—*school* PA-2
Glass Post Office (historical)—*building* TN-4
Glass Ranch—*locale* (3) TX-5
**Glass Rock**—*pop pl* OH-6
Glass Rock Knob—*summit* NC-3
Glass Run—*stream* PA-2
Glass Spring—*spring* AL-4
Glass Spring—*spring* OR-9
Glass Spring—*spring* TN-4
Glass Springs—*spring* CA-9
Glass Tank—*reservoir* AZ-5
Glass Tank—*reservoir* TX-5
**Glasston**—*pop pl* ND-7
Glasston Cem—*cemetery* MO-7
*Glasston Lake* MT-8
Glasston Sch—*school* MT-8
Glasston Sch (abandoned)—*school* MO-7
Glass (Township of)—*fmr MCD* AR-4
Glass Window Cem—*cemetery* LA-4
*Glass Works* IL-6
*Glass Works* PA-2
**Glassworks**—*pop pl* PA-2
**Glassy**—*pop pl* SC-3
Glassy Knob—*summit* GA-3
Glassy Mountain Ch—*church* (2) SC-3
Glassy Mtn—*summit* GA-3
Glassy Mtn—*summit* NC-3
Glassy Mtn—*summit* (2) SC-3
Glassy Pond—*lake* NH-1
Glassy Rock—*cliff* SC-3
Glassyrock Creek—*stream* NC-3
*Glassy Rock Mountain* SC-3
Glassyrock Mtn—*summit* NC-3
Glassyrock Ridge—*ridge* NC-3
*Glastenbury* CT-1
Glastenbury Camp—*locale* VT-1
Glastenbury Mtn—*summit* VT-1
Glastenbury River—*stream* VT-1
Glastenbury (Town of)—*fmr MCD* VT-1
**Glaston**—*pop pl* MS-4
**Glastonbury**—*pop pl* CT-1
*Glastonbury Cove* CT-1
Glastonbury Ferry—*other* CT-1
Glastonbury Green Cem—*cemetery* CT-1
Glastonbury Hist Dist—*hist pl* CT-1
Glastonbury Meadows—*flat* CT-1
Glastonbury Monastery—*church* MA-1
**Glastonbury (Town of)**—*pop pl* CT-1
Glaston Post Office (historical)—*building* MS-4
Glastowbury Lake—*reservoir* TN-4
Glastowbury Lake Dam—*dam* TN-4
Glasva Branch—*stream* MD-2
Glat Co Lake—*lake* PA-2
G Lateral—*canal* CA-9
G Lateral Two—*canal* CA-9
**Glatfelter**—*pop pl* PA-2
Glatfelter Memorial Field—*park* PA-2
**Glatfelters**—*pop pl* PA-2
Glau Canyon—*valley* CA-9
Glaucophane Ridge—*ridge* CA-9
*Glaucus Island* MO-7
Glaus Pond—*reservoir* TN-4
Glaus Ranch—*locale* MT-8
Glaus Ranch—*locale* SD-7
Glaves Sch—*school* MO-7
Glawe Lake—*lake* MN-6
Glawes Airp—*airport* SD-7
Glawe Sch—*school* MI-6
Glawson Creek—*stream* GA-3
Glaydin Sch—*school* VA-3
*Glaze* AR-4
Glaze Bridge—*bridge* TN-4
Glaze Cem—*cemetery* MO-7
Glaze Cem—*cemetery* OH-6
Glaze Cem—*cemetery* (2) TN-4
Glaze Ch—*church* AR-4
Glaze Ch (historical)—*church* MO-7
Glaze City—*locale* TX-5
*Glaze Creek* MO-7
Glaze Creek—*stream* AL-4
Glaze Creek—*stream* AR-4
Glaze Creek—*stream* LA-4
Glaze Creek—*stream* MO-7
Glaze Creek—*stream* OR-9
Glaze Creek Ch—*church* AR-4
*Glazed Alder Creek* OR-9
Glaze Ferry (historical)—*locale* AL-4
Glaze Lake—*lake* OR-9
Glaze Lake—*lake* TX-5
Glaze Meadow—*flat* OR-9
Glazener Cem—*cemetery* NC-3
Glazener Gap—*gap* NC-3
Glaze Ranch—*locale* NM-5
Glazer Creek—*stream* CA-9
*Glazer Ridge* CA-9
Glazer Ridge—*ridge* CA-9
Glazer Sch—*school* MI-6
Glaze Rsvr—*reservoir* NM-5
Glaze Sch (abandoned)—*school* MO-7
Glaze Sch (abandoned)—*school* PA-2
Glaze Tank—*reservoir* NM-5

Glaze Township—*civil* MO-7
Glaze Well—*well* NM-5
Glaze Windmill—*locale* (2) NM-5
Glazewood Manor—*uninc pl* MD-2
**Glazier**—*pop pl* TX-5
*Glazier Brook* ME-1
Glazier Brook—*stream* (2) ME-1
Glazier Brook Mtn—*summit* ME-1
*Glazier Canyon* CA-9
Glazier Creek—*stream* ID-8
*Glazier Hill* MA-1
Glazier Lake—*lake* ME-1
Glazier Park—*park* CA-9
Glazier Peau Ch—*church* AR-4
Glazier Pond—*lake* ME-1
Glazier Pond Brook—*stream* ME-1
Glazier Ranch—*locale* MT-8
Glazier Sch—*school* CA-9
Glazier Sch—*school* NE-7
Glazon, Lake—*lake* MI-6
Glazypeau Creek—*stream* AR-4
Glazypeau Mountain—*ridge* AR-4
*Gleabiski Lake* WI-6
Gleade Branch—*stream* AL-4
Gleam Lake—*lake* MN-6
Gleaners Hall—*locale* MI-6
**Gleanings**—*pop pl* KY-4
*Glean Lake* IN-6
Gleason—*locale* AR-4
Gleason—*locale* PA-2
Gleason—*locale* WY-8
**Gleason**—*pop pl* TN-4
**Gleason**—*pop pl* WI-6
Gleason, Dr. Edward Francis, House—*hist pl* MA-1
Gleason, Edmund, House—*hist pl* OH-6
Gleason, F. C. House—*hist pl* ID-8
Gleason, Lake—*lake* FL-3
Gleason, Mount—*summit* CA-9
Gleason Basin—*basin* NV-8
Gleason Bay—*bay* WI-6
Gleason Beach—*beach* CA-9
Gleason Bldg—*hist pl* MA-1
Gleason Branch—*stream* MO-7
Gleason Brook—*stream* ME-1
Gleason Brook—*stream* MI-6
Gleason Brook—*stream* NH-1
Gleason Brook—*stream* VT-1
Gleason Butte—*summit* OR-9
Gleason Canyon—*valley* CA-9
Gleason Canyon—*valley* CO-8
Gleason Canyon—*valley* NM-5
Gleason Canyon Wash—*stream* NV-8
Gleason (CCD)—*cens area* TN-4
Gleason Cem—*cemetery* MI-6
Gleason Cem—*cemetery* NH-1
Gleason Cem—*cemetery* OR-9
Gleason Cem—*cemetery* WI-6
Gleason City Hall—*building* TN-4
Gleason Cove—*bay* ME-1
Gleason Creek—*stream* AK-9
Gleason Creek—*stream* CA-9
Gleason Creek—*stream* (2) MI-6
Gleason Creek—*stream* MT-8
Gleason Creek—*stream* NV-8
Gleason Creek—*stream* OR-9
Gleason Creek—*stream* TN-4
**Gleasondale**—*pop pl* MA-1
**Gleasondale (sta.)**—*pop pl* MA-1
**Gleasondale Station**—*pop pl* MA-1
Gleason Division—*civil* TN-4
Gleason Drain—*stream* MI-6
Gleason First Baptist Ch—*church* TN-4
Gleason Flat—*flat* AZ-5
Gleason Flat Catchment—*reservoir* AZ-5
Gleason Grove Cem—*cemetery* MS-4
Gleason Grove Ch—*church* MS-4
Gleason Gulch—*valley* CO-8
Gleason Hill—*summit* PA-2
Gleason Hill—*summit* WA-9
Gleason Hollow—*valley* NY-2
Gleason Hollow—*valley* (3) PA-2
Gleason Island—*island* VT-1
Gleason Lake—*lake* MI-6
Gleason Lake—*lake* MN-6
Gleason Lake—*lake* MT-8
Gleason Marsh—*swamp* VA-3
Gleason Meadow—*flat* ID-8
*Gleason Mountain* CA-9
Gleason Mtn—*summit* ME-1
Gleason Mtn—*summit* NY-2
Gleason Mtn—*summit* WA-9
Gleason Park—*park* IN-6
Gleason Park—*park* TX-5
Gleason Peak—*summit* CA-9
Gleason Point—*cape* ME-1
Gleason Point—*cape* NY-2
Gleason Pond—*lake* MA-1
Gleason Pond—*reservoir* MA-1
Gleason Pond Dam—*dam* MA-1
Gleason Post Office—*building* TN-4
Gleason Resort—*locale* MT-8
Gleasons Canyon—*valley* NM-5
Gleason Sch—*school* MA-1
Gleason Sch—*school* NV-8
Gleason Sch—*school* TN-4
Gleason Sch (historical)—*school* MS-4
Gleasons Gap—*gap* VA-3
Gleasons Mill—*locale* NY-2
*Gleasons Pond* MA-1
Gleason Spring—*spring* OR-9
Gleason Spring One—*spring* NV-8
Gleason Springs—*spring* NV-8
Gleason Spring Two—*spring* NV-8
Gleasonton—*locale* PA-2
Gleaton-Johnson Slough—*stream* GA-3
Gleaves Knob—*summit* VA-3
*Glebe* VA-3
*Glebe* WV-2
**Glebe**—*pop pl* WV-2
Glebe, The—*bay* VA-3
Glebe, The—*hist pl* VA-3
Glebe, The—*ridge* VT-1
Glebe Bay—*bay* MD-2
Glebe Branch—*stream* (2) MD-2
Glebe Brook—*stream* NH-1
Glebe Burying Ground—*hist pl* VA-3
Glebe Cem—*cemetery* DE-2
Glebe Cem—*cemetery* VA-3
Glebe Ch—*church* VA-3

Glebe Church—*hist pl* VA-3
Glebe Creek—*bay* MD-2
Glebe Creek—*stream* MD-2
Glebe Creek—*stream* NC-3
Glebe Creek—*stream* (3) VA-3
Glebe Creek Marsh—*swamp* MD-2
Glebe Harbor—*locale* VA-3
**Glebe Heights**—*pop pl* MD-2
Glebe House—*hist pl* CT-1
Glebe House—*hist pl* DE-2
Glebe House—*hist pl* NY-2
Glebe House of Southwark Parish—*hist pl* VA-3
Glebe House of St. Anne's Parish—*hist pl* VA-3
Glebe Landing Ch—*church* VA-3
Glebe Mills—*locale* VA-3
Glebe Mtn—*summit* VT-1
Glebe Neck—*cape* VA-3
Glebe of Hungar's Parish—*hist pl* VA-3
Glebe of Shelburne Parish—*hist pl* VA-3
Glebe of Westover Parish—*hist pl* VA-3
*Glebe Point* VA-3
Glebe Point—*cape* (3) VA-3
Glebe Pond—*reservoir* VA-3
Glebe Run—*stream* MD-2
Glebe Run—*stream* (2) VA-3
Glebe Schoolhouse—*hist pl* VA-3
*Glebe Station* WV-2
Glebe Swamp—*stream* (2) VA-3
Glebe View Cem—*cemetery* VT-1
**Glecker**—*pop pl* TX-5
Gledhill Draw—*valley* CO-8
Gledhill Street Sch—*school* CA-9
*Glee* AL-4
**Gleed**—*pop pl* WA-9
*Gleed Cow Camp* MT-8
Gleed Ditch—*canal* WA-9
Gleeden Branch—*stream* AL-4
Gleedsville—*locale* VA-3
Gleed Tank—*reservoir* AZ-5
Glee Lake—*lake* MN-6
Glee Lake—*lake* SD-7
*Glee Mill* MD-2
**Glee Mill**—*pop pl* MD-2
*Gleen Spring* AZ-5
*Gleenwood* IN-6
Gleenwood Cem—*cemetery* TX-5
Gleenwood Ch (abandoned)—*church* MO-7
**Gleeson**—*pop pl* AZ-5
Gleeson Diggings—*locale* CA-9
*Gleeson Lake* MN-6
*Gleeson Station Post Office* TN-4
Gleeson Substation—*locale* AZ-5
Gleeten Sch (abandoned)—*school* PA-2
Gleghorn (Township of)—*fmr MCD* AR-4
*Gleichenia* MH-9
*Gleichenia Beach* MH-9
*Gleichenia Cliffs* MH-9
*Gleichenia Grasslands* MH-9
*Gleichenia Mtn* MH-9
*Gleichenia Point* MH-9
**Glemont Forest**—*pop pl* MD-2
Glemont Sch—*school* MD-2
*Glen* IL-6
*Glen* MP-9
Glen—*locale* AK-9
Glen—*locale* MD-2
Glen—*locale* PA-2
Glen—*locale* TN-4
Glen—*locale* WV-2
Glen—*other* WI-6
**Glen**—*pop pl* CT-1
**Glen**—*pop pl* MN-6
**Glen**—*pop pl* MT-8
**Glen**—*pop pl* NE-7
**Glen**—*pop pl* NH-1
**Glen**—*pop pl* NY-2
Glen, Lake—*lake* AL-4
Glen, Lake—*reservoir* OH-6
**Glen, The**—*pop pl* NH-1
**Glen, The**—*pop pl* NY-2
Glen, The—*valley* (2) NY-2
Glen, The—*valley* RI-1
Glen Abbey Cem—*cemetery* CA-9
Glen Abbey Memorial Gardens—*cemetery* (2) FL-3
Glen Abbey Memorial Gardens—*cemetery* OK-5
*Glen Acres* IL-6
Glen Acres—*locale* WA-9
**Glen Acres**—*pop pl* PA-2
**Glen Acres (subdivision)**—*pop pl* AL-4
**Glen Acres (subdivision)**—*pop pl* NC-3
**Glenada**—*pop pl* OR-9
Glenada, Lake—*lake* FL-3
Glenada Ponds—*lake* OR-9
Glenaddie Baptist Ch—*church* AL-4
Glen Addie Volunteer Hose Company Fire Hall—*hist pl* AL-4
Glen Aiken Creek—*stream* OR-9
**Glenaire**—*pop pl* MO-7
**Glen Aire Subdivision**—*pop pl* (2) UT-8
**Glen Alden**—*pop pl* VA-3
*Glenalice* TN-4
**Glen Alice**—*pop pl* TN-4
Glen Alice Christian Ch—*church* TN-4
*Glen Alice Post Office* TN-4
Glenalice Post Office (historical)—*building* TN-4
*Glen Alice School* TN-4
**Glen Allan**—*pop pl* MS-4
Glen Allan Attendance Center (historical)—*school* MS-4
**Glen Allen**—*pop pl* AL-4
**Glenallen**—*pop pl* AK-9
**Glenallen**—*pop pl* MD-2
**Glenallen**—*pop pl* MA-1
**Glenallen**—*pop pl* MO-7
**Glen Allen**—*pop pl* VA-3
**Glen Allen Heights**—*pop pl* VA-3
Glenallen Lodge—*locale* AK-9
Glen Alpin—*locale* NJ-2
*Glen Alpine* NJ-2
**Glen Alpine**—*pop pl* NC-3
**Glen Alpine**—*pop pl* TN-4
Glen Alpine Ch—*church* TN-4
Glen Alpine Creek—*stream* CA-9
Glen Alpine Elementary and JHS—*school* NC-3
Glen Alpine JHS—*school* TN-4

Glen Alpine Plantation (historical)—*locale* AL-4
Glen Alpine Spring—*spring* CA-9
Glen Alps—*uninc pl* AK-9
Glen Alta—*locale* GA-3
Glen Alternate Sch—*school* CA-9
*Glen Alum* WV-2
Glen Alum—*locale* WV-2
**Glenalum**—*pop pl* WV-2
Glen Alum Junction—*locale* WV-2
Glen Alum Mtn—*summit* WV-2
**Glen Alum (sta.)**—*pop pl* WV-2
**Glen Anna**—*pop pl* NC-3
*Glen Anne Canyon* CA-9
Glen Annie Canyon—*valley* CA-9
Glen Annie Rsvr—*reservoir* CA-9
**Glen Arbor**—*pop pl* CA-9
**Glen Arbor**—*pop pl* MI-6
**Glen Arbor (Township of)**—*pop pl* MI-6
**Glen Arden**—*pop pl* GA-3
**Glenarden**—*pop pl* MD-2
**Glen Arden**—*pop pl* TN-4
Glen Arden Elem Sch—*school* NC-3
Glenarden Woods Sch—*school* MD-2
*Glenarm* (2) MD-2
Glenarm—*locale* KY-4
**Glenarm**—*pop pl* IL-6
**Glen Arm**—*pop pl* MD-2
**Glen Arm (Glenarm)**—*pop pl* MD-2
Glenarm Place Historic Residential District—*hist pl* CO-8
**Glen Arms**—*pop pl* IL-6
Glenartney—*locale* MD-2
Glen Arven Country Club—*other* GA-3
Glen Arvon—*hist pl* VA-3
**Glen Ashton Farms**—*pop pl* PA-2
Glen Aubin—*hist pl* MS-4
**Glen Aubin**—*pop pl* MS-4
Glen Aubin Oil Field—*oilfield* MS-4
**Glen Aubrey**—*pop pl* NY-2
Glen Aulin—*basin* CA-9
Glen Aulin High Sierra Camp—*locale* CA-9
Glen Avon—*locale* IL-6
**Glen Avon**—*pop pl* CA-9
**Glenavon**—*pop pl* IL-6
**Glen Avon**—*pop pl* OR-9
Glen Avon (census name for Glen Avon Heights)—*CDP* CA-9
Glen Avon Golf Course—*other* CA-9
Glen Avon Heights (census name Glen Avon)—*uninc pl* CA-9
Glen Avon Sch—*school* CA-9
**Glenayr**—*pop pl* IN-6
*Glenayre* IL-6
**Glen Ayre**—*pop pl* IN-6
**Glen Ayre**—*pop pl* NC-3
*Glenayre Gardens* IL-6
Glen Ayre Sch—*school* NC-3
Glenays—*hist pl* PA-2
Glen Baker Irrigation Dam—*dam* SD-7
**Glenbar**—*pop pl* AZ-5
Glenbar Cem—*cemetery* AZ-5
Glenbard East HS—*school* IL-6
Glenbard HS—*school* IL-6
Glen Barker Dam—*dam* TN-4
Glen Barker Lake—*reservoir* TN-4
**Glenbeg (historical)**—*pop pl* MT-8
Glen Bench—*bench* UT-8
*Glenberg* MT-8
**Glen Berne Estate**—*pop pl* DE-2
**Glen Berne Estates**—*pop pl* DE-2
Glenberry Lake—*lake* CA-9
**Glenbeulah**—*pop pl* WI-6
Glenbeulah Mill/Grist Mill—*hist pl* WI-6
Glenblair—*locale* CA-9
*Glen Blair Junction* CA-9
**Glen Blair Junction**—*pop pl* CA-9
Glen Bldg—*hist pl* NY-2
Glen Boulder—*rock* NH-1
Glen Boulder Trail—*trail* NH-1
Glen Brake—*swamp* AR-4
Glen Branch—*stream* NC-3
Glenbrier Country Club—*other* WV-2
Glen Bringman Dam—*dam* SD-7
*Glenbrook* CT-1
*Glen Brook* NY-2
*Glen Brook* OR-9
**Glenbrook**—*pop pl* (2) CA-9
**Glenbrook**—*pop pl* CT-1
**Glenbrook**—*pop pl* KY-4
**Glen Brook**—*pop pl* MD-2
**Glenbrook**—*pop pl* MD-2
**Glenbrook**—*pop pl* NV-8
**Glenbrook**—*pop pl* (2) OR-9
Glen Brook—*stream* CT-1
Glen Brook—*stream* MA-1
Glen Brook—*stream* (2) NY-2
Glen Brook—*stream* PA-2
Glenbrook, The—*hist pl* NV-8
Glenbrook Bay—*bay* NV-8
**Glenbrook Countryside**—*pop pl* IL-6
Glenbrook Creek—*stream* CA-9
Glenbrook Creek—*stream* NV-8
Glenbrook Creek—*stream* OR-9
Glenbrook Golf Course—*locale* NV-8
**Glenbrook Heights**—*pop pl* CA-9
**Glenbrook Hills**—*pop pl* VA-3
**Glenbrook Knoll**—*pop pl* MD-2
Glenbrook Log Pond—*reservoir* OR-9
Glenbrook North HS—*school* IL-6
Glen Brook Number Four Dam—*dam* PA-2
Glenbrook Park Golf Course—*other* TX-5
Glenbrook Pond—*reservoir* VA-3
*Glenbrook Rocks* NV-8
Glen Brook Rsvr—*reservoir* PA-2
Glenbrook Sch—*school* CA-9
Glenbrook Sch—*school* CT-1
Glenbrook Sch—*school* OH-6
Glenbrook Sch—*school* WI-6
Glenbrook South HS—*school* IL-6
**Glenbrook Square**—*pop pl* IN-6
**Glenbrook (subdivision)**—*pop pl* NC-3
**Glenbrook Village**—*pop pl* MD-2
Glen Brown Place—*locale* OR-9
**Glenburine (historical)**—*pop pl* NC-3
Glenburn—*locale* CA-9
Glenburn—*locale* IL-6
**Glenburn**—*pop pl* ND-7
**Glenburn**—*pop pl* PA-2
**Glenburn Center**—*pop pl* ME-1
Glen Burn Colliery Station—*locale* PA-2

Glenburn Creek—*stream* IL-6
Glenburn Dam—*dam* PA-2
*Glenburnie* MD-2
Glen Burnie—*hist pl* KY-4
Glenburnie—*hist pl* MS-4
Glen Burnie—*hist pl* VA-3
Glenburnie—*hist pl* WV-2
**Glen Burnie**—*pop pl* MD-2
**Glenburnie**—*pop pl* NY-2
Glen Burnie—*valley* NY-2
Glenburnie Gardens—*other* NC-3
Glen Burnie HS—*school* MD-2
Glenburnie Park—*park* NC-3
**Glen Burnie Park**—*pop pl* MD-2
Glen Burnie Sch—*school* NY-2
**Glenburnie (subdivision)**—*pop pl* NC-3
Glenburn Municipal Airp—*airport* ND-7
Glenburn Pond—*reservoir* PA-2
Glenburn Sch—*school* ME-1
**Glenburn (subdivision)**—*pop pl* NC-3
**Glenburn (Town of)**—*pop pl* ME-1
**Glenburn (Township of)**—*pop pl* PA-2
Glenburny Plantation (historical)—*locale* MS-4
Glen Burr Landing (historical)—*locale* MS-4
Glen Burr Race Track Sch—*school* MS-4
Glenbyrne Center—*locale* OH-6
Glen Cabin Creek—*stream* UT-8
Glen Cabin Gap—*gap* PA-2
Glen Cabin Trail—*trail* PA-2
Glencairn—*hist pl* PA-2
Glencairn—*hist pl* VA-3
Glencairn—*locale* KY-4
Glencairn—*locale* NY-2
Glencairn—*locale* PA-2
**Glen Campbell**—*pop pl* PA-2
Glen Campbell Borough—*civil* PA-2
Glen Campbell Fire Tower—*tower* PA-2
Glen Campground—*locale* (2) CA-9
Glen Canal—*canal* UT-8
Glencannon Falls—*falls* NC-3
**Glen Cannon (subdivision)**—*pop pl* NC-3
**Glen Canyon**—*pop pl* UT-8
Glen Canyon—*valley* AZ-5
Glen Canyon—*valley* AR-4
Glen Canyon—*valley* CA-9
Glen Canyon—*valley* ID-8
Glen Canyon—*valley* UT-8
**Glen Canyon City**—*pop pl* UT-8
Glen Canyon Covered Bridge—*hist pl* CA-9
Glen Canyon Dam—*dam* AZ-5
Glen Canyon Dam Visitor Center—*building* AZ-5
Glen Canyon Generating Station—*locale* AZ-5
Glen Canyon Natl Rec Area—*park* AZ-5
Glen Canyon Natl Rec Area(Also UT)—*park* AZ-5
Glen Canyon Natl Recreation Area—*park* (4) UT-8
Glen Canyon Park—*park* CA-9
*Glen Canyon Reservoir* AZ-5
*Glen Canyon Reservoir* UT-8
Glen Canyon Spring—*spring* ID-8
Glen Canyon Substation—*locale* AZ-5
Glen Canyon Trailer Park—*locale* AZ-5
Glen Carbon—*locale* PA-2
**Glen Carbon**—*pop pl* AL-4
**Glen Carbon**—*pop pl* IL-6
Glen Carbon Crossing—*locale* IL-6
Glen Carbon Mine (underground)—*mine* AL-4
**Glencarlyn**—*pop pl* VA-3
Glencarlyn Park—*park* VA-3
Glencarlyn Sch—*school* VA-3
Glen Cary Ch—*church* MN-6
**Glen Castle**—*pop pl* NY-2
Glen Castle Creek—*stream* NY-2
Glencastle Mine—*mine* OH-6
Glen Cem—*cemetery* IL-6
Glen Cem—*cemetery* (2) OH-6
Glen Ch—*church* MD-2
Glen Ch—*church* MN-6
Glen Chapel—*church* CO-8
Glen Chapel—*church* MS-4
Glen Charlie Pond—*reservoir* MA-1
Glen Charlie Pond Dam—*dam* MA-1
Glenchrest—*hist pl* NH-1
**Glen City**—*pop pl* AL-4
Glen City Sch—*school* CA-9
*Glencliff* TN-4
**Glencliff**—*pop pl* GA-3
**Glen Cliff**—*pop pl* IN-6
**Glencliff**—*pop pl* NH-1
**Glencliff**—*pop pl* TN-4
Glencliff HS—*school* TN-4
Glencliff State Sanatorium—*hospital* NH-1
Glencliff Trail—*trail* NH-1
Glenclyffe—*locale* NY-2
Glenco Baptist Ch—*church* IN-6
Glencoe—*hist pl* IN-6
Glencoe—*hist pl* MD-2
Glencoe—*locale* AR-4
Glencoe—*locale* GA-3
Glencoe—*locale* MD-2
Glencoe—*locale* MI-6
Glencoe—*locale* NM-5
**Glencoe**—*pop pl* (2) AL-4
**Glencoe**—*pop pl* CA-9
**Glencoe**—*pop pl* FL-3
**Glencoe**—*pop pl* ID-8
**Glencoe**—*pop pl* IL-6
**Glencoe**—*pop pl* KY-4
**Glencoe**—*pop pl* LA-4
**Glencoe**—*pop pl* MD-2
**Glencoe**—*pop pl* MN-6
**Glencoe**—*pop pl* MO-7
**Glencoe**—*pop pl* NC-3
**Glencoe**—*pop pl* (2) OH-6
**Glencoe**—*pop pl* OK-5
**Glencoe**—*pop pl* OR-9
**Glencoe**—*pop pl* PA-2
**Glencoe**—*pop pl* WV-2
Glencoe Bible Methodist Ch—*church* AL-4
Glencoe Canyon—*valley* UT-8
Glencoe Cem—*cemetery* AR-4
Glencoe Cem—*cemetery* NM-5
Glencoe Cem—*cemetery* OK-5
Glencoe Cem—*cemetery* VA-3
Glencoe Cem—*cemetery* WI-6
Glencoe Ch—*church* GA-3
Glencoe Ch—*church* NE-7
Glencoe Ch—*church* NC-3

Glencoe Creek—*stream* ND-7
Glencoe Cumberland Presbyterian Ch—*church* AL-4
Glencoe Ditch—*canal* CO-8
Glencoe Elem Sch—*school* AL-4
Glencoe First Baptist Ch—*church* AL-4
Glencoe First Methodist Ch—*church* AL-4
Glencoe Golf Club—*other* IL-6
**Glencoe Hills Apartments**—*pop pl* MI-6
Glencoe HS—*school* AL-4
Glencoe HS—*school* OR-9
Glencoe Junction—*locale* WY-8
**Glencoe Mills**—*pop pl* NY-2
Glencoe Mill Village Hist Dist—*hist pl* NC-3
Glencoe Mine—*mine* UT-8
Glencoe Mine—*mine* WY-8
Glencoe MS—*school* AL-4
Glencoe Post Office (historical)—*building* ND-7
Glencoe Ridge—*ridge* WI-6
Glencoe Road Ch—*church* NC-3
Glencoe Sch—*school* OR-9
Glencoe Sloan Ch—*church* ND-7
Glencoe Spring—*spring* AL-4
Glencoe Spring—*spring* AR-4
Glencoe Swamp—*swamp* GA-3
**Glencoe (Town of)**—*pop pl* WI-6
**Glencoe Township**—*pop pl* (2) KS-7
**Glencoe (Township of)**—*pop pl* MN-6
Glenco Hollow—*valley* WV-2
Glenco Lake—*reservoir* MO-7
Glencoma Lake—*reservoir* NY-2
**Glen Comfort**—*pop pl* CO-8
**Glenco Mills**—*pop pl* NY-2
*Glen Consolidated School* MS-4
Glenco Spring—*spring* NV-8
Glen Cove—*bay* CA-9
Glen Cove—*bay* MD-2
Glen Cove—*bay* MI-6
Glen Cove—*bay* (2) NY-2
Glencove—*bay* UT-8
Glen Cove—*bay* (2) WA-9
Glen Cove—*locale* CO-8
Glen Cove—*locale* TX-5
Glencove—*locale* WA-9
**Glencove**—*pop pl* CA-9
**Glen Cove**—*pop pl* ME-1
**Glen Cove**—*pop pl* MD-2
**Glen Cove**—*pop pl* NJ-2
**Glen Cove**—*pop pl* NY-2
**Glen Cove**—*pop pl* NC-3
**Glen Cove**—*pop pl* TX-5
**Glen Cove**—*pop pl* WA-9
Glen Cove—*uninc pl* GA-3
Glen Cove—*valley* NC-3
Glencove Cem—*cemetery* IN-6
Glen Cove Cem—*cemetery* NY-2
Glen Cove Cem—*cemetery* TX-5
Glen Cove Creek—*channel* NY-2
Glen Cove Creek—*stream* CO-8
Glen Cove Creek—*stream* ID-8
Glencove Hotel—*hist pl* WA-9
Glen Cove Landing—*locale* NY-2
Glen Cove Pumping Station—*other* TX-5
*Glen Creek* MT-8
*Glen Creek* WI-6
Glen Creek—*stream* AK-9
Glen Creek—*stream* CA-9
Glen Creek—*stream* ID-8
Glen Creek—*stream* IN-6
Glen Creek—*stream* MS-4
Glen Creek—*stream* (2) MT-8
Glen Creek—*stream* (3) NY-2
Glen Creek—*stream* OK-5
Glen Creek—*stream* OR-9
Glen Creek—*stream* TX-5
Glen Creek—*stream* WY-8
Glencrest—*uninc pl* TX-5
Glencrest JHS—*school* IL-6
Glencrest Sch—*school* TX-5
**Glencross**—*pop pl* SD-7
**Glen Crouse**—*pop pl* KS-7
**Glencullen**—*pop pl* OR-9
Glenda Cem—*cemetery* MO-7
*Glendale* CA-9
*Glendale* IL-6
*Glendale* IN-6
*Glen Dale* KS-7
*Glendale* MS-4
*Glendale* PA-2
*Glen Dale* WV-2
Glendale—*locale* CO-8
Glendale—*locale* MO-7
Glendale—*locale* MT-8
Glendale—*locale* NH-1
Glendale—*locale* NJ-2
Glendale—*locale* OK-5
Glendale—*locale* (2) PA-2
Glendale—*locale* RI-1
Glendale—*locale* TN-4
Glendale—*locale* (2) VA-3
**Glendale**—*pop pl* AL-4
**Glendale**—*pop pl* AZ-5
**Glendale**—*pop pl* AR-4
**Glendale**—*pop pl* (2) CA-9
**Glendale**—*pop pl* CO-8
**Glendale**—*pop pl* DE-2
**Glendale**—*pop pl* FL-3
**Glendale**—*pop pl* GA-3
**Glendale**—*pop pl* (2) ID-8
**Glendale**—*pop pl* (2) IL-6
**Glendale**—*pop pl* (2) IN-6
**Glendale**—*pop pl* KS-7
**Glendale**—*pop pl* KY-4
**Glen Dale**—*pop pl* LA-4
**Glendale**—*pop pl* MD-2
**Glendale**—*pop pl* MA-1
**Glendale**—*pop pl* MI-6
**Glendale**—*pop pl* MN-6
**Glendale**—*pop pl* MS-4
**Glendale**—*pop pl* MO-7
**Glendale**—*pop pl* (2) NV-8
**Glendale**—*pop pl* NJ-2
**Glendale**—*pop pl* (3) NY-2
**Glendale**—*pop pl* (2) OH-6
**Glendale**—*pop pl* (2) OR-9
**Glendale**—*pop pl* (2) PA-2
**Glendale**—*pop pl* SC-3
**Glendale**—*pop pl* (5) TN-4
**Glendale**—*pop pl* TX-5
**Glendale**—*pop pl* UT-8

**Glendale**—pop pl VA-3
**Glendale**—pop pl WA-9
**Glendale**—pop pl (2) WV-2
**Glendale**—pop pl (2) WI-6
Glendale—post sta NY-2
Glendale—uninc pl MD-2
Glendale—uninc pl TN-4
Glendale, Lake—reservoir IL-6
Glendale Acad—school FL-3
**Glendale Acres**—pop pl IA-7
**Glendale Acres**—pop pl TN-4
Glendale Acres Elem Sch—school NC-3
**Glendale Acres (subdivision)**—pop pl NC-3
**Glendale Addition (subdivision)**—pop pl UT-8
Glendale Baptist Ch—church FL-3
Glendale Baptist Ch—church MS-4
Glendale Baptist Ch—church UT-8
Glendale Bench—bench UT-8
Glendale Branch—stream AR-4
Glendale Bridge—bridge MD-2
Glendale Brook—stream MA-1
Glendale Butte—summit MT-8
Glen Dale Canal—canal LA-4
Glendale Canyon—valley NM-5
Glendale (CCD)—cens area CA-9
Glendale (CCD)—cens area TX-5
Glendale Cem—cemetery AL-4
Glendale Cem—cemetery CO-8
Glendale Cem—cemetery FL-3
Glendale Cem—cemetery (3) IL-6
Glendale Cem—cemetery IN-6
Glendale Cem—cemetery (2) IA-7
Glendale Cem—cemetery (4) KS-7
Glendale Cem—cemetery MD-2
Glendale Cem—cemetery MN-6
Glendale Cem—cemetery (2) NE-7
Glendale Cem—cemetery NJ-2
Glendale Cem—cemetery (3) OH-6
Glendale Cem—cemetery PA-2
Glendale Cem—cemetery (4) TX-5
Glendale Cem—cemetery WV-2
Glendale Ch—church (3) AL-4
Glendale Ch—church AR-4
Glendale Ch—church FL-3
Glendale Ch—church KS-7
Glendale Ch—church (2) KY-4
Glendale Ch—church (2) MD-2
Glendale Ch—church MS-4
Glendale Ch—church ND-7
Glendale Ch—church SC-3
Glendale Ch—church (2) TN-4
Glendale Ch—church WA-9
Glendale Ch—church (2) WV-2
Glendale Chapel Sch—school NC-3
Glendale Ch (historical)—church AL-4
Glendale Ch (historical)—church OH-6
Glendale Ch (historical)—church TN-4
Glen Dale Childrens Home—building KY-4
Glendale Ch of Christ (historical)—church AL-4
Glendale Ch of God—church IN-6
Glendale City Cem—cemetery UT-8
Glendale City Hall—building AZ-5
Glendale Coll—school CA-9
**Glendale Colony**—pop pl SD-7
Glendale Community Coll—school AZ-5
Glendale Community Park—park AZ-5
**Glen Dale (corporate and RR name for Glendale)**—pop pl WV-2
Glendale Country Club—other IL-6
Glendale Dam—dam MA-1
Glendale Dam—dam PA-2
Glendale Ditch—canal CO-8
Glendale East Campground—park UT-8
*Glendale Elementary School* AL-4
*Glendale Elementary School* MS-4
Glendale Elem Sch—school IN-6
**Glendale Estates**—pop pl TN-4
**Glendale Estates (subdivision)**—pop pl AL-4
Glendale Falls—falls MA-1
Glendale Farms—locale (2) AL-4
Glendale Fork—stream MO-7
**Glendale Gardens**—pop pl IL-6
Glendale Gardens—uninc pl PA-2
**Glendale Gardens (subdivision)**—pop pl AL-4
**Glendale Gardens Subdivision**—pop pl (2) UT-8
Glendale Golf Club—other WA-9
Glendale Gulch—valley CO-8
**Glendale Heights**—pop pl IL-6
**Glendale Heights**—pop pl IN-6
**Glendale Heights**—pop pl MD-2
**Glendale Heights**—pop pl WV-2
*Glendale Hills* NC-3
Glendale Hist Dist—hist pl KY-4
Glendale Hist Dist—hist pl OH-6
Glendale (historical)—locale KS-7
Glendale (historical)—locale (2) SD-7
**Glendale (historical)**—pop pl (2) MS-4
**Glendale (historical)**—pop pl PA-2
Glendale (historical P.O.)—locale IA-7
Glendale Hollow—valley MN-6
Glendale Hosp and Sanitarium—hospital CA-9
Glendale HS—school CA-9
Glendale HS—school MO-7
Glendale Intermediate Sch—school UT-8
**Glendale (Jones Station)**—pop pl TN-4
Glendale Junction—locale CA-9
**Glendale Junction**—pop pl KY-4
**Glendale Junction**—pop pl OR-9
*Glendale Junior High School* UT-8
*Glendale-Kenly Elem Sch* NC-3
Glendale Kingdom Hall—church IN-6
**Glendale Lake**—pop pl IN-6
Glendale Lake—reservoir IN-6
Glendale Lake—reservoir NY-2
Glendale Lake—reservoir PA-2
Glendale Lake Dam—dam IN-6
*Glendale Landing* MS-4
Glendale Main Post Office—building CA-9
Glendale Masonic Cem—cemetery OR-9
Glendale Memorial Cem—cemetery AZ-5
Glendale Memorial Cem—cemetery IL-6
Glendale Memorial Gardens—cemetery MO-7
Glendale Mine—mine SD-7
Glendale Mines—mine KY-4
Glendale Montessori Sch—school FL-3
Glendale Municipal Airp—airport AZ-5
*Glendale Muscatine Junction* IA-7
Glendale Natl Cem—cemetery VA-3
Glendale Oil Field—oilfield MS-4
Glendale Park—park (2) DE-2
Glendale Park—park MA-1
Glendale Park—park MI-6
Glendale Park—park NY-2
Glendale Park—park TX-5
**Glendale Park**—pop pl UT-8
**Glendale Park Plat A Subdivision (central)**—pop pl UT-8
**Glendale Park Plat A Subdivision (East)**—pop pl UT-8
**Glendale Park Plat A Subdivision (North)**—pop pl UT-8
**Glendale Park Plat A Subdivision (West)**—pop pl UT-8
Glendale Park Sch—school UT-8
Glendale Playground—park NY-2
Glendale Plaza—locale AZ-5
Glendale Plaza Shop Ctr—locale AZ-5
Glendale Police Station—hist pl OH-6
Glendale Ponds—lake OR-9
Glendale Post Office—building AZ-5
Glendale Post Office—building UT-8
Glendale Power House—hist pl MA-1
Glendale Presbyterian Ch (historical)—church AL-4
Glendale Reservoir Dam—dam IN-6
Glendale River Archaeol Site (12 Da 86)—hist pl IN-6
Glendale Rsvr—reservoir ID-8
Glendale Rsvr—reservoir OR-9
*Glendale Sch* AL-4
Glendale Sch—hist pl NV-8
Glendale Sch—school AL-4
Glendale Sch—school ID-8
Glendale Sch—school (2) IL-6
Glendale Sch—school (3) IA-7
Glendale Sch—school KS-7
Glendale Sch—school MD-2
Glendale Sch—school MI-6
Glendale Sch—school MN-6
Glendale Sch—school MS-4
Glendale Sch—school (7) MO-7
Glendale Sch—school (6) NE-7
Glendale Sch—school NY-2
Glendale Sch—school (2) OH-6
Glendale Sch—school SC-3
Glendale Sch—school (3) TN-4
Glendale Sch—school WA-9
Glendale Sch—school WV-2
Glendale Sch—school WI-6
Glendale Sch (abandoned)—school MO-7
Glendale Sch (historical)—school MS-4
Glendale Sch (historical)—school (2) MO-7
Glendale Sch (historical)—school (10) TN-4
Glendale Sch Number Four—school AZ-5
Glendale Sch Number One—school AZ-5
Glendale Sch Number Two—school AZ-5
*Glendale School* ID-8
Glendale Seventh Day Adventist Ch—church IN-6
Glendale Shop Ctr—locale AZ-5
Glendale Shop Ctr—locale IN-6
Glendale Shopping Plaza—locale UT-8
**Glendale Springs**—pop pl NC-3
Glendale Springs Inn—hist pl NC-3
*Glendale State Fish and Game Preserve* IN-6
Glendale State Fish and Wildlife Area—park IN-6
*Glendale Station* KS-7
**Glendale (subdivision)**—pop pl MA-1
**Glendale (subdivision)**—pop pl MS-4
**Glendale Subdivision**—pop pl UT-8
**Glendale (Town of)**—pop pl WI-6
**Glendale Township**—pop pl KS-7
**Glendale Township**—pop pl ND-7
**Glendale Township**—pop pl SD-7
Glendale Township Hall—building SD-7
Glendale (Township of)—other OH-6
Glendale United Methodist Ch—church MS-4
*Glendale United Methodist Church* TN-4
Glendale Water Tank Triangulation Station—locale AZ-5
Glendale West Mobile Home Park—locale AZ-5
*Glen Dam Reservoir* CT-1
**Glen Daniel**—pop pl WV-2
**Glen Daniel Junction**—pop pl WV-2
**Glen Dean**—pop pl KY-4
Glendean—uninc pl AL-4
Glendean Shop Ctr—locale AL-4
Glendenen Run—stream PA-2
Glendening Creek—stream NY-2
Glendenning Brook—stream ME-1
Glendenning Creek—stream CA-9
Glendenning Creek—stream OR-9
Glendenning Creek—stream WI-6
Glendenning Ditch—canal IN-6
Glendenning Fork—stream CA-9
Glendenning Gulch—valley CA-9
Glendenning Lake—lake WI-6
Glendenning Sch (historical)—school MO-7
Glendennon Lake—lake WI-6
**Glendevey**—pop pl CO-8
Glendevey Post Office—locale CO-8
Glen D. Hale Sch—school OR-9
Glendie—locale VA-3
**Glendive**—pop pl MT-8
Glendive City Water Filtration Plant—hist pl MT-8
Glendive Coulee—valley MT-8
Glendive Creek—stream MT-8
Glendive Heat, Light and Power Company Power Plant—hist pl MT-8
Glendive Oil Field—oilfield MT-8
**Glendo**—pop pl WY-8
Glendo Dam—dam WY-8
Glendo (historical)—locale SD-7
**Glendola**—pop pl NJ-2
Glendola Reservoir Dam—dam NJ-2
Glendola Rsvr—reservoir NJ-2
Glendola Sch—school NJ-2
Glendon—locale ME-1
Glendon—locale OH-6
**Glendon**—pop pl IA-7
**Glendon**—pop pl NC-3
**Glendon**—pop pl (2) PA-2
**Glendon**—pop pl WV-2
Glendon Borough—civil PA-2
Glendon Ch—church PA-2
Glendon (historical)—locale AL-4
Glendon Road Beach—beach MA-1
**Glendora**—pop pl CA-9
**Glendora**—pop pl (2) IN-6
**Glendora**—pop pl MI-6
**Glendora**—pop pl MS-4
**Glendora**—pop pl NJ-2
Glendora Bougainvillea—hist pl CA-9
Glendora Cem—cemetery MI-6
**Glendorado**—pop pl MN-6
Glendorado Ch—church MN-6
**Glendorado (Township of)**—pop pl MN-6
Glendora HS—school CA-9
Glendora Lake—lake MT-8
Glendora Landing—locale MS-4
Glendora Mine (underground)—mine AL-4
Glendora Mtn—summit CA-9
Glendora School (Abandoned)—locale CA-9
Glendo Rsvr—reservoir WY-8
Glendo Sch—school SD-7
Glendo State Park—park WY-8
**Glendo Township**—pop pl SD-7
Glendoveer Golf Course—other OR-9
Glendover Sch—school KY-4
*Glendower* OH-6
*Glen Dower* PA-2
Glendower—hist pl OH-6
Glendower—locale PA-2
Glendower—locale VA-3
**Glen Dower**—pop pl PA-2
Glen Draper HS—school MA-1
*Glendwell* OH-6
Glendye Branch—stream VA-3
Gleneagles Country Club—other IL-6
**Glen Easton**—pop pl WV-2
Glen Easton Ridge—ridge WV-2
Glen Ebon—locale OH-6
*Glen Echo* MO-7
Glen Echo—hist pl GA-3
Glen Echo—hist pl TN-4
Glen Echo—locale VA-3
**Glen Echo**—pop pl CO-8
**Glen Echo**—pop pl MD-2
**Glen Echo**—pop pl MA-1
**Glen Echo**—pop pl OH-6
**Glen Echo**—pop pl OR-9
**Glen Echo**—pop pl VA-3
Glen Echo Cem—cemetery AL-4
Glen Echo Ch—church AL-4
Glen Echo Ch—church NE-7
Glen Echo Country Club—other MO-7
Glen Echo Creek—stream CA-9
**Glen Echo Heights**—pop pl MD-2
*Glenecho Lake* MA-1
Glen Echo Lake—lake TN-4
Glen Echo Lake—lake VA-3
Glen Echo Lake—reservoir MA-1
Glen Echo Lake—reservoir TN-4
Glen Echo Lake Dam—dam MA-1
Glen Echo Lake Dam—dam TN-4
Glen Echo Park—park OH-6
**Glen Echo Park**—pop pl MO-7
Glen Echo Park Hist Dist—hist pl MD-2
Glen Echo Pond—lake MA-1
Glen Echo Pond—lake NH-1
Glen Echo Resort—locale MI-6
Glen Echo Sch—school VA-3
Glen Echo Sch (historical)—school AL-4
Glen Eden—locale CO-8
Glen Eden—locale PA-2
**Glen Eden**—pop pl IN-6
**Gleneden Beach**—pop pl OR-9
Gleneden Beach Wayside—park OR-9
Glen Eden Cem—cemetery MI-6
Glen Eden Community Center—building KY-4
Gleneden County Park—park OR-9
Gleneden Lake—lake OR-9
Glen Eden Sch—school CA-9
**Glen Eden (subdivision)**—pop pl NC-3
**Glen Edith**—pop pl NY-2
Gleneida, Lake—reservoir NY-2
**Glen Elder**—pop pl KS-7
Glen Elder Dam—dam KS-7
Glen Elder Rsvr—reservoir KS-7
Glenelder Sch—school CA-9
Glen Elder State Park—park KS-7
**Glen Elder Township**—pop pl KS-7
Glen Elder Wildlife Area—park KS-7
Glen Eldridge Point—cape NY-2
Glen Eldridge Tug Hollow—valley NY-2
Glenelg—locale MD-2
Glenelg Manor—hist pl MD-2
**Glenelk**—pop pl CO-8
**Glen Elk**—pop pl WV-2
*Glen Ellen* IN-6
**Glen Ellen**—pop pl CA-9
**Glen Ellen**—pop pl IA-7
**Glen Ellen**—pop pl MD-2
Glenellen Post Office (historical)—building TN-4
*Glenellen Sch* TN-4
Glen Ellen Sch—school TN-4
Glen Ellen Ski Area—other VT-1
Glen Ellis Falls—falls NH-1
**Glen Ellyn**—pop pl IL-6
**Glen Ellyn Countryside**—pop pl IL-6
Glen Ellyn Main Street Hist Dist—hist pl IL-6
**Glen Ellyn Woods**—pop pl IL-6
**Glenerie**—pop pl NY-2
Glenerie Falls—falls NY-2
**Glenerie Lake Park**—pop pl NY-2
Glen Erin Creek—stream SD-7
**Glen Essex**—pop pl CA-9
**Glen Este**—pop pl OH-6
Glen Eyie—locale CO-8
Glen Eyre—locale PA-2
Glen Eyrie—hist pl CO-8
*Glen Eyrie Canyon* CO-8
*Glen Eyrie Creek* CO-8
Glen Eyrie Rsvr—reservoir CO-8
Gleneyrie Sch—school KY-4
Glenfair Sch—school OR-9
Glen Fairs Shop Ctr—locale AZ-5
Glen Falls—falls NY-2
Glen Falls—falls NC-3
Glen Falls—locale MD-2
**Glen Falls**—pop pl WV-2
Glen Falls Brook—stream VT-1
**Glen Farms**—pop pl MD-2
Glenfawn—locale TX-5
Glenfawn Cem—cemetery TX-5
Glen Feliz Blvd Sch—school CA-9
**Glen Ferris**—pop pl WV-2
**Glenfield**—pop pl MS-4
**Glenfield**—pop pl NJ-2
**Glenfield**—pop pl NY-2
**Glenfield**—pop pl NC-3
**Glenfield**—pop pl ND-7
**Glenfield**—pop pl PA-2
Glenfield Baptist Ch—church MS-4
Glenfield Borough—civil PA-2
Glenfield Cem—cemetery MS-4
Glenfield Cem—cemetery ND-7
Glenfield Crossroads—locale NC-3
Glenfield JHS—school NJ-2
Glenfield Park—park NJ-2
Glenfield Post Office (historical)—building MS-4
Glenfields—hist pl NY-2
**Glenfield Township**—pop pl ND-7
**Glen Flora**—pop pl TX-5
**Glen Flora**—pop pl WI-6
Glen Flora Park—park IL-6
Glen Flora Sch—school IL-6
Glen Flora Sch—school TX-5
Glen Foerd at Torresdale—hist pl PA-2
Glenford—locale VA-3
**Glenford**—pop pl NY-2
**Glenford**—pop pl OH-6
Glenford Cem—cemetery AL-4
Glenford Fort—hist pl OH-6
**Glen Forest**—pop pl NC-3
**Glen Forest**—pop pl VA-3
Glen Forest Sch—school VA-3
**Glen Forest (subdivision)**—pop pl AL-4
**Glen Forest (subdivision)**—pop pl NC-3
*Glenfork* WV-2
Glenfork—other WV-2
**Glen Fork**—pop pl WV-2
Glen Fork—stream WV-2
**Glen Fork (Glenfork)**—pop pl WV-2
**Glen Forney**—pop pl PA-2
Glen Frazer—locale CA-9
Glen Gale Park—park MN-6
Glen Gap—gap WV-2
Glen Gap Branch—stream NC-3
Glen Garden Ch—church TX-5
Glen Garden Country Club—other TX-5
**Glen Gardens**—pop pl MD-2
**Glen Gardner**—pop pl NJ-2
Glen Gardner Pony Pratt Truss Bridge—hist pl NJ-2
Glengarry—locale MT-8
**Glengarry**—pop pl IL-6
Glengarry Gulch—valley OR-9
Glengarry Mines—mine MT-8
Glengarry Sch—school TN-4
Glengarry Sch—school WI-6
Glengary—locale ID-8
Glengary—locale MI-6
**Glengary**—pop pl KY-4
**Glengary**—pop pl MI-6
**Glengary**—pop pl OR-9
**Glen Gary**—pop pl VA-3
**Glengary**—pop pl WV-2
Glengary Country Club—other OH-6
**Glengary Heights**—pop pl OH-6
Glengary Lake—reservoir TN-4
Glengary Lake Dam—dam TN-4
**Glengary Township**—pop pl NE-7
**Glen (Glen), The**—pop pl MD-2
Glen Gray Camp—locale NJ-2
Glen Grouse Cem—cemetery KS-7
Glen Grouse (historical)—locale KS-7
Glen Grove—locale NY-2
**Glen Grove**—pop pl MA-1
Glen Grove—uninc pl NM-5
**Glen Grove Annex**—pop pl MA-1
Glen Grove Cem—cemetery CO-8
Glen Grove Ch—church GA-3
Glengrove Ch—church NC-3
Glen Grove Sch—hist pl CO-8
Glen Grove Sch—school CO-8
Glen Grove Sch—school IL-6
Glen Gulch—valley AK-9
Glen Gulch—valley MT-8
Glenhall—locale PA-2
**Glenhall**—pop pl IN-6
**Glenham**—pop pl NY-2
**Glenham**—pop pl SD-7
Glenham Sch—school NY-2
**Glenharold**—pop pl ND-7
*Glenhaven* WI-6
Glen Haven—locale GA-3
Glen Haven—locale MI-6
Glen Haven—locale NY-2
**Glenhaven**—pop pl CA-9
**Glen Haven**—pop pl CO-8
**Glen Haven**—pop pl MD-2
**Glen Haven**—pop pl NY-2
**Glenhaven**—pop pl NY-2
**Glen Haven**—pop pl WI-6
Glenhaven—uninc pl GA-3
Glen Haven Cem—cemetery OH-6
Glen Haven Memorial Cem—cemetery OH-6
Glenhaven Memorial Garden Cem—cemetery MN-6
Glen Haven Memorial Garden (cemetery)—cemetery GA-3
Glen Haven Memorial Gardens—cemetery IN-6
Glen Haven Memorial Park—cemetery IN-6
**Glen Haven Memorial Park**—pop pl IN-6
Glen Haven Memorial Park Cem—cemetery FL-3
Glen Haven Memorial Park (Cemetery)—cemetery CA-9
Glen Haven Memorial Park (Cemetery)—cemetery MD-2
Glen Haven Memory Gardens—cemetery VA-3
Glenhaven Park—park CA-9
Glenhaven Park—park OR-9
Glen Haven Picnic Ground—locale CO-8
Glenhaven Roadside Park—park MS-4
Glenhaven Sch—school GA-3
Glen Haven Sch—school MD-2
Glenhaven Sch—school OR-9
**Glen Haven (subdivision)**—pop pl (2) AL-4
**Glenhaven (subdivision)**—pop pl NC-3
**Glenhaven (subdivision)**—pop pl TN-4
**Glen Haven (Town of)**—pop pl WI-6
Glen Haven Village Hist Dist—hist pl MI-6
**Glenhayes**—pop pl WV-2
Glen Hazel—locale PA-2
*Glenhead* NY-2
**Glen Head**—pop pl NY-2
Glen Head Country Club—other NY-2
**Glen Heather Subdivision**—pop pl UT-8
*Glen Hedrick* WV-2
**Glen Hedrick**—pop pl WV-2
**Glen Heights**—pop pl MA-1
**Glen Heights (subdivision)**—pop pl NC-3
Glen Helen Regional Park—park CA-9
Glen Helen Rehabilitation Facility—other CA-9
**Glen High Estates**—pop pl NC-3
*Glen Hill* IL-6
Glen Hill—locale TX-5
Glen Hill—summit AR-4
Glen Hill Ch—church AL-4
Glen Hill Ch—church VA-3
**Glen Hills**—pop pl AL-4
**Glen Hills**—pop pl MD-2
Glen Hill Sch (historical)—school AL-4
Glen Hills County Park—park WI-6
Glen-Hire Ranch Airp—airport IN-6
**Glen (historical)**—pop pl OR-9
Glen Holloway Dam—dam SD-7
Glen Hollow Camp—locale GA-3
**Glen Hope**—pop pl PA-2
Glen Hope Borough—civil PA-2
Glen Hope Cem—cemetery NY-2
**Glen Hope (corporate name for Glenhope)**—pop pl PA-2
*Glenhope (corporate name Glen Hope)* PA-2
Glen Hope Covered Bridge—hist pl PA-2
**Glen Hope (historical)**—pop pl PA-2
**Glen House**—pop pl NH-1
Glenhurst—uninc pl PA-2
Glenhurst Golf Course—other MI-6
Gleniffer Hill Elem Sch—school KS-7
**Glen Ilah**—pop pl AZ-5
**Glenila Township**—pop pl ND-7
Glen Iris Campground—locale AL-4
Glen Iris Ch—church AL-4
Glen Iris Park—park AL-4
Glen Iris Park Hist Dist—hist pl AL-4
*Glen Iris Sch* AL-4
**Glen Iron**—pop pl PA-2
**Gleniron (Glen Iron)**—pop pl PA-2
Glen Island—island AK-9
Glen Island—island (2) NY-2
**Glen Island**—pop pl NY-2
Glen Island Park—park NY-2
Glenisle—hist pl CO-8
Glen Isle—island MD-2
**Glenisle**—pop pl CO-8
**Glen Isle**—pop pl MD-2
*Glenita* VA-3
Glenita Ch—church VA-3
**Glenita (Natural Tunnel)**—pop pl VA-3
Glen Ivy Hot Springs—locale CA-9
Glen Ivy Substation—other CA-9
Glen Jean—locale OH-6
**Glen Jean**—pop pl WV-2
Glen Junction—locale PA-2
**Glen Junction**—pop pl WV-2
**Glen Karn**—pop pl OH-6
Glen Karn Ditch—canal OH-6
Glen Kirk Ch—church VA-3
Glenkirk Island—island TN-4
Glenkirk Landing—locale TN-4
Glen Kirk Sch—school IL-6
Glenkirk Sch—school PA-2
**Glen Kyle**—pop pl MD-2
*Glen Lake* MN-6
Glen Lake—lake (2) CA-9
Glen Lake—lake (2) MI-6
Glen Lake—lake (2) MN-6
Glen Lake—lake (2) MT-8
Glen Lake—lake NJ-2
Glen Lake—lake (2) NY-2
Glen Lake—lake TX-5
Glen Lake—lake VT-1
Glen Lake—lake WI-6
Glenlake—locale PA-2
**Glenlake**—pop pl AR-4
**Glen Lake**—pop pl MN-6
**Glen Lake**—pop pl NY-2
Glen Lake—reservoir CT-1
Glen Lake—reservoir MO-7
Glen Lake—reservoir NH-1
Glen Lake—reservoir (2) NJ-2
Glen Lake—reservoir TX-5
Glen Lake—reservoir WI-6
Glen Lake Camp—locale TX-5
Glen Lake HS—school MI-6
Glen Lakes Country Club—other TX-5
Glen Lakes Golf Course—other AZ-5
Glen Lake State Sanatorium—hospital MN-6
**Glenland**—pop pl VA-3
**Glenlaurel**—pop pl NC-3
Glen Lawrence Lake Dam—dam AL-4
Glen L Downs Sch—school AZ-5
Glen Lea Sch—school VA-3
Glen Leigh—area PA-2
Glen Leigh Valley—valley PA-2
**Glen Lennox**—pop pl NC-3
Glenlevit (historical)—locale SD-7
*Glen Lewis Pond* MA-1
Glen Lily—locale KY-4
Glen Lily Ch—church (2) KY-4
Glen Livet Dam—dam AZ-5
Glen Livet Rsvr—reservoir AZ-5
*Glen Loch* PA-2
Glenloch—locale GA-3
Glenloch—locale PA-2
Glenloch Post Office (historical)—building TN-4
**Glenloch (RR name Glen)**—pop pl PA-2
Glenloch Village—uninc pl GA-3
Glenlock—locale KS-7
Glen Lock Lake—reservoir WI-6
Glen Loe Dam—dam AZ-5
Glen Lonely—valley CA-9
Glen Lookout Tower—locale MN-6
Glen Lookout Tower—locale MS-4
**Glen Lord**—pop pl MI-6
Glen Lore Golf Club—other MI-6
Glenlove Post Office (historical)—building TN-4
**Glen Lyn**—pop pl VA-3
Glenlynn Post Office (historical)—building MS-4
Glenlyon—hist pl MI-6
**Glen Lyon**—pop pl PA-2
Glenlyon Shoal—bar MI-6
Glen Lyon Station—locale PA-2
**Glenmar**—pop pl (2) MD-2
Glen Mar Ch—church MD-2
**Glenmar Gardens**—pop pl PA-2
**Glenmar Hills (subdivision)**—pop pl TN-4
Glen Marie Gulch—valley MT-8
Glenmark—locale NY-2
**Glenmar Manor**—pop pl MD-2
**Glen Mar Park**—pop pl MD-2
Glenmar Sch—school MD-2
**Glen Martin**—pop pl CA-9
Glen Martin Creek—stream CA-9
Glen Martin Sch—school CA-9
*Glenmary* AL-4
*Glenmary* OH-6
*Glen Mary* TN-4
Glen Mary—hist pl GA-3
**Glen Mary**—pop pl AL-4
**Glen Mary**—pop pl TN-4
**Glenmary**—pop pl TN-4
Glenmary Baptist Ch—church TN-4
Glen Mary Cem—cemetery LA-4
**Glen Mary Heights**—pop pl MD-2
Glenmary Mission Sch—school OH-6
Glen Mary Plantation and Tenant House—hist pl MS-4
Glenmary Post Office (historical)—building TN-4
Glenmary Sch (historical)—school TN-4
Glen Maury—hist pl VA-3
Glen Mawr—locale PA-2
**Glen Meade (subdivision)**—pop pl NC-3
Glen Meadow—flat CA-9
Glen Meadow Creek—stream CA-9
Glenmere—locale ME-1
**Glenmere**—pop pl NH-1
Glenmere Country Club—other NY-2
*Glenmere Lake* MA-1
Glenmere Lake—reservoir NY-2
Glenmere Park—park CO-8
*Glenmere Pond* MA-1
Glen Mills—locale PA-2
**Glen Mills**—pop pl MA-1
*Glen Mills Farm School* PA-2
Glen Mills Sch—school (2) PA-2
Glen Mine—mine MN-6
**Glenmont**—pop pl (2) MD-2
**Glenmont**—pop pl NY-2
**Glenmont**—pop pl OH-6
Glenmont Ch—church MD-2
**Glenmont Forest**—pop pl MD-2
**Glenmont Heights**—pop pl MD-2
**Glenmont Hills**—pop pl MD-2
Glenmont Sch—school OH-6
**Glenmont Village**—pop pl MD-2
**Glenmoor**—pop pl OH-6
**Glenmoor Country Estates Subdivision**—pop pl UT-8
Glenmoore—locale NJ-2
**Glenmoore**—pop pl PA-2
**Glen Moore**—pop pl PA-2
Glenmoor Sch—school CA-9
**Glenmora**—pop pl LA-4
Glenmora Cem—cemetery LA-4
*Glenmore* PA-2
Glenmore—hist pl TN-4
Glenmore—locale KY-4
Glenmore—locale LA-4
Glenmore—locale NY-2
Glenmore—locale VA-3
**Glenmore**—pop pl GA-3
**Glenmore**—pop pl MD-2
**Glenmore**—pop pl NY-2
**Glenmore**—pop pl OH-6
**Glenmore**—pop pl WV-2
**Glenmore**—pop pl WI-6
Glenmore Creek—stream MN-6
**Glenmore Estates**—pop pl TN-4
Glenmore Lake—lake MN-6
**Glenmore Park**—pop pl MD-2
Glenmore Sch—school ND-7
Glenmore Sch—school TX-5
**Glenmore Township**—pop pl ND-7
**Glen Morgan**—pop pl WV-2
**Glenmorrie**—pop pl OR-9
**Glen Morris**—pop pl MD-2
Glen Mountains—range OK-5
Glenmount Sch—school MD-2
*Glenn* IN-6
*Glenn* NC-3
*Glenn* OH-6
*Glenn* MP-9
Glenn—locale (2) IL-6
Glenn—locale MO-7
Glenn—locale NV-8
Glenn—locale TX-5
**Glenn**—pop pl CA-9
**Glenn**—pop pl GA-3
**Glenn**—pop pl MI-6
**Glenn**—pop pl OK-5
Glenn, Abram, House—hist pl TN-4
Glenn, Dr. John, House—hist pl SC-3
Glenn, Mount—summit AK-9
Glenn, Mount—summit AZ-5
*Glenn, The* NH-1
**Glenn Acres (subdivision)**—pop pl PA-2
*Glenn Addie Baptist Church* AL-4
Glennallen—CDP AK-9
Glenn Alpine Spring—spring TN-4
*Glennan Gulch* CA-9
**Glenn Ayr**—pop pl IN-6
Glenn Bald—summit NC-3
Glenn Branch—stream FL-3
Glenn Branch—stream TN-4
Glenn Bridge—bridge AL-4
Glenn Bridge—bridge NC-3
**Glenn Brook (subdivision)**—pop pl NC-3
Glenn Canyon—valley OR-9
Glenn Cave—cave AL-4
Glenn Cem—cemetery AL-4
Glenn Cem—cemetery KY-4
Glenn Cem—cemetery MS-4
Glenn Cem—cemetery (2) MO-7
Glenn Cem—cemetery OH-6
Glenn Cem—cemetery TN-4

Glenn Cem—*cemetery* (2) TX-5
Glenn Ch—*church* NC-3
Glenn Chapel—*church* KY-4
Glenn Chapel—*church* MS-4
Glenn Chapel—*church* TN-4
Glenn-Colusa Canal—*canal* CA-9
*Glenn-Colusa Irrigation Canal* CA-9
**Glenn (County)**—*pop pl* CA-9
Glenn County Fairground—*locale* CA-9
*Glenn Creek* TX-5
Glenn Creek—*stream* AL-4
Glenn Creek—*stream* (3) AK-9
Glenn Creek—*stream* AR-4
Glenn Creek—*stream* IL-6
Glenn Creek—*stream* MT-8
Glenn Creek—*stream* NC-3
Glenn Creek—*stream* (2) OR-9
Glenn Creek—*stream* WI-6
*Glenndale* MD-2
Glenn Dale—*CDP* MD-2
**Glenn-Dale**—*pop pl* ME-1
**Glenn Dale**—*pop pl* MD-2
**Glenndale**—*pop pl* MD-2
Glenndale Airp—*airport* IN-6
Glenn Dale Golf Club—*other* MD-2
Glenndale Hosp—*hospital* MD-2
Glenndale Sch—*school* MD-2
Glenndale Sch (historical)—*school* TN-4
Glenndale Shop Ctr—*locale* MS-4
Glenn Drain—*canal* NE-7
Glenn Draw—*valley* TX-5
Glenn D. Walker Lake—*reservoir* MS-4
Glen Nell—*locale* OH-6
Glennell RR Station (historical)—*locale* FL-3
Glennen Gulch—*valley* CA-9
Glennette Lake—*lake* CA-9
**Glennfarm Estates (subdivision)**—*pop pl* NC-3
Glenn Field—*locale* GA-3
Glenn Flint Lake—*reservoir* IN-6
*Glenn Gap* AL-4
Glenn Gap—*gap* NC-3
Glenn Gap—*gap* TN-4
Glenn Gulch—*valley* AK-9
Glenn Hammock—*island* FL-3
**Glenn Heights**—*pop pl* MD-2
**Glenn Heights**—*pop pl* TX-5
*Glenn High School* IN-6
*Glenn High School* NC-3
Glenn Hill—*summit* IN-6
Glenn Hill—*summit* TN-4
Glenn (historical)—*locale* AL-4
Glenn (historical)—*locale* KS-7
**Glenn (historical)**—*pop pl* OR-9
*Glenn Hollow* KY-4
Glenn House—*hist pl* AR-4
Glenn House—*hist pl* MO-7
Glenn HS—*school* MI-6
**Glennie**—*pop pl* MI-6
Glennie Cem—*cemetery* MI-6
Glennie Creek—*stream* MI-6
Glennie Ditch—*canal* MT-8
Glennie Sch—*school* MI-6
Glenn Islands—*island* PA-2
Glennison Gap—*gap* CA-9
Glennis Saddle—*gap* NM-5
Glenn Lake—*lake* AK-9
Glenn Lake—*lake* MI-6
Glenn Lake—*lake* (2) MN-6
Glenn Lake Park—*park* GA-3
Glenn Lakes—*lake* AZ-5
Glenn Lawrence Lake—*reservoir* AL-4
Glenn L Martin JHS—*school* TN-4
Glennmary—*hist pl* VA-3
Glenn Mason Spring—*spring* UT-8
Glenn Meadows—*flat* KY-4
Glenn Miller Ditch—*canal* IN-6
Glenn Miller Park—*park* IN-6
Glenn Mills—*other* NC-3
Glenn Mtn—*summit* VA-3
Glenn Neal Sch (Variety Childrens Hospital)—*school* FL-3
**Glenn Oaks Beach**—*pop pl* WI-6
Glenn Oaks Golf Club—*locale* NC-3
**Glennon**—*pop pl* MO-7
Glennon, Mount—*summit* CO-8
Glennon Cem—*cemetery* LA-4
Glennon Coulee—*stream* ND-7
Glennon Heights Cottage Sch No 1—*school* CO-8
Glennon Heights Cottage Sch No. 2—*school* CO-8
Glennon Heights Sch—*school* CO-8
Glennon HS—*school* MO-7
Glennon Memorial Hosp—*hospital* MO-7
**Glennonville**—*pop pl* MO-7
Glenn Orms Spring—*spring* UT-8
Glenn Park—*park* IL-6
Glenn Park Christian Ch—*church* KS-7
Glenn Pond—*reservoir* GA-3
Glenn Ranch—*locale* CA-9
Glenn Ranch—*locale* (2) NM-5
Glenn Ranch—*locale* (2) SD-7
Glenn Ridge—*ridge* OR-9
Glenn Ridge—*ridge* TN-4
Glenn Run—*stream* OH-6
*Glenns* OH-6
Glenns—*locale* VA-3
**Glenns**—*pop pl* GA-3
Glenns Branch—*stream* GA-3
Glenns Bridge—*bridge* SC-3
Glenns Cabin—*locale* MT-8
Glenn Sch—*school* MN-6
Glenn Sch—*school* NC-3
Glenn Sch—*school* TN-4
Glenn Sch—*school* TX-5
Glenn Sch (abandoned)—*school* PA-2
Glenns Chapel—*church* AL-4
*Glenns Chapel Ch* AL-4
Glenn Sch (historical)—*school* AL-4
Glenn Sch (historical)—*school* PA-2
Glenns Creek—*stream* KY-4
Glenns Creek Ch—*church* KY-4
**Glenns Ferry**—*pop pl* ID-8
Glenns Ferry Sch—*hist pl* ID-8
*Glennshire* IL-6
Glenn Shoals, Lake—*reservoir* IL-6
Glenns Hole—*lake* OR-9
Glenns Lake—*lake* MT-8
Glenns Lake—*reservoir* SC-3
Glenn Slough—*stream* AR-4
Glenns Mill (historical)—*locale* AL-4
Glenn Spring—*locale* TX-5
Glenn Spring—*spring* AZ-5
Glenn Spring—*spring* AR-4
Glenn Spring—*spring* CA-9
Glenn Spring—*spring* TN-4
Glenn Spring—*spring* (2) TX-5
Glenn Springs—*locale* SC-3
**Glenn Springs**—*pop pl* SC-3
*Glenn Springs Draw* TX-5
Glenn Springs Hist Dist—*hist pl* SC-3
*Glenns Run* WV-2
**Glenns Run**—*pop pl* OH-6
Glenns Run—*stream* OH-6
Glenns Run—*stream* WV-2
**Glenn Stores**—*pop pl* MI-6
**Glenn Subdivision**—*pop pl* UT-8
*Glenns Valley* IN-6
**Glenns Valley**—*pop pl* IN-6
Glenn Tank—*reservoir* (2) AZ-5
Glenn-Thompson Plantation—*hist pl* AL-4
Glenn Township—*civil* SD-7
**Glenn (University)**—*pop pl* NC-3
Glenn Valley—*valley* WI-6
Glenn Valley Slough—*stream* CA-9
**Glenn Valley (subdivision)**—*pop pl* AL-4
*Glennville* AL-4
Glennville—*locale* PA-2
**Glennville**—*pop pl* CA-9
**Glennville**—*pop pl* GA-3
Glennville Adobe—*locale* CA-9
Glennville (CCD)—*cens area* GA-3
Glennville Cem—*cemetery* AL-4
*Glennville Collegiate Institute* AL-4
Glennville Female Acad (historical)—*school* AL-4
Glennville Hist Dist—*hist pl* AL-4
Glennville HS—*school* GA-3
Glennville Male Acad (historical)—*school* AL-4
Glennville Military Acad (historical)—*school* AL-4
Glenn Vocational HS—*school* AL-4
Glenn Walters Dam—*dam* OR-9
Glenn Wishard Dam—*dam* SD-7
**Glennwood Acres (subdivision)**—*pop pl* NC-3
Glennwood Ditch—*canal* MT-8
Glen Oak—*hist pl* TN-4
Glenoak—*locale* OK-5
Glen Oak—*locale* WI-6
**Glen Oak**—*pop pl* IL-6
Glen Oak Cem—*cemetery* (2) IL-6
Glen Oak Country Club—*locale* PA-2
Glen Oak Country Club—*other* IL-6
**Glenoak (Glen Oak)**—*pop pl* WI-6
Glen Oak Hotel—*hist pl* MD-2
Glen Oak-Kimbrough House—*hist pl* MS-4
Glen Oak Park—*park* IL-6
Glenoak Park—*park* MI-6
Glen Oaks—*locale* AZ-5
**Glen Oaks**—*pop pl* (2) AL-4
**Glen Oaks**—*pop pl* CA-9
**Glen Oaks**—*pop pl* MD-2
**Glen Oaks**—*pop pl* NY-2
**Glen Oaks**—*pop pl* VA-3
Glenoaks—*uninc pl* CA-9
Glen Oak Sch—*school* CA-9
Glenoak Sch—*school* FL-3
Glen Oak Sch—*school* (2) IL-6
Glenoak School—*locale* MI-6
Glen Oaks Golf Club—*other* NY-2
Glen Oaks HS—*school* LA-4
Glen Oaks JHS—*school* LA-4
Glenoaks Park—*park* CA-9
Glen Oaks Park—*park* TX-5
Glen Oaks Sch—*school* CA-9
Glenoaks Sch—*school* CA-9
Glen Oaks Sch—*school* IL-6
Glen Oaks Sch—*school* NY-2
Glen Oaks Sch—*school* TX-5
Glen Oaks Sch—*school* WI-6
Glen Oaks Spring—*spring* AZ-5
**Glen Oaks Subdivision**—*pop pl* UT-8
Glen Oak United Methodist Ch—*church* TN-4
Glenoak Valley—*valley* CA-9
Glenobey—*locale* TN-4
Glenobey Post Office (historical)—*building* TN-4
Glen Oil Field—*oilfield* TX-5
**Glenola**—*pop pl* NC-3
*Glen Olden* PA-2
**Glenolden**—*pop pl* PA-2
Glenolden Borough—*civil* PA-2
Glen Olden Mills—*locale* PA-2
Glen Olden Station—*building* PA-2
Glen Olive Mine—*mine* CA-9
Glenoma—*locale* WA-9
**Glen Onoko**—*pop pl* PA-2
Glen Onoko—*valley* PA-2
Glen Onoko Station—*locale* PA-2
*Glenora* PA-2
Glenora—*locale* VA-3
**Glenora**—*pop pl* NY-2
Glenora Falls—*falls* NY-2
**Glenora Hills**—*pop pl* MD-2
Glenora Landing—*locale* MS-4
*Glen Osborne* PA-2
*Glenosburn* PA-2
*Glenover* PA-2
**Glenover**—*pop pl* NE-7
*Glenoyer* PA-2
*Glen Park* IN-6
*Glenpark* IN-6
Glen Park—*park* CA-9
Glen Park—*park* MO-7
Glen Park—*park* NY-2
Glen Park—*park* WI-6
**Glen Park**—*pop pl* CO-8
**Glen Park**—*pop pl* IL-6
**Glen Park**—*pop pl* IN-6
**Glen Park**—*pop pl* NY-2
Glen Park—*uninc pl* KS-7
Glen Park Ch—*church* TN-4
Glen Park East—*post sta* IN-6
Glen Park Sch—*school* CA-9
Glen Park Sch—*school* IN-6
Glen Park Sch—*school* TX-5
**Glen Park (subdivision)**—*pop pl* AL-4
**Glen Park West (alternate name West Glen Park)**—*pop pl* IN-6
Glen Pass—*gap* CA-9
Glen Point—*cape* MI-6
*Glen Pond* MA-1
**Glenpool**—*pop pl* OK-5
Glen Post Office (historical)—*building* SD-7
Glen Post Office (historical)—*building* TN-4
Glen Providence Park—*park* PA-2
Glen Raven—*hist pl* TN-4
**Glen Raven**—*pop pl* NC-3
**Glenraven (historical)**—*pop pl* TN-4
Glenraven Post Office (historical)—*building* TN-4
**Glenray**—*pop pl* WV-2
Glen Rest Cem—*cemetery* OH-6
Glen Rest Cem—*cemetery* TX-5
**Glen Richey**—*pop pl* PA-2
Glen Riddle—*locale* PA-2
**Glen Riddle-Lima**—*pop pl* PA-2
Glenriddle Station—*bulding* PA-2
*Glen Ridge* CT-1
*Glen Ridge* IL-6
*Glenridge* IL-6
Glenridge—*other* IL-6
**Glen Ridge**—*pop pl* CT-1
**Glen Ridge**—*pop pl* FL-3
**Glenridge**—*pop pl* MA-1
**Glen Ridge**—*pop pl* NJ-2
**Glenridge**—*pop pl* NY-2
**Glen Ridge Acres**—*pop pl* OH-6
Glen Ridge Borough (Township of)—*civ div* NJ-2
Glenridge Cem—*cemetery* MO-7
Glen Ridge Ch—*church* NJ-2
Glen Ridge Club—*other* PA-2
Glenridge Country Club—*locale* SD-7
Glen Ridge Country Club—*other* NJ-2
Glenridge Hall—*hist pl* GA-3
Glen Ridge Hist Dist—*hist pl* NJ-2
Glen Ridge Hist Dist (Boundary Increase)—*hist pl* NJ-2
Glenridge JHS—*school* MD-2
Glen Ridge Park—*park* NY-2
Glenridge Recreation Center—*park* MD-2
Glenridge Sanatorium—*hospital* NY-2
Glenridge Sch—*school* FL-3
Glenridge Sch—*school* MO-7
Glen Ridge Station—*locale* NJ-2
**Glen Ridge (subdivision)**—*pop pl* TN-4
**Glenrio**—*pop pl* NM-5
**Glenrio**—*pop pl* TX-5
**Glenrio (sta.)**—*pop pl* TX-5
Glen Road Brook—*stream* NY-2
Glen Road Sch—*school* MA-1
**Glen Robbins**—*pop pl* OH-6
**Glenrochie**—*pop pl* VA-3
Glenrochie Country Club—*other* VA-3
*Glen Rock* NE-7
*Glen Rock* TN-4
Glen Rock—*fmr MCD* NE-7
Glen Rock—*pillar* WY-8
**Glenrock**—*pop pl* NE-7
**Glen Rock**—*pop pl* NJ-2
**Glen Rock**—*pop pl* PA-2
**Glen Rock**—*pop pl* VA-3
**Glenrock**—*pop pl* WY-8
Glenrock—*uninc pl* NC-3
Glen Rock Borough—*civil* PA-2
Glenrock Branch—*stream* TN-4
Glen Rock Brook—*stream* RI-1
Glenrock Buffalo Jump—*hist pl* WY-8
Glen Rock Cem—*cemetery* PA-2
*Glenrock Cemetery* TN-4
Glen Rock Ch—*church* SC-3
Glen Rock Creek—*stream* KS-7
Glenrock Gravel Pit—*other* WY-8
Glen Rock Reservoir Dam—*dam* RI-1
Glen Rock Rsvr—*reservoir* RI-1
Glenrock Spring—*spring* ME-1
Glen Rock Valley—*valley* PA-2
**Glen Rogers**—*pop pl* WV-2
Glen Rogers HS—*school* WV-2
Glenrose—*locale* PA-2
Glenrose—*locale* WA-9
**Glen Rose**—*pop pl* AR-4
**Glen Rose**—*pop pl* PA-2
**Glen Rose**—*pop pl* TX-5
Glenrose—*uninc pl* KS-7
Glen Rose (CCD)—*cens area* TX-5
Glen Rose Cem—*cemetery* TX-5
Glen Rose Ch—*church* AR-4
Glen Rose Hist Dist—*hist pl* PA-2
Glenrose Park—*park* IN-6
Glenrose Prairie—*flat* WA-9
Glenrose Spring—*spring* CA-9
*Glenroy* PA-2
Glen Roy—*locale* OH-6
**Glen Roy**—*pop pl* PA-2
Glen Roy Cem—*cemetery* OH-6
Glen Roy Estates—*locale* VA-3
Glen (RR name for Glenloch)—*other* PA-2
**Glen (RR name Glens)**—*pop pl* MS-4
Glen Rsvr—*reservoir* CO-8
Glen Rsvr—*reservoir* MT-8
**Glenruadh**—*pop pl* PA-2
Glen Run—*locale* OH-6
Glen Run—*stream* IN-6
Glen Run—*stream* OH-6
Glen Run—*stream* PA-2
Glens, The—*valley* PA-2
**Glen Saint Mary**—*pop pl* FL-3
Glen Savage—*locale* PA-2
**Glensboro**—*pop pl* KY-4
Glen Sch—*school* NC-3
Glen Sch—*school* PA-2
Glens Chapel—*church* NC-3
Glens Creek—*stream* KY-4
Glens Creek Cem—*cemetery* KY-4
**Glens Falls**—*pop pl* NY-2
Glens Falls Cem—*cemetery* NY-2
Glens Falls Country Club—*other* NY-2
Glens Falls Feeder Canal—*hist pl* NY-2
Glens Falls Home for Aged Women—*hist pl* NY-2
Glens Falls HS—*hist pl* NY-2
Glens Falls North—*CDP* NY-2
**Glens Fork**—*pop pl* KY-4
Glens Fork—*stream* KY-4
Glens Fork (CCD)—*cens area* KY-4
**Glens Glen (Post Office)**—*pop pl* (2) MS-4
*Glensharold* KS-7
Glen Sharrald (historical)—*locale* KS-7
**Glenshaw**—*pop pl* PA-2
Glenshaw Community Ch—*church* PA-2
Glenshaw Valley Sch—*school* PA-2
Glenshellah—*uninc pl* VA-3
*Glenshire* IL-6
**Glenshire**—*pop pl* CA-9
**Glenside**—*pop pl* NJ-2
**Glenside**—*pop pl* PA-2
Glenside—*post sta* MI-6
Glenside Cem—*cemetery* ME-1
Glen Side Cem—*cemetery* NY-2
Glenside Cem—*cemetery* NY-2
Glenside Elem Sch—*school* PA-2
**Glenside Farms (subdivision)**—*pop pl* DE-2
*Glenside Gardens* MI-6
**Glenside Gardens**—*pop pl* PA-2
**Glenside Heights**—*pop pl* PA-2
Glenside Mine Station—*locale* PA-2
Glenside Park—*park* PA-2
**Glenside Park**—*pop pl* MD-2
Glenside Sch—*school* MI-6
Glenside Sch—*school* PA-2
Glenside Weldon JHS—*school* PA-2
Glen Silver Pit No.1—*mine* ID-8
Glen Silver Pit No.2—*mine* ID-8
Glens Peak—*summit* ID-8
**Glen Spey**—*pop pl* NY-2
*Glen Spring* TX-5
Glen Spring—*spring* AL-4
Glen Spring—*spring* TN-4
Glen Spring—*spring* UT-8
*Glen Spring Draw* TX-5
*Glen Springs* TX-5
Glen Springs—*locale* KY-4
Glen Springs Elem Sch—*school* FL-3
Glen Springs Hill—*summit* KY-4
Glens (RR name for Glen)—*other* MS-4
*Glens Run* WV-2
**Glens (subdivision), The**—*pop pl* AL-4
**Glensted**—*pop pl* MO-7
Glensted Sch—*school* MO-7
*Glenstone* MO-7
**Glenstone (subdivision)**—*pop pl* TN-4
Glen Street—*uninc pl* NY-2
**Glen Summit**—*pop pl* PA-2
**Glen Summit (Glen Summit Springs)**—*pop pl* PA-2
*Glen Summit Springs* PA-2
Glen Summit Springs—*other* PA-2
Glen Summit Station—*locale* PA-2
**Glen Summitt**—*pop pl* OH-6
Glens Well—*well* NM-5
**Glentana**—*pop pl* MT-8
Glen Tank—*reservoir* TX-5
Glen Tavern Hotel—*hist pl* CA-9
**Glentivar**—*pop pl* CO-8
Glen Town—*locale* MO-7
**Glen (Town of)**—*pop pl* NY-2
**Glen Township**—*pop pl* ND-7
**Glen Township**—*pop pl* SD-7
**Glen (Township of)**—*pop pl* MN-6
Glentzer Perry Ditch—*canal* IN-6
**Glen Ullin**—*pop pl* ND-7
Glen Ullin Municipal Airp—*airport* ND-7
Glen Ullin RR Dam—*dam* ND-7
Glen Union—*locale* PA-2
**Glenvale**—*pop pl* PA-2
*Glen Valley* IN-6
*Glen Valley* KS-7
**Glen Valley**—*pop pl* CA-9
Glen Valley Cem—*cemetery* MA-1
Glen Valley Sch—*school* KS-7
**Glenvar**—*pop pl* VA-3
**Glenvar Heights**—*pop pl* FL-3
Glenvar Lake—*lake* FL-3
*Glen View* IL-6
*Glenview* NJ-2
Glenview—*locale* CA-9
**Glenview**—*pop pl* AL-4
**Glenview**—*pop pl* (2) CA-9
**Glenview**—*pop pl* (2) IL-6
**Glenview**—*pop pl* IN-6
**Glenview**—*pop pl* KY-4
**Glenview**—*pop pl* MD-2
**Glenview**—*pop pl* NJ-2
**Glenview**—*pop pl* NC-3
**Glenview**—*pop pl* PA-2
**Glenview**—*pop pl* (2) TN-4
**Glen View**—*pop pl* WV-2
Glenview—*uninc pl* AR-4
**Glenview Acres**—*pop pl* KY-4
Glenview Cem—*cemetery* NY-2
Glenview Cem—*cemetery* NC-3
Glenview Cem—*cemetery* (2) OH-6
Glenview Cem—*cemetery* WI-6
Glenview Ch—*church* KS-7
Glenview Ch—*church* KY-4
Glen View Ch—*church* SD-7
Glenview Country Club—*other* IL-6
**Glenview Countryside**—*pop pl* IL-6
**Glenview Estates**—*pop pl* IL-6
**Glenview Estates (subdivision)**—*pop pl* (2) AZ-5
**Glenview Heights**—*pop pl* KY-4
**Glenview Hills**—*pop pl* KY-4
Glenview Hist Dist—*hist pl* KY-4
Glenview JHS—*school* IL-6
Glenview Lake—*reservoir* TN-4
Glenview Lake Dam—*dam* TN-4
**Glenview Manor**—*pop pl* KY-4
Glenview Memorial Gardens—*cemetery* IL-6
Glenview Memorial Gardens—*church* WI-6
Glenview Naval Air Station—*military* IL-6
Glenview Orchard Ensemble—*hist pl* OR-9
Glenview Park—*park* OH-6
Glenview Park—*park* TN-4
Glenview Sch—*school* AR-4
Glenview Sch—*school* CA-9
Glen View Sch—*school* CA-9
Glenview Sch—*school* CA-9
Glenview Sch—*school* IL-6
Glenview Sch—*school* KY-4
Glenview Sch—*school* (2) OH-6
Glenview Sch—*school* TX-5
*Glenview School* ND-7
*Glenview Terrace* IL-6
**Glenview Township**—*pop pl* ND-7
**Glenview Woodlands**—*pop pl* IL-6
**Glenvil**—*pop pl* NE-7
Glenvil Cem—*cemetery* NE-7
*Glenville* NE-7
*Glenville* OH-6
*Glenville* PA-2
Glenville—*hist pl* AL-4
Glenville—*locale* AR-4
Glenville—*locale* KY-4
Glenville—*locale* MD-2
Glenville—*locale* MS-4
Glenville—*locale* NY-2
Glenville—*obs name* NE-7
**Glenville**—*pop pl* AL-4
**Glenville**—*pop pl* CT-1
**Glenville**—*pop pl* DE-2
**Glenville**—*pop pl* KS-7
**Glenville**—*pop pl* MN-6
**Glenville**—*pop pl* (2) NY-2
**Glenville**—*pop pl* NC-3
**Glenville**—*pop pl* PA-2
**Glenville**—*pop pl* WV-2
Glenville—*uninc pl* KS-7
Glenville Baptist Ch—*church* MS-4
Glenville Bible Baptist Ch—*church* KS-7
Glenville Cem—*cemetery* AL-4
Glenville Cem—*cemetery* MS-4
Glenville Cem—*cemetery* OH-6
**Glenville Center**—*pop pl* NY-2
Glenville Ch—*church* KY-4
*Glenville Dam* NC-3
Glenville Dam—*dam* NC-3
Glenville Hill—*summit* (2) NY-2
Glenville HS—*school* OH-6
*Glenville Lake* NC-3
Glenville Lake—*reservoir* NC-3
Glenville Lake Dam—*dam* NC-3
Glenville Lookout Tower—*locale* AR-4
Glenville Lookout Tower—*tower* MS-4
Glenville (Magisterial District)—*fmr MCD* WV-2
Glenville Pond—*reservoir* CT-1
Glenville Post Office (historical)—*building* MS-4
*Glenville Reservoir* NC-3
Glenville Sch—*school* WI-6
Glenville State Coll—*school* WV-2
**Glenville (Town of)**—*pop pl* NY-2
**Glenvil Township**—*pop pl* NE-7
**Glenwall Village**—*pop pl* PA-2
**Glenwaye Gardens**—*pop pl* MD-2
Glenway Golf Course—*other* WI-6
Glenway Park—*park* IA-7
Glenway Park—*park* OH-6
**Glen Westover**—*pop pl* MD-2
**Glen White**—*pop pl* WV-2
Glen White Dam—*dam* IN-6
**Glen White Junction**—*pop pl* WV-2
Glen White Lake—*reservoir* IN-6
Glenwhite Run—*stream* PA-2
*Glenwild* NY-2
Glenwild—*locale* NY-2
**Glenwild**—*pop pl* LA-4
**Glenwild**—*pop pl* MS-4
**Glen Wild**—*pop pl* NY-2
Glenwild Cem—*cemetery* MO-7
**Glenwild (Clear Creek Ranch)**—*pop pl* MS-4
**Glenwilde (Glen Wilde)**—*pop pl* TN-4
Glen Wild Lake—*reservoir* NJ-2
Glen Wild Lake Dam—*dam* NJ-2
Glen Wild Methodist Church—*hist pl* NY-2
Glenwild Sch—*school* IL-6
**Glenwillard**—*pop pl* PA-2
**Glenwillard (Shousetown)**—*pop pl* PA-2
Glen Williams Mine—*mine* CO-8
Glen Willis—*hist pl* KY-4
**Glenwillow**—*pop pl* OH-6
**Glen Willow**—*pop pl* PA-2
Glen Willow Lake—*reservoir* OH-6
**Glen Wilton**—*pop pl* VA-3
*Glenwood* ID-8
*Glenwood* KS-7
*Glenwood* NC-3
*Glenwood* PA-2
*Glenwood* WI-6
Glenwood—*hist pl* NY-2
Glenwood—*hist pl* (2) NC-3
Glenwood—*locale* FL-3
Glenwood—*locale* ID-8
Glenwood—*locale* KY-4
Glenwood—*locale* ME-1
Glenwood—*locale* MD-2
Glenwood—*locale* OH-6
Glenwood—*locale* TN-4
Glenwood—*locale* (2) WA-9
**Glenwood**—*pop pl* AL-4
**Glenwood**—*pop pl* AR-4
**Glenwood**—*pop pl* CA-9
**Glenwood**—*pop pl* (2) FL-3
**Glenwood**—*pop pl* (2) GA-3
**Glenwood**—*pop pl* HI-9
**Glenwood**—*pop pl* IL-6
**Glenwood**—*pop pl* IN-6
**Glenwood**—*pop pl* IA-7
**Glenwood**—*pop pl* LA-4
**Glenwood**—*pop pl* (2) MD-2
**Glenwood**—*pop pl* MA-1
**Glenwood**—*pop pl* MI-6
**Glenwood**—*pop pl* MN-6
**Glenwood**—*pop pl* MO-7
**Glenwood**—*pop pl* NJ-2
**Glenwood**—*pop pl* NM-5
**Glenwood**—*pop pl* (3) NY-2
**Glenwood**—*pop pl* (3) NC-3
**Glenwood**—*pop pl* OH-6
**Glenwood**—*pop pl* (3) OR-9
**Glenwood**—*pop pl* (4) PA-2
**Glenwood**—*pop pl* SC-3
**Glenwood**—*pop pl* (2) TN-4
**Glenwood**—*pop pl* TX-5
**Glenwood**—*pop pl* UT-8
**Glenwood**—*pop pl* VA-3
**Glenwood**—*pop pl* WA-9
**Glenwood**—*pop pl* (3) WV-2
Glenwood—*uninc pl* TX-5
**Glenwood Acres**—*pop pl* IN-6
**Glenwood Acres (subdivision)**—*pop pl* NC-3
Glenwood Airp—*airport* CO-8
Glenwood Ave Sch—*school* OH-6
Glenwood Baptist Ch—*church* (2) TN-4
Glenwood Basin—*basin* CA-9
Glenwood Beach—*beach* NY-2
**Glenwood Beach**—*pop pl* MI-6
Glenwood Branch—*stream* (2) KY-4
Glenwood Bridge—*bridge* PA-2
Glenwood Camp—*locale* WI-6
Glenwood Canal—*canal* LA-4
Glenwood Canyon—*valley* CO-8
Glenwood Cave—*cave* IA-7
Glenwood (CCD)—*cens area* GA-3
Glenwood Cem—*cemetery* (2) AL-4
Glenwood Cem—*cemetery* AR-4
Glenwood Cem—*cemetery* DC-2
Glenwood Cem—*cemetery* FL-3
Glenwood Cem—*cemetery* GA-3
Glenwood Cem—*cemetery* (3) IL-6
Glenwood Cem—*cemetery* IN-6
Glenwood Cem—*cemetery* (2) IA-7
Glenwood Cem—*cemetery* (2) KS-7
Glenwood Cem—*cemetery* (2) KY-4
Glenwood Cem—*cemetery* (4) MA-1
Glenwood Cem—*cemetery* (2) MI-6
Glenwood Cem—*cemetery* (2) MN-6
Glenwood Cem—*cemetery* MS-4
Glenwood Cem—*cemetery* MO-7
Glenwood Cem—*cemetery* (3) NH-1
Glenwood Cem—*cemetery* (2) NJ-2
Glenwood Cem—*cemetery* (12) NY-2
Glenwood Cem—*cemetery* (2) OH-6
Glenwood Cem—*cemetery* (2) OK-5
Glenwood Cem—*cemetery* OR-9
Glenwood Cem—*cemetery* (2) PA-2
Glenwood Cem—*cemetery* (2) TN-4
Glenwood Cem—*cemetery* (5) TX-5
Glenwood Cem—*cemetery* (2) UT-8
Glenwood Cem—*cemetery* (3) WI-6
Glenwood Cem North Sector—*cemetery* TX-5
Glenwood Cem South Sector—*cemetery* TX-5
Glenwood Ch—*church* AL-4
Glenwood Ch—*church* (2) IL-6
Glenwood Ch—*church* IN-6
Glenwood Ch—*church* IA-7
Glenwood Ch—*church* KY-4
Glenwood Ch—*church* MO-7
Glenwood Ch—*church* (2) NC-3
Glenwood Ch—*church* ND-7
Glenwood Ch—*church* (3) PA-2
Glenwood Ch—*church* (2) TN-4
Glenwood Ch—*church* TX-5
Glenwood Ch—*church* (5) VA-3
Glenwood Chapel—*church* NY-2
Glenwood Ch of Christ—*church* FL-3
**Glenwood City**—*pop pl* WI-6
Glenwood Cooperative Store—*hist pl* UT-8
*Glenwood Creek* OR-9
Glenwood Creek—*stream* (2) NY-2
Glenwood Creek—*stream* OR-9
Glenwood Creek—*stream* TX-5
Glenwood Crossroads—*locale* NC-3
Glenwood Ditch—*canal* CO-8
Glenwood-Downing—*uninc pl* WI-6
Glenwood-Dyer Interchange—*other* IL-6
Glenwood Elementary and JHS—*school* IN-6
*Glenwood Elementary School* TN-4
Glenwood Elem Sch—*school* NC-3
Glenwood Elem Sch—*school* PA-2
*Glenwood Estates* IL-6
**Glenwood Estates**—*pop pl* ND-7
**Glenwood Farms**—*pop pl* VA-3
Glenwood Fish Hatchery—*locale* UT-8
*Glenwood Forest* MI-6
Glenwood Furnace (Ruins)—*locale* VA-3
Glenwood Golf Club—*other* VA-3
**Glenwood Heights**—*pop pl* FL-3
Glenwood Heights Sch—*school* WA-9
Glenwood Hills—*locale* GA-3
Glenwood Hills—*uninc pl* NC-3
Glenwood Hills Ch—*church* (2) GA-3
Glenwood Hills Hosp—*hospital* MN-6
**Glenwood Hills (subdivision)**—*pop pl* NC-3
Glenwood (historical)—*locale* KS-7
**Glenwood (historical)**—*pop pl* OR-9
**Glenwood (historical)**—*pop pl* SD-7
Glenwood HS—*school* GA-3
Glenwood HS—*school* OH-6
Glenwoodie Country Club—*other* IL-6
Glenwood JHS—*school* OH-6
*Glenwood Junction* MN-6
Glenwood Junction—*LOCALE* MN-6
Glenwood Junction—*locale* MO-7
Glenwood Junction—*uninc pl* PA-2
*Glenwood Lake* NC-3
Glenwood Lake—*lake* AR-4
Glenwood Lake—*lake* MT-8
Glenwood Lake—*reservoir* NJ-2
Glenwood Lake—*reservoir* (2) NY-2
*Glenwood Lake Dam* NC-3
Glenwood Lake Dam—*dam* NJ-2
Glenwood Lake Dam—*dam* PA-2
Glenwood Lake Park—*park* IA-7
**Glenwood Landing**—*pop pl* NY-2
Glenwood Mall—*locale* KS-7
Glenwood Manor Motor Hotel Airp—*airport* KS-7
Glenwood Memorial Cem—*cemetery* FL-3
Glenwood Memorial Gardens—*cemetery* WI-6
Glenwood Memorial Park—*cemetery* NC-3
Glenwood Mtn—*summit* UT-8
Glenwood Park—*park* FL-3
Glenwood Park—*park* IL-6
Glenwood Park—*park* KS-7
Glenwood Park—*park* MD-2
Glenwood Park—*park* MO-7
Glenwood Park—*park* OH-6
Glenwood Park—*park* (2) OK-5
Glenwood Park—*park* (2) PA-2
Glenwood Park—*park* (2) TX-5
**Glenwood Park**—*pop pl* IN-6
**Glenwood Park**—*pop pl* NE-7
**Glenwood Park**—*pop pl* NY-2
**Glenwood Park**—*pop pl* VA-3
**Glenwood Park (Buena)**—*pop pl* MD-2
**Glenwood Park (Glenwood)**—*pop pl* WV-2
**Glenwood Park (subdivision)**—*pop pl* AL-4
Glenwood Park Zoo—*locale* PA-2
Glenwood (Plantation of)—*civ div* ME-1
Glenwood Plaza Shop Ctr—*locale* AZ-5
Glenwood Point—*cape* NY-2
Glenwood Public Library—*hist pl* MN-6
Glenwood Racetrack—*other* VA-3
Glenwood Ranger Station—*locale* NM-5

Gold Dust Mine—*mine* ... MT-8
Gold Dust Mine—*mine* ... NM-5
Gold Dust Peak—*summit* ... CO-8
Gold Dust Plantation (historical)—*locale* ... MS-4
Golddust Post Office (historical)—*building* ... AL-4
Golddust Post Office (historical)—*building* ... TN-4
Gold Dust Sch—*school* ... MO-7
Golddust Sch (historical)—*school* ... AL-4
Golddust Sch (historical)—*school* ... TN-4
*Gold Dust School* ... TN-4
Gold Eagle Mine—*mine* ... AZ-5
Gold Edge Mine—*mine* ... CO-8
Golden—*locale* (2) ... MI-6
Golden—*locale* ... NV-8
Golden—*locale* ... OR-9
Golden—*locale* (2) ... WV-2
**Golden**—*pop pl* ... CO-8
**Golden**—*pop pl* ... ID-8
**Golden**—*pop pl* ... IL-6
**Golden**—*pop pl* ... IA-7
**Golden**—*pop pl* ... MS-4
**Golden**—*pop pl* ... MO-7
**Golden**—*pop pl* ... NM-5
**Golden**—*pop pl* ... NC-3
**Golden**—*pop pl* ... OK-5
**Golden**—*pop pl* ... TX-5
Golden, Frank, Block—*hist pl* ... NV-8
Golden, Lake—*lake* ... WY-8
*Golden Acres* ... IL-6
**Golden Acres**—*pop pl* (2) ... IL-6
**Golden Acres**—*pop pl* ... IN-6
**Golden Acres**—*pop pl* ... TX-5
Golden Acres—*post sta* ... CO-8
Golden Acres Baptist Ch—*church* ... AL-4
Golden Acres Cem—*cemetery* ... MD-2
Golden Acres Ch—*church* ... AL-4
Golden Acres Country Club—*other* ... IL-6
Golden Acres Country Club—*other* ... TX-5
**Golden Acres Estates**—*pop pl* ... PA-2
Golden Acres Home—*building* ... TX-5
Golden Acres Methodist Ch—*church* ... AL-4
Golden Acres Sch—*school* ... TX-5
**Golden Acres (subdivision)**—*pop pl* ... AL-4
**Golden Acres Subdivision**—*pop pl* (2) ... UT-8
Golden Age Hill—*summit* ... CO-8
Golden Age Home—*building* ... TX-5
Golden Age Mine—*mine* ... CA-9
Golden Age Mine—*mine* ... ID-8
Golden Age Mine—*mine* ... MT-8
*Golden Amethyst* ... NV-8
Golden Amythest Mine—*mine* ... NV-8
Golden Anchor—*mine* ... NV-8
Golden Anchor Mine—*mine* ... ID-8
Golden Anchor Mine—*mine* ... MT-8
Golden and Silver Falls State Park—*park* ... OR-9
Golden Anniversary State For—*forest* ... MN-6
Golden Arrow—*locale* ... NV-8
Golden Arrow Sch—*school* ... IL-6
**Golden Ash**—*pop pl* ... KY-4
Golden Aster Creek—*stream* ... AZ-5
Golden Ave Sch—*school* ... CA-9
Golden Ball Park—*park* ... GA-3
Golden Ball Tavern—*hist pl* ... MA-1
Golden Basin—*basin* ... OR-9
**Golden Beach**—*pop pl* (2) ... FL-3
**Golden Beach**—*pop pl* ... MD-2
Golden Beach Campsite—*locale* ... NY-2
Golden Bear Creek Bridge—*bridge* ... MS-4
Golden Bear Lake—*lake* ... CA-9
Golden Bear Mine—*mine* ... CA-9
Golden Bee Mine—*mine* ... CA-9
Golden Bell Guest Ranch—*locale* ... CO-8
Golden Bell Mine—*mine* ... AZ-5
Golden Bell Mine—*mine* ... CA-9
Golden Belt Hist Dist—*hist pl* ... NC-3
Golden Belt Memorial Park—*cemetery* ... KS-7
Golden Belt Mine—*mine* ... AZ-5
Golden Belt Spur—*uninc pl* ... KS-7
**Golden Belt Township**—*pop pl* ... KS-7
Golden Belt Tunnel—*tunnel* ... CO-8
Golden Bomber Mine—*mine* ... NV-8
Golden Box Mine—*mine* ... OR-9
Golden Branch—*stream* ... IA-7
Golden Branch—*stream* ... VA-3
Golden Branch—*stream* ... WV-2
*Goldenbridge* ... NY-2
Golden Bridge—*bridge* ... AL-4
Golden Brook—*stream* ... NH-1
Golden Brothers, Founders and Machinsts—*hist pl* ... GA-3
*Golden Buckle of the Cotton Belt* ... MS-4
Golden Bucksin Mine—*mine* ... AZ-5
Goldenburg Draw—*valley* ... NM-5
Golden Cabin—*locale* ... WY-8
Golden Canyon—*valley* (2) ... CA-9
Golden Canyon—*valley* ... OR-9
Golden Castle Gulch—*valley* ... CO-8
Golden Cem—*cemetery* ... AR-4
Golden Cem—*cemetery* ... GA-3
Golden Cem—*cemetery* (2) ... KS-7
Golden Cem—*cemetery* ... PA-2
Golden Cem—*cemetery* ... SC-3
Golden Ch—*church* ... IL-6
Golden Ch—*church* ... IA-7
Golden Ch—*church* ... NC-3
Golden Chain Camp—*locale* ... NJ-2
Golden Chain Ch—*church* ... LA-4
Golden Chapel United Methodist Ch—*church* ... MS-4
Golden Chariot Mine—*mine* ... CA-9
Golden Chariot Mine—*mine* (2) ... ID-8
Golden Chariot Mine—*mine* ... NV-8
Golden Charm Mine—*mine* ... MT-8
Golden Chest Mine—*mine* ... ID-8
Golden Chief Mine—*mine* ... CA-9
*Golden Circle* ... ME-1
Golden Circle Valley Country Club—*other* ... CA-9
*Golden City* ... KS-7
Golden City—*locale* ... AR-4
**Golden City**—*pop pl* ... MO-7
Golden City (Abandoned)—*locale* ... AK-9
Golden City Hall—*building* ... MS-4
**Golden City Township**—*pop pl* ... MO-7
Golden Clover Mine—*mine* ... WY-8
Golden Clover Rsvr No 1—*reservoir* ... WY-8
Golden Clover Rsvr No 2—*reservoir* ... WY-8
Golden Corners—*locale* ... WI-6
**Golden Corners**—*pop pl* ... OH-6
Golden Cove—*post sta* ... CA-9
Golden Cove Brook—*stream* ... MA-1
*Golden Creek* ... MT-8
*Golden Creek* ... NC-3
*Golden Creek* ... OH-6
*Golden Creek* ... TX-5
Golden Creek—*stream* ... AL-4
Golden Creek—*stream* ... AK-9
Golden Creek—*stream* (2) ... CA-9
Golden Creek—*stream* (4) ... GA-3
Golden Creek—*stream* ... ID-8
Golden Creek—*stream* (2) ... MI-6
Golden Creek—*stream* ... MS-4
Golden Creek—*stream* ... NC-3
Golden Creek—*stream* ... OR-9
Golden Creek—*stream* ... SC-3
Golden Creek—*stream* ... TN-4
Golden Creek—*stream* ... WA-9
Golden Creek—*stream* (2) ... WI-6
Golden Creek Ch—*church* ... SC-3
**Golden Crest**—*pop pl* ... NJ-2
Golden Crest Mine—*mine* ... SD-7
Golden Cross Cem—*cemetery* ... TN-4
Golden Cross Mine—*mine* ... NM-5
Golden Crown Mine—*mine* ... ID-8
Golden Crown Mine—*mine* ... SD-7
Golden Cup Mine—*mine* ... ID-8
Golden Curry Creek—*stream* ... OR-9
Golden Cycle Mine—*mine* (2) ... CO-8
Golden Cycle Mine—*mine* (2) ... ID-8
**Goldendale**—*pop pl* ... WA-9
Goldendale Airp—*airport* ... WA-9
Goldendale (CCD)—*cens area* ... WA-9
Goldendale Free Public Library—*hist pl* ... WA-9
Goldendale Trout Hatchery—*locale* ... WA-9
Golden Dam—*dam* ... AL-4
Golden Dam Tank—*reservoir* ... AZ-5
Golden Days Montessori Sch—*school* ... FL-3
Golden Ditch—*canal* ... MT-8
Golden Door Mine—*mine* ... AZ-5
Golden Drainage Ditch—*canal* ... MI-6
Golden Draw—*valley* ... WY-8
Golden Dream Mine—*mine* ... AZ-5
Golden Dream Mine—*mine* ... CA-9
Golden Dreams Mine (abandoned)—*mine* ... OR-9
Golden Eagle—*locale* ... IL-6
Golden Eagle Cliff—*cliff* ... KY-4
Golden Eagle Ferry—*locale* ... IL-6
Golden Eagle Ferry—*locale* ... MO-7
Golden Eagle Lake—*reservoir* ... MO-7
Golden Eagle Mine—*mine* (2) ... AZ-5
Golden Eagle Mine—*mine* ... CA-9
Golden Eagle Mine—*mine* (3) ... NV-8
Golden Eagle Mine—*mine* (2) ... NM-5
Golden Eagle Mine—*mine* (2) ... OR-9
Golden Eagle Mine (abandoned)—*mine* ... OR-9
Golden Eagle-Toppmeyer Site—*hist pl* ... IL-6
Golden Eagle Trail—*trail* ... PA-2
Golden Eagle Wine Cellars—*hist pl* ... OH-6
Golden East Crossing Shop Ctr—*locale* ... NC-3
Golden Egg Mine—*mine* ... CA-9
Golden Ella Mine—*mine* ... CA-9
Golden Empire Mine—*mine* ... NV-8
Golden Ensign Mine—*mine* ... NV-8
Golden Era Mine—*mine* ... MT-8
Goldeneye Lake—*lake* ... MN-6
Goldeneye Lake—*lake* ... OR-9
Goldeneye Lake—*lake* ... WA-9
Goldeneye Pond—*reservoir* ... IN-6
Golden Falls—*falls* ... OR-9
Golden Fawn Ranch—*locale* ... TX-5
Golden Field Pond—*reservoir* ... MA-1
Golden Field Pond Dam—*dam* ... MA-1
Golden Fleece Mine—*mine* ... CA-9
Golden Fleece Mine—*mine* ... CO-8
Golden Fleece Mine—*mine* ... NV-8
Golden Fleece Tunnel—*mine* ... CA-9
Golden Ford (historical)—*locale* ... MO-7
**Golden Forest (subdivision)**—*pop pl* ... NC-3
**Golden Gardens**—*pop pl* ... IL-6
Golden Gardens Park—*park* ... OR-9
Golden Gate—*channel* ... CA-9
Golden Gate—*gap* ... WY-8
Golden Gate—*locale* ... WA-9
Golden Gate—*other* ... CA-9
**Golden Gate**—*pop pl* (2) ... FL-3
**Golden Gate**—*pop pl* ... IL-6
Golden Gate—*post sta* ... NC-3
Golden Gate—*summit* ... UT-8
Golden Gate Acad—*school* ... CA-9
Golden Gate Bridge—*bridge* ... CA-9
*Golden Gate Brook* ... MA-1
Golden Gate Campground—*locale* ... ID-8
Golden Gate Canal—*canal* (2) ... ID-8
Golden Gate Canal—*canal* ... OR-9
Golden Gate Canyon—*valley* ... CO-8
Golden Gate Canyon—*valley* ... WY-8
Golden Gate Canyon State Park—*park* ... CO-8
Golden Gate Cem—*cemetery* ... MN-6
Golden Gate Cem—*cemetery* ... OH-6
Golden Gate Ch—*church* ... MO-7
Golden Gate Ch—*church* ... TX-5
Golden Gate Ch—*church* ... WV-2
Golden Gate Ch of Christ—*church* ... FL-3
Golden Gate Club—*other* ... CA-9
*Goldengate (corporate and RR name Golden Gate)* ... IL-6
Goldengate Creek—*stream* ... AK-9
Golden Gate Creek—*stream* ... CA-9
Golden Gate Drain—*canal* ... MI-6
Golden Gate Drop—*other* ... ID-8
Golden Gate Elem Sch—*school* ... FL-3
Golden Gate Estates—*other* ... FL-3
Golden Gate Falls—*falls* ... AK-9
Golden Gate Fields—*flat* ... CA-9
Golden Gate (Golden Gate Estates)—*CDP* ... FL-3
Golden Gate Hill—*summit* ... CA-9
Golden Gate Hill—*summit* ... ID-8
Golden Gate Hill—*summit* ... NV-8
Golden Gate JHS—*school* ... CA-9
Golden Gate Mine—*mine* (2) ... AZ-5
Golden Gate Mine—*mine* (2) ... CA-9
Golden Gate Mine—*mine* ... OR-9
Golden Gate Mine—*mine* ... UT-8
Golden Gate MS—*school* ... FL-3
Golden Gate Mtn—*summit* ... AZ-5
Golden Gate Natl Cem—*cemetery* ... CA-9
Golden Gate Natl Rec Area—*park* ... CA-9
Golden Gate North Oil Field—*other* ... IL-6
Golden Gate Number One Mine—*mine* ... CA-9
Golden Gate Oil Field—*other* ... IL-6
Golden Gate Park—*park* ... CA-9
Golden Gate Park Conservatory—*hist pl* ... CA-9
Golden Gate Point—*cape* ... FL-3
Golden Gate Prospect—*mine* ... WY-8
Golden Gate Range—*range* ... NV-8
Golden Gate Ravine—*valley* ... CA-9
Goldengate Sch—*school* ... KS-7
**Golden Gates Estates (subdivision)**—*pop pl* ... FL-3
Golden Gate Shop Ctr—*locale* ... FL-3
Golden Gate (Shop Ctr)—*locale* ... FL-3
Golden Gate Speedway—*locale* ... FL-3
Golden Gate Theater—*hist pl* ... CA-9
Golden Gate United Methodist Ch—*church* ... FL-3
Golden Gate Villa—*hist pl* ... CA-9
Golden Gateway—*gap* ... TN-4
Golden Gateway Shop Ctr—*locale* ... TN-4
Golden Gate Windmill—*locale* ... NM-5
Golden Gem Mine—*mine* ... AZ-5
Golden Glades—*CDP* ... FL-3
Golden Glades Ch—*church* ... FL-3
Golden Glades Interchange 1—*crossing* ... FL-3
Golden Glades Sch—*school* ... FL-3
Golden Glades Shop Ctr—*locale* ... FL-3
Golden Glen Gulch—*valley* ... CO-8
Golden Glen Mine—*mine* ... CO-8
**Golden Glen Township**—*pop pl* ... ND-7
**Golden Glow Heights**—*pop pl* ... NY-2
Golden Goose Canyon—*valley* ... ID-8
Golden Goose Cove—*bay* ... MO-7
Golden Grades Day Sch—*school* ... FL-3
Golden Grove—*locale* ... MS-4
**Golden Grove**—*pop pl* ... SC-3
**Golden Grove**—*pop pl* ... VI-3
Golden Grove Cem—*cemetery* ... MS-4
Golden Grove Ch—*church* ... AL-4
Golden Grove Ch—*church* (2) ... MS-4
Golden Grove Ch—*church* (2) ... SC-3
Golden Grove Sch—*school* ... MN-6
Golden Grove School (Abandoned)—*locale* ... WI-6
Golden Gulch—*valley* ... MT-8
Golden Gulch—*valley* ... OR-9
Golden Hammock Thorofare—*channel* ... NJ-2
Golden Hand Mine—*mine* ... ID-8
Golden Harp Mine—*mine* ... AZ-5
Golden Harvest Creek—*stream* ... WA-9
Golden Harvest Ministries Ch—*church* ... MS-4
Golden Harvest Trail—*trail* ... WA-9
**Golden Heights**—*pop pl* ... FL-3
Golden Heights Ch of Christ—*church* ... FL-3
*Golden Highridge* ... IL-6
Golden Hill—*locale* ... MD-2
Golden Hill—*locale* ... PA-2
**Golden Hill**—*pop pl* ... IN-6
**Golden Hill**—*pop pl* ... MN-6
Golden Hill—*summit* (2) ... CT-1
Golden Hill—*summit* (2) ... MA-1
Golden Hill—*summit* ... NY-2
Golden Hill—*summit* ... PA-2
Golden Hill—*uninc pl* ... CA-9
Golden Hill Branch—*stream* ... VA-3
Golden Hill Canal—*canal* ... CO-8
**Golden Hill Canyon Subdivision**—*pop pl* ... UT-8
Golden Hill Cem—*cemetery* ... CO-8
Golden Hill Cem—*cemetery* ... MS-4
Golden Hill Cem—*cemetery* ... NE-7
Golden Hill Ch—*church* ... MS-4
Golden Hill Ch—*church* ... TX-5
Golden Hill Ch—*church* ... VA-3
Golden Hill Creek—*stream* ... NY-2
Golden Hill Hist Dist—*hist pl* ... CT-1
Golden Hill Ind Res—*reserve* ... CT-1
Golden Hill Lake—*lake* ... ND-7
Golden Hill Park—*park* ... IN-6
*Golden Hills* ... MN-6
**Golden Hills**—*pop pl* ... FL-3
Golden Hills Acad—*school* ... FL-3
**Golden Hills (Apache Country Club)**—*pop pl* ... AZ-5
Golden Hill Sch—*school* ... CA-9
Golden Hill Sch—*school* ... IA-7
Golden Hills Golf Course—*other* ... AZ-5
Golden Hills Golf Course—*other* ... CA-9
Golden Hillside Mines—*mine* ... AZ-5
**Golden Hills Subdivision**—*pop pl* ... UT-8
Golden Hills Turf and Country Club—*locale* ... FL-3
Golden (historical)—*locale* ... KS-7
**Golden (historical)**—*pop pl* ... PA-2
Golden Hole—*cave* ... AL-4
Golden Hollow—*valley* ... IN-6
Golden Hollow—*valley* ... TN-4
Golden Horn—*bay* ... AK-9
Golden Horn—*pillar* ... AK-9
Golden Horn—*summit* ... CO-8
Golden Horn—*summit* ... WA-9
*Goldenhorn Branch* ... TN-4
Golden Horn Branch—*stream* ... AL-4
Golden Horn Creek—*stream* ... MS-4
Goldenhorn Creek—*stream* ... TN-4
Golden Hub Mine—*mine* ... CA-9
Golden Idol Mine—*mine* ... AZ-5
**Golden Isles**—*pop pl* ... FL-3
Golden Isles Lake—*lake* ... FL-3
Golden Isles Park—*park* ... FL-3
Golden Key Mine—*mine* ... AZ-5
Golden Key Mine—*mine* ... CA-9
Golden Key Mine—*mine* ... WY-8
Golden King Mine—*mine* ... NV-8
Golden King Mine—*mine* ... WA-9
Golden Lady Mine—*mine* ... CA-9
*Golden Lake* ... NE-7
*Golden Lake* ... OR-9
Golden Lake—*lake* ... AL-4
Golden Lake—*lake* (3) ... CA-9
Golden Lake—*lake* (2) ... FL-3
Golden Lake—*lake* (2) ... ID-8
Golden Lake—*lake* ... IN-6
Golden Lake—*lake* ... IA-7
Golden Lake—*lake* ... MI-6
Golden Lake—*lake* ... MN-6
Golden Lake—*lake* ... MT-8
Golden Lake—*lake* ... NM-5
Golden Lake—*lake* ... ND-7
Golden Lake—*lake* ... OR-9
Golden Lake—*lake* (2) ... WI-6
Golden Lake—*lake* (3) ... WY-8
**Golden Lake**—*pop pl* ... AR-4
**Golden Lake**—*pop pl* ... IN-6
Golden Lake—*reservoir* ... AL-4
Golden Lake—*reservoir* ... ID-8
Golden Lake Cem—*cemetery* ... AR-4
Golden Lake Ch—*church* ... AR-4
Golden Lake Crevasse—*basin* ... AR-4
Golden Lake Lookout Tower—*locale* ... MI-6
Golden Lake Revetment—*dam* ... AR-4
Golden Lakes—*lake* ... WA-9
Golden Lakes—*lake* (2) ... WY-8
Golden Lake Sch—*school* ... WI-6
Golden Lake State Wildlife Mngmt Area—*park* ... ND-7
Golden Lake Town Hall—*building* ... ND-7
**Golden Lake Township**—*pop pl* ... ND-7
Golden Lake (Township of)—*fmr MCD* ... AR-4
Golden Lamb—*hist pl* ... OH-6
Golden Lateral—*canal* ... ID-8
Golden Leaf Center (Shop Ctr)—*locale* ... NC-3
Golden Leaf Mine—*mine* ... MT-8
Golden Light Ch (historical)—*church* ... MO-7
**Golden Lilly**—*pop pl* ... IL-6
**Golden Lily**—*pop pl* ... IL-6
Golden Link Cabin—*locale* ... NM-5
Golden Link Cem—*cemetery* ... MS-4
Golden Link Trail (Pack)—*trail* ... NM-5
Golden Lodge Cem—*cemetery* ... OK-5
*Golden Manor* ... IL-6
Golden Meadow—*flat* ... WA-9
**Golden Meadow**—*pop pl* ... LA-4
Golden Meadow Farms—*locale* ... LA-4
Golden Meadow Oil and Gas Field—*oilfield* ... LA-4
**Golden Meadows**—*pop pl* ... KY-4
**Golden Meadows**—*pop pl* ... TN-4
**Golden Meadows Subdivision**—*pop pl* ... UT-8
Golden Memorial Ch—*church* ... FL-3
Golden Memorial Park Lake—*reservoir* ... MS-4
Golden Memorial State Park—*park* ... MS-4
Golden Memorial State Park Dam—*dam* ... MS-4
Golden Messenger Mine—*mine* ... MT-8
Golden Mile Mine—*mine* ... AZ-5
Golden Mine—*hist pl* ... DE-2
Golden Moss Mine—*mine* ... MT-8
Golden Mountain—*ridge* ... NV-8
Golden Mount Ch—*church* ... MS-4
Golden Mtn—*summit* ... MT-8
Golden Mtn—*summit* ... TX-5
Golden Nugget Mine (area)—*mine* ... NM-5
Golden Number 1 Dam—*dam* ... SD-7
*Golden Oak* ... MO-7
**Golden Oaks Estates (subdivision)**—*pop pl* ... TN-4
Golden Oaks Memorial Gardens—*cemetery* ... KY-4
Golden Oaks Sch—*school* ... MO-7
Golden Oaks Spring—*spring* ... CA-9
**Golden Oaks Subdivision**—*pop pl* ... UT-8
Golden Park—*park* ... NJ-2
Golden Park—*park* ... NY-2
**Golden Park Subdivision**—*pop pl* (2) ... UT-8
Golden Pen Mine—*mine* ... NV-8
Golden Pheasant Country Club—*other* ... NJ-2
Golden Pipe Mine—*mine* ... NV-8
**Golden Place**—*pop pl* ... NC-3
Golden Plains Cem—*cemetery* ... KS-7
Golden Plains Elem Sch—*school* ... KS-7
Golden Plains HS—*school* ... KS-7
Golden Plains JHS—*school* ... KS-7
*Golden Pond* ... NH-1
Golden Pond—*lake* ... KY-4
Golden Pond—*lake* ... NY-2
Golden Pond—*locale* ... KY-4
Golden Pond Sch—*school* ... TX-5
Golden Prairie America Ch—*church* ... WY-8
Golden Prairie Sch—*school* ... NE-7
Golden Quarter Neck—*cape* ... MD-2
Golden Queen Mine—*mine* (2) ... CA-9
Golden Ranch—*locale* ... NE-7
Golden Ranch—*locale* ... TX-5
Golden Rapids—*rapids* ... ME-1
Golden Ray Mine—*mine* ... UT-8
Golden Reef Mine—*mine* ... UT-8
Golden Relief Mine—*mine* ... UT-8
Golden Reservoir Dam—*dam* ... MA-1
Golden Reward Mine—*mine* ... SD-7
Golden Reward Mine (historical)—*mine* ... SD-7
Golden Ridge—*locale* ... MT-8
**Goldenridge**—*pop pl* ... PA-2
**Golden Ridge**—*pop pl* ... WV-2
Golden Ridge—*ridge* ... ME-1
Golden Ridge—*ridge* ... MO-7
Golden Ridge—*ridge* ... NC-3
Golden Ridge—*ridge* ... OR-9
Golden Ridge—*ridge* ... UT-8
Golden Ridge Cem—*cemetery* ... ID-8
Golden Ridge Tunnel—*mine* ... WY-8
Golden Riffle Mine—*mine* ... CA-9
**Golden Ring**—*pop pl* ... MD-2
**Golden Ring Camp**—*pop pl* ... MA-1
Golden Ring Mine—*mine* ... OR-9
Golden River Mine—*mine* ... CA-9
Golden River Tunnel—*mine* ... CA-9
Golden Rock—*locale* ... VI-3
*Goldenrod* ... MP-9
GOLDENROD—*hist pl* ... MO-7
Goldenrod—*locale* ... KS-7
Goldenrod—*locale* ... MN-6
**Goldenrod**—*pop pl* ... FL-3
Goldenrod Ave Baptist Ch—*church* ... AL-4
Goldenrod Baptist Ch—*church* (2) ... FL-3
Goldenrod Cem—*cemetery* ... WA-9
Goldenrod Creek—*stream* ... TX-5
**Golden Rod Farms**—*pop pl* ... PA-2
Goldenrod Mine—*mine* ... CA-9
Goldenrod Mine—*mine* ... NV-8
Goldenrod Mine—*mine* ... NM-5
Golden Rod Mines—*mine* ... CO-8
Goldenrod Plaza (Shop Ctr)—*locale* ... FL-3
Goldenrod Point—*cape* ... IN-6
Golden Rod (RR name for Goldenrod)—*other* ... FL-3
Goldenrod (RR name Golden Rod)—*CDP* ... FL-3
Golden Rod Sch—*school* ... KS-7
Goldenrod Sch—*school* (3) ... NE-7
Goldenrod Sch—*school* ... SD-7
Goldenrod Sch—*school* ... WI-6
Goldenrod Schoolhouse—*hist pl* ... IA-7
Goldenrod Spring—*spring* ... CA-9
*Golden Rod Station* ... FL-3
Goldenrod Trail—*trail* ... PA-2
Golden Roll Dam—*dam* ... AZ-5
Golden Roll Spring—*spring* ... AZ-5
Golden Roll Tank—*reservoir* ... AZ-5
Golden Rose Mine—*mine* ... CO-8
Golden Rsvr—*reservoir* ... CO-8
Golden Rule Baptist Ch—*church* ... IN-6
Golden Rule Department Store—*hist pl* ... SD-7
Golden Rule Mine—*mine* (2) ... AZ-5
Golden Rule Mine—*mine* (2) ... CA-9
Golden Rule Peak—*summit* ... AZ-5
Golden Rule Placer Mine—*mine* ... ID-8
Golden Rule Sch—*school* ... IL-6
Golden Rule Sch—*school* ... KS-7
Golden Rule Sch—*school* ... TX-5
Golden Rule Sch—*school* ... WI-6
*Golden Run* ... VA-3
Golden Run—*stream* ... PA-2
Golden Rush Lake—*lake* ... ND-7
Golden Russian Lake—*lake* ... CA-9
**Goldens Bridge**—*pop pl* ... NY-2
Golden Scepter Mine—*mine* ... CA-9
Golden Sch—*school* ... AR-4
Golden Sch—*school* ... IL-6
Golden Sch—*school* ... MA-1
Golden Sch—*school* ... MI-6
Golden Sch—*school* ... NE-7
Golden Sch—*school* ... TN-4
Goldens Creek—*stream* ... GA-3
Goldens Creek—*stream* ... KY-4
Goldens Creek Sch—*school* ... KY-4
Golden Seal Mine—*mine* ... CA-9
Golden Sheaf Bakery—*hist pl* ... CA-9
**Golden Shores**—*pop pl* ... FL-3
Golden Siren Mine—*mine* ... CA-9
Golden (Site)—*locale* ... AK-9
Goldens Landing (historical)—*locale* ... MS-4
*Golden Slipper Mine* ... SD-7
Golden Slipper Mine—*mine* ... CO-8
Golden Slipper Mine—*mine* ... SD-7
Golden Slipper Mine (historical)—*mine* ... SD-7
Golden Slipper Sch—*school* ... FL-3
Goldens Mtn—*summit* ... KY-4
Golden Spike Monmt—*park* ... UT-8
Golden Spike Natl Historic Site—*park* ... UT-8
Golden Spike Oil Field—*oilfield* ... CO-8
Goldens Point Ch—*church* ... IL-6
Goldens Pond—*reservoir* ... GA-3
**Golden Springs**—*pop pl* ... AL-4
Golden Springs—*spring* ... AL-4
Golden Springs Baptist Ch—*church* ... AL-4
Golden Springs Community Center—*building* ... AL-4
Golden Springs Sch—*school* ... AL-4
Golden Springs Sch—*school* ... CA-9
Golden Springs Shop Ctr—*locale* ... AL-4
**Golden Spur**—*pop pl* ... CT-1
Golden Stair Creek—*stream* ... NY-2
Golden Stair Mtn—*summit* ... NY-2
Golden Stairs—*locale* ... MT-8
Golden Stairs, The—*trail* ... UT-8
Golden Stairs Canyon—*valley* ... UT-8
Golden Stairs Trail—*trail* ... CA-9
Golden Stairs Trail—*trail* ... OR-9
Golden Stairway Trail—*trail* ... NM-5
Golden Stairway Trail—*trail* ... WA-9
Golden Standard Sch—*school* ... NE-7
Golden Star Mine—*mine* ... AZ-5
Golden Star Mine—*mine* ... ID-8
**Golden Star Plantation**—*pop pl* ... LA-4
Golden State Christian Acad—*school* ... FL-3
Golden State Island—*island* ... CA-9
Golden State Sch—*school* ... CA-9
Golden Streak Mine—*mine* ... CA-9
Golden Stream Fishing Club—*locale* ... AL-4
Golden Stream Lake Dam—*dam* ... AL-4
Golden Sucker Gulch—*valley* ... MT-8
Golden Sugar Mine—*mine* ... CA-9
Golden Summit Mine—*mine* ... SD-7
Golden Sunset Mine—*mine* ... MT-8
Golden Sunset Mine—*mine* ... UT-8
Golden Sun Tunnel—*mine* ... CO-8
Golden Tee Country Club—*other* ... MN-6
**Goldenthal**—*pop pl* ... WI-6
Goldenthal—*uninc pl* ... WI-6
Golden Thicket (historical)—*area* ... DE-2
Golden Throne—*summit* ... UT-8
Golden Town Hall—*building* ... ND-7
**Golden Township**—*pop pl* ... NE-7
**Golden Township**—*pop pl* ... ND-7
Golden Township (historical)—*civil* ... SD-7
**Golden (Township of)**—*pop pl* ... MI-6
Golden Treasure—*mine* ... UT-8
Golden Treasure Mine—*mine* ... AZ-5
Golden Treasure Mine—*mine* ... CA-9
Golden Trend Oil Field—*oilfield* ... OK-5
Golden Triangle—*locale* ... PA-2
Golden Triangle Industrial Park—*locale* ... MS-4
Golden Triangle Regional Airp—*airport* ... MS-4
Golden Triangle Regional Med Ctr—*hospital* ... MS-4
Golden Triangle Shop Ctr—*locale* ... FL-3
Golden Triangle Shop Ctr—*locale* ... PA-2
Golden Triangle Vocational Technical Sch—*school* ... MS-4
*Golden Triangle Vocational Training Center* ... MS-4
Golden Trout Camp—*locale* ... CA-9
*Golden Trout Creek* ... CA-9
Golden Trout Creek—*stream* ... CA-9
Golden Trout Crossing—*locale* ... CA-9
Golden Trout Lake—*lake* (2) ... CA-9
Golden Trout Lake—*lake* ... ID-8
Golden Trout Lakes—*lake* ... MT-8
Golden Turkey Mine—*mine* ... AZ-5
Goldenvale Creek—*stream* ... VA-3
**Golden Valley**—*pop pl* ... MN-6
**Golden Valley**—*pop pl* ... ND-7
Golden Valley—*post sta* ... CA-9
Golden Valley—*valley* ... NV-8
Golden Valley—*valley* ... OR-9
Golden Valley—*valley* (2) ... WI-6
Golden Valley Cem—*cemetery* ... MN-6
Golden Valley Cem—*cemetery* ... OK-5
Golden Valley Ch—*church* ... KS-7
Golden Valley Ch—*church* ... NC-3
Golden Valley Ch—*church* ... ND-7
Golden Valley Ch—*church* ... SD-7
Golden Valley Coll—*school* ... MN-6
Golden Valley Country Club—*other* ... MN-6
Golden Valley County—*civil* ... ND-7
Golden Valley County Courthouse—*hist pl* ... ND-7
Golden Valley HS—*school* ... MN-6
Golden Valley JHS—*school* ... CA-9
Golden Valley Norwegian Lutheran Church—*hist pl* ... SD-7
Golden Valley Ranch—*locale* ... NH-1
Golden Valley Sch—*school* ... IL-6
Golden Valley Sch—*school* (2) ... MT-8
**Golden Valley Township**—*pop pl* ... ND-7
Golden Valley (Township of)—*civ div* ... MN-6
Golden Valley (Township of)—*fmr MCD* ... NC-3
**Golden View Subdivision**—*pop pl* ... UT-8
**Goldenville**—*pop pl* ... PA-2
Golden Wash—*stream* ... NV-8
Golden Wedge Mine (abandoned)—*mine* ... OR-9
Golden West Cem—*cemetery* ... MT-8
Golden West Cemetery—*hist pl* ... MS-4
Golden West Ch—*church* ... MT-8
**Golden West Estates (subdivision)**—*pop pl* (2) ... AZ-5
Golden West Mine—*mine* ... MT-8
Golden West Mine—*mine* ... OR-9
Golden West Mine—*mine* ... SD-7
Golden West Sch—*school* ... CA-9
**Golden West Subdivision**—*pop pl* ... UT-8
**Golden West Villa Subdivision**—*pop pl* ... UT-8
Golden Willows Sch—*school* ... WI-6
Golden Windmill—*locale* ... NM-5
Golden Window Sch—*school* ... FL-3
Golden Wonder Mine—*mine* ... AZ-5
Golden Wonder Mine—*mine* (2) ... CO-8
**Golden Wood Estates Subdivision**—*pop pl* ... UT-8
Golden Zone Mine—*mine* ... AK-9
Golden Zone Mine—*mine* ... WA-9
Golder Cem—*cemetery* ... ME-1
Golder Dam—*dam* ... AZ-5
Goldern Cove—*stream* ... MA-1
*Golders Creek* ... VA-3
Golders Point—*cape* ... NJ-2
*Goldfield* ... MS-4
Goldfield—*locale* ... AZ-5
**Goldfield**—*pop pl* ... CO-8
**Goldfield**—*pop pl* ... IA-7
**Goldfield**—*pop pl* ... MS-4
**Goldfield**—*pop pl* ... NV-8
Goldfield Airp—*airport* ... NV-8
Goldfield Branch—*stream* ... AL-4
Goldfield City Hall and Fire Station—*hist pl* ... CO-8
Goldfield Hills—*summit* ... NV-8
Goldfield Hist Dist—*hist pl* ... NV-8
Goldfield (historical)—*locale* ... SD-7
Goldfield Mill—*locale* ... WA-9
Goldfield Mine—*mine* ... AZ-5
Goldfield Mine Water Tower—*tower* ... AZ-5
*Gold Field Mountains* ... AZ-5
Goldfield Mountains—*summit* ... AZ-5
Goldfield Plantation—*locale* ... MS-4
Goldfield Post Office (historical)—*building* ... MS-4
*Goldfield Substation* ... AZ-5
Goldfield Summit—*summit* ... NV-8
Goldfield Switching Substation—*locale* ... AZ-5
**Goldfield Township**—*pop pl* ... ND-7
**Goldfinch**—*pop pl* ... TX-5
Goldfinch Mine (active)—*mine* ... MT-8
Goldfinch Towhead (historical)—*island* ... ND-7
Goldfish Campground—*locale* ... CA-9
Goldfish Creek—*stream* ... FL-3
Gold Fish Group Mine—*mine* ... SD-7
Goldfish Lake—*lake* ... AK-9
Goldfish Point—*cape* ... CA-9
Goldfish Pond—*lake* ... MA-1
Goldfish Pond—*lake* ... NY-2
Goldfish Tank—*reservoir* ... AZ-5
Gold Flat—*flat* (2) ... CA-9
Gold Flat—*flat* ... NV-8
**Gold Flat**—*pop pl* ... CA-9
Gold Flat Well Number One—*well* ... NV-8
Gold Flat Well Number Two (historical)—*well* ... NV-8
Goldflint Mtn—*summit* ... MT-8
Gold Fork—*stream* ... AK-9
Gold Fork—*stream* ... ID-8
*Gold Fork Canal* ... ID-8
Gold Fork Canal—*canal* ... ID-8
Gold Fork Hot Spring—*spring* ... ID-8
Gold Fork Lookout—*locale* ... ID-8
Gold Fork Meadow—*flat* ... ID-8
Gold Fork River—*stream* ... ID-8
Gold Fork Rock—*pillar* ... ID-8
Gold Fork Trail—*trail* ... ID-8
Gold Fund Mine—*mine* ... NV-8
Gold Granite Lake—*lake* ... CA-9
**Gold Gulch**—*pop pl* ... CA-9
Gold Gulch—*stream* ... OR-9
Gold Gulch—*valley* (2) ... AK-9
Gold Gulch—*valley* (8) ... AZ-5
Gold Gulch—*valley* ... CA-9
Gold Gulch—*valley* ... ID-8
Gold Gulch—*valley* ... MT-8
Gold Gulch—*valley* (2) ... NM-5
Gold Gulch—*valley* (2) ... UT-8
Gold Gulch Corral—*locale* ... AZ-5
Gold Gulch Dam—*dam* ... AZ-5
Goldhammer Cem—*cemetery* ... NE-7
Goldhammer Mine—*mine* ... CA-9
Gold Harbor—*bay* ... AK-9
Gold Head Branch—*stream* ... FL-3
Gold Head Branch State Park—*park* ... FL-3
*Goldhill* ... AL-4
Gold Hill—*locale* (2) ... CA-9
Gold Hill—*locale* (2) ... NC-3
**Gold Hill**—*pop pl* ... AL-4
**Gold Hill**—*pop pl* ... CO-8
**Gold Hill**—*pop pl* ... NV-8
**Gold Hill**—*pop pl* ... NC-3
**Gold Hill**—*pop pl* ... OR-9
**Gold Hill**—*pop pl* ... UT-8
**Gold Hill**—*pop pl* ... VA-3
Gold Hill—*ridge* ... NV-8
Gold Hill—*summit* (4) ... AK-9
Gold Hill—*summit* (6) ... AZ-5
Gold Hill—*summit* (5) ... CA-9
Gold Hill—*summit* (3) ... CO-8
Gold Hill—*summit* (7) ... ID-8
Gold Hill—*summit* ... IL-6

Goose Lake Branch Canal—*canal* WI-6
Goose Lake Canal—*canal* CA-9
*Goose Lake Creek* ID-8
Goose Lake Drain—*canal* MI-6
Goose Lake Flats—*flat* MS-4
Goose Lake (historical)—*lake* (2) IA-7
Goose Lake (historical)—*lake* MS-4
Goose Lake (historical)—*lake* (2) MO-7
Goose Lake (Lower)—*reservoir* UT-8
Goose Lake Lower Dam—*dam* UT-8
Goose Lake Outlet—*stream* MI-6
Goose Lake Prairie State Park—*park* IL-6
Goose Lake Quarry—*other* IA-7
Goose Lake Ranch—*locale* CA-9
Goose Lake Ridge—*ridge* NM-5
Goose Lakes—*lake* AR-4
Goose Lakes—*lake* UT-8
Goose Lakes—*lake* VA-3
Goose Lake Sch—*school* IL-6
Goose Lake Slough—*stream* CA-9
**Goose Lake (sta.)**—*pop pl* IL-6
Goose Lake State Preserve—*park* IA-7
Goose Lake State Public Shooting Area—*park* SD-7
Goose Lake State Wildlife Area—*park* IA-7
Goose Lakes (Upper)—*reservoir* UT-8
Goose Lake Swamp—*swamp* MN-6
**Goose Lake Township**—*pop pl* SD-7
**Goose Lake (Township of)**—*pop pl* IL-6
Goose Lake Trail—*trail* OR-9
Goose Landing—*locale* NV-8
Goose Ledge—*bar* ME-1
Goose Marsh—*swamp* AK-9
Goose Marsh—*swamp* ME-1
Goose Marsh—*swamp* MI-6
Goose Marsh Pond—*lake* ME-1
Goose Mtn—*summit* CA-9
Goose Neck—*bend* TN-4
Goose Neck—*bend* UT-8
Goose Neck—*cape* MO-7
Goose Neck—*cape* NY-2
Goose Neck—*locale* GA-3
Gooseneck—*locale* NC-3
Gooseneck—*locale* TN-4
Gooseneck—*locale* WA-9
**Gooseneck**—*pop pl* TN-4
*Gooseneck, The* UT-8
Gooseneck, The—*bend* AZ-5
Gooseneck, The—*bend* OR-9
Gooseneck, The—*bend* PA-2
Gooseneck, The—*bend* TN-4
Gooseneck, The—*ridge* WA-9
Goose Neck Bend—*bend* AL-4
Goose Neck Bend—*bend* OK-5
Gooseneck Bend—*bend* OK-5
Gooseneck Bend—*bend* TX-5
Gooseneck Bend—*bend* WV-2
*Gooseneck Boat Access* UT-8
*Goose Neck Boat Camp* UT-8
Gooseneck Boat Camp—*locale* UT-8
Gooseneck Branch—*stream* AL-4
Gooseneck Branch—*stream* (2) KY-4
Gooseneck Branch—*stream* MO-7
Gooseneck Branch—*stream* NC-3
Gooseneck Bridge—*bridge* TX-5
Gooseneck Cave—*cave* TN-4
Goose Neck Cem—*cemetery* OK-5
Gooseneck Cem—*cemetery* TX-5
Goose Neck Cove—*bay* RI-1
Gooseneck Cove Campground—*locale* CA-9
Gooseneck Creek—*stream* MI-6
Gooseneck Creek—*stream* NY-2
Gooseneck Creek—*stream* OR-9
Goose Neck Dam—*dam* VA-3
Gooseneck Flat—*flat* CA-9
Gooseneck Glacier—*glacier* AK-9
Gooseneck Glacier—*glacier* WY-8
Gooseneck Harbor—*bay* AK-9
Gooseneck Hill—*summit* NM-5
Gooseneck Hollow—*valley* GA-3
Gooseneck Hollow—*valley* MO-7
Gooseneck Hollow—*valley* (2) TN-4
Gooseneck Island—*island* ME-1
*Gooseneck Island Shoals* NY-2
Goose Neck Islands Shoals—*bar* NY-2
Gooseneck Lake—*lake* AK-9
Gooseneck Lake—*lake* FL-3
Gooseneck Lake—*lake* ID-8
Gooseneck Lake—*lake* IN-6
Gooseneck Lake—*lake* (2) MI-6
Gooseneck Lake—*lake* NY-2
Goose Neck Lake—*lake* OK-5
Gooseneck Lake—*lake* WI-6
Gooseneck Pass—*channel* FL-3
Gooseneck Pinnacle—*pillar* WY-8
*Gooseneck Point* UT-8
Gooseneck Point—*cape* AK-9
Gooseneck Point—*cape* CA-9
Gooseneck Point—*cape* NJ-2
Gooseneck Point—*cape* UT-8
Gooseneck Pond—*lake* (2) MI-6
Gooseneck Pond—*lake* NY-2
Gooseneck Ridge—*ridge* UT-8
Gooseneck River Access—*locale* MO-7
Gooseneck River Campground—*park* MO-7
Gooseneck Rock—*pillar* TN-4
Gooseneck Run—*stream* WV-2
*Goosenecks* UT-8
Goosenecks—*bend* UT-8
Goosenecks, The—*bend* UT-8
Gooseneck School (abandoned)—*locale* OR-9
Goose Neck Shoals—*rapids* TN-4
Goosenecks of San Juan Campground—*locale* UT-8
*Goosenecks of the San Juan, The* UT-8
*Goosenecks of the San Juan river* UT-8
Goosenecks of the San Juan River State Park—*park* UT-8
Goosenecks Overlook—*locale* UT-8
*Goosenecks State Park* UT-8
Goosenecks State Park—*park* UT-8
**Gooseneck Township**—*pop pl* ND-7
Goose Neck Trick Tank—*reservoir* AZ-5
Goose Nest—*basin* UT-8
Goose Nest—*island* ME-1
Goose Nest—*locale* WV-2
Goosenest—*summit* CA-9
Goose Nest—*summit* OR-9
*Goosenest Butte* CA-9
Goosenest Canyon—*valley* UT-8
*Goose Nest Creek* NC-3
Goosenest Hollow—*valley* TN-4
Goose Nest Ledge—*bar* ME-1
*Goosenest Mtn* CA-9
*Goose Nest Mtn* OR-9
Goosenest Run—*stream* WV-2
Goose Nest (Township of)—*fmr MCD* NC-3
Goosenest Trail—*trail* CA-9
Goosen Sch—*school* MN-6
Goose Point—*cape* OR-9
Goose Pan Slough—*lake* ND-7
Goose Pasture—*flat* FL-3
Goose Pasture—*flat* ID-8
Goose Pasture—*swamp* CO-8
Goose Pasture Draw—*valley* SD-7
Goose Pasture Lake—*lake* IL-6
Goose Pasture Tarn—*reservoir* CO-8
Goose Pen—*gut* TN-4
Goosepen Run—*stream* WV-2
**Goose Pimple Junction**—*pop pl* VA-3
Goose Platter Creek—*stream* SC-3
Goose Pocket—*bay* TN-4
*Goose Point* DE-2
Goose Point—*cape* (2) AK-9
Goose Point—*cape* (2) DE-2
Goose Point—*cape* FL-3
Goose Point—*cape* LA-4
Goose Point—*cape* ME-1
Goose Point—*cape* (5) MD-2
Goose Point—*cape* MA-1
Goose Point—*cape* MN-6
Goose Point—*cape* MS-4
Goose Point—*cape* NY-2
Goose Point—*cape* NC-3
Goose Point—*cape* OR-9
Goose Point—*cape* RI-1
Goose Point—*cape* UT-8
Goose Point—*cape* VT-1
Goose Point—*cape* (2) VA-3
Goose Point—*cape* (2) WA-9
Goose Point—*locale* DE-2
Goose Point Channel—*channel* MA-1
Goose Point Marsh—*swamp* MD-2
*Goose Pond* AL-4
*Goose Pond* ME-1
Goose Pond—*bay* MD-2
Goose Pond—*bay* WI-6
Goose Pond—*lake* (4) AL-4
Goose Pond—*lake* (5) AR-4
Goose Pond—*lake* (2) DE-2
Goose Pond—*lake* (5) FL-3
Goose Pond—*lake* GA-3
Goose Pond—*lake* (3) IL-6
Goose Pond—*lake* (7) IN-6
Goose Pond—*lake* IA-7
Goose Pond—*lake* (2) KY-4
Goose Pond—*lake* (2) LA-4
Goose Pond—*lake* (6) ME-1
Goose Pond—*lake* (2) MD-2
Goose Pond—*lake* (5) MA-1
Goose Pond—*lake* (2) MI-6
Goose Pond—*lake* (3) MS-4
Goose Pond—*lake* (2) MO-7
Goose Pond—*lake* (3) NH-1
Goose Pond—*lake* (4) NJ-2
Goose Pond—*lake* (6) NY-2
Goose Pond—*lake* NC-3
Goose Pond—*lake* (3) PA-2
Goose Pond—*lake* (3) SC-3
Goose Pond—*lake* (5) TN-4
Goose Pond—*lake* VT-1
Goose Pond—*lake* VA-3
Goose Pond—*lake* WA-9
Goose Pond—*lake* (2) WI-6
**Goose Pond**—*pop pl* NC-3
Goose Pond—*reservoir* MD-2
Goose Pond—*reservoir* MA-1
Goose Pond—*reservoir* NH-1
Goose Pond—*reservoir* VA-3
Goose Pond—*swamp* AL-4
Goose Pond—*swamp* (2) AR-4
Goose Pond—*swamp* (2) FL-3
Goose Pond—*swamp* (2) GA-3
Goose Pond—*swamp* IL-6
Goose Pond—*swamp* IN-6
Goose Pond—*swamp* NH-1
Goose Pond—*swamp* (2) NC-3
*Goose Pond Baptist Church* MS-4
Goose Pond Bayou—*gut* LA-4
Goose Pond Bayou—*stream* LA-4
*Goose Pond Branch* AL-4
Goose Pond Branch—*stream* AL-4
Goose Pond Branch—*stream* TN-4
*Goose Pond Brook* MA-1
Goose Pond Brook—*stream* MA-1
Goose Pond Brook—*stream* NH-1
Goose Pond Brook—*stream* NY-2
Goose Pond Ch—*church* AL-4
Goose Pond Colony Park—*park* AL-4
Goose Pond Creek—*stream* AL-4
Goosepond Creek—*stream* GA-3
Goose Pond Creek—*stream* MS-4
Goose Pond Crossroads—*locale* AL-4
*Goosepond Cumberland Presbyterian Church* AL-4
Goose Pond Dam—*dam* MA-1
*Goose Pond Ditch* IN-6
Goose Pond Ditch—*canal* IN-6
Goose Pond Ditch—*canal* KY-4
Goose Pond Ditch—*canal* MO-7
Goose Pond Drain—*canal* MI-6
Goose Pond Heath—*swamp* ME-1
Goose Pond Hill—*summit* NY-2
Goose Pond Hills—*other* MO-7
Goose Pond (historical)—*lake* AL-4
Goose Pond (historical)—*lake* IN-6
Goose Pond (historical)—*lake* IA-7
**Goose Pond (historical)**—*pop pl* MS-4
Goose Pond Island—*island* AL-4
Goose Pond Island—*island* NC-3
Goose Pond Landing—*locale* NC-3
*Goosepond Methodist Ch* TN-4
Goose Pond Methodist Ch—*church* TN-4
Goosepond Mtn—*summit* AR-4
Goose Pond Mtn—*summit* ME-1
Goose Pond Mtn—*summit* NY-2
*Goose Pond Run* PA-2
Goose Pond Run—*stream* PA-2
Goose Pond Run Dam—*dam* PA-2
Goose Pond Scatters—*swamp* IL-6
*Goosepond Sch* TN-4
Goose Pond Sch—*school* TN-4
*Goose Pond Scool* MS-4
Goose Pond Slough—*stream* AR-4
Goose Pond Slough (inundated)—*gut* AL-4
*Goose Pond Stream* MA-1
Goose Pond Swamp—*swamp* IL-6
Goose Pond Swamp—*swamp* IN-6
Goose Pond Swamp—*swamp* TN-4
Goose Pond Swamp (historical)—*swamp* TN-4
Goose Pool—*reservoir* WI-6
**Gooseport**—*pop pl* IN-6
Goose Prairie—*bay* TX-5
Goose Prairie—*flat* TX-5
Goose Prairie—*flat* WA-9
**Gooseprairie**—*pop pl* WA-9
**Goose Prairie (Gooseprairie PO)**—*pop pl* WA-9
Goose Prairie State Wildlife Mngmt Area—*park* MN-6
Goose Prairie (Township of)—*civ div* MN-6
Goose Prairie Trail—*trail* WA-9
Goosepuddle Pond—*lake* NY-2
Goose Ranch—*locale* OR-9
Goose Ranch Slough—*stream* OR-9
Goose Ridge—*ridge* ID-8
Goose Ridge—*ridge* ME-1
*Goose River* ND-7
Goose River—*stream* (3) ME-1
Goose River—*stream* ND-7
Goose River Bank—*hist pl* ND-7
Goose River Ch—*church* ND-7
*Goose Rock* ME-1
Goose Rock—*bar* ME-1
Goose Rock—*bar* NH-1
Goose Rock—*cliff* OR-9
Goose Rock—*island* (4) ME-1
Goose Rock—*locale* KY-4
Goose Rock—*pillar* MT-8
Goose Rock—*pillar* TX-5
Goose Rock—*pillar* WY-8
Goose Rock—*summit* IA-7
Goose Rock—*summit* WA-9
*Goose Rock Bay* ME-1
*Goose Rock Beach* ME-1
Goose Rock Flat—*flat* MT-8
Goose Rock Ledge—*bar* ME-1
Goose Rock Passage—*channel* ME-1
Goose Rocks—*bar* AK-9
Goose Rocks—*island* CT-1
Goose Rocks—*locale* ME-1
Goose Rocks Beach—*beach* ME-1
**Goose Rocks Beach**—*pop pl* ME-1
Gooserock Sch—*school* KY-4
Goose Rocks Creek—*stream* ME-1
Goose Rocks Light Station—*hist pl* ME-1
Goose Rsvr—*reservoir* OR-9
*Goose Run* OH-6
Goose Run—*stream* (2) IL-6
Goose Run—*stream* (4) IN-6
Goose Run—*stream* IA-7
Goose Run—*stream* (7) OH-6
Goose Run—*stream* (2) PA-2
Goose Run—*stream* VA-3
Goose Run—*stream* (5) WV-2
Goose Run Ch—*church* WV-2
Goose Run Creek—*stream* GA-3
*Goose Ry Creek* ID-8
Goose Shoals—*bar* AL-4
Goose Shoals Bridge—*bridge* AL-4
Goose Shoals Ford—*locale* AL-4
Goose Slough—*gut* AK-9
Goose Slough—*gut* IL-6
*Goose Spit* WA-9
Goose Spring—*spring* AZ-5
Goose Spring—*spring* NV-8
Goose Spring—*spring* OR-9
Goose Springs—*spring* NV-8
Goose Swale—*valley* OR-9
Goosetail Rock—*summit* WA-9
Goose Tongue Island—*island* AK-9
Goosetown—*locale* PA-2
**Goosetown**—*pop pl* TN-4
Goosetown Ridge—*ridge* (2) IN-6
Goosetree—*locale* NY-2
Goose Valley—*valley* (2) CA-9
Goose Valley—*valley* NE-7
Goose Valley Ranch—*locale* CA-9
Goose Valley Ranger Station—*locale* CA-9
Goose Valley Sch—*school* NE-7
Gooseville—*locale* WI-6
Gooseville Corners—*locale* NY-2
Gooseville Creek—*stream* WI-6
Gooseville Mill/Grist Mill—*hist pl* WI-6
Goose Windmill—*locale* TX-5
*Goose Wing Beach* RI-1
Goosewing Creek—*stream* WY-8
Goosewing Guard Station—*locale* WY-8
Goosey Fork—*stream* KY-4
Goosey Lake Creek—*stream* NV-8
Goosey Lake Flat—*flat* NV-8
Gooseys Landing—*locale* MS-4
*Gooskee Prairie* FL-3
*Gooskie Prairie* FL-3
Gooski Prairie—*swamp* FL-3
*Goosky Prairie* FL-3
Goosmus Creek—*stream* WA-9
**Goosport**—*pop pl* LA-4
Goosport Park—*park* LA-4
Goostaa—*bay* FM-9
Goostree Lake—*reservoir* IL-6
*Gootch Mill* MO-7
*Gootchs Mill* MO-7
*Gooto* MP-9
*Gopher* KS-7
Gopher—*locale* IA-7
**Gopher**—*pop pl* OR-9
Gopher Branch—*stream* SC-3
Gopher Canyon—*valley* CA-9
Gopher Canyon—*valley* ID-8
Gopher Cave—*cave* AL-4
Gopher Creek—*stream* (2) CA-9
Gopher Creek—*stream* CO-8
Gopher Creek—*stream* FL-3
Gopher Creek—*stream* NV-8
Gopher Creek—*stream* OR-9
Gopher Creek—*stream* TX-5
Gopher Den Hollow—*valley* KY-4
Gopher Gulch—*valley* AK-9
Gopher Gulch—*valley* (2) CA-9
Gopher Gulch—*valley* CO-8
Gopher Gulch Airstrip—*airport* OR-9
Gopher Gully—*stream* FL-3
Gopher Hill—*locale* AL-4
Gopher Hill—*summit* (2) CA-9
Gopher Hill—*summit* MT-8
Gopher Hill—*summit* WI-6
Gopher Hill Cem—*cemetery* IN-6
*Gopher Hill Fire Tower* AL-4
Gopher Hill Mine—*mine* CA-9
Gopher Hills Sch—*school* IL-6
Gopher Island—*island* FL-3
Gopher Island—*island* MS-4
Gopher Key—*island* (2) FL-3
Gopher Key Bay—*bay* FL-3
Gopher Key Creek—*gut* FL-3
Gopher Keys—*island* FL-3
Gopher Knoll—*summit* ID-8
*Gopher Lake* MI-6
Gopher Lake—*lake* MI-6
Gopher Lake—*reservoir* MO-7
Gopher Lake—*swamp* MI-6
Gopher Landing (historical)—*locale* AL-4
Gopher Lope—*locale* GA-3
*Gopher Mine* SD-7
Gopher Mine—*mine* CA-9
Gopher Mine—*mine* OR-9
Gopher Mountian—*summit* WA-9
Gopher Pumping Station—*locale* WY-8
Gopher Ridge—*locale* FL-3
Gopher Ridge—*ridge* AL-4
Gopher Ridge—*ridge* (2) CA-9
Gopher Ridge—*ridge* (2) FL-3
Gopher Ridge—*ridge* OR-9
Gopher Ridge Tower—*tower* FL-3
Gopher River—*stream* FL-3
Gopher Rsvr—*reservoir* CO-8
Gopher Sch—*school* SD-7
Gopher Sch Number 4—*school* ND-7
Gopher Slough—*gut* FL-3
Gopher Spring—*spring* (2) AZ-5
Gopher Spring—*spring* OR-9
*Gopher Station* KS-7
Gopher Swamp—*swamp* FL-3
Gopher Tail Lake—*lake* ND-7
Gopher Tank—*reservoir* AZ-5
Gopher Tank—*reservoir* NM-5
Gopher Valley—*valley* OR-9
Gophner Ravine—*valley* CA-9
Goplin Ridge—*ridge* WI-6
Goqchol—*locale* FM-9
*Goragel* PW-9
*Goragel Island* PW-9
*Gorak* PW-9
*Gorakbald Passage* PW-9
*Gorakibad Einfahrt* PW-9
*Gorak Island* PW-9
*Goraklbad* PW-9
Goraklbad Passage—*channel* PW-9
*Goraklbad Reef* PW-9
*Goraku* PW-9
*Goraku To* PW-9
Goram—*locale* PA-2
**Goram**—*pop pl* PA-2
*Gorangiday* PW-9
*Goran Pond* PA-2
Goray Spring—*spring* AL-4
Gorbetts Ch—*church* IN-6
Gorbon Canyon—*valley* NM-5
Gorbon Well—*well* NM-5
*Gorbs Branch* IN-6
Gorbutt Lake—*lake* WI-6
Gorbutt Pond—*reservoir* GA-3
Gorby—*locale* AR-4
Gorby Opera Theater—*hist pl* ID-8
Gorby Run—*stream* PA-2
Gorby Run—*stream* WV-2
Gorcum Ch—*church* WI-6
Gorda—*locale* CA-9
Gordan Cem—*cemetery* MS-4
Gordan Cem—*cemetery* MO-7
Gordan Chapel—*church* LA-4
*Gordan Hills* IN-6
Gordan Hunter Dam—*dam* TN-4
Gordan Hunter Lake—*reservoir* TN-4
Gordan Peak—*summit* OR-9
Gordan Peak Trail—*trail* OR-9
*Gordans Point* ME-1
Gordans Pond—*reservoir* AL-4
Gorda Rock—*island* CA-9
*Gorday* GA-3
**Gorday**—*pop pl* GA-3
*Gorday Station* GA-3
Gordear Ditch—*canal* LA-4
Gorden Cem—*cemetery* GA-3
Gorden Cem—*cemetery* MO-7
Gorden Chapel Ch—*church* MS-4
*Gordens Butte* MT-8
Gorden Sch—*school* MN-6
**Gorder**—*pop pl* UT-8
Gorder Creek—*stream* UT-8
Gorder Lake—*lake* MN-6
Gordey Creek—*stream* OR-9
Gordie Branch—*stream* LA-4
*Gordilsau* PW-9
Gordner Cem—*cemetery* PA-2
**Gordo**—*pop pl* AL-4
Gordo, Cerro—*summit* OR-9
Gordo (CCD)—*cens area* AL-4
Gordo Ch of God of Prophecy—*church* AL-4
Gordo City Cem—*cemetery* AL-4
Gordo Division—*civil* AL-4
Gordo Elem Sch—*school* AL-4
Gordo HS—*school* AL-4
Gordola—*locale* CA-9
*Gordon* IA-7
*Gordon* ND-7
*Gordon* PA-2
Gordon—*locale* CA-9
Gordon—*locale* CO-8
Gordon—*locale* KY-4
Gordon—*locale* LA-4
Gordon—*locale* MI-6
Gordon—*locale* MS-4
Gordon—*locale* MT-8
Gordon—*locale* TX-5
Gordon—*locale* WA-9
**Gordon**—*pop pl* AL-4
**Gordon**—*pop pl* FL-3
**Gordon**—*pop pl* GA-3
**Gordon**—*pop pl* IL-6
**Gordon**—*pop pl* KS-7
**Gordon**—*pop pl* (2) LA-4
**Gordon**—*pop pl* NE-7
**Gordon**—*pop pl* OH-6
**Gordon**—*pop pl* PA-2
**Gordon**—*pop pl* TN-4
**Gordon**—*pop pl* TX-5
**Gordon**—*pop pl* WV-2
**Gordon**—*pop pl* WI-6
Gordon, Cornelia, House—*hist pl* KY-4
Gordon, David, House and Collins Log Cabin—*hist pl* MO-7
Gordon, Jervis, Grist Mill Hist Dist—*hist pl* PA-2
Gordon, J. M., House—*hist pl* DE-2
Gordon, John, House—*hist pl* TN-4
Gordon, Lake—*lake* (2) FL-3
Gordon, Lake—*lake* MI-6
Gordon, Lake—*lake* WI-6
Gordon, Lake—*reservoir* PA-2
Gordon, Lake—*reservoir* VA-3
Gordon, Mount—*summit* AK-9
Gordon, Mount Lyon—*summit* AK-9
Gordon, Troy, House—*hist pl* AR-4
Gordon (Aban'd)—*locale* AK-9
Gordon Acad—*school* LA-4
Gordon Airp—*airport* GA-3
Gordon Airp—*airport* IN-6
Gordon Arroyo—*stream* CO-8
Gordon Ave Apartments—*hist pl* GA-3
Gordon Ave Hist Dist—*hist pl* GA-3
Gordon Babcock Dam—*dam* SD-7
Gordon-Banks House—*hist pl* GA-3
Gordon Bar—*bar* AL-4
**Gordon Beach**—*pop pl* MI-6
Gordon Bend Ch—*church* AL-4
Gordon Bibb Sch—*school* AL-4
Gordon Bldg—*hist pl* CA-9
Gordon Borough—*civil* PA-2
*Gordon Branch* TN-4
Gordon Branch—*stream* AL-4
Gordon Branch—*stream* DE-2
Gordon Branch—*stream* (2) MS-4
Gordon Branch—*stream* MO-7
Gordon Branch—*stream* (4) TN-4
Gordon Branch—*stream* TX-5
Gordon Brook—*stream* (3) ME-1
Gordon Brook—*stream* NY-2
Gordon Butte—*summit* MT-8
Gordon Butte—*summit* (3) OR-9
Gordon Butte Trail—*trail* OR-9
Gordon Camp—*locale* AZ-5
Gordon Camp—*locale* PA-2
Gordon Canyon—*valley* (2) AZ-5
Gordon Canyon—*valley* (3) CA-9
Gordon Canyon—*valley* NM-5
Gordon Canyon—*valley* OR-9
Gordon Canyon—*valley* SD-7
Gordon Canyon Creek—*stream* AZ-5
Gordon Canyon Ranch—*locale* AZ-5
Gordon Canyon Spring—*spring* AZ-5
Gordon (CCD)—*cens area* AL-4
Gordon (CCD)—*cens area* (2) GA-3
*Gordon Cem* MO-7
Gordon Cem—*cemetery* (3) AL-4
Gordon Cem—*cemetery* FL-3
Gordon Cem—*cemetery* GA-3
Gordon Cem—*cemetery* IL-6
Gordon Cem—*cemetery* IN-6
Gordon Cem—*cemetery* IA-7
Gordon Cem—*cemetery* (2) ME-1
Gordon Cem—*cemetery* (5) MS-4
Gordon Cem—*cemetery* (2) MO-7
Gordon Cem—*cemetery* NE-7
Gordon Cem—*cemetery* OH-6
Gordon Cem—*cemetery* PA-2
Gordon Cem—*cemetery* (2) TN-4
Gordon Cem—*cemetery* VA-3
Gordon Cem—*cemetery* WI-6
Gordon-Center House—*hist pl* VT-1
Gordon Ch—*church* GA-3
Gordon Ch—*church* MN-6
Gordon Ch—*church* NC-3
Gordon Ch—*church* WV-2
Gordon Chapel—*church* FL-3
Gordon Chapel—*church* (3) GA-3
Gordon Chapel—*church* OH-6
Gordon Chapel—*church* WV-2
**Gordon Chapel**—*pop pl* FL-3
Gordon Chapel Ch—*church* FL-3
Gordon Coll—*school* MA-1
Gordon-Conwell Theological Seminary—*facility* MA-1
Gordon Corner—*locale* ME-1
Gordon Corner—*locale* VA-3
**Gordon (County)**—*pop pl* GA-3
*Gordon Creek* CA-9
*Gordon Creek* GA-3
*Gordon Creek* NV-8
**Gordon Creek**—*pop pl* UT-8
Gordon Creek—*stream* (3) CA-9
Gordon Creek—*stream* (5) CO-8
Gordon Creek—*stream* ID-8
Gordon Creek—*stream* KS-7
Gordon Creek—*stream* (2) MI-6
Gordon Creek—*stream* (3) MS-4
Gordon Creek—*stream* MO-7
Gordon Creek—*stream* (2) MT-8
Gordon Creek—*stream* NE-7
Gordon Creek—*stream* (2) NV-8
Gordon Creek—*stream* NY-2
Gordon Creek—*stream* (2) OH-6
Gordon Creek—*stream* (5) OR-9
Gordon Creek—*stream* PA-2
Gordon Creek—*stream* TX-5
Gordon Creek—*stream* (2) UT-8
Gordon Creek—*stream* VA-3
Gordon Creek—*stream* WA-9
Gordon Creek—*stream* WI-6
Gordon Creek—*stream* WY-8
Gordon Creek Fire Guard—*locale* NV-8
Gordon Creek Station—*locale* UT-8
Gordon Creek Wildlife Mngmt Area—*park* UT-8
Gordon Crossing—*locale* VA-3
Gordon Crowell Memorial Hosp—*hospital* NC-3
Gordon Dam—*dam* MA-1
Gordon Dam—*dam* UT-8
*Gordon Ditch* IN-6
Gordon Ditch—*canal* (2) IN-6
Gordon Division—*civil* AL-4
Gordon Drain—*canal* MI-6
*Gordon Falls* OR-9
Gordon Falls—*falls* ME-1
Gordon Falls—*falls* NH-1
Gordon Farm—*locale* WA-9
*Gordon Ferry* IA-7
Gordon Ferry Bridge—*bridge* TN-4
Gordon Flats—*flat* UT-8
Gordon Flats Airp—*airport* UT-8
Gordon Flowage Campground—*locale* WI-6
Gordon Ford—*locale* KY-4
Gordon Ford—*other* MO-7
Gordon Gap—*gap* TX-5
Gordon Gordons Lake—*reservoir* TN-4
Gordon Gordons Lake Dam—*dam* TN-4
**Gordon (Gordonsville)**—*pop pl* MN-6
Gordon Grove Ch—*church* (2) GA-3
Gordon Gulch—*valley* (2) CA-9
Gordon Gulch—*valley* (2) CO-8
Gordon Gulch—*valley* MT-8
Gordon Gulch—*valley* OR-9
Gordon Gulch—*valley* SD-7
Gordon Hall—*hist pl* MI-6
**Gordon Heights**—*pop pl* AL-4
**Gordon Heights**—*pop pl* DE-2
**Gordon Heights**—*pop pl* NY-2
Gordon Heights Ch—*church* GA-3
Gordon Hill—*summit* CA-9
Gordon Hill—*summit* KY-4
Gordon Hill—*summit* ME-1
Gordon Hill—*summit* NH-1
Gordon Hill—*summit* (2) TN-4
Gordon Hill Ch—*church* GA-3
Gordon Hill Road Hist Dist—*hist pl* KY-4
Gordon Hills—*range* IN-6
Gordon Hills—*ridge* CA-9
Gordon (historical)—*locale* ME-1
*Gordon Hollow* OR-9
Gordon Hollow—*valley* AR-4
Gordon Hollow—*valley* KY-4
Gordon Hollow—*valley* (3) MO-7
Gordon Hollow—*valley* OR-9
Gordon Hollow—*valley* (3) TN-4
Gordon Hotel—*hist pl* LA-4
Gordon House—*hist pl* MT-8
Gordon House—*hist pl* SD-7
Gordon HS—*school* SC-3
Gordonia Alatamaha State Park—*park* GA-3
Gordonier Sch—*school* MI-6
*Gordon Island* NH-1
Gordon Island—*island* (2) ME-1
Gordon Island—*island* VA-3
Gordon JHS—*school* DC-2
Gordon Junction—*locale* TX-5
Gordon Junior Coll—*school* GA-3
*Gordon Lake* DE-2
Gordon Lake—*lake* AR-4
Gordon Lake—*lake* (2) CA-9
Gordon Lake—*lake* (2) MI-6
Gordon Lake—*lake* MN-6
Gordon Lake—*lake* (2) ND-7
Gordon Lake—*lake* (2) TX-5
Gordon Lake—*lake* WA-9
Gordon Lake—*lake* (2) WI-6
Gordon Lake—*reservoir* CO-8
Gordon Lake—*reservoir* GA-3
Gordon Lake—*reservoir* OR-9
Gordon Lake—*reservoir* (2) TX-5
Gordon Lake Dam—*dam* MS-4
Gordon Lakes—*lake* (2) OR-9
**Gordon Lakes**—*pop pl* NJ-2
Gordon Lakes—*reservoir* NJ-2
Gordon Lakes Dam—*dam* NJ-2
Gordon Landing—*locale* AL-4
Gordon Landing—*locale* VT-1
Gordon-Lee House—*hist pl* GA-3
Gordon Lee Sch—*school* GA-3
Gordon Lick Knob—*summit* KY-4
Gordon (Magisterial District)—*fmr MCD* VA-3
Gordon Meadow—*flat* CA-9
Gordon Meadows—*flat* OR-9
Gordon Mill (historical)—*locale* MS-4
Gordon Mine—*mine* (2) CO-8
Gordon Mountain, Cerro—*summit* AZ-5
Gordon MS—*school* PA-2
Gordon Mtn—*summit* CA-9
Gordon Mtn—*summit* (2) MT-8
Gordon Mtn—*summit* (2) NC-3
Gordon Mtn—*summit* OK-5
Gordon Mtn—*summit* (2) TX-5
Gordon-Nash Library—*hist pl* NH-1
Gordon Oil and Gas Field—*oilfield* LA-4
Gordon Oil Field—*oilfield* TX-5
Gordon Park—*park* (2) OH-6
Gordon Park—*park* WI-6
Gordon Pass—*channel* FL-3
Gordon Pass—*gap* MT-8
Gordon Payne Site (31MR15)—*hist pl* NC-3
*Gordon Peak* OR-9
Gordon Point—*cape* ME-1
Gordon Point—*cape* MD-2
Gordon Point—*cape* UT-8
Gordon Point—*cape* WA-9
Gordon Point—*summit* CA-9
*Gordon Pond* CT-1
*Gordon Pond* VA-3
Gordon Pond—*lake* FL-3
Gordon Pond—*lake* GA-3
Gordon Pond—*lake* ME-1
Gordon Pond—*lake* (2) NH-1
Gordon Pond—*reservoir* AZ-5
Gordon Pond—*reservoir* GA-3
Gordon Pond—*reservoir* NJ-2
Gordon Pond—*swamp* DE-2
Gordon Pond Brook—*stream* NH-1
Gordon Pond Trail—*trail* NH-1
Gordon Pond Wildlife Area—*park* DE-2
*Gordon Post Office* MS-4
Gordon Post Office—*building* AL-4
Gordon Post Office (historical)—*building* SD-7
Gordon Ranch—*locale* MT-8
Gordon Ranch—*locale* UT-8
Gordon Ranch—*locale* WY-8
Gordon Ridge—*ridge* (2) CA-9
Gordon Ridge—*ridge* NH-1
Gordon Ridge—*ridge* OR-9
Gordon Ridge—*ridge* WA-9
Gordon Ridge Sch (historical)—*school* MS-4
Gordon River—*stream* FL-3
**Gordon Road**—*pop pl* GA-3

Gordon Road Ch—*church* GA-3
Gordon Rock—*rock* MA-1
Gordon Rsvr—*reservoir* CO-8
Gordon Rsvr—*reservoir* PA-2
Gordon Rsvr—*reservoir* UT-8
Gordon Run—*stream* OH-6
Gordon Run—*stream* PA-2
*Gordons* IL-6
*Gordon's* IA-7
**Gordons**—*pop pl* IL-6
Gordons Branch—*stream* WV-2
Gordons Bridge—*bridge* SC-3
Gordons Brook—*stream* NY-2
Gordonsburg—*locale* TN-4
Gordonsburg Cem—*cemetery* TN-4
Gordonsburg Ch of Christ—*church* TN-4
Gordonsburg Post Office (historical)—*building* TN-4
Gordons Cabin—*locale* CA-9
Gordons Camp—*locale* WY-8
Gordons Ch—*church* SC-3
Gordon Sch—*school* (2) CA-9
Gordon Sch—*school* CO-8
Gordon Sch—*school* GA-3
Gordon Sch—*school* LA-4
Gordon Sch—*school* (3) MI-6
Gordon Sch—*school* MS-4
Gordon Sch—*school* (4) MO-7
Gordon Sch—*school* MT-8
Gordon Sch—*school* NY-2
Gordon Sch—*school* (2) OH-6
Gordon Sch—*school* PA-2
Gordon Sch—*school* SC-3
Gordon Sch—*school* SD-7
Gordon Sch—*school* TN-4
Gordon Sch—*school* TX-5
Gordon Sch—*school* WI-6
Gordon Sch (abandoned)—*school* PA-2
Gordons Chapel—*church* AR-4
Gordons Chapel—*church* GA-3
Gordon-Schaust Site—*hist pl* MN-6
Gordon Sch (historical)—*school* MO-7
*Gordon School* AL-4
Gordons Corner—*locale* NJ-2
**Gordons Corner**—*pop pl* MD-2
Gordon's Corner (alternate name: Gordons Corner)—*CDP* NJ-2
Gordons Cowcamp—*locale* WY-8
*Gordons Creek* MI-6
Gordons Creek—*stream* MN-6
Gordons Creek—*stream* MS-4
Gordons Creek—*stream* NY-2
Gordons Dam—*dam* AL-4
Gordons Ferry—*locale* IA-7
Gordons Ferry (Site)—*locale* CA-9
Gordons Hill—*summit* NH-1
Gordons Peak—*summit* VA-3
*Gordons Point* ME-1
Gordon Spring—*spring* AL-4
Gordon Spring—*spring* AZ-5
Gordon Spring—*spring* GA-3
Gordon Spring—*spring* OR-9
Gordon Spring—*spring* TN-4
Gordon Spring—*spring* UT-8
Gordon Spring Creek—*stream* GA-3
**Gordon Springs**—*pop pl* GA-3
Gordon Square Bldg—*hist pl* OH-6
Gordons Run—*stream* VA-3
**Gordons South Lawn Addition (subdivision)**—*pop pl* UT-8
*Gordon Station Post* MS-4
**Gordonston**—*pop pl* GA-3
Gordon Street Ch—*church* GA-3
*Gordonsville* PA-2
Gordonsville—*locale* AL-4
**Gordonsville**—*pop pl* KY-4
**Gordonsville**—*pop pl* MN-6
**Gordonsville**—*pop pl* TN-4
**Gordonsville**—*pop pl* VA-3
Gordonsville, Lake—*reservoir* VA-3
Gordonsville Cem—*cemetery* TN-4
*Gordonsville Center Church* AL-4
Gordonsville Ch—*church* VA-3
Gordonsville First Baptist Ch—*church* TN-4
Gordonsville Hist Dist—*hist pl* VA-3
Gordonsville HS—*school* TN-4
Gordonsville Post Office—*building* TN-4
Gordons Well—*locale* CA-9
Gordon Tank—*reservoir* AZ-5
Gordon Tank—*reservoir* (2) NM-5
Gordon Tank—*reservoir* TX-5
Gordon Technical HS—*school* IL-6
*Gordonton* NC-3
Gordonton—*locale* NC-3
**Gordontown**—*pop pl* NC-3
**Gordon (Town of)**—*pop pl* (2) WI-6
**Gordon Township**—*pop pl* ND-7
**Gordon (Township of)**—*pop pl* MN-6
Gordon Tract Archeol Site—*hist pl* MO-7
Gordon Tri-County Ditch—*canal* OH-6
Gordon Valley—*valley* (2) CA-9
Gordon Valley Ch—*church* NE-7
Gordon Valley Creek—*stream* CA-9
Gordon Valley Dam—*dam* CA-9
Gordon Valley Ranch—*locale* NE-7
Gordon Valley Sch—*school* CA-9
*Gordonville* MS-4
Gordonville—*locale* MI-6
Gordonville—*locale* SC-3
**Gordonville**—*pop pl* FL-3
**Gordonville**—*pop pl* KY-4
**Gordonville**—*pop pl* MO-7
**Gordonville**—*pop pl* PA-2
**Gordonville**—*pop pl* TX-5
Gordonville Ch—*church* NC-3
Gordonville Post Office (historical)—*building* PA-2
Gordonville Sch (abandoned)—*school* MO-7
Gordon Well—*well* CA-9
Gordo Post Office—*building* AL-4
Gordo Public Library—*building* AL-4
Gordo Tank—*reservoir* AZ-5
Gordo Tank—*reservoir* NM-5
Gordy—*locale* GA-3
Gordy—*locale* LA-4
Gordy Branch—*stream* MS-4
Gordy Cem—*cemetery* GA-3
**Gordy Estates**—*pop pl* DE-2
Gordy Grove Ch—*church* GA-3
Gordy Lake—*lake* IN-6
Gordy Marsh—*swamp* TX-5
Gordy Memorial Gardens—*cemetery* GA-3
Gordy Mill Creek—*stream* AL-4
Gordy Park—*park* KS-7
Gordy Pond—*reservoir* GA-3
Gordy Ranch—*locale* ID-8
Gordys Branch—*stream* MD-2
Gordys Cove—*bay* NV-8
*Gordys Fork* PA-2
*Gordys Landing* AL-4
*Gordys Millpond* VA-3
Gordys Pond—*reservoir* GA-3
Gore—*locale* CO-8
Gore—*locale* GA-3
Gore—*locale* MO-7
**Gore**—*pop pl* OH-6
**Gore**—*pop pl* OK-5
**Gore**—*pop pl* VA-3
**Gore**—*pop pl* WV-2
Gore, Lake—*lake* FL-3
*Gore, The* NY-2
Gore, The—*summit* VT-1
Goreau, Bayou—*gut* LA-4
Gore Branch—*stream* FL-3
Gore Branch—*stream* NH-1
Gore Branch—*stream* NC-3
Gore Brook—*stream* MA-1
Gore Canyon—*valley* CO-8
Gore Canyon—*valley* NM-5
Gore Cem—*cemetery* AL-4
Gore Cem—*cemetery* KY-4
Gore Cem—*cemetery* MA-1
Gore Cem—*cemetery* MI-6
Gore Cem—*cemetery* MO-7
Gore Cem—*cemetery* NC-3
Gore Cem—*cemetery* OK-5
Gore Cem—*cemetery* (2) TN-4
Gore Cem—*cemetery* TX-5
Gore Cem—*cemetery* (2) VT-1
Gore Cem—*cemetery* WV-2
Gore Chapel—*church* NC-3
Gore Creek—*stream* (2) CO-8
Gore Creek—*stream* NC-3
Gore Creek—*stream* OR-9
Gore Creek Campground—*locale* CO-8
Gore Creek Spring—*spring* CO-8
Goreczky, Anton, House—*hist pl* ID-8
Gore Draft—*valley* PA-2
**Goree**—*pop pl* AL-4
**Goree**—*pop pl* TX-5
Goree (CCD)—*cens area* TX-5
Goree Cem—*cemetery* TX-5
Goree Coal Bed Branch—*stream* AL-4
Goree Coalbed Number 1 Mine (underground)—*mine* AL-4
Goree Drift Mine (underground)—*mine* AL-4
Goree Mill (historical)—*locale* AL-4
Goree Oil Field—*oilfield* TX-5
Goree State Prison Farm—*other* TX-5
Gore Fork—*stream* WV-2
Gore Gulch—*valley* ID-8
Gore Hill—*summit* MT-8
Gore Lake—*lake* CO-8
Gore Lake—*lake* FL-3
Gore Lake—*lake* MN-6
Gore Lake—*lake* NC-3
Gore Lake—*lake* TX-5
Gore Lake—*reservoir* NC-3
Gore Landing—*locale* OK-5
Gore Landing—*locale* TX-5
Gore (Magisterial District)—*fmr MCD* WV-2
Gore Mtn—*summit* CO-8
Gore Mtn—*summit* NH-1
Gore Mtn—*summit* NY-2
Gore Mtn—*summit* TX-5
Gore Mtn—*summit* VT-1
Gorenflo Elem Sch—*school* MS-4
Gore Notch—*gap* NH-1
Gore Oil Field—*oilfield* (2) TX-5
*Goreor* PW-9
Gore Park—*park* HI-9
Gore Park—*park* OK-5
Gore Pass—*gap* CO-8
Gore Peak—*summit* AK-9
Gore Pit District—*hist pl* OK-5
Gore Place—*building* MA-1
Gore Place—*hist pl* MA-1
Gore Point—*cape* AK-9
*Gore Pond* MA-1
Gore Pond—*lake* MA-1
Gore Pond Dam—*dam* MA-1
Gore Range—*range* CO-8
Gore Range Overlook—*locale* CO-8
Gore Range Trail—*trail* CO-8
Gore Rapids—*rapids* ME-1
Gore Rock—*bar* AK-9
Gores Branch—*stream* AL-4
Gore Sch—*school* GA-3
Gore Sch—*school* IL-6
Gore Sch—*school* NH-1
Gore Sch—*school* OK-5
Gore Sch—*school* OR-9
Gores Landing—*locale* FL-3
Gores Landing—*locale* NC-3
Gores Mill—*locale* MD-2
Gores Peak—*summit* AR-4
Gore Spring Ch—*church* GA-3
**Gore Springs**—*pop pl* MS-4
Gore Springs Baptist Ch—*church* MS-4
Gore Springs Cem—*cemetery* MS-4
Gore Springs HS—*school* MS-4
Gores Spring Ch—*church* MS-4
Gore Stump Knob—*summit* KY-4
Gore Towhead—*flat* TN-4
Gore Towhead Bar—*bar* TN-4
*Gore Town* SC-3
**Goretown**—*pop pl* SC-3
**Gore Township**—*pop pl* KS-7
**Gore (Township of)**—*pop pl* MI-6
Gore Trail—*trail* VT-1
**Goreville**—*pop pl* IL-6
Goreville No. 1 (Election Precinct)—*fmr MCD* IL-6
Goreville No. 2 (Election Precinct)—*fmr MCD* IL-6
Gorfinkle Camp—*locale* ME-1
**Gorgas**—*pop pl* (2) AL-4
Gorgas Bridge—*bridge* AL-4
Gorgas Cem—*cemetery* MO-7
Gorgas Elem Sch—*school* AL-4
*Gorgas HS* AL-4
Gorgas-Manly Hist Dist—*hist pl* AL-4
Gorgas Mine (surface)—*mine* AL-4
Gorgas Mine (underground)—*mine* AL-4
Gorgas Park—*park* AL-4
Gorgas Park—*park* (2) PA-2
Gorgas Post Office (historical)—*building* AL-4
Gorgas Power Plant—*building* AL-4
Gorgas Sch—*school* (3) AL-4
Gorgas Sch (historical)—*school* AL-4
Gorge, The—*channel* AK-9
Gorge, The—*channel* CA-9
Gorge, The—*channel* MN-6
Gorge, The—*cliff* ME-1
Gorge, The—*gap* VA-3
Gorge, The—*valley* AL-4
Gorge, The—*valley* (2) AK-9
Gorge, The—*valley* AZ-5
Gorge, The—*valley* AR-4
Gorge, The—*valley* (2) CA-9
Gorge, The—*valley* GA-3
Gorge, The—*valley* (3) MA-1
Gorge, The—*valley* NM-5
Gorge, The—*valley* NY-2
Gorge, The—*valley* UT-8
Gorge, The—*valley* VA-3
Gorge, The—*valley* WA-9
Gorge Brook—*stream* NH-1
Gorge Brook Trail—*trail* NH-1
Gorge Camp—*locale* OR-9
Gorge Camp—*locale* WA-9
Gorge Canyon—*valley* (2) UT-8
*Gorge Creek* AR-4
*Gorge Creek* MT-8
Gorge Creek—*stream* (2) AK-9
Gorge Creek—*stream* CA-9
Gorge Creek—*stream* (4) MT-8
Gorge Creek—*stream* OR-9
Gorge Creek—*stream* UT-8
Gorge Creek—*stream* WA-9
Gorge Dam—*dam* WA-9
Gorge Draw—*valley* UT-8
Gorge Falls—*falls* MI-6
Gorge Forest Camp—*locale* OR-9
Gorge Gulch—*valley* ID-8
Gorge Gulch—*valley* NV-8
Gorge Hills—*range* CO-8
Gorge Lake—*lake* WY-8
Gorge Lake—*reservoir* WA-9
Gorge Lakes—*lake* CO-8
Gorge Lakes—*lake* MT-8
Gorge Metropolitan Park—*park* OH-6
Gorge of Despair—*valley* CA-9
Gorge Powerhouse—*other* WA-9
Gorges, The—*valley* NC-3
Gorge Spring—*spring* UT-8
Gorginski Creek—*stream* MI-6
*Gorgora Hill* TX-5
*Gorgorza* UT-8
Gorgosa—*locale* UT-8
**Gorham**—*pop pl* IL-6
**Gorham**—*pop pl* KS-7
**Gorham**—*pop pl* ME-1
**Gorham**—*pop pl* NH-1
**Gorham**—*pop pl* NY-2
**Gorham**—*pop pl* ND-7
Gorham Bridge—*bridge* VT-1
Gorham Brook—*stream* NH-1
Gorham Butte—*summit* OR-9
Gorham Campus Hist Dist—*hist pl* ME-1
Gorham Cem—*cemetery* KS-7
Gorham Cem—*cemetery* MO-7
Gorham Center (census name Gorham)—*other* ME-1
**Gorham Compact (census name Gorham)**—*pop pl* NH-1
Gorham Covered Bridge—*hist pl* VT-1
Gorham Dam Number 2—*dam* MA-1
Gorham Farm Pond—*reservoir* RI-1
Gorham Farm Pond Dam—*dam* RI-1
Gorham Gore—*unorg* ME-1
Gorham Gulch—*valley* OR-9
Gorham House—*hist pl* NY-2
Gorham HS—*school* KS-7
Gorham Island—*island* CT-1
Gorham Lodge—*building* VT-1
Gorham Mtn—*summit* ME-1
Gorham Oil Field—*oilfield* KS-7
Gorham Park—*park* MT-8
Gorham Playground—*park* MI-6
Gorham Pond—*lake* NH-1
Gorham Raceway—*other* ME-1
Gorham Sch—*school* IL-6
Gorham Sch—*school* NC-3
Gorham Sch—*school* ND-7
Gorham Sch Number 4—*school* ND-7
Gorhams Pond—*lake* CT-1
**Gorham Spur**—*pop pl* MN-6
Gorham Swamp—*stream* NC-3
Gorham Swamp Ch—*church* NC-3
Gorhamtown—*locale* VT-1
**Gorhamtown**—*pop pl* LA-4
Gorham Town Farm—*locale* ME-1
**Gorham (Town of)**—*pop pl* ME-1
**Gorham (Town of)**—*pop pl* NH-1
**Gorham (Town of)**—*pop pl* NY-2
**Gorham (Township of)**—*pop pl* OH-6
Gorilla Spring—*spring* NM-5
Gorilon Sch—*school* MI-6
*Goring Ditch* IN-6
Goring Pond—*lake* UT-8
Goring Post Office (historical)—*building* AL-4
Gorin Park—*park* KY-4
**Gorin (South Gorin)**—*pop pl* MO-7
Gorinth Ch—*church* NC-3
Gori Point—*cape* AK-9
Goris Gulch—*valley* MT-8
*Goritoru Mountain* PW-9
Gorke Drain—*canal* MI-6
Gorley Creek—*stream* ID-8
Gorley Lake—*lake* AK-9
Gorley Ranch—*locale* NE-7
Gorley Ridge—*ridge* IN-6
*Gorleys Lake* PA-2
Gorlock Bldg—*hist pl* MO-7
Gorma Mine—*mine* CO-8
*Gorman* TN-4
Gorman—*locale* IL-6
Gorman—*locale* SD-7
**Gorman**—*pop pl* CA-9
**Gorman**—*pop pl* MD-2
**Gorman**—*pop pl* NC-3
**Gorman**—*pop pl* TN-4
**Gorman**—*pop pl* TX-5
Gorman, Lake—*reservoir* AL-4
*Gorman Branch* TX-5
Gorman Branch—*stream* AR-4
Gorman Branch—*stream* GA-3
Gorman Canyon—*valley* CA-9
Gorman (CCD)—*cens area* TX-5
Gorman Cem—*cemetery* MN-6
Gorman Cem—*cemetery* MS-4
Gorman Cem—*cemetery* MO-7
Gorman Cem—*cemetery* PA-2
Gorman Chapel—*church* AR-4
Gorman Coulee—*valley* MT-8
Gorman Creek—*stream* CA-9
Gorman Creek—*stream* ID-8
Gorman Creek—*stream* LA-4
Gorman Creek—*stream* MN-6
Gorman Creek—*stream* (2) MT-8
Gorman Creek—*stream* OR-9
Gorman Creek—*stream* TX-5
Gorman Creek Siphon—*canal* CA-9
Gorman Dam—*dam* SD-7
Gorman Draft—*valley* PA-2
Gorman Draw—*valley* TX-5
Gorman Falls—*falls* TX-5
Gorman Gulch—*valley* SD-7
Gorman Hill—*summit* ID-8
Gorman Hill—*summit* NV-8
**Gorman (historical)**—*pop pl* OR-9
**Gormania**—*pop pl* WV-2
Gormania Branch—*stream* PA-2
Gorman Lake—*lake* MI-6
Gorman Lake—*lake* MN-6
Gorman Lake—*lake* MS-4
Gorman Lake—*reservoir* MN-6
Gorman Lakes—*lake* MI-6
Gorman Memorial Ch of the Nazarene—*church* FL-3
Gorman Park—*park* MN-6
Gorman Pit—*mine* CA-9
Gorman Post Office (historical)—*building* TN-4
Gorman Ranch—*locale* CA-9
Gormans Branch—*stream* MS-4
Gorman Sch—*school* CA-9
Gorman Sch—*school* IL-6
Gorman Sch—*school* MN-6
Gorman Sch—*school* OH-6
Gorman Sch (historical)—*school* PA-2
Gorman School—*locale* IL-6
*Gormans Depot* TN-4
*Gormans Depot Post Office* TN-4
*Gormans Eddy* TN-4
Gorman Spring—*spring* (2) TX-5
Gorman Strait—*channel* AK-9
Gorman Summit—*locale* PA-2
Gorman Summit—*summit* PA-2
**Gorman (Township of)**—*pop pl* MN-6
*Gormely Lake* WI-6
**Gormer**—*pop pl* MI-6
Gormer Canyon—*valley* ID-8
Gormer Sch—*school* MI-6
Gormley—*locale* WV-2
Gormley Branch—*stream* GA-3
Gormley Ridge—*ridge* AL-4
Gormleys Stock Yard Post Office (historical)—*building* TN-4
Gormons Trading Post—*locale* AZ-5
Gornik Ranch—*locale* WY-8
Gornoi Island—*island* AK-9
Gorn Sch—*school* KY-4
Gornto Cem—*cemetery* GA-3
Gornto Lake—*lake* FL-3
*Gorokblbad Durchfahrt* PW-9
*Gorokottan* PW-9
*Gorokottan Island* PW-9
*Gorokottan To* PW-9
**Gorom**—*pop pl* CO-8
*Goror* FM-9
*Goror* PW-9
*Gororu* FM-9
*Gororuro To* PW-9
Gorow—*summit* FM-9
*Gorra Island* MP-9
Gorrel Lake—*lake* MI-6
Gorrell Cem—*cemetery* IN-6
Gorrell Cem—*cemetery* OH-6
Gorrell Run—*stream* WV-2
Gorrell Run Ch—*church* WV-2
Gorrell Sch—*school* OH-6
*Gorrells Run* WV-2
Gorres Lake—*lake* WI-6
Gorret Rock—*island* VI-3
Gorrie JHS—*school* FL-3
Gorrie Sch—*school* FL-3
Gorrilla Creek—*stream* UT-8
Gorrindo Ranch—*locale* CA-9
Gorr Island—*island* OR-9
Gorr Lake—*lake* MI-6
*Gorror* FM-9
*Gorrur* FM-9
Gorsett Farmstead—*hist pl* SD-7
Gorsich Sch (abandoned)—*school* PA-2
Gorson Dam—*dam* PA-2
**Gorst**—*pop pl* WA-9
Gorst Creek—*stream* WA-9
Gorst Creek Pump Plant—*other* WA-9
Gorsuch—*other* PA-2
Gorsuch, Ernest J., House—*hist pl* OH-6
Gorsuch Cem—*cemetery* OH-6
Gorsuch Creek—*stream* ID-8
Gortemoller Cem—*cemetery* FL-3
*Gorten Chute* LA-4
**Gorthey Corners**—*pop pl* NY-2
Gort Knob—*summit* TN-4
**Gortner**—*pop pl* MD-2
Gorton—*locale* PA-2
Gorton, Caleb, House—*hist pl* RI-1
Gorton, William, Farm—*hist pl* CT-1
Gorton Brook—*stream* NY-2
Gorton Cem—*cemetery* IN-6
Gorton Cem—*cemetery* NY-2
Gorton Chute—*lake* LA-4
Gorton Creek—*stream* AK-9
Gorton Creek—*stream* NY-2
Gorton Creek—*stream* OR-9
Gorton Dam—*dam* AZ-5
*Gorton Heights* PA-2
Gorton Hill—*summit* NY-2
Gorton Lake—*lake* NY-2
Gorton Memorial Ch—*church* IN-6
Gorton Pond—*lake* NY-2
Gorton Pond—*lake* RI-1
Gorton Pond—*reservoir* CT-1
Gorton Pond—*reservoir* RI-1
Gorton Pond Dam—*dam* RI-1
Gorton Sch—*school* IL-6
Gortons Corner—*locale* RI-1
*Gortons Pond* RI-1
**Gorton (Township of)**—*pop pl* MN-6
**Gorum**—*pop pl* LA-4
Gorum, Bayou—*gut* LA-4
Gorum Cem—*cemetery* LA-4
Gorus—*locale* MT-8
Gorus Gulch—*valley* MT-8
*Gorwuied* PW-9
Gory Brook—*stream* NY-2
Gory Creek—*stream* MT-8
Gosa—*locale* AL-4
Gosage Creek—*stream* OR-9
*Gosak Island* PW-9
Gosby Cem—*cemetery* VA-3
Gosby House Inn—*hist pl* CA-9
Gosch Athletic Field—*park* TX-5
Gosche Hollow—*valley* KY-4
Goschke Dam—*dam* ND-7
*Gosch School* IN-6
Gosch Spring—*spring* CA-9
*Gose* KS-7
**Gose**—*pop pl* WA-9
Gose Branch—*stream* (2) KY-4
Gose Branch—*stream* VA-3
Gose Cem—*cemetery* TN-4
Gose Cem—*cemetery* (3) VA-3
Gose Ch—*church* VA-3
Gose Creek—*stream* IN-6
Gosee Swamp—*stream* VA-3
*Gosegasu Island* PW-9
*Gosegosu* PW-9
Gose Hollow—*valley* VA-3
Gose Knob—*summit* VA-3
Gose Mill—*locale* VA-3
Gosen Ch—*church* MN-6
Gosen Lake—*lake* MN-6
Gose Oil Field—*oilfield* TX-5
Goses Landing—*locale* TN-4
Gosey Cem—*cemetery* TN-4
Gosey Hill—*summit* TN-4
Gosey Well—*well* NM-5
Gosford—*locale* CA-9
**Gosford**—*pop pl* PA-2
Gosha Creek—*stream* AR-4
Goshawk Dam—*dam* CO-8
*Goshen* IN-6
*Goshen* NH-1
*Goshen* NJ-2
Goshen—*locale* GA-3
Goshen—*locale* KY-4
Goshen—*locale* MD-2
Goshen—*locale* MO-7
Goshen—*locale* NC-3
Goshen—*locale* OH-6
Goshen—*locale* PA-2
Goshen—*locale* SC-3
Goshen—*locale* TN-4
Goshen—*locale* TX-5
Goshen—*locale* WA-9
**Goshen**—*pop pl* AL-4
**Goshen**—*pop pl* AR-4
**Goshen**—*pop pl* CA-9
**Goshen**—*pop pl* CT-1
**Goshen**—*pop pl* ID-8
**Goshen**—*pop pl* (2) IN-6
**Goshen**—*pop pl* MA-1
**Goshen**—*pop pl* MS-4
**Goshen**—*pop pl* NH-1
**Goshen**—*pop pl* NJ-2
**Goshen**—*pop pl* NY-2
**Goshen**—*pop pl* (2) NC-3
**Goshen**—*pop pl* OH-6
**Goshen**—*pop pl* OR-9
**Goshen**—*pop pl* PA-2
**Goshen**—*pop pl* TX-5
**Goshen**—*pop pl* UT-8
**Goshen**—*pop pl* (2) VT-1
**Goshen**—*pop pl* VA-3
**Goshen**—*pop pl* WV-2
Goshen Annex Training Sch—*school* NY-2
Goshen Baptist Ch (historical)—*church* TN-4
Goshen Bayou—*stream* MS-4
*Goshen Branch* GA-3
Goshen Branch—*stream* (2) GA-3
Goshen Branch—*stream* MD-2
Goshen Branch—*stream* MS-4
Goshen Branch—*stream* (2) NC-3
Goshen Branch—*stream* VA-3
*Goshen Bridge* VA-3
Goshen Brook—*stream* CT-1
Goshen Brook—*stream* (2) VT-1
Goshen Canyon—*valley* UT-8
Goshen Carnegie Public Library—*hist pl* IN-6
Goshen Cave—*cave* AL-4
Goshen (CCD)—*cens area* KY-4
Goshen Cem—*cemetery* (2) AL-4
Goshen Cem—*cemetery* (2) CT-1
Goshen Cem—*cemetery* (2) KY-4
Goshen Cem—*cemetery* MA-1
Goshen Cem—*cemetery* (3) MS-4
Goshen Cem—*cemetery* MO-7
Goshen Cem—*cemetery* (3) TN-4
Goshen Cem—*cemetery* (3) TX-5
Goshen Cem—*cemetery* UT-8
Goshen Cem—*cemetery* VA-3
Goshen Center—*locale* OH-6
Goshen Ch—*church* AL-4
Goshen Ch—*church* CT-1
Goshen Ch—*church* (5) GA-3
Goshen Ch—*church* (2) IN-6
Goshen Ch—*church* IA-7
Goshen Ch—*church* (6) KY-4
Goshen Ch—*church* (3) MS-4
Goshen Ch—*church* (2) MO-7
Goshen Ch—*church* (5) NC-3
Goshen Ch—*church* ND-7
Goshen Ch—*church* (2) OH-6
Goshen Ch—*church* (2) PA-2
Goshen Ch—*church* (5) TN-4
Goshen Ch—*church* (3) VA-3
Goshen Ch—*church* WV-2
Goshen Chapel—*church* IN-6
Goshen Ch (historical)—*church* AL-4
Goshen Christian Sch—*school* NY-2
Goshen Church—*hist pl* VT-1
Goshen Coll—*school* IN-6
*Goshen Corners* VT-1
Goshen Cove—*bay* CT-1
*Goshen Creek* NC-3
*Goshen Creek* WY-8
Goshen Creek—*stream* GA-3
Goshen Creek—*stream* IN-6
Goshen Creek—*stream* NJ-2
Goshen Creek—*stream* OH-6
Goshen Creek—*stream* TN-4
Goshen Creek—*stream* TX-5
Goshen Crossing—*locale* NJ-2
Goshen Cross Road—*locale* VA-3
*Goshen Cumberland Presbyterian Church* TN-4
Goshen Dam—*dam* VT-1
*Goshen Dam Pond* IN-6
Goshen Dam Pond—*reservoir* IN-6
Goshen Ditch—*canal* IA-7
Goshen Division—*civil* UT-8
Goshen Elem Sch—*school* AL-4
Goshen Elem Sch—*school* PA-2
**Goshen Estates**—*pop pl* MD-2
Goshen Four Corners—*locale* VT-1
**Goshen Four Corners**—*pop pl* NH-1
Goshen Gap—*gap* UT-8
Goshen (Goshen Junction)—*CDP* CA-9
Goshen Grange 561 Cem—*cemetery* OR-9
**Goshen Grove**—*pop pl* NC-3
*Goshen Hill* AL-4
**Goshen Hill**—*pop pl* SC-3
Goshen Hill—*summit* CT-1
Goshen Hill—*summit* NC-3
Goshen Hill—*summit* UT-8
Goshen Hill Cem—*cemetery* OH-6
**Goshen Hills**—*pop pl* CT-1
**Goshen Hills**—*pop pl* NY-2
Goshen Hills—*summit* NY-2
Goshen Hist Dist—*hist pl* CT-1
Goshen (historical)—*locale* AL-4
Goshen (historical)—*locale* IA-7
Goshen (historical)—*locale* KS-7
**Goshen (historical)**—*pop pl* MS-4
**Goshen (historical)**—*pop pl* TN-4
Goshen Historic Distriict—*hist pl* IN-6
Goshen Hole—*basin* WY-8
Goshen Hole—*cens area* WY-8
*Goshen Hole Basin* WY-8
Goshen Hole Ditch—*canal* WY-8
*Goshen Hole Lowland* WY-8
Goshen Hole Rim—*cliff* WY-8
Goshen Hole Rsvr—*reservoir* WY-8
Goshen Hollow—*valley* AL-4
Goshen Hollow—*valley* TN-4
Goshen Hollow Cave—*cave* AL-4
Goshenhoppen Creek—*stream* PA-2
Goshen Junction—*locale* ID-8
*Goshen Junction (Goshen)* CA-9
Goshen Lake—*lake* MS-4
Goshen Lampster Sch—*school* NH-1
Goshen Land Company Bridge—*hist pl* VA-3
Goshen Lane Sch—*school* OH-6
Goshen Ledge—*bar* CT-1
*Goshen Methodist Church* MS-4
Goshen Mountain—*ridge* TN-4
Goshen Mtn—*summit* GA-3
Goshen Mtn—*summit* NY-2
Goshen Mtn—*summit* VT-1
Goshen Municipal Airp—*airport* IN-6
Goshen Number Two Rsvr—*reservoir* NY-2
Goshen Pass—*gap* UT-8
Goshen Pass—*gap* VA-3
Goshen Point—*cape* CT-1
Goshen Point—*cape* SC-3
Goshen Pond—*reservoir* IN-6
Goshen Pond Camping Area—*park* NJ-2
Goshen Pond Dam—*dam* IN-6
Goshen Post Office—*building* UT-8
Goshen Post Office (historical)—*building* PA-2
Goshen Post Office (historical)—*building* TN-4
Goshen Primitive Baptist Church—*hist pl* KY-4
Goshen Prong—*stream* TN-4
*Goshen Reservoir* WY-8
Goshen Ridge—*ridge* (2) TN-4
Goshen Ridge—*ridge* WV-2
Goshen Rsvr—*reservoir* NY-2
Goshen Rsvr—*reservoir* UT-8
Goshen Run—*stream* OH-6
Goshen Sch—*school* CA-9
Goshen Sch—*school* (2) IL-6
Goshen Sch—*school* IA-7
Goshen Sch—*school* MO-7
Goshen Sch—*school* NC-3
Goshen Sch—*school* OR-9
Goshen Sch—*school* UT-8
Goshen Sch—*school* WV-2
Goshen Sch (historical)—*school* MS-4
Goshen Sch (historical)—*school* PA-2
Goshen-Shady Grove (CCD)—*cens area* AL-4
Goshen-Shady Grove Division—*civil* AL-4
*Goshen Slope* UT-8
Goshen Springs—*locale* MS-4
Goshen Springs Cem—*cemetery* MS-4
Goshen Springs Pilgrim Branch Cem—*cemetery* MS-4
Goshen Springs Post Office (historical)—*building* MS-4
Goshen Springs Station—*locale* MS-4
Goshen Swamp—*stream* NC-3
Goshen Swamp—*swamp* GA-3
Goshen Swamp—*swamp* NC-3
**Goshen (Town of)**—*pop pl* CT-1
**Goshen (Town of)**—*pop pl* MA-1
**Goshen (Town of)**—*pop pl* NH-1
**Goshen (Town of)**—*pop pl* NY-2
**Goshen (Town of)**—*pop pl* VT-1
Goshen Township—*fmr MCD* IA-7
**Goshen Township**—*pop pl* KS-7
Goshen (Township of)—*fmr MCD* AR-4
**Goshen (Township of)**—*pop pl* IL-6
**Goshen (Township of)**—*pop pl* (7) OH-6
**Goshen (Township of)**—*pop pl* PA-2
Goshen United Methodist Ch—*church* DE-2
*Goshen United Methodist Church* MS-4
Goshen Valley—*valley* TN-4
Goshen Valley—*valley* UT-8

Gourdneck Pit—*cave* TN-4
Gourdneck Sch—*school* IL-6
Gourdneck State Game Area—*park* MI-6
Gourdneck Valley—*valley* AL-4
Gourdshell Ponds—*lake* NY-2
Gourds Point—*cape* VA-3
Gourd Spring—*spring* NV-8
Gourd Springs Ch—*church* NC-3
Gourdsville—*locale* AL-4
Gourdvine Creek—*stream* MS-4
Gourdvine Creek—*stream* NC-3
Gourd Vine Eddy—*rapids* TX-5
*Gourd Wine Creek* NC-3
Gourlay Creek—*stream* OR-9
Gourley—*locale* MI-6
Gourley Dam—*dam* NC-3
Gourley Ford—*locale* TN-4
Gourley Meadows—*flat* WY-8
Gourley Oil Field—*oilfield* TX-5
Gourley Ranch—*locale* MT-8
Gourley Ranch—*locale* TX-5
Gourley Rsvr—*reservoir* CA-9
*Gourleys Bridge* TN-4
Gourleys Bridge Post Office (historical)—*building* TN-4
Gourleys Corners—*locale* PA-2
*Gourleys Land Creek* TN-4
Gourley's Opera House—*hist pl* NE-7
Gourley Spring—*spring* TN-4
**Gourley (Township of)**—*pop pl* MI-6
Gourlie Point—*cape* NY-2
Gourney Lake—*swamp* LA-4
Gouster Cem—*cemetery* OH-6
**Gouverneur**—*pop pl* NY-2
Gouverneur Hosp—*hist pl* NY-2
**Gouverneur (Town of)**—*pop pl* NY-2
Govalle Playground—*park* TX-5
Govalle Sch—*school* TX-5
Govalle Shop Ctr—*locale* TX-5
Govan—*locale* WA-9
**Govan**—*pop pl* SC-3
Govans—*uninc pl* MD-2
Govan Slough—*stream* AR-4
Govans Sch—*school* MD-2
**Govanstown**—*pop pl* MD-2
Govatos'/McVey Bldg—*hist pl* DE-2
Gove—*locale* CO-8
**Gove**—*pop pl* CO-8
**Gove**—*pop pl* KS-7
Gove, The—*swamp* NH-1
*Gove Brook* MA-1
Gove Brook—*stream* (2) NH-1
Gove Cem—*cemetery* KS-7
Gove Cem—*cemetery* ME-1
Gove Cem—*cemetery* NH-1
Gove Cem—*cemetery* NY-2
*Gove City* KS-7
**Gove City**—*pop pl* KS-7
Gove County—*civil* KS-7
Gove Creek—*stream* CO-8
Gove Creek—*stream* KS-7
Gove Elem Sch—*school* KS-7
Gove Hill—*summit* (3) NH-1
Gove Hill—*summit* VT-1
Gove JHS—*school* CO-8
*Gove Lake* MI-6
*Govenors Pond* NH-1
Govenors Punchbowl—*lake* ID-8
Govenor Winslow House—*building* MA-1
Gove Peak—*summit* WA-9
Gove Point—*cape* ME-1
Gover—*locale* TX-5
Gover Branch—*stream* MO-7
Gover Cem—*cemetery* MS-4
Gover (historical)—*locale* SD-7
Goverment Canyon—*valley* CA-9
Goverment Canyon Trail—*trail* CA-9
Goverment Peak—*summit* CA-9
Government—*fmr MCD* NE-7
**Government**—*pop pl* VA-3
Government Bay—*bay* MI-6
Government Bird Rock—*pillar* UT-8
Government Brake—*swamp* MS-4
Government Bridge—*bridge* IA-7
Government Bridge—*bridge* WY-8
Government Cable Office—*hist pl* AK-9
Government Camp—*locale* CA-9
**Government Camp**—*pop pl* OR-9
*Government Canal* WA-9
Government Canyon—*valley* (2) AZ-5
Government Canyon—*valley* CA-9
Government Canyon—*valley* (2) NE-7
Government Canyon—*valley* (4) TX-5
Government Canyon—*valley* (3) UT-8
Government Canyon—*valley* WY-8
Government Canyon Sch—*school* WY-8
Government Canyon Spring—*spring* AZ-5
Government Cem—*cemetery* SC-3
Government Cem—*cemetery* TN-4
Government Corral—*locale* NV-8
Government Corral Creek—*stream* CO-8
Government Corral Spring—*spring* OR-9
Government Coulee—*valley* MT-8
Government Cove—*bay* OR-9
Government Cove—*bay* TX-5
*Government Creek* MT-8
Government Creek—*stream* (3) AK-9
Government Creek—*stream* (2) CO-8
Government Creek—*stream* ID-8
Government Creek—*stream* (4) MT-8
Government Creek—*stream* (2) ND-7
Government Creek—*stream* (3) UT-8
Government Creek—*stream* (2) WY-8
Government Creek Supply Ditch—*canal* CO-8
Government Cut—*channel* FL-3
Government Cut—*gut* FL-3
Government Cypress Slough—*gut* AR-4
Government Dam—*dam* WY-8
Government Dead Lake—*lake* FL-3
Government Ditch—*canal* IN-6
Government Ditch—*canal* LA-4
Government Ditch—*canal* MT-8
Government Ditch—*canal* TX-5
Government Ditch Camp—*locale* WY-8
Government Ditch No. 1—*canal* CO-8
Government Ditch No. 2—*canal* CO-8
Government Draw—*valley* AZ-5
Government Draw—*valley* CO-8
Government Draw—*valley* SD-7
Government Draw—*valley* (2) TX-5
Government Draw—*valley* (3) WY-8
Government Eighteen Oil Field—*oilfield* CA-9
*Government Farm Dam* SD-7
Government Field Rsvr—*reservoir* MT-8
Government Flat—*flat* OR-9
Government Flat—*flat* UT-8
Government Flat—*locale* CA-9
Government Floyd Monument—*other* WV-2
Government Ford (historical)—*locale* SD-7
Government Fork—*stream* ID-8
Government Gap—*gap* WY-8
Government Gulch—*valley* CA-9
Government Gulch—*valley* ID-8
Government Gulch—*valley* OR-9
Government Gulch—*valley* WY-8
Government Gully—*valley* WY-8
Government Harvey Pass—*gap* OR-9
Government Heights Sch—*school* AZ-5
Government Highline Canal—*canal* CO-8
*Government Hi-line Canal* CO-8
*Government Hill* KS-7
*Government Hill* WI-6
**Government Hill**—*pop pl* AZ-5
Government Hill—*summit* (2) AZ-5
Government Hill—*summit* KS-7
Government Hill—*summit* MT-8
Government Hill—*summit* OR-9
Government Hill—*summit* SD-7
Government Hill—*summit* WY-8
Government Hill—*summit* VI-3
Government Hills—*range* MS-4
Government Hole—*reservoir* AZ-5
Government Holes—*locale* CA-9
Government House—*building* GU-9
Government House—*hist pl* AS-9
Government Indian Sch—*hist pl* AK-9
Government Indian Sch (historical)—*school* SD-7
*Government Island* CA-9
Government Island—*cape* MA-1
Government Island—*island* MI-6
Government Island—*island* MT-8
Government Island—*island* OR-9
Government Island—*island* VA-3
Government Island—*island* WI-6
Government Island—*uninc pl* CA-9
Government Knob—*summit* AR-4
*Government Knoll* AZ-5
*Government Knolls* AZ-5
Government Knolls—*summit* AZ-5
*Government Lake* MN-6
Government Lake—*lake* MI-6
Government Lake—*lake* UT-8
Government Light Slough—*stream* WI-6
*Government Low Line Canal* NE-7
Government Meadow—*flat* WA-9
Government Meadows—*flat* WY-8
Government Meadows Draw—*locale* WY-8
Government Meadows Draw—*valley* WY-8
Government Meadows Windmill—*locale* WY-8
Government Mesa—*summit* AZ-5
Government Mill Dam—*dam* MA-1
Government Mineral Springs—*locale* WA-9
Government Mtn—*summit* (2) AZ-5
Government Mtn—*summit* MT-8
Government Mtn—*summit* OR-9
Government Park—*flat* (2) CO-8
Government Park—*flat* UT-8
*Government Parks* UT-8
Government Pass—*gap* UT-8
Government Peak—*summit* AK-9
Government Peak—*summit* AZ-5
Government Peak—*summit* CA-9
Government Peak—*summit* MI-6
Government Peak—*summit* (2) NV-8
Government Peak—*summit* UT-8
Government Peak—*summit* WY-8
Government Pier—*locale* MH-9
Government Point—*cape* CA-9
Government Point—*cape* IN-6
Government Point—*cape* (3) MN-6
Government Point—*cape* OR-9
Government Point—*cape* UT-8
Government Pond—*reservoir* CO-8
Government Prairie—*flat* AZ-5
Government Printing Office—*building* DC-2
Government Rapids—*rapids* UT-8
Government Reservoir—*lake* AZ-5
Government Ridge—*ridge* CA-9
Government Rock—*bar* AK-9
Government Rock—*summit* IL-6
Government Rsvr—*reservoir* CA-9
Government Rsvr—*reservoir* CO-8
Government Rsvr—*reservoir* (2) WY-8
Government Sch—*school* MO-7
Government Slide Draw—*valley* WY-8
Government Slough—*stream* AK-9
Government Slough—*stream* SD-7
Government Slough—*swamp* MN-6
Government Smallwood House—*building* MD-2
Government Spring—*spring* (8) AZ-5
Government Spring—*spring* (4) CA-9
Government Spring—*spring* (2) CO-8
Government Spring—*spring* (4) NV-8
Government Spring—*spring* (4) OR-9
Government Spring—*spring* (3) TX-5
Government Spring—*spring* (2) UT-8
Government Spring—*spring* WA-9
Government Spring—*spring* WY-8
Government Spring Forest Camp—*locale* AZ-5
Government Spring Gulch—*valley* AZ-5
Government Springs—*spring* CA-9
Government Springs—*spring* CO-8
Government Springs—*spring* OK-5
Government Springs—*spring* WA-9
Government Spring Wash—*stream* AZ-5
Government Street Methodist Ch—*church* AL-4
Government Street Presbyterian Ch—*church* AL-4
Government Tank—*reservoir* (7) AZ-5
Government Tank—*reservoir* (6) NM-5
Government Tank—*reservoir* (4) TX-5
*Government Tank Canyon* AZ-5
Government Tank Windmill—*locale* NM-5
*Government Town* MT-8
Government Trail—*trail* UT-8
Government Trail Canyon—*valley* CA-9
Government Trail Canyon—*valley* NV-8
Government Trail Pass—*gap* ID-8
Government Trail Ridge—*ridge* WA-9
Government Trick Tank—*reservoir* AZ-5
Government Valley—*valley* WY-8
Government Valley Sch—*school* WY-8
Government Wash—*stream* AZ-5
Government Wash—*stream* NV-8
Government Water Hole—*lake* NM-5
*Government Well* UT-8
Government Well—*well* (2) AZ-5
Government Well—*well* (3) NV-8
Government Well—*well* OR-9
Government Well—*well* TX-5
Government Well—*well* (2) UT-8
Government Well No 36—*well* UT-8
Government Well No 52—*well* UT-8
Government Well No 82—*well* UT-8
Government Wells Creek—*stream* TX-5
Government Wells Oil Field—*oilfield* TX-5
Government Windmill—*locale* (3) TX-5
Governor—*mine* UT-8
Governor Bacon Health Center—*hospital* DE-2
Governor Basin—*basin* CO-8
Governor Bond Lake—*reservoir* IL-6
Governor Bradleys House (historical)—*locale* NV-8
Governor Bridge—*bridge* MD-2
Governor Brook—*stream* MA-1
Governor Burke Grave—*cemetery* NC-3
*Governor Creek* VA-3
Governor Creek—*stream* ID-8
Governor Creek—*stream* MT-8
Governor Dern Lake—*lake* UT-8
Governor Dick Hill—*summit* PA-2
Governor Dodge State Park—*park* WI-6
Governor Drain—*canal* MI-6
Governor Dummer Acad—*school* MA-1
Governor Gorton Farm—*locale* RI-1
Governor Gulch—*valley* CO-8
Governor Harvey Canyon—*valley* KS-7
Governor Hill—*summit* NY-2
Governor Hill Lake—*lake* FL-3
Governor Hunt Tomb—*cemetery* AZ-5
*Governor Island* MN-6
Governor Island—*island* CT-1
Governor Island—*island* NE-7
Governor Matthews Cem—*cemetery* MS-4
Governor Mifflin HS—*school* PA-2
Governor Mifflin Sch—*school* PA-2
Governor Mine—*mine* CA-9
Governor Mine—*mine* NV-8
Governor Patterson Memorial State Park—*park* OR-9
Governor Pennypacker Monument—*locale* PA-2
Governor Pond—*lake* MT-8
Governor Printz Park—*park* PA-2
*Governor Reeders Town* KS-7
**Governor Run**—*pop pl* MD-2
Governor Run—*stream* MD-2
Governors Bay—*bay* OR-9
Governors Bayou—*stream* FL-3
Governors Branch—*stream* AL-4
Governors Branch—*stream* NJ-2
Governors Brook—*stream* NH-1
Governors Cem—*cemetery* KY-4
Governors Channel—*channel* MA-1
Governors Creek—*stream* FL-3
Governors Creek—*stream* NC-3
Governors Creek—*stream* SC-3
Governors Drive Ch of God—*church* AL-4
**Governors Estates (subdivision)**—*pop pl* AL-4
Governors Field—*park* NV-8
**Governor's Hill**—*pop pl* CT-1
Governors Hill—*ridge* NH-1
Governor's House—*hist pl* DE-2
Governor's House—*hist pl* ME-1
Governor's House—*hist pl* NY-2
Governor's Inn—*hist pl* OH-6
*Governor's Island* MN-6
*Governor's Island* NY-2
Governors Island—*cape* MA-1
Governor's Island—*hist pl* NY-2
Governor's Island—*hist pl* NC-3
Governors Island—*island* CT-1
Governors Island—*island* (2) NH-1
Governors Island—*island* (2) NY-2
Governors Island—*island* NC-3
Governors Island—*island* OH-6
Governors Island—*island* RI-1
Governors Island—*island* WI-6
**Governors Island**—*pop pl* NC-3
Governors Island—*uninc pl* NY-2
Governors Island Ch—*church* NC-3
Governors Island Flats—*flat* MA-1
*Governor's Lake* UT-8
Governors Lake—*lake* NH-1
Governor's Land Archeol District—*hist pl* VA-3
Governors Mansion—*building* FL-3
Governors Mansion—*building* GA-3
Governors Mansion—*building* PA-2
Governor's Mansion—*hist pl* AL-4
Governor's Mansion—*hist pl* MI-6
Governor's Mansion—*hist pl* NV-8
Governors Mansion—*hist pl* OK-5
Governor's Mansion—*hist pl* TX-5
Governor's Mansion—*hist pl* VA-3
Governor's Mansion—*hist pl* WY-8
Governor's Mansion Hist Dist—*hist pl* AR-4
Governor's Mansion Hist Dist (Boundary Increase)—*hist pl* AR-4
Governors Manson—*building* TN-4
Governors Mtn—*summit* VT-1
Governors Palace—*locale* VA-3
Governors Park—*park* AL-4
Governors Park—*park* OR-9
Governors Peak—*summit* AZ-5
Governors Point—*cape* ME-1
Governors Point—*cape* WA-9
Governors Pond—*lake* NH-1
Governors Ranch—*post sta* CO-8
Governors Ridge—*ridge* AK-9
Governors Ridge—*ridge* WA-9
Governors Right Sch—*school* VT-1
**Governors Run**—*pop pl* MD-2
Governors Spring—*spring* UT-8
**Governors Square Condominium**—*pop pl* UT-8
Governors Square Mall—*locale* FL-3
Governors Square Mall Shop Ctr—*locale* TN-4
Governors Square Shop Ctr—*locale* AL-4
Governors Stables—*cave* PA-2
Governor Swamp—*stream* VA-3
Governor Thomas Wells Sch—*school* CT-1
Governor Williams Cem—*cemetery* SC-3
Governor Wolf Elem Sch—*school* PA-2
*Governor Wolf Sch* PA-2
Gover Rsvr—*reservoir* OR-9
Govert Sch—*school* SD-7
Gove Sch—*school* FL-3
Gove Sch—*school* IA-7
Goves Hill—*summit* NH-1
Goves Mtn—*summit* NH-1
**Gove Township**—*pop pl* KS-7
Govina Canyon—*valley* NM-5
Govina Canyon Tank No 1—*reservoir* NM-5
Govina Canyon Tank No 8—*reservoir* NM-5
Govorushka Lake—*lake* AK-9
Gov. Smith Homestead—*hist pl* CT-1
Govtilden Mine—*mine* MT-8
Gov Troup Grave—*cemetery* GA-3
**Gow**—*pop pl* OK-5
Gowan—*locale* LA-4
**Gowan**—*pop pl* MN-6
Gowan Branch—*stream* MS-4
Gowan Cem—*cemetery* AL-4
Gowan Creek—*stream* CA-9
Gowanda—*locale* CO-8
**Gowanda**—*pop pl* NY-2
Gowanda Country Club—*other* NY-2
Gowanda State Homeopathic Hospital—*other* NY-2
Gowanda State Hosp—*hospital* NY-2
Gowanda State Hosp Annex—*hospital* NY-2
Gowanda Village Hist Dist—*hist pl* NY-2
Gowanda Waterworks—*other* NY-2
**Gowango (historical)**—*pop pl* PA-2
Gowan Hollow—*valley* NY-2
Gowanie Country Club—*other* MI-6
Gowan Lake—*lake* MN-6
Gowan Mine—*mine* AZ-5
Gowan Ranch—*locale* NM-5
Gowans Cave—*cave* AL-4
Gowans Cem—*cemetery* NC-3
Gowans Cove—*valley* NC-3
Gowans Hollow—*valley* ID-8
Gowans Hollow—*valley* UT-8
*Gowansville* IL-6
Gowanus Bay—*bay* NY-2
Gowanus Canal—*canal* NY-2
Gowanus Flats—*bar* NY-2
**Gowards Corner**—*pop pl* MA-1
Gowden Park—*park* TX-5
Gowder Branch—*stream* AL-4
Gowdeysville Ch—*church* SC-3
*Gowdgen Gap* AL-4
Gowdy—*locale* MO-7
**Gowdy**—*pop pl* IN-6
Gowdy Creek—*stream* IL-6
Gowdy Park—*park* OH-6
Gowdy Pond—*lake* NY-2
Gowdy Ranch—*locale* NM-5
Gowdy Ranch—*locale* OR-9
*Gowdys Brook* CT-1
Gowed Point—*cape* VI-3
Gowell Sch—*school* ME-1
Gowen—*locale* PA-2
**Gowen**—*pop pl* MI-6
**Gowen**—*pop pl* OK-5
**Gowen Breaker Station**—*pop pl* PA-2
Gowen Cave—*cave* TN-4
Gowen Cem—*cemetery* IA-7
Gowen Cem—*cemetery* KY-4
Gowen Cem—*cemetery* OK-5
Gowen Cem—*cemetery* TN-4
**Gowen City**—*pop pl* PA-2
Gowen Colliery—*building* PA-2
Gowen Knob—*summit* TN-4
Gowen Lake—*lake* NM-5
Gowen Meadow Brook—*stream* ME-1
Gowens Canyon—*valley* CO-8
Gowen Sch—*school* TX-5
Gowen Sch No 1—*school* IA-7
Gowen Sch No 3—*school* IA-7
Gowens Creek—*stream* SC-3
Gowens Mtn—*summit* SC-3
**Gowensville**—*pop pl* SC-3
Gowensville Ch—*church* SC-3
**Gower**—*pop pl* MO-7
Gower, Mount—*summit* CA-9
Gower Branch—*stream* MO-7
Gower Cem—*cemetery* ME-1
Gower Cem—*cemetery* OK-5
Gower Cem—*cemetery* TN-4
Gower Creek—*stream* IA-7
Gower Field Airp—*airport* WA-9
Gower Gulch—*valley* CA-9
Gower Gulch—*valley* CO-8
**Gower (historical)**—*pop pl* TN-4
Gower House—*hist pl* KY-4
Gower Island—*island* TN-4
Gower Point—*cliff* AR-4
Gower Run—*stream* WV-2
Gower Sch—*school* IL-6
Gower Sch—*school* TN-4
Gower Sch (abandoned)—*school* PA-2
**Gowers Corners**—*pop pl* FL-3
Gowers Fy—*locale* IA-7
Gowers Hill—*summit* WA-9
Gower Township—*fmr MCD* IA-7
Gower Truck Trail—*trail* CA-9
Gow Hill—*summit* GA-3
Gowing, James, Farm—*hist pl* NH-1
Gowing, Joseph, Farm—*hist pl* NH-1
Gowing Creek—*stream* OR-9
Gowing Drain—*canal* MI-6
Gowing Spring—*spring* OR-9
*Gowings Swamp* MA-1
Gowin-Kesecker Lake—*reservoir* WY-8
Gowins—*locale* IL-6
Gowler Ridge—*ridge* OH-6
Gowman Ditch—*canal* OH-6
**Gowrie**—*pop pl* IA-7
Gowrie Creek—*stream* GA-3
Gowrie Island—*island* GA-3
Gowrie Park—*uninc pl* VA-3
*Gowrie Swamp* GA-3
Gowrie Swamp—*swamp* GA-3
Gowrie Township—*fmr MCD* IA-7
Gowrie Township Cem—*cemetery* IA-7
Gow Sch—*school* NY-2
G Owsley Windmill—*locale* NM-5
*Gowuied* PW-9
Go Ye Mission Campground—*locale* OK-5
Goyeneche Ranch—*locale* NV-8
Goyen Memorial (reduced usage)—*other* TX-5
Goyens Hill Ch—*church* TX-5
Goyer Drain—*canal* MI-6
Goyer Shop Ctr—*locale* MS-4
Goyhenex Ranch—*locale* WY-8
Goymes Family Cem—*cemetery* AL-4
Goza Branch—*stream* MS-4
Gozad Ranch (abandoned)—*locale* MT-8
Goza Post Office (historical)—*building* MS-4
Gozar—*locale* TX-5
Gozem Peak—*summit* CA-9
Gozey Hollow—*valley* KY-4
Gozzard Flat—*flat* SD-7
G P Bar Ranch—*locale* WY-8
G Pena—*locale* TX-5
G Peterson Ranch—*locale* (2) NE-7
G Pierce Wood Memorial Hosp—*hospital* FL-3
G Pierce Wood Memorial Hospital—*school* FL-3
G P I-2—*locale* UT-8
G P I-3—*locale* UT-8
G P Joens Dam—*dam* SD-7
G P O—*post sta* NY-2
G Pool—*reservoir* MI-6
G Portal ( Conda Mine)—*mine* ID-8
G P Rsvr—*reservoir* OR-9
**Graafschap**—*pop pl* MI-6
Graafschap Cem—*cemetery* MI-6
Grab—*locale* KY-4
*Grabal* TN-4
Graball—*locale* GA-3
Graball—*locale* TN-4
Graball—*locale* TX-5
**Graball**—*pop pl* AL-4
**Graball**—*pop pl* (2) TN-4
Graball Canyon—*valley* UT-8
Graball (historical)—*locale* MS-4
Grab All (historical)—*locale* MS-4
Graball Landing—*locale* MS-4
Grabast Canyon—*valley* CA-9
Grabb Creek—*stream* OR-9
Grabbert Cabin—*locale* WY-8
Grabbert Corral—*locale* WY-8
Grabb Lake—*lake* PA-2
Grab Creek—*stream* CA-9
Grab Creek—*stream* TN-4
Grabemeyer Lake—*lake* MI-6
Grabenheim Creek—*stream* OR-9
Grabenhorst Corner—*locale* OR-9
Grabens, The—*area* UT-8
Graber Cem—*cemetery* (2) IN-6
Graber Elem Sch—*school* KS-7
**Graber Heights (subdivision)**—*pop pl* NC-3
Graber Oil Field—*oilfield* KS-7
Grabhorns Airstrip—*airport* OR-9
**Grabill**—*pop pl* IN-6
Grabin Cem—*cemetery* IA-7
**Grable**—*pop pl* IA-7
Grable Branch—*stream* (2) TN-4
Grable Branch—*stream* VA-3
Grable Cem—*cemetery* IN-6
Grable Cem—*cemetery* TN-4
Grable Cem—*cemetery* TX-5
Grable Coulee—*valley* MT-8
Grable Coulee Spring—*spring* MT-8
Grable Creek—*stream* TX-5
Grable Ditch—*canal* IN-6
Grable Ranch—*locale* CA-9
Grabler Manufacturing Company (Plant)—*facility* OH-6
Grable Spring—*spring* IN-6
Grable Tank—*reservoir* TX-5
Grab Mill Creek—*stream* AL-4
Grabner Ditch—*canal* IN-6
**Grabners**—*pop pl* CA-9
Grabtown—*locale* CA-9
Grabtown—*locale* NC-3
Grabtown Gulch—*valley* CA-9
Grabun (historical)—*locale* AL-4
Grace—*fmr MCD* NE-7
Grace—*locale* AL-4
Grace—*locale* KY-4
Grace—*locale* MO-7
Grace—*locale* MT-8
Grace—*locale* WA-9
Grace—*locale* (2) WV-2
**Grace**—*pop pl* ID-8
**Grace**—*pop pl* MI-6
**Grace**—*pop pl* MS-4
**Grace**—*pop pl* NC-3
**Grace**—*pop pl* OK-5
**Grace**—*pop pl* SC-3
**Grace**—*pop pl* TX-5
Grace, Lake—*lake* AL-4
Grace, Lake—*lake* AK-9
Grace, Lake—*lake* (2) FL-3
Grace, Lake—*lake* WA-9
Grace, Mount—*summit* MA-1
Grace, Perry, House—*hist pl* WI-6
Grace, W. R. Company—*facility* KY-4
Graceada Park—*park* CA-9
Grace American Methodist Episcopol—*church* NJ-2
Grace and Thomaston Buildings—*hist pl* NY-2
Grace And Truth Bible Camp—*locale* NC-3
Grace and Truth Ch—*church* NC-3
Grace and Truth Chapel—*church* AK-9
Grace and Truth Gospel Chapel—*church* KS-7
Grace Apostolic Pentecostal Ch—*church* IN-6
Grace Assembly Ch—*church* IN-6
Grace Assembly of God Ch—*church* UT-8
Grace Ave Ch—*church* PA-2
Grace Ave Park—*park* NY-2
Grace Ave Sch—*school* NY-2
Grace Baptist Acad—*school* FL-3
*Grace Baptist Ch* AL-4
*Grace Baptist Ch* TN-4
Grace Baptist Ch—*church* (6) AL-4
Grace Baptist Ch—*church* (9) FL-3
Grace Baptist Ch—*church* MT-8
Grace Baptist Ch—*church* NC-3
Grace Baptist Ch—*church* (4) TN-4
*Grace Baptist Chapel* MS-4
Grace Baptist Ch (Bountiful)—*church* UT-8
Grace Baptist Ch (Delta)—*church* UT-8
Grace Baptist Ch of Hollywood—*church* FL-3
Grace Baptist Ch (Orem)—*church* UT-8
Grace Baptist Ch (Salt Lake City)—*church* UT-8
Grace Baptist Chuch—*church* KS-7
*Grace Baptist Church* MS-4
Grace Baptist Church and Sch—*school* NC-3
Grace Baptist Ch (Vernal)—*church* UT-8
Grace Baptist Ch (Washington)—*church* UT-8
Grace Baptist Sch—*school* NC-3
*Grace Baptist School* AL-4
*Grace Baptist Tabernacle* TN-4
Grace Baptist Temple—*church* AL-4
Grace Bently Camp—*locale* MI-6
*Grace Bible Ch* MS-4
Grace Bible Ch—*church* AL-4
Grace Bible Ch—*church* (2) FL-3
Grace Bible Ch—*church* (2) IN-6
Grace Bible Ch—*church* MS-4
Grace Bible Ch—*church* (2) TN-4
Grace Bible Coll—*school* MI-6
*Grace Bleachery* SC-3
Grace Branch—*stream* (2) GA-3
Grace Branch—*stream* TN-4
Grace Brethren Bible Ch—*church* FL-3
Grace Brethren Ch—*church* FL-3
Grace Brethren Ch—*church* IN-6
Grace Brethren Ch—*church* KS-7
Grace Brethren Ch—*church* PA-2
Grace Brethren Ch of Maitland—*church* FL-3
Grace Brethren Ch of North Lauderdale—*church* FL-3
Grace Brethren Ch of Orlando—*church* FL-3
Grace Brethren Christian Sch—*school* FL-3
Grace Brethren Sch—*school* AZ-5
Grace Brook—*stream* MA-1
Grace Calvary Mission—*church* GA-3
Grace Cathederal—*church* OH-6
Grace Cem—*cemetery* AL-4
Grace Cem—*cemetery* AR-4
Grace Cem—*cemetery* GA-3
Grace Cem—*cemetery* ID-8
Grace Cem—*cemetery* (2) IL-6
Grace Cem—*cemetery* IA-7
Grace Cem—*cemetery* KS-7
Grace Cem—*cemetery* (2) KY-4
Grace Cem—*cemetery* LA-4
Grace Cem—*cemetery* MD-2
Grace Cem—*cemetery* MI-6
Grace Cem—*cemetery* (4) MN-6
Grace Cem—*cemetery* MO-7
Grace Cem—*cemetery* (2) NE-7
Grace Cem—*cemetery* NY-2
Grace Cem—*cemetery* (2) ND-7
Grace Cem—*cemetery* (2) OH-6
Grace Cem—*cemetery* PA-2
Grace Cem—*cemetery* SD-7
Grace Cem—*cemetery* TN-4
Grace Cem—*cemetery* TX-5
Grace Cem—*cemetery* (2) VA-3
*Grace Ch* AL-4
*Grace Ch* DE-2
Grace Ch—*church* (13) AL-4
Grace Ch—*church* (3) AR-4
Grace Ch—*church* CA-9
Grace Ch—*church* CO-8
Grace Ch—*church* DE-2
Grace Ch—*church* DC-2
Grace Ch—*church* (11) FL-3
Grace Ch—*church* (4) GA-3
Grace Ch—*church* (5) IL-6
Grace Ch—*church* (6) IN-6
Grace Ch—*church* IA-7
Grace Ch—*church* (2) KS-7
Grace Ch—*church* (5) KY-4
Grace Ch—*church* (2) LA-4
Grace Ch—*church* (9) MD-2
Grace Ch—*church* MA-1
Grace Ch—*church* (12) MI-6
Grace Ch—*church* (8) MN-6
Grace Ch—*church* (5) MS-4
Grace Ch—*church* (2) MO-7
Grace Ch—*church* MT-8
Grace Ch—*church* (3) NE-7
Grace Ch—*church* NH-1
Grace Ch—*church* (5) NJ-2
Grace Ch—*church* NM-5
Grace Ch—*church* (11) NY-2
Grace Ch—*church* (23) NC-3
Grace Ch—*church* (11) OH-6
Grace Ch—*church* (28) PA-2
Grace Ch—*church* (7) SC-3
Grace Ch—*church* (2) SD-7
Grace Ch—*church* (14) TN-4
Grace Ch—*church* (9) TX-5
Grace Ch—*church* (29) VA-3
Grace Ch—*church* (6) WV-2
Grace Ch—*church* (4) WI-6
Grace Ch—*church* WY-8
Grace Chapel—*church* (4) AL-4
Grace Chapel—*church* FL-3
Grace Chapel—*church* (4) GA-3
Grace Chapel—*church* IL-6
Grace Chapel—*church* IN-6
Grace Chapel—*church* (3) KY-4
Grace Chapel—*church* MN-6
Grace Chapel—*church* (2) MS-4
Grace Chapel—*church* MO-7
Grace Chapel—*church* (5) NC-3
Grace Chapel—*church* (2) OH-6
Grace Chapel—*church* (2) OK-5
Grace Chapel—*church* (5) PA-2
Grace Chapel—*church* (3) SC-3
Grace Chapel—*church* (3) TN-4
Grace Chapel—*church* VA-3
Grace Chapel—*church* (3) WV-2
**Grace Chapel**—*pop pl* NC-3
*Grace Chapel Assembly of God Ch* AL-4
*Grace Chapel Baptist Ch* MS-4
Grace Chapel Cave—*cave* TN-4
Grace Chapel Cem—*cemetery* SC-3
Grace Chapel Cem—*cemetery* TN-4
Grace Chapel Cem—*cemetery* VA-3
*Grace Chapel Ch* AL-4
*Grace Chapel Ch of The Nazarene* AL-4
Grace Chapel Primitive Baptist Ch—*church* AL-4
*Grace Chapel United Methodist Church* TN-4
Grace Ch Assemblies of God—*church* FL-3
Grace Ch (historical)—*church* (2) MO-7
Grace Ch (historical)—*church* PA-2
Grace Ch (historical)—*church* TN-4
Grace Ch of Christ—*church* MS-4
Grace Ch of Jackson—*church* MS-4

Grace Ch of Kendall—*church* ... FL-3
Grace Ch of Tallahassee—*church* ... FL-3
*Grace Ch of the Nazarene* ... TN-4
Grace Ch of the Nazarene—*church* ... AL-4
Grace Ch of the Nazarene—*church* ... KS-7
Grace Ch of the Nazarene—*church* ... MS-4
Grace Ch of the Nazarene—*church* ... TN-4
Grace Christian Acad—*school* ... AL-4
Grace Christian Elem Sch—*school* ... MS-4
Grace Christian Fellowship—*church* ... FL-3
Grace Christian Sch—*school* (2) ... FL-3
Grace Christian Sch—*school* ... MS-4
Grace Church—*church* ... IN-6
Grace Church—*hist pl* ... GA-3
Grace Church—*hist pl* ... NJ-2
Grace Church—*hist pl* ... OH-6
Grace Church—*hist pl* ... RI-1
Grace Church—*hist pl* (3) ... VA-3
Grace Church and Dependencies—*hist pl* ... NY-2
Grace Church Complex—*hist pl* ... NY-2
Grace Church Rectory—*hist pl* ... CT-1
Grace Church Van Vorst—*hist pl* ... NJ-2
**Grace City**—*pop pl* ... ND-7
Grace City Cem—*cemetery* ... ND-7
Grace Coll—*school* ... IN-6
Grace Community Baptist Ch—*church* ... KS-7
Grace Community Ch—*church* ... FL-3
Grace Community Ch—*church* ... KS-7
Grace Community Ch—*church* ... NY-2
Grace Community Ch—*church* ... PA-2
Grace Community Park—*park* ... WV-2
Grace Coolidge Creek—*stream* ... SD-7
Grace Cove—*bay* ... RI-1
Grace Covenant Ch—*church* ... MS-4
Grace Covenant Ch of Central Florida—*church* ... FL-3
Grace Covenant Presbyterian Ch—*church* ... AL-4
Grace Covenant Presbyterian Ch—*church* ... FL-3
Grace Creek—*bay* ... MD-2
Grace Creek—*stream* (2) ... AK-9
Grace Creek—*stream* ... AR-4
Grace Creek—*stream* ... CA-9
Grace Creek—*stream* ... CO-8
Grace Creek—*stream* ... KY-4
Grace Creek—*stream* (2) ... MI-6
Grace Creek—*stream* ... MT-8
Grace Creek—*stream* ... NV-8
Grace Creek—*stream* ... TN-4
Grace Creek—*stream* ... TX-5
Grace Creek—*stream* ... WY-8
Grace Creek Ditch—*canal* ... CO-8
Grace Creek Ranch—*locale* ... CO-8
**Gracedale**—*pop pl* ... PA-2
Gracedale County Home—*hospital* ... PA-2
Grace Ditch—*canal* ... OH-6
Grace E Loucks Elem Sch—*school* ... PA-2
Grace Episcopal Cathedral—*church* ... KS-7
Grace Episcopal Ch—*church* (4) ... AL-4
Grace Episcopal Ch—*church* ... DE-2
Grace Episcopal Ch—*church* (2) ... FL-3
Grace Episcopal Ch—*church* ... IA-7
Grace Episcopal Ch—*church* ... MS-4
*Grace Episcopal Church* ... TN-4
Grace Episcopal Church—*hist pl* (2) ... AL-4
Grace Episcopal Church—*hist pl* (2) ... CO-8
Grace Episcopal Church—*hist pl* (2) ... KY-4
Grace Episcopal Church—*hist pl* ... LA-4
Grace Episcopal Church—*hist pl* (2) ... MA-1
Grace Episcopal Church—*hist pl* ... MI-6
Grace Episcopal Church—*hist pl* ... MS-4
Grace Episcopal Church—*hist pl* ... MO-7
Grace Episcopal Church—*hist pl* ... NY-2
Grace Episcopal Church—*hist pl* ... NC-3
Grace Episcopal Church—*hist pl* ... OH-6
Grace Episcopal Church—*hist pl* ... TN-4
Grace Episcopal Church—*hist pl* (3) ... TX-5
Grace Episcopal Church—*hist pl* ... WI-6
Grace Episcopal Church and Bldg—*hist pl* ... MO-7
Grace Episcopal Church and Rectory—*hist pl* ... OR-9
Grace Episcopal Church Complex—*hist pl* ... MD-2
Grace Episcopal Church Complex—*hist pl* ... NY-2
Grace Episcopal Day Sch—*school* ... FL-3
Grace Episcopal Sch—*school* ... FL-3
Grace Evangelical and Reformed Church—*hist pl* ... NC-3
Grace Evangelical Brethren Ch—*church* ... PA-2
Grace Evangelical Free Ch—*church* (2) ... FL-3
Grace Evangelical Lutheran Church—*hist pl* ... MI-6
Grace Evangelical Sch—*school* ... MI-6
Grace Falls—*falls* ... CO-8
Grace Fellowship Baptist Ch—*church* ... FL-3
Grace Fellowship Baptist Ch—*church* ... MS-4
Grace Fellowship Ch—*church* ... AL-4
Grace Freewill Baptist Ch—*church* ... AL-4
Grace Furnace (Ruins)—*locale* ... VA-3
Grace Gospel Ch—*church* ... MO-7
Grace Gospel Chapel—*church* ... PA-2
**Grace (Grace Bleachery)**—*pop pl* ... SC-3
Grace Gulch—*valley* ... AK-9
**Graceham**—*pop pl* ... MD-2
Graceham Moravian Church And Parsonage—*hist pl* ... MD-2
*Grace Harbor* ... MI-6
Grace Harbor—*bay* ... AK-9
Grace Harbor—*bay* ... MI-6
*Grace Harbour* ... MI-6
Grace Hartley Memorial Hosp—*hospital* ... NC-3
**Grace Hill**—*pop pl* ... IA-7
Grace Hill—*summit* ... CA-9
Grace Hill Cem—*cemetery* ... AL-4
Grace Hill Cem—*cemetery* (2) ... IA-7
Grace Hill Cem—*cemetery* ... KS-7
Grace Hill Cem—*cemetery* ... OK-5
Grace Hill Cem—*cemetery* ... SD-7
Grace Hill Cem—*cemetery* ... TX-5
Grace Hill Ch—*church* ... KS-7
Gracehill Moravian Church and Cemetery—*hist pl* ... IA-7
**Grace (historical)**—*pop pl* ... TN-4
Grace Hollow—*valley* ... OH-6
Grace Hosp—*hospital* ... KS-7
Grace Hosp—*hospital* (2) ... MI-6
Grace Hosp—*hospital* ... NC-3
Grace Hosp—*hospital* ... OH-6
Grace Hosp—*hospital* ... TX-5
Grace House—*building* ... VA-3
Grace Howard Mission (historical)—*church* ... SD-7
Grace HS—*school* ... MN-6
Grace Island—*island* ... AK-9
Grace Island—*island* ... MI-6
Grace Island—*island* ... SC-3
Grace Island Campground—*locale* ... MI-6
Grace James Sch—*school* ... AR-4
Grace Lake—*lake* ... CA-9
Grace Lake—*lake* ... FL-3
Grace Lake—*lake* (2) ... MI-6
Grace Lake—*lake* (2) ... MN-6
Grace Lake—*lake* (4) ... MT-8
Grace Lake—*lake* ... WY-8
Grace Lake—*reservoir* ... CO-8
Grace Lake—*reservoir* ... SC-3
Grace Lakes—*lake* ... WA-9
Graceland—*hist pl* ... WV-2
**Graceland**—*pop pl* ... MD-2
**Graceland**—*pop pl* ... SC-3
**Graceland**—*pop pl* ... VA-3
**Graceland Acres (subdivision)**—*pop pl* ... AL-4
Graceland Cem—*cemetery* ... AR-4
Graceland Cem—*cemetery* (3) ... IL-6
Graceland Cem—*cemetery* (4) ... IN-6
Graceland Cem—*cemetery* (10) ... IA-7
Graceland Cem—*cemetery* (2) ... KS-7
Graceland Cem—*cemetery* ... MI-6
Graceland Cem—*cemetery* ... MN-6
Graceland Cem—*cemetery* (3) ... MO-7
Graceland Cem—*cemetery* ... NE-7
Graceland Cem—*cemetery* ... NY-2
Graceland Cem—*cemetery* ... ND-7
Graceland Cem—*cemetery* ... OH-6
Graceland Cem—*cemetery* ... SC-3
Graceland Cem—*cemetery* (7) ... SD-7
Graceland Cem—*cemetery* ... TX-5
Graceland Cem—*cemetery* ... WV-2
Graceland Cem—*cemetery* (5) ... WI-6
Graceland Cemetery Chapel—*hist pl* ... IA-7
Graceland Ch—*church* ... SD-7
Graceland Ch—*church* ... TN-4
Graceland Ch—*church* ... VA-3
Graceland Chapel—*church* ... PA-2
*Graceland Heights* ... IN-6
Graceland Heights Park (historical)—*park* ... FL-3
Graceland Mausoleum—*cemetery* ... MI-6
Graceland Memorial Gardens—*cemetery* ... OH-6
Graceland Memorial Park—*cemetery* ... FL-3
Graceland Memorial Park (Cemetery)—*cemetery* ... NJ-2
Graceland Park—*park* ... AL-4
**Graceland Park**—*pop pl* ... MD-2
**Graceland Park**—*pop pl* ... MA-1
Graceland Park Cem—*cemetery* ... IA-7
Graceland Park Cem—*cemetery* ... NE-7
Graceland Park-O'Donnel Heights Sch—*school* ... MD-2
Graceland Sch—*school* ... MO-7
Graceland Sch—*school* ... TN-4
**Graceland Township**—*pop pl* ... SD-7
Gracelawn Cem—*cemetery* ... AR-4
Grace Lawn Cem—*cemetery* ... AR-4
Grace Lawn Cem—*cemetery* (2) ... IN-6
Gracelawn Cem—*cemetery* ... MI-6
Grace Lawn Cem—*cemetery* ... OK-5
Gracelawn Memorial Park—*cemetery* ... DE-2
Gracelawn Memorial Park—*cemetery* ... ME-1
Gracelock—*locale* ... MN-6
Gracelon Field—*park* ... ME-1
Grace Lord Park—*park* ... NJ-2
*Grace Love Elementary School* ... MS-4
Grace-Lower Stone Ch—*church* ... NC-3
Grace Lutheran Ch—*church* (3) ... AL-4
Grace Lutheran Ch—*church* (3) ... FL-3
Grace Lutheran Ch—*church* ... IN-6
Grace Lutheran Ch—*church* ... KS-7
Grace Lutheran Ch—*church* ... MS-4
Grace Lutheran Ch—*church* ... TN-4
Grace Lutheran Ch (Moab)—*church* ... UT-8
Grace Lutheran Ch (Mo Synod)—*church* ... FL-3
Grace Lutheran Ch (Sandy)—*church* ... UT-8
Grace Lutheran Church of Barber—*hist pl* ... MT-8
Grace Lutheran Church Sch—*school* ... FL-3
Grace Lutheran Learning Center—*school* ... FL-3
Grace Lutheran Sch—*school* ... FL-3
Grace Lutheran Sch—*school* ... KS-7
Grace Meadow—*flat* ... CA-9
*Grace Memorial Baptist Ch* ... AL-4
Grace Memorial Baptist Ch—*church* (2) ... MS-4
Grace Memorial Bridge—*bridge* ... SC-3
Grace Memorial Cem—*cemetery* ... TX-5
Grace Memorial Ch—*church* ... AL-4
Grace Memorial Ch—*church* ... VA-3
Grace Memorial Chapel—*church* ... MA-1
Grace Memorial Episcopal Church—*hist pl* ... LA-4
Grace Memorial Episcopal Church—*hist pl* ... MN-6
Grace Memorial Gardens—*cemetery* ... FL-3
Grace Methodist Ch—*church* ... AL-4
Grace Methodist Episcopal Church—*hist pl* ... MI-6
Grace Methodist Episcopal Church—*hist pl* ... TX-5
Grace Miller Sch—*school* ... CA-9
Grace Mine—*mine* ... PA-2
Grace Mine Diversion Dam—*dam* ... PA-2
Grace Mine Tailings Dam—*dam* ... PA-2
Grace Mine Tailings Rsvr—*reservoir* ... PA-2
Grace Mine (underground)—*mine* ... AL-4
Grace Mission—*church* ... NC-3
Grace Mission—*church* ... VA-3
Grace Missionary Baptist Ch—*church* ... AL-4
Grace Missionary Baptist Ch—*church* ... IN-6
Grace Missionary Ch—*church* ... IN-6
Grace Mission Ch—*church* ... VA-3
**Gracemont**—*pop pl* ... OK-5
Gracemont Cem—*cemetery* ... OK-5
Gracemount Sch—*school* ... OH-6
Grace Mtn—*summit* ... AK-9
Grace Mtn—*summit* ... MT-8
Grace Mtn—*summit* ... OK-5
Gracen Chapel—*church* ... MS-4
Grace Park—*park* ... NC-3
Grace Park—*park* ... OH-6
**Grace Park**—*pop pl* ... PA-2
Grace Park Elem Sch—*school* ... PA-2
*Grace Park Sch* ... PA-2
Grace Point—*bay* ... VA-3
Grace Point—*cape* ... LA-4
Grace Point—*cape* ... NC-3
Grace Point—*cape* ... RI-1
Grace Pond—*lake* ... ME-1
Grace Pond Camp—*locale* ... ME-1
Grace Post Office (historical)—*building* (2) ... TN-4
Grace Power Plant—*other* ... ID-8
Grace Presbyterian Ch—*church* ... AL-4
Grace Presbyterian Ch Associate Reformed Synod—*church* ... FL-3
Grace Protestant Episcopal Church—*hist pl* ... DC-2
Grace Protestant Episcopal Church—*hist pl* ... NE-7
Grace Reformed Church—*hist pl* ... OH-6
Grace Regular Baptist Ch—*church* ... IN-6
Grace Ridge—*ridge* ... KY-4
Grace Rock—*bar* (2) ... ME-1
Grace Run—*stream* ... IN-6
Grace Run—*stream* ... OH-6
*Graces* ... MS-4
Grace S Beck Elem Sch—*school* ... PA-2
Grace Sch—*school* (2) ... AL-4
Grace Sch—*school* (3) ... CA-9
Grace Sch—*school* ... CO-8
Grace Sch—*school* ... FL-3
Grace Sch—*school* ... GA-3
Grace Sch—*school* ... ID-8
Grace Sch—*school* (2) ... IL-6
Grace Sch—*school* ... IN-6
Grace Sch—*school* ... MI-6
Grace Sch—*school* ... MO-7
Grace Sch—*school* ... NE-7
Grace Sch—*school* (2) ... NY-2
Grace Sch—*school* (2) ... OH-6
Grace Sch—*school* ... WI-6
Grace School—*locale* ... MI-6
*Graces Cove* ... RI-1
Graces Gap—*gap* ... AL-4
Graces (historical)—*locale* ... AL-4
Graces Lake—*lake* ... MN-6
*Graces Point* ... RI-1
Grace Spring—*spring* ... ID-8
Graces Quarters—*locale* ... MD-2
Graces Tank—*reservoir* ... NM-5
Grace Street Ch of God—*church* ... FL-3
Grace Tabernacle—*church* ... IN-6
Grace Tabernacle—*church* ... MS-4
Grace Tabernacle—*church* ... NC-3
*Grace Tabernacle Church* ... AL-4
Grace Temple Ch—*church* (2) ... TX-5
Graceton—*locale* ... MD-2
Graceton—*locale* ... TX-5
**Graceton**—*pop pl* ... MN-6
**Graceton**—*pop pl* ... PA-2
Graceton Cem—*cemetery* ... MN-6
Graceton Dam—*dam* ... PA-2
Grace Town Hall—*building* ... ND-7
Gracetown Rsvr—*reservoir* ... PA-2
**Grace Township**—*pop pl* ... ND-7
**Grace (Township of)**—*pop pl* ... MN-6
Grace Union Ch—*church* ... KY-4
Grace Union Ch—*church* ... VA-3
Grace United Methodist Ch—*church* (4) ... FL-3
Grace United Methodist Ch—*church* ... IN-6
Grace United Methodist Ch—*church* ... KS-7
Grace United Methodist Ch—*church* (4) ... MS-4
Grace United Methodist Church—*hist pl* ... DE-2
Grace United Methodist Church—*hist pl* ... FL-3
Grace United Methodist Church—*hist pl* ... NH-1
Grace United Methodist Church Preschool—*school* ... DE-2
*Grace Valley* ... AZ-5
*Graceville* ... DE-2
**Graceville**—*pop pl* ... FL-3
**Graceville**—*pop pl* ... MN-6
**Graceville**—*pop pl* ... PA-2
Graceville (CCD)—*cens area* ... FL-3
Graceville Cem—*cemetery* ... MN-6
Graceville Cem—*cemetery* ... MT-8
Graceville Colony—*locale* ... SD-7
Graceville Elem Sch—*school* ... FL-3
Graceville HS—*school* ... FL-3
Graceville Post Office (historical)—*building* ... AL-4
**Graceville (Township of)**—*pop pl* ... MN-6
Gracewil Lawns Golf Course—*other* ... MI-6
**Gracewood**—*pop pl* ... GA-3
Gracewood (CCD)—*cens area* ... GA-3
Gracewood Ch—*church* ... GA-3
Gracey—*locale* ... OH-6
Gracey—*locale* ... PA-2
**Gracey**—*pop pl* ... KY-4
Gracey Cave—*cave* ... TN-4
Gracey Corners—*locale* ... NY-2
*Gracey Creek* ... MO-7
Gracey Creek—*stream* ... AK-9
Gracey Creek—*stream* ... MO-7
Gracey Creek Glacier—*glacier* ... AK-9
Grace Young Park—*park* ... NE-7
Gracey Ranch—*locale* ... TX-5
Gracey Sch (historical)—*school* ... PA-2
Gracey Trail—*trail* ... PA-2
Gracey-Woodward Furnace (40MT378)—*hist pl* ... TN-4
Gracia Cem—*cemetery* ... TX-5
Gracian Well—*well* ... NV-8
Gracie—*locale* ... NY-2
Gracie—*uninc pl* ... NY-2
Gracie, Archibald, Mansion—*hist pl* ... NY-2
Gracie, Lake—*lake* ... FL-3
Gracie Branch—*stream* ... WV-2
Gracie Creek—*stream* ... NE-7
Gracie Flats—*flat* ... NE-7
Gracie House—*hist pl* ... AR-4
Gracie Mine—*mine* ... CA-9
Gracik Trail—*trail* ... VA-3
Graciosa Ridge—*ridge* ... CA-9
*Graciosa Ridge* ... CA-9
Grack Lake—*swamp* ... MN-6
Gracy—*fmr MCD* ... NE-7
Gracy Ave Baptist Ch—*church* ... TN-4
Gracy Wash—*arroyo* ... NV-8
Gradatim Post Office (historical)—*building* ... PA-2
Graddock Gulch—*valley* ... CA-9
Graddy Blue Hole—*lake* ... AR-4
Graddy Gin (historical)—*locale* ... AL-4
Grade—*other* ... KY-4
Grade, The—*locale* ... NV-8
Grade, The—*slope* ... IN-6
Grade Canyon—*valley* ... WY-8
Grade Canyon Creek—*stream* ... WY-8
*Grade Creek* ... WY-8
Grade Creek—*stream* ... CO-8
Grade Creek—*stream* ... ID-8
Grade Creek—*stream* ... OR-9
Grade Creek—*stream* (2) ... WA-9
*Grade Creek Canyon* ... WY-8
Grade Ditch—*canal* ... ID-8
Grade Gulch—*valley* ... CO-8
**Grade (historical)**—*pop pl* ... OR-9
Grade Lake—*lake* ... MN-6
Grade Lake, The—*reservoir* ... IA-7
Graden Sch—*school* ... MO-7
Grader Creek—*stream* ... WA-9
Grader Gulch—*valley* ... CA-9
Grader Gulch—*valley* ... ID-8
Graders Ridge—*ridge* ... PA-2
Grade Rsvr—*reservoir* ... OR-9
Grade Sch—*school* (2) ... TX-5
Grade Siding Station (historical)—*locale* ... SD-7
Grade Tank—*reservoir* (2) ... AZ-5
Gradewood Cem—*cemetery* ... GA-3
**Gradney Island**—*pop pl* ... LA-4
Gradon Canyon—*valley* ... OR-9
Gradual Point—*cape* ... AK-9
Graduate Hosp—*hospital* ... PA-2
**Gradwohl Terrace**—*pop pl* ... PA-2
Grady—*locale* ... FL-3
Grady—*locale* ... MS-4
Grady—*locale* ... TN-4
Grady—*locale* (2) ... TX-5
Grady—*locale* ... VA-3
**Grady**—*pop pl* ... AL-4
**Grady**—*pop pl* ... AR-4
**Grady**—*pop pl* ... GA-3
**Grady**—*pop pl* ... NM-5
**Grady**—*pop pl* ... OK-5
Grady, Henry W., House—*hist pl* ... GA-3
Grady Camp—*locale* ... AR-4
Grady Cem—*cemetery* ... AR-4
Grady Cem—*cemetery* ... MO-7
Grady Cem—*cemetery* ... OK-5
Grady Cem—*cemetery* (2) ... TX-5
**Grady (County)**—*pop pl* ... GA-3
**Grady (County)**—*pop pl* ... OK-5
Grady Creek—*stream* ... OR-9
Grady Ditch—*canal* ... MT-8
Grady Elem Sch—*school* ... FL-3
Grady Gammage Memorial Auditorium—*hist pl* ... AZ-5
Grady Hall Creek—*stream* ... AL-4
**Grady Heights (subdivision)**—*pop pl* ... NC-3
Grady Hosp—*hist pl* ... GA-3
Grady HS—*school* ... NY-2
Grady HS—*school* ... NC-3
Grady Lake—*reservoir* ... AL-4
Grady Memorial Hosp—*hospital* ... GA-3
Grady Memorial Hosp—*hospital* ... OK-5
Grady Mill Hollow—*valley* ... MO-7
Grady Monmt park—*park* ... NC-3
*Gradyns Point* ... NJ-2
Grady Park—*park* ... TX-5
Grady Park—*park* ... WI-6
Grady Pond—*lake* ... FL-3
Grady Pond—*lake* ... MA-1
Grady Post Office (historical)—*building* ... MS-4
Grady Post Office (historical)—*building* ... TN-4
**Gradys**—*pop pl* ... NC-3
Gradys Cem—*cemetery* ... NC-3
Grady Sch—*school* ... GA-3
Grady Sch—*school* ... NY-2
Grady Sch—*school* ... TX-5
Gradys Chapel—*church* ... MS-4
Gradys Chapel—*church* ... NC-3
Gradys Chapel—*church* ... TN-4
*Gradys Chapel United Methodist Ch* ... MS-4
Grady Sch (historical)—*school* ... MS-4
**Gradys Crossroads**—*pop pl* ... NC-3
Gradys Lake—*reservoir* ... GA-3
*Gradys Landing* ... AL-4
Grady Smith Pond Dam—*dam* ... MS-4
Grady Street Yard—*locale* ... TX-5
Grady (Township of)—*fmr MCD* ... NC-3
Gradyville—*locale* ... PA-2
**Gradyville**—*pop pl* ... KY-4
Gradyville (CCD)—*cens area* ... KY-4
Gradyville Ch—*church* ... KY-4
**Graeagle**—*pop pl* ... CA-9
**Graeagle (sta.)**—*pop pl* ... CA-9
**Graebers Post Office Addition (subdivision)**—*pop pl* ... UT-8
Graeb Hollow—*valley* ... WV-2
Graebner Sch—*school* ... TX-5
Graefe, Henry, House—*hist pl* ... OH-6
**Graefenburg**—*pop pl* ... KY-4
**Graefenburg**—*pop pl* ... PA-2
Graefenburg Hill—*summit* ... PA-2
Graefenburg Post Office—*building* ... PA-2
Graef Ranch—*locale* ... TX-5
Graehl—*uninc pl* ... AK-9
Graehl Canyon—*valley* ... ID-8
Graeme (historical site)—*park* ... PA-2
Graeme Park—*hist pl* ... PA-2
Graeme State Park—*park* ... PA-2
Graeser Drain—*canal* ... CA-9
Graesers Run—*stream* ... PA-2
**Graettinger**—*pop pl* ... IA-7
**Graf**—*pop pl* ... IA-7
**Graf**—*pop pl* ... NE-7
**Graf**—*pop pl* ... WI-6
Graf, Andreas, House—*hist pl* ... OR-9
Grafa Park—*park* ... TX-5
Graf Bldg—*hist pl* ... MT-8
Graf Canal—*canal* ... NE-7
Grafe Branch—*stream* ... TX-5
Graff—*locale* ... MN-6
Graff—*locale* ... MO-7
Graffam Development Hist Dist—*hist pl* ... MA-1
Graffa Mill Dam—*dam* ... PA-2
Graffam Island—*island* ... ME-1
Graffam Pond—*reservoir* ... PA-2
Graff Brook—*stream* ... NY-2
Graff Cem—*cemetery* ... IL-6
Graff Cem—*cemetery* ... IN-6
Graff Creek—*stream* ... WA-9
Graff Ditch—*canal* ... IN-6
Graffenburg Cem—*cemetery* ... NY-2
Graffenburg Rsvr—*reservoir* ... NY-2
Graff Hollow—*valley* ... PA-2
Graff House—*building* ... PA-2
Graffis Ditch—*canal* ... IN-6
Graffius Run—*stream* ... PA-2
Graffin Sch—*school* ... NY-2
Graff Point—*cliff* ... UT-8
Graff's Market—*hist pl* ... PA-2
Grafft Cem—*cemetery* ... IA-7
*Graffum Island* ... ME-1
Graff Woolever Trail—*trail* ... PA-2
*Graf Heyden* ... MP-9
Grafius Run—*stream* ... PA-2
Graf Lake—*lake* ... WI-6
Graflin Gulch—*valley* ... CO-8
**Graford**—*pop pl* ... TX-5
Graford (CCD)—*cens area* ... TX-5
Graf Ranch—*canal* ... CO-8
Graf Ranch—*locale* ... WY-8
Grafried Cem—*cemetery* ... TN-4
Grafried Landing (historical)—*locale* ... TN-4
Graf Sch—*school* ... WI-6
Graft—*locale* ... CO-8
*Grafton* ... MD-2
*Grafton* ... PA-2
Grafton—*locale* ... KS-7
Grafton—*locale* ... MI-6
Grafton—*locale* ... NM-5
Grafton—*locale* ... UT-8
**Grafton**—*pop pl* ... IL-6
**Grafton**—*pop pl* ... IN-6
**Grafton**—*pop pl* ... IA-7
**Grafton**—*pop pl* ... KY-4
**Grafton**—*pop pl* ... MA-1
**Grafton**—*pop pl* ... NE-7
**Grafton**—*pop pl* ... NH-1
**Grafton**—*pop pl* ... NY-2
**Grafton**—*pop pl* ... ND-7
**Grafton**—*pop pl* ... OH-6
**Grafton**—*pop pl* ... PA-2
**Grafton**—*pop pl* ... VT-1
**Grafton**—*pop pl* (2) ... VA-3
**Grafton**—*pop pl* ... WV-2
**Grafton**—*pop pl* ... WI-6
Grafton, Mount—*summit* ... NV-8
Grafton, The—*hist pl* ... CO-8
Grafton-Bethel Sch—*school* ... VA-3
Grafton Cem—*cemetery* ... IA-7
Grafton Cem—*cemetery* ... MI-6
Grafton Cem—*cemetery* ... NE-7
Grafton Cem—*cemetery* ... OH-6
Grafton Cem—*cemetery* ... TX-5
Grafton Cemter Sch—*school* ... MA-1
*Grafton Center* ... MA-1
Grafton Center—*other* ... MA-1
**Grafton Center**—*pop pl* ... NH-1
*Grafton Centre* ... MA-1
Grafton Ch—*church* ... OH-6
Grafton Ch—*church* ... VA-3
Grafton Common Hist Dist—*hist pl* ... MA-1
**Grafton County**—*pop pl* ... NH-1
Grafton Dam—*dam* ... ND-7
Grafton Downtown Commercial Hist Dist—*hist pl* ... WV-2
Grafton Flour Mill—*hist pl* ... WI-6
*Grafton Gate* ... VA-3
*Grafton Ghost Town* ... UT-8
*Grafton Gore* ... MA-1
**Grafton (Grafton Center)**—*pop pl* ... MA-1
Grafton Hall Sch (historical)—*school* ... MS-4
Grafton HS—*school* ... MA-1
Grafton Inn—*hist pl* ... MA-1
*Grafton Island* ... ME-1
Grafton JHS—*school* ... MA-1
Grafton-Kennedy Sch—*school* ... OH-6
Grafton (Magisterial District)—*fmr MCD* ... VA-3
Grafton Mesa—*summit* ... UT-8
Grafton Municipal Airp—*airport* ... ND-7
Grafton Natl Cemetery—*hist pl* ... WV-2
Grafton Notch—*gap* ... ME-1
Grafton Oil Field—*oilfield* ... MS-4
Grafton Park—*park* ... IL-6
Grafton Pond—*lake* ... NH-1
Grafton Post Office (historical)—*building* ... AL-4
Grafton Road Sch—*school* ... OH-6
Grafton Sch—*school* ... VA-3
Graftons Lake Dam—*dam* ... MS-4
**Graftons Square**—*pop pl* ... NY-2
Grafton State Farm—*locale* ... OH-6
Grafton State Forest—*forest* ... VT-1
Grafton State Hosp—*hospital* (2) ... MA-1
Grafton Street Sch—*hist pl* ... MA-1
Grafton Street Sch—*school* ... MA-1
**Grafton (Town of)**—*pop pl* ... MA-1
**Grafton (Town of)**—*pop pl* ... NH-1
**Grafton (Town of)**—*pop pl* ... NY-2
**Grafton (Town of)**—*pop pl* ... VT-1
**Grafton (Town of)**—*pop pl* ... WI-6
**Grafton Township**—*pop pl* ... NE-7
**Grafton Township**—*pop pl* ... ND-7
**Grafton Township**—*pop pl* ... SD-7
Grafton Township (historical)—*civil* ... ND-7
**Grafton (Township of)**—*pop pl* ... IL-6
**Grafton (Township of)**—*pop pl* ... MN-6
**Grafton (Township of)**—*pop pl* ... OH-6
Grafton (Township of)—*unorg* ... ME-1
**Grafton Village**—*pop pl* ... VA-3
Grafton Wash—*valley* ... UT-8
Grafton Well—*well* ... OR-9
**Graf Township**—*pop pl* ... ND-7
*Grafts* ... NH-1
*Grafts Island* ... PA-2
*Grafty Creek* ... NC-3
*Grafy Creek* ... NC-3
Gragenitos Windmill—*locale* ... TX-5
Grage Tank—*reservoir* ... NM-5
**Gragg**—*pop pl* ... NC-3
Gragg Canyon—*valley* ... CA-9
Gragg Cem—*cemetery* ... MO-7
Gragg Cem—*cemetery* (4) ... NC-3
Gragg Cem—*cemetery* ... WV-2
Gragg Chapel—*church* ... TN-4
Gragg Field (airport)—*airport* ... AL-4
Gragg Gap—*gap* ... NC-3
Gragg Hollow—*valley* ... TN-4
Gragg Hollow—*valley* ... TX-5
Gragg House—*hist pl* ... NC-3
Gragg Park—*park* ... TN-4
Gragg Prong—*stream* (2) ... NC-3
Gragg Ranch—*locale* ... NE-7
Gragg Sch—*school* ... IL-6
Gragg Sch—*school* ... TN-4
Graggs Chapel Cem—*cemetery* ... KS-7
*Graggs Mill* ... AL-4
Gragg Well—*locale* ... NM-5
Gragreen (historical)—*locale* ... ND-7
Gragston Ch—*church* ... WV-2
Gragston Creek—*stream* ... WV-2
*Graham* ... TN-4
*Graham* ... WV-2
Graham—*locale* ... ID-8
Graham—*locale* (2) ... MS-4
Graham—*locale* ... OH-6
Graham—*locale* ... PA-2
Graham—*locale* ... WA-9
**Graham**—*pop pl* ... AL-4
**Graham**—*pop pl* ... AZ-5
**Graham**—*pop pl* ... FL-3
**Graham**—*pop pl* ... GA-3
**Graham**—*pop pl* (2) ... IN-6
**Graham**—*pop pl* ... IA-7
**Graham**—*pop pl* ... KY-4
**Graham**—*pop pl* ... MO-7
**Graham**—*pop pl* ... NY-2
**Graham**—*pop pl* ... NC-3
**Graham**—*pop pl* ... OK-5
**Graham**—*pop pl* ... OR-9
**Graham**—*pop pl* ... PA-2
**Graham**—*pop pl* ... TN-4
**Graham**—*pop pl* (2) ... TX-5
Graham—*uninc pl* ... CA-9
Graham, Col. James, House—*hist pl* ... WV-2
Graham, Dr. L. H., House—*hist pl* ... TX-5
Graham, John, House—*hist pl* ... KY-4
Graham, Lake—*reservoir* ... TX-5
Graham, Maj. David, House—*hist pl* ... VA-3
Graham, Mentor, House—*hist pl* ... SD-7
Graham, Mount—*summit* ... AZ-5
Graham, Robert C., House—*hist pl* ... IN-6
Graham, William, House—*hist pl* ... OH-6
Graham, William A., Jr., Farm—*hist pl* ... NC-3
Graham, William H. H., House—*hist pl* ... IN-6
Graham, William J., House—*hist pl* ... NV-8
Graham Airp—*airport* ... KS-7
Graham And Farmsley Ditch No 1—*canal* ... WY-8
Graham And Farmsley Ditch No 2—*canal* ... WY-8
Graham and Laird, Schober and Mitchell Factories—*hist pl* ... PA-2
Graham Baptist Ch—*church* ... FL-3
Graham Bay—*swamp* ... FL-3
Graham Bayou—*stream* ... AL-4
Graham Beach—*uninc pl* ... NY-2
Graham Bible Coll—*school* ... TN-4
Graham Bldg—*hist pl* ... IL-6
Graham Branch—*stream* (3) ... AL-4
Graham Branch—*stream* ... AR-4
Graham Branch—*stream* ... DE-2
Graham Branch—*stream* ... KY-4
Graham Branch—*stream* ... MO-7
Graham Branch—*stream* (2) ... NC-3
Graham Branch—*stream* (3) ... TN-4
Graham Branch—*stream* (2) ... TX-5
Graham Branch—*stream* ... VA-3
Graham Bridge—*bridge* ... AL-4
Graham Bridge—*bridge* ... OR-9
Graham Bridge Campground—*locale* ... ID-8
Graham Bridge (historical)—*bridge* ... NC-3
Graham Brook—*stream* ... NH-1
Graham Butte—*summit* ... OR-9
Graham Cabin—*locale* ... MT-8
Graham Canal—*canal* ... AZ-5
Graham Canyon—*valley* ... CA-9
Graham Canyon—*valley* ... OR-9
Graham Cave—*cave* ... MO-7
Graham Cave—*hist pl* ... MO-7
Graham Cave State Park—*park* ... MO-7
Graham (CCD)—*cens area* ... TX-5
Graham Cem—*cemetery* (6) ... AL-4
Graham Cem—*cemetery* ... AZ-5
Graham Cem—*cemetery* (3) ... GA-3
Graham Cem—*cemetery* ... IL-6
Graham Cem—*cemetery* ... IN-6
Graham Cem—*cemetery* (4) ... KY-4
Graham Cem—*cemetery* (2) ... LA-4
Graham Cem—*cemetery* ... MN-6
Graham Cem—*cemetery* (4) ... MS-4
Graham Cem—*cemetery* (5) ... MO-7
Graham Cem—*cemetery* (2) ... NM-5
Graham Cem—*cemetery* (2) ... NC-3
Graham Cem—*cemetery* (5) ... OH-6
Graham Cem—*cemetery* ... PA-2
Graham Cem—*cemetery* (3) ... SC-3
Graham Cem—*cemetery* (7) ... TN-4
Graham Cem—*cemetery* (2) ... TX-5
Graham Cem—*cemetery* (5) ... VA-3
Graham Cem—*cemetery* ... WV-2
Graham Ch—*church* ... IN-6
Graham Ch—*church* ... MI-6
Graham Ch—*church* ... MN-6
Graham Ch—*church* ... PA-2
Graham Ch—*church* (2) ... SC-3
Graham Ch—*church* ... TN-4
Graham Ch—*church* ... TX-5
Graham Ch—*church* ... WV-2
*Graham Chapel* ... AL-4
*Graham Chapel* ... TN-4
Graham Chapel—*church* ... AR-4
Graham Chapel—*church* ... IL-6
Graham Chapel—*church* ... MS-4
Graham Chapel—*church* ... NC-3
Graham Chapel—*church* ... OH-6
Graham Chapel—*church* (2) ... SC-3
**Graham Chapel**—*pop pl* ... TX-5
Graham Chapel Cem—*cemetery* ... TN-4
Graham Chapel Cem—*cemetery* ... TX-5
Graham Chapel (historical)—*church* ... AL-4
Graham Ch (historical)—*church* ... TN-4
Graham-Ginestra House—*hist pl* ... IL-6
Graham City Lake Number One—*reservoir* ... NC-3
Graham City Lake Number One Dam—*dam* ... NC-3
Graham City Lake Number Two Dam—*dam* ... NC-3
Graham Corners—*locale* ... OH-6
**Graham Corners**—*pop pl* ... WI-6
Graham Corral—*locale* ... OR-9
Graham Coulee—*valley* (3) ... MT-8
Graham County—*civil* ... KS-7

**Graham County**—pop pl ... AZ-5
**Graham County**—pop pl ... NC-3
Graham County Courthouse—hist pl ... AZ-5
Graham County Dam—dam ... KS-7
Graham County Fair Ground—locale ... AZ-5
Graham County Fairgrounds—locale ... KS-7
Graham County Highway Maintenance Yard—other ... AZ-5
Graham Cove—valley ... AL-4
Graham Cove—valley ... TN-4
Graham Cove Branch—stream ... TN-4
*Graham Creek* ... AL-4
*Graham Creek* ... AR-4
*Graham Creek* ... GA-3
Graham Creek—gut ... SC-3
Graham Creek—stream ... AL-4
Graham Creek—stream ... AK-9
Graham Creek—stream ... AR-4
Graham Creek—stream (5) ... CA-9
Graham Creek—stream ... CO-8
Graham Creek—stream ... FL-3
Graham Creek—stream ... GA-3
Graham Creek—stream (3) ... ID-8
Graham Creek—stream (2) ... IN-6
Graham Creek—stream ... MD-2
Graham Creek—stream ... MI-6
Graham Creek—stream (2) ... MT-8
Graham Creek—stream ... NY-2
Graham Creek—stream (2) ... NC-3
Graham Creek—stream (5) ... OR-9
Graham Creek—stream ... TN-4
Graham Creek—stream (3) ... TX-5
Graham Creek—stream ... VA-3
Graham Creek—stream ... WA-9
Graham Creek—stream ... WI-6
Graham Creek Campground—locale ... CO-8
Graham-Crocker House—hist pl ... MD-2
**Graham Crossing**—pop pl ... PA-2
Graham Dam—dam ... ME-1
Graham Dam—dam ... OR-9
Graham Ditch—canal ... CO-8
Graham Ditch—canal (3) ... IN-6
Graham Ditch—canal ... MT-8
Graham Ditch—canal ... OH-6
Graham Ditch—canal (3) ... WY-8
Graham Drain—canal ... MI-6
Graham Draw—valley (2) ... WY-8
Graham-Eckes Palm Beach Acad—school ... FL-3
Grahame House—hist pl ... MD-2
Graham Elem Sch—school ... AL-4
Graham Elem Sch—school ... FL-3
Graham Farms Airp—airport ... KS-7
Graham Farms Auxiliary Airp—airport ... KS-7
Graham Ferry—locale ... MS-4
Graham Field—park ... PA-2
Graham Field (airport)—airport ... SD-7
Graham Fishing Camp—locale ... MS-4
Graham Flat—flat ... OK-5
*Graham Forest Reserve* ... AZ-5
*Graham Forge* ... VA-3
*Graham Fork Muscatatuck River* ... IN-6
*Graham Fork Muscatuck River* ... IN-6
Graham Gap—gap ... TX-5
Graham-Gaughan-Betts House—hist pl ... AR-4
**Graham (Graham Station)**—pop pl ... WV-2
Graham Guard Station—locale ... ID-8
*Graham Gulch* ... CO-8
Graham Gulch—valley (2) ... CA-9
Graham Gulch—valley (2) ... CO-8
Graham Gulch—valley ... MT-8
Graham Gymnasium—hist pl ... NM-5
Graham Harbor—bay ... WA-9
Graham Harbor Campground—locale ... WA-9
Graham Harbor Creek—stream ... WA-9
Grahamhaven Lake—reservoir ... AL-4
**Graham Heights**—pop pl ... WV-2
Graham Heights Ch—church ... TN-4
**Graham Hill**—pop pl ... KY-4
Graham Hill—summit ... KY-4
Graham Hill—summit ... VT-1
Graham Hill—summit ... WA-9
Graham Hills County Park—park ... NY-2
Graham Hist Dist—hist pl ... NC-3
Graham (historical P.O.)—locale ... IN-6
*Graham Hollow* ... WI-6
Graham Hollow—valley (2) ... ID-8
Graham Hollow—valley ... IL-6
Graham Hollow—valley ... KY-4
Graham Hollow—valley (2) ... MO-7
Graham Hollow—valley ... TN-4
Graham Hollow—valley ... VA-3
Graham Hollow—valley ... WI-6
Graham Hollow Spring—spring ... ID-8
Graham Hosp—hospital ... IL-6
Graham Hosp—hospital ... IA-7
Graham Hotel—hist pl ... OK-5
Graham House—hist pl ... KY-4
Graham House—hist pl ... MI-6
Graham HS—school ... NC-3
Graham HS—school ... VA-3
Graham Island (historical)—island ... NC-3
Graham JHS—school ... NC-3
Graham-Kivette House—hist pl ... TN-4
Graham Knob—summit ... MO-7
Graham Lake—lake ... CA-9
Graham Lake—lake (4) ... MI-6
Graham Lake—lake (4) ... MN-6
Graham Lake—lake ... MS-4
Graham Lake—lake ... NM-5
Graham Lake—lake ... NC-3
Graham Lake—lake ... OR-9
Graham Lake—lake ... TX-5
Graham Lake—lake ... WI-6
**Graham Lake**—pop pl ... MI-6
Graham Lake—reservoir ... KY-4
Graham Lake—reservoir ... ME-1
Graham Lake—reservoir (2) ... TX-5
Graham Lake—swamp ... MN-6
Graham Lake Dam—dam (2) ... MS-4
Graham Lake (historical)—lake ... MS-4
*Graham Lakes* ... MI-6
Graham Lakes—lake ... MI-6
Graham Lakes (Township of)—civ div ... MN-6
Graham Lateral—canal ... AZ-5
Graham Lateral—canal ... ID-8
Graham Local HS—school ... OH-6
Graham (Magisterial District)—fmr MCD ... WV-2
Graham Marsh—swamp ... FL-3
Graham McCulloch Ditch—canal ... IN-6
Graham McCulloch Ditch Number Four—canal ... IN-6
Graham McCulloch Ditch Number One—canal ... IN-6
Graham Meadow—area ... CA-9
Graham Memorial Cem—cemetery ... OK-5
Graham Memorial Ch—church ... GA-3
Graham Memorial Park—cemetery ... MD-2
Graham Memorial Park—cemetery ... NC-3
Graham Memorial Park—park ... CO-8
Graham Mesa—summit ... CO-8
*Graham Mesa Ditch* ... CO-8
Graham Mill—locale ... TN-4
Graham Mill Bridge (historical)—bridge ... MO-7
Graham Mill Creek—stream (2) ... MS-4
Graham Mill (Site)—locale ... ID-8
Graham Mine—mine ... CA-9
Graham Mission—church ... FL-3
*Graham Mountain* ... AZ-5
*Graham Mountains* ... AZ-5
Graham MS—school ... NC-3
Graham Mtn—summit ... CA-9
Graham Mtn—summit ... ID-8
Graham Mtn—summit ... MT-8
Graham Mtn—summit ... NY-2
Graham Mtn—summit ... OR-9
Graham Municipal Park—park ... NC-3
Graham Oil Field—oilfield ... KS-7
Graham Oil Field—oilfield ... TX-5
Graham-Osborn Ditch—canal ... CA-9
Graham Park—park ... FL-3
Graham Park—park ... IA-7
Graham Park—park ... KS-7
Graham Park—park ... NM-5
Graham Park—park ... TX-5
Graham Park JHS—school ... VA-3
Graham Pass—gap ... CA-9
Graham Pass—gap ... OR-9
*Graham Peak* ... AZ-5
Graham Peak—summit ... CO-8
Graham Peak—summit (2) ... ID-8
Graham Peak—summit ... UT-8
Graham Peak—summit ... WY-8
Graham Pinery—woods ... CA-9
Graham Pit—cave ... AL-4
Graham Place—locale ... CA-9
Graham Point—cape ... AR-4
Graham Point—cape ... ID-8
Graham Point—cape (2) ... MI-6
Graham Point—cape ... TX-5
Graham Point—cape ... WA-9
Graham Point—locale ... WA-9
Graham Point Cem—cemetery ... TX-5
Graham Pond—lake ... CT-1
Graham Pond—lake ... NY-2
Graham Pond—lake ... PA-2
Graham Pond—reservoir ... MA-1
Graham Pond Dam—dam ... MA-1
Graham Pond Dam—dam ... MS-4
Graham Ponds—lake ... GA-3
Graham (Post Office)—locale ... TN-4
Graham Post Office (historical)—building ... TN-4
Graham Power Plant—locale ... TX-5
Graham Ranch—locale ... AZ-5
Graham Ranch—locale ... CA-9
Graham Ranch—locale ... MT-8
Graham Ranch—locale (2) ... NE-7
Graham Ranch—locale (4) ... NM-5
Graham Ranch—locale ... SD-7
Graham Ranch—locale ... TX-5
Graham Ranch—locale (3) ... WY-8
Graham Ranch (historical)—locale ... SD-7
Graham Ridge—ridge ... AR-4
Graham Ridge—ridge ... CA-9
Graham Ridge—ridge ... ID-8
Graham Ridge—ridge (2) ... OH-6
Graham Road Sch—school ... VA-3
Graham Roughs—area ... WY-8
Graham Row—hist pl ... WI-6
Graham Rsvr—reservoir (2) ... OR-9
Graham Rsvr—reservoir (3) ... WY-8
Graham Rsvr No 1—reservoir ... WY-8
Graham Run—stream ... PA-2
Grahams—locale ... WA-9
Grahams Cave—cave ... PA-2
Grahams Cem—cemetery ... AR-4
Grahams Ch—church ... NY-2
Graham Sch—school (3) ... CA-9
Graham Sch—school ... FL-3
Graham Sch—school ... GA-3
Graham Sch—school (4) ... IL-6
Graham Sch—school ... IN-6
Graham Sch—school (3) ... MI-6
Graham Sch—school (2) ... NY-2
Graham Sch—school (2) ... NC-3
Graham Sch—school (2) ... ND-7
Graham Sch—school ... OK-5
Graham Sch—school (2) ... TN-4
Graham Sch—school ... WA-9
Grahams Chapel—church ... AL-4
Graham Sch (historical)—school ... AL-4
Graham Sch (historical)—school (2) ... MS-4
Graham Sch (historical)—school ... NC-3
Graham Sch (historical)—school ... TN-4
Graham School—locale ... WA-9
Grahams Crawl Cave—cave ... AL-4
*Grahams Creek* ... IN-6
Grahams Crossroads—locale ... SC-3
Grahams Day Care Center—school ... FL-3
Graham Seep—canal ... CO-8
Grahams Ferry (historical)—locale ... TN-4
**Grahams Forge**—pop pl ... VA-3
*Grahams Fork* ... IN-6
Grahams Hill—summit ... OR-9
Grahams Island—island ... ND-7
Grahams Lake—reservoir ... TX-5
Grahams Landing—locale ... WA-9
*Grahams Mill* ... MS-4
Grahams Mill (historical)—locale ... AL-4
Grahams Mill (historical)—locale ... MS-4
Grahams Neck—cape ... SC-3
Grahams Place—locale ... MT-8
*Graham Spring* ... NV-8
Graham Spring—spring ... ID-8
Graham Spring—spring ... MO-7
Graham Spring—spring ... NV-8
Graham Spring—spring ... NM-5
Graham Spring—spring ... OR-9
Graham Spring—spring ... TN-4
Graham Spring—spring ... WA-9
*Graham Springs* ... NV-8
Graham Springs—spring ... AL-4
Grahams Rsvr—reservoir ... WY-8
*Grahams Spur* ... WA-9
Grahams Stand (historical)—locale ... TN-4
**Graham (sta.)**—pop pl ... KY-4
**Graham (sta.)**—pop pl ... TN-4
Graham Station—locale ... WV-2
Graham Store (historical)—locale (2) ... MS-4
Graham Street Sch—school ... GA-3
Grahamsville—locale ... FL-3
**Grahamsville**—pop pl ... NY-2
Grahamsville Cem—cemetery ... OH-6
Grahamsville Hist Dist—hist pl ... NY-2
Grahamsville (historical)—locale ... MS-4
Graham Swamp—swamp ... FL-3
Graham Swamp—swamp ... SC-3
Graham Tabernacle—church ... NC-3
Graham-Thrift (CCD)—cens area ... WA-9
Grahamton—locale ... KY-4
Graham Top—summit ... NC-3
**Grahamtown**—pop pl ... MD-2
Graham Township—fmr MCD ... IA-7
**Graham Township**—pop pl ... KS-7
**Graham (Township of)**—pop pl ... IN-6
**Graham (Township of)**—pop pl ... MN-6
**Graham (Township of)**—pop pl ... PA-2
Graham Trail—trail ... CA-9
Graham Trail—trail ... MT-8
Graham Triangle Park—park ... NE-7
Graham Tunnel—tunnel ... MD-2
*Graham United Methodist Church* ... TN-4
**Graham Valley**—pop pl ... IN-6
**Grahamville**—pop pl ... KY-4
**Grahamville**—pop pl (2) ... SC-3
**Grahamville**—pop pl ... VT-1
Grahamville Cem—cemetery ... SC-3
Grahamville Landing—locale ... FL-3
Grahamville Reservoir Dam—dam ... PA-2
Grahamville Rsvr—reservoir ... PA-2
Grahamville Sch—school ... VT-1
Graham Well—well ... AZ-5
Graham Well—well ... CA-9
Graham Well—well (3) ... NM-5
Graham Wildlife Mngmt Area—park ... MS-4
Graham Windmill—locale ... TX-5
**Graham Woods**—pop pl ... IN-6
Grahamwood Sch—school ... TN-4
Grah Cem—cemetery ... IL-6
Grahl Cem—cemetery ... TN-4
Grahm Creek—stream ... AR-4
**Grahms**—pop pl ... PA-2
**Grahn**—pop pl ... KY-4
Grahn (CCD)—cens area ... KY-4
Grahn Fork—stream ... KY-4
Graif Sch—school ... CT-1
*Graig* ... IN-6
**Graig Dale Subdivision**—pop pl ... UT-8
**Grail Township**—pop pl ... ND-7
Grain and Lumber Exchange Bldg—hist pl ... MN-6
Grainbelt Cem—cemetery ... MT-8
Grainbelt Sch—school ... MT-8
**Grainbelt Township**—pop pl ... ND-7
Grain Camp Dam—dam ... OR-9
Grain Creek—stream ... IN-6
Grainer Ridge—ridge ... MO-7
Grainery Rock—pillar ... UT-8
**Grainfield**—pop pl ... KS-7
Grainfield Cem—cemetery ... KS-7
Grainfield Elem Sch—school ... KS-7
Grainfield Opera House—hist pl ... KS-7
**Grainfield Township**—pop pl ... KS-7
**Grainfield Township**—pop pl ... ND-7
*Grainger* ... NC-3
Grainger Cem—cemetery ... MO-7
Grainger Cem—cemetery (2) ... SC-3
Grainger Cem—cemetery ... TN-4
**Grainger County**—pop pl ... TN-4
*Grainger County Cemetery* ... TN-4
Grainger County Farm (historical)—locale ... TN-4
Grainger County Park—park (2) ... TN-4
*Grainger Point* ... NC-3
**Graingers**—pop pl ... NC-3
Graino—locale ... CA-9
**Grainola**—pop pl ... OK-5
Grain Run—stream ... IN-6
*Grains Chapel* ... AL-4
**Grainton**—pop pl ... NE-7
**Grain Valley**—pop pl ... MO-7
Grain Valley Cem—cemetery ... MO-7
Grainville—locale ... ID-8
Grainville—locale ... OK-5
**Grainwood**—pop pl ... MN-6
Gram, Hans, House—hist pl ... WI-6
Grama—locale ... NM-5
Grama Canyon—valley ... AZ-5
Grama Draw—valley ... AZ-5
Grama Flat—flat ... OK-5
Grama Grass Bottom—bend ... TX-5
Grama Lake—reservoir ... OK-5
Gramann House—hist pl ... TX-5
Grama Point—cliff ... AZ-5
Grama Ridge—ridge ... AZ-5
Grama Ridge—ridge ... NM-5
Grama Spring—spring ... AZ-5
Grama Tank—reservoir ... AZ-5
Grama Trick Tank—reservoir ... AZ-5
Grambauer Mtn—summit ... MT-8
Gramble Mill (historical)—locale ... AL-4
**Grambling**—pop pl ... LA-4
Grambling Coll—school ... LA-4
Grambling Corners—locale ... LA-4
*Grambling Creek* ... SC-3
Grambokola Hill—summit ... VI-3
Gramelspacher-Gutzweiler House—hist pl ... IN-6
**Gramercy**—pop pl ... LA-4
Gramercy Park Hist Dist—hist pl ... NY-2
**Gramercy Park (subdivision)**—pop pl ... FL-3
Gramercy Sch—school ... UT-8
Gramercy Town Canal—canal ... LA-4
**Gramere**—pop pl ... PA-2
Gramfield Ch—church ... TX-5
Gramies Run—stream ... MD-2
Gramis Ranch—locale ... CA-9
Gramley Gap—gap ... PA-2
**Gramlin**—pop pl ... FL-3
**Gramling**—pop pl ... SC-3
Gramling (CCD)—cens area ... SC-3
Gramling Creek—stream ... SC-3
Gramlin Number 2—locale ... FL-3
**Gramm**—pop pl ... WY-8
Gramma Valley—valley ... NM-5
Gramm Creek—stream ... WY-8
**Grammer**—pop pl ... IN-6
Grammer Branch—stream ... TN-4
Grammer Cem—cemetery ... IL-6
Grammer Cem—cemetery ... MO-7
Grammercy Park—park ... NY-2
**Grammer Estates (subdivision)**—pop pl ... TN-4
Grammer Grove County Wildlife Area—park ... IA-7
Grammer Hill—summit ... IL-6
Grammer Spring—spring ... TN-4
*Gramm Mountain* ... AZ-5
*Gramp Creek* ... MI-6
Gramp Creek—stream ... ID-8
**Grampian**—pop pl ... PA-2
Grampian Borough—civil ... PA-2
Grampian Hill—summit ... UT-8
**Grampian Hills**—pop pl ... PA-2
Grampian Hills—range ... OR-9
Grampian Hills—summit ... MI-6
Grampian Lake—lake ... MI-6
Gramp Rock—island ... AK-9
Gramps Bluff—cliff ... MT-8
Gramps Oil Field—oilfield ... CO-8
Grampus Branch—stream ... KY-4
Grampuses, The—bar ... MA-1
Grampus Lake—lake ... NY-2
Grampus Lake Mtn—summit ... NY-2
Grampus Point—cape ... AK-9
Gramse—locale ... UT-8
Gramtham Branch—stream ... MS-4
Gran, Frank, Farmstead—hist pl ... MN-6
**Granada**—pop pl ... CO-8
**Granada**—pop pl ... KS-7
**Granada**—pop pl ... MN-6
*Granada Beach* ... CA-9
Granada Cem—cemetery ... CO-8
Granada Cem—cemetery ... KS-7
Granada Christian—school ... FL-3
Granada Creek—stream ... CO-8
Granada Ditch—canal ... CO-8
Granada Golf Course—locale ... FL-3
Granada Golf Course—locale ... NC-3
Granada Heights Sch—school ... CA-9
**Granada Hills**—pop pl ... CA-9
Granada Hills HS—school ... CA-9
Granada Hills Park—park ... CA-9
**Granada Hills Subdivision**—pop pl ... UT-8
Granada JHS—school ... CA-9
Granada Mines—mine ... NM-5
Granada Park—park ... AZ-5
Granada Park—park ... CA-9
Granada Plaza (Shop Ctr)—locale ... FL-3
Granada Presbyterian Ch—church ... FL-3
Granada Santa Fe Trail—trail ... CO-8
Granada Sch—school ... AZ-5
Granada Sch—school (2) ... CA-9
Granada Shoppes and Studios—hist pl ... CA-9
Granada Terrace Park—park ... FL-3
Granada Theater—hist pl ... KS-7
Granada Towers—hist pl ... NY-2
**Granada Township**—pop pl ... KS-7
**Granada (trailer park)**—pop pl ... DE-2
Granado Cave—hist pl ... TX-5
Granard—locale ... VI-3
Granary Burying Ground—cemetery ... MA-1
Granary Creek—bay ... MD-2
Granary Creek—stream ... IL-6
Granary Draw—valley ... WY-8
Granary Ranch—locale ... UT-8
Granary Spring—spring ... UT-8
**Granato Estates (subdivision)**—pop pl ... AL-4
Granberry Branch—stream ... TX-5
*Granberrys Crossroads* ... NC-3
Granbery Cem—cemetery ... TN-4
Granbery Sch—school ... TN-4
**Granbrook Park**—pop pl ... CT-1
**Granbury**—pop pl ... TX-5
Granbury, Lake—reservoir ... TX-5
Granbury Cem—cemetery (2) ... TX-5
Granbury East (CCD)—cens area ... TX-5
Granbury West (CCD)—cens area ... TX-5
Granby—CDP ... CT-1
**Granby**—pop pl ... CO-8
**Granby**—pop pl ... CT-1
**Granby**—pop pl ... MA-1
**Granby**—pop pl ... MO-7
**Granby**—pop pl ... VT-1
Granby, Lake—reservoir ... CO-8
Granby Bog—swamp ... VT-1
Granby Brook—stream ... VT-1
Granby Cem—cemetery ... CT-1
Granby (census name for Granby Center)—CDP ... MA-1
**Granby Center**—pop pl ... NY-2
Granby Center (census name Granby)—other ... MA-1
**Granby Center (Granby)**—pop pl ... NY-2
Granby Center Hist Dist—hist pl ... CT-1
Granby Dam—dam ... CO-8
Granby Ditch—canal ... CO-8
*Granby Hollow* ... MA-1
Granby HS—school ... MA-1
Granby HS—school ... VA-3
*Granby Lake* ... CO-8
Granby Memorial Cem—cemetery ... MO-7
Granby Mesa—summit ... CO-8
Granby Mtn—summit ... VT-1
Granby Pump Canal—canal ... CO-8
Granby Pumping Plant—other ... CO-8
*Granby Reservoir* ... CO-8
Granby Reservoirs—reservoir ... CO-8
Granby Rsvr No. 1—reservoir ... CO-8
Granby Rsvr No. 11—reservoir ... CO-8
Granby Rsvr No. 12—reservoir ... CO-8
Granby Rsvr No. 2—reservoir ... CO-8
Granby Rsvr No. 3—reservoir ... CO-8
Granby Rsvr No. 4—reservoir ... CO-8
Granby Rsvr No. 5—reservoir ... CO-8
Granby Rsvr No. 7—reservoir ... CO-8
Granby Rsvr No. 8—reservoir ... CO-8
Granby Rsvr No. 9—reservoir ... CO-8
Granby Sch (historical)—school ... MS-4
Granby Shores—uninc pl ... VA-3
Granby Station—locale ... CT-1
Granby Stream—stream ... VT-1
Granby Townhall—building ... MA-1
**Granby (Town of)**—pop pl ... CT-1
**Granby (Town of)**—pop pl ... MA-1
**Granby (Town of)**—pop pl ... NY-2
**Granby (Town of)**—pop pl ... VT-1
Granby Township—civil ... MO-7
**Granby (Township of)**—pop pl ... MN-6
**Granby Woods**—pop pl ... MD-2
*Gran Canal de Nuestra Senora del Rosario la Marinera* ... WA-9
Gran Cem—cemetery ... MN-6
**Grancen**—pop pl ... AZ-5
Grancen RR Station—building ... AZ-5
Grancer—locale ... KY-4
Grancer Creek—stream ... KY-4
Grancer Hollow—valley ... TN-4
Gran Ch—church ... MN-6
Gran Creek—stream ... IA-7
*Grand* ... IA-7
*Grand* ... MO-7
**Grand Acres (subdivision)**—pop pl ... AL-4
Grandad Campsite—locale ... ID-8
Grandad Creek—stream ... ID-8
Grandaddy Branch—stream ... FL-3
Grandaddy Branch—stream ... TN-4
*Grandaddy Creek* ... TN-4
Grandaddy Lake—lake ... UT-8
Grandaddy Run—stream ... WV-2
Grandad Gut—gut ... NJ-2
Grandad Meadows—swamp ... NJ-2
*Grandad Peak* ... UT-8
Grandad Run—stream ... PA-2
Grandad Trail—trail ... PA-2
*Granda Flora Church of Christ* ... AL-4
**Grandale Gardens**—pop pl ... MI-6
*Grandalles* ... WA-9
*Grand Anglais Creek* ... MO-7
*Grand Anglaise Creek* ... MO-7
**Grand Annse**—pop pl ... LA-4
*Grand Arch* ... UT-8
Grand Army Memorial Home—hist pl ... ME-1
Grand Army of Republic Mine—mine ... AZ-5
Grand Army of the Republic Bldg—hist pl ... PA-2
Grand Army of the Republic Cem—cemetery ... OK-5
Grand Army of the Republic Hall—hist pl ... MN-6
Grand Army of the Republic Hall—hist pl ... PA-2
Grand Army of the Republic Memorial Hall—hist pl ... IL-6
Grand Army Plaza—locale (2) ... NY-2
Grand Auditorium and Hotel Block—hist pl ... IA-7
**Grand Ave**—pop pl ... CA-9
Grand Ave Ch—church ... IA-7
Grand Ave Ch—church ... TX-5
Grand Ave Congregational Church—hist pl ... WI-6
Grand Ave JHS—school ... NY-2
Grand Ave Park—park ... FL-3
**Grand Ave Park**—pop pl ... WI-6
Grand Ave Sch—school ... AZ-5
Grand Ave Sch—school ... CA-9
Grand Ave Sch—school ... FL-3
Grand Ave Sch—school ... MT-8
Grand Ave Sch—school ... NE-7
Grand Ave Sch—school ... NY-2
Grand Ave Sch—school ... WI-6
Grand Ave Shop Ctr—locale ... AZ-5
Grand Ave Temple and Grand Avenue Temple Bldg—hist pl ... MO-7
Grand Ave Water Tower—hist pl ... MO-7
Grand Avoille Cove—lake ... LA-4
Grand Bank Bayou—channel ... LA-4
*Grand Bateur Spit* ... MS-4
*Grand Batture Island* ... MS-4
*Grand Batture Islands* ... MS-4
*Grand Bay* ... AL-4
Grand Bay—bay (2) ... AL-4
Grand Bay—bay ... CO-8
Grand Bay—bay ... GA-3
Grand Bay—bay ... LA-4
Grand Bay—bay ... MS-4
Grand Bay—lake (2) ... LA-4
**Grand Bay**—pop pl ... AL-4
Grand Bay—swamp ... FL-3
Grand Bay (CCD)—cens area ... AL-4
Grand Bay Cem—cemetery ... AL-4
Grand Bay Ch—church ... AL-4
Grand Bay Creek—stream ... GA-3
*Grand Bay Creek - in part* ... FL-3
*Grand Bay Creek - in part* ... GA-3
Grand Bay Division—civil ... AL-4
*Grand Bay Free Methodist Church* ... AL-4
Grand Bay Oil Field—oilfield ... LA-4
*Grand Bayou* ... LA-4
Grand Bayou—bay ... AL-4
Grand Bayou—channel ... LA-4
Grand Bayou—gut (6) ... LA-4
Grand Bayou—locale ... LA-4
**Grand Bayou**—pop pl (2) ... LA-4
Grand Bayou—stream (7) ... LA-4
Grand Bayou—stream (2) ... MS-4
Grand Bayou, Lac—lake ... LA-4
Grand Bayou Blue—gut ... LA-4
Grand Bayou Bourbeux—gut ... LA-4
Grand Bayou Canal—canal (2) ... LA-4
Grand Bayou Carrion Crow—gut ... LA-4
Grand Bayou Ch—church ... LA-4
*Grand Bayou des Acadiens* ... LA-4
Grand Bayou du Large—gut ... LA-4
Grand Bayou Felicity—gut ... LA-4
Grand Bayou Mission—church ... LA-4
Grand Bayou Pass—channel ... LA-4
*Grand Bayou Village* ... LA-4
Grand Bay Swamp—swamp ... AL-4
**Grand Beach**—pop pl (2) ... ME-1
**Grand Beach**—pop pl ... MI-6
**Grand Bel Manor**—pop pl ... MD-2
Grand Bench—bench ... UT-8
Grand Bench Neck—cape ... UT-8
*Grand Bend* ... KY-4
Grand Bend—bend ... LA-4
*Grandberry Branch* ... AL-4
Grandberry Branch—stream ... AL-4
Grandberry Crossroads—locale ... AL-4
Grandberry Plantation (historical)—locale ... MS-4
**Grand Blanc**—pop pl ... MI-6
**Grand Blanc (Township of)**—pop pl ... MI-6
Grand Bluff—cliff ... CA-9
**Grand Bluff**—pop pl ... TX-5
Grand Bluff Cem—cemetery ... TX-5
**Grandbois**—pop pl ... LA-4
Grand Branch—stream ... AR-4
Grand Branch—stream ... TN-4
Grand Caillou, Bayou—gut ... LA-4
Grand Caillou, Bayou—stream ... LA-4
**Grand Caillou (Boudreaux)**—pop pl ... LA-4
Grand Calumet River—stream ... IL-6
Grand Calumet River—stream ... IN-6
Grand Camp Run—stream ... WV-2
Grandcamp Run—stream ... WV-2
Grand Canal—canal ... AZ-5
Grand Canal—canal ... CA-9
Grand Canal—canal (3) ... FL-3
Grand Canal—canal (2) ... LA-4
Grand Canal—canal (2) ... NY-2
**Grand Cane**—pop pl ... LA-4
**Grand Cane**—pop pl ... TX-5
Grand Cane, Bayou—stream ... LA-4
Grand Cane Lookout Tower—locale ... LA-4
Grand Cane Oil Field—oilfield ... LA-4
*Grand Canon* ... AZ-5
*Grand Canon of the Colorado* ... AZ-5
**Grand Canyon**—pop pl ... AZ-5
Grand Canyon—valley ... AK-9
Grand Canyon—valley ... AZ-5
Grand Canyon—valley (3) ... CA-9
Grand Canyon—valley ... IL-6
Grand Canyon—valley ... SD-7
Grand Canyon—valley ... WA-9
Grand Canyon—valley (3) ... WY-8
*Grand Canyon, The* ... OR-9
*Grand Canyon Bridge* ... AZ-5
Grand Canyon Caverns—cave ... AZ-5
**Grand Canyon Caverns**—pop pl ... AZ-5
Grand Canyon Caverns Airp—airport ... AZ-5
**Grand Canyon Caverns (Dinosaur City)**—pop pl ... AZ-5
Grand Canyon Coll—school ... AZ-5
Grand Canyon Elem Sch—school ... AZ-5
**Grand Canyon Estates**—pop pl ... AZ-5
*Grand Canyon Forest Reserve* ... AZ-5
Grand Canyon Hills—range ... CO-8
Grand Canyon Hosp—hospital ... AZ-5
Grand Canyon HS—school ... AZ-5
Grand Canyon Inn and Campground—hist pl ... AZ-5
Grand Canyon Lodge—building ... AZ-5
Grand Canyon Lodge—hist pl ... AZ-5
Grand Canyon Natl Park—park ... AZ-5
Grand Canyon Natl Park Airp—airport ... AZ-5
Grand Canyon Natl Park Visitor Center—building ... AZ-5
Grand Canyon Natural Game Preserve—park ... AZ-5
Grand Canyon Navajo Tribal Park—park ... AZ-5
Grand Canyon North Rim HQ—hist pl ... AZ-5
Grand Canyon of Pennsylvania—locale ... PA-2
*Grand Canyon of Pennsylvania, The* ... PA-2
*Grand Canyon of Santa Elena* ... TX-5
*Grand Canyon of Santa Helena* ... TX-5
*Grand Canyon of Snake River* ... OR-9
*Grand Canyon of the Colorado* ... AZ-5
Grand Canyon of the Snake River—valley ... OR-9
Grand Canyon of the Tuolumne River—valley ... CA-9
Grand Canyon Of The Yellowstone—valley ... WY-8
Grand Canyon Park Operations Bldg—hist pl ... AZ-5
Grand Canyon Power House—hist pl ... AZ-5
Grand Canyon RR Station—hist pl ... AZ-5
*Grand Canyon Snake River* ... OR-9
Grand Canyon State Airp—airport ... PA-2
Grand Canyon Tank—reservoir ... AZ-5
Grand Canyon Trading Post (historical)—locale ... AZ-5
*Grand Canyon Village* ... AZ-5
Grand Canyon Village—CDP ... AZ-5
Grand Canyon Village Hist Dist—hist pl ... AZ-5
Grand Castle—pillar ... UT-8
*Grand Caverns* ... TN-4
Grand Caverns—cave ... VA-3
Grand Cem—cemetery ... OK-5
*Grand Center* ... IA-7
Grand Center—locale ... MO-7
Grand Center Cem—cemetery ... KS-7
Grand Center Ch—church ... GA-3
Grand Central—mine ... UT-8
**Grand Central**—pop pl ... PA-2
Grand Central—uninc pl ... CA-9
Grand Central Mine—hist pl ... UT-8
Grand Central Mine—mine ... OR-9
Grand Central River—stream ... AK-9
**Grand Central (RR name Grand Central Terminal)**—pop pl ... NY-2
Grand Central Sch—school ... KS-7
Grand Central Sch—school ... SD-7
Grand Central Station—hist pl ... OR-9
Grand Central Terminal—building ... NY-2
Grand Central Terminal—hist pl ... NY-2
Grand Central Terminal (Boundary Increase: Park Ave Viaduct)—hist pl ... NY-2
Grand Central Terminal (RR name for Grand Central)—other ... NY-2
Grand Ch—church ... IA-7
Grand Chain—channel ... KY-4
**Grand Chain**—pop pl ... IL-6
*Grand Chain (corporate name New Grand Chain)* ... IL-6
Grand Chain (Election Precinct)—fmr MCD ... IL-6
Grand Chain Landing—locale ... IL-6
Grand Chain Rapids—rapids ... IL-6
Grand Chain Rapids—rapids ... IN-6
Grandchamp House—hist pl ... MT-8
**Grand Chenier**—pop pl ... LA-4
*Grand Cheniere* ... LA-4
Grand Cheniere Ferry—locale ... LA-4
*Grand Cheniere Ridge* ... LA-4
Grand Cheniere Sch—school ... LA-4
Grand Chenier Ridge—ridge (2) ... LA-4
*Grand Chenlere Ridge* ... LA-4
**Grand Chute (Town Of)**—pop pl ... WI-6
*Grand Circus Park* ... MI-6
Grand Circus Park—park ... MI-6
Grand Circus Park Hist Dist—hist pl ... MI-6
Grand City Plaza—locale ... MA-1
*Grand Cliff Range* ... AZ-5

*Grand Valley* CO-8
**Grand Valley**—*pop pl* CO-8
**Grand Valley**—*pop pl* MI-6
**Grand Valley**—*pop pl* PA-2
Grand Valley—*valley* UT-8
Grand Valley—*valley* WA-9
Grand Valley Canal—*canal* CO-8
Grand Valley Cem—*cemetery* UT-8
Grand Valley Ch—*church* ND-7
Grand Valley Ch—*church* OH-6
Grand Valley Ch—*church* SD-7
Grand Valley Dam Number Two—*dam* TN-4
Grand Valley Ditch—*canal* WY-8
Grand Valley Diversion Dam—*dam* CO-8
Grand Valley Lake—*reservoir* TN-4
*Grand Valley Lake Number One* TN-4
Grand Valley Lake Number One Dam—*dam* TN-4
Grand Valley Lake Number Two—*reservoir* TN-4
Grand Valley Sch—*school* CO-8
Grand Valley Sch—*school* SD-7
**Grand Valley State College**—*pop pl* MI-6
Grand Valley Town Hall—*building* ND-7
**Grand Valley Township**—*pop pl* ND-7
**Grand Valley Township**—*pop pl* SD-7
Grand Victory Ch—*church* OH-6
*Grandvies* VA-3
*Grandview* AL-4
*Grandview* CA-9
*Grandview* IN-6
*Grand View* IN-6
*Grandview* (2) IN-6
*Grand View* IA-7
*Grand View* KS-7
*Grandview* OH-6
*Grand View* SD-7
*Grand View* TN-4
*Grandview* WI-6
Grandview—*locale* AL-4
Grandview—*locale* AK-9
Grand View—*locale* AZ-5
Grandview—*locale* AR-4
Grand View—*locale* CO-8
Grandview—*locale* FL-3
Grandview—*locale* GA-3
Grandview—*locale* KY-4
Grandview—*locale* NC-3
Grand View—*locale* PA-2
Grandview—*locale* (2) TN-4
Grandview—*locale* TX-5
**Grandview**—*pop pl* AR-4
**Grandview**—*pop pl* CA-9
**Grandview**—*pop pl* CO-8
**Grandview**—*pop pl* (2) ID-8
**Grand View**—*pop pl* ID-8
**Grandview**—*pop pl* (4) IL-6
**Grandview**—*pop pl* (3) IN-6
**Grandview**—*pop pl* IA-7
**Grandview**—*pop pl* KS-7
**Grandview**—*pop pl* KY-4
**Grand View**—*pop pl* (2) MI-6
**Grandview**—*pop pl* MO-7
**Grandview**—*pop pl* NY-2
**Grandview**—*pop pl* OH-6
**Grand View**—*pop pl* PA-2
**Grandview**—*pop pl* (5) PA-2
**Grandview**—*pop pl* SD-7
**Grandview**—*pop pl* (3) TN-4
**Grandview**—*pop pl* (2) TX-5
**Grand View**—*pop pl* VA-3
**Grandview**—*pop pl* WA-9
**Grandview**—*pop pl* WV-2
**Grand View**—*pop pl* WI-6
Grandview—*post sta* WA-9
Grand View—*summit* ND-7
Grand View—*summit* PA-2
Grand View—*summit* UT-8
Grandview—*uninc pl* KS-7
**Grand View Acres**—*pop pl* MI-6
**Grandview Acres (subdivision)**—*pop pl* PA-2
**Grandview Acres Subdivision**—*pop pl* (2) UT-8
**Grandview Acres (subdivision)**—*pop pl* UT-8
Grandview Assembly of God Ch—*church* AL-4
Grandview Baptist Ch—*church* AL-4
Grandview Baptist Ch—*church* TN-4
*Grand View Baptist Church* MS-4
Grandview Bay—*bay* NY-2
**Grandview Bay**—*pop pl* NY-2
Grandview Bay Golf Course—*other* NY-2
**Grand View Beach**—*pop pl* MI-6
**Grandview Beach**—*pop pl* MI-6
**Grand View Beach**—*pop pl* NY-2
Grand View Blvd Sch—*school* CA-9
Grandview Branch—*stream* AL-4
Grandview Branch—*stream* MO-7
Grand View Burial Park—*cemetery* MO-7
Grandview Butte—*summit* WA-9
*Grandview Campground* UT-8
Grandview Campground—*park* OR-9
Grandview Canyon—*valley* CA-9
Grand View Canyon—*valley* ID-8
Grandview Canyon—*valley* NM-5
Grandview (CCD)—*cens area* OR-9
Grandview (CCD)—*cens area* TX-5
Grandview Cem—*cemetery* AR-4
Grandview Cem—*cemetery* (2) CO-8
Grandview Cem—*cemetery* (2) ID-8
Grandview Cem—*cemetery* IL-6
Grand View Cem—*cemetery* IL-6
Grandview Cem—*cemetery* (2) IN-6
Grandview Cem—*cemetery* (6) IA-7
Grandview Cem—*cemetery* (3) KS-7
Grandview Cem—*cemetery* (2) KY-4
Grandview Cem—*cemetery* MO-7
Grand View Cem—*cemetery* (2) NE-7
Grandview Cem—*cemetery* (2) NE-7
Grand View Cem—*cemetery* NE-7
Grandview Cem—*cemetery* NM-5
Grandview Cem—*cemetery* (2) NY-2
Grandview Cem—*cemetery* (11) OH-6
Grand View Cem—*cemetery* OK-5
Grandview Cem—*cemetery* OK-5
Grandview Cem—*cemetery* OR-9
Grandview Cem—*cemetery* (9) PA-2
Grandview Cem—*cemetery* SC-3
Grandview Cem—*cemetery* (3) SD-7
Grandview Cem—*cemetery* TN-4
Grandview Cem—*cemetery* (4) TX-5
Grandview Cem—*cemetery* (2) VT-1
Grandview Cem—*cemetery* (2) WA-9
Grandview Cem—*cemetery* WI-6
Grandview Cemetery—*hist pl* OH-6
*Grandview Ch* MO-7
Grand View Ch—*church* (2) AR-4
Grandview Ch—*church* (2) IN-6
Grandview Ch—*church* IA-7
Grandview Ch—*church* (2) KS-7
Grandview Ch—*church* KY-4
Grand View Ch—*church* MS-4
Grandview Ch—*church* MS-4
Grand View Ch—*church* MO-7
Grandview Ch—*church* (2) MO-7
Grandview Ch—*church* NE-7
Grand View Ch—*church* (2) NC-3
Grandview Ch—*church* ND-7
Grandview Ch—*church* OH-6
Grandview Ch—*church* (2) OK-5
Grand View Ch—*church* PA-2
Grandview Ch—*church* (2) TN-4
Grandview Ch—*church* TX-5
Grandview Ch—*church* (2) WV-2
Grand View Ch (abandoned)—*church* MO-7
Grand View Chapel—*church* PA-2
Grandview Christian Ch—*church* TN-4
Grandview Coll—*school* IA-7
Grand View College (Old Main)—*hist pl* IA-7
Grandview Community Center—*locale* OK-5
Grand View Country Club—*locale* MA-1
Grandview Country Club—*locale* OH-6
Grandview Country Club—*other* IN-6
Grandview Creek—*stream* OR-9
Grandview Dam—*dam* IN-6
Grand View Ditch—*canal* CO-8
Grandview Ditch—*canal* CO-8
Grand View Ditch—*canal* CO-8
*Grandview Elementary School* AL-4
*Grandview Elem Sch* PA-2
Grandview Elem Sch—*school* (3) IN-6
Grandview Elem Sch—*school* (2) KS-7
Grandview Elem Sch—*school* (4) PA-2
**Grandview Estates**—*pop pl* CO-8
**Grandview Estates Subdivision**—*pop pl* UT-8
Grand View Fire Tower—*tower* PA-2
Grandview Flats—*flat* WA-9
Grandview Gas Storage Field—*oilfield* KY-4
*Grandview Golf Course* PA-2
Grand View Golf Course—*locale* PA-2
Grandview Golf Course—*locale* PA-2
Grandview Golf Course—*other* MO-7
Grandview Golf Lake—*reservoir* NC-3
Grandview Golf Lake Dam—*dam* NC-3
Grandview Green—*locale* NM-5
Grand View Health Resort—*hist pl* WI-6
**Grand View Heights**—*pop pl* MN-6
**Grand View Heights**—*pop pl* NY-2
**Grandview Heights**—*pop pl* NC-3
**Grandview Heights**—*pop pl* (2) OH-6
**Grandview Heights**—*pop pl* OK-5
**Grandview Heights**—*pop pl* PA-2
**Grand View Heights**—*pop pl* PA-2
**Grandview Heights**—*pop pl* PA-2
Grandview Heights—*uninc pl* KY-4
Grandview Heights Sch—*school* TN-4
Grandview Heights Sch—*school* WA-9
**Grandview Heights (subdivision)**—*pop pl* MS-4
**Grandview Heights (subdivision)**—*pop pl* TN-4
Grandview Heights (Township of)—*other* OH-6
Grandview Herald Bldg—*hist pl* WA-9
Grand View Hill—*summit* KS-7
Grandview Hill—*summit* ME-1
Grandview Hill—*summit* NY-2
Grandview Hill—*summit* SD-7
Grandview (historical)—*locale* KS-7
**Grandview (historical)**—*pop pl* OR-9
**Grandview (historical)**—*pop pl* SD-7
**Grandview Homes**—*pop pl* OH-6
Grandview Hosp—*hospital* MI-6
Grandview Hosp—*hospital* OH-6
Grandview Hosp—*hospital* PA-2
Grandview Hosp—*hospital* TX-5
Grandview Hosp—*hospital* WI-6
Grandview HS—*hist pl* WA-9
Grand View Intl Airp—*airport* WA-9
Grand View Irrigation District Canal—*canal* (2) ID-8
Grandview Island—*island* WV-2
Grandview JHS—*school* NC-3
Grandview Lake—*lake* GA-3
**Grandview Lake**—*pop pl* IN-6
Grandview Lake—*reservoir* IN-6
Grandview Lake—*reservoir* KY-4
Grandview Lake—*reservoir* VA-3
Grand View Lake—*reservoir* VA-3
Grand View Landing (historical)—*locale* MS-4
Grand View Lodge—*hist pl* MN-6
Grandview Lookout Tower—*locale* AL-4
Grandview Lookout Tower—*tower* AZ-5
Grandview Lookout Tower and Cabin—*hist pl* AZ-5
Grand View Memorial Cem—*cemetery* MN-6
Grandview Memorial Cem—*cemetery* WV-2
Grandview Memorial Garden—*cemetery* IN-6
Grandview Memorial Gardens—*cemetery* IL-6
Grand View Memorial Gardens—*cemetery* MN-6
Grandview Memorial Gardens—*cemetery* MN-6
Grand View Memorial Gardens—*cemetery* MN-6
Grandview Memorial Park—*park* PA-2
Grandview Memorial Park—*park* TX-5
Grand View Memorial Park (Cemetery)—*cemetery* CA-9
Grandview Memory Gardens—*cemetery* VA-3
Grandview Mesa—*bench* NM-5
Grandview Mine—*hist pl* AZ-5
Grand View Mine—*mine* CA-9
Grandview Mine—*mine* CA-9
Grandview Mine—*mine* NV-8
Grandview Mine—*mine* WA-9
Grand View Mine (historical)—*mine* ID-8
Grandview Mines—*mine* NM-5
Grandview Missionary Ch—*church* TX-5
Grandview Mobile Home Park—*locale* AZ-5
Grandview Mtn—*summit* NH-1
Grandview Mtn—*summit* WA-9
Grand View Mutual Irrigation Canal—*canal* ID-8
Grandview Normal Institute (historical)—*school* TN-4
Grandview Oil and Gas Field—*oilfield* MT-8
**Grand View-on-Hudson**—*pop pl* NY-2
**Grand View-on-Hudson (Grand View)**—*pop pl* NY-2
Grandview Overlook—*locale* AZ-5
Grandview Overlook—*locale* ID-8
Grandview Overlook—*locale* NC-3
Grandview-Palos Verdes—*uninc pl* CA-9
*Grandview Park* IL-6
*Grand View Park* NY-2
*Grandview Park* PA-2
Grandview Park—*CDP* PA-2
Grand View Park—*park* AL-4
Grandview Park—*park* CA-9
Grand View Park—*park* CA-9
Grand View Park—*park* IL-6
Grandview Park—*park* (4) IA-7
Grandview Park—*park* (2) KS-7
Grandview Park—*park* MN-6
Grandview Park—*park* OH-6
Grandview Park—*park* PA-2
Grandview Park—*park* TN-4
Grandview Park—*park* TX-5
Grandview Park—*park* WI-6
**Grandview Park**—*pop pl* NY-2
**Grand View Park**—*pop pl* PA-2
Grand View Park Ch—*church* NC-3
Grand View Peak—*summit* AZ-5
Grand View Peak—*summit* ID-8
Grandview Peak—*summit* UT-8
**Grandview Pines (subdivision)**—*pop pl* AL-4
Grandview Pit—*summit* WA-9
Grandview Plaza—*locale* PA-2
**Grandview Plaza**—*pop pl* KS-7
Grandview Plaza Shop Ctr—*locale* AZ-5
Grand View Point—*cape* IA-7
Grandview Point—*cape* MN-6
Grandview Point—*cape* ND-7
Grand View Point—*cape* TX-5
Grandview Point—*cliff* AZ-5
Grandview Point—*cliff* ID-8
Grand View Point—*summit* CA-9
Grand View Point—*summit* UT-8
Grand View Point Overlook—*locale* UT-8
Grandview Post Office—*building* TN-4
Grandview Recreation Center—*park* WA-9
Grandview Resort—*locale* CO-8
Grandview Ridge—*ridge* TN-4
Grandview Ridge—*ridge* WV-2
Grandview Rock—*pillar* CO-8
Grandview (RR name for Grand View)—*other* WI-6
Grand View RR Station—*building* AZ-5
Grandview Sanitarium—*hospital* CA-9
*Grandview Sch* PA-2
Grandview Sch—*school* AL-4
Grandview Sch—*school* AZ-5
Grandview Sch—*school* AR-4
Grandview Sch—*school* (3) CA-9
Grand View Sch—*school* (2) CA-9
Grandview Sch—*school* CO-8
Grandview Sch—*school* (2) IL-6
Grand View Sch—*school* IA-7
Grand View Sch—*school* (2) KS-7
Grandview Sch—*school* KS-7
Grandview Sch—*school* KY-4
Grandview Sch—*school* MI-6
Grandview Sch—*school* MO-7
Grandview Sch—*school* MT-8
Grand View Sch—*school* MT-8
Grandview Sch—*school* MT-8
Grandview Sch—*school* (2) NE-7
Grand View Sch—*school* NE-7
Grandview Sch—*school* (2) OK-5
Grandview Sch—*school* (3) PA-2
Grandview Sch—*school* (2) SD-7
Grandview Sch—*school* TN-4
Grandview Sch—*school* (2) TX-5
Grandview Sch—*school* (2) UT-8
Grandview Sch—*school* (3) WV-2
Grandview Sch—*school* WI-6
Grand View Sch—*school* WI-6
Grandview Sch—*school* WI-6
Grand View Sch (abandoned)—*school* MO-7
Grandview Sch (abandoned)—*school* SD-7
Grand View Sch (historical)—*school* MO-7
Grandview Sch (historical)—*school* (2) MO-7
Grandview Sch (historical)—*school* (2) SD-7
Grandview Sch (historical)—*school* TN-4
Grand View Sch (historical)—*school* (2) TN-4
Grandview Sch Number 1—*school* ND-7
Grandview Shaft—*mine* CO-8
Grandview (site)—*locale* OR-9
Grandview Spring—*spring* OR-9
Grandview State Bank—*hist pl* WA-9
Grandview State Institution—*other* MN-6
Grandview State Park—*park* WV-2
Grandview State Wildlife Mngmt Area—*park* MN-6
**Grandview (subdivision)**—*pop pl* TN-4
**Grand View Subdivision**—*pop pl* UT-8
**Grand View Subdivision Lot 162**—*pop pl* UT-8
Grandview Tank—*reservoir* AZ-5
**Grandview Terrace**—*pop pl* PA-2
**Grandview Terrace**—*pop pl* TN-4
**Grand View (Town of)**—*pop pl* WI-6
Grandview Township—*civil* SD-7
Grand View Township—*civil* (2) SD-7
Grandview Township—*fmr MCD* IA-7
Grandview Township—*obs name* SD-7
**Grandview Township**—*pop pl* KS-7
**Grandview Township**—*pop pl* ND-7
**Grandview Township**—*pop pl* (4) SD-7
**Grandview (Township of)**—*pop pl* IL-6
**Grandview (Township of)**—*pop pl* MN-6
**Grandview (Township of)**—*pop pl* OH-6
Grandview Track—*other* OH-6
*Grand View Trail* AZ-5
Grandview Trail—*trail* AZ-5
**Grandview (Trailer Park)**—*pop pl* IL-6
Grandview Trailhead—*locale* UT-8
Grandview Transfer Camp—*locale* UT-8
**Grandview Village**—*pop pl* IN-6
Grand Village of the Natchez Indians—*hist pl* MS-4
*Grandville* WV-2
**Grandville**—*pop pl* MI-6
Grandville Bridge—*bridge* IN-6
Grandville Sch—*school* MI-6
**Grandville (Township of)**—*pop pl* IL-6
Grand Vision Sch—*school* NH-1
Grand Vista Draw—*valley* SD-7
Grand Vrew Mesa—*summit* CO-8
Grandvue Hosp—*hospital* MI-6
*Grand Wash* AZ-5
Grand Wash—*stream* AZ-5
Grand Wash—*valley* UT-8
Grand Wash Archeol District—*hist pl* AZ-5
Grand Wash Bay—*bay* AZ-5
Grand Wash Canyon—*valley* AZ-5
*Grand Wash Cliffs* AZ-5
Grand Wash Cliffs—*cliff* AZ-5
*Grand Wash Fault* AZ-5
Grand Wash River—*stream* AK-9
Grand Wash Valley—*valley* AZ-5
**Grandwood Park**—*pop pl* IL-6
**Grandy**—*pop pl* MN-6
**Grandy**—*pop pl* NC-3
**Grandy**—*pop pl* VA-3
Grandy, Caleb, House—*hist pl* NC-3
Grandy Brook—*stream* NH-1
Grandy Cem—*cemetery* NE-7
Grandy Creek—*stream* WA-9
Grandy Drain—*canal* MI-6
Grandy Hill—*ridge* MA-1
Grandy Hollow—*valley* ID-8
Grandy Lake—*lake* WA-9
*Grandyle* NY-2
**Grandyle Village**—*pop pl* NY-2
**Grandy Park**—*pop pl* VA-3
Grandy Rsvr—*reservoir* WY-8
Grandy Sch—*school* NE-7
Grandy Sch—*school* NC-3
Grandy Street Bridge—*bridge* VA-3
Grane Creek—*stream* KY-4
Graneer Drain—*canal* MI-6
*Grane Hill* MA-1
Graner Bottom—*bend* ND-7
Graner Cem—*cemetery* IA-7
Graneros Creek—*stream* CO-8
Graneros Flats—*flat* CO-8
Graneros Gorge—*valley* CO-8
Graneros Sch—*school* CO-8
Granes Cabin—*locale* CA-9
Gran Evangelical Lutheran Church—*hist pl* MN-6
Graney—*locale* IL-6
Graney Bridge—*bridge* IA-7
Graney Creek—*stream* ID-8
Graney Creek—*stream* NM-5
*Granfills Gap* TX-5
*Grange* (2) IL-6
*Grange* KY-4
Grange—*locale* AR-4
Grange—*locale* GA-3
Grange—*locale* MS-4
Grange—*locale* PA-2
**Grange**—*pop pl* NH-1
**Grange**—*pop pl* VI-3
Grange, The—*hist pl* KY-4
Grange, The—*hist pl* MA-1
Grange, The—*hist pl* PA-2
Grange, The, (Boundary Increase)—*hist pl* MA-1
*Grangeburg* IN-6
**Grangeburg**—*pop pl* AL-4
Grangeburg Post Office (historical)—*building* AL-4
Grange Cem—*cemetery* MO-7
Grange Cem—*cemetery* VA-3
*Grange Center* PA-2
Grange Centre—*locale* PA-2
Grange Ch—*church* IL-6
Grange Ch—*church* IA-7
**Grange City**—*pop pl* KY-4
Grange Corner—*locale* ME-1
**Grange Corner**—*pop pl* (2) IN-6
Grange Corner Covered Bridge—*bridge* IN-6
*Grange Corners* PA-2
**Grange Corners**—*pop pl* MI-6
**Grange Corners**—*pop pl* PA-2
Grange Creek—*stream* OR-9
*Grange Hall* DE-2
*Grange Hall* PA-2
Grange Hall—*locale* (2) IL-6
Grange Hall—*locale* (2) MI-6
Grange Hall—*locale* MS-4
Grange Hall—*locale* NY-2
Grange Hall—*other* CA-9
**Grange Hall**—*pop pl* OH-6
**Grange Hall**—*pop pl* TX-5
**Grange Hall**—*pop pl* WI-6
Grange Hall Cem—*cemetery* MO-7
Grange Hall Cem—*cemetery* (2) TX-5
**Grange Hall Center**—*pop pl* PA-2
*Grange Hall Ch* TN-4
Grange Hall Ch—*church* TX-5
Grange Hall Chapel—*church* TN-4
Grange Hall Sch—*school* IL-6
Grange Hall Sch—*school* TN-4
Grange Hall Sch—*school* (2) TX-5
Grange Hall Sch—*school* VA-3
Grange Hall Sch (historical)—*school* (2) MS-4
Grange Hall Sch (historical)—*school* TN-4
Grange Hall United Methodist Ch—*church* TN-4
Grange Hill—*summit* NY-2
Grange Hill Cem—*cemetery* TX-5
*Grange Hill School* TN-4
Grange Hole—*valley* UT-8
Grange Island—*island* FL-3
Grange Island—*island* OH-6
**Grange Landing**—*pop pl* NY-2
Grangemont—*locale* ID-8
Grange Park—*park* ID-8
Grange Pond—*swamp* TX-5
*Granger* AL-4
*Granger* IA-7
Granger—*locale* IL-6
Granger—*locale* (2) NY-2
Granger—*locale* (2) OR-9
Granger—*other* TX-5
**Granger**—*pop pl* FL-3
**Granger**—*pop pl* IN-6
**Granger**—*pop pl* IA-7
**Granger**—*pop pl* MN-6
**Granger**—*pop pl* MO-7
**Granger**—*pop pl* OH-6
**Granger**—*pop pl* TX-5
**Granger**—*pop pl* UT-8
**Granger**—*pop pl* WA-9
**Granger**—*pop pl* WY-8
Granger, Francis, House—*hist pl* NY-2
Granger Branch—*stream* NC-3
Granger Bridge—*bridge* CO-8
Granger Brook—*stream* MA-1
*Grangerburg* AL-4
Granger Butte—*summit* ID-8
Granger Canyon—*valley* UT-8
Granger (CCD)—*cens area* TX-5
Granger Cem—*cemetery* LA-4
Granger Cem—*cemetery* MI-6
Granger Cem—*cemetery* MO-7
Granger Cem—*cemetery* SC-3
Granger Cem—*cemetery* (2) TX-5
Granger Community Christian Ch—*church* UT-8
Granger Cottage—*hist pl* NY-2
Granger Creek—*stream* CA-9
Granger Creek—*stream* ID-8
Granger Creek—*stream* IA-7
Granger Creek—*stream* KS-7
Granger Creek—*stream* MT-8
Granger Creek—*stream* SD-7
Granger Creek—*stream* TX-5
Granger Ditch—*canal* MT-8
Granger Ditch—*canal* OH-6
Granger Ditch—*canal* OR-9
Granger Drain—*canal* MI-6
Granger Drain—*stream* MI-6
Granger Draw—*valley* TX-5
Granger Fork—*stream* MT-8
**Granger Gardens Subdivision**—*pop pl* UT-8
Granger Hall—*hist pl* CA-9
**Granger Heights Subdivision**—*pop pl* UT-8
Granger Hill—*summit* IA-7
Granger Hollow—*valley* NY-2
*Granger Homestead* IA-7
**Granger Homesteads**—*pop pl* IA-7
Granger House—*hist pl* IA-7
Granger HS—*school* UT-8
*Granger-Hunter* UT-8
**Granger-Hunter**—*pop pl* UT-8
Granger JHS—*school* CA-9
Granger Junction—*locale* WY-8
Granger Lake—*lake* MI-6
Granger Lake—*lake* OH-6
Granger Lake—*lake* (2) WI-6
**Grangerland**—*pop pl* TX-5
Granger Lateral—*canal* WA-9
Granger Meadow—*flat* MT-8
Granger Missionary Ch—*church* IN-6
Granger Mtn—*summit* NC-3
Granger Mtn—*summit* UT-8
*Grangero Banco Number Forty-Four* TX-5
**Granger Park Subdivision**—*pop pl* UT-8
Granger Point—*cape* NY-2
Granger Pond—*lake* ME-1
Granger Pond—*lake* SC-3
*Granger Post Office* AL-4
Granger Ranch—*locale* WY-8
Granger Ridge—*ridge* UT-8
Granger Rsvr—*reservoir* WY-8
Grangers Bar—*bar* AL-4
Granger Sch—*school* IA-7
Granger Sch—*school* MA-1
Granger Sch—*school* MI-6
Granger Sch—*school* NM-5
Granger Sch—*school* OH-6
Granger Sch—*school* SC-3
Granger Sch—*school* UT-8
Granger Service Area—*locale* IN-6
Granger Shop Ctr—*locale* UT-8
*Grangers Landing* AL-4
**Grangers Mill**—*pop pl* FL-3
Grangers Point—*cape* MI-6
Granger Spring—*spring* CA-9
Granger Spring—*spring* NV-8
Granger Stage Station Historical Marker—*locale* WY-8
Granger Station—*hist pl* WY-8
Granger Tank—*reservoir* AZ-5
Granger Tank—*reservoir* (2) TX-5
**Grangertown**—*pop pl* KY-4
**Granger (Town of)**—*pop pl* NY-2
Granger Township—*civil* SD-7
**Granger (Township of)**—*pop pl* OH-6
Grangerville—*locale* GA-3
**Grangerville**—*pop pl* NY-2
Granger Well—*well* AZ-5
**Granger West Subdivision**—*pop pl* UT-8
Grange Sch—*school* NH-1
Grange Sch—*school* WI-6
Grange Sch (historical)—*school* MS-4
Grange Sch (historical)—*school* TN-4
Granges Coulee—*stream* LA-4
Grange Township—*fmr MCD* IA-7
**Grange Township**—*pop pl* SD-7
**Grange (Township of)**—*pop pl* MN-6
**Grange Villa Subdivision**—*pop pl* UT-8
Grangeville—*locale* VA-3
**Grangeville**—*pop pl* CA-9
**Grangeville**—*pop pl* ID-8
**Grangeville**—*pop pl* LA-4
**Grangeville**—*pop pl* PA-2
**Grangeville**—*pop pl* WV-2
Grangeville Golf and Country Club—*other* ID-8
Grangeville Mine—*mine* ID-8
Grangeville Sch—*school* WV-2
Gran Grae Creek—*stream* WI-6
Granicus Bayou—*stream* MS-4
Graning Lake—*lake* MN-6
Graniss Pond—*lake* CT-1
Granite—*locale* AZ-5
Granite—*locale* (3) ID-8
Granite—*locale* IA-7
Granite—*locale* MT-8
Granite—*locale* TN-4
Granite—*locale* WY-8
**Granite**—*pop pl* CO-8
**Granite**—*pop pl* MD-2
**Granite**—*pop pl* NH-1
**Granite**—*pop pl* NY-2
**Granite**—*pop pl* OK-5
**Granite**—*pop pl* OR-9
**Granite**—*pop pl* UT-8
**Granite**—*pop pl* VA-3
Granite—*uninc pl* VA-3
Granite Adit—*tunnel* CO-8
Granite Airp—*airport* AZ-5
Granite Basin—*basin* AK-9
Granite Basin—*basin* (5) AZ-5
Granite Basin—*basin* (3) CA-9
Granite Basin—*basin* CO-8
Granite Basin—*basin* (2) ID-8
Granite Basin—*basin* (2) NV-8
Granite Basin—*basin* WY-8
Granite Basin Campground—*park* AZ-5
Granite Basin Dam—*dam* AZ-5
Granite Basin Lake—*reservoir* AZ-5
Granite Basin Lakes—*lake* WY-8
Granite Basin Picnic Area—*park* AZ-5
Granite Basin Spring—*spring* AZ-5
**Granite Basin Summer Homes**—*pop pl* AZ-5
Granite Basin Viewpoint—*area* AZ-5
Granite Bay—*bay* (2) AK-9
Granite Bay—*bay* CA-9
Granite Bay—*bay* MN-6
Granite Bay—*bay* WI-6
**Granite Bay**—*pop pl* CT-1
Granite Bay Golf Course—*other* CA-9
**Granite Bay Vista**—*pop pl* CA-9
Granite Bend—*bend* MO-7
Granite Bldg—*hist pl* NY-2
Granite Bluff—*locale* MI-6
Granite Boulder Creek—*stream* OR-9
Granite Branch—*stream* KY-4
Granite Branch—*stream* MD-2
*Granite Butte* WA-9
Granite Butte—*summit* AZ-5
Granite Butte—*summit* CA-9
Granite Butte—*summit* MT-8
Granite Butte—*summit* (2) OR-9
Granite Butte—*summit* WA-9
Granite Butte Dam—*dam* AZ-5
Granite Butte Lookout Tower—*locale* MT-8
Granite Butte Tank—*reservoir* AZ-5
Granite Cabin—*locale* MT-8
*Granite Canon* WY-8
Granite Canon—*locale* WY-8
*Granite Canyon* AZ-5
*Granite Canyon* UT-8
*Granite Canyon* WY-8
Granite Canyon—*valley* AK-9
Granite Canyon—*valley* (2) AZ-5
Granite Canyon—*valley* (5) CA-9
Granite Canyon—*valley* CO-8
Granite Canyon—*valley* (4) NV-8
Granite Canyon—*valley* (2) NM-5
Granite Canyon—*valley* UT-8
Granite Canyon—*valley* WY-8
Granite Canyon Trail—*trail* WY-8
Granite Cape—*cape* AK-9
Granite (CCD)—*cens area* OK-5
Granite Cem—*cemetery* CO-8
Granite Cem—*cemetery* ME-1
Granite Cem—*cemetery* OK-5
Granite Chief—*summit* CA-9
*Granite City* UT-8
**Granite City**—*pop pl* IL-6
Granite City—*ridge* NC-3
Granite City Cem—*cemetery* UT-8
Granite City (Township of)—*civ div* IL-6
Granite Cliff—*cliff* OR-9
Granite Column Cave—*cave* TN-4
Granite Column Pit—*cave* TN-4
Granite Country—*area* CO-8
Granite County Jail—*hist pl* MT-8
Granite Cove—*bay* (2) AK-9
Granite Cove—*bay* AZ-5
Granite Cove—*valley* CA-9
*Granite Creek* CO-8
*Granite Creek* ID-8
*Granite Creek* MT-8
Granite Creek—*stream* (12) AK-9
Granite Creek—*stream* AZ-5
Granite Creek—*stream* (14) CA-9
Granite Creek—*stream* (4) CO-8
Granite Creek—*stream* (17) ID-8
Granite Creek—*stream* KS-7
Granite Creek—*stream* (11) MT-8
Granite Creek—*stream* (7) NV-8
Granite Creek—*stream* (15) OR-9
Granite Creek—*stream* TX-5
Granite Creek—*stream* (4) UT-8
Granite Creek—*stream* (8) WA-9
Granite Creek—*stream* (5) WY-8
Granite Creek Campground—*locale* CA-9
Granite Creek Campground—*locale* ID-8
Granite Creek Campground—*locale* (2) WY-8
Granite Creek Cem—*cemetery* KS-7
Granite Creek Cow Camp—*locale* ID-8
Granite Creek Dam—*dam* AZ-5
*Granite Creek Desert* NV-8
Granite Creek Guard Station—*locale* AK-9
Granite Creek Guard Station—*locale* WA-9
*Granite Creek Lakes* MT-8
Granite Creek Meadow—*flat* NV-8
Granite Creek Mine—*mine* NV-8
Granite Creek Overpass—*crossing* AZ-5
Granite Creek Park—*park* AZ-5
Granite Creek Ranch—*locale* NV-8
Granite Creek Rec Area—*park* AK-9
Granite Creek Rsvr—*reservoir* NV-8
Granite Creek Rsvr—*reservoir* OR-9
Granite Creek Saddle—*gap* CA-9
Granite Creek Trail—*trail* ID-8
Granite Creek Trail—*trail* MT-8
Granite Creek Trail—*trail* WA-9
**Granite Crest Subdivision**—*pop pl* UT-8
Granite Dam—*dam* AZ-5
Granite Dells—*locale* AZ-5
Granite Dells—*valley* AZ-5
Granite Ditch—*canal* MT-8
Granite Dome—*summit* CA-9
Granite Draw—*valley* TX-5
*Granite Falls* AZ-5
Granite Falls—*falls* CO-8
Granite Falls—*falls* (2) WA-9
Granite Falls—*falls* WY-8
**Granite Falls**—*pop pl* MN-6
**Granite Falls**—*pop pl* NC-3
**Granite Falls**—*pop pl* WA-9

**Grasonville**—pop pl MD-2
Grasonville Cem—cemetery MD-2
Gras Point ME-1
Grass IN-6
Grass MI-6
Grass—locale CT-1
Grass, Bay—bay AL-4
Grassay Gap Sch—school AR-4
Grass Bay—bay MI-6
Grass Bay—bay NY-2
Grass Bay—swamp FL-3
Grass Bay—swamp SC-3
Grass Branch—stream NC-3
Grass Brook MA-1
Grass Butte—summit OR-9
Grass Canyon—valley (2) AZ-5
Grass Canyon—valley CA-9
Grass Canyon—valley CO-8
Grass Canyon—valley OR-9
Grass Cay—island VI-3
Grass Cem—cemetery MO-7
Grass Corner—locale ME-1
Grass Coulee—valley MT-8
Grasscreek (2) IN-6
Grass Creek MO-7
Grass Creek OK-5
Grass Creek TN-4
Grass Creek TX-5
**Grass Creek**—pop pl IN-6
**Grass Creek**—pop pl WY-8
Grass Creek—stream AK-9
Grass Creek—stream (3) CO-8
Grass Creek—stream FL-3
Grass Creek—stream GA-3
Grass Creek—stream (2) ID-8
Grass Creek—stream (5) MI-6
Grass Creek—stream MT-8
Grass Creek—stream NY-2
Grass Creek—stream NC-3
Grass Creek—stream (4) OR-9
Grass Creek—stream SD-7
Grass Creek—stream TN-4
Grass Creek—stream (2) UT-8
Grass Creek—stream VA-3
Grass Creek—stream WA-9
Grass Creek—stream WI-6
Grass Creek—stream (6) WY-8
Grass Creek Basin—basin WY-8
Grass Creek Canyon—valley WY-8
Grass Creek Cem—cemetery IN-6
Grass Creek Channel—channel WA-9
Grass Creek (Site)—locale UT-8
Grass Dale—hist pl TN-4
Grassdale—hist pl VA-3
Grassdale—locale GA-3
Grassdale Cem—cemetery TX-5
Grasse Isle LA-4
Grasselli IN-6
Grasselli—locale AL-4
Grasselli—locale NJ-2
**Grasselli (Grasselli Heights)**—pop pl AL-4
Grasselli Mine—mine TN-4
Grasselli Station—locale NJ-2
Grassemount—hist pl VT-1
Grasser Creek—stream ID-8
Grasse River NY-2
Grasse River Club—locale NY-2
Grasser Lake—lake WI-6
Grasses, The—swamp FL-3
Grassey Canyon—valley CA-9
Grassey Lake MN-6
Grassey Valley Cemetery TN-4
Grassey Wash UT-8
Grassfield—locale VA-3
Grass Field Tank—reservoir TX-5
Grass Flat PA-2
Grass Flat—locale CA-9
**Grassflat**—pop pl PA-2
Grass Flat Island—island PA-2
Grass Flat Rsvr—reservoir UT-8
Grassflat Run—stream PA-2
Grass Flats Run—stream PA-2
**Grass Flat (sta.)**—pop pl PA-2
Grass Flat Tank—reservoir (2) AZ-5
Grass-ground River MA-1
Grass Gulch—valley CO-8
Grass Gulch—valley ID-8
Grass Gulch Park—flat CO-8
Grass Gulch Spring—spring CO-8
Grassham Hollow—valley KY-4
Grass Hassock Channel—channel NY-2
Grass Hill—summit CT-1
Grass Hill—summit (2) MA-1
Grass Hill—summit MO-7
Grass Hill—summit NY-2
Grass Hill Brook—stream MA-1
Grass Hill Cem—cemetery PA-2
Grass Hills—hist pl KY-4
Grass (historical)—locale KS-7
Grass Hollow—valley (2) UT-8
Grass Hollow Branch—stream NJ-2
Grasshopper—locale AZ-5
Grasshopper—locale TN-4
Grasshopper Butte—summit AZ-5
Grasshopper Butte—summit WY-8
Grasshopper Campground—locale (2) MT-8
Grasshopper Canyon—valley CA-9
Grasshopper Canyon—valley NV-8
Grasshopper Canyon—valley (2) NM-5
Grasshopper Cemetery AL-4
Grasshopper Coulee—valley MT-8
Grasshopper Creek KS-7
Grasshopper Creek—stream (3) CA-9
Grasshopper Creek—stream CO-8
Grasshopper Creek—stream (4) ID-8
Grasshopper Creek—stream (2) MT-8
Grasshopper Creek—stream (2) OR-9
Grasshopper Creek—stream TN-4
Grasshopper Creek—stream TX-5
Grasshopper Creek—stream WY-8
Grasshopper Creek Rec Area—park TN-4
Grass Hopper Falls KS-7
Grasshopper Fire Control Station—locale CA-9
Grasshopper Flat—flat AZ-5
Grasshopper Flat—flat (4) CA-9
Grasshopper Flat—flat (5) OR-9
Grasshopper Flat—flat UT-8
Grasshopper Flat Campground—locale CA-9
Grasshopper Flats—other AZ-5
Grasshopper Flat Spring—spring OR-9
Grasshopper Flat Tank—reservoir AZ-5
Grasshopper Glacier—glacier (3) MT-8
Grasshopper Glacier—glacier WY-8
Grasshopper Gulch—valley NV-8
Grasshopper Hill—summit CA-9
Grasshopper Hill—summit (2) NY-2
Grasshopper Hill—summit TN-4
Grasshopper Hills—range ND-7
Grasshopper Hollow—valley MO-7
Grasshopper Hollow—valley WV-2
Grasshopper Island—island FL-3
Grasshopper Junction—locale AZ-5
Grasshopper Lake—lake MN-6
Grasshopper Meadows Campground—locale WA-9
Grasshopper Mine—mine UT-8
Grasshopper Mtn—summit CA-9
Grasshopper Mtn—summit (2) OR-9
Grasshopper Park—flat CO-8
Grasshopper Park Campground—locale CO-8
Grasshopper Point—area AZ-5
Grasshopper Point—cape OR-9
Grasshopper Point—summit OR-9
Grasshopper Prairie—area CA-9
Grasshopper Ridge—ridge (2) CA-9
Grasshopper River KS-7
Grasshopper Rsvr—reservoir MT-8
Grasshopper Ruin—hist pl AZ-5
Grasshoppers Camp—locale CA-9
Grasshoppers Creek—stream IL-6
Grasshopper Slough—stream CA-9
Grasshopper Spring—reservoir OR-9
Grasshopper Spring—spring AZ-5
Grasshopper Spring—spring ID-8
Grasshopper Spring—spring NV-8
Grasshopper Spring—spring NM-5
Grasshopper Spring—spring (3) OR-9
Grasshopper Tank—reservoir (2) AZ-5
Grasshopper Tank—reservoir NM-5
Grasshopper Tank Number Two—reservoir AZ-5
**Grasshopper Township**—pop pl KS-7
Grasshopper Trail—trail CA-9
Grasshopper Trail—trail ID-8
Grasshopper Trail—trail OR-9
Grasshopper Valley—valley AK-9
Grasshopper Valley—valley CA-9
Grasshopper Valley—valley MT-8
Grassie Place—locale NM-5
Grassie Point Rsvr—reservoir AZ-5
Grassies, The—area UT-8
Grass Inlet—bay FL-3
Grass Island AL-4
Grass Island WA-9
Grass Island—island AL-4
Grass Island—island (2) AK-9
Grass Island—island CA-9
Grass Island—island (2) CT-1
Grass Island—island (3) FL-3
Grass Island—island IL-6
Grass Island—island (2) LA-4
Grass Island—island (2) ME-1
Grass Island—island (2) MI-6
Grass Island—island MN-6
Grass Island—island (4) NY-2
Grass Island—island (3) TX-5
Grass Island—island WA-9
Grass Island Bar—bar AK-9
Grass Island Breaker—area PA-2
Grass Island Reefs—bar TX-5
Grass JHS—school MN-6
Grass Knob KY-4
Grass Knoll—summit UT-8
Grass Lake CA-9
Grass Lake MI-6
Grass Lake MN-6
Grasslake MS-4
Grass Lake PA-2
Grass Lake WI-6
Grass Lake—CDP IL-6
Grass Lake—lake (3) AK-9
Grass Lake—lake (7) CA-9
Grass Lake—lake CO-8
Grass Lake—lake (7) FL-3
Grass Lake—lake (3) IL-6
Grass Lake—lake IN-6
Grass Lake—lake (40) MI-6
Grass Lake—lake (24) MN-6
Grass Lake—lake MS-4
Grass Lake—lake MT-8
Grass Lake—lake NE-7
Grass Lake—lake NV-8
Grass Lake—lake NY-2
Grass Lake—lake (5) ND-7
Grass Lake—lake (2) OR-9
Grass Lake—lake PA-2
Grass Lake—lake (4) SD-7
Grass Lake—lake (2) TX-5
Grass Lake—lake (4) UT-8
Grass Lake—lake (5) WA-9
Grass Lake—lake (16) WI-6
Grass Lake—lake (2) WY-8
Grass Lake—locale CA-9
Grass Lake—locale MN-6
Grass Lake—locale MS-4
**Grass Lake**—pop pl MI-6
Grass Lake—swamp AK-9
Grass Lake—swamp CA-9
Grass Lake—swamp FL-3
Grass Lake—swamp IN-6
Grass Lake—swamp (4) MI-6
Grass Lake—swamp (3) MN-6
Grass Lake—swamp WI-6
Grass Lake Campground—park OR-9
Grass Lake Campground No. 2—park OR-9
Grass Lake Cem—cemetery IL-6
Grass Lake Cem—cemetery MI-6
Grass Lake Cem—cemetery MN-6
Grass Lake Creek—stream CA-9
Grass Lake Creek—stream MI-6
Grass Lake Drain—canal MI-6
Grass Lake (historical)—lake IA-7
Grass Lake Lookout Tower—locale MI-6
Grass Lake Park—park MI-6
Grass Lake Public Sch—hist pl MI-6
Grass Lakes—lake UT-8
Grass Lake Sch—school IL-6
Grass Lake Sch—school MN-6
Grass Lake Sch—school ND-7
Grass Lake State Game Mngmt Area—park IA-7
**Grass Lake Township**—pop pl ND-7
**Grass Lake (Township of)**—pop pl MI-6
**Grass Lake (Township of)**—pop pl MN-6
Grass Lake Trail—trail MI-6
Grassland—hist pl MD-2
Grassland—locale AL-4
Grassland—locale KY-4
Grassland—locale TX-5
Grassland—locale VA-3
**Grassland**—pop pl PA-2
**Grassland**—pop pl TN-4
**Grassland Addition (subdivision)**—pop pl TN-4
Grassland Cem—cemetery TX-5
Grassland Ch—church KY-4
Grassland Elem Sch—school TN-4
**Grassland Estates**—pop pl TN-4
Grassland Farm—hist pl TN-4
Grassland Farm—locale AL-4
Grassland Farm (University of Tennessee)—school TN-4
Grassland MS TN-4
Grassland Mtn—summit NC-3
Grassland Post Office (historical)—building AL-4
Grassland Post Office (historical)—building TN-4
Grassland Ridge—ridge NC-3
Grasslands—hist pl KY-4
Grassland Sch—school TN-4
Grassland Sch (abandoned)—school MO-7
Grassland Sch Number 1—school ND-7
Grassland Sch Number 2—school ND-7
Grasslands Hosp—hospital NY-2
**Grasslands (subdivision)**—pop pl TN-4
**Grassland Township**—pop pl ND-7
Grass Ledge—bar ME-1
Grasslick Branch—stream WV-2
Grasslick Ch—church WV-2
Grasslick Creek—stream WV-2
Grass Lick Run—stream OH-6
Grasslick Run—stream (6) WV-2
Grass Lot Cave—cave AL-4
Grassman Peak AZ-5
Grassman Valley—valley WI-6
Grass Meadow Brook NH-1
Grassmere NY-2
Grassmere PA-2
Grassmere—hist pl TN-4
Grassmere—locale WA-9
Grassmere—other PA-2
**Grassmere**—pop pl MI-6
Grassmere, Lake—lake FL-3
Grassmere Lake FL-3
Grassmere Lake LA-4
**Grassmere Park**—pop pl PA-2
**Grassmere Park (Grassmere)**—pop pl PA-2
Grassmere Station—locale MI-6
Grass Mesa—summit CO-8
Grass Mine—mine NV-8
Grassmont Rsvr—reservoir CA-9
Grass Mountain AZ-5
Grass Mountain ID-8
Grass Mountain Lakes—lake ID-8
Grass Mountain Leona Divide Truck Trail—trail CA-9
Grass Mountains UT-8
Grass Mountain Ski Area—locale MT-8
Grass Mountain Spring—spring ID-8
Grass Mountain Trail—trail OR-9
Grass Mountian—summit PA-2
Grass Mountian Trail—trail PA-2
Grass Mtn—summit CA-9
Grass Mtn—summit (2) ID-8
Grass Mtn—summit MT-8
Grass Mtn—summit NV-8
Grass Mtn—summit NM-5
Grass Mtn—summit NY-2
Grass Mtn—summit (3) OR-9
Grass Mtn—summit PA-2
Grass Mtn—summit SD-7
Grass Mtn—summit VT-1
Grass Mtn—summit (2) WA-9
Grass Mtns—range ID-8
**Grassna**—pop pl ND-7
Grasso Mine—mine CO-8
Grasso Plaza—locale MO-7
Grass Park—flat CO-8
Grass Park—park KS-7
Grass Patch Branch—stream MS-4
Grass Patch Lake—lake MS-4
Grass Patch Springs—spring TX-5
Grass Peak—island AK-9
Grass Point ME-1
Grass Point—cape MI-6
Grass Point—cape NY-2
Grass Point—cape VI-3
Grass Point State Park—park NY-2
Grass Pond MA-1
Grass Pond NY-2
Grass Pond—lake (5) FL-3
Grass Pond—lake GA-3
Grass Pond—lake (6) ME-1
Grass Pond—lake (2) MA-1
Grass Pond—lake NH-1
Grass Pond—lake NJ-2
Grass Pond—lake (14) NY-2
Grass Pond—lake RI-1
Grass Pond—lake VT-1
Grass Pond—swamp FL-3
Grass Pond Bog—swamp MA-1
Grass Pond Colony—locale TX-5
Grass Pond Interchange—other NH-1
Grass Pond Mtn—summit NY-2
Grass Pond Outlet—stream NY-2
Grass Ponds—lake TX-5
Grass Ponds—swamp TX-5
Grass Pond Slough—swamp TX-5
Grass Prairie—flat FL-3
Grass Range MT-8
**Grass Range**—pop pl MT-8
**Grassrange**—pop pl MT-8
**Grass Ridge**—pop pl VA-3
Grass Ridge—ridge AR-4
Grass Ridge—ridge NC-3
Grass River—stream AK-9
Grass River—stream MI-6
Grass River—stream NY-2
Grass River Flow—channel NY-2
Grass River Flow—reservoir NY-2
Grass Rock—island AK-9
Grassroots Oil Field—oilfield TX-5
Grass Rsvr—reservoir MT-8
Grass Run OH-6
Grass Run PA-2
Grass Run—stream (5) OH-6
Grass Run—stream (7) WV-2
Grass Run Cem—cemetery WV-2
Grass Run Ch—church WV-2
Grass Shack Spring—spring AZ-5
Grass Slough—lake MI-6
Grass Spring—spring CA-9
Grass Spring—spring OR-9
Grass Spring Canyon—valley NV-8
Grass Spring Run—stream WV-2
Grass Springs—spring NV-8
Grass Tank—reservoir AZ-5
Grass Tank—reservoir NM-5
**Grasston**—pop pl MN-6
Grasstop Rock—island AK-9
**Grass (Township of)**—pop pl IN-6
Grass Valley CA-9
Grass Valley UT-8
Grass Valley—basin CA-9
Grass Valley—basin NV-8
Grass Valley—basin UT-8
Grass Valley—locale MT-8
**Grass Valley**—pop pl CA-9
**Grass Valley**—pop pl OR-9
Grass Valley—valley (2) AK-9
Grass Valley—valley (5) CA-9
Grass Valley—valley CO-8
Grass Valley—valley NV-8
Grass Valley—valley TX-5
Grass Valley—valley (4) UT-8
Grass Valley—valley WA-9
**Grass Valley Acres Subdivision**—pop pl UT-8
Grass Valley Bald Mtn—summit CA-9
Grass Valley Canal—canal CO-8
Grass Valley Canyon—valley NV-8
Grass Valley Canyon—valley OR-9
Grass Valley Canyon—valley UT-8
Grass Valley (CCD)—cens area CA-9
Grass Valley Creek—stream (3) CA-9
Grass Valley Creek—stream (2) NV-8
Grass Valley Creek—stream UT-8
Grass Valley Dam—dam UT-8
Grass Valley Ditch—canal CA-9
Grass Valley Elem Sch—school OR-9
Grass Valley French Ditch—canal MT-8
Grass Valley (historical)—valley AZ-5
Grass Valley Lake—lake CA-9
Grass Valley Memorial Hosp—hospital CA-9
Grass Valley Ranch—locale (3) NV-8
Grass Valley Rsvr—reservoir CA-9
Grass Valley Rsvr—reservoir CO-8
Grass Valley Rsvr—reservoir NV-8
Grass Valley Rsvr—reservoir UT-8
Grass Valley Sch—school MT-8
Grass Valley Springs—spring NV-8
Grass Valley Trail—trail UT-8
Grass Valley Wash—arroyo NV-8
Grass Wash—stream AZ-5
Grassy AR-4
Grassy GA-3
Grassy OR-9
Grassy—locale AL-4
Grassy—locale UT-8
**Grassy**—pop pl AL-4
**Grassy**—pop pl MO-7
Grassy Bald—summit NC-3
Grassy Bay—bay FL-3
Grassy Bay—bay MN-6
Grassy Bay—bay NJ-2
Grassy Bay—bay (2) NY-2
Grassy Bay—bay SC-3
Grassy Bay—swamp FL-3
Grassy Bay Ch—church SC-3
Grassy Bayou—gut (3) LA-4
Grassy Bayou—locale MO-7
Grassy Bayou—stream (3) LA-4
Grassy Bend—bend TN-4
Grassy Bend—bend UT-8
Grassy Bottom Branch—stream SC-3
Grassy Branch GA-3
Grassy Branch NC-3
Grassy Branch TN-4
Grassy Branch VA-3
Grassy Branch—stream FL-3
Grassy Branch—stream IL-6
Grassy Branch—stream (2) IN-6
Grassy Branch—stream (16) KY-4
Grassy Branch—stream MO-7
Grassy Branch—stream (11) NC-3
Grassy Branch—stream OH-6
Grassy Branch—stream OK-5
Grassy Branch—stream (10) TN-4
Grassy Branch—stream TX-5
Grassy Branch—stream (4) VA-3
Grassy Branch—stream (3) WV-2
Grassy Branch Cove—valley GA-3
Grassy Branch Sch (historical)—school TN-4
Grassy Branch Trail—trail TN-4
Grassy Brook—stream (2) NH-1
Grassy Brook—stream NY-2
Grassy Brook—stream PA-2
Grassy Brook—stream VT-1
**Grassy Butte**—pop pl ND-7
Grassy Butte—summit (2) MT-8
Grassy Butte—summit (2) ND-7
Grassy Butte—summit (3) OR-9
Grassy Butte Ch—church ND-7
Grassy Butte Creek—stream OR-9
Grassy Butte Post Office—hist pl ND-7
Grassy Butte Rsvr—reservoir OR-9
Grassy Camp Creek—stream NC-3
Grassy Canyon AZ-5
Grassy Canyon—valley (2) CA-9
Grassy Canyon—valley (4) NV-8
Grassy Canyon—valley NM-5
Grassy Canyon—valley (4) UT-8
Grassy Canyon Spring—spring NV-8
Grassy Cem—cemetery IN-6
Grassy Ch—church (2) AL-4
Grassy Ch—church VA-3
Grassy Ch (historical)—church AL-4
Grassy Cone—summit ID-8
Grassy Cove—basin UT-8
Grassy Cove—bay FL-3
Grassy Cove—locale TN-4
Grassy Cove—valley TN-4
Grassy Cove Acad (historical)—school TN-4
Grassy Cove Baptist Ch (historical)—church TN-4
Grassy Cove Cem—cemetery TN-4
Grassy Cove Creek—stream TN-4
Grassy Cove Gap—gap NC-3
Grassy Cove Methodist Ch—church TN-4
Grassy Cove Post Office (historical)—building TN-4
Grassy Cove Ridge—ridge NC-3
Grassy Cove Saltpeter Cave TN-4
Grassy Cove Top—summit NC-3
Grassy Creek GA-3
Grassy Creek IN-6
Grassy Creek KY-4
Grassy Creek NC-3
Grassy Creek TX-5
Grassy Creek VA-3
Grassy Creek—gut FL-3
Grassy Creek—locale KY-4
Grassy Creek—locale NC-3
Grassy Creek—locale VA-3
**Grassy Creek**—pop pl (2) NC-3
**Grassy Creek**—pop pl TN-4
**Grassy Creek**—pop pl VA-3
Grassy Creek—stream (4) AR-4
Grassy Creek—stream (3) CA-9
Grassy Creek—stream (3) CO-8
Grassy Creek—stream (4) FL-3
Grassy Creek—stream GA-3
Grassy Creek—stream (4) IL-6
Grassy Creek—stream (6) IN-6
Grassy Creek—stream (8) KY-4
Grassy Creek—stream MI-6
Grassy Creek—stream (7) MO-7
Grassy Creek—stream MT-8
Grassy Creek—stream NM-5
Grassy Creek—stream (13) NC-3
Grassy Creek—stream (3) OH-6
Grassy Creek—stream (3) OK-5
Grassy Creek—stream (2) OR-9
Grassy Creek—stream (6) TN-4
Grassy Creek—stream (5) TX-5
Grassy Creek—stream (2) UT-8
Grassy Creek—stream (11) VA-3
Grassy Creek—stream (3) WV-2
Grassy Creek—stream WI-6
Grassy Creek—stream WY-8
Grassy Creek Cave—cave TN-4
Grassy Creek (CCD)—cens area KY-4
Grassy Creek Cem—cemetery IL-6
Grassy Creek Ch—church KY-4
Grassy Creek Ch—church MO-7
Grassy Creek Ch—church (4) NC-3
Grassy Creek Ch—church VA-3
Grassy Creek Diversion Channel—channel OH-6
Grassy Creek Elem Sch—school IN-6
Grassy Creek Falls—falls NC-3
Grassy Creek Hist Dist—hist pl NC-3
Grassy Creek No. 1 (Township of)—fmr MCD NC-3
Grassy Creek No. 2 (Township of)—fmr MCD NC-3
Grassy Creek Rec Area—park NC-3
Grassy Creek Sch—school KY-4
Grassy Creek Sch (historical)—school TN-4
Grassy Creek (Township of)—fmr MCD NC-3
Grassy Dell Creek—stream OR-9
Grassy Draw—valley CO-8
Grassy Draw—valley WY-8
Grassy (Election Precinct)—fmr MCD IL-6
Grassy Falls—locale WV-2
Grassy Field Hollow—valley VA-3
Grassy Flat—flat (2) CA-9
Grassy Flat—flat GA-3
Grassy Flat—flat (2) ID-8
Grassy Flat—flat (3) UT-8
Grassy Flat Camp Ground—locale CA-9
Grassy Flat Canyon—valley UT-8
Grassy Flat Creek—stream (2) AR-4
Grassy Flat Creek—stream CA-9
Grassy Flats—flat TN-4
Grassy Fork KY-4
Grassy Fork—locale TN-4
Grassy Fork—stream (4) IN-6
Grassy Fork—stream (6) KY-4
Grassy Fork—stream (2) NC-3
Grassy Fork—stream (3) OH-6
Grassy Fork—stream (3) TN-4
Grassy Fork—stream (3) VA-3
Grassy Fork—stream (3) WV-2
Grassy Fork Creek IN-6
Grassy Fork Elem Sch—school TN-4
Grassyfork Farm Number Three Dam IN-6
**Grassy Fork (Township of)**—pop pl IN-6
Grassy Gap—gap AR-4
Grassy Gap—gap CO-8
Grassy Gap—gap GA-3
Grassy Gap—gap (2) KY-4
Grassy Gap—gap (11) NC-3
Grassy Gap—gap (5) TN-4
Grassy Gap—gap VA-3
Grassy Gap Branch—stream GA-3
Grassy Gap Branch—stream KY-4
Grassy Gap Cem—cemetery KY-4
Grassy Gap Creek—stream NC-3
Grassy Gap Fork—stream KY-4
Grassy Gap Ridge—ridge KY-4
Grassy Gap Trail—trail TN-4
Grassy Glade—flat OR-9
Grassy Glade—flat TN-4
Grassy Glade Ridge—ridge TN-4
Grassy Granulated Mtn—summit MT-8
Grassy Gulch—valley (5) CO-8
Grassy Hammock Rocks—island CT-1
**Grassy Hill**—pop pl CT-1
Grassy Hill—summit AZ-5
Grassy Hill—summit CA-9
Grassy Hill—summit (3) CT-1
Grassy Hill—summit MA-1
Grassy Hill—summit NV-8
Grassy Hill—summit NH-1
Grassy Hill—summit (2) NY-2
Grassy Hill—summit OH-6
Grassy Hill—summit VA-3
Grassy Hill—summit WA-9
Grassy Hill Brook—stream CT-1
Grassy Hill Ch—church CT-1
Grassy Hills—range CO-8
Grassy Hills—summit MT-8
Grassy Hills Cabin—locale MT-8
Grassy Hollow—basin NY-2
Grassy Hollow—valley (4) AR-4
Grassy Hollow—valley CA-9
Grassy Hollow—valley GA-3
Grassy Hollow—valley ID-8
Grassy Hollow—valley KY-4
Grassy Hollow—valley (7) MO-7
Grassy Hollow—valley (2) OK-5
Grassy Hollow—valley PA-2
Grassy Hollow—valley (3) TN-4
Grassy Hollow—valley TX-5
Grassy Hollow—valley UT-8
Grassy Hollow—valley VA-3
Grassy Hollow—valley WY-8
Grassy Hollow Cem—cemetery MO-7
Grassy Hollow Ch—church MO-7
Grassy Hollow Creek—stream TN-4
Grassy Hollow Creek—stream WY-8
Grassy Island NC-3
Grassy Island—island (3) AK-9
Grassy Island—island CT-1
Grassy Island—island FL-3
Grassy Island—island (2) GA-3
Grassy Island—island (2) LA-4
Grassy Island—island (2) MA-1
Grassy Island—island MI-6
Grassy Island—island MN-6
Grassy Island—island NY-2
Grassy Island—island NC-3
Grassy Island—island OH-6
Grassy Island—island (2) OR-9
Grassy Island—island TN-4
Grassy Island—island WA-9
Grassy Island—island WI-6
Grassy Island—island WY-8
**Grassy Island**—pop pl PA-2
Grassy Island Breaker—building PA-2
Grassy Island Creek—stream (2) PA-2
Grassy Island (historical)—island FL-3
Grassy Island Ledge Light—locale MA-1
Grassy Islands—island ME-1
Grassy Islands—island NC-3
Grassy Island Shaft—mine PA-2
Grassy Junior High School AL-4
Grassy Key FL-3
Grassy Key—island (4) FL-3
**Grassy Key**—pop pl FL-3
Grassy Key Bank—bar FL-3
Grassy Knob GA-3
Grassy Knob—summit GA-3
Grassy Knob—summit IL-6
Grassy Knob—summit (2) KY-4
Grassy Knob—summit MO-7
Grassy Knob—summit (18) NC-3
Grassy Knob—summit OR-9
Grassy Knob—summit SC-3
Grassy Knob—summit (2) TN-4
Grassy Knob—summit TX-5
Grassy Knob—summit VA-3
Grassy Knob—summit (3) WV-2
Grassy Knob Branch—stream NC-3
Grassy Knob Ch—church AR-4
Grassy Knob Ch—church (2) NC-3
Grassy Knob Lookout Tower—locale TN-4
Grassy Knob Ridge—ridge (2) NC-3
Grassy Knobs—summit NC-3
Grassy Knob Trail—trail OR-9
Grassy Knoll—summit OR-9
Grassy Knoll—summit VA-3
Grassy Knoll Lake—lake WI-6
Grassy Knoll Lookout—locale WA-9
Grassy Knolls—summit AZ-5
Grassy Knoll Tank—reservoir AZ-5
Grassy Lake AR-4
Grassy Lake CA-9
Grassy Lake FL-3
Grassy Lake TX-5
Grassy Lake WI-6
Grassy Lake—bend AR-4
Grassy Lake—lake (3) AK-9
Grassy Lake—lake (10) AR-4
Grassy Lake—lake (4) CA-9
Grassy Lake—lake CO-8
Grassy Lake—lake (10) FL-3
Grassy Lake—lake GA-3
Grassy Lake—lake IL-6
Grassy Lake—lake KY-4
Grassy Lake—lake (13) LA-4
Grassy Lake—lake (5) MI-6
Grassy Lake—lake (3) MN-6
Grassy Lake—lake (6) MS-4
Grassy Lake—lake (3) MO-7
Grassy Lake—lake (6) MT-8
Grassy Lake—lake (3) OK-5
Grassy Lake—lake (3) OR-9
Grassy Lake—lake (2) SC-3
Grassy Lake—lake (2) TN-4
Grassy Lake—lake (9) TX-5
Grassy Lake—lake (3) WI-6
Grassy Lake—lake (2) WY-8
**Grassy Lake**—pop pl AR-4
Grassy Lake—reservoir MS-4
Grassy Lake—reservoir MT-8
Grassy Lake—reservoir OK-5
Grassy Lake—reservoir TX-5
Grassy Lake—reservoir (2) UT-8
Grassy Lake—stream MS-4
Grassy Lake—swamp (4) AR-4
Grassy Lake—swamp (2) FL-3
Grassy Lake—swamp LA-4
Grassy Lake—swamp OK-5
Grassy Lake—swamp OR-9
Grassy Lake Bay—bay MN-6
**Grassy Lake Bottom**—pop pl AR-4
Grassy Lake Canal—canal LA-4
Grassy Lake Creek—stream OR-9
Grassy Lake Cut-Off—bend MS-4
Grassy Lake Dam—dam (2) UT-8
Grassy Lake Drain—canal TN-4
Grassy Lake (historical)—lake TN-4
Grassy Lake Hollow—valley OK-5
Grassy Lake Rsvr—reservoir WY-8
Grassy Lakes UT-8
Grassy Lakes WY-8
Grassy Lakes—lake CA-9
Grassy Lakes—lake MI-6
Grassy Lake Trail—trail CO-8

Grassy Lake Trail—*trail* MT-8
Grassy Landing—*locale* ME-1
Grassy Lane Sch—*school* IA-7
Grassylead Ch—*church* AR-4
Grassy Ledge—*bar* ME-1
**Grassy Lick**—*pop pl* KY-4
Grassy Lick—*stream* WV-2
Grassy Lick Branch—*stream* KY-4
Grassy Lick Ch—*church* KY-4
Grassy Lick Creek—*stream* (2) KY-4
Grassy Lick Run—*stream* WV-2
Grassy Lick Sch—*school* WV-2
Grassy Lookout—*pillar* NM-5
Grassy Lot Gap—*gap* NC-3
Grassy Lot Hollow—*valley* WV-2
Grassy Marsh—*swamp* FL-3
*Grassy Meadow* WV-2
Grassy Meadow Run—*stream* PA-2
Grassy Meadows—*locale* WV-2
Grassy Memorial Chapel Ch—*church* AL-4
Grassy Mountain—*ridge* (2) TN-4
Grassy Mountain Ch—*church* AL-4
Grassy Mountain Rsvr—*reservoir* OR-9
Grassy Mountain Spring—*spring* OR-9
Grassy Mountain Tank—*reservoir* AZ-5
Grassy Mountain Windmill—*locale* AZ-5
*Grassy Mtn* GA-3
Grassy Mtn—*summit* AL-4
Grassy Mtn—*summit* (3) AZ-5
Grassy Mtn—*summit* AR-4
Grassy Mtn—*summit* CA-9
Grassy Mtn—*summit* (3) CO-8
Grassy Mtn—*summit* (2) GA-3
Grassy Mtn—*summit* (2) ID-8
Grassy Mtn—*summit* KY-4
Grassy Mtn—*summit* (3) MO-7
Grassy Mtn—*summit* (3) MT-8
Grassy Mtn—*summit* (2) NV-8
Grassy Mtn—*summit* (3) NC-3
Grassy Mtn—*summit* (4) OR-9
Grassy Mtn—*summit* SC-3
Grassy Mtn—*summit* (5) TN-4
Grassy Mtn—*summit* UT-8
Grassy Mtn—*summit* (3) VA-3
Grassy Mtn—*summit* WA-9
Grassy Mtn—*summit* WV-2
*Grassy Mtn Divide* OR-9
*Grassy Mtn Lake* GA-3
Grassy Mtns—*summit* UT-8
Grassy Narrows—*channel* MN-6
Grassy Nook—*summit* MA-1
Grassy Nook Pond—*lake* MA-1
Grassy Notch—*gap* NY-2
Grassy Pass—*gap* CO-8
Grassy Pass—*gap* NV-8
Grassy Patch—*flat* CA-9
Grassy Patch—*flat* TN-4
Grassy Peak—*summit* AZ-5
**Grassy Plain**—*pop pl* CT-1
Grassy Plain Sch—*school* CT-1
*Grassy Point* FL-3
Grassy Point—*cape* AL-4
Grassy Point—*cape* (2) AK-9
Grassy Point—*cape* (7) FL-3
Grassy Point—*cape* (2) LA-4
Grassy Point—*cape* (2) ME-1
Grassy Point—*cape* (3) MN-6
Grassy Point—*cape* MS-4
Grassy Point—*cape* NJ-2
Grassy Point—*cape* (2) NY-2
Grassy Point—*cape* (3) NC-3
Grassy Point—*cape* RI-1
Grassy Point—*cape* TN-4
Grassy Point—*cape* (3) TX-5
Grassy Point—*cape* VA-3
Grassy Point—*cliff* WA-9
Grassy Point—*locale* OH-6
**Grassy Point**—*pop pl* NY-2
Grassy Point—*summit* CO-8
Grassy Point—*summit* ID-8
Grassy Point Bayou—*gut* FL-3
Grassy Point Trail—*trail* AR-4
*Grassy Pond* FL-3
*Grassy Pond* ME-1
*Grassy Pond* MA-1
*Grassy Pond* PA-2
Grassy Pond—*lake* (7) FL-3
Grassy Pond—*lake* GA-3
Grassy Pond—*lake* IN-6
Grassy Pond—*lake* KY-4
Grassy Pond—*lake* (9) ME-1
Grassy Pond—*lake* (10) MA-1
Grassy Pond—*lake* MI-6
Grassy Pond—*lake* MO-7
Grassy Pond—*lake* NH-1
Grassy Pond—*lake* (7) NY-2
Grassy Pond—*lake* OH-6
Grassy Pond—*lake* OR-9
Grassy Pond—*lake* (2) PA-2
Grassy Pond—*lake* RI-1
Grassy Pond—*lake* TN-4
Grassy Pond—*lake* (2) TX-5
**Grassy Pond**—*pop pl* SC-3
Grassy Pond—*swamp* FL-3
Grassy Pond—*swamp* NH-1
Grassy Pond—*swamp* (3) TX-5
Grassy Pond Creek—*stream* AR-4
Grassy Pond Island—*island* GA-3
Grassy Pond Rec Area—*park* FL-3
Grassy Ponds—*lake* NY-2
Grassy Pond Slough—*swamp* KY-4
Grassy Pond Slough—*swamp* TX-5
Grassy Prairie—*lake* FL-3
Grassy Ranch—*locale* NV-8
Grassy Ranch Camp—*locale* OR-9
Grassy Ranch Trail—*trail* OR-9
Grassy Range—*range* OR-9
Grassy Ravine—*valley* CA-9
Grassy Ridge—*ridge* AL-4
Grassy Ridge—*ridge* AZ-5
Grassy Ridge—*ridge* AR-4
Grassy Ridge—*ridge* (2) GA-3
Grassy Ridge—*ridge* (2) ID-8
Grassy Ridge—*ridge* (8) NC-3
Grassy Ridge—*ridge* OR-9
Grassy Ridge—*ridge* PA-2
Grassy Ridge—*ridge* (2) TN-4
Grassy Ridge—*ridge* (2) VA-3
Grassy Ridge—*ridge* (2) WV-2
Grassy Ridge Bald—*summit* NC-3
Grassy Ridge Branch—*stream* NC-3
Grassy Ridge Cem—*cemetery* IL-6
Grassy Ridge Mine—*mine* NC-3
Grassy Ridge Sch—*school* IL-6
Grassy Ridge Spring—*spring* AZ-5
Grassy Rock—*island* AK-9
Grassy Rock—*island* CT-1
Grassy Rock—*summit* NV-8
Grassy Rsvr—*reservoir* OR-9
Grassy Run—*stream* CO-8
Grassy Run—*stream* (2) KY-4
Grassy Run—*stream* MO-7
Grassy Run—*stream* (3) OH-6
Grassy Run—*stream* PA-2
Grassy Run—*stream* VA-3
Grassy Run—*stream* (7) WV-2
Grassy Run Branch—*stream* SC-3
Grassy Run Cem—*cemetery* OH-6
Grassy Run Ch—*church* OH-6
**Grassy Run Junction**—*pop pl* PA-2
Grassy Run Sch—*school* WV-2
Grassy Run Trail—*trail* CO-8
Grassy Saddle Picnic Grounds—*locale* CO-8
Grassy Sch—*school* AL-4
Grassy Sch—*school* KY-4
Grassy Sch (historical)—*school* AL-4
Grassy Sch (historical)—*school* MO-7
Grassy Shoal Branch—*stream* KY-4
Grassy Slough—*gut* (2) IN-6
Grassy Slough—*stream* (3) AR-4
Grassy Slough—*stream* (2) TX-5
Grassy Slough—*swamp* OK-5
Grassy Sound—*bay* NJ-2
**Grassy Sound**—*pop pl* NJ-2
Grassy Sound Channel—*channel* NJ-2
Grassy Sound Meadow—*swamp* NJ-2
Grassy Sprain Brook—*stream* NY-2
Grassy Sprain Rsvr—*reservoir* NY-2
Grassy Spring—*spring* AZ-5
Grassy Spring—*spring* ID-8
Grassy Spring—*spring* (4) NV-8
Grassy Spring—*spring* (2) OR-9
Grassy Spring—*spring* (2) TN-4
Grassy Spring—*spring* UT-8
Grassy Spring Branch—*stream* VA-3
Grassy Springs Ch—*church* (2) KY-4
Grassy Springs Ch—*church* TN-4
Grassy Springs Sch—*school* TN-4
Grassy Spur Ch—*church* VA-3
Grassy Swale—*valley* CA-9
Grassy Swamp—*swamp* NY-2
Grassy Swamp Brook—*stream* NY-2
Grassy Swamp Creek—*stream* VA-3
Grassy Swamp Pond—*lake* NY-2
Grassy Tank—*reservoir* (2) AZ-5
Grassy Top—*summit* MT-8
Grassy Top—*summit* (4) NC-3
Grassy Top—*summit* TN-4
Grassy Top Mtn—*summit* NC-3
Grassy Top Mtn—*summit* SC-3
Grassy Top Mtn—*summit* WA-9
Grassy Tower Site State Public Hunting Area—*park* MO-7
Grassy (Township of)—*fmr MCD* AR-4
Grassy Trail Creek—*stream* UT-8
Grassy Trail Dam—*dam* UT-8
Grassy Trail Oil and Gas Field—*area* UT-8
Grassy Trail Rsvr—*reservoir* UT-8
Grassy Troughs—*spring* UT-8
Grassy Valley—*locale* TN-4
Grassy Valley—*valley* (4) TN-4
*Grassy Valley Baptist Church* TN-4
Grassy Valley Cem—*cemetery* TN-4
Grassy Valley Ch—*church* TN-4
Grassy Valley Sch (historical)—*school* TN-4
Grassy Wash—*valley* UT-8
Grassy Well—*well* NV-8
Grassy West Pond—*lake* MA-1
Graston Windmill—*locale* TX-5
Grasty Sch—*school* IL-6
Grasty Sch—*school* VA-3
Gratatum Sch—*school* IL-6
Grate—*locale* CO-8
Grate Ranch—*locale* NE-7
Grater Butte—*summit* OR-9
**Graterford**—*pop pl* PA-2
Graterford Ch—*church* PA-2
*Graterford Prison* PA-2
**Graterford (RR name Graters Ford)**—*pop pl* PA-2
*Graters Ford* PA-2
Graters Ford (RR name for Graterford)—*other* PA-2
Gratigny—*uninc pl* FL-3
Gratigny Park—*park* FL-3
Gratigny Plateau Park—*park* FL-3
Gratigny Sch—*school* FL-3
**Gratio**—*pop pl* TN-4
Gratio Post Office (historical)—*building* TN-4
*Gratiot* MI-6
**Gratiot**—*pop pl* MO-7
**Gratiot**—*pop pl* OH-6
**Gratiot**—*pop pl* WI-6
Gratiot, Lake—*lake* MI-6
Gratiot, Point—*cape* NY-2
Gratiot Cem—*cemetery* WI-6
**Gratiot (County)**—*pop pl* MI-6
Gratiot County Courthouse—*hist pl* MI-6
Gratiot House—*hist pl* WI-6
Gratiot Mine—*mine* MI-6
Gratiot Mtn—*summit* MI-6
Gratiot Park—*park* MI-6
Gratiot River—*stream* MI-6
Gratiot - Saginaw State Game Mngmt Area—*park* MI-6
Gratiot Sch—*school* MI-6
**Gratiot (Town of)**—*pop pl* WI-6
Gratis—*locale* GA-3
**Gratis**—*pop pl* OH-6
**Gratis**—*pop pl* TX-5
**Gratis (Township of)**—*pop pl* OH-6
**Gratitude**—*pop pl* MD-2
Gratitude Ch—*church* TN-4
**Graton**—*pop pl* CA-9
Grato Park—*park* AZ-5
Gratsinger Run—*stream* NY-2
**Grattam (historical)**—*pop pl* MS-4
**Grattan**—*pop pl* MI-6
**Grattan**—*pop pl* MN-6
Grattan Cem—*cemetery* MN-6
*Grattan Center* MI-6
Grattan Center—*other* MI-6
Grattan Ditch—*canal* WY-8
Grattan Massacre Historical Monmt—*park* WY-8
Grattan Sch—*school* CA-9
Grattan Sch—*school* MI-6
**Grattan Township**—*pop pl* NE-7
**Grattan (Township of)**—*pop pl* MI-6
**Grattan (Township of)**—*pop pl* MN-6
Gratt Cem—*cemetery* LA-4
Gratten Creek—*stream* CA-9
Gratten Flat—*flat* CA-9
Gratten Mine—*mine* NM-5
*Gratton* PA-2
**Gratton**—*pop pl* PA-2
**Gratton**—*pop pl* VA-3
Gratton Congregational Church and Chapel—*hist pl* VT-1
*Gratton Gulch* MT-8
Gratton Gulch—*valley* MT-8
Gratton Post Office (historical)—*building* TN-4
Gratton Sch—*school* CA-9
Gratton Sch—*school* VA-3
Gratton Station (historical)—*locale* TN-4
Gratuity Brook—*stream* MA-1
Gratwick Sch—*school* NY-2
Gratwick Waterfront Park—*park* NY-2
**Gratz**—*pop pl* KY-4
**Gratz**—*pop pl* PA-2
Gratz Borough—*civil* PA-2
Gratz Cem—*cemetery* OH-6
Gratz HS—*school* PA-2
Gratz Park Hist Dist—*hist pl* KY-4
**Gratztown**—*pop pl* PA-2
Gratztown Sch—*school* PA-2
Graue Mill—*hist pl* IL-6
Grauer, Gustav, Farm—*hist pl* MO-7
Grauer Lake—*reservoir* NM-5
Grauf Drain—*stream* MI-6
Grau Mine—*mine* CA-9
Graus Lake—*reservoir* MO-7
Grauthier Bayou—*gut* LA-4
Grauwyler Park—*park* TX-5
Gravatts Millpond—*reservoir* VA-3
*Grave* OR-9
*Grave, The* MH-9
Grave Ajax Mine—*mine* ID-8
Grave Branch—*stream* TN-4
Grave Butte—*summit* ID-8
Grave Canyon—*valley* NM-5
Grave Cem—*cemetery* TX-5
Grave Cem—*cemetery* VA-3
*Grave Cliffs* MH-9
*Grave Creek* AR-4
*Grave Creek* ID-8
*Grave Creek* IN-6
*Grave Creek* MI-6
*Grave Creek* OK-5
*Grave Creek* OR-9
**Grave Creek**—*pop pl* WV-2
Grave Creek—*stream* AK-9
Grave Creek—*stream* (6) ID-8
Grave Creek—*stream* KS-7
Grave Creek—*stream* MN-6
Grave Creek—*stream* (2) MT-8
Grave Creek—*stream* OH-6
Grave Creek—*stream* OK-5
Grave Creek—*stream* (5) OR-9
Grave Creek—*stream* PA-2
Grave Creek—*stream* WV-2
Grave Creek—*stream* WY-8
**Grave Creek (Big Grave Creek)**—*pop pl* WV-2
Grave Creek Bridge—*bridge* OR-9
Grave Creek Bridge—*hist pl* OR-9
Grave Creek Ch—*church* OK-5
Grave Creek Falls—*falls* OR-9
**Grave Creek (historical)**—*pop pl* OR-9
Grave Creek Indian Mound—*summit* WV-2
Grave Creek Meadow—*flat* MT-8
Grave Creek Mound—*hist pl* WV-2
Grave Creek Range—*range* MT-8
Grave Creek Riffle—*rapids* OR-9
Grave Creek Saddle—*gap* ID-8
Grave Creek Trail—*trail* OR-9
Grave Fork—*stream* WV-2
Grave Gap—*gap* NC-3
Grave Gap—*gap* TN-4
*Grave Hill* AL-4
Grave Hill—*summit* TN-4
Grave Hill—*summit* VA-3
*Grave Hill Baptist Church* TN-4
Grave Hill Cem—*cemetery* KY-4
Grave Hill Cem—*cemetery* MS-4
Grave Hill Cem—*cemetery* OH-6
Grave Hill Cem—*cemetery* (2) TN-4
Grave Hill Ch—*church* KY-4
Grave Hill Ch—*church* (2) TN-4
Grave Hill Sch—*school* NE-7
Grave Hollow—*valley* MO-7
Grave Hollow—*valley* TX-5
Grave Hollow—*valley* VA-3
*Grave Island* WA-9
Grave Island—*island* (2) AK-9
Grave Island—*island* MN-6
Grave Island—*island* OH-6
Gravel—*locale* LA-4
Grave Lake—*lake* (3) MN-6
Grave Lake—*lake* WY-8
Grave Lawn Cem—*cemetery* IN-6
*Gravelbank* OH-6
Gravel Bank—*other* OH-6
Gravel Bar—*bar* ME-1
Gravelbar Creek—*stream* WY-8
Gravel Bayou—*stream* MS-4
**Gravel Beach**—*pop pl* IN-6
Gravel Bluff—*cliff* MO-7
Gravel Bottom—*bend* WV-2
Gravel Bottom Lake—*lake* ND-7
*Gravel Branch* TN-4
Gravel Branch—*stream* AL-4
Gravel Branch—*stream* KY-4
Gravel Branch—*stream* NC-3
Gravel Brook—*stream* MI-6
Gravel Brook—*stream* VT-1
Gravel Butte—*summit* OR-9
Gravel Canyon—*valley* (2) NV-8
Gravel Canyon—*valley* NM-5
Gravel Canyon—*valley* (2) UT-8
Gravel Canyon Rsvr—*reservoir* NV-8
Gravel Cem—*cemetery* KY-4
**Gravel Center**—*pop pl* WA-9
Gravel Coulee—*valley* MT-8
*Gravel Creek* CA-9
*Gravel Creek* DE-2
*Gravel Creek* OH-6
*Gravel Creek* OR-9
*Gravel Creek* PA-2
*Gravel Creek* SD-7
Gravel Creek—*stream* (2) AL-4
Gravel Creek—*stream* (3) AK-9
Gravel Creek—*stream* AR-4
Gravel Creek—*stream* CA-9
Gravel Creek—*stream* ID-8
Gravel Creek—*stream* IL-6
Gravel Creek—*stream* IN-6
Gravel Creek—*stream* KY-4
Gravel Creek—*stream* LA-4
Gravel Creek—*stream* MI-6
Gravel Creek—*stream* NE-7
Gravel Creek—*stream* (2) NV-8
Gravel Creek—*stream* (4) OR-9
Gravel Creek—*stream* WA-9
Gravel Creek—*stream* WY-8
Gravel Creek Campground—*locale* ID-8
Gravel Creek Ch—*church* AL-4
Gravel Creek Patrol Cabin—*locale* WY-8
Gravel Crossing—*locale* UT-8
Gravel Ditch—*canal* WY-8
Gravel Draw—*valley* WY-8
Gravel Draw Pond—*reservoir* AZ-5
Gravel Dug Well—*well* AZ-5
Graveled Hill—*summit* AZ-5
Gravel Field Hollow—*valley* TN-4
Gravel Flat—*flat* OR-9
Gravelford—*locale* OR-9
Gravel Ford Bridge—*bridge* KY-4
Gravelford Cem—*cemetery* OR-9
Gravel Fork—*stream* WV-2
Gravel Gulch—*valley* MT-8
Gravel Gulch Shelter Cabin—*locale* AK-9
Gravel Gully—*valley* SC-3
Gravel Gully Sch—*school* SC-3
Gravel Gut—*gut* DE-2
*Gravel Hill* AR-4
*Gravel Hill* NJ-2
Gravel Hill—*locale* AL-4
Gravel Hill—*locale* (2) AR-4
Gravel Hill—*locale* DE-2
Gravel Hill—*locale* MD-2
Gravel Hill—*locale* NJ-2
Gravel Hill—*locale* TN-4
Gravel Hill—*locale* (2) VA-3
**Gravel Hill**—*pop pl* AL-4
**Gravel Hill**—*pop pl* AR-4
**Gravel Hill**—*pop pl* IN-6
**Gravel Hill**—*pop pl* MS-4
**Gravelhill**—*pop pl* MO-7
**Gravel Hill**—*pop pl* MO-7
**Gravel Hill**—*pop pl* PA-2
**Gravel Hill**—*pop pl* SC-3
**Gravel Hill**—*pop pl* TN-4
**Gravel Hill**—*pop pl* VA-3
Gravel Hill—*summit* AR-4
Gravel Hill—*summit* IL-6
Gravel Hill—*summit* KY-4
Gravel Hill—*summit* MD-2
Gravel Hill—*summit* MT-8
Gravel Hill—*summit* NJ-2
Gravel Hill—*summit* OH-6
Gravel Hill—*summit* PA-2
Gravel Hill—*summit* SC-3
Gravel Hill—*summit* TN-4
Gravel Hill—*summit* UT-8
Gravel Hill—*summit* VA-3
Gravel Hill—*uninc pl* VA-3
Gravel Hill Baptist Ch—*church* TN-4
Gravel Hill Baptist Ch (historical)—*church* TN-4
*Gravel Hill Baptist Church* AL-4
Gravel Hill Bend—*bend* AZ-5
Gravel Hill Branch—*stream* VA-3
Gravel Hill Cave—*cave* TN-4
Gravel Hill Cem—*cemetery* (3) AL-4
Gravel Hill Cem—*cemetery* AR-4
Gravel Hill Cem—*cemetery* GA-3
Gravel Hill Cem—*cemetery* IN-6
Gravel Hill Cem—*cemetery* (3) MO-7
Gravel Hill Cem—*cemetery* OH-6
Gravel Hill Cem—*cemetery* SC-3
Gravel Hill Cem—*cemetery* (4) TN-4
Gravel Hill Cem—*cemetery* TX-5
*Gravel Hill Ch* TN-4
Gravel Hill Ch—*church* (7) AL-4
Gravel Hill Ch—*church* (3) AR-4
Gravel Hill Ch—*church* LA-4
Gravel Hill Ch—*church* MS-4
Gravel Hill Ch—*church* MO-7
Gravel Hill Ch—*church* NC-3
Gravel Hill Ch—*church* PA-2
Gravel Hill Ch—*church* (2) TN-4
Gravel Hill Ch—*church* (3) TX-5
Gravel Hill Ch—*church* (8) VA-3
Gravel Hill Ch (abandoned)—*church* MO-7
Gravel Hill Ch (historical)—*church* TN-4
Gravel Hill Church—*locale* AR-4
Gravel Hill Plantation—*hist pl* SC-3
*Gravel Hill Post Office* TN-4
Gravelhill Post Office (historical)—*building* TN-4
Gravel Hill Post Office (historical)—*building* TN-4
Gravel Hills—*other* NM-5
Gravel Hills—*range* CA-9
*Gravel Hill Sch* AL-4
Gravel Hill Sch—*school* AL-4
Gravel Hill Sch—*school* IL-6
Gravel Hill Sch—*school* KS-7
Gravel Hill Sch—*school* MO-7
Gravel Hill Sch—*school* OH-6
Gravel Hill Sch (abandoned)—*school* MO-7
Gravel Hill Sch (abandoned)—*school* (2) PA-2
Gravel Hill Sch (historical)—*school* AL-4
Gravel Hill Sch (historical)—*school* (2) MS-4
Gravel Hill Sch (historical)—*school* (5) TN-4
Gravel Hill Swamp—*stream* SC-3
Gravel Hill (Township of)—*fmr MCD* AR-4
Gravel Hole—*lake* TX-5
Gravel Hollow—*valley* TN-4
Gravelick Branch—*stream* WV-2
Graveline Bay—*bay* AL-4
Graveline Bay—*bay* MS-4
Graveline Bayou—*gut* MS-4
Graveline Gulch—*valley* CO-8
Graveline Mound Site (22JK503)—*hist pl* MS-4
Graveling Point—*cape* NJ-2
Gravel Island—*island* ME-1
Gravel Island—*island* (2) MA-1
Gravel Island—*island* (2) MI-6
Gravel Island—*island* (2) WI-6
Gravel Island Natl Wildlife Ref—*park* WI-6
Gravel Islands—*island* MA-1
Gravel Junction—*locale* AR-4
Gravel Knob—*summit* KY-4
Gravel Knob—*summit* NC-3
Gravel Knob—*summit* TN-4
*Gravel Lake* MN-6
Gravel Lake—*lake* IN-6
Gravel Lake—*lake* (4) MI-6
Gravel Lake—*lake* (2) MN-6
Gravel Lake—*lake* ND-7
Gravel Lake—*lake* WA-9
Gravel Lake—*lake* WY-8
**Gravel Lake**—*pop pl* MI-6
Gravel Lake Campground—*locale* ND-7
Gravelle Creek—*stream* MT-8
Gravelles—*locale* WA-9
Gravel Lick—*locale* (2) PA-2
**Gravel Lick**—*pop pl* VA-3
Gravel Lick—*stream* (2) KY-4
Gravel Lick—*stream* (2) PA-2
Gravel Lick Branch—*stream* (2) KY-4
Gravel Lick Ch—*church* VA-3
Gravel Lick Creek—*stream* VA-3
Gravel Lick Dam—*dam* PA-2
Gravel Lick Run—*stream* (4) PA-2
Gravel Lick Run—*stream* WV-2
Gravel Lick Sch—*school* KY-4
Gravel Lick Trail—*trail* (3) PA-2
*Gravellines Bay* AL-4
**Gravelly**—*pop pl* AR-4
Gravelly Bar Creek—*stream* CA-9
Gravelly Bay—*bay* WI-6
*Gravelly Branch* DE-2
Gravelly Branch—*stream* (2) AR-4
Gravelly Branch—*stream* (2) DE-2
Gravelly Branch—*stream* (2) MD-2
Gravelly Branch—*stream* (2) NC-3
Gravelly Branch—*stream* TN-4
Gravelly Branch—*stream* TX-5
Gravelly Brook—*stream* CT-1
Gravelly Brook—*stream* MA-1
Gravelly Brook—*stream* NJ-2
Gravelly Brook—*stream* (2) WI-6
*Gravelly Buttes* CA-9
Gravelly Buttes—*summit* CA-9
Gravelly Ch—*church* AR-4
Gravelly Cliff—*cliff* KY-4
Gravelly Cove—*basin* OR-9
Gravelly Creek—*stream* GA-3
Gravelly Creek—*stream* NJ-2
Gravelly Creek—*stream* NC-3
Gravelly Creek—*stream* TN-4
Gravelly Creek—*stream* TX-5
Gravelly Ditch—*stream* DE-2
Gravelly Flat—*flat* (3) CA-9
Gravelly Ford—*locale* CA-9
Gravelly Ford—*locale* NV-8
Gravelly Ford Canal—*canal* CA-9
Gravelly Ford Canal (Abandoned)—*canal* CA-9
Gravelly Ford Ranch—*locale* CA-9
*Gravelly Fork* DE-2
*Gravelly Fork* MD-2
Gravelly Gap—*gap* GA-3
Gravelly Gulch—*valley* OR-9
**Gravelly Hill**—*pop pl* TN-4
Gravelly Hill Ch—*church* AR-4
Gravelly Hill Ch—*church* VA-3
**Gravelly Hills**—*pop pl* TN-4
Gravelly Hill Sch (historical)—*school* TN-4
Gravelly Hill (Township of)—*fmr MCD* AR-4
Gravelly Hollow—*valley* AR-4
Gravelly Hollow—*valley* (2) MO-7
Gravelly Hollow—*valley* TN-4
*Gravelly Island* MA-1
Gravelly Island—*island* (2) MI-6
*Gravelly Islands* MA-1
Gravelly Island Shoals—*bar* MI-6
Gravelly Knobs—*summit* TN-4
Gravelly Lake—*lake* (2) CA-9
Gravelly Lake—*lake* WA-9
**Gravelly Lake**—*pop pl* WA-9
Gravelly Mtn—*summit* TN-4
*Gravelly Point* MI-6
Gravelly Point—*cape* AR-4
Gravelly Point—*cape* ME-1
Gravelly Point—*cape* MD-2
Gravelly Point—*cape* (2) NY-2
Gravelly Point—*cape* VA-3
Gravelly Point—*cliff* ID-8
**Gravelly Point**—*pop pl* VA-3
Gravelly Pond—*lake* MA-1
Gravelly Range—*range* MT-8
Gravelly Range Lake—*lake* MT-8
Gravelly Ridge—*ridge* AL-4
Gravelly Ridge—*ridge* CA-9
Gravelly Ridge—*ridge* TN-4
Gravelly Ridge—*ridge* VA-3
Gravelly Ridges Artificial Revegetation Plot—*other* NM-5
Gravelly Rock—*rock* MA-1
Gravelly Run—*locale* NJ-2
Gravelly Run—*stream* DE-2
Gravelly Run—*stream* (2) MD-2
Gravelly Run—*stream* (5) NJ-2
Gravelly Run—*stream* PA-2
Gravelly Run—*stream* TN-4
Gravelly Run—*stream* (2) VA-3
Gravelly Run Ch—*church* IN-6
Gravelly Run Dam—*dam* NJ-2
Gravelly Run Pond—*reservoir* NJ-2
Gravelly Sch—*school* TN-4
Gravelly Spring—*spring* CA-9
Gravelly Spring—*spring* NV-8
**Gravelly Springs**—*pop pl* AL-4
Gravelly Springs—*spring* (2) AL-4
*Gravelly Springs Branch* AL-4
Gravelly Springs Cave—*cave* AL-4
Gravelly Springs Creek—*stream* CA-9
Gravelly Springs Missionary Baptist Ch—*church* AL-4
Gravelly Spur—*valley* TN-4
Gravelly Valley—*basin* CA-9
Gravelly Valley—*valley* (2) TN-4
Gravel Mtn—*summit* AK-9
Gravel Mtn—*summit* (2) CO-8
Gravel Mtn—*summit* WY-8
Gravel Neck—*cape* VA-3
**Gravelotte**—*pop pl* TN-4
Gravel Pass—*gap* UT-8
Gravel Peak—*summit* WY-8
Gravel Pile Oil Field—*oilfield* UT-8
Gravel Pit—*locale* ID-8
Gravel Pit—*locale* NM-5
Gravel Pit—*locale* WA-9
**Gravel Pit**—*pop pl* AR-4
**Gravel Pit**—*pop pl* IA-7
**Gravel Pit**—*pop pl* PA-2
Gravel Pit—*ridge* TN-4
Gravel Pit Coulee—*valley* MT-8
Gravel Pit Creek—*stream* MI-6
Gravel Pit Lake—*lake* CA-9
Gravel Pit Lake—*lake* IN-6
Gravel Pit Lake—*lake* MI-6
Gravel Pit Lake—*reservoir* MS-4
Gravel Pit Lakes—*lake* NM-5
Gravel Pit Sch—*school* IL-6
Gravel Pit Site (39WW203)—*hist pl* SD-7
Gravel Pit Spur (historical)—*locale* NV-8
*Gravel Pit Station* PA-2
Gravel Pit Station—*locale* PA-2
Gravel Pit Tank—*reservoir* AZ-5
Gravel Pit Tank—*reservoir* (3) TX-5
**Gravel Place**—*pop pl* PA-2
*Gravel Point* ME-1
Gravel Point—*bend* CA-9
Gravel Point—*cape* (2) AK-9
Gravel Point—*cape* MI-6
Gravel Point—*cape* NY-2
Gravel Point—*cape* OR-9
Gravel Point—*summit* WA-9
Gravel Point Bridge—*bridge* LA-4
Gravel Point Cem—*cemetery* WA-9
Gravel Point Sch—*school* MO-7
*Gravel Pond* MA-1
Gravel Pond—*lake* NY-2
Gravel Pond—*lake* PA-2
Gravel Pond—*reservoir* PA-2
Gravel Prairie—*flat* LA-4
Gravel Range—*range* CA-9
Gravel Range Creek—*stream* CA-9
*Gravel Reservoir* NV-8
Gravelridge—*locale* AR-4
Gravel Ridge—*locale* VA-3
**Gravel Ridge**—*pop pl* AR-4
Gravel Ridge—*ridge* AL-4
Gravel Ridge—*ridge* AR-4
Gravel Ridge—*ridge* OR-9
Gravel Ridge—*ridge* VA-3
Gravel Ridge—*ridge* WY-8
Gravel Ridge Ch—*church* MO-7
Gravel Ridge Ch—*church* TX-5
*Gravel Ridge Church* AL-4
Gravel Ridges—*ridge* OR-9
Gravel Ridge Sch—*school* AL-4
Gravel Ridge Sch (historical)—*school* MO-7
Gravel Ridge Sch (reduced usage)—*school* TX-5
Gravel Road Windmill—*locale* NV-8
*Gravel Run* DE-2
Gravel Run—*stream* ID-8
Gravel Run—*stream* (2) IN-6
Gravel Run—*stream* (2) MD-2
Gravel Run—*stream* (2) NY-2
Gravel Run—*stream* OH-6
Gravel Run—*stream* (3) PA-2
Gravel Run—*stream* SC-3
Gravel Run—*stream* (2) VA-3
Gravel Run—*stream* WV-2
Gravel Run Airp—*airport* PA-2
Gravel Run Cem—*cemetery* PA-2
Gravel Run Ch—*church* PA-2
Gravel Run Ch—*church* VA-3
Gravel Shoals Sluice—*hist pl* NC-3
Gravel Sholes Park—*park* WI-6
Gravel Siding—*locale* MS-4
Gravel Slough—*locale* TX-5
Gravel Slough—*stream* MS-4
Gravel Slough—*stream* TX-5
Gravel Spit Anchorage—*channel* AK-9
Gravels Pond—*lake* MI-6
Gravel Spring—*spring* ID-8
Gravel Spring—*spring* MO-7
Gravel Spring—*spring* (2) NV-8
Gravel Spring—*spring* (3) OR-9
Gravel Spring—*spring* (2) TN-4
Gravel Spring—*spring* (3) UT-8
Gravel Spring—*spring* WY-8
*Gravel Spring Canyon* AZ-5
Gravel Spring Hollow—*valley* MO-7
Gravel Springs—*locale* MS-4
Gravel Springs—*locale* VA-3
Gravel Springs Cem—*cemetery* MS-4
Gravel Springs Cem—*cemetery* VA-3
Gravel Springs Ch—*church* GA-3
Gravel Springs Ch—*church* MS-4
Gravel Springs Creek—*stream* MS-4
Gravel Springs Gap—*gap* VA-3
Gravel Springs Run—*stream* VA-3
Gravel Springs Sch—*school* AL-4
Gravel Springs Shelter—*locale* VA-3
Gravel Springs Trail—*trail* VA-3
Gravelstand Top—*summit* TN-4
Gravel Switch—*locale* KY-4
**Gravel Switch**—*pop pl* KY-4
Gravel Switch (CCD)—*cens area* KY-4
Gravel Tank—*reservoir* (2) AZ-5
Gravel Tank—*reservoir* (3) NM-5
Gravel Tank—*reservoir* (6) TX-5
**Gravelton**—*pop pl* IN-6
**Gravelton**—*pop pl* MO-7
**Gravelton**—*pop pl* NC-3
Gravelton Hollow—*valley* MO-7
**Graveltown**—*pop pl* TN-4
Gravel Wall Sch (historical)—*school* MO-7
*Gravel Wash* CA-9
Gravel Wash—*stream* AZ-5
Gravel Wash—*stream* CA-9
Gravel Wash—*stream* NV-8

Gravel Waterhole—*lake* OR-9
Gravel Waterhole—*lake* TX-5
Gravel Well—*well* CA-9
Gravel Windmill—*locale* TX-5
Gravely Bay—*bay* NY-2
*Gravely Branch* DE-2
*Gravely Branch* TN-4
Gravely Branch—*stream* TN-4
Gravely Branch—*stream* VA-3
*Gravely Elementary School* TN-4
Gravely Gap—*gap* KY-4
Gravely Gully—*stream* SC-3
Gravely Hill—*summit* TN-4
Gravely Mine—*mine* MT-8
Gravely Mtn—*summit* MT-8
Gravely Run—*stream* MD-2
Gravely Valley—*valley* TN-4
Grave Meadow—*flat* ID-8
Grave Meadow Peak—*summit* ID-8
*Gravemore Creek* FL-3
Grave Mtn—*summit* PA-2
Grave Mtn—*summit* VA-3
Gravenburg, Bayou—*stream* LA-4
Graven Lake—*lake* MN-6
Graven Point—*cape* VA-3
Graven Ridge—*ridge* CA-9
Graven Rsvr—*reservoir* CA-9
Gravenstein—*locale* CA-9
Gravenstein Union Sch—*school* CA-9
Gravens Thorofare—*channel* NJ-2
Grave of Myles Standish—*cemetery* MA-1
Grave of N B Kinnear—*cemetery* WY-8
Grave of President Harrison—*cemetery* IN-6
Grave Of Red Eagle (Weatherford)—*cemetery* AL-4
Grave of the Legendary Giantess—*hist pl* WA-9
*Grave of William Weatherford* AL-4
Grave Peak—*summit* ID-8
*Grave Point* MH-9
Grave Point—*cape* (3) AK-9
Grave Point—*cape* MT-8
Grave Point—*summit* ID-8
Graveraet HS—*school* MI-6
Graveraet River—*stream* MI-6
Graver Creek—*stream* OR-9
*Gravereat River* MI-6
*Grave Ridge* PA-2
Grave Ridge—*ridge* PA-2
Grave Riffle—*rapids* OR-9
Graver Park—*park* IL-6
Gravers—*locale* PA-2
Gravers Grove—*woods* CA-9
Graver's Lane Station—*hist pl* PA-2
*Grave Run* PA-2
Grave Run—*stream* MD-2
Grave Run Ch—*church* MD-2
Graver Wash—*arroyo* AZ-5
Graver Wash—*stream* AZ-5
*Graves* MA-1
*Graves* MS-4
Graves—*locale* CA-9
Graves—*locale* GA-3
Graves—*locale* MS-4
**Graves**—*pop pl* SC-3
Graves—*post sta* TX-5
Graves, Abbott, House—*hist pl* ME-1
Graves, Dr. Harry S., House—*hist pl* SD-7
Graves, Lulu, Farm—*hist pl* ID-8
Graves, Sereno W., House—*hist pl* WI-6
Graves, The—*bar* ME-1
Graves, The—*island* MA-1
Graves Atterberry Ditch—*canal* NM-5
Graves Bar—*bar* AL-4
Graves Bayou—*gut* AR-4
Graves Beach—*beach* MA-1
**Gravesboro**—*pop pl* CA-9
Graves Branch—*stream* (4) TN-4
Graves Bridge—*bridge* VA-3
Graves Brook—*stream* MA-1
Graves Brook—*stream* NY-2
Graves Brook—*stream* (2) VT-1
Graves Butte—*summit* OR-9
Graves Cabin—*building* CA-9
Graves Cabin—*locale* CA-9
Graves Camp—*locale* CO-8
Graves Canyon—*valley* CA-9
Graves Cave—*cave* AL-4
Graves Cem—*cemetery* (3) AL-4
Graves Cem—*cemetery* (2) AR-4
Graves Cem—*cemetery* CA-9
Graves Cem—*cemetery* IN-6
Graves Cem—*cemetery* KY-4
Graves Cem—*cemetery* (6) MS-4
Graves Cem—*cemetery* (2) MO-7
Graves Cem—*cemetery* NY-2
Graves Cem—*cemetery* OH-6
Graves Cem—*cemetery* (3) TN-4
Graves Cem—*cemetery* (2) TX-5
Graves Cem—*cemetery* VT-1
Graves Cem—*cemetery* WI-6
Graves Chapel—*church* GA-3
Graves Chapel—*church* MS-4
Graves Chapel—*church* MO-7
Graves Chapel—*church* NC-3
Graves Chapel—*church* (2) TN-4
Graves Chapel—*church* VA-3
**Graves Chapel**—*pop pl* AR-4
Graves Chapel Cem—*cemetery* MS-4
Graves Chapel Sch—*school* TN-4
Graves Corner—*locale* VA-3
Graves Corners—*locale* NY-2
**Graves (County)**—*pop pl* KY-4
*Graves Creek* AL-4
*Graves Creek* ID-8
*Graves Creek* MT-8
*Graves Creek* TX-5
Graves Creek—*stream* (3) AL-4
Graves Creek—*stream* (3) AR-4
Graves Creek—*stream* (2) CA-9
Graves Creek—*stream* CO-8
Graves Creek—*stream* (2) FL-3
Graves Creek—*stream* (4) ID-8
Graves Creek—*stream* MS-4
Graves Creek—*stream* (2) MT-8
Graves Creek—*stream* OH-6
Graves Creek—*stream* OK-5
Graves Creek—*stream* (2) OR-9
Graves Creek—*stream* SD-7
Graves Creek—*stream* (2) WA-9
Graves Creek—*stream* WY-8
Graves Creek Ch—*church* MS-4
Graves Creek Falls—*falls* MT-8
Graves Creek Guard Station—*locale* WA-9
Graves Creek Inn—*locale* WA-9
Graves Creek Trail—*trail* MT-8
Graves Ditch—*canal* WY-8
Graves Ditch—*channel* LA-4
Graves Drain—*canal* MI-6
**Gravesend**—*pop pl* NY-2
Gravesend Bay—*bay* NY-2
Gravesend Cem—*cemetery* NY-2
Gravesend Park—*park* NY-2
*Graves Ferry* TN-4
Graves-Fisher-Strong House—*hist pl* OR-9
Graves Gap—*gap* TN-4
Graves Gap Branch—*stream* TN-4
Graves Gap Cem—*cemetery* AL-4
Graves Gap Ch—*church* AL-4
Graves Gap Ch—*church* TN-4
Graves Gap Mine (underground)—*mine* TN-4
Graves Harbor—*bay* AK-9
Graves Hill—*ridge* OH-6
Graves Hill—*summit* ME-1
Graves Hill—*summit* NH-1
Graves Hill—*summit* VT-1
Graves Hill Cem—*cemetery* NY-2
Graves (historical)—*locale* KS-7
Graves Hollow—*valley* (4) TN-4
Graves Hollow—*valley* TX-5
Graves Hotel—*hist pl* MT-8
Graves House—*hist pl* NC-3
Graves HS—*school* AL-4
Graves Island—*island* MA-1
Graves Island—*island* OR-9
Graves JHS—*school* VA-3
Graves Knob—*summit* KY-4
Graves Lake—*lake* MS-4
Graves Lake—*lake* MT-8
Graves Lake—*lake* SC-3
Graves Lake—*lake* WY-8
Graves Landing—*locale* VA-3
Graves Landing (historical)—*locale* MS-4
Graves Landing Strip—*airport* IN-6
*Graves Ledge* MA-1
Graves Light, The—*locale* MA-1
Graves Light Station—*hist pl* MA-1
Graves Meadow—*flat* ID-8
Graves Meadows—*flat* MT-8
Graves Mill—*locale* VA-3
Graves Mill Hist Dist—*hist pl* DE-2
Graves Millpond—*reservoir* SC-3
Graves Mines (underground)—*mine* AL-4
Graves Mine (underground)—*mine* AL-4
Graves Mound—*summit* MO-7
Graves Mountain State For—*forest* (2) MO-7
Graves Mtn—*summit* GA-3
Graves Mtn—*summit* MO-7
Graves Mtn—*summit* NY-2
Graves Mtn—*summit* VA-3
Graves Mtn—*summit* WA-9
Graves Neck—*cape* RI-1
Graves Park—*park* NM-5
Graves Peak—*summit* ID-8
Graves Peak—*summit* (2) MT-8
Graves Point—*cape* RI-1
Graves Pond—*lake* CT-1
Graves Pond—*lake* MA-1
Graves Pond—*lake* NH-1
Graves Pond—*lake* NY-2
Graves Pond—*lake* (2) PA-2
Graves Pond—*reservoir* PA-2
Graves Pond—*reservoir* SC-3
Grave Spring—*spring* WY-8
Graves Prospect—*mine* TN-4
Graves Ranch—*locale* (2) WY-8
Graves Ridge—*ridge* TN-4
Graves Rocks—*area* AK-9
Graves Rsvr—*reservoir* CA-9
Graves Sch—*school* AR-4
Graves Sch—*school* CA-9
Graves Sch—*school* (2) IL-6
Graves Sch—*school* IA-7
Graves Sch—*school* ME-1
Graves Sch—*school* TN-4
Graves Sch—*school* VA-3
Graves Sch (abandoned)—*school* MO-7
Graves School (abandoned)—*locale* WY-8
Graves Spring—*spring* GA-3
Graves Spring—*spring* ID-8
Graves Spring—*spring* TN-4
Graves Station Sch—*school* SC-3
Graves-Stewart House—*hist pl* NC-3
Graves Store—*locale* VA-3
**Graveston**—*pop pl* TN-4
Gravestone Brook—*stream* NY-2
Graveston Mill Pond—*lake* TN-4
Graveston Post Office (historical)—*building* TN-4
**Gravestown**—*pop pl* MS-4
Graves Valley—*stream* CA-9
*Gravesville* TN-4
**Gravesville**—*pop pl* AR-4
**Gravesville**—*pop pl* NY-2
**Gravesville**—*pop pl* WI-6
Gravesville Cem—*cemetery* NY-2
Graves Vly—*swamp* NY-2
Graves Windmill—*locale* TX-5
Grave Tank—*reservoir* NM-5
*Gravet Islands* MA-1
Gravett Branch—*stream* TN-4
**Gravette**—*pop pl* AR-4
Grave Wash—*stream* CA-9
Grave Well—*well* NM-5
Grave Yard Bank Mine—*mine* TN-4
Graveyard Bay—*swamp* SC-3
*Graveyard Bayou* LA-4
Graveyard Bayou—*stream* (3) LA-4
Graveyard Bayou—*stream* MS-4
Graveyard Branch—*stream* (3) AL-4
Graveyard Branch—*stream* FL-3
Graveyard Branch—*stream* (2) KY-4
Graveyard Branch—*stream* MO-7
Graveyard Branch—*stream* NC-3
Graveyard Branch—*stream* (5) TX-5
Graveyard Butte—*summit* OR-9
Graveyard Butte Cem—*cemetery* OR-9
Graveyard Camp—*locale* WA-9
Graveyard Canyon—*valley* (2) AZ-5
Graveyard Canyon—*valley* CA-9
Graveyard Canyon—*valley* ID-8
Graveyard Canyon—*valley* (10) NM-5
Graveyard Canyon—*valley* OR-9
Graveyard Canyon—*valley* TX-5
Graveyard Canyon—*valley* UT-8
Graveyard Canyon—*valley* WY-8
Graveyard Coulee—*valley* MT-8
Graveyard Cove—*bay* (2) AK-9
Graveyard Cove—*bay* MD-2
*Graveyard Creek* MD-2
Graveyard Creek—*stream* AL-4
Graveyard Creek—*stream* (2) AK-9
Graveyard Creek—*stream* (2) CA-9
Graveyard Creek—*stream* (2) CO-8
Graveyard Creek—*stream* (2) FL-3
Graveyard Creek—*stream* MD-2
Graveyard Creek—*stream* (2) MT-8
Graveyard Creek—*stream* NC-3
Graveyard Creek—*stream* TX-5
Graveyard Creek—*stream* WI-6
Graveyard Crossing Cem—*cemetery* TX-5
Graveyard Drain—*canal* NV-8
Graveyard Draw—*valley* NM-5
Graveyard Draw—*valley* UT-8
Graveyard Flat—*flat* UT-8
Graveyard Flat—*flat* WA-9
Graveyard Flats—*flat* CO-8
Graveyard Gap—*gap* NC-3
Graveyard Gap—*gap* TN-4
*Graveyard Gulch* CO-8
Graveyard Gulch—*valley* AZ-5
Graveyard Gulch—*valley* CA-9
Graveyard Gulch—*valley* (3) CO-8
Graveyard Gulch—*valley* ID-8
Graveyard Gulch—*valley* MT-8
Graveyard Gulch—*valley* NM-5
Graveyard Gulch—*valley* (2) OR-9
Graveyard Gulch—*valley* SD-7
Graveyard Gulch Wasteway—*canal* ID-8
Graveyard High Top—*summit* NC-3
*Grave Yard Hill* AL-4
Graveyard Hill—*cemetery* PA-2
Graveyard Hill—*cliff* TX-5
Graveyard Hill—*summit* (4) AL-4
Graveyard Hill—*summit* IL-6
Graveyard Hill—*summit* KY-4
Graveyard Hill—*summit* (2) MO-7
Graveyard Hill—*summit* MT-8
Graveyard Hill—*summit* NC-3
Graveyard Hill—*summit* (3) TN-4
Graveyard Hill—*summit* TX-5
Graveyard Hill—*summit* WY-8
Graveyard Hill Cem—*cemetery* MT-8
Graveyard Hill Cem—*cemetery* SC-3
Graveyard Hill Cem—*cemetery* TN-4
*Graveyard Hills* CA-9
Graveyard Hollow—*valley* AL-4
Graveyard Hollow—*valley* (2) AR-4
Graveyard Hollow—*valley* IN-6
Graveyard Hollow—*valley* (3) KY-4
Graveyard Hollow—*valley* (10) MO-7
Graveyard Hollow—*valley* PA-2
Graveyard Hollow—*valley* (6) TN-4
Graveyard Hollow—*valley* (2) TX-5
Graveyard Hollow—*valley* (3) UT-8
Graveyard Hollow—*valley* VA-3
Graveyard Hollow—*valley* (2) WV-2
Graveyard Island—*island* AK-9
Graveyard Island—*island* LA-4
Graveyard Island—*island* NC-3
Graveyard Island—*island* OH-6
Graveyard Knob—*summit* KY-4
Graveyard Knob—*summit* VA-3
Graveyard Lake—*lake* AR-4
Graveyard Lake—*lake* FL-3
Graveyard Lake—*lake* (2) GA-3
Graveyard Lake—*lake* MN-6
Graveyard Lakes—*lake* AK-9
Graveyard Lakes—*lake* CA-9
Graveyard Meadow—*locale* CA-9
Graveyard Meadows—*flat* CA-9
Graveyard Mesa—*summit* NM-5
Graveyard Mound—*summit* KS-7
Graveyard Mtn—*summit* NC-3
Graveyard Mtn—*summit* TX-5
*Graveyard of Ships* NC-3
*Graveyard of the Atlantic* NC-3
Grave Yard Ore Bank—*mine* TN-4
Graveyard Peak—*summit* CA-9
Graveyard Pocket—*basin* NM-5
*Graveyard Point* VT-1
Graveyard Point—*cape* (4) AK-9
Graveyard Point—*cape* CA-9
Graveyard Point—*cape* IA-7
Graveyard Point—*cape* ME-1
Graveyard Point—*cape* (2) MD-2
Graveyard Point—*cape* (3) NC-3
Graveyard Point—*cape* (2) OR-9
Graveyard Point—*cape* TN-4
Graveyard Point—*cape* TX-5
Graveyard Point—*cape* VT-1
Graveyard Point—*summit* ID-8
Graveyard Pole Lookout—*locale* FL-3
Graveyard Pond—*lake* FL-3
Graveyard Prairie—*flat* CA-9
Graveyard Ridge—*ridge* AL-4
Graveyard Ridge—*ridge* AR-4
Graveyard Ridge—*ridge* (2) NC-3
Graveyard Ridge—*ridge* (3) TN-4
Graveyard Ridge Cem—*cemetery* TN-4
Graveyard Rim—*cliff* OR-9
Graveyard Run—*stream* PA-2
Graveyard Run—*stream* VA-3
Graveyard Run—*stream* (2) WV-2
Graveyard Slough—*bay* TX-5
Graveyard Slough—*gut* AK-9
Graveyard Slough—*gut* AR-4
Graveyard Spit—*bar* WA-9
Graveyard Spring—*spring* SD-7
Graveyard Springs—*spring* WI-6
Graveyard Tank—*reservoir* NM-5
Graveyard Wash—*stream* (2) AZ-5
Graveyard Wash—*valley* UT-8
*Graveyard Wash Dam* AZ-5
Graveyard Wash Retarding Dam—*dam* AZ-5
Graveyard Well—*well* NM-5
*Gravey Creek* MT-8
Gravey Creek—*stream* ID-8
Gravey Flat—*flat* NV-8
Gravier Slough—*gut* TX-5
Gravina Island—*island* (2) AK-9
Gravina Point—*cape* (2) AK-9
Gravina River—*stream* AK-9
Gravina Rocks—*bar* AK-9
Gravine Island—*island* AL-4
Gravitt Chapel—*church* AL-4
*Gravitt Chapel Ch* AL-4
Gravity—*locale* TX-5
**Gravity**—*pop pl* IA-7
**Gravity**—*pop pl* PA-2
Gravity Ditch—*canal* WA-9
Gravity (historical P.O.)—*locale* IA-7
Gravity Lateral—*canal* CA-9
Gravity Point Ch—*church* AR-4
Gravlee Cem—*cemetery* AL-4
Gravlee Junction—*locale* AL-4
Gravleeton (historical)—*locale* AL-4
Gravleeton Post Office (historical)—*building* AL-4
Gravley Ch—*church* VA-3
*Gravley Elementary School* TN-4
*Gravline Bay* AL-4
Gravning Sch (historical)—*school* SD-7
Gravois Arm—*bay* MO-7
Gravois Ave Sch—*school* CA-9
Gravois Camp—*locale* MO-7
Gravois Creek—*stream* (2) MO-7
**Gravois Mills**—*pop pl* MO-7
Gravois Park—*park* MO-7
**Gravois (sta.)**—*pop pl* MO-7
Gravois Township—*civil* MO-7
Gravy Branch—*stream* KY-4
*Gravy Creek* ID-8
Gravy Creek—*stream* OR-9
Gravy Gulch—*valley* OR-9
**Grawn**—*pop pl* MI-6
Gray—*locale* KS-7
Gray—*locale* MD-2
Gray—*locale* MS-4
Gray—*locale* (2) OK-5
Gray—*locale* (2) PA-2
Gray—*locale* TX-5
Gray—*locale* VA-3
**Gray**—*pop pl* GA-3
**Gray**—*pop pl* ID-8
**Gray**—*pop pl* IA-7
**Gray**—*pop pl* KY-4
**Gray**—*pop pl* LA-4
**Gray**—*pop pl* ME-1
**Gray**—*pop pl* NY-2
**Gray**—*pop pl* (2) PA-2
**Gray**—*pop pl* TN-4
Gray, Asa, House—*hist pl* MA-1
Gray, Benajah, Log House—*hist pl* TN-4
Gray, Capt. J. H. D., House—*hist pl* OR-9
Gray, Capt. Thomas, House—*hist pl* MA-1
Gray, Charles, Printing Shop—*hist pl* DE-2
Gray, David, House—*hist pl* MA-1
Gray, Garret and Julia, Cottage—*hist pl* CO-8
Gray, Henry P., House—*hist pl* TN-4
Gray, Isaac, House—*hist pl* TN-4
Gray, John, House—*hist pl* PA-2
Gray, John, Springhouse—*hist pl* KY-4
Gray, John P. and Stella, House—*hist pl* ID-8
Gray, Joseph H., House—*hist pl* NV-8
Gray, Levins D., House—*hist pl* UT-8
Gray, Rev. John H., House—*hist pl* AL-4
Gray, Walter, House—*hist pl* AR-4
Gray Aaf Airp—*airport* WA-9
Gray Acad—*school* MS-4
**Gray Acres**—*pop pl* TN-4
Gray and Ligon Ranch—*locale* NM-5
Gray Ave Sch—*school* CA-9
*Grayback* CA-9
**Grayback**—*pop pl* TX-5
Grayback—*summit* AZ-5
Grayback—*summit* NV-8
Grayback—*summit* OR-9
Grayback Branch—*stream* TN-4
Grayback Clapboard Trail—*trail* OR-9
*Grayback Creek* ID-8
Grayback Creek—*stream* CO-8
Grayback Creek—*stream* ID-8
Grayback Creek—*stream* OR-9
Gray Back Creek—*stream* TX-5
Grayback Forest Camp—*locale* OR-9
Grayback Glades—*flat* OR-9
Grayback Gulch—*stream* NM-5
Grayback Gulch—*valley* CO-8
Grayback Gulch—*valley* ID-8
Grayback Hills—*summit* UT-8
Grayback Mount—*summit* OR-9
*Gray Back Mountain* UT-8
Grayback Mountains—*range* AZ-5
*Grayback Mtn* AZ-5
*Grayback Mtn* OR-9
Grayback Mtn—*summit* AK-9
Grayback Mtn—*summit* AZ-5
Grayback Mtn—*summit* CO-8
Grayback Mtn—*summit* OR-9
Grayback Mtn—*summit* WA-9
*Grayback Peak* CA-9
Gray Back Peak—*summit* CO-8
Grayback Ridge—*ridge* CA-9
Grayback Ridge—*ridge* CO-8
Grayback Ridge—*ridge* OR-9
Grayback Ridge—*ridge* WY-8
Grayback Shelter—*locale* OR-9
Grayback Trail—*trail* OR-9
Grayback Well Number One—*well* NV-8
Grayback Well Number Two (dry)—*well* NV-8
Gray Baptist Ch—*church* TN-4
Gray Bay—*bay* SC-3
Gray Bay—*swamp* SC-3
Gray Bayou—*stream* MS-4
Gray Beach—*beach* MA-1
Graybeal Branch—*stream* NC-3
Graybeal Cem—*cemetery* (2) NC-3
Gray Beal Spring—*spring* CO-8
Graybeard Creek—*stream* NC-3
Graybeard Mtn—*summit* NC-3
**Gray (Beattieville)**—*pop pl* LA-4
Graybell Spring—*spring* TN-4
Graybill—*locale* PA-2
Graybill Canyon—*valley* NM-5
Graybill Cem—*cemetery* IA-7
Graybill Cem—*cemetery* (2) OH-6
Graybill Creek—*stream* IA-7
Graybill Hollow—*valley* WV-2
Graybills Ch—*church* PA-2
Gray Blanket Creek—*stream* SD-7
*Gray Branch* NC-3
Gray Branch—*stream* (3) AL-4
Gray Branch—*stream* AR-4
Gray Branch—*stream* (2) GA-3
Gray Branch—*stream* KS-7
Gray Branch—*stream* KY-4
Gray Branch—*stream* (2) LA-4
Gray Branch—*stream* (3) MO-7
Gray Branch—*stream* (3) NC-3
Gray Branch—*stream* OH-6
Gray Branch—*stream* (2) TN-4
Gray Branch—*stream* TX-5
Gray Branch—*stream* (2) VA-3
Gray Branch Ch—*church* NC-3
Gray Brook—*stream* IN-6
Gray Brook—*stream* (2) ME-1
Gray Brook—*stream* OH-6
Gray Brook—*stream* VT-1
Gray-Brownlow-Wilcox House—*hist pl* NC-3
**Grayburg**—*pop pl* TX-5
Grayburg Cem—*cemetery* TX-5
*Gray Butte* CA-9
Gray Butte—*summit* CA-9
Gray Butte—*summit* OR-9
Gray Butte—*summit* (2) SD-7
Gray Butte—*summit* WY-8
Gray Butte Cem—*cemetery* OR-9
Gray Butte Creek—*stream* OR-9
Gray Buttes—*range* SD-7
Gray Buttes—*ridge* OR-9
Gray Cabin Draw—*valley* WY-8
Gray Cactus Mesa—*summit* AZ-5
Gray Camp Branch—*stream* NC-3
Gray Canal—*canal* LA-4
Gray Canyon—*valley* ID-8
Gray Canyon—*valley* UT-8
Gray Canyon—*valley* WA-9
Gray Casstevens Lake—*reservoir* NC-3
Gray Casstevens Lake Dam—*dam* NC-3
Gray Castle—*pillar* AZ-5
*Gray Cave* AL-4
Gray Cave—*cave* TN-4
Gray (CCD)—*cens area* KY-4
Grayce Farms Airp—*airport* PA-2
*Gray Cem* AL-4
Gray Cem—*cemetery* (3) AL-4
Gray Cem—*cemetery* (3) AR-4
Gray Cem—*cemetery* (2) IL-6
Gray Cem—*cemetery* IN-6
Gray Cem—*cemetery* IA-7
Gray Cem—*cemetery* (9) KY-4
Gray Cem—*cemetery* (6) MS-4
Gray Cem—*cemetery* (6) MO-7
Gray Cem—*cemetery* NE-7
Gray Cem—*cemetery* NC-3
Gray Cem—*cemetery* (2) OK-5
Gray Cem—*cemetery* (2) PA-2
Gray Cem—*cemetery* SC-3
Gray Cem—*cemetery* (16) TN-4
Gray Cem—*cemetery* (2) TX-5
Gray Cem—*cemetery* (4) VA-3
Gray Cem—*cemetery* WV-2
Gray Center—*locale* KS-7
Gray Ch—*church* LA-4
Gray Chapel—*church* TN-4
Gray Chapel—*church* TX-5
Gray Chapel (historical)—*church* TN-4
Gray Cliff—*cliff* AK-9
Gray Cliff—*cliff* CA-9
Gray Cliff Campground—*park* UT-8
Gray Cliff Hist Dist—*hist pl* MA-1
Gray Cliffs—*ridge* UT-8
Gray Cliff Spring—*spring* UT-8
Gray Coat Sch (historical)—*school* MS-4
Gray Cobb Lake Dam—*dam* MS-4
Gray Colony Ditch—*canal* CA-9
Gray Community Cem—*cemetery* TN-4
Gray Cone—*summit* NV-8
Gray Copper Falls—*falls* CO-8
Gray Copper Gulch—*valley* CO-8
Gray Corners—*locale* NY-2
Gray-Coulton House—*hist pl* OH-6
Gray County—*civil* KS-7
**Gray (County)**—*pop pl* TX-5
Gray County Free Fair—*locale* KS-7
**Gray Court**—*pop pl* SC-3
Gray Court (CCD)—*cens area* SC-3
Gray Court-Owings Sch—*school* SC-3
Gray Cove—*basin* TN-4
Gray Cove—*bay* (2) ME-1
Gray Cow Camp—*locale* CO-8
*Gray Creek* AL-4
*Gray Creek* CT-1
*Gray Creek* KS-7
*Gray Creek* LA-4
*Gray Creek* TN-4
Gray Creek—*stream* AL-4
Gray Creek—*stream* (5) CA-9
Gray Creek—*stream* CO-8
Gray Creek—*stream* GA-3
Gray Creek—*stream* (2) ID-8
Gray Creek—*stream* IA-7
Gray Creek—*stream* (2) KY-4
Gray Creek—*stream* (2) LA-4
Gray Creek—*stream* MI-6
Gray Creek—*stream* MS-4
Gray Creek—*stream* (2) MT-8
Gray Creek—*stream* NV-8
Gray Creek—*stream* (7) OR-9
Gray Creek—*stream* TN-4
Gray Creek—*stream* TX-5
Gray Creek—*stream* VA-3
Gray Creek—*stream* WY-8
Graycroft Ridge—*ridge* MT-8
Gray Crossing—*locale* TX-5
Gray Dam—*dam* (2) AL-4
Grayden—*locale* WV-2
Grayden Mine—*mine* CO-8
Gray Ditch—*canal* CA-9
Gray Ditch—*canal* IN-6
Gray Ditch—*canal* NC-3
Graydon—*locale* PA-2
**Graydon**—*pop pl* WV-2
Graydon Branch—*stream* AL-4
Graydon House—*hist pl* AL-4
Graydon Park—*park* NJ-2
**Graydon Springs**—*pop pl* MO-7
Gray Duck Hole—*lake* TN-4
*Gray Eagle* MN-6
*Grayeagle* WV-2
Gray Eagle Bar—*bar* CA-9
Gray Eagle Canyon—*valley* CA-9
Gray Eagle Creek—*stream* CA-9
Gray Eagle Creek—*stream* ID-8
Gray Eagle Lodge—*locale* CA-9
Gray Eagle Mine—*mine* AZ-5
Gray Eagle Mine—*mine* (3) CA-9
Gray Eagle Mine—*mine* CO-8
Gray Eagle Mine—*mine* MT-8
Gray Eagle Mine—*mine* (3) NV-8
Gray Eagle Mine—*mine* NM-5
Gray Eagle Mine—*mine* (2) OR-9
Gray Eagle Quarry—*mine* TN-4
Gray Eagletail Creek—*stream* SD-7
Gray Elem Sch—*school* TN-4
Gray Eye Run—*stream* OH-6
Gray Family Cem—*cemetery* GA-3
Gray Farms—*locale* TX-5
Gray Field Airp—*airport* IN-6
Grayfield Hollow—*valley* TN-4
Gray Flat—*flat* OR-9
Gray Ford—*locale* IL-6
**Grayford**—*pop pl* IN-6
*Grayford Church* MS-4
Grayford Sch (historical)—*school* MS-4
Grayfox—*locale* KY-4
Gray Friends Ch—*church* IN-6
Gray Gables—*hist pl* MD-2
Gray Gables—*hist pl* NC-3
Gray Gables—*locale* WA-9
**Gray Gables**—*pop pl* MA-1
Gray Gables Cem—*cemetery* MA-1
Gray Gables Ch—*church* FL-3
Gray Gap—*gap* NC-3
Gray Gardens East and West Hist Dist—*hist pl* MA-1
Gray Glacier—*glacier* AK-9
Gray Goose—*locale* SD-7
Gray Goose Mine—*mine* AZ-5
Gray Grass Bench—*bench* AZ-5
Gray-Griswold (CCD)—*cens area* GA-3
Gray Grove Sch (historical)—*school* MO-7
Gray Gulch—*valley* (2) MT-8
Gray Gulch—*valley* OR-9
Gray Gut—*bay* NC-3
Gray-Hackett House—*hist pl* OR-9
Grayham Branch—*stream* KY-4
Grayham Cem—*cemetery* GA-3
Gray Hammock—*island* TX-5
**Gray Haven**—*pop pl* MD-2
**Gray Hawk**—*pop pl* KY-4
Gray Head—*summit* CO-8
*Grayhead Peak* UT-8
Gray Head Peak—*summit* UT-8
Gray Hill—*locale* AL-4
Gray Hill—*locale* GA-3
Gray Hill—*summit* AL-4
Gray Hill—*summit* AR-4
Gray Hill—*summit* GA-3
Gray Hill—*summit* KY-4
Gray Hill—*summit* ME-1
Gray Hill—*summit* MI-6
Gray Hill—*summit* NM-5
Gray Hill—*summit* (2) NY-2
Gray Hill—*summit* PA-2
Gray Hill—*summit* TN-4
Gray Hill Cem—*cemetery* GA-3
Gray Hill Ch—*church* AL-4
Gray Hill Ch—*church* GA-3
Gray Hills—*range* CO-8
Gray Hills—*range* UT-8
Gray Hills—*ridge* WY-8
Gray Hills—*summit* AZ-5
Gray Hills—*summit* (2) NV-8
Gray Hills—*summit* UT-8
Grayhill Sch—*school* OH-6
Gray Hill Sch (historical)—*school* AL-4
Gray Hills Tank—*reservoir* AZ-5
Gray (historical)—*locale* AL-4
**Gray (historical)**—*pop pl* OR-9
Gray Hollow—*valley* (4) AR-4
Gray Hollow—*valley* KY-4
Gray Hollow—*valley* MS-4
Gray Hollow—*valley* MO-7
Gray Hollow—*valley* PA-2
Gray Hollow—*valley* (5) TN-4
Gray Hollow—*valley* VA-3
Gray Hollow—*valley* WV-2
Gray Hollow Cem—*cemetery* VA-3
**Gray Horse**—*pop pl* OK-5
Grayhorse Canyon—*valley* AZ-5
Gray Horse Cem—*cemetery* OK-5
Gray Horse Creek—*stream* CA-9
Grayhorse Creek—*stream* CA-9
Grayhorse Creek—*stream* MT-8
Gray Horse Creek—*stream* (2) OK-5
Grayhorse Dam—*dam* AZ-5
Gray Horse Isle—*island* LA-4
Grayhorse Valley—*valley* CA-9
*Grayhound Ridge* ID-8
Gray House—*hist pl* KY-4
Gray HS—*school* NC-3
Gray HS—*school* OK-5
Graying—*locale* MT-8
Gray Island—*island* ME-1
Gray JHS—*school* WA-9
Gray Jockey Mine—*mine* MT-8
Gray Jockey Peak—*summit* MT-8
**Gray Junction**—*pop pl* IN-6
Gray Knoll—*summit* (3) UT-8
Gray Knolls—*summit* UT-8
Gray Knox Quarry—*mine* TN-4
*Gray Lake* WI-6
Gray Lake—*lake* (5) MI-6
Gray Lake—*lake* (2) MN-6
Gray Lake—*lake* NV-8
Gray Lake—*lake* NY-2
Gray Lake—*lake* WI-6
Gray Lake—*stream* MS-4
Gray Lake Dam—*dam* MS-4
Gray Lakes—*lake* WY-8
*Grayland* IL-6
**Grayland**—*pop pl* WA-9
Grayland Ave Sch—*school* CA-9
Grayland Ch Number 1—*church* TX-5
Grayland Park—*park* WA-9
Gray Lateral—*canal* CA-9
Gray Lateral—*canal* OR-9
Gray Ledge Dam Trail—*trail* ME-1

Gray Ledge Deadwater—lake ME-1
Graylime Creek—stream AK-9
Grayline Lake—lake AK-9
Grayling—locale MN-6
Grayling—locale MT-8
**Grayling**—pop pl AK-9
**Grayling**—pop pl MI-6
Grayling Arm—bay MT-8
Grayling Cem—cemetery MN-6
Grayling Creek—stream (4) AK-9
Grayling Creek—stream MT-8
Grayling Creek—stream WY-8
Grayling Fork Black River—stream AK-9
Grayling Golf Club—other MI-6
Grayling Hill—summit AK-9
Grayling Lake—lake (3) AK-9
Grayling Lake—lake CA-9
Grayling Lake—lake (2) MT-8
Grayling Lake—lake UT-8
Grayling Lake—lake WY-8
Grayling Lake Number One—lake MT-8
Grayling Lake Number Two—lake MT-8
Grayling Sch—school MI-6
Grayling State Wildlife Mngmt Area—park MN-6
**Grayling (Township of)**—pop pl MI-6
Grayling Winter Rec Area—park MI-6
Graylin Sch—school CO-8
Graylock Butte—summit OR-9
Gray Lodge Waterfowl Mngmt Area—park CA-9
Graylyn—hist pl NC-3
Graylyn Conference Center—locale NC-3
**Graylyn Crest**—pop pl DE-2
Gray Manor—locale MD-2
Gray Manor Sch—school MD-2
Gray Mare Branch—stream KY-4
Gray Mare Hill—summit CT-1
Graymare Hollow—valley SC-3
Gray Mare Tank—reservoir AZ-5
Gray Marsh Point MD-2
Gray Meadow—swamp ME-1
Gray Memorial Ch—church FL-3
Gray Memorial Field—cemetery PA-2
Gray Memorial United Methodist Ch—church FL-3
Graymere Golf and Country Club—locale TN-4
**Graymere Manor**—pop pl TN-4
Gray Mesa UT-8
Gray Mesa—summit (2) AZ-5
Gray Mill Branch LA-4
Gray Mill (site)—locale CA-9
Gray Mine TN-4
Gray Mine—mine KY-4
Gray Mine—mine TN-4
Graymont—locale CO-8
**Graymont**—pop pl AL-4
**Graymont**—pop pl IL-6
Graymont—uninc pl GA-3
Graymont Sch—school AL-4
Graymoor IL-6
Graymoor KY-4
Graymoor—locale NY-2
**Graymoor**—pop pl KY-4
**Graymoor-Devondale**—pop pl KY-4
Graymound Cem—cemetery MS-4
Gray Mountain AZ-5
Gray Mountain WA-9
**Gray Mountain**—pop pl AZ-5
Gray Mountain—ridge CA-9
Gray Mountain Canal—canal UT-8
Gray Mountain Pumping Station—other AZ-5
**Gray Mountain (Trading Post)**—pop pl AZ-5
Gray Mtn—summit AK-9
Gray Mtn—summit (2) AZ-5
Gray Mtn—summit AR-4
Gray Mtn—summit CA-9
Gray Mtn—summit CO-8
Gray Mtn—summit KY-4
Gray Mtn—summit MO-7
Gray Mtn—summit NV-8
Gray Mtn—summit OK-5
Gray Mtn—summit TN-4
Gray Mtn—summit (2) TX-5
Gray Mule—locale TX-5
Gray Mule Cem—cemetery TX-5
Gray Needle—summit CO-8
Gray Oaks—uninc pl NY-2
Gray Oil Field—oilfield OK-5
Gray Park—park FL-3
Gray Park—park MS-4
Gray Park—park OR-9
Gray Peak—summit AK-9
Gray Peak—summit CA-9
Gray Peak—summit NY-2
Gray Peak—summit WA-9
Gray Peak—summit WY-8
Gray Point—cape MD-2
Gray Point—cape NC-3
Gray Point—cape TX-5
Gray Point—cliff (2) AZ-5
**Gray Point**—pop pl LA-4
Gray Point—summit UT-8
Gray Pond—lake ME-1
Gray Post Office (historical)—building MS-4
Gray Prairie—flat OR-9
Gray Ranch—locale AZ-5
Gray Ranch—locale CA-9
Gray Ranch—locale MT-8
Gray Ranch—locale NM-5
Gray Ranch—locale TX-5
Gray Ranch Airp—airport WA-9
Gray Ridge MO-7
Gray Ridge—ridge AL-4
Gray Ridge—ridge (2) AZ-5
Gray Ridge—ridge IL-6
Gray Ridge—ridge ME-1
Gray Ridge—ridge OR-9
Gray Ridge—ridge UT-8
Gray Ridge Ch—church OH-6
**Grayridge (Gray Ridge Station)**—pop pl MO-7
Grayridge Post Office (historical)—building TN-4
Gray Ridge Sch—school AL-4
Gray RLA Airp—airport IN-6
Gray Road Baptist Ch—church IN-6
Gray Road Ch IN-6
Gray Rock—island AK-9
**Gray Rock**—pop pl AR-4
**Gray Rock**—pop pl MD-2
Gray Rock—summit OR-9
Gray Rock Cem—cemetery AL-4
Gray Rock Cem—cemetery AR-4
Grayrock Cem—cemetery TX-5
Gray Rock Ch—church AL-4
Gray Rock Ch—church MS-4
Gray Rock Lake CA-9
Gray Rock Lake—lake CA-9
Gray Rock Lakes CA-9
Grayrock Peak—summit CO-8
Gray Rocks CA-9
Gray Rocks—pillar WY-8
**Gray Rocks**—pop pl CA-9
Gray Rocks—summit (2) CA-9
Gray Rock Sch (historical)—school AL-4
Gray Rocks (historical)—locale SD-7
Gray Rock United Methodist Ch MS-4
**Gray (RR name Steff)**—pop pl KY-4
Gray Rsvr—reservoir CO-8
Gray Rsvr—reservoir OR-9
Gray Rsvr No. 3—reservoir CO-8
Gray Run—stream IN-6
Gray Run—stream PA-2
Grays AL-4
Grays—locale VA-3
**Grays**—pop pl AR-4
**Grays**—pop pl LA-4
**Grays**—pop pl OH-6
**Grays**—pop pl PA-2
**Grays**—pop pl SC-3
**Grays**—pop pl WA-9
Grays Arch—arch KY-4
Graysarch Trail—trail KY-4
Grays Basin—basin CO-8
Grays Bay—bay IL-6
Grays Bay—bay MN-6
Grays Bay—bay WA-9
Grays Bay—swamp NC-3
Grays Bay Light—locale OR-9
Grays Bayou—stream LA-4
Grays Bayou—stream TX-5
Grays Beach—beach ME-1
Grays Beach—beach MA-1
Grays Bend—bend CA-9
Grays Bend—bend TN-4
Grays Bend Cem—cemetery TN-4
Grays Bluff—cliff LA-4
Grays Bluff—cliff (2) TN-4
Grays Box (historical)—locale MS-4
Grays Branch AL-4
Grays Branch DE-2
**Grays Branch**—pop pl KY-4
Grays Branch—stream DE-2
Grays Branch—stream (6) KY-4
Grays Branch—stream MS-4
Grays Branch—stream NC-3
Grays Branch—stream (2) TN-4
Grays Branch—stream (2) TX-5
Grays Branch—stream VA-3
Grays Branch Sch—school KY-4
Grays Brook—stream ME-1
Graysburg—locale TN-4
Graysburge Post Office (historical)—building TN-4
Graysburgh TN-4
Graysburg Hills—range TN-4
Graysburgh Post Office (historical)—building TN-4
Graysburg Knobs—ridge TN-4
Grays Butte—summit OR-9
Grays Butte—summit WA-9
Grays Camp—locale LA-4
**Grays Camp**—pop pl TN-4
Grays Campsite—locale CA-9
Grays Canal—canal LA-4
Grays Canyon—valley CA-9
Grays Canyon—valley NV-8
Grays Cem MS-4
Grays Cem—cemetery (2) IN-6
Grays Cem—cemetery ME-1
Grays Cem—cemetery (2) MS-4
Grays Cem—cemetery PA-2
Grays Cem—cemetery TX-5
Grays Ch—church KY-4
Grays Ch—church PA-2
Gray Sch—school AZ-5
Gray Sch—school DE-2
Gray Sch—school GA-3
Gray Sch—school (2) IL-6
Gray Sch—school KS-7
Gray Sch—school MI-6
Gray Sch—school NM-5
Gray Sch—school NY-2
Gray Sch—school OR-9
Gray Sch—school PA-2
Gray Sch (abandoned)—school MO-7
Grays Chapel TN-4
Grays Chapel—church (2) AL-4
Grays Chapel—church AR-4
Grays Chapel—church KY-4
Grays Chapel—church MS-4
Grays Chapel—church (2) NC-3
Grays Chapel—church (2) TN-4
**Grays Chapel**—pop pl AL-4
**Grays Chapel**—pop pl NC-3
**Grays Chapel**—pop pl TX-5
Grays Chapel Cem—cemetery GA-3
Grays Chapel Ch (historical)—church AL-4
Grays Chapel Elem Sch—school NC-3
Grays Chapel Freewill Baptist Ch AL-4
Grays Chapel Presbyterian Ch TN-4
Grays Chapel Sch (historical)—school AL-4
Grays Chapel School TN-4
Gray Sch (historical)—school MS-4
Gray Sch (historical)—school (3) TN-4
Gray School—locale IL-6
Gray School—locale MI-6
Grays Corner—locale (2) ME-1
Grays Corner—locale NY-2
Grays Corner—locale (2) VA-3
**Grays Corner**—pop pl IL-6
**Grays Corner**—pop pl MD-2
Grays Corners—locale NY-2
**Grays Corners**—pop pl NY-2
Grays Cove—bay ME-1
Grays Cove—bay MD-2
Gray's Creek CT-1
Grays Creek GA-3
Grays Creek ID-8
Grays Creek LA-4
Grays Creek MI-6
Grays Creek TN-4
Grays Creek—gut CT-1
Grays Creek—locale NC-3
Grays Creek—stream (2) CO-8
Grays Creek—stream (2) GA-3
Grays Creek—stream (4) ID-8
Grays Creek—stream IA-7
Grays Creek—stream LA-4
Grays Creek—stream (3) MD-2
Grays Creek—stream MI-6
Grays Creek—stream (3) MS-4
Grays Creek—stream MO-7
Grays Creek—stream (3) NC-3
Grays Creek—stream (2) OR-9
Grays Creek—stream (3) SC-3
Grays Creek—stream (3) TN-4
Grays Creek—stream (2) TX-5
Grays Creek—stream VA-3
Grays Creek Baptist Church MS-4
Grays Creek Canal—canal TN-4
Grays Creek Ch—church LA-4
Grays Creek Ch—church (2) NC-3
Grays Creek Ch—church TN-4
Grays Creek Lake—lake LA-4
Grays Creek Marina—other VA-3
Grays Creek Sch—school IA-7
Grays Creek Sch—school NC-3
Grays Creek (Township of)—fmr MCD NC-3
Grays Creek Watershed Structure Number 11 Dam—dam MS-4
Grays Creek Watershed Structure Number 9 Dam—dam MS-4
Grays Crossing—locale CA-9
Grays Crossing—locale TN-4
**Grays Crossing**—pop pl TN-4
Grays Ditch—canal LA-4
Grays Eddy—locale PA-2
Grays Ferry—locale TN-4
Grays Ferry—uninc pl PA-2
Grays Flat CA-9
Grays Flat—flat CA-9
Grays Flat—locale CA-9
Grays Ford—locale VA-3
Grays Fork—stream KY-4
Grays Fork—stream MT-8
Grays Fork—stream PA-2
Grays Fork—stream VA-3
Grays Grove Ch—church GA-3
Grays Grove Sch—school GA-3
Grays Gulch—valley AZ-5
Grays Gulch—valley CO-8
Grays Gulch—valley (2) MT-8
Grays Gulch—valley OR-9
Grays Gulch Mine—mine AZ-5
Grays Harbor—bay WA-9
**Grays Harbor City**—pop pl WA-9
Grays Harbor Coll—school WA-9
**Grays Harbor County**—pop pl WA-9
Grays Harbor Light Station—hist pl WA-9
Grays Hill TN-4
**Grays Hill**—pop pl SC-3
Grays Hill—summit ME-1
Grays Hill—summit MD-2
Grays Hill—summit NH-1
Grays Hill Cem—cemetery ME-1
Grays Hill Ch—church SC-3
Grays Hill Post Office (historical)—building TN-4
**Grays Hill Village**—pop pl VA-3
Grays Hollow—valley OK-5
**Gray Shores**—pop pl NY-2
Graysill Creek—stream CO-8
Graysill Mine—mine CO-8
Graysill Mtn—summit CO-8
Gray Sink—basin FL-3
Grays Inn Creek—stream MD-2
Grays Inn Point—cape MD-2
Grays Island—island TN-4
Grays Island—island VA-3
Grays Island Marsh—swamp MD-2
Grays Island Shoal—bar AL-4
Grays Knob—summit KY-4
Grays Knob—summit VA-3
Grays Knob (Wilsonberger Station)—locale KY-4
Grays Lake ID-8
Grays Lake—lake AR-4
Grays Lake—lake ID-8
Grays Lake—lake IL-6
Grays Lake—lake IA-7
**Grayslake**—pop pl IL-6
Grays Lake—reservoir (2) AL-4
Grays Lake (corporate name Grayslake) IL-6
Grays Lake Guard Station—locale ID-8
Grays Lake Natl Wildlife Ref—park ID-8
Grays Lake Outlet—stream ID-8
Grays Landing NC-3
Grays Landing TN-4
Grays Landing—locale GA-3
Grays Landing—locale SC-3
Grays Landing—locale VA-3
Grays Landing—locale WA-9
**Grays Landing**—pop pl PA-2
Grays Landing (historical)—locale AL-4
Grays Landing Lake Access Area—park TN-4
Gray Slough—lake KY-4
Grays Marsh—swamp WA-9
Grays Marsh—swamp WI-6
Grays Meadow—flat CA-9
Grays Mill MS-4
Grays Mill TN-4
Grays Mill (historical)—locale AL-4
Grays Mill Pond—lake MA-1
Grays Mill Pond—lake RI-1
Grays Millpond—reservoir NY-2
Grays Millpond—reservoir NC-3
Grays Millpond Dam—dam NC-3
Grays Mills Station—locale PA-2
Grays Mtn—summit ME-1
Grays Mtn—summit NY-2
Grays Mtn—summit VT-1
Grays Number Two Landing—locale FL-3
Grays Number 1 Landing—locale FL-3
Grayson—locale AR-4
Grayson—locale NC-3
Grayson—locale OH-6
Grayson—locale VA-3
**Grayson**—pop pl AL-4
**Grayson**—pop pl CA-9
**Grayson**—pop pl GA-3
**Grayson**—pop pl KY-4
**Grayson**—pop pl LA-4
**Grayson**—pop pl MO-7
**Grayson**—pop pl OK-5
Grayson Bayou—gut LA-4
Grayson Branch—stream (2) TN-4
Grayson Canyon—valley NV-8
Grayson (CCD)—cens area KY-4
Grayson Cem—cemetery (2) AL-4
Grayson Cem—cemetery CA-9
Grayson Cem—cemetery KY-4
Grayson Cem—cemetery MO-7
Grayson Cem—cemetery (3) OK-5
Grayson Cem—cemetery TN-4
Grayson Cem—cemetery TX-5
Grayson Ch—church OK-5
**Grayson (County)**—pop pl KY-4
**Grayson (County)**—pop pl TX-5
**Grayson (County)**—pop pl VA-3
Grayson County Courthouse—hist pl VA-3
Grayson Creek—stream AR-4
Grayson Creek—stream CA-9
Grayson Creek—stream NC-3
Grayson Creek—stream OK-5
Grayson Dam—dam KY-4
Grayson Gap—gap WV-2
Grayson Highlands State Park—park VA-3
Grayson (historical)—locale KS-7
Grayson House—hist pl LA-4
Graysonia—locale AR-4
Grayson Lake—reservoir AL-4
Grayson Lake—reservoir KY-4
Grayson Lake Dam—dam AL-4
Grayson Lake State Park—park KY-4
Grayson Lake Wildlife Mngmt Area—park KY-4
Grayson Mill Creek—stream TN-4
Grayson Mountain AR-4
Grayson Oil Field—oilfield OK-5
Grayson Point—cape AL-4
Grayson Pond—lake AR-4
Grayson Post Office (historical)—building AL-4
Grayson Ranch—locale NV-8
Grayson Reservoir KY-4
Grayson Ridge—ridge TN-4
Grayson Sch—school CA-9
Grayson Sch—school KS-7
Grayson Sch—school (2) MI-6
Grayson Sch—school PA-2
Grayson Sch (abandoned)—school MO-7
Graysons Mill (historical)—locale TN-4
Grayson Spring—spring (2) AL-4
Grayson Spring—spring NV-8
Grayson Spring Cave—cave AL-4
Grayson Springs—hist pl KY-4
Grayson Springs—locale KY-4
Graysons Sch (historical)—school MS-4
**Graysontown**—pop pl VA-3
Grayson Valley Ch—church AL-4
Grayson Valley Country Club—locale AL-4
Graysonville MD-2
**Grays Park**—pop pl KS-7
Grays Park—uninc pl KS-7
Grays Pasture UT-8
Grays Pasture—flat UT-8
Grays Peak—summit (2) CA-9
Grays Peak—summit CO-8
Grays Peak—summit (3) ID-8
Grays Peak—summit NV-8
Grays Peak—summit OR-9
Grays Peak Trail—trail CO-8
Grays Point ME-1
Grays Point—cape DE-2
Grays Point—cape ME-1
Grays Point—cape (2) MD-2
Grays Point—cape MO-7
Grays Point—cape NY-2
Grays Point—cape NC-3
Grays Point—cape TN-4
Grays Point—cape WA-9
**Grays Point**—pop pl MO-7
Grays Point Cem—cemetery (2) MO-7
Grays Point Light—locale WA-9
Grays Pond—lake IN-6
Grays Pond—lake VT-1
Grays Pond—reservoir CT-1
Grays Pond Brook—stream CT-1
Graysport—locale MS-4
Graysport Crossing—locale MS-4
Graysport Post Office (historical)—building MS-4
Gray Spot Rock—summit UT-8
Gray Spot Wash—stream AZ-5
Grays Prairie—locale TX-5
**Grays Prairie (Peede's Mill)**—pop pl TX-5
Gray Spring—spring (2) AL-4
Gray Spring—spring AZ-5
Gray Spring—spring AR-4
Gray Spring—spring SD-7
Gray Spring—spring UT-8
Gray Springs Branch—stream TX-5
Grays Prong DE-2
Grays Prong—canal DE-2
Grays Prong—stream DE-2
Gray Squirrel Hollow—valley OK-5
Grays Ranch—locale AZ-5
Grays Range—range ID-8
Grays Ridge—ridge KY-4
Grays Ridge—ridge (2) NC-3
Grays Ridge—ridge OH-6
**Grays River**—pop pl WA-9
Grays River—stream WA-9
Grays River (CCD)—cens area WA-9
Grays River Covered Bridge—hist pl WA-9
Grays River Divide—ridge WA-9
Grays Road Recreation Center—hist pl PA-2
Grays Rock—island ME-1
Grays Rock—rock MA-1
Grays Run PA-2
Grays Run—stream (2) KY-4
Grays Run—stream MD-2
Grays Run—stream (2) OH-6
Grays Run—stream PA-2
Grays Run—stream WV-2
Grays Sch—school MS-4
Grays Sch—school NY-2
Grays Sch (historical)—school MS-4
Grays Shaft Mine (underground)—mine AL-4
Grays Siding—locale VA-3
**Grays Siding**—pop pl IL-6
Grays Slough—gut OR-9
Grays Slough Dam—dam OR-9
Grays Slough Rsvr—reservoir OR-9
Grays Spring—spring AZ-5
Grays Spring Rec Area—park AR-4
Grays Station TN-4
Gray Station—locale ME-1
Grays-Tillman (CCD)—cens area SC-3
Graystone KS-7
**Graystone**—pop pl AL-4
**Graystone**—pop pl MD-2
Graystone Cliff—cliff AK-9
Graystone Creek—stream AK-9
**Graystone Estates (subdivision)**—pop pl TN-4
Graystone Peak—summit CO-8
Graystone Presbyterian Ch—church TN-4
Graystone Quarry—mine TN-4
Graystone Sch—school NE-7
Gray Street Sch—school GA-3
Gray Stud Rsvr—reservoir OR-9
Gray Stud Spring—spring ID-8
**Gray Summit**—pop pl MO-7
Grays Valley—valley CA-9
Grays Valley Post Office (historical)—building PA-2
Grays Valley Well—well CA-9
Graysville IL-6
Graysville—locale KY-4
**Graysville**—pop pl AL-4
**Graysville**—pop pl GA-3
**Graysville**—pop pl (2) IN-6
**Graysville**—pop pl MO-7
**Graysville**—pop pl OH-6
**Graysville**—pop pl (2) PA-2
**Graysville**—pop pl TN-4
**Graysville**—pop pl VA-3
**Graysville**—pop pl WV-2
Graysville-Adamsville (CCD)—cens area AL-4
Graysville-Adamsville Division—civil AL-4
Graysville Cemetery TN-4
Graysville Elem Sch—school IN-6
Graysville Elem Sch—school TN-4
**Graysville Heights (subdivision)**—pop pl AL-4
Graysville Post Office—building TN-4
Graysville Sch—school AL-4
Graysville Sch—school GA-3
Graysville Springs—spring GA-3
**Graysville (Township name Gray)**—pop pl PA-2
Gray Swamp—swamp (2) NC-3
Grays Well (Site)—locale CA-9
Grays Wharf (historical)—locale NC-3
Gray Tank—reservoir (2) AZ-5
Gray Tanks—reservoir AZ-5
Gray-Taylor House—hist pl PA-2
Grayton—locale AL-4
Grayton—locale MD-2
**Grayton Beach**—pop pl FL-3
Grayton Beach State Park—park FL-3
Grayton JHS—school AL-4
Grayton Lake—lake TX-5
Graytop—summit TX-5
Gray Top Mtn—summit NV-8
**Graytown**—pop pl OH-6
**Graytown**—pop pl TN-4
**Graytown**—pop pl TX-5
**Graytown**—pop pl WI-6
**Gray (Town of)**—pop pl ME-1
Graytown Post Office (historical)—building TN-4
**Gray Township**—pop pl ND-7
Gray (Township of)—fmr MCD (2) AR-4
**Gray (Township of)**—pop pl IL-6
**Gray (Township of)**—pop pl MN-6
**Gray (Township of)**—pop pl PA-2
Gray Valley Sch—school PA-2
**Grayvik**—pop pl FL-3
**Grayville**—pop pl (2) IL-6
Grayville Church TN-4
Gray Wall—cliff WY-8
Gray Wash—stream (2) AZ-5
Gray-Watkins Mill—hist pl IL-6
Gray Well AZ-5
Gray Well—well AZ-5
Gray Well—well (2) TX-5
Gray Well Draw—valley TX-5
Gray Whiskers—summit AZ-5
Gray Windmill—locale (2) TX-5
Gray Wolf Glacier—glacier MT-8
Gray Wolf Lake—lake MT-8
Gray Wolf Mine—mine ID-8
Gray Wolf Mountain UT-8
Gray Wolf Mtn—summit CO-8
Graywolf Pass WA-9
Gray Wolf Pass—gap WA-9
Gray Wolf Peak—summit MT-8
Gray Wolf Ridge—ridge WA-9
Graywolf River WA-9
Gray Wolf River—stream WA-9
Gray Wolf Shelter—locale WA-9
**Graywood**—pop pl NY-2
Gray-Wood Buildings—hist pl MO-7
Graze Branch—stream SC-3
Graze Creek—stream SC-3
Graze Creek—stream TX-5
Graze Mtn—summit TX-5
Graze Point—cape FL-3
Grazide Ranch—locale CA-9
Grazide Sch—school CA-9
**Grazier**—pop pl PA-2
Grazier Mill—locale PA-2
Grazier Park—park MN-6
**Grazierville**—pop pl PA-2
Grba Field—park MI-6
G R Barbour Pond—reservoir NC-3
G R Barbour Pond Dam—dam NC-3
G R Cummings Mine (Abandoned)—mine AL-4
Grdina Sch—school OH-6
Greacen Point—cape NY-2
Greager Flats—flat CO-8
Grealey Ch—church TX-5
**Greaney**—pop pl MN-6
Greaney Cem—cemetery MN-6
Greany Bldg—hist pl MA-1
Grear Hope Pond—lake FL-3
Grear Prehistoric Village Site—hist pl MD-2
Grears Corners—locale DE-2
Greaseboat Island LA-4
Grease Bucket Tank—reservoir AZ-5
Grease Creek—stream VA-3
Grease Creek—stream WA-9
Greaser Basin—basin OR-9
Greaser Canyon—valley OR-9
Greaser Creek CO-8
Greaser Creek—stream KS-7
Greaser Creek—stream MO-7
Greaser Gulch—valley CA-9
Greaser Lake OR-9
Greaser Lake—lake OR-9
Greaser Lake Dam—dam OR-9
Greaser Petroglyph Site—hist pl OR-9
Greaser Ranch—locale WY-8
Greaser Ridge—ridge OR-9
Greaser Rsvr—reservoir OR-9
Greaser Wash—stream AZ-5
Greasewood AZ-5
**Greasewood**—pop pl AZ-5
Greasewood Arroyo—stream CO-8
Greasewood Basin—basin CA-9
Greasewood Basin—basin NV-8
Greasewood Bottom—bend MT-8
Greasewood Canyon—valley (2) CO-8
Greasewood Canyon—valley OR-9
Greasewood Canyon—valley UT-8
Greasewood Canyon—valley WY-8
Greasewood Cem—cemetery OR-9
Greasewood Creek—stream CO-8
Greasewood Creek—stream (2) MT-8
Greasewood Creek—stream OR-9
Greasewood Creek—stream (3) WY-8
Greasewood Draw—valley CO-8
Greasewood Draw—valley SD-7
Greasewood Draw—valley UT-8
Greasewood Draw—valley (2) WY-8
Greasewood Finnish Apostolic Lutheran Church—hist pl OR-9
Greasewood Flat—flat AZ-5
Greasewood Flat—flat CO-8
Greasewood Flat—flat MT-8
Greasewood Flat—flat UT-8
Greasewood Flat Rsvr—reservoir CO-8
Greasewood Flats—flat CO-8
Greasewood Flats—flat WY-8
Greasewood Gulch—valley (2) CO-8
Greasewood Hill—summit CA-9
Greasewood Hills—summit NM-5
Greasewood Knoll—summit WY-8
Greasewood Lake—flat AZ-5
Greasewood Lake—lake CO-8
Greasewood Lake—lake WY-8
Greasewood Mtn—summit AZ-5
Greasewood Mtn—summit CA-9
Greasewood Place—area AZ-5
Greasewood Pond—lake UT-8
Greasewood Ranch—locale (2) WY-8
Greasewood Rsvr—reservoir WY-8
Greasewood Spring—spring AZ-5
Greasewood Spring—spring NV-8
Greasewood Spring—spring UT-8
Greasewood Spring—spring WY-8
**Greasewood Springs**—pop pl AZ-5
Greasewood Tank—reservoir AZ-5
Greasewood Tank—reservoir NM-5
Greasewood Tank—reservoir UT-8
Greasewood Wash—stream AZ-5
Greasewood Wash—valley WY-8
Greasewood Windmill—locale TX-5
**Greason**—pop pl PA-2
Greason Hollow TN-4
Greaswood Airp—airport AZ-5
Greaswood Gulch CO-8
Greasy—locale OK-5
Greasy Bayou Landing—locale MS-4
Greasy Bottom—bend AR-4
Greasy Branch—stream AR-4
Greasy Branch—stream GA-3
Greasy Branch—stream (4) KY-4
Greasy Branch—stream LA-4
Greasy Branch—stream (3) NC-3
Greasy Branch—stream (3) TN-4
Greasy Branch Dock (Floating moorage)—locale NC-3
Greasy Branch Island—island GA-3
Greasy Canyon—valley NM-5
**Greasy Corner**—pop pl AR-4
Greasy Cove—valley (2) AL-4
Greasy Cove—valley (2) NC-3
Greasy Cove—valley (3) TN-4
Greasy Cove Prong—stream NC-3
Greasy Cove Spring—spring AL-4
Greasy Creek AR-4
Greasy Creek MS-4
Greasy Creek OK-5
Greasy Creek TX-5
**Greasy Creek**—pop pl KY-4
Greasy Creek—stream AL-4
Greasy Creek—stream (7) AR-4
Greasy Creek—stream CA-9
Greasy Creek—stream GA-3
Greasy Creek—stream (2) IL-6
Greasy Creek—stream (3) IN-6
Greasy Creek—stream (13) KY-4
Greasy Creek—stream LA-4
Greasy Creek—stream MI-6
Greasy Creek—stream (4) MS-4
Greasy Creek—stream (10) MO-7
Greasy Creek—stream (8) NC-3
Greasy Creek—stream (4) OK-5
Greasy Creek—stream OR-9
Greasy Creek—stream (6) TN-4
Greasy Creek—stream (2) TX-5
Greasy Creek—stream (5) VA-3
Greasy Creek Acad (historical)—school TN-4
Greasy Creek Baptist Ch—church TN-4
Greasy Creek Cem—cemetery AR-4
Greasy Creek Cem—cemetery TN-4
Greasy Creek Ch—church (2) KY-4
Greasy Creek Ch—church VA-3
Greasy Creek Church—church IN-6
Greasy Creek Sch—school KY-4
Greasy Creek Sch—school TN-4
Greasy Creek Watershed LT-1a-1 Dam—dam MS-4
Greasy Creek Watershed LT-1a-10 Dam—dam MS-4

Greasy Creek Watershed LT-1a-11 Dam—dam MS-4
Greasy Creek Watershed LT-1a-13 Dam—dam MS-4
Greasy Creek Watershed LT-1a-14 Dam—dam MS-4
Greasy Creek Watershed LT-1a-15 Dam—dam MS-4
Greasy Creek Watershed LT-1a-16 Dam—dam MS-4
Greasy Creek Watershed LT-1a-2 Dam—dam MS-4
Greasy Creek Watershed LT-1a-3 Dam—dam MS-4
Greasy Creek Watershed LT-1a-4 Dam—dam MS-4
Greasy Creek Watershed LT-1a-5 Dam—dam MS-4
Greasy Creek Watershed LT-1a-6-7 Dam—dam MS-4
Greasy Creek Watershed LT-1a-8 Dam—dam MS-4
Greasy Creek Watershed LT-1a-9 Dam—dam MS-4
Greasy Ditch—canal KY-4
Greasy Falls—falls VA-3
Greasy Fork KY-4
Greasy Fork—stream KY-4
Greasy Gap—gap KY-4
Greasy Head Branch—stream AL-4
Greasy Head Swamp—swamp AL-4
Greasy Hill—summit MT-8
Greasy Hills—range MO-7
Greasy Hollow TN-4
Greasy Hollow—valley AL-4
Greasy Hollow—valley (2) IN-6
Greasy Hollow—valley (2) KY-4
Greasy Hollow—valley (3) TN-4
Greasy Hollow Cem—cemetery TN-4
Greasy Jim Lake—lake MI-6
Greasy Lake—lake MS-4
Greasy Lake—reservoir OK-5
Greasy Mtn—summit GA-3
Greasy Mtn—summit NC-3
Greasy Point Ch—church IL-6
Greasy Ridge—locale OH-6
Greasy Ridge—ridge KY-4
Greasy Ridge—ridge OH-6
Greasy Ridge Ch—church WV-2
Greasy Rock Creek—stream TN-4
Greasy Rock Hollow—valley VA-3
Greasy Run IN-6
Greasy Run—stream (3) OH-6
Greasy Run—stream VA-3
Greasy Run Creek—stream TN-4
Greasy Run Valley—valley TN-4
Greasy Sch—school OK-5
Greasy Spoon Tank—reservoir AZ-5
Greasy Spring Branch—stream VA-3
Greasy Valley—basin VA-3
Greasy Valley—valley (2) AR-4
Great Alamance Creek NC-3
Great American Mortgage Dam—dam TN-4
Great American Mortgage Lake—reservoir TN-4
Great Androscoggin Falls ME-1
Great Antioch Ch—church LA-4
Great Aquavitae—bar MA-1
Great Arch, The—arch UT-8
Great Arm—bay AK-9
Great Asnaconcomick Pond MA-1
Great Atlantic and Pacific Tea Company Warehouse—hist pl NJ-2
Great Aughwick Creek PA-2
Great Averill lake VT-1
Great Averill Pond—lake VT-1
Great Back Bay—bay VT-1
Great Back Bone MD-2
Great Back Bone WV-2
Great Balds Central Peak, The TN-4
Great Balds South Peak TN-4
Great Balsam Range NC-3
Great Bank—island MA-1
Great Bar—bar ME-1
Great Barcut Island NY-2
Great Barn Island NY-2
**Great Barrington**—pop pl MA-1
**Great Barrington Center**—pop pl MA-1
Great Barrington State For—forest MA-1
**Great Barrington (Town of)**—pop pl MA-1
Great Basin—basin ME-1
**Great Basin Addition**—pop pl UT-8
Great Basin Experiment Station—other UT-8
Great Basin Natl Park—park NV-8
Great Bass Lake—lake WI-6
Great Bay MA-1
Great Bay NH-1
Great Bay—bay ME-1
Great Bay—bay NH-1
Great Bay—bay NJ-2
Great Bay—bay VI-3
Great Bay—lake MI-6
Great Bay de Noquet MI-6
Great Bay des Noquets MI-6
Great Bay Fish and Wildlife Mngmt Area—park NJ-2
Great Bay Point MD-2
Great Beach MA-1
Great Beach Hill—summit MA-1
Great Beach Pond—lake NC-3
Great Bear Creek—stream MT-8
Great Bear Lake—lake MI-6
Great Bear Mtn—summit MT-8
Great Bear Siding—locale NY-2
Great Bear Springs—spring NY-2
Great Bear Swamp MA-1
Great Bear Swamp—swamp CT-1
Great Bear Swamp—swamp NJ-2
Great Beds—bar NJ-2
Great Beds Lighthouse—locale NJ-2
Great Beds Reach—channel NJ-2
**Great Belt**—pop pl PA-2
Greatbend KS-7
Great Bend—bend AL-4
Great Bend—bend AK-9
Great Bend—bend NM-5
Great Bend—bend OH-6
Great Bend—locale OH-6
**Great Bend**—pop pl KS-7
**Great Bend**—pop pl NY-2
**Great Bend**—pop pl ND-7
**Great Bend**—pop pl PA-2
Great Bend, The—bend WA-9
Great Bend Airport KS-7
Great Bend Bomb Scoring Site—military NY-2
Great Bend Borough—civil PA-2
Great Bend Cem—cemetery KS-7
Great Bend Ch—church OH-6
Great Bend (historical)—bend ND-7
Great Bend HS—school KS-7
Great Bend Lowland KS-7
Great Bend Municipal Airp—airport KS-7
Great Bend of the San Juan River—bend UT-8
Great Bend Plaza—locale KS-7
Great Bend Prairie—plain KS-7
**Great Bend Township**—pop pl KS-7
**Great Bend Township**—pop pl SD-7
**Great Bend (Township of)**—pop pl MN-6
**Great Bend (Township of)**—pop pl PA-2
Great Bend Village PA-2
Great Bethel Baptist Ch—church AL-4
Great Bethel Cemetery AL-4
Great Black River ME-1
Great Black Swamp—swamp MA-1
Great Blue Hill—summit MA-1
Great Blue Hill Observation Tower—hist pl MA-1
Great Blue Hill Weather Observatory—hist pl MA-1
Great Blue River IN-6
**Great Boars Head**—pop pl NH-1
Great Bog—swamp NH-1
Great Bohemia Creek—stream DE-2
Great Bohemia Creek—stream MD-2
Great Boiling Spring Park—park NV-8
Great Bond PA-2
**Great Branch**—pop pl SC-3
Great Branch—stream (4) NC-3
Great Branch—stream SC-3
Great Branch—stream (2) VA-3
Great Branch Community Ch—church NC-3
Great Branch Meadow Branch—stream NC-3
Great Branch Sch—school SC-3
Great Break, The—other CA-9
Great-Brewster Island MA-1
Great Brewster Island—island MA-1
Great Brewster Spit—flat MA-1
**Great Bridge**—pop pl VA-3
Great Bridge Battle Site—hist pl VA-3
Great Bridge Lock—other VA-3
Great Britain Mine—mine CO-8
Great Brook CT-1
Great Brook MA-1
Great Brook—stream (6) CT-1
Great Brook—stream (8) ME-1
Great Brook—stream (4) MA-1
Great Brook—stream (14) NH-1
Great Brook—stream NJ-2
Great Brook—stream (2) NY-2
Great Brook—stream (3) VT-1
Great Brook Hill—summit ME-1
Great Brook Lake—lake ME-1
Great Brook Rsvr—reservoir CT-1
Great Brook Trail—trail ME-1
**Great Brook Valley (subdivision)**—pop pl MA-1
Great Bruster Island MA-1
Great Burnt Ship Creek NY-2
Great Butte—summit CA-9
**Great Cacapon**—pop pl WV-2
Great Cacapon River WV-2
Great Cain Creek NC-3
Great Calf Island MA-1
Great Calfpasture River VA-3
Great Canal FL-3
Great Canyon AZ-5
Great Canyon MT-8
Great Capon River WV-2
Great Captain Island—island CT-1
Great Captain Rocks—island CT-1
Great Captain's Island Harbor CT-1
Great Catawba River NC-3
Great Cedar Swamp MA-1
Great Cedar Swamp—swamp (4) MA-1
Great Cedar Swamp—swamp NJ-2
Great Cedar Swamp—swamp RI-1
Great Central Mound—summit TN-4
Great Channel—channel NJ-2
Great Channel—channel VA-3
Great Chauncy Pond MA-1
Great Chazy River—stream NY-2
Great Chebeague Island—island ME-1
Great Cherry Portage—trail MN-6
Great Cliff, The—cliff VT-1
Great Cliff of Jokaj FM-9
Great Cliffs—cliff CA-9
Great Coharie Creek—stream NC-3
Great Colorado Valley—basin AZ-5
Great Commission Sch—school IN-6
Great Conewago Presbyterian Church—hist pl PA-2
Great Conglomerate Falls—falls MI-6
Great Contentnea Creek NC-3
Great Corn Lake—lake WI-6
Great Cotecktney Creek NC-3
Great Cove NY-2
Great Cove—bay (2) ME-1
Great Cove—bay (2) MD-2
Great Cove—bay NJ-2
Great Cove—bay NY-2
Great Cove—bay VA-3
Great Cove Creek—bay MD-2
Great Cove Island—island MD-2
Great Cove Point—cape MD-2
Great Crack—other HI-9
Great Craggy Mountains—range NC-3
Great Cranberry Island—island ME-1
Great Creek MA-1
Great Creek NC-3
Great Creek—stream CT-1
Great Creek—stream ME-1
Great Creek—stream (3) NC-3
Great Creek—stream RI-1
Great Creek—stream (3) VA-3
Great Creek Ch—church VA-3
**Great Crossing**—pop pl KY-4
Great Crossing Ch—church MD-2
Great Cruz Bay—bay VI-3
Great Crystal KY-4
Great Cypress Ch—church SC-3
Great Cypress Swamp AL-4
Great Cypress Swamp, The SC-3
Great Dane Tank—reservoir AZ-5
Great Desert—flat NC-3
Great Diamond Island ME-1
Great Diamond Island—island ME-1
Great Diamond Island Landing—locale ME-1
Great Dismal Swamp—swamp NC-3
Great Dismal Swamp—swamp VA-3
Great Dismal Swamp Canal—canal VA-3
Great Dismal Swamp Natl Wildlife Ref—park VA-3
Great Ditch—canal (2) NJ-2
Great Ditch—channel NC-3
Great Divide—locale CO-8
Great Divide—ridge CO-8
Great Divide Basin—basin (2) WY-8
Great Dome—summit MA-1
Great Dome Mountain CA-9
Great Dover Swamp—swamp NC-3
Great Drain—stream MA-1
Great-Drain Brook MA-1
Great Drum Drain VA-3
Great Duck Creek DE-2
Great Duck Island—island ME-1
Great Duck Island Light Station—hist pl ME-1
Great Duck Pond MA-1
Great Eastern—mine UT-8
Great Eastern Cem—cemetery IN-6
Great Eastern Ditch—canal KS-7
Great Eastern Hollow—valley UT-8
Great Eastern Mine—mine AZ-5
Great Eastern Mine—mine NV-8
Great Eastern Ravine—valley CA-9
Great East Lake—lake ME-1
Great East Lake—lake NH-1
Great East Neck—cape NY-2
Great Eddy—bay ME-1
Great Eddy Covered Bridge—hist pl VT-1
Great Egg Bay NJ-2
Great Egg Harbor NJ-2
Great Egg Harbor Bay—bay NJ-2
Great Egg Harbor Inlet—bay NJ-2
Great Egg Harbor River—stream NJ-2
Great Egg Harbour NJ-2
Great Egging Beach—beach MD-2
Great Egg Inlet NJ-2
Great Egg River NJ-2
Great Egg Rock MA-1
Great Egg Rock—island MA-1
Great Elizabeth Ch—church LA-4
Greater Allen Temple AME Ch—church MS-4
Greater Allenville Ch of God—church AL-4
Greater Alpha and Omega Ch—church MS-4
Greater Antioch Ch AL-4
Greater Bass Lake—lake WI-6
Greater Baton Rouge Port—harbor LA-4
Greater Bell Ch—church FL-3
Greater Bells Chapel—church AL-4
Greater Bethel African Methodist Episcopal Ch—church FL-3
Greater Bethel Apostolic Temple—church MS-4
Greater Bethel Ch—church GA-3
Greater Bethlehem Temple Apostolic Faith Ch—church MS-4
Greater Bethlehem Baptist Ch—church FL-3
Greater Blair Street AME Zion Ch—church MS-4
Greater Buffalo International Airp—airport NY-2
Greater Bush Grove Ch—church TN-4
Greater Calvary Baptist Ch—church MS-4
Greater Calvary Ch—church SC-3
Greater Canaan Baptist Ch—church IN-6
**Greater Capitol Heights**—pop pl MD-2
Greater Cincinnati International Airp—airport KY-4
Greater Clark Street Baptist Ch—church MS-4
Greater Community Temple Ch—church MS-4
Greater Cross Roads—locale NJ-2
Greater Dunn Chapel—church AL-4
Greater Ebenezer Baptist Ch—church AL-4
Greater Ebenezer Baptist Ch—church TN-4
Greater Ebenezer Ch—church AL-4
Greater Emmanuel Mission—church AL-4
Greater Fairview Baptist Ch—church MS-4
Greater Faith Baptist Ch—church IN-6
Greater Fatherland Baptist Ch—church MS-4
Greater First Apostolic Temple—church MS-4
Greater First Baptist Ch of Cantonment—church FL-3
Greater Fort Worth Tabernacle—church TX-5
Greater Fountain Chapel African Methodist Episcopal Ch—church FL-3
Greater Friendship Baptist Ch—church FL-3
Greater Friendship Ch—church AL-4
Greater Friendship Ch—church TX-5
Greater Friendship Missionary Baptist Ch—church TN-4
Greater Galilee Ch—church MS-4
Greater Gethsemane Baptist Ch—church IN-6
Greater Gethsemane Missionary Baptist Ch—church MS-4
Greater Gratiot Sch—school MI-6
Greater Gulf State Fair—locale AL-4
Greater Hendersonville—uninc pl TN-4
Greater Hope Ch—church GA-3
Greater Hopewell Baptist Ch—church FL-3
Greater Jerusalem Ch—church AR-4
Greater Johnstown Water Authority Dam—dam PA-2
Greater Keys Baptist Ch—church FL-3
Greater King Solomon Baptist Ch—church IN-6
Greater Latrobe Senior HS—school PA-2
Greater Leech Lake Ind Res—other MN-6
Greater Liberty Hill Ch—church FL-3
Greater Liberty Hill United Methodist Ch—church FL-3
Greater Life Tabernacle—church MS-4
Greater Lily Star Baptist Ch—church AL-4
Greater Little Rock Baptist Ch—church FL-3
Greater Little Zion Ch—church VA-3
Greater Love Ch of God in Christ—church FL-3
Greater Macedonia Baptist Ch—church AL-4
Greater Macedonia Ch—church GA-3
Greater Maysville Ch of God—church AL-4
Greater Mer Baptist Ch—church MS-4
Greater Miami Acad—school FL-3
Greater Morning Star Baptist Ch—church (2) FL-3
Greater Morning Star Baptist Ch—church IN-6
Greater Mount Calvary Baptist—church MS-4
Greater Mount Calvary Ch—church AL-4
Greater Mount Canaan Ch—church GA-3
Greater Mount Carmel Baptist Ch—church AL-4
Greater Mount Carmel Ch—church TX-5
Greater Mount Hebron Baptist Ch—church AL-4
Greater Mount Herman Baptist Ch—church MS-4
Greater Mount Hermon Ch—church OK-5
Greater Mount Lilly Baptist Ch—church FL-3
Greater Mount Mariah Baptist Ch—church MS-4
Greater Mount Moriah Ch—church AL-4
Greater Mount Moriah Ch—church TN-4
Greater Mount Olive Baptist Ch Number 1—church AL-4
Greater Mount Olive Baptist Ch Number 2—church AL-4
Greater Mount Olive Ch—church AL-4
Greater Mount Olive Ch—church MS-4
Greater Mount Olive Church, The—church GA-3
Greater Mount Sinai Baptist Ch—church (2) MS-4
Greater Mount Zion Ch—church OK-5
Greater Mount Zion Missionary Baptist Ch—church AL-4
Greater Mount Zion Primitive Baptist Ch—church FL-3
Greater Nashville Junior Acad—school TN-4
Greater Nazarene Baptist Ch—church AL-4
Greater Nazarene Ch—church AL-4
Greater Newark (CCD)—cens area DE-2
Greater New Bethel Baptist Ch—church FL-3
Greater New Bethel Ch—church FL-3
Greater New Bethel Missionary Baptist Ch—church FL-3
Greater New Bethlehem Baptist Ch—church MS-4
Greater New Bethlehem Kindergarten—school FL-3
Greater New Home Baptist Ch—church TN-4
Greater New Hope Ch—church (2) GA-3
Greater New Hope Ch—church TX-5
Greater New Mount Zion Missionary Baptist Ch—church FL-3
Greater New Orleans Bridge—bridge LA-4
Greater New Providence Ch—church FL-3
Greater New Zion Baptist Ch—church MS-4
Greater New Zion Primitive Baptist Ch—church FL-3
Greater Northeast Congregation—church PA-2
Greater North Mountain VA-3
Greater North Mountain WV-2
Greater North Mountains VA-3
Greater North Mountains WV-2
Greater Northside Freewill Baptist Ch—church MS-4
Greater Oak Grove Ch—church TX-5
Greater Old Salem Ch AL-4
Greater Olive Branch Ch—church SC-3
Greater Palestine Ch—church TX-5
Greater Parks AME Chapel—church AL-4
Greater Peoria Airp—airport IL-6
Greater Pine Grove AME Ch—church AL-4
Greater Pine Grove Ch—church AL-4
Greater Pine Hill Church, The—church AL-4
Greater Pine Level Ch AL-4
Greater Pittsburgh Air Natl Guard Base—building PA-2
Greater Pittsburgh Airport Cove—cove PA-2
Greater Pittsburgh Int. Airport—mil airp PA-2
Greater Pittsburgh International Airp—airport PA-2
Greater Pleasant Grove Ch—church AL-4
Greater Pleasant View Ch—church TN-4
Greater Pleasant View Missionary Baptist Ch TN-4
**Greater Point Marion**—pop pl PA-2
Greater Powell Chapel African Methodist Episcopal Ch—church MS-4
Greater Prayer Tabernacle Ch of God—church AL-4
Greater Richland Area (P.O. name for Richland Hills)—other TX-5
Greater Richmond Grove Missionary Baptist Ch—church MS-4
Greater Rising Star Ch—church TX-5
Greater Ruth Chapel AME Ch—church AL-4
Greater Saint James Baptist Ch MS-4
Greater Saint James Missionary Baptist Ch—church FL-3
Greater Saint John African Methodist Episcopal Ch—church MS-4
Greater Saint John Baptist Ch—church TN-4
Greater Saint John Ch—church AL-4
Greater Saint Johns Ch—church NC-3
Greater Saint Lukes Baptist Ch—church TN-4
Greater Saint Lukes Ch—church SC-3
Greater Saint Marks Baptist Ch MS-4
Greater Saint Marks Ch—church LA-4
Greater Saint Marys Baptist Ch—church KS-7
Greater Saint Matthew Baptist Ch—church FL-3
Greater Saint Paul African Methodist Episcopal Ch—church FL-3
Greater Saint Paul AME Ch AL-4
Greater Saint Paul AME Ch—church (2) AL-4
Greater Saint Paul Baptist Missionary Ch—church FL-3
Greater Saint Peter Ch—church GA-3
Greater Samuel Chapel AME Ch—church AL-4
Greater Second Missionary Baptist Ch—church TN-4
Greater South Baptist Ch—church TN-4
Greater Southern Baptist Ch—church IN-6
Greater Springfield Missionary Baptist Ch—church MS-4
Greater St. Paul AME Church—hist pl TX-5
Greater Timber Ridge Ch—church GA-3
Greater Tried Stone Baptist Ch—church IN-6
Greater Union Baptist Ch—church AL-4
Greater Union Baptist Ch—church FL-3
Greater Union First Baptist Ch—church FL-3
Greater View Spring—spring CA-9
**Greaterville**—pop pl (3) AZ-5
Greaterville Gulch AZ-5
Greaterville Gulch—valley AZ-5
Greater Warner Tabernacle African Methodist Episcopal Ch—church TN-4
**Greater Washington Park (subdivision)**—pop pl AL-4
Greater Wesley Chapel—church AL-4
Greater Wilmington Airp—airport DE-2
Greater Wyatt Chapel—church TX-5
Greater Zion Baptist Ch—church IN-6
Greater Zion Brighter Day Spiritual Ch—church IN-6
Greater Zion Brighter Day Spritual Ch Number Four IN-6
Greater Zion Ch—church NC-3
Greater Zion Ch—church TN-4
Greater Zion Chapel—church MS-4
Greater Zion Hope Primitive Baptist Ch—church AL-4
Greater Zion Travel Ch—church LA-4
Great Falls NJ-2
Great Falls NC-3
Great Falls—falls (2) AL-4
Great Falls—falls CT-1
Great Falls—falls (3) ME-1
Great Falls—falls MD-2
Great Falls—falls NC-3
Great Falls—falls TN-4
Great Falls—falls VA-3
Great Falls—locale MD-2
**Great Falls**—pop pl MT-8
**Great Falls**—pop pl SC-3
**Great Falls**—pop pl VA-3
Great Falls—post sta ME-1
Great Falls, The ME-1
Great Falls Basin—basin CA-9
Great Falls Branch—stream ME-1
Great Falls Bridge—bridge ME-1
Great Falls (CCD)—cens area SC-3
Great Falls Central HS—hist pl MT-8
Great Falls (community)—CDP VA-3
Great Falls Cotton Mill—hist pl TN-4
Great Falls Creek—stream MT-8
Great Falls Creek—stream WA-9
Great Falls Dam—dam (2) TN-4
Great Falls Depot—hist pl SC-3
Great Falls Hydro Plant—building TN-4
Great Falls International Airport—airport MT-8
Great Falls Lake—reservoir (2) TN-4
Great Falls North—cens area MT-8
Great Falls of Paterson/S.U.M. Hist Dist—hist pl NJ-2
Great Falls of the Lehigh—falls PA-2
Great Falls of the Passaic and Society for Useful Manufactures Hist Dist—hist pl NJ-2
Great Falls Of The Passaic River NJ-2
Great Falls Park—park (2) VA-3
**Great Falls (P.O.)**—pop pl VA-3
Great Falls Pond—reservoir NC-3
Great Falls Portage—hist pl MT-8
Great Falls Rsvr TN-4
Great Falls Rsvr—reservoir SC-3
Great Falls Sch—school NC-3
Great Farm Brook—stream ME-1
Great Faun—bar MA-1
Great Faun Bar MA-1
Great Field MA-1
Great Fields MA-1
Great Fire of 1911 Hist Dist—hist pl ME-1
Great Flat—flat CT-1
Great Flat—flat NJ-2
Great Flat—island MA-1
Great Flat Thorofare—channel NJ-2
Great Flint River AL-4
Great Fork Ch—church VA-3
Great Forks Creek NY-2
Great Fountain Geyser—geyser WY-8
Great Fox Island—island VA-3
Great Fresh Kills—stream NY-2
Great Gallery Pictographs—other UT-8
Great Gap Channel—channel VA-3
Great Geneva—hist pl DE-2
Great Geneva—park DE-2
**Great Good Place**—pop pl DE-2
Great Goosenecks of the San Juan UT-8
Great Gorge, The—valley AK-9
Great Gorge Trail—trail PA-2
Great Gott Island—island ME-1
Great Grass Pond—lake RI-1
Great Gulch—valley NV-8
Great Gulf—valley NH-1
Great Gulf Creek—stream NY-2
Great Gulf Island NY-2
Great Gulf Trail—trail NH-1
Great Gull Island—island NY-2
Great Gully—valley NY-2
Great Gut VA-3
Great Gut—gut (3) NC-3
Great Gut—gut (4) VA-3
Great Gut Bay—bay NC-3
Great Gut Cove—bay VA-3
Great Hall—hist pl OH-6
**Great Hammock**—pop pl CT-1
Great Hammock Beach—beach CT-1
Great Hammock Swash NC-3
Great Harbor MA-1
Great Harbor—bay MA-1
**Great Harbor**—pop pl CT-1
Great Harbor, Town of MA-1
Great Harbor Cove—bay ME-1
Great Harbor Ferry Slip Light—locale MA-1
Great Harbor Range Light—locale MA-1
Great Harbour MA-1
Great Harvest Baptist Church—school FL-3
Great Haste Island—island MA-1
Great Head MA-1
Great Head—cliff (2) ME-1
Great Head—summit (2) ME-1
Great Head Reef ME-1
Greatheart Mesa—summit UT-8
Great Heart of Timpanogos—cave UT-8
Great Heath ME-1
Great Heath—swamp ME-1
Great Hell Gate ME-1
Great Hemlock—summit MA-1
Great Hen Island ME-1
Great Herring Pond—lake MA-1
Great Hill CT-1
Great Hill MA-1
Great Hill—summit (7) CT-1
Great Hill—summit (5) ME-1
Great Hill—summit (7) MA-1
Great Hill—summit (6) NH-1
Great Hill Brook—stream CT-1
Great Hill Cem—cemetery CT-1
Great Hill Place—hist pl GA-3
Great Hill Point—cape MA-1
Great Hill Pond—reservoir CT-1
Great Hill Pond—reservoir NH-1
Great Hill Pond Brook—stream CT-1
Great Hill Rsvr—reservoir CT-1
Great Hogback NC-3
Great Hog Island ME-1
Great Hog Neck—cape NY-2
Great Hollow—valley MA-1
Great Hollow—valley NH-1
Great Hollow Beach—beach MA-1
Great Hollow JHS—school NY-2
Great Hope Cem—cemetery OK-5
Great Hope Ch—church AL-4
Great Hope Ch—church (2) NC-3
Great Hope Sch—school AL-4
Great Hosmer Pond—lake VT-1
Great House—hist pl MD-2
Greathouse Branch TX-5
Greathouse Branch—stream TX-5
Greathouse Branch—stream WV-2
Greathouse Cem—cemetery (2) IL-6
Greathouse Cem—cemetery KY-4
Greathouse Cem—cemetery MO-7
Greathouse Cem—cemetery (2) TX-5
Greathouse Creek—stream AR-4
Greathouse Creek—stream IL-6
Greathouse Creek—stream KS-7
Greathouse Ford—locale IL-6
Greathouse Gulch—valley CO-8
Greathouse Hollow—valley (3) WV-2
Greathouse Island—island IN-6
Greathouse Mountain MT-8
Greathouse Mtn—summit AL-4
Greathouse Peak—summit MT-8
Great House Point—cape VA-3
Greathouse Sch—school KY-4
Greathouse Spring—spring AR-4
Greathouse Well—well NM-5
Great Hunting Creek VA-3
Great Hurl Gate ME-1
Great Icefall—falls AK-9
Great Indian Pond MA-1
Great Indian War Trail Monmt—park TN-4
Great Island CT-1
Great Island ME-1
Great Island NH-1
Great Island TN-4
Great Island VA-3
Great Island—cape (2) MA-1
Great Island—island (2) CT-1
Great Island—island (5) MA-1
Great Island—island (2) NH-1
Great Island—island NJ-2
Great Island—island (3) NY-2
Great Island—island (8) NC-3
Great Island—island PA-2
Great Island—island VA-3
Great Island Bay—bay NC-3
Great Island Channel NY-2
Great Island Channel—channel NY-2
Great Island Creek—channel NC-3
Great Island Creek—stream MA-1
Great Island Narrows—channel NC-3
Great Island Point—cape NC-3
Great James Pond MA-1
Great Jebeig Island ME-1
Great Kanhawa River WV-2
Great Kanhaway River WV-2
Great Kehhawa River WV-2
Great Kenhawa River WV-2
Great Kill NY-2
Great Kill Point NY-2
Great Kills NY-2
**Great Kills**—pop pl NY-2
Great Kills Harbor—harbor NY-2
Great Kills Park—park NY-2
Great Kills Yacht Club—other NY-2
Great Knobs—range VA-3
Great Kobuk Sand Dunes—area AK-9
Great Konhaway River WV-2
Great Lake ME-1
Great Lake MA-1
Great Lake—lake NC-3
**Great Lake Beach**—pop pl MI-6
**Great Lake Estates (subdivision)**—pop pl MS-4
Great Lake Recreation Site—park NC-3
Great Lakes—post sta IL-6
**Great Lakes Beach**—pop pl MI-6
Great Lakes Camp—locale PA-2
Great Lakes Dragaway—other WI-6
Great Lakes Marina—harbor MI-6
Great Lakes Naval Public Works Center—military IL-6
Great Lakes Naval Regional Med Ctr—military IL-6
Great Lakes Naval Training Center—other IL-6
Great Lakes Naval Training Station—hist pl IL-6
Great Lakes Pumping Station—other MO-7
Great Lameshur Bay—bay VI-3
Great Lava Fissure HI-9
Great Lechau PA-2
Great Lechau River PA-2
Great Ledge—bar ME-1
Great Ledge—bar MA-1
Great Ledge—bench RI-1
Great Ledge—rock (2) MA-1
Great Ledge, The—cliff VT-1
Great Ledge Cove—bay ME-1
Great Machipongo Channel—channel VA-3
Great Machipongo Inlet—bay VA-3
Great Machipongo River VA-3
Great Maring Pond—lake MA-1
Great Mark Island—island ME-1
Great Marsh CT-1
Great Marsh MA-1
Great Marsh NC-3
Great Marsh PA-2
Great Marsh—swamp (2) CT-1
Great Marsh—swamp DE-2
Great Marsh—swamp (3) MD-2
Great Marsh—swamp NC-3
Great Marsh Ch—church NC-3
Great Marsh Creek—channel NC-3

Great Marsh Creek—*gut* ... MD-2
Great Marshes—*swamp* ... MA-1
*Great Marshes, The* ... MA-1
Great Marsh Island—*island* ... FL-3
Great Marsh Island—*island* ... NC-3
*Great Marsh Point* ... MD-2
*Great Marsh Point* ... NC-3
Great Marsh Point—*cape* (2) ... MD-2
*Great Marsh River* ... MA-1
*Great Masterpiece, The* ... FL-3
Great Masterpiece Gardens—*park* ... FL-3
Great Meadow—*bench* ... MA-1
Great Meadow—*flat* ... CT-1
Great Meadow—*flat* ... NH-1
Great Meadow—*swamp* (3) ... ME-1
Great Meadow Brook—*stream* ... CT-1
Great Meadow Hill—*summit* ... MA-1
Great Meadow Riffles—*rapids* ... ME-1
*Great Meadow Run* ... PA-2
*Great Meadows* ... MA-1
**Great Meadows**—*pop pl* ... CT-1
**Great Meadows**—*pop pl* ... NJ-2
Great Meadows—*swamp* ... CT-1
Great Meadows—*swamp* (2) ... MA-1
Great Meadows—*swamp* (2) ... NH-1
Great Meadows Correctional Institution—*other* ... NY-2
Great Meadows Natl Wildlife Ref—*park* (2) ... MA-1
Great Meadows State Prison—*other* ... NY-2
Great Meadow Stream—*stream* ... ME-1
Great Miami River—*stream* ... IN-6
Great Miami River—*stream* ... OH-6
*Great Mill Brook* ... MA-1
**Great Mills**—*pop pl* ... MD-2
Great Mink Hole—*lake* ... MA-1
*Great Mink Pond* ... MA-1
*Great Mioxes Pond* ... MA-1
Great Misery Island—*island* ... MA-1
Great Mogul Mine—*mine* ... SD-7
Great Mohave Wall—*cliff* ... AZ-5
Great Moose Hill—*summit* ... MA-1
Great Moose Lake—*lake* ... ME-1
*Great Moose Pond* ... ME-1
Great Morning Star Missionary Baptist Ch—*church* ... AL-4
*Great Morse Hill* ... MA-1
*Great Moshier Island* ... ME-1
Great Mound—*hist pl* ... OH-6
*Great Mountain* ... PA-2
Great Mount Gilliard Baptist Ch—*church* ... AL-4
Great Mtn—*summit* ... CT-1
Great Mtn—*summit* ... MA-1
Great Narrows—*gut* ... VA-3
*Great Neck* ... MA-1
Great Neck—*cape* (2) ... CT-1
Great Neck—*cape* (4) ... MA-1
Great Neck—*cape* (2) ... NY-2
Great Neck—*cape* ... NC-3
Great Neck—*cape* (3) ... VA-3
Great Neck—*cliff* ... MA-1
Great Neck—*locale* ... NC-3
**Great Neck**—*pop pl* ... MA-1
**Great Neck**—*pop pl* ... NY-2
Great Neck—*summit* ... RI-1
Great Neck Cem—*cemetery* ... CT-1
Great Neck Ch—*church* ... WV-2
*Great Neck Creek* ... VA-3
Great Neck Creek—*stream* ... NY-2
Great Neck Creek—*stream* ... NC-3
Great Neck Creek—*stream* ... VA-3
**Great Neck Estates**—*pop pl* ... NY-2
**Great Neck Estates**—*pop pl* ... VA-3
Great Neck Estates Park—*park* ... NY-2
Great Neck Gardens—*other* ... NY-2
Great Neck (historical)—*civil* ... MA-1
Great Neck (historical)—*isthmus* ... MA-1
Great Neck HS—*school* ... NY-2
Great Neck JHS—*school* ... NY-2
Great Neck Lake—*reservoir* ... VA-3
Great Neck Landing—*locale* ... NC-3
**Great Neck Manor**—*pop pl* ... VA-3
**Great Neck Plaza**—*pop pl* ... NY-2
*Great Neck Point* ... MA-1
Great Neck Point—*cape* ... NC-3
Great Neck Point—*cape* ... VA-3
Great Neck Road Sch—*school* ... NY-2
Great Neck Sch—*school* ... CT-1
Great Neck (Village) (P.O. Sta. name Old Village)—*other* ... NY-2
*Great Nemaha River* ... NE-7
*Great Nesenkeag Brook* ... NH-1
*Great Nine Mile Pond* ... MA-1
*Great Noquet Bay* ... MI-6
*Great Northern Cascade Tunnel* ... WA-9
Great Northern Depot—*hist pl* (2) ... MN-6
Great Northern Depot—*hist pl* ... WA-9
Great Northern Flats—*flat* ... MT-8
Great Northern Lake—*lake* ... MN-6
Great Northern Mine—*mine* ... CA-9
Great Northern Mine—*mine* ... CO-8
Great Northern Mine—*mine* ... OR-9
Great Northern Mtn—*summit* (2) ... MT-8
Great Northern Passenger Depot—*hist pl* . MN-6
Great Northern Passenger Station—*hist pl* ... WA-9
Great Northern Railway Buildings—*hist pl* ... MT-8
Great Northern Railway Company Bridge—*hist pl* ... MN-6
Great Northern Railway Depot—*hist pl* ... ND-7
Great Northern Railway Passenger and Freight Depot—*hist pl* ... SD-7
Great Northern RR Depot—*hist pl* ... MN-6
Great Northern Rsvr—*reservoir* ... MT-8
Great Northern Sch—*school* ... WA-9
*Great North Mountain* ... WV-2
Great North Mountain—*ridge* ... WV-2
*Great North Mtn* ... VA-3
Great North Mtn—*range* (2) ... VA-3
Great North Mtn—*summit* ... VA-3
**Great Notch**—*pop pl* ... NJ-2
Great Notch Reservoir Dam—*dam* ... NJ-2
Great Notch Rsvr—*reservoir* ... NJ-2
Great Notch Station—*locale* ... NJ-2
Great Nunatak—*summit* ... AK-9
**Great Oak Farms (subdivision)**—*pop pl* ... DE-2
Great Oak (historical P.O.)—*locale* ... IA-7
**Great Oak Landing**—*pop pl* ... MD-2
Great Oak Manor—*locale* ... MD-2
Great Oaks—*hist pl* ... FL-3
Great Oak Sch—*school* ... MA-1
Great Oaks Country Club—*other* ... VA-3
**Great Oaks (subdivision)**—*pop pl* ... AL-4
Great Oak Townhall—*building* ... IA-7
Great Oak Township—*fmr MCD* ... IA-7
Great Oasis Lakebed—*flat* ... MN-6
Great Oasis State Wildlife Mngmt Area—*park* ... MN-6
*Great Ogeechee River* ... GA-3
Great Oil Basin Shop Ctr—*locale* ... TX-5
Great Onyx Cave—*cave* ... KY-4
Great Onyx Cave Pumphouse—*other* ... KY-4
Great Onyx Job Corps Conservation Center—*other* ... KY-4
*Great Organ, The* ... UT-8
*Great Oval Arch* ... UT-8
Great Owl Cavern—*cave* ... ID-8
Great Paimiut Island—*island* ... AK-9
Great Patchogue Lake—*reservoir* ... NY-2
*Great Peconic Bay* ... NY-2
Great Peconic Bay—*bay* ... NY-2
*Great Pee Dee* ... NC-3
*Great Pee Dee* ... SC-3
*Great Peedee River* ... NC-3
*Great Pee Dee River* ... SC-3
Great Pee Dee River—*stream* ... SC-3
*Great Peede River* ... SC-3
Great Piece Meadows—*swamp* ... NJ-2
*Great Pigeon Creek* ... IN-6
Great Pig Rocks—*bar* ... MA-1
*Great Pine Dam* ... AL-4
Great Pine Lake—*lake* ... AL-4
Great Pine Point—*cape* ... ME-1
*Great Piute Wash* ... CA-9
Great Plain, The—*plain* ... AZ-5
Great Plain Brook—*stream* ... CT-1
Great Plain Cem—*cemetery* ... CT-1
Great Plains—*plain* ... KS-7
Great Plains—*plain* ... MA-1
Great Plain Sch—*school* ... CT-1
Great Planes Field (airport)—*airport* ... SD-7
Great Pleasant Sch—*school* ... SC-3
Great Pocket—*lake* ... FL-3
Great Point—*cape* ... MD-2
Great Point—*cape* (2) ... MA-1
Great Point—*cape* ... RI-1
*Great Point Au Sable* ... MI-6
Great Point Clear—*cape* ... AL-4
*Great Point Light* ... MA-1
Great Point Pond—*lake* ... MD-2
*Great Pond* ... ME-1
*great Pond* ... MA-1
*Great Pond* ... NH-1
*Great Pond* ... NY-2
*Great Pond* ... RI-1
Great Pond—*bay* ... MA-1
Great Pond—*lake* (3) ... CT-1
Great Pond—*lake* (5) ... ME-1
Great Pond—*lake* ... MD-2
Great Pond—*lake* (6) ... MA-1
Great Pond—*lake* ... NH-1
Great Pond—*lake* (2) ... NY-2
Great Pond—*lake* (2) ... NC-3
Great Pond—*lake* ... VI-3
Great Pond—*locale* ... VI-3
**Great Pond**—*pop pl* ... ME-1
Great Pond—*reservoir* ... CT-1
Great Pond—*reservoir* ... ME-1
Great Pond Archeol Site—*hist pl* ... VI-3
Great Pond Bay—*bay* ... VI-3
Great Pond Cem—*cemetery* ... ME-1
Great Pond Cove—*bay* ... ME-1
Great Pond Dam—*dam* ... MA-1
*Great Pond Hill* ... ME-1
Great Pond Island—*island* ... ME-1
Great Pond Mtn—*summit* ... ME-1
Great Pond Rsvr—*reservoir* ... MA-1
**Great Pond (Town of)**—*pop pl* ... ME-1
Great Pond Upper Reservoir Dam—*dam* ... MA-1
Great Pond Upper Rsvr—*reservoir* ... MA-1
*Great Porcupine Creek* ... MT-8
*Great Porcupine Island* ... ME-1
*Great Quabin Mountain* ... MA-1
Great Quittacas Pond—*lake* ... MA-1
*Great Quittacus Pond* ... MA-1
*Great Ram Pasture Point* ... MA-1
*Great Rattlesnake Bend* ... AL-4
Great Redoubt (historical)—*locale* ... MS-4
Great Reef—*bar* ... CT-1
Great Republic Mine—*mine* ... WA-9
Great Ridge—*ridge* ... AK-9
Great Ridge—*ridge* ... ME-1
Great Rift—*valley* ... ID-8
Great Rip—*bar* ... MA-1
*Great River* ... CT-1
*Great River* ... MA-1
*Great River* ... NH-1
*Great River* ... RI-1
Great River—*bay* ... MA-1
**Great River**—*pop pl* ... NY-2
Great River Marshes—*swamp* ... MA-1
**Great River (sta.)**—*pop pl* ... NY-2
Great Road Hist Dist—*hist pl* ... RI-1
Great Road Shop Ctr, The—*locale* ... MA-1
Great Roaring Brook—*stream* ... VT-1
*Great Rock* ... MA-1
Great Rock—*rock* ... MA-1
Great Rock—*summit* ... MA-1
*Great Rock House Cave* ... AL-4
Great Rocks—*island* ... CT-1
Great Rock Sch—*school* ... NH-1
*Great Round Pond* ... MA-1
Great Round Shoal—*bar* (2) ... MA-1
Great Round Shoal Channel—*channel* ... MA-1
Great Run—*stream* ... IN-6
Great Run—*stream* (3) ... VA-3
*Great Sable River* ... MI-6
Great Sacandaga Lake—*reservoir* ... NY-2
Great Saint James Island—*island* ... VI-3
Great Salt Lake—*lake* ... UT-8
Great Salt Lake Desert—*plain* ... UT-8
Great Salt Lake State Park—*park* ... UT-8
Great Salt Lake State Park - Saltair Beach (inundated)—*park* ... UT-8
*Great Saltpeter Cave* ... AL-4
Great Saltpeter Cave—*cave* ... KY-4
Great Salt Plains Lake—*reservoir* ... OK-5
*Great Salt Plains Rsvr* ... OK-5
Great Salt Plains State Park—*park* ... OK-5
*Great Salt Pond* ... RI-1
Great Salt Pond—*bay* ... RI-1
*Great Salts* ... KY-4
Great Sand Bay—*bay* ... MI-6
Great Sand Creek—*stream* ... NY-2
Great Sand Dunes Natl Monument—*park* .. CO-8
Great Sand Hill—*summit* ... MS-4
*Great Sands* ... MI-6
Great Sandy Bottom Pond—*lake* ... MA-1
*Great Sandy Desert* ... OR-9
Great Sandy Desert—*plain* ... OR-9
*Great Sandy Pond* ... MA-1
Great Sandy Run Pocosin—*swamp* ... NC-3
*Great Sawokli* ... AL-4
**Great Scott (Township of)**—*pop pl* ... MN-6
Great Seal Park Archeol District—*hist pl* ... OH-6
Great Seneca Creek—*stream* ... MD-2
*Great Sheebage* ... ME-1
Great Shoal—*bar* ... NC-3
Great Shoal—*bar* ... VA-3
Great Shoals Light—*locale* ... MD-2
Great Sidney Bog—*swamp* ... ME-1
Great Sierra Mine—*mine* ... CA-9
Great Sierra Mine Historic Site—*hist pl* ... CA-9
Great Sierra Wagon Road—*hist pl* ... CA-9
Great Silver Mine—*mine* ... AZ-5
Great Sippewisset Creek—*stream* ... MA-1
Great Sippewisset Marsh—*swamp* ... MA-1
Great Sippewisset Rock—*bar* ... MA-1
*Great Sippewissett Creek* ... MA-1
*Great Sippowisset Creek* ... MA-1
*Great Sippowisset Swamp* ... MA-1
*Great Sitilla River* ... GA-3
Great Sitkin Island—*island* ... AK-9
Great Sitkin Pass—*channel* ... AK-9
*Great Sky Lake* ... MS-4
*Great Sloop Creek* ... NJ-2
Great Smokies Hilton—*locale* ... NC-3
Great Smoky Mountains Natl Park (Also NC)—*park* ... TN-4
Great Smoky Mountains Natl Park (Also TN)—*park* ... NC-3
*Great Smoky Valley* ... NV-8
Great Snake Pond—*lake* ... MA-1
*Great Snake River* ... OR-9
*Great Sodus Bay* ... NY-2
Great Sound—*bay* ... NJ-2
Great South Bay—*bay* ... NY-2
*Great South Beach* ... NY-2
Great South Beach—*beach* ... NY-2
Great Southern Hotel and Theatre—*hist pl* ... OH-6
Great Southern Mine—*mine* ... AZ-5
Great Southern Paper Company—*facility* ... GA-3
Great Southern Shop Ctr—*locale* ... MS-4
Great Southern Shop Ctr—*locale* ... OH-6
Great South Pond—*lake* ... MA-1
Great Southwest—*uninc pl* ... TX-5
Great Southwest Industrial Park—*facility* .. GA-3
Great Spirit Spring—*spring* ... KS-7
Great Spoon Island—*island* ... ME-1
*Great Spring* ... PA-2
Great Spring—*spring* ... AZ-5
Great Spring—*spring* ... OR-9
*Great Spring Creek* ... PA-2
Great Spring Creek—*stream* ... NY-2
Great Spring Tank—*reservoir* ... AZ-5
Great Spruce Head—*cliff* ... ME-1
*Great Sprucehead Island* ... ME-1
Great Spruce Head Island—*island* ... ME-1
Great Spruce Island—*island* ... ME-1
Great Spruce Ledges—*bar* ... ME-1
*Great Stone Dam* ... MA-1
Great Stone Dam—*hist pl* ... MA-1
*Great Stone Door State Environmental Educational Area* ... TN-4
Great Stone Face—*summit* ... UT-8
Great Stone Face—*summit* ... WY-8
Great Stone Face Park—*park* ... CA-9
Greatstone Sch Number 2—*school* ... ND-7
**Greatstone Township**—*pop pl* ... ND-7
*Great Sucker Brook* ... NY-2
*Great Swamp* ... CT-1
*Great Swamp* ... NC-3
**Great Swamp**—*pop pl* ... MA-1
Great Swamp—*stream* ... NC-3
Great Swamp—*stream* ... SC-3
Great Swamp—*stream* ... VA-3
Great Swamp—*swamp* (2) ... CT-1
Great Swamp—*swamp* (9) ... MA-1
Great Swamp—*swamp* (2) ... NJ-2
Great Swamp—*swamp* ... NY-2
Great Swamp—*swamp* ... NC-3
Great Swamp—*swamp* (3) ... RI-1
Great Swamp—*swamp* (3) ... SC-3
Great Swamp, The—*swamp* ... NY-2
Great Swamp Branch—*stream* ... NJ-2
Great Swamp Bridge—*bridge* ... SC-3
*Great-swamp Brook* ... MA-1
Great Swamp Brook—*stream* (2) ... MA-1
Great Swamp Ch—*church* ... PA-2
Great Swamp Ch—*church* (2) ... SC-3
Great Swamp Goose Marsh—*reservoir* ... RI-1
Great Swamp Goose Marsh Dam—*dam* ... RI-1
Great Swamp Natl Wildlife Ref—*park* ... NJ-2
Great Swamp (Township of)—*fmr MCD* ... NC-3
Great Swan Pond—*bay* ... NJ-2
Great Swap—*swamp* ... MA-1
*Great Swash* ... NC-3
Great Swash, The—*swamp* ... NC-3
*Great Thatcher Island* ... MA-1
Great Thatch Island—*island* ... MA-1
Great Thorofare—*channel* (2) ... NJ-2
Great Thumb Mesa—*summit* ... AZ-5
Great Thumb Point—*cape* ... AZ-5
*Great Thunb Cove* ... MA-1
*Great-Tisbury Pond* ... MA-1
*Great Tonoloway Creek* ... MD-2
*Great Tonoloway Creek* ... PA-2
*Great Track* ... CO-8
Great Trail Camp—*locale* ... OH-6
Great Trough Creek—*stream* ... PA-2
Great Unknown Creek—*stream* ... AK-9
**Great Valley**—*pop pl* ... NY-2
Great Valley Ch—*church* ... PA-2
Great Valley Creek—*stream* ... NY-2
Great Valley Mill—*hist pl* ... PA-2
Great Valley Mills—*locale* ... PA-2
Great Valley Mine—*mine* ... NV-8
Great Valley Overlook—*locale* ... VA-3
**Great Valley (Town of)**—*pop pl* ... NY-2
Great Vly—*swamp* ... NY-2
Great Walker Sch—*school* ... ND-7
Great Wall, The—*cliff* ... UT-8
Great Wanamingo Mine—*mine* ... CA-9
Great Warren Dune—*summit* ... MI-6
Great Wass Island—*island* ... ME-1
*Great Watatic* ... MA-1
*Great Watatick Mountain* ... MA-1
Great West Canyon—*valley* ... UT-8
*Great Western* ... MI-6
**Great Western**—*pop pl* ... OH-6
*Great Western and Porter Canal* ... ID-8
Great Western Canal—*canal* ... ID-8
Great Western Coal and Coke Company Bldg—*hist pl* ... OK-5
Great Western Coal and Coke Company Mine No. 3—*hist pl* ... OK-5
Great Western Divide—*ridge* ... CA-9
Great Western Iron Furnace (historical)—*locale* ... TN-4
Great Western King Mine—*mine* ... UT-8
Great Western Lake—*lake* ... WA-9
Great Western Mine—*mine* ... CA-9
Great Western Mine—*mine* ... MT-8
Great Western Mine—*mine* ... UT-8
Great Western Mine—*mine* ... WA-9
Great Western Post Office (historical)—*building* ... TN-4
Great Western Rsvr—*reservoir* ... CO-8
Great Western Sch—*school* ... CA-9
Great Western Schoolhouse—*hist pl* ... OH-6
Great West Mine—*mine* ... AZ-5
**Great Westside Subdivision**—*pop pl* ... UT-8
Great White Heron Natl Wildlife Ref—*park* ... FL-3
Great White Throne, The—*summit* ... UT-8
*Great Wicomico River* ... MD-2
Great Wicomico River—*stream* ... VA-3
Great Wood Island—*island* ... MA-1
Great Wood Island River—*channel* ... MA-1
Great Woods—*woods* ... MA-1
*Great Work Pond* ... ME-1
*Great Works* ... ME-1
Great Works—*locale* ... ME-1
**Great Works**—*pop pl* (2) ... ME-1
Great Works Pond—*lake* ... ME-1
Great Works River—*stream* ... ME-1
Great Works Stream—*stream* ... ME-1
Greaver Hollow—*valley* ... TN-4
Greavers Ridge—*ridge* ... VA-3
Greaves-Deakin House—*hist pl* ... UT-8
Grebe Bay—*bay* ... AZ-5
Grebe Cem—*cemetery* ... MO-7
Grebe Creek—*stream* ... OR-9
*Grebe Lake* ... MN-6
Grebe Lake—*lake* ... AK-9
Grebe Lake—*lake* ... MI-6
Grebe Lake—*lake* ... WY-8
Grebe Pond—*lake* ... NJ-2
Grebe Ranch—*locale* ... MT-8
**Greble**—*pop pl* ... PA-2
Grecian Bend Sch—*school* ... NE-7
*Grecian Hollow* ... TN-4
Grecian Shelter—*hist pl* ... NY-2
Greco Island—*island* ... CA-9
Greco JHS—*school* ... FL-3
Grecos Canal—*canal* ... DE-2
Gredlein Pond—*lake* ... PA-2
Gredler-Gramins House—*hist pl* ... WI-6
Greear—*locale* ... KY-4
Greear Branch—*stream* ... KY-4
Greear Cem—*cemetery* (3) ... VA-3
**Greece**—*pop pl* ... NY-2
Greece Arcadia HS—*school* ... NY-2
Greece Athena HS—*school* ... NY-2
**Greece City**—*pop pl* ... PA-2
Greece Olympia HS—*school* ... NY-2
Greece Park—*park* ... NY-2
**Greece (Town of)**—*pop pl* ... NY-2
Greedville Sch—*school* ... TN-4
Greeg Mtn—*summit* ... CA-9
Greehill Presbyterian Ch—*church* ... DE-2
Greek American Mine—*mine* ... NV-8
Greek Canyon—*valley* ... UT-8
Greek Catholic Cem—*cemetery* ... PA-2
Greek Cem—*cemetery* ... NH-1
Greek Cem—*cemetery* ... PA-2
Greek Ch—*church* ... ND-7
Greek Ch—*church* ... PA-2
Greek Creek—*stream* ... ID-8
Greek Creek—*stream* ... MT-8
Greek Creek—*stream* ... WA-9
Greek Creek Camp—*locale* ... MT-8
Greek Island—*island* ... TX-5
*Greek Lake* ... NE-7
Greek Legation Bldg—*building* ... DC-2
Greek Orthodox Cathedral of New England—*hist pl* ... MA-1
Greek Orthodox Ch Holy Mother of God—*church* ... FL-3
Greek Orthodox Ch of the Annunciation—*church* ... FL-3
Greek Orthodox Ch of the Holy Trinity—*church* ... FL-3
Greek Orthodox Ch of Transfiguration—*church* ... UT-8
Greek Orthodox Ch (Price)—*church* ... UT-8
Greek Orthodox Church—*hist pl* ... MA-1
Greek Orthodox Church, The—*church* ... FL-3
Greek Orthodox Church of the Assumption—*hist pl* ... CA-9
Greek Peak—*summit* ... UT-8
Greek Revival Commercial Bldg—*hist pl* ... OH-6
Greek Revival Cottage—*hist pl* ... IL-6
Greek Revival Cottage—*hist pl* ... MA-1
Greek Revival Farmhouse, Old—*hist pl* ... OH-6
Greek Revival Houses of Mercer County: Lynnwood, Walnut Hall, Glenworth—*hist pl* ... KY-4
Greek Spring—*spring* ... NV-8
Greek Store Guard Station—*locale* ... CA-9
Greek Theater—*building* (2) ... CA-9
Greektown Hist Dist—*hist pl* ... MI-6
*Greeley* ... AL-4
*Greeley* ... GA-3
*Greeley* ... IN-6
Greeley—*locale* ... KY-4
Greeley—*locale* ... MO-7
**Greeley**—*pop pl* ... AL-4
**Greeley**—*pop pl* ... CA-9
**Greeley**—*pop pl* ... CO-8
**Greeley**—*pop pl* ... GA-3
**Greeley**—*pop pl* ... IA-7
**Greeley**—*pop pl* ... KS-7
**Greeley**—*pop pl* ... MI-6
**Greeley**—*pop pl* ... NE-7
**Greeley**—*pop pl* ... PA-2
Greeley, Lake—*reservoir* ... PA-2
Greeley, Mount—*summit* ... MT-8
Greeley Bar—*bar* ... OR-9
Greeley Brook—*stream* ... ME-1
Greeley Brook—*stream* (2) ... NH-1
Greeley Camp—*locale* ... NH-1
Greeley Cattleguard—*locale* ... NV-8
Greeley Cem—*cemetery* ... IN-6
*Greeley Center* ... NE-7
**Greeley Center**—*pop pl* ... NE-7
Greeley Center (historical)—*locale* ... KS-7
Greeley Ch—*church* ... MI-6
Greeley Ch—*church* ... MO-7
Greeley Ch (historical)—*church* ... AL-4
Greeley Country Club—*other* ... CO-8
Greeley County—*civil* ... KS-7
Greeley County Courthouse—*hist pl* ... KS-7
Greeley County Elem Sch—*school* ... KS-7
Greeley County HS—*school* ... KS-7
Greeley Creek—*stream* ... MT-8
Greeley Crossing—*crossing* ... NV-8
Greeley Dam—*dam* ... AZ-5
Greeley Farm—*locale* ... PA-2
Greeley Farm (historical)—*locale* ... AL-4
Greeley Filtration Plant—*other* ... CO-8
Greeley Flat—*flat* ... NV-8
Greeley Hill—*locale* ... CA-9
Greeley Hill—*summit* ... CA-9
Greeley Hill—*summit* ... ME-1
Greeley Hill—*summit* ... UT-8
Greeley Hollow—*valley* ... MO-7
Greeley Hosp—*hospital* ... IA-7
Greeley House—*hist pl* ... NH-1
Greeley House—*hist pl* ... NY-2
Greeley HS—*school* ... NY-2
Greeley HS and Grade Sch—*hist pl* ... CO-8
Greeley Island—*island* ... ME-1
Greeley Junction—*locale* ... CO-8
Greeley Lake—*lake* ... MN-6
Greeley Lake—*lake* (2) ... WI-6
*Greeley Landing* ... ME-1
**Greeley Landing**—*pop pl* ... ME-1
Greeley Mtn—*summit* ... ID-8
Greeley No 2 Canal—*canal* ... CO-8
Greeley No. 3 Ditch—*canal* ... CO-8
Greeley Oil Field—*oilfield* ... CA-9
Greeley Park—*park* ... NH-1
Greeley Pass—*gap* ... UT-8
Greeley Point—*cliff* ... WY-8
Greeley Pond—*lake* ... ME-1
Greeley Ponds—*lake* ... NH-1
Greeley Ponds Trail—*trail* ... NH-1
Greeley Rsvr—*reservoir* ... OR-9
Greeley Sch—*school* (3) ... CA-9
Greeley Sch—*school* (4) ... IL-6
Greeley Sch—*school* ... MN-6
Greeley Sch—*school* ... PA-2
Greeley Sch (abandoned)—*school* (2) ... PA-2
Greeleys Landing—*locale* ... ME-1
Greeley Square—*uninc pl* ... NY-2
Greeley Tank—*reservoir* ... AZ-5
Greeley Township—*fmr MCD* (2) ... IA-7
**Greeley Township**—*pop pl* (2) ... KS-7
**Greeleyville**—*pop pl* ... SC-3
Greeleyville (CCD)—*cens area* ... SC-3
Greeleyville Ch—*church* ... SC-3
*Greely* ... CO-8
*Greely* ... KS-7
Greely—*locale* ... GA-3
**Greely**—*pop pl* ... MN-6
*Greely Brook* ... NH-1
Greely Brook—*stream* ... ME-1
Greely Cem—*cemetery* ... NY-2
Greely Ch—*church* ... ME-1
Greely Ch—*church* ... MN-6
Greely Corner—*locale* ... ME-1
Greely County Cem—*cemetery* ... KS-7
Greely Creek—*stream* ... OR-9
Greely Elem Sch—*school* ... KS-7
Greely Hall—*building* ... AZ-5
Greely Helipad—*airport* ... NJ-2
Greely Institute—*school* ... ME-1
Greely Point—*cape* ... AK-9
Greely Pond—*lake* ... ME-1
Greely Sch—*school* ... ME-1
**Greely Township**—*pop pl* ... ND-7
Greeman Field—*park* ... CA-9
*Green* ... IN-6
*Green* ... KS-7
*Green* ... MA-1
*Green* ... MS-4
Green—*locale* ... KY-4
Green—*locale* (2) ... OK-5
Green—*locale* ... TX-5
**Green**—*pop pl* ... KS-7
**Green**—*pop pl* (2) ... LA-4
**Green**—*pop pl* ... MI-6
**Green**—*pop pl* ... MT-8
**Green**—*pop pl* ... OH-6
**Green**—*pop pl* ... OR-9
Green—*uninc pl* ... CA-9
Green, Alanson, Farm House—*hist pl* ... MI-6
Green, Albert and Letha, House and Barn—*hist pl* ... WA-9
Green, Duff, House—*hist pl* ... MS-4
Green, Garner Wynn, House—*hist pl* ... MS-4
Green, Harley E., House—*hist pl* ... AR-4
Green, Jacob, House—*hist pl* ... AL-4
Green, James, House—*hist pl* ... UT-8
Green, John, Archaeol Sites—*hist pl* ... VA-3
Green, John, House—*hist pl* ... NY-2
Green, John, Mausoleum—*hist pl* ... ID-8
Green, John A., Estate—*hist pl* ... IA-7
Green, John Bunyan, Farm—*hist pl* ... NC-3
Green, Jonathan, House—*hist pl* ... MA-1
Green, Joseph, Farmhouse—*hist pl* ... NY-2
Green, Lake in the—*lake* ... MI-6
Green, Lucius, House—*hist pl* ... OH-6
Green, Mary and Moses, House—*hist pl* ... AZ-5
Green, Mitchell J., Plantation—*hist pl* ... GA-3
Green, Rufus A., House—*hist pl* ... TX-5
Green, Samuel, House—*hist pl* ... UT-8
Green, Sherwood, House—*hist pl* ... TN-4
Green, The—*hist pl* ... SC-3
Green, The—*park* ... DE-2
**Green, The**—*pop pl* ... MA-1
Green, William, House—*hist pl* ... NJ-2
Greenacre—*hist pl* ... ME-1
Green Acre—*locale* ... ME-1
Green Acre Branch—*stream* ... MO-7
Green Acre Farm Sewage Pond Dam—*dam* ... MS-4
Green Acre Park—*park* ... NM-5
*Greenacres* ... OR-9
Green Acres—*locale* ... GA-3
Greenacres—*locale* ... KY-4
Green Acres—*locale* ... MD-2
Green Acres—*locale* ... PA-2
Green Acres—*other* ... OH-6
Green Acres—*other* ... WA-9
**Green Acres**—*pop pl* (2) ... AL-4
**Greenacres**—*pop pl* ... CA-9
**Green Acres**—*pop pl* ... CA-9
**Green Acres**—*pop pl* ... DE-2
**Green Acres**—*pop pl* (2) ... GA-3
**Green Acres**—*pop pl* ... IL-6
**Green Acres**—*pop pl* ... IN-6
**Green Acres**—*pop pl* ... IA-7
**Green Acres**—*pop pl* ... KY-4
**Green Acres**—*pop pl* (3) ... LA-4
**Green Acres**—*pop pl* ... MD-2
**Green Acres**—*pop pl* ... NJ-2
**Green Acres**—*pop pl* ... NY-2
**Green Acres**—*pop pl* ... NC-3
**Green Acres**—*pop pl* ... OH-6
**Green Acres**—*pop pl* ... OR-9
**Greenacres**—*pop pl* ... OR-9
**Green Acres**—*pop pl* ... OR-9
**Green Acres**—*pop pl* (2) ... PA-2
**Green Acres**—*pop pl* (8) ... TN-4
**Green Acres**—*pop pl* (2) ... VA-3
**Greenacres**—*pop pl* ... WA-9
Green Acres—*uninc pl* ... KY-4
Greenacres—*uninc pl* ... LA-4
Green Acres—*uninc pl* ... NY-2
Green Acres—*uninc pl* ... TX-5
Green Acres Air Park—*airport* ... OR-9
*Greenacres Airport* ... NC-3
Green Acres Cem—*cemetery* ... GA-3
Green Acres Cem—*cemetery* ... NC-3
Green Acres Cem—*cemetery* ... TN-4
Green Acres Ch—*church* ... AL-4
Green Acres Ch—*church* ... KY-4
Green Acres Ch—*church* ... TN-4
Green Acre Sch—*school* ... WI-6
Greenacres Christian Acad—*school* ... FL-3
**Greenacres City**—*pop pl* ... FL-3
Green Acres Country Club—*other* ... IL-6
Greenacres Country Club—*other* ... NJ-2
Greenacres Country Day Sch—*school* (3) ... FL-3
Greenacres Country Dayschool—*school* ... FL-3
Greenacres Elem Sch—*school* ... FL-3
Greenacres Elem Sch—*school* ... IN-6
Green Acres Elem Sch—*school* ... MS-4
Green Acres Estate—*uninc pl* ... GA-3
**Green Acres Estates**—*pop pl* ... AL-4
**Green Acres Estates**—*pop pl* ... ND-7
**Green Acres Estates (subdivision)**—*pop pl* ... UT-8
Green Acres Golf Course—*locale* (2) ... PA-2
Greenacres Golf Range—*other* ... OR-9
Green Acres Heliport—*airport* ... PA-2
Greenacres JHS—*school* ... LA-4
Green Acres Lake—*reservoir* ... AL-4
Green Acres Lake—*reservoir* ... TN-4
*Green Acres Lake Dam* ... AL-4
Green Acres Memorial Gardens Cem—*cemetery* ... AZ-5
Green Acres Memorial Gardens (Cemetery)—*cemetery* ... CA-9
Green Acres Memorial Park—*cemetery* ... AL-4
Greenacres Memorial Park—*cemetery* ... TX-5
Green Acres Memorial Park—*cemetery* ... WA-9
Green Acres Mobile and Recreational Vehicle Park—*locale* ... AZ-5
Greenacres Park—*park* ... AL-4
Green Acres Park—*park* ... IA-7
Green Acres Park—*park* (2) ... MI-6
Green Acres Park—*park* ... MO-7
Green Acres Rest Home—*other* ... MO-7
Green Acres Rsvr—*reservoir* ... OR-9
Green Acres Sch—*school* ... AL-4
Green Acres Sch—*school* ... CA-9
Green Acres Sch—*school* ... CT-1
Green Acres Sch—*school* ... ID-8
Green Acres Sch—*school* ... IA-7
Green Acres Sch—*school* ... MD-2
Green Acres Sch—*school* ... MI-6
Green Acres Sch—*school* ... NH-1
Green Acres Sch—*school* ... NY-2
Greenacres Sch—*school* ... NY-2
Green Acres Sch—*school* (2) ... OR-9
Green Acres Sch—*school* ... UT-8
Green Acres Sch—*school* ... VA-3
Green Acres Shop Ctr—*locale* (2) ... TN-4
**Green Acres (subdivision)**—*pop pl* (2) ... AL-4
**Green Acres (subdivision)**—*pop pl* ... MS-4
**Greenacres (subdivision)**—*pop pl* ... MS-4
**Green Acres (subdivision)**—*pop pl* (3) .. MS-4
**Green Acres (subdivision)**—*pop pl* (3) .. NC-3
**Green Acres (subdivision)**—*pop pl* ... TN-4
**Greenacres (subdivision)**—*pop pl* ... TN-4
**Green Acres Subdivision**—*pop pl* ... UT-8
Green Acres Trailer Court—*locale* ... AZ-5
**Green Acres (trailer park)**—*pop pl* ... DE-2
**Green Acres (Trailer Park)**—*pop pl* ... IL-6
**Green Acres Valley**—*pop pl* ... NY-2
Green Airp—*airport* ... IN-6
Green and Faris Buildings—*hist pl* ... TX-5
Green and Ford Cem—*cemetery* ... TX-5
Green Apple Creek—*stream* ... OR-9
Green Ash Greentree Rsvr—*reservoir* ... MS-4
Green Ave Canal—*canal* ... LA-4
*Greenawald* ... PA-2
Greenawald—*locale* ... PA-2
**Greenawalds**—*pop pl* ... PA-2
Greenawalt Bldg—*hist pl* ... PA-2
Greenawalt Gap—*gap* ... WV-2
Greenback—*locale* ... PA-2
**Greenback**—*pop pl* ... TN-4
*Greenback Butte* ... AZ-5

Greendale Cem—*cemetery* PA-2
Greendale Cem—*cemetery* WI-6
Greendale Ch—*church* MI-6
Greendale Ch—*church* MS-4
Greendale Creek—*stream* VA-3
Greendale Junction—*locale* UT-8
Greendale Lake—*reservoir* IL-6
**Greendale Manor**—*pop pl* VA-3
*Greendale Methodist Ch* MS-4
Greendale Sch—*school* MD-2
Greendale Sch—*school* MA-1
Green Dale Sch—*school* NE-7
Greendale Sch—*school* (2) PA-2
Greendale Sch—*school* SC-3
Greendale Sch—*school* VA-3
**Greendale (subdivision)**—*pop pl* MA-1
Greendale Town Hall—*building* ND-7
**Greendale Township**—*pop pl* ND-7
Greendale Township (historical)—*civil* ND-7
**Greendale (Township of)**—*pop pl* MI-6
Greendale Village Improvement Society
Bldg—*hist pl* MA-1
Green Dam—*dam* AL-4
Green Dead River—*gut* MS-4
**Greendell**—*pop pl* NJ-2
Greendell Park—*park* IL-6
Greendell Sch—*school* CA-9
Green Dell Sch—*school* KS-7
Green-Dickson Lake—*reservoir* TX-5
Green-Dickson Park—*park* TX-5
Green Ditch—*canal* (3) IN-6
Green Ditch—*canal* NM-5
Green Ditch—*canal* (2) OH-6
Green Ditch—*canal* WY-8
Green Dome—*summit* AK-9
Green Double House—*hist pl* MO-7
Green Drain—*canal* (2) MI-6
Green Drain—*stream* (3) MI-6
Green Draw—*valley* (2) SD-7
Green Draw—*valley* UT-8
Green Draw—*valley* WY-8
*Greene* AL-4
*Greene* OH-6
Greene—*locale* RI-1
**Greene**—*pop pl* IN-6
**Greene**—*pop pl* IA-7
**Greene**—*pop pl* ME-1
**Greene**—*pop pl* NY-2
**Greene**—*pop pl* ND-7
**Greene**—*pop pl* OH-6
Greene, Benjamin F., House—*hist pl* RI-1
Greene, Caleb, House—*hist pl* RI-1
Greene, Gen. Nathanael,
Homestead—*hist pl* RI-1
Greene, James, House—*hist pl* WA-9
Greene, John T., House—*hist pl* CA-9
Greene, Moses, House—*hist pl* RI-1
Greene, Nelson H., House—*hist pl* WA-9
Greene, Peter, House—*hist pl* RI-1
Greene, Richard Wickes, House—*hist pl* RI-1
Greene Acad—*hist pl* PA-2
Greene-Bowen House—*hist pl* RI-1
Greene Branch—*stream* MD-2
Greene Branch—*stream* NC-3
Greene Branch—*stream* PA-2
Greene Brook—*stream* MA-1
Greene Canal—*stream* AZ-5
Greene Canyon—*valley* WA-9
Greene Cem—*cemetery* (2) IL-6
Greene Cem—*cemetery* (2) KY-4
Greene Cem—*cemetery* LA-4
Greene Cem—*cemetery* MI-6
Greene Cem—*cemetery* (5) NC-3
Greene Cem—*cemetery* OH-6
Greene Cem—*cemetery* PA-2
Greene Cem—*cemetery* (4) TN-4
Greene Cem—*cemetery* (2) VA-3
**Greene Center**—*pop pl* OH-6
Greene Central HS—*school* NC-3
Greene Central JHS—*school* NC-3
Greene Central Sch—*school* ME-1
**Greene Corner**—*pop pl* ME-1
Greene Coulee—*valley* MT-8
Greene Country Club—*other* OH-6
*Greene County* KS-7
**Greene County**—*pop pl* AL-4
**Greene (County)**—*pop pl* AR-4
**Greene (County)**—*pop pl* GA-3
**Greene (County)**—*pop pl* IL-6
**Greene County**—*pop pl* IN-6
**Greene County**—*pop pl* MS-4
**Greene County**—*pop pl* MO-7
**Greene (County)**—*pop pl* NY-2
**Greene County**—*pop pl* NC-3
**Greene (County)**—*pop pl* OH-6
**Greene County**—*pop pl* PA-2
**Greene County**—*pop pl* TN-4
**Greene (County)**—*pop pl* VA-3
Greene County Agricultural HS
(historical)—*school* MS-4
Greene County Airp—*airport* PA-2
Greene County Area Vocational
Center—*school* AL-4
Greene County Ch—*church* AR-4
Greene County Courthouse—*building* TN-4
Greene County Courthouse—*hist pl* AL-4
Greene County Courthouse—*hist pl* AR-4
Greene County Courthouse—*hist pl* GA-3
Greene County Courthouse—*hist pl* IA-7
Greene County Courthouse—*hist pl* NC-3
Greene County Courthouse—*hist pl* VA-3
Greene County Courthouse Square
District—*hist pl* AL-4
Greene County Fairgrounds—*locale* TN-4
Greene County Home—*building* IA-7
Greene County Hosp—*hospital* MS-4
Greene County HS—*school* AR-4
Greene County Industrial Park—*locale* TN-4
Greene County Memorial Hosp—*hospital* PA-2
Greene County Steam Plant—*facility* AL-4
*Greene County Training School* AL-4
Greene County Vocational Sch—*school* MS-4
*Greene Cove* RI-1
**Greene Cove**—*pop pl* NC-3
Greene Cove Creek—*stream* NC-3
*Greene Creek* IN-6
Greene Creek—*stream* AK-9
Greene Creek—*stream* GA-3
Greene Creek—*stream* MI-6
Greene Creek—*stream* NC-3
Greene Creek—*stream* (2) SC-3
*Greene Crossing* MS-4
Greene Crossing Post Office
(historical)—*building* MS-4
Green Eddy—*rapids* MS-4
Greene Dreher Dam—*dam* PA-2
Greene-Durfee House—*hist pl* RI-1
Greene Elem Sch—*school* IN-6
Greene Elem Sch—*school* NC-3
**Greene (Fairfield)**—*pop pl* PA-2
Greene Gene Number 2 Dam—*dam* SD-7
**Greene High**—*pop pl* AR-4
Greene Hill—*summit* TN-4
Greene Hills Farm—*hist pl* PA-2
Greene Hills Memorial Cem—*cemetery* AL-4
Greene Hills Sch—*school* CT-1
Greene Hist Dist—*hist pl* NY-2
Greene Hollow—*valley* (3) MO-7
Greene Hollow—*valley* NY-2
Greene Hollow—*valley* WI-6
Greene Inn—*hist pl* RI-1
Greene Island—*island* RI-1
Greene Joint Vocational Sch—*school* OH-6
Greene Junction—*uninc pl* PA-2
Greene Knob—*summit* NC-3
*Greene Lake* MI-6
*Greene Lake* NY-2
Greene Lake—*lake* AK-9
*Green Elementary School* MS-4
*Green Elementary School* TN-4
Green Elem Sch—*school* KS-7
Green Elm Cem—*cemetery* TX-5
Green Elm Ch—*church* KS-7
Green Elm (historical)—*locale* KS-7
Greene Mansion—*hist pl* NY-2
Greene-Marston House—*hist pl* AL-4
Greene Mill Hill—*summit* IN-6
Greene Mountain—*ridge* TN-4
Greene Mountain Trail—*trail* TN-4
Green End Pond—*lake* RI-1
Green End Pond—*reservoir* RI-1
*Green End Pond Dam* RI-1
Greene Number 2 Dam—*dam* AL-4
Greene Park—*park* FL-3
Greene Park—*park* IL-6
Greene Park—*park* IA-7
Greene Park—*park* WI-6
Greene Place—*locale* WY-8
Greene Plaza (Shop Ctr)—*locale* PA-2
Greene Point—*cape* MN-6
Greene Point—*cape* (2) NY-2
Greene Point—*cape* RI-1
Greene Ranch—*locale* AZ-5
Greene Ranch Ditch—*canal* MT-8
Greener Cem—*cemetery* TN-4
Greene Rec Area—*park* IA-7
Greene Reservoir Dam—*dam* AZ-5
Greener Mill Pond—*lake* GA-3
Greener Road Trail (jeep)—*trail* OR-9
Greener Rsvr—*reservoir* UT-8
Greener Sch—*school* OH-6
Greene Rsvr—*reservoir* AZ-5
Greenes Bay—*bay* MI-6
Greenes Branch—*stream* (2) NC-3
Greene Sch—*school* IL-6
Greene Sch—*school* MN-6
Greene Sch—*school* MO-7
Greene Sch—*school* (2) NC-3
Greene Sch—*school* OH-6
Greene Sch—*school* TX-5
Greene Sch—*school* VA-3
Greenes Corner—*locale* VA-3
*Greenes Creek* MA-1
*Greenes Island* RI-1
Greenes Lake—*lake* MI-6
Greenes Lake—*lake* NJ-2
Greenes Lake—*lake* SC-3
Greenes Lake—*reservoir* (2) TX-5
Greenes Landing—*locale* PA-2
*Greenes Point* RI-1
Greenes Pond—*reservoir* MA-1
Greenes Pond—*reservoir* NC-3
Greenes Pond Dam—*dam* MA-1
*Greene Spring* AL-4
Greene Springs Acad (historical)—*school* AL-4
*Greenes Reservoir* AZ-5
*Greenes River* RI-1
*Greenes Run* PA-2
Greene Statue—*park* DC-2
Greene Street Hist Dist—*hist pl* GA-3
Greene-Sullivan State For—*forest* IN-6
Greene Swamp—*swamp* MA-1
*Greenes Wash* AZ-5
**Greene (Town of)**—*pop pl* ME-1
**Greene (Town of)**—*pop pl* NY-2
*Greene Township* KS-7
Greene Township—*civil* MO-7
Greene Township—*civil* PA-2
Greene Township—*fmr MCD* IA-7
**Greene Township**—*pop pl* IN-6
**Greene Township**—*pop pl* KS-7
**Greene Township**—*pop pl* ND-7
Greene Township Center—*hist pl* OH-6
Greene (Township of)—*fmr MCD* MO-7
Greene (Township of)—*fmr MCD* NC-3
**Greene (Township of)**—*pop pl* (2) IL-6
**Greene (Township of)**—*pop pl* (3) IN-6
**Greene (Township of)**—*pop pl* OH-6
**Greene (Township of)**—*pop pl* (7) PA-2
*Greene Township School* IN-6
*Greene Valley Developmental Center* TN-4
*Greene Valley Hospital* TN-4
Greene Valley Mental Hosp—*hospital* TN-4
**Greenevers**—*pop pl* NC-3
*Greeneville* GA-3
*Greeneville* OH-6
*Greeneville* PA-2
**Greeneville**—*pop pl* TN-4
Greeneville (CCD)—*cens area* TN-4
Greeneville City Hall—*building* TN-4
*Greeneville Dam* TN-4
Greeneville Division—*civil* TN-4
Greeneville First Freewill Baptist
Ch—*church* TN-4
Greeneville Hist Dist—*hist pl* TN-4
Greeneville Hosp—*hospital* TN-4
Greeneville HS—*school* TN-4
Greeneville MS—*school* TN-4
Greeneville Municipal Airp—*airport* TN-4
Greeneville Post Office—*building* TN-4
Greeneville Square Shop Ctr—*locale* TN-4
Greene Vocational Center—*school* TN-4
Greene Wash—*stream* AZ-5
Green Fall Pond—*lake* CT-1
Green Fall River—*stream* CT-1
Green Fall River—*stream* RI-1
Green Falls—*falls* ME-1
Green Farm—*locale* ME-1
Greenfeild HS—*school* TN-4
*Greenfield* IN-6
*Greenfield* NY-2
*Greenfield* PA-2
*Greenfield* WI-6
Greenfield—*hist pl* VA-3
Greenfield—*locale* AL-4
Greenfield—*locale* (3) FL-3
Greenfield—*locale* LA-4
Greenfield—*locale* MS-4
Greenfield—*locale* NM-5
Greenfield—*locale* NY-2
Greenfield—*locale* ND-7
Greenfield—*locale* SD-7
Greenfield—*locale* (4) VA-3
**Greenfield**—*pop pl* AR-4
**Greenfield**—*pop pl* CA-9
**Greenfield**—*pop pl* IL-6
**Greenfield**—*pop pl* IN-6
**Greenfield**—*pop pl* IA-7
**Greenfield**—*pop pl* ME-1
**Greenfield**—*pop pl* MD-2
**Greenfield**—*pop pl* MA-1
**Greenfield**—*pop pl* MN-6
**Greenfield**—*pop pl* MO-7
**Greenfield**—*pop pl* MT-8
**Greenfield**—*pop pl* NH-1
**Greenfield**—*pop pl* NJ-2
**Greenfield**—*pop pl* NC-3
**Greenfield**—*pop pl* OH-6
**Greenfield**—*pop pl* OK-5
**Greenfield**—*pop pl* (4) PA-2
**Green Field**—*pop pl* TN-4
**Greenfield**—*pop pl* TN-4
**Greenfield**—*pop pl* VA-3
**Greenfield**—*pop pl* WI-6
Greenfield Acad—*school* GA-3
**Greenfield Acres**—*pop pl* TX-5
Greenfield Acres Ch—*church* TX-5
**Greenfield Addition**—*pop pl* MS-4
Greenfield Artesian Recorder Well—*well* NM-5
Greenfield Bayou—*gut* IN-6
Greenfield Bayou—*stream* MS-4
*Greenfield Bench* MT-8
Greenfield Bend—*bend* PA-2
Greenfield Bend—*bend* TN-4
**Greenfield Bend**—*pop pl* TN-4
Greenfield Bend Revetment
(historical)—*levee* MO-7
Greenfield Branch—*stream* KY-4
Greenfield Branch—*stream* NC-3
Greenfield (CCD)—*cens area* CA-9
Greenfield (CCD)—*cens area* TN-4
Greenfield Cem—*cemetery* AR-4
Greenfield Cem—*cemetery* CA-9
Greenfield Cem—*cemetery* IA-7
Greenfield Cem—*cemetery* (2) KS-7
Greenfield Cem—*cemetery* (2) MN-6
Greenfield Cem—*cemetery* MS-4
Greenfield Cem—*cemetery* MO-7
Greenfield Cem—*cemetery* NY-2
Greenfield Cem—*cemetery* NC-3
Greenfield Cem—*cemetery* TN-4
Greenfield Cem—*cemetery* VA-3
Greenfield Cem—*cemetery* WI-6
**Greenfield Center**—*pop pl* NY-2
Greenfield Center—*uninc pl* MA-1
Greenfield Center Sch—*school* NY-2
Greenfield-Central HS—*school* IN-6
Greenfield Ch—*church* (2) AL-4
Greenfield Ch—*church* GA-3
Greenfield Ch—*church* (2) LA-4
Greenfield Ch—*church* (5) MS-4
Greenfield Ch—*church* NE-7
Greenfield Ch—*church* NC-3
Greenfield Ch—*church* OK-5
Greenfield Ch—*church* (2) PA-2
Greenfield City Hall—*building* TN-4
Greenfield Community Coll—*school* (2) MA-1
Greenfield Conservation Club—*other* IN-6
**Greenfield Corners**—*pop pl* CA-9
Greenfield Country Club—*other* IN-6
Greenfield Courthouse Square Hist
Dist—*hist pl* IN-6
Greenfield Creek—*stream* FL-3
Greenfield Creek—*stream* VA-3
**Greenfield (delkern Post
Office)**—*pop pl* CA-9
Greenfield Division—*civil* TN-4
*Greenfield Electric And Power Dam* MA-1
Greenfield Electric Light and Power
Dam—*dam* MA-1
Greenfield Elem Sch—*hist pl* PA-2
Greenfield Elem Sch—*school* PA-2
Greenfield Elem Sch—*school* TN-4
**Greenfield Estates**—*pop pl* IN-6
**Greenfield Estates (subdivision)**—*pop pl*
(2) AZ-5
**Greenfield Farms**—*pop pl* VA-3
**Greenfield Farms Subdivision**—*pop pl* UT-8
Greenfield Fire Tower—*locale* WI-6
Greenfield First Baptist Ch—*church* TN-4
Greenfield Flat—*flat* ID-8
Greenfield Hall—*hist pl* NJ-2
**Greenfield Heights**—*pop pl* NJ-2
**Greenfield Heights
(subdivision)**—*pop pl* TN-4
**Greenfield Hill**—*pop pl* CT-1
Greenfield Hill—*summit* AR-4
Greenfield Hill—*summit* MN-6
Greenfield Hill Cem—*cemetery* CT-1
Greenfield Hill Hist Dist—*hist pl* CT-1
**Greenfield (historical)**—*pop pl* MS-4
Greenfield HS—*school* IN-6
Greenfield HS—*school* MA-1
Greenfield HS—*school* PA-2
Greenfield Island—*island* MI-6
Greenfield Island—*island* TN-4
Greenfield Islands—*island* FL-3
Greenfield JHS—*school* AZ-5
Greenfield JHS—*school* (2) CA-9
Greenfield JHS—*school* MA-1
*Greenfield Lake* MT-8
Greenfield Lake—*lake* KS-7
Greenfield Lake—*lake* NY-2
Greenfield Lake—*reservoir* NC-3
Greenfield Lake Dam—*dam* NC-3
*Greenfield Lower Dam* MA-1
Greenfield Main Canal—*canal* MT-8
**Greenfield Manor**—*pop pl* PA-2
Greenfield Manor—*uninc pl* FL-3
Greenfield Meadows—*flat* MA-1
**Greenfield Meadows
Subdivision**—*pop pl* UT-8
Greenfield Meeting House—*hist pl* NH-1
Greenfield Memorial Cem—*cemetery* TN-4
*Greenfield Methodist Ch* AL-4
*Greenfield Methodist Church* MS-4
Greenfield Mills—*locale* MD-2
**Greenfield Mills**—*pop pl* IN-6
*Greenfield Mills Millpond Dam* IN-6
Greenfield Mtn—*summit* MA-1
Greenfield Mtn—*summit* NY-2
Greenfield Normal Coll
(historical)—*school* TN-4
Greenfield-Panama (CCD)—*cens area* CA-9
Greenfield Park—*cemetery* WI-6
Greenfield Park—*park* AZ-5
Greenfield Park—*park* MI-6
Greenfield Park—*park* MN-6
**Greenfield Park**—*pop pl* MI-6
**Greenfield Park**—*pop pl* NY-2
Greenfield Park Sch—*school* MI-6
**Greenfield Park (subdivision)**—*pop pl*
(2) AZ-5
Greenfield Plantation—*hist pl* NC-3
Greenfield Plantation—*locale* SC-3
Greenfield Plantation—*locale* VA-3
Greenfield Plaza—*locale* MA-1
**Greenfield Plaza**—*pop pl* IA-7
Greenfield Point—*cape* VA-3
Greenfield Pond—*lake* NY-2
Greenfield Post Office—*building* TN-4
Greenfield Post Office
(historical)—*building* AL-4
Greenfield Post Office
(historical)—*building* MS-4
Greenfield Public Use Area—*park* MO-7
Greenfield Ranch—*locale* (2) CA-9
Greenfield Rec Area—*park* AR-4
Greenfield Reservoir Dam—*dam* IN-6
Greenfield Reservoir Dam—*dam* MA-1
Greenfield Ridge—*ridge* WV-2
Greenfield Rsvr—*reservoir* IN-6
Greenfield Rsvr—*reservoir* MA-1
Greenfield Rsvr - Lower Glen—*reservoir* MA-1
Greenfields—*hist pl* MD-2
**Green-Fields**—*pop pl* NJ-2
**Green Fields**—*pop pl* PA-2
**Greenfields**—*pop pl* TN-4
Greenfields Bench—*bench* MT-8
Greenfield Sch—*school* CT-1
Greenfield Sch—*school* FL-3
Greenfield Sch—*school* MI-6
Greenfield Sch—*school* NC-3
Greenfield Sch—*school* SD-7
Greenfield Sch—*school* (2) WI-6
Greenfield Sch (historical)—*school* (2) AL-4
Greenfield Sch (historical)—*school* MS-4
*Greenfield School Number 18* SD-7
**Green Fields Estates**—*pop pl* KY-4
Greenfield Sewage Lagoon Dam—*dam* TN-4
Greenfield Sewage Lagoon
Lake—*reservoir* TN-4
**Greenfields Heights
(subdivision)**—*pop pl* NC-3
*Greenfields Lake* MT-8
Greenfield South Canal—*canal* MT-8
Greenfields Park—*park* IL-6
Greenfield Spring—*spring* ID-8
Green Fields Sch—*school* AZ-5
Green Fields Sch—*school* NY-2
**Greenfields (subdivision)**—*pop pl* TN-4
Greenfield Station—*locale* PA-2
**Greenfield (subdivision)**—*pop pl* NC-3
**Greenfield Subdivision**—*pop pl* (2) UT-8
**Greenfields Village**—*pop pl* NJ-2
**Greenfield Terrace
(subdivision)**—*pop pl* NC-3
Greenfield Town Hall—*building* ND-7
Greenfield (Town of)—*civ div* WI-6
**Greenfield (Town of)**—*pop pl* ME-1
**Greenfield (Town of)**—*pop pl* MA-1
**Greenfield (Town of)**—*pop pl* NH-1
**Greenfield (Town of)**—*pop pl* NY-2
**Greenfield (Town of)**—*pop pl* (3) WI-6
*Greenfield Township* KS-7
Greenfield Township—*fmr MCD* (4) IA-7
**Greenfield Township**—*pop pl* KS-7
**Greenfield Township**—*pop pl* (2) ND-7
**Greenfield Township**—*pop pl* SD-7
Greenfield Township Elem Sch—*school* PA-2
Greenfield Township Hall—*building* SD-7
Greenfield Township (historical)—*civil* SD-7
Greenfield (Township of)—*fmr MCD* (3) AR-4
**Greenfield (Township of)**—*pop pl* IL-6
**Greenfield (Township of)**—*pop pl* (2) IN-6
**Greenfield (Township of)**—*pop pl* MN-6
**Greenfield (Township of)**—*pop pl* (3) OH-6
**Greenfiled (Township of)**—*pop pl* (3) PA-2
Greenfield Training Sch
(historical)—*school* TN-4
Greenfield Union Sch—*school* MI-6
Greenfield United Methodist Ch—*church* TN-4
*Greenfield Village* MI-6
**Greenfield Village**—*pop pl* MI-6
**Greenfield Village**—*pop pl* OH-6
**Greenfield Village**—*pop pl* UT-8
Greenfield Village and Henry Ford
Museum—*hist pl* MI-6
**Greenfield Village
Subdivision**—*pop pl* UT-8
**Greenfiled (Delkern Post
Office)**—*pop pl* CA-9
Green Flat—*flat* CA-9
Green Flat—*flat* (2) UT-8
Green Flat Camp—*locale* CA-9
Green Flat Campground—*locale* ID-8
Green Flat Rsvr—*reservoir* OR-9
Green Flats—*bar* (2) NY-2
Green Flats—*flat* NY-2
Green Fly Canyon—*valley* WA-9
Green Fly Tanks—*reservoir* NM-5
Green Fly Trail—*trail* NM-5
**Greenford**—*pop pl* OH-6
Green Ford Bridge—*bridge* AL-4
Green Ford Ch—*church* KY-4
**Green Forest**—*pop pl* AR-4
**Green Forest**—*pop pl* MO-7
Green Forest Ch—*church* MO-7
Green Forest Sch—*school* MO-7
Green Forest Sch (historical)—*school* MO-7
Green Fork—*stream* (3) WA-9
Green Fork Ch—*church* GA-3
Green Fork Creek—*stream* AR-4
Green Fork Creek—*stream* MO-7
Green Fork Guard Station—*locale* MT-8
Green Fork New Canyon—*valley* UT-8
Green Fork Rsvr—*reservoir* UT-8
*Green Forks* NC-3
Green Forks—*flat* TN-4
Green Fork Sink—*lake* UT-8
Green Fork Straight Creek—*stream* MT-8
*Green Gables* CO-8
**Green Gables**—*pop pl* LA-4
Green Gables Country Club—*other* CO-8
Green Gables-Fleischhacker, Mortimer, Country
House—*hist pl* CA-9
Green Gables Lodge—*locale* MO-7
Green Gables Sch—*school* CA-9
Green Gables Sch—*school* CO-8
Green Gap—*gap* GA-3
Green Gap—*gap* (2) NC-3
Green Gap—*gap* (3) PA-2
Green Gap—*gap* TN-4
Green Gap Trail—*trail* (2) PA-2
*Greengarden* KS-7
Green Garden—*fmr MCD* NE-7
Green Garden—*locale* MI-6
Green Garden—*locale* PA-2
Green Garden Cem—*cemetery* MI-6
Green Garden Cem—*cemetery* NE-7
Green Garden Ch—*church* IL-6
Green Garden Oil Field—*oilfield* KS-7
Green Garden Plaza—*locale* PA-2
**Green Garden Township**—*pop pl* KS-7
Green Garden (Township of)—*civ div* IL-6
Greengate Lake—*lake* MS-4
Greengate Lake—*reservoir* MS-4
Greengate Mall—*locale* PA-2
Greengate Park—*park* NY-2
Green Gate Well—*well* AZ-5
Green Gate Windmill—*locale* TX-5
**Green Glade**—*pop pl* MD-2
Green Glade Cem—*cemetery* IA-7
Green Glade Cove—*bay* MD-2
Greenglade Elem Sch—*school* FL-3
Green Glade Run—*stream* MD-2
Greenglen Golf Club—*other* KS-7
Green Gold Mine—*mine* NV-8
Green Gorge Park—*park* TN-4
Green Gose Branch—*stream* KY-4
Green Goshen Cem—*cemetery* MS-4
Green Goshen Ch—*church* MS-4
Green Granite Lake—*lake* CA-9
*Green Grant* NH-1
**Green Grass**—*pop pl* SD-7
Green Grass Cem—*cemetery* SD-7
Green Grass Ch (historical)—*church* SD-7
Green Grass Creek—*stream* SD-7
Green Grass Valley—*valley* UT-8
Green Griffin Hollow—*valley* AR-4
Green Griffin Knob—*summit* AR-4
Green Grotto—*cave* AL-4
*Greengrove* AL-4
*Greengrove* MS-4
Green Grove—*locale* KY-4
Green Grove—*locale* MS-4
Green Grove—*locale* MO-7
Green Grove—*locale* TN-4
**Green Grove**—*pop pl* NJ-2
**Green Grove**—*pop pl* (2) PA-2
*Green Grove Baptist Church* TN-4
Green Grove Cem—*cemetery* AL-4
Green Grove Cem—*cemetery* (2) AR-4
Green Grove Cem—*cemetery* NH-1
Green Grove Cem—*cemetery* NJ-2
Green Grove Cem—*cemetery* PA-2
Green Grove Cem—*cemetery* WI-6
Green Grove Ch—*church* AL-4
Green Grove Ch—*church* AR-4
Green Grove Ch—*church* (11) GA-3
Green Grove Ch—*church* (3) KY-4
Green Grove Ch—*church* (3) LA-4
Greengrove Ch—*church* LA-4
Green Grove Ch—*church* (7) MS-4
Greengrove Ch—*church* MS-4
Green Grove Ch—*church* MS-4
Green Grove Ch—*church* MO-7
Green Grove Ch—*church* NJ-2
Green Grove Ch—*church* (2) NC-3
Green Grove Ch—*church* (2) TN-4
Green Grove Ch (historical)—*church* MS-4
Green Grove Hill—*summit* KY-4
Green Grove (historical)—*locale* AL-4
Green Grove Hollow—*valley* UT-8
Green Grove Missionary Baptist
Ch—*church* AL-4
*Greengrove Plantation* MS-4
Greengrove Post Office
(historical)—*building* AL-4
*Green Grove Primitive Baptist Ch* TN-4
Green Grove Sch—*school* AR-4
Green Grove Sch—*school* FL-3
Green Grove Sch—*school* (2) GA-3
Green Grove Sch—*school* IL-6
Green Grove Sch—*school* MS-4
Green Grove Sch—*school* (2) MO-7
Green Grove Sch—*school* NC-3
Green Grove Sch—*school* PA-2
Green Grove Sch—*school* WI-6
Green Grove Sch (abandoned)—*school*
(2) PA-2
Green Grove Sch (historical)—*school* (2) MO-7
Green Grove Sch (historical)—*school* TN-4
**Green Grove (subdivision)**—*pop pl* AL-4
**Green Grove (subdivision)**—*pop pl* FL-3
**Green Grove (Town of)**—*pop pl* WI-6
Green Grove United Methodist
Ch—*church* TN-4
*Green Gulch* CA-9
*Green Gulch* TX-5
Green Gulch—*valley* (2) AK-9
Green Gulch—*valley* AZ-5
Green Gulch—*valley* (4) CA-9
Green Gulch—*valley* (2) CO-8
Green Gulch—*valley* (2) MT-8
Green Gulch—*valley* (3) OR-9
Green Gulch—*valley* TX-5
Green Gulch—*valley* WA-9
Green Gulch Spring—*spring* AZ-5
Green Gulch Spring—*spring* OR-9
Green Gulch Tank—*reservoir* AZ-5
Green Gully—*valley* NY-2
Greengurst Sch—*school* ID-8
*Greenhagen Bay* WI-6
Greenhalge Point—*cape* MA-1
Greenhalge Sch—*school* MA-1
Greenhalgh Mtn—*summit* CO-8
Green Hall—*locale* KY-4
Green Hall, Univ of Kansas—*hist pl* KS-7
Green Hall Cem—*cemetery* NC-3
Greenhall Creek—*stream* KS-7
*Greenhall School* TN-4
Greenhall Spring—*spring* TN-4
Green Ham Hollow—*valley* IN-6
Green Hammock—*island* GA-3
*Green Harbor* MA-1
**Green Harbor**—*pop pl* MA-1
Green Harbor Brook—*stream* MA-1
Green Harbor Island—*island* VA-3
Green Harbor Marsh—*swamp* MA-1
Green Harbor Point—*cape* MA-1
*Green Harbor River* MA-1
Green Harbor River—*stream* MA-1
Green Harbor River Harshes—*swamp* MA-1
Green Harbor Village (historical
P.O.)—*locale* MA-1
Green Hatley Branch—*stream* TN-4
Greenhaven—*locale* KY-4
**Green Haven**—*pop pl* MD-2
**Green Haven**—*pop pl* MI-6
**Greenhaven**—*pop pl* NJ-2
**Green Haven**—*pop pl* NJ-2
**Green Haven**—*pop pl* NY-2
**Greenhaven**—*pop pl* NY-2
Greenhaven, Lake—*lake* CA-9
Green Haven Ch—*church* MD-2
Greenhaven Country Club—*other* MN-6
Greenhaven Mobile Park—*locale* AZ-5
Greenhaven Park—*park* MN-6
Greenhaven Sch—*school* MN-6
Greenhaven Seventy—*uninc pl* CA-9
Green Haven State Prison—*other* NY-2
**Greenhaven (subdivision)**—*pop pl* NC-3
Greenhaw—*locale* TN-4
*Green Haw Branch* MS-4
Greenhaw Branch—*stream* AR-4
Greenhaw Branch—*stream* MS-4
Greenhaw Cem—*cemetery* AR-4
Greenhaw Cem—*cemetery* MS-4
Greenhaw Ch—*church* AR-4
Greenhaw Creek—*stream* TN-4
Green Haw Hollow—*valley* AR-4
Greenhaw Lake—*lake* TX-5
Greenhaw Sch (historical)—*school* TN-4
Greenhaw Spring—*spring* AL-4
Green Head—*cape* ME-1
Greenhead—*locale* FL-3
Green Head Branch—*stream* FL-3
Greenhead Branch—*stream* FL-3
Green Head Branch—*stream* MS-4
Greenhead Cem—*cemetery* FL-3
*Greenhead Cemetery* AL-4
*Greenhead Church* AL-4
Greenhead Creek—*stream* TX-5
Greenhead Duck Club—*locale* NV-8
Greenhead Gully—*stream* LA-4
Greenhead Lake—*reservoir* TX-5
Greenhead Rec Area—*park* TN-4
Greenhead Sch—*school* FL-3
Green Head Sch (historical)—*school* MS-4
Greenhead State Wildlife Mngmt
Area—*park* MN-6
Greenhead Tank—*reservoir* AZ-5
*Greenhill* AL-4
*Green Hill* HI-9
*Green Hill* ME-1
*Greenhill* PA-2
*Greenhill* RI-1
*Greenhill* TN-4
Green Hill—*hist pl* VA-3
Green Hill—*locale* AR-4
Green Hill—*locale* DE-2
Green Hill—*locale* KY-4
Greenhill—*locale* KY-4
Greenhill—*locale* MD-2
Green Hill—*locale* (2) SC-3
Green Hill—*locale* TN-4
Green Hill—*locale* TX-5
Green Hill—*locale* VA-3
**Green Hill**—*pop pl* AL-4
**Green Hill**—*pop pl* IN-6
**Greenhill**—*pop pl* IN-6
**Green Hill**—*pop pl* MD-2
**Greenhill**—*pop pl* NC-3
**Green Hill**—*pop pl* (2) NC-3
**Green Hill**—*pop pl* (3) PA-2
**Green Hill**—*pop pl* RI-1
**Greenhill**—*pop pl* TN-4
**Green Hill**—*pop pl* TN-4
**Green Hill**—*pop pl* WV-2
Green Hill—*summit* AK-9
Green Hill—*summit* CA-9
Green Hill—*summit* CT-1
Green Hill—*summit* (2) GA-3
Green Hill—*summit* KY-4
Green Hill—*summit* (4) ME-1
Green Hill—*summit* MD-2
Green Hill—*summit* (8) MA-1
Green Hill—*summit* (2) NV-8
Green Hill—*summit* (4) NH-1
Green Hill—*summit* NJ-2
Green Hill—*summit* (4) NY-2
Green Hill—*summit* OR-9
Greenhill—*summit* OR-9
Green Hill—*summit* (2) PA-2
Green Hill—*summit* RI-1
Green Hill—*summit* TN-4
Green Hill—*summit* (2) TX-5
Green Hill—*summit* UT-8
Green Hill—*summit* VT-1

Greenmead—uninc pl ... CA-9
Greenmead Farms—hist pl ... MI-6
Green Meadow ... OR-9
Green Meadow—flat ... CA-9
**Green Meadow**—pop pl ... DE-2
**Green Meadow**—pop pl (2) ... TN-4
Green Meadow—swamp ... SC-3
Green Meadow Cem—cemetery ... MD-2
Green Meadow Ch—church ... TN-4
Green Meadow Ch of Christ ... TN-4
Green Meadow Country Club—locale ... TN-4
Green Meadow Creek ... SC-3
Green Meadow Creek—stream ... WI-6
Green Meadow Golf Club—other ... NH-1
Green Meadow Lake—lake ... NM-5
**Green Meadow Point**—pop pl ... VA-3
Green Meadow Res—reserve ... MT-8
Green Meadows (2) ... IL-6
Green Meadows ... SC-3
Green Meadows—area ... NM-5
Green Meadows—CDP ... OH-6
Green Meadows—locale ... PA-2
**Green Meadows**—pop pl (2) ... IN-6
**Green Meadows**—pop pl (2) ... MD-2
**Green Meadows**—pop pl ... NE-7
**Green Meadows**—pop pl ... OR-9
Green Meadows—uninc pl ... NM-5
Green Meadows Ch—church ... KY-4
Green Meadow Sch—school ... MA-1
Green Meadow Sch—school (2) ... MI-6
Green Meadow Sch—school ... NY-2
Green Meadow Sch—school (2) ... WI-6
Green Meadows Country Club—locale ... NC-3
**Green Meadows Estates (subdivision)**—pop pl ... UT-8
Green Meadows Golf Course—locale (2) ... PA-2
Green Meadows JHS—school ... NY-2
Green Meadows Playground—park ... CA-9
Green Meadows Point—uninc pl ... VA-3
Green Meadows Sch (historical)—school ... TN-4
Green Meadows School (Abandoned)—locale ... ID-8
**Green Meadows (subdivision)**—pop pl (2) ... NC-3
**Green Meadows Subdivision**—pop pl (3) ... UT-8
**Green Meadow (subdivision)**—pop pl ... MS-4
Green Meadow (Township of)—civ div ... MN-6
**Greenmead (subdivision)**—pop pl ... NC-3
Green-Meldrim House—hist pl ... GA-3
Green Memorial A.M.E. Zion Church—hist pl ... ME-1
Green Memorial Ch—church ... NC-3
Green Memorial Park—cemetery ... TX-5
Green Mercantile Store—hist pl ... CO-8
Green Mesa Ranch—locale ... CO-8
Green Mine—mine ... AZ-5
Green Mine—mine ... CA-9
Green Mine—mine ... IL-6
Green Mine—mine ... KY-4
Green Mine (Inactive)—mine ... CA-9
Green Mine (underground)—mine ... TN-4
Green Monarch Mine—mine ... ID-8
Green Monarch Mtn—summit ... ID-8
Green Monarch Ridge—ridge ... ID-8
Greenmond Cem—cemetery ... OH-6
Green Monster Canyon—valley ... NV-8
Green Monster Mine—mine (2) ... CA-9
Green Monster Mine—mine ... NV-8
Green Monster Mtn—summit ... AK-9
Greenmont Cem—cemetery ... NY-2
Greenmont Cem—cemetery ... OH-6
Greenmonte Ch—church ... VA-3
Greenmont Post Office (historical)—building ... SD-7
Greenmont Sch—school ... OH-6
Greenmont Sch—school ... WV-2
Green-Moore Ch—church ... AL-4
Greenmore ... AL-4
Greenmore Sch (historical)—school ... AL-4
Green Moss Ch—church ... IL-6
Greenmoss Ferry (historical)—crossing ... TN-4
Green Moss Sch—school ... IL-6
Green Mound Cem—cemetery ... IA-7
Green Mound Cem—cemetery (2) ... KS-7
Green Mound Cem—cemetery ... NE-7
Greenmound Cem—cemetery ... OH-6
Green Mound Cem—cemetery ... OH-6
Greenmound Cem—cemetery ... OH-6
Green Mound Cem—cemetery ... OH-6
Green Mound Cem—cemetery ... SD-7
Green Mound Cem—cemetery ... WA-9
Green Mound Cem—cemetery ... WI-6
Green Mound Ch—church ... IA-7
Green Mound Ch—church ... KS-7
Green Mound Ch—church ... MO-7
**Green Mound Ridge**—pop pl ... MO-7
Green Mound Ridge—ridge ... MO-7
Green Mound Sch—school (2) ... MO-7
Greenmount ... OH-6
Green Mount—locale ... AR-4
Greenmount—locale ... KY-4
Green Mount—locale ... VA-3
**Greenmount**—pop pl ... MD-2
**Greenmount**—pop pl ... PA-2
**Greenmount**—pop pl ... VA-3
Greenmount—uninc pl ... PA-2
Green Mountain ... AL-4
Green Mountain ... AR-4
Green Mountain (2) ... CO-8
Green Mountain ... MA-1
Green Mountain ... MT-8
Green Mountain ... WY-8
Green Mountain—locale ... NC-3
**Green Mountain**—pop pl ... IA-7
**Green Mountain**—pop pl ... MO-7
**Greenmountain**—pop pl ... NC-3
**Green Mountain**—pop pl ... WA-9
Green Mountain—ridge ... MT-8
Green Mountain—ridge (3) ... NC-3
Green Mountain—ridge ... OR-9
Green Mountain Arrow Site (48FR96)—hist pl ... WY-8
Green Mountain Arroyo—stream ... NM-5
Green Mountain Beach—locale ... MI-6
Green Mountain Branch—stream ... TN-4
Green Mountain Cabins—locale ... VT-1
Green Mountain Camp—locale ... VT-1
**Green Mountain Camp**—pop pl ... CO-8
Green Mountain Canon Creek - in part ... NV-8
Green Mountain Cem—cemetery ... CO-8
Green Mountain Cem—cemetery ... IL-6
Green Mountain Cem—cemetery ... NJ-2
Green Mountain Cem—cemetery ... NC-3
Green Mountain Cem—cemetery ... PA-2
Green Mountain Cem—cemetery (2) ... WY-8
Green Mountain Ch—church ... CO-8
Green Mountain Ch—church ... MO-7
Green Mountain Ch—church ... NC-3
Green Mountain Ch—church (2) ... VA-3
Green Mountain Community Center—locale ... TX-5
Green Mountain Creek ... PA-2
Green Mountain Creek—stream (2) ... CO-8
Green Mountain Creek—stream ... ID-8
Green Mountain Creek—stream ... NV-8
Green Mountain Creek—stream ... NC-3
Green Mountain Creek—stream (2) ... OR-9
Green Mountain Creek—stream ... WA-9
Green Mountain Dam—dam ... AZ-5
Green Mountain Draw—valley ... WY-8
Green Mountain Estates ... CO-8
**Green Mountain Estates Subdivision**—pop pl ... UT-8
**Green Mountain Falls**—pop pl ... CO-8
Green Mountain Gap—gap ... NC-3
Green Mountain Gulch ... CO-8
Green Mountain Gulch—valley ... CO-8
Green Mountain (historical P.O.)—locale ... IA-7
Green Mountain Lake—lake ... MN-6
Green Mountain Lake—lake ... NY-2
Green Mountain Lake—lake ... WA-9
Green Mountain Lookout—hist pl ... WA-9
Green Mountain Memorial Park—cemetery ... CO-8
Green Mountain Mine—mine (2) ... CO-8
Green Mountain Mine—mine ... MT-8
Green Mountain Natl For—forest ... VT-1
Green Mountain Pasture—flat ... WA-9
Green Mountain Pond—lake ... ME-1
Green Mountain Ranch—hist pl ... CO-8
Green Mountain Ranch—locale (2) ... CO-8
Green Mountain Range ... VT-1
Green Mountain Range ... WA-9
Green Mountain Ridge—ridge ... OR-9
Green Mountain Rsvr—reservoir ... CO-8
Green Mountain Rsvr No 1—reservoir ... CO-8
Green Mountains ... WY-8
Green Mountains—range ... VT-1
Green Mountain Sch—school ... CA-9
Green Mountain Sch—school ... CO-8
Green Mountain Sch—school ... MT-8
Green Mountain Sch—school ... NH-1
Green Mountain Sch—school ... OR-9
Green Mountain Sch—school ... VT-1
Green Mountain Sch—school ... WA-9
Green Mountain Sch (abandoned)—school ... PA-2
Green Mountain Seminary—hist pl ... VT-1
**Greenmountain (sta.)**—pop pl ... NC-3
Green Mountain Tank—reservoir ... AZ-5
Green Mountain (Township of)—fmr MCD ... NC-3
Green Mountain Trail—trail (4) ... CO-8
Green Mountain Trail—trail ... ID-8
Green Mountain Trail—trail (2) ... MT-8
Green Mountain Trail—trail ... WV-2
Green Mountain Trail—trail ... WY-8
**Green Mountain (Trailer Park)**—pop pl ... VT-1
Green Mountain Union HS—school ... VT-1
**Green Mountain Village**—pop pl ... CO-8
Green Mount Cem—cemetery ... AL-4
Green Mount Cem—cemetery ... AR-4
Green Mount Cem—cemetery (2) ... IL-6
Greenmount Cem—cemetery ... MD-2
Green Mount Cem—cemetery ... NY-2
Greenmount Cem—cemetery (2) ... OH-6
Green Mount Cem—cemetery (2) ... PA-2
Greenmount Cem—cemetery (2) ... PA-2
Greenmount Cem—cemetery ... VT-1
Green Mount Cem—cemetery (2) ... VT-1
Green Mount Cem—cemetery ... VA-3
Green Mount Cem—cemetery ... WV-2
Green Mount Cemetery—hist pl ... MD-2
Green Mount Ch—church ... GA-3
Green Mount Ch—church ... VA-3
Greenmount-Langnau (CCD)—cens area ... KY-4
Green Mount Post Office—building ... PA-2
Greenmount Sch—school ... PA-2
**Greenmount (subdivision)**—pop pl ... DE-2
Green Mtn ... ME-1
Green Mtn ... OR-9
Green Mtn ... WA-9
Green Mtn—range ... WA-9
Green Mtn—summit (2) ... AK-9
Green Mtn—summit ... AZ-5
Green Mtn—summit (9) ... CA-9
Green Mtn—summit (15) ... CO-8
Green Mtn—summit ... CT-1
Green Mtn—summit ... GA-3
Green Mtn—summit (8) ... ID-8
Green Mtn—summit ... KY-4
Green Mtn—summit (3) ... ME-1
Green Mtn—summit (2) ... MO-7
Green Mtn—summit (12) ... MT-8
Green Mtn—summit (2) ... NV-8
Green Mtn—summit (5) ... NH-1
Green Mtn—summit (2) ... NM-5
Green Mtn—summit (3) ... NY-2
Green Mtn—summit (5) ... NC-3
Green Mtn—summit (18) ... OR-9
Green Mtn—summit (5) ... PA-2
Green Mtn—summit ... SC-3
Green Mtn—summit (4) ... SD-7
Green Mtn—summit (2) ... TN-4
Green Mtn—summit (7) ... TX-5
Green Mtn—summit ... UT-8
Green Mtn—summit (2) ... VT-1
Green Mtn—summit (6) ... VA-3
Green Mtn—summit (13) ... WA-9
Green Mtn—summit ... WV-2
Green Mtn—summit (9) ... WY-8
Green Mtn (historical)—summit ... SD-7
Green Mtn Peak—summit ... MI-6
Green Mtns—range ... WY-8
Green Neal Branch—stream ... TX-5
**Green Needles (subdivision)**—pop pl ... NC-3
Green No. 5 (41OL257)—hist pl ... TX-5
Green Nubble—island ... ME-1
Green Number Three Beach ... MH-9
Greenoak ... IN-6
Greenoak—locale ... IL-6
Green Oak—locale ... PA-2
**Greenoak**—pop pl ... IN-6
**Green Oak**—pop pl ... NJ-2
**Green Oak**—pop pl ... MI-6
Green Oak Cem—cemetery (2) ... LA-4
Green Oak Cem—cemetery ... MI-6
Green Oak Ch—church ... MI-6
Green Oak Ch (historical)—church ... AL-4
Green Oak Church ... AL-4
Green Oak Lake—lake (2) ... MI-6
**Green Oaks**—pop pl ... IL-6
**Green Oaks**—pop pl ... MO-7
**Green Oaks**—pop pl ... PA-2
Green Oaks—uninc pl ... VA-3
Green Oak Sch—school ... MI-6
Green Oak Sch (historical)—school ... AL-4
Green Oak Sch Number 1 ... AL-4
Green Oaks County Park—park ... OR-9
Green Oaks Creek—stream ... CA-9
**Green Oaks Estates Subdivision**—pop pl ... UT-8
Green Oaks Memorial Park—cemetery ... LA-4
Green Oaks Ranch—locale ... CA-9
Green Oaks Ranch House—hist pl ... CA-9
Green Oaks Sch—school (2) ... CA-9
**Green Oaks (subdivision)**—pop pl ... MS-4
**Green Oak (Township of)**—pop pl ... MI-6
Greenock—locale ... TX-5
**Greenock**—pop pl ... MD-2
**Greenock**—pop pl ... PA-2
Greenock Country Club—locale ... MA-1
Greenock Elem Sch—school ... PA-2
Greenock Station—building ... PA-2
Green Olive Ch—church ... AR-4
Green Olive Ch—church ... SC-3
Greenon Cem—cemetery ... AL-4
Greenon HS—school ... OH-6
Greenop Cem—cemetery ... MI-6
Greenough—locale ... GA-3
Greenough—locale ... MT-8
Greenough—uninc pl ... KY-4
Greenough, Byron, Block—hist pl ... ME-1
Greenough, Mount—summit ... AK-9
Greenough Brook—stream ... NH-1
Greenough Coulee—valley ... MT-8
Greenough Creek—stream ... MT-8
Greenough Lake—lake ... MT-8
Greenough Lookout Tower—locale ... GA-3
Greenough Mtn—summit ... NY-2
Greenough Park—park ... MT-8
Greenough Pond—lake ... MA-1
Greenough Pond—lake (2) ... NH-1
Greenough Pond—reservoir ... MA-1
Greenough Pond Dam—dam ... MA-1
Greenough Post Office—locale ... MT-8
Greenough Ranch—locale ... MT-8
Greenough Ridge—ridge ... CA-9
Greenough Roughs—ridge ... CA-9
Greenpark ... PA-2
Green Park—flat ... WA-9
Greenpark—other ... PA-2
Green Park—park ... MN-6
Green Park—park ... PA-2
Green Park Cem—cemetery ... IN-6
**Green Park (Greenpark)**—pop pl ... PA-2
Green Park Inn—hist pl ... NC-3
Green Park Playground—locale ... WA-9
Green Park Sch—school ... LA-4
Green Park Sch—school ... NC-3
Green Park Sch—school ... WA-9
Green Pass—gap ... ID-8
Green Pass—gap ... WA-9
Green Pass Spring—spring ... ID-8
Green Pasture Camp—locale ... MI-6
Green Pasture Ch—church ... TX-5
Green Pastures—hist pl ... TX-5
**Green Pastures**—pop pl ... OK-5
Green Pastures Plantation (historical)—locale ... TN-4
**Green Pastures Subdivision**—pop pl ... UT-8
Green Peak ... HI-9
Green Peak ... VT-1
Green Peak—locale ... OR-9
Green Peak—summit ... CA-9
Green Peak—summit (2) ... OR-9
Green Peak—summit (2) ... WA-9
Green Peak Lake—lake ... OR-9
Green Persimmon Sch—school ... IL-6
Green Peter—summit ... OR-9
Green Peter Creek—stream ... OR-9
Green Peter Dam—dam ... OR-9
Green Peter Lake—lake ... OR-9
Green Peter Lake—reservoir ... OR-9
Green Peter Rsvr ... OR-9
Green Pine—locale ... TN-4
Green Pine Baptist Church ... TN-4
Green Pine Ch—church ... NC-3
Green Pine Ch—church ... TN-4
Green Pine Creek ... ID-8
Green Pine Creek—stream ... ID-8
Green Pine Lake—lake ... MI-6
Green Pine Sch (historical)—school ... TN-4
**Green Pines (subdivision)**—pop pl ... NC-3
Green Plain—locale ... VA-3
**Green Plain**—pop pl ... VA-3
Green Plain Cem—cemetery ... IL-6
Green Plain Monthly Meetinghouse—hist pl ... OH-6
Green Plains Cem—cemetery ... KY-4
Green Plains Ch—church ... AR-4
Green Plains Ch—church ... KY-4
Green Plain Sch—school ... IA-7
Green Plains Post Office (historical)—building ... MS-4
Green Playground—park ... FL-3
Green Playground—park ... MI-6
Green-Poe House—hist pl ... GA-3
Green Point ... MN-6
Green Point ... NY-2
Green Point ... SD-7
Green Point—cape (5) ... AK-9
Green Point—cape (6) ... FL-3
Green Point—cape ... LA-4
Green Point—cape (2) ... ME-1
Green Point—cape (2) ... MD-2
Green Point—cape (2) ... MA-1
Green Point—cape (4) ... NY-2
Green Point—cape (5) ... NC-3
Green Point—cape (2) ... OR-9
Green Point—cape ... VT-1
Green Point—cape (4) ... VA-3
Green Point—cape (4) ... WA-9
Green Point—island ... MI-6
Green Point—locale (2) ... PA-2
**Green Point**—pop pl ... FL-3
**Greenpoint**—pop pl ... NY-2
Green Point—summit ... CA-9
Green Point—summit ... ME-1
Green Point Ch—church ... GA-3
Green Point Ch—church ... SC-3
Green Point Cove—bay ... NC-3
Green Point Creek—stream ... OR-9
Green Point Creek—stream ... WA-9
Green Point Farm—locale ... MD-2
Green Point Feeder Canal ... OR-9
Greenpoint Glacier—glacier ... AK-9
Greenpoint Hist Dist—hist pl ... NY-2
Greenpoint Hosp—hospital ... NY-2
Green Point Lower Rsvr—reservoir ... OR-9
Green Point Mtn—summit ... OR-9
Green Point Ridge—ridge ... CA-9
Green Point Shoal—bar ... ME-1
Green Point Station—locale ... PA-2
Green Point Upper Rsvr—reservoir ... OR-9
Green Point Wharf—locale ... MD-2
Green Pole Canyon—valley ... MT-8
Greenpole Creek—stream ... MT-8
Green Pond ... FL-3
Green Pond ... NH-1
Green Pond ... NJ-2
Greenpond ... TN-4
Green Pond—bay ... MA-1
Green Pond—lake ... CT-1
Green Pond—lake (2) ... FL-3
Green Pond—lake ... GA-3
Green Pond—lake (4) ... ME-1
Green Pond—lake (2) ... MA-1
Green Pond—lake ... MI-6
Green Pond—lake ... NJ-2
Green Pond—lake (9) ... NY-2
Green Pond—lake ... PA-2
Green Pond—lake ... TN-4
Green Pond—lake ... TX-5
Green Pond—lake ... UT-8
Green Pond—lake ... VA-3
Greenpond—locale ... IL-6
Green Pond—locale ... TN-4
Green Pond—locale ... VA-3
**Green Pond**—pop pl ... AL-4
**Green Pond**—pop pl ... FL-3
**Green Pond**—pop pl ... NJ-2
**Green Pond**—pop pl ... NC-3
**Green Pond**—pop pl (2) ... SC-3
Green Pond—reservoir ... GA-3
Green Pond—reservoir ... PA-2
Green Pond—swamp ... FL-3
Green Pond Baptist Ch—church ... AL-4
Green Pond Bayou ... TX-5
Green Pond Branch—stream ... MS-4
Green Pond Brook—stream ... NJ-2
Green Pond (CCD)—cens area ... SC-3
Green Pond Ch—church ... FL-3
Green Pond Ch—church (5) ... SC-3
Green Pond Ch—church ... TN-4
Greenpond Ch—church ... TX-5
Green Pond Christian Sch—school ... AL-4
Green Pond Country Club ... PA-2
Green Pond Golf Course—locale ... PA-2
Green Pond Gully—valley ... TX-5
Green Pond Harbor Light—locale ... MA-1
Green Pond Junction—locale ... NJ-2
Green Pond Mtn—summit ... CT-1
Green Pond Mtn—summit ... NJ-2
Green Pond Mtn—summit ... NY-2
Green Pond Mtn—summit ... TN-4
Greenpond Post Office (historical)—building ... TN-4
Green Pond Ranch—locale ... CA-9
Green Pond Ridge—ridge ... KY-4
Green Ponds—lake ... FL-3
Green Pond Sch—school ... KY-4
Green Pond Sch—school ... SC-3
Green Pond Swamp—swamp ... FL-3
Greenport ... AL-4
**Greenport**—pop pl (2) ... NY-2
**Greenport Center**—pop pl ... NY-2
Greenport Harbor—bay ... NY-2
**Greenport (Town of)**—pop pl ... NY-2
Greenport Village Hist Dist—hist pl ... NY-2
Greenport West—CDP ... NY-2
Green Posey Cave—cave ... AL-4
Green Post Office (historical)—building ... TN-4
Green Prairie—area ... OR-9
Green Prairie Fish Lake—lake ... MN-6
Green Prairie Sch—school ... IL-6
Green Prairie (Township of)—civ div ... MN-6
Green Pump Well—well ... TX-5
Green Quarry Site—hist pl ... MI-6
Green Quartz Mine—mine ... AZ-5
Greenquist Lake ... WI-6
Green Ranch—locale ... CO-8
Green Ranch—locale (2) ... MT-8
Green Ranch—locale ... NE-7
Green Ranch—locale ... NV-8
Green Ranch—locale (2) ... NM-5
Green Ranch—locale ... WY-8
Green Ranch (abandoned)—locale ... MT-8
Green Ravine—valley ... UT-8
Green Reservoir ... AZ-5
Green Reservoir Dam ... AZ-5
Green Reservoir Outlet ... AZ-5
Green Ridge ... OR-9
Green Ridge ... PA-2
Greenridge—locale ... IL-6
Green Ridge—locale ... MD-2
Green Ridge—locale ... WV-2
**Green Ridge**—pop pl ... MD-2
**Greenridge**—pop pl ... MD-2
**Green Ridge**—pop pl ... MO-7
**Greenridge**—pop pl ... NY-2
**Green Ridge**—pop pl (4) ... PA-2
**Greenridge**—pop pl ... PA-2
Green Ridge—ridge ... AR-4
Green Ridge—ridge (2) ... CA-9
Green Ridge—ridge (5) ... CO-8
Green Ridge—ridge ... FL-3
Green Ridge—ridge (2) ... ID-8
Green Ridge—ridge (2) ... MD-2
Green Ridge—ridge (3) ... NC-3
Green Ridge—ridge ... OH-6
Green Ridge—ridge (2) ... OR-9
Green Ridge—ridge (5) ... PA-2
Green Ridge—ridge (2) ... TN-4
Green Ridge—ridge (2) ... VA-3
Green Ridge—ridge (2) ... WA-9
Green Ridge—ridge ... WV-2
Green Ridge—ridge ... WY-8
Green Ridge—summit ... AK-9
Green Ridge Branch—stream ... NC-3
Green Ridge Breaker—building ... PA-2
Greenridge Cem—cemetery ... IA-7
Green Ridge Cem—cemetery ... KS-7
Greenridge Cem—cemetery ... MO-7
Greenridge Cem—cemetery ... MT-8
Greenridge Cem—cemetery ... NY-2
Greenridge Cem—cemetery ... OH-6
Green Ridge Cem—cemetery ... PA-2
Greenridge Cem—cemetery ... WI-6
Greenridge Ch—church ... AL-4
Green Ridge Ch—church ... IL-6
Green Ridge Ch—church (3) ... MO-7
Green Ridge Ch—church ... TN-4
Green Ridge Chapel—church ... MI-6
Green Ridge Creek—stream ... ID-8
Green Ridge Creek—stream ... OR-9
Green Ridge Elem Sch—school ... PA-2
**Greenridge Farms**—pop pl ... PA-2
Green Ridge Glade—valley ... CO-8
Greenridge KLA Airp—airport ... IN-6
Green Ridge Knob—summit ... NC-3
Green Ridge Lake—lake ... WA-9
Green Ridge Lake—reservoir ... NJ-2
Green Ridge Memorial Park (Cemetery)—cemetery ... PA-2
**Green Ridge Park**—pop pl ... MA-1
**Greenridge Park**—pop pl ... WI-6
Greenridge Point—cape ... FL-3
Green Ridge Sch—school ... KS-7
Greenridge Sch—school ... KY-4
Greenridge Sch—school ... MO-7
Green Ridge Sch—school ... NE-7
Green Ridge Sch—school (2) ... PA-2
Green Ridge Station—building ... PA-2
Green Ridge Station—locale ... PA-2
Green Ridge Township—civil ... MO-7
Green Ridge Trail—trail ... CO-8
Green Ridge Trail—trail ... PA-2
Green Ridge Trail—trail ... WY-8
Green Ridge Vista—locale ... PA-2
Green River ... AR-4
Green River ... ND-7
Greenriver ... TN-4
Green River ... WI-6
Green River—locale ... MI-6
Green River—locale ... WA-9
**Green River**—pop pl ... IL-6
**Green River**—pop pl ... MS-4
**Green River**—pop pl ... NY-2
**Greenriver**—pop pl ... NC-3
**Green River**—pop pl ... UT-8
**Green River**—pop pl ... VT-1
**Green River**—pop pl ... WY-8
Green River—stream ... CT-1
Green River—stream (2) ... IL-6
Green River—stream ... KY-4
Green River—stream (4) ... MA-1
Green River—stream (2) ... MI-6
Green River—stream ... MO-7
Green River—stream ... NY-2
Green River—stream ... NC-3
Green River—stream ... ND-7
Green River—stream ... OR-9
Green River—stream ... TN-4
Green River—stream ... TX-5
Green River—stream (2) ... UT-8
Green River—stream (3) ... VT-1
Green River—stream (2) ... WA-9
Green River—stream (2) ... WY-8
Green River—summit ... CO-8
Green River Airp—airport ... UT-8
Green River Airp Heliport—airport ... UT-8
Green River Baptist Church ... TN-4
Green River Bible Ch—church ... TN-4
Green River Bluffs Trail—trail ... KY-4
Green River Boys Camp—locale ... KY-4
Green River Campground—park (2) ... UT-8
Green River Cem—cemetery ... MA-1
Green River Cem—cemetery ... NY-2
Green River Ch—church ... AR-4
Green River Ch—church (3) ... KY-4
Green River Ch—church ... MS-4
Green River Ch—church (2) ... NC-3
Green River Ch—church ... TN-4
Green River Chapel—church ... KY-4
Green River Community Coll—school ... WA-9
Green River Country Club—other ... SC-3
Green River Cove—valley ... NC-3
Green River Covered Bridge—hist pl ... VT-1
Green River Dam—dam ... ND-7
Green River Desert ... UT-8
Green River Division—civil ... UT-8
Green River Gap—gap ... NC-3
Green River Gap—gap ... UT-8
Green River Glacier ... WY-8
Green River Gorge—stream ... WA-9
Green River Guard Station—locale ... WA-9
Green River Hill—summit ... KY-4
Green River Hill Confederate Cem—cemetery ... KY-4
Green River (historical)—locale ... MS-4
**Green River (historical)**—pop pl ... TN-4
Green River HS—school ... UT-8
Green River Island—cape ... KY-4
Green River Island Ditch—canal ... WY-8
Green River Knob—summit ... KY-4
Green River Lake—reservoir ... KY-4
Green River Lakes—lake ... WY-8
Green River Lake State Park—park ... KY-4
Green River Memorial Ch—church ... KY-4
**Green River (Mog)**—pop pl ... KY-4
Green River North—cens area ... WY-8
Green River Ordnance Plant—other ... IL-6
Green River Overlook—locale ... UT-8
Green River Pass—gap ... WY-8
Green River Plantation—hist pl ... NC-3
Green River Plantation—locale ... AR-4
Green River Plaza—locale ... IN-6
Green River Post Office—building ... UT-8
Greenriver Post Office (historical)—building ... TN-4
Green River Power Plant—other ... KY-4
Green River Ranch—locale ... MI-6
Green River Ranger Station—locale ... UT-8
Green River Reservoir ... KY-4
Green River Retention Dam No 5—dam ... WY-8
Green River Retention Dam No 6—dam ... WY-8
Green River Rsvr—reservoir ... VT-1
Green River Run—stream ... GA-3
Green River Salmon Hatchery—other ... WA-9
Green River Sch—school ... IL-6
Green River Sch—school ... MA-1
Green River Sch—school ... WI-6
Green River Sch Number 4—school ... ND-7
Green River Slope—flat ... CO-8
Green River South—cens area ... WY-8
Green River State Park—park ... UT-8
Green River State Rec Area ... UT-8
Green River State Rec Area—park ... UT-8
Green River Station ... ND-7
Green River Supply Canal—canal ... WY-8
Green River Supply Canal Lateral No 1—canal ... WY-8
Green River (Township of)—fmr MCD ... NC-3
Green River Union Ch—church ... KY-4
Green River Valley—valley ... UT-8
Green River Valley Ch—church ... KY-4
Green River Watershed (City of Tacoma)—area ... WA-9
Green River Wildlife Ref—park ... IL-6
Green Road—locale ... KY-4
Green Road Ch—church ... KY-4
Green Rock ... AK-9
Green Rock—island ... CA-9
Green Rock—island ... ME-1
**Green Rock**—pop pl ... IL-6
Green Rock—rock ... MA-1
Green Rock Branch—stream ... NC-3
Green Rock Branch—stream ... VA-3
Green Rock Ch—church ... NC-3
Greenrock Fork—stream ... KY-4
Green Rock Hollow—valley ... KY-4
Green Rock Mine—mine ... CA-9
Green Rock Mine—mine ... OR-9
Green Rocks Lake—lake ... AK-9
Green Rocks Light—locale ... AK-9
Green Rsvr—reservoir (2) ... OR-9
Green Rsvr—reservoir ... WY-8
Green Run ... DE-2
**Green Run**—pop pl ... WV-2
Green Run—stream (3) ... IN-6
Green Run—stream ... MD-2
Green Run—stream ... OH-6
Green Run—stream (4) ... PA-2
Green Run Bay—bay ... MD-2
Green Run Inlet Bay ... MD-2
Green Run Sch (historical)—school ... PA-2
Green Run Trail—trail ... PA-2
Greens ... AL-4
Greens ... NC-3
Greens—locale ... NV-8
**Greens**—pop pl ... AL-4
**Greens**—pop pl ... MS-4
Green Saddle—gap (2) ... ID-8
Green Saint Sch—school ... DE-2
Greensand—locale ... NJ-2
Green Sandstone Rsvr—reservoir ... WY-8
Green Savannah Lake—swamp ... SC-3
Green Savanna Lake ... SC-3
Greens Baber Well—well ... NM-5
Greens Bar—bar ... AL-4
Greens Basin—basin ... UT-8
Greens Basin—bay ... NH-1
Greens Bay ... MI-6
Greens Bayou ... TX-5
Greens Bayou—bay ... FL-3
Greens Bayou—bay ... TX-5
Greens Bayou—gut ... LA-4
Greens Bayou—gut ... TX-5
**Greens Bayou**—pop pl ... TX-5
Greens Bayou—stream (4) ... LA-4
Greens Bayou—stream ... MS-4
Greens Bayou—stream (2) ... TX-5
Greens Bayou Oil Field—oilfield ... MS-4
Greens Bayou Park—park ... TX-5
Greens Bear Hole—basin ... FL-3
Greens Bench—bench ... MT-8
Greens Bluff ... TX-5
Greens Bluff—cliff ... AL-4
Greens Bluff—locale ... TX-5
Greens Bluff Bar (historical)—bar ... AL-4
Greensboro ... IN-6
**Greensboro**—pop pl ... AL-4
**Greensboro**—pop pl ... FL-3
**Greensboro**—pop pl ... GA-3
**Greensboro**—pop pl ... IN-6
**Greensboro**—pop pl ... MD-2
**Greensboro**—pop pl ... NC-3
**Greensboro**—pop pl ... PA-2
**Greensboro**—pop pl ... VT-1
Greensboro Baptist Ch—church ... AL-4
Greensboro Baptist Church ... MS-4
**Greensboro Bend**—pop pl ... VT-1
Greensboro Borough—civil ... PA-2
Greensboro Branch—stream ... GA-3
Greensboro Brook—stream ... VT-1
Greensboro (CCD)—cens area ... AL-4
Greensboro (CCD)—cens area ... FL-3
Greensboro (CCD)—cens area ... GA-3
Greensboro Ch—church ... FL-3
Greensboro Ch of Christ—church ... AL-4
Greensboro Coll—school ... NC-3
Greensboro Commercial Hist Dist—hist pl ... GA-3
Greensboro Country Club ... AL-4
Greensboro Country Club—locale ... NC-3
Greensboro Country Park—park ... NC-3
Greensboro Country Park Lake Five A—reservoir ... NC-3
Greensboro Country Park Lake Five A Dam—dam ... NC-3
Greensboro Country Park Lake Five B—reservoir ... NC-3
Greensboro Country Park Lake Five B Dam—dam ... NC-3
Greensboro Depot—hist pl ... GA-3
Greensboro Depot—hist pl ... VT-1
Greensboro Division—civil ... AL-4
Greensboro Elem Sch—school ... FL-3
Greensboro Female Acad (historical)—school ... AL-4

Greensboro-High Point-Winston Salem Regional Airport—airport ... NC-3
Greensboro Hist Dist—hist pl ... AL-4
Greensboro (historical)—locale ... MS-4
Greensboro Historical Museum—hist pl ... NC-3
Greensboro Hosp (historical)—hospital ... AL-4
Greensboro HS ... NC-3
Greensboro HS—school ... FL-3
Greensboro HS—school ... NC-3
Greensboro Lake—reservoir ... GA-3
Greensboro Methodist Ch (historical)—church ... MS-4
Greensboro Municipal Airp—airport ... AL-4
Greensboro Presbyterian Ch—church ... AL-4
Greensboro Public East Sch—school ... AL-4
Greensboro Public West Sch—school ... AL-4
Greensboro Sch—school ... FL-3
Greensboro Sch (historical)—school ... MS-4
Greensboro (sta.) (RR name for Greensboro Bend)—other ... VT-1
Greensboro Street Hist Dist—hist pl ... MS-4
Greensboro (Town of)—pop pl ... VT-1
Greensboro (Township of)—pop pl ... IN-6
Greensborough ... IN-6
Greensborough ... MS-4
Greensboro Waterworks—locale ... NC-3
Greens Bottom—bend ... MO-7
Greens Branch ... NJ-2
Greens Branch ... WV-2
Greens Branch—stream ... DE-2
Greens Branch—stream (3) ... KY-4
Greens Branch—stream ... LA-4
Greens Branch—stream ... TN-4
Greens Branch—stream ... WV-2
Greens Bridge—bridge ... OR-9
Greens Bridge—bridge ... SC-3
Greens Bridge—uninc pl ... NJ-2
Greens Brook ... CT-1
Greens Brook—stream ... MA-1
Greens Brook—stream ... VT-1
Greensburg ... IN-6
Greensburg ... OH-6
Greensburg—locale ... WV-2
Greensburg—pop pl ... IN-6
Greensburg—pop pl ... KS-7
Greensburg—pop pl ... KY-4
Greensburg—pop pl ... LA-4
Greensburg—pop pl ... MD-2
Greensburg—pop pl ... MO-7
Greensburg—pop pl ... OH-6
Greensburg—pop pl ... PA-2
Greensburg Acad—hist pl ... KY-4
Greensburg Airp—airport ... IN-6
Greensburg Bank Bldg—hist pl ... KY-4
Greensburg (CCD)—cens area ... KY-4
Greensburg Cem—cemetery ... OH-6
Greensburg City—civil ... PA-2
Greensburg City Park—park ... IN-6
Greensburg Community HS—school ... IN-6
Greensburg Corners ... OH-6
Greensburg Country Club—other ... PA-2
Greensburg Cumberland Presbyterian Church—hist pl ... KY-4
Greensburg Ferry—locale ... PA-2
Greensburgh ... KS-7
Greensburg Junior-Senior HS—school ... KS-7
Greensburg Land Office—hist pl ... LA-4
Greensburg Public Fishing Area ... IN-6
Greensburg RR Station—hist pl ... PA-2
Greensburg Sch—school ... MD-2
Greensburg Township—civil ... MO-7
Greensburg (Township of)—pop pl ... OH-6
Greensburg Well—hist pl ... KS-7
Greensburg YMCA Camp—locale ... PA-2
Greens Camp—locale ... NV-8
Greens Canyon—valley ... CA-9
Greens Canyon—valley (2) ... UT-8
Greens Canyon—valley (2) ... WA-9
Greens Canyon—valley ... WY-8
Greens Cave—cave ... MO-7
Greens Cem—cemetery ... GA-3
Greens Cem—cemetery ... MI-6
Green Sch—school (3) ... CA-9
Green Sch—school ... CT-1
Green Sch—school ... DC-2
Green Sch—school (4) ... IL-6
Green Sch—school ... IN-6
Green Sch—school ... IA-7
Green Sch—school (2) ... MA-1
Green Sch—school (8) ... MI-6
Green Sch—school ... MS-4
Green Sch—school (2) ... MO-7
Green Sch—school ... MT-8
Green Sch—school ... NC-3
Green Sch—school ... ND-7
Green Sch—school (4) ... OH-6
Green Sch—school ... OR-9
Green Sch—school (2) ... PA-2
Green Sch—school (2) ... SC-3
Green Sch—school (3) ... TN-4
Green Sch—school ... TX-5
Green Sch—school ... VT-1
Green Sch (abandoned)—school (2) ... MO-7
Green Sch (abandoned)—school ... PA-2
Greens Chapel ... AL-4
Greens Chapel—church (2) ... AL-4
Greens Chapel—church ... AR-4
Greens Chapel—church ... KY-4
Greens Chapel—church ... NC-3
Greens Chapel—church ... TN-4
Greens Chapel—church (2) ... VA-3
Greens Chapel—locale ... AL-4
Greens Chapel Cem—cemetery ... AL-4
Greens Chapel Ch ... AL-4
Greens Chapel Ch—church ... AL-4
Greens Chapel Methodist Ch ... AL-4
Greens Chapel Sch—school ... TX-5
Green Sch (historical)—school ... MO-7
Green School (abandoned)—locale ... MT-8
Greens Chute—gut ... MO-7
Greens Cliff—cliff ... NH-1
Greens Corner—locale ... DE-2
Greens Corner—locale ... ME-1
Greens Corner—locale ... VA-3
Greens Corner—pop pl ... UT-8
Greens Corners—locale ... DE-2
Greens Corners—locale ... WI-6
Greens Corners—pop pl ... VT-1
Greens Coulee—valley ... MT-8
Green's Cove ... NY-2
Greens Cove—bay ... NY-2
Greens Creek ... CO-8
Greens Creek ... MA-1
Greens Creek ... MI-6
Greens Creek ... PA-2
Greens Creek—pop pl ... NC-3
Greens Creek—stream ... AL-4
Greens Creek—stream ... AK-9
Greens Creek—stream ... AR-4
Greens Creek—stream ... CA-9
Greens Creek—stream ... FL-3
Greens Creek—stream ... LA-4
Greens Creek—stream ... MI-6
Greens Creek—stream (4) ... MS-4
Greens Creek—stream ... MO-7
Greens Creek—stream ... NY-2
Greens Creek—stream (2) ... NC-3
Greens Creek—stream ... OR-9
Greens Creek—stream ... SC-3
Greens Creek—stream ... TX-5
Greens Creek—stream (2) ... VA-3
Greens Creek Baptist Church ... MS-4
Greens Creek Campground—locale ... CA-9
Greens Creek Ch—church (2) ... MS-4
Greens Creek Lookout Tower—locale ... MS-4
Greens Creek Mountain—ridge ... AL-4
Greens Creek Mtn—summit ... AL-4
Greens Creek Oil Field—oilfield ... MS-4
Greens Creek Sch—school ... NC-3
Greens Creek Sch (historical)—school ... MS-4
Greens Creek (Township of)—fmr MCD (2) ... NC-3
Greens Cross Ch—church ... NC-3
Greens Crossing—locale ... GA-3
Greens Crossing—locale ... NY-2
Greens Crossing—locale ... TX-5
Greens Crossroad—locale ... TN-4
Greens Cut—locale ... GA-3
Greens Cut Branch ... GA-3
Greens Cut (CCD)—cens area ... GA-3
Greens Ditch ... OH-6
Greens Ditch—canal ... MI-6
Greens Ditch—canal ... OH-6
Greens Ditch—pop pl ... LA-4
Greens Drain—canal ... MI-6
Greens Draw—valley ... UT-8
Green Sea—pop pl ... SC-3
Green Sea—swamp ... VA-3
Green Sea, The ... VA-3
Green Sea Bay—swamp ... SC-3
Green Sea Branch—stream ... TN-4
Green Sedge Point—cape ... NY-2
Green Sergeant Covered Bridge—bridge ... NJ-2
Green Sergeants Covered Bridge—hist pl ... NJ-2
Green Settlement—locale ... NY-2
Greens Farm Park—park ... KS-7
Greens Farms—pop pl ... CT-1
Greens Farms Brook—stream ... CT-1
Greensfelder, Delia, House—hist pl ... MO-7
Greens Ferry ... AL-4
Greens Ford (historical)—crossing ... TN-4
Greensfork ... IN-6
Greens Fork—locale ... NC-3
Greens Fork—pop pl ... IN-6
Greens Fork—stream ... IN-6
Greens Fork—stream ... KY-4
Greens Fork Cem—cemetery ... IN-6
Greensfork (Township of)—pop pl ... IN-6
Greens Gap—gap ... NM-5
Greens Gap—gap ... NC-3
Greens Grant—civil ... NH-1
Greens Grove Ch—church ... IA-7
Greens Gulch—valley (2) ... MT-8
Greens Gulch—valley ... OR-9
Greens Gulch—valley ... SD-7
Green Shack Cove—slope ... TX-5
Green Shade Cem—cemetery ... GA-3
Green Shadow Dam—dam ... TN-4
Green Shadow Lake—reservoir ... TN-4
Green Shanty Hollow—valley ... TN-4
Greens Harbor—bay ... CT-1
Greenshaw Creek—stream ... OR-9
Greenshaw Mtn—summit ... AR-4
Greens Head ... ME-1
Greens Head—summit ... AK-9
Greens Hill—summit ... NY-2
Greenshire (subdivision)—pop pl ... DE-2
Green Shoals Branch—stream ... WV-2
Green Shoals Ch—church ... WV-2
Green Shoals Mtn—summit ... WV-2
Greens Hollow—valley ... AR-4
Greens Hollow—valley (2) ... MO-7
Greens Hollow—valley ... PA-2
Greens Hollow—valley ... TN-4
Greens Hollow—valley ... TX-5
Greens Hollow—valley ... UT-8
Greens Hollow Greers Hollow ... PA-2
Greenshores—pop pl ... TX-5
Green Shutters—hist pl ... LA-4
Greenside—locale ... IA-7
Greenside Butte—summit ... ID-8
Green Siding—pop pl ... WV-2
Green's Inheritance—hist pl ... MD-2
Greens Island—island ... GA-3
Greens Island—island ... ME-1
Greens Island Marsh—swamp ... MD-2
Greens Knob—summit ... VA-3
Greensky Ch—church ... MI-6
Greensky Hill Mission—hist pl ... MI-6
Greens Lake ... AL-4
Greens Lake ... LA-4
Greens Lake ... MI-6
Greens Lake ... TX-5
Greens Lake ... UT-8
Greens Lake—lake ... CA-9
Greens Lake—lake ... LA-4
Greens Lake—lake (2) ... MI-6
Greens Lake—lake ... NY-2
Greens Lake—lake ... TX-5
Greens Lake—reservoir ... TX-5
Greens Lake Campground (UT-M9)—locale ... UT-8
Greens Lake Debris Basin Number Three—reservoir ... UT-8
Greens Lake Debris Basin Number Three Dam—dam ... UT-8
Greens Lake Debris Basin Number Two—reservoir ... UT-8
Greens Lake Debris Basin Number Two Dam—dam ... UT-8
Greens Lake Oil Field—oilfield ... TX-5
Greens Lake Retarding Basin Number Four—reservoir ... UT-8
Greens Lake Retarding Dam Number Four—dam ... UT-8
Greens Lake Road Ch of Christ—church ... TN-4
Greens Lakes—lake ... UT-8
Greens Landing ... PA-2
Greens Landing—locale ... DE-2
Greens Landing—locale ... WA-9
Greens Landing—pop pl ... NY-2
Greens Landing—pop pl ... PA-2
Greens Landing (historical)—locale (2) ... AL-4
Greens Ledge—bar ... CT-1
Greens Ledge—bar (2) ... ME-1
Greens Ledge—bench ... NH-1
Greens Ledge Lighthouse—locale ... CT-1
Green Slough—gut ... AR-4
Green Slough—gut ... CA-9
Green Slough—gut ... WA-9
Green Slough—stream ... AK-9
Green Slough—stream ... OR-9
Green Slough—swamp ... FL-3
Greens Mill—locale ... CA-9
Greens Mill—locale (2) ... GA-3
Greens Mill—pop pl ... TN-4
Greens Mill (historical)—locale ... AL-4
Greens Mill (historical)—locale ... MS-4
Greens Mill Run—stream ... NC-3
Greens Mine—mine ... CA-9
Green Smoke Cave—cave ... AL-4
Greens (North Shore Trace), The—pop pl ... IL-6
Greens of Dover (subdivision)—pop pl ... DE-2
Greens of Woodgate, The ... IL-6
Green Spar Mine—mine ... NM-5
Greens Peak—summit ... AZ-5
Greens Peak—summit ... CA-9
Greens Peak Tank—reservoir ... AZ-5
Green Special Sch—school ... OH-6
Greens Pine Island—island ... LA-4
Greens Pocket—basin ... WA-9
Greens Point—cape ... MI-6
Greens Point—cape ... NC-3
Greens Pond ... MA-1
Greens Pond ... NJ-2
Greens Pond—lake ... GA-3
Greens Pond—lake ... NH-1
Greens Pond—lake ... NY-2
Greens Pond—reservoir ... AL-4
Greens Pond—reservoir ... NC-3
Greens Pond—reservoir ... VA-3
Greens Pond—swamp ... DE-2
Greens Pond Dam—dam ... NC-3
Greensport Ch—church ... AL-4
Greensport Ferry (historical)—locale ... AL-4
Greensport (historical)—locale ... AL-4
Greensport Marina—locale ... AL-4
Green Spot—area ... AZ-5
Green Spot—pop pl ... AZ-5
Greenspot—pop pl (2) ... CA-9
Green Spot Picnic Area—park ... CA-9
Green Spot Spring—spring ... OR-9
Green Spot Well—well ... AZ-5
Greens Prairie—swamp ... FL-3
Greens Prairie Cem—cemetery ... WI-6
Green Spring ... OH-6
Green Spring—hist pl ... VA-3
Green Spring—locale ... DE-2
Green Spring—locale (2) ... VA-3
Green Spring—pop pl ... KY-4
Green Spring—pop pl ... PA-2
Greenspring—pop pl ... PA-2
Green Spring—pop pl ... WV-2
Green Spring—spring ... AL-4
Green Spring—spring (3) ... AZ-5
Green Spring—spring (4) ... CA-9
Green Spring—spring ... CO-8
Green Spring—spring ... ME-1
Green Spring—spring (2) ... MO-7
Green Spring—spring (2) ... NV-8
Green Spring—spring ... NM-5
Green Spring—spring (3) ... OR-9
Green Spring—spring ... PA-2
Green Spring—spring (2) ... TN-4
Green Spring—spring (2) ... TX-5
Green Spring—spring (3) ... UT-8
Green Spring—spring ... WA-9
Green Spring Bay—swamp ... SC-3
Green Spring Branch—stream ... AL-4
Green Spring Branch—stream ... DE-2
Green Spring Branch—stream ... GA-3
Green Spring Branch—stream ... SC-3
Green Spring Canyon ... AZ-5
Green Spring Canyon—valley ... AZ-5
Green Spring Cem—cemetery ... GA-3
Green Spring Cem—cemetery ... MD-2
Green Spring Ch—church ... GA-3
Green Spring Ch—church ... NC-3
Green Spring Ch—church ... PA-2
Green Spring Ch—church ... VA-3
Green Spring Ch (historical)—church ... PA-2
Green Spring Creek ... GA-3
Green Spring Creek—stream ... CA-9
Green Spring Creek—stream ... PA-2
Green Spring Crossing ... DE-2
Greenspring Draw—valley ... OR-9
Green Spring Draw—valley ... OR-9
Green Spring Farm (subdivision)—pop pl ... DE-2
Green Spring Furnace—locale ... MD-2
Green Spring Golf Course—other ... MD-2
Green Spring Hills—pop pl ... MD-2
Green Spring Junction—locale ... MD-2
Green Spring Junction (Kirk)—pop pl ... MD-2
Green Spring (Magisterial District)—fmr MCD ... VA-3
Green Spring Mine—mine ... CA-9
Green Spring Mountain ... OR-9
Green Spring Point—cape ... NC-3
Green Spring Ridge—ridge ... WV-2
Green Spring Run—stream ... CA-9
Green Spring Run—stream ... MD-2
Green Spring Run—stream ... VA-3
Green Spring Run—stream ... WV-2
Green Springs ... VA-3
Green Springs—hist pl ... VA-3
Green Springs—pop pl ... NC-3
Green Springs—pop pl ... OH-6
Green Springs—pop pl ... PA-2
Green Springs—pop pl ... VA-3
Greensprings—pop pl ... VA-3
Green Springs—pop pl ... VA-3
Green Springs—spring ... CA-9
Green Springs—spring ... MT-8
Green Springs—spring ... NV-8
Green Springs—spring ... OR-9
Green Springs—spring ... TX-5
Green Springs—spring ... VA-3
Green Springs—uninc pl ... AL-4
Green Springs Cem—cemetery ... AL-4
Green Springs Ch—church ... AL-4
Green Springs Ch—church ... MD-2
Green Springs Ch—church ... WV-2
Green Springs Depot Post Office ... VA-3
Green Springs Hist Dist—hist pl ... VA-3
Green Springs Missionary Baptist Ch ... AL-4
Green Springs Mobile Park (subdivision)—pop pl ... NC-3
Green Springs Mtn—summit ... OR-9
Green Springs Park—park ... NC-3
Green Springs Rsvr—reservoir ... NV-8
Green Springs Run—stream ... PA-2
Green Springs Sch—school ... MO-7
Green Springs Sch—school ... VA-3
Green Springs Shop Ctr—locale ... AL-4
Green Springs State Nursery—park ... OH-6
Green Springs Summit—summit ... OR-9
Green Spring Trail—trail ... PA-2
Green Spring Valley—valley ... MD-2
Green Spring Valley Hist Dist—hist pl ... MD-2
Green Spring Valley Hunt Club—other ... MD-2
Green Spur—summit (2) ... VA-3
Greens Reservoir Outlet ... AZ-5
Greens Rest Run—stream ... MD-2
Greens Ridge—ridge ... NC-3
Greens Ridge—ridge ... UT-8
Greens Rocks ... RI-1
Greens Run—locale ... OH-6
Greens Run—pop pl ... WV-2
Greens Run—stream ... OH-6
Greens Run—stream ... PA-2
Greens Run—stream (2) ... WV-2
Green's Shell Enclosure—hist pl ... SC-3
Greens Spring ... AL-4
Greens Station—locale ... AL-4
Greens Station Ch—church ... AL-4
Greens Store ... VA-3
Greens Store—locale ... VA-3
Greens Store—pop pl ... OH-6
Greens (subdivision), The—pop pl ... NC-3
Green's Switch ... IL-6
Greens Switch—locale ... IL-6
Green Star Sch—school ... TX-5
Green Station ... KS-7
Green-sterling Sch—school ... OH-6
Greens Thorofare—channel ... NC-3
Greenstone Apartments—hist pl ... TN-4
Greenstone Beach—beach ... MI-6
Greenstone Creek—stream (2) ... AK-9
Greenstone Falls—falls ... MI-6
Greenstone Gulch—valley ... MT-8
Greenstone Lake—lake ... CA-9
Greenstone Lake—lake ... MN-6
Greenstone Mine—mine ... CA-9
Greenstone Mine—mine ... MT-8
Greenstone Mtn—summit ... MT-8
Greenstone Overlook—locale ... VA-3
Greenstone Ridge—ridge ... AK-9
Greenstone Ridge—ridge ... MI-6
Greenstone Ridge Trail—trail ... MI-6
Greenstone (RR name Gladhill)—pop pl ... PA-2
Green Store (historical)—locale ... AL-4
Greenstown—pop pl ... WV-2
Greenstown (Greentown)—pop pl ... WV-2
Greens Trading Post ... AL-4
Greenstreet ... AL-4
Greenstreet—locale ... WI-6
Green Street—pop pl ... AL-4
Greenstreet—pop pl ... MO-7
Green Street—pop pl ... NY-2
Green Street Baptist Ch—church ... AL-4
Green Street-Brenau Hist Dist—hist pl ... GA-3
Green Street Brook—stream ... NY-2
Green Street Cem—cemetery ... MA-1
Green Street Ch—church ... AL-4
Green Street Ch—church ... GA-3
Greenstreet Creek—stream ... CO-8
Green Street District—hist pl ... GA-3
Green Street Elementary School ... MS-4
Greenstreet Elem Sch—school ... IN-6
Green Street Hist Dist—hist pl ... AL-4
Green Street Sch—hist pl ... NH-1
Green Street Sch—school ... IL-6
Green Street Sch—school ... MA-1
Green Street Sch—school ... MS-4
Greenstreet School (historical)—locale ... MO-7
Greenstreets Mtn—summit ... NC-3
Green Stump Pool—reservoir ... MN-6
Green-Sullivan State Forest ... IN-6
Green Sulphur Springs—pop pl ... WV-2
Green Summit Cem—cemetery ... OH-6
Greens Valley—valley (2) ... PA-2
Greens Valley Stream—stream ... PA-2
Greens Valley Trail—trail ... PA-2
Greens View—locale ... TN-4
Greens Village ... IN-6
Greensville Community Center—building ... VA-3
Greensville (County)—pop pl ... VA-3
Greensville County Courthouse Complex—hist pl ... VA-3
Greensville Creek—stream ... VA-3
Greensville Memorial Cem—cemetery ... VA-3
Greensville Memorial Hosp—hospital ... VA-3
Greensville Water Supply—locale ... TN-4
Green Swamp—stream ... SC-3
Green Swamp—stream ... VA-3
Green Swamp—swamp ... FL-3
Green Swamp—swamp (2) ... GA-3
Green Swamp—swamp (2) ... MI-6
Green Swamp—swamp ... MN-6
Green Swamp—swamp ... NJ-2
Green Swamp—swamp ... NY-2
Green Swamp—swamp (2) ... NC-3
Green Swamp—swamp ... SC-3
Green Swamp Branch—stream ... VA-3
Green Swamp Brook—stream ... CT-1
Green Swamp Brook—stream ... NJ-2
Green Swamp Creek—stream ... VA-3
Green Swamp Dam—dam ... NJ-2
Green Swamp Hunting Lodge—locale ... SC-3
Green Swamp Run—swamp ... FL-3
Green Swamp Wildlife Mngmt Area—park ... FL-3
Greensward (historical)—locale ... KS-7
Greens Waterhole—lake ... FL-3
Greens Well—well ... CA-9
Greens Well Cave—cave ... AL-4
Green Tank—reservoir (5) ... AZ-5
Green Tank—reservoir ... CA-9
Green Tank—reservoir (6) ... NM-5
Green Tank—reservoir (4) ... TX-5
Green Tanks—reservoir ... AZ-5
Green Tank Windmill—locale ... AZ-5
Green-Tanner Rsvr—reservoir ... UT-8
Green Three Beach ... MH-9
Green Timber Basin—basin ... MT-8
Green Timber Creek—stream ... MT-8
Green Timber Creek—stream ... OR-9
Green Timber Creek—stream ... WY-8
Green Timber Gulch—valley ... CO-8
Green Timber Gulch—valley ... MT-8
Green Timber Hollow—valley ... PA-2
Green Timber Reservoir Number Four—swamp ... MS-4
Green Timber Reservoir Number One—swamp ... MS-4
Green Timber Reservoir Number Three—swamp ... MS-4
Green Timber Reservoir Number Two—swamp ... MS-4
Green Timbers—locale ... MI-6
Greenton Ch—church ... MO-7
Green Top ... MO-7
Greentop—pop pl ... DE-2
Green Top—summit ... ME-1
Green Top—summit ... NY-2
Green Top—summit ... NC-3
Greentop—summit ... OR-9
Green Top—summit (2) ... OR-9
Green Top—summit ... SD-7
Greentop—summit ... TN-4
Green Top—summit ... TX-5
Greentop Harbor—bay ... AK-9
Green Top (historical)—locale ... KS-7
Greentop Manor—pop pl ... MD-2
Green Top Mtn—summit ... WY-8
Greentop (RR name Green Top)—pop pl ... MO-7
Green Top Sch—school ... MO-7
Green Towers—pop pl ... CO-8
Green Tower Windmill—locale ... TX-5
Greentown ... WV-2
Greentown—locale ... TN-4
Greentown—locale ... VA-3
Greentown—other ... WV-2
Greentown—pop pl ... IN-6
Green Town—pop pl ... MO-7
Greentown—pop pl ... NC-3
Greentown—pop pl (2) ... OH-6
Greentown—pop pl ... PA-2
Greentown Branch—stream ... VA-3
Greentown Cem—cemetery ... IL-6
Green Townhall—building ... IA-7
Greentown Park—park ... OH-6
Green Township ... IN-6
Green Township ... KS-7
Green Township—civil (3) ... MO-7
Green Township—fmr MCD (2) ... IA-7
Green Township—pop pl ... KS-7
Green Township—pop pl (2) ... MO-7
Green Township—pop pl ... NE-7
Green Township—pop pl ... ND-7
Green Township Elem Sch—school ... IN-6
Green (Township of) ... IN-6
Green (Township of)—pop pl (7) ... IN-6
Green (Township of)—pop pl (2) ... MI-6
Green (Township of)—pop pl ... NJ-2
Green (Township of)—pop pl (17) ... OH-6
Green (Township of)—pop pl (2) ... PA-2
Greentrock—locale ... AL-4
Green Trail—trail (2) ... PA-2
Greentrails (subdivision)—pop pl (2) ... AZ-5
Green Treble Lake—lake ... CA-9
Greentree ... IL-6
Greentree ... PA-2
Green Tree ... TN-4
Green Tree—locale ... NJ-2
Green Tree—locale ... PA-2
Green Tree—pop pl ... AL-4
Greentree—pop pl ... MD-2
Greentree—pop pl ... PA-2
Green Tree—pop pl (3) ... PA-2
Green Tree Borough—civil ... PA-2
Green Tree Cem—cemetery ... PA-2
Green Tree Ch—church ... PA-2
Greentree Corners—pop pl ... OH-6
Green Tree Country Club—other ... CA-9
Green Tree Creek—stream ... NE-7
Green Tree Estates—locale ... PA-2
Greentree Grove Creek ... KY-4
Greentree Grove Creek ... TN-4
Green Tree (historical)—locale ... AL-4
Green Tree Mall—locale ... IN-6
Green Tree Manor—pop pl ... MD-2
Greentree Manor—pop pl ... MD-2
Green Tree Mobile Home Park—locale ... AZ-5
Green Tree Post Office ... TN-4
Greentree Post Office (historical)—building ... TN-4
Greentree Rsvr—reservoir ... MS-4
Green Trees—locale ... CA-9
Green Tree Sch—school ... WI-6
Green Tree Sch (historical)—school ... AL-4
Green Tree School ... PA-2
Greentree Spring—spring ... CA-9
Green Trees Ranch Airstrip, The—airport ... OR-9
Green Trees Subdivision (subdivision)—pop pl ... SD-7
Greentree State Waterfowl Production Area—park ... MS-4
Greentree (subdivision)—pop pl ... DE-2
Green Tree (subdivision)—pop pl ... NC-3
Green Tree Subdivision—pop pl ... UT-8
Green Tree Tank—reservoir ... NM-5
Green Tree Tavern—hist pl ... PA-2
Greentree Village—pop pl ... NJ-2
Greentree Waterfowl Area ... MS-4
Green Turtle Lake—lake ... NJ-2
Greenup—pop pl ... IL-6
Greenup—pop pl ... KY-4
Greenup—pop pl ... OK-5
Greenup (CCD)—cens area ... KY-4
Greenup (County)—pop pl ... KY-4
Greenup Creek—stream ... KY-4
Greenup Dam ... KY-4
Greenup Fork Ch—church ... KY-4
Greenup Locks And Dam—other ... KY-4
Greenup Masonic Lodge—hist pl ... KY-4
Greenup Siding—locale ... OK-5
Greenup (Township of)—pop pl ... IL-6
Greenvale—locale ... TN-4
Greenvale—pop pl ... NY-2
Greenvale—pop pl ... TN-4
Greenvale Baptist Ch ... TN-4
Greenvale Baptist Ch—church ... TN-4
Greenvale Cem—cemetery ... MN-6
Greenvale Cem—cemetery ... NH-1
Greenvale Cem—cemetery ... TN-4
Greenvale Ch—church ... TN-4
Green Vale Ch—church ... TN-4
Greenvale Cove—bay ... ME-1
Greenvale Creek—stream ... VA-3
Greenvale Farm—hist pl ... RI-1
Greenvale (historical)—locale ... IA-7
Greenvale (historical)—locale ... KS-7
Greenvale (historical P.O.)—locale ... IA-7
Greenvale (North Roslyn)—pop pl ... NY-2
Greenvale Post Office (historical)—building ... TN-4
Greenvale Sch—school ... IA-7
Greenvale Sch—school ... ME-1
Greenvale Sch—school (2) ... NY-2
Greenvale Sch (historical)—school ... TN-4
Greenvale (Township of)—pop pl ... MN-6
Greenvale Village—pop pl ... MD-2
Green Valley ... IL-6
Green Valley—basin (2) ... NE-7
Green Valley—basin ... TX-5
Green Valley—locale ... MD-2
Green Valley—locale ... TN-4
Green Valley—locale ... TX-5
Green Valley—locale ... VA-3
Green Valley—pop pl (2) ... AL-4
Green Valley—pop pl ... AZ-5
Green Valley—pop pl ... CA-9
Green Valley—pop pl ... IL-6
Greenvalley—pop pl ... IN-6
Green Valley—pop pl ... IN-6
Green Valley—pop pl ... MN-6
Green Valley—pop pl ... MO-7
Green Valley—pop pl ... NC-3
Green Valley—pop pl (2) ... OH-6
Green Valley—pop pl (2) ... PA-2
Green Valley—pop pl (5) ... TN-4
Green Valley—pop pl ... VA-3
Green Valley—pop pl (2) ... WV-2
Green Valley—pop pl ... WI-6
Green Valley—valley ... AL-4
Green Valley—valley ... AZ-5
Green Valley—valley (13) ... CA-9
Green Valley—valley ... IN-6
Green Valley—valley ... IA-7
Green Valley—valley ... NC-3
Green Valley—valley (3) ... OR-9
Green Valley—valley (2) ... PA-2
Green Valley—valley ... TX-5
Green Valley—valley ... VA-3
Green Valley—valley ... WA-9
Green Valley—valley (3) ... WV-2
Green Valley Acres—locale ... CO-8
Green Valley Acres—pop pl ... PA-2
Green Valley Acres (subdivision)—pop pl ... NC-3
Green Valley Airfield Airp—airport ... WA-9
Green Valley Area Campground—locale ... CA-9
Green Valley Baptist Ch—church (2) ... AL-4
Green Valley Campground—locale ... CA-9
Green Valley Cave—cave ... AL-4
Green Valley Cem—cemetery ... IL-6
Green Valley Cem—cemetery ... IA-7
Green Valley Cem—cemetery (3) ... KS-7
Green Valley Cem—cemetery ... MN-6
Green Valley Cem—cemetery (2) ... MS-4
Green Valley Cem—cemetery ... MO-7
Green Valley Cem—cemetery ... NE-7
Green Valley Cem—cemetery ... NC-3
Green Valley Cem—cemetery ... OK-5
Green Valley Cem—cemetery ... PA-2
Green Valley Cem—cemetery ... WI-6
Green Valley Cemetery ... AL-4
Green Valley Ch—church (2) ... AL-4
Green Valley Ch—church ... KS-7
Green Valley Ch—church ... KY-4
Green Valley Ch—church ... MN-6
Green Valley Ch—church (3) ... MS-4
Green Valley Ch—church (3) ... MO-7
Green Valley Ch—church (3) ... NC-3
Green Valley Ch—church (2) ... OH-6
Green Valley Ch—church ... OK-5
Green Valley Ch—church ... TN-4
Green Valley Ch—church (4) ... VA-3
Green Valley Ch—church (4) ... WV-2
Greenvalley Ch—church ... WV-2
Green Valley Chapel—church ... WV-2
Green Valley Christian Holiness Ch—church ... AL-4
Green Valley Congregational Methodist Ch ... MS-4
Green Valley Country Club—other ... KY-4
Green Valley Country Club—other ... NY-2
Green Valley Country Club—other ... PA-2
Green Valley Creek—stream ... AZ-5
Green Valley Creek—stream (5) ... CA-9
Green Valley Creek—stream (2) ... IN-6
Green Valley Creek—stream ... MO-7
Green Valley Creek—stream ... WA-9
Green Valley Dam—dam ... SD-7
Green Valley Ditch—canal ... MN-6
Green Valley Elementary School ... NC-3
Green Valley Elem Sch—school ... IN-6
Green Valley Elem Sch—school ... PA-2
Green Valley Estates—pop pl ... CA-9
Green Valley Estates—pop pl ... TN-4
Green Valley Estates (subdivision)—pop pl (2) ... NC-3
Green Valley Falls—falls (2) ... CA-9
Green Valley Farm—locale ... TX-5
Green Valley Farm Lake—reservoir ... TN-4
Green Valley Farm Lake Dam—dam ... TN-4

Greenwood Lake—*lake* (3) MN-6
Greenwood Lake—*lake* OH-6
Greenwood Lake—*lake* VT-1
Greenwood Lake—*lake* (2) WA-9
Greenwood Lake—*lake* WI-6
**Greenwood Lake**—*pop pl* NY-2
Greenwood Lake—*reservoir* IN-6
Greenwood Lake—*reservoir* MA-1
Greenwood Lake—*reservoir* NJ-2
Greenwood Lake—*reservoir* NM-5
Greenwood Lake—*reservoir* NY-2
Greenwood Lake—*reservoir* NC-3
Greenwood Lake—*reservoir* OK-5
Greenwood Lake—*reservoir* PA-2
Greenwood Lake Dam—*dam* IN-6
Greenwood Lake Dam—*dam* MA-1
Greenwood Lake Dam—*dam* NJ-2
Greenwood Lake Dam—*hist pl* PA-2
Greenwood Lake Junction—*uninc pl* NJ-2
Greenwood Leflore, Lake—*reservoir* MS-4
Greenwood-Leflore Airp—*airport* (2) MS-4
Greenwood LeFlore Cem—*cemetery* MS-4
Greenwood-Leflore Civic Center—*building* MS-4
Greenwood-Leflore Hosp—*hospital* MS-4
Greenwood-Leflore Library—*building* MS-4
Greenwood Lookout Tower—*locale* LA-4
Greenwood Mall—*locale* IN-6
Greenwood Mall—*locale* PA-2
Greenwood Mall Shop Ctr—*locale* MS-4
**Greenwood Manor**—*pop pl* NJ-2
**Greenwood Manor Estates**—*pop pl* MA-1
Greenwood Mausoleum—*building* PA-2
**Greenwood Meadows**—*pop pl* IL-6
**Greenwood Meadows Subdivision**—*pop pl* UT-8
Greenwood Memorial Cem—*cemetery* CA-9
Greenwood Memorial Gardens—*cemetery* SC-3
Greenwood Memorial Gardens Cem—*cemetery* VA-3
Greenwood Memorial Park—*cemetery* MS-4
Greenwood Memorial Park—*cemetery* WV-2
Greenwood Memorial Park Cem—*cemetery* LA-4
Greenwood Memorial Park Cem—*cemetery* PA-2
Greenwood Memorial Terrace (cemetery)—*cemetery* WA-9
Greenwood Mennonite Ch—*church* DE-2
Greenwood Mennonite Sch—*school* DE-2
*Greenwood Methodist Church* TN-4
**Greenwood Mine Junction**—*pop pl* MI-6
Greenwood Mine (underground)—*mine* AL-4
*Greenwood Missionary Baptist Church* MS-4
*Greenwood Missionary Baptist Church* TN-4
*Greenwood Mount* MA-1
*Greenwood Mountain* NJ-2
Greenwood Mountain Cem—*cemetery* ME-1
Greenwood MS—*school* IN-6
Greenwood MS—*school* TN-4
Greenwood Mtn—*summit* (2) ME-1
Greenwood Mtn—*summit* NY-2
Greenwood Mtn—*summit* TX-5
Greenwood Mtn—*summit* WV-2
Greenwood Northeast Elem Sch—*school* IN-6
Greenwood Nursery—*locale* PA-2
Greenwood Oil Field—*oilfield* NE-7
Greenwood Park—*park* CA-9
Greenwood Park—*park* (2) IA-7
Greenwood Park—*park* LA-4
Greenwood Park—*park* MA-1
Greenwood Park—*park* MI-6
Greenwood Park—*park* (2) TX-5
Greenwood Park—*park* (2) WI-6
**Greenwood Park**—*pop pl* LA-4
Greenwood Park Sch—*school* MA-1
**Greenwood Park Subdivision**—*pop pl* UT-8
Greenwood Pasture—*flat* KS-7
Greenwood Peak—*summit* AZ-5
Greenwood Plantation—*hist pl* GA-3
Greenwood Plantation—*hist pl* LA-4
Greenwood Plantation—*other* LA-4
Greenwood Playground—*park* OK-5
*Greenwood P.O.* AL-4
Greenwood Point—*cape* OR-9
Greenwood Point—*cape* WA-9
Greenwood Pond—*lake* ME-1
Greenwood Pond—*lake* MA-1
Greenwood Pond—*lake* NH-1
Greenwood Pond—*lake* NJ-2
Greenwood Pond—*reservoir* MA-1
Greenwood Post Office—*building* MS-4
Greenwood Post Office (historical)—*building* TN-4
Greenwood Raceway—*other* IA-7
Greenwood Ranch—*locale* (2) NM-5
Greenwood Ridge—*ridge* CA-9
*Greenwood River* MN-6
Greenwood River—*stream* (2) MN-6
Greenwood Rsvr—*reservoir* CO-8
Greenwood Rsvr—*reservoir* MI-6
Greenwood Rsvr No 1—*reservoir* WA-9
Greenwood Rsvr No 2—*reservoir* WA-9
*Greenwood Sch* DE-2
Greenwood Sch—*hist pl* PA-2
Greenwood Sch—*school* AR-4
Greenwood Sch—*school* (3) CA-9
Greenwood Sch—*school* CO-8
Greenwood Sch—*school* DE-2
Greenwood Sch—*school* (7) IL-6
Greenwood Sch—*school* IA-7
Greenwood Sch—*school* (2) KS-7
Greenwood Sch—*school* (2) KY-4
Greenwood Sch—*school* LA-4
Greenwood Sch—*school* MD-2
Greenwood Sch—*school* (8) MI-6
Greenwood Sch—*school* (6) MO-7
Greenwood Sch—*school* NE-7
Greenwood Sch—*school* (3) NC-3
Greenwood Sch—*school* OH-6
Greenwood Sch—*school* OK-5
Greenwood Sch—*school* (2) OR-9
Greenwood Sch—*school* (2) PA-2
Greenwood Sch—*school* TN-4
Greenwood Sch—*school* (2) TX-5
Greenwood Sch—*school* UT-8
Greenwood Sch—*school* (3) VA-3
Greenwood Sch—*school* WA-9
Greenwood Sch—*school* WV-2
Greenwood Sch—*school* (3) WI-6
Greenwood Sch (abandoned)—*school* (3) MO-7
Greenwood Sch (abandoned)—*school* PA-2
Greenwood Sch (historical)—*school* AL-4
Greenwood Sch (historical)—*school* (2) MS-4
Greenwood Sch (historical)—*school* (3) MO-7
Greenwood Sch (historical)—*school* NC-3
Greenwood Sch (historical)—*school* (2) PA-2
Greenwood Sch (historical)—*school* (4) TN-4
Green Woods Country Club—*other* CT-1
Greenwood Seminary (historical)—*school* TN-4
Greenwood Sewage Lagoon Dam—*dam* MS-4
*Greenwood's Hill* MA-1
Greenwood Shopping Centre—*locale* FL-3
**Greenwood Shores**—*pop pl* SC-3
*Greenwoods Island* MS-4
Greenwood Slough—*gut* IL-6
Greenwood Slough—*gut* UT-8
Greenwood Southwest Elem Sch—*school* IN-6
Greenwood Spring—*spring* AZ-5
Greenwood Spring Branch—*stream* AL-4
**Greenwood Springs**—*pop pl* MS-4
Greenwood Springs Baptist Ch—*church* MS-4
Greenwood Springs Ch—*church* MS-4
Greenwood Springs Sch—*school* MS-4
*Greenwood Springs United Methodist Church* MS-4
**Greenwood (sta.)**—*pop pl* VA-3
Greenwood State Park—*park* SC-3
Greenwood State Wildlife Ref—*park* WI-6
Greenwood Station (historical)—*locale* KS-7
Greenwood Station (historical)—*locale* MA-1
Greenwood Store (historical)—*locale* AL-4
Greenwood Stream—*stream* ME-1
**Greenwood (subdivision)**—*pop pl* (2) NC-3
Greenwood Swamp—*swamp* WI-6
Greenwood Tank—*reservoir* NM-5
Greenwood Tower—*tower* PA-2
**Greenwood (Town of)**—*pop pl* ME-1
**Greenwood (Town of)**—*pop pl* NY-2
**Greenwood (Town of)**—*pop pl* (2) WI-6
Greenwood Township—*fmr MCD* IA-7
**Greenwood Township**—*pop pl* (2) KS-7
**Greenwood Township**—*pop pl* SD-7
Greenwood Township (historical)—*civil* ND-7
Greenwood (Township of)—*fmr MCD* (2) AR-4
**Greenwood (Township of)**—*pop pl* (2) IL-6
**Greenwood (Township of)**—*pop pl* (5) MI-6
**Greenwood (Township of)**—*pop pl* (2) MN-6
**Greenwood (Township of)**—*pop pl* (5) PA-2
Greenwood Union Cem—*cemetery* KS-7
Greenwood Union Cem—*cemetery* MN-6
Greenwood Union Cem—*cemetery* NY-2
Greenwood Union Ch—*church* PA-2
Greenwood United Methodist Ch—*church* DE-2
*Greenwood United Methodist Church* TN-4
Greenwood Valley—*valley* MO-7
Greenwood Valley—*valley* PA-2
Greenwood Valley—*valley* WI-6
Greenwood Valley Cem—*cemetery* WI-6
Greenwood Valley Ranch—*locale* TX-5
Greenwood Valley Sch—*school* KS-7
**Greenwood Village**—*pop pl* CO-8
**Greenwood Village**—*pop pl* NJ-2
**Greenwood Village**—*pop pl* PA-2
**Greenwood Village**—*pop pl* SC-3
**Greenwood Village**—*pop pl* TX-5
Greenwood Village Ch—*church* TX-5
**Greenwood Village Subdivision**—*pop pl* UT-8
Greenwood Well—*well* AZ-5
Greenwreath—*hist pl* NC-3
**Greenwycke Village**—*pop pl* AL-4
Green Wycke Village—*uninc pl* AL-4
Green Young Cem—*cemetery* NC-3
Greenzweig Sch (abandoned)—*school* PA-2
*Greer* AR-4
Greer—*locale* IL-6
Greer—*other* MS-4
**Greer**—*pop pl* AL-4
**Greer**—*pop pl* AZ-5
**Greer**—*pop pl* ID-8
**Greer**—*pop pl* MO-7
**Greer**—*pop pl* OH-6
**Greer**—*pop pl* SC-3
**Greer**—*pop pl* TX-5
**Greer**—*pop pl* (2) WV-2
Greer, R. T., and Company—*hist pl* KY-4
*Greer Branch* TX-5
Greer Branch—*stream* AL-4
Greer Branch—*stream* KY-4
Greer Branch—*stream* MS-4
Greer Branch—*stream* MO-7
Greer Branch—*stream* NC-3
Greer Branch—*stream* (2) TN-4
Greer Branch—*stream* TX-5
Greer Bridge—*bridge* NC-3
Greer Brook—*stream* VT-1
Greer Campground—*park* AZ-5
Greer (CCD)—*cens area* (2) SC-3
Greer Cem—*cemetery* (3) AL-4
Greer Cem—*cemetery* IL-6
Greer Cem—*cemetery* IA-7
Greer Cem—*cemetery* KY-4
Greer Cem—*cemetery* LA-4
Greer Cem—*cemetery* MS-4
Greer Cem—*cemetery* (2) MO-7
Greer Cem—*cemetery* (4) NC-3
Greer Cem—*cemetery* OH-6
Greer Cem—*cemetery* (11) TN-4
Greer Cem—*cemetery* (4) TX-5
Greer Cem—*cemetery* (2) VA-3
Greer Cem—*cemetery* WV-2
*Greer Chapel* TN-4
Greer Chapel—*church* LA-4
Greer Chapel Cem—*cemetery* TN-4
Greer Childrens Home—*other* NY-2
Greer Country Club—*other* SC-3
**Greer (County)**—*pop pl* OK-5
Greer County Courthouse—*hist pl* OK-5
*Greer Creek* NC-3
Greer Creek—*stream* AL-4
Greer Creek—*stream* LA-4
Greer Creek—*stream* MO-7
Greer Creek—*stream* NC-3
Greer Creek—*stream* TX-5
Greer Depot—*hist pl* SC-3
Greer Ditch—*canal* IN-6
Greer Downs—*other* OK-5
Greer Draw—*valley* WY-8
Greer Ford—*locale* TN-4
Greer Gulch—*valley* AK-9
Greer Gulch—*valley* ID-8
Greer Gulch—*valley* MT-8
Greer Hill—*summit* FL-3
Greer (historical)—*locale* AL-4
*Greer Hollow* TN-4
Greer Hollow—*valley* MO-7
Greer Hollow—*valley* OH-6
Greer Hollow—*valley* (3) TN-4
Greer HS—*school* MS-4
Greer Island—*island* TX-5
Greer JHS—*school* AL-4
Greer JHS—*school* IL-6
Greer Knob—*summit* NC-3
Greer Knob—*summit* VA-3
Greer Lake—*lake* KY-4
Greer Lake—*lake* MN-6
Greer Lake—*reservoir* AL-4
Greer Lake—*reservoir* TN-4
Greer Lakes—*reservoir* AZ-5
Greer Lakes Campground—*park* AZ-5
Greer Lateral—*canal* AZ-5
Greer Mill—*uninc pl* SC-3
Greer Miller Landing Strip—*airport* KS-7
Greer Mitchell Sch (abandoned)—*school* PA-2
*Greer Mountain* TX-5
Greer Mountains—*summit* TX-5
Greer Mtn—*summit* TN-4
*Greer Paw Creek* NC-3
Greer Peak—*summit* WY-8
Greer Pit Cave—*cave* AL-4
Greer Place—*locale* AZ-5
Greer Place—*locale* AR-4
*Greer P.O.* AL-4
Greer Pond—*lake* PA-2
Greer Post Office (historical)—*building* TN-4
Greer Ranch—*locale* NM-5
Greer Ranch—*locale* TX-5
Greer Ranch—*locale* WY-8
Greer Rsvr—*reservoir* SC-3
Greers Bog—*swamp* ME-1
Greersburg Acad—*hist pl* PA-2
Greersburg City Park Lake—*reservoir* IN-6
Greersburg City Park Lake Dam—*dam* IN-6
Greers Ch—*church* AL-4
Greers Ch—*church* AR-4
Greers Ch—*church* NC-3
Greer Sch—*school* CA-9
Greer Sch—*school* (2) GA-3
Greer Sch—*school* IL-6
Greer Sch—*school* NY-2
Greer Sch—*school* TN-4
Greer Sch—*school* TX-5
Greers Chapel—*church* GA-3
Greers Chapel—*church* TN-4
*Greers Chapel Missionary Baptist Ch* TN-4
*Greers Chapel United Methodist Ch* TN-4
Greers Corner—*locale* ME-1
*Greers Creek* AL-4
*Greers Creek* MS-4
**Greers Ferry**—*pop pl* AR-4
Greers Ferry Dam—*dam* AR-4
Greers Ferry Lake—*reservoir* AR-4
*Greers Ferry Rsvr* AR-4
*Greers Hollow* PA-2
Greers Lake Dam—*dam* MS-4
Greers Landing—*locale* AL-4
Greer Slough—*stream* TX-5
Greer Spring—*spring* AZ-5
Greer Spring—*spring* CA-9
Greer Spring—*spring* MO-7
Greer Spring Branch—*stream* MO-7
Greers Sch (historical)—*school* TN-4
*Greers Stand* TN-4
Greerton (historical)—*locale* AL-4
**Greer (Township of)**—*pop pl* IN-6
Greer Tunnel—*tunnel* PA-2
Greer Tunnel—*tunnel* TN-4
*Greer Valley* WV-2
Greer Well—*well* NM-5
Greer Windmill—*well* AZ-5
Greesman Ditch—*canal* OH-6
Greeson, Lake—*reservoir* AR-4
Greeson Chapel—*church* TN-4
Greeson Chapel Cem—*cemetery* TN-4
*Greeson Cumberland Presbyterian Church* TN-4
Greeson Drain—*canal* CA-9
Greeson Drain Three—*canal* CA-9
Greeson Drain Two—*canal* CA-9
Greeson Family Cem—*cemetery* TN-4
Greeson Hollow—*valley* TN-4
Greeson Nursery Pond, Lake—*reservoir* AR-4
**Greesons Crossroads**—*pop pl* NC-3
Greeson Wash—*stream* CA-9
*Greesy Creek* TN-4
*Greetingsville* IN-6
**Greetingville**—*pop pl* IN-6
Greever Branch—*stream* VA-3
Greever Cem—*cemetery* VA-3
*Greever Chapel Baptist Church* TN-4
Greeves Cem—*cemetery* IL-6
Greewild Sch (historical)—*school* TN-4
**Grefco (General Refractories Co.)**—*pop pl* KY-4
*Gregan* MH-9
Gregeory Creek—*stream* GA-3
*Gregersen Lake* WI-6
Gregerson Basin—*basin* NV-8
Gregerson Hill—*summit* MT-8
Gregerson Lake—*lake* WI-6
Gregg—*locale* CA-9
Gregg—*locale* PA-2
**Gregg**—*pop pl* OH-6
**Gregg**—*pop pl* TX-5
Gregg, Andrew, Homestead—*hist pl* PA-2
Gregg, Dr. Benjamin, House—*hist pl* SC-3
Gregg, Edward M., Farm—*hist pl* ID-8
Gregg, William L., House—*hist pl* IL-6
Gregg Airp—*airport* PA-2
Gregg Basin—*basin* AZ-5
Gregg Basin—*basin* NV-8
Gregg Bay—*swamp* SC-3
Gregg Boat Dock—*locale* TN-4
Gregg Branch—*stream* NC-3
Gregg Branch—*stream* TN-4
Gregg Branch—*stream* TX-5
**Gregg Camp**—*pop pl* SC-3
*Gregg Canyon* CA-9
Gregg Canyon—*valley* CO-8
Gregg Canyon—*valley* NV-8
Gregg Canyon—*valley* NM-5
Gregg Cem—*cemetery* IN-6
Gregg Cem—*cemetery* IA-7
Gregg Cem—*cemetery* OH-6
Gregg Cem—*cemetery* PA-2
Gregg Cem—*cemetery* TN-4
Gregg Cem—*cemetery* (2) TX-5
Gregg Cem—*cemetery* WV-2
Gregg Chapel—*church* TN-4
**Gregg (County)**—*pop pl* TX-5
*Gregg Creek* KS-7
Gregg Creek—*stream* CA-9
Gregg Creek—*stream* MI-6
Gregg Creek—*stream* MT-8
Gregg Creek—*stream* OR-9
Gregg Creek—*stream* TN-4
Gregg Draw—*valley* WY-8
Gregg Fork—*stream* WY-8
Gregg Hill—*summit* NH-1
Gregg Hill—*summit* PA-2
Gregg Hill—*summit* VT-1
Gregg House—*hist pl* (2) AR-4
Gregg House—*hist pl* OH-6
Gregg Knob—*summit* (2) WV-2
Gregg Lake—*lake* MI-6
Gregg Lake—*lake* MN-6
Gregg Lake—*lake* NH-1
Gregg Lake—*lake* NY-2
Gregg Mtn—*summit* ME-1
**Gregg Neck**—*pop pl* MD-2
Gregg Park—*park* IN-6
Gregg Park—*park* (2) SC-3
Gregg Peak—*summit* NV-8
Gregg Ranch—*locale* TX-5
Gregg Run—*stream* OH-6
Gregg Run—*stream* PA-2
Greggs—*locale* GA-3
Greggs—*locale* OH-6
*Greggs Basin* NV-8
Greggs Brook—*stream* MI-6
Gregg Sch—*school* IN-6
Gregg Sch—*school* KY-4
Gregg Sch—*school* MI-6
Gregg Sch—*school* MN-6
Gregg Sch—*school* MO-7
Gregg Sch—*school* TX-5
Gregg Sch (historical)—*school* PA-2
Gregg Sch (historical)—*school* TN-4
*Gregg Sch Number 15* IN-6
*Greggs Creek* KS-7
Greggs Creek—*stream* MO-7
Greggs Creek—*stream* OR-9
Greggs Ferry (historical)—*locale* NV-8
Greggs Ferry (submerged ruin)—*locale* AZ-5
Greggs Hideout—*bay* AZ-5
Greggs Hill—*locale* OH-6
Greggs Hill Cem—*cemetery* OH-6
Gregg Shoals—*bar* GA-3
Greggs Landing—*locale* SC-3
Greggs Mill (historical)—*locale* TN-4
Greggsport Sch—*school* NE-7
*Greggsville* DE-2
**Greggsville**—*pop pl* WV-2
Gregg Tank—*reservoir* AZ-5
**Greggton**—*pop pl* TX-5
**Gregg (Township of)**—*pop pl* IN-6
**Gregg (Township of)**—*pop pl* (2) PA-2
Gregg Wash—*stream* NV-8
Gregg Well—*well* NM-5
Greg Hills—*other* NM-5
Greg Lake—*lake* AL-4
Gregler Swamp—*swamp* SC-3
Greg Mace Peak—*summit* CO-8
*Gregoire Island* FM-9
Gregoria Tank—*reservoir* AZ-5
Gregorie, Bayou—*stream* LA-4
Gregorie Neck—*cape* SC-3
*Gregories Neck* SC-3
Gregor Lake—*lake* MT-8
Gregor Mine—*mine* ID-8
*Gregorson Lkae* WI-6
Gregorson Number 1 Dam—*dam* SD-7
Gregorville—*locale* WI-6
*Gregory* TN-4
Gregory—*locale* GA-3
Gregory—*locale* KY-4
Gregory—*locale* MN-6
Gregory—*locale* NC-3
Gregory—*locale* OH-6
Gregory—*locale* OR-9
Gregory—*locale* WV-2
**Gregory**—*pop pl* AR-4
**Gregory**—*pop pl* MI-6
**Gregory**—*pop pl* PA-2
**Gregory**—*pop pl* SD-7
**Gregory**—*pop pl* TX-5
Gregory, Lake—*lake* CA-9
Gregory, Lake—*reservoir* TX-5
Gregory, Willoughby, House—*hist pl* FL-3
*Gregory Arch* UT-8
Gregory Bald—*summit* NC-3
Gregory Bald—*summit* TN-4
Gregory Bar—*bar* VA-3
Gregory Basin—*basin* UT-8
Gregory Branch—*stream* AR-4
Gregory Branch—*stream* IL-6
Gregory Branch—*stream* (6) KY-4
Gregory Branch—*stream* NC-3
Gregory Branch—*stream* TN-4
*Gregory Bridge* UT-8
Gregory Butte—*summit* (2) UT-8
Gregory Canyon—*valley* CO-8
*Gregory Cape* OR-9
*Gregory Cave* TN-4
Gregory (CCD)—*cens area* KY-4
Gregory Cem—*cemetery* AR-4
Gregory Cem—*cemetery* IL-6
Gregory Cem—*cemetery* (5) KY-4
Gregory Cem—*cemetery* (2) MS-4
Gregory Cem—*cemetery* (9) MO-7
Gregory Cem—*cemetery* NY-2
Gregory Cem—*cemetery* (3) OH-6
Gregory Cem—*cemetery* SC-3
Gregory Cem—*cemetery* (5) TN-4
Gregory Cem—*cemetery* (2) TX-5
Gregory Cem—*cemetery* VA-3
Gregory Cem—*cemetery* WV-2
Gregory Ch—*church* OK-5
Gregory Ch—*church* TN-4
Gregory Chapel—*church* AR-4
Gregory Chapel—*church* MS-4
Gregory Chapel—*church* (2) TN-4
Gregory Corner—*locale* VA-3
Gregory Corners—*locale* NY-2
Gregory Coulee—*valley* MT-8
Gregory County—*civil* SD-7
Gregory Cove—*bay* GA-3
*Gregory Creek* TN-4
Gregory Creek—*stream* CA-9
Gregory Creek—*stream* (2) CO-8
Gregory Creek—*stream* ID-8
Gregory Creek—*stream* NC-3
Gregory Creek—*stream* OH-6
Gregory Creek—*stream* (2) OR-9
Gregory Creek—*stream* SC-3
Gregory Creek—*stream* TX-5
Gregory Creek Campground—*locale* CA-9
Gregory Creek Rsvr—*reservoir* OR-9
*Gregory Cross Roads* NC-3
**Gregory Crossroads**—*pop pl* NC-3
Gregory Ditch—*canal* IN-6
Gregory Drain—*canal* MI-6
Gregory Drain—*stream* MI-6
Gregory Drive Elem Sch—*school* FL-3
Gregory Field—*park* TX-5
Gregory Flats—*flat* NV-8
**Gregory Forks**—*pop pl* NC-3
Gregory Gap—*gap* AL-4
Gregory Gap—*gap* GA-3
Gregory Gardens Sch—*school* CA-9
Gregory Gulch—*valley* CO-8
Gregory Gulch—*valley* ID-8
Gregory Heights Sch—*school* OR-9
Gregory Hill—*summit* CO-8
Gregory Hill Sch—*school* CO-8
Gregory (historical)—*locale* AL-4
Gregory (historical)—*locale* KS-7
**Gregory (historical)**—*pop pl* MS-4
**Gregory (historical)**—*pop pl* SD-7
Gregory Hollow—*valley* KY-4
Gregory Hollow—*valley* (2) MO-7
Gregory Hollow—*valley* (2) NY-2
Gregory Hollow—*valley* TN-4
Gregory Hollow Cave—*cave* TN-4
Gregory House—*hist pl* NY-2
Gregory House—*hist pl* OH-6
Gregory Island—*cliff* MA-1
Gregory Island—*island* VA-3
Gregory JHS—*school* LA-4
Gregory Knob—*summit* GA-3
Gregory Lake—*lake* (2) MI-6
Gregory Lake—*lake* NM-5
Gregory Lake—*reservoir* NC-3
Gregory Lake Dam—*dam* (2) MS-4
Gregory Lake Dam—*dam* NC-3
Gregory Landing—*locale* NY-2
Gregory Landing (Gregory Station)—*locale* MO-7
Gregory Lateral—*canal* SD-7
**Gregory (local name Gregory Landing)**—*pop pl* MO-7
Gregory Memorial Chapel—*church* VA-3
Gregory Mill Creek—*stream* FL-3
Gregory Mine—*mine* MT-8
Gregory Mtn—*summit* CA-9
Gregory Mtn—*summit* MT-8
Gregory Municipal Airp—*airport* SD-7
Gregory Natural Bridge—*arch* UT-8
*Gregory Neck* SC-3
Gregory Oil And Gas Field—*oilfield* OK-5
*Gregory Plantation* MS-4
Gregory Point—*cape* CT-1
Gregory Point—*cape* LA-4
Gregory Point—*cape* OR-9
Gregory Pond—*lake* NY-2
Gregory Pond—*lake* PA-2
Gregory Pond—*reservoir* SC-3
Gregory-Portland (CCD)—*cens area* TX-5
Gregory-Portland HS—*school* TX-5
Gregory-Portland JHS—*school* TX-5
Gregory Post Office (historical)—*building* MS-4
Gregory Ranch—*locale* WY-8
Gregory Ridge—*ridge* TN-4
Gregory Ridge—*ridge* VA-3
Gregory Rsvr—*reservoir* OR-9
Gregory Run—*stream* PA-2
Gregory Run—*stream* WV-2
*Gregorys Bald* NC-3
*Gregorys Bald* TN-4
Gregorys Cave—*cave* TN-4
Gregory Sch—*school* AL-4
Gregory Sch—*school* (7) IL-6
Gregory Sch—*school* (2) MI-6
Gregory Sch—*school* MO-7
Gregory Sch—*school* (3) NJ-2
Gregory Sch—*school* OK-5
Gregory Sch—*school* TX-5
*Gregorys Chapel Baptist Church* MS-4
*Gregorys Chapel Baptist Church* TN-4
Gregory Sch (historical)—*school* MO-7
Gregorys Child Development Center—*school* FL-3
Gregory School (historical)—*locale* MO-7
Gregorys Corner—*locale* ME-1
Gregorys Creek—*stream* SC-3
Gregorys Ford—*locale* AL-4
*Gregorys Gap* WV-2
Gregorys Lake—*reservoir* NC-3
Gregorys Lake—*reservoir* SC-3
Gregorys Lake Dam—*dam* NC-3
Gregorys Little Bald—*summit* TN-4
Gregory Slough—*bay* TN-4
*Gregorys Mill* GA-3
Gregorys Monument—*summit* CA-9
*Gregorys Neck* SC-3
Gregorys Pond—*reservoir* VA-3
Gregory Spring—*spring* OR-9
Gregory Spring—*spring* TN-4
Gregory Spring—*spring* WA-9
Gregorys Ruby Mine—*mine* NC-3
Gregorys State Game Area—*park* MI-6
Gregory State Wildlife Mngmt Area—*park* MN-6
**Gregory Subdivision**—*pop pl* TN-4
**Gregorytown**—*pop pl* NY-2
Gregorytown Cem—*cemetery* NY-2
Gregory (Township of)—*fmr MCD* AR-4
**Gregory (Township of)**—*pop pl* MN-6
Gregoryville—*locale* KY-4
Gregoryville Post Office (historical)—*building* TN-4
Gregory Well—*well* NM-5
Gregovich, John, House—*hist pl* NV-8
*Gregs Island* NY-2
*Gregson* MT-8
Gregson—*locale* MT-8
Gregson Creek—*stream* MT-8
Gregson-Hadley House—*hist pl* NC-3
**Gregson Hot Springs**—*pop pl* MT-8
Gregson Island—*island* AK-9
Gregs Peak—*summit* CA-9
Greg Spring—*spring* NM-5
Gregs Run—*stream* PA-2
*Greguan* MH-9
*Gregville* AL-4
Greider Creek—*stream* WA-9
Greider Lake—*lake* IN-6
*Greiders Mill* PA-2
Greiffenstein Elem Sch—*school* KS-7
Greig—*locale* LA-4
**Greig**—*pop pl* NY-2
Greig—*uninc pl* OK-5
Greig, Cape—*cape* AK-9
Greig, Mount—*summit* AK-9
Greiger Ditch—*canal* (2) IN-6
Greig Hill—*summit* VI-3
Greig Lake—*lake* MI-6
Greigs Lake—*lake* MN-6
**Greigsville**—*pop pl* NY-2
Greigsville Cem—*cemetery* NY-2
Greigsville (sta.) (RR name for Wadsworth)—*other* NY-2
**Greig (Town of)**—*pop pl* NY-2
Greil Hosp—*hospital* AL-4
Greilich Camp—*locale* CA-9
**Greilickville (Rennies Station)**—*pop pl* MI-6
Greiner, Frederick, House—*hist pl* MN-6
Greiner Canyon—*valley* OR-9
Greinwich Terrace—*uninc pl* LA-4
**Greinwich Village**—*pop pl* LA-4
Greisemer's Mill Bridge—*hist pl* PA-2
Greisemersville—*locale* PA-2
*Greisemore* PA-2
Greisenheim Home—*building* MD-2
Greisinger Dam—*dam* PA-2
Greisinger Pond—*reservoir* PA-2
Greisin Pond—*reservoir* OH-6
Greison Drain—*canal* MI-6
Greis Park—*park* NY-2
Greitl Draw—*valley* WY-8
Greivers Chapel—*church* TN-4
Greivertown—*locale* TN-4
Greives Sch—*school* SD-7
*Grelder Hollow* MA-1
Grell Cem—*cemetery* MO-7
Grellet Sch—*school* KS-7
Grellett Cem—*cemetery* KS-7
Grell Pond—*reservoir* IA-7
Grell Pond Dam—*dam* IA-7
Grells Airfield—*airport* OR-9
Grellton—*locale* WI-6
Grel Ranch—*locale* CA-9
**Grelton**—*pop pl* OH-6
Grelton Cem—*cemetery* OH-6
Gremel Drain—*canal* MI-6
Gremer JHS—*school* TX-5
Gremes Cem—*cemetery* IN-6
Gremlin Cove—*bay* NE-7
Gremmert Coulee—*valley* MT-8
Gremm Sch—*school* NE-7
Gremo Hill—*summit* UT-8
Gremore Lake—*lake* WI-6
**Grenada**—*pop pl* CA-9
**Grenada**—*pop pl* MS-4
Grenada Bank—*hist pl* MS-4
Grenada Butte—*summit* OR-9
Grenada Ch of Christ—*church* MS-4
Grenada City Colored HS (historical)—*school* MS-4
Grenada Coll (historical)—*school* MS-4
**Grenada County**—*pop pl* MS-4
Grenada County Courthouse—*building* MS-4
Grenada Dam—*dam* MS-4
Grenada Farms Pond Dam—*dam* MS-4
Grenada Female Acad (historical)—*school* MS-4
Grenada Female Coll (historical)—*school* MS-4
*Grenada Free Sch* MS-4
Grenada HS—*school* MS-4
Grenada JHS—*school* MS-4
Grenada Junction—*locale* MS-4
Grenada Lake—*reservoir* MS-4
Grenada Lake Med Ctr—*hospital* MS-4
Grenada Landing—*locale* MS-4
Grenada Male Acad (historical)—*school* MS-4
Grenada Masonic Temple—*hist pl* MS-4
*Grenada Methodist District HS* MS-4
Grenada Municipal Airp—*airport* MS-4
Grenada Normal Sch (historical)—*school* MS-4
Grenada Plaza (Shop Ctr)—*locale* FL-3
Grenada Plaza Shop Ctr—*locale* MS-4
Grenada Post Office (historical)—*building* AL-4
Grenada Public Sch (historical)—*school* MS-4
*Grenada Reservoir* MS-4
Grenada Shop Ctr—*locale* FL-3
Grenada (Shop Ctr)—*locale* FL-3
Grenada State Waterfowl Mngmt Area—*park* MS-4
Grenada Vocational Complex—*school* MS-4
Grenada Yacht Basin—*locale* MS-4
Grenade Ch—*church* AR-4
Grenade Chapel—*church* AR-4
*Grenade Creek* ID-8
Grenade Creek—*stream* ID-8
Grenade Crossing—*locale* OK-5
**Grenadier**—*pop pl* SC-3
Grenadier Island—*island* NY-2
Grenadier Range—*range* CO-8
Grena Lake—*lake* MN-6
*Grenda Butte* WY-8
Grendah Mtn—*summit* MT-8
Grendell Brook—*stream* ME-1
**Grendel Mills**—*pop pl* SC-3
**Grendel Village**—*pop pl* SC-3
**Grendon Farms**—*pop pl* DE-2
Grendra Airfield—*airport* ND-7
*Grenego Canyon* AZ-5
Grenelefe—*post sta* FL-3
**Grenell**—*pop pl* NY-2

Griffing Cem—cemetery MS-4
Griffin Give Ch—church GA-3
Griffing Park TX-5
Griffing Park—park FL-3
Griffing Park—park MN-6
**Griffing Park**—pop pl TX-5
GRIFFING'S, FREDERICK, (ship)—hist pl CA-9
Griffin Gulch—valley CA-9
Griffin Gulch—valley MT-8
Griffin Gulch—valley OR-9
Griffin Gulf—valley AL-4
Griffin Harris Lake—reservoir AL-4
Griffin Harris Lake Dam—dam AL-4
**Griffin Heights (subdivision)**—pop pl AL-4
Griffin Hill—summit NH-1
Griffin Hill—summit NY-2
Griffin Hill—summit PA-2
Griffin Hill—summit TN-4
Griffin (historical)—locale (2) AL-4
**Griffin (historical)**—pop pl TN-4
Griffin Hollow—valley (2) AR-4
Griffin Hollow—valley (2) KY-4
Griffin Hollow—valley MO-7
Griffin Hollow—valley (2) TN-4
Griffin Hollow—valley WI-6
Griffin Homestead—locale WY-8
Griffin Hosp—hospital GA-3
Griffin House—hist pl ME-1
Griffin House—hist pl MS-4
Griffin HS—school IL-6
Griffin Island—island ME-1
Griffin Island—island NY-2
Griffin Island—island TX-5
Griffin Island—summit MA-1
Griffin JHS—school FL-3
Griffin JHS—school MS-4
Griffin Junior Lake Dam—dam MS-4
Griffin Lake MA-1
Griffin Lake WA-9
Griffin Lake—lake (2) GA-3
Griffin Lake—lake (2) TX-5
Griffin Lake—reservoir GA-3
Griffin Lake—reservoir (2) NC-3
Griffin Lake—reservoir TX-5
Griffin Lake—swamp MN-6
Griffin Lake Number Two—reservoir NC-3
Griffin Lake Number Two Dam—dam NC-3
Griffin Lakes—lake AL-4
Griffin Landing (historical)—locale MS-4
Griffin Ledge—bar ME-1
Griffin Meadow—flat OR-9
Griffin Memorial Gardens—cemetery (2) GA-3
Griffin Memorial Hosp Annex—hospital OK-5
Griffin Mill AL-4
Griffin Mill Pond—lake FL-3
Griffin Mine—mine TN-4
Griffin Monument—cemetery CO-8
Griffin Mtn GA-3
Griffin Mtn—summit AR-4
Griffin Mtn—summit GA-3
Griffin Mtn—summit ME-1
Griffin Mtn—summit OK-5
Griffin Mtn—summit VA-3
Griffin Mtn—summit WA-9
Griffin North Ranch—locale TX-5
Griffin No 2 Ditch—canal WY-8
Griffin Park TX-5
Griffin Park—park FL-3
Griffin Park—park MT-8
Griffin Park—park SD-7
Griffin Park—park TX-5
Griffin Pass—gap MT-8
Griffin Pass—gap OR-9
Griffin Pass Rsvr—reservoir MT-8
Griffin Peak—summit WA-9
Griffin Place—locale CA-9
Griffin Point—cape AK-9
Griffin Point—cape MS-4
Griffin Point—summit UT-8
Griffin Pond CT-1
Griffin Pond WA-9
Griffin Pond—reservoir AL-4
Griffin Pond—reservoir TX-5
Griffin Ranch—locale AZ-5
Griffin Ranch—locale CO-8
Griffin Ranch—locale NM-5
Griffin Ranch—locale OR-9
Griffin Ranch—locale TX-5
Griffin Ranch—locale UT-8
Griffin Rapids—rapids NY-2
Griffin Ridge—ridge AL-4
Griffin Ridge—ridge GA-3
Griffin Ridge—ridge ME-1
Griffin Ridge—ridge OH-6
Griffin Road Ch—church FL-3
Griffin Rocks—bar WA-9
Griffin Rsvr—reservoir (2) PA-2
Griffin Run—stream OH-6
Griffin Run—stream (2) WV-2
**Griffins**—pop pl CT-1
Griffins Beach—locale VA-3
**Griffins Beach**—pop pl VA-3
Griffinsburg—locale VA-3
Griffin Sch—school IN-6
Griffin Sch—school (2) MI-6
Griffin Sch—school TN-4
Griffin Sch—school TX-5
Griffin Sch—school WA-9
Griffin Sch (abandoned)—school PA-2
Griffins Chapel—church TN-4
Griffins Chapel Cem—cemetery TN-4
Griffins Chapel Methodist Church TN-4
Griffin Sch (historical)—school AL-4
Griffin Sch (historical)—school (3) MS-4
Griffin Sch (historical)—school MO-7
Griffin Sch (historical)—school TN-4
Griffin School—locale MT-8
Griffins Corner—locale FL-3
**Griffins Corners**—pop pl NY-2
Griffins Creek TX-5
Griffins Creek—stream SC-3
Griffins Crossroads—locale (2) NC-3
Griffins Day Care Nursery Sch—school FL-3
Griffins Gulch OR-9
Griffin Shoals—bar AL-4
Griffins Island MA-1
Griffin Site (410L246)—hist pl TX-5
Griffins Lake MA-1
Griffins Lake—reservoir NC-3
Griffins Lake—reservoir SC-3
Griffins Lake Dam—dam NC-3
Griffins Landing—locale GA-3
Griffins Landing—locale TN-4
Griffins Landing—locale VA-3
Griffins Landing (historical)—locale AL-4
Griffin Slough—gut MS-4
**Griffins Mills**—pop pl NY-2
Griffins Point TX-5
Griffins Pond—lake CT-1
Griffins Precinct (historical)—locale MS-4
Griffin Spring—spring AL-4
Griffin Spring—spring MT-8
Griffin Spring—spring UT-8
Griffin Spring—spring WA-9
Griffin Spring Branch—stream MS-4
Griffin Springs—locale AL-4
Griffin Spur AL-4
Griffins Store (historical)—locale MS-4
Griffins Store P.O. (historical)—building MS-4
Griffins (Township of)—fmr MCD (2) NC-3
Griffin Street Baptist Ch—church MS-4
**Griffin (subdivision)**—pop pl AL-4
Griffinsville—locale IA-7
Griffin Tank—reservoir AZ-5
Griffin Tank—reservoir NM-5
Griffin Temple COGIC—church UT-8
Griffin Top—summit UT-8
**Griffintown**—pop pl TN-4
**Griffin Township**—pop pl ND-7
Griffin (Township of)—fmr MCD (2) AR-4
Griffin Tunnels—mine CO-8
Griffin United Methodist Ch—church MS-4
Griffin Wash—stream AZ-5
Griffin Whirl—bend NC-3
Griffin Windmill—locale TX-5
Griffis Bay—bay FL-3
Griffis Canal—canal SD-7
Griffis Canyon—valley SD-7
Griffis Cem—cemetery (2) GA-3
Griffis Cem—cemetery IA-7
Griffis Cem—cemetery SC-3
Griffis Creek—stream TX-5
Griffis Creek Trail—trail OR-9
Griffis Lake Dam—dam MS-4
Griffis-Patton House—hist pl NC-3
Griffiss AFB—military NY-2
Griffiss AFB Camden Test
Annex—military NY-2
Griffis Well—well SD-7
Griffith OH-6
Griffith—locale AZ-5
Griffith—locale KY-4
Griffith—locale NC-3
Griffith—locale (2) TX-5
Griffith—locale VA-3
**Griffith**—pop pl GA-3
**Griffith**—pop pl IN-6
**Griffith**—pop pl MS-4
**Griffith**—pop pl OH-6
**Griffith**—pop pl TN-4
Griffith—uninc pl CA-9
Griffith, David Jefferson, House—hist pl SC-3
Griffith, D. W., House—hist pl KY-4
Griffith, James Turk, House—hist pl TN-4
Griffith, William R., House—hist pl PA-2
Griffith Airp—airport IN-6
Griffith and Wallace Number 4 Mine
(underground)—mine TN-4
Griffith Ball Park—building KS-7
Griffith Bend AL-4
Griffith Bldg—hist pl NJ-2
Griffith Bluff—cliff KY-4
Griffith Branch TN-4
Griffith Branch—stream GA-3
Griffith Branch—stream (5) KY-4
Griffith Branch—stream (2) NC-3
Griffith Branch—stream (4) TN-4
Griffith Branch—stream (2) WV-2
Griffith Brook—stream VT-1
Griffith Cabin—locale MT-8
Griffith Canyon—valley NV-8
Griffith Cem—cemetery FL-3
Griffith Cem—cemetery (2) GA-3
Griffith Cem—cemetery (4) IL-6
Griffith Cem—cemetery (2) IN-6
Griffith Cem—cemetery (2) KS-7
Griffith Cem—cemetery (2) KY-4
Griffith Cem—cemetery MS-4
Griffith Cem—cemetery (2) MO-7
Griffith Cem—cemetery (7) TN-4
Griffith Cem—cemetery TX-5
Griffith Cem—cemetery (2) WV-2
Griffith Cem—cemetery WI-6
Griffith Ch—church MD-2
Griffith Chapel—church TX-5
Griffith Chapel—church WV-2
Griffith Christian Ch—church MS-4
Griffith Church TN-4
Griffith Corners—locale NY-2
Griffith Court Sch—school MI-6
**Griffith Creek**—pop pl TN-4
Griffith Creek—stream CA-9
Griffith Creek—stream IL-6
Griffith Creek—stream (2) MT-8
Griffith Creek—stream (2) OR-9
Griffith Creek—stream TN-4
Griffith Creek—stream UT-8
Griffith Creek—stream VA-3
Griffith Creek—stream WV-2
Griffith Creek Cem—cemetery TN-4
Griffith Creek Ch—church TN-4
Griffith Creek Ch—church WV-2
Griffith Creek Sch—school TN-4
Griffith Draw—valley WY-8
Griffith Elem Sch—school KS-7
Griffith Elem Sch—school TN-4
Griffith Ferry Stretch—channel FL-3
Griffith-Franklin House—hist pl KY-4
Griffith Gulch—valley MT-8
Griffith Head Ledge—bar ME-1
Griffith Hill CA-9
Griffith Hollow—valley TN-4
Griffith House—hist pl CA-9
Griffith House—hist pl KY-4
Griffith House—hist pl MD-2
Griffith Institute—school NY-2
Griffith Interchange—crossing AZ-5
Griffith Knob—summit TN-4
Griffith Knob—summit (2) VA-3
Griffith Knoll—summit AZ-5
Griffith Lake DE-2
Griffith Lake—lake IL-6
Griffith Lake—lake MI-6
Griffith Lake—lake VT-1
Griffith Lake—reservoir AL-4
Griffith Lake—reservoir CO-8
Griffith Lake—reservoir DE-2
Griffith Lake Dam—dam DE-2
Griffith Lakes—reservoir NC-3
Griffith Landing (historical)—locale NC-3
Griffith Manor Park—park CA-9
Griffith Memorial Baptist Ch—church (2) MS-4
Griffith Mine—mine TN-4
Griffith Mine (underground)—mine AL-4
Griffith Mtn—summit AR-4
Griffith Mtn—summit CO-8
Griffith Mtn—summit TN-4
Griffith Neck—cape MD-2
**Griffith (Oasis)**—pop pl TX-5
Griffith Observatory—building CA-9
Griffit Hollow—valley KY-4
Griffith Park NC-3
Griffith Park—park CA-9
Griffith Park Boys Camp—locale CA-9
Griffith Peak—summit ID-8
Griffith Peak—summit NV-8
Griffith Peak Trail—trail NV-8
Griffith Peak Trailhead—trail NV-8
Griffith Placer—mine OR-9
Griffith Pond MA-1
Griffith Pond—reservoir NJ-2
Griffith Pond—reservoir PA-2
Griffith Pond Dam—dam NJ-2
Griffith Post Office (historical)—building TN-4
Griffith Quarry—hist pl CA-9
Griffith Ranch—locale (2) WY-8
Griffith Ranch Historical Monmt—park CA-9
Griffith Ridge—ridge KY-4
Griffith Ridge—ridge OH-6
Griffith Rsvr—reservoir (2) OR-9
Griffiths—locale PA-2
**Griffiths**—pop pl NY-2
Griffith's, Evan, Grocery—hist pl KY-4
Griffiths, John W., Mansion—hist pl IL-6
Griffiths, J. W., House—hist pl WA-9
Griffiths Cave—cave AL-4
Griffiths Cem—cemetery NH-1
Griffith Sch—school AZ-5
Griffith Sch—school KY-4
Griffith Sch—school MI-6
Griffith Sch—school NV-8
Griffith Sch—school NC-3
Griffith Sch—school (2) TN-4
Griffith's Chapel—hist pl DE-2
**Griffiths Corner**—pop pl VA-3
Griffiths Dam PA-2
Griffith Senior HS—school IN-6
Griffiths Ferry (historical)—locale AL-4
Griffiths House—hist pl FL-3
Griffith Siding—locale GA-3
Griffith Slough Ditch—canal KY-4
Griffiths Pond—lake MA-1
**Griffith Spring**—pop pl AR-4
Griffith Spring—spring ID-8
Griffith Spring—spring UT-8
Griffith Spring—spring WA-9
Griffith Spring Rsvr—reservoir OR-9
Griffith Springs—spring AR-4
Griffith Springs—spring ID-8
Griffiths Reservoir MT-8
Griffiths Spring—spring AZ-5
Griffith Stadium—park DC-2
Griffiths Tank—reservoir AZ-5
Griffith State Wildlife Area—park MO-7
Griffiths Traps (historical)—locale AL-4
**Griffithsville**—pop pl WV-2
Griffith Tank—reservoir AZ-5
**Griffithtown**—pop pl AR-4
**Griffithtown**—pop pl PA-2
Griffith Trail—trail PA-2
Griffith Tunnel—mine CO-8
Griffithville AR-4
**Griffithville**—pop pl AR-4
Griffith Wash—stream AZ-5
Griffith Well—locale NM-5
Griffitt Bend—bend AL-4
Griffitts Branch—stream (2) TN-4
**Griffitts (historical)**—pop pl TN-4
**Griffitts Lake Shore
Subdivision**—pop pl AL-4
Griffitts Mill (historical)—locale TN-4
Griffitts Post Office (historical)—building TN-4
Griff Lake—lake PA-2
Griffon Hollow—valley MO-7
Griffon Park—park NY-2
Griff Peak—summit WA-9
Griffus Cem—cemetery MI-6
Griffus Creek—stream MI-6
Griffy Branch—stream (2) KY-4
Griffy Branch—stream VA-3
Griffy Creek—stream IN-6
Griffy Rsvr—reservoir IN-6
Griffy Run—stream OH-6
**Griffytown**—pop pl KY-4
Grifka Drain—canal MI-6
Griftlo Park—park PA-2
**Grifton**—pop pl NC-3
Grifton Country Club NC-3
Grifton Sch—school NC-3
Grifton (Township of)—fmr MCD NC-3
Grigby Cem—cemetery TN-4
Grigg—locale IL-6
Grigg Cem—cemetery TN-4
Grigger Hollow—valley KY-4
Grigg Farm Airp—airport WA-9
Grigg Lake—lake ND-7
Grigg Lake—reservoir VA-3
Griggs IL-6
Griggs OH-6
Griggs SD-7
Griggs—locale AZ-5
Griggs—locale OK-5
Griggs—locale OR-9
Griggs, Clark R., House—hist pl IL-6
Griggs, Mount—summit AK-9
Griggs Branch—stream NC-3
Griggsby Cem—cemetery AL-4
Griggs Cem AL-4
Griggs Cem TN-4
Griggs Cem—cemetery (2) MO-7
Griggs Cem—cemetery SC-3
Griggs Cem—cemetery (2) TN-4
Griggs Cem—cemetery TX-5
Griggs Chapel—church GA-3
Griggs Chapel—church IL-6
Griggs Corners—locale OH-6
Griggs County—civil ND-7
Griggs County Courthouse—hist pl ND-7
Griggs Creek—stream AR-4
Griggs Creek—stream OH-6
Griggs Ditch—canal IN-6
Griggs Drain—stream MI-6
Griggs-Erwin House—hist pl GA-3
Griggs Field—park TX-5
**Griggs (Griggs Corners)**—pop pl OH-6
Griggs Gulch—valley SD-7
Griggs Hollow—valley TN-4
Griggs Lateral—canal IN-6
Griggs Mtn—summit VT-1
Griggs Park—park MA-1
Griggs Park—park TX-5
Griggs Place Cem AL-4
Griggs Pond—reservoir AL-4
Griggs Pond—reservoir CT-1
Griggs Pond—reservoir SC-3
Griggs Pond—reservoir VT-1
Griggs Pond—reservoir VA-3
Griggs Ponds—reservoir AL-4
Griggs Rsvr—reservoir OH-6
**Griggstown**—pop pl NJ-2
Griggstown Hist Dist—hist pl NJ-2
Griggs Township—fmr MCD IA-7
Griggs (Township of)—fmr MCD (2) AR-4
**Griggsville**—pop pl IL-6
Griggsville Hist Dist—hist pl IL-6
**Griggsville (Township of)**—pop pl IL-6
Grignon, Augustin, Hotel—hist pl WI-6
Grignon, Charles A., House—hist pl WI-6
Grignon Lake—lake WI-6
Grignon Park—park WI-6
Grigsby KS-7
Grigsby—locale KY-4
Grigsby—locale TN-4
**Grigsby**—pop pl TX-5
Grigsby Branch—stream KY-4
Grigsby Camp—locale CA-9
Grigsby Canyon—valley CA-9
Grigsby Canyon—valley TX-5
Grigsby Cem—cemetery (2) AL-4
Grigsby Cem—cemetery VA-3
Grigsby Chapel—church TN-4
Grigsby Creek—stream CA-9
Grigsby Creek—stream KY-4
Grigsby Draw—valley CA-9
Grigsby Estate—hist pl IL-6
Grigsby Ferry (historical)—locale AL-4
Grigsby Rock—pillar OR-9
Grigsby Sch (historical)—school TN-4
Grigsbys Ferry (historical)—locale MS-4
Grigsby Spring—spring CA-9
Grigsbys Springs—spring MS-4
Grigston—locale KS-7
Grijalva, Luciana B., House—hist pl NM-5
Grijes MH-9
Grikhdalitna Creek—stream AK-9
Grilk, Charles, House—hist pl IA-7
**Grill**—pop pl PA-2
Grill Cove—valley NC-3
**Grilley Township**—pop pl ND-7
Grill Lake—lake MN-6
Grill Lake—reservoir NY-2
Grill Sch—school OH-6
Grim WV-2
Grim—locale LA-4
Grimaud Creek—stream CA-9
Grimball, Paul, House Ruins—hist pl SC-3
Grimball Creek—stream GA-3
**Grimball Park**—pop pl GA-3
Grimball Point—cape GA-3
Grim Bldg—hist pl MO-7
Grim Branch Sch—school MS-4
Grim Cem—cemetery WV-2
Grim Chapel—church AL-4
Grim Chapel—church NC-3
Grim Chapel—church OH-6
Grime Lake ID-8
Grime Lake—lake LA-4
Grime Point—cape NV-8
Grimes—locale AL-4
Grimes—locale MD-2
Grimes—locale OK-5
Grimes—locale TX-5
Grimes—locale VA-3
**Grimes**—pop pl AL-4
**Grimes**—pop pl CA-9
**Grimes**—pop pl IA-7
**Grimes**—pop pl LA-4
Grimes, Dr. C. A., House—hist pl TX-5
Grimes, Felix, House—hist pl KY-4
Grimes, Jonathan Taylor, House—hist pl MN-6
**Grimes Addition**—pop pl IL-6
Grimes Airp—airport PA-2
Grimes Bay—swamp FL-3
Grimes Bottom—bend CO-8
Grimes Branch—stream AL-4
Grimes Branch—stream TN-4
Grimes Brook—stream CT-1
Grimes Brook—stream NH-1
Grimes Brooks Rsvr—reservoir CO-8
Grimes Canyon—valley (2) CA-9
Grimes Canyon—valley NV-8
Grimes Canyon—valley OR-9
Grimes Cem—cemetery (4) AL-4
Grimes Cem—cemetery FL-3
Grimes Cem—cemetery GA-3
Grimes Cem—cemetery MS-4
Grimes Cem—cemetery (2) NC-3
Grimes Cem—cemetery OK-5
Grimes Cem—cemetery PA-2
Grimes Cem—cemetery TN-4
Grimes Cem—cemetery (3) TX-5
Grimes Ch—church AL-4
Grimes Chapel—church AL-4
Grimes Chapel Cem—cemetery AL-4
Grimes Chapel Church AL-4
Grimes Church PA-2
**Grimes (County)**—pop pl TX-5
Grimes Covered Bridge—hist pl PA-2
Grimes Creek ID-8
Grimes Creek TX-5
Grimes Creek—stream CO-8
Grimes Creek—stream ID-8
Grimes Creek—stream MD-2
Grimes Creek—stream (3) MT-8
Grimes Creek—stream NY-2
Grimes Creek—stream OR-9
Grimes Creek—stream SC-3
Grimes Creek—stream TX-5
Grimes Creek—stream UT-8
Grimes Creek—stream VA-3
Grimes Creek—stream WA-9
Grimes Crossroads NC-3
Grimes-Crotts Mill—hist pl NC-3
**Grimesdale**—pop pl NC-3
Grimes Ditch—canal IN-6
Grimes Drain—stream ID-8
Grimes Farm Strip—airport IN-6
Grimes Flat—flat (2) OR-9
Grimes Ford—crossing TN-4
Grimes Garage—hist pl TX-5
Grimes Gasoline Plant—oilfield TX-5
Grimes Gulch—valley MT-8
Grimes Hill—summit NY-2
Grimes Hill Road—trail NH-1
Grimes Hills—summit NV-8
Grimes (historical)—locale MS-4
**Grimes (historical)**—pop pl NC-3
Grimes Homestead—hist pl NJ-2
Grimes House—hist pl TX-5
Grimes House and Mill Complex—hist pl KY-4
Grimes Island—island IL-6
Grimes Lake—lake FL-3
Grimes Lake—lake ID-8
Grimes Lake—lake IN-6
Grimes Lake—lake MI-6
Grimes Lake—lake TX-5
Grimes Lake—lake WA-9
Grimes Lake—reservoir TX-5
**Grimesland**—pop pl NC-3
Grimes Landing—locale VA-3
Grimes Landing (historical)—locale NC-3
Grimesland Plantation—hist pl NC-3
Grimesland (Township of)—fmr MCD NC-3
Grimes Lateral—canal CA-9
Grimes Mill ME-1
Grimes Mill—hist pl NC-3
Grimes Mill—locale MO-7
Grimes Mill—park NC-3
**Grimes Mill**—pop pl ME-1
Grimes Monmt—park ID-8
Grimes Nose—cliff GA-3
Grimes Octagon Barn—hist pl IA-7
Grimes Pass—gap ID-8
**Grimes Pass**—pop pl ID-8
Grimes Point—cape CA-9
Grimes Point—hist pl NV-8
Grimes Pond—lake UT-8
Grimes Portal—mine PA-2
Grimes Prairie Sch—school TX-5
Grimes Primary School NC-3
Grimes Ranch—locale CO-8
Grimes Ranch—locale NV-8
Grimes Run—stream (3) PA-2
Grimes Run—stream WV-2
Grimes Sch—hist pl NC-3
Grimes Sch—school CA-9
Grimes Sch—school (2) IL-6
Grimes Sch—school IA-7
Grimes Sch—school MO-7
Grimes Sch—school NY-2
Grimes Sch—school NC-3
Grimes Sch—school OK-5
Grimes Sch—school (2) TX-5
Grimes-Shull Cemetery TN-4
Grimes Spring—spring AZ-5
Grimestown (historical)—locale AL-4
Grimes Township—fmr MCD IA-7
Grimes Valley—valley WI-6
Grimesville MD-2
**Grimesville**—pop pl MD-2
**Grimesville**—pop pl PA-2
Grimes Wash—valley UT-8
Grimes Windmill—locale NM-5
Grimh Flowage—reservoir WI-6
Grim Hollow—valley PA-2
Grimhs Lake—lake WI-6
Grim Independent Sch
(abandoned)—school PA-2
Griminger—locale CA-9
Grimke, Charolette Forten,
House—hist pl DC-2
Grimke Sch—school DC-2
Grimland, Gunsten and Lofise,
House—hist pl TX-5
Grimland, Keddel and Liv, Farm—hist pl TX-5
Grimm, Wendelin, Farmstead—hist pl MN-6
Grimm Book Bindery—hist pl WI-6
Grimm Cem—cemetery AL-4
Grimm Cem—cemetery AR-4
Grimm Cem—cemetery NE-7
Grimm Chapel AL-4
Grimm Creek—stream AK-9
Grimmer Sch—school CA-9
Grimmet—locale MO-7
Grimmet Ch (historical)—church MO-7
Grimmet Creek—stream ID-8
Grimmet Lateral—canal ID-8
Grimmet Sch (historical)—school MO-7
Grimmet Spring—spring OR-9
Grimmet Springs—spring AR-4
Grimmett, John, Jr., House and
Outbuildings—hist pl ID-8
Grimmett, Orson, Bungalow—hist pl ID-8
Grimmett Bridge—other MO-7
Grimmett Cem—cemetery MO-7
Grimmette Cem—cemetery AR-4
Grimmett Hill—summit TN-4
Grimmett School (abandoned)—locale MO-7
Grimmetts Gulch—valley WY-8
Grimm Fork—stream WV-2
Grimm Lake—lake MI-6
Grimm Lake—lake ND-7
Grimms—locale WI-6
**Grimms Bridge**—pop pl OH-6
Grimm Sch—school IL-6
Grimms Crossing WV-2
**Grimms Crossroads**—pop pl PA-2
**Grimms Landing**—pop pl WV-2
Grimm Spring—spring AL-4
Grimms Run—stream WV-2
Grimms Trail—trail PA-2
Grimoud Creek CA-9
Grim Run—stream PA-2
**Grimsby**—pop pl IL-6
Grim Sch—school TX-5
Grim Sch (abandoned)—school PA-2
Grims Creek SC-3
Grims Crossroads NC-3
Grimsgard Lake—lake MN-6
Grimshaw—locale GA-3
Grimshaw, Duckworth, House—hist pl UT-8
Grimshaw, John, House—hist pl UT-8
**Grimshawes**—pop pl NC-3
Grimshaw Lake—lake CA-9
Grimshaw MS—school NY-2
Grimshaw Silk Mill—hist pl PA-2
Grims Island OR-9
Grims Lake—reservoir PA-2
Grims Landing (historical)—locale AL-4
**Grimsley**—pop pl TN-4
Grimsley Cem—cemetery SC-3
Grimsley Cem—cemetery TX-5
Grimsley Ch—church NC-3
Grimsley Cove—bay FL-3
Grimsley Creek—stream MT-8
Grimsley Ditch—canal WY-8
Grimsley Elem Sch—school TN-4
Grimsley Mill Branch—stream GA-3
Grimsley Neck—cape FL-3
Grimsley Park—flat MT-8
Grimsley Post Office—building TN-4
Grimsley Sch—school AL-4
Grimsleyville—locale VA-3
Grims Mill Bridge—bridge PA-2
**Grimstad (Township of)**—pop pl MN-6
**Grimstead**—pop pl VA-3
Grimsville PA-2
Grimton Cem—cemetery NE-7
Grimton Sch—school NE-7
**Grim (Township of)**—pop pl MI-6
Grimville—locale PA-2
Grimy Gulch—valley NV-8
Grinager Mercantile Bldg—hist pl ND-7
Grinage Run—stream PA-2
Grin Creek AL-4
**Grindall Creek**—pop pl VA-3
Grindall Creek—stream VA-3
Grindall Island—island AK-9
Grindall Passage—channel AK-9
Grindall Point—cape AK-9
Grindel Point—cape ME-1
Grindel's Point ME-1
Grinder Bluff—cliff (2) TN-4
Grinder Lake—lake MN-6
Grinders TN-4
**Grinders**—pop pl TN-4
Grinders Branch TN-4
Grinders Creek—stream TN-4
Grinders Creek Cem—cemetery (2) TN-4
Grinders Creek Ch—church TN-4
Grinders Inn (historical)—locale TN-4
Grinders Marsh TX-5
Grinders Switch—locale TN-4
Grinders Wharf—locale MD-2
Grindestaff Cem—cemetery MO-7
Grinding Rock Hill—summit MA-1
Grindle MO-7
Grindle Brook—stream CT-1
Grindle Chapel Baptist Ch NC-3
Grindle Creek—stream NC-3
Grindle Creek Ch—church NC-3
Grindle Hills—other AK-9
Grindle Hole—bay AL-4
Grindle Hole—lake AR-4
Grindle Lake IN-6
Grindle Lake—lake AR-4
Grindle Lake—lake IN-6
Grindle Lake—lake WI-6
Grindle Pocosin—swamp NC-3
Grindle Point—cape ME-1
Grindle Point Light Station—hist pl ME-1
Grindle Pond AL-4
Grindle Pond—lake AL-4
Grindles Eddy—bay ME-1
Grindool NC-3
Grindstaff Branch—stream TN-4
Grindstaff Cave—cave TN-4
Grindstaff Cem—cemetery NC-3
Grindstaff Cem—cemetery (4) TN-4
Grindstaff Hollow—valley IL-6
Grindstaff Hollow—valley TN-4
Grindstaff Prospect—mine (2) TN-4
Grindstaff Ridge—ridge TN-4
Grindstff Prospect—mine TN-4
Grindstone—locale (2) ME-1
Grindstone—locale NY-2
**Grindstone**—pop pl PA-2
**Grindstone**—pop pl SD-7
**Grindstone**—pop pl TX-5
Grindstone Bay—bay (2) NY-2
Grindstone Bend—bend KY-4
Grindstone Branch—stream AL-4
Grindstone Branch—stream GA-3
Grindstone Branch—stream IN-6
Grindstone Branch—stream KY-4
Grindstone Branch—stream MS-4
Grindstone Branch—stream MO-7
Grindstone Branch—stream (2) NC-3
Grindstone Branch—stream (2) TN-4
Grindstone Branch—stream (3) VA-3
Grindstone Brook—stream ME-1
Grindstone Brook—stream MA-1
Grindstone Brook—stream (2) NY-2
Grindstone Brook—stream VT-1
Grindstone Butte—summit ID-8
Grindstone Butte—summit SD-7
Grindstone Camp—locale CA-9
Grindstone Camp—locale OR-9
Grindstone Canyon—valley NM-5
Grindstone Canyon—valley UT-8
Grindstone Cem—cemetery CA-9
**Grind Stone City**—pop pl MI-6
Grindstone City Hist Dist—hist pl MI-6
Grindstone County Park—park MI-6
Grindstone Creek—stream (2) AL-4
Grindstone Creek—stream AK-9
Grindstone Creek—stream (2) CA-9
Grindstone Creek—stream (2) CO-8
Grindstone Creek—stream ID-8
Grindstone Creek—stream (4) IL-6

Grindstone Creek—stream IN-6
Grindstone Creek—stream KS-7
Grindstone Creek—stream (2) KY-4
Grindstone Creek—stream (2) MI-6
Grindstone Creek—stream (3) MO-7
Grindstone Creek—stream MT-8
Grindstone Creek—stream (2) NY-2
Grindstone Creek—stream NC-3
Grindstone Creek—stream OK-5
Grindstone Creek—stream OR-9
Grindstone Creek—stream SD-7
Grindstone Creek—stream (3) TX-5
Grindstone Creek—stream WA-9
Grindstone Creek—stream WI-6
Grindstone Creek—stream WY-8
**Grindstone Creek Rancheria (Indian Reservation)**—pop pl CA-9
Grindstone Creek State Wildlife Mngmt Area—park WI-6
Grindstone Dam—dam OR-9
Grindstone Draw—valley WY-8
Grindstone Falls—falls ME-1
Grindstone Flat—flat UT-8
Grindstone Ford—locale MS-4
Grindstone Forest Camp—locale OR-9
Grindstone Fork—stream KY-4
Grindstone Gap—gap KY-4
Grindstone Gap—gap PA-2
Grindstone Gulch—valley MT-8
Grindstone Harbor—bay WA-9
Grindstone Hill—summit AR-4
Grindstone Hill—summit KY-4
Grindstone Hill—summit PA-2
Grindstone Hollow PA-2
Grindstone Hollow—valley AL-4
Grindstone Hollow—valley PA-2
Grindstone Hollow—valley (4) TN-4
Grindstone Hollow—valley TX-5
Grindstone Hollow—valley VA-3
Grindstone Hollow—valley (3) WV-2
Grindstone Island—island MN-6
Grindstone Island—island NY-2
Grindstone Knob—summit KY-4
Grindstone Knob—summit NC-3
Grindstone Knob—summit TN-4
Grindstone Knob—summit (2) VA-3
Grindstone Knob—summit WV-2
Grindstone Lake—lake MN-6
Grindstone Lake—lake WI-6
Grindstone Lake—reservoir CO-8
Grindstone Ledge—bar (2) ME-1
Grindstone Mesa—summit NM-5
Grindstone Mtn—summit AZ-5
Grindstone Mtn—summit (3) AR-4
Grindstone Mtn—summit MA-1
Grindstone Mtn—summit NV-8
Grindstone Mtn—summit NC-3
Grindstone Mtn—summit OR-9
Grindstone Mtn—summit (2) TN-4
Grindstone Mtn—summit (2) TX-5
Grindstone Mtn—summit (3) VA-3
Grindstone Mtn—summit WA-9
Grindstone Neck—cape ME-1
**Grindstone Neck**—pop pl ME-1
Grindstone Openings—flat CA-9
Grindstone Park—flat WY-8
Grindstone Pass—gap WA-9
Grindstone Point—cape ME-1
Grindstone Pond—lake (2) ME-1
Grindstone Prairie—area AL-4
Grindstone Rancheria—locale CA-9
Grindstone Ridge—ridge (2) NC-3
Grindstone Ridge—ridge OR-9
Grindstone Ridge—ridge (6) TN-4
Grindstone Ridge—ridge (2) UT-8
Grindstone Ridge—ridge VA-3
Grindstone Ridge—ridge WV-2
Grindstone River—stream MN-6
Grindstone Rsvr—reservoir OR-9
Grindstone Run—stream KY-4
Grindstone Run—stream MD-2
Grindstone Run—stream PA-2
Grindstone Sch (historical)—school MO-7
Grindstone Spring—spring AZ-5
Grindstone Spring—spring ID-8
Grindstone Spring—spring NV-8
Grindstone Spring—spring UT-8
Grindstone Spring—spring WI-6
Grindstone Spring—spring WY-8
Grindstone Tank—reservoir (2) AZ-5
Grindstone Tank—reservoir TX-5
Grindstone Township (historical)—civil SD-7
Grindstone (Township of)—unorg ME-1
Grindstone Valley TN-4
Grindstone Wash AZ-5
Grindstone Wash—stream AZ-5
Grindstone Wash—valley UT-8
Grindstone Wash—valley WY-8
Grindstuen Cem—cemetery MI-6
Grindy Creek—stream OR-9
Grinell Mountain CA-9
Grinell Sch (historical)—school PA-2
Grinels—locale VA-3
Grinem MP-9
Grinem—island MP-9
Grinem Island MP-9
Griner Cem—cemetery GA-3
Griner Cem—cemetery TN-4
Griner Ditch—canal IN-6
Griner Peak—summit CA-9
Griner Pond—lake GA-3
Griner School—locale MI-6
Griners Marsh—swamp TX-5
Gring Creek—stream MT-8
Gringer Branch—stream NC-3
**Gringo**—pop pl PA-2
Gringo Gulch—valley AZ-5
Gringo Lake—lake NM-5
Gringo Peak—summit NM-5
Gringras Creek MO-7
Gringres Creek MO-7
Grinlin Lake—reservoir AL-4
Grinnage Run—stream PA-2
Grinnel IL-6
Grinnell NY-2
Grinnell—locale IL-6
Grinnell—locale WA-9
**Grinnell**—pop pl IA-7
**Grinnell**—pop pl KS-7
Grinnell, Lake—lake NJ-2
Grinnell, Levi P., House—hist pl IA-7
Grinnell, Mount—summit MT-8
Grinnel Lake—lake TX-5
Grinnell Brothers Music House—hist pl MI-6
Grinnell Cem—cemetery KS-7
Grinnell Coll—school IA-7
Grinnell Corporation—facility KY-4
Grinnell Creek—stream MT-8
Grinnell Creek—stream (3) WY-8
Grinnell Ditch—canal (2) WY-8
Grinnell Drain—canal MI-6
Grinnell Falls—falls MT-8
Grinnell Glacier—glacier AK-9
Grinnell Glacier—glacier MT-8
Grinnell Glacier Trail—trail MT-8
Grinnell Hill—locale NC-3
Grinnell HS—school IA-7
Grinnell HS—school KS-7
Grinnell Island NY-2
Grinnell Lake—lake CA-9
Grinnell Lake—lake MT-8
Grinnell Lake—lake WY-8
Grinnell Livestock Company Ditch—canal WY-8
Grinnell Meadows—flat WY-8
Grinnell Mill Hist Dist—hist pl OH-6
Grinnell Mtn—summit CA-9
Grinnell Point—cliff MT-8
Grinnell Rock—rock MA-1
Grinnell Sch—school NH-1
Grinnell School SD-7
Grinnells Landing (historical)—locale ND-7
Grinnell Station AZ-5
**Grinnell Township**—pop pl KS-7
Grinnel Pond—lake AL-4
Grinnel Pond—swamp AR-4
Grinnel Pond, The—lake TN-4
Grinnel Slough—gut IL-6
Grinnel Slough—stream NC-3
Grinnin Hollow—valley MO-7
Grinsell Branch—stream WI-6
Grinslade Ditch—canal IN-6
Grinter Chapel—church KS-7
**Grinter Heights**—pop pl KS-7
Grinter Heights—uninc pl KS-7
Grinter (historical)—locale KS-7
Grinter Place—hist pl KS-7
Grinwell Pond—lake AR-4
Grip—locale PA-2
**Gripe**—pop pl AZ-5
Gripe Canyon—valley NM-5
Gripe Inspection Station AZ-5
Gripe Rsvr—reservoir UT-8
**Gripinas**—pop pl PR-3
**Grippe**—pop pl (2) WV-2
Grippen Hill—summit NY-2
Grip Pit—cave AL-4
Grippy Branch—stream VA-3
Grisamore House—hist pl IN-6
Grisby Cem—cemetery IL-6
Grisby Hollow—valley VA-3
Griscom Creek—stream NJ-2
Griscom Creek—stream PA-2
Griscom Swamp—swamp NJ-2
Grisco Swamp—swamp PA-2
**Grisdale**—pop pl WA-9
Grisdale Hill—summit WA-9
Grise Bourbe Island—island LA-4
Grise Cemetery TN-4
Griselda Sch—school GA-3
**Grisemore**—pop pl PA-2
Grisgris, Bayou—gut LA-4
Grisham—locale MO-7
Grisham—locale TX-5
**Grisham**—pop pl TX-5
Grisham Branch—stream MS-4
Grisham Branch—stream TX-5
Grisham Cem—cemetery WA-9
Grisham Cemetery AL-4
Grisham Hollow—valley MO-7
Grisham Hollow—valley (2) TN-4
Grisham Knob—summit MO-7
**Grisham Pumping Station**—pop pl TX-5
**Grisham (Township of)**—pop pl IL-6
Grisinger Sch Number 3 (historical)—school SD-7
Grisly Creek—stream AR-4
**Grismore**—pop pl IN-6
Grissel Branch—stream TN-4
Grissel Knob—summit TN-4
Grisset Pond—lake FL-3
**Grissett**—pop pl SC-3
Grissett Lake—lake SC-3
**Grissettown**—pop pl NC-3
Grissett Swamp—stream NC-3
Grissim Branch—stream TN-4
Grissim Ch—church TN-4
Grissims Corner Ch of Christ TN-4
Grissinger Sch—school IL-6
Grissley Slough CA-9
Grissley Slough—gut CA-9
Grisso, W. E., Mansion—hist pl OK-5
**Grissom**—pop pl NC-3
Grissom, Island—island CA-9
Grissom AFB—military IN-6
Grissom Branch—stream AL-4
Grissom Branch—stream KY-4
Grissom Branch—stream SC-3
Grissom Cem—cemetery (2) AL-4
Grissom Cem—cemetery OK-5
Grissom Cem—cemetery TN-4
Grissom Chapel—church MS-4
Grissom Creek—stream TX-5
Grissom Creek—stream VA-3
Grissom Ditch—canal IN-6
Grissom Ferry (historical)—locale AL-4
Grissom Hole—bay FL-3
Grissom Island—island AL-4
Grissom Island—island TN-4
Grissom Island Ch—church TN-4
Grissom Park—park AL-4
Grissom Quarry—mine TN-4
Grissom Quarry Cave—cave TN-4
Grissom Sch—school VA-3
Grissom Sch (historical)—school AL-4
Grissoms Island TN-4
Grissoms Island Baptist Church TN-4
Grissoms Mill MS-4
Grissum Creek—stream MS-4
Grissum Creek—stream TN-4
**Grist**—pop pl NC-3
Grist Branch—stream SC-3
Grist Creek TX-5
Grist Creek—stream CA-9
Grist Flat—flat PA-2
Grist Island—island IL-6
Grist Mill—locale PA-2
Grist Mill Branch—stream NC-3
Grist Mill Covered Bridge—hist pl VT-1
Gristmill Creek—stream MI-6
Gristmiller's House—hist pl PA-2
Grist Mill Peak—summit CA-9
Grist Mill Pond—lake RI-1
Gristmill Pond—reservoir ME-1
Grist Mill Pond—reservoir ME-1
Grist Millpond—reservoir MA-1
**Gristmill Woods (subdivision)**—pop pl DE-2
Grist Mtn—summit NC-3
Grist Run—stream IN-6
Griswald Lake IL-6
Griswell Ch—church PA-2
Griswell Creek TX-5
Griswell Creek—stream OR-9
Griswells (historical)—locale AZ-5
Griswold GA-3
Griswold—locale IL-6
Griswold—locale (2) NY-2
**Griswold**—pop pl IA-7
**Griswold**—pop pl ME-1
Griswold, John, House—hist pl RI-1
Griswold, Maj. Joseph, House—hist pl MA-1
Griswold, Peck, House—hist pl OH-6
Griswold Bldg—hist pl MI-6
Griswold Canyon—valley (2) CA-9
Griswold Cem—cemetery CT-1
Griswold Cem—cemetery (2) IL-6
Griswold Cem—cemetery IA-7
Griswold Cem—cemetery NY-2
Griswold Cem—cemetery ND-7
Griswold Ch—church ND-7
Griswold Civic Center Hist Dist—hist pl MI-6
Griswold Creek CA-9
Griswold Creek NV-8
Griswold Creek—stream AL-4
Griswold Creek—stream (2) CA-9
Griswold Creek—stream NV-8
Griswold Creek—stream (2) OH-6
**Griswold (Griswoldville)**—pop pl GA-3
Griswold Hill—summit GA-3
Griswold Hill—summit NH-1
Griswold Hills—other CA-9
Griswold (historical)—locale ND-7
Griswold House—hist pl CA-9
Griswold House—hist pl CT-1
Griswold HS—school NY-2
Griswold Island—island CT-1
Griswold Island—island ME-1
Griswold Lake—lake IL-6
Griswold Lake—lake NV-8
Griswold Mine—mine ND-7
Griswold Mtn—summit MI-6
Griswold Natl Bank—hist pl IA-7
Griswold Park—park IA-7
Griswold Point—cape CT-1
Griswold Pond—lake (2) CT-1
Griswold Pond—lake FL-3
Griswold Pond—lake NY-2
Griswold Pond—reservoir MA-1
Griswold Pond Dam—dam MA-1
Griswold Ranch—locale CA-9
Griswold Sch—school CA-9
Griswold Sch—school CT-1
Griswold Sch—school IL-6
Griswold Sch—school (3) MI-6
Griswolds Creek—stream NV-8
Griswolds Mills NY-2
**Griswold Station**—pop pl IN-6
Griswoldsville GA-3
**Griswold (Town of)**—pop pl CT-1
Griswold Union HS—school OR-9
Griswoldville—locale GA-3
**Griswoldville**—pop pl CT-1
**Griswoldville**—pop pl MA-1
Griswoldville Dam MA-1
Griswold Well—well NV-8
Griswould Cem—cemetery AR-4
Griswould Creek—stream AR-4
Grit—locale TX-5
Grit—locale VA-3
**Grit**—pop pl TX-5
Grit Cem—cemetery TX-5
Grit Creek—stream ID-8
Grit Hill Sch—school VA-3
Grithy Branch—stream KY-4
Gritman Pond—reservoir CT-1
Grit Mine—mine CA-9
Gritney—locale FL-3
Gritney Ch—church FL-3
Grit Post Office (historical)—building TN-4
Grits Spring—spring UT-8
Gritta Ridge Sch—school NE-7
Gritten Cem—cemetery KS-7
Gritter Creek—stream IA-7
Gritter Hollow—valley WV-2
Gritt Hill—summit VT-1
Gritts Cem—cemetery OK-5
Gritts Hill—summit OK-5
Gritty Gulch—valley NV-8
Gritty Reservoir Dam—dam IN-6
Grives Ranch—locale WY-8
Grizelle, Lake—lake FL-3
Grizzard—locale TN-4
Grizzard—locale VA-3
Grizzard Branch—stream AL-4
Grizzard Cem—cemetery AL-4
Grizzard Cem—cemetery AR-4
Grizzard Post Office (historical)—building TN-4
Grizzard Spring—spring TN-4
Grizzie Hollow—valley VA-3
Grizzle Cem—cemetery KY-4
Grizzle Cem—cemetery (2) VA-3
Grizzle Creek—stream GA-3
Grizzle-Gunter Cem—cemetery TN-4
Grizzle Hollow—valley (2) KY-4
Grizzle Ocean—lake NY-2
Grizzle Ocean Mtn—summit NY-2
Grizzles Branch—stream VA-3
Grizzles Orchard—locale AZ-5
**Grizzletown**—pop pl GA-3
Grizzley Creek WY-8
Grizzley Creek—stream CO-8
Grizzley Park—flat CO-8
Grizzlie Place—locale CA-9
Grizzly—locale CO-8
Grizzly—locale OR-9
Grizzly Bar—bar AK-9
Grizzly Basin—basin ID-8
Grizzly Basin—basin (2) MT-8
Grizzly Basin—basin (2) WY-8
Grizzly Bay—bay CA-9
Grizzly Bear Creek—stream SD-7
Grizzly Bear Falls—falls CA-9
Grizzly Bear House—locale CA-9
Grizzly Bear Lake—lake WY-8
Grizzly Bear Mine—mine AK-9
Grizzly Bear Mine—mine CO-8
Grizzly Bear Mine—mine SD-7
Grizzly Bear Mountain MT-8
Grizzly Bear Ridge—ridge OR-9
Grizzly Bear Ridge—ridge (2) WA-9
Grizzly Bear Spring—spring AZ-5
Grizzly Bend—bend CA-9
Grizzly Bluff Sch—hist pl CA-9
Grizzly Bluff Sch—school CA-9
Grizzly Bluffs (historical)—cliff ND-7
Grizzly Butte—summit CA-9
Grizzly Butte—summit (2) OR-9
Grizzly Camp—locale CA-9
Grizzly Camp—locale OR-9
Grizzly Campground—locale CA-9
Grizzly Campground—locale MT-8
Grizzly Canyon CA-9
Grizzly Canyon—valley (4) CA-9
Grizzly Canyon—valley OR-9
Grizzly Canyon Trail—trail CA-9
Grizzly Cattle Ranch—locale CO-8
Grizzly Cem—cemetery OR-9
Grizzly Cow Camp—locale CO-8
Grizzly Creek CA-9
Grizzly Creek SD-7
Grizzly Creek WY-8
Grizzly Creek—stream (4) AK-9
Grizzly Creek—stream (17) CA-9
Grizzly Creek—stream (3) CO-8
Grizzly Creek—stream (6) ID-8
Grizzly Creek—stream (8) MT-8
Grizzly Creek—stream (8) OR-9
Grizzly Creek—stream (4) WA-9
Grizzly Creek—stream (6) WY-8
Grizzly Creek Campground—locale CO-8
Grizzly Creek Guard Station—locale CO-8
Grizzly Creek Redwoods State Park—park CA-9
Grizzly Creek Trail—trail MT-8
Grizzly Ditch—canal CO-8
Grizzly Dome—summit CA-9
Grizzly Extension Ditch—canal CO-8
Grizzly Flat—flat (3) CA-9
Grizzly Flat—flat (2) OR-9
Grizzly Flats—flat CA-9
Grizzly Flats—flat OR-9
**Grizzly Flats**—pop pl CA-9
Grizzly Flat Station—locale CA-9
Grizzly Forebay—reservoir CA-9
Grizzly Giant Tree—other CA-9
Grizzly Gulch—valley (9) CA-9
Grizzly Gulch—valley (7) CO-8
Grizzly Gulch—valley ID-8
Grizzly Gulch—valley (2) MT-8
Grizzly Gulch—valley OR-9
Grizzly Gulch—valley SD-7
Grizzly Gulch—valley (2) UT-8
Grizzly Helena Trail—trail CO-8
Grizzly Hill CA-9
Grizzly Hill—summit ID-8
Grizzly Hill—summit MT-8
Grizzly Hill—summit NV-8
Grizzly Hollow—valley UT-8
Grizzly Ice Pond—reservoir CA-9
Grizzly Island—island CA-9
Grizzly Island Club—other CA-9
Grizzly Lake—lake (2) AK-9
Grizzly Lake—lake (5) CA-9
Grizzly Lake—lake (4) CO-8
Grizzly Lake—lake MT-8
Grizzly Lake—lake (2) WA-9
Grizzly Lake—lake (2) WY-8
Grizzly Lakes—lake CA-9
Grizzly Land Club—other CA-9
Grizzly Lodge—locale CA-9
Grizzly Meadow—flat (3) CA-9
Grizzly Meadows—flat CA-9
Grizzly Mine—mine (2) CA-9
Grizzly Mine—mine OR-9
Grizzly Mountain CA-9
Grizzly Mountain Canyon—valley OR-9
Grizzly Mtn CA-9
Grizzly Mtn—summit AK-9
Grizzly Mtn—summit AZ-5
Grizzly Mtn—summit (2) CA-9
Grizzly Mtn—summit CO-8
Grizzly Mtn—summit ID-8
Grizzly Mtn—summit MT-8
Grizzly Mtn—summit (4) OR-9
Grizzly Mtn—summit (2) WA-9
Grizzly Park CA-9
Grizzly Park—flat MT-8
Grizzly Peak OR-9
Grizzly Peak WA-9
Grizzly Peak—summit (9) CA-9
Grizzly Peak—summit (5) CO-8
Grizzly Peak—summit MT-8
Grizzly Peak—summit (4) OR-9
Grizzly Peak—summit UT-8
Grizzly Peak—summit WA-9
Grizzly Peak—summit WY-8
Grizzly Point—ridge MT-8
Grizzly Point—summit CA-9
Grizzly Point—summit MT-8
Grizzly Prairie—flat OR-9
Grizzly Ranch—locale WY-8
Grizzly Ridge UT-8
Grizzly Ridge—ridge CA-9
Grizzly Ridge—ridge ID-8
Grizzly Ridge—ridge (2) OR-9
Grizzly Ridge—summit CO-8
Grizzly Ridges—ridge UT-8
Grizzly Ridge Winter Sports Area—area UT-8
Grizzly Rock—pillar ID-8
Grizzly Rsvr—reservoir CO-8
Grizzly Saddle—gap ID-8
Grizzly Slough—gut (2) CA-9
Grizzly Slough—stream OR-9
Grizzly Spring—spring (2) CA-9
Grizzly Spring—spring ID-8
Grizzly Summit—summit CA-9
Grizzly Tooth—pillar NM-5
Grizzly Tunnel—mine CO-8
Grizzly Valley—valley CA-9
Grizzly Valley Dam—dam CA-9
**Grnderville (historical)**—pop pl PA-2
Groahs Ridge—ridge VA-3
Groaner Spring—spring CA-9
Groat—locale IL-6
Groat Creek—stream MT-8
Groat Creek—stream VT-1
Groat Mtn—summit WA-9
Groat Point—cape WA-9
Grobe (historical)—locale SD-7
Grobe Post Office (historical)—building SD-7
Grober Mtn—summit AR-4
Grobes Branch—stream WV-2
Grob Lake—lake MT-8
Grob Sch—school IL-6
Groce Branch—stream TX-5
Groce Hill—summit PA-2
Groce Lake—reservoir AL-4
Groce-Montgomery Cem—cemetery AL-4
Grocer Lake—lake LA-4
Grocery Bottom—flat TN-4
Grocery Branch—stream MO-7
Grocery Gap—gap KY-4
Grocery Hollow—valley (2) TN-4
Grocery Island FL-3
Grocery Place—locale FL-3
Grocery Swamp—swamp TN-4
Groce Spring Branch—stream KY-4
Groceville—locale TX-5
Grodey Ridge—ridge IN-6
**Grodis Corner**—pop pl OH-6
Groedocker Ranch—locale NE-7
Groenendyke Cem—cemetery IN-6
Groenfeldt Site—hist pl CA-9
Groe Run PA-2
**Groesbeck**—pop pl OH-6
**Groesbeck**—pop pl TX-5
Groesbeck (CCD)—cens area TX-5
Groesbeck Creek TX-5
Groesbeck Creek—stream TX-5
Groesbeck Hills Sch—school MI-6
Groesbeck Municipal Golf Course—other MI-6
Groesbeck Park—park MI-6
Groesbeck Sch—school MI-6
Groesbeeck TX-5
Groesbuck TX-5
Groezinger Wine Cellars—hist pl CA-9
Groff Cem—cemetery MO-7
Groff Creek—stream NY-2
Groff Creek—stream PA-2
**Groffdale**—pop pl PA-2
Groffdale Ch—church PA-2
Groff Ditch—canal IN-6
Groff Island PA-2
Groff Mtn—summit NY-2
Groff Oil Field—oilfield KS-7
Groff Park—park MA-1
Groff Run—stream PA-2
Groff Sch—school MO-7
Groff Sch—school PA-2
Groffs Corner—locale PA-2
Groff Spring—spring CO-8
Grogan OH-6
Grogan—locale MO-7
**Grogan**—pop pl GA-3
**Grogan**—pop pl MN-6
Grogan Canyon—valley NM-5
Grogan Cem—cemetery TN-4
Grogan Creek—stream NC-3
Grogan Estate Lake—reservoir NC-3
Grogan Estate Lake Dam—dam NC-3
Grogan Hill—summit TN-4
Grogan Hole CA-9
Grogan Hollow—valley WV-2
Grogan Lake—lake FL-3
Grogan Mtn—summit GA-3
Grogan Oil Field—oilfield LA-4
Grogan Sch (historical)—school MO-7
Grogans Hollow—valley AR-4
Grogans Spring—spring AL-4
Grog Branch—stream FL-3
Grog Branch—stream KY-4
Grog Creek—stream NC-3
Grogen Branch—stream VA-3
G Rogers—locale TX-5
Grogg Creek—stream AK-9
Grogg Creek—stream MS-4
Groggin Drain UT-8
Groggins Creek—stream TN-4
Grogg Lake—lake AK-9
Groggs Point—cape MD-2
Groggy Rustic PA-2
Grog Hall Creek AL-4
Grog Harbor—bay NY-2
Grog Island—island ME-1
Grog Island—island VA-3
Grog Island Ledge ME-1
Grog Ledge—bar ME-1
Grognon Gulch—valley AK-9
Grog Run—stream (2) OH-6
Grog Run—stream WV-2
Grogtown DE-2
Grogue Town DE-2
Groh Drain—stream MI-6
Grohe Creek—stream OR-9
Grohl Meadow—flat CA-9
Grohs Dam—dam OR-9
Grohs Ranch—locale CA-9
Grohs Rsvr—reservoir (2) OR-9
Grolemund Run—stream PA-2
Gromeaux Ditch—canal IN-6
Gromes Chapel—church KY-4
Grommund Creek—stream WY-8
**Gromore**—pop pl WA-9
Grompau Branch—stream AL-4
**Gronanville**—pop pl TN-4
Gronden Creek—stream (2) MI-6
Gronemus Valley—valley WI-6
Gronendyke Ditch—canal IN-6
Groner Rsvr—reservoir ID-8
Grone Tarn—lake WA-9
Grong Cem—cemetery ND-7
Grong Ch—church MN-6
**Groningen**—pop pl MN-6
Gronning Canal—canal UT-8
Gronosho Cave—cave AL-4
Gronseth Slough—stream SD-7
Gronvold, Just C., House—hist pl MN-6
Gronvold Ridge—ridge WI-6
Groo Canyon—valley WY-8
**Groom**—pop pl TX-5
Groom Branch—stream TN-4
Groom Cem—cemetery TX-5
Groom Ch—church NY-2
**Groom Creek**—pop pl AZ-5
Groom Creek—stream AZ-5
Groom Creek—stream MT-8
Groom Creek Horse Camp—locale AZ-5
Groom Creek Loop Number Three Hundred Seven—trail AZ-5
Groom Creek Loop Trail—trail AZ-5
Groom Creek Work Center—locale AZ-5
**Groome**—pop pl UT-8
Groomer Branch—stream MO-7
Groomer Canyon—valley CO-8
Groome Siding—locale UT-8
**Groometown**—pop pl NC-3
Groome United Methodist Ch—church DE-2
Grooming Spring—spring AZ-5
Groom Lake—lake NV-8
Groom Mine—mine NV-8
Groom Pass—gap NV-8
Groom Peak AZ-5
Groom Peak—summit AZ-5
Groom Range—range NV-8
Groom Ridge—ridge TN-4
Grooms—locale OH-6
Grooms Branch—stream KY-4
Grooms Branch—stream NC-3
Grooms Branch—stream TX-5
Grooms Bridge—bridge TN-4
Grooms Cave—cave AL-4
Grooms Cem—cemetery SC-3
Grooms Cem—cemetery TN-4
Groom Sch—school VA-3
Groom Sch—school WI-6
Grooms Chapel—church NC-3
**Grooms Corners**—pop pl NY-2
Grooms Creek—stream FL-3
Grooms Hill—summit AZ-5
Grooms Hill—summit CA-9
Grooms Hollow—valley AR-4
Groom Slash LA-4
Groom Slash—stream LA-4
Grooms Peak AZ-5
Grooms Pocket—bay TN-4
Groom Spring—spring AZ-5
Groom Spring—spring KY-4
Groom Spring—spring TN-4
Groom Spring Wash—stream AZ-5
Grooms Ridge—ridge VA-3
Grooms Ridge Trail—trail VA-3
**Groomsville**—pop pl IN-6
Groomsville Ch—church SC-3
Groomtown NC-3
**Groomtown**—pop pl NC-3
Groomville IN-6
**Groos**—pop pl MI-6
Groose Creek—stream AL-4
Groothousen Bay—bay WI-6
Grootpan Bay—bay VI-3
Groove Hollow—valley AR-4
Groover Branch—stream FL-3
Groover Branch—stream GA-3
Groover Cem—cemetery GA-3
Groover Cem—cemetery IN-6
Groover Cem—cemetery PA-2
Groover Landing—locale SC-3
Groover Lateral—canal AZ-5
Groover Mine—mine CA-9
Groover Pond—reservoir GA-3
Groovers Lake—reservoir GA-3
Groover Spring—spring OR-9
Grooverville—locale GA-3
**Grooverville**—pop pl GA-3
Grooverville Sch—school GA-3
Grooves Lake—reservoir AL-4
Grooves Lake Dam—dam AL-4
**Grooville**—pop pl NY-2
Grophes Island—island LA-4
Gropius House—building MA-1
Gropp Ditch—canal IN-6
Gropper Lake—reservoir AR-4
Gropp Lake—reservoir NJ-2
Gropp Lake Dam—dam NJ-2
Grosbeak, Bayou—stream LA-4
Grosbec, Bayou—gut (2) LA-4
Grosbec, Bayou—stream LA-4
Gros Bec, Cypriere—swamp LA-4
Grosbeck Creek—stream MI-6
**Groscap**—pop pl MI-6
Gros Cap Archaeol District—hist pl MI-6
Gros Cap Cemetery—hist pl MI-6
Groschen Cabin OR-9
**Grosclose**—pop pl VA-3
Grosco Cem—cemetery TX-5
Grose, Gen. William, House—hist pl IN-6
Grose Cem—cemetery AR-4
Grose Cem—cemetery WV-2
Groseclose—locale VA-3
**Groseclose**—pop pl VA-3
Groseclose Cem—cemetery TN-4
Groseclose Chapel—church VA-3
**Groseclose Store**—pop pl VA-3
Grose Hollow—valley TN-4
Grose Mtn—summit AR-4
Grosen Sch—school MO-7
Grose Ranch—locale MT-8
Grose Spring—spring VA-3
Grosfield Ditch—canal MT-8
Grosfield Homestead—locale MT-8
Grosfield Ranch—locale MT-8
**Gros Gap**—pop pl MI-6
Gros Gap Cem—cemetery MI-6
**Grosh**—pop pl FL-3
Grosh, Mount—summit NV-8
Groshans Ditch—canal IN-6
Groshen Cabin—locale OR-9
Groshen Trail—trail OR-9
**Gros (historical)**—pop pl SD-7
Groshon Creek—stream WY-8
Groshong Branch—stream MO-7

Groshong Gulch—*valley* CA-9
Groshong Mine—*mine* SD-7
Grosilliers Lake—*lake* MN-6
*Gross* TN-4
Gross—*locale* FL-3
Gross—*locale* ID-8
Gross—*locale* IL-6
**Gross**—*pop pl* KS-7
**Gross**—*pop pl* NE-7
Gross, Courtlandt, House—*hist pl* CA-9
Gross, Lake—*lake* FL-3
Gross And Taylor Drain—*canal* MI-6
Gross Bar—*bar* AL-4
Gross Bayou—*gut* MS-4
Gross Branch—*stream* (2) AL-4
Gross Bridge—*hist pl* PA-2
Gross Brook—*stream* ME-1
Gross Cem—*cemetery* (2) AL-4
Gross Cem—*cemetery* AR-4
Gross Cem—*cemetery* GA-3
Gross Cem—*cemetery* IN-6
Gross Cem—*cemetery* KY-4
Gross Cem—*cemetery* (2) MO-7
Gross Cem—*cemetery* NE-7
Gross Cem—*cemetery* PA-2
Gross Cem—*cemetery* (2) TN-4
Gross Cove—*valley* TN-4
*Gross Creek* MT-8
Gross Creek—*bay* MD-2
Gross Creek—*stream* AR-4
Gross Creek—*stream* CO-8
Gross Creek—*stream* KY-4
Gross Creek—*stream* OR-9
Gross Creek—*stream* VA-3
Gross Creek—*stream* WY-8
Gross Crossroad—*locale* TN-4
**Grosscup**—*pop pl* WA-9
Grosscup Road Hist Dist—*hist pl* WV-2
Grossdale Station—*hist pl* IL-6
Gross Ditch—*canal* IN-6
Grosse—*locale* SD-7
Grosse Cem—*cemetery* WI-6
Grosse (historical)—*locale* SD-7
Grosse Ile—*CDP* MI-6
Grosse Ile—*island* MI-6
Grosse Ile Ch—*church* MI-6
Grosse Ile Country Club—*other* MI-6
Grosse Ile HS—*school* MI-6
Grosse Ile JHS—*school* MI-6
Grosse Ile Naval Air Station—*military* MI-6
**Grosse Ile (Township of)**—*pop pl* MI-6
Grosse Isle—*locale* LA-4
Grosse Isle Point—*cape* LA-4
Grosse Lake—*lake* MI-6
*G Ross Elementary School* PA-2
Grossen Canyon—*valley* ID-8
*Grosse Point* MI-6
Grosse Point—*cape* (2) MI-6
Grosse Point—*cape* VT-1
*Grosse Pointe* AL-4
*Grossepointe* MI-6
Grosse Pointe—*cape* LA-4
**Grosse Pointe**—*pop pl* MI-6
Grosse Pointe Club—*other* MI-6
**Grosse Pointe Farms**—*pop pl* MI-6
Grosse Pointe HS—*school* MI-6
Grosse Pointe North HS—*school* MI-6
**Grosse Pointe Park**—*pop pl* MI-6
Grosse Pointe Plaza (Shop Ctr)—*locale* FL-3
**Grosse Pointe Shores**—*pop pl* MI-6
Grosse Pointe (Township of)—*civ div* MI-6
**Grosse Pointe Woods**—*pop pl* MI-6
Grosse Pointe Yacht Club—*other* MI-6
Grosse Point Lighthouse—*hist pl* IL-6
Grosse Savanne—*cape* LA-4
Grosses Creek—*stream* VA-3
Grosses Creek Ch—*church* VA-3
Grosses Gap Trail—*trail* PA-2
Grosses Mtn—*summit* VA-3
**Grosse Tete**—*pop pl* LA-4
Grosse Tete, Bayou—*stream* LA-4
Grosse Tete Bay Sch—*school* LA-4
*Grossett Canyon* WY-8
Gross Fork—*stream* KY-4
Gross Golf Course—*other* MN-6
Gross Hill—*summit* KY-4
Gross Hill—*summit* MA-1
Gross Hill—*summit* NY-2
Gross Hill Sch—*school* NY-2
Gross Hole—*cave* AL-4
Gross Hollow—*valley* AL-4
Gross Hollow—*valley* MD-2
Gross Hollow—*valley* (2) PA-2
Gross Hollow—*valley* WV-2
Gross HS—*school* TX-5
Grosshuesch Lake—*lake* WI-6
**Grossinger**—*pop pl* NY-2
Grossingers Lake—*lake* NY-2
*Gross Island* MI-6
Gross Knob—*summit* KY-4
Gross Lake—*lake* SD-7
Gross Lake—*lake* WI-6
Gross Lake—*reservoir* AL-4
Gross Lake—*reservoir* TN-4
Gross Lake Dam—*dam* AL-4
Gross Lake State Public Shooting Area—*park* SD-7
Gross Landing (historical)—*locale* AL-4
Grossman Creek—*stream* OR-9
Grossman Hammock—*island* FL-3
Grossman Hammock State Park—*park* FL-3
**Grossman (historical)**—*pop pl* OR-9
*Grossman Peak* AZ-5
Grossman Point—*cape* NY-2
Grossman Ridge—*ridge* FL-3
Grossman Slough—*lake* MN-6
Gross -Marble Mine—*mine* MN-6
*Gross Mesa* WY-8
**Grossmont**—*pop pl* CA-9
Grossmont Coll—*school* CA-9
Grossmont Hosp—*hospital* CA-9
Grossmont HS—*school* CA-9
Gross Mtn—*summit* OR-9
Gross Mtn—*summit* WA-9
Gross Neck—*cape* ME-1
Grossnickle Ch—*church* MD-2
Grossnickle Ditch—*canal* OH-6
*Gross Plains* AL-4
Gross Playground—*park* IL-6
*Gross Point* AL-4
*Gross' Point* ME-1
*Grosspoint* MI-6
Gross Point—*cape* ME-1
Gross Point—*cape* MO-7
**Gross Point**—*pop pl* IL-6
Gross Point Cem—*cemetery* ME-1
Grosspoint Lighthouse—*locale* IL-6
Gross Pond—*lake* GA-3
Gross Pond—*lake* ME-1
Gross Post Office (historical)—*building* TN-4
Gross Ranch—*locale* MT-8
Gross Ridge—*ridge* TN-4
*Gross-Rong* MP-9
Gross Rsvr—*reservoir* CO-8
Gross Rsvr—*reservoir* WY-8
Gross Run—*stream* PA-2
Gross Sch—*school* IL-6
Gross Skeleton Cave—*cave* AL-4
Gross Spring—*spring* AL-4
Gross Spring—*spring* (2) AZ-5
Gross Tank—*reservoir* TX-5
Grosstown—*locale* MD-2
Gross Valley—*basin* NE-7
Gross Valley—*valley* WI-6
Grossville—*locale* TX-5
Grosvenor—*locale* OH-6
Grosvenor—*locale* TX-5
**Grosvenor**—*pop pl* MI-6
Grosvenor, E. O., House—*hist pl* MI-6
Grosvenor, Lake—*lake* AK-9
Grosvenor, Mount—*summit* AK-9
Grosvenor Arch—*arch* UT-8
Grosvenor Bay—*bay* NY-2
**Grosvenor Corner**—*pop pl* MA-1
**Grosvenor Dale**—*pop pl* CT-1
*Grosvenordale (Grosvenor Dale)* CT-1
Grosvenor Drain—*canal* MI-6
Grosvenor Hills—*summit* AZ-5
Grosvenor Reservoir—*lake* MA-1
Grosvenor Sch—*school* MD-2
Grosvenor Square—*park* MN-6
Gros Ventre Campground—*locale* WY-8
Gros Ventre Falls—*falls* MT-8
Gros Ventre Junction—*locale* WY-8
*Gros Ventre Lake* WY-8
*Gros Ventre Mountains* WY-8
Gros Ventre Range—*range* WY-8
Gros Ventre River—*stream* WY-8
Gros Ventre Rsvr—*reservoir* MT-8
Gros Ventres Island (historical)—*island* ND-7
Gros Ventre Slide Geological Area—*area* WY-8
Grosvold Bay—*bay* AK-9
Grosz, Martin and Wilhelminn, House-Barn—*hist pl* SD-7
*Grotan Creek* UT-8
Grotan Fairgrounds—*locale* MA-1
*Grotch Lake* MI-6
**Grote**—*pop pl* CO-8
Grote Cem—*cemetery* TX-5
Grotee Sch—*school* LA-4
Grotes Pond—*lake* MN-6
Groth Drain—*stream* MI-6
Grothoff Cem—*cemetery* IL-6
Groth State Wildlife Mngmt Area—*park* MN-6
**Groton**—*pop pl* CT-1
**Groton**—*pop pl* MA-1
**Groton**—*pop pl* NH-1
**Groton**—*pop pl* NY-2
**Groton**—*pop pl* SD-7
**Groton**—*pop pl* VT-1
Groton, Lake—*lake* VT-1
Groton Bank Hist Dist—*hist pl* CT-1
Groton Beach—*beach* CT-1
Groton Cem—*cemetery* MA-1
Groton Cem—*cemetery* SD-7
Groton (census name for Groton Center)—*CDP* MA-1
Groton Center (census name Groton)—*other* MA-1
*Groton Centre* MA-1
**Groton City**—*pop pl* NY-2
*Groton Heights* CT-1
Groton Heights Sch—*school* CT-1
Groton Hollow—*valley* NH-1
Groton HS—*school* MA-1
Groton Inn—*hist pl* MA-1
Groton Island—*island* NH-1
Groton JHS—*school* MA-1
**Groton Lake Shores**—*pop pl* CT-1
*Groton Leatherboard Company Dam* MA-1
Groton Long Point—*cape* CT-1
**Groton Long Point**—*pop pl* CT-1
Groton Municipal Airp—*airport* SD-7
*Groton Pond* VT-1
Groton Rsvr—*reservoir* CT-1
Grotons—*locale* VA-3
Groton Sch—*school* MA-1
Groton School Camp—*locale* NH-1
Groton School Pond—*lake* MA-1
Groton State For—*forest* VT-1
Groton Town—*locale* VA-3
**Groton (Town of)**—*pop pl* CT-1
**Groton (Town of)**—*pop pl* MA-1
**Groton (Town of)**—*pop pl* NH-1
**Groton (Town of)**—*pop pl* NY-2
**Groton (Town of)**—*pop pl* VT-1
**Groton Township**—*pop pl* SD-7
**Groton (Township of)**—*pop pl* OH-6
Grots Pond—*lake* MO-7
*Grotto* MH-9
**Grotto**—*pop pl* NY-2
**Grotto**—*pop pl* WA-9
Grotto, Petit Jean No. 8—*hist pl* AR-4
Grotto, The—*cave* (3) UT-8
Grotto, The—*falls* PA-2
Grotto, The—*other* CA-9
Grotto Campground—*locale* UT-8
Grotto Camping Ground North Comfort Station—*hist pl* UT-8
Grotto Camping Ground South Comfort Station—*hist pl* UT-8
Grotto Canyon—*valley* CA-9
Grotto Canyon—*valley* UT-8
Grotto Cove—*bay* OR-9
Grotto Creek—*stream* (2) AK-9
Grotto Creek—*stream* CA-9
Grotto Creek—*stream* ID-8
**Grottoes**—*pop pl* VA-3
*Grotto Falls* ID-8
*Grotto Falls* OR-9
Grotto Falls—*falls* MT-8
Grotto Falls—*falls* OR-9
Grotto Geyser—*geyser* WY-8
Grotto Hill—*summit* ME-1
Grotto Hills—*other* CA-9
Grotto Lake—*lake* MN-6
Grotto Lake—*lake* WA-9
Grotto Mtn—*summit* AK-9
Grotto Mtn—*summit* WA-9
Grotto Park—*park* OK-5
*Grotto Picnic Area* UT-8
Grotto Pit—*cave* TN-4
Grotto Pond—*lake* MA-1
Grottos, The—*valley* CO-8
Grottos Campground—*locale* CO-8
Grotto Spring—*spring* CA-9
Grotto Springs—*spring* UT-8
Grottos Trail—*trail* WI-6
Grotzman Creek—*stream* CA-9
Grou Camp—*locale* WA-9
Grouch Creek—*stream* AK-9
Grouch Drain—*canal* ID-8
Groudy Creek—*stream* AK-9
Ground Bend—*bend* AR-4
Ground Bridge Gully—*valley* TX-5
Ground Brook—*stream* MA-1
Ground Creek—*stream* NJ-2
*Grounder Creek* MO-7
*Ground Gully* TX-5
Ground Hemlock Lake—*lake* WI-6
Groundhog, Lake—*lake* PA-2
Groundhog Bar—*bar* ID-8
Groundhog Basin—*basin* AK-9
Groundhog Basin—*basin* CO-8
Groundhog Branch—*stream* IN-6
Groundhog Branch—*stream* (2) KY-4
Groundhog Branch—*stream* (2) NC-3
Groundhog Branch—*stream* TN-4
Groundhog Branch—*stream* (2) WV-2
Ground Hog Brook—*stream* NJ-2
Groundhog Canyon—*valley* NV-8
*Ground Hog Creek* CO-8
*Groundhog Creek* ID-8
*Groundhog Creek* IN-6
*Ground Hog Creek* TN-4
Groundhog Creek—*stream* (2) AK-9
Groundhog Creek—*stream* (3) CO-8
Ground Hog Creek—*stream* ID-8
Groundhog Creek—*stream* NV-8
Groundhog Creek—*stream* NC-3
Groundhog Creek—*stream* OH-6
Groundhog Creek—*stream* TN-4
Groundhog Falls—*falls* IN-6
Groundhog Falls—*falls* OR-9
Groundhog Flat—*flat* CO-8
Ground Hog Fork—*ridge* TN-4
Groundhog Fork—*stream* (2) KY-4
*Ground Hog Gulch* OR-9
Groundhog Gulch—*valley* (3) CO-8
Groundhog Gulch—*valley* OR-9
Groundhog Hill—*summit* NY-2
Groundhog Hill—*summit* VA-3
Ground Hog (historical)—*locale* AL-4
Groundhog Hollow—*valley* (4) KY-4
Ground Hog Hollow—*valley* KY-4
Groundhog Hollow—*valley* (2) OH-6
Groundhog Hollow—*valley* OK-5
Groundhog Hollow—*valley* VA-3
Groundhog Knoll—*summit* OR-9
Groundhog Meadow—*flat* (2) CA-9
Groundhog Meadows—*flat* CA-9
Groundhog Meadows—*flat* NV-8
Ground Hog Mine—*mine* CO-8
Groundhog Mine—*mine* CO-8
Ground Hog Mine—*mine* MT-8
*Ground Hog Mountain* CO-8
*Ground Hog Mtn* TN-4
Groundhog Mtn—*summit* AK-9
Groundhog Mtn—*summit* CO-8
Groundhog Mtn—*summit* OR-9
Groundhog Mtn—*summit* TN-4
Groundhog Mtn—*summit* VA-3
Groundhog North Shaft (Active)—*mine* NM-5
Groundhog No 1 Shaft—*mine* NM-5
Groundhog No 5 Shaft (Active)—*mine* NM-5
Groundhog Park—*flat* CO-8
Groundhog Point Rsvr—*reservoir* CO-8
*Ground Hog Reservoir* CO-8
Groundhog Ridge—*ridge* NC-3
Groundhog Ridge—*ridge* (2) TN-4
Groundhog Ridge—*ridge* WV-2
Groundhog Rock—*pillar* CA-9
Groundhog Rsvr—*reservoir* CO-8
Groundhog Rsvr—*reservoir* NV-8
Groundhog Rsvr—*reservoir* OR-9
Groundhog Slough—*gut* IL-6
Ground Hog Spring—*spring* ID-8
Ground Hog Stock Driveway—*trail* CO-8
*Ground Hog Valley* PA-2
Groundhop Branch—*stream* NC-3
Groundhop Hollow—*valley* TN-4
Groundhouse River—*stream* MN-6
Ground Lump Bar—*bar* AR-4
Groundnut Creek—*stream* NC-3
Groundnut Hill—*summit* ME-1
Ground Oak Trail—*trail* PA-2
Grounds Cem—*cemetery* TX-5
*Grounds Church* TX-5
Grounds Creek—*stream* MO-7
Ground Squirrel Branch—*stream* NC-3
Ground Squirrel Bridge—*bridge* VA-3
Ground Squirrel Gap—*gap* GA-3
Ground Tank—*reservoir* AZ-5
**Grounts Corner**—*pop pl* MA-1
Group Camp—*locale* NC-3
Group Camping Area Lake—*reservoir* PA-2
*Group Camp Lake* GA-3
*Groupe de Ralik* MP-9
*Groupe de Ratak* MP-9
Grouper Creek—*gut* FL-3
Grouper Point—*cape* VI-3
Grouping of Religious Buildings at Trinity—*hist pl* IN-6
*Grouse* ID-8
**Grouse**—*pop pl* ID-8
**Grouse**—*pop pl* OR-9
Grouse Bay—*bay* MN-6
Grouse Brook—*stream* NJ-2
Grouse Butte—*summit* ID-8
Grouse Butte—*summit* (2) OR-9
Grouse Butte—*summit* WA-9
Grouse Camp—*locale* WA-9
Grouse Campground—*locale* ID-8
Grouse Canyon—*valley* (2) CA-9
Grouse Canyon—*valley* CO-8
Grouse Canyon—*valley* ID-8
Grouse Canyon—*valley* MT-8
Grouse Canyon—*valley* (2) NV-8
Grouse Canyon—*valley* NM-5
Grouse Canyon—*valley* (2) OR-9
Grouse Coulee—*valley* MT-8
*Grouse Creek* CO-8
*Grouse Creek* ID-8
*Grouse Creek* UT-8
**Grouse Creek**—*pop pl* UT-8
Grouse Creek—*stream* (4) AK-9
Grouse Creek—*stream* (15) CA-9
Grouse Creek—*stream* (9) CO-8
Grouse Creek—*stream* (32) ID-8
Grouse Creek—*stream* KS-7
Grouse Creek—*stream* MN-6
Grouse Creek—*stream* (11) MT-8
Grouse Creek—*stream* (3) NV-8
Grouse Creek—*stream* (11) OR-9
Grouse Creek—*stream* SD-7
Grouse Creek—*stream* TN-4
Grouse Creek—*stream* (2) UT-8
Grouse Creek—*stream* (9) WA-9
Grouse Creek—*stream* (6) WY-8
*Grouse Creek Butte* ID-8
Grouse Creek Campground—*locale* WA-9
Grouse Creek Cem—*cemetery* UT-8
Grouse Creek Club—*locale* KS-7
Grouse Creek Falls—*falls* ID-8
Grouse Creek Gap—*gap* OR-9
Grouse Creek Junction—*locale* UT-8
Grouse Creek Lake—*lake* CA-9
Grouse Creek Lake—*reservoir* ID-8
Grouse Creek Mine—*mine* CA-9
Grouse Creek Mtn—*summit* ID-8
Grouse Creek Mtns—*range* UT-8
Grouse Creek Oil Field—*oilfield* KS-7
Grouse Creek Peak—*summit* ID-8
Grouse Creek Point—*summit* ID-8
Grouse Creek Sch—*school* UT-8
*Grouse Creek School* ID-8
Grouse Creek School (historical)—*locale* ID-8
Grouse Creek Sinks—*basin* UT-8
Grouse Creek Spring—*spring* ID-8
Grouse Creek Township—*civil* SD-7
Grouse Creek Tractor Trail—*trail* CA-9
Grouse Creek Tractor Way—*trail* CA-9
Grouse Creek Trail—*trail* CA-9
Grouse Creek Trail—*trail* ID-8
Grouse Creek Valley—*valley* UT-8
Grouse Draw—*valley* (4) WY-8
Grouse Flat—*flat* (2) OR-9
Grouse Flat—*flat* WA-9
Grouse Flats—*flat* WA-9
Grouse Flat Spring—*spring* UT-8
Grouse Gulch—*valley* AK-9
Grouse Gulch—*valley* CO-8
Grouse Gulch—*valley* (3) ID-8
Grouse Gulch—*valley* (2) MT-8
Grouse Gulch—*valley* NM-5
Grouse Gulch—*valley* OR-9
Grouse Gulch—*valley* WA-9
Grouse Gulch Cave—*cave* MT-8
Grouse Hall Pond—*reservoir* PA-2
Grousehaven Lake—*lake* MI-6
Grouse Heaven—*flat* WA-9
Grouse Hill—*summit* CA-9
Grouse Hill—*summit* MT-8
Grouse Hill—*summit* OR-9
Grouse (historical)—*locale* NV-8
Grouse Hollow—*valley* CA-9
Grouse Hollow—*valley* CO-8
Grouse Hollow—*valley* MT-8
Grouse Hollow—*valley* UT-8
Grouse Hollow—*valley* WA-9
Grouse Hollow Creek—*stream* CA-9
*Grouse Island* SD-7
Grouse Knob—*summit* OR-9
Grouse Knob—*summit* WA-9
Grouse Knoll—*summit* ID-8
Grouse Lake—*lake* AK-9
Grouse Lake—*lake* (7) CA-9
Grouse Lake—*lake* CO-8
Grouse Lake—*lake* (2) ID-8
Grouse Lake—*lake* MN-6
Grouse Lake—*lake* (2) MT-8
Grouse Lake—*lake* OR-9
Grouse Lake—*lake* WA-9
Grouse Lake—*lake* WI-6
Grouse Lake—*lake* WY-8
Grouse Lakes—*lake* CA-9
Grouse Lakes—*lake* ID-8
Grouse Lakes—*lake* MT-8
**Grouseland**—*pop pl* IN-6
Grouselands—*hist pl* VT-1
Grouse Meadow—*flat* (5) CA-9
Grouse Meadows—*flat* (2) CA-9
Grouse Mesa—*summit* NM-5
Grouse Mine—*mine* MT-8
*Grouse Mountain* MT-8
Grouse Mountain Campground—*locale* WA-9
Grouse Mountain Falls—*falls* OR-9
Grouse Mountain Mine—*mine* MT-8
Grouse Mountain Point—*cape* ID-8
Grouse Mountain Spring—*spring* WA-9
Grouse Mountain Trail—*trail* ID-8
Grouse Mountain Trail—*trail* MT-8
*Grouse Mtn* WA-9
Grouse Mtn—*summit* (5) CA-9
Grouse Mtn—*summit* (7) CO-8
Grouse Mtn—*summit* (3) ID-8
Grouse Mtn—*summit* (4) MT-8
Grouse Mtn—*summit* NM-5
Grouse Mtn—*summit* (3) OR-9
Grouse Mtn—*summit* (3) WA-9
Grouse Mtn—*summit* (2) WY-8
Grouse Peak—*summit* AK-9
Grouse Peak—*summit* CA-9
Grouse Peak—*summit* ID-8
Grouse Peak—*summit* UT-8
Grouse Point—*cape* CA-9
Grouse Point—*cliff* CO-8
Grouse Point—*summit* OR-9
Grouse Prairie—*flat* CA-9
Grouse Prairie—*flat* OR-9
*Grouse Ridge* WA-9
Grouse Ridge—*ridge* (4) CA-9
Grouse Ridge—*ridge* (2) ID-8
Grouse Ridge—*ridge* (2) MT-8
Grouse Ridge—*ridge* OR-9
Grouse Ridge—*ridge* (5) WA-9
Grouse Ridge Lake—*reservoir* IN-6
Grouse Ridge Lake Dam—*dam* IN-6
Grouse Ridge Public Fishing Area—*park* IN-6
*Grouse Ridge State Fishing Area* IN-6
Grouse Ridge Trail—*trail* CA-9
Grouse Rincon—*valley* CO-8
Grouse Rsvr—*reservoir* CO-8
Grouse Run—*stream* WV-2
Grouse Sch—*school* ID-8
Grouse Sch—*school* OH-6
Grouse Spring—*spring* (9) CA-9
Grouse Spring—*spring* (3) CO-8
Grouse Spring—*spring* (2) ID-8
Grouse Spring—*spring* NV-8
Grouse Spring—*spring* (6) OR-9
Grouse Spring—*spring* UT-8
Grouse Spring—*spring* WA-9
Grouse Spring Creek—*stream* CO-8
Grouse Springs—*spring* WA-9
Grouse Spring Trail (historical)—*trail* OR-9
Grouse Valley—*basin* (2) CA-9
Grouslous Mtn—*summit* OR-9
**Grout**—*pop pl* VT-1
Grout Athletic Field—*park* NY-2
Grout Bay—*bay* CA-9
Grout Brook—*stream* NY-2
Grout Cem—*cemetery* MI-6
Grout Creek—*stream* CA-9
Grout Ditch—*canal* OR-9
Grout Ditch—*canal* WY-8
Grout Hill—*summit* NH-1
Grout Hill—*summit* VT-1
**Grout Mill**—*pop pl* NY-2
Grout Mtn—*summit* VT-1
Grout Oil Field—*other* MI-6
Grout Park Sch—*school* NY-2
Grout Pond—*lake* VT-1
Grout Sch—*school* IL-6
Grout Sch—*school* IA-7
Grout Sch—*school* OR-9
Grout Sch—*school* VT-1
Grout Station—*locale* NH-1
**Grout (Township of)**—*pop pl* MI-6
Grovania—*locale* PA-2
**Grovania**—*pop pl* GA-3
**Grovania**—*pop pl* PA-2
*Grove* IN-6
*Grove* OH-6
Grove—*fmr MCD* NE-7
Grove—*locale* CA-9
Grove—*locale* (2) KS-7
Grove—*locale* KY-4
Grove—*locale* LA-4
Grove—*locale* ME-1
Grove—*locale* (2) MD-2
Grove—*locale* PA-2
Grove—*locale* VT-1
Grove—*locale* WV-2
**Grove**—*pop pl* NJ-2
**Grove**—*pop pl* OK-5
**Grove**—*pop pl* OR-9
**Grove**—*pop pl* (2) TN-4
**Grove**—*pop pl* VA-3
Grove, Benjamin, House—*hist pl* KY-4
Grove, E. W. Henry County HS—*hist pl* TN-4
Grove, John A., House—*hist pl* IN-6
Grove, Lake—*lake* FL-3
Grove, The—*area* MS-4
Grove, The—*hist pl* FL-3
Grove, The—*hist pl* MI-6
Grove, The—*hist pl* NY-2
Grove, The—*hist pl* NC-3
Grove, The—*locale* MO-7
**Grove, The**—*pop pl* CA-9
**Grove, The**—*pop pl* TX-5
Grove, The—*woods* NY-2
**Grove Addition (subdivision)**—*pop pl* UT-8
Grove AME Ch—*church* MS-4
Groveania Ch—*church* OK-5
Grove Baptist Ch—*church* MS-4
Grove Beach—*beach* CT-1
**Grove Beach**—*pop pl* CT-1
Grove Beach Point—*cape* CT-1
**Grove Beach Point**—*pop pl* CT-1
**Grove Beach Terrace**—*pop pl* CT-1
Grove Bible Ch—*church* MI-6
Grove Branch—*stream* IL-6
Grove Branch—*stream* KY-4
Grove Branch—*stream* MO-7
Grove Branch Ditch—*canal* IA-7
Grove Brook—*stream* IN-6
Grove Brook—*stream* NH-1
Grove Brook—*stream* NY-2
Grove (CCD)—*cens area* OK-5
Grove Cem—*cemetery* AL-4
Grove Cem—*cemetery* (3) CT-1
Grove Cem—*cemetery* IN-6
Grove Cem—*cemetery* (2) IA-7
Grove Cem—*cemetery* (2) ME-1
Grove Cem—*cemetery* MD-2
Grove Cem—*cemetery* MA-1
Grove Cem—*cemetery* MN-6
Grove Cem—*cemetery* MO-7
Grove Cem—*cemetery* (2) NE-7
Grove Cem—*cemetery* NH-1
Grove Cem—*cemetery* (6) NY-2
Grove Cem—*cemetery* (3) OH-6
Grove Cem—*cemetery* SC-3
Grove Cem—*cemetery* (4) TN-4
Grove Cem—*cemetery* (2) VT-1
Grove Cem—*cemetery* WV-2
Grove Cem—*cemetery* WI-6
Grove Center—*locale* TN-4
**Grove Center**—*pop pl* KS-7
**Grove Center**—*pop pl* KY-4
Grove Center—*uninc pl* KS-7
Grove Center Cem—*cemetery* IA-7
Grove Center Ch—*church* IA-7
Grovecenter Sch—*school* CA-9
*Grove Ch* AL-4
Grove Ch—*church* AL-4
Grove Ch—*church* AR-4
Grove Ch—*church* (2) GA-3
Grove Ch—*church* (2) KY-4
Grove Ch—*church* MN-6
Grove Ch—*church* NY-2
Grove Ch—*church* NC-3
Grove Ch—*church* (3) OH-6
Grove Ch—*church* PA-2
Grove Ch—*church* TN-4
Grove Ch—*church* (3) VA-3
Grove Chapel—*church* IN-6
Grove Chapel—*church* NJ-2
Grove Chapel—*church* PA-2
**Grove Chapel**—*pop pl* PA-2
Grove Chapel—*uninc pl* NJ-2
Grove Chapel Ch—*church* GA-3
Grove Church, The—*church* AL-4
Grove Church Cem—*cemetery* NJ-2
Grove Churches—*church* VA-3
Grove City—*locale* IA-7
**Grove City**—*pop pl* FL-3
**Grove City**—*pop pl* IL-6
**Grove City**—*pop pl* MN-6
**Grove City**—*pop pl* OH-6
**Grove City**—*pop pl* PA-2
Grove City Airp—*airport* PA-2
Grove City Area HS—*school* PA-2
Grove City Area JHS—*school* PA-2
Grove City Borough—*civil* PA-2
Grove City Cem—*cemetery* ID-8
Grove City Coll—*school* PA-2
Grove City Country Club—*other* PA-2
**Grove City Country Club**—*pop pl* OH-6
Grove City Landing Area—*airport* PA-2
Grove City-Rotonda (CCD)—*cens area* FL-3
Grove Cleveland HS—*school* NY-2
Grove Club Lake—*reservoir* TX-5
**Grove Controls**—*pop pl* TX-5
Grove Cottage Post Office (historical)—*building* AL-4
*Grove Creek* AZ-5
*Grove Creek* ID-8
Grove Creek—*stream* CO-8
Grove Creek—*stream* (2) GA-3
Grove Creek—*stream* (2) ID-8
Grove Creek—*stream* (5) IL-6
Grove Creek—*stream* (2) IN-6
Grove Creek—*stream* IA-7
Grove Creek—*stream* (2) MD-2
Grove Creek—*stream* MN-6
Grove Creek—*stream* (2) MO-7
Grove Creek—*stream* (3) MT-8
Grove Creek—*stream* NC-3
Grove Creek—*stream* (2) OR-9
Grove Creek—*stream* (2) SC-3
Grove Creek—*stream* (2) TX-5
Grove Creek—*stream* UT-8
Grove Creek—*stream* VA-3
Grove Creek—*stream* WY-8
Grove Creek Canal—*canal* MT-8
Grove Creek Cem—*cemetery* IA-7
Grove Creek Debris Basin Dam—*dam* UT-8
Grove Creek Debris Basin Rsvr—*reservoir* UT-8
Grove Creek Mine—*mine* MT-8
Grove Creek Village—*uninc pl* SC-3
Grovecrest Sch—*school* UT-8
Grovedale Cem—*cemetery* MO-7
Grovedale Sch—*school* CA-9
Grove Draw—*valley* WY-8
Grove Drive Park—*park* PA-2
Grove Farm—*hist pl* HI-9
Grove Farm (Boundary Increase)—*hist pl* HI-9
Grove Farm Company Locomotives—*hist pl* HI-9
Grove Field Airp—*airport* WA-9
Grove Gate—*locale* CA-9
Grove Gate Shop Ctr—*locale* FL-3
Grove Gulch—*valley* MT-8
Grove Gulch—*valley* OR-9
Grove Gulch Creek—*stream* MT-8
**Grove Hall**—*pop pl* SC-3
**Grove Hall (subdivision)**—*pop pl* MA-1
Grove Haven Ch—*church* TX-5
**Grove Highlands**—*pop pl* CA-9
*Grove Hill* AL-4
Grove Hill—*locale* IA-7
Grove Hill—*locale* VA-3
**Grove Hill**—*pop pl* AL-4
**Grove Hill**—*pop pl* MD-2
**Grove Hill**—*pop pl* NC-3
Grove Hill—*summit* AL-4
Grove Hill—*summit* CA-9
Grove Hill—*summit* ME-1
Grove Hill—*summit* (2) PA-2
Grove Hill Acad—*school* AL-4
*Grove Hill Baptist Ch* TN-4
Grove Hill Baptist Ch—*church* AL-4
Grove Hill (CCD)—*cens area* AL-4
Grove Hill Cem—*cemetery* CT-1
Grove Hill Cem—*cemetery* IA-7
Grove Hill Cem—*cemetery* KY-4
Grove Hill Cem—*cemetery* MA-1
Grove Hill Cem—*cemetery* NE-7
Grove Hill Cem—*cemetery* NH-1
Grove Hill Cem—*cemetery* OH-6
Grove Hill Cem—*cemetery* (2) PA-2
Grove Hill Cem—*cemetery* SC-3
Grove Hill Cem—*cemetery* TN-4
Grove Hill Cemetery Chapel—*hist pl* KY-4
Grove Hill Ch—*church* (3) AL-4
Grove Hill Ch—*church* NC-3
Grove Hill Ch—*church* (2) TN-4
Grove Hill Ch—*church* TX-5
Grove Hill Ch (abandoned)—*church* LA-4
Grove Hill Ch (historical)—*church* (2) AL-4
Grove Hill Ch (historical)—*church* MO-7
Grove Hill Division—*civil* AL-4
Grove Hill Elem Sch—*school* AL-4
Grove Hill (historical P.O.)—*locale* IA-7
Grove Hill Landing—*locale* VA-3
Grove Hill Lookout Tower—*locale* AL-4
Grove Hill Mansion—*hist pl* MA-1
Grove Hill Memorial Hosp—*hospital* AL-4
Grove Hill Memorial Park—*cemetery* TX-5
Grove Hill Municipal Airp—*airport* AL-4
*Grove Hill Municipal Hospital* AL-4
Grove Hill New Mission Church—*hist pl* MI-6
Grove Hill Sch—*school* IL-6
Grove Hill Sch—*school* PA-2
Grove Hill Sch (historical)—*school* MO-7
**Grove Hill (subdivision)**—*pop pl* AL-4
Grove Hill United Methodist Ch—*church* AL-4
Grove Hist Dist—*hist pl* PA-2

Grove (historical P.O.)—*locale* IA-7
Grove Hollow—*valley* KY-4
Grove Hollow—*valley* (2) VA-3
Grove Holman Park—*park* MI-6
Grove HS—*school* IA-7
Grove Island Cem—*cemetery* TX-5
Grove Island Creek—*stream* TX-5
Grove Isle—*island* FL-3
*Grove Junior High School* TN-4
*Grove Lake* MI-6
Grove Lake—*lake* (2) MN-6
**Grove Lake**—*pop pl* MN-6
Grove Lake—*reservoir* NE-7
Grove Lake Cem—*cemetery* MN-6
Grove Lake Ch—*church* (2) MN-6
Grove Lakes—*lake* TX-5
**Grove Lake (Township of)**—*pop pl* MN-6
*Groveland* NY-2
Groveland—*locale* KS-7
Groveland—*locale* MT-8
**Groveland**—*pop pl* CA-9
**Groveland**—*pop pl* FL-3
**Groveland**—*pop pl* (2) GA-3
**Groveland**—*pop pl* ID-8
**Groveland**—*pop pl* IL-6
**Groveland**—*pop pl* IN-6
**Groveland**—*pop pl* MA-1
**Groveland**—*pop pl* MN-6
**Groveland**—*pop pl* NY-2
**Groveland**—*pop pl* VA-3
Groveland Acad—*school* (2) FL-3
Groveland (CCD)—*cens area* CA-9
Groveland Cem—*cemetery* ID-8
Groveland Cem—*cemetery* IN-6
Groveland Cem—*cemetery* KS-7
Groveland Cem—*cemetery* MA-1
**Groveland Corners**—*pop pl* MI-6
**Groveland Corners**—*pop pl* NY-2
Groveland Elem Sch—*school* FL-3
Groveland (historical)—*locale* SD-7
**Groveland (historical)**—*pop pl* IA-7
Groveland (historical P.O.)—*locale* IA-7
Groveland HS—*school* FL-3
*Grove Landing Ch* AL-4
Groveland-Mascotte (CCD)—*cens area* FL-3
Groveland Mills—*locale* MI-6
Groveland Mine—*mine* MI-6
Groveland MS—*school* FL-3
Groveland Northeast Oil Field—*oilfield* KS-7
Groveland Park—*uninc pl* GA-3
Groveland Park Sch—*school* MN-6
Groveland Ranger Station—*locale* CA-9
Groveland Sch—*school* MA-1
Groveland Sch—*school* PA-2
*Groveland Siding* MT-8
Groveland South Oil Field—*oilfield* KS-7
*Groveland Station* NY-2
Groveland Tower—*tower* FL-3
**Groveland (Town of)**—*pop pl* MA-1
**Groveland (Town of)**—*pop pl* NY-2
**Groveland Township**—*pop pl* KS-7
**Groveland Township**—*pop pl* SD-7
**Groveland (Township of)**—*pop pl* (2) IL-6
**Groveland (Township of)**—*pop pl* MI-6
Grovelawn Cem—*cemetery* IN-6
Grove Level—*locale* GA-3
Grove Level Ch—*church* (2) GA-3
Grove-Linden-St. John's Hist Dist—*hist pl* NY-2
Grove Mansion—*hist pl* PA-2
Grove Meadow—*flat* OR-9
Grove Mill—*locale* PA-2
Grove Mill (historical)—*locale* PA-2
Grove Mini Park—*park* FL-3
Grove Missionary Ch—*church* TX-5
*Grovemon* NC-3
*Grovemont* NC-3
**Grovemont**—*pop pl* NC-3
Grove Mount Cem—*cemetery* NY-2
**Grovena Township**—*pop pl* SD-7
Grovenburg Ch—*church* MI-6
Grovenburg Drain—*canal* MI-6
Grove Neck—*cape* MD-2
**Grovenor Corners**—*pop pl* NY-2
*Groveoak* AL-4
**Grove Oak**—*pop pl* AL-4
**Groveoak**—*pop pl* AL-4
Grove Oak Sch—*school* AL-4
Grove of the Aspen Giants Scenic
Area—*locale* UT-8
Grove Of The Patriarchs—*woods* WA-9
Grove Park—*park* GA-3
Grove Park—*park* MI-6
Grove Park—*park* NJ-2
Grove Park—*park* NY-2
Grove Park—*park* NC-3
Grove Park—*park* PA-2
**Grove Park**—*pop pl* (2) AL-4
**Grove Park**—*pop pl* (2) FL-3
**Grove Park**—*pop pl* (3) GA-3
**Grove Park**—*pop pl* NC-3
**Grove Park**—*pop pl* VA-3
Grove Park—*uninc pl* (2) FL-3
Grove Park Ch—*church* FL-3
Grove Park Christian Ch—*church* FL-3
Grove Park Elem Sch—*school* (2) FL-3
**Grove Park Estates**—*pop pl* FL-3
Grove Park Inn—*hist pl* NC-3
Grove Park Sch—*school* NC-3
Grove Park Sch—*school* VA-3
Grove Park Shop Ctr—*locale* FL-3
Grove Park Shop Ctr—*locale* NC-3
**Grove Park (subdivision)**—*pop pl* AL-4
**Grove Park (subdivision)**—*pop pl* MS-4
**Grove Park (subdivision)**—*pop pl* (3) NC-3
**Grove Park (Township of)**—*pop pl* MN-6
Grove Park Vista—*uninc pl* FL-3
**Grove Place**—*pop pl* VI-3
Grove Place Cem—*cemetery* NY-2
Grove Place Hist Dist—*hist pl* NY-2
Grove Plantation—*hist pl* SC-3
Grove Point—*cape* CT-1
Grove Point—*cape* MD-2
Grove Point—*cape* NY-2
Grove Point—*cape* RI-1
Grove Point—*cape* TN-4
Grove Point—*locale* GA-3
Grove Point Rock—*pillar* RI-1
Grove Pond—*lake* MA-1
Grove Pond—*swamp* TX-5
Groveport—*locale* OH-6
**Groveport**—*pop pl* OH-6
Groveport Log Houses—*hist pl* OH-6
Groveport Town Hall Historic
Group—*hist pl* OH-6
Grove Post Office (historical)—*building* TN-4
Grove Prairie Cem—*cemetery* WI-6
Grove Prairie Sch—*school* WI-6
*Grover* AL-4
*Grover* IN-6
Grover—*hist pl* IN-6
Grover—*locale* AL-4
Grover—*locale* KS-7
Grover—*locale* SD-7
Grover—*locale* UT-8
**Grover**—*pop pl* CO-8
**Grover**—*pop pl* MO-7
**Grover**—*pop pl* NE-7
**Grover**—*pop pl* NY-2
**Grover**—*pop pl* NC-3
**Grover**—*pop pl* PA-2
**Grover**—*pop pl* SC-3
**Grover**—*pop pl* WY-8
Grover, Emery, Bldg—*hist pl* MA-1
Grover Anton Spring—*spring* CA-9
Grover Brook—*stream* CT-1
Grover Brook—*stream* ME-1
Grover Brown Lake Dam—*dam* MS-4
Grover Canyon—*valley* AZ-5
Grover Canyon—*valley* ID-8
Grover Canyon—*valley* NV-8
*Grover C Barton Subdivision* UT-8
Grover Cem—*cemetery* ME-1
Grover Cem—*cemetery* NC-3
Grover Cem—*cemetery* TX-5
Grover Cem—*cemetery* WY-8
**Grover City**—*pop pl* CA-9
**Grover City (Grover)**—*pop pl* CA-9
Grover Cleveland House Site—*locale* MA-1
Grover Cleveland Park—*park* NJ-2
Grover Cleveland Park—*park* NY-2
Grover Cleveland Sch—*school* CA-9
Grover Cleveland Sch—*school* NJ-2
**Grover Cleveland Terrace**—*pop pl* NY-2
*Grover Cliff* MA-1
Grover Creek—*gut* GA-3
Grover Creek—*stream* MD-2
Grover Creek—*stream* WY-8
Grover Ditch—*canal* IN-6
Grover Draw—*valley* WY-8
Grover Elem Sch—*school* NC-3
**Grover Estates Subdivision**—*pop pl* UT-8
Grover Grimes Catfish Ponds Dam—*dam* MS-4
*Grover (Grover City)* CA-9
Grover Gulch—*valley* CA-9
Grover Heights Sch—*school* CA-9
*Grover Hill* CT-1
**Grover Hill**—*pop pl* CT-1
**Grover Hill**—*pop pl* OH-6
Grover Hill—*summit* ME-1
Grover Hill Cem—*cemetery* PA-2
**Grover Hills**—*pop pl* NY-2
Grover Hollow—*valley* PA-2
Grover Hollow—*valley* TN-4
Grover Hollow—*valley* UT-8
Grover Hot Springs State Park—*park* CA-9
Grove Ridge—*ridge* KY-4
Grove Ridge Ch—*church* KY-4
Grover Island—*island* GA-3
Grove River—*stream* GA-3
Grover Lake—*lake* ME-1
Grover Lake Rsvr—*reservoir* ID-8
Grover Lewis Mine (Underground)—*mine* TN-4
*Grover Memorial Church* NC-3
*Grover Mill* NJ-2
**Grovernor Corners**—*pop pl* NY-2
Grover Park—*park* MO-7
Grover Park—*park* WY-8
Grover Point—*summit* AZ-5
Grover Point Well—*well* NV-8
Grover Post Office (historical)—*building* AL-4
Grover Rsvr—*reservoir* OR-9
Grover Rsvr—*reservoir* WY-8
Grovers Bend—*bend* TX-5
Grover Sch—*hist pl* UT-8
Grover Sch Number 2—*school* (2) ND-7
Grovers Cliff—*cliff* MA-1
Grovers Creek—*stream* KY-4
Grovers Creek—*stream* MD-2
*Grover's Lake* IA-7
Grovers Lake—*lake* IA-7
Grovers Lake—*lake* MN-6
**Grovers Mill**—*pop pl* NJ-2
Grovers Mill Dam—*dam* NJ-2
Grovers Mill (historical)—*locale* TN-4
Grovers Mill Pond—*reservoir* NJ-2
*Grovers Mills* NJ-2
**Grovers Mills**—*pop pl* NJ-2
*Grovers Point* FL-3
Grover Spring—*spring* AZ-5
Grover Spring Canyon—*valley* AZ-5
*Groverton* TX-5
**Grovertown**—*pop pl* IN-6
**Grover (Town of)**—*pop pl* (2) WI-6
Grover Township—*civil* MO-7
**Grover Township**—*pop pl* ND-7
Grover (Township of)—*fmr MCD* (2) AR-4
**Grover (Township of)**—*pop pl* IL-6
Grove Run—*locale* PA-2
Grove Run—*stream* (2) IN-6
Grove Run—*stream* OH-6
Grove Run—*stream* (4) PA-2
Grove Run Spring—*spring* PA-2
Grove Run Trail—*trail* PA-2
Groverware Spring Hollow—*valley* AR-4
Grover Wash—*valley* UT-8
Grover Wash Rsvr—*reservoir* UT-8
Grover Well—*well* NM-5
Grover Willis Lake Dam—*dam* MS-4
*Groves* OH-6
Groves—*locale* WV-2
**Groves**—*pop pl* NC-3
**Groves**—*pop pl* TX-5
**Groves, The**—*pop pl* SC-3
Groves Branch—*stream* TN-4
Groves Branch—*stream* TX-5
Groves Branch Lateral—*canal* ID-8
Groves-Cabell House—*hist pl* KY-4
*Groves Cem* TN-4
Groves Cem—*cemetery* AR-4
Groves Cem—*cemetery* IL-6
Groves Cem—*cemetery* (2) IN-6
Groves Cem—*cemetery* IA-7
Groves Cem—*cemetery* KY-4
Groves Cem—*cemetery* MO-7
Groves Cem—*cemetery* OH-6
Groves Cem—*cemetery* (3) TN-4
Groves Cem—*cemetery* TX-5
Groves Cem—*cemetery* (2) WV-2
Grove Sch—*school* AL-4
Grove Sch—*school* (2) CA-9
Grove Sch—*school* CT-1
Grove Sch—*school* (8) IL-6
Grove Sch—*school* IA-7
Grove Sch—*school* KY-4
Grove Sch—*school* MD-2
Grove Sch—*school* (2) MN-6
Grove Sch—*school* MS-4
Grove Sch—*school* ND-7
Grove Sch—*school* OK-5
Grove Sch—*school* SC-3
Grove Sch—*school* SD-7
Grove Sch—*school* TN-4
Grove Sch—*school* (2) WI-6
Grove Sch (abandoned)—*school* PA-2
Groves Chapel—*church* (2) KY-4
Groves Chapel—*church* NC-3
Groves Chapel Cem—*cemetery* KY-4
Groves Chapel Sch—*school* KY-4
Grove Sch (historical)—*school* TN-4
*Groves Creek* IN-6
Groves Creek—*stream* GA-3
Groves Creek—*stream* KY-4
Groves Creek—*stream* NY-2
Groves Creek—*stream* TX-5
Groves Creek—*stream* UT-8
Groves Creek—*stream* WV-2
Groves Creek Ch—*church* WV-2
Grove-Sharpe Cem—*cemetery* GA-3
Groves Hill—*summit* IN-6
**Groves (historical)**—*pop pl* TN-4
Grove Shop Ctr—*locale* TN-4
Groves HS—*school* MI-6
Groveside Sch—*school* NY-2
Groves Lake—*lake* NE-7
Groves Lake—*lake* WA-9
Groves Lake—*reservoir* NV-8
Groves Lake—*reservoir* NC-3
Grove Slough—*stream* WA-9
*Groves Meadow* CA-9
Groves Memorial Ch—*church* VA-3
Groves Park, The—*park* AZ-5
Groves Prairie—*area* CA-9
Groves Prairie Creek—*stream* CA-9
*Grove Spring* MO-7
*Grove Spring* OR-9
**Grovespring**—*pop pl* MO-7
Grove Spring—*spring* NV-8
Grove Spring—*spring* OR-9
Grove Spring—*spring* WY-8
*Grove Spring Branch* TX-5
*Grove Spring Cemetery* TN-4
**Grove Spring (historical)**—*pop pl* OR-9
*Grove Springs* MO-7
**Grove Springs**—*pop pl* NY-2
Grove Springs Cem—*cemetery* TN-4
Grove Springs Ch (historical)—*church* TN-4
Groves Ridge—*ridge* OH-6
Groves Run—*stream* WV-2
Groves Sch (historical)—*school* PA-2
Groves Shop Ctr, The—*locale* AZ-5
Groves Spring Branch—*stream* WV-2
Groves Stadium—*park* NC-3
*Groves Subdivision* UT-8
**Groves Subdivision, The**—*pop pl* UT-8
Grove Station Ch—*church* SC-3
**Grovestone**—*pop pl* NC-3
*Grovestown* IN-6
Grove Street—*uninc pl* NJ-2
Grove Street Cem—*cemetery* CT-1
*Grove Street Elem Sch* MS-4
Grove Street Elem Sch—*hist pl* RI-1
Grove Street Elem Sch—*school* PA-2
Grove Street Hist Dist—*hist pl* WI-6
Grove Street Houses—*hist pl* MS-4
Grove Street Pier—*locale* CA-9
Grove Street Sch—*school* MS-4
Grove Street Sch—*school* (2) NJ-2
Grove Street Station—*locale* NJ-2
Groves Valley Plantation
(historical)—*locale* MS-4
Groves Windmill—*locale* TX-5
Grove Tank—*reservoir* AZ-5
*Groveton* MS-4
Groveton—*locale* MI-6
Groveton—*locale* VA-3
**Groveton**—*pop pl* NH-1
**Groveton**—*pop pl* PA-2
**Groveton**—*pop pl* TX-5
**Groveton**—*pop pl* VA-3
Groveton (CCD)—*cens area* TX-5
Groveton Ch—*church* MS-4
Groveton Confederate Cem—*cemetery* VA-3
**Groveton Gardens**—*pop pl* VA-3
**Groveton Heights**—*pop pl* VA-3
Groveton HS—*school* VA-3
Groveton Sch—*school* VA-3
**Grovetown**—*pop pl* GA-3
**Grove (Town of)**—*pop pl* NY-2
Grove Township—*fmr MCD* (8) IA-7
**Grove Township**—*pop pl* (2) KS-7
Grove Township Cem—*cemetery* IA-7
Grove (Township of)—*fmr MCD* AR-4
Grove (Township of)—*fmr MCD* NC-3
**Grove (Township of)**—*pop pl* IL-6
**Grove (Township of)**—*pop pl* MN-6
**Grove (Township of)**—*pop pl* PA-2
*Grove Union Ch* MS-4
Grove Valley—*basin* NE-7
**Grove View Acres
(subdivision)**—*pop pl* AL-4
**Groveville**—*pop pl* ME-1
**Groveville**—*pop pl* NJ-2
**Groveville**—*pop pl* NY-2
Grovewood—*hist pl* SC-3
Grovewood Post Office
(historical)—*building* TN-4
**Grovewood (subdivision)**—*pop pl* AL-4
**Grovont**—*pop pl* WY-8
Grow—*locale* TX-5
Grow Block—*hist pl* MI-6
Grow Cem—*cemetery* NY-2
Growcock Branch—*stream* IN-6
Grow Creek—*stream* MI-6
Growden Cem—*cemetery* PA-2
Growden Guard Station—*locale* WA-9
Growden Memorial Park—*park* AK-9
Growden Run—*stream* PA-2
Grower Hot Spring—*spring* CA-9
*Growers Crossroads* NC-3
**Growers Crossroads**—*pop pl* NC-3
Growey Creek—*stream* OR-9
Growing House Sch—*school* FL-3
*Growing Island* FM-9
Growing Valley Cem—*cemetery* LA-4
Growing Valley Ch—*church* LA-4
Growing Valley Sch—*school* LA-4
Grow Lake—*swamp* SD-7
Growler—*locale* AZ-5
Growler Bay—*bay* AK-9
Growler Canyon—*valley* AZ-5
*Growler Creek* AZ-5
Growler Mine Area—*hist pl* AZ-5
*Growler Mountains* AZ-5
Growler Mountains—*summit* AZ-5
Growler Pass—*gap* AZ-5
Growler Peak—*summit* AZ-5
Growler Rapids—*rapids* ID-8
Growler RR Station—*building* AZ-5
Growler Trail—*trail* CA-9
Growler Valley—*valley* AZ-5
*Growler Wash* AZ-5
Growler Wash—*stream* AZ-5
*Growl Hill* MA-1
Grow Ranch—*locale* NE-7
**Growstown**—*pop pl* ME-1
**Grow (Town of)**—*pop pl* WI-6
Grow (Township of)—*civ div* MN-6
*Grox School* TN-4
*Grozier* LA-4
G R Patterson Lake Dam—*dam* MS-4
G Rsvr—*reservoir* OR-9
Grubaugh Sch—*school* OH-6
Grubb—*locale* VA-3
Grubb, A., House—*hist pl* KY-4
Grubb, Conrad, Homestead—*hist pl* PA-2
Grubb, Jacob L., Store—*hist pl* TN-4
Grubb Bend—*bend* KY-4
Grubb Branch—*stream* (2) KY-4
Grubb Cem—*cemetery* NC-3
Grubb Cem—*cemetery* (3) VA-3
Grubb Creek—*stream* TN-4
Grubb Creek—*stream* TX-5
Grubbe—*locale* TX-5
Grubbes Creek—*stream* CA-9
Grubb Flat—*flat* NV-8
Grubb Gulch—*valley* MT-8
Grubb Hill—*summit* MS-4
Grubb Hill—*summit* WI-6
Grubb Hill Cem—*cemetery* MS-4
Grubb Hill Ch (historical)—*church* MS-4
Grubb Hollow—*valley* IL-6
Grubb Hollow—*valley* KY-4
Grubb Hollow—*valley* PA-2
Grubb Hollow Branch Settling
Basin—*basin* IL-6
Grubbing Hoe Ranch—*locale* WY-8
Grubb Islands—*island* TN-4
Grubb Lake—*lake* MI-6
Grubb Lake—*lake* MN-6
Grubb Lake—*lake* ND-7
*Grubbler Creek* MO-7
Grubb Mtn—*summit* MT-8
Grubb Mtn—*summit* OK-5
Grub Box Gap—*gap* OR-9
Grubb Run—*stream* IA-7
*Grubbs* DE-2
Grubbs—*locale* GA-3
**Grubbs**—*pop pl* AR-4
*Grubbsberg* PA-2
Grubbs Branch—*stream* TX-5
Grubbs Canyon—*valley* NV-8
Grubbs Cem—*cemetery* IN-6
Grubbs Cem—*cemetery* MS-4
Grubbs Cem—*cemetery* TN-4
Grubbs Ch—*church* PA-2
Grubb Sch—*school* MI-6
Grubb Sch (abandoned)—*school* PA-2
Grubbs Chapel—*church* VA-3
*Grubbs Church* AL-4
Grubbs Corner—*locale* DE-2
**Grubbs Corner**—*pop pl* WV-2
**Grubbs Corner (subdivision)**—*pop pl* DE-2
Grubbs Cove—*bay* WA-9
Grubbs Ditch—*canal* IN-6
Grubbs Hollow—*valley* KY-4
Grubbs Knob—*summit* VA-3
Grubbs Lake—*reservoir* NC-3
Grubbs Lake Dam—*dam* NC-3
Grubbs Landing—*locale* DE-2
Grubbs Mission—*church* SC-3
**Grubb Springs**—*pop pl* AR-4
*Grubb Springs Church* MS-4
**Grubb Springs (historical)**—*pop pl* MS-4
**Grubbs Store**—*pop pl* VA-3
Grubbs (Township of)—*fmr MCD* AR-4
Grubby Creek—*stream* GA-3
Grubby Neck Branch—*stream* DE-2
Grub Canyon—*valley* WA-9
Grub Creek—*stream* (2) CA-9
Grub Creek—*stream* MI-6
Grub Creek—*stream* OR-9
Grub Drain—*canal* MI-6
Grub Draw—*valley* WY-8
Grube Airp—*airport* PA-2
Grube Dam—*dam* ND-7
Grube Ditch—*canal* IN-6
Grube Hill—*summit* MI-6
Grubel Spring—*spring* WA-9
Gruber Hill—*summit* OK-5
Gruber Oil Field—*oilfield* TX-5
*Grubers Creek* CO-8
Grubers Lake—*reservoir* PA-2
Grubers Lake Dam—*dam* PA-2
Gruber State Game Mngmt Area—*park* OK-5
*Grubertown* PA-2
Gruber Wagon Works—*hist pl* PA-2
Grube Sch (historical)—*school* PA-2
*Grub Flat* NV-8
Grub Flat Rsvr—*reservoir* CA-9
Grub Gulch—*basin* CA-9
Grub Gulch—*bay* AK-9
Grub Gulch—*valley* AK-9
Grub Gulch—*valley* (3) CA-9
Grub Gulch—*valley* NV-8
Grub Gulch—*valley* OR-9
Grub Hill—*locale* TX-5
Grub Hill Ch—*church* VA-3
Grub Hoe Lake—*lake* WI-6
Grub Hollow—*valley* MO-7
Grub Hollow—*valley* WV-2
Grub Hollow Creek—*stream* OR-9
Grubin Neck—*cape* MD-2
Grubisich Place—*locale* NM-5
Grub Lake—*lake* MN-6
Grubny Lake—*lake* NE-7
Grub Ridge Ch—*church* KY-4
*Grubs Berg* PA-2
Grubs Canyon—*valley* TX-5
Grubs Island—*island* TX-5
Grub Spring Rsvr—*reservoir* OR-9
Grub Springs Branch—*stream* MS-4
Grub Springs Ch—*church* MS-4
Grubstake Creek—*stream* (2) AK-9
Grubstake Gulch—*valley* (2) AK-9
Grubstake Gulch—*valley* ID-8
Grubstake Gulch—*valley* MT-8
Grubstake Lake—*lake* MN-6
Grubstake Mine—*mine* MT-8
Grubstake Mine—*mine* OR-9
Grubstake Mtn—*summit* MT-8
Grub Tank—*reservoir* NM-5
**Grubville**—*pop pl* MO-7
Grubville Sch—*school* MO-7
Grudge Ditch—*canal* LA-4
Grudge Ditch—*stream* TN-4
Grudging Cabin—*locale* NM-5
Grue, Bayou—*stream* LA-4
Grue Ch—*church* MN-6
Grue Ch—*church* ND-7
Gruel Ditch—*canal* MT-8
Gruells Bar—*bar* MT-8
Gruenau—*locale* TX-5
Gruendyke Mill Dam—*dam* NJ-2
**Gruene**—*pop pl* TX-5
Gruene Hist Dist—*hist pl* TX-5
Gruene Siding—*locale* TX-5
Gruenewald House—*hist pl* IN-6
Gruenhagen Bay—*bay* WI-6
Gruenhagen Flat—*flat* CA-9
Gruenheim Cem—*cemetery* KY-4
Gruenig Dam—*dam* SD-7
Gruenig Ranch—*locale* WY-8
Gruenwald Convent—*hist pl* OH-6
Gruenwalt Cem—*cemetery* PA-2
Grues, Coulee des —*stream* LA-4
Gruesbeck Drain—*canal* MI-6
Grueser Hollow—*valley* OH-6
*Grueti Cemetery* TN-4
Gruetli—*locale* TN-4
Gruetli Ch—*church* NE-7
Gruetli Ch—*church* TN-4
Gruetli Gas Field—*oilfield* TN-4
**Gruetli-Laager**—*pop pl* (2) TN-4
Gruetli-Laager City Hall—*building* TN-4
*Gruetli Post Office* TN-4
Gruetli Sch (historical)—*school* TN-4
Gruetli Station—*locale* TN-4
Gruetlli-Laager Post Office—*building* TN-4
Gruff Lake—*lake* CA-9
Grugan Hollow—*valley* PA-2
**Grugan (Township of)**—*pop pl* PA-2
Gruger Hollow Trail—*trail* PA-2
Grugin Cem—*cemetery* KY-4
Gruhlkey—*locale* TX-5
Gruhl State Wildlife Mngmt Area—*park* MN-6
*Gruise Creek* TN-4
*Gruiser Creek* MT-8
**Grulla (alternate name
LaGrulla)**—*pop pl* TX-5
Grulla Natl Wildlife Ref—*park* NM-5
*Grullo Bayou* TX-5
Gruman Creek—*stream* WI-6
Grumble Gulch—*valley* NM-5
Grumblethorpe—*hist pl* PA-2
Grumblethorpe Tenant House—*hist pl* PA-2
Grumble Wells—*well* AZ-5
Grumell Well—*well* AZ-5
**Grumman (Aircraft Factory)**—*pop pl* NY-2
Grumman Hill—*summit* CT-1
Grummett Creek—*stream* CA-9
*Grummis Creek* WV-2
Grummit Canyon Creek—*stream* SD-7
Grummit Canyon Creek—*stream* WY-8
Grummond Cem—*cemetery* MO-7
Grummond Highway—*channel* MI-6
Grump Pond—*swamp* FL-3
Grumpton Hills—*summit* AL-4
Grumpy Ledge—*bar* ME-1
Grunard Lake—*lake* MN-6
Grunch Rapids, The—*rapids* TN-4
Grun Creek (historical)—*stream* PA-2
Grundell Creek—*stream* CO-8
Grunder Cabin and Outbuildings—*hist pl* ID-8
Grunder Hill—*summit* NY-2
Grunder Hollow—*valley* ID-8
Grunder Run—*stream* PA-2
Grundge Hole—*cave* AL-4
Grundman Drain—*stream* MI-6
Grundy—*locale* KY-4
**Grundy**—*pop pl* VA-3
Grundy Ave Sch—*school* NY-2
Grundy Canyon—*valley* WI-6
**Grundy Center**—*pop pl* IA-7
Grundy Center Cem—*cemetery* IA-7
Grundy Center Ch—*church* MO-7
Grundy Center Sch (abandoned)—*school* MO-7
Grundy Ch—*church* KY-4
**Grundy (County)**—*pop pl* IL-6
**Grundy County**—*pop pl* MO-7
**Grundy County**—*pop pl* TN-4
Grundy County Courthouse—*building* TN-4
Grundy County Courthouse—*hist pl* IA-7
Grundy County Fairgounds—*locale* TN-4
Grundy County Home
(abandoned)—*building* MO-7
Grundy County HS—*school* TN-4
Grundy Forest State Natural Area—*park* TN-4
Grundy Hill—*summit* KY-4
Grundy Houses—*hist pl* KY-4
Grundy HS—*school* VA-3
*Grundy Knob* KY-4
Grundy Lake Dam Number Four—*dam* TN-4
Grundy Lake Number Four—*reservoir* TN-4
Grundy Lake Number One—*reservoir* TN-4
Grundy Lake Number One Dam—*dam* TN-4
Grundy Lake Number Two—*reservoir* TN-4
Grundy Lake Number Two Dam—*dam* TN-4
Grundy Lakes Game Preserve—*park* TN-4
Grundy Lakes Hist Dist—*hist pl* TN-4
*Grundy Lakes State Game Preserve* TN-4
*Grundy Lakes State Park* TN-4
Grundy Mill Complex—*hist pl* PA-2
Grundy Sch—*school* KY-4
**Grundys Corner**—*pop pl* PA-2
Grundy State For—*forest* TN-4
Grundy Street Ch of Christ—*church* TN-4
Grundyville Ch—*church* TX-5
Gruner Creek—*stream* CO-8
Grunigen Creek—*stream* CA-9
Gruninger, W. A., Bldg—*hist pl* AZ-5
Grun Island—*island* NC-3
Grunland Creek—*gut* VA-3
Grunland Point—*cape* VA-3
Grunley Creek—*stream* NY-2
Grunnel Slough—*gut* AR-4
*Grunot Settlement* PA-2
Grunow, Lois, Memorial Clinic—*hist pl* AZ-5
Grunow Memorial Clinic—*hospital* AZ-5
Grunsky Sch—*school* CA-9
Grunter Mine—*mine* ID-8
Grunting Spring Gap—*gap* NC-3
Grunting Spring Gap—*gap* SC-3
Grunt Lake—*lake* MN-6
Grunt Point—*cape* AK-9
Grupes Rsvr—*reservoir* CT-1
Grus Cone—*summit* AK-9
Grusher Branch—*stream* GA-3
Grush Gulch—*valley* MT-8
Gruskka Lake—*lake* AK-9
Grus Lake—*lake* AK-9
*Grutorukkuru* PW-9
Grutt Island—*island* WI-6
**Gruver**—*pop pl* IA-7
**Gruver**—*pop pl* TX-5
Gruver (CCD)—*cens area* TX-5
Gruver Cem—*cemetery* TX-5
Gruver Sch (historical)—*school* PA-2
Gruvers Memorial Ch—*church* NC-3
Gruvers Mesa—*summit* UT-8
Gruversville—*locale* (2) PA-2
Gruvertown—*locale* PA-2
Gruwell and Crew General Store—*hist pl* IA-7
Gruwell Canyon—*valley* AZ-5
Gruwell Spring—*spring* AZ-5
Gruwell Well—*well* AZ-5
Gruyer Windmill—*locale* TX-5
*G R Whitfield School* NC-3
Gryder Camp—*locale* GA-3
Gryder Camp Trail—*trail* GA-3
Gryder Cem—*cemetery* LA-4
Gryder-Teague Airp—*airport* NC-3
Gryer Branch—*stream* SC-3
**Grygla**—*pop pl* MN-6
Grygla State Wildlife Mngmt Area—*park* MN-6
**Grymes Hill**—*pop pl* NY-2
Grymes Sch—*school* VA-3
Grytal Lake—*lake* MN-6
GSA Regional Office Bldg—*building* DC-2
G S Barr—*locale* TX-5
Gschwend Creek—*stream* CA-9
**G S Holmes Addition
(subdivision)**—*pop pl* UT-8
*Gspco Dam* AL-4
G Spring—*spring* CO-8
G S Skiff Sch—*school* AZ-5
G Strom Ranch—*locale* ND-7
G Sutton—*locale* TX-5
GS 51 Ditch—*canal* MT-8
G Tank—*reservoir* TX-5
GTE-Sylvania, Incorporated—*facility* NC-3
G-Three Canal—*canal* OR-9
G Turnquist Ranch—*locale* ND-7
Gua'a'—*slope* MH-9
*Guaban* MH-9
Guacamalla Canyon—*valley* NM-5
Guacamayo Site (FS0572, LA-
189)—*hist pl* NM-5
Gu Achi Childrens Shrine—*church* AZ-5
*Gu Achi Mountains* AZ-5
Gu Achi Peak—*summit* AZ-5
**Gu Achi (Santa Rosa)**—*pop pl* AZ-5
Gu Achi Wash—*stream* AZ-5
**Guachupangue**—*pop pl* NM-5
Guacio (Barrio)—*fmr MCD* PR-3
Guacluluyao—*area* GU-9
*Guadabusu To* PW-9
Guadacanal Mine—*mine* CO-8
Guadalasca—*civil* CA-9
Guadalcanal Village—*locale* CA-9
*Guadaloupe Peak* TX-5
*Guadalupe* AZ-5
Guadalupe—*civil* CA-9
Guadalupe—*locale* (2) NM-5
**Guadalupe**—*pop pl* AZ-5
**Guadalupe**—*pop pl* CA-9
**Guadalupe**—*pop pl* CO-8
**Guadalupe**—*pop pl* TX-5
Guadalupe Administrative Site—*other* NM-5
Guadalupe Arroyo—*stream* NM-5
Guadalupe Arroyo—*valley* TX-5
Guadalupe Artesian Well—*well* TX-5
Guadalupe Bay—*bay* TX-5
Guadalupe Box—*other* NM-5
Guadalupe Bridge—*bridge* TX-5
Guadalupe Canon—*valley* NM-5
Guadalupe Canyon—*valley* AZ-5
Guadalupe Canyon—*valley* (3) NM-5
Guadalupe Canyon—*valley* TX-5
Guadalupe (CCD)—*cens area* CA-9
Guadalupe Cem—*cemetery* AZ-5
Guadalupe Cem—*cemetery* (4) NM-5
Guadalupe Cem—*cemetery* (10) TX-5
Guadalupe Ch—*church* NM-5
Guadalupe Ch—*church* OH-6
Guadalupe Ch—*church* (2) TX-5
Guadalupe Church Camp—*locale* NM-5
Guadalupe Coll—*school* CA-9
**Guadalupe (County)**—*pop pl* NM-5
**Guadalupe (County)**—*pop pl* TX-5

Guadalupe County Courthouse in Santa Rosa—*hist pl* NM-5
*Guadalupe Creek* CA-9
Guadalupe Creek—*stream* (3) CA-9
Guadalupe Creek—*stream* TX-5
Guadalupe Cruz (historical)—*locale* AZ-5
Guadalupe Dam—*dam* AZ-5
Guadalupe Dam—*dam* CA-9
Guadalupe Ditch—*canal* CO-8
Guadalupe Draw—*valley* NM-5
**Guadalupe Heights**—*pop pl* TX-5
Guadalupe Hotel—*hist pl* TX-5
Guadalupe Lateral—*canal* TX-5
Guadalupe Lookout—*locale* CA-9
Guadalupe Meadows—*flat* OR-9
Guadalupe Mine—*mine* CA-9
Guadalupe Mine—*mine* (3) NM-5
Guadalupe Mines—*mine* CA-9
*Guadalupe Mountains* AZ-5
*Guadalupe Mountains* (2) NM-5
*Guadalupe Mountains* TX-5
Guadalupe Mountains—*other* NM-5
Guadalupe Mountains—*range* AZ-5
Guadalupe Mountains—*range* NM-5
Guadalupe Mountains—*summit* CA-9
Guadalupe Mountains Natl Park—*park* TX-5
Guadalupe Mtn—*summit* AZ-5
Guadalupe Mtn—*summit* (2) NM-5
*Guadalupe Oil Field* CA-9
Guadalupe Park—*park* UT-8
Guadalupe Pass—*gap* NM-5
Guadalupe Pass—*gap* TX-5
Guadalupe Peak—*summit* NM-5
Guadalupe Peak—*summit* TX-5
*Guadalupe Point* TX-5
Guadalupe Pumping Station—*other* (2) TX-5
Guadalupe Ranch—*hist pl* TX-5
Guadalupe Ranch—*locale* TX-5
Guadalupe Range—*range* AZ-5
Guadalupe Ranger Station—*locale* NM-5
Guadalupe Ridge—*ridge* NM-5
*Guadalupe River* CA-9
Guadalupe River—*stream* CA-9
Guadalupe River—*stream* TX-5
Guadalupe Rsvr—*reservoir* CA-9
Guadalupe Ruin—*hist pl* NM-5
Guadalupe Sch—*school* CA-9
Guadalupe Sch—*school* (4) TX-5
Guadalupe Sch—*school* UT-8
*Guadalupe Slough* CA-9
Guadalupe Slough—*gut* CA-9
Guadalupe Spring—*spring* (2) NM-5
Guadalupe Spring—*spring* TX-5
Guadalupe Springs—*spring* NM-5
Guadalupe Tank—*reservoir* (3) NM-5
Guadalupe Tank—*reservoir* TX-5
Guadalupe Toreros Ch—*church* TX-5
Guadalupe Valley—*basin* CA-9
Guadalupe Valley—*valley* CA-9
Guadalupe Valley Hosp—*hospital* TX-5
Guadalupe Valley Memorial Park—*cemetery* TX-5
Guadalupe Windmill—*locale* (3) TX-5
Guadalupe Y Llanitos De Los Correos—*civil* CA-9
**Guadalupita**—*pop pl* NM-5
Guadalupita Canyon—*valley* NM-5
Guadalupita Mesa—*summit* NM-5
Guaddey Lake—*lake* MI-6
*Guadeloupe* TX-5
*Guadeloupe River* TX-5
Guadiana (Barrio)—*fmr MCD* PR-3
*Guadichaud* FM-9
*Guadobusu Island* PW-9
Guae—*area* GU-9
*Guagan* MH-9
Guage—*locale* KY-4
Guagial Windmill—*locale* TX-5
**Guagolotes**—*pop pl* NM-5
Guagua—*other* GU-9
Guagus Stream—*stream* ME-1
Guaifan—*area* GU-9
Guaifan Point—*cape* GU-9
*Gua Island* PW-9
Guajalote Park—*flat* NM-5
Guajalote Windmill—*locale* (3) TX-5
Guajataca (Barrio)—*fmr MCD* (2) PR-3
*Guajatah Creek* CO-8
*Guajatolla Creek* CO-8
Guajatoyah Creek—*stream* CO-8
*Guajatoyan Creek* CO-8
Guaje Canyon—*valley* NM-5
Guaje Mtn—*summit* NM-5
Guajes, Arroyo Los—*valley* TX-5
Guaje Site—*hist pl* NM-5
**Guajillo**—*pop pl* TX-5
Guajillo Creek—*stream* TX-5
Guajillo Tank—*reservoir* (2) TX-5
Guajillo Well—*well* TX-5
Guajolote Flat—*flat* AZ-5
Guajolote Ranch—*locale* TX-5
Guajolotes Enramada—*lake* TX-5
Guajolote Windmill—*locale* (4) TX-5
Guajome—*civil* CA-9
Guajome Lake—*reservoir* CA-9
Guajome Ranch House—*hist pl* CA-9
**Gualala**—*pop pl* CA-9
Gualala Mtn—*summit* CA-9
Gualala Point—*cape* CA-9
Gualala Point County Park—*park* CA-9
Gualala Point Island—*island* CA-9
*Gualala River* CA-9
Gualala River—*stream* CA-9
Gualett Branch—*stream* GA-3
*Gualo Rai* MH-9
Gualo'Rai—*slope* MH-9
Gualo' Rai, Okso'—*summit* MH-9
*Gualpi* AZ-5
Gualt JHS—*school* WA-9
Gualtney Cem—*cemetery* TN-4
Guam—*island* GU-9
Guam—*locale* MO-7
Guama (Barrio)—*fmr MCD* PR-3
Guamaguamlap—*island* MP-9
Guam Air Terminal—*building* GU-9
Guamani (Barrio)—*fmr MCD* PR-3
Guam Congress—*building* GU-9
Guam (County-equivalent)—*civil* GU-9
Guam Detention Home—*other* GU-9
Guam Institute—*hist pl* GU-9
Guam Memorial Hosp—*hospital* GU-9
Guam Mission Acad—*school* GU-9
Guam Naval Facility—*military* GU-9
Guam Naval Magazine—*military* GU-9
Guam Naval Public Works Center—*military* GU-9
Guam Naval Regional Med Ctr—*hospital* GU-9
Guam Naval Ship Repair Facility—*military* GU-9
Guam Naval Station—*military* GU-9
Guam Naval Supply Depot—*military* GU-9
Guam Observatory—*other* GU-9
Guam Penitentiary—*other* GU-9
Guam Trade and Technical Sch—*school* GU-9
*Guamudokku To* PW-9
**Guanabana**—*pop pl* (2) PR-3
Guanabano (Barrio)—*fmr MCD* PR-3
Guana Dam—*dam* FL-3
Guana Draw—*valley* NM-5
**Guanaiibo**—*pop pl* PR-3
**Guanajibo**—*pop pl* PR-3
Guanajibo (Barrio)—*fmr MCD* (3) PR-3
**Guanajibo Castillo**—*pop pl* PR-3
Guanajuato Windmill—*locale* TX-5
Guana River—*stream* FL-3
Guanella Pass—*gap* CO-8
Guanica—*CDP* PR-3
**Guanica**—*pop pl* PR-3
Guanica, Bahia de—*bay* PR-3
Guanica (Municipio)—*civil* PR-3
Guanica (Pueblo)—*fmr MCD* PR-3
**Guaniquilla**—*pop pl* PR-3
Guaniquilla (Barrio)—*fmr MCD* PR-3
Guano Bridge—*bridge* CA-9
Guano Canyon—*valley* OR-9
Guano Canyon Dam—*dam* OR-9
*Guano Creek* WY-8
Guano Creek—*stream* OR-9
Guano Creek—*stream* WV-2
*Guano Lake* FL-3
Guano Lake—*flat* OR-9
Guano Lake—*reservoir* FL-3
Guano Rim—*cliff* NV-8
Guano Rim—*cliff* OR-9
*Guano River* FL-3
Guano River Wildlife Mngmt Area—*park* FL-3
Guano Rock—*ISLAND* MN-6
Guano Rock—*island* OR-9
Guano Rsvr—*reservoir* OR-9
Guano Slough—*stream* OR-9
Guano Valley—*valley* NV-8
Guano Valley—*valley* OR-9
Guaonica (Barrio)—*fmr MCD* PR-3
*Guap* FM-9
*Guapatsu-To* PW-9
**Guaraguao**—*pop pl* PR-3
Guaraguao Abajo (Barrio)—*fmr MCD* PR-3
Guaraguao Arriba (Barrio)—*fmr MCD* PR-3
Guaraguao (Barrio)—*fmr MCD* (2) PR-3
Guaranteed Pond—*reservoir* AZ-5
Guaranto Spring—*spring* FL-3
Guaranty Bldg—*hist pl* CA-9
Guaranty Bldg—*hist pl* WV-2
Guaraquao—*post sta* PR-3
Guarcahe Windmill—*locale* TX-5
**Guard**—*pop pl* AL-4
Guardarraya—*post sta* PR-3
Guardarraya (Barrio)—*fmr MCD* PR-3
Guard Cem—*cemetery* IN-6
Guard Corral—*locale* (2) NV-8
Guard Corral Rsvr—*reservoir* NV-8
Guard Creek—*stream* (2) ID-8
Guard Creek—*stream* MT-8
Guarden Angel Cem—*cemetery* MO-7
Guard Gate Number 1—*other* NY-2
Guard Gate Number 2—*other* NY-2
Guard Hill—*summit* AK-9
Guard Hill—*summit* NY-2
Guard Hill—*summit* VA-3
Guardhouse, The—*summit* MT-8
Guardhouse Branch—*stream* FL-3
Guardhouse Point—*cape* CT-1
Guardia Canyon—*valley* NM-5
**Guardian**—*pop pl* WV-2
Guardian, Mount—*summit* NY-2
Guardian, The—*summit* CO-8
Guardian, The—*summit* WY-8
Guardian Angel Camp—*locale* MI-6
Guardian Angel Cem—*cemetery* MN-6
Guardian Angel Cem—*cemetery* TX-5
Guardian Angel Cem—*cemetery* (2) WI-6
Guardian Angel Ch—*church* PA-2
Guardian Angel Pass—*gap* UT-8
*Guardian Angel Peak* UT-8
Guardian Angels Ch—*church* MI-6
Guardian Angel Sch—*school* CA-9
Guardian Angel Sch—*school* (2) MN-6
Guardian Angel Sch—*school* MO-7
Guardian Angel Sch—*school* NH-1
Guardian Angels Sch—*school* CO-8
Guardian Angels Sch—*school* KY-4
Guardian Angels Sch—*school* (2) MI-6
Guardian Angels Sch—*school* NY-2
Guardian Care Convalescent Center—*building* NC-3
Guardian Industries—*facility* MI-6
Guardian Mtn—*summit* AK-9
Guardian Peak—*summit* NV-8
Guarding Mtn—*summit* CT-1
Guardipee Lake—*lake* MT-8
*Guard Island* MI-6
Guard Islands—*area* AK-9
Guard Knoll—*summit* UT-8
Guard Lake—*lake* IA-7
Guard Lake—*lake* (2) MI-6
Guard Lake—*lake* MN-6
Guard Locks—*dam* MA-1
Guard Peak—*summit* ID-8
Guard Point—*cape* ME-1
Guard Pond—*reservoir* OR-9
Guards Hill—*summit* MD-2
Guard Shore—*beach* VA-3
Guards Island—*island* OH-6
Guardsman Pass—*gap* UT-8
Guard Station—*locale* CA-9
Guard Station—*locale* OR-9
Guard Station Park—*flat* WY-8
*Guarolai* MH-9
*Guarorai* MH-9
Guasaon—*area* GU-9
Guase Landing Creek—*gut* NC-3
Guasimas (Barrio)—*fmr MCD* PR-3
*Guasquet* CA-9
**Guasti**—*pop pl* CA-9
Guatata—*summit* GU-9
**Guatay**—*pop pl* CA-9
Guatay Campground—*locale* CA-9
Guatay Mtn—*summit* CA-9
Guatemala (Barrio)—*fmr MCD* PR-3
Guatemalan Legation Bldg—*building* DC-2
*Guat Island* PW-9
Guaturche Tank—*reservoir* TX-5
Guaturche Windmill—*locale* TX-5
Guava Hammock—*island* FL-3
Guava Island—*island* FL-3
Guavate (Barrio)—*fmr MCD* PR-3
**Guayabal**—*pop pl* PR-3
Guayabal (Barrio)—*fmr MCD* PR-3
Guayabo (Barrio)—*fmr MCD* PR-3
**Guayabo Dulce**—*pop pl* PR-3
Guayabo Dulce (Barrio)—*fmr MCD* PR-3
Guayabos (Barrio)—*fmr MCD* PR-3
Guayabota (Barrio)—*fmr MCD* PR-3
Guayacan (Barrio)—*fmr MCD* PR-3
Guayacan Well (Windmill)—*locale* TX-5
Guaya Canyon—*valley* CA-9
**Guayama**—*pop pl* PR-3
Guayama (Municipio)—*civil* PR-3
Guayama (Pueblo)—*fmr MCD* PR-3
**Guayanilla**—*pop pl* PR-3
Guayanilla, Bahia de—*bay* PR-3
Guayanilla (Municipio)—*civil* PR-3
Guayanilla (Pueblo)—*fmr MCD* PR-3
Guay Creek—*stream* ID-8
Guay Creek—*stream* NY-2
**Guaydia**—*pop pl* (2) PR-3
*Guaymas Creek* CA-9
*Guaymas River* CA-9
**Guaynabo**—*pop pl* PR-3
Guaynabo (Municipio)—*civil* PR-3
Guaynabo (Pueblo)—*fmr MCD* PR-3
**Guayo**—*pop pl* PR-3
Guayo (Barrio)—*fmr MCD* PR-3
*Guayotoyo Creek* CO-8
**Guaypao**—*pop pl* PR-3
*Guayuco Arroyo* TX-5
Guayule Creek—*stream* TX-5
Guayule Mtn—*summit* TX-5
*Guazaza* FL-3
*Gubahatchee Creek* AL-4
Gube Mtn—*summit* CA-9
Guber Hollow—*valley* MO-7
Gubic Gas Field—*other* AK-9
Gubler Canyon—*valley* NV-8
Gubler Wash—*stream* NV-8
Gubler Well—*well* NV-8
Gubser Mill—*locale* KY-4
**Gubser Mill (Gubser Mills)**—*pop pl* KY-4
Gubser Mine—*mine* WA-9
Gubser-Schuchter Farm—*hist pl* KY-4
Gu Chuapo—*locale* AZ-5
Guchuth—*bay* FM-9
**Guckeen**—*pop pl* MN-6
Guckolds Branch—*stream* SC-3
Guck Spring—*spring* NM-5
Guda—*locale* TX-5
Gudalupe Toreros Cem—*cemetery* TX-5
Gudat Gulch—*valley* SD-7
Gudat Ranch—*locale* SD-7
Gudde Ridge—*ridge* CA-9
Gude—*locale* TX-5
**Gude**—*pop pl* TX-5
Gude Branch—*stream* FL-3
Gudegast Creek—*stream* WI-6
Gudegast Lake—*lake* MI-6
Gudex Cem—*cemetery* WI-6
Gudgel—*locale* KY-4
**Gudgel**—*pop pl* IN-6
Gudgel Ranch—*locale* NE-7
Gudgeonville Covered Bridge—*hist pl* PA-2
**Gudger**—*pop pl* TN-4
Gudger Cem—*cemetery* NC-3
Gudger Cem—*cemetery* TN-4
Gudger Chapel—*church* NC-3
Gudger Mine—*mine* NC-3
Gudger Post Office (historical)—*building* TN-4
Gudger Well—*well* AZ-5
*Gudinger Spring* WY-8
Gudith Drain—*stream* MI-6
*Gudju* FM-9
Gudrum Mtn—*summit* AK-9
*Guebabi* AZ-5
*Guebabi Canyon* AZ-5
*Guebadi Canyon* AZ-5
Guebara Tank—*reservoir* NM-5
*Guebavi* AZ-5
*Guebavi Canyon* AZ-5
Gueck Ranch—*locale* NE-7
Guedry Cem—*cemetery* TX-5
*Guegon* MH-9
Guejito—*civil* CA-9
Guejito Creek—*stream* CA-9
Guejito Truck Trail—*trail* CA-9
**Guelph**—*pop pl* ND-7
Guelph (historical)—*locale* KS-7
Guelph Oil Field—*oilfield* KS-7
**Guelph Township**—*pop pl* KS-7
Guemes—*locale* WA-9
Guemes Channel—*channel* WA-9
**Guemes (Guemes Island)**—*pop pl* WA-9
Guemes Island—*island* WA-9
Guemes Island—*other* WA-9
*Guendaloo Creek* SC-3
Guendalose Creek—*stream* SC-3
Guendel Island—*island* NE-7
Guenevere, Lake—*reservoir* PA-2
Guenoc—*civil* CA-9
Guenot Settlement—*locale* PA-2
Guenser Park—*park* CA-9
Guenther, Richard, House—*hist pl* WI-6
Guenther Cem—*cemetery* AR-4
Guenther & Handel's Block—*hist pl* MA-1
Guenther Hogg Camp—*locale* KY-4
Guenther Post Office (historical)—*building* TN-4
**Guenther (Town of)**—*pop pl* WI-6
Guentzel Cem—*cemetery* TX-5
Guenyon—*area* GU-9
Gueras Windmill—*locale* TX-5
Guerengeh Canal—*canal* LA-4
**Guerette**—*pop pl* ME-1
Guerette Camp—*locale* ME-1
Guericke Dam—*dam* SD-7
Guerilla Hollow—*valley* KY-4
Guerin, Lake—*lake* AK-9
Guerin Bridge—*bridge* SC-3
Guerin Creek—*stream* (2) OR-9
Guerin Creek—*stream* SC-3
Guerin Glacier—*glacier* AK-9
Guerin Slough—*gut* AK-9
**Guerne**—*pop pl* OH-6
Guernesy Slough—*gut* CA-9
**Guerneville**—*pop pl* CA-9
**Guernewood**—*pop pl* CA-9
**Guernewood Park**—*pop pl* CA-9
Guernsey—*locale* PA-2
**Guernsey**—*pop pl* AR-4
**Guernsey**—*pop pl* CA-9
**Guernsey**—*pop pl* IN-6
**Guernsey**—*pop pl* IA-7
**Guernsey**—*pop pl* OH-6
**Guernsey**—*pop pl* WY-8
Guernsey Brook—*stream* ME-1
Guernsey Brook—*stream* (2) VT-1
Guernsey Cem—*cemetery* IN-6
Guernsey Cem—*cemetery* IA-7
Guernsey Cem—*cemetery* NY-2
Guernsey Ch—*church* AR-4
Guernsey Ch—*church* IN-6
**Guernsey (County)**—*pop pl* OH-6
Guernsey County Courthouse—*hist pl* OH-6
Guernsey Creek—*stream* CO-8
Guernsey Creek—*stream* IN-6
Guernsey Creek—*stream* MI-6
Guernsey Creek Trail—*trail* MI-6
Guernsey Dairy Milk Depot—*hist pl* ID-8
Guernsey Gulch—*valley* CO-8
Guernsey Hill—*summit* CT-1
Guernsey HS—*school* AR-4
*Guernsey Island* NH-1
Guernsey Lake—*lake* (2) MI-6
Guernsey Lake—*lake* MN-6
Guernsey Lake Park—*hist pl* WY-8
**Guernsey Mill**—*pop pl* CA-9
Guernsey Sch—*school* AR-4
Guernsey Slough—*stream* CA-9
Guero, Mount—*summit* CO-8
**Guerra**—*pop pl* TX-5
Guerra Banco Number 119—*levee* TX-5
Guerra Cem—*cemetery* TX-5
Guerra Farm—*locale* TX-5
Guerrant—*locale* KY-4
Guerrant Springs Ch—*church* NC-3
Guerrart Cem—*cemetery* MO-7
Guerra Windmill—*locale* TX-5
Guerrero (Barrio)—*fmr MCD* (2) PR-3
Guerrero Canyon—*valley* NM-5
Guerricabita Ranch—*locale* NV-8
**Guerrier**—*pop pl* WA-9
Guerrieri-Decunto House—*hist pl* CO-8
Guerritas Windmill—*locale* TX-5
Guerry-Mitchell House—*hist pl* GA-3
Guerryton—*locale* AL-4
Guerryton Sch—*school* AL-4
*Guertie* OK-5
Guertin Island—*island* AK-9
Guertler House—*hist pl* IL-6
Guertz Well—*well* AZ-5
Guesisosi—*civil* CA-9
Gues Meadow Brook—*stream* NH-1
Guess—*locale* SC-3
Guess Cave—*cave* AL-4
Guess Cem—*cemetery* (2) MS-4
*Guess Creek* TN-4
Guess Creek—*stream* AL-4
Guess Creek—*stream* (2) KY-4
Guess Creek Cave—*cave* AL-4
Guess Creek Ch—*church* AL-4
Guess Creek Sch (historical)—*school* AL-4
Guesses Creek—*stream* AR-4
Guess Fork—*stream* VA-3
Guess Gulch—*valley* (2) ID-8
Guess Place—*locale* NM-5
Guess Pond—*lake* SC-3
Guess Ranch—*locale* NM-5
**Guest**—*pop pl* AL-4
Guest, Henry, House—*hist pl* NJ-2
Guest Assembly Cem—*cemetery* SC-3
Guest Branch—*stream* AR-4
Guest Bridge—*bridge* AL-4
Guest Cem—*cemetery* TX-5
*Guest Creek* AL-4
Guest Creek—*stream* AL-4
Guest Creek—*stream* SC-3
Guest Creek—*stream* TN-4
Guest Drain—*canal* MI-6
Guest Flowers Oil Field—*oilfield* TX-5
Guest JHS—*school* MI-6
Guest Lake—*lake* CA-9
Guest Lake—*lake* FL-3
Guest Millpond—*lake* GA-3
Guest Mtn—*summit* VA-3
Guest Point—*cape* MD-2
Guest River—*stream* VA-3
Guest Run—*stream* OH-6
Guest Sch—*school* (2) MI-6
Guestwell Windmill—*locale* TX-5
Guettler, Philip, House—*hist pl* MN-6
Guevavi Canyon—*valley* AZ-5
Guevavi Mission (historical)—*locale* AZ-5
Guevavi Mission Ruins—*hist pl* AZ-5
**Guevavi Mission (ruins)**—*pop pl* AZ-5
Guevavi Ranch—*locale* AZ-5
**Gueydan**—*pop pl* LA-4
Gueydan Canal—*canal* LA-4
Gueydan House Windmill—*locale* TX-5
Gueydan Oil and Gas Field—*oilfield* LA-4
Gueydan Tank—*reservoir* TX-5
Gueydon Cem—*cemetery* LA-4
*Gueyetta Meadows* CA-9
Guffey—*locale* (2) PA-2
Guffey—*locale* TX-5
**Guffey**—*pop pl* CO-8
**Guffey**—*pop pl* KY-4
Guffey, Joe, House—*hist pl* AR-4
Guffey Butte—*summit* ID-8
Guffey Butte-Black Butte Archeol District—*hist pl* ID-8
Guffey Cem—*cemetery* PA-2
Guffey Creek—*stream* KY-4
Guffey Creek—*stream* VA-3
Guffey Hollow—*valley* AL-4
Guffey Hollow—*valley* KY-4
Guffey Hollow—*valley* PA-2
Guffey Mtn—*summit* KY-4
Guffey Oil Field—*oilfield* PA-2
Guffey Spring—*spring* AL-4
Guffie—*locale* KY-4
Guffin Bay—*bay* NY-2
Guffin Creek—*stream* NY-2
Guffords Branch—*stream* NC-3
Guffra Ranch—*locale* CA-9
Guffy Bluff—*cliff* MO-7
Guffy Branch—*stream* NC-3
Guffy Branch—*stream* TN-4
Guffy Camp—*locale* CA-9
Guffy Cave—*cave* AL-4
Guffy Cem—*cemetery* AL-4
Guffy Creek—*stream* MO-7
Guffy Hill—*summit* IN-6
*Guffy Island* MN-6
*Guffy Lake* AR-4
Guffy Peak—*summit* WY-8
Guffy Pit—*cave* AL-4
Guffy Ranch—*locale* WY-8
Guffy Run—*stream* PA-2
Gufmut—*locale* AK-9
Gugae—*summit* GU-9
Gugagon—*area* GU-9
Gugagon—*valley* GU-9
*Gugan* MH-9
*Gugecgue To* MP-9
*Gugeegue Island* MP-9
*Gugeegue To* MP-9
*Gugegue* MP-9
Gugegwe—*island* MP-9
*Gugegwe Island* MP-9
*Gugegwe-to* MP-9
Gugelman Hollow—*valley* TN-4
Gugenheim, Simon, House—*hist pl* TX-5
Gugenheim Pond—*lake* NY-2
Guggenheim, Murry, House—*hist pl* NJ-2
Guggenheim Creek—*stream* AK-9
Guggenheim Lakes—*lake* NY-2
Guggenheim Museum—*building* NY-2
Guggenheim Sch—*school* NY-2
Guggins Brook—*stream* MA-1
*Gugua* MH-9
Guguak Bay—*bay* AK-9
*Guguam* MH-9
Guguan—*island* MH-9
*Guguan Insel* MH-9
*Guguan Island* MH-9
Gugugee (not verified)—*island* MP-9
*Guguwan* MH-9
*Gugwan-to* MH-9
*Gui Achi* AZ-5
Guiberson Canal—*canal* CA-9
Guiberson House—*hist pl* IA-7
Guibert Islets—*area* AK-9
Guibors Battery—*locale* MO-7
Guibourd, Jacques Dubreuil, House—*hist pl* MO-7
*Guicatic Run* VA-3
*Guice Branch* AL-4
Guice Branch—*stream* LA-4
Guice Cem—*cemetery* MS-4
*Guice Creek* TN-4
Guice Creek—*stream* MS-4
Guice Lake—*lake* LA-4
*Guiceland* TX-5
Guiceland Sch (historical)—*school* TX-5
Guice Mtn—*summit* NC-3
Guices Creek—*stream* TN-4
Guices Creek Rec Area—*park* TN-4
Guichard Canal—*canal* LA-4
Guida Lake—*lake* MN-6
**Guide**—*pop pl* NC-3
Guideboard—*locale* NY-2
Guide Board Brook—*stream* NY-2
Guide Board Corners—*locale* NY-2
Guideboard Hill—*summit* (2) NY-2
Guide Creek—*stream* MT-8
Guide Island—*island* (2) AK-9
*Guide Mountain* TN-4
Guide Peak—*summit* CA-9
Guide Peak—*summit* TX-5
Guider House—*hist pl* MS-4
Guide Rock—*other* AK-9
**Guide Rock**—*pop pl* NE-7
Guide Rock—*summit* WY-8
Guide Rock, The—*pillar* NE-7
Guide Rock Cem—*cemetery* NE-7
Guide Rocks—*area* AK-9
Guide Rock Sch—*school* NE-7
Guide Saddle—*gap* MT-8
Guides Lake—*lake* MI-6
Guide Star Sch (abandoned)—*school* MO-7
**Guideway**—*pop pl* NC-3
Guideway Elem Sch—*school* NC-3
Guidici Cowcamp—*locale* MT-8
Guidici Ditch—*canal* MT-8
Guiding Ch—*church* WV-2
Guidinger Dam—*dam* SD-7
Guidinger Rsvr—*reservoir* SD-7
Guidinger Spring—*spring* WY-8
Guiding Light Cem—*cemetery* MS-4
Guiding Light Ch—*church* AL-4
Guiding Light Ch—*church* MS-4
Guiding Light Ch—*church* OK-5
Guiding Light Ch—*church* VA-3
Guiding Light Ch—*church* (2) WV-2
*Guiding Light Pentecostal Ch* MS-4
Guiding Light Temple—*church* NC-3
Guiding Star Ch—*church* IL-6
Guiding Star Ch—*church* (2) MS-4
Guiding Star Ch—*church* NC-3
Guiding Star Ch—*church* TN-4
Guiding Star Memorial Cem—*cemetery* IL-6
Guidiville Rancheria—*locale* CA-9
Guido Canyon—*valley* NM-5
Guidotti Ranch—*locale* CA-9
Guidry And Huval Canal—*canal* LA-4
Guier Branch—*stream* KY-4
Guier Cem—*cemetery* PA-2
**Guignard**—*pop pl* SC-3
Guignard Park—*park* SC-3
Guignard Pond—*reservoir* SC-3
Guijada Tank—*reservoir* AZ-5
Guijarral Hills—*other* CA-9
*Guijarral Hills Oil Field* CA-9
*Guijas Mountains* AZ-5
Guijas Mountains, Las—*range* AZ-5
Guijas Wash, Las—*stream* AZ-5
Guijen Point—*cape* GU-9
Guijen Rock—*island* GU-9
*Gui Kangulas* AK-9
*Gui Kangulas Island* AK-9
Guilarte (Barrio)—*fmr MCD* PR-3
Guilbeau—*uninc pl* TX-5
*Guilbert Creek* SD-7
*Guild* TN-4
Guild—*locale* CA-9
Guild—*locale* TX-5
**Guild**—*pop pl* GA-3
**Guild**—*pop pl* NH-1
Guild, John, House—*hist pl* HI-9
Guild-Bovard Mine—*mine* NV-8
Guild Cem—*cemetery* MA-1
Guild Ditch—*canal* IN-6
Guild Elem Sch—*school* TN-4
Guilder Brook—*stream* MA-1
Guilder Hollow—*valley* (2) MA-1
**Guilderland**—*pop pl* NY-2
Guilderland Cem—*cemetery* (2) NY-2
Guilderland Cemetery Vault—*hist pl* NY-2
**Guilderland Center**—*pop pl* NY-2
**Guilderland Gardens**—*pop pl* NY-2
**Guilderland (Town of)**—*pop pl* NY-2
Guilder Peak—*summit* UT-8
Guilder Pond—*reservoir* MA-1
Guilder Pond Dam—*dam* MA-1
*Guilders Brook* MA-1
Guilders Creek—*stream* NC-3
*Guildersleeve Canyon* UT-8
Guilder Sleeve Canyon—*valley* UT-8
*Guilders Pond* MA-1
*Guilder Steve Canyon* UT-8
Guildfield Corner—*locale* VA-3
Guild First Baptist Ch—*church* TN-4
*Guildford Creek* VA-3
*Guildford Flats* VA-3
**Guild (Haletown)**—*pop pl* TN-4
**Guildhall**—*pop pl* VT-1
Guildhall Station—*locale* VT-1
**Guildhall (Town of)**—*pop pl* VT-1
Guildhall Village Hist Dist—*hist pl* VT-1
Guild Hill—*summit* NH-1
Guild Hollow—*valley* (2) WY-8
*Guild Lateral* IN-6
Guild Lateral—*canal* IN-6
Guild Placer Mines—*mine* NV-8
Guild Pond—*reservoir* CT-1
Guild Post Office (historical)—*building* TN-4
Guild Rsvr—*reservoir* CO-8
Guild Rsvr—*reservoir* WY-8
Guild Sch (historical)—*school* ME-1
Guild Sch (historical)—*school* TN-4
**Guilds Woods (subdivision)**—*pop pl* AL-4
Guild-Verner House—*hist pl* AL-4
Guild Wash—*stream* AZ-5
*Guile Brook* NY-2
Guile Lake—*lake* MN-6
Guiles Lake—*lake* OR-9
*Guiley Creek* MI-6
Guiley Creek—*stream* MI-6
Guiley Creek—*stream* OR-9
Guiley Pond—*lake* MI-6
Guilfield Ch—*church* VA-3
Guilfoil Village Site (15FA176)—*hist pl* KY-4
*Guilford* KS-7
Guilford—*hist pl* MD-2
Guilford—*locale* FL-3
Guilford—*locale* IL-6
Guilford—*locale* KS-7
Guilford—*locale* PA-2
**Guilford**—*pop pl* CT-1
**Guilford**—*pop pl* IN-6
**Guilford**—*pop pl* ME-1
**Guilford**—*pop pl* (2) MD-2
**Guilford**—*pop pl* MO-7
**Guilford**—*pop pl* NY-2
**Guilford**—*pop pl* NC-3
**Guilford**—*pop pl* OH-6
**Guilford**—*pop pl* VT-1
**Guilford**—*pop pl* (2) VA-3
Guilford Branch—*stream* IN-6
Guilford Bridge—*bridge* KS-7
Guilford Cem—*cemetery* OH-6
Guilford Center—*locale* ME-1
**Guilford Center**—*pop pl* NY-2
**Guilford Center**—*pop pl* VT-1
**Guilford Center (census name Guilford)**—*pop pl* CT-1
Guilford Center Meetinghouse—*hist pl* VT-1
Guilford Center Sch—*school* (2) IL-6
Guilford Ch—*church* (2) VA-3
*Guilford-Chester Reservoir* CT-1
Guilford Church Branch—*stream* VA-3
Guilford Coll—*school* NC-3
**Guilford College**—*pop pl* NC-3
Guilford College (sta.) (RR name for Guilford)—*other* NC-3
Guilford Compact (census name Guilford)—*other* ME-1
Guilford County—*civil* NC-3
Guilford County Courthouse—*hist pl* NC-3
Guilford County Office and Court Bldg—*hist pl* NC-3
Guilford Courthouse Natl Military Park—*hist pl* NC-3
Guilford Creek—*stream* NY-2
Guilford Creek—*stream* VA-3
**Guilford Downs**—*pop pl* MD-2
Guilford Flats—*flat* VA-3
Guilford Harbor—*bay* CT-1
**Guilford Hills**—*pop pl* PA-2
Guilford Hills Elem Sch—*school* PA-2
**Guilford Hills (subdivision)**—*pop pl* NC-3
Guilford Historic Town Center—*hist pl* CT-1
Guilford HS—*school* CT-1
Guilford HS—*school* IL-6
*Guilford Lake* CT-1
Guilford Lake—*lake* MI-6
Guilford Lake—*lake* NY-2
Guilford Lake—*reservoir* OH-6
Guilford Lakes—*reservoir* CT-1
Guilford Lakes Sch—*school* CT-1
Guilford Lake State Res—*park* OH-6
Guilford Lookout Tower—*locale* CT-1

Guilford (Magisterial District)—fmr MCD (2) ... VA-3
Guilford Memorial Library—hist pl ... ME-1
Guilford Memorial Park Cem—cemetery ... NC-3
Guilford Middle School ... NC-3
Guilford Mill—hist pl ... NC-3
Guilford Mtn—summit ... ME-1
Guilford Point—cape ... CT-1
Guilford Primary Sch—school ... NC-3
Guilford Road Ch—church ... MD-2
**Guilford (RR name Guilford College (sta.))**—pop pl ... NC-3
Guilford Sch—school ... MD-2
Guilford Sch—school ... NE-7
Guilford Sch—school ... NC-3
Guilford Sch—school ... PA-2
Guilford Sch—school ... VA-3
**Guilford Springs**—pop pl ... PA-2
Guilford Station—locale ... CT-1
Guilford Station—locale ... NC-3
**Guilford (Town of)**—pop pl ... CT-1
**Guilford (Town of)**—pop pl ... ME-1
**Guilford (Town of)**—pop pl ... NY-2
**Guilford (Town of)**—pop pl ... VT-1
Guilford Township—fmr MCD ... IA-7
**Guilford Township**—pop pl ... KS-7
**Guilford (Township of)**—pop pl ... IL-6
**Guilford (Township of)**—pop pl ... IN-6
**Guilford (Township of)**—pop pl ... OH-6
**Guilford (Township of)**—pop pl ... PA-2
Guilford Union Cem—cemetery ... IL-6
Guilita Windmill—locale ... TX-5
Guillaume, Bayou—stream (2) ... LA-4
Guillaume, Lac a —lake ... LA-4
Guillaume Cem—cemetery ... IN-6
Guillaume Slough—stream ... LA-4
Guillebeau House—hist pl ... SC-3
**Guillemette (Trailer Park)**—pop pl ... ME-1
Guillemot Island—island ... AK-9
Guillermo, Canada De —valley ... CA-9
Guillermo Canyon—valley ... NM-5
Guillermo Windmill—locale ... TX-5
Guilliam Landing ... MS-4
Guilliard Lake—lake ... SC-3
Guillmettes Pond—lake ... VT-1
Guillory Cem—cemetery (3) ... LA-4
Guillot Springs—spring ... MT-8
Guilmette Gulch—valley ... UT-8
**Guilquarry**—pop pl ... NC-3
Guilrock Camp—locale ... NC-3
Guimond Sch—school ... ND-7
**Guin**—pop pl ... AL-4
Guinan Drain—canal ... MI-6
Guinard ... FM-9
Guinavah Amphitheater—locale ... UT-8
Guinavah Campground—locale ... UT-8
Guin Branch—stream ... MS-4
Guin Branch—stream ... TN-4
Guin (CCD)—cens area ... AL-4
Guin Cem—cemetery ... AL-4
Guin Cem—cemetery ... LA-4
Guin Ch of Christ—church ... AL-4
Guin City Cem—cemetery ... AL-4
**Guinda**—pop pl ... CA-9
Guindani Canyon—valley ... AZ-5
Guin Division—civil ... AL-4
Guinea—locale ... AL-4
**Guinea**—pop pl ... VA-3
Guinea Brook—stream ... CT-1
Guinea Ch—church ... VA-3
Guinea Church ... AL-4
Guinea Corner ... ME-1
**Guinea Corner**—pop pl ... ME-1
Guinea Corners Ch—church ... OH-6
Guinea Creek—stream ... DE-2
Guinea Creek—stream ... FL-3
Guinea Creek—stream ... SC-3
Guinea Gap—gap ... TN-4
Guinea Gulf—valley ... MA-1
Guinea Gut—stream ... VI-3
Guinea Hill—summit ... NH-1
Guinea Hill—summit ... NY-2
Guinea Hill Knob—summit ... TN-4
Guinea Jim Hollow—valley ... TN-4
Guinea Jim Spring—spring ... TN-4
Guinea Marsh—swamp ... MD-2
Guinea Marshes—swamp ... VA-3
Guinea Meadow—swamp ... MA-1
Guinea Meadow Swamp—swamp ... MA-1
Guinea Mill Run Canal—canal ... NC-3
Guinea Mills—locale ... VA-3
Guinea Mtn—summit ... VA-3
Guinea Neck—cape ... VA-3
Guinea Pond—lake ... NH-1
Guinea Pond Trail—trail ... NH-1
Guinea Ridge—ridge ... NH-1
Guinea School ... AL-4
Guinea Town ... DE-2
Guin Elem Sch—school ... AL-4
Guinevere Castle—summit ... AZ-5
Guinn—locale ... MO-7
Guinn Bottom—flat ... OK-5
Guinn Branch ... VA-3
Guinn Branch—stream ... AL-4
Guinn Canyon—valley ... ID-8
Guinn Cem—cemetery ... AR-4
Guinn Cem—cemetery ... IL-6
Guinn Cem—cemetery ... MS-4
Guinn Ch—church ... AL-4
Guinn Cove—valley ... AL-4
Guinn Cove Cemetery ... AL-4
Guinn Creek ... MO-7
Guinn Creek ... TN-4
Guinn Creek—stream ... ID-8
Guinn Creek—stream ... MS-4
Guinn Cross Roads—locale ... AL-4
Guinne Creek ... MO-7
Guinn Field—park ... TX-5
Guinn Island—island ... TN-4
Guinn JHS—school ... TX-5
Guinn Lake—reservoir ... MS-4
Guinn Memorial Methodist Ch—church ... MS-4
Guinn Mine—mine ... WA-9
Guinn Mtn—summit ... CO-8
Guinn Narrows—gap ... TN-4
Guinn Ranch—locale ... CA-9
Guinn Ridge—ridge ... TN-4
Guinn Ridge—ridge ... WV-2
Guinn Road Park—park ... TN-4
Guinn Sch—school ... CA-9
Guinn Sch (historical)—school ... TN-4
Guinns Cove Cem—cemetery ... AL-4
Guinns Creek—stream ... MO-7
Guinns Mill Pond—reservoir ... NC-3
Guins Creek ... AL-4
Guins Creek ... MO-7
Guins Creek—stream ... TN-4
Guins Slough ... AL-4
Guinston Ch—church ... PA-2
Guinston United Presbyterian Church—hist pl ... PA-2
**Guion**—pop pl ... AR-4
**Guion**—pop pl ... IN-6
Guion Creek—stream ... IN-6
Guion Park—park ... AR-4
Guionsville ... IN-6
Guionsville (historical P.O.)—locale ... IN-6
Guion (Township of)—fmr MCD ... AR-4
Guiou ... ME-1
Gui Pond—lake ... NY-2
**Guique**—pop pl ... NM-5
Guiraud Ditch—canal ... CO-8
Guiry and Schillestad Bldg—hist pl ... WA-9
Guise Bay—swamp ... SC-3
Guise Creek ... MT-8
Guise Creek ... TN-4
**Guise Park**—pop pl ... IN-6
Guiser Creek ... MT-8
Guises Creek ... TN-4
Guises Creek Rec Area ... TN-4
Guishiemana Lake—lake ... AK-9
Guisinger Bldg—hist pl ... AR-4
Guist Creek—stream ... KY-4
Guist Creek Lake—lake ... KY-4
Guist Creek Lake State Park—park ... KY-4
Guitar Lake—lake ... AK-9
Guitar Lake—lake ... WY-8
Guiteau Ch—church ... MO-7
Guiterrez Peak—summit ... WY-8
Guitman Ranch—locale ... CO-8
Guiton Crossing—locale ... SC-3
Guiton Run—stream ... PA-2
**Guitonville**—pop pl ... PA-2
Guitroz Bayou—stream ... LA-4
Guittard ... KS-7
Guittard Cem—cemetery ... KS-7
Guittard Station—locale ... KS-7
**Guittard Township**—pop pl ... KS-7
Guittar Hollow—valley ... MO-7
Gukenheimer Pond ... NY-2
Gukhzna Creek—stream ... AK-9
Gukien Cohee Ditch—canal ... IN-6
Gu Komelik ... AZ-5
**Gu Komelik**—pop pl ... AZ-5
Gu Kui Chuchg (Baboquivari Camp)—locale ... AZ-5
Gukyuk Slough—gut ... AK-9
Gulager Spring Branch—stream ... OK-5
Gula Point—cape ... AK-9
Gulay Island—island ... NH-1
Gulbrandson Creek—gut ... FL-3
Gulceville Cem—cemetery ... TX-5
Gulch, Lake—lake ... WA-9
Gulch, The—valley ... CA-9
Gulch, The—valley (4) ... UT-8
Gulch Branch ... LA-4
Gulch Brook—stream (2) ... ME-1
Gulch Brook—stream ... NH-1
Gulch Canyon—valley ... NE-7
Gulch Creek ... OR-9
Gulch Creek ... TN-4
Gulch Creek—stream (2) ... AK-9
Gulch Creek—stream ... CA-9
Gulch Creek—stream ... MN-6
Gulch Creek—stream ... UT-8
Gulch Creek—stream ... WI-6
Gulch Dam—dam ... OR-9
Gulch Eight—valley ... CA-9
Gulch Eleven—valley ... CA-9
Gulch Fifteen—valley ... CA-9
Gulch Five—valley (2) ... CA-9
Gulch Four—valley ... CA-9
Gulch House Creek—stream ... CA-9
Gulch Lakes—lake ... WA-9
Gulch Lateral—canal ... ID-8
Gulch Nine—valley ... CA-9
Gulch One—valley (3) ... CA-9
Gulch Outstanding Natural Area, The—area ... UT-8
Gulch Quartz ... OR-9
Gulch Rsvr—reservoir ... OR-9
Gulch Seven—valley (2) ... CA-9
Gulch Six—valley ... CA-9
Gulch Sixteen—valley ... CA-9
Gulch Spring—spring ... NV-8
Gulch Thirtyone—valley ... CA-9
Gulch Three—valley (2) ... CA-9
Gulch Two—valley (2) ... CA-9
Gulde—locale ... MS-4
Gulde Cem—cemetery ... MS-4
Gulde Ch—church ... MS-4
Gulden Cem—cemetery ... TN-4
Gulden Creek—stream ... NC-3
Gulden Lake—lake ... MN-6
**Guldens**—pop pl ... PA-2
Guldin Hill—summit ... PA-2
**Guler**—pop pl ... WA-9
Guler Mtn—summit ... WA-9
Gulf—locale ... CA-9
Gulf—locale (2) ... TX-5
**Gulf**—pop pl ... NC-3
Gulf, Colorado and Sante Fe RR Passenger Station—hist pl ... TX-5
Gulf, Mobile, and Ohio Passenger Terminal—hist pl ... AL-4
Gulf, Mobile & Ohio Freight Depot—hist pl ... MS-4
Gulf, The ... NY-2
Gulf, The ... TN-4
Gulf, The—basin ... MO-7
Gulf, The—bay ... CT-1
Gulf, The—bay ... NH-1
Gulf, The—bay ... NY-2
Gulf, The—bay ... VA-3
Gulf, The—channel ... NY-2
Gulf, The—gap ... KY-4
Gulf, The—gap ... MA-1
Gulf, The—stream ... MA-1
Gulf, The—stream ... NH-1
Gulf, The—stream ... NY-2
Gulf, The—valley ... AL-4
Gulf, The—valley (2) ... NH-1
Gulf, The—valley (8) ... NY-2
Gulf, The—valley ... OH-6
Gulf, The—valley (3) ... VT-1
Gulf, The—valley ... WV-2
Gulf Atlantic Ship Canal ... FL-3
Gulf Ave Sch—school ... CA-9
Gulf Bays—locale ... AL-4
Gulf Beach—beach ... CT-1
Gulf Beach—locale ... FL-3
Gulf Beach Baptist Ch—church ... FL-3
Gulf Beaches Elem Sch—school ... FL-3
**Gulf Beach Heights**—pop pl ... FL-3
Gulf Bldg—hist pl ... TX-5
Gulf Branch—stream ... AL-4
Gulf Branch—stream ... GA-3
Gulf Branch—stream ... KY-4
Gulf Branch—stream (2) ... NC-3
Gulf Branch—stream ... TN-4
Gulf Branch—stream ... VA-3
Gulf Branch—stream ... WV-2
**Gulf Breeze**—pop pl ... FL-3
Gulf Breeze Elem Sch—school ... FL-3
Gulf Breeze-Harold (CCD)—cens area ... FL-3
Gulf Breeze Hosp—hospital ... FL-3
Gulf Breeze Sch—school ... FL-3
Gulf Breeze Senior HS—school ... FL-3
Gulf Breeze Shop Ctr—locale ... FL-3
Gulf Breeze United Methodist Ch—church ... FL-3
**Gulf Bridge**—pop pl ... NY-2
Gulf Brook ... CT-1
Gulf Brook ... MA-1
Gulf Brook—stream (2) ... CT-1
Gulf Brook—stream (5) ... MA-1
Gulf Brook—stream (8) ... NH-1
Gulf Brook—stream (3) ... NY-2
Gulf Brook—stream ... PA-2
Gulf Brook—stream (3) ... VT-1
Gulf Brook, The—stream ... NY-2
**Gulf Camp**—pop pl ... TX-5
Gulf Camp Windmill—locale ... TX-5
Gulf Canyon—valley ... OR-9
Gulf Cem—cemetery ... NY-2
**Gulf City**—pop pl ... FL-3
Gulf City Rescue Mission—church ... AL-4
Gulfco—uninc pl ... KY-4
Gulf Coast Baptist Ch—church ... FL-3
Gulf Coast Bible Camp—locale ... MS-4
Gulf Coast Center for the Arts—hist pl ... MS-4
Gulf Coast Center (Shop Ctr)—locale ... FL-3
Gulf Coast Christian Ch—church ... FL-3
Gulf Coast Christian Sch—school ... FL-3
Gulf Coast Community Coll—school ... FL-3
Gulf Coast Community Hosp—hospital ... FL-3
Gulf Coast Community Hosp—hospital ... MS-4
Gulf Coast Community Hospital-Emergency Helipad—airport ... MS-4
Gulf Coast Experiment Station—other ... AL-4
Gulf Coast Military Acad—school ... MS-4
Gulf Coast Research Laboratory—building ... MS-4
**Gulf County**—pop pl ... FL-3
Gulf County Adult Sch—school ... FL-3
Gulf County Canal—canal ... FL-3
Gulf County Guidance Clinic—school ... FL-3
Gulf Cove—post sta ... FL-3
Gulf Creek ... NY-2
Gulf Creek ... OK-5
Gulf Creek ... PA-2
Gulf Creek—stream ... AL-4
Gulf Creek—stream ... AR-4
Gulf Creek—stream ... GA-3
Gulf Creek—stream (7) ... NY-2
Gulf Creek—stream ... NC-3
Gulf Crest ... AL-4
**Gulfcrest**—pop pl ... AL-4
**Gulf Crest**—pop pl ... AL-4
Gulf Crest Ch—church ... AL-4
Gulf Crossing—locale ... LA-4
Gulf Dale Shop Ctr—locale ... AL-4
**Gulf Dale (subdivision)**—pop pl ... AL-4
Gulf Elem Sch—school ... FL-3
Gulf Fishing and Hunting Club—other ... AL-4
Gulf Fork—stream ... KY-4
Gulf Fork—stream ... NC-3
Gulf Fork—stream ... WV-2
Gulf Fork Big Creek—stream ... TN-4
Gulf Gardens Baptist Ch—church ... MS-4
Gulf Gate Baptist Ch—church ... FL-3
Gulf Gate East—post sta ... FL-3
Gulf Gate Estates—CDP ... FL-3
Gulf Gate Mall—locale ... FL-3
Gulf Gate-Osprey (CCD)—cens area ... FL-3
Gulf Gate Sch—school ... FL-3
Gulfgate Shopping City—locale ... TX-5
Gulf Hagas Brook—stream ... ME-1
Gulf Hagas Mtn—summit ... ME-1
Gulf Hagas Trail—trail ... ME-1
Gulf Hammock—island (2) ... FL-3
**Gulf Hammock**—pop pl ... FL-3
Gulf Hammock—swamp ... FL-3
Gulf Hammock Wildlife Mngmt Area—park ... FL-3
**Gulf Harbors**—pop pl ... FL-3
**Gulf Harbor (subdivision)**—pop pl ... FL-3
Gulf Haven Ch—church ... MS-4
Gulf Haven Park ... AL-4
Gulf Highlands—locale ... AL-4
Gulf Hill—locale ... TX-5
Gulf Hill—summit ... CT-1
Gulf Hill—summit ... ME-1
Gulf Hill—summit ... NH-1
Gulf Hill—summit ... NY-2
**Gulf Hills**—pop pl ... MS-4
Gulf Hills Baptist Ch—church ... AL-4
Gulf Hills Golf Course—locale ... MS-4
Gulf Hollow ... AR-4
Gulf Hollow—valley ... AL-4
Gulf Hollow—valley (3) ... AR-4
Gulf Hollow—valley ... KY-4
Gulf HS—school ... FL-3
Gulf Island ... MA-1
Gulf Island—cape ... MA-1
Gulf Island—island ... NJ-2
Gulf Island Dam—dam ... ME-1
Gulf Island Pond—reservoir ... ME-1
Gulf Islands Natl Seashore—park ... MS-4
Gulf Islands Natl Seashore (Also Fl)—park ... MS-4
Gulf Islands Natl Seashore (Also MS)—park ... FL-3
Gulf JHS—school ... FL-3
Gulf Junction—locale ... MO-7
Gulf Junction—locale ... OK-5
Gulf Junction—uninc pl ... OK-5
Gulf Knob—summit ... GA-3
Gulf Lagoon Beach ... FL-3
**Gulf Lagoon Beach**—pop pl ... FL-3
Gulf Lake—lake ... MN-6
Gulf Marine State Park—park ... MS-4
Gulf Mart Shop Ctr—locale ... MS-4
Gulf Meadows—swamp ... MA-1
Gulf Mills ... PA-2
Gulf MS—school ... FL-3
Gulf Mtn—summit ... AR-4
Gulf Mtn—summit ... GA-3
Gulf Mtn—summit ... TN-4
Gulf Mtn—summit ... VA-3
Gulf Oaks Hosp—hospital ... MS-4
Gulf Of Alaska—bay ... AK-9
Gulf Of Esquibel—bay ... AK-9
Gulf of Florida ... FL-3
Gulf of Georgia ... WA-9
Gulf Of Mexico—bay ... LA-4
Gulf of Mexico Brook—stream ... NY-2
Gulf of New Spain ... MS-4
Gulf Of Slides—valley ... NH-1
Gulf of the Farallones—bay ... CA-9
**Gulfoil**—pop pl ... NE-7
**Gulf Park**—pop pl ... TN-4
**Gulf Park**—pop pl ... TX-5
Gulfpark Airp—airport ... MS-4
Gulf Park Coll—school ... MS-4
**Gulf Park Estates (subdivision)**—pop pl ... MS-4
Gulf Peak—summit ... NH-1
Gulf Peninsula—cape ... TX-5
**Gulf Pine**—pop pl ... FL-3
Gulf Pines—locale ... FL-3
Gulf Pines Golf Course—locale ... AL-4
Gulf Pines Hosp—hospital ... FL-3
Gulf Pines Memorial—cemetery ... FL-3
Gulf Pines Memorial Park—cemetery ... FL-3
Gulf Plaza (Shop Ctr)—locale ... FL-3
Gulf Plaza Shop Ctr—locale ... MS-4
Gulf Point—cape ... NJ-2
Gulf Points Square (Shop Ctr)—locale ... FL-3
Gulf Pond—lake ... CT-1
Gulf Pond—swamp ... PA-2
Gulf Port ... FL-3
Gulfport—locale ... NY-2
**Gulfport**—pop pl ... FL-3
**Gulfport**—pop pl ... IL-6
**Gulfport**—pop pl ... MS-4
Gulfport-Biloxi Regional Airp—airport ... MS-4
Gulfport Channel—channel ... MS-4
Gulfport Channel Range Front Light—locale ... FL-3
Gulfport City Hall—building ... MS-4
Gulfport Elem Sch—school ... FL-3
**Gulf Port (Gulfport)**—pop pl ... IL-6
Gulfport Harbor—harbor ... MS-4
Gulfport-Harrison County Library—building ... MS-4
Gulfport HS—school ... MS-4
Gulfport Memorial Hosp—hospital ... MS-4
Gulfport Middle Ground—island ... FL-3
Gulfport Naval Construction Battalion Center—military ... MS-4
Gulfport Post Office—building ... MS-4
Gulfport Reach—channel ... NJ-2
Gulfport Reach—channel ... NY-2
Gulfport Recreation Center—park ... MS-4
Gulf Port (RR name for Gulfport)—other ... FL-3
**Gulfport (RR name Gulf Port)**—pop pl ... FL-3
Gulf Post Office (historical)—building ... AL-4
Gulfpost Plaza-Disston Shop Ctr—locale ... FL-3
Gulf Prairie Ch—church ... TX-5
Gulf Presbyterian Ch—church ... FL-3
Gulf Prong—stream ... NC-3
**Gulf Resort Beach**—pop pl ... FL-3
Gulf Ridge—ridge ... KY-4
Gulf Run—stream ... PA-2
Gulf Run—stream (3) ... WV-2
Gulf Sch—school ... NY-2
**Gulf Shores**—pop pl ... AL-4
Gulf Shores—uninc pl ... FL-3
Gulf Shores Presbyterian Ch—church ... AL-4
Gulf Shores United Methodist Ch—church ... AL-4
**Gulfside**—pop pl ... MS-4
Gulfside Elem Sch—school ... FL-3
Gulfside Park—park ... TX-5
Gulfside Trail—trail ... NH-1
Gulf Spring—spring (2) ... TN-4
Gulf Springs Branch—stream ... TN-4
Gulf State Park—park ... AL-4
Gulf States Columbiana SW Dam—dam ... AL-4
Gulf States Columbiana SW Lake—reservoir ... AL-4
Gulf States Paper Company Dam—dam ... AL-4
Gulf States Paper Company Lake—reservoir ... AL-4
Gulf Stream ... CT-1
Gulf Stream ... NY-2
**Gulf Stream**—pop pl ... FL-3
Gulf Stream—school ... FL-3
Gulf Stream—stream (2) ... CT-1
Gulf Stream—stream (4) ... ME-1
Gulf Stream—stream (2) ... NY-2
Gulf Stream—stream ... VT-1
Gulfstream Elem Sch—school ... FL-3
Gulf Stream Hotel—hist pl ... FL-3
Gulfstream Mall—locale ... FL-3
Gulfstream Park Racetrack—locale ... FL-3
Gulf Stream School Library—building ... FL-3
**Gulf Summit**—pop pl ... NY-2
Gulf Summit Ch—church ... NY-2
Gulf Tank—reservoir ... TX-5
Gulf-to-Bay Plaza (Shop Ctr)—locale ... FL-3
**Gulfton**—pop pl ... MO-7
Gulftown—locale ... OK-5
Gulf (Township of)—fmr MCD ... NC-3
Gulf Trail, The—trail ... OH-6
Gulfview Elementary School ... MS-4
Gulfview JHS—school ... FL-3
Gulfview MS—school ... FL-3
Gulf View Sch—school ... MS-4
Gulf View Square Mall—locale ... FL-3
Gulfway—post sta ... TX-5
Gulfway Shop Ctr—locale ... TX-5
Gulf Well—locale ... NM-5
Gulf Well—well (2) ... NV-8
Gulf Windmill—locale (2) ... TX-5
Gulf Wind Shop Ctr—locale ... FL-3
**Gulfwood**—pop pl ... TN-4
Gulgotha Butte ... WA-9
**Gulich (Township of)**—pop pl ... PA-2
Gulick—locale ... NY-2
Gulick Cem—cemetery ... OH-6
Gulick Creek—stream ... CA-9
Gulick House—hist pl ... NJ-2
Gulick Lake—lake ... MI-6
Gulick Park—park ... KS-7
Gulick-Rowell House—hist pl ... HI-9
Gulifield Ch—church ... VA-3
Guliiq—summit ... FM-9
**Gulkana**—pop pl ... AK-9
Gulkana ANV797—reserve ... AK-9
Gulkana Glacier—glacier ... AK-9
Gulkana River—stream ... AK-9
Gullage Lake Dam—dam ... MS-4
Gullat Cem—cemetery ... LA-4
Gullatte Dam—dam ... AL-4
Gullatts Lake—reservoir ... AL-4
Gull Bay—bay (2) ... NY-2
Gull Brook ... NY-2
Gull Brook—stream ... NY-2
Gull Cem—cemetery ... OH-6
Gull Cove—bay ... AK-9
Gull Creek—stream ... AK-9
Gull Creek—stream ... MI-6
Gull Creek—stream ... MN-6
Gull Creek—stream ... WI-6
Gull Creek Springs—lake ... WI-6
Gulledge—locale ... AR-4
Gulledge Branch—stream ... TN-4
Gulledge Cem—cemetery ... MS-4
Gulledge Cem—cemetery (2) ... TN-4
Gulledge HS—school ... MS-4
Gulledge Sch (historical)—school ... MS-4
Gulledge (Township of)—fmr MCD ... NC-3
Guller Creek—stream ... CO-8
Gullers Lake—reservoir ... NC-3
Gullers Lake Dam—dam ... NC-3
Gullet Cem—cemetery ... TN-4
Gullet Chute—channel ... TN-4
Gullet Mtn—summit ... TN-4
Gullet Ridge—ridge ... AL-4
Gullett—locale ... KY-4
**Gullett**—pop pl ... LA-4
Gullett, Benjamin D., House—hist pl ... AL-4
Gullett Bluff—cliff ... AL-4
Gullett Branch—stream (3) ... KY-4
Gullett Cem—cemetery ... KY-4
Gullettes Bluff ... AL-4
Gullettes Bluff Landing (historical)—locale ... AL-4
Gulletts Bluff Ch—church ... AL-4
Gulletts Bluff Park—park ... AL-4
Gullett Sch—school ... TX-5
Gulletts Creek—stream ... IN-6
Gulley, The—stream ... SC-3
Gulley Bay—swamp ... FL-3
Gulley Branch—stream (3) ... FL-3
Gulley Branch—stream ... GA-3
Gulley Branch—stream ... SC-3
Gulley Branch—stream ... TX-5
Gulley Cem—cemetery (2) ... AR-4
Gulley Cem—cemetery ... IL-6
Gulley Cem—cemetery ... TN-4
Gulley Creek ... MS-4
Gulley Farm—hist pl ... KY-4
Gulley Park—park ... PA-2
Gulley Run—stream ... PA-2
Gulley Run—stream ... VA-3
Gulley Spring Creek—stream ... AR-4
Gulley Spring Creek—stream ... MO-7
Gulley-Vickery-Blackwell House—hist pl ... GA-3
Gull Harbor—bay ... WA-9
Gull Harbor—hist pl ... NC-3
Gull Hill ... ME-1
Gulliams Cem—cemetery ... MO-7
Gullian Gerig's Mill—hist pl ... KY-4
Gullick Park—park ... OK-5
Gullicks Lake—reservoir ... MS-4
Gullickson's Glen—hist pl ... WI-6
Gulliday Well (Dry)—well ... CA-9
Gullied Peak—summit ... AK-9
Gulliford Crossing—locale ... OR-9
Gulliford Spring—spring ... OR-9
Gulling—locale ... OR-9
Gullion Creek—stream ... KY-4
Gullion Fork—stream ... VA-3
Gullion Mtn—summit ... AL-4
Gull Island ... CA-9
Gull Island ... MA-1
Gull Island ... MI-6
Gull Island ... MN-6
Gull Island ... NV-8
Gull Island ... OR-9
Gull Island—island ... AL-4
Gull Island—island (10) ... AK-9
Gull Island—island ... CA-9
Gull Island—island ... CO-8
Gull Island—island ... DE-2
Gull Island—island ... FL-3
Gull Island—island ... ID-8
Gull Island—island (4) ... MA-1
Gull Island—island (10) ... MI-6
Gull Island—island ... MN-6
Gull Island—island ... MT-8
Gull Island—island (3) ... NJ-2
Gull Island—island (3) ... NY-2
Gull Island—island (2) ... NC-3
Gull Island—island ... OR-9
Gull Island—island ... TN-4
Gull Island—island ... VT-1
Gull Island—island ... WI-6
Gull Island Bay—bay ... NC-3
Gull Island Channel—channel ... OR-9
Gull Island Channel—channel ... WA-9
Gull Island Reef—bar ... MI-6
Gull Islands—island ... AK-9
Gull Islands—island ... MI-6
Gull Islands—island ... NV-8
Gull Island Shoal—bar ... WI-6
Gull Island Thorofare—channel ... NJ-2
Gull Islet—island ... AK-9
Gullivan Bay—bay ... FL-3
Gullivan Key—island ... FL-3
**Gulliver**—pop pl ... MI-6
Gulliver Acad—school ... FL-3
Gulliver Brook—stream (4) ... ME-1
Gulliver Creek—bay ... MA-1
Gulliver Lake—lake ... MI-6
Gulliver Lake Outlet—stream ... MI-6
Gulliver Preparatory Sch—school (2) ... FL-3
Gulliver Ridge—ridge ... MO-7
Gullivers Castle—pillar ... UT-8
Gulliver Sch—school ... FL-3
Gull Keys—island ... FL-3
Gull Lake ... MN-6
Gull Lake—lake (2) ... AK-9
Gull Lake—lake ... CA-9
Gull Lake—lake (2) ... MI-6
Gull Lake—lake (5) ... MN-6
Gull Lake—lake (3) ... NY-2
Gull Lake—lake ... UT-8
Gull Lake—lake (2) ... WI-6
**Gull Lake**—pop pl ... MI-6
Gull Lake—reservoir ... MN-6
Gull Lake—stream ... MN-6
Gull Lake Lookout Tower—locale ... MN-6
Gull Lake Mounds Site—hist pl ... MN-6
Gull Lake Outlet—stream ... NY-2
Gull Lakes—lake ... NY-2
**Gull Lake (Town of)**—pop pl ... WI-6
Gull Ledge—bar ... ME-1
Gull Ledges—cliff ... ME-1
Gull Marsh—swamp ... VA-3
Gull Marsh Channel—channel ... VA-3
Gull Neck Rock—summit ... CA-9
Gull Pass—gap ... AK-9
Gull Point ... FL-3
Gull Point—cape (2) ... AK-9
Gull Point—cape ... IA-7
Gull Point—cape ... MA-1
Gull Point—cape (2) ... MI-6
Gull Point—cape (2) ... NY-2
Gull Point—cape ... RI-1
Gull Point—cliff ... IN-6
Gull Point—cliff ... WY-8
Gull Point—uninc pl ... FL-3
Gull Point State Park—park ... IA-7
**Gull Point (subdivision)**—pop pl ... DE-2
Gull Pond—bay ... NY-2
Gull Pond—lake ... ME-1
Gull Pond—lake ... MA-1
Gull Pond—lake (2) ... NY-2
Gull Ranch—locale ... SD-7
Gull Reef—bar ... WA-9
Gull River—stream (2) ... MN-6
Gull River Cem—cemetery ... MN-6
Gull Rock ... OR-9
Gull Rock—bar ... ME-1
Gull Rock—bar ... MI-6
Gull Rock—cape ... AK-9
Gull Rock—island (2) ... AK-9
Gull Rock—island (2) ... CA-9
Gull Rock—island ... CT-1
Gull Rock—island (2) ... ME-1
Gull Rock—island (4) ... MN-6
Gull Rock—island ... NY-2
Gull Rock—island (3) ... OR-9
Gull Rock—island ... VT-1
Gull Rock—island ... WA-9
Gull Rock—other ... AK-9
Gull Rock—pillar ... MI-6
Gull Rock—pillar ... NH-1
Gull Rock—pillar ... RI-1
Gull Rock—rock ... MA-1
Gull Rock Ledge—bar ... ME-1
Gull Rock Light—locale ... NY-2
Gull Rock Light Station—hist pl ... MI-6
Gull Rock Point—cape ... NY-2
Gull Rocks—bar ... AK-9
Gull Rocks—bar ... MI-6
Gull Rocks—bar ... WA-9
Gull Rocks—island ... CT-1
Gull Rocks—pillar ... RI-1
Gull Sch—school ... SD-7
Gull Sch (abandoned)—school ... SD-7
**Gulls Flight (subdivision)**—pop pl ... NC-3
**Gulls Nest (subdivision)**—pop pl ... DE-2
Gull Street Sch—school ... MI-6
Gullway General Hosp—hospital ... TX-5
Gullwing Rsvr—reservoir ... MT-8
**Gully**—pop pl ... MN-6
Gully, The—stream ... SC-3
Gully Bay—swamp ... NC-3
Gully Branch ... AL-4
Gully Branch—stream (2) ... AL-4
Gully Branch—stream (10) ... FL-3
Gully Branch—stream (3) ... GA-3
Gully Branch—stream (4) ... MS-4
Gully Branch—stream ... NC-3
Gully Branch—stream (4) ... SC-3
Gully Brook—stream (2) ... ME-1
Gully Brook—stream ... NH-1
Gully Brook—stream ... VT-1
Gully Camp—locale ... DE-2
Gully Camp Ditch—stream ... DE-2
Gully Creek ... WI-6
Gully Creek—stream ... AL-4
Gully Creek—stream ... FL-3
Gully Creek—stream (2) ... GA-3
Gully Creek—stream ... KY-4
Gully Creek—stream (2) ... MS-4
Gully Creek—stream ... MT-8
Gully Creek—stream ... NC-3
Gully Creek—stream ... SC-3
Gully Creek Ch—church ... KY-4
Gully Homestead—hist pl ... CO-8
Gully Lake—lake (2) ... FL-3
Gully Ledge—bar ... ME-1
Gully Meadow—flat ... CA-9
Gully Mill—hist pl ... NC-3
Gully Mtn—summit ... VA-3
Gully Point—cape ... MA-1
Gully Pond ... FL-3
Gully Pond—lake ... OR-9
Gully Ponds ... FL-3
Gully Ranch—locale ... NV-8
Gully Run—stream ... SC-3
Gully Sch—school ... OK-5
Gully Spring—spring ... OR-9
Gully Springs Ch—church ... FL-3
Gullys Slough—gut ... ND-7
Gully State Wildlife Mngmt Area—park ... MN-6

Gullysville—*locale* VA-3
Gully Tank—*reservoir* AZ-5
**Gully (Township of)**—*pop pl* MN-6
Gully View Sch (historical)—*school* TN-4
Gulnac Peak—*summit* CA-9
Gulnare—*locale* CO-8
Gulnare—*locale* KY-4
Gulo Creek—*stream* AK-9
Gulp Cem—*cemetery* MI-6
Gulph—*locale* NY-2
*Gulph, The* MA-1
Gulpha Creek—*stream* AR-4
Gulpha Gorge Campground—*park* AR-4
Gulph Creek—*stream* PA-2
**Gulph Mills**—*pop pl* PA-2
Gulph Mills Golf Course—*locale* PA-2
**Gulph Mills Village**—*pop pl* PA-2
Gulph Station—*locale* PA-2
**Culph Terrace** *pop pl* PA-2
Gulpins Branch—*stream* SC-3
Gulp Sch (historical)—*school* AL-4
Gulps Gap—*gap* TX-5
Gulrock—*locale* NC-3
Gulskoog Creek—*stream* MI-6
*Gulston* KY-4
**Gulston (Pansy)**—*pop pl* KY-4
*Gulteman Bayou* FL-3
*Gult Gulch* MT-8
**Gulthrie Beach**—*pop pl* KY-4
*Gultonville* PA-2
Gulvey—*locale* VA-3
Gum—*locale* CA-9
Gum—*locale* VA-3
**Gum**—*pop pl* TN-4
Gumaer Brook—*stream* NY-2
Gumaer Island—*island* NY-2
Gumaer Memorial Park—*park* MI-6
Gum Arm—*bay* TN-4
Gum Arm Ditch—*canal* TN-4
Gumayas Caves—*cave* GU-9
*Gumbar Creek* WI-6
Gum Bar Point—*cape* VA-3
Gum Bay—*swamp* (2) FL-3
Gum Bayou—*gut* MS-4
Gum Bayou—*stream* (4) LA-4
Gum Bayou—*stream* MS-4
Gum Bayou Landing—*locale* LA-4
Gum Bayou Oil Field—*oilfield* TX-5
*Gumb Creek* OR-9
Gumbel Bldg—*hist pl* MO-7
**Gumberry**—*pop pl* NC-3
Gumberry Sch—*school* NC-3
Gumberry Swamp—*stream* (2) NC-3
Gumbert Hill—*summit* PA-2
Gumble Brothers Dam—*dam* PA-2
Gumble Sch—*school* IL-6
**Gumbo**—*pop pl* (2) MO-7
Gumboat Basin—*basin* AK-9
Gumbo Butte—*summit* MT-8
Gumbo Ch—*church* MO-7
Gumbo Creek—*stream* MT-8
Gumbo Creek—*stream* ND-7
Gumbo Creek—*stream* WY-8
Gumbo Draw—*valley* (2) WY-8
Gumbo Flat—*flat* SD-7
*Gumbo Flats* ND-7
Gumbo Gulch—*valley* OR-9
Gumbo Hills—*range* WY-8
Gumbo (historical)—*locale* SD-7
Gumbo Lake—*lake* WY-8
Gumbo Lake—*swamp* AL-4
Gumbo Limbo Hammock—*island* FL-3
Gumboot Butte—*summit* OR-9
Gum Boot Canyon—*valley* OR-9
Gum Boot Creek—*stream* CA-9
Gumboot Creek—*stream* CA-9
Gumboot Creek—*stream* OR-9
Gumboot Lake—*flat* NV-8
Gumboot Lake—*lake* CA-9
Gum Boot Mine—*mine* CA-9
Gumboot Mine—*mine* CA-9
Gumboot Mtn—*summit* WA-9
*Gumboot Run* PA-2
Gum Boot Run—*stream* PA-2
Gumbo Point—*cliff* NM-5
Gumbo Point Archeol Site—*hist pl* MO-7
Gumbo Point Spring—*spring* MT-8
Gumbo Ridge—*ridge* MT-8
Gumboro—*locale* DE-2
Gumboro Ch—*church* DE-2
Gumboro Hundred—*civil* DE-2
Gumbo Rsvr—*reservoir* MT-8
Gum Bottom—*basin* AL-4
Gum Bottom—*bend* AR-4
*Gumbottom Branch* MD-2
Gum Bottom Branch—*stream* KY-4
Gumbottom Branch—*stream* MD-2
Gumbottom Sch—*school* AR-4
Gum Brake—*swamp* AR-4
*Gum Branch* TX-5
Gum Branch—*gut* FL-3
Gum Branch—*locale* GA-3
**Gumbranch**—*pop pl* GA-3
**Gumbranch**—*pop pl* NC-3
**Gum Branch**—*pop pl* NC-3
Gum Branch—*stream* (4) AL-4
Gum Branch—*stream* (2) AR-4
Gum Branch—*stream* (3) DE-2
Gum Branch—*stream* (2) FL-3
Gum Branch—*stream* (9) GA-3
Gum Branch—*stream* (2) IL-6
Gum Branch—*stream* (5) KY-4
Gum Branch—*stream* (4) LA-4
Gum Branch—*stream* (6) MS-4
Gum Branch—*stream* (8) NC-3
Gum Branch—*stream* (5) SC-3
Gum Branch—*stream* (5) TN-4
Gum Branch—*stream* (12) TX-5
Gum Branch—*stream* (3) VA-3
Gum Branch—*stream* WV-2
Gum Branch Canal—*canal* NC-3
Gum Branch Ch—*church* NC-3
Gumbridge Branch—*stream* MD-2
Gum Bridge Pond—*lake* TX-5
*Gum Brook* DE-2
Gum Brook—*stream* PA-2
*Gumbs Lake* MI-6
**Gumbud**—*pop pl* AL-4
*Gumbud Church* AL-4
Gumbud Creek—*stream* AL-4
Gum Cabin Hollow—*valley* WV-2
Gum Cave—*cave* AL-4
Gum Cem—*cemetery* (2) KY-4
Gum Cem—*cemetery* MO-7
Gum Cem—*cemetery* TN-4
Gum Ch—*church* MS-4
Gum Chapel—*church* NC-3
*Gum Ch of Christ* MS-4
*Gum Corner* MS-4
Gum Corner—*locale* NC-3
*Gum Corner Hollow* VA-3
Gum Corner Hollow—*valley* VA-3
Gum Corners—*locale* KY-4
Gum Cove—*bay* TX-5
Gum Cove Ferry—*locale* LA-4
Gum Cove Oil and Gas Field—*oilfield* LA-4
Gum Cove Ridge—*ridge* LA-4
*Gum Creek* MS-4
*Gum Creek* OR-9
*Gum Creek* SC-3
**Gum Creek**—*pop pl* TN-4
Gum Creek—*stream* AL-4
Gum Creek—*stream* (5) AR-4
Gum Creek—*stream* (8) FL-3
Gum Creek—*stream* (9) GA-3
Gum Creek—*stream* IL-6
Gum Creek—*stream* KY-4
Gum Creek—*stream* LA-4
Gum Creek—*stream* MS-4
Gum Creek—*stream* MO-7
Gum Creek—*stream* NC-3
Gum Creek—*stream* OK-5
Gum Creek—*stream* OR-9
Gum Creek—*stream* TN-4
Gum Creek—*stream* (6) TX-5
Gum Creek—*swamp* FL-3
Gum Creek Bay—*swamp* FL-3
Gum Creek Cem—*cemetery* TN-4
Gum Creek Ch—*church* FL-3
Gum Creek Ch—*church* (4) GA-3
Gum Creek Ch—*church* OK-5
Gum Creek Cumberland Presbyterian Ch—*church* TN-4
Gum Creek Landing—*locale* FL-3
Gum Creek Oil And Gas Field—*oilfield* AR-4
Gum Creek Sch—*school* TX-5
Gum Creek Sch (historical)—*school* TN-4
Gum Creek Swamp—*swamp* FL-3
Gum Crossroads—*locale* DE-2
Gum Cypress Lake (historical)—*lake* AL-4
**Gumdale**—*pop pl* TN-4
Gumdale Dewatering Area—*basin* TN-4
Gumdale Sch (historical)—*school* TN-4
Gum Draft—*valley* PA-2
Gum Drift Slough—*gut* FL-3
Gumdrop Hills—*range* NV-8
**Gum Flat**—*pop pl* TN-4
Gum Flat Bay—*swamp* NC-3
Gum Flat Bayou—*stream* AR-4
Gum Flat Bayou—*swamp* AR-4
Gum Flats—*flat* AL-4
Gum Flats—*flat* AR-4
Gum Flat Sch (historical)—*school* TN-4
Gumflats Creek—*stream* NC-3
Gum Fork—*locale* VA-3
Gum Fork—*stream* AL-4
Gum Fork—*stream* NC-3
Gum Fork—*stream* TN-4
Gum Fork Ch—*church* TN-4
*Gum Fork Creek* TN-4
Gum Fork Mine (surface)—*mine* TN-4
Gumfork Post Office (historical)—*building* TN-4
Gum Forks—*locale* NC-3
Gum Fork Sch—*school* TN-4
Gum Gap—*gap* KY-4
Gum Gap—*gap* NC-3
Gum Gap—*gap* SC-3
Gum Gap—*gap* TN-4
Gum Grove—*locale* AR-4
**Gum Grove**—*pop pl* MS-4
**Gum Grove**—*pop pl* TX-5
*Gum Grove Baptist Church* MS-4
Gum Grove Cem—*cemetery* (2) AR-4
Gum Grove Ch—*church* MS-4
Gum Grove Ch (historical)—*church* MS-4
Gum Grove Ch (historical)—*church* TN-4
Gum Grove Landing (historical)—*locale* MS-4
Gum Grove Sch—*school* KY-4
Gum Grove Sch—*school* LA-4
Gum Grove Sch—*school* MS-4
Gum Grove Sch (historical)—*school* MS-4
Gum Grove Sch (historical)—*school* TN-4
Gum Gully—*stream* (2) LA-4
Gum Gully—*valley* (3) TX-5
Gum Hammock Creek—*gut* VA-3
Gum Hill—*summit* MD-2
Gum Hill—*summit* NV-8
Gum Hill—*summit* UT-8
Gumhill, The—*ridge* UT-8
Gum Hill Ch—*church* VA-3
Gum Hollow—*valley* (2) AR-4
Gum Hollow—*valley* KY-4
Gum Hollow—*valley* (3) MO-7
Gum Hollow—*valley* OH-6
Gum Hollow—*valley* TN-4
Gum Hollow—*valley* TX-5
Gum Hollow—*valley* (2) WV-2
Gum Hollow Branch—*stream* (2) TN-4
*Gum Island* AL-4
Gum Island—*island* AL-4
Gum Island—*island* AR-4
Gum Island—*island* DE-2
Gum Island—*island* (3) LA-4
Gum Island—*island* MD-2
Gum Island—*island* MO-7
Gum Island—*island* (2) TX-5
Gumjuwac Creek—*stream* OR-9
Gumjuwac Saddle—*gap* OR-9
Gum Lake—*lake* FL-3
Gum Lake—*lake* LA-4
Gum Lake—*lake* MS-4
Gum Lake—*lake* NC-3
Gum Lake—*lake* TX-5
Gum Landing—*locale* FL-3
Gum Landing—*locale* MS-4
Gum Lick—*stream* KY-4
Gumlick Branch—*stream* KY-4
Gum Lick Ch—*church* KY-4
Gum Lick Creek—*stream* IN-6
Gum Lick Creek—*stream* KY-4
Gumlick Hollow—*valley* KY-4
Gum Lick Hollow—*valley* VA-3
Gumlick Run—*stream* WV-2
Gum Log—*locale* AR-4
**Gum Log**—*pop pl* GA-3
*Gum Log Baptist Church* MS-4
Gumlog Bayou—*gut* LA-4
Gum Log Branch—*stream* GA-3
Gum Log Branch—*stream* KY-4
Gum Log Branch—*stream* (2) NC-3
Gum Log Canal—*canal* NC-3
Gum Log Cem—*cemetery* MS-4
Gum Log Ch—*church* GA-3
Gum Log Ch—*church* MS-4
Gum Log Creek—*stream* AR-4
Gum Log Creek—*stream* GA-3
Gumlog Creek—*stream* GA-3
Gumlog Creek—*stream* (2) NC-3
Gumlog Gap—*gap* GA-3
Gumlog Lead—*ridge* GA-3
Gumlog Mountain—*ridge* GA-3
Gumlog Mtn—*summit* GA-3
Gum Log (Township of)—*fmr MCD* AR-4
Gumm Creek—*stream* GA-3
Gumm Creek—*stream* OR-9
Gummel Branch—*stream* KY-4
Gummer House—*hist pl* OH-6
Gumm Hill Ch—*church* GA-3
Gum Mill Creek—*stream* MD-2
Gumm Pond—*lake* GA-3
Gum Mtn—*summit* VA-3
Gum Neck—*cape* NC-3
Gum Neck—*locale* NC-3
Gum Neck Creek—*stream* NC-3
Gum Neck Landing—*locale* NC-3
Gum Neck (Township of)—*fmr MCD* NC-3
Gumoje—*ridge* GU-9
Gum Orchard Ch—*church* NC-3
**Gump**—*pop pl* PA-2
Gumpas Cem—*cemetery* NH-1
Gumpas Hill—*summit* NH-1
Gumpas Pond—*lake* NH-1
Gumpas Pond Brook—*stream* NH-1
Gump Branch—*stream* MO-7
Gump House—*hist pl* IN-6
Gump Lake—*lake* MI-6
Gump Lake—*lake* MN-6
Gum Pocket—*bay* TN-4
Gum Point—*cape* AR-4
Gum Point—*cape* (3) MD-2
Gum Point—*cape* (3) NC-3
Gum Point—*cape* TN-4
Gum Point—*cape* VA-3
Gum Point—*cliff* AZ-5
**Gum Point**—*pop pl* AR-4
Gumpoint Gully—*stream* LA-4
*Gum Pond* MS-4
Gum Pond—*lake* (2) AL-4
Gum Pond—*lake* (2) AR-4
Gum Pond—*lake* (3) FL-3
Gum Pond—*lake* GA-3
Gum Pond—*lake* LA-4
Gum Pond—*lake* (2) MS-4
Gum Pond—*lake* (2) TN-4
Gum Pond—*locale* AL-4
Gum Pond—*locale* MS-4
Gum Pond—*reservoir* FL-3
Gum Pond—*swamp* AL-4
Gum Pond—*swamp* (2) FL-3
Gum Pond—*swamp* GA-3
Gum Pond—*swamp* LA-4
Gum Pond—*swamp* MS-4
Gum Pond—*swamp* SC-3
Gum Pond Branch—*stream* AL-4
Gum Pond Branch—*stream* MS-4
Gum Pond Branch—*stream* NC-3
Gum Pond Cem—*cemetery* (2) AL-4
Gum Pond Ch—*church* AL-4
Gum Pond Ch (historical)—*church* AL-4
Gum Pond Ditch—*canal* AR-4
Gum Pond (historical)—*lake* TN-4
Gum Pond (historical)—*locale* AL-4
*Gum Pond Primitive Baptist Church* AL-4
*Gum Pond Run* NC-3
Gum Pond Sch—*school* SC-3
Gum Pond Sch (historical)—*school* AL-4
Gum Pond Slough—*stream* AL-4
Gum Pond (Township of)—*fmr MCD* AR-4
Gump Sch—*school* AZ-5
Gump Tank—*reservoir* AZ-5
Gum Pudding Branch—*stream* NC-3
Gum Reed Brake—*stream* MS-4
**Gum Ridge**—*pop pl* LA-4
Gum Ridge—*ridge* (3) AR-4
Gum Ridge—*ridge* IL-6
Gum Ridge—*ridge* LA-4
Gum Ridge Chute—*stream* LA-4
Gum Ridge Chute—*stream* MS-4
**Gum Ridge (historical)**—*pop pl* MS-4
Gum Ridge P.O. (historical)—*building* MS-4
Gum Ridge Sch—*school* SC-3
Gum River—*gut* FL-3
Gum Road Ditch—*canal* IL-6
Gumroot Branch—*stream* LA-4
Gum Root Creek—*stream* SC-3
Gum Root Swamp—*swamp* FL-3
*Gum Run* VA-3
Gum Run—*locale* PA-2
Gum Run—*stream* OH-6
Gum Run—*stream* (2) PA-2
Gum Run—*stream* VA-3
Gum Run—*stream* (3) WV-2
Gum Run Canal—*canal* NC-3
**Gums**—*pop pl* MS-4
Gum Sch (abandoned)—*school* MO-7
Gum Sch (historical)—*school* AL-4
Gums Crossing—*locale* MS-4
*Gums Crossroad* DE-2
*Gums Crossroads* DE-2
*Gum Slough* AR-4
Gum Slough—*gut* (2) AR-4
Gum Slough—*gut* (4) FL-3
Gum Slough—*gut* GA-3
Gum Slough—*gut* (2) TN-4
Gum Slough—*gut* (4) TX-5
Gum Slough—*stream* AL-4
Gum Slough—*stream* (2) AR-4
Gum Slough—*stream* (3) FL-3
Gum Slough—*stream* (3) LA-4
Gum Slough—*stream* (2) TX-5
Gum Slough—*swamp* FL-3
Gum Slough—*swamp* TX-5
Gum Slough Ditch—*canal* (2) AR-4
Gum Slough (historical)—*stream* TN-4
*Gumspring* AL-4
Gum Spring—*locale* AL-4
Gum Spring—*locale* TN-4
Gum Spring—*locale* WV-2
**Gum Spring**—*pop pl* AL-4
**Gum Spring**—*pop pl* MS-4
**Gum Spring**—*pop pl* TN-4
**Gum Spring**—*pop pl* VA-3
Gum Spring—*spring* (2) AL-4
Gum Spring—*spring* (2) KY-4
Gum Spring—*spring* MS-4
Gum Spring—*spring* (4) MO-7
Gum Spring—*spring* (2) OK-5
Gum Spring—*spring* PA-2
Gum Spring—*spring* (8) TN-4
Gum Spring—*spring* (2) TX-5
Gum Spring—*stream* (2) NJ-2
Gum Spring Branch—*stream* AL-4
Gum Spring Branch—*stream* KY-4
Gum Spring Branch—*stream* MO-7
Gum Spring Branch—*stream* SC-3
Gum Spring Branch—*stream* (2) TN-4
Gum Spring Branch—*stream* TX-5
Gum Spring Branch—*stream* VA-3
Gum Spring Camp—*locale* PA-2
Gum Spring Canyon—*valley* NM-5
Gum Spring Cem—*cemetery* AR-4
Gum Spring Cem—*cemetery* OK-5
Gum Spring Ch—*church* (2) AR-4
Gum Spring Ch—*church* NC-3
Gum Spring Ch—*church* OK-5
Gumspring Ch—*church* SC-3
Gum Spring Ch—*church* (3) TN-4
Gum Spring Ch (historical)—*church* AL-4
Gum Spring Creek—*stream* AL-4
Gum Spring Hollow—*valley* (2) AR-4
Gum Spring Hollow—*valley* (2) MO-7
*Gum Spring Missionary Baptist Ch* TN-4
Gum Spring Mtn—*summit* TN-4
*Gum Springs* MS-4
*Gum Springs* TN-4
Gum Springs—*locale* AR-4
Gum Springs—*locale* GA-3
Gum Springs—*locale* (2) TN-4
Gum Springs—*locale* (2) TX-5
**Gum Springs**—*pop pl* AL-4
**Gum Springs**—*pop pl* (2) AR-4
**Gum Springs**—*pop pl* (3) MS-4
**Gum Springs**—*pop pl* NC-3
**Gum Springs**—*pop pl* TN-4
**Gum Springs**—*pop pl* TX-5
**Gum Springs**—*pop pl* VA-3
Gum Springs—*spring* (2) AL-4
Gum Springs—*spring* AR-4
Gum Springs—*spring* FL-3
*Gum Springs Baptist Church* TN-4
Gum Springs Bible Ch—*church* KY-4
Gum Springs Branch—*stream* (2) AL-4
Gum Springs Branch—*stream* AR-4
Gum Springs Branch—*stream* FL-3
Gum Springs Branch—*stream* SC-3
Gum Springs Branch—*stream* (2) TN-4
Gum Springs Branch—*stream* TX-5
Gum Springs Branch—*stream* VA-3
Gum Springs Cem—*cemetery* AL-4
Gum Springs Cem—*cemetery* (2) AR-4
Gum Springs Cem—*cemetery* (2) TN-4
Gum Springs Ch—*church* (5) AL-4
Gum Springs Ch—*church* (2) AR-4
Gum Springs Ch—*church* GA-3
Gum Springs Ch—*church* (2) MS-4
Gum Springs Ch—*church* MO-7
Gum Springs Ch—*church* (2) NC-3
Gum Springs Ch—*church* (3) SC-3
Gum Springs Ch—*church* (4) TN-4
Gum Springs Ch—*church* TX-5
Gum Springs Ch—*church* VA-3
Gum Springs Ch—*church* WV-2
Gum Spring Sch—*school* AR-4
Gum Spring Sch—*school* OK-5
Gum Springs Ch (historical)—*church* TN-4
*Gum Spring School* AL-4
Gum Spring School—*locale* MO-7
Gum Springs Creek—*stream* AR 4
Gum Springs Hill—*summit* AR-4
Gum Springs (historical)—*locale* AL-4
Gum Springs Lookout Tower—*locale* LA-4
*Gum Springs Missionary Baptist Ch* TN-4
Gum Springs Mountain—*ridge* AL-4
Gum Springs Sch—*school* (2) KY-4
Gum Springs Sch—*school* TX-5
Gum Springs Sch (historical)—*school* (2) AL-4
Gum Springs Sch (historical)—*school* MS-4
Gum Springs Sch (historical)—*school* (4) TN-4
Gum Springs (Township of)—*fmr MCD* AR-4
Gum Springs Trail—*trail* TN-4
Gum Spring Trail—*trail* PA-2
Gums Run—*stream* PA-2
Gum Stand—*gap* VA-3
Gumstand Branch—*stream* NC-3
Gum Stand Ch—*church* TN-4
Gumstand Gap—*gap* NC-3
Gumstock Branch—*stream* NC-3
**Gum Stump**—*pop pl* PA-2
Gum Stump Hollow—*valley* OH-6
Gum Stump Landing—*locale* GA-3
Gum Stump Point—*cape* GA-3
Gumstump Pool—*swamp* MO-7
Gumsuck Branch—*stream* AL-4
Gum Suck Hollow—*valley* AL-4
**Gum Sulphur**—*pop pl* KY-4
*Gum Swamp* NC-3
*Gum Swamp* SC-3
Gum Swamp—*locale* (2) MD-2
Gum Swamp—*stream* GA-3
Gum Swamp—*stream* (8) NC-3
Gum Swamp—*swamp* (4) AL-4
Gum Swamp—*swamp* (6) FL-3
Gum Swamp—*swamp* (2) LA-4
Gum Swamp—*swamp* MD-2
Gum Swamp—*swamp* NY-2
Gum Swamp—*swamp* (8) NC-3
Gum Swamp—*swamp* (2) SC-3
Gum Swamp—*swamp* VA-3
*Gum Swamp Bay* NC-3
Gum Swamp Bay—*basin* SC-3
Gum Swamp Bay—*swamp* NC-3
Gum Swamp Branch—*stream* FL-3
Gum Swamp Branch—*stream* GA-3
Gum Swamp Branch—*stream* SC-3
Gum Swamp Branch—*stream* TN-4
Gum Swamp Canal—*canal* NC-3
Gum Swamp Ch—*church* SC-3
*Gum Swamp Creek* GA-3
Gum Swamp Creek—*stream* FL-3
Gum Swamp Creek—*stream* GA-3
Gum Swamp Creek—*stream* MS-4
Gum Swamp Creek—*stream* (2) NC-3
Gum Swamp Creek—*stream* (2) SC-3
Gum Swamp Lake—*reservoir* NC-3
Gum Swamp Lake Dam—*dam* NC-3
Gum Swamp Run—*stream* (3) NC-3
Gum Thicket—*flat* NC-3
Gum Thicket Creek—*stream* NC-3
Gum Thicket Shoal—*bar* NC-3
*Gumtree* NC-3
*Gumtree* PA-2
Gum Tree—*locale* AR-4
Gum Tree—*locale* KY-4
Gum Tree—*locale* NC-3
Gum Tree—*locale* PA-2
**Gumtree**—*pop pl* NC-3
**Gum Tree**—*pop pl* VA-3
Gum Tree Branch—*stream* AL-4
Gumtree Branch—*stream* SC-3
Gum Tree Branch—*stream* TX-5
Gum Tree Corner—*locale* NJ-2
Gum Tree Cove—*bay* CA-9
Gumtree Cove—*bay* MD-2
*Gum Tree Creek* TX-5
Gum Tree Mtn—*summit* VA-3
*Gumwood* MS-4
**Gumwood**—*pop pl* DE-2
Gumwood Ch—*church* AR-4
Gumwood Plantation—*locale* MS-4
Gumwood Post Office (historical)—*building* MS-4
Gum Woods (Township of)—*fmr MCD* AR-4
Gunari Gulch—*valley* CA-9
Gunbarrel—*CDP* CO-8
Gunbarrel Bay—*bay* TX-5
Gunbarrel Camp—*locale* WA-9
Gunbarrel Canyon—*valley* CO-8
**Gun Barrel City**—*pop pl* TX-5
Gunbarrel Cove—*bay* MD-2
Gunbarrel Creek—*stream* CA-9
Gunbarrel Creek—*stream* CO-8
Gunbarrel Creek—*stream* ID-8
Gunbarrel Creek—*stream* OR-9
Gunbarrel Creek—*stream* WA-9
Gunbarrel Creek—*stream* WY-8
**Gunbarrel Estates**—*pop pl* CO-8
Gunbarrel Gulf—*valley* NY-2
Gun Barrel Hill—*summit* CO-8
Gun Barrel Hill—*summit* KS-7
Gunbarrel Hollow—*valley* WV-2
**Gunbarrel Meadows**—*pop pl* CO-8
Gunbarrel Mine—*mine* CA-9
Gunbarrel Point—*cape* MD-2
Gunbarrel Spring—*spring* MT-8
Gun Barrel Windmill—*locale* TX-5
Gun Bayou Landing (historical)—*locale* MS-4
Gunbert Sch—*school* PA-2
Gunboat Island—*island* AK-9
Gunboat Island—*island* FL-3
Gunboat Island—*island* SC-3
Gunboat Lake—*lake* WY-8
Gunboat Lakes—*area* AK-9
Gunboat Mtn—*summit* TX-5
Gunboat Point—*cape* VA-3
Gunboat Rock—*bar* NY-2
Gunboat Rock—*island* AK-9
*Gun Branch* TX-5
Gun Branch—*stream* FL-3
Gun Branch—*stream* NJ-2
Gunby Ch—*church* MD-2
Gunby Creek—*stream* MD-2
Gunckel Park—*park* OH-6
Gunckel Sch—*school* OH-6
Gunckel's Town Plan Hist Dist—*hist pl* OH-6
Gun Club Canyon—*valley* OR-9
*Gunclub Lake* MN-6
Gun Club Lake—*lake* MN-6
Gun Club Pond *reservoir* MA-1
Gun Club Pond Dam—*dam* MA-1
Gun Creek—*stream* AZ-5
Gun Creek—*stream* ID-8
Gun Creek—*stream* IL-6
Gun Creek—*stream* IN-6
Gun Creek—*stream* KY-4
Gun Creek—*stream* NY-2
Gun Creek—*stream* OR-9
Gun Creek Cem—*cemetery* MS-4
Gun Creek Ch—*church* KY-4
Gun Creek Corral—*locale* AZ-5
Gun Creek Public Use Area—*locale* IL-6
Gun Creek Sch—*school* KY-4
Gundaker Hill—*summit* NV-8
Gundar Lake—*lake* MN-6
Gundby Draw—*valley* WY-8
Gund Cem—*cemetery* IL-6
Gundell Island—*island* ME-1
**Gunder**—*pop pl* IA-7
Gunderland Park—*park* TX-5
*Gunderson* MN-6
Gunderson, Endre B., Farmstead—*hist pl* SD-7
Gunderson, Jos., House—*hist pl* MA-1
Gunderson, Martin T., House—*hist pl* MN-6
Gunderson Creek—*stream* (2) MT-8
Gunderson Creek—*stream* ND-7
Gunderson Creek—*stream* OR-9
Gunderson Creek—*stream* WA-9
Gunderson Elevator—*locale* MT-8
*Gunderson Hill* WA-9
*Gunderson Lake* MN-6
Gunderson Lake—*lake* MN-6
Gunderson Lake—*lake* ND-7
Gunderson Mtn—*summit* WA-9
Gunderson Park—*park* SD-7
Gunderson Ridge—*ridge* WI-6
Gunderson Rock—*island* CA-9
Gunderson Strip (airport)—*airport* NV-8
Gunderson Valley—*valley* WI-6
Gundigut Valley—*valley* PA-2
*Gundlach Creek* IA-7
Gundlach-Grosse House—*hist pl* IL-6
*Gundlach Lookout Tower* MS-4
Gundlach Sch—*school* MO-7
Gund Ranch—*locale* NV-8
*Gundrum* IN-6
Gundry Sch—*school* MI-6
**Gundy**—*pop pl* IL-6
Gundy Cem—*cemetery* IL-6
Gundy Cem—*cemetery* OH-6
Gundy Creek—*stream* SC-3
Gundy Ditch—*canal* IN-6
Gundy Hollow—*valley* KY-4
Gundy Hollow—*valley* UT-8
Gundy Knob—*summit* OH-6
Gunerson Lateral—*canal* ID-8
Gunflint Camp—*locale* MN-6
Gunflint Lake—*lake* MN-6
Gunflint Lookout Tower—*locale* MN-6
Gun Flint Mtn—*summit* AL-4
Gunflint Trail—*trail* MN-6
*Gungen* FM-9
Gung'l, John, House—*hist pl* AZ-5
Gungywamp Hill—*summit* CT-1
Gun Hill Cem—*cemetery* GA-3
Gun Hollow—*valley* NY-2
Gun Hollow—*valley* TN-4
Gun Hollow—*valley* TX-5
Gunhouse Chute—*channel* MS-4
Gunhouse Hill—*summit* NY-2
*Gun Inlet* NC-3
Gunion Ch—*church* IL-6
*Gun Island* NH-1
Gun Island—*island* AL-4
Gun Island—*island* AR-4
Gun Island—*island* NH-1
*Gunkan* MH-9
*Gunkan Island* MH-9
Gunkel Ranch—*locale* ND-7
Gunkel Ranch—*locale* OR-9
**Gunkel Township**—*pop pl* ND-7
Gun Lake—*lake* GA-3
Gun Lake—*lake* (2) MI-6
Gun Lake—*lake* (3) MN-6
**Gun Lake**—*pop pl* MI-6
Gun Lake Chapel—*church* MI-6
*Gun Landing* VA-3
*Gunleeta Creek* NC-3
Gunlock—*locale* KY-4
Gunlock—*locale* UT-8
Gunlock Campground—*park* UT-8
Gunlock Cem—*cemetery* UT-8
Gunlock Creek—*stream* MO-7
Gunlock Dam—*dam* UT-8
*Gunlock Lake* UT-8
Gunlock Lake—*lake* WI-6
*Gunlock Lake State Beach* UT-8
**Gunlock (Mid)**—*pop pl* KY-4
Gunlock Ranch—*locale* CA-9
Gunlock Ridge—*ridge* NC-3
Gunlock Rsvr—*reservoir* (2) UT-8
*Gunlock State* UT-8
Gunlock State Park—*park* UT-8
Gunlow Point—*cape* MD-2
*Gunmear Island* NY-2
Gunmetal Mine—*mine* NV-8
Gun Mtn—*summit* (2) NH-1
Gun Mtn—*summit* VA-3
*Gunn* MS-4
**Gunn**—*pop pl* MN-6
**Gunn**—*pop pl* MS-4
Gunn, Cornelius, House—*hist pl* NJ-2
Gunna Creek—*stream* NC-3
Gunnals—*locale* FL-3
Gunn and Hubbard Blocks—*hist pl* MA-1
Gunn And Ramsey Drain—*canal* MI-6
Gunnard Anderson Ditch—*canal* IN-6
Gunnary Sch—*school* MN-6
Gunn Ave Park—*park* CA-9
Gunn Branch—*stream* MI-6
Gunn Branch—*stream* MS-4
Gunn Brook—*stream* CT-1
Gunn Brook—*stream* MA-1
Gunn Canyon—*valley* CA-9
Gunn Canyon—*valley* NM-5
Gunn Cem—*cemetery* (2) AL-4
Gunn Cem—*cemetery* GA-3
Gunn Cem—*cemetery* LA-4
Gunn Cem—*cemetery* OH-6
Gunn Cem—*cemetery* (2) TN-4
Gunn Cem—*cemetery* TX-5
Gunn Chute—*channel* AL-4
**Gunn City**—*pop pl* MO-7
Gunn City Cem—*cemetery* MO-7
Gunn City (Station)—*locale* MO-7
Gunn Creek—*stream* AK-9
Gunn Creek—*stream* CO-8
Gunn Creek—*stream* FL-3
Gunn Ditch—*canal* WA-9
Gunn Drain—*canal* MI-6
Gunn-Dyer Park—*park* MI-6
*Gunnear Island* NY-2
*Gunnel Creek* SC-3
Gunnel Fork—*stream* AR-4
Gunnel Hollow—*valley* KY-4
Gunnell Cem—*cemetery* MO-7
Gunnell Guard Station—*locale* ID-8
Gunnell Hollow—*valley* WV-2
Gunnell House—*hist pl* MS-4
Gunnels Landing Strip—*airport* MO-7
Gunneltree Run—*stream* WV-2
*Gunner Branch* TN-4
Gunner Branch—*stream* KY-4
*Gunner Creek* SC-3
Gunner Creek—*stream* AR-4
Gunner Hollow—*valley* AR-4
Gunner Hollow—*valley* TN-4
Gunner Mtn—*summit* VA-3
Gunner Pool Rec Area—*park* AR-4
Gunners Branch—*stream* MD-2
Gunners Brook—*stream* VT-1
Gunners Cove—*bay* AK-9
Gunners Cove—*bay* MD-2
Gunners Ditch—*channel* NJ-2
Gunners Exchange Pond—*lake* MA-1
Gunners Hill—*summit* RI-1
*Gunners Island* DE-2
Gunners Island—*island* MD-2
Gunners Lakes—*reservoir* OR-9
Gunner Slough—*stream* (2) AR-4
Gunnerson Draw—*valley* MT-8
*Gunners Point* MA-1

Gunners Point—cape ... MD-2
Gunners Point—cape ... NJ-2
Gunners Rapids—rapids ... WI-6
Gunners Run—stream ... WV-2
Gunners Run (historical)—stream ... PA-2
Gunnerville—locale ... OH-6
Gunnery Hill—summit ... OK-5
Gunnery Sch—school ... CT-1
Gunnesons Creek ... AL-4
Gunn Hall Manor—locale ... VA-3
Gunn Hill—summit ... GA-3
Gunn Hill—summit ... PA-2
Gunn Hill Branch—stream ... GA-3
Gunn Hollow—valley (2) ... TN-4
Gunn Hollow Branch—stream ... TN-4
Gunn House—hist pl ... OH-6
Gunn HS—school ... CA-9
Gunnie, Bayou—stream ... LA-4
Gunning Bedford JHS—school ... DE-2
Gunning Cem—cemetery ... KY-4
Gunning Creek—stream ... CA-9
Gunning Hammock Island—island ... NC-3
Gunning Island—island ... MA-1
Gunning Island—island ... NJ-2
Gunning Marsh ... ME-1
Gunning Playground—park ... OH-6
Gunning Point—cape ... MA-1
Gunning Point—cape ... NY-2
Gunning River—stream ... NJ-2
Gunning Rock—bar ... ME-1
Gunning Rock—pillar ... RI-1
Gunning Rocks—island ... ME-1
Gunning Rock Shoal—bar ... ME-1
Gunning Run—stream ... PA-2
Gunnings—locale ... TN-4
Gunnings Acad (historical)—school ... TN-4
Gunnings Cem—cemetery ... TN-4
Gunnings Special Education Sch—school ... TN-4
Gunnis Creek—stream ... MO-7
Gunnison—pop pl ... CO-8
Gunnison—pop pl ... MS-4
Gunnison—pop pl ... UT-8
Gunnison, Capt. John, House—hist pl ... NH-1
Gunnison, Mount—summit ... CO-8
Gunnison and Vulcan Mine—mine ... SD-7
Gunnison Bay—lake ... UT-8
Gunnison Bend—bend ... UT-8
Gunnison Bend Dam—dam ... UT-8
Gunnison Bend Rsvr—reservoir ... UT-8
Gunnison Brook—stream ... NH-1
Gunnison Butte—summit ... UT-8
Gunnison Cem—cemetery ... CO-8
Gunnison Cem—cemetery ... MS-4
Gunnison Cem—cemetery ... UT-8
Gunnison City Cemetery ... UT-8
Gunnison County Airport—airport ... CO-8
Gunnison Creek—stream ... AL-4
Gunnison Creek—stream (2) ... AK-9
Gunnison Cut—gut ... FL-3
Gunnison Dam—dam ... UT-8
Gunnison Division—civil ... UT-8
Gunnison Fayette Canal—canal ... UT-8
Gunnison Gulch ... CO-8
Gunnison Gulch—valley ... CO-8
Gunnison Highline Canal—canal ... CO-8
Gunnison Hills—summit ... AZ-5
Gunnison Island—island ... UT-8
Gunnison Lake—lake ... CO-8
Gunnison Massacre Historical Monmt—park ... UT-8
Gunnison Massacre Site ... UT-8
Gunnison Massacre Site—hist pl ... UT-8
Gunnison Massacre Site—locale ... UT-8
Gunnison Natl For—forest ... CO-8
Gunnison Plateau ... UT-8
Gunnison Post Office—building ... UT-8
Gunnison River—stream ... CO-8
Gunnison Rsvr—reservoir ... UT-8
Gunnison (Siding)—locale ... UT-8
Gunnison's Island ... UT-8
Gunnison Trail—trail ... CO-8
Gunnison Trail—trail ... UT-8
Gunnison Tunnel—hist pl ... CO-8
Gunnison Tunnel—tunnel ... CO-8
Gunnison Valley—basin ... UT-8
Gunnison Valley—valley ... UT-8
Gunnison Valley Hosp—hospital ... UT-8
Gunnison Valley HS—school ... UT-8
Gunnison Valley Sch—school ... UT-8
Gunnisonville—pop pl ... MI-6
Gunn Lake—lake ... MN-6
Gunn Lake—lake ... NM-5
Gunn Lake—lake ... OK-5
Gunn Lake—lake ... WA-9
Gunn Lakes—lake ... AK-9
Gunn Landing—locale (3) ... FL-3
Gunn Mesa—summit ... NM-5
Gunnoes Cem—cemetery ... WV-2
Gunn Park—park ... KS-7
Gunn Peak—summit ... WA-9
Gunn Place Abandoned)—locale ... NM-5
Gunn Ranch—locale ... CA-9
Gunns Bayou—stream ... MS-4
Gunns Branch—stream ... MO-7
Gunn Sch—school ... IA-7
Gunn Sch—school ... NC-3
Gunn Sch—school ... SD-7
Gunns Chapel—church ... KY-4
Gunns Chapel (Chapel)—pop pl ... KY-4
Gunns Church ... AL-4
Gunns Corners—locale ... NY-2
Gunns Creek ... MO-7
Gunns Hill—summit ... VA-3
Gunn Spring—spring ... GA-3
Gunn Square—park ... MA-1
Gunns Run—stream ... VA-3
Gunn Tank—reservoir ... NM-5
Gunnuk Creek—stream ... AK-9
Gunn (Whiteoak)—pop pl ... MS-4
Gunn Windmill—locale ... NM-5
Gunny Sack Bottom—bend ... SD-7
Gunnysack Creek—stream ... AK-9
Gunnysack Creek—stream ... WY-8
Gunny Sack Lake—lake ... MN-6
Gunoe Hill ... WI-6
Gun Plains—flat ... MI-6
Gunplain (Township of)—pop pl ... MI-6
Gun Point—cape ... FL-3
Gun Point—cape ... ME-1
Gun Point—cape ... MN-6
Gun Point—cape ... WA-9
Gun Point—cliff ... AZ-5
Gun Point Cove—bay ... ME-1
Gun Point Key—island ... FL-3
Gunpowder—pop pl ... MD-2
Gunpowder—post sta ... MD-2
Gunpowder Ch—church ... MD-2
Gunpowder Creek—stream ... KY-4
Gunpowder Creek—stream ... NC-3
Gunpowder Estates—pop pl ... MD-2
Gunpowder Falls—stream ... MD-2
Gunpowder Falls—stream ... PA-2
Gunpowder Lake—lake ... MI-6
Gunpowder Meetinghouse—hist pl ... MD-2
Gunpowder Meetinghouse—locale ... MD-2
Gunpowder Neck—cape ... MD-2
Gunpowder Ridge—ridge ... WV-2
Gunpowder Rifle Range—other ... MD-2
Gunpowder River—stream ... MD-2
Gunpowder State Park—park ... MD-2
Gunpowder Youth Camps—locale ... MD-2
Gun Rack Hollow—valley ... KY-4
Gunrack Ridge—ridge ... CA-9
Gunright Creek ... CO-8
Gun River—stream ... MI-6
Gun Rock—rock ... MA-1
Gun Rock Point—cape ... FL-3
Gun Rock Pond ... MA-1
Gunsaulus HS—school ... IL-6
Gunsight ... AZ-5
Gunsight—locale ... AZ-5
Gunsight—locale ... MT-8
Gunsight—locale ... TX-5
Gunsight—pillar ... CA-9
Gunsight—summit ... AZ-5
Gunsight—summit ... CA-9
Gunsight, The—gap ... ID-8
Gunsight Bar—bar ... UT-8
Gunsight Bay—bay ... UT-8
Gunsight Bench ... UT-8
Gunsight Butte—summit ... AZ-5
Gunsight Butte—summit ... OR-9
Gunsight Butte—summit (2) ... UT-8
Gunsight Canyon—valley (2) ... AZ-5
Gunsight Canyon—valley ... NM-5
Gunsight Canyon—valley ... UT-8
Gunsight Cem—cemetery ... AZ-5
Gunsight Creek—stream (3) ... AK-9
Gunsight Creek—stream (3) ... ID-8
Gunsight Draw—valley ... TX-5
Gunsight Flat—flat ... UT-8
Gunsight Gap—gap ... AZ-5
Gunsight Gap—gap ... CO-8
Gunsight Hills—summit ... AZ-5
Gunsight Hills—summit ... TX-5
Gunsight Lake—lake ... ID-8
Gunsight Lake—lake (2) ... MT-8
Gunsight Mine—mine ... CA-9
Gunsight Mountains ... AZ-5
Gunsight Mtn—summit (3) ... AK-9
Gunsight Mtn—summit ... AZ-5
Gunsight Mtn—summit (2) ... MT-8
Gunsight Mtn—summit ... OR-9
Gunsight Mtn—summit ... TN-4
Gunsight Mtn—summit (2) ... TX-5
Gunsight Notch—gap ... AZ-5
Gunsight Pass—gap (2) ... AK-9
Gunsight Pass—gap ... AZ-5
Gunsight Pass—gap ... CA-9
Gunsight Pass—gap (3) ... CO-8
Gunsight Pass—gap ... MT-8
Gunsight Pass—gap ... OR-9
Gunsight Pass—gap (2) ... UT-8
Gunsight Pass—gap (3) ... WY-8
Gunsight Pass Shelter—hist pl ... MT-8
Gunsight Pass Trail—trail (2) ... MT-8
Gunsight Peak—summit (2) ... CA-9
Gunsight Peak—summit (2) ... ID-8
Gunsight Peak—summit ... MT-8
Gunsight Peak—summit ... NM-5
Gunsight Peak—summit ... UT-8
Gunsight Peak—summit ... WA-9
Gunsight Point—cliff ... AZ-5
Gunsight Point—cliff ... UT-8
Gunsight Ranch ... AZ-5
Gunsight Ranch—locale ... AZ-5
Gunsight Ranch—locale ... TX-5
Gunsight Range ... AZ-5
Gunsight Rock—summit ... MT-8
Gunsight Spring—spring (2) ... UT-8
Gunsight Tank—reservoir (2) ... AZ-5
Gunsight Tank—reservoir ... TX-5
Gunsight Tank—reservoir ... UT-8
Gunsight Trail—trail ... CO-8
Gunsight Trail—trail ... MT-8
Gunsight Valley—valley ... AZ-5
Gunsight Wash—stream ... AZ-5
Gunsight Well ... AZ-5
Gunsmoke Trail—trail ... OK-5
Gunsolas Sch—school ... IL-6
Gunsolus Creek—stream ... TX-5
Gunson Ridge—ridge ... TN-4
Gun Spring—spring ... TN-4
Gun Spring—spring ... UT-8
Gunsten Lake—lake ... MN-6
Gunstock Branch—stream ... FL-3
Gunstock Branch—stream ... GA-3
Gunstock Branch—stream ... KY-4
Gunstock Branch—stream ... MS-4
Gunstock Branch—stream (2) ... TN-4
Gunstock Creek—stream ... VA-3
Gunstocker Creek—stream ... TN-4
Gunstock Hollow—valley ... MO-7
Gunstock Knob—summit ... WV-2
Gunstock Lake—lake ... MN-6
Gunstock Mountains ... NH-1
Gunstock Mtn—summit ... NH-1
Gunstock River—stream ... NH-1
Gunston Cove—bay ... VA-3
Gunston Hall—building ... VA-3
Gunston Hall—hist pl ... VA-3
Gunston Hall Ch—church ... VA-3
Gunston Heights—pop pl ... VA-3
Gunston JHS—school ... VA-3
Gunston Manor—pop pl ... VA-3
Gunston Sch—school ... VA-3
Gunston-Temple Ch—church ... MD-2
Gunstream Lakes—reservoir ... TX-5
Gunst Rsvr—reservoir ... WY-8
Gun Tank—reservoir (2) ... AZ-5
Gunter ... MO-7
Gunter—locale ... OR-9
Gunter—locale ... TX-5
Gunter—pop pl (2) ... TX-5
Gunter AFB—military ... AL-4
Gunter Bay—swamp ... SC-3
Gunter Branch—stream ... AR-4
Gunter Branch—stream (2) ... NC-3
Gunter Cem—cemetery ... AL-4
Gunter Cem—cemetery ... AR-4
Gunter Cem—cemetery ... IL-6
Gunter Cem—cemetery (2) ... NC-3
Gunter Cem—cemetery ... SC-3
Gunter Cem—cemetery (4) ... TN-4
Gunter Cem—cemetery (3) ... TX-5
Gunter Ch—church ... MO-7
Gunter Cove—valley ... NC-3
Gunter Creek—stream ... CA-9
Gunter Creek—stream ... MO-7
Gunter Field (Gunter Air Force Base)—other ... AL-4
Gunter Fork—stream ... NC-3
Gunter Gap—gap ... NC-3
Gunter Grove (subdivision)—pop pl ... AL-4
Gunter-Harris Island—island ... NC-3
Gunter Hill—summit ... AL-4
Gunter Hill—summit ... TX-5
Gunter Hollow—valley ... MO-7
Gunter Hollow—valley (3) ... TN-4
Gunter Industrial Park—locale ... AL-4
Gunter Island—island ... SC-3
Gunter Island Sch—school ... SC-3
Gunter Lake—lake ... SC-3
Gunter Lake—reservoir ... TX-5
Gunter Lake Dam—dam ... MS-4
Gunterman Cem—cemetery ... IL-6
Gunter Mill Creek—stream ... AL-4
Gunter Mtn—summit ... TN-4
Gunterpole Branch—stream ... TN-4
Gunter Post Office (historical)—building ... TN-4
Gunter Recreation Site—park ... OR-9
Gunter Reservation—reserve ... AL-4
Gunter Ridge—ridge ... TN-4
Gunter Ridge—ridge ... VA-3
Gunter Ridge Trail—trail ... VA-3
Gunters Bar—bar ... AL-4
Gunters Big Spring ... MO-7
Gunters Cove ... TN-4
Gunter's Creek ... AL-4
Gunters Creek—stream ... NC-3
Gunters Farm—locale ... AL-4
Gunters Hollow ... TN-4
Gunters Millpond—reservoir ... SC-3
Gunters Mtn—summit ... AL-4
Gunters Pond—reservoir ... AL-4
Gunters Reef—bar ... AL-4
Gunter-Summers House—hist pl ... SC-3
Gunters Valley—valley ... MO-7
Gunters Village ... AL-4
Guntersville—pop pl ... AL-4
Guntersville Caverns—cave ... AL-4
Guntersville (CCD)—cens area ... AL-4
Guntersville City Cem—cemetery ... AL-4
Guntersville Dam—dam ... AL-4
Guntersville Division—civil ... AL-4
Guntersville Hosp—hospital ... AL-4
Guntersville HS—school ... AL-4
Guntersville Lake—reservoir ... AL-4
Guntersville Lake—reservoir ... TN-4
Guntersville Lake Yacht Club—other ... AL-4
Guntersville Marina—locale ... AL-4
Guntersville Municipal Airp—airport ... AL-4
Guntersville Municipal Park—park ... AL-4
Guntersville Recreation Center—building ... AL-4
Guntersville Reservoir ... AL-4
Guntersville Shores (subdivision)—pop pl ... AL-4
Guntertown—pop pl ... NC-3
Gunter Trail—trail ... AR-4
Gunter Valley—valley ... PA-2
Gunter Valley Dam—dam ... PA-2
Gunter Valley Rsvr—reservoir ... PA-2
Gunterville Dam—pop pl ... AL-4
Gunther Branch—stream ... VA-3
Gunther Cabin Springs—spring ... OR-9
Gunther Castle—summit ... AZ-5
Gunther Creek—stream ... CA-9
Gunther Creek—stream ... OR-9
Gunther Field—park ... NY-2
Gunther Hollow—valley ... MO-7
Gunther Island ... CA-9
Gunther Island Site 67—hist pl ... CA-9
Gunther Park—pop pl ... NY-2
Gunther Sch—school ... NY-2
Gunther Sch—school ... OH-6
Gunther Sch—school ... SD-7
Gunther Spring—spring ... OR-9
Gunther Tank—reservoir ... AZ-5
Gunthertown—locale ... AL-4
Gunthrop ... ND-7
Guntley Ranch—locale ... CA-9
Guntner Place—locale ... MT-8
Gunton Park—locale ... VA-3
Gunton Sch—school ... MI-6
Guntown—pop pl ... MS-4
Guntown—pop pl ... TN-4
Guntown Acad (historical)—school ... MS-4
Guntown Baptist Ch—church ... MS-4
Guntown Cem—cemetery ... CT-1
Guntown Cem—cemetery ... MS-4
Guntown Sch—school ... MS-4
Guntown United Methodist Ch—church ... MS-4
Gun Tube Islands—island ... FL-3
Gunville—locale ... WV-2
Gunville Ranch—locale ... SD-7
Gunville Ridge—ridge ... WV-2
Gunwald ... IA-7
Gunwald—pop pl ... IA-7
Gunwale Run—stream ... WV-2
Gunyon Hollow—valley ... OH-6
Gu Oidak—pop pl ... AZ-5
Gu Oidak Valley—valley ... AZ-5
Gu Oidak Wash ... AZ-5
Gu Oidak Wash—arroyo ... AZ-5
G U Parker Wildlife Mngmt Area—park ... FL-3
Gupsaw Lake Dam—dam ... NJ-2
Guptil Gulch—valley ... CA-9
Guptill—locale ... ND-7
Guptill Cem—cemetery ... ME-1
Guptill Hill—summit ... ME-1
Guptill Point—cape ... ME-1
Gupton—locale ... NC-3
Gupton Branch—stream ... MS-4
Gupton Branch—stream ... TN-4
Gupton Cem—cemetery (2) ... TN-4
Gupton Run—stream ... VA-3
Guptons Lake—reservoir ... NC-3
Guptons Lake Dam—dam ... NC-3
Gur ... MH-9
Gurabo—pop pl ... PR-3
Gurabo Abajo (Barrio)—fmr MCD ... PR-3
Gurabo Arriba (Barrio)—fmr MCD ... PR-3
Gurabo (Municipio)—civil ... PR-3
Gurabo (Pueblo)—fmr MCD ... PR-3
Guradian Angel Ch—church ... TX-5
Gurapan ... MH-9
Gurdane—locale ... OR-9
Gurdane Cem—cemetery ... OR-9
Gurdane Creek—stream ... OR-9
Gurdon—pop pl ... AR-4
Gurdon Bill Park—park ... MA-1
Gurdon Golf Course—other ... AR-4
Gurdon Pond No 1—reservoir ... AR-4
Gurdon Pond No 2—reservoir ... AR-4
Gurdy Run—stream ... PA-2
Guren Cem—cemetery ... MO-7
Gurer—island ... MP-9
Gurer Island ... MP-9
Gurer Island ... PW-9
Gurganius ... AL-4
Gurganius Post Office (historical)—building ... AL-4
Gurganus—pop pl ... NC-3
Gurganus Cem—cemetery (2) ... NC-3
Gurganus Ch—church ... NC-3
Gurgle Creek—stream ... MI-6
Gurgling Run—stream ... PA-2
Gurgling Spring—spring ... TN-4
Gurguam Point ... MH-9
Gurholt Lake—lake ... WI-6
Gurikeru-Yageru ... PW-9
Gurkin Creek—stream ... AK-9
Gurkin Creek—stream ... OR-9
Gurler, George H., House—hist pl ... IL-6
Gurley—pop pl (2) ... AL-4
Gurley—pop pl ... LA-4
Gurley—pop pl ... NE-7
Gurley—pop pl ... SC-3
Gurley Airp—airport ... AL-4
Gurley Branch—stream ... GA-3
Gurley Canyon—valley ... CO-8
Gurley Canyon—valley ... OR-9
Gurley Cave—cave ... AL-4
Gurley (CCD)—cens area ... AL-4
Gurley Cem—cemetery ... CT-1
Gurley Cem—cemetery ... IL-6
Gurley Cem—cemetery ... NC-3
Gurley Ch—church ... SC-3
Gurley Corner—pop pl ... IN-6
Gurley Creek ... AL-4
Gurley Creek—stream ... AL-4
Gurley Creek—stream ... GA-3
Gurley Creek—stream ... ID-8
Gurley Creek—stream ... TN-4
Gurley Creek Gap—gap ... AL-4
Gurley Creek Mine (underground)—mine ... AL-4
Gurley Ditch—canal (2) ... CO-8
Gurley Ditch—canal ... IL-6
Gurley Division—civil ... AL-4
Gurley Draw—valley ... TX-5
Gurley Gulch—valley ... CA-9
Gurley Gulch—valley ... CO-8
Gurley Hollow—valley ... TN-4
Gurley Hughs Mtn—summit ... AL-4
Gurley Lake—lake ... MI-6
Gurley Lake Drain—canal ... MI-6
Gurley Landing—locale ... IN-6
Gurley Mtn—summit (2) ... AL-4
Gurley Post Office—building ... AL-4
Gurley Road Baptist Ch—church ... AL-4
Gurley Rsvr—reservoir ... CO-8
Gurley Sch—school ... LA-4
Gurley Sch—school ... TX-5
Gurleysville ... AL-4
Gurleysville Post Office ... AL-4
Gurleyville—locale ... CT-1
Gurleyville Hist Dist—hist pl ... CT-1
Gurley Windmill—locale ... TX-5
Gurlick Run ... PA-2
Gurlie Bayou—gut ... MS-4
Gurli Put Vo—locale ... AZ-5
Gurman Canyon—valley ... NM-5
Gurneau Lake—lake ... MN-6
Gurnee—locale ... PA-2
Gurnee—pop pl ... AL-4
Gurnee—pop pl ... IL-6
Gurnee Junction—locale ... AL-4
Gurnee Lake—lake ... NY-2
Gurnee Mine (underground)—mine ... AL-4
Gurnet—locale ... PA-2
Gurnet, The ... ME-1
Gurnet, The ... MA-1
Gurnet, The—cape ... MA-1
Gurnet Bridge Strait ... ME-1
Gurnet Point—cape ... MA-1
Gurnet Rock (historical)—bar ... MA-1
Gurnet Rocks ... MA-1
Gurnet Strait—channel ... ME-1
Gurnett Creek—stream ... MT-8
Gurney ... PA-2
Gurney—locale ... IL-6
Gurney—pop pl ... WI-6
Gurney, Charles, Hotel—hist pl ... SD-7
Gurney, Mount—summit ... OR-9
Gurney Bay—bay ... AK-9
Gurney Bogs—swamp ... MA-1
Gurney Creek—stream ... MI-6
Gurney Creek—stream ... MT-8
Gurney Gulch—valley ... MT-8
Gurney Hill—locale ... PA-2
Gurney Hill—summit ... ME-1
Gurney-Kochheiser House—hist pl ... OH-6
Gurney Peak—summit ... AK-9
Gurney Peak—summit ... WY-8
Gurney Sch—school ... IL-6
Gurney Sch—school ... MA-1
Gurneys Corner—pop pl ... MA-1
Gurney Spring—spring ... SD-7
Gurneys Ranch (historical)—locale ... SD-7
Gurney (Town of)—pop pl ... WI-6
Gurneyville—pop pl ... OH-6
Gurnie Creek ... MI-6
Gurno Lake—lake ... WI-6
Gurnsey Creek—stream ... CA-9
Gurnsey Creek Campground—locale ... CA-9
Gurn Spring—pop pl ... NY-2
Guro—island ... MP-9
Guro Island ... MP-9
Guroor—pop pl ... FM-9
Guroor—summit ... FM-9
Guror ... FM-9
Guro-to ... MP-9
Gurow ... FM-9
Gurrant Park—park ... FL-3
Gurr Lateral—canal ... CA-9
Gurry Well—well ... AZ-5
Gurtis Creek—stream ... OR-9
Gurtman Rock—pillar ... MO-7
Gurue Cem—cemetery ... SD-7
Gurule, Delfinia, House—hist pl ... NM-5
Gurule Arroyo—stream ... CO-8
Gurule Canyon—valley (2) ... NM-5
Gurule Spring—spring ... NM-5
Gurule Tank—reservoir ... NM-5
Gurum ... FM-9
Gurun ... FM-9
Gurung ... FM-9
Gurur Island ... PW-9
Gururoan Island ... PW-9
Guruung—locale ... FM-9
Gus—locale ... KY-4
Gus—locale ... TX-5
Gus Allen 1 Dam—dam ... SD-7
Gus Allen 2 Dam—dam ... SD-7
Gusano Mesa—summit ... NM-5
Gusano Pass ... AZ-5
Gus Bottom—valley ... MS-4
Gus Brink Mtn—summit ... MT-8
Gus Creek ... MT-8
Gus Creek—stream ... ID-8
Gus Creek—stream ... MO-7
Gus Creek—stream ... MT-8
Gus Creek—stream (2) ... OR-9
Gusdagane Point—cape ... AK-9
Guse Arm—canal ... IN-6
Guseman—locale ... WV-2
Gus Gaston Dam One—dam ... AL-4
Gus Gaston Dam Two—dam ... AL-4
Gushaw-Mudgett House—hist pl ... CA-9
Gushdoiman Lake—lake ... AK-9
Gushee Pond—lake ... MA-1
Gushees Corner—locale ... ME-1
Gus Henry Branch ... AL-4
Gusher—pop pl ... UT-8
Gusher Cem—cemetery ... UT-8
Gusher Knob—summit ... NC-3
Gusher Knob Dam—dam ... NC-3
Gusher Knob Lake—reservoir ... NC-3
Gusher Knob Mine—mine ... NC-3
Gusher Spring—spring ... NE-7
Gushiate Lake—lake ... AK-9
Gushing Creek—stream ... IN-6
Gushnee Pond ... MA-1
Gushwa Ditch—canal ... IN-6
Gus Johnson Branch—stream ... AL-4
Gus Johnson Creek—stream ... WI-6
Guskie Pond—lake ... CT-1
Guski Pond ... CT-1
Gus Lake—lake ... NE-7
Gus Lake—lake ... WA-9
Gusler Airp—airport ... PA-2
Gusler Creek—stream ... MI-6
Guslers Creek ... MI-6
Gus Lind Flat—flat ... UT-8
Gus Mitchell Brook—stream ... ME-1
Gus Pit—cave ... AL-4
Gus Point—cape ... FL-3
Guss—locale ... IA-7
Guss Cem—cemetery ... IA-7
Guss Creek ... AL-4
Gusses Creek—stream ... AR-4
Gussettville Cem—cemetery ... TX-5
Gussie Creek—stream ... OR-9
Gussie Draw—valley ... UT-8
Gussie Tank—reservoir ... TX-5
Guss Island—island ... WA-9
Guss Knoll—summit ... UT-8
Guss Lake—lake ... ND-7
Gusslers Gulch ... KS-7
Guss Picnic Area—locale ... PA-2
Gus Spring—spring ... AZ-5
Gus Spring—spring ... WA-9
Gus Steven Slough—gut ... AK-9
Gus Still Creek—stream ... AR-4
Gust, Lake—lake ... MN-6
Gustad, Bernt, House—hist pl ... SD-7
Gustaf Bay—bay ... FL-3
Gustafson Creek—stream ... MN-6
Gustafson Hill—summit ... MN-6
Gustafson Lake—lake ... MI-6
Gustafson Lake—lake ... MN-6
Gustafson Lateral—canal ... ID-8
Gustafson Marsh—swamp ... MI-6
Gustafson Sch—school ... IL-6
Gustafson Sch—school ... MI-6
Gustafson Sch—school ... SD-7
Gustafsons Dam—dam ... SD-7
Gustafson Spring—spring ... WA-9
Gustafva Cem—cemetery ... MN-6
Gust Anderson Lake ... MN-6
Gus Tank—reservoir (2) ... AZ-5
Gusta Point—cape ... LA-4
Gustave—locale ... SD-7
Gustave Aman Dam—dam ... SD-7
Gustave Butte—summit ... SD-7
Gustave Cem—cemetery ... SD-7
Gustave (historical)—locale (2) ... SD-7
Gustave Lake—lake ... WY-8
Gustavson Lake ... MN-6
Gustavus—pop pl ... AK-9
Gustavus—pop pl (2) ... OH-6
Gustavus Adolphus Coll—school ... MN-6
Gustavus Center Hist Dist—hist pl ... OH-6
Gustavus (Township of)—pop pl ... OH-6
Gust Cem—cemetery ... NE-7
Guste Sch—school ... LA-4
Gustin ... LA-4
Gustin—locale ... MI-6
Gustin Cem—cemetery ... PA-2
Gustin Ditch—canal ... OH-6
Gustine—pop pl ... CA-9
Gustine—pop pl ... TX-5
Gustine (CCD)—cens area ... CA-9
Gustine (CCD)—cens area ... TX-5
Gustine Gun Club—other ... CA-9
Gustine Lake—lake ... PA-2
Gustin Homestead—locale ... WY-8
Gustin No 2 Rsvr—reservoir ... WY-8
Gustin Pond—lake ... NH-1
Gustin Ranch—locale ... NM-5
Gustin Rsvr—reservoir ... WY-8
Gustin Sch—school ... MI-6
Gustin Spring—spring ... WA-9
Gustins Ranch—locale ... NM-5
Gustin (Township of)—pop pl ... MI-6
Gust James Wash—stream ... AZ-5
Gust Lake—lake ... WI-6
Gust Mtn—summit ... MT-8
Gust Natl Cem—cemetery ... MN-6
Guston—locale ... CO-8
Guston—pop pl ... KY-4
Guston—pop pl ... WV-2
Guston Run—stream ... WV-2
Gust Sch—school ... CO-8
Gustwiller Ditch—canal ... OH-6
Gusty Bay—bay ... AK-9
Gusty Branch—stream ... KY-4
Gusty Hollow—valley ... MO-7
Gusty Spring—spring ... MO-7
Gusubac ... AZ-5
Gus Well—well ... OR-9
Gus Well—well ... TX-5
Guswert Canyon—valley ... AZ-5
Gut, The ... CT-1
Gut, The ... NY-2
Gut, The—cape ... MA-1
Gut, The—channel (2) ... ME-1
Gut, The—gap ... UT-8
Gut, The—gut (2) ... ME-1
Gut, The—gut ... MA-1
Gut, The—gut ... NC-3
Gut, The—gut ... PA-2
Gut, The—gut ... RI-1
Gut, The—gut ... VT-1
Gut Ache Mesa—bend ... NM-5
Gut Ache Mesa Tank ... NM-5
Gut Bay—bay ... AK-9
Gut Branch—stream (2) ... TN-4
Gut Bridge—bridge ... DE-2
Gut Canyon—valley ... CO-8
Gutches Creek—stream ... NC-3
Gutches Grove—pop pl ... MN-6
Gutchi Creek—stream ... AK-9
Gut Creek—stream ... AR-4
Gut Creek—stream ... CA-9
Gut Creek—stream ... MT-8
Gut Creek—stream ... OR-9
Gut Gulch—valley ... MT-8
Guth—pop pl ... PA-2
Guthard, Charles, House—hist pl ... MI-6
Guth Cem—cemetery ... IL-6
Gutherie Prairie—flat ... OR-9
Gutheries Chapel—church ... AL-4
Gutherie School ... AL-4
Guthery Cem—cemetery ... OH-6
Guthery Creek—stream ... ID-8
Guthery Crossroads—pop pl ... AL-4
Guthie Island ... AR-4
Guthiel Ditch—canal ... OH-6
Guthmiller Lake—lake ... SD-7
Guthoerl Cave—cave ... MO-7
Guthrey Archeol Site—hist pl ... MO-7
Guthridge Elem Sch—school ... KS-7
Guthridge Ranch—locale ... MT-8
Guthridge Rsvr—reservoir ... WY-8
Guthridge Sch—school ... MO-7
Guthrie—locale ... AZ-5
Guthrie—locale ... MI-6
Guthrie—pop pl ... IL-6
Guthrie—pop pl ... IN-6
Guthrie—pop pl ... KY-4
Guthrie—pop pl ... LA-4
Guthrie—pop pl ... MN-6
Guthrie—pop pl ... MO-7
Guthrie—pop pl ... NC-3
Guthrie—pop pl ... ND-7
Guthrie—pop pl ... OK-5
Guthrie—pop pl ... TX-5
Guthrie—pop pl ... WV-2
Guthrie—pop pl ... WI-6
Guthrie, George W., Sch—hist pl ... PA-2
Guthrie, Woody, House—hist pl ... OK-5
Guthrie Bluff—cliff ... MO-7
Guthrie Branch—stream ... DE-2
Guthrie Branch—stream ... KY-4
Guthrie Branch—stream ... NC-3
Guthrie Branch—stream ... TN-4
Guthrie Branch—stream ... VA-3
Guthrie Canyon—valley ... AZ-5
Guthrie Canyon—valley ... CA-9
Guthrie (CCD)—cens area ... KY-4
Guthrie (CCD)—cens area ... OK-5
Guthrie (CCD)—cens area ... TX-5
Guthrie Cem ... AL-4
Guthrie Cem—cemetery ... AL-4
Guthrie Cem—cemetery ... AR-4
Guthrie Cem—cemetery ... GA-3
Guthrie Cem—cemetery ... MN-6
Guthrie Cem—cemetery (3) ... MO-7
Guthrie Cem—cemetery ... TN-4
Guthrie Cem—cemetery ... TX-5
Guthrie Cem—cemetery ... WV-2
Guthrie Center—pop pl ... IA-7
Guthrie Ch—church ... GA-3
Guthrie Ch—church ... WV-2
Guthrie Community Park—park ... OR-9
Guthrie Country Club—other ... OK-5
Guthrie County Care Facility—building ... IA-7
Guthrie County Park—park ... IA-7
Guthrie Cove—bay ... WA-9
Guthrie Creek ... IN-6
Guthrie Creek—stream (2) ... AL-4
Guthrie Creek—stream ... CA-9
Guthrie Creek—stream (2) ... GA-3
Guthrie Creek—stream ... IN-6
Guthrie Creek—stream ... OH-6
Guthrie Creek—stream ... VA-3
Guthrie Creek Ch—church ... IN-6
Guthrie Cut Ch—church ... AL-4
Guthrie Draw—valley (2) ... TX-5

Guthrie Elem Sch—*hist pl* ... TN-4
Guthrie Gap—*gap* ... TN-4
Guthrie Gap Ch—*church* ... TN-4
Guthrie Gas And Oil Field—*oilfield* ... OK-5
Guthrie Grove Camp—*locale* ... IA-7
Guthrie Hall—*hist pl* ... VA-3
Guthrie Hammock—*island* ... NC-3
Guthrie Hist Dist—*hist pl* ... OK-5
Guthrie Hollow—*valley* ... MO-7
Guthrie Hollow—*valley* ... TN-4
Guthrie Hosp—*hospital* ... WV-2
Guthrie House—*hist pl* ... CA-9
Guthrie Island—*island* ... AR-4
Guthrie Lake—*lake* ... AR-4
Guthrie Lake—*lake* ... CO-8
Guthrie Lake—*lake* ... LA-4
Guthrie Lake—*lake* ... MI-6
Guthrie Lake—*lake* ... TX-5
Guthrie Lake—*reservoir* ... IN-6
Guthrie Lake—*reservoir* ... OK-5
Guthrie Lake Dam—*dam* ... IN-6
*Guthrie Lake No. 2* ... OK-5
Guthrie Mine (underground)—*mine* ... AL-4
Guthrie Mtn—*summit* (2) ... AZ-5
Guthrie Mtn—*summit* ... KS-7
Guthrie Park—*park* ... IN-6
Guthrie Peak—*summit* ... AZ-5
Guthrie Point—*cape* ... NC-3
Guthrie Pond—*lake* ... CT-1
Guthrie Ranch—*locale* ... AZ-5
Guthrie Ranch—*locale* ... CA-9
Guthrie RR Station—*building* ... AZ-5
Guthrie Rsvr—*reservoir* ... OR-9
*Guthrie Run* ... DE-2
**Guthries**—*pop pl* ... SC-3
Guthrie Sch—*school* ... IL-6
Guthrie Sch—*school* ... KS-7
Guthrie Sch—*school* ... TN-4
Guthrie Sch (historical)—*school* ... AL-4
Guthrie Sch (historical)—*school* ... MO-7
Guthrie Sch (historical)—*school* ... PA-2
*Guthries Creek* ... IN-6
Guthrie Smith Park—*park* ... AL-4
Guthrie Spring—*spring* ... TN-4
**Guthrie's Ridge (Tanbark)**—*pop pl* ... KY-4
Guthries Sch—*school* ... KY-4
*Guthriesville* ... SC-3
**Guthriesville**—*pop pl* ... PA-2
**Guthriesville**—*pop pl* ... SC-3
Guthrie Tank—*reservoir* ... AZ-5
Guthrie Township—*civil* ... MO-7
Guthrie (Township of)—*fmr MCD* (2) ... AR-4
**Guthrie (Township of)**—*pop pl* ... IN-6
**Guthrie (Township of)**—*pop pl* ... MN-6
*Guthrieville* ... PA-2
*Guthrieville* ... SC-3
Guthrie Well—*well* ... WY-8
*Guths* ... PA-2
Guths Bay—*bay* ... WI-6
*Guth Station* ... PA-2
**Guthsville**—*pop pl* ... PA-2
Gutierez And Sedillo Grant (Tract No 1)—*civil* ... NM-5
Gutierrez Alto Windmill—*locale* ... TX-5
Gutierrez And Sedillo Grant (Tract No 2)—*civil* ... NM-5
Gutierrez Canyon—*valley* ... CO-8
Gutierrez Canyon—*valley* ... NM-5
Gutierrez House—*hist pl* ... NM-5
Gutierrez Spring—*spring* ... NM-5
Gutierrezville—*locale* ... NM-5
Gutierrez Windmill—*locale* ... NM-5
Gutierrez Windmill—*locale* ... TX-5
Gut Lake—*lake* ... AR-4
Gut Lake—*lake* (2) ... MI-6
Gut Lake—*lake* ... MN-6
Gut Lick Branch—*stream* ... KY-4
Gutman—*locale* ... OH-6
Gut Marsh—*swamp* ... MD-2
Gutnecht Drain—*stream* ... MI-6
Gutoer—*bay* ... FM-9
*Gutor* ... FM-9
Gutosky Park—*park* ... CA-9
Gut Point—*cape* ... DE-2
Gut Pond—*lake* ... VT-1
Gut Port—*bay* ... MI-6
Gutridge Creek—*stream* ... OR-9
Gutridge Mine—*mine* ... OR-9
*Guts Canyon* ... UT-8
**Gutschmidt Township**—*pop pl* ... ND-7
Gutshall Gulch—*valley* ... CO-8
Gutshall Hollow—*valley* ... PA-2
Gutshall Spring—*spring* (2) ... CO-8
Guts Lake—*lake* ... ID-8
**Guttenberg**—*pop pl* ... IA-7
**Guttenberg**—*pop pl* ... NJ-2
Guttenberg Cem—*cemetery* ... IA-7
Guttenberg Cem—*cemetery* ... SD-7
Guttenberg Corn Canning Co.—*hist pl* ... IA-7
Guttenberg State Bank—*hist pl* ... IA-7
*Gutter Branch* ... AL-4
Gutter Branch—*stream* ... NC-3
Gutter Creek—*gut* ... NC-3
Gutter Inlet—*bay* ... NY-2
Gutter Rock Creek—*stream* ... AR-4
Gutters Branch—*stream* ... AL-4
Guttery Spring—*spring* ... OR-9
Gutzman Dam—*dam* ... SD-7
Gutz Peak—*summit* ... UT-8
Guungean—*cape* ... FM-9
*Guvernors Branch* ... AL-4
**Gu Vo**—*pop pl* ... AZ-5
Gu Vo Hills—*summit* ... AZ-5
Gu Vo Pass—*gap* ... AZ-5
Gu Vo Wash—*stream* ... AZ-5
Guvspuny Island—*island* ... ME-1
**Gu-Win**—*pop pl* ... AL-4
Gu -Win Ch—*church* ... AL-4
*Guy* ... KS-7
*Guy* ... MS-4
*Guy* ... WA-9
Guy—*locale* ... KY-4
Guy—*locale* ... NM-5
Guy—*locale* ... TX-5
**Guy**—*pop pl* ... AR-4
**Guy**—*pop pl* ... IN-6
**Guy**—*pop pl* ... LA-4
Guy, Bayou—*stream* ... LA-4
Guy, Finley, Bldg—*hist pl* ... IA-7
Guyago, Bayou—*gut* ... LA-4
*Guyan* ... WV-2
Guyan—*locale* ... WV-2
Guyan Ch—*church* ... WV-2
Guyan Country Club—*other* ... WV-2
Guyan Creek—*stream* ... WV-2
*Guyandot* ... WV-2
*Guyandot Mountain* ... WV-2
*Guyandot River* ... WV-2
*Guyandotte* ... OH-6
**Guyandotte**—*pop pl* ... WV-2
Guyandotte Ch—*church* ... WV-2
Guyandotte (Magisterial District)—*fmr MCD* ... WV-2
Guyandotte Mtn—*range* ... WV-2
*Guyandotte River* ... WV-2
Guyandotte River—*stream* ... WV-2
**Guyan Estates**—*pop pl* ... WV-2
Guyan (Magisterial District)—*fmr MCD* ... WV-2
**Guyanoga**—*pop pl* ... NY-2
Guyanoga Valley—*valley* ... NY-2
Guyan Ridge—*ridge* ... WV-2
*Guyan River* ... WV-2
Guyan Run—*stream* ... OH-6
**Guyan Terrace**—*pop pl* ... WV-2
**Guyan (Township of)**—*pop pl* ... OH-6
Guyan Valley Ch—*church* ... OH-6
Guyastuta Station—*building* ... PA-2
**Guyasuta**—*pop pl* ... PA-2
Guyasuta Run—*stream* ... PA-2
*Guyaux* ... PA-2
Guyaux—*other* ... PA-2
Guy A West Bridge—*bridge* ... CA-9
Guyaz—*locale* ... ID-8
Guy Branch—*stream* ... AL-4
Guy Branch—*stream* ... FL-3
Guy Branch—*stream* ... GA-3
Guy Brown Pond Dam—*dam* ... MS-4
Guy Camp Branch—*stream* ... KY-4
Guy Canyon—*valley* ... ID-8
Guy Cem—*cemetery* ... AL-4
Guy Cem—*cemetery* ... IL-6
Guy Cem—*cemetery* ... LA-4
Guy Cem—*cemetery* (2) ... MS-4
Guy Cem—*cemetery* ... NC-3
Guy Cem—*cemetery* ... OH-6
Guy Cem—*cemetery* (2) ... TN-4
Guy Cem—*cemetery* ... TX-5
Guy Cem—*cemetery* ... WA-9
Guy C Irving House—*locale* ... PA-2
Guy Cove—*valley* ... KY-4
Guy Creek—*stream* ... CA-9
Guy Creek—*stream* ... OK-5
Guy Dickerson Lake—*dam* ... MS-4
Guy Ditch—*canal* ... IN-6
**Guyencourt**—*pop pl* ... DE-2
Guye Peak—*summit* ... WA-9
Guyer Branch—*stream* ... AL-4
Guyer Cem—*cemetery* ... IL-6
Guyer Cove—*valley* ... AL-4
Guyer Creek—*stream* ... MI-6
Guyer Creek—*stream* ... OR-9
Guyer Hot Springs—*spring* ... ID-8
Guyer Opera House—*hist pl* ... IN-6
Guyer Spring—*spring* ... AL-4
Guyes Lake—*lake* ... ND-7
Guyette Ditch No 1—*canal* ... WY-8
Guy Gap Sch—*school* ... TN-4
Guy Gray Lake Dam—*dam* ... MS-4
Guy Gulch—*valley* ... CO-8
Guy Hill—*summit* ... CO-8
Guy Hollow—*valley* ... PA-2
Guy Hollow—*valley* (2) ... VA-3
Guy House—*hist pl* ... LA-4
Guy Hyde Pond Dam—*dam* ... MS-4
*Guy Jones Dam* ... AL-4
Guy Jones Lake—*lake* ... TN-4
Guy Jones Lake Dam—*dam* ... MS-4
Guy Kinyon Cabin—*locale* ... ID-8
Guy Knob—*summit* ... NC-3
Guy Lake—*lake* ... CA-9
Guy Lake Dam—*dam* ... MS-4
Guy Lee Windmill—*locale* ... TX-5
Guyler Hill—*locale* ... NY-2
Guyman Seep—*spring* ... UT-8
Guymanton Lake—*lake* ... NC-3
Guyman Well—*well* ... UT-8
**Guymard**—*pop pl* ... NY-2
Guymard Lake—*lake* ... NY-2
*Guy Mills* ... PA-2
Guy Mine (underground)—*mine* ... TN-4
**Guymon**—*pop pl* ... OK-5
Guymon (CCD)—*cens area* ... OK-5
Guymon Lake—*reservoir* ... TN-4
Guymon Lake Dam—*dam* ... TN-4
Guymon Pond—*lake* ... UT-8
Guymon Spring—*spring* ... MT-8
Guymon Wash—*valley* ... UT-8
Guyn, Robert, Jr., House—*hist pl* ... KY-4
Guynes—*locale* ... LA-4
Guynes Cem—*cemetery* ... LA-4
Guyn's Mill Hist Dist—*hist pl* ... KY-4
Guyo Canyon—*valley* ... UT-8
Guyon Basin—*basin* ... OR-9
Guyon Hotel—*hist pl* ... IL-6
Guyonmoore Creek—*stream* ... SC-3
Guyon Spring—*spring* ... OR-9
Guyo Spring—*spring* ... UT-8
Guyot, Mount—*summit* ... CA-9
Guyot, Mount—*summit* ... CO-8
Guyot, Mount—*summit* ... NH-1
Guyot, Mount—*summit* ... TN-4
Guyot Bay—*bay* ... AK-9
Guyot Creek—*stream* ... CA-9
Guyot Flat—*flat* ... CA-9
Guyot Glacier—*glacier* ... AK-9
Guyot Hill—*summit* ... CO-8
Guyot Hill—*summit* ... NY-2
Guyot Hills—*other* ... AK-9
*Guyot Mountains* ... UT-8
Guyot Spur—*ridge* ... TN-4
Guy Park—*hist pl* ... NY-2
Guy Park Ave Sch—*school* ... NY-2
Guy Plaza (Shop Ctr)—*locale* ... FL-3
Guy Pond—*swamp* ... FL-3
Guy Pugh Dam—*dam* ... AL-4
*Guyre Cove* ... AL-4
Guyre Creek—*stream* ... CA-9
Guy Rife Ranch—*locale* ... WY-8
*Guy Roberts Dam* ... AL-4
*Guy Rock* ... MH-9
Guy Rowe Creek—*stream* ... AK-9
Guy Run—*stream* ... WV-2
*Guys* ... MD-2
**Guys**—*pop pl* ... SC-3
**Guys**—*pop pl* ... TN-4
*Guy Sandy Creek* ... OK-5
Guy Sandy Creek—*stream* ... OK-5
Guysbarger Run—*stream* ... WV-2
*Guys Branch* ... SC-3
Guys Branch—*stream* ... KY-4
Guys Branch—*stream* ... NC-3
Guys Cave—*cave* ... AL-4
Guys Cem—*cemetery* ... TN-4
Guys Chapel—*church* ... AL-4
Guys Chapel—*church* ... MO-7
Guy Sch (historical)—*school* ... MS-4
Guys Creek—*stream* ... NC-3
Guys Crossroads—*locale* ... AL-4
Guy Senter Pond Dam—*dam* ... MS-4
*Guyser Creek* ... OR-9
Guyser Hollow—*valley* ... MO-7
Guyses Run—*stream* ... WV-2
*Guys Gap School* ... TN-4
Guys Gulch—*valley* ... CA-9
Guys Hollow—*valley* ... PA-2
Guy (Siding)—*locale* ... TX-5
Guysie—*locale* ... GA-3
*Guys Mill* ... PA-2
**Guys Mills**—*pop pl* ... PA-2
Guy Smith Park—*park* ... NC-3
**Guyson**—*pop pl* ... ND-7
Guys Point—*cape* ... VA-3
Guys Point Gut—*gut* ... MD-2
Guys Point Gut—*stream* ... VA-3
Guys Pond—*reservoir* ... AL-4
Guys Pond—*reservoir* ... NC-3
Guys Pond Dam—*dam* ... NC-3
Guys Post Office—*building* ... TN-4
Guys Ranch—*locale* ... CA-9
Guys Run—*stream* ... PA-2
Guys Run—*stream* (2) ... VA-3
Guys Sch (historical)—*school* ... TN-4
Guys Spring—*spring* ... AL-4
Guys Store—*locale* ... TX-5
Guys Tank—*reservoir* ... AZ-5
Guys Tank—*reservoir* ... NM-5
Guys Tank—*reservoir* ... TX-5
Guyst Fork—*stream* ... OH-6
Guys Village Ch—*church* ... AL-4
Guys Village Sch—*school* ... AL-4
**Guysville**—*pop pl* ... OH-6
Guys Well—*well* ... AZ-5
Guyton—*locale* ... MO-7
**Guyton**—*pop pl* ... GA-3
**Guyton**—*pop pl* ... NC-3
Guyton Canyon—*valley* ... OR-9
Guyton Cem—*cemetery* (2) ... GA-3
Guyton Cem—*cemetery* ... MS-4
Guyton Creek—*stream* ... LA-4
Guyton Creek—*stream* ... MS-4
*Guyton Cut* ... TX-5
Guyton Hill—*summit* ... MI-6
Guyton Hist Dist—*hist pl* ... GA-3
Guyton (historical)—*locale* ... MS-4
Guyton (reduced usage)—*locale* ... LA-4
Guyton Sch—*school* ... MI-6
Guytons Lake—*reservoir* ... AL-4
Guytons Lake Dam—*dam* ... AL-4
Guyton-Springfield (CCD)—*cens area* ... GA-3
Guy Wash—*valley* ... UT-8
Guy W Talbot State Park—*park* ... OR-9
Guzman Abajo (Barrio)—*fmr MCD* ... PR-3
Guzman Arriba (Barrio)—*fmr MCD* ... PR-3
Guzman Rsvr—*reservoir* ... NM-5
Guzmans Lookout Mtn—*summit* ... NM-5
Guzzier—*other* ... CA-9
Guzzle Hollow—*valley* ... TN-4
*Guzzler Gulch* ... KS-7
Guzzlers Gulch—*valley* ... KS-7
G V Creek—*stream* ... CO-8
Gvernsey Rsvr—*reservoir* ... WY-8
G V Spring—*spring* ... CO-8
*Gwadobusu-To* ... PW-9
Gwaltney Cem—*cemetery* ... TN-4
Gwaltney Corner—*locale* ... VA-3
Gwaltney Memorial Cem—*cemetery* ... IN-6
Gwaltneys (Township of)—*fmr MCD* ... NC-3
G Wammen Ranch—*locale* ... SD-7
G Wash—*stream* ... AZ-5
G Wash—*valley* ... CO-8
G Wash Tank—*reservoir* ... AZ-5
**Gwathmey**—*pop pl* ... VA-3
Gwathmey, Richard, House—*hist pl* ... KY-4
G W Baker Dam—*dam* ... AL-4
G W Carver Sch—*school* ... TX-5
G W Chapman—*locale* ... TX-5
Gweek River—*stream* ... AK-9
G Wellhausen—*locale* ... TX-5
G Welter Dam—*dam* ... SD-7
Gwenah Mine—*mine* ... NV-8
Gwen Cherry Park—*park* ... FL-3
**Gwendale**—*pop pl* ... PA-2
Gwendolen—*locale* ... OR-9
Gwendolen Canyon—*valley* ... OR-9
Gwendolen Lake—*lake* ... CO-8
*Gwenford* ... ID-8
**Gwenford**—*pop pl* ... ID-8
Gwen Lake—*lake* ... AK-9
Gwen Lake—*lake* ... FL-3
Gwen Lake—*lake* ... TX-5
**Gwen Mill (subdivision)**—*pop pl* ... AL-4
Gwent Cove—*bay* ... AK-9
G William Holmes Research Station—*locale* ... AK-9
Gwills Branch—*stream* ... KY-4
Gwills Corners—*locale* ... NY-2
*Gwin* ... MS-4
**Gwin**—*pop pl* ... KY-4
**Gwin**—*pop pl* ... MS-4
Gwin Airp—*airport* ... PA-2
Gwin Cem—*cemetery* ... IN-6
Gwin Cem—*cemetery* (3) ... TN-4
Gwin Gulch—*valley* ... CA-9
Gwin Hollow—*valley* ... TN-4
**Gwinhurst**—*pop pl* ... DE-2
Gwin Landing (historical)—*locale* ... MS-4
Gwin Mine—*mine* ... CA-9
Gwin Mine (underground)—*mine* ... AL-4
Gwin Mtn—*summit* ... VA-3
Gwinn—*locale* ... WV-2
**Gwinn**—*pop pl* ... MI-6
Gwinna Falls—*falls* ... WY-8
Gwinn Branch—*stream* ... KY-4
Gwinn Cem—*cemetery* ... IA-7
Gwinn Cem—*cemetery* ... KY-4
Gwinn Cem—*cemetery* ... MI-6
Gwinn Cem—*cemetery* ... TN-4
Gwinn Cove—*valley* ... TN-4
Gwinn Cove Cave—*cave* ... TN-4
Gwinn Ditch—*canal* ... IN-6
Gwinn Draw—*valley* ... WY-8
**Gwinner**—*pop pl* ... ND-7
Gwinner Cem—*cemetery* ... ND-7
Gwinner Municipal Airfield—*airport* ... ND-7
*Gwinners Island* ... PA-2
Gwinn Estate—*hist pl* ... OH-6
**Gwinnett (County)**—*pop pl* ... GA-3
Gwinnett County Courthouse—*hist pl* ... GA-3
Gwinnett County Park—*park* ... GA-3
Gwinnett Memorial Gardens—*cemetery* ... GA-3
Gwinn Fork—*stream* ... WY-8
Gwinn Fork Dick Creek—*stream* ... WY-8
Gwinn Island—*island* ... KY-4
**Gwinn Island**—*pop pl* ... KY-4
Gwinn Lookout Tower—*locale* ... MI-6
Gwinn Mine—*mine* ... MI-6
Gwinn Mtn—*summit* ... WV-2
*Gwinns Creek* ... AL-4
Gwinns Crossing (Historical)—*locale* ... TX-5
Gwinn Spring—*spring* ... OR-9
Gwinn Tank—*reservoir* ... NM-5
**Gwinntown (historical)**—*pop pl* ... TN-4
*Gwinport Airfield* ... PA-2
Gwin River—*stream* ... AR-4
Gwin Sch—*school* ... AL-4
Gwins Lodge—*locale* ... AK-9
Gwins Post Office (historical)—*building* ... TN-4
Gwin Spring—*spring* ... ID-8
Gwinville—*locale* ... MS-4
Gwinville Branch—*stream* ... MS-4
Gwinville Oil And Gas Field—*oilfield* ... MS-4
G W Perpall Grant—*civil* (3) ... FL-3
G Wright Ranch—*locale* (2) ... ND-7
G W Sewell Pond—*lake* ... FL-3
G W Trotter Lake Dam—*dam* ... MS-4
G W Trotters Lake Dam—*dam* ... MS-4
Gwydyr Bay—*bay* ... AK-9
Gwyn, James M., House—*hist pl* ... NC-3
Gwyn, Lake—*lake* ... FL-3
Gwyna Sch—*school* ... MS-4
Gwyn Creek—*stream* ... OR-9
Gwynedd—*locale* ... PA-2
Gwynedd Hall—*hist pl* ... PA-2
**Gwynedd Heights**—*pop pl* ... PA-2
Gwynedd-Mercy Coll—*school* ... PA-2
*Gwynedd-Mercy Junior Coll* ... PA-2
**Gwynedd Square**—*pop pl* ... PA-2
Gwynedd Valley—*locale* ... PA-2
Gwyneth Ham Elem Sch—*school* ... AZ-5
Gwynn—*other* ... MD-2
**Gwynn**—*pop pl* ... VA-3
**Gwynn Acres (Gwynn)**—*pop pl* ... MD-2
Gwynnbrook—*locale* ... MD-2
Gwynnbrook State Game Farm—*park* ... MD-2
Gwynn Camp—*locale* ... NM-5
Gwynn Canyon—*valley* ... NM-5
Gwynn Cem—*cemetery* ... NC-3
Gwynn Cem—*cemetery* ... TN-4
Gwynn Cienega—*stream* ... NM-5
Gwynn Creek—*stream* ... OR-9
Gwynne Bldg—*hist pl* ... OH-6
Gwynne-Love House—*hist pl* ... CO-8
Gwynne Mine—*mine* ... CA-9
Gwynne Sch—*school* ... FL-3
**Gwynneville**—*pop pl* ... IN-6
Gwynn Island—*island* ... VA-3
Gwynn Island Landing—*locale* ... VA-3
Gwynn Knoll—*summit* ... OR-9
Gwynn Oak—*locale* ... MD-2
Gwynn Oak Park—*park* ... MD-2
Gwynn Park Sch—*school* ... MD-2
Gwynns Chapel—*church* ... NC-3
Gwynns Falls—*stream* ... MD-2
Gwynns Falls Park—*park* ... MD-2
**Gwynn's Island**—*pop pl* ... VA-3
Gwynns Ranch—*locale* ... WY-8
Gwynns Run—*stream* ... MD-2
Gwynn's Run—*uninc pl* ... MD-2
Gwyn Ridge—*ridge* ... NC-3
Gwyns Branch—*stream* ... VA-3
Gwyn Spring—*spring* ... TN-4
Gwynville Point—*cape* ... VA-3
*Gwyther* ... ND-7
Gyberg Tank—*reservoir* ... AZ-5
Gyetta Tank—*reservoir* ... AZ-5
Gyger Bend—*bend* ... IN-6
Gygi and Engle Rsvr—*reservoir* ... OR-9
Gygnes, Lac aux—*lake* ... LA-4
Gyle Lake Dam—*dam* ... MS-4
Gyles, Stella Pepper, House—*hist pl* ... DE-2
Gyles Cem—*cemetery* ... AR-4
Gyles Lake—*lake* ... MN-6
Gymnasium—*hist pl* ... AZ-5
Gymnasium, Vanderbilt Univ—*hist pl* ... TN-4
Gymon Cem—*cemetery* ... IL-6
Gym Peak—*summit* ... NM-5
*Gympsum Canyon* ... UT-8
Gyon Bluffs—*cliff* ... CA-9
**Gyp**—*pop pl* ... OK-5
Gyp Arroyo—*stream* ... NM-5
Gyp Basin—*basin* ... MT-8
Gyp Bend—*bend* ... NM-5
Gyp Canyon—*valley* ... TX-5
Gyp Cem—*cemetery* ... OK-5
*Gyp Creek* ... OK-5
*Gyp Creek* ... TX-5
Gyp Creek—*stream* ... KS-7
Gyp Creek—*stream* (2) ... MT-8
Gyp Creek—*stream* (5) ... OK-5
Gyp Creek—*stream* ... OR-9
Gyp Creek—*stream* (8) ... TX-5
Gyp Creek Tank—*reservoir* ... TX-5
Gyp Draw—*valley* (2) ... TX-5
Gyp Flat—*flat* ... WY-8
Gyp Flats Windmill—*locale* ... TX-5
Gyp Hill—*summit* ... CO-8
Gyp Hill—*summit* ... TX-5
Gyp Hill Oil Field—*oilfield* ... TX-5
Gyp Hills—*other* ... NM-5
Gyp Hills—*range* ... AZ-5
Gyp Mine—*mine* ... CO-8
Gyp Mtn—*summit* ... MT-8
Gypo Creek—*stream* ... ID-8
Gypo Creek—*stream* ... MI-6
Gypo Creek—*stream* ... WA-9
Gypo Lake—*lake* ... MN-6
*Gyp Peak* ... NV-8
Gyp Pocket—*basin* ... AZ-5
Gyp Pocket Tank—*reservoir* ... AZ-5
Gyppo Creek—*stream* ... ID-8
Gyppo Creek—*stream* ... OR-9
Gyp Point—*cape* ... OR-9
Gyp Rsvr—*reservoir* ... AZ-5
Gypsite—*locale* ... CA-9
*Gypsom Canyon* ... CA-9
Gyp Spring—*spring* (3) ... NM-5
Gyp Spring—*spring* ... WY-8
Gyp Spring Canyon—*valley* ... NM-5
Gypsum—*locale* ... AK-9
**Gypsum**—*pop pl* ... CO-8
**Gypsum**—*pop pl* ... IA-7
**Gypsum**—*pop pl* ... KS-7
**Gypsum**—*pop pl* ... MI-6
**Gypsum**—*pop pl* ... NY-2
**Gypsum**—*pop pl* ... OH-6
**Gypsum**—*pop pl* ... TX-5
Gypsum Beds—*bay* ... NV-8
Gypsum Bluff—*cliff* ... CO-8
Gypsum Buttes—*summit* ... WY-8
Gypsum Canyon—*valley* (2) ... CA-9
Gypsum Canyon—*valley* ... UT-8
Gypsum Cave—*cave* ... NV-8
Gypsum Cem—*cemetery* ... KS-7
*Gypsum City* ... KS-7
*Gypsum Creek* ... KS-7
Gypsum Creek—*stream* (2) ... AK-9
Gypsum Creek—*stream* ... AZ-5
Gypsum Creek—*stream* ... CO-8
Gypsum Creek—*stream* ... IA-7
Gypsum Creek—*stream* (3) ... KS-7
Gypsum Creek—*stream* ... MT-8
Gypsum Creek—*stream* (2) ... OK-5
Gypsum Creek—*stream* ... TX-5
Gypsum Creek—*stream* ... UT-8
Gypsum Creek—*stream* (2) ... WY-8
Gypsum Creek Campground—*locale* ... CO-8
Gypsum Creek Oil Field—*oilfield* ... KS-7
Gypsum Creek Rapids—*rapids* ... UT-8
**Gypsum Creek Township**—*pop pl* ... KS-7
Gypsum Dam—*dam* ... TN-4
Gypsum Draw—*valley* ... WY-8
Gypsum Gap—*gap* ... CO-8
Gypsum Hill—*summit* ... WY-8
Gypsum Hill Cem—*cemetery* ... KS-7
Gypsum Hills—*summit* ... KS-7
Gypsum Hollow—*valley* ... AR-4
Gypsum Ledges—*bench* ... AZ-5
*Gypsum Mill* ... NV-8
Gypsum Mill—*locale* ... UT-8
Gypsum Mine—*mine* ... AZ-5
Gypsum Mine—*mine* ... NV-8
Gypsum Mines (abandoned)—*mine* ... AZ-5
Gypsum Mtn—*summit* ... WY-8
Gypsum Park—*flat* ... WY-8
*Gypsum Point* ... AZ-5
Gypsum Pond—*reservoir* ... TN-4
*Gypsum Pond Dam* ... TN-4
Gypsum Reefs—*bar* ... AZ-5
Gypsum Ridge—*ridge* ... CA-9
Gypsum Sinkhole—*basin* ... UT-8
Gypsum Spring—*spring* ... NV-8
Gypsum Spring—*spring* ... WY-8
Gypsum Tabernacle—*church* ... OH-6
Gypsum Tank—*reservoir* ... NM-5
**Gypsum Township**—*pop pl* (2) ... KS-7
Gypsum Trail—*trail* ... AR-4
*Gypsum Triangulation* ... NV-8
Gypsum Wash—*stream* ... NV-8
Gypsum Wash Debris Basin Dam—*dam* ... UT-8
Gypsum Wash Debris Basin Rsvr—*reservoir* ... UT-8
Gypsum Well (Site)—*well* ... CA-9
Gypsy—*locale* ... KY-4
Gypsy—*locale* ... OK-5
**Gypsy**—*pop pl* ... LA-4
**Gypsy**—*pop pl* ... WV-2
Gypsy, Lake—*reservoir* ... AL-4
Gypsy Camp Hist Dist—*hist pl* ... AR-4
Gypsy Ch—*church* ... OK-5
Gypsy Creek—*stream* ... CA-9
Gypsy Creek—*stream* ... ID-8
Gypsy Creek—*stream* ... SC-3
Gypsy Creek—*stream* ... WA-9
Gypsy Fork—*stream* ... OR-9
Gypsy Hill Park—*park* ... VA-3
Gypsy Island—*island* ... NY-2
Gypsy Lake—*lake* ... MI-6
Gypsy Lake—*lake* ... MN-6
Gypsy Lake Lookout Tower—*locale* ... MI-6
Gypsy Lakes—*lake* ... WA-9
Gypsy Lookout Tower—*locale* ... MO-7
Gypsy Meadows—*flat* ... WA-9
Gypsy Mine—*mine* ... CA-9
Gypsy Park—*flat* ... CO-8
Gypsy Park—*park* ... WI-6
Gypsy Peak—*summit* ... WA-9
Gypsy Queen Canyon—*valley* ... NM-5
Gypsy Queen Mine—*mine* ... CA-9
Gypsy Queen Mine—*mine* ... NM-5
Gypsy Ridge—*ridge* ... WA-9
Gypsy Run—*stream* ... PA-2
Gypsy Sch—*school* ... KY-4
Gypsy Spring—*spring* ... OR-9
Gypsy Valley—*basin* ... NE-7
Gypsy Well—*well* ... NM-5
Gyp Tank—*reservoir* (2) ... NM-5
Gyp Tank—*reservoir* (2) ... TX-5
Gyp Wash—*valley* ... AZ-5
Gyp Well—*well* ... TX-5
Gyp Williams Hollow—*valley* ... IL-6
Gyp Windmill—*locale* ... NM-5
Gyp Windmill—*locale* ... TX-5
Gyrfalcon Lake—*lake* ... MT-8
Gyte Chester Pond—*lake* ... FL-3
Gyttja Lake—*lake* ... MI-6
Gyurman Rsvr—*reservoir* ... CO-8
G Z Canyon—*valley* ... NV-8
G-2 Shaft—*mine* ... CO-8
G 20 Lateral—*canal* ... ID-8
G4 Canyon—*valley* ... TX-5

# H

*H* .... MS-4
*H* .... NC-3
H—*mine* .... NM-5
H—*mine* .... WA-9
H—*park* .... CA-9
H, Lateral—*canal* .... MT-8
Haa, Puu—*summit* .... HI-9
Haack Cem—*cemetery* .... MO-7
Haacke Creek—*stream* .... MT-8
Haack Lake—*lake* .... WI-6
Haada Is Taani Di Wash—*stream* .... AZ-5
*Haaeleele Ridge* .... HI-9
*Haaeleele Valley* .... HI-9
Haafsville—*locale* .... PA-2
Haag, J.H., House—*hist pl* .... IN-6
Haag Cove—*bay* .... WA-9
Haag Cove Campground—*locale* .... WA-9
Haag Creek—*stream* .... TX-5
Haag Ditch—*canal* .... IN-6
Haagen Creek—*stream* .... OR-9
Haagen Sch (abandoned)—*school* .... PA-2
Haag Ranch—*locale* .... TX-5
Haags Hollow—*valley* .... AR-4
**Haags Mill**—*pop pl* .... PA-2
**Haag Township**—*pop pl* .... ND-7
Haa-guar Shop Ctr—*locale* .... IN-6
**Haaheo**—*pop pl* .... HI-9
Haaheo Sch—*school* .... HI-9
*Haaibusu Sanhir* .... MH-9
*Haainiya Misaki* .... MH-9
Haake Hollow Branch—*stream* .... AL-4
Haake Mound—*summit* .... MO-7
*Haakenson Creek* .... WI-6
Haakers Camp—*locale* .... CA-9
Haakoa Stream—*stream* .... HI-9
Haakon County—*civil* .... SD-7
Haaks Ch—*church* .... PA-2
Ha-ak Va-ak Intaglio Site—*hist pl* .... AZ-5
**Haakwood**—*pop pl* .... MI-6
**Haaland Township**—*pop pl* .... ND-7
Haalelepaakai—*summit* .... HI-9
*Haal-Muihedak* .... AZ-5
Ha Amar Creek—*stream* .... CA-9
*Haanadrois Creek* .... NY-2
Haan Hill—*summit* .... MI-6
*Haaniya Cape* .... MH-9
*Haaniya Point* .... MH-9
**Haanka Ullah (historical)**—*pop pl* .... MS-4
*Haanomu* .... MH-9
*Haanomu Saki* .... MH-9
Haan Sch—*school* .... IN-6
*Haao* .... HI-9
Haao Springs—*spring* .... HI-9
Haao Valley—*valley* .... HI-9
Haara Ditch—*canal* .... MT-8
Haaren HS—*school* .... NY-2
Haarer Ditch—*canal* .... IN-6
Haarley Lake—*reservoir* .... GA-3
*Haarstad* .... ND-7
Haarstick State Wildlife Mngmt Area—*park* .... MN-6
Haarstick-Whittemore Houses—*hist pl* .... MO-7
Haas—*locale* .... LA-4
Haas—*locale* .... PA-2
Haas, Bernard, House—*hist pl* .... ID-8
Haas, Herman, House—*hist pl* .... ID-8
Haas Ave Missionary Baptist Ch—*church* .... AL-4
Haas Canyon—*valley* .... AZ-5
Haas Cave—*cave* .... PA-2
Haas Cem—*cemetery* .... ND-7
Haas Ch—*church* .... ND-7
Haas Chapel—*church* .... IN-6
*Haas Creek* .... PA-2
Haas Creek—*stream* .... NC-3
Haas Creek—*stream* .... WA-9
Haas Ditch—*canal* .... OH-6
Haase Cem—*cemetery* .... MO-7
Haasen Creek—*stream* .... PA-2
Haas Grove—*woods* .... CA-9
Haas Hill—*summit* .... PA-2
Haas Hollow—*valley* .... OR-9
Haas JHS—*school* .... TX-5
*Haas Knob* .... PA-2
Haas Lake—*lake* .... AL-4
Haas Lake—*lake* .... ID-8
Haas-Lilienthal House—*hist pl* .... CA-9
Haas Oil and Gas Field—*oilfield* .... LA-4
Haas Park—*park* .... IL-6
Haas Park—*park* .... MI-6
Haas Pond—*reservoir* .... PA-2
Haas Ridge—*ridge* .... OR-9
Haas-Rush Lake Dam—*dam* .... MS-4
Haas Sch—*school* .... ID-8
Haas Sch—*school* .... MI-6
Haas Sch—*school* .... SD-7
Haas Slough—*stream* .... CA-9
Haas Well—*well* .... NM-5
**Haaswood**—*pop pl* .... LA-4
Habakkuk Ch—*church* .... GA-3
H A Baldwin Park—*park* .... HI-9
Habberton—*locale* .... AR-4
*Habeck Creek* .... WI-6
Habecker Airp—*airport* .... PA-2
Habecker Bridge—*other* .... IL-6
Habecker Cem—*cemetery* .... TX-5
Habecker Ch—*church* .... PA-2
Habegger Ditch—*canal* .... IN-6
Habel Sch—*school* .... MT-8
*Haber De Venture* .... MD-2
Haberkorn Creek—*stream* .... IA-7
Haberkorn House and Farmstead—*hist pl* .... IA-7
Haberle Sch—*school* .... NY-2
Haberman—*locale* .... NY-2
Haberman Lake—*lake* .... MN-6
Haberman State Wildlife Mngmt Area—*park* .... MN-6
Haber Pond—*lake* .... NY-2
**Habersham**—*pop pl* .... GA-3
**Habersham**—*pop pl* .... TN-4
Habersham (CCD)—*cens area* .... TN-4
Habersham Cem—*cemetery* .... SC-3
Habersham Ch—*church* .... GA-3
**Habersham (County)**—*pop pl* .... GA-3
Habersham Creek—*stream* (2) .... GA-3
Habersham Creek—*stream* .... SC-3
Habersham Division—*civil* .... TN-4
Habersham Memorial Hall—*hist pl* .... GA-3
Habersham Mills Lake—*reservoir* .... GA-3
Habersham Mountains—*range* .... NC-3
Habershon Field—*park* .... CT-1
Haberstock Hill—*summit* .... AZ-5
Haberstock Wash—*stream* .... AZ-5
Habe Sch—*school* .... NE-7
*Habgood* .... AL-4
Habicht-Cohn-Crow House—*hist pl* .... AR-4
Habig Draw—*valley* .... WY-8
Habig Lake—*reservoir* .... IN-6
Habig Lake Dam—*dam* .... IN-6
Habig Spring—*spring* .... WY-8
**Habit**—*pop pl* .... KY-4
*Habitat Trail* .... MO-7
Habit Creek—*stream* .... ID-8
*Habnab* .... MD-2
*Habo Canyon* .... AZ-5
**Habor Bluffs**—*pop pl* .... FL-3
*Habredeventure* .... MD-2
Habre-de-Venture—*hist pl* .... MD-2
Habre De Venture—*locale* .... MD-2
Habron Elementary and JHS—*school* .... IN-6
Habron Gap—*gap* .... VA-3
Habron Hollow—*valley* .... OH-6
Ha Brook Creek—*stream* .... IN-6
Haby Cem—*cemetery* .... TX-5
Haby Crossing—*locale* .... TX-5
Haby Ranch—*locale* (2) .... TX-5
Habys Cove—*bay* .... TX-5
Haby Spring—*spring* .... AZ-5
*Hacadorn Lake* .... MT-8
*Hacedore Lake* .... MT-8
Hacha Island—*island* .... AK-9
Hacha Windmill—*locale* .... TX-5
*Hachcha Osi River* .... MS-4
Hachemedega Creek—*stream* .... AL-4
*Hachemedego Creek* .... AL-4
Hacheney Spring—*spring* .... OR-9
Hachers Run—*stream* (2) .... NC-3
Hachie Shoal—*bar* .... TN-4
**Hachita**—*pop pl* .... NM-5
Hachita Canyon—*valley* .... NM-5
Hachita Peak—*summit* .... NM-5
Hachita Valley—*valley* .... NM-5
*Hacienda* .... FL-3
Hacienda—*locale* .... TX-5
**Hacienda**—*pop pl* .... CA-9
Hacienda Aana Maria—*locale* .... PR-3
**Hacienda Acres**—*pop pl* .... NM-5
Hacienda Aldea—*locale* .... PR-3
Hacienda Alicia—*locale* .... PR-3
Hacienda Alomar—*locale* .... PR-3
Hacienda Altura—*locale* .... PR-3
Hacienda Amelia—*locale* .... PR-3
Hacienda Americo—*locale* .... PR-3
Hacienda Anadon—*locale* .... PR-3
Hacienda Arbela—*locale* .... PR-3
Hacienda Arbona—*locale* .... PR-3
Hacienda Arcadia—*locale* .... PR-3
Hacienda Arms Apartments—*hist pl* .... CA-9
Hacienda Artau—*locale* .... PR-3
Hacienda Asuncion—*locale* .... PR-3
Hacienda Azucarera la Esperanza—*hist pl* .... PR-3
Hacienda Balare—*locale* .... PR-3
Hacienda Ballester—*locale* .... PR-3
Hacienda Barrancas—*locale* .... PR-3
Hacienda Batiz—*locale* .... PR-3
Hacienda Beatriz Soledad—*locale* .... PR-3
Hacienda Belgodere—*locale* .... PR-3
Hacienda Bermudez—*locale* .... PR-3
Hacienda Bianchi—*locale* .... PR-3
Hacienda Buena Union—*hist pl* .... PR-3
Hacienda Buena Vista—*locale* .... PR-3
Hacienda Burenes—*locale* .... PR-3
Hacienda Butler—*locale* .... PR-3
Hacienda Candelaria—*locale* .... PR-3
Hacienda Cano Verde—*locale* .... PR-3
Hacienda Carbonell—*locale* .... PR-3
Hacienda Carmelita—*locale* .... PR-3
Hacienda Carmen—*locale* .... PR-3
Hacienda Casa del Frances—*hist pl* .... PR-3
Hacienda Casanova—*locale* .... PR-3
Hacienda Casey—*locale* .... PR-3
Hacienda Catalina—*locale* .... PR-3
Hacienda Cem—*cemetery* .... CA-9
Hacienda Channel—*canal* .... CA-9
Hacienda Chesari—*locale* .... PR-3
Hacienda Cintrona Primera—*locale* .... PR-3
Hacienda Cipriano—*locale* .... PR-3
Hacienda Clavell—*locale* .... PR-3
Hacienda Colom—*locale* .... PR-3
Hacienda Concepcion—*locale* .... PR-3
Hacienda Constancia—*locale* .... PR-3
Hacienda Constanza—*locale* .... PR-3
Hacienda Corcega—*locale* .... PR-3
Hacienda Cortada—*locale* .... PR-3
Hacienda Coto—*locale* .... PR-3
Hacienda Cristina—*locale* .... PR-3
Hacienda de la Tordilla—*locale* .... TX-5
Hacienda Del Florasol—*locale* .... CA-9
Hacienda Delicias—*locale* .... PR-3
Hacienda de los Muchachos—*school* .... NM-5
Hacienda del Santa Rita (historical)—*locale* .... AZ-5
Hacienda Desengano—*locale* .... PR-3
Hacienda de Valencia (trailer park)—*locale* .... AZ-5
**Hacienda De Valencia (Trailer Park)**—*pop pl* .... AZ-5
Hacienda El Banco—*locale* .... PR-3
Hacienda El Fenix—*locale* .... PR-3
Hacienda El Progreso—*locale* .... PR-3
Hacienda El Semil—*locale* .... PR-3
Hacienda El Tesoro—*locale* .... PR-3
Hacienda Esmeralda—*locale* .... PR-3
Hacienda Esperanza—*locale* .... PR-3
Hacienda Espino—*locale* .... PR-3
Hacienda Eugenia—*locale* .... PR-3
Hacienda Fajardo—*locale* .... PR-3
Hacienda Fe—*locale* .... PR-3
Hacienda Felicia—*locale* .... PR-3
**Hacienda Felicita**—*pop pl* (2) .... PR-3
Hacienda Fernandez Rosal—*locale* .... PR-3
Hacienda Figueroa—*locale* .... PR-3
Hacienda Flor de Alba—*locale* .... PR-3
Hacienda Florida—*locale* .... PR-3
Hacienda Fortuna—*locale* .... PR-3
Hacienda Garau—*locale* .... PR-3
Hacienda Gloria—*locale* .... PR-3
Hacienda Golf Club—*other* .... CA-9
Hacienda Grande—*locale* .... PR-3
Hacienda Gripinas—*locale* .... PR-3
Hacienda Guayo—*locale* .... PR-3
**Hacienda Heights**—*pop pl* (2) .... CA-9
**Hacienda Heights**—*pop pl* .... TX-5
Hacienda Hotel Heliport—*airport* .... NV-8
Hacienda Hucar—*locale* .... PR-3
Hacienda Iberia—*locale* .... PR-3
Hacienda Indiera—*locale* .... PR-3
Hacienda Iruena Manor House—*hist pl* .... PR-3
Hacienda Jauca—*locale* .... PR-3
Hacienda Josefa—*locale* .... PR-3
Hacienda Juanita—*locale* .... PR-3
Hacienda Julia—*locale* .... PR-3
Hacienda Jurutungo—*locale* .... PR-3
Hacienda La Balear—*locale* .... PR-3
Hacienda La Catalana—*locale* .... PR-3
Hacienda La Concordia—*locale* .... PR-3
Hacienda La Delfina—*locale* .... PR-3
Hacienda La Esperanza—*locale* .... PR-3
Hacienda La Gloria—*locale* .... PR-3
Hacienda La Isolina—*locale* .... PR-3
Hacienda La Juanita—*locale* .... PR-3
Hacienda La Luisa—*locale* .... PR-3
Hacienda La Marina—*locale* .... PR-3
Hacienda Lamberti—*locale* .... PR-3
Hacienda La Milagrosa—*locale* .... PR-3
Hacienda La Mocha—*locale* .... PR-3
Hacienda La Ratina—*locale* .... PR-3
Hacienda La Rosita—*locale* .... PR-3
Hacienda La Sabana—*hist pl* .... PR-3
Hacienda Las Abras—*locale* .... PR-3
Hacienda Las Magas—*locale* .... PR-3
Hacienda Las Pinas—*locale* .... PR-3
Hacienda La Vega—*locale* .... PR-3
Hacienda Lealtad—*locale* .... PR-3
Hacienda Leonor—*locale* .... PR-3
Hacienda Limon—*locale* .... PR-3
Hacienda Llanada—*locale* .... PR-3
Hacienda Los Encino—*locale* .... AZ-5
Hacienda Los Planes—*locale* .... PR-3
Hacienda Loyola—*locale* .... PR-3
Hacienda Luciana—*locale* .... PR-3
Hacienda Luisa—*locale* .... PR-3
Hacienda Mallorquina—*locale* .... PR-3
Hacienda Manuela—*locale* .... PR-3
Hacienda Maraguez—*locale* .... PR-3
Hacienda Margarita—*locale* .... PR-3
Hacienda Maria—*locale* .... PR-3
Hacienda Maria Antonia—*locale* .... PR-3
Hacienda Marques—*locale* .... PR-3
Hacienda Mata—*locale* .... PR-3
Hacienda Matilde—*locale* .... PR-3
Hacienda Mejias—*locale* .... PR-3
Hacienda Mercado—*locale* .... PR-3
Hacienda Merle—*locale* .... PR-3
Hacienda Miramar—*locale* .... PR-3
Hacienda Miranda—*locale* .... PR-3
Hacienda Mogote—*locale* .... PR-3
Hacienda Molina—*locale* .... PR-3
Hacienda Monserrate—*locale* .... PR-3
Hacienda Morales—*locale* .... PR-3
Hacienda Noez—*locale* .... PR-3
Hacienda Oliva—*locale* .... PR-3
Hacienda Olivieri—*locale* .... PR-3
Hacienda Pales—*locale* .... PR-3
Hacienda Paraiso—*locale* .... PR-3
Hacienda Penonales—*locale* .... PR-3
Hacienda Piedra Gorda—*locale* .... PR-3
Hacienda Pietri—*locale* .... PR-3
Hacienda Pintado—*locale* .... PR-3
Hacienda Plato Indio—*locale* .... PR-3
Hacienda Polmares—*locale* .... PR-3
Hacienda Poncena—*locale* .... PR-3
Hacienda Porvenir—*locale* .... PR-3
Hacienda Potala—*locale* .... PR-3
Hacienda Ralate—*locale* .... PR-3
Hacienda Ranch—*locale* .... CA-9
Hacienda Recurso—*locale* .... PR-3
Hacienda Resolucion—*locale* .... PR-3
Hacienda Restaurada—*locale* .... PR-3
Hacienda Rest Home—*hospital* .... MO-7
Hacienda Resurreccion—*locale* .... PR-3
Hacienda Retiro—*locale* .... PR-3
Hacienda Reynes—*locale* .... PR-3
Hacienda Ripoll—*locale* .... PR-3
Hacienda Rivera—*locale* .... PR-3
Hacienda Roig—*locale* .... PR-3
Hacienda Rolon—*locale* .... PR-3
Hacienda Rosali—*locale* .... PR-3
Hacienda Rosario—*locale* .... PR-3
Hacienda Salome—*locale* .... PR-3
Hacienda San Alberto—*locale* .... PR-3
Hacienda San Antonio—*locale* .... PR-3
Hacienda San Carlos—*locale* .... PR-3
Hacienda San Clemente—*locale* .... PR-3
Hacienda San Isidoro—*locale* .... PR-3
Hacienda San Jose—*locale* .... PR-3
Hacienda San Lorenzo—*locale* .... PR-3
Hacienda San Narciso—*locale* .... PR-3
Hacienda San Pedro—*locale* .... PR-3
Hacienda Santa Anita—*locale* .... PR-3
Hacienda Santa Barbara—*locale* .... PR-3
Hacienda Santa Clara—*locale* .... PR-3
Hacienda Santa Elena—*locale* .... PR-3
Hacienda Santa Maria—*locale* .... PR-3
Hacienda Santa Rita—*hist pl* .... PR-3
Hacienda Santa Rita—*locale* .... PR-3
Hacienda Santa Rosa—*locale* .... PR-3
Hacienda Santiago—*locale* .... PR-3
Hacienda Sch—*school* (3) .... CA-9
**Haciendas del Lago (subdivision)**—*pop pl* (2) .... AZ-5
Hacienda Solano Park (trailer park)—*locale* .... AZ-5
**Hacienda Solano Park (trailer park)**—*pop pl* .... AZ-5
Hacienda Spillway—*canal* .... CA-9
**Haciendas (subdivision), The**—*pop pl* (2) .... AZ-5
Hacienda Tabonuco—*locale* .... PR-3
Hacienda Teresa—*locale* .... PR-3
Hacienda Tetuan—*locale* .... PR-3
Hacienda Tres Hermanas—*locale* .... PR-3
Hacienda Tunnel—*tunnel* .... CA-9
Hacienda Ursula—*locale* .... PR-3
Hacienda Usera—*locale* .... PR-3
Hacienda Vaquinas—*locale* .... PR-3
Hacienda Vega Grande—*locale* .... PR-3
Hacienda Veremos—*locale* .... PR-3
Hacienda Vertedero—*locale* .... PR-3
Hacienda Vicario—*locale* .... PR-3
Hacienda Vilella—*locale* .... PR-3
**Hacienda Village**—*pop pl* .... FL-3
**Hacienda Village**—*pop pl* .... IN-6
Hacienda Village (Hacienda)—*other* .... FL-3
Hacienda Vista Alegre—*locale* .... PR-3
Hacienda Yani—*locale* .... PR-3
Haciendita Cem—*cemetery* .... TX-5
Hackaberry Sch—*school* .... AR-4
Hackamore—*locale* .... CA-9
*Hackamore Creek* .... WY-8
Hackamore Creek—*stream* .... WA-9
Hackamore Creek—*stream* .... WY-8
Hackamore Ranch—*locale* .... CO-8
Hackamore Rsvr—*reservoir* .... CA-9
Hackamore Spring—*spring* .... UT-8
Hack and Keary Drain—*canal* .... MI-6
*Hackasofkee Creek* .... GA-3
*Hackataia* .... AZ-5
Hackberry—*fmr MCD* .... NE-7
Hackberry—*locale* (4) .... TX-5
**Hackberry**—*pop pl* .... AZ-5
**Hackberry**—*pop pl* .... LA-4
**Hackberry**—*pop pl* .... TN-4
**Hackberry**—*pop pl* .... TX-5
Hackberry—*uninc pl* .... TX-5
Hackberry, Lake—*lake* .... LA-4
Hackberry Arroyo—*valley* .... TX-5
Hackberry Basin—*basin* (2) .... AZ-5
Hackberry Basin Spring—*spring* .... AZ-5
Hackberry Bay—*bay* (2) .... LA-4
Hackberry Bayou—*gut* .... LA-4
Hackberry Bayou—*stream* (2) .... LA-4
Hackberry Beach—*beach* .... LA-4
Hackberry Branch—*stream* .... MO-7
Hackberry Branch—*stream* (3) .... TX-5
Hackberry Branch—*stream* .... WV-2
*Hackberry Butte* .... AZ-5
Hackberry Butte—*summit* .... AZ-5
Hackberry Camp—*locale* .... TX-5
*Hackberry Canyon* .... WY-8
Hackberry Canyon—*valley* (7) .... AZ-5
Hackberry Canyon—*valley* .... CO-8
Hackberry Canyon—*valley* .... NV-8
Hackberry Canyon—*valley* (4) .... NM-5
Hackberry Canyon—*valley* (3) .... TX-5
Hackberry Canyon—*valley* .... UT-8
Hackberry Cem—*cemetery* (2) .... KS-7
Hackberry Cem—*cemetery* .... MS-4
Hackberry Cem—*cemetery* .... MO-7
Hackberry Cem—*cemetery* (2) .... OK-5
Hackberry Cem—*cemetery* .... TX-5
Hackberry Ch—*church* (2) .... VA-3
*Hackberry Creek* .... CO-8
*Hackberry Creek* .... OK-5
*Hackberry Creek* .... TX-5
*Hackberry Creek* .... UT-8
Hackberry Creek—*stream* (4) .... AZ-5
Hackberry Creek—*stream* .... AR-4
Hackberry Creek—*stream* .... CO-8
Hackberry Creek—*stream* (6) .... KS-7
Hackberry Creek—*stream* .... MT-8
Hackberry Creek—*stream* (2) .... NE-7
Hackberry Creek—*stream* (8) .... OK-5
Hackberry Creek—*stream* (34) .... TX-5
Hackberry Creek—*stream* .... UT-8
Hackberry Creek Bridge—*hist pl* .... KS-7
Hackberry Crossing—*locale* .... TX-5
Hackberry Draw—*valley* (2) .... AZ-5
Hackberry Draw—*valley* (6) .... NM-5
Hackberry Draw—*valley* (11) .... TX-5
Hackberry Elem Sch—*school* .... AZ-5
Hackberry Flat—*flat* .... OK-5
*Hackberry Gulch* .... AZ-5
Hackberry Gulch—*valley* (2) .... AZ-5
Hackberry Gulch—*valley* .... WA-9
Hackberry Gully—*valley* .... TX-5
Hackberry Hill—*summit* .... NM-5
Hackberry Hills—*range* .... NM-5
Hackberry Hill Sch—*school* .... CO-8
Hackberry (historical)—*locale* .... KS-7
Hackberry Hollow—*valley* (2) .... TX-5
Hackberry Island—*island* .... IL-6
Hackberry Lake—*lake* (2) .... LA-4
Hackberry Lake—*lake* (3) .... NE-7
Hackberry Lake—*lake* (2) .... NM-5
Hackberry Lake—*lake* (4) .... TX-5
Hackberry Mesa—*summit* (2) .... AZ-5
Hackberry Mesa—*summit* .... TX-5
Hackberry Mine—*mine* (2) .... AZ-5
Hackberry Mine—*mine* .... TX-5
Hackberry Mine Dump—*other* .... AZ-5
Hackberry Mine Spring—*spring* .... AZ-5
Hackberry Mtn—*summit* (2) .... AZ-5
Hackberry Mtn—*summit* .... AR-4
Hackberry Mtn—*summit* .... CA-9
Hackberry Park—*park* .... TX-5
Hackberry Point—*cape* .... LA-4
Hackberry Point—*cape* .... MN-6
Hackberry Point—*cape* .... NE-7
Hackberry Post Office—*building* .... AZ-5
Hackberry Post Office (historical)—*building* .... TN-4
Hackberry Ranch—*locale* .... AZ-5
Hackberry Ranch—*locale* .... NM-5
Hackberry Ranch—*locale* .... TX-5
*Hackberry Ridge* .... TN-4
Hackberry Ridge—*ridge* (2) .... LA-4
*Hackberry Ridge Mine* .... TN-4
Hackberry RR Station—*building* .... AZ-5
Hackberry Rsvr—*reservoir* .... CO-8
Hackberry Rsvr—*reservoir* .... ID-8
Hackberry Ruins—*locale* .... CO-8
Hackberry Sch—*school* .... IL-6
Hackberry Sch—*school* .... LA-4
Hackberry Sch—*school* .... MO-7
Hackberry Sch (historical)—*school* .... AL-4
Hackberry Sch (historical)—*school* .... MS-4
Hackberry (siding)—*locale* .... AZ-5
Hackberry Slope—*area* .... NM-5
Hackberry Slough—*bay* .... TX-5
Hackberry Slough—*stream* .... IL-6
*Hackberry Spring* .... AZ-5
Hackberry Spring—*spring* (20) .... AZ-5
Hackberry Spring—*spring* .... CA-9
Hackberry Spring—*spring* (2) .... NV-8
Hackberry Spring—*spring* .... NM-5
Hackberry Spring—*spring* (3) .... TX-5
Hackberry Springs—*spring* .... AZ-5
Hackberry Springs—*spring* .... CO-8
Hackberry Springs—*spring* .... NM-5
**Hackberry (Stewart)**—*pop pl* .... TX-5
Hackberry Tank—*reservoir* (3) .... AZ-5
Hackberry Tank—*reservoir* (4) .... NM-5
Hackberry Tank—*reservoir* (13) .... TX-5
Hackberry Tank Number One—*reservoir* .... AZ-5
Hackberry Tank Number Two—*reservoir* .... AZ-5
**Hackberry Township**—*pop pl* .... KS-7
*Hackberry Wash* .... AZ-5
Hackberry Wash—*stream* (6) .... AZ-5
Hackberry Wash Well—*well* .... AZ-5
Hackberry Waterhole—*lake* (2) .... TX-5
Hackberry Well—*locale* .... NM-5
Hackberry Well—*well* .... AZ-5
Hackberry Well—*well* (3) .... NM-5
Hackberry Well—*well* .... TX-5
Hackberry Windmill—*locale* (2) .... AZ-5
Hackberry Windmill—*locale* (5) .... NM-5
Hackberry Windmill—*locale* (8) .... TX-5
Hackbill Hollow—*valley* .... MO-7
Hack Canyon—*valley* .... AZ-5
Hack Canyon Mine—*mine* .... AZ-5
Hack Cem—*cemetery* .... IL-6
Hack Cem—*cemetery* .... IN-6
*Hack Creek* .... TX-5
Hack Creek—*stream* .... CO-8
Hack Creek—*stream* .... VA-3
Hack Ditch—*canal* .... IN-6
Hack Drain—*canal* .... MI-6
Hacke Cem—*cemetery* .... IL-6
Hackelbarney Run—*stream* .... WV-2
Hackelbender Run—*stream* .... PA-2
Hackelbernie—*uninc pl* .... PA-2
Hackelton Lake—*lake* .... AR-4
Hackenberg, Harvey, House—*hist pl* .... OH-6
*Hackenburg Airport* .... PA-2
Hackenburg Lake—*lake* .... IN-6
Hackenburg-Penny Hill Airp—*airport* .... PA-2
*Hackendequa* .... PA-2
Hacken Run—*stream* .... VA-3
*Hackensac* .... NJ-2
**Hackensack**—*pop pl* .... MN-6
**Hackensack**—*pop pl* .... NJ-2
Hackensack Cem—*cemetery* .... NJ-2
Hackensack Golf Club—*other* .... NJ-2
Hackensack Hosp—*hospital* .... NJ-2
Hackensack Mtn—*summit* .... NY-2
Hackensack River—*stream* .... NJ-2
Hackensack River—*stream* .... NY-2
Hackensack Rsvr Number One—*reservoir* .... NJ-2
Hackensack Rsvr Number Two—*reservoir* .... NJ-2
Hackensack Water Company Complex—*hist pl* .... NJ-2
*Hackens Draw* .... CO-8
Hacker Branch—*stream* .... KY-4
Hacker Brook—*stream* .... ME-1
Hacker Camp Run—*stream* .... WV-2
Hacker Cem—*cemetery* .... KY-4
Hacker Creek—*stream* .... CA-9
Hacker Creek—*stream* .... OR-9
Hacker Flat—*flat* .... CA-9
Hacker Fork—*stream* .... KY-4
Hacker Gap—*gap* .... TN-4
Hacker Gulch—*valley* .... OR-9
**Hacker (historical)**—*pop pl* .... TN-4
Hacker Lick Run—*stream* .... WV-2
Hacker Mtn—*summit* .... CA-9
*Hacker Pond* .... MA-1
Hacker Ridge—*ridge* .... KY-4
Hacker Run—*stream* .... WV-2
*Hackerry Creek* .... TX-5
Hackers Branch—*stream* .... KY-4
Hackers Branch Sch—*school* .... KY-4
Hackers Bridge—*bridge* .... AR-4
Hacker Sch—*school* (2) .... KY-4
Hacker Sch—*school* .... WI-6
Hackers Creek—*stream* .... AR-4
Hackers Creek—*stream* .... SC-3
Hackers Creek—*stream* (2) .... WV-2
Hackers Creek Ch—*church* .... WV-2
Hackers Creek (Magisterial District)—*fmr MCD* .... WV-2
*Hackers Fork* .... AR-4
Hacker Smith Mtn—*summit* .... KY-4
*Hackers Pond* .... MA-1
Hackers Sch—*school* .... WV-2
Hackert Lake—*lake* .... MI-6
**Hacker Valley**—*pop pl* .... WV-2
Hacker Valley Ch—*church* .... WV-2
Hacker Valley (Magisterial District)—*fmr MCD* .... WV-2
Hackery Brook—*stream* .... NJ-2
Hacket Canyon—*valley* .... WA-9
Hacket Hollow—*valley* .... PA-2
*Hacketstown* .... NJ-2
Hacketsville—*locale* .... CA-9
Hackett—*locale* .... MN-6
**Hackett**—*pop pl* .... AR-4
**Hackett**—*pop pl* .... PA-2
Hackett, Edward M., House—*hist pl* .... WI-6
Hackett, Roy, House—*hist pl* .... AZ-5
Hackett Branch—*stream* .... IL-6
Hackett Branch—*stream* .... MO-7
Hackett Branch—*stream* .... TX-5
Hackett Branch—*stream* .... WI-6
Hackett Brook—*stream* (2) .... NH-1
Hackett Butte—*summit* .... MT-8
Hackett Cabin—*locale* .... ID-8
Hackett Canal—*canal* .... LA-4
Hackett Canyon—*valley* .... NV-8
Hackett Canyon—*valley* .... NM-5
Hackett Cem—*cemetery* .... MO-7
Hackett Cem—*cemetery* .... NV-8
Hackett Cem—*cemetery* .... VA-3
Hackett Cem—*cemetery* .... WI-6
Hackett Corners—*locale* .... MD-2
*Hackett Creek* .... WI-6
Hackett Creek—*stream* .... AK-9
Hackett Creek—*stream* .... AR-4
Hackett Creek—*stream* .... CA-9
Hackett Creek—*stream* .... MT-8
Hackett Creek—*stream* .... OK-5
Hackett Creek—*stream* .... OR-9
Hackett Creek—*stream* .... VA-3
Hackett Creek—*stream* .... WV-2
Hackett Creek—*stream* .... WI-6
Hackett Creek—*stream* .... WY-8
Hackett Dam Cem—*cemetery* .... VT-1
Hackett Ditch—*canal* .... IA-7
Hackett Fork—*stream* .... PA-2
Hackett Gulch—*valley* .... CO-8
Hackett Hill—*summit* (2) .... ME-1
Hackett Hill—*summit* .... VA-3
Hackett (historical)—*locale* .... ND-7
Hackett Hollow—*valley* .... PA-2
Hackett Hollow—*valley* .... TN-4
Hackett House—*hist pl* .... CA-9
Hackett HS—*school* .... MI-6
Hackett JHS—*school* .... NY-2
Hackett Lake—*lake* (2) .... MI-6
Hackett Lake—*reservoir* .... NC-3
Hackett Lake Sch—*school* .... MI-6
**Hackett Mills**—*pop pl* .... ME-1
Hackett Mountain—*valley* .... CO-8
Hackett Mtn—*summit* .... OK-5
Hackett Park—*park* .... PA-2
Hackett Peak—*summit* .... TX-5

Hackett Playground—*park* MI-6
Hackett Point—*cape* MD-2
Hackett Pond—*reservoir* MA-1
Hackett Pond Dam—*dam* MA-1
Hackett Ridge—*ridge* WV-2
Hackett Sch—*school* ME-1
Hackett Sch—*school* PA-2
Hackett Sch—*school* WI-6
Hackett Sch Number 2 (abandoned)—*school* ND-7
Hackett Sch Number 4—*school* ND-7
**Hacketts Mills**—*pop pl* ME-1
*Hackett's Point* MD-2
Hackett Spring—*spring* WY-8
*Hackettstown* NJ-2
**Hackettstown**—*pop pl* NJ-2
Hackettstown Community Hospital—*airport* NJ-2
Hackettstown Storage Reservoir Dam—*dam* NJ-2
Hackettstown Storage Rsvr—*reservoir* NJ-2
Hackett Tank—*reservoir* TX-5
**Hackett (Town of)**—*pop pl* WI-6
Hackett Trail—*trail* PA-2
Hackett Well—*well* NM-5
Hack Flats—*flat* NY-2
Hack Gap—*gap* NC-3
Hack Hollow—*valley* OR-9
*Hackientachqua* PA-2
Hacking Lake—*lake* UT-8
Hacking Rsvr—*reservoir* UT-8
Hacking Run—*stream* WV-2
Hackings Draw—*valley* CO-8
Hackings Springs—*spring* CO-8
Hack Inlet—*stream* ME-1
Hack Knob—*summit* NC-3
Hack Lake—*lake* CO-8
Hack Lake—*lake* FL-3
Hack Lake—*lake* MN-6
*Hacklan Branch* NC-3
Hacklander Site—*hist pl* MI-6
*Hacklebarney* PA-2
Hacklebarney—*locale* NJ-2
Hacklebarney Ch—*church* GA-3
Hacklebarney Creek—*stream* GA-3
Hacklebarney State Park—*park* NJ-2
**Hacklebernie**—*pop pl* PA-2
*Hackleberry Spring* AZ-5
**Hackleburg**—*pop pl* AL-4
Hackleburg (CCD)—*cens area* AL-4
Hackleburg Ch of Christ—*church* AL-4
Hackleburg Ch of God of Prophecy—*church* AL-4
Hackleburg Division—*civil* AL-4
Hackleburg Freewill Baptist Ch—*church* AL-4
Hackleburg HS—*school* AL-4
*Hackleburg United Methodist Church* AL-4
Hackle Creek—*stream* MO-7
Hackle Knob—*summit* TN-4
**Hackleman**—*pop pl* IN-6
Hackleman Cem—*cemetery* IN-6
Hackleman Cem—*cemetery* MO-7
Hackleman Corner—*locale* MO-7
Hackleman Corner Lake—*reservoir* MO-7
Hackleman Creek—*stream* OR-9
Hackleman Hist Dist—*hist pl* OR-9
Hackler Cem—*cemetery* MS-4
Hackler Cem—*cemetery* TN-4
Hackler Ford (historical)—*locale* MO-7
Hackler Ford State For—*forest* MO-7
Hackler Gap—*gap* TN-4
Hackler Sch—*school* MO-7
Hacklers Store—*locale* VA-3
Hackler Tank—*reservoir* NM-5
Hackleshin Hollow—*valley* OH-6
Hackleshin Ridge—*ridge* OH-6
Hackleton Hollow—*valley* MO-7
*Hackletooth Post Office* TN-4
Hackley—*locale* KY-4
**Hackley**—*pop pl* KY-4
**Hackley**—*pop pl* LA-4
Hackley, Charles H., House—*hist pl* MI-6
*Hackley Branch* NC-3
Hackley Branch—*stream* AR-4
Hackley Cem—*cemetery* MO-7
*Hackley Creek* VA-3
Hackley Creek—*stream* MT-8
Hackley Creek—*stream* TX-5
Hackley Ditch—*canal* CO-8
Hackley Hosp—*hospital* MI-6
Hackley Island—*island* IL-6
Hackley Ranch—*locale* CO-8
Hackley Rsvr—*reservoir* CO-8
Hackley Sch—*school* MO-7
Hackley Sch—*school* NY-2
*Hackleys Creek* VA-3
Hackleys Crossroad—*locale* VA-3
Hackley Spring—*spring* MT-8
Hackley Swamp—*stream* NC-3
Hacklin Cem—*cemetery* AL-4
Hacklin Island—*island* WI-6
**Hackman**—*pop pl* ID-8
Hackman Creek—*stream* OR-9
*Hackman Lake* MI-6
Hackmans Falls—*falls* CA-9
Hackmans Ravine—*valley* CA-9
Hackmaster Ditch—*canal* WY-8
Hackmatack Bog—*swamp* ME-1
Hackmatack Pond—*lake* ME-1
Hackmatack Swamp—*swamp* MA-1
Hackmetack Pond—*lake* MA-1
Hackmeyer Park—*park* AL-4
*Hack Neck* VA-3
Hack Neck—*cape* VA-3
Hackney—*locale* MT-8
**Hackney**—*pop pl* KS-7
**Hackney**—*pop pl* NC-3
**Hackney**—*pop pl* OH-6
**Hackney**—*pop pl* PA-2
Hackney, W. P., House—*hist pl* KS-7
Hackney Branch—*stream* GA-3
Hackney Branch—*stream* KY-4
Hackney Cem—*cemetery* FL-3
Hackney Cem—*cemetery* MO-7
Hackney Cem—*cemetery* VA-3
Hackney Cem—*cemetery* WV-2
Hackney Chapel—*church* TN-4
Hackney Creek—*stream* AL-4
Hackney Creek—*stream* AR-4
Hackney Creek—*stream* KY-4
Hackney Creek—*stream* VA-3
Hackney Creek Cem—*cemetery* KY-4
Hackney Hollow—*valley* VA-3
*Hackney Island* WA-9
Hackney Lake—*lake* MS-4
Hackney Lake—*lake* TX-5
Hackney Lake Inlet—*canal* TX-5
Hackney Mill Bridge—*other* MO-7
Hackney Pond—*reservoir* CT-1
*Hackneys* PA-2
Hackneys Mill Pond—*reservoir* NC-3
Hackneys Millpond Dam—*dam* NC-3
Hackneys Pier—*locale* NJ-2
Hackney Spring—*spring* GA-3
**Hackneyville**—*pop pl* AL-4
Hackneyville Cem—*cemetery* AL-4
Hackneyville Ch—*church* AL-4
Hackneyville HS—*school* AL-4
Hackneyville Presbyterian Cem—*cemetery* AL-4
Hackneyville Presbyterian Ch—*church* AL-4
Hackney Windmill—*locale* TX-5
**Hack Point**—*pop pl* MD-2
Hack Rsvr—*reservoir* AZ-5
Hacksaw Canyon—*valley* NV-8
Hacks Bayou—*gut* LA-4
Hacks Hill—*summit* AR-4
Hacks Neck—*cape* VA-3
Hacksneck—*locale* VA-3
**Hacks Point Acre**—*pop pl* MD-2
Hackwell Branch—*stream* AL-4
Hackwood Ranch—*locale* NV-8
Hackworth Branch—*stream* KY-4
Hackworth Cem—*cemetery* AL-4
Hackworth Cem—*cemetery* (3) KY-4
Hackworth Cem—*cemetery* OH-6
Hackworth Cem—*cemetery* TN-4
Hackworth Hollow—*valley* (2) KY-4
Hackworth Hollow—*valley* MO-7
**Hacoda**—*pop pl* AL-4
Hacoda Union Ch—*church* AL-4
*Hacq Island* FM-9
*Hacquehila Mountains* AZ-5
H A Creek—*stream* (2) WY-8
Hadacol Corners—*other* TX-5
**Hadar**—*pop pl* NE-7
Hadar Creek—*stream* NE-7
*Hadassah Island* NY-2
Hadaway Chapel—*church* MD-2
Hadaway Creek—*stream* MS-4
Hadaway Sch—*school* MI-6
Hadaway Slough—*stream* IL-6
**Haddam**—*pop pl* CT-1
**Haddam**—*pop pl* KS-7
Haddam Cem—*cemetery* KS-7
Haddam Island State Park—*park* CT-1
Haddam JHS—*school* CT-1
Haddam Meadows State Park—*park* CT-1
Haddam Neck—*cape* CT-1
Haddam Neck—*locale* CT-1
Haddam Neck Ch—*church* (2) CT-1
**Haddam (Town of)**—*pop pl* CT-1
**Haddam Township**—*pop pl* KS-7
*Haddanfield* NJ-2
*Haddaway Bay* MD-2
Haddaway Hall—*hist pl* WA-9
Hadday Hollow—*valley* MO-7
Hadden Branch—*stream* GA-3
Haddenbrock Hill—*summit* TX-5
Hadden Canyon—*valley* UT-8
Hadden Cem—*cemetery* (2) IL-6
Hadden Cem—*cemetery* IA-7
Hadden Ch—*church* AL-4
**Hadden Crossroads**—*pop pl* SC-3
*Haddenfield* NJ-2
Hadden Flat—*flat* UT-8
**Hadden Heights**—*pop pl* SC-3
**Hadden Hill**—*pop pl* IA-7
Hadden Hill—*summit* IN-6
Hadden Hills—*summit* UT-8
Hadden Holes—*spring* UT-8
Hadden Hollow—*valley* OH-6
Hadden Pit—*lake* UT-8
Hadden Pond—*reservoir* GA-3
Hadden Ranch—*locale* NM-5
Hadden Reef—*ridge* UT-8
Hadden Rsvr—*reservoir* UT-8
Hadden Run—*stream* PA-2
Haddens—*locale* LA-4
Hadden Sch—*school* OH-6
Hadden Site (15TO1)—*hist pl* KY-4
**Haddenville**—*pop pl* PA-2
Hadding Cem—*cemetery* OH-6
**Haddington**—*pop pl* PA-2
Haddington Hist Dist—*hist pl* PA-2
Haddington Recreation Center—*park* PA-2
**Haddix**—*pop pl* KY-4
Haddix (CCD)—*cens area* KY-4
Haddix Cem—*cemetery* (2) KY-4
Haddix Fork—*stream* KY-4
Haddix Fork Ch—*church* KY-4
Haddix Run—*stream* WV-2
*Haddley Gulch* CO-8
**Haddock**—*pop pl* GA-3
**Haddock**—*pop pl* PA-2
**Haddock**—*pop pl* SC-3
*Haddock Arroyo* CO-8
Haddock Cem—*cemetery* AR-4
Haddock Cem—*cemetery* FL-3
Haddock Cem—*cemetery* KY-4
Haddock Creek—*stream* AR-4
Haddock Creek—*stream* GA-3
Haddock Creek—*stream* MO-7
Haddock Fork—*stream* KY-4
Haddock Hill—*summit* FL-3
Haddock (historical)—*locale* AL-4
Haddock Island—*island* ME-1
Haddock Island Kelp Ledge—*bar* ME-1
Haddock Island Ledge—*bar* ME-1
Haddock Landing—*locale* GA-3
Haddock Ledge—*bar* (2) ME-1
*Haddock P.O.* AL-4
Haddock Rock—*island* ME-1
Haddock Sch—*school* IL-6
**Haddocks Crossroads**—*pop pl* NC-3
Haddock Slough—*gut* MN-6
Haddock Spring—*spring* MO-7
**Haddon**—*pop pl* NJ-2
Haddon Ave Sch—*school* CA-9
Haddon Cem—*cemetery* AL-4
Haddon Cem—*cemetery* IN-6
Haddonfield—*locale* VA-3
**Haddonfield**—*pop pl* NJ-2
Haddonfield Ch—*church* VA-3
Haddonfield Hist Dist—*hist pl* NJ-2
Haddon Fortnightly Club House—*hist pl* NJ-2
Haddon Hall—*hist pl* OH-6
**Haddon Heights**—*pop pl* NJ-2
Haddon Heights Park—*park* NJ-2
**Haddon Hills**—*pop pl* NJ-2
Haddon Hollow—*valley* AL-4
Haddon Lake—*lake* GA-3
Haddon Lake—*reservoir* NJ-2
Haddon Lake Dam—*dam* NJ-2
Haddon Lake Park—*park* NJ-2
**Haddon Leigh**—*pop pl* NJ-2
Haddon Sch—*school* WA-9
Haddon Spring—*spring* AL-4
**Haddon Towne**—*pop pl* NJ-2
**Haddontowne**—*pop pl* NJ-2
**Haddon (Township of)**—*pop pl* IN-6
**Haddon (Township of)**—*pop pl* NJ-2
Haddonville—*locale* GA-3
Haddow Creek—*stream* MT-8
Haddow Sch—*school* OH-6
Haddox Branch—*stream* VA-3
Haddox Ferry—*locale* KY-4
Haddrell Point—*cape* SC-3
Hade Fork—*stream* KY-4
Haden—*locale* AL-4
Haden—*locale* VA-3
Haden Bald—*summit* MO-7
Haden Branch—*stream* TN-4
Haden Bridge—*bridge* VA-3
Haden Canal—*canal* ID-8
Haden Cem—*cemetery* ID-8
Haden Cem—*cemetery* MO-7
Haden Cem—*cemetery* VA-3
Haden Chapel—*church* VA-3
Haden Creek—*stream* MN-6
Haden Creek—*stream* OR-9
Haden Creek—*stream* WA-9
Hadenfield Branch—*stream* TX-5
Haden Grove Ch—*church* NC-3
Haden Hill—*summit* VT-1
Haden House—*hist pl* TX-5
Haden Mtn—*summit* VA-3
Haden Place—*hist pl* NC-3
Haden Post Office (historical)—*building* AL-4
Haden Run—*stream* PA-2
Haden Sch (abandoned)—*school* MO-7
**Hadens Store**—*pop pl* VA-3
Hadensville—*locale* VA-3
**Hadensville**—*pop pl* KY-4
Hader—*locale* MN-6
Haderlie Creek—*stream* ID-8
Haderlie Knoll—*summit* ID-8
Haderlie Knoll—*summit* WY-8
Hade-Rose Cem—*cemetery* KY-4
Hades Campground—*locale* UT-8
Hades Canyon—*valley* UT-8
Hades Creek—*stream* AK-9
Hades Creek—*stream* UT-8
Hades Creek—*stream* WA-9
Hades Gulch—*valley* OR-9
Hades Highway—*glacier* AK-9
Hades Knoll—*summit* AZ-5
Hades Lake—*lake* AZ-5
Hades Lake—*lake* AR-4
Hades Lake—*lake* UT-8
Hades Pass—*gap* UT-8
Hadfield Company Lime Kilns—*hist pl* WI-6
Hadfield Island—*island* CO-8
Hadfield Sch—*school* WI-6
Hadicks Lake—*lake* MI-6
H A Dillon—*locale* TX-5
H A Divide—*ridge* WY-8
Hadland Fishing Camp—*hist pl* WI-6
Hadland Park—*park* NV-8
Hadler—*locale* MN-6
*Hadley* SD-7
Hadley—*locale* CO-8
Hadley—*locale* (2) IL-6
Hadley—*locale* KY-4
Hadley—*locale* MO-7
Hadley—*locale* WA-9
**Hadley**—*pop pl* AK-9
**Hadley**—*pop pl* (2) IN-6
**Hadley**—*pop pl* MA-1
**Hadley**—*pop pl* MI-6
**Hadley**—*pop pl* MN-6
**Hadley**—*pop pl* NH-1
**Hadley**—*pop pl* NY-2
**Hadley**—*pop pl* NC-3
**Hadley**—*pop pl* PA-2
Hadley, Denny P., House—*hist pl* TN-4
*Hadley, Town of* MA-1
Hadley, Walter, House—*hist pl* OK-5
Hadley Barrett IX Ranch—*locale* NE-7
**Hadley Bay**—*pop pl* NY-2
Hadley Bend—*bend* TN-4
Hadley Bottom—*valley* OH-6
Hadley Branch—*stream* MO-7
Hadley Branch—*stream* TN-4
Hadley Brook—*stream* ME-1
Hadley Brook—*stream* NH-1
Hadley Butte—*summit* OR-9
Hadley Canyon—*valley* ID-8
Hadley Canyon—*valley* NM-5
Hadley Cem—*cemetery* GA-3
Hadley Cem—*cemetery* (2) IL-6
Hadley Cem—*cemetery* IA-7
Hadley Cem—*cemetery* LA-4
Hadley Cem—*cemetery* (2) ME-1
Hadley Cem—*cemetery* (2) MI-6
Hadley Cem—*cemetery* NH-1
Hadley Center Hist Dist—*hist pl* MA-1
Hadley Ch—*church* GA-3
Hadley Corners Sch—*school* MI-6
*Hadley Creek* CA-9
Hadley Creek—*stream* GA-3
Hadley Creek—*stream* IL-6
Hadley Creek—*stream* OR-9
Hadley Creek—*stream* TX-5
Hadley Creek—*stream* WI-6
Hadley Dam (Pa-489)—*dam* PA-2
Hadley Dam Rsvr—*reservoir* PA-2
Hadley-Dean Glass Company—*hist pl* MO-7
Hadley Draw—*valley* NM-5
*Hadley East* MA-1
*Hadley East Precinct* MA-1
Hadley Falls Company Housing District—*hist pl* MA-1
Hadley Field—*locale* MA-1
Hadley Flour and Feed Mill—*hist pl* MI-6
Hadley Glacier—*glacier* WA-9
*Hadley Gulch* CO-8
Hadley Gulch—*valley* CO-8
Hadley Harbor—*bay* MA-1
Hadley Hill—*summit* VT-1
Hadley Hills—*range* MI-6
Hadley (historical)—*locale* KS-7
Hadley (historical)—*locale* MS-4
Hadley Hosp—*hospital* DC-2
Hadley Hosp—*hospital* KS-7
Hadley House—*hist pl* OK-5
Hadley House and Grist Mill—*hist pl* NC-3
Hadley Island—*island* AK-9
Hadley JHS—*school* KS-7
Hadley Lake—*lake* IN-6
Hadley Lake—*lake* ME-1
Hadley Lake—*lake* MN-6
Hadley Lake—*lake* MS-4
Hadley Lake—*lake* WI-6
Hadley Lakes—*lake* ME-1
Hadley Lake Sch—*school* ME-1
Hadley Landing Public Access Area—*locale* IL-6
Hadley Lateral—*canal* CA-9
Hadley-Locke House—*hist pl* OR-9
Hadley-McCraney Diversion Ditch—*canal* IL-6
Hadley Millpond Dam—*dam* NC-3
Hadley Mine—*mine* MN-6
Hadley Mtn—*summit* NY-2
Hadley Mtn—*summit* OK-5
Hadley Mtn—*summit* VT-1
Hadley Parabolic Bridge—*hist pl* NY-2
Hadley Park—*flat* MT-8
Hadley Park—*park* FL-3
Hadley Park—*park* TN-4
Hadley Peak—*summit* CA-9
Hadley Peak—*summit* WA-9
Hadley Point—*cape* ME-1
Hadley Point—*summit* CO-8
Hadley Pond—*lake* NY-2
Hadley Rock—*bar* MA-1
Hadley Rsvr—*reservoir* CO-8
Hadley Rsvr—*reservoir* MA-1
Hadleys Cem—*cemetery* KY-4
Hadley Sch—*school* FL-3
Hadley Sch—*school* MA-1
Hadley Sch—*school* PA-2
Hadley Sch—*school* TN-4
Hadley Sch for the Blind—*school* IL-6
Hadleys Mill Pond—*reservoir* NC-3
*Hadleys Point* ME-1
Hadley Spring—*spring* WA-9
Hadleys Purchase—*fmr MCD* NH-1
Hadleys Windmill—*locale* NV-8
Hadley Technical HS—*school* MO-7
*Hadley Third Precinct* MA-1
**Hadley (Town of)**—*pop pl* MA-1
**Hadley (Town of)**—*pop pl* NY-2
Hadley Township—*civil* MO-7
Hadley (Township of)—*fmr MCD* AR-4
Hadley (Township of)—*fmr MCD* NC-3
**Hadley (Township of)**—*pop pl* IL-6
**Hadley (Township of)**—*pop pl* MI-6
Hadley Valley—*valley* MN-6
Hadley Valley Sch—*school* MN-6
Hadley Village Barn Shops—*locale* MA-1
**Hadleyville**—*pop pl* OR-9
Hadleyville Cem—*cemetery* NY-2
Hadleyville Cem—*cemetery* WI-6
Hadleyville Sch—*school* OR-9
*Hadleywood Plantation* TN-4
**Hadlock**—*pop pl* VA-3
**Hadlock**—*pop pl* WA-9
Hadlock Airp—*airport* WA-9
Hadlock Brook—*stream* ME-1
Hadlock Cove—*bay* (2) ME-1
Hadlock-Irondale—*CDP* WA-9
Hadlock Point—*cape* ME-1
Hadlock Pond—*reservoir* NY-2
*Hadlock's Cove* ME-1
Hadlock's Crow Canyon No. 1 (LA 55830)—*hist pl* NM-5
**Hadlow**—*pop pl* NC-3
**Hadlyme**—*pop pl* CT-1
Hadlyme Ch—*church* CT-1
Hadlyme North Hist Dist—*hist pl* CT-1
Hadnot Bar—*bar* AL-4
Hadnot Cem—*cemetery* TX-5
Hadnot Ch—*church* NC-3
Hadnot Creek—*stream* NC-3
Hadnot Point—*cape* NC-3
Hadokhten Lake—*lake* AK-9
Hadonbrook Country Club—*other* NJ-2
Hadorn Bridge Access Area—*locale* MO-7
Hadotohedan Lake—*lake* AK-9
*Hadrells Point* SC-3
Hadsall Creek—*stream* OR-9
Hadsell—*locale* MO-7
Hadsell—*locale* WY-8
Hadsell Cabin—*locale* WY-8
Hadsell Corral—*locale* WY-8
Hadsell Place—*locale* WY-8
Hadsell Ranch—*locale* WY-8
Hadsell Rsvr—*reservoir* WY-8
Hadsell Slough—*stream* WY-8
Hadsells Pond—*lake* MI-6
Hadsell Spring—*spring* WY-8
Hadselville Creek—*stream* CA-9
Hadson Creek—*stream* OR-9
Hads Point—*ridge* CO-8
Hadstadt Drain—*canal* MI-6
Hadweenzic River—*stream* AK-9
Hadwen Park—*park* MA-1
*Hady Creek* TX-5
*Hadzard Cave* TN-4
Haeckel, Mount—*summit* CA-9
**Haeckerville**—*pop pl* TX-5
Haedge Cem—*cemetery* TX-5
Haedicke Cem—*cemetery* IL-6
Haefele Ranch—*locale* WY-8
Haefner Ditch—*canal* OH-6
**Haegers Bend**—*pop pl* IL-6
Haegler Ranch—*locale* CO-8
Haeg Park—*park* MN-6
*Haehl Creek* CA-9
Haehl Creek—*stream* CA-9
Haehnel Bldg—*hist pl* TX-5
Haehule Creek—*stream* WA-9
Haeleele Ridge—*ridge* HI-9
Haeleele Valley—*valley* HI-9
Haelleck Canyon—*valley* CA-9
*Haena* HI-9
Haena—*civil* HI-9
Haena—*locale* HI-9
**Haena**—*pop pl* HI-9
Haena Archeol Complex—*hist pl* HI-9
Haena Dry Cave—*cave* HI-9
Haena Point—*cape* (2) HI-9
Haena (Site)—*locale* HI-9
Haenke Glacier—*glacier* AK-9
Haenke Island—*island* AK-9
Haen Sch—*school* WI-6
Haerr Field Airp—*airport* MO-7
Haese Memorial Village Hist Dist—*hist pl* WI-6
**Haevers Corners**—*pop pl* WI-6
Hafed—*locale* NV-8
Hafel Drain—*stream* MI-6
Hafen, John, House—*hist pl* UT-8
**Hafer**—*pop pl* IL-6
Hafer, Edgar F., House—*hist pl* OR-9
Hafer Ch—*church* IL-6
Hafer Flat—*flat* OR-9
Hafer Run—*stream* KS-7
Hafers Mill (historical)—*locale* PA-2
*Hafetna Point* MH-9
Hafey Brook—*stream* ME-1
Hafey Mtn—*summit* ME-1
Hafey Pond—*lake* ME-1
Haffaw Mine (Inactive)—*mine* KY-4
Haffen Park—*park* NY-2
Haffenreffer Brewery—*hist pl* MA-1
Haffer Cem—*cemetery* MO-7
**Haffey (Milltown)**—*pop pl* PA-2
Haffner Cem—*cemetery* TN-4
Hafford Brook—*stream* (2) ME-1
*Haffstadt Creek* WA-9
Hafften Lake—*lake* MN-6
Hafla Sch—*school* MT-8
Haflin Canyon—*valley* CO-8
Haflinger Creek—*stream* OR-9
Hafner Creek—*stream* OR-9
Hafner Dam—*dam* SD-7
Hafner Ducklake Dam—*dam* SD-7
Hafner Grocery Warehouse—*hist pl* MO-7
Hafslo Cem—*cemetery* MN-6
Hafslo Chapel—*church* MN-6
*Haften Lake* MN-6
Haga Ch—*church* OH-6
Haga Creek—*stream* ID-8
Hagadone Brook—*stream* NY-2
Hagador Canyon—*valley* CA-9
Hagadore Lake—*lake* MT-8
Hagadorn Waterhole—*reservoir* OR-9
Hagali Lake—*lake* MN-6
**Hagali (Township of)**—*pop pl* MN-6
Hagaman—*locale* IL-6
**Hagaman**—*pop pl* NY-2
Hagaman Cem—*cemetery* (2) MI-6
Hagaman Cem—*cemetery* NE-7
Hagaman Gulch—*valley* CA-9
Hagaman Heights Sch—*school* NJ-2
Hagaman Lake—*reservoir* TX-5
Hagaman Mills Cem—*cemetery* NY-2
Hagaman Park—*park* CA-9
Haga Mission—*church* OH-6
Hagamon Spring (historical)—*spring* SD-7
Hagan—*locale* SC-3
Hagan—*locale* VA-3
**Hagan**—*pop pl* GA-3
**Hagan**—*pop pl* MN-6
Hagan, Mount—*summit* OR-9
**Hagan Addition**—*pop pl* OH-6
Hagan Branch—*stream* MO-7
Hagan Branch—*stream* TN-4
Hagan Cem—*cemetery* TX-5
Hagan Cem—*cemetery* VA-3
*Hagan Creek* NC-3
Hagan Creek—*stream* LA-4
Hagan Ditch—*canal* KY-4
Hagan Field—*park* MN-6
Hagan Flat—*flat* MT-8
Hagan Fork—*stream* NC-3
Hagan (ghost Town)—*locale* NM-5
Hagan Hall—*locale* VA-3
Hagan Hill—*summit* AL-4
Hagan Hollow—*valley* TN-4
Hagan House—*hist pl* KY-4
Hagan Island—*island* SC-3
Hagan Lake—*lake* CA-9
Hagan Lake—*lake* NE-7
Hagan Landing—*locale* SC-3
Hagan Mtn—*summit* WA-9
Hagan Pond—*lake* MT-8
**Hagans**—*pop pl* WV-2
Hagans Cem—*cemetery* WV-2
Hagan Sch (abandoned)—*school* MO-7
Hagans Chapel—*church* LA-4
Hagans Crossing—*locale* MT-8
**Hagans (Hagan)**—*pop pl* VA-3
Hagans Hammock—*island* FL-3
Hagan Shanty Ridge—*ridge* KY-4
Hagans Landing—*locale* MS-4
**Hagansport**—*pop pl* TX-5
Hagansport Cem—*cemetery* TX-5
Hagan Spring Branch—*stream* VA-3
Hagans Slough—*gut* FL-3
Hagan Stone Park—*park* NC-3
Hagan Swamp—*swamp* AL-4
Hagar Cem—*cemetery* MO-7
Hagar Creek—*stream* CT-1
Hagar Creek—*stream* MI-6
Hagar Creek—*stream* OR-9
*Hagar Hill* MA-1
Hagar Hill—*summit* MA-1
Hagar Hill—*summit* VT-1
Haga Ridge—*ridge* OH-6
Hagar Mtn—*summit* CO-8
Hagar Ridge—*ridge* OR-9
Hagar Sch—*school* MI-6
*Hagar Shores* MI-6
Hagar Shores (census name Lake Michigan Beach)—*other* MI-6
**Hagarstown**—*pop pl* IL-6
**Hagar (Township of)**—*pop pl* MI-6
**Hagarville**—*pop pl* AR-4
Hagata Canyon—*valley* CA-9
Hagata Rsvr—*reservoir* CA-9
Hag Creek—*stream* MN-6
*Hagebone Lake* MI-6
Hagedons Lake—*lake* GA-3
**Hagedorns Mills**—*pop pl* NY-2
Hage Hollow—*valley* AR-4
Hagelbarger Pass—*gap* AK-9
Hagel Creek—*stream* ND-7
Hagelstein Commercial Bldg—*hist pl* TX-5
Hagelstein Park—*park* OR-9
Hagelstein Ranch—*locale* (2) TX-5
**Hagel Township**—*pop pl* ND-7
Hageman—*locale* OH-6
Hageman Cem—*cemetery* IL-6
Hageman Cem—*cemetery* NY-2
Hageman Elem Sch—*school* KS-7
Hageman Mine—*mine* CA-9
Hagemann, John, House—*hist pl* TX-5
Hagemann Creek—*stream* IL-6
Hagemann Ranch—*locale* CA-9
*Hageman Run* PA-2
Hageman Slough—*lake* SD-7
*Hagemans Run* PA-2
*Hageman Station* OH-6
Hagemeister, Mount—*summit* AK-9
Hagemeister Island—*island* AK-9
Hagemeister Lake—*lake* MI-6
Hagemeister Ranch—*locale* WY-8
Hagemeister Strait—*channel* AK-9
*Hagen* MN-6
Hagenbarth Coulee—*valley* WI-6
Hagenbaugh Ranch—*locale* CA-9
Hagen Branch—*stream* MS-4
Hagenbuch Ranch—*locale* NV-8
Hagen Canyon—*valley* AZ-5
Hagen Cem—*cemetery* IL-6
Hagen Cem—*cemetery* IN-6
Hagen Cem—*cemetery* NC-3
Hagen Coulee—*valley* MT-8
*Hagen Creek* OR-9
Hagen Creek—*stream* AZ-5
Hagen Creek—*stream* GA-3
Hagen Creek—*stream* ID-8
Hagen Creek—*stream* NM-5
Hagen Creek—*stream* OR-9
Hagen Creek—*stream* WA-9
Hagen Draw—*valley* AZ-5
Hagen Draw—*valley* ID-8
Hagener—*locale* IL-6
**Hagener (Township of)**—*pop pl* IL-6
Hagen Flat—*flat* CA-9
Hagen Gap—*gap* MT-8
Hagen Hill—*summit* MO-7
Hagen Lake—*lake* AK-9
Hagen Lake—*lake* (2) MN-6
Hagen Lake—*lake* WA-9
Hagen Lake—*lake* WI-6
Hagen Ranch—*locale* (2) AZ-5
Hagen Ranch—*locale* MT-8
Hagen Ridge—*ridge* OR-9
Hagen Run—*stream* PA-2
*Hagens Branch* LA-4
Hagen Sch—*school* FL-3
Hagen Sch—*school* MN-6
Hagens Cove—*bay* FL-3
*Hagens Dam* ND-7
Hagens Dam—*dam* ND-7
Hagen Site—*hist pl* MT-8
Hagens Point—*cliff* AZ-5
Hagensville—*locale* MI-6
Hagensville Hunting Club—*other* MI-6
Hagen Tank—*reservoir* AZ-5
**Hagen (Township of)**—*pop pl* MN-6
Hagen Well—*well* AZ-5
Hager—*locale* KY-4
Hager—*locale* OR-9
Hager—*locale* WV-2
Hager, C., and Sons Hinge Co.—*hist pl* MO-7
Hager, Otto J., House—*hist pl* IA-7
Hager Airstrip—*airport* PA-2
Hage Ranch—*locale* NM-5
Hager Basin—*basin* CA-9
Hager Basin Rsvr—*reservoir* CA-9
Hager Bldg—*hist pl* PA-2
Hager Branch—*stream* KY-4
Hager Brook—*stream* VT-1
Hager Cem—*cemetery* MO-7
Hager Cem—*cemetery* NY-2
Hager Cem—*cemetery* (6) WV-2
**Hager City**—*pop pl* WI-6
Hager Community Hall—*locale* MI-6
Hager Creek—*stream* (2) NC-3
Hager Creek—*stream* OK-5
Hager Creek—*stream* TX-5
Hager Creek—*stream* WA-9
Hager Dam—*dam* ND-7
Hagerdon Lake—*reservoir* NM-5
Hager Farm—*hist pl* VT-1
Hager Fork—*stream* WV-2
**Hagerhill**—*pop pl* KY-4
Hager Hill—*summit* MA-1
Hager Hill—*summit* PA-2
Hager Hill (RR name for Hagerhill)—*other* KY-4
**Hagerhill (RR name Hager Hill)**—*pop pl* KY-4
Hager Hollow—*valley* WV-2
Hagerhorst Mountains—*range* OR-9
Hager House—*hist pl* IN-6
Hager House—*hist pl* MD-2
Hager Lake—*lake* ID-8
Hager Lake—*lake* MI-6
Hager Lake—*lake* WA-9
Hager Lake Shelter—*locale* WA-9
*Hagerman* OH-6
**Hagerman**—*pop pl* ID-8
**Hagerman**—*pop pl* NM-5
**Hagerman**—*pop pl* NY-2
Hagerman Branch—*stream* TX-5
Hagerman Branch—*stream* WV-2
Hagerman Canal—*canal* NM-5
Hagerman Canyon—*valley* CA-9
Hagerman (CCD)—*cens area* NM-5
Hagerman Cem—*cemetery* NM-5
Hagerman Cem—*cemetery* TX-5
Hagerman Cem—*cemetery* WV-2
Hagerman Ch—*church* TX-5
Hagerman Creek—*stream* MI-6
Hagerman Creek—*stream* OH-6
Hagerman Drain—*canal* MI-6

**Hagerman Heights**—pop pl ... NM-5
Hagerman Lake—lake ... CO-8
Hagerman Lake—lake ... MI-6
**Hagerman Lake**—pop pl ... MI-6
Hagerman Lake—reservoir ... PA-2
Hagerman Mansion—hist pl ... CO-8
Hagerman Natl Wildlife Ref—park ... TX-5
Hagerman Pass—gap ... CO-8
Hagerman Peak—summit ... CA-9
Hagerman Peak—summit ... CO-8
Hagerman Ranch—locale (2) ... NM-5
Hagerman Rsvr—reservoir ... WY-8
Hagerman Run ... PA-2
Hagerman Run—stream ... PA-2
Hagerman Run Dam ... PA-2
Hagerman Sch—school ... WV-2
Hagerman's run ... PA-2
Hagermans Run—stream ... PA-2
Hagermans Run Rsvr—reservoir ... PA-2
Hagerman Tunnel—tunnel ... CO-8
Hager Mine—mine ... AL-4
Hager Mtn—summit ... OR-9
Hagero—locale ... PA-2
Hager Park—park ... OR-9
Hager Park—park ... TX-5
Hager Pond—reservoir ... MA-1
Hager Pond—reservoir ... MN-6
Hager Post Office (historical)—building ... TN-4
Hager Ranch—locale ... CA-9
Hager Ranch—locale ... MT-8
Hager (RR name for Hager City)—other ... WI-6
Hagers Camp—locale ... KY-4
Hager Sch—school ... KY-4
Hager Sch—school ... MO-7
Hagers Corners—locale ... NY-2
**Hagers Grove**—pop pl ... MO-7
Hager Slough—gut ... IL-6
Hagers Mtn—summit ... NC-3
Hager Spring—spring ... OR-9
Hagers Town ... NJ-2
**Hagerstown**—pop pl ... IN-6
**Hagerstown**—pop pl ... MD-2
Hagerstown Airp—airport ... IN-6
Hagerstown Armory—hist pl ... MD-2
Hagerstown Charity Sch—hist pl ... MD-2
Hagerstown Commercial Core Hist Dist—hist pl ... MD-2
Hagerstown I.O.O.F. Hall—hist pl ... IN-6
Hagerstown Rsvr—reservoir ... MD-2
Hagersville ... NJ-2
**Hagersville**—pop pl ... PA-2
**Hagerty**—pop pl (2) ... IA-7
Hagerty Butte—summit ... WA-9
Hagerty Gulch—valley ... MT-8
Hagerty House—hist pl ... TX-5
Hagerty Ranch—locale ... CA-9
Hagerty Ridge—ridge ... OR-9
Hagerty Run ... PA-2
Hagerud Sch—school ... MN-6
Hagerville—locale ... TX-5
**Hagerville**—pop pl ... NJ-2
Hagerville Baptist Ch (historical)—church ... TX-5
Hagerville Branch—stream ... TN-4
Hagerville Hollow ... TN-4
Hagerville Post Office (historical)—building ... TX-5
Hagerville Sch—school ... TX-5
Hagestad 1 Drill Hole—well ... NV-8
Hagevo ... PA-2
**Hagewood**—pop pl ... LA-4
Hagewood Cem—cemetery (2) ... TN-4
Hagewood Chapel—church ... TN-4
Hagey, Levi, House—hist pl ... OR-9
Hagey Branch—stream ... MO-7
Hagey Bridge ... TN-4
Hagey Sch—school ... MO-7
Haggai Creek—stream ... TX-5
Haggard—mine ... OR-9
**Haggard**—pop pl ... KS-7
Haggard, Nathaniel, House—hist pl ... KY-4
Haggard Branch—stream ... KY-4
Haggard Branch—stream (2) ... TN-4
Haggard Cem—cemetery ... IL-6
Haggard Cem—cemetery ... TN-4
Haggard Creek ... TN-4
Haggard Creek—stream ... AL-4
Haggard Creek—stream ... AK-9
Haggard Hollow—valley (2) ... TN-4
Haggards Ferry (historical)—locale ... TN-4
Haggarty Creek ... WY-8
Haggarty Creek—stream ... WY-8
Haggar Udden ... DE-2
Hagge County Park—park ... IA-7
Hagged Mtn—summit ... CO-8
Haggen Hollow ... TN-4
Hagger Creek—stream ... MS-4
Haggerman Creek—stream ... OK-5
Haggert ... ND-7
Haggert Creek ... MI-6
Haggerty, Dennis J., House—hist pl ... MI-6
Haggerty Camp Lake—lake ... LA-4
Haggerty Cem—cemetery ... AL-4
Haggerty Creek ... WY-8
Haggerty Creek—stream ... ID-8
Haggerty Creek—stream ... LA-4
Haggerty Creek—stream ... TX-5
Haggerty Creek—stream ... WA-9
Haggerty Drain—canal ... MI-6
Haggerty Gulch—valley ... CA-9
Haggerty Hollow—valley ... PA-2
Haggerty Hollow—valley ... TN-4
Haggerty Lake—lake ... MN-6
Haggerty Road Sch—school ... MI-6
Haggerty Sch—school ... ME-1
Haggerty Sch—school ... MA-1
Haggerty Spring—spring ... NV-8
Haggerty Wash—stream ... NV-8
Haggets Pond ... MA-1
Haggett ... MA-1
Haggett Hill—summit ... ME-1
Haggett Pond ... MA-1
**Haggetts**—pop pl ... MA-1
Haggetts Pond—reservoir ... MA-1
Haggetts Pond Dam—dam ... MA-1
Haggey Spring—spring ... WA-9
Haggieville Hollow—valley ... TN-4
Haggin, Mount—summit ... MT-8
Haggin Farm—hist pl ... KY-4
Haggin Hill ... AL-4
Haggin Lake—lake ... MT-8
Haggin Museum—building ... CA-9
Haggin Oaks Golf Course—other ... CA-9
Haggins Branch—stream ... SC-3
Haggin State Wildlife Mngmt Area, Mount—park ... MT-8
Haggin Well—well ... CA-9
**Hagginwood**—pop pl ... CA-9
Hagginwood Park—park ... CA-9
Hagginwood Sch—school ... CA-9
Haggle Branch—stream ... WV-2
Haggy Cem—cemetery ... WV-2
Hag Hill—summit ... TX-5
Hagin Branch—stream ... GA-3
Hagin Creek—stream ... MS-4
Haginsack ... NJ-2
Hagins Cem—cemetery ... KY-4
Hagins Peak—summit ... NM-5
Hagins Prong—stream ... SC-3
Hagist Ranch—locale ... TX-5
Hagist Ranch Gas Plant—oilfield ... TX-5
Hagist Ranch Oil Field—oilfield ... TX-5
Hag Lake—lake ... MN-6
Hagler—locale ... AL-4
Hagler—locale ... AR-4
Hagler—locale ... OH-6
Hagler, John L., House—hist pl ... TN-4
Hagler, William, House—hist pl ... NC-3
Hagler AAF Airp—airport ... MS-4
Hagler Canyon—valley ... TX-5
Hagler Cem—cemetery (2) ... IL-6
Hagler Cem—cemetery ... OH-6
Hagler Cem—cemetery ... TN-4
Hagler-Cole Cabin—hist pl ... AR-4
Hagler Creek—stream ... AR-4
Hagler Creek—stream ... ID-8
Hagler Creek—stream ... MI-6
Hagler Mill ... AL-4
**Hagler Mill Estates (subdivision)**—pop pl ... AL-4
Hagler Mill Pond ... AL-4
Hagler Mill Pond Dam—dam ... AL-4
Hagler Oil Field—oilfield ... TX-5
Haglers ... AL-4
Haglers Cypress Brake—swamp ... AR-4
Haglers Mill (historical)—locale ... AL-4
Haglers Millpond—reservoir ... AL-4
Haglersville ... TN-4
Haglersville Post Office (historical)—building ... TN-4
**Haglerville (historical)**—pop pl ... TN-4
Hagley Hollow—valley ... OH-6
Hagley Lake—lake ... MI-6
Hagley Museum—building ... DE-2
Hagley Plantation—locale ... SC-3
Haglofs Dam—dam ... MT-8
**Haglund**—pop pl ... IN-6
Haglund Cem—cemetery ... MI-6
Haglund Ditch—canal ... WY-8
Haglund Ranch—locale ... WY-8
Hagman ... MH-9
Hagman Beach ... MH-9
Hagman Cliffs ... MH-9
Hagney Spring—spring ... OR-9
Hagoi—lake ... MH-9
Hagoi Chalan ... MH-9
Hagoi Chalan Kanoa ... MH-9
Hagoi Susupe ... MH-9
Hagoi Susupi—lake ... MH-9
Hagons Branch ... LA-4
Hagood ... VA-3
**Hagood**—pop pl ... SC-3
**Hagood**—pop pl ... VA-3
Hagood Branch—stream ... SC-3
Hagood Creek—stream ... AL-4
Hagood Creek—stream ... AR-4
Hagood Creek—stream ... VA-3
Hagood Mill—hist pl ... SC-3
Hagoods Crossroads ... AL-4
Hagoods Mill—locale ... SC-3
Hagoods Store (historical)—locale ... AL-4
Hagood Station ... VA-3
Hagoy Chalan Kanoa ... MH-9
Hagoy Susupe ... MH-9
Hag Peak—summit ... AK-9
Haguaba ... AZ-5
Hagua Hali ... AZ-5
**Hague**—pop pl ... FL-3
**Hague**—pop pl ... NY-2
**Hague**—pop pl ... ND-7
**Hague**—pop pl ... VA-3
Hague, Mount—summit ... AK-9
Hague, Mount—summit ... MT-8
Hague Brook—stream ... NY-2
Hague Cem—cemetery ... SD-7
Hague Channel—channel ... AK-9
Hague Creek—stream ... CO-8
Hague Creek—stream ... WY-8
Hague Crossing—locale ... NY-2
Hague Hill—summit ... WY-8
Hague Mtn—summit ... WY-8
Hague Point ... SC-3
Hague Point—cape ... NY-2
Hague Ranch—locale ... NE-7
Hague Rock—island ... AK-9
Hague Run—stream ... PA-2
Hagues Peak—summit ... CO-8
**Hague (Town of)**—pop pl ... NY-2
**Hague Township**—pop pl ... SD-7
Haguge Township—civil ... SD-7
Haguman-Misaki ... MH-9
Haguman Point ... MH-9
Hagwood Ch—church ... AL-4
Hagwood Creek ... AL-4
Hagwood Dam—dam ... AL-4
Hagwood Lake—reservoir ... AL-4
Hagy Bridge—locale ... TN-4
Hagy Cem—cemetery ... MO-7
Hagy Cem—cemetery ... VA-3
**Hagys Corner**—pop pl ... TN-4
Ha Ha, Bayou—stream ... LA-4
Haha Bay—lake ... LA-4
Haha Bayou—stream ... LA-4
Haha Branch—stream ... MD-2
Haha Creek—stream ... AK-9
Hahaeule—summit ... HI-9
Haha Falls—falls ... HI-9
Hahaha Bay—bay ... HI-9
Hahaimoa Gulch ... HI-9
Hahaione Sch—school ... HI-9
Hahaione Valley—valley ... HI-9
Hahakea—civil ... HI-9
Hahakea Gulch—valley ... HI-9
Hahalawe—civil ... HI-9
Hahalawe Gulch—valley ... HI-9
Hahalawe Stream ... HI-9
Ha Hand, Lake—lake ... MT-8
Hahanudan Lake—lake ... AK-9
Ha Ha Tonka ... MO-7
Hahatonka—locale ... MO-7
Hahatonka Castle—locale ... MO-7
Ha Ha Tonka State Park—park ... MO-7
**Hahira**—pop pl ... GA-3
Hahira (CCD)—cens area ... GA-3
Ha-hi-yalin Wash ... AZ-5
Hahl Memorial Cem—cemetery ... TX-5
Hahn—locale ... ID-8
Hahn—locale ... TX-5
**Hahn**—pop pl ... MO-7
**Hahn**—pop pl ... NM-5
**Hahn**—pop pl ... NC-3
Hahnaman—locale ... IL-6
**Hahnaman (Township of)**—pop pl ... IL-6
Hahn Bottoms—bend ... TX-5
Hahn Branch—stream ... KS-7
Hahn Branch—stream ... MO-7
Hahn Canyon—valley ... OR-9
Hahn Cem—cemetery ... MO-7
Hahn Cem—cemetery ... TX-5
Hahn Chapel—church ... MO-7
Hahn Coulee ... MT-8
Hahn Creek—stream ... CO-8
Hahn Creek—stream (2) ... MT-8
Hahn Creek Guard Station—locale ... MT-8
Hahn Creek Pass—gap ... MT-8
Hahn Ditch—canal ... IN-6
Hahn Drain—canal (2) ... MI-6
Hahn Drain—stream ... MI-6
Hahnemann Hosp—hospital ... MA-1
Hahnemann Medical Coll—school ... PA-2
Hahnemann Memorial—park ... DC-2
Hahnert Ditch—canal ... IN-6
Hahn Field Archeol District—hist pl ... OH-6
Hahn Gulch—valley ... ID-8
Hahn Lake—lake ... MN-6
Hahn Peak—summit ... MT-8
Hahn Reservoir Dam—dam ... IN-6
Hahn Rsvr—reservoir ... IN-6
Hahns Airport*—airport ... SD-7
Hahns Lake—lake ... WI-6
Hahns Mill—locale ... MO-7
Hahns Peak—locale ... CO-8
Hahns Peak—summit ... CO-8
Hahns Peak Lake—reservoir ... CO-8
Hahns Peak Reservoir ... CO-8
Hahns Peak Schoolhouse—hist pl ... CO-8
Hahn Springs ... PA-2
Hahns Reservoir ... CO-8
**Hahns Switch**—pop pl ... IA-7
Hahnstown ... PA-2
**Hahnstown**—pop pl ... PA-2
**Hahntown**—pop pl ... PA-2
**Hahnville**—pop pl ... LA-4
Hahomu-Saki ... MH-9
Ha Ho No Geh Canyon—valley ... AZ-5
Hah-quah-sa eel ... AZ-5
**Haid**—pop pl ... TX-5
Haida Mine—mine ... AK-9
Haida Point—cape ... WA-9
Haid Cem—cemetery ... MO-7
Haidee Mine (inactive)—mine ... ID-8
Haidusek Cem—cemetery ... TX-5
Haidyjz McNeil Drain—canal ... MI-6
Haieone—summit ... HI-9
Haifley Ditch—canal ... IN-6
**Haig**—pop pl ... AR-4
**Haig**—pop pl ... NE-7
**Haig**—pop pl ... OR-9
Haig Ch—church ... AL-4
Haig Creek ... GA-3
Haig Creek—stream ... SC-3
Haig Creek—stream ... WA-9
Haigh Cem—cemetery ... OH-6
Haigh Sch—school ... MI-6
Haigh Sch—school ... NH-1
Haight—locale ... CA-9
Haight, Hector C., House—hist pl ... UT-8
Haight Bench Canal—canal ... UT-8
Haight Canyon—valley ... CA-9
Haight Cem—cemetery (2) ... NY-2
Haight Creek—stream ... OR-9
Haight Creek—stream ... UT-8
Haight Creek Mound Group (47-Je-38)—hist pl ... WI-6
Haight Creek Picnic Area—park ... OR-9
Haight Hill—summit ... NY-2
Haight Mtn—summit ... CA-9
Haight Park—park ... IL-6
Haight Rsvr—reservoir ... CO-8
Haight Rsvr—reservoir ... WA-9
Haights Bay—bay ... WI-6
Haights Branch—stream ... MD-2
Haight Sch—school ... CA-9
Haight Sch—school ... IL-6
Haights Corners—locale ... NY-2
Haights Creek—stream ... NY-2
**Haight (Township of)**—pop pl ... MI-6
Haight Village Hist Dist—hist pl ... IL-6
Haight Wells—well ... CO-8
Haigis Beach—beach ... MA-1
**Haigler**—pop pl ... NE-7
Haigler, Lake—reservoir ... SC-3
Haigler Branch—stream ... TN-4
Haigler Camp Branch—stream ... NC-3
Haigler Canal—canal ... CO-8
Haigler Canal—canal ... NE-7
Haigler Canyon—valley ... AZ-5
Haigler Cem—cemetery ... AL-4
Haigler Cem—cemetery ... NC-3
Haigler Creek—stream ... AZ-5
Haigler Ditch ... CO-8
**Haigler Ridge**—pop pl ... TN-4
Haigler Township—civ div ... NE-7
Haig Mill Creek—stream ... GA-3
Haig Mill Lake—reservoir ... GA-3
Haig Mtn—summit ... WA-9
Haig Point—cape ... SC-3
Haig Point Cem—cemetery ... SC-3
Haig Pond—reservoir ... PA-2
Haigs Lake—lake ... WA-9
Haigwood Branch—stream ... AL-4
Haigwood Ch—church ... AL-4
Haikey Cem—cemetery ... OK-5
Haikey Chapel—church ... OK-5
Haiku—canal (2) ... HI-9
Haiku—civil (2) ... HI-9
**Haiku**—pop pl ... HI-9
Haiku Ditch—canal ... HI-9
Haiku Iki—civil ... HI-9
Haiku Mill—hist pl ... HI-9
Haiku Nui—civil ... HI-9
Haiku-Pauwela (CCD)—cens area ... HI-9
Haiku Point—cape ... HI-9
Haiku Rsvr—reservoir ... HI-9
Haiku Sch—school ... HI-9
Haikuua—cape ... HI-9
Haiku Uka—civil ... HI-9
Haiku Valley—valley ... HI-9
Hail—locale ... KY-4
**Hail**—pop pl ... TX-5
Hail and Waite Hill—summit ... ME-1
Hail Canyon—valley ... NM-5
Hail Cem—cemetery ... TX-5
Hail Columbia Gulch—valley ... MT-8
Hail Creek ... TN-4
Hail Creek—stream ... MD-2
Hail Creek—stream ... NE-7
Haile—locale ... FL-3
**Haile**—pop pl ... LA-4
Haile, Joseph, House—hist pl ... RI-1
Haile Cave—cave ... NY-2
Haile Cave—cave ... TN-4
Haile Cem—cemetery ... MS-4
Haile Cem—cemetery ... MO-7
Haile Cem—cemetery ... OK-5
Haile Ch—church ... TX-5
Haile Creek—stream ... LA-4
Haile Gold Mine Ch—church ... SC-3
Haile Gold Mine Creek—stream ... SC-3
Haile Hollow—valley ... TN-4
**Hailesboro**—pop pl ... NY-2
Hailes Hopyard—summit ... NY-2
Hailey—locale ... MO-7
**Hailey**—pop pl ... ID-8
Hailey-Bellevue—cens area ... ID-8
Hailey Branch—stream ... TN-4
Hailey Cem—cemetery ... AR-4
Hailey Cem—cemetery ... LA-4
Hailey Cem—cemetery ... MS-4
Hailey Cem—cemetery ... TN-4
Hailey Creek—stream (3) ... ID-8
Hailey Hollow—valley ... AR-4
Hailey Hollow—valley ... TX-5
Hailey Hot Springs—spring ... ID-8
Hailey Lake—lake ... WY-8
Haileys Branch—stream ... NC-3
Hailey Spring—spring ... MO-7
**Haileyville**—pop pl ... OK-5
Hail Hollow—valley ... MO-7
Hail Hollow—valley ... OK-5
Haili Congressional Cem—cemetery ... HI-9
Hailies Prairie Ditch—canal ... IN-6
Haili Gulch—valley ... HI-9
Hail Island ... FM-9
Hail Island—island ... FL-3
Hailmann Elem Sch—school ... IN-6
Hailman Sch ... IN-6
Hail Mtn—summit ... NY-2
Hail Point—cape ... MD-2
Hail Point—cape (2) ... TX-5
Hail Ridge Sch—school ... MO-7
Hailstone—locale ... UT-8
Hailstone Basin—basin ... MT-8
Hailstone Butte—summit ... ND-7
Hailstone Camp—locale ... CA-9
Hailstone Creek—stream ... MT-8
Hailstone Creek—stream ... ND-7
Hailstone Hollow—valley ... PA-2
Hailstone Natl Wildlife Ref—park ... MT-8
Hailstone Rsvr—reservoir ... MT-8
Hailstone Spring—spring ... MT-8
Hailville Cem—cemetery ... NY-2
Hailwell—locale ... KY-4
Hailwood Golf Course—locale ... PA-2
Haily Pass—gap ... WY-8
Haina—civil ... HI-9
**Haina**—pop pl ... HI-9
Ha'ina, Puntan—cape ... MH-9
Hainer Branch—stream ... WV-2
Hainer Cem—cemetery ... WV-2
Hainer Creek ... KY-4
Hainer Creek—stream ... IA-7
Hainers Run—stream ... PA-2
Haines—locale ... CA-9
Haines—locale ... IL-6
**Haines**—pop pl ... AK-9
**Haines**—pop pl ... OR-9
**Haines**—pop pl ... PA-2
Haines, Frank, House—hist pl ... OH-6
Haines, Hanson, House—hist pl ... PA-2
Haines, John, House—hist pl ... ID-8
Haines, Jonathan, House—hist pl ... NJ-2
Haines, Lake—lake (2) ... FL-3
**Haines Acres**—pop pl ... PA-2
Haines Acres Shop Ctr—locale ... PA-2
Haines Barranca—valley ... CA-9
Haines (Borough)—civil ... AK-9
Haines Branch—stream ... AL-4
Haines Branch—stream ... MD-2
Haines Branch—stream ... NE-7
Haines Branch—stream ... PA-2
Haines Branch—stream ... TN-4
Haines Branch Buffalo Creek—stream ... OH-6
Haines Bridge—bridge ... VA-3
Haines Brook—stream (3) ... NH-1
**Hainesburg**—pop pl ... NJ-2
Hainesburg Station—locale ... NJ-2
Haines Cabin—locale ... OR-9
Haines Canyon—valley ... CA-9
Haines Canyon—valley ... NV-8
Haines Canyon Channel—canal ... CA-9
Haines Cem—cemetery ... MO-7
Haines Cem—cemetery ... OH-6
Haines Cem—cemetery ... TN-4
Haines (Census Subarea)—cens area ... AK-9
Haines Ch—church ... OH-6
Haines Chapel—church ... VA-3
Haines Chapel Cem—cemetery ... AL-4
**Haines City**—pop pl ... FL-3
Haines City (CCD)—cens area ... FL-3
Haines City Mall—locale ... FL-3
Haines City Plaza (Shop Ctr)—locale ... FL-3
Haines City Senior HS—school ... FL-3
Haines Corner—locale ... ME-1
Haines Corner—locale ... NJ-2
**Haines Corner**—pop pl ... NJ-2
**Haines Corners**—pop pl ... NY-2
Haines Coulee—valley ... MT-8
Haines Creek ... NV-8
Haines Creek—stream ... FL-3
Haines Creek—stream ... IN-6
Haines Creek—stream ... LA-4
Haines Creek—stream ... NY-2
Haines Creek—stream ... OK-5
Haines Creek—stream (3) ... OR-9
Haines Creek—stream ... TX-5
Haines Creek—stream ... WV-2
Haines Creek Ch—church ... FL-3
Haines Ditch—canal (2) ... IN-6
Haines Ditch—canal ... WY-8
Haines Drain—canal ... MI-6
Haines Eyebrow—ridge ... NC-3
Haines Falls—falls ... OR-9
**Haines Falls**—pop pl ... NY-2
Haines Flat—flat ... AZ-5
Haines Flat—flat ... CA-9
Haines Flat—flat ... WY-8
Haines Flat, The ... AZ-5
Haines Flat Creek—stream ... TX-5
Haines Gap—gap ... PA-2
Haines Gap Trail ... PA-2
Haines Grove Sch—school ... MO-7
Haines Gulch—valley ... MT-8
Haines Hill—summit ... CT-1
Haines Hill—summit ... ME-1
Haines Hollow—valley ... NY-2
Haines House—hist pl ... OH-6
Haines Island ... TN-4
Haines Island—island ... AL-4
Haines Island—island ... AK-9
Haines Island Park—park ... AL-4
Haines JHS—school ... IL-6
Haines Junction—locale ... PA-2
Haines Knob—summit ... WV-2
Haines Lake—flat ... OR-9
Haines Lake—lake ... MI-6
Haines Lake—lake ... NE-7
Haines Lake—lake ... TX-5
Haines Landing Field—airport ... KS-7
Haines Mill—hist pl ... PA-2
Haines Mill (historical)—locale ... MS-4
Haines Neck—cape ... NJ-2
Haines Neck Ch—church ... NJ-2
Haines Pass—gap ... MT-8
Haines Path—trail ... PA-2
Haines Point—cape ... ME-1
Haines Point—cape ... MD-2
Haines Point—summit ... MT-8
Haines Pond—lake ... MD-2
Haines Pond—lake (2) ... NY-2
Haines Pond—lake ... VA-3
Haines Pond Number One—lake ... OR-9
Haines Pond Number Two—lake ... OR-9
**Hainesport**—pop pl ... NJ-2
**Hainesport (Township of)**—pop pl ... NJ-2
Haines Ranch—locale (2) ... WY-8
Haines Ridge—ridge ... MT-8
Haines Road Ch—church ... FL-3
Haines Rsvr—reservoir ... MT-8
Haines Rsvr—reservoir ... OR-9
Haines Rsvr—reservoir ... WY-8
Haines Sch—school (2) ... IL-6
Haines Sch—school ... MO-7
Haines Sch—school ... NH-1
Haines Sch—school ... NJ-2
Haines Sch (historical)—school ... PA-2
Haines Taverns ... PA-2
**Haines (Township of)**—pop pl ... IL-6
**Haines (Township of)**—pop pl ... PA-2
Hainesville—locale ... NJ-2
Hainesville—locale ... TX-5
**Hainesville**—pop pl ... IL-6
**Hainesville**—pop pl ... WV-2
Hainesville Cem—cemetery ... NJ-2
Hainesville Cem—cemetery ... WI-6
Hainesville Fish and Wildlife Mngmt Area—park ... NJ-2
Hainesville Sch—school ... WI-6
Haines Well—locale ... NM-5
Haines Wharf ... WA-9
**Hainesworth**—pop pl ... FL-3
Hainey Sch Number 4 (historical)—school ... SD-7
Haining Cem—cemetery ... MT-8
Haining Ranch—locale ... MT-8
Hainiya-misaki ... MH-9
Hainiya Point ... MH-9
Hain Lake ... KS-7
Hainline Cem—cemetery ... KY-4
Hainline Cem—cemetery ... OK-5
Hainlin Park—park ... MN-6
Hainoa—summit ... HI-9
Hainoa Crater—crater ... HI-9
Hains Branch—stream ... TX-5
Hains Ch—church ... PA-2
Hains Creek ... IN-6
Hains Lake—reservoir ... KS-7
Hains Lake Dam*—dam ... KS-7
Hains Point—cape ... DC-2
Hains Point—ridge ... CA-9
Hain Spring—spring ... WY-8
Hain State Fishing Lake And Wildlife Area—park ... KS-7
Hainty Branch—stream ... TX-5
Haipuaena Falls—falls ... HI-9
Haipuaena Stream—stream ... HI-9
Hair Bench—bench ... UT-8
Hair Bend—bend ... AL-4
Hairbino ... NE-7
Hair Canal—canal ... NC-3
Hair Cem—cemetery ... SC-3
Hair Clipper Wash—stream ... AZ-5
Haircomb Gap—gap ... NC-3
Hair Creek—stream ... LA-4
Haire Cem—cemetery (2) ... TN-4
Haire Draw—valley ... WY-8
Haire Rsvr—reservoir ... WY-8
**Haires**—pop pl ... MI-6
**Haire (Wright)**—pop pl ... LA-4
Hair Farm—locale ... WA-9
Hair Hill ... ND-7
Hair Hills ... ND-7
Hair Lake—lake ... GA-3
Hairnakraus Kill ... NY-2
Hair Park—park ... TX-5
Hairpin, The—locale ... TN-4
Hairpin Branch—stream ... VA-3
Hairpin Creek—stream ... CO-8
Hairpin Curve Lookout Tower—locale ... MI-6
Hairpin Ditch—canal ... CO-8
Hairpin Hollow—valley ... AR-4
Hairpin Ranch—locale ... MT-8
Hairpin Spring—dam ... AZ-5
Hairpin Spring—spring ... AZ-5
Hairpin Turn—locale ... MA-1
Hairpin Turn—locale ... WY-8
Hair Schoolhouse (historical)—school ... PA-2
Hairs Creek ... TN-4
Hair Seal Rock—island ... CA-9
Hair Spring—spring ... GA-3
Hairston ... AL-4
Hairston Bend—bend ... MS-4
Hairston Bend Cutoff—channel ... MS-4
Hairston Branch—stream ... VA-3
Hairston Cem—cemetery (2) ... MS-4
Hairston Creek—stream ... TX-5
Hairston Island—island ... GA-3
Hairston Place (historical)—locale ... MS-4
Hairston Sch—school ... VA-3
**Hairtown**—pop pl ... NC-3
Hairy Bear Mountain ... NC-3
Hairy Head Pond—lake ... VA-3
Hairy Hill—summit ... IL-6
Hairy Johns Picnic Area—area ... PA-2
Hairy John Trail—trail ... PA-2
Hairy Knob—summit ... TX-5
Hairy Lake—lake ... MN-6
Hairy Pit—cave ... AL-4
Hairy Spring—spring ... PA-2
Hairy Spring Hollow ... PA-2
Hairy Springs Hollow—valley ... PA-2
Haisch Lake—reservoir ... SD-7
Haish Memorial Library—hist pl ... IL-6
Haish Sch—school ... IL-6
Haislet Creek ... VA-3
Haislets Creek ... VA-3
Haislett Creek—stream ... MT-8
Haisley Sch—school ... MI-6
Haislip Branch—stream ... TN-4
Haislip Hollow—valley (2) ... TN-4
Haislip House—hist pl ... FL-3
Haislip Pond—lake ... VA-3
Haislip Sch (historical)—school ... TN-4
Haislup Cem—cemetery ... IN-6
Haist Mine—mine ... AZ-5
Hait, Benjamin, House—hist pl ... CT-1
Hait, Thaddeus, Farm—hist pl ... NY-2
Haitema Sch—school ... MI-6
Haithcock Branch—stream ... AL-4
Haithcock Pond—reservoir ... SC-3
Haithcock Sch—school ... CT-1
Haitian Apostolate—church ... FL-3
Haitian Baptist Mission—church ... FL-3
Haitian Catholic Center—church ... FL-3
Haitian Legation Bldg—building ... DC-2
Haiti Cem—cemetery ... KY-4
Haiti Hollow—valley ... IN-6
Haiti Island—island ... NY-2
Hait Rsvr—reservoir ... ID-8
Haitz Ditch—canal ... IA-7
**Haivana Nakya**—pop pl ... AZ-5
Haivan Vaya—locale ... AZ-5
Haiwahine ... HI-9
Haiwee Creek—stream ... CA-9
**Haiwee (L.A. City Power Plant)**—pop pl ... CA-9
Haiwee Pass—gap ... CA-9
Haiwee Powerhouse—building ... CA-9
Haiwee Rsvr—reservoir ... CA-9
Haiwee Spring—spring ... CA-9
Haiyaha, Lake—lake ... CO-8
Hajdukovich, Mount—summit ... AK-9
Hajdukovich Creek—stream ... AK-9
Hakaaana ... HI-9
Hakaaano—summit ... HI-9
Hakalaoa Falls—falls ... HI-9
**Hakalau**—pop pl ... HI-9
Hakalau Bay—bay ... HI-9
Hakalau Gulch ... HI-9
Hakalau Homesteads—civil ... HI-9
Hakalau Iki—civil ... HI-9
Hakalau Nui—civil ... HI-9
Hakalau Sch—school ... HI-9
Hakalau Stream—stream ... HI-9
Hakatai Canyon—valley ... AZ-5
Hakatai Rapids—rapids ... AZ-5
Hakel Gulch—valley ... MT-8
Hakel Spring—spring ... OR-9
Hakepuu ... HI-9
Hakert Draw—valley ... WY-8
Hake Sch—school ... PA-2
**Hakes Corners**—pop pl ... OH-6
Hakes Hollow—valley ... PA-2
Hakihokake Creek—stream ... NJ-2
Hakina Gulch—valley ... HI-9
Hakioawa—bay ... HI-9
Hakipuu—civil ... HI-9
Hakki Creek—stream ... OR-9
Hakl, John, Chalkrock House—hist pl ... SD-7
Hakmang—bench ... MH-9
Hakmang, Laderan—cliff ... MH-9
Hakmang, Puntan—cape ... MH-9
Hakmang, Sabanan—slope ... MH-9
Hakmang, Unai—beach ... MH-9
Haku Cliff ... MH-9
Hakuhee ... HI-9
Hakuhee Point—cape ... HI-9
Hakuma Point—cape ... HI-9
Hakumiyo To ... FM-9
Hakuola Gulch—valley ... HI-9
Hakusha Shima ... FM-9
Hala, Moku—island ... HI-9
Halabaugh Hills ... MI-6
Halabaugh Bottom—flat ... TN-4
Halabaugh Branch—stream ... TN-4
Hala Cem—cemetery ... IA-7
Hal Adams Bridge—bridge ... FL-3
Halagow Creek—stream ... CA-9
Hala Grove—woods ... HI-9
Halahii Lake—lake ... HI-9
Halahol Point ... PW-9
Halai—summit ... HI-9

**Half Hollow Hills**—*pop pl* NY-2
Half Hollow Hills—*summit* NY-2
Half Hollow Hills HS—*school* NY-2
Half H Windmill—*locale* TX-5
*Half Island* AL-4
Half Lake—*lake* CA-9
Halfman Sch—*school* MI-6
*Half Mile Branch* TN-4
Halfmile Branch—*stream* KY-4
Halfmile Branch—*stream* NC-3
Half Mile Branch—*stream* NC-3
Halfmile Branch—*stream* NC-3
Halfmile Branch—*stream* TN-4
Halfmile Branch—*stream* VA-3
Halfmile Brook—*stream* ME-1
Half Mile Brook—*stream* NY-2
Halfmile Canyon—*valley* UT-8
Half Mile Ch—*church* MS-4
Halfmile Cliff—*cliff* VA-3
Halfmile Creek—*stream* AK-9
Half Mile Creek—*stream* CO-8
Half Mile Creek—*stream* ID-8
Halfmile Creek—*stream* IL-6
Halfmile Creek—*stream* VA-3
Half Mile Creek—*stream* WY-8
Halfmile Gulch—*valley* (2) CO-8
Halfmile Hill—*summit* RI-1
Halfmile Island—*island* NH-1
Half Mile Lake—*lake* LA-4
Halfmile Lake—*lake* MI-6
Halfmile Lake—*lake* MS-4
Half Mile Park—*park* MS-4
*Half Mile Point* NJ-2
Halfmile Point—*cape* NJ-2
*Half Mile Point Meadow* NJ-2
Halfmile Point Meadow—*swamp* NJ-2
Half Mile Pond—*lake* IL-6
Halfmile Pond—*lake* (2) ME-1
Halfmile Pond—*lake* NH-1
*Half Mile River* MA-1
Halfmile Rock—*island* CA-9
Halfmile Rock—*rock* MA-1
Half Mile Run—*stream* PA-2
Halfmile Shoals—*rapids* AL-4
Half Mile Trail—*trail* PA-2
**Half Moon**—*pop pl* AR-4
**Half Moon**—*pop pl* FL-3
**Halfmoon**—*pop pl* MT-8
**Halfmoon**—*pop pl* NY-2
**Half Moon**—*pop pl* NC-3
Half Moon, Lake—*lake* WI-6
Halfmoon, The—*bend* GA-3
Half Moon, The—*ridge* VA-3
Halfmoon Anchorage—*bay* AK-9
Half Moon Arch—*arch* KY-4
Half Moon Bar—*bar* OR-9
Half Moon Basin—*basin* CO-8
Half Moon Basin—*bay* TN-4
Halfmoon Bay—*bay* AK-9
Half Moon Bay—*bay* CA-9
Halfmoon Bay—*bay* OR-9
Half Moon Bay—*bay* WY-8
Halfmoon Bay—*lake* LA-4
**Half Moon Bay**—*pop pl* CA-9
Half Moon Bay—*swamp* SC-3
*Half Moon Bay Harbor* CA-9
Half Moon Bayou—*stream* LA-4
Half Moon Bayou—*stream* MS-4
Half Moon Bayou—*stream* MO-7
Halfmoon Beach—*beach* CA-9
Halfmoon Beach—*beach* MA-1
**Halfmoon Beach**—*pop pl* NY-2
Halfmoon Bend—*bend* MO-7
Half Moon Bend—*bend* OR-9
Half Moon Bluff—*cliff* FL-3
Halfmoon Bluff—*cliff* (3) GA-3
Halfmoon Branch—*stream* (2) SC-3
Half Moon Brook—*stream* MA-1
Halfmoon Campground—*locale* CO-8
Half Moon Campground—*locale* CO-8
Half Moon Campground—*locale* MT-8
Half Moon Campground—*locale* WY-8
Half Moon Canyon—*valley* MT-8
Half Moon Ch—*church* AR-4
Halfmoon Cove—*bay* (2) ME-1
Halfmoon Cove—*bay* VT-1
Halfmoon Creek—*stream* AK-9
Half Moon Creek—*stream* AR-4
Halfmoon Creek—*stream* CA-9
Halfmoon Creek—*stream* (2) CO-8
Half Moon Creek—*stream* ID-8
Halfmoon Creek—*stream* IN-6
Half Moon Creek—*stream* MS-4
Halfmoon Creek—*stream* MT-8
Half Moon Creek—*stream* MT-8
Halfmoon Creek—*stream* NC-3
Half Moon Creek—*stream* NC-3
Halfmoon Creek—*stream* PA-2
Half Moon Creek—*stream* UT-8
Half Moon Creek—*stream* (2) WA-9
Halfmoon Dearborn River Trail—*trail* MT-8
Halfmoon Ditch—*canal* IN-6
Halfmoon Flat—*island* MA-1
Halfmoon Gap—*gap* VA-3
Halfmoon Gulch—*valley* CO-8
**Half Moon Heights (subdivision)**—*pop pl* NC-3
Half Moon Hill—*summit* MT-8
Half Moon Hollow—*valley* UT-8
Half-Moon Inn—*hist pl* PA-2
Half Moon Island—*is* MA-1
Halfmoon Island—*island* FL-3
Halfmoon Island—*island* IL-6
Half Moon Island—*island* LA-4
Halfmoon Island—*island* ME-1
Half Moon Island—*island* MA-1
Half Moon Island—*island* MN-6
Halfmoon Island—*island* SC-3
Halfmoon Island—*island* VA-3
Half Moon Island Boat Dock—*locale* TN-4
Half Moon Island (historical)—*island* TN-4
*Half Moon Island Post Office* TN-4
Halfmoon Island Post Office (historical)—*building* TN-4
Halfmoon Islands—*island* IL-6
**Halfmoon Junction**—*pop pl* NY-2
Halfmoon Key—*island* FL-3
*Half Moon Lake* LA-4
*Halfmoon Lake* MI-6
*Half Moon Lake* MN-6
*Half Moon Lake* WI-6
Halfmoon Lake—*lake* AK-9
Half Moon Lake—*lake* (3) AR-4
Half Moon Lake—*lake* (2) CA-9
Halfmoon Lake—*lake* CA-9
Halfmoon Lake—*lake* CO-8
Half Moon Lake—*lake* CO-8
Halfmoon Lake—*lake* (3) FL-3
Half Moon Lake—*lake* (2) FL-3
Halfmoon Lake—*lake* FL-3
Half Moon Lake—*lake* (3) GA-3
Halfmoon Lake—*lake* (5) IL-6
Half Moon Lake—*lake* IN-6
Half Moon Lake—*lake* IA-7
Halfmoon Lake—*lake* KS-7
Half Moon Lake—*lake* LA-4
Halfmoon Lake—*lake* LA-4
Half Moon Lake—*lake* LA-4
Halfmoon Lake—*lake* LA-4
Half Moon Lake—*lake* (2) MI-6
Halfmoon Lake—*lake* (3) MI-6
Half Moon Lake—*lake* (3) MI-6
Halfmoon Lake—*lake* (3) MI-6
Half Moon Lake—*lake* MI-6
Halfmoon Lake—*lake* MN-6
Half Moon Lake—*lake* (2) MN-6
Halfmoon Lake—*lake* MN-6
Half Moon Lake—*lake* MN-6
Halfmoon Lake—*lake* (2) MT-8
Halfmoon Lake—*lake* NH-1
Halfmoon Lake—*lake* (2) NY-2
Halfmoon Lake—*lake* PA-2
Halfmoon Lake—*lake* TX-5
Halfmoon Lake—*lake* UT-8
Halfmoon Lake—*lake* VT-1
Halfmoon Lake—*lake* (2) WA-9
Half Moon Lake—*lake* WA-9
Half Moon Lake—*lake* WI-6
Halfmoon Lake—*lake* WI-6
Half Moon Lake—*lake* WI-6
Halfmoon Lake—*lake* WI-6
Half Moon Lake—*lake* (2) WI-6
Halfmoon Lake—*lake* WI-6
Halfmoon Lake—*lake* WY-8
Half Moon Lake—*lake* WY-8
Half Moon Lake—*reservoir* PA-2
Half Moon Lake—*swamp* MI-6
Half Moon Lake (Township of)—*fmr MCD* AR-4
Half Moon Landing—*locale* GA-3
Halfmoon Landing—*locale* GA-3
Halfmoon Lookout Trail—*trail* WV-2
Halfmoon Meadow—*flat* (2) CA-9
Halfmoon Meadow—*swamp* ME-1
Halfmoon Meadow Brook—*stream* MA-1
Half Moon Mine—*mine* NV-8
*Halfmoon Mountain* WY-8
*Half Moon Mountains* WY-8
*Half Moon Mtn* NH-1
Half Moon Mtn—*summit* AR-4
Halfmoon Mtn—*summit* NH-1
Halfmoon Mtn—*summit* WV-2
Half Moon Mtn—*summit* WY-8
Half Moon Oil Field—*oilfield* WY-8
Half Moon Oil Field—*other* IL-6
Halfmoon Park—*flat* MT-8
Halfmoon Park—*flat* NM-5
Half Moon Park—*flat* UT-8
Halfmoon Park—*park* FL-3
Halfmoon Park—*park* WI-6
Half Moon Pass—*gap* CO-8
Halfmoon Pass—*gap* CO-8
Half Moon Pass—*gap* ID-8
Half Moon Pass—*gap* MT-8
Halfmoon Pass—*lake* LA-4
Halfmoon Pass Bay—*lake* LA-4
Halfmoon Peak—*summit* MT-8
Half Moon Pocosin—*swamp* NC-3
Halfmoon Point—*cape* ID-8
Halfmoon Point—*cape* VA-3
*Halfmoon Pond* NH-1
Half Moon Pond—*lake* (3) FL-3
Half Moon Pond—*lake* (2) IL-6
Half Moon Pond—*lake* IN-6
Halfmoon Pond—*lake* IN-6
Halfmoon Pond—*lake* KY-4
Halfmoon Pond—*lake* (4) ME-1
Half Moon Pond—*lake* ME-1
Halfmoon Pond—*lake* ME-1
Halfmoon Pond—*lake* (4) NH-1
Half Moon Pond—*lake* NH-1
Halfmoon Pond—*lake* NY-2
Halfmoon Pond—*lake* VT-1
Halfmoon Pond Brook—*stream* NH-1
Half Moon Prairie—*area* TX-5
Half Moon Prairie—*flat* WA-9
Half Moon Ranch—*locale* CA-9
*Halfmoon Reef* TX-5
Halfmoon Reef—*bar* FL-3
Halfmoon Reef—*bar* TX-5
Half Moon Ridge—*ridge* AZ-5
Halfmoon River—*stream* GA-3
Halfmoon Run—*stream* (2) WV-2
*Half Moon Run Valley* PA-2
Half Moon Sand Hills—*summit* SC-3
Half Moon Sch—*school* MI-6
Halfmoon Sch—*school* MT-8
*Half Moon Shoal* TX-5
Halfmoon Shoal—*bar* FL-3
Halfmoon Shoal—*bar* MA-1
Halfmoon Shoal—*bar* TX-5
Half Moon Shoals—*bar* (2) TN-4
*Halfmoon Shores* TN-4
Half Moon Shores—*locale* TN-4
*Halfmoon Slough* AR-4
Half Moon Slough—*gut* AR-4
Half Moon Slough—*gut* IL-6
Halfmoon Slough—*gut* IL-6
Half Moon Slough—*gut* MT-8
Half Moon Spring—*spring* (2) AZ-5
Half Moon Spring—*spring* ID-8
Half Moon Spring—*spring* MT-8
Half Moon Spring—*spring* OR-9
Halfmoon Springs—*spring* IN-6
Halfmoon Stream—*stream* (2) ME-1
Halfmoon Swamp—*swamp* PA-2
Half Moon Swamp—*swamp* PA-2
Halfmoon Tank—*reservoir* (2) AZ-5
Half Moon Tank—*reservoir* AZ-5
**Halfmoon (Town of)**—*pop pl* NY-2
**Halfmoon (Township of)**—*pop pl* PA-2
Half Moon Trail—*trail* CO-8
Half Moon Trail—*trail* WY-8
Halfmoon Valley—*valley* AZ-5
Half Moon Valley—*valley* NM-5
Halfmoon Valley—*valley* PA-2
**Half Mound**—*pop pl* KS-7
Half Mtn—*summit* CO-8
Half Open Pond—*lake* FL-3
Halford—*locale* WA-9
**Halford**—*pop pl* KS-7
Halford Camp—*locale* MT-8
Halford Cem—*cemetery* IL-6
Halford Chapel—*church* IL-6
Halford Creek—*stream* MI-6
Halford Creek—*stream* MT-8
**Halford Hills**—*pop pl* PA-2
Halford Independent Ditch—*canal* (2) NM-5
Halford Lake—*lake* FL-3
Halford Spring—*spring* MO-7
Hal Foss Peak—*summit* WA-9
Half Ounce Creek—*stream* WY-8
Half Penny Barn Tunnel—*tunnel* PA-2
Halfpenny Bay—*bay* VI-3
Half-pint Creek—*stream* OR-9
Halfpint Range—*range* NV-8
Halfpint Rsvr—*reservoir* MT-8
Half Pint Tank—*reservoir* AZ-5
Half Pone Branch—*stream* TN-4
Half Pone Creek—*stream* TN-4
Half Pone Hollow—*valley* TN-4
*Half Pone Hollow Branch* TN-4
Half Pone Point—*cape* MD-2
Half Rock—*locale* MO-7
Halfrock Cave—*cave* AL-4
Half Rock Ridge—*ridge* ME-1
Half Round Bay—*bay* ID-8
Half Section Tank—*reservoir* AZ-5
Halfshot Cave—*cave* AL-4
Half Step Cave—*cave* AL-4
Half Tide Ledge—*bar* ME-1
Halftide Ledge—*bar* (4) ME-1
Halftide Ledges—*bar* ME-1
*Halftide Rock* MA-1
Halftide Rock—*bar* AK-9
Halftide Rock—*bar* (2) ME-1
Halftide Rock—*bar* NH-1
Halftide Rock—*island* CT-1
Halftide Rock—*rock* (3) MA-1
Half Tide Rock—*rock* MA-1
*Halftide Rocks* MA-1
Half Tide Rocks—*bar* MA-1
Halftide Rocks—*bar* (2) MA-1
Halftide Rocks—*bar* WA-9
Half Timber Butte—*summit* ND-7
Half Township Cem—*cemetery* ME-1
**Half Tree MHP (subdivision)**—*pop pl* NC-3
Halfturn Creek—*stream* WY-8
**Halfville**—*pop pl* PA-2
Halfway—*locale* AR-4
Halfway—*locale* IL-6
Halfway—*locale* (2) KY-4
Halfway—*locale* LA-4
Halfway—*locale* NM-5
Halfway—*locale* TN-4
Halfway—*locale* VA-3
Half Way—*locale* WV-2
Halfway—*locale* WY-8
Halfway—*other* MI-6
**Half Way**—*pop pl* LA-4
**Halfway**—*pop pl* ME-1
**Halfway**—*pop pl* MD-2
**Half Way**—*pop pl* MO-7
**Halfway**—*pop pl* NY-2
**Halfway**—*pop pl* OR-9
**Halfway**—*pop pl* PA-2
**Halfway**—*pop pl* TX-5
Halfway Bayou—*stream* (3) LA-4
Halfway Bayou—*swamp* AR-4
Halfway Bench—*bench* UT-8
Halfway Bend—*bend* AZ-5
Halfway Bend—*bend* SC-3
Halfway Branch—*stream* AL-4
Half Way Branch—*stream* GA-3
Halfway Branch—*stream* (5) KY-4
Halfway Branch—*stream* (2) SC-3
Halfway Branch—*stream* TN-4
Halfway Branch—*stream* VA-3
Halfway Branch Sch—*school* NC-3
Halfway Bridge—*bridge* HI-9
Halfway Brook—*stream* CT-1
Halfway Brook—*stream* (10) ME-1
Halfway Brook—*stream* MA-1
Halfway Brook—*stream* (3) NH-1
Halfway Brook—*stream* (5) NY-2
Halfway Brook—*stream* VT-1
*Halfway Buttes* OR-9
Halfway Camp—*locale* CA-9
Halfway Camp—*locale* NV-8
Halfway Canyon—*valley* CA-9
Halfway Canyon—*valley* CO-8
Halfway Canyon—*valley* MT-8
Halfway Canyon—*valley* (2) UT-8
Halfway Canyon—*valley* WY-8
Halfway (CCD)—*cens area* KY-4
Halfway (CCD)—*cens area* OR-9
Halfway Cem—*cemetery* LA-4
Halfway Cem—*cemetery* TX-5
Half Way Ch—*church* MO-7
Halfway Corners—*locale* MI-6
**Halfway (corporate name for Half Way)**—*pop pl* MO-7
*Half Way (corporate name Halfway)* MO-7
Halfway Corral—*locale* AZ-5
Halfway Coulee—*valley* (2) MT-8
Halfway Cove—*bay* CA-9
*Halfway Creek* DE-2
*Halfway Creek* MS-4
Halfway Creek—*stream* AK-9
Halfway Creek—*stream* AR-4
Half Way Creek—*stream* CO-8
Halfway Creek—*stream* (2) FL-3
Halfway Creek—*stream* GA-3
Halfway Creek—*stream* (4) ID-8
Halfway Creek—*stream* IN-6
Halfway Creek—*stream* IA-7
Halfway Creek—*stream* LA-4
Halfway Creek—*stream* (4) MI-6
Halfway Creek—*stream* MS-4
Halfway Creek—*stream* (4) MT-8
Halfway Creek—*stream* NJ-2
Halfway Creek—*stream* NY-2
Halfway Creek—*stream* OH-6
Halfway Creek—*stream* (2) OR-9
Halfway Creek—*stream* (2) SC-3
Half Way Creek—*stream* SC-3
Halfway Creek—*stream* TX-5
Halfway Creek—*stream* UT-8
Halfway Creek—*stream* (3) VA-3
Halfway Creek—*stream* WA-9
Halfway Creek—*stream* WI-6
Halfway Creek Access Area—*park* MS-4
Halfway Creek Cem—*cemetery* WI-6
Halfway Creek Sch—*school* SC-3
Halfway Creek Site—*hist pl* FL-3
Halfway Dam—*dam* PA-2
Halfway Detention Dam—*dam* AZ-5
Halfway Diner—*hist pl* NY-2
Halfway Draw—*valley* WY-8
Halfway Flat Campground—*locale* WA-9
Half Way Ground—*flat* TN-4
Halfway Gulch—*valley* CA-9
Half Way Gulch—*valley* CA-9
Halfway Gulch—*valley* CO-8
Halfway Gulch—*valley* (3) ID-8
Halfway Gut Creek—*stream* SC-3
Halfway Hill—*summit* CA-9
Halfway Hill—*summit* ID-8
Halfway Hill—*summit* OR-9
Halfway Hill—*summit* UT-8
Halfway Hill—*summit* WY-8
Halfway Hills—*summit* UT-8
Halfway Hill Wildlife Mngmt Area—*park* UT-8
Half Way (historical)—*locale* KS-7
Halfway Hollow—*valley* (4) UT-8
Halfway Hollow—*valley* WV-2
Halfway Hollow—*valley* WY-8
*Half Way House* PA-2
*Halfway House* UT-8
Halfway House—*CDP* PA-2
Half-Way House—*hist pl* MD-2
Half Way House—*hist pl* MA-1
Halfway House—*hist pl* WV-2
Halfway House—*hist pl* WI-6
Halfway House—*locale* AZ-5
Halfway House—*locale* (2) CO-8
Halfway House—*locale* HI-9
Halfway House—*locale* (2) ID-8
Halfway House—*locale* OR-9
Halfway House—*locale* VT-1
**Halfway House**—*pop pl* CA-9
**Halfway House**—*pop pl* MA-1
**Half Way House**—*pop pl* PA-2
Halfway House Archeol Site—*hist pl* NM-5
Halfway House Campground—*locale* ID-8
Halfway House Corners—*locale* NY-2
Halfway House Coulee—*valley* MT-8
Halfway House Gulch—*valley* CA-9
Halfway House (historical)—*locale* NV-8
Halfway House Historical Site—*locale* MT-8
Halfway House Ranch—*locale* NM-5
Halfway House Tank—*reservoir* AZ-5
Halfway Inn—*locale* CA-9
Halfway Island—*island* (2) AK-9
Halfway Island—*island* (4) NY-2
*Halfway Lake* WI-6
Halfway Lake—*lake* (2) AK-9
Halfway Lake—*lake* (3) FL-3
Halfway Lake—*lake* ID-8
Halfway Lake—*lake* LA-4
Halfway Lake—*lake* (2) MI-6
Halfway Lake—*lake* MT-8
Halfway Lake—*lake* OR-9
Halfway Lake—*lake* PA-2
Halfway Lake—*lake* WA-9
Halfway Lake Dam—*hist pl* PA-2
Half-Way Lake Natl Wildlife Ref—*park* ND-7
Halfway Ledge—*bench* RI-1
Halfway Mtn—*summit* (2) AK-9
Halfway Mtn—*summit* ME-1
Halfway Mtn—*summit* NY-2
*Half Way Park* PA-2
Halfway Park—*flat* MT-8
Halfway Park—*park* TX-5
Halfway Peak—*summit* ID-8
Halfway Picnic Area—*park* AZ-5
Half-Way Pillar—*pillar* AK-9
*Half Way Point* AL-4
*Halfway Point* AK-9
Halfway Point—*cape* AK-9
Halfway Point—*cape* (2) FL-3
Halfway Point—*cape* ME-1
Halfway Point—*cape* NY-2
Halfway Point—*cape* (2) NC-3
Halfway Point—*cape* OR-9
*Halfway Pond* MA-1
Halfway Pond—*lake* (3) FL-3
Halfway Pond—*lake* (3) MA-1
Halfway Pond—*lake* VT-1
**Halfway Pond**—*pop pl* MA-1
Halfway Pond—*reservoir* OK-5
Halfway Pond—*swamp* TX-5
*Halfway Pond Brook* MA-1
Halfway Post Office (historical)—*building* TN-4
Halfway Prairie Creek—*stream* WI-6
Halfway Prairie Sch—*school* IA-7
Halfway Ranch—*locale* AZ-5
Halfway Ranger Station—*locale* OR-9
Halfway Retaining Pit—*reservoir* MT-8
Halfway Ridge—*ridge* CA-9
*Halfway River* MI-6
Halfway River—*stream* CT-1
Halfway Rock—*bar* (2) ME-1
Halfway Rock—*island* AK-9
Halfway Rock—*island* CA-9
Halfway Rock—*island* ME-1
Halfway Rock—*pillar* (2) RI-1
Halfway Rock—*rock* MA-1
Halfway Rock—*summit* WA-9
Halfway Rock Light Station—*hist pl* ME-1
Halfway Rocks—*bar* NH-1
Halfway Rsvr—*reservoir* (2) MT-8
Halfway Rsvr—*reservoir* (3) OR-9
Halfway Run—*stream* PA-2
Halfway Run—*stream* (2) WV-2
Halfway Sch—*school* KY-4
Halfway Sch—*school* NY-2
Halfway Sch—*school* WI-6
Halfway Sch (historical)—*school* MO-7
Halfway Slough—*stream* LA-4
Halfway Spring—*spring* CA-9
Halfway Spring—*spring* ID-8
Halfway Spring—*spring* NV-8
Halfway Spring—*spring* (4) OR-9
Halfway Spring—*spring* UT-8
Halfway Spring—*spring* WA-9
Halfway Spring Campground—*locale* CA-9
Halfway Station—*locale* CO-8
Halfway Station—*locale* ID-8
Halfway Summit—*summit* UT-8
Halfway Swamp—*stream* (2) SC-3
Halfway Swamp Creek—*stream* (2) SC-3
Halfway Tank—*basin* AZ-5
Halfway Tank—*reservoir* (5) AZ-5
**Halfway Town (historical)**—*pop pl* TN-4
Halfway Truck Trail—*trail* CA-9
Halfway Wash—*stream* NV-8
Halfway Wash—*valley* (2) UT-8
Halfway Well—*well* AZ-5
Halfway Well—*well* NM-5
Halfway Whirlpool—*other* AK-9
Halfway Windmill—*locale* NM-5
Halfway Windmill—*locale* (2) TX-5
Half White Mtn—*summit* AZ-5
Half Windmill—*locale* TX-5
Halgaitoh Spring—*spring* UT-8
Halgaitoh Wash—*valley* UT-8
Halgan, Cape—*cape* FM-9
*Halgers Creek* GA-3
*Halgtr Branch* TX-5
Hal Henard Elem Sch—*school* TN-4
Hal Henderson Elem Sch—*school* AL-4
Haliburton Ch—*church* MS-4
Halibut Bay—*bay* (2) AK-9
Halibut Cove—*bay* (2) AK-9
Halibut Cove—*CDP* AK-9
Halibut Cove Lagoon—*bay* AK-9
Halibut Creek—*stream* (3) AK-9
Halibut Harbor—*bay* AK-9
Halibut Hole—*channel* ME-1
Halibut Island—*island* AK-9
Halibut Mtn—*summit* VT-1
Halibut Nose—*cape* AK-9
Halibut Point—*cape* (2) AK-9
Halibut Point—*cape* MA-1
Halibut Point Recreation Center—*locale* AK-9
Halibut Point Reservation—*park* MA-1
Halibut Rock—*bar* ME-1
Halibut Rock—*other* AK-9
Halibut Rocks—*bar* (2) ME-1
Halice, Lake—*lake* IA-7
*Haliday* MD-2
Halie Turner Sch—*school* AL-4
*Halifax* KS-7
*Halifax* MA-1
Halifax—*locale* KY-4
Halifax—*mine* NV-8
**Halifax**—*pop pl* GA-3
**Halifax**—*pop pl* MA-1
**Halifax**—*pop pl* MO-7
**Halifax**—*pop pl* NC-3
**Halifax**—*pop pl* PA-2
**Halifax**—*pop pl* VA-3
Halifax Acad—*school* NC-3
Halifax Banks Island—*island* FL-3
**Halifax Beach**—*pop pl* MA-1
Halifax Borough—*civil* PA-2
Halifax Canal—*canal* FL-3
Halifax Center—*other* VT-1
Halifax Community Hosp—*hospital* VA-3
**Halifax County**—*pop pl* NC-3
**Halifax (County)**—*pop pl* VA-3
Halifax County Acad—*school* VA-3
Halifax County Airp—*airport* NC-3
Halifax County Courthouse—*hist pl* NC-3
Halifax County Courthouse—*hist pl* VA-3
Halifax County Home and Tubercular Hosp—*hist pl* NC-3
Halifax Creek—*stream* ID-8
Halifax Creek—*stream* OR-9
Halifax Creek—*stream* TX-5
**Halifax Crossing**—*pop pl* NC-3
**Halifax Estates**—*pop pl* FL-3
**Halifax (Halifax Beach)**—*pop pl* MA-1
**Halifax (Halifax Center)**—*pop pl* VT-1
Halifax Hist Dist—*hist pl* NC-3
Halifax (historical)—*locale* MS-4
Halifax (historical P.O.)—*locale* MA-1
Halifax Hollow—*valley* TN-4
Halifax Hollow—*valley* VT-1
Halifax Hosp—*hospital* FL-3
Halifax Hosp Med Ctr—*hospital* FL-3
Halifax Island—*island* ME-1
Halifax Memorial Gardens—*cemetery* VA-3
Halifax Mtn—*summit* KY-4
Halifax Ranch—*locale* TX-5
Halifax River—*stream* FL-3
Halifax Shop Ctr—*locale* FL-3
**Halifax (Town of)**—*pop pl* MA-1
**Halifax (Town of)**—*pop pl* VT-1
Halifax (Township of)—*fmr MCD* NC-3
**Halifax (Township of)**—*pop pl* PA-2
Halifax Trail—*trail* OR-9
Halifax Zion Ch—*church* OH-6
Haligan Branch—*stream* AR-4
**Halihan Hill**—*pop pl* NY-2
Halihan Hill—*summit* NY-2
Halii—*area* HI-9
Halii Falls—*falls* HI-9
Haliimaile—*civil* HI-9
**Haliimaile**—*pop pl* HI-9
*Haliimaile Camp* HI-9
Halii Paakai—*cape* HI-9
Haliipalala—*area* HI-9
Halii Stream—*stream* HI-9
Halimecek Cem—*cemetery* TX-5
Hali Murk—*locale* AZ-5
Hali Murk Wash—*stream* AZ-5
Halissee Hall—*hist pl* FL-3
Halivah—*locale* UT-8
Haliwa Indian Sch—*school* NC-3
Halk Cem—*cemetery* AR-4
Halk Creek—*stream* AR-4
*Halketstown* NJ-2
Halkey Ditch—*canal* IN-6
Hal Kirby Junior Park—*park* AL-4
*Hall* KS-7
Hall—*fmr MCD* (2) NE-7
Hall—*locale* CO-8
Hall—*locale* KY-4
Hall—*locale* NC-3
Hall—*locale* PA-2
Hall—*locale* (2) TX-5
Hall—*locale* (2) WV-2
**Hall**—*pop pl* CA-9
**Hall**—*pop pl* IN-6
**Hall**—*pop pl* KY-4
**Hall**—*pop pl* MD-2
**Hall**—*pop pl* MS-4
**Hall**—*pop pl* MT-8
**Hall**—*pop pl* NY-2
Hall—*uninc pl* CA-9
Hall—*uninc pl* NY-2
Hall, Ainsley, House—*hist pl* SC-3
Hall, Chauncey, Bldg—*hist pl* WI-6
Hall, Chauncey, House—*hist pl* WI-6
Hall, Col. David, House—*hist pl* DE-2
Hall, Dr. Leonard, House—*hist pl* MI-6
Hall, Dr. Orrin I., House—*hist pl* MN-6
Hall, Edward, House—*hist pl* MA-1
Hall, Frank A., House—*hist pl* NY-2
Hall, Gen. Robinson, House—*hist pl* VT-1
Hall, Gov. Luther, House—*hist pl* LA-4
Hall, Howard A., House—*hist pl* OR-9
Hall, Isaac, House—*hist pl* MA-1
Hall, Israel, House—*hist pl* IA-7
Hall, James, Office—*hist pl* NY-2
Hall, James Norman, House—*hist pl* IA-7
Hall, Joseph E., House—*hist pl* MI-6
Hall, Joseph E., House—*hist pl* PA-2
Hall, Lake—*lake* (2) FL-3
Hall, Lake—*reservoir* TX-5
Hall, Lewis, Mansion—*hist pl* WV-2
Hall, Nels G., House—*hist pl* UT-8
Hall, R. A., House—*hist pl* TX-5
Hall, Ralph, Farm District—*hist pl* ND-7
Hall, Robert, House—*hist pl* TX-5
Hall, S.A., House—*hist pl* MA-1
Hall, Stephen, House—*hist pl* MA-1
Hall, William P., House—*hist pl* MO-7
**Hall Acres (subdivision)**—*pop pl* UT-8
Hallada Lake—*lake* (2) WI-6
Halladay Brook—*stream* VT-1
Halladay Creek—*stream* WI-6
Halladay Farmhouse—*hist pl* NY-2
Halladay Gulch—*valley* OR-9
Halladay Spring—*spring* OR-9
**Hall Addition**—*pop pl* OK-5
**Hall Addition**—*pop pl* VA-3
Hall Airfield—*airport* KS-7
Hall Air Natl Guard Station—*building* AL-4
Hall Airp—*airport* IN-6
Hall Airp—*airport* MO-7
Hall Airp—*airport* NC-3
*Hallalla* AL-4
Hallam—*locale* KY-4
**Hallam**—*pop pl* NE-7
Hallam Borough—*civil* PA-2
Hallam Branch—*stream* NC-3
Hallam Cem—*cemetery* NE-7
**Hallam (corporate name for Hellam)**—*pop pl* PA-2
Hallam Creek—*stream* WA-9
**Hallam (Hellam Post Office)**—*pop pl* PA-2
Hallam Sch Two (abandoned)—*school* PA-2
Hallam Station—*building* PA-2
Hallanan Oil Field—*oilfield* TX-5
**Hallandale**—*pop pl* FL-3
Hallandale Adult and Community Center—*school* FL-3
Hallandale Adult Community Center—*locale* FL-3
Hallandale (CCD)—*cens area* FL-3
Hallandale City Park—*park* FL-3
Hallandale Elem Sch—*school* FL-3
Hallandale HS—*school* FL-3
Hallandale Sch—*school* FL-3
Hallandale Shop Ctr—*locale* FL-3
Hall and Primm Ranch—*locale* NM-5
Hall and Rivers Cem—*cemetery* AL-4
Hallanger Coulee—*valley* MT-8
Hallar Rsvr—*reservoir* CO-8
Hallars Cem—*cemetery* KY-4
Hallaway Hill—*summit* KY-4
Hallaway Hollow—*valley* MO-7
Hallaway State Park—*park* MD-2
Hall Barret Lake Dam—*dam* MS-4
Hall Basin—*basin* WY-8
Hall Bay—*bay* FL-3
Hall Bay—*bay* ME-1
Hall Bay—*bay* MI-6
Hall Bay—*bay* VT-1
Hall Beckley Canyon—*valley* CA-9
Hall Bend—*bend* TN-4
Hall-Benedict Drug Company Bldg—*hist pl* CT-1
Hallberg Hill—*summit* WI-6
Hall Bottom—*basin* VA-3
*Hall Branch* AL-4
Hall Branch—*stream* (4) AL-4
Hall Branch—*stream* (3) AR-4
Hall Branch—*stream* (2) FL-3
Hall Branch—*stream* (3) GA-3
Hall Branch—*stream* IN-6
Hall Branch—*stream* (9) KY-4
Hall Branch—*stream* LA-4
Hall Branch—*stream* (2) MD-2
Hall Branch—*stream* (3) MS-4
Hall Branch—*stream* (3) MO-7
Hall Branch—*stream* (5) NC-3
Hall Branch—*stream* (2) SC-3
Hall Branch—*stream* (9) TN-4
Hall Branch—*stream* (6) TX-5
Hall Branch—*stream* (3) VA-3
*Hall Branch Hollow* TN-4
Hall Bridge—*bridge* FL-3
Hall Bridge—*bridge* GA-3
*Hall Brook* CT-1
*Hall Brook* MA-1
*Hall Brook* NH-1
**Hallbrook**—*pop pl* TN-4
Hall Brook—*stream* CT-1
Hall Brook—*stream* (4) ME-1
Hall Brook—*stream* NH-1
Hall Brook—*stream* NY-2
Hall Brook—*stream* (4) VT-1
*Hallbrook Gut* MD-2
Hallbrook Lake Dam—*dam* MS-4
*Hallbrooks Gut* MD-2
Hallbrooks Gut—*gut* MD-2
Hallburg—*locale* WV-2

Hall Burlew Ditch—*canal* ... IN-6
Hallburn Ridge—*ridge* ... AZ-5
Hall Butte—*summit* ... AZ-5
Hall Butte—*summit* ... CA-9
Hall Butte—*summit* ... WY-8
Hall Cabin—*hist pl* ... NC-3
Hall Cabin—*locale* (2) ... CA-9
Hall Cabin—*locale* ... OR-9
*Hall Camp Gap* ... TN-4
*Hall Canyon* ... AZ-5
Hall Canyon—*valley* (5) ... CA-9
Hall Canyon—*valley* ... CO-8
Hall Canyon—*valley* (2) ... UT-8
Hall Cave—*cave* ... AL-4
Hall Cave—*cave* ... TN-4
Hall Cem—*cemetery* (8) ... AL-4
Hall Cem—*cemetery* (4) ... AR-4
Hall Cem—*cemetery* ... CT-1
Hall Cem—*cemetery* (8) ... GA-3
Hall Cem—*cemetery* (9) ... IL-6
Hall Cem—*cemetery* (4) ... IN-6
Hall Cem—*cemetery* (2) ... KS-7
Hall Cem—*cemetery* (14) ... KY-4
Hall Cem—*cemetery* ... LA-4
Hall Cem—*cemetery* (2) ... ME-1
Hall Cem—*cemetery* ... MA-1
Hall Cem—*cemetery* (4) ... MS-4
Hall Cem—*cemetery* (7) ... MO-7
Hall Cem—*cemetery* ... NH-1
Hall Cem—*cemetery* ... NY-2
Hall Cem—*cemetery* (8) ... NC-3
Hall Cem—*cemetery* (6) ... OH-6
Hall Cem—*cemetery* ... OK-5
Hall Cem—*cemetery* ... SC-3
Hall Cem—*cemetery* (26) ... TN-4
Hall Cem—*cemetery* (11) ... TX-5
Hall Cem—*cemetery* ... VT-1
Hall Cem—*cemetery* (6) ... VA-3
Hall Cem—*cemetery* (10) ... WV-2
Hall Cem—*cemetery* ... WI-6
Hall Center Cem—*cemetery* ... NY-2
Hall Ch—*church* ... KS-7
Hall Ch—*church* ... MO-7
Hall Ch—*church* ... PA-2
Hall Ch—*church* ... TN-4
Hall-Chaney House—*hist pl* ... OR-9
Hall Chapel—*church* ... AR-4
Hall Chapel—*church* (2) ... GA-3
Hall Chapel—*church* (2) ... KY-4
Hall Chapel—*church* ... NC-3
Hall Chapel—*church* ... TN-4
*Hall Chapel Congregational Holiness Church* ... AL-4
Hall Chapel Sch (historical)—*school* ... AL-4
Hall Ch (historical)—*church* ... TX-5
*Hall Ch of Christ* ... TN-4
Hall Cienega—*flat* ... AZ-5
Hall City—*locale* ... FL-3
Hall City Cave—*cave* ... CA-9
*Hall City Caves* ... CA-9
Hall City Creek—*stream* ... CA-9
Hall Community Well—*well* ... MT-8
Hall Corner—*locale* ... ME-1
Hall Corners—*locale* (2) ... NY-2
Hall Coulee—*valley* (2) ... MT-8
**Hall (County)**—*pop pl* ... GA-3
**Hall (County)**—*pop pl* ... TX-5
Hall County Courthouse—*hist pl* ... NE-7
Hall County Jail—*hist pl* ... GA-3
Hall County Memorial Park
(cemetery)—*cemetery* ... GA-3
Hall County Regional Airp—*airport* ... NE-7
Hall Cove—*bay* ... AK-9
Hall Cove—*bay* (2) ... ME-1
Hall Cove—*valley* ... TN-4
Hall Covered Bridge—*hist pl* ... VT-1
*Hallcraft Town Houses* ... CO-8
*Hall Creek* ... CA-9
*Hall Creek* ... GA-3
*Hall Creek* ... IN-6
*Hall Creek* ... OR-9
*Hall Creek* ... TN-4
*Hall Creek* ... WI-6
Hall Creek—*locale* ... AL-4
Hall Creek—*locale* ... IA-7
Hall Creek—*stream* (3) ... AL-4
Hall Creek—*stream* ... AK-9
Hall Creek—*stream* ... AZ-5
Hall Creek—*stream* (6) ... AR-4
Hall Creek—*stream* (4) ... CA-9
Hall Creek—*stream* ... CO-8
Hall Creek—*stream* (2) ... FL-3
Hall Creek—*stream* ... GA-3
Hall Creek—*stream* (4) ... ID-8
Hall Creek—*stream* ... IN-6
Hall Creek—*stream* ... IA-7
Hall Creek—*stream* (3) ... MD-2
Hall Creek—*stream* ... MI-6
Hall Creek—*stream* (2) ... MS-4
Hall Creek—*stream* (5) ... MT-8
Hall Creek—*stream* (2) ... NV-8
Hall Creek—*stream* ... NJ-2
Hall Creek—*stream* (4) ... NY-2
Hall Creek—*stream* (2) ... NC-3
Hall Creek—*stream* (8) ... OR-9
Hall Creek—*stream* ... RI-1
Hall Creek—*stream* (4) ... TN-4
Hall Creek—*stream* (2) ... TX-5
Hall Creek—*stream* ... UT-8
Hall Creek—*stream* ... VA-3
Hall Creek—*stream* (8) ... WA-9
Hall Creek—*stream* ... WI-6
Hall Creek—*stream* (2) ... WY-8
Hall Creek Ch—*church* ... AL-4
Hall Creek Flat—*flat* ... WA-9
Hall Creek Lake—*reservoir* ... GA-3
Hall Creek Ranch—*locale* ... NV-8
Hall Creek Sch (historical)—*school* ... AL-4
Hall Creek Spring—*spring* ... MT-8
Hall Creek Tabernacle—*church* ... NC-3
Hall-Cromer Cem—*cemetery* ... SC-3
*Hall Crossroad* ... TN-4
Hall-Crull Octagonal House—*hist pl* ... IN-6
Halldale—*locale* ... ME-1
Halldale Ave Sch—*school* ... CA-9
Hall Dam—*dam* (2) ... AL-4
Hall Deadening Hollow—*valley* ... TN-4
Hall Ditch—*canal* ... IL-6
Hall Ditch—*canal* (2) ... IN-6
Hall Ditch—*canal* ... NV-8
Hall Divide—*gap* ... UT-8

Hall Drain—*canal* (2) ... MI-6
Hall Drain—*stream* ... MI-6
Hall Draw—*valley* ... CO-8
Hall Draw—*valley* ... NM-5
Hall Draw—*valley* ... SD-7
Hall Draw Rsvr—*reservoir* ... CO-8
Halle Bldg—*hist pl* ... OH-6
**Halleck**—*pop pl* ... NV-8
**Halleck**—*pop pl* ... WV-2
Halleck Canyon—*valley* ... WY-8
Halleck Ch—*church* ... MO-7
Halleck Creek—*stream* ... CA-9
Halleck Creek—*stream* (2) ... WY-8
Halleck Harbor—*bay* ... AK-9
Halleck Hill—*summit* ... CA-9
Halleck Interchange—*crossing* ... NV-8
Halleck Island—*island* ... AK-9
Halleck Point—*cape* ... AK-9
Halleck Range—*summit* ... AK-9
Halleck Ridge—*ridge* ... WY-8
*Hallegate* ... NY-2
*Hall Elementary School* ... MS-4
Hall Elem Sch—*school* ... IN-6
Hallelujah Junction—*locale* ... CA-9
Hallelujah Keys—*island* ... FL-3
Hallenback Cem—*cemetery* ... IL-6
Hallenback Creek—*stream* ... IL-6
*Hallenback River* ... CT-1
Hallenbeck Cow Camp—*locale* ... CO-8
Hallenbeck Creek—*stream* ... NY-2
Hallenbeck Hill—*summit* (2) ... NY-2
*Hallenbeck River* ... CT-1
Hallenbeck Rsvr—*reservoir* ... CO-8
Hallenbeck Sch—*school* ... MI-6
Hallen Sch—*school* ... CT-1
Haller Cem—*cemetery* ... AR-4
*Haller Creek* ... WA-9
Haller Creek—*stream* ... WA-9
Haller Creek—*stream* ... WI-6
Haller-Gibboney Rock House—*hist pl* ... VA-3
Haller Lake—*lake* ... WA-9
**Haller Lake**—*pop pl* ... WA-9
Haller Lake—*reservoir* ... AR-4
Haller Lake Sch—*school* ... WA-9
Haller Pass—*gap* ... WA-9
**Hallers Corners**—*pop pl* ... MI-6
**Hallersville**—*pop pl* ... AK-9
Hallersville Creek—*stream* ... AK-9
Halle Sch—*school* ... OH-6
**Hall Estates**—*pop pl* ... DE-2
*Hallet* ... KS-7
*Hallet* ... NY-2
*Hallet Glacier* ... CO-8
Hallet Ranch—*locale* ... UT-8
Hallet River—*stream* ... AK-9
Hallets Cove—*bay* ... NY-2
Hallets Millpond—*lake* ... MA-1
Hallets Point—*cape* ... NY-2
Hallet Spring—*spring* ... OR-9
Hallets Rock—*bar* ... MA-1
*Halletsville* ... TX-5
*Hallett* ... KS-7
Hallett—*locale* ... OH-6
**Hallett**—*pop pl* ... OK-5
Hallett, Capt. William, House—*hist pl* ... MA-1
Hallett, Samuel I., House—*hist pl* ... CO-8
Hallett, Seth, House—*hist pl* ... MA-1
Hallett Cem—*cemetery* ... AR-4
Hallett Cem—*cemetery* ... NY-2
Hallett Creek—*stream* ... CO-8
**Hallett Heights**—*pop pl* ... MD-2
Hallett House—*hist pl* ... WA-9
Hallett Interchange—*other* ... OK-5
Hallett Meadow—*flat* ... CA-9
**Hallet Township**—*pop pl* ... KS-7
Hallett Peak—*summit* ... CO-8
**Halletts**—*pop pl* ... OR-9
Hallett Sch—*school* ... CO-8
Hallett Siding—*locale* ... OK-5
*Halletts Mill Pond* ... MA-1
**Hallettsville**—*pop pl* ... TX-5
Hallettsville (CCD)—*cens area* ... TX-5
Hallettsville Oil Field—*oilfield* ... TX-5
*Halley* ... MO-7
**Halley**—*pop pl* ... AR-4
Halley, Capt. Robert, House—*hist pl* ... TX-5
Halley Bayou—*stream* ... LA-4
Halley Bluffs—*cliff* ... MO-7
Halley Brake (historical)—*swamp* ... LA-4
Halley Branch—*stream* ... LA-4
Halley Cem—*cemetery* ... MO-7
Halley Creek—*stream* ... TN-4
Halley Creek—*stream* ... WI-6
**Halley Estates**—*pop pl* ... MD-2
Halley Gas Plant—*oilfield* ... TX-5
Halley Grade—*trail* ... CA-9
**Halley Junction**—*pop pl* ... AR-4
Halley-Liles Cem—*cemetery* ... MO-7
Halley Oil Field—*oilfield* ... TX-5
Halley Park—*park* ... SD-7
Halley Place—*hist pl* ... KY-4
Halley Placer Mine—*mine* ... ID-8
Halleys Bluff Site—*hist pl* ... MO-7
Halley Sch—*school* ... NH-1
Halley Sch (abandoned)—*school* ... MO-7
*Halleys Creek* ... TX-5
Halley Spring—*spring* ... CA-9
Halleys Ridge Ch—*church* ... OH-6
Halleytown—*locale* ... SC-3
Halley (Township of)—*fmr MCD* ... AR-4
Hall Family House—*hist pl* ... NC-3
Hall Farms Airp—*airport* ... KS-7
Hall Ferry (historical)—*locale* ... TN-4
**Hall Ferry Junction**—*pop pl* ... NC-3
Hall Field Draw—*valley* ... WY-8
Hallfield Pond—*lake* ... MA-1
Hall Fletcher Sch—*school* ... NC-3
Hall Ford—*locale* ... TN-4
Hall Ford—*locale* ... VA-3
Hall Ford (historical)—*locale* ... TN-4
Hall Forest Camp—*locale* ... AZ-5
Hall Fork—*stream* ... KY-4
Hall Fork—*stream* ... OH-6
Hall Fork—*stream* ... WV-2
Hall-Fowler Memorial Library—*hist pl* ... MI-6
Hall Gap—*gap* ... GA-3
Hall Gap—*gap* ... TN-4
Hall Gap—*gap* ... VA-3
Hall Gate—*other* ... CA-9
Hall-Gott Cem—*cemetery* ... WV-2

**Hall Grove**—*pop pl* ... AL-4
Hall Grove Ch—*church* ... GA-3
Hall Grove Ch—*church* ... LA-4
Hall Grove Sch—*school* ... LA-4
*Hall Gulch* ... CO-8
Hall Gulch—*valley* (2) ... CA-9
Hall Gulch—*valley* (2) ... CO-8
Hall Gulch—*valley* (2) ... ID-8
Hall Gulch—*valley* ... MT-8
Hall Gulch—*valley* ... WY-8
Hall-Gurney Oil and Gas Field—*oilfield* ... KS-7
Hall Gurney Oil Field—*oilfield* ... KS-7
Hall-Halsell Sch—*school* ... OK-5
Hall-Henderson House—*hist pl* ... MS-4
*Hall Hill* ... NY-2
Hall Hill—*summit* ... CT-1
Hall Hill—*summit* ... KY-4
Hall Hill—*summit* (3) ... ME-1
Hall Hill—*summit* ... NY-2
Hall Hill—*summit* ... ND-7
Hall Hill—*summit* ... OR-9
Hall Hill—*summit* ... VT-1
Hall Hill Brook—*stream* ... CT-1
Hall Hill Ch—*church* ... MS-4
Hall Hill Ch—*church* ... OK-5
Hall Hill Ch—*church* ... SC-3
Hall Hill Gap—*gap* ... KY-4
Hall Hollow—*valley* ... AL-4
Hall Hollow—*valley* ... GA-3
Hall Hollow—*valley* (3) ... KY-4
Hall Hollow—*valley* (5) ... MO-7
Hall Hollow—*valley* (2) ... OH-6
Hall Hollow—*valley* ... PA-2
Hall Hollow—*valley* (5) ... TN-4
Hall Hollow—*valley* ... TX-5
Hall Hollow—*valley* (2) ... VA-3
Hall Hotel—*hist pl* ... NM-5
Hall House—*hist pl* ... AR-4
Hall House—*hist pl* ... KY-4
Hall HS—*school* ... AR-4
Hall HS—*school* ... CT-1
Hall HS—*school* ... KY-4
**Halliahurst Park**—*pop pl* ... VA-3
Halliburton Branch—*stream* ... AR-4
Halliburton Cave—*cave* ... TN-4
Halliburton Cem—*cemetery* ... MS-4
Halliburton Ch—*church* ... MS-4
Halliburton House—*hist pl* ... AR-4
Halliburton Sch (historical)—*school* ... MS-4
Halliburton Town Houses—*hist pl* ... AR-4
Hallicom Cove—*bay* ... ME-1
**Halliday**—*pop pl* ... AR-4
**Halliday**—*pop pl* ... ND-7
**Hallidayboro**—*pop pl* ... IL-6
Halliday Creek—*stream* ... AL-4
Halliday Drain—*canal* ... OR-9
Halliday Flowing Well—*well* ... ND-7
Halliday Island—*island* ... NY-2
Hallidays Pond—*reservoir* ... GA-3
Hallidie Bldg—*hist pl* ... CA-9
Hallie—*locale* ... KY-4
**Hallie**—*pop pl* ... WI-6
Hallie, Lake—*reservoir* ... WI-6
Hallie Ditch—*canal* ... WY-8
Hallieford—*locale* ... VA-3
Hallie State Public Hunting
Grounds—*park* ... WI-6
**Hallie (Town of)**—*pop pl* ... WI-6
Hallie Turner Private Sch—*school* ... AL-4
Halligan Mesa—*summit* ... NV-8
Halligan Rsvr—*reservoir* ... CO-8
Hallihan Ditch—*canal* ... IN-6
Hallinan Dam—*dam* ... OR-9
Halling Cem—*cemetery* ... ND-7
Halling Creek—*stream* ... KS-7
Hallings Spring—*spring* ... UT-8
Hallin Lake—*lake* ... WA-9
Halliock Inn—*hist pl* ... NY-2
*Hallis Cemetery* ... AL-4
*Hall Island* ... AL-4
*Hall Island* ... ME-1
Hall Island—*island* (2) ... AK-9
Hall Island—*island* ... CA-9
Hall Island—*island* ... CT-1
Hall Island—*island* ... FL-3
Hall Island—*island* (3) ... ME-1
Hall Island—*island* ... MN-6
Hall Island—*island* (2) ... NY-2
Hall Island—*island* ... WA-9
Hall Island—*island* ... WI-6
Hall Islands—*island* ... FM-9
*Hallison* ... NC-3
Hallison—*other* ... NC-3
*Hallisterville* ... PA-2
Halliwell Well—*locale* ... NM-5
*Hall-Kent Elem Sch* ... AL-4
Hall-Kent Sch—*school* ... AL-4
Hall Knob—*summit* ... NC-3
Hall Knob—*summit* ... VA-3
Hall Knob—*summit* ... WV-2
*Hall Lake* ... MI-6
Hall Lake—*lake* ... FL-3
Hall Lake—*lake* ... IN-6
Hall Lake—*lake* (7) ... MI-6
Hall Lake—*lake* (2) ... MN-6
Hall Lake—*lake* (2) ... MT-8
Hall Lake—*lake* ... NY-2
Hall Lake—*lake* ... OR-9
Hall Lake—*lake* ... TX-5
Hall Lake—*lake* ... WA-9
Hall Lake—*reservoir* (3) ... AL-4
Hall Lake—*reservoir* ... NC-3
Hall Lake—*reservoir* (3) ... TN-4
Hall Lake—*reservoir* ... TX-5
Hall Lake Dam—*dam* (5) ... MS-4
Hall Lake Dam—*dam* ... NC-3
Hall Lake Dam—*dam* (2) ... TN-4
*Hall Lakes* ... MI-6
Hall Landing—*locale* ... NC-3
Hall-London House—*hist pl* ... NC-3
Hall Lot Brook—*stream* ... CT-1
Hallman—*locale* ... PA-2
Hallman Branch—*stream* ... MS-4
Hallman Cem—*cemetery* ... SC-3
Hallman Hollow—*valley* ... AL-4
Hallman Millpond—*reservoir* ... SC-3
Hallman Sch (historical)—*school* ... AL-4
*Hallmans Creek* ... AR-4
Hallmans Lake—*reservoir* ... AL-4
*Hallmans Millpond* ... SC-3

Hallmark—*post sta* ... TX-5
*Hallmark Branch* ... MS-4
Hallmark Cem—*cemetery* ... AL-4
Hallmark Creek—*stream* ... AL-4
Hallmark Crossing—*locale* ... TX-5
**Hallmark Estates**
**(subdivision)**—*pop pl* ... TN-4
Hallmark Hollow—*valley* ... AR-4
Hallmark Hollow—*valley* ... TN-4
Hallmark Lake—*reservoir* ... AL-4
Hallmark Lake Dam—*dam* ... AL-4
Hallmark Pond—*reservoir* ... AZ-5
Hallmark Sch—*school* ... FL-3
Hallmark Shop Ctr—*locale* ... AL-4
Hall Meadow—*flat* ... CA-9
Hall Meadow—*swamp* ... CT-1
Hall Meadow Brook—*stream* ... CT-1
Hall Meadow Brook Dam—*dam* ... CT-1
Hall Meadow Brook Rsvr—*reservoir* ... CT-1
Hall Meadow Cem—*cemetery* ... CT-1
Hall Memorial Cem—*cemetery* ... AL-4
Hall Memorial Ch—*church* ... GA-3
Hall Memorial Library—*hist pl* ... NH-1
Hall Memorial Park—*park* ... IL-6
Hallmere Rsvr—*reservoir* ... CT-1
Hall Mesa—*summit* ... UT-8
Hall Mill—*locale* ... GA-3
*Hall Mills* ... NC-3
Hall Mine—*mine* (2) ... NV-8
Hall Mitchell Ch—*church* ... AL-4
Hall Mountain Cem—*cemetery* ... AR-4
Hall Mountain Marsh—*lake* ... NH-1
Hall Mountain Trail—*trail* ... ID-8
Hall Mtn—*summit* ... AL-4
Hall Mtn—*summit* (3) ... AR-4
Hall Mtn—*summit* ... CA-9
Hall Mtn—*summit* ... ID-8
Hall Mtn—*summit* ... ME-1
Hall Mtn—*summit* ... NH-1
Hall Mtn—*summit* (2) ... NC-3
Hall Mtn—*summit* ... PA-2
Hall Mtn—*summit* (2) ... TN-4
Hall Mtn—*summit* ... VA-3
Hall Mtn—*summit* ... WA-9
*Hallo* ... PA-2
Hallo Bay—*bay* ... AK-9
Halloca Creek—*stream* ... GA-3
Hallock—*locale* ... IL-6
**Hallock**—*pop pl* ... MN-6
**Hallock**—*pop pl* ... OH-6
Hallock Basin—*basin* ... CO-8
Hallock Brook—*stream* ... CT-1
Hallock Brook—*stream* ... VT-1
Hallock Cem—*cemetery* ... IL-6
Hallock Cem—*cemetery* ... MI-6
Hallock Cem—*cemetery* ... VT-1
Hallock Creek—*stream* ... IL-6
Hallock Homestead—*hist pl* ... NY-2
Hallock Landing—*locale* ... NY-2
Hallocks Mill Brook—*stream* ... NY-2
*Hallocks Point* ... NY-2
Hallocks Pond—*lake* ... CT-1
Hallocks Pond—*lake* ... NY-2
Hallock Spring—*spring* ... OR-9
**Hallock (Township of)**—*pop pl* ... IL-6
**Hallock (Township of)**—*pop pl* ... MN-6
**Hallockville**—*pop pl* ... MA-1
Hallockville Pond—*reservoir* ... MA-1
Hallockville Pond Dam—*dam* ... MA-1
Hallo Creek—*stream* ... AK-9
Hall of Crucifixion—*building* ... CA-9
Hall of Fame Complex—*hist pl* ... NY-2
Hall of Justice—*building* ... CA-9
Hall of Languages, Syracuse
Univ—*hist pl* ... NY-2
Hall of Waters—*hist pl* ... MO-7
Hallo Glacier—*glacier* ... AK-9
Hall Oil Field—*oilfield* ... TX-5
Halloran—*locale* ... NE-7
Halloran, Lake—*lake* ... MI-6
Halloran-Matthews-Brady House—*hist pl* ... SD-7
Halloran Park—*park* ... OH-6
Halloran Sch—*school* ... NJ-2
Halloran Sch (historical)—*school* ... MO-7
Hallorans Draw—*valley* ... SD-7
Halloran Spring—*spring* ... CA-9
**Halloran Springs**—*pop pl* ... CA-9
Halloran Wash—*stream* ... CA-9
*Hallo Strand Creek* ... ND-7
Hallot Lake—*lake* ... MN-6
*Hallowall Island* ... ME-1
Hallowat Creek—*stream* ... MT-8
Halloway Bayou—*bay* ... FL-3
Halloway Branch—*stream* ... MD-2
Halloway Gap—*gap* ... GA-3
Halloway Hill—*summit* ... TN-4
Halloway Island—*island* ... FL-3
Halloway Sch (historical)—*school* ... MO-7
Halloway Spring—*spring* ... NV-8
*Hallowayville* ... IL-6
**Hallowell**—*pop pl* ... KS-7
**Hallowell**—*pop pl* ... ME-1
**Hallowell**—*pop pl* ... PA-2
Hallowell Cem—*cemetery* ... WI-6
Hallowell Ch—*church* ... PA-2
Hallowell Elem Sch—*school* ... PA-2
Hallowell Hist Dist—*hist pl* ... ME-1
*Hallowell Park* ... CO-8
Hallowes Cove—*bay* ... FL-3
Hallowing Point—*cape* ... MD-2
Hallowing Point—*cape* ... VA-3
**Hallowing Point River Estates**—*pop pl* ... VA-3
Hallowing Run—*stream* ... PA-2
Hallowood Lake—*reservoir* ... PA-2
*Hall Park* ... AZ-5
Hall Park—*park* ... CA-9
Hall Park—*park* ... SD-7
Hall Park—*park* ... TN-4
**Hall Park**—*pop pl* ... OK-5
Hall Park Sch—*school* ... MI-6
*Hall Pass* ... WA-9
Hall Peak—*summit* ... AK-9
Hall Peak—*summit* ... MT-8
Hall Peak—*summit* ... WA-9
Hall Pioneer Cem—*cemetery* ... WI-6
Hall Pocosin—*swamp* ... NC-3
Hall P O (historical)—*building* ... PA-2
*Hall Point* ... RI-1
Hall Point—*cape* ... ME-1
Hall Point—*cape* ... MD-2

Hall Point—*cape* ... MI-6
Hall Point—*cape* (3) ... NC-3
Hall Point—*cape* ... RI-1
Hall Point—*cape* ... TX-5
Hall Point—*summit* ... AZ-5
Hall Pond—*lake* ... FL-3
Hall Pond—*lake* (4) ... ME-1
Hall Pond—*lake* ... MD-2
Hall Pond—*lake* ... MA-1
Hall Pond—*lake* ... NY-2
Hall Pond—*lake* ... PA-2
Hall Pond—*reservoir* ... NH-1
Hall Pond—*reservoir* ... NC-3
Hall Pond—*reservoir* ... PA-2
Hall Pond Brook—*stream* ... MA-1
Hall Pond Hollow—*valley* ... MO-7
Hall Ponds—*lake* ... KY-4
Hall Ponds—*lake* ... ME-1
Hall Ponds—*lake* ... NH-1
Hall Post Office (historical)—*building* ... PA-2
Hall Prairie—*area* ... OR-9
**Hall Quarry**—*pop pl* ... ME-1
Hallquist Lake—*lake* ... MN-6
Hall Ranch—*locale* ... CA-9
Hall Ranch—*locale* ... MT-8
Hall Ranch—*locale* (2) ... NE-7
Hall Ranch—*locale* (2) ... NV-8
Hall Ranch—*locale* (2) ... NM-5
Hall Ranch—*locale* ... OR-9
Hall Ranch—*locale* (3) ... TX-5
Hall Ranch—*locale* ... UT-8
Hall Ranch—*locale* (4) ... WY-8
Hall Ranch Oil Field—*oilfield* ... TX-5
Hall Ranch (Site)—*locale* ... WA-9
Hall-Raynor Stopping Place—*hist pl* ... WI-6
Hall Ridge—*ridge* ... CA-9
Hall Ridge—*ridge* ... KY-4
Hall Ridge—*ridge* ... ME-1
Hall Ridge—*ridge* ... NC-3
Hall Ridge—*ridge* (2) ... OR-9
Hall Ridge—*ridge* ... VA-3
Hall Ridge—*ridge* ... WA-9
Hall Ridge Ch—*church* ... TN-4
Hall Ridge Dock—*locale* ... TN-4
Hall-Roberson House—*hist pl* ... MS-4
Hall Rsvr—*reservoir* ... CO-8
Hall Rsvr—*reservoir* ... MT-8
Hall Run—*stream* ... IN-6
Hall Run—*stream* ... OH-6
Hall Run—*stream* (3) ... PA-2
Hall Run—*stream* ... WV-2
*Halls* ... AR-4
*Halls* ... GA-3
*Halls* ... MD-2
*Halls* ... TN-4
Halls—*CDP* ... TN-4
Halls—*locale* ... NC-3
Halls—*locale* ... PA-2
**Halls**—*pop pl* ... GA-3
**Halls**—*pop pl* ... MO-7
**Halls**—*pop pl* ... NC-3
**Halls**—*pop pl* (2) ... TN-4
Hall-Sayers-Perkins House—*hist pl* ... TX-5
Halls Bar (inundated)—*bar* ... UT-8
Halls Basin—*basin* ... CO-8
Halls Bayou—*stream* (2) ... TX-5
Halls Bayou Camp—*locale* ... TX-5
*Halls Bend Cave* ... TN-4
Halls Bluff—*cliff* ... MO-7
Halls Bluff—*locale* ... TX-5
Halls Bluff Landing (historical)—*locale* ... TX-5
Halls Bluff Post Office
(historical)—*building* ... TX-5
**Halls Bluff Town (historical)**—*pop pl* ... TX-5
Hallsboro—*locale* ... VA-3
**Hallsboro**—*pop pl* ... NC-3
Hallsboro Elem Sch—*school* ... NC-3
Hallsboro HS—*school* ... NC-3
Hallsborough Tavern—*hist pl* ... VA-3
Halls Brake—*swamp* ... LA-4
*Halls Branch* ... FL-3
Halls Branch—*stream* (2) ... AL-4
Halls Branch—*stream* ... FL-3
Halls Branch—*stream* ... IL-6
Halls Branch—*stream* (2) ... IN-6
Halls Branch—*stream* (2) ... KY-4
Halls Branch—*stream* (2) ... MO-7
Halls Branch—*stream* (2) ... TN-4
Halls Branch—*stream* (2) ... TX-5
Halls Branch—*stream* (3) ... VA-3
Halls Branch—*stream* ... WI-6
Hall's Bridge—*hist pl* ... PA-2
*Halls Brook* ... CT-1
*Halls Brook* ... MA-1
Halls Brook—*stream* ... CT-1
Halls Brook—*stream* (2) ... MA-1
Halls Brook—*stream* ... NH-1
Halls Brook—*stream* (2) ... VT-1
Halls Brook Dam—*dam* ... MA-1
Halls Brook Rsvr—*reservoir* ... MA-1
**Hallsburg**—*pop pl* ... TX-5
Halls Butt—*summit* ... KY-4
Halls Butte—*summit* ... WY-8
Halls Cabin—*locale* ... OR-9
Halls Canyon—*valley* ... CA-9
Halls Canyon—*valley* ... NM-5
Halls Canyon Channel—*canal* ... CA-9
Halls (CCD)—*cens area* (2) ... TN-4
Halls Cem—*cemetery* ... FL-3
Halls Cem—*cemetery* ... IL-6
Halls Cem—*cemetery* ... KY-4
Halls Cem—*cemetery* ... MS-4
Halls Cem—*cemetery* ... NC-3
Halls Cem—*cemetery* ... VA-3
*Hall Sch* ... TN-4
Halls Ch—*church* ... LA-4
Halls Ch—*church* (2) ... NC-3
Halls Ch—*church* ... VA-3
Hall Sch—*school* ... AR-4
Hall Sch—*school* (5) ... CA-9
Hall Sch—*school* ... CT-1
Hall Sch—*school* ... FL-3
Hall Sch—*school* ... GA-3
Hall Sch—*school* (5) ... IL-6
Hall Sch—*school* (4) ... KY-4
Hall Sch—*school* (2) ... MI-6
Hall Sch—*school* ... MN-6
Hall Sch—*school* (2) ... MS-4
Hall Sch—*school* (2) ... MO-7
Hall Sch—*school* (2) ... NE-7

Hall Sch—*school* (2) ... NY-2
Hall Sch—*school* ... PA-2
Hall Sch—*school* ... SC-3
Hall Sch—*school* (2) ... SD-7
Hall Sch—*school* ... TN-4
Hall Sch—*school* (3) ... TX-5
Hall Sch (abandoned)—*school* ... MO-7
Hall Sch (Abandoned)—*school* ... MO-7
Hall Sch (abandoned)—*school* ... SD-7
*Halls Chapel* ... TN-4
Halls Chapel—*church* (3) ... AL-4
Halls Chapel—*church* ... GA-3
Halls Chapel—*church* ... MS-4
Halls Chapel—*church* ... OH-6
Halls Chapel—*church* ... TN-4
Halls Chapel—*church* ... VA-3
Halls Chapel—*church* ... WV-2
**Halls Chapel**—*pop pl* ... AL-4
Halls Chapel Cem—*cemetery* ... AL-4
*Halls Chapel Church* ... AL-4
Halls Chapel (historical)—*church* ... TN-4
Halls Chapel Sch (historical)—*school* ... TN-4
Hall Sch (historical)—*school* ... AL-4
Hall Sch (historical)—*school* ... MO-7
Hall Sch (historical)—*school* (3) ... TN-4
Hall School—*locale* ... IL-6
Hall School (abandoned)—*locale* ... MO-7
Hall-Schultz Canal—*canal* ... LA-4
*Halls Corner* ... IN-6
Halls Corner—*locale* (2) ... ME-1
Halls Corner—*locale* ... MI-6
Halls Corner—*locale* (3) ... NY-2
Halls Corner—*locale* ... TN-4
**Halls Corner**—*pop pl* ... CA-9
**Halls Corner**—*pop pl* ... MI-6
**Halls Corner**—*pop pl* ... NY-2
Halls Corners—*locale* ... MI-6
Halls Corners—*locale* ... NJ-2
Halls Corners—*locale* (4) ... NY-2
Halls Corners—*locale* ... PA-2
**Halls Corners**—*pop pl* ... IN-6
**Halls Corners**—*pop pl* ... OH-6
Halls Cove—*valley* ... VA-3
*Halls Creek* ... AL-4
*Halls Creek* ... LA-4
*Halls Creek* ... RI-1
*Halls Creek* ... VA-3
Halls Creek—*locale* ... TN-4
Halls Creek—*stream* (5) ... AL-4
Halls Creek—*stream* ... GA-3
Halls Creek—*stream* ... IN-6
Halls Creek—*stream* (2) ... KY-4
Halls Creek—*stream* ... MA-1
Halls Creek—*stream* ... MI-6
Halls Creek—*stream* (3) ... MS-4
Halls Creek—*stream* ... MO-7
Halls Creek—*stream* ... NY-2
Halls Creek—*stream* (2) ... NC-3
Halls Creek—*stream* ... OH-6
Halls Creek—*stream* ... RI-1
Halls Creek—*stream* (2) ... TN-4
Halls Creek—*stream* ... TX-5
Halls Creek—*stream* ... UT-8
Halls Creek—*stream* (2) ... WI-6
Halls Creek—*stream* ... WY-8
*Halls Creek Baptist Church* ... AL-4
Halls Creek Bay—*bay* ... UT-8
Halls Creek Ch—*church* ... NC-3
Halls Creek Ch—*church* ... TN-4
*Halls Creek Church* ... AL-4
Halls Creek Church Cem—*cemetery* ... AL-4
Halls Creek Post Office
(historical)—*building* ... TN-4
Halls Creek Sch (historical)—*school* ... TN-4
Halls Crossing—*locale* ... GA-3
Halls Crossing—*locale* ... UT-8
Halls Crossing Airp—*airport* ... UT-8
*Halls Crossing Bar* ... UT-8
Halls Crossing Campground—*park* ... UT-8
Halls Crossing Marina—*locale* ... UT-8
Halls Crossing RV Campground—*park* ... UT-8
*Halls Crossroads* ... AL-4
*Halls Cross Roads* ... TN-4
**Halls Crossroads**—*pop pl* ... AL-4
**Halls Crossroads**—*pop pl* ... NC-3
**Halls Crossroads**—*pop pl* ... TN-4
Halls Cross Roads Post Office
(historical)—*building* ... TN-4
Halls Crossroads Sch—*school* ... MD-2
Halls Dam—*dam* ... AL-4
Halls Ditch—*canal* ... ID-8
*Halls Divide* ... UT-8
Halls Division—*civil* (2) ... TN-4
Halls Dock—*locale* ... NY-2
Halls Double Rsvr—*reservoir* ... UT-8
Halls Elem Sch—*school* (2) ... TN-4
*Halls Ferry* ... MO-7
*Halls Ferry* ... NC-3
Halls Ferry—*locale* ... ID-8
Halls Ferry—*locale* ... OR-9
Halls Ferry Cem—*cemetery* ... OR-9
*Halls Ferry ElementarySchool* ... MS-4
Halls Ferry (historical)—*locale* (2) ... AL-4
Halls Ferry (historical)—*locale* ... MS-4
Halls Ferry (historical)—*locale* (3) ... TN-4
**Halls Ferry Junction**—*pop pl* ... NC-3
Halls Ferry Landing—*locale* ... GA-3
Halls Ferry Sch—*school* ... MS-4
Halls Field Cem—*cemetery* ... TX-5
**Halls Fifth Ave Condominium**—*pop pl* ... UT-8
Halls First Baptist Ch—*church* ... TN-4
Halls Flat—*flat* ... CA-9
Halls Flat—*locale* ... CA-9
Halls Ford—*locale* ... IL-6
Halls Ford—*locale* ... NC-3
Halls Fork—*stream* ... KY-4
Halls Fork—*stream* ... UT-8
Halls Fork—*stream* ... WV-2
Halls Fork Ch—*church* ... AL-4
Halls Fork Sch—*school* ... AL-4
Halls Gap—*gap* ... AL-4
**Halls Gap**—*pop pl* ... KY-4
*Halls Grove* ... AL-4
Halls Grove Ch—*church* ... AL-4
Halls Grove Sch—*school* ... PA-2
Halls Gulch—*valley* (3) ... CA-9
Halls Gulch—*valley* (2) ... CO-8
Halls Gulch—*valley* (2) ... ID-8
Halls Gulch—*valley* ... WY-8
Halls Gut—*gut* ... AL-4

Hancock Cem—*cemetery* ... MS-4
Hancock Cem—*cemetery* ... MO-7
Hancock Cem—*cemetery* ... OH-6
Hancock Cem—*cemetery* ... TN-4
Hancock Cem—*cemetery* (2) ... TX-5
Hancock Cem—*cemetery* ... WI-6
Hancock Cemetery—*hist pl* ... MA-1
Hancock Central Elem Sch—*school* ... TN-4
Hancock Central HS—*school* ... GA-3
Hancock Central Sch—*school* ... MA-1
Hancock Ch—*church* ... AL-4
Hancock Ch—*church* ... NC-3
Hancock Ch—*church* ... PA-2
**Hancock Chapel**—*pop pl* ... IN-6
**Hancock Circle (subdivision)**—*pop pl* ... MS-4
Hancock-Clarke House—*building* ... MA-1
Hancock-Clarke House—*hist pl* ... MA-1
**Hancock Corner**—*pop pl* ... IN-6
Hancock Coulee—*valley* ... MT-8
*Hancock County* ... AL-4
**Hancock (County)**—*pop pl* ... GA-3
**Hancock (County)**—*pop pl* ... IL-6
**Hancock County**—*pop pl* ... IN-6
**Hancock (County)**—*pop pl* ... KY-4
**Hancock (County)**—*pop pl* ... ME-1
**Hancock County**—*pop pl* ... MS-4
**Hancock (County)**—*pop pl* ... OH-6
**Hancock County**—*pop pl* ... TN-4
**Hancock (County)**—*pop pl* ... WV-2
Hancock County Courthouse—*building* ... MS-4
Hancock County Courthouse—*building* ... TN-4
Hancock County Courthouse—*hist pl* ... IA-7
Hancock County Courthouse—*hist pl* ... KY-4
Hancock County Courthouse—*hist pl* ... OH-6
Hancock County Fairgrounds—*locale* ... MS-4
Hancock County Hosp—*hospital* ... TN-4
Hancock County Library—*building* ... MS-4
*Hancock County School* ... TN-4
Hancock Cove—*area* ... UT-8
*Hancock Creek* ... OR-9
Hancock Creek—*stream* ... AL-4
Hancock Creek—*stream* (2) ... CA-9
Hancock Creek—*stream* ... FL-3
Hancock Creek—*stream* ... KY-4
Hancock Creek—*stream* ... LA-4
Hancock Creek—*stream* ... MD-2
Hancock Creek—*stream* ... MI-6
Hancock Creek—*stream* ... NC-3
Hancock Creek—*stream* (2) ... OR-9
Hancock Creek—*stream* ... TX-5
Hancock Creek—*stream* ... UT-8
Hancock Creek—*stream* (2) ... WA-9
**Hancock Crossroads**—*pop pl* ... AL-4
Hancock Dam—*dam* ... UT-8
Hancock Ditch—*canal* (2) ... IN-6
Hancock Draw—*valley* ... WY-8
*Hancock Elementary School* ... PA-2
Hancock Field (Syracuse Hancock Int Airport)—*airport* ... NY-2
Hancock Field United States Air Force—*military* ... NY-2
Hancock Flat—*flat* (2) ... UT-8
Hancock Fork—*stream* ... UT-8
Hancock General Hosp—*hospital* ... MS-4
Hancock-Greenfield Bridge—*hist pl* ... NH-1
Hancock-Grigory Cem—*cemetery* ... AL-4
Hancock Gulch—*valley* (2) ... CO-8
Hancock Gut—*gut* ... VA-3
*Hancock Height* ... MA-1
*Hancock Heights* ... MA-1
Hancock Hill—*summit* ... IN-6
Hancock Hill—*summit* ... KS-7
Hancock Hill—*summit* (2) ... MA-1
Hancock Hill—*summit* ... MS-4
Hancock Hill—*summit* ... TX-5
Hancock (historical)—*locale* ... KS-7
Hancock Hole—*lake* ... MO-7
Hancock Hole (historical)—*lake* ... MO-7
Hancock Hollow—*valley* ... AR-4
Hancock Hollow—*valley* ... MO-7
Hancock Hollow—*valley* ... PA-2
Hancock House—*hist pl* ... KY-4
Hancock House—*hist pl* ... NJ-2
Hancock House—*hist pl* ... NY-2
Hancock HS—*school* ... TN-4
Hancock JHS—*school* ... OH-6
Hancock Junction—*locale* ... AR-4
**Hancock Junction**—*pop pl* ... IA-7
Hancock Knoll—*summit* ... AZ-5
Hancock Knolls—*summit* ... AZ-5
*Hancock Lake* ... AL-4
Hancock Lake—*lake* ... CA-9
Hancock Lake—*lake* ... CO-8
Hancock Lake—*lake* (3) ... FL-3
Hancock Lake—*lake* ... ID-8
Hancock Lake—*lake* ... MN-6
Hancock Lake—*lake* ... NE-7
Hancock Lake—*lake* ... TX-5
Hancock Lake—*lake* ... WI-6
Hancock Lake—*reservoir* ... NC-3
Hancock Lake Dam—*dam* ... NC-3
Hancock Landing—*locale* ... GA-3
Hancock Landing Strip—*airport* ... KS-7
Hancock Lateral—*canal* ... UT-8
Hancock Licklog Branch—*stream* ... TN-4
Hancock Loop Trail—*trail* ... NH-1
Hancock Med Ctr—*hospital* ... MS-4
Hancock Millpond—*reservoir* ... GA-3
Hancock Mtn—*summit* ... OK-5
Hancock Mtn—*summit* ... VT-1
Hancock North Central HS—*school* ... MS-4
Hancock Notch—*gap* ... NH-1
Hancock Notch Trail—*trail* ... NH-1
Hancock Park—*park* ... CA-9
Hancock Park—*park* ... DC-2
Hancock Park—*park* ... TX-5
Hancock Park—*park* ... WI-6
Hancock Park Sch—*school* ... CA-9
Hancock Pass—*gap* ... AK-9
Hancock Pass—*gap* ... CO-8
Hancock Peak—*summit* ... AK-9
Hancock Peak—*summit* ... CO-8
Hancock Peak—*summit* ... NH-1
Hancock Peak—*summit* (2) ... UT-8
Hancock Picnic Area—*park* ... NH-1
Hancock Point—*cape* ... ME-1
Hancock Point—*cape* ... NC-3
**Hancock Point**—*pop pl* ... ME-1
Hancock Pond—*lake* ... CT-1
Hancock Pond—*lake* (3) ... ME-1
Hancock Pond—*lake* ... VT-1
Hancock Pond—*reservoir* ... GA-3
Hancock Post Office (historical)—*building* ... AL-4
Hancock Ranch—*locale* ... AZ-5
Hancock Ranch—*locale* ... ID-8
Hancock Ranch—*locale* ... UT-8
Hancock Ranch—*locale* ... WY-8
Hancock Rapids—*rapids* (2) ... ID-8
Hancock Rsvr—*reservoir* ... NY-2
Hancock Rsvr—*reservoir* ... UT-8
Hancock Run—*stream* ... MD-2
Hancock Savings Bank—*hist pl* ... IA-7
Hancocks Bar—*bar* ... AL-4
**Hancocks Bridge**—*pop pl* ... NJ-2
Hancock Sch—*hist pl* ... MA-1
Hancock Sch—*school* (3) ... IL-6
Hancock Sch—*school* ... KY-4
Hancock Sch—*school* (3) ... MA-1
Hancock Sch—*school* (2) ... MN-6
Hancock Sch—*school* ... NV-8
Hancock Sch—*school* ... OH-6
Hancock Sch—*school* (2) ... PA-2
Hancock Sch—*school* ... WV-2
Hancock Shaker Village—*hist pl* ... MA-1
Hancocks (historical P.O.)—*locale* ... IN-6
Hancock Shoals—*bar* ... AL-4
Hancock Shop Ctr—*locale* ... TX-5
Hancock Slough—*gut* ... IL-6
Hancocks Mill (historical)—*locale* ... TN-4
Hancock Spring—*spring* (2) ... UT-8
Hancock's Resolution—*hist pl* ... MD-2
*Hancocks Store* ... AL-4
*Hancock Station* ... AR-4
Hancock Stream—*stream* ... ME-1
Hancock Summit—*gap* ... NV-8
Hancock Tank—*reservoir* (2) ... AZ-5
Hancock Town Hall—*hist pl* ... MA-1
Hancock Town Hall and Fire Hall—*hist pl* ... MI-6
**Hancock (Town of)**—*pop pl* ... ME-1
**Hancock (Town of)**—*pop pl* ... MA-1
**Hancock (Town of)**—*pop pl* ... NH-1
**Hancock (Town of)**—*pop pl* ... NY-2
**Hancock (Town of)**—*pop pl* ... VT-1
**Hancock (Town of)**—*pop pl* ... WI-6
Hancock Township—*civil* ... SD-7
Hancock Township—*fmr MCD* ... IA-7
**Hancock Township**—*pop pl* ... KS-7
Hancock Township (historical)—*civil* ... SD-7
**Hancock (Township of)**—*pop pl* ... IL-6
**Hancock (Township of)**—*pop pl* ... MI-6
**Hancock (Township of)**—*pop pl* ... MN-6
Hancock Tunnel—*tunnel* ... VT-1
*Hancock Village* ... MA-1
Hancock Village Hist Dist—*hist pl* ... NH-1
**Hancock Village (subdivision)**—*pop pl* ... MA-1
**Hancock Village (subdivision)**—*pop pl* ... NC-3
Hancock Well—*well* ... CA-9
Hancock-Wirt-Caskie House—*hist pl* ... VA-3
Hancorne Prairie—*area* ... CA-9
Hand—*locale* ... MI-6
Hand—*locale* ... SC-3
**Hand**—*pop pl* ... AR-4
**Hand**—*pop pl* ... MS-4
Hand, Gen. Edward, House—*hist pl* ... PA-2
**Hand B Junction**—*pop pl* ... SC-3
Handboy Creek—*stream* ... SD-7
H and B Ranch—*locale* ... TX-5
Hand Branch—*stream* ... FL-3
Hand Branch—*stream* ... IN-6
Hand Branch—*stream* (2) ... TN-4
Hand Brook—*stream* ... PA-2
Hand Cabin—*locale* ... ID-8
Hand Camp—*locale* ... ID-8
Handcart Gulch—*valley* ... CO-8
Handcart Peak—*summit* ... CO-8
Hand Cem—*cemetery* ... AR-4
Hand Cem—*cemetery* ... IL-6
Hand Cem—*cemetery* ... LA-4
Hand Cem—*cemetery* ... MO-7
Handchew Cem—*cemetery* ... AR-4
Hand City Sch—*school* ... SD-7
Handco Branch—*stream* ... GA-3
Handcock Cem—*cemetery* ... KY-4
Handcock Cem—*cemetery* ... TX-5
Handcock Creek—*stream* ... AR-4
Handcock Creek—*stream* ... KY-4
Handcock Lake—*lake* ... FL-3
Handcock Ridge—*ridge* ... WA-9
Handcock Tank—*reservoir* ... AZ-5
Hand County—*civil* ... SD-7
Hand Cove—*bay* ... FL-3
Hand Creek—*stream* ... ID-8
Hand Creek—*stream* ... MN-6
Hand Creek—*stream* ... MT-8
Hand Creek—*stream* ... OR-9
Handcuff Canyon—*valley* ... NV-8
Hand Dam—*dam* ... SD-7
Hand Drain—*stream* ... MI-6
Hand Draw—*valley* ... TX-5
Hande Creek—*stream* ... WA-9
Handel Sch—*school* ... SD-7
Hande Meadow—*flat* ... WA-9
Hand Flat—*flat* ... CA-9
Handford, Charles R., House—*hist pl* ... AR-4
Handford, James S., House—*hist pl* ... AR-4
Handford Bluff—*cliff* ... AR-4
Handgardner Cem—*cemetery* ... WV-2
H and G Mine (Inactive)—*mine* ... CA-9
Hand-Hale Hist Dist—*hist pl* ... NY-2
H and H Commercial Park Subdivision—*locale* ... UT-8
**H and H Corner**—*pop pl* ... DE-2
Hand Hill—*summit* ... NY-2
Hand Hill—*summit* ... OK-5
Hand Hillside Cem—*cemetery* ... MI-6
Hand (historical)—*locale* ... SD-7
H and H Lake—*reservoir* ... TX-5
H and H Lakes—*reservoir* ... MO-7
H And H Mine—*mine* ... CA-9
Hand House—*hist pl* ... MS-4
Hand HS—*school* ... CT-1
Handies Peak—*summit* ... CO-8
Hand in Hand Creek—*stream* ... WY-8
Hand JHS—*school* ... PA-2
Hand JHS—*school* ... SC-3
Handkerchief Creek—*stream* ... MT-8
Handkerchief Knob—*summit* ... WV-2
Handkerchief Lake—*lake* ... MT-8
Handkerchief Mesa—*summit* ... CO-8
Handkerchief Shoal—*bar* ... MA-1
Handkins Landing Strip—*airport* ... KS-7
Hand Lake—*lake* (3) ... MN-6
Hand Lake—*lake* (2) ... OR-9
Hand Lake Trail—*trail* ... OR-9
Hand Landing—*locale* ... AR-4
**Handle**—*pop pl* ... MS-4
Handle Factory Hollow—*valley* ... WV-2
Handle Lake—*lake* ... MN-6
Handley—*locale* ... MO-7
**Handley**—*pop pl* ... MO-7
**Handley**—*pop pl* ... TX-5
**Handley**—*pop pl* ... WV-2
**Handley Acres (subdivision)**—*pop pl* ... NC-3
Handley Branch—*stream* ... AL-4
Handley Branch—*stream* ... KY-4
Handley Branch—*stream* ... OH-6
Handley Canyon—*valley* ... CA-9
Handley Cem—*cemetery* (2) ... TX-5
*Handley Creek* ... KY-4
Handley Elem Sch—*school* ... IN-6
*Handley Grade School* ... AL-4
Handley House—*building* ... OH-6
Handley HS—*school* ... AL-4
Handley HS—*school* ... TX-5
Handley HS—*school* ... VA-3
*Handley JHS* ... AL-4
Handley Library—*hist pl* ... VA-3
Handley Loop Ch—*church* ... LA-4
*Handley MS* ... AL-4
Handley Park—*park* ... FL-3
Handley Park—*park* ... TX-5
Handley Prairie—*area* ... MO-7
Handley Public Hunting And Fishing Area—*park* ... WV-2
Handley Ranch—*locale* ... MT-8
*Handleys Branch* ... KY-4
Handley Sch—*school* ... AL-4
Handley Sch—*school* ... MI-6
Handley Spring—*spring* ... MT-8
**Handleyton**—*pop pl* ... TN-4
Handleyton Post Office (historical)—*building* ... TN-4
Handlin Valley—*basin* ... NE-7
Handlon Hill—*summit* ... MT-8
Handly Creek—*stream* ... AR-4
Handmaul Branch—*stream* ... KY-4
*Hand Meadow* ... ID-8
Hand Meadows—*flat* ... ID-8
Hand-me-down Creek—*stream* ... NV-8
Hand-me-down Spring—*spring* ... NV-8
Hand Mtn—*summit* ... AR-4
Hando Draw—*valley* ... WY-8
Hand Park—*park* ... KS-7
Hand Place—*locale* ... ID-8
Handpointers—*locale* ... NJ-2
Hand Pole Branch—*stream* ... AL-4
Handpole Branch—*stream* (2) ... NC-3
Handpole Creek—*stream* ... VA-3
Hand Rock—*summit* ... WA-9
Hand (RR name for Handsom)—*other* ... VA-3
H and R Skylane Airp—*airport* ... IN-6
Handsaw Creek—*stream* ... WI-6
**Handsboro**—*pop pl* ... MS-4
Handsboro Baptist Ch—*church* ... MS-4
Handsboro Bridge—*bridge* ... MS-4
Handsboro Cem—*cemetery* ... MS-4
Handsboro Female Acad (historical)—*school* ... MS-4
Hands Branch—*stream* ... TN-4
H and S Cem—*cemetery* ... KS-7
Hand Sch—*school* ... MI-6
Handschumacher Cem—*cemetery* ... WV-2
Hands Cove—*bay* ... VT-1
Hand's Cove—*hist pl* ... VT-1
*Hands Creek* ... WV-2
Hands Creek—*bay* ... NY-2
Hands Creek—*stream* ... OR-9
Hands Creek Landing—*locale* ... NY-2
Hands Ditch—*canal* ... MT-8
H and S Drain—*canal* ... MI-6
Handshaw Coulee—*valley* ... MN-6
Handshoe—*locale* ... KY-4
Hands Lake—*lake* ... NJ-2
Hands Marsh—*swamp* ... MN-6
Hands Millpond—*reservoir* ... NJ-2
Hands Mill Pond Dam—*dam* ... NJ-2
Handsom—*locale* ... VA-3
Handsome Brook—*stream* (2) ... NY-2
Handsome Cem—*cemetery* ... TX-5
**Handsome Eddy**—*pop pl* ... NY-2
Handsome Hollow—*valley* ... NY-2
Handsome Lake—*lake* ... MI-6
Handsome Lake Campground—*locale* ... PA-2
Handsome Pond—*lake* ... NY-2
Handsome Pond—*lake* ... PA-2
*Handsom Hand* ... VA-3
*Handsom Post Office* ... VA-3
**Handsom (RR name Hand)**—*pop pl* ... VA-3
Hands Pass—*gap* ... AZ-5
Hands Pond—*reservoir* ... NJ-2
Hand Springs—*spring* ... CO-8
Hands Run—*stream* ... VA-3
Hands Run—*stream* ... WV-2
Hands Spring—*spring* ... ID-8
Hands Store (historical)—*locale* ... AL-4
*Hand Station* ... VA-3
Hands Well—*well* ... TX-5
Hand Valley—*locale* ... AR-4
Hand Valley Cem—*cemetery* ... AR-4
Handwerk Peak—*summit* ... ID-8
Handwork Sch (historical)—*school* ... PA-2
Handworks Corners—*locale* ... OH-6
Handwrought—*hist pl* ... PA-2
Handy—*locale* ... GA-3
Handy—*locale* ... MO-7
**Handy**—*pop pl* (2) ... IN-6
**Handy**—*pop pl* ... NC-3
**Handy**—*pop pl* ... TX-5
Handy-Andy Memorial Park—*park* ... WI-6
Handy Brake—*swamp* ... LA-4
Handy Branch—*stream* (2) ... NC-3
H and Y Cabin—*locale* ... OR-9
Handy Camp—*locale* (2) ... CA-9
Handy Camp Gulch—*valley* ... CA-9
Handy Camp Run—*stream* ... WV-2
Handy Cem—*cemetery* ... AL-4
Handy Ch—*church* ... MO-7
Handy Chapel African Methodist Episcopal Ch—*church* ... AL-4
**Handy Corner**—*pop pl* ... MS-4
Handy Creek—*stream* ... CA-9
Handy Creek—*stream* ... ID-8
Handy Creek—*stream* (2) ... MI-6
Handy Creek—*stream* ... OR-9
Handy Creek—*stream* ... VA-3
Handy Ditch—*canal* ... CO-8
Handy Drain No 5—*canal* ... MI-6
**Handy Four Corners**—*pop pl* ... MA-1
Handy Gap—*gap* ... NC-3
Handy (historical)—*locale* (2) ... KS-7
**Handy (historical)**—*pop pl* ... OR-9
Handy Hollow—*valley* ... MO-7
Handy Howell Drain No 1—*canal* ... MI-6
Handy HS—*school* ... MI-6
H and Y Hunting Lodge—*locale* ... AL-4
Handy Iosco Drain No 1—*canal* ... MI-6
*Handy Island* ... SD-7
Handy Lake—*lake* ... IN-6
Handy Lake—*lake* (2) ... MI-6
Handy Memorial Ch—*church* ... MD-2
Handy Mtn—*summit* ... NC-3
Handy Museum—*building* ... AL-4
Handy Park—*park* ... TN-4
Handy Point—*cape* (2) ... MA-1
Handys Bend—*bend* ... KY-4
Handy Sch—*school* ... AL-4
Handy Sch—*school* ... CA-9
Handys Hammock—*island* ... MD-2
Handyside Gulf—*valley* ... NY-2
*Handys Lake* ... SD-7
*Handys Point* ... MA-1
Handys Point—*cape* ... MD-2
Handys Point—*cape* ... NC-3
Handys Point (historical)—*cliff* ... SD-7
Handy Spring—*spring* ... NV-8
Handy Spring—*spring* ... OR-9
Handy Spring—*spring* ... WA-9
**Handy (Township of)**—*pop pl* ... MI-6
Handyville—*locale* ... KY-4
Handy Water Creek—*stream* ... ND-7
Hane, Gottfried, House—*hist pl* ... MI-6
*Hanegras Plain* ... AZ-5
Hanehoi—*civil* ... HI-9
Hanehoi Point—*cape* ... HI-9
Hanehoi Stream—*stream* ... HI-9
Hanel Field (airport)—*airport* ... OR-9
Haneline Cem—*cemetery* ... IL-6
Haneman Lake—*lake* ... WI-6
Hanenkrat Creek—*stream* ... OR-9
Hanen Run—*stream* ... PA-2
Haneoo—*civil* ... HI-9
Haneoo Gulch—*valley* ... HI-9
Haner, William, Polygonal Barn—*hist pl* ... IA-7
Haner Butte—*summit* ... OR-9
Haner Cem—*cemetery* ... OK-5
**Hanersville**—*pop pl* ... OH-6
Hanerville—*locale* ... WI-6
Haner Windmill—*locale* ... TX-5
**Hanes**—*pop pl* ... NC-3
Hanes Airp—*airport* ... WA-9
Hanes Branch—*stream* ... AL-4
Hanes Branch—*stream* ... TN-4
Hanes Cem—*cemetery* ... IL-6
Hanes Cem—*cemetery* ... MS-4
Hanes Cem—*cemetery* ... TN-4
Hanes Cem—*cemetery* ... WV-2
Hanes Ch—*church* ... MO-7
Hanes Chapel—*church* ... VA-3
Hanes Cheaha Lake—*reservoir* ... AL-4
Hanes Ditch—*canal* ... IN-6
Hanes Flat—*flat* ... MO-7
*Hanes Flat, The* ... AZ-5
Hanes Fork—*stream* ... WY-8
Hanes Grove Ch—*church* ... NC-3
*Hane Shima* ... MP-9
Hanes Hollow—*valley* (2) ... AR-4
Hanes Home—*hist pl* ... OK-5
Hanes HS—*school* ... NC-3
*Hanes Island* ... AL-4
Hanes Lake—*lake* ... MI-6
Hanes Lake—*reservoir* ... NC-3
Hanes Lake Dam—*dam* ... NC-3
Hanes Mall Shop Ctr—*locale* ... NC-3
Hanes Park—*park* ... NC-3
Hanes Ridge—*ridge* ... CA-9
Hanes Rsvr—*reservoir* ... WY-8
Hanes Sch—*school* ... TX-5
*Hanes School* ... NC-3
Hanesville—*locale* ... OH-6
**Hanesville**—*pop pl* ... MD-2
Haney—*locale* ... GA-3
Haney—*locale* ... MS-4
Haney—*locale* ... TN-4
Haney—*locale* ... TX-5
Haney Airp—*airport* ... PA-2
Haney Bar—*bar* ... ID-8
Haney Bottoms—*flat* ... AL-4
*Haney Branch* ... TN-4
Haney Branch—*stream* ... AL-4
Haney Branch—*stream* (3) ... KY-4
Haney Branch—*stream* ... MS-4
Haney Branch—*stream* ... NC-3
Haney Branch—*stream* ... TN-4
Haney Bridge—*bridge* ... AL-4
Haney Brook—*stream* ... ME-1
Haney Canyon—*valley* ... CO-8
Haney Cem—*cemetery* ... AL-4
Haney Cem—*cemetery* ... GA-3
Haney Cem—*cemetery* ... LA-4
Haney Cem—*cemetery* ... MO-7
Haney Cem—*cemetery* ... NC-3
Haney Cem—*cemetery* ... SC-3
Haney Cem—*cemetery* ... TX-5
Haney Ch—*church* ... OK-5
Haney Ch—*church* ... WV-2
Haney Chapel—*church* ... AL-4
Haney Chapel—*church* ... TX-5
Haney Chapel Cem—*cemetery* ... AL-4
*Haney Church* ... AL-4
**Haney Corner**—*pop pl* ... IN-6
Haney Creek—*stream* ... AL-4
Haney Creek—*stream* (2) ... AR-4
Haney Creek—*stream* ... IL-6
Haney Creek—*stream* ... MT-8
Haney Creek—*stream* ... NC-3
Haney Creek—*stream* (2) ... OR-9
Haney Creek Ch—*church* ... AR-4
Haney Draw—*valley* ... CO-8
Haney Fork—*stream* ... WV-2
Haney Grove Ch—*church* ... GA-3
Haney Hill—*summit* ... IL-6
Haney Hill—*summit* ... MO-7
Haney Hollow—*valley* ... AL-4
Haney Hollow—*valley* (2) ... AR-4
Haney Hollow—*valley* ... KY-4
Haney Hollow—*valley* ... TN-4
Haney Lake—*lake* (2) ... MI-6
Haney Lake—*lake* (2) ... NE-7
Haney Marsh—*swamp* ... MI-6
Haney Meadow—*flat* ... WA-9
Haney Meadow Campground—*locale* ... WA-9
Haney Mtn—*summit* ... AL-4
Haney Mtn—*summit* (2) ... CA-9
Haney Ridge—*ridge* ... IN-6
Haney Ridge—*ridge* ... OH-6
Haney Ridge—*ridge* ... OR-9
Haney Ridge—*ridge* ... WI-6
Haney Ridge Ch—*church* ... WI-6
*Haney Run* ... PA-2
Haneys—*locale* ... IA-7
Haneys Branch—*stream* ... WV-2
Haneys Branch Ch—*church* ... WV-2
Haney Sch—*school* ... KY-4
Haney Sch—*school* ... MI-6
Haney Sch—*school* ... NE-7
Haney Sch—*school* ... WV-2
Haney Sch—*school* ... WI-6
Haney Sch (historical)—*school* ... MS-4
Haney Sch (historical)—*school* ... TN-4
*Haneys Church* ... AL-4
Haneys Corner (historical P.O.)—*locale* ... IN-6
Haneys Creek—*stream* ... GA-3
Haneys Mill—*locale* ... NJ-2
Haney Spring—*spring* ... MT-8
Haneytown—*locale* ... VA-3
Haneytown Creek—*stream* ... VA-3
**Haney (Town of)**—*pop pl* ... WI-6
Haney Valley—*basin* ... WI-6
Haney Valley Cem—*cemetery* ... WI-6
Haneyville—*locale* ... PA-2
Haneyville Ch—*church* ... PA-2
Haney Well—*well* (3) ... NM-5
Hanff Draw—*valley* ... WY-8
Hanff Rsvr—*reservoir* ... WY-8
**Hanfield**—*pop pl* ... IN-6
*Hanford* ... OH-6
Hanford—*locale* ... ME-1
Hanford—*locale* ... NJ-2
Hanford—*locale* ... WA-9
**Hanford**—*pop pl* ... CA-9
**Hanford**—*pop pl* ... IA-7
**Hanford**—*pop pl* ... MS-4
**Hanford**—*pop pl* ... OH-6
Hanford, Edwin H., House—*hist pl* ... WA-9
Hanford Carnegie Library—*hist pl* ... CA-9
Hanford (CCD)—*cens area* ... CA-9
Hanford Cem—*cemetery* ... CA-9
Hanford Cem—*cemetery* ... IL-6
Hanford Christian Sch—*school* ... CA-9
Hanford Ditch—*canal* ... WA-9
Hanford HS—*school* ... WA-9
Hanford Island Archeol Site—*hist pl* ... WA-9
Hanford Mill—*hist pl* ... NY-2
Hanford North Archeol District—*hist pl* ... WA-9
Hanford Northeast (CCD)—*cens area* ... CA-9
**Hanford Northwest (census name Short Acres)**—*pop pl* ... CA-9
Hanford Park—*park* ... IA-7
Hanford Reservation—*area* ... WA-9
Hanford Road Barricade—*locale* ... WA-9
**Hanfords Bay**—*pop pl* ... NY-2
**Hanford South**—*pop pl* ... CA-9
Hanford Union HS—*school* ... CA-9
Hanford Works(U.S. Dept. of Energy)—*building* ... WA-9
Hangaard State Wildlife Mngmt Area—*park* ... MN-6
**Hangaard (Township of)**—*pop pl* ... MN-6
*Hangamn Islet* ... MA-1
Hangar, The—*hist pl* ... OH-6
Hangar Lake—*lake* ... AK-9
Hangar No. 1, Lakehurst Naval Air Station—*hist pl* ... NJ-2
Hangar 9—*hist pl* ... TX-5
Hang Dog Creek—*stream* ... UT-8
Hanger—*locale* ... TX-5
Hanger, Frederick, House—*hist pl* ... AR-4
Hanger Cem—*cemetery* ... OH-6
Hanger Cem—*cemetery* ... WV-2
Hanger Cotton Gin—*hist pl* ... AR-4
Hanger Ditch—*canal* ... IN-6
Hanger Gulch—*valley* ... WA-9
Hanger Hollow—*valley* ... VA-3
*Hangerman Reservoir* ... WY-8
Hangerman Valley—*bend* ... ID-8
Hanger Rsvr—*reservoir* ... WY-8
Hanger Tank—*reservoir* ... TX-5
Hanging Basket Lake—*lake* ... CA-9
Hanging Birds Nest—*valley* ... NY-2
Hanging Bog—*swamp* ... NY-2
Hanging Bog Game Mngmt Area—*park* ... NY-2
Hanging Canyon—*valley* ... WY-8
Hanging Dog Ch—*church* ... NC-3
Hanging Dog Creek—*stream* ... NC-3
Hanging Dog Creek—*stream* ... OK-5
Hanging Dog Gap—*gap* ... NC-3
Hanging Dog Island—*island* ... IL-6
Hanging Dog Mtn—*summit* ... NC-3
Hanging Flume—*hist pl* ... CO-8
*Hanging Fork* ... KY-4
Hanging Fork Ch—*church* ... KY-4
Hanging Fork Creek—*stream* ... KY-4
Hanging Gardens—*basin* ... MT-8
Hanging Glacier—*glacier* ... AK-9
Hanging Glacier—*glacier* (2) ... WA-9
Hanging Glacier Mtn—*summit* ... AK-9
**Hanging Grove**—*pop pl* ... IN-6
Hanging Grove (Township of)—*civ div* ... IN-6
Hanging Hills—*range* ... CT-1
Hanging Horn Lake—*lake* ... MN-6
*Hanging Kettle Creek* ... MS-4
Hanging Kettle Lake—*lake* ... MN-6
*Hanging Lake* ... MN-6
*Hanging Lake* ... WY-8
Hanging Lake—*lake* ... AK-9
Hanging Lake—*lake* (2) ... CO-8
Hanging Lake—*lake* ... WA-9
Hanging Lake—*lake* ... WY-8
Hanging Lake Park—*park* ... CO-8
**Hanging Limb**—*pop pl* ... TN-4
Hanging Limb Baptist Ch—*church* ... TN-4
Hanging Limb Cem—*cemetery* ... TN-4
Hanging Limb Post Office (historical)—*building* ... TN-4
Hanging Limb Sch (historical)—*school* ... TN-4
Hanging Log Cave—*cave* ... AL-4
Hanging Mesa—*summit* ... NV-8
Hanging Moss Creek—*stream* (3) ... MS-4
Hanging Moss Plaza Shop Ctr—*locale* ... MS-4
Hanging Moss Village Shop Ctr—*locale* ... MS-4
*Hanging Mount* ... MA-1
Hanging Mountain Pond—*lake* ... MA-1
Hanging Mtn—*summit* ... GA-3
Hanging Mtn—*summit* (2) ... MA-1
*Hanging Rock* ... RI-1
Hanging Rock—*cliff* ... IL-6
Hanging Rock—*cliff* ... IN-6
Hanging Rock—*cliff* ... OK-5
Hanging Rock—*cliff* (2) ... WV-2
Hanging Rock—*locale* ... KY-4
Hanging Rock—*locale* ... WV-2
Hanging Rock—*pillar* ... CA-9
Hanging Rock—*pillar* ... GA-3
Hanging Rock—*pillar* ... IN-6
Hanging Rock—*pillar* ... KY-4
Hanging Rock—*pillar* ... MD-2
Hanging Rock—*pillar* ... NC-3
Hanging Rock—*pillar* ... OR-9
Hanging Rock—*pillar* ... RI-1
Hanging Rock—*pillar* (2) ... VA-3
Hanging Rock—*pillar* ... WY-8
**Hanging Rock**—*pop pl* ... OH-6
**Hanging Rock**—*pop pl* ... VA-3
Hanging Rock—*summit* ... IN-6
Hanging Rock—*summit* (2) ... KY-4
Hanging Rock—*summit* (2) ... NC-3
Hanging Rock—*summit* ... VA-3
Hanging Rock—*summit* (2) ... WV-2
Hanging Rock Battleground—*other* ... SC-3
Hanging Rock Branch—*stream* ... NC-3
Hanging Rock Branch—*stream* ... TN-4
Hanging Rock Branch—*stream* (2) ... WV-2
Hanging Rock Campground—*locale* ... WY-8
Hanging Rock Campground—*park* ... UT-8
Hanging Rock Canyon—*valley* ... CA-9
Hanging Rock Canyon—*valley* ... NV-8
Hanging Rock Canyon—*valley* ... UT-8
Hanging Rock Cave—*cave* ... AL-4
Hanging Rock Cem—*cemetery* ... OH-6
Hanging Rock Ch—*church* (2) ... KY-4
Hanging Rock Ch—*church* ... SC-3
Hanging Rock Chapel—*church* ... NC-3
Hanging Rock Christian Assembly—*church* ... IN-6
Hanging Rock Creek—*stream* ... NC-3
Hanging Rock Creek—*stream* ... SC-3
Hanging Rock Falls—*falls* ... NY-2
Hanging Rock Gap—*gap* ... GA-3
Hanging Rock Gap—*gap* ... NC-3
*Hanging Rock Gulch* ... CO-8
Hanging Rock Hollow—*valley* ... AR-4
Hanging Rock Hollow—*valley* ... TN-4
Hanging Rock Hollow—*valley* ... UT-8
Hanging Rock Hollow—*valley* ... VA-3
*Hanging Rock Island* ... TN-4
Hanging Rock Park Lake—*reservoir* ... NC-3
Hanging Rock Park Lake Dam—*dam* ... NC-3
Hanging Rock Ridge—*ridge* ... NC-3
Hanging Rock Ridge—*ridge* ... WV-2
Hanging Rock Sch—*school* ... WV-2
Hanging Rock Spring—*spring* ... AZ-5
Hanging Rock Spring—*spring* ... OR-9
Hanging Rock Spring—*spring* ... TX-5
Hanging Rock Spring—*spring* ... UT-8
Hanging Rocks Tank—*reservoir* ... NM-5
Hanging Rock State Park—*park* ... NC-3
Hanging Rock Trail—*trail* ... NC-3
Hanging Rock Trail—*trail* ... WV-2
Hanging Rock Trail (Pack)—*trail* ... NM-5
Hanging Rock Valley—*valley* ... VA-3
Hanging Run—*stream* ... WV-2
Hanging Spear Falls—*falls* ... NY-2
Hanging Springs—*spring* ... AZ-5
Hanging Tank—*reservoir* ... AZ-5
Hanging Tree Campground—*locale* ... WA-9
Hanging Tree Draw—*valley* ... CO-8
Hanging Trees Historical Marker—*park* ... ID-8
Hanging Valley—*basin* ... MT-8
Hanging Valley—*valley* ... CO-8
Hanging Valley—*valley* ... MA-1
Hanging Valley—*valley* ... MT-8
Hanging Valley—*valley* ... NC-3
Hanging Valley—*valley* ... PA-2
Hanging Valley Mine—*mine* ... CA-9
Hanging Valley Ridge—*ridge* ... CA-9
Hanging Water Well—*well* ... AZ-5
*Hanging Woman Creek* ... WY-8
Hanging Woman Creek—*stream* ... MT-8
Hanging Woman Creek—*stream* ... WY-8
*Hang Kettle Creek* ... MS-4
Hang Kettle Creek—*stream* ... MS-4
Hang Lake—*lake* ... CO-8
*Hangman Creek* ... ID-8
*Hangman Creek* ... WA-9
Hangman Creek—*stream* ... ID-8
Hangman Creek—*stream* (2) ... WA-9
**Hangman Crossing**—*pop pl* ... IN-6
Hangman Gulch—*valley* ... CO-8
Hangman Gulch—*valley* ... ID-8
Hangman Hill—*summit* ... SD-7
Hangman Island—*island* ... MA-1
Hangman Run—*stream* ... VA-3
Hangmans Bridge—*locale* ... CA-9
Hangmans Cabin—*locale* ... CO-8
Hangmans Canyon—*valley* ... AZ-5
*Hangmans Creek* ... ID-8
*Hangmans Creek* ... WA-9
Hangmans Creek—*stream* ... MT-8
Hangmans Draw—*valley* ... AZ-5
Hangman's Gulch—*valley* ... CO-8
Hangmans Gulch—*valley* ... MT-8
Hangmans Hollow—*valley* ... TX-5
*Hangmans Island* ... MA-1
Hangmans Rock—*cliff* ... CO-8
Hangmans Run—*stream* ... DE-2
Hangmans Tank—*reservoir* ... AZ-5
Hangman Tree—*locale* ... ID-8
Hangman Valley—*valley* ... WA-9
Hangman Valley Golf Course—*other* ... WA-9
**Hangore Heights**—*pop pl* ... MI-6
Hangout Ridge—*ridge* ... WY-8

Happy Jack Peak—*summit* ... NE-7
Happy Jack Ranger Station—*locale* ... AZ-5
Happy Jack Ridge—*ridge* ... OR-9
Happy Jack Spring—*spring* ... CA-9
Happy Jack Spring—*spring* ... CO-8
Happy Jack Spring—*spring* ... OR-9
Happy Jack Tank—*reservoir* ... AZ-5
Happy Jack Underpass—*crossing* ... AZ-5
Happy Jack Wash—*stream* ... AZ-5
Happy Jack Winter Sports Area—*park* ... WY-8
Happy Knoll Sch—*school* ... MN-6
*Happy Lake* ... MI-6
*Happy Lake* ... MN-6
*Happy Lake* ... WI-6
Happy Lake—*lake* ... MI-6
Happy Lake—*lake* ... ND-7
Happy Lake—*lake* ... OR-9
Happy Lake—*lake* ... WA-9
Happy Lake—*reservoir* ... MS-4
Happy Lake—*reservoir* ... OK-5
Happy Lake Creek—*stream* ... WA-9
Happy Lake Dam—*dam* ... MS-4
Happy Lake Ridge—*ridge* ... WA-9
Happy Lake Ridge Trail—*trail* ... WA-9
*Happyland* ... AL-4
Happyland—*locale* ... CT-1
Happyland—*locale* ... OK-5
Happy Land—*other* ... MN-6
Happyland Camp No 5—*locale* ... VA-3
Happyland Day Sch—*school* ... FL-3
**Happyland (Happy Land)**—*pop pl* ... MN-6
Happy Landing—*locale* ... GA-3
Happy Landing—*locale* ... KY-4
Happy Landing Lake—*reservoir* ... IN-6
Happyland Lake—*reservoir* ... VA-3
Happy Land Lookout Tower—*locale* ... MN-6
Happyland Sanitarium—*hospital* ... CA-9
Happy Mine—*mine* ... CO-8
Happy Mine—*mine* ... NV-8
Happy Nest Learning Center—*school* ... FL-3
Happy New Year Creek—*stream* ... AK-9
Happy Old Folks Home—*building* ... TX-5
Happy Prairie—*flat* (2) ... OR-9
Happy Prairie Way—*trail* ... OR-9
Happy Reach—*channel* ... FL-3
Happy Retreat—*locale* ... PA-2
Happy Ridge—*ridge* (2) ... KY-4
Happy Ridge—*ridge* ... OR-9
Happy Ridge—*ridge* ... TN-4
Happy Ridge Ch—*church* ... MO-7
Happy River—*stream* ... AK-9
Happy Rsvr—*reservoir* ... OR-9
Happy Run—*stream* ... IA-7
Happys Hill—*summit* ... AK-9
**Happys Inn**—*pop pl* ... MT-8
Happys Lake—*reservoir* ... NC-3
Happy Slough—*stream* ... AK-9
Happy Sock Creek—*stream* ... MO-7
Happy Spring—*spring* (2) ... OR-9
Happy Spring—*spring* ... WY-8
Happy Spring Creek—*reservoir* ... WY-8
Happy Spring Creek—*stream* ... WY-8
Happy Spring Sheep Camp—*locale* ... WY-8
Happy Springs Oil Field—*oilfield* ... WY-8
Happy Tank—*reservoir* ... AZ-5
Happy Time Sch—*school* ... OH-6
**Happy Top**—*pop pl* ... TN-4
Happy Top—*summit* ... GA-3
Happy Top—*summit* ... KY-4
Happy Top Ch—*church* ... TN-4
Happy Top Ch (historical)—*church* (2) ... TN-4
Happy Top Mtn—*summit* ... KY-4
Happytown Oil and Gas Field—*oilfield* ... LA-4
**Happy Township**—*pop pl* ... KS-7
Happy Union—*locale* ... TX-5
Happy Union Ch—*church* ... TX-5
Happy Union Community Center—*locale* ... TX-5
Happy Valley—*area* ... CA-9
Happy Valley—*area* ... NM-5
Happy Valley—*basin* ... AZ-5
Happy Valley—*basin* ... UT-8
Happy Valley—*flat* ... CA-9
Happy Valley—*flat* ... WA-9
Happy Valley—*locale* ... AK-9
Happy Valley—*locale* ... CA-9
Happy Valley—*locale* ... FL-3
Happy Valley—*locale* (2) ... NY-2
Happy Valley—*locale* (2) ... TX-5
Happy Valley—*locale* ... WA-9
**Happy Valley**—*pop pl* ... CA-9
**Happy Valley**—*pop pl* ... HI-9
**Happy Valley**—*pop pl* ... MT-8
**Happy Valley**—*pop pl* ... NH-1
**Happy Valley**—*pop pl* ... NM-5
**Happy Valley**—*pop pl* ... NC-3
**Happy Valley**—*pop pl* ... OR-9
**Happy Valley**—*pop pl* ... PA-2
**Happy Valley**—*pop pl* ... TN-4
**Happy Valley**—*pop pl* ... WA-9
Happy Valley—*valley* ... AR-4
Happy Valley—*valley* (4) ... CA-9
Happy Valley—*valley* ... MT-8
Happy Valley—*valley* (2) ... NC-3
Happy Valley—*valley* (6) ... OR-9
Happy Valley—*valley* (4) ... TN-4
Happy Valley—*valley* ... WA-9
Happy Valley—*valley* ... WI-6
Happy Valley—*valley* ... AS-9
Happy Valley Bar—*bar* ... TN-4
Happy Valley Branch—*stream* ... MD-2
Happy Valley Brook—*stream* ... VT-1
Happy Valley Camp—*locale* ... AK-9
*Happy Valley Cem* ... OR-9
Happy Valley Cem—*cemetery* ... NY-2
Happy Valley Cem—*cemetery* ... OR-9
Happy Valley Cem—*cemetery* ... TN-4
Happy Valley Ch—*church* (2) ... AL-4
Happy Valley Ch—*church* ... AR-4
Happy Valley Ch—*church* (3) ... GA-3
Happy Valley Ch—*church* ... NC-3
Happy Valley Ch—*church* ... OH-6
Happy Valley Ch—*church* ... TN-4
Happy Valley Conference Ground—*locale* ... CA-9
Happy Valley Country Club—*locale* ... NC-3
Happy Valley Creek—*stream* ... IN-6
Happy Valley Ditch—*canal* ... OR-9
*Happy Valley Elementary School* ... TN-4
Happy Valley Game Mngmt Area—*park* ... NY-2
Happy Valley Gap—*gap* ... TN-4
Happy Valley Golf Course—*locale* ... PA-2
Happy Valley HS—*school* ... TN-4
Happy Valley Interchange—*crossing* ... AZ-5
Happy Valley Irrigation Canal—*canal* ... CA-9
Happy Valley Landing—*locale* ... TN-4
Happy Valley Lookout—*locale* ... AZ-5
Happy Valley Memorial Park—*cemetery* ... TN-4
*Happy Valley Missionary Baptist Ch* ... AL-4
Happy Valley Missionary Baptist Ch—*church* ... TN-4
Happy Valley MS—*school* ... TN-4
Happy Valley Post Office (historical)—*building* ... TN-4
Happy Valley Ranch—*locale* ... CA-9
**Happy Valley Ranch (subdivision)**—*pop pl* (2) ... AZ-5
Happy Valley Revetment—*levee* ... TN-4
Happy Valley Ridge—*ridge* ... TN-4
Happy Valley Rsvr—*reservoir* ... OR-9
Happy Valley Saddle—*gap* ... AZ-5
Happy Valley Sch—*school* (3) ... CA-9
Happy Valley Sch—*school* ... GA-3
Happy Valley Sch—*school* ... ID-8
Happy Valley Sch—*school* ... KY-4
Happy Valley Sch—*school* ... NC-3
Happy Valley Sch—*school* ... OK-5
Happy Valley Sch—*school* ... OR-9
Happy Valley Sch—*school* ... SD-7
Happy Valley Sch—*school* ... TN-4
Happy Valley School—*locale* ... OK-5
**Happy Valley (subdivision)**—*pop pl* ... NC-3
**Happy Valley Subdivision**—*pop pl* ... UT-8
Happy Windmill—*locale* ... TX-5
Happy Woods Ch—*church* ... LA-4
Hap Rsvr—*reservoir* ... CO-8
Haps Airp—*airport* ... IN-6
Hapuna Bay—*bay* ... HI-9
Hapuna Beach Park—*park* ... HI-9
Haputo Beach—*beach* ... GU-9
Haputo Beach Site—*hist pl* ... GU-9
Haputo Point—*summit* ... GU-9
*Hapuua Bay* ... HI-9
*Ha Puu a Pele* ... HI-9
Hapuu Bay—*bay* ... HI-9
Hapuu Camp—*locale* ... HI-9
Hapworth Brook—*stream* ... ME-1
Hapworth Cem—*cemetery* ... ME-1
*Haquequenunck* ... NJ-2
Hara Arena—*building* ... OH-6
Harada House—*hist pl* ... CA-9
Haraguchi Rice Mill—*hist pl* ... HI-9
**Harahan**—*pop pl* ... LA-4
Harahan Bridge—*bridge* ... AR-4
Harahan Bridge—*bridge* ... TN-4
Harahan Elem Sch—*hist pl* ... LA-4
Harahan Junction—*locale* ... LA-4
Harahan Sch—*school* ... LA-4
Harakleys Pond—*reservoir* ... CT-1
**Haralson**—*pop pl* (2) ... GA-3
Haralson, Lake—*reservoir* ... GA-3
**Haralson (County)**—*pop pl* ... GA-3
Haralson County Courthouse—*hist pl* ... GA-3
Haralson HS—*school* ... GA-3
Haralson Memory Gardens—*cemetery* ... GA-3
Haralson Recreation Center—*locale* ... GA-3
Haram Branch—*stream* ... MS-4
Haram Creek—*stream* ... SD-7
Haram (historical)—*locale* ... SD-7
**Haram Township**—*pop pl* ... ND-7
Harantis Lake—*lake* ... NH-1
Ha-Ra Oil Field—*oilfield* ... TX-5
*Harappu* ... MP-9
Harappu—*island* ... MP-9
*Harappu Island* ... MP-9
*Harappu-To* ... MP-9
*Haraseket River* ... ME-1
Haraszthy Creek—*stream* ... CA-9
Haraszthy Falls—*falls* ... CA-9
Haraway Cem—*cemetery* ... AL-4
Haraway Sch—*school* ... AR-4
Harb—*locale* ... MT-8
*Harba* ... SD-7
Harbach, Gerald, Round Barn—*hist pl* ... IL-6
Harbach, John, House—*hist pl* ... MA-1
Harban Creek—*stream* ... OH-6
Harbar Acres Lake—*lake* ... PA-2
Harbargar Hollow—*valley* ... OH-6
*Harbatos Creek* ... IN-6
Harbaugh Cem—*cemetery* ... KS-7
Harbaugh Ch—*church* ... PA-2
Harbaugh Run—*stream* ... PA-2
Harbaugh Sch (historical)—*school* ... PA-2
Harbaugh Valley—*valley* ... MD-2
Harbean Slough—*stream* ... CA-9
Harbecke Ranch—*locale* ... NV-8
Harbeck-Fruitdale—*CDP* ... OR-9
Harbeck Windmill—*locale* ... CO-8
Harbell—*locale* ... KY-4
Harben Lake—*reservoir* ... NM-5
**Harber**—*pop pl* ... KY-4
Harber Ditch—*canal* ... IN-6
Harber Fork Turkey Creek—*stream* ... OH-6
Harber Hollow—*valley* ... TN-4
Harberson Hollow—*valley* ... TN-4
*Harbert* ... MI-6
Harbert—*locale* ... WA-9
**Harbert**—*pop pl* ... MI-6
Harbert Ch—*church* ... MI-6
Harbert Dam—*dam* ... AL-4
Harbert Hills Acad—*school* ... TN-4
Harbert Lake—*reservoir* (2) ... AL-4
Harbert Landing—*locale* ... MS-4
*Harbert Point* ... MS-4
*Harberts* ... MS-4
Harberts Creek—*stream* ... IN-6
**Harbertson Subdivision**—*pop pl* ... UT-8
**Harbeson**—*pop pl* ... DE-2
**Harbeson (Broadkill)**—*pop pl* ... DE-2
Harbeson City (abandoned)—*locale* ... FL-3
Harbeston Sink—*basin* ... MO-7
Harbet Airp—*airport* ... MO-7
Harbin—*locale* ... GA-3
Harbin—*locale* ... TX-5
**Harbin**—*pop pl* ... TN-4
Harbin Artesian Well—*well* ... TX-5
Harbin Branch—*stream* (2) ... TN-4
*Harbin Community* ... TX-5
Harbin Creek—*stream* ... CA-9
Harbin Creek—*stream* ... IN-6
Harbin Creek—*stream* ... SC-3
**Harbine**—*pop pl* ... KS-7
**Harbine**—*pop pl* ... NE-7
Harbine Cem—*cemetery* ... NE-7
**Harbinger**—*pop pl* ... NC-3
Harbin Hollow—*valley* ... TN-4
Harbin Lake—*lake* ... MT-8
Harbin Mtn—*summit* ... CA-9
Harbin Pit—*cave* ... AL-4
Harbin Rsvr—*reservoir* ... TX-5
**Harbins**—*pop pl* ... GA-3
Harbins Landing—*locale* ... MS-4
Harbin Spring—*spring* ... TN-4
**Harbin Springs**—*pop pl* ... CA-9
**Harbin Springs Annex**—*pop pl* ... CA-9
**Harbinwood Estates**—*pop pl* ... FL-3
*Harbison* ... TN-4
**Harbison**—*pop pl* ... PA-2
**Harbison**—*pop pl* ... TN-4
Harbison Branch—*stream* ... VA-3
**Harbison Canyon**—*pop pl* ... CA-9
Harbison Canyon—*valley* ... CA-9
Harbison Cem—*cemetery* ... IN-6
Harbison College President's Home—*hist pl* ... SC-3
**Harbison Crossroads**—*pop pl* ... TN-4
Harbison Ditch—*canal* ... CO-8
Harbison Gulch—*valley* ... WA-9
Harbison Hills—*range* ... IN-6
Harbison House—*hist pl* ... KY-4
Harbison Institute—*school* ... SC-3
Harbison Sch—*school* ... CA-9
Harbison Sch (abandoned)—*school* ... MO-7
*Harbisons Crossroads* ... TN-4
Harbisons Pond—*reservoir* ... AL-4
Harbisons Pond Dam—*dam* ... AL-4
Harbison Spring—*spring* ... OR-9
Harbison Tank—*reservoir* ... AZ-5
**Harbison (Township of)**—*pop pl* ... IN-6
Harble Ridge—*ridge* ... OH-6
Harbnson Bridge—*bridge* ... TN-4
*Harboaton* ... VA-3
Harbolds Sch—*school* ... PA-2
Harbon Cove—*valley* ... NC-3
*Harbon School* ... MS-4
*Harbor* ... IN-6
*Harbor* ... ME-1
*Harbor* ... NC-3
**Harbor**—*pop pl* ... CA-9
**Harbor**—*pop pl* ... NY-2
**Harbor**—*pop pl* ... OH-6
**Harbor**—*pop pl* ... OR-9
**Harbor**—*pop pl* ... PA-2
Harbor—*uninc pl* ... WI-6
*Harbor, The* ... MA-1
*Harbor, The* ... RI-1
**Harbor, The**—*pop pl* ... AK-9
Harbor Acres—*uninc pl* ... NY-2
*Harbor Acres Lake* ... PA-2
Harbor Bar—*bar* ... MA-1
Harbor Basin—*harbor* ... MI-6
Harbor Basin—*harbor* ... PA-2
Harbor Bay—*bay* ... TX-5
**Harbor Beach**—*pop pl* ... FL-3
**Harbor Beach**—*pop pl* ... MA-1
**Harbor Beach**—*pop pl* ... MI-6
Harbor Beach Lighthouse—*hist pl* ... MI-6
Harbor Beach Plaza (Shop Ctr)—*locale* ... FL-3
Harbor Bluff—*cape* ... MA-1
**Harbor Bluffs**—*pop pl* ... FL-3
Harbor Bluffs Center (Shop Ctr)—*locale* ... FL-3
**Harbor Branch Junction**—*pop pl* ... NJ-2
Harbor Bridge—*locale* ... PA-2
Harbor Brook—*stream* ... CT-1
Harbor Brook—*stream* ... NY-2
Harbor Canal—*canal* ... NJ-2
Harbor (CCD)—*cens area* ... OR-9
Harbor Cem—*cemetery* ... ME-1
Harbor Cem—*cemetery* ... MS-4
Harbor Cem—*cemetery* ... TN-4
**Harbor Center**—*pop pl* ... WA-9
Harbor Centre (Shop Ctr)—*locale* ... FL-3
Harbor Ch—*church* ... SC-3
Harbor Channel—*channel* ... CA-9
Harbor Channel—*channel* ... FL-3
Harbor Channel—*channel* ... NC-3
Harbor Channel—*channel* ... TN-4
Harbor Chapel Sch (historical)—*school* ... TN-4
Harbor Church Cem—*cemetery* ... PA-2
**Harbor City**—*pop pl* ... CA-9
Harbor City Christian Sch—*school* ... CA-9
Harbor City Elem Sch—*school* ... FL-3
Harbor City Sch—*school* ... CA-9
Harbor Cove—*bay* ... MD-2
Harbor Cove—*cove* ... MA-1
*Harbor Creek* ... PA-2
Harbor Creek—*bay* ... NC-3
**Harborcreek**—*pop pl* ... PA-2
Harborcreek Junior-Senior HS—*school* ... PA-2
Harborcreek Mall—*locale* ... PA-2
Harbor Creek (RR name for Harborcreek)—*other* ... PA-2
**Harborcreek (RR name Harbor Creek)**—*pop pl* ... PA-2
Harborcreek Sch For Boys—*school* ... PA-2
**Harborcreek (Township of)**—*pop pl* ... PA-2
Harbor Crest Shop Ctr—*locale* ... FL-3
**Harbord**—*pop pl* ... CO-8
Harbordale Arroyo—*stream* ... CO-8
Harbordale Pond—*reservoir* ... CO-8
Harbordale Sch—*school* ... FL-3
**Harbor Dell**—*pop pl* ... IL-6
Harbord Field Airp—*airport* ... WA-9
**Harbor East**—*pop pl* ... FL-3
**Harbor Estates**—*pop pl* ... IL-6
Harborfields HS—*school* ... NY-2
Harbor Grace—*bay* ... ME-1
**Harbor Green**—*pop pl* ... NY-2
**Harbor Grove**—*pop pl* ... TX-5
Harbor Gut—*gut* ... VA-3
Harbor Hall Sch—*school* ... PA-2
Harbor Hat Point—*cape* ... AK-9
*Harbor Haven* ... MI-6
Harbor Head—*lake* ... MA-1
Harbor Heights—*locale* (2) ... WA-9
**Harbor Heights**—*pop pl* ... FL-3
**Harbor Heights**—*pop pl* ... TN-4
**Harbor Heights Park**—*pop pl* ... NY-2
Harbor Heights Sch—*school* ... WA-9
**Harbor Heights Subdivision**—*pop pl* ... UT-8
Harbor Highlands Ski Club—*other* ... MI-6
Harbor Hill—*summit* (2) ... NY-2
Harbor Hill—*summit* ... RI-1
*Harbor Hills* ... MI-6
**Harbor Hills**—*pop pl* ... CA-9
**Harbor Hills**—*pop pl* ... NY-2
**Harbor Hills**—*pop pl* ... OH-6
**Harbor Hills**—*pop pl* ... TN-4
Harbor Hills—*range* ... OH-6
Harbor Hills Country Club—*other* ... NY-2
Harbor (historical), The—*locale* ... NC-3
Harbor HS—*school* ... CA-9
*Harbor Island* ... MI-6
*Harbor Island* ... MN-6
*Harbor Island* ... TN-4
Harbor Island—*island* (3) ... AK-9
Harbor Island—*island* (2) ... CA-9
Harbor Island—*island* (2) ... FL-3
Harbor Island—*island* ... ID-8
Harbor Island—*island* (7) ... ME-1
Harbor Island—*island* (2) ... MI-6
Harbor Island—*island* ... MN-6
Harbor Island—*island* ... NJ-2
Harbor Island—*island* ... NY-2
Harbor Island—*island* (2) ... NC-3
Harbor Island—*island* ... SC-3
Harbor Island—*island* (2) ... TX-5
Harbor Island—*island* ... WA-9
Harbor Island—*uninc pl* ... CA-9
Harbor Island—*uninc pl* ... NC-3
*Harbor Island East Basin* ... CA-9
Harbor Island Ledge—*bar* ... ME-1
Harbor Island Park—*park* ... NY-2
Harbor Island Point—*cape* ... ME-1
Harbor Island Reach—*channel* ... CA-9
Harbor Island Reef—*bar* ... MI-6
Harbor Island Rock—*bar* ... ME-1
Harbor Islands—*island* ... NY-2
*Harbor Island West Basin* ... CA-9
**Harbor Isle**—*pop pl* ... NY-2
*Harbor Junction (Harbor Junction Wharf)* ... RI-1
*Harbor Junction Wharf* ... RI-1
Harbor Key—*island* ... FL-3
Harbor Key Bank—*bar* ... FL-3
Harbor Lake—*lake* ... CA-9
Harbor Lake—*lake* ... FL-3
Harbor Lake—*lake* ... ID-8
Harbor Lake—*lake* ... MN-6
Harbor Lake—*lake* ... WA-9
Harbor Ledge—*bar* (2) ... ME-1
Harbor Ledge—*rock* ... MA-1
Harbor Ledges—*bar* ... ME-1
Harborlight Mall (Shop Ctr)—*locale* ... MA-1
Harbor Lights Boat Dock—*locale* ... TN-4
Harbor Mills Sch (historical)—*school* ... PA-2
*Harbor Mtn* ... PA-2
Harbor Mtn—*summit* ... PA-2
Harbor Neck—*cape* ... RI-1
Harboro—*locale* ... CO-8
**Harbor Oaks**—*pop pl* ... FL-3
Harbor Oaks Residential District—*hist pl* ... FL-3
*Harbor of Refuge* ... MI-6
Harbor of Refuge—*bay* ... DE-2
Harbor of Refuge—*bay* ... MI-6
*Harbor of Saint James* ... MI-6
*Harbor of Saipan* ... MH-9
**Harbor Palms**—*pop pl* ... FL-3
*Harbor Park* ... MI-6
Harbor Park—*park* ... CA-9
Harbor Plaza (Shop Ctr)—*locale* ... FL-3
Harbor Point—*cape* (4) ... AK-9
Harbor Point—*cape* ... FL-3
Harbor Point—*cape* ... ME-1
Harbor Point—*cape* ... MD-2
Harbor Point—*cape* ... MI-6
Harbor Point—*cape* ... VI-3
**Harbor Point**—*pop pl* ... FL-3
**Harbor Point**—*pop pl* ... MI-6
*Harbor Pond* ... NY-2
Harbor Pond—*bay* ... RI-1
Harbor Pond—*reservoir* ... MA-1
Harbor Rest Memorial Park (Cemetery)—*park* ... CA-9
Harbor Ridge—*summit* ... AK-9
Harbor Ridge Ch—*church* ... PA-2
Harbor River—*stream* (2) ... SC-3
Harbor Road Hist Dist—*hist pl* ... NY-2
Harbor Road Park—*park* ... IA-7
Harbor Road Sch—*school* ... IA-7
Harbor Road Sch—*school* ... NY-2
Harbor Rock—*bar* (2) ... WA-9
Harbor Rock—*rock* ... MA-1
*Harbor (RR name Ashtabula Harbor)* ... OH-6
Harbor Run—*stream* ... PA-2
Harbor Sch—*school* ... CA-9
Harbor Sch—*school* ... MS-4
Harbor Sch—*school* ... NY-2
Harbor Sch (historical)—*school* ... MO-7
Harbor Sch (historical)—*school* ... TN-4
Harbor Shop Ctr—*locale* ... CA-9
Harbor Shores—*locale* ... FL-3
**Harbor Side**—*pop pl* ... CA-9
**Harborside**—*pop pl* ... ME-1
Harborside Hosp—*hospital* ... FL-3
Harborside Sch—*school* ... CA-9
Harbor Springs—*locale* ... WI-6
**Harbor Springs**—*pop pl* ... MI-6
Harbor Square Hist Dist—*hist pl* ... MS-4
Harbor Square Park—*park* ... MS-4
Harbor Square (Shop Ctr)—*locale* ... FL-3
Harbor Street Sch—*school* ... CT-1
Harborth Hill—*summit* ... TX-5
**Harborton**—*pop pl* ... OR-9
**Harborton**—*pop pl* ... VA-3
*Harbortown* ... NJ-2
Harbor Track—*uninc pl* ... OR-9
Harbor Tunnel—*tunnel* ... MD-2
Harbor Turning Basin—*harbor* ... PA-2
*Harborview* ... CT-1
Harbor View—*hospital* ... FL-3
**Harborview**—*pop pl* ... CT-1
**Harbor View**—*pop pl* ... CT-1
**Harbor View**—*pop pl* (3) ... FL-3
**Harborview**—*pop pl* (2) ... MD-2
**Harbor View**—*pop pl* ... MD-2
**Harbor View**—*pop pl* ... MA-1
**Harbor View**—*pop pl* ... MI-6
**Harbor View**—*pop pl* ... OH-6
**Harbor View**—*pop pl* ... TN-4
**Harbor View**—*pop pl* ... VA-3
Harborview—*uninc pl* ... FL-3
Harbor View Cem—*cemetery* ... MA-1
Harborview Hosp—*hospital* ... WA-9
Harborview Med Ctr Heliport—*airport* ... WA-9
Harbor View Memorial Park—*cemetery* ... CA-9
Harbor View Sch—*school* (2) ... CA-9
Harbor View Sch—*school* ... FL-3
**Harbor Village**—*pop pl* ... FL-3
**Harbor Woods**—*pop pl* ... PA-2
**Harbour**—*pop pl* ... TN-4
Harbour Bay Plaza (Shop Ctr)—*locale* ... FL-3
*Harbour Cem* ... TN-4
Harbour Cem—*cemetery* ... AL-4
Harbour Cem—*cemetery* ... IA-7
Harbour Cem—*cemetery* (2) ... OH-6
Harbour Cem—*cemetery* ... TN-4
*Harbour Creek* ... PA-2
**Harbour Heights**—*pop pl* ... FL-3
Harbour Homes—*uninc pl* ... VA-3
Harbour Island—*island* ... FL-3
Harbour Island—*island* ... RI-1
Harbour Island—*island* ... TN-4
Harbour-Longmire Bldg—*hist pl* ... OK-5
Harbour Mall—*locale* ... MA-1
Harbour Post Office (historical)—*building* ... TN-4
*Harbour School* ... TN-4
Harbour Spring—*spring* ... AL-4
Harbourton—*locale* ... NJ-2
Harbourton Hist Dist—*hist pl* ... NJ-2
Harbour Town—*post sta* ... SC-3
**Harbourview (subdivision)**—*pop pl* ... MS-4
**Harbour Woods**—*pop pl* ... TN-4
*Har Brack High School* ... PA-2
Har Brac Trail—*trail* ... PA-2
Harbridge Run—*stream* ... PA-2
Harbstreit Hill—*summit* ... IN-6
Harbuck—*locale* ... TN-4
Harbuck Branch—*stream* ... TX-5
Harbuck Creek—*stream* ... AL-4
Harbucks Chapel—*church* ... TX-5
Harchenko Field—*airport* ... ND-7
Harchenko Indusdrial Airfield—*airport* ... OR-9
Harcklerodes Towhead—*island* ... AR-4
Harck Sch—*school* ... IL-6
**Harco**—*pop pl* ... GA-3
**Harco**—*pop pl* (2) ... IL-6
**Harco**—*pop pl* ... SC-3
Harcourt—*locale* ... KY-4
**Harcourt**—*pop pl* ... IA-7
Harcourt Elem Sch—*school* ... IN-6
Harcourt Lake—*lake* ... MI-6
Harcourt Sch—*school* ... MI-6
Harcourt Swamp—*swamp* ... MI-6
**Harcrow (Draper)**—*pop pl* ... KY-4
Harcrow Lake—*lake* ... TX-5
Harcum—*locale* ... VA-3
Harcum Creek—*stream* ... MD-2
Harcum Junior Coll—*school* ... PA-2
Harcums Wharf—*locale* ... MD-2
**Harcuvar**—*pop pl* (2) ... AZ-5
*Harcuvar Mountains* ... AZ-5
Harcuvar Mountains—*range* (2) ... AZ-5
Harcuvar Peak—*summit* ... AZ-5
Harcuvar RR Station—*building* ... AZ-5
Harcuvar Tank—*reservoir* ... AZ-5
Hard—*locale* ... OH-6
Hard, Zera, House—*hist pl* ... VT-1
Hardage—*locale* ... MO-7
Hardage Creek—*stream* ... AK-9
Hardage Creek—*stream* ... TX-5
Hardage Ford Creek—*stream* ... GA-3
*Hardage School* ... MS-4
Hardaman Lake—*lake* ... TX-5
Hardamon Cem—*cemetery* ... LA-4
Hardanger Cem—*cemetery* ... MN-6
**Hardaway**—*pop pl* ... AL-4
**Hardaway**—*pop pl* ... FL-3
Hardaway Baptist Ch—*church* ... AL-4
Hardaway Branch—*stream* ... TN-4
Hardaway Cem—*cemetery* ... AL-4
Hardaway Cem—*cemetery* (2) ... MS-4
Hardaway Ch—*church* ... AL-4
Hardaway Ch—*church* ... MS-4
Hardaway Draw—*valley* ... CO-8
Hardaway Pond—*lake* ... MS-4
Hardaway Post Office—*building* ... AL-4
Hardaway Sch—*school* ... MS-4
Hardaway Site (31ST4)—*hist pl* ... NC-3
Hardaway Street Ch of God—*church* ... AL-4
Hard Bargain—*hist pl* ... VA-3
*Hard Bargain Branch* ... NC-3
Hard Bargain Cem—*cemetery* ... AL-4
Hard Boil Bar—*bar* ... ID-8
Hard Bottom Tank—*reservoir* ... NM-5
Hard Branch—*stream* ... KY-4
*Hardbrick Hill* ... MA-1
*Hard Burgain* ... NC-3
Hardburgain Branch—*stream* ... NC-3
**Hardburly**—*pop pl* ... KY-4
Hard Butte—*summit* ... ID-8
Hard Butte Lake—*lake* ... ID-8
Hardcamp Run—*stream* ... WV-2
Hardcamp Sch—*school* ... WV-2
Hard Cash—*locale* ... GA-3
Hard Cash—*locale* ... MS-4
Hard Cash Cutoff—*bend* ... MS-4
Hardcash Gulch—*valley* ... CA-9
Hard Cash Lake—*lake* ... MS-4
Hardcash Mine—*mine* ... MT-8
*Hard Cash Plantation* ... MS-4
Hardcastle—*locale* ... KY-4
Hardcastle Canyon—*valley* (2) ... NM-5
Hardcastle Cem—*cemetery* ... AR-4
Hardcastle Creek—*stream* ... TN-4
Hard Cem—*cemetery* ... KY-4
Hard Climb Mine—*mine* ... CA-9
Hard Corner—*locale* ... VA-3
Hard Creek—*stream* (2) ... ID-8
Hard Creek—*stream* (2) ... WA-9
Hard Creek Basin—*basin* ... ID-8
Hard Creek Guard Station—*locale* ... ID-8
Hard Creek Lake—*lake* ... ID-8
Hard Creek Meadow—*flat* ... ID-8
*Hardee* ... NC-3
**Hardee**—*pop pl* ... MS-4
**Hardee Acres (subdivision)**—*pop pl* ... NC-3
Hardee Cabins—*locale* ... WY-8
Hardee Cem—*cemetery* ... FL-3
Hardee Cem—*cemetery* (2) ... NC-3
Hardee Cem—*cemetery* ... SC-3
**Hardee County**—*pop pl* ... FL-3
Hardee County Community Education Center—*school* ... FL-3
**Hardee Cross Roads**—*pop pl* ... NC-3
**Hardee Heights (subdivision)**—*pop pl* ... NC-3
Hardee JHS—*school* ... FL-3
Hardee Lake—*lake* ... MS-4
Hardee (Magisterial District)—*fmr MCD* ... WV-2
Hardee Memorial Hosp—*hospital* ... FL-3
Hardee Mill Branch—*stream* ... NC-3
**Hardees**—*pop pl* ... FL-3
*Hardees Cross Road* ... NC-3
**Hardees Cross Road**—*pop pl* ... NC-3
Hardee Senior HS—*school* ... FL-3
Hardees Pond—*reservoir* ... NC-3
Hardees Pond Dam—*dam* ... NC-3
Hardees RR Station—*locale* ... FL-3
Hardee Swamp—*swamp* ... GA-3
**Hardeetown (subdivision)**—*pop pl* ... FL-3
**Hardeeville**—*pop pl* ... SC-3
Hardeeville (CCD)—*cens area* ... SC-3
Hardegree Cem—*cemetery* ... GA-3
Hardell Creek—*stream* ... WI-6
Hardeman—*locale* ... MO-7
Hardeman, Franklin, House—*hist pl* ... TN-4
Hardeman, Lake—*reservoir* ... TN-4
Hardeman Bend—*bend* ... TX-5
Hardeman Branch—*stream* ... TX-5
Hardeman Cem—*cemetery* ... MS-4
Hardeman Cem—*cemetery* ... TN-4
**Hardeman County**—*pop pl* ... TN-4
**Hardeman (County)**—*pop pl* ... TX-5
Hardeman county Courthouse—*building* ... TN-4
Hardeman County Golf Course—*locale* ... TN-4
Hardeman County Library—*building* ... TN-4
Hardeman Creek—*stream* ... GA-3
Hardeman Slough—*stream* ... TX-5
Hardemen Cem—*cemetery* ... IA-7
*Harden* ... OK-5
Hardenbergh Lake—*reservoir* ... AL-4
Hardenbergh Mine—*mine* ... CA-9
Harden Branch—*stream* (2) ... MS-4
Harden Branch—*stream* ... SC-3
Harden Branch—*stream* ... TX-5
Harden Bridge—*bridge* ... GA-3
Hardenbrook Creek—*stream* ... OR-9
Hardenbrook Dam—*dam* ... NE-7
Hardenbrook Playground—*locale* ... MI-6
Hardenburg—*locale* ... NY-2
Hardenburg Bay—*bay* ... AK-9
*Hardenburgh* ... IN-6
Hardenburgh Falls—*falls* ... NY-2
**Hardenburgh (Town of)**—*pop pl* ... NY-2
Harden Cem—*cemetery* ... AL-4
Harden Cem—*cemetery* ... GA-3
Harden Cem—*cemetery* (2) ... MS-4
Harden Cem—*cemetery* ... WV-2
Harden Chapel—*church* ... GA-3
Harden Cienega—*locale* ... NM-5
Harden Cienega Creek—*stream* ... AZ-5
Harden Cienega Creek—*stream* ... NM-5
**Harden City**—*pop pl* ... OK-5
Harden Creek—*stream* ... FL-3
Harden Creek—*stream* (2) ... GA-3
Harden Creek—*stream* ... WY-8
**Harden Flat**—*pop pl* ... CA-9
*Harden Hill* ... MA-1
Harden Hill—*summit* ... WA-9
Harden Hollow—*valley* ... AL-4
Harden Hollow—*valley* ... IN-6
Harden Hollow—*valley* ... TN-4
Harden Lake—*lake* ... CA-9
Hardens—*hist pl* ... VA-3
Hardens Bluff—*cliff* ... VA-3
Harden Sch—*school* ... WV-2
Hardens Chapel—*church* ... GA-3
Hardens Dead River—*gut* ... SC-3
*Hardens Graveyard* ... TN-4
Hardens Hill Cem—*cemetery* ... VA-3
Hardens Pond—*reservoir* ... AL-4
Hardens Pond (historical)—*reservoir* ... NC-3
*Hardentown* (2) ... IN-6
*Harden Valley* ... TN-4
*Harden Valley School* ... TN-4
**Hardenville**—*pop pl* ... MO-7
Harder—*locale* ... WA-9
Harder Cem—*cemetery* ... KS-7
Harder Cem—*cemetery* (2) ... NY-2
Harder Cem—*cemetery* (3) ... TN-4
Harder Creek—*stream* ... WI-6
Harder Drain—*stream* ... MI-6
Harder Hollow—*valley* ... TN-4
Harder Lake—*lake* ... MI-6
Harder Lake—*lake* ... MN-6
Harder Ranch—*locale* ... WA-9
Harder Ranch Airp—*airport* ... WA-9
Harder Sch—*school* ... CA-9
Harder Sch—*school* ... NY-2
Harderwyk Ch—*church* ... MI-6
Hardes Hollow—*valley* ... PA-2
Hard Estate-West Sayville County Park—*park* ... NY-2
Hardester Hollow—*valley* ... MO-7
*Hardesty* ... VA-3
Hardesty—*locale* ... KY-4
**Hardesty**—*pop pl* ... OK-5
**Hardesty**—*pop pl* ... VA-3
Hardesty, Ralph, Stone House—*hist pl* ... OH-6
Hardesty Branch—*stream* ... MO-7
Hardesty Canyon—*valley* ... NM-5
Hardesty Cem—*cemetery* ... OH-6
Hardesty Cem—*cemetery* ... OK-5
Hardesty Coulee—*valley* ... WA-9
Hardesty Creek—*stream* ... NV-8
Hardesty Creek—*stream* ... UT-8
Hardesty Draw—*valley* ... CO-8
Hardesty Homestead Mine—*mine* ... SD-7
Hardesty Lake—*lake* ... FL-3
Hardesty Mesa—*summit* ... CO-8
Hardesty Mesa—*summit* ... NM-5
Hardesty Mtn—*summit* ... OR-9
Hardesty Park—*park* ... OH-6
Hardesty Peak—*summit* ... SD-7
Hardesty Ranch—*locale* ... CO-8
Hardesty Ranch—*locale* ... OR-9
Hardesty Rsvr—*reservoir* ... CO-8
Hardesty Sch—*school* ... MO-7
Hardestys Cove—*bay* ... MD-2
Hardesty Trail—*trail* ... OR-9
Hardesty Way—*trail* ... OR-9
Hardesty Well—*locale* ... NM-5

Hard Fish Creek—stream KS-7
Hard Fork—stream KY-4
Hard Fortune Creek—stream GA-3
Hardge Island TN-4
Hardgrave Ranch—locale (2) TX-5
Hardgraves Cem—cemetery (2) AR-4
Hard Ground Canyon—valley NM-5
Hard Ground Flats—flat NM-5
Hardgrove Cem—cemetery MO-7
Hardgrove Creek—stream MT-8
Hardgrove Rim—cliff CO-8
Hardhack Hill—summit NY-2
Hardhack Ridge—ridge NY-2
Hardhead Hill—summit NH-1
Hardhead Island—island ME-1
Hardhead Water Spring—spring UT-8
Hardie, Harrison, House—hist pl WI-6
Hardies Ch—church WI-6
Hardies Creek—stream WI-6
Hardies Creek State Forest—park WI-6
Hardies Grove Ch—church NC-3
Hardies Lake—reservoir PA-2
Hardigan Hill—summit VT-1
Hardigan Lake—lake WY-8
Hardigan Pond—lake NY-2
Hardig Brook—stream RI-1
Hardigree Cem—cemetery (2) GA-3
Hardikner Creek—stream TX-5
Hardilee (historical)—locale KS-7
Hardiman Branch—stream AL-4
Hardiman Cem—cemetery AL-4
Hardiman Cem—cemetery MS-4
Hardiman Chapel—church MS-4
Hardiman Spring—spring ID-8
Hardimui AZ-5
Hardin NC-3
Hardin—locale CO-8
Hardin—locale NC-3
**Hardin**—pop pl AR-4
**Hardin**—pop pl IL-6
**Hardin**—pop pl IA-7
**Hardin**—pop pl KY-4
**Hardin**—pop pl MO-7
**Hardin**—pop pl MT-8
**Hardin**—pop pl (2) OH-6
**Hardin**—pop pl (2) TX-5
Hardin Airp—airport IN-6
Hardin Barn Landing—locale TN-4
Hardin-Baylor Coll—school TX-5
Hardin Beauty Ch—church TN-4
Hardin Beauty Sch (historical)—school TN-4
Hardin-Bennett Cem—cemetery TN-4
Hardin Bottom—bend KY-4
Hardin Bottom—bend TN-4
Hardin Branch—stream AL-4
Hardin Branch—stream KY-4
Hardin Branch—stream (5) TN-4
Hardin Branch—stream (2) TX-5
Hardin Branch—stream VA-3
Hardin Bridge—bridge AL-4
Hardin Bridge—bridge NE-7
Hardin Brook—stream NY-2
Hardin Butte—summit CA-9
Hardin Canal—canal GA-3
Hardin Cem—cemetery AL-4
Hardin Cem—cemetery (5) AR-4
Hardin Cem—cemetery (2) IN-6
Hardin Cem—cemetery (3) IA-7
Hardin Cem—cemetery (3) KY-4
Hardin Cem—cemetery (2) MO-7
Hardin Cem—cemetery NC-3
Hardin Cem—cemetery SC-3
Hardin Cem—cemetery (8) TN-4
Hardin Ch—church IA-7
Hardin Ch—church TX-5
Hardin Chapel—church (2) TN-4
Hardin Chapel Cem—cemetery MS-4
Hardin Chapel United Methodist Ch TN-4
Hardin City—locale NV-8
Hardin City Bridge—bridge IA-7
Hardin Company Dock—locale TN-4
**Hardin (County)**—pop pl IL-6
**Hardin (County)**—pop pl KY-4
**Hardin (County)**—pop pl OH-6
**Hardin County**—pop pl TN-4
**Hardin (County)**—pop pl TX-5
Hardin County Courthouse—hist pl IA-7
Hardin County Courthouse—hist pl OH-6
Hardin County General Hosp—hospital TN-4
Hardin County Health Care
Center—hospital IA-7
Hardin County Home—building IA-7
Hardin County Home Cem—cemetery IA-7
Hardin County Memory
Gardens—cemetery TN-4
Hardin Creek AL-4
Hardin Creek IN-6
Hardin Creek KY-4
Hardin Creek—stream CA-9
Hardin Creek—stream GA-3
Hardin Creek—stream IA-7
Hardin Creek—stream MS-4
Hardin Creek—stream MO-7
Hardin Creek—stream (2) OH-6
Hardin Creek—stream (2) TN-4
Hardin Creek—stream TX-5
Hardin Creek—stream WY-8
Hardin Creek Ch—church OH-6
Hardin Cut-Off (1942)—channel AR-4
Hardin Dam AL-4
Hardin Dam—dam AL-4
Hardin Ditch IN-6
Hardin Ditch—canal IL-6
Hardin Ditch—canal IN-6
Hardin (Election Precinct)—fmr MCD IL-6
**Hardin Estates**—pop pl TN-4
Hardin Field Airp—airport MO-7
Hardin Flat CA-9
Hardin Ford—locale (2) TN-4
Harding—locale GA-3
Harding—locale KY-4
Harding—locale NJ-2
Harding—locale ND-7
Harding—locale SD-7
Harding—locale UT-8
**Harding**—pop pl GA-3
**Harding**—pop pl IL-6
**Harding**—pop pl KS-7
**Harding**—pop pl ME-1
**Harding**—pop pl MA-1
**Harding**—pop pl MN-6
**Harding**—pop pl OH-6
**Harding**—pop pl PA-2
**Harding**—pop pl WV-2
Harding, Benjamin, House—hist pl KS-7
Harding, Benjamin F., House—hist pl OR-9
Harding, Chester, House—hist pl MA-1
Harding, Lake—lake MN-6
Harding, Lake—reservoir AL-4
Harding, Lake—reservoir GA-3
Harding, Mount—summit (2) AK-9
Harding, Mount—summit MT-8
Harding, P. M., House—hist pl MS-4
Harding, Sarah H., House—hist pl MA-1
Harding, Warren G., House—hist pl OH-6
Harding, Warren G., JHS—hist pl PA-2
Harding Acad—school CA-9
Harding Acad—school (2) TN-4
Harding and Miller Music
Company—hist pl IN-6
Harding Ave Sch—school NY-2
Harding Beach—beach MA-1
Harding Beach Point—cape MA-1
Harding Bottoms—swamp AL-4
Harding Bridge—bridge FL-3
Harding Brook RI-1
Harding Brook—stream (2) ME-1
Harding Brook Ridge—ridge ME-1
Harding Butte—summit OR-9
Harding Canyon—valley CA-9
Harding Cem—cemetery GA-3
Harding Cem—cemetery IL-6
Harding Cem—cemetery IN-6
Harding Cem—cemetery (2) KY-4
Harding Cem—cemetery (2) ME-1
Harding Cem—cemetery OH-6
Harding Cem—cemetery PA-2
Harding Coll—school AR-4
Harding Coll—school TN-4
Harding Corners—locale PA-2
Harding County—civil SD-7
**Harding (County)**—pop pl NM-5
Harding County Airp—airport SD-7
Harding County Courthouse—hist pl NM-5
Harding Cove—bay ME-1
Harding Creek—stream AR-4
Harding Creek—stream (2) MI-6
Harding Creek—stream MO-7
Harding Creek—stream SD-7
Harding Creek—stream TN-4
**Harding Crossing**—pop pl NY-2
Harding Ditch—canal IL-6
Harding Ditch—canal IN-6
Harding Drain—canal MI-6
Harding Drain—stream AR-4
Harding Elem Sch—school PA-2
Hardinger Draw—valley UT-8
**Harding Estates**—pop pl MA-1
Harding Flats—flat IN-6
Harding Gateway—channel AK-9
Harding Golf Course—other CA-9
Harding Grove Sch—school SD-7
Harding Gulch—valley WY-8
Harding Heights OH-6
Harding Hill—summit (2) ME-1
Harding Hill—summit MA-1
Harding (historical)—locale SD-7
Harding Hole—bend CO-8
Harding Hole Overlook—cliff CO-8
Harding Hollow—valley WY-8
Harding House-Walker Missionary
Home—hist pl MA-1
Harding HS—school CT-1
Harding HS—school MN-6
Harding HS—school NC-3
Harding HS—school (3) OH-6
Harding Ice Field—glacier AK-9
Harding Island—island NY-2
Harding JHS—school (2) IA-7
Harding JHS—school (3) OH-6
Harding JHS—school OK-5
Harding JHS—school PA-2
Harding-Jones Paper Company
District—hist pl OH-6
Harding Lake—CDP AK-9
Harding Lake—lake AK-9
Harding Lake—lake (2) MI-6
Harding Lake—lake MN-6
Harding Lake—reservoir TX-5
**Harding Lakes**—pop pl NJ-2
Harding Lake State Rec Area—park AK-9
Harding Lateral—canal UT-8
Harding Ledge—bar ME-1
Harding Ledge—bar MA-1
Harding Memorial Park—cemetery OH-6
Harding Mine—mine NM-5
Harding Mtn—summit WA-9
Harding Museum—building IL-6
Harding Museum—building OH-6
Harding Park—park CA-9
Harding Park—park IN-6
Harding Park—park MI-6
Harding Park—park OH-6
Harding Park (historical)—park FL-3
Harding Peak—summit SD-7
Harding Point—cape AK-9
Harding Point—cliff AZ-5
Harding Point—summit CA-9
Harding Pond—lake PA-2
Harding Pond—reservoir IN-6
Harding Pond—swamp KY-4
Harding Ranch—locale NM-5
Harding Ridge—ridge AR-4
Harding River—stream AK-9
Harding Rock—bar CA-9
**Hardingrove**—pop pl IN-6
Hardingrove (historical)—locale SD-7
Harding RR Car—hist pl AK-9
Hardings—locale VA-3
**Hardings**—pop pl ME-1
Hardings Bayou—stream MS-4
Hardings Beach MA-1
Harding Sch PA-2
Harding Sch—school AZ-5
Harding Sch—school (6) CA-9
Harding Sch—school IA-7
Harding Sch—school LA-4
Harding Sch—school (2) ME-1
Harding Sch—school (3) MI-6
Harding Sch—school MN-6
Harding Sch—school NE-7
Harding Sch—school NJ-2
Harding Sch—school (2) OH-6
Harding Sch—school OR-9
Harding Sch—school (3) PA-2
Harding Sch—school SD-7
Harding Sch No 70—school NE-7
Harding School IN-6
Hardings Ledge MA-1
Harding Slough—gut KY-4
Harding Spring—spring AL-4
Harding Spring—spring AZ-5
Harding Spring—spring CA-9
Harding Spring Pond—reservoir MD-2
Hardings Run—stream PA-2
Harding Street Sch—school MA-1
Harding Swamp—stream NC-3
Harding Tomb—hist pl OH-6
**Harding (Town of)**—pop pl WI-6
**Harding Township**—pop pl (2) ND-7
Harding Township (historical)—civil (2) SD-7
**Harding (Township of)**—pop pl NJ-2
**Harding (Township of)**—pop pl OH-6
Harding Truck Trail—trail CA-9
Hardingville—locale NJ-2
Harding-Winter Street Manufacturing
District—hist pl MA-1
**Hardin Heights**—pop pl FL-3
Hardin Hill—summit AR-4
Hardin Hill—summit MA-1
Hardin Hills—summit TX-5
**Hardin (historical)**—pop pl OR-9
Hardin Hole Ridge—ridge CA-9
Hardin Hole Spring—spring CA-9
Hardin Hollow—valley KY-4
Hardin Hollow—valley PA-2
Hardin Hollow—valley (3) TN-4
Hardin Island—island VA-3
Hardin Junior High School AL-4
Hardin Knob—summit KY-4
Hardin Lake CA-9
Hardin Lake—lake GA-3
Hardin Lake—lake TX-5
Hardin Lake—lake WI-6
Hardin Lake—reservoir AL-4
Hardin Lake—reservoir AR-4
Hardin Lake—reservoir NC-3
Hardin Lake Dam—dam MS-4
Hardin Lake Dam—dam NC-3
Hardin Landing—locale TN-4
Hardin Landing Strip MS-4
Hardin Mine—mine TN-4
Hardin Mtn—summit CA-9
Hardin Northern Sch—school OH-6
Hardin Oil Field—oilfield TX-5
Hardin Park Elem Sch—school NC-3
Hardin Point—cape AR-4
Hardin Point Lodge—locale AR-4
Hardin Properties Mine—mine SD-7
Hardin Prospect—mine TN-4
Hardin Ranch—locale NM-5
Hardin Ranch—locale TX-5
Hardin Ranch—locale WY-8
Hardin Reynolds Memorial Sch—school VA-3
Hardin Ridge—ridge CA-9
Hardin Ridge—ridge IN-6
Hardin Ridge Rec Area—park IN-6
Hardin Rsvr—reservoir CA-9
Hardin Rsvr—reservoir CO-8
Hardin Run—stream WV-2
Hardin-Russell Creek TX-5
Hardin Russell Creek—stream TX-5
Hardin-Rye (CCD)—cens area TX-5
**Hardins**—pop pl NC-3
Hardins Bluff VA-3
**Hardinsburg**—pop pl (2) IN-6
**Hardinsburg**—pop pl KY-4
Hardinsburg (CCD)—cens area KY-4
Hardinsburgh IN-6
Hardins Ch—church MS-4
Hardin Sch—school AL-4
Hardin Sch—school CA-9
Hardin Sch—school IL-6
Hardin Sch—school LA-4
Hardin Sch—school MO-7
Hardin Sch—school OH-6
Hardin Sch—school (3) TX-5
Hardins Chapel AL-4
Hardins Chapel—church KY-4
Hardin Sch (historical)—school TN-4
Hardin School (historical)—locale MO-7
**Hardins Corner**—pop pl VA-3
Hardins Creek AL-4
Hardins Creek TN-4
Hardins Creek—stream (2) KY-4
Hardins Creek Fire Tower—tower TN-4
Hardin-Simmons (Hardin-Simmons
University)—uninc pl TX-5
Hardin-Simmons Univ—school TX-5
Hardins Lake CA-9
Hardin Slough—gut TN-4
Hardin Slough—stream TN-4
Hardin Slough—stream TX-5
Hardin's Point AR-4
Hardin Spring—spring OR-9
Hardin Spring—spring (2) TN-4
Hardin Springs—locale KY-4
Hardin Springs Sch—hist pl KY-4
Hardin Square—park IL-6
Hardins Station NC-3
Hardin Station—locale OH-6
Hardin Store (historical)—locale TN-4
Hardins View Material Center TN-4
Hardins View School TN-4
Hardinsville TN-4
Hardin Swamp—swamp GA-3
Hardin Tank—reservoir NM-5
Hardin Tank No 2—reservoir NM-5
Hardintown IN-6
Hardin Township—civil MO-7
Hardin Township—fmr MCD (5) IA-7
Hardin Township Cem—cemetery IA-7
Hardin (Township of)—fmr MCD AR-4
**Hardin (Township of)**—pop pl IL-6
**Hardin Valley**—pop pl TN-4
Hardin Valley—valley TN-4
Hardin Valley (CCD)—cens area TN-4
Hardin Valley Division—civil TN-4
Hardin Valley Post Office
(historical)—building TN-4
Hardin Valley Sch—school TN-4
Hardin View Sch—school TN-4
**Hardinville**—pop pl IL-6
Hardinville Cem—cemetery IL-6
Hardin Well—locale NM-5
Hardin Well—well NM-5
Hardison Cem—cemetery (3) TN-4
Hardison Ch—church GA-3
Hardison Ch—church NC-3
Hardison Crossroads—locale NC-3
Hardison Elementary School TN-4
Hardison Hollow—valley TN-4
Hardison Lake—lake TX-5
Hardison Mill—locale TN-4
Hardison Mill Creek—stream NC-3
Hardison Mound—summit TX-5
Hardison Sch—school TN-4
Hardison Shelter, Petit Jean No.
3—hist pl AR-4
Hardister Creek NV-8
Hardister Creek UT-8
Hardistonville—locale NJ-2
Hardisty Lake FL-3
Hard Labor Ch—church FL-3
Hard Labor Creek FL-3
Hard Labor Creek—stream AL-4
Hard Labor Creek—stream FL-3
Hard Labor Creek—stream GA-3
Hard Labor Creek—stream SC-3
Hard Labor Creek State Park—park GA-3
**Hard Labour**—pop pl VI-3
Hardland Windmill—locale TX-5
Hardley Creek—stream AL-4
Hardley Creek—stream GA-3
Hardley Lake—lake MI-6
Hardleys Purchase—civil NH-1
Hard Lodging—hist pl MD-2
Hard Luck—locale MI-6
Hardluck Bay—bay AK-9
Hardluck Campground—locale CA-9
Hard Luck Creek—stream (2) AK-9
Hard Luck Crossing—locale NM-5
Hard Luck Draw—valley TX-5
Hard Luck Hammock—island FL-3
Hardluck Island—island AK-9
Hard Luck Mine—mine CA-9
Hard Luck Mine—mine MT-8
Hardluck Mtn—summit WY-8
Hard Luck Ranch—locale AZ-5
Hardluck Rsvr—reservoir WY-8
Hardluck Slough—stream AK-9
Hard Luck Tank—reservoir AZ-5
Hard Luck Tank—reservoir NM-5
Hard Luck Tank—reservoir (2) TX-5
Hard Luck Well—well MT-8
Hard Luck Well—well NM-5
Hardluck Well—well TX-5
Hardluck Windmill—locale NM-5
Hardly Corp—locale TX-5
Hardman—locale CO-8
Hardman—locale (2) WV-2
**Hardman**—pop pl OR-9
**Hardman**—pop pl WV-2
Hardman, Governor L. G., House—hist pl GA-3
Hardman Bend—bend WV-2
Hardman Cem—cemetery AL-4
Hardman Cem—cemetery OR-9
Hardman Cem—cemetery WV-2
Hardman Center—uninc pl CA-9
Hardman Ch—church (2) WV-2
Hardman Chapel—church WV-2
Hardman Ditch—canal WY-8
Hardman Fork—stream (2) WV-2
Hardman IOOF Cem—cemetery OR-9
Hardmans Fork—stream WV-2
Hardmans Hollow—valley ID-8
Hardmans Hollow—valley WY-8
Hardman Springfield Ch—church GA-3
Hard Mill Pond MS-4
**Hard Money**—pop pl KY-4
**Hardmoney**—pop pl KY-4
Hardmoney Ch—church KY-4
Hardnack Creek—stream CO-8
Hardon Hill WA-9
Hardover Point—cape AK-9
Hardpac Creek—stream AK-9
Hardpan KS-7
Hardpan, The—flat UT-8
Hardpan Coulee—valley MT-8
Hardpan Creek—stream (2) ID-8
Hard Pan Creek—stream MT-8
Hardpan Creek—stream WY-8
Hardpan Lake—lake WY-8
Hardpan Point—summit ID-8
Hardpan Ridge—ridge IL-6
Hardpan Rsvr—reservoir MT-8
Hard Pan Rsvr—reservoir OR-9
Hardpan Rsvr—reservoir UT-8
Hardpan Sch—school WY-8
Hardpans Flat—flat NV-8
Hard Pan Well—well NV-8
Hardpan Windmill—locale NM-5
Hard Pass—gap WA-9
Hardpen—other PA-2
Hard Pinch Reserve—reservoir SC-3
**Hard Point**—pop pl NY-2
Hard Pond—reservoir AZ-5
Hardquartz Mine—mine CA-9
Hard Ridge—ridge NC-3
Hardridge Creek—stream AL-4
Hardridge Creek Public Use Area—park AL-4
Hardrobe Creek—stream MT-8
Hardrobe Spring—spring MT-8
Hardrobe Water Gap—gap MT-8
Hardrock Cem—cemetery KS-7
Hardrock Gulch—valley ID-8
Hard Rock Mesa—summit AZ-5
Hardrock Queen Spring—spring CA-9
Hard Rock Ridge—ridge NM-5
Hard Rock Rsvr—reservoir OR-9
Hard Rocks—locale AZ-5
Hard Rocks Dam—dam AZ-5
Hardrock Windmill—locale NM-5
Hards Branch—stream SC-3
Hard Sch—school AL-4
Hardscrabble—flat CA-9
Hardscrabble—flat UT-8
Hardscrabble—hist pl NC-3
Hardscrabble—locale DE-2
Hardscrabble—locale NV-8
Hardscrabble—locale NH-1
Hardscrabble—locale (2) NY-2
Hardscrabble—locale TN-4
Hardscrabble—locale VA-3
**Hardscrabble**—pop pl IN-6
**Hardscrabble**—pop pl (2) OH-6
**Hardscrabble**—pop pl VT-1
Hardscrabble, The—flat UT-8
Hardscrabble Bluff—cliff TN-4
Hardscrabble Bottom—bend UT-8
Hardscrabble Branch—stream NC-3
Hardscrabble Campground—locale ID-8
Hardscrabble Canyon—valley AZ-5
Hardscrabble Canyon—valley ID-8
Hardscrabble Canyon—valley NM-5
Hardscrabble Canyon—valley (4) UT-8
Hardscrabble Cem—cemetery IL-6
Hardscrabble Cem—cemetery NY-2
Hardscrabble Cem—cemetery OH-6
**Hardscrabble Corner**—pop pl VT-1
Hard Scrabble County Park—park IA-7
Hardscrabble Creek—stream (2) AK-9
Hardscrabble Creek—stream AZ-5
Hardscrabble Creek—stream (2) CA-9
Hardscrabble Creek—stream CO-8
Hardscrabble Creek—stream ID-8
Hardscrabble Creek—stream (3) MT-8
Hardscrabble Creek—stream NV-8
Hardscrabble Creek—stream OR-9
Hardscrabble Creek—stream TX-5
Hardscrabble Creek—stream (2) UT-8
Hardscrabble Creek—stream (2) WA-9
Hardscrabble Creek—stream WI-6
Hardscrabble Creek—stream WY-8
Hard Scrabble Falls—falls WA-9
Hard Scrabble Falls Creek—stream WA-9
Hard Scrabble Falls Gulch—valley WA-9
Hardscrabble Golf Course—other AR-4
Hardscrabble Guard Station
(historical)—locale ID-8
Hardscrabble Gulch—valley (2) CA-9
Hardscrabble Gulch—valley CO-8
Hardscrabble Gulch—valley ID-8
Hardscrabble Hill OR-9
Hardscrabble Hill—summit (2) NY-2
Hardscrabble Hill—summit (2) OH-6
Hardscrabble Hill—summit OR-9
**Hardscrabble (historical)**—pop pl MS-4
Hardscrabble Hollow—valley IL-6
Hardscrabble Hollow—valley PA-2
Hardscrabble Hollow—valley TN-4
Hardscrabble Hollow—valley UT-8
Hardscrabble Hollow—valley VA-3
Hardscrabble Island—island ME-1
Hardscrabble Knob VA-3
Hardscrabble Knob—summit VA-3
Hardscrabble Lake—lake (2) NY-2
Hardscrabble Lake—reservoir CO-8
Hardscrabble Lakes—lake WA-9
Hardscrabble Mesa—summit AZ-5
Hard Scrabble Mine SD-7
Hardscrabble Mine—mine NM-5
Hardscrabble Mountains—range NM-5
Hardscrabble Mtn—summit (2) CO-8
Hardscrabble Mtn—summit ME-1
Hardscrabble Mtn—summit OR-9
Hardscrabble Mtn—summit UT-8
Hardscrabble Mtn—summit VT-1
Hardscrabble Mtn—summit VA-3
Hardscrabble Mtn—summit WA-9
Hardscrabble Peak—summit MT-8
Hardscrabble Pinnacle—pillar TN-4
Hardscrabble Plantation
(historical)—locale MS-4
Hardscrabble Point—cape ME-1
Hardscrabble Point—cape MN-6
Hardscrabble Point—cape NY-2
Hardscrabble Quarry—mine OR-9
Hard Scrabble Ridge—ridge IN-6
Hardscrabble Ridge—ridge (2) OR-9
Hardscrabble River—stream ME-1
Hardscrabble Saddle—gap CO-8
Hardscrabble Sch—school (2) NE-7
Hard Scrabble Sch—school NE-7
Hardscrabble Sch—school NE-7
Hard Scrabble Sch (historical)—school MS-4
Hardscrabble School (Abandoned)—locale NE-7
Hardscrabble Spring—spring AZ-5
Hardscrabble Spring—spring (2) NM-5
Hardscrabble Tank—reservoir AZ-5
Hardscrabble Tank—reservoir NM-5
**Hardscrabble Township**—pop pl ND-7
Hardscrabble Wash—stream AZ-5
Hardscrabble Well—well NM-5
Hardscrable Creek KS-7
Hardscrable Creek—stream OR-9
Hardscrable Creek—stream WA-9
Hard Scramble Cem—cemetery GA-3
Hardscramble Spring—spring UT-8
Hardscrapple Hill UT-8
**Hard Scratch**—pop pl IA-7
Hard Scratch Hill—summit TN-4
Hardscratch Point CA-9
Hardscratch Point—cape AK-9
Hardscribble Sch—school MI-6
Hardshell—locale KY-4
Hardshell Baptist Ch (historical)—church AL-4
Hardshell (CCD)—cens area KY-4
Hard Shell Cem—cemetery LA-4
Hardshell Cem—cemetery LA-4
Hardshell Cem—cemetery MS-4
Hardshell Cem—cemetery (3) TX-5
Hardshell Ch—church AL-4
Hard Shell Ch—church MD-2
Hardshell Ch (historical)—church AL-4
Hardshell Church MO-7
Hardshell Church TN-4
Hardshell Creek—stream TX-5
Hardshell Mine—mine AZ-5
Hardshift Branch MD-2
Hardship Branch—stream MD-2
Hardside Church TN-4
Hard Sink—basin AL-4
Hardslate Gap—gap GA-3
Hard Slate Gap—gap NC-3
Hard Spring—spring AZ-5
Hard Spring—spring CA-9
Hardstein Playground—park MI-6
Hardstrable Hollow—valley IN-6
Hardtack Island—island OR-9
Hardtack Lake—lake MN-6
Hardtack Lake—lake WA-9
Hardt Cem—cemetery AL-4
Hardt Creek—stream AZ-5
Hardt Creek Well—well AZ-5
Hardtime Bayou—gut MS-4
Hardtime Creek—stream WA-9
Hardtime Lake—lake MS-4
Hard Time Rsvr—reservoir OR-9
Hard Times Bend—bend MS-4
Hardtimes Branch—stream MS-4
Hard Times Landing—locale MS-4
Hard Times Landing (historical)—locale AL-4
Hardtimes Mine—mine AZ-5
Hard Time Spring—spring NV-8
Hardtna KS-7
**Hardtner**—pop pl KS-7
Hard to Beat Canyon—valley UT-8
Hard To Find Mine—mine NV-8
Hard-To-Get-To Ridge—ridge WA-9
Hardtrigger Creek—stream ID-8
Hardt Tank—reservoir AZ-5
Hardt Well—locale NM-5
Hardup—locale UT-8
Hard Up Cem—cemetery GA-3
Hard Up Gulch—valley ID-8
Hardup Key—island FL-3
Hard Up Point—cape OR-9
Hardville (historical)—locale KS-7
Hardware—locale VA-3
Hardware Bldg—hist pl IA-7
Hardware Ch—church VA-3
Hardware Ranch—locale UT-8
Hardware Ranch Game Mngmt
Area—park UT-8
Hardware Ranch Trail—trail UT-8
Hardware River—stream VA-3
Hardware River State Wildlife Mngmt
Are—park VA-3
Hardwater Lake—lake LA-4
**Hardway**—pop pl FL-3
Hardway Branch—stream WV-2
Hardway Creek—stream AK-9
Hardway Run—stream WV-2
Hard West Well—well NM-5
Hardwich GA-3
Hardwick PA-2
Hardwick—locale AL-4
Hardwick—locale KY-4
Hardwick—locale NJ-2
**Hardwick**—pop pl CA-9
**Hardwick**—pop pl GA-3
**Hardwick**—pop pl MA-1
**Hardwick**—pop pl MN-6
**Hardwick**—pop pl VT-1
**Hardwickburg**—pop pl AL-4
Hardwick Cem TN-4
Hardwick Cem—cemetery KY-4
Hardwick Cem—cemetery MS-4
Hardwick Cem—cemetery TN-4
Hardwick Center—locale NJ-2
Hardwick Center—other MA-1
**Hardwick Center**—pop pl VT-1
Hardwick Centre MA-1
Hardwick Creek—stream KY-4
Hardwick Creek Ch—church KY-4
Hardwick Ferry (historical)—locale AL-4
Hardwick Field (airport)—airport TN-4
**Hardwick (Hardwick Center)**—pop pl MA-1
**Hardwick (historical)**—pop pl TN-4
Hardwick Island (historical)—island TN-4
Hardwick Lake—reservoir VT-1
Hardwick (Midway)—uninc pl GA-3
Hardwick Mine—mine (2) TN-4
Hardwick Mtn—summit VA-3
Hardwick Point—cape WA-9
Hardwick Pond—reservoir MA-1
Hardwick Pond Dam—dam MA-1
Hardwick Ranch—locale NM-5
Hardwicksburg Post Office
(historical)—building AL-4
Hardwicks Ditch—canal LA-4
Hardwick Spit WA-9
Hardwick Spring—spring TN-4
**Hardwick Steet**—pop pl VT-1
**Hardwick Street**—pop pl VT-1
Hardwick Street Hist Dist—hist pl VT-1
**Hardwick Subdivision**—pop pl TN-4
**Hardwick (Town of)**—pop pl MA-1
**Hardwick (Town of)**—pop pl VT-1
**Hardwick (Township of)**—pop pl NJ-2
Hardwick Tunnel—tunnel AL-4
Hardwick Well—well OR-9
Hardwood MO-7
**Hardwood**—pop pl LA-4
**Hardwood**—pop pl MI-6
**Hardwood**—pop pl VA-3
Hardwood Brook—stream (2) ME-1
Hardwood Brook—stream VT-1
Hardwood Creek—stream MI-6
Hardwood Creek—stream MN-6
Hardwood Creek—stream VA-3
Hardwood Creek—stream WA-9
Hardwood Ditch—canal VA-3
Hardwood Flats—flat VT-1
Hardwood Flats Sch—school VT-1
Hardwood Gap—gap TN-4
Hardwood Hill—summit (5) ME-1
Hardwood Hill—summit MS-4
Hardwood Hill—summit (4) NY-2
Hardwood Hill—summit VT-1
Hardwood Hills—summit NY-2
Hardwood Island ME-1
Hardwood Island—island (7) ME-1
Hardwood Island—island MI-6
Hardwood Island—island NY-2
Hardwood Island—ridge NY-2
Hardwood Island Ledge—bar ME-1
Hardwood Lake—lake (5) MI-6
Hardwood Lake—lake (2) MN-6
Hardwood Lake—lake TX-5
Hardwood Lake—lake WI-6
Hardwood Lake—swamp FL-3
Hardwood Leg—canal VA-3
Hardwood Mtn—summit (2) ME-1
Hardwood Mtn—summit VT-1
Hardwood Point MI-6
Hardwood Point—cape (2) ME-1
Hardwood Point—cape (3) MI-6
Hardwood Point—cape MN-6

Hardwood Pond—*lake* VT-1
Hardwood Ridge—*ridge* (2) ME-1
Hardwood Ridge—*ridge* (2) NH-1
Hardwood Ridge—*ridge* (2) NY-2
Hardwood Ridge—*ridge* PA-2
Hardwood Ridge—*ridge* VT-1
Hardwood State For—*forest* MI-6
Hardwood Trail—*trail* (2) PA-2
Hardwood Trail—*trail* WI-6
Hardwork Ditch—*canal* CO-8
Hardworking Bayou—*lake* FL-3
Hard Working Lumps—*island* NC-3
*Hardy* TN-4
Hardy—*locale* AZ-5
Hardy—*locale* CA-9
Hardy—*locale* KY-4
Hardy—*locale* ME-1
Hardy—*locale* MT-8
Hardy—*locale* OK-5
Hardy—*locale* OR-9
Hardy—*locale* TX-5
Hardy—*locale* UT-8
Hardy—*locale* VA-3
**Hardy**—*pop pl* (2) AL-4
**Hardy**—*pop pl* AR-4
**Hardy**—*pop pl* IA-7
**Hardy**—*pop pl* KY-4
**Hardy**—*pop pl* MS-4
**Hardy**—*pop pl* NE-7
**Hardy**—*pop pl* PA-2
**Hardy**—*pop pl* SC-3
**Hardy**—*pop pl* TN-4
**Hardy**—*pop pl* TX-5
**Hardy**—*pop pl* VA-3
**Hardy**—*pop pl* WV-2
Hardy, Lake—*lake* UT-8
Hardy, Mount—*summit* WA-9
Hardy, Richard, JHS—*hist pl* TN-4
Hardy, Richard, Memorial Sch—*hist pl* TN-4
Hardy, Robert Lee, House—*hist pl* AR-4
Hardy, Thomas P., House—*hist pl* WI-6
Hardy, Urias, House—*hist pl* MA-1
**Hardy Acres**—*pop pl* TN-4
Hardy-Anders Field Natchez-Adams County Airp—*airport* MS-4
Hardy Baptist Ch—*church* MS-4
Hardy Bar Island—*island* IL-6
**Hardy Beet Siding**—*pop pl* ND-7
Hardy Beet Spur—*locale* UT-8
Hardy Bluff Sch—*school* MS-4
*Hardy Branch* VA-3
Hardy Branch—*stream* GA-3
Hardy Branch—*stream* KY-4
Hardy Branch—*stream* LA-4
Hardy Branch—*stream* SC-3
Hardy Branch—*stream* TN-4
Hardy Branch—*stream* TX-5
Hardy Bridge—*bridge* MT-8
Hardy Bridge—*bridge* VA-3
Hardy Bridge—*other* VA-3
Hardy Brook—*stream* (2) ME-1
Hardy Brook—*stream* (3) NH-1
Hardy Canyon—*valley* CO-8
Hardy Canyon—*valley* NV-8
Hardy Canyon—*valley* NM-5
Hardy Canyon—*valley* WA-9
Hardy Cem—*cemetery* AL-4
Hardy Cem—*cemetery* AR-4
Hardy Cem—*cemetery* (3) GA-3
Hardy Cem—*cemetery* KY-4
Hardy Cem—*cemetery* ME-1
Hardy Cem—*cemetery* MO-7
Hardy Cem—*cemetery* NC-3
Hardy Cem—*cemetery* SC-3
Hardy Cem—*cemetery* (3) TX-5
Hardy Cem—*cemetery* VA-3
*Hardy Cemetery* MS-4
Hardy Central Ch—*church* VA-3
Hardy Ch—*church* MI-6
Hardy Corners—*locale* NY-2
**Hardy Corners**—*pop pl* NY-2
**Hardy (County)**—*pop pl* WV-2
Hardy Court Shop Ctr—*locale* MS-4
Hardy Creek—*stream* (2) AK-9
Hardy Creek—*stream* CA-9
Hardy Creek—*stream* KY-4
Hardy Creek—*stream* MS-4
Hardy Creek—*stream* MT-8
Hardy Creek—*stream* NV-8
Hardy Creek—*stream* (2) NC-3
Hardy Creek—*stream* OK-5
Hardy Creek—*stream* (2) OR-9
Hardy Creek—*stream* (2) TX-5
Hardy Creek—*stream* VA-3
Hardy Creek—*stream* WA-9
Hardy Creek Ch—*church* VA-3
*Hardy Crossroads* NC-3
Hardy Dam—*dam* MI-6
*Hardy Dam Number 1* AL-4
Hardy Dam Pond—*reservoir* MI-6
Hardy Ditch—*canal* IN-6
Hardy Ditch—*canal* MT-8
Hardy-Durham Cem—*cemetery* GA-3
Hardy Field—*other* OK-5
Hardy Flats—*flat* NM-5
Hardy Fork—*stream* KY-4
Hardy Guard Station—*locale* SD-7
Hardy Gulch—*valley* ID-8
**Hardy Heights**—*pop pl* TX-5
**Hardy Hill**—*pop pl* ME-1
**Hardy Hill**—*pop pl* PA-2
Hardy Hill—*summit* AZ-5
Hardy Hill—*summit* NH-1
Hardy Hill—*summit* NY-2
Hardy Hill—*summit* VT-1
Hardy Hill—*summit* WA-9
Hardy Hill Brook—*stream* NH-1
Hardy Hill Sch—*school* NH-1
Hardy Hollow—*valley* MO-7
Hardy Hollow—*valley* (2) TN-4
Hardy Hollow—*valley* UT-8
Hardy Hollow—*valley* VA-3
Hardy House—*hist pl* AR-4
Hardy House—*hist pl* HI-9
Hardy Island—*island* ME-1
Hardy JHS—*school* MS-4
*Hardy Lake* MI-6
Hardy Lake—*lake* LA-4
Hardy Lake—*lake* (2) MN-6
Hardy Lake—*reservoir* IN-6
Hardy Lake Dam—*dam* (3) MS-4
Hardy Lake Number 1—*reservoir* AL-4
Hardy (Magisterial District)—*fmr MCD* VA-3
Hardy Mill Creek—*stream* GA-3
Hardy Millpond—*reservoir* GA-3
Hardy Millpond—*reservoir* NC-3
*Hardy Mill Run* NC-3
Hardy Mill Run—*stream* NC-3
Hardy Mine—*mine* CA-9
Hardy Mtn—*summit* AZ-5
Hardy Neck—*bay* GA-3
Hardy Oak Cem—*cemetery* KS-7
Hardy Oil Field—*oilfield* OK-5
Hardy Place—*locale* CA-9
Hardy Point—*cape* FL-3
Hardy Point—*cape* ME-1
*Hardy Pond* ME-1
*Hardy Pond* MA-1
*Hardy Pond* MI-6
Hardy Pond—*lake* ME-1
**Hardy Pond**—*pop pl* ME-1
Hardy Pond Trail—*trail* ME-1
Hardy Post Office (historical)—*building* TN-4
Hardy Ranch—*locale* NE-7
Hardy Ranch—*locale* WY-8
*Hardy Ridge* WA-9
Hardy Ridge—*ridge* CA-9
Hardy Ridge—*ridge* NM-5
Hardy Ridge—*ridge* OR-9
Hardy Rock—*island* CA-9
Hardy Rocks—*bar* MA-1
*Hardy Rsvr* MI-6
Hardy Run—*channel* MN-6
Hardy Run—*stream* OH-6
Hardy Run—*stream* VA-3
Hardy Run—*stream* WV-2
*Hardys* AL-4
*Hardys* MS-4
Hardys—*locale* NY-2
Hardy Sand Company Dam—*dam* TN-4
Hardy Sand Company Lake—*reservoir* TN-4
*Hardy's Bluff* VA-3
Hardys Bridge—*bridge* NC-3
Hardy Sch—*school* CA-9
Hardy Sch—*school* DC-2
Hardy Sch—*school* ME-1
Hardy Sch—*school* (2) MA-1
Hardy Sch—*school* NY-2
Hardys Chapel—*church* GA-3
Hardys Chapel Sch (historical)—*school* TN-4
Hardy-Schell Tank—*reservoir* AZ-5
*Hardy School* MS-4
Hardy School—*locale* MI-6
Hardy School, The—*school* CA-9
Hardy School (Abandoned)—*locale* TX-5
Hardys Creek—*stream* GA-3
Hardys Creek—*stream* VA-3
Hardys Crossroads—*locale* GA-3
Hardy Shoal—*bar* MA-1
Hardy Sink—*lake* FL-3
Hardys Lake—*lake* IN-6
Hardys Lake—*lake* MO-7
Hardys Mill Pond—*reservoir* NC-3
Hardys Mill Pond Dam—*dam* NC-3
Hardys Pond—*reservoir* MA-1
Hardy Spring—*spring* NM-5
Hardy Spring—*spring* OR-9
Hardy Spring—*spring* TN-4
Hardy Spring Branch—*stream* VA-3
Hardy Spring Brook—*stream* NH-1
Hardy Springs—*spring* NV-8
Hardys Rsvr—*reservoir* WY-8
Hardys Sandy Creek—*stream* TX-5
Hardys Station (historical)—*locale* NV-8
Hardys Steam Mill (historical)—*locale* AL-4
Hardys Store (historical)—*locale* AL-4
*Hardy Station* MS-4
Hardy Station—*locale* CA-9
Hardy Station Post Office (historical)—*building* MS-4
Hardyston Cem—*cemetery* NJ-2
**Hardyston (Township of)**—*pop pl* NJ-2
*Hardystonville* NJ-2
Hardy Stream—*stream* ME-1
Hardy Street Mart Shop Ctr—*locale* MS-4
Hardy Street Yard—*locale* TX-5
*Hardy Swamp* GA-3
Hardy (Township of)—*fmr MCD* (2) AR-4
**Hardy (Township of)**—*pop pl* OH-6
Hardy Trail—*trail* TN-4
Hardy Union Sch—*school* WV-2
Hardy Valley—*basin* NE-7
*Hardyville* AL-4
Hardyville—*locale* MO-7
**Hardyville**—*pop pl* KY-4
**Hardyville**—*pop pl* VA-3
Hardyville (CCD)—*cens area* KY-4
**Hardyville (historical)**—*pop pl* AZ-5
Hardyville Mill (ruins)—*locale* AZ-5
Hardy-Williams Bldg—*hist pl* TX-5
Hardy Wilson Memorial Hosp—*hospital* MS-4
Hardy Winter Camp—*locale* AZ-5
Hardy Young Cem—*cemetery* AL-4
Hare—*locale* NC-3
Hare—*locale* TX-5
**Hare**—*pop pl* KY-4
Harebell Creek—*stream* WY-8
Harebell Creek Patrol Cabin—*locale* WY-8
Harebell Trail—*trail* WY-8
Hare Branch—*stream* MS-4
Hare Branch—*stream* OK-5
Hare Brook—*stream* NY-2
Hare Canyon—*valley* (2) CA-9
Hare Canyon—*valley* NV-8
Hare Cem—*cemetery* OK-5
Hare Cem—*cemetery* TN-4
Hare Cem—*cemetery* VA-3
*Hare Creek* TN-4
Hare Creek—*stream* (2) CA-9
Hare Creek—*stream* NY-2
Hare Creek—*stream* PA-2
Hare Ditch—*canal* IN-6
Harefarm Cem—*cemetery* AR-4
Harefarm Creek—*stream* AR-4
Hare Gulch—*valley* OR-9
**Hare (historical)**—*pop pl* OR-9
*Hare Island* FM-9
Hare Island—*island* AK-9
Hare Island—*island* SC-3
Hare Island—*island* FM-9
Hare Lake—*lake* FL-3
Hare Lake—*lake* MN-6
Hare Lake—*lake* UT-8
**Harelson**—*pop pl* LA-4
Harelson Cem—*cemetery* LA-4
Harelson Cem—*cemetery* MO-7
Harelson Cem—*cemetery* TN-4
Harelson Sch—*school* AZ-5
Harem Hill—*summit* WY-8
Harem Rock—*island* AK-9
Harems Store (historical)—*locale* TN-4
Hare Mtn—*summit* AR-4
Haren Run—*stream* OH-6
Hare Plantation House—*hist pl* NC-3
Hare Pond—*lake* MI-6
Hare Prong—*stream* TX-5
Harer—*locale* ID-8
Harer Canyon—*valley* OR-9
Harer Farm Strip (airport)—*airport* SD-7
Hare Rock—*island* CA-9
Harer Point—*cape* ID-8
Hares Branch—*stream* NC-3
Hares Canyon—*valley* OR-9
Hare Sch—*school* CA-9
Hare Sch—*school* NC-3
Hare Sch—*school* PA-2
*Hare School Dam* SD-7
Hares Corner—*locale* DE-2
*Hares Corner Station* DE-2
Hares Creek—*stream* NC-3
**Hares Crossroads**—*pop pl* NC-3
Hare's Hill Road Bridge—*hist pl* PA-2
**Hares (historical)**—*pop pl* OR-9
Hare Snipe Creek—*stream* NC-3
Hares Valley—*valley* PA-2
Hares Valley Creek—*stream* PA-2
Haretown—*locale* AR-4
Hare Valley—*basin* UT-8
**Hare Valley**—*pop pl* VA-3
Hare Valley Sch—*school* VA-3
*Harewood* MD-2
Harewood—*hist pl* WV-2
Harewood—*locale* (2) WV-2
**Harewood**—*pop pl* MD-2
**Harewood Acres**—*pop pl* OH-6
Harewood and Beechwood—*hist pl* PA-2
Harewood Cem—*cemetery* VA-3
**Harewood Park**—*pop pl* (2) MD-2
Harewood Station—*locale* MD-2
**Harfield**—*pop pl* NJ-2
**Harfield**—*pop pl* VA-3
**Harford**—*pop pl* PA-2
Harford Boat Club—*other* MD-2
Harford Canyon—*valley* CA-9
Harford Cem—*cemetery* MI-6
**Harford (County)**—*pop pl* MD-2
**Harford Estates**—*pop pl* MD-2
**Harford Farms**—*pop pl* MD-2
**Harford Furnace**—*pop pl* MD-2
Harford Furnace Sch—*school* MD-2
**Harford Heights**—*pop pl* PA-2
**Harford Hills**—*pop pl* MD-2
**Harford Mills**—*pop pl* NY-2
**Harford Mills (RR name Mills)**—*pop pl* NY-2
Harford Natl Bank—*hist pl* MD-2
**Harford (North Harford Station)**—*pop pl* NY-2
**Harford Park**—*pop pl* MD-2
Harford Road—*uninc pl* MD-2
Harfords Point—*cape* ME-1
Harfords Point (Township of)—*unorg* ME-1
Harford Spring—*spring* CA-9
Harfords Swamp—*swamp* TN-4
**Harford (Town of)**—*pop pl* NY-2
**Harford (Township of)**—*pop pl* PA-2
Harg—*locale* MO-7
Hargadine Cem—*cemetery* OR-9
Hargadine-McKittrick Dry Goods Bldg—*hist pl* MO-7
Hargadine Spring—*spring* OR-9
Hargan Mine—*mine* AZ-5
Hargens Sch—*school* SD-7
Harger Cem—*cemetery* MI-6
Harger Cem—*cemetery* OH-6
Harger Creek—*stream* NY-2
Hargett—*locale* KY-4
Hargett Branch—*stream* AL-4
Hargett Cem—*cemetery* AL-4
Hargett Creek—*stream* AL-4
*Hargetts* NC-3
Hargett Sch—*school* KY-4
Hargetts Creek—*stream* NC-3
**Hargetts Cross Roads**—*pop pl* NC-3
**Hargetts Crossroads**—*pop pl* NC-3
*Hargetts Store* NC-3
Hargetts Store—*other* NC-3
**Hargill**—*pop pl* TX-5
Hargill (CCD)—*cens area* TX-5
Hargill Cem—*cemetery* TX-5
Hargill Rsvr—*reservoir* TX-5
Hargis—*locale* (2) KY-4
Hargis—*locale* NM-5
**Hargis**—*pop pl* LA-4
Hargis, Andrew M., House—*hist pl* NE-7
Hargis Arroyo—*stream* NM-5
Hargis Bayou—*stream* LA-4
Hargis Branch—*stream* (2) KY-4
Hargis Canyon—*valley* UT-8
*Hargis Cem* TN-4
Hargis Cem—*cemetery* IL-6
Hargis Cem—*cemetery* TN-4
Hargis Christian Retreat—*locale* AL-4
Hargis Creek—*stream* (2) KS-7
Hargis Creek—*stream* KY-4
Hargis Creek—*stream* TN-4
Hargis Hollow—*valley* KY-4
Hargis Hollow—*valley* TN-4
Hargis Lake—*reservoir* AL-4
Hargis-Mitchell-Cochran House—*hist pl* OK-5
*Hargis Retreat* AL-4
Hargiss—*locale* TN-4
Hargiss Cem—*cemetery* (2) TN-4
Hargiss Cove—*valley* TN-4
Hargiss Cove Branch—*stream* TN-4
Hargiss Ridge—*ridge* TN-4
Hargiss Slough—*gut* LA-4
Hargitt Sch—*school* CA-9
Hargove Bridge—*other* MO-7
Hargrave—*locale* KS-7
Hargrave Branch—*stream* MO-7
Hargrave Cem—*cemetery* MO-7
Hargrave Chapel—*church* GA-3
**Hargrave Corner**—*pop pl* AR-4
Hargrave Creek—*stream* ID-8
Hargrave Hollow—*valley* IL-6
Hargrave House—*hist pl* NC-3
Hargrave Military Acad—*school* VA-3
**Hargraves**—*pop pl* VA-3
**Hargraves Bench (subdivision)**—*pop pl* NC-3
Hargraves Canyon—*valley* WY-8
Hargraves Cem—*cemetery* TX-5
*Hargraves Junction* AR-4
**Hargraves Junction**—*pop pl* AR-4
Hargraves Mill No. 1—*hist pl* MA-1
*Hargrave Store* MS-4
Hargreave Knob—*summit* WV-2
Hargret Ridge—*ridge* GA-3
**Hargrove**—*pop pl* LA-4
**Hargrove**—*pop pl* MO-7
Hargrove Branch—*stream* AL-4
Hargrove Branch—*stream* KY-4
Hargrove Branch—*stream* TN-4
Hargrove Cem—*cemetery* (2) AL-4
Hargrove Cem—*cemetery* LA-4
Hargrove Cem—*cemetery* (2) TN-4
Hargrove Cem—*cemetery* TX-5
Hargrove Ch—*church* AL-4
Hargrove Ch—*church* LA-4
*Hargrove Creek* AL-4
Hargrove Creek—*stream* TX-5
Hargrove Crossroads—*locale* NC-3
Hargrove (historical)—*locale* AL-4
Hargrove Hollow—*valley* (2) TN-4
Hargrove Lake—*lake* TX-5
Hargrove Memorial Methodist Ch—*church* AL-4
*Hargrove Mill Creek* AL-4
Hargrove Mine (underground)—*mine* AL-4
Hargrove Pivot Bridge—*hist pl* MO-7
Hargrove Post Office (historical)—*building* TN-4
Hargroves Branch—*stream* LA-4
Hargrove Sch—*school* NC-3
Hargrove Sch (historical)—*school* AL-4
*Hargroves Church* AL-4
*Hargroves Ferry* AL-4
Hargrove Store (historical)—*locale* MS-4
Hargrove Windmill—*locale* TX-5
*Hargua Hala* AZ-5
*Hargus Brook* NY-2
Hargus Creek—*stream* KY-4
Hargus Creek—*stream* OH-6
Hargus Creek—*stream* PA-2
Hargus Eddy—*other* MO-7
Hargus Lake—*reservoir* OH-6
Hargus Post Office (historical)—*building* TN-4
Hargus Ranch—*locale* TX-5
*Harian Mountain* TN-4
Harica Lake—*lake* MN-6
*Harietta* MI-6
Harihokake Creek—*stream* NJ-2
Harild Mikuoik Dam—*dam* SD-7
Harim Jordan Lake Dam—*dam* MS-4
**Haring**—*pop pl* MI-6
Haring, Abraham A., House—*hist pl* NJ-2
Haring, Frederick, House—*hist pl* NJ-2
Haring, Gerrit, House—*hist pl* NJ-2
Haring, Nicholas, House—*hist pl* NJ-2
Haring, Teunis, House—*hist pl* NJ-2
Haring-Auryanson House—*hist pl* NJ-2
Haring-Blauvelt-Demarest House—*hist pl* NJ-2
Haring-Blauvelt House—*hist pl* NJ-2
Haring Cem—*cemetery* OR-9
Haring-Corning House—*hist pl* NJ-2
Haring Creek—*stream* OR-9
Haring-DeWolf House—*hist pl* NJ-2
Haring Swamp—*stream* VA-3
**Haring (Township of)**—*pop pl* MI-6
Haring-Vervalen House—*hist pl* NJ-2
*Hariots Island* NC-3
Har Jehuda Cem—*cemetery* PA-2
Harjo—*locale* OK-5
Harjo Cem—*cemetery* (4) OK-5
Harjo Hills Camp—*locale* OK-5
Harju State Public Shooting Area—*park* SD-7
*Harkan Creek* MT-8
Harkcom Creek—*stream* MN-6
Harkell Canyon—*valley* TX-5
Harkens Lake—*lake* OR-9
Harker—*locale* FL-3
Harker Canyon—*valley* UT-8
Harker Canyon—*valley* WA-9
Harker Cem—*cemetery* IA-7
**Harker Heights**—*pop pl* TX-5
*Harker Lake* ND-7
Harker Lake—*lake* ND-7
Harker Park Lake—*lake* CO-8
Harker Run—*stream* WV-2
Harkers Canyon—*valley* (2) UT-8
Harkers Ch—*church* PA-2
Harker Sch—*school* CA-9
Harker Sch—*school* WI-6
Harkers Corner Cem—*cemetery* IL-6
Harkers Hollow Golf Course—*other* NJ-2
*Harkers Island* NC-3
Harkers Island—*island* NC-3
**Harkers Island**—*pop pl* NC-3
Harkers Island Sch—*school* NC-3
Harkers Island (Township of)—*fmr MCD* NC-3
Harkers Point—*cape* NC-3
Harkers Run—*stream* OH-6
**Harker Village**—*pop pl* NJ-2
Harkes—*locale* MO-7
Harkey-Banner Windmill—*locale* TX-5
Harkey Cem—*cemetery* AL-4
Harkey Cem—*cemetery* AR-4
Harkey Crossing—*locale* NM-5
Harkey Double Mills—*locale* NM-5
Harkey Draw—*valley* TX-5
Harkey Knobs—*summit* TX-5
Harkey Ranch—*locale* NM-5
Harkeys Cem—*cemetery* MO-7
Harkeys Chapel—*church* AL-4
Harkeys Chapel—*church* MO-7
Harkey Site—*hist pl* OK-5
Harkey Valley—*valley* AR-4
Harkeyville—*locale* TX-5
Harkey Windmill—*locale* TX-5
Hark Hill—*summit* NH-1
Harkin, Alexander, Store—*hist pl* MN-6
Harkin Branch—*stream* AL-4
Harkin Fork—*stream* KY-4
Harkin Franklin Creek—*stream* OK-5
Harkin Lake—*lake* MI-6
Harkins—*locale* MD-2
Harkins Cem—*cemetery* AL-4
Harkins Cem—*cemetery* GA-3
Harkins Cem—*cemetery* NC-3
Harkins Cem—*cemetery* (2) TN-4
Harkins Chapel—*church* OH-6
Harkins Creek—*stream* GA-3
**Harkins Crossroads**—*pop pl* AL-4
Harkins Dam—*dam* AL-4
Harkins Lake—*reservoir* (2) AL-4
Harkins Lake Dam—*dam* AL-4
Harkins Ranch—*locale* TX-5
Harkins Sch—*school* MN-6
*Harkins School* AL-4
Harkins Slough—*stream* CA-9
**Harkle Road**—*pop pl* AR-4
Harkleroad Hollow—*valley* VA-3
Harkless Flat—*flat* CA-9
Harkley Mtn—*summit* UT-8
*Harkness* AL-4
Harkness—*locale* NY-2
Harkness—*locale* PA-2
Harkness, H. O., Stable Bldg—*hist pl* ID-8
Harkness, Mount—*summit* CA-9
Harkness Branch—*gut* IL-6
Harkness Branch—*stream* AL-4
*Harknessburg Cemetery* PA-2
Harkness Cem—*cemetery* PA-2
Harkness Center—*school* NY-2
Harkness Creek—*stream* ID-8
Harkness Creek—*stream* MT-8
Harkness Crossroads—*locale* AL-4
Harkness Drain—*stream* MI-6
Harkness Grove Sch—*school* IL-6
Harkness Hill—*summit* NY-2
Harkness Home—*building* NY-2
Harkness Lake—*lake* NY-2
Harkness Lakes—*lake* MT-8
Harkness Memorial State Park—*park* CT-1
Harkness Mine—*mine* CA-9
Harkness Point—*cape* PA-2
Harkness Sch—*school* CA-9
Harkness Sch (historical)—*school* AL-4
Harkness Sch (historical)—*school* PA-2
Harkness Spring—*spring* MT-8
Harkness Spring—*spring* NM-5
*Harkness Wood Church* AL-4
Harkney Hill—*summit* RI-1
Harkridge Lake—*lake* MN-6
*Harks Creek* NV-8
Harksdale Sch—*school* TN-4
Harkum Slough—*stream* AL-4
Harky Hollow—*valley* TX-5
Harky Well—*well* NM-5
Harlacher Bridge—*bridge* PA-2
Harlam Camp—*locale* PA-2
Harlan—*locale* PA-2
**Harlan**—*pop pl* IN-6
**Harlan**—*pop pl* IA-7
**Harlan**—*pop pl* KS-7
**Harlan**—*pop pl* KY-4
**Harlan**—*pop pl* MI-6
**Harlan**—*pop pl* OR-9
**Harlan**—*pop pl* PA-2
Harlan, Elijah, House—*hist pl* KY-4
Harlan, Lake—*lake* FL-3
Harlan, Mount—*summit* CA-9
Harlan and Hollingsworth Office Bldg—*hist pl* DE-2
Harlan Bend—*bend* TN-4
Harlan Branch—*stream* KY-4
Harlan Branch—*stream* MO-7
Harlan Branch—*stream* TN-4
Harlan-Bruce House—*hist pl* KY-4
Harlan Butlerville Sch—*school* OH-6
Harlan Canyon—*valley* CA-9
Harlan Cave—*cave* TN-4
Harlan (CCD)—*cens area* KY-4
Harlan Cem—*cemetery* IA-7
Harlan Cem—*cemetery* MI-6
Harlan Cem—*cemetery* MO-7
Harlan Cem—*cemetery* OR-9
Harlan Ch—*church* IN-6
Harlan Commercial District—*hist pl* KY-4
**Harlan (County)**—*pop pl* KY-4
Harlan County Dam—*dam* NE-7
Harlan County Lake—*reservoir* KS-7
Harlan County Lake—*reservoir* NE-7
*Harlan County Reservoir* NE-7
Harlan Creek—*stream* CA-9
Harlan Creek—*stream* (3) ID-8
Harlan Creek—*stream* MT-8
Harlan Creek—*stream* OR-9
Harlan Creek—*stream* WA-9
**Harlan Crossroads**—*pop pl* KY-4
Harlandale—*uninc pl* TX-5
Harlandale Creek—*stream* TX-5
Harlandale HS—*school* TX-5
Harlandale JHS—*school* TX-5
Harlandale Park—*park* TX-5
Harlandale Sch—*school* TX-5
Harlan Davis Canyon—*valley* CA-9
Harland Cabin—*locale* CO-8
Harland Canyon—*valley* TX-5
Harland Cem—*cemetery* MS-4
Harland Cem—*cemetery* WV-2
Harland Creek—*stream* MS-4
Harland Creek Ch—*church* MS-4
Harland Flat—*flat* WY-8
Harlan Ditch—*canal* CO-8
Harlan Ditch—*canal* NM-5
Harlan Drain—*canal* MI-6
Harland Ridge—*ridge* WV-2
Harlands Bayou—*stream* LA-4
*Harlands Creek* MS-4
Harlands Creek—*stream* NC-3
Harlands Creek Cem—*cemetery* MS-4
Harland Slough—*stream* OR-9
**Harlan Gas**—*pop pl* KY-4
Harlan Gulch—*valley* CO-8
Harlan Hill—*summit* CA-9
Harlan (historical)—*locale* AL-4
**Harlan (historical)**—*pop pl* MS-4
Harlan House—*hist pl* PA-2
Harlan House Hotel—*hist pl* IA-7
Harlan HS—*school* IL-6
**Harlan Junction (historical)**—*pop pl* IA-7
*Harlan Knob* TN-4
Harlan Knobs—*ridge* TN-4
Harlan Lake—*lake* MN-6
Harlan Lateral—*canal* NM-5
Harlan-Lincoln House—*hist pl* IA-7
Harlan Log House—*hist pl* PA-2
Harlan Meadows—*flat* ID-8
Harlan Mtn—*summit* TN-4
*Harlan Park* OH-6
**Harlan Park**—*pop pl* OH-6
Harlan Post Office (historical)—*building* MS-4
Harlan Ranch—*locale* CA-9
Harlan Rock—*island* CA-9
Harlan Run—*stream* IN-6
Harlan Run—*stream* WV-2
**Harlansburg**—*pop pl* IN-6
**Harlansburg**—*pop pl* PA-2
*Harlan Sch* DE-2
Harlan Sch—*school* (2) AL-4
Harlan Sch—*school* IA-7
Harlan Sch—*school* MI-6
Harlan Sch (abandoned)—*school* MO-7
Harlan Sch (historical)—*school* MO-7
Harlan Spring—*spring* CA-9
Harlan Spring—*spring* WV-2
Harlan Spring Hist Dist—*hist pl* WV-2
Harlans Run—*stream* OH-6
Harlan's Station Site—*hist pl* KY-4
Harlan Stevens Ditch—*canal* CA-9
Harlan Swamp—*swamp* ME-1
Harlan Tank—*reservoir* NM-5
Harlan Tank Farm—*other* TX-5
Harlan Township—*fmr MCD* (2) IA-7
**Harlan Township**—*pop pl* (2) KS-7
**Harlan (Township of)**—*pop pl* OH-6
Harlan Trail Camp—*locale* NM-5
Harl Butte—*summit* OR-9
Harl Creek—*stream* TX-5
Harle Cem—*cemetery* TN-4
Harlech Castle Rock—*bar* CA-9
**Harleigh**—*pop pl* PA-2
Harleigh Cem—*cemetery* NJ-2
Harleigh Junction—*locale* PA-2
Harle Island (historical)—*island* TN-4
Harlem—*locale* CA-9
Harlem—*locale* ID-8
Harlem—*locale* LA-4
Harlem—*locale* PA-2
Harlem—*locale* TX-5
**Harlem**—*pop pl* FL-3
**Harlem**—*pop pl* GA-3
**Harlem**—*pop pl* IL-6
**Harlem**—*pop pl* MI-6
**Harlem**—*pop pl* MO-7
**Harlem**—*pop pl* MT-8
**Harlem**—*pop pl* (2) NY-2
**Harlem**—*pop pl* OH-6
Harlem—*uninc pl* LA-4
Harlem Acad—*school* FL-3
*Harlem Avenue* IL-6
Harlem Bridge—*other* IL-6
Harlem Canal—*canal* MT-8
Harlem Canal—*canal* NC-3
Harlem (CCD)—*cens area* GA-3
Harlem Cem—*cemetery* IL-6
Harlem Cem—*cemetery* ND-7
Harlem Cem—*cemetery* TN-4
Harlem Center Cem—*cemetery* IL-6
Harlem Ch—*church* IL-6
Harlem Ch—*church* MI-6
Harlem Courthouse—*hist pl* NY-2
Harlem Creek—*stream* AK-9
Harlem Drain—*canal* MI-6
Harlem Elementary JHS—*school* GA-3
Harlem Fire Watchtower—*hist pl* NY-2
**Harlem Heights**—*pop pl* AL-4
**Harlem Heights**—*pop pl* FL-3
**Harlem Heights**—*pop pl* NC-3
**Harlem Heights**—*pop pl* WV-2
**Harlem Heights (Labor Camp)**—*pop pl* FL-3
**Harlem (historical)**—*pop pl* ND-7
Harlem Hosp—*hospital* NY-2
Harlem HS—*school* IL-6
Harlem-Irving Shop Ctr—*locale* IL-6
Harlem Meer—*lake* NY-2
Harlem Park—*park* MD-2
Harlem Plantation House—*hist pl* LA-4
Harlem Reef—*bar* MI-6
Harlem River—*stream* NY-2
Harlem River—*uninc pl* NY-2
Harlem River Houses—*hist pl* NY-2
Harlem Sch—*school* IL-6
**Harlem Springs**—*pop pl* CA-9
**Harlem Springs**—*pop pl* OH-6
Harlem Town Hall—*building* ND-7
**Harlem Township**—*pop pl* ND-7
**Harlem (Township of)**—*pop pl* (2) IL-6
**Harlem (Township of)**—*pop pl* OH-6
**Harlemtown (subdivision)**—*pop pl* DE-2
*Harlemuheta* AZ-5
Harlem Valley State Hosp—*hospital* NY-2
**Harlemville**—*pop pl* NY-2
Harlemville Cem—*cemetery* NY-2
Harlen Sch—*school* TN-4
*Harlens Creek* MS-4
*Harlequin Hills* NV-8
Harlequin Lake—*lake* AK-9
Harlequin Lake—*lake* OR-9
Harlequin Lake—*lake* WY-8
Harlequin Park—*park* LA-4
Harles Branch—*stream* VA-3
Harles Cem—*cemetery* AL-4
Harles Hill—*summit* VA-3
*Harless* VA-3
**Harless**—*pop pl* VA-3
Harless Airp—*airport* IN-6
Harless Branch—*stream* WV-2
*Harless Cem* AL-4
Harless Cem—*cemetery* MS-4
Harless Cem—*cemetery* TX-5
Harless Cem—*cemetery* (4) WV-2
Harless Creek—*stream* KY-4
Harless Creek—*stream* MO-7
Harless Creek Sch—*school* KY-4
Harless Fork—*stream* (2) WV-2
Harless Lake—*reservoir* AL-4
Harless Lake Dam—*dam* AL-4
**Harleston**—*pop pl* MS-4
Harleston Dam Creek—*stream* SC-3

Harleston Post Office (historical)—*building* ... MS-4
**Harleton**—*pop pl* ... TX-5
Harleton (CCD)—*cens area* ... TX-5
Harleton Receiving Station—*other* ... TX-5
*Harley* ... IL-6
*Harley* ... IN-6
Harley—*locale* ... NC-3
Harley—*locale* ... OH-6
Harley—*locale* ... WV-2
**Harley**—*pop pl* ... IN-6
Harley Anderson Ditch—*canal* ... AR-4
Harley Ave Sch—*school* ... NY-2
*Harley Branch* ... SC-3
Harley Branch—*stream* ... NC-3
Harley Cem—*cemetery* ... KS-7
Harley Cem—*cemetery* ... PA-2
**Harley Corners**—*pop pl* ... PA-2
Harley Creek—*stream* ... MT-8
Harley Dome—*locale* ... UT-8
Harley Dome Gas Field—*oilfield* ... UT-8
Harley Gap—*summit* ... GA-3
Harley Gulch—*valley* ... CA-9
Harley Holben Elem Sch—*school* ... IN-6
Harley Lake—*lake* ... MN-6
Harley Millpond—*lake* ... MA-1
Harley Mtn—*summit* ... NM-5
Harley Park—*flat* ... MT-8
Harley Park Archeol Site—*hist pl* ... MO-7
Harleys Bridge—*bridge* ... SC-3
Harley Sch—*school* ... NY-2
**Harley Siding**—*pop pl* ... IN-6
Harleys Millpond—*reservoir* ... SC-3
Harley Spring—*spring* ... VA-3
**Harley Subdivision**—*pop pl* ... TN-4
**Harleysville**—*pop pl* ... PA-2
**Harleyville**—*pop pl* ... SC-3
Harleyville (CCD)—*cens area* ... SC-3
Harleyville Cem—*cemetery* ... SC-3
Harleyville-Ridgeville HS—*school* ... SC-3
**Harlin**—*pop pl* ... WV-2
**Harlin Addition (subdivision)**—*pop pl* ... SD-7
Harlin Chapel Cem—*cemetery* ... TX-5
Harlin Chapel Ch—*church* ... TX-5
Harlin Creek—*stream* ... OR-9
Harling Cem—*cemetery* ... SC-3
**Harlingen**—*pop pl* ... NJ-2
**Harlingen**—*pop pl* ... TX-5
Harlingen, Lake—*lake* ... TX-5
Harlingen Industrial Airp—*airport* ... TX-5
Harlingen Main Canal—*canal* ... TX-5
Harlingen Municipal Golf Course—*other* ... TX-5
Harlingen Pumping Station—*other* ... TX-5
Harlingen Reform Cem—*cemetery* ... NJ-2
Harlingen-San Benito (CCD)—*cens area* ... TX-5
Harlington Cem—*cemetery* ... IA-7
Harling Trail—*trail* ... NH-1
Harlin Lake—*lake* ... WA-9
Harlin Morgan And Rilie Reservations—*park* ... AL-4
**Harlin (Morgans Run)**—*pop pl* ... WV-2
Harlin Robinson Ditch—*canal* ... WY-8
Harlis—*locale* ... MN-6
Harlis and Broady Mine—*mine* ... CA-9
Harliss—*locale* ... MN-6
Harliss Creek—*stream* ... OR-9
**Harllee**—*pop pl* ... GA-3
Harlocker Hill—*summit* ... OR-9
Harlock Pond—*lake* ... MA-1
Harlon Block Park—*park* ... TX-5
*Harlow* ... MS-4
Harlow—*locale* ... AR-4
Harlow—*locale* ... GA-3
**Harlow**—*pop pl* ... ND-7
Harlow, Elmer, House—*hist pl* ... OR-9
Harlow, Fred, House—*hist pl* ... OR-9
Harlow, Mount—*summit* ... MT-8
Harlow, Sgt. William, Family Homestead—*hist pl* ... MA-1
Harlow Block—*hist pl* ... MI-6
Harlow Block—*hist pl* ... OR-9
Harlow Branch—*stream* ... FL-3
Harlow Bridge Sch—*school* ... VT-1
Harlow Brook—*stream* (2) ... MA-1
Harlow Brook—*stream* ... VT-1
Harlow Brook Number 1 Dam—*dam* ... MA-1
Harlow Brook Number 2 Dam—*dam* ... MA-1
Harlow Brook Rsvr—*reservoir* ... MA-1
Harlow Cem—*cemetery* ... AL-4
Harlow Cem—*cemetery* (2) ... AR-4
Harlow Cem—*cemetery* ... KY-4
Harlow Cem—*cemetery* ... MO-7
Harlow Chapel—*church* ... KY-4
Harlow Creek—*stream* ... IL-6
Harlow Creek—*stream* ... MI-6
Harlow Creek—*stream* ... OK-5
Harlow Creek—*stream* (2) ... WA-9
**Harlowe**—*pop pl* ... NC-3
Harlowe Canal—*canal* ... NC-3
Harlowe Ch—*church* ... NC-3
Harlowe Creek—*stream* ... NC-3
Harlowe (Township of)—*fmr MCD* ... NC-3
Harlow Farmstead—*hist pl* ... SD-7
Harlow Fay Lakes—*lake* ... MO-7
Harlow Ford—*locale* ... MO-7
Harlow Hill—*summit* ... WA-9
Harlow Hollow—*valley* ... AR-4
Harlow Homestead—*hist pl* ... MA-1
Harlow Island—*island* ... MO-7
Harlow Lake—*lake* (2) ... MI-6
Harlow Old Fort House—*hist pl* ... MA-1
Harlow Park—*park* ... CO-8
Harlow Place—*locale* ... CA-9
Harlow Point—*cape* ... ID-8
Harlow Pond—*lake* ... ME-1
Harlow Pond—*lake* ... MA-1
Harlow Pond—*reservoir* ... MA-1
Harlow Pond—*reservoir* ... PA-2
Harlow Ridge—*ridge* ... ME-1
Harlow Ridge—*ridge* ... WA-9
Harlow Row—*hist pl* ... NY-2
Harlow Sch—*school* ... NY-2
Harlow Sch—*school* ... SD-7
Harlow Sch (abandoned)—*school* ... SD-7
*Harlows Hill* ... MA-1
*Harlows Island* ... MO-7
**Harlows Landing**—*pop pl* ... MA-1
Harlow Street Sch—*school* ... ME-1
**Harlowton**—*pop pl* ... MT-8
Harlow-Wright Cem—*cemetery* ... MO-7
Harlson, Eugene, House—*hist pl* ... TX-5
Harl Tank—*mine* ... AZ-5
Harmac Oil Field—*oilfield* ... KS-7
Harman—*locale* ... VA-3
**Harman**—*pop pl* ... VA-3
**Harman**—*pop pl* ... WV-2
Harman, James, Bldg—*hist pl* ... SC-3
Harman, Lake—*lake* ... ND-7
Harman Ave Sch—*school* ... OH-6
Harman Branch—*stream* ... SC-3
Harman Branch—*stream* ... WV-2
Harman Cem—*cemetery* ... IN-6
Harman Cem—*cemetery* ... NC-3
*Harman Church* ... TN-4
*Harman Creek* ... MT-8
Harman Creek—*stream* ... ID-8
Harman Creek—*stream* ... MO-7
Harman Ditch—*canal* ... WY-8
Harman Gap—*locale* ... MD-2
*Harman (Harmans)* ... MD-2
Harman Heights—*locale* ... WA-9
**Harman Junction**—*pop pl* ... VA-3
Harman Knob—*summit* ... WV-2
Harman Marsh Pond—*lake* ... MA-1
Harman Run—*stream* ... OH-6
**Harmans**—*pop pl* ... MD-2
Harman School—*locale* ... MI-6
*Harmans Gap* ... MD-2
**Harmans (Harman)**—*pop pl* ... MD-2
*Harman Spring* ... OR-9
Harmans Sch—*school* ... MD-2
**Harmans Station**—*pop pl* ... IN-6
Harman Tank—*reservoir* ... AZ-5
*Harmanville* ... PA-2
Harman-Watson-Matthews House—*hist pl* ... GA-3
Harman Windmill—*locale* ... NM-5
Harmany Ch—*church* ... WV-2
**Harmar**—*pop pl* ... OH-6
**Harmar Heights**—*pop pl* ... PA-2
Harmar Hist Dist—*hist pl* ... OH-6
Harmar (RR name for Harmarville)—*other* ... PA-2
Harmar Sch—*school* ... IN-6
**Harmar (Township of)**—*pop pl* ... PA-2
**Harmarville**—*pop pl* ... PA-2
Harmarville Ch—*church* ... PA-2
**Harmarville (RR name Harmar)**—*pop pl* ... PA-2
Harmaston—*locale* ... TX-5
Harmattan Strip Mine—*mine* ... IL-6
Harmco—*uninc pl* ... WV-2
Harm Coat Bayou—*gut* ... AR-4
Harm Creek—*stream* ... NC-3
Harmen Cem—*cemetery* ... TN-4
*Harmer* ... OH-6
Har-Mer Elem Sch—*school* ... PA-2
*Harmer Hill* ... MS-4
Harmersville—*locale* ... NJ-2
Harmes Canyon—*valley* ... UT-8
*Harmeson Heights* ... IN-6
**Harmeson Heights**—*pop pl* ... IN-6
Harmes Spring—*spring* ... CA-9
Harmiller Gap—*gap* ... NC-3
Harmin Lake—*lake* ... WI-6
*Harmon* ... VA-3
Harmon—*locale* ... AL-4
Harmon—*locale* (2) ... AR-4
Harmon—*locale* ... ND-7
**Harmon**—*pop pl* ... AL-4
**Harmon**—*pop pl* ... IL-6
**Harmon**—*pop pl* ... LA-4
**Harmon**—*pop pl* ... MS-4
**Harmon**—*pop pl* ... OH-6
**Harmon**—*pop pl* ... OK-5
**Harmon**—*pop pl* ... TN-4
**Harmon**—*pop pl* ... TX-5
Harmon, Francis E., House—*hist pl* ... OH-6
Harmon, Isaac, Farmhouse—*hist pl* ... DE-2
Harmon, William, House—*hist pl* ... MT-8
Harmon Barranca—*valley* ... CA-9
**Harmon Beach**—*pop pl* ... ME-1
*Harmon Branch* ... MO-7
*Harmon Branch* ... VA-3
Harmon Branch—*stream* (2) ... MO-7
Harmon Branch—*stream* ... VA-3
Harmon Branch—*stream* (5) ... WV-2
Harmon Branch Ch—*church* ... WV-2
*Harmon Brook* ... ME-1
Harmon Brook—*stream* (2) ... ME-1
Harmon Brook—*stream* ... MA-1
Harmon Brook—*stream* ... OH-6
Harmon Canyon—*valley* ... CA-9
Harmon Canyon—*valley* ... UT-8
Harmon Cem—*cemetery* ... AL-4
Harmon Cem—*cemetery* ... AR-4
Harmon Cem—*cemetery* (2) ... IL-6
Harmon Cem—*cemetery* ... KY-4
Harmon Cem—*cemetery* (2) ... MS-4
Harmon Cem—*cemetery* (3) ... OH-6
Harmon Cem—*cemetery* ... OK-5
Harmon Cem—*cemetery* ... SC-3
Harmon Cem—*cemetery* (5) ... TN-4
Harmon Cem—*cemetery* (2) ... VA-3
Harmon Cem—*cemetery* ... WI-6
Harmon Ch—*church* ... AR-4
Harmon Ch—*church* ... MS-4
Harmon Ch—*church* ... VA-3
Harmon Chapel—*church* ... IL-6
Harmon Chapel Cumberland Presbyterian Ch—*church* ... TN-4
**Harmon City Heights**—*pop pl* ... MI-6
**Harmon (County)**—*pop pl* ... OK-5
Harmon County Courthouse—*hist pl* ... OK-5
Harmon Cove—*bay* ... VA-3
Harmon Creek—*stream* ... AR-4
Harmon Creek—*stream* ... KY-4
Harmon Creek—*stream* ... MO-7
Harmon Creek—*stream* ... MT-8
Harmon Creek—*stream* ... NC-3
Harmon Creek—*stream* ... OH-6
Harmon Creek—*stream* ... OR-9
Harmon Creek—*stream* ... PA-2
Harmon Creek—*stream* ... SC-3
Harmon Creek—*stream* (3) ... TN-4
Harmon Creek—*stream* ... TX-5
Harmon Creek—*stream* ... UT-8
Harmon Creek—*stream* ... WV-2
*Harmon Creek Baptist Church* ... TN-4
Harmon Creek Boat Dock—*locale* ... TN-4
Harmon Creek Ch—*church* ... TN-4
Harmon Creek Resort—*locale* ... TN-4
Harmon Creek Sch (historical)—*school* ... TN-4
Harmon Crossroads—*locale* ... AL-4
Harmond Branch—*stream* ... KY-4
Harmond Cem—*cemetery* ... AL-4
Harmond Creek—*stream* ... WV-2
Harmon Den Mtn—*summit* ... NC-3
Harmon Den Wildlife Mngmt Area—*park* ... NC-3
Harmon Ditch—*canal* ... IN-6
Harmon Ditch—*canal* ... UT-8
Harmond Park—*park* ... LA-4
Harmon Drain—*canal* ... NV-8
Harmon Field—*park* ... AL-4
Harmon Field—*park* ... GA-3
Harmon Field—*park* ... LA-4
Harmon Field—*park* ... MI-6
Harmon Field—*park* ... NC-3
Harmon Field—*park* (4) ... OH-6
Harmon Field—*park* ... OK-5
Harmon Field—*park* ... SC-3
Harmon Field—*park* ... TN-4
Harmon Field—*park* ... WA-9
Harmon Field Park—*park* ... OH-6
*Harmon Gulch* ... TX-5
Harmon Gulch—*valley* ... CO-8
Harmon Harbor—*bay* ... ME-1
Harmon Heath—*swamp* ... ME-1
Harmon Heights—*summit* ... WY-8
Harmon-Herman Sch (historical)—*school* ... AL-4
Harmon Hill—*summit* ... VT-1
Harmon Hollow—*valley* (2) ... KY-4
Harmon Hollow—*valley* (3) ... MO-7
Harmon Hollow—*valley* ... TN-4
Harmonia Cem—*cemetery* (2) ... MS-4
Harmonia Ch—*church* (2) ... GA-3
Harmonia Ch—*church* ... MS-4
Harmonia Ch (historical)—*church* ... MS-4
Harmonia (historical)—*locale* ... KS-7
*Harmonia Methodist Ch* ... MS-4
Harmonia Park—*park* ... WI-6
Harmonia Sch—*school* ... PA-2
*Harmonia Villa* ... AZ-5
Harmonica Creek—*stream* ... CA-9
Harmonica Lake—*lake* ... UT-8
Harmonica Point—*cape* ... UT-8
*Harmonie* ... IN-6
Harmonie Ch—*church* ... MO-7
Harmonie Club, The—*hist pl* ... MI-6
Harmonie Park—*park* ... TX-5
Harmonie State Park—*park* ... IN-6
*Harmonie State Rec Area* ... IN-6
Harmonious Ch—*church* ... MS-4
**Harmonious Township**—*pop pl* ... ND-7
Harmon Island—*island* ... PA-2
Harmonist Cem—*cemetery* ... IN-6
*Harmon Junction* ... VA-3
Harmon Knob—*summit* ... NC-3
Harmon Lake—*lake* ... AL-4
Harmon Lake—*lake* ... IA-7
Harmon Lake—*lake* ... LA-4
Harmon Lake—*lake* ... ME-1
Harmon Lake—*lake* ... MI-6
Harmon Lake—*lake* ... MS-4
Harmon Lake—*lake* ... TX-5
Harmon Lake—*lake* ... WI-6
Harmon Lake—*reservoir* ... LA-4
Harmon Lake State Game Mngmt Area—*park* ... IA-7
Harmon Landing—*locale* ... MD-2
Harmon Lateral—*canal* ... AZ-5
Harmon-McNeil House—*hist pl* ... CA-9
Harmon Memorial Park—*park* ... OH-6
Harmon Mine—*mine* ... TN-4
Harmon Mtn—*summit* (2) ... ME-1
Harmon-Neils House—*hist pl* ... OR-9
Harmon Number One Drain—*canal* ... NV-8
Harmon-on-Hudson—*uninc pl* ... NY-2
Harmon Park—*park* ... AL-4
Harmon Park—*park* ... AZ-5
Harmon Park—*park* ... ID-8
Harmon Park—*park* ... MN-6
Harmon Park—*park* ... NE-7
Harmon Park—*park* ... ND-7
Harmon Park—*park* ... OK-5
Harmon Park—*park* ... TX-5
**Harmon Park**—*pop pl* ... NY-2
*Harmon Peak* ... CA-9
Harmon Peak—*summit* ... CA-9
Harmon Playground—*park* ... OH-6
*Harmon Pond* ... MA-1
Harmon Pond—*lake* ... CT-1
Harmon Pond—*lake* ... MA-1
Harmon Pond—*reservoir* ... SC-3
Harmon Powerplant—*other* ... GU-9
Harmon Prospect—*mine* ... TN-4
Harmon Pye Branch—*stream* ... GA-3
Harmon Ranch—*locale* ... AZ-5
Harmon Ranch—*locale* ... MT-8
Harmon Refuse Bank Dam—*dam* ... PA-2
Harmon Ridge—*ridge* ... MO-7
Harmon Ridge—*ridge* (2) ... OH-6
Harmon Ridge—*ridge* ... WV-2
Harmon Rocks—*summit* ... WV-2
Harmon Rsvr—*reservoir* ... OR-9
Harmon Run—*stream* ... VA-3
Harmon's—*post sta* ... UT-8
Harmon-Salt Creek Ch—*church* ... OH-6
**Harmonsburg**—*pop pl* ... PA-2
Harmonsburg Station—*locale* ... PA-2
Harmon Sch—*hist pl* ... DE-2
Harmon Sch—*school* ... AL-4
Harmon Sch—*school* ... DE-2
Harmon Sch—*school* ... IL-6
Harmon Sch—*school* ... MI-6
Harmon Sch—*school* ... NV-8
Harmon Sch—*school* ... TX-5
Harmon Sch (historical)—*school* ... MO-7
Harmon Sch (historical)—*school* ... TN-4
*Harmons Corner* ... ME-1
**Harmons Corner**—*pop pl* ... ME-1
Harmon's Covered Bridge—*hist pl* ... PA-2
*Harmons Creek* ... TN-4
*Harmons Creek* ... TX-5
*Harmons Crossroads* ... NC-3
*Harmon's Harbor* ... ME-1
Harmon Sink—*basin* ... GU-9
Harmons Island—*island* ... AL-4
Harmon Site—*hist pl* ... KS-7
Harmon Site No. 2 (14LT323)—*hist pl* ... KS-7
Harmons Lake—*reservoir* ... IN-6
Harmons Lick—*stream* ... KY-4
Harmonson Corners—*locale* ... PA-2
Harmons Pond—*lake* ... SC-3
Harmon Spring—*spring* ... MO-7
Harmon Spring—*spring* ... NV-8
Harmon Spring—*spring* ... OR-9
Harmon Spring—*spring* ... WA-9
Harmon Spring Campground—*locale* ... MO-7
Harmon Springs—*spring* (2) ... WY-8
*Harmon Spring Trail Campground* ... MO-7
*Harmons Run* ... VA-3
Harmons School—*locale* ... DE-2
Harmon Stream—*stream* ... ME-1
**Harmon (subdivision)**—*pop pl* ... AL-4
**Harmon Subdivision**—*pop pl* ... MS-4
Harmon Subdivision Hist Dist—*hist pl* ... MS-4
*Harmons Valley United Methodist Church* ... TN-4
Harmon Tank—*reservoir* ... AZ-5
Harmon Tank Farm—*other* ... GU-9
Harmon Telephone Exchange—*other* ... GU-9
Harmontown—*locale* ... AR-4
Harmontown—*locale* ... PA-2
**Harmontown**—*pop pl* ... MS-4
Harmontown Baptist Ch—*church* ... MS-4
Harmontown Cem—*cemetery* ... MS-4
Harmontown Post Office (historical)—*building* ... MS-4
**Harmon Township**—*pop pl* ... KS-7
**Harmon Township**—*pop pl* ... SD-7
Harmon Township Hall—*building* ... SD-7
Harmon (Township of)—*fmr MCD* ... AR-4
**Harmon (Township of)**—*pop pl* ... IL-6
Harmon Trail—*trail* ... UT-8
Harmon Tunnel—*other* ... IA-7
Harmon Valley Ch—*church* ... TN-4
**Harmon Village**—*pop pl* ... GU-9
**Harmonville**—*pop pl* ... PA-2
Harmonville Impounding Basin—*basin* ... PA-2
Harmon Wildlife Area—*park* ... KS-7
*Harmony* ... AL-4
*Harmony* ... IN-6
*Harmony* ... NJ-2
*Harmony* ... OH-6
*Harmony* ... UT-8
Harmony—*locale* (4) ... AR-4
Harmony—*locale* ... CA-9
Harmony—*locale* ... DE-2
Harmony—*locale* (2) ... GA-3
Harmony—*locale* ... IL-6
Harmony—*locale* ... KY-4
Harmony—*locale* ... LA-4
Harmony—*locale* ... MS-4
Harmony—*locale* ... NJ-2
Harmony—*locale* ... OR-9
Harmony—*locale* ... RI-1
Harmony—*locale* ... SC-3
Harmony—*locale* (2) ... TN-4
Harmony—*locale* (9) ... TX-5
Harmony—*locale* ... VA-3
Harmony—*locale* ... WA-9
**Harmony**—*pop pl* (5) ... AL-4
**Harmony**—*pop pl* (3) ... AR-4
**Harmony**—*pop pl* ... CO-8
**Harmony**—*pop pl* ... IL-6
**Harmony**—*pop pl* ... IN-6
**Harmony**—*pop pl* ... ME-1
**Harmony**—*pop pl* (2) ... MD-2
**Harmony**—*pop pl* ... MN-6
**Harmony**—*pop pl* (3) ... MS-4
**Harmony**—*pop pl* ... MO-7
**Harmony**—*pop pl* (4) ... NJ-2
**Harmony**—*pop pl* ... NC-3
**Harmony**—*pop pl* ... OH-6
**Harmony**—*pop pl* (2) ... OR-9
**Harmony**—*pop pl* (3) ... PA-2
**Harmony**—*pop pl* ... SC-3
**Harmony**—*pop pl* (2) ... TN-4
**Harmony**—*pop pl* ... TX-5
**Harmony**—*pop pl* ... VA-3
**Harmony**—*pop pl* ... WV-2
**Harmony**—*pop pl* ... WI-6
**Harmony**—*pop pl* ... WY-8
Harmony—*unorg reg* ... SD-7
Harmony, Lake—*reservoir* ... PA-2
**Harmony Acres**—*pop pl* ... CA-9
*Harmony and the Union Church* ... AL-4
*Harmony Baptist Ch* ... MS-4
*Harmony Baptist Ch* ... TN-4
Harmony Baptist Ch—*church* ... KS-7
Harmony Baptist Ch—*church* ... MS-4
Harmony Baptist Ch—*church* ... TN-4
*Harmony Baptist Church* ... AL-4
*Harmony Baptist Institute* ... MS-4
Harmony Bay—*bay* ... OR-9
*Harmony Bethel Church* ... PA-2
Harmony Borax Works—*hist pl* ... CA-9
Harmony Borax Works (Ruins)—*locale* ... CA-9
Harmony Borough—*civil* ... PA-2
Harmony Branch—*stream* ... AL-4
Harmony Branch—*stream* ... MS-4
Harmony Brook—*stream* ... NJ-2
*Harmony Brook Dam* ... NJ-2
Harmony Canal—*canal* ... LA-4
*Harmony Canyon* ... NV-8
Harmony Canyon—*valley* ... NV-8
Harmony (CCD)—*cens area* ... TN-4
*Harmony Cem* ... AL-4
*Harmony Cem* ... MS-4
Harmony Cem—*cemetery* (8) ... AL-4
Harmony Cem—*cemetery* (4) ... AR-4
Harmony Cem—*cemetery* ... CO-8
Harmony Cem—*cemetery* ... DE-2
Harmony Cem—*cemetery* ... DC-2
Harmony Cem—*cemetery* (2) ... GA-3
Harmony Cem—*cemetery* (3) ... IL-6
Harmony Cem—*cemetery* ... IN-6
Harmony Cem—*cemetery* ... IA-7
Harmony Cem—*cemetery* (4) ... KS-7
Harmony Cem—*cemetery* ... KY-4
Harmony Cem—*cemetery* ... ME-1
Harmony Cem—*cemetery* ... MA-1
Harmony Cem—*cemetery* ... MI-6
Harmony Cem—*cemetery* (13) ... MS-4
Harmony Cem—*cemetery* ... MO-7
Harmony Cem—*cemetery* (2) ... NE-7
Harmony Cem—*cemetery* ... NJ-2
Harmony Cem—*cemetery* ... NC-3
Harmony Cem—*cemetery* (5) ... OH-6
Harmony Cem—*cemetery* ... OK-5
Harmony Cem—*cemetery* (2) ... PA-2
Harmony Cem—*cemetery* (5) ... TN-4
Harmony Cem—*cemetery* (3) ... TX-5
Harmony Cem—*cemetery* (2) ... WV-2
Harmony Cem—*cemetery* (2) ... WI-6
Harmony Cemetery—*hist pl* ... WV-2
*Harmony Centre* ... PA-2
*Harmony Ch* ... AL-4
*Harmony Ch* ... MS-4
*Harmony Ch* ... TN-4
Harmony Ch—*church* (24) ... AL-4
Harmony Ch—*church* (9) ... AR-4
Harmony Ch—*church* ... DE-2
Harmony Ch—*church* (4) ... FL-3
Harmony Ch—*church* (27) ... GA-3
Harmony Ch—*church* (5) ... IL-6
Harmony Ch—*church* (3) ... IN-6
Harmony Ch—*church* (7) ... KY-4
Harmony Ch—*church* (4) ... LA-4
Harmony Ch—*church* ... MD-2
Harmony Ch—*church* ... MI-6
Harmony Ch—*church* (17) ... MS-4
Harmony Ch—*church* (14) ... MO-7
Harmony Ch—*church* (8) ... NC-3
Harmony Ch—*church* (9) ... OH-6
Harmony Ch—*church* (2) ... OK-5
Harmony Ch—*church* (4) ... PA-2
Harmony Ch—*church* (8) ... SC-3
Harmony Ch—*church* ... SD-7
Harmony Ch—*church* (9) ... TN-4
Harmony Ch—*church* (10) ... TX-5
Harmony Ch—*church* (4) ... VA-3
Harmony Ch—*church* (5) ... WV-2
*Harmony Chapel* ... TN-4
Harmony Chapel—*church* ... AR-4
Harmony Chapel—*church* ... LA-4
Harmony Chapel—*church* ... MD-2
Harmony Chapel—*church* ... MI-6
Harmony Chapel—*church* ... OH-6
Harmony Chapel—*church* ... VA-3
Harmony Chapel and Cemetery—*hist pl* ... RI-1
Harmony Ch (historical)—*church* (2) ... AL-4
Harmony Ch (historical)—*church* ... GA-3
Harmony Ch (historical)—*church* (2) ... MS-4
Harmony Ch (historical)—*church* ... PA-2
Harmony Ch of God—*church* ... AL-4
Harmony Church—*hist pl* ... DE-2
**Harmony Church**—*pop pl* ... GA-3
Harmony Church Cem—*cemetery* ... AR-4
Harmony Church Oil Field—*oilfield* ... LA-4
Harmony Community Center—*locale* ... TX-5
Harmony Community Ch—*church* ... NC-3
Harmony Community Hall—*locale* ... WA-9
*Harmony Corners* ... WI-6
**Harmony Corners**—*pop pl* ... NY-2
**Harmony Corners**—*pop pl* ... WI-6
Harmony Creek—*stream* ... ID-8
Harmony Creek—*stream* ... IN-6
Harmony Creek—*stream* ... MO-7
Harmony Creek—*stream* ... TX-5
Harmony Creek—*stream* ... WA-9
Harmony Creek—*stream* ... WY-8
Harmony Cumberland Presbyterian Ch—*church* ... TN-4
Harmony Ditch—*canal* ... WY-8
Harmony Ditch No 1—*canal* ... CO-8
Harmony Ditch No 2—*canal* ... CO-8
Harmony Ditch No 3—*canal* ... CO-8
Harmony Division—*civil* ... TN-4
Harmony Drain—*stream* ... IN-6
Harmony Falls—*falls* ... WA-9
Harmony Falls Landing—*locale* ... WA-9
Harmony Falls Lodge—*locale* ... WA-9
Harmony Farms Preschool—*school* ... DE-2
Harmony Ferry (historical)—*locale* ... PA-2
Harmony Flat—*flat* ... UT-8
Harmony Forge Mansion—*hist pl* ... PA-2
Harmony Freewell Ch—*church* ... MD-2
*Harmony Freewill Baptist Ch* ... AL-4
Harmony Freewill Baptist Ch—*church* ... MS-4
Harmony Grange—*locale* ... PA-2
Harmony Grove—*locale* ... TN-4
**Harmony Grove**—*pop pl* ... AR-4
**Harmony Grove**—*pop pl* ... CA-9
**Harmony Grove**—*pop pl* ... MD-2
**Harmony Grove**—*pop pl* ... NC-3
**Harmony Grove**—*pop pl* ... PA-2
**Harmony Grove**—*pop pl* ... WV-2
**Harmony Grove**—*pop pl* ... WI-6
*Harmony Grove Baptist Ch* ... AL-4
Harmony Grove Cem—*cemetery* ... AL-4
Harmony Grove Cem—*cemetery* ... AR-4
Harmony Grove Cem—*cemetery* ... CA-9
Harmony Grove Cem—*cemetery* (2) ... GA-3
Harmony Grove Cem—*cemetery* ... KY-4
Harmony Grove Cem—*cemetery* ... ME-1
Harmony Grove Cem—*cemetery* ... MA-1
Harmony Grove Cem—*cemetery* (2) ... MO-7
Harmony Grove Cem—*cemetery* ... PA-2
Harmony Grove Ch—*church* (4) ... AL-4
Harmony Grove Ch—*church* (2) ... AR-4
Harmony Grove Ch—*church* (10) ... GA-3
Harmony Grove Ch—*church* ... LA-4
Harmony Grove Ch—*church* ... MD-2
Harmony Grove Ch—*church* ... MO-7
Harmony Grove Ch—*church* (2) ... NC-3
Harmony Grove Ch—*church* ... PA-2
Harmony Grove Ch—*church* ... TX-5
Harmony Grove Ch—*church* (2) ... VA-3
Harmony Grove Ch—*church* (2) ... WV-2
Harmony Grove Meeting House—*hist pl* ... WV-2
**Harmony Grove (Religious Camp)**—*pop pl* ... CA-9
Harmony Grove Sch—*school* ... AR-4
Harmony Grove Sch—*school* ... CA-9
Harmony Grove Sch (historical)—*school* ... AL-4
Harmony Grove Sch (historical)—*school* ... TN-4
Harmony Grove School (historical)—*locale* ... MO-7
Harmony Hall—*hist pl* ... MD-2
Harmony Hall—*hist pl* ... NC-3
Harmony Hall—*locale* ... NC-3
Harmony Hall—*locale* ... PA-2
**Harmony Hall**—*pop pl* ... MD-2
Harmony Hall Ch—*church* ... GA-3
Harmony Hall Sch (abandoned)—*school* ... PA-2
Harmony Heights—*flat* ... WY-8
Harmony Heights—*summit* ... WA-9
**Harmony Heights (subdivision)**—*pop pl* ... FL-3
**Harmony Hill**—*pop pl* ... PA-2
**Harmony Hill**—*pop pl* ... TX-5
Harmony Hill—*summit* ... CT-1
Harmony Hill—*summit* ... PA-2
Harmony Hill—*summit* ... TX-5
Harmony Hill Cem—*cemetery* ... TX-5
Harmony Hill Ch—*church* ... AR-4
Harmony Hill Ch—*church* ... NC-3
Harmony Hill Ch—*church* ... TX-5
Harmony Hill Elem Sch—*school* ... KS-7
Harmony Hill HS—*school* ... SD-7
**Harmony Hills**—*pop pl* ... DE-2
**Harmony Hills**—*pop pl* ... MD-2
**Harmony Hills**—*pop pl* ... PA-2
**Harmony Hills**—*pop pl* ... TN-4
**Harmony Hills**—*pop pl* ... TX-5
Harmony Hill Sch—*school* ... IL-6
Harmony Hill Sch—*school* ... NE-7
Harmony Hills Community Park—*park* ... TX-5
Harmony Hill Site—*hist pl* ... TX-5
Harmony Hills Sch—*school* ... MD-2
Harmony Hills Sch—*school* ... TX-5
Harmony Hill United Methodist Church—*hist pl* ... NJ-2
Harmony Hist Dist—*hist pl* ... PA-2
Harmony (historical)—*locale* ... AL-4
Harmony (historical)—*locale* ... KS-7
Harmony (historical)—*locale* ... MS-4
Harmony Hollow—*valley* ... OH-6
Harmony Hollow—*valley* ... VA-3
Harmony HS—*school* ... IA-7
Harmony Industrial Park—*locale* ... DE-2
Harmony Islands—*area* ... AK-9
**Harmony Junction**—*pop pl* ... PA-2
Harmony Lake—*lake* ... MN-6
Harmony Lake—*lake* ... NJ-2
Harmony Lake—*lake* (2) ... WI-6
Harmony Lake—*reservoir* ... NY-2
Harmony Lake Estates—*locale* ... KY-4
Harmony Landing—*locale* ... KY-4
Harmony Landing Country Club—*other* ... KY-4
**Harmony Lane Subdivision**—*pop pl* ... UT-8
Harmony Leland Sch—*school* ... GA-3
Harmony Lookout Tower—*locale* ... WI-6
*Harmony Meeting House* ... AL-4
Harmony Metaphysical Ch—*church* ... FL-3
*Harmony Methodist Church* ... AL-4
*Harmony Methodist Church* ... MS-4
Harmony Mill Hist Dist—*hist pl* ... NY-2
Harmony Mill No. 3—*hist pl* ... NY-2
Harmony Mine—*mine* ... NV-8
Harmony Mine—*mine* ... SD-7
Harmony Mine (Inactive)—*mine* ... ID-8
*Harmony Missionary Baptist Church* ... AL-4
*Harmony Missionary Baptist Church* ... MS-4
*Harmony Mountain* ... UT-8
Harmony Mtn—*summit* ... AR-4
Harmony Mtns—*summit* (2) ... UT-8
Harmony Oil Field—*oilfield* ... MS-4
Harmony Park—*flat* ... UT-8
Harmony Park—*park* ... IN-6
Harmony Park—*park* ... UT-8
**Harmony Park**—*pop pl* ... NJ-2
**Harmony Park Subdivision**—*pop pl* ... UT-8
**Harmony Point**—*pop pl* ... OR-9
Harmony Point Sch—*school* ... IA-7
Harmony Post Office (historical)—*building* ... TN-4
*Harmony Presbyterian Church* ... AL-4
*Harmony Primitive Baptist Ch* ... TN-4
Harmony Primitive Baptist Ch—*church* ... TN-4
*Harmony Primitive Baptist Church* ... AL-4
Harmony Private Sch (historical)—*school* ... MS-4
Harmony Ranch—*locale* ... TX-5
*Harmony Reservoir* ... NJ-2
Harmony Ridge—*ridge* ... CA-9
Harmony Ridge—*ridge* ... PA-2
Harmony Sch—*school* ... AL-4
Harmony Sch—*school* ... CO-8
Harmony Sch—*school* ... DE-2
Harmony Sch—*school* (2) ... GA-3
Harmony Sch—*school* (10) ... IL-6
Harmony Sch—*school* (3) ... IA-7
Harmony Sch—*school* (3) ... KS-7
Harmony Sch—*school* (2) ... KY-4
Harmony Sch—*school* ... MN-6
Harmony Sch—*school* ... MS-4
Harmony Sch—*school* (3) ... MO-7
Harmony Sch—*school* ... MT-8
Harmony Sch—*school* (3) ... NE-7
Harmony Sch—*school* ... NJ-2
Harmony Sch—*school* ... NC-3
Harmony Sch—*school* (3) ... OK-5
Harmony Sch—*school* ... OR-9
Harmony Sch—*school* ... PA-2
Harmony Sch—*school* (3) ... SD-7
Harmony Sch—*school* (3) ... TX-5
Harmony Sch—*school* ... WA-9
Harmony Sch—*school* ... WI-6
Harmony Sch—*school* ... WY-8
Harmony Sch (abandoned)—*school* ... MO-7
Harmony Sch (historical)—*school* ... AL-4
Harmony Sch (historical)—*school* (3) ... MS-4
Harmony Sch (historical)—*school* ... PA-2
Harmony Sch (historical)—*school* ... SD-7
Harmony Sch (historical)—*school* (6) ... TN-4
Harmony School—*locale* (2) ... WA-9
Harmony School (Abandoned)—*locale* ... CA-9
Harmony School (historical)—*locale* (2) ... MO-7
Harmony Shop Ctr—*locale* ... MO-7
Harmony Spring—*spring* (2) ... TN-4
Harmony Springs—*spring* ... GA-3
Harmony Star—*locale* ... OK-5
*Harmony State Rec Area* ... IN-6
Harmony Station—*locale* ... NJ-2
**Harmony (Town of)**—*pop pl* ... ME-1
**Harmony (Town of)**—*pop pl* ... NY-2
**Harmony (Town of)**—*pop pl* (3) ... WI-6
Harmony Township—*CDP* ... PA-2
Harmony Township—*civil* ... KS-7
Harmony Township—*civil* ... MO-7
Harmony Township—*civil* ... SD-7
**Harmony Township**—*pop pl* ... ND-7
**Harmony Township**—*pop pl* (3) ... SD-7
**Harmony (Township of)**—*pop pl* ... IL-6
**Harmony (Township of)**—*pop pl* (2) ... IN-6
**Harmony (Township of)**—*pop pl* ... MN-6
**Harmony (Township of)**—*pop pl* ... NJ-2
**Harmony (Township of)**—*pop pl* ... OH-6
**Harmony (Township of)**—*pop pl* (3) ... PA-2
Harmony Union Sch—*school* ... CA-9

Harrell-Kirkland Cem—cemetery MS-4
Harrell Lake—lake LA-4
Harrell Lake—reservoir AL-4
Harrell Lake Dam—dam MS-4
Harrell-Martin Cem—cemetery MS-4
Harrell Park—park OK-5
Harrell Park—park TN-4
Harrell Park—park TX-5
Harrell Place—locale ID-8
Harrell Prairie Botanical Area—park MS-4
Harrell Prairie Hill—summit MS-4
Harrell Ranch—locale (2) TX-5
Harrells—locale TX-5
**Harrells**—pop pl NC-3
Harrells Bay—swamp NC-3
Harrells Ch—church NC-3
Harrell Sch—school TX-5
Harrell Sch (abandoned)—school MO-7
Harrells Chapel—church NC-3
**Harrells (Harrells Store)**—pop pl NC-3
Harrell Shop Ctr—locale MS-4
Harrell Siding—locale VA-3
Harrell Site—hist pl TX-5
Harrells Lake—reservoir NC-3
Harrells Lake Dam—dam NC-3
Harrells Lake One—reservoir AL-4
Harrells Mill—locale NC-3
Harrells Mill—locale VA-3
Harrells Mill (historical)—locale NC-3
Harrells Pond—reservoir (2) VA-3
Harrells Quarter—locale NC-3
Harrells Quarters—locale AL-4
Harrells Store NC-3
Harrells Store—other NC-3
Harrell Store NC-3
Harrells Town NC-3
Harrell Strand—swamp FL-3
**Harrellsville**—pop pl NC-3
Harrellsville (Township of)—fmr MCD NC-3
Harrell Swamp VA-3
Harrell Swamp—stream NC-3
Harrell Temple Ch of God in Christ—church MS-4
Harrell (Township of)—fmr MCD NC-3
Harrel Mill Creek—stream GA-3
Harrel Ranch—locale TX-5
Harrel Rsvr—reservoir WY-8
Harrel Sch—school TX-5
Harrel Slough TX-5
Harrelson—locale MO-7
Harrelson Branch—stream SC-3
Harrelson Cem—cemetery GA-3
Harrelson Cem—cemetery (2) SC-3
Harrelson Dam—dam AL-4
Harrelson Lake—reservoir AL-4
Harrelson Pond—reservoir AL-4
Harrelson Ranch—locale TX-5
Harrelsonville NC-3
**Harrelsonville**—pop pl NC-3
**Harrelsonville Crossroads**—pop pl NC-3
Harrel Square Shop Ctr—locale FL-3
Harrence Lake—lake CO-8
Harrer Bldg—hist pl IL-6
Harrer Sch (historical)—school PA-2
Harres Cem—cemetery IL-6
Harrett Cem—cemetery IL-6
Harr Hollow—valley TN-4
Harrible, Mount—summit WA-9
Harrican Branch LA-4
Harrican Creek AL-4
Harrican Creek—stream OK-5
Harricane TN-4
Harricane Creek AL-4
Harricane Creek—stream WA-9
**Harrican (historical)**—pop pl TN-4
Harrican Post Office (historical)—building TN-4
Harricks Ravine—valley CA-9
Harrie Creek—stream OR-9
Harrier Creek—stream WA-9
Harrier Hollow—valley PA-2
**Harries**—pop pl OH-6
Harriet—locale TX-5
Harriet—locale WV-2
**Harriet**—pop pl AR-4
Harriet—reservoir OR-9
Harriet—uninc pl NY-2
Harriet, Lake—lake CA-9
Harriet, Lake—lake FL-3
Harriet, Lake—lake MN-6
Harriet, Lake Hunt—lake AK-9
Harriet Beecher Stowe Elementary School—school CT-1
Harriet Beecher Stowe Elem Sch—school IN-6
Harriet Beecher Stowe Sch CT-1
Harriet Beecher Stowe Sch—school CT-1
Harriet Branch—stream KY-4
Harriet Brook—stream ME-1
Harriet Cem—cemetery TX-5
Harriet Ch—church NC-3
Harriet Cove—valley NC-3
Harriet Creek—stream (2) AK-9
Harriet Creek—stream MN-6
Harriet Creek—stream TX-5
Harriet Creek—stream WA-9
Harriete MI-6
Harriet Field Airp—airport NV-8
Harriet Island—island MN-6
Harriet Lake—lake CA-9
Harriet Lake—lake (2) MN-6
Harriet Lake—lake ND-7
Harriet Lake—lake (3) WI-6
Harriet Lou Creek MT-8
Harriet Lou Creek—stream MT-8
Harriet Mine—mine UT-8
Harriet Point—cape AK-9
Harriet Ranch HQ—locale NM-5
Harriet School (Abandoned)—locale TX-5
Harriet Spring—spring UT-8
Harriet Spring Number One—spring MT-8
Harriet Spring Number Two—spring MT-8
**Harrietstown**—pop pl NY-2
**Harrietstown (Town of)**—pop pl NY-2
Harriett TX-5
Harriett—hist pl IN-6
**Harriett**—pop pl (2) OH-6
Harriett, Lake—lake WI-6
**Harrietta**—pop pl MI-6
Harrietta Cem—cemetery MI-6
Harrietta Plantation—hist pl SC-3
Harrietta Plantation—locale SC-3
Harriette MI-6
Harriette, Lake—lake OR-9
Harriett Lake—lake MN-6
**Harriet Township**—pop pl ND-7
**Harrietts Bluff**—pop pl GA-3
**Harriettsville**—pop pl (2) OH-6
Harriet Tubman Home for the Aged—hist pl NY-2
Harriet Wallace Park—park CT-1
Harriet Well—well NM-5
Harrigan—locale NY-2
Harrigan Branch—stream AL-4
Harrigan Branch—stream IN-6
Harrigan Branch—stream MS-4
Harrigan Canyon CA-9
Harrigan Creek AL-4
Harrigan Creek—stream AL-4
Harrigan Creek—stream CO-8
Harrigan Hollow—valley AK-4
Harrigan Lake—lake MN-6
Harrigan Point—cape WA-9
Harrigan Pond—lake MA-1
Harrigan Ridge ND-7
Harrigate Sch—school NY-2
Harrigton Trail—trail PA-2
Harrill Ford—crossing TN-4
Harrill Ford—locale MO-7
**Harrill Hills**—pop pl TN-4
Harriman OR-9
Harriman—locale WY-8
**Harriman**—pop pl NY-2
**Harriman**—pop pl PA-2
**Harriman**—pop pl TN-4
Harriman, Dr. O. B., House—hist pl IA-7
Harriman, John, House—hist pl WV-2
Harriman, L. F., House—hist pl SD-7
Harriman, Mount—summit OR-9
Harriman Canal—canal CO-8
Harriman (CCD)—cens area TN-4
Harriman Ch—church MO-7
Harriman Chandler State For—forest NH-1
Harriman Ch of Christ—church TN-4
Harriman Circle Park—park FL-3
Harriman City Hall—building TN-4
Harriman City Hall—hist pl TN-4
Harriman City Hosp—hospital TN-4
Harriman Cove—bay ME-1
Harriman Dam—dam VT-1
Harriman Division—civil TN-4
Harriman Fiord—bay AK-9
Harriman Glacier—glacier AK-9
Harriman Hill—summit VT-1
Harriman Hist Dist—hist pl PA-2
Harriman Hosp—hospital CA-9
Harriman HS—school TN-4
**Harriman Junction**—pop pl TN-4
Harriman Lake—reservoir CO-8
Harriman Ledge—bar ME-1
Harriman Lodge—locale OR-9
Harriman Mine—mine CA-9
Harriman Occupational Sch—school TN-4
Harriman Park—park IA-7
Harriman Park—park NH-1
**Harriman Park**—pop pl AL-4
Harriman Point—cape ME-1
Harriman Pond—lake (2) ME-1
Harriman Pond—lake VT-1
Harriman Post Office—building TN-4
Harriman Power Plant—other VT-1
**Harriman (Recreational Area)**—pop pl OR-9
Harriman Red Ash Mine (surface)—mine TN-4
Harriman Rsvr—reservoir VT-1
Harriman Sch—school ME-1
Harriman Sch—school MA-1
Harriman South—CDP NY-2
**Harrimans Point**—pop pl ME-1
Harriman Spring—spring CO-8
Harriman Spring—spring OR-9
Harriman United Methodist Ch—church TN-4
Harrine Hill TN-4
Harringan, Lake—reservoir AL-4
Harring Cem—cemetery OH-6
Harringdeane MI-6
Harring Swamp VA-3
Harrington—hist pl MD-2
Harrington—locale CA-9
Harrington—locale SD-7
Harrington—locale VA-3
**Harrington**—pop pl DE-2
**Harrington**—pop pl GA-3
**Harrington**—pop pl ME-1
**Harrington**—pop pl WA-9
Harrington, Lake—lake MN-6
Harrington, Mount—summit CA-9
Harrington Airp—airport NC-3
Harrington Archaeol Site—hist pl AL-4
Harrington Baptist Ch—church DE-2
Harrington Bay—bay ME-1
Harrington Bayou—lake MI-6
Harrington Beaverdam Ditch—stream DE-2
Harrington Beaverdam Ditch—stream MD-2
Harrington-Birchett House—hist pl AZ-5
Harrington Branch—stream AL-4
Harrington Branch—stream OK-5
Harrington Branch—stream TN-4
Harrington Branch—stream TX-5
Harrington Brook—stream CT-1
Harrington Brook—stream NY-2
Harrington Canyon—valley NM-5
Harrington Canyon—valley OR-9
Harrington (CCD)—cens area DE-2
Harrington Cem—cemetery CT-1
Harrington Cem—cemetery IA-7
Harrington Cem—cemetery KS-7
Harrington Cem—cemetery LA-4
Harrington Cem—cemetery MI-6
Harrington Cem—cemetery (2) MS-4
Harrington Cem—cemetery (2) MO-7
Harrington Cem—cemetery NC-3
Harrington Cem—cemetery (2) OH-6
Harrington Cem—cemetery (4) TN-4
Harrington Cem—cemetery TX-5
Harrington Cem—cemetery VA-3
Harrington Church AL-4
Harrington Cobble—summit VT-1
Harrington Corner—building MA-1
**Harrington Corner**—pop pl ME-1
Harrington Cove—basin TX-5
Harrington Cove—bay ME-1
Harrington Covered Bridge—hist pl PA-2
Harrington Creek ID-8
Harrington Creek MI-6
Harrington Creek—stream AK-9
Harrington Creek—stream (2) CA-9
Harrington Creek—stream ID-8
Harrington Creek—stream NV-8
Harrington Creek—stream (2) OK-5
Harrington Creek—stream (2) OR-9
Harrington Creek—stream TN-4
Harrington Ditch—canal CO-8
Harrington Ditch—canal IN-6
**Harrington Donnelly and Newells Subdivision**—pop pl UT-8
Harrington Drain—stream MI-6
Harrington Flat—flat CA-9
Harrington Fork—stream ID-8
Harrington Fork Birch Creek—stream AK-9
Harrington Fork Picnic Ground—locale ID-8
Harrington Gulch—valley CO-8
Harrington Heights Ch—church AL-4
Harrington-Hickory Mine—mine UT-8
Harrington Hill—summit MA-1
Harrington Hills—range MN-6
Harrington (historical)—locale SD-7
Harrington Hollow PA-2
Harrington Hollow—valley TN-4
Harrington Hotel—hist pl MI-6
Harrington House—hist pl MA-1
Harrington House—hist pl OR-9
Harrington House—hist pl VT-1
Harrington Island—island MI-6
Harrington Lagoon—bay WA-9
Harrington Lake WI-6
Harrington Lake—lake CA-9
Harrington Lake—reservoir ME-1
Harrington Lake Dam—dam MS-4
Harrington Machine Shop—hist pl PA-2
**Harrington Manor**—pop pl MD-2
Harrington Meetinghouse—church ME-1
Harrington Meetinghouse—hist pl ME-1
Harrington Memorial Hosp—hospital MA-1
Harrington Mtn—summit CA-9
Harrington Mtn—summit ID-8
Harrington Mtn—summit NY-2
**Harrington Park**—pop pl NJ-2
Harrington Peak—summit (2) ID-8
Harrington Place—locale AZ-5
Harrington Point—cape AK-9
Harrington Point—cape WA-9
Harrington Point Range—channel OR-9
Harrington Pond—lake ME-1
Harrington Pond—lake MA-1
Harrington Pond—lake NH-1
Harrington Pond—lake NY-2
Harrington Pool—lake MA-1
Harrington Ranch—locale CA-9
Harrington Ranch—locale CO-8
Harrington Ridge—ridge ID-8
Harrington Ridge—ridge TN-4
Harrington-Rikard Ditch—canal CO-8
Harrington River—stream ME-1
Harrington Rock—other AK-9
Harrington Rock—pillar WA-9
Harrington Run MD-2
Harrington Saddle—gap ID-8
Harrington Sch—school CO-8
Harrington Sch—school IL-6
Harrington Sch—school ME-1
Harrington Sch—school (3) MA-1
Harrington Sch—school (2) MI-6
Harrington Sch—school PA-2
Harrington Sch—school SD-7
Harrington-Smith Block—hist pl NH-1
Harrington South Ditch—canal CO-8
Harrington's Pond—reservoir NC-3
Harringtons Pond Dam—dam NC-3
Harrington Spring ID-8
Harrington Spring OR-9
Harrington Spring—spring CA-9
Harrington Spring—spring ID-8
Harrington Spring—spring OR-9
Harrington Spring Branch—stream AR-4
Harrington's Run MD-2
Harrington Street Hist Dist—hist pl SC-3
**Harrington (Town of)**—pop pl ME-1
Harrington Well—well NM-5
Harrington Windmill—locale NM-5
Harris AL-4
Harris GA-3
Harris IN-6
Harris—locale AL-4
Harris—locale AZ-5
Harris—locale CA-9
Harris—locale (2) IL-6
Harris—locale KY-4
Harris—locale LA-4
Harris—locale MI-6
Harris—locale OR-9
Harris—locale RI-1
**Harris**—pop pl AL-4
**Harris**—pop pl AR-4
**Harris**—pop pl CO-8
**Harris**—pop pl GA-3
**Harris**—pop pl IN-6
**Harris**—pop pl IA-7
**Harris**—pop pl KS-7
**Harris**—pop pl MA-1
**Harris**—pop pl MN-6
**Harris**—pop pl MO-7
**Harris**—pop pl NY-2
**Harris**—pop pl (2) NC-3
**Harris**—pop pl OH-6
**Harris**—pop pl OK-5
**Harris**—pop pl OR-9
**Harris**—pop pl SC-3
**Harris**—pop pl TN-4
**Harris**—pop pl WV-2
Harris, Abner L., House—hist pl WI-6
Harris, Capt. Thomas C., House—hist pl MO-7
Harris, Col. John, House—hist pl MO-7
Harris, Dr. J. H., House—hist pl NC-3
Harris, Dr. John, Dental Sch—hist pl OH-6
Harris, E. M., House—hist pl TX-5
Harris, Fred S., House—hist pl SD-7
Harris, Joel Chandler, House—hist pl GA-3
Harris, John, House and Farm—hist pl MA-1
Harris, John, Mansion—hist pl PA-2
Harris, Jonathan Newton, House—hist pl CT-1
Harris, Joseph, House—hist pl MI-6
Harris, Joseph D., House—hist pl UT-8
Harris, Lake—lake FL-3
Harris, Lake—reservoir AL-4
Harris, Lake—reservoir TX-5
Harris, Louis W., Flour Mill—hist pl UT-8
Harris, Louis W., House—hist pl UT-8
Harris, Martin, Gravesite—hist pl UT-8
Harris, Mount—summit AK-9
Harris, Mount—summit ME-1
Harris, Mount—summit OR-9
Harris, Nathan and Susannah, House—hist pl MD-2
Harris, Robert C., House—hist pl TN-4
Harris, Sarah Eliza, House—hist pl UT-8
Harris, Senator William A., House—hist pl KS-7
Harris, Stephen R., House—hist pl OH-6
Harris, V. R., House—hist pl TN-4
Harris, W. C., House—hist pl CO-8
Harris, William, Family Farmstead—hist pl GA-3
Harris, William, House—hist pl VT-1
Harris, William B., House—hist pl OH-6
Harris, William H., House—hist pl UT-8
**Harris Acres**—pop pl PA-2
Harris Airp—airport (2) NC-3
Harris Airp—airport PA-2
Harris Airp—airport (2) WA-9
Harris And Spang Ditch—canal WY-8
Harris Arm—canal IN-6
Harris Arnett Branch—stream KY-4
Harris-Banks House—hist pl MS-4
Harris-Barrett Sch (historical)—school AL-4
Harris Bay AK-9
Harris Bay—bay (2) AK-9
Harris Bay—bay NY-2
Harris Bay—swamp (2) FL-3
Harris Bayou AR-4
Harris Bayou—gut FL-3
Harris Bayou—gut LA-4
Harris Bayou—stream AR-4
Harris Bayou—stream MS-4
Harris Beach State Park—park OR-9
Harris Bear Camp—locale NM-5
Harris Bend—bend MO-7
Harris Bend Cem—cemetery MO-7
Harris Bend Cut Off—bend TX-5
Harris Bend Sch—school MO-7
Harris Bldg—hist pl OR-9
Harris Bluff—cliff TN-4
Harris Bluff Cave—cave TN-4
Harris Bottom—bend AR-4
Harris Brake—reservoir AR-4
Harris Branch AL-4
Harris Branch VA-3
Harris Branch—stream (3) AL-4
Harris Branch—stream (4) GA-3
Harris Branch—stream IL-6
Harris Branch—stream (6) KY-4
Harris Branch—stream LA-4
Harris Branch—stream (2) MS-4
Harris Branch—stream (2) MO-7
Harris Branch—stream NJ-2
Harris Branch—stream NC-3
Harris Branch—stream (2) SC-3
Harris Branch—stream (9) TN-4
Harris Branch—stream (4) TX-5
Harris Branch—stream (2) VA-3
Harris Branch—stream (3) WV-2
Harris Bridge—bridge (2) AL-4
Harris Bridge—bridge FL-3
Harris Bridge—bridge OR-9
Harris Bridge—bridge PA-2
Harris Bridge—bridge SC-3
Harris Bridge—hist pl KS-7
Harris Bridge—hist pl OR-9
Harris Bridge—locale VA-3
Harris Bridge—locale WY-8
Harris Bridge—other IL-6
Harris Brook MA-1
Harris Brook—stream (3) CT-1
Harris Brook—stream (2) ME-1
Harris Brook—stream (4) MA-1
Harris Brook—stream (2) NH-1
Harris Brook—stream NY-2
Harris Brook—stream RI-1
Harris Brook—stream VT-1
Harris Brothers Ranch—locale CA-9
Harrisburg IN-6
Harrisburg TN-4
Harrisburg—locale CA-9
Harrisburg—locale FL-3
Harrisburg—locale GA-3
Harrisburg—locale ID-8
Harrisburg—locale NM-5
Harrisburg—locale OH-6
Harrisburg—locale OK-5
Harrisburg—locale TX-5
Harrisburg—locale UT-8
Harrisburg—locale VA-3
**Harrisburg**—pop pl (2) AL-4
**Harrisburg**—pop pl AR-4
**Harrisburg**—pop pl GA-3
**Harrisburg**—pop pl IL-6
**Harrisburg**—pop pl IN-6
**Harrisburg**—pop pl IA-7
**Harrisburg**—pop pl MI-6
**Harrisburg**—pop pl MO-7
**Harrisburg**—pop pl NE-7
**Harrisburg**—pop pl NM-5
**Harrisburg**—pop pl (2) NY-2
**Harrisburg**—pop pl NC-3
**Harrisburg**—pop pl (2) OH-6
**Harrisburg**—pop pl OR-9
**Harrisburg**—pop pl (2) PA-2
**Harrisburg**—pop pl SD-7
**Harrisburg**—pop pl TN-4
**Harrisburg**—pop pl TX-5
Harrisburg Acad—school PA-2
Harrisburg Area Community Coll—school PA-2
Harrisburg Baptist Ch—church MS-4
Harrisburg Bench—bench UT-8
Harrisburg Bend—bend OR-9
Harrisburg Canyon—valley UT-8
Harrisburg (CCD)—cens area OR-9
Harrisburg Cem—cemetery AZ-5
Harrisburg Cem—cemetery AR-4
Harrisburg Cem—cemetery IA-7
Harrisburg Cem—cemetery PA-2
Harrisburg Cemetery—hist pl PA-2
Harrisburg Central RR Station and Trainshed—hist pl PA-2
Harrisburg Ch—church GA-3
Harrisburg Christian Sch—school PA-2
Harrisburg City—civil PA-2
Harrisburg Community Park—park NC-3
Harrisburg Corner (2) AR-4
Harrisburg Country Club—other PA-2
Harrisburg Covered Bridge—hist pl TN-4
Harrisburg Creek UT-8
Harrisburg Creek—stream UT-8
Harrisburg Dome—summit UT-8
**Harrisburg East End**—pop pl PA-2
Harrisburg-East Interchange PA-2
Harrisburg East Mall—locale PA-2
Harrisburg Flat—flat UT-8
Harrisburg Flats—flat CA-9
Harrisburg Gap—gap GA-3
Harrisburg Gap—gap UT-8
Harrisburg Gulf—valley GA-3
Harrisburgh IN-6
Harrisburgh PA-2
**Harrisburg Heights (subdivision)**—pop pl MS-4
Harrisburg Hist Dist—hist pl PA-2
Harrisburg (historical)—locale MS-4
**Harrisburg (historical)**—pop pl ND-7
Harrisburgh Lake NY-2
Harrisburg Hollow—valley NY-2
Harrisburgh Station TN-4
Harrisburgh Station Post Office TN-4
Harrisburg Industrial Park—locale PA-2
Harrisburg International Airport-Olmsted Field—airport PA-2
Harrisburg Junction—locale UT-8
Harrisburg Lake—lake NY-2
Harrisburg Reservoir PA-2
Harrisburg Rsvr—reservoir IL-6
Harrisburg Run—stream NY-2
Harrisburg Run—stream PA-2
Harrisburg Sch—school TX-5
Harrisburg Shop Ctr—locale PA-2
Harrisburg Sportsman Club—locale PA-2
Harrisburg Substation—locale OR-9
Harrisburg Technical HS—hist pl PA-2
Harrisburg Townhall—building IA-7
**Harrisburg (Town of)**—pop pl NY-2
Harrisburg Township—fmr MCD IA-7
**Harrisburg (Township of)**—pop pl IL-6
Harrisburg Valley—valley AZ-5
Harrisburg Water Supply PA-2
Harrisburg-West Shore Interchange PA-2
Harris Butte—summit OR-9
Harris Buttes—spring MT-8
Harris Camp—locale FL-3
Harris Camp Canyon—valley AZ-5
Harris Camp Spring—spring AZ-5
Harris Canyon—valley (2) CA-9
Harris Canyon—valley MT-8
Harris Canyon—valley (2) NV-8
Harris Canyon—valley (4) NM-5
Harris Canyon—valley (3) OR-9
Harris Canyon—valley UT-8
Harris Canyon Dam—dam NV-8
Harris Cave—cave AL-4
Harris Cave—cave AZ-5
Harris Cave—cave (2) TN-4
Harris Cem AL-4
Harris Cem—cemetery (13) AL-4
Harris Cem—cemetery (15) AR-4
Harris Cem—cemetery (12) GA-3
Harris Cem—cemetery (9) IL-6
Harris Cem—cemetery (2) IN-6
Harris Cem—cemetery IA-7
Harris Cem—cemetery (4) KY-4
Harris Cem—cemetery ME-1
Harris Cem—cemetery (4) MI-6
Harris Cem—cemetery MN-6
Harris Cem—cemetery (7) MS-4
Harris Cem—cemetery (10) MO-7
Harris Cem—cemetery NE-7
Harris Cem—cemetery (2) NY-2
Harris Cem—cemetery NC-3
Harris Cem—cemetery (4) OH-6
Harris Cem—cemetery (4) OK-5
Harris Cem—cemetery OR-9
Harris Cem—cemetery SC-3
Harris Cem—cemetery (32) TN-4
Harris Cem—cemetery (4) TX-5
Harris Cem—cemetery (4) VA-3
Harris Cem—cemetery (2) WV-2
Harris Cem (historical)—cemetery AL-4
Harris Ch TN-4
Harris Ch—church AR-4
Harris Ch—church TX-5
Harris Channel—channel FL-3
Harris Chapel—church (4) AL-4
Harris Chapel—church (3) AR-4
Harris Chapel—church GA-3
Harris Chapel—church IN-6
Harris Chapel—church (2) LA-4
Harris Chapel—church (4) MS-4
Harris Chapel—church (5) NC-3
Harris Chapel—church (4) TN-4
Harris Chapel—church (3) TX-5
Harris Chapel—church VA-3
Harris Chapel—locale AR-4
Harris Chapel African Methodist Episcopal Zion Ch—church TN-4
Harris Chapel Baptist Ch TN-4
Harris Chapel Cem—cemetery FL-3
Harris Chapel Cem—cemetery LA-4
Harris Chapel Cem—cemetery MS-4
Harris Chapel Cem—cemetery (3) TN-4
Harris Chapel Cem—cemetery TX-5
Harris Chapel Ch AL-4
Harris Chapel Church MS-4
Harris Chapel Methodist Church MS-4
Harris Chapel Missionary Baptist Ch AL-4
Harris Chapel United Ch—church TN-4
Harris Chapel United Methodist Ch TN-4
Harris Ch (historical)—church MI-6
Harris-Chilton-Ruble House—hist pl MO-7
**Harris City**—pop pl GA-3
**Harris City**—pop pl IN-6
Harris Coll—school MO-7
Harris Corner MA-1
Harris Corners—locale PA-2
**Harris Corners**—pop pl NY-2
**Harris (County)**—pop pl GA-3
**Harris (County)**—pop pl TX-5
Harris County Boys Sch—school TX-5
Harris County Boy's Sch Site—hist pl TX-5
Harris County Cem—cemetery TX-5
Harris County Courthouse—hist pl GA-3
Harris County Courthouse of 1910—hist pl TX-5
Harris County Lookout Tower—locale GA-3
Harris Cove TN-4
Harris Cove—basin GA-3
Harris Cove—bay (2) ME-1
Harris Cove—valley NC-3
Harris Cove—valley (2) VA-3
Harris Cove Utz Gap Trail—trail VA-3
Harris Creek AL-4
Harris Creek NC-3
Harris Creek TX-5
Harris Creek VA-3
Harris Creek—stream (5) AL-4
Harris Creek—stream (2) AK-9
Harris Creek—stream (5) AR-4
Harris Creek—stream (4) CA-9
Harris Creek—stream FL-3
Harris Creek—stream (7) GA-3
Harris Creek—stream (2) ID-8
Harris Creek—stream IL-6
Harris Creek—stream IN-6
Harris Creek—stream KS-7
Harris Creek—stream (2) KY-4
Harris Creek—stream MD-2
Harris Creek—stream (2) MI-6
Harris Creek—stream MN-6
Harris Creek—stream (3) MS-4
Harris Creek—stream MO-7
Harris Creek—stream (8) MT-8
Harris Creek—stream (9) NC-3
Harris Creek—stream OH-6
Harris Creek—stream (2) OK-5
Harris Creek—stream (7) OR-9
Harris Creek—stream SC-3
Harris Creek—stream (3) TN-4
Harris Creek—stream (6) TX-5
Harris Creek—stream (6) VA-3
Harris Creek—stream (5) WA-9
Harris Creek—stream WI-6
Harris Creek—stream (2) WY-8
Harris Creek Canyon UT-8
Harris Creek Cem—cemetery OH-6
Harris Creek Ch—church OH-6
Harris Creek Ch—church SC-3
Harris Creek Ch—church (3) TX-5
Harris Creek Rsvr—reservoir ID-8
Harris Creek Spring No 1—spring WA-9
Harris Creek Spring No 2—spring WA-9
Harris Creek Summit—summit ID-8
Harris Crossing Bridge—bridge MS-4
**Harris Crossroads**—pop pl (2) NC-3
Harris-Currin House—hist pl NC-3
**Harrisdale**—pop pl RI-1
**Harrisdale**—pop pl TX-5
Harrisdale Ch—church TX-5
Harris Dam PA-2
Harris Dam—dam ID-8
Harris Dam—dam ME-1
Harris Ditch—canal (2) OH-6
Harris Ditch—canal TN-4
Harris Ditch—canal UT-8
Harris Ditch—canal WY-8
Harris Dome—summit AK-9
Harris Drain—canal MI-6
Harris Drain—stream (4) MI-6
Harris Draw—valley KS-7
Harris Elem Sch—school IN-6
Harris Elem Sch—school KS-7
Harris Elem Sch—school NC-3
Harrisena Ch—church NY-2
Harris Falls ME-1
Harris Family Cem—cemetery OR-9
Harris Ferry—locale WV-2
Harris Field—park FL-3
Harris Field—park MA-1
Harris Flat—flat CA-9
Harris Flat—flat (2) UT-8
Harris Ford—locale TN-4
Harris Fork—stream KY-4
Harris Fork—stream UT-8
Harris Fork—stream (2) WV-2
Harris Fork Creek—stream KY-4
Harris Fork Creek—stream TN-4
Harris Gap—gap GA-3
Harris Gap—gap KY-4
Harris Gap—gap (2) NC-3
Harris Gap—gap WV-2
Harris Gap Channel—channel FL-3
Harris Glacier—glacier MT-8
Harris Grade Spring—spring CA-9
Harris Grove—locale KY-4
**Harris Grove**—pop pl VA-3
Harris Grove Cem—cemetery TN-4
Harris Grove Ch—church IA-7
Harris Grove Ch—church NC-3
Harris Grove Ch—church SC-3
Harris Grove Ch—church TN-4
Harris Grove Creek—stream IA-7
Harris Gubler Dam—dam UT-8
Harris Gubler Rsvr—reservoir UT-8
Harris Gulch—valley (2) CO-8
Harris Gulch—valley (2) MT-8
Harris Gulch—valley NV-8
Harris Gulch—valley OR-9
Harris Hall—hist pl MI-6
Harris Harbor—bay NJ-2
Harris Heights Park—park OR-9
Harris Hereford Ranch—locale CO-8
**Harris Hill**—pop pl NY-2
Harris Hill—summit CA-9
Harris Hill—summit KY-4
Harris Hill—summit ME-1
Harris Hill—summit MA-1
Harris Hill—summit MT-8
Harris Hill—summit (6) NY-2
Harris Hill—summit VT-1
Harris Hill Brook—stream NY-2
Harris Hill Ford—locale KY-4
**Harris Hill Manor**—pop pl NY-2
**Harris Hills**—pop pl TN-4
Harris Hill Sch—school NY-2
**Harris Hills (subdivision)**—pop pl TN-4
Harris-Holden House—hist pl TN-4
Harris Hollow—valley (2) AL-4

Harris Hollow—*valley* (3) AR-4
Harris Hollow—*valley* KY-4
Harris Hollow—*valley* MO-7
Harris Hollow—*valley* (9) TN-4
Harris Hollow—*valley* (2) TX-5
Harris Hollow—*valley* UT-8
Harris Hollow—*valley* VA-3
Harris Hollow—*valley* WV-2
Harris Homestead—*locale* CO-8
*Harris-Hooks Cemetery* AL-4
Harris Hosp—*hospital* AR-4
Harris Hosp—*hospital* TX-5
Harris House—*hist pl* AR-4
Harris House—*hist pl* MO-7
Harris House—*hist pl* MT-8
Harris House—*hist pl* NE-7
Harris House—*hist pl* OK-5
Harris House—*hist pl* WI-6
Harris HS—*school* (2) MS-4
Harris HS—*school* NC-3
Harris HS—*school* PA-2
Harris HS—*school* VA-3
Harris Inn—*building* MT-8
Harris Island—*island* (2) AK-9
Harris Island—*island* FL-3
Harris Island—*island* LA-4
Harris Island—*island* ME-1
Harris Island—*island* MI-6
Harris Island—*island* MN-6
Harris Island—*island* OR-9
Harris Island—*island* (2) PA-2
Harris Island—*island* WI-6
Harris JHS—*school* LA-4
Harris JHS—*school* TX-5
Harris-Jobe Sch—*school* OK-5
Harris Junior Acad—*school* OR-9
Harris Kiddie Kollege and Elem Sch—*school* DE-2
Harris Knob—*summit* MO-7
Harris Knoll—*summit* UT-8
*Harris Lake* AL-4
*Harris Lake* MA-1
*Harris Lake* MI-6
*Harris Lake* SD-7
*Harris Lake* UT-8
Harris Lake—*lake* AZ-5
Harris Lake—*lake* CO-8
Harris Lake—*lake* (2) ID-8
Harris Lake—*lake* LA-4
Harris Lake—*lake* (5) MI-6
Harris Lake—*lake* (3) MN-6
Harris Lake—*lake* NE-7
Harris Lake—*lake* NM-5
Harris Lake—*lake* NY-2
Harris Lake—*lake* SC-3
Harris Lake—*lake* TX-5
Harris Lake—*lake* WI-6
Harris Lake—*reservoir* AL-4
Harris Lake—*reservoir* MO-7
Harris Lake—*reservoir* (2) NC-3
Harris Lake—*reservoir* (2) TX-5
Harris Lake—*reservoir* WV-2
Harris Lake—*swamp* MS-4
*Harris Lake Dam* AL-4
Harris Lake Dam—*dam* AL-4
Harris Lake Dam—*dam* MS-4
Harris Landing—*locale* ID-8
Harris Landing—*locale* LA-4
Harris Landing—*locale* (2) NC-3
Harris Landing—*locale* TN-4
Harris Landing (historical)—*locale* AL-4
Harris Lateral—*canal* AZ-5
Harris-Lord Cem—*cemetery* GA-3
Harris Lot—*locale* MD-2
Harris (Magisterial District)—*fmr MCD* WV-2
Harris-Marsh Mine (underground)—*mine* AL-4
Harris Meadow—*flat* CA-9
Harris Memorial Ch—*church* IN-6
Harris Memorial Ch—*church* NC-3
Harris Memorial Methodist Ch—*church* AL-4
Harris-Merrick House—*hist pl* MA-1
Harris Mesa—*summit* NM-5
Harris Mill—*locale* TN-4
*Harris Mill Creek* AL-4
Harris Mill Creek—*stream* AL-4
Harris Mill Creek—*stream* MD-2
Harris Mill (historical)—*locale* AL-4
Harris Mill (historical)—*locale* TN-4
Harris Millpond—*lake* NC-3
Harris Millpond (historical)—*reservoir* NC-3
Harris Mill Run—*stream* NC-3
*Harris Mills* RI-1
Harris Mine—*mine* CA-9
Harris Mine—*mine* UT-8
*Harris Mountains* UT-8
Harris Mountains—*summit* AR-4
Harris MS—*school* NC-3
Harris MS—*school* TN-4
*Harris Mtn* NC-3
Harris Mtn—*summit* AL-4
Harris Mtn—*summit* AZ-5
Harris Mtn—*summit* (2) AR-4
Harris Mtn—*summit* CA-9
Harris Mtn—*summit* GA-3
Harris Mtn—*summit* (2) MT-8
Harris Mtn—*summit* NV-8
Harris Mtn—*summit* (3) NC-3
Harris Mtn—*summit* OK-5
Harris Mtn—*summit* TN-4
Harris Mtn—*summit* UT-8
Harris Mtn—*summit* VT-1
Harris Mtn—*summit* VA-3
Harris Neck—*cape* GA-3
Harris Neck Creek—*stream* GA-3
Harris Neck Natl Wildlife Ref—*park* GA-3
Harris Oil Field—*oilfield* TX-5
*Harrison* IN-6
*Harrison* MS-4
*Harrison* NJ-2
*Harrison* OH-6
*Harrison* PA-2
Harrison—*fmr MCD* (4) NE-7
Harrison—*locale* FL-3
Harrison—*locale* GA-3
Harrison—*locale* IA-7
Harrison—*locale* OK-5
Harrison—*locale* (2) WV-2
Harrison—*locale* WI-6
**Harrison**—*pop pl* AR-4
**Harrison**—*pop pl* GA-3
**Harrison**—*pop pl* ID-8
**Harrison**—*pop pl* (2) IL-6
**Harrison**—*pop pl* IN-6
**Harrison**—*pop pl* IA-7
**Harrison**—*pop pl* ME-1
**Harrison**—*pop pl* MI-6
**Harrison**—*pop pl* MT-8
**Harrison**—*pop pl* NE-7
**Harrison**—*pop pl* NJ-2
**Harrison**—*pop pl* NY-2
**Harrison**—*pop pl* OH-6
**Harrison**—*pop pl* PA-2
**Harrison**—*pop pl* SD-7
**Harrison**—*pop pl* TN-4
**Harrison**—*pop pl* TX-5
**Harrison**—*pop pl* WI-6
Harrison—*unorg reg* SD-7
Harrison, Benjamin, House—*hist pl* IN-6
Harrison, Daniel, House—*hist pl* VA-3
Harrison, E. H., House—*hist pl* IA-7
Harrison, Gen. William Henry, HQ—*hist pl* OH-6
Harrison, Lake—*reservoir* VA-3
Harrison, Mount—*summit* ID-8
Harrison, Mount—*summit* TN-4
Harrison, Samuel Orton, House—*hist pl* NJ-2
Harrison, Sen. James A., House—*hist pl* AZ-5
Harrison, Thomas, House—*hist pl* CT-1
Harrison, Thomas, House—*hist pl* VA-3
Harrison, Wallace K., Estate—*hist pl* NY-2
Harrison, William H., Sch—*hist pl* PA-2
Harrison, William Henry, Home—*hist pl* IN-6
Harrison, William Henry, Tomb State Memorial—*hist pl* OH-6
**Harrison Addition (subdivision)**—*pop pl* TN-4
Harrison Airp—*airport* MO-7
Harrison Ave Bridge—*hist pl* PA-2
Harrison Ave Sch—*school* CT-1
Harrison Ave Sch—*school* GA-3
Harrison Ave Sch—*school* (2) NY-2
Harrison Basin—*basin* MT-8
Harrison Basin Ridge—*ridge* MT-8
Harrison Bay—*bay* AK-9
Harrison Bay—*bay* (2) MN-6
Harrison Bay—*bay* TN-4
Harrison Bayou—*bay* FL-3
Harrison Bayou—*stream* TX-5
Harrison Bay State Park—*park* TN-4
Harrison Bay Vocational Technical Center—*school* TN-4
**Harrison Beach**—*pop pl* MI-6
Harrison Bend—*bend* TN-4
Harrison Bluff—*cliff* TN-4
**Harrison Bluff**—*pop pl* TN-4
*Harrison Bluff Cabin Site Area* TN-4
Harrison Bluff Caves—*cave* TN-4
Harrison Blvd Hist Dist—*hist pl* ID-8
*Harrison Branch* MS-4
Harrison Branch—*stream* (2) GA-3
Harrison Branch—*stream* IL-6
Harrison Branch—*stream* KS-7
Harrison Branch—*stream* KY-4
Harrison Branch—*stream* MS-4
Harrison Branch—*stream* (2) MO-7
Harrison Branch—*stream* (2) NC-3
Harrison Branch—*stream* SC-3
Harrison Branch—*stream* (9) TN-4
Harrison Branch—*stream* VA-3
Harrison Branch—*stream* WV-2
Harrison Branch Boat Launching Ramp—*locale* TN-4
Harrison Branch Rec Area—*park* TN-4
Harrison Brook—*stream* ME-1
*Harrisonburg* AZ-5
**Harrisonburg**—*pop pl* LA-4
**Harrisonburg (ind. city)**—*pop pl* VA-3
Harrisonburg Oil Field—*oilfield* LA-4
Harrisonburg Rsvr—*reservoir* VA-3
Harrison Cabin—*locale* CA-9
Harrison Camp—*locale* LA-4
Harrison Camp—*locale* WA-9
Harrison Canal—*canal* ID-8
Harrison Canyon—*valley* AZ-5
Harrison Canyon—*valley* MT-8
Harrison Canyon—*valley* NV-8
Harrison Canyon Dam—*dam* AZ-5
*Harrison Cave* AL-4
Harrison (CCD)—*cens area* GA-3
Harrison Cem—*cemetery* (6) AL-4
Harrison Cem—*cemetery* (3) AR-4
Harrison Cem—*cemetery* (2) GA-3
Harrison Cem—*cemetery* (4) IL-6
Harrison Cem—*cemetery* IN-6
Harrison Cem—*cemetery* (3) IA-7
Harrison Cem—*cemetery* KY-4
Harrison Cem—*cemetery* (2) LA-4
Harrison Cem—*cemetery* MI-6
Harrison Cem—*cemetery* MS-4
Harrison Cem—*cemetery* (2) MO-7
Harrison Cem—*cemetery* MT-8
Harrison Cem—*cemetery* NE-7
Harrison Cem—*cemetery* (2) NC-3
Harrison Cem—*cemetery* OH-6
Harrison Cem—*cemetery* (2) OK-5
Harrison Cem—*cemetery* OR-9
Harrison Cem—*cemetery* PA-2
Harrison Cem—*cemetery* (2) SC-3
Harrison Cem—*cemetery* SD-7
Harrison Cem—*cemetery* (9) TN-4
Harrison Cem—*cemetery* (4) TX-5
Harrison Cem—*cemetery* (2) VA-3
Harrison Cem—*cemetery* WI-6
Harrison Center Sch—*school* MO-7
Harrison Central HS—*school* MS-4
Harrison Ch—*church* AL-4
Harrison Ch—*church* AR-4
Harrison Ch—*church* IN-6
Harrison Ch—*church* KS-7
Harrison Ch—*church* MN-6
Harrison Ch—*church* NC-3
Harrison Ch—*church* (2) OH-6
*Harrison Chapel* AL-4
Harrison Chapel—*church* (3) AR-4
Harrison Chapel—*church* NC-3
Harrison Chapel—*church* TN-4
Harrison Chapel Cem—*cemetery* AR-4
Harrison Chapel Cem—*cemetery* TN-4
Harrison Chapel Cem—*cemetery* TX-5
*Harrison Chapel United Methodist Church* AL-4
*Harrison Chatman Branch* VA-3
Harrison Chilhowee Acad—*school* (2) TN-4
*Harrison Church of Christ* TN-4
**Harrison City**—*pop pl* PA-2
Harrison Country Club—*other* AR-4
**Harrison County**—*pop pl* IN-6
**Harrison (County)**—*pop pl* KY-4
**Harrison County**—*pop pl* MS-4
**Harrison County**—*pop pl* MO-7
**Harrison (County)**—*pop pl* OH-6
**Harrison (County)**—*pop pl* TX-5
**Harrison (County)**—*pop pl* WV-2
Harrison County Courthouse—*building* MS-4
Harrison County Courthouse—*hist pl* IA-7
Harrison County Courthouse—*hist pl* KY-4
Harrison County Courthouse—*hist pl* OH-6
Harrison County Courthouse—*hist pl* TX-5
Harrison County Elem Sch—*school* MS-4
Harrison County Farm—*locale* MO-7
Harrison County Farm (historical)—*locale* MS-4
Harrison County Farm Lake Dam—*dam* MS-4
Harrison County Infirmary (historical)—*hospital* IN-6
Harrison Cove—*basin* AL-4
Harrison-Crawford State For—*forest* IN-6
*Harrison Creek* MO-7
*Harrison Creek* MT-8
*Harrison Creek* VA-3
Harrison Creek—*stream* (3) AK-9
Harrison Creek—*stream* AZ-5
Harrison Creek—*stream* AR-4
Harrison Creek—*stream* (2) CO-8
Harrison Creek—*stream* (2) FL-3
Harrison Creek—*stream* (2) ID-8
Harrison Creek—*stream* IL-6
Harrison Creek—*stream* IN-6
Harrison Creek—*stream* KS-7
Harrison Creek—*stream* (2) KY-4
Harrison Creek—*stream* MI-6
Harrison Creek—*stream* (2) MN-6
Harrison Creek—*stream* (3) MO-7
Harrison Creek—*stream* (5) MT-8
Harrison Creek—*stream* (2) NY-2
Harrison Creek—*stream* NC-3
Harrison Creek—*stream* OH-6
Harrison Creek—*stream* (2) OR-9
Harrison Creek—*stream* TN-4
Harrison Creek—*stream* (2) VA-3
Harrison Creek—*stream* (4) WA-9
Harrison Creek—*stream* (2) WI-6
Harrison Creek—*stream* (2) WY-8
Harrison Creek Bay—*swamp* NC-3
Harrison Creek Ch—*church* NC-3
Harrison Creek Picnic Area—*locale* CO-8
**Harrison Cross Roads**—*pop pl* NC-3
Harrison Cut—*stream* MD-2
Harrison Dam—*dam* OR-9
Harrison-District Six Township—*civil* KS-7
Harrison Ditch—*canal* MT-8
Harrison Drain—*canal* (2) MI-6
Harrison Drain—*stream* (3) MI-6
Harrison Duck Club—*other* UT-8
Harrison Elem Sch—*school* AL-4
Harrison Elem Sch—*school* (2) IN-6
Harrison Elem Sch—*school* TN-4
**Harrison Ferry**—*pop pl* MD-2
Harrison Ferry Bridge—*bridge* MD-2
Harrison Ferry (historical)—*crossing* TN-4
Harrison Ferry Mtn—*summit* TN-4
Harrison Flat—*flat* CA-9
Harrison Flat—*flat* CO-8
Harrison Flat—*flat* SD-7
Harrison Flats—*flat* ID-8
Harrison Flats—*flat* KS-7
Harrison Flat Sch—*school* SD-7
Harrison Flats Sch—*school* KS-7
Harrison Fork—*stream* AK-9
Harrison Furnace—*locale* OH-6
Harrison Furnace Ch—*church* OH-6
Harrison Furnace Creek—*stream* OH-6
Harrison Gap—*gap* AL-4
Harrison Gap—*gap* (2) NC-3
Harrison Gap—*gap* TN-4
Harrison-Gibson House—*hist pl* GA-3
Harrison Glacier—*glacier* MT-8
**Harrison Grange**—*pop pl* IN-6
Harrison Grist Mill—*hist pl* NY-2
**Harrison Grove**—*pop pl* NY-2
Harrison Grove Cem—*cemetery* WV-2
Harrison Grove Ch—*church* MS-4
Harrison Grove Ch—*church* SC-3
Harrison Grove Ch—*church* (2) VA-3
Harrison Grove Mine—*mine* NV-8
Harrison Grove Sch—*school* MS-4
*Harrison Gulch* CA-9
Harrison Gulch—*valley* (2) CA-9
Harrison Gulch—*valley* CO-8
Harrison Gulch—*valley* (2) MT-8
Harrison Gulch—*valley* OR-9
Harrison Gulch Ranger Station—*locale* CA-9
Harrison Gulf Branch—*stream* TN-4
Harrison-Harlan Ditch—*canal* IN-6
Harrison Hill—*summit* (2) IN-6
Harrison Hill—*summit* MO-7
Harrison Hill—*summit* NY-2
Harrison Hill—*summit* TX-5
Harrison Hill—*summit* WA-9
Harrison Hill Elementary South—*school* IN-6
Harrison Hill Elem Sch—*school* IN-6
*Harrison Hills* IN-6
**Harrison Hills**—*pop pl* (2) TN-4
Harrison Hills—*summit* WI-6
Harrison Hills Cem—*cemetery* IN-6
Harrison Hills Country Club—*other* IN-6
Harrison (historical)—*locale* IA-7
Harrison (historical)—*locale* KS-7
Harrison (historical)—*locale* MS-4
**Harrison (historical)**—*pop pl* NC-3
**Harrison (historical)**—*pop pl* OR-9
Harrison Hollow—*valley* IN-6
Harrison Hollow—*valley* KY-4
Harrison Hollow—*valley* (3) MO-7
Harrison Hollow—*valley* OH-6
Harrison Hollow—*valley* PA-2
Harrison Hollow—*valley* (2) TN-4
Harrison Hollow—*valley* TX-5
Harrison Hosp—*hospital* KY-4
Harrison House—*hist pl* CA-9
Harrison House—*hist pl* PA-2
Harrison House—*hist pl* TN-4
Harrison House Mansion—*building* TN-4
Harrison HS—*school* CO-8
Harrison HS—*school* GA-3
Harrison HS—*school* IL-6
Harrison HS—*school* NJ-2
Harrison HS—*school* NC-3
Harrison-Hughes Cem—*cemetery* KY-4
Harrison Hump—*summit* CO-8
Harrison Island—*island* FL-3
Harrison Island—*island* MD-2
Harrison Island—*island* NY-2
Harrison Island—*island* (2) TN-4
Harrison Islands (historical)—*island* TN-4
Harrison JHS—*school* KS-7
Harrison JHS—*school* PA-2
Harrison Johnson Draw—*valley* ID-8
Harrison Knob—*summit* KY-4
Harrison Knob—*summit* TN-4
Harrison Lagoon—*bay* AK-9
*Harrison Lake* AL-4
*Harrison Lake* IN-6
*Harrison Lake* MN-6
Harrison Lake—*lake* AK-9
Harrison Lake—*lake* (2) FL-3
Harrison Lake—*lake* ID-8
Harrison Lake—*lake* IN-6
Harrison Lake—*lake* (2) LA-4
Harrison Lake—*lake* (2) MN-6
Harrison Lake—*lake* MS-4
Harrison Lake—*lake* (2) MT-8
Harrison Lake—*lake* ND-7
Harrison Lake—*lake* (2) OR-9
Harrison Lake—*lake* WA-9
Harrison Lake—*lake* (2) WI-6
**Harrison Lake**—*pop pl* (2) IN-6
Harrison Lake—*reservoir* MO-7
Harrison Lake—*reservoir* OH-6
Harrison Lake—*swamp* MI-6
Harrison Lake Country Club—*other* IN-6
Harrison Lake Natl Fish Hatchery—*other* VA-3
Harrison Lakes—*area* AK-9
Harrison Lake State Reservation—*park* OH-6
Harrison-Landers House—*hist pl* OH-6
*Harrison Landing* VA-3
Harrison Landing Field—*airport* KS-7
Harrison Learning Center—*school* AR-4
Harrison Lookout—*locale* PA-2
Harrison Lookout Tower—*locale* MI-6
Harrison Lookout Tower—*locale* MS-4
Harrison (Magisterial District)—*fmr MCD* (2) VA-3
Harrison Mall—*locale* AZ-5
Harrison Manns Choice Community Center—*building* PA-2
Harrison Marsh—*swamp* NY-2
Harrison Memorial Hosp—*hospital* WA-9
*Harrison Middle School* PA-2
Harrison Mill—*locale* MT-8
Harrison Mill Creek—*stream* AL-4
Harrison Mill (historical)—*locale* TN-4
**Harrison Mills**—*pop pl* OH-6
Harrison Mine—*mine* CA-9
Harrison Mine—*mine* MN-6
Harrison Mine—*mine* MT-8
Harrison Mine—*mine* SD-7
Harrison-Morton HS—*school* PA-2
Harrison Mountain Lake—*reservoir* NJ-2
Harrison Mountain Lake—*uninc pl* NJ-2
Harrison Mountain Lake Dam—*dam* NJ-2
Harrison Mtn—*summit* CA-9
Harrison Mtn—*summit* OR-9
Harrison Narrows—*gap* MN-6
*Harrison North Lake* IN-6
Harrison North Lake Dam—*dam* IN-6
Harrison Number 1 Dam—*dam* SD-7
Harrison Park—*flat* MT-8
Harrison Park—*park* AL-4
Harrison Park—*park* CT-1
Harrison Park—*park* (2) IL-6
Harrison Park—*park* (3) IN-6
Harrison Park—*park* MI-6
Harrison Park—*park* (2) MN-6
Harrison Park—*park* MO-7
Harrison Park—*park* NE-7
Harrison Park—*park* OK-5
**Harrison Park**—*pop pl* CA-9
Harrison Park JHS—*school* MI-6
Harrison Pass—*gap* CA-9
Harrison Pass—*gap* NV-8
*Harrison Pass Administrative Site* NV-8
Harrison Pass Creek—*stream* NV-8
Harrison Pass Guard Station—*locale* NV-8
Harrison Peak—*summit* CO-8
Harrison Peak—*summit* ID-8
Harrison Peak—*summit* UT-8
**Harrison Place (historical)**—*pop pl* IN-6
Harrison Point—*cape* CT-1
Harrison Point—*cape* (2) VA-3
**Harrison Point**—*pop pl* TN-4
Harrison Pond—*lake* NY-2
Harrison Pond—*reservoir* GA-3
Harrison Pond—*reservoir* SC-3
Harrison Pool—*reservoir* UT-8
Harrison Post Office—*building* TN-4
Harrison Prospect—*mine* TN-4
Harrison Ranch—*locale* MT-8
Harrison Ranch—*locale* TX-5
Harrison Ranch—*locale* WY-8
Harrison Reach—*channel* NJ-2
Harrison Reservation—*reserve* AL-4
Harrison Ridge—*ridge* (2) CA-9
Harrison Ridge—*ridge* KY-4
Harrison Ridge—*ridge* TN-4
Harrison Ridge—*ridge* WA-9
Harrison Ridge—*ridge* WI-6
Harrison Road Creek—*stream* FL-3
Harrison (RR name for Quecreek)—*other* PA-2
Harrison Rsvr—*reservoir* CO-8
Harrison Rsvr—*reservoir* OR-9
Harrison Run—*stream* PA-2
Harrison Run—*stream* VA-3
Harrisons—*locale* CT-1
Harrison Sawmill—*locale* SC-3
Harrisons Brook—*stream* NJ-2
*Harrison Sch* IN-6
Harrison Sch—*hist pl* VA-3
Harrison Sch—*school* (2) CA-9
Harrison Sch—*school* CT-1
Harrison Sch—*school* DC-2
Harrison Sch—*school* ID-8
Harrison Sch—*school* (3) IL-6
Harrison Sch—*school* (4) IN-6
Harrison Sch—*school* (4) IA-7
Harrison Sch—*school* (3) KY-4
Harrison Sch—*school* (5) MI-6
Harrison Sch—*school* (3) MN-6
Harrison Sch—*school* (2) MO-7
Harrison Sch—*school* NE-7
Harrison Sch—*school* NV-8
Harrison Sch—*school* NJ-2
Harrison Sch—*school* NY-2
Harrison Sch—*school* (6) OH-6
Harrison Sch—*school* (5) OK-5
Harrison Sch—*school* PA-2
Harrison Sch—*school* SD-7
Harrison Sch—*school* VA-3
Harrison Sch—*school* (3) WI-6
Harrison Sch (abandoned)—*school* (2) PA-2
*Harrisons Chapel* TN-4
Harrison Sch (historical)—*school* MS-4
Harrison Sch (historical)—*school* TN-4
*Harrison Sch Number 2* IN-6
Harrison School (historical)—*locale* MO-7
*Harrison's Creek* MN-6
*Harrisons Creek* NC-3
*Harrison's Creek* VA-3
Harrisons Creek—*stream* NC-3
**Harrisons Crossroads**—*pop pl* NC-3
*Harrisons Ford* TN-4
*Harrison Shoals* TN-4
Harrison Shoals—*bar* TN-4
Harrison Shoals—*rapids* SC-3
*Harrisons Island* TN-4
Harrisons Lake—*lake* GA-3
Harrisons Landing—*locale* VA-3
Harrisons Mill—*locale* GA-3
*Harrison South Lake* IN-6
Harrison South Lake Dam—*dam* IN-6
Harrison Spring—*spring* CA-9
Harrison Spring—*spring* ID-8
Harrison Spring—*spring* IN-6
Harrison Spring—*spring* NV-8
Harrison Spring—*spring* (2) OR-9
Harrison Spring—*spring* TN-4
Harrison Spring—*spring* UT-8
*Harrison Square* MA-1
*Harrisons Shoals* TN-4
Harrison State Forest—*park* SC-3
Harrison State Park—*park* OH-6
*Harrison Station* MS-4
Harrison Station—*locale* NJ-2
*Harrison (sta.) (West Harrison)* IN-6
Harrison St. Bridge—*hist pl* IL-6
Harrison Store (historical)—*locale* AL-4
Harrison Store (historical)—*locale* MS-4
Harrison Street Hollow—*valley* TN-4
Harrison Street Sch—*school* IL-6
Harrison Switch (historical)—*locale* AL-4
Harrison Tank—*reservoir* AZ-5
Harrison Tank—*reservoir* TX-5
Harrison-Thornton-Griggs Cem—*cemetery* MS-4
Harrison Tower—*pillar* LA-4
**Harrison Town**—*pop pl* TX-5
Harrison Townhall—*building* IA-7
**Harrison (Town of)**—*pop pl* ME-1
**Harrison (Town of)**—*pop pl* NY-2
**Harrison (Town of)**—*pop pl* (5) WI-6
Harrison Township—*CDP* PA-2
Harrison Township—*civ div* NE-7
Harrison Township—*civil* KS-7
Harrison Township—*civil* (2) MO-7
Harrison Township—*civil* (3) SD-7
Harrison Township—*fmr MCD* (8) IA-7
**Harrison Township**—*pop pl* (6) KS-7
**Harrison Township**—*pop pl* (4) MO-7
**Harrison Township**—*pop pl* (3) NE-7
**Harrison Township**—*pop pl* ND-7
**Harrison Township**—*pop pl* SD-7
Harrison (Township of)—*fmr MCD* (3) AR-4
**Harrison (Township of)**—*pop pl* IL-6
**Harrison (Township of)**—*pop pl* (24) IN-6
**Harrison (Township of)**—*pop pl* MI-6
**Harrison (Township of)**—*pop pl* MN-6
**Harrison (Township of)**—*pop pl* NJ-2
**Harrison (Township of)**—*pop pl* (19) OH-6
**Harrison (Township of)**—*pop pl* (3) PA-2
Harrison Trestle—*other* KY-4
Harrison Tunnel—*mine* UT-8
Harrison-Tutor Cem—*cemetery* MS-4
Harrison United Methodist Ch—*church* TN-4
**Harrison Valley**—*pop pl* PA-2
Harrison Valley—*valley* MO-7
Harrison Village Mall—*locale* IN-6
*Harrisonville* IN-6
*Harrisonville* PA-2
**Harrisonville**—*pop pl* GA-3
**Harrisonville**—*pop pl* (2) IL-6
**Harrisonville**—*pop pl* KY-4
**Harrisonville**—*pop pl* MD-2
**Harrisonville**—*pop pl* MO-7
**Harrisonville**—*pop pl* (2) NJ-2
**Harrisonville**—*pop pl* OH-6
**Harrisonville**—*pop pl* PA-2
Harrisonville—*uninc pl* GA-3
Harrisonville (CCD)—*cens area* KY-4
Harrisonville Cem—*cemetery* KS-7
Harrisonville Ch—*church* MS-4
Harrisonville City Lake—*reservoir* MO-7
Harrisonville Dam—*dam* NJ-2
Harrisonville (historical)—*locale* KS-7
Harrisonville Lake—*reservoir* NJ-2
Harrisonville Landing—*locale* IL-6
Harrisonville Landing Strip—*airport* MO-7
Harrisonville Sch—*school* MS-4
Harrisonville Station—*locale* NJ-2
Harrison Well—*well* (2) NM-5
Harrison White Brook—*stream* ME-1
**Harrisonwood Estates (subdivision)**—*pop pl* UT-8
Harrison Wright Falls—*falls* PA-2
Harrison Yates School (historical)—*locale* MO-7
Harrison Young Brook—*stream* OR-9
Harris Park—*flat* AZ-5
Harris Park—*flat* WY-8
Harris Park—*park* IL-6
Harris Park—*park* KY-4
Harris Park—*park* MI-6
Harris Park—*park* NY-2
**Harris Park**—*pop pl* CO-8
Harris Park Sch—*school* CO-8
Harris Peak—*summit* AK-9
Harris Peak—*summit* TX-5
Harris-Pearson-Walker House—*hist pl* GA-3
Harris Peninsula—*cape* AK-9
Harris Point—*cape* (2) AK-9
Harris Point—*cape* CA-9
Harris Point—*cape* NC-3
Harris Point—*cape* PA-2
Harris Point—*cape* RI-1
Harris Point—*cliff* AR-4
Harris Point—*summit* KY-4
Harris Point—*summit* UT-8
*Harris Pond* MA-1
Harris Pond—*lake* AR-4
Harris Pond—*lake* FL-3
Harris Pond—*lake* IN-6
Harris Pond—*lake* (2) NH-1
Harris Pond—*lake* (2) TN-4
Harris Pond—*reservoir* AL-4
Harris Pond—*reservoir* (2) MA-1
Harris Pond—*reservoir* NH-1
Harris Pond—*reservoir* PA-2
Harris Pond—*reservoir* (2) RI-1
Harris Pond—*reservoir* VA-3
Harris Pond—*reservoir* WI-6
Harris Pond—*swamp* FL-3
Harris Pond Dam—*dam* MA-1
Harris Pond Dam—*dam* PA-2
Harris Pond Number Three—*reservoir* NC-3
Harris Pond Number Three Dam—*dam* NC-3
Harris Pond Number Two—*reservoir* NC-3
Harris Pond Number Two Dam—*dam* NC-3
Harris Post Office—*locale* CA-9
Harris Post Office (historical)—*building* AL-4
Harris Post Office (historical)—*building* TN-4
Harris Prairie Cem—*cemetery* IN-6
Harris Prairie Ch—*church* IN-6
Harris Preschool Nursery—*school* FL-3
Harris Ranch—*locale* (2) AZ-5
Harris Ranch—*locale* (3) CA-9
Harris Ranch—*locale* CO-8
Harris Ranch—*locale* MT-8
Harris Ranch—*locale* NM-5
Harris Ranch—*locale* OR-9
Harris Ranch—*locale* SD-7
Harris Ranch—*locale* (3) WY-8
Harris Ranch Catfish Pond Dam—*dam* MS-4
Harris Ranch Petroglyph Site 41 CX 110—*hist pl* TX-5
Harris Ridge—*ridge* CA-9
Harris Ridge—*ridge* ID-8
Harris Ridge—*ridge* MO-7
Harris Ridge—*ridge* OH-6
Harris Ridge—*ridge* TN-4
Harris Ridge—*ridge* WV-2
Harris Ridge—*ridge* WI-6
Harris Ridge Cem—*cemetery* MO-7
Harris Ridge Sch (historical)—*school* MO-7
Harris Ridge Trail—*trail* MT-8
Harris Rift Mtn—*summit* NY-2
Harris River—*stream* AK-9
Harris River—*stream* VA-3
Harris Rsvr—*reservoir* CO-8
Harris Rsvr—*reservoir* OR-9
Harris Rsvr—*reservoir* TX-5
Harris Rsvr—*reservoir* UT-8
*Harris Run* OH-6
*Harris Run* WV-2
Harris Saxon Bridge—*bridge* FL-3
*Harris Sch* AL-4
Harris Sch—*school* AL-4
Harris Sch—*school* AR-4
Harris Sch—*school* (2) CA-9
Harris Sch—*school* CO-8
Harris Sch—*school* CT-1
Harris Sch—*school* DC-2
Harris Sch—*school* (2) FL-3
Harris Sch—*school* (2) IL-6
Harris Sch—*school* KY-4
Harris Sch—*school* LA-4
Harris Sch—*school* (2) MA-1
Harris Sch—*school* MI-6
Harris Sch—*school* NE-7
Harris Sch—*school* NJ-2
Harris Sch—*school* (3) NC-3
Harris Sch—*school* OH-6
Harris Sch—*school* OK-5
Harris Sch—*school* (2) OR-9
Harris Sch—*school* PA-2
Harris Sch—*school* (3) SD-7
Harris Sch—*school* TN-4
Harris Sch—*school* (5) TX-5
Harris Sch—*school* UT-8
Harris Sch—*school* WI-6
Harris Sch (abandoned)—*school* MO-7
Harris Sch (historical)—*school* (2) AL-4
Harris Sch Number 4—*school* ND-7
Harris Shoals—*bar* TN-4
Harris Siding—*locale* WV-2
**Harris Siding**—*pop pl* ID-8
**Harris Siding**—*pop pl* NC-3
Harris Siding Run—*stream* WV-2
Harris Siding Trail—*trail* WV-2
Harris Site—*hist pl* KS-7
Harris Slope Mine (underground)—*mine* AL-4
Harris Slough—*gut* LA-4
Harris Slough—*stream* IL-6
Harris Slough—*stream* WY-8
*Harrisson Creek* MN-6
Harrisson Gray Otis House Museum—*building* MA-1
Harris Spring—*spring* (2) AL-4
Harris Spring—*spring* AZ-5
Harris Spring—*spring* (3) CA-9
Harris Spring—*spring* ID-8
Harris Spring—*spring* (2) MT-8
Harris Spring—*spring* TN-4
Harris Spring—*spring* (2) TX-5
Harris Spring—*spring* UT-8
Harris Spring—*spring* (2) WY-8
Harris Spring Branch—*stream* TN-4
Harris Spring Ch—*church* TX-5
Harris Spring Hollow—*valley* UT-8
Harris Springs—*locale* SC-3
Harris Springs—*spring* NV-8
Harris Springs—*spring* UT-8
Harris Springs—*spring* VA-3
Harris Springs Canyon—*valley* NV-8
Harris Springs Ch—*church* GA-3
*Harris Station* IN-6

Harris Station ... NJ-2
Harris Station ... TN-4
Harris Station—locale ... AL-4
Harris Station Post Office ... AL-4
Harris Station Post Office ... TN-4
Harris Store—locale ... VA-3
Harris Store (historical)—locale ... AL-4
Harris Store (historical)—locale ... TN-4
Harris Street Bridge—hist pl ... MA-1
Harris Street Sch—school ... GA-3
**Harris Subdivision**—pop pl ... UT-8
Harris Swamp—stream ... NC-3
Harris Swamp—stream ... VA-3
Harris Swamp—swamp ... MA-1
Harris-Sweetwater Dewatering Area—swamp ... AL-4
Harris-Sweetwater Dewatering Project ... AL-4
Harris Tank ... NM-5
Harris Tank—mine ... AZ-5
Harris Tank—reservoir (2) ... AZ-5
Harris Tank—reservoir (2) ... NM-5
Harris Temple—church ... LA-4
**Harriston**—pop pl ... MS-4
**Harriston**—pop pl ... VA-3
**Harriston Township**—pop pl ... ND-7
Harris Top—summit (2) ... NC-3
Harristown—locale ... SC-3
**Harristown**—pop pl ... IL-6
**Harristown**—pop pl ... IN-6
**Harristown**—pop pl ... MD-2
**Harristown**—pop pl ... PA-2
**Harris (Town of)**—pop pl ... WI-6
Harris Township—civil ... MO-7
Harris (Township of)—fmr MCD ... AR-4
Harris (Township of)—fmr MCD ... NC-3
**Harris (Township of)**—pop pl ... IL-6
**Harris (Township of)**—pop pl ... IN-6
**Harris (Township of)**—pop pl ... MI-6
**Harris (Township of)**—pop pl ... MN-6
**Harris (Township of)**—pop pl ... OH-6
**Harris (Township of)**—pop pl ... PA-2
**Harristown (Township of)**—pop pl ... IL-6
Harris Valley—valley ... CA-9
Harris Valley—valley ... NM-5
Harrisville ... MA-1
Harrisville ... NJ-2
Harrisville ... RI-1
Harrisville—locale ... IL-6
Harrisville—locale (2) ... MD-2
Harrisville—locale ... NJ-2
Harrisville—locale ... VA-3
**Harrisville**—pop pl ... AL-4
**Harrisville**—pop pl ... CT-1
**Harrisville**—pop pl ... IN-6
**Harrisville**—pop pl ... MD-2
**Harrisville**—pop pl ... MA-1
**Harrisville**—pop pl ... MI-6
**Harrisville**—pop pl ... MS-4
**Harrisville**—pop pl ... NH-1
**Harrisville**—pop pl (2) ... NY-2
**Harrisville**—pop pl ... NC-3
**Harrisville**—pop pl ... OH-6
**Harrisville**—pop pl ... PA-2
**Harrisville**—pop pl ... RI-1
**Harrisville**—pop pl ... UT-8
**Harrisville**—pop pl ... VT-1
**Harrisville**—pop pl ... WV-2
**Harrisville**—pop pl ... WI-6
Harrisville Attendance Center (historical)—school ... MS-4
Harrisville Baptist Ch—church ... MS-4
Harrisville Borough—civil ... PA-2
Harrisville Brook—stream ... VT-1
Harrisville Dam—dam ... NJ-2
Harrisville Golf Club—other ... CT-1
**Harrisville Heights**—pop pl ... UT-8
Harrisville Hist Dist—hist pl ... NH-1
Harrisville Hist Dist—hist pl ... RI-1
Harrisville Lookout Tower—locale ... NC-3
Harrisville Pond—lake ... NH-1
Harrisville Pond—reservoir ... NJ-2
Harrisville Pond—reservoir ... RI-1
Harrisville Pond Dam—dam ... RI-1
Harrisville Rural District—hist pl ... NH-1
Harrisville State Park—park ... MI-6
Harrisville Station (RR name for Forestville)—locale ... PA-2
**Harrisville (Town of)**—pop pl ... NH-1
**Harrisville (Township of)**—pop pl ... MI-6
**Harrisville (Township of)**—pop pl ... OH-6
Harris Warehouse—hist pl ... RI-1
Harris Wash—stream ... AZ-5
Harris Wash—valley ... UT-8
Harris Well—well ... AZ-5
Harris Well—well ... NV-8
Harris Well—well (2) ... NM-5
Harris Wharf—locale ... MD-2
Harris Windmill—locale ... TX-5
Harris Windmills—locale ... NM-5
Harriswood Crescent—hist pl ... MA-1
Harris Yard—locale ... OH-6
Harriton—hist pl ... PA-2
Harriton HS—school ... PA-2
Harriton Senior HS ... PA-2
Harritt Sch—school ... CA-9
Harrity—locale ... PA-2
Harrity Elementary School ... PA-2
Harrity Sch—school ... PA-2
**Harrock Hall**—pop pl ... GA-3
**Harrod**—pop pl ... OH-6
Harrod, Ephraim, House—hist pl ... KY-4
Harrod Cem—cemetery ... IN-6
Harrod Cem—cemetery (2) ... OH-6
Harrod Run—stream ... OH-6
**Harrodsburg**—pop pl ... IN-6
**Harrodsburg**—pop pl ... KY-4
Harrodsburg (CCD)—cens area ... KY-4
Harrodsburg Commercial District—hist pl ... KY-4
Harrodsburgh ... IN-6
**Harrods Creek**—pop pl ... KY-4
Harrods Creek—stream (2) ... KY-4
Harrods Creek Baptist Church and Rev. William Kellar House—hist pl ... KY-4
Harrods Creek Cem—cemetery ... KY-4
Harrods Creek Ch—church ... KY-4
Harrods Fork—stream ... KY-4
Harrods Fork Ch—church ... KY-4
Harrods (RR name for Harrod)—other ... OH-6
Harroff Lake—reservoir ... IN-6
**Harrogate**—pop pl ... TN-4

Harrogate Cem—cemetery ... TN-4
Harrogate Church ... TN-4
Harrogate Post Office—building ... TN-4
Harrogate-Shawanee—CDP ... TN-4
**Harrogate Springs**—pop pl ... AL-4
Harrogate United Methodist Ch—church ... TN-4
**Harrold**—pop pl ... SD-7
**Harrold**—pop pl ... TX-5
Harrold Airp—airport ... IN-6
Harrold Cem—cemetery ... TN-4
Harrold Ditch—canal ... IN-6
Harrold Hollow—valley ... TN-4
Harrold JHS—school ... PA-2
Harrold JHS—school ... TN-4
Harrold Mtn—summit ... NC-3
Harrold Municipal Airp—airport ... SD-7
Harrold-Oklaunion (CCD)—cens area ... TX-5
Harrold Run ... PA-2
Harrolds Cem—cemetery ... PA-2
Harrold Township—civil ... SD-7
Harrol Hollow—valley ... TX-5
Harroum Coulee—valley ... MT-8
Harroun Canal—canal ... NM-5
Harroun Canyon—valley ... ID-8
Harroun Crossing—locale ... NM-5
Harroun Dam—dam ... NM-5
Harroun Ditch—canal ... NM-5
Harroun Ditch—canal ... OH-6
Harroun Sch—school ... NM-5
Harrow—locale ... PA-2
Harrow Brook—stream ... ME-1
Harrow Canyon—valley ... CA-9
Harrow Creek—stream ... CA-9
Harrowed Trail—trail ... PA-2
**Harrower**—pop pl ... NY-2
Harrower Glacier—glacier ... WY-8
Harrower Peak—summit ... WY-8
Harrower Pond—reservoir ... NY-2
**Harrowgate**—pop pl ... VA-3
Harrowgate Sch—school ... VA-3
Harrow Hall HS (historical)—school ... TN-4
Harrow Lake—lake ... ME-1
Harrow Mtn—summit ... ME-1
Harrow Prairie—flat ... CA-9
Harrow Run—stream ... NJ-2
Harrows Branch—stream ... IA-7
Harrow Sch—school ... MI-6
Harr-Pinti Field—park ... NY-2
Harr Post Office (historical)—building ... TN-4
Harrison County Jail—hist pl ... IA-7
**Harrs Place (historical)**—pop pl ... MS-4
**Harrtown**—pop pl ... TN-4
Harrts Run (historical)—stream ... PA-2
**Harrubs Corner**—pop pl ... MA-1
Harr Valley—basin ... NE-7
Harr Wills Ditch—canal ... IN-6
Harry ... MN-6
Harry, Lake—lake ... FL-3
Harry, Lake—lake ... MN-6
Harry-Anna Sch—school ... FL-3
**Harryat**—pop pl ... GA-3
Harry Bay—bay ... AK-9
Harry Bickel Dam ... SD-7
Harry Bickel Dam—dam ... SD-7
Harry Birch Springs—spring ... CA-9
Harry Bivins Airp—airport ... KS-7
Harry Branch ... WV-2
Harry Branch—stream ... AL-4
Harry Branch—stream ... VA-3
Harry Bremmer Canyon—valley ... NM-5
Harry Brook—stream ... NH-1
Harry Brown Ranch—locale ... WY-8
Harry Canyon—valley ... ID-8
Harry Canyon—valley ... NV-8
Harry Canyon Creek ... NV-8
Harry Cem—cemetery (2) ... WV-2
Harry Coleman Ranch—locale ... WY-8
Harry Colwes Draw—valley ... UT-8
Harry Colwes Spring—spring ... UT-8
Harry Cool Ditch—canal ... IN-6
Harry Creek ... NV-8
Harry Creek—stream ... AK-9
Harry Creek—stream ... CO-8
Harry Creek—stream ... MD-2
Harry Creek—stream ... MN-6
Harry Creek—stream (2) ... OR-9
Harry Davis Camp—locale ... NH-1
Harry Davis Landing—locale ... AL-4
Harry Dayton Ranch—locale ... WY-8
Harry Debutts Yards (Southern)—locale ... TN-4
Harry Diamond Laboratories—military ... MD-2
Harry Diamond Laboratories—other ... MD-2
Harry E Braker Dam Number One—dam ... PA-2
Harry E Breaker Station—locale ... PA-2
Harry E Dobbins Memorial State For—forest ... NY-2
Harry Evans Bridge—hist pl ... IN-6
Harry Evans Covered Bridge—bridge ... IN-6
**Harry Floyd Terrace**—pop pl ... CA-9
Harry George Creek—stream ... VA-3
Harry Hall Gulch—valley ... CA-9
Harry Hammock—island ... GA-3
Harry Harding High School ... NC-3
Harry Head Cove—swamp ... SC-3
Harryhogan ... VA-3
**Harryhogan**—pop pl ... VA-3
**Harryhogan Point**—pop pl ... VA-3
Harry Hollow ... TN-4
Harry Hollow—valley ... TN-4
Harry Holy Bottom—bend ... CO-8
Harry H Russell Pond Dam—dam ... MS-4
Harry Island—island ... AK-9
Harry James Creek—bay ... MD-2
Harry Kaul Spring—spring ... NV-8
Harry K Brown Park—park ... HI-9
Harry Knight Spring—spring ... AZ-5
Harry Lake—lake ... LA-4
Harry Lake—lake ... MS-4
Harry Lake—lake ... WA-9
Harry L. Englebright Lake ... CA-9
Harry L Englebright Lake—reservoir ... CA-9
Harry L. Englebright Rsvr ... CA-9
Harry Madison Pond Dam—dam ... MS-4
Harrymans Cem—cemetery ... IL-6
Harry M Arnot MS—school ... NC-3
Harry Marr Ranch—locale ... CA-9
Harry M Ayres State Technical Sch—school ... AL-4
Harry M. Hewitt Memorial Park—park ... OR-9
Harry Miller Creek—stream ... NE-7

Harry O. Eisenberg Elem Sch—school ... DE-2
Harry Page Rsvr—reservoir ... OR-9
Harry Parker Place—locale ... CO-8
Harry Payne Spring—spring ... CA-9
Harry Pond—lake ... NJ-2
Harry Ponds—lake ... NY-2
Harry Rocks ... MA-1
Harry Rowe Trail—trail ... OK-5
Harrys—uninc pl ... TX-5
Harry Saddle—other ... AK-9
Harrys Branch—stream ... WV-2
Harrys Brook—stream ... NJ-2
Harry Sch—school ... WV-2
Harrys Creek ... NV-8
Harrys Creek—stream ... FL-3
Harrys Creek—stream ... MT-8
Harrys Flat Campground—locale ... MT-8
Harrys Gulch—valley ... AK-9
Harrys Gulch—valley ... MT-8
Harrys Hollow—valley ... ID-8
Harrys Island (historical)—island ... AL-4
Harrys Lake—lake ... AK-9
Harrys Pond—bay ... LA-4
Harry Spring—spring ... CA-9
Harry Spring—spring ... NV-8
Harry Spring—spring ... OR-9
Harry Spring—spring ... SD-7
Harrys Ridge—ridge ... WA-9
Harrys Rock—rock ... MA-1
Harrys Rock Light—locale ... MA-1
Harrys Spring—spring ... NV-8
Harry Stone Park—park ... TX-5
Harry Street Ch of God—church ... KS-7
Harry Street Elem Sch—school ... KS-7
Harry S Truman ... MO-7
Harry S. Truman Airp—airport ... VI-3
Harry S Truman Bridge—other ... MO-7
Harry S Truman Dam—dam ... MO-7
Harry S Truman Elem Sch—school ... PA-2
Harry S Truman HS—school ... PA-2
Harry S Truman Library ... MO-7
Harry S Truman Natl Historic Site—hist pl ... MO-7
Harry S Truman Regional Airp—airport ... MO-7
Harry S. Truman Reservoir ... AR-4
Harry S Truman RR Station—locale ... MO-7
Harry S Truman Rsvr ... MO-7
Harry S Truman Rsvr—reservoir ... MO-7
Harry S Truman Sch—school ... UT-8
Harry S Truman Sports Complex—other ... MO-7
Harry S Truman State Park—park ... MO-7
Harry Strunk Lake—reservoir ... NE-7
Harrys Valley—valley ... PA-2
Harry Tank—reservoir (2) ... TX-5
Harry Truman JHS—school ... TX-5
Harry White Reservoirs—reservoir ... CO-8
Harry W Lockley Elementary School ... PA-2
Harry W Nice Memorial Bridge—bridge ... MD-2
Harry W Nice Memorial Bridge—bridge ... VA-3
Harry Wrights Lake—reservoir ... NJ-2
Harsco Airp—airport ... PA-2
Hars Creek—stream ... AR-4
Harsens Island ... MI-6
Harsens Island—island ... MI-6
Harsens Island Drain—canal ... MI-6
**Harsens Island (Sans Souci)**—pop pl ... MI-6
Harsens Island Sch—school ... MI-6
Harsha—locale ... WA-9
Harsha Canyon—valley ... OK-5
Harsha Gulch—valley ... CO-8
**Harshasville**—pop pl ... OH-6
**Harshaville**—pop pl ... PA-2
Harshaville Covered Bridge—hist pl ... OH-6
**Harshaw**—pop pl ... AZ-5
**Harshaw**—pop pl ... WI-6
Harshaw Bottom—bend ... NC-3
Harshaw Branch—stream ... NC-3
Harshaw Ch—church ... NC-3
Harshaw Chapel and Cemetery—hist pl ... NC-3
Harshaw Creek—stream ... AZ-5
Harshaw Gap—gap ... NC-3
Harshaw-Stovall House—hist pl ... GA-3
Harshbarger Cem—cemetery (2) ... IN-6
Harshbarger Sch—school ... IL-6
Harshberger Gap—gap ... VA-3
Harsh Ch—church ... OH-6
Harsh Ch—church ... TN-4
Harsh Ditch—canal (2) ... IN-6
Harshey, John, Residence—hist pl ... OH-6
Harshfield Ranch—locale ... NE-7
Harshfield Spring—spring ... KY-4
Harsh Lake Dam—dam ... MS-4
Harshman, Charles, House—hist pl ... OH-6
Harshman Canyon—valley ... OR-9
Harshman Covered Bridge—hist pl ... OH-6
Harshman Creek—stream ... IN-6
Harshman Ditch—canal (2) ... IN-6
Harshman Sch—school ... OH-6
Harshman School Number 101 ... IN-6
Harsimus Cove—bay ... NJ-2
Harsimus Cove Hist Dist—hist pl ... NJ-2
Harson Ranch—locale ... WY-8
Harsons Island ... MI-6
Harstad Park—park ... WI-6
Harstad Slough—lake ... MN-6
Harstene ... WA-9
Harsten Flat—flat ... MT-8
Harstine ... WA-9
**Harstine**—pop pl ... WA-9
Harstine Island ... WA-9
Harston Branch—stream ... AR-4
Harston Coulee—valley ... MT-8
Hart ... WV-2
Hart—locale ... AR-4
Hart—locale ... CA-9
Hart—locale ... MO-7
Hart—locale ... OK-5
**Hart**—pop pl ... ID-8
**Hart**—pop pl ... IL-6
**Hart**—pop pl ... IA-7
**Hart**—pop pl ... KY-4
**Hart**—pop pl ... MI-6
**Hart**—pop pl ... MN-6
**Hart**—pop pl ... MO-7
**Hart**—pop pl ... SC-3
**Hart**—pop pl ... TX-5
Hart, Charles Walter, House—hist pl ... IA-7
Hart, Dr. Franklin, Farm—hist pl ... NC-3
Hart, Eleazer, House—hist pl ... NY-2
Hart, F. H., House—hist pl ... KS-7

Hart, Gen. Thomas, House—hist pl ... KY-4
Hart, Gen. William, House—hist pl ... CT-1
Hart, Gideon, House—hist pl ... OH-6
Hart, Jeremiah, House—hist pl ... NH-1
Hart, John, House—hist pl ... NH-1
Hart, John D., House—hist pl ... NJ-2
Hart, John L., House—hist pl ... SC-3
Hart, Lake—lake (3) ... FL-3
Hart, Maurice, House—hist pl ... NC-3
Hart, Meredith, House—hist pl ... TX-5
Hart, Phoebe, House—hist pl ... NH-1
Hart, Rodney G., House—hist pl ... MI-6
Hart, Thomas B., House—hist pl ... WI-6
Hart, Wilson A., House—hist pl ... CO-8
Hartab Lake ... WI-6
Hart Airp—airport ... MO-7
Hart and Hart Mine (Inactive—mine ... KY-4
Hartbarger Cem—cemetery ... VA-3
Hartbauer Creek—stream ... WA-9
Hartbauer Orchard—area ... WA-9
Hart Bay—bay ... VI-3
Hart Bed Mine (underground)—mine ... AL-4
Hart Bench—bench ... MT-8
Hart Bend—bend ... TX-5
Hart Bldg—hist pl ... CA-9
Hart Bldg—hist pl ... PA-2
Hart Branch—canal ... MI-6
Hart Branch—stream ... FL-3
Hart Branch—stream (3) ... KY-4
Hart Branch—stream ... MO-7
Hart Branch—stream ... NC-3
Hart Branch—stream ... TX-5
Hart Brook ... MA-1
Hart Brook—stream ... CT-1
Hart Brook—stream ... ME-1
Hart Brook—stream (2) ... NH-1
**Hartburg**—pop pl ... TX-5
Hart Butte ... OR-9
Hart Camp—locale ... ME-1
Hart Camp—locale ... NV-8
Hart Camp—locale (2) ... TX-5
Hart Canyon—valley ... AZ-5
Hart Canyon—valley ... CA-9
Hart Canyon—valley ... CO-8
Hart Canyon—valley (4) ... NM-5
Hart Canyon—valley ... OR-9
Hart Cem—cemetery (2) ... AR-4
Hart Cem—cemetery (2) ... FL-3
Hart Cem—cemetery ... GA-3
Hart Cem—cemetery (3) ... IL-6
Hart Cem—cemetery ... KS-7
Hart Cem—cemetery (4) ... KY-4
Hart Cem—cemetery (2) ... ME-1
Hart Cem—cemetery ... MI-6
Hart Cem—cemetery ... MS-4
Hart Cem—cemetery (6) ... MO-7
Hart Cem—cemetery ... NM-5
Hart Cem—cemetery ... NC-3
Hart Cem—cemetery ... OH-6
Hart Cem—cemetery ... OK-5
Hart Cem—cemetery ... SC-3
Hart Cem—cemetery (8) ... TN-4
Hart Cem—cemetery (5) ... TX-5
Hart Cem—cemetery ... VA-3
Hart Cem—cemetery ... WV-2
Hart Ch—church ... KY-4
Hart Ch—church ... LA-4
Hart Chapel—church (2) ... WV-2
Hart Chapel Cem—cemetery ... TN-4
Hart Chapel School ... TN-4
Hart Childress Cem—cemetery ... MS-4
Hart Church ... PA-2
Hart-Cluett Mansion—hist pl ... NY-2
Hart Coal Mine—mine ... NM-5
Hart Corner—locale ... VA-3
Hart Corners—locale ... NY-2
**Hart (County)**—pop pl ... GA-3
**Hart (County)**—pop pl ... KY-4
Hart County Courthouse—hist pl ... KY-4
Hart County Deposit Bank and Trust Company Bldg—hist pl ... KY-4
Hart County Jail—hist pl ... GA-3
Hart Cove—bay ... GA-3
Hart Cove—bay ... NY-2
Hart Creek ... AR-4
Hart Creek ... PA-2
Hart Creek ... WV-2
Hart Creek—stream ... AL-4
Hart Creek—stream ... AK-9
Hart Creek—stream ... AR-4
Hart Creek—stream ... GA-3
Hart Creek—stream ... ID-8
Hart Creek—stream ... IL-6
Hart Creek—stream ... LA-4
Hart Creek—stream ... MO-7
Hart Creek—stream (5) ... MT-8
Hart Creek—stream (2) ... OR-9
Hart Creek—stream ... TN-4
Hart Creek—stream ... TX-5
Hart Creek—stream ... VA-3
Hart Creek—stream ... WA-9
Hart Creek Rsvr—reservoir ... OR-9
Hart Ditch ... IL-6
Hart Ditch ... IN-6
Hart Ditch—canal ... CO-8
Hart Ditch—canal ... IN-6
Hart Ditch—canal ... MS-4
Hart Ditch—canal ... MO-7
Hart Ditch—canal ... MT-8
Hart Ditch—canal ... OH-6
Hart Drain—stream ... MI-6
Hart Draw ... UT-8
Hart Draw—valley ... KS-7
Hart Draw—valley ... MT-8
Hart Draw—valley ... NM-5
Hart Draw—valley (2) ... TX-5
Hart Draw—valley (2) ... WY-8
Harte, H.W., Block-Chrystal Falls Village Hall—hist pl ... MI-6
Hartel Drain—stream ... MI-6
Harten Slough—gut ... TX-5
Hartens Pond—lake ... CT-1
Hartenstein Lake—lake ... CO-8
Hartenstine Creek—stream ... PA-2
Harter—locale ... WA-9
Harter—locale ... WV-2
**Harter**—pop pl ... CA-9
Harte Ranch—locale ... CO-8
Harter Cem—cemetery ... KS-7
Harter Cem—cemetery ... OH-6

Harter Creek—stream ... IA-7
Harter Creek—stream ... MI-6
Harter Creek—stream ... OR-9
Harter Ditch ... IN-6
Harter Gulch—valley ... AK-9
Harter Hill—summit (2) ... NY-2
Harter Hill—summit ... WA-9
Harter Hill Ch—church ... WV-2
Harter Hill Sch—school ... WV-2
Harter Marsh—swamp ... WI-6
Harter Mtn—summit ... OR-9
Harter Sch—school ... OH-6
Harter Sch—school ... PA-2
**Harters Hill**—pop pl ... WV-2
Harters Pond—lake ... SC-3
**Harter (Township of)**—pop pl ... IL-6
Harte Run—stream ... OH-6
Harte Sch—school ... IL-6
Harte Spring—spring ... CO-8
Hartex—locale ... TX-5
Hartfield ... PA-2
**Hartfield**—pop pl ... NY-2
**Hartfield**—pop pl ... PA-2
**Hartfield**—pop pl ... VA-3
Hartfield Bay—bay ... NY-2
Hartfield Cem—cemetery ... KY-4
Hartfield Cem—cemetery (2) ... MS-4
Hartfield Creek—stream ... MS-4
Hartfield Mill Creek—stream ... MS-4
Hartfiel State Wildlife Mngmt Area—park ... MN-6
Hartford ... IN-6
Hartford ... NC-3
Hartford ... PA-2
Hartford ... WV-2
Hartford—locale ... IL-6
Hart Ford—locale ... TN-4
Hartford—locale ... VA-3
Hartford—other ... OH-6
**Hartford**—pop pl ... AL-4
**Hartford**—pop pl ... AR-4
**Hartford**—pop pl ... CT-1
**Hartford**—pop pl ... GA-3
**Hartford**—pop pl ... IL-6
**Hartford**—pop pl ... IN-6
**Hartford**—pop pl ... IA-7
**Hartford**—pop pl ... KS-7
**Hartford**—pop pl ... KY-4
**Hartford**—pop pl ... ME-1
**Hartford**—pop pl ... MI-6
**Hartford**—pop pl ... MO-7
**Hartford**—pop pl ... NJ-2
**Hartford**—pop pl ... NY-2
**Hartford**—pop pl ... OH-6
**Hartford**—pop pl ... SD-7
**Hartford**—pop pl ... TN-4
**Hartford**—pop pl ... VT-1
**Hartford**—pop pl ... WI-6
Hartford—uninc pl ... WA-9
Hartford, John A., House—hist pl ... NY-2
**Hartford Beach**—pop pl ... SD-7
Hartford Beach Creek—stream ... SD-7
Hartford Beach State Park—park ... SD-7
Hartford Brook—stream (2) ... NH-1
Hartford Buffalo P O & Station ... OH-6
Hartford Camp—locale ... ME-1
Hartford Canyon ... CA-9
Hartford Canyon—valley ... NM-5
Hartford (CCD)—cens area ... AL-4
Hartford (CCD)—cens area ... GA-3
Hartford (CCD)—cens area ... KY-4
Hartford (CCD)—cens area ... TN-4
Hartford Cem—cemetery ... GA-3
Hartford Cem—cemetery ... IN-6
Hartford Cem—cemetery ... KS-7
Hartford Cem—cemetery ... ME-1
Hartford Cem—cemetery ... SD-7
Hartford Center Cem—cemetery ... ME-1
Hartford Ch—church ... GA-3
Hartford Church—locale ... IL-6
**Hartford City**—pop pl ... IN-6
**Hartford City**—pop pl ... WV-2
**Hartford City (corporate name for Hartford)**—pop pl ... WV-2
Hartford Club—hist pl ... CT-1
Hartford Collegiate Institute—hist pl ... KS-7
**Hartford (corporate name for Croton)**—pop pl ... OH-6
Hartford (corporate name Hartford City) ... WV-2
Hartford Country Club—other ... CT-1
**Hartford County**—pop pl ... CT-1
**Hartford Croton Post Office**—pop pl ... OH-6
Hartford Division—civil ... AL-4
Hartford Division—civil ... TN-4
Hartford Elem Sch—school ... AZ-5
Hartford Elem Sch—school ... TN-4
Hartford Golf Club Hist Dist—hist pl ... CT-1
Hartford Heights Elem Sch—school ... PA-2
Hartford Heights Sch ... PA-2
Hartford Hill—summit ... NV-8
Hartford (historical)—locale (2) ... MS-4
Hartford Hosp—hospital ... CT-1
Hartford HS—school ... AL-4
Hartford HS—school ... KS-7
Hartford Lake—lake ... AL-4
Hartford Lake Number 1 Dam—dam ... AL-4
Hartford Lake Number 2 Dam—dam ... AL-4
Hartford Memorial Cem—cemetery ... AR-4
Hartford Memorial Sch—school ... VT-1
Hartford & New Haven Railroad-Freight Depot—hist pl ... CT-1
Hartford & New Haven RR Depot—hist pl ... CT-1
Hartford Picnic Grove ... SD-7
Hartford Place ... IN-6
Hartford Post Office—building ... TN-4
Hartford Rec Area—park ... KS-7
Hartford Rsvr—reservoir ... CO-8
Hartford Rsvr No 1—reservoir ... CT-1
Hartford Rsvr No 2—reservoir ... CT-1
Hartford Rsvr No 3—reservoir ... CT-1
Hartford Rsvr No 5—reservoir ... CT-1
Hartford Rsvr No 6—reservoir ... CT-1
Hartford Sch—school ... IL-6
Hartford Sch—school ... OH-6
Hartford Sch (historical)—school ... MO-7
Hartford School ... TN-4
Hartford Seminary—hist pl ... KY-4
Hartford Seminary—school ... CT-1
Hartford Seminary Foundation—hist pl ... CT-1
**Hartford Siding**—pop pl ... WV-2

Hartford Spring ... CA-9
Hartford State Technical Institute—school ... CT-1
Hartford (Town of)—civ div ... CT-1
**Hartford (Town of)**—pop pl ... ME-1
**Hartford (Town of)**—pop pl ... NY-2
**Hartford (Town of)**—pop pl ... VT-1
**Hartford (Town of)**—pop pl ... WI-6
Hartford Township—civil ... MO-7
Hartford Township—civil ... SD-7
Hartford Township—fmr MCD ... IA-7
**Hartford Township**—pop pl ... SD-7
Hartford Township (historical)—civil ... SD-7
Hartford (Township of)—fmr MCD ... AR-4
**Hartford (Township of)**—pop pl ... IN-6
**Hartford (Township of)**—pop pl ... MI-6
**Hartford (Township of)**—pop pl ... MN-6
**Hartford (Township of)**—pop pl (2) ... OH-6
Hartford Union Station—hist pl ... CT-1
Hartgrave Creek—stream ... IA-7
Hartgraves Creek ... IA-7
Hartgraves Place—locale ... NE-7
Hartgrove Ranch—locale ... TX-5
Hart Gulch—valley ... CA-9
Hart Gulch—valley ... CO-8
Hart Gulch—valley ... MT-8
Hart Gulf—valley ... TN-4
**Harth Addition (subdivision)**—pop pl ... TN-4
Hart Hammock—island ... FL-3
Harthaven—lake ... MA-1
**Hart Haven**—pop pl ... FL-3
**Harthaven**—pop pl ... MA-1
Harthegig Run—stream ... PA-2
Hart Hill ... NY-2
Hart Hill—summit ... CT-1
Hart Hill—summit ... MN-6
Hart Hill—summit ... NH-1
Harthill Cem—cemetery ... MO-7
Hart Hill Sch—school ... NY-2
**Hart (historical)**—pop pl ... TN-4
**Hartho**—pop pl ... MI-6
Hart-Hoch House—hist pl ... NJ-2
Hart Hollow—valley ... KY-4
Hart Hollow—valley ... MO-7
Hart Hollow—valley ... TN-4
Hart Hollow—valley ... VT-1
Harthorne Ledge—bar ... ME-1
Harthorn Playground—locale ... MA-1
Hart House—hist pl ... DE-2
Hart House—hist pl (2) ... LA-4
Hart House—hist pl ... SC-3
Hartill Creek—stream ... WA-9
Hartill Meadows—flat ... WA-9
Hart Industrial Park—locale ... NC-3
Harting Ditch—canal ... IN-6
**Hartington**—pop pl ... NE-7
**Hartington and Williams (subdivision)**—pop pl ... NC-3
Hartington Cem—cemetery ... NE-7
Hartis Grove Ch—church ... NC-3
Hart Island ... MD-2
Hart Island ... NY-2
Hart Island—island ... ME-1
Hart Island—island ... MI-6
Hart Island—island ... NH-1
Hart Island—island ... NY-2
Hart Island—island ... WA-9
Hart Island—uninc pl ... NY-2
Hart Island Ledges—bar ... ME-1
Hartje Cem—cemetery ... AR-4
Hart JHS—school ... DC-2
Hart JHS—school ... IL-6
Hart JHS—school ... OH-6
Hartke Cem—cemetery ... KS-7
Hartkopf Park—park ... MN-6
Hart Lake ... MI-6
Hart Lake ... MN-6
Hart Lake ... PA-2
Hart Lake ... WY-8
Hart Lake—lake ... AK-9
Hart Lake—lake ... AR-4
Hart Lake—lake ... FL-3
Hart Lake—lake (5) ... MI-6
Hart Lake—lake (8) ... MN-6
Hart Lake—lake (2) ... MT-8
Hart Lake—lake ... NE-7
Hart Lake—lake (2) ... WA-9
Hart Lake—lake (2) ... WI-6
Hart Lake—reservoir ... AL-4
Hart Lake—reservoir ... IN-6
Hart Lake—reservoir ... MI-6
Hart Lake—reservoir ... NC-3
Hart Lake—reservoir ... OR-9
Hart Lake—swamp ... MN-6
Hart Lake Dam—dam ... IN-6
Hart Lake Dam—dam ... NC-3
Hart Lake Dam—dam ... OR-9
Hart Lake Geyser Basin ... WY-8
Hart Lake Number One—lake ... TN-4
Hart Lake Number Two—lake ... TN-4
Hart Lakes—lake ... CA-9
**Hart Lake (Township of)**—pop pl ... MN-6
Hartland—hist pl ... KY-4
Hartland—hist pl ... WV-2
Hartland—locale ... CT-1
Hartland—locale ... KS-7
Hartland—locale ... TX-5
**Hartland**—pop pl ... CA-9
**Hartland**—pop pl ... IL-6
**Hartland**—pop pl ... ME-1
**Hartland**—pop pl ... MI-6
**Hartland**—pop pl ... MN-6
**Hartland**—pop pl ... NY-2
**Hartland**—pop pl ... NC-3
**Hartland**—pop pl ... ND-7
**Hartland**—pop pl ... OH-6
**Hartland**—pop pl ... VT-1
**Hartland**—pop pl ... WA-9
**Hartland**—pop pl ... WV-2
**Hartland**—pop pl ... WI-6
Hartland Cem—cemetery ... KS-7
Hartland Cem—cemetery ... WA-9
**Hartland Center**—pop pl ... OH-6
Hartland Central Cem—cemetery ... NY-2
Hartland Ch—church ... IL-6
Hartland Ch—church ... NY-2
Hartland Ch—church (2) ... WI-6
Hartland Ditch—canal ... CO-8
**Hartland Estates**—pop pl ... TN-4
**Hartland Four Corners**—pop pl ... VT-1
Hartland Hill—summit ... VT-1

Hart Landing—*locale* MS-4
Hartland Millpond—*lake* MI-6
Hartland Pond—*lake* CT-1
Hartland Ridge Cem—*cemetery* OH-6
Hartland RR Depot—*hist pl* WI-6
Hartland Sch—*school* IL-6
Hartland Sch—*school* MI-6
**Hartland Station**—*pop pl* OH-6
**Hartland (Town of)**—*pop pl* CT-1
**Hartland (Town of)**—*pop pl* ME-1
**Hartland (Town of)**—*pop pl* NY-2
**Hartland (Town of)**—*pop pl* VT-1
**Hartland (Town of)**—*pop pl* (2) WI-6
Hartland Township—*fmr MCD* IA-7
**Hartland Township**—*pop pl* KS-7
**Hartland Township**—*pop pl* (2) SD-7
**Hartland (Township of)**—*pop pl* IL-6
**Hartland (Township of)**—*pop pl* MI-6
**Hartland (Township of)**—*pop pl* MN-6
**Hartland (Township of)**—*pop pl* OH-6
Hart Lateral—*canal* CO-8
Hartlaub Lake—*lake* WI-6
Hartle Cem—*cemetery* MO-7
Hart Ledge—*bar* ME-1
Hart Ledge—*bench* NH-1
Hartle Ford—*locale* MO-7
Hartle Hollow—*valley* PA-2
Hartle Sch (historical)—*school* MO-7
Hartless Branch—*stream* TX-5
Hartless Guard Station—*locale* CA-9
**Hartleton**—*pop pl* PA-2
Hartleton Borough—*civil* PA-2
Hartleton Cem—*cemetery* PA-2
*Hartley* DE-2
Hartley—*locale* AR-4
Hartley—*locale* CA-9
Hartley—*locale* GA-3
Hartley—*locale* KY-4
Hartley—*locale* MI-6
Hartley—*locale* WV-2
**Hartley**—*pop pl* IA-7
**Hartley**—*pop pl* PA-2
**Hartley**—*pop pl* SD-7
**Hartley**—*pop pl* TX-5
Hartley, Lake—*lake* FL-3
Hartley, Roland, House—*hist pl* WA-9
Hartley Airp—*airport* WA-9
Hartley Branch—*stream* GA-3
Hartley Branch—*stream* IL-6
Hartley Branch—*stream* MS-4
Hartley Branch—*stream* MO-7
Hartley Branch—*stream* TN-4
Hartley Branch Prospect—*mine* TN-4
*Hartley Brohard* WV-2
Hartley Burt Mine—*mine* MN-6
Hartley Butte—*summit* CA-9
*Hartley Canyon* AZ-5
*Hartley Canyon* UT-8
Hartley Canyon—*valley* ID-8
Hartley Canyon—*valley* WA-9
Hartley Cem—*cemetery* AL-4
Hartley Cem—*cemetery* CA-9
Hartley Cem—*cemetery* IN-6
Hartley Cem—*cemetery* KY-4
Hartley Cem—*cemetery* MS-4
Hartley Cem—*cemetery* MO-7
Hartley Cem—*cemetery* NC-3
Hartley Cem—*cemetery* OR-9
Hartley Cem—*cemetery* (2) SC-3
Hartley Cem—*cemetery* (2) TN-4
Hartley Cem—*cemetery* TX-5
Hartley Cem—*cemetery* WV-2
**Hartley (County)**—*pop pl* TX-5
Hartley County Courthouse and Jail—*hist pl* TX-5
Hartley Creek—*stream* NC-3
Hartley Creek—*stream* OR-9
Hartley Draw—*valley* NE-7
Hartley Forest Preserve—*park* IL-6
Hartley Gap—*gap* NC-3
Hartley Hill—*summit* CA-9
Hartley Hill—*summit* PA-2
Hartley Hill—*summit* VT-1
Hartley Hill Ch—*church* NC-3
Hartley (historical)—*locale* SD-7
Hartley House—*hist pl* SC-3
Hartley House—*hist pl* TX-5
Hartley HS—*school* IA-7
Hartley Island—*island* CA-9
*Hartley Lake* PA-2
Hartley Lake—*lake* (2) MI-6
Hartley Lake—*lake* (2) MN-6
Hartley Lake—*lake* ND-7
Hartley Lateral—*canal* CA-9
Hartley Mill Pond—*reservoir* MA-1
Hartley Mine—*mine* MN-6
Hartley Mine—*mine* MT-8
Hartley Mound—*hist pl* OH-6
Hartley Outdoor Recreation Center—*park* MI-6
Hartley Park—*park* MN-6
Hartley Park—*park* NY-2
Hartley Peak—*summit* ID-8
Hartley Point—*cape* MN-6
Hartley Pond—*lake* GA-3
Hartley Pond—*lake* PA-2
Hartley Ridge—*ridge* NC-3
Hartley-Rose Belting Company Bldg—*hist pl* PA-2
Hartley Rsvr—*reservoir* CO-8
Hartley Rsvr—*reservoir* OR-9
Hartley Run—*stream* IN-6
Hartley Run—*stream* (3) WV-2
Hartley Saw Mill Dam—*dam* MA-1
Hartleys Canyon—*valley* UT-8
Hartley Sch—*school* KY-4
Hartley Sch—*school* NE-7
Hartley Sch—*school* OH-6
Hartley Sch—*school* WV-2
Hartley Sch—*school* WI-6
*Hartleys Creek* AL-4
*Hartleys Creek* NC-3
*Hartleys Lake* PA-2
Hartleys Landing (historical)—*locale* TN-4
Hartley Slough—*stream* CA-9
Hartleys Pond—*reservoir* AL-4
Hartley Springs—*spring* CA-9
Hartley Spur—*locale* MN-6
Hartley Sugar Camp—*hist pl* MN-6
Hartley Township—*fmr MCD* IA-7
**Hartley (Township of)**—*pop pl* PA-2
**Hartleyville**—*pop pl* IN-6
**Hartleyville**—*pop pl* OH-6
Hartley Wash—*stream* NM-5
Hartliben Cem—*cemetery* IA-7
Hartlin Cem—*cemetery* IL-6
**Hartline**—*pop pl* WA-9
Hartline Camp—*locale* PA-2
Hartline Cem—*cemetery* AL-4
Hartline Cem—*cemetery* OH-6
Hartline Creek—*stream* IL-6
Hart Lookout Tower—*locale* MI-6
**Hart Lot (RR name Skaneateles Junction)**—*pop pl* NY-2
Hart Loucks Ditch—*canal* IN-6
*Hartlubs Lake* WI-6
**Hartly**—*pop pl* DE-2
Hartly Elem Sch—*school* DE-2
Hartly Meadows—*flat* ID-8
*Hartlys Canyon* UT-8
*Hartly Sch* DE-2
Hartman—*locale* MI-6
Hartman—*locale* MS-4
Hartman—*locale* NE-7
Hartman—*locale* NY-2
Hartman—*locale* NC-3
Hartman—*locale* TX-5
**Hartman**—*pop pl* AR-4
**Hartman**—*pop pl* CO-8
**Hartman**—*pop pl* IN-6
**Hartman**—*pop pl* MT-8
Hartman, George, House—*hist pl* PA-2
Hartman Bar—*bar* CA-9
Hartman Bar Ridge—*ridge* (2) CA-9
Hartman Branch—*stream* LA-4
Hartman Branch—*stream* NC-3
Hartman Branch—*stream* TN-4
Hartman Branch Dayton Lateral—*canal* CO-8
Hartman Camp—*locale* MI-6
Hartman Canyon—*valley* CO-8
Hartman Canyon—*valley* NM-5
Hartman Cem—*cemetery* CO-8
Hartman Cem—*cemetery* IL-6
Hartman Cem—*cemetery* IN-6
Hartman Cem—*cemetery* (2) IA-7
Hartman Cem—*cemetery* (3) OH-6
Hartman Cem—*cemetery* (2) TN-4
Hartman Cem—*cemetery* VA-3
Hartman Center Ch—*church* PA-2
Hartman Ch—*church* NC-3
Hartman Ch—*church* TN-4
Hartman Cider Press—*hist pl* PA-2
Hartman Coll—*school* MO-7
*Hartman Creek* MO-7
*Hartman Creek* WA-9
Hartman Creek—*stream* CA-9
Hartman Creek—*stream* MO-7
Hartman Creek—*stream* (2) MT-8
Hartman Creek—*stream* WA-9
Hartman Creek—*stream* WI-6
Hartman Creek State Park—*park* WI-6
Hartman Ditch—*canal* (3) IN-6
Hartman Divide—*gap* CO-8
Hartman Drain—*canal* MI-6
Hartman Draw—*valley* (2) CO-8
Hartman Farms Field Airp—*airport* IN-6
Hartman Guard Station—*locale* CA-9
Hartman Gulch—*valley* CO-8
Hartman Hollow—*valley* PA-2
Hartman Homestake Mines—*mine* AZ-5
Hartman Island—*island* AK-9
Hartman Island—*island* NE-7
Hartman Island—*island* PA-2
Hartman JHS—*school* PA-2
Hartman JHS—*school* TX-5
Hartman Knob—*summit* VA-3
Hartman Lake—*lake* AK-9
Hartman Lake—*lake* AR-4
Hartman Lake—*lake* (2) MI-6
Hartman Lake—*lake* WI-6
Hartman Mine Number One—*mine* TN-4
Hartman Mine Number Two—*mine* TN-4
Hartman Natural Bridge—*arch* AZ-5
Hartmann Gulch—*valley* UT-8
Hartmann Hollow—*valley* TX-5
Hartmanns Deep Valley Golf Course—*locale* PA-2
Hartman Park—*park* TN-4
Hartman Park—*park* TX-5
Hartman Pond—*lake* IA-7
Hartman Ranch—*locale* CA-9
Hartman Ranch—*locale* NE-7
Hartman River—*stream* AK-9
Hartman Rsvr—*reservoir* CO-8
Hartman Rsvr—*reservoir* OR-9
Hartman Run—*stream* (2) PA-2
Hartman Run—*stream* WV-2
Hartmans Cem—*cemetery* IN-6
Hartman Sch—*school* (2) IL-6
Hartman Sch—*school* IN-6
Hartman Sch—*school* MO-7
Hartman Sch—*school* PA-2
Hartman Sch—*school* WV-2
Hartman Sch (abandoned)—*school* (2) PA-2
Hartman Sch (historical)—*school* PA-2
*Hartman School* TN-4
**Hartmans Corners**—*pop pl* NY-2
*Hartman's Creek* WI-6
Hartman Slough—*stream* OR-9
Hartman Spring—*spring* AZ-5
Hartman Spring—*spring* TN-4
Hartmans Sch (historical)—*school* TN-4
Hartman Stock Farm Hist Dist—*hist pl* OH-6
**Hartman Subdivision**—*pop pl* TN-4
**Hartman Subdivision**—*pop pl* UT-8
**Hartmansville**—*pop pl* WV-2
Hartman Tank—*reservoir* NV-8
Hartmantown—*locale* TN-4
Hartman Trail—*trail* CO-8
Hartman Trail—*trail* PA-2
Hartman Wash—*stream* AZ-5
Hartman Wildlife Area—*park* IA-7
Hart Meadow—*flat* CA-9
Hart Meadow—*swamp* CT-1
Hart Memorial Park—*cemetery* GA-3
Hart Memorial Unit—*other* CA-9
Hartmens Sch (abandoned)—*school* PA-2
Hart-Miller Island—*island* MD-2
*Hart Mills* IN-6
Hart Mine—*mine* AZ-5
Hart Mine—*mine* CO-8
Hart Mine Wash—*stream* AZ-5
Hart Monmt—*park* GA-3
Hart Mountain Natl Antelope Refuge—*reserve* OR-9
*Hart Mtn* OR-9
Hart Mtn—*summit* NV-8
Hart Mtn—*summit* NM-5
Hart Mtn—*summit* OR-9
Hart Mtn—*summit* TX-5
Hartnan Lake—*lake* WI-6
Hart Neck—*cape* ME-1
Hartnell Coll—*school* CA-9
Hartnell Coll (East Campus)—*school* CA-9
Hartner—*locale* CO-8
Hartness House—*hist pl* VT-1
Hartnet, The—*area* UT-8
Hartnet Draw—*valley* UT-8
Hartnet Island—*island* AK-9
Hartnet Tank—*reservoir* TX-5
Hartnette Lake—*lake* MN-6
*Hartnett School* KS-7
Hartney Bay—*bay* AK-9
*Hartney Creek* OR-9
Hartney Creek—*stream* AK-9
Hartney Lake—*lake* MI-6
Hartney Lake—*lake* UT-8
*Hartnig Lake* MI-6
Hart Oil Field—*oilfield* NE-7
Harton Davis Canal—*canal* ID-8
Harton House—*hist pl* AR-4
Hartov Cove—*bay* AK-9
Hart Park—*park* CT-1
Hart Park—*park* MO-7
Hart Parker Ditch—*canal* MT-8
Hart Peak—*summit* CA-9
*Hart Point* UT-8
Hart Point—*summit* AZ-5
*Hart Pond* AL-4
*Hart Pond* MA-1
Hart Pond—*lake* CT-1
Hart Pond—*lake* FL-3
Hart Ponds—*reservoir* CT-1
Hart Post Office (historical)—*building* TN-4
Hart Prairie—*flat* AZ-5
Hart Prairie Tank—*reservoir* AZ-5
Hart Ranch—*locale* ID-8
Hart Ranch—*locale* NM-5
Hart Ranch—*locale* TX-5
Hart Ranch—*locale* (2) WY-8
Hart Ranch Airp—*airport* WA-9
Hartranet Station—*locale* PA-2
**Hartranft**—*pop pl* PA-2
Hartranft Post Office (historical)—*building* TN-4
Hartranft Sch—*school* PA-2
Hart-Ransom Union Sch—*school* CA-9
Hart-Rice House—*hist pl* NH-1
Hart Ridge—*ridge* (2) AR-4
Hart Ridge—*ridge* CO-8
Hart Ridge—*ridge* WV-2
Hartridge, Lake—*lake* FL-3
Hartridge Sch—*school* NJ-2
Hartridge (Site)—*locale* WV-2
Hart Riggs Cem—*cemetery* OR-9
*Hart River* WY-8
Hart Rsvr—*reservoir* OR-9
Hart Rsvr—*reservoir* (2) WY-8
Hart Run—*stream* (2) PA-2
**Harts**—*pop pl* (2) GA-3
**Harts**—*pop pl* WV-2
Hartsaw Cem—*cemetery* TN-4
Hartsaw Cove—*valley* TN-4
Harts Basin—*basin* CO-8
Harts Bluff—*locale* TX-5
**Harts Bluff**—*pop pl* SC-3
Harts Bluff Sch—*school* TX-5
Hartsboro—*locale* NC-3
Harts Branch—*stream* SC-3
Harts Branch—*stream* TN-4
Harts Branch—*stream* WV-2
Harts Bridge—*bridge* VA-3
Harts Brook—*stream* MA-1
**Hartsburg**—*pop pl* IL-6
**Hartsburg**—*pop pl* MO-7
**Hartsburg**—*pop pl* OH-6
Harts Butte—*summit* AZ-5
Harts Camp—*locale* CA-9
Harts Cem—*cemetery* KY-4
Hart Sch—*school* CA-9
Hart Sch—*school* CT-1
Hart Sch—*school* (2) IL-6
Hart Sch—*school* KS-7
Hart Sch—*school* KY-4
Hart Sch—*school* (2) LA-4
Hart Sch—*school* MI-6
Hart Sch—*school* MO-7
Hart Sch—*school* PA-2
Hart Sch—*school* TN-4
Hart Sch (abandoned)—*school* MO-7
Harts Chapel—*church* AR-4
Harts Chapel—*church* KY-4
Harts Chapel—*church* MS-4
Harts Chapel (historical)—*church* TN-4
Harts Chapel Presbyterian Ch (historical)—*church* TN-4
Harts Chapel Sch (historical)—*school* TN-4
Harts Ch (historical)—*church* MS-4
Hart Sch (historical)—*school* TN-4
Harts Corner—*locale* NJ-2
Hart's Corner Hist Dist—*hist pl* CT-1
Harts Corners—*locale* ME-1
Harts Coulee—*valley* MT-8
Hart Scout Camp—*locale* PA-2
*Harts Cove* NY-2
*Harts Creek* GA-3
Harts Creek—*stream* ID-8
Harts Creek—*stream* MS-4
Harts Creek—*stream* NC-3
Harts Creek—*stream* PA-2
Harts Creek—*stream* (2) TX-5
Harts Creek (Magisterial District)—*fmr MCD* WV-2
*Harts Crossroads* AL-4
*Hartsdale* IN-6
**Hartsdale**—*pop pl* IN-6
**Hartsdale**—*pop pl* NY-2
Harts Draw—*valley* UT-8
*Harts Draw Reservoir* UT-8
**Hartsease**—*pop pl* NC-3
**Hartsel**—*pop pl* CO-8
Hartsell Bridge—*bridge* ID-8
Hartsell Cem—*cemetery* TN-4
Hartsell Ch—*church* LA-4
Hartsell Creek—*stream* ID-8
**Hartselle**—*pop pl* AL-4
Hartselle (CCD)—*cens area* AL-4
Hartselle Division—*civil* AL-4
Hartselle HS—*school* AL-4
Hartselle JHS—*school* AL-4
Hartselle Memory Gardens—*cemetery* AL-4
Hartselle Natural Bridge—*arch* AL-4
Hartselle Post Office—*building* AL-4
*Hartselle Public School* AL-4
Hartselle Water Supply—*other* AL-4
Hartsell Hollow—*valley* TN-4
*Hartsells* AL-4
Hartsell Sch—*school* NC-3
*Hartsells Post Office* AL-4
Hartsell (Township of)—*fmr MCD* AR-4
Hartsel Ranch—*locale* CO-8
Hart Senate Bldg—*building* DC-2
Harts Falls—*falls* IN-6
Harts Falls Creek—*stream* IN-6
Harts Ferry Bridge—*bridge* LA-4
Harts Ferry (historical)—*locale* TN-4
**Hartsfield**—*pop pl* GA-3
**Hartsfield**—*pop pl* PA-2
Hartsfield, William P., Atlanta International Airport—*airport* GA-3
Hartsfield Branch—*stream* MS-4
Hartsfield Cem—*cemetery* AR-4
Hartsfield Cem—*cemetery* KY-4
Hartsfield Cem—*cemetery* TN-4
Hartsfield Sch—*school* FL-3
Hartsfield Sch—*school* TX-5
Harts Ford Bridge—*bridge* GA-3
Harts Fork—*stream* KY-4
**Hartsgrove**—*pop pl* OH-6
Harts Grove Cem—*cemetery* GA-3
Harts Grove Ch—*church* GA-3
**Hartsgrove (Township of)**—*pop pl* OH-6
*Harts Harbor* MA-1
*Harts Haven* MA-1
**Hartshaw Subdivision**—*pop pl* TN-4
**Harts Hill**—*pop pl* NY-2
Harts Hill—*summit* MA-1
Harts Hill—*summit* NY-2
**Harts (historical)**—*pop pl* NC-3
*Hartshorn* FL-3
**Hartshorn**—*pop pl* IL-6
**Hartshorn**—*pop pl* MO-7
**Hartshorn**—*pop pl* OH-6
Hartshorn, Timothy, House—*hist pl* MA-1
Hartshorn Brook—*stream* NH-1
Hartshorn Brook—*stream* NY-2
Hartshorn Butte—*summit* OR-9
Hartshorn Cem—*cemetery* OH-6
Hartshorn Drain—*canal* MI-6
**Hartshorne**—*pop pl* OK-5
Hartshorne Lake—*reservoir* OK-5
Hartshorne Mill Stream—*stream* NJ-2
Hartshorn Lookout Tower—*locale* MO-7
Hartshorn Pond—*reservoir* NH-1
*Hartshorn Ridge* OH-6
Hartshorn Ridge—*ridge* OH-6
Hartshorn Ridge Ch—*church* OH-6
Hartshorn Run—*stream* PA-2
Hartshorn State For—*forest* MO-7
Harts HS—*school* WV-2
Hartsig JHS—*school* MI-6
*Harts Island* MD-2
*Harts Island* NY-2
Harts Island—*cape* ID-8
Harts Island—*island* LA-4
Harts Lake—*lake* FL-3
Harts Lake—*lake* MI-6
Harts Lake—*lake* ND-7
Harts Lake—*lake* WA-9
*Harts Landing* MS-4
**Harts Location**—*pop pl* NH-1
Hartslog Valley—*valley* PA-2
Harts Meadow—*flat* CA-9
*Harts Mill* KS-7
Harts Mill—*locale* PA-2
Harts Mill Creek*—*stream* IA-7
Harts Mill (historical)—*locale* AL-4
Harts Mill Run—*stream* NC-3
*Harts Mills* IN-6
**Harts Neck (Elmore)**—*pop pl* ME-1
Hartsock Branch—*stream* KY-4
Hartsock Cem—*cemetery* (3) VA-3
Hartsock Sch—*school* IA-7
*Hartsocks Hairy Hole* PA-2
Hartsoe Cem—*cemetery* AR-4
Hartson Lake—*lake* CA-9
**Hartson Point**—*pop pl* NY-2
Hartson Sand Ridge—*summit* CA-9
Hartson Slough—*stream* CA-9
Hartson Swamp—*swamp* NY-2
*Hartsook* KS-7
Hartsook Creek—*stream* CA-9
Hartsook Giant—*ridge* CA-9
Hartsook Ranch—*locale* MT-8
Harts Park—*locale* IL-6
Harts Pass—*gap* WA-9
Harts Place—*locale* CA-9
Harts Point—*cape* FL-3
Harts Point—*cape* MD-2
Harts Point—*cape* UT-8
Harts Pond—*lake* (2) MA-1
Harts Pond—*lake* WV-2
Harts Pond—*swamp* FL-3
*Hart Spring* UT-8
Hart Spring—*spring* (2) CO-8
Hart Spring—*spring* (3) OR-9
Hart Spring—*spring* TN-4
Hart Spring Ch—*church* SC-3
*Hart Spring Draw* UT-8
Hart Springs—*spring* FL-3
Hart Springs—*spring* NM-5
Hart Spur—*locale* TX-5
*Harts Run* PA-2
Harts Run—*locale* WV-2
Harts Run—*stream* KY-4
Harts Run—*stream* (3) PA-2
Harts Run—*stream* (2) WV-2
Harts Run Camping Area—*locale* WV-2
Harts Sch—*school* IL-6
**Harts Shop**—*pop pl* VA-3
Harts Spring—*spring* UT-8
Harts Spring Draw—*valley* UT-8
**Harts Store**—*pop pl* NC-3
Harts Swamp—*swamp* WA-9
Hartstack Cem—*cemetery* TX-5
*Harts Tavern* PA-2
*Hartstein Island* WA-9
Hartstene—*locale* WA-9
Hartstene Island—*island* WA-9
Hartstern Sch—*school* KY-4
*Hartstine* WA-9
*Hartstine Island* WA-9
**Hartstown**—*pop pl* PA-2
Hartstown Golf Course—*locale* PA-2
Harts Trail—*trail* PA-2
*Hartstrand Gulch* CA-9
*Hartstrings* MP-9
Hartsugg Creek—*stream* AR-4
Hartsugg (Township of)—*fmr MCD* AR-4
Harts Valley—*valley* CA-9
Hartsville—*locale* IL-6
**Hartsville**—*pop pl* IN-6
**Hartsville**—*pop pl* (2) MA-1
**Hartsville**—*pop pl* NY-2
**Hartsville**—*pop pl* PA-2
**Hartsville**—*pop pl* SC-3
**Hartsville**—*pop pl* TN-4
Hartsville Access Area—*park* TN-4
Hartsville Baptist Ch—*church* TN-4
Hartsville (CCD)—*cens area* SC-3
Hartsville (CCD)—*cens area* TN-4
Hartsville Cem—*cemetery* OK-5
Hartsville Center Cem—*cemetery* NY-2
Hartsville Ch—*church* NY-2
Hartsville Ch—*church* VA-3
Hartsville City Hall—*building* TN-4
Hartsville College Cem—*cemetery* IN-6
Hartsville Depot—*hist pl* TN-4
Hartsville Division—*civil* TN-4
Hartsville General Hosp—*hospital* TN-4
Hartsville Hill—*summit* NY-2
Hartsville Hill Cem—*cemetery* NY-2
Hartsville Island—*island* TN-4
Hartsville Junction—*locale* TN-4
Hartsville Landing—*locale* TN-4
Hartsville Nuclear Power Plant—*building* TN-4
Hartsville Passenger Station—*hist pl* SC-3
Hartsville Post Office—*building* TN-4
**Hartsville (Town of)**—*pop pl* NY-2
Hart Table—*summit* SD-7
Hart Tank—*reservoir* (3) AZ-5
Hartt Cabin Draw—*valley* WY-8
Hartt Cabin Spring—*spring* WY-8
Hartt Cem—*cemetery* TX-5
Hartt Creek—*stream* WY-8
Hart Town Cem—*cemetery* MS-4
Hart Township—*civ div* ND-7
**Hart Township**—*pop pl* MO-7
**Hart Township**—*pop pl* SD-7
**Hart (Township of)**—*pop pl* IN-6
**Hart (Township of)**—*pop pl* MI-6
**Hart (Township of)**—*pop pl* MN-6
Hart Tree—*locale* CA-9
Hartts Creek—*stream* TX-5
Hartung—*airport* NJ-2
Hartung, Lake—*lake* NJ-2
Hartung Cem—*cemetery* NE-7
Hartung Lake—*lake* NJ-2
**Hartville**—*pop pl* MO-7
**Hartville**—*pop pl* OH-6
**Hartville**—*pop pl* WY-8
Hartville Canyon—*valley* WY-8
Hartville Cem—*cemetery* TX-5
Hartville Ch—*church* FL-3
Hartville Ch—*church* OH-6
Hartville Hotel—*hist pl* OH-6
Hartville Sch (historical)—*school* MO-7
Hart Vly Lake—*lake* NY-2
Hart Vly Stream—*stream* NY-2
*Hartwell* NE-7
*Hartwell* OH-6
*Hartwell* WV-2
Hartwell—*building* MA-1
Hartwell—*locale* AR-4
**Hartwell**—*pop pl* GA-3
**Hartwell**—*pop pl* IN-6
**Hartwell**—*pop pl* MO-7
**Hartwell**—*pop pl* OH-6
Hart Well—*well* AZ-5
Hart Well—*well* WY-8
Hartwell, W. W., House & Dependencies—*hist pl* NY-2
Hartwell Brook—*stream* MA-1
*Hartwell Canyon* AZ-5
Hart Well Canyon—*valley* AZ-5
Hartwell (CCD)—*cens area* GA-3
Hartwell Cem—*cemetery* WV-2
Hartwell Ch—*church* MO-7
Hartwell City Sch—*hist pl* GA-3
Hartwell Commercial Hist Dist—*hist pl* GA-3
Hartwell Dam—*dam* GA-3
Hartwell Dam—*dam* SC-3
Hartwell Draw—*valley* OR-9
Hartwell Field—*park* AL-4
Hartwell Hollow—*valley* AR-4
Hartwell House—*hist pl* MA-1
Hartwell Intervale—*basin* ME-1
*Hartwell Junction* IN-6
**Hartwell Junction**—*pop pl* IN-6
Hartwell Lake—*reservoir* GA-3
Hartwell Lake—*reservoir* SC-3
Hartwell Lookout Tower—*tower* IN-6
Hartwell Methodist Episcopal Church, South—*hist pl* GA-3
Hartwell Mtn—*summit* ME-1
Hartwell Pond—*lake* VT-1
Hartwell Pumping Station—*other* IL-6
Hartwell Ranch—*flat* IL-6
Hartwell Ranch—*locale* IL-6
*Hartwell Reservoir* GA-3
Hartwell (RR name for Vallscreek)—*other* WV-2
*Hartwell Rsvr* SC-3
*Hartwells Brook* MA-1
Hartwell Sch—*school* MA-1
Hartwell Sch—*school* TX-5
Hartwells Hill—*summit* MA-1
Hartwell Swamp—*swamp* NY-2
**Hartwellville**—*pop pl* VT-1
Hartwic Cem—*cemetery* AL-4
*Hartwick* MN-6
Hartwick—*locale* IA-7
**Hartwick**—*pop pl* IA-7
**Hartwick**—*pop pl* NY-2
*Hartwick Cem* AL-4
Hartwick Coll—*school* NY-2
Hartwick Creek—*stream* MI-6
Hartwick Ditch—*canal* IN-6
Hartwick Lake—*reservoir* IA-7
Hartwick Lookout Tower—*locale* MI-6
Hartwick Pines State Park—*park* MI-6
*Hartwick Pine State Park* MI-6
Hartwick Reservoir—*lake* NY-2
Hartwick Rsvr—*reservoir* OR-9
Hartwick Sch—*school* MT-8
**Hartwick Seminary**—*pop pl* NY-2
**Hartwick (Town of)**—*pop pl* NY-2
**Hartwick (Township of)**—*pop pl* MI-6
Hartwig, Ferdinand C., House—*hist pl* WI-6
Hartwig Lake—*lake* MI-6
*Hartwood* MA-1
Hartwood—*locale* NY-2
Hartwood—*locale* VA-3
Hartwood Ch—*church* AL-4
Hartwood Ch—*church* OH-6
**Hartwood Club**—*pop pl* NY-2
*Hartwood Plantation* MA-1
Harty Pond—*lake* AL-4
Harty Sch—*school* IL-6
Hartz Drain—*canal* MI-6
Hartzel—*locale* WV-2
**Hartzel**—*pop pl* IN-6
Hartzel Ditch—*canal* IN-6
**Hartzell**—*pop pl* MO-7
Hartzell Cem—*cemetery* OH-6
**Hartzell (historical)**—*pop pl* PA-2
*Hartzells* PA-2
Hartzell Sch—*school* CA-9
Hartzell Sch—*school* NE-7
Hartzell Sch—*school* PA-2
Hartzell Sch (abandoned)—*school* PA-2
**Hartzells Ferry**—*pop pl* PA-2
Hartzells Ferry (historical)—*locale* PA-2
*Hartzellstown* PA-2
*Hartzels* PA-2
Hartzfelt Mtn—*summit* NY-2
Hartzig Sch—*school* MI-6
Hartz Lake—*lake* IN-6
**Hartz Lake**—*pop pl* IN-6
Hartzler Cem—*cemetery* PA-2
Hartzler Hollow—*valley* PA-2
Hartzler Sch—*school* OH-6
**Hartzo**—*pop pl* TX-5
Hartzog Branch—*stream* SC-3
Hartzog Drain—*canal* MI-6
Hartzog Draw—*valley* WY-8
Hartzog Pond—*reservoir* AL-4
Haruff Cem—*cemetery* OH-6
**Harundale**—*pop pl* MD-2
*Haru-Shima* FM-9
*Haru-Sima* FM-9
*Harvard* CO-8
*Harvard* MA-1
Harvard—*locale* AR-4
Harvard—*locale* CA-9
Harvard—*locale* TX-5
**Harvard**—*pop pl* FL-3
**Harvard**—*pop pl* ID-8
**Harvard**—*pop pl* IL-6
**Harvard**—*pop pl* IA-7
**Harvard**—*pop pl* MA-1
**Harvard**—*pop pl* MI-6
**Harvard**—*pop pl* NE-7
**Harvard**—*pop pl* NY-2
Harvard, David, House—*hist pl* PA-2
Harvard, Mount—*summit* CA-9
Harvard, Mount—*summit* CO-8
Harvard Arm—*bay* AK-9
Harvard Ave Fire Station—*hist pl* MA-1
Harvard-Belmont District—*hist pl* WA-9
Harvard Boathouse—*other* CT-1
Harvard Branch—*stream* CA-9
Harvard Brook—*stream* NH-1
Harvard Cem—*cemetery* NY-2
Harvard Center Cem—*cemetery* MA-1
*Harvard Centre* MA-1
Harvard Club of New York City—*hist pl* NY-2
Harvard Company-Weber Dental Manufacturing Company—*hist pl* OH-6
Harvard Coop—*building* MA-1
Harvard Creek—*stream* OR-9
Harvard Ferry (historical)—*locale* MS-4
Harvard For—*forest* MA-1
Harvard Forest Administration Bldg—*building* MA-1
Harvard Glacier—*glacier* AK-9
Harvard Grove Cem—*cemetery* OH-6
Harvard Gulch—*valley* CO-8
Harvard Hill—*summit* CA-9
**Harvard Hills**—*pop pl* IL-6
Harvard Houses Hist Dist—*hist pl* MA-1
Harvard Lake—*lake* MI-6
Harvard Lakes—*lake* CO-8
Harvard Lampoon Bldg—*hist pl* MA-1
Harvard Marsh—*swamp* NE-7
Harvard Mine—*mine* CA-9
Harvard Mtn—*summit* WA-9
Harvard Observatory—*building* MA-1
Harvard Park—*park* WA-9
Harvard Park Sch—*school* IL-6
**Harvard Park Subdivision**—*pop pl* UT-8
Harvard Playground—*park* CA-9
Harvard Pond—*reservoir* MA-1
Harvard Sch—*school* CA-9
Harvard Sch—*school* IL-6
Harvard Sch—*school* IA-7
Harvard Sch—*school* MO-7
Harvard Sch—*school* (2) OH-6
Harvard Sch—*school* TX-5
Harvard Sch—*school* WA-9
Harvard Sch (historical)—*school* MS-4
Harvard Square—*park* MA-1
Harvard Square Hist Dist—*hist pl* MA-1
Harvard Square Hist Dist (Boundary Increase)—*hist pl* MA-1
Harvard Square Subway Kiosk—*hist pl* MA-1
Harvard Stadium—*locale* MA-1
**Harvard Station**—*pop pl* MA-1
*Harvard Stream* MA-1
Harvard Street Hist Dist—*hist pl* MA-1
Harvard Street Station (historical)—*locale* MA-1

**Harvard (Town of)**—pop pl MA-1
**Harvard Township**—pop pl NE-7
Harvard Trail—trail CO-8
Harvard Union—hist pl MA-1
Harvard Univ—school MA-1
Harvard University Observatory—building MA-1
Harvard Yard—park MA-1
Harvard Yard Hist Dist—hist pl MA-1
Harvat Ranch—hist pl MT-8
Harve Clark Cove—valley GA-3
Harve Creek—stream NC-3
Harve Creek—stream OR-9
Harve Hollow—valley AR-4
**Harvel**—pop pl IL-6
Harvel Canyon—valley CA-9
Harvel Cem—cemetery AR-4
Harvel Creek—stream VA-3
Harvell Branch—stream MS-4
Harvell Canyon NV-8
Harvell Cave—cave TN-4
Harvell Hollow—valley TN-4
Harvell Park—park NC-3
Harvells Bay (Carolina Bay)—swamp NC-3
Harvells Branch—stream VA-3
Harvell Spring NV-8
Harvells Store (historical)—locale AL-4
**Harvel Park Condo**—pop pl UT-8
Harvel Pond—lake GA-3
Harvels Branch—stream TN-4
**Harvel (Township of)**—pop pl IL-6
Harvel Windmill—locale TX-5
Harver Sch—school MI-6
Harverson Mill Creek—stream MS-4
Harversons Cross Roads TN-4
Harves River Rsvr—reservoir UT-8
Harvest—locale GA-3
**Harvest**—pop pl AL-4
Harvest Baptist Ch—church AL-4
Harvest Baptist Ch—church (2) FL-3
Harvest Bible Ch—church MS-4
Harvest Bible Fellowship (Foursquares Gospel)—church UT-8
Harvest Chapel—church NC-3
Harvest Ch of Christ—church AL-4
Harvest Christian Acad—school FL-3
Harvest Creek IN-6
**Harvester**—pop pl MO-7
Harvester Island—island AK-9
Harvester Square—locale MO-7
**Harvest Estates Subdivision**—pop pl UT-8
Harvest Farms Lake—reservoir TN-4
Harvest Farms Lake Dam—dam TN-4
**Harvest Heights**—pop pl TX-5
**Harvest Hill**—pop pl OH-6
Harvest Hills—locale PA-2
**Harvest Hills (subdivision)**—pop pl PA-2
Harvest Home Park—park OH-6
Harvest Lake—lake FL-3
**Harvestland Estates**—pop pl UT-8
**Harvestland Estates Condo**—pop pl UT-8
**Harvest Lane Condo**—pop pl UT-8
Harvest Mission—church AZ-5
Harvest MS—school AL-4
Harvest Mtn—summit GA-3
**Harvest Park Estates (subdivision)**—pop pl UT-8
Harvest Post Office—building AL-4
Harvest Scene Pictograph—hist pl UT-8
Harvest Temple Ch—church FL-3
Harvest Temple Ch of God—church FL-3
Harvest Time Ch—church AL-4
Harvest Time Christian Sch—school FL-3
Harvestwood Ch—church VA-3
Harve (Township of)—fmr MCD AR-4
Harvey MO-7
Harvey—locale AR-4
Harvey—locale KY-4
Harvey—locale ME-1
Harvey—locale TX-5
Harvey—locale WA-9
**Harvey**—pop pl IL-6
**Harvey**—pop pl IA-7
**Harvey**—pop pl LA-4
**Harvey**—pop pl MI-6
**Harvey**—pop pl MS-4
**Harvey**—pop pl MO-7
**Harvey**—pop pl ND-7
**Harvey**—pop pl VT-1
**Harvey**—pop pl VA-3
**Harvey**—pop pl WV-2
Harvey—uninc pl CA-9
Harvey, Belen, House—hist pl NM-5
Harvey, Eli, House—hist pl OH-6
Harvey, Elizabeth, Free Negro Sch—hist pl OH-6
Harvey, Fred, House—hist pl KS-7
Harvey, John, House—hist pl KY-4
Harvey, Lake—lake FL-3
Harvey, Lake—lake MI-6
Harvey, Lake—lake MN-6
Harvey, Nathan, House—hist pl PA-2
Harvey, Nathaniel Burwell, House—hist pl VA-3
Harvey, Peter, House and Barn—hist pl PA-2
Harvey, William, House—hist pl PA-2
Harvey, William H., House—hist pl CT-1
Harvey and Phebus Cem—cemetery IN-6
Harvey Basin—basin WY-8
Harvey Bayou TX-5
Harvey Bayou—stream LA-4
Harvey Branch—stream AL-4
Harvey Branch—stream (2) AR-4
Harvey Branch—stream GA-3
Harvey Branch—stream IN-6
Harvey Branch—stream (3) KY-4
Harvey Branch—stream LA-4
Harvey Branch—stream (2) TN-4
Harvey Branch—stream TX-5
Harvey Bridge—other MI-6
Harvey Brook—stream CT-1
Harvey Brook—stream (5) ME-1
Harvey Brook—stream (2) NH-1
Harvey Brook—stream NJ-2
Harvey Brook—stream NY-2
Harvey Brook—stream VT-1
Harvey Buttes—summit NE-7
Harvey Cabin—locale MT-8
Harvey Canal Number One—canal LA-4
Harvey Canal Number Two—canal LA-4
Harvey Canyon—valley NV-8
Harvey Canyon—valley OR-9
Harvey Cave—cave KY-4
**Harvey Cedars**—pop pl NJ-2
Harvey Cem—cemetery AL-4
Harvey Cem—cemetery AR-4
Harvey Cem—cemetery FL-3
Harvey Cem—cemetery IL-6
Harvey Cem—cemetery (3) IN-6
Harvey Cem—cemetery KS-7
Harvey Cem—cemetery (2) KY-4
Harvey Cem—cemetery ME-1
Harvey Cem—cemetery MS-4
Harvey Cem—cemetery (2) MO-7
Harvey Cem—cemetery NY-2
Harvey Cem—cemetery ND-7
Harvey Cem—cemetery OH-6
Harvey Cem—cemetery OR-9
Harvey Cem—cemetery (7) TN-4
Harvey Cem—cemetery (3) TX-5
Harvey Cem—cemetery VA-3
Harvey Cem—cemetery WV-2
Harvey Center Ch—church ND-7
Harvey Ch—church LA-4
Harvey Chapel—church MS-4
Harvey Chapel—church WV-2
Harvey Clarke Sch—school OR-9
Harvey County—civil KS-7
Harvey County Park—park KS-7
Harvey Creek MI-6
Harvey Creek PA-2
Harvey Creek TX-5
Harvey Creek—stream AK-9
Harvey Creek—stream (3) CA-9
Harvey Creek—stream (2) FL-3
Harvey Creek—stream GA-3
Harvey Creek—stream (3) ID-8
Harvey Creek—stream IL-6
Harvey Creek—stream KS-7
Harvey Creek—stream MI-6
Harvey Creek—stream (2) MT-8
Harvey Creek—stream NV-8
Harvey Creek—stream NY-2
Harvey Creek—stream NC-3
Harvey Creek—stream (7) OR-9
Harvey Creek—stream TN-4
Harvey Creek—stream (2) TX-5
Harvey Creek—stream VA-3
Harvey Creek—stream (4) WA-9
Harvey Creek—stream WV-2
Harvey Creek—stream (3) WI-6
Harvey Creek Ch—church IN-6
Harvey Creek Ch—church WV-2
Harvey Creek Sch—school (2) WV-2
Harvey Cut—channel GA-3
Harvey Cutoff—canal LA-4
Harvey Dam—dam ND-7
Harvey Divide—ridge WY-8
Harvey Draw—valley WY-8
Harvey Falls—falls WV-2
Harvey Farm—locale ME-1
**Harvey Farm Estates Subdivision**—pop pl UT-8
Harvey Fear UT-8
Harvey Field Airp—airport WA-9
Harvey Flat—flat OR-9
Harvey Flat Ch—church IN-6
Harvey Fork—stream WV-2
Harvey Gap—gap CO-8
Harvey Gap—gap OR-9
Harvey Grove—cemetery WA-9
Harvey Gray Creek—stream CA-9
Harvey Gulch—valley CA-9
Harvey Gulch—valley NM-5
Harvey Gulch—valley WY-8
**Harvey Heights**—pop pl FL-3
Harvey Hill—summit KS-7
Harvey Hill—summit MA-1
Harvey Hills—range ND-7
Harvey Hodge Mtn—summit AR-4
**Harvey Hollow**—pop pl VT-1
Harvey Hollow—valley MO-7
Harvey Hollow—valley TN-4
Harvey Hollow—valley WV-2
Harvey Hotel—hist pl NM-5
Harvey House—hist pl KS-7
Harvey House—hist pl VA-3
Harvey House—hist pl WV-2
Harvey House RR Depot—hist pl CA-9
Harvey Howze Pond Dam—dam MS-4
Harvey HS—school OH-6
Harvey Island GA-3
Harvey Island—island CO-8
Harvey Jones Butte—summit CA-9
Harvey Junction IL-6
Harvey Junction—locale PA-2
Harvey Junction Station—locale PA-2
Harvey Knob TN-4
Harvey Knob—summit VA-3
Harvey Knob—summit WV-2
Harvey Knobs—summit TN-4
Harvey Knoll—summit UT-8
Harvey Lake PA-2
Harvey Lake—lake (2) AK-9
Harvey Lake—lake AR-4
Harvey Lake—lake (2) CA-9
Harvey Lake—lake CO-8
Harvey Lake—lake (5) MI-6
Harvey Lake—lake MN-6
Harvey Lake—lake NH-1
Harvey Lake—lake (2) OR-9
Harvey Lake—lake (2) TX-5
Harvey Lake—lake VT-1
Harvey Lake—lake WI-6
Harvey Lake—reservoir MT-8
Harvey Lake Dam—dam MS-4
Harvey (Magisterial District)—fmr MCD WV-2
Harvey Mansion—hist pl NC-3
Harvey Martin Tank—reservoir TX-5
Harvey Meadow—flat AZ-5
Harvey Meadow—flat UT-8
Harvey Mill Stream—stream ME-1
Harvey Mill Well—well AZ-5
Harvey Mine—mine AZ-5
Harvey Mine (surface)—mine AL-4
Harvey Mountain Quarry—hist pl ID-8
Harvey Mtn—summit AK-9
Harvey Mtn—summit CA-9
Harvey Mtn—summit ID-8
Harvey Mtn—summit MA-1
Harvey Mtn—summit (2) NY-2
Harvey Mtn—summit OK-5
Harvey Mtn—summit OR-9
Harvey Mtn—summit VT-1
Harvey Municipal Airp—airport ND-7
Harvey-Niemeyer House—hist pl AZ-5
Harvey O. Banks Delta Pumping Plant—other CA-9
Harvey Oil Field—oilfield KS-7
Harvey Park—park CO-8
Harvey Peak—summit CA-9
Harvey Peninsula—cape MD-2
Harvey Pete Brook—stream CT-1
Harvey Place—locale ID-8
Harvey Point—cape ID-8
Harvey Point—cape NC-3
Harvey Point—ridge OR-9
Harvey Point—summit AR-4
Harvey Point—summit MI-8
Harvey Pond PA-2
Harvey Pond—lake CT-1
Harvey Pond—lake (2) ME-1
Harvey Pond—lake NH-1
Harvey Pond—reservoir AR-4
Harvey Post Office (historical)—building MS-4
Harvey Prong—stream FL-3
Harvey Ranch—locale NE-7
Harvey Ranch—locale (2) NM-5
Harvey Ranch—locale SD-7
Harvey Ranch—locale TX-5
Harvey Ranch HQ—locale NM-5
Harvey Ridge—ridge AR-4
Harvey Ridge—ridge CA-9
Harvey Ridge—ridge KY-4
Harvey Ridge—ridge ME-1
Harvey Ridge—ridge MT-8
Harvey R Newlin Elem Sch—school NC-3
Harvey Road Ch—church OK-5
Harvey Run—stream IN-6
Harvey Run—stream PA-2
Harvey Run—stream WV-2
Harveys PA-2
Harveys—locale VA-3
Harveys Brook ME-1
Harveys Burg IN-6
**Harveysburg**—pop pl IN-6
**Harveysburg**—pop pl OH-6
Harveysburgh IN-6
Harveys Canyon Rsvr—reservoir ID-8
Harveys Sch—school CA-9
Harvey Sch—school IL-6
Harvey Sch—school LA-4
Harvey Sch—school MA-1
Harvey Sch—school MI-6
Harvey Sch—school (2) OH-6
Harvey Sch—school TX-5
Harvey Sch—school VT-1
Harvey Sch—school WI-6
Harveys Chapel—church (2) AR-4
Harveys Chapel—church IN-6
Harvey Sch (historical)—school PA-2
Harvey's Creek PA-2
Harveys Creek—stream PA-2
Harveys Creek—stream TX-5
Harveys Creek—stream VA-3
Harveys Cross Roads P. O. AL-4
Harvey Sedges—island NJ-2
Harveys Fear Cliff—cliff UT-8
Harveys Five Points PA-2
Harvey's Hill Hist Dist—hist pl KY-4
Harveys Hammock NJ-2
Harveys Island—island GA-3
Harveys Knob—summit VA-3
Harveys Knob Overlook—locale VA-3
Harvey's Lake PA-2
**Harveys Lake**—pop pl PA-2
Harveys Lake—reservoir PA-2
Harveys Lake Borough—civil PA-2
Harveys Landing—locale FL-3
Harvey Slough—stream CA-9
Harveys Mtn—summit NC-3
Harveys Neck—cape NC-3
Harveys Neck—cape VA-3
Harveys Point—cape NC-3
Harveys Point Ch—church IL-6
Harveys Pond—lake ME-1
Harveys Pond—reservoir MS-4
Harvey Spring—spring AZ-5
Harvey Spring—spring OR-9
Harvey Spring—spring SD-7
Harvey Spring—spring WY-8
Harvey Spring Creek—stream CA-9
Harvey Spring Ridge—ridge CA-9
**Harvey Spur**—pop pl IL-6
Harveys Ranch KS-7
**Harveys Redwood Estates Subdivision**—pop pl UT-8
Harveys Run—locale PA-2
Harveys Run—stream (2) PA-2
Harveys Store (historical)—locale MS-4
Harveys Store (historical)—locale TN-4
Harvey Stream—stream ME-1
Harvey Street Building—school NC-3
Harveys V Rsvr—reservoir ID-8
Harveys Swell—summit NH-1
Harveys Well—well NM-5
Harvey Swell Sch—school NH-1
Harveys Whaling Station NJ-2
Harvey Tank—reservoir AZ-5
**Harveyton**—pop pl KY-4
**Harveytown**—pop pl NC-3
**Harveytown**—pop pl SC-3
**Harveytown**—pop pl WV-2
Harvey Township—civil KS-7
**Harvey Township**—pop pl (2) KS-7
**Harvey Township**—pop pl ND-7
**Harvey (Township of)**—pop pl MN-6
Harvey Trail Draw—valley WY-8
Harvey Valley—basin NE-7
Harvey Valley—valley CA-9
Harveyville IA-7
Harveyville—locale PA-2
**Harveyville**—pop pl KS-7
**Harveyville**—pop pl PA-2
Harveyville Elem Sch—school KS-7
Harvey West Stadium—locale CA-9
Harvey-Wilson Cem—cemetery MD-2
**Harvie**—pop pl KY-4
Harvieland—locale KY-4
Harvieland Ch—church KY-4
**Harviell**—pop pl MO-7
Harviell Ditch—canal (2) MO-7
Harvik Ranch—locale TX-5
Harvill Cem—cemetery MO-7
Harvill Cem—cemetery TN-4
Harville Branch—stream MS-4
Harville Canyon NV-8
**Harvin**—pop pl SC-3
Harvin Bay—basin SC-3
Harvin Ridge—ridge AR-4
Harvin Sch—school SC-3
Harvison Lake Dam—dam MS-4
Harv's Squaw WY-8
Harvstack Rsvr—reservoir OR-9
**Harvy**—pop pl KY-4
Harvy Draw WY-8
Harwards—locale ME-1
Harwelden—hist pl OK-5
Harwell—locale TN-4
Harwell Cem—cemetery AL-4
Harwell Cem—cemetery MS-4
Harwell Cem—cemetery MO-7
Harwell Cem—cemetery (2) TN-4
Harwell Chapel Ch—church TN-4
**Harwell Hills (subdivision)**—pop pl AL-4
Harwell Hollow—valley TN-4
Harwell Lake—lake MI-6
Harwell Lake—lake WI-6
Harwell Mill Creek—stream AL-4
Harwell Mtn—summit MS-4
Harwell Pond Dam—dam MS-4
Harwell Ranch—locale NM-5
Harwells Bar—bar AL-4
Harwell Sch—school TX-5
Harwells Landing (historical)—locale AL-4
Harwell Spring—spring TN-4
Harwell Windmill—locale (2) TX-5
Harwi, A. J., House—hist pl KS-7
**Harwich**—pop pl MA-1
Harwich, Town of MA-1
Harwich Bogs—swamp MA-1
**Harwich Center**—pop pl MA-1
Harwich Centre MA-1
Harwich Hist Dist—hist pl MA-1
Harwich HS—school MA-1
Harwich Lower Reservoir Dam—dam MA-1
Harwichport MA-1
**Harwich Port**—pop pl MA-1
Harwich Rsvr—reservoir MA-1
Harwich Station (historical)—building MA-1
**Harwich (Town of)**—pop pl MA-1
Harwich Upper Reservoir Dam—dam MA-1
**Harwick**—pop pl PA-2
Harwick Cem—cemetery MI-6
Harwick Ferry AL-4
Harwinton—locale CT-1
Harwinton, Lake—lake CT-1
Harwinton Sch—school CT-1
**Harwinton (Town of)**—pop pl CT-1
Harwood PA-2
Harwood TX-5
Harwood—locale AZ-5
Harwood—locale AR-4
Harwood—locale MD-2
**Harwood**—pop pl IN-6
**Har-Wood**—pop pl MD-2
**Harwood**—pop pl MO-7
**Harwood**—pop pl ND-7
**Harwood**—pop pl OH-6
**Harwood**—pop pl TX-5
**Harwood**—pop pl WA-9
Harwood, Mount—summit CA-9
Harwood Bench—bench MT-8
Harwood Block—hist pl OH-6
Harwood Branch—stream NC-3
Harwood Branch—stream (2) TN-4
Harwood Cabin—locale CA-9
Harwood Canyon—valley ID-8
Harwood Cem—cemetery MO-7
Harwood Cem—cemetery OH-6
Harwood Ch—church NM-5
Harwood Creek—stream CA-9
Harwood Creek—stream MI-6
Harwood Ditch—canal IN-6
Harwood Elementary and JHS—school IN-6
Harwood Flat—flat SD-7
Harwood Foundation—hist pl NM-5
Harwood Girls Sch—school NM-5
Harwood Gulf—valley TN-4
**Harwood (Harwood Mines Post Office)**—pop pl (2) PA-2
**Harwood Heights**—pop pl IL-6
**Harwood Heights (subdivision)**—pop pl AL-4
Harwood Hill Sch—school VT-1
Harwood Hollow—basin MD-2
Harwood Island ME-1
**Harwood Junction**—pop pl PA-2
Harwood Junction Station—locale PA-2
Harwood Lake—lake (2) MI-6
Harwood Lake—lake MT-8
Harwood Lake—reservoir NC-3
Harwood Lake Dam—dam NC-3
Harwood Lakes—lake WI-6
Harwood Lakes—reservoir NC-3
Harwood Lateral—canal NM-5
Harwood Mines PA-2
**Harwood Mines**—pop pl PA-2
Harwood Park—park NY-2
**Harwood Park**—pop pl MD-2
**Harwood Park**—pop pl PA-2
Harwood Point—cape MI-6
**Harwood (RR name Littleton (sta.))**—pop pl WV-2
Harwoods Brook MA-1
Harwood Sch—hist pl NM-5
Harwood Sch—school MT-8
Harwood Sch—school ND-7
**Harwoods Mill**—pop pl VA-3
Harwoods Mill Rsvr—reservoir VA-3
**Harwood Township**—pop pl ND-7
**Harwood (Township of)**—pop pl IL-6
Harwoodville KS-7
Harwoodville Township KS-7
**Harworth**—pop pl MS-4
Harx Creek AR-4
Har Zion Cem—cemetery PA-2
Har Zion Temple—church PA-2
Hasadiah Ch—church VA-3
Hasan—locale FL-3
Hasbidi To Creek AZ-5
Hasbidito Creek—stream AZ-5
Hasbidi To Spring AZ-5
Hasbidito Spring—spring AZ-5
Hasbidito Valley—valley AZ-5
Has-bi-di-to Wash—stream NM-5
Hasbrook IL-6
Hasbrook Lake—lake WI-6
Hasbrook Park—park IL-6
**Hasbrouck**—pop pl NY-2
Hasbrouck, Jean, House—hist pl NY-2
Hasbrouck Bldg—hist pl ID-8
**Hasbrouck Heights**—pop pl NJ-2
Hasbrouck Hill—summit PA-2
Hasbrouck House—hist pl NY-2
Hasbrouck Mine—mine (2) NV-8
Hasbrouck Park—park NY-2
Hasbrouck Peak—summit NV-8
**Hasbroucks**—pop pl NY-2
Hasbrouck Sch—school NY-2
Hasby KS-7
Hascall Cem—cemetery MO-7
Hascall Creek—stream MO-7
Hascall Spring—spring OR-9
Haschel Ditch—canal IN-6
Haschke Cem—cemetery TX-5
Hascue TN-4
Hascue Cem—cemetery WV-2
Haselden Cem—cemetery SC-3
Hasell Lake—lake OK-5
Hasell Point Site—hist pl SC-3
Haselrodt Spring—spring SD-7
**Haseltine**—pop pl MO-7
Haseltine, Edward Knox, House—hist pl OR-9
Haseltine Branch—stream MO-7
Haseltine Cobblestone House—hist pl WI-6
Haseltine Corner—locale ME-1
Haseltine Millpond NH-1
Haseltine Sch—school ME-1
Haselton OH-6
Haselton—locale NY-2
Haselton—other KY-4
**Haselton**—pop pl OH-6
Haselton—uninc pl NY-2
Haselton Brook—stream NH-1
Haselton Cem—cemetery NY-2
Hasenclever Hill—summit NY-2
Hasenclever Mtn—summit NY-2
Hasen Creek—stream AK-9
Hasenjaeger Lake—lake FL-3
Hasenwinkel Creek—stream TX-5
Hasenwinkel Ranch—locale TX-5
Haserway (historical)—locale MS-4
Hasete Ranch—locale TX-5
**Haseville**—pop pl MO-7
Haseville Ch—church MO-7
Hasfords Sawmill—locale AK-9
Hasgox Point—cape AK-9
Hash, Boys, Site—hist pl NC-3
Hashamomuck Beach—beach NY-2
Hashamomuck Pond—lake NY-2
Hashan Chuchg—locale AZ-5
Hash Cem—cemetery IL-6
Hash Cem—cemetery (2) VA-3
Hash Creek—stream AK-9
Hash Ford (historical)—crossing TN-4
Hash Hollow—valley VA-3
Hash Homestead—locale MT-8
Hashhooker Creek MS-4
Hashknife Tank—reservoir AZ-5
Hashlupbacher Creek MS-4
Hashlupbatcher Creek MS-4
Hashluphatcher Creek MS-4
Hash Mtn—summit MT-8
Hashngug MH-9
Hash Ranch—locale MT-8
Hash Rock—summit OR-9
Hash Rock Creek—stream OR-9
Hash Spring—spring ID-8
Hash Spring—spring NV-8
**Hashtown**—pop pl IN-6
Hashuqua Creek MS-4
Hashuphatchee River MS-4
Hashuqua Creek—stream MS-4
**Hashuqua (historical)**—pop pl MS-4
Hashuqua Post Office (historical)—building MS-4
Hasiamp AZ-5
Hasiamp River AZ-5
Hasima—locale TX-5
Hasion Ch—church NC-3
Haska Creek—stream AK-9
Haskel VA-3
Haskel Creek NY-2
Haskel Creek—stream CO-8
Haskel Flats NY-2
Haskell KS-7
Haskell—locale MT-8
Haskell—locale VA-3
**Haskell**—pop pl AR-4
**Haskell**—pop pl IN-6
**Haskell**—pop pl MT-8
**Haskell**—pop pl NJ-2
**Haskell**—pop pl OK-5
**Haskell**—pop pl TX-5
Haskell, Charles, House—hist pl MA-1
Haskell, Squire Ignatius, House—hist pl ME-1
Haskell Ave Sch—school CA-9
Haskell Bogs MA-1
Haskell Branch—stream KY-4
Haskell Branch—stream VA-3
Haskell Brook MA-1
Haskell Brook—stream NH-1
Haskell Brook Reservoir MA-1
Haskell Canyon—valley CA-9
Haskell (CCD)—cens area OK-5
Haskell (CCD)—cens area TX-5
Haskell Cem—cemetery AR-4
Haskell Cem—cemetery KS-7
Haskell Cem—cemetery (2) ME-1
Haskell Cem—cemetery (2) OK-5
Haskell Cem—cemetery TX-5
Haskell Corner ME-1
**Haskell Corner**—pop pl ME-1
Haskell County—civil KS-7
**Haskell (County)**—pop pl OK-5
**Haskell (County)**—pop pl TX-5
Haskell County Courthouse—hist pl OK-5
Haskell Creek—stream CA-9
Haskell Creek—stream ID-8
Haskell Creek—stream KS-7
Haskell Creek*—stream NE-7
Haskell Creek—stream NE-7
Haskell Creek—stream NV-8
Haskell Creek—stream NY-2
Haskell Creek Homesites—locale CA-9
Haskell Creek Sch—school NE-7
Haskell Deadwater—lake ME-1
Haskell Falls NY-2
**Haskell Flats**—pop pl NY-2
Haskell Foster Lake—reservoir TN-4
Haskell Foster Lake Dam—dam TN-4
Haskell Free Library and Opera House—hist pl VT-1
**Haskell Heights**—pop pl SC-3
Haskell Hill—summit (2) ME-1
Haskell Hill—summit MA-1
Haskell Hollow—valley PA-2
Haskell House—hist pl CO-8
Haskell House—hist pl NY-2
Haskell Indian Junior Coll—school KS-7
Haskell (Indian Junior College)—uninc pl KS-7
Haskell Institute KS-7
Haskell Institute—hist pl KS-7
Haskell Island—island ME-1
Haskell Island—island MA-1
Haskell Lake—lake (2) MI-6
Haskell Lake—lake MN-6
Haskell Lake—lake WI-6
Haskell Lake—reservoir OK-5
Haskell Lands MA-1
Haskell Ledge—bar ME-1
Haskell Meadow—flat CA-9
Haskell Mine—mine TN-4
Haskell Noyes Park—park WI-6
Haskell Oil Field—oilfield TX-5
Haskell Park—park IL-6
Haskell Pass MT-8
Haskell Peak—summit (2) CA-9
Haskell Peak Trail—trail CA-9
Haskell Playhouse—hist pl IL-6
Haskell Point—cape ME-1
Haskell Pond—lake ME-1
Haskell Pond—lake NJ-2
Haskell Pond—reservoir MA-1
Haskell Pond Dam—dam MA-1
Haskell Prock Lake Dam—dam IN-6
Haskell Ridge—ridge NY-2
Haskell Ridge Cem—cemetery NY-2
Haskell Rincon—valley CO-8
Haskell Rock Pitch—rapids ME-1
Haskell Rsvr—reservoir OR-9
Haskell Run—stream OH-6
Haskells IN-6
Haskell's Bloomfield Villa—hist pl NJ-2
Haskell Sch—school CA-9
Haskell Sch—school NY-2
Haskell Sch—school OK-5
Haskell Sch—school TN-4
**Haskells (Haskell)**—pop pl IN-6
Haskell Sims Cave—cave TN-4
Haskells Island MA-1
Haskells Mill Pond NJ-2
Haskells Pond MA-1
Haskell Spring—spring AZ-5
Haskell State Sch of Agriculture—hist pl OK-5
Haskell Station IN-6
Haskell Station—locale NJ-2
Haskell Swamp—swamp ME-1
Haskell Swamp—swamp MA-1
**Haskell Township**—pop pl KS-7
Haskell (Township of)—fmr MCD AR-4
Haskel Slough—stream WA-9
Haskel Spring AZ-5
Haskens Branch—stream TN-4
Hasken Tank—reservoir AZ-5
Hasker and Marcuse Factory—hist pl VA-3
Hasker Flat—flat SC-3
Hasker Hollow—valley PA-2
Hasket Bay—swamp NC-3
Hasket Creek NY-2
Hasket Spring AZ-5
Hasket Spring—spring AZ-5
Haskett Cem—cemetery IN-6
Haskett Court—hist pl CA-9
Hasketts Creek—stream NC-3
**Haskew**—pop pl OK-5
Haskew Cem—cemetery OK-5
**Haskill**—pop pl PA-2
Haskill Basin—basin MT-8
Haskill Creek NY-2
Haskill Creek—stream MT-8
Haskill Hill—cliff CO-8
Haskill Mtn—summit MT-8
Haskill Pass—gap MT-8
Haskill Station—locale PA-2
Haskin MI-6
Haskin Butte—summit OR-9
Haskin Cem—cemetery AR-4
Haskin Creek WY-8
Haskin Creek—stream ID-8
Haskin Creek—stream LA-4
Haskin Creek—stream MI-6
Haskin Creek Campground WY-8
Haskind Cem—cemetery OH-6
Haskings Gulch—valley CO-8
Haskingsville—locale KY-4
Haskin Gulch OR-9
Haskin Lake—reservoir OH-6
Haskin Park—park TX-5
Haskin Run—stream IN-6
Haskins GA-3
Haskins MI-6
**Haskins**—pop pl GA-3
**Haskins**—pop pl IA-7
**Haskins**—pop pl OH-6
Haskins, Liberty Whitcomb, House—hist pl OH-6
Haskins, Sarah A., House—hist pl MA-1
Haskins, W. H., House—hist pl KY-4
Haskins Cem—cemetery GA-3
Haskins Cem—cemetery MA-1
Haskins Cem—cemetery OH-6
Haskins Cem—cemetery (2) TN-4
Haskins Cem—cemetery WI-6
Haskin Sch—school IL-6
Haskins Chapel—church TN-4
Haskins Chapel Sch—school TN-4
Haskins Cove—bay MD-2
Haskins Creek OR-9

Haskins Creek—*stream* ... CA-9
Haskins Creek—*stream* (2) ... OR-9
Haskins Creek—*stream* ... TN-4
Haskins Creek—*stream* ... WY-8
Haskins Creek Campground—*locale* ... WY-8
Haskins Creek Dam—*dam* ... OR-9
Haskins Creek Rsvr—*reservoir* ... OR-9
Haskins Crossing—*locale* ... GA-3
Haskins Dam—*dam* ... MA-1
Haskins Elem Sch—*school* ... KS-7
Haskins Ferry (historical)—*locale* ... MS-4
Haskins Ford (historical)—*locale* ... TN-4
Haskins Gulch—*valley* (2) ... OR-9
Haskins Hill—*summit* ... CA-9
Haskins Landing Strip—*airport* ... ND-7
Haskins Number 1 Dam—*dam* ... SD-7
Haskins Pond—*reservoir* ... AZ-5
Haskins Saw Mill (historical)—*locale* ... MS-4
Haskins Sch—*school* ... MA-1
Haskins Valley—*valley* ... CA-9
*Haskinsville* ... NY-2
Haskins Wells—*well* ... NM-5
Haskins Windmill—*locale* ... NM-5
**Haskinville**—*pop pl* ... NY-2
Haslam—*locale* ... TX-5
**Haslam Estates Subdivision**—*pop pl* ... UT-8
Haslam Point—*cape* ... MN-6
Haslem Cabin—*locale* ... CO-8
Hasler, Emelia, House—*hist pl* ... TX-5
Hasler, T. A., House—*hist pl* ... TX-5
Hasler Cem—*cemetery* ... IN-6
Hasler Creek—*stream* (2) ... MI-6
Hasler Inlet—*gut* ... MI-6
*Hasler Mill* ... GA-3
**Haslet**—*pop pl* ... TX-5
Haslets Corner—*locale* ... PA-2
**Haslett**—*pop pl* ... MI-6
Haslett Basin—*basin* ... CA-9
Haslett Run—*stream* ... PA-2
*Hasletts Corners* ... PA-2
Haslett (Township of)—*fmr MCD* ... NC-3
*Haslettville* ... DE-2
Haslett Warehouse—*hist pl* ... CA-9
Hasley Basin—*basin* ... CO-8
Hasley Canyon—*valley* ... CA-9
*Hasley Canyon Oil Field* ... CA-9
Hasley Cem—*cemetery* ... LA-4
Hasley Creek—*stream* ... WI-6
Hasley Lake—*lake* ... MI-6
Haslie Lake—*lake* ... MN-6
Haslin Corner—*locale* ... NC-3
**Haslin Corners**—*pop pl* ... NC-3
Haslir Sch (historical)—*school* ... NC-3
Hasloe Mine—*mine* ... CA-9
Hasmer Lake—*lake* ... WI-6
Hasngot, I—*slope* ... MH-9
Hasngot, Saddok I—*stream* ... MH-9
Hasngot, Unai I—*beach* ... MH-9
*Hasngot Beach* ... MH-9
*Hasngot Stream* ... MH-9
*Hasngug* ... MH-9
Hasn Hollow—*valley* ... VA-3
Hasotino—*hist pl* ... ID-8
Hasouse, Bayou—*gut* ... LA-4
*Hasparos Canyon* ... NM-5
Hasperos Canyon—*valley* ... NM-5
Hasppy Hollow—*valley* ... TN-4
H A Spring—*spring* ... WY-8
*Hassamp* ... AZ-5
*Hassamp River* ... AZ-5
*Hassanamesitt* ... MA-1
*Hassanamisco* ... MA-1
Hassanamisco Ind Res—*reserve* ... MA-1
*Hassan Lowah* ... MS-4
**Hassan (Township of)**—*pop pl* ... MN-6
Hassan Valley (Township of)—*civ div* ... MN-6
Hassard—*locale* ... MO-7
*Hassas Canyon* ... OR-9
*Hassayamp* ... AZ-5
Hassayampa—*locale* ... AZ-5
Hassayampa Airp—*airport* ... AZ-5
Hassayampa Check Dam—*dam* ... AZ-5
Hassayampa Cotton Gin—*locale* ... AZ-5
Hassayampa Country Club—*other* ... AZ-5
*Hassayampa Creek* ... AZ-5
Hassayampa Hotel—*hist pl* ... AZ-5
Hassayampa Lake—*reservoir* ... AZ-5
Hassayampa Plain—*plain* ... AZ-5
Hassayampa River—*stream* ... AZ-5
Hassayampa River Bridge—*hist pl* ... AZ-5
Hassayampa Windmill—*locale* ... AZ-5
*Hassayamp River* ... AZ-5
Hass Cem—*cemetery* ... KS-7
Hass Creek—*stream* ... OR-9
Hass Dam—*dam* ... ND-7
Hasse—*locale* ... TX-5
Hasse Creek—*stream* ... TX-5
Hasseib Lake—*lake* ... MI-6
Hassel—*locale* ... MT-8
Hassel, Lake—*lake* ... MN-6
Hasselborg Creek—*stream* ... AK-9
Hasselborg Homestead—*locale* ... AK-9
Hasselborg Lake—*lake* ... AK-9
Hasselbring Park—*park* ... MI-6
Hassel Cem—*cemetery* ... AR-4
Hassel Creek—*stream* ... MN-6
Hassel Island—*hist pl* ... VI-3
Hassel Island—*island* ... VI-3
Hassel Island Hist Dist (Boundary Increase)—*hist pl* ... VI-3
Hassell—*locale* ... NM-5
**Hassell**—*pop pl* ... NC-3
Hassell, John, House—*hist pl* ... AL-4
Hassel Lake—*lake* ... MN-6
Hassell Cem—*cemetery* (2) ... TN-4
Hassell Creek—*stream* ... TN-4
Hassell Field (airport)—*airport* ... TN-4
Hassell Gap—*locale* ... AL-4
**Hassell Heights Subdivision**—*pop pl* ... UT-8
Hassell Lake—*lake* ... CO-8
Hassell Landing—*locale* ... TN-4
Hassell Ridge—*ridge* ... MO-7
Hassells Brook—*stream* ... NH-1
Hassel Ranch—*locale* ... UT-8
Hasselstrom, John, House—*hist pl* ... MI-6
Hassel Tank—*reservoir* ... AZ-5
Hasselton State Wildlife Mngmt Area—*park* ... MN-6
Hassen Branch—*stream* ... LA-4
*Hassencleaver Hill* ... NY-2
Hassenfuss Field—*other* ... NY-2
**Hassen Heights**—*pop pl* ... VA-3
Hassenplug Bridge—*hist pl* ... PA-2
Hasser Ranch—*locale* ... CO-8
Hasse Sch—*school* ... TX-5
Hassiah Inlet—*bay* ... AK-9
Hassiamp (historical)—*locale* ... AZ-5
Hassic Cem—*cemetery* ... MI-6
Hassie Hunt Gas Plant—*oilfield* ... TX-5
**Hassier Mill**—*pop pl* ... GA-3
Hassinger Drain—*canal* ... MI-6
Hassingers Ch—*church* ... PA-2
Hassinger Sch (abandoned)—*school* ... PA-2
Hassion Hill Ch—*church* ... SC-3
Hassle Branch—*stream* ... TX-5
Hassler Bluff—*cliff* ... MO-7
Hassler Harbor—*bay* ... AK-9
Hassler Island—*island* ... AK-9
**Hassler Meadows (subdivision)**—*pop pl* ... PA-2
*Hassler Mill* ... GA-3
Hassler Mill—*locale* ... GA-3
Hassler Mine (Underground)—*mine* ... TN-4
Hassler Pass—*channel* ... AK-9
Hassler Point—*cape* ... AK-9
Hassler Post Office (historical)—*building* ... TN-4
Hassler Reef—*bar* ... AK-9
Hassler Run—*stream* ... PA-2
Hasslers Mill—*locale* ... GA-3
Hassley-Herron Lake—*reservoir* ... MS-4
Hassley-Herron Lake Dam—*dam* ... MS-4
Hassman—*locale* ... MN-6
Hassmer Hill—*summit* ... IN-6
Hassock, The—*island* ... NY-2
Hassock Creek—*channel* ... NY-2
Hasson Cave—*cave* ... TN-4
Hasson Cem—*cemetery* ... OH-6
*Hasson Gap* ... PA-2
Hasson Heights—*CDP* ... PA-2
*Hasson Heights Elementary School* ... PA-2
Hasson Heights Sch—*school* ... PA-2
Hasson Pond Dam—*dam* ... MS-4
Hass Sch (historical)—*school* ... MO-7
*Hass Slough* ... CA-9
*HastabuchaRiver* ... MS-4
Hastain—*locale* ... MO-7
Hastain Cem—*cemetery* ... MO-7
Hast-clog-toh—*spring* ... AZ-5
*Hastehatchee River* ... MS-4
*Haste Island* ... MA-1
Hasten Sch (abandoned)—*school* ... MO-7
Haste Rock—*rock* ... MA-1
Haster Retarding Basin—*reservoir* ... CA-9
Haste Shoal—*bar* ... MA-1
Hastie—*locale* ... IA-7
Hastie Lake—*lake* ... AL-4
Hastie Lake—*lake* ... WA-9
Hastiin Akahibito—*spring* ... AZ-5
*Hastillos Brook* ... CT-1
*Hasting* ... MI-6
Hasting Airpark—*airport* ... MS-4
Hasting Cem—*cemetery* ... AL-4
Hasting Cem—*cemetery* ... IA-7
Hasting Cem—*cemetery* ... TN-4
Hasting Cove—*valley* ... TN-4
Hasting Creek—*stream* ... TX-5
**Hasting Estates (trailer park)**—*pop pl* ... DE-2
**Hasting Hill**—*pop pl* ... OH-6
Hasting Lake—*lake* ... NC-3
*Hasting Pass* ... UT-8
*Hastings* ... AZ-5
*Hastings* ... KS-7
*Hastings* ... NY-2
*Hastings* ... NC-3
Hastings—*locale* ... GA-3
Hastings—*locale* ... IL-6
Hastings—*locale* ... ME-1
Hastings—*locale* ... PA-2
Hastings—*locale* ... TX-5
Hastings—*locale* ... WV-2
**Hastings**—*pop pl* ... FL-3
**Hastings**—*pop pl* ... IL-6
**Hastings**—*pop pl* ... IN-6
**Hastings**—*pop pl* ... IA-7
**Hastings**—*pop pl* ... MA-1
**Hastings**—*pop pl* ... MI-6
**Hastings**—*pop pl* ... MN-6
**Hastings**—*pop pl* ... NE-7
**Hastings**—*pop pl* ... NH-1
**Hastings**—*pop pl* ... NY-2
**Hastings**—*pop pl* ... ND-7
**Hastings**—*pop pl* ... OH-6
**Hastings**—*pop pl* ... OK-5
**Hastings**—*pop pl* ... PA-2
Hastings, Lake—*lake* ... NE-7
Hastings, Mount—*summit* ... ME-1
Hastings, Oliver, House—*hist pl* ... MA-1
Hastings Adobe—*hist pl* ... CA-9
Hastings Borough—*civil* ... PA-2
Hastings Brake—*swamp* ... AR-4
Hastings Branch—*stream* ... PA-2
Hastings Branch—*stream* (2) ... TN-4
Hastings Brook—*stream* ... ME-1
Hastings Camp Ground Cem—*cemetery* ... TN-4
Hastings Canyon—*valley* ... CA-9
Hastings (CCD)—*cens area* ... FL-3
*Hastings Cem* ... AL-4
Hastings Cem—*cemetery* (2) ... IL-6
Hastings Cem—*cemetery* ... NY-2
Hastings Cem—*cemetery* (3) ... OH-6
Hastings Cem—*cemetery* ... OK-5
Hastings Cem—*cemetery* (2) ... TN-4
**Hastings Center**—*pop pl* ... NY-2
Hastings Center Sch—*school* ... MI-6
Hasting Sch—*school* ... AR-4
Hastings Chapel (historical)—*church* ... TN-4
Hastings Coll—*school* ... NE-7
**Hastings Corner**—*pop pl* ... NC-3
Hastings Cove—*cove* ... MA-1
Hastings Creek—*stream* (2) ... AK-9
Hastings Creek—*stream* (2) ... CA-9
Hastings Creek—*stream* ... IL-6
Hastings Cut—*canal* ... CA-9
Hastings Cut-Off (California Emigrant Trail)—*trail* ... NV-8
*Hastings Cut-Offs California Trail* ... NV-8
Hastings Elementary/MS—*school* ... FL-3
Hastings Fish Pond—*lake* ... GA-3
Hastings Foundry-Star Iron Works—*hist pl* ... MN-6
Hastings Gulch—*valley* ... WA-9
Hastings Hill—*summit* ... CT-1
Hastings Hill Hist Dist—*hist pl* ... CT-1
Hastings (historical)—*locale* ... SD-7
Hastings Hollow—*valley* ... OK-5
Hastings Island—*island* ... ME-1
Hastings Island—*island* ... MI-6
Hastings Lake—*lake* ... IL-6
Hastings Lake—*lake* ... MI-6
*Hastings Landing* ... ND-7
Hastings Landing—*locale* ... IL-6
Hastings-Locke Ferry—*hist pl* ... TN-4
Hasting Slough—*gut* ... CA-9
Hastings-McKinnie House—*hist pl* ... NC-3
Hastings Mesa—*summit* ... CO-8
Hastings Methodist Episcopal Church—*hist pl* ... MN-6
Hastings Mtn—*summit* ... OK-5
Hastings Municipal Airp—*airport* ... NE-7
Hastings Natural History State Reservation—*park* ... CA-9
Hastings Oil Field—*oilfield* ... TX-5
*Hastings On Hudson* ... NY-2
**Hastings-On-Hudson**—*pop pl* ... NY-2
*Hastings On The Hudson* ... NY-2
**Hastings Park (trailer park)**—*pop pl* ... DE-2
Hastings Pass—*gap* ... UT-8
Hastings Peak—*summit* ... OR-9
Hastings Pond—*lake* ... ME-1
Hastings Pond—*lake* ... MA-1
Hastings Post Office (historical)—*building* ... TN-4
Hasting Spring—*spring* ... OR-9
Hastings Ranch—*locale* ... CA-9
Hastings Ranch—*locale* ... CO-8
Hastings Run—*stream* ... PA-2
Hastings Run—*stream* ... WV-2
Hastings Sch—*school* (2) ... MA-1
Hastings Sch—*school* ... OH-6
Hastings Siding—*locale* (2) ... TX-5
Hastings Slough—*stream* ... CA-9
Hastings Square Hist Dist—*hist pl* ... MA-1
Hastings State Hosp—*hospital* ... NE-7
*Hastings Station* ... IN-6
Hastings Store (historical)—*locale* ... TN-4
Hastings Swamp—*swamp* ... VT-1
Hastings Tank—*reservoir* ... NM-5
**Hastings (Town of)**—*pop pl* ... NY-2
**Hastings Township**—*pop pl* ... ND-7
**Hastings (Township of)**—*pop pl* ... MI-6
Hastings Tract—*civil* ... CA-9
Hastings Trail—*trail* ... ME-1
Hastings Trail—*trail* ... NH-1
Hastins, John, Cottage—*hist pl* ... MA-1
Haston Cem—*cemetery* ... TN-4
Haston Chapel—*church* ... TN-4
Haston JHS—*school* ... MI-6
Haston Mine (surface)—*mine* ... TN-4
Haston Point—*cape* ... TN-4
Hastons Cave—*cave* ... TN-4
*Hastons Chapel Church of God* ... TN-4
Haston Sch (historical)—*school* ... TN-4
Hastons Pit—*cave* ... TN-4
Hasty—*locale* ... AR-4
Hasty—*locale* ... GA-3
Hasty—*locale* ... KS-7
**Hasty**—*pop pl* ... CO-8
**Hasty**—*pop pl* ... MN-6
**Hasty**—*pop pl* ... NC-3
Hasty, Bogue—*stream* ... MS-4
Hasty, Lake—*reservoir* ... CO-8
Hasty Branch—*stream* ... GA-3
Hasty Branch—*stream* ... TN-4
Hasty Brook—*stream* ... MN-6
Hasty Cem—*cemetery* ... MO-7
Hasty Corner—*locale* ... ME-1
Hasty Creek—*stream* ... TX-5
Hasty Ditch—*canal* ... IN-6
Hasty Hollow—*valley* ... TN-4
*Hasty Lake* ... WA-9
Hasty Point—*cape* ... MD-2
Hasty Point Plantation—*locale* ... SC-3
Hasty Pond—*swamp* ... FL-3
Hasty Pond Ch—*church* ... FL-3
Hasty Pond Sch—*school* ... FL-3
Hasty Pudding Club—*hist pl* ... MA-1
Hasty Pudding Hollow—*valley* ... MO-7
Hasty Sch—*school* ... NC-3
Hasty (Township of)—*fmr MCD* ... AR-4
*Hasunlovieasha Creek* ... MS-4
**Haswell**—*pop pl* ... CO-8
Haswell, Isaac M., House—*hist pl* ... NY-2
Haswell Cem—*cemetery* ... GA-3
Haswell Memorial Park—*park* ... TX-5
Hat, The—*summit* ... CA-9
Hat, The—*summit* ... CO-8
Hat, The—*summit* ... ID-8
Hat, The—*summit* ... NE-7
Hat, The—*summit* ... UT-8
Hatahley Biay Well—*well* ... AZ-5
Hatalacva Ruin—*hist pl* ... AZ-5
Hatana Falls—*falls* ... WA-9
H A Tank—*reservoir* ... AZ-5
Hat-A Ranch—*locale* ... TX-5
Hatband Creek—*stream* ... AL-4
Hat Bar Well—*well* ... NM-5
Hatbill Park (county park)—*park* ... FL-3
**Hatboro**—*pop pl* ... PA-2
Hatboro Borough—*civil* ... PA-2
Hatboro Cem—*cemetery* ... PA-2
Hatboro-Horsham Senior HS—*school* ... PA-2
**Hatboro West**—*pop pl* ... PA-2
Hatbox Mesa—*summit* ... AK-9
Hat Branch—*stream* ... KY-4
*Hat Butte* ... OR-9
Hat Butte—*summit* ... ID-8
Hat Butte—*summit* ... OR-9
Hat Butte—*summit* ... WY-8
Hat Butte Lateral—*canal* ... ID-8
Hat Butte Waterhole—*lake* ... OR-9
Hatcase Pond—*lake* ... ME-1
Hatch—*locale* ... CA-9
Hatch—*locale* ... ID-8
Hatch—*locale* ... MO-7
Hatch—*locale* ... OH-6
Hatch—*locale* ... WA-9
**Hatch**—*pop pl* ... NM-5
**Hatch**—*pop pl* ... UT-8
Hatch, Abram, House—*hist pl* ... UT-8
Hatch, Alfred, Place at Arcola—*hist pl* ... AL-4
Hatch, Barbara Rutherford, House—*hist pl* ... NY-2
Hatch, Horace W., House—*hist pl* ... WI-6
Hatch, Lake—*lake* ... LA-4
Hatch, L. H., House—*hist pl* ... ID-8
Hatch, Seneca W. & Bertha, House—*hist pl* ... WI-6
Hatch Airfield—*airport* ... OR-9
*Hatcha-Lucha Creek* ... MS-4
*Hatchaoose River* ... MS-4
*Hatchapalog Creek* ... MS-4
Hatchapaloo Creek—*stream* ... MS-4
*Hatcha River* ... AL-4
*Hatcha River* ... MS-4
Hatchbend—*locale* ... FL-3
Hatchbend Ch—*church* ... FL-3
Hatch Bridge—*bridge* ... NY-2
Hatch Brook—*stream* (2) ... CT-1
Hatch Brook—*stream* ... IN-6
Hatch Brook—*stream* ... NH-1
Hatch Brook—*stream* (2) ... NY-2
Hatch Brothers Tank—*reservoir* ... AZ-5
**Hatchcakamocha (historical)**—*pop pl* ... FL-3
*Hatchcalamocha* ... FL-3
Hatch Canal—*canal* ... NM-5
Hatch Canyon—*valley* ... TX-5
Hatch Canyon—*valley* (2) ... UT-8
*Hatch Canyon Creek* ... UT-8
Hatch Canyon Draw—*valley* ... TX-5
Hatch (CCD)—*cens area* ... NM-5
Hatch Cem—*cemetery* ... AL-4
Hatch Cem—*cemetery* ... AR-4
Hatch Cem—*cemetery* ... IL-6
Hatch Cem—*cemetery* ... KS-7
Hatch Cem—*cemetery* ... NM-5
Hatch Cem—*cemetery* (3) ... NY-2
Hatch Cem—*cemetery* ... OH-6
Hatch Cem—*cemetery* ... PA-2
Hatch Cem—*cemetery* ... UT-8
Hatch Cem—*cemetery* ... VT-1
*Hatch-chi-chubba* ... AL-4
Hatch Corners—*locale* ... OH-6
Hatch Corners—*locale* ... PA-2
Hatch Cove—*bay* (2) ... ME-1
Hatch Creek—*stream* ... AK-9
Hatch Creek—*stream* ... CA-9
Hatch Creek—*stream* ... MT-8
Hatch Creek—*stream* (2) ... NY-2
Hatch Creek—*stream* ... WY-8
Hatch Ditch—*canal* ... CA-9
Hatch Ditch—*canal* ... IN-6
Hatch Drain—*canal* ... CA-9
Hatch Drain—*canal* ... NM-5
Hatch Draw—*valley* ... AZ-5
Hatche Cem—*cemetery* ... AL-4
*Hat-che Chub-bau Creek* ... AL-4
*Hatchechubbee* ... AL-4
**Hatchechubbee**—*pop pl* ... AL-4
Hatchechubbee Ch—*church* ... AL-4
Hatchechubbee Creek—*stream* ... AL-4
Hatchechubbee Creek Park—*park* ... AL-4
Hatched Lake—*lake* ... AK-9
*Hatchee* ... MS-4
Hatchee Bluff—*cliff* ... MO-7
Hatchee Branch—*stream* ... AL-4
*Hatchee Chubbee Creek* ... AL-4
*Hatchee Creek* ... AL-4
Hatchee Creek—*stream* ... MO-7
*Hatchee River* ... TN-4
*Hatcheesofka Creek* ... GA-3
*Hatcheesofkee Creek* ... AL-4
*Hatcheetigbee Bar* ... AL-4
Hatcheetigbee Landing (historical)—*locale* ... AL-4
Hatche (historical)—*locale* ... AL-4
Hatchel—*locale* ... TX-5
Hatchel Creek—*stream* ... TN-4
Hatchell Branch—*stream* ... KY-4
*Hatche Oose River* ... MS-4
*Hatcher* ... VA-3
Hatcher—*locale* ... GA-3
Hatcher—*locale* ... KY-4
Hatcher—*locale* ... NC-3
Hatcher—*locale* ... VA-3
Hatcher—*locale* ... WV-2
Hatcher—*other* ... LA-4
**Hatcher**—*pop pl* ... WV-2
Hatcher Ave Baptist Ch—*church* ... AL-4
Hatcher Bayou—*stream* ... MS-4
Hatcher Bluff—*cliff* ... AL-4
Hatcher Branch—*stream* (2) ... KY-4
Hatcher Cave—*cave* ... TN-4
Hatcher Cem—*cemetery* ... AR-4
Hatcher Cem—*cemetery* ... FL-3
Hatcher Cem—*cemetery* ... MO-7
Hatcher Cem—*cemetery* ... NY-2
Hatcher Cem—*cemetery* ... OH-6
Hatcher Cem—*cemetery* (2) ... TN-4
Hatcher Cem—*cemetery* ... VA-3
Hatcher Cem—*cemetery* ... WV-2
*Hatcher Creek* ... KY-4
*Hatcher Creek* ... VA-3
Hatcher Creek—*stream* ... AK-9
Hatcher Creek—*stream* ... KY-4
Hatcher Creek—*stream* (2) ... OR-9
Hatcher Creek—*stream* (2) ... TN-4
Hatcher Creek—*stream* (2) ... VA-3
Hatcher Creek Ch—*church* ... KY-4
Hatcher Field—*flat* ... MT-8
Hatcher Flat—*flat* ... MT-8
Hatcher-Groover-Schwartz House—*hist pl* ... GA-3
Hatcher Gully—*valley* ... TX-5
Hatcher Hall Cem—*cemetery* ... TN-4
Hatcher Hall Ch—*church* ... TN-4
Hatcher (historical)—*locale* ... MS-4
*Hatcher Hollow* ... TN-4
Hatcher Hollow—*valley* (3) ... TN-4
Hatcher Hollow—*valley* ... WV-2
Hatcher HS—*school* ... AL-4
Hatcher Island—*island* ... VA-3
Hatcher Lakes—*lake* ... CO-8
Hatcher Mesa—*summit* ... WY-8
Hatcher Mine—*mine* ... AK-9
Hatcher Mountain—*ridge* (2) ... TN-4
Hatcher Mtn—*range* ... TN-4
Hatcher Pass—*gap* ... AK-9
Hatcher Pass—*gap* ... MT-8
Hatcher P.O. (historical)—*locale* ... AL-4
Hatcher Point—*cape* ... AL-4
Hatcher Prospect—*mine* ... TN-4
Hatcher Pyrite Mine—*mine* ... TN-4
Hatcher Rsvr—*reservoir* ... CO-8
Hatcher Run—*stream* ... VA-3
Hatchers—*locale* ... VA-3
*Hatchers Bluff* ... AL-4
Hatchers Branch—*stream* (2) ... GA-3
Hatchers Branch Ch—*church* ... GA-3
Hatcher Sch—*school* ... AR-4
Hatcher Sch—*school* ... KY-4
Hatchers Chapel—*church* ... VA-3
Hatchers Creek—*stream* ... NC-3
Hatchers Hall Sch (historical)—*school* ... TN-4
Hatchers Lake—*lake* ... MN-6
Hatchers Landing (historical)—*locale* ... AL-4
Hatchers Memorial Ch—*church* ... VA-3
Hatchers Millpond—*reservoir* ... GA-3
Hatcher Spring—*spring* ... TN-4
**Hatchersville**—*pop pl* ... LA-4
Hatcher Swamp—*swamp* ... NC-3
**Hatchertown**—*pop pl* ... TN-4
Hatcher Valley—*basin* ... KY-4
Hatcher Village Shop Ctr—*locale* ... AZ-5
Hatcher Windmill—*locale* ... NM-5
**Hatcher Woods**—*pop pl* ... IL-6
Hatchery Brook—*stream* ... CT-1
Hatchery Brook—*stream* (2) ... ME-1
Hatchery Brook—*stream* ... NY-2
Hatchery Butte—*summit* ... ID-8
*Hatchery Creek* ... CA-9
Hatchery Creek—*stream* (2) ... AK-9
Hatchery Creek—*stream* (2) ... CA-9
Hatchery Creek—*stream* ... IN-6
Hatchery Creek—*stream* (4) ... OR-9
Hatchery Creek—*stream* (3) ... WA-9
Hatchery Creek—*stream* ... WI-6
Hatchery Ford—*locale* ... ID-8
Hatchery Grange—*locale* ... WA-9
Hatchery (historical)—*locale* ... PA-2
Hatchery Hollow—*valley* ... NY-2
Hatchery Lake—*lake* ... AK-9
Hatchery Peak—*summit* ... AK-9
Hatchery Sch—*school* ... WI-6
Hatchery Spring—*spring* ... OR-9
**Hatches**—*pop pl* ... LA-4
Hatche Sch (historical)—*school* ... AL-4
Hatches Creek—*stream* ... MA-1
*Hatches Crossing* ... MI-6
Hatches Harbor—*cove* ... MA-1
Hatches Pond Dam—*dam* ... NC-3
Hatches Wharf—*locale* ... MA-1
Hatchet Branch—*stream* ... GA-3
Hatchet Branch—*stream* ... VA-3
Hatchet Brook—*stream* ... CT-1
Hatchet Brook—*stream* ... MA-1
Hatchet Camp Branch—*stream* ... SC-3
Hatchet Campground—*locale* ... WY-8
Hatchet Canyon—*valley* ... AZ-5
Hatchet Canyon—*valley* ... CO-8
Hatchet Cem—*cemetery* ... AL-4
Hatchet Cem—*cemetery* ... MS-4
Hatchet Cove—*bay* ... ME-1
**Hatchet Creek**—*pop pl* ... AL-4
Hatchet Creek—*stream* ... AL-4
Hatchet Creek—*stream* (2) ... CA-9
Hatchet Creek—*stream* ... FL-3
Hatchet Creek—*stream* ... GA-3
Hatchet Creek—*stream* ... MS-4
Hatchet Creek—*stream* ... MT-8
Hatchet Creek—*stream* ... OR-9
Hatchet Creek—*stream* ... VA-3
Hatchet Creek—*stream* ... WY-8
Hatchet Creek Ch—*church* ... AL-4
Hatchet Creek (reduced usage)—*stream* ... AL-4
Hatchet Ditch—*canal* ... AR-4
Hatchet Flat—*flat* ... CA-9
Hatchet Gap—*gap* ... NM-5
Hatchet Grove Ch—*church* ... NC-3
Hatchet Hill—*summit* ... MA-1
Hatchetigbee Hills—*summit* ... AL-4
Hatchetigbee Lake—*lake* ... AL-4
Hatchetigbee Landing (historical)—*locale* ... AL-4
Hatchet Island—*island* ... NY-2
Hatchet Lake—*bay* ... LA-4
Hatchet Lake—*lake* ... AK-9
Hatchet Lake—*lake* ... ID-8
Hatchet Lake—*lake* ... MI-6
Hatchet Lake—*lake* (2) ... MN-6
Hatchet Lake—*lake* ... WA-9
Hatchet Lake—*lake* ... WY-8
Hatchet Lake Campground—*locale* ... MI-6
Hatchet Mountain Pass—*gap* ... CA-9
Hatchet Mtn—*summit* ... CA-9
Hatchet Mtn—*summit* ... ME-1
Hatchet Mtn—*summit* ... WA-9
Hatchet New Well—*well* ... NM-5
Hatchet Pass—*channel* ... AK-9
Hatchet Peak—*summit* (2) ... CA-9
*Hatchet Point* ... AL-4
Hatchet Point—*cape* ... AK-9
Hatchet Pond—*lake* ... CT-1
Hatchet Ranch—*locale* ... NM-5
Hatchet (reduced usage)—*locale* ... AL-4
Hatchet Slough—*stream* ... OR-9
Hatchet Spring—*spring* ... NM-5
Hatchet Spring—*spring* ... SD-7
Hatchet Springs Ch—*church* ... AL-4
Hatchet Springs Sch—*school* ... AL-4
*Hatchett* ... AL-4
Hatchett Cem—*cemetery* (2) ... AL-4
Hatchett Cem—*cemetery* (2) ... TN-4
Hatchett Cem—*cemetery* ... TX-5
*Hatchett Creek* ... AL-4
Hatchett Creek—*stream* ... FL-3
Hatchett Creek Golf Club—*locale* ... AL-4
Hatchett Creek Hunting Club—*locale* ... AL-4
**Hatchette (historical)**—*pop pl* ... MS-4
Hatchett Hill—*summit* ... CT-1
Hatchett Hollow—*valley* (4) ... TN-4
Hatchett Oil Field—*oilfield* ... TX-5
Hatchett Point—*cape* ... CT-1
Hatchett Reef—*bar* ... CT-1
Hatchett Sch (historical)—*school* ... TN-4
*Hatchett's Reef* ... CT-1
Hatchetville—*locale* ... OK-5
Hatchetville—*locale* ... TX-5
Hatchet Well—*well* ... NM-5
Hatcheys Store—*locale* ... NC-3
Hatch Falls—*falls* ... ME-1
Hatch Flat—*flat* ... CA-9
Hatch Flats—*flat* ... CO-8
Hatch Fork Big Run—*stream* ... OH-6
Hatch Four Corners—*locale* ... CT-1
Hatch Gulch—*valley* (2) ... CO-8
Hatch Gulf—*valley* ... NY-2
Hatch Hill—*summit* (2) ... ME-1
Hatch Hill—*summit* (2) ... NY-2
Hatch (historical P.O.)—*locale* ... IA-7
Hatch Hollow—*valley* ... IL-6
Hatch Hollow Ch—*church* ... PA-2
Hatch Hollow Sch (abandoned)—*school* ... PA-2
Hatch House—*hist pl* ... ME-1
Hatch HS—*school* ... AL-4
Hatchichapa (historical)—*locale* ... AL-4
*Hatchie* ... TN-4
**Hatchie**—*pop pl* ... TN-4
*Hatchie Baptist Church* ... TN-4
Hatchie Bottom—*basin* ... TN-4
Hatchie Branch—*stream* ... MS-4
Hatchie Cem—*cemetery* ... AR-4
Hatchie Cem—*cemetery* ... TN-4
Hatchie Chapel—*church* ... MS-4
*Hatchie Church* ... TN-4
**Hatchie Coon**—*pop pl* ... AR-4
Hatchie Coon Hunting Lodge—*locale* ... AR-4
Hatchie Coon Island—*flat* ... AR-4
Hatchie Coon Lake—*swamp* ... AR-4
*Hatchie Creek* ... MS-4
Hatchie Hills—*ridge* ... MS-4
Hatchie (historical)—*locale* ... MS-4
Hatchie Island—*flat* ... TN-4
*Hatchie Island Bar* ... TN-4
Hatchie Natl Wildlife Ref—*park* ... TN-4
*Hatchiepeloc Creek* ... MS-4
Hatchie Post Office (historical)—*building* ... MS-4
Hatchie Post Office (historical)—*building* (2) ... TN-4
Hatchie River—*stream* ... MS-4
Hatchie River—*stream* ... TN-4
Hatchie Towhead—*island* ... TN-4
Hatchineha, Lake—*lake* ... FL-3
Hatchineha Canal—*canal* ... FL-3
Hatching House Brook—*stream* ... CT-1
Hatching Pond—*lake* ... NY-2
*Hatch Island* ... MA-1
Hatchitchada (historical)—*locale* ... AL-4
Hatchitigbee Bar—*bar* ... AL-4
*Hatchitigbee Landing* ... AL-4
Hatch JHS—*school* ... NJ-2
Hatch Lake—*lake* ... CA-9
Hatch Lake—*lake* ... MI-6
Hatch Lake—*lake* (2) ... MN-6
Hatch Lake—*lake* ... MS-4
Hatch Lake—*lake* ... NM-5
Hatch Lake—*lake* ... NY-2
Hatch Lake—*lake* ... VA-3
Hatch Lake—*lake* ... WA-9
Hatch Lake—*lake* ... WI-6
Hatch Landing—*locale* ... WI-6
*Hatch Ledge* ... ME-1
Hatch Meadow—*flat* ... MT-8
Hatch Memorial Shell—*building* ... MA-1
Hatch Mesa—*summit* ... UT-8
Hatch Mtn—*summit* ... PA-2
Hatch Mtn—*summit* ... UT-8
*Hatchoose River* ... AL-4
*Hatch Oose River* ... MS-4
Hatch Park—*park* ... CA-9
Hatch Point—*cape* ... ME-1
Hatch Point—*cape* ... NY-2
Hatch Point—*cape* ... NC-3
Hatch Point—*cape* ... UT-8
Hatch Point—*flat* ... LA-4
Hatch Point Campground—*park* ... UT-8
*Hatch Point-Canyon Rims Campground* ... UT-8
Hatch Pond—*lake* ... CT-1
Hatch Pond—*lake* (3) ... MA-1
Hatch Pond—*lake* ... NH-1
Hatch Pond—*lake* ... NY-2
Hatch Pond—*reservoir* ... CT-1
Hatch Post Office (historical)—*building* ... TN-4
Hatch Ranch—*locale* ... NE-7
Hatch Ranch—*locale* ... TX-5
Hatch Ranch—*locale* (3) ... UT-8
Hatch Ranch Canyon—*valley* ... UT-8
Hatch Rock—*bar* ... NY-2
Hatch Rock—*island* ... NC-3
Hatch Rock—*summit* ... UT-8
Hatch Rsvr—*reservoir* ... UT-8
Hatch Run—*stream* ... MI-6
Hatch Run—*stream* ... PA-2
**Hatchs**—*pop pl* ... MI-6
Hatchs Camp—*locale* ... UT-8
Hatch Sch—*school* ... IL-6
Hatch Sch—*school* ... MA-1
Hatch Sch—*school* ... NE-7
Hatch Sch—*school* (3) ... PA-2
**Hatchs Corner**—*pop pl* ... ME-1
**Hatch's Corner (Owens Corners)**—*pop pl* ... NY-2
**Hatchs Corners**—*pop pl* ... NY-2
**Hatch's Corner (South Dresden)**—*pop pl* ... ME-1
*Hatch's Creek* ... MA-1
*Hatchs Crossing* ... MI-6
Hatch Show Print Company Bldg—*hist pl* ... TN-4
Hatch Siphon—*other* ... NM-5
Hatchs Pond—*reservoir* ... NC-3
Hatch Spring—*spring* (2) ... NM-5
Hatch Spring—*spring* (2) ... UT-8
Hatch State Experimental Station (abandoned)—*locale* ... MO-7
**Hatch Subdivision**—*pop pl* ... UT-8
Hatch Tank—*reservoir* ... AZ-5
Hatchtown—*locale* ... PA-2
Hatch Trading Post—*locale* ... UT-8
Hatch Trailer Sch—*school* ... UT-8
*Hatchushe Creek* ... MS-4
**Hatchville**—*pop pl* ... MA-1
**Hatchville**—*pop pl* ... WI-6
Hatch Wash—*valley* ... UT-8
*Hatch Wash Creek* ... UT-8
Hatch Well—*locale* ... NM-5
Hatch Well—*well* ... UT-8
*Hat Creek* ... ID-8
Hat Creek—*fmr MCD* ... NE-7
Hat Creek—*locale* ... VA-3
Hat Creek—*locale* ... WY-8
**Hat Creek**—*pop pl* ... CA-9
Hat Creek—*stream* ... CA-9
Hat Creek—*stream* ... CO-8

Hauser Property Cem—*cemetery* ... TX-5
*Hausers* ... NC-3
Hauser Sch—*school* ... MT-8
Hauser (siding)—*locale* ... ID-8
Hauser Spring—*spring* ... TN-4
Hauser Spring Branch—*stream* ... TN-4
Hauser Substation—*locale* ... OR-9
*Hausertown* ... IN-6
Hause Sch—*school* ... PA-2
Hausgen House—*hist pl* ... KY-4
Hausgen Island—*island* ... MO-7
Haushalter Creek—*stream* ... IL-6
Haushalter Hollow—*valley* ... IL-6
Haushar Ranch—*locale* ... WY-8
*Haus Hill* ... PA-2
Hauskin Branch—*stream* ... AL-4
Hauskins Creek—*stream* ... CO-8
Hausle Ranch—*locale* ... SD-7
Hausler Creek—*stream* ... TX-5
*Hausman Lake* ... MN-6
*Hausmanns Lake* ... MN-6
*Hausmans Lake* ... MN-6
Hausman Spring—*spring* ... AZ-5
Hausner Canyon—*valley* ... NM-5
Haus Park—*park* ... IA-7
*Hauss Church* ... PA-2
Haustrup Cem—*cemetery* ... WI-6
*Haut* ... ME-1
Haut, Isle Au—*island* ... ME-1
Hautala Corner—*locale* ... MI-6
**Hauto**—*pop pl* ... PA-2
Hauto Dam—*reservoir* ... PA-2
Hauton Lee Intermediate Sch—*school* ... OR-9
Hauto Station—*locale* ... PA-2
**Hauula**—*pop pl* ... HI-9
Hauula Beach Park—*beach* ... HI-9
Hauula For Res—*forest* ... HI-9
Hauula Homesteads—*civil* ... HI-9
*Hauxhurst Creek* ... CO-8
**Havaco**—*pop pl* ... WV-2
Hava Lakatu Lake Dam Number
One—*dam* ... TN-4
Hava Lakatu Lake Number
One—*reservoir* ... TN-4
Hava-Lakatu Lakes—*lake* ... TN-4
Havala Spring—*spring* ... CA-9
*Havalau Gulch* ... NV-8
*Havana* ... NY-2
Havana—*locale* ... OR-9
Havana—*locale* ... TN-4
Havana—*locale* ... TX-5
Havana—*other* ... WV-2
**Havana**—*pop pl* ... AL-4
**Havana**—*pop pl* ... AR-4
**Havana**—*pop pl* ... FL-3
**Havana**—*pop pl* ... IL-6
**Havana**—*pop pl* ... KS-7
**Havana**—*pop pl* ... MN-6
**Havana**—*pop pl* ... ND-7
**Havana**—*pop pl* ... OH-6
Havana, The—*hist pl* ... TX-5
Havana (CCD)—*cens area* ... FL-3
Havana Cem—*cemetery* ... AL-4
Havana Cem—*cemetery* ... AR-4
Havana Cem—*cemetery* ... MN-6
Havana Cem—*cemetery* ... ND-7
Havana Cem—*cemetery* ... SD-7
Havana Ch—*church* ... AL-4
Havana Creek—*stream* ... KY-4
Havana Day Care Center—*school* ... FL-3
Havana Elem Sch—*school* ... FL-3
Havana Glen—*valley* ... NY-2
*Havanaki* ... AZ-5
Havana Lake—*reservoir* ... KS-7
Havana Lookout Tower—*locale* ... AL-4
Havana MS—*school* ... FL-3
*Havana Nakya* ... AZ-5
**Havana Nakya**—*pop pl* ... AZ-5
Havana Northside HS—*school* ... FL-3
**Havana (Parshallburg)**—*pop pl* ... MI-6
Havana Tank—*reservoir* ... AZ-5
Havana Tower (fire tower)—*tower* ... FL-3
**Havana Township**—*pop pl* ... SD-7
**Havana (Township of)**—*pop pl* ... IL-6
**Havana (Township of)**—*pop pl* ... MN-6
Havard Cem—*cemetery* (2) ... TX-5
Havard Lake—*lake* ... LA-4
Havard Univ—*school* ... MA-1
*Havasa Lake* ... CA-9
Havasau Natl Wildlife Ref—*park* (3) ... CA-9
Havash Lake—*reservoir* ... AZ-5
Havasu, Lake—*reservoir* ... AZ-5
Havasu, Lake—*reservoir* ... CA-9
*Havasu Canyon* ... AZ-5
Havasu Canyon—*valley* ... AZ-5
Havasu Cove—*bay* ... AZ-5
*Havasu Creek* ... AZ-5
Havasu Creek—*stream* ... AZ-5
Havasu Falls—*falls* ... AZ-5
*Havasu Lake* ... AZ-5
**Havasu Lake**—*pop pl* ... CA-9
**Havasu Lake (Havasu
Landing)**—*pop pl* ... CA-9
*Havasu Landing* ... CA-9
Havasu Natl Wildlife Ref—*park* (2) ... AZ-5
Havasu Natl Wildlife Ref—*park* ... CA-9
Havasu Natl Wildlife Ref—*park* ... NV-8
Havasupai (CCD)—*cens area* ... AZ-5
Havasupai Elem Sch—*school* ... AZ-5
**Havasupai Ind Res**—*pop pl* ... AZ-5
Havasupai Point—*cliff* ... AZ-5
*Havasupai Reservation* ... AZ-5
Havasupai Trail Thirty—*trail* ... AZ-5
Havasupai Wash—*stream* ... AZ-5
Havasu Palms—*locale* ... CA-9
Havasu Rapids—*rapids* ... AZ-5
Havasu Spring—*spring* ... AZ-5
Havasu Springs—*spring* ... AZ-5
Havasu Springs Campground—*park* ... AZ-5
Havatagvitch Canyon—*valley* ... AZ-5
H A Vaughan Junior Dam—*dam* ... AL-4
H A Vaughn Junior Number 1 Dam—*dam* ... AL-4
Have, The—*bay* ... MD-2
*Havel Creek* ... WI-6
*Havelock* ... MN-6
Havelock—*locale* ... VA-3
**Havelock**—*pop pl* ... IA-7
**Havelock**—*pop pl* (2) ... NE-7
**Havelock**—*pop pl* ... NC-3
**Havelock**—*pop pl* ... ND-7
Havelock Cem—*cemetery* ... MN-6
Havelock Cem—*cemetery* ... ND-7
Havelock Ch—*church* ... MN-6
Havelock Ch—*church* ... NC-3
Havelock Key—*island* ... FL-3
**Havelock Manor (subdivision)**—*pop pl* ... NC-3
Havelock Park—*park* ... NE-7
**Havelock Park (subdivision)**—*pop pl* ... NC-3
Havelock Sch—*school* ... NE-7
Havelock Shop Ctr—*locale* ... NC-3
**Havelock Station**—*pop pl* ... NC-3
**Havelock Township**—*pop pl* ... ND-7
**Havelock (Township of)**—*pop pl* ... MN-6
Havely Cem—*cemetery* ... PA-2
Havely Rock Garden—*area* ... WY-8
Havely Run—*stream* ... OH-6
Havemeyer Brook—*stream* ... NJ-2
Havemeyer Hollow—*valley* ... NJ-2
Havemeyer Rsvr—*reservoir* ... NJ-2
Havemeyer-Willcox Canal Pumphouse and
Forebay—*hist pl* ... CO-8
Haven—*locale* ... VA-3
**Haven**—*pop pl* ... IA-7
**Haven**—*pop pl* ... KS-7
**Haven**—*pop pl* ... ME-1
**Haven**—*pop pl* ... NY-2
**Haven**—*pop pl* ... WI-6
Haven, George H., House—*hist pl* ... MN-6
Haven, Lake—*lake* ... WA-9
Haven, Lake—*reservoir* (2) ... AL-4
Haven, Lake—*reservoir* ... IN-6
*Haven, The* ... NC-3
**Haven Acres (subdivision)**—*pop pl* ... MS-4
Haven Airp—*airport* ... KS-7
Haven And Max Lake Drain—*stream* ... MI-6
Haven Ashe Bridge—*bridge* ... FL-3
**Haven Beach**—*pop pl* ... NJ-2
Haven Beach—*uninc pl* ... FL-3
Haven Branch—*stream* ... KY-4
Haven Canyon—*valley* ... SD-7
Haven Cem—*cemetery* ... FL-3
Haven Cem—*cemetery* ... IN-6
Haven Cem—*cemetery* ... KS-7
Haven Cem—*cemetery* ... VT-1
Haven Ch—*church* ... IA-7
Haven Chapel—*church* ... AR-4
Haven Chapel—*church* (2) ... GA-3
Haven Chapel—*church* ... TN-4
Haven Chapel Cem—*cemetery* ... TN-4
Haven Chapel Methodist Ch—*church* ... AL-4
*Haven Chapel Methodist Episcopal Ch* ... AL-4
Haven Chapel United Methodist
Ch—*church* ... MS-4
Haven Creek—*stream* ... AK-9
Haven Creek—*stream* (2) ... OR-9
Haven Creek Ch—*church* ... NC-3
**Haven Croft (subdivision)**—*pop pl* ... PA-2
**Havendale**—*pop pl* ... MS-4
Havendale Plaza Shop Ctr—*locale* ... FL-3
Haven Dam—*dam* ... AL-4
Haven Drive Sch—*school* ... CA-9
Haven Elem Sch—*school* ... KS-7
Havener Cove—*bay* ... ME-1
Havener Hollow—*valley* ... AR-4
Havener Hollow—*valley* ... TN-4
Havener Lake—*lake* ... WI-6
Havener Ledge—*bar* ... ME-1
Havener Point—*cape* ... ME-1
Havener Pond—*lake* ... ME-1
*Havener's Ledge* ... ME-1
**Haven Grove PUD Subdivision**—*pop pl* ... UT-8
**Haven Heights**—*pop pl* ... VA-3
*Haven Hill* ... NH-1
Haven Hill—*summit* ... MI-6
Haven Hill—*summit* ... NH-1
*Haven Hill Baptist Church* ... MS-4
Haven Hill Cem—*cemetery* ... IL-6
Haven Hill Cem—*cemetery* ... MS-4
Haven Hill Cem—*cemetery* ... NH-1
Haven Hill Ch—*church* ... MS-4
Haven Hill Lake—*lake* ... MI-6
Haven Hill Pond—*lake* ... OR-9
**Haven Homes**—*pop pl* ... NJ-2
Haven Home Sch—*school* ... GA-3
Haven Hosp—*hospital* ... AL-4
Haven Hosp—*hospital* ... CT-1
Haven HS—*school* ... KS-7
**Havenhurst**—*pop pl* ... MO-7
Haven Island—*island* ... MI-6
Haven Island—*island* ... OR-9
Haven Lake—*lake* ... CA-9
Haven Lake—*lake* ... MI-6
Haven Lake—*lake* ... MN-6
Haven Lake—*lake* ... WA-9
Haven Lake—*lake* ... WI-6
Haven Lake—*reservoir* ... DE-2
*Haven Lake Acres* ... DE-2
Haven Lake Dam—*dam* ... DE-2
**Haven Lake Estates**—*pop pl* ... DE-2
Haven Memorial Park—*park* ... KS-7
Haven Methodist Ch—*church* ... AL-4
Haven Methodist Ch—*church* ... DE-2
*Havenner Ledge* ... ME-1
Haven of Memories Cem—*cemetery* ... TX-5
Haven of Rest Cem—*cemetery* ... AL-4
Haven of Rest Cem—*cemetery* ... AR-4
Haven of Rest Cem—*cemetery* ... KS-7
Haven of Rest Cem—*cemetery* ... ND-7
Haven of Rest Cem—*cemetery* ... TX-5
Haven of Rest Tabernacle—*church* ... AR-4
Havenor Lateral—*canal* ... ID-8
Havenor Siphon—*canal* ... ID-8
Haven Park—*park* ... AL-4
**Haven Park**—*pop pl* ... OH-6
**Haven Park (subdivision)**—*pop pl* ... FL-3
**Haven Park Subdivision**—*pop pl* ... UT-8
Haven Place—*locale* ... CA-9
**Haven Place Subdivision**—*pop pl* ... UT-8
*Haven Point* ... NY-2
Haven Point—*cape* ... FL-3
Haven Reach—*channel* ... NJ-2
Haven Rest Cem—*cemetery* ... AR-4
*Havens* ... KS-7
Havens—*locale* ... ID-8
Havens—*locale* ... OH-6
**Havens**—*pop pl* ... NE-7
Havens, Bert and Fay, House—*hist pl* ... ID-8
Havens, James, Homestead—*hist pl* ... NY-2
Havens, William, House—*hist pl* ... SD-7
Havens Anchorage—*bay* ... CA-9
Haven Sanitarium, The—*hospital* ... MI-6
Havens Branch—*stream* ... KY-4
*Havens Brook* ... PA-2
Havens Cave—*cave* ... TN-4
Havens Cem—*cemetery* ... LA-4
Haven Sch—*school* ... IL-6
Haven Sch—*school* ... KY-4
Haven Sch—*school* ... WI-6
Havens Chapel—*church* ... NE-7
Havens Chapel—*church* ... VA-3
Haven Sch (historical)—*school* ... FL-3
Havens Corner—*locale* ... NY-2
**Havens Corners**—*pop pl* ... OH-6
Havenscourt JHS—*school* ... CA-9
Havens Cove—*bay* ... NJ-2
*Havens Fresh Pond* ... NJ-2
Havens Green Valley Shopping
Mall—*locale* ... AZ-5
Havensight Point—*cape* ... VI-3
Havens Island—*island* ... FL-3
Havens Lake—*lake* ... MI-6
Havens Lateral—*canal* ... AZ-5
Havens Ledge Brook—*stream* ... CT-1
Havens Neck—*cape* ... CA-9
Havens-Page House—*hist pl* ... NE-7
Havens Point—*cape* ... NJ-2
Havens Point—*cape* ... NY-2
Havens Pond—*lake* ... CT-1
**Havensport**—*pop pl* ... OH-6
Havens Ranch—*locale* ... NM-5
Havens Run—*stream* ... PA-2
Havens Sch—*school* ... IN-6
Havens Spur—*ridge* ... VA-3
Havens State Game Ref—*park* ... VA-3
Havens Tank—*reservoir* ... NM-5
Havenstrite Ridge—*ridge* ... AK-9
**Havensville**—*pop pl* ... KS-7
Havensville Cem—*cemetery* ... KS-7
Havensville Elem Sch—*school* ... KS-7
**Haven Township**—*pop pl* ... KS-7
**Haven Township**—*pop pl* ... ND-7
**Haven (Township of)**—*pop pl* ... MN-6
Haven Trail Tank—*reservoir* ... AZ-5
Haven United Methodist Ch—*church* ... AL-4
Haven United Methodist Ch—*church* (2) ... MS-4
**Haven View**—*pop pl* ... OH-6
Havenview Ch—*church* ... TN-4
Haven View Sch—*school* ... CA-9
Havenview Sch—*school* ... TN-4
**Havenville**—*pop pl* ... MA-1
Haven-White House—*hist pl* ... NH-1
Haven Winquipin—*lake* ... FL-3
**Havenwood**—*pop pl* ... MD-2
Haven Wood Airp—*airport* ... MO-7
**Havenwood Hills**—*pop pl* ... MD-2
Havenwood Sch—*school* ... VT-1
Haver—*locale* ... CO-8
*Haver Church* ... PA-2
**Haverford**—*pop pl* ... DE-2
**Haverford**—*pop pl* ... MD-2
**Haverford**—*pop pl* ... PA-2
Haverford Coll—*school* ... PA-2
Haverford Community Hosp—*hospital* ... PA-2
*Haverford General Hosp* ... PA-2
Haverford HS—*school* ... PA-2
Haverford Moravian Ch—*church* ... IN-6
Haverford MS—*school* ... PA-2
Haverford Post Office
(historical)—*building* ... PA-2
Haverford State Hosp—*hospital* ... PA-2
Haverford Station—*building* ... PA-2
Haverford Township—*CDP* ... PA-2
**Haverford (Township of)**—*pop pl* ... PA-2
**Haverhill**—*pop pl* ... FL-3
**Haverhill**—*pop pl* ... IA-7
**Haverhill**—*pop pl* ... KS-7
**Haver Hill**—*pop pl* ... MD-2
**Haverhill**—*pop pl* ... MA-1
**Haverhill**—*pop pl* ... NH-1
**Haverhill**—*pop pl* (2) ... OH-6
Haverhill Baptist Day Sch—*school* ... FL-3
Haverhill-Bath Covered Bridge—*hist pl* ... NH-1
Haverhill Cem—*cemetery* ... MN-6
Haverhill City Cem—*cemetery* ... MA-1
Haverhill City Hall—*building* ... MA-1
*Haverhill Corner* ... NH-1
Haverhill Corner Hist Dist—*hist pl* ... NH-1
Haverhill Country Club—*locale* ... MA-1
Haverhill HS—*school* ... MA-1
Haverhill Lake—*lake* ... FL-3
Haverhill Oil Field—*oilfield* ... KS-7
Haverhill Sch—*school* ... KS-7
Haverhill Sch—*school* ... MI-6
Haverhill Sch—*school* ... MN-6
Haverhill Stadium—*locale* ... MA-1
Haverhill Street Milestone—*hist pl* ... MA-1
Haverhill (Town of)—*civil* ... MA-1
**Haverhill (Town of)**—*pop pl* ... NH-1
**Haverhill (Township of)**—*pop pl* ... MN-6
Haverland Meadows—*flat* ... WA-9
Haverland Pond—*lake* ... CO-8
Haverling Farm House—*hist pl* ... NY-2
**Haverling Heights**—*pop pl* ... NY-2
Haverling HS—*school* ... NY-2
Havermale Island—*island* ... WA-9
Havermale JHS—*school* ... WA-9
*Haveron Chapel* ... TN-4
Havers Creek—*stream* ... AL-4
*Haversham* ... RI-1
**Haversham**—*pop pl* ... RI-1
**Haversons (historical)**—*pop pl* ... TN-4
Haverstick, Hiram A., Farmstead—*hist pl* ... IN-6
Haverstick Creek—*stream* ... IN-6
Haverstick Creek—*stream* ... MO-7
Haverstick Ditch—*canal* ... IN-6
Haverstock Creek—*stream* ... MI-6
Haverstock Ditch—*canal* ... IN-6
**Haverstraw**—*pop pl* ... NY-2
Haverstraw Bay—*bay* ... NY-2
**Haverstraw (Town of)**—*pop pl* ... NY-2
**Havertown**—*pop pl* ... PA-2
**Havertown (RR name
Llanerch)**—*pop pl* ... PA-2
Havey Brook—*stream* ... CT-1
Havey Hill—*summit* ... ME-1
Havice Creek—*stream* ... PA-2
Havice Gap—*gap* ... PA-2
Havice Mtn—*summit* ... PA-2
Havice Spring—*spring* ... PA-2
Havice Valley—*valley* ... PA-2
Havie Brook—*stream* ... NH-1
Havilah—*locale* ... CA-9
Havilah Canyon—*valley* ... CA-9
Havilah Forest Service Station—*locale* ... CA-9
Havilah Gulch—*valley* ... NV-8
**Havilah Hills Estates
(subdivision)**—*pop pl* ... AL-4
Havilah Well—*well* ... NV-8
Haviland—*CDP* ... NY-2
Haviland—*locale* ... AZ-5
**Haviland**—*pop pl* ... KS-7
**Haviland**—*pop pl* ... OH-6
Haviland and Elizabeth Streets-Hanford Place
Hist Dist—*hist pl* ... CT-1
Haviland Brook—*stream* ... CT-1
Haviland Cem—*cemetery* ... KS-7
Haviland Cem—*cemetery* ... NY-2
Haviland Cove Beach—*beach* ... NY-2
Haviland Hall—*hist pl* ... CA-9
Haviland Hollow—*locale* ... NY-2
Haviland Hollow Brook—*stream* ... NY-2
Haviland House—*hist pl* ... KY-4
Haviland HS—*school* ... KS-7
Haviland JHS—*school* ... NY-2
Haviland Lake—*reservoir* ... CO-8
Haviland Lake Campground—*locale* ... CO-8
*Haviland Meadows* ... WA-9
Haviland Millpond—*lake* ... CT-1
Haviland Pond—*lake* ... MA-1
Haviland's, Widow, Tavern—*hist pl* ... NY-2
Haviland Sch—*school* ... MI-6
Havillah—*locale* ... WA-9
Havill Canyon—*valley* ... NM-5
Havingdon Peak—*summit* ... NV-8
Havirdsville—*other* ... SC-3
Havis Chapel—*church* ... AR-4
*Havise Valley* ... PA-2
Havison Cem—*cemetery* ... AR-4
**Havley Springs**—*pop pl* ... TN-4
Havley Springs Branch—*stream* ... TN-4
Havlicek Sch—*school* ... IL-6
Havoc Branch—*stream* ... AL-4
**Havoline**—*pop pl* ... IL-6
Havord Creek—*stream* ... ID-8
*Havre* ... MS-4
**Havre**—*pop pl* ... IA-7
**Havre**—*pop pl* ... MT-8
Havre Air Force Station—*military* ... MT-8
Havre City-County Airport—*airport* ... MT-8
**Havre De Grace**—*pop pl* ... MD-2
Havre de Grace Consolidated
Sch—*school* ... MD-2
**Havre de Grace Heights**—*pop pl* ... MD-2
Havre de Grace Hist Dist—*hist pl* ... MD-2
Havre de Grace Lighthouse—*hist pl* ... MD-2
Havre Irrigation Ditch—*canal* ... MT-8
*Havrell* ... NH-1
**Havre North**—*pop pl* ... MT-8
Havre Point—*summit* ... NM-5
Havron Chapel—*church* ... TN-4
**Havron Chapel**—*pop pl* ... TN-4
Havron Chapel Cem—*cemetery* ... TN-4
Havy Branch—*stream* ... AR-4
*Haw* ... NC-3
*Haw* ... VA-3
Haw—*locale* ... TN-4
**Haw**—*pop pl* ... NC-3
Haw, John Stoddert, House—*hist pl* ... DC-2
Hawaii—*island* ... HI-9
Hawaii Agricultural Experiment
Station—*locale* ... HI-9
Hawaiian Ave Sch—*school* ... CA-9
Hawaiian Baptist Acad—*school* ... HI-9
**Hawaiian Gardens**—*pop pl* ... CA-9
Hawaiian Homes—*civil* ... HI-9
Hawaiian Island—*island* ... MO-7
Hawaiian Islands Natl Wildlife Ref—*park* ... HI-9
Hawaiian Memorial Park
(Cemetery)—*cemetery* ... HI-9
Hawaiian Mission Acad—*school* ... HI-9
**Hawaiian Ocean View Estates**—*pop pl* ... HI-9
Hawaiian Sch—*school* ... CA-9
**Hawaiian-Spanish Village**—*pop pl* ... HI-9
Hawaiian Sugar Planters
Association—*building* ... HI-9
**Hawaiian Village**—*pop pl* (2) ... HI-9
Hawaiian Village Mobile Home
Park—*locale* ... AZ-5
Hawaii Capital Hist Dist—*hist pl* ... HI-9
*Hawaii Channel* ... HI-9
Hawaii Country Club—*other* ... HI-9
**Hawaii (County)**—*pop pl* ... HI-9
Hawaii Falls—*falls* ... HI-9
*Hawaii Island* ... HI-9
**Hawaii Kai**—*pop pl* ... HI-9
Hawaii Kai Golf Course—*other* ... HI-9
Hawaiilanui Gulch—*valley* ... HI-9
*Hawaii Loa* ... HI-9
*Hawaiiloa Hill* ... HI-9
Hawaiiloa Ridge—*ridge* ... HI-9
Hawaii Natl Guard Rifle Range—*military* ... HI-9
Hawaii Natl Park—*post sta* ... HI-9
Hawaii Technical Sch—*school* ... HI-9
Hawaii Theatre—*hist pl* ... HI-9
Hawaii Volcanoes Natl Park—*park* ... HI-9
Hawald Drain—*stream* ... MI-6
Hawaloa—*cape* ... HI-9
Hawarden—*hist pl* ... UT-8
**Hawarden**—*pop pl* ... IA-7
**Hawarden Estates
(subdivision)**—*pop pl* ... UT-8
Hawarden Hall—*locale* ... MT-8
**Hawarden Heights
Subdivision**—*pop pl* ... UT-8
Hawarth Ch—*church* ... MI-6
Haw Bluff—*cliff* ... KY-4
Haw Bluff Ch—*church* ... NC-3
Haw Bluff Landing—*locale* ... MS-4
**Hawbottom**—*pop pl* ... MD-2
Haw Branch—*hist pl* ... VA-3
Haw Branch—*locale* ... NC-3
Haw Branch—*locale* ... VA-3
**Haw Branch**—*pop pl* ... NC-3
Haw Branch—*stream* (2) ... AL-4
Haw Branch—*stream* (6) ... AR-4
Haw Branch—*stream* ... FL-3
Haw Branch—*stream* ... IL-6
Haw Branch—*stream* ... MS-4
Haw Branch—*stream* (3) ... MO-7
Haw Branch—*stream* (8) ... NC-3
Haw Branch—*stream* (3) ... TN-4
Haw Branch—*stream* (4) ... TX-5
Haw Branch—*stream* (2) ... VA-3
Haw Branch Ch—*church* ... NC-3
Haw Branch Sch (abandoned)—*school* ... MO-7
Hawbuck Creek—*stream* ... IL-6
Hawbush Point—*cape* ... MD-2
Hawbush Spring—*spring* ... UT-8
Haw Cabin—*locale* ... OR-9
Hawchen Hollow—*valley* ... WV-2
Haw Cove—*bay* ... NC-3
*Haw Creek* ... TX-5
Haw Creek—*locale* ... OK-5
**Haw Creek**—*pop pl* ... NC-3
Haw Creek—*stream* (6) ... AR-4
Haw Creek—*stream* ... CA-9
Haw Creek—*stream* (2) ... FL-3
Haw Creek—*stream* ... GA-3
Haw Creek—*stream* ... ID-8
Haw Creek—*stream* (2) ... IL-6
Haw Creek—*stream* (3) ... IN-6
Haw Creek—*stream* (3) ... LA-4
Haw Creek—*stream* (4) ... MO-7
Haw Creek—*stream* ... NV-8
Haw Creek—*stream* (2) ... NC-3
Haw Creek—*stream* ... OK-5
Haw Creek—*stream* ... TX-5
Haw Creek Cem—*cemetery* ... GA-3
Haw Creek Ch—*church* ... AR-4
Haw Creek Ch—*church* ... GA-3
Haw Creek Ch—*church* (2) ... IN-6
Haw Creek Ch—*church* ... TX-5
Haw Creek Community Center—*building* ... FL-3
**Haw Creek Siding**—*pop pl* ... IN-6
Haw Creek Slough—*stream* ... MO-7
Haw Creek Township—*civil* ... MO-7
**Haw Creek (Township of)**—*pop pl* ... IL-6
**Haw Creek (Township of)**—*pop pl* ... IN-6
*Haw Crossroad* ... TN-4
**Hawdon Junction (Hawdon)**—*pop pl* ... TX-5
Hawea—*cape* ... HI-9
Hawea Point—*cape* ... HI-9
Hawe Creek—*stream* ... SC-3
Hawe Creek Camping Area—*locale* ... SC-3
Hawe Fork—*stream* ... OH-6
Haweleau Gulch—*valley* ... HI-9
Hawelewele Gulch—*valley* ... HI-9
*Hawels Crossroads* ... AL-4
Hawels Crossroads Post Office
(historical)—*building* ... AL-4
Hawes Branch—*stream* ... GA-3
*Hawes Brook* ... MA-1
Hawes Brook—*stream* ... MA-1
Hawes Cem—*cemetery* ... NC-3
Hawes Chapel—*church* ... NC-3
*Hawes Creek* ... SC-3
Hawes Creek—*stream* ... NV-8
*Hawes Cross Roads* ... TN-4
Hawes Cross Roads Post Office
(historical)—*building* ... TN-4
Hawes Ditch—*canal* ... IN-6
Hawes Drift Mine (underground)—*mine* ... AL-4
Hawes Fork—*stream* (2) ... KY-4
Hawes Fork Sch—*school* ... KY-4
Hawes Hill—*summit* ... MA-1
Hawes Hill—*summit* ... NY-2
Hawes Hollow—*valley* ... WV-2
Hawes Homestead—*hist pl* ... NY-2
Hawes Marsh—*swamp* ... NC-3
*Hawes Meadow Brook* ... ME-1
*Hawes Memorial Campground* ... MO-7
*Hawes Mill Creek* ... NC-3
Hawes Millrace—*stream* ... VA-3
Hawes Park—*park* ... KY-4
Hawes Pasture—*flat* ... ID-8
*Hawes Peak* ... CA-9
Hawes Peak—*summit* ... CA-9
Hawes Point—*cape* ... ME-1
*Hawes Pond* ... MA-1
Hawes Pond—*reservoir* ... MA-1
Hawes Pond Dam—*dam* ... MA-1
Hawes Ranch—*locale* ... CA-9
Hawes Rec Area—*locale* ... MO-7
Hawes Run—*stream* ... WV-2
Hawes Sch—*school* ... CA-9
Hawes Shoal—*bar* ... MA-1
Hawes Stream—*stream* ... ME-1
Hawes-Taylor Cem—*cemetery* ... KY-4
**Hawes (Township of)**—*pop pl* ... MI-6
**Hawesville**—*pop pl* ... KY-4
Hawesville (CCD)—*cens area* ... KY-4
Hawesville Hist Dist—*hist pl* ... KY-4
Hawes Windmill—*locale* ... TX-5
**Hawfields**—*pop pl* ... NC-3
Hawfields Ch—*church* ... NC-3
Hawfields Presbyterian Church—*hist pl* ... NC-3
Hawfields United Ch—*church* ... NC-3
Hawflat Knob—*summit* ... WV-2
*Haw Fork* ... OH-6
Haw Gap—*gap* ... AR-4
Haw Gap—*gap* (4) ... NC-3
Haw Gap—*gap* ... TN-4
Haw Gap Branch—*stream* ... NC-3
*Haw Gap Creek* ... NC-3
Hawgood—*locale* ... ID-8
*Haw Grove Baptist Church* ... AL-4
*Hawgrove Ch* ... AL-4
Haw Grove Ch—*church* ... AL-4
Haw Gulch—*valley* (2) ... MT-8
Hawhammock Ch—*church* ... GA-3
*Haw Haw Creek* ... MO-7
Haw Hill—*summit* ... KY-4
Hawhill Cem—*cemetery* ... AL-4
*Hawhill Ch* ... AL-4
Haw Hill Ch—*church* ... AL-4
Ha-whi-yalin Wash—*stream* ... AZ-5
Haw Hollow—*valley* ... TN-4
Haw Hollow—*valley* (2) ... TX-5
Hawi—*civil* ... HI-9
**Hawi**—*pop pl* ... HI-9
**Hawi Camp 17 (Camp 17)**—*pop pl* ... HI-9
**Hawick**—*pop pl* ... MN-6
Hawikuh—*hist pl* ... NM-5
*Hawiliwili* ... HI-9
*Hawk* ... OH-6
Hawk—*locale* ... AL-4
Hawk—*locale* ... VA-3
**Hawk**—*pop pl* ... KS-7
**Hawk**—*pop pl* ... NC-3
Hawk, William, Cabin—*hist pl* ... UT-8
Hawkbill Creek—*stream* ... NC-3
*Hawkbill Mountain* ... NC-3
Hawkbill Rock—*summit* ... NC-3
Hawk Bluff—*cliff* (2) ... AK-9
Hawk Branch—*locale* ... NC-3
Hawk Branch—*stream* ... KY-4
Hawk Branch—*stream* ... NC-3
Hawk Butte—*summit* ... CA-9
Hawk Camp—*locale* ... CA-9
Hawk Campground—*locale* ... WV-2
Hawk Canyon—*valley* (2) ... AZ-5
Hawk Canyon—*valley* ... CA-9
Hawk Canyon—*valley* ... CO-8
Hawk Canyon—*valley* ... OR-9
Hawk Canyon—*valley* ... SD-7
Hawk Cave—*cave* ... TN-4
Hawk Cem—*cemetery* ... AR-4
Hawk Cem—*cemetery* ... IN-6
Hawk Cem—*cemetery* ... NY-2
Hawk Cem—*cemetery* ... OH-6
Hawk Cem—*cemetery* ... WV-2
Hawk Channel—*channel* (3) ... FL-3
Hawk Cliff—*cliff* ... GA-3
Hawk Coulee—*valley* (2) ... MT-8
Hawk Cove—*bay* ... MD-2
Hawk Cove—*bay* ... TX-5
*Hawk Creek* ... IN-6
*Hawk Creek* ... TX-5
*Hawk Creek* ... WA-9
Hawk Creek—*stream* (2) ... CA-9
Hawk Creek—*stream* ... CO-8
Hawk Creek—*stream* ... GA-3
Hawk Creek—*stream* ... IA-7
Hawk Creek—*stream* ... KY-4
Hawk Creek—*stream* ... MN-6
Hawk Creek—*stream* (3) ... MT-8
Hawk Creek—*stream* ... NJ-2
Hawk Creek—*stream* ... NC-3
Hawk Creek—*stream* ... ND-7
Hawk Creek—*stream* (5) ... OR-9
Hawk Creek—*stream* ... SC-3
Hawk Creek—*stream* ... SD-7
Hawk Creek—*stream* (2) ... WA-9
Hawk Creek Ch—*church* ... KY-4
Hawk Creek Ch—*church* ... MN-6
Hawk Creek Station—*locale* ... OR-9
**Hawk Creek (Township of)**—*pop pl* ... MN-6
Hawk Draw—*valley* ... WY-8
Hawken House—*hist pl* ... MO-7
Hawken Sch—*school* (2) ... OH-6
Hawker Branch—*stream* ... MO-7
Hawker Ch—*church* ... OH-6
Hawker Creek—*stream* ... MO-7
Hawker Point Public Use Area—*locale* ... MO-7
Hawkers Bluff—*cliff* ... KY-4
Hawkersmith Cem—*cemetery* ... TN-4
*Hawkersville* ... PA-2
Hawkes—*locale* ... MS-4
Hawkes, Z. T. (Tip), House—*hist pl* ... TX-5
Hawkes Branch—*stream* ... TN-4
*Hawke's Brook* ... MA-1
Hawkes Brook—*stream* (3) ... MA-1
Hawkes Cem—*cemetery* ... TN-4
Hawkes Children's Library—*hist pl* ... GA-3
Hawkes Hill—*summit* ... ME-1
Hawkes House—*building* ... MA-1
Hawkes Lake—*lake* ... MN-6
Hawkes Library—*hist pl* ... GA-3
*Hawkes Mountain* ... MA-1
Hawkes Pond—*lake* ... ME-1
Hawkes Pond—*reservoir* ... MA-1
Hawkes Pond Outlet Dam—*dam* ... MA-1
Hawkes Store—*locale* ... VA-3
**Hawkey**—*pop pl* ... PA-2
Hawkey Branch—*stream* ... DE-2
Hawkey Creek—*stream* ... MT-8
*Hawk Eye* ... IA-7
Hawkeye—*locale* ... MD-2
Hawkeye—*locale* ... MO-7
Hawkeye—*locale* ... NY-2
Hawkeye—*locale* ... WY-8
**Hawkeye**—*pop pl* ... IA-7
**Hawkeye**—*pop pl* ... PA-2
Hawkeye Canyon—*valley* ... NM-5
Hawkeye Cem—*cemetery* (2) ... IA-7
Hawkeye Cem—*cemetery* ... KS-7
Hawkeye Cem—*cemetery* ... MO-7
Hawkeye Ch—*church* ... MD-2
Hawkeye Creek—*stream* ... IA-7
Hawkeye Creek—*stream* ... MT-8
Hawkeye-Dolbee Diversion
Channel—*canal* ... IA-7
Hawkeye Downs—*locale* ... IA-7
Hawkeye Downs Park—*park* ... IA-7
Hawkeye (historical)—*locale* ... KS-7
Hawkeye Hunt Club—*other* ... TX-5
Hawkeye Insurance Company
Bldg—*hist pl* ... IA-7
Hawkeye Lake—*lake* ... SD-7
Hawkeye McHenry—*mine* ... UT-8
Hawkeye Mine—*mine* ... CA-9
Hawkeye Mine—*mine* ... MT-8
Hawkeye Natural Bridge—*arch* ... UT-8
Hawkeye-Pluma Mine—*mine* ... SD-7
Hawkeye Point—*cape* ... WA-9
*Hawkeye Pond* ... PA-2
Hawkeye Sch—*school* ... IL-6
Hawkeye Sch—*school* ... IA-7
Hawkeye Sch—*school* ... KS-7
Hawkeye Sch—*school* ... MO-7
Hawkeye Sch—*school* (2) ... ND-7
Hawkeye State Wildlife Area—*park* ... IA-7
Hawkeye Tank—*reservoir* ... TX-5
**Hawkeye Township**—*pop pl* ... KS-7
**Hawkeye Township**—*pop pl* (2) ... ND-7
Hawkeye Valley—*valley* ... SD-7
Hawkey Pond—*lake* ... PA-2
Hawkey Run—*stream* ... PA-2
Hawkey Well—*well* ... AZ-5
Hawk Falls—*falls* ... PA-2
Hawk Gap—*gap* ... TN-4
Hawk Gulch—*valley* ... ID-8
Hawk Gulch—*valley* ... OR-9
*Hawk Head* ... MI-6
Hawkhead—*locale* ... MI-6
**Hawk Head**—*pop pl* ... MI-6
Hawk Hill—*cliff* ... NJ-2
Hawk Hill—*summit* ... MA-1
Hawk Hill—*summit* (2) ... NY-2
Hawk Hill—*summit* ... VT-1

**Heathrow (subdivision)**—*pop pl* AL-4
**Heathrow (subdivision)**—*pop pl* TN-4
Heath Run—*stream* PA-2
**Heaths Blocks 39 and 40**—*pop pl* UT-8
Heath Sch—*school* CA-9
Heath Sch—*school* VT-1
Heath Sch (historical)—*school* MO-7
*Heath's Corners* OH-6
Heaths Creek—*stream* MO-7
Heaths Creek Ch—*church* MO-7
Heaths Creek Township—*civil* MO-7
Heathside Cottage—*hist pl* PA-2
Heaths Peak—*summit* WY-8
*Heath Spring* NV-8
Heath Spring—*spring (2)* CA-9
Heath Spring—*spring (2)* ID-8
Heath Spring—*spring* TN-4
**Heath Springs**—*pop pl* SC-3
Heath Springs—*spring* NV-8
Heath Springs (CCD)—*cens area* SC-3
**Heaths Store**—*pop pl* VA-3
Heath Station—*locale* MT-8
**Heath Station**—*pop pl* PA-2
Heath Station (historical)—*locale* MA-1
**Heath Subdivision**—*pop pl* UT-8
Heathsville—*locale* NC-3
**Heathsville**—*pop pl* IL-6
**Heathsville**—*pop pl* VA-3
Heathsville (Magisterial District)—*fmr MCD* VA-3
Heath Tank Number One—*reservoir* AZ-5
Heath Tank Number Two—*reservoir* AZ-5
**Heath (Town of)**—*pop pl* MA-1
**Heath (Township of)**—*pop pl* MI-6
**Heath (Township of)**—*pop pl* PA-2
Heath Trail—*trail* PA-2
Heath Valley—*basin* NE-7
Heathville—*locale* PA-2
Heathville (historical)—*locale* MS-4
Heath Wash—*valley* UT-8
Heathwood—*uninc pl* SC-3
Heathwood Hall Sch—*school* SC-3
Heathwood Park—*park* SC-3
**Heathwood Park**—*pop pl* SC-3
**Heathwood (subdivision)**—*pop pl* TN-4
Heating Plant—*hist pl* KY-4
Heating Plant—*hist pl* NM-5
Heatley Branch—*stream* TX-5
*Heaton* SD-7
Heaton—*locale* AZ-5
Heaton—*locale* IL-6
Heaton—*locale* PA-2
Heaton—*locale* TX-5
**Heaton**—*pop pl* NC-3
**Heaton**—*pop pl* ND-7
Heaton Bay—*bay* CO-8
Heaton Branch—*stream* TN-4
Heaton Bridge—*bridge* NC-3
Heaton Bridge—*bridge* ND-7
Heaton Campground—*locale* CO-8
Heaton Canyon—*valley* NM-5
Heaton Cem—*cemetery* AL-4
Heaton Cem—*cemetery* IL-6
Heaton Cem—*cemetery (2)* IN-6
Heaton Cem—*cemetery* MO-7
Heaton Cem—*cemetery* ND-7
Heaton Cem—*cemetery* TN-4
**Heatoncreek**—*pop pl* TN-4
**Heaton Creek**—*pop pl* TN-4
Heaton Creek—*stream* OR-9
Heaton Creek—*stream* TN-4
Heaton Creek Ridge—*ridge* TN-4
Heaton Creek Sch (historical)—*school* TN-4
Heaton Flat—*flat* CA-9
Heaton Flat Trail—*trail* CA-9
Heaton Gulch—*valley* WA-9
Heaton Hill—*summit* WA-9
Heaton Hollow—*valley* TX-5
Heaton House—*hist pl* LA-4
Heaton JHS—*school* CO-8
Heaton Knolls—*summit* AZ-5
Heaton Knolls Catchment—*basin* AZ-5
Heaton Lake—*lake* IN-6
**Heaton Lake**—*pop pl* IN-6
Heaton Mine—*mine* NM-5
Heaton Private Airp—*airport* IN-6
Heaton Ridge—*ridge* TN-4
Heaton Ridge Cem—*cemetery* TN-4
Heaton Rsvr—*reservoir* AZ-5
*Heatons Brook* CT-1
Heaton Sch—*school* SC-3
Heatons Creek—*stream* IA-7
Heaton Station—*building* PA-2
Heaton Station—*locale* PA-2
**Heatonville**—*pop pl* MO-7
Heat String Creek—*stream* MO-7
Heatwole—*locale* MN-6
**Heavener**—*pop pl* OK-5
Heavener (CCD)—*cens area* OK-5
Heavener Fork—*stream* WV-2
**Heavener Grove**—*pop pl* WV-2
Heavener Memorial Park—*cemetery* OK-5
Heavener Mtn—*summit* WV-2
Heavener Run—*stream* WV-2
Heaveners Creek—*stream* NC-3
**Heaven Heights**—*pop pl* MA-1
Heaven Hill—*summit* NY-2
Heaven Hill—*summit* SC-3
Heavenly Branch—*stream* TX-5
Heavenly Branch Cem—*cemetery* TX-5
Heavenly Ch of First Born—*church* FL-3
Heavenly Heights Baptist Ch—*church* FL-3
Heavenly Hills Lake—*lake* IL-6
Heavenly Hollow—*valley* TN-4
Heavenly Rest Cem—*cemetery* MI-6
Heavenly Rest Ch—*church* SC-3
Heavenly Rest Ch—*church* VA-3
Heavenly Rest Memorial Park—*cemetery* LA-4
Heavenly Rest Memorial Park—*park* MS-4
Heavenly Ridge—*ridge* AK-9
Heavenly Twin Lakes—*lake* OR-9
Heavenly Twins—*summit* MT-8
Heavenly Valley—*basin* CA-9
Heavenly Valley Creek—*stream* CA-9
Heavenly Valley Ski Lodge—*building* CA-9
Heavenly View Ch—*church* TN-4
Heavenly Waters—*stream* MD-2
Heaven Point—*cape* VA-3
*Heaven Pond* NY-2
Heavens Gate—*gap* CA-9
Heavens Gate—*summit* ID-8
Heavens Gate Trail—*trail* ID-8
Heavens Lake—*lake* NY-2
Heavens Peak—*summit* MT-8
Heaven's Peak Fire Lookout—*hist pl* MT-8
Heavens Pond—*lake* NY-2
Heavens Well—*well* NV-8
*Heaven Well* NV-8
Heavey Gulch—*valley* CA-9
Heavey Mtn—*summit* CA-9
Heavey Sheep Camp—*locale* CA-9
Heaviest Corner on Earth—*hist pl* AL-4
Heavilon Ditch—*canal* IN-6
Heaviside Cem—*cemetery* MO-7
Heavisides Sch—*school* IL-6
*Heavner's Ledge* ME-1
Heavy Boy Mine—*mine* AZ-5
Heavy Burn Tank—*reservoir* AZ-5
Heavy Rock Mine—*mine* NV-8
Heavy Runner Mtn—*summit* MT-8
*Heavy Runner Peak* MT-8
Heavy Weight Mine—*mine* AZ-5
Hebard, Alfred, House—*hist pl* IA-7
Hebard-Ford Summer House—*hist pl* MI-6
Hebard Hill—*summit* VT-1
Hebards—*locale* MI-6
Hebard Sch—*school* WY-8
**Hebardville**—*pop pl* GA-3
**Hebardville**—*pop pl* OH-6
*Hebbardsville* OH-6
**Hebbardsville**—*pop pl* KY-4
**Hebbardsville**—*pop pl* OH-6
Hebbardsville-Robards (CCD)—*cens area* KY-4
Hebbardsville Sch—*school* KY-4
Hebbertsburg—*locale* TN-4
Hebbertsburg Cem—*cemetery* TN-4
*Hebbertsburgh* TN-4
*Hebbertsburgh Post Office* TN-4
Hebbertsburg Post Office (historical)—*building* TN-4
Hebbertsburg Sch (historical)—*school* TN-4
Hebbingston Hollow—*valley* TX-5
*Hebbiza Church* MS-4
Hebbiza Sch (historical)—*school* MS-4
Hebble Creek—*stream* OH-6
**Hebbronville**—*pop pl* TX-5
**Hebbville**—*pop pl* MD-2
Hebden Cove—*bay* VA-3
*Hebdon Creek* WY-8
**Hebe**—*pop pl* PA-2
*Hebeardsville* OH-6
*Hebe Canyon* UT-8
Hebe Canyon—*valley* UT-8
H E Beck Junior Memorial Branch—*other* CA-9
Hebeisen, Jacob, Hardware Store—*hist pl* MN-6
Hebeisen, Jacob, House—*hist pl* MN-6
*Hebel* WI-6
**Hebel**—*pop pl* WI-6
Hebels Corners—*locale* WI-6
He Bend—*bend* MO-7
*Heber* UT-8
Heber—*locale* NE-7
**Heber**—*pop pl* AZ-5
**Heber**—*pop pl* CA-9
**Heber**—*pop pl* UT-8
Heber Ch—*church* KS-7
*Heber Christian Fellowship* UT-8
**Heber City**—*pop pl* UT-8
Heber City Airp—*airport* UT-8
Heber City Cem—*cemetery* UT-8
Heber City Post Office—*building* UT-8
Heber Division—*civil* UT-8
Heber Drain—*canal* CA-9
Heber Dump—*other* AZ-5
Heberers Branch—*stream* IL-6
Heber (historical)—*locale* KS-7
Heber Hunt Sch—*school* MO-7
Heber Job Corp Conservation Center—*building* AZ-5
Heberle Sch—*school* OH-6
**Heberlig**—*pop pl* PA-2
**Heberling**—*pop pl* PA-2
Heberling Sch—*school* PA-2
Heberling Sch (historical)—*school* PA-2
*Heberlin Mine* TN-4
Heberly Run—*stream* PA-2
Heber Mtn—*summit* UT-8
Heber Park—*park* NE-7
Heber Ranger Station—*locale* AZ-5
Heber Road Tank—*reservoir* AZ-5
Heber Second Ward Meetinghouse—*hist pl* UT-8
Heber Spring—*spring* UT-8
**Heber Springs**—*pop pl* AR-4
Heber Springs Marina—*locale* AR-4
Heber Springs Rec Area—*park* AR-4
Hebert—*locale* TX-5
**Hebert**—*pop pl* LA-4
Hebert, Bayou—*stream (2)* LA-4
Hebert, Louis, House—*hist pl* IA-7
Heber Tank—*reservoir* AZ-5
Hebert Canal—*canal (2)* LA-4
Hebert Cem—*cemetery (6)* LA-4
Hebert Cem—*cemetery* TX-5
Hebert Ch—*church* LA-4
Hebert HS—*school* TX-5
Hebert Island—*island* LA-4
Hebert Lake—*lake* LA-4
Hebert Lake—*lake* MI-6
Heber (Township of)—*fmr MCD* AR-4
Hebert Park—*park* TX-5
Heber Trick Tank—*reservoir* AZ-5
Hebert Sch—*school* LA-4
Heber Valley—*valley* UT-8
*Heber Valley Airport* UT-8
Heber Valley Bible Ch—*church* UT-8
Hebes Mtn—*summit* UT-8
Hebgen Dam—*dam* MT-8
Hebgen Lake—*reservoir* MT-8
*Hebgen Reservoir* MT-8
Hebgen Ridge—*ridge* MT-8
Hebing Post Office (historical)—*building* TN-4
Hebner (historical)—*locale* SD-7
**Hebo**—*pop pl* OR-9
Hebo, Mount—*summit* OR-9
Hebo Lake—*reservoir* OR-9
Hebo Lake Campground—*park* OR-9
Hebo Mtn—*summit* NC-3
Hebo Ranger Station—*locale* OR-9
Hebo Work Camp—*locale* OR-9
Hebraica Miami Community Center—*locale* FL-3
Hebrew Acad—*school (2)* NY-2
Hebrew Acad—*school* OH-6
*Hebrew Cem* MS-4
Hebrew Cem—*cemetery* CA-9
Hebrew Cem—*cemetery (2)* CT-1
Hebrew Cem—*cemetery* GA-3
Hebrew Cem—*cemetery (2)* IN-6
Hebrew Cem—*cemetery* MD-2
Hebrew Cem—*cemetery (2)* MA-1
Hebrew Cem—*cemetery* MS-4
Hebrew Cem—*cemetery* MO-7
Hebrew Cem—*cemetery* NH-1
Hebrew Cem—*cemetery* NY-2
Hebrew Cem—*cemetery* NC-3
Hebrew Cem—*cemetery* ND-7
Hebrew Cem—*cemetery* OH-6
Hebrew Cem—*cemetery (2)* TX-5
Hebrew Cem—*cemetery (3)* VA-3
Hebrew Cem—*cemetery (3)* WI-6
Hebrew Cemeteries—*cemetery* DC-2
Hebrew Center—*school* NY-2
*Hebrew Ch* MS-4
Hebrew Ch—*church* GA-3
Hebrew Ch—*church* LA-4
Hebrew Ch—*church* MS-4
Hebrew Ch—*church* TN-4
*Hebrew Church* AL-4
Hebrew Day Sch of Central Florida—*school* FL-3
Hebrew Day Sch of Fort Lauderdale—*school* FL-3
Hebrew Home—*building* NY-2
Hebrew Home and Hosp—*hospital* NY-2
Hebrew Home for the Aged—*building* CA-9
Hebrew Hosp—*hospital* NY-2
Hebrew Institute—*school* OH-6
Hebrew Memorial Park—*cemetery* MI-6
Hebrew Orthodox Congregation—*church* KS-7
Hebrew Rest Cem—*cemetery (3)* LA-4
Hebrew Rest Cem—*cemetery* TX-5
Hebrew Sch—*school* MO-7
Hebrew Sch—*school (2)* NY-2
Hebrew Sch—*school* OH-6
Hebrew Sch—*school* PA-2
Hebrew Sch—*school* TN-4
Hebrew Theological Coll—*school* IL-6
Hebrew Union Coll—*school* OH-6
Hebrion Ch—*church* SC-3
*Hebrom Church* AL-4
*Hebron* AL-4
*Hebron* GA-3
*Hebron* PA-2
Hebron—*hist pl* MD-2
Hebron—*hist pl* MO-7
Hebron—*locale* CO-8
Hebron—*locale (2)* GA-3
Hebron—*locale* IA-7
Hebron—*locale* MS-4
Hebron—*locale* NM-5
Hebron—*locale* PA-2
Hebron—*locale* UT-8
Hebron—*locale* VA-3
Hebron—*other* WV-2
**Hebron**—*pop pl (2)* AL-4
**Hebron**—*pop pl* AR-4
**Hebron**—*pop pl* CA-9
**Hebron**—*pop pl* CT-1
**Hebron**—*pop pl* IL-6
**Hebron**—*pop pl* IN-6
**Hebron**—*pop pl* KY-4
**Hebron**—*pop pl* ME-1
**Hebron**—*pop pl* MD-2
**Hebron**—*pop pl (3)* MS-4
**Hebron**—*pop pl* MO-7
**Hebron**—*pop pl* NE-7
**Hebron**—*pop pl* NH-1
**Hebron**—*pop pl (2)* NC-3
**Hebron**—*pop pl* ND-7
**Hebron**—*pop pl* OH-6
**Hebron**—*pop pl* PA-2
**Hebron**—*pop pl* SC-3
**Hebron**—*pop pl* TN-4
**Hebron**—*pop pl* TX-5
**Hebron**—*pop pl (2)* VA-3
**Hebron**—*pop pl* WV-2
**Hebron**—*pop pl* WI-6
Hebron, Lake—*lake* ME-1
Hebron, Mount—*summit* CA-9
Hebron Acad—*hist pl* MS-4
Hebron Acad—*school* ME-1
Hebron Acad (historical)—*school* MS-4
Hebron Access Point—*locale* MO-7
Hebron Ave Sch—*school* CT-1
Hebron Baptist Ch—*church* TN-4
*Hebron Baptist Church* AL-4
*Hebron Baptist Church* MS-4
Hebron Bay—*bay* NH-1
Hebron Branch—*stream* LA-4
Hebron Branch—*stream* TN-4
Hebron (CCD)—*cens area* KY-4
Hebron (CCD)—*cens area* TX-5
*Hebron Cem* MS-4
Hebron Cem—*cemetery (6)* AL-4
Hebron Cem—*cemetery (2)* GA-3
Hebron Cem—*cemetery* IL-6
Hebron Cem—*cemetery (3)* IN-6
Hebron Cem—*cemetery* IA-7
Hebron Cem—*cemetery* KS-7
Hebron Cem—*cemetery (2)* KY-4
Hebron Cem—*cemetery* MI-6
Hebron Cem—*cemetery (2)* MN-6
Hebron Cem—*cemetery (9)* MS-4
Hebron Cem—*cemetery (3)* MO-7
Hebron Cem—*cemetery* NE-7
Hebron Cem—*cemetery* OH-6
Hebron Cem—*cemetery* OK-5
Hebron Cem—*cemetery* PA-2
Hebron Cem—*cemetery (2)* TN-4
Hebron Cem—*cemetery* TX-5
Hebron Cem—*cemetery* UT-8
Hebron Cem—*cemetery* VA-3
Hebron Cem—*cemetery* WI-6
**Hebron Center**—*pop pl* PA-2
*Hebron Ch* AL-4
*Hebron Ch* TN-4
Hebron Ch—*church (9)* AL-4
Hebron Ch—*church (3)* AR-4
Hebron Ch—*church* DE-2
Hebron Ch—*church (2)* FL-3
Hebron Ch—*church (9)* GA-3
Hebron Ch—*church (4)* IL-6
Hebron Ch—*church (2)* IN-6
Hebron Ch—*church (3)* KS-7
Hebron Ch—*church (5)* KY-4
Hebron Ch—*church (9)* LA-4
Hebron Ch—*church* MN-6
Hebron Ch—*church (21)* MS-4
Hebron Ch—*church* MO-7
Hebron Ch—*church* NY-2
Hebron Ch—*church (10)* NC-3
Hebron Ch—*church* OH-6
Hebron Ch—*church* OR-9
Hebron Ch—*church (2)* PA-2
Hebron Ch—*church (11)* SC-3
Hebron Ch—*church (8)* TN-4
Hebron Ch—*church (8)* TX-5
Hebron Ch—*church (14)* VA-3
Hebron Ch—*church (4)* WV-2
Hebron Chapel—*church* MS-4
Hebron Ch (historical)—*church* MS-4
*Hebron Ch of Christ* TN-4
*Hebron Christian School* MS-4
Hebron Church—*hist pl* SC-3
Hebron Church, Cemetery, and Acad—*hist pl* GA-3
Hebron Church Cem—*cemetery (2)* AL-4
Hebron Church Cem—*cemetery* IN-6
*Hebron Church of Christ* AL-4
Hebron Colony Ch—*church* NC-3
**Hebron Crossroads**—*pop pl* SC-3
Hebron Elementary—*school* PA-2
Hebron Elem Sch—*school* IN-6
**Hebron Estates**—*pop pl* KY-4
Hebron Hill—*summit* NY-2
Hebron Hill—*summit* SC-3
Hebron Hill Cem—*cemetery* MS-4
Hebron (historical)—*locale* AL-4
Hebron (historical)—*locale (2)* MS-4
**Hebron (historical)**—*pop pl* NC-3
*Hebron Historical Site* UT-8
Hebron Hollow—*valley* MO-7
Hebron HS (historical)—*school* MS-4
Hebron Junior-Senior HS—*school* IN-6
Hebron Lodge Cem—*cemetery* MS-4
Hebron Lookout Tower—*locale* MI-6
Hebron Lutheran Church—*hist pl* VA-3
*Hebron Methodist Ch* MS-4
Hebron Methodist Ch—*church* MS-4
*Hebron Methodist Church* AL-4
Hebron Methodist Church—*hist pl* NC-3
Hebron Mill Pond Dam—*dam* MA-1
*Hebron Missionary Baptist Ch* MS-4
*Hebron Mtn* CA-9
Hebron Mtn—*summit* NY-2
Hebron Mtn—*summit* NC-3
Hebron Municipal Airp—*airport* ND-7
*Hebron Presbyterian Ch* TN-4
*Hebron Ridge Baptist Ch* MS-4
Hebron Ridge Ch—*church* MS-4
Hebron Ridge Sch (historical)—*school* MS-4
*Hebron Sch* IN-6
Hebron Sch—*school* AL-4
Hebron Sch—*school* CT-1
Hebron Sch—*school* IL-6
Hebron Sch—*school* IN-6
Hebron Sch—*school* KS-7
Hebron Sch—*school (2)* KY-4
Hebron Sch—*school* LA-4
Hebron Sch—*school* MI-6
Hebron Sch—*school* MS-4
Hebron Sch—*school* SC-3
Hebron Sch—*school* TX-5
Hebron Sch (abandoned)—*school* MO-7
Hebron Sch (historical)—*school* AL-4
Hebron Sch (historical)—*school (3)* MS-4
Hebron Sch (historical)—*school* PA-2
Hebron Sch (historical)—*school* TN-4
Hebron Springs—*spring* AL-4
Hebron Station—*locale* ME-1
Hebron Station (historical)—*locale* AL-4
**Hebron (Town of)**—*pop pl* CT-1
**Hebron (Town of)**—*pop pl* ME-1
**Hebron (Town of)**—*pop pl* NH-1
**Hebron (Town of)**—*pop pl* NY-2
**Hebron (Town of)**—*pop pl* WI-6
Hebron Township—*fmr MCD* IA-7
**Hebron Township**—*pop pl* ND-7
**Hebron (Township of)**—*pop pl* IL-6
**Hebron (Township of)**—*pop pl* MI-6
**Hebron (Township of)**—*pop pl* PA-2
Hebron Village Hist Dist—*hist pl* NH-1
Hebronville Mill Hist Dist—*hist pl* MA-1
Hebronville Post Office (historical)—*building* TN-4
Hebronville (RR name for Twin Village)—*other* MA-1
H E Butt Park—*park* TX-5
Heceta Bank—*bar* OR-9
**Heceta Beach**—*pop pl* OR-9
Heceta Beach County Rec Area—*park* OR-9
Heceta Head—*cliff* OR-9
Heceta Head Lighthouse and Keepers Quarters—*hist pl* OR-9
Heceta Island—*island* AK-9
**Heceta Junction**—*pop pl* OR-9
Heceta Junction Lake—*lake* OR-9
Hechenbleikner Lake—*lake* NC-3
Hechicera, Cerro De La—*ridge* CA-9
Hechinger Mall—*post sta* DC-2
*Hechla* KY-4
**Hechler Village**—*pop pl* VA-3
Hecht And Ferrall Ditch—*canal* WY-8
Hecht Creek—*stream* MO-7
Hecht Creek—*stream* WY-8
Hecht Drain—*canal* MI-6
Hechtman Creek—*stream* WY-8
Hechtman Lake—*lake* WY-8
Hecht Sch—*school* PA-2
*Heckadorn Gap* PA-2
Heck and Gone—*locale (2)* OR-9
Heck-Andrews House—*hist pl* NC-3
Heckard Creek—*stream* OR-9
Heckathorn Ch—*church* PA-2
Heck Branch—*stream* TN-4
Heck Branch—*stream* WV-2
Heck Bridge—*bridge* OH-6
Heck Canyon—*valley* CA-9
Heck Cem—*cemetery* TN-4
Heck Cem—*cemetery* WV-2
Heck Cotton Gin—*locale* TX-5
Heck Creek—*stream* CA-9
Heck Creek—*stream* NC-3
Heck Creek Cem—*cemetery* NC-3
Heckel Creek*—*stream* NE-7
Heckel Creek—*stream* SD-7
Heckel Hill—*summit* NH-1
Heckendorn Gap—*gap* PA-2
Hecker—*locale* LA-4
**Hecker**—*pop pl* IL-6
Hecker, Col. Frank J., House—*hist pl* MI-6
Hecker Freedom Cem—*cemetery* IL-6
Hecker Pass—*gap* CA-9
Hecker Ranch—*locale* MT-8
Hecker Sch—*school (2)* ND-7
Heckers Lake—*lake* ND-7
Heckert Gap—*gap* PA-2
*Heckertown* PA-2
**Heckescherville**—*pop pl* PA-2
Heckethorn Cem—*cemetery* IL-6
*Heckethorn Hills* UT-8
Heckethorn Tank—*reservoir (2)* AZ-5
Heckethorn Well—*well* NV-8
Heck Gulch—*valley* CO-8
Heck Hill—*summit* OH-6
Heck Hollow—*valley* MO-7
Heck Hollow—*valley* TN-4
Heck Hollow Branch—*stream* TN-4
*Heckla Station* MS-4
Heck-Lee, Heck-Wynne, and Heck-Pool Houses—*hist pl* NC-3
Heckle Ranch—*locale* CA-9
Heckler Farmhouse—*hist pl* OH-6
Heckler Knob—*summit* TN-4
Heckler Sch (abandoned)—*school* PA-2
**Heckler Village**—*pop pl* VA-3
Heckletooth Mtn—*summit* OR-9
Heckman Bend—*bend* MO-7
Heckman Camp—*locale* TX-5
Heckman Cem—*cemetery* OH-6
Heckman Cem—*cemetery* PA-2
Heckman Hollow—*valley* PA-2
Heckman Island—*island* MO-7
Heckman Lake—*lake* AK-9
Heckman Lake—*lake* IN-6
Heckman Memorial Cem—*cemetery* IN-6
Heckman Point—*cape* AK-9
Heckman Ridge—*ridge* PA-2
Heckman Rsvr—*reservoir* OR-9
Heckman Rsvr Number One—*reservoir* OR-9
*Heckman Rsvr Number 2* OR-9
Heckman Sch—*school* PA-2
Heckman Sch (abandoned)—*school* MO-7
Heckman Siding—*locale* MT-8
*Heckmans Island* MO-7
Heck Point—*cape* WI-6
Heck Pond—*lake* TN-4
Heck Ridge—*ridge* AL-4
Heck Rock—*summit* OR-9
Hecks Camp—*locale* CA-9
Heckscher Canal—*canal* NY-2
Heckscher Drive Ch—*church* FL-3
Heckscher Park—*hist pl* NY-2
Heckscher State Park—*park* NY-2
Heckscherville—*locale* PA-2
Hecks Grove Ch—*church* NC-3
Hecks Grove Sch—*school* NC-3
Hecksher Park—*park* NY-2
*Heckshevville* PA-2
Hecks Knob—*summit* WV-2
Hecks Lake—*reservoir* IL-6
Hecks Shop Ctr—*locale* TN-4
Heck Table—*summit* SD-7
**Heckton**—*pop pl* PA-2
Heckton Ch—*church* PA-2
*Heckton Mills* PA-2
**Hecktown**—*pop pl* PA-2
Hecktown Sch (abandoned)—*school* PA-2
Heckville—*locale* TX-5
*Hecla* IN-6
Hecla—*locale* AZ-5
Hecla—*locale* MO-7
Hecla—*locale* NE-7
Hecla—*other* PA-2
**Hecla**—*pop pl* IN-6
**Hecla**—*pop pl* KS-7
**Hecla**—*pop pl* KY-4
**Hecla**—*pop pl* NY-2
**Hecla**—*pop pl* OH-6
**Hecla**—*pop pl* PA-2
**Hecla**—*pop pl* SD-7
**Hecla**—*pop pl* WY-8
Hecla Branch Storms Creek—*stream* OH-6
Hecla Canal—*canal* MA-1
*Hecla Furnace* PA-2
*Hecla Furnace Gap* PA-2
Hecla Gap—*gap* PA-2
Hecla Mine—*mine* NV-8
Hecla Mine—*mine* UT-8
Hecla Mine—*mine* WA-9
Hecla Mines—*mine* MT-8
*Hecla Park* PA-2
Hecla Park—*park* PA-2
Hecla Pond—*lake* MA-1
*Heclar* PA-2
Hecla Rsvr—*reservoir* CO-8
Hecla Shaft—*mine* UT-8
**Hecla Township**—*pop pl* SD-7
He Creek—*stream* NC-3
He Creek—*stream* TN-4
Hecs Hole—*basin* AZ-5
Hecta Mine—*mine* ID-8
Hectic Savannas—*flat* SC-3
*Hector* IN-6
*Hector* OK-5
Hector—*locale* AL-4
Hector—*locale* CA-9
Hector—*locale* KY-4
Hector—*locale* PA-2
**Hector**—*pop pl* AR-4
**Hector**—*pop pl* MN-6
**Hector**—*pop pl* NY-2
**Hector**—*pop pl* OH-6
**Hector A Pinero**—*pop pl (2)* PR-3
Hector Backbone—*ridge* NY-2
Hector Branch—*stream* AL-4
Hector Branch—*stream* KY-4
Hector Cem—*cemetery* MN-6
Hector Creek—*stream (2)* NC-3
Hector Falls—*falls* NY-2
Hector Falls Creek—*stream* NY-2
Hector Falls Point—*cape* NY-2
Hector Field—*airport* ND-7
Hector Gap—*gap* KY-4
**Hector Heights Subdivision**—*pop pl* UT-8
*Hector Hollow* PA-2
Hector Hollow—*valley* UT-8
Hector Knob—*summit* WV-2
Hector Land Use Area (U S Forest Service)—*park* NY-2
Hector Lookout Tower—*locale* KY-4
**Hector Park Condominium**—*pop pl* UT-8
**Hector Park Subdivision**—*pop pl* UT-8
Hector P O—*locale* NY-2
Hectors Creek (Township of)—*fmr MCD* NC-3
Hector Station—*locale* CA-9
**Hector (Town of)**—*pop pl* NY-2
Hector (Township of)—*fmr MCD* AR-4
**Hector (Township of)**—*pop pl* MN-6
**Hector (Township of)**—*pop pl* PA-2
**Hector Village Subdivision**—*pop pl* UT-8
Hectorville—*locale* OK-5
**Hectorville**—*pop pl (2)* VT-1
Hectorville Ch—*church* OK-5
Hectorville Covered Bridge—*hist pl* VT-1
*Hectown* PA-2
Hedd Canyon—*valley* CA-9
Hedden Bluff Landing—*locale* NC-3
Hedden Cem—*cemetery* GA-3
Hedden Cem—*cemetery* IN-6
*Hedden Corners* NY-2
Hedden Creek—*stream* GA-3
Hedden Ditch—*canal* OH-6
Hedden Hall—*hist pl* MI-6
Hedden House—*hist pl* KY-4
Hedden Pond—*lake* CT-1
Heddens Lake—*reservoir* NY-2
*Heddens Point* NY-2
Heddin Creek—*stream* OR-9
**Hedding**—*pop pl* NH-1
**Hedding**—*pop pl* NJ-2
Hedding Ch—*church* IN-6
Hedding Ch—*church* NJ-2
**Hedding (Three Tuns)**—*pop pl* NJ-2
Heddon Chapel—*church* AR-4
*Heddonfield* NJ-2
Heddrick Knob—*summit* NC-3
*Heddricks Point* FL-3
Heddrick Tank—*reservoir* NM-5
Heddy Creek—*stream* GA-3
Heddy Gutter Creek—*stream* SC-3
Heddy Hollow—*valley* TN-4
Heddy Run—*stream* IN-6
Heddy Run—*stream* KY-4
Hedell Memorial Park—*cemetery* NC-3
Hedemarken Ch—*church* MN-6
Hedemen Springs—*spring* MO-7
Hederman Brothers Pond Dam—*dam* MS-4
He Devil—*summit* ID-8
He Devil Lake—*lake* ID-8
*He Devil Mountain* ID-8
Hedge—*locale* IA-7
Hedge, Cape—*cape* MA-1
Hedge Block—*hist pl* IA-7
Hedge Bridge—*other* IL-6
*Hedge Brook* MA-1
Hedge Brook—*stream* CT-1
*Hedge Cape* MA-1
Hedge Cem—*cemetery (2)* IN-6
Hedge Cem—*cemetery (2)* TN-4
Hedge City—*locale* MO-7
Hedgecock Windmill—*locale* CO-8
Hedge Coll Sch—*school* IL-6
Hedge Coll Sch—*school* IA-7
Hedge Coll Sch—*school* MO-7
Hedge Corner Sch—*school* NE-7
Hedgecoth Cem—*cemetery* TN-4
**Hedgecoth (historical)**—*pop pl* TN-4
Hedgecoth Post Office (historical)—*building* TN-4
Hedge Creek—*stream* CA-9
Hedge Ditch—*canal* MT-8
Hedge Fence—*bar* MA-1
Hedge Hill—*area* CA-9
Hedge Hill Sch—*school* NE-7
Hedgehog Bay—*bay* NY-2
Hedgehog Brook—*stream* NH-1
Hedgehog Brook—*stream* VT-1
Hedgehog Cove—*bay* NH-1
Hedgehog Creek—*stream* OH-6
Hedgehog Harbor—*bay* WI-6
Hedgehog Hill—*ridge* NH-1
Hedgehog Hill—*summit* CT-1
Hedgehog Hill—*summit (13)* ME-1
Hedgehog Hill—*summit (6)* NH-1
Hedgehog Hill—*summit (3)* NY-2
Hedgehog Hill—*summit (5)* VT-1
Hedgehog Hollow—*valley (2)* PA-2
Hedgehog Island—*island* ME-1
Hedgehog Knoll—*summit* VT-1
Hedgehog Ledge—*cliff* ME-1
*Hedgehog Mtn* ME-1
Hedgehog Mtn—*summit (8)* ME-1
Hedgehog Mtn—*summit* NH-1
Hedgehog Mtn—*summit (5)* NY-2
Hedgehog Mtn—*summit (2)* VT-1
Hedgehog Nubble—*summit* NH-1
Hedgehog Point—*cape* ME-1
Hedgehog Point—*summit* PA-2
Hedgehog Pond—*lake (3)* ME-1
Hedgehog Pond—*lake* NH-1
Hedgehog Pond—*lake (3)* NY-2
Hedgehog Rapids—*rapids* NY-2
Hedgehog Run—*stream* PA-2
Hedgehog Trail—*trail* PA-2
Hedge Hollow—*valley* TN-4
Hedgeland Ditch—*canal* IN-6
Hedgeland Landing—*locale* LA-4
Hedgelawn—*hist pl* DE-2
Hedge Lawn—*hist pl* NY-2
**Hedgemoor (subdivision)**—*pop pl* MS-4
Hedge Neck—*cape* MD-2
Hedgepath Creek—*stream* OR-9
Hedgepeth Cem—*cemetery* NC-3
*Hedgepeth Cemetery* TN-4
Hedgepeth Pond—*reservoir* NC-3
Hedgepeth Pond Dam—*dam* NC-3
*Hedge Pond* MA-1

Hedge Providence Ch—church ... AR-4
Hedger Branch—stream ... KY-4
Hedger Chapel—church ... KY-4
Hedger Hollow—valley ... KY-4
Hedger House—locale ... NJ-2
Hedge Ridge—ridge ... PA-2
**Hedgerow Hollow (trailer park)**—pop pl ... DE-2
Hedge Row Sch—school ... IL-6
Hedger Sch—school ... CA-9
Hedger's Ranch—locale ... MT-8
**Hedges**—pop pl ... FL-3
**Hedges**—pop pl ... GA-3
**Hedges**—pop pl ... KY-4
**Hedges**—pop pl ... OH-6
**Hedges**—pop pl ... WA-9
Hedges, Decatur, House—hist pl ... WV-2
Hedges, Samuel, House—hist pl ... WV-2
Hedges Arroyo—stream ... NM-5
Hedges Bank—cliff ... NY-2
Hedges Bog—swamp ... MA-1
Hedges-Boyer Park—park ... OH-6
Hedges Branch—stream ... NJ-2
Hedges Cem—cemetery ... CA-9
Hedges Cem—cemetery ... IN-6
Hedges Cem—cemetery ... OH-6
Hedges Cem—cemetery ... VA-3
Hedges Central Elem Sch—school ... IN-6
Hedges Chapel—church ... OH-6
Hedges Chapel—church ... WV-2
Hedge Sch (historical)—school ... MO-7
Hedges Creek—stream ... MT-8
Hedges Creek—stream ... NY-2
Hedges Creek—stream ... OR-9
Hedges Fork—stream ... WV-2
Hedges-Hunter-Keller-Bacon Gristmill—hist pl ... OH-6
Hedges Island—island ... OH-6
Hedges Lake—lake ... NY-2
Hedges Lakes—reservoir ... PA-2
Hedges Mtn—summit ... MT-8
Hedges Mtn—summit ... WV-2
Hedges North Dam—dam ... NM-5
Hedges Peak—summit ... WY-8
Hedgespeth Cem—cemetery ... KY-4
*Hedges Pond* ... MA-1
Hedges Pond—lake ... FL-3
Hedges Pond—lake (2) ... MA-1
Hedges-Robinson-Myers House—hist pl ... WV-2
Hedges Run—stream ... KY-4
Hedges Sch—school ... IL-6
Hedges Sch—school ... MA-1
Hedges Sch—school ... MT-8
Hedges Sch—school ... OH-6
Hedges (Site)—locale ... CA-9
Hedge Substation—other ... CA-9
Hedgesville—locale ... MT-8
**Hedgesville**—pop pl ... NY-2
**Hedgesville**—pop pl ... WV-2
Hedgesville Ch—church ... WV-2
Hedgesville Hist Dist—hist pl ... WV-2
Hedgesville (Magisterial District)—fmr MCD ... WV-2
Hedges Well—well ... AZ-5
**Hedgeview**—pop pl ... WV-2
Hedgeville—locale ... KY-4
Hedgewood (historical)—locale ... KS-7
Hedging, The—summit ... CT-1
Hedgpeth Cem—cemetery ... NC-3
Hedgpeth Cem—cemetery ... TN-4
*Hedgpeth Hills* ... AZ-5
Hedgpeth Hills—summit ... AZ-5
Hedgpeth Hills Petroglyph Site—hist pl ... AZ-5
Hedgpeth Lake—reservoir ... CA-9
Hediendilla—locale ... AZ-5
Hedin And Slate Ditch—canal ... WY-8
Hedin Lake—lake ... WA-9
Hediondo Creek—stream ... TX-5
Hedke Sch—school ... MI-6
**Hedley**—pop pl ... TX-5
Hedley (CCD)—cens area ... TX-5
Hedley Knob—summit ... MO-7
Hedlund Bridge—bridge ... WA-9
Hedlund Lake—lake (2) ... MN-6
Hedlund Motor Company Bldg—hist pl ... OK-5
Hedman Lake—lake ... MN-6
Hedman Number 1 Dam—dam ... SD-7
Hedmons Pond—lake ... CT-1
*Hedneys Creek* ... MD-2
*Hedoes Creek* ... MT-8
He Dog Dam—dam ... SD-7
He Dog Day Sch—school ... SD-7
He Dog Lake—lake ... SD-7
He Dog Village (historic site)—locale ... SD-7
*Hedona* ... AL-4
Hedrich Cem—cemetery ... MS-4
**Hedrick**—pop pl ... IN-6
**Hedrick**—pop pl ... IA-7
Hedrick, John W., House—hist pl ... IN-6
Hedrick Branch—stream ... TX-5
Hedrick Branch—stream ... WV-2
Hedrick Cem—cemetery ... LA-4
Hedrick Cem—cemetery ... MO-7
Hedrick Ch—church ... KY-4
Hedrick Chapel—church ... WV-2
Hedrick Creek—stream ... WA-9
Hedrick Dam—dam ... NC-3
**Hedrick Estates (subdivision)**—pop pl ... NC-3
**Hedrick Grove**—pop pl ... NC-3
Hedrick Hollow—valley ... MO-7
Hedrick Lake—reservoir ... NC-3
Hedrick Meadow—flat ... CA-9
Hedrick Mtn—summit ... NC-3
Hedrick Point—cape ... TN-4
Hedrick Pond—lake ... WY-8
Hedricks Canyon—valley ... AZ-5
Hedrick Sch—school ... CA-9
Hedrick Sch—school ... IA-7
Hedricks Creek—stream ... WV-2
Hedricks Number 5 Dam—dam ... SD-7
Hedrix—locale ... NE-7
Hedstrom Lake—reservoir ... MT-8
Hedstroms Ponds—lake ... CT-1
Hedum Draw—valley ... MT-8
Hedum Spring—spring ... MT-8
**Hedville**—pop pl ... KS-7
*Hedwig* ... TX-5
Hedwigs Hill—locale ... TX-5
**Hedwig Village**—pop pl ... TX-5
*Hedy Creek* ... SD-7
Hee-A-Han Park (cemetery)—cemetery ... AZ-5
Heebeecheeche, Lake—lake ... WY-8
Heebnerville—locale ... PA-2
Heeb Sch—school ... MT-8
Hee Creek—stream ... OK-5
Heedie Spring—spring ... OR-9
Heed Univ—school ... FL-3
Hee Haw Creek—stream ... WA-9
Hee Hee Creek—stream ... WA-9
Hee Hee Mtn—summit ... WA-9
Hee Hee Stone—pillar ... WA-9
*Heeia* ... HI-9
Heeia—civil ... HI-9
**Heeia**—pop pl ... HI-9
Heeia Bay—bay ... HI-9
Heeia Fishpond—hist pl ... HI-9
Heeia Pond—lake ... HI-9
Heeia Sch—school ... HI-9
Heeia Stream—stream ... HI-9
Heeka Point—cape ... HI-9
Heekin—locale ... KY-4
Heekin Park—park ... IN-6
Heekla Mine (underground)—mine ... AL-4
Heel, The—summit ... UT-8
Heelan HS—school ... IA-7
Heel Creek—stream ... WA-9
Heeley Ditch—canal ... CO-8
Heeley Ditch—canal ... WY-8
Heelfly Creek—stream ... NV-8
Heel Fly Draw—valley ... TX-5
Heel Fly Tank—reservoir ... TX-5
Heel Point—RIDGE ... MP-9
Heelstring—locale ... AR-4
Heeltap Branch—stream ... TX-5
Heely Cem—cemetery ... AR-4
Heely Creek—stream ... SD-7
Hee Mtn—summit ... OK-5
*Heenan Creek* ... CA-9
*Heenan Creek* ... NV-8
Heenan Creek—stream ... CA-9
Heenan Drain—canal ... MI-6
Heenan Lake—reservoir ... CA-9
*Heenan Rsvr* ... CA-9
Heenanville Sch—school ... IL-6
**Heeney**—pop pl ... CO-8
Heenon—locale ... KY-4
Heer Hill—summit ... IL-6
Heermance Farmhouse—hist pl ... NY-2
Heermance House and Law Office—hist pl ... NY-2
Heerten Cem—cemetery ... NE-7
Heery Woods State Park—park ... IA-7
Heesacker Rsvr—reservoir ... OR-9
Heeter Ditch—canal ... IN-6
Heeter-Russo House—hist pl ... OH-6
Heetland Ranch—locale ... WY-8
Hefel Ridge—summit ... IA-7
Hefel School(Abandoned)—locale ... IA-7
Hefferan Sch—school ... IL-6
Heffernan Gulch—valley ... CO-8
Heffers Brook—stream ... CT-1
Heffington—locale ... AR-4
Heffington Cem—cemetery ... AR-4
Hefflefinger Gulch—valley ... WA-9
Hefflen Draw—valley ... WY-8
Heffner Canyon—valley ... NM-5
Heffner Gap—gap ... NC-3
Heffner Lake—lake ... ND-7
Heffner Landing—locale ... TN-4
Heffners Bridge—bridge ... PA-2
Heffners Mill (historical)—locale ... TN-4
Heffner Spring—spring ... OR-9
Heffner Street Sch—school ... OH-6
Heffner Tank—reservoir ... NM-5
*Heffren* ... IN-6
*Heffron* ... IN-6
Heffron—locale ... WI-6
Heffron Lake—lake ... MN-6
Hefley Cabin—locale ... CO-8
Hefley Cem—cemetery ... OK-5
Hefley Cem—cemetery ... TX-5
Hefley Cow Camp—locale ... CO-8
*Hefley Knob* ... AR-4
Heflin—locale ... KY-4
Heflin—locale ... NC-3
Heflin—locale ... VA-3
**Heflin**—pop pl ... AL-4
**Heflin**—pop pl ... LA-4
Heflin, Lake—reservoir ... AL-4
Heflin AME Ch—church ... AL-4
Heflin-Beda (CCD)—cens area ... KY-4
Heflin (CCD)—cens area ... AL-4
Heflin Cem—cemetery (2) ... AL-4
Heflin Cem—cemetery ... AR-4
Heflin Cem—cemetery (3) ... TN-4
Heflin Cem—cemetery ... TX-5
Heflin City Hall—building ... AL-4
Heflin Creek—stream ... CO-8
Heflin Creek—stream ... KY-4
Heflin Creek—stream ... OR-9
Heflin Dam—dam ... AL-4
Heflin Division—civil ... AL-4
Heflin Grammar Sch (historical)—school ... AL-4
Hefling Run—stream ... OH-6
Heflin Sch (historical)—school ... AL-4
Heflin Spring—spring ... OR-9
Heflin Spring No 1—spring ... CO-8
Heflin Spring No 2—spring ... CO-8
Heflin Training Sch—school ... AL-4
*Heflin Water Supply Dam* ... AL-4
**He Flys Subdivision**—pop pl ... UT-8
Hefner—locale ... TX-5
Hefner, Lake—reservoir ... OK-5
Hefner Branch—stream ... TX-5
Hefner Cem—cemetery ... OH-6
Hefner Ch—church ... OK-5
Hefner Tank—reservoir ... NM-5
*Hefren Run* ... PA-2
Hefren Run—stream ... PA-2
Hefta Lake—lake ... MN-6
Heft Brook—stream ... CT-1
Hefty, Mount—summit ... AK-9
Hefty, Mount—summit ... MT-8
*Hefty Creek* ... WI-6
Hefty Creek—stream ... OR-9
Hefty Creek—stream ... WI-6
Hefty Tank—reservoir ... AZ-5
Hegan Cem—cemetery ... MS-4
Hegan Creek—stream ... OR-9
*Hegani Lake* ... WI-6
Hegar—locale ... TX-5
Hegar Branch—stream ... TX-5
Hegar Cem—cemetery ... TX-5
Hegari Windmills—locale ... TX-5
*Hegarty Cross Roads* ... PA-2
Hegarty Crossroads—locale ... PA-2
**Hegbert (Township of)**—pop pl ... MN-6
Hegdal Homestead—locale ... MT-8
Hegeler—locale ... IL-6
**Hegeler**—pop pl ... IL-6
Hegeler Park—park ... IL-6
Hegel Road Hist Dist—hist pl ... MI-6
Hegel Spring—spring ... OR-9
**Hegemanns Landing**—pop pl ... OH-6
**Hegemans Landing**—pop pl ... OH-6
*Hege Ridge* ... PA-2
*Hegewisch* ... IL-6
**Hegewisch**—pop pl ... IL-6
**Hegg**—pop pl ... WI-6
Hegge Coulee—valley ... WI-6
Heggen Mine—mine ... MT-8
Hegge Ranch—locale ... WY-8
Heggerman Hollow—valley ... MO-7
*Hegginson Ditch* ... KY-4
Hegg Lake State Wildlife Mngmt Area—park ... MN-6
Hegg Sch—school ... SD-7
Heggs Lake—lake ... SD-7
Heginbotham, W. E., House—hist pl ... CO-8
**Hegins**—pop pl ... PA-2
Hegins-Hubley Sch—school ... PA-2
**Hegins (Township of)**—pop pl ... PA-2
Hegira—locale ... KY-4
Hegland Cem—cemetery ... MN-6
Hegland Ch—church (2) ... MN-6
Heglar—locale ... ID-8
Heglar Canyon—valley ... ID-8
Heglar Chapel Cem—cemetery ... TN-4
Heglars Shoals—bar ... TN-4
Hegler Branch—stream ... TN-4
Hegler Creek—stream ... WA-9
Hegler Ford—locale ... TN-4
Hegler Mine—mine ... CA-9
*Heglers* ... OH-6
Hegleys Mill (historical)—locale ... TN-4
*Hegman Lake* ... MN-6
Hegmeister Lake—lake ... WI-6
Heg Memorial Park—park ... WI-6
*Hegna Creek* ... SD-7
**Hegne (Township of)**—pop pl ... MN-6
Hegralle Tank—reservoir ... TX-5
Hegre Cem—cemetery ... MN-6
*Hegre Cemetery* ... SD-7
Hegre Church Cem—cemetery ... MN-6
Hegre Lake—lake ... MN-6
Hegren Branch—stream ... TX-5
Hegrey Cem—cemetery ... SD-7
Hegton Town Hall—building ... ND-7
**Hegton Township**—pop pl ... ND-7
*Hegwer* ... KS-7
Hegwer Cabin—locale ... CO-8
Hegwood Bayou—stream ... LA-4
Hegwood Branch—stream ... SC-3
Hegwood Cem—cemetery ... SC-3
Hegwood Ch—church ... LA-4
*Hegwood Creek* ... AL-4
Hegwood Creek—stream ... AR-4
Hegwood Creek—stream ... OK-5
Hegwood Island—island ... LA-4
Hegwood Landing—locale ... TN-4
He Hanken Spring—spring ... MO-7
Hehe Butte—summit ... OR-9
Hehe Creek—stream ... OR-9
Hehe Lake—lake ... MI-6
*Hehe Mountain* ... WA-9
Hehe Mtn—summit ... OR-9
*Hehe Rock* ... WA-9
Hehn Draw—valley ... MT-8
He Hollow—valley ... WV-2
Hehr Cem—cemetery ... TX-5
H E Hults Lake Dam—dam ... MS-4
Heiau—locale (2) ... HI-9
Heiau in Kukuipahu—hist pl ... HI-9
Heiberg—locale ... MN-6
Heiberger—locale ... CO-8
**Heiberger**—pop pl ... AL-4
Heiberger (CCD)—cens area ... AL-4
Heiberger Cem—cemetery ... AL-4
Heiberger Division—civil ... AL-4
*Heiberger Elementary School* ... AL-4
Heiberger Methodist Ch—church ... AL-4
Heiberger Post Office (historical)—building ... AL-4
Heiberger Sch—school ... AL-4
Heibuhr Well—well ... CO-8
Heichel Run—stream ... PA-2
*Heida Drain* ... MI-6
Heide Drain—stream ... MI-6
Heidegger Hill—summit ... WA-9
**Heidelberg**—pop pl ... KY-4
**Heidelberg**—pop pl ... MN-6
**Heidelberg**—pop pl ... MS-4
**Heidelberg**—pop pl ... PA-2
**Heidelberg**—pop pl ... TX-5
**Heidelberg Beach**—pop pl ... OH-6
Heidelberg Borough—civil ... PA-2
Heidelberg Branch—stream ... FL-3
Heidelberg Cem—cemetery (3) ... MS-4
Heidelberg Cem—cemetery ... PA-2
Heidelberg Ch—church ... IN-6
Heidelberg Ch—church ... OH-6
Heidelberg Ch—church (2) ... PA-2
Heidelberg Coll—school ... OH-6
*Heidelberg Elementary School* ... MS-4
Heidelberg Hotel—hist pl ... LA-4
Heidelberg HS—school ... MS-4
Heidelberg Lookout Tower—locale ... MS-4
*Heidelberg Meeting House* ... PA-2
Heidelberg Mine—mine ... MT-8
Heidelberg Post Office—building ... MS-4
Heidelberg Sch—school ... MS-4
Heidelberg Sch—school ... PA-2
Heidelberg Sch (historical)—school ... PA-2
Heidelberg Shaft (historical)—mine ... PA-2
**Heidelberg (Township of)**—pop pl (4) ... PA-2
**Heidelburg Beach**—pop pl ... OH-6
Heidemann Coulee—valley ... ND-7
Heideman Sch—SCHOOL ... MN-6
Heiden Canyon—valley ... AK-9
Heiden Creek—stream ... AK-9
Heiden Glacier—glacier ... AK-9
**Heidenheimer**—pop pl ... TX-5
Heidepriem and Cattles Mine—mine ... SD-7
Heider Ditch—canal ... OH-6
Heider Tank—reservoir ... TX-5
*Heidi Lake* ... UT-8
Heidi Rock—island ... AK-9
Heidlebaugh Cem—cemetery ... IA-7
Heidle Cem—cemetery ... TX-5
**Heidlersburg**—pop pl ... PA-2
Heidley Park—park ... WY-8
Heidmann Lake—lake ... WI-6
*Heidmans Lake* ... WI-6
*Heidra Springs* ... AL-4
**Heidrich**—pop pl ... GA-3
Heidrich Creek—stream ... CO-8
Heidrich Creek—stream ... WY-8
Heidrich Scales Station—locale ... PA-2
Heidrich Slough—gut ... ND-7
Heidrich Station—locale ... PA-2
**Heidrick**—pop pl ... KY-4
**Heidrick**—pop pl ... PA-2
Heid Sch—school ... CO-8
Heidt Draw—valley ... WY-8
*Heidtman Canyon* ... OR-9
Heidtmann Canyon—valley ... OR-9
Heidtmann Mtn—summit ... OR-9
Heidtman Sch—school ... MI-6
Heierding Bldg—hist pl ... OK-5
Heier's Hotel—hist pl ... IN-6
Heiert Farm—hist pl ... KY-4
**Heier (Township of)**—pop pl ... MN-6
Heifer Basin—basin ... NM-5
Heifer Branch Beaver Creek—stream ... AZ-5
Heifer Camp Creek—stream ... CA-9
Heifer Canyon—valley ... NM-5
Heifer Canyon—valley ... OR-9
Heifer Creek—stream ... ID-8
Heifer Creek—stream ... KY-4
Heifer Creek—stream (2) ... MT-8
Heifer Creek—stream ... OK-5
Heifer Creek—stream ... OR-9
Heifer Creek—stream ... TX-5
Heifer Creek—stream ... WA-9
Heifer Creek—stream ... WY-8
Heiferhorn Creek—stream ... GA-3
Heifer Lake—lake ... AR-4
Heifer Lick Trail—trail ... PA-2
Heifer Pasture Tank—reservoir ... AZ-5
Heifer Pasture Well—well ... AZ-5
Heifer Pasture Windmill—locale ... WY-8
Heifer Point—cape ... NM-5
Heifer Ridge—ridge ... CA-9
Heifer Rsvr—reservoir ... ID-8
Heifers Delight Canyon—valley ... NM-5
Heifers Delight Tank—reservoir ... NM-5
Heifer Spring—spring ... AZ-5
Heifer Spring—spring ... ID-8
Heifer Springs—spring ... ID-8
Heifer Springs Creek—stream ... ID-8
Heifer Tank—reservoir (4) ... AZ-5
Heifer Tank—reservoir (2) ... NM-5
Heifer Well—well (2) ... NM-5
Heifer Well—well ... TX-5
Heifer Windmill—locale ... NM-5
Heifer Windmill—locale ... TX-5
Heiffel Branch—stream ... TX-5
Heiffer Mound—summit ... FL-3
Heiffer Tank—reservoir ... AZ-5
Heiffner Cem—cemetery ... OH-6
Heigho, Col. E. M., House—hist pl ... ID-8
Height—locale ... VA-3
*Height Gulch* ... CA-9
Height Hill—summit ... TX-5
*Height Of Land* ... MN-6
Height of Land—hist pl ... MN-6
Height Of Land Lake—lake ... MN-6
Height of Land Lookout Tower—locale ... MN-6
Height of Land Mtn—summit ... NY-2
Height of Land Portage—trail ... MN-6
Height of Land Sch—school ... NH-1
Height Of Land (Township of)—civ div ... MN-6
Heighton Hill Cem—cemetery ... IN-6
Heights—other ... PA-2
**Heights**—pop pl ... GA-3
**Heights**—pop pl ... TX-5
**Heights**—pop pl ... VA-3
**Heights**—pop pl ... WV-2
Heights—post sta ... TX-5
*Heights, The* ... MI-6
*Heights, The* ... NH-1
Heights, The—hist pl ... VT-1
Heights, The—locale ... TX-5
Heights, The—other ... MI-6
**Heights, The**—pop pl ... MI-6
Heights Baptist Ch—church ... FL-3
Heights Blvd Esplanade—hist pl ... TX-5
Heights Bridge—bridge ... PA-2
Heights Ch—church ... NM-5
Heights Christian Church—hist pl ... TX-5
**Heights Condominium, The**—pop pl ... UT-8
**Heights Corner**—pop pl ... IN-6
Heights Elem Sch—school ... FL-3
**Heights (Granite Heights)**—pop pl ... WI-6
Height Shoals—bar ... IL-6
Heights Hosp—hospital ... TX-5
Heights HS—school ... OH-6
Heights Murray Elem Sch—school ... PA-2
Heights Park—park ... MN-6
Heights Rockfeller Bldg—hist pl ... OH-6
Heights Sch—school ... CA-9
Heights Sch—school ... TX-5
Heights Sch—school ... VT-1
Heights State Bank Bldg—hist pl ... TX-5
Heights Windmill—locale ... NM-5
Heigh Valley—basin ... NE-7
*Heigstadt* ... SD-7
Heihei—summit ... HI-9
Heiheiahulu—summit ... HI-9
*Heiheiahulu Crater* ... HI-9
*Heiheihula* ... HI-9
**Heijahs Town (historical)**—pop pl ... FL-3
Heiken North Oil Field—oilfield ... KS-7
Heiken Oil Field—oilfield ... KS-7
Heiken Ranch—locale ... MT-8
Heikes Covered Bridge—hist pl ... PA-2
Heikkala Lake—lake ... MN-6
Heikkila Creek—stream ... MN-6
Heikkila Lake—lake ... MN-6
Heikkila Lake (Unorganized Territory of)—unorg ... MN-6
Heikkilla Lake—lake ... MN-6
Heikkinen Sch—school ... MI-6
**Heil**—pop pl ... ND-7
Heiland View Cem—cemetery ... PA-2
Heilberger Lake—lake ... MN-6
Heilbron House—hist pl ... CA-9
**Heilbronn**—pop pl ... FL-3
Heilbronn Spring—spring ... FL-3
**Heilbron Springs (Hillburn Spring)**—pop pl ... FL-3
Heiler Creek—stream ... WI-6
Heiliger Kanzel Overlook—locale ... WV-2
Heiliqmann Canyon—valley ... TX-5
*Heil Lake* ... WI-6
**Heil Leah (subdivision)**—pop pl ... NC-3
Heilman—locale ... PA-2
**Heilman**—pop pl ... IN-6
Heilman Ch—church ... PA-2
**Heilmandale**—pop pl ... PA-2
*Heilmandale Station* ... PA-2
Heilman Dam—dam ... PA-2
Heilman Ditch—canal ... OH-6
Heilmann Memorial Playground—park ... MI-6
**Heilmans Mill**—pop pl ... NC-3
Heilman State Public Shooting Area—park ... SD-7
Heil Park—park ... PA-2
Heilsberg, Gustave, Farm—hist pl ... WA-9
Heil Sch—school ... NE-7
Heil Sch—school ... WI-6
Heils Creek—stream ... NY-2
Heilsher Ditch—canal ... IN-6
Heilwield Corner—locale ... CT-1
**Heilwood**—pop pl ... PA-2
Heimandale Sch—school ... OH-6
Heiman Field Airp—airport ... MO-7
Heimann Ranch—locale ... NM-5
Heimanns Hill—summit ... IL-6
Heimanns Levee—levee ... IL-6
Heimbaugh Creek—stream ... CO-8
Heimberg Ditch—canal ... IN-6
Heim Bridge—bridge ... CA-9
Heim Creek—stream ... AK-9
**Heimdal**—pop pl ... ND-7
**Heimdal Township**—pop pl ... ND-7
Heimer Cem—cemetery ... TX-5
Heimer Spring—spring ... MO-7
Heimes Sch—school ... ND-7
**Heimforth**—pop pl ... MI-6
Heimforth Cem—cemetery ... MI-6
Heim Gulch—valley ... ID-8
*Heimond* ... IN-6
Heimple Park—park ... PA-2
Heimsath Cem—cemetery ... TX-5
Heim Sch—school ... CA-9
Heims Lake—lake ... MN-6
Heinaman Creek—stream ... ID-8
Heinan Flats—flat ... CO-8
Heinan Lake—lake ... CO-8
Heinatz Flat—flat ... TX-5
Heinbaugh Creek—stream ... WY-8
Heindel Drain—canal ... MI-6
Heindel Elem Sch (abandoned)—school ... PA-2
*Heindel Sch* ... PA-2
Heinecke Coulee—valley ... MT-8
Heineck Farm Airp—airport ... WA-9
Heine Creek—locale ... AK-9
Heine Creek—stream ... AK-9
*Heine Gulch* ... CA-9
Heineke Spring—spring ... NV-8
**Heineman**—pop pl ... SC-3
Heineman Airp—airport ... PA-2
Heineman Ditch—canal ... CO-8
Heineman Hill—summit ... NY-2
Heinemann Sch—school ... SD-7
*Heinemann Spring* ... WI-6
*Heinemansville* ... PA-2
*Heinemeyer Gulch* ... ID-8
Heinen, Mount—summit ... ID-8
Heinen Lake—lake ... MN-6
Heinen Pond—lake ... OR-9
Heiner—locale ... UT-8
Heiner, Daniel, House—hist pl ... UT-8
**Heiner (Pioneer)**—pop pl ... KY-4
*Heiners Creek* ... UT-8
Heiners Creek—stream ... UT-8
*Heiner Spring* ... CO-8
*Heines Bay* ... TX-5
Heine Sublateral—canal ... ID-8
Heiney Bar—bar ... CA-9
Heiney Cem—cemetery ... OH-6
Heiney Creek—stream ... OR-9
Heiney Gulch—valley ... CA-9
Heineys Bend—bend ... IN-6
Heiney's Meat Market—hist pl ... WI-6
Heiniger Lake—lake ... FL-3
Heinish Hollow—valley ... KY-4
Heinks State Wildlife Mngmt Area—park ... MN-6
*Heinlen* ... CA-9
Heinlen Lake—lake ... WA-9
Heinly Sch—school ... PA-2
Heinmann Brake—swamp ... AR-4
Heinola—locale ... MN-6
Heinold JHS—school ... OH-6
Hein Park Hist Dist—hist pl ... TN-4
Hein Post Office (historical)—building ... SD-7
Heinrich Airstrip—airport ... SD-7
Heinrich Ditch—canal ... IN-6
Heinrich Lake—lake ... MT-8
Heinrich-Martin Dam—dam ... ND-7
Heinricy Lake—reservoir ... CO-8
Heinrude Creek—stream ... MT-8
*Heinsaw Creek* ... WY-8
Heinsbergen Decorating Company Bldg—hist pl ... CA-9
Heins Creek—stream ... WA-9
Heins Creek—stream ... WI-6
Heins Lake—lake ... WA-9
Heintein Pond—lake ... NY-2
Heintooga Bald—summit ... NC-3
Heintooga Creek—stream ... NC-3
Heintooga Overlook—locale ... NC-3
Heintooga Ridge—ridge ... NC-3
Heints Bar—bar ... AL-4
Heints Landing (historical)—locale ... AL-4
Heintzelman Mine—mine ... AZ-5
Heintzen Sch—school ... MI-6
Heintz Lake—lake ... MI-6
Heintzleman Ridge—ridge ... AK-9
Heintzlemans—locale ... PA-2
Heintz Number 1 Dam—dam ... SD-7
Heintz Park—park ... OH-6
Heintz Trail—trail ... PA-2
Heinz, Bonaventura, House (first)—hist pl ... IA-7
Heinz, Bonaventura, House (second)—hist pl ... IA-7
Heinz Camp—locale ... PA-2
Heinz Canyon—valley ... UT-8
Heinz Creek—stream ... CA-9
Heinze Dam—dam ... ND-7
Heinzelman Canyon—valley ... KS-7
Heinz Gilbert Mine—mine ... CA-9
Heinz Hall—building ... PA-2
Heinz Hall Memorial Chapel—church ... PA-2
Heinz Hill—summit ... PA-2
Heinz Lake—lake ... MI-6
Heinzman Airp—airport ... IN-6
Heinz Oil Field—oilfield ... KS-7
Heinz Springs—spring ... WI-6
Heinz Well—well ... NM-5
Heipsy Hills—summit ... MS-4
Heir Airp—airport ... KS-7
*Heird Pond* ... MA-1
Heiress Lake—lake ... WI-6
Heirline Covered Bridge—hist pl ... PA-2
Heirs Branch—stream ... AR-4
Heirs of A E Ferguson Grant—civil ... FL-3
Heirs of Ambrose Hull Grant—civil ... FL-3
Heirs of F P Fatio Grant—civil ... FL-3
Heirs of Hudnall Grant—civil ... FL-3
Heirs of John H McIntosh Grant—civil ... FL-3
Heirs of Joseph Hogans Grant—civil ... FL-3
Heirs of Juan Garcia—civil ... FL-3
Heirs of Paul Dupont Grant—civil ... FL-3
Heirs of Peter Bagley Grant—civil ... FL-3
Heirs of Thomas Fitch Grant—civil ... FL-3
Heirs of Wiggins Grant—civil ... FL-3
Heirs of Wm Williams Grant—civil ... FL-3
Heise—locale ... ID-8
Heise Company Ditch—canal ... NV-8
Heisel Lake—lake ... WI-6
Heisen, Henry, House—hist pl ... WA-9
Heise Park—park ... OH-6
*Heise Pond* ... SC-3
Heiser, Rosenfeld, and Strauss Buildings—hist pl ... MD-2
Heiser Canyon—valley ... CA-9
Heiser Cem—cemetery ... KS-7
Heiser Corners—locale ... OH-6
*Heiser Creek* ... CA-9
Heiser Hill—summit ... IN-6
Heiser Hollow—valley ... TX-5
Heiser Lake—lake ... CA-9
Heiserman Coulee—valley ... MT-8
Heiser Pond Dam—dam ... SD-7
Heiser Slough—gut ... IL-6
Heiser Spring—spring ... AZ-5
Heise Run—locale ... PA-2
Heise Run—stream ... PA-2
Heise Run Sch—school ... PA-2
Heiser Valley—valley ... WI-6
Heiser Wash—stream ... AZ-5
Heisetts Hollow—valley ... UT-8
Heisey House—hist pl ... PA-2
Heishman Ch—church ... WV-2
Heisic Cem—cemetery ... TX-5
**Heisig**—pop pl ... MN-6
**Heiskell**—pop pl ... TN-4
Heiskell Branch—stream ... TN-4
Heiskell Cem—cemetery ... TN-4
Heiskell Ch—church ... TN-4
Heiskell Hollow—valley ... VA-3
Heiskell Mine—mine ... TN-4
Heiskell Pit—cave ... TN-4
Heiskell Post Office—building ... TN-4
*Heiskells* ... TN-4
Heiskell Sch—school ... TN-4
Heiskells Mill (historical)—locale ... TN-4
Heiskell United Methodist Ch—church ... TN-4
Heisler Cem—cemetery ... IA-7
Heisler Creek—stream ... IA-7
Heisler Creek—stream ... OR-9
Heisler Park—park ... CA-9
Heisler Sch—school ... IL-6
Heislers Creek—stream ... WA-9
Heisler Station (site)—locale ... OR-9
**Heislerville**—pop pl ... NJ-2
Heislerville Fish and Wildlife Mngmt Area—park ... NJ-2
Heison (RR name for Heisson)—other ... WA-9
Heiss, William A., House and Buggy Shop—hist pl ... PA-2
Heissner Ranch—locale ... TX-5
**Heisson**—pop pl ... WA-9
**Heisson (RR name Heison)**—pop pl ... WA-9
Heisspitz, The—summit ... CO-8
Heist—locale ... UT-8
Heistand Cem—cemetery ... IN-6
Heist Creek—stream ... MT-8
*Heisterburg* ... PA-2
Heister Gulch—valley ... CO-8
Heisterman Island—island ... MI-6
**Heistersburg**—pop pl ... PA-2
Heisters Creek—stream ... PA-2
*Heister Valley* ... PA-2
Heiston-Strickler House—hist pl ... VA-3
Heiter Cem—cemetery ... KY-4
Heitholt Cem—cemetery ... OK-5
Heitman Cem—cemetery ... TX-5
Heitman Lake—lake ... AK-9
Heitman Lake—lake ... MI-6
Heitman Mtn—summit ... AK-9
Heitman Sch—school ... MI-6
Heitmiller Creek—stream ... OR-9
Heitz Meadow Guard Station—locale ... CA-9
Heitz Place Courthouse—hist pl ... NY-2
Heitz Sch—school ... MT-8
Heitz Sch—school ... WI-6
**Heizer**—pop pl ... KS-7
**Heizer**—pop pl ... WV-2
Heizer Creek—stream ... WV-2
Heizer JHS—school ... NM-5
Heizer Park—park ... NM-5
*Heizerton* ... KS-7
Hekili Point—cape ... HI-9
*Hekton* ... ND-7
*Heku Point* ... HI-9
Helane, Lake—lake ... WI-6

Helani—*summit* HI-9
Helani Ridge—*ridge* HI-9
*Hela River* AZ-5
Helberg Park—*park* TX-5
Helbert Cem—*cemetery* TN-4
Helbig—*locale* TX-5
Helbing Ranch—*locale* CA-9
Helbing Sch—*school* TX-5
**Held**—*pop pl* IL-6
*Held Creek* MI-6
Held Creek—*stream* WY-8
Helde Lake—*lake* ND-7
Heldeno Well (Flowing)—*well* TX-5
Helderberg Lake—*lake* NY-2
Helderberg Mountains—*range* NY-2
Helderberg Reformed Dutch Church—*hist pl* NY-2
Helderbrand Ford—*locale* TN-4
Helderman Creek—*stream* MO-7
*Heldermann Creek* MO-7
Heldermann Sch (abandoned)—*school* MO-7
Heldman Ditch—*canal* OH-6
Heldman Homestead—*locale* CO-8
Heldnfelt—*locale* TX-5
Held-Poage House—*hist pl* CA-9
Held Ranch—*locale* NE-7
Heldreth Hollow—*valley* VA-3
Helds Cove—*bay* NY-2
Helds Island—*island* MO-7
Helds Island Public Access—*locale* MO-7
Heldt—*locale* NE-7
Heldt—*locale* WY-8
Heldt Creek—*stream* WA-9
*Heleakala* HI-9
*Heleakala Mountain* HI-9
*Heleakala Peak* HI-9
Helean Camp—*locale* MT-8
Helebore Creek—*stream* WA-9
**Helechal**—*pop pl* PR-3
Helechal (Barrio)—*fmr MCD* PR-3
Helechawa—*locale* KY-4
Helechawa Interchange—*other* KY-4
Heleleikeoha Stream—*stream* HI-9
*Helemano Ditch* HI-9
*Helemano Gulch* HI-9
Helemano Radio Station—*military* HI-9
Helemano Reservoir Ditch—*canal* HI-9
Helemano Sch—*school* HI-9
Helemano Stream—*stream* HI-9
Helem Lake—*lake* MO-7
*Helems Creek* FL-3
*Helen* PA-2
*Helen* MP-9
Helen—*locale* FL-3
Helen—*locale* PA-2
Helen—*locale* WA-9
**Helen**—*pop pl* GA-3
**Helen**—*pop pl* MD-2
**Helen**—*pop pl* WV-2
Helen, Lake—*lake* (2) AK-9
Helen, Lake—*lake* (4) CA-9
Helen, Lake—*lake* (4) FL-3
Helen, Lake—*lake* GA-3
Helen, Lake—*lake* (2) MN-6
Helen, Lake—*lake* NE-7
Helen, Lake—*lake* NY-2
Helen, Lake—*lake* ND-7
Helen, Lake—*lake* WA-9
Helen, Lake—*lake* (2) WI-6
Helen, Lake—*lake* WY-8
Helen, Lake—*reservoir* AL-4
Helen, Mount—*summit* CA-9
Helen, Mount—*summit* CO-8
Helen, Mount—*summit* KS-7
Helen, Mount—*summit* MT-8
Helen, Mount—*summit* NV-8
Helen, Mount—*summit* WY-8
*Helena* MS-4
*Helena* NC-3
*Helena* ND-7
Helena—*fmr MCD* NE-7
Helena—*locale* AZ-5
Helena—*locale* ID-8
Helena—*locale* IL-6
Helena—*locale* IA-7
Helena—*locale* KS-7
Helena—*locale* LA-4
Helena—*locale* MI-6
Helena—*locale* OH-6
**Helena**—*pop pl* AL-4
**Helena**—*pop pl* AR-4
**Helena**—*pop pl* CA-9
**Helena**—*pop pl* GA-3
**Helena**—*pop pl* KY-4
**Helena**—*pop pl* MI-6
**Helena**—*pop pl* MS-4
**Helena**—*pop pl* MO-7
**Helena**—*pop pl* MT-8
**Helena**—*pop pl* NY-2
**Helena**—*pop pl* OH-6
**Helena**—*pop pl* OK-5
**Helena**—*pop pl* SC-3
**Helena**—*pop pl* TN-4
**Helena**—*pop pl* TX-5
**Helena**—*pop pl* WI-6
Helena, Lake—*reservoir* MT-8
Helena, Mount—*summit* MT-8
Helena Airport—*airport* MT-8
Helena Campground—*locale* CO-8
Helena Canyon—*valley* CO-8
Helena (CCD)—*cens area* OK-5
Helena Cem—*cemetery* IA-7
Helena Cem—*cemetery* LA-4
Helena Cem—*cemetery* NE-7
Helena Cem—*cemetery* TX-5
*Helena Cemetery* AL-4
Helena Ch—*church* MS-4
*Helena Church* AL-4
Helena Creek—*stream* AK-9
Helena Creek—*stream* WA-9
**Helena Crossing**—*pop pl* AR-4
Helena Cumberland Presbyterian Ch—*church* AL-4
Helena Depot—*hist pl* AR-4
Helena Elem Sch—*school* AL-4
Helena Flat Sch—*school* MT-8
Helena Gulch—*valley* MT-8
Helena Hist Dist—*hist pl* CA-9
Helena Hist Dist—*hist pl* MT-8
Helena (historical)—*locale* MS-4
Helena (historical P.O.)—*locale* IA-7
Helena Island Number Sixty—*island* MS-4
Helena Lake—*lake* MI-6
Helena Lake—*lake* (2) WA-9
Helena Lake—*swamp* MN-6
Helena Library and Museum—*hist pl* AR-4
Helena Mine—*mine* AZ-5
Helena Mine—*mine* OR-9
Helena Mine (underground)—*mine* AL-4
Helena Natl For—*forest* MT-8
Helena Number Two Mine (underground)—*mine* AL-4
Helena Oil Field—*oilfield* LA-4
Helena Peak—*summit* WA-9
Helena Post Office (historical)—*building* TN-4
Helena Reach—*channel* (2) MS-4
Helena Reach—*stream* AR-4
Helena Revet—*levee* AR-4
Helena Ridge—*ridge* WA-9
Helena (RR name for Timberlake)—*other* NC-3
Helena RR Station—*building* AZ-5
Helena Run—*stream* FL-3
Helena Saddle—*gap* OR-9
Helena Sch—*school* NC-3
Helena Sch—*school* TN-4
Helena South-Central Hist Dist—*hist pl* MT-8
Helena State Sch for Boys—*school* OK-5
Helena Towhead—*island* AR-4
**Helena Township**—*pop pl* ND-7
Helena Township (historical)—*civil* ND-7
**Helena (Township of)**—*pop pl* MI-6
**Helena (Township of)**—*pop pl* MN-6
Helena Valley Canal—*canal* MT-8
Helena Valley Canal Tunnel—*tunnel* MT-8
Helena Valley Regulating Rsvr—*reservoir* MT-8
Helena-West Helena Central HS—*school* AR-4
Helen Baller Sch—*school* WA-9
Helen Bay—*bay* AK-9
Helen Beryl Mine—*mine* SD-7
Helen Buttes—*summit* WA-9
Helen (CCD)—*cens area* GA-3
Helen Channel—*channel* PW-9
Helen Chapel—*hist pl* OH-6
Helen Creek—*stream* (3) AK-9
Helen Creek—*stream* (2) ID-8
Helen Creek—*stream* MT-8
Helen Creek—*stream* OR-9
Helen Creek—*stream* WA-9
Helen Creek—*stream* WI-6
Helen Creek Trail—*trail* MT-8
Helen Creek Way—*trail* OR-9
**Helendale**—*pop pl* CA-9
Helendale Church*—*church* ND-7
Helendale Reservation—*reserve* CA-9
**Helendale Township**—*pop pl* ND-7
Helen D Cohen Preschool of Temple Judea—*school* FL-3
Helende Campground—*locale* ID-8
Helende Creek—*stream* ID-8
Helene—*locale* NV-8
Helene, Lake—*lake* CO-8
Helene, Lake—*lake* FL-3
Helene, Lake—*lake* MD-2
Helene Lake—*lake* MN-6
Helene Mine—*mine* MT-8
Helene Wash—*stream* NV-8
Helen Furnace—*locale* PA-2
Helen Glacier—*glacier* WY-8
Helen Gohlke Oil Field—*oilfield* TX-5
Helen Gulch—*valley* AK-9
Helen Hunt Falls—*falls* CO-8
Helen Island—*island* AK-9
Helen Island—*island* MI-6
Helen Island—*island* PW-9
Helen Keller Home—*building* AL-4
Helen Keller HS—*school* MI-6
Helen Keller Park—*park* CA-9
Helen Keller Sch—*school* CA-9
Helen Keller Sch of Alabama—*school* AL-4
Helen Key—*island* FL-3
*Helen Lake* CA-9
*Helen Lake* MN-6
Helen Lake—*lake* (3) CA-9
Helen Lake—*lake* (3) MI-6
Helen Lake—*lake* MN-6
Helen Lake—*lake* MT-8
Helen Lake—*lake* (2) OR-9
Helen Lake—*lake* UT-8
Helen Lake—*lake* WI-6
Helen Lake—*reservoir* MS-4
Helen Lake Trail—*trail* MT-8
**Helen Mills**—*pop pl* PA-2
Helen Mine—*mine* CA-9
Helen Mine—*mine* MN-6
Helenmode Pyrite Mine—*mine* TN-4
Helen Mtn—*summit* MT-8
Helen of Troy, Lake—*lake* CA-9
Helen Peak—*summit* AK-9
*Helen Place* MS-4
Helen Pond—*lake* ME-1
Helen Rae Mine—*mine* NM-5
Helen Reef—*bar* PW-9
*Helens Bluff School* TN-4
**Helens Crossroads**—*pop pl* NC-3
Helens Dome—*summit* (2) AZ-5
Helen Shaft—*mine* NV-8
**Helens Run**—*pop pl* WV-2
Helens Run—*stream* WV-2
Helens Spring—*spring* OR-9
Helen Street Sch—*school* CT-1
Helentown Hist Dist—*hist pl* KY-4
**Helen (Township of)**—*pop pl* MN-6
**Helenville**—*pop pl* WI-6
**Helenwood**—*pop pl* TN-4
Helenwood Baptist Ch—*church* TN-4
Helenwood Post Office—*building* TN-4
Helenwood Sch (historical)—*school* TN-4
*Hele Run* PA-2
Helester Point—*summit* CA-9
*Heleu* PW-9
Heley Lake—*lake* FL-3
**Helfenstein**—*pop pl* (2) PA-2
*Helfer Creek* TX-5
Helfer Creek Tank—*reservoir* TX-5
Helfer Hill—*summit* ME-1
Helfer Log Landing—*locale* AR-4
Helfrich, Michael D., House—*hist pl* IN-6
Helfrich And Hoppe Ditch—*canal* IN-6
Helfrich Landing Park—*park* OR-9
Helfrich Park—*park* IN-6
Helfrich Park Elementary and JHS—*school* IN-6
*Helfrich Park Sch* IN-6
*Helfrichs Cave* PA-2
*Helfrich Spring* PA-2
Helfrich Springs Cave—*cave* PA-2
Helfrichs Spring—*spring* PA-2
Helfrich's Springs Grist Mill—*hist pl* PA-2
**Helfrichsville**—*pop pl* PA-2
*Helfrick Airport* PA-2
Helfricks Heliport—*airport* PA-2
Helga Lake—*lake* MN-6
**Helga (Township of)**—*pop pl* MN-6
**Helgeland (Township of)**—*pop pl* MN-6
Helgen Cem—*cemetery* SD-7
Helgen (historical)—*locale* SD-7
Helger Ranch—*locale* MT-8
Helgerson Ridge—*ridge* WI-6
Helgesen Park—*park* IL-6
Helgeson Lake—*lake* MN-6
*Helgramite Lake* CA-9
Helianthus Cove—*bay* AK-9
HELIANTHUS III (yacht)—*hist pl* MD-2
Helianthus Passage—*channel* AK-9
Helias HS—*school* MO-7
*Helicon* AL-4
**Helicon**—*pop pl* (2) AL-4
Helicon Ch—*church* (2) AL-4
Helicon Sch—*school* AL-4
Helicopter Airways of Indiana—*airport* IN-6
Helio Creek—*stream* MT-8
Heliograph Hill—*summit* TX-5
Heliograph Lookout Complex—*hist pl* AZ-5
Heliograph Peak—*summit* AZ-5
Heliograph Ranger Lookout—*locale* AZ-5
Heliograph Spring—*spring* AZ-5
*Helio Mountain* OR-9
Helios Ranch—*hist pl* CA-9
Heliotrope Ave Sch—*school* CA-9
Heliotrope Creek—*stream* WA-9
Heliotrope Mtn—*summit* UT-8
Heliotrope Point—*summit* UT-8
Heliotrope Post Office (historical)—*building* TN-4
Heliotrope Ridge—*ridge* WA-9
*Helisma (sta. (Burson)* CA-9
**Helix**—*pop pl* OR-9
Helix, Mount—*summit* CA-9
Helix Cem—*cemetery* OR-9
Helix Creek—*stream* ID-8
Helix Cross—*locale* CA-9
Helix HS—*school* CA-9
**Helixville**—*pop pl* PA-2
Hell—*locale* CA-9
**Hell**—*pop pl* MI-6
Hell, The—*area* NY-2
*Hellam* PA-2
*Hellam (corporate name Hallam)* PA-2
Hellam Hills—*range* PA-2
**Hellam (Township of)**—*pop pl* PA-2
Helland, Mount—*summit* TX-5
Hell and Gone Creek—*stream* OK-5
Hell and Purgatory Airp—*airport* NC-3
Hellard Branch—*stream* KY-4
Hellard Cem—*cemetery* OK-5
Hell Bays—*bay* FL-3
Hellbeck Sch—*school* CO-8
Hell Bend—*bend* TN-4
Hellbent Creek—*stream* AK-9
Hellberg Spring—*spring* MO-7
Hellbore Spring—*spring* OR-9
Hell Bottom Swamp—*swamp* ME-1
Hellbranch Run—*stream* OH-6
*Hell Canyon* AZ-5
*Hell Canyon* UT-8
Hell Canyon—*gap* AZ-5
Hell Canyon—*valley* (2) AZ-5
Hell Canyon—*valley* (4) CO-8
Hell Canyon—*valley* (2) ID-8
Hell Canyon—*valley* (3) NM-5
Hell Canyon—*valley* (2) SD-7
Hell Canyon—*valley* TX-5
Hell Canyon—*valley* (6) UT-8
Hell Canyon—*valley* WY-8
Hell Canyon Bridge—*hist pl* AZ-5
Hell Canyon Drain—*canal* NM-5
Hell Canyon Wash—*stream* NM-5
Hell Canyon Wasteway—*canal* NM-5
Hellcat Bay—*swamp* FL-3
Hell Cat Bay—*swamp* FL-3
Hell Cat Bay—*swamp* NC-3
*Hell Cat Lake* AL-4
Hellcat Lake—*lake* AL-4
Hell Cat Rock—*summit* OR-9
Hell Cem—*cemetery* AR-4
Hell Cem—*cemetery* KY-4
Hell Coulee—*valley* MN-6
*Hell Creek* AL-4
*Hell Creek* VA-3
*Hell Creek* WY-8
Hell Creek—*stream* AR-4
Hell Creek—*stream* (2) CA-9
Hell Creek—*stream* (7) CO-8
Hell Creek—*stream* (6) ID-8
Hell Creek—*stream* (2) KS-7
Hell Creek—*stream* KY-4
Hell Creek—*stream* MS-4
Hell Creek—*stream* (6) MT-8
Hell Creek—*stream* NE-7
Hell Creek—*stream* NV-8
Hell Creek—*stream* OK-5
Hell Creek—*stream* PA-2
Hell Creek—*stream* (4) WA-9
Hell Creek—*stream* WV-2
Hell Creek—*stream* WY-8
Hell Creek Ditch—*canal* CO-8
Hell Creek Rec Area—*park* MT-8
*Hell Creek Spring* NV-8
Hell Creek Structure LT-9b-2 Dam—*dam* MS-4
Hell Creek Watershed LT-9b-3 Dam—*dam* MS-4
Hell Creek Watershed LT-9b-4 Dam—*dam* MS-4
Hell Creek Watershed LT-9b-5 Dam—*dam* MS-4
Hell Creek Watershed LT-9b-6 Dam—*dam* MS-4
Helldiver Lake—*lake* ID-8
Helldiver Lake—*swamp* MI-6
Hell Diver Lakes—*lake* CA-9
Helldiver Pond—*lake* NY-2
Helldive Spring—*spring* AZ-5
Helle Lake—*lake* MN-6
*Hellen* MD-2
*Hellen* PA-2
Hellena Mine—*mine* CO-8
Hellen Bar—*bar* MD-2
Hellen Blazes, Lake—*lake* FL-3
Hellen Creek—*stream* MD-2
Hellendale Town Hall—*building* ND-7
Hellendale Township—*civil* ND-7
*Hellen Gut* MD-2
Hellenic American Sch—*school* MA-1
Hellenic Orthodox Church of the Assumption—*hist pl* UT-8
**Hellen Mills**—*pop pl* PA-2
Hellens Bluff Sch—*school* TN-4
*Hellens Creek* MD-2
*Hellen's Gut* MD-2
Heller, Edward, Residence—*hist pl* OH-6
Heller, Isadore H., House—*hist pl* IL-6
Heller, Mount—*summit* CA-9
Heller, William Jacob, House—*hist pl* PA-2
Heller Butte—*summit* NV-8
Heller Cem—*cemetery* (2) OH-6
Heller Ch—*church* PA-2
Heller Coulee—*valley* WI-6
Heller Creek—*stream* ID-8
Heller Creek—*stream* NY-2
Heller Creek—*stream* WA-9
Heller Creek Recreation Site—*locale* ID-8
Heller Ditch—*canal* OH-6
Heller Estate—*hist pl* CA-9
Heller Grave—*cemetery* ID-8
Heller Hill—*summit* WI-6
Heller Hotel—*hist pl* KY-4
Heller Lake—*lake* TX-5
Heller Lake—*lake* UT-8
Heller Lake—*reservoir* UT-8
Heller Lake Dam—*dam* UT-8
Heller Parkway Station—*locale* NJ-2
Heller Rsvr—*reservoir* OR-9
*Hellers* PA-2
Hellers Bend—*bend* CA-9
Hellers Branch—*stream* TX-5
Heller Sch—*school* (2) IL-6
Heller Sch—*school* MT-8
Hellers Creek—*stream* SC-3
Hellers Hill—*summit* TX-5
Hellers Peak—*summit* MT-8
Heller Spring—*spring* CA-9
*Hellerstown* PA-2
Heller Tank—*reservoir* NM-5
**Hellertown**—*pop pl* PA-2
Hellertown Borough—*civil* PA-2
*Hellertown Cave* PA-2
*Hellertown Cemetery* PA-2
Hellertown Ch—*church* PA-2
Hellertown Park—*park* PA-2
Hellertown Rsvr—*reservoir* PA-2
Hellertown Union Cem—*cemetery* PA-2
*Hellerville* PA-2
Helle Slough—*lake* ND-7
Helley Bluffs Ch—*church* MO-7
*Helleys Creek* TN-4
Hell Fire Flat—*flat* OR-9
Hellfire Run—*stream* PA-2
*Hell for Brush Creek* OR-9
Hell For Certain Branch—*stream* WV-2
Hell For Certain Creek—*stream* (2) KY-4
Hell For Slim Draw—*valley* OR-9
Hell For Sure—*ridge* CA-9
Hell For Sure Canyon—*valley* CA-9
Hell for Sure Lake—*lake* CA-9
Hell For Sure Pass—*gap* CA-9
Hell Gap—*gap* CO-8
Hell Gap—*gap* WY-8
*Hellgate* MT-8
Hell Gate—*bay* FL-3
Hell Gate—*cape* SC-3
Hell Gate—*channel* (2) FL-3
Hell Gate—*channel* GA-3
Hell Gate—*channel* NY-2
Hellgate—*gap* CO-8
Hell Gate—*gap* MT-8
Hellgate—*gap* OR-9
Hell Gate—*locale* FL-3
Hell Gate—*locale* NH-1
Hell Gate—*stream* NY-2
Hell Gate—*uninc pl* NY-2
Hell Gate Bridge—*bridge* NY-2
Hellgate Brook—*stream* (2) NH-1
Hellgate Campground—*locale* MT-8
*Hellgate Canyon* SD-7
Hellgate Canyon—*valley* MT-8
Hellgate Canyon—*valley* OR-9
Hell Gate Canyon—*valley* WA-9
Hellgate Coulee—*valley* MT-8
*Hellgate Creek* VA-3
Hell Gate Creek—*gut* NC-3
Hellgate Creek—*stream* ID-8
*Hellgate Gulch* SD-7
Hellgate Gulch—*valley* CO-8
Hellgate Gulch—*valley* MT-8
Hellgate HS—*school* MT-8
Hellgate Mtn—*summit* AZ-5
Hell Gate Point—*cape* FL-3
Hellgate Pond—*lake* GA-3
Hellgate Ridge—*ridge* VA-3
*Hell Gate River* ID-8
*Hell Gate River* WA-9
Hell Gate Rsvr—*reservoir* MT-8
Hellgate Sch—*school* MT-8
Hellgate Spring—*spring* UT-8
Hellgate Swamp—*swamp* GA-3
**Hellgate Villa Condominiums**—*pop pl* UT-8
Hell Gate Yard—*locale* NY-2
Hellgrammite Lake—*lake* CA-9
*Hell Hole* LA-4
*Hell Hole* UT-8
Hell Hole—*area* AZ-5
Hell Hole—*area* NM-5
Hellhole—*basin* (2) TN-4
Hell Hole—*basin* TN-4
Hellhole—*basin* (2) UT-8
Hell Hole—*bay* LA-4
Hell Hole—*bay* NY-2
Hell Hole—*bay* WY-8
Hell Hole—*bend* (2) UT-8
Hellhole—*cave* TN-4
Hellhole—*locale* ID-8
Hell Hole—*swamp* CA-9
Hell Hole—*valley* (2) CA-9
Hell Hole—*valley* ID-8
Hell Hole—*valley* (2) UT-8
Hell Hole Basin—*basin* UT-8
Hellhole Bay—*lake* LA-4
Hellhole Bay—*swamp* SC-3
*Hell Hole Bayou* LA-4
Hellhole Bayou—*gut* LA-4
Hell Hole Bayou—*stream* LA-4
Hell Hole Bayou Gas Field—*oilfield* LA-4
Hellhole Bend—*bend* AZ-5
Hellhole Branch—*stream* GA-3
Hellhole Branch—*stream* TN-4
Hellhole Canyon—*valley* (2) CA-9
Hell Hole Canyon—*valley* ID-8
Hellhole Canyon—*valley* UT-8
Hell Hole Canyon—*valley* (2) UT-8
Hellhole Canyon—*valley* UT-8
Hell Hole Coulee—*valley* MT-8
*Hellhole Creek* MS-4
Hell Hole Creek—*stream* AL-4
Hell Hole Creek—*stream* CA-9
Hell Hole Creek—*stream* ID-8
Hell Hole Creek—*stream* MS-4
Hellhole Creek—*stream* OR-9
Hellhole Creek—*stream* SC-3
Hell Hole Creek—*stream* SC-3
Hell Hole Creek—*stream* UT-8
Hell Hole Creek—*stream* WI-6
Hellhole Flat—*flat* CA-9
Hell Hole Hollow—*valley* MO-7
*Hellhole Lake* CA-9
Hellhole Lake—*lake* CA-9
Hell Hole Lake—*lake* UT-8
Hell Hole Meadow—*flat* CA-9
Hellhole Mtn—*summit* GA-3
Hellhole Mtn—*summit* TN-4
Hellhole Palms—*locale* CA-9
Hell Hole Ridge—*ridge* CA-9
Hell Hole Ridge—*ridge* UT-8
Hell Hole Rsvr—*reservoir* CA-9
Hell Hole Rsvr—*reservoir* UT-8
*Hell Holes* AZ-5
Hell Hole Sink Cave—*cave* TN-4
Hellhole Spring—*spring* UT-8
Hell Hole Swale—*basin* UT-8
Hellhole Swamp—*stream* SC-3
Hell Hole Valley—*valley* AZ-5
Hell Hollow—*basin* OH-6
Hell Hollow—*locale* NH-1
Hell Hollow—*valley* CA-9
Hell Hollow—*valley* CT-1
Hell Hollow—*valley* MT-8
Hell Hollow—*valley* (2) NY-2
Hell Hollow—*valley* OR-9
Hell Hollow—*valley* PA-2
Hell Hollow—*valley* (2) TN-4
Hell Hollow—*valley* WI-6
Hell Hollow Brook—*stream* VT-1
Hell Hollow Trail—*trail* PA-2
Hell Hook Marsh—*swamp* MD-2
Hellican, The—*summit* TN-4
Hellick Lake—*lake* ND-7
Hellickson Ranch—*locale* ND-7
*Hellicon Creek* MS-4
**Hellier**—*pop pl* KY-4
Hellier (CCD)—*cens area* KY-4
Helling Cem—*cemetery* MO-7
Helling Creek—*stream* WI-6
Hellings Corner—*locale* PA-2
Hellings Lakes—*lake* MO-7
*Hellings Mill* AZ-5
Hellion Canyon—*valley* NM-5
Hellion Canyon—*valley* OR-9
*Hellion Creek* MS-4
Hellion Rapids—*rapids* OR-9
Hellion Ridge—*ridge* OR-9
Hell Island Site—*hist pl* DE-2
Hellkamp Creek—*stream* MN-6
Hell Kitchen Gap—*gap* PA-2
Hell Lake—*lake* WA-9
Hellman Sch Number 2—*school* ND-7
Hellman Sch Number 4—*school* ND-7
*Hellmans Lake* WI-6
Hellmans Point—*cliff* IN-6
Hellman Spring—*spring* NV-8
Hellmers Park—*park* CA-9
Hell Mtn—*summit* NJ-2
Hell Neck—*cape* VA-3
Hell'n Maria Canyon—*valley* UT-8
Hell'n Maria Kitchen—*basin* UT-8
Hello Bay Spring—*spring* OR-9
Hello Canyon—*valley* CA-9
*Hello Ditch* AR-4
*Hell of Bush Creek* OR-9
Helloff Creek—*stream* OR-9
**Helloff (historical)**—*pop pl* OR-9
Hello Lake—*lake* CA-9
Hell Pass Coast—*beach* LA-4
*Hell Peckish Bay* FL-3
Hell Pocosin—*swamp* NC-3
Hell Point—*cliff* AZ-5
Hell Point Creek—*gut* VA-3
*Hell Pond* MA-1
Hell Rapids—*rapids* ME-1
Hell Roaring Basin—*basin* MT-8
Hell Roaring Canyon—*valley* MT-8
Hellroaring Canyon—*valley* MT-8
Hell Roaring Canyon—*valley* MT-8
Hellroaring Canyon—*valley* OR-9
Hellroaring Canyon—*valley* UT-8
Hell Roaring Canyon—*valley* UT-8
*Hellroaring Creek* MT-8
*Hell Roaring Creek* OK-5
*Hell Roaring Creek* WY-8
Hell Roaring Creek—*stream* AK-9
Hell Roaring Creek—*stream* CO-8
Hellroaring Creek—*stream* (2) ID-8
Hell Roaring Creek—*stream* ID-8
Hell Roaring Creek—*stream* (2) MT-8
Hellroaring Creek—*stream* (2) MT-8
Hell Roaring Creek—*stream* (4) MT-8
Hellroaring Creek—*stream* (3) MT-8
Hell Roaring Creek—*stream* MT-8
Hellroaring Creek—*stream* MT-8
Hellroaring Creek—*stream* (2) OK-5
Hellroaring Creek—*stream* OR-9
Hell Roaring Creek—*stream* TX-5
Hell Roaring Creek—*stream* WA-9
Hellroaring Creek—*stream* WA-9
Hellroaring Creek—*stream* WY-8
Hellroaring Ditch—*canal* WA-9
Hell Roaring Gulch—*valley* CA-9
Hell Roaring Hollow—*valley* TX-5
Hell Roaring Lake—*lake* ID-8
Hell Roaring Lake—*lake* MT-8
Hellroaring Lakes—*lake* MT-8
Hellroaring Meadow—*flat* WA-9
Hellroaring Mesa—*summit* (2) NM-5
Hell Roaring Mesa—*summit* NM-5
Hell Roaring Mesa Tank—*reservoir* NM-5
*Hell Roaring Mountain* MT-8
Hellroaring Mtn—*summit* MT-8
Hellroaring Pass—*gap* MT-8
*Hell Roaring Plateau* MT-8
Hellroaring Plateau—*plain* MT-8
Hell Roaring Point—*cape* MT-8
Hellroaring Ranger Station—*locale* MT-8
Hellroaring Ranger Station—*locale* WY-8
Hellroaring Ridge—*ridge* ID-8
Hellroaring Ridge Trail—*trail* ID-8
Hellroaring Spring—*spring* MO-7
Hell Roaring Spring—*spring* MT-8
*Hell RR Hollow* TX-5
Hell Run—*stream* PA-2
Hell Run—*stream* WV-2
Hells Acres Gulch—*valley* NV-8
Hells Acre Springs—*spring* WI-6
Hellsapoppin Well—*well* AZ-5
Hells Backbone—*ridge* UT-8
Hells Basin—*basin* WA-9
Hells Bay—*bay* FL-3
Hells Bay—*swamp* FL-3
Hells Bay Canoe Trail—*trail* FL-3
Hells Bellows—*basin* UT-8
*Hells Bend* TN-4
Hells Bend—*bend* VA-3
Hells Bottom Run—*stream* MD-2
Hells Branch—*stream* IL-6
*Hells Canyon* OR-9
Hells Canyon—*valley* (4) AZ-5
Hells Canyon—*valley* (2) CA-9
Hells Canyon—*valley* (3) CO-8
Hells Canyon—*valley* (2) ID-8
Hells Canyon—*valley* KS-7
Hells Canyon—*valley* MT-8
Hells Canyon—*valley* (5) NM-5
Hells Canyon—*valley* OR-9
Hells Canyon—*valley* SD-7
Hells Canyon—*valley* TX-5
Hells Canyon—*valley* (3) UT-8
Hells Canyon—*valley* WA-9
Hells Canyon—*valley* (3) WY-8
Hells Canyon Archeol District—*hist pl* ID-8
Hells Canyon Archeol District—*hist pl* OR-9
Hells Canyon Creek—*stream* MT-8
Hells Canyon Creek—*stream* OR-9
Hells Canyon Dam—*dam* OR-9
Hells Canyon Draw—*valley* WY-8
Hells Canyon Guard Station—*locale* MT-8
Hells Canyon Natl Rec Area—*reserve* OR-9
Hells Canyon Ranch—*locale* MT-8
Hells Canyon Rapids—*rapids* OR-9
Hells Canyon Rsvr—*reservoir* OR-9
Hells Canyon Spring—*spring* AZ-5
Hells Canyon Tank—*reservoir* (3) AZ-5
Hells Canyon Well—*well* NM-5
Hells Canyon Wilderness Area—*reserve* OR-9
Hells Corner Sch—*school* NE-7
*Hells Creek* MI-6
Hells Creek—*stream* AL-4
Hells Creek—*stream* ID-8
Hells Crossing Campground—*locale* WA-9
Hells Delight Canyon—*valley* CA-9
Hells Delight Creek—*stream* CA-9
Hells Delight Valley—*basin* CA-9
Hells Dive Spring—*spring* AZ-5
Hells Gate—*channel* FL-3
Hells Gate—*channel* GA-3
Hells Gate—*channel* TX-5
Hells Gate—*channel* WA-9
Hells Gate—*cliff* CO-8
Hells Gate—*gap* (2) AZ-5
Hells Gate—*gap* NV-8
Hells Gate—*locale* CA-9
Hells Gate—*locale* GA-3
Hellsgate—*valley* AK-9
Hells Gate Bayou—*stream* LA-4
*Hellsgate Canyon* OR-9
Hells Gate Canyon—*valley* AZ-5
Hells Gate Canyon—*valley* WA-9
Hells Gate Channel Range B—*channel* OR-9
Hells Gate Creek—*stream* ID-8
Hellsgate Gulch—*valley* SD-7
Hells Gate Point—*cape* WA-9
Hells Gate Ridge—*ridge* AZ-5
Hells Gate Trail—*trail* AZ-5
Hells Gate Trail Tank—*reservoir* AZ-5
Hells Gorge—*valley* WA-9
Hells Gulch—*valley* (2) ID-8
Hells Gulch—*valley* (2) MT-8
*Hells Half Acre* AL-4
*Hells Half Acre* MS-4
*Hells Half Acre* WY-8
Hells Half Acre—*area* (4) AZ-5
Hells Half Acre—*area* NM-5
Hells Half Acre—*area* OR-9
Hells Half Acre—*bar* ME-1
Hells Half Acre—*basin* TX-5
Hells Half Acre—*bay* FL-3
Hells Half Acre—*bench* CA-9
Hells Half Acre—*flat* (5) CA-9
Hells Half Acre—*flat* CO-8
Hells Half Acre—*flat* NV-8
Hells Half Acre—*flat* UT-8
Hells Halfacre—*gut* MS-4
Hells Half Acre—*island* FL-3
Hells Half Acre—*island* ME-1
Hells Half Acre—*locale* FL-3
Hells Halfacre—*locale* KY-4
Hells Half Acre—*locale* WY-8
Hells Half Acre—*range* WY-8
Hells Half Acre—*summit* TX-5
Hells Halfacre—*summit* TX-5
Hells Half Acre—*swamp* TX-5
Hells Half Acre Canyon—*valley* AZ-5
Hells Half Acre Canyon—*valley* WY-8
Hells Half Acre Creek—*stream* CA-9
Hells Half Acre Creek—*stream* ID-8

Hells Half Acre Mtn—summit ID-8
Hells Half Acre Saddle—gap ID-8
Hells Half Mile—rapids CO-8
Hells Hall Acre—area OR-9
Hells Hill—summit OR-9
Hells Hip Pocket—flat CO-8
Hells Hip Pocket—valley AZ-5
Hells Hole CO-8
Hells Hole—area NM-5
Hells Hole—basin (2) AZ-5
Hells Hole—basin CA-9
Hells Hole—basin (4) CO-8
Hells Hole—basin (2) UT-8
Hells Hole—basin (2) WA-9
Hells Hole—bay AK-9
Hells Hole—bend AZ-5
Hells Hole—bend CO-8
Hells Hole—bend MT-8
Hells Hole—flat CO-8
Hells Hole—stream CO-8
Hells Hole—stream NM-5
Hells Hole—summit AZ-5
Hells Hole—valley (3) AZ-5
Hells Hole—valley CO-8
Hells Hole—valley ID-8
Hells Hole—valley NM-5
Hells Hole Branch—stream TN-4
Hells Hole Canyon—valley (2) AZ-5
Hells Hole Canyon—valley (3) CO-8
Hells Hole Canyon—valley NM-5
Hells Hole Canyon—valley (2) UT-8
Hells Hole Creek—stream AZ-5
Hells Hole Gap—gap TN-4
Hells Hole Gulch—valley CO-8
Hells Hole Peak—summit AZ-5
Hells Hole Rsvr—reservoir CO-8
Hells Hole Spring—spring AZ-5
Hells Hole Tank—reservoir AZ-5
Hells Hole Well—well TX-5
Hells Hole Windmill—locale NM-5
Hells Hollow—valley (2) AZ-5
Hells Hollow—valley CA-9
Hells Hollow—valley GA-3
Hells Hollow—valley IA-7
Hells Hollow—valley OK-5
Hells Hollow—valley PA-2
Hells Hollow—valley TX-5
Hells Hollow—valley UT-8
Hells Hollow Creek—stream CA-9
Hells Hollow Ridge—ridge CA-9
Hells Hollow Tank—reservoir AZ-5
Hellsing Bluff—ridge WI-6
Hellsinger Canyon—valley CA-9
Hells Island—ridge OR-9
Hells Kitchen—area UT-8
Hells Kitchen—area WA-9
Hells Kitchen—basin NV-8
Hells Kitchen—basin PA-2
Hells Kitchen—basin (2) UT-8
Hells Kitchen—flat (2) CA-9
Hells Kitchen—valley CO-8
Hells Kitchen—valley MA-1
Hells Kitchen Canyon UT-8
Hells Kitchen Canyon—valley NV-8
Hells Kitchen Canyon—valley (2) UT-8
Hells Kitchen Gulch—valley AK-9
Hells Kitchen Lake—lake WI-6
Hells Kitchen Park—flat UT-8
Hells Kitchen Spring—spring ID-8
Hells Kitchen Vista—locale CA-9
Hells Meadows—flat CA-9
Hells Mesa—summit NM-5
Hells Mtn—summit CA-9
Hells Neck—cape DE-2
Hellsneck Hollow—valley TN-4
Hells Neck Ridge—ridge AZ-5
Hells Peak—summit CA-9
Hells Peak—summit OR-9
Hells Pocket PW-9
Hells Pocket—basin AZ-5
Hells Pocket—basin CO-8
Hells Pocket—bay FL-3
Hells Point—cape IN-6
Hells Point Ridge—ridge TN-4
Hells Swamp Branch—stream AL-4
Hells Tank—reservoir AZ-5
Hells Thicket Creek—stream MT-8
Hells Uncle Tank—reservoir AZ-5
Hells Valley MS-4
Hell Swamp—swamp MA-1
Hell Swamp—swamp NC-3
Hells Well—well AZ-5
Helltack Base—locale CA-9
Hell Tank—reservoir (2) AZ-5
Hell to Pay WA-9
Helltown IN-6
Helltown—locale CA-9
Hell Town (historical)—locale AL-4
Hellum Ford—locale AL-4
Hellum Hollow—valley TN-4
Hellum Mill Branch—stream AL-4
Hellums, Lake—reservoir OK-5
Hellums Hollow—valley MO-7
Hellwegs Creek MN-6
Hellwegs River MN-6
Hellwig Cem—cemetery WI-6
Hellwig Creek—stream MN-6
Hellyer Drain—canal ID-8
Hellyer Sch—school CA-9
Hellzapoppin Canyon—valley AZ-5
Hellzapoppin Creek—stream AZ-5
Helm—locale IL-6
Helm—locale KY-4
**Helm**—pop pl CA-9
**Helm**—pop pl MS-4
**Helm**—pop pl MO-7
**Helm**—pop pl VA-3
Helm, Benjamin, House—hist pl KY-4
Helm, John B., House—hist pl KY-4
Helman Ditch—canal IN-6
Helmans Swamp PA-2
Helman Swamp—swamp PA-2
**Helmar**—pop pl IL-6
Helmar Cem—cemetery IL-6
Helmar Lake MI-6
Helm Bay—bay AK-9
Helm Bay—locale AK-9
Helmbold Island—island IL-6
Helmbold Slough—stream IL-6
Helm Branch—stream KY-4
Helm Canal—canal (2) CA-9
Helm Canyon—valley OR-9
Helm Cem—cemetery IN-6
Helm Cem—cemetery (2) IA-7
Helm Cem—cemetery MN-6
Helm Cem—cemetery MS-4
Helm Cem—cemetery MO-7
Helm Cem—cemetery TN-4
Helm Cem—cemetery TX-5
Helm Ch—church TN-4
Helm Colonial Ditch—canal CA-9
Helm Corner—locale CA-9
Helm Creek—stream IN-6
Helm Creek—stream WA-9
Helm Creek—stream WY-8
Helmcrest IN-6
**Helmcrest**—pop pl IN-6
Helm Ditch—canal (2) CA-9
Helm Drain—canal CA-9
Helme—locale LA-4
Helme, G. W., Snuff Mill District—hist pl NJ-2
Helm-Engleman House—hist pl KY-4
Helment VA-3
**Helmer**—pop pl ID-8
**Helmer**—pop pl IN-6
**Helmer**—pop pl MI-6
Helmer Cem—cemetery (2) NY-2
Helmer Creek NY-2
Helmer Creek—stream IA-7
Helmer Creek—stream (2) MI-6
Helmer Creek—stream NY-2
Helmer Creek—stream WA-9
Helmer Gulch—valley CO-8
Helmer Hill—summit CA-9
Helmerich, Lake—reservoir IN-6
Helmer Lake MI-6
Helmer Mtn—summit MT-8
Helmer Mtn—summit WA-9
Helmer Ranch—locale WY-8
Helmer Sch—school MI-6
Helmer Sch—school NY-2
Helmers Ranch—locale TX-5
Helmer Valley—basin NE-7
Helmer-Winnett-White Flats—hist pl NE-7
Helmet—locale VA-3
Helmet, The MT-8
Helmet, The—summit MT-8
Helmet Butte—summit WA-9
Helmet Mtn—summit (2) AK-9
Helmet Peak—summit AZ-5
Helmet Peak—summit CO-8
Helmet Peak Interchange—crossing AZ-5
Helmet Point—summit MT-8
Helmet Rock—island CA-9
**Helmetta**—pop pl NJ-2
Helmetta Dam—dam NJ-2
**Helmetta Park**—pop pl NJ-2
Helmetta Pond—reservoir NJ-2
Helm Fork TN-4
Helm Fork—stream KY-4
Helm Gap—gap GA-3
Helm Gulch—valley CO-8
Helm Hollow—valley AR-4
Helm-Hout House—hist pl OR-9
Helmic—locale TX-5
Helmic Bridge—bridge OH-6
Helmick—locale OH-6
Helmick—other OK-5
**Helmick**—pop pl KS-7
**Helmick**—pop pl OR-9
Helmick Covered Bridge—hist pl OH-6
Helmick Hill—summit OR-9
Helmick (historical)—locale SD-7
Helmick Point—cape AK-9
Helmick Rock—cliff WV-2
Helmick Run—stream WV-2
Helmick State Park—park OR-9
Helmick Station—locale OH-6
Helmic Sch—school KS-7
Helming Ditch—canal MT-8
Helmintoller Cem—cemetery VA-3
Helmke Pond—lake CA-9
Helmke Spring—spring CA-9
Helm Lake—lake AK-9
Helm Lateral—canal ID-8
Helm-Lewis Ditch—canal CA-9
Helmley Pond—lake GA-3
Helm Mission AL-4
Helm Mountain VA-3
Helm Oil Field CA-9
Helm Park—park MO-7
**Helm Park Subdivision**—pop pl UT-8
Helm Place—hist pl (2) KY-4
Helm Point—cape (2) AK-9
Helm Post Office (historical)—building MS-4
Helm Ranch—locale CA-9
Helm Ranch—locale NM-5
Helm Rock—other AK-9
Helms IN-6
Helms WV-2
Helms—locale TX-5
Helms Apartments—hist pl UT-8
Helms Bend TN-4
Helms Branch—stream FL-3
Helms Branch—stream TN-4
Helms Branch—stream TX-5
**Helmsburg**—pop pl IN-6
Helmsburg Elem Sch—school IN-6
Helms Canyon OR-9
Helms Cem—cemetery AL-4
Helms Cem—cemetery MO-7
Helms Cem—cemetery TN-4
Helms Cove—bay DE-2
Helms Cove—bay NJ-2
Helms Cove—bay OR-9
Helms Creek OR-9
Helms Creek—stream (2) CA-9
Helms Creek—stream OR-9
Helms Creek—stream TX-5
Helms Dam—dam OR-9
Helms Fork KY-4
Helms Hall—building NC-3
Helms Hollow—valley MO-7
Helms House—hist pl FL-3
Helms-Jacobs Airp—airport IN-6
Helms JHS—school CA-9
Helms Lake—reservoir AL-4
Helms Lake—reservoir NC-3
Helms Lake Dam—dam NC-3
**Helms Landing (subdivision)**—pop pl DE-2
Helms Meadow—flat CA-9
Helms Mill Creek—stream AL-4
Helms Mills NJ-2
Helms Mtn—summit TX-5
**Helms Park (subdivision)**—pop pl NC-3
Helms Pond—lake NY-2
Helms Pond—reservoir AL-4
Helm Springs—spring OR-9
Helms Ranch—locale SD-7
Helms Rsvr—reservoir OR-9
Helms Sch—school FL-3
Helms Sch—school TX-5
Helm Stores and Apartments—hist pl FL-3
**Helm Subdivision**—pop pl UT-8
Helms West Well—well TX-5
Helm Tank—reservoir NM-5
Helm-Turner Cem—cemetery CA-9
**Helmuth (Gowanda State Homeopathic Hospital)**—pop pl NY-2
**Helmville**—pop pl MT-8
Helmwheel Ranch—locale AZ-5
Helmwood Hall—hist pl KY-4
Helmwood Heights Sch—school KY-4
Heloise—locale TN-4
Heloise, Lake—lake NY-2
Heloise Landing—locale TN-4
Heloise Post Office (historical)—building TN-4
Heloise Revetment—levee TN-4
**Helotes**—pop pl (2) TX-5
Helotes Cem—cemetery TX-5
Helotes Creek—stream TX-5
**Helotes Park Estates**—pop pl TX-5
**Helotes Ranch Acres**—pop pl TX-5
Helotes Windmill—locale TX-5
Helpenstell Cem—cemetery TX-5
**Helper**—pop pl UT-8
Helper, Hinton Rowan, House—hist pl NC-3
Helper Canyon—valley UT-8
Helper City Cemetery UT-8
Helper Commercial District—hist pl UT-8
Helper Division—civil UT-8
Helper Mine—mine MT-8
Helper Rescue Mission UT-8
Helpful Spring—spring OR-9
Helphenstein Creek—stream OR-9
Helphrey Cem—cemetery MO-7
Helphrey Hill—summit MO-7
Helping Hands Cem—cemetery LA-4
Helpmejack Creek—stream AK-9
Helpmejack Hills—other AK-9
Helpmejack Lakes—lake AK-9
Help Post Office (historical)—building TN-4
Helps—locale MI-6
Helps Branch—stream MO-7
Helps Creek—stream MI-6
Helsa Lake NE-7
Helsel Ch—church OH-6
Helsel Corners—locale OH-6
Helsel Creek—stream OK-5
Helsels Plum Creek Dam—dam SD-7
Helsene State Wildlife Mngmt Area—park MN-6
Helser Drain—stream MI-6
Helseth Sch—school ND-7
Helsingborg NJ-2
Helsing Junction—locale WA-9
Helsley Cem—cemetery MO-7
Helster Draw—valley SD-7
Helton—locale KY-4
Helton—locale MO-7
Helton—locale TN-4
**Helton**—pop pl NC-3
**Helton**—pop pl TN-4
Helton Bay—swamp AL-4
Helton Bluff—cliff AR-4
Helton Branch—stream GA-3
Helton Branch—stream (3) KY-4
Helton Branch—stream MO-7
Helton Cem—cemetery AL-4
Helton Cem—cemetery (3) KY-4
Helton Cem—cemetery (5) TN-4
Helton Cem—cemetery TX-5
Helton Cem—cemetery (3) VA-3
Helton Ch—church MO-7
Helton Ch—church (2) NC-3
Helton Creek—stream (2) GA-3
Helton Creek—stream MS-4
Helton Creek—stream NM-5
Helton Creek—stream NC-3
Helton Creek—stream TN-4
Helton Creek—stream (2) TX-5
Helton Creek—stream VA-3
Helton Creek Baptist Church TN-4
Helton Creek Ch—church TN-4
Helton Creek Falls—falls GA-3
Helton Ditch—canal NM-5
Helton Hollow—valley IN-6
Helton Hollow—valley (4) TN-4
Helton Hollow—valley (2) VA-3
Helton Knob—summit NC-3
Helton Memorial Ch—church AL-4
Helton Primitive Baptist Ch (historical)—church TN-4
Helton Road Baptist Ch—church AL-4
Helton Sch—school NC-3
Helton Sch—school TN-4
Heltons Island—island ID-8
Helton Springs Baptist Church TN-4
Helton Springs Cem—cemetery TN-4
Helton Springs Ch—church TN-4
Heltons Store (historical)—locale TN-4
Heltonsville IN-6
Helton Tank—reservoir NM-5
Helton (Township of)—fmr MCD NC-3
Helton Valley Ch—church VA-3
Heltonville TN-4
**Heltonville**—pop pl IN-6
**Heltonville**—pop pl TN-4
Heltonville Elem Sch—school IN-6
Heltsley Cem—cemetery KY-4
Helts Prairie Cem—cemetery IN-6
**Helt (Township of)**—pop pl IN-6
Heltzel Ditch—canal IN-6
Heltzell Hollow—valley MO-7
Helu—summit HI-9
Heluma Oil Field—oilfield TX-5
Helum Cem—cemetery MO-7
Helverson Creek—stream (2) FL-3
Helverson Island—island FL-3
Helveston MS-4
Helvetia IN-6
Helvetia—hist pl WV-2
Helvetia—locale AZ-5
Helvetia—locale LA-4
**Helvetia**—pop pl OR-9
**Helvetia**—pop pl PA-2
**Helvetia**—pop pl WV-2
Helvetia Cem—cemetery AZ-5
Helvetia Cem—cemetery OR-9
Helvetia Cem—cemetery WV-2
Helvetia Dam—dam PA-2
**Helvetia (Helvetia Mines)**—pop pl PA-2
Helvetia (historical)—locale KS-7
Helvetia Mine AZ-5
Helvetia Mine—mine AZ-5
Helvetia Mine—mine CA-9
Helvetia Mine Camp AZ-5
Helvetian Gun Club—other CA-9
Helvetia Spring AZ-5
Helvetia Spring—spring AZ-5
**Helvetia (Town of)**—pop pl WI-6
**Helvetia (Township of)**—pop pl IL-6
Helvey—locale NE-7
Helvey Cem—cemetery MO-7
Helvey Draw—valley WY-8
Helveys Mill Creek—stream VA-3
Helvic Cem—cemetery OH-6
Helvie Ditch—canal IN-6
Helvingston Creek FL-3
Helvingston Island FL-3
Helvy Cem—cemetery KY-4
Helwick Gulch—valley MT-8
Helwick Hollow—valley TN-4
Helwick Peak—summit MT-8
Helwig Cem—cemetery IA-7
Helwig Drain—canal MI-6
Helwig Hollow—valley IN-6
Helwig Hollow Pond—lake IN-6
Hely Creek—stream CA-9
Heman—locale ID-8
Heman—locale IL-6
Heman—locale OK-5
Hemann, Joseph A., House—hist pl OH-6
Heman Park MO-7
Heman Park—park MO-7
Hemans—locale MI-6
Hemans Drain—canal MI-6
Hematite—locale TN-4
Hematite—locale WI-6
**Hematite**—pop pl MO-7
**Hematite**—pop pl VA-3
Hematite Basin—basin CO-8
Hematite Branch—stream GA-3
Hematite Cem—cemetery MI-6
Hematite Ch—church KY-4
Hematite Creek—stream NM-5
Hematite Gulch—valley CO-8
Hematite Lake—lake CO-8
Hematite Lake—reservoir KY-4
Hematite Mine—mine ID-8
Hematite Mtn—summit VA-3
Hematite Park—flat NM-5
Hematite Peak—summit MT-8
Hematite Rec Area—park TN-4
**Hematite (Township of)**—pop pl MI-6
Hematite Trail—trail KY-4
Hembeck River RI-1
Hembling Drain—canal MI-6
Hembre Creek—stream OR-9
Hembree—locale TN-4
Hembree Cem—cemetery MS-4
Hembree Cem—cemetery (2) TN-4
Hembree Creek—stream SC-3
Hembree Mill (historical)—locale TN-4
Hembrees Bar—bar AL-4
Hembree Sch (historical)—school TN-4
Hembrees Landing (historical)—locale AL-4
Hembree Spring—spring GA-3
Hembre Lookout—locale OR-9
Hembre Mtn—summit WA-9
Hembre Ridge—ridge OR-9
Hembrey Creek CA-9
Hembrey Creek—stream CA-9
Hembrillo Canyon—valley NM-5
Hembrillo Pass—gap NM-5
Hembrillo Wash—stream NM-5
**Hemby**—pop pl NC-3
Hemby Branch—stream MS-4
Hemby Branch—stream TN-4
**Hemby Bridge**—pop pl NC-3
Hemby Bridge Elem Sch—school NC-3
Hemby Cem—cemetery MS-4
Hemby Cem—cemetery TN-4
Hemby Sch (historical)—school MS-4
Hem Cem—cemetery IA-7
Hem Creek—stream ID-8
Hemelline Cem—cemetery TX-5
Hemen Town Hall—building ND-7
**Hemen Township**—pop pl ND-7
Hemenway NV-8
Hemenway—locale MO-7
**Hemenway**—pop pl IN-6
Hemenway Campground—locale NV-8
Hemenway Drain—canal MI-6
Hemenway Furniture Co. Bldg—hist pl LA-4
Hemenway Harbor—bay NV-8
Hemenway Hill—summit MA-1
Hemenway House—locale CO-8
Hemenway Pond—lake MA-1
Hemenway Ridge—ridge ME-1
Hemenway Sch—school (2) MA-1
Hemenway State Reservation—reserve NH-1
Hemenway Wall—cliff NV-8
Hemenway Wash—stream NV-8
Hemenz Golf Course—locale PA-2
**Hemet**—pop pl CA-9
Hemet, Lake—reservoir CA-9
Hemet Butte—summit CA-9
**Hemet East**—pop pl CA-9
Hemeter Cem—cemetery MS-4
Hemet Reservoir CA-9
Hemet-San Jacinto (CCD)—cens area CA-9
Hemet Valley—valley CA-9
Heminger Sch—school OH-6
**Hemingford**—pop pl NE-7
Hemingford Cem—cemetery NE-7
Hemingford Creek—stream NE-7
**Hemingway**—pop pl SC-3
Hemingway, Ernest, Cottage—hist pl MI-6
Hemingway, Ernest, House—hist pl FL-3
Hemingway Butte—summit ID-8
Hemingway (CCD)—cens area SC-3
Hemingway Chapel—church SC-3
Hemingway Creek—stream CT-1
Hemingway Creek—stream MN-6
Hemingway Draw—valley WY-8
Hemingway Hill—summit VT-1
Hemingway (historical)—locale MS-4
Hemingway House—hist pl AR-4
Hemingway House and Barn—hist pl AR-4
Hemingway Lake ND-7
Hemingway Lake—lake (3) MI-6
Hemingway Mtn—summit ME-1
Hemingway Point—cape MI-6
Hemingway Pond—lake MA-1
Hemingway Sch—school IL-6
Hemingway Swamp—swamp MA-1
Heminway Park Sch—school CT-1
Heminway Pond—lake CT-1
HemisFair Plaza—locale TX-5
Hemler Creek—stream MT-8
Hemler Rsvr—reservoir WY-8
Hemlock RI-1
Hemlock TN-4
Hemlock—locale NC-3
Hemlock—locale PA-2
Hemlock—locale (2) WV-2
Hemlock—locale WI-6
**Hemlock**—pop pl IN-6
**Hemlock**—pop pl KY-4
**Hemlock**—pop pl (2) MI-6
**Hemlock**—pop pl NY-2
**Hemlock**—pop pl OH-6
**Hemlock**—pop pl (3) OR-9
**Hemlock**—pop pl PA-2
**Hemlock**—pop pl TN-4
**Hemlock**—pop pl VA-3
**Hemlock**—pop pl WV-2
Hemlock, David, J., House—hist pl WI-6
Hemlock Bluff TVA Small Wild Area—park TN-4
Hemlock Branch—stream NC-3
Hemlock Branck—stream VA-3
Hemlock Bridge—bridge TN-4
Hemlock Bridge—hist pl ME-1
Hemlock Brook CT-1
Hemlock Brook—stream (2) CT-1
Hemlock Brook—stream (2) MA-1
Hemlock Brook—stream NY-2
Hemlock Brook—stream (2) RI-1
**Hemlock Brook (historical)**—pop pl MA-1
Hemlock Butte—summit (2) ID-8
Hemlock Butte—summit (3) OR-9
Hemlock Butte Beaver Creek ID-8
Hemlock Camp—locale WA-9
Hemlock Canal—canal CA-9
Hemlock Cem—cemetery CT-1
Hemlock Cem—cemetery ME-1
**Hemlock (census name Eureka)**—pop pl SC-3
**Hemlock Center**—pop pl NH-1
Hemlock Ch—church VA-3
Hemlock Ch—church WV-2
Hemlock Cliffs—cliff IN-6
Hemlock Cobble—summit NY-2
Hemlock Cove—bay NY-2
Hemlock Creek PA-2
Hemlock Creek—stream AK-9
Hemlock Creek—stream CA-9
Hemlock Creek—stream (4) ID-8
Hemlock Creek—stream (2) MI-6
Hemlock Creek—stream (3) MT-8
Hemlock Creek—stream (2) NY-2
Hemlock Creek—stream (3) OR-9
Hemlock Creek—stream (3) PA-2
Hemlock Creek—stream TN-4
Hemlock Creek—stream (4) WA-9
Hemlock Creek—stream (4) WI-6
Hemlock Crossing—locale CA-9
Hemlock District—locale NY-2
Hemlock Drain—canal CA-9
Hemlock Drain One—canal CA-9
Hemlock Draw—valley WI-6
Hemlock Falls—falls OR-9
Hemlock Falls Dam—dam MI-6
**Hemlock Farms**—pop pl PA-2
Hemlock Flats Run—stream PA-2
Hemlock Flats Trail—trail PA-2
Hemlock Forest Trail—trail TN-4
Hemlock Glen—locale NJ-2
Hemlock Gorge—gap MA-1
Hemlock Grove—locale PA-2
**Hemlock Grove**—pop pl OH-6
**Hemlock Grove**—pop pl PA-2
Hemlock Gulch—valley MT-8
Hemlock Gully—valley NY-2
Hemlock Heights—summit PA-2
Hemlock Hill—summit ME-1
Hemlock Hill—summit MA-1
Hemlock Hill—summit NH-1
Hemlock Hill—summit NY-2
Hemlock Hill—summit NC-3
Hemlock Hill—summit PA-2
Hemlock Hill—summit VT-1
**Hemlock Hollow**—pop pl WV-2
Hemlock Hollow—valley TN-4
Hemlock Hollow—valley WV-2
Hemlock Hollow Run—stream PA-2
Hemlock Island NY-2
Hemlock Island—island AK-9
Hemlock Island—island (2) ME-1
Hemlock Island—island (2) MA-1
Hemlock Island—island NY-2
Hemlock Island—island (2) PA-2
Hemlock Island—island VT-1
Hemlock Knob—summit NC-3
Hemlock Knob—summit (2) TN-4
Hemlock Knoll—summit ME-1
Hemlock Knoll—summit NY-2
Hemlock Lake—lake (3) CA-9
Hemlock Lake—lake (9) MI-6
Hemlock Lake—lake MT-8
Hemlock Lake—lake (2) NY-2
Hemlock Lake—lake (3) OR-9
Hemlock Lake—lake (5) WI-6
Hemlock Lake—reservoir (2) NJ-2
Hemlock Lake—reservoir NC-3
Hemlock Lake—reservoir OR-9
Hemlock Lake—reservoir (2) PA-2
Hemlock Lake Campground—park (2) OR-9
Hemlock Lake County Park—park PA-2
Hemlock Lake Dam—dam (2) NJ-2
Hemlock Lake Dam—dam (2) PA-2
Hemlock Lake Park—park NY-2
Hemlock Lakes—lake IN-6
Hemlock Lakes—lake (2) PA-2
**Hemlock Lakes**—pop pl IN-6
Hemlock Lakes Dam North—dam IN-6
Hemlock Lakes Dam South—dam IN-6
Hemlock Lake Trail—trail OR-9
Hemlock Lateral Four Waste—canal CA-9
Hemlock Lateral Two B—canal CA-9
Hemlock Ledges—bench RI-1
Hemlock Meadow—flat UT-8
Hemlock Meadows Dam—dam OR-9
Hemlock Meadows Lake OR-9
Hemlock Mine—mine CA-9
Hemlock Mine—mine MT-8
Hemlock Mountain MA-1
Hemlock Mountain OR-9
Hemlock Mtn—summit ID-8
Hemlock Mtn—summit MT-8
Hemlock Mtn—summit NY-2
Hemlock Outlet—stream NY-2
Hemlock Park—park MI-6
**Hemlock Park**—pop pl TN-4
Hemlock Pass—gap (2) WA-9
Hemlock Playground—park NY-2
Hemlock Point MA-1
Hemlock Point—cape AK-9
Hemlock Point—cape (2) ME-1
Hemlock Point—cape MA-1
Hemlock Point—cape NY-2
Hemlock Point—summit MT-8
Hemlock Point Gun Club—other MI-6
Hemlock Post Office (historical)—building TN-4
Hemlock Ranch—locale CA-9
Hemlock Ranger Station—locale WA-9
Hemlock Rapids—rapids MI-6
Hemlock Rapids—rapids WI-6
Hemlock Ridge—ridge CA-9
Hemlock Ridge—ridge ID-8
Hemlock Ridge—ridge NY-2
Hemlock Ridge—ridge TN-4
Hemlock Ridge—ridge VA-3
Hemlock River—stream MI-6
Hemlock Road Ch—church MI-6
Hemlock Rsvr—reservoir CT-1
Hemlock Run PA-2
Hemlock Run—stream NY-2
Hemlock Run—stream (5) PA-2
Hemlock Run—stream WV-2
**Hemlocks**—pop pl MA-1
Hemlock-Sauk County Park—park WI-6
Hemlocks Camp, The—locale PA-2
Hemlock Sch—school (2) CA-9
Hemlock Sch—school (2) NY-2
Hemlock Sch (abandoned)—school (2) PA-2
Hemlock Sch (historical)—school (2) PA-2
Hemlock(Site)—locale WA-9
Hemlock Slough—gut WI-6
Hemlock Sluice Drain—canal CA-9
Hemlocks Natural Area—area PA-2
Hemlock Spring—spring ID-8
Hemlock Spring—spring OR-9
Hemlock Spring—spring PA-2
Hemlock Spring Creek—stream ID-8
Hemlock Springs Overlook—locale VA-3
Hemlock Spur Creek—stream WI-6
Hemlock Station—locale PA-2
Hemlock Station (historical)—locale MA-1
Hemlock Stream—stream ME-1
Hemlock Swamp—swamp MA-1
Hemlock Three Drain—canal CA-9
**Hemlock (Township of)**—pop pl PA-2
Hemlock Trail—trail ID-8
Hemlock Trail—trail (3) PA-2
Hemlock Trail—trail TN-4
Hemlock Trail—trail VA-3
Hemlock Valley—valley CT-1
Hemlock Valley Brook—stream CT-1
Hemm Ditch—canal OH-6
Hemmed-In Hollow—valley AR-4
Hemmed Island—island NC-3
Hemme Hills—range CA-9
Hemmelberg, William, House—hist pl MN-6
Hemmer Hill—summit NY-2
Hemmerling Sch—school CA-9
Hemmert Canyon—valley WY-8
Hemmeter Sch—school MI-6
Hemming—locale TX-5
Hemming Ditch—canal OH-6
Hemminger Saloon—hist pl OH-6
Hemming Lake—lake ND-7
Hemming Park—park FL-3
Hemming Point—cape FL-3
Hemmingson Airfield—airport OR-9
Hemmingway and Whipple Drain—stream MI-6
Hemmingway Lake—lake (2) MI-6
Hemmingway Slough—stream TX-5
Hemmy Cabin—locale OR-9
Hemnes Cem—cemetery MN-6
Hemnes Ch—church MN-6
Hemore Brook—stream ME-1
Hemp NC-3
Hemp VA-3
Hemp—locale GA-3
Hemp Branch—stream SC-3
Hemp Ch—church GA-3
Hempel Creek—stream WA-9
Hempel Lake—lake WA-9
Hemperly Sch (abandoned)—school PA-2
Hempfield PA-2
Hempfield—locale PA-2
Hempfield Elem Sch—school PA-2
Hempfield HS—school PA-2
Hempfield Lake—lake MI-6
Hempfield Post Office (historical)—building PA-2
Hempfield Senior High School PA-2
Hempfield Shop Ctr—locale PA-2
**Hempfield Township**—pop pl PA-2
**Hempfield (Township of)**—pop pl PA-2
Hempfling, Barth, House—hist pl AR-4
Hemp Fork—stream VA-3
Hemphilis PA-2
Hemphill—locale LA-4
**Hemphill**—pop pl TX-5
**Hemphill**—pop pl WV-2

*Hendricks Pond* AL-4
*Hendricks Pond* DE-2
Hendricks Pond—*reservoir* NJ-2
Hendricks Pond—*reservoir* NC-3
Hendrick Spring—*spring* UT-8
Hendricks Ranch—*locale* CO-8
Hendricks Ranch Airp—*airport* NC-3
Hendricks Reef (historical)—*bar* AL-4
Hendricks Rsvrs—*reservoir* OR-9
Hendricks Sch—*school* IL-6
Hendricks Sch—*school* KY-4
*Hendricks School* IN-6
*Hendricks School Number 37* IN-6
Hendricks Spring—*spring* WA-9
Hendricks State Wildlife Mngmt Area—*park* MN-6
Hendricks Store—*locale* VA-3
Hendricks Township—*civil* KS-7
**Hendricks (Township of)**—*pop pl* IN-6
**Hendricks (Township of)**—*pop pl* MI-6
**Hendricks (Township of)**—*pop pl* MN-6
Hendricks Trail—*trail* PA-2
**Hendricksville**—*pop pl* IN-6
Hendricks Well—*well* AZ-5
Hendricks Windmills—*locale* TX-5
Hendrick Tank—*reservoir* NM-5
Hendrick Trail—*trail* WV-2
Hendrickville (historical)—*locale* AL-4
Hendrics Lake—*lake* FL-3
Hendrie and Bolthoff Warehouse Bldg—*hist pl* CO-8
Hendrie River—*stream* MI-6
Hendrie River Camp—*locale* MI-6
Hendrik Bay—*bay* VI-3
*Hendrix* GA-3
Hendrix—*locale* IL-6
Hendrix—*locale* MS-4
Hendrix—*locale* TX-5
**Hendrix**—*pop pl* AL-4
**Hendrix**—*pop pl* NC-3
**Hendrix**—*pop pl* OK-5
Hendrix, Henry Franklin, House—*hist pl* SC-3
Hendrix, John Solomon, House—*hist pl* SC-3
Hendrix Bay—*swamp* GA-3
Hendrix Branch—*stream* AR-4
Hendrix Branch—*stream* KY-4
Hendrix Branch—*stream* (2) TN-4
Hendrix Cem—*cemetery* (2) AL-4
Hendrix Cem—*cemetery* AR-4
Hendrix Cem—*cemetery* GA-3
Hendrix Cem—*cemetery* KY-4
Hendrix Cem—*cemetery* MO-7
Hendrix Cem—*cemetery* (8) TN-4
Hendrix Cem—*cemetery* TX-5
Hendrix Ch—*church* AL-4
*Hendrix Chapel Church of Christ* AL-4
Hendrix Coll—*school* AR-4
Hendrix Creek—*bay* NY-2
Hendrix Creek—*stream* TN-4
Hendrix Crossroad—*locale* AL-4
*Hendrix Crossroads* AL-4
Hendrix Gap—*gap* PA-2
Hendrix Gap Trail—*trail* PA-2
Hendrix Hollow—*valley* TN-4
Hendrix Mine (surface)—*mine* AL-4
Hendrix Mtn—*summit* GA-3
Hendrix Park—*park* IN-6
Hendrix Post Office (historical)—*building* TN-4
Hendrix Siphon—*other* OR-9
Hendrixson Cem—*cemetery* OH-6
**Hendrix Spur**—*pop pl* WA-9
**Hendrixville**—*pop pl* AL-4
**Hendron**—*pop pl* KY-4
**Hendron**—*pop pl* TN-4
Hendron Chapel—*church* TN-4
*Hendrons Chapel* TN-4
*Hendrons United Methodist Ch* TN-4
Hendronsville Cem—*cemetery* KY-4
**Hendrum**—*pop pl* MN-6
Hendrum City Park—*park* MN-6
**Hendrum (Township of)**—*pop pl* MN-6
Hendry, Francis, House—*hist pl* OH-6
*Hendry and Knight Channel* FL-3
Hendry Cem—*cemetery* FL-3
Hendry Cem—*cemetery* GA-3
**Hendry County**—*pop pl* FL-3
Hendry Creek—*stream* FL-3
**Hendry Estates**—*pop pl* MD-2
Hendry Frierson Cem—*cemetery* FL-3
Hendry General Hosp—*hospital* FL-3
Hendry Hosp—*hospital* FL-3
Hendry Point—*cape* TX-5
Hendry Ranch—*locale* WY-8
**Hendrysburg**—*pop pl* OH-6
Hendrys Creek—*stream* CA-9
Hendrys Creek—*stream* NV-8
Hendrys Creek—*stream* UT-8
**Hendryx Manor**—*pop pl* IL-6
Hendryx Sch—*school* IL-6
Hendy Ave Sch—*school* NY-2
*Hendy Creek* NY-2
**Hendy Creek**—*pop pl* NY-2
Hendy Creek—*stream* NY-2
Hendy Memorial Playground—*park* OH-6
Hendy Woods State Park—*park* CA-9
**Henefer**—*pop pl* UT-8
Henefer Cem—*cemetery* UT-8
Henefer-Echo Wildlife Mngmt Area—*park* UT-8
Henefer Valley—*valley* UT-8
Henegan Lake—*lake* SC-3
Henegar Bend—*bend* TN-4
Henegar Bluff—*cliff* TN-4
Henegar Branch—*stream* TN-4
Henegar Cem—*cemetery* TN-4
Henegar Ch—*church* TN-4
Henegar Dam—*dam* TN-4
Henegar House—*hist pl* TN-4
Henegar Lake—*reservoir* TN-4
Henegartown—*locale* VA-3
Hen Egg Mtn—*summit* TX-5
Heneheneula—*civil* HI-9
**Henekes Corner**—*pop pl* MD-2
Heneman Cem—*cemetery* KY-4
Henen Cem—*cemetery* LA-4
Henery—*locale* CO-8
Henery Cem—*cemetery* MO-7
Henery Ditch—*canal* OH-6
Henery Lake Rsvr—*reservoir* CO-8
*Henery Run* PA-2
Henery Tanks—*reservoir* NM-5

Henessey, Dr. Edwin, House—*hist pl* CA-9
Henesy Branch—*stream* TX-5
Heney, Lake—*lake* FL-3
Heney Creek—*stream* AK-9
Heney Glacier—*glacier* AK-9
Heney Peak—*summit* AK-9
Heney Range—*ridge* AK-9
*Heneys Landing* CA-9
**Hen Farm Estates Subdivision**—*pop pl* UT-8
**Henfer Park**—*pop pl* LA-4
Hengst Peak—*summit* CA-9
Henhawk Ledge—*bench* ME-1
Hen Hollow—*valley* TN-4
Henholt Canyon—*valley* UT-8
Henhouse Hollow—*valley* MO-7
Henifin Ranch—*locale* AZ-5
Henifin Well—*well* AZ-5
Heninger Branch—*stream* VA-3
Heninger Gap—*gap* VA-3
*Hening Lake* WI-6
Hening Sch—*school* VA-3
Henio Dam—*dam* NM-5
Henion Cem—*cemetery* WI-6
Henion Pond—*reservoir* NJ-2
Henion Pond Dam—*dam* NJ-2
*Hen Island* NY-2
Hen Island—*island* AK-9
Hen Island—*island* CT-1
Hen Island—*island* (8) ME-1
Hen Island—*island* MD-2
Hen Island—*island* MI-6
Hen Island—*island* (2) NH-1
Hen Island—*island* NY-2
Hen Island—*island* RI-1
Hen Island—*island* VT-1
Hen Island Creek—*stream* MD-2
Hen Island Ledge—*bar* ME-1
*Hen Islands* ME-1
Henjna Farmstead—*hist pl* SD-7
Hen Johnson Hollow—*valley* TN-4
Henke Hill—*summit* TX-5
Henkel—*locale* CO-8
Henkel—*locale* IL-6
Henkel, Mount—*summit* MT-8
Henke Lake—*reservoir* IN-6
Henke Lake Dam—*dam* IN-6
Henkel-Duke Mercantile Company Warehouse—*hist pl* CO-8
Henkel Lake—*lake* MI-6
Henkes Brook—*stream* MA-1
**Henke Spur**—*pop pl* IL-6
Henke Windmill—*locale* TX-5
Henkhaus—*locale* TX-5
Henking Hotel and Cafe—*hist pl* MA-1
Henkle Branch—*stream* IL-6
Henkle Butte—*summit* OR-9
Henkle Canyon—*valley* KS-7
Henkle Cem—*cemetery* MS-4
Henkle Park—*park* CO-8
*Hen Lake* MN-6
**Henlawson**—*pop pl* WV-2
Hen Lee Bench—*bench* UT-8
Henlein—*locale* PA-2
*Henlein Station* PA-2
Henlen Sch—*school* PA-2
Henleranch Number 1 Dam—*dam* SD-7
Henley—*locale* TN-4
Henley—*locale* VA-3
**Henley**—*pop pl* CA-9
**Henley**—*pop pl* MS-4
**Henley**—*pop pl* MO-7
**Henley**—*pop pl* OH-6
**Henley**—*pop pl* OR-9
**Henley**—*pop pl* PA-2
Henley, Benjamin Franklin, House—*hist pl* AR-4
Henley Basin—*basin* (2) ID-8
Henley Branch—*stream* AR-4
*Henley Bridge* TN-4
Henley Bridge—*bridge* AL-4
Henley Canal—*canal* FL-3
Henley Canyon—*valley* CA-9
Henley Cay—*island* VI-3
Henley Cem—*cemetery* AL-4
Henley Cem—*cemetery* AR-4
Henley Cem—*cemetery* IL-6
Henley Cem—*cemetery* (6) TN-4
Henley Cem—*cemetery* (2) VA-3
Henley Cem—*cemetery* WV-2
Henley Ch—*church* OH-6
Henley Creek—*stream* ID-8
Henley Creek—*stream* IN-6
Henley Creek—*stream* MT-8
Henley Creek—*stream* SC-3
Henley Creek—*stream* TN-4
Henley Creek—*stream* VA-3
Henley Field—*park* FL-3
**Henleyfield**—*pop pl* MS-4
*Henley Field Church* MS-4
Henleyfield Sch (historical)—*school* MS-4
Henley Fork—*locale* VA-3
Henley-Heflin Cem—*cemetery* GA-3
Henley Hollow—*valley* MO-7
Henley Hollow—*valley* (2) TN-4
Henley Hollow—*valley* VA-3
Henley Knob—*summit* MO-7
Henley Lake—*reservoir* MO-7
Henley Mtn—*summit* VA-3
Henley Roberts—*locale* AL-4
Henleys Cem—*cemetery* MS-4
Henley Sch—*school* AL-4
Henley Sch—*school* DC-2
Henley Sch—*school* IL-6
Henley Sch—*school* ME-1
Henley Sch—*school* NY-2
Henley Sch—*school* VA-3
*Henleys Creek* SC-3
Henleys Ford—*locale* TN-4
Henleys Fork—*locale* VA-3
Henley Site—*hist pl* WA-9
Henleys Mill (historical)—*locale* TN-4
Henley Spring—*spring* ID-8
Henleys Store—*locale* VA-3
Henleys Store (historical)—*locale* TN-4
*Henleys Switch* TN-4
Henley Station—*locale* PA-2
Henley Street Bridge—*bridge* TN-4
Henley Tank—*reservoir* NM-5
Henleyville—*locale* CA-9

Henline Creek—*stream* IL-6
Henline Creek—*stream* OR-9
Henline Mountain Lookout—*locale* OR-9
Henline Mtn—*summit* OR-9
Henline Spring—*spring* UT-8
Henlopen, Cape—*cape* DE-2
**Henlopen Acres**—*pop pl* DE-2
Henlopen Acres Yacht Basin—*harbor* DE-2
**Henlopen Keys (subdivision)**—*pop pl* DE-2
Henly—*locale* TX-5
Henly Branch—*stream* TX-5
Henly Cem—*cemetery* TX-5
Henly Creek—*stream* CA-9
Hen Magee Cem—*cemetery* MS-4
Henmison Sch—*school* TX-5
*Hen Mountain* TX-5
*Hennan Creek* NV-8
Hennard Cave—*cave* TN-4
Hennard Creek—*stream* TN-4
*Hennard Mill* TN-4
Hennard Mtn—*summit* TN-4
Henne, Lake—*reservoir* CA-9
Henne, Robert, House—*hist pl* IA-7
Henneberry Gulch—*valley* MT-8
Henneberry Ranch—*locale* MT-8
Henneberry Ridge—*ridge* MT-8
Henne Drain—*canal* MI-6
*Hennegers Chapel* TN-4
Hennegers Chapel Cem—*cemetery* TN-4
Henneman Lake—*lake* WI-6
Hennen Bldg—*hist pl* LA-4
Hennen Canyon—*valley* NV-8
Hennen Run—*stream* PA-2
Henne Oil Field—*oilfield* KS-7
Hennepin—*park* IL-6
**Hennepin**—*pop pl* IL-6
**Hennepin**—*pop pl* OK-5
Hennepin, Point—*cape* MI-6
Hennepin Canal—*canal* IL-6
Hennepin Canal Hist Dist—*hist pl* IL-6
Hennepin Canyon—*valley* IL-6
Hennepin Cem—*cemetery* OK-5
**Hennepin (County)**—*pop pl* MN-6
Hennepin County Library—*hist pl* MN-6
Hennepin Creek—*stream* MN-6
Hennepin Feeder Canal—*canal* IL-6
Hennepin Island—*island* (2) MN-6
Hennepin Lake—*lake* MN-6
Hennepin Park—*park* (2) NY-2
**Hennepin (sta.)**—*pop pl* IL-6
**Hennepin (Township of)**—*pop pl* IL-6
Hennequin Creek—*stream* CO-8
*Hennercroix Creek* NY-2
*Hennerville Peak* CA-9
Hennery Island—*island* PA-2
Hennesey Brook—*stream* NY-2
Hennesey Creek—*stream* MT-8
Hennesey Ranch—*locale* CA-9
Henneside, Lake—*lake* NY-2
Henness Cem—*cemetery* IA-7
Hennessee Bridge—*bridge* TN-4
Hennesset Ford—*crossing* TN-4
Hennessey—*locale* TX-5
**Hennessey**—*pop pl* OK-5
Hennessey, Lake—*reservoir* CA-9
Hennessey (CCD)—*cens area* OK-5
Hennessey Creek—*stream* CA-9
Hennessey Lake—*lake* MN-6
Hennessey Meadow—*flat* ID-8
Hennessey Park—*park* TX-5
Hennesseys Bayou—*stream* MS-4
Hennessey Sch—*school* CA-9
Hennessey Spring—*spring* WI-6
Henness Pass—*gap* CA-9
Hennessy Buttes—*summit* AZ-5
Hennessy Creek—*stream* CA-9
Hennessy Field—*park* NY-2
Hennessy Lake—*lake* MN-6
Hennessy Mtn—*summit* NY-2
Hennessy Peak—*summit* CA-9
Hennessy Point—*summit* UT-8
Hennessy Ridge—*ridge* CA-9
Hennesy Cem—*cemetery* LA-4
Henney Sch—*school* IL-6
Henn Gulch—*valley* MT-8
Hennican Cem—*cemetery* LA-4
Hennick Draw—*valley* WY-8
Hennicksons Ridge—*ridge* CA-9
Hennicksons Ridge Trail—*trail* CA-9
Hennigan Cem—*cemetery* (2) AL-4
Hennigan Sch (historical)—*school* AL-4
*Hennigar Bluff* TN-4
Hennig Creek—*stream* WI-6
Henniger Farm Covered Bridge—*hist pl* PA-2
*Hennig Lake* WI-6
Hennig Lake—*lake* WI-6
Hennig Rock—*bar* AK-9
Henni Hall—*hist pl* WI-6
**Henniker**—*pop pl* NH-1
**Henniker Junction**—*pop pl* NH-1
Henniker Town Hall—*hist pl* NH-1
**Henniker (Town of)**—*pop pl* NH-1
**Henning**—*pop pl* IL-6
**Henning**—*pop pl* MN-6
**Henning**—*pop pl* TN-4
**Henning**—*pop pl* TX-5
**Henning**—*pop pl* WV-2
Henning (CCD)—*cens area* TN-4
Henning Cem—*cemetery* MO-7
Henning Creek—*stream* TX-5
Henning Division—*civil* TN-4
Henning Drain—*stream* MI-6
Henninger Ditch—*canal* IN-6
Henninger Flats—*flat* CA-9
Henningers Mill—*locale* NJ-2
Henning Grove Ch—*church* TN-4
Henning Grove Sch (historical)—*school* TN-4
Henning Hill Sch (historical)—*school* PA-2
Henning Lake—*lake* WI-6
Henning Lakes—*lake* WA-9
Henning Mine—*mine* CA-9
Henning Post Office—*building* TN-4
*Hennings* TN-4
Hennings Canyon—*valley* UT-8
Henning Sch—*school* CA-9
Henning Sch—*school* IL-6
Henning Sch—*school* TN-4
**Hennings Mill**—*pop pl* OH-6
*Hennings Mills* OH-6
Hennings Mine—*mine* CA-9

Henningson Dam—*dam* UT-8
Henningson Rsvr—*reservoir* UT-8
Henningson Slough—*stream* NV-8
Henningsville—*locale* PA-2
Hennington Cem—*cemetery* TX-5
Hennington-Flowers Cem—*cemetery* MS-4
Hennington Lake—*reservoir* MS-4
**Henning (Township of)**—*pop pl* MN-6
*Henningville* PA-2
Hennink Sch (historical)—*school* SD-7
Hennion House—*hist pl* NJ-2
Hennis, Edgar Harvey, House—*hist pl* NC-3
Henn Mansion—*hist pl* IA-7
Hennon Branch—*stream* AL-4
Hennon Cem—*cemetery* AL-4
Hennon Chapel—*church* NC-3
Hennon Creek—*stream* WI-6
Hennsey Tank—*reservoir* AZ-5
Henny Barn—*hist pl* OH-6
*Henolerson* AL-4
*Henpeck* IL-6
Henpeck—*locale* IL-6
Henpeck—*locale* KY-4
Henpeck—*other* OH-6
**Henpeck**—*pop pl* MO-7
Henpeck Corners—*locale* OH-6
*Henpeck Creek* MO-7
Henpeck Creek—*stream* MO-7
Henpeck Hollow—*valley* MO-7
Henpeck Mill Cave—*cave* TN-4
Henpeck Mill (historical)—*locale* (2) TN-4
Henpen Branch—*stream* KY-4
Henquent, Mount—*summit* OK-5
Henredon Dam—*dam* NC-3
Henredon Lake—*reservoir* NC-3
Henrich Lake—*lake* WI-6
Henrich Ranch—*locale* CO-8
**Henrici**—*pop pl* OR-9
*Henrici Bar* OR-9
Henrici Lake—*lake* OR-9
Henrici Range—*channel* WA-9
*Henrick Mountain* GA-3
Henricks Gap—*gap* GA-3
Henrico—*hist pl* VA-3
Henrico—*locale* VA-3
**Henrico**—*pop pl* NC-3
Henrico Central Sch—*school* VA-3
**Henrico (County)**—*pop pl* VA-3
Henrico County Courthouse—*building* VA-3
Henrico HS—*school* VA-3
Henrico Revetment—*levee* AR-4
Henrie Ditch—*canal* UT-8
Henrie Knolls—*summit* UT-8
Henries Hollow—*valley* UT-8
Henrie Tank—*reservoir* AZ-5
Henrietta—*locale* KY-4
Henrietta—*locale* NC-3
**Henrietta**—*pop pl* FL-3
**Henrietta**—*pop pl* MO-7
**Henrietta**—*pop pl* NY-2
**Henrietta**—*pop pl* NC-3
**Henrietta**—*pop pl* OH-6
**Henrietta**—*pop pl* PA-2
**Henrietta**—*pop pl* TN-4
**Henrietta**—*pop pl* TX-5
**Henrietta**—*pop pl* WV-2
Henrietta Canyon—*valley* AZ-5
Henrietta (CCD)—*cens area* TX-5
Henrietta Cem—*cemetery* MN-6
Henrietta Cem—*cemetery* OH-6
Henrietta Cem—*cemetery* TX-5
Henrietta Ch—*church* LA-4
Henrietta Ch—*church* OH-6
Henrietta Ch—*church* TX-5
Henrietta Creek—*stream* TX-5
Henrietta Gulch—*valley* CO-8
Henrietta Lake—*lake* WI-6
Henrietta Mine—*mine* AZ-5
Henrietta Mine—*mine* ID-8
Henrietta Park—*park* IL-6
Henrietta Peak—*summit* CA-9
Henrietta Post Office (historical)—*building* TN-4
Henrietta Rock—*rock* MA-1
Henrietta Sch—*school* IL-6
Henrietta Sch—*school* MI-6
Henrietta Sch—*school* WI-6
Henrietta Spring—*spring* AZ-5
Henrietta Station—*locale* MI-6
Henrietta Substation—*other* CA-9
**Henrietta (Town of)**—*pop pl* NY-2
**Henrietta (Town of)**—*pop pl* WI-6
**Henrietta Township**—*pop pl* ND-7
**Henrietta (Township of)**—*pop pl* MI-6
**Henrietta (Township of)**—*pop pl* MN-6
**Henrietta (Township of)**—*pop pl* OH-6
**Henriette**—*pop pl* MN-6
**Henrieville**—*pop pl* UT-8
Henrieville Cem—*cemetery* UT-8
*Henrieville Creek* UT-8
Henrieville Creek—*stream* UT-8
Henriod Seeding Well—*well* NV-8
Henriques, Edgar and Lucy, House—*hist pl* HI-9
*Henrixy River* NC-3
Hen Rock—*island* CA-9
*Henrod Creek* AR-4
*Henrods Creek* AR-4
Henroost Fork—*stream* KY-4
Hen Run—*stream* OH-6
Hen Run—*stream* PA-2
*Henry* MI-6
*Henry* UT-8
*Henry* MP-9
Henry—*locale* CA-9
Henry—*locale* NV-8
Henry—*locale* SC-3
Henry—*locale* VA-3
Henry—*locale* WV-2
**Henry**—*pop pl* CO-8
**Henry**—*pop pl* GA-3
**Henry**—*pop pl* ID-8
**Henry**—*pop pl* IL-6
**Henry**—*pop pl* IN-6
**Henry**—*pop pl* LA-4
**Henry**—*pop pl* MI-6
**Henry**—*pop pl* NE-7
**Henry**—*pop pl* NC-3
**Henry**—*pop pl* SD-7
**Henry**—*pop pl* TN-4

**Henry**—*pop pl* VA-3
Henry, Bayou—*stream* LA-4
Henry, Cape—*cape* VA-3
Henry, C. D., House—*hist pl* AZ-5
Henry, Charles Wolcott, Sch—*hist pl* PA-2
Henry, C. K., Bldg—*hist pl* OR-9
Henry, Hugh, House—*hist pl* OK-5
Henry, Jacob, House—*hist pl* NC-3
Henry, Jacob H., House—*hist pl* IL-6
Henry, Joseph, House—*hist pl* NJ-2
Henry, Lake—*lake* (4) FL-3
Henry, Lake—*lake* (3) MN-6
Henry, Lake—*lake* MS-4
Henry, Lake—*lake* ND-7
Henry, Lake—*lake* (3) SD-7
Henry, Lake—*reservoir* (2) AL-4
Henry, Lake—*reservoir* CO-8
Henry, Lake—*reservoir* GA-3
Henry, Lake—*reservoir* MS-4
Henry, Lake—*reservoir* PA-2
Henry, Lake—*reservoir* SD-7
Henry, Lake—*reservoir* TX-5
Henry, Lake—*reservoir* WI-6
Henry, Matthew, House—*hist pl* KY-4
Henry, Mount—*summit* CA-9
Henry, Mount—*summit* ME-1
Henry, Mount—*summit* (3) MT-8
Henry, Point—*summit* ID-8
Henry, Robert W., House—*hist pl* OH-6
Henry, William, House—*hist pl* VT-1
Henry A Bradshaw HS—*school* AL-4
Henry Adkins Hollow—*valley* TN-4
Henry Anderson Creek—*stream* MT-8
*Henry Attens Island* PA-2
Henry Ave Bridge—*bridge* PA-2
Henry Ayers Cem—*cemetery* TN-4
Henry Bandelier Ditch—*canal* IN-6
Henry Baptist Ch—*church* TN-4
Henry Barnard Hollow—*valley* TN-4
Henry Basin—*basin* OR-9
*Henry Bell Creek* CA-9
Henry Bell Gulch—*valley* CA-9
*Henry Bend* PA-2
Henry Bend—*bend* TN-4
Henry Bowlin Gap—*gap* KY-4
Henry Brake—*stream* MS-4
*Henry Branch* TN-4
Henry Branch—*stream* AL-4
Henry Branch—*stream* (3) AR-4
Henry Branch—*stream* GA-3
Henry Branch—*stream* (4) KY-4
Henry Branch—*stream* MO-7
Henry Branch—*stream* (2) NC-3
Henry Branch—*stream* (3) TN-4
Henry Branch—*stream* WV-2
Henry Bridge—*bridge* TN-4
**Henrybro**—*pop pl* WA-9
Henry Brook—*stream* IN-6
Henry Brook—*stream* MA-1
Henry Brown Lake Dam—*dam* MS-4
Henry Brown Meadow—*flat* WA-9
Henry Brown Tank—*reservoir* AZ-5
Henry Camp—*locale* WV-2
Henry Camp Run—*stream* WV-2
Henry Canyon—*valley* AZ-5
Henry Canyon—*valley* NM-5
Henry Canyon—*valley* OR-9
Henry (CCD)—*cens area* TN-4
*Henry Cem* TN-4
Henry Cem—*cemetery* (3) AL-4
Henry Cem—*cemetery* AR-4
Henry Cem—*cemetery* IL-6
Henry Cem—*cemetery* (2) IN-6
Henry Cem—*cemetery* KS-7
Henry Cem—*cemetery* KY-4
Henry Cem—*cemetery* (2) LA-4
Henry Cem—*cemetery* MN-6
Henry Cem—*cemetery* (4) MS-4
Henry Cem—*cemetery* (3) NC-3
Henry Cem—*cemetery* (3) OH-6
Henry Cem—*cemetery* OK-5
Henry Cem—*cemetery* (7) TN-4
Henry Cem—*cemetery* (4) TX-5
Henry Cem—*cemetery* (2) VA-3
Henry Cem—*cemetery* WV-2
Henry Ch—*church* NC-3
Henry Ch—*church* VA-3
Henry Chisholm—*hist pl* MI-6
**Henry Clay**—*pop pl* DE-2
**Henry Clay**—*pop pl* KY-4
Henry Clay—*uninc pl* KY-4
Henry Clay, Mount—*summit* AK-9
Henry Clay Birthplace—*building* VA-3
Henry Clay Furnace—*hist pl* WV-2
**Henry Clay Heights**—*pop pl* VA-3
Henry Clay Hotel—*hist pl* KY-4
Henry Clay HS—*school* KY-4
Henry Clay Mine—*mine* CO-8
Henry Clay Mine—*mine* NM-5
Henry Clay Sch—*school* (3) KY-4
Henry Clay Sch—*school* PA-2
Henry Clay Sch—*school* VA-3
**Henry Clay (Township of)**—*pop pl* PA-2
Henry Cool Memorial Park—*cemetery* SD-7
**Henry County**—*pop pl* AL-4
**Henry (County)**—*pop pl* GA-3
**Henry (County)**—*pop pl* IL-6
**Henry County**—*pop pl* IN-6
**Henry (County)**—*pop pl* KY-4
**Henry County**—*pop pl* MO-7
**Henry (County)**—*pop pl* OH-6
**Henry County**—*pop pl* TN-4
**Henry (County)**—*pop pl* VA-3
Henry County Airp—*airport* TN-4
Henry County Courthouse—*building* TN-4
Henry County Courthouse—*hist pl* GA-3
Henry County Courthouse—*hist pl* IN-6
Henry County Courthouse—*hist pl* IA-7
Henry County Courthouse—*hist pl* OH-6
Henry County Courthouse, Jail, and Warden's House—*hist pl* KY-4
Henry County Fairgrounds—*locale* IL-6
Henry County General Hosp—*hospital* TN-4
Henry County Home—*building* IL-6
Henry County Home—*building* IA-7
Henry County Hosp—*hospital* AL-4
Henry County Hospital Airp—*airport* AL-4
Henry County Hospital Airp—*airport* TN-4
Henry County HS—*school* TN-4
Henry County Industrial Sch—*school* AL-4

*Henry County Library* AL-4
*Henry County Med Ctr* TN-4
Henry County Memorial Gardens—*cemetery* TN-4
Henry County Rod and Gun Club Lake—*reservoir* KY-4
Henry County Sheriff's Residence and Jail—*hist pl* OH-6
Henry County Training Sch—*school* TN-4
Henry Cove—*bay* ME-1
Henry Cove—*valley* TN-4
Henry Cove Cem—*cemetery* TN-4
Henry Covered Bridge—*hist pl* PA-2
Henry Covered Bridge—*hist pl* VT-1
Henry Cowell Redwoods State Park—*park* CA-9
*Henry Creek* IN-6
*Henry Creek* UT-8
*Henry Creek* WA-9
Henry Creek—*stream* AL-4
Henry Creek—*stream* (4) AK-9
Henry Creek—*stream* CA-9
Henry Creek—*stream* FL-3
Henry Creek—*stream* (4) ID-8
Henry Creek—*stream* (3) IL-6
Henry Creek—*stream* IN-6
Henry Creek—*stream* IA-7
Henry Creek—*stream* (2) KS-7
Henry Creek—*stream* MS-4
Henry Creek—*stream* (2) MO-7
Henry Creek—*stream* (4) MT-8
Henry Creek—*stream* NE-7
Henry Creek—*stream* (2) NC-3
Henry Creek—*stream* OH-6
Henry Creek—*stream* (6) OR-9
Henry Creek—*stream* SC-3
Henry Creek—*stream* TN-4
Henry Creek—*stream* (2) WA-9
Henry Creek—*stream* WY-8
Henry Creek Sch—*school* ID-8
Henry Crossing—*locale* TN-4
*Henry Crossroads* VA-3
Henry Crossroads—*locale* TN-4
**Henry Crossroads**—*pop pl* VA-3
Henry Culp Family Plot—*cemetery* TN-4
Henry Dam—*dam* (2) SD-7
Henry DeTonty Woods—*woods* IL-6
*Henry Ditch* IN-6
Henry Ditch—*canal* (3) IN-6
Henry Ditch—*canal* WY-8
Henry Division—*civil* TN-4
Henry Dover Pond—*lake* FL-3
Henry D Perry MS—*school* FL-3
Henry Drain—*canal* (2) MI-6
Henry Drain—*stream* MI-6
Henry Draw—*valley* WY-8
Henry Eaton Sch (abandoned)—*school* MO-7
Henry Elem Sch—*school* TN-4
*Henryellen* AL-4
Henry Ellen—*locale* AL-4
Henry Ellen Mine (surface)—*mine* AL-4
Henry Ellen Mine (underground)—*mine* AL-4
**Henryetta**—*pop pl* OK-5
Henryetta, Lake—*reservoir* OK-5
Henryetta (CCD)—*cens area* OK-5
Henryetta Oil And Gas Field—*oilfield* OK-5
Henry Evans Mine (background)—*mine* AL-4
Henry E. Wallace Dam—*dam* IA-7
Henry Fannin Branch—*stream* KY-4
Henry Ferguson Branch—*stream* WV-2
Henry-Field Ch—*church* AL-4
Henry Fietzer Landing Field—*airport* ND-7
Henry F Kite Elem Sch—*school* FL-3
Henry Ford—*locale* TN-4
Henry Ford Coll—*school* MI-6
Henry Ford Community Coll—*school* MI-6
Henry Ford Dam—*dam* MI-6
Henry Ford Dam—*dam* WI-6
Henry Ford Field—*park* MI-6
Henry Ford II Sch—*school* IL-6
Henry Ford Rock—*pillar* WY-8
Henry Ford Sch—*school* CA-9
Henry Ford Sch—*school* (4) MI-6
*Henry Fork* ID-8
**Henry Fork**—*pop pl* VA-3
Henry Fork—*stream* (2) KY-4
Henry Fork—*stream* NC-3
Henry Fork—*stream* WV-2
Henry Fork Ch—*church* (2) WV-2
Henry Gap—*gap* GA-3
Henry Gap—*gap* NC-3
*Henry G Cliff High School* AL-4
Henry George Canyon—*valley* CO-8
Henry Gilbert Ditch—*canal* IN-6
Henry Glacier—*glacier* AK-9
Henry G Mtn—*summit* OK-5
Henry Grady Sch—*school* GA-3
Henry Grady Sch (historical)—*school* MS-4
Henry-Grant Cem—*cemetery* MS-4
Henry Grove Sch—*school* NC-3
Henry Gulch—*valley* MT-8
Henry Gulch—*valley* OR-9
Henry Gulch Spring—*spring* OR-9
Henry Hagg Lake—*lake* OR-9
Henry Hagg Lake—*reservoir* OR-9
Henry Halls Landing (historical)—*locale* MS-4
Henry Hardin Hollow—*valley* TN-4
Henry Harris Dam—*dam* NC-3
Henry Harris Lake—*reservoir* NC-3
Henry Hartley Grant—*civil* FL-3
Henry H Buckman Bridge—*bridge* FL-3
Henry Heights Sch—*school* LA-4
Henry Hill—*summit* NY-2
Henry Hill—*summit* VA-3
Henry Hills Harbor—*bay* NC-3
Henry (historical)—*locale* KS-7
*Henry Hollow* PA-2
Henry Hollow—*valley* AR-4
Henry Hollow—*valley* KY-4
Henry Hollow—*valley* MO-7
Henry Hollow—*valley* OH-6
Henry Hollow—*valley* TN-4
Henry Hollow—*valley* WV-2
Henry Holwenger Dam—*dam* SD-7
Henry Horton Bridge—*bridge* TN-4
Henry Horton State Park—*park* TN-4
Henry House—*building* VA-3
Henry House—*hist pl* AL-4
Henry House—*hist pl* TN-4
Henry House—*hist pl* WI-6

Henry House Creek—*stream* ... OK-5
Henry House Falls—*falls* ... OK-5
Henry HS—*school* ... MN-6
Henry Hudson Bridge—*bridge* ... NY-2
Henry Hudson JHS—*school* ... NY-2
Henry Hudson Regional HS—*school* ... NJ-2
*Henry Hunt Ditch* ... IN-6
*Henry Island* ... AL-4
Henry Island—*island* ... AK-9
Henry Island—*island* ... PA-2
Henry Island—*island* ... WA-9
Henry Islands—*island* ... ME-1
Henry-Jarman Cem—*cemetery* ... TN-4
Henry Jim Canal—*canal* ... UT-8
*Henry Johnson Elementary School* ... TN-4
Henry Johnson Sch—*school* ... TN-4
Henry Jones Creek—*bay* ... NC-3
Henry-Jordan House—*hist pl* ... AL-4
Henry Junior Dam—*dam* ... CA-9
Henry Key—*island* ... FL-3
Henry Knob—*summit* ... GA-3
Henry Knob—*summit* ... NC-3
Henry Knob—*summit* ... SC-3
Henry Kock Ditch—*canal* ... IN-6
Henry Lake—*lake* ... CO-8
Henry Lake—*lake* ... FL-3
Henry Lake—*lake* ... ID-8
Henry Lake—*lake* ... IN-6
Henry Lake—*lake* ... LA-4
Henry Lake—*lake* (2) ... MI-6
Henry Lake—*lake* (6) ... MN-6
Henry Lake—*lake* ... TX-5
Henry Lake—*lake* ... WA-9
Henry Lake—*lake* ... WI-6
Henry Lake—*reservoir* ... CO-8
Henry Lake—*reservoir* ... PA-2
Henry Lake—*swamp* ... MN-6
Henry Lake Branch—*stream* ... TX-5
Henry Lake Dam—*dam* ... MS-4
Henry Landing—*locale* ... AL-4
Henry Landing—*locale* ... NC-3
Henry Lateral—*canal* ... AZ-5
*Henry L Barger Elem Sch* ... TN-4
Henry L Barger Sch—*school* ... TN-4
Henry Lee Pond—*lake* ... FL-3
Henry Lott Brook—*stream* ... PA-2
Henry L Porter Evangelistic
Association—*church* ... FL-3
Henrylyn Canal—*canal* ... CO-8
*Henry Magee Run* ... PA-2
Henry Maggard Branch—*stream* ... KY-4
Henry (Magisterial District)—*fmr MCD* (2) ... VA-3
Henry (Magisterial District)—*fmr MCD* ... WV-2
Henry Martin Island—*island* ... AK-9
Henry-Martinson House—*hist pl* ... SD-7
Henry Meadow—*flat* ... ID-8
Henry Memorial Cem—*cemetery* ... PA-2
Henry Memorial Park—*cemetery* ... VA-3
Henry Meyer Canyon—*valley* ... NV-8
Henry Meyer Spring—*spring* ... NV-8
Henry Michalet Grant—*civil* ... FL-3
Henry Miller Field—*flat* ... CA-9
Henry Miller Sch—*school* ... CA-9
Henry Mine—*mine* ... ID-8
Henry Mitchell Brook—*stream* ... ME-1
Henry Moore Spring—*spring* ... ID-8
Henry Mountain—*ridge* ... AR-4
Henry Mtn—*summit* ... CO-8
Henry Mtn—*summit* ... KY-4
Henry Mtn—*summit* ... NC-3
Henry Mtns—*range* ... UT-8
**Henry Oleson Subdivision**—*pop pl* ... UT-8
Henry Olsen Draw—*valley* ... UT-8
Henry O'Neal Grant—*civil* ... FL-3
Henry Ott Hill—*summit* ... IN-6
Henry Park—*park* ... CT-1
Henry Park—*park* ... KS-7
Henry Peak—*summit* ... AK-9
Henry Peak—*summit* ... CA-9
Henry Peak—*summit* ... ID-8
Henry Peak—*summit* ... MT-8
Henry Peak—*summit* ... WY-8
Henry P Fieler Elem Sch—*school* ... IN-6
Henry Place—*locale* ... WY-8
Henry Platt Springs—*spring* ... AZ-5
Henry Point—*cape* (2) ... ME-1
Henry Post Office—*building* ... TN-4
Henry Prairie Ch—*church* ... TX-5
Henry Prescott Pond—*lake* ... FL-3
Henry Ranch—*locale* ... NM-5
Henry Ranch—*locale* ... WY-8
Henry-Remsen House—*hist pl* ... NY-2
Henry Ridge—*ridge* (2) ... CA-9
Henry Ridge—*ridge* ... TN-4
Henry Ridge—*ridge* (2) ... VA-3
**Henry River**—*pop pl* ... NC-3
Henry River Dam—*dam* ... NC-3
Henry River Lake—*reservoir* ... NC-3
**Henry Road Estates**
**(subdivision)**—*pop pl* ... AL-4
Henry Run—*stream* (4) ... PA-2
Henry Run—*stream* (2) ... WV-2
**Henrys**—*pop pl* ... WA-9
Henry Sands Canyon—*valley* ... CA-9
Henrys Arm—*bay* ... AK-9
Henrys Bar—*bar* ... AL-4
**Henrys Bend**—*pop pl* ... PA-2
Henrys Branch—*stream* ... KY-4
*Henrysburg* ... PA-2
Henrys Cabin—*locale* ... NM-5
Henrys Cem—*cemetery* ... OH-6
Henrys Ch—*church* ... TX-5
Henry Sch—*school* ... AZ-5
Henry Sch—*school* ... AR-4
Henry Sch—*school* ... CA-9
Henry Sch—*school* (3) ... IL-6
Henry Sch—*school* ... MI-6
Henry Sch—*school* ... MS-4
Henry Sch—*school* ... NY-2
Henry Sch—*school* ... OH-6
Henry Sch—*school* ... OK-5
Henry Sch—*school* (3) ... PA-2
Henry Sch—*school* ... TX-5
Henry Sch—*school* ... WI-6
Henry Sch (abandoned)—*school* ... PA-2
Henry Schacht Lake—*lake* ... FL-3
Henrys Chapel—*church* ... MS-4
Henrys Chapel—*church* ... TN-4
Henrys Chapel—*locale* ... TX-5
Henrys Chapel Cem—*cemetery* ... MS-4
Henrys Chapel Cem—*cemetery* ... TX-5
Henry Sch (historical)—*school* ... PA-2
Henrys Corners—*locale* ... NY-2
*Henrys Cove* ... ME-1
Henrys Creek—*stream* ... AR-4
Henrys Creek—*stream* ... NC-3
Henrys Creek—*stream* ... VA-3
Henrys Crossroads—*locale* ... MD-2
**Henrys Crossroads**—*pop pl* ... TN-4
Henrys Diggings—*locale* ... CA-9
Henry Seale Cem—*cemetery* ... MS-4
Henry S Evans Elem Sch—*school* ... IN-6
Henrys Falls—*falls* ... OR-9
Henrys Ferry (historical)—*crossing* ... TN-4
Henrys Flat—*flat* ... CA-9
*Henry's Fork* ... UT-8
*Henry's Fork* ... WY-8
Henrys Fork—*stream* ... ID-8
Henrys Fork—*stream* (2) ... UT-8
Henrys Fork—*stream* ... WY-8
Henrys Fork Campground—*locale* ... UT-8
*Henrys Fork Green River* ... UT-8
*Henrys Fork Green River* ... WY-8
Henrys Fork Lake—*lake* ... UT-8
*Henry's Fork of Green River* ... UT-8
*Henry's Fork of Green River* ... WY-8
*Henrys Fork Of Snake River* ... ID-8
*Henry's Fork of the Green River* ... UT-8
*Henry's Fork of the Green River* ... WY-8
Henrys Fork Park—*park* ... UT-8
Henrys Fork Trailhead—*locale* ... UT-8
*Henrys Fork Trail Head Campground* ... UT-8
Henrys Fort (historical)—*locale* (2) ... TN-4
Henry's Grove—*hist pl* ... MD-2
Henrys Gulch—*valley* ... CA-9
Henry Shackleford Lake Dam—*dam* ... MS-4
*Henry Shaw Arboretum* ... MO-7
Henry Short Hollow—*valley* ... KY-4
*Henry's Hunting Ground* ... WA-9
Henry Siebrasse Dam—*dam* ... SD-7
Henry Slacks Log House
(historical)—*locale* ... SD-7
Henry Slade Spring—*spring* ... AZ-5
Henrys Lake—*reservoir* ... ID-8
Henrys Lake Flat—*flat* ... ID-8
*Henry's Lake Mountains* ... ID-8
Henrys Lake Mtns—*range* ... ID-8
Henrys Lake Mtns—*range* ... MT-8
Henrys Landing (historical)—*locale* ... MS-4
*Henrys Mill* ... PA-2
Henrys Mill—*locale* ... VA-3
**Henrys Mill**—*pop pl* ... PA-2
Henrys Mill (historical)—*locale* ... AL-4
Henrys Mills—*locale* ... PA-2
Henry Smith Branch—*stream* ... WV-2
Henry Soap Ridge—*ridge* ... VA-3
Henryson Coulee—*valley* ... MT-8
*Henrys Point* ... MD-2
*Henrys Pond* ... MA-1
Henry Spring—*spring* ... AZ-5
Henry Spring—*spring* ... CA-9
Henry Spring—*spring* (2) ... NV-8
Henry Spring—*spring* ... TX-5
Henry Spring—*spring* (2) ... UT-8
*Henrys River* ... NC-3
Henrys Rsvr—*reservoir* ... OR-9
Henrys Run—*stream* ... PA-2
*Henrys Station* ... TN-4
Henrys Store (historical)—*locale* ... AL-4
Henrys Tank—*reservoir* (2) ... AZ-5
*Henry Station* ... TN-4
*Henry Station Post Office* ... TN-4
Henry Statue—*park* ... DC-2
*Henry Street* ... MI-6
Henry Street—*uninc pl* ... TN-4
Henry Street Park—*park* ... IL-6
Henry Street Park—*park* ... NY-2
Henry Street Sch (historical)—*school* ... AL-4
Henry Street Settlement and Neighborhood
Playhouse—*hist pl* ... NY-2
Henry Street Station Morristown Post
Office—*building* ... TN-4
Henry Studebaker Elem Sch—*school* ... IN-6
Henrysville—*locale* ... WI-6
*Henrys Well* ... AZ-5
Henrys Well—*well* ... NV-8
Henry S West Laboratory Elem
Sch—*school* ... FL-3
Henry Tank—*reservoir* (3) ... AZ-5
Henry Thomas Branch—*stream* ... TX-5
Henry-Thompson House—*hist pl* ... AR-4
Henry Tin Mine—*mine* ... SD-7
Henryton—*locale* ... MD-2
**Henryton (Henryton State**
**Hospital)**—*pop pl* ... MD-2
Henryton State Hosp—*hospital* ... MD-2
*Henryton State Hospital* ... MD-2
Henrytown—*locale* ... VA-3
**Henrytown**—*pop pl* ... MN-6
**Henrytown**—*pop pl* ... NC-3
Henry Township—*fmr MCD* (2) ... IA-7
**Henry Township**—*pop pl* ... KS-7
**Henry Township**—*pop pl* ... MO-7
**Henry Township**—*pop pl* ... ND-7
**Henry Township**—*pop pl* (2) ... SD-7
Henry Township Hall—*building* ... SD-7
**Henry (Township of)**—*pop pl* ... IL-6
**Henry (Township of)**—*pop pl* (2) ... IN-6
**Henry (Township of)**—*pop pl* ... OH-6
Henry U. Payne Cotton Gin
(historical)—*building* ... TX-5
Henry-Vernon House—*hist pl* ... NC-3
Henryville—*locale* ... PA-2
**Henryville**—*pop pl* ... AL-4
**Henryville**—*pop pl* ... IN-6
**Henryville**—*pop pl* ... KY-4
**Henryville**—*pop pl* ... TN-4
*Henryville Baptist Church* ... MS-4
Henryville Cem—*cemetery* ... AL-4
Henryville Cem—*cemetery* ... TN-4
Henryville Ch—*church* ... AL-4
Henryville Ch of Christ—*church* ... TN-4
Henryville Elem Sch—*school* ... IN-6
**Henryville (historical)**—*pop pl* ... OR-9
Henryville House—*hist pl* ... PA-2
Henryville Junior and Senior HS—*school* ... IN-6
Henryville Methodist Ch—*church* ... TN-4
Henryville Post Office
(historical)—*building* ... TN-4
Henryville Sch (historical)—*school* ... TN-4
**Henryville (Township of)**—*pop pl* ... MN-6
Henry W Breyer Camp—*locale* ... PA-2
Henry W Darden Lake Dam—*dam* ... MS-4
Henry Weathers Sch (historical)—*school* ... MS-4
Henry Whitehead Cabin—*locale* ... TN-4
Henry White Mtn—*summit* ... TX-5
Henry Widener Branch—*stream* ... VA-3
Henry Willard Coe State Park—*park* ... CA-9
Henry Wilson Dam—*dam* ... SD-7
Henry Windmill—*locale* ... NM-5
Henry W Longfellow JHS—*school* ... IN-6
Henry Woods Mtn—*summit* ... MT-8
Henry W. Wheeler—*post sta* ... MO-7
Henry X State Wildlife Mngmt
Area—*park* ... MN-6
Henry Z Mine—*mine* ... CO-8
Hensarling Cem—*cemetery* ... TX-5
Hensby Spring—*spring* ... TN-4
Henschel Lake—*lake* ... CO-8
Henschel Park—*park* ... CA-9
Henschen Branch—*stream* ... IN-6
Henschen Ditch—*canal* ... IN-6
Henschen Hill—*summit* ... IN-6
Henschien Lake—*lake* ... MN-6
Hen Scratch—*locale* ... FL-3
Hense Branch—*stream* ... TN-4
Hense Branch—*stream* ... WV-2
Hensel—*locale* ... PA-2
**Hensel**—*pop pl* ... ND-7
Hensel Airp—*airport* ... ND-7
Hensel Cem—*cemetery* ... TX-5
Hensel Fork—*stream* ... PA-2
Hensel Hollow—*valley* ... PA-2
Hensel Park—*park* ... TX-5
Hensel Sch (historical)—*school* ... MO-7
*Hensen* ... CO-8
*Hensen Creek* ... AL-4
*Hensenger* ... PA-2
Hensen Sch (historical)—*school* ... AL-4
Hensen Tank—*reservoir* ... AZ-5
Hensen Tank One—*reservoir* ... AZ-5
Hensey Cem—*cemetery* ... FL-3
Hensey Sch—*school* ... IL-6
**Hensfoot**—*pop pl* ... NJ-2
Hen Shanty Run—*stream* ... WV-2
Hen Shate Hollow—*valley* ... KY-4
**Henshaw**—*pop pl* ... IA-7
**Henshaw**—*pop pl* ... KY-4
Henshaw, Lake—*reservoir* ... CA-9
Henshaw Bend—*bend* ... IN-6
Henshaw Cabin—*locale* ... AK-9
Henshaw Cem—*cemetery* ... AL-4
Henshaw Cem—*cemetery* ... IL-6
Henshaw Cove—*valley* ... AL-4
Henshaw Creek—*stream* (2) ... TX-5
**Henshaw (historical)**—*pop pl* ... TN-4
Henshaw Lake—*lake* ... MN-6
Henshaw Oil Field—*other* ... NM-5
Henshaw Playground—*park* ... NJ-2
Henshaw Pond—*lake* ... MA-1
Henshaw Post Office (historical)—*building* ... TN-4
*Henshaw Rsvr* ... CA-9
Henshaw Run—*stream* ... VA-3
Henshaw (Sozhekla)—*stream* ... AK-9
Henshaw Spring Cave—*cave* ... AL-4
Henshaw Tank—*reservoir* ... NM-5
Henshaw Truck Trail—*trail* ... CA-9
Henshaw Well—*well* ... TX-5
Hens Hole Flat—*flat* ... UT-8
Hens Hole Peak—*summit* ... UT-8
Hensingersville—*locale* ... PA-2
Hensingersville Dam—*dam* ... PA-2
*Hensingerville* ... PA-2
**Hensingerville**—*pop pl* ... PA-2
Hen Skin Lake—*lake* ... WA-9
Henski Rsvr—*reservoir* ... CA-9
Henslee Chapel—*church* ... TX-5
**Henslee Heights**—*pop pl* ... AR-4
Hensleigh Coulee—*valley* ... MT-8
**Hensler**—*pop pl* ... ND-7
Hensler Cem—*cemetery* ... ND-7
**Henslertown**—*pop pl* ... PA-2
Hensley—*locale* (2) ... KY-4
**Hensley**—*pop pl* ... AR-4
**Hensley**—*pop pl* ... WV-2
Hensley and Glover Cem—*cemetery* ... MS-4
Hensley Bar Cutoff—*bend* ... AR-4
Hensley Big Branch—*stream* ... WV-2
Hensley Branch—*stream* (4) ... KY-4
Hensley Branch—*stream* ... MS-4
Hensley Branch—*stream* (3) ... NC-3
Hensley Branch—*stream* ... WV-2
Hensley Bridge—*bridge* ... CA-9
Hensley Butte—*ridge* ... OR-9
*Hensley Cem* ... TN-4
Hensley Cem—*cemetery* ... GA-3
Hensley Cem—*cemetery* (5) ... KY-4
Hensley Cem—*cemetery* ... MO-7
Hensley Cem—*cemetery* (2) ... NC-3
Hensley Cem—*cemetery* (8) ... TN-4
Hensley Cem—*cemetery* (2) ... VA-3
Hensley Cem—*cemetery* (2) ... WV-2
Hensley Ch—*church* ... VA-3
Hensley Chapel—*church* ... TN-4
Hensley Chapel—*locale* ... TN-4
Hensley Chapel Cave Number One—*cave* ... TN-4
Hensley Chapel Cave Number Two—*cave* ... TN-4
Hensley Church Trail—*trail* ... VA-3
*Hensley Claren* ... WV-2
Hensley Creek—*stream* (2) ... CA-9
Hensley Creek—*stream* ... IN-6
Hensley Creek—*stream* (3) ... MT-8
Hensley Creek—*stream* ... OR-9
Hensley Creek—*stream* ... TN-4
Hensley Creek—*stream* ... WV-2
Hensley Creek Ch—*church* ... TN-4
Hensley Creek Sch (historical)—*school* ... TN-4
Hensley Draw—*valley* ... TX-5
Hensley Draw—*valley* ... WY-8
*Hensley Draw Creek* ... WY-8
*Hensley Field* ... TX-5
Hensley Flats—*flat* ... KY-4
Hensley Ford—*locale* ... AR-4
Hensley Ford—*locale* ... KY-4
Hensley Glade—*flat* ... CA-9
Hensley Gulch—*valley* ... MT-8
**Hensley Heights**—*pop pl* ... WV-2
Hensley Hill—*summit* ... MT-8
Hensley Hist Dist—*hist pl* ... CA-9
Hensley Hollow—*valley* ... AR-4
Hensley Hollow—*valley* ... KY-4
Hensley Hollow—*valley* (7) ... TN-4
Hensley Hollow—*valley* (2) ... VA-3
Hensley Hollow Overlook—*locale* ... VA-3
Hensley Hollow Trail—*trail* ... VA-3
Hensley Island—*island* ... AR-4
Hensley Knob—*summit* ... WV-2
Hensley Lake—*reservoir* ... TX-5
Hensley Mountain—*ridge* ... AL-4
Hensley Mtn—*summit* ... NC-3
Hensley Mtn—*summit* ... OK-5
Hensley Pond—*reservoir* ... MS-4
Hensley Ridge—*ridge* (3) ... NC-3
Hensley Ridge—*ridge* ... TN-4
Hensley Ridge—*ridge* ... VA-3
Hensley Ridge Cem—*cemetery* ... TN-4
**Hensley Ridge (historical)**—*pop pl* ... TN-4
Hensley Ridge Sch (historical)—*school* ... TN-4
**Hensley (RR name Claren)**—*pop pl* ... WV-2
*Hensley Sch* ... TN-4
Hensley Sch—*school* ... IL-6
Hensley Sch—*school* ... KY-4
Hensley Sch—*school* ... TN-4
Hensley Sch—*school* ... WV-2
*Hensleys Chapel Free Will Christian Baptist*
*Church* ... TN-4
*Hensleys Creek* ... TN-4
Hensley Settlement—*hist pl* ... KY-4
Hensley Spring—*spring* ... TX-5
Hensley Springs—*spring* ... CA-9
*Hensleys Sch* ... TN-4
**Hensleytown**—*pop pl* ... KY-4
**Hensley (Township of)**—*pop pl* ... IL-6
**Hensley (Township of)**—*pop pl* ... IN-6
Hensley Windmill—*locale* (2) ... TX-5
Henslin Creek—*stream* ... MN-6
Hens Nest, The—*basin* ... UT-8
Hens Nest Cliff—*cliff* ... KY-4
Hens Nest Creek—*stream* ... KY-4
Hens Nest Rock—*summit* ... KY-4
Henson—*locale* ... CO-8
Henson—*locale* ... MO-7
**Henson**—*pop pl* ... KS-7
Henson, Alfred W., House—*hist pl* ... AR-4
Henson, Matthew, Residence—*hist pl* ... NY-2
*Henson Branch* ... MO-7
Henson Branch—*stream* ... AL-4
Henson Branch—*stream* ... GA-3
Henson Branch—*stream* ... MO-7
Henson Branch—*stream* ... NC-3
Henson Branch—*stream* ... TN-4
Hensonburg Sch—*school* ... IN-6
Henson Cave—*cave* ... AL-4
Henson Cem—*cemetery* (3) ... AL-4
Henson Cem—*cemetery* ... GA-3
Henson Cem—*cemetery* (2) ... IL-6
Henson Cem—*cemetery* (2) ... KY-4
Henson Cem—*cemetery* ... LA-4
Henson Cem—*cemetery* (2) ... MO-7
Henson Cem—*cemetery* (2) ... TN-4
Henson Cem—*cemetery* (2) ... TX-5
*Henson Cemetery* ... MS-4
Henson Chapel Cem—*cemetery* ... NC-3
Henson Cove—*valley* ... GA-3
Henson Cove—*valley* (2) ... NC-3
Henson Creek—*stream* (2) ... AL-4
Henson Creek—*stream* ... AR-4
Henson Creek—*stream* ... CO-8
Henson Creek—*stream* ... GA-3
Henson Creek—*stream* ... KY-4
Henson Creek—*stream* ... MD-2
Henson Creek—*stream* (2) ... NC-3
Henson Creek—*stream* (3) ... TN-4
Henson Creek—*stream* (3) ... TX-5
Henson Creek Ch—*church* ... NC-3
Henson Dam—*dam* ... AL-4
Henson Gap—*gap* ... GA-3
Henson Gap—*gap* (2) ... NC-3
Henson Gap—*gap* ... TN-4
Henson Gulf—*valley* ... GA-3
Henson Hollow—*valley* ... AL-4
Henson Hollow—*valley* ... MO-7
Henson Hollow—*valley* ... NC-3
Henson Hollow—*valley* (2) ... TN-4
Henson Island (historical)—*island* ... TN-4
Henson Knob—*summit* ... KY-4
Henson Lake—*lake* (2) ... MN-6
Henson Lake—*lake* ... MO-7
Henson Lake—*lake* ... WI-6
Henson Lake—*reservoir* ... NC-3
Henson Lake Dam—*dam* ... NC-3
Henson Mine (underground)—*mine* ... AL-4
Henson Mountain—*ridge* ... TN-4
Henson Mountains—*summit* ... TX-5
Henson Mtn—*summit* ... NC-3
Henson No 1 Windmill—*locale* ... NM-5
Henson No 2 Windmill—*locale* ... NM-5
Henson Pond—*lake* ... IL-6
Henson Pond—*reservoir* ... AL-4
Henson Ridge—*ridge* ... NC-3
Henson Ridge—*ridge* ... PA-2
Hensons Cem—*cemetery* ... MS-4
Henson Sch—*school* ... IL-6
Henson Sch (abandoned)—*school* (2) ... MO-7
*Hensons Creek* ... AL-4
Hensons Creek—*stream* ... NC-3
*Hensons Gap* ... TN-4
Henson Spring—*spring* (2) ... AL-4
Henson Spring—*spring* ... TN-4
Henson Spring Branch—*stream* ... TN-4
Henson Springs—*locale* ... AL-4
Henson Springs Cem—*cemetery* ... AL-4
*Hensons Spring Branch* ... TN-4
Hensons Springs Post Office
(historical)—*building* ... AL-4
Hensons Store—*locale* ... VA-3
**Hensonville**—*pop pl* ... NY-2
Hens Peak Spring—*spring* ... UT-8
Hen Spring—*spring* ... NV-8
Henstep Run—*stream* ... PA-2
Henstep Trail—*trail* ... PA-2
Henstep Valley—*valley* ... PA-2
Henstep Valley Trail—*trail* ... PA-2
Henthorn Branch—*stream* ... IN-6
Henthorn Cem—*cemetery* ... OH-6
Henthorne Lake—*lake* ... CA-9
*Henthorne Lakes* ... CA-9
Henthorn Fork—*stream* ... WV-2
Henthorn Gulch—*valley* ... CO-8
*Henton* ... IA-7
**Henton**—*pop pl* ... IL-6
Henton Cem—*cemetery* ... MO-7
Henton (historical)—*locale* ... AL-4
Henton Lake—*lake* ... WA-9
Henton Ranch—*locale* ... WY-8
*Henton's* ... IA-7
Henton Sch—*school* ... IL-6
Henton School (historical)—*locale* ... MO-7
**Hentons (historical)**—*pop pl* ... IA-7
Hentons Lodge—*locale* ... AK-9
Henton (Township of)—*fmr MCD* ... AR-4
**Hentown**—*pop pl* ... GA-3
Hentz Ditch—*canal* ... IN-6
Hentzels Lake—*lake* ... IL-6
Hen Valley—*valley* ... TN-4
Hen Wallow Creek—*stream* ... TN-4
Hen Wilder Branch—*stream* ... KY-4
Hen Windmill—*locale* ... NM-5
Henyon Hollow—*valley* ... NY-2
Henyon Hollow—*valley* ... PA-2
Henze, LeRoy A., House—*hist pl* ... WI-6
Henzel Park—*park* ... OR-9
Henze Oil Field—*oilfield* ... TX-5
Heola Mine—*mine* ... AZ-5
Hepbron—*locale* ... MD-2
**Hepburn**—*pop pl* ... IN-6
**Hepburn**—*pop pl* ... IA-7
**Hepburn**—*pop pl* ... OH-6
Hepburn, Col. William Peters,
House—*hist pl* ... IA-7
Hepburn Ch—*church* ... PA-2
Hepburn Creek—*stream* ... OR-9
**Hepburn Heights**—*pop pl* ... PA-2
**Hepburnia**—*pop pl* ... PA-2
Hepburn Lycoming Sch—*school* ... PA-2
Hepburn Peninsula—*cape* ... AK-9
**Hepburn (Township of)**—*pop pl* ... PA-2
**Hepburnville**—*pop pl* ... PA-2
**Hepco**—*pop pl* ... NC-3
Hepepa Island—*island* ... FM-9
*Hepes* ... UT-8
Hephzibah—*locale* ... PA-2
**Hephzibah**—*pop pl* ... AL-4
**Hephzibah**—*pop pl* ... GA-3
*Hephzibah Baptist Church* ... AL-4
Hephzibah (CCD)—*cens area* ... GA-3
Hephzibah Cem—*cemetery* ... AL-4
Hephzibah Cem—*cemetery* ... GA-3
Hephzibah Cem—*cemetery* ... MS-4
Hephzibah Ch—*church* (3) ... AL-4
Hephzibah Ch—*church* ... AR-4
Hephzibah Ch—*church* ... GA-3
Hephzibah Ch—*church* ... IN-6
Hephzibah Ch—*church* ... MS-4
Hephzibah Ch—*church* (3) ... NC-3
Hephzibah Ch—*church* ... SC-3
Hephzibah Ch (historical)—*church* ... TN-4
**Hephzibah Heights**—*pop pl* ... MA-1
*Hephzibah Primitive Baptist Ch* ... AL-4
Hephzibah Sch (historical)—*school* ... AL-4
*Hepikoft Hill* ... PA-2
Hepler—*locale* ... PA-2
**Hepler**—*pop pl* ... KS-7
Hepler Airp—*airport* ... IN-6
Hepler Ditch—*canal* ... IN-6
Hepler Ranch—*locale* (2) ... NM-5
Heplers Ch—*church* ... PA-2
Heplers Summer Ch—*church* ... PA-2
Hepner Cem—*cemetery* ... IN-6
Hepner Creek—*stream* ... ID-8
Hepners—*locale* ... VA-3
Hepner Sch—*school* ... PA-2
Hepp Cow Camp—*locale* ... WY-8
Hepp Creek—*stream* ... WI-6
Heppe Cave—*cave* ... CA-9
Heppe Chimney—*pillar* ... CA-9
Hepplers Ponds—*lake* ... UT-8
Heppner—*locale* ... SD-7
**Heppner**—*pop pl* ... OR-9
Heppner (CCD)—*cens area* ... OR-9
Heppner City Well—*well* ... OR-9
Heppner Dam, The—*dam* ... SD-7
Heppner Draw—*valley* ... WY-8
Heppner Hotel—*hist pl* ... OR-9
Heppner Junction—*locale* ... OR-9
Heppsie Mtn—*summit* ... OR-9
Hepsabah Ch—*church* ... AL-4
Hepseby Cem—*cemetery* ... AR-4
*Hepseby Ch* ... AL-4
Hepsedam Creek—*stream* ... CA-9
Hepsedam Peak—*summit* ... CA-9
Hepsedam Ranch—*locale* ... CA-9
Hepsedam Spring—*spring* ... CA-9
Hepsibah Baptist Ch—*church* ... TX-5
Hepsibah Cem—*cemetery* ... TX-5
Hepsibah Ch—*church* ... SC-3
Hepsibah Ch—*church* ... TX-5
Hepsibah Sch (historical)—*school* ... MS-4
*Hepsiby Ch* ... AL-4
Hepsida Ch—*church* ... MO-7
**Hepsidam**—*pop pl* ... AL-4
Hepton Union Ch—*church* ... IN-6
Hepworth Wash—*valley* ... UT-8
Hepzibah—*locale* ... WV-2
**Hepzibah**—*pop pl* ... AL-4
**Hepzibah**—*pop pl* ... WV-2
Hepzibah Baptist Ch—*church* ... AL-4
Hepzibah Baptist Ch (historical)—*church* ... AL-4
Hepzibah Cem—*cemetery* (2) ... AL-4
Hepzibah Cem—*cemetery* ... GA-3
Hepzibah Cem—*cemetery* ... MS-4
Hepzibah Ch—*church* (2) ... GA-3
Hepzibah Ch—*church* ... MS-4
Hequembourg House—*hist pl* ... FL-3
Hequy Well—*well* ... NV-8
Herald—*locale* ... CA-9
**Herald**—*pop pl* ... IL-6
**Herald**—*pop pl* ... VA-3
Herald Bldg—*hist pl* ... UT-8
Herald Block—*hist pl* ... MN-6
Herald Branch—*stream* ... MO-7
Herald Cem—*cemetery* ... IL-6
Herald Cem—*cemetery* ... KY-4
**Herald Harbor**—*pop pl* ... MD-2
Herald Hollow—*valley* ... AR-4
Herald Hotel—*hist pl* ... CA-9
Herald Knob—*summit* ... WV-2
Herald Mine—*mine* ... CO-8
Heralds Prairie (Township of)—*civ div* ... IL-6
Herald Square—*locale* ... NY-2
Herard, Mount—*summit* ... CO-8
*Herard Peak* ... CO-8
Herarradura Tank—*reservoir* ... TX-5
**Herbamount**—*pop pl* ... IN-6
Herb Creek—*stream* ... AK-9
Herb Creek—*stream* ... OR-9
Herbeck Flat—*flat* ... CA-9
Herber Ditch—*canal* ... SD-7
Herberger Lake—*lake* ... MN-6
Herberger Lake State Wildlife Mngmt
Are—*park* ... MN-6
Herberger Park Number Two—*park* ... AZ-5
Herberger Park One—*park* ... AZ-5
Herberger Spring—*spring* ... OR-9
Herberg Lake—*reservoir* ... TX-5
Herberg Sch—*school* ... ND-7
Herberg Town Hall—*building* ... ND-7
**Herberg Township**—*pop pl* ... ND-7
Herber JHS—*school* ... NY-2
*Herbert* ... OK-5
*Herbert* ... TN-4
*Herbert* ... VA-3
*Herbert* ... WV-2
Herbert—*locale* ... AL-4
Herbert—*locale* ... AR-4
Herbert—*locale* ... ID-8
Herbert—*locale* ... KY-4
Herbert—*locale* ... TX-5
**Herbert**—*pop pl* ... AR-4
**Herbert**—*pop pl* ... IL-6
**Herbert**—*pop pl* ... MD-2
**Herbert**—*pop pl* ... PA-2
**Herbert**—*pop pl* ... SC-3
Herbert, John, House—*hist pl* ... TN-4
Herbert, Mount—*summit* ... AK-9
Herbert, Rev. Walter I., House—*hist pl* ... SC-3
Herberta Siding—*locale* ... SC-3
*Herbert Baptist Ch* ... MS-4
Herbert Brook—*stream* ... NY-2
*Herbert C Bonner Bridge* ... NC-3
Herbert C Bonner Bridge—*bridge* ... NC-3
Herbert Cem—*cemetery* ... AL-4
Herbert Cem—*cemetery* ... LA-4
Herbert Cem—*cemetery* ... MS-4
Herbert Cem—*cemetery* ... NY-2
Herbert Ch—*church* ... MS-4
Herbert Ch—*church* ... VA-3
Herbert C Hoover JHS—*school* ... FL-3
Herbert Cooper Pond Dam—*dam* ... MS-4
**Herbert Corners**—*pop pl* ... OH-6
*Herbert Creek* ... KS-7
Herbert Creek—*stream* ... AR-4
Herbert Creek—*stream* ... CA-9
Herbert Creek—*stream* ... SD-7
**Herbert Domain**—*pop pl* ... TN-4
Herbert E Gowdy Pond Dam—*dam* ... MS-4
Herbert Glacier—*glacier* ... AK-9
Herbert Graves Island—*island* ... AK-9
Herbert G West, Lake—*reservoir* ... WA-9
Herbert Hill—*summit* ... AR-4
**Herbert (historical)**—*pop pl* ... MS-4
Herbert Hoover Dyke—*levee* ... FL-3
Herbert Hoover Elem Sch—*school* ... PA-2
Herbert Hoover JHS—*school* (2) ... CA-9
Herbert Hoover Natl Historic Site—*hist pl* ... IA-7
Herbert Hoover Natl Historic Site—*park* ... IA-7
*Herbert Hoover Sch* ... PA-2
Herbert Hoover Sch—*school* ... CA-9
Herbert House—*hist pl* ... VA-3
Herbert Island—*island* ... AK-9
*Herbert Lake* ... MI-6
Herbert Lee Lake Dam—*dam* ... MS-4
*Herbert L Sloan Ditch* ... IN-6
Herbert Mine—*mine* ... MT-8
Herbert Mine—*mine* ... NM-5
Herbert Mission Ch (historical)—*church* ... AL-4
Herbert Mullins Senior Citizen
Center—*building* ... MS-4
*Herberton* ... NJ-2
Herbert Post Office (historical)—*building* ... TN-4
Herbert Ranch—*locale* ... CA-9
Herbert Ranch—*locale* ... UT-8
*Herbert Rhea* ... TN-4
Herbert River—*stream* ... AK-9
*Herbert Run* ... MD-2
Herbert Run—*stream* (2) ... MD-2
**Herberts**—*pop pl* ... NJ-2
Herbert Sch—*school* ... IL-6
Herbert Sch—*school* ... LA-4
Herbert Sch (abandoned)—*school* ... MO-7
Herberts Chapel—*church* ... GA-3
*Herbert School* ... KS-7
Herberts Corner—*locale* ... NJ-2
Herberts Corner—*locale* ... VA-3
**Herberts Corner**—*pop pl* ... NJ-2
*Herberts Creek* ... VA-3
Herberts Creek—*stream* ... VA-3
Herbert Slater JHS—*school* ... CA-9
Herbert Smart Downtown Municipal
Airp—*airport* ... GA-3
**Herbert Springs**—*pop pl* ... MS-4
Herbert Stoick Dam—*dam* ... SD-7
**Herbertsville**—*pop pl* ... NJ-2
Herbert Temple Ch—*church* ... AL-4
Herbert Wilson Recreation Center—*park* ... MS-4
Herbert Windmill—*locale* (2) ... TX-5
Herbes, Isle aux—*island* ... AL-4
Herbes, Point aux—*cape* ... LA-4
Herb Eyre Hollow—*valley* ... UT-8
Herbine—*locale* ... AR-4
Herb Lake—*lake* ... MN-6
Herb Lake—*lake* ... OR-9
Herb Lake—*lake* ... WA-9
Herblengths Cave—*cave* ... PA-2
Herb Martyr Forest Camp—*locale* ... AZ-5
**Herbonville**—*pop pl* ... MA-1
**Herborn**—*pop pl* ... IL-6
Herb Parsons Lake—*reservoir* ... TN-4
Herb Parsons Lake Dam—*dam* ... TN-4
Herbrandt Branch—*stream* ... MO-7
Herb River—*stream* ... GA-3
Herbruger Pond—*reservoir* ... OR-9
Herbs Lagoon—*bay* ... AK-9
Herbs Lake—*lake* ... MI-6
Herbs Point—*cape* ... UT-8
**Herbst**—*pop pl* ... IN-6
Herbst Cem—*cemetery* ... MO-7
**Herbster**—*pop pl* ... WI-6
Herbster Cem—*cemetery* ... WI-6
Herbst Glacier—*glacier* ... MT-8

Herbst Place—*locale* OR-9
Herbst Sch—*school* MI-6
Herburger Cabin—*locale* OR-9
Herby Ch—*church* ND-7
*Herby Chapel* MS-4
Herby Lake—*lake* WI-6
Herchberger Cem—*cemetery* IN-6
*Herculaneum* IN-6
**Herculaneum**—*pop pl* MO-7
Herculean Mine—*mine* OR-9
*Hercules* PA-2
Hercules—*locale* MO-7
**Hercules**—*pop pl* CA-9
**Hercules**—*pop pl* DE-2
**Hercules**—*pop pl* FL-3
**Hercules**—*pop pl* MO-7
**Hercules**—*pop pl* VA-3
Hercules—*uninc pl* PA-2
Hercules, Incorporated—*facility* NC-3
Hercules and Coach No. 2—*hist pl* KY-4
Hercules Bacchas Works Heliport—*airport* UT-8
Hercules Canyon—*valley* NV-8
Hercules Country Club—*locale* DE-2
Hercules Creek—*stream* MT-8
Hercules Creek—*stream* NV-8
Hercules Creek—*stream* SC-3
Hercules Gap—*gap* NV-8
Hercules Gap Well—*well* NV-8
Hercules Glades Wilderness—*forest* MO-7
Hercules Glades Wilderness—*locale* MO-7
Hercules Hollow—*valley* PA-2
Hercules Lookout Tower—*locale* MO-7
Hercules Mine—*mine* AK-9
Hercules Mine—*mine* (2) AZ-5
Hercules Mine—*mine* (2) ID-8
Hercules Mine—*mine* NV-8
Hercules Parlin—*airport* NJ-2
Hercules (site)—*locale* NV-8
**Hercules Station**—*pop pl* MS-4
HERCULES (tugboat)—*hist pl* CA-9
Hercules Village—*hist pl* CA-9
Hercules Wharf—*locale* CA-9
Herd—*locale* KY-4
Herd—*locale* OK-5
Herd Branch—*stream* AR-4
Herd Branch—*stream* KY-4
Herd Branch—*stream* TX-5
Herd Camp Creek—*stream* (2) SD-7
Herd Cem—*cemetery* AR-4
Herd Creek—*stream* ID-8
Herde Lake—*lake* WI-6
*Herden Creek* OH-6
Herder Bridge—*bridge* NY-2
Herder Creek—*stream* NV-8
Herder Mtn—*summit* AZ-5
Herder Spring—*spring* OR-9
Herder Spring—*spring* PA-2
Herd Fork—*stream* KY-4
Herd Hollow—*valley* (2) UT-8
Herd House—*locale* UT-8
Herdhouse Wash—*stream* UT-8
Herdic, Peter, House—*hist pl* PA-2
*Herdina Arch* UT-8
Herdina Park—*area* UT-8
Herd Island—*island* AR-4
Herd Lake—*lake* ID-8
Herd Lake—*lake* ND-7
Herdland Township—*fmr MCD* IA-7
**Herdlyn**—*pop pl* CA-9
Herdman Brook—*stream* NY-2
Herdman Hollow—*valley* AR-4
Herdman Run—*stream* WV-2
Herd Mtn—*summit* UT-8
Herdon Lake Dam—*dam* MS-4
Herdon Park—*park* AL-4
Herd Pass—*gap* UT-8
Herd Pasture Tub—*reservoir* NM-5
*Herd Peak* UT-8
Herd Peak—*summit* CA-9
Herd Peak—*summit* ID-8
Herd Pen Branch—*stream* TX-5
Herd Pen Creek—*stream* TX-5
Herdrick Ridge—*ridge* WY-8
Herd Rock—*bar* AK-9
Herds Branch—*stream* TX-5
Herd Sch (historical)—*school* PA-2
Herds Creek—*stream* GA-3
Herds Creek—*stream* NC-3
*Herds Gap* AL-4
Herds Mtn—*summit* AL-4
Herds Pass—*valley* TX-5
*Herds Pass Draw* TX-5
Herds Pass Draw—*valley* TX-5
Herds Pass Spring—*spring* TX-5
Herds Pond—*reservoir* GA-3
*Herds Quarry* AL-4
Herds V—*summit* ID-8
Herd (Township of)—*fmr MCD* AR-4
Herd Well—*locale* NM-5
Heredura Tank—*reservoir* NM-5
*Herefoid* TX-5
Hereford—*locale* MO-7
Hereford—*locale* PA-2
Hereford—*locale* SD-7
Hereford—*locale* VA-3
Hereford—*locale* WV-2
**Hereford**—*pop pl* AZ-5
**Hereford**—*pop pl* CO-8
**Hereford**—*pop pl* MD-2
**Hereford**—*pop pl* (2) OR-9
**Hereford**—*pop pl* TX-5
Hereford Airstrip—*airport* AZ-5
Hereford Branch—*stream* TX-5
Hereford Bridge—*hist pl* AZ-5
Hereford Canyon—*valley* CO-8
Hereford (CCD)—*cens area* OR-9
Hereford Cem—*cemetery* (2) AL-4
Hereford Cem—*cemetery* MN-6
Hereford Cem—*cemetery* TN-4
Hereford Cem—*cemetery* TX-5
Hereford Creek—*stream* OK-5
Hereford Creek—*stream* WY-8
Hereford Dairy Ranch—*locale* AZ-5
Hereford Ditch—*canal* OR-9
Hereford Drain—*canal* CA-9
Hereford East (CCD)—*cens area* TX-5
Hereford Elem Sch—*school* PA-2
Hereford Field—*flat* NV-8
Hereford Gulch—*valley* MT-8
Hereford Hills Ranch (Headquarters)—*locale* TX-5
Hereford (historical)—*locale* SD-7
Hereford Hollow—*valley* PA-2
Hereford Inlet—*bay* NJ-2
Hereford Lighthouse—*hist pl* NJ-2
Hereford Manor Lake—*reservoir* PA-2
Hereford Meadow—*flat* WA-9
Hereford Pens—*locale* TX-5
Hereford Ranch—*locale* CA-9
Herefords Bend—*bend* KY-4
Hereford Sch—*school* MO-7
Hereford Sch—*school* SD-7
**Herefordshire Condominium**—*pop pl* UT-8
**Herefordshire Subdivision**—*pop pl* UT-8
Herefords Mill (historical)—*locale* TN-4
Hereford Spring—*spring* OR-9
Hereford Spring—*spring* UT-8
**Hereford (Township of)**—*pop pl* PA-2
Hereford Valley Ranch—*locale* NV-8
Hereford Well—*well* TX-5
Hereford West (CCD)—*cens area* TX-5
Hereford Windmill—*locale* TX-5
**Herefork**—*pop pl* OH-6
Hereim Creek—*stream* MT-8
Hereim Homestead—*locale* MT-8
**Hereim (Township of)**—*pop pl* MN-6
Herein Creek—*stream* MT-8
Herendeen Bay—*bay* AK-9
Herendeen Bay—*locale* AK-9
Herendeene Lake—*lake* MI-6
Herendeen Island—*island* AK-9
*Herendeen Lake* MI-6
Heren Park—*park* MT-8
*Herenton Hollow* TN-4
Hererra Park—*park* TX-5
Herff Park Fairground—*locale* TX-5
Herff Sch—*school* TX-5
Herford Lake Dam—*dam* SD-7
**Hergas**—*pop pl* NC-3
Hergert Quarry—*mine* OR-9
**Herget**—*pop pl* AR-4
Herget Bottoms—*flat* IL-6
Herget Drainage Ditch—*canal* IL-6
*Hergett* AR-4
**Hergett**—*pop pl* AR-4
Herget Turquoise Mine—*mine* AZ-5
Herien Hollow—*valley* MO-7
Herig Sch—*school* MI-6
*Heriman* UT-8
Herin Cem—*cemetery* SC-3
Herinckx Pond—*reservoir* OR-9
Heringa Ranch—*locale* NM-5
Hering Cave—*cave* AL-4
Hering Creek—*stream* OR-9
Hering Lake—*lake* WY-8
**Herington**—*pop pl* KS-7
Herington, Lake—*reservoir* KS-7
Herington Carnegie Public Library—*hist pl* KS-7
Herington Cem—*cemetery* GA-3
Herington City Dam—*dam* KS-7
Herington HS—*school* KS-7
Herington Municipal Airp—*airport* KS-7
Heriot Creek—*stream* GA-3
Heriot Mtn—*summit* CA-9
**Heriots Crossroads**—*pop pl* SC-3
*Herit* FM-9
*Heritage* IL-6
**Heritage**—*pop pl* DE-2
Heritage—*post sta* CO-8
Heritage—*post sta* NY-2
Heritage, Lake—*lake* PA-2
Heritage, Lake—*lake* WA-9
Heritage Acad—*school* MS-4
Heritage Baptist Ch—*church* AL-4
Heritage Baptist Ch—*church* TN-4
Heritage Baptist Ch Cantonment—*church* FL-3
Heritage Baptist Temple—*church* FL-3
Heritage Cem—*cemetery* OH-6
Heritage Center—*post sta* OK-5
Heritage Ch—*church* MN-6
Heritage Ch—*church* VA-3
Heritage Ch of Jesus Christ—*church* MS-4
Heritage Christian Acad—*school* FL-3
Heritage Christian Sch—*school* (2) FL-3
Heritage Coll—*school* NC-3
**Heritage Colony (subdivison)**—*pop pl* MS-4
Heritage Country Club—*locale* MA-1
**Heritage Court (subdivision)**—*pop pl* (2) AZ-5
Heritage Creek—*stream* MN-6
Heritage Elem Sch—*school* AZ-5
**Heritage Estates**—*pop pl* TN-4
**Heritage Estates (subdivision)**—*pop pl* MS-4
**Heritage Estates (subdivision)**—*pop pl* TN-4
**Heritage Estates Subdivision**—*pop pl* UT-8
**Heritage Farm**—*pop pl* MD-2
**Heritage Farms**—*pop pl* DE-2
**Heritage Grove Subdivision**—*pop pl* UT-8
Heritage Hall—*hist pl* IN-6
**Heritage Harbor**—*pop pl* MD-2
**Heritage Heights (subdivision)**—*pop pl* NC-3
**Heritage Heights Subdivision**—*pop pl* UT-8
**Heritage Highlands (subdivision)**—*pop pl* (2) AZ-5
Heritage Hill Acad—*school* SC-3
Heritage Hill Hist Dist—*hist pl* IA-7
Heritage Hill Hist Dist—*hist pl* MI-6
**Heritage Hills**—*pop pl* PA-2
**Heritage Hills**—*pop pl* (4) TN-4
**Heritage Hills**—*pop pl* TX-5
Heritage Hill Sch—*school* OH-6
Heritage Hills Historic and Architectural District—*hist pl* OK-5
**Heritage Hills (subdivision)**—*pop pl* AL-4
Heritage House—*hist pl* CA-9
Heritage HS—*school* CA-9
Heritage HS—*school* TN-4
Heritage JHS—*school* NJ-2
*Heritage Lake* WA-9
Heritage Lake—*lake* MN-6
Heritage Lake—*reservoir* IN-6
Heritage Lake—*reservoir* PA-2
Heritage Lake Dam—*dam* IN-6
Heritage Lake Dam—*dam* MS-4
Heritage Landing Strip—*airport* MO-7
Heritage Lookout Tower—*locale* MN-6
Heritage Mall—*locale* MA-1
Heritage MS—*school* IN-6
**Heritage North Ranch (subdivision)**—*pop pl* (2) AZ-5
Heritage Park—*park* AZ-5
Heritage Park—*park* CA-9
Heritage Park Plaza—*locale* MA-1
**Heritage Park (subdivision)**—*pop pl* AL-4
**Heritage Park (subdivision)**—*pop pl* TN-4
Heritage Plantation of Sandwich—*locale* MA-1
Heritage Preparatory Sch—*school* FL-3
Heritage Private Sch—*school* FL-3
Heritage Private Sch of Hardee County—*school* FL-3
Heritage Reservation Dam—*dam* PA-2
Heritage Sch—*school* AL-4
Heritage Sch—*school* CA-9
Heritage Sch—*school* (2) FL-3
Heritage Sch—*school* NY-2
Heritage Square—*park* AZ-5
**Heritage Square**—*pop pl* VA-3
Heritage Square Shop Ctr—*other* CO-8
**Heritage Square Subdivision**—*pop pl* (2) UT-8
Heritage Square Village Mall—*locale* NC-3
**Heritage Terrace (subdivision)**—*pop pl* (2) AZ-5
**Heritage Village**—*pop pl* DE-2
**Heritage Village**—*pop pl* NJ-2
**Heritage Village**—*pop pl* VA-3
**Heritage Village (subdivision)**—*pop pl* (2) NC-3
**Heritage Villa Subdivision**—*pop pl* UT-8
Heritage Vocational Sch—*school* TN-4
*Herit Island* FM-9
Herkey Creek—*stream* CA-9
Herkey Creek Camp—*locale* CA-9
Herkimer—*mine* UT-8
**Herkimer**—*pop pl* KS-7
**Herkimer**—*pop pl* NY-2
Herkimer Cem—*cemetery* (2) NY-2
**Herkimer (County)**—*pop pl* NY-2
Herkimer County Courthouse—*hist pl* NY-2
Herkimer County Historical Society—*hist pl* NY-2
Herkimer County Jail—*hist pl* NY-2
Herkimer County Trust Company Bldg—*hist pl* NY-2
Herkimer Creek—*stream* NY-2
Herkimer Drain—*stream* MI-6
Herkimer House—*hist pl* NY-2
Herkimer Lake—*lake* AK-9
Herkimer Landing—*locale* NY-2
Herkimer Mine—*mine* CA-9
Herkimer Rsvr—*reservoir* NY-2
Herkimer Sch—*school* MI-6
**Herkimer (Town of)**—*pop pl* NY-2
**Herkimer Township**—*pop pl* KS-7
Herkless Ditch—*canal* IN-6
Her-La-Co Park—*park* NC-3
Her Lake—*lake* WY-8
Herlan—*locale* OH-6
Herlan Lake—*lake* MI-6
Herlan Peak—*summit* NV-8
Herlick Canyon—*valley* CO-8
Herlickson Cem—*cemetery* ND-7
Herlihy Canyon—*valley* OR-9
*Herlihy Island* IL-6
**Herling (historical)**—*pop pl* OR-9
Herlong—*locale* CA-9
**Herlong**—*pop pl* CA-9
Herlong Cem—*cemetery* MS-4
Herlong Junction—*locale* CA-9
Herlong (sta.) (Sierra Army Depot)—*other* CA-9
**Herl Township**—*pop pl* KS-7
Herma—*locale* AR-4
Hermagos Islands—*area* AK-9
Hermam Number 6 Dam—*dam* SD-7
*Herman* WI-6
Herman—*locale* ID-8
Herman—*locale* NJ-2
Herman—*locale* TX-5
**Herman**—*pop pl* (2) AR-4
**Herman**—*pop pl* KY-4
**Herman**—*pop pl* MI-6
**Herman**—*pop pl* MN-6
**Herman**—*pop pl* NE-7
**Herman**—*pop pl* PA-2
**Herman**—*pop pl* VA-3
Herman, Joseph, Chalkrock House—*hist pl* SD-7
Herman, Joseph, Log Stable—*hist pl* SD-7
Herman, Joseph, Rubblestone Barn—*hist pl* SD-7
Herman, Lake—*lake* SD-7
Herman, Lake—*reservoir* CA-9
Herman, Lake—*reservoir* IL-6
Herman, Lake—*reservoir* LA-4
Herman, Lake—*reservoir* NC-3
Herman, Mount—*summit* AK-9
Herman, Mount—*summit* CO-8
Herman, Mount—*summit* NY-2
Hermanas—*locale* NM-5
Hermanas Draw—*valley* NM-5
Hermanas Windmill—*locale* TX-5
Herman Ave Sch—*school* PA-2
Herman Ave Seventh Day Adventist Ch—*church* AL-4
Herman Bay—*bay* FL-3
Herman Bay Point—*cape* FL-3
Herman Branch—*stream* NC-3
Herman Canyon—*valley* WY-8
Herman Cem—*cemetery* MI-6
Herman Cem—*cemetery* NE-7
Herman Cem—*cemetery* NC-3
Herman Cem—*cemetery* ND-7
**Herman Center**—*pop pl* WI-6
Herman Ch—*church* AL-4
Herman Ch—*church* MS-4
Herman Ch—*church* (3) NC-3
Herman Ch—*church* (2) VA-3
*Herman City* IN-6
*Herman City* NJ-2
Herman Coulee—*valley* WI-6
*Herman Creek* TX-5
Herman Creek—*stream* AK-9
Herman Creek—*stream* CA-9
Herman Creek—*stream* ID-8
Herman Creek—*stream* MS-4
Herman Creek—*stream* (4) OR-9
Herman Creek—*stream* WA-9
Herman Creek—*stream* WI-6
*Herman Creek Campground* OR-9
Herman Creek Recreation Site—*park* OR-9
Herman Creek Trail (Skyline Trail)—*trail* OR-9
Herman Direk Memorial Park—*cemetery* AR-4
Herman Farm—*locale* VI-3
Herman Gibson Dam—*dam* AL-4
Herman Gibson Lake—*reservoir* AL-4
Herman Gibson Number 2 Dam—*dam* AL-4
Herman Gulch—*valley* CO-8
Herman Gulch—*valley* (3) MT-8
*Herman Harbor* ME-1
**Herman Heights**—*pop pl* PA-2
Herman Hill—*locale* VI-3
Herman Hill—*summit* GA-3
Herman Hill—*summit* IL-6
Herman Hill—*summit* NJ-2
Herman (historical)—*locale* KS-7
Herman Hoiness Ranch—*locale* MT-8
Herman House—*hist pl* MI-6
Herman Kaubish Dam—*dam* SD-7
Herman Lake—*lake* (2) AK-9
Herman Lake—*lake* CO-8
Herman Lake—*lake* ID-8
Herman Lake—*lake* MI-6
Herman Lake—*lake* NE-7
Herman Lake—*lake* WA-9
Herman Lake—*lake* WI-6
Herman Lookout Tower Radio Tower—*locale* MI-6
Herman Matt Ranch—*locale* SD-7
Herman Mine—*mine* CA-9
Herman Moeller 1 Dam—*dam* SD-7
Herman Mtn—*summit* AZ-5
*Hermann* IN-6
**Hermann**—*pop pl* MO-7
Hermann, Mount—*summit* WA-9
Hermann Area Hospital Heliport—*airport* MO-7
Hermann Cem—*cemetery* OR-9
Hermann Cem—*cemetery* TX-5
Hermann Country Club—*other* MO-7
*Hermann Creek* OR-9
Hermann-Grima House—*hist pl* LA-4
Hermann Hist Dist—*hist pl* MO-7
**Hermann (historical)**—*pop pl* OR-9
Hermann Hosp—*hospital* TX-5
Hermann Hospital Lake—*lake* TX-5
Hermann House—*hist pl* MS-4
Hermann I Heliport—*airport* MO-7
Hermann II Heliport—*airport* MO-7
Hermann Island—*island* IN-6
Hermann Monmt—*hist pl* MN-6
Hermann Monument—*locale* MN-6
Hermann Municipal Airp—*airport* MO-7
Hermann Park—*park* (2) TX-5
Hermann Sons Cem—*cemetery* TX-5
Herman Number 1 Dam—*dam* SD-7
Herman Number 10 Dam—*dam* SD-7
Herman Number 11 Dam—*dam* SD-7
Herman Number 12 Dam—*dam* SD-7
Herman Number 13 Dam—*dam* SD-7
Herman Number 14 Dam—*dam* SD-7
Herman Number 15 Dam—*dam* SD-7
Herman Number 17 Dam—*dam* SD-7
Herman Number 18 Dam—*dam* SD-7
Herman Number 2 Dam—*dam* SD-7
Herman Number 20 Dam—*dam* SD-7
Herman Number 3 Dam—*dam* SD-7
Herman Number 4 Dam—*dam* SD-7
Herman Number 5 Dam—*dam* SD-7
Herman Number 6 Dam—*dam* SD-7
Herman Number 7 Dam—*dam* SD-7
Herman Number 8 Dam—*dam* SD-7
Herman Number 9 Dam—*dam* SD-7
Herman Nusbaum Dam—*dam* OR-9
Hermano Cem—*cemetery* TX-5
*Hermano Peak* CO-8
Hermanos Island—*area* AK-9
Hermanos Windmill—*locale* TX-5
Herman Park—*park* IA-7
Herman Park—*park* NC-3
Herman Passiflora Mine—*mine* CO-8
Herman Peak—*summit* OR-9
Herman Playground—*park* OH-6
Herman Point—*cape* ME-1
Herman Point—*cape* MT-8
Herman Point—*cliff* PA-2
Herman Pond—*lake* GA-3
*Herman Presbyterian Church* MS-4
Herman Ranch—*locale* CO-8
Herman Ranch—*locale* NE-7
Herman Ranch—*locale* WY-8
Herman Ridge—*ridge* MT-8
Herman Rsvr—*reservoir* CO-8
**Hermans**—*pop pl* OR-9
Herman-Sadlier Dam—*dam* UT-8
Herman-Sadlier Rsvr—*reservoir* UT-8
Hermansberg—*locale* KS-7
Herman Sch—*school* IL-6
Herman Sch—*school* MI-6
Herman Sch—*school* NY-2
Herman Sch—*school* WI-6
Herman Sch (historical)—*school* PA-2
*Herman School* PA-2
*Hermans Church* AL-4
Hermansfort Sch—*school* WI-6
*Herman's Harbor* ME-1
**Herman Siding**—*pop pl* KY-4
*Hermans Island* IN-6
*Hermans Lake* MI-6
*Hermans Lake* WI-6
Hermans Landing—*locale* WI-6
Herman Slough—*lake* SD-7
Hermans Point—*summit* TX-5
Herman Spring—*spring* AZ-5
Herman Spring—*spring* OR-9
Hermans Sch—*school* PA-2
**Hermansville**—*pop pl* MI-6
Hermansville Lake—*reservoir* MI-6
Hermantano Springs Ranch—*locale* NM-5
**Hermantown**—*pop pl* MN-6
Hermantown Cem—*cemetery* MN-6
Herman Town Hall—*building* ND-7
Hermantown HS—*school* MN-6
**Herman (Town of)**—*pop pl* (3) WI-6
**Herman Township**—*pop pl* ND-7
**Herman Township**—*pop pl* SD-7
Herman (Township of)—*other* MN-6
Hermanutz, Eugene, House—*hist pl* MN-6
Herman Van Den Berg Dam—*dam* SD-7
Hermanville—*locale* MD-2
**Hermanville**—*pop pl* MS-4
**Hermanville**—*pop pl* OH-6
Hermanville Baptist Ch—*church* MS-4
*Hermanville Consolidated Elementary School* MS-4
Hermanville Methodist Ch—*church* MS-4
Hermanville Presbyterian Ch (historical)—*church* MS-4
Hermanville Sch—*school* MS-4
*Hermaphrodite Creek* SD-7
Hermaphrodite Creek—*stream* SD-7
*Hermes Creek* KS-7
Hermes Creek—*stream* KS-7
Hermesprota Creek—*stream* PA-2
*Hermesprota Run* PA-2
Hermes Sch—*school* IL-6
Hermes Sch—*school* TX-5
Hermess Ridge—*ridge* CA-9
**Hermine No. 2**—*pop pl* PA-2
Hermin Hill Park—*park* KS-7
**Herminie**—*pop pl* PA-2
**Herminie Number Two**—*pop pl* PA-2
Herminie Waterworks—*other* PA-2
Hermione Plantation House—*hist pl* LA-4
**Hermiston**—*pop pl* OR-9
Hermiston Butte—*summit* OR-9
Hermiston Ditch—*canal* OR-9
*Hermiston Drain* OR-9
Hermiston Junction—*locale* OR-9
Hermiston Municipal Airp—*airport* OR-9
Hermiston State Game Farm—*park* OR-9
Hermit, The—*summit* CA-9
*Hermitage* LA-4
Hermitage—*hist pl* LA-4
Hermitage—*locale* GA-3
Hermitage—*locale* VA-3
Hermitage—*locale* (2) VI-3
**Hermitage**—*pop pl* (2) AR-4
**Hermitage**—*pop pl* FL-3
**Hermitage**—*pop pl* LA-4
**Hermitage**—*pop pl* MO-7
**Hermitage**—*pop pl* (2) NY-2
**Hermitage**—*pop pl* (2) PA-2
**Hermitage**—*pop pl* TN-4
**Hermitage**—*pop pl* UT-8
Hermitage, The—*building* TN-4
Hermitage, The—*hist pl* DE-2
Hermitage, The—*hist pl* KY-4
Hermitage, The—*hist pl* NJ-2
Hermitage, The—*hist pl* (2) NC-3
Hermitage, The—*hist pl* TN-4
Hermitage, The—*locale* CA-9
Hermitage, The—*locale* ME-1
Hermitage, The—*locale* NV-8
Hermitage Airp—*airport* PA-2
Hermitage Apartments—*hist pl* IL-6
*Hermitage Area Pomme de Terre State Park - in part* MO-7
Hermitage Bayou—*gut* LA-4
Hermitage Cem—*cemetery* WI-6
Hermitage Ch—*church* SC-3
Hermitage Ch—*church* VA-3
Hermitage Church of Nuestra Senora de Valvanera of Coamo—*hist pl* PR-3
Hermitage Country Club—*other* VA-3
**Hermitage Court**—*pop pl* VA-3
**Hermitage Estates (subdivision)**—*pop pl* TN-4
Hermitage- Ethelwood Country Club—*other* VA-3
**Hermitage Farms**—*pop pl* VA-3
Hermitage Forest Camp—*locale* AZ-5
**Hermitage Hills**—*pop pl* KY-4
**Hermitage Hills**—*pop pl* TN-4
Hermitage (historical)—*locale* MS-4
Hermitage Home For The Aged—*building* VA-3
Hermitage Hotel—*hist pl* TN-4
Hermitage HS—*school* VA-3
Hermitage Island—*island* GA-3
*Hermitage Lake* MN-6
Hermitage Lookout Tower—*locale* GA-3
Hermitage Memorial Gardens—*cemetery* TN-4
Hermitage Mill—*locale* SC-3
Hermitage Mill Pond—*lake* SC-3
Hermitage Mill Pond—*reservoir* SC-3
Hermitage Motor Inn—*hist pl* WV-2
Hermitage of Our Lady of Kursk—*church* NY-2
Hermitage of San Antonio de Padua de la Tuna—*hist pl* PR-3
Hermitage Park—*park* AL-4
Hermitage Park—*park* IL-6
**Hermitage Park**—*pop pl* MD-2
**Hermitage Park**—*pop pl* VA-3
Hermitage Plantation Hist Dist—*hist pl* VI-3
Hermitage Plantation (historical)—*locale* MS-4
Hermitage Point—*cape* FL-3
Hermitage Point—*cape* GA-3
Hermitage Point—*cape* WY-8
Hermitage Point Trail—*trail* WY-8
Hermitage Sch—*school* PA-2
Hermitage Sch—*school* TN-4
Hermitage Sch (historical)—*school* PA-2
**Hermitage Springs**—*pop pl* TN-4
Hermitage Springs (CCD)—*cens area* TN-4
Hermitage Springs Ch of Christ—*church* TN-4
Hermitage Springs Division—*civil* TN-4
Hermitage Springs HS—*school* TN-4
Hermitage Springs Post Office (historical)—*building* TN-4
**Hermitage (subdivision)**—*pop pl* NC-3
**Hermitage Subdivision, The**—*pop pl* UT-8
Hermitage Swamp—*swamp* GA-3
Hermitage Township—*civil* PA-2
Hermitage Wharf—*locale* NC-3
Hermit Basin—*basin* AZ-5
Hermit Branch—*stream* NC-3
Hermit Brook—*stream* NH-1
Hermit Butte—*summit* CA-9
Hermit Cave—*cave* TN-4
Hermit Creek—*stream* AZ-5
Hermit Falls—*falls* NH-1
Hermit Gulch—*valley* AK-9
Hermit Hollow—*valley* NJ-2
Hermit Island—*island* ME-1
Hermit Island—*island* MD-2
Hermit Island—*island* NH-1
Hermit Island—*island* NC-3
Hermit Island—*island* WI-6
Hermit Jones Lake Dam—*dam* MS-4
*Hermit Lake* CO-8
*Hermit Lake* MI-6
Hermit Lake—*lake* CO-8
Hermit Lake—*lake* IN-6
Hermit Lake—*lake* MI-6
Hermit Lake—*lake* (2) MT-8
Hermit Lake—*lake* (2) NH-1
Hermit Lake (historical)—*flat* UT-8
*Hermit Lakes* CO-8
Hermit Lakes—*reservoir* CO-8
Hermit Lake Trail—*trail* CO-8
Hermit Mine—*mine* CA-9
Hermit Mine—*mine* ID-8
Hermit Mtn—*summit* MA-1
Hermit Park—*flat* CO-8
Hermit Park—*park* IN-6
Hermit Pass—*gap* CO-8
Hermit Peak—*summit* (2) CO-8
Hermit Peak—*summit* NM-5
*Hermit Point* AZ-5
Hermit Point—*cape* IL-6
*Hermit Pond* MA-1
Hermit Rapids—*rapids* AZ-5
Hermit Ridge—*ridge* AK-9
Hermit Rock—*pillar* CA-9
Hermit Rock—*summit* WY-8
Hermit Rock Creek—*stream* WY-8
Hermit Rock Valley Ditch—*canal* WY-8
Hermits Bench—*bench* CA-9
Hermits Cabin—*locale* CA-9
Hermits Cove—*locale* TX-5
*Hermits Hill* RI-1
Hermits Home Mine—*mine* AZ-5
*Hermits Mtn* MA-1
Hermit Spring—*locale* PA-2
Hermit Spring—*spring* CA-9
*Hermit Springs* PA-2
Hermits Rest—*locale* AZ-5
Hermits Rest Concession Bldg—*hist pl* AZ-5
Hermit Tract State Public Hunting Area—*park* MO-7
Hermit Trail—*trail* AZ-5
Hermit Valley—*basin* CA-9
**Hermleigh**—*pop pl* TX-5
Hermleigh (CCD)—*cens area* TX-5
Hermleigh Cem—*cemetery* TX-5
*Hermo Mountain* CO-8
*Hermon* NJ-2
**Hermon**—*pop pl* IL-6
**Hermon**—*pop pl* KY-4
**Hermon**—*pop pl* ME-1
**Hermon**—*pop pl* NY-2
**Hermon**—*pop pl* TN-4
Hermon, Mount—*summit* (2) MA-1
Hermon Bog—*swamp* ME-1
Hermon Cem—*cemetery* KY-4
**Hermon Center**—*pop pl* ME-1
Hermon Ch—*church* IN-6
Hermon Ch—*church* MD-2
Hermon Ch—*church* TN-4
Hermon Ch—*church* (2) VA-3
*Hermon Church* AL-4
Hermon Creek—*stream* IL-6
**Hermondale**—*pop pl* MO-7
Hermon Farm Airp—*airport* KS-7
Hermon Hill—*summit* ME-1
Hermon Jackson Lake Dam—*dam* MS-4
Hermon Parkman Lake Dam—*dam* MS-4
Hermon Pond—*lake* ME-1
Hermon Pond—*locale* ME-1
Hermon Sch—*school* ME-1
*Hermon Slough* IL-6
**Hermon (Town of)**—*pop pl* ME-1
**Hermon (Town of)**—*pop pl* NY-2
*Hermon United Methodist Ch* TN-4
*Hermosa* IL-6
Hermosa—*locale* NM-5
Hermosa—*locale* TX-5
Hermosa—*locale* VA-3
**Hermosa**—*pop pl* CO-8
**Hermosa**—*pop pl* SD-7
**Hermosa**—*pop pl* WY-8
Hermosa, Lake—*lake* (2) FL-3
Hermosa Beach—*beach* WA-9
**Hermosa Beach**—*pop pl* CA-9
Hermosa Canyon—*valley* AZ-5
Hermosa Cem—*cemetery* CA-9
Hermosa Cem—*cemetery* CO-8
Hermosa Cem—*cemetery* NM-5
Hermosa Cliffs—*cliff* CO-8
Hermosa Creek—*stream* CO-8
Hermosa Dam—*reservoir* CO-8
Hermosa Drive Sch—*school* CA-9
Hermosa Green—*park* NM-5
Hermosa Heights Sch—*school* NM-5
Hermosa Hill—*summit* AZ-5
Hermosa JHS—*school* NM-5
Hermosa Mine—*mine* AZ-5
Hermosa Mine—*mine* NV-8
*Hermosa Mountain* CO-8
Hermosa Mtn—*summit* NM-5
Hermosa Park—*flat* CO-8
Hermosa Park—*park* IL-6
Hermosa Peak—*summit* CO-8
Hermosa Point—*cape* WA-9
Hermosa Sch—*school* CA-9
Hermosa Sch—*school* CO-8
Hermosa Terrace Park—*park* CA-9
Hermosa Tunnel—*tunnel* WY-8
Hermoso Park—*park* AZ-5
Hermsmyer Raymond Ditch—*canal* MT-8
Hern—*locale* PA-2
Hernage Creek—*stream* CO-8
Hernage Ditch—*canal* CO-8
Hernandex Point—*cape* FL-3
**Hernandez**—*pop pl* CA-9
**Hernandez**—*pop pl* NM-5
Hernandez Cem—*cemetery* TX-5
Hernandez Ditch—*canal* NM-5
Hernandez Draw—*valley* NM-5
Hernandez Lake—*lake* NM-5
Hernandez Peak—*summit* AL-4
Hernandez Rsvr—*reservoir* CA-9
Hernandez Valley—*valley* CA-9
Hernandez Windmill—*locale* TX-5
**Hernando**—*pop pl* FL-3
**Hernando**—*pop pl* MS-4

**Heshbon**—pop pl ... PA-2
Heshbon Park—park ... PA-2
Heshbon Sch (abandoned)—school ... PA-2
Hesher Creek—stream ... WI-6
Hesi Island—island ... FM-9
Hesitation Point—cape ... IN-6
Hesketh Island—island ... AK-9
Heskett Lake—lake ... NE-7
Heslep House—hist pl ... SC-3
**Hesler**—pop pl ... KY-4
Hesler-Noble Field (airport)—airport ... MS-4
Hesley Spring—spring ... MO-7
Heslington Canyon—valley ... UT-8
Heslip Creek—stream ... ID-8
Heslip Lake—lake ... ID-8
Heslop—locale ... OH-6
Heslop Hollow—valley ... WV-2
Heslops Corner—locale ... NY-2
**Hesnault**—pop pl ... ND-7
Hesnnann Spring—spring ... AZ-5
HES No 138—civil ... AK-9
HES No 144—civil ... AK-9
Heson Bluff ... WI-6
Hespeotus Mine—mine ... UT-8
Hesper—locale ... MT-8
**Hesper**—pop pl ... IA-7
**Hesper**—pop pl ... KS-7
**Hesper**—pop pl ... ND-7
Hesper Cem—cemetery ... IA-7
Hesper Cem—cemetery ... ND-7
**Hesperia**—pop pl ... CA-9
**Hesperia**—pop pl ... MI-6
Hesperia (historical P.O.)—locale ... IA-7
Hesperian Sch—school ... CA-9
Hesperia Pond—lake ... MI-6
Hesperia Sch—school ... CA-9
**Hesperides**—pop pl ... FL-3
Hesper Township—fmr MCD ... IA-7
**Hesper Township**—pop pl ... ND-7
**Hesperus**—pop pl ... CO-8
Hesperus, Mount—summit ... AK-9
Hesperus Cem—cemetery ... CO-8
Hesperus Mine—mine ... CO-8
Hesperus Mtn—summit ... CO-8
Hesperus Ski Center—other ... CO-8
Hess—locale ... KS-7
Hess—locale ... MD-2
**Hess**—pop pl ... OK-5
Hess, A. B., Cigar Factory, and Warehouses—hist pl ... PA-2
Hess, Binks, House and Barn—hist pl ... AR-4
Hess, Elmer, House—hist pl ... OH-6
Hess, Lake—lake ... AK-9
Hess, Thomas E., House—hist pl ... AR-4
Hess, Thomas M., House—hist pl ... AR-4
Hessa Inlet—bay ... AK-9
Hessa Island—island ... AK-9
Hessa Lake—lake ... AK-9
Hessa Narrows—channel ... AK-9
Hessan Cassel ... IN-6
Hessan Castle ... IN-6
Hess Archeol Site—hist pl ... MO-7
Hess Bayou—stream ... IL-6
Hess Branch ... OR-9
Hess Branch—stream ... KY-4
Hess Cabin—locale ... WY-8
Hess Canyon ... TX-5
Hess Canyon—valley ... AZ-5
Hess Canyon—valley (2) ... TX-5
Hess Cem—cemetery ... AR-4
Hess Cem—cemetery (2) ... IN-6
Hess Cem—cemetery ... IA-7
Hess Cem—cemetery ... NY-2
Hess Cem—cemetery ... TN-4
Hess Cem—cemetery ... VA-3
Hess Cem—cemetery (3) ... WV-2
Hess Ch—church ... PA-2
Hess Creek ... AZ-5
Hess Creek ... OR-9
Hess Creek ... TN-4
Hess Creek ... TX-5
Hess Creek—stream ... AK-9
Hess Creek—stream ... AZ-5
Hess Creek—stream ... AR-4
Hess Creek—stream ... MO-7
Hess Creek—stream ... OR-9
Hess Creek—stream ... VA-3
Hess Creek Draw—valley ... WY-8
**Hessdale**—pop pl ... KS-7
**Hessdale**—pop pl ... PA-2
Hessdale Post Office (historical)—building ... PA-2
Hessdorfer Sch Number 5 (historical)—school ... SD-7
Hess Drain—stream ... MI-6
Hess Draw—valley ... AZ-5
Hess Draw—valley ... WY-8
Hesse—hist pl ... VA-3
Hesse Brook—stream ... ME-1
Hesse Cassel ... IN-6
Hesse Cem—cemetery ... TN-4
Hesse Creek—stream ... TN-4
Hesse Creek—stream ... WY-8
Hesse Ditch—canal ... WY-8
Hesse Flat—flat ... CA-9
Hesseky Brook—stream ... CT-1
Hesseky Meadow Pond—lake ... CT-1
**Hessel**—pop pl ... CA-9
**Hessel**—pop pl ... MI-6
Hesse Lake—reservoir ... TN-4
Hesse Lake Dam—dam ... TN-4
Hesse Lateral—canal ... CA-9
Hessel Bay—bay ... MI-6
**Hesselberg**—pop pl ... VI-3
Hessel Gessel Millstone ... PA-2
Hessel Gesser Millstone—other ... PA-2
Hessel Park—park ... IL-6
Hessel Point—cape ... MI-6
Hessel Rsvr—reservoir ... OR-9
**Hesseltine**—pop pl ... WA-9
Hessel Tractor Airstrip—airport ... OR-9
Hessemer Number One Mine—mine ... TN-4
Hessemer Number Two Mine—mine ... TN-4
Hesse Mtn—summit ... WY-8
**Hessen Cassel**—pop pl ... IN-6
Hessen Kassel ... IN-6
Hessen Oil Field—other ... MI-6
Hesser Gap—gap ... PA-2
Hesse Sch—school ... GA-3
Hesse Sch—school ... MI-6
Hesses Creek ... TN-4
Hesses Mill (historical)—locale ... TN-4
Hessey Branch—stream ... TN-4
Hessey Lake—lake ... NE-7
Hessey Mill (historical)—locale ... TN-4
Hess Flat—flat ... AZ-5
Hess Flat—flat ... CA-9
Hess Hammock—island ... FL-3
Hess Hill—summit ... GA-3
Hess Hill—summit ... PA-2
Hess (historical)—locale ... KS-7
Hess Hollow—valley ... AR-4
Hess Hollow—valley ... PA-2
Hess Hollow—valley ... VA-3
Hessian Barracks—hist pl ... MD-2
Hessian Camp—locale ... PA-2
Hessian Hill—summit ... NY-2
**Hessian Hills**—pop pl ... VA-3
Hessian Lake—lake ... NY-2
Hessian Meadow—flat ... CA-9
Hessian Powder Magazine—hist pl ... PA-2
Hessian Ridge—ridge ... TN-4
Hessian Run—stream ... NJ-2
Hessian Run Park—park ... NJ-2
Hessians Hole—swamp ... RI-1
Hessick Trail—trail ... PA-2
Hessie—locale ... CO-8
Hessie, Lake—lake ... UT-8
Hessie Lake—lake ... MN-6
Hessig Ranch—locale ... CA-9
Hess Island—island (2) ... PA-2
Hess Knob—summit ... AR-4
**Hessl**—pop pl ... PA-2
Hess Lake ... MI-6
Hess Lake—lake ... AK-9
Hess Lake—lake (4) ... MI-6
Hess Lake—lake ... WA-9
Hess Lake—lake (2) ... WI-6
Hesslan Canyon—valley ... OR-9
Hessler Branch—stream ... PA-2
Hessler Court Wooden Pavement—hist pl ... OH-6
Hessler Ditch—canal ... IN-6
Hessler Lake—lake ... MI-6
Hessler Ridge—ridge ... MT-8
Hesslon Speedway—other ... PA-2
Hess-McKeown Airp—airport ... MO-7
**Hessmer**—pop pl ... LA-4
Hess Mill ... TN-4
Hess Mill—locale ... CA-9
Hess Mill Creek ... OR-9
Hess Mine—mine (2) ... CA-9
Hess Mtn—summit ... AK-9
Hess Mtn—summit ... PA-2
Hesson Cem—cemetery ... IN-6
Hesson Cem—cemetery ... OH-6
Hessong Rock—peak ... WA-9
Hesson Ridge—ridge ... TN-4
Hess Park—park ... IL-6
Hess Park—park ... WA-9
Hess Point ... OR-9
Hess Point—cape ... ID-8
Hess Pond—lake ... NY-2
Hess Pond Number 1 Dam—dam ... SD-7
Hess Ranch—locale ... CA-9
Hess Ranch—locale ... OR-9
Hess Ranch—locale (2) ... TX-5
Hess Ranch—locale ... WY-8
Hess Road Ch—church ... NY-2
Hess Run—stream (2) ... PA-2
Hess Sch—school ... IL-6
Hess Sch—school ... IA-7
Hess Sch—school (2) ... MI-6
Hess Sch—school ... TN-4
Hess Sch—school ... WV-2
Hess Shelter Cave—cave ... PA-2
Hess Spring—spring ... CA-9
Hess Spring—spring ... ID-8
Hess Spring—spring ... NV-8
Hess Spring—spring ... NM-5
Hess Tank—reservoir ... AZ-5
**Hesston**—pop pl ... IN-6
**Hesston**—pop pl ... KS-7
**Hesston**—pop pl ... PA-2
Hesston Coll—school ... KS-7
Hesston Elem Sch—school ... KS-7
Hesston High School ... KS-7
Hesston MS—school ... KS-7
Hesstown—locale ... NJ-2
Hessville ... IN-6
Hessville ... NJ-2
Hessville—locale ... NY-2
**Hessville**—pop pl ... IN-6
**Hessville**—pop pl ... OH-6
Hess Wash—stream ... AZ-5
Hess Well—well ... NM-5
Hess Windmill—locale ... CO-8
Hess Windmill—locale (2) ... TX-5
**Hest**—pop pl ... MO-7
**Hestand**—pop pl ... KY-4
Hestand Creek—stream ... TX-5
Hestand Sch—school ... KY-4
Hester—locale ... MO-7
Hester—locale ... OK-5
Hester—locale ... SC-3
**Hester**—pop pl (2) ... LA-4
**Hester**—pop pl ... NC-3
**Hester**—pop pl ... TX-5
Hester, Lake—lake ... FL-3
Hester, Lake—lake ... ND-7
Hester Airp—airport ... MO-7
Hester Airstrip—airport ... OR-9
Hester A Mine—mine ... SD-7
Hester Bay—swamp ... NC-3
Hester Branch—stream (4) ... AL-4
Hester Branch—stream ... GA-3
Hester Branch—stream ... LA-4
Hester Branch—stream ... MS-4
Hester Branch—stream (2) ... TN-4
Hester Branch—stream (2) ... TX-5
Hester Bridge—bridge ... AL-4
Hesterburg Creek—stream ... IL-6
Hester Canal—canal ... SC-3
Hester Cave Number One—cave ... AL-4
Hester Cave Number Two—cave ... AL-4
Hester Cem—cemetery ... AL-4
Hester Cem—cemetery (2) ... AR-4
Hester Cem—cemetery ... GA-3
Hester Cem—cemetery (2) ... KY-4
Hester Cem—cemetery (3) ... MS-4
Hester Cem—cemetery ... NC-3
Hester Cem—cemetery ... OH-6
Hester Cem—cemetery ... OK-5
Hester Cem—cemetery ... SC-3
Hester Cem—cemetery (4) ... TN-4
Hester Cem—cemetery (2) ... TX-5
Hester Ch—church ... FL-3
Hester Ch—church ... NC-3
Hester Chapel—church ... AL-4
Hester Chapel—church ... AR-4
Hester Chapel—church ... MS-4
Hester Cove—bay ... VA-3
Hester Creek ... MS-4
Hester Creek ... NC-3
Hester Creek—stream ... AL-4
Hester Creek—stream ... AR-4
Hester Creek—stream ... CA-9
Hester Creek—stream ... MS-4
Hester Creek—stream ... OR-9
Hester Creek—stream ... TN-4
Hester Creek Ch—church ... CA-9
Hestere Creek ... AL-4
Hester Gap—gap ... GA-3
**Hester Heights**—pop pl ... AL-4
Hester House—locale ... TX-5
Hester Knob—summit ... TN-4
Hester Lake—lake ... CA-9
Hester Lake—lake ... FL-3
Hester Lake—lake ... NC-3
Hester Lake—lake ... TX-5
Hester Lake—lake ... WA-9
Hester Lake—reservoir ... NC-3
Hester Lake Dam—dam ... MS-4
Hester Lake Number One Dam—dam ... NC-3
**Hester Landing**—pop pl ... LA-4
Hesterlee Creek—stream ... GA-3
Hester Millpond—reservoir ... NC-3
Hester Millpond Dam—dam ... NC-3
Hester Mills Post Office (historical)—building ... TN-4
Hester Mtn—summit ... SC-3
Hester Park—park ... MN-6
Hester Plantation—locale ... LA-4
Hester Pond—reservoir ... NC-3
Hester Pond Dam—dam ... NC-3
Hester Ranch—locale ... TX-5
Hester Ranch—locale ... WY-8
Hesters Branch—stream ... NJ-2
Hester Sch—school ... CA-9
Hesters Chapel Cem—cemetery ... AL-4
Hesters Chapel Cem—cemetery ... MS-4
Hesters Chapel Church of Christ ... AL-4
Hester Sch (historical)—school ... MS-4
Hesters Creek ... AL-4
Hester Sedge—island ... NJ-2
Hesters Ferry (historical)—locale ... MS-4
Hesters Grove Ch—church ... NC-3
Hesters Lake—reservoir ... NC-3
Hesters Lake Dam—dam ... NC-3
Hesters Store—locale ... NC-3
Hesters Store (historical)—locale ... AL-4
Hester-Standifer Creek Site—hist pl ... MS-4
**Hestertown**—pop pl ... NC-3
Hester Valley—basin ... PA-2
**Hesterville**—pop pl ... MS-4
Hesterville Ch of Christ—church ... MS-4
Hesterville Post Office (historical)—building ... MS-4
Hestle—locale ... AL-4
Hestness Park—park ... OR-9
**Heston**—pop pl ... OH-6
Heston Ditch—canal ... IN-6
Heston Sch—school ... PA-2
Hestonville—locale ... PA-2
Hestoria ... OH-6
Hestor Oil and Gas Field—oilfield ... LA-4
HES 1242—civil ... AK-9
HES 1255—civil ... AK-9
HES 1599—civil ... AK-9
HES 205—civil ... AK-9
HES 206—civil ... AK-9
HES 207—civil ... AK-9
HES 208—civil ... AK-9
HES 2716—civil ... AK-9
HES 690—civil ... AK-9
HES 735—civil ... AK-9
HES 785—civil ... AK-9
HES 977—civil ... AK-9
Hetchel Swamp—swamp ... CT-1
Hetchel Swamp Brook—stream ... CT-1
Hetch Hetchy Aqueduct—canal ... CA-9
Hetch Hetchy Dam ... CA-9
Hetch Hetchy Dome—summit ... CA-9
Hetch Hetchy Junction—locale ... CA-9
Hetch Hetchy RR Engine No.6—hist pl ... CA-9
Hetch Hetchy Rsvr—reservoir ... CA-9
Hetch Hetchy Trail—trail ... CA-9
Heter Farm—hist pl ... OH-6
**Heth**—pop pl ... AR-4
Hethcoe Bottoms—bend ... IN-6
Hethcoe Cem—cemetery ... IN-6
Heth Drain—canal ... MI-6
Hetherington, W. W., House—hist pl ... KS-7
Hetherington Cem—cemetery ... PA-2
Hetherly Height—summit ... NC-3
Hetherton—locale ... MI-6
Het Hollow—valley ... KY-4
Heth Ranch—locale ... NE-7
Heth Run—stream ... PA-2
Heth (Township of)—fmr MCD ... AR-4
**Heth (Township of)**—pop pl ... IN-6
Heth-Washington Elem Sch—school ... IN-6
**Hetland**—pop pl ... SD-7
Hetland Cem—cemetery ... SD-7
**Hetlerville**—pop pl ... PA-2
Hetley Grove Ch—church ... PA-2
Hetrick Cem—cemetery ... PA-2
Hetrick Ditch—canal ... IN-6
Hetrick Hill—summit ... PA-2
Hetrick Hollow—valley ... KY-4
Hetrick Run—stream ... PA-2
Hetta—locale ... AK-9
Hetta Cove—bay ... AK-9
Hetta Creek—stream ... AK-9
Hetta Inlet—bay ... AK-9
Hetta Lake—lake ... AK-9
Hetta Mtn—summit ... AK-9
Hetta Point—cape ... AK-9
Hettenchaw Valley ... CA-9
Hettenchow Valley ... CA-9
Hetten Cove—bay ... CA-9
Hetten Creek—stream ... CA-9
Hetten Ridge—ridge ... CA-9
Hetten Rock—pillar ... CA-9
Hettenshaw Peak—summit ... CA-9
Hettenshaw Valley—valley ... CA-9
**Hettesheimer Corners**—pop pl ... PA-2
Hettesheimer Run—stream ... PA-2
Hettich Branch—stream ... MO-7
**Hettick**—pop pl ... IL-6
Hettick Point Sch—school ... IL-6
Hettie—locale ... WV-2
Hettie Cem—cemetery ... TN-4
Hettie Creek—stream ... TN-4
Hettie Hollow—valley ... TN-4
Hettie Pond—lake ... FL-3
**Hettinger**—pop pl ... ND-7
Hettinger Cem—cemetery ... ND-7
Hettinger Country Club—locale ... ND-7
Hettinger County—civil ... ND-7
Hettinger County Courthouse—hist pl ... ND-7
Hettinger Creek—stream ... MI-6
Hettinger Hollow ... VA-3
Hettinger Municipal Airp—airport ... ND-7
Hettinger Picnic Area—locale ... WY-8
**Hettinger Township**—pop pl ... ND-7
Hett Number 1 Dam—dam ... SD-7
Hett Number 2 Dam—dam ... SD-7
Hetty Branch—stream ... TX-5
Hetty Brook—stream ... NH-1
Hetty Creek—channel ... NJ-2
Hetty Fisher Glade—gut ... DE-2
Hetty Fisher Pond—lake ... DE-2
Hettys Creek ... NJ-2
Hetzel—locale ... WV-2
Hetzel Pond—reservoir ... PA-2
Hetzel Ranch—locale ... MT-8
Hetzel Shoal—bar ... FL-3
Hetzer Cem—cemetery ... IL-6
Hetzler Cem—cemetery ... IL-6
Hetzler Cem—cemetery ... IA-7
Heublein Tower—hist pl ... CT-1
Heubler Creek—stream ... WI-6
Heubler Lake—lake ... WI-6
**Heubner**—pop pl ... AR-4
**Heucks**—pop pl ... MS-4
Heucks Lookout Tower—locale ... MS-4
Heucks Retreat—locale ... MS-4
Heucks Retreat Baptist Ch—church ... MS-4
Heuer Cem—cemetery ... MO-7
Heuer Valley—valley ... WI-6
Heugh Canyon Subdivision ... UT-8
Heughs Canyon—valley ... UT-8
**Heughs Canyon Subdivision**—pop pl ... UT-8
Heule Ranch—locale ... MT-8
Heulings-Coles Sch—school ... NJ-2
Heun—locale ... NE-7
Heupel Lake—lake ... SD-7
Heupscup Knobs—summit ... TN-4
Heups Homestead—locale ... MT-8
Heurich, Christian, Mansion—hist pl ... DC-2
Heusing Cem—cemetery ... IL-6
**Heusler**—pop pl ... IN-6
Heusner, George F., House—hist pl ... OR-9
Heusner Elem Sch—school ... KS-7
Heuss Ditch ... IN-6
Heuss Ditch—canal ... IN-6
Heusser Mtn—summit ... NV-8
Heusser Spring ... NV-8
Heusser Springs—spring ... NV-8
Heussner Drain—canal ... MI-6
Heustis Prairie—area ... CA-9
Heuter Hollow—valley ... OH-6
Heutt Cem—cemetery ... AR-4
**Heuvelton**—pop pl ... NY-2
Hevener, John and Julia, House—hist pl ... MI-6
Hevener Ch—church ... WV-2
Hevener Lateral—canal ... AZ-5
Hevener Run—stream ... VA-3
Hevener Sch—school ... IL-6
Heverly—locale (2) ... PA-2
Hevner Run—stream ... PA-2
Heward Creek—stream ... UT-8
Heward Ranch—locale (2) ... WY-8
Heward Rsvr—reservoir ... NV-8
Heward Rsvr—reservoir ... WY-8
Heward Troughs—spring ... NV-8
Hewas Cem—cemetery ... FL-3
Hewasse River ... TN-4
H E Watson Rsvr—reservoir ... RI-1
Hewed Log Creek—stream ... OR-9
Hewed Log Gap—gap ... NC-3
Hewed Log Ridge—ridge ... ID-8
Hewed Log Spring—spring ... OR-9
Hewell Creek—stream ... GA-3
Hewell Island ... ME-1
Hewell Island Rocks ... ME-1
Hewell Mine (underground)—mine ... AL-4
Hewell's Island ... ME-1
Hewens Drain—stream ... MI-6
**Hewes**—pop pl ... LA-4
Hewes Bldg—hist pl ... MS-4
Hewes Brook—stream ... ME-1
Hewes Brook—stream ... NH-1
Hewes Brook Pond—lake ... ME-1
Hewes Hill—summit ... NH-1
Hewes House—building ... NC-3
Hewes Lake—lake ... MI-6
Hewes Ledge—bar ... ME-1
Hewes Point—cape ... LA-4
Hewes Point—cape ... ME-1
Hewes Square Shop Ctr—locale ... MS-4
Hewetson Sch—school ... NV-8
**Hewett**—pop pl ... WV-2
Hewett Bayou—stream ... FL-3
Hewett Cem—cemetery ... OH-6
Hewett Cove ... MA-1
Hewett Creek—stream ... IA-7
Hewett Creek—stream ... WV-2
Hewett Fork—stream ... OH-6
Hewett Fork—stream ... WV-2
Hewett Head—stream ... FL-3
Hewett House—hist pl ... KY-4
Hewett Island—island ... ME-1
Hewett Island Rocks—bar ... ME-1
Hewett Lake—lake ... WA-9
Hewett Mine (underground)—mine ... AL-4
Hewetts Corners ... VT-1
Hewett Slope Mine (underground)—mine ... AL-4
Hewetts Mill (historical)—locale ... AL-4
Hewett Spring—spring ... GA-3
**Hewett (Town of)**—pop pl ... WI-6
Hewey Cem—cemetery ... ME-1
Hewey Creek—stream ... VA-3
Hewey Knob—summit ... KY-4
Hewey Lake—lake ... MI-6
Hewey Valley—valley ... CA-9
Hewhannee ... MS-4
Hew Hope Missionary Baptist Church ... MS-4
Hewick—hist pl ... VA-3
Hewing Branch—stream ... AR-4
Hewins—locale ... KS-7
Hewins Cem—cemetery ... MA-1
Hewins Park—park ... KS-7
Hewinta Forest Service Station ... UT-8
Hewinta Guard Station—locale ... UT-8
Hewitt ... ND-7
Hewitt ... PA-2
Hewitt—locale ... CA-9
Hewitt—locale ... NJ-2
Hewitt—locale ... NC-3
Hewitt—locale ... OH-6
Hewitt—locale ... OK-5
Hewitt—locale (2) ... PA-2
**Hewitt**—pop pl ... MN-6
**Hewitt**—pop pl ... TX-5
**Hewitt**—pop pl ... WI-6
Hewitt, Austin, Home—hist pl ... TN-4
Hewitt, Dr. Charles, Laboratory—hist pl ... MN-6
Hewitt, Edwin H., House—hist pl ... MN-6
Hewitt Bluff—cliff ... TN-4
Hewitt Branch—stream ... TN-4
Hewitt Bridge—bridge ... AL-4
Hewitt Brook—stream ... CT-1
Hewitt Brook—stream ... ME-1
Hewitt Brook—stream ... NJ-2
Hewitt Brook—stream ... VT-1
Hewitt Camp—locale ... TX-5
Hewitt Canyon—valley ... AZ-5
Hewitt Carroll Drain—canal ... MI-6
Hewitt Cem—cemetery ... AR-4
Hewitt Cem—cemetery (3) ... IA-7
Hewitt Cem—cemetery ... LA-4
Hewitt Cem—cemetery ... MN-6
Hewitt Cem—cemetery ... NE-7
Hewitt Cem—cemetery ... NY-2
Hewitt Cem—cemetery ... OH-6
Hewitt Cem—cemetery (2) ... OK-5
Hewitt Cem—cemetery ... SC-3
Hewitt Cem—cemetery ... VA-3
Hewitt Covered Bridge—hist pl ... PA-2
Hewitt Creek—stream ... AK-9
Hewitt Creek—stream ... IA-7
Hewitt Creek—stream ... MI-6
Hewitt Creek—stream ... OR-9
Hewitt Creek—stream ... WV-2
Hewitt Drain—canal (2) ... MI-6
Hewitt Eddy—rapids ... NY-2
Hewitt Elem Sch—school ... AL-4
**Hewitt Farm**—pop pl ... VA-3
Hewitt Gap—gap ... NC-3
Hewitt Gordon Cem—cemetery ... MS-4
Hewitt House—hist pl ... NH-1
Hewitt Island ... ME-1
Hewitt Island—island ... NE-7
Hewitt Lake ... WI-6
Hewitt Lake—lake ... AK-9
Hewitt Lake—lake ... LA-4
Hewitt Lake—lake ... MI-6
Hewitt Lake—lake ... WA-9
Hewitt Lake—lake ... WI-6
Hewitt Lake—reservoir ... MT-8
Hewitt Lake Natl Wildlife Ref—park ... MT-8
Hewitt Lakes—lake ... FL-3
Hewitt Mtn—summit ... OK-5
Hewitt Park—locale ... NY-2
Hewitt Park—park ... CA-9
Hewitt Park—park ... IA-7
Hewitt Place—locale ... NM-5
Hewitt Place—locale ... WY-8
Hewitt Point—cape ... NY-2
Hewitt Point—cape ... WI-6
Hewitt Pond—lake ... CT-1
Hewitt Pond—lake ... MA-1
Hewitt Pond—lake ... NY-2
Hewitt Pond—reservoir ... NC-3
Hewitt Pond Brook—stream ... NY-2
Hewitt Pond Dam—dam ... NC-3
Hewitt Pond Mtn—summit ... NY-2
Hewitt Post Office ... AL-4
Hewitt Ranch—locale ... AZ-5
Hewitt Ridge—ridge ... AZ-5
Hewitt Run—stream ... OH-6
Hewitt Run—stream ... PA-2
Hewitt Run—stream ... WV-2
Hewitts Branch—stream ... NC-3
Hewitt Sch—school ... AL-4
Hewitt Sch—school ... CT-1
Hewitt Sch—school ... IL-6
Hewitt Sch—school ... IA-7
Hewitt Sch—school ... MI-6
Hewitt Sch—school ... NY-2
Hewitt Sch (historical)—school ... AL-4
**Hewitts Corners**—pop pl ... VT-1
Hewitts Cove—cove ... MA-1
Hewitt's Island ... ME-1
Hewitts Pond ... NJ-2
Hewitt Spring—spring ... AR-4
Hewitt Spring—spring ... OR-9
Hewitt Spring—spring ... WA-9
Hewitt Station—locale ... AZ-5
Hewittsville ... IL-6
**Hewittsville**—pop pl ... IL-6
Hewitt Tank—reservoir ... AZ-5
Hewitt Texas Sch—school ... WI-6
**Hewitt (Town of)**—pop pl ... WI-6
Hewitt-Trussville HS—school ... AL-4
Hewitt-Trussville JHS—school ... AL-4
Hewitt Tunnel—tunnel ... VA-3
Hewitt Valley—flat ... CA-9
Hewitt Valley—valley ... CA-9
**Hewittville**—pop pl ... NY-2
Hewlet—locale ... WV-2
Hewlet Branch—stream ... KY-4
Hewlet Creek ... NC-3
Hewlett ... WV-2
**Hewlett**—pop pl ... NY-2
**Hewlett**—pop pl ... VA-3
Hewlett, Lester F. and Margaret Stewart, Ranch House—hist pl ... UT-8
Hewlett, Verner O., Ranch House—hist pl ... UT-8
Hewlett Bay—bay ... NY-2
**Hewlett Bay Park**—pop pl ... NY-2
Hewlett Branch—stream ... MO-7
Hewlett Branch—stream ... TN-4
Hewlett Canal—canal ... CA-9
Hewlett Cem—cemetery (2) ... AL-4
Hewlett Creek—stream ... KY-4
Hewlett Gulch—valley ... CO-8
**Hewlett Harbor**—pop pl ... NY-2
Hewlett House—hist pl ... NY-2
**Hewlett Neck**—pop pl ... NY-2
Hewlett Point—cape ... NY-2
Hewlett Point—cape ... WA-9
Hewlett's ... VA-3
Hewlett Sch—school (2) ... NY-2
Hewletts Creek—stream ... NC-3
Hewlett's Point ... NY-2
Hewlett Spring—spring ... MT-8
Hewling Ridge—ridge ... KY-4
Hewolf Creek—stream ... MT-8
Hewolf Mtn—summit ... MT-8
Hewossa River ... TN-4
Hewson-Gutting House—hist pl ... OH-6
Hewson Lanoe Drain—canal ... MI-6
Hewson Ranch—locale (2) ... ND-7
Hewsten Ridge ... WY-8
**Hew-Wood Estates (subdivision)**—pop pl ... UT-8
Hewwtt Pond ... MA-1
Hexa Creek—stream ... TX-5
Hexagon Barn—hist pl ... ME-1
Hexagon House—hist pl ... VA-3
Hex Creek—stream ... WA-9
Hexenkopf Hill—summit ... PA-2
Hexenkopf Rock—pillar ... PA-2
Hexenkopt ... PA-2
Hexenkoup Hill ... PA-2
Hexie Mountains—range ... CA-9
**Hexlena**—pop pl ... NC-3
Hex Mtn—summit ... WA-9
Hex Sch—school ... IN-6
Hexsite Cem—cemetery ... OH-6
Hext—locale ... OK-5
Hext—locale ... TX-5
Hext Cem—cemetery ... TX-5
Hexter, Levi, House—hist pl ... OR-9
Hexter Sch—school ... TX-5
Hext Place (site)—locale ... NM-5
Hext Spring—spring ... TX-5
Heybrook Ridge—ridge ... WA-9
Heyburn—locale ... OK-5
**Heyburn**—pop pl ... ID-8
Heyburn, Lake—reservoir ... OK-5
Heyburn Bldg—hist pl ... KY-4
Heyburn Ditch—canal ... NV-8
Heyburn Mountain Campground—locale ... ID-8
Heyburn Mtn—summit ... ID-8
Heyburn Rsvr—reservoir ... OK-5
Heyburn State Park—park ... ID-8
Heyburn Youth Camp—locale ... ID-8
Heydecker Draw—valley ... WY-8
**Heyden**—pop pl ... NJ-2
Heyden Baldy—summit ... CO-8
Heyden Gulch—valley ... CO-8
Heydenreich Drain—stream ... MI-6
Heydlauff Canyon—valley ... ID-8
Hey Dog Tank—reservoir ... AZ-5
Heydon Sch—school ... MO-7
Heye Foundation Museum—building ... NY-2
**Heyer**—pop pl ... CA-9
Heyer, Point—cape ... WA-9
Heyer Cem—cemetery ... MO-7
Heyer Island—island ... MN-6
Heyers Gulch—valley ... MT-8
Heyes Hollow—valley ... TN-4
Hey Field—airport ... PA-2
Hey Joe Canyon—valley ... UT-8
Hey Joe Mine—mine ... UT-8
Heyl Ave Sch—school ... OH-6
Heylmun Run—stream ... PA-2
Heyls Hill—summit ... OK-5
Heyls Hole—bay ... OK-5
Heymans Creek—stream ... MN-6
Heyne-Zimmerman House—hist pl ... OH-6
Hey Point—cape ... MD-2
Heyser—locale ... TX-5
Heyser Oil Field—oilfield ... TX-5
Heyville—locale ... PA-2
Heyward, Dubose, House—hist pl ... SC-3
Heyward Ch—church (2) ... SC-3
Heyward-Washington House—hist pl ... SC-3
Heywood—uninc pl ... MA-1
Heywood, John H., Elem Sch—hist pl ... KY-4
Heywood, Levi, Memorial Library Bldg—hist pl ... MA-1
Heywood, Phineas, House—hist pl ... ME-1
Heywood Ave Sch—school ... NJ-2
Heywood Chair Factory—hist pl ... PA-2
Heywood Creek—stream ... ID-8
Heywood Creek—stream ... VA-3
Heywood Memorial Hosp—hospital ... MA-1
Heywood Reservoir Dam—dam ... MA-1
Heywood Rsvr—reservoir ... MA-1
Heywood Sch—school ... OH-6
Heywoods Pond ... MA-1
Heywoods Station—locale ... MA-1
Heywood-Wakefield Company Complex—hist pl ... MA-1
**Heyworth**—pop pl ... IL-6
Hezel Township—civil ... SD-7
Hezron Camp—locale ... CO-8
Hezron Gulch—valley ... CO-8
Hezron Mines—mine ... CO-8
H F Bar Ranch—locale ... WY-8
HF Bar Ranch Hist Dist—hist pl ... WY-8
H Feist Ranch—locale ... SD-7
H F Gierke III Ranch—locale ... ND-7
H Fields Ranch—locale ... TX-5
H Four Cem—cemetery ... AZ-5
H Four Tank—reservoir ... AZ-5
H Freeze Dam—dam ... SD-7
H Fritz Ranch—locale ... ND-7
H F Sojourner Lake Dam—dam ... MS-4
H Garcia—locale ... TX-5
H G Davis Landing ... AL-4
H G Davis Lodge—locale ... AL-4
H G F Airp—airport ... PA-2
H G Horman Dam Number 1—dam ... SD-7
H Goldens Landing (historical)—locale ... MS-4
H G Quinnelly Dam—dam ... AL-4
H G Quinnelly Lake—reservoir ... AL-4

*H. Greenlands Brook* ... NJ-2
H G Rsvr—*reservoir* ... WY-8
H Guy Child Sch—*school* ... UT-8
H&H Airp (private)—*airport* ... PA-2
H Harrison Dam—*dam* ... SD-7
H Heart Ranch—*locale* ... CO-8
H Hewson Ranch—*locale* ... ND-7
H Hillderbrand Pond Dam—*dam* ... MS-4
H Hinton Ranch—*locale* ... NE-7
H Holm Dam—*dam* ... SD-7
H Hotchkiss Ranch—*locale* ... SD-7
H Howie Ranch—*locale* ... ND-7
H Hoyt Ranch—*locale* ... NE-7
H H Pepper Lake Dam—*dam* ... MS-4
H H Raulerson Junior Memorial Hosp—*hospital* ... FL-3
H.H. Richardson Hist Dist of North Easton—*hist pl* ... MA-1
HH Rsvr No 1—*reservoir* ... WA-9
HH Rsvr No 2—*reservoir* ... WA-9
H H Swisher Pond—*lake* ... FL-3
H Hulm Dam—*dam* ... SD-7
H H Webb Dam—*dam* ... AL-4
H H Wheeler Historical Marker—*other* ... OR-9
Hi, Lae—*cape* ... HI-9
Hiack Creek—*stream* ... OR-9
**Hi-Acres**—*pop pl* ... KY-4
Hi Acres—*uninc pl* ... KY-4
*Hiaggee Creek* ... AL-4
Hiagi (historical)—*locale* ... AL-4
Hiah Lake—*lake* ... AK-9
**Hialeah**—*pop pl* ... FL-3
Hialeah, Lake—*lake* ... FL-3
Hialeah Baptist Temple—*church* ... FL-3
Hialeah (CCD)—*cens area* ... FL-3
Hialeah Drive Shop Ctr—*locale* ... FL-3
Hialeah Elem Sch—*school* ... FL-3
**Hialeah Estates**—*pop pl* ... FL-3
Hialeah First United Methodist Sch—*school* ... FL-3
**Hialeah Gardens**—*pop pl* ... FL-3
Hialeah Gardens Acad—*school* ... FL-3
Hialeah Hosp—*hospital* ... FL-3
Hialeah JHS—*school* ... FL-3
Hialeah Lakes—*uninc pl* ... FL-3
Hialeah Metrorail Station—*locale* ... FL-3
Hialeah Miami Lakes HS—*school* ... FL-3
Hialeah-Miami Lakes Senior HS—*school* ... FL-3
*Hialeah Park* ... FL-3
Hialeah Park Race Track—*hist pl* ... FL-3
Hialeah Race Track—*locale* ... FL-3
Hialeah Senior HS—*school* ... FL-3
Hialeah Speedway—*locale* ... FL-3
Hialeah Springs—*spring* ... CA-9
Hialeah Yards—*locale* ... FL-3
Hi Allen Ridge—*ridge* ... WY-8
Hi Allen Spring—*lake* ... WY-8
**Hiamonee (historical)**—*pop pl* ... FL-3
Hiamovi Mtn—*summit* ... CO-8
*Hiampum* ... CA-9
Hianaula Point—*cape* ... HI-9
**Hiara Heights**—*pop pl* ... TN-4
Hiatt—*locale* ... KS-7
**Hiatt**—*pop pl* ... KY-4
Hiatt, Bennett, Log House—*hist pl* ... KY-4
Hiatt Airp—*airport* ... NC-3
Hiatt Branch—*stream* ... NC-3
Hiatt Canyon—*valley* ... CA-9
Hiatt Cem—*cemetery* ... KY-4
Hiatt Cem—*cemetery* ... WV-2
Hiatt Creek—*stream* ... MT-8
Hiatt House—*hist pl* ... AZ-5
Hiatt JHS—*school* ... IA-7
Hiatt Lake—*lake* ... CA-9
Hiatt Run—*stream* ... VA-3
Hiatt Sch—*school* ... IL-6
*Hiatts Run* ... VA-3
**Hiattsville**—*pop pl* ... IA-7
**Hiattville**—*pop pl* ... KS-7
Hiattville Cem—*cemetery* ... KS-7
*Hiattville Cemetery* ... KS-7
Hiaupe Stream—*stream* ... HI-9
Hiawana Creek—*stream* ... OK-5
Hiawana Prairie—*flat* ... OK-5
Hiawassa, Lake—*lake* ... FL-3
Hiawassa Bible Chapel—*church* ... FL-3
Hiawassee—*locale* ... TN-4
**Hiawassee**—*pop pl* ... GA-3
Hiawassee (CCD)—*cens area* ... GA-3
Hiawassee Ch of Christ—*church* ... TN-4
Hiawassee Elem Sch—*school* ... FL-3
*Hiawassee River* ... GA-3
*Hiawassee River* ... NC-3
*Hiawassee River* ... TN-4
Hiawata Creek—*stream* ... WA-9
*Hiawatha* ... MI-6
*Hiawatha* ... NC-3
Hiawatha—*locale* ... IA-7
Hiawatha—*locale* ... MI-6
Hiawatha—*locale* ... OK-5
Hiawatha—*locale* ... WV-2
**Hiawatha**—*pop pl* ... CO-8
**Hiawatha**—*pop pl* ... IA-7
**Hiawatha**—*pop pl* ... KS-7
**Hiawatha**—*pop pl* ... PA-2
**Hiawatha**—*pop pl* ... UT-8
Hiawatha, Lake—*lake (5)* ... FL-3
Hiawatha, Lake—*lake* ... MN-6
Hiawatha, Lake—*reservoir* ... KS-7
Hiawatha, Lake—*reservoir (2)* ... MA-1
Hiawatha, Lake—*reservoir* ... NJ-2
Hiawatha, Lake—*reservoir* ... ND-7
Hiawatha, Lake—*reservoir* ... TX-5
**Hiawatha Beach**—*pop pl* ... SD-7
*Hiawatha Camp* ... CO-8
**Hiawatha Camp**—*pop pl* ... CO-8
Hiawatha Campground—*locale* ... CA-9
Hiawatha Canal—*canal* ... ID-8
Hiawatha Cem—*cemetery* ... NE-7
Hiawatha Cem—*cemetery* ... NY-2
Hiawatha City Dam—*dam* ... KS-7
*Hiawatha City Lake* ... KS-7
Hiawatha Club—*other* ... PA-2
Hiawatha Country Club—*other* ... KS-7
Hiawatha Creek—*stream (2)* ... MI-6
Hiawatha Creek—*stream* ... PA-2
Hiawatha Creek—*stream* ... WA-9
Hiawatha Dam—*dam* ... PA-2
Hiawatha HS—*school* ... KS-7
Hiawatha Hunt Club—*locale* ... MI-6
Hiawatha Island—*island (2)* ... NY-2
*Hiawatha Lake* ... MN-6
Hiawatha Lake—*lake* ... NY-2
Hiawatha Lake—*lake (2)* ... PA-2
Hiawatha Lake—*lake (2)* ... WI-6
Hiawatha Lake—*reservoir* ... CO-8
Hiawatha Lake—*reservoir* ... PA-2
**Hiawatha Location**—*pop pl* ... MI-6
Hiawatha Memorial Auditorium—*hist pl* ... KS-7
Hiawatha Mine—*mine* ... UT-8
Hiawatha Mine No. One Complex—*hist pl* ... MI-6
Hiawatha Mission—*church* ... MI-6
Hiawatha Municipal Airp—*airport* ... KS-7
Hiawatha Municipal Golf Course—*other* ... MN-6
Hiawatha Natl For—*forest* ... MI-6
Hiawatha Number One Mine—*mine* ... MI-6
Hiawatha Number Two Mine—*mine* ... MI-6
Hiawatha Park—*park* ... IL-6
Hiawatha Point—*cape* ... NY-2
Hiawatha Run—*stream* ... MI-6
Hiawatha Sch—*school* ... IL-6
Hiawatha Sch—*school* ... IN-6
Hiawatha Sch—*school (2)* ... MI-6
Hiawatha Sch—*school (2)* ... MN-6
Hiawatha Sch—*school* ... MT-8
Hiawatha Sch—*school* ... NY-2
Hiawatha Sch—*school (2)* ... OH-6
Hiawatha Sch—*school* ... SC-3
Hiawatha Sch—*school (3)* ... WI-6
Hiawatha Sch (historical)—*school* ... PA-2
Hiawatha Sch (historical)—*school* ... TN-4
Hiawatha Shores—*locale* ... MI-6
*Hiawatha Spur* ... MN-6
Hiawatha (Station)—*locale* ... MI-6
**Hiawatha Subdivision**—*pop pl* ... TN-4
**Hiawatha Township**—*pop pl* ... KS-7
**Hiawatha (Township of)**—*pop pl* ... MI-6
Hiawatha Valley—*basin* ... WA-9
Hiawatha Well—*well* ... WY-8
Hiawawtha Lake—*reservoir* ... TN-4
Hibank Ch—*church* ... AR-4
Hibank Creek—*stream* ... AR-4
Hi Banks—*cliff* ... NY-2
Hibard Hollow—*valley* ... PA-2
Hibbard—*locale* ... AZ-5
**Hibbard**—*pop pl* ... ID-8
**Hibbard**—*pop pl* ... IN-6
Hibbard, Benjamin, Residence—*hist pl* ... MA-1
Hibbard, Charles H., House—*hist pl* ... IL-6
Hibbard, Enoch, House and Grannis, George, House—*hist pl* ... CT-1
Hibbard Apartment Bldg—*hist pl* ... MI-6
Hibbard Bay—*bay* ... VT-1
Hibbard Branch—*stream* ... KY-4
Hibbard Brook—*stream* ... MA-1
Hibbard Brook—*stream* ... NH-1
Hibbard Brook—*stream* ... VT-1
*Hibbard Corner* ... NY-2
Hibbard Creek—*stream* ... CA-9
Hibbard Creek—*stream* ... MT-8
Hibbard Creek—*stream* ... OR-9
Hibbard Creek—*stream* ... WA-9
Hibbard Creek—*stream* ... WI-6
Hibbard Draw—*valley* ... WY-8
Hibbard Gulch—*valley* ... OR-9
Hibbard Hill—*summit* ... VT-1
Hibbard Interchange—*crossing* ... AZ-5
*Hibbard Lake* ... MI-6
Hibbard Lake—*lake* ... MI-6
Hibbard Mtn—*summit* ... NH-1
Hibbard Point—*cape* ... OR-9
Hibbard Point—*cape* ... VT-1
Hibbard Sch—*school* ... IL-6
Hibbard Sch—*school* ... ME-1
*Hibbard School* ... IN-6
**Hibbards Corner**—*pop pl* ... NY-2
*Hibbard's Corners* ... NY-2
Hibbards Run—*stream* ... PA-2
Hibben Ch—*church* ... SC-3
Hibben Tank—*reservoir* ... AZ-5
Hibberd JHS—*school* ... IN-6
Hibbert, William, House—*hist pl* ... OR-9
Hibbert Branch—*stream* ... NC-3
Hibbert Cem—*cemetery* ... OR-9
Hibbert Mtn—*summit* ... NC-3
Hibberts Corner—*locale* ... ME-1
Hibberts Gore—*fmr MCD* ... ME-1
**Hibbetts**—*pop pl* ... OH-6
Hibbett Sch—*school* ... AL-4
**Hibbing**—*pop pl* ... MN-6
Hibbing City Hall—*hist pl* ... MN-6
Hibbing HS—*hist pl* ... MN-6
Hibbing Park—*park* ... MN-6
Hibbing Point—*cape* ... MN-6
Hibbing State Junior Coll—*school* ... MN-6
*Hibbins* ... MN-6
Hibbin Tank—*reservoir* ... AZ-5
Hibbit Ch—*church* ... TX-5
Hibbitts Cem—*cemetery* ... VA-3
Hibbitts Gap—*gap* ... VA-3
Hibble Gulch—*valley* ... ID-8
Hibbler Branch—*stream* ... SC-3
Hibbler Lake—*lake* ... NE-7
**Hibbs**—*pop pl* ... PA-2
Hibbs Bayou—*stream* ... LA-4
*Hibbs Cabin* ... ID-8
Hibbs Cem—*cemetery* ... AL-4
Hibbs Cem—*cemetery* ... IN-6
Hibbs Cow Camp—*locale* ... ID-8
Hibbs Draw—*valley* ... SD-7
Hibbs Island—*island* ... TN-4
Hibbs Lake—*lake* ... LA-4
Hibbs Ranch—*locale* ... ID-8
Hibbs Ridge—*ridge* ... OH-6
Hibbs Run—*stream* ... OH-6
Hibbs Run—*stream* ... WV-2
Hibbsville—*locale* ... IA-7
Hibbsville Cem—*cemetery* ... IA-7
Hibdon Hollow—*valley* ... MO-7
Hibenthal Rsvr—*reservoir* ... OR-9
Hiberian Block—*hist pl* ... MA-1
Hiberlee Sch—*school* ... MI-6
Hibernia—*locale* ... FL-3
Hibernia—*locale* ... KY-4
Hibernia—*locale* ... NJ-2
Hibernia—*locale* ... SC-3
**Hibernia**—*pop pl (2)* ... IN-6
**Hibernia**—*pop pl* ... NY-2
Hibernia Brook—*stream* ... NJ-2
Hibernia Canyon—*valley* ... AZ-5
Hibernia Cem—*cemetery* ... NJ-2
Hibernia Ch—*church* ... PA-2
Hibernia Hall—*hist pl* ... IA-7
Hibernia House—*hist pl* ... PA-2
Hibernia Junction—*uninc pl* ... NJ-2
*Hibernia Mills* ... IN-6
**Hibernia Mills**—*pop pl* ... IN-6
Hibernian Hall—*hist pl* ... SC-3
Hibernia Peak—*summit* ... AZ-5
Hibernia Point—*cape* ... FL-3
Hibernia Public Use Area—*park* ... NC-3
Hibiscus Apartments—*hist pl* ... FL-3
*Hibiscus Island* ... FM-9
Hibiscus Island—*island* ... FL-3
**Hibiscus Mobile Park**—*pop pl* ... FL-3
Hibiscus Point—*cape* ... NY-2
Hibiscus Sch—*school* ... FL-3
Hiblar Tank—*reservoir* ... NM-5
Hibler Cem—*cemetery* ... MO-7
Hibler Ditch—*canal* ... IN-6
Hibler Ranch—*locale* ... NM-5
Hiblers Bar—*bar* ... AL-4
Hiblers Landing—*locale* ... AL-4
*Hiblertown* ... PA-2
*Hi Box Lake* ... WA-9
Hibox Lake—*lake* ... WA-9
Hibriten Ch—*church* ... NC-3
**Hibriten (historical)**—*pop pl* ... NC-3
Hibriten HS—*school* ... NC-3
Hibriten Mtn—*summit* ... NC-3
Hibrooten Lake—*lake* ... MN-6
Hibsaw—*locale* ... OK-5
**Hibsaw**—*pop pl* ... OK-5
Hibshman Farm—*hist pl* ... PA-2
Hi Bug Hist Dist—*hist pl* ... MT-8
*Hicaholahala* ... MS-4
*Hicaholahia* ... MS-4
HIC Cem—*cemetery* ... TX-5
Hiccock Mtn—*summit* ... NY-2
Hice Branch—*stream* ... GA-3
Hice Branch—*stream* ... TN-4
Hice Hill Cem—*cemetery* ... NC-3
Hice Mine—*mine* ... NV-8
Hice Spring—*spring* ... NV-8
Hichborn, Nathan G., House—*hist pl* ... ME-1
*Hichita* ... OK-5
Hichitee Bridge—*bridge* ... AL-4
Hichitee Creek—*stream* ... GA-3
Hi Chute Ridge—*ridge* ... CA-9
Hickahala Creek—*stream* ... MS-4
Hickahala Creek Bridge—*hist pl* ... MS-4
Hickahala Creek Watershed C-34-9 Dam—*dam* ... MS-4
Hickahala Creek Watershed Y-6-11 Dam—*dam* ... MS-4
Hickahala Creek Watershed Y-6-15 Dam—*dam* ... MS-4
Hickahala Creek Watershed Y-6-16 Dam—*dam* ... MS-4
Hickahala Creek Watershed Y-6-3 Dam—*dam* ... MS-4
Hickahala Creek Watershed Y-6-4 Dam—*dam* ... MS-4
Hickahala Creek Watershed Y-6-5 Dam—*dam* ... MS-4
Hickahala Creek Watershed Y-6-6 Dam—*dam* ... MS-4
*Hickahall* ... MS-4
*Hickahate* ... MS-4
Hickam AFB—*military* ... HI-9
Hickam Cem—*cemetery* ... MO-7
Hickam Cem—*cemetery (3)* ... VA-3
Hickam Field—*hist pl* ... HI-9
Hickam Harbor—*bay* ... HI-9
**Hickam Housing (Hickam Village)**—*pop pl* ... HI-9
Hickam Lateral—*canal* ... IN-6
Hickam Sch—*school* ... HI-9
**Hickam Village**—*pop pl* ... HI-9
Hickaneck Swamp—*stream* ... VA-3
Hick Branch—*stream* ... TX-5
Hick Cem—*cemetery* ... AL-4
Hick Cem—*cemetery* ... TN-4
Hickenbottom Cem—*cemetery* ... KY-4
Hickenbottom Cem—*cemetery* ... WV-2
Hicken Ditch—*canal* ... UT-8
Hicken Hollow—*valley* ... UT-8
*Hickens Dam* ... SD-7
*Hickens Rock* ... MA-1
**Hickernell**—*pop pl* ... PA-2
Hickernell Spring—*spring* ... PA-2
Hickerson—*locale* ... TN-4
Hickerson Bayou—*stream* ... LA-4
Hickerson Branch—*stream* ... TN-4
Hickerson Branch—*stream* ... VA-3
Hickerson Cem—*cemetery* ... MO-7
Hickerson Cem—*cemetery (4)* ... TN-4
*Hickerson Elementary School* ... TN-4
Hickerson Gulch—*valley* ... OR-9
Hickerson Hollow—*valley* ... AR-4
Hickerson Hollow—*valley* ... TN-4
Hickerson Hollow—*valley* ... VA-3
Hickerson Lake—*lake* ... AK-9
Hickerson Mtn—*summit* ... VA-3
Hickerson Park—*flat* ... UT-8
Hickerson Post Office (historical)—*building* ... TN-4
*Hickerson School* ... TN-4
Hickerson Spring Branch—*stream* ... TN-4
Hickersons Store (historical)—*locale* ... TN-4
*Hickerson Station* ... TN-4
Hickerson Station Ch—*church* ... TN-4
*Hickerson Station Ch of Christ* ... TN-4
Hickerson Station Sch—*school* ... TN-4
*Hickey* ... TN-4
Hickey—*locale* ... TN-4
Hickey—*locale* ... TX-5
**Hickey**—*pop pl* ... TN-4
Hickey Basin—*basin* ... OR-9
Hickey Basin Rsvr—*reservoir* ... OR-9
Hickey Beaver Meadow—*flat* ... NY-2
Hickey Branch—*stream* ... FL-3
Hickey Branch—*stream* ... MS-4
Hickey Branch—*stream* ... NC-3
Hickey Branch—*stream* ... TX-5
Hickey Bridge—*bridge* ... CO-8
Hickey Brook—*stream* ... NH-1
Hickey Canyon—*valley* ... AZ-5
Hickey Canyon—*valley* ... CA-9
Hickey Cem—*cemetery* ... AR-4
Hickey Cem—*cemetery* ... IL-6
Hickey Cem—*cemetery* ... NC-3
Hickey Cem—*cemetery (4)* ... TN-4
Hickey Cem—*cemetery (2)* ... TX-5
Hickey Cem—*cemetery* ... VT-1
Hickey Ch—*church* ... TN-4
*Hickey Creek* ... OK-5
Hickey Creek—*stream* ... AK-9
Hickey Creek—*stream* ... FL-3
Hickey Creek—*stream (3)* ... MI-6
Hickey Creek—*stream* ... MT-8
Hickey Creek—*stream (3)* ... OR-9
Hickey Creek—*stream* ... WI-6
Hickey Creek Canal—*canal* ... FL-3
Hickey Creek Swamp—*swamp* ... FL-3
Hickey Dam—*dam* ... OR-9
Hickey Draw—*valley* ... WY-8
Hickey Field—*park* ... NY-2
Hickey Fork—*stream* ... NC-3
Hickey Gap—*gap* ... GA-3
Hickey Grove—*woods* ... CA-9
Hickey Gulch—*valley* ... CA-9
Hickey Hill—*summit* ... DC-2
Hickey Hill—*summit* ... MI-6
Hickey Hill—*summit* ... MT-8
Hickey Hill—*summit* ... NH-1
Hickey Hump—*summit* ... WA-9
Hickey Island—*island* ... ME-1
Hickey Knob—*summit* ... GA-3
Hickey Lake—*lake (2)* ... MN-6
Hickey Lake—*lake* ... WI-6
Hickey Meadow—*flat* ... OR-9
Hickey Mine—*mine (2)* ... CA-9
Hickey Mine (underground)—*mine* ... TN-4
Hickey Mountain Rsvr—*reservoir* ... WY-8
Hickey Mtn—*summit* ... AZ-5
Hickey Mtn—*summit* ... WY-8
Hickey No 1 Mine—*mine* ... NM-5
Hickey-Osborne Block—*hist pl* ... MA-1
Hickey Park—*park* ... MO-7
Hickey Post Office (historical)—*building* ... TN-4
Hickey Ranch—*locale* ... OR-9
*Hickey Ridge* ... WY-8
Hickey Rsvr—*reservoir (2)* ... OR-9
Hickey Run—*stream* ... DC-2
Hickey School(Abandoned)—*locale* ... IA-7
Hickeys Corners—*locale* ... NY-2
*Hickeys Lake* ... MN-6
Hickey Spring—*spring* ... AZ-5
Hickey Spring—*spring* ... OR-9
Hickey Springs—*spring* ... WI-6
Hickey Tanks—*reservoir* ... AZ-5
Hickeytown—*locale* ... AR-4
Hickey (Township of)—*fmr MCD* ... AR-4
Hickeyville—*locale* ... OR-9
Hick Hill Branch—*stream* ... TN-4
Hick Hollow Ch—*church* ... WV-2
Hickie Cem—*cemetery* ... TN-4
Hickison Pasture—*flat* ... NV-8
Hickison Summit—*gap* ... NV-8
**Hickiwan**—*pop pl* ... AZ-5
Hickiwan Peak—*summit* ... AZ-5
Hickiwan Valley—*valley* ... AZ-5
Hickiwan Wash—*stream* ... AZ-5
*Hickkins Rock* ... MA-1
*Hick Lake* ... WA-9
Hickland Butte—*summit* ... OR-9
Hickland Canyon—*valley* ... NM-5
Hickland Spring—*spring* ... NM-5
Hickle Cem—*cemetery* ... OH-6
Hickle Hollow—*valley* ... WV-2
Hicklen, William, House—*hist pl* ... DE-2
Hicklen Cem—*cemetery* ... KY-4
Hicklen Run—*stream* ... PA-2
Hickler Creek—*stream* ... MI-6
Hickleson Ditch—*canal* ... IN-6
Hickley Field Park—*park* ... WI-6
Hicklin Branch—*stream* ... MO-7
Hicklin Branch—*stream* ... SC-3
Hicklin Creek—*stream* ... MO-7
Hicklin Crossing—*locale* ... SC-3
Hicklin Hearthstone—*hist pl* ... MO-7
Hicklin Lake—*lake* ... MO-7
Hicklin Sch—*school* ... MO-7
*Hickman* ... AL-4
*Hickman* ... MS-4
*Hickman* ... NC-3
*Hickman* ... PA-2
Hickman—*locale* ... IL-6
Hickman—*locale* ... MO-7
Hickman—*locale* ... PA-2
Hickman—*locale* ... VA-3
**Hickman**—*pop pl* ... AR-4
**Hickman**—*pop pl* ... CA-9
**Hickman**—*pop pl* ... DE-2
**Hickman**—*pop pl* ... KY-4
**Hickman**—*pop pl* ... MD-2
**Hickman**—*pop pl* ... NE-7
**Hickman**—*pop pl* ... OH-6
**Hickman**—*pop pl* ... TN-4
Hickman, William, House—*hist pl* ... KY-4
Hickman Baptist Ch—*church* ... TN-4
Hickman Bar—*bar* ... TN-4
Hickman Bay—*swamp* ... MS-4
Hickman Bayou—*stream* ... LA-4
*Hickman Bend* ... AR-4
Hickman Bottom—*valley* ... LA-4
Hickman Branch—*stream (2)* ... AR-4
Hickman Branch—*stream* ... IN-6
Hickman Branch—*stream* ... KY-4
Hickman Branch—*stream* ... NE-7
Hickman Branch—*stream* ... NC-3
Hickman Branch—*stream (3)* ... TN-4
Hickman Branch—*stream (2)* ... TX-5
*Hickman Bridge* ... UT-8
Hickman Butte—*summit* ... OR-9
Hickman Canyon—*valley* ... NE-7
Hickman Canyon—*valley* ... UT-8
Hickman (CCD)—*cens area* ... KY-4
Hickman Cem—*cemetery (2)* ... AR-4
Hickman Cem—*cemetery* ... GA-3
Hickman Cem—*cemetery* ... IL-6
Hickman Cem—*cemetery* ... KY-4
Hickman Cem—*cemetery (4)* ... MS-4
Hickman Cem—*cemetery (5)* ... MO-7
Hickman Cem—*cemetery* ... OH-6
Hickman Cem—*cemetery* ... PA-2
Hickman Cem—*cemetery (5)* ... TN-4
Hickman Ch—*church* ... AL-4
*Hickman Chapel* ... AL-4
Hickman Chapel—*church* ... PA-2
Hickman Chapel Cem—*cemetery* ... AL-4
Hickman Chapel Sch (historical)—*school* ... MS-4
**Hickman (County)**—*pop pl* ... KY-4
**Hickman County**—*pop pl* ... TN-4
Hickman County Courthouse—*building* ... TN-4
Hickman County Courthouse—*hist pl* ... KY-4
Hickman County Fairgrounds—*locale* ... TN-4
Hickman County Farm (historical)—*locale* ... TN-4
Hickman County Hosp—*hospital* ... TN-4
Hickman County HS—*school* ... TN-4
Hickman County MS—*school* ... TN-4
Hickman Cove—*valley* ... NC-3
Hickman Creek—*stream* ... CA-9
Hickman Creek—*stream* ... GA-3
Hickman Creek—*stream* ... ID-8
Hickman Creek—*stream* ... IL-6
Hickman Creek—*stream (2)* ... KY-4
Hickman Creek—*stream* ... MS-4
Hickman Creek—*stream* ... OR-9
Hickman Creek—*stream (2)* ... TN-4
Hickman Creek—*stream (2)* ... TX-5
Hickman Creek—*stream* ... UT-8
Hickman Creek Hill—*summit* ... TN-4
Hickman Creek Rec Area—*park* ... TN-4
Hickman Dam—*dam* ... AL-4
Hickman Dam—*dam* ... SD-7
Hickman Ditch—*canal (3)* ... IN-6
Hickman Ditch—*stream* ... DE-2
Hickman Ditch—*stream* ... MD-2
Hickman Draft—*valley (2)* ... VA-3
Hickman Fork—*stream* ... KY-4
Hickman Forks—*locale* ... GA-3
Hickman Gulf—*valley* ... GA-3
Hickman Gun Club (historical)—*locale* ... TN-4
Hickman Hights Ch—*church* ... IN-6
Hickman Hill—*summit* ... IN-6
Hickman Hill—*summit* ... KY-4
Hickman Hill—*summit* ... MO-7
Hickman Hill—*summit* ... TN-4
Hickman (historical)—*locale* ... FL-3
Hickman (historical)—*locale* ... KS-7
*Hickman Hollow* ... TN-4
Hickman Hollow—*valley* ... WV-2
Hickman HS—*school* ... MO-7
Hickman Hunting Club (historical)—*locale* ... TN-4
Hickman Island—*island* ... GA-3
Hickman Knob—*summit* ... AR-4
Hickman Knob—*summit* ... TX-5
Hickman Knolls—*summit (2)* ... UT-8
Hickman Lake—*lake* ... IN-6
Hickman Lake—*lake* ... MI-6
Hickman Lake—*lake* ... OR-9
Hickman Lake—*reservoir* ... AL-4
Hickman Lake—*reservoir* ... SD-7
Hickman Landing—*locale* ... AR-4
Hickman Landing—*locale* ... MS-4
Hickman-Lockhart Bridge—*bridge* ... TN-4
Hickman Lookout Tower—*locale* ... MS-4
*Hickman Mills* ... MO-7
**Hickman Mills**—*pop pl* ... MO-7
Hickman Mtn—*summit* ... MO-7
Hickman Natural Bridge—*other* ... UT-8
Hickman Number 1 Dam—*dam* ... SD-7
Hickman Number 2 Dam—*dam* ... SD-7
Hickman Pass—*gap* ... UT-8
Hickman Pasture—*flat* ... UT-8
Hickman Post Office—*building* ... TN-4
Hickman Prairie—*flat* ... FL-3
Hickman Ranch—*locale* ... NE-7
Hickman Ranch—*locale* ... NM-5
Hickman Ridge—*ridge* ... TN-4
Hickman Road—*post sta* ... IA-7
**Hickman Run**—*pop pl* ... WV-2
Hickman Run—*stream* ... OH-6
Hickman Run—*stream* ... PA-2
Hickman Run—*stream* ... VA-3
Hickman Run—*stream (3)* ... WV-2
Hickman Run Sch—*school* ... WV-2
*Hickmans* ... AL-4
Hickmans Bar—*bar* ... AL-4
Hickmans Branch—*stream* ... NC-3
Hickmans Branch—*stream* ... VA-3
Hickman Sch—*school* ... MO-7
Hickman Sch—*school (2)* ... SC-3
Hickman Sch—*school* ... TN-4
Hickman Sch—*school* ... TX-5
Hickman Sch—*school* ... WV-2
Hickman Sch (historical)—*school* ... TN-4
*Hickmans Church* ... AL-4
*Hickmans Creek Baptist Church* ... TN-4
Hickmans Cross Roads—*locale* ... NC-3
**Hickmans Crossroads**—*pop pl* ... NC-3
*Hickman's Landing* ... AR-4
Hickmans Landing—*locale* ... FL-3
Hickman Slide Hollow—*valley* ... WV-2
Hickmans Mill—*locale* ... PA-2
Hickman Spring—*spring* ... MO-7
Hickman Spring—*spring* ... TN-4
Hickman Spring—*spring* ... UT-8
*Hickman Springs* ... TN-4
Hickman Springs Cave—*cave* ... TN-4
Hickman Springs Hollow—*valley* ... TN-4
*Hickman Station* ... AL-4
Hickman Street Sch—*school* ... KY-4
**Hickman Subdivision**—*pop pl* ... TN-4
*Hickmans X-Roads* ... NC-3
Hickman Tank—*reservoir* ... NM-5
**Hickman Township**—*pop pl* ... SD-7
Hickman Township (historical)—*civil* ... SD-7
Hickman (Township of)—*fmr MCD (2)* ... AR-4
**Hickman Village Estates (trailer park)**—*pop pl* ... DE-2
*Hickmuntown* ... TX-5
**Hickmuntown**—*pop pl* ... TX-5
Hickneytown (historical)—*locale* ... NV-8
Hickock Point—*cape* ... NY-2
Hickok—*locale* ... KS-7
Hickok Brook—*stream (2)* ... NY-2
Hickok Canyon—*valley* ... CO-8
Hickok Cem—*cemetery* ... CT-1
Hickok Cem—*cemetery* ... OH-6
Hickok Drain—*canal* ... MI-6
Hickok Hollow—*valley* ... PA-2
Hickok Run—*stream* ... PA-2
*Hickon Creek* ... PA-2
**Hickoria**—*pop pl* ... AR-4
*Hickories* ... DE-2
Hickories Park, The—*park* ... NY-2
*Hickory* ... FL-3
*Hickory* ... NC-3
*Hickory* ... PA-2
*Hickory* ... TN-4
Hickory—*locale* ... AL-4
Hickory—*locale* ... VA-3
**Hickory**—*pop pl* ... KY-4
**Hickory**—*pop pl (2)* ... LA-4
**Hickory**—*pop pl* ... MD-2
**Hickory**—*pop pl* ... MS-4
**Hickory**—*pop pl (2)* ... NC-3
**Hickory**—*pop pl* ... OK-5
**Hickory**—*pop pl* ... PA-2
**Hickory**—*pop pl* ... TN-4
**Hickory**—*pop pl* ... WV-2
Hickory, Lake—*reservoir (2)* ... NC-3
Hickory, The—*locale* ... NJ-2
**Hickory Acres (subdivision)**—*pop pl (2)* ... NC-3
Hickory Attendance Center—*school* ... MS-4
*Hickory Bar Point* ... MD-2
**Hickory Barren**—*pop pl* ... MO-7
Hickory Barren School (abandoned)—*locale* ... MO-7
Hickory Basin—*basin* ... NC-3
Hickory Bay—*bay* ... SC-3
Hickory Bayou—*stream* ... AL-4
Hickory Bearpen Run—*stream* ... WV-2
Hickory Bend—*uninc pl* ... TN-4
Hickory Bend Cem—*cemetery* ... AL-4
Hickory Bend Ch—*church* ... TN-4
Hickory Block Cem—*cemetery* ... MS-4
Hickory Block Ch—*church* ... MS-4
Hickory Bluff—*cliff* ... TX-5
**Hickory Bluff**—*pop pl* ... GA-3
**Hickory Bluff**—*pop pl* ... SC-3
Hickory Bluff Cem—*cemetery* ... MS-4
Hickory Bluff Landing—*locale* ... MS-4
Hickory Bluff Trail—*trail* ... MO-7
Hickory Bottom—*flat* ... NC-3
Hickory Bottom Branch—*stream (2)* ... NC-3
Hickory Bottom Creek—*stream* ... PA-2
Hickory Bottom Sch (abandoned)—*school* ... PA-2
Hickory Branch—*stream* ... AL-4
Hickory Branch—*stream (5)* ... FL-3
Hickory Branch—*stream (2)* ... GA-3
Hickory Branch—*stream* ... IN-6
Hickory Branch—*stream (4)* ... LA-4
Hickory Branch—*stream (8)* ... MO-7
Hickory Branch—*stream (4)* ... NC-3
Hickory Branch—*stream* ... OH-6
Hickory Branch—*stream* ... OK-5
Hickory Branch—*stream* ... TX-5
Hickory Branch—*stream (5)* ... WV-2
Hickory Branch Canal—*canal* ... LA-4
Hickory Branch (historical P.O.)—*locale* ... IN-6
Hickory Brook—*stream* ... CT-1
**Hickorybush**—*pop pl* ... NY-2
Hickory Bush—*uninc pl* ... NY-2
Hickory Camp—*locale* ... FL-3
Hickory Camp—*locale* ... WV-2
Hickory Camp Branch—*stream* ... WV-2
Hickory Camp Creek—*stream* ... KY-4
Hickory Camp Run—*stream* ... KY-4
Hickory Cane Mine—*mine* ... KY-4
Hickory Cem—*cemetery* ... DE-2
Hickory Cem—*cemetery* ... IL-6
Hickory Cem—*cemetery (2)* ... IA-7
Hickory Cem—*cemetery* ... MS-4
Hickory Cem—*cemetery (2)* ... OK-5
Hickory Cem—*cemetery* ... WI-6
Hickory Center—*locale* ... PA-2
Hickory Ch—*church* ... IN-6
Hickory Ch—*church* ... IA-7
Hickory Ch—*church* ... KY-4
Hickory Ch—*church* ... WI-6
Hickory Chapel—*church* ... AL-4
Hickory Chapel—*church* ... MO-7
Hickory Chapel—*church (2)* ... NC-3
Hickory Chapel—*church* ... WV-2
*Hickory Chapel Ch* ... AL-4
Hickory Chute—*stream* ... MO-7
Hickory Coll—*school* ... IL-6
Hickory College Ch—*church* ... KY-4
Hickory Corner—*locale* ... KY-4
Hickory Corner—*locale* ... NJ-2
Hickory Corner—*locale (2)* ... PA-2
Hickory Corner—*locale* ... TN-4
**Hickory Corner**—*pop pl* ... IN-6
*Hickory Corners* ... PA-2
Hickory Corners—*locale* ... IL-6
Hickory Corners—*locale* ... PA-2
**Hickory Corners**—*pop pl* ... IL-6
**Hickory Corners**—*pop pl* ... MI-6
**Hickory Corners**—*pop pl* ... NY-2
**Hickory Corners**—*pop pl* ... OH-6
**Hickory Corners**—*pop pl (2)* ... PA-2
**Hickory Corners**—*pop pl* ... TN-4
**Hickory Corners**—*pop pl* ... WI-6
Hickory Corner Sch—*school* ... IL-6
Hickory Corner Sch (historical)—*school* ... TN-4
Hickory Corners Sch—*school* ... MI-6
Hickory Coulee—*valley* ... MT-8
**Hickory County**—*pop pl* ... MO-7
*Hickory Cove* ... MD-2
Hickory Cove—*bay* ... DE-2
Hickory Cove—*bay* ... MD-2
Hickory Cove—*bay (2)* ... TX-5
Hickory Cove—*valley (3)* ... NC-3
Hickory Cove—*valley* ... TN-4
Hickory Cove—*valley* ... VA-3
*Hickory Cove Baptist Church* ... TN-4
*Hickory Cove Church* ... TN-4
Hickory Cove Creek—*stream* ... NC-3
**Hickory Cove (historical)**—*pop pl* ... TN-4
*Hickory Creek* ... MS-4
*Hickory Creek* ... TX-5
Hickory Creek—*locale (2)* ... MO-7
Hickory Creek—*locale* ... TX-5
**Hickory Creek**—*pop pl* ... AR-4
**Hickory Creek**—*pop pl (2)* ... TX-5
Hickory Creek—*stream (6)* ... AR-4
Hickory Creek—*stream* ... CA-9
Hickory Creek—*stream* ... FL-3
Hickory Creek—*stream* ... GA-3
Hickory Creek—*stream (10)* ... IL-6
Hickory Creek—*stream (2)* ... IN-6
Hickory Creek—*stream (8)* ... IA-7
Hickory Creek—*stream (5)* ... KS-7
Hickory Creek—*stream* ... KY-4

Hickory Creek—stream (2) ... LA-4
Hickory Creek—stream ... MI-6
Hickory Creek—stream (7) ... MS-4
Hickory Creek—stream (12) ... MO-7
Hickory Creek—stream (5) ... NC-3
Hickory Creek—stream ... OH-6
Hickory Creek—stream (7) ... OK-5
Hickory Creek—stream (2) ... PA-2
Hickory Creek—stream (4) ... TN-4
Hickory Creek—stream (17) ... TX-5
Hickory Creek—stream (3) ... VA-3
Hickory Creek Arm—bay ... TX-5
Hickory Creek Bay—bay ... NC-3
Hickory Creek Bend—bend ... TN-4
Hickory Creek Cem—cemetery ... AR-4
Hickory Creek Cem—cemetery ... OK-5
Hickory Creek Ch—church ... MS-4
Hickory Creek Ch (historical)—church ... MO-7
*Hickory Creek Church* ... TN-4
Hickory Creek East Rec Area—park ... KS-7
Hickory Creek Island—island ... OK-5
Hickory Creek Park—locale ... TX-5
Hickory Creek Park—park ... NC-3
Hickory Creek Park—park ... TN-4
*Hickory Creek Post Office* ... TN-4
Hickory Creek Post Office (historical)—building ... TN-4
Hickory Creek Sch—school ... AR-4
Hickory Creek Sch (abandoned)—school ... MO-7
Hickory Creek Shop Ctr—locale ... NC-3
Hickory Creek Stone Arch Bridge—hist pl ... TN-4
Hickory Creek West Rec Area—park ... KS-7
*Hickory Cross* ... NC-3
*Hickory Cross Roads* ... NC-3
*Hickory Cross Roads* ... PA-2
Hickory Crossroads—locale ... NC-3
Hickory Cross Roads—other ... NC-3
**Hickory Crossroads**—pop pl ... NC-3
**Hickory Dale Acres**—pop pl ... DE-2
Hickorydale Sch—school ... OH-6
Hickory Donnick—other ... AR-4
*Hickory Drain* ... MI-6
Hickory East (census name East Hickory)—other ... NC-3
Hickory Falls—falls ... OK-5
**Hickory Falls**—pop pl ... IL-6
*Hickory Flat* ... MO-7
*Hickory Flat* ... TN-4
Hickory Flat—flat ... AR-4
Hickory Flat—flat ... IN-6
Hickory Flat—flat ... KY-4
Hickory Flat—flat ... MO-7
Hickory Flat—flat ... OK-5
Hickory Flat—flat (2) ... TN-4
Hickory Flat—flat ... WV-2
Hickory Flat—flat ... WI-6
Hickory Flat—gap ... AL-4
Hickory Flat—gap ... WV-2
Hickory Flat—locale ... AL-4
Hickory Flat—locale ... KY-4
**Hickory Flat**—pop pl ... AR-4
**Hickory Flat**—pop pl (2) ... GA-3
**Hickory Flat**—pop pl ... MS-4
**Hickory Flat**—pop pl ... TN-4
**Hickory Flat**—pop pl ... VA-3
*Hickory Flat Branch* ... MS-4
Hickory Flat Branch—stream ... MS-4
Hickory Flat Branch—stream (2) ... NC-3
Hickory Flat Branch—stream ... SC-3
Hickory Flat Branch—stream ... TN-4
Hickory Flat Cem—cemetery ... KY-4
Hickory Flat Cem—cemetery ... MS-4
Hickory Flat Cem—cemetery ... TN-4
Hickory Flat Ch—church (3) ... AL-4
Hickory Flat Ch—church ... GA-3
Hickory Flat Ch—church ... MS-4
Hickory Flat Ch—church ... OH-6
Hickory Flat Ch—church (2) ... TN-4
Hickory Flat Cove—valley ... GA-3
Hickory Flat Cove—valley ... NC-3
*Hickory Flat Creek* ... MS-4
Hickory Flat Creek—stream ... MO-7
Hickory Flat Creek—stream ... NC-3
Hickory Flat Creek—stream ... TN-4
*Hickory Flat Freewill Baptist Ch* ... AL-4
**Hickory Flat (historical)**—pop pl ... MS-4
Hickory Flat Hollow—valley ... AR-4
Hickory Flat Knob—summit ... NC-3
Hickory Flat Mtn—summit ... AL-4
Hickory Flat Mtn—summit ... KY-4
Hickory Flat Run—stream ... WV-2
Hickory Flats—flat ... NC-3
Hickory Flats—flat ... VA-3
Hickory Flats—flat ... WV-2
**Hickory Flats**—pop pl (2) ... TN-4
Hickory Flats—summit ... NC-3
Hickory Flats Branch—stream ... TN-4
Hickory Flats Cem—cemetery ... GA-3
Hickory Flat Sch—school ... AR-4
Hickory Flat Sch—school ... IA-7
Hickory Flat Sch—school ... KY-4
Hickory Flat Sch—school (2) ... MS-4
Hickory Flat Sch—school ... TN-4
Hickory Flat Sch (abandoned)—school ... MO-7
Hickory Flat Sch (historical)—school ... MS-4
Hickory Flat Sch (historical)—school (3) ... TN-4
*Hickory Flats Church* ... AL-4
Hickory Flats Lookout Tower—locale ... KY-4
*Hickory Flats Methodist Church* ... TN-4
Hickory Flats Sch (historical)—school ... TN-4
Hickory Flats Slough—gut ... AR-4
*Hickory Flatt Sch* ... TN-4
Hickory Forest Creek—stream ... VA-3
**Hickory Forest (subdivision)**—pop pl ... AL-4
*Hickory Fork* ... NC-3
Hickory Fork—locale ... VA-3
Hickory Fork—stream (2) ... WV-2
Hickory Forks—locale ... TN-4
Hickory Gap—gap ... KY-4
Hickory Gap—gap (3) ... NC-3
Hickory Gap—gap ... SC-3
Hickory Gap—gap ... TN-4
Hickory Gap—locale ... WV-2
Hickory Gap Branch—stream ... WV-2
Hickory Gap Ch—church ... KY-4
Hickory Gas Storage Field—oilfield ... KY-4
**Hickory Glen (subdivision)**—oop pl ... MS-4
*Hickory Ground* ... AL-4
*Hickory Ground* ... VA-3
Hickory Ground—hist pl ... AL-4
Hickory Ground—locale ... VA-3
Hickory Ground (Hickory)—uninc pl ... VA-3
Hickory Ground No 1 Ch—church ... OK-5
Hickory Ground No 2 Ch—church ... OK-5
*Hickory Grove* ... KY-4
*Hickory Grove* ... MS-4
Hickory Grove—locale ... AL-4
Hickory Grove—locale ... AR-4
Hickory Grove—locale ... IA-7
Hickory Grove—locale ... KY-4
Hickory Grove—locale ... MS-4
Hickory Grove—locale ... NC-3
Hickory Grove—locale ... SC-3
Hickory Grove—locale (3) ... TN-4
Hickory Grove—locale (2) ... VA-3
Hickory Grove—locale ... WV-2
Hickory Grove—locale ... WI-6
**Hickory Grove**—pop pl ... AL-4
**Hickory Grove**—pop pl ... IL-6
**Hickory Grove**—pop pl ... IA-7
**Hickory Grove**—pop pl ... KY-4
**Hickory Grove**—pop pl ... LA-4
**Hickory Grove**—pop pl ... MS-4
**Hickory Grove**—pop pl ... NY-2
**Hickory Grove**—pop pl (2) ... NC-3
**Hickory Grove**—pop pl ... OH-6
**Hickory Grove**—pop pl ... PA-2
**Hickory Grove**—pop pl (2) ... SC-3
**Hickory Grove**—pop pl (2) ... TN-4
**Hickory Grove**—pop pl ... TX-5
**Hickory Grove**—pop pl ... WI-6
Hickory Grove Baptist Ch—church ... AL-4
*Hickory Grove Baptist Church* ... MS-4
*Hickory Grove Baptist Church* ... TN-4
Hickory Grove Branch—stream ... TN-4
Hickory Grove Camp—locale ... IA-7
**Hickory Grove (Cary Ridge)**—pop pl ... KY-4
Hickory Grove (CCD)—cens area ... KY-4
Hickory Grove (CCD)—cens area ... SC-3
Hickory Grove Cem—cemetery (5) ... AL-4
Hickory Grove Cem—cemetery (6) ... AR-4
Hickory Grove Cem—cemetery ... DE-2
Hickory Grove Cem—cemetery ... GA-3
Hickory Grove Cem—cemetery (2) ... IL-6
Hickory Grove Cem—cemetery (2) ... IN-6
Hickory Grove Cem—cemetery (4) ... IA-7
Hickory Grove Cem—cemetery (9) ... MS-4
Hickory Grove Cem—cemetery (8) ... MO-7
Hickory Grove Cem—cemetery (2) ... OH-6
Hickory Grove Cem—cemetery (2) ... OK-5
Hickory Grove Cem—cemetery ... PA-2
Hickory Grove Cem—cemetery (7) ... TN-4
Hickory Grove Cem—cemetery (7) ... TX-5
Hickory Grove Cem—cemetery ... WI-6
*Hickory Grove Ch* ... AL-4
*Hickory Grove Ch* ... MO-7
Hickory Grove Ch—church (12) ... AL-4
Hickory Grove Ch—church (12) ... AR-4
Hickory Grove Ch—church (3) ... FL-3
Hickory Grove Ch—church (4) ... GA-3
Hickory Grove Ch—church (2) ... IL-6
Hickory Grove Ch—church (4) ... IN-6
Hickory Grove Ch—church ... IA-7
Hickory Grove Ch—church (6) ... KY-4
Hickory Grove Ch—church (3) ... LA-4
Hickory Grove Ch—church (10) ... MS-4
Hickory Grove Ch—church (12) ... MO-7
Hickory Grove Ch—church (16) ... NC-3
Hickory Grove Ch—church (3) ... OH-6
Hickory Grove Ch—church (2) ... OK-5
Hickory Grove Ch—church ... PA-2
Hickory Grove Ch—church (5) ... SC-3
Hickory Grove Ch—church (12) ... TN-4
Hickory Grove Ch—church (2) ... TX-5
Hickory Grove Ch—church (2) ... VA-3
Hickory Grove Ch—church (2) ... WV-2
Hickory Grove Chapel—church ... AL-4
Hickory Grove Ch (historical)—church (4) ... MS-4
Hickory Grove Ch (historical)—church (2) ... TN-4
*Hickory Grove Ch of Christ* ... MS-4
Hickory Grove Church and Sch—hist pl ... AR-4
Hickory Grove Country Club—other ... IA-7
Hickory Grove County Park—park ... IA-7
Hickory Grove Creek—stream ... AR-4
Hickory Grove Creek—stream ... IL-6
Hickory Grove Crossroads—locale ... NC-3
Hickory Grove Ditch—canal ... IL-6
Hickory Grove Elem Sch—school ... NC-3
Hickory Grove Elem Sch—school ... PA-2
**Hickory Grove Estates (subdivision)**—pop pl ... MS-4
Hickory Grove Hill—summit ... IL-6
Hickory Grove (historical)—locale ... MS-4
**Hickory Grove (historical)**—pop pl ... NC-3
Hickory Grove Lake—lake ... IA-7
Hickory Grove Lake Dam—dam ... IA-7
Hickory Grove Market—locale ... NC-3
Hickory Grove Memorial Cem—cemetery ... VA-3
Hickory Grove Picnic Area—locale ... AR-4
Hickory Grove P. O. (historical)—locale ... AL-4
Hickory Grove Pond—lake ... IN-6
Hickory Grove (reduced usage)—locale ... IL-6
Hickory Grove Sanatorium—hospital ... WI-6
*Hickory Grove Sch* ... AL-4
Hickory Grove Sch—school ... AL-4
Hickory Grove Sch—school (9) ... IL-6
Hickory Grove Sch—school (2) ... IA-7
Hickory Grove Sch—school (3) ... KS-7
Hickory Grove Sch—school (2) ... KY-4
Hickory Grove Sch—school ... MI-6
Hickory Grove Sch—school ... MS-4
Hickory Grove Sch—school (8) ... MO-7
Hickory Grove Sch—school ... NE-7
Hickory Grove Sch—school ... OK-5
Hickory Grove Sch—school ... PA-2
Hickory Grove Sch—school (2) ... SC-3
Hickory Grove Sch—school ... TN-4
Hickory Grove Sch—school ... WV-2
Hickory Grove Sch—school (3) ... WI-6
Hickory Grove Sch (abandoned)—school (4) ... MO-7
Hickory Grove Sch (historical)—school (2) ... AL-4
Hickory Grove Sch (historical)—school (6) ... MS-4
Hickory Grove Sch (historical)—school (3) ... MO-7
Hickory Grove Sch (historical)—school (8) ... TN-4
Hickory Grove School (abandoned)—locale (2) ... MO-7
Hickory Grove School (historical)—locale ... MO-7
**Hickory Grove (subdivision)**—pop pl ... NC-3
Hickory Grove Township—civil ... MO-7
Hickory Grove Township—fmr MCD (2) ... IA-7
Hickory Grove (Township of)—civ div ... IN-6
Hickory Grove (Township of)—fmr MCD ... AR-4
*Hickory Grove United Methodist Church* ... TN-4
Hickory Gulch—valley ... AZ-5
Hickory Gully—stream ... LA-4
Hickory Gut—gut ... MD-2
Hickory Hall (historical)—locale ... AL-4
Hickory Hammock—island ... FL-3
Hickory Hammock—island ... GA-3
Hickory Hammock Ch—church ... FL-3
Hickory Hammock Grove—locale ... FL-3
Hickory Hammock Lake—lake ... FL-3
Hickory Haven—locale ... CT-1
**Hickory Haven**—pop pl ... VA-3
Hickory Head—stream ... FL-3
Hickory Head—valley ... FL-3
Hickory Head Branch—stream ... AL-4
Hickory Head Ch—church ... GA-3
**Hickory Heights**—pop pl ... MI-6
**Hickory Heights**—pop pl ... PA-2
**Hickory Heights**—pop pl (2) ... TN-4
Hickory Heights Ch of Christ—church ... TN-4
Hickory Heights Sch—school ... PA-2
**Hickory (Hickory Ground)**—pop pl ... VA-3
Hickory Highland Cem—cemetery ... MI-6
*Hickory Hill* ... MT-8
*Hickoryhill* ... PA-2
*Hickory Hill* ... VA-3
Hickory Hill—hist pl ... GA-3
Hickory Hill—hist pl ... NY-2
Hickory Hill—hist pl ... NC-3
Hickory Hill—hist pl ... VA-3
Hickory Hill—hist pl ... WV-2
Hickory Hill—locale ... AR-4
Hickory Hill—locale ... DE-2
Hickory Hill—locale ... FL-3
Hickory Hill—locale ... PA-2
Hickory Hill—locale ... TX-5
Hickory Hill—locale ... VA-3
**Hickory Hill**—pop pl (2) ... DE-2
**Hickory Hill**—pop pl ... KY-4
**Hickory Hill**—pop pl ... MO-7
**Hickory Hill**—pop pl ... OK-5
**Hickory Hill**—pop pl ... PA-2
**Hickoryhill**—pop pl ... PA-2
**Hickory Hill**—pop pl (2) ... SC-3
**Hickory Hill**—pop pl ... TN-4
Hickory Hill—summit ... CT-1
Hickory Hill—summit (2) ... FL-3
Hickory Hill—summit ... MI-6
Hickory Hill—summit ... MN-6
Hickory Hill—summit (2) ... NY-2
Hickory Hill—summit (2) ... TN-4
Hickory Hill—summit ... TX-5
Hickory Hill—summit (2) ... VA-3
Hickory Hill Airp—airport ... NC-3
Hickory Hill Baptist Ch—church ... TN-4
Hickory Hill Branch—stream ... TX-5
Hickory Hill Cem—cemetery ... AL-4
Hickory Hill Cem—cemetery ... IL-6
Hickory Hill Cem—cemetery ... IN-6
Hickory Hill Cem—cemetery ... MS-4
Hickory Hill Cem—cemetery ... TN-4
Hickory Hill Cem—cemetery (2) ... TX-5
Hickory Hill Ch—church ... DE-2
Hickory Hill Ch—church (3) ... FL-3
Hickory Hill Ch—church (5) ... IL-6
Hickory Hill Ch—church ... KY-4
Hickory Hill Ch—church ... OK-5
Hickory Hill Ch—church (2) ... SC-3
Hickory Hill Ch—church (3) ... TN-4
Hickory Hill Ch—church (3) ... TX-5
Hickory Hill Ch—church (2) ... VA-3
Hickory Hill Ch (historical)—church ... AL-4
*Hickory Hill Church* ... AL-4
*Hickory Hill Club* ... AL-4
Hickory Hill Crossing—bridge ... SC-3
**Hickory Hill Estates**—pop pl ... TN-4
Hickory Hill Farm Dam—dam ... OR-9
Hickory Hill Farm Rsvr—reservoir ... OR-9
Hickory Hill Farms Airp—airport ... PA-2
Hickory Hill Fire Tower (historical)—tower ... AL-4
Hickory Hill Girl Scout Camp—locale ... WI-6
Hickory Hill Golf Club—other ... MI-6
Hickory Hill Golf Course—locale ... MS-4
Hickory Hill (historical)—locale ... AL-4
Hickory Hill Hollow—valley ... VA-3
*Hickory Hill Hunting Club* ... AL-4
Hickory Hill Lake—lake ... SC-3
Hickory Hill Lake—reservoir ... KY-4
Hickory Hill Lookout Tower—locale ... LA-4
*Hickory Hill Methodist Church* ... TN-4
Hickory Hill Plantation (historical)—locale ... AL-4
Hickory Hill Rsvr—reservoir ... OR-9
**Hickory Hills**—pop pl (2) ... AL-4
**Hickory Hills**—pop pl ... IL-6
**Hickory Hills**—pop pl ... IN-6
**Hickory Hills**—pop pl (2) ... PA-2
**Hickory Hills**—pop pl (5) ... TN-4
Hickory Hills—uninc pl ... MD-2
Hickory Hills Ch—church ... TN-4
Hickory Hill Sch—school ... AR-4
Hickory Hill Sch—school ... GA-3
Hickory Hill Sch—school ... IL-6
Hickory Hill Sch—school ... MO-7
Hickory Hill Sch—school ... NY-2
Hickory Hill Sch—school ... NC-3
Hickory Hill Sch—school ... PA-2
Hickory Hill Sch—school (3) ... SC-3
Hickory Hill Sch—school ... VA-3
Hickory Hill Sch—school ... WI-6
Hickory Hill Sch (historical)—school ... MO-7
Hickory Hill Sch (historical)—school ... TN-4
*Hickory Hill School* ... AL-4
Hickory Hills Country Club—other ... MO-7
Hickory Hills Country Club—other ... WI-6
Hickory Hills Golf Club—other ... IL-6
Hickory Hills Golf Club—other ... MI-6
Hickory Hills Lake—reservoir ... MA-1
Hickory Hills Lake Dam—dam ... MA-1
Hickory Hills Plaza Shop Ctr—locale ... AL-4
Hickory Hills Recreation Dam—dam ... IA-7
Hickory Hills Sch—school ... MO-7
Hickory Hills Shop Ctr—locale ... MO-7
**Hickory Hills (subdivision)**—pop pl ... AL-4
**Hickory Hills (subdivision)**—pop pl (2) ... NC-3
**Hickory Hills (subdivision)**—pop pl (2) ... TN-4
Hickory Hill Strip Mine—mine ... OK-5
**Hickory Hill (subdivision)**—pop pl (2) ... NC-3
**Hickory Hills West Trailer Park**—pop pl ... NC-3
Hickory Hills Woods—woods ... IL-6
Hickory Hill (Township of)—civ div ... IL-6
Hickory (historical)—locale ... AL-4
*Hickory Hollow* ... VA-3
Hickory Hollow—valley ... AL-4
Hickory Hollow—valley (2) ... AR-4
Hickory Hollow—valley (4) ... KY-4
Hickory Hollow—valley ... LA-4
Hickory Hollow—valley ... MS-4
Hickory Hollow—valley (9) ... MO-7
Hickory Hollow—valley ... OK-5
Hickory Hollow—valley ... PA-2
Hickory Hollow—valley ... SC-3
Hickory Hollow—valley (6) ... TN-4
Hickory Hollow—valley ... TX-5
Hickory Hollow—valley (4) ... VA-3
Hickory Hollow—valley (2) ... WV-2
Hickory Hollow Branch—stream ... LA-4
Hickory Hollow Branch—stream ... VA-3
Hickory Hollow Golf Course—other ... MI-6
**Hickory Hollow (subdivision)**—pop pl ... NC-3
Hickory HS—school ... PA-2
Hickory Hunting Club—locale ... AL-4
Hickory Institute (historical)—school ... MS-4
*Hickory Island* ... MI-6
Hickory Island—island (2) ... GA-3
Hickory Island—island ... IL-6
Hickory Island—island ... MI-6
Hickory Island—island (2) ... NJ-2
Hickory Island—island ... NC-3
Hickory Island—island ... OH-6
Hickory Island—island (2) ... SC-3
**Hickory Island**—pop pl ... IN-6
**Hickory Island**—pop pl ... MI-6
Hickory Island Gully—valley ... TX-5
Hickory Junction—locale ... VA-3
Hickory King Branch—stream ... TN-4
Hickory Knob—summit ... AL-4
Hickory Knob—summit (2) ... AR-4
Hickory Knob—summit (2) ... GA-3
Hickory Knob—summit ... KS-7
Hickory Knob—summit (3) ... KY-4
Hickory Knob—summit (5) ... NC-3
Hickory Knob—summit (4) ... PA-2
Hickory Knob—summit ... TN-4
Hickory Knob—summit (3) ... VA-3
Hickory Knob—summit (4) ... WV-2
Hickory Knob Ch—church ... KY-4
*Hickory Knoll* ... NC-3
**Hickory Knoll**—pop pl ... NC-3
Hickory Knoll Ch—church ... NC-3
Hickory Knoll Creek—stream ... NC-3
Hickory Lake—lake ... FL-3
Hickory Lake—lake ... IL-6
Hickory Lake—lake ... IN-6
Hickory Lake—lake ... MI-6
Hickory Lake—lake ... MN-6
Hickory Lake—lake ... NY-2
Hickory Lake—lake ... PA-2
Hickory Lake—lake ... TX-5
Hickory Lake—reservoir (2) ... IN-6
Hickory Lake—reservoir ... IA-7
Hickory Lake—reservoir ... VA-3
Hickory Lake Creek—stream ... LA-4
Hickory Lake Dam—dam ... IN-6
Hickory Lake Dam—dam ... IA-7
**Hickory Lake (subdivision)**—pop pl ... TN-4
Hickory Landing—locale (2) ... FL-3
Hickory Landing—locale ... MO-7
Hickory Landing—locale ... TN-4
Hickory Landing Creek—stream ... MD-2
Hickory Landing (historical)—locale ... TN-4
Hickoryland Mtn—summit ... GA-3
Hickory Level—locale ... GA-3
Hickory Level Ch—church ... FL-3
Hickory Level Creek—stream ... GA-3
**Hickory Lick**—pop pl ... WV-2
Hickory Lick—stream ... KY-4
Hickory Lick—stream ... VA-3
Hickory Lick Branch—stream ... KY-4
Hickory Lick Creek—stream ... IN-6
Hickory Lick Creek—stream ... MO-7
Hickory Lick Ridge—ridge ... KY-4
Hickory Lick Run—stream ... WV-2
Hickorylick Run—stream ... WV-2
Hickory Lodge (historical)—locale ... MO-7
Hickory Log Branch—stream ... KY-4
Hickorylog Branch—stream ... NC-3
Hickory Log Ch—church ... GA-3
Hickory Log Creek—stream ... GA-3
Hickory Log Gully—valley ... LA-4
Hickory Log Hollow—valley ... KY-4
Hickory Log Hollow—valley ... VA-3
Hickory Log Mtn—summit ... GA-3
Hickory Log Sch—school ... IL-6
Hickory Log Vocational Sch—school ... GA-3
Hickory Lookout Tower—locale ... LA-4
**Hickory Meadows (subdivision)**—pop pl ... NC-3
Hickory Mill Hollow—valley ... AL-4
Hickory Mill Spring—spring ... TN-4
*Hickory Mountain* ... AZ-5
Hickory Mountain Branch—stream ... NC-3
Hickory Mountain Branch—stream ... TX-5
Hickory Mountain Ch—church ... NC-3
Hickory Mountain (Township of)—fmr MCD ... NC-3
Hickory Mtn—summit ... GA-3
Hickory Mtn—summit ... MA-1
Hickory Mtn—summit ... NJ-2
Hickory Mtn—summit ... NY-2
Hickory Mtn—summit (4) ... NC-3
Hickory Mtn—summit ... TX-5
Hickory Municipal Airp—airport ... NC-3
Hickory Neck Church—hist pl ... VA-3
Hickory Neek Ch—church ... VA-3
Hickory North—locale ... NC-3
Hickory Number 1 Mine Station—locale ... PA-2
Hickorynut—other ... KY-4
Hickorynut Branch—stream ... GA-3
Hickorynut Branch—stream (2) ... NC-3
Hickory Nut Branch—stream ... SC-3
Hickorynut Cove—bay ... VA-3
Hickorynut Cove—valley ... GA-3
Hickorynut Creek—stream ... KY-4
Hickorynut Falls—falls ... NC-3
Hickorynut Gap—gap (2) ... GA-3
Hickorynut Gap—gap (5) ... NC-3
Hickory Nut Gap—gap ... NC-3
Hickorynut Gap—gap ... TN-4
**Hickory Nut Gap**—pop pl ... NC-3
Hickorynut Knob—summit ... NC-3
Hickorynut Lake—lake ... FL-3
Hickorynut Lead—ridge ... GA-3
Hickorynut Lookout Tower—locale ... AR-4
Hickory Nut Lower Dam—dam ... NC-3
Hickory Nut Lower Lake—reservoir ... NC-3
Hickorynut Mountain—ridge ... AR-4
Hickorynut Mountain—ridge ... NC-3
Hickory Nut Mtn—summit ... GA-3
Hickorynut Mtn—summit (2) ... GA-3
Hickorynut Mtn—summit (2) ... NC-3
Hickory Nut Mtn—summit ... SC-3
Hickorynut Mtn—summit ... SC-3
Hickory Nut Mtn—summit ... TN-4
Hickorynut Ridge—ridge ... GA-3
Hickory Nut Ridge—ridge (3) ... KY-4
Hickorynut Ridge—ridge ... MO-7
Hickorynut Ridge—ridge ... OK-5
*Hickory Nut Saddle Gap* ... TN-4
Hickory Nut Upper Dam—dam ... NC-3
Hickory Nut Upper Lake—reservoir ... NC-3
Hickory Park—park ... NJ-2
Hickory Pass—gap ... TX-5
**Hickory Plains**—pop pl ... AR-4
Hickory Plains Ch—church ... TN-4
Hickory Plains Creek—stream ... AR-4
Hickory Plains Sch—school ... AR-4
Hickory Plain (Township of)—fmr MCD ... AR-4
*Hickory Point* ... KS-7
Hickory Point—cape ... FL-3
Hickory Point—cape (3) ... MD-2
Hickory Point—cape ... NY-2
Hickory Point—cape (3) ... NC-3
Hickory Point—cape ... OK-5
Hickory Point—cape (2) ... VA-3
Hickory Point—cape (2) ... WI-6
Hickory Point—locale ... TN-4
**Hickory Point**—pop pl ... NC-3
**Hickory Point**—pop pl ... TN-4
Hickory Point Cem—cemetery ... IL-6
Hickory Point Ch—church (2) ... MO-7
Hickory Point Gut—gut ... MD-2
Hickory Point Hollow—valley ... PA-2
Hickory Point Post Office (historical)—building ... TN-4
Hickory Point Rec Area—park ... OK-5
Hickory Point Sch—school ... IL-6
Hickory Point Sch—school ... IA-7
Hickory Point Sch—school ... PA-2
Hickory Point Sch (abandoned)—school ... MO-7
Hickory Point Sch (historical)—school (2) ... MO-7
Hickory Point Sch (historical)—school ... TN-4
**Hickory Point (sta.)**—pop pl ... TN-4
Hickory Point (Township of)—civ div ... IL-6
*Hickory Pond* ... PA-2
Hickory Pond—lake ... FL-3
*Hickory Ridge* ... GA-3
*Hickory Ridge* ... TN-4
Hickory Ridge—church ... DE-2
Hickory Ridge—locale ... TX-5
Hickory Ridge—other ... PA-2
**Hickory Ridge**—pop pl ... AR-4
**Hickory Ridge**—pop pl ... DE-2
**Hickory Ridge**—pop pl ... IN-6
**Hickory Ridge**—pop pl ... MI-6
Hickory Ridge—ridge (2) ... AL-4
Hickory Ridge—ridge (4) ... AR-4
Hickory Ridge—ridge ... CT-1
Hickory Ridge—ridge ... FL-3
Hickory Ridge—ridge (2) ... GA-3
Hickory Ridge—ridge (4) ... IN-6
Hickory Ridge—ridge (5) ... KY-4
Hickory Ridge—ridge ... MD-2
Hickory Ridge—ridge ... MO-7
Hickory Ridge—ridge ... NY-2
Hickory Ridge—ridge ... NC-3
Hickory Ridge—ridge ... OH-6
Hickory Ridge—ridge ... OK-5
Hickory Ridge—ridge (5) ... PA-2
Hickory Ridge—ridge (3) ... TN-4
Hickory Ridge—ridge ... VT-1
Hickory Ridge—ridge (2) ... VA-3
Hickory Ridge—ridge ... WV-2
Hickory Ridge—ridge (2) ... WI-6
Hickory Ridge—uninc pl ... GA-3
Hickory Ridge Branch—stream ... NC-3
*Hickory Ridge Cem* ... MS-4
Hickory Ridge Cem—cemetery (2) ... AR-4
Hickory Ridge Cem—cemetery ... KY-4
Hickory Ridge Cem—cemetery ... MS-4
Hickory Ridge Cem—cemetery ... TX-5
Hickory Ridge Cem—cemetery ... WV-2
Hickory Ridge Ch—church (2) ... AR-4
Hickory Ridge Ch—church (2) ... MS-4
Hickory Ridge Ch—church ... MO-7
Hickory Ridge Ch—church ... NC-3
Hickory Ridge Ch—church ... OH-6
Hickory Ridge Ch (historical)—church ... AL-4
Hickory Ridge Ch of Christ—church ... TN-4
Hickory Ridge Christian Sch—school ... DE-2
Hickory Ridge Lake—lake ... IL-6
Hickory Ridge Lateral—canal ... IN-6
Hickory Ridge Lookout Tower—locale ... IL-6
Hickory Ridge Lookout Tower—tower ... IN-6
Hickory Ridge Point—locale ... TN-4
Hickory Ridge Post Office (historical)—building ... TN-4
Hickory Ridge Sch—school ... IL-6
Hickory Ridge Sch—school ... IN-6
Hickory Ridge Sch—school (2) ... KY-4
Hickory Ridge Sch (historical)—school (3) ... MS-4
Hickory Ridge School (historical)—locale ... MO-7
**Hickory Ridge (subdivision)**—pop pl (2) ... DE-2
**Hickory Ridge (subdivision)**—pop pl ... NC-3
**Hickory Ridge (subdivision)**—pop pl ... PA-2
Hickory Ridge (Township of)—fmr MCD (2) ... AR-4
Hickory Ridge Trail—trail ... PA-2
Hickory Ridge Trail—trail ... VA-3
Hickory Ridge Trail—trail ... WI-6
Hickory River—stream ... TX-5
Hickory Rock—pillar ... TX-5
**Hickory Rock**—pop pl ... NC-3
Hickory Rock Ch—church ... NC-3
Hickory Rock Sch (historical)—school ... AL-4
Hickory Run—locale ... VA-3
**Hickory Run**—pop pl ... PA-2
Hickory Run—stream ... IL-6
Hickory Run—stream ... IN-6
Hickory Run—stream (2) ... PA-2
Hickory Run—stream (2) ... VA-3
Hickory Run—stream (2) ... WV-2
**Hickory Run (historical)**—pop pl ... PA-2
Hickory Run Lake—reservoir ... PA-2
Hickory Run Sch (abandoned)—school ... PA-2
Hickory Run State Park—park ... PA-2
Hickory Saint Ch—church ... AR-4
Hickory Sch—school ... CA-9
Hickory Sch—school (10) ... IL-6
Hickory Sch—school ... MI-6
Hickory Sch—school ... PA-2
Hickory Sch (historical)—school ... MO-7
Hickory Sch (historical)—school ... PA-2
Hickory Shade Sch—school ... WI-6
*Hickory Shadows II* ... AZ-5
Hickory Shed Landing (historical)—locale ... TN-4
Hickory Shoals—bar ... TN-4
**Hickory Sign Post**—pop pl ... VA-3
Hickory Sink—basin ... FL-3
Hickory Slough—gut (2) ... AR-4
Hickory Slough—gut ... FL-3
Hickory Slough—gut ... IL-6
Hickory Slough—gut ... TX-5
Hickory Slough—stream ... FL-3
Hickory Slough—stream ... IL-6
Hickory Speedway—locale ... NC-3
Hickory Spring—spring ... TN-4
Hickory Spring—spring ... TX-5
Hickory Spring—spring ... VA-3
Hickory Spring Branch—stream ... TN-4
Hickory Spring Ch—church ... AR-4
*Hickory Springs* ... AL-4
*Hickory Springs Baptist Church* ... MS-4
Hickory Springs Cem—cemetery ... MS-4
Hickory Springs Ch—church ... GA-3
Hickory Springs Ch—church ... LA-4
Hickory Springs Ch—church (2) ... MS-4
Hickory Springs Sch—school ... MS-4
Hickory Spur—ridge ... NC-3
Hickory Square Ch—church ... PA-2
Hickory Stand—gap ... VA-3
Hickory Stand Ch—church ... AL-4
Hickory Stand Ch—church ... NC-3
Hickory Stand Sch—school ... KY-4
Hickory Stand Sch (historical)—school ... AL-4
Hickory Star Boat Dock—locale ... TN-4
*Hickory Star Landing* ... TN-4
**Hickory Star Landing**—pop pl ... TN-4
Hickory Sticks—building ... MS-4
Hickory Sticks—hist pl ... MS-4
Hickory Street Cem—cemetery ... CT-1
Hickory Street District—hist pl ... MO-7
*Hickory Street Drain* ... MI-6
Hickory Street Drain—canal ... MI-6
Hickory Street Sch—school ... NJ-2
Hickory Stump Hollow—valley ... MO-7
Hickory Swale—swamp ... PA-2
Hickory Swale—valley ... PA-2
Hickory Swamp—stream ... VA-3
**Hickory Tavern**—pop pl ... SC-3
Hickory Thicket—locale ... MD-2
Hickory Top—summit ... NC-3
Hickory Top—summit ... SC-3
Hickory Top—summit (2) ... TN-4
*Hickory Town* ... AL-4
*Hickorytown* ... PA-2
**Hickorytown**—pop pl (2) ... PA-2
Hickory Township—civil ... MO-7
Hickory Township—civil ... PA-2
**Hickory Township**—pop pl ... KS-7
Hickory (Township of)—fmr MCD ... AR-4
Hickory (Township of)—fmr MCD ... NC-3
**Hickory (Township of)**—pop pl ... IL-6
**Hickory (Township of)**—pop pl ... MN-6
**Hickory (Township of)**—pop pl (2) ... PA-2
Hickory Trail—trail ... PA-2
**Hickory Tree**—pop pl ... NJ-2
**Hickory Tree**—pop pl ... TN-4
Hickory Tree Branch—stream ... TN-4
Hickory Tree Ch—church ... GA-3
Hickory Tree Elem Sch—school ... FL-3
Hickory Tree Flat Slough—gut ... FL-3
Hickory Tree Gap—gap ... TN-4
Hickory Tree Sch (historical)—school ... MS-4
Hickory Tunnel—tunnel ... PA-2
Hickory Turn Branch—stream ... TN-4
Hickory Turn Ridge—ridge ... TN-4
Hickory Union Cem—cemetery ... IL-6
Hickory Valley—locale ... AR-4
**Hickory Valley**—pop pl ... LA-4
**Hickory Valley**—pop pl (3) ... TN-4
Hickory Valley—valley (3) ... TN-4
*Hickory Valley Baptist Ch* ... TN-4
Hickory Valley Baptist Ch—church ... TN-4
Hickory Valley Branch—stream ... TN-4
Hickory Valley Ch—church ... AR-4
Hickory Valley Ch—church (4) ... TN-4
Hickory Valley Ch (historical)—church ... TN-4
*Hickory Valley Ch of Christ* ... TN-4
Hickory Valley Christian Ch—church ... TN-4
**Hickory Valley Estates Subdivision**—pop pl ... UT-8
Hickory Valley Golf Course—locale ... PA-2
Hickory Valley Golf Course—locale ... TN-4
Hickory Valley Hist Dist—hist pl ... SC-3
Hickory Valley Post Office—building ... TN-4
*Hickory Valley Presbyterian Church* ... TN-4
Hickory Valley Sch—school (3) ... TN-4
Hickory Valley Shop Ctr—locale ... TN-4
**Hickory Valley Subdivision**—pop pl ... UT-8
Hickory View Cem—cemetery ... WV-2
**Hickoryville**—pop pl ... OH-6
Hickory Wash—valley ... UT-8
Hickory With Branch—stream ... KY-4
**Hickory Withe**—pop pl ... TN-4
Hickory Withe First Baptist Ch—church ... TN-4
Hickory Withe Post Office—building ... TN-4
*Hickory Withe Springs* ... TN-4
Hickory Withe Station—locale ... TN-4
**Hickory Woods**—pop pl ... TN-4
**Hickory Woods (subdivision)**—pop pl ... DE-2
**Hickory Woods (subdivision)**—pop pl ... TN-4
Hickox—locale ... PA-2

**Hickox**—pop pl GA-3
Hickox, Virgil, House—hist pl IL-6
Hickox, Warren, House—hist pl IL-6
Hickox Apartments—hist pl IL-6
**Hickox (Perryville)**—pop pl PA-2
Hicks OK-5
Hicks—locale AL-4
Hicks—locale (2) AR-4
Hicks—locale GA-3
Hicks—locale IA-7
Hicks—locale NY-2
Hicks—locale OH-6
Hicks—locale TX-5
**Hicks**—pop pl IL-6
**Hicks**—pop pl IN-6
**Hicks**—pop pl LA-4
**Hicks**—pop pl MS-4
**Hicks**—pop pl TX-5
Hicks, Joseph, House—hist pl RI-1
Hicks, Mount—summit NV-8
Hicks, William House—hist pl KY-4
**Hicks Addition**—pop pl OK-5
Hicks and Duncan Canyon—valley AZ-5
Hicks and Duncan Tank—reservoir AZ-5
Hicks Bar—bar AL-4
Hicksbaugh—locale TX-5
Hicksbaugh Ch—church TX-5
Hicksbaugh Oil Field—oilfield TX-5
Hicks Bay—bay WA-9
Hicks Beach—beach NY-2
Hicks Bend—bend (2) TN-4
Hicks Block—hist pl KS-7
Hicks Bluff—cliff TN-4
Hicks Bluff—cliff TX-5
Hicks Branch—stream AR-4
Hicks Branch—stream IL-6
Hicks Branch—stream (5) KY-4
Hicks Branch—stream LA-4
Hicks Branch—stream (5) NC-3
Hicks Branch—stream OK-5
Hicks Branch—stream SC-3
Hicks Branch—stream (9) TN-4
Hicks Branch Dam TN-4
Hicks Branch Sch—school IL-6
Hicks Bridge—bridge SC-3
Hicks Brook—stream ME-1
Hicks-Brown Spring—spring TN-4
Hicksburg—locale MD-2
Hicksburg Sch—school MD-2
Hicks Butte—summit WA-9
Hicks Butte Trail—trail WA-9
Hicks Canyon—valley AZ-5
Hicks Canyon—valley CA-9
Hicks Canyon—valley (2) CO-8
Hicks Canyon—valley UT-8
Hicks Canyon—valley WA-9
Hicks Canyon Wash—stream CA-9
Hicks Cem AL-4
Hicks Cem TN-4
Hicks Cem—cemetery (2) AL-4
Hicks Cem—cemetery (5) AR-4
Hicks Cem—cemetery CO-8
Hicks Cem—cemetery GA-3
Hicks Cem—cemetery (3) IN-6
Hicks Cem—cemetery (2) KY-4
Hicks Cem—cemetery MI-6
Hicks Cem—cemetery (2) MS-4
Hicks Cem—cemetery (3) MO-7
Hicks Cem—cemetery NM-5
Hicks Cem—cemetery NY-2
Hicks Cem—cemetery (3) NC-3
Hicks Cem—cemetery (16) TN-4
Hicks Cem—cemetery VA-3
Hicks Cem—cemetery (2) WV-2
Hicks Ch—church AR-4
Hicks Ch—church (2) IN-6
Hicks Ch—church NY-2
Hicks Ch—church SC-3
Hicks Chapel MS-4
Hicks Chapel—church KS-7
Hicks Chapel—church NC-3
Hicks Chapel—church TX-5
**Hicks Chapel**—pop pl TN-4
Hicks Chapel Cem—cemetery OK-5
Hicks Chapel (historical)—church TN-4
Hicks Chapel Sch (historical)—school TN-4
Hicks Corner—locale ME-1
Hicks Corners—locale NY-2
Hicks Cove—cove MA-1
Hicks Cove—valley AL-4
Hicks Creek AL-4
Hicks Creek—stream AL-4
Hicks Creek—stream AK-9
Hicks Creek—stream (2) AR-4
Hicks Creek—stream CO-8
Hicks Creek—stream (2) FL-3
Hicks Creek—stream GA-3
Hicks Creek—stream IL-6
Hicks Creek—stream KS-7
Hicks Creek—stream ME-1
Hicks Creek—stream MI-6
Hicks Creek—stream NE-7
Hicks Creek—stream NV-8
Hicks Creek—stream NC-3
Hicks Creek—stream (2) OR-9
Hicks Creek—stream (2) PA-2
Hicks Creek—stream SC-3
Hicks Creek—stream (3) TN-4
Hicks Creek—stream (2) TX-5
Hicks Creek—stream UT-8
Hicks Creek—stream VA-3
Hicks Crossing—locale LA-4
Hicks Crossing—locale TN-4
Hicks Crossing—locale TX-5
Hicks Crossroads—locale NC-3
**Hicks Crossroads**—pop pl NC-3
Hicks Ditch—canal OH-6
Hicks Dome—summit IL-6
Hicks-Dugan-Deener House—hist pl AR-4
**Hicks Ferry**—pop pl PA-2
Hicks Ferry (historical)—crossing (2) TN-4
Hicks Ferry (historical)—locale NC-3
Hicks Ferry Station—locale PA-2
Hicks Field—airport TX-5
Hicks Ford—crossing TN-4
Hicksford (Magisterial District)—fmr MCD VA-3
Hicks Fork—stream KY-4
Hicks Gap—gap GA-3
Hicks Gap—gap (2) TN-4
Hicks Gap Branch—stream GA-3
Hicks Gap Ridge—ridge GA-3
Hicks Gin (historical)—locale AL-4
Hicks Grove Ch—church NC-3
Hicks Gulch—valley (2) CA-9
Hicks Gulch—valley (2) CO-8
Hicks Gulch—valley UT-8
Hicks Gully—valley NY-2
Hicks Head—valley FL-3
**Hicks Hill**—pop pl AL-4
**Hicks Hill**—pop pl PA-2
Hicks Hill—summit FL-3
Hicks Hill—summit (2) NH-1
Hicks Hill—summit (2) NY-2
Hicks Hill—summit OK-5
Hicks Hill—summit TN-4
Hicks Hollow TN-4
Hicks Hollow—valley IL-6
Hicks Hollow—valley KY-4
Hicks Hollow—valley MS-4
Hicks Hollow—valley (3) MO-7
Hicks Hollow—valley (2) PA-2
Hicks Hollow—valley (5) TN-4
Hicks Hollow—valley TX-5
Hicks Hollow—valley (2) WV-2
Hicks House—hist pl CA-9
Hicks HS—school LA-4
Hickside Cem—cemetery IN-6
Hicks Island—island FL-3
Hicks Island—island NY-2
Hicks Island—island VA-3
Hicksite Cem—cemetery NY-2
Hicksite Cem—cemetery OH-6
Hicksite Friends Meetinghouse (Wayne County Museum)—hist pl IN-6
Hicks Lake WI-6
Hicks Lake—lake AK-9
Hicks Lake—lake AR-4
Hicks Lake—lake (2) FL-3
Hicks Lake—lake GA-3
Hicks Lake—lake KY-4
Hicks Lake—lake (2) MI-6
Hicks Lake—lake MN-6
Hicks Lake—lake MT-8
Hicks Lake—lake OR-9
Hicks Lake—lake WA-9
Hicks Lake—lake WI-6
Hicks Lake—reservoir GA-3
Hicks Lake—reservoir VA-3
Hicks Landing (historical)—locale TN-4
Hicks Lead—ridge TN-4
Hicks Ledge—bar NY-2
Hicks Lookout Tower—locale LA-4
Hicks Lumber Company Store—hist pl NY-2
Hicks Memorial Ch—church NC-3
Hicks Mill—locale (2) VA-3
Hicks Millpond—reservoir GA-3
Hicks Mills Cem—cemetery IL-6
Hicks Mine—mine CO-8
Hicks Mine—mine TX-5
Hicks Mtn—summit CA-9
Hicks Mtn—summit CO-8
Hicks Mtn—summit MT-8
Hicks Mtn—summit (2) NC-3
Hicks Mtn—summit OK-5
Hicks Mtn—summit TN-4
Hicks Old Bay—swamp FL-3
Hickson TN-4
**Hickson**—pop pl ND-7
Hickson Community Hall—locale WA-9
Hickson Dam ND-7
Hickson Ditch—canal IN-6
Hickson Grove Sch—school SC-3
Hickson Hollow—valley TX-5
Hickson Lake—lake AR-4
Hickson Ranch—locale MT-8
Hicks Park—flat UT-8
Hicks Park Corral—locale UT-8
Hicks Peak—summit MT-8
Hicks Pit—cave TN-4
Hicks Pocket—bay LA-4
Hicks Point—cape AL-4
Hicks Point—cape AK-9
Hicks Point—cape MA-1
Hicks Point—cape NY-2
Hicks Pond FL-3
Hicks Pond MA-1
Hicks Pond—lake (2) ME-1
Hicks Pond—lake NY-2
Hicks Pond—reservoir NY-2
Hicks Pond—reservoir NC-3
Hicks Post Office (historical)—building TN-4
Hick Springs—spring TX-5
Hicks Ranch—locale AZ-5
Hicks Ranch—locale CA-9
Hicks Ranch—locale NM-5
Hicks Ranch, A—locale MT-8
Hicks Ridge—ridge GA-3
Hicks Ridge—ridge IN-6
Hicks Ridge—ridge WV-2
Hicks River PA-2
Hicks Rock—rock TN-4
Hicks Rocks—bar ME-1
Hicks Run PA-2
Hicks Run—locale PA-2
Hicks Run—stream NC-3
Hicks Run—stream PA-2
Hicks Run—stream (2) WV-2
Hicks Run Camping Area—area PA-2
Hicks Run Cem—cemetery PA-2
Hicks Sch—school AZ-5
Hicks Sch—school (4) MI-6
Hicks Sch—school (3) MO-7
Hicks Sch—school NY-2
Hicks Sch—school SC-3
Hicks Sch—school VT-1
Hicks Sch (abandoned)—school MO-7
Hicks Sch (historical)—school (3) TN-4
Hicks School AL-4
Hicks Spring—spring AL-4
Hicks Spring—spring CA-9
Hicks Spring—spring NV-8
Hicks Spring—spring OR-9
Hicks Spring—spring TN-4
Hicks Spring Branch—stream VA-3
Hicks Springs—spring ID-8
**Hicks Station**—pop pl AR-4
Hicks Station (Site)—locale NV-8
Hicks Station Wash—stream NV-8
Hicks Store—locale VA-3
**Hicks Store**—pop pl SC-3
Hicks Summit—summit NV-8
Hicks Swamp—swamp GA-3
Hicks Tank—reservoir (2) AZ-5
Hicks Tank—reservoir NM-5
Hickston—locale TX-5
Hickstown—locale NJ-2
Hicks Valley—basin CA-9
Hicks Valley—valley WI-6
**Hicks Village**—pop pl NC-3
Hicksville MA-1
Hicksville—locale KY-4
Hicksville—locale VA-3
**Hicksville**—pop pl MA-1
**Hicksville**—pop pl NY-2
**Hicksville**—pop pl OH-6
**Hicksville**—pop pl PA-2
**Hicksville**—pop pl TN-4
Hicksville Cem—cemetery CA-9
Hicksville Sch—school KY-4
Hicksville Station (historical)—locale MA-1
Hicksville (Township of)—fmr MCD AR-4
**Hicksville (Township of)**—pop pl OH-6
Hicks Wash—stream AZ-5
Hicks Well—well AZ-5
Hick Thomas Sch (historical)—school TN-4
Hicktom Lake—lake LA-4
**Hickton**—pop pl PA-2
Hicky Hump WA-9
Hi-Cliff Park—park WI-6
Hico—locale KY-4
Hico—locale TN-4
**Hico**—pop pl LA-4
**Hico**—pop pl TX-5
**Hico**—pop pl WV-2
Hico, Lake—reservoir MS-4
Hico Bridge—other MO-7
Hico (CCD)—cens area TX-5
Hico Cem—cemetery TX-5
Hico Ch—church NC-3
Hico Ch—church TN-4
Hico Gas Field—oilfield LA-4
Hico (historical P.O.)—locale AL-4
Hico Post Office (historical)—building TN-4
Hi Corbett Field—park AZ-5
Hi Corbett Sch—school AZ-5
Hicoria—locale FL-3
**Hicoria**—pop pl FL-3
Hico Sch—school LA-4
Hico Sch (historical)—school (2) TN-4
Hico Square Shop Ctr—locale MS-4
Hico Station—locale TN-4
Hico (Township of)—fmr MCD AR-4
**Hi Country Estates Subdivision**—pop pl UT-8
Hicox Draw—valley WY-8
Hicpochee, Lake—lake FL-3
Hicrest—post sta KS-7
Hicson ND-7
Hictons Big Spring—spring TN-4
**Hicumbottom**—pop pl WV-2
Hicumbottom Ch—church WV-2
Hicumbottom Run—stream WV-2
Hidalgo—locale KY-4
**Hidalgo**—pop pl IL-6
**Hidalgo**—pop pl TX-5
Hidalgo and Willacy Counties Water District—other TX-5
Hidalgo Beach—beach AK-9
Hidalgo Bluffs—cliff TX-5
Hidalgo Canyon—valley CA-9
Hidalgo Cem—cemetery CA-9
Hidalgo Cem—cemetery IL-6
**Hidalgo (County)**—pop pl NM-5
**Hidalgo (County)**—pop pl TX-5
Hidalgo County Courthouse—hist pl NM-5
Hidalgo County Water District Number 1—other TX-5
Hidalgo County Water District Number 15—other TX-5
Hidalgo County Water District Number 16—other TX-5
Hidalgo Falls—falls TX-5
Hidalgo Gas Field—oilfield TX-5
Hidalgo Mtn—summit CA-9
Hidalgo Park—park (3) TX-5
Hidalgo Sch—school CA-9
Hida Point—cape ID-8
Hida Ridge—ridge ID-8
Hidatsa Bay—bay ND-7
Hidaway Creek—stream OR-9
Hidaway Lake OR-9
Hidaway Meadows—flat OR-9
Hidaway Spring—spring OR-9
**Hidaway Springs**—pop pl OR-9
Hiday Cem—cemetery IN-6
**Hidden Acres**—pop pl TX-5
Hidden Acres Country Club—other NE-7
Hidden Acres Mobile Home Park—locale AZ-5
Hidden Acres Pond—reservoir SC-3
**Hidden Acres (subdivision)**—pop pl DE-2
**Hidden Acres (subdivision)**—pop pl TN-4
Hidden Acres Township Park—park NJ-2
Hidden Anchorage—bay CA-9
Hidden Arch UT-8
Hidden Basin—basin (2) WY-8
Hidden Basin—bay AK-9
Hidden Basin Creek—stream WY-8
Hidden Basin Mine—mine CO-8
Hidden Basin Tank—reservoir CA-9
Hidden Bay—bay (3) AK-9
Hidden Branch—stream OR-9
**Hiddenbrook**—pop pl VA-3
**Hiddenbrook (subdivision)**—pop pl TN-4
Hidden Cabin—locale AZ-5
Hidden Camp—locale WA-9
Hidden Canyon—valley (2) AZ-5
Hidden Canyon—valley CA-9
Hidden Canyon—valley (2) NV-8
Hidden Canyon—valley UT-8
Hidden Canyon Trail—hist pl UT-8
Hidden Canyon Trail—trail UT-8
Hidden Cave—cave (2) AL-4
Hidden Cave—cave NV-8
Hidden Cave—cave NM-5
Hidden Cliff—cliff NV-8
Hidden Corners NY-2
Hidden Corral Basin—basin WY-8
Hidden Cove IL-6
Hidden Cove—bay (2) AK-9
Hidden Cove—bay CO-8
Hidden Cove Lake—reservoir TN-4
Hidden Cove Lake Dam—dam TN-4
**Hidden Cove Subdivision - Number 2**—pop pl UT-8
**Hidden Cove Subdivision - Number 3**—pop pl UT-8
**Hidden Creek**—pop pl IL-6
Hidden Creek—stream (7) AK-9
Hidden Creek—stream AR-4
Hidden Creek—stream CA-9
Hidden Creek—stream (5) ID-8
Hidden Creek—stream (8) MT-8
Hidden Creek—stream (2) OR-9
Hidden Creek—stream (3) WA-9
Hidden Creek—stream (2) WY-8
Hidden Creek Campground—locale ID-8
Hidden Creek Lake—lake AK-9
Hidden Creek Rec Area—locale GA-3
Hidden Creek Ridge—ridge ID-8
Hidden Dome Oil And Gas Field—oilfield WY-8
Hidden Dome Rsvr—reservoir WY-8
Hidden Dome Rsvr No 1—reservoir WY-8
Hidden Echo—locale TX-5
Hidden Falls—falls AK-9
Hidden Falls—falls CA-9
Hidden Falls—falls MN-6
Hidden Falls—falls MT-8
Hidden Falls—falls NC-3
Hidden Falls—falls UT-8
Hidden Falls—falls WA-9
Hidden Falls Horse Trail—trail WY-8
Hidden Falls Lake—lake AK-9
Hidden Forest Cabin—hist pl NV-8
Hidden Forest Cabin—locale NV-8
Hidden Forest Campground—park OR-9
Hidden Forest Ridge—ridge NV-8
**Hidden Forest (subdivision)**—pop pl AL-4
Hidden Fork—stream CA-9
Hidden Form—stream NV-8
Hidden Glacier—glacier (2) AK-9
Hidden Glacier—glacier MT-8
Hidden Glen—valley CA-9
Hidden Gold Camp—locale CA-9
Hidden Gold Mine—mine CA-9
Hidden Gulch—valley WY-8
Hidden Hand Creek—stream WA-9
Hidden Hand Mine—mine MT-8
Hidden Hand Mine—mine WY-8
Hidden Hand Pass—gap WA-9
Hidden Harbor—bay AK-9
**Hidden Harbor (subdivision)**—pop pl TN-4
Hidden Haven Camp—locale KS-7
Hidden Haven Campground—park UT-8
**Hidden Hideaway Condominium**—pop pl UT-8
Hidden Hill—locale TX-5
Hidden Hill—summit CA-9
Hidden Hill Lake—reservoir OH-6
**Hidden Hills**—pop pl CA-9
**Hidden Hills**—pop pl IL-6
**Hidden Hills**—pop pl TN-4
Hidden Hills—range AZ-5
Hidden Hills Airp—airport NV-8
Hidden Hills Golf Club—other NE-7
Hidden Hills Ranch—locale NV-8
**Hidden Hills (subdivision)**—pop pl NC-3
**Hidden Hills Subdivision**—pop pl UT-8
Hidden Hole No 2 Mine—mine UT-8
Hidden Hole No 3 Mine—mine UT-8
Hidden Hollow—valley AZ-5
Hidden Hollow—valley TN-4
Hidden Hollow—valley UT-8
Hidden Hollow—valley WV-2
Hidden Hollow Camp—locale OH-6
**Hidden Hollow Estates (subdivision)**—pop pl TN-4
Hidden Hollow Lake—lake FL-3
Hidden Hollow Sch—school NE-7
**Hidden Hollow Subdivision**—pop pl UT-8
Hidden Hollow Tank—reservoir AZ-5
Hidden Houses—hist pl WA-9
Hidden Inlet—bay AK-9
Hidden Inlet Lake—lake AK-9
Hidden Island—island AK-9
Hidden Island Coulee—valley ND-7
**Hiddenite**—pop pl NC-3
Hiddenite Elem Sch—school NC-3
Hidden Johnson Creek—stream FL-3
Hidden Lake CA-9
Hidden Lake MT-8
Hidden Lake WA-9
Hidden Lake—lake (3) AK-9
Hidden Lake—lake (8) AZ-5
Hidden Lake—lake (18) CA-9
Hidden Lake—lake (2) CO-8
Hidden Lake—lake CT-1
Hidden Lake—lake (6) FL-3
Hidden Lake—lake GA-3
Hidden Lake—lake (14) ID-8
Hidden Lake—lake ME-1
Hidden Lake—lake (11) MI-6
Hidden Lake—lake (2) MN-6
Hidden Lake—lake (19) MT-8
Hidden Lake—lake NV-8
Hidden Lake—lake NJ-2
Hidden Lake—lake (6) NM-5
Hidden Lake—lake (4) NY-2
Hidden Lake—lake (6) OR-9
Hidden Lake—lake (3) PA-2
Hidden Lake—lake TX-5
Hidden Lake—lake (10) UT-8
Hidden Lake—lake VT-1
Hidden Lake—lake (7) WA-9
Hidden Lake—lake (3) WI-6
Hidden Lake—lake (6) WY-8
**Hidden Lake**—pop pl CT-1
Hidden Lake—reservoir AZ-5
Hidden Lake—reservoir CO-8
Hidden Lake—reservoir GA-3
Hidden Lake—reservoir NC-3
Hidden Lake—reservoir OH-6
Hidden Lake—reservoir (2) PA-2
Hidden Lake—reservoir VA-3
Hidden Lake—swamp CA-9
Hidden Lake Bench—bench MT-8
Hidden Lake Camp—locale NY-2
Hidden Lake Camp Ground—locale MT-8
**Hidden Lake Condominium**—pop pl UT-8
Hidden Lake Creek—stream WA-9
Hidden Lake Dam—dam (2) PA-2
Hidden Lake Divide—gap CA-9
Hidden Lake Hill—summit MT-8
Hidden Lake Lookout—locale WA-9
Hidden Lake Mine—mine MT-8
Hidden Lake Park—park FL-3
Hidden Lake Park—park MI-6
Hidden Lake Pass—gap MT-8
Hidden Lake Peak Lookout—hist pl WA-9
Hidden Lake Peaks WA-9
Hidden Lake Peaks—summit WA-9
Hidden Lake Ranch—locale CA-9
Hidden Lake Rsvr—reservoir ID-8
Hidden Lake Rsvr—reservoir OR-9
Hidden Lakes—lake AK-9
Hidden Lakes—lake (2) CA-9
Hidden Lakes—lake (2) CO-8
Hidden Lakes—lake (2) MT-8
Hidden Lakes—lake NV-8
Hidden Lakes—lake UT-8
Hidden Lakes—lake WA-9
Hidden Lakes—lake WY-8
**Hidden Lakes**—pop pl KS-7
Hidden Lakes—reservoir OH-6
Hidden Lakes Peaks WA-9
Hidden Lake Trail—trail MT-8
Hidden Lake Trail—trail OR-9
Hidden Lake Trail—trail WA-9
Hidden Lake Trick Tank—reservoir AZ-5
Hidden Log Tank—reservoir AZ-5
Hidden Meadow—flat MT-8
Hidden Meadow—flat NV-8
Hidden Meadow—swamp OR-9
Hidden Meadows—flat WA-9
**Hidden Meadows**—pop pl CA-9
**Hidden Meadows Subdivision**—pop pl UT-8
Hidden Mines—mine AZ-5
Hidden Mountain Dam Number One—dam TN-4
Hidden Mountain Dam Number Two—dam TN-4
Hidden Mountain Lake Number One—reservoir TN-4
Hidden Mouth Cave—cave ID-8
Hidden Mt Lake Number Two—reservoir TN-4
Hidden Mtn—summit NV-8
Hidden Mtn—summit NM-5
**Hidden Oak Estates Subdivision**—pop pl UT-8
**Hidden Oaks PUD Subdivision**—pop pl UT-8
Hidden Pair Canyon—valley CA-9
Hidden Palms—locale CA-9
Hidden Park—park WA-9
Hidden Passage Canyon—valley UT-8
Hidden Passage Trail—trail TN-4
Hidden Pasture—flat AZ-5
Hidden Pasture—flat NM-5
Hidden Pasture Canyon—valley NM-5
Hidden Pasture Creek—stream MT-8
Hidden Pastures Creek MT-8
Hidden Pasture Trail—trail MT-8
Hidden Peak—summit ID-8
Hidden Playa Well—well NV-8
Hidden Pocket—valley WY-8
Hidden Point—cape AK-9
Hidden Point—locale MD-2
Hidden Pond—lake CA-9
Hidden Pond—lake IL-6
Hidden Pond—lake ME-1
Hidden Pond—lake MD-2
Hidden Pond—lake NY-2
Hidden Pond Slough—gut IL-6
Hidden Pond Woods—woods IL-6
Hidden Potrero—flat CA-9
Hidden Pump Station—other AZ-5
Hidden Ranch—locale CA-9
Hidden Ranch—locale WA-9
Hidden Ridge—ridge OR-9
Hidden Ridge—ridge WA-9
Hidden Rim—cliff AZ-5
Hidden River—locale FL-3
**Hidden River**—pop pl CA-9
Hidden River—stream AK-9
Hidden River—stream CO-8
Hidden River Cave—cave KY-4
Hidden River Lake—lake AK-9
Hidden Rock Spring—spring ID-8
Hidden Rsvr—reservoir ID-8
Hidden Rsvr—reservoir (2) OR-9
Hidden Rsvr—reservoir WY-8
Hidden Seep—spring NM-5
Hidden Seep—spring OR-9
Hidden Slough—gut AR-4
Hidden Slough—lake ND-7
Hidden Smith Ravine Spring—spring AZ-5
Hidden Spring NM-5
Hidden Spring—spring (16) AZ-5
Hidden Spring—spring AR-4
Hidden Spring—spring (6) CA-9
Hidden Spring—spring CO-8
Hidden Spring—spring MT-8
Hidden Spring—spring NV-8
Hidden Spring—spring (4) NM-5
Hidden Spring—spring (5) OR-9
Hidden Spring—spring PA-2
Hidden Spring—spring TX-5
Hidden Spring—spring (6) UT-8
Hidden Spring—spring (2) WA-9
Hidden Spring—spring (2) WY-8
Hidden Spring Canyon UT-8
Hidden Spring Canyon—valley CA-9
Hidden Springs—locale CA-9
Hidden Springs—spring OR-9
Hidden Springs Campground—locale CA-9
Hidden Springs Canyon—valley NM-5
Hidden Springs Golf Course—locale PA-2
Hidden Springs Mission—church AZ-5
**Hidden Springs Mission**—pop pl AZ-5
**Hidden Springs Mission (Willow Springs)**—pop pl AZ-5
Hidden Spring Trail—trail CA-9
Hidden Spring Trail—trail MD-2
Hidden Tank—reservoir (23) AZ-5
Hidden Tank—reservoir CA-9
Hidden Tank—reservoir (5) NM-5
Hidden Tank—reservoir TX-5
Hidden Tepee Creek—stream WY-8
Hidden Timber—locale SD-7
Hidden Timber Dam—dam SD-7
**Hidden Township**—pop pl ND-7
Hidden Treasure Gulch—valley WY-8
Hidden Treasure Mine—mine (3) AZ-5
Hidden Treasure Mine—mine (2) CA-9
Hidden Treasure Mine—mine (3) CO-8
Hidden Treasure Mine—mine MT-8
Hidden Treasure Mine—mine NV-8
Hidden Treasure Mine—mine NM-5
Hidden Treasure Mine—mine OR-9
Hidden Treasure Mine—mine (2) SD-7
Hidden Treasure Mine—mine UT-8
Hidden Treasure Mine—mine WA-9
Hidden Treasure Spring—spring NV-8
Hidden Treasure Spring—spring UT-8
Hidden Tunnel Spring—spring AZ-5
Hidden Valley CA-9
Hidden Valley—basin AZ-5
Hidden Valley—basin (3) CA-9
Hidden Valley—basin ID-8
Hidden Valley—basin (2) NV-8
Hidden Valley—basin OR-9
Hidden Valley—basin UT-8
Hidden Valley—flat VA-3
Hidden Valley—hist pl VA-3
**Hidden Valley**—pop pl AR-4
**Hidden Valley**—pop pl CA-9
**Hidden Valley**—pop pl CO-8
**Hidden Valley**—pop pl MN-6
**Hidden Valley**—pop pl NV-8
**Hidden Valley**—pop pl PA-2
**Hidden Valley**—pop pl (3) TN-4
**Hidden Valley**—pop pl TX-5
Hidden Valley—valley (4) AZ-5
Hidden Valley—valley (8) CA-9
Hidden Valley—valley (3) CO-8
Hidden Valley—valley (2) ID-8
Hidden Valley—valley MT-8
Hidden Valley—valley NE-7
Hidden Valley—valley NV-8
Hidden Valley—valley (2) NM-5
Hidden Valley—valley (3) OR-9
Hidden Valley—valley (2) UT-8
Hidden Valley—valley WA-9
Hidden Valley—valley WY-8
Hidden Valley Airstrip—airport AZ-5
Hidden Valley Boy Scout Camp—locale PA-2
Hidden Valley Boy Scouts East Camp—locale PA-2
Hidden Valley Boy Scouts West Camp PA-2
Hidden Valley Camp PA-2
Hidden Valley Camp—locale MS-4
Hidden Valley Camp—locale NY-2
Hidden Valley Camp—locale TN-4
Hidden Valley Camp—locale WA-9
Hidden Valley Campground—locale CA-9
Hidden Valley Campground—locale CO-8
Hidden Valley Canal—canal UT-8
Hidden Valley Cem—cemetery VA-3
Hidden Valley Club—other MI-6
Hidden Valley Country Club—locale FL-3
Hidden Valley Country Club—locale NC-3
Hidden Valley Country Club—other SC-3
Hidden Valley Country Club—other UT-8
Hidden Valley Country Club—other VA-3
Hidden Valley Country Club—other WV-2
**Hidden Valley Country Club Estates**—pop pl UT-8
Hidden Valley County Park—park NV-8
Hidden Valley Creek—stream CO-8
Hidden Valley Creek—stream ID-8
Hidden Valley Creek—stream OR-9
Hidden Valley Dam—dam TN-4
**Hidden Valley Estates (subdivision)**—pop pl NC-3
**Hidden Valley Estates Subdivision**—pop pl UT-8
Hidden Valley Farm—hist pl MD-2
Hidden Valley Golf Course—locale (2) PA-2
Hidden Valley Hills—summit AZ-5
**Hidden Valley Hills Subdivision**—pop pl UT-8
Hidden Valley Hot Springs CA-9
Hidden Valley HS—school OR-9
Hidden Valley Incorporated Lake Dam—dam MS-4
Hidden Valley Interchange—crossing AZ-5
Hidden Valley Interchange—crossing NV-8
Hidden Valley Lake WI-6
Hidden Valley Lake—lake NJ-2
Hidden Valley Lake—reservoir AL-4
Hidden Valley Lake—reservoir (2) IN-6
Hidden Valley Lake*—reservoir KS-7
Hidden Valley Lake—reservoir (2) MO-7
Hidden Valley Lake—reservoir OH-6
Hidden Valley Lake—reservoir SC-3
Hidden Valley Lake—reservoir TN-4
Hidden Valley Lake Dam—dam (2) IN-6
Hidden Valley Lake Dam—dam KS-7
Hidden Valley Meadows CA-9
Hidden Valley Park—park MO-7
Hidden Valley Ranch—locale AZ-5
Hidden Valley Ranch—locale (4) CA-9
Hidden Valley Ranch—locale (2) CO-8
Hidden Valley Ranch—locale (2) MT-8
Hidden Valley Ranch—locale TX-5
Hidden Valley Ranch—locale WA-9
Hidden Valley Ranch—locale WY-8
Hidden Valley Resort Community and Conference Center PA-2
Hidden Valley Rock Shelter (44BA31)—hist pl VA-3
Hidden Valley Sch—school NC-3
Hidden Valley Sch—school SD-7
Hidden Valley Sch—school TX-5
Hidden Valley Ski Area—other PA-2
Hidden Valley Spring AZ-5
Hidden Valley Spring—spring AZ-5
Hidden Valley Spring—spring TN-4
**Hidden Valley (subdivision)**—pop pl (4) NC-3
Hidden Valley Tank—reservoir AZ-5
Hidden Valley Tanks—reservoir AZ-5
Hidden Valley Trail—trail CO-8
**Hidden Village PUD Subdivision**—pop pl UT-8
**Hidden Village Subdivision**—pop pl UT-8
Hidden Wash—arroyo NV-8
Hidden Wash—stream NV-8
Hidden Wash—valley AZ-5
Hidden Water Creek—stream MT-8
Hidden Water Creek—stream WY-8
Hidden Waterhole Canyon—valley NM-5

Hidden Water Spring—spring AZ-5
Hidden Water Windmill—locale TX-5
Hidden Well—well (2) AZ-5
Hidden Well—well NV-8
Hidden Well—well NM-5
Hidden Windmill—locale TX-5
Hiddenwood Cem—cemetery ND-7
*Hidden Wood Creek* SD-7
Hiddenwood Creek—stream SD-7
Hiddenwood Gulch—valley SD-7
Hiddenwood Lake—lake SD-7
Hiddenwood Lake—reservoir ND-7
Hiddenwood Natl Wildlife Ref—park ND-7
Hiddenwood Sch Number 2—school ND-7
Hiddenwood Sch Number 3—school ND-7
Hiddenwood Sch Number 4—school ND-7
Hiddenwood Township—civil SD-7
**Hiddenwood Township**—pop pl ND-7
Hidder Cove Lake—reservoir TN-4
Hiddleson Sch—school IL-6
Hide and Seek Creek—stream OR-9
Hideaway, Lake—lake AK-9
Hideaway, Lake—reservoir IN-6
Hide-A-Way, Lake—reservoir MS-4
**Hideaway Acres**—pop pl DE-2
**Hide Away Acres (subdivision)**—pop pl AL-4
Hideaway Brook—stream NC-3
Hide-A-Way Camp—locale SC-3
Hideaway Canyon—valley CA-9
Hideaway Coulee—valley MT-8
Hideaway Cove—bay NV-8
**Hideaway Estates (subdivision)**—pop pl NC-3
Hideaway Falls—falls OR-9
**Hideaway Hill**—pop pl TX-5
**Hideaway Hills**—pop pl AL-4
**Hideaway Hills**—pop pl MS-4
**Hide-A-Way Hills**—pop pl OH-6
**Hideaway Hills**—pop pl OH-6
**Hide-A-Way Hills**—pop pl TN-4
**Hideaway Hills**—pop pl TN-4
Hideaway Hollow—valley ID-8
Hideaway Lake—lake CA-9
Hideaway Lake—lake OR-9
Hide-Away Lake—lake PA-2
**Hideaway Lake**—pop pl IN-6
Hide-A-Way Lake—reservoir TX-5
Hideaway Lake—reservoir VA-3
Hideaway Lake Campground—park OR-9
Hide-A-Way Lake Dam—dam MS-4
Hide-A-Way Lake Number Two—reservoir TX-5
Hideaway Lakes—reservoir TX-5
Hideaway Marina—locale MO-7
Hideaway Mountain Lake—reservoir NC-3
Hideaway Mountain Lake Dam—dam NC-3
**Hideaway Park**—pop pl CO-8
Hideaway Pond—reservoir VA-3
Hideaway Ranch—locale CA-9
Hideaway Spring—spring (2) OR-9
Hideaway Tank—reservoir TX-5
Hide Bayou—stream LA-4
Hidebound Branch—stream TN-4
Hide Branch—stream NC-3
*Hide Creek* AZ-5
*Hide Creek* OR-9
*Hide Creek* TX-5
*Hide Creek Mountain* AZ-5
Hide Lake—lake MN-6
Hidens Branch—stream VA-3
Hiden Spring—spring VA-3
**Hidenwood**—pop pl VA-3
Hideout, The—area UT-8
Hideout, The—locale AZ-5
Hideout, The—locale UT-8
*Hideout Campground* UT-8
Hideout Canyon—valley CA-9
Hideout Canyon—valley (5) UT-8
Hideout Canyon Campground—locale UT-8
Hideout Creek—stream WY-8
Hideout Draw—valley UT-8
Hideout Eagle Basin Trail—trail UT-8
Hideout Hill—summit AK-9
Hideout Hollow—valley AR-4
Hideout Hollow—valley TN-4
Hideout Mesa—summit UT-8
Hideout Pond—lake MO-7
Hide Out Slough—bay TN-4
Hideout Trail—trail AR-4
Hideout Windmill—locale NM-5
Hiderbrand Cem—cemetery OK-5
Hider Hollow—valley OK-5
Hidershide Valley—valley MN-6
Hi Desert Ski Area—area OR-9
Hide Tank—reservoir AZ-5
**Hidetown**—pop pl NC-3
Hideway Lake—lake ID-8
*Hideway Park* CO-8
Hidewood Creek—stream SD-7
Hidewoods—woods SD-7
Hidewood Townhall (historical)—building SD-7
**Hidewood Township**—pop pl SD-7
Hidi—locale MS-4
Hidi Landing (historical)—locale MS-4
Hiding Canyon—valley CA-9
Hiding Canyon Camp—locale CA-9
Hiding Lake—lake AK-9
Hiding Rocks—island CT-1
Hidi Nursery and Kindergarten Sch—school FL-3
Hidlay Ch—church PA-2
*Hidle School* AL-4
Hidley, James P., Cottage—hist pl OH-6
Hidout Rsvr—reservoir OR-9
Hid Pond—lake ME-1
Hid Reef—bar AK-9
Hidy Canyon—valley NE-7
Hidy Cem—cemetery OH-6
Hi Early Cem—cemetery OK-5
Hi Early Mtn—summit OK-5
Hieatt, Samuel, House—hist pl KY-4
Hieber Park—park IA-7
Hieb Sch—school SD-7
Hiedelberg Elem Sch—school PA-2
Hiekkila Lake—lake MN-6
Hiem Cem—cemetery NE-7
Hienaloli One-Six—civil HI-9
Hieneken Tank—reservoir AZ-5
Hier Creek—stream MN-6
Hierlihy Ranch—locale CA-9
Hierly Ditch—canal IN-6
*Hieroglphic Hills* AZ-5
Hieroglyphic Canyon—valley (2) AZ-5
Hieroglyphic Canyon—valley CO-8
Hieroglyphic Mountains—range AZ-5
Hieroglyphic Spring—spring AZ-5
Hieroglyphic Tanks—reservoir AZ-5
Hieronymus Cem—cemetery IL-6
Hieronymus Hollow—valley MO-7
Hier Park—park IN-6
Hierr Lick Run—stream WV-2
Hierro—locale CO-8
Hiersche Drain—canal NE-7
Hiers Lakes—lake NE-7
Hiesel Ranch—locale NE-7
*Hiesen Creek* ID-8
Hiestand—locale PA-2
Hiestand, Jacob, House—hist pl KY-4
Hiestand Cem—cemetery IN-6
Hiestand Ch—church OH-6
Hiestand Community Hall—locale OH-6
Hiestand Sch—school WI-6
Hiestand Sch (abandoned)—school PA-2
Hiester Valley—valley PA-2
Hi Estes Windmill—locale TX-5
**Hiett**—pop pl OH-6
Hiett Chapel Cem—cemetery OH-6
Hiett Run—stream WV-2
Hiett Spring—spring TN-4
Hi Foster Hollow—valley PA-2
Hi Fuller Canyon—valley AZ-5
Hi Fuller Spring—spring AZ-5
HIG—airport NJ-2
*Higashi* FM-9
*Higashi* MH-9
*Higashi* MP-9
*Higashi* PW-9
Higashi Camp—locale HI-9
*Higashi Kakku* MP-9
*Higashi-Kaku* MP-9
*Higashi-manto-to* FM-9
*Higashi Mura* MH-9
*Higashi-shima* MH-9
*Higashi-suido* MP-9
*Higashi Suido* PW-9
*Higashi To* MH-9
**Higate Hamlet Subdivision**—pop pl UT-8
Higate Square (Shop Ctr)—locale FL-3
Higbee—locale CO-8
Higbee—locale PA-2
**Higbee**—pop pl MO-7
Higbee Beach—beach NJ-2
Higbee Cem—cemetery CO-8
Higbee Cem—cemetery MI-6
Higbee Cem—cemetery (2) MO-7
Higbee Community Hall—locale OK-5
Higbee Corner—locale MI-6
Higbee Draw—valley ID-8
Higbee Ravine—valley IL-6
Higbee Sch—school (2) PA-2
*Higbeetown* NJ-2
**Higbee Town**—pop pl NJ-2
Higbee Valley Sch—school CO-8
Higbeeville—locale NJ-2
Higbie Cem—cemetery (2) IN-6
Higbie Lane Sch—school NY-2
Higby—locale CA-9
Higby—locale CO-8
Higby—locale OH-6
Higby Branch—stream TN-4
Higby Cave—cave ID-8
Higby Creek—stream KS-7
Higby Creek—stream WY-8
Higby House—hist pl OH-6
Higby Mtn—summit CT-1
Higby Ranch—locale WY-8
Higby Run—stream WV-2
Higby Sch (historical)—school PA-2
Higby Twin Ponds—lake NY-2
**Higdem (Township of)**—pop pl MN-6
**Higden**—pop pl AR-4
Higden Bay—bay AR-4
Higden Ch—church AR-4
Higden-McLahaney Chapel—church AR-4
Higdon—locale GA-3
Higdon—locale KY-4
Higdon—locale MS-4
Higdon—locale MO-7
**Higdon**—pop pl AL-4
Higdon Branch—stream AL-4
Higdon Branch—stream NC-3
Higdon Branch—stream TN-4
Higdon Cem—cemetery (2) AL-4
Higdon Cem—cemetery GA-3
Higdon Cem—cemetery MS-4
Higdon Cem—cemetery NC-3
Higdon Ch—church (2) AL-4
Higdon Ch—church MS-4
Higdon Cove—valley GA-3
*Higdon Creek* GA-3
Higdon Creek—stream AL-4
Higdon Creek—stream GA-3
Higdon Creek—stream LA-4
Higdon Lookout Tower—locale MO-7
*Higdon Memorial Cemetery* AL-4
Higdon Mill (historical)—locale GA-3
Higdon-Mobile (CCD)—cens area GA-3
Higdon Mtn—summit NC-3
Higdon Point—cape AL-4
Higdon Post Office (historical)—building MS-4
*Higdons* GA-3
Higdon Sch—school NC-3
Higdon Spring—spring AL-4
*Higdons Store* GA-3
Higdons Store Post Office (historical)—building TN-4
*Higdon Store* GA-3
Higdonville—locale NC-3
Higganbotham Cem—cemetery AL-4
**Higganum**—pop pl CT-1
Higganum Creek—stream CT-1
Higganum Reservoir State Park—park CT-1
Higganum Rsvr—reservoir CT-1
Higgason Sch (historical)—school MS-4
Higgenbotham Branch—stream TX-5
Higgenbotham Creek—gut FL-3
Higgenbotham Spring—spring TN-4
Higgenbottom Bend—bend TN-4
Higgenbottom Cem—cemetery TN-4
*Higgenbottomn* GA-3
Higgens Cem—cemetery AL-4
Higgens Creek—stream AR-4
Higgens Ditch—canal IN-6
Higgensport—locale IA-7
*Higgens Spring* CA-9
Higgens Spring—spring NV-8
Higgin, Kate Douglas, House—hist pl ME-1
Higginbotham—locale TX-5
**Higginbotham**—pop pl LA-4
Higginbotham Cem—cemetery FL-3
Higginbotham Cem—cemetery GA-3
Higginbotham Cem—cemetery MS-4
Higginbotham Cem—cemetery MO-7
Higginbotham Cem—cemetery VA-3
Higginbotham Cem—cemetery WV-2
Higginbotham Creek—stream VA-3
Higginbotham Ditch—canal IN-6
Higginbotham Field Airp—airport IN-6
Higginbotham Lake—lake FL-3
Higginbotham Mine (underground)—mine AL-4
Higginbotham Number 7 Mine (underground)—mine AL-4
Higginbotham Ridge—ridge TN-4
Higginbotham Run—stream WV-2
Higginbotham Sch—school MI-6
*Higginbothams Ferry* MS-4
Higginbothams Ferry—locale MO-7
Higginbothams Lake—reservoir AL-4
Higginbothon Store (historical)—locale MS-4
Higginbottom Creek—stream AR-4
Higgin Cem—cemetery OH-6
*Higgin Mountain* WA-9
*Higgin Point* MD-2
*Higgins* LA-4
Higgins—locale MS-4
Higgins—locale MT-8
Higgins—locale OK-5
**Higgins**—pop pl AR-4
**Higgins**—pop pl IL-6
**Higgins**—pop pl (2) NY-2
**Higgins**—pop pl NC-3
**Higgins**—pop pl SC-3
**Higgins**—pop pl (2) TX-5
Higgins, Aldus Chapin, House—hist pl MA-1
Higgins, E. H., House—hist pl KY-4
Higgins, Francis B., House—hist pl SC-3
Higgins, H. A., Bldg—hist pl OH-6
Higgins, Jedediah, House—hist pl MA-1
Higgins, Lake—reservoir NC-3
Higgins, Mount—summit WA-9
Higgins, Point—cape AK-9
Higgins, S., Farm—hist pl DE-2
Higgins Armory Museum—hist pl MA-1
Higgins Bald—ridge NC-3
Higgins Bay—bay KY-4
Higgins Bay—bay NY-2
**Higgins Bay**—pop pl NY-2
**Higgins Beach**—pop pl ME-1
Higgins Block—hist pl KY-4
Higgins Block—hist pl MT-8
*Higgins Branch* KY-4
*Higgins Branch* NE-7
Higgins Branch—stream IN-6
Higgins Branch—stream (5) KY-4
Higgins Branch—stream (2) NC-3
Higgins Branch—stream TX-5
Higgins Bridge—bridge IN-6
Higgins Bridge—bridge MT-8
Higgins Bridge—bridge SC-3
*Higgins Brook* ME-1
Higgins Brook—stream (3) ME-1
Higgins Brook—stream NH-1
Higgins Bros Ranch—locale NE-7
Higgins Camp—locale CA-9
Higgins Canyon—valley (3) CA-9
Higgins Canyon—valley (2) NM-5
Higgins Canyon Spring—spring NM-5
Higgins (CCD)—cens area TX-5
*Higgins Cem* AL-4
Higgins Cem—cemetery AL-4
Higgins Cem—cemetery AR-4
Higgins Cem—cemetery (2) IL-6
Higgins Cem—cemetery KY-4
Higgins Cem—cemetery (2) MS-4
Higgins Cem—cemetery NC-3
Higgins Cem—cemetery OH-6
Higgins Cem—cemetery PA-2
Higgins Cem—cemetery TN-4
Higgins Cem—cemetery TX-5
Higgins Chapel—church TN-4
Higgins Chapel—church WV-2
*Higgins Chapel Baptist Ch* TN-4
Higgins Chapel Methodist Ch (historical)—church AL-4
Higgins Chapel Sch—school TN-4
Higgins Corner—locale CA-9
Higgins Corner—locale (2) ME-1
**Higgins Corner**—pop pl PA-2
*Higgins Corners* PA-2
**Higgins Corners**—pop pl PA-2
*Higgins Creek* KY-4
*Higgins Creek* MT-8
*Higgins Creek* TN-4
Higgins Creek—stream CA-9
Higgins Creek—stream (2) ID-8
Higgins Creek—stream (2) IL-6
Higgins Creek—stream ME-1
Higgins Creek—stream MO-7
Higgins Creek—stream NC-3
Higgins Creek—stream OK-5
Higgins Creek—stream (2) OR-9
Higgins Creek—stream (2) TN-4
Higgins Creek—stream WA-9
Higgins Crossroads—locale VA-3
Higgins Dam—dam AL-4
Higgins Dam—dam OR-9
Higgins Ditch—canal IN-6
Higgins Ditch—canal MO-7
Higgins Duplex—hist pl FL-3
Higgins Family Cem—cemetery AL-4
Higgins Ferry (historical)—locale AL-4
Higgins Flat—flat CA-9
Higgins Flat—flat KY-4
Higgins Flat—flat NM-5
Higgins Flat Tank No 1—reservoir NM-5
Higgins Flat Tank No 2—reservoir NM-5
Higgins Gulch—valley SD-7
Higgins Hill—ridge AZ-5
Higgins-Hodgeman House—hist pl MA-1
Higgins Hollow—valley MA-1
Higgins Hollow—valley (2) TN-4
Higgins Hollow—valley UT-8
Higgins Hollow Cave—cave TN-4
Higgins Hollow Rsvr—reservoir UT-8
Higgins Homestead (abandoned)—locale MT-8
Higgins HS—school (2) MS-4
Higgins Hump—summit ID-8
*Higgins Island* MA-1
Higgins Island—island WA-9
Higgins Knob—summit NC-3
Higgins Knob—summit WV-2
*Higgins Lake* IN-6
*Higgins Lake* MA-1
Higgins Lake—lake CA-9
Higgins Lake—lake MI-6
Higgins Lake—lake MN-6
**Higgins Lake**—pop pl MI-6
Higgins Lake—reservoir AL-4
Higgins Lake—reservoir CO-8
Higgins Lake—reservoir NC-3
Higgins Lake Dam—dam NC-3
Higgins Lake State For—forest MI-6
Higgins Lake State Nursery—other MI-6
Higgins Lake State Park—park MI-6
Higgins Landing (historical)—locale TN-4
Higgins-McEwen Mine—mine MN-6
Higgins Mill—locale GA-3
Higgins Millpond—reservoir MD-2
Higgins Mine (underground)—mine TN-4
Higgins Mtn—summit ME-1
Higgins Mtn—summit NM-5
Higgins Mtn—summit NC-3
**Higginson**—pop pl AR-4
Higginson, Col. Thomas Wentworth, House—hist pl MA-1
Higginson Creek—stream MI-6
Higginson Ditch—canal KY-4
Higginson-Henry Wildlife Mngmt Area—park KY-4
Higginson Homestead—locale WY-8
Higginson (Township of)—fmr MCD AR-4
Higgins Park—flat CO-8
Higgins Park—flat MT-8
Higgins Place (abandoned)—locale NM-5
*Higgins Point* MD-2
Higgins Point—cape WY-8
Higgins Pond—lake (2) MA-1
*Higginsport* KY-4
**Higginsport**—pop pl OH-6
*Higginsport Station* KY-4
Higgins Post Office (historical)—building MS-4
Higgins Ranch—locale (2) MT-8
Higgins Ranch—locale NE-7
Higgins Ridge—ridge (2) TN-4
Higgins Rsvr—reservoir MT-8
Higgins Rsvr—reservoir OR-9
Higgins Run—stream OH-6
Higgins Run—stream PA-2
Higgins Run—stream WV-2
Higgins Sch—school CT-1
Higgins Sch—school IL-6
Higgins Sch—school MI-6
Higgins Sch—school MT-8
Higgins Sch (historical)—school MO-7
Higgins School—locale LA-4
Higgins Shoal—bar FL-3
Higgins Slough—gut WA-9
Higgins Slough—stream WA-9
Higgins Spring—spring AZ-5
Higgins Spring—spring CA-9
Higgins Spring—spring CO-8
Higgins Spring—spring OR-9
Higgins Spring—spring SD-7
Higgins Springs—spring TN-4
**Higgins Spur**—pop pl MT-8
Higgins Stream—stream ME-1
Higgins Swamp—stream VA-3
Higgins Swamp—swamp MA-1
Higgins Tank—reservoir AZ-5
Higgins (Township of)—fmr MCD AR-4
Higgins (Township of)—fmr MCD NC-3
**Higgins (Township of)**—pop pl MI-6
Higginsville—locale IL-6
Higginsville—locale WV-2
**Higginsville**—pop pl ME-1
**Higginsville**—pop pl MO-7
**Higginsville**—pop pl NJ-2
**Higginsville**—pop pl NY-2
Higginsville Cem—cemetery IL-6
Higginsville Ch—church GA-3
Higginsville Industrial Municipal Airp—airport MO-7
Higginsville Rsvr—reservoir MO-7
Higgins Well—well NM-5
Higgland Cem—cemetery MS-4
Higgmson Homestead—locale WY-8
Higgon, Cape—cape MA-1
Higgs, Walter J., House—hist pl TX-5
Higgs Branch—stream TN-4
Higgs Cem—cemetery (2) TN-4
Higgs Chapel—church TN-4
Higgs Ford (historical)—crossing TN-4
Higgs Mtn—summit AR-4
*Higgs Point* SC-3
Higgs Post Office (historical)—building TN-4
**Higgs (subdivision)**—pop pl NC-3
**Higgston**—pop pl GA-3
Higgs Well (abandoned)—well NM-5
**High**—pop pl IA-7
**High**—pop pl TX-5
High, Mount—summit MT-8
High Acre Ridge—ridge VA-3
High Acres Ranch—locale WY-8
**High Amana**—pop pl IA-7
Higham Ditch—canal MT-8
Higham Peak—summit ID-8
Higham Well—well MT-8
High and Dry Rsvr—reservoir SD-7
**High Ave Subdivision**—pop pl UT-8
*High Bald Peak* NV-8
High Bald Peaks—summit NV-8
Highball Signal—hist pl DE-2
Highball Spring—spring AZ-5
High Band Bend—bend AR-4
High Bands Lodge—locale AR-4
High Bank—locale NY-2
**Highbank**—pop pl TX-5
Highbank Branch—stream AR-4
High Bank Campsite—locale (2) ME-1
High Bank Cem—cemetery OH-6
High Bank Ch—church WI-6
High Bank Creek—stream GA-3
High Bank Creek—stream MI-6
Highbank Creek—stream MI-6
Highbank Creek—stream SD-7
Highbank Creek—stream TX-5
Highbank Farm—hist pl OH-6
High Bank Island—island WI-6
Highbank Lake—lake MI-6
High Bank Lake—lake MN-6
Highbank Lake—lake MN-6
High Bank Landing—locale NJ-2
High Bank Landing—locale TN-4
High Bank Lodge—locale MI-6
Highbank Park Works—hist pl OH-6
Highbank Run—stream WV-2
High Banks—cliff IN-6
High Banks—levee FL-3
**Highbanks**—pop pl IN-6
High Banks, The—cliff MI-6
Highbanks Campgrounds—locale NY-2
High Bank Sch—school KY-4
High Bank Sch—school MO-7
*Highbanks Lake* MI-6
Highbanks Lake—lake MI-6
Highbank Slough—gut TX-5
Highbanks Metropolitan Park Mounds I and II—hist pl OH-6
Highbanks Rec Area—park NY-2
High Banks Works—hist pl OH-6
**Highbank Town**—pop pl IN-6
High Bar—bar OR-9
High Basin—basin ID-8
Highbee Cem—cemetery OH-6
Highberger Ditch—canal OR-9
High Blevens Spring—spring AZ-5
High Bliss Pond—lake AZ-5
*Highbluff* AL-4
High Bluff—cliff CA-9
High Bluff—cliff FL-3
High Bluff—locale FL-3
**High Bluff**—pop pl AL-4
**Highbluff**—pop pl AL-4
**High Bluff**—pop pl TN-4
High Bluff Ch—church GA-3
High Bluff Creek—stream FL-3
High Bluff (historical)—locale AL-4
High Bluff Landing—locale FL-3
High Bluffs—cliff AK-9
High Bluffs, The—cliff ME-1
High Bluff Sch—school AL-4
*High Bluff School* TN-4
Highboy Mtn—summit MT-8
High Breaks—range ID-8
High Breaks Creek—stream ID-8
High Bridge—bridge (2) CA-9
High Bridge—bridge IN-6
High Bridge—bridge IA-7
High Bridge—bridge KY-4
High Bridge—bridge MD-2
High Bridge—bridge NY-2
High Bridge—bridge OR-9
High Bridge—bridge PA-2
High Bridge—bridge VA-3
High Bridge—bridge WA-9
High Bridge—hist pl PA-2
High Bridge—locale IA-7
High Bridge—locale NJ-2
High Bridge—locale (2) NY-2
High Bridge—locale OK-5
High Bridge—other (2) MI-6
**High Bridge**—pop pl KY-4
**High Bridge**—pop pl MD-2
**High Bridge**—pop pl NH-1
**High Bridge**—pop pl NJ-2
**High Bridge**—pop pl (2) NY-2
**High Bridge**—pop pl WI-6
High Bridge Aqueduct and Water Tower—hist pl NY-2
High Bridge Brook—stream VT-1
High Bridge Campground—locale CA-9
High Bridge Cem—cemetery IL-6
High Bridge Cem—cemetery VA-3
High Bridge Ch—church (2) VA-3
Highbridge Creek—stream CA-9
High Bridge Creek—stream PA-2
High Bridge Creek—stream (2) WA-9
High Bridge Dam—dam PA-2
**High Bridge Estates**—pop pl MD-2
High Bridge Guard Station—locale WA-9
High Bridge Gulch—valley CO-8
High Bridge Lake—lake GA-3
Highbridge Lake—lake MI-6
Highbridge Mill (Ruins)—locale NV-8
High Bridge Park—park MD-2
High Bridge Park—park NY-2
High Bridge Park—park WA-9
High Bridge Reformed Church—hist pl NJ-2
High Bridge Sch—school MD-2
Highbridge Shaft—mine NV-8
Highbridge Spring—spring WA-9
High Brook—stream IN-6
*High Brush Island* MA-1
High Bunk—summit MA-1
High Burning Ridge—ridge KY-4
High Bush Island—island MA-1
High Butte—summit OR-9
High Butte—summit VA-3
High Butte Cem—cemetery NE-7
High Butte Effigy and Village Site (32ME13)—hist pl ND-7
High Butte Rsvr—reservoir OR-9
High Cache—locale AK-9
High Camp—locale OR-9
High Camp—locale WA-9
High Camp Creek—stream CA-9
High Camp Creek—stream OR-9
High Camp Lookout—locale OR-9
High Camp Trail—trail OR-9
High Cannon Trail—trail NH-1
High Castle Island—island AK-9
High Cedar Creek—stream VA-3
High Cem—cemetery IN-6
High Cem—cemetery LA-4
High Cem—cemetery (2) TX-5
High Center Rsvr—reservoir WY-8
Highchair Mtn—summit WA-9
**High Chaparral (subdivision)**—pop pl TN-4
**High Chateau Ranches**—pop pl CO-8
High Clam Ledge—bar ME-1
High Clark Canyon—valley NM-5
High Class Food Company—hist pl AZ-5
High Cliff—cliff MA-1
High Cliff—cliff WI-6
**Highcliff**—pop pl PA-2
**Highcliff**—pop pl TN-4
High Cliff Cem—cemetery WI-6
High Cliff Country Club—other WI-6
*High Cliff Elem Sch* PA-2
High Cliff Elem Sch—school PA-2
**High Cliff (Highcliff)**—pop pl WI-6
**High Cliff Junction**—pop pl WI-6
Highcliff Post Office (historical)—building TN-4
High Cliff Ridge—ridge NC-3
High Cliff State Park—park WI-6
**High Cliff (subdivision)**—pop pl AL-4
High Climb Mine—mine SD-7
*Highcoal* WV-2
High Coal—locale WV-2
High Coal Hollow—valley WV-2
High Cobble—summit PA-2
*High Cock* VA-3
*High Cock Knob* VA-3
Highcock Knob—summit VA-3
High Commission—summit CA-9
Highco Mtn—summit VA-3
High Cove Ridge—ridge GA-3
*High Creek* AL-4
*High Creek* MT-8
**High Creek**—pop pl IA-7
High Creek—stream (2) AK-9
High Creek—stream AZ-5
High Creek—stream AR-4
High Creek—stream CA-9
High Creek—stream (2) CO-8
High Creek—stream (3) ID-8
High Creek*—stream IA-7
High Creek—stream MO-7
High Creek—stream (2) OR-9
High Creek—stream UT-8
High Creek—stream WA-9
High Creek Campground—locale UT-8
High Creek Ch—church MO-7
High Creek Ditch—canal MO-7
High Creek (historical P.O.)—locale IA-7
High Creek Lake—lake UT-8
High Creek Sch (historical)—school MO-7
High Creek Spring—spring AZ-5
High Creek Trail—trail WA-9
High Crest Air Park—airport KS-7
High Crest Lake—reservoir NJ-2
High Crest Lake Dam—dam NJ-2
High Crest Sch—school IL-6
**Highcroft**—pop pl CA-9
**High Crossing**—pop pl NJ-2
**High Crossroads**—pop pl NC-3
High Cut—summit ME-1
**High Danish Condominium**—pop pl UT-8
High Davey Mtn—summit AR-4
High Deck—summit OR-9
High Desert—plain OR-9
High Ditch—canal (2) IN-6
High Ditch—canal MT-8
High Ditch—canal NV-8
High Ditch—canal WY-8
High Divide—ridge CA-9
High Divide—ridge WA-9
High Divide Trail—trail OR-9
High Dome—summit CA-9
High Drain—canal (2) MI-6
High Drive Parkway—park WA-9
High Dry Hollow—valley PA-2
High Dune Trail—trail VA-3
High Eagle—summit NC-3
High Elk Ranch—locale SD-7
High Emigrant Lake—lake CA-9
**High-Energy**—pop pl KY-4
*Higher Brook* MA-1
Higher Brook—stream MA-1
Higher Ground Camp—locale NH-1
Higher Pond—lake ME-1
Highers Cem—cemetery TN-4
*Highest Blue Mountain* CA-9
Highest Lake—lake CO-8
**Highets Corner**—pop pl IN-6
High Fall Branch—stream AL-4
Highfall Branch—stream NC-3
*High Falls* MN-6
High Falls—falls (2) AL-4
High Falls—falls (9) NY-2
High Falls—falls (3) NC-3
High Falls—falls (2) PA-2
High Falls—falls SC-3
High Falls—falls WV-2
Highfalls—locale AL-4
High Falls—locale GA-3
High Falls—locale KY-4
High Falls—locale NY-2
**Highfalls**—pop pl GA-3
**High Falls**—pop pl (2) NY-2
**Highfalls**—pop pl NC-3
**High Falls**—pop pl NC-3
High Falls Brook—stream (2) NY-2
High Falls Cem—cemetery NY-2
Highfalls Ch—church AL-4
High Falls Ch—church NC-3
High Falls Ch—church SC-3
High Falls Creek—stream MT-8
High Falls Dam—dam WI-6
High Falls Elem Sch—school NC-3
High Falls Gorge—gap NY-2
High Falls Lake—reservoir GA-3
*High Falls Pond* GA-3
High Falls Pond—reservoir NY-2
High Falls Rsvr—reservoir WI-6
High Falls State Park—park GA-3
Highfield—hist pl KY-4
**Highfield**—pop pl (2) MD-2
**Highfield**—pop pl PA-2
Highfield Anchorage—area AK-9
Highfield Branch—stream AL-4
Highfield Creek—stream AL-4
Highfield Sch—school PA-2
**Highfill**—pop pl AR-4
Highfill Cem—cemetery AR-4
Highfill Chapel—church IN-6
Highfill Creek—stream IN-6
Highfill Ranch—locale CO-8
High Flat Ridge—ridge CA-9
High Flats—locale NY-2

Highland Park NV-8
Highland Park PA-2
Highland Park—flat CO-8
Highland Park—hist pl CO-8
Highland Park—hist pl MS-4
Highland Park—locale ME-1
Highland Park—park AL-4
Highland Park—park CO-8
Highland Park—park FL-3
Highland Park—park ID-8
Highland Park—park IL-6
Highland Park—park IN-6
Highland Park—park (2) IA-7
Highland Park—park (2) KS-7
Highland Park—park LA-4
Highland Park—park (3) MA-1
Highland Park—park MI-6
Highland Park—park (3) MN-6
Highland Park—park MS-4
Highland Park—park (2) NE-7
Highland Park—park NM-5
Highland Park—park (2) NY-2
Highland Park—park (2) NC-3
Highland Park—park (3) OH-6
Highland Park—park OK-5
Highland Park—park (2) PA-2
Highland Park—park SD-7
Highland Park—park (2) TN-4
Highland Park—park (2) TX-5
Highland Park—park UT-8
Highland Park—park (2) VA-3
Highland Park—park WA-9
Highland Park—park WI-6
Highland Park—park WY-8
**Highland Park**—pop pl AK-9
**Highland Park**—pop pl (2) AZ-5
**Highland Park**—pop pl (2) CA-9
**Highland Park**—pop pl (2) CO-8
**Highland Park**—pop pl CT-1
**Highland Park**—pop pl (2) FL-3
**Highland Park**—pop pl (2) GA-3
**Highland Park**—pop pl (3) IL-6
**Highland Park**—pop pl IA-7
**Highland Park**—pop pl KS-7
**Highland Park**—pop pl (2) KY-4
**Highland Park**—pop pl LA-4
**Highland Park**—pop pl (2) MD-2
**Highland Park**—pop pl (2) MI-6
**Highland Park**—pop pl (2) NJ-2
**Highland Park**—pop pl NY-2
**Highland Park**—pop pl NC-3
**Highland Park**—pop pl (3) OH-6
**Highland Park**—pop pl (7) PA-2
**Highland Park**—pop pl (2) SC-3
**Highland Park**—pop pl (6) TN-4
**Highland Park**—pop pl (3) VA-3
**Highland Park**—pop pl WA-9
**Highland Park**—pop pl WV-2
**Highland Park**—pop pl WI-6
**Highland Park**—pop pl PR-3
Highland Park—uninc pl AL-4
Highland Park—uninc pl FL-3
Highland Park—uninc pl KS-7
Highland Park—uninc pl LA-4
Highland Park—uninc pl MA-1
Highland Park—uninc pl NC-3
Highland Park—uninc pl OK-5
Highland Park—uninc pl VA-3
**Highland Park Addition**—pop pl UT-8
Highland Park Assembley of God KS-7
Highland Park Baptist Ch—church KS-7
Highland Park Baptist Ch—church MS-4
Highland Park Baptist Ch—church (3) TN-4
Highland Park Bridge—bridge PA-2
Highland Park Campground—locale WY-8
Highland Park Cave—cave PA-2
Highland Park Cave—cave TN-4
Highland Park Cem—cemetery (2) KS-7
Highland Park Cem—cemetery KY-4
Highland Park Cem—cemetery LA-4
Highland Park Cem—cemetery MI-6
Highland Park Cem—cemetery MO-7
Highland Park Cem—cemetery (2) OH-6
Highland Park (Cem)—cemetery TX-5
Highland Park Central Elem Sch—school KS-7
Highland Park Ch—church AL-4
Highland Park Ch—church MO-7
Highland Park Ch—church SC-3
Highland Park Ch—church TX-5
Highland Park Ch—church (2) WV-2
Highland Park Ch of Christ—church AL-4
Highland Park Ch of God—church KS-7
Highland Park Christian Ch—church KS-7
Highland Park Church TN-4
Highland Park Dentzel Carousel and Shelter Bldg—hist pl MS-4
Highland Park Ditch—canal NM-5
Highland Park Elem Sch—school PA-2
Highland Park Elem Sch—school (3) TN-4
Highland Park General Hosp—hist pl MI-6
Highland Park General Hosp—hospital FL-3
Highland Park Golf Club—other NY-2
**Highland Park Heights**—pop pl LA-4
Highland Park Hist Dist—hist pl CO-8
Highland Park (historical)—park FL-3
Highland Park HS—school KS-7
Highland Park JHS—school OR-9
Highland Park Lakes WY-8
Highland Park Lakes—lake WY-8
Highland Park Landing—locale FL-3
**Highland Park Magna Subdivision**—pop pl UT-8
Highland Park Manufacturing Company Mill No. 3—hist pl NC-3
Highland Park Methodist Ch—church AL-4
Highland Park Methodist Ch—church TX-5
Highland Park Methodist Episcopal church—hist pl TN-4
Highland Park North Elem Sch—school KS-7
Highland Park Plant, Ford Motor Company—hist pl MI-6
Highland Park Police Station—hist pl CA-9
Highland Park Post Office—building TN-4
Highland Park Presbyterian Ch—church TX-5
Highland Park Presbyterian Ch (historical)—church AL-4
Highland Park Presbyterian Church—hist pl MI-6
Highland Park Public Use Area—park AL-4
Highland Park Run—gut FL-3
Highland Park Sch—school AL-4
Highland Park Sch—school CO-8
Highland Park Sch—school CT-1
Highland Park Sch—school FL-3
Highland Park Sch—school IA-7
Highland Park Sch—school MD-2
Highland Park Sch—school MI-6
Highland Park Sch—school (2) MT-8
Highland Park Sch—school NE-7
Highland Park Sch—school OH-6
Highland Park Sch—school (3) OK-5
Highland Park Sch—school (3) TX-5
Highland Park Sch—school UT-8
Highland Park Sch—school (2) VA-3
Highland Park Sch—school WY-8
Highland Park Sch (historical)—school FL-3
Highland Park School TN-4
Highland Park South Elem Sch—school KS-7
**Highland Park (subdivision)**—pop pl AL-4
**Highland Park (subdivision)**—pop pl MA-1
**Highland Park (subdivision)**—pop pl MS-4
**Highland Park (subdivision)**—pop pl (3) NC-3
**Highland Park (subdivision)**—pop pl TX-5
Highland Park Tower—hist pl MN-6
Highland Park Trailer Park—locale FL-3
Highland Park United Methodist Ch—church KS-7
Highland Park Water Tower—hist pl IL-6
**Highland Park West**—pop pl NC-3
Highland Peak—summit CA-9
Highland Peak—summit CO-8
Highland Peak—summit NV-8
**Highland Pines**—pop pl AZ-5
**Highland Pines**—pop pl GA-3
**Highland Pines**—pop pl NC-3
Highland Pines Ch—church NC-3
**Highland Pit (Highland)**—pop pl WA-9
Highland Plantation—locale LA-4
Highland (Plantation of)—civ div ME-1
Highland Plateau WY-8
Highland Playground—park MA-1
Highland Plaza—locale TN-4
Highland Plaza Apartments—hist pl AL-4
Highland Plaza (Shop Ctr)—locale FL-3
Highland Plaza (Shop Ctr)—locale MA-1
Highland P.O. (historical)—locale AL-4
Highland Point—cape (2) FL-3
Highland Pond—lake AL-4
Highland Pond—lake CT-1
Highland Pond—lake NC-3
Highland Pond—lake TN-4
Highland Pond—lake TX-5
Highland Pond—reservoir SC-3
Highland Pond Branch—stream TX-5
Highland Post Office (historical)—building TN-4
Highland Prairie Ch—church MN-6
Highland Prairie Ch—church MO-7
Highland Prong—stream NC-3
Highland Queen Mine—mine NV-8
Highland Ranch—locale MT-8
Highland Range NV-8
Highland Range—range NV-8
Highland Range Crucial Bighorn Habitat Area—park NV-8
Highland Regional HS—school NJ-2
Highland Reservoir CA-9
Highland Ridge—ridge CA-9
Highland Ridge—ridge NV-8
Highland Ridge—ridge NC-3
Highland Ridge—ridge TN-4
Highland Ridge—ridge (2) WV-2
Highland Ridge CAbin Site—locale TN-4
Highland Ridge Cem—cemetery NE-7
Highland Ridge Hosp—hospital UT-8
Highland Ridge Trail—trail NV-8
Highland Rim TN-4
**Highland Rim**—pop pl TN-4
Highland Rim Elem Sch—school TN-4
**Highland Rim Falls Subdivision**—pop pl TN-4
Highland Rim Plateau TN-4
**Highland Rim Terrace (subdivision)**—pop pl TN-4
Highland-Riverside Sch—school IL-6
Highland Road—post sta LA-4
Highland Road Hist Dist—hist pl NH-1
Highland Rsvr—reservoir NV-8
Highland Rsvr No. 2—reservoir CO-8
Highlands CA-9
Highlands CO-8
Highlands (2) IL-6
Highlands MA-1
Highlands—building DC-2
Highlands—hist pl KY-4
**Highlands**—pop pl FL-3
**Highlands**—pop pl ID-8
**Highlands**—pop pl (2) KY-4
**Highlands**—pop pl ME-1
**Highlands**—pop pl MD-2
**Highlands**—pop pl MA-1
**Highlands**—pop pl NH-1
**Highlands**—pop pl NJ-2
**Highlands**—pop pl NC-3
**Highlands**—pop pl PA-2
**Highlands**—pop pl TX-5
**Highlands**—pop pl VA-3
Highlands—uninc pl FL-3
Highlands, The—hist pl DC-2
Highlands, The—hist pl PA-2
**Highlands, The**—pop pl (2) AL-4
**Highlands, The**—pop pl DE-2
**Highlands, The**—pop pl ME-1
**Highlands, The**—pop pl OH-6
**Highlands, The**—pop pl WA-9
Highlands, The—summit ME-1
Highlands, The—summit (2) MA-1
Highlands, The—summit OH-6
Highlands, The—summit UT-8
Highland Sacred Garden—cemetery MO-7
Highland Sanitarium—hospital CA-9
Highlands Baptist Ch—church AL-4
Highlands Baptist Ch—church FL-3
Highlands Bay—bay MD-2
Highlands Beach—beach NJ-2
Highlands Cem—cemetery LA-4
Highlands Cem—cemetery NC-3
Highland Sch IN-6
Highland Sch PA-2
Highlands Ch—church CO-8
Highlands Ch—church MI-6
Highland Sch—hist pl CO-8
Highland Sch—hist pl MA-1
Highland Sch—school (2) AL-4
Highland Sch—school (10) CA-9
Highland Sch—school (4) CO-8
Highland Sch—school (2) CT-1
Highland Sch—school (2) GA-3
Highland Sch—school (11) IL-6
Highland Sch—school (2) IN-6
Highland Sch—school (5) IA-7
Highland Sch—school (3) KS-7
Highland Sch—school (4) KY-4
Highland Sch—school (2) LA-4
Highland Sch—school ME-1
Highland Sch—school MD-2
Highland Sch—school (8) MA-1
Highland Sch—school (3) MI-6
Highland Sch—school (2) MN-6
Highland Sch—school MS-4
Highland Sch—school (6) MO-7
Highland Sch—school (3) MT-8
Highland Sch—school (8) NE-7
Highland Sch—school NV-8
Highland Sch—school NH-1
Highland Sch—school (2) NM-5
Highland Sch—school NY-2
Highland Sch—school (2) NC-3
Highland Sch—school ND-7
Highland Sch—school (4) OH-6
Highland Sch—school OK-5
Highland Sch—school (2) OR-9
Highland Sch—school (7) PA-2
Highland Sch—school (5) SD-7
Highland Sch—school TN-4
Highland Sch—school (4) TX-5
Highland Sch—school VT-1
Highland Sch—school VA-3
Highland Sch—school (5) WA-9
Highland Sch—school (2) WV-2
Highland Sch—school (2) WI-6
Highland Sch (Abandoned)—school CA-9
Highland Sch (abandoned)—school (3) MO-7
Highland Sch (abandoned)—school (2) PA-2
Highland Sch (historical)—school (5) MO-7
Highland Sch (historical)—school PA-2
Highland Sch (historical)—school (5) TN-4
Highland Sch Number 1—school (2) ND-7
Highland Sch Number 2—school ND-7
Highland Sch Number 3—school ND-7
Highland Sch Number 4—school ND-7
Highland School DE-2
Highland School—locale KS-7
Highland School—locale OK-5
Highland School (Abandoned)—locale CA-9
Highland School(Abandoned)—locale IA-7
Highland School (abondoned)—locale CA-9
Highlands Christian Acad—school FL-3
Highlands City Elem Sch—school FL-3
Highlands City (RR name for Highland City)—other FL-3
Highlands Country Club—locale NC-3
Highlands Country Club—other GA-3
Highlands Country Club—other NY-2
**Highlands County**—pop pl FL-3
Highlands County Achievement Center—school FL-3
Highlands Elem Sch—school AL-4
Highlands Elem Sch—school DE-2
Highlands Elem Sch—school (2) FL-3
Highland Senior HS—school IN-6
Highland Seventh Day Adventist Ch—church TN-4
Highlands Falls—falls NC-3
Highlands Farm Dam—dam PA-2
Highlands Forge Lake—lake NY-2
Highlands Hammock State Park—park FL-3
Highlands (Highland) IN-6
Highlands Hill—summit MA-1
Highlands Hist Dist—hist pl KY-4
Highlands Hist Dist—hist pl MA-1
Highlands Hist Dist—hist pl MS-4
**Highlands (historical)**—pop pl MA-1
**Highlands (historical)**—pop pl TN-4
Highland Shop Ctr—locale MS-4
**Highland Shore**—pop pl WI-6
**Highland Shores**—pop pl IL-6
Highlands HS—school CA-9
Highlands HS—school TX-5
Highland Silver Lake—reservoir IL-6
Highlands Intermediate Sch—school HI-9
Highlands JHS—school FL-3
Highlands JHS—school IL-6
Highlands JHS—school PA-2
Highlands JHS—school WA-9
Highlands Lake NY-2
Highlands Lake—reservoir NC-3
Highlands Masonic Temple—other CO-8
Highlands Methodist Ch—church (2) AL-4
**Highlands of Hidden Valley Subdivision**—pop pl UT-8
Highlands of Neversink NJ-2
Highlands Park—park AL-4
Highlands Park—park CA-9
Highlands Park—park FL-3
Highlands Park—park MN-6
Highlands Park—park WA-9
**Highlands Park**—pop pl IN-6
**Highlands Park Estates**—pop pl FL-3
**Highlands Park Estates (subdivision)**—pop pl FL-3
**Highland Spring**—pop pl KY-4
Highland Spring—spring AL-4
Highland Spring—spring ME-1
Highland Spring—spring (2) NV-8
Highland Spring—spring OR-9
Highland Springs—locale CA-9
Highland Springs—locale KY-4
Highland Springs—locale TN-4
**Highland Springs**—pop pl CA-9
**Highland Springs**—pop pl VA-3
Highland Springs Branch—stream TN-4
Highland Springs Cove Dam—dam TN-4
Highland Springs Cove Lake—reservoir TN-4
Highland Square Park—park IA-7
Highland Square (Shop Ctr)—locale (2) FL-3
Highlands Ranch—locale CO-8
Highlands Reach—channel NJ-2
Highlands Regional Med Ctr—hospital FL-3
Highlands (Renton Highlands)—uninc pl WA-9
Highlands Rsvr—reservoir NC-3
Highlands Rsvr—reservoir TX-5
Highlands Sch—school (3) CA-9
Highlands Sch—school FL-3
Highlands Sch—school ID-8
Highlands Sch—school (3) IL-6
Highlands Sch—school MA-1
Highlands Sch—school NY-2
Highlands Sch—school OH-6
Highlands Sch—school PA-2
Highlands Sch—school TX-5
Highlands Shop Ctr—locale FL-3
**Highlands (subdivision)**—pop pl (2) MA-1
**Highlands Subdivision**—pop pl UT-8
**Highlands (subdivision), The**—pop pl AL-4
**Highlands (subdivision), The**—pop pl NC-3
**Highland (sta.)**—pop pl OH-6
Highland State Rec Area—park MI-6
Highland State Training Sch—school NY-2
Highland State Wildlife Mngmt Area—park MN-6
Highland Station KS-7
Highland Station (historical)—locale (2) MA-1
**Highland Stone**—pop pl MD-2
**Highlands (Town of)**—pop pl NY-2
Highlands (Township of)—fmr MCD NC-3
Highland Street Elem Sch—school PA-2
**Highland Subdivision**—pop pl UT-8
Highland Switch—locale MO-7
**Highland Terrace**—pop pl DE-2
**Highland Terrace**—pop pl OH-6
Highland Terrace Mobile Home Park—locale AZ-5
Highland Terrace Shop Ctr—locale FL-3
Highland Towers Apartments—hist pl PA-2
**Highlandtown**—pop pl MD-2
**Highlandtown**—pop pl OH-6
Highland Townhall—building (2) IA-7
**Highland (Town of)**—pop pl NY-2
**Highland (Town of)**—pop pl (2) WI-6
Highlandtown Rsvr—reservoir OH-6
Highlandtown Sch—school MD-2
Highland Township KS-7
Highland Township SD-7
Highland Township—civil (2) MO-7
Highland Township—civil (3) SD-7
Highland Township—fmr MCD (10) IA-7
**Highland Township**—pop pl (6) KS-7
**Highland Township**—pop pl (2) NE-7
**Highland Township**—pop pl (3) ND-7
**Highland Township**—pop pl (8) SD-7
Highland Township—unorg reg KS-7
Highland Township Hall—building SD-7
Highland Township (historical)—civil ND-7
Highland Township HS (historical)—school PA-2
Highland (Township of)—fmr MCD AR-4
**Highland (Township of)**—pop pl IL-6
**Highland (Township of)**—pop pl (3) IN-6
**Highland (Township of)**—pop pl (2) MI-6
**Highland (Township of)**—pop pl MN-6
**Highland (Township of)**—pop pl (2) OH-6
**Highland (Township of)**—pop pl (4) PA-2
Highlandtown Wildlife Area—park OH-6
Highland Trail DC-2
Highland Trail—trail (2) CA-9
Highland Trail—trail MT-8
Highland Trail (pack)—trail OR-9
**Highland Trails (subdivision)**—pop pl NC-3
Highland Tunnel—mine UT-8
Highland United Methodist Ch—church MS-4
Highland United Methodist Church—hist pl MI-6
Highland United Presbyterian—church FL-3
Highland Univ—school NM-5
Highland U. S. Life Saving Station (historical)—locale MA-1
Highland Valley—valley CA-9
Highland Valley—valley ID-8
Highland Valley Park—park NV-8
Highland Valley Summit—summit ID-8
Highland View MI-6
**Highland View**—pop pl FL-3
**Highland View**—pop pl MD-2
**Highland View**—pop pl PA-2
**Highlandview**—pop pl TN-4
**Highland View**—pop pl (2) TN-4
Highland View Baptist Ch—church MT-8
Highlandview Ch—church AL-4
Highland View Ch—church NC-3
Highland View Ch—church TN-4
Highland View Ch of Christ—church TN-4
Highland View County Hosp—hospital OH-6
Highland View Elem Sch—school FL-3
Highland View JHS—school OR-9
Highland View Memorial Gardens—cemetery CA-9
Highland View Overlook—locale CO-8
Highland View Sch—school MD-2
Highland View Sch—school NE-7
Highland View Sch—school SD-7
Highland View Sch—school (2) TN-4
Highland View Sch—school VA-3
Highland View Sch—school WI-6
**Highland View Subdivision**—pop pl UT-8
Highland Village IN-6
Highland Village—locale KS-7
**Highland Village**—pop pl IN-6
**Highland Village**—pop pl (2) TX-5
Highland Village Park—park FL-3
Highland Village Shop Ctr—locale KS-7
Highland Village Shop Ctr—locale MS-4
Highland Village Shop Ctr—locale TX-5
**Highland Village (subdivision)**—pop pl AL-4
**Highland Village (subdivision)**—pop pl NC-3
Highlandville MA-1
**Highlandville**—pop pl IA-7
**Highlandville**—pop pl MA-1
**Highlandville**—pop pl MO-7
Highlandville Station (historical)—locale MA-1
Highland Vista Park—park AZ-5
**Highland Waters**—pop pl TX-5
Highland Well—well NM-5
**Highland West**—pop pl DE-2
Highland Wildlife Mngmt Area—park VA-3
Highland Windmill—locale (3) TX-5
**Highland Woods**—pop pl DE-2
High Laurel Branch—stream NC-3
Highlawn IL-6
**Highlawn**—pop pl WV-2
Highlawn—uninc pl NY-2
High Lawn Memorial Park—cemetery WV-2
Highlawns—uninc pl WV-2
Highlawn Sch—school (2) WV-2
High Lawn Sch—school WI-6
Highleap, The—cliff UT-8
Highleap Canyon—valley UT-8
High Ledge—island ME-1
High Ledge—ridge MA-1
Highlevel AL-4
High Level—locale AL-4
High Level Mine (underground)—mine AL-4
Highley Cem—cemetery MO-7
Highley Heights MO-7
**Highley Heights**—pop pl MO-7
Highley Spring—spring MO-7
Highlife Lake—lake MN-6
High Life Lake—lake WI-6
Highlift Canal—canal WA-9
High Lift Lateral—canal CA-9
High Lift Line—other ID-8
Highline—canal MT-8
High Line Canal AZ-5
High Line Canal CO-8
Highline Canal NE-7
Highline Canal WA-9
Highline Canal—canal AZ-5
Highline Canal—canal CA-9
High Line Canal—canal CA-9
Highline Canal—canal (3) CO-8
High Line Canal—canal ID-8
Highline Canal—canal ID-8
High Line Canal—canal ID-8
Highline Canal—canal ID-8
Highline Canal—canal MT-8
High Line Canal—canal NE-7
Highline Canal—canal NV-8
High Line Canal—canal NV-8
Highline Canal—canal NM-5
High Line Canal—canal (2) OR-9
Highline Canal—canal OR-9
Highline Canal—canal TX-5
High Line Canal—canal UT-8
Highline Canal—canal (4) UT-8
High Line Canal—canal UT-8
Highline Canal—canal UT-8
Highline Canal—canal WA-9
High Line Canal—canal WA-9
Highline Canal—canal (2) WY-8
Highline Canal—valley NE-7
Highline Canal Feeder—canal ID-8
Highline Canal (historical)—canal AZ-5
Highline Canyon—valley TX-5
Highline Creek—stream ID-8
Highline Dich—canal CO-8
Highline Ditch—canal CA-9
Highline Ditch—canal (4) CO-8
Highline Ditch—canal ID-8
Highline Ditch—canal (2) MT-8
High Line Ditch—canal NM-5
Highline Ditch—canal NM-5
High Line Ditch—canal (2) OR-9
Highline Ditch—canal OR-9
High Line Ditch—canal (2) OR-9
Highline Ditch—canal OR-9
Highline Ditch—canal TX-5
Highline Ditch—canal UT-8
High Line Ditch—canal WA-9
Highline Ditch—canal (2) WY-8
High Line Ditch—canal WY-8
Highline Ditch—canal (2) WY-8
High Line Diversion Dam—dam NV-8
Highline Draw—valley WY-8
Highline Gulch—valley MT-8
Highline HS—school WA-9
Highline Lake—reservoir CO-8
Highline Lakes—lake ID-8
Highline Lake State Rec Area—park CO-8
Highline Lateral—canal (3) CO-8
Highline Lateral—canal OR-9
Highline Mine—mine CO-8
Highline Mine—mine WY-8
High Line North Canal—canal ID-8
Highline Pumping Plant—other AZ-5
Highline Ridge—ridge (2) ID-8
Highline Rsvr—reservoir CO-8
Highline Saddle—gap CA-9
High Line Sch—school ID-8
Highline Sch—school MT-8
High Line Spring—spring UT-8
Highline Stock Driveway—trail CO-8
Highline Substation—locale AZ-5
Highline Tank—reservoir NM-5
Highline Tank—reservoir (3) TX-5
Highline Trail—trail AZ-5
Highline Trail—trail (5) CO-8
High Line Trail—trail ID-8
Highline Trail—trail MT-8
Highline Trail—trail NM-5
Highline Trail—trail UT-8
High Line Trail—trail UT-8
Highline Trail—trail UT-8
Highline Trail—trail WA-9
Highline Trail—trail WY-8
High Line Trail—trail WY-8
Highline Trail—trail WY-8
Highline Trail Head Campground—locale UT-8
Highline Trail Lakes—lake WY-8
Highline Windmill—locale TX-5
High Loaf Mtn—summit NC-3
High Loch Leven Lake—lake CA-9
High Lode Mine—mine SD-7
High Log AL-4
Highlog Branch—stream GA-3
High Log Creek—stream AL-4
High Log Creek—stream WA-9
Highlog (historical)—locale AL-4
Highlog Lake—lake FL-3
Highlog Run—stream WV-2
High Lonesome—locale NM-5
High Lonesome Camp—locale TX-5
High Lonesome Canyon—valley AZ-5
High Lonesome Canyon—valley NM-5
High Lonesome Draw—valley TX-5
High Lonesome Hill—summit NM-5
High Lonesome Mine—mine CO-8
High Lonesome Mtn—summit TX-5
High Lonesome Peak—summit NM-5
High Lonesome Peak—summit TX-5
High Lonesome Ranch—locale (2) TX-5
High Lonesome Sch (abandoned)—school MO-7
High Lonesome Spring—spring AZ-5
High Lonesome Stage Station—locale TX-5
High Lonesome Tank—reservoir AZ-5
High Lonesome Tank—reservoir (2) NM-5
High Lonesome Tank—reservoir (2) TX-5
High Lonesome Trail—trail CO-8
High Lonesome Water Tank—reservoir NM-5
High Lonesome Well—locale AZ-5
High Lonesome Well—well (3) NM-5
High Lonesome Well—well (4) TX-5
High Lonesome Wells—locale NM-5
High Lonesome Windmill—locale AZ-5
High Lonesome Windmill—locale (9) NM-5
High Lonesome Windmill—locale (19) TX-5
High-Lonesome Windmill—well AZ-5
High Lookout—locale MO-7
High Low Gap—gap SC-3
Highly Creek—stream MO-7
Highlys Beach—locale MD-2
High Mangrove Point—cape FL-3
High-Mar CO-8
High Market—locale NY-2
High Market (Town of)—other NY-2
High Meadow—flat NY-2
High Meadow—flat WY-8
High Meadow Creek—stream WY-8
High Meadow Farms—airport NJ-2
High Meadow Lake—lake WY-8
High Meadows—flat (2) CA-9
High Meadows—hist pl VA-3
**High Meadows**—pop pl IL-6
**High Meadows**—pop pl MD-2
**High Meadows**—pop pl PA-2
**High Meadows**—pop pl VA-3
High Meadow Sch—school MI-6
High Meadows Dam—dam NC-3
High Meadows Lake—reservoir NC-3
High Meadow Springs—spring CA-9
**High Meadows (subdivision)**—pop pl (2) NC-3
High Meadows Trail—trail VA-3
High Mesa CO-8
High Mesa—summit AZ-5
High Mesa—summit (3) CO-8
High Mesa—summit NM-5
High Mesa Rsvr No 2—reservoir WY-8
**High Mills**—pop pl NY-2
High Moon Rsvr—reservoir MT-8
**Highmoor**—pop pl IL-6
**Highmore**—pop pl SD-7
Highmore Cem—cemetery SD-7
Highmore Municipal Airp—airport SD-7
Highmore Township—civil SD-7
High Morning Ch—church TX-5
High Mound AL-4
**Highmound**—pop pl AL-4
Highmound Ch—church AL-4
Highmound Park Training Track—other TX-5
**Highmount**—pop pl NY-2
**Highmount**—pop pl PA-2
High Mount—uninc pl LA-4
High Mountain MT-8
High Mountain Brook NJ-2
High Mountain Brook—stream NJ-2
High Mountain Campground—park UT-8
High Mountains AZ-5
High Mountains UT-8
**Highmount (Grand Hotel)**—pop pl NY-2
High Mowing Sch—school NH-1
High Mtn—summit (2) AK-9
High Mtn—summit (2) CA-9
High Mtn—summit (2) NJ-2
High Mtn—summit NY-2
High Mtn—summit OR-9
High Mtn—summit PA-2
High Mtn—summit UT-8
High Mtn—summit WV-2
High Museum—building GA-3
Highnite Hollow AR-4
High Noon Mine—mine WA-9
High Noon Ridge—ridge CO-8
High Nopit—summit NY-2
Highnote—locale AL-4
Higho Ditch—canal CO-8
High Ore Creek—stream MT-8
Higho Sch—school CO-8
High Park—flat (6) CO-8
High Park—flat MT-8
High Park—park CT-1
High Park—park WY-8
**High Park**—pop pl PA-2
High Park Creek—stream CO-8
High Park Lake—lake CO-8
High Park Lake—lake MT-8
High Park Lookout—locale WY-8
High Park Peak—summit MT-8
**High Park (subdivision)**—pop pl NC-3
High Park Windmill—locale TX-5
High Pass—gap ID-8
High Pass—gap (2) WA-9
**High Pasture**—pop pl ME-1
High Peak AZ-5
High Peak CA-9
High Peak NC-3
High Peak—cliff NY-2
High Peak—summit AZ-5
High Peak—summit (3) AR-4
High Peak—summit (3) CA-9
High Peak—summit CO-8
High Peak—summit (2) MT-8
High Peak—summit (2) NV-8
High Peak—summit NM-5
High Peak—summit NY-2
High Peak—summit (5) NC-3
Highpeak—summit NC-3
High Peak—summit NC-3
High Peak—summit (2) OK-5
High Peak—summit OR-9
High Peak—summit UT-8
High Peak—summit VT-1
High Peak—summit (3) VA-3
High Peak Ch—church NC-3
High Peak Cienega—spring AZ-5
High Peak Mine—mine CA-9
High Peaks Trail—trail CA-9
High Pig Tank—reservoir AZ-5
High Pine AL-4
High Pine ME-1

**High Water**—pop pl OH-6
**Highwater**—pop pl OH-6
High Water Canal—canal UT-8
Highwater Ch—church MN-6
Highwater Cienega—flat AZ-5
Highwater Creek—stream MN-6
High Water Drain—stream GA-3
Highwater Island—island AK-9
Highwater Mark Sch—school IL-6
Highwater Rock—hist pl IA-7
Highwater Rock—island CT-1
High Water Slough—stream OR-9
**Highwater (Township of)**—pop pl MN-6
Highwater Trail—trail ME-1
Highwater Trail—trail NH-1
Highwater Well—well NM-5
Highway—locale NM-5
**Highway**—pop pl KY-4
**Highway**—pop pl MI-6
**Highway**—pop pl OR-9
**Highway**—pop pl TN-4
**Highway**—pop pl TX-5
**Highway**—pop pl VA-3
Highway Assembly Ch—church MO-7
Highway Bible Ch—church IN-6
Highway Canyon—valley AZ-5
Highway Cave—cave AL-4
Highway Ch—church (2) AL-4
Highway Ch—church GA-3
Highway Ch—church KY-4
Highway Ch—church LA-4
Highway Ch—church MD-2
Highway Ch—church (2) MS-4
Highway Ch—church MO-7
Highway Ch—church (2) NC-3
Highway Ch—church OH-6
Highway Ch—church OK-5
Highway Ch—church SC-3
Highway Ch—church (2) TN-4
Highway Ch—church (2) TX-5
Highway Chapel—church TX-5
Highway Ch of Christ—church FL-3
Highway Christian Ch of Christ of the Apostolic Faith—church FL-3
Highway Christian Church MS-4
**Highway City**—pop pl CA-9
Highway Dam—dam AZ-5
Highway Dam—dam IN-6
Highway Department Number 2 Dam—dam SD-7
Highway Department Number 3 Dam—dam SD-7
Highway Drift Fence Tank—reservoir AZ-5
Highway Fifty Access Area—park MS-4
Highway Fiftyone Landing—locale MS-4
Highway Five Ch—church AL-4
Highway Forty Mine—mine CA-9
**Highway Four Forty One**—pop pl SC-3
Highway Gospel Ch—church MI-6
Highway Highlands—uninc pl CA-9
Highway Holy Ch—church SC-3
Highway I-80-N Embankment—dam OR-9
**Highway Junction**—pop pl TN-4
Highway K Public Use Area—park MO-7
Highway Lake—reservoir TX-5
Highway Lake Waterhole—spring OR-9
Highway Mill—locale NM-5
Highway Mission—church (2) KY-4
Highway Mission Ch—church OK-5
Highway Mission Ch—church VA-3
Highway M Public Use Area—locale MO-7
Highway One Hundred—uninc pl TN-4
Highway Park—park AZ-5
**Highway Park**—pop pl LA-4
Highway Pass—gap AK-9
Highway Pasture—flat KS-7
Highway Patro Acad—school CA-9
Highway Patrol Troop C HQ Heliport—airport MO-7
Highway Pit Tank—reservoir TX-5
Highway Pond—lake IL-6
Highway Ranch—locale UT-8
Highway Ridge Memorial Gardens—cemetery AL-4
Highway Rsvr—reservoir UT-8
Highway Sch—school CA-9
Highway Sch—school MO-7
Highway Sch—school NE-7
Highway Sch—school ND-7
Highway Sch—school TX-5
Highway Sch—school WY-8
Highway Sch (historical)—school AL-4
Highway Seeding Well—well NV-8
Highway Seventyone Ch—church TX-5
Highway Sixtyeight Cave—cave AL-4
Highway Sixty Tank—reservoir AZ-5
Highway Spring—spring AZ-5
Highway Spring—spring NV-8
Highway Spring—spring OR-9
Highway Spring Campground—locale CO-8
Highway Spring Cave—cave TN-4
Highway Tabernacle—church MI-6
Highway Tabernacle—church PA-2
Highway Tabernacle—church (2) VA-3
Highway Tank—lake TX-5
Highway Tank—reservoir (9) AZ-5
Highway Tank—reservoir (6) NM-5
Highway Tank—reservoir (6) TX-5
Highway Tank Dam—dam AZ-5
Highway Tanks—reservoir (2) AZ-5
Highway Thirteen Park—park MO-7
Highway Thirteen Public Use Area—park MO-7
Highway View Sch—school KS-7
Highway View Sch—school NE-7
Highway View Sch—school WI-6
Highway Village IL-6
**Highway Village**—pop pl HI-9
**Highway Village**—pop pl IL-6
**Highway Village**—pop pl MS-4
**Highway Village**—pop pl TX-5
Highway Village Ch—church MS-4
Highway Well NV-8
Highway Well—well NV-8
Highway Well—well (3) NM-5
Highway Well—well TX-5
Highway Well—well UT-8
Highway Well Number Seventy-eight (dry)—well NV-8
Highway Windmill—locale AZ-5
Highway Windmill—locale (4) NM-5
Highway Windmill—locale (6) TX-5
Highway 10 State Public Shooting Area—park SD-7
Highway 109 North Industrial Area—locale TN-4
Highway 11 Bridge over Chunky River—hist pl MS-4
Highway 125 Public Use Area—park AR-4
Highway 203 Pond—lake OR-9
Highway 31 Landing Rec Area—park OK-5
Highway 36 Ch—church AL-4
Highway 44 Dam—dam SD-7
Highway 44 Number 4 Dam—dam SD-7
Highway 44 Number 6 Dam—dam SD-7
Highway 45 Baptist Ch—church AL-4
Highway 51 Senior HS—school NC-3
Highway 58 Shop Ctr—locale TN-4
Highway 70 Landing Public Use Area—park AR-4
Highway 71 Ch—church AR-4
Highway 75 Dam—dam MN-6
Highway 79 Bridge—hist pl AR-4
Highway 9 Landing—locale OK-5
Highway 96 Ch—church AR-4
High Well—well MT-8
High Well—well (2) NM-5
High Well—well (2) TX-5
High White Valley—valley AZ-5
High Wide and Handsome Tank—reservoir TX-5
High Windmill—locale NM-5
High Windmill—locale (9) TX-5
High Windy—summit NC-3
Highwood IN-6
Highwood—locale MI-6
**Highwood**—pop pl CT-1
**Highwood**—pop pl (2) IL-6
**Highwood**—pop pl MN-6
**Highwood**—pop pl MT-8
**Highwood**—pop pl NJ-2
Highwood Baldy—summit MT-8
Highwood Branch—stream IN-6
Highwood Cem—cemetery PA-2
Highwood Creek—stream MT-8
Highwood Creek Community Hall—locale MT-8
Highwood Guard Station—locale MT-8
Highwood Industrial Park—locale NC-3
Highwood Lake—lake WA-9
Highwood Lake—reservoir PA-2
Highwood Mountains—spring MT-8
Highwood Park—park CA-9
Highwood Park—park MN-6
Highwood Peak MT-8
**Highwoods**—pop pl IN-6
**High Woods**—pop pl NY-2
**High Woods**—pop pl VA-3
Highwood Sch—school MD-2
Highwood Terrace IL-6
Highwood Trail—trail PA-2
Higinbotham Woods—woods IL-6
Higinbottom Cem—cemetery IN-6
**Higley**—pop pl AZ-5
Higley Brook—stream CT-1
Higley Brook—stream MA-1
Higley Brook Dam—dam MA-1
Higley Cem—cemetery IA-7
Higley Cem—cemetery MI-6
Higley Cem—cemetery OH-6
Higley Creek—stream WA-9
Higley Falls—falls NY-2
Higley Flow State Park—park NY-2
Higley Hill—summit GA-3
Higley Hill—summit MA-1
Higley Hill—summit VT-1
Higley Mtn—summit NY-2
Higley Peak—summit WA-9
Higley Post Office—building AZ-5
Higley Sch—school AZ-5
Higley Sch—school VT-1
Higley Spring—spring ID-8
Higley Substation—locale AZ-5
Higley Tank AZ-5
Higley Twin Tanks—reservoir AZ-5
Higlon Ridge—ridge NC-3
Higman Hill—summit NY-2
**Higman Park**—pop pl MI-6
**Hignite**—pop pl KY-4
Hignite Branch—stream TN-4
Hignite Cem—cemetery AR-4
Hignite Cem—cemetery KY-4
Hignite Creek—stream KY-4
Hignite Gap—gap AR-4
Hignite Hollow—valley AR-4
Higo, Lake—reservoir OK-5
Higuera Grocery—hist pl AZ-5
**Higuey**—pop pl (2) PR-3
**Higuillals**—pop pl PR-3
**Higuillar**—pop pl PR-3
Higuillar (Barrio)—fmr MCD PR-3
Higway Tank—reservoir AZ-5
Hihat KY-4
**Hi Hat**—pop pl KY-4
Hi Hat Ranch—locale FL-3
Hihimanu—summit HI-9
Hihimanu Mtn HI-9
Hihiu—civil HI-9
Hihn Bldg—hist pl CA-9
Hi - Ho Ditch—canal CO-8
Hi Hunt Creek—stream UT-8
Hiiaka, Lae o—cape HI-9
Hiiaka Crater—crater HI-9
Hii Flats—flat HI-9
Hiilawe Falls—falls HI-9
Hiilawe Stream—stream HI-9
Hiiliula Stream HI-9
Hi Isle—island AZ-5
Hijacker Lake—lake MI-6
Hijadero Spring—spring NM-5
Hijinio Draw—valley NM-5
Hi Jolly Monument—locale AZ-5
Hika—uninc pl WI-6
Hika Island WA-9
**Hikapoloa**—pop pl HI-9
Hikauhi—cape HI-9
Hikauhi Gulch—valley HI-9
Hike Lake—lake MI-6
Hiker Park—park WI-6
Hikers Lake—lake AK-9
Hiker Trace IN-6
Hikes Family Houses—hist pl KY-4
Hikes-Hunsinger House—hist pl KY-4
Hikes Point—cape KY-4
Hikes Point—uninc pl KY-4
Hike Spring—spring NV-8
Hikes Sch—school KY-4
Hikiau Falls—falls HI-9
Hikiau Heiau—locale HI-9
Hikibon AZ-5
Hikilei Valley—valley HI-9
Hikimoe Ridge—ridge HI-9
Hikimoe Valley—valley HI-9
Hikina o ka la Heiau—locale HI-9
Hikinegitto-To FM-9
Hikiro AZ-5
Hikiula Gulch—valley HI-9
Hikjorn AZ-5
**Hiko**—pop pl NV-8
Hiko-Bukta Bay AK-9
Hiko Canyon—valley NV-8
Hiko Narrows—valley NV-8
Hiko Range—range NV-8
Hiko Spring—spring NV-8
Hiko Springs—spring NV-8
Hikuwan AZ-5
Hilaan Point—summit GU-9
Hiland TN-4
Hiland—locale WY-8
**Hi-Land**—pop pl LA-4
**Hi-Land Acres**—pop pl CO-8
Hiland Cem—cemetery OH-6
Hiland Ch—church PA-2
Hiland Chapel—church OH-6
**Hilander Park**—pop pl VA-3
Hiland HS—school OH-6
Hiland Lake MI-6
Hi-Land Lake—lake MI-6
Hi Land Lake—other MI-6
Hiland Lake—reservoir PA-2
**Hiland Park**—pop pl FL-3
**Hiland Park**—pop pl VA-3
Hiland Park Assembly of God Ch—church FL-3
Hiland Park Elem Sch—school FL-3
Hiland Public Golf Course—locale PA-2
Hiland Rsvr—reservoir WY-8
Hilands Golf Club—other MT-8
**Hiland Shores**—pop pl TX-5
Hilands Overlook State Park—park IN-6
**Hiland Township**—pop pl SD-7
Hiland Township Hall—building SD-7
Hil'ardin/Sharp-Hardin-Wright House—hist pl GA-3
Hilario Spring—spring OR-9
**Hilarita**—pop pl CA-9
Hil-A-Wa Lake—reservoir TN-4
**Hilbert**—pop pl WI-6
Hilbert Branch—stream MO-7
Hilbert Cem—cemetery TN-4
Hilbert Farm—hist pl KY-4
Hilbert JHS—school MI-6
Hilbert Junction—locale WI-6
Hilbert Junction—uninc pl WI-6
Hilbert Lake WI-6
Hilbert Lake—lake WI-6
Hilbert Sch (historical)—school MS-4
Hilborn—locale PA-2
Hilborn Creek—stream PA-2
Hilborn Park—park MI-6
Hilborn Run—stream PA-2
Hilbrand Drain—canal MI-6
Hilbun Cem—cemetery LA-4
Hilburn—locale TX-5
Hilburn—locale WI-6
Hilburn Cem—cemetery TX-5
Hilburn Creek—stream MT-8
Hilburn Park—park GA-3
Hilburn Ranch—locale NM-5
Hilburn Spring—spring KY-4
Hilburns Run PA-2
Hilburn (Township of)—fmr MCD AR-4
Hilchey Pond—reservoir MA-1
**Hilcrest**—pop pl IL-6
Hilcrest Shop Ctr—locale MO-7
Hilda—locale KY-4
Hilda—locale TX-5
Hilda—locale VA-3
Hilda—locale WA-9
**Hilda**—pop pl MS-4
**Hilda**—pop pl MO-7
**Hilda**—pop pl SC-3
Hilda, Lake—lake FL-3
Hilda, Lake—lake OR-9
Hilda Cem—cemetery WI-6
Hilda Creek—stream (3) AK-9
Hilda Creek—stream MN-6
Hilda Creek—stream MT-8
Hildago TX-5
**Hildale**—pop pl UT-8
Hildalgo Mountain CA-9
Hilda Lookout Tower—locale MS-4
Hilda Lookout Tower—locale MO-7
Hilda Mine—mine CA-9
HILDA M. WILLING—hist pl MD-2
Hilda-Ross Memorial Park—cemetery OH-6
Hildas Basin Creek—stream UT-8
**Hilda Siding**—pop pl TX-5
Hildbrandt Branch—stream LA-4
**Hildebran**—pop pl NC-3
Hildebran Creek—stream NC-3
Hildebrand—locale OR-9
Hildebrand—locale PA-2
**Hildebrand**—pop pl WV-2
Hildebrand, Lake—lake WA-9
Hildebrand Bayou TX-5
Hildebrand Bend—bend TN-4
Hildebrand Bluff—cliff MO-7
Hildebrand Branch—stream SC-3
Hildebrand Canyon—valley (2) NV-8
Hildebrand Cem—cemetery MO-7
Hildebrand Cem—cemetery VA-3
Hildebrand Ch—church VA-3
Hildebrand Creek—stream ID-8
Hildebrand Creek—stream WA-9
Hildebrand Dam—dam ND-7
Hildebrand Ditch—canal WY-8
Hildebrande Ranch—hist pl CO-8
Hildebrand Lake—lake IN-6
Hildebrand Lake—lake WI-6
Hildebrand Mill—hist pl OK-5
Hildebrand Run—stream OH-6
Hildebrand Sch (historical)—school PA-2
Hildebrand Spring—spring MT-8
Hildebrandt Bayou TX-5
Hildebrandt Creek—stream WI-6
Hildebrandt Ditch—canal IN-6
Hildebrandt Drain—canal MI-6
Hildebrandt Drain—stream MI-6
**Hildebrand Village**—pop pl IN-6
Hildebran Mtn—summit NC-3
Hildebran Sch—school NC-3
Hildebran View Ch—church NC-3
Hildebright Sch (abandoned)—school MO-7
**Hilden**—pop pl FL-3
Hildene—hist pl VT-1
Hilderbrand—locale WV-2
Hilderbrand Cem—cemetery MS-4
Hilderbrand Creek—stream SD-7
Hilderbrand Lake—lake WI-6
Hilderbrand Lock and Dam—dam WV-2
Hilderbrant Drain MI-6
**Hilderorand**—pop pl MO-7
Hilderth Hollow TN-4
Hilde Township—civil SD-7
Hildreth—locale CA-9
Hildreth—locale FL-3
Hildreth—locale IL-6
**Hildreth**—pop pl NE-7
Hildreth Cem—cemetery KY-4
Hildreth Cem—cemetery MA-1
Hildreth Cem—cemetery NE-7
Hildreth Cem—cemetery WV-2
Hildreth Ch—church KY-4
Hildreth Covered Bridge—hist pl OH-6
Hildreth Creek—stream CA-9
Hildreth Creek—stream MT-8
Hildreth Dam—dam NH-1
Hildreth Ditch—canal IN-6
Hildreth Hill—summit MA-1
Hildreth Hollow—valley TN-4
Hildreth Knob—summit TN-4
Hildreth Meadow—swamp NJ-2
Hildreth Mtn—summit CA-9
Hildreth Oil Field—oilfield TX-5
Hildreth Peak—summit CA-9
Hildreth Sch—school MA-1
Hildreth Sch—school NY-2
Hildreths Mill—locale ME-1
Hildur Lake—lake WI-6
Hilea—locale HI-9
Hilea Gulch—valley HI-9
Hilea Iki—civil HI-9
Hilea Nui—civil HI-9
Hile Cem—cemetery WV-2
Hile Creek—stream NE-7
Hileman Cem—cemetery TN-4
Hileman Cem—cemetery VA-3
Hileman Draw—valley WY-8
**Hileman Heights**—pop pl PA-2
Hileman Landing County Park—park OR-9
Hileman Sch—school NE-7
Hiler—uninc pl NY-2
Hiler Cem—cemetery MN-6
Hile Run—stream WV-2
**Hiles**—pop pl WI-6
Hiles Bridge (historical)—bridge TN-4
Hiles Canyon—valley NE-7
Hiles Cem—cemetery MO-7
Hiles Cem—cemetery WI-6
Hile Sch—school MI-6
Hiles Creek AL-4
Hiles Creek TN-4
Hiles Hollow—valley OH-6
**Hiles Junction**—pop pl WI-6
Hiles Lookout Tower—locale WI-6
Hiles Millpond—lake WI-6
Hiles Run—stream PA-2
**Hiles (Town of)**—pop pl (2) WI-6
Hi Level Golf Course—locale PA-2
Hi Lewis Branch—stream KY-4
Hiley Meadows—swamp MA-1
**Hilford**—pop pl KS-7
**Hilgard**—pop pl OR-9
Hilgard, Mount—summit CA-9
Hilgard Basin—basin MT-8
Hilgard Branch—stream CA-9
Hilgard Cem—cemetery OR-9
Hilgard Creek—stream MT-8
Hilgard Creek—stream WA-9
Hilgard Hall—hist pl CA-9
Hilgard Junction State Park—park OR-9
Hilgard Lake—lake CA-9
Hilgard Lake—lake MT-8
Hilgard Lodge—locale MT-8
Hilgard Mtn—summit UT-8
Hilgard Peak—summit MT-8
Hilgen and Wittenberg Woolen Mill—hist pl WI-6
Hilger—locale TX-5
**Hilger**—pop pl MT-8
Hilger Camp—locale MI-6
Hilger Coulee—valley MT-8
Hilger Lake—lake WI-6
Hilger Ranch—locale MT-8
Hilgers Gulch—valley SD-7
Hilger Southwest Oil Field—oilfield KS-7
Hilger Valley—valley MT-8
Hilger Well—well MT-8
Hilger Windmill—locale TX-5
Hilgo Coast NY-2
**Hilham**—pop pl TN-4
Hilham (CCD)—cens area TN-4
Hilham Cem—cemetery TN-4
Hilham Ch of Christ—church TN-4
Hilham Division—civil TN-4
Hilham Elem Sch—school TN-4
Hilham Post Office—building TN-4
Hilham United Methodist Ch—church TN-4
Hilhon Airp—airport IN-6
Hilight—locale WY-8
Hilight Gas Plant—oilfield WY-8
Hilight Oil And Gas Field—oilfield WY-8
Hilight Oil and Gas Field—oilfield WY-8
Hi-Li International Boys Camp—locale NY-2
Hilina Pali—cliff HI-9
Hilina Pali Trail—trail HI-9
Hiline—locale NV-8
Hi-Line Airp—airport PA-2
Hiline Heliport—airport WA-9
Hiline Lake—lake AK-9
Hi Line Lateral—canal CA-9
Hiline Lateral—canal CO-8
Hi Line Lodge Airp—airport PA-2
Hi Line Trail—trail MT-8
Hiline Trail—trail MT-8
Hilkey Pond—lake CO-8
Hilkey Run—stream WV-2
Hill AL-4
Hill KS-7
Hill SD-7
Hill—locale IL-6
Hill—locale OK-5
Hill—locale VA-3
**Hill**—pop pl ME-1
**Hill**—pop pl MT-8
**Hill**—pop pl NH-1
**Hill**—pop pl NM-5
**Hill**—pop pl NC-3
**Hill**—pop pl TN-4
Hill, Aaron, House—hist pl MA-1
Hill, A. B., Elem Sch—hist pl TN-4
Hill, Abraham Wiley, House—hist pl TX-5
Hill, Addison, House—hist pl MA-1
Hill, A. P., Boyhood Home—hist pl VA-3
Hill, A. P., House—hist pl GA-3
Hill, Ben, House—hist pl TX-5
Hill, Buckner, House—hist pl NC-3
Hill, Burwell O., House—hist pl GA-3
Hill, Dr. Oliver Perry, House—hist pl KY-4
Hill, Dr. S. W., Drug Store—hist pl ND-7
Hill, Gov. John F., Mansion—hist pl ME-1
Hill, Hiram Warner, House—hist pl GA-3
Hill, James J., House—hist pl MN-6
Hill, Jediah, Covered Bridge—hist pl OH-6
Hill, John, House—hist pl PA-2
Hill, John, Ranch-Keltomaki—hist pl SD-7
Hill, John B., House—hist pl TX-5
Hill, John Sprunt, House—hist pl NC-3
Hill, J. S., House—hist pl NC-3
Hill, Lake—lake (2) FL-3
Hill, Lake—reservoir TN-4
Hill, Lake of the—lake MN-6
Hill, Matt N., Homestead Barn—hist pl ID-8
Hill, Moran, House—hist pl TX-5
Hill, Mount—summit AK-9
Hill, Mount—summit KY-4
Hill, Nathaniel, Brick House—hist pl NY-2
Hill, Ray, Archeol Site—hist pl KY-4
Hill, Robert, House—hist pl DE-2
Hill, Sam, Hardware—hist pl AZ-5
Hill, Samuel, Hardware Company Warehouse—hist pl AZ-5
Hill, Samuel, House—hist pl WA-9
Hill, Samuel E., House—hist pl KY-4
Hill, Sidney A., House—hist pl MA-1
Hill, The—hist pl LA-4
Hill, The—summit NY-2
Hill, The—uninc pl GA-3
Hill, W. R., House—hist pl TX-5
Hillabahatchee Creek—stream AL-4
Hillabahatchee Creek—stream GA-3
Hillabee AL-4
Hillabee Campground Cem—cemetery AL-4
Hillabee Campground Ch—church AL-4
Hillabee Campground Methodist Ch AL-4
Hillabee Ch AL-4
Hillabee Ch—church AL-4
Hillabee Creek AL-4
Hillabee Creek—stream (2) AL-4
Hillabeehago Branch—stream AL-4
Hillabee-Hatchee Creek AL-4
Hillabee Mill AL-4
Hillabee P.O. (historical)—locale AL-4
Hillabee Ridge—ridge AL-4
Hillabi (historical)—locale AL-4
Hillabrandt Vly—swamp NY-2
**Hill Acres**—pop pl TN-4
**Hill Acres Subdivision**—pop pl (2) UT-8
**Hill Addition**—pop pl OH-6
Hill AFB—military (3) UT-8
Hill AFB Heliport—airport UT-8
Hill AFB Rec Area—locale UT-8
Hill AFB Recreation Camp—locale UT-8
Hillaire Sch—school WA-9
Hill Airy—hist pl NC-3
Hillake—reservoir AL-4
Hillaker Drain—canal MI-6
**Hilland**—pop pl SD-7
**Hillandale**—pop pl AL-4
**Hillandale**—pop pl MD-2
Hillandale Center—locale TN-4
Hillandale Ch—church MD-2
Hillandale Country Club—locale MS-4
Hillandale Country Club—other CT-1
**Hillandale Forest**—pop pl MD-2
Hillandale Golf Course—other SC-3
**Hillandale Heights**—pop pl MD-2
Hillandale Lake—reservoir MS-4
Hillandale Sch—school MD-2
Hillandale Sch—school (2) NC-3
**Hillandale (subdivision)**—pop pl (2) NC-3
Hill and Brush Ditch—canal CO-8
Hill and Crouter Ditch—canal CO-8
**Hill and Dale**—pop pl FL-3
**Hill And Dale**—pop pl IN-6
Hill and Dale Country Club—other NY-2
Hill and Dale Golf Club—locale ND-7
Hilland Dam—dam SD-7
Hill and Hill Dam—dam AL-4
Hill and Hill Lake—reservoir AL-4
Hill and Hill Tank—reservoir AZ-5
Hill and Hill Wells—well TX-5
Hill And Hollow OH-6
**Hill and Park**—pop pl CO-8
Hill and Sons Lake Dam—dam MS-4
Hill and Tracey Lateral—canal CO-8
Hill Annex Mine—hist pl MN-6
Hill -Annex Mine—mine MN-6
Hillard—locale TX-5
**Hillard**—pop pl AL-4
**Hillard**—pop pl TN-4
Hillard Branch—stream TN-4
Hillard Chapel—church VA-3
Hillard Drift Mine (underground)—mine AL-4
Hillard Island—island FL-3
Hillard Island—island GA-3
Hillard-Ladd Cem—cemetery TN-4
Hillard Lake PA-2
Hillard Mine (underground)—mine AL-4
Hillard Nolley Cem—cemetery TN-4
Hillard Peak—summit AK-9
Hillard Sch (historical)—school TN-4
Hillards Cross Roads—locale AL-4
Hillardsville (historical)—locale AL-4
**Hillaryville**—pop pl LA-4
**Hillaryville (Marchandville)**—pop pl LA-4
Hill Bayou—stream (4) AR-4
Hill Bayou—stream (2) LA-4
Hill Bench—bench OR-9
Hillbern Creek—stream SC-3
Hillberry Mtn—summit CO-8
Hillberry Rim—cliff WY-8
Hillbilly Windmill—locale (2) TX-5
Hill Bluff—cliff KY-4
**Hillborough Heights**—pop pl UT-8
Hill Branch—stream AL-4
Hill Branch—stream IL-6
Hill Branch—stream IN-6
Hill Branch—stream (2) KY-4
Hill Branch—stream (2) MS-4
Hill Branch—stream (2) NC-3
Hill Branch—stream SC-3
Hill Branch—stream (3) TN-4
Hill Branch—stream TX-5
Hill Branch—stream (2) WV-2
Hill Branch Cucharas River—stream CO-8
Hill Branch Lick Fork KY-4
Hill Bridge—bridge GA-3
Hill Brook MA-1
Hillbrook—CDP SC-3
**Hillbrook**—pop pl VA-3
Hill Brook—stream (2) CT-1
Hill Brook—stream (2) IN-6
Hill Brook—stream (4) ME-1
Hill Brook—stream NH-1
**Hillbrook Forest**—pop pl VA-3
**Hillbrook (subdivision)**—pop pl MS-4
Hillbun Ditch—canal NV-8
Hillburn FL-3
**Hillburn**—pop pl NY-2
Hillburn Branch—stream NC-3
**Hillburn City**—pop pl NM-5
Hillburn Rsvr—reservoir NY-2
Hillburn Spring—other FL-3
Hill Cabin Tank—reservoir AZ-5
Hill Camp Spring—spring OR-9
Hill Canal—canal ID-8
Hill Canyon—valley CA-9
Hill Canyon—valley CO-8
Hill Canyon—valley (2) NM-5
Hill Canyon—valley TX-5
Hill-Carrillo Adobe—hist pl CA-9
Hill Cave—cave (2) TN-4
Hill Cem AL-4
Hill Cem TN-4
Hill Cem—cemetery (13) AL-4
Hill Cem—cemetery (6) AR-4
Hill Cem—cemetery FL-3
Hill Cem—cemetery (2) GA-3
Hill Cem—cemetery ID-8
Hill Cem—cemetery (8) IL-6
Hill Cem—cemetery IA-7
Hill Cem—cemetery (6) KY-4
Hill Cem—cemetery LA-4
Hill Cem—cemetery ME-1
Hill Cem—cemetery (2) MA-1
Hill Cem—cemetery MI-6
Hill Cem—cemetery (7) MS-4
Hill Cem—cemetery (11) MO-7
Hill Cem—cemetery NE-7
Hill Cem—cemetery NY-2
Hill Cem—cemetery (3) NC-3
Hill Cem—cemetery (5) OH-6
Hill Cem—cemetery OK-5
Hill Cem—cemetery (2) OR-9
Hill Cem—cemetery PA-2
Hill Cem—cemetery (3) SC-3
Hill Cem—cemetery (20) TN-4
Hill Cem—cemetery (10) TX-5
Hill Cem—cemetery VT-1
Hill Cem—cemetery (6) VA-3
Hill Cem—cemetery (9) WV-2
Hill Cem—cemetery (2) WI-6
Hill Cemetery, The TN-4
**Hill Center**—pop pl NH-1
Hill Center Church—hist pl NH-1
Hill Ch AL-4
Hill Ch—church (3) AR-4
Hill Ch—church LA-4
Hill Ch—church PA-2
Hill Ch—church SD-7
Hill Channel—channel MI-6
Hill Chapel AL-4
Hill Chapel—church AL-4
Hill Chapel—church AR-4
Hill Chapel—church GA-3
Hill Chapel—church IN-6
Hill Chapel—church (2) MS-4
Hill Chapel—church (2) NC-3
Hill Chapel—church SC-3
Hill Chapel—church TN-4
Hill Chapel—church VA-3
Hill Chapel—locale KY-4
**Hill Chapel**—pop pl OK-5
Hill Chapel Cem—cemetery PA-2
Hill Chapel Ch AL-4
Hill Chapel (historical)—church MO-7
Hill Chapel Sch—school KY-4
Hill Ch Number 1—church PA-2
Hill Ch Number 2—church PA-2
Hill Church—locale PA-2
**Hill Church**—pop pl PA-2
Hill City KS-7
Hill City ND-7
Hill City SD-7
Hill City—locale MO-7
Hill City—locale PA-2
Hill City—locale TX-5
**Hill City**—pop pl GA-3
**Hill City**—pop pl ID-8
**Hill City**—pop pl KS-7
**Hill City**—pop pl MN-6
**Hill City**—pop pl SD-7
Hill City Cem—cemetery ID-8
Hill City Cem—cemetery KS-7
Hill City Elem Sch—school KS-7
Hill City HS—school KS-7
Hill City Municipal Airp—airport KS-7
Hill City Sch—school IL-6
**Hill City Township**—pop pl KS-7
Hill Cliff Mine—mine WA-9
Hillcoat—locale FL-3

Hillcoke—*other* PA-2
**Hill Corners**—*pop pl* NY-2
**Hill Country (subdivision)**—*pop pl* TN-4
**Hill Country Village**—*pop pl* TX-5
**Hill (County)**—*pop pl* TX-5
Hill County Courthouse—*hist pl* TX-5
Hill County Jail—*hist pl* TX-5
Hill County Wayside—*park* OR-9
Hill Cow Camp—*locale* CO-8
**Hill Craft Acres**—*pop pl* OH-6
*Hill Creek* AZ-5
*Hill Creek* AR-4
*Hill Creek* ID-8
*Hill Creek* MN-6
*Hill Creek* OR-9
*Hill Creek* PA-2
*Hill Creek* TX-5
*Hill Creek* VA-3
*Hill Creek* WA-9
Hill Creek—*locale* AR-4
Hill Creek—*stream* (2) AL-4
Hill Creek—*stream* (2) AK-9
Hill Creek—*stream* AZ-5
Hill Creek—*stream* (3) AR-4
Hill Creek—*stream* CA-9
Hill Creek—*stream* (4) CO-8
Hill Creek—*stream* (5) ID-8
Hill Creek—*stream* (3) IL-6
Hill Creek—*stream* IN-6
Hill Creek—*stream* KS-7
Hill Creek—*stream* ME-1
Hill Creek—*stream* (4) MI-6
Hill Creek—*stream* MN-6
Hill Creek—*stream* NE-7
Hill Creek—*stream* NY-2
Hill Creek—*stream* (8) OR-9
Hill Creek—*stream* PA-2
Hill Creek—*stream* SC-3
Hill Creek—*stream* (2) TN-4
Hill Creek—*stream* (7) TX-5
Hill Creek—*stream* UT-8
Hill Creek—*stream* (3) WA-9
Hill Creek—*stream* WV-2
Hill Creek—*stream* (2) WI-6
Hill Creek—*stream* (4) WY-8
Hill Creek Cave—*cave* TN-4
Hill Creek Ch—*church* (2) VA-3
Hill Creek Marina—*locale* AR-4
Hill Creek Mine (underground)—*mine* (3) AL-4
Hill Creek Point—*summit* UT-8
Hill Creek Ranger Station—*locale* UT-8
Hill Creek Rec Area—*park* AR-4
Hill Creek Youth Camp—*locale* UT-8
*Hillcrest* (3) IN-6
*Hillcrest* PA-2
Hillcrest—*CDP* PA-2
Hillcrest—*hist pl* GA-3
Hillcrest—*hist pl* KY-4
Hillcrest—*hist pl* NY-2
Hillcrest—*locale* AL-4
Hillcrest—*locale* CA-9
Hill Crest—*locale* CA-9
Hillcrest—*locale* ID-8
Hillcrest—*locale* OH-6
Hillcrest—*locale* TN-4
Hillcrest—*locale* TX-5
Hill Crest—*locale* VA-3
Hillcrest—*locale* WA-9
Hillcrest—*locale* WI-6
Hillcrest—*other* AR-4
**Hillcrest**—*pop pl* (2) AR-4
**Hillcrest**—*pop pl* CA-9
**Hillcrest**—*pop pl* CT-1
**Hillcrest**—*pop pl* DE-2
**Hillcrest**—*pop pl* DC-2
**Hillcrest**—*pop pl* GA-3
**Hillcrest**—*pop pl* (3) IL-6
**Hillcrest**—*pop pl* (6) IN-6
**Hillcrest**—*pop pl* KS-7
**Hillcrest**—*pop pl* KY-4
**Hillcrest**—*pop pl* MA-1
**Hillcrest**—*pop pl* (2) MI-6
**Hill Crest**—*pop pl* MO-7
**Hillcrest**—*pop pl* (2) NJ-2
**Hillcrest**—*pop pl* (3) NY-2
**Hill Crest**—*pop pl* NC-3
**Hillcrest**—*pop pl* (2) NC-3
**Hillcrest**—*pop pl* (5) OH-6
**Hill Crest**—*pop pl* PA-2
**Hillcrest**—*pop pl* PA-2
**Hill Crest**—*pop pl* PA-2
**Hillcrest**—*pop pl* (2) PA-2
**Hillcrest**—*pop pl* (2) SC-3
**Hillcrest**—*pop pl* (6) TN-4
**Hillcrest**—*pop pl* TX-5
**Hill Crest**—*pop pl* TX-5
**Hillcrest**—*pop pl* VA-3
**Hillcrest**—*pop pl* WV-2
Hillcrest—*post sta* CA-9
Hill Crest—*uninc pl* MD-2
Hillcrest—*uninc pl* (2) NJ-2
Hillcrest—*uninc pl* TX-5
Hillcrest Acad—*school* MN-6
Hillcrest Acad—*school* MS-4
**Hillcrest Acres**—*pop pl* MA-1
**Hillcrest Acres**—*pop pl* SC-3
**Hillcrest Acres (trailer park)**—*pop pl* DE-2
**Hillcrest Addition (subdivision)**—*pop pl* UT-8
Hillcrest-Allen Clinic and Hosp—*hist pl* GA-3
Hillcrest Apartment—*hist pl* IL-6
Hillcrest Apartments—*hist pl* UT-8
**Hillcrest Apts (subdivision)**—*pop pl* NC-3
Hillcrest Ave Sch—*school* NC-3
*Hillcrest Baptist Ch* AL-4
*Hillcrest Baptist Ch* TN-4
Hillcrest Baptist Ch—*church* AL-4
Hillcrest Baptist Ch—*church* FL-3
Hillcrest Baptist Ch—*church* IN-6
Hillcrest Baptist Ch—*church* (2) MS-4
Hill Crest Baptist Ch—*church* MO-7
Hillcrest Baptist Ch—*church* (2) TN-4
Hillcrest-Bellefont Methodist Ch—*church* DE-2
*Hillcrest-Beverly Nursing Institute* TN-4
Hillcrest Brook—*stream* IN-6
Hillcrest Cabana Club—*other* NY-2
Hillcrest Camp—*locale* WI-6
Hillcrest Canyon—*valley* CA-9
Hillcrest (CCD)—*cens area* GA-3
*Hillcrest Cem* TN-4
Hillcrest Cem—*cemetery* (6) AL-4
Hillcrest Cem—*cemetery* AR-4
Hillcrest Cem—*cemetery* CA-9
Hillcrest Cem—*cemetery* CO-8
Hill Crest Cem—*cemetery* GA-3
Hillcrest Cem—*cemetery* (5) GA-3
Hillcrest Cem—*cemetery* (2) ID-8
Hillcrest Cem—*cemetery* (2) IL-6
Hill Crest Cem—*cemetery* IN-6
Hillcrest Cem—*cemetery* (2) IN-6
Hill Crest Cem—*cemetery* IN-6
Hillcrest Cem—*cemetery* (2) IA-7
Hillcrest Cem—*cemetery* (3) KS-7
Hillcrest Cem—*cemetery* (3) KY-4
Hill Crest Cem—*cemetery* KY-4
Hillcrest Cem—*cemetery* (3) ME-1
Hillcrest Cem—*cemetery* (2) MA-1
Hillcrest Cem—*cemetery* (2) MI-6
Hillcrest Cem—*cemetery* (6) MN-6
Hillcrest Cem—*cemetery* (5) MS-4
Hillcrest Cem—*cemetery* (4) MO-7
Hillcrest Cem—*cemetery* (2) MT-8
Hillcrest Cem—*cemetery* (2) NE-7
Hillcrest Cem—*cemetery* NV-8
Hillcrest Cem—*cemetery* NH-1
Hillcrest Cem—*cemetery* NM-5
Hill Crest Cem—*cemetery* NY-2
Hillcrest Cem—*cemetery* (3) NY-2
Hill Crest Cem—*cemetery* NY-2
Hillcrest Cem—*cemetery* NY-2
Hill Crest Cem—*cemetery* NC-3
Hillcrest Cem—*cemetery* (5) NC-3
Hill Crest Cem—*cemetery* OH-6
Hillcrest Cem—*cemetery* OH-6
Hillcrest Cem—*cemetery* OK-5
Hillcrest Cem—*cemetery* (2) OR-9
Hillcrest Cem—*cemetery* (2) PA-2
Hillcrest Cem—*cemetery* SC-3
Hillcrest Cem—*cemetery* SD-7
Hillcrest Cem—*cemetery* TN-4
Hill Crest Cem—*cemetery* TN-4
Hillcrest Cem—*cemetery* TX-5
Hill Crest Cem—*cemetery* TX-5
Hillcrest Cem—*cemetery* (2) TX-5
Hill Crest Cem—*cemetery* TX-5
Hillcrest Cem—*cemetery* (4) TX-5
Hillcrest Cem—*cemetery* VT-1
Hillcrest Cem—*cemetery* VA-3
Hillcrest Cem—*cemetery* WA-9
Hillcrest Cem—*cemetery* WV-2
Hillcrest Cem—*cemetery* (8) WI-6
Hillcrest Cemetery—*hist pl* MS-4
**Hillcrest Center**—*pop pl* CA-9
Hillcrest Ch—*church* (3) AL-4
Hill Crest Ch—*church* AL-4
Hillcrest Ch—*church* AR-4
Hillcrest Ch—*church* (2) FL-3
Hillcrest Ch—*church* (2) GA-3
Hillcrest Ch—*church* IL-6
Hillcrest Ch—*church* (2) IN-6
Hillcrest Ch—*church* (2) KS-7
Hillcrest Ch—*church* KY-4
Hillcrest Ch—*church* (2) MI-6
Hillcrest Ch—*church* (5) MS-4
Hillcrest Ch—*church* NY-2
Hillcrest Ch—*church* (6) NC-3
Hillcrest Ch—*church* OH-6
Hillcrest Ch—*church* (4) SC-3
Hillcrest Ch—*church* (6) TN-4
Hill Crest Ch—*church* TX-5
Hillcrest Ch—*church* (4) TX-5
Hillcrest Ch—*church* VA-3
Hillcrest Ch—*church* WV-2
Hillcrest Chapel—*church* AR-4
Hillcrest Childrens Home—*building* OH-6
Hillcrest Childrens Home—*locale* DC-2
*Hillcrest Ch of Christ* MS-4
Hillcrest Ch of God—*church* FL-3
Hill Crest Christian Sch—*school* PA-2
Hillcrest Clinic—*locale* OH-6
Hillcrest Country Club—*locale* FL-3
Hillcrest Country Club—*locale* NE-7
Hillcrest Country Club—*other* AL-4
Hillcrest Country Club—*other* CA-9
Hillcrest Country Club—*other* ID-8
Hillcrest Country Club—*other* IL-6
Hillcrest Country Club—*other* IN-6
Hillcrest Country Club—*other* (2) IA-7
Hillcrest Country Club—*other* KS-7
Hillcrest Country Club—*other* MI-6
Hillcrest Country Club—*other* (2) MO-7
Hillcrest Country Club—*other* OH-6
Hillcrest Country Club—*other* OK-5
Hillcrest Country Club—*other* (2) TX-5
Hillcrest Country Club—*other* WI-6
Hillcrest Creek—*stream* IN-6
Hillcrest Creek—*stream* (2) OR-9
Hillcrest Detention Home—*building* (2) CA-9
Hillcrest Drive Sch—*school* CA-9
*Hillcrest Elem Sch* TN-4
Hillcrest Elem Sch—*school* FL-3
Hillcrest Elem Sch—*school* IN-6
Hillcrest Elem Sch—*school* KS-7
Hillcrest Elem Sch—*school* MO-7
Hillcrest Elem Sch—*school* NC-3
Hillcrest Elem Sch—*school* (2) PA-2
Hillcrest Elem Sch—*school* (2) TN-4
Hill Crest Estate—*locale* PA-2
**Hillcrest Estates**—*pop pl* TN-4
**Hillcrest Estates**—*pop pl* VA-3
**Hillcrest Farms (subdivision)**—*pop pl* NC-3
**Hillcrest Farm (subdivision)**—*pop pl* NC-3
Hillcrest Fire Control Station—*locale* CA-9
Hillcrest Floral Gardens—*cemetery* OK-5
Hillcrest Garden ( Cemetery)—*cemetery* AL-4
Hillcrest Garden of Memory Cem—*cemetery* TX-5
**Hillcrest Gardens**—*pop pl* VA-3
*Hillcrest Gardens Cem* AL-4
Hillcrest Golf and Country Club—*locale* TN-4
Hillcrest Golf Club—*locale* NC-3
Hillcrest Golf Club—*other* MN-6
Hillcrest Golf Course—*other* AZ-5
Hill Crest Golf Course—*other* IL-6
Hillcrest Golf Course—*other* TX-5
Hillcrest Grange—*locale* PA-2
Hillcrest Gun Club—*other* CA-9
**Hillcrest Heights**—*pop pl* FL-3
**Hillcrest Heights**—*pop pl* (2) MD-2
**Hillcrest Heights**—*pop pl* SC-3
Hillcrest Heights Sch—*school* MD-2
**Hillcrest Heights Subdivision**—*pop pl* UT-8
Hillcrest (historical)—*locale* SD-7
Hillcrest Hosp—*hospital* CA-9
Hillcrest Hosp—*hospital* IA-7
Hillcrest Hosp—*hospital* MA-1
Hillcrest Hosp—*hospital* (2) OK-5
Hillcrest HS—*school* AL-4
Hillcrest HS—*school* MO-7
Hillcrest HS—*school* TN-4
Hillcrest HS—*school* TX-5
Hillcrest HS—*school* UT-8
Hillcrest JHS—*school* KS-7
Hillcrest JHS—*school* UT-8
Hillcrest Lake—*reservoir* PA-2
*Hillcrest Manor* NV-8
Hillcrest Medical Nursing Institute—*hospital* TN-4
Hillcrest Memorial Cem—*cemetery* FL-3
Hillcrest Memorial Cem—*cemetery* MD-2
Hillcrest Memorial Cem—*cemetery* OR-9
Hill Crest Memorial Cem—*cemetery* TN-4
Hillcrest Memorial Gardens—*cemetery* AL-4
Hillcrest Memorial Gardens—*cemetery* (2) FL-3
Hillcrest Memorial Gardens—*cemetery* ID-8
Hillcrest Memorial Gardens—*cemetery* MI-6
Hillcrest Memorial Gardens—*cemetery* MN-6
Hillcrest Memorial Gardens—*cemetery* MS-4
Hillcrest Memorial Gardens—*cemetery* MO-7
Hillcrest Memorial Gardens—*cemetery* (2) NC-3
Hillcrest Memorial Gardens—*cemetery* TN-4
Hillcrest Memorial Gardens—*cemetery* TX-5
Hillcrest Memorial Gardens—*cemetery* WV-2
Hillcrest Memorial Gardens Cem—*cemetery* NM-5
Hillcrest Memorial Gardens Cem—*cemetery* TN-4
Hillcrest Memorial Gardens (Cemetery)—*cemetery* SC-3
Hillcrest Memorial Hosp—*hospital* TX-5
Hillcrest Memorial Park—*cemetery* FL-3
Hillcrest Memorial Park—*cemetery* IA-7
Hillcrest Memorial Park—*cemetery* KS-7
Hillcrest Memorial Park—*cemetery* KY-4
Hillcrest Memorial Park—*cemetery* LA-4
Hillcrest Memorial Park—*cemetery* MD-2
Hill Crest Memorial Park—*cemetery* NJ-2
Hillcrest Memorial Park—*cemetery* PA-2
Hillcrest Memorial Park—*cemetery* SC-3
Hillcrest Memorial Park—*cemetery* TX-5
Hillcrest Memorial Park—*cemetery* VA-3
Hillcrest Memorial Park—*locale* TX-5
Hillcrest Memorial Park Cem—*cemetery* GA-3
Hillcrest Memorial Park Cem—*cemetery* IL-6
Hillcrest Memorial Park Cem—*cemetery* MI-6
Hillcrest Memorial Park (Cemetery)—*cemetery* TX-5
Hillcrest Memory Gardens—*cemetery* VA-3
*Hillcrest Missionary Baptist Church* MS-4
**Hillcrest Mobile Home Subdivision**—*pop pl* NC-3
Hillcrest MS—*school* NC-3
*Hillcrest Nursing Home* TN-4
Hillcrest Observation Point—*locale* TX-5
**Hillcrest Orchard**—*pop pl* MI-6
Hillcrest Orchard Hist Dist—*hist pl* OR-9
Hillcrest Park—*park* CA-9
Hillcrest Park—*park* IA-7
Hillcrest Park—*park* KS-7
Hillcrest Park—*park* MD-2
Hillcrest Park—*park* MN-6
Hillcrest Park—*park* MO-7
Hillcrest Park—*park* NM-5
Hillcrest Park—*park* OH-6
Hillcrest Park—*park* OK-5
Hillcrest Park—*park* PA-2
Hillcrest Park—*park* SD-7
Hillcrest Park—*park* TX-5
Hillcrest Park—*park* WA-9
**Hillcrest Park**—*pop pl* CA-9
Hillcrest Park Cem—*cemetery* MA-1
Hillcrest Park Cem—*cemetery* TX-5
Hillcrest Park Ch—*church* TX-5
**Hillcrest Park Subdivision**—*pop pl* UT-8
Hillcrest Point—*summit* CA-9
Hillcrest Pond—*reservoir* AL-4
*Hillcrest Pond Number One* AL-4
*Hillcrest Pond Number Two* AL-4
Hillcrest Pond Number 1 Dam—*dam* AL-4
Hillcrest Pond Number 2 Dam—*dam* AL-4
Hillcrest Ponds—*reservoir* AL-4
Hillcrest Ranch—*locale* TX-5
Hillcrest Receiving Home—*building* CA-9
Hillcrest Rsvr—*reservoir* CO-8
Hillcrest Sanitarium—*hospital* AL-4
Hillcrest Sanitarium—*hospital* WV-2
*Hill Crest Sch* IN-6
*Hillcrest Sch* PA-2
*Hill Crest Sch* TN-4
Hillcrest Sch—*school* AL-4
Hillcrest Sch—*school* (8) CA-9
Hillcrest Sch—*school* (2) CO-8
Hillcrest Sch—*school* (2) FL-3
Hillcrest Sch—*school* (2) GA-3
Hillcrest Sch—*school* ID-8
Hill Crest Sch—*school* IL-6
Hillcrest Sch—*school* (3) IL-6
Hillcrest Sch—*school* IN-6
Hillcrest Sch—*school* (2) KS-7
Hillcrest Sch—*school* MA-1
Hillcrest Sch—*school* (7) MI-6
Hillcrest Sch—*school* MN-6
Hillcrest Sch—*school* MS-4
Hillcrest Sch—*school* MO-7
Hill Crest Sch—*school* MO-7
Hillcrest Sch—*school* NE-7
Hill Crest Sch—*school* NE-7
Hillcrest Sch—*school* NE-7
Hillcrest Sch—*school* (2) NJ-2
Hillcrest Sch—*school* (2) OH-6
Hillcrest Sch—*school* (2) OK-5
Hillcrest Sch—*school* (2) OR-9
Hillcrest Sch—*school* (2) PA-2
Hillcrest Sch—*school* (2) SC-3
Hillcrest Sch—*school* (2) SD-7
Hillcrest Sch—*school* (2) TN-4
Hillcrest Sch—*school* (3) TX-5
Hillcrest Sch—*school* (2) UT-8
Hillcrest Sch—*school* VA-3
Hillcrest Sch—*school* WA-9
Hillcrest Sch—*school* (4) WI-6
Hill Crest Sch—*school* WI-6
Hillcrest Sch—*school* (2) WI-6
Hillcrest Sch—*school* WY-8
Hillcrest Sch (abandoned)—*school* MO-7
Hillcrest Sch (historical)—*school* TN-4
Hillcrest Shop Ctr—*locale* KS-7
Hillcrest Shop Ctr—*locale* UT-8
Hillcrest Special Education Sch—*school* FL-3
Hillcrest Special Education Sch—*school* IN-6
Hillcrest Spring—*spring* WY-8
**Hillcrest (subdivision)**—*pop pl* (3) AL-4
**Hillcrest (subdivision)**—*pop pl* (2) MS-4
**Hillcrest (subdivision)**—*pop pl* (3) NC-3
**Hillcrest (subdivision)**—*pop pl* TN-4
**Hillcrest Subdivision**—*pop pl* UT-8
**Hillcrest Terrace**—*pop pl* IN-6
*Hillcrest (Trailer Park)* IL-6
Hillcrest United Methodist Ch—*church* TN-4
Hillcrest West Sch—*school* CO-8
**Hillcroft**—*pop pl* PA-2
*Hilldale* UT-8
Hilldale—*locale* KS-7
Hilldale—*locale* MO-7
**Hilldale**—*pop pl* DE-2
**Hilldale**—*pop pl* (3) PA-2
**Hilldale**—*pop pl* WV-2
Hilldale—*uninc pl* FL-3
Hilldale—*uninc pl* TN-4
Hilldale—*uninc pl* WI-6
Hilldale Baptist Ch—*church* AL-4
Hill Dale Cem—*cemetery* IN-6
Hilldale Cem—*cemetery* KY-4
Hilldale Cem—*cemetery* MA-1
Hilldale Cem—*cemetery* NE-7
Hilldale Ch—*church* AL-4
Hilldale Ch—*church* KY-4
Hilldale Ch—*church* MO-7
Hilldale Colony—*locale* MT-8
**Hilldale Estates**—*pop pl* TN-4
Hilldale Farm Lake—*reservoir* AL-4
Hilldale Farm Lake Dam—*dam* AL-4
Hill & Dale Mall—*locale* MA-1
Hilldale Pond—*lake* NY-2
Hilldale Sch—*school* CA-9
Hilldale Sch—*school* OK-5
Hilldale South—*locale* KS-7
*Hilldale Villages* IL-6
Hill Dam—*dam* AL-4
Hill Dannatt Bowers Cem—*cemetery* IA-7
Hill Dee Park—*park* MN-6
Hill Detention—*reservoir* AZ-5
**Hill Distrct**—*pop pl* PA-2
Hill Ditch—*canal* (2) IN-6
Hill Ditch—*canal* (3) OH-6
Hill Ditch—*canal* WY-8
Hill Ditch No. 1—*canal* CO-8
Hill Ditch No. 2—*canal* CO-8
Hill Drain—*canal* (2) MI-6
Hill Drain—*stream* MI-6
Hill Draw—*valley* WY-8
Hilleary, William, House—*hist pl* MD-2
Hillebrands Lake—*lake* SD-7
**Hillebrandt**—*pop pl* TX-5
Hillebrandt Bayou—*stream* TX-5
Hillebrandt Cem—*cemetery* TX-5
*Hillebrant Bayou* TX-5
Hilledgeville Cem—*cemetery* IA-7
Hillegas Run—*stream* PA-2
Hillegass—*locale* PA-2
Hillel Acad—*school* CO-8
Hille Lake—*lake* WA-9
Hillel Sch—*school* MI-6
Hillel Sch—*school* NY-2
Hillel Sch of Tampa—*school* FL-3
**Hillemann**—*pop pl* AR-4
Hillen—*uninc pl* MD-2
Hillenbrand Industries Airp—*airport* IN-6
Hillenburg Airp—*airport* IN-6
Hillenburg Cem—*cemetery* IN-6
Hillen Canyon—*valley* NV-8
**Hillendale**—*pop pl* DE-2
**Hillendale**—*pop pl* MD-2
Hillendale Country Club—*other* MD-2
**Hillendale Farms**—*pop pl* MD-2
Hillendale Golf Course—*other* MD-2
**Hillendale Park**—*pop pl* MD-2
**Hillendale (subdivision)**—*pop pl* NC-3
Hill End Sch (abandoned)—*school* PA-2
Hillen Junction—*uninc pl* MD-2
Hillen Station—*locale* MD-2
**Hiller**—*pop pl* PA-2
Hiller, Col. Hiram M., House—*hist pl* MO-7
**Hillerage**—*pop pl* NE-7
Hiller Bldg—*hist pl* IA-7
*Hiller Brook* PA-2
Hiller Brook—*stream* NY-2
Hiller Canyon—*valley* NV-8
Hiller Cove—*cove* MA-1
Hiller Cove Marshes—*swamp* MA-1
Hiller Elem Sch—*school* PA-2
Hillerest Sch—*school* WI-6
Hiller House—*hist pl* TX-5
**Hillerman**—*pop pl* IL-6
Hillerman Ch—*church* IL-6
Hillerman (Election Precinct)—*fmr MCD* IL-6
Hiller Mtns—*range* NV-8
Hiller Park Rec Area—*park* MS-4
Hiller Ridge—*ridge* ME-1
Hillers, Mount—*summit* UT-8
Hillers Butte—*summit* AZ-5
Hillers Cem—*cemetery* MI-6
Hiller Sch—*school* IL-6
Hiller Sch—*school* MI-6
Hiller Sch—*school* NY-2
*Hillers Cove* MA-1
Hillers Creek—*stream* MO-7
Hillers Sch—*school* NJ-2
Hiller Street Cem—*cemetery* NY-2
Hillert Cem—*cemetery* TX-5
*Hillery* GA-3
**Hillery**—*pop pl* IL-6
Hillery Chapel—*church* (2) TX-5
Hillery Creek—*channel* GA-3
Hillery Creek—*stream* IL-6
Hillerys Cove—*bay* NC-3
Hillery Slough—*channel* GA-3
Hilles Lake—*lake* ND-7
Hillesland Lake—*lake* ND-7
Hillestad Cem—*cemetery* SD-7
Hille State Game Mngmt Area—*park* ND-7
Hilley Branch—*stream* AL-4
Hilley Point—*cape* AL-4
*Hill Family Cemetery* AL-4
Hill Farm—*locale* PA-2
*Hillfield Baptist Church* TN-4
Hillfield Catholic Chapel—*church* UT-8
Hillfield Ch—*church* TN-4
Hillfield Hollow—*valley* WV-2
Hillfield Protestant Chapel—*church* UT-8
Hill Field Sch—*school* UT-8
Hillfield Sch (historical)—*school* TN-4
Hill Fifteen—*summit* IL-6
Hill Fifty-seven—*summit* MT-8
Hillforest (Forest Hill)—*hist pl* IN-6
Hill Fork—*stream* WV-2
Hill Gap—*gap* TN-4
Hillgate Shop Ctr—*locale* UT-8
**Hill Gate Subdivision**—*pop pl* UT-8
Hillger Sch—*school* MI-6
**Hillgirt**—*pop pl* NC-3
*Hillgoss Lake* MN-6
Hill Grade Sch—*hist pl* KS-7
*Hillgrove* CA-9
Hillgrove—*locale* KY-4
Hill Grove—*locale* VA-3
**Hillgrove**—*pop pl* CA-9
**Hillgrove**—*pop pl* IN-6
**Hill Grove**—*pop pl* OH-6
**Hillgrove**—*pop pl* WA-9
Hillgrove Cem—*cemetery* IN-6
Hill Grove Cem—*cemetery* (2) OH-6
Hill Grove Cem—*cemetery* PA-2
Hill Grove Cem—*cemetery* WI-6
Hillgrove Ch—*church* IN-6
Hill Grove Ch—*church* NC-3
Hill Grove Ch—*church* VA-3
Hillgrove Filtration Park—*locale* NC-3
Hillgrove Park—*park* MI-6
Hillgrove Sch—*school* CA-9
Hillgrove Sch—*school* PA-2
Hill Grove Sch—*school* TN-4
Hill Grove Sch—*school* (2) WV-2
Hill Grove Sch—*school* WI-6
Hill Gulch—*valley* AK-9
Hill Gulch—*valley* (2) CO-8
Hill H—*summit* WI-6
Hill Hall at Savannah State College—*hist pl* GA-3
*Hillham* TN-4
**Hillham**—*pop pl* IN-6
Hill-Hance House—*hist pl* TN-4
Hillhaven Convalescent Center—*hospital* TN-4
**Hillhaven Estates Subdivision**—*pop pl* UT-8
Hill Haven Memory Gardens—*cemetery* KY-4
**Hillhead**—*pop pl* SD-7
**Hill (Hills Prairie)**—*pop pl* TX-5
Hill Hole—*lake* TX-5
Hill Hollow—*valley* AR-4
Hill Hollow—*valley* (2) KY-4
Hill Hollow—*valley* MO-7
Hill Hollow—*valley* NC-3
Hill Hollow—*valley* PA-2
Hill Hollow—*valley* (2) TN-4
Hill Hotel—*hist pl* NE-7
*Hillhouse* MO-7
Hill House—*hist pl* AZ-5
Hill House—*hist pl* MD-2
Hill House—*hist pl* PA-2
Hillhouse—*locale* CA-9
**Hillhouse**—*pop pl* MS-4
*Hillhouse Addition* MO-7
**Hillhouse Addition**—*pop pl* MO-7
**Hillhouse Addition (subdivision)**—*pop pl* MO-7
Hillhouse Ave Hist Dist—*hist pl* CT-1
Hillhouse Branch—*stream* MO-7
Hillhouse Canyon—*valley* ID-8
Hillhouse Cem—*cemetery* AR-4
Hillhouse Cem—*cemetery* MS-4
Hillhouse Cem—*cemetery* MO-7
Hillhouse Drift Mine (underground)—*mine* AL-4
Hillhouse Hill—*summit* GA-3
Hillhouse Hollow—*valley* MO-7
Hillhouse HS—*school* CT-1
*Hillhouse Island* NY-2
Hillhouse Lake—*lake* AL-4
*Hillhouse Lake Dam* AL-4
Hillhouse Landing—*locale* MS-4
Hillhouse Post Office (historical)—*building* MS-4
Hillhouse Sch—*school* IL-6
Hill-Howard House—*hist pl* TX-5
Hill HS—*school* CA-9
Hill HS—*school* MI-6
Hill HS—*school* MN-6
Hill HS—*school* MS-4
Hillhurst—*locale* WA-9
Hillhurst Lake—*lake* WA-9
Hillhurst Park—*park* NY-2
Hillian Store (historical)—*locale* AL-4
*Hilliard* NJ-2
*Hilliard* PA-2
Hilliard—*locale* AL-4
**Hilliard**—*pop pl* FL-3
**Hilliard**—*pop pl* MO-7
**Hilliard**—*pop pl* NJ-2
**Hilliard**—*pop pl* OH-6
**Hilliard**—*pop pl* WY-8
Hilliard—*uninc pl* TN-4
Hilliard, David, House—*hist pl* KY-4
Hilliard AME Zion Ch—*church* AL-4
Hilliard Apartment Bldg—*hist pl* OH-6
Hilliard Branch—*stream* TN-4
Hilliard Brook—*stream* NH-1
Hilliard Canal—*canal* UT-8
Hilliard Cem—*cemetery* CT-1
Hilliard Cem—*cemetery* NC-3
Hilliard Coulee—*valley* MT-8
Hilliard Creek—*stream* TX-5
Hilliard Drain—*canal* MI-6
Hilliard East Fork Canal—*canal* UT-8
Hilliard East Fork Canal—*canal* WY-8
Hilliard Elem Sch—*school* FL-3
Hilliard Falls—*falls* TN-4
Hilliard Flat—*flat* WY-8
Hilliard House—*hist pl* MS-4
Hilliard Island—*island* GA-3
Hilliard Junior-Senior HS—*school* FL-3
*Hilliard Knob* MA-1
Hilliard Methodist Episcopal Church—*hist pl* OH-6
Hilliard Pond—*lake* NH-1
Hilliard Pond—*reservoir* VA-3
Hilliard Ranch—*locale* CA-9
*Hilliards* OH-6
*Hilliard's* PA-2
**Hilliards**—*pop pl* MI-6
**Hilliards**—*pop pl* PA-2
Hilliard Sch—*school* (2) OH-6
Hilliard Sch—*school* (2) TX-5
Hilliard Sch (historical)—*school* MS-4
Hilliard Sch (historical)—*school* TN-4
Hilliards Grove Ch—*church* NC-3
*Hilliards Knob* MA-1
Hilliards Mill (historical)—*locale* TN-4
*Hilliards Millpond* NC-3
Hilliards Pond—*lake* CT-1
Hilliards Pond—*lake* GA-3
Hilliards (RR name for Hilliard)—*other* OH-6
Hilliard Station Ch—*church* GA-3
Hilliardston—*locale* NC-3
*Hilliardsville* AL-4
Hilliardsville Post Office (historical)—*building* AL-4
Hilliardville—*locale* CT-1
Hilliardville—*locale* FL-3
Hilliard Westside Canal—*canal* UT-8
Hilliard Westside Canal—*canal* WY-8
**Hilliar (Township of)**—*pop pl* OH-6
*Hilliby Creek* OK-5
Hilliby Creek—*stream* OK-5
*Hilligross Lake* MN-6
Hilliker Gulch—*valley* OR-9
Hillingdon Ranch—*locale* TX-5
Hillington Cem—*cemetery* NY-2
Hillin Ranch—*locale* TX-5
Hill Institute—*school* MA-1
Hill Interchange—*crossing* ND-7
**Hillisburg**—*pop pl* IN-6
Hillis Cem—*cemetery* AR-4
Hillis Cem—*cemetery* MO-7
Hillis Cem—*cemetery* (2) TN-4
Hillis (census name for Hillis Terrace)—*CDP* NY-2
**Hillis (historical)**—*pop pl* TN-4
Hillis Holes—*cave* TN-4
Hillis Lake—*lake* WI-6
Hill Island—*island* AK-9
Hill Island—*island* MI-6
Hill Island—*island* PA-2
Hill Island—*island* SC-3
Hillis Pond—*reservoir* GA-3
Hillis Sch—*school* IL-6
Hillis Sch—*school* IA-7
**Hillister**—*pop pl* TX-5
**Hillis Terrace (census name Hillis)**—*pop pl* NY-2
**Hillje**—*pop pl* TX-5
Hillje Oil Field—*oilfield* TX-5
Hill JHS—*school* CA-9
Hill JHS—*school* CO-8
Hill JHS—*school* IL-6
Hill JHS—*school* ND-7
Hill-Johnson Rsvr—*reservoir* OR-9
Hill Junior Coll—*school* TX-5
Hill-Kinder Mound—*hist pl* OH-6
Hill King Ch—*church* NC-3
Hill Knob—*summit* KY-4
Hill-Kurtz House—*hist pl* GA-3
*Hill Lake* AR-4
*Hill Lake* CT-1
*Hill Lake* MI-6
*Hill Lake* MN-6
Hill Lake—*lake* (2) AR-4
Hill Lake—*lake* CO-8
Hill Lake—*lake* IN-6
Hill Lake—*lake* (3) MI-6
Hill Lake—*lake* (5) MN-6
Hill Lake—*lake* MS-4
Hill Lake—*lake* NE-7
Hill Lake—*lake* SD-7
Hill Lake—*lake* (2) TX-5
Hill Lake—*lake* (2) WA-9
Hill Lake—*lake* (3) WI-6
Hill Lake—*reservoir* AL-4
Hill Lake—*reservoir* GA-3
Hill Lake—*reservoir* NY-2
Hill Lake—*reservoir* NC-3
Hill Lake—*reservoir* TN-4
Hill Lake—*reservoir* TX-5
Hill Lake Cem—*cemetery* MN-6
Hill Lake Creek—*stream* IL-6
Hill Lake Dam—*dam* MS-4
Hill Lake Dam—*dam* NC-3
Hill Lake Number One—*reservoir* TN-4
Hill Lake Number One Dam—*dam* TN-4
Hill Lake Number Two—*reservoir* AL-4
Hill Lakes—*lake* OH-6
**Hill Lake (Township of)**—*pop pl* MN-6
Hill Landing—*locale* VA-3
Hill-Lassonde House—*hist pl* NH-1
Hill Lateral—*canal* NM-5
Hill Lookout Tower—*tower* FL-3
Hillmaid—*locale* CA-9
Hillman—*locale* GA-3
Hillman—*locale* ME-1
Hillman—*locale* MS-4
Hillman—*locale* MT-8
Hillman—*locale* PA-2
**Hillman**—*pop pl* AL-4
**Hillman**—*pop pl* MI-6
**Hillman**—*pop pl* MN-6
**Hillman**—*pop pl* OH-6
Hillman-Berry Park—*park* MS-4
Hillman Bluff—*cliff* KY-4
Hillman Bridge—*bridge* ND-7
Hillman Cem—*cemetery* LA-4
Hillman Cem—*cemetery* ME-1
Hillman Cem—*cemetery* MI-6
Hillman Cem—*cemetery* MS-4
Hillman Cem—*cemetery* TX-5
Hillman Cem—*cemetery* (3) VA-3
Hillman Ch—*church* MN-6
Hillman Ch—*church* NJ-2
Hillman Coll (historical)—*school* MS-4
Hillman Creek—*stream* (2) ID-8
Hillman Creek—*stream* MN-6
Hillman Dead River—*lake* MS-4

Hillman Ditch—*canal* ... IN-6
Hillman Ferry Camping Area—*locale* ... KY-4
Hillman Ferry (historical)—*locale* ... AL-4
Hillman Fish Pond—*lake* ... WA-9
**Hillman Gardens**—*pop pl* ... AL-4
Hillman Hills—*ridge* ... MS-4
Hillman Hollow—*valley* ... UT-8
Hillman Hosp House—*hist pl* ... NJ-2
*Hillman Hospital* ... AL-4
Hillman Ice Pond—*reservoir* ... MA-1
Hillman Ice Pond Dam—*dam* ... MA-1
Hillman Lake—*lake* ... MI-6
Hillman Lake—*lake* ... WI-6
Hillman Mine—*mine* ... ID-8
*Hillman Park* ... CO-8
**Hillman Park**—*pop pl* ... AL-4
Hillman Peak—*summit* ... OR-9
Hillman Pond—*lake* ... AL-4
Hillman Pond—*reservoir* ... AR-4
Hillman Ranch—*locale* ... CA-9
Hillman Ridge—*ridge* ... OH-6
Hillman Ridge Cem—*cemetery* ... OH-6
Hillman Sch—*school* ... MI-6
*Hillmans Ferry* ... AL-4
Hill Mansion—*hist pl* ... VA-3
Hillmans Island (historical)—*island* ... AL-4
Hillmans Landing—*locale* ... MS-4
Hillman State Park—*park* ... PA-2
*Hillmanton* ... NJ-2
**Hillman (Township of)**—*pop pl* ... MI-6
**Hillman (Township of)**—*pop pl* (2) ... MN-6
*Hillmar* ... CA-9
Hill Marsh—*swamp* ... VA-3
**Hillmead**—*pop pl* ... MD-2
**Hillmeade**—*pop pl* ... MD-2
Hillmeade Lookout Tower—*locale* ... MD-2
**Hillmeade Manor**—*pop pl* ... MD-2
Hill Meadow—*flat* ... MT-8
Hill Meadow—*swamp* ... NE-7
Hill Meadow Cem—*cemetery* ... MA-1
Hill Memorial—*hist pl* ... NJ-2
Hill Memorial Ch—*church* ... LA-4
Hill Memorial Park—*cemetery* ... TX-5
**Hill (Middletown State Hospital)**—*pop pl* ... NY-2
Hill Military Acad—*school* ... OR-9
Hill Mine—*mine* ... IL-6
Hillmons Grove Ch—*church* ... NC-3
Hillmont—*hist pl* ... NC-3
**Hillmont Heights (subdivision)**—*pop pl* ... TN-4
**Hillmont (subdivision)**—*pop pl* ... AL-4
Hillmoor Country Club—*other* ... WI-6
Hill Mtn—*summit* (2) ... AL-4
**Hill N Dale**—*pop pl* ... FL-3
**Hill-n-Dale**—*pop pl* ... PA-2
**Hill-N-Dale (subdivision)**—*pop pl* ... TN-4
Hill No 8—*summit* ... NY-2
**Hill Number 1**—*pop pl* ... AL-4
**Hill Number 2**—*pop pl* ... AL-4
Hillocher Lake—*lake* ... MI-6
Hillockburn Guard Station—*locale* ... OR-9
Hillockburn Spring—*spring* ... OR-9
Hillock Dam—*dam* ... PA-2
Hill Of Gold Mine—*mine* ... NV-8
*Hill of Hoath Plantation* ... AL-4
*Hill of Hoth Plantation* ... AL-4
*Hill of Howth Plantation* ... AL-4
Hill of Knowledge Sch (historical)—*school* ... AL-4
Hill of Pines—*summit* ... NY-2
Hill of Rest Cem—*cemetery* ... FL-3
Hill of Rest Cem—*cemetery* ... TX-5
Hill of Zion Ch—*church* ... MS-4
Hill Oil Field—*oilfield* ... TX-5
Hill One—*summit* ... AZ-5
Hill Opening Mine (underground)—*mine* ... AL-4
Hill Orchard Cem—*cemetery* ... TN-4
*Hillover Airport* ... PA-2
Hillover/Sekol Airp—*airport* ... PA-2
Hill Park—*park* ... GA-3
Hill Park—*park* ... IL-6
Hill Park—*park* ... MO-7
Hill Park—*park* (3) ... TX-5
Hill Pasture—*flat* ... ID-8
Hill Pasture Bottom Windmill—*locale* ... NM-5
Hill Pasture Middle Windmill—*locale* ... NM-5
Hill Pasture Point—*cape* ... ID-8
Hill Pasture Top Windmill—*locale* ... NM-5
Hill-Physick House—*hist pl* ... PA-2
Hill-Physick-Keith House—*building* ... PA-2
Hillpine Park—*park* ... GA-3
Hill Pippin Cem—*cemetery* ... TX-5
Hill Place Cem—*cemetery* ... AL-4
Hill-Place Lake—*reservoir* ... IN-6
*Hill Plantation* ... MS-4
Hill Point—*cape* ... AK-9
Hill Point—*cape* ... MD-2
Hill Point—*cape* ... MI-6
Hill Point—*cape* ... MN-6
Hill Point—*cape* ... VT-1
Hill Point—*cape* ... VA-3
**Hill Point**—*pop pl* ... WI-6
**Hillpoint**—*pop pl* ... WI-6
Hill Point—*summit* ... AK-9
Hill Point Creek—*stream* ... WI-6
*Hill Pond* ... IN-6
*Hill Pond* ... NY-2
Hill Pond—*lake* ... ME-1
Hill Pond—*reservoir* ... AL-4
Hill Pond—*reservoir* ... MA-1
Hill Pond—*reservoir* ... MO-7
Hill Pond Dam—*dam* ... AL-4
Hill Pond Dam—*dam* ... MA-1
Hill Post Office (historical)—*building* (2) ... AL-4
Hillpot Cem—*cemetery* ... PA-2
Hill Prairie Cem—*cemetery* ... IL-6
Hill Prong Badger Creek—*stream* ... WY-8
Hill Pumping Station—*other* ... PA-2
Hill Push Mine (underground)—*mine* ... AL-4
Hill Ranch—*locale* (2) ... CA-9
Hill Ranch—*locale* ... CO-8
Hill Ranch—*locale* ... MT-8
Hill Ranch—*locale* (2) ... NE-7
Hill Ranch—*locale* (2) ... NM-5
Hill Ranch—*locale* ... OR-9
Hill Ranch—*locale* (2) ... TX-5
Hill Ranch—*locale* (2) ... WY-8
Hill Ranch Canyon—*valley* ... NV-8
Hill Ranch Dam—*dam* ... AL-4
Hill Ranch Pond—*reservoir* ... AL-4
*Hill Reformed Church* ... PA-2
Hillrest Cem—*cemetery* ... ME-1
Hill Ridge—*ridge* ... ME-1
Hill Ridge—*ridge* ... VA-3
Hill Ridge Ch—*church* ... LA-4
Hill Ridge Ch—*church* ... VA-3
**Hill Ridge Development (subdivision)**—*pop pl* ... SD-7
**Hillrise (subdivision)**—*pop pl* ... TN-4
*Hill River* ... MN-6
Hill River—*stream* (2) ... MN-6
Hill River Ditch—*canal* ... MN-6
Hill River Lake—*lake* ... MN-6
Hill River State For—*forest* ... MN-6
Hill River State Wildlife Mngmt Area—*park* ... MN-6
**Hill River (Township of)**—*pop pl* ... MN-6
Hi!l Road Ch—*church* ... MI-6
Hill Road Ruin (LA 55833)—*hist pl* ... NM-5
**Hillrose**—*pop pl* ... CO-8
**Hillrose**—*pop pl* ... TN-4
Hill Rsvr—*reservoir* ... MA-1
Hill Rsvr—*reservoir* ... MT-8
Hill Rsvr—*reservoir* ... OR-9
Hill Rsvr—*reservoir* (2) ... WY-8
Hill Rsvr Number One—*reservoir* ... OR-9
Hill Rsvr Number Two—*reservoir* ... OR-9
Hill Run—*stream* ... MD-2
Hill Run—*stream* (2) ... PA-2
Hill Run—*stream* ... WV-2
*Hill Run Reservoir* ... PA-2
Hill-Rupp Site—*hist pl* ... NE-7
*Hills* ... PA-2
Hills—*locale* ... OH-6
Hills—*locale* ... OR-9
Hills—*locale* ... TX-5
Hills—*locale* ... UT-8
**Hills**—*pop pl* ... GA-3
**Hills**—*pop pl* ... IA-7
**Hills**—*pop pl* ... ME-1
**Hills**—*pop pl* ... MN-6
**Hills**—*pop pl* ... NC-3
Hills, Ebenezer, Jr., Farmhouse—*hist pl* ... NY-2
Hills, Lake—*reservoir* ... NC-3
**Hills, Lake in the**—*pop pl* ... IL-6
Hills, Lake Of The—*lake* ... WI-6
Hills, Lake of the—*reservoir* ... MI-6
Hills, Lewis S., House—*hist pl* ... UT-8
Hills, The—*range* ... GA-3
Hills, The—*range* ... RI-1
Hills, W. S., Commercial Structure—*hist pl* ... TX-5
Hill's Acad—*hist pl* ... CT-1
Hills Acad (historical)—*school* ... TN-4
**Hills And Dales**—*pop pl* ... IN-6
**Hills and Dales**—*pop pl* ... KY-4
**Hills and Dales**—*pop pl* ... MI-6
**Hills and Dales**—*pop pl* ... OH-6
**Hills and Dales**—*pop pl* ... TN-4
**Hills And Dales**—*pop pl* ... TX-5
Hills And Dales Park—*park* ... OH-6
Hill Savannah Ditch—*stream* ... DE-2
Hills Bay—*bay* ... VA-3
*Hills Beach* ... ME-1
Hills Beach—*beach* ... ME-1
**Hills Beach**—*pop pl* ... ME-1
*Hillsboro* ... AL-4
*Hillsboro* ... NJ-2
*Hillsboro* ... NC-3
*Hillsboro* ... OH-6
*Hillsboro* ... TN-4
Hillsboro—*locale* ... AL-4
Hillsboro—*locale* ... CO-8
Hillsboro—*locale* ... MT-8
Hillsboro—*locale* ... NY-2
Hillsboro—*locale* ... PA-2
Hillsboro—*other* ... TN-4
**Hillsboro**—*pop pl* ... AL-4
**Hillsboro**—*pop pl* ... AR-4
**Hillsboro**—*pop pl* ... GA-3
**Hillsboro**—*pop pl* ... IL-6
**Hillsboro**—*pop pl* (2) ... IN-6
**Hillsboro**—*pop pl* (2) ... IA-7
**Hillsboro**—*pop pl* ... KS-7
**Hillsboro**—*pop pl* ... KY-4
**Hillsboro**—*pop pl* ... MD-2
**Hillsboro**—*pop pl* ... MS-4
**Hillsboro**—*pop pl* ... MO-7
**Hillsboro**—*pop pl* ... NH-1
**Hillsboro**—*pop pl* ... NM-5
**Hillsboro**—*pop pl* ... ND-7
**Hillsboro**—*pop pl* ... OH-6
**Hillsboro**—*pop pl* ... OR-9
**Hillsboro**—*pop pl* ... PA-2
**Hillsboro**—*pop pl* ... TN-4
**Hillsboro**—*pop pl* ... TX-5
**Hillsboro**—*pop pl* ... VA-3
**Hillsboro**—*pop pl* ... WV-2
**Hillsboro**—*pop pl* ... WI-6
Hillsboro—*summit* ... NM-5
Hillsboro—*uninc pl* ... FL-3
Hillsboro, Lake—*reservoir* ... IL-6
Hillsboro Acad (historical)—*school* ... TN-4
**Hillsboro Acres**—*pop pl* ... TN-4
*Hillsboro Baptist Ch* ... TN-4
Hillsboro Baptist Ch—*church* ... TN-4
*Hillsboro Bay* ... FL-3
Hillsboro Bay—*bay* ... FL-3
*Hillsboro Bay Channel* ... FL-3
**Hillsboro Beach**—*pop pl* ... FL-3
Hillsboro Branch—*stream* ... KY-4
Hillsboro Camp—*locale* ... NH-1
Hillsboro Canal—*canal* ... FL-3
Hillsboro (CCD)—*cens area* ... AL-4
Hillsboro (CCD)—*cens area* ... GA-3
Hillsboro (CCD)—*cens area* ... KY-4
Hillsboro (CCD)—*cens area* ... TN-4
Hillsboro (CCD)—*cens area* ... TX-5
Hillsboro Cem—*cemetery* ... GA-3
Hillsboro Cem—*cemetery* ... KY-4
Hillsboro Cem—*cemetery* ... TN-4
Hillsboro Cem—*cemetery* ... VT-1
Hillsboro Cem—*cemetery* ... VA-3
*Hillsboro Cemetery* ... AL-4
**Hillsboro Center**—*pop pl* ... NH-1
Hillsboro Ch—*church* ... GA-3
Hillsboro Ch—*church* ... KY-4
Hillsboro Ch—*church* ... MO-7
Hillsboro Ch—*church* (2) ... TN-4
Hillsboro Ch—*church* (2) ... VA-3
*Hillsboro Channel* ... FL-3
Hillsboro Ch of Christ—*church* ... TN-4
Hillsboro Cotton Mills—*hist pl* ... TX-5
Hillsboro Cove Public Use Area—*park* ... KS-7
Hillsboro Covered Bridge—*hist pl* ... KY-4
*Hillsboro Creek* ... KY-4
Hillsboro Cumberland Presbyterian Ch—*church* ... TN-4
Hillsboro Dam—*dam* ... ND-7
Hillsboro Day Sch—*school* ... FL-3
Hillsboro Ditch—*canal* ... CO-8
Hillsboro Division—*civil* ... AL-4
Hillsboro Division—*civil* ... TN-4
*Hillsboro Elem Sch* ... TN-4
Hillsboro Elem Sch—*school* ... AL-4
Hillsboro Elem Sch—*school* ... KS-7
Hillsboro Elem Sch—*school* ... TN-4
*Hillsboro Heights Baptist Church* ... AL-4
Hillsboro Heights Ch—*church* ... AL-4
**Hillsboro Heights (subdivision)**—*pop pl* ... TN-4
Hillsboro Hist Dist—*hist pl* ... VA-3
Hillsboro Historic Business District—*hist pl* ... OH-6
Hillsboro HS—*school* ... KS-7
Hillsboro HS—*school* ... OR-9
Hillsboro HS—*school* ... TN-4
Hillsboro Inlet—*channel* ... FL-3
Hillsboro Inlet Bridge—*bridge* ... FL-3
Hillsboro Inlet Light—*locale* ... FL-3
Hillsboro Inlet Light Station—*hist pl* ... FL-3
Hillsboro Lake—*reservoir* ... GA-3
**Hillsboro Lower Village**—*pop pl* ... NH-1
Hillsboro Memorial Gardens—*cemetery* ... FL-3
Hillsboro Methodist Ch—*church* ... TN-4
Hillsboro MS—*school* ... KS-7
Hillsboro Mtn—*summit* ... VT-1
Hillsboro Municipal Airp—*airport* ... KS-7
Hillsboro Municipal Airp—*airport* ... ND-7
Hillsboro Peak Lookout Tower and Cabin—*hist pl* ... NM-5
*Hillsboro Post Office* ... TN-4
Hillsboro Post Office—*building* ... AL-4
Hillsboro Post Office—*building* ... TN-4
Hillsboro Residential Hist Dist—*hist pl* ... TX-5
*Hillsboro River* ... FL-3
Hillsboro River—*channel* ... FL-3
Hillsboro RR Station—*locale* ... FL-3
Hillsboro Rsvr—*reservoir* ... CO-8
Hillsboro Rsvr—*reservoir* ... OR-9
Hillsboro Sch—*school* ... TN-4
Hillsboro State Bank Bldg—*hist pl* ... FL-3
Hillsboro Town Hall—*building* ... ND-7
**Hillsboro (Town of)**—*pop pl* ... WI-6
**Hillsboro Township**—*pop pl* ... ND-7
**Hillsboro (Township of)**—*pop pl* ... IL-6
*Hillsborough* ... AL-4
*Hillsborough* ... IN-6
*Hillsborough* ... KS-7
*Hillsborough* ... NH-1
*Hillsborough* ... OH-6
*Hillsborough* ... PA-2
*Hillsborough* ... TN-4
Hillsborough—*CDP* ... NH-1
Hillsborough—*hist pl* ... VA-3
**Hillsborough**—*pop pl* ... CA-9
**Hillsborough**—*pop pl* ... MD-2
**Hillsborough**—*pop pl* ... NJ-2
**Hillsborough**—*pop pl* ... NC-3
Hillsborough Bay—*bay* ... FL-3
*Hillsborough Canal* ... FL-3
Hillsborough Cem—*cemetery* ... IL-6
*Hillsborough Center* ... NH-1
**Hillsborough Center**—*pop pl* ... NH-1
Hillsborough Ch—*church* ... KY-4
Hillsborough Channel—*channel* ... FL-3
Hillsborough Community Coll—*school* ... FL-3
**Hillsborough Compact (census name Hillsborough)**—*pop pl* ... NH-1
**Hillsborough County**—*pop pl* ... FL-3
Hillsborough County Courthouse—*hist pl* ... NH-1
Hillsborough County Hosp—*hospital* ... FL-3
**Hillsborough County(in (P)MSA 4560, 4760,5350)**—*pop pl* ... NH-1
*Hillsborough Drainage Canal* ... FL-3
**Hillsborough Estates**—*pop pl* ... MD-2
**Hillsborough Estates Subdivision**—*pop pl* ... UT-8
*Hillsborough (Hillsboro)* ... IN-6
Hillsborough Hist Dist—*hist pl* ... NC-3
Hillsborough HS—*school* ... FL-3
*Hillsborough Inlet* ... FL-3
*Hillsborough Lower Village* ... NH-1
**Hillsborough Lower Village**—*pop pl* ... NH-1
**Hillsborough Park**—*pop pl* ... CA-9
*Hillsborough Plantation* ... SC-3
Hillsborough Plaza (Shop Ctr)—*locale* ... FL-3
*Hillsborough Post Office* ... AL-4
*Hillsborough Post Office* ... TN-4
*Hillsborough River* ... FL-3
Hillsborough River—*stream* ... FL-3
Hillsborough River—*swamp* ... FL-3
Hillsborough River State Park—*park* ... FL-3
Hillsborough RR Bridge—*hist pl* ... NH-1
Hillsborough Sch—*school* ... NJ-2
Hillsborough Square Shop Ctr—*locale* ... FL-3
**Hillsborough (Town of)**—*pop pl* ... NH-1
Hillsborough (Township of)—*fmr MCD* ... NC-3
**Hillsborough (Township of)**—*pop pl* ... NJ-2
*Hillsborough Upper Village* ... NH-1
**Hillsborough Upper Village**—*pop pl* ... NH-1
Hillsborough Wildlife Mngmt Area—*park* ... FL-3
**Hillsboro Upper Village**—*pop pl* ... NH-1
**Hillsboro Valley**—*pop pl* ... TN-4
*Hills Branch* ... GA-3
Hills Branch—*stream* ... GA-3
Hills Branch—*stream* ... IL-6
Hills Branch—*stream* ... IN-6
Hills Branch—*stream* ... TX-5
Hills Bridge—*bridge* ... MD-2
Hills Bridge—*bridge* ... NC-3
Hillsbrook Hosp—*hospital* ... CT-1
Hillsbury Slough—*stream* ... IL-6
Hills Cem—*cemetery* ... ME-1
Hills Cem—*cemetery* ... NY-2
*Hill Sch* ... AL-4
Hills Ch—*church* ... IN-6
Hills Ch—*church* ... NC-3
Hills Ch—*church* ... OH-6
Hill Sch—*hist pl* ... MA-1
Hill Sch—*school* ... AL-4
Hill Sch—*school* ... AR-4
Hill Sch—*school* (2) ... CA-9
Hill Sch—*school* ... CO-8
Hill Sch—*school* ... FL-3
Hill Sch—*school* ... GA-3
Hill Sch—*school* (4) ... IL-6
Hill Sch—*school* ... IA-7
Hill Sch—*school* ... ME-1
Hill Sch—*school* (6) ... MI-6
Hill Sch—*school* ... MN-6
Hill Sch—*school* (2) ... MO-7
Hill Sch—*school* ... MT-8
Hill Sch—*school* ... NJ-2
Hill Sch—*school* ... NC-3
Hill Sch—*school* (2) ... OH-6
Hill Sch—*school* ... OR-9
Hill Sch—*school* (2) ... PA-2
Hill Sch—*school* ... SC-3
Hill Sch—*school* ... SD-7
Hill Sch—*school* (3) ... TN-4
Hill Sch—*school* ... VT-1
Hill Sch—*school* (2) ... VA-3
Hill Sch—*school* (2) ... WV-2
Hill Sch—*school* ... WI-6
Hill Sch—*school* ... WY-8
Hill Sch (abandoned)—*school* ... PA-2
*Hills Chapel* ... TN-4
Hills Chapel—*church* (4) ... AL-4
Hills Chapel—*church* (2) ... GA-3
Hills Chapel—*church* ... KY-4
Hills Chapel—*church* (2) ... NC-3
Hills Chapel—*church* ... OH-6
Hills Chapel—*church* ... TN-4
Hills Chapel—*church* (2) ... TX-5
Hills Chapel—*church* ... WV-2
**Hills Chapel**—*pop pl* ... MS-4
*Hills Chapel Attendance Center* ... MS-4
Hills Chapel Cem—*cemetery* ... AL-4
Hills Chapel Cem—*cemetery* ... AR-4
Hills Chapel Cem—*cemetery* ... KY-4
*Hills Chapel Ch* ... AL-4
Hills Chapel Ch—*church* ... AL-4
Hills Chapel Ch of Christ—*church* ... MS-4
Hills Chapel CME Ch—*church* ... AL-4
*Hills Chapel Grammar School* ... MS-4
Hills Chapel (historical)—*church* (3) ... TN-4
Hills Chapel (historical)—*locale* ... MO-7
Hills Chapel Sch—*school* ... KY-4
Hills Chapel Sch—*school* ... MS-4
Hills Chapel Sch—*school* ... OK-5
Hills Chapel Sch—*school* ... TN-4
Hills Chapel Sch (historical)—*school* ... AL-4
Hill Sch (historical)—*school* ... AL-4
Hill Sch (historical)—*school* ... MS-4
Hill Sch (historical)—*school* ... PA-2
Hill Sch (historical)—*school* (3) ... TN-4
Hill Sch No 44—*school* ... NE-7
Hill School (historical)—*locale* ... MO-7
*Hills Church* ... AL-4
Hills Consolidated Sch—*school* ... PA-2
Hills Corner—*locale* ... NH-1
Hills Corner—*locale* ... VA-3
**Hills Corner**—*pop pl* ... NH-1
Hills Corners—*locale* ... NY-2
**Hills Corners**—*pop pl* ... MI-6
Hills Cove—*bay* ... ME-1
*Hills Creek* ... AL-4
*Hills Creek* ... OR-9
*Hills Creek* ... TN-4
Hills Creek—*stream* (2) ... AL-4
Hills Creek—*stream* ... CA-9
Hills Creek—*stream* ... GA-3
Hills Creek—*stream* ... IL-6
Hills Creek—*stream* ... MI-6
Hills Creek—*stream* ... NV-8
Hills Creek—*stream* ... NY-2
Hills Creek—*stream* (3) ... NC-3
Hills Creek—*stream* (2) ... OR-9
Hills Creek—*stream* ... PA-2
Hills Creek—*stream* (2) ... SC-3
Hills Creek—*stream* (2) ... TN-4
Hills Creek—*stream* ... TX-5
Hills Creek—*stream* (4) ... VA-3
Hills Creek—*stream* ... WV-2
Hills Creek—*stream* ... WI-6
Hills Creek Ch—*church* ... GA-3
Hills Creek Ch—*church* ... PA-2
Hills Creek Ch—*church* ... TN-4
Hills Creek Dam—*dam* ... OR-9
Hills Creek Dam—*dam* ... PA-2
Hills Creek Lake—*lake* ... OR-9
Hills Creek Lake—*reservoir* ... OR-9
Hills Creek Lake—*reservoir* ... PA-2
*Hills Creek Rsvr* ... OR-9
Hills Creek State Park—*park* ... PA-2
Hills Creek Trail—*trail* ... OR-9
Hills Crossing—*locale* ... WV-2
Hills Crossing Ch—*church* ... GA-3
**Hills Crossroads**—*pop pl* (2) ... NC-3
Hillsdale—*locale* ... AL-4
Hillsdale—*locale* ... GA-3
Hillsdale—*locale* ... IA-7
Hillsdale—*locale* ... KY-4
Hillsdale—*locale* ... MS-4
Hillsdale—*locale* ... NY-2
Hillsdale—*locale* ... UT-8
Hillsdale—*locale* ... WV-2
**Hillsdale**—*pop pl* ... AL-4
**Hillsdale**—*pop pl* ... CA-9
**Hillsdale**—*pop pl* ... IL-6
**Hillsdale**—*pop pl* (2) ... IN-6
**Hillsdale**—*pop pl* ... KS-7
**Hillsdale**—*pop pl* ... LA-4
**Hillsdale**—*pop pl* ... MI-6
**Hillsdale**—*pop pl* ... MO-7
**Hillsdale**—*pop pl* (2) ... NJ-2
**Hillsdale**—*pop pl* ... NY-2
**Hillsdale**—*pop pl* (2) ... NC-3
**Hillsdale**—*pop pl* ... OK-5
**Hillsdale**—*pop pl* ... OR-9
**Hillsdale**—*pop pl* (2) ... PA-2
**Hillsdale**—*pop pl* ... RI-1
**Hillsdale**—*pop pl* ... TN-4
**Hillsdale**—*pop pl* ... WA-9
**Hillsdale**—*pop pl* ... WV-2
**Hillsdale**—*pop pl* ... WI-6
**Hillsdale**—*pop pl* ... WY-8
Hillsdale—*post sta* ... CA-9
Hillsdale—*uninc pl* ... MD-2
Hillsdale—*uninc pl* ... VA-3
**Hillsdale Acres (subdivision)**—*pop pl* ... PA-2
Hillsdale Archeol District—*hist pl* ... KS-7
*Hillsdale Baptist Church* ... TN-4
Hillsdale Brick Store—*hist pl* ... NC-3
Hillsdale Brook—*stream* ... NJ-2
Hillsdale Canyon—*valley* ... UT-8
Hillsdale Cem—*cemetery* (2) ... IA-7
Hillsdale Cem—*cemetery* (2) ... KS-7
Hillsdale Cem—*cemetery* ... LA-4
Hillsdale Cem—*cemetery* ... NE-7
Hillsdale Cem—*cemetery* (2) ... NY-2
Hillsdale Cem—*cemetery* ... SD-7
Hillsdale Cem—*cemetery* ... TX-5
Hillsdale Cem—*cemetery* ... WA-9
Hillsdale Ch—*church* ... IN-6
Hillsdale Ch—*church* ... NC-3
Hillsdale Ch—*church* ... ND-7
Hillsdale Ch—*church* ... PA-2
Hillsdale Ch—*church* ... TN-4
Hillsdale Ch—*church* ... WV-2
Hillsdale Coll—*school* ... MI-6
Hillsdale Country Club—*other* ... MI-6
**Hillsdale (County)**—*pop pl* ... MI-6
Hillsdale County Courthouse—*hist pl* ... MI-6
Hillsdale Elem Sch—*school* ... KS-7
Hillsdale Elem Sch—*school* ... PA-2
**Hillsdale Forest (subdivision)**—*pop pl* ... NC-3
Hillsdale Heights Ch of God—*church* ... AL-4
Hillsdale Heights Park—*park* ... AL-4
**Hillsdale Heights (subdivision)**—*pop pl* ... AL-4
Hillsdale (historical)—*locale* ... SD-7
Hillsdale Historic and Archeol District—*hist pl* ... RI-1
Hillsdale HS—*school* ... CA-9
**Hillsdale Junction**—*pop pl* ... IN-6
Hillsdale Lake—*lake* ... KS-7
Hillsdale Lake—*reservoir* ... MS-4
Hillsdale Lake Dam—*dam* ... NC-3
**Hillsdale Manor**—*pop pl* ... NJ-2
Hillsdale Memorial Park—*park* ... NJ-2
*Hillsdale Methodist Church* ... AL-4
Hillsdale Mine—*mine* ... CA-9
*Hillsdale Park* ... OR-9
Hillsdale Park—*park* ... KS-7
Hillsdale Park and Golf Course—*other* ... MD-2
**Hillsdale Park (subdivision)**—*pop pl* ... NC-3
**Hillsdale Pit**—*pop pl* ... TX-5
Hillsdale Post Office (historical)—*building* ... MS-4
Hillsdale Post Office (historical)—*building* ... TN-4
Hillsdale Presbyterian Ch—*church* ... AL-4
Hillsdale Run—*stream* ... IN-6
Hillsdale Sch—*school* ... AL-4
Hillsdale Sch—*school* ... CA-9
Hillsdale Sch—*school* ... IL-6
Hillsdale Sch—*school* (3) ... NE-7
Hillsdale Sch—*school* ... OH-6
Hillsdale Sch—*school* ... PA-2
Hillsdale Sch—*school* ... TX-5
Hillsdale Sch—*school* ... UT-8
Hillsdale Sch—*school* ... WI-6
Hillsdale Sch Number 3—*school* ... ND-7
Hillsdale Sch Number 31—*school* ... ND-7
Hillsdale School(Abandoned)—*locale* ... ID-8
Hillsdale Shop Ctr—*locale* ... KS-7
Hillsdale Station—*hist pl* ... NJ-2
**Hillsdale (subdivision)**—*pop pl* ... AL-4
**Hillsdale (subdivision)**—*pop pl* (4) ... NC-3
**Hillsdale (subdivision)**—*pop pl* (2) ... TN-4
**Hillsdale Subdivision**—*pop pl* (2) ... UT-8
**Hillsdale (Town of)**—*pop pl* ... NY-2
**Hillsdale Township**—*pop pl* (2) ... ND-7
**Hillsdale Township**—*pop pl* ... SD-7
**Hillsdale (Township of)**—*pop pl* ... MI-6
**Hillsdale (Township of)**—*pop pl* ... MN-6
**Hillsdale Twin Homes Subdivision**—*pop pl* ... UT-8
Hillsde Cem—*cemetery* ... MA-1
**Hillsden Addition Subdivision**—*pop pl* ... UT-8
Hills Ditch—*canal* ... CO-8
Hill Settlement Sch—*school* ... WI-6
Hill Seven—*summit* ... MT-8
Hill Seventyone—*summit* ... CO-8
Hills Farms Cem—*cemetery* ... NH-1
Hills Ferry—*locale* ... NC-3
**Hills Ferry**—*pop pl* ... CA-9
Hills Ferry (historical)—*locale* ... NC-3
**Hills Flat**—*pop pl* ... CA-9
Hills Fork—*stream* ... OH-6
*Hills Grove* ... PA-2
*Hillsgrove* ... RI-1
*Hills Grove* ... RI-1
**Hillsgrove**—*pop pl* ... PA-2
**Hillsgrove**—*pop pl* ... RI-1
Hills Grove Cem—*cemetery* ... IL-6
Hills Grove Ch—*church* ... IL-6
Hills Grove Ch—*church* ... NC-3
Hillsgrove Covered Bridge—*hist pl* ... PA-2
**Hillsgrove (Township of)**—*pop pl* ... PA-2
Hills Gulch—*valley* ... CO-8
Hills Hans Park—*park* ... IN-6
Hills Hill—*summit* ... AR-4
**Hillshire Subdivision**—*pop pl* ... UT-8
Hills (historical)—*locale* ... MS-4
Hills Hollow—*valley* ... NY-2
Hills Home Ranch—*locale* ... NM-5
Hills House—*hist pl* ... NH-1
*Hillside* ... CT-1
*Hillside* ... KS-7
*Hillside* ... MN-6
*Hill Side* ... PA-2
*Hillside* ... SD-7
Hillside—*hist pl* ... CT-1
Hillside—*hist pl* ... IA-7
Hillside—*hist pl* ... MA-1
Hillside—*hist pl* ... MS-4
Hillside—*hist pl* ... NC-3
Hillside—*hist pl* ... SC-3
Hillside—*hist pl* ... WV-2
Hillside—*locale* ... AZ-5
Hillside—*locale* ... CO-8
Hillside—*locale* ... ME-1
Hillside—*locale* ... MT-8
Hillside—*locale* ... OR-9
Hill Side—*locale* ... SD-7
Hillside—*locale* ... SD-7
Hillside—*locale* ... UT-8
**Hillside**—*pop pl* ... CO-8
**Hillside**—*pop pl* (2) ... IL-6
**Hillside**—*pop pl* ... IN-6
**Hillside**—*pop pl* ... KY-4
**Hillside**—*pop pl* ... LA-4
**Hillside**—*pop pl* ... ME-1
**Hillside**—*pop pl* (2) ... MD-2
**Hillside**—*pop pl* ... NJ-2
**Hillside**—*pop pl* (2) ... NY-2
**Hillside**—*pop pl* (5) ... PA-2
**Hillside**—*pop pl* ... SC-3
**Hillside**—*pop pl* ... TN-4
**Hillside**—*pop pl* (2) ... WA-9
**Hillside**—*pop pl* ... WI-6
Hillside—*uninc pl* ... KS-7
Hillside—*uninc pl* ... NY-2
**Hillside Acres (subdivision)**—*pop pl* ... DE-2
**Hillside Addition Subdivision**—*pop pl* ... UT-8
Hillside Airp—*airport* ... KS-7
Hillside Ave Hist Dist—*hist pl* ... MA-1
Hillside Ave Hist Dist—*hist pl* ... NJ-2
Hillside Ave Sch—*school* ... NJ-2
Hillside Ave Sch—*school* ... NY-2
Hillside Beach Dam—*dam* ... MA-1
*Hillside-Berkeley* ... IL-6
Hillside Bone Cave—*cave* ... PA-2
Hillside Branch—*stream* ... NC-3
Hillside Brook—*stream* ... IN-6
Hillside Brook—*stream* ... NH-1
Hillside Camp—*locale* ... WY-8
*Hillside Canal* ... NE-7
Hillside Canal—*canal* ... ID-8
Hillside Cave—*cave* ... AL-4
Hillside Cem—*cemetery* ... AL-4
Hillside Cem—*cemetery* (2) ... CA-9
Hillside Cem—*cemetery* (4) ... CO-8
Hillside Cem—*cemetery* (9) ... CT-1
Hillside Cem—*cemetery* ... FL-3
Hillside Cem—*cemetery* (3) ... IN-6
Hillside Cem—*cemetery* (8) ... IA-7
Hillside Cem—*cemetery* (3) ... KS-7
Hillside Cem—*cemetery* (16) ... ME-1
Hillside Cem—*cemetery* (10) ... MA-1
Hillside Cem—*cemetery* (7) ... MI-6
Hillside Cem—*cemetery* (19) ... MN-6
Hillside Cem—*cemetery* (3) ... MT-8
Hillside Cem—*cemetery* (2) ... NE-7
Hillside Cem—*cemetery* (5) ... NH-1
Hillside Cem—*cemetery* (6) ... NJ-2
Hillside Cem—*cemetery* ... NM-5
Hillside Cem—*cemetery* (19) ... NY-2
Hillside Cem—*cemetery* ... NC-3
Hillside Cem—*cemetery* (2) ... ND-7
Hill Side Cem—*cemetery* ... ND-7
Hillside Cem—*cemetery* (3) ... ND-7
Hillside Cem—*cemetery* (4) ... OH-6
Hillside Cem—*cemetery* ... OK-5
Hillside Cem—*cemetery* ... OR-9
Hillside Cem—*cemetery* (4) ... PA-2
Hillside Cem—*cemetery* (6) ... SD-7
Hillside Cem—*cemetery* ... TX-5
Hillside Cem—*cemetery* (5) ... VT-1
Hillside Cem—*cemetery* (15) ... WI-6
Hillside Cemetery—*hist pl* ... AL-4
Hillside Ch—*church* (2) ... AR-4
Hillside Ch—*church* (3) ... GA-3
Hillside Ch—*church* ... IA-7
Hillside Ch—*church* ... KS-7
Hillside Ch—*church* ... LA-4
Hillside Ch—*church* ... MS-4
Hillside Ch—*church* ... NJ-2
Hillside Ch—*church* (2) ... NY-2
Hillside Ch—*church* (4) ... NC-3
Hillside Ch—*church* (4) ... OK-5
Hillside Ch—*church* ... PA-2
Hillside Ch—*church* ... SC-3
Hillside Chapel—*church* ... AL-4
Hillside Chapel—*church* ... OH-6
Hillside Christian Ch—*church* ... KS-7
Hillside Colliery (historical)—*mine* ... PA-2
**Hillside Colony**—*pop pl* ... MT-8
**Hillside Colony**—*pop pl* (2) ... SD-7
Hillside Community Hosp—*hospital* ... CA-9
Hillside Cottage—*hist pl* ... KS-7
Hillside Cottages—*locale* ... GA-3
Hillside Creek—*stream* ... ID-8
Hillside Ditch—*canal* ... CO-8
Hillside Ditch—*canal* (2) ... MT-8
Hillside Diversion Terrace—*other* ... TX-5
Hillside Drain—*stream* ... AZ-5
Hillside Draw—*valley* ... MT-8
*Hillside Elementary School* ... PA-2
Hillside Elem Sch—*school* ... KS-7
**Hillside Estates Subdivision**—*pop pl* ... UT-8
Hill Side Farm—*locale* ... MI-6
**Hillside Gardens**—*pop pl* ... MI-6
**Hillside Gardens**—*pop pl* ... TX-5
**Hillside Gardens Subdivision**—*pop pl* ... UT-8
Hillside Gospel Chapel—*church* ... PA-2
Hillside Grove Sch—*school* ... KS-7
Hillside Grove Sch—*school* ... WI-6
Hillside Haven Mound—*hist pl* ... OH-6
**Hillside Heights**—*pop pl* ... DE-2
**Hillside Heights**—*pop pl* ... NY-2
**Hillside Heights Subdivision**—*pop pl* ... UT-8
Hillside Hist Dist—*hist pl* ... CT-1
Hillside (historical)—*locale* ... AL-4
Hillside (historical P.O.)—*locale* ... MS-4
Hill Side Home—*locale* ... CT-1
Hillside Hosp—*hospital* ... NY-2
Hillside Hosp—*hospital* ... TN-4
Hillside Hotel—*hist pl* ... WI-6
Hillside HS—*school* ... NJ-2
Hillside HS—*school* ... NC-3
Hillside HS—*school* ... SC-3
Hillside Intermediate Sch—*school* ... UT-8
Hillside JHS—*school* ... ID-8
Hillside JHS—*school* ... MI-6
Hillside JHS—*school* ... NH-1
Hillside JHS—*school* ... NJ-2
Hillside JHS—*school* ... OH-6
Hillside Junction—*locale* ... PA-2
*Hillside Junction Station* ... PA-2
*Hillside Junior High School* ... UT-8
Hillside Lake—*CDP* ... NY-2
Hillside Lake—*lake* ... AK-9
Hillside Lake—*lake* ... ID-8
Hillside Lake—*lake* (2) ... NY-2
Hillside Lake—*lake* ... WV-2
Hillside Lake—*reservoir* (2) ... NC-3
Hillside Lake Dam—*dam* ... NC-3

**Hillside Manor**—pop pl IL-6
**Hillside Manor**—pop pl NY-2
**Hillside Manor Subdivision**—pop pl (2) UT-8
**Hillside Meadow Subdivision**—pop pl UT-8
Hillside Memorial Gardens—cemetery AL-4
Hillside Memorial Gardens—cemetery LA-4
Hillside Memorial Park (Cemetery)—cemetery CA-9
Hillside Memory Gardens—cemetery ND-7
Hillside Methodist Church—hist pl NY-2
Hillside Mine—mine AZ-5
Hillside Mine—mine NV-8
Hillside Mission—church GA-3
Hillside Natl Wildlife Ref—park MS-4
**Hillside Oaks Subdivision Number One**—pop pl UT-8
**Hillside Oaks Subdivision Number Two**—pop pl UT-8
Hillside Palms RV Park—park UT-8
Hillside Park—park CA-9
Hillside Park—park IL-6
Hillside Park—park ND-7
Hillside Park—park (2) TX-5
Hillside Park—uninc pl NY-2
Hillside Peak—summit AZ-5
Hillside Placer Mine—mine MT-8
Hillside Pond—lake MA-1
Hillside Primary Sch—school CA-9
Hillside Quarry—mine ME-1
Hillside Ranch—locale CO-8
Hillside Resort—locale MI-6
Hillside Rest Cem—cemetery NY-2
Hillside Rocks—summit AZ-5
Hillside RR Station—building AZ-5
Hillside Rsvr—reservoir MT-8
Hillside Rsvr—reservoir OR-9
Hillside Run PA-2
Hillside Run—stream PA-2
Hillside Run Dam PA-2
Hillside Sch—hist pl CA-9
Hillside Sch—school AL-4
Hillside Sch—school AR-4
Hillside Sch—school (6) CA-9
Hillside Sch—school CO-8
Hillside Sch—school CT-1
Hillside Sch—school (5) IL-6
Hillside Sch—school (2) ME-1
Hillside Sch—school (3) MA-1
Hillside Sch—school MI-6
Hillside Sch—school (3) MN-6
Hillside Sch—school (2) MO-7
Hillside Sch—school (5) NE-7
Hillside Sch—school (3) NJ-2
Hillside Sch—school (2) NY-2
Hillside Sch—school (2) OK-5
Hillside Sch—school (4) PA-2
Hillside Sch—school (2) SD-7
Hill Side Sch—school SD-7
Hillside Sch—school TX-5
Hillside Sch—school VT-1
Hillside Sch—school (7) WI-6
Hillside Sch (abandoned)—school PA-2
Hillside Sch (historical)—school (2) SD-7
Hillside Sch Number 1—school ND-7
Hillside Sch Number 2—school ND-7
Hillside Sch Number 4—school ND-7
Hillside School UT-8
Hillside School (Abandoned)—locale WI-6
Hillside Siding—locale WA-9
Hillside Slough—gut TX-5
Hillside Spring—spring AL-4
Hillside Spring—spring (6) AZ-5
Hillside Spring—spring CO-8
Hillside Spring—spring ID-8
Hillside Spring—spring (5) NV-8
Hillside Spring—spring NM-5
Hillside Spring—spring OR-9
Hillside Springs—spring AZ-5
Hillside Springs—spring NV-8
Hillside Springs—spring OK-5
Hillside Springs—spring (2) WY-8
**Hillside (sta.)**—pop pl ME-1
**Hillside Subdivision**—pop pl UT-8
Hillside Tank—reservoir AZ-5
Hillside Tank—reservoir NM-5
Hillside Tank—reservoir TX-5
**Hillside Terrace**—pop pl NJ-2
Hillside Terrace Acres—locale PA-2
Hillside Thomas Ditch—canal NM-5
**Hillside Townhouse Condominium**—pop pl UT-8
Hillside Township—civil SD-7
**Hillside Township**—pop pl SD-7
**Hillside (Township of)**—pop pl NJ-2
Hillside View Lake—reservoir MO-7
**Hillside Village**—pop pl PA-2
Hillside Village Shop Ctr—locale MO-7
**Hillside Village (subdivision)**—pop pl PA-2
**Hillside Village Subdivision**—pop pl UT-8
Hill Siding—locale MN-6
Hills Island—island AK-9
Hills Island—island GA-3
Hills Island—island MD-2
Hills Island—island TN-4
**Hillsite Addition, The**—pop pl UT-8
Hills Lake AL-4
Hills Lake—lake AR-4
Hills Lake—lake GA-3
Hills Lake—lake MI-6
Hills Lake—lake NE-7
Hills Lake—lake (2) WI-6
Hills Lake—reservoir (2) AL-4
Hills Lake—reservoir GA-3
Hills Lake (historical)—lake IA-7
Hills Landing—locale NC-3
Hills Landing (historical)—locale AL-4
**Hills (Lawrence Post Office)**—pop pl PA-2
Hill Slough—gut WI-6
Hill Slough—stream (2) AR-4
Hill Slough—stream CA-9
**Hillsman Corner**—pop pl VA-3
Hillsman Gap—gap AL-4
Hillsman House—building VA-3
Hillsman House—hist pl TN-4
Hillsman Taylor Ch (abandoned)—church MO-7
Hills Meadow—flat WA-9
Hills Memorial Library—hist pl NH-1
**Hillsmere Shores**—pop pl MD-2
Hills Mill Creek—stream WI-6
Hills Mill (historical)—locale (3) TN-4
Hills Millpond—reservoir (2) GA-3
Hills Mills (historical)—locale AL-4
Hills Mill Tunnel—tunnel VA-3
Hills Mine—mine CA-9
Hills Mtn—summit TN-4
Hills Mtn—summit VA-3
Hills of Calvary Cem—cemetery TN-4
Hills of Eternity Memorial Park—cemetery CA-9
**Hills of Homes**—pop pl UT-8
Hills Of Judea—summit OH-6
Hills Of Rest Cem—cemetery IL-6
Hills of Rest Cem—cemetery SD-7
**Hills of Skyline, The**—pop pl DE-2
Hills of Storms, Hill of Churches—cemetery MA-1
Hills of the Moon Wash—stream CA-9
Hills Park—park IA-7
Hills Park—uninc pl GA-3
Hill Spaulding Ditch—canal OH-6
Hills Peak—summit (2) OR-9
Hill's Point MD-2
Hills Point—cape ME-1
Hills Point—cape MD-2
Hills Point—cape NC-3
Hills Point—cape WI-6
**Hills Point**—pop pl MD-2
Hills Point Cove—bay MD-2
Hills Point Neck—cape MD-2
Hills Pond CT-1
Hills Pond—lake CT-1
Hills Pond—lake ME-1
Hills Pond—lake NH-1
Hills Pond—lake NY-2
Hills Pond—lake WI-6
Hills Pond—reservoir GA-3
Hills Pond—reservoir MA-1
Hills Pond—reservoir OH-6
Hills Pond—reservoir OR-9
Hills Pond Creek—stream WI-6
Hills Pond No 1—lake CT-1
Hills Pond No 2—lake CT-1
Hills Ponds—lake UT-8
Hills Prairie—flat MS-4
Hills Prairie—flat TX-5
Hills Prairie—other TX-5
Hills Prairie Cem—cemetery WI-6
Hills Precinct (historical)—locale MS-4
Hill Spring KS-7
Hill Spring—spring ID-8
Hill Spring—spring NV-8
Hill Spring—spring (2) OR-9
Hill Spring—spring SD-7
Hill Spring—spring TN-4
Hill Spring—spring UT-8
Hill Spring Baptist Church AL-4
Hill Spring Branch—stream AL-4
Hill Spring Ch—church AL-4
Hill Springs Cem—cemetery MS-4
Hill Springs Ch—church MS-4
Hill Springs (historical)—locale AL-4
Hills Ranch—locale CA-9
Hills Ranch—locale CO-8
Hills Ranch—locale NE-7
Hills Ridge—ridge WV-2
Hills (RR name for Lawrence)—other PA-2
Hills Rsvr—reservoir OR-9
Hills Run—stream WV-2
Hill's Sawmill—hist pl PA-2
Hills Sch—school IA-7
Hills Sch—school OH-6
Hills School, The—school NY-2
Hills Shoals—bar TN-4
Hills Shop Ctr—locale PA-2
Hills Shop Ctr—locale TN-4
Hills Shop Ctr - West—locale PA-2
Hills Shopping Plaza—locale MA-1
Hills Slough—stream AK-9
Hills Station (historical)—locale PA-2
Hills Store—locale GA-3
**Hills Store**—pop pl MO-7
Hills Store (historical)—locale AL-4
**Hills Subdivisions, The**—pop pl UT-8
Hill Stadium—other PA-2
Hill's Tavern—hist pl PA-2
Hillstead Cem—cemetery ND-7
Hill Stead Museum—building CT-1
Hills Terrace—locale PA-2
**Hillstream**—pop pl DE-2
Hill Street JHS—school GA-3
Hill Street Sch—school NC-3
Hill Street Sch—school PA-2
**Hill Street Subdivision**—pop pl MS-4
Hills Union Cem—cemetery TN-4
Hills Union Ch—church TN-4
Hills Union United Methodist Ch TN-4
Hills Upper Landing (historical)—locale AL-4
Hills Valley—valley CA-9
Hillsview—locale TN-4
**Hillsview**—pop pl OR-9
**Hillsview**—pop pl PA-2
**Hillsview**—pop pl SD-7
**Hills View**—pop pl TN-4
Hillsview Lake—lake MI-6
Hillsview Sanatorium—hospital PA-2
Hillsview Sch (historical)—school TN-4
Hillsview Township—civil SD-7
**Hillsville**—pop pl MA-1
**Hillsville**—pop pl PA-2
**Hillsville**—pop pl VA-3
Hillsville (historical)—locale AL-4
Hillsville Station (historical)—locale PA-2
Hills West Dam—dam IN-6
**Hillswood (subdivision)**—pop pl AL-4
Hill Tank—reservoir (5) AZ-5
Hill Tank—reservoir (5) NM-5
Hill Tank—reservoir (4) TX-5
Hill Technical Sch—school MI-6
Hill To Hill Bridge—bridge PA-2
**Hilltonia**—pop pl GA-3
Hilltonia Bridge—bridge GA-3
Hilltonia (CCD)—cens area GA-3
Hilltonia JHS—school OH-6
Hillton Lake—lake WA-9
Hillton Point—cape ME-1
Hillton Ranch—locale AZ-5
Hillton Run—stream MD-2
Hill Top KS-7
Hilltop MD-2
Hilltop MO-7
Hilltop OH-6
Hilltop SD-7
Hilltop—hist pl VA-3
Hilltop—locale (2) AR-4
Hilltop—locale IL-6
Hilltop—locale IA-7
Hilltop—locale KS-7
Hilltop—locale (3) KY-4
Hill Top—locale MD-2
Hilltop—locale MI-6
Hill Top—locale MO-7
Hilltop—locale NV-8
Hilltop—locale PA-2
Hilltop—locale (2) TN-4
Hilltop—locale TX-5
Hill Top—locale UT-8
Hilltop—locale WA-9
Hill Top—locale WA-9
Hill Top—locale WV-2
**Hilltop**—pop pl AL-4
**Hill Top**—pop pl AL-4
**Hilltop**—pop pl AZ-5
**Hilltop**—pop pl CA-9
**Hilltop**—pop pl CO-8
**Hill Top**—pop pl IL-6
**Hilltop**—pop pl IL-6
**Hill Top**—pop pl (2) KY-4
**Hilltop**—pop pl KY-4
**Hilltop**—pop pl LA-4
**Hilltop**—pop pl MN-6
**Hill Top**—pop pl MO-7
**Hilltop**—pop pl MO-7
**Hilltop**—pop pl NJ-2
**Hilltop**—pop pl (2) NC-3
**Hilltop**—pop pl (2) OH-6
**Hill Top**—pop pl OK-5
**Hilltop**—pop pl SC-3
**Hilltop**—pop pl (2) TN-4
**Hill Top**—pop pl TN-4
**Hilltop**—pop pl TX-5
**Hilltop**—pop pl WA-9
**Hilltop**—pop pl WV-2
Hilltop—summit MT-8
Hilltop—summit TX-5
Hill Top—uninc pl NC-3
Hill Top—uninc pl VA-3
Hilltop—uninc pl VA-3
Hilltop—uninc pl WI-6
Hilltop—uninc pl WY-8
Hilltop Acres OH-6
**Hilltop Acres**—pop pl MA-1
**Hill Top Acres**—pop pl OH-6
**Hilltop Acres**—pop pl PA-2
**Hill Top Acres**—pop pl PA-2
**Hilltop Acres**—pop pl TN-4
**Hilltop Acres (subdivision)**—pop pl DE-2
**Hilltop Acres (subdivision)**—pop pl (2) NC-3
Hill Top Airp PA-2
Hilltop Airp—airport IN-6
Hilltop Airp—airport MO-7
Hill Top Airp—airport PA-2
Hilltop Airp—airport PA-2
Hilltop Barium Mine NV-8
Hilltop Camp—park IN-6
Hilltop Campground—locale MT-8
Hilltop Campground—locale NV-8
Hilltop Campground—park AZ-5
Hilltop Canyon—valley NV-8
Hilltop Cem—cemetery AR-4
Hilltop Cem—cemetery CO-8
Hilltop Cem—cemetery KS-7
Hilltop Cem—cemetery KY-4
Hilltop Cem—cemetery ME-1
Hill Top Cem—cemetery MO-7
Hilltop Cem—cemetery NY-2
Hill Top Cem—cemetery TN-4
Hilltop Cem—cemetery VT-1
Hilltop Cem—cemetery (2) WV-2
Hilltop Cem—cemetery WI-6
Hilltop Center Sch—school KY-4
Hilltop Ch AL-4
Hilltop Ch—church (2) AL-4
Hilltop Ch—church (2) AR-4
Hilltop Ch—church IN-6
Hill Top Ch—church (2) IN-6
Hill Top Ch—church KY-4
Hilltop Ch—church (3) KY-4
Hilltop Ch—church MI-6
Hilltop Ch—church (2) NC-3
Hill Top Ch—church NC-3
Hilltop Ch—church (2) OH-6
Hilltop Ch—church (2) OK-5
Hill Top Ch—church SC-3
Hilltop Ch—church TN-4
Hill-Top Ch—church TN-4
Hill Top Ch—church TN-4
Hilltop Ch—church TN-4
Hilltop Ch—church TX-5
Hill Top Ch—church VA-3
Hilltop Ch—church WV-2
Hill Top Ch—church (2) WV-2
Hilltop Chapel—church AR-4
Hilltop Chapel—church CA-9
Hilltop Chapel—church KY-4
Hill Top Chapel—church MN-6
Hill Top Chapel—church MO-7
Hill Top Country Club—other MI-6
Hilltop Country Club—other NE-7
Hilltop Country Club—other TX-5
Hilltop Creek—stream WA-9
Hilltop Downs—other TX-5
Hilltop Drive Sch—school CA-9
Hilltop Elem Sch—school IN-6
Hilltop Elem Sch—school PA-2
**Hilltop Estates**—pop pl NJ-2
Hilltop Fork MD-2
Hill Top Fork—stream MD-2
**Hilltop Gardens Subdivision**—pop pl UT-8
Hilltop Girls Home—other MO-7
Hilltop Hall—hist pl MN-6
Hill Top (historical)—locale AL-4
Hilltop Holiness Ch—church MO-7
Hilltop House—locale NM-5
Hilltop HS—school CA-9
Hill Top Inn—locale TX-5
Hill Top JHS—school CA-9
Hilltop Lake PA-2
Hilltop Lake—lake IL-6
Hilltop Lake—lake (2) MI-6
Hilltop Lake—lake MT-8
Hill Top Lake—reservoir NY-2
Hill Top Lake—reservoir NC-3
Hill Top Lake Dam—dam NC-3
Hilltop Lakes—lake OH-6
**Hilltop Lakes**—pop pl TX-5
Hill Top Lookout Tower—locale MO-7
**Hilltop Manor**—pop pl DE-2
Hilltop Memorial Park—cemetery TX-5
Hilltop Mine NV-8
Hill Top Mine—mine AZ-5
Hilltop Mine—mine AZ-5
Hilltop Mine—mine CO-8
Hilltop Mine—mine ID-8
Hill Top Mine—mine (2) NV-8
Hilltop Mine—mine NM-5
Hill Top Mine—mine NM-5
Hilltop Mine—mine (2) UT-8
Hilltop Mission MO-7
Hilltop Mission—church AR-4
Hill Top Mission—church NC-3
Hilltop Mission—church OH-6
Hill Top Mission—church TN-4
Hilltop Montessori Sch—school (2) FL-3
Hilltop Mound—summit MO-7
Hilltop Nursing Home—hospital KS-7
Hilltop-Oceana—post sta VA-3
Hill Top Open Door Mission—church NC-3
Hilltop Park—park AL-4
Hilltop Park—park CA-9
Hilltop Park—park (4) MN-6
Hilltop Park—park WV-2
Hilltop Park Speedway—other PA-2
Hilltop Plaza (Shop Ctr)—locale MA-1
Hilltop Pond—reservoir CT-1
Hilltop Ranch—locale AZ-5
Hilltop Ranch—locale CA-9
Hilltop Ranch—locale (2) CO-8
Hilltop Ranch—locale (2) TX-5
Hilltop Ranger Station—locale CO-8
Hilltop (reduced Usage)—locale MN-6
Hilltop Rsvr—reservoir CO-8
Hilltop Rsvr—reservoir (2) OR-9
Hilltop Run—stream IN-6
Hilltop Sch—school CA-9
Hilltop Sch—school FL-3
Hilltop Sch—school GA-3
Hilltop Sch—school IL-6
Hilltop Sch—school IA-7
Hill Top Sch—school KS-7
Hilltop Sch—school KS-7
Hilltop Sch—school MA-1
Hilltop Sch—school (3) MN-6
Hilltop Sch—school (3) NE-7
Hilltop Sch—school NY-2
Hilltop Sch—school (2) OH-6
Hilltop Sch—school OK-5
Hilltop Sch—school SD-7
Hilltop Sch—school (2) TX-5
Hilltop Sch—school WA-9
Hilltop Sch—school (2) WI-6
Hilltop Sch (historical)—school SD-7
Hilltop Sch (historical)—school TN-4
Hilltop School AL-4
Hilltop School (Abandoned)—locale NE-7
Hilltop Silo—locale MT-8
Hilltop (Site)—locale AZ-5
Hilltop Spring—spring CA-9
Hilltop Stadium—other CO-8
**Hilltop Subdivision**—pop pl (2) UT-8
**Hill Top Subdivision**—pop pl UT-8
Hill Top Tank—reservoir AZ-5
Hilltop Tank—reservoir (2) AZ-5
Hilltop Tank—reservoir NM-5
**Hilltop Terrace**—pop pl NJ-2
Hill Top Trail—trail WV-2
Hilltop United Methodist Ch—church UT-8
Hilltop View Sch—school IA-7
Hill Top Village Home—building TX-5
Hilltop Village Shop Ctr—locale NC-3
Hilltop Well—well AZ-5
Hilltop Well—well (2) NM-5
Hilltop Wildlife Mngmt Area—park UT-8
Hilltop Windmill—locale TX-5
Hilltown NJ-2
Hilltown PA-2
Hilltown SD-7
Hilltown—locale PA-2
**Hilltown**—pop pl IN-6
**Hilltown**—pop pl NJ-2
**Hilltown**—pop pl (2) PA-2
**Hilltown**—pop pl VA-3
Hilltown Cem—cemetery IA-7
Hilltown Ch—church IA-7
Hill Town Ch—church TN-4
Hilltown Dam—dam PA-2
Hilltown Farms—locale PA-2
Hilltown Industrial Park—locale PA-2
Hilltown Manor—locale PA-2
**Hill (Town of)**—pop pl NH-1
**Hill (Town of)**—pop pl WI-6
Hilltown Sch—school PA-2
**Hill Township**—pop pl MO-7
**Hill Township**—pop pl NE-7
**Hill Township**—pop pl ND-7
Hill (Township of)—fmr MCD (3) AR-4
**Hill (Township of)**—pop pl MI-6
**Hill (Township of)**—pop pl MN-6
Hilltown Shop Ctr—locale PA-2
**Hilltown (subdivision)**—pop pl PA-2
**Hilltown (Township of)**—pop pl PA-2
Hill Trail Flowage—lake WI-6
Hill Trap Windmill—locale TX-5
Hill Trumbull Mine—mine MN-6
**Hillvale**—pop pl TN-4
Hillvale Canyon—valley CA-9
Hillvale Country Club—locale TN-4
Hill Valley—valley CA-9
Hill Valley—valley PA-2
Hill Valley Ch (abandoned)—church PA-2
Hill Valley Creek—stream PA-2
Hill Valley Sch—school WV-2
Hillview ID-8
Hillview NY-2
Hillview—locale KY-4
**Hillview**—pop pl AL-4
**Hillview**—pop pl IL-6
**Hillview**—pop pl KY-4
**Hillview**—pop pl MN-6
**Hillview**—pop pl NY-2
**Hill View**—pop pl NC-3
**Hillview**—pop pl (2) WV-2
Hillview—post sta CA-9
**Hillview Acres (subdivision)**—pop pl AL-4
**Hill View Acres Subdivision**—pop pl UT-8
Hillview Cem—cemetery AL-4
Hill View Cem—cemetery GA-3
Hillview Cem—cemetery MI-6
Hillview Cem—cemetery NY-2
Hillview Cem—cemetery (2) PA-2
Hillview Cem—cemetery (2) SD-7
Hillview Ch—church AL-4
Hill View Ch—church KY-4
Hillview Ch—church (2) KY-4
Hillview Ch—church LA-4
Hillview Ch—church NY-2
Hillview Ch—church NC-3
Hillview Ch—church (2) PA-2
Hillview Ch—church (3) TN-4
Hill View Country Club—locale MA-1
Hillview Country Club—other IN-6
Hillview Crest Sch—school CA-9
Hillview Elem Sch—school AL-4
Hillview Elem Sch—school NE-7
Hillview Elem Sch—school PA-2
**Hillview Estates**—pop pl IN-6
**Hillview Estates**—pop pl TN-4
**Hillview Estates (subdivision)**—pop pl TN-4
Hillview Home—locale WY-8
Hillview Junior HS—school CA-9
Hillview Lake—reservoir IN-6
Hill View Lake—reservoir MO-7
Hillview Lake Dam—dam IN-6
Hillview Memorial Gardens—cemetery MO-7
Hillview Pumping Station—other IL-6
Hillview Rsvr—reservoir NY-2
Hillview RV Park Campground—park UT-8
Hillview Sch—school (4) CA-9
Hillview Sch—school MO-7
Hillview Sch—school (3) NE-7
Hillview Sch—school NJ-2
Hillview Sch—school NY-2
Hillview Sch—school SD-7
Hillview Sch—school UT-8
Hillview Sch (abandoned)—school PA-2
Hill View Sch (abandoned)—school SD-7
Hill View School UT-8
**Hillview (subdivision)**—pop pl AL-4
**Hillview (subdivision)**—pop pl TN-4
**Hillview Terrace**—pop pl WV-2
**Hill Villa Subdivision**—pop pl UT-8
Hillville—locale MD-2
**Hillville**—pop pl PA-2
**Hillville**—pop pl TN-4
Hillville (CCD)—cens area TN-4
Hillville Division—civil TN-4
**Hillville (Lower Hillville)**—pop pl PA-2
**Hillville (Mount Pleasant)**—pop pl TN-4
Hillville Post Office (historical)—building TN-4
Hillville Sch—school OH-6
Hillvue Heights Ch—church KY-4
Hill-Webb Grain Elevator—hist pl TX-5
Hill Well—locale NM-5
Hill Well—well AZ-5
Hill Well—well (2) NM-5
Hill Well—well TX-5
**Hillwest Subdivision**—pop pl UT-8
Hill Windmill—locale NM-5
Hill Windmill—locale (4) TX-5
Hill Windmill—summit WY-8
Hillwood—locale AL-4
**Hillwood**—pop pl TN-4
**Hillwood**—pop pl (2) VA-3
Hillwood—uninc pl TN-4
**Hillwood Acres**—pop pl TN-4
Hillwood Baptist Church AL-4
Hillwood Ch—church AL-4
Hillwood Ch—church TN-4
Hillwood Estates IL-6
**Hillwood Estates**—pop pl TN-4
Hillwood HS—school TN-4
**Hillwood Lakes**—pop pl NJ-2
Hillwood Private School-Montessori—school FL-3
**Hillwood (subdivision)**—pop pl (2) AL-4
**Hillwood (subdivision)**—pop pl (2) TN-4
**Hillwood West (subdivision)**—pop pl AL-4
**Hilly**—pop pl LA-4
**Hill Yard**—pop pl PA-2
**Hillyard**—pop pl WA-9
Hillyard Branch—stream KY-4
Hillyard Canyon—valley ID-8
Hillyard Sch—school MO-7
Hillyard Spring—spring ID-8
**Hillyard (Township of)**—pop pl IL-6
Hilly Branch Sch—school NC-3
Hilly Creek—stream VA-3
Hillyer, Mount—summit CA-9
Hillyer Branch—stream SC-3
Hillyer Ravine—valley NY-2
Hilly Haven Golf Course—other WI-6
Hilly Lake MI-6
Hilly Lake—lake MN-6
Hilly Lookout Tower—locale LA-4
**Hillymeade (subdivision)**—pop pl PA-2
Hilly Mill Creek—stream GA-3
Hilly Upland Run—stream WV-2
Hill Zion Ch—church AL-4
Hill 16—summit NY-2
Hill 36—summit ID-8
Hill 40—hist pl GU-9
Hill 640 Milit Reservation—military CA-9
Hilma NC-3
Hilman Creek—stream WY-8
Hilman Gap AL-4
Hilman Lake—lake CO-8
Hilman Lake—lake MN-6
Hilman Park—flat CO-8
Hilmans Lake WI-6
**Hilma Park (subdivision)**—pop pl NC-3
**Hilmar**—pop pl CA-9
Hilmar Drain—canal CA-9
Hilmar HS—school CA-9
Hilmar-Irwin—CDP CA-9
Hilmar-Irwin (CCD)—cens area CA-9
**Hilmoe Township**—pop pl SD-7
Hilo—locale AR-4
**Hilo**—pop pl HI-9
**Hilo**—pop pl KY-4
Hilo Bay—bay HI-9
Hilo Breakwater—dam HI-9
Hilo (CCD)—cens area HI-9
Hilo Cem—cemetery MO-7
Hilo Country Club—other HI-9
Hilo Creek—stream ID-8
Hilo For Res—forest HI-9
Hilo Golf Course—other HI-9
Hilo Hill—summit WA-9
Hilo Hosp—hospital HI-9
Hilo HS—school HI-9
Hilokee Creek—stream GA-3
Hilolo—locale FL-3
Hi Lonesome Windmill—locale TX-5
Hilo Oil Field—oilfield MS-4
Hilo Park—summit NM-5
Hilo Peak—summit ID-8
Hilo Ridge—ridge (2) MO-7
**Hilorn (historical)**—pop pl NC-3
Hilo Trail—trail (2) HI-9
Hi Low Lake—lake UT-8
Hi-Low Lake—lake WA-9
Hilp Creek—stream OR-9
**Hilshire Village**—pop pl TX-5
Hilsman Park—park GA-3
Hilson Bay—swamp SC-3
Hilson Lake—lake WI-6
**Hilt**—pop pl CA-9
Hiltabidels Opening—flat CA-9
Hilt Brook—stream ME-1
Hilt Creek—stream WA-9
Hilt Lake—lake WA-9
Hiltman Creek—stream CO-8
Hilton VA-3
Hilton—hist pl GA-3
Hilton—hist pl MD-2
Hilton—locale CO-8
Hilton—locale GA-3
Hilton—locale KS-7
Hilton—locale TX-5
Hilton—other VA-3
**Hilton**—pop pl AR-4
**Hilton**—pop pl CA-9
**Hilton**—pop pl KY-4
**Hilton**—pop pl NJ-2
**Hilton**—pop pl NY-2
**Hilton**—pop pl PA-2
**Hilton**—pop pl SC-3
**Hilton**—pop pl WI-6
Hilton, Adam, House—hist pl NY-2
Hilton, Martin, House—hist pl KY-4
Hilton, Mount—summit CA-9
Hilton Branch—stream KY-4
Hilton Bridge—bridge ME-1
Hilton Brook—stream (4) ME-1
Hilton Canyon—valley CA-9
Hilton Canyon—valley NM-5
Hilton Cem—cemetery KY-4
Hilton Cem—cemetery (2) ME-1
Hilton Cem—cemetery MI-6
Hilton Cem—cemetery MO-7
Hilton Cem—cemetery PA-2
Hilton Cem—cemetery TN-4
Hilton Ch—church KY-4
Hilton Cove—bay ME-1
Hilton Creek VA-3
Hilton Creek—stream (2) CA-9
Hilton Creek—stream ID-8
Hilton Creek—stream IA-7
Hilton Creek Lakes—lake CA-9
Hilton Creek Mine—mine CA-9
Hilton Ditch—canal NV-8
Hilton Draw—valley WY-8
Hilton Farm—locale ME-1
Hilton Gap VA-3
Hilton Gulch—valley OR-9
Hiltonhead SC-3
Hilton Head—cape SC-3
Hilton Head Harbor—locale SC-3
Hilton Head Island—island SC-3
**Hilton Head Island**—pop pl SC-3
Hilton Head JHS—school SC-3
Hilton Head Rear Range—other SC-3
Hilton Head Sch—school SC-3
Hilton Heights—uninc pl GA-3
Hilton Hill—summit (2) ME-1
**Hilton (historical)**—pop pl MS-4
**Hilton (historical)**—pop pl TN-4
Hilton Hollow—valley MO-7
Hilton Hotel—hist pl (2) TX-5
Hilton House—hist pl NM-5
Hiltonia GA-3
Hilton Lake—lake MI-6
Hilton Lake—lake WA-9
Hilton Mckee Lake—reservoir AL-4
Hilton Mckee Lake Dam—dam AL-4
Hilton Mine—mine AZ-5
Hilton Mine—mine SD-7
Hilton Northwood Sch—school NY-2
**Hilton Park**—pop pl VA-3
Hilton Pond ME-1
Hilton Ponds—lake ME-1
Hilton Post Office (historical)—building MS-4
Hilton Ridge—ridge OR-9
Hiltons TN-4
**Hiltons**—pop pl VA-3
Hilton Sch—school DC-2
Hilton Sch—school IA-7
Hilton Sch—school MI-6
Hilton Sch—school VA-3
Hilton Sch Number 1—school ND-7
Hilton Sch Number 2—school ND-7
Hilton Sch Number 3—school ND-7
Hilton Sch Number 4—school ND-7
Hilton Sch Number 5—school ND-7
Hiltons Creek—stream VA-3
Hiltons Gap—gap VA-3
**Hiltons (Hilton)**—pop pl VA-3
Hiltons Post Office (historical)—building TN-4
Hilton Spring—spring MO-7
Hilton Springs Church TN-4
Hilton State Park—park NH-1
Hilton Station—locale CA-9
Hilton Township—civil SD-7
Hilton Township—fmr MCD IA-7
**Hilton Township**—pop pl ND-7
Hilton Village—hist pl VA-3
**Hilton Village**—pop pl VA-3
**Hilton Village**—pop pl WV-2
**Hilton Villa Subdivision**—pop pl UT-8
Hiltonville—locale NY-2

Hilton Wash—*stream* AZ-5
Hilton Zumbro Lake Dam—*dam* MS-4
*Hilts* CA-9
Hiltscher Park—*park* CA-9
Hilts Creek—*stream* ID-8
*Hilts Hammocks* DE-2
Hilts Lake—*lake* WI-6
Hiltsley Creek—*stream* ID-8
Hilts Shoals—*bar* TN-4
Hilt Tank—*reservoir* NM-5
Hilt Well—*locale* NM-5
Hilty Cem—*cemetery* OH-6
Hilty Mine—*mine* (2) MO-7
Hiltz Cem—*cemetery* KS-7
Hiltz Creek—*stream* MI-6
Hilukea, Lae o—*cape* HI-9
Hilview Ch—*church* AL-4
Hilyard Cem—*cemetery* IL-6
Hilyard Cem—*cemetery* OH-6
Hilyard Ch—*church* GA-3
*Hilyards Canyon* ID-8
**Hilyer**—*pop pl* GA-3
Hilyn Lake—*reservoir* IL-6
**Hima**—*pop pl* KY-4
Hima Branch—*stream* TN-4
Himalaya—*locale* LA-4
Himalaya Canal—*canal* LA-4
Himalaya Mine—*mine* CA-9
Himan Cem—*cemetery* MS-4
Himango Sch (abandoned)—*school* SD-7
Himebaugh Drain—*canal* MI-6
Himebaugh Sch (abandoned)—*school* PA-2
Himell Cem—*cemetery* KY-4
Himes—*locale* WY-8
Himes Cem—*cemetery* (2) TN-4
Himes Creek—*stream* MT-8
Himes Creek Trail—*trail* MT-8
*Himes Methodist Church* TN-4
Himes Park—*park* OR-9
Himes Pass—*gap* MT-8
Himes Peak—*summit* CO-8
Himes Peak Campground—*locale* CO-8
Hime Spring—*spring* SD-7
Himes Sch—*school* IL-6
Himes Sch (historical)—*school* PA-2
**Himesville**—*pop pl* TN-4
Himesville Ch—*church* TN-4
Himesville Post Office
(historical)—*building* TN-4
Himley Cem—*cemetery* TX-5
Himley Lake—*lake* WI-6
Himmel—*locale* MO-7
Himmel Canyon—*valley* CA-9
Himmel Park—*park* AZ-5
Himmels Ch—*church* PA-2
Himmel's Church Covered Bridge—*hist pl* PA-2
Himmel Springs—*spring* NV-8
Himmelwright Run—*stream* WV-2
Himmelwright Spring—*spring* OR-9
Himmershee Canal—*canal* FL-3
Himont Lookout Tower—*locale* MO-7
Hi Mountain Campground—*locale* CA-9
Hi Mountain Spring—*spring* CA-9
Hi Mountain Trail—*trail* CA-9
Hi-Mount Boulvard Sch—*school* WI-6
*Himphill Landing* AL-4
Himple Lake—*lake* WI-6
Himrod—*locale* IL-6
**Himrod**—*pop pl* NY-2
**Himrod (RR name Seneca
Lake)**—*pop pl* NY-2
**Himrods Junction**—*pop pl* NY-2
Hi Mtn—*summit* CA-9
Hi Mtn Potrero—*summit* CA-9
Himyar—*locale* KY-4
Hina, Mauna—*summit* HI-9
Hina Falls—*falls* HI-9
Hina Gulch—*valley* HI-9
*Hinai Hill* HI-9
Hinakapoula—*summit* HI-9
Hinalele Falls—*falls* HI-9
Hinalenale Point—*cape* HI-9
Hinaman Acres Airp—*airport* PA-2
Hinaman Creek—*stream* MT-8
Hinanaulua—*cape* HI-9
Hinao Gulch—*valley* HI-9
*Hinashisu* MH-9
*Hinasusu* MH-9
Hinau—*summit* HI-9
*Hincel Creek* OR-9
Hinch—*locale* MO-7
**Hinch**—*pop pl* WV-2
Hincha Creek—*stream* AR-4
Hinch Branch—*stream* MO-7
Hinch Cem—*cemetery* (2) TN-4
**Hinchcliff**—*pop pl* MS-4
Hinchcliff Cem—*cemetery* IL-6
Hinch Creek—*stream* MT-8
Hinchee House—*hist pl* TX-5
Hinchey, Franklin, House—*hist pl* NY-2
Hinchey Cem—*cemetery* TN-4
Hinchey Hollow—*valley* TN-4
Hincheyville Hist Dist—*hist pl* TN-4
Hinch Gap—*gap* TN-4
Hinchinbrook Brook—*stream* NY-2
Hinchinbrook Entrance—*channel* AK-9
Hinchinbrook Island—*island* AK-9
Hinchinbrook Lighthouse Reserve—*other* AK-9
Hinchingham—*hist pl* MD-2
Hinchings Pond—*lake* NY-2
Hinchley Canyon—*valley* NM-5
Hinchley Ranch—*locale* NM-5
Hinchley Sch—*school* NE-7
**Hinchman**—*pop pl* MI-6
**Hinchman**—*pop pl* NJ-2
Hinchman Cem—*cemetery* (2) IN-6
*Hinchman Hollow* WV-2
Hinchman Oil Field—*oilfield* KS-7
Hinchman Pond—*lake* NJ-2
Hinchman Ravine—*valley* CA-9
Hinchman Rsvr—*reservoir* CO-8
Hinchman Sch—*school* MI-6
Hinchman Sch—*school* NJ-2
*Hinchmans Pond* NJ-2
Hinch Mill (historical)—*locale* TN-4
Hinch Mtn—*summit* TN-4
Hinch Sch (historical)—*school* TN-4
*Hinchs Mill* TN-4
Hinchwood Creek—*stream* MT-8
Hinchy Mine (Inactive)—*mine* CA-9
*Hinckel Creek* OR-9
**Hinckley**—*pop pl* ID-8
**Hinckley**—*pop pl* IL-6
**Hinckley**—*pop pl* ME-1
**Hinckley**—*pop pl* MN-6
**Hinckley**—*pop pl* NY-2
**Hinckley**—*pop pl* OH-6
**Hinckley**—*pop pl* TX-5
**Hinckley**—*pop pl* UT-8
Hinckley, Capt. Joseph, House—*hist pl* MA-1
Hinckley, Col. J., House—*hist pl* MI-6
Hinckley, Mount—*summit* AK-9
Hinckley, Nymphus, House—*hist pl* MA-1
Hinckley, S. Alexander, House—*hist pl* MA-1
Hinckley, Ward, House—*hist pl* ME-1
Hinckley Bend—*bend* MO-7
Hinckley Brook—*stream* CT-1
Hinckley Brook—*stream* (2) ME-1
Hinckley Cem—*cemetery* OH-6
Hinckley City Cem—*cemetery* UT-8
Hinckley Corner—*locale* ME-1
Hinckley Cove—*bay* ME-1
Hinckley-Creamer Dairy—*hist pl* AK-9
Hinckley Creek—*stream* CA-9
Hinckley Creek—*stream* ID-8
Hinckley Fire Relief House—*hist pl* MN-6
Hinckley Good Will Home Hist
Dist—*hist pl* ME-1
Hinckley Hill—*summit* ME-1
Hinckley Homestead—*hist pl* MA-1
Hinckley HS Gymnasium—*hist pl* UT-8
*Hinckley Lake* NY-2
Hinckley Lake—*reservoir* OH-6
*Hinckley Pond* MA-1
Hinckley Pond—*lake* MA-1
Hinckley Reservation—*park* OH-6
Hinckley Ridge—*ridge* CA-9
Hinckley Ridge—*ridge* ME-1
Hinckley Ridge Cem—*cemetery* OH-6
Hinckley Ridge Ch—*church* OH-6
Hinckley Rock—*rock* MA-1
Hinckley Rsvr—*reservoir* NY-2
*Hinckleys Bend* MO-7
Hinckleys Pond—*lake* MA-1
**Hinckley (Township of)**—*pop pl* MN-6
**Hinckley (Township of)**—*pop pl* OH-6
Hinckley Trail Rsvr—*reservoir* UT-8
**Hinckleyville**—*pop pl* NY-2
Hinckston Run—*stream* PA-2
Hinckston Run Dam—*dam* PA-2
Hinckston Run Rsvr—*reservoir* PA-2
Hincle Lake—*reservoir* AL-4
Hinda—*locale* CA-9
**Hinda Heights**—*pop pl* KY-4
*Hind Creek* TN-4
Hinde, James J., House—*hist pl* OH-6
Hinde & Dauch Paper Co.—*hist pl* OH-6
*Hinden Lake* OR-9
Hinden Lake—*lake* FL-3
Hinde Oil Field—*oilfield* TX-5
Hinder Creek—*stream* WI-6
Hinderlider Cem—*cemetery* IN-6
Hinderlider Ditch—*canal* IN-6
Hinderlider Lift Canal—*canal* CO-8
Hinderlie Cem—*cemetery* SD-7
Hinder Sch—*school* PA-2
Hindes—*locale* TX-5
Hindes Ranch—*locale* TX-5
Hindley Sch—*school* CT-1
Hindman—*locale* TX-5
**Hindman**—*pop pl* KY-4
Hindman Airp—*airport* MO-7
Hindman Bottom—*bend* TN-4
Hindman Branch—*stream* TN-4
Hindman (CCD)—*cens area* KY-4
Hindman Cem—*cemetery* AR-4
Hindman Cem—*cemetery* IL-6
Hindman Cem—*cemetery* MS-4
Hindman Creek—*stream* MO-7
Hindman Ditch—*canal* IN-6
Hindman Gulch—*valley* CO-8
**Hindman (historical)**—*pop pl* OR-9
Hindman Hollow—*valley* TN-4
Hindman Lake—*lake* ID-8
Hindman Lake—*reservoir* IN-6
Hindman Park—*park* AR-4
Hindman (Township of)—*fmr MCD* AR-4
**Hindoo**—*pop pl* CA-9
*Hindoo Amphitheater* AZ-5
Hindoo Creek—*stream* WA-9
*Hindostan* IN-6
**Hindostan**—*pop pl* IN-6
Hindostan Ch—*church* IN-6
Hindostan Falls—*falls* IN-6
**Hindostan Falls**—*pop pl* IN-6
Hindostan Falls Public Fishing Area—*park* IN-6
Hinds, A. J., House—*hist pl* CA-9
Hinds Bluff—*cliff* AR-4
**Hindsboro**—*pop pl* IL-6
Hinds Brook—*stream* NH-1
**Hindsburg**—*pop pl* NY-2
Hinds Cem—*cemetery* (3) MS-4
Hinds Cem—*cemetery* OH-6
Hinds Cem—*cemetery* (2) TN-4
Hinds Chapel—*church* TN-4
Hinds Chapel Sch (historical)—*school* TN-4
**Hinds County**—*pop pl* MS-4
Hinds County Agricultural HS—*school* MS-4
Hinds County Courthouse—*hist pl* MS-4
Hinds County Penal Farm—*locale* MS-4
Hinds County Vocational Technical
Sch—*school* MS-4
**Hindscreek**—*pop pl* TN-4
Hinds Creek—*stream* MS-4
Hinds Creek—*stream* TN-4
*Hinds Creek Baptist Church* TN-4
Hinds Creek Ch—*church* TN-4
**Hinds Creek (historical)**—*pop pl* TN-4
Hinds Creek Post Office
(historical)—*building* TN-4
**Hinds Creek Valley**—*pop pl* TN-4
Hinds Field Branch—*stream* TN-4
Hindsfield Ridge—*ridge* KY-4
Hindsfield Sch—*school* KY-4
Hinds Gap—*gap* TN-4
Hinds General Hosp—*hospital* MS-4
Hinds Hotel—*hist pl* CA-9
Hinds Junior Coll—*school* MS-4
Hinds Lake—*lake* MN-6
Hinds Lateral—*canal* (2) CA-9
Hindsman Cem—*cemetery* WV-2
*Hinds Pond* NY-2
Hinds Ranch—*locale* TX-5
Hinds Ridge—*ridge* TN-4
Hinds Sch—*school* MI-6
Hinds Street Baptist Ch—*church* MS-4
*Hinds Valley* TN-4
Hinds Valley—*valley* (2) TN-4
Hinds Valley Cem—*cemetery* TN-4
*Hinds Valley - in part* TN-4
**Hindsville**—*pop pl* AR-4
Hinds Well—*well* NM-5
Hindu Amphitheater—*basin* AZ-5
Hindu Canyon—*valley* AZ-5
Hindu Lake—*lake* WI-6
**Hindustan**—*pop pl* IN-6
Hindu Temple—*church* PA-2
Hindu Temples—*cliff* UT-8
Hine—*locale* MO-7
Hine, Horace L., House—*hist pl* OH-6
Hine Airstrip—*airport* AZ-5
Hinebaugh Creek—*stream* CA-9
*Hinegars Baptist Church* TN-4
Hine JHS—*school* DC-2
Hine Lake—*reservoir* CO-8
Hi-Nella—*locale* NJ-2
**Hi-Nella (Hi Nella)**—*pop pl* NJ-2
Hineman Branch—*stream* TN-4
Hineman Cave—*cave* PA-2
Hineman Spring—*spring* TN-4
Hiner Cem—*cemetery* IN-6
Hiner Cem—*cemetery* TX-5
Hiner Ch—*church* VA-3
Hiner Hollow—*valley* VA-3
Hinerman Cem—*cemetery* MO-7
Hiner Ranch—*locale* NE-7
Hiner Spring—*spring* CO-8
Hiner Spring—*spring* VA-3
Hinerville Sch—*school* KS-7
Hines—*locale* AL-4
Hines—*locale* IL-6
Hines—*locale* WI-6
**Hines**—*pop pl* FL-3
**Hines**—*pop pl* MN-6
**Hines**—*pop pl* OR-9
**Hines**—*pop pl* TX-5
**Hines**—*pop pl* WV-2
Hines, E. M., House—*hist pl* TX-5
Hines Airp—*airport* MO-7
Hines Airstrip—*airport* OR-9
*Hines Bay* TX-5
Hines Branch—*stream* AR-4
Hines Branch—*stream* KY-4
Hines Branch—*stream* MS-4
Hines Branch—*stream* MO-7
Hines Branch—*stream* TN-4
Hines Branch—*stream* (3) TX-5
Hines Branch—*stream* VA-3
Hines Branch Ch—*church* VA-3
*Hinesburg* VT-1
**Hinesburg**—*pop pl* (2) VT-1
Hinesburg Brook—*stream* VT-1
**Hinesburg (Town of)**—*pop pl* VT-1
Hines Camp—*locale* CA-9
Hines Cave—*cave* AL-4
*Hines Cem* MS-4
Hines Cem—*cemetery* (2) AL-4
Hines Cem—*cemetery* IL-6
Hines Cem—*cemetery* KY-4
Hines Cem—*cemetery* MS-4
Hines Cem—*cemetery* NC-3
Hines Cem—*cemetery* (2) OH-6
Hines Cem—*cemetery* SD-7
Hines Cem—*cemetery* TN-4
Hines Cem—*cemetery* (2) TX-5
Hines Ch—*church* GA-3
Hines Chapel—*church* MS-4
Hines Chapel—*church* (2) NC-3
Hines Chapel—*church* OH-6
Hines Chapel—*church* TX-5
Hines Chapel Cem—*cemetery* TX-5
Hines Corners—*locale* PA-2
*Hines Creek* TN-4
*Hines Creek* WI-6
Hines Creek—*stream* AL-4
Hines Creek—*stream* AK-9
Hines Creek—*stream* CA-9
Hines Creek—*stream* KY-4
Hines Creek—*stream* OK-5
Hines Creek—*stream* SD-7
Hines Creek—*stream* (2) TN-4
Hines Creek—*stream* TX-5
Hines Creek—*stream* WI-6
Hines Creek Shoals—*bar* TN-4
Hines Crossroads—*locale* NC-3
*Hinesdale* MN-6
Hinesdale—*locale* KY-4
Hines Ditch—*canal* (2) IN-6
Hines Gap—*gap* AL-4
Hines Gap—*gap* GA-3
Hines (historical P.O.)—*locale* AL-4
Hines Hollow—*valley* MO-7
Hines Hollow—*valley* TN-4
Hines House—*hist pl* KY-4
Hines House—*hist pl* MT-8
Hines Island—*island* VA-3
Hines Junction—*locale* NC-3
Hines Lake—*lake* KS-7
Hines Lake—*lake* NC-3
Hines Lake—*lake* TX-5
Hines Lake—*reservoir* AL-4
Hines Landing—*locale* AL-4
Hines Landing—*locale* MO-7
Hinesley Cem—*cemetery* GA-3
Hinesley Spring—*spring* AR-4
Hines Log Pond—*reservoir* OR-9
Hines Lookout Tower—*tower* FL-3
Hines Mansion—*hist pl* UT-8
Hines Mare Cave—*cave* AL-4
Hines Meadow—*flat* NH-1
Hines Memorial Baptist Ch—*church* AL-4
Hines Memorial Cem—*cemetery* MS-4
*Hines Mill Creek* AL-4
Hines Mill (historical)—*locale* AL-4
Hines Millpond—*lake* OR-9
Hines Mill Pond—*reservoir* OR-9
Hines Mtn—*summit* AL-4
Hines Peak—*summit* CA-9
Hines Point—*cape* MA-1
Hines Point—*cape* NC-3
Hines Pond—*lake* NY-2
Hines Pond—*lake* TN-4
Hines Pond—*reservoir* NJ-2
Hines Ponds—*lake* MD-2
Hines Ranch—*locale* CO-8
Hines Ranch—*locale* MT-8
Hines Round Barn—*hist pl* OK-5
Hines Rsvr—*reservoir* CA-9
Hines Run—*stream* OH-6
Hines Sch—*school* IL-6
Hines Sch—*school* MS-4
Hines Sch—*school* TX-5
Hines Spring—*locale* SD-7
Hines Spring—*spring* CA-9
Hines Spring—*spring* SD-7
Hines Spring—*spring* TN-4
Hines Tank—*reservoir* NM-5
**Hineston**—*pop pl* LA-4
Hineston Branch—*stream* LA-4
Hineston Lookout Tower—*locale* LA-4
Hinestown Ch—*church* TN-4
**Hines (Township of)**—*pop pl* MN-6
*Hinestown United Methodist Ch* TN-4
Hines Trail—*trail* PA-2
Hines Valley—*valley* TN-4
Hines Valley Ch—*church* TN-4
Hinesville—*locale* VA-3
**Hinesville**—*pop pl* GA-3
Hinesville (CCD)—*cens area* GA-3
Hinesville Cem—*cemetery* GA-3
Hiney Ch—*church* WV-2
**Hingham**—*pop pl* MA-1
**Hingham**—*pop pl* MT-8
**Hingham**—*pop pl* WI-6
Hingham Bay—*bay* MA-1
**Hingham Center**—*pop pl* MA-1
Hingham Center Central JHS—*school* MA-1
Hingham Center (historical P.O.)—*locale* MA-1
*Hingham Centre* MA-1
Hingham Coulee—*valley* MT-8
Hingham Harbor—*harbor* MA-1
Hingham Lake—*lake* MT-8
Hingham Mill Pond—*reservoir* WI-6
Hingham Shipyard—*locale* MA-1
Hingham Shopping Plaza—*locale* MA-1
Hingham Station (historical)—*locale* MA-1
**Hingham (Town of)**—*pop pl* MA-1
Hingham Yacht Club—*locale* MA-1
Hingle Bend—*gut* LA-4
Hingle Pass—*gut* LA-4
Hingle Pond—*bay* LA-4
Hinke Gulch—*valley* ID-8
Hinkel, Jacob, House—*hist pl* MN-6
*Hinkel Creek* OR-9
Hinkel Lake—*reservoir* WV-2
Hinken Cem—*cemetery* MO-7
Hinken Creek—*stream* MN-6
Hinkey Summit—*summit* NV-8
Hinkie Park—*flat* NM-5
*Hinkle* GA-3
*Hinkle* WV-2
Hinkle—*locale* AR-4
Hinkle—*locale* KY-4
Hinkle—*locale* OR-9
**Hinkle**—*pop pl* LA-4
**Hinkle**—*pop pl* TN-4
Hinkle, W. R., and Co.—*hist pl* IN-6
*Hinkle Bend* MO-7
Hinkle Bend—*bend* AR-4
Hinkle Branch—*stream* IL-6
Hinkle Branch—*stream* KY-4
Hinkle Branch—*stream* MO-7
Hinkle Branch—*stream* TN-4
Hinkle Branch—*stream* WV-2
Hinkle Branch Trail—*trail* WV-2
*Hinkle Butte* OR-9
Hinkle Butte—*summit* OR-9
Hinkle Cem—*cemetery* (2) IL-6
Hinkle Cem—*cemetery* OH-6
Hinkle Cem—*cemetery* (2) TN-4
Hinkle Cem—*cemetery* WV-2
Hinkle Ch—*church* TN-4
Hinkle Chapel—*church* WV-2
*Hinkle Creek* IN-6
Hinkle Creek—*stream* IN-6
Hinkle Creek—*stream* IA-7
Hinkle Creek—*stream* (2) KY-4
Hinkle Creek—*stream* MS-4
Hinkle Creek—*stream* OR-9
*Hinkle Creek Baptist Church* MS-4
Hinkle Creek Ch—*church* IN-6
Hinkle Creek Ch—*church* MS-4
**Hinkledale**—*pop pl* TN-4
Hinkle Dam—*dam* AL-4
*Hinkle Ferry* TX-5
Hinkle Gap—*gap* KY-4
Hinkle Gap—*gap* WV-2
Hinkle Gulch—*valley* CO-8
Hinkle Gulch—*valley* OR-9
Hinkle (historical)—*locale* MS-4
Hinkle Hollow—*valley* (2) AR-4
Hinkle Hollow—*valley* MD-2
Hinkle Hollow—*valley* NY-2
Hinkle Hollow—*valley* TN-4
Hinkle Lake—*lake* OR-9
Hinkleman Canyon—*valley* WA-9
Hinkleman Spring—*spring* WA-9
Hinkle Mine—*mine* CO-8
Hinkle Mountain Ch—*church* WV-2
Hinkle-Murphy House—*hist pl* MN-6
Hinkle Ranch—*locale* OR-9
Hinkle Run—*stream* MD-2
Hinkle Run—*stream* WV-2
**Hinkles**—*pop pl* GA-3
*Hinkles Bend* MO-7
Hinkle Sch—*school* MS-4
Hinkles Ferry—*other* TX-5
*Hinkles Mills* WV-2
Hinkle Spring—*spring* AZ-5
Hinkle Spring Canyon—*valley* AZ-5
Hinkles Valley—*valley* PA-2
Hinkle Tinkle Creek—*stream* WA-9
Hinkletown—*locale* PA-2
**Hinkletown**—*pop pl* PA-2
Hinkletown Post Office
(historical)—*building* PA-2
Hinkle Trail—*trail* PA-2
Hinkleville—*locale* KY-4
**Hinkleville**—*pop pl* WV-2
Hinkleville Foot (historical P.O.)—*locale* IA-7
**Hinkley**—*pop pl* CA-9
Hinkley, Ahira R., House—*hist pl* WI-6
Hinkle Yards—*locale* OR-9
Hinkley Brook—*stream* ME-1
Hinkley Brook—*stream* VT-1
Hinkley Cabin—*locale* ID-8
Hinkley Corners—*locale* PA-2
Hinkley Creek—*stream* OH-6
Hinkley Ditch—*canal* IN-6
Hinkley Hill—*summit* CT-1
Hinkley Hill—*summit* ME-1
Hinkley Hill—*summit* NY-2
Hinkley Hollow—*valley* OH-6
Hinkley HS—*school* CO-8
Hinkley Lake—*reservoir* CO-8
Hinkley Shoal—*bar* ME-1
*Hinkleys Pond* MA-1
Hinkley Union Sch—*school* CA-9
Hinkley Valley—*valley* CA-9
**Hinkleyville**—*pop pl* NY-2
Hinkly, R. B., House—*hist pl* MN-6
Hinks Cem—*cemetery* MI-6
Hinks Cem—*cemetery* TX-5
Hinkson, John, House—*hist pl* KY-4
Hinkson Brook—*stream* NH-1
**Hinkson Corner**—*pop pl* PA-2
Hinkson Cors—*locale* PA-2
Hinkson Creek—*stream* MO-7
Hinkson Creek—*stream* WI-6
Hinkson Creek Cem—*cemetery* MO-7
Hinkson High Lonesome
Windmill—*locale* NM-5
Hinksons Corners—*locale* PA-2
Hinkson Slough—*gut* NV-8
Hinks Sch—*school* MI-6
Hinkston Creek—*stream* KY-4
Hinkston Park—*park* IL-6
Hinkum Pond—*lake* VT-1
*Hinleys Lake* WI-6
Hinman—*fmr MCD* NE-7
Hinman, Lake—*reservoir* CA-9
Hinman, Mount—*summit* WA-9
Hinman Apartments—*hist pl* IL-6
Hinman Campground—*locale* CO-8
Hinman Canyon—*valley* CO-8
Hinman Cem—*cemetery* MI-6
Hinman Cem—*cemetery* (2) NY-2
*Hinman Corner* NY-2
*Hinman Corners* NY-2
Hinman Creek—*stream* CO-8
Hinman Ditch—*canal* CO-8
Hinman Glacier—*glacier* WA-9
Hinman Hollow—*valley* NY-2
Hinman Island—*island* NH-1
Hinman Lake—*lake* CO-8
Hinman Lake—*lake* MI-6
Hinman Park—*flat* CO-8
Hinman Pond—*lake* NH-1
Hinman Ranch—*locale* NM-5
Hinman Rsvr—*reservoir* CO-8
Hinman Sch—*school* IL-6
*Hinmans Corner* NY-2
**Hinmans Corners**—*pop pl* NY-2
**Hinmansville**—*pop pl* NY-2
Hinman Swamp—*swamp* NY-2
Hinman Valley—*valley* NY-2
Hinmon Cem—*cemetery* AR-4
Hinnant Oil Field—*oilfield* (2) TX-5
Hinnants Lake—*reservoir* NC-3
Hinnants Lake Dam—*dam* NC-3
Hinnes Crossroads—*locale* NC-3
*Hinnicksons Ridge* CA-9
Hinnom—*locale* VA-3
Hinojosa Cem—*cemetery* (2) TX-5
Hinojosa Site—*hist pl* TX-5
Hinojoseno Artesian Well—*well* TX-5
*Hinole* HI-9
Hi-Notch—*gap* NY-2
Hinote Cem—*cemetery* AL-4
*Hinsacho Cove* TX-5
*Hinsacho Creek* TX-5
*Hinsaw Creek* WY-8
**Hinsburg**—*pop pl* NY-2
Hinsdale—*locale* CA-9
Hinsdale—*locale* MN-6
**Hinsdale**—*pop pl* IL-6
**Hinsdale**—*pop pl* MA-1
**Hinsdale**—*pop pl* MT-8
**Hinsdale**—*pop pl* NH-1
**Hinsdale**—*pop pl* (2) NY-2
Hinsdale Animal Cem—*cemetery* IL-6
Hinsdale Brook—*stream* MA-1
Hinsdale Cem—*cemetery* NY-2
**Hinsdale Compact (census name
Hinsdale)**—*pop pl* NH-1
**Hinsdale Estates**—*pop pl* MA-1
Hinsdale Island—*island* MN-6
Hinsdale Sch—*school* IL-6
Hinsdale Slough—*stream* OR-9
**Hinsdale (Town of)**—*pop pl* MA-1
**Hinsdale (Town of)**—*pop pl* NH-1
**Hinsdale (Town of)**—*pop pl* NY-2
Hinsdellville Cem—*cemetery* VT-1
Hinsdill, Henry M., House—*hist pl* UT-8
Hinshall Ditch—*canal* IN-6
Hinshaw, Elias, House—*hist pl* IN-6
Hinshaw Airp—*airport* (2) NC-3
*Hinshaw Cove* AL-4
Hinshaw Creek—*stream* WY-8
Hinshaw Ditch—*canal* (2) IN-6
Hinshaw Street Ch—*church* NC-3
Hinson—*locale* NC-3
**Hinson**—*pop pl* FL-3
*Hinson Branch* AR-4
Hinson Branch—*stream* AR-4
Hinson Branch—*stream* KY-4
Hinson Cem—*cemetery* FL-3
Hinson Cem—*cemetery* (4) GA-3
Hinson Cem—*cemetery* LA-4
Hinson Cem—*cemetery* MS-4
Hinson Cem—*cemetery* NC-3
Hinson Cem—*cemetery* OK-5
Hinson Cem—*cemetery* TX-5
*Hinson Church* AL-4
Hinson Creek—*stream* TN-4
Hinson Crossing—*locale* GA-3
*Hinson Crossroads* FL-3
Hinson Cross Roads—*locale* NC-3
**Hinson Cross Roads**—*pop pl* FL-3
Hinson Gap—*gap* AR-4
Hinson Hollow—*valley* (2) TN-4
Hinson Hollow Branch—*stream* VA-3
Hinson House—*hist pl* AL-4
*Hinson JHS* AL-4
Hinson-Knippers Cem—*cemetery* MS-4
Hinson Lake—*reservoir* NC-3
Hinson Mill (historical)—*locale* AL-4
Hinson Mounds—*hist pl* FL-3
Hinson Pond—*reservoir* NC-3
Hinson Pond Dam—*dam* NC-3
Hinson Run—*stream* PA-2
Hinsons Cross Roads—*locale* FL-3
**Hinsons Crossroads**—*pop pl* NC-3
*Hinson Spring* TN-4
Hinson Spring—*spring* TN-4
*Hinsonsprings* TN-4
**Hinson Springs**—*pop pl* TN-4
Hinsonsprings Post Office
(historical)—*building* TN-4
Hinsons Store (historical)—*locale* AL-4
**Hinsonton**—*pop pl* GA-3
Hinspeter Sch—*school* IL-6
*Hinstons Run* PA-2
**Hinswood**—*pop pl* IL-6
Hinter Cem—*cemetery* MS-4
Hinter Lake—*lake* WA-9
Hinterleiter—*locale* PA-2
Hinterleiter Sch (abandoned)—*school* PA-2
Hinterlong For Preserve—*forest* IL-6
Hinton—*locale* AL-4
Hinton—*locale* CA-9
Hinton—*locale* KY-4
Hinton—*locale* OH-6
**Hinton**—*pop pl* GA-3
**Hinton**—*pop pl* IA-7
**Hinton**—*pop pl* MO-7
**Hinton**—*pop pl* OK-5
**Hinton**—*pop pl* VA-3
**Hinton**—*pop pl* WV-2
Hinton, James, House—*hist pl* MO-7
Hinton, Mount—*summit* CA-9
Hinton Bay—*bay* WI-6
Hinton Branch—*stream* GA-3
Hinton Branch—*stream* (2) KY-4
Hinton Canyon—*valley* AZ-5
*Hinton Cem* AL-4
Hinton Cem—*cemetery* AL-4
Hinton Cem—*cemetery* AZ-5
Hinton Cem—*cemetery* GA-3
Hinton Cem—*cemetery* (2) KY-4
Hinton Cem—*cemetery* MI-6
Hinton Cem—*cemetery* (6) MS-4
Hinton Cem—*cemetery* MO-7
Hinton Cem—*cemetery* NC-3
Hinton Cem—*cemetery* OK-5
Hinton Ch—*church* AL-4
Hinton Ch—*church* AR-4
Hinton Ch—*church* MI-6
Hinton Ch—*church* MS-4
Hinton Chapel—*church* AR-4
Hinton-Coleman Hill—*summit* SD-7
*Hinton Creek* OR-9
Hinton Creek—*stream* AZ-5
Hinton Creek—*stream* (3) GA-3
Hinton Creek—*stream* KS-7
Hinton Creek—*stream* (2) MI-6
Hinton Creek—*stream* NC-3
Hinton Creek—*stream* (4) OR-9
Hinton Creek—*stream* (2) TX-5
Hinton Crossing—*locale* TN-4
Hinton Drain—*canal* MI-6
Hinton Farm Cem—*cemetery* OH-6
**Hinton Hills**—*pop pl* KY-4
Hinton Hist Dist—*hist pl* WV-2
Hinton Hollow—*valley* OK-5
Hinton Knob—*summit* KY-4
*Hinton Methodist Ch* MS-4
*Hinton Point* OR-9
Hinton Point—*cape* ME-1
Hinton Ranch—*locale* AZ-5
Hinton Ranch—*locale* OR-9
Hinton Rsvr—*reservoir* ID-8
Hinton Rural Life Center—*building* NC-3
Hinton Sch—*school* AL-4
Hinton Sch—*school* NE-7
Hinton Sch—*school* VT-1
Hinton Sch (historical)—*school* (2) MS-4
Hinton School—*locale* KS-7
*Hintons Grove* AL-4
Hinton Shoals—*bar* GA-3
Hinton Shoals Bridge—*bridge* GA-3
Hinton Slough—*stream* OR-9
Hintons Mill (historical)—*locale* AL-4
Hintons Mill (historical)—*locale* TN-4
Hinton Spring—*spring* AZ-5
Hinton Spring—*spring* ID-8
Hinton Spring—*spring* (2) OR-9
Hinton Springs—*spring* AZ-5
**Hinton (subdivision)**—*pop pl* NC-3
Hinton Surnuf Mine—*mine* CA-9
**Hintonsville (historical)**—*pop pl* NC-3
**Hinton (Township of)**—*pop pl* MI-6
Hintonville—*locale* MS-4
Hinton-Ward Ranch—*locale* OR-9
Hint Reservoirs—*reservoir* MT-8
Hintshon Ridge—*ridge* OH-6
*Hintugee* NC-3
**Hintz**—*pop pl* WI-6
Hintze-Anders House—*hist pl* UT-8
Hintz Lake—*lake* WI-6
Hintzville—*locale* WA-9
Hinuhinu Pali—*cliff* HI-9
Hinze—*locale* MS-4
*Hinze Baptist Church* MS-4
Hinze Cem—*cemetery* MS-4
Hinze Ch—*church* MS-4
Hinze Lake—*lake* LA-4
Hinz Fork—*stream* NE-7
Hinz Lake—*lake* MN-6
*Hio Hill* MA-1
Hio Hill—*summit* ME-1
Hio Hill—*summit* MA-1
Hionaa—*civil* HI-9
Hionamoa—*civil* HI-9
Hionamoa Gulch—*valley* HI-9
Hio Ridge—*ridge* ME-1
Hio Ridge Cem—*cemetery* ME-1
**Hiorra**—*pop pl* WV-2
**Hiouchi**—*pop pl* CA-9
Hiouchi Bridge—*bridge* CA-9

Hockman (West Graham)—uninc pl VA-3
Hockmock Bay ME-1
Hock Mock Swamp MA-1
Hock Mtn—summit WA-9
Hockney Hollow—valley PA-2
Hockomack River MA-1
Hockomack Swamp MA-1
Hockomock Bay ME-1
Hockomoch Channel ME-1
Hockomock ME-1
Hockomock Bay—bay ME-1
Hockomock Channel—channel ME-1
Hockomock Peninsula ME-1
Hockomock Point ME-1
Hockomock Point—cape (2) ME-1
Hockomock River—stream MA-1
Hockomock Swamp—swamp MA-1
Hockosofkee Creek GA-3
Hock Ridge Sch (abandoned)—school MO-7
Hock Run PA-2
Hock Spring—spring AZ-5
Hock Swale—valley UT-8
Hocomo—locale MO-7
Hocomoc Channel ME-1
Hocomock Channel ME-1
Hocomoco Pond MA-1
Hocomonco Pond—lake MA-1
Hocomonock Pond MA-1
Hoconuco Alto (Barrio)—fmr MCD PR-3
Hoconuco Bajo (Barrio)—fmr MCD PR-3
H O Cook State For—forest MA-1
Hocter Pond—lake ME-1
Hocum Hollow—valley MO-7
Hocumville Ch—church NY-2
Hocutt Cem—cemetery (2) NC-3
Hocutt Memorial Ch—church NC-3
**Hocutts Crossroads**—pop pl NC-3
Hocutts Mill (historical)—locale AL-4
Hodag Creek—stream MT-8
Hodag Lake—lake WI-6
Hodag Park—park WI-6
Hodag Trail—trail PA-2
Hodam—locale WV-2
Hodam Creek—stream WV-2
Hodam Mtn—summit WV-2
Hodapp Creek—stream CA-9
Hodatic River—stream AK-9
H O Davis Ranch—locale AZ-5
Hodchodkee Creek—stream GA-3
Hodchodkee Pond—reservoir GA-3
Hodding Creek CO-8
Hodding Creek—stream CO-8
Hode—locale KY-4
Hodegaden Creek—stream AK-9
Hodenpyl Dam—dam MI-6
Hodenpyl Dam Pond—reservoir MI-6
Hodes Park—park IL-6
Hodgden, Perry, House—hist pl KS-7
**Hodgdon**—pop pl ME-1
Hodgdon Brook—stream ME-1
**Hodgdon Corners**—pop pl ME-1
Hodgdon Hill—summit NH-1
Hodgdon Hill Sch—school NH-1
Hodgdon Homestead Cabin—hist pl CA-9
Hodgdon Island—island (2) ME-1
Hodgdon Ledge—bar ME-1
Hodgdon Pond—lake ME-1
Hodgdon Ranch—locale CA-9
Hodgdon Site—hist pl ME-1
**Hodgdon (Town of)**—pop pl ME-1
Hodgdor Cove—bay ME-1
Hodge—locale AL-4
**Hodge**—pop pl CA-9
**Hodge**—pop pl IA-7
**Hodge**—pop pl LA-4
**Hodge**—pop pl MO-7
Hodge—uninc pl TX-5
Hodge, Lake—lake FL-3
Hodge Bayou FL-3
Hodge Bend—bend TN-4
Hodge Branch—stream IN-6
Hodge Branch—stream KY-4
Hodge Branch—stream MS-4
Hodge Branch—stream (4) TN-4
Hodge Branch—stream TX-5
Hodge brook MA-1
Hodge Brook—stream MA-1
Hodge Canyon—valley NM-5
Hodge Cem—cemetery (2) IL-6
Hodge Cem—cemetery (2) KY-4
Hodge Cem—cemetery LA-4
Hodge Cem—cemetery MI-6
Hodge Cem—cemetery (2) MS-4
Hodge Cem—cemetery (2) MO-7
Hodge Cem—cemetery OH-6
Hodge Cem—cemetery (5) TN-4
Hodge Cem—cemetery TX-5
Hodge Cem—cemetery (2) WV-2
Hodge Cem—cemetery WI-6
Hodge Ch—church AL-4
Hodge Chapel Church AL-4
Hodge Creek GA-3
Hodge Creek—stream AL-4
Hodge Creek—stream KY-4
Hodge Creek—stream MI-6
Hodge Creek—stream MO-7
Hodge Creek—stream MT-8
Hodge Creek—stream NY-2
Hodge Creek—stream OK-5
Hodge Creek—stream WY-8
Hodge Crest—ridge OR-9
Hodge Dam—dam NC-3
Hodge Ditch—canal (3) IN-6
Hodgedon Brook—stream NH-1
Hodgedon Sch—school ME-1
Hodge Ferry (historical)—crossing TN-4
Hodge Hall—hist pl SC-3
Hodge Hill—summit ME-1
Hodge Hill—summit MO-7
Hodge Hill Cem—cemetery MS-4
Hodge Hollow—valley (3) MO-7
Hodge Hollow—valley TN-4
Hodge Island—island AL-4
Hodge Island—island TN-4
Hodge Junction—uninc pl TX-5
Hodge Lake MI-6
Hodge Lake—lake AL-4
Hodge Lake—lake GA-3
Hodge Lake—lake MI-6
Hodge Lake—lake SC-3
Hodge Lake—lake WA-9
Hodge Lake—lake WI-6
Hodge Lake—reservoir NC-3
Hodgeman Centre (historical)—locale KS-7
Hodgeman Community Ch—church KS-7
Hodgeman County—civil KS-7
Hodgeman County Dam—dam KS-7
Hodgeman County State Lake—reservoir KS-7
Hodgeman County State Lake Dam—dam KS-7
Hodgeman County State Park—park KS-7
Hodgeman Hill—summit NH-1
Hodgeman (historical)—locale KS-7
Hodgeman Ranch—locale CA-9
Hodgeman Rock—rock MA-1
Hodgeman State Fishing Lake And Wildlife Area—park KS-7
Hodge Memorial Ch—church WV-2
Hodge Mine—mine KY-4
Hodge Mine—mine TN-4
Hodge Mtn—summit AL-4
Hodge Mtn—summit GA-3
**Hodgen**—pop pl OK-5
Hodgen Cem—cemetery OK-5
Hodgen Ditch MT-8
Hodge Nibley Creek—stream ID-8
**Hodgen (RR name Hodgens)**—pop pl OK-5
Hodgens OK-5
Hodgen's Cemetery Mound—hist pl OH-6
Hodgens Creek—stream AL-4
Hodgens (RR name for Hodgen)—other OK-5
Hodgens Sch (historical)—school MO-7
**Hodgenville**—pop pl KY-4
Hodgenville (CCD)—cens area KY-4
Hodgenville Christian Church—hist pl KY-4
Hodgenville Commercial Hist Dist—hist pl KY-4
Hodge Park—park CT-1
Hodge Pass—gap OR-9
Hodge Podge Lodge—locale TX-5
Hodge Pond MA-1
Hodge Pond—lake CT-1
Hodge Pond—lake NH-1
Hodge Pond—lake NY-2
Hodge Prospect—mine TN-4
Hodge Ranch Spring—spring UT-8
Hodger Branch—stream TN-4
Hodge Rock MA-1
Hodgers Pond—lake TN-4
Hodge Run—stream PA-2
Hodges AL-4
Hodges—locale KS-7
Hodges—locale TX-5
**Hodges**—pop pl AL-4
**Hodges**—pop pl MT-8
**Hodges**—pop pl SC-3
**Hodges**—pop pl TN-4
**Hodges**—pop pl VA-3
**Hodges**—pop pl WV-2
Hodges, Lake—reservoir CA-9
Hodges, Peter B., House—hist pl AZ-5
Hodges Bayou—bay FL-3
Hodges Branch—channel FL-3
Hodges Branch—stream LA-4
Hodges Branch—stream MO-7
Hodges Branch—stream SC-3
Hodges Branch—stream TN-4
Hodges Branch—stream WV-2
Hodges Brook—stream MA-1
Hodges Cabin—locale CA-9
Hodges Canal—canal LA-4
Hodges Canyon—valley CA-9
Hodges Canyon—valley NV-8
Hodges Canyon—valley UT-8
Hodges Cem—cemetery (5) AL-4
Hodges Cem—cemetery (5) GA-3
Hodges Cem—cemetery KS-7
Hodges Cem—cemetery KY-4
Hodges Cem—cemetery LA-4
Hodges Cem—cemetery MS-4
Hodges Cem—cemetery MO-7
Hodges Cem—cemetery NC-3
Hodges Cem—cemetery SC-3
Hodges Cem—cemetery (9) TN-4
Hodges Cem—cemetery TX-5
Hodges Cem—cemetery VA-3
Hodges Cem—cemetery WV-2
Hodges Ch—church GA-3
Hodges Ch—church TX-5
Hodges Sch—school AR-4
Hodges Sch—school CA-9
Hodges Sch—school OH-6
Hodges Chapel—church AL-4
Hodges Chapel—church KY-4
Hodges Chapel—church MS-4
Hodges Chapel—church (2) NC-3
Hodges Chapel—church TN-4
Hodges Chapel Cem—cemetery MS-4
Hodges Chapel Cem—cemetery TN-4
Hodges Chapel Methodist Church MS-4
Hodges Cherry Mound Airp—airport TN-4
Hodges Ch (historical)—church MS-4
Hodges Sch (historical)—school PA-2
Hodges Sch (historical)—school TN-4
Hodges Cove—bay VA-3
Hodges Creek NC-3
Hodges Creek—stream AL-4
Hodges Creek—stream (2) IL-6
Hodges Creek—stream KY-4
Hodges Creek—stream MI-6
Hodges Creek—stream MT-8
Hodges Creek—stream (3) NC-3
Hodges Creek—stream OR-9
Hodges Creek—stream TN-4
Hodges Creek—stream VA-3
Hodges Dam—dam AL-4
Hodges Ditch VA-3
Hodges Ditch—canal IN-6
Hodges Ditch—canal MT-8
Hodges Ditch—canal OH-6
Hodges Draft—valley VA-3
Hodges Drain—canal CA-9
Hodges Draw—valley WY-8
Hodges Family Cem—cemetery AL-4
Hodges Ferry TN-4
**Hodges Ferry**—pop pl VA-3
Hodges Ferry Bridge—bridge VA-3
Hodges Ferry (historical)—locale AL-4
Hodges Gap—gap NC-3
**Hodges Gap**—pop pl NC-3
Hodges-Hardy-Chambers House—hist pl TX-5
Hodges Heights Park—park PA-2
**Hodges Heights (subdivision)**—pop pl PA-2
Hodges Hill—summit NY-2
Hodges Hill Ch—church GA-3
Hodges Horse Pasture—flat WA-9
Hodges House—hist pl IL-6
Hodges House—hist pl LA-4
Hodges House—hist pl MA-1
Hodges Island—island FL-3
Hodge Site—hist pl OK-5
Hodges Lake AL-4
Hodges Lake NY-2
Hodges Lake—lake AR-4
Hodges Lake—lake LA-4
Hodges Lake—lake MI-6
Hodges Lake—lake MS-4
Hodges Lake—lake SC-3
Hodges Lake—lake TN-4
**Hodges Lake**—pop pl AL-4
Hodges Lake—reservoir (2) GA-3
Hodges Lake Dam AL-4
Hodges Library—building TN-4
Hodges Lookout Tower—locale SC-3
Hodge Slough—stream TX-5
**Hodges Manor**—pop pl VA-3
Hodges Manor Sch—school VA-3
Hodges Mathis Mill Creek—stream AL-4
Hodges Mill TN-4
Hodges Mill—locale VA-3
Hodges Mill Creek NC-3
Hodges Millpond—lake NH-1
Hodges Mission—church LA-4
Hodges Mtn—summit MT-8
Hodge's Narrows VA-3
Hodges Narrows—gut VA-3
Hodges New Pond—lake GA-3
Hodgeson Brook—stream ME-1
Hodgeson Sch—school MT-8
Hodges Park (RR name for Unity)—other IL-6
Hodges Peak—summit WY-8
Hodges Pond MA-1
Hodges Pond—lake AL-4
Hodges Pond—lake CT-1
Hodges Pond—lake (2) GA-3
Hodges Pond—reservoir GA-3
Hodges Post Office (historical)—building TN-4
Hodge Spring Corral—locale WY-8
Hodges Ranch—locale MT-8
Hodges Ranch—locale NV-8
Hodges Ranch—locale NM-5
Hodges Ranch—locale WA-9
Hodges Rock—rock MA-1
Hodges-Runyan-Brainard House—hist pl NM-5
Hodges Sch—school AL-4
Hodges Sch—school MI-6
Hodges Sch—school TN-4
Hodges Sch—school TX-5
Hodges Sch—school WV-2
Hodges-Sipple House—hist pl NM-5
Hodges (Site)—locale NM-5
Hodges Slough—gut ID-8
Hodges Spring—spring ID-8
Hodges Spring—spring TN-4
Hodges Spring—spring UT-8
Hodges Store (2) AL-4
**Hodges Store**—pop pl AL-4
Hodges Tank—reservoir AZ-5
**Hodges (Township of)**—pop pl MN-6
**Hodges Village**—pop pl MA-1
Hodges Village Dam—dam MA-1
Hodges Village Pond—reservoir MA-1
**Hodgesville**—pop pl AL-4
**Hodgesville**—pop pl VA-3
**Hodgesville**—pop pl WV-2
Hodgesville Ch—church AL-4
**Hodgetown**—pop pl TN-4
Hodgetown Branch—stream TN-4
Hodgets Canyon—valley AZ-5
Hodge Village MA-1
Hodgeville—locale IL-6
**Hodgewood**—pop pl AL-4
Hodgin Hall—hist pl NM-5
Hodgin, Abner F., House—hist pl MN-6
Hodgin Sch—school NM-5
Hodgins Lake—lake SC-3
Hodgins Pond—reservoir NC-3
Hodgins Pond Dam—dam NC-3
Hodgins Slough—gut AK-9
Hodgkin Cove MA-1
**Hodgkins**—pop pl IL-6
Hodgkins Brook—stream ME-1
Hodgkins Cem—cemetery ME-1
Hodgkins Cove—cove MA-1
Hodgkins Gulch—valley AZ-5
Hodgkins House—hist pl KY-4
Hodgkins JHS—school CO-8
Hodgkins Park—park IL-6
Hodgkins Park—park WI-6
Hodgkins Peak—summit AK-9
Hodgkins Point—cape AK-9
Hodgkins Sch—school MA-1
Hodgkins Windmill—locale AZ-5
Hodgman Canyon—valley MT-8
Hodgman Hill—summit ME-1
Hodgmans Creek—stream NY-2
Hodgman State For—forest NH-1
Hodgoods AL-4
Hodgsen Pond—lake UT-8
Hodgskiss Ranch—locale MT-8
Hodgson—locale FL-3
**Hodgson**—pop pl TX-5
Hodgson, Lake—lake OH-6
Hodgson, W. B., Hall—hist pl GA-3
Hodgson Bridge—other IL-6
Hodgson Brook—stream NH-1
Hodgson Canyon—valley OR-9
Hodgson Cem—cemetery VA-3
Hodgson Creek—stream WA-9
Hodgson Ditch—canal CO-8
Hodgson-Harris Rsvr—reservoir CO-8
Hodgson Hill—summit FL-3
Hodgson Lake—lake (2) MN-6
Hodgson Mill Spring—spring MO-7
Hodgson Point—cape MD-2
Hodgson Run—stream PA-2
Hodgsons Island—island ME-1
Hodikof Bay—bay AK-9
Hodikof Point—cape AK-9
Hodister Run—stream MD-2
Hod Main Coulee—valley MT-8
Hodnett Creek—stream AL-4
Hodnett Mill Creek—stream AL-4
Hodo Gap—gap GA-3
Hodo Hollow—valley MO-7
Hodo Spring—spring MO-7
Hodsden Bridge—bridge TN-4
Hodsdon Flats—flat MT-8
**Hods Hollow Subdivision**—pop pl UT-8
Hodson—locale TN-4
Hodson Cem—cemetery (2) IN-6
Hodson Creek—stream ID-8
Hodson Creek—stream (2) OR-9
Hodson Ditch—canal IN-6
**Hodson Estates Subdivision**—pop pl UT-8
Hodson Sch—school ME-1
Hodson Sch—school SD-7
Hods Ranch—locale UT-8
Hodstradt Lake—lake WI-6
**Hodunk**—pop pl MI-6
Hodunk Pond—lake MI-6
Hodzana River—stream AK-9
Hodzana Slough—stream AK-9
Hoe TN-4
Hoea Camp—locale HI-9
**Hoea (Hoea Camp)**—pop pl HI-9
Hoea - Kaao Tract—civil HI-9
Hoea Valley—valley HI-9
Hoeb Mine—mine IL-6
Hoebuck NJ-2
Hoecake Village Archeol Site—hist pl MO-7
Hoecker—locale MO-7
Hoeckers Cove—bay TX-5
Hoeckers Point—cape TX-5
Hoecradle Canyon—valley NM-5
Hoecradle Tank—reservoir (2) NM-5
Hoe Creek—stream WY-8
Hoedapp Creek MO-7
Hoedapp Creek—stream MO-7
Hoefeld Ch—church MO-7
Hoefer—locale TX-5
Hoeffken Lake—swamp MN-6
Hoeffkens Lake MN-6
Hoefle Dulin Rec Area—park IA-7
Hoefle Oil Field—oilfield TX-5
Hoef-Scheer Ranch—locale NE-7
Hoefs Ranch—locale TX-5
Hoegee Campground—locale CA-9
Hoegle Drain—canal MI-6
Hoehammer Branch—stream KY-4
**Hoehne**—pop pl CO-8
Hoehne Ditch—canal CO-8
Hoehnes CO-8
Hoehn Mine (underground)—mine AL-4
Hoehns Lake—reservoir VA-3
Hoeh Sch (abandoned)—school PA-2
Hoe Island—island ME-1
Hoekaday Sch—school TX-5
Hoekman School SD-7
Hoekstre Rsvr—reservoir OR-9
Hoekstre Slough—stream OR-9
Hoekwater Park—park MI-6
Hoe Lake—lake MN-6
Hoe Lick Run—stream WV-2
Hoel Pond—lake NY-2
Hoelscher Elem Sch—school TX-5
Hoelsher Creek—stream AK-9
Hoeltz, Herbert, House—hist pl WI-6
Hoelz, Alfred M., House—hist pl WI-6
Hoelzle Place—locale ID-8
Hoemako Co-Operative Hosp—hospital AZ-5
Hoen—locale TX-5
Hoene Drift Mine (underground)—mine AL-4
**Hoene Spring**—pop pl MO-7
Hoene-Werle House—hist pl PA-2
Hoen Slough (historical)—swamp MO-7
Ho-e Park—park AZ-5
Hoepa (Site)—locale HI-9
Hoepker Cem—cemetery WI-6
Hoe Pond—lake CT-1
Hoe Post Office TN-4
Hoe Ranch—locale WY-8
Hoe Ranch Arroyo—stream CO-8
Hoere-kil DE-2
Hoere Kill County DE-2
Hoeren-Kil DE-2
Hoerenkil County DE-2
**Hoernerstown**—pop pl PA-2
Hoerners Waldorf Pond Dam—dam NC-3
Hoerner Waldorf Corporation—facility IL-6
Hoerner Waldorf Pond—reservoir NC-3
Hoersch, John, House—hist pl IA-7
Hoerth Lake—lake WI-6
**Hoeseville**—pop pl NY-2
Hoe Spring—spring (2) WY-8
Hoe Swamp—stream NC-3
Hoe Tank—reservoir AZ-5
Hoevens Gulch—valley ND-7
Hoevet Creek—stream OR-9
Hoeye Ranch—locale SD-7
Hoey Point—cape OR-9
**Hofa Park**—pop pl WI-6
Hofeld Lake—lake NE-7
Hofeldt Ranch—locale WY-8
Hofer, Enoch, House-Barn—hist pl SD-7
Hofer, Michael, House—hist pl SD-7
Hofer Dam—dam SD-7
Hofer Landing Field—airport SD-7
Hofer Pond—reservoir OR-9
Hofer Ranch—locale MT-8
Hofer Sch—school SD-7
Hofer State Public Shooting Area—park SD-7
Hofert-Arcade Prospect Mine SD-7
Hoffa Cem—cemetery MS-4
Hoffacker Sch—school PA-2
**Hoffasville (historical)**—pop pl TN-4
Hoffasville Post Office (historical)—building TN-4
Hoffa Trail—trail PA-2
Hoff Cem—cemetery MN-6
Hoff Cem—cemetery (2) ND-7
Hoff Ch—church (2) ND-7
Hoff Coulee—valley MT-8
Hoffecker-Lockwood House—hist pl DE-2
Hoffelder Ditch—canal IN-6
**Hoffer**—pop pl PA-2
Hoffer Butte—summit OR-9
Hoffer Cem—cemetery NE-7
Hoffer Creek—stream (2) PA-2
Hoffer Hill—summit OH-6
Hoffer Hill Ch—church OH-6
Hoffer Hollow—valley TX-5
Hoffer Lakes—lake OR-9
Hoffey Sch (historical)—school PA-2
Hoff Gap—gap WY-8
Hoff Lake—lake (2) MN-6
Hoff Lake—lake WY-8
Hoffland—locale NE-7
Hoffland Lateral—canal MT-8
Hoff Lateral—canal ID-8
Hoffler Creek—stream VA-3
Hofflin & Greentree Bldg—hist pl GA-3
Hofflins—locale MO-7
Hofflund Bay—bay ND-7
Hofflund Gas and Oil Field—oilfield ND-7
Hofflund Sch—school ND-7
Hofflund State Game Mngmt Area—park ND-7
**Hofflund Township**—pop pl ND-7
Hoffman AL-4
Hoffman NJ-2
Hoffman PA-2
Hoffman TN-4
Hoffman—locale MS-4
Hoffman—locale MO-7
Hoffman—locale MT-8
Hoffman—locale NJ-2
Hoffman—locale VI-3
**Hoffman**—pop pl IL-6
**Hoffman**—pop pl MD-2
**Hoffman**—pop pl MN-6
**Hoffman**—pop pl NY-2
**Hoffman**—pop pl NC-3
**Hoffman**—pop pl OK-5
**Hoffman**—pop pl PA-2
Hoffman, Amos, House—hist pl SD-7
Hoffman, Charles, House—hist pl MT-8
Hoffman, George, House—hist pl PA-2
Hoffman, George P., House—hist pl SC-3
Hoffman, Isaac, House—hist pl MD-2
Hoffman, Mount—summit AK-9
Hoffman, Mount—summit (3) CA-9
Hoffman, Samuel, Jr., House—hist pl IA-7
Hoffman Airp—airport PA-2
Hoffman Airstrip—airport OR-9
Hoffman Arm—canal IN-6
Hoffman Barn—hist pl ID-8
Hoffman Bldg—hist pl IA-7
Hoffman Boston JHS—school VA-3
Hoffman-Bowers-Josey-Riddick House—hist pl NC-3
Hoffman Branch AL-4
Hoffman Branch—stream TX-5
Hoffman Brook—stream (2) NY-2
Hoffman Campground—locale ID-8
Hoffman Canal—canal NJ-2
Hoffman Canyon—valley (2) CA-9
Hoffman Canyon—valley NV-8
Hoffman Cem—cemetery AL-4
Hoffman Cem—cemetery IL-6
Hoffman Cem—cemetery IN-6
Hoffman Cem—cemetery KY-4
Hoffman Cem—cemetery LA-4
Hoffman Cem—cemetery NJ-2
Hoffman Cem—cemetery OH-6
Hoffman Cem—cemetery OK-5
Hoffman Cem—cemetery PA-2
Hoffman Cem—cemetery (2) TX-5
Hoffman Cem—cemetery VA-3
Hoffman Cem—cemetery WV-2
Hoffman Cem—cemetery (2) WI-6
Hoffman Cemeteries—cemetery WV-2
Hoffman Ch—church PA-2
Hoffman Chapel—church NC-3
Hoffman Corners—locale WI-6
Hoffman Coulee—valley MT-8
Hoffman Cove—bay WA-9
Hoffman Creek CA-9
Hoffman Creek PA-2
Hoffman Creek—stream (3) CA-9
Hoffman Creek—stream CO-8
Hoffman Creek—stream FL-3
Hoffman Creek—stream IL-6
Hoffman Creek—stream IN-6
Hoffman Creek—stream IA-7
Hoffman Creek—stream LA-4
Hoffman Creek—stream MT-8
Hoffman Creek—stream (2) OR-9
Hoffman Creek—stream TX-5
Hoffman Creek—stream UT-8
Hoffman Creek—stream (3) WI-6
Hoffman Creek—stream WY-8
**Hoffman Crossing**—pop pl IN-6
Hoffman Dam—dam OR-9
Hoffman Dam—dam SD-7
Hoffman Ditch IN-6
Hoffman Ditch—canal (3) IN-6
Hoffman Ditch—canal OR-9
Hoffman Drain MI-6
Hoffman Drain—canal MI-6
Hoffman Drain—stream MI-6
Hoffman Draw—valley MT-8
Hoffman Elem Sch—school NC-3
**Hoffman Estates**—pop pl IL-6
Hoffman Falls KS-7
Hoffman Falls—falls IN-6
Hoffman Farm Camp—locale PA-2
Hoffman Flat—flat CA-9
Hoffman Gulch—valley MT-8
Hoffman Heights CO-8
**Hoffman Heights Subdivision**—pop pl UT-8
**Hoffman Heights Subdivision - Numbers 12 and 13**—pop pl UT-8
Hoffman Hill—summit MD-2
Hoffman Hill—summit OR-9
Hoffman Hill—summit WA-9
Hoffman (historical)—locale PA-2
Hoffman Hollow AL-4
Hoffman Hollow—valley MO-7
Hoffman Hollow—valley NY-2
Hoffman Hollow—valley (2) WV-2
Hoffman Hotel—hist pl IN-6
Hoffman House—hist pl KY-4
Hoffman House—hist pl OH-6
Hoffman House Hotel—hist pl WI-6
Hoffman Iron Deposit Mine—mine SD-7
Hoffman Island—island IL-6
Hoffman Island—island NY-2
Hoffman Islands TN-4
Hoffman JHS—school MI-6
Hoffman Junction—locale MO-7
Hoffman Lake—lake CO-8
Hoffman Lake—lake IN-6
Hoffman Lakes—lake (2) MI-6
Hoffman Lake—lake (2) MN-6
Hoffman Lake—lake WI-6
**Hoffman Lake**—pop pl IN-6
Hoffman Lake—reservoir NC-3
Hoffman Lake Dam—dam NC-3
Hoffman Lepper Ditch—canal IN-6
Hoffman Meadow—flat CA-9
Hoffman Memorial State Wayside—park OR-9
Hoffman Mid Sch—school IL-6
Hoffman Mill (historical)—locale TN-4
Hoffman Mill (Site)—locale CA-9
Hoffman Mtn—summit CA-9
Hoffman Mtn—summit NY-2
Hoffmann Creek CA-9
Hoffmann Creek—stream CA-9
Hoffmann Niedhardt Ditch—canal CO-8
Hoffmann Island NY-2
Hoffmann-La Roche Incorporated—airport NJ-2
Hoffman Notch—gap NY-2
Hoffman Notch Brook—stream NY-2
Hoffmann Township—civil SD-7
Hoffman Oil Field—oilfield TX-5
Hoffman Oil Field—other IL-6
Hoffman Orphanage—building PA-2
Hoffman Park—flat CO-8
Hoffman Park—park AZ-5
Hoffman Park—park CA-9
Hoffman Park—park MN-6
Hoffman Park—park NM-5
Hoffman Pits—mine CA-9
Hoffman Place—locale MT-8
Hoffman Point OR-9
Hoffman Point—locale CA-9
Hoffman Pond—reservoir MI-6
Hoffman Ranch—locale NV-8
Hoffman Ranch—locale OR-9
Hoffman Rhyne Lake—reservoir AL-4
Hoffman Rhyne Lake Dam AL-4
Hoffman Ridge—ridge PA-2
Hoffman Ridge—ridge WV-2
Hoffman Roadside Park—park SD-7
Hoffman Run—stream IN-6
Hoffman Run—stream OH-6
Hoffman Run—stream (3) PA-2
Hoffman Run—stream WV-2
Hoffman's NY-2
Hoffmans PA-2
Hoffmans—locale NJ-2
**Hoffmans**—pop pl IN-6
**Hoffmans**—pop pl NY-2
Hoffman Sch—school (2) CA-9
Hoffman Sch—school (3) IL-6
Hoffman Sch—school LA-4
Hoffman Sch—school MA-1
Hoffman Sch—school (2) NY-2
Hoffman Sch—school OH-6
Hoffman Sch—school TX-5
Hoffman Sch—school WV-2
Hoffman Sch (abandoned)—school PA-2
Hoffman Sch (historical)—school MO-7
Hoffman Sch (Maxey School)—school MT-8
Hoffman School (Abandoned)—locale WI-6
Hoffmans Church PA-2
**Hoffmans Corner**—pop pl MN-6
Hoffmans Corners MN-6
Hoffmans Ferry TN-4
Hoffmans Lake IN-6
Hoffmans Mill KS-7
Hoffmans Mill—locale MD-2
Hoffmans Mill—locale NJ-2
Hoffmans Mill Dam—dam NJ-2
Hoffmans Mill Pond—reservoir NJ-2
Hoffman Spring—spring NM-5
Hoffman Spring—spring (2) OR-9
Hoffman State Park OR-9
Hoffman Station NJ-2
Hoffman Station NY-2
**Hoffmans Trailer Court (subdivision)**—pop pl SD-7
Hoffman Summit—gap CA-9
Hoffmansville PA-2
**Hoffmansville**—pop pl PA-2
Hoffman Tank—reservoir (2) AZ-5
Hoffman Tank—reservoir NM-5
Hoffman Thorofare—channel NJ-2
**Hoffman Town**—pop pl NM-5
Hoffmantown—uninc pl NM-5
**Hoffman Township**—pop pl ND-7
**Hoffman Township**—pop pl SD-7
Hoffmanville—locale MD-2
Hoffmanville—locale MT-8
Hoffman Well (Dry)—well CA-9
Hoffman Windmill—locale CO-8
Hoffman Woods—woods WA-9
Hoffman Zion Ch—church PA-2
**Hoffmeister**—pop pl NY-2
Hoffmeister Cem—cemetery IA-7
Hoffmeister Creek—stream CA-9
Hoffmeister Spring—spring MO-7
**Hoffmeyer Crossing**—pop pl SC-3
Hoffmyer Creek—stream MI-6
Hoffmyer Drain—canal MI-6
Hoffner Hist Dist—hist pl OH-6
Hoffners Lake—reservoir NC-3
Hoffners Lake Dam—dam NC-3
Hoffnugstahl Cem—cemetery SD-7
Hoffnungberg Cem—cemetery SD-7
Hoffnungsay Ch—church KS-7
Hoffnungs Cem—cemetery SD-7
Hoffnungsfeld Cem—cemetery ND-7
Hoffnungsfeld Township—civil SD-7
Hoffnungs Gemeinde Cem—cemetery SD-7
Hoffnungstahl Cem—cemetery SD-7
Hoffnungstal Cem—cemetery (2) SD-7
Hoff Pond—reservoir AL-4
Hoff Pond Dam—dam AL-4
Hoff Ranch—locale WY-8
Hoff Run—stream OH-6
Hoff Sch—school IN-6
Hoff Sch—school SD-7
Hoff Sch (abandoned)—school PA-2
Hoffse Point—cape ME-1
Hoffse's Point ME-1
Hoffs Gulch—valley CA-9
Hoffs Point ME-1
Hoffs Slough—lake MN-6
Hoffstadt Creek—stream WA-9
Hoffstadt Creek Park—park WA-9

Hoffstadt Mtn—*summit* WA-9
Hoffstadt Viewpoint Heliport—*airport* WA-9
*Hoffstead Creek* WA-9
*Hoffstedt Creek* WA-9
Hoffstetter, Jacob, House—*hist pl* MI-6
**Hoff Subdivision**—*pop pl* UT-8
Hofftowe Meadows—*flat* WY-8
**Hoff (Township of)**—*pop pl* MN-6
Hoff-Ulland Farm—*hist pl* TX-5
Hoff Valley—*valley* WI-6
Hofheimer Cem—*cemetery* NJ-2
Hofheintz-Reissig Store—*hist pl* TX-5
Hofheinz, Augusta, House—*hist pl* TX-5
Hofheinz, Walter, House—*hist pl* TX-5
Hofherr Chapel—*church* IN-6
Hoflanda Ch—*church* MN-6
*Hoflar's Creek* VA-3
**Hoflers Fork**—*pop pl* NC-3
Hofmann Cem—*cemetery* WV-2
Hofmann For—*forest* NC-3
Hofmann Ranch—*locale* CO-8
Hofmann Rsvr—*reservoir* CO-8
Hofmann Tower—*hist pl* IL-6
*Hofman Peak* WA-9
Hofma Park—*park* MI-6
*Hofs* NJ-2
Hofschulte Hill—*summit* OK-5
Hofstad Creek—*stream* AK-9
Hofstetter Sch—*school* WA-9
Hofstra Coll—*school* NY-2
Hofstra Univ Old Westbury Campus—*school* NY-2
Hofva Ch—*church* ND-7
Hofwyl-Broadfield Plantation—*hist pl* GA-3
Hogadero Draw—*valley* NM-5
Hogadon Basin Ski Area—*area* WY-8
*Hogaerikku-To* MP-9
*Hogairikku-to* MP-9
Hogala Lake—*lake* MI-6
*Hogamockock Point* ME-1
Hogan—*locale* AR-4
Hogan—*locale* GA-3
Hogan—*locale* NV-8
Hogan—*locale* OR-9
**Hogan**—*pop pl* FL-3
**Hogan**—*pop pl* GA-3
**Hogan**—*pop pl* MO-7
Hogan, Lake—*reservoir* NC-3
Hogan, Mount—*summit* AK-9
Hogan Airp—*airport* NC-3
*Hogan Basin* UT-8
Hogan Basin—*valley* UT-8
*Hogan Bay* SC-3
Hogan Bay—*bay* AK-9
Hogan-Borger Mound Archeol District—*hist pl* OH-6
*Hogan Branch* SC-3
Hogan Branch—*stream* GA-3
Hogan Branch—*stream* NC-3
Hogan Branch—*stream* (2) TN-4
Hogan Branch—*stream* VA-3
Hogan Cabin—*locale* AZ-5
Hogan Cabin—*locale* NM-5
Hogan Cabin Trail—*trail* NM-5
*Hogan Canyon* UT-8
Hogan Cave—*cave* AL-4
Hogan Cem—*cemetery* (2) AR-4
Hogan Cem—*cemetery* IL-6
Hogan Cem—*cemetery* KY-4
Hogan Cem—*cemetery* OK-5
Hogan Cem—*cemetery* TX-5
Hogan Cem—*cemetery* (2) VA-3
Hogan Ch—*church* FL-3
Hogan Ch—*church* UT-8
Hogan Chapel Sch (historical)—*school* MS-4
*Hogan Corner* GA-3
Hogan Cove—*valley* NC-3
*Hogan Creek* AR-4
*Hogan Creek* IN-6
*Hogan Creek* NC-3
Hogan Creek—*stream* AL-4
Hogan Creek—*stream* AR-4
Hogan Creek—*stream* CA-9
Hogan Creek—*stream* CO-8
Hogan Creek—*stream* IN-6
Hogan Creek—*stream* MS-4
Hogan Creek—*stream* MO-7
Hogan Creek—*stream* (5) MT-8
Hogan Creek—*stream* NC-3
Hogan Creek—*stream* OR-9
Hogan Creek—*stream* TN-4
Hogan Creek—*stream* (2) TX-5
Hogan Creek—*stream* (2) VA-3
Hogan Creek—*stream* WA-9
Hogan Creek Ch—*church* NC-3
Hogan Creek Ch—*church* TN-4
Hogan Creek Sch (historical)—*school* TN-4
Hogan Dam—*dam* CA-9
Hog and Homing Cove—*bay* FL-3
Hogan Ditch—*canal* IN-6
Hogan Ditch—*canal* (3) MT-8
Hogan Fork—*stream* MO-7
Hogan Grove Ch—*church* GA-3
Hogan Gulch—*valley* ID-8
Hogan Hill—*summit* AK-9
Hogan Hill—*summit* FL-3
Hogan Hill—*summit* NY-2
Hogan Hill—*summit* VT-1
Hogan Hill Ch—*church* IN-6
Hogan Hollow—*valley* AR-4
Hogan Hollow—*valley* IN-6
Hogan Hollow—*valley* MO-7
Hogan Hollow—*valley* (4) TN-4
Hogan Hollow Sch (historical)—*school* MO-7
Hogan HS—*school* MO-7
Hogan Island—*island* AK-9
Hogan Island—*island* FL-3
Hogan JHS—*school* CA-9
Hogan Lake—*lake* AK-9
Hogan Lake—*lake* CA-9
Hogan Lake—*reservoir* AZ-5
Hogan Lake—*reservoir* GA-3
Hogan Lake—*reservoir* (2) NC-3
Hogan Lake—*reservoir* VA-3
Hogan Lake Dam—*dam* NC-3
*Hogan Meadow* CA-9
Hogan Mesa—*summit* UT-8
Hogan Mine—*mine* CA-9
Hogan Mtn—*summit* AR-4
Hogan Mtn—*summit* CA-9
Hogan Mtn—*summit* MO-7
Hogan Park—*park* MS-4
Hogan Park—*park* TX-5
**Hogan Park Subdivision**—*pop pl* UT-8
Hogan Pass—*gap* UT-8
Hogan Point—*cape* IL-6
Hogan Point—*cape* WA-9
Hogan Pond—*lake* FL-3
Hogan Pond—*lake* ME-1
Hogan Pond—*lake* TN-4
Hogan Ponds—*lake* MA-1
Hogan Quarters—*hist pl* KY-4
*Hogan Reservoir* CA-9
Hogan Ridge—*ridge* (2) AZ-5
Hogan Ridge—*ridge* NC-3
Hogan Ridge—*ridge* TX-5
Hogan Rsvr—*reservoir* WY-8
*Hogan Sa-ani Spring* AZ-5
Hogansaani Spring—*spring* AZ-5
Hogansaani Wash—*stream* AZ-5
Hogans Alley—*valley* NV-8
Hogans Alley—*valley* UT-8
*Hogan Say-ani Spring* AZ-5
Hogans Bottoms—*flat* IL-6
Hogans Branch—*stream* FL-3
Hogans Branch—*stream* GA-3
Hogans Branch—*stream* IA-7
Hogans Brook—*stream* ME-1
**Hogansburg**—*pop pl* NY-2
Hogan Sch—*school* IL-6
Hogan Sch—*school* MT-8
Hogan Sch—*school* (2) WI-6
Hogan Sch (abandoned)—*school* MO-7
Hogan's Corner Airp—*airport* WA-9
*Hogans Creek* MO-7
*Hogans Creek* TN-4
Hogans Creek—*stream* AR-4
Hogans Creek—*stream* (3) NC-3
*Hogans Creek Baptist Church* TN-4
Hogans Guard Station—*locale* MT-8
Hogans Hill—*locale* VA-3
Hogans HS—*school* TX-5
Hogans Island—*island* GA-3
Hogans Lake—*lake* MN-6
Hogan Slough—*gut* KY-4
Hogan Slough—*stream* MT-8
*Hogans Meadow* CA-9
Hogans Millpond—*reservoir* VA-3
Hogan Spring—*spring* (3) AZ-5
Hogan Spring—*spring* NV-8
Hogan Spring—*spring* NM-5
Hogan Spring—*spring* OR-9
Hogan Spring—*spring* UT-8
Hogans Slough—*stream* MT-8
*Hogans Spring* AL-4
Hogans Spring—*spring* GA-3
Hogansville—*locale* TX-5
**Hogansville**—*pop pl* GA-3
Hogansville (CCD)—*cens area* GA-3
Hogans Wash—*valley* UT-8
Hogan Tank—*reservoir* NM-5
Hogan Tank Number One—*reservoir* AZ-5
Hogan Tank Number Two—*reservoir* AZ-5
Hogan (Township of)—*fmr MCD* AR-4
**Hogan (Township of)**—*pop pl* IN-6
Hogan View Point—*cliff* AZ-5
*Hoganville* KS-7
Hogan Well—*well* AZ-5
Hogan Well—*well* ID-8
Hogan Well—*well* NM-5
Hogan Windmill—*locale* NM-5
Hogard Ch—*church* KY-4
Hogard Creek—*stream* (2) MO-7
Hogards Chapel—*church* KY-4
Hogar Estatal de Ninos—*other* PR-3
Hogarth Hill—*summit* MI-6
**Hogarty**—*pop pl* WI-6
*Hogarty Creek* WY-8
Hogarty Creek—*stream* WA-9
Hogarty Rsvr—*reservoir* CO-8
*Hogate Island* MD-2
Hogatza—*locale* AK-9
Hogatza Hills—*other* AK-9
Hogatzakhotak Creek—*stream* AK-9
Hogatza River—*stream* AK-9
*Hogback* KS-7
*Hog Back* UT-8
*Hog Back* VT-1
Hogback—*island* CA-9
Hog Back—*locale* KS-7
Hogback—*ridge* CA-9
Hogback—*ridge* (2) CO-8
Hogback—*ridge* GA-3
Hogback—*ridge* MT-8
Hogback—*ridge* (2) NC-3
Hogback—*ridge* OH-6
Hogback—*ridge* PA-2
Hogback—*ridge* UT-8
Hogback—*ridge* VA-3
Hogback—*ridge* (2) WV-2
Hogback—*ridge* WY-8
Hog Back—*summit* CA-9
Hog Back—*summit* IN-6
Hogback—*summit* (2) NY-2
Hogback—*summit* UT-8
Hogback—*summit* VT-1
Hogback—*summit* VA-3
Hogback—*summit* WY-8
Hogback, The—*ridge* (2) CA-9
Hogback, The—*ridge* (5) CO-8
Hogback, The—*ridge* CT-1
Hogback, The—*ridge* IN-6
Hogback, The—*ridge* KY-4
Hogback, The—*ridge* (2) MT-8
Hogback, The—*ridge* (3) NM-5
Hogback, The—*ridge* NY-2
Hogback, The—*ridge* ND-7
Hogback, The—*ridge* (2) OR-9
Hogback, The—*ridge* PA-2
Hogback, The—*ridge* TN-4
Hogback, The—*ridge* (3) UT-8
Hogback, The—*ridge* WI-6
Hogback, The—*ridge* WY-8
Hogback, The—*summit* IA-7
Hogback, The—*summit* MI-6
Hogback, The—*summit* NM-5
Hogback, The—*summit* PA-2
Hogback, The—*summit* WY-8
Hogback Bend—*bend* GA-3
*Hogback Branch* TN-4
Hogback Branch—*stream* TN-4
Hogback Bridge—*hist pl* PA-2
Hogback Brook—*stream* (2) NY-2
Hogback Butte—*summit* NM-5
Hogback Butte—*summit* OR-9
Hogback Canal—*canal* NM-5
Hogback Covered Bridge—*hist pl* IA-7
Hogback Creek—*stream* (4) CA-9
Hogback Creek—*stream* ID-8
Hogback Creek—*stream* KY-4
Hogback Creek—*stream* MT-8
Hogback Creek—*stream* NC-3
Hogback Creek—*stream* (2) OR-9
Hogback Creek—*stream* VA-3
Hogback Dam—*dam* NC-3
Hogback Dam—*dam* UT-8
Hogback Ditch—*canal* CO-8
Hogback Draw—*valley* NM-5
Hogback Draw—*valley* WY-8
Hogback Field—*other* NM-5
Hogback Gap—*gap* NC-3
Hogback Glacier—*glacier* AK-9
Hogback Hill—*ridge* IN-6
Hogback Hill—*ridge* NM-5
Hogback Hill—*summit* AK-9
Hog Back Hill—*summit* IN-6
Hogback Hill—*summit* KS-7
Hogback Hill—*summit* KY-4
Hogback Hill—*summit* MN-6
Hogback Hill—*summit* (3) NY-2
Hogback Hill—*summit* (2) PA-2
Hogback Hill—*summit* WI-6
Hogback Hollow—*valley* PA-2
Hogback Island—*island* IL-6
Hogback Island—*island* IA-7
Hogback Island—*island* ME-1
Hogback Island—*island* NY-2
Hogback Island Recreation Facility—*park* CA-9
Hogback Knob—*summit* NC-3
Hogback Lake—*lake* IN-6
Hogback Lake—*lake* (2) MI-6
Hogback Lake—*lake* WI-6
Hogback Lake—*lake* WY-8
Hogback Lake—*reservoir* NC-3
Hogback Ledge—*cliff* ME-1
Hogback Mesa—*summit* CO-8
Hogback Mine—*mine* TN-4
Hogback Mountain—*ridge* CA-9
Hogback Mountain—*ridge* GA-3
Hogback Mountain—*ridge* OR-9
Hogback Mountains—*ridge* VT-1
*Hogback Mtn* NY-2
Hogback Mtn—*summit* (2) CA-9
Hogback Mtn—*summit* (2) CO-8
Hogback Mtn—*summit* GA-3
Hogback Mtn—*summit* ME-1
Hogback Mtn—*summit* MA-1
Hogback Mtn—*summit* MI-6
Hogback Mtn—*summit* (2) MT-8
Hogback Mtn—*summit* NE-7
Hogback Mtn—*summit* (2) NH-1
Hogback Mtn—*summit* NM-5
Hogback Mtn—*summit* (4) NY-2
Hog Back Mtn—*summit* NY-2
Hogback Mtn—*summit* (6) NC-3
Hogback Mtn—*summit* OR-9
Hogback Mtn—*summit* PA-2
Hogback Mtn—*summit* (2) SC-3
Hogback Mtn—*summit* TN-4
Hogback Mtn—*summit* (4) VT-1
Hogback Mtn—*summit* (3) VA-3
Hogback Mtn—*summit* WA-9
Hogback Peak—*summit* CA-9
Hogback Point—*summit* MT-8
Hogback Pond—*lake* NH-1
Hogback Ravine—*valley* CA-9
Hogback Reef—*bar* VT-1
*Hogback Ridge* IN-6
Hogback Ridge—*ridge* (4) CA-9
Hogback Ridge—*ridge* (2) ID-8
Hogback Ridge—*ridge* IN-6
Hogback Ridge—*ridge* (2) KY-4
Hogback Ridge—*ridge* MT-8
Hogback Ridge—*ridge* (2) NY-2
Hogback Ridge—*ridge* NC-3
Hogback Ridge—*ridge* ND-7
Hog Back Ridge—*ridge* OH-6
Hogback Ridge—*ridge* OR-9
Hog Back Ridge—*ridge* PA-2
Hogback Ridge—*ridge* (2) TN-4
Hogback Ridge—*ridge* UT-8
Hogback Ridge—*ridge* (2) WA-9
Hogback Ridge—*ridge* (2) WV-2
Hogback Ridge—*ridge* WY-8
Hogback Ridge State Rec Area—*park* IN-6
Hogback Ridge Trail—*trail* MT-8
Hogback Rsvr—*reservoir* UT-8
*Hogback Run* PA-2
Hogback Run—*stream* OH-6
Hogback Run—*stream* (2) PA-2
Hogback Run—*stream* WV-2
Hogbacks—*summit* CA-9
Hogback Shelter—*locale* NY-2
Hogback Ski Area—*area* VT-1
Hog Back Station (historical)—*locale* KS-7
Hogback Summit—*summit* UT-8
Hogback Tank—*reservoir* AZ-5
Hogback Tank—*reservoir* NM-5
Hogback (Township of)—*fmr MCD* NC-3
Hogback Trail—*trail* PA-2
Hogback Trail—*trail* TN-4
Hogback Trail—*trail* WA-9
Hogback Tunnel—*tunnel* PA-2
Hogback Well—*well* OR-9
Hog Basin—*basin* AZ-5
Hog Basin Tank—*reservoir* AZ-5
Hog Bay—*bay* ME-1
Hog Bay—*stream* FL-3
Hog Bay—*swamp* FL-3
Hog Bay—*swamp* GA-3
Hog Bay—*swamp* NC-3
Hog Bay—*swamp* (2) SC-3
Hog Bay (Carolina Bay)—*swamp* NC-3
*Hog Bayou* TX-5
Hog Bayou—*gut* (2) AL-4
Hog Bayou—*gut* LA-4
Hog Bayou—*stream* (11) LA-4
Hog Bayou—*stream* (2) TX-5
Hog Bayou Lake—*lake* LA-4
Hog Bayou Oil and Gas Field—*oilfield* LA-4
Hog Bed Branch—*stream* GA-3
Hogbed Branch—*stream* KY-4
*Hog Bed Creek* AL-4
Hogbed Creek—*stream* AL-4
Hogbed Hollow—*valley* KY-4
Hog Bend—*bend* TX-5
*Hog Branch* MS-4
*Hog Branch* TX-5
*Hog Branch* VA-3
Hog Branch—*stream* (3) AL-4
Hog Branch—*stream* AR-4
Hog Branch—*stream* (2) FL-3
Hog Branch—*stream* (2) GA-3
Hog Branch—*stream* IL-6
Hog Branch—*stream* IN-6
Hog Branch—*stream* IA-7
Hog Branch—*stream* KS-7
Hog Branch—*stream* (6) KY-4
Hog Branch—*stream* (3) LA-4
Hog Branch—*stream* (5) MS-4
Hog Branch—*stream* (4) MO-7
Hog Branch—*stream* (3) NC-3
Hog Branch—*stream* (5) SC-3
Hog Branch—*stream* (3) TN-4
Hog Branch—*stream* (16) TX-5
Hog Branch—*stream* VA-3
Hog Branch—*valley* NM-5
Hog Branch Black Creek—*stream* FL-3
Hog Brook—*stream* CT-1
Hog Brook—*stream* MA-1
Hog Brook—*stream* NY-2
Hog Camp—*locale* CA-9
Hog Camp Branch—*stream* (2) KY-4
Hog Camp Branch—*stream* NC-3
Hogcamp Branch—*stream* TN-4
Hogcamp Branch—*stream* VA-3
Hog Camp Canyon—*valley* NM-5
Hog Camp Creek—*stream* KY-4
Hog Camp Gap—*gap* VA-3
Hog Camp Run—*stream* WV-2
Hogcamp Run—*stream* WV-2
Hog Camp Spring—*spring* CA-9
Hogcamp Trail—*trail* VA-3
Hog Canal—*canal* ID-8
*Hog Canyon* CA-9
Hog Canyon—*valley* (13) AZ-5
Hog Canyon—*valley* (11) CA-9
Hog Canyon—*valley* CO-8
Hog Canyon—*valley* NV-8
Hog Canyon—*valley* (2) NM-5
Hog Canyon—*valley* (4) TX-5
Hog Canyon—*valley* (4) UT-8
Hog Canyon—*valley* (2) WA-9
Hog Canyon Creek—*stream* WA-9
Hog Canyon Spring—*spring* (2) AZ-5
Hog Canyon Spring—*spring* UT-8
Hog Canyon Tank—*reservoir* (3) AZ-5
Hog Canyon Wash—*stream* AZ-5
Hog Cave Hollow—*valley* (2) MO-7
Hog Chain (historical)—*locale* MS-4
Hog Chute Bridge—*other* IL-6
Hog Cliff Hollow—*valley* MO-7
Hog Cove—*bay* ME-1
Hog Cove—*bay* NC-3
Hog Cove—*valley* (2) NC-3
Hog Cove Butte—*summit* ID-8
Hog Cove Creek—*stream* ID-8
Hog Cove Ledge—*bar* ME-1
Hog Crawl Creek—*stream* GA-3
Hogcrawl Creek—*stream* GA-3
Hog Crawl Swamp—*swamp* SC-3
*Hog Creek* AR-4
*Hog Creek* GA-3
*Hog Creek* ID-8
*Hog Creek* IL-6
*Hog Creek* IN-6
*Hog Creek* MI-6
*Hog Creek* OH-6
*Hog Creek* TX-5
Hog Creek—*gut* NY-2
Hog Creek—*stream* (6) AL-4
Hog Creek—*stream* (2) AR-4
Hog Creek—*stream* CA-9
Hog Creek—*stream* (4) FL-3
Hog Creek—*stream* (8) GA-3
Hog Creek—*stream* (4) ID-8
Hog Creek—*stream* (3) IL-6
Hog Creek—*stream* (2) IN-6
Hog Creek—*stream* (2) IA-7
Hog Creek—*stream* (2) KS-7
Hog Creek—*stream* KY-4
Hog Creek—*stream* LA-4
Hog Creek—*stream* (2) MD-2
Hog Creek—*stream* (3) MI-6
Hog Creek—*stream* MN-6
Hog Creek—*stream* (2) MS-4
Hog Creek—*stream* (6) MO-7
Hog Creek—*stream* (2) OH-6
Hog Creek—*stream* (9) OK-5
Hog Creek—*stream* (11) OR-9
Hog Creek—*stream* (3) TN-4
Hog Creek—*stream* (30) TX-5
Hog Creek—*stream* (3) VA-3
Hog Creek—*stream* WI-6
Hog Creek Archeol District—*hist pl* TX-5
Hog Creek Bay—*swamp* GA-3
Hog Creek Butte—*summit* ID-8
Hog Creek Cem—*cemetery* AR-4
Hog Creek Cem—*cemetery* TN-4
Hog Creek Cem—*cemetery* TX-5
Hog Creek Ditch—*canal* OH-6
Hog Creek Hollow—*valley* AL-4
*Hog Creek Lake* MI-6
Hog Creek Point—*cape* NY-2
Hog Creek Ridge—*ridge* OR-9
Hog Creek Rsvr Number One—*reservoir* OR-9
Hog Creek Rsvr Number Two—*reservoir* OR-9
Hog Creek Sch—*school* IL-6
Hog Creek Sch (historical)—*school* MS-4
Hog Creek Sch (historical)—*school* TN-4
Hog Creek Spring—*spring* ID-8
Hog Creek Tank—*reservoir* TX-5
Hog Cypress—*swamp* FL-3
Hogdon Cove—*bay* ME-1
Hoge—*locale* KS-7
Hoge, Arista, House—*hist pl* VA-3
Hoge, John, House—*hist pl* VA-3
Hoge, Walter, House—*hist pl* ID-8
*Hoge Airport* PA-2
Hoge Bldg—*hist pl* WA-9
Hoge Branch—*stream* TN-4
Hoge Cem—*cemetery* MS-4
Hoge Cem—*cemetery* (3) TN-4
Hoge Farm Airp—*airport* PA-2
*Hoge Hollow* AL-4
Hoge Island—*island* PA-2
**Hogeland**—*pop pl* MT-8
Hogeland Cave—*cave* AL-4
Hogeland Creek—*stream* AL-4
Hogelee Spring Number One—*lake* WI-6
Hogelee Spring Number Two—*lake* WI-6
*Hogem* ID-8
Hoge Mine—*mine* CA-9
Hoge Mine (underground)—*mine* AL-4
Hogen Camp Mine—*mine* NY-2
Hogencamp Mtn—*summit* NY-2
Hogendobler Cem—*cemetery* IL-6
Hogensborg—*locale* VI-3
Hoge Pond—*reservoir* VA-3
Hoge Ranch (site)—*locale* AZ-5
Hogers Bayou—*bay* WI-6
*Hogers Creek* TX-5
Hoge Run—*stream* PA-2
Hoge Run—*stream* VA-3
**Hoges Chapel**—*pop pl* VA-3
Hoges Chapel Cem—*cemetery* VA-3
*Hoges Crossroads* AL-4
Hoge Spring—*spring* TN-4
*Hoges Store* VA-3
*Hoge Station* KS-7
**Hogestown**—*pop pl* PA-2
Hogestown Run—*stream* PA-2
Hogetown—*locale* NC-3
*Hog Eye* AL-4
*Hogeye* MS-4
Hogeye—*locale* AR-4
Hogeye—*locale* TX-5
Hog Eye Branch—*stream* MO-7
Hogeye Branch—*stream* NC-3
Hog Eye Branch—*stream* SC-3
Hogeye Cem—*cemetery* LA-4
Hog Eye Cem—*cemetery* TX-5
Hogeye Ch—*church* TN-4
*Hogeye Community* MS-4
*Hog Eye Creek* AR-4
Hogeye Creek—*stream* AR-4
Hog Eye Creek—*stream* OK-5
Hogeye Creek—*stream* OK-5
Hog Eye Creek—*stream* OR-9
Hogeye Creek—*stream* UT-8
**Hogeye Crossroads**—*pop pl* SC-3
Hogeye Gulch—*valley* CA-9
*Hogeye Hollow* WA-9
Hogeye Hollow—*valley* OK-5
Hogeye Hollow—*valley* WA-9
Hog Eye Lake—*lake* TX-5
Hogeye Mesa—*summit* NM-5
Hogeye Mtn—*summit* NM-5
Hogeye Mtn—*summit* TX-5
Hog Eye Point—*cape* FL-3
Hogeye Sink—*lake* FL-3
Hogeye Spring—*spring* NM-5
Hog Eye Windmill—*locale* TX-5
Hogfat Hill—*summit* ME-1
Hog Flat—*flat* OR-9
Hog Flat—*flat* UT-8
Hog Flat Resevoir—*reservoir* CA-9
Hog Flat Spring—*spring* OR-9
*Hog Foot Creek* AR-4
Hog Foot Creek—*stream* AL-4
Hog Fork—*stream* GA-3
Hog Fork—*stream* (2) WV-2
Hogfork Branch—*stream* SC-3
Hog Fork Indian Cem—*cemetery* AL-4
Hogg—*locale* (2) TX-5
Hogg, William, House—*hist pl* MA-1
Hog Gallus Island—*island* GA-3
Hog Gap Hollow—*valley* KY-4
Hoggard Bridge—*bridge* NC-3
Hoggard Bridge (historical)—*bridge* NC-3
Hoggard Cem—*cemetery* NC-3
Hoggard HS—*school* NC-3
Hoggard Mill Creek—*stream* NC-3
*Hoggards Mill* NC-3
Hoggard Swamp—*swamp* NC-3
Hoggatt Bay—*bay* AK-9
Hoggatt Branch—*stream* IN-6
Hoggatt Branch—*stream* MS-4
Hoggatt Cem—*cemetery* MS-4
Hoggatt Island—*island* AK-9
Hoggatt Reefs—*bar* AK-9
Hogg Bay—*bay* AK-9
Hogg Bldg—*hist pl* TX-5
Hogg Bluff Creek—*stream* TX-5
Hogg Branch—*stream* TX-5
Hogg Cem—*cemetery* IL-6
Hogg Cem—*cemetery* MO-7
Hogg Cem—*cemetery* TN-4
Hogg Cem—*cemetery* TX-5
Hogg Creek—*stream* AR-4
Hogg Creek—*stream* IL-6
Hogg Creek—*stream* MI-6
Hogg Creek—*stream* MO-7
Hogge Branch—*stream* KY-4
Hogge Cem—*cemetery* KY-4
Hoggem Lake—*lake* CA-9
Hogger Branch—*stream* WV-2
Hogger Run—*stream* WV-2
Hogge Sch—*school* IL-6
Hogg Hill—*summit* NH-1
Hogg Hollow—*valley* TX-5
*Hoggins Island* MA-1
*Hogg Island* MA-1
Hogg Island—*island* AK-9
Hogg Island—*island* TX-5
Hogg JHS—*school* (2) TX-5
Hog Glade—*flat* LA-4
Hoggle Cem—*cemetery* AL-4
Hoggle Ch—*church* AL-4
Hoggle Ridge—*ridge* AL-4
**Hogglesville**—*pop pl* AL-4
Hogg Mtn—*summit* GA-3
Hogg Park—*park* TX-5
*Hogg Pass* OR-9
Hogg Place—*locale* NM-5
Hogg Point—*cape* AK-9
Hogg Rock—*pillar* OR-9
*Hoggs Bayou* TX-5
Hoggs Bayou—*stream* TX-5
Hogg Sch—*school* (2) TX-5
Hogg Sch (abandoned)—*school* MO-7
Hoggs Cove—*bay* FL-3
**Hoggtown**—*pop pl* TN-4
Hoggtown Branch—*stream* TN-4
*Hoggtown Post Office* TN-4
Hog Gulch—*valley* (4) CA-9
Hog Gulch—*valley* NV-8
Hog Gulch—*valley* OR-9
Hog Gulch—*valley* UT-8
Hog Gully—*stream* LA-4
Hogg Windmill—*locale* TX-5
Hoggy John Tank—*reservoir* AZ-5
Hoghair Hollow—*valley* MO-7
Hog Hammock—*island* GA-3
Hog Hammock—*swamp* FL-3
Hog Head Bluff—*cliff* TX-5
Hoghead Creek—*stream* AR-4
Hoghead Mtn—*summit* SC-3
Hog Head Trail—*trail* FL-3
Hog Heaven—*summit* AL-4
Hog Heaven Branch—*stream* TN-4
Hog Heaven Lookout Tower—*locale* MT-8
Hog Heaven Range—*spring* MT-8
Hog Hill—*summit* (2) AZ-5
Hog Hill—*summit* (2) CA-9
Hog Hill—*summit* CT-1
Hog Hill—*summit* ME-1
Hog Hill—*summit* MD-2
Hog Hill—*summit* (2) MA-1
Hog Hill—*summit* (3) NH-1
Hog Hill—*summit* NM-5
Hog Hill—*summit* NY-2
Hog Hill—*summit* NC-3
Hog Hill Brook—*stream* NH-1
Hog Hill Cem—*cemetery* CT-1
Hog Hill Island—*island* RI-1
Hog Hill Pond—*lake* NH-1
Hog Hill Swamp—*swamp* NH-1
Hog Hole—*lake* CA-9
Hog Hole—*reservoir* AZ-5
Hog Hole—*ridge* CA-9
Hog Hole—*valley* UT-8
Hog Hole Branch—*stream* NC-3
Hoghole Creek—*bay* MD-2
Hog Hole Ridge—*ridge* CA-9
Hoghole Run—*stream* MD-2
Hog Hole Spring—*spring* CA-9
*Hog Hollow* AL-4
Hog Hollow—*valley* (2) AL-4
Hog Hollow—*valley* AR-4
Hog Hollow—*valley* ID-8
Hog Hollow—*valley* (2) IN-6
Hog Hollow—*valley* IA-7
Hog Hollow—*valley* (5) KY-4
Hog Hollow—*valley* MA-1
Hog Hollow—*valley* (3) MO-7
Hog Hollow—*valley* MT-8
Hog Hollow—*valley* (2) NY-2
Hog Hollow—*valley* (2) OH-6
Hog Hollow—*valley* OK-5
Hog Hollow—*valley* OR-9
Hog Hollow—*valley* PA-2
Hog Hollow—*valley* (3) TN-4
Hog Hollow—*valley* (6) TX-5
Hog Hollow—*valley* UT-8
Hog Hollow—*valley* (3) WV-2
Hog Hollow—*valley* WI-6
Hog Hollow Creek—*stream* CA-9
Hog Hollow Sch—*school* NE-7
Hoghouse Canyon—*valley* OR-9
*Hog House Creek* AL-4
Hoghouse Creek—*stream* AL-4
Hoghouse Point—*cape* AL-4
Hoghouse Run—*stream* PA-2
Hogin Cem—*cemetery* TN-4
Hog Inlet—*bay* SC-3
*Hog Island* AL-4
*Hog Island* FL-3
*Hog Island* ME-1
*Hog Island* MD-2
*Hog Island* MA-1
*Hog Island* MI-6
*Hog Island* NY-2
*Hog Island* VT-1
*Hog Island* FM-9
Hog Island—*cape* SC-3
Hog Island—*cliff* MA-1
Hog Island—*island* AL-4
Hog Island—*island* (2) AK-9
Hog Island—*island* AR-4
Hog Island—*island* (4) CA-9
Hog Island—*island* (8) FL-3
Hog Island—*island* (3) GA-3
Hog Island—*island* (2) ID-8
Hog Island—*island* IA-7
Hog Island—*island* (5) LA-4
Hog Island—*island* (14) ME-1
Hog Island—*island* (4) MD-2
Hog Island—*island* (2) MA-1
Hog Island—*island* MI-6
Hog Island—*island* MN-6
Hog Island—*island* MS-4
Hog Island—*island* NE-7
Hog Island—*island* NH-1
Hog Island—*island* (3) NY-2
Hog Island—*island* (7) NC-3
Hog Island—*island* (2) OR-9
Hog Island—*island* PA-2
Hog Island—*island* RI-1
Hog Island—*island* SC-3
Hog Island—*island* (4) TX-5
Hog Island—*island* UT-8
Hog Island—*island* VT-1
Hog Island—*island* (5) VA-3
Hog Island—*island* (3) WI-6
**Hog Island**—*pop pl* MD-2
**Hog Island**—*pop pl* NC-3
**Hog Island**—*pop pl* RI-1
Hog Island—*summit* MI-6
Hog Island Bar—*bar* ME-1
*Hog Island Bay* NC-3
Hog Island Bay—*bay* VA-3
Hog Island Campground—*locale* MI-6
Hog Island Channel—*channel* MA-1
Hog Island Channel—*channel* NY-2
Hog Island Channel—*channel* SC-3
Hog Island Cranes—*hist pl* NJ-2
Hog Island Creek—*gut* MA-1
Hog Island Creek—*gut* NC-3
Hog Island Creek—*gut* VA-3

Hog Island Creek—stream ... FL-3
Hog Island Creek—stream ... MI-6
Hog Island Cut—canal ... CA-9
Hog Island Gully—stream ... LA-4
Hog Island Hammock—island ... FL-3
Hog Island Harbor ... MA-1
Hog Island (historical)—island ... AL-4
Hog Island (historical)—island ... PA-2
Hog Island (historical)—locale ... AL-4
Hog Island Lake—lake ... FL-3
Hog Island Ledge—bar ... ME-1
Hog Island Marsh ... GA-3
Hog Island Marsh—swamp ... MD-2
Hog Island Narrows—channel ... NC-3
Hog Island Pass—channel ... LA-4
Hog Island Point ... MD-2
Hog Island Point ... NC-3
Hog Island Point—cape ... MD-2
Hog Island Point—cape ... MA-1
Hog Island Point—cape ... MI-6
Hog Island Point—cape (2) ... NC-3
Hog Island Point—cape ... VT-1
Hog Island Pond—lake ... FL-3
Hog Island Reach—channel ... SC-3
Hog Islands—island ... MA-1
Hog Islands—island ... NJ-2
Hog Islands—island ... NC-3
Hog Island Shoal Lighthouse—hist pl ... RI-1
Hog Island State Waterfowl Ref—park ... VA-3
Hog Island Swamp—swamp ... NC-3
Hog Jaw—locale ... AR-4
**Hog Jaw**—pop pl ... AL-4
**Hogjaw**—pop pl ... AL-4
**Hog Jaw**—pop pl ... AR-4
Hog Jaw Creek ... AL-4
Hog Jaw Creek ... TN-4
Hogjaw Creek—stream ... AL-4
Hog Jaw Creek—stream ... AL-4
Hogjaw Creek—stream ... TN-4
Hogjaw Gap—gap ... NC-3
Hogjaw Gap—gap ... TN-4
Hog Jaw Mtn—summit ... AR-4
Hogjaw Ridge—ridge ... AL-4
Hogjaw Ridge—ridge ... TN-4
Hog Jaw Valley ... AL-4
Hog Jaw Valley ... TN-4
Hogjaw Valley—valley ... AL-4
Hogjaw Valley—valley ... TN-4
Hog John Gulch—valley ... CO-8
Hog John Ranch (historical)—locale ... NV-8
Hog John Rsvr—reservoir ... NV-8
Hog Joint Hollow—valley ... TN-4
Hogjowl Creek—stream ... GA-3
Hog Jowl Mtn—summit ... KY-4
Hogjowl Valley—valley ... GA-3
Hog Key—island (3) ... FL-3
Hog Knob—summit ... KY-4
Hog Knob—summit (3) ... WV-2
Hog Lake ... FL-3
Hog Lake ... IN-6
Hog Lake ... MI-6
Hog Lake ... OR-9
Hog Lake—lake ... AR-4
Hog Lake—lake (4) ... CA-9
Hog Lake—lake ... CO-8
Hog Lake—lake ... FL-3
Hog Lake—lake ... IL-6
Hog Lake—lake (2) ... IN-6
Hog Lake—lake (4) ... LA-4
Hog Lake—lake ... MI-6
Hog Lake—lake ... MN-6
Hog Lake—lake ... MO-7
Hog Lake—lake ... NM-5
Hog Lake—lake ... SC-3
Hog Lake—lake (2) ... TX-5
Hog Lake—lake ... WA-9
Hog Lake—stream ... LA-4
Hog Lake—swamp ... LA-4
Hog Lake—swamp ... TX-5
Hogland Drift Mine (underground)—mine ... AL-4
Hog Landing—locale ... AK-9
Hogland Run ... OH-6
Hogland Run—stream ... WV-2
Hogland Slough—gut ... KY-4
Hoglan Run—stream ... WV-2
Hog Lat Draw—valley ... CO-8
Hoglaw Gap—gap ... TN-4
Hogle And Miller Ditch—canal ... MI-6
Hog Leg Rsvr—reservoir ... OR-9
Hoglen Branch—stream ... NC-3
Hoglen Gap—gap ... NC-3
Hogles Creek—stream ... MO-7
Hogles Creek Ch (historical)—church ... MO-7
Hogles Creek Sch (historical)—school ... MO-7
Hogley Wood Church ... AL-4
Hogle Zoological Gardens—area ... UT-8
Hog Lick Run—stream ... WV-2
Hoglot Branch—stream ... NC-3
Hoglot Hollow—valley ... TN-4
Hoglot Springs—lake ... WI-6
Hoglund Lake—lake ... MI-6
Hoglund State Wildlife Mngmt Area—park ... MN-6
Hog Marsh Creek—bay ... MD-2
Hog Marsh Creek—stream ... TX-5
Hog Marsh Gut—gut ... MD-2
Hog Marsh Island—island ... GA-3
Hog Meadow—flat ... ID-8
Hog Meadow Creek—stream ... ID-8
Hog Meadow Swamp—swamp ... SC-3
Hogmire-Berryman Farm—hist pl ... MD-2
Hogmire Sch—school ... MI-6
Hog Mountain—locale ... GA-3
Hog Mountain—ridge ... AL-4
Hog Mountain Ch—church ... GA-3
Hog Mountain Dam—dam ... AZ-5
Hog Mountain Dam Number Two—dam ... AZ-5
Hog Mountain Goldmine—mine ... AL-4
Hog Mountains ... UT-8
Hog Mountains—summit ... TX-5
Hog Mountain Spring—spring ... AZ-5
Hog Mountain Tanks—reservoir ... AZ-5
Hog Mtn ... TX-5
Hog Mtn—summit (2) ... AL-4
Hog Mtn—summit (2) ... AZ-5
Hog Mtn—summit (2) ... CA-9
Hog Mtn—summit (3) ... GA-3
Hog Mtn—summit ... KY-4
Hog Mtn—summit (2) ... MA-1
Hog Mtn—summit ... NY-2
Hog Mtn—summit (2) ... OR-9
Hog Mtn—summit (7) ... TX-5
Hog Mtn—summit ... VA-3
Hog Narrows ... VA-3
Hog Neck ... MA-1
Hog Neck ... NY-2
Hog Neck ... VA-3
Hog Neck—cape (2) ... MD-2
Hog Neck—cape ... MA-1
Hog Neck—cape (2) ... VA-3
Hog Neck Bay—bay ... NY-2
Hog Neck Creek—stream (2) ... VA-3
Hognose Creek—stream ... MS-4
Hognose Point—cape ... GA-3
Hogohegee Creek ... AL-4
Hogoleu Islands ... FM-9
Hogolu Islands ... FM-9
Hog Park—flat ... CO-8
Hog Park—park ... WY-8
Hog Park Creek—stream ... WY-8
Hog Park Guard Station—locale ... CO-8
Hog Park Wash—stream ... CO-8
Hog Pass—gap ... TX-5
Hog Path - in part ... PA-2
Hog Peak—summit ... TX-5
Hogpen Bay—bay ... NC-3
Hog Pen Bay—bay ... SC-3
Hog Pen Branch ... MS-4
Hogpen Branch—stream ... AL-4
Hog Pen Branch—stream (2) ... AL-4
Hogpen Branch—stream (2) ... FL-3
Hog Pen Branch—stream ... FL-3
Hogpen Branch—stream (2) ... FL-3
Hog Pen Branch—stream ... FL-3
Hogpen Branch—stream (3) ... GA-3
Hogpen Branch—stream (2) ... LA-4
Hogpen Branch—stream (4) ... MS-4
Hogpen Branch—stream (8) ... NC-3
Hogpen Branch—stream (2) ... SC-3
Hogpen Branch—stream (2) ... TN-4
Hogpen Branch—stream (3) ... TX-5
Hog Pen Creek ... AR-4
Hogpen Creek—bay ... NC-3
Hogpen Creek—stream ... AL-4
Hogpen Creek—stream (2) ... AR-4
Hogpen Creek—stream (2) ... FL-3
Hogpen Creek—stream ... MD-2
Hogpen Creek—stream ... MS-4
Hogpen Creek—stream ... TX-5
Hog Pen Creek—stream ... TX-5
Hogpen Crossing—locale ... TX-5
Hogpen Dingle Brook ... MA-1
Hogpen Gap—gap ... GA-3
Hogpen Gap—gap (3) ... NC-3
Hogpen Gap—gap ... TN-4
Hogpen Gulch—valley ... ID-8
Hogpen Hill—summit ... CT-1
Hog Pen Hole—lake ... AR-4
Hogpen Hollow—valley ... AL-4
Hogpen Hollow—valley ... AR-4
Hogpen Hollow—valley ... KY-4
Hogpen Hollow—valley ... MO-7
Hog Pen Hollow—valley ... MO-7
Hogpen Hollow—valley ... OH-6
Hogpen Hollow—valley ... PA-2
Hogpen Hollow—valley (3) ... TN-4
Hogpen Hollow—valley (2) ... TX-5
Hogpen Hollow—valley ... WV-2
Hogpen Island—island ... MS-4
Hog Pen Lake—lake ... LA-4
Hogpen Lake—lake ... MS-4
Hogpen Lake—lake ... OK-5
Hog Pen Lake—lake ... TX-5
Hog Pen Mtn ... AR-4
Hogpen Mtn—summit ... AR-4
Hogpen Mtn—summit ... GA-3
Hog Pen Mtn—summit ... TX-5
Hogpen Mtn—summit (2) ... VA-3
Hog Pen Neck—cape ... VA-3
Hogpen Point—cape ... NC-3
Hog Pen Point—cape ... NC-3
Hogpen Pond—lake (2) ... FL-3
Hogpen Pond—lake ... TX-5
Hog Pen Pond—swamp ... FL-3
Hog Pen Public Access—park ... OK-5
Hogpen Ridge—ridge (2) ... AR-4
Hogpen Ridge—ridge ... MO-7
Hogpen Ridge—ridge ... WV-2
Hogpen Run—stream ... VA-3
Hogpen Run—stream (2) ... WV-2
Hogpen Slough—channel ... GA-3
Hogpen Slough—gut ... AR-4
Hogpen Slough—gut ... CA-9
Hogpen Slough—gut ... FL-3
Hogpen Slough—gut ... KY-4
Hogpen Slough—gut ... LA-4
Hog Pen Slough—gut ... MS-4
Hogpen Slough—gut ... TN-4
Hogpen Slough—gut ... TX-5
Hogpen Slough—stream ... AR-4
Hog Pen Slough—swamp ... FL-3
Hogpen Spring—spring ... AZ-5
Hog Pen Spring—spring ... CA-9
Hog Pen Trail—trail ... KY-4
Hog Pen Wells—well ... TX-5
Hog Point—cape (2) ... FL-3
Hog Point—cape (3) ... LA-4
Hog Point—cape (2) ... MD-2
Hog Point—cape ... NC-3
Hog Point—cape ... TN-4
Hog Point—cape (2) ... VA-3
Hog Point—summit ... CA-9
Hog Point—summit ... CO-8
Hog Point Cove—bay ... FL-3
Hog Pond—lake ... AR-4
Hog Pond—lake ... CT-1
Hog Pond—lake (7) ... FL-3
Hog Pond—lake ... MS-4
Hog Pond—lake ... NY-2
Hog Pond—swamp ... TX-5
Hog Pond Brook—stream ... CT-1
Hog Ponds—lake ... MA-1
Hog Pond Swamp—swamp ... FL-3
Hog Pond Village ... MA-1
Hog Quarter Landing—locale ... NC-3
Hog Ranch—locale (4) ... CA-9
Hog Ranch—locale ... CO-8
Hog Ranch—locale ... NM-5
Hog Ranch Buttes—range ... WA-9
Hog Ranch Canyon—valley ... CO-8
Hog Ranch Creek—stream ... CA-9
Hog Ranch Creek—stream ... NV-8
Hog Ranch Creek—stream ... OR-9
Hog Ranch Mtn—summit ... NV-8
Hog Ranch Prairie—area ... CA-9
Hog Ranch Ridge—ridge (2) ... CA-9
Hog Ranch Spring—spring ... UT-8
Hog Ranch Tank—reservoir ... AZ-5
Hog Ranch Well—well ... AZ-5
Hog Range—flat ... MD-2
Hog Range—ridge ... CA-9
Hog Range Marsh—swamp ... MD-2
Hog Ridge—ridge ... CA-9
Hog Ridge—ridge ... IN-6
Hog Ridge—ridge ... MO-7
Hog Ridge—ridge ... OR-9
Hog Ridge—ridge ... VA-3
Hog Ridge—ridge ... WV-2
Hog River ... CT-1
Hog River ... OH-6
Hog River—stream ... IL-6
Hog Rock—pillar ... NC-3
Hog Rock—rock ... MA-1
Hog Rock Branch ... VA-3
Hog Rock Branch—stream ... VA-3
Hog Rock Branch—stream ... WV-2
Hog Rocks—area ... AK-9
Hog Rooting Pond—lake ... MD-2
Hog Run ... OH-6
Hog Run—stream ... IL-6
Hog Run—stream (2) ... IN-6
Hog Run—stream (3) ... IA-7
Hog Run—stream ... KY-4
Hog Run—stream (8) ... OH-6
Hog Run—stream (2) ... PA-2
Hog Run—stream ... VA-3
Hog Run—stream (6) ... WV-2
Hog Run Creek—stream ... IL-6
Hogsback—cape ... WA-9
Hogsback—ridge ... CA-9
Hogs Back—ridge ... CA-9
Hogs Back—ridge ... MT-8
Hogs Back—ridge (3) ... UT-8
Hogsback—summit ... NY-2
Hogsback, The—ridge ... CA-9
Hogsback, The—ridge ... NH-1
Hogs Back, The—ridge ... NY-2
Hogsback, The—ridge ... UT-8
Hogs Back, The—ridge ... UT-8
Hogsback, The—ridge (3) ... WY-8
Hogs Back Buttes—ridge ... ND-7
Hogs Back Creek—stream ... NY-2
Hogsback Creek—stream ... NY-2
Hogsback Creek—stream ... WI-6
Hogsback Dam Reservoir ... CT-1
Hogsback Dam Reservoir ... MA-1
Hogsback Exclosure—locale ... UT-8
Hogsback Island ... NY-2
Hogsback Lakes—lake ... MN-6
Hogsback Marsh Public Hunting Area—area ... IA-7
Hogsback Mount—summit ... PA-2
Hogsback O'Brien Trail—trail ... MN-6
Hogsback Park—park ... IA-7
Hogsback Park Annex—park ... IA-7
Hogsback Pond—lake ... NY-2
Hogsback Ridge—ridge ... ID-8
Hogsback Ridge—ridge ... UT-8
Hogsback Ridge—ridge ... WI-6
Hogsback Ridge—ridge ... WY-8
Hogsback Spring No 1—spring ... WY-8
Hogsback Spring No 2—spring ... WY-8
Hogsback Springs—spring ... WI-6
Hogsback State Game Mngmt Area—park ... IA-7
Hogsback Tunnel—mine ... CA-9
Hogscald Hollow—valley ... AR-4
Hogs Canyon—valley ... CA-9
Hogs Defeat Creek—stream ... IN-6
Hogs Den Hollow—valley ... IA-7
Hogsed Cove—valley ... NC-3
Hogsed Creek—stream ... NC-3
Hogset Lake—lake ... MI-6
**Hogsett**—pop pl ... PA-2
**Hogsett**—pop pl ... WV-2
Hogsett Sch—school ... KY-4
Hogshead, The—bar ... ME-1
Hogshead Canyon—valley ... NV-8
Hogshead Hollow—valley ... KY-4
Hogshead Point—cape ... CT-1
Hogshead Rock—rock ... MA-1
Hogs Heaven—summit ... UT-8
Hogshed Creek—stream ... CA-9
Hogshooter—locale ... OK-5
**Hog Shooter**—pop pl ... OK-5
Hogshooter Bluff—cliff ... OK-5
Hogshooter Creek—stream (2) ... OK-5
Hogsick Creek—stream ... AL-4
Hogskin Bottoms—flat ... IL-6
Hogskin Branch—stream ... KY-4
Hogskin Branch—stream ... NC-3
Hogskin Branch—stream (3) ... TN-4
Hogskin Creek—stream ... AL-4
Hogskin Creek—stream (2) ... AR-4
Hogskin Creek—stream ... IL-6
Hogskin Creek—stream ... OK-5
Hogskin Creek—stream ... SC-3
Hogskin Creek—stream ... TN-4
Hogskin Hollow—valley ... AR-4
Hogskin Hollow—valley ... OK-5
Hogskin Lake—lake ... WI-6
Hogskin Ridge—ridge ... KY-4
Hogskin Slough—gut ... FL-3
Hogskin Valley—valley ... TN-4
Hog Slough—gut ... CA-9
Hog Slough—gut (2) ... IL-6
Hog Slough—stream ... AR-4
Hog Slough—stream ... CA-9
Hog Slough—stream ... LA-4
Hog Slough—stream ... MO-7
Hogs Neck—cape ... SC-3
Hog Spring—spring (4) ... AZ-5
Hog Spring—spring (5) ... CA-9
Hog Spring—spring ... NV-8
Hog Spring—spring (2) ... NM-5
Hog Spring—spring ... UT-8
Hog Spring Canyon—valley ... AZ-5
Hog Spring Canyon—valley ... CA-9
Hog Spring Canyon—valley ... NM-5
Hog Spring Hollow—valley ... MO-7
Hog Springs—spring ... CO-8
Hog Springs Campground—park ... UT-8
Hog Springs Picnic Area—locale ... UT-8
Hog Springs Rec Area ... UT-8
Hog Spring Tank—reservoir (2) ... AZ-5
Hogsted Ranch—locale ... MT-8
Hogstock Run—stream ... PA-2
Hogston Branch—stream ... KY-4
Hogston Hollow—valley ... KY-4
Hogstrom—other ... MI-6
Hog Sup Spring—spring ... NM-5
Hog Swamp—swamp ... CT-1
Hog Swamp—swamp ... MA-1
Hog Swamp—swamp (2) ... NC-3
Hog Swamp—swamp ... WA-9
Hog Swamp Brook ... NJ-2
Hog Swamp Ch—church ... NC-3
Hogtail Canyon ... AZ-5
Hogtail Saddle ... AZ-5
Hog Tank—reservoir (5) ... AZ-5
Hog Tank—reservoir (2) ... NM-5
Hog Tank—reservoir (2) ... TX-5
Hogtan Run—stream ... WV-2
Hog Theif Creek—stream ... IA-7
Hog Thief Creek—stream ... AR-4
Hogthief Creek—stream ... IL-6
Hog Thief Creek—stream ... TX-5
Hog Thief Hollow—valley ... OH-6
Hog Thief Lake—lake ... AR-4
Hog Tommy Spring—spring ... NV-8
Hogton ... NC-3
Hog Tongue Brook—stream ... NH-1
Hogtown ... AZ-5
Hog Town ... NC-3
**Hogtown**—pop pl ... IN-6
**Hogtown**—pop pl ... NY-2
Hogtown Bayou—bay ... FL-3
Hogtown Creek—stream ... FL-3
Hogtown Knob—summit ... KY-4
Hogtown Prairie—flat ... FL-3
Hog Town Slough—swamp ... FL-3
Hogtrail Canyon—valley ... AZ-5
Hogtrail Run—stream ... WV-2
Hogtrail Saddle—gap ... AZ-5
Hog Trap Windmill—locale ... TX-5
Hog Trough—basin ... CO-8
Hogtrough Brook—stream ... VT-1
Hog Trough Creek—stream ... MT-8
Hog Trough Fork—stream ... WV-2
Hogtrough Hollow—valley ... KY-4
Hogtrough Hollow—valley ... TN-4
Hogtrough Hollow—valley ... VA-3
Hog Trough Hollow—valley ... WV-2
Hog Trough Spring—spring ... AZ-5
Hog Trough Tank—reservoir ... AZ-5
Hog Tusk Creek—stream ... AR-4
Hogue—locale ... KY-4
Hogue, Mount—summit ... CA-9
Hogue, Robert M., House—hist pl ... PA-2
Hogue Allen Cem—cemetery ... OH-6
Hogue Branch—stream ... MS-4
Hogue Canyon—valley ... TX-5
Hogue Cem—cemetery ... AR-4
Hogue Cem—cemetery ... IL-6
Hogue Cem—cemetery (2) ... TN-4
Hogue Channel—channel ... FL-3
Hogue Creek—stream ... AL-4
Hogue Creek—stream ... VA-3
Hogue Farm Airp—airport ... MO-7
Hogue Hill ... OH-6
Hogue Hills ... NM-5
Hogue Hollow—valley ... OH-6
Hogue House—hist pl ... OK-5
Hogue Mtn—summit ... ID-8
Hogue Ranch—locale ... CA-9
Hogue Run—stream ... PA-2
Hogue Sch—school ... KY-4
Hogue's Hill ... OH-6
Hogues Lake ... MI-6
Hogue Tank—reservoir ... TX-5
Hogue Town—locale ... IL-6
**Hoguetown**—pop pl ... PA-2
Hogue Well—well ... NM-5
Hogue Well (Dry)—well ... TX-5
Hogum—locale ... NV-8
Hogum Bay—bay ... WA-9
Hogum Creek—stream ... MT-8
Hogum Creek—stream ... OR-9
Hogum Fork—stream ... UT-8
Hogum Hollow—valley ... TN-4
Hogun Cem—cemetery ... NC-3
Hogup—locale ... UT-8
Hogup Bar—flat ... UT-8
Hogup Cave (42BO36)—hist pl ... UT-8
Hogup Mtns—range ... UT-8
Hogup Point—ridge ... UT-8
Hogup Pump Station Heliport—airport ... UT-8
Hogup Ridge—ridge ... UT-8
Hogup Siding ... UT-8
Hogup Well—well ... UT-8
Hog Valley—basin ... NE-7
**Hog Valley**—pop pl ... FL-3
Hog Valley—valley ... CA-9
Hog Valley Rsvr—reservoir ... CA-9
Hogville Landing—locale ... IL-6
Hog Wallow—valley ... ID-8
Hogwallow Branch—stream ... IL-6
Hogwallow Branch—stream ... VA-3
Hog Wallow Cranberry Bogs—swamp ... NJ-2
Hog Wallow Creek ... TX-5
Hog Wallow Creek—stream ... GA-3
Hogwallow Creek—stream ... TN-4
Hog Wallow Dam—dam ... AZ-5
Hogwallow Flat—flat ... VA-3
Hogwallow Flat Overlook—locale ... VA-3
Hog Wallow Hollow—valley ... KY-4
Hog Wallow Lake—lake ... AZ-5
Hog Wallow Ridge—ridge ... AL-4
Hog Wallow Ridge—ridge ... TN-4
Hog Wallow Slough ... TX-5
Hog Wallow Slough—stream ... LA-4
Hog Wallow Slough—stream ... TX-5
Hogwallow Spring—spring ... AZ-5
Hogwallow Spring—spring ... OR-9
Hog Wallow Spring—spring ... OR-9
Hogwarten Slough—stream ... OR-9
Hog Wash—stream ... AZ-5
Hogwash Slough—gut ... IL-6
Hog Windmill—locale ... TX-5
Hogwood Branch—stream ... AL-4
Hogyard Ridge—ridge ... AL-4
Hoh Creek—stream (2) ... WA-9
Hohe Insel ... MP-9
Hohenberger Cem—cemetery ... OH-6
Hohenlinden ... AL-4
**Hohenlinden**—pop pl ... MS-4
Hohenlinden Baptist Ch—church ... MS-4
Hohenlinden Plantation (historical)—locale ... AL-4
Hohenlinden Post Office (historical)—building ... MS-4
Hohen Point—cape ... IN-6
**Hohen Solms**—pop pl ... LA-4
**Hohenwald**—pop pl ... TN-4
Hohenwald (CCD)—cens area ... TN-4
Hohenwald Ch of Christ—church ... TN-4
Hohenwald cumberland Presbyterian Ch—church ... TN-4
Hohenwald Division—civil ... TN-4
Hohenwald Elementary School ... TN-4
Hohenwald First Baptist Ch—church ... TN-4
Hohenwald First Methodist Ch—church ... TN-4
Hohenwald First United Pentecostal Ch—church ... TN-4
Hohenwald Post Office—building ... TN-4
Hohenwald RR Depot—hist pl ... TN-4
Hoh Glacier—glacier ... WA-9
Hoh Head—summit ... WA-9
H O Hill—summit ... TX-5
**Hoh Ind Res**—pop pl ... WA-9
**Ho (historical)**—pop pl ... TN-4
Hoh Lake—lake ... WA-9
Hohlfeld Coulee—valley ... WI-6
Hohl Sch—school ... TX-5
Hohls Crossing—locale ... PA-2
Hohman ... IN-6
Hohman—locale ... OH-6
Hohman Cem—cemetery ... KS-7
Hohman Lake—reservoir ... IL-6
Hohman Ridge—ridge ... OH-6
Hohneck ... KS-7
Hohnen Draw—valley ... WY-8
Hohnes Island ... ME-1
Hohnholz Lake ... CO-8
Hohnholz Lakes Campground—locale ... CO-8
Hohn Sch—school ... WI-6
Hohoghee River ... MS-4
Ho Ho Kam Country Club—other ... AZ-5
Hohokam Elem Sch—school ... AZ-5
Ho Ho Kam Park—park ... AZ-5
Hohokam-Pima Irrigation Sites ... AZ-5
Hohokam-Pima Irrigation Sites—hist pl ... AZ-5
Hohokam-Pima Natl Monmt—hist pl ... AZ-5
Hohokam Pima Natl Monmt—park ... AZ-5
**Hohokam Village (subdivision)**—pop pl (2) ... AZ-5
Hohokus ... NJ-2
**Ho-Ho-Kus**—pop pl ... NJ-2
Ho-ho-kus Brook ... NJ-2
Hohokus Brook—stream ... NJ-2
Hohokus Creek ... NJ-2
Hohokus (Ho-Ho-Kus) ... NJ-2
**Ho-Ho-Kus (Hohokus)**—pop pl ... NJ-2
Hoholitna River—stream ... AK-9
Ho-Hos-Keli Wash ... AZ-5
Hoh Peak—summit ... WA-9
Hoh Ranger Station—locale ... WA-9
Hoh River—stream ... WA-9
Hoh River Trail—trail ... WA-9
Hohstadt Rsvr—reservoir ... OR-9
**Hoicks Hollow**—pop pl ... MA-1
Hoidal Sch—school ... MN-6
Hoiland Township (historical)—civil ... ND-7
Hoil Creek—stream ... CA-9
Hoile Sch—school ... WI-6
Hoimadelehesuh ... PW-9
Hoinakaunalehua Stream—stream ... HI-9
Hointville Lake—lake ... WI-6
Hoinville Lake ... WI-6
Hoi Oidak—locale ... AZ-5
Hoise Branch ... TN-4
Hoisey Cem—cemetery ... AR-4
**Hoisington**—pop pl ... KS-7
Hoisington Brook—stream ... NY-2
Hoisington Cem—cemetery ... VT-1
Hoisington HS—school ... KS-7
Hoisington Lake—lake ... MI-6
Hoisington Mtn—summit ... NY-2
Hoisington Sch—school ... IL-6
Hoisington Sch—school ... NY-2
Hoist Bay—bay (3) ... MN-6
Hoist Creek—stream ... MN-6
Hoister Lake ... MI-6
Hoister Lake—lake ... MI-6
Hoister Lake—lake ... MN-6
Hoist Lake ... MI-6
Hoist Lake—lake ... MI-6
Hoist Lake—lake ... MN-6
Hoist Lake—lake (2) ... WI-6
Hoist Lakes—lake ... MI-6
Hoist Ridge—ridge ... CA-9
Hoit Camp—locale ... ME-1
Hoit Creek ... GA-3
Hoithlewalli (historical)—locale ... AL-4
Ho-ith-le-wau-le Creek ... AL-4
Hoits Ch—church ... IL-6
Hoits Point—cape ... NH-1
Hojitas, Las—bar ... PR-3
Hok, The—bay ... FL-3
**Hokah**—pop pl ... MN-6
**Hokah (Township of)**—pop pl ... MN-6
**Hokamahoe House Lot (Hokumahoe)**—pop pl ... HI-9
Hoka Tiki Mobile Village—locale ... AZ-5
**Ho-Kay-Gan**—pop pl ... AZ-5
Hok Canyon—valley ... NM-5
Hokdoloni Hills—other ... AK-9
Hoke—locale ... NC-3
Hoke, Andrew, House—hist pl ... KY-4
Hoke Bldg—hist pl ... OK-5
Hoke Cem—cemetery (2) ... IN-6
Hoke Cem—cemetery ... MO-7
Hoke Cem—cemetery ... NY-2
Hoke Cem—cemetery ... VA-3
Hoke Chapel—church ... VA-3
**Hoke County**—pop pl ... NC-3
Hoke County Ch—church ... NC-3
Hoke County Courthouse—hist pl ... NC-3
Hoke County HS—school ... NC-3
Hoke Creek—stream ... MS-4
Hoke Creek—stream ... MT-8
Hoke Ditch—canal ... IN-6
Hokeley Gulch—valley ... AK-9
Hokely Creek ... VA-3
**Hokendauqua**—pop pl ... PA-2
Hokendauqua Creek—stream ... PA-2
Hokenson Fishing Dock—hist pl ... WI-6
Hokenstad Sch—school ... SD-7
Hokeo Point—cape ... HI-9
Hoke Run—stream ... WV-2
Hokes—locale ... PA-2
**Hokes Bluff**—pop pl ... AL-4
Hokes Bluff (CCD)—cens area ... AL-4
Hokes Bluff Division—civil ... AL-4
Hokes Bluff Elem Sch—school ... AL-4
Hokes Bluff Ferry (historical)—locale ... AL-4
Hokes Bluff First Baptist Ch—church ... AL-4
Hokes Bluff HS—school ... AL-4
Hokes Bluff Male and Female Coll ... AL-4
Hokes Bluff Male and Female Institute ... AL-4
Hokes Bluff Methodist Church ... AL-4
Hokes Bluff MS—school ... AL-4
Hoke Sch—school ... IL-6
Hoke Sch (abandoned)—school ... PA-2
Hokes Creek ... TX-5
Hokes Meeting House—locale ... PA-2
Hokes Mill—locale ... WV-2
Hokes Mill Covered Bridge—hist pl ... WV-2
Hoke-Smith HS—school ... GA-3
Hokes Mtn—summit ... WV-2
Hokes Pond—reservoir ... NC-3
Hokes Pond Dam—dam ... NC-3
Hokes Sch—school ... PA-2
Hoke Valley—valley ... CA-9
Hokey Lake—lake ... FL-3
Hokey Pokey Ridge—ridge ... CA-9
Hokey's Drugstore—hist pl ... OK-5
Hok Farm Canyon—valley ... NM-5
Hokit Cem—cemetery ... OK-5
Hoknede Mtn—summit ... AK-9
**Hoko**—pop pl ... WA-9
Hoko Camp—locale ... WA-9
Hoko Falls—falls ... WA-9
Hokola Ditch—canal ... MT-8
Hoko River—stream ... WA-9
Hoko River Archeol Site—hist pl ... WA-9
Hoko River Rockshelter Archeol Site—hist pl ... WA-9
Hoko-Wash Lake ... MN-6
Hoko-wWsh-Te Lake ... MN-6
Hok Ranch—locale ... NM-5
Hokshela Creek—stream ... SD-7
Hoktaheen Cove—bay ... AK-9
Hoktaheen Creek—stream ... AK-9
Hoktaheen Lake—lake ... AK-9
Hokualele—summit ... HI-9
Hokukano—civil ... HI-9
Hokukano—summit ... HI-9
Hokukano Cone ... HI-9
Hokukano Heiau—locale ... HI-9
Hokukano Mauka Tract—civil ... HI-9
Hokukano One-Two—civil ... HI-9
Hokukano-Ualapue Complex—hist pl ... HI-9
Hokulani Sch—school ... HI-9
Hokulei Peak—summit ... HI-9
Hokumahoe ... HI-9
Hokumahoe—civil ... HI-9
Hokum Rock—summit ... MA-1
Hokunui ... HI-9
Hokunui—summit ... HI-9
Hoku Point—cape ... HI-9
Hokusei ... MP-9
Hokusei Sho ... PW-9
Hokusei Suido ... MP-9
Hokuto ... MP-9
Hokuto Suido ... FM-9
Hokuto-suido ... MP-9
Hokuula—civil ... HI-9
Hokuula—locale ... HI-9
Hokuula—summit (2) ... HI-9
**Holabird**—pop pl ... SD-7
Holabird—uninc pl ... MD-2
Holabird House—hist pl ... CT-1
Holabird Township—civil ... SD-7
Holaday Chapel—church ... MS-4
Holaday Hill—ridge ... NM-5
**Holaday Hills and Dales**—pop pl ... IN-6
Holadays (historical)—locale ... IA-7
Holadays (historical P.O.)—locale ... IA-7
Holaki Knob—summit ... ID-8
Holana Bay—bay ... HI-9
Holan Cem—cemetery ... IA-7
Holanna Creek—stream ... GA-3
Holap Island ... FM-9
Holaway Sch—school ... AZ-5
Holban Yards—locale ... NY-2
Holbeck Creek ... SC-3
Holben Creek—stream ... MT-8
Holben Creek—stream ... WY-8
Holben Sch—school ... IL-6
Holben School ... IN-6
Holbensville ... PA-2
Holbenville ... PA-2
Holberg Cem—cemetery ... MN-6
Holbert Branch (historical)—stream ... TN-4
Holbert Cabin—locale ... CO-8
Holbert Cem—cemetery (5) ... WV-2
Holbert Cemetery ... TN-4
Holbert Ch—church ... KY-4
Holbert Creek—stream ... PA-2
Holbert Creek—stream ... TN-4
Holbert Gap—gap ... TN-4
Holbert Hall—building ... NC-3
Holbert Park—park ... IA-7
Holbert Run—stream ... WV-2
Holbert Spring—spring ... TN-4
Holbert Springs ... AL-4
Holbert Springs Ch—church ... AL-4
Holborn—locale ... NV-8
Holborn Field—flat ... NV-8
Holbrecht Cem—cemetery ... TX-5
Holbrock Ditch—canal ... IN-6
Holbrook—locale ... AK-9
Holbrook—locale ... IA-7
Holbrook—locale ... KY-4
Holbrook—locale ... PA-2
**Holbrook**—pop pl ... AZ-5
**Holbrook**—pop pl ... GA-3
**Holbrook**—pop pl ... ID-8
**Holbrook**—pop pl ... IL-6
**Holbrook**—pop pl ... MD-2

Hole Windmill—locale TX-5
Holey Flat—flat SD-7
Holey Land Wildlife Mngmt Area—park FL-3
Holey Meadow—flat CA-9
Holey Run—stream IN-6
Holf Oak Grove NC-3
**Holgate**—pop pl NJ-2
**Holgate**—pop pl OH-6
Holgate Arm—bay AK-9
Holgate Glacier—glacier AK-9
Holgate Head—summit AK-9
Holguin Creek—stream TX-5
Holibaugh Hills—summit MI-6
Holice Powell Elementary School TN-4
**Holicong**—pop pl PA-2
Holicong Post Office (historical)—building PA-2
Holicong Village Hist Dist—hist pl PA-2
Holida IN-6
**Holida**—pop pl IN-6
Holiday PA-2
Holiday—other IL-6
**Holiday**—pop pl FL-3
**Holiday**—pop pl IN-6
**Holiday**—pop pl TX-5
Holiday—post sta CA-9
Holiday, Lake—lake MN-6
Holiday, Lake—reservoir IL-6
Holiday, Lake—reservoir IN-6
Holiday, Lake—reservoir TN-4
**Holiday Acres**—pop pl DE-2
**Holiday Acres**—pop pl MD-2
**Holiday Acres**—pop pl OH-6
Holiday Acres—uninc pl NM-5
Holiday Acres Golf Course—locale PA-2
Holiday Acres Lake—reservoir MO-7
Holiday Acres Lake—reservoir NC-3
Holiday Acres Lake Dam—dam NC-3
Holiday Airstrip—airport OR-9
Holiday Beach—beach AK-9
Holiday Beach—beach TX-5
Holiday Beach—park AL-4
**Holiday Beach**—pop pl ME-1
**Holiday Beach**—pop pl MD-2
**Holiday Beach**—pop pl OR-9
**Holiday Beach**—pop pl TX-5
Holiday Branch—stream TX-5
Holiday Bridge—bridge SC-3
Holiday Camp—locale WA-9
Holiday Campground—locale MT-8
Holiday Cem—cemetery GA-3
Holiday Cem—cemetery MI-6
Holiday Cem—cemetery MO-7
**Holiday Center Addition**
**Subdivision**—pop pl UT-8
Holiday Center Shop Ctr—locale IN-6
Holiday Ch—church FL-3
Holiday Chapel MS-4
**Holiday City**—pop pl NJ-2
Holiday City—uninc pl TN-4
Holiday City-Berkeley—CDP NJ-2
Holiday Country Club—other OH-6
Holiday Cove—cove FL-3
Holiday Creek MO-7
Holiday Creek TX-5
Holiday Creek—stream AK-9
Holiday Creek—stream ID-8
Holiday Creek—stream IN-6
Holiday Creek—stream MS-4
Holiday Creek—stream VA-3
Holiday Creek Structure 4 Dam—dam MS-4
Holiday Creek Watershed Structure 3
Dam—dam MS-4
Holiday (Crooked Creek)—other PA-2
Holiday Day Sch—school FL-3
Holiday Draw—valley WY-8
Holiday Drive Ch—church OH-6
**Holiday Estates**—pop pl NJ-2
**Holiday Estates**—pop pl TX-5
**Holiday Estates (subdivision)**—pop pl DE-2
Holiday Ford—locale KY-4
**Holiday Forest**—pop pl CA-9
**Holiday Gardens**—pop pl AL-4
**Holiday Gardens**—pop pl FL-3
Holiday Golf Course—locale MS-4
Holiday Gulch—valley MT-8
Holiday Harbor—harbor VA-3
Holiday Harbor—locale NC-3
**Holiday Harbor**—pop pl FL-3
Holiday Harbor Marina—locale FL-3
**Holiday Heights**—pop pl FL-3
**Holiday Heights**—pop pl WI-6
Holiday Hide-away, Lake—reservoir IN-6
Holiday Hide-A-Way Cabin Site—locale TN-4
Holiday Hill—summit FL-3
Holiday Hill—summit MA-1
Holiday Hill—summit PA-2
Holiday Hill—summit TX-5
Holiday Hill—summit VT-1
Holiday Hill Park—park FL-3
Holiday Hill Public Use Area—locale KS-7
Holiday Hills—locale TN-4
**Holiday Hills**—pop pl CO-8
**Holiday Hills**—pop pl DE-2
**Holiday Hills**—pop pl FL-3
**Holiday Hills**—pop pl IL-6
**Holiday Hills**—pop pl KY-4
**Holiday Hills**—pop pl MD-2
**Holiday Hills**—pop pl (4) TN-4
**Holiday Hills**—pop pl TX-5
**Holiday Hills**—pop pl VA-3
**Holiday Hills**—pop pl WI-6
Holiday Hills Camp—locale KY-4
Holiday Hills Campground—park UT-8
Holiday Hills Ch—church AR-4
Holiday Hill Ski Lift—other CA-9
**Holiday Hills (subdivision)**—pop pl TN-4
Holiday Hole—cave AL-4
Holiday Homes CT-1
Holiday Homes—uninc pl AL-4
Holiday Homestead (abandoned)—locale WY-8
Holiday House—locale NY-2
Holiday House Kindergarten and
Nursery—school FL-3
Holiday Industrial Park—facility MS-4
Holiday Inn Of New Hope Airp—airport PA-2
Holiday Inn Westport Heliport—airport MO-7
Holiday Island—island AK-9
Holiday Island—island NY-2
**Holiday Island**—pop pl AR-4
**Holiday Island**—pop pl NC-3
Holiday Lake—lake CA-9
Holiday Lake—lake IA-7
Holiday Lake—lake MN-6
Holiday Lake—lake NJ-2
Holiday Lake—lake PA-2
Holiday Lake—lake TX-5
Holiday Lake—other IL-6
**Holiday Lake**—pop pl IA-7
Holiday Lake—reservoir IL-6
Holiday Lake—reservoir IN-6
Holiday Lake—reservoir MS-4
Holiday Lake—reservoir MO-7
Holiday Lake—reservoir (2) NJ-2
Holiday Lake—reservoir NC-3
Holiday Lake—reservoir OH-6
Holiday Lake—reservoir PA-2
Holiday Lake—reservoir TN-4
Holiday Lake—reservoir VA-3
Holiday Lake Dam—dam IN-6
Holiday Lake Dam—dam IA-7
Holiday Lake Dam—dam MS-4
Holiday Lake Dam—dam NJ-2
Holiday Lake Dam—dam TN-4
Holiday Lake Dam Lower—dam NC-3
Holiday Lakes—lake IN-6
**Holiday Lakes**—pop pl TX-5
Holiday Lake State Rec Area—park VA-3
Holiday Lake Upper—reservoir NC-3
Holiday Lake Upper Dam—dam NC-3
Holiday Liquors, Incorporated—facility IL-6
Holiday Mall—locale FL-3
**Holiday Manor**—pop pl FL-3
Holiday Manor—uninc pl NY-2
Holiday Marina and Resort—locale TN-4
Holiday Mesa—bench NM-5
Holiday Mesa—summit UT-8
Holiday Mine—mine CA-9
**Holiday Mobile Home City**—pop pl NC-3
Holiday-on-Lake Lanier Marina—other GA-3
Holiday Palms Mobile Home Park—locale AZ-5
Holiday Park—park AL-4
Holiday Park—park AZ-5
Holiday Park—park CA-9
Holiday Park—park FL-3
Holiday Park—park IA-7
Holiday Park—park TX-5
Holiday Park—park WA-9
Holiday Park—park WV-2
**Holiday Park**—pop pl MD-2
**Holiday Park**—pop pl PA-2
**Holiday Park Estates**—pop pl AL-4
Holiday Park Peak—summit UT-8
Holiday Park Sch—school AZ-5
Holiday Park Sch—school MD-2
Holiday Park Site (20GR91)—hist pl MI-6
**Holiday Park (subdivision)**—pop pl
(2) NC-3
**Holiday Park (subdivision)**—pop pl PA-2
**Holiday Pines**—pop pl DE-2
**Holiday Pines (trailer park)**—pop pl DE-2
Holiday Plaza—locale PA-2
Holiday Plaza Shop Ctr—locale AL-4
Holiday Plaza (Shop Ctr)—locale FL-3
Holiday Plaza (Shop Ctr)—post sta FL-3
**Holiday Poconos**—pop pl PA-2
Holiday Point VA-3
Holiday Point—cape CT-1
Holiday Point—cape VT-1
Holiday Point—uninc pl VA-3
**Holiday Point Estates**—pop pl VA-3
Holiday Pond—lake NY-2
Holiday Raceway—locale AL-4
Holiday Ranch—locale MT-8
Holiday Ranch—locale WY-8
Holiday Resort—locale TN-4
Holiday Run—stream PA-2
Holidays Bridge AL-4
Holidaysburg KS-7
Holidaysburg PA-2
Holiday Sch—school KY-4
Holiday Sch—school OH-6
Holiday Sch (historical)—school MS-4
**Holidays Cove**—pop pl WV-2
Holidays Creek MS-4
Holiday Shop Ctr—locale AL-4
Holiday Shop Ctr—locale TN-4
Holiday Shores—locale TN-4
**Holiday Shores**—pop pl IL-6
**Holiday Shores**—pop pl MO-7
**Holiday Shores (subdivision)**—pop pl
(2) AL-4
Holidays Island—island NC-3
Holiday Spa Mobile Home Park—locale AZ-5
Holiday Springs UT-8
Holiday Springs Shop Ctr—locale FL-3
Holiday Station—locale PA-2
Holiday Trail—trail FL-3
**Holiday (Trailer Park)**—pop pl AZ-5
**Holiday Valley**—pop pl OH-6
Holiday Valley Ski Club—other NY-2
Holiday Village Mobile Home
Park—locale AZ-5
Holiday Village Shopping Mall—locale UT-8
**Holifield**—pop pl KY-4
Holifield Playground—park CA-9
Holifield Store (historical)—locale MS-4
Holihan Gulf—valley NY-2
**Holihtasha (historical)**—pop pl MS-4
**Holikachuk**—pop pl AK-9
Holikachuk Slough—gut AK-9
Holiman Ranch—locale TX-5
Holiman Sch—school TX-5
Holimont Ski Club—other NY-2
Holin Creek—stream WY-8
Holiness Camp—locale IL-6
Holiness Camp—locale MD-2
Holiness Camp—locale NJ-2
Holiness Camp—locale OK-5
Holiness Camp—locale PA-2
Holiness Campground—locale MI-6
Holiness Cem—cemetery MN-6
Holiness Cem—cemetery MO-7
Holiness Ch AL-4
Holiness Ch NC-3
Holiness Ch—church (10) AL-4
Holiness Ch—church AR-4
Holiness Ch—church FL-3
Holiness Ch—church (4) GA-3
Holiness Ch—church (2) LA-4
Holiness Ch—church MN-6
Holiness Ch—church (9) MS-4
Holiness Ch—church (2) MO-7
Holiness Ch—church (3) NC-3
Holiness Ch—church ND-7
Holiness Ch—church OH-6
Holiness Ch—church OK-5
Holiness Ch—church PA-2
Holiness Ch—church (2) SC-3
Holiness Ch—church (5) TN-4
Holiness Ch—church (7) TX-5
Holiness Ch—church (2) VA-3
Holiness Ch—church (2) WV-2
Holiness Chapel—church NC-3
Holiness Chapel—church OH-6
Holiness Chapel (historical)—church AL-4
Holiness Ch (historical)—church (2) AL-4
Holiness Ch (historical)—church (3) MS-4
Holiness Ch (historical)—church (4) TN-4
Holiness Ch Number 2—church AL-4
Holiness Ch of God Number 1—church MS-4
Holiness Christian Ch—church PA-2
Holiness Church Camp—locale OK-5
Holiness Gospel Ch—church MI-6
Holiness Hollow—valley KY-4
Holiness Indian Mission—church NM-5
Holiness Tabernacle—church AL-4
Holiness Tabernacle—church IL-6
Holiness Tabernacle—church SC-3
Holiness Tabernacle (historical)—church AL-4
Holiness Temple AL-4
Holiness Temple—church GA-3
Holiness Temple of Alexandria—church AL-4
Holisters Creek PA-2
Holita Ditch—canal CO-8
Holita Rsvr—reservoir CO-8
Holitna River—stream AK-9
Holi-Tuska Creek—stream OK-5
Holiville Schenk Eleven Drain—canal CA-9
Holkeo Creek—stream NM-5
Holker—locale (2) MT-8
Holkham Bay—bay AK-9
Holkums Branch—stream VA-3
Holky Creek MS-4
Hollabaugh Cem—cemetery TN-4
Hollabaugh Hollow—valley AR-4
Holla Bend—locale AR-4
Holla Bend Cutoff—channel AR-4
Holla Bend Natl Wildlife Ref—park AR-4
Holladay—locale VA-3
**Holladay**—pop pl MS-4
**Holladay**—pop pl (2) TN-4
**Holladay**—pop pl UT-8
**Holladay Acres Subdivision**—pop pl UT-8
Holladay Baptist Ch—church UT-8
Holladay Branch—stream VA-3
Holladay Branch Post Office—building UT-8
Holladay (CCD)—cens area TN-4
Holladay Cem—cemetery IN-6
Holladay Cem—cemetery MS-4
Holladay Cem—cemetery MO-7
Holladay Cem—cemetery TN-4
Holladay Ch—church TN-4
Holladay Ch (historical)—church TN-4
**Holladay Circle Subdivision**—pop pl UT-8
Holladay Congregational Methodist Ch
(historical)—church MS-4
**Holladay Creek Condominium**—pop pl UT-8
Holladay Division—civil TN-4
**Holladay East Subdivision**—pop pl UT-8
**Holladay Edgehill Subdivision**—pop pl UT-8
Holladay Elem Sch—school TN-4
**Holladay Estates Subdivision**—pop pl UT-8
**Holladay Gardens**
**Subdivision**—pop pl UT-8
**Holladay Grove Subdivision**—pop pl UT-8
**Holladay Haven**
**Condominium**—pop pl UT-8
**Holladay Heights Subdivision**—pop pl UT-8
**Holladay Highlands**
**Subdivision**—pop pl UT-8
**Holladay Highlands Subdivision**
**Three**—pop pl UT-8
**Holladay Hills Subdivision**—pop pl UT-8
Holladay Hot Springs AZ-5
Holladay Independent Normal Coll
(historical)—school TN-4
**Holladay Manor Subdivision**—pop pl UT-8
**Holladay Meadows**
**Condominium**—pop pl UT-8
Holladay Memorial Park
(Cem)—cemetery UT-8
Holladay Mtn—summit MO-7
Holladay Park—park OR-9
Holladay Park Hosp—hospital OR-9
**Holladay Park Subdivision**—pop pl UT-8
**Holladay Pines Condominium**—pop pl UT-8
Holladay Post Office—building TN-4
Holladay Post Office
(historical)—building MS-4
Holladay Ranch—locale AZ-5
Holladay Sch—school AZ-5
Holladay Sch—school OR-9
Holladay Sch—school TN-4
Holladay Sch—school UT-8
Holladay Sch (historical)—school MS-4
Holladay Springs—spring UT-8
Holladay United Ch of Christ—church UT-8
**Holladay Village**
**Condominium**—pop pl UT-8
**Holladay Villa Homes**
**Condominium**—pop pl UT-8
Hollam NE-7
Hollaman Lake—reservoir NC-3
Holland—locale AR-4
Holland—locale FL-3
Holland—locale GA-3
Holland—locale MT-8
**Holland**—pop pl AR-4
**Holland**—pop pl IL-6
**Holland**—pop pl IN-6
**Holland**—pop pl IA-7
**Holland**—pop pl KS-7
**Holland**—pop pl KY-4
**Holland**—pop pl MA-1
**Holland**—pop pl MI-6
**Holland**—pop pl MN-6
**Holland**—pop pl MO-7
**Holland**—pop pl NE-7
**Holland**—pop pl (3) NJ-2
**Holland**—pop pl (2) NY-2
**Holland**—pop pl NC-3
**Holland**—pop pl OH-6
**Holland**—pop pl OR-9
**Holland**—pop pl PA-2
**Holland**—pop pl SC-3
**Holland**—pop pl TX-5
**Holland**—pop pl VT-1
**Holland**—pop pl VA-3
**Holland**—pop pl WA-9
**Holland**—pop pl WI-6
Holland, Benjamin Franklin,
House—hist pl FL-3
Holland, Captain, House—hist pl ME-1
Holland, Lake—lake MA-1
Holland, Ora, House—hist pl IA-7
**Hollandale**—pop pl MN-6
**Hollandale**—pop pl MS-4
**Hollandale**—pop pl WI-6
Hollandale Baptist Ch—church MS-4
Hollandale Junction—locale MN-6
Hollandale Municipal Airp—airport MS-4
Hollandale Sch (historical)—school MS-4
Hollandale United Methodist Ch—church MS-4
Holland Apartments—hist pl IL-6
Holland Bay—swamp FL-3
Holland Branch—stream (2) AL-4
Holland Branch—stream AR-4
Holland Branch—stream (2) FL-3
Holland Branch—stream (3) KY-4
Holland Branch—stream MO-7
Holland Branch—stream NC-3
Holland Branch—stream (2) TN-4
Holland Branch—stream TX-5
Holland Brook—stream CT-1
Holland Brook—stream ME-1
Holland Brook—stream NJ-2
Holland Brook—stream VT-1
Holland Camp—locale CA-9
Holland Camp Spring—spring SD-7
Holland Canyon—valley CA-9
Holland Canyon—valley ID-8
Holland (CCD)—cens area KY-4
Holland Cem AL-4
Holland Cem TN-4
Holland Cem—cemetery (4) AL-4
Holland Cem—cemetery (3) AR-4
Holland Cem—cemetery (2) GA-3
Holland Cem—cemetery IL-6
Holland Cem—cemetery IA-7
Holland Cem—cemetery (3) KY-4
Holland Cem—cemetery (2) MN-6
Holland Cem—cemetery MO-7
Holland Cem—cemetery NE-7
Holland Cem—cemetery NJ-2
Holland Cem—cemetery (3) NY-2
Holland Cem—cemetery OK-5
Holland Cem—cemetery SD-7
Holland Cem—cemetery (11) TN-4
Holland Cem—cemetery (4) TX-5
Holland Cem—cemetery (2) VA-3
Holland Cem—cemetery WA-9
Holland Ch—church NJ-2
Holland Ch—church ND-7
Holland Chapel—church AL-4
Holland Chapel—church NC-3
Holland Cliff—locale MD-2
**Holland Cliff Shores**—pop pl MD-2
Holland Congregational Church—hist pl VT-1
Holland Cove—bay GA-3
**Holland Cove**—pop pl NY-2
Holland Cove—valley AL-4
Holland Creek VA-3
Holland Creek—bay MD-2
Holland Creek—stream (3) AL-4
Holland Creek—stream (2) AK-9
Holland Creek—stream CA-9
Holland Creek—stream (2) GA-3
Holland Creek—stream IA-7
Holland Creek—stream KS-7
Holland Creek—stream MD-2
Holland Creek—stream MI-6
Holland Creek—stream (2) MT-8
Holland Creek—stream NC-3
Holland Creek—stream OR-9
Holland Creek—stream (2) TN-4
Holland Creek—stream TX-5
Holland Creek—stream WV-2
Holland Creek—stream WY-8
Holland Creek Baptist Ch—church AL-4
Holland Crossroads—locale FL-3
Holland Cut—canal CA-9
Holland Dam—dam TX-5
Holland Ditch—canal CO-8
Holland Ditch—canal MI-6
Holland Ditch—canal OR-9
Holland Ditch—canal WY-8
Holland Drain—canal CA-9
Holland Drain—canal MI-6
Holland Drain—stream MI-6
Holland Draw—valley CO-8
Holland Draw—valley TX-5
Holland-Drew House—hist pl ME-1
Holland Elem Sch—school IN-6
Hollander Branch AL-4
Hollander Branch—stream TN-4
Hollander Sch (historical)—school TN-4
Hollanders Creek—stream PA-2
Holland Farm—locale CA-9
Holland Flying Sch—school GA-3
Holland Ford—locale TN-4
Holland Fork—stream OH-6
Holland Gin—locale AL-4
Holland Glade DE-2
Holland Glade—stream DE-2
Holland Glen—valley MA-1
Holland Gordon Trail—trail MT-8
Holland Gulch—valley CO-8
Holland Gulch—valley ID-8
Holland Hall Sch—school OK-5
Holland Harbor Lighthouse—hist pl MI-6
**Holland Heights**—pop pl PA-2
Holland Heights Sch—school MI-6
Holland Hill—summit AR-4
Holland Hill—summit PA-2
Holland Hill Cem—cemetery TN-4
Holland Hill Church TN-4
Holland Hill Sch—school CT-1
Holland Hist Dist—hist pl MI-6
**Holland (historical)**—pop pl OR-9
Holland Hollow—valley TN-4
Holland Hollow—valley TX-5
Holland Homestead—locale MT-8
**Hollandia**—pop pl IL-6
Holland Island—island MD-2
Holland Island Bar MD-2
Holland Island Bar Lighthouse—locale MD-2
Holland Island Bay—bay MD-2
Holland Island Creek—stream SC-3
Holland JHS—school PA-2
Holland Lake MA-1
Holland Lake—lake (2) MI-6
Holland Lake—lake (3) MN-6
Holland Lake—lake MT-8
Holland Lake—reservoir IN-6
Holland Lake—reservoir NC-3
Holland Lake—reservoir TN-4
Holland Lake Campground—locale MT-8
Holland Lake Park (Private)—locale TX-5
Holland Landing—locale GA-3
Holland Landing—locale MS-4
Holland Land Office—hist pl NY-2
Holland-Lucy Lake—lake MN-6
Holland Meadows—flat OR-9
Holland Meadows Trail—trail OR-9
Holland Memorial Ch—church NC-3
**Holland Mill**—pop pl TN-4
Holland Mill Creek DE-2
Holland Mill Creek—stream NC-3
Holland Mill Pond DE-2
Holland Mine—mine AZ-5
Holland Mine—mine CA-9
Holland Mtn—summit NC-3
Holland Mtn—summit TX-5
Holland Neck—cape DE-2
Holland Neck—cape MD-2
Holland New Water Supply Lake IN-6
Holland Northlake Day Sch—school FL-3
Holland Old City Hall and Fire
Station—hist pl MI-6
Holland Old Water Supply Dam Number
1—dam IN-6
Holland Park—park MO-7
**Holland Patent**—pop pl NY-2
Holland Peak—summit MT-8
Holland Pit—cave AL-4
Holland Place—locale WY-8
**Holland Place (subdivision)**—pop pl AL-4
Holland Point—cape DE-2
Holland Point—cape (6) MD-2
Holland Point—cape (4) NC-3
Holland Point—cape VA-3
Holland Point—summit OR-9
Holland Pond ME-1
Holland Pond—lake DE-2
Holland Pond—lake FL-3
Holland Pond—lake ME-1
Holland Pond—lake MA-1
Holland Pond—lake TN-4
Holland Pond—lake VT-1
Holland Post Office (historical)—building PA-2
Holland Prospect—mine AK-9
Holland Quarters—locale TX-5
Holland Ranch—locale NV-8
Holland Ranch—locale NM-5
Holland Ranch—locale (3) TX-5
Holland Reformed Ch—church IA-7
Holland Ridge—ridge IN-6
Holland Road Chapel—church VA-3
Holland Rsvr—reservoir WY-8
Holland Run—stream PA-2
Holland Run Trail—trail PA-2
Hollands—locale NC-3
Hollands Branch—stream MD-2
**Hollandsburg**—pop pl IN-6
Hollands Cem—cemetery VA-3
Hollands Ch—church NC-3
Holland Sch—school CA-9
Holland Sch—school IL-6
Holland Sch—school (3) MI-6
Holland Sch—school MN-6
Holland Sch—school MO-7
Holland Sch—school NC-3
Holland Sch—school (2) PA-2
Holland Sch—school TX-5
Holland Sch—school WI-6
Hollands Chapel AL-4
Hollands Chapel—church AL-4
Hollands Chapel—church NC-3
Holland Sch (historical)—school AL-4
Holland Sch (historical)—school (2) TN-4
Hollands Creek NC-3
Hollands Creek—stream IL-6
Hollands Creek—stream NC-3
Hollands Crossroads—locale MD-2
**Hollands Crossroads**—pop pl NC-3
Holland Settlement Cem—cemetery MT-8
Hollands Grist Mill—hist pl SD-7
Hollands Grove Cem—cemetery IL-6
**Hollands (historical)**—pop pl MS-4
Holland's Island MD-2
Hollands Landing MS-4
Holland's Ledge ME-1
Hollands Pasture Island—island VT-1
Hollands Point—cape NY-2
Holland Spring Ch—church GA-3
Hollands River MD-2
Hollands Run PA-2
Hollands Store—locale GA-3
**Hollands Store**—pop pl SC-3
Hollands Store (historical)—locale TN-4
**Holland (sta.)**—pop pl NJ-2
Holland Stand (historical)—locale TN-4
Holland State Park—park MI-6
Holland State Wildlife Area—park WI-6
Holland State Wildlife Mngmt
Area—park MN-6
Holland Station GA-3
Holland Station PA-2
Holland Station—locale PA-2
Holland Straits—channel MD-2
**Holland Subdivision**—pop pl UT-8
Holland-Summers House—hist pl NC-3
Hollandsville—locale DE-2
Hollandsworth Hollow—valley TN-4
Hollandsworth Post Office
(historical)—building TN-4
**Holland (Town of)**—pop pl MA-1
**Holland (Town of)**—pop pl NY-2
**Holland (Town of)**—pop pl VT-1
**Holland (Town of)**—pop pl (3) WI-6
Holland Township—civil MO-7
Holland Township—fmr MCD IA-7
**Holland Township**—pop pl KS-7
**Holland Township**—pop pl SD-7
Holland (Township of)—fmr MCD AR-4
**Holland (Township of)**—pop pl IL-6
**Holland (Township of)**—pop pl (2) MI-6
**Holland (Township of)**—pop pl MN-6
**Holland (Township of)**—pop pl NJ-2
Holland Tract—civil CA-9
Holland Tunnel—tunnel NJ-2
Holland Tunnel—tunnel NY-2
Hollandville ME-1
**Hollandville**—pop pl ME-1
Holland Winter Camp—locale WY-8
**Hollansburg**—pop pl OH-6
Hollar Creek—stream TX-5
Hollard Mill—locale TN-4
Hollars Cem—cemetery NC-3
**Hollars Hill**—pop pl PA-2
Hollaway Bridge—bridge MS-4
Hollaway Cem—cemetery KY-4
Hollaway Cem—cemetery TX-5
Hollaway Point—cape AL-4
Hollberg Hotel—hist pl GA-3
Hollecker Lake—reservoir MT-8
Hollekonk Well Cave—cave PA-2
Holleman Bend—bend TN-4
Holleman Cem—cemetery AR-4
Holleman Cem—cemetery (2) TX-5
Holleman Chapel—church TX-5
Holleman Park FL-3
Hollemans NC-3
**Hollemans Crossroads**—pop pl NC-3
**Hollenback**—pop pl IL-6
**Hollenback**—pop pl PA-2
Hollenback Cem—cemetery IN-6
Hollenback Creek—stream IL-6
Hollenback Creek—stream NM-5
Hollenback Hollow—valley PA-2
Hollenback Point—summit AZ-5
Hollenback Spring—spring MO-7
**Hollenback (Township of)**—pop pl PA-2
Hollenbeak Swamp—swamp CA-9
Hollenbeck—locale CA-9
Hollenbeck, Lake—reservoir MO-7
Hollenbeck Butte—summit CA-9
Hollenbeck Canyon—valley CA-9
Hollenbeck Cem—cemetery MI-6
Hollenbeck Cem—cemetery NM-5
Hollenbeck Creek—stream OR-9
Hollenbeck Ditch—canal CO-8
Hollenbeck Draw—valley MT-8
Hollenbeck Flat—flat CA-9
Hollenbeck Hollow—valley NY-2
Hollenbeck JHS—school CA-9
Hollenbeck Park—park (2) CA-9
Hollenbeck Point AZ-5
Hollenbeck Pond—reservoir CT-1
Hollenbeck Reservoir Number One CO-8
Hollenbeck River—stream CT-1
Hollenbeck Rsvr No. 2—reservoir CO-8
Hollenbeck Run—stream WV-2
Hollenbeck Sch—school NY-2
Hollenbeck Spring—spring CO-8
Hollenbeck Spring—spring OR-9
**Hollenberg**—pop pl KS-7
Hollenberg Pony Express Station—hist pl KS-7
Hollenberg Ranch State Park—park KS-7
Hollencamp House—hist pl OH-6
Hollencrest Sch—school CA-9
Hollendale IL-6
Hollene—locale NM-5
Hollenfelz House—hist pl IA-7
Hollens Draw—valley SD-7
Hollensteiner Gulch—valley MT-8
Hollenstein Wagon and Carriage
Factory—hist pl WI-6
**Hollentown**—pop pl PA-2
Holleque Lake—reservoir MN-6
Holleran Swamp—swamp CT-1
Hollerberg Floodway—canal MN-6
Hollerberg Lake—lake MN-6
Hollerberg Lake State Wildlife Mngmt
Ar—park MN-6
Holler Draw—valley (2) WY-8
Hollering Point—cape MD-2
Hollernan Cem—cemetery PA-2
Holler Park—park WI-6
Hollers Cem—cemetery KY-4
Hollers Cem—cemetery MO-7
Holler Sch—school MN-6
**Hollers Hill**—pop pl PA-2
Hollets NY-2
Holletts Corners—locale DE-2
**Holley**—pop pl FL-3
**Holley**—pop pl NY-2
**Holley**—pop pl OR-9
**Holley Acres Subdivision**—pop pl UT-8
Holley And Day Drain—canal MI-6
**Holley and Whitney**
**Subdivision**—pop pl UT-8
Holley Branch—stream AL-4
Holley Branch—stream FL-3
Holley Branch—stream KY-4
Holley Branch—stream NC-3
Holley Cem—cemetery (3) AL-4
Holley Cem—cemetery ME-1
Holley Cem—cemetery MS-4
Holley Chapel—church MI-6
Holley Corners—locale NY-2
Holley Coulee—valley WI-6
Holley Creek SC-3
**Holley Creek**—pop pl OK-5
Holley Creek—stream (2) AL-4
Holley Creek—stream AR-4
Holley Creek—stream FL-3
Holley Creek—stream TN-4
Holley Creek Landing—locale AL-4
Holley Crossroads—locale AL-4
Holley Crossroads Missionary Baptist
Ch—church AL-4
Holley Dusting Field FL-3
Holley-Globe Grain and Milling Company
Elevator—hist pl UT-8
**Holley Heights**—pop pl PA-2
Holley Hill—summit AL-4
Holley Hills Estate—hist pl WV-2
**Holley (Holly)**—pop pl OR-9
Holley Landing Strip—airport FL-3

Homestead Hills Country Club—other ... IL-6
Homestead Hole—lake ... OR-9
Homestead Hollow—valley ... AR-4
Homestead Hollow—valley (2) ... MO-7
Homestead Hollow—valley ... PA-2
Homestead Home—locale ... NE-7
**Homestead (Homestead Village)**—pop pl ... NC-3
Homestead House—building ... NC-3
Homestead HS—school ... CA-9
Homestead HS (historical)—school ... TN-4
Homestead Hump—summit ... ID-8
Homestead Hunting Club—other ... MI-6
Homestead Island—island ... WA-9
Homestead JHS—school ... FL-3
Homestead Junior Acad—school ... FL-3
Homestead Knoll—summit ... UT-8
Homestead Lake—lake ... MI-6
Homestead Lake—lake (2) ... MN-6
Homestead Lake—lake (2) ... NE-7
Homestead Lake—lake (4) ... WI-6
Homestead Lake—reservoir ... KY-4
Homestead Lake—reservoir ... MT-8
Homestead Lake—reservoir ... OR-9
Homestead Manor—hist pl ... TN-4
Homestead Manor Plantation (historical)—locale ... TN-4
Homestead Mc Intyre Ditch—canal ... CO-8
Homestead Mine—mine ... NV-8
Homestead Mine—mine ... WI-6
Homestead Natl Monmt of America—hist pl ... NE-7
Homestead Natl Monmt Of America—park ... NE-7
Homestead Naval Security Group—military ... FL-3
Homestead Number 2 Prospect Mine—mine ... SD-7
Homestead Number 3 Prospect Mine—mine ... SD-7
Homestead Opening—flat ... CA-9
Homestead Park—park ... WI-6
**Homestead Park**—pop pl ... NJ-2
**Homestead Park**—pop pl ... NY-2
*Homestead Park School* ... PA-2
**Homestead Park (subdivision)**—pop pl ... PA-2
Homestead Pennsylvania RR Station—hist pl ... PA-2
Homestead Plantation Complex—hist pl ... LA-4
Homestead Plaza (Shop Ctr)—locale ... FL-3
Homestead Pond—lake ... FL-3
Homestead Public School-Neva King Cooper Sch—hist pl ... FL-3
Homestead Ranch—locale ... WY-8
Homestead Ridge—locale ... FL-3
Homestead Ridge—ridge ... CA-9
Homestead Ridge—ridge (2) ... OR-9
Homestead Rsvr—reservoir ... CO-8
Homestead Rsvr—reservoir ... MT-8
Homestead Rsvr—reservoir ... OR-9
Homestead Rsvr—reservoir ... WY-8
Homestead Run—stream ... PA-2
*Homesteads* ... HI-9
Homestead Sch—school ... CA-9
Homestead Sch—school ... MA-1
Homestead Sch—school ... NY-2
Homestead Sch—school ... TN-4
Homestead Sch—school ... WV-2
Homestead Sch—school ... WI-6
Homestead Sch (abandoned)—school ... MO-7
Homestead Sch (historical)—school ... TN-4
Homestead Senior HS—school ... FL-3
Homestead Shop Ctr—locale ... FL-3
Homestead Spring—spring (2) ... AZ-5
Homestead Spring—spring ... CA-9
Homestead Spring—spring ... CO-8
Homestead Spring—spring ... ID-8
Homestead Spring—spring ... NV-8
Homestead Spring—spring (3) ... OR-9
Homestead Spring—spring ... WA-9
Homestead Springs—spring ... NV-8
**Homestead (subdivision)**—pop pl ... AL-4
**Homestead (subdivision)**—pop pl (2) ... AZ-5
**Homestead (subdivision)**—pop pl (2) ... NC-3
*Homestead Tank* ... AZ-5
*Homestead Tank* ... NM-5
Homestead Tank—reservoir (7) ... AZ-5
Homestead Tank—reservoir (5) ... NM-5
Homestead Tank—reservoir ... TX-5
**Homestead Township**—pop pl ... KS-7
**Homestead Township**—pop pl ... ND-7
**Homestead (Township of)**—pop pl ... MI-6
**Homestead (Township of)**—pop pl ... MN-6
Homestead Trail—trail ... VA-3
**Homestead (Trailer Homes)**—pop pl ... OR-9
**Homestead Trailer Park**—pop pl ... DE-2
Homestead Transfer Station—building ... PA-2
Homestead Valley—uninc pl ... CA-9
Homestead Valley—valley (2) ... CA-9
*Homestead Village* ... NC-3
**Homestead Village**—pop pl ... NJ-2
Homestead Well—locale ... CA-9
Homestead Well—well (2) ... NM-5
Homestead Windmill—locale (2) ... AZ-5
Homestead Windmill—locale ... CO-8
Homestead Windmill—locale (3) ... NM-5
Homestead Yard—locale ... OH-6
**Homestown**—pop pl ... MO-7
*Homestrad* ... OR-9
Homes Trail—trail ... WA-9
Home Supply Ditch—canal (2) ... CO-8
Homes Valley—valley ... NM-5
*Homesville* ... LA-4
**Homesville**—pop pl ... PA-2
Home Swamp—stream ... SC-3
Home Sweet Home Cem—cemetery ... TN-4
Home Sweet Home Ch—church ... OK-5
Home Sweet Home Creek—stream ... ID-8
Home Sweet Home Shelter—locale ... WA-9
Home Sweet Home Spring—spring ... OR-9
Home Tank—reservoir (3) ... AZ-5
Home Tank—reservoir ... NM-5
Home Tank—reservoir (4) ... TX-5
Home Tank Draw—valley ... AZ-5
Home Tank Number One—reservoir ... AZ-5
Home Tank Number Two—reservoir ... AZ-5
*Homet Creek* ... ND-7
Home Ticket Mine—mine ... CA-9
*Home Town* ... MO-7
**Hometown**—pop pl ... IL-6
**Hometown**—pop pl ... PA-2
**Hometown**—pop pl ... WV-2
Hometown Mall—locale ... PA-2
Hometown Sch—school ... IL-6
**Home Township**—pop pl ... KS-7
**Home Township**—pop pl ... SD-7
**Home (Township of)**—pop pl (2) ... MI-6
**Home (Township of)**—pop pl ... MN-6
**Homets Ferry**—pop pl ... PA-2
Home Union Sch—school ... LA-4
**Home Valley**—pop pl ... WA-9
Home Valley Knoll—summit ... UT-8
*Home Valley Lake* ... NE-7
Home Valley Lake—lake (2) ... NE-7
*Homeville* ... LA-4
Homeville—locale ... VA-3
**Homeville**—pop pl ... OH-6
**Homeville**—pop pl (2) ... PA-2
Homeville Elem Sch—school ... PA-2
*Homeville JHS* ... PA-2
Homeward Cem—cemetery ... GA-3
Homewater Spring—spring ... UT-8
Homeway Village—uninc pl ... TN-4
Home Well—well (3) ... NM-5
Home Windmill—locale ... NM-5
Homewood—hist pl ... MD-2
Homewood—locale ... AL-4
Homewood—locale ... AR-4
Homewood—locale ... MS-4
Homewood—locale ... VA-3
**Homewood**—pop pl ... AL-4
**Homewood**—pop pl ... CA-9
**Homewood**—pop pl ... IL-6
**Homewood**—pop pl ... KS-7
**Homewood**—pop pl (2) ... MD-2
**Homewood**—pop pl ... NY-2
**Homewood**—pop pl (2) ... OH-6
**Homewood**—pop pl (3) ... PA-2
**Homewood**—pop pl ... SC-3
**Homewood**—pop pl ... VA-3
**Homewood**—pop pl (2) ... WV-2
Homewood—uninc pl (2) ... MD-2
**Homewood Acres**—pop pl ... IL-6
Homewood Borough—civil ... PA-2
Homewood Canyon—valley (2) ... CA-9
Homewood Cem—cemetery ... IA-7
Homewood Cem—cemetery ... PA-2
Homewood Ch—church ... IL-6
Homewood Ch—church ... MS-4
Homewood Ch—church ... NC-3
Homewood Ch—church ... PA-2
Homewood Ch of Christ—church ... AL-4
Homewood City Hall—building ... AL-4
**Homewood (corporate name for Racine)**—pop pl ... PA-2
Homewood Creek—stream ... VA-3
Homewood Falls—falls ... PA-2
Homewood-Flossmoor HS—school ... IL-6
Homewood Golf Course—other ... IA-7
Homewood Heights Sch—school ... IL-6
Homewood JHS—school ... AL-4
Homewood Junction (RR name for Racine)—other ... PA-2
**Homewood (Lower Homewood)**—pop pl ... MD-2
*Homewood Methodist Ch* ... MS-4
Homewood Oil Field—oilfield ... MS-4
Homewood Park—park ... TX-5
**Homewood Park**—pop pl ... CO-8
**Homewood Park**—pop pl ... NY-2
Homewood Public Library—building ... AL-4
Homewood Ridge—ridge ... WV-2
Homewood Sch—school ... OH-6
Homewood Sch—school ... SC-3
Homewood Senior HS—school ... AL-4
*Homewood Shores* ... IL-6
*Homewood Terrace* ... IL-6
**Homewood Township**—pop pl ... KS-7
*Homewood Valley* ... WI-6
Home Woolen Company—hist pl ... CT-1
**Homeworth**—pop pl ... OH-6
Homeymeyer Mtn—summit ... TX-5
**Homine**—pop pl ... FL-3
*Homing Creek* ... WY-8
Homing Creek—stream ... KY-4
Homing Creek—stream ... MO-7
Homing Mill Branch—stream ... KY-4
Hominsto Cem—cemetery ... MT-8
**Hominy**—pop pl ... NC-3
**Hominy**—pop pl ... OK-5
Hominy, Lake—reservoir ... OK-5
Hominy Branch—stream ... FL-3
Hominy Branch—stream ... KY-4
Hominy Branch—stream ... MO-7
Hominy Branch—stream ... TN-4
Hominy (CCD)—cens area ... OK-5
Hominy Cem—cemetery ... AR-4
Hominy Cem—cemetery ... OK-5
Hominy Ch—church ... NC-3
Hominy Creek—stream ... GA-3
Hominy Creek—stream ... KY-4
Hominy Creek—stream (2) ... MS-4
Hominy Creek—stream ... MO-7
Hominy Creek—stream (2) ... NC-3
Hominy Creek—stream ... OH-6
Hominy Creek—stream (2) ... OK-5
Hominy Creek—stream ... OR-9
Hominy Creek—stream ... UT-8
Hominy Creek—stream ... WV-2
Hominy Creek—stream ... WY-8
Hominy Creek Rapids—rapids ... OR-9
**Hominy Falls**—pop pl ... WV-2
**Hominy Heights (subdivision)**—pop pl ... NC-3
Hominy Hill—summit ... WV-2
Hominy Hills—range ... NJ-2
Hominy Mill Branch—stream ... NC-3
Hominy Mortar—summit ... IN-6
Hominy Oil Field—oilfield ... OK-5
Hominy Osage Round House—hist pl ... OK-5
Hominy Peak—summit ... WY-8
Hominy Ridge—ridge ... IN-6
Hominy Ridge—ridge (2) ... PA-2
Hominy Ridge—ridge ... TN-4
Hominy Ridge Cem—cemetery ... PA-2
Hominy Ridge Lake—reservoir ... IN-6
Hominy Ridge Lake Dam—dam ... IN-6
Hominy Saddle—gap ... OR-9
Hominy Sch—hist pl ... OK-5
Hominy Swamp—stream ... NC-3
Homler Hollow—valley ... PA-2
Homly—locale ... OR-9
*Homly Cemetery* ... OR-9
Homme Dam—dam ... ND-7
Homme Home For Boys—locale ... WI-6
Homme Lake—lake ... MN-6
Homme Lake—reservoir ... ND-7
Homme Pond—reservoir ... WI-6
*Homme Reservoir* ... ND-7
Homme Rsvr—reservoir ... ND-7
Hommon Mtn—summit ... WV-2
Homnear Ch—church ... AR-4
Homo, Bogue—stream (2) ... MS-4
**Homochitto**—pop pl ... MS-4
Homochitto Cutoff—channel ... MS-4
*Homochitto Game Mngmt Area* ... MS-4
**Homochitto (historical)**—pop pl ... MS-4
Homochitto Natl Forest—park ... MS-4
Homochitto Post Office (historical)—building ... MS-4
Homochitto River—stream ... MS-4
Homochitto River Bridge—hist pl ... MS-4
Homochitto State Wildlife Mngmt Area—park ... MS-4
*Homo Cypress Bayou* ... MS-4
Homolovi Four (IV)—hist pl ... AZ-5
Homolovi II—hist pl ... AZ-5
Homolovi III—hist pl ... AZ-5
Homolovi I Ruin—hist pl ... AZ-5
**Homosassa**—pop pl ... FL-3
Homosassa Bay—bay ... FL-3
Homosassa Bay Entrance—locale ... FL-3
Homosassa Elem Sch—school ... FL-3
*Homosassa Islands* ... FL-3
*Homosassa Point* ... FL-3
Homosassa Point—cape ... FL-3
Homosassa River—stream ... FL-3
**Homosassa Springs**—pop pl ... FL-3
Homosassa Springs—spring ... FL-3
Homosassa Springs Shop Ctr—locale ... FL-3
Homosassa Square (Shop Ctr)—locale ... FL-3
*Homossa* ... FL-3
Homowack Kill—stream ... NY-2
*Hompeg Falls* ... WA-9
Hompegg Falls—falls ... WA-9
Homstad Sch—school ... WI-6
**Hon**—pop pl ... AR-4
Honaker—locale ... KY-4
**Honaker**—pop pl ... VA-3
Honaker Branch—stream ... VA-3
Honaker Cem—cemetery ... VA-3
Honaker Cem—cemetery (2) ... WV-2
Honaker Gap—gap ... VA-3
Honaker Gap—gap ... WV-2
**Honaker Junction**—pop pl ... VA-3
Honaker Ridge—ridge ... VA-3
Honakers Cem—cemetery ... KY-4
Honaker Sch—school ... VA-3
Honakers Ferry—locale ... KY-4
Honaker Trail—trail ... UT-8
*Honalo* ... HI-9
Honalo—civil ... HI-9
Honalo—locale ... HI-9
**Honalo**—pop pl ... HI-9
Honam, John, House—hist pl ... OH-6
Honanana Gulch—valley ... HI-9
Honan Park Two—park ... AZ-5
Honan Point—cliff ... AZ-5
Honaunau—civil ... HI-9
**Honaunau**—pop pl ... HI-9
Honaunau Bay—bay ... HI-9
Honaunau Field—park ... HI-9
Honaunau For Res—forest ... HI-9
**Honaunau Post Office**—pop pl ... HI-9
Honaunau Sch—school ... HI-9
Honawan Lake—lake ... MI-6
Honberger Sch—school ... IL-6
*Hon Branch* ... AR-4
Hon Branch—stream ... AR-4
Honby—locale ... CA-9
Hon Cem—cemetery (2) ... AR-4
Honcho Creek—stream ... OR-9
Hon Creek—stream ... WY-8
Honcut—civil ... CA-9
**Honcut**—pop pl ... CA-9
Honcut Cem—cemetery ... CA-9
Honda—locale ... CA-9
Honda, Canada —stream ... TX-5
Honda, Canada —valley ... TX-5
Honda, Lake—lake ... CA-9
Honda Barranca—valley ... CA-9
Honda Cove—bay ... CA-9
*Honda Creek* ... WY-8
Honda Creek, Canada —stream ... CA-9
*Honda Key* ... FL-3
Honda of America Manufacturing—facility ... OH-6
Honda Valley—valley ... CA-9
**Hondin (historical)**—pop pl ... MO-7
Hondius Park—flat ... CO-8
Hondo—locale ... NM-5
**Hondo**—pop pl ... TX-5
Hondo, Arroyo—arroyo ... AZ-5
Hondo, Arroyo—stream (5) ... CA-9
Hondo, Arroyo—valley (2) ... CA-9
Hondo, Canon—valley ... CO-8
Hondo, Rito—stream ... CO-8
Hondo Cabin—locale ... NM-5
Hondo Canyon—valley ... CA-9
Hondo Canyon—valley (9) ... NM-5
Hondo (CCD)—cens area ... NM-5
Hondo (CCD)—cens area ... TX-5
Hondo Creek—stream (5) ... TX-5
Hondo Creek—stream ... WY-8
Hondo Creek, Rito—stream ... CO-8
Hondo Creek Oil Field—oilfield ... TX-5
Hondo Ditch—canal ... NM-5
Hondo Irrigation Project (Abandoned)—other ... NM-5
*Hondoo Arch* ... UT-8
Hondo Park—park ... NM-5
Hondo Reservoir Diversion Canal—canal ... NM-5
*Hondo River* ... TX-5
Hondo Rsvr—reservoir ... CO-8
Hondo Rsvr (Abandoned)—reservoir ... NM-5
Hondo Tank—reservoir (2) ... NM-5
Hondo Tank—reservoir (2) ... TX-5
Hondo Valley Sch—school ... NM-5
Hondu, The—arch ... UT-8
Hondu Country—area ... UT-8
**Honduras**—pop pl ... IN-6
**Honduras**—pop pl ... PR-3
Honduras (Barrio)—fmr MCD (2) ... PR-3
Honduras Branch—stream ... AR-4
Honduras Sch—school ... LA-4
Hondu Rsvr—reservoir ... MT-8
Hondu Spring—spring ... OR-9
Honea—locale ... TX-5
Honea Cem—cemetery ... MS-4
Honea (historical)—locale ... AL-4
Honea Hollow—valley ... AL-4
Honea Island—island ... AR-4
**Honea Path**—pop pl ... SC-3
Honea Path (CCD)—cens area ... SC-3
Honea Post Office (historical)—building ... AL-4
*Honea Reservoir* ... TX-5
Hone Creek—locale ... IA-7
Hone Cypress Ditch No 2—canal ... AR-4
*Honed Island* ... AR-4
**Honegger**—pop pl ... IL-6
*Honek* ... KS-7
**Honeoye**—pop pl ... NY-2
**Honeoye**—pop pl ... PA-2
Honeoye Creek—stream (2) ... NY-2
Honeoye Creek—stream ... PA-2
**Honeoye Falls**—pop pl ... NY-2
Honeoye Inlet—stream ... NY-2
Honeoye Lake—lake ... NY-2
**Honeoye Park**—pop pl ... NY-2
*Hone Quarry Branch* ... VA-3
Hone Quarry Dam—dam ... VA-3
Hone Quarry Rec Area—park ... VA-3
Hone Quarry Ridge—ridge ... VA-3
Hone Quarry Ridge Trail—trail ... VA-3
Hone Quarry Run—stream ... VA-3
*Hone Range* ... UT-8
Honerine Mine—mine ... UT-8
Honer Plaza Shop Ctr—locale ... CA-9
Honer Sch—school ... MI-6
**Honesdale**—pop pl ... PA-2
Honesdale Borough—civil ... PA-2
Honesdale Catholic Sch—school ... PA-2
Honesdale HS—school ... PA-2
Honess Creek—stream ... WA-9
Honess Mtn—summit ... OK-5
Honest Branch—stream ... KY-4
Honest Brook—stream ... NY-2
Honest Fork—stream ... KY-4
**Honest Hill**—pop pl ... NY-2
Honest Hollow—valley ... PA-2
Honest John Lake—lake ... WI-6
Honest John Well—well ... NV-8
Honest Point—cape ... VA-3
Honest Ridge—ridge ... TX-5
Honest Ridge Cem—cemetery ... TX-5
Honestville Ch—church ... TN-4
Honesty—locale ... OH-6
**Honey**—pop pl ... PA-2
Honey Acre—locale ... KY-4
Honey Bay—swamp ... NC-3
Honey Bayou—gut ... LA-4
Honey Bayou—stream (2) ... LA-4
Honeybee—locale ... KY-4
Honey Bee—summit ... HI-9
Honeybee Campground—locale ... CA-9
Honey Bee Canyon—valley ... AZ-5
*Honey Bee Creek* ... GA-3
Honeybee Creek—stream ... CA-9
Honey Bee Creek—stream ... GA-3
Honeybee Lake—lake ... AK-9
Honey Bee Mine—mine ... UT-8
Honey Bee Tank—reservoir ... AZ-5
Honey Bee Well—well ... NM-5
Honey Bend—locale ... IL-6
Honey Bluff—cliff ... AL-4
Honey Bluff—cliff ... GA-3
Honey Bov Mine—mine ... UT-8
Honey Bowl Stadium—other ... TX-5
Honey Boy Ranch—locale ... NM-5
Honey Brake Bayou—stream ... LA-4
Honey Brake Lake—lake ... LA-4
*Honey Branch* ... IL-6
*Honey Branch* ... TN-4
**Honey Branch**—pop pl ... VA-3
Honey Branch—stream ... AL-4
Honey Branch—stream ... IL-6
Honey Branch—stream (3) ... KY-4
Honey Branch—stream ... LA-4
Honey Branch—stream ... MD-2
Honey Branch—stream ... MS-4
Honey Branch—stream ... MO-7
Honey Branch—stream ... NJ-2
Honey Branch—stream ... NC-3
Honey Branch—stream (3) ... TN-4
Honey Branch—stream (3) ... VA-3
Honey Branch—stream (2) ... WV-2
Honey Branch Caves—cave ... MO-7
Honey Branch Cem—cemetery ... KY-4
**Honey Brook**—pop pl ... PA-2
Honey Brook—stream ... MA-1
Honey Brook—stream ... NH-1
Honey Brook—stream ... NY-2
Honey Brook—stream ... PA-2
Honey Brook—stream ... VT-1
Honey Brook Borough—civil ... PA-2
Honey Brook Colliery (historical)—building ... PA-2
Honey Brook State For—forest ... NH-1
**Honeybrook (subdivision)**—pop pl ... TN-4
**Honey Brook (Township of)**—pop pl ... PA-2
Honey Butte—summit ... AZ-5
Honey Butte Tank—reservoir ... AZ-5
Honey Butte Well—well ... AZ-5
Honey Camp—locale ... VA-3
**Honeycamp**—pop pl ... VA-3
Honey Camp Branch—stream ... GA-3
Honeycamp Branch—stream (2) ... KY-4
Honeycamp Branch—stream ... NC-3
Honey Camp Branch—stream ... SC-3
Honeycamp Branch—stream (2) ... VA-3
Honeycamp Branch—stream ... WV-2
Honeycamp Fork—stream ... WV-2
Honey Camp Run—stream ... WV-2
Honey Canyon—valley ... NM-5
Honey Cem—cemetery ... AL-4
Honey Cem—cemetery ... IL-6
Honey Cem—cemetery ... MO-7
Honeycomb—valley ... ID-8
Honeycomb Branch—stream ... VA-3
*Honey Comb Buttes* ... UT-8
Honeycomb Buttes—range ... WY-8
Honeycomb Cem—cemetery ... AL-4
Honeycomb Ch—church ... AL-4
Honeycomb Ch—church ... IL-6
Honeycomb Cliffs—cliff ... UT-8
Honeycomb Creek—stream ... AL-4
Honeycomb Creek—stream ... MT-8
Honeycomb Creek—stream ... TN-4
Honeycomb Fork—valley ... UT-8
Honeycomb Glacier—glacier ... WA-9
*Honey Comb Hill* ... UT-8
*Honey Comb Hills* ... UT-8
Honeycomb Hills—spring ... MT-8
Honeycomb Hollow—valley ... OH-6
Honeycomb Mtn—summit ... TN-4
**Honeycomb Park (subdivision)**—pop pl ... AL-4
Honeycomb Rock Campground—locale ... UT-8
Honeycomb Rocks—cliff ... UT-8
*Honey Combs* ... OR-9
Honeycombs—summit ... OR-9
Honeycombs, The—area ... WY-8
Honeycombs, The—summit ... UT-8
Honeycomb School Cave—cave ... AL-4
Honeycomb Shaft—mine ... NM-5
Honeycomb Snug Harbor—locale ... AL-4
Honeycomb Spring—spring ... AL-4
Honey Cove Branch—stream ... TN-4
*Honey Creek* ... AL-4
*Honey Creek* ... IN-6
*Honey Creek* ... MO-7
*Honey Creek* ... OH-6
*Honey Creek* ... OR-9
*Honey Creek* ... TX-5
*Honey Creek* ... WI-6
Honey Creek—locale ... IA-7
Honey Creek—locale ... TX-5
**Honey Creek**—pop pl ... IL-6
**Honey Creek**—pop pl ... IN-6
**Honey Creek**—pop pl ... MO-7
**Honey Creek**—pop pl ... PA-2
**Honey Creek**—pop pl ... WI-6
Honey Creek—stream (2) ... AL-4
Honey Creek—stream ... AK-9
Honey Creek—stream ... AZ-5
Honey Creek—stream (3) ... AR-4
Honey Creek—stream (2) ... CA-9
Honey Creek—stream (2) ... FL-3
Honey Creek—stream (3) ... GA-3
Honey Creek—stream (3) ... ID-8
Honey Creek—stream (7) ... IL-6
Honey Creek—stream (13) ... IN-6
Honey Creek—stream (4) ... IA-7
Honey Creek*—stream ... IA-7
Honey Creek—stream (17) ... IA-7
Honey Creek—stream (7) ... KS-7
Honey Creek—stream ... KY-4
Honey Creek—stream (4) ... MI-6
Honey Creek—stream (13) ... MO-7
Honey Creek—stream ... MT-8
Honey Creek—stream (4) ... NE-7
Honey Creek—stream (7) ... OH-6
Honey Creek—stream (5) ... OK-5
Honey Creek—stream (4) ... OR-9
Honey Creek—stream (2) ... PA-2
Honey Creek—stream (2) ... TN-4
Honey Creek—stream (22) ... TX-5
Honey Creek—stream ... WA-9
Honey Creek—stream (5) ... WI-6
Honey Creek—stream ... WY-8
Honey Creek Bar—bar ... IL-6
Honey Creek Bay—bay ... IN-6
Honey Creek Bridge—bridge ... KS-7
Honey Creek Cem—cemetery ... IA-7
Honey Creek Cem—cemetery ... KS-7
Honey Creek Cem—cemetery ... MO-7
Honey Creek Cem—cemetery (4) ... TX-5
Honey Creek Cem—cemetery ... WI-6
Honey Creek Ch—church ... GA-3
Honey Creek Ch—church (2) ... IN-6
Honey Creek Ch—church (3) ... OH-6
Honey Creek Ch—church ... OK-5
Honey Creek Ch—church ... TN-4
Honey Creek Ch—church ... TX-5
Honey Creek Childrens Home—building ... MI-6
Honey Creek Divide—ridge ... AZ-5
Honey Creek Falls—falls ... OR-9
Honey Creek Friends' Meetinghouse—hist pl ... IA-7
Honey Creek JHS—school ... IN-6
Honey Creek Overlook—locale ... TN-4
Honey Creek Pocket Wilderness Area—park ... TN-4
Honey Creek Quarry Cave—cave ... PA-2
Honey Creek Ranch—locale (2) ... TX-5
Honey Creek Rec Area—park ... OK-5
Honey Creek Ridge—ridge ... WI-6
*Honey Creek Sch* ... IN-6
Honey Creek Sch—hist pl ... IN-6
Honey Creek Sch—school ... IL-6
Honey Creek Sch—school ... KS-7
Honey Creek Sch—school ... MO-7
Honey Creek Sch—school ... NE-7
Honey Creek Sch—school ... TN-4
Honey Creek Sch (abandoned)—school ... MO-7
Honey Creek Square Shop Ctr—locale ... IN-6
Honey Creek State Wildlife Area—locale ... MO-7
Honey Creek Station (historical)—locale ... IA-7
**Honey Creek (Town of)**—pop pl ... WI-6
Honey Creek Township—fmr MCD (2) ... IA-7
**Honey Creek Township**—pop pl ... MO-7
**Honey Creek (Township of)**—pop pl (2) ... IL-6
**Honey Creek (Township of)**—pop pl (3) ... IN-6
*Honey Creek United Baptist Church* ... TN-4
Honey Cut Bayou—stream ... LA-4
*Honeycut Branch* ... TN-4
Honeycut Branch—stream ... IL-6
Honeycut Branch—stream ... KY-4
Honeycut Branch—stream ... NC-3
Honeycut Cove—valley ... NC-3
*Honeycut Creek* ... TN-4
Honeycut Creek—stream ... AL-4
Honey Cut Gap—gap ... AR-4
Honey Cut (historical)—locale ... MS-4
Honeycut Hollow—valley ... IN-6
Honeycut Lake—lake ... FL-3
Honeycut Mine (underground)—mine ... TN-4
*Honeycutt* ... TN-4
Honeycutt—locale ... TN-4
**Honeycutt**—pop pl ... NC-3
Honeycutt Branch—stream ... LA-4
Honeycutt Cave—cave ... TN-4
Honeycutt Cem—cemetery ... NC-3
Honeycutt Cem—cemetery (5) ... TN-4
Honeycutt Cem—cemetery ... TX-5
Honeycutt Ch—church ... NC-3
Honeycutt Creek—stream ... AL-4
Honeycutt Creek—stream (2) ... NC-3
Honeycutt Creek—stream (2) ... TN-4
**Honeycutt Estates**—pop pl ... TN-4
Honeycutt (historical)—locale ... AL-4
Honeycutt Institute (historical)—school ... AL-4
Honeycutt Lake—reservoir ... TX-5
Honeycutt Lake Dam—dam ... MS-4
Honeycutt Mtn—summit ... NC-3
Honeycutt Mtn—summit ... TN-4
Honeycutt Post Office (historical)—building ... TN-4
Honeycutt Ranch—locale ... TX-5
Honeycutt Run—stream ... WV-2
*Honeycutts Creek* ... AL-4
Honey Cutts Mill (historical)—locale ... AL-4
Honeycutt Spring—spring ... AZ-5
Honeycutts (Township of)—fmr MCD ... NC-3
Honeycutt Tunnel—tunnel ... NC-3
Honey Cypress Ditch No 34—canal ... MO-7
Honey Cypress Ditch No 4—canal ... AR-4
Honeydew—locale ... CA-9
*Honeydew Creek* ... CA-9
Honeydew Creek—stream ... CA-9
Honey Ferry (historical)—locale ... AL-4
Honey Field—locale ... NC-3
Honey Flat—flat ... MT-8
**Honeyford**—pop pl ... ND-7
Honeyford Cem—cemetery ... SC-3
Honeyford Ch—church ... SC-3
*Honey Fork* ... TN-4
Honey Fork—locale ... KY-4
Honey Fork—stream (2) ... KY-4
Honey Fork—stream ... OH-6
*Honey Fork Branch* ... TN-4
Honeyfork Creek—stream ... MS-4
Honey Fork Creek—stream ... TN-4
Honeyfork Lake—reservoir ... MS-4
*Honeygal Creek* ... GA-3
*Honeygal Landing* ... GA-3
*Honey Gall Creek* ... GA-3
Honeygall Creek—stream ... GA-3
Honeygall Landing—locale ... GA-3
Honeygall Swamp—swamp ... GA-3
Honey Gap Hollow—valley ... KY-4
Honeygo Run—stream ... MD-2
*Honeygrove* ... PA-2
**Honey Grove**—pop pl ... KY-4
**Honey Grove**—pop pl ... PA-2
**Honey Grove**—pop pl ... TX-5
*Honey Grove Baptist Church Number 2* ... AL-4
Honey Grove (CCD)—cens area ... TX-5
Honey Grove Cem—cemetery ... IA-7
Honey Grove Cem—cemetery ... MO-7
Honey Grove Ch—church ... AR-4
Honey Grove Ch—church ... TX-5
Honey Grove Ch—church ... VA-3
Honey Grove Creek—stream ... OR-9
Honey Grove Creek—stream ... TX-5
Honey Grove Sch—school ... OK-5
Honey Grove Sch (historical)—school ... MO-7
Honey Heart Sch—school ... IL-6
*Honeyhill* ... SC-3
Honey Hill—island ... FL-3
Honey Hill—locale ... NC-3
**Honey Hill**—pop pl ... SC-3
Honey Hill—summit (2) ... CT-1
Honey Hill—summit (2) ... MA-1
Honey Hill—summit ... NH-1
Honey Hill—summit (3) ... NY-2
Honey Hill—summit ... SC-3
Honey Hill Bay—swamp ... FL-3
Honey Hill Branch—stream ... OK-5
Honey Hill Ch—church ... AR-4
Honey Hill Ch—church ... NC-3
Honey Hill Ch—church ... OK-5
Honey Hill Ch—church ... SC-3
Honey Hill Lookout Tower—locale ... SC-3
Honey Hill Plantation (historical)—locale ... MS-4
Honey Hill Ridge—ridge ... AR-4
Honey Hill Sch—school ... CT-1
Honey Hill Swamp—swamp ... SC-3
**Honey Hole**—pop pl ... PA-2
Honeyhole Dam—dam ... PA-2
*Honey Hollow* ... TN-4
Honey Hollow—basin ... NY-2
Honey Hollow—valley (2) ... AL-4
Honey Hollow—valley ... AR-4
Honey Hollow—valley ... OH-6
Honey Hollow—valley ... TN-4
Honey Hollow—valley ... VT-1
Honey Hollow Cem—cemetery ... NY-2
Honey Hollow Pond—reservoir ... PA-2
Honey Hollow Sch—school ... NY-2
Honey Hollow Watershed—hist pl ... PA-2
Honeyhook Sch—school ... IL-6
Honey Island—island (2) ... GA-3
Honey Island—island (2) ... LA-4
Honey Island—island ... MS-4
Honey Island—island ... NC-3
Honey Island—island ... WI-6
Honey Island—locale ... NC-3
**Honey Island**—pop pl ... MS-4
**Honey Island**—pop pl ... TX-5
Honey Island Flowage—reservoir ... WI-6
Honey Island Prairie—swamp ... GA-3
Honey Island Swamp—swamp ... NC-3
Honey Jones Mill Creek—stream ... AL-4
Honey Jones Peak—summit ... ID-8
Honey Lake—lake ... AR-4
Honey Lake—lake ... CA-9
Honey Lake—lake ... IL-6
Honey Lake—lake ... LA-4
Honey Lake—lake (2) ... MI-6
Honey Lake—lake ... OR-9
Honey Lake—lake ... SC-3
Honey Lake—lake ... TX-5
Honey Lake—lake ... WA-9
Honey Lake—lake ... WI-6
**Honey Lake**—pop pl ... WI-6
Honey Lake—reservoir ... MO-7
Honey Lake—reservoir ... WI-6

Honey Lake—*swamp* ... KY-4
Honey Lake (CCD)—*cens area* ... CA-9
Honey Lake Cem—*cemetery* ... CA-9
Honey Lake Ch—*church* ... MO-7
Honey Lake Drain—*canal* ... MI-6
Honey Lake (historical)—*lake* ... IA-7
Honey Lake Hollow—*valley* ... MO-7
Honey Lake Mine—*mine* ... CA-9
Honey Lakes—*lake* ... OR-9
Honey Lake State Wildlife Area—*park* ... CA-9
Honey Lake Valley—*basin* ... NV-8
Honey Lake Valley—*valley* ... CA-9
Honey Landing (historical)—*locale* ... AL-4
Honey Locust Bayou—*gut* ... AR-4
Honey Locust Bayou—*stream* ... AR-4
Honey Locust Branch—*stream* ... VA-3
Honey Locust Creek—*stream* ... KY-4
Honey Locust Knobs—*range* ... VA-3
Honey Locust Lake—*reservoir* ... KY-4
Honeyman, David T. and Nan Wood, House—*hist pl* ... OR-9
Honeyman, Jessie M., Memorial State Park Hist Dist—*hist pl* ... OR-9
Honeyman, John S., House—*hist pl* ... OR-9
Honeyman Cem—*cemetery* ... OH-6
Honeyman Creek—*stream* ... NV-8
Honeyman Creek—*stream* ... OR-9
*Honeymans Creek* ... NV-8
Honeyman State Park—*park* ... OR-9
Honeymoon Basin—*basin* ... MT-8
Honeymoon Basin—*basin* ... OR-9
Honeymoon Bay—*bay* (2) ... WA-9
Honeymoon Brook—*stream* ... ME-1
*Honeymoon Cabin* ... AZ-5
Honeymoon Campground—*locale* ... WA-9
Honeymoon Campground—*park* ... AZ-5
Honeymoon Canyon—*valley* ... AZ-5
Honeymoon Canyon—*valley* ... CO-8
Honeymoon Canyon—*valley* ... OR-9
Honeymoon Cove—*bay* ... CA-9
Honeymoon Creek—*stream* ... AK-9
Honeymoon Creek—*stream* ... GA-3
Honeymoon Creek—*stream* ... ID-8
Honeymoon Creek—*stream* ... MN-6
Honeymoon Creek—*stream* ... MT-8
Honeymoon Creek—*stream* (4) ... OR-9
Honeymoon Creek—*stream* ... WA-9
Honeymoon Creek—*stream* ... WY-8
Honeymoon Flat—*flat* ... CA-9
Honeymoon Flat Campground—*locale* ... CA-9
*Honeymoon Island* ... MN-6
Honeymoon Island—*island* ... FL-3
Honeymoon Island—*island* (2) ... MN-6
Honeymoon Island—*island* ... VA-3
Honeymoon Island—*island* ... WI-6
Honeymoon Island State Rec Area—*park* ... FL-3
*Honeymoon Isle* ... FL-3
Honeymoon Lake—*lake* ... CA-9
Honeymoon Lake—*lake* ... FL-3
Honeymoon Lake—*lake* ... ID-8
Honeymoon Lake—*lake* ... MI-6
Honeymoon Lake—*lake* ... MT-8
Honeymoon Lake—*lake* ... OR-9
Honeymoon Lake—*lake* ... UT-8
Honeymoon Lake—*lake* ... WY-8
Honeymoon Lookout Tower—*locale* ... MN-6
Honeymoon Meadows—*flat* ... WA-9
Honeymoon Mine—*mine* ... CO-8
Honeymoon Mine—*mine* ... WA-9
Honeymoon Park—*flat* ... MT-8
*Honeymoon Ranch* ... AZ-5
Honeymoon Ridge—*ridge* ... CA-9
Honeymoon Seep—*spring* ... AZ-5
Honeymoon Slough—*stream* ... AK-9
Honeymoon Spring—*spring* ... AZ-5
Honeymoon Spring—*spring* ... CA-9
Honeymoon Spring—*spring* ... CO-8
Honeymoon Spring—*spring* ... TX-5
*Honeymoon Springs* ... CA-9
Honeymoon Springs—*spring* ... MT-8
Honeymoon Tank—*reservoir* ... AZ-5
Honeymoon Trail—*trail* ... AZ-5
Honey Moon Trail—*trail* ... WV-2
Honeymoon Trail (pack)—*trail* ... AZ-5
Honeymoon Wash—*stream* ... CA-9
Honeymoon Windmill—*locale* ... NM-5
Honeymoon Windmill—*locale* (2) ... TX-5
*Honey Mountain* ... ID-8
Honey Mtn—*summit* ... ID-8
Honey Mud Pond—*reservoir* ... PA-2
Honeyoey Creek—*stream* ... MI-6
Honey Point—*cliff* ... TN-4
Honey Point Post Office (historical)—*building* ... TN-4
**Honey Point (Township of)**—*pop pl* ... IL-6
*Honey Pond* ... PA-2
Honey Pond—*lake* ... FL-3
Honey Pond—*lake* ... NY-2
Honey Pond—*lake* ... VA-3
Honey Pond—*locale* ... NC-3
Honey Pot—*summit* ... PA-2
Honey Pot—*uninc pl* ... PA-2
Honeypot Brook—*stream* ... CT-1
**Honeypot Glen**—*pop pl* ... CT-1
Honeypot Hill—*summit* ... MA-1
Honey Pot Pond—*lake* ... NH-1
Honey Pot Swamp—*swamp* ... NC-3
Honeypot Swamp—*swamp* ... RI-1
Honey Prong—*stream* ... TN-4
Honey Rock Camp—*locale* ... WI-6
Honey Run—*gut* ... FL-3
Honey Run—*stream* ... CA-9
Honey Run—*stream* (2) ... IN-6
Honey Run—*stream* ... KY-4
Honey Run—*stream* ... MO-7
Honey Run—*stream* ... NJ-2
Honey Run—*stream* ... NY-2
Honey Run—*stream* (7) ... OH-6
Honey Run—*stream* (2) ... PA-2
Honey Run—*stream* ... TN-4
Honey Run—*stream* (4) ... VA-3
Honey Run—*stream* (5) ... WV-2
Honey Run Branch—*stream* ... NJ-2
Honey Run Cave—*cave* ... TN-4
Honey Run Cem—*cemetery* ... OH-6
Honey Run Covered Bridge—*hist pl* ... CA-9
*Honey Run Creek* ... IN-6
Honey Run Creek—*stream* ... MT-8
Honey Run Creek—*stream* ... TN-4
Honey School Lookout Tower—*locale* ... IL-6
Honey Scrub Island—*island* ... GA-3
Honeysett Sch—*school* ... NE-7
**Honeys Hill (subdivison)**—*pop pl* ... TN-4
Honey Sink—*basin* ... IN-6
Honey Slough—*gut* ... IA-7
Honeyspot Sch—*school* ... CT-1
Honey Spring—*spring* ... AZ-5
Honey Spring—*spring* ... IN-6
Honey Spring—*spring* ... TX-5
Honey Spring Mtn—*summit* ... TN-4
Honey Spring Patrol Cabin—*locale* ... VA-3
Honey Springs—*spring* ... OK-5
Honey Springs Battlefield—*hist pl* ... OK-5
Honey Springs Branch—*stream* ... OK-5
Honey Springs Branch—*stream* ... TX-5
Honey Springs Cem—*cemetery* ... OK-5
Honey Springs Cem—*cemetery* ... TN-4
Honey Spring Sch (abandoned)—*school* ... MO-7
Honey Springs Ranch—*locale* ... CA-9
Honeysuckle Bay—*bay* ... ID-8
Honeysuckle Beach—*beach* ... ID-8
Honeysuckle Campground—*locale* ... ID-8
Honeysuckle Creek—*stream* ... AL-4
Honeysuckle Creek—*stream* (3) ... OR-9
Honeysuckle Gate—*locale* ... VA-3
Honeysuckle Hill—*hist pl* ... KY-4
**Honeysuckle Hills**—*pop pl* ... ID-8
Honeysuckle Hills Park—*park* ... AL-4
Honeysuckle Lake—*lake* ... MI-6
Honeysuckle Lake—*lake* ... WI-6
Honeysuckle MS—*school* ... AL-4
Honeysuck Prospect—*mine* ... TN-4
Honey Swamp—*swamp* ... GA-3
Honeys Windmill—*locale* ... CO-8
Honeytown—*locale* ... PA-2
**Honey Town**—*pop pl* ... NC-3
**Honeytown**—*pop pl* ... OH-6
Honeytown Ch—*church* ... IN-6
Honeytrace Fork—*stream* ... WV-2
Honeytree—*other* ... IL-6
Honey Tunnel—*mine* ... CA-9
Honey Valley Sch—*school* ... KS-7
Honeyville—*locale* (2) ... VA-3
**Honeyville**—*pop pl* ... FL-3
**Honeyville**—*pop pl* ... IN-6
**Honeyville**—*pop pl* ... NY-2
**Honeyville**—*pop pl* ... UT-8
Honeyville Cem—*cemetery* ... NY-2
Honeyville Cem—*cemetery* ... UT-8
Honeyville Elem Sch—*school* ... IN-6
Honeyville Sch—*school* ... UT-8
Honeyville Springs—*spring* ... UT-8
**Honeywell Corners**—*pop pl* ... NY-2
Honeywell Country Club—*other* ... MN-6
Honeywell Creek—*stream* ... MI-6
Honeywell Ditch—*canal* ... MI-6
*Honeywell Island* ... ME-1
Honeywell Lake—*lake* ... MI-6
Honeywell Memorial Community Center—*hist pl* ... IN-6
Honeywell Sch—*school* ... IL-6
**Honeywood Cove PUD Subdivision**—*pop pl* ... UT-8
**Honeywood Hills Subdivision**—*pop pl* ... UT-8
**Hong**—*pop pl* ... ND-7
**Honga**—*pop pl* ... MD-2
Honga River—*stream* ... MD-2
Honga River Light—*locale* ... MD-2
Honga Springs—*spring* ... AZ-5
Honghton Sch—*school* ... GA-3
Hongkong Bend—*bend* ... AK-9
Hong Kong Sch—*school* ... IL-6
Hongkong Sch (historical)—*school* ... TN-4
*Hong Kong School* ... TN-4
**Hongore Bay**—*pop pl* ... MI-6
Hongore Heights—*other* ... MI-6
Hon Gulch—*valley* ... OR-9
Hongwanji Mission Sch—*school* ... HI-9
Honhosa River—*stream* ... AK-9
Honig Cem—*cemetery* ... TX-5
Honig Sch (historical)—*school* ... AL-4
Honiss Sch—*school* ... NJ-2
Honker Bay—*bay* ... CA-9
Honker Bay—*bay* ... KY-4
*Honker Cove Waterfowl Refuge* ... MO-7
Honker Creek—*stream* ... AK-9
Honker Cut—*canal* ... CA-9
Honker Duck Club—*locale* ... NV-8
Honker Lake—*lake* ... MN-6
Honker Lake—*reservoir* ... KY-4
Honker Lake Tract—*civil* ... CA-9
Honkers Hollow Dam—*dam* ... NC-3
Honkers Hollow Lake—*reservoir* ... NC-3
Honk Hill—*locale* ... NY-2
Honk Lake—*lake* ... MI-6
Honk Lake—*reservoir* ... NY-2
Honky Tonk Picnic Area—*park* ... CA-9
Honky Tonk Well—*well* ... TX-5
Hon Lateral—*canal* ... ID-8
*Honlin* ... PA-2
*Honlookato Creek* ... MS-4
Honnas Ranch—*locale* ... AZ-5
Honn Creek—*stream* ... CA-9
Honn Creek Camp Ground—*locale* ... CA-9
Honnedaga—*locale* ... NY-2
Honnedaga Brook—*stream* ... NY-2
Honnedaga Lake—*lake* ... NY-2
**Honnedaga Lake**—*pop pl* ... NY-2
Honner, Martin, Chalkrock House—*hist pl* ... SD-7
Honner Station (historical)—*locale* ... KS-7
**Honner (Township of)**—*pop pl* ... MN-6
Honness Mtn—*summit* ... NY-2
Honn Farm Airp—*airport* ... WA-9
Honnoll Mill Creek—*stream* ... MS-4
Honnor-Hosken House—*hist pl* ... MN-6
Honno Two Sch (historical)—*school* ... MS-4
Honn Spring—*spring* ... OR-9
*Hono* ... HI-9
**Honobia**—*pop pl* (2) ... OK-5
Honobia Creek—*stream* ... OK-5
Honobia Mtn—*summit* ... OK-5
Honobia Sch—*school* ... OK-5
Honobia Trail—*trail* ... OK-5
Honohina—*civil* ... HI-9
**Honohina**—*pop pl* ... HI-9
Honohina Gulch—*valley* ... HI-9
Honoipu—*civil* ... HI-9
Honoipu Landing (Site)—*locale* ... HI-9
**Honokaa**—*pop pl* ... HI-9
Honokaa-Kukuihaele (CCD)—*cens area* ... HI-9
Honokaa Landing—*locale* ... HI-9
*Honokaape* ... HI-9
*Honokahau* ... HI-9
*Honokahau Bay* ... HI-9
*Honokahau Stream* ... HI-9
Honokaheka Point—*cape* ... HI-9
Honokahua—*civil* ... HI-9
Honokahua—*summit* ... HI-9
Honokahua Bay—*bay* ... HI-9
*Honokahua Camp* ... HI-9
*Honokahua Gulch* ... HI-9
**Honokahua (Honokohua Post Office)**—*pop pl* ... HI-9
Honokahua Stream—*stream* ... HI-9
Honokaia—*civil* ... HI-9
Honokaia Gulch—*valley* ... HI-9
**Honokai Hale**—*pop pl* ... HI-9
Honokala Gulch—*valley* ... HI-9
*Honokalani* ... HI-9
Honokalani—*civil* ... HI-9
Honokalani Village—*hist pl* ... HI-9
Honokala Point—*cape* ... HI-9
Honokanaia—*bay* ... HI-9
Honokanaia—*locale* ... HI-9
*Honokane* ... HI-9
Honokane—*civil* ... HI-9
Honokane Iki Stream—*stream* ... HI-9
Honokane Nui Stream—*stream* ... HI-9
*Honokane Stream* ... HI-9
Honokaope Bay—*bay* ... HI-9
*Honokau* ... HI-9
*Honokawai* ... HI-9
*Honokawai Ditch* ... HI-9
*Honokawai Stream* ... HI-9
*Honokea Gulch* ... HI-9
Honokeana—*civil* ... HI-9
Honokeana Bay—*bay* ... HI-9
Honokea Stream—*stream* ... HI-9
*Honokes Creek* ... HI-9
Honokoa Bay—*bay* ... HI-9
Honokoa Gulch—*valley* ... HI-9
*Honokohau* ... HI-9
Honokohau—*civil* ... HI-9
**Honokohau**—*pop pl* (2) ... HI-9
Honokohau Bay—*bay* (2) ... HI-9
Honokohau One—*civil* ... HI-9
Honokohau One-Two—*civil* ... HI-9
Honokohau Sch—*school* ... HI-9
Honokohau Settlement—*hist pl* ... HI-9
Honokohau Stream—*stream* ... HI-9
Honokohau Tunnel—*tunnel* ... HI-9
Honokohau Two—*civil* ... HI-9
Honokoi Gulch—*valley* ... HI-9
*Honokokau* ... HI-9
Honokowai—*civil* ... HI-9
**Honokowai**—*pop pl* ... HI-9
*Honokowai Camp* ... HI-9
Honokowai Ditch—*canal* ... HI-9
Honokowai Point—*cape* ... HI-9
Honokowai Rsvr—*reservoir* ... HI-9
Honokowai Stream—*stream* ... HI-9
Honokowai Tunnel—*tunnel* ... HI-9
Honokua—*civil* ... HI-9
Honokua Lava Flow Of 1950—*lava* ... HI-9
*Honokus Brook* ... NJ-2
Honolewa Stream—*stream* ... HI-9
Honolii Cove—*bay* ... HI-9
Honolii Stream—*stream* ... HI-9
Honolua—*civil* ... HI-9
**Honolua**—*pop pl* ... HI-9
Honolua Bay—*bay* ... HI-9
Honolua Stream—*stream* ... HI-9
Honolulu—*civil* ... HI-9
Honolulu—*locale* ... AK-9
Honolulu—*locale* ... NC-3
**Honolulu**—*pop pl* ... HI-9
Honolulu Acad of Arts—*hist pl* ... HI-9
Honolulu Acad of Arts—*school* ... HI-9
Honolulu (CCD)—*cens area* ... HI-9
Honolulu Channel—*canal* ... HI-9
Honolulu Community Coll—*school* ... HI-9
**Honolulu (County)**—*pop pl* ... HI-9
Honolulu Creek—*stream* ... AK-9
Honolulu Harbor—*bay* ... HI-9
Honolulu House—*hist pl* ... MI-6
Honolulu II Main Camp—*locale* ... CA-9
Honolulu International Airp—*airport* ... HI-9
Honolulu Junior Acad—*school* ... HI-9
Honolulu Landing—*locale* ... HI-9
Honolulunui—*civil* ... HI-9
Honolulunui Bay—*bay* ... HI-9
Honolulu Observatory (NOS)—*locale* ... HI-9
Honolulu Pass—*gap* ... AK-9
Honolulu Sch—*school* ... CA-9
Honolulu Stadium—*other* ... HI-9
Honolulu Watershed For Res—*forest* ... HI-9
Honolulu Zoo—*other* ... HI-9
Honomaele—*locale* ... HI-9
Honomaele Gulch—*valley* ... HI-9
Honomainoa—*civil* ... HI-9
Honomakau—*civil* ... HI-9
**Honomakau**—*pop pl* ... HI-9
*Honomalina Bay* ... HI-9
Honomalino—*civil* ... HI-9
Honomalino Bay—*bay* ... HI-9
Honomalino Camp—*locale* ... HI-9
Honomanu—*civil* ... HI-9
Honomanu Bay—*bay* ... HI-9
Honomanu Stream—*stream* ... HI-9
*Honomilino* ... HI-9
Honomu—*civil* ... HI-9
**Honomu**—*pop pl* ... HI-9
Honomu Homesteads—*civil* ... HI-9
Honomuni—*civil* ... HI-9
Honomuni Gulch—*valley* ... HI-9
Honomu Stream—*stream* ... HI-9
Hononegah—*school* ... IL-6
Hononegah For Preserve—*forest* ... IL-6
**Hononegah Heights**—*pop pl* ... IL-6
Honono Point—*cape* ... HI-9
Hono o Na Pali—*summit* ... HI-9
Honopou—*civil* ... HI-9
Honopou Point—*cape* ... HI-9
Honopou Stream—*stream* ... HI-9
Honopu—*civil* ... HI-9
Honopu—*locale* ... HI-9
Honopu Bay—*bay* ... HI-9
Honopue—*civil* ... HI-9
*Honopue Gulch* ... HI-9
Honopueo—*civil* ... HI-9
Honopue Stream—*stream* ... HI-9
Honopue Valley—*valley* ... HI-9
Honopu Gulch—*valley* ... HI-9
Honopu Trail—*trail* ... HI-9
Honopu Valley—*valley* ... HI-9
**Honor**—*pop pl* ... MI-6
Honora—*locale* ... GA-3
**Honoraville**—*pop pl* ... AL-4
Honoraville Ch—*church* ... AL-4
Honoraville JHS—*school* ... AL-4
Honor Branch—*stream* ... AL-4
Honor Camp Number Four—*locale* ... AL-4
Honor Camp Number Seven (iron mine)—*mine* ... CA-9
Honore—*locale* ... FL-3
**Honore**—*pop pl* ... LA-4
Honor Farm—*locale* ... CA-9
Honor Grove—*woods* ... CA-9
Honor Heights Park—*park* ... OK-5
Honor Island Park—*park* ... AZ-5
Honor Lookout Tower—*locale* ... MI-6
*Honor Rancho Oil Field* ... CA-9
*Honoruru* ... HI-9
Honorville Sch—*school* ... MN-6
Honoulimaloo—*civil* ... HI-9
Honoulimaloo Stream—*stream* ... HI-9
*Honouliul* ... HI-9
Honouliuli—*civil* ... HI-9
**Honouliuli**—*pop pl* ... HI-9
Honouliuli Contour Trail—*trail* ... HI-9
Honouliuli For Res—*forest* ... HI-9
Honouliuli Gulch—*valley* ... HI-9
Honouliuli Stream—*stream* ... HI-9
*Honouliuul* ... HI-9
*Honouliuuli* ... HI-9
Honouliwai—*civil* ... HI-9
Honouliwai Stream—*stream* ... HI-9
Honour Lake—*lake* ... WA-9
Honowae—*beach* ... HI-9
Honowewe—*bay* ... HI-9
Honsapple Ditch—*canal* ... OH-6
Honse Cem—*cemetery* ... MO-7
*Honsen* ... CO-8
Honsinger Creek—*stream* ... CA-9
Honslinger Creek—*stream* ... UT-8
Honsocker Knob—*summit* ... WV-2
Hontokalo Creek—*stream* ... MS-4
Hontone Mine (historical)—*mine* ... NV-8
Hontoon Dead River—*stream* ... FL-3
Hontoon Island—*island* ... FL-3
Hontoon Island State Park—*park* ... FL-3
Hontoon Landing—*locale* ... FL-3
*Hontoun Dead River* ... FL-3
*Hontoun Island* ... FL-3
Hon (Township of)—*fmr MCD* ... AR-4
**Hontubby**—*pop pl* ... OK-5
Hontubby Creek—*stream* ... OK-5
Hontubby Falls—*falls* ... OK-5
Honuaino Four—*civil* ... HI-9
Honuaino One-Two—*civil* ... HI-9
Honuaino Three—*civil* ... HI-9
Honuapo—*civil* ... HI-9
**Honuapo**—*pop pl* ... HI-9
Honuapo Bay—*bay* ... HI-9
*Honuapo Harbor* ... HI-9
Honua Stream—*stream* ... HI-9
*Honuaula* ... HI-9
Honuaula—*civil* ... HI-9
*Honuaula Crater* ... HI-9
Honuaula For Res—*forest* ... HI-9
Honuaula Point—*cape* ... HI-9
Honuaula Tract Three—*civil* ... HI-9
Honuaula Tract Two—*civil* ... HI-9
Honuaula Valley—*valley* (2) ... HI-9
Honukanaenae—*bay* ... HI-9
Honu Point—*cape* ... HI-9
Honwee Mtn—*summit* ... MA-1
Hony Hill—*summit* ... NY-2
Hooam Cem—*cemetery* ... WV-2
Hooch Creek—*stream* ... CO-8
*Hooch Head* ... WA-9
*Hooch River* ... WA-9
Hooch Spring—*spring* ... UT-8
*Hoock Spring* ... UT-8
*Hood* ... CA-9
*Hood* ... MS-4
Hood—*locale* ... GA-3
Hood—*locale* ... PA-2
Hood—*locale* ... TX-5
Hood—*locale* ... VA-3
Hood—*locale* ... WA-9
**Hood**—*pop pl* ... AL-4
**Hood**—*pop pl* ... CA-9
**Hood**—*pop pl* ... LA-4
**Hood**—*pop pl* ... MD-2
Hood, Col. O. R., House—*hist pl* ... AL-4
Hood, John, House—*hist pl* ... ID-8
Hood, Mount—*summit* ... CA-9
Hood, Mount—*summit* ... MA-1
Hood, Mount—*summit* ... OR-9
Hood Arroyo—*stream* ... NM-5
Hood Bay—*bay* ... AK-9
**Hood Bay**—*pop pl* ... AK-9
Hood Branch—*stream* (3) ... GA-3
Hood Branch—*stream* (2) ... KY-4
Hood Branch—*stream* (3) ... MS-4
Hood Branch—*stream* (2) ... SC-3
Hood Branch—*stream* (5) ... TN-4
Hood Brook—*stream* ... ME-1
Hood Brothers Bldg—*hist pl* ... NC-3
**Hood Camp**—*pop pl* ... LA-4
Hood Canal—*bay* ... WA-9
Hood Cem—*cemetery* ... AL-4
Hood Cem—*cemetery* ... AR-4
Hood Cem—*cemetery* ... GA-3
Hood Cem—*cemetery* ... KY-4
Hood Cem—*cemetery* (2) ... MO-7
Hood Cem—*cemetery* (2) ... PA-2
Hood Cem—*cemetery* (5) ... TN-4
Hood Cem—*cemetery* (3) ... TX-5
Hood Cem—*cemetery* ... WV-2
*Hood Cemetery* ... MS-4
Hood Chapel—*church* ... MS-4
Hood Chapel—*church* (3) ... NC-3
Hood Coll—*school* ... MD-2
**Hood (County)**—*pop pl* ... TX-5
Hood County Courthouse Hist Dist—*hist pl* ... TX-5
*Hood Creek* ... OR-9
Hood Creek—*stream* ... AL-4
Hood Creek—*stream* ... ID-8
Hood Creek—*stream* (2) ... KY-4
Hood Creek—*stream* ... MT-8
Hood Creek—*stream* ... NC-3
Hood Creek—*stream* ... OR-9
Hood Creek Ch—*church* ... KY-4
Hood Creek Landing—*locale* ... NC-3
Hood Drain—*canal* ... MI-6
Hood Drain—*stream* ... MI-6
Hood Draw—*valley* ... CO-8
Hood Draw—*valley* ... WY-8
Hooded Creek—*stream* ... MI-6
Hooded Fireplace Ruin (LA 5662)—*hist pl* ... NM-5
Hoodelmier Ditch—*canal* ... IN-6
Hooders Run—*stream* ... PA-2
Hood Fork Ch—*church* ... KY-4
Hood Gap—*gap* ... NC-3
Hood Gulch—*valley* ... ID-8
Hood Hafassienda—*locale* ... AZ-5
Hood Head—*island* ... WA-9
*Hood Hill* ... MA-1
Hood Hill—*summit* ... MO-7
Hood Hollow—*valley* ... OH-6
Hood Hollow—*valley* (3) ... TN-4
Hood Hollow—*valley* ... VA-3
Hood Hollow—*valley* ... WI-6
Hood-Holt Cem—*cemetery* ... TN-4
Hoodin Bldg—*hist pl* ... OH-6
Hood JHS—*school* (2) ... TX-5
Hood Junction—*locale* ... CA-9
Hood Lake—*lake* ... AK-9
Hood Lake—*lake* (2) ... AR-4
Hood Lake—*lake* ... MN-6
Hood Lake—*lake* ... SC-3
**Hood Lake**—*pop pl* ... TN-4
Hood Lake—*reservoir* ... IN-6
Hood Lake—*reservoir* ... TN-4
Hood Lake—*swamp* ... FL-3
Hood Lake Campground—*locale* ... MT-8
Hood Lake Dam—*dam* ... IN-6
Hood Lake Dam—*dam* ... TN-4
Hood Landing Ferry (historical)—*locale* ... TN-4
Hood Landing (historical)—*locale* ... TN-4
Hoodle Creek—*stream* ... UT-8
Hoodley Branch—*stream* ... TN-4
Hood Lumber Company Dam—*dam* ... MS-4
Hoodlum Canyon—*valley* ... OR-9
Hoodlum Creek—*stream* ... AK-9
Hoodlum Ridge—*ridge* ... AR-4
Hood Memorial Sch—*school* ... NH-1
Hood Mendel Arena—*building* ... TX-5
Hood Mesa—*summit* ... NM-5
Hood Mtn—*summit* ... NY-2
Hood Mtn—*summit* ... OR-9
Hoodon Gap—*gap* ... CO-8
**Hoodoo**—*pop pl* ... TN-4
Hoodoo Basin—*basin* ... WY-8
Hoodoo Butte—*summit* (2) ... OR-9
Hoodoo Canyon—*valley* ... NV-8
Hoodoo Canyon—*valley* ... NM-5
Hoodoo Canyon—*valley* ... UT-8
Hoodoo Canyon—*valley* ... WA-9
Hoodoo Cascade—*falls* ... MT-8
*Hoodoo Cascades* ... MT-8
Hoodoo Coulee—*valley* ... MT-8
Hoodoo Creek—*stream* ... CA-9
Hoodoo Creek—*stream* ... CO-8
Hoodoo Creek—*stream* (7) ... ID-8
Hoodoo Creek—*stream* ... MN-6
Hoodoo Creek—*stream* (4) ... MT-8
Hoodoo Creek—*stream* (4) ... OR-9
Hoodoo Creek—*stream* ... UT-8
Hoodoo Creek—*stream* ... WA-9
Hoodoo Creek—*stream* (3) ... WY-8
Hoodoo Draw—*valley* ... TX-5
Hoodoo Gulch—*valley* ... AK-9
Hoodoo Gulch—*valley* (2) ... CA-9
Hoodoo Gulch—*valley* ... ID-8
Hoodoo Gulch—*valley* (2) ... MT-8
Hoodoo Gulch—*valley* ... SD-7
Hoodoo Hill—*summit* ... AK-9
Hoodoo Hill—*summit* ... MT-8
Hoodoo Hills—*range* ... CA-9
*Hoodoo Island* ... OR-9
Hoodoo Island—*island* ... MN-6
Hoodoo Knoll—*summit* ... AZ-5
Hoodoo Knoll—*summit* ... UT-8
Hoodoo Lake—*lake* (3) ... ID-8
Hoodoo Lake—*lake* ... MN-6
Hoodoo Lake—*lake* ... MT-8
Hoodoo Lake—*lake* ... WI-6
Hoodoo Lake Campground—*locale* ... ID-8
Hoodoo Lookout Tower—*locale* ... OR-9
Hoodoo Meadows—*flat* ... ID-8
Hoodoo Meadows—*flat* ... MT-8
Hoodoo Methodist Ch—*church* ... TN-4
Hoodoo Mine—*mine* ... NV-8
*Hoodoo Mountain* ... MT-8
Hoodoo Mtn—*summit* ... AK-9
Hoodoo Mtn—*summit* (2) ... ID-8
Hoodoo Mtn—*summit* ... MT-8
Hoodoo Mtn—*summit* ... NM-5
Hoodoo Mtn—*summit* ... OR-9
Hoodoo Mtn—*summit* ... WA-9
Hoodoo Mtns—*range* ... ID-8
Hoodoo Pass—*gap* ... ID-8
Hoodoo Pass—*gap* (2) ... MT-8
Hoodoo Pass—*gap* ... WA-9
Hoodoo Peak—*summit* ... ID-8
Hoodoo Peak—*summit* ... WA-9
Hoodoo Peak—*summit* ... WY-8
Hoodoo Point—*cape* ... MN-6
Hoodoo Ranch—*locale* ... WY-8
Hoodoo Ridge—*ridge* ... ID-8
Hoodoo Ridge—*ridge* ... OR-9
Hoodoos, The—*pillar* ... AK-9
Hoodoos, The—*pillar* ... WY-8
Hoodoo Ski Bowl—*other* ... OR-9
Hoodoo Spring—*spring* ... ID-8
Hoodoo Spring—*spring* ... NM-5
Hoodoo Spring—*spring* (3) ... OR-9
Hoodoo Trail (pack)—*trail* ... OR-9
Hoodoo-Union Hill Mine—*mine* ... SD-7
Hoodoo Wash—*stream* ... AZ-5
Hoodoo Water Tank—*reservoir* ... TX-5
Hoodoo Well—*well* ... AZ-5
Hood Park—*park* ... KS-7
Hood Park—*park* ... NH-1
Hood Park—*park* ... WA-9
Hood Point—*cape* ... AK-9
Hood Point—*cape* ... MD-2
Hood Point—*cape* ... WA-9
Hood Pond—*reservoir* ... GA-3
Hood Pond—*reservoir* ... MA-1
Hood Pond—*reservoir* ... NJ-2
Hood Pond Dam—*dam* ... MA-1
Hood Ranch—*locale* ... NE-7
Hood Ranch—*locale* ... TX-5
Hood Ridge—*ridge* ... TN-4
*Hood River* ... OR-9
**Hood River**—*pop pl* ... OR-9
Hood River—*stream* ... OR-9
Hood River Airp—*airport* ... OR-9
Hood River (CCD)—*cens area* ... OR-9
**Hood River County**—*pop pl* ... OR-9
Hood River Hatchery—*locale* ... OR-9
*Hood River Irrigation District Canal* ... OR-9
Hood River Meadows—*flat* ... OR-9
Hood River MS—*school* ... OR-9
Hood River Mtn—*summit* ... OR-9
Hood River Valley—*valley* ... OR-9
Hood River Valley Ranger Station—*locale* ... OR-9
**Hoods**—*pop pl* ... NC-3
Hood Sand Pond—*lake* ... FL-3
Hoods Cem—*cemetery* ... KY-4
Hood Sch—*school* (2) ... KS-7
Hood Sch—*school* (2) ... MA-1
*Hoods Creek* ... AL-4
*Hoods Creek* ... GA-3
*Hoods Creek* ... TN-4
Hoods Creek—*stream* ... AL-4
Hoods Creek—*stream* ... CA-9
Hoods Creek—*stream* ... GA-3
Hoods Creek—*stream* (2) ... KY-4
Hoods Creek—*stream* ... NC-3
Hoods Creek—*stream* ... WI-6
Hoods Creek Sch—*school* ... WI-6
*Hoods Cross Roads* ... AL-4
*Hoods Crossroads* ... NC-3
**Hoods Crossroads**—*pop pl* ... AL-4
**Hoods Crossroads**—*pop pl* ... NC-3
**Hoods Crossroads (Murphree Valley)**—*pop pl* ... AL-4
Hoods Crossroads Shop Ctr—*locale* ... NC-3
Hoods Fork—*stream* ... KY-4
**Hoods (historical)**—*pop pl* ... NC-3
Hoods Hollow—*valley* ... PA-2
Hood-Simmons House—*hist pl* ... OH-6
Hoods Island—*island* ... DE-2
*Hoods Landing* ... TN-4
Hoods Landing Post Office (historical)—*building* ... TN-4
*Hoods Mill* ... MS-4
Hoods Mill—*locale* ... MD-2
**Hood's Mill**—*pop pl* ... MD-2
Hoods Mill Lookout Tower—*locale* ... LA-4
*Hoods Point* ... MD-2
Hoods Point Ch—*church* ... TX-5
*Hoods Pond* ... MA-1
Hoods Pond—*lake* ... NH-1
**Hoodsport**—*pop pl* ... WA-9
Hood Spring—*spring* ... AL-4
Hood Spring—*spring* ... TX-5
Hood Springs—*spring* ... TN-4
Hoods Run—*stream* ... KY-4
Hoods Run Sch—*school* ... KY-4
Hoods Sch—*school* ... AL-4
Hoods Temple—*church* ... NC-3
Hood Street Rsvr—*reservoir* ... WA-9
Hoodsville—*locale* ... WV-2
**Hood Swamp**—*pop pl* ... NC-3
Hood Tank—*reservoir* (3) ... NM-5
Hoodtown—*locale* ... MS-4
**Hoodtown**—*pop pl* ... SC-3
Hoodtown Lookout Tower—*locale* ... MS-4
Hood Tunnel—*tunnel* ... SD-7
**Hoodview**—*pop pl* ... OR-9
Hood View Campground—*park* ... OR-9
Hood View Sch—*school* ... OR-9
Hoodville—*locale* ... PA-2
**Hoodville**—*pop pl* ... IL-6
Hood Well—*well* ... NM-5
Hood Windmill—*locale* ... AZ-5
Hood Windmill—*locale* ... NM-5
Hooe Ch—*church* ... MO-7
Hooes—*locale* ... VA-3
Hooes Run—*stream* ... VA-3
Hooff Run—*stream* ... VA-3
Hoof Hill—*summit* ... AK-9
Hoof Inn (historical)—*building* ... NC-3
Hooflander Mtn—*summit* ... PA-2
Hoofnagle Gap—*gap* ... PA-2
Hoof Point—*cape* ... AK-9
Hoogdal—*locale* ... WA-9
Hoogie Doogie Mtn—*summit* ... OR-9
Hoogstraat Sch—*school* ... MI-6
*Hoo Hoo* ... WV-2
**Hoohoo**—*pop pl* ... WV-2
Hoo Hoo Gulch—*valley* ... ID-8
Hoo Hoo Lake—*lake* ... WA-9
Hooie Cem—*cemetery* ... AL-4
Hoojah Branch—*stream* ... GA-3
Hoojah Branch Site (9RA34)—*hist pl* ... GA-3
*Hook* ... AL-4
*Hook* ... OK-5
Hook, Lake—*lake* ... MN-6
Hook, Mary Rockwell, House—*hist pl* ... MO-7
Hook, The—*bend* ... PA-2
Hook, The—*locale* ... NY-2
*Hook and Ladder Canyon* ... UT-8
Hook and Ladder Company No. 2—*hist pl* ... KY-4
Hook and Ladder Company No. 3—*hist pl* ... KY-4
Hook and Ladder Company No. 4—*hist pl* ... KY-4
Hook and Ladder Company No. 5—*hist pl* ... KY-4
Hook and Ladder Gulch—*valley* ... UT-8
Hook and Ladder No. 1 and Hose Co. No. 2—*hist pl* ... ND-7
Hook and Line Ranch—*locale* ... AZ-5
Hook and Moore Glade—*flat* ... CO-8
Hook Arm—*bay* ... AK-9
Hook Bay—*bay* (2) ... AK-9
Hook Branch—*stream* ... SC-3
Hook Branch—*stream* ... VA-3
Hook Branch Creek—*stream* ... WA-9
Hook Bridge—*bridge* ... NE-7

Hoppy Field (airport)—*airport* MS-4
Hoppy Gulch—*valley* MT-8
Hoppy Lake—*lake* MI-6
Hoppy Lake—*lake* MN-6
Hoppy Spring—*spring* OR-9
Hoppy Tank—*reservoir* NM-5
**Hoprig**—*pop pl* IA-7
Hop River—*locale* CT-1
Hop River—*stream* CT-1
Hops Bayou—*stream* LA-4
Hopsewee—*hist pl* SC-3
Hopsicker Pond—*lake* NY-2
Hopson—*locale* TN-4
**Hopson**—*pop pl* KY-4
**Hopson**—*pop pl* MS-4
*Hopson Bayou* MS-4
Hopson Bayou—*stream* MS-4
*Hopson Bayou Elementary School* MS-4
Hopson Bayou Sch—*school* MS-4
Hopson Bluff—*cliff* TN-4
Hopson Cem—*cemetery* (2) AR-4
Hopson Cem—*cemetery* TN-4
Hopson Ch—*church* TN-4
Hopson Ch (historical)—*church* MS-4
Hopson Creek—*stream* KY-4
Hopson House—*hist pl* LA-4
Hopson Lake—*lake* KY-4
Hopson Lake—*reservoir* AL-4
Hopson Mill Creek—*stream* TX-5
*Hopson Plantation* MS-4
Hopson Post Office (historical)—*building* TN-4
Hopsons Bay—*bay* NY-2
Hopson Sch—*school* TN-4
**Hopsons (Hopson Spur)**—*pop pl* MS-4
*Hopson Spur* MS-4
Hopspinike Lake—*lake* AR-4
Hopspinike Slough—*stream* AR-4
Hop Spring—*spring* AZ-5
Hop Spring—*spring* SD-7
Hops Shoals—*bar* TN-4
Hops Spring—*spring* UT-8
Hops Wash—*stream* ND-7
Hopukani Springs—*spring* HI-9
**Hopuwai**—*pop pl* HI-9
Hop Valley—*valley* UT-8
Hop Valley Trail—*trail* UT-8
Hopville—*locale* OR-9
Hopwell Cem—*cemetery* IL-6
Hopwell Missionary Baptist Ch—*church* MS-4
Hopwell Sch (historical)—*school* TN-4
Hop Williams Mine—*mine* NM-5
**Hopwood**—*pop pl* PA-2
**Hopwood Acres**—*pop pl* MI-6
Hopwood Cem—*cemetery* AL-4
Hopwood Cem—*cemetery* MO-7
Hopwood Cem—*cemetery* TN-4
Hopwood Christian Ch—*church* TN-4
Hopwood Creek—*stream* ID-8
*Hop Yard* VA-3
**Hop Yard**—*pop pl* CA-9
Hop Yard (historical)—*civil* DC-2
Hop Yard Landing—*locale* VA-3
*Hopyard Wharf* VA-3
*Hoquarton Slough* OR-9
**Hoquiam**—*pop pl* WA-9
Hoquiam, Mount—*summit* WA-9
*Hoquiam Creek* WA-9
Hoquiam Radio Range Station—*other* WA-9
*Hoquiam River* WA-9
Hoquiam River—*stream* WA-9
Hoquiam River Bridge—*hist pl* WA-9
Hoquiam's Castle—*hist pl* WA-9
*Hoquiamts River* WA-9
Hoquiam Water Works—*other* WA-9
Hor, Mount—*summit* VT-1
Horace—*locale* NC-3
**Horace**—*pop pl* IL-6
**Horace**—*pop pl* IN-6
**Horace**—*pop pl* KS-7
**Horace**—*pop pl* NE-7
**Horace**—*pop pl* ND-7
*Horace Aarnold Brook* MA-1
*Horace Arnold Brook* RI-1
Horace B Rowland State Heliport—*airport* PA-2
Horace Caldwell Pier—*locale* TX-5
Horace Cem—*cemetery* ND-7
Horace Chapel—*church* TX-5
Horace Chapel (historical)—*church* MS-4
Horace Greeley, Mount—*summit* MI-6
Horace Greeley Birthplace—*building* NH-1
Horace Gulch—*valley* WY-8
Horace Harding—*uninc pl* NY-2
Horace (historical)—*locale* IA-7
**Horace (historical)**—*pop pl* TN-4
Horace Island—*island* RI-1
Horace Mann Alternative JHS—*school* KS-7
*Horace Mann Elementary School* PA-2
Horace Mann Elem Sch—*school* (2) IN-6
Horace Mann JHS—*school* (2) CO-8
Horace Mann JHS—*school* FL-3
Horace Mann JHS—*school* OK-5
Horace Mann JHS—*school* (2) TX-5
Horace Mann Memorial Monmt—*park* OH-6
Horace Mann Public Sch No. 13—*hist pl* IN-6
*Horace Mann Sch* FL-3
Horace Mann Sch—*school* AZ-5
Horace Mann Sch—*school* (4) CA-9
Horace Mann Sch—*school* DC-2
Horace Mann Sch—*school* (2) IL-6
Horace Mann Sch—*school* IN-6
Horace Mann Sch—*school* MN-6
Horace Mann Sch—*school* (2) MO-7
Horace Mann Sch—*school* NJ-2
Horace Mann Sch—*school* (3) NY-2
Horace Mann Sch—*school* ND-7
Horace Mann Sch—*school* (6) OH-6
Horace Mann Sch—*school* (2) OK-5
Horace Mann Sch—*school* SD-7
Horace Mann Sch—*school* TX-5
Horace Mann Sch—*school* UT-8
Horace Mann Sch—*school* WV-2
Horace Mann Sch—*school* WI-6
Horace Mann Sch—*school* VI-3
Horace Maynard HS—*school* TN-4
Horace Mesa—*summit* NM-5
Horace Mtn—*summit* AK-9
Horace Obryant MS—*school* FL-3
Horace Post Office (historical)—*building* TN-4
Horace W Elrod Sch—*school* TX-5
Horace Williams Airp—*airport* NC-3
*Horace Williams Landing* AL-4
Horaito Windmill—*locale* TX-5
Horak Airp—*airport* AL-4
Ho Ranch—*locale* NE-7
Horan Head—*summit* ME-1
Horanif (historical)—*locale* KS-7
Horanif Sch—*school* KS-7
Horan Lake—*lake* MN-6
Horan Park—*park* IL-6
Horan Sch—*school* IA-7
Horath Corral Spring—*spring* NV-8
Horatio—*locale* MS-4
Horatio—*locale* PA-2
**Horatio**—*pop pl* AR-4
**Horatio**—*pop pl* OH-6
**Horatio**—*pop pl* SC-3
**Horatio Gardens**—*pop pl* IL-6
Horatio Rock—*summit* WY-8
Horatio West Court—*hist pl* CA-9
Horcado Ranch—*locale* NM-5
Horcones Windmill—*locale* TX-5
Horcon Tract—*civil* TX-5
Hord—*locale* NE-7
**Hord**—*pop pl* IL-6
Hord, Heber, House—*hist pl* NE-7
Hord, Robert, House—*hist pl* KY-4
Hord Cem—*cemetery* (2) TN-4
Hord Creek—*stream* TN-4
Hord Creek—*stream* TX-5
*Horde Creek* TX-5
Horde Mtn—*summit* NC-3
*Horden Brook* RI-1
*Hordes Creek* TX-5
Hordes Creek Gas Field—*oilfield* TX-5
Hordeum Rsvr—*reservoir* WY-8
Hord Ford—*locale* TN-4
Hord Gulch—*valley* ID-8
Hord Island—*island* TN-4
Hord Lake—*lake* WI-6
Hord Lake State Rec Area—*park* NE-7
Hord Mill—*locale* TN-4
Hords Bend—*bend* TN-4
Hord Sch—*school* NE-7
Hord Sch (abandoned)—*school* MO-7
Hords Chapel—*church* TN-4
*Hords Creek* TX-5
Hords Creek—*stream* TX-5
Hords Creek Lake—*reservoir* TX-5
Hords Islands—*island* TN-4
Hord Slough—*stream* TX-5
Hord Tank—*reservoir* NM-5
**Hordville**—*pop pl* NE-7
Hordville (historical)—*locale* MS-4
*Horeb* AL-4
**Horeb**—*pop pl* SC-3
Horeb, Mount—*summit* OR-9
*Horeb Baptist Church* AL-4
Horeb Branch—*stream* SC-3
Horeb Cem—*cemetery* IN-6
Horeb Cem—*cemetery* OH-6
Horeb Cem—*cemetery* WV-2
Horeb Ch—*church* AL-4
Horeb Ch—*church* GA-3
Horeb Ch—*church* (2) OH-6
Horeb Ch—*church* (2) SC-3
Horeb Ch—*church* VA-3
Horeb Ch—*church* WV-2
Horeb Christian Sch—*school* FL-3
Horeb Spring Park—*park* WI-6
Horehound Springs—*spring* NV-8
*Horekill* DE-2
*Horekill Road* DE-2
Horen Drain—*stream* MI-6
Horesepen Lake—*reservoir* VA-3
*Horeshoe Lake* MI-6
Horgan Ridge—*ridge* ND-7
Horgan Rsvr—*reservoir* MT-8
Horgen Lake—*lake* WI-6
Horger Pond (historical)—*reservoir* SC-3
Horger Sch—*school* MI-6
*Horicon* NY-2
**Horicon**—*pop pl* WI-6
Horicon, Lake—*lake* MI-6
Horicon Ch—*church* MN-6
Horicon Island—*island* NY-2
Horicon Lake—*reservoir* NJ-2
Horicon Marsh—*swamp* WI-6
Horicon Marsh Wildlife Area—*park* WI-6
Horicon Natl Wildlife Ref—*park* WI-6
Horicon Sch—*school* CA-9
Horicon Site—*hist pl* WI-6
*Horicon Stream* NJ-2
**Horicon (Town of)**—*pop pl* NY-2
**Horine**—*pop pl* MO-7
Horine Cem—*cemetery* KY-4
Horine Cem—*cemetery* MO-7
Horine Mtn—*summit* AR-4
Horizan—*island* FM-9
**Horizon Circle Subdivision**—*pop pl* UT-8
**Horizon City**—*pop pl* TX-5
Horizon Elem Sch—*school* FL-3
Horizon Heliport—*airport* NV-8
**Horizon Hills**—*pop pl* CA-9
**Horizon Hills**—*pop pl* VA-3
Horizon Hosp—*hospital* FL-3
Horizon Park—*park* AZ-5
Horizon Park—*park* MT-8
Horizon Park (Shop Ctr)—*locale* FL-3
Horizon Ridge—*ridge* CA-9
**Horizon Run**—*pop pl* MD-2
Horizon Sch—*school* (2) FL-3
Horizon Sch—*school* UT-8
**Horizon Subdivision**—*pop pl* UT-8
*Horizon View* NV-8
**Horizon View**—*pop pl* WA-9
Horizon Viewsite—*locale* NV-8
Horizon West Industrial Park (subdivision)—*locale* UT-8
*Horjes Cove* WA-9
*Horkan Creek* MT-8
Horkan Creek—*stream* MT-8
Horkan Creek Sch—*school* MT-8
Horkelia Meadow—*flat* OR-9
Horlbeck Creek—*stream* SC-3
Horlick—*locale* WA-9
Horlick HS—*school* WI-6
Horlick Park—*park* WI-6
Horman Ranch—*locale* SD-7
*Hormans Creek* PA-2
Hormblower Point—*cape* NC-3
Hormel Park—*park* NE-7
Hormel Stadium—*locale* MA-1
Hormiga, Monte—*cape* PR-3
Hormigas Lake—*swamp* TX-5
Hormigas Windmill—*locale* TX-5
Hormigoso Diversion Dam—*dam* NM-5
**Hormigueros**—*pop pl* PR-3
Hormigueros (Municipio)—*civil* PR-3
Hormigueros (Pueblo)—*fmr MCD* PR-3
Horm Run—*stream* PA-2
Horm Run Sch (historical)—*school* PA-2
**Hormtown**—*pop pl* PA-2
Horn—*locale* AZ-5
Horn—*locale* MS-4
Horn—*locale* NE-7
**Horn**—*pop pl* MO-7
Horn, Cape—*cape* (3) CA-9
Horn, Cape—*cape* (2) ID-8
Horn, Cape—*cape* NJ-2
Horn, Cape—*cape* (2) OR-9
Horn, Cape—*cape* (3) WA-9
Horn, Cape—*summit* CA-9
Horn, Cape—*summit* NV-8
Horn, Cape—*summit* OR-9
Horn, George L., Sch—*hist pl* PA-2
Horn, Lake—*lake* MN-6
Horn, The—*cape* CA-9
Horn, The—*falls* OR-9
Horn, The—*gut* AR-4
Horn, The—*other* AK-9
Horn, The—*ridge* UT-8
Horn, The—*ridge* WY-8
Horn, The—*summit* CO-8
Horn, The—*summit* ID-8
Horn, The—*summit* ME-1
Horn, The—*summit* MT-8
Horn, The—*summit* NH-1
Horn, The—*summit* PA-2
Horn, The—*summit* (3) UT-8
Horn, The—*summit* WA-9
Hornaday, Mount—*summit* WY-8
Hornaday Creek—*stream* WY-8
Hornaday-Miles Cem—*cemetery* TN-4
Hornaday-Proby Cem—*cemetery* TN-4
Hornady—*locale* AL-4
Hornady Park—*park* IN-6
Hornady Pleasant Union Ch—*church* NC-3
Horn and Meason Rsvr—*reservoir* WY-8
Horn Arroyo—*stream* NM-5
Hornback, Emily, House—*hist pl* IA-7
Hornback Cem—*cemetery* (2) IL-6
Hornback Creek—*stream* CA-9
Hornback Creek—*stream* OK-5
Horn Back Mill—*locale* KY-4
Hornback Ranch—*locale* CA-9
Hornbaker Airp—*airport* KS-7
Hornbarn Cove—*bay* ME-1
Horn Basin—*basin* NV-8
**Hornbeak**—*pop pl* TN-4
Hornbeak Cem—*cemetery* (2) TN-4
Hornbeak Post Office—*building* TN-4
Hornbeak-Samburg (CCD)—*cens area* TN-4
Hornbeak-Samburg Division—*civil* TN-4
Hornbeak Sch (historical)—*school* TN-4
Hornbeam Branch—*stream* NC-3
Hornbeam Chapel—*summit* RI-1
*Hornbeam Hill* ME-1
Hornbeam Hill—*summit* ME-1
Hornbeam Mtn—*summit* ME-1
*Horn Beam Swamp* NC-3
Hornbeam Swamp—*swamp* NH-1
**Hornbeck**—*pop pl* LA-4
*Hornbeck Cemetery* TN-4
Hornbeck Draw—*valley* WY-8
Hornbeck Hollow—*valley* AR-4
Hornbeck Sch—*school* IL-6
Hornbeck Sch—*school* SD-7
Hornbecks Creek—*stream* PA-2
Hornbeck Spring—*spring* OR-9
Hornbek House—*hist pl* CO-8
Horn Bench—*bench* AR-4
Hornbine Baptist Church—*hist pl* MA-1
Hornbine Ch—*church* MA-1
Hornbine Sch—*hist pl* MA-1
*Hornblende Camp* SD-7
*Hornblower* NC-3
Hornblower, Edward, House and Barn—*hist pl* MA-1
Hornbostel Branch—*stream* IL-6
*Horn Branch* GA-3
Horn Branch—*stream* (4) AL-4
Horn Branch—*stream* (4) AR-4
Horn Branch—*stream* (3) KY-4
Horn Branch—*stream* (3) MO-7
Horn Branch—*stream* (3) TN-4
Horn Branch—*stream* (2) TX-5
Horn Branch Ch—*church* KY-4
*Horn Brook* PA-2
Hornbrook—*locale* PA-2
**Hornbrook**—*pop pl* CA-9
**Horn Brook**—*pop pl* PA-2
Horn Brook—*stream* (3) NH-1
Horn Brook—*stream* PA-2
Hornbrook Cem—*cemetery* PA-2
*Hornbrook Creek* CA-9
Hornbrook-Hilt (CCD)—*cens area* CA-9
Hornbrook Mtn—*summit* NM-5
Hornbuckle Branch—*stream* NC-3
Hornbuckle Creek—*stream* NC-3
Hornbuckle Creek—*stream* SC-3
Hornbuckle Draw—*valley* WY-8
Hornbuckle Hollow—*valley* AL-4
Hornbuckle Ranch—*locale* WY-8
Hornbuckle Valley Overlook—*locale* NC-3
Hornburg, Harold, House—*hist pl* WI-6
Hornburger Lake—*lake* NE-7
Horn Butte—*summit* (2) OR-9
Hornby—*locale* MN-6
Hornby—*locale* PA-2
**Hornby**—*pop pl* NY-2
*Hornby Creek* WI-6
Hornby Creek—*stream* ID-8
Hornby Creek—*stream* MN-6
Hornby Creek—*stream* WI-6
*Hornby Ferry* TN-4
Hornby Hollow—*valley* PA-2
Hornby Hollow—*valley* WI-6
Hornby Lake—*lake* MN-6
Hornby Mine—*mine* CA-9
**Hornby (Town of)**—*pop pl* NY-2
Horn Camp Run—*stream* WV-2
Horn Camp Swamp—*stream* NC-3
Horn Canyon—*valley* CA-9
Horn Canyon—*valley* CO-8
Horn Canyon—*valley* NM-5
Horn Canyon Well—*well* WY-8
*Horn Cem* TN-4
Horn Cem—*cemetery* (3) AR-4
Horn Cem—*cemetery* CO-8
Horn Cem—*cemetery* IA-7
Horn Cem—*cemetery* KS-7
Horn Cem—*cemetery* (2) KY-4
Horn Cem—*cemetery* LA-4
Horn Cem—*cemetery* MS-4
Horn Cem—*cemetery* MO-7
Horn Cem—*cemetery* OH-6
Horn Cem—*cemetery* PA-2
Horn Cem—*cemetery* (4) TN-4
Horn Cem—*cemetery* TX-5
Horn Cem—*cemetery* (2) VA-3
Horn Cem—*cemetery* (2) WV-2
Horn Cem (historical)—*cemetery* MO-7
Horn Ch—*church* MS-4
Horn Chapel—*church* KY-4
*Horn Church* AL-4
Horn Cliffs—*cliff* AK-9
*Horncold Swamp* MI-6
Horn Coral Cave—*cave* AL-4
Horn Cotton Gin—*locale* AZ-5
*Horn Creek* AL-4
*Horn Creek* MS-4
*Horn Creek* TX-5
Horn Creek—*stream* AL-4
Horn Creek—*stream* (2) AK-9
Horn Creek—*stream* AZ-5
Horn Creek—*stream* CA-9
Horn Creek—*stream* CO-8
Horn Creek—*stream* (5) ID-8
Horn Creek—*stream* (2) IN-6
Horn Creek—*stream* KY-4
Horn Creek—*stream* MN-6
Horn Creek—*stream* MO-7
Horn Creek—*stream* (3) MT-8
Horn Creek—*stream* (5) OR-9
Horn Creek—*stream* SC-3
Horn Creek—*stream* TN-4
Horn Creek—*stream* TX-5
Horn Creek—*stream* WA-9
Horn Creek—*stream* WV-2
Horn Creek—*stream* WY-8
Horn Creek Baptist Church—*hist pl* SC-3
Horn Creek Ch—*church* SC-3
Horn Creek Ch—*church* WV-2
Horn Creek Ditch—*canal* WY-8
Horn Creek Gap—*gap* CA-9
Horn Creek Ranch—*locale* CO-8
Horn Creek Rapids—*rapids* AZ-5
Horn Creek Rsvr—*reservoir* WY-8
Horncrist Spring—*spring* OR-9
Horn Crossing Ch—*church* TX-5
Horn Ditch—*canal* (2) IN-6
Horn Ditch—*canal* OH-6
Horn Draw—*valley* SD-7
*Horne* MS-4
*Horne* PA-2
Horne, Cape—*cape* CA-9
Horne Airfield—*airport* OR-9
Horne Airp—*airport* PA-2
Horne Branch—*stream* KS-7
Horne Branch—*stream* KY-4
Horne Branch—*stream* MS-4
Horne Branch—*stream* MO-7
Horne Branch—*stream* TX-5
Horne Brook—*stream* (2) NH-1
Horne Cem—*cemetery* GA-3
Horne Cem—*cemetery* KY-4
Horne Cem—*cemetery* MS-4
Horne Cem—*cemetery* (2) NC-3
Horne Cem—*cemetery* SC-3
Horne Cem—*cemetery* TX-5
Horne Cem—*cemetery* (3) VA-3
Horne Cem—*cemetery* WV-2
Horne Ch—*church* PA-2
Hornecker Creek—*stream* WY-8
Horne Creek—*stream* NC-3
Horne Dam—*dam* AL-4
Horned Owl Gulch—*valley* CA-9
Horned Owl Retention Dam—*dam* CO-8
Horned Toad Hills—*range* CA-9
*Horne Falls* MN-6
Horne Flats—*flat* WY-8
Horne Knob—*summit* VA-3
*Horne Lake* WY-8
Horne Lake—*lake* WY-8
Horne Landing Strip—*airport* OR-9
**Hornell**—*pop pl* NY-2
Hornell Armory—*hist pl* NY-2
Hornell Country Club—*other* NY-2
Hornell JHS—*school* NY-2
Hornell Public Library—*hist pl* NY-2
Hornell Rsvr Number One—*reservoir* NY-2
Hornell Rsvr Number Three—*reservoir* NY-2
Hornell Rsvr Number Two—*reservoir* NY-2
Hornell Senior HS—*school* NY-2
**Hornellsville (Town of)**—*pop pl* NY-2
Horne Mill Pond—*reservoir* MS-4
Horne Mission Ch—*church* GA-3
Horne Park—*park* IN-6
Horne Park—*park* KS-7
Horne Pond—*lake* ME-1
Horne Post Office (historical)—*building* MS-4
Horner—*locale* TN-4
**Horner**—*pop pl* NC-3
**Horner**—*pop pl* WV-2
Horner, John Scott, House—*hist pl* WI-6
Horner, Sidney H., House—*hist pl* AR-4
Horne Ranch—*locale* CA-9
Horner Bay—*lake* AR-4
Horner Branch Upper Twin Creek—*stream* OH-6
Horner Brook—*stream* NH-1
Horner Cabin Spring—*spring* AZ-5
Horner Cave—*cave* TN-4
Horner Cem—*cemetery* IN-6
Horner Cem—*cemetery* (2) MO-7
Horner Cem—*cemetery* OH-6
Horner Cem—*cemetery* PA-2
Horner Cem—*cemetery* (2) TN-4
Horner Ch—*church* MO-7
Horner Ch—*church* PA-2
Horner Ch—*church* TN-4
Horner Cove—*bay* MD-2
Horner Creek—*stream* AK-9
Horner Creek—*stream* OR-9
Horner Creek—*stream* WY-8
Horner Drain—*stream* MI-6
Horner Fork—*stream* KY-4
Horner Fork—*stream* WV-2
Horner Fork Ch—*church* WV-2
Horner Gulch—*valley* AZ-5
Horner Gut—*stream* MD-2
**Horner Hill**—*pop pl* OH-6
Horner Hill—*summit* OH-6
Horner Hill Cem—*cemetery* OH-6
Horner Hollow—*valley* (2) MO-7
Horner Hollow—*valley* (3) TN-4
Horner Hot Springs—*locale* AK-9
Horner House—*hist pl* KY-4
Horner House—*hist pl* NJ-2
Horner Houses—*hist pl* NC-3
Horner-Hyde House—*hist pl* SD-7
Horne Ridge—*ridge* AL-4
Horner Island—*island* MI-6
Horner Knoll—*summit* UT-8
Horner Lake—*lake* LA-4
Horner Lake—*reservoir* TX-5
*Horner Mountain* WV-2
Horner Mountain Tank—*reservoir* AZ-5
Horner Mtn—*summit* AZ-5
Horner Park—*park* (2) IL-6
*Horner P3nd* MA-1
Horner Ranch—*locale* OR-9
Horner Rsvr—*reservoir* HI-9
*Horner Run* PA-2
Horner Run—*stream* OH-6
Horner Run—*stream* PA-2
Horner Run—*stream* VA-3
Horner Run—*stream* (2) WV-2
Horners—*locale* VA-3
Horners Branch—*stream* VA-3
Horners Cem—*cemetery* (2) MO-7
Horners Ch—*church* PA-2
Horner Sch—*school* CA-9
Horner Sch—*school* IL-6
Horner Sch—*school* OK-5
Horner Sch—*school* PA-2
Horner Sch (abandoned)—*school* MO-7
Horners Chapel—*church* IN-6
Horners Ferry (historical)—*locale* MS-4
Horner Site—*hist pl* WY-8
Horners Mill—*locale* PA-2
Horners Pond—*reservoir* VA-3
Horner Spring—*spring* TN-4
Horner Springs—*spring* ID-8
Horners Run—*stream* VA-3
Horners Run—*stream* WV-2
Horners Sch (abandoned)—*school* PA-2
Horners Sch (historical)—*school* PA-2
Horners Store Post Office (historical)—*building* TN-4
Horner State Game Ref—*park* WV-2
*Hornerston* NJ-2
**Hornerstown**—*pop pl* NJ-2
**Hornerstown**—*pop pl* PA-2
**Hornersville**—*pop pl* MO-7
Hornersville Cem—*cemetery* MO-7
Hornersville Gage—*other* MO-7
Hornersville Junction—*locale* MO-7
Hornersville Memorial Airp—*airport* MO-7
Hornersville Swamp State Wildlife Area—*park* MO-7
*Horner Swamp Creek* VA-3
Horner Tank—*reservoir* (2) NM-5
Hornertown—*locale* TN-4
Hornertown Lookout Tower—*locale* TN-4
Horne Run—*stream* NJ-2
Horne Run—*stream* PA-2
*Hornes* GA-3
Hornes Ch—*church* NC-3
Horne Sch (historical)—*school* MS-4
Hornes Lakes—*reservoir* AL-4
Hornes Mill (historical)—*locale* NC-3
**Horne Spur**—*pop pl* KS-7
**Horne Subdivision**—*pop pl* UT-8
Horne Swamp—*swamp* NC-3
*Hornet* NC-3
**Hornet**—*pop pl* ID-8
**Hornet**—*pop pl* MO-7
**Hornet**—*pop pl* TN-4
Hornet Branch—*stream* TX-5
Hornet Butte—*summit* OR-9
Hornet Canyon—*valley* (2) ID-8
Hornet Cem—*cemetery* MO-7
Hornet Cobbles—*summit* NY-2
Hornet Cove—*bay* NH-1
Hornet Creek—*stream* AL-4
Hornet Creek—*stream* AK-9
Hornet Creek—*stream* (2) ID-8
Hornet Creek—*stream* MT-8
Hornet Creek—*stream* UT-8
Hornet Creek—*stream* WA-9
Hornet Creek Trail—*trail* ID-8
Hornet Draw—*valley* WA-9
Hornet Gulch—*valley* (2) CA-9
Hornet Gulch—*valley* UT-8
*Hornet Hollow* WV-2
Hornet Hollow—*valley* TN-4
Hornet Lake—*lake* MS-4
Hornet Lookout—*hist pl* MT-8
Hornet Mine—*mine* ID-8
Hornet Mtn—*summit* MT-8
Hornet Nest Branch—*stream* NC-3
Hornet Nest Hill—*summit* CA-9
Hornet Nest Ridge—*ridge* CA-9
Hornet Nest Spring—*spring* CA-9
Hornet Notch—*gap* NY-2
**Hornetown**—*pop pl* NH-1
Hornet Point—*cape* UT-8
Hornet Point—*summit* ID-8
Hornet Ponds—*lake* NY-2
Hornet Ranger Station—*locale* ID-8
Hornet Ridge—*ridge* ID-8
Hornet Ridge—*ridge* MT-8
Hornet Ridge—*ridge* (2) WA-9
Hornet Rsvr—*reservoir* ID-8
Hornet Rsvr—*reservoir* OR-9
*Hornet's Ferry* PA-2
Hornets Nest—*locale* VA-3
**Hornets Nest (historical)**—*pop pl* NC-3
Hornets Nest Point—*cape* NH-1
Hornet Spring—*spring* ID-8
Hornet Spring—*spring* NV-8
Hornet Stadium—*other* TX-5
Hornet Stadium—*park* AL-4
Hornet Swamp—*stream* NC-3
Hornet Swamp—*stream* VA-3
**Hornet (Township of)**—*pop pl* MN-6
Hornet Tree Top—*summit* TN-4
Horney, Lake—*lake* FL-3
Horney Branch—*stream* IL-6
Horney Branch—*stream* NC-3
Horney Camp Run—*stream* PA-2
Horney Cem—*cemetery* IN-6
Horney Park—*park* FL-3
Horney Ranch—*locale* NM-5
Horney Sch—*school* IL-6
Horney Tank—*reservoir* AZ-5
**Horneytown**—*pop pl* NC-3
Horn Field—*flat* CA-9
*Horn Fire Tower* AL-4
Horn Fork Basin—*basin* CO-8
Horn Fork Creek—*stream* CO-8
Horn Fork Trail—*trail* CO-8
Horn Gap—*gap* OR-9
Horn Gulch—*valley* CO-8
Horn Gulch—*valley* ID-8
Horn Gulch—*valley* (2) OR-9
*Horn Gulch Creek* NE-7
Horn Harbor—*bay* (2) VA-3
Horn Harbor Cem—*cemetery* VA-3
Horn Harbor Nursing Home—*building* VA-3
Horn Hill—*locale* TX-5
**Horn Hill**—*pop pl* AL-4
Horn Hill—*summit* (3) ME-1
Horn Hill—*summit* NH-1
Horn Hill—*summit* RI-1
Horn Hill—*summit* TX-5
Horn Hill Cem—*cemetery* KY-4
Horn Hill Cem—*cemetery* TX-5
Horn Hill Ch—*church* TX-5
Horn (historical)—*locale* IA-7
Horn Hollow—*valley* (2) AR-4
Horn Hollow—*valley* IL-6
Horn Hollow—*valley* KY-4
Horn Hollow—*valley* MO-7
Horn Hollow—*valley* PA-2
Horn Hollow—*valley* (2) TN-4
Horn House—*hist pl* IA-7
Horn-Hudson Cem—*cemetery* TN-4
*Horniblows* NC-3
Hornibrook House—*hist pl* AR-4
Hornica Creek—*stream* TX-5
**Hornick**—*pop pl* IA-7
**Hornig**—*pop pl* PA-2
**Horning**—*pop pl* AL-4
**Horning**—*pop pl* PA-2
Horning Cem—*cemetery* NE-7
Horningford—*locale* PA-2
Horning Gap—*gap* (2) OR-9
Horning Hollow—*valley* (2) PA-2
Horning Memorial—*cemetery* GA-3
Horning Rsvr—*reservoir* (3) OR-9
*Horning Run* MD-2
Horning Run—*stream* (2) PA-2
Hornings Pit State Wildlife Mngmt Ar—*park* MN-6
Horning Swamp—*swamp* GA-3
Hornin Hollow—*valley* KY-4
Horn Island—*island* ME-1
Horn Island—*island* MD-2
Horn Island—*island* MI-6
Horn Island—*island* MS-4
Horn Island Natl Wildlife Ref—*park* MS-4
Horn Island Pass—*channel* MS-4
**Hornitos**—*pop pl* CA-9
Hornitos Cone—*summit* NV-8
Hornitos Creek—*stream* CA-9
Hornitos Sch—*school* CA-9
*Horn Kil* DE-2
*Horn Kill* DE-2
*Hornkohl Marsh* MI-6
Hornkohl Swamp—*swamp* MI-6
Horn Lake—*lake* (2) AR-4
Horn Lake—*lake* MI-6
Horn Lake—*lake* (2) MN-6
Horn Lake—*lake* (2) MS-4
Horn Lake—*lake* MT-8
Horn Lake—*lake* NY-2
Horn Lake—*lake* (2) WI-6
**Horn Lake**—*pop pl* MS-4
Horn Lake Bend—*bend* TN-4
Horn Lake City Hall—*building* MS-4
Horn Lake Community Park—*park* MS-4
Horn Lake Creek—*stream* MS-4
Horn Lake Creek—*stream* TN-4
Horn Lake Cutoff—*bend* MS-4
Horn Lake Cutoff—*canal* (2) TN-4
Horn Lake Elem Sch—*school* MS-4
Horn Lake HS—*school* MS-4
Horn Lake JHS—*school* MS-4
Horn Lake Pass—*canal* TN-4
Horn Lake Pass—*stream* MS-4
Horn Lakes—*lake* CO-8
Horn Lateral—*canal* AZ-5
Horn Mesa—*summit* NM-5
Horn Mill Branch—*stream* TX-5
Horn Mound—*hist pl* OH-6
*Horn Mountain* MT-8
Horn Mountain—*ridge* AK-9
Horn Mountain Cow Camp—*locale* UT-8
Horn Mountain Lookout Tower—*tower* AL-4
Horn Mountains—*other* AK-9
Horn Mountains—*ridge* AK-9
Horn Mountains—*spring* MT-8
Horn Mountain Sch—*school* AR-4
Horn Mtn—*summit* AL-4
Horn Mtn—*summit* (5) AK-9
Horn Mtn—*summit* AR-4
Horn Mtn—*summit* CA-9
Horn Mtn—*summit* GA-3
Horn Mtn—*summit* ID-8
Horn Mtn—*summit* MT-8
Horn Mtn—*summit* VA-3
Horno Canyon—*valley* CA-9
Horno Creek—*stream* CA-9
Horn of the Moon Pond—*lake* VT-1
Horno Hill—*summit* CA-9
Hornolucka Creek—*stream* MS-4
Hornor (Township of)—*fmr MCD* AR-4
Horno Summit—*gap* CA-9
*Horn Passage* FL-3

Horn Peak—summit (2) ... CA-9
Horn Peak—summit ... CO-8
Horn Peaks, The—summit ... AK-9
Hornpipe Branch—stream ... NC-3
Horn Place Landing—locale ... MS-4
Horn Point—cape ... AK-9
Horn Point—cape (2) ... MD-2
Horn Point—cape ... VA-3
Horn-Polk House—hist pl ... TX-5
Horn Pond ... MA-1
Horn Pond—lake (2) ... ME-1
Horn Pond—lake (2) ... MA-1
Horn Pond—lake ... NH-1
Horn Pond—lake ... NY-2
Horn Pond—lake ... OR-9
Horn Pond—reservoir ... MA-1
Horn Pond Brook—stream ... MA-1
Horn Pond Dam—dam ... MA-1
Hornpond Mtn ... MA-1
Horn Pond Mtn—summit ... MA-1
Horn Quarter—hist pl ... VA-3
Hornquarter Creek—stream ... VA-3
Horn Quater Creek—stream ... VA-3
Horn Ranch—locale (2) ... CO-8
Horn Ranch—locale ... WY-8
Horn Rapids—rapids ... MN-6
Horn Rapids—rapids ... WA-9
Horn Rapids Canal—canal ... WA-9
Horn Rapids County Park—park ... WA-9
Horn Rapids Dam—dam ... WA-9
Horn Rapids Ditch—canal ... WA-9
Horn Ridge—ridge ... AR-4
Horn Ridge Cem—cemetery ... TN-4
Hornridge Methodist Ch
(historical)—church ... TN-4
Horn RR Station—building ... AZ-5
Horn Rsvr—reservoir ... WY-8
Horn Run—stream ... PA-2
Horns—pop pl ... GA-3
Horns, The—summit ... CO-8
Horns, The—summit ... ME-1
Horns Bluff—summit ... TN-4
Hornsboro—locale ... SC-3
Horns Branch—stream ... AL-4
Horns Bridge (historical)—bridge ... AL-4
Hornsby ... TX-5
Hornsby—locale ... IL-6
Hornsby—pop pl ... TN-4
Hornsby, John A., House—hist pl ... KY-4
Hornsby Baptist Ch—church ... TN-4
Hornsby Bend—bend ... TX-5
Hornsby Bend—pop pl ... TX-5
Hornsby Branch—stream ... LA-4
Hornsby Branch—stream ... MO-7
Hornsby Bridge—hist pl ... KY-4
Hornsby (CCD)—cens area ... TN-4
Hornsby Cem ... TN-4
Hornsby Cem—cemetery ... AL-4
Hornsby Cem—cemetery ... GA-3
Hornsby Cem—cemetery ... MO-7
Hornsby Cem—cemetery (2) ... TN-4
Hornsby Cem—cemetery ... TX-5
Hornsby Chapel ... TN-4
Hornsby Chapel—cemetery ... TN-4
Hornsby Creek—stream ... GA-3
Hornsby Creek—stream ... LA-4
Hornsby Creek—stream (2) ... TX-5
Hornsby Division—civil ... TN-4
Hornsby Elem Sch—school ... TN-4
Hornsby Hollow—valley ... KY-4
Hornsby Hollow Rec Area—park ... TN-4
Hornsby Post Office—building ... TN-4
Hornsby Ranch—locale (2) ... NM-5
Hornsby Sch—school ... GA-3
Hornsbys Chapel Methodist Ch
(historical)—church ... TN-4
Hornsbys Ferry ... TN-4
Hornsby Spring—spring ... FL-3
Hornsby Spring—spring ... TN-4
Hornsbytown—pop pl ... AL-4
Hornsbyville—pop pl ... VA-3
Hornsbyville (Tampico)—pop pl ... VA-3
Horn Sch—school ... KY-4
Horn Sch—school ... PA-2
Horn Sch—school ... TX-5
Horn Sch (abandoned)—school ... MO-7
Horns Chapel Sch—school ... TX-5
Horn Sch (historical)—school ... AL-4
Horn Sch (historical)—school ... PA-2
Horns Corner—pop pl ... WI-6
Horns Corners—pop pl ... WI-6
Horns Creek—stream (2) ... FL-3
Horns Creek—stream ... TN-4
Horns Creek Sch (historical)—school ... TN-4
Horn Shanty Branch—stream ... PA-2
Horn Shanty Run ... PA-2
Horns Hill Park—park ... OH-6
Horn Siding—pop pl ... PA-2
Hornsilver Campground—locale ... CO-8
Horn Silver Gulch—valley ... UT-8
Horn Silver Mine ... NV-8
Horn Silver Mine—mine ... AZ-5
Hornsilver Mine—mine ... CO-8
Horn Silver Mine—mine ... ID-8
Horn Silver Mine—mine ... UT-8
Horn Silver Mine—mine ... WA-9
Hornsilver Mtn—summit ... CO-8
Horn Silver Wash ... UT-8
Horns Memorial Church ... AL-4
Horns Mill—pop pl ... OH-6
Horns Millrace—stream ... NC-3
Horns Mobile Village (trailer
park)—pop pl ... DE-2
Horns Mtn—summit ... WA-9
Horns Old Millpond—reservoir ... NC-3
Horn Spire—summit ... AK-9
Horns Pond—lake ... NH-1
Horns Pond, The—lake ... ME-1
Horn Spring ... NM-5
Horn Spring ... PA-2
Horn Spring—spring ... AZ-5
Horn Spring—spring ... CA-9
Horn Spring—spring ... CO-8
Horn Spring—spring ... FL-3
Horn Spring—spring ... GA-3
Horn Spring—spring ... ID-8
Horn Spring—spring ... NM-5
Horn Spring—spring ... OR-9
Horn Spring—spring ... TX-5
Horn Spring Branch—stream ... LA-4
Horn Spring Canyon—valley ... CO-8
Horn Spring Number Two—spring ... TN-4
Hornsprings ... TN-4
Horn Springs—locale ... TN-4
Horn Springs—spring ... CA-9
Horn Springs—spring ... PA-2
Horn Springs Branch—stream ... TN-4
Hornsprings Post Office
(historical)—building ... TN-4
Horns Ranch—locale ... TX-5
Horns River—stream ... KY-4
Hornstra Sch—school ... SD-7
Horns Valley—valley ... AL-4
Hornsville—locale ... FL-3
Hornswoggle Creek—stream ... CA-9
Horntavern Spring—spring ... TN-4
Hornton ... KY-4
Horntown ... PA-2
Horntown—locale (2) ... KY-4
Horntown—other ... PA-2
Horntown—pop pl ... OK-5
Horntown—pop pl ... VA-3
Horntown Bay—bay ... VA-3
Horntown Landing—locale ... VA-3
Horn Trail—trail ... PA-2
Horn Valley—valley ... AL-4
Horn Valley Ch—church ... AL-4
Hornville Mine—mine ... TN-4
Horn Waterhole—lake ... OR-9
Horn Well—well ... TX-5
Hornyhead Branch—stream ... AL-4
Hornyhead Branch—stream ... TN-4
Horny Head Creek—stream ... TN-4
Hornyhead Mtn—summit ... NC-3
Horotman Number 1 Dam—dam ... SD-7
Horowitz, Joe, House—hist pl ... AZ-5
Horp Cem—cemetery ... KY-4
Horr—locale ... MI-6
Horr, Benjamin, House—hist pl ... MO-7
Horr, Mount—summit ... CT-1
Horrace Williams Landing
(historical)—locale ... AL-4
Horr Cow Camp—locale ... WY-8
Horrel Hill—pop pl ... SC-3
Horrell—fmr MCD ... NE-7
Horrell—pop pl ... PA-2
Horrell Cem—cemetery ... MO-7
Horrell Creek—stream ... AZ-5
Horrell Creek—stream ... MO-7
Horrell Hill ... SC-3
Horrell Hill (CCD)—cens area ... SC-3
Horrell Ranch—locale ... AZ-5
Horrell Sch—school ... PA-2
Horrell Spring—spring (2) ... AZ-5
Horrel Ranch—locale ... AZ-5
Horrel Well—well ... AZ-5
Horrible Mine—mine ... AK-9
Horricks Spring—spring ... UT-8
Horrid, Mount—summit ... VT-1
Horrid Brook—stream ... VT-1
Horrigan—pop pl ... MI-6
Horrigan Hill—summit ... MN-6
Horrigan Ridge ... ND-7
Horrigan Ridge—ridge ... WI-6
Horrigans Siding—locale ... MI-6
Horring Cem—cemetery ... MS-4
Horris—pop pl ... SC-3
Horr Island ... FL-3
Horrock—locale ... WV-2
Horr Pond—lake ... CA-9
H Orr Ranch—locale ... NE-7
Horrs Four Corners—locale ... CA-9
Horrs Island—island ... FL-3
Horry—pop pl ... SC-3
Horry (County)—pop pl ... SC-3
Horry-Guignard House—hist pl ... SC-3
Horse and Black Creek Reservoir ... CO-8
Horse and Chaise Point—cape ... FL-3
Horse and Cow Meadow—flat ... CA-9
Horse and Poplar Branch—stream ... IN-6
Horseapple Cove—valley ... AL-4
Horseapple Creek—stream ... KY-4
Horseback ... PA-2
Horseback—ridge (2) ... ME-1
Horseback, The—ridge (3) ... ME-1
Horseback Cave—cave ... AL-4
Horseback Knob—summit ... OH-6
Horseback Pond—lake ... ME-1
Horseback Ridge—ridge ... CA-9
Horseback Ridge—ridge ... PA-2
Horseback Ridge—ridge ... TN-4
Horseback Ridge—ridge ... VT-1
Horse Barn—hist pl ... ID-8
Horse Barn Spring—spring ... CO-8
Horse Basin—basin ... AZ-5
Horse Basin—basin ... CO-8
Horse Basin—basin (4) ... ID-8
Horse Basin—basin (2) ... NV-8
Horse Basin Creek—stream ... CO-8
Horse Basin Creek—stream ... ID-8
Horse Basin Creek—stream ... OR-9
Horse Basin Rsvr—reservoir ... NV-8
Horse Basin Spring—spring (2) ... ID-8
Horse Basin Spring No 1—spring ... ID-8
Horse Basin Spring No 2—spring ... ID-8
Horse Basin Tanks—reservoir ... AZ-5
Horse Bay—gut ... LA-4
Horse Bay—swamp (2) ... SC-3
Horse Bayou—gut (2) ... LA-4
Horse Bayou—stream (2) ... LA-4
Horse Beef Point—cape ... ME-1
Horse Bench—bench (7) ... UT-8
Horse Bench Dam—dam ... UT-8
Horse Bench Rsvr—reservoir ... UT-8
Horse Bend—bend ... ID-8
Horse Bend Bluff ... GA-3
Horsebend Creek—stream ... SC-3
Horseblock Mountain—ridge ... AL-4
Horse Bluff—cliff ... NC-3
Horse Bluff—cliff ... SC-3
Horse Bluff—cliff ... WI-6
Horse Bluff Landing—locale ... NC-3
Horse Bluff Landing—pop pl ... LA-4
Horsebone—channel ... NC-3
Horse Bone Branch—stream ... SC-3
Horse Bone Branch—stream ... TN-4
Horse Bone Creek—stream ... OK-5
Horse Bone Flat—flat ... AZ-5
Horsebone Gap—gap ... GA-3
Horsebone Gap—gap ... NC-3
Horsebone Gap—gap ... WV-2
Horsebone Hollow—valley ... WV-2
Horsebone Ridge—ridge ... CA-9
Horsebone Ridge—ridge ... TN-4
Horse Bottom Creek—stream ... NC-3
Horse Bottom Ridge—ridge ... NC-3
Horse Branch ... GA-3
Horse Branch ... IL-6
Horse Branch—pop pl ... KY-4
Horse Branch—stream (4) ... AL-4
Horse Branch—stream (2) ... AR-4
Horse Branch—stream ... FL-3
Horse Branch—stream (5) ... GA-3
Horse Branch—stream ... IL-6
Horse Branch—stream (6) ... KY-4
Horse Branch—stream (6) ... LA-4
Horse Branch—stream (3) ... MS-4
Horse Branch—stream (12) ... NC-3
Horse Branch—stream ... OK-5
Horse Branch—stream (6) ... SC-3
Horse Branch—stream (3) ... TN-4
Horse Branch—stream (2) ... TX-5
Horse Branch—stream (3) ... VA-3
Horse Branch—stream (2) ... WV-2
Horse Branch (CCD)—cens area ... KY-4
Horse Branch Creek—stream ... NC-3
Horse Bridge Creek ... VA-3
Horsebridge Creek—stream ... MD-2
Horse Brook ... MA-1
Horse Brook—stream ... CT-1
Horse Brook—stream (2) ... ME-1
Horse Brook—stream (2) ... NH-1
Horse Brook—stream (2) ... NY-2
Horsebrook Sch—school ... MI-6
Horse Butte—crater ... ID-8
Horse Butte—summit ... AZ-5
Horse Butte—summit (2) ... ID-8
Horse Butte—summit (3) ... MT-8
Horse Butte—summit (3) ... OR-9
Horse Butte—summit (2) ... WY-8
Horse Butte Peninsula—cape ... MT-8
Horse Butte Sch—school ... SD-7
Horse Butte Township (historical)—civil ... SD-7
Horse Camp—locale (5) ... AZ-5
Horsecamp—locale ... AZ-5
Horse Camp—locale ... CA-9
Horse Camp—locale ... ID-8
Horsecamp—locale ... ID-8
Horse Camp—locale ... ID-8
Horse Camp—locale ... NC-3
Horse Camp Basin—basin ... AZ-5
Horse Camp Campsite—locale ... MO-7
Horse Camp Canyon—valley (2) ... AZ-5
Horsecamp Canyon—valley ... AZ-5
Horse Camp Canyon—valley ... CA-9
Horse Camp Canyon—valley ... NM-5
Horse Camp Corral—locale ... AZ-5
Horse Camp Coulee—valley ... MT-8
Horse Camp Coulee—valley ... ND-7
Horse Camp Creek—stream ... AZ-5
Horsecamp Creek—stream ... ID-8
Horse Camp Ditch—canal ... MT-8
Horse Camp Draw—arroyo ... AZ-5
Horse Camp Draw—valley (2) ... NM-5
Horse Camp Draw—valley ... SD-7
Horse Camp Mesa—summit ... AZ-5
Horse Camp Mesa Tank—reservoir ... AZ-5
Horsecamp Mtn—summit ... CA-9
Horse Camp Peak—summit ... NM-5
Horse Camp Peak—summit ... TX-5
Horse Camp Rim—cliff ... OR-9
Horse Camp Rsvr—reservoir ... CA-9
Horse Camp Rsvr—reservoir ... OR-9
Horsecamp Run—stream (2) ... WV-2
Horse Camp Seep—spring (2) ... AZ-5
Horse Camp Spring—spring (4) ... AZ-5
Horse Camp Spring—spring ... CA-9
Horse Camp Spring—spring ... NM-5
Horse Camp Spring—spring ... OR-9
Horse Camp Spring—spring ... TX-5
Horse Camp Springs—spring ... NV-8
Horse Camp Tank—reservoir ... AZ-5
Horse Camp Tank—reservoir ... TX-5
Horse Camp Tanks—reservoir ... AZ-5
Horse Camp Trail—trail ... MT-8
Horse Camp Wash—stream ... NV-8
Horse Camp Waterhole—lake ... TX-5
Horse Camp Well—well ... NV-8
Horse Camp Well—well ... NM-5
Horse Camp Wells—locale ... NM-5
Horse Camp Wells—well ... NM-5
Horse Camp Windmill—locale ... NM-5
Horse Canyon ... CA-9
Horse Canyon ... CO-8
Horse Canyon ... TX-5
Horse Canyon ... UT-8
Horse Canyon—pop pl ... UT-8
Horse Canyon—valley (12) ... AZ-5
Horse Canyon—valley (20) ... CA-9
Horse Canyon—valley (7) ... CO-8
Horse Canyon—valley ... ID-8
Horse Canyon—valley ... MT-8
Horse Canyon—valley ... NE-7
Horse Canyon—valley (20) ... NV-8
Horse Canyon—valley (17) ... NM-5
Horse Canyon—valley ... OK-5
Horse Canyon—valley ... OR-9
Horse Canyon—valley (5) ... TX-5
Horse Canyon—valley (20) ... UT-8
Horse Canyon—valley (2) ... WA-9
Horse Canyon—valley ... WY-8
Horse Canyon Agate Beds—flat ... CA-9
Horse Canyon Creek—stream ... MT-8
Horse Canyon Ranch—locale ... NM-5
Horse Canyon Ridge Tank—reservoir ... AZ-5
Horse Canyon Rsvr—reservoir ... UT-8
Horse Canyon Saddle—gap ... CA-9
Horse Canyon Spring—spring ... CA-9
Horse Canyon Spring—spring ... NV-8
Horse Canyon Spring—spring ... OR-9
Horse Canyon Springs—spring ... NV-8
Horse Canyon Tank—lake ... NM-5
Horse Canyon Tank—reservoir (3) ... AZ-5
Horse Canyon Tank—reservoir ... NM-5
Horse Canyon Trail Number Two hundred fifty
four—trail ... AZ-5
Horse Canyon Trail Thirty-six—trail ... AZ-5
Horse Canyon Well—well ... CA-9
Horse Canyon Well—well ... NM-5
Horse Cave ... TN-4
Horse Cave—cave ... AL-4
Horse Cave—cave ... OR-9
Horse Cave—pop pl ... KY-4
Horse Cave (CCD)—cens area ... KY-4
Horse Cave Creek—stream ... OH-6
Horse Cave Lookout Tower—locale ... KY-4
Horse Cave Run—stream ... WV-2
Horse Channel—channel ... NY-2
Horse Chock Brook—stream ... NY-2
Horse Chock Mtn—summit ... NY-2
Horsechoe Canyon Extension ... UT-8
Horse Cliffs ... UT-8
Horsecollar Branch—stream ... AL-4
Horse Collar Rock—pillar ... ID-8
Horse Collar Ruin—cave ... UT-8
Horse Collar Ruin—locale ... UT-8
Horse Collar Slough—swamp ... IL-6
Horsecorn Canyon—valley ... UT-8
Horse Corner—pop pl ... NH-1
Horse Corral Creek—stream ... CA-9
Horse Corral Meadow—flat ... CA-9
Horse Corral Pass—gap ... NV-8
Horse Corral Point—cliff ... AZ-5
Horse Corral Spring—spring (2) ... NV-8
Horse Coulee—valley (3) ... MT-8
Horse Cove ... ME-1
Horse Cove—basin ... NC-3
Horse Cove—bay ... ME-1
Horse Cove—valley ... AL-4
Horse Cove—valley (2) ... GA-3
Horse Cove—valley (4) ... NC-3
Horse Cove—valley (2) ... TN-4
Horse Cove Branch—stream ... KY-4
Horse Cove Branch—stream ... NC-3
Horsecove Branch—stream ... NC-3
Horse Cove Branch—stream ... NC-3
Horse Cove Cem—cemetery ... NC-3
Horse Cove Gap—gap ... NC-3
Horse Cove Gap—gap ... TN-4
Horse Cove Ridge—ridge (2) ... NC-3
Horse Creek ... AL-4
Horse Creek ... AZ-5
Horse Creek ... CA-9
Horse Creek ... CO-8
Horse Creek ... FL-3
Horse Creek ... GA-3
Horse Creek ... ID-8
Horse Creek ... LA-4
Horse Creek ... MT-8
Horse Creek ... NV-8
Horse Creek ... OR-9
Horsecreek ... TN-4
Horse Creek ... TX-5
Horse Creek ... UT-8
Horse Creek ... WV-2
Horse Creek ... WY-8
Horse Creek—locale ... TN-4
Horse Creek—pop pl ... CA-9
Horse Creek—pop pl ... TN-4
Horse Creek—pop pl ... WI-6
Horse Creek—pop pl ... WY-8
Horse Creek—stream (11) ... AL-4
Horse Creek—stream (3) ... AK-9
Horse Creek—stream (3) ... AZ-5
Horse Creek—stream (2) ... AR-4
Horse Creek—stream (20) ... CA-9
Horse Creek—stream (18) ... CO-8
Horse Creek—stream (3) ... FL-3
Horse Creek—stream (10) ... GA-3
Horse Creek—stream (18) ... ID-8
Horse Creek—stream (7) ... IL-6
Horse Creek—stream ... IN-6
Horse Creek—stream ... IA-7
Horse Creek—stream (5) ... KS-7
Horse Creek—stream (5) ... KY-4
Horse Creek—stream (3) ... LA-4
Horse Creek—stream ... MD-2
Horse Creek—stream ... MI-6
Horse Creek—stream (8) ... MS-4
Horse Creek—stream (4) ... MO-7
Horse Creek—stream (40) ... MT-8
Horse Creek*—stream ... NE-7
Horse Creek—stream (5) ... NE-7
Horse Creek—stream (10) ... NV-8
Horse Creek—stream ... NM-5
Horse Creek—stream ... NY-2
Horse Creek—stream (8) ... NC-3
Horse Creek—stream (7) ... ND-7
Horse Creek—stream ... OH-6
Horse Creek—stream (10) ... OK-5
Horse Creek—stream (24) ... OR-9
Horse Creek—stream ... PA-2
Horse Creek—stream (7) ... SC-3
Horse Creek—stream (8) ... SD-7
Horse Creek—stream (8) ... TN-4
Horse Creek—stream (24) ... TX-5
Horse Creek—stream (11) ... UT-8
Horse Creek—stream ... VA-3
Horse Creek—stream (4) ... WA-9
Horse Creek—stream (7) ... WV-2
Horse Creek—stream (3) ... WI-6
Horse Creek—stream (28) ... WY-8
Horse Creek—valley ... TX-5
Horse Creek and Black Draw
Ditch—canal ... CO-8
Horse Creek and Black Draw
Rsvr—reservoir ... CO-8
Horse Creek Arena—locale ... WY-8
Horse Creek Basin—basin ... WY-8
Horse Creek Basin Rsvr—reservoir ... MT-8
Horse Creek Boat Dock—locale ... TN-4
Horse Creek Bridge—bridge ... ID-8
Horse Creek Butte—summit ... ID-8
Horse Creek Butte—summit ... WY-8
Horse Creek Buttes—spring ... MT-8
Horse Creek Cabin—locale ... OR-9
Horse Creek Campground—locale ... TN-4
Horse Creek Cave—cave ... AL-4
Horse Creek Cem—cemetery ... AL-4
Horse Creek Cem—cemetery ... IL-6
Horse Creek Ch—church ... KY-4
Horse Creek Ch—church ... NC-3
Horse Creek Ch—church (2) ... TN-4
Horse Creek Ch—church ... WV-2
Horse Creek Cove—bay ... OK-5
Horse Creek Cow Camp—locale ... WY-8
Horse Creek Crossing Well—well ... MT-8
Horse Creek Ditch—canal ... IA-7
Horse Creek Ditch—canal ... MT-8
Horse Creek Ditch No 1—canal ... WY-8
Horse Creek Ditch No 2—canal ... WY-8
Horse Creek Ditch No 3—canal ... WY-8
Horse Creek Forest Camp—locale ... OR-9
Horse Creek Gap—gap ... NC-3
Horse Creek Grove—woods ... CA-9
Horse Creek Hill—summit ... MT-8
Horse Creek Hogback—summit ... WY-8
Horse Creek Junction—locale ... WV-2
Horse Creek Junction—pop pl ... KY-4
Horse Creek Lake—reservoir ... WV-2
Horse Creek Lakes—lake ... WY-8
Horse Creek Mesa—summit ... WY-8
Horse Creek Mine ... AL-4
Horse Creek Oil Field—oilfield ... WY-8
Horse Creek Pass—gap ... ID-8
Horse Creek Pass—gap ... MT-8
Horse Creek Pawnee Village—hist pl ... NE-7
Horse Creek Picnic Area—locale ... WY-8
Horse Creek Post Office
(historical)—building ... TN-4
Horse Creek Prairie—lake ... FL-3
Horse Creek Quarries—locale ... WY-8
Horse Creek Ranch—locale ... NV-8
Horse Creek Ranger Station—locale ... WY-8
Horse Creek Rec Area ... TN-4
Horse Creek Reservoir—lake ... CO-8
Horse Creek Reservoir Inlet Ditch—canal ... CO-8
Horse Creek Reservoir Outlet
Ditch—canal ... CO-8
Horse Creek Ridge ... CA-9
Horse creek Ridge ... TN-4
Horse Creek Ridge—ridge ... NC-3
Horse Creek Ridge—ridge ... WY-8
Horse Creek Rsvr—reservoir ... CO-8
Horse Creek Rsvr—reservoir ... WY-8
Horse Creek Sch—school ... CO-8
Horse Creek Sch—school ... ND-7
Horse Creek Sch—school ... SD-7
Horse Creek Sch—school ... TN-4
Horse Creek Siding—pop pl ... WY-8
Horse Creek Spring—spring (2) ... NV-8
Horse Creek Spring—spring ... NM-5
Horse Creek Spring—spring ... OR-9
Horse Creek Spring—spring ... TN-4
Horse Creek Springs—spring ... CO-8
Horse Creek Springs—spring ... WY-8
Horse Creek Supply Canal—canal ... CO-8
Horse Creek Tank—reservoir ... AZ-5
Horse Creek Top—summit ... UT-8
Horse Creek Township—pop pl ... SD-7
Horse Creek (Township of)—fmr MCD ... NC-3
Horse Creek Trail—trail (2) ... OR-9
Horse Creek Trail—trail ... WY-8
Horse Creek Valley—basin ... NV-8
Horse Creek Valley—valley ... AL-4
Horse Creek Well—well ... MT-8
Horse Creek Well—well ... NM-5
Horse Crossing—locale ... AZ-5
Horse Crossing Trail—trail ... AZ-5
Horse Ditch—gut ... MD-2
Horse Drain—canal ... CA-9
Horse Draw—valley (2) ... CO-8
Horse Draw—valley (2) ... NM-5
Horse Draw—valley (2) ... WY-8
Horse Draw Well—well ... CO-8
Horsefall Canyon—valley ... AZ-5
Horse Fall Creek—stream ... TX-5
Horse Falls Creek ... TX-5
Horsefish Lake—lake ... MN-6
Horse Flat ... CA-9
Horse Flat—flat ... AZ-5
Horse Flat—flat ... CA-9
Horse Flat—flat (4) ... ID-8
Horse Flat—flat (2) ... OR-9
Horse Flat—flat (5) ... UT-8
Horse Flat—pop pl ... CA-9
Horse Flat Canyon ... AZ-5
Horse Flat Canyon—valley ... AZ-5
Horseflat Canyon—valley ... UT-8
Horse Flat Creek—stream ... ID-8
Horse Flat Rsvr—reservoir ... OR-9
Horse Flats—flat ... CA-9
Horse Flats Campground—locale ... CA-9
Horse Flat Tank—reservoir ... AZ-5
Horsefly Bench—bench ... CO-8
Horse Fly Creek ... MT-8
Horsefly Creek—stream ... AK-9
Horsefly Creek—stream ... CO-8
Horsefly Creek—stream ... ID-8
Horsefly Creek—stream ... MT-8
Horsefly Ditch—canal ... WY-8
Horsefly Gulch—valley ... ID-8
Horsefly Hill—summit ... WA-9
Horsefly Lake—lake ... OR-9
Horsefly Meadows—flat ... ID-8
Horsefly Mtn—summit ... OR-9
Horsefly Park—flat ... CO-8
Horsefly Pass—gap ... WA-9
Horsefly Peak—summit ... CO-8
Horsefly Ridge—ridge ... CO-8
Horsefly Rsvr—reservoir ... OR-9
Horsefly Spring—spring ... ID-8
Horsefly Spring—spring ... MT-8
Horsefly Trail—trail ... CO-8
Horsefly Trail Rsvr No 1—reservoir ... CO-8
Horsefly Trail Rsvr No 2—reservoir ... CO-8
Horsefly Valley—flat ... OR-9
Horsefolds Brook ... MA-1
Horse Foot Cove—bay ... NJ-2
Horsefoot Mtn—summit ... AZ-5
Horse Foot Ranch—locale ... AZ-5
Horse Foot Wash—stream ... AZ-5
Horse Ford—locale ... GA-3
Horseford Branch—stream ... FL-3
Horse Ford Bridge—bridge ... SC-3
Horse Ford Creek—gut ... NC-3
Horse Ford Creek—gut ... SC-3
Horseford Creek—stream ... KY-4
Horseford Creek—stream ... NC-3
Horseford Hollow—valley ... TN-4
Horse Ford Lake—lake ... GA-3
Horsefords Brook—stream ... MA-1
Horse Fork—stream (3) ... KY-4
Horse Fork—stream ... MO-7
Horse Fork—stream ... PA-2
Horse Fork—stream ... TN-4
Horse Fork—stream ... UT-8
Horse Fork—stream (3) ... WV-2
Horse Fork Branch—stream ... WV-2
Horsefork Mtn—summit ... NC-3
Horsegall—pop pl ... SC-3
Horsegall Creek—stream ... SC-3
Horse Gap—gap ... GA-3
Horse Gap—gap ... NC-3
Horse Gap—gap ... PA-2
Horse Gap—gap (2) ... SC-3
Horse Gap—gap (2) ... TN-4
Horse Gap—locale ... VA-3
Horse Gap Mtn—summit ... SC-3
Horse Gap Ridge—ridge ... TN-4
Horse Gap Trail—trail ... PA-2
Horse Glade ... OR-9
Horse Glade—flat ... OR-9
Horse Glade Camp—locale ... CA-9
Horse Glade Spring ... OR-9
Horseglade Spring—spring ... OR-9
Horse Grove Point—cape ... TX-5
Horse Gulch ... WY-8
Horse Gulch—valley (4) ... CA-9
Horse Gulch—valley (8) ... CO-8
Horse Gulch—valley (5) ... MT-8
Horse Gulch—valley ... NV-8
Horse Gulch—valley (2) ... OR-9
Horse Gulch—valley ... WA-9
Horse Gulch—valley (2) ... WY-8
Horse Gulch Draw ... WY-8
Horse Gulch Spring—spring ... WA-9
Horse Hammock—island ... GA-3
Horse Hammock—island ... MD-2
Horse Hammock—island ... VA-3
Horse Hammock Gut—gut ... VA-3
Horse Hammock Point—cape ... VA-3
Horse Haven ... NM-5
Horse Haven Canyon ... NM-5
Horse Haven Summit—summit ... UT-8
Horsehead ... AL-4
Horsehead—locale ... AR-4
Horsehead—locale ... MD-2
Horse Head—pop pl ... VA-3
Horsehead Bay—bay ... WA-9
Horsehead Bayou—stream ... LA-4
Horse Head Branch ... AR-4
Horsehead Branch—stream ... AR-4
Horsehead Branch—stream ... MD-2
Horsehead Branch—stream ... SC-3
Horsehead Canyon—valley ... NM-5
Horsehead Canyon—valley ... TX-5
Horsehead Canyon—valley (2) ... UT-8
Horsehead Cem—cemetery ... SD-7
Horsehead Ch (historical)—church ... AL-4
Horsehead Cliffs—cliff ... VA-3
Horsehead Creek—gut ... SC-3
Horsehead Creek—stream (2) ... AL-4
Horsehead Creek—stream (4) ... AR-4
Horsehead Creek—stream ... FL-3
Horsehead Creek—stream ... GA-3
Horsehead Creek—stream (2) ... LA-4
Horsehead Creek*—stream ... NE-7
Horsehead Creek—stream ... NE-7
Horsehead Creek—stream ... ND-7
Horsehead Creek—stream ... OK-5
Horse Head Creek—stream ... OK-5
Horsehead Creek—stream (2) ... OR-9
Horse Head Creek—stream ... SD-7
Horsehead Creek—stream ... SD-7
Horsehead Creek—stream (2) ... WI-6
Horsehead Crossing—locale ... TX-5
Horsehead Draw—valley ... TX-5
Horsehead Gate—gap ... CA-9
Horsehead Hollow—valley ... PA-2
Horse Head Island ... ME-1
Horsehead Island—island ... ME-1
Horsehead Island—island ... SC-3
Horsehead Island—summit ... OR-9
Horsehead Knob—summit ... TN-4
Horsehead Knoll—summit ... MO-7
Horse Head Lake ... MI-6
Horsehead Lake ... UT-8
Horsehead Lake—lake (3) ... MI-6
Horsehead Lake—lake (3) ... MN-6
Horsehead Lake—lake ... ND-7
Horsehead Lake—lake ... OR-9
Horsehead Lake—lake (4) ... WI-6
Horsehead Lake—reservoir ... AR-4
Horsehead Lake—reservoir ... GA-3
Horsehead Lake—reservoir ... MS-4
Horsehead Mountain Overlook—locale ... VA-3
Horsehead Mtn—summit (2) ... CA-9
Horsehead Mtn—summit ... OK-5
Horsehead Mtn—summit ... OR-9
Horsehead Mtn—summit ... VA-3
Horsehead Oil Field—oilfield ... AR-4
Horsehead Pass—gap ... WA-9
Horsehead Peak—summit ... MT-8
Horsehead Peak—summit ... UT-8
Horsehead Point ... MD-2
Horsehead Point—cape ... MD-2
Horse Head Point—cape ... NY-2
Horse Head Point—cape ... VA-3
Horsehead Point—cliff ... UT-8
Horsehead Pond—lake ... FL-3
Horsehead Ranch—locale ... NE-7
Horsehead Ridge—ridge ... CA-9
Horsehead Rock—summit ... UT-8
Horsehead Run—stream ... FL-3
Horsehead Run—stream ... MD-2
Horseheads—pop pl ... NY-2
Horsehead Slough—gut ... AR-4
Horseheads North—CDP ... NY-2
Horsehead Spring—spring ... AZ-5
Horsehead Spring—spring ... CA-9
Horsehead Spring—spring ... FL-3
Horsehead Spring—spring (2) ... ID-8
Horsehead Spring—spring (2) ... OR-9
Horsehead Spring—spring ... UT-8
Horseheads (Town of)—pop pl ... NY-2
Horseheads 1855 Extension Hist
Dist—hist pl ... NY-2
Horsehead Tank—reservoir ... NM-5
Horsehead (Township of)—fmr MCD ... AR-4
Horsehead Tump—island ... MD-2
Horsehead Valley—valley ... ND-7
Horse Heaven—basin ... ID-8
Horse Heaven—basin ... NM-5
Horse Heaven—basin (3) ... UT-8
Horse Heaven—flat ... CA-9
Horse Heaven—flat (4) ... NV-8
Horse Heaven—flat ... OR-9
Horse Heaven—pop pl ... CT-1
Horseheaven—pop pl ... OR-9

Horseshoe Bend Landing (historical)—locale MS-4
Horseshoe Bend Mtn—summit CA-9
Horseshoe Bend Natl Military Park—hist pl AL-4
Horseshoe Bend Oil and Gas Field—oilfield UT-8
Horseshoe Bend Oil Field—oilfield UT-8
Horseshoe Bend Placer Claim—hist pl WA-9
Horseshoe Bend Pond—lake NE-7
Horse Shoe Bend Post Office (historical)—building TN-4
Horseshoe Bend Public Use Area—park AR-4
Horseshoe Bend Public Use Area—park OK-5
Horseshoe Bend Ranch—locale CO-8
Horseshoe Bend Rapids—rapids TN-4
Horseshoe Bend Sch—school SD-7
Horseshoe Bend Spring—spring OR-9
Horseshoe Bend Trail—trail PA-2
Horseshoe Bend Wash—stream AZ-5
Horseshoe Bend Windmill—locale NM-5
Horseshoe Bluff—cliff IL-6
Horseshoe Bluff—cliff IA-7
Horseshoe Bluff—cliff WI-6
Horseshoe Bog—swamp ME-1
Horseshoe Bottom—bend IL-6
Horse Shoe Brake MS-4
Horseshoe Brake—lake TX-5
Horseshoe Brake—swamp (2) AR-4
Horseshoe Brake—swamp LA-4
Horseshoe Brake—swamp (2) MS-4
Horseshoe Branch—stream AL-4
Horseshoe Branch—stream AR-4
Horseshoe Branch—stream FL-3
Horseshoe Branch—stream (2) KY-4
Horseshoe Branch—stream MS-4
Horseshoe Branch—stream MO-7
Horseshoe Branch—stream (2) TN-4
Horseshoe Branch—stream (4) VA-3
Horseshoe Branch—stream WV-2
Horseshoe Bridge—bridge (2) SC-3
Horseshoe Bridge—bridge VA-3
Horseshoe Brook—stream ME-1
Horseshoe Brook—stream NY-2
Horseshoe Butte—summit (2) ND-7
Horseshoe Butte—summit (2) OR-9
Horseshoe Butte—summit SD-7
Horseshoe Butte—summit TX-5
Horseshoe Butte—summit WY-8
Horseshoe Campground—locale CO-8
Horseshoe Canal—channel MI-6
Horseshoe Canyon UT-8
Horseshoe Canyon—valley (3) AZ-5
Horseshoe Canyon—valley CA-9
Horseshoe Canyon—valley CO-8
Horseshoe Canyon—valley ID-8
Horseshoe Canyon—valley IL-6
Horseshoe Canyon—valley NE-7
Horseshoe Canyon—valley NV-8
Horseshoe Canyon—valley OK-5
Horseshoe Canyon—valley TX-5
Horseshoe Canyon—valley (3) UT-8
Horseshoe Canyon—valley (2) WA-9
Horseshoe Canyon—valley WY-8
Horseshoe Canyon Camp—locale OK-5
Horseshoe Canyon Unit- Canyonlands Natl Park—park UT-8
Horseshoe Cave AL-4
Horseshoe Cave—cave AL-4
Horseshoe Cave—cave GA-3
Horseshoe Cave—cave ID-8
Horseshoe Cave—cave TN-4
Horseshoe Cave Canyon—valley NM-5
Horseshoe Cem—cemetery WY-8
Horseshoe Ch—church AR-4
Horseshoe Ch—church LA-4
Horseshoe Ch—church MS-4
Horseshoe Ch—church NC-3
Horseshoe Ch—church TN-4
Horseshoe Chapel—church MS-4
Horseshoe Chapel—church TN-4
Horseshoe Cienega—flat AZ-5
Horseshoe Cienega—swamp AZ-5
Horseshoe Cienega Lake—reservoir AZ-5
Horseshoe Cienega Lake Campground—park AZ-5
Horseshoe Cienega Lake Dam—dam AZ-5
Horseshoe Cliff—cliff TN-4
Horseshoe-Comet Mine—mine SD-7
Horseshoe Coulee—valley ND-7
Horseshoe Cove—bay AK-9
Horseshoe Cove—bay (2) CA-9
Horseshoe Cove—bay (2) FL-3
Horseshoe Cove—bay (3) ME-1
Horseshoe Cove—bay NJ-2
Horseshoe Cove—bay NY-2
Horseshoe Cove—valley CT-1
Horseshoe Crater—crater NM-5
Horseshoe Creek WY-8
Horseshoe Creek—gut FL-3
Horseshoe Creek—stream AL-4
Horseshoe Creek—stream (2) AK-9
Horseshoe Creek—stream AZ-5
Horseshoe Creek—stream CA-9
Horseshoe Creek—stream (3) CO-8
Horseshoe Creek—stream (2) FL-3
Horseshoe Creek—stream (4) ID-8
Horseshoe Creek—stream IL-6
Horseshoe Creek—stream KS-7
Horseshoe Creek—stream LA-4
Horseshoe Creek—stream (3) MI-6
Horseshoe Creek—stream MO-7
Horseshoe Creek—stream (2) MT-8
Horseshoe Creek*—stream NE-7
Horseshoe Creek—stream (7) OR-9
Horseshoe Creek—stream SC-3
Horseshoe Creek—stream TX-5
Horseshoe Creek—stream (2) WA-9
Horseshoe Creek—stream (2) WV-2
Horseshoe Creek—stream (2) WY-8
Horseshoe Creek Ch—church WV-2
Horseshoe Curve—bend OR-9
Horseshoe Curve—hist pl PA-2
Horseshoe Curve—locale MD-2
Horseshoe Curve—locale PA-2
Horseshoe Cutoff—bend IL-6
Horseshoe Cutoff—bend IN-6
Horseshoe Cutoff—lake TN-4
Horseshoe Dam SD-7
Horseshoe Dam—dam AZ-5
Horseshoe Dam—dam RI-1
Horseshoe Ditch—canal CO-8
Horseshoe Ditch—canal UT-8
Horseshoe Drainage Canal—canal LA-4
Horseshoe Drainage Ditch—canal NE-7
Horseshoe Draw—valley CO-8
Horseshoe Draw—valley NM-5
Horseshoe Draw—valley (2) TX-5
Horseshoe Draw—valley WY-8
Horseshoe Drive Sch—school LA-4
Horseshoe Falls TN-4
Horseshoe Falls—falls CO-8
Horseshoe Falls—falls IN-6
Horseshoe Falls—falls NE-7
Horseshoe Falls—falls NY-2
Horseshoe Falls—falls (2) OR-9
Horseshoe Falls—falls TX-5
Horseshoe Falls—falls WA-9
Horseshoe Falls—falls WI-6
Horseshoe Falls Dam—dam RI-1
**Horseshoe Falls (historical)**—pop pl TN-4
Horseshoe Falls Light—locale OR-9
Horse Shoe Falls Post Office (historical)—building TN-4
Horseshoe Flat NE-7
Horseshoe Flat—flat CA-9
Horseshoe Flat—flat UT-8
Horse Shoe Ford TN-4
Horseshoe Ford (historical)—crossing TN-4
Horseshoe Gap—gap AL-4
Horseshoe Gap—gap KY-4
Horseshoe Gap—gap VA-3
Horseshoe Grove (historical)—locale SD-7
Horseshoe Gulch—valley AZ-5
Horseshoe Gulch—valley (2) CA-9
Horseshoe Gulch—valley (2) CO-8
Horseshoe Gulch—valley ID-8
Horseshoe Gulch—valley OR-9
Horseshoe Gully—valley TX-5
Horseshoe Harbor—bay MI-6
Horseshoe Harbor—bay NY-2
Horseshoe Head—island FL-3
**Horseshoe Heights**—pop pl PA-2
Horseshoe Hill SD-7
**Horseshoe Hill**—pop pl DE-2
**Horseshoe Hill**—pop pl NY-2
Horseshoe Hill—summit AZ-5
Horseshoe Hill—summit DE-2
Horseshoe Hill—summit KS-7
Horseshoe Hill—summit TN-4
Horseshoe Hill—summit TX-5
Horseshoe Hill—summit UT-8
Horseshoe Hill—summit WY-8
Horseshoe Hills—range WY-8
Horseshoe Hills—spring MT-8
Horseshoe Hollow—valley IL-6
Horseshoe Hollow—valley TN-4
Horseshoe Hollow—valley UT-8
Horseshoe House—locale CO-8
Horseshoe Island—cape OR-9
Horseshoe Island—island (2) AK-9
Horseshoe Island—island (2) FL-3
Horseshoe Island—island (2) GA-3
Horseshoe Island—island ME-1
Horseshoe Island—island (2) MI-6
Horseshoe Island—island (3) MN-6
Horseshoe Island—island NH-1
Horseshoe Island—island NY-2
Horseshoe Island—island OH-6
Horseshoe Island—island (2) OR-9
Horseshoe Island—island (2) WI-6
Horseshoe Key FL-3
Horseshoe Key—island FL-3
Horseshoe Keys—island (2) FL-3
Horseshoe Lagoon—lake CT-1
Horseshoe Lake AR-4
Horseshoe Lake LA-4
Horseshoe Lake MI-6
Horseshoe Lake MN-6
Horse Shoe Lake MS-4
Horse Shoe Lake NM-5
Horseshoe Lake OR-9
Horseshoe Lake WA-9
Horseshoe Lake WI-6
Horseshoe Lake—lake AL-4
Horseshoe Lake—lake (4) AK-9
Horseshoe Lake—lake AZ-5
Horseshoe Lake—lake (22) AR-4
Horseshoe Lake—lake (10) CA-9
Horseshoe Lake—lake (4) CO-8
Horseshoe Lake—lake (12) FL-3
Horseshoe Lake—lake (4) ID-8
Horseshoe Lake—lake (14) IL-6
Horseshoe Lake—lake IN-6
Horseshoe Lake—lake IA-7
Horse Shoe Lake—lake IA-7
Horseshoe Lake—lake (3) IA-7
Horseshoe Lake—lake (3) KS-7
Horseshoe Lake—lake KY-4
Horseshoe Lake—lake (24) LA-4
Horseshoe Lake—lake (3) ME-1
Horseshoe Lake—lake (30) MI-6
Horseshoe Lake—lake (57) MN-6
Horseshoe Lake—lake (27) MS-4
Horseshoe Lake—lake (17) MO-7
Horseshoe Lake—lake (5) MT-8
Horse Shoe Lake—lake MT-8
Horseshoe Lake—lake (3) MT-8
Horseshoe Lake—lake (2) NE-7
Horseshoe Lake—lake NJ-2
Horse Shoe Lake—lake NM-5
Horseshoe Lake—lake (3) NM-5
Horseshoe Lake—lake (2) NY-2
Horseshoe Lake—lake NC-3
Horseshoe Lake—lake (9) ND-7
Horseshoe Lake—lake (7) OK-5
Horseshoe Lake—lake (5) OR-9
Horseshoe Lake—lake (3) SC-3
Horseshoe Lake—lake (3) SD-7
Horse Shoe Lake—lake SD-7
Horseshoe Lake—lake (5) SD-7
Horseshoe Lake—lake (6) TN-4
Horseshoe Lake—lake (32) TX-5
Horseshoe Lake—lake (3) UT-8
Horseshoe Lake—lake (19) WA-9
Horseshoe Lake—lake (11) WI-6
Horse Shoe Lake—lake WI-6
Horseshoe Lake—lake (14) WI-6
Horseshoe Lake—lake (4) WY-8
**Horseshoe Lake**—pop pl AR-4
**Horseshoe Lake**—pop pl WA-9
Horseshoe Lake—reservoir CA-9
Horseshoe Lake—reservoir CO-8
Horseshoe Lake—reservoir IN-6
Horseshoe Lake—reservoir LA-4
Horseshoe Lake—reservoir NE-7
Horseshoe Lake—reservoir NY-2
Horseshoe Lake—reservoir NC-3
Horseshoe Lake—reservoir OR-9
Horseshoe Lake—reservoir PA-2
Horseshoe Lake—reservoir (3) TX-5
Horseshoe Lake—reservoir VA-3
Horseshoe Lake—swamp (3) AR-4
Horseshoe Lake—swamp (2) LA-4
Horseshoe Lake—swamp MI-6
Horseshoe Lake—swamp MS-4
Horseshoe Lake—swamp NE-7
Horseshoe Lake—swamp TX-5
Horseshoe Lake Bayou—gut AR-4
Horseshoe Lake Club—other AR-4
Horseshoe Lake Cut -Off—bend MS-4
Horseshoe Lake Dam—dam NC-3
Horseshoe Lake Lookout Tower—locale ID-8
Horseshoe Lake Mound and Village Site—hist pl IL-6
Horseshoe Lake Ranger Station—hist pl CA-9
Horseshoe Lakes AR-4
Horseshoe Lakes MS-4
Horseshoe Lakes—lake CA-9
Horseshoe Lakes—lake IN-6
Horseshoe Lake State Conservation Area—park IL-6
Horseshoe Lake State Public Shooting Area—park (2) SD-7
Horseshoe Lake Trail—trail WY-8
Horseshoe Lead—channel VA-3
Horseshoe Lead Creek—stream SC-3
Horseshoe Ledge—bar ME-1
Horseshoe Little Oak Flat, The—flat CA-9
Horseshoe Lode—mine OR-9
Horseshoe Lookout Tower—tower FL-3
Horseshoe Lot—bend NY-2
Horseshoe Marsh—swamp FL-3
Horseshoe Marsh—swamp MI-6
Horseshoe Marsh—swamp NV-8
Horseshoe Marsh—swamp TX-5
Horseshoe Meadow—flat CA-9
Horseshoe Meadow—flat NE-7
Horseshoe Meadow—flat OR-9
Horseshoe Meadow—flat WA-9
Horseshoe Meadows—flat CA-9
Horseshoe Mesa—flat CO-8
Horseshoe Mesa—summit AZ-5
Horseshoe Mesa—summit (2) TX-5
Horseshoe Mesa Caves—cave AZ-5
Horseshoe Mine—mine AZ-5
Horseshoe Mine—mine CA-9
Horseshoe Mine—mine ID-8
Horseshoe Mine—mine NV-8
Horseshoe Mine—mine NM-5
Horseshoe Mine—mine WA-9
Horseshoe Mobile Home Park—locale AZ-5
Horseshoe Mound—hist pl OH-6
Horseshoe Mound—summit IL-6
Horseshoe Mountain—ridge (2) AR-4
Horseshoe Mountain Lookout Tower—locale ME-1
Horseshoe Mtn NC-3
Horseshoe Mtn—summit AL-4
Horseshoe Mtn—summit AK-9
Horseshoe Mtn—summit (4) AR-4
Horseshoe Mtn—summit (3) CO-8
Horseshoe Mtn—summit ME-1
Horseshoe Mtn—summit MT-8
Horseshoe Mtn—summit NV-8
Horseshoe Mtn—summit NM-5
Horseshoe Mtn—summit NY-2
Horseshoe Mtn—summit NC-3
Horse Shoe Mtn—summit NC-3
Horseshoe Mtn—summit OK-5
Horseshoe Mtn—summit SC-3
Horseshoe Mtn—summit (3) TN-4
Horseshoe Mtn—summit VA-3
Horseshoe Mtn—summit (2) WA-9
Horseshoe Mtn—summit WV-2
Horseshoe Mtn—summit WY-8
Horseshoe Mud Lake—lake FL-3
Horseshoe Neck—bend NC-3
Horseshoe Oil Field—oilfield LA-4
Horseshoe Park—flat (2) CO-8
Horseshoe Park—flat UT-8
Horseshoe Park—park SD-7
Horseshoe Pass AZ-5
Horseshoe Pass—gap AZ-5
Horseshoe Pass—gap WA-9
Horseshoe Peak AZ-5
Horseshoe Peak—summit ID-8
Horseshoe Peak—summit MT-8
Horseshoe Peak—summit WA-9
Horseshoe Point—cape AK-9
Horseshoe Point—cape CA-9
Horseshoe Point—cape (3) FL-3
Horseshoe Point—cape (3) MD-2
Horseshoe Point—cape (2) RI-1
Horseshoe Point—cape TN-4
Horseshoe Point—cape VA-3
Horseshoe Point—cape WI-6
Horseshoe Point—cliff AZ-5
Horseshoe Point—summit WA-9
Horse Shoe Pond IN-6
Horseshoe Pond NV-8
Horse Shoe Pond PA-2
Horseshoe Pond—bay LA-4
Horseshoe Pond—lake AL-4
Horseshoe Pond—lake AR-4
Horseshoe Pond—lake CT-1
Horseshoe Pond—lake DE-2
Horseshoe Pond—lake FL-3
Horseshoe Pond—lake (4) IL-6
Horseshoe Pond—lake (2) IN-6
Horseshoe Pond—lake (2) KY-4
Horseshoe Pond—lake (19) ME-1
Horseshoe Pond—lake MA-1
Horseshoe Pond—lake MI-6
Horseshoe Pond—lake (4) NH-1
Horseshoe Pond—lake (8) NY-2
Horseshoe Pond—lake PA-2
Horseshoe Pond—lake TN-4
Horseshoe Pond—lake UT-8
Horseshoe Pond—lake VA-3
Horseshoe Pond—lake WA-9
Horseshoe Pond—reservoir MA-1
Horseshoe Pond Brook—stream NY-2
Horseshoe Pond Dam—dam MA-1
Horseshoe Pond (historical)—lake TN-4
Horseshoe Pony Express Station—locale WY-8
Horseshoe Prairie—flat OR-9
Horseshoe Ranch NV-8
Horseshoe Ranch—locale (2) AZ-5
Horseshoe Ranch—locale (2) CA-9
Horseshoe Ranch—locale NV-8
Horseshoe Ranch—locale OK-5
Horseshoe Ranch—locale WY-8
Horseshoe Range—channel PA-2
Horseshoe Ranger Station—locale CO-8
Horseshoe Rapids—rapids AZ-5
Horseshoe Reef NY-2
Horseshoe Reef—bar CT-1
Horseshoe Reef—bar MI-6
Horseshoe Reef—bar NY-2
Horseshoe Reef—bar WI-6
Horseshoe Reefs—bar WI-6
Horseshoe Revetment—levee MS-4
Horseshoe Ridge—ridge GA-3
Horseshoe Ridge—ridge (2) NC-3
Horseshoe Ridge—ridge OK-5
Horseshoe Ridge—ridge (3) OR-9
Horseshoe Ridge—ridge (2) TN-4
Horseshoe Ridge—ridge UT-8
Horseshoe Ridge—ridge WA-9
Horseshoe Ridge—ridge WY-8
Horseshoe Ridge Trail—trail OR-9
Horseshoe Ridge Trail—trail WA-9
Horseshoe Rim—cliff OR-9
Horseshoe River ME-1
Horseshoe Rock—cliff NC-3
Horseshoe Rock—pillar NV-8
Horseshoe Rsvr—reservoir (2) AZ-5
Horseshoe Rsvr—reservoir (2) ID-8
Horseshoe Rsvr—reservoir NV-8
Horseshoe Rsvr—reservoir (2) OR-9
Horseshoe Run WV-2
**Horse Shoe Run**—pop pl WV-2
Horseshoe Run—stream (2) WV-2
Horseshoe Run YMCA Camp—locale WV-2
Horseshoe Sch—school MI-6
Horseshoe Sch (historical)—school TN-4
Horseshoe Shoal—bar (2) MA-1
Horseshoe Shoal—bar NC-3
Horseshoe Shoal—bar PA-2
Horseshoe Shoal—bar VT-1
Horseshoe Shoals—bar GA-3
Horseshoe Slough—gut (2) AR-4
Horseshoe Slough—gut IL-6
Horseshoe Slough—gut (3) TX-5
Horseshoe Slough—gut WA-9
Horseshoe Slough—lake TX-5
Horseshoe Slough—stream AR-4
Horseshoe Slough—stream MO-7
Horseshoe Sloughs—lake UT-8
Horseshoe Spring—spring (2) AZ-5
Horseshoe Spring—spring (3) CA-9
Horseshoe Spring—spring ID-8
Horseshoe Spring—spring (2) NM-5
Horseshoe Spring—spring (4) OR-9
Horseshoe Spring—spring UT-8
Horseshoe Spring—spring WA-9
Horseshoe Spring—spring WY-8
Horseshoe Springs—spring TX-5
Horseshoe Springs—spring UT-8
Horseshoe Springs Campground—locale NM-5
Horseshoe Stream—stream ME-1
Horseshoe Sulfur Trail—trail CO-8
Horseshoe Swamp MS-4
Horseshoe Swamp—stream NC-3
Horseshoe Swamp—swamp GA-3
Horse Shoe Swamp—swamp PA-2
Horseshoe Swamp—swamp (2) PA-2
Horseshoes Windmill—locale TX-5
Horseshoe Tank—lake NM-5
Horseshoe Tank—reservoir (11) AZ-5
Horseshoe Tank—reservoir (2) NM-5
Horse Shoe Tank—reservoir NM-5
Horseshoe Tank—reservoir (2) NM-5
Horseshoe Tank—reservoir (12) TX-5
Horseshoe Tank Number Four—reservoir AZ-5
Horseshoe Tank Number One—reservoir AZ-5
Horseshoe Tank Number Three—reservoir AZ-5
Horseshoe Tank Number Two—reservoir AZ-5
Horseshoe Terrace Dam—dam NM-5
Horseshoe Trail—trail (5) PA-2
Horseshoe Tunnel—tunnel UT-8
Horseshoe Valley—valley MO-7
Horseshoe Valley—valley NE-7
Horseshoe Valley—valley ND-7
**Horseshoe Valley Township**—pop pl ND-7
Horseshoe Wash—stream NM-5
Horseshoe Wash—valley WY-8
Horseshoe Well—well AZ-5
Horseshoe Well—well NV-8
Horseshoe Windmill—locale (5) TX-5
Horseshoe 4—lake GA-3
Horseshoe 5—lake GA-3
Horseshor Bend Lake—lake NE-7
Horseshutem Springs—spring NV-8
Horse Sign Butte—summit OR-9
Horse Sign Creek—stream OR-9
Horse Sign Creek Rapids—rapids OR-9
Horseskull Bay—swamp SC-3
Horse Skull Cave—cave AL-4
Horse Spring CA-9
Horse Spring NM-5
Horse Spring—spring (10) AZ-5
Horse Spring—spring (2) CA-9
Horse Spring—spring (2) CO-8
Horse Spring—spring (3) ID-8
Horse Spring—spring (13) NV-8
Horse Spring—spring (4) NM-5
Horse Spring—spring (8) OR-9
Horse Spring—spring (3) UT-8
Horse Spring—spring WY-8
Horse Spring Branch TN-4
Horse Spring Camp—locale OR-9
Horse Spring Campground—locale CA-9
Horse Spring Canyon—valley AZ-5
Horse Spring Canyon—valley TX-5
Horse Spring Canyon—valley UT-8
Horse Spring Draw UT-8
Horse Spring Gulch—valley ID-8
Horse Spring Hills—summit NV-8
Horse Spring Point—cliff AZ-5
Horse Springs—spring AZ-5
Horse Springs—spring CA-9
Horse Springs—spring CO-8
Horse Springs—spring ID-8
Horse Springs—spring (2) NV-8
Horse Springs Canyon—valley NV-8
Horse Springs Coulee—valley WA-9
Horse Springs Draw—valley WY-8
**Horse Springs (Old Horse Springs)**—pop pl NM-5
Horse Springs Store—locale NM-5
Horsespring Tank—reservoir AZ-5
Horse Spring Trail—trail CA-9
Horse Spring Wash—stream NV-8
Horse Stable Mtn—summit NY-2
Horse Stable Rock—summit NY-2
Horse Stamp Cem—cemetery GA-3
Horse Stamp Ch—church GA-3
Horse Stomp Gap—gap NC-3
Horse State Wildlife Mngmt Area—park MN-6
Horse Stomp Campground—locale AL-4
**Horse Store, The**—pop pl UT-8
Horse Swamp—stream NC-3
Horse Swamp—swamp (2) NC-3
Horse Swamp—swamp SC-3
Horse Swamp—swamp VA-3
Horsetail Creek—stream AK-9
Horsetail Creek—stream CO-8
Horsetail Creek—stream (2) OR-9
Horsetail Creek—stream WA-9
Horsetail Creek—stream WY-8
Horse Tail Falls MT-8
Horsetail Falls WA-9
Horsetail Falls—falls (2) CA-9
Horsetail Falls—falls MT-8
Horsetail Falls—falls OR-9
Horsetail Falls—falls WA-9
Horsetail Falls Creek—stream AK-9
Horsetail Gulch—valley CA-9
Horsetail Lake—lake IL-6
Horsetail Rapids—RAPIDS MN-6
Horsetail Rsvr—reservoir (2) OR-9
Horsetail Run—stream OH-6
Horse Tank—reservoir (14) AZ-5
Horse Tank—reservoir (5) NM-5
Horse Tank Creek—stream AZ-5
Horse Tank Number Two—reservoir AZ-5
Horse Tanks—reservoir AZ-5
Horse Tanks—reservoir UT-8
Horse Tank Wash AZ-5
Horsetank Wash—stream AZ-5
Horse Tavern Branch—stream MD-2
Horse Tavern Brook—stream CT-1
Horse Theif Mesa—summit AZ-5
**Horse Thief**—pop pl AZ-5
Horsethief Basin—basin AZ-5
Horsethief Basin—basin ID-8
Horsethief Basin—basin WA-9
Horsethief Basin Rec Area—park AZ-5
Horsethief Bench—bench AZ-5
Horsethief Bluff—cliff MO-7
Horsethief Bottom—bend UT-8
Horsethief Butte—summit CA-9
Horsethief Butte—summit WA-9
Horsethief Canyon—valley (3) AZ-5
Horsethief Canyon—valley (2) CA-9
Horse Thief Canyon—valley CA-9
Horsethief Canyon—valley (10) CA-9
Horse Thief Canyon—valley CO-8
Horsethief Canyon—valley CO-8
Horsethief Canyon—valley ID-8
Horse Thief Canyon—valley KS-7
Horsethief Canyon—valley KS-7
Horsethief Canyon—valley MT-8
Horsethief Canyon—valley (2) NV-8
Horse Thief Canyon—valley OK-5
Horse Thief Canyon—valley TX-5
Horsethief Canyon—valley (2) UT-8
Horsethief Canyon—valley WA-9
Horsethief Canyon—valley (3) WY-8
Horsethief Canyons—valley NE-7
Horsethief Cave—cave KS-7
Horsethief Cave—cave WA-9
Horse Thief Cave—cave WY-8
Horsethief Coulee—valley MT-8
Horse Thief Coulee—valley WI-6
Horsethief Cove—valley TX-5
Horse Thief Creek MT-8
Horsethief Creek—stream AZ-5
Horsethief Creek—stream (3) CA-9
Horsethief Creek—stream (2) CO-8
Horsethief Creek—stream (3) ID-8
Horse Thief Creek—stream ID-8
Horsethief Creek—stream MT-8
Horsethief Creek—stream NM-5
Horsethief Creek—stream SD-7
Horse Thief Creek—stream TX-5
Horsethief Dam—dam AZ-5
Horsethief Draw—valley KS-7
Horsethief Flat—flat (2) CA-9
Horse Thief Gap—gap NM-5
Horsethief Guard Station—locale AZ-5
Horsethief Gulch—valley CO-8
Horsethief Gulch—valley NV-8
Horsethief Gulch—valley (2) WY-8
Horsethief Lake SD-7
Horse Thief Lake—dam SD-7
Horsethief Lake—lake CO-8
Horsethief Lake—reservoir AZ-5
Horse Thief Lake—reservoir SD-7
Horsethief Lake State Park—park WA-9
Horsethief Lookout Tower—tower AZ-5
Horsethief Meadow—area NM-5
Horsethief Meadows—flat OR-9
Horse Thief Mountain MT-8
Horsethief Mtn—summit CA-9
Horsethief Mtn—summit (2) CO-8
Horsethief Mtn—summit MT-8
Horsethief Mtn—summit NV-8
Horse Thief Mtn—summit TX-5
Horsethief Opening—flat CA-9
Horsethief Park—flat CO-8
Horse Thief Park—flat (2) CO-8
Horsethief Park—flat CO-8
Horsethief Park—flat MT-8
Horsethief Pass—gap CO-8
Horse Thief Pasture—flat CO-8
Horse Thief Peak—summit CO-8
Horsethief Point—ridge UT-8
Horsethief Point—summit WA-9
Horsethief Ridge—ridge CA-9
Horsethief Ridge—summit MT-8
Horsethief Ridge Trail—trail CA-9
Horsethief Rsvr—reservoir ID-8
Horse Thief Run—stream PA-2
Horse Thief Spring—spring CA-9
Horsethief Spring—spring CO-8
Horsethief Spring—spring MT-8
Horsethief Spring—spring NV-8
Horse Thief Spring—spring TX-5
Horsethief Spring—spring UT-8
Horse Thief Springs—spring CA-9
Horsethief Springs—spring WY-8
Horsethief Tank—reservoir (2) AZ-5
Horsethief Trail—trail CA-9
Horsethief Trail—trail CO-8
Horsethief Trail—trail UT-8
Horse Tie, The—ridge TN-4
Horse Tied Creek—stream MT-8
Horse Tied Creek—stream ND-7
Horse Tooth—pillar WY-8
Horsetooth Dam—dam CO-8
Horsetooth Gully—valley TX-5
**Horsetooth Heights**—pop pl CO-8
Horsetooth Mtn—summit CO-8
Horsetooth Peak—summit CO-8
Horsetooth Rsvr—reservoir CO-8
Horse Track Canyon—valley AZ-5
Horse Track Ridge—ridge WY-8
Horse Track Spring—spring NV-8
Horse Track Spring—spring WY-8
Horse Trail—trail CA-9
Horse Trail—trail UT-8
Horse Trail Campground—locale CA-9
Horse Trail Canyon—valley (2) UT-8
Horse Trail Gap—gap NC-3
Horse Trail Lake—lake AK-9
Horse Trail Ridge—ridge CA-9
Horse Trail Valley—valley AZ-5
Horse Trap Canyon—valley (2) AZ-5
Horse Trap Draw—valley WY-8
Horse Trap Hill—summit AZ-5
Horse Trap Lake—lake AZ-5
Horse Trap Mesa—summit AZ-5
Horse Trap Mtn—summit SD-7
Horsetrap Rsvr—reservoir UT-8
Horse Trap Rsvr—reservoir WY-8
Horse Trap Sink—reservoir AZ-5
Horse Trap Spring—spring OR-9
Horsetrap Spring—spring TX-5
Horsetrap Tank—reservoir AZ-5
Horse Trap Tank—reservoir (2) AZ-5
Horse Trap Tank—reservoir NM-5
Horse Trap Tank—reservoir (4) TX-5
Horse Trap Well—well NM-5
Horse Trough Canyon—valley WA-9
Horsetrough Creek—stream AL-4
Horse Trough Creek—stream CA-9
Horse Trough Creek—stream LA-4
Horsetrough Falls—falls GA-3
Horse Trough Hollow—valley MO-7
Horse Trough Hollow—valley TN-4
Horse Trough Hollow—valley VA-3
Horse Trough Mtn GA-3
Horsetrough Mtn—summit GA-3
Horse Trough Ridge—ridge CA-9
Horsetrough Ridge—ridge NC-3
Horsetrough Ridge Overlook—locale NC-3
Horse Trough Spring—spring AZ-5
Horsetrough Spring—spring CA-9
Horse Valley AZ-5
Horse Valley—basin AZ-5
Horse Valley—basin (6) UT-8
Horse Valley—valley (3) CA-9
Horse Valley—valley ID-8
Horse Valley—valley NV-8
Horse Valley—valley (2) PA-2
Horse Valley—valley (4) UT-8
Horse Valley Bridge—hist pl PA-2
Horse Valley Cem—cemetery PA-2
Horse Valley Ch—church PA-2
Horse Valley Creek—stream CA-9
Horse Valley Peak—summit (2) UT-8
Horse Valley Ranch—hist pl AZ-5
Horse Valley Ranch—locale TX-5
Horse Valley Run—stream PA-2
Horse Valley Wash—valley UT-8
Horse Wallow—basin ID-8
Horse Wash—stream AZ-5
Horse Wash—stream NV-8
Horse Wash Springs—spring AZ-5
Horsewater Ridge—ridge AR-4
Horse Water Tanks—reservoir AZ-5
Horseway Swamp—stream NC-3
Horse Well—well NM-5
Horse Well—well TX-5
Horse Well Draw—valley TX-5
Horse Wells—well TX-5
Horse Windmill—locale TX-5
Horsey—locale VA-3
Horsey-Barthelmas Farm—hist pl OH-6
Horsey Ch—church DE-2
Horseys DE-2
Horseys Cross Roads DE-2
Horseys Pond—reservoir DE-2
Horsfall Lake—lake OR-9
Horsfeld Creek—stream AK-9
Horsford Spring—spring MT-8
**Horsham**—pop pl PA-2
Horsham-Montgomery Bridge—hist pl PA-2
Horsham Ridge Industrial Center—locale PA-2
**Horsham (Township of)**—pop pl PA-2
Horsham Township Police Airp—airport PA-2
Horsham Valley Golf Course—locale PA-2
Horsham Valley Golf Course Airp—airport PA-2
Horsham Valley Industrial Park—locale PA-2
Horsham Valley Township Park—park PA-2
Horshamville PA-2
Horshoe Lake (historical)—lake AL-4
Horshoe Meadow OR-9
Horshoe Mine—mine CA-9
Horsley TN-4
Horsley Branch—stream (2) KY-4
Horsley Cem—cemetery KY-4
Horsley Chapel—church KY-4
Horsley Creek—stream TX-5
Horsley Creek—stream VA-3
Horsley Draw—valley WY-8
Horsley Lake—reservoir AL-4

Horsleys—locale TN-4
Horsley Sch (historical)—school TN-4
Horsleys Number 2 Mine (underground)—mine AL-4
Horsman Ditch—canal CA-9
Horsman Ditch—canal KY-4
Horst, Martin, House—hist pl AL-4
Horst Airp—airport PA-2
Horst Cove—cave PA-2
Horst Cem—cemetery CO-8
Horst Cem—cemetery TN-4
Horstman Creek—stream MO-7
Horstman Drain—canal ID-8
Horstmann Lake—lake IL-6
Horstmann Peak—summit ID-8
Horstman Sch—school IA-7
Horst Pond—reservoir AL-4
**Horstville**—pop pl CA-9
Horswill Sch—school WI-6
Horten Lake—lake WI-6
Hortense—locale TN-4
Hortense—locale TX-5
**Hortense**—pop pl GA-3
**Hortense**—pop pl MO-7
Hortense Bridge—hist pl CO-8
Hortense Ch—church TX-5
Hortense Hot Spring—spring CO-8
Hortense Lake—lake CA-9
Hortense Lake—lake OR-9
Hortense Memorial Ch—church GA-3
Hortense Mine—mine CO-8
Hortense Post Office (historical)—building TN-4
Hortense Sch—school MO-7
Hortenstine Cem—cemetery VA-3
Horte Rsvr—reservoir MT-8
Horticulture and Agricultural Physics and Soil Science Bldg—hist pl WI-6
Horticulture Bldg—hist pl MN-6
Horticulture Hall—building MA-1
Hortill Creek—stream OR-9
Horting Run—stream PA-2
Hortin Lake—lake MI-6
Hortin Slough—gut IL-6
Horti Point—cape FL-3
Hortman—locale LA-4
*Horton* IN-6
Horton—locale AL-4
Horton—locale KY-4
Horton—locale MN-6
Horton—locale MT-8
Horton—locale NY-2
Horton—locale (2) OH-6
Horton—locale OR-9
Horton—locale (2) TX-5
Horton—locale VA-3
Horton—locale WV-2
**Horton**—pop pl AL-4
**Horton**—pop pl IA-7
**Horton**—pop pl KS-7
**Horton**—pop pl MI-6
**Horton**—pop pl MO-7
**Horton**—pop pl OR-9
**Horton**—pop pl TX-5
**Horton**—pop pl WY-8
Horton, Joseph, House—hist pl NY-2
Horton, Welcome, Farm—hist pl MA-1
Horton, William, Farmhouse—hist pl MI-6
Horton-Bailey Cem—cemetery MS-4
Horton Bay—bay MI-6
Horton Bay—bay NC-3
**Horton Bay**—pop pl MI-6
Horton Bay—swamp FL-3
Horton Bayou—stream LA-4
*Horton Bend* AL-4
Horton Bend—bend GA-3
Horton Bend—bend TN-4
*Horton Bend Church* AL-4
Horton Branch—stream (3) AL-4
Horton Branch—stream AR-4
Horton Branch—stream (3) NC-3
Horton Branch—stream SC-3
Horton Branch—stream TN-4
Horton Branch—stream VA-3
Horton Brook—stream NY-2
Horton Brook—stream VT-1
Horton Brook Ch—church NY-2
*Hortonburg* KS-7
*Hortonburgh* KS-7
Horton Butte—summit WA-9
Horton Campground—park AZ-5
Horton Canyon—valley AZ-5
Horton Canyon—valley CA-9
Horton Canyon—valley NM-5
Horton Canyon—valley OR-9
Horton Cave—cave TN-4
*Horton Caves* MS-4
*Horton Cem* MO-7
*Horton Cem* TN-4
Horton Cem—cemetery (2) AL-4
Horton Cem—cemetery AR-4
Horton Cem—cemetery GA-3
Horton Cem—cemetery IN-6
Horton Cem—cemetery IA-7
Horton Cem—cemetery (2) KY-4
Horton Cem—cemetery LA-4
Horton Cem—cemetery (4) MI-6
Horton Cem—cemetery (2) MS-4
Horton Cem—cemetery (2) MO-7
Horton Cem—cemetery NE-7
Horton Cem—cemetery NY-2
Horton Cem—cemetery NC-3
Horton Cem—cemetery OH-6
Horton Cem—cemetery (5) TN-4
Horton Cem—cemetery (2) TX-5
Horton Cem—cemetery VT-1
Horton Cem—cemetery (2) VA-3
Horton Chapel—church VA-3
Horton Chapel (historical)—church TN-4
**Horton City**—pop pl PA-2
*Horton City Dam* KS-7
Horton Cove—bay CT-1
*Horton Creek* OR-9
Horton Creek—stream AL-4
Horton Creek—stream AK-9
Horton Creek—stream (3) AZ-5
Horton Creek—stream AR-4
Horton Creek—stream CA-9
Horton Creek—stream (2) GA-3
Horton Creek—stream ID-8
Horton Creek—stream IL-6
Horton Creek—stream (2) IA-7
Horton Creek—stream MI-6
Horton Creek—stream MS-4
Horton Creek—stream NY-2
Horton Creek—stream (2) NC-3
Horton Creek—stream OR-9
Horton Creek—stream (2) PA-2
Horton Creek—stream SC-3
Horton Creek—stream (2) TX-5
Horton Creek—stream WI-6
Horton Creek Trail—trail AZ-5
Horton Crossing—locale NY-2
Horton Dam—dam OR-9
Horton Drain—stream MI-6
Horton Draw—valley WY-8
Horton-duBignon House, Brewery Ruins, duBignon Cemetery—hist pl GA-3
Horton-Dutch Creek Settling Basin—basin IL-6
Horton Elem Sch—school KS-7
**Horton Estates**—pop pl NY-2
Horton Family Cem—cemetery TN-4
Horton Ford—locale TN-4
Horton Gap—gap AL-4
Horton Gap—gap NC-3
Horton Graham Drain—stream MI-6
Horton Gristmill—hist pl NY-2
Horton Grove Complex—hist pl NC-3
Horton Gulch—valley CO-8
Horton Gulch—valley SD-7
Horton Heights Ch—church TN-4
Horton Hill—summit IL-6
Horton Hill—summit NY-2
Horton Hill—summit NC-3
Horton Hill Ch—church NC-3
Horton (historical)—locale MS-4
Horton Hollow—valley AL-4
Horton Hollow—valley IN-6
Horton Hollow—valley MO-7
Horton Hollow—valley MT-8
Horton Hollow—valley (3) TN-4
Horton Hollow—valley TX-5
**Horton (Hortonville)**—pop pl IN-6
Horton Hosp—hospital NY-2
Horton HS—school KS-7
Horton HS—school NC-3
**Hortonia**—pop pl VT-1
Hortonia, Lake—lake VT-1
**Hortonia (Town of)**—pop pl WI-6
Horton Island—island AR-4
Horton Jeep Trail—trail PA-2
Horton Knob—summit NC-3
Horton Lake—lake CA-9
Horton Lake—lake ID-8
Horton Lake—lake (2) MI-6
Horton Lake—reservoir PA-2
Horton Lake Dam—dam PA-2
Horton Lane Beach—beach NY-2
Horton Lateral—canal ID-8
Horton Marsh—swamp VT-1
*Horton Memorial Baptist Church* MS-4
Horton Memorial Ch—church MS-4
Horton Mill Bridge—bridge AL-4
Horton Mill Covered Bridge—hist pl AL-4
Horton Mtn—summit AL-4
Horton Municipal Airp—airport KS-7
Horton Neck—cape NY-2
Horton Park—park MN-6
Horton Pass—gap OR-9
Horton Peak—summit ID-8
Horton Place—locale NM-5
Horton Point—cape CT-1
Horton Point—cape NY-2
Horton Point—cape NC-3
*Horton Pond* VT-1
Horton Pond—reservoir SC-3
Horton Pond Dam Number One—dam NC-3
Horton Pond Number One—reservoir NC-3
Horton Ponds—lake NY-2
Horton Post Office (historical)—building TN-4
Horton Ranch—locale SD-7
Horton Ridge—ridge (2) CA-9
Horton Ridge—ridge ID-8
Horton Ridge Ch—church VA-3
Horton Rim—cliff OR-9
Horton Riverton Trail—trail WV-2
Horton Rsvr—reservoir MT-8
Horton Rsvr—reservoir OR-9
Horton Run—stream (3) PA-2
Horton Run Trail—trail PA-2
Horton Run Vista—summit PA-2
Hortons—other PA-2
Hortons Bridge—bridge MA-1
Hortons Ch—church NC-3
Horton Sch—school CA-9
Horton Sch—school NY-2
Horton Sch—school TX-5
Horton Sch (abandoned)—school MO-7
Horton Sch (abandoned)—school PA-2
Hortons Chapel—church OK-5
Horton Sch (historical)—school AL-4
**Hortons Corners**—pop pl PA-2
*Hortons Creek* MI-6
*Hortons Creek* PA-2
Horton Shoal—rapids AL-4
Horton Shoal Branch—stream AL-4
Hortons Island—island TN-4
Hortons Landing—locale AR-4
**Hortons Mill**—pop pl AL-4
Hortons Mill Cave—cave AL-4
Hortons Mill Creek—stream MS-4
Hortons Mill (historical)—locale AL-4
Hortons Millpond—reservoir GA-3
*Horton's Neck* NY-2
Horton Sog—swamp FL-3
Hortons Place—locale AZ-5
*Horton's Point* NY-2
Hortons Pond—lake NH-1
Hortons Pond—lake NJ-2
Horton Spring—spring (2) AL-4
Horton Spring—spring AZ-5
Horton Spring Branch—stream AL-4
Horton Spring Branch—stream SC-3
*Hortons Run* PA-2
**Horton Subdivision**—pop pl MS-4
Horton-Suiter House—hist pl IA-7
Horton Summit (Post Office)—locale VA-3
**Horton Summit (Post Office)**—pop pl VA-3
Horton Tank—reservoir AZ-5
Horton Tank—reservoir NM-5
Horton Tank—reservoir TX-5
**Hortontown**—pop pl MS-4
**Hortontown**—pop pl (2) NY-2
Horton Township—fmr MCD IA-7
**Horton (Township of)**—pop pl MI-6
**Horton (Township of)**—pop pl MN-6
**Horton (Township of)**—pop pl PA-2
Horton Valley—valley VA-3
Horton-Vickery House—hist pl GA-3
*Hortonville* KS-7
*Hortonville* VT-1
**Hortonville**—pop pl IN-6
**Hortonville**—pop pl MA-1
**Hortonville**—pop pl NY-2
**Hortonville**—pop pl VT-1
**Hortonville**—pop pl WI-6
*Hortonville Church* AL-4
Hortonville Community Hall—hist pl WI-6
*Hortonville Mill Pond* WI-6
Hort Sch—school CA-9
Horttor Airp—airport KS-7
Hortt Sch—school FL-3
*Horu* FM-9
Horus Temple—summit AZ-5
*Horvels Branch* TN-4
Horville Sch—school KS-7
Horway Cem—cemetery TN-4
Hosack House—hist pl OH-6
Hosack Run—stream PA-2
*Hosacks Run* PA-2
Hosac Mtn—summit ME-1
*Hosacock Creek* PA-2
Hosama Ch—church GA-3
Hosanger Cem—cemetery SD-7
Hosanna Ch—church FL-3
Hosanna Ch—church LA-4
Hosanna Ch—church MD-2
Hosannah Ch—church (2) SC-3
*Hosapoligee Creek* AL-4
Hoschar Cem—cemetery WV-2
Hoschover Cem—cemetery OH-6
**Hoschton**—pop pl GA-3
Hosea, Lake—reservoir NC-3
Hosea Cem—cemetery AL-4
Hosea Creek—stream CA-9
Hosea Lake—reservoir IN-6
Hosea Lake—reservoir NC-3
Hosea Lake Dam—dam IN-6
Hosea Mathis Dam—dam AL-4
Hosea Mathis Lake—reservoir AL-4
Hose and Hook and Ladder Truck Bldg—hist pl CT-1
Hosea Pug Lake—lake ME-1
Hosea Ridge—ridge CA-9
Hosea Rsvr—reservoir CO-8
Hosea Sch—school MO-7
Hosea Tank—reservoir AZ-5
**Hoseaville**—pop pl NY-2
Hose Creek—stream AR-4
*Hose Hill* AZ-5
Hose House No. 10—hist pl IN-6
Hose House No. 12—hist pl IN-6
Hose House No. 2—hist pl MA-1
Hoselton Creek—stream OR-9
Hose Mill Branch—stream KY-4
Hose Mine—mine CA-9
Hosensack—locale PA-2
**Hosensack**—pop pl PA-2
Hosensack Ch—church PA-2
Hosensack Creek—stream PA-2
Hosensack Number Four Dam—dam PA-2
Hosensack Station—locale PA-2
**Hosensock**—pop pl PA-2
Hosensock Creek—stream PA-2
Hosensock Dam—dam PA-2
Hose Point—cape AK-9
Hoses Cem—cemetery GA-3
Hose Station No. 1—hist pl IA-7
Hose Station No. 6—hist pl IA-7
Hose Station No. 7—hist pl IA-7
Hoseville—locale NY-2
Hosey Branch—stream AR-4
Hosey Cem—cemetery OK-5
Hosey Hollow—valley TN-4
Hosey Lake Dam—dam MS-4
Hosey Mine—mine AZ-5
Hosey P. O. (historical)—building MS-4
Hosey Tank—reservoir AZ-5
**Hosford**—pop pl FL-3
Hosford, Emmett, House—hist pl ID-8
Hosford, John, House—hist pl OH-6
Hosford Branch—stream FL-3
Hosford Branch—swamp FL-3
Hosford Camp—locale MT-8
Hosford Creek—stream AK-9
Hosford (historical)—locale KS-7
Hosford House—hist pl OH-6
Hosford Lookout Tower—tower FL-3
Hosford Park Sch—school IN-6
Hosford Pond—lake NY-2
Hosford Pond—swamp FL-3
Hosford Sch—school OR-9
Hosford Sch Number 7—school NY-2
*Hoshi-Jima* FM-9
*Hoshi Shima* FM-9
Hoshoni Park—park AZ-5
Hoshow Coulee—valley MT-8
Hosick Creek—stream IL-6
H O Siding—locale SD-7
*Hosier Lake* MN-6
Hosier Sch (abandoned)—school MO-7
**Hosiery Mill**—pop pl NC-3
*Hoska Island* WA-9
Hoskaninni Company Road—trail UT-8
Hoskaninni Dredge, The (inundated)—other UT-8
Hoskin Branch—stream KY-4
*Hoskin Creek* MS-4
Hoskin Creek—stream AR-4
Hoskin Fork—stream NC-3
Hosking Creek—stream (2) MI-6
Hoskininni Mesa—summit AZ-5
*Hoskininn Monument* UT-8
Hoskin Lake—lake WI-6
*Hoskin Lakes* MT-8
Hoskinnini Mesa—summit (2) UT-8
Hoskinnini Monmt—pillar UT-8
Hoskins—locale (2) TX-5
**Hoskins**—pop pl CT-1
**Hoskins**—pop pl NE-7
**Hoskins**—pop pl OR-9
Hoskins, Caesar, Log Cabin—hist pl NJ-2
Hoskins, Lake—lake ND-7
Hoskins Basin Archeol District—hist pl MT-8
Hoskins Branch—stream KY-4
Hoskins Branch—stream TX-5
Hoskins Bridge—bridge OH-6
Hoskins Canyon—valley OR-9
Hoskins Cem—cemetery GA-3
Hoskins Cem—cemetery IA-7
Hoskins Cem—cemetery (4) KY-4
Hoskins Cem—cemetery MO-7
Hoskins Cem—cemetery (3) TN-4
Hoskins Cem—cemetery TX-5
Hoskins Ch—church TX-5
Hoskins Creek—stream IA-7
Hoskins Creek—stream MS-4
Hoskins Creek—stream OH-6
Hoskins Creek—stream OR-9
Hoskins Creek—stream VA-3
Hoskins Dam—dam TN-4
Hoskins Ditch—canal IN-6
Hoskins Fork—stream KY-4
Hoskins Gulch—valley WA-9
Hoskins (historical)—locale IA-7
Hoskins (historical)—locale KS-7
Hoskins Hollow—valley TN-4
Hoskins House Hist Dist—hist pl NC-3
**Hoskins Junction**—pop pl TX-5
Hoskins Lake—lake MI-6
Hoskins Lake—lake MT-8
Hoskins Lake—reservoir TN-4
Hoskins Library—building TN-4
Hoskins Mill—hist pl NC-3
Hoskins Mound—summit TX-5
Hoskinson Cottage Sch—school CO-8
Hoskinson Drain—canal IN-6
Hoskins Park—park NC-3
Hoskins Pits—basin IN-6
Hoskins Pond—lake NH-1
Hoskins Ranch—locale TX-5
Hoskins Sch—school IL-6
Hoskins Sch—school NC-3
Hoskins Spring—spring CA-9
Hoskins Spring—spring (2) OR-9
Hoskins Spring—spring TN-4
**Hoskins (subdivision)**—pop pl NC-3
Hoskinston—locale KY-4
Hoskins Valley—valley TN-4
**Hoskinsville**—pop pl (2) OH-6
Hosler Ditch—canal IN-6
Hosler JHS—school CA-9
Hosley—locale OR-9
Hosley Brook—stream NH-1
Hosley Hill—summit VT-1
Hosley Memorial Chapel—church VA-3
*Hosma* MS-4
**Hosman**—pop pl KY-4
Hosman and Wheeler Meat Market—hist pl MI-6
Hosman Ch—church KY-4
Hosman Sch (historical)—school MO-7
*Hosmer* IN-6
Hosmer—other IN-6
**Hosmer**—pop pl SD-7
*Hosmer Brook* VT-1
Hosmer Brook—stream NY-2
Hosmer Cem—cemetery MI-6
Hosmer Cem—cemetery WI-6
**Hosmer Corner**—pop pl MA-1
Hosmer Creek—stream AK-9
Hosmer Creek—stream WA-9
Hosmer Drain—stream MI-6
Hosmer Grove—woods HI-9
Hosmer Lake—lake OR-9
Hosmer Lake Trail—trail OR-9
Hosmer Mtn—summit CT-1
Hosmer Pond—lake ME-1
Hosmer Run—stream PA-2
Hosmer Sch—school (2) MA-1
Hosmer Sch—school (2) MI-6
Hosmer State Public Shooting Area—park SD-7
*Hosmer Town* IN-6
**Hosmer Township**—pop pl SD-7
Hosner Mtn—summit NY-2
*Hospa* SC-3
*Hospa Creek* SC-3
*Hospah* SC-3
**Hospah**—pop pl NM-5
Hospah Oil Field—other NM-5
**Hospers**—pop pl IA-7
Hospers Cem—cemetery IA-7
Hospers Memorial Cem—cemetery IA-7
Hospilika Creek—stream AL-4
*Hospillka Creek* AL-4
*Hospital* IL-6
Hospital—hist pl MT-8
Hospital—hist pl NM-5
Hospital, Bayou—stream LA-4
Hospital, State Sch for the Feeble Minded—hist pl MN-6
Hospital, The—hospital FL-3
Hospital and Benevolent Ass'n—hist pl AR-4
Hospital and Homebound—school (4) FL-3
Hospital Bar—bar ID-8
Hospital Bay—bay LA-4
Hospital Bayou—gut LA-4
Hospital Bella Visto—hospital PR-3
Hospital (Binghamton State Hospital)—hospital NY-2
*Hospital Branch* VA-3
Hospital (Bryce Hospital)—uninc pl AL-4
Hospital Canyon—valley CA-9
Hospital Canyon—valley CO-8
Hospital Canyon—valley NM-5
Hospital Canyon—valley TX-5
Hospital Cem—cemetery MT-8
Hospital Cem—cemetery (2) VA-3
Hospital Chapel Cem—cemetery MD-2
*Hospital Cove* CA-9
Hospital Cove—cove MA-1
Hospital Cove—valley GA-3
*Hospital Creek* MI-6
Hospital Creek—stream (3) CA-9
Hospital Creek—stream FL-3
Hospital Creek—stream OR-9
Hospital Creek—stream PA-2
Hospital Creek—stream VT-1
Hospital Creek—stream WA-9
Hospital (Crownsville State Hospital)—hospital MD-2
Hospital del Maestro—hospital PR-3
Hospital Flat—flat (2) AZ-5
Hospital Flat Campground—park AZ-5
Hospital Flat Rec Area—park AZ-5
Hospital for the Mentally Retarded—hospital DE-2
Hospital General Rodriguez—hospital PR-3
Hospital Gulch—valley WY-8
Hospital Hill—summit CO-8
Hospital Hill—summit MA-1
Hospital Hill—summit OR-9
Hospital Hill Springs—spring WY-8
Hospital Hot Spring—spring ID-8
Hospital in the Pines—hospital TX-5
Hospital Island—island ME-1
Hospital Island—island NY-2
Hospitality Branch—stream NJ-2
Hospitality Brook—stream NJ-2
Hospitality Creek—stream NJ-2
Hospitality Lake—lake NJ-2
*Hospital Key* FL-3
Hospital Key—island FL-3
Hospital Lake—lake AK-9
Hospital Lake—lake CA-9
Hospital Lake—lake IL-6
*Hospital Mine* AL-4
Hospital Mtn—summit CA-9
Hospital (Norristown State Hospital)—hospital PA-2
Hospital Park—park WY-8
Hospital Pass—gut LA-4
Hospital Point—cape HI-9
Hospital Point—cape (2) ME-1
Hospital Point—cape MA-1
Hospital Point—cape NC-3
Hospital Point—cape VA-3
Hospital Point—locale ID-8
Hospital Point Light Station—hist pl MA-1
Hospital Point Range Light—locale MA-1
Hospital Pond—bay LA-4
Hospital Pond—reservoir MA-1
Hospital Property Heliport—airport MO-7
Hospital Ranch—locale TX-5
Hospital Ridge—ridge AZ-5
Hospital Ridge—ridge CA-9
Hospital Rock—hist pl CA-9
Hospital Rock—pillar CA-9
Hospital Rock Army Camp Site—hist pl CA-9
Hospital Rock Ranger Station—locale CA-9
Hospital Run—stream WV-2
Hospital Sagrado Corazon—hospital PR-3
Hospital San Martin—hospital PR-3
Hospital Sch—school TN-4
Hospital Shoal—bar MA-1
Hospital Spring—spring CA-9
Hospital Spring—spring NM-5
Hospital Spring—spring UT-8
**Hospital Station**—pop pl NY-2
Hospital Tank—reservoir AZ-5
Hospital Valley—valley NE-7
Hospital Valley*—valley NE-7
**Hospital Village**—pop pl HI-9
Hospital Windmill—locale NM-5
*Hospitito Creek* AZ-5
*Hospitito Spring* AZ-5
*Hospitito Valley* AZ-5
Hosposki Creek—stream OR-9
Hoss, Henry, House—hist pl TN-4
Hossack, John, House—hist pl IL-6
Hossack Creek—stream CA-9
Hossack Meadow—flat CA-9
Hoss Cem—cemetery IN-6
Hoss Cem—cemetery TN-4
Hoss Creek—stream IN-6
Hoss Creek—stream LA-4
*Hossek* MA-1
Hosselkus Creek—stream CA-9
Hossick Creek—stream CO-8
Hossick Lake—lake CO-8
Hosspen Creek—stream MS-4
Hoss-Ray-Miller Cem—cemetery MO-7
*Hoss Run* IN-6
*Hosstetter Creek* TX-5
**Hosston**—pop pl LA-4
Hosston Cem—cemetery LA-4
Hosston Lake—reservoir LA-4
Hosston Oil and Gas Field—oilfield LA-4
Host—locale AL-4
Host—locale PA-2
Hosta Butte—summit NM-5
Hostage Branch—stream FL-3
Host Cem—cemetery PA-2
*Host Crossroads* AL-4
*Hostedler Spring* WA-9
*Hosted Mtn* CT-1
Hosteen Begay Well—well AZ-5
Hosteen Tso Canyon—valley AZ-5
Hosteen Tso Canyon—valley UT-8
*Hosteen Tso Wash* AZ-5
*Hosteen Tso Wash* UT-8
Hosteen Tso Wash—stream AZ-5
Hosterman—locale WV-2
Hosterman Gap—gap PA-2
Hosterman JHS—school MN-6
*Hosterra Creek* TX-5
Hostess House—hist pl CA-9
Hostetler Airp—airport PA-2
Hostetler Ditch—canal IN-6
Hostetler Gap—gap PA-2
Hostetler Spring—spring WA-9
Hostetler Trail—trail PA-2
**Hostetter**—pop pl PA-2
Hostetter Airp—airport PA-2
Hostetter and Johnson Spring—spring CA-9
Hostetter Cem—cemetery MO-7
Hostetter Ch—church PA-2
Hostetter Creek—stream TX-5
Hostetter Inn—hist pl OH-6
Hostetter Sch (abandoned)—school PA-2
*Hostetters Creek* TX-5
Hostetter Tank—reservoir AZ-5
*Host Farm and Corral Golf Course* PA-2
Host Farm Resort Golf Course—locale PA-2
Hostility Branch—stream TN-4
Hostler Branch—stream NC-3
Hostler Creek—stream AL-4
Hostler Creek—stream CA-9
Hostler Point—cape CA-9
Hostler Ridge—ridge CA-9
Hostler Trail—trail PA-2
*Hostrassers Lake* WI-6
Hostrawser Lake—lake WI-6
*Hostter Creek* TX-5
**Hostyn**—pop pl TX-5
Hostyn Sch—school TX-5
*Hot Air* MS-4
Hot Air Canyon—valley AZ-5
Hot Air Tank—reservoir AZ-5
Hot Air Trail Fifteen—trail AZ-5
*Hotaling Island* NY-2
Hotaling (Site)—locale CA-9
Hotamville—locale AL-4
*Hotaru Jima* FM-9
*Hotaru S* FM-9
*Hotaru Shima* FM-9
*Hotashonevo* AZ-5
*Hota Son Vo* AZ-5
**Hotason Vo**—pop pl AZ-5
Hotauta Amphitheater—basin AZ-5
Hotauta Canyon—valley AZ-5
Hot Boy Mine—mine AZ-5
Hot Brook—stream (2) ME-1
Hot Brook—stream SD-7
Hot Brook Canyon—valley SD-7
*Hot Brook Lake* ME-1
Hotcake Channel—channel AK-9
Hot Canyon—valley UT-8
*Hotch City* SD-7
Hotchkiss—locale VA-3
**Hotchkiss**—pop pl CO-8
**Hotchkiss**—pop pl WV-2
Hotchkiss, David, House—hist pl CT-1
Hotchkiss, H. G., Essential Oil Company Plant—hist pl NY-2
Hotchkiss, Jedediah, House—hist pl NY-2
Hotchkiss Bend—channel MO-7
Hotchkiss Bridge—hist pl CO-8
Hotchkiss Cem—cemetery MI-6
Hotchkiss Creek—stream NY-2
Hotchkiss Creek—stream TN-4
Hotchkiss Ditch—canal OR-9
Hotchkiss Field—locale VA-3
Hotchkiss Grove Beach—beach CT-1
Hotchkiss Hill—summit (2) CA-9
Hotchkiss Hollow—valley NY-2
Hotchkiss Hotel—hist pl CO-8
Hotchkiss House—hist pl AR-4
Hotchkiss Landing—locale MO-7
Hotchkiss Park—park CA-9
Hotchkiss Ranch—locale CO-8
Hotchkiss Ranch—locale OR-9
Hotchkiss Rsvr—reservoir CO-8
Hotchkiss Run—stream NY-2
Hotchkiss Sch—school OH-6
Hotchkiss Sch (abandoned)—school PA-2
Hotchkiss School, The—school CT-1
**Hotchkiss School (Prep School)**—pop pl CT-1
Hotchkiss Sheep Camp—locale CO-8
Hotchkiss Springs—spring OR-9
Hotchkiss Valley—valley TN-4
**Hotchkissville**—pop pl CT-1
Hotcoal—locale WV-2
**Hot Coal**—pop pl WV-2
Hot Coffee—locale MS-4
*Hot Creek* NV-8
*Hot Creek* OR-9
Hot Creek—stream (4) CA-9
Hot Creek—stream CO-8
Hot Creek—stream (6) ID-8
Hot Creek—stream (8) NV-8
Hot Creek—stream (2) OR-9
Hot Creek Butte—summit NV-8
Hot Creek Campground—locale NV-8
Hot Creek Canyon—valley NV-8
*Hot Creek Mountains* NV-8
Hot Creek Pass—gap NV-8
Hot Creek Ranch—locale CA-9
Hot Creek Ranch—locale NV-8
Hot Creek Range—range NV-8
Hot Creek Spring—spring NV-8
*Hot Creek Springs* NV-8
Hot Creek Springs—spring NV-8
Hot Creek Stock Driveway—trail (2) CO-8
*Hot Creek Valley* NV-8
Hot Creek Valley—valley NV-8
*Hotei Creek* OR-9
Hotel Adelaide—hist pl MA-1
Hotel Adolphus—hist pl TX-5
Hotel Albert—hist pl UT-8
Hotel Aldridge—hist pl OK-5
Hotel Arcata—hist pl CA-9
Hotel Argonne—hist pl OH-6
Hotel Ashtabula—hist pl OH-6
Hotel Atwater—hist pl MN-6
Hotel Aurora—hist pl IL-6
Hotel Baker—hist pl IL-6
Hotel Baxter—hist pl MT-8
Hotel Beach—hist pl CT-1
Hotel Beecher—hist pl KY-4
Hotel Benton—hist pl OR-9
Hotel Berry—hist pl ND-7
Hotel Blanca—hist pl AZ-5
Hotel Blessing—hist pl TX-5
Hotel Bottom—bend UT-8
Hotel Breakers—hist pl OH-6
Hotel Breeding—hist pl KY-4
Hotel Broz—hist pl MN-6
Hotel Buhl—hist pl ID-8
Hotel Burlington—hist pl IA-7
Hotel Camp—locale CA-9
Hotel Capital—hist pl NE-7
Hotel Cem—cemetery (2) AL-4
Hotel Charlotte—hist pl NC-3
Hotel Chelsea—hist pl NY-2
Hotel Cherry—building NC-3
Hotel Chester—hist pl MS-4
Hotel Claridge—hist pl TN-4
Hotel Clovis—hist pl NM-5
Hotel Colorado—hist pl CO-8
Hotel Cortez—hist pl TX-5
Hotel Courtland—hist pl OH-6
Hotel Creek—stream CA-9
Hotel Creek—stream ID-8
Hotel Creek—stream NY-2
Hotel Creek—stream WA-9
Hotel Danville—hist pl VA-3
Hotel de Bum Camp—locale OR-9

House at 1025 RR—*hist pl* ... NM-5
House at 103 Roslyn Ave—*hist pl* ... NY-2
House at 104 Kaufman—*hist pl* ... TX-5
House at 10410 Stanley Road—*hist pl* ... MI-6
House at 105 Marion Street—*hist pl* ... MA-1
House at 105 Spring St.—*hist pl* ... AZ-5
House at 106 East Denton—*hist pl* ... TX-5
House at 106 Kaufman—*hist pl* ... TX-5
House at 107 Stroud Street—*hist pl* ... NY-2
House at 107 Waban Hill Road—*hist pl* ... MA-1
House at 107 William Street—*hist pl* ... MA-1
House at 108-112 Quarry Street—*hist pl* ... MA-1
House at 109 N. Sterling—*hist pl* ... TX-5
House at 11 Beach Street—*hist pl* ... MA-1
House at 110 S. 3rd West—*hist pl* ... UT-8
House at 1101 Norfolk Ave—*hist pl* ... UT-8
House at 1105 Hill—*hist pl* ... TX-5
House at 1108 Hill—*hist pl* ... TX-5
House at 111 Brown—*hist pl* ... TX-5
House at 111 Maple Ave—*hist pl* ... CT-1
House at 111 Williams—*hist pl* ... TX-5
House at 1111 Heights Blvd—*hist pl* ... TX-5
House at 1112 Bowen Ave—*hist pl* ... MS-4
House at 1114 10th—*hist pl* ... NM-5
House at 1116 Columbia—*hist pl* ... NM-5
House at 112 Park Street—*hist pl* ... MT-8
House at 112 Sea Cliff Ave—*hist pl* ... NY-2
House at 112 W. 4th Street—*hist pl* ... TX-5
House at 113 East Ross—*hist pl* ... TX-5
House at 113-115 Center Street—*hist pl* ... MA-1
House at 114 Marble Street—*hist pl* ... MA-1
House at 115 Central Ave—*hist pl* ... NY-2
House at 115 South Main Street—*hist pl* ... NY-2
House at 115-117 Jewett Street—*hist pl* ... MA-1
House at 116 Main Street—*hist pl* ... NY-2
House at 1170 San Bernard Street—*hist pl* ... TX-5
House at 1177 Main Street—*hist pl* ... MA-1
House at 119 RR—*hist pl* ... NM-5
House at 12 Grand—*hist pl* ... NM-5
House at 12 Linden Street—*hist pl* ... MA-1
House at 12 Vernon Street—*hist pl* ... MA-1
House at 121 W. Water Street—*hist pl* ... MS-4
House at 1210 Harvard Street—*hist pl* ... TX-5
House at 12-16 Corey Road—*hist pl* ... MA-1
House at 1217 Harvard—*hist pl* ... TX-5
House at 122 East Fifth Street—*hist pl* ... TX-5
House at 1220 Harvard—*hist pl* ... TX-5
House at 1221 San Francisco—*hist pl* ... NM-5
House at 1227 Rutland Street—*hist pl* ... TX-5
House at 123 Allen—*hist pl* ... TX-5
House at 1230 Oxford Street—*hist pl* ... TX-5
House at 1237 Rutland Street—*hist pl* ... TX-5
House at 1239-1245 Scott Street—*hist pl* ... CA-9
House at 1249-1251 Scott Street—*hist pl* ... CA-9
House at 1254-1256 Montgomery Street—*hist pl* ... CA-9
House at 129 High Street—*hist pl* ... MA-1
House at 13 Annis Street—*hist pl* ... MA-1
House at 130 Hayden Station Road—*hist pl* ... CT-1
House at 1301 East Marvin—*hist pl* ... TX-5
House at 1301 Hill—*hist pl* ... TX-5
House at 1303 W. Louisiana—*hist pl* ... TX-5
House at 1304 Cortlandt Street—*hist pl* ... TX-5
House at 1308 Fayette—*hist pl* ... TX-5
House at 1316 Farm—*hist pl* ... TX-5
House at 1321 Scott Street—*hist pl* ... CA-9
House at 1325 South David—*hist pl* ... TX-5
House at 1331-1335 Scott Street—*hist pl* ... CA-9
House at 1339 Cummings Road—*hist pl* ... MI-6
House at 1343 Allston Street—*hist pl* ... TX-5
House at 136 Hampstead Street—*hist pl* ... MA-1
House at 137 Prospect Ave—*hist pl* ... NY-2
House at 140 Allen—*hist pl* ... TX-5
House at 140 and 144 Retreat Ave—*hist pl* ... CT-1
House at 1400 Canterbury Street—*hist pl* ... TX-5
House at 1401 Baker—*hist pl* ... TX-5
House at 1410 Bowen Ave—*hist pl* ... MS-4
House at 1421 Harvard St.—*hist pl* ... TX-5
House at 1421 Heights Blvd—*hist pl* ... TX-5
House at 1421-1423 Waverly Street—*hist pl* ... TX-5
House at 1423 Sycamore—*hist pl* ... TX-5
House at 1435 Heights Blvd—*hist pl* ... TX-5
House at 1437 Heights Blvd—*hist pl* ... TX-5
House at 1437 Waverly Street—*hist pl* ... TX-5
House at 1443 Allston Street—*hist pl* ... TX-5
House at 147 Park Street—*hist pl* ... NJ-2
House at 15 Davis Ave—*hist pl* ... MA-1
House at 1509 Allston Street—*hist pl* ... TX-5
House at 1513 8th—*hist pl* ... NM-5
House at 1514 N. Michigan Street—*hist pl* ... MI-6
House at 1515 Allston Street—*hist pl* ... TX-5
House at 1517 Cortland Street—*hist pl* ... TX-5
House at 152 Suffolk Road—*hist pl* ... MA-1
House at 1537 Tulane Street—*hist pl* ... TX-5
House at 155 Reservoir—*hist pl* ... MA-1
House at 156 Mason Terrace—*hist pl* ... MA-1
House at 16 Grand—*hist pl* ... NM-5
House at 16 Mineral Street—*hist pl* ... MA-1
House at 160 Apache—*hist pl* ... AZ-5
House at 1602 North Moody—*hist pl* ... TX-5
House at 161 Damascus Road—*hist pl* ... CT-1
House at 1616 8th—*hist pl* ... NM-5
House at 1621 North Chadbourne—*hist pl* ... TX-5
House at 1640 Harvard Street—*hist pl* ... TX-5
House at 1646 W. Second Street—*hist pl* ... IA-7
House at 17 Cranston Street—*hist pl* ... MA-1
House at 17 West 16th Street—*hist pl* ... NY-2
House at 170 Center—*hist pl* ... AZ-5
House at 170 Otis Street—*hist pl* ... MA-1
House at 1717 8th—*hist pl* ... NM-5
House at 1723 Holcomb Street—*hist pl* ... WA-9
House at 173 Sixteenth Ave—*hist pl* ... NY-2
House at 173-175 Ward Street—*hist pl* ... MA-1
House at 175 Belden Street—*hist pl* ... NY-2
House at 176 Prospect Ave—*hist pl* ... NY-2
House at 18 Brunswick Road—*hist pl* ... NJ-2
House at 18 Seventeenth Ave—*hist pl* ... NY-2
House at 185 Washington—*hist pl* ... AZ-5
House at 19 Linden Street—*hist pl* ... MA-1
House at 19 Locust Place—*hist pl* ... NY-2
House at 19 Tremont Street—*hist pl* ... MA-1
House at 1907 Southwest Ben Jordan—*hist pl* ... TX-5
House at 195 Prospect Ave—*hist pl* ... NY-2
House at 197 Hornbine Road—*hist pl* ... MA-1
House at 199 Prospect Ave—*hist pl* ... NY-2
House at 199 Summer Ave—*hist pl* ... MA-1
House at 200 Bay Ave—*hist pl* ... NY-2
House at 200 West North Ave—*hist pl* ... PA-2
House at 201 N. Graves—*hist pl* ... TX-5
House at 201 W. 15th Street—*hist pl* ... TX-5
House at 2017-2023 Ave I—*hist pl* ... TX-5
House at 203 East 29 Street—*hist pl* ... NY-2
House at 203 Islington Road—*hist pl* ... MA-1
House at 203 Prince Street—*hist pl* ... NY-2
House at 2035 Rutland Street—*hist pl* ... TX-5
House at 205 North Main Street—*hist pl* ... NY-2
House at 206 Park Street—*hist pl* ... KY-4
House at 206 West Street—*hist pl* ... MA-1
House at 207 Carpenter Ave—*hist pl* ... NY-2
House at 209-211 S. Ninth Street—*hist pl* ... IN-6
House at 21 Stonebridge Road—*hist pl* ... NJ-2
House at 2123 W. Second Street—*hist pl* ... IA-7
House at 214 W. Univ—*hist pl* ... TX-5
House at 215 Brookline Street—*hist pl* ... MA-1
House at 216 Warren Street—*hist pl* ... NY-2
House at 217 E. 5th Street—*hist pl* ... TX-5
House at 22 West Lamme—*hist pl* ... MT-8
House at 220 Walnut Street—*hist pl* ... AZ-5
House at 2203 New Mexico—*hist pl* ... NM-5
House at 221 North Magdalen—*hist pl* ... TX-5
House at 2212 Commonwealth Ave—*hist pl* ... MA-1
House at 2212 W. River Drive—*hist pl* ... IA-7
House at 23 East Street—*hist pl* ... MA-1
House at 230 Melrose Street—*hist pl* ... MA-1
House at 230 Winchester Street—*hist pl* ... MA-1
House at 233 James Street—*hist pl* ... NY-2
House at 235-237 Reynolds Street—*hist pl* ... NY-2
House at 240 Sea Cliff Ave—*hist pl* ... NY-2
House at 2402 Rutland Street—*hist pl* ... TX-5
House at 242 Summer Ave—*hist pl* ... MA-1
House at 2437 Fifteenth Street, NW—*hist pl* ... DC-2
House at 244 Park Ave—*hist pl* ... NY-2
House at 25 Stanton Road—*hist pl* ... MA-1
House at 2501 Taos Alley—*hist pl* ... NM-5
House at 2528 Postoffice St.—*hist pl* ... TX-5
House at 26 Center Ave—*hist pl* ... MA-1
House at 262-264 Pelham Street—*hist pl* ... MA-1
House at 269 Green Street—*hist pl* ... MA-1
House at 285 Sea Cliff Ave—*hist pl* ... NY-2
House at 29 Flat Rock Road—*hist pl* ... CT-1
House at 3 Crown Street—*hist pl* ... NY-2
House at 3 Davis Ave—*hist pl* ... MA-1
House at 30 Kelton Street—*hist pl* ... MA-1
House at 30 Tremont Street—*hist pl* ... WA-9
House at 301 Eighth Avenue, South—*hist pl* ... MT-8
House at 301 E. Lamar—*hist pl* ... TX-5
House at 301 Turner—*hist pl* ... TX-5
House at 3023A Kalakaua Ave—*hist pl* ... HI-9
House at 3023B Kalakaua Ave—*hist pl* ... HI-9
House at 3023 Kalakaua Ave—*hist pl* ... HI-9
House at 3027 Kalakaua Ave—*hist pl* ... HI-9
House at 3033B Kalakaua Ave—*hist pl* ... HI-9
House at 3033 Kalakaua Ave—*hist pl* ... HI-9
House at 304 West Stayton—*hist pl* ... TX-5
House at 305 E. Ashley—*hist pl* ... AR-4
House at 306 Broadway—*hist pl* ... MA-1
House at 306 East Forrest—*hist pl* ... TX-5
House at 307 Lexington Street—*hist pl* ... MA-1
House at 308 South Street—*hist pl* ... AL-4
House at 309 RR—*hist pl* ... NM-5
House at 309 Waltham Street—*hist pl* ... MA-1
House at 31 Woodbine Street—*hist pl* ... MA-1
House at 310 South Beaver—*hist pl* ... AZ-5
House at 311 Pecan—*hist pl* ... TX-5
House at 312 Tecolote—*hist pl* ... NM-5
House at 313 North Main Street—*hist pl* ... NY-2
House at 314 W. King St.—*hist pl* ... MI-6
House at 318-332 Marquette Street—*hist pl* ... IA-7
House at 320 East Marvin—*hist pl* ... TX-5
House at 322 Haven Street—*hist pl* ... MA-1
House at 325 S. Main St.—*hist pl* ... UT-8
House at 326 North Peterboro Street—*hist pl* ... NY-2
House at 328 North Peterboro Street—*hist pl* ... NY-2
House at 332 Franklin Ave—*hist pl* ... NY-2
House at 3325 Via de la Reiva—*hist pl* ... FL-3
House at 3335 Via de la Reina—*hist pl* ... FL-3
House at 334-338 Walnut Street—*hist pl* ... AZ-5
House at 343 Park Ave—*hist pl* ... UT-8
House at 3500 Via de la Reina—*hist pl* ... FL-3
House at 36 Forest Street—*hist pl* ... CT-1
House at 3609 Via de la Reina—*hist pl* ... FL-3
House at 362 Sea Cliff Ave—*hist pl* ... NY-2
House at 364 Cedar Ave—*hist pl* ... NJ-2
House at 3685 Via de la Reina—*hist pl* ... FL-3
House at 37 Center Street—*hist pl* ... NY-2
House at 37 East 4th Street—*hist pl* ... NY-2
House at 3703 Via de la Reina—*hist pl* ... FL-3
House at 3764 Ponce de Leon Ave—*hist pl* ... FL-3
House at 378 Glen Ave—*hist pl* ... NY-2
House at 379 West State Street—*hist pl* ... NJ-2
House at 38-40 Webster Place—*hist pl* ... MA-1
House at 391 Williams Street—*hist pl* ... MA-1
House at 4 Birch Ave—*hist pl* ... MA-1
House at 4 Perry Street—*hist pl* ... MA-1
House at 401 East Stayton—*hist pl* ... TX-5
House at 402 E. 11th Street—*hist pl* ... TX-5
House at 404 East Crockett—*hist pl* ... TX-5
House at 404 Stockdale—*hist pl* ... TX-5
House at 405 Preusser—*hist pl* ... TX-5
House at 407 East Convent—*hist pl* ... TX-5
House at 407 East Howard Ave—*hist pl* ... MS-4
House at 407 N. Parker—*hist pl* ... TX-5
House at 41 Middlesex Road—*hist pl* ... MA-1
House at 4109 Black Point Road—*hist pl* ... HI-9
House at 418 North College—*hist pl* ... TX-5
House at 419 West Ave C—*hist pl* ... TX-5
House at 42 Salem Street—*hist pl* ... MA-1
House at 421 West Twohig—*hist pl* ... TX-5
House at 4305 South Linden Road—*hist pl* ... MI-6
House at 4344 Frances Road—*hist pl* ... MI-6
House at 44 Court Street—*hist pl* ... CT-1
House at 44 Linden Street—*hist pl* ... MA-1
House at 44 Stanton Road—*hist pl* ... MA-1
House at 44 Temple Street—*hist pl* ... MA-1
House at 4402 East Juan Linn—*hist pl* ... TX-5
House at 444 West 24th Street—*hist pl* ... TX-5
House at 45 Claremont Ave—*hist pl* ... MA-1
House at 47 Sargent Street—*hist pl* ... MA-1
House at 483 Summer Ave—*hist pl* ... MA-1
House at 491 Prospect Street—*hist pl* ... MA-1
House at 5 Lincoln Road—*hist pl* ... MA-1
House at 5 Willow Court—*hist pl* ... MA-1
House at 50 Pelham Street—*hist pl* ... MA-1
House at 500 North Main, East—*hist pl* ... TX-5
House at 501 North Grand—*hist pl* ... TX-5
House at 501 North Swenson—*hist pl* ... TX-5
House at 5011 Sunset Drive—*hist pl* ... MO-7
House at 502 South Orient—*hist pl* ... TX-5
House at 503 Fir Street—*hist pl* ... WA-9
House at 505 W. 18th Street—*hist pl* ... TX-5
House at 508 North Dallas—*hist pl* ... TX-5
House at 508 Univ—*hist pl* ... NM-5
House at 509 West Brown—*hist pl* ... TX-5
House at 51 Market St.—*hist pl* ... NY-2
House at 511 Watertown Street—*hist pl* ... MA-1
House at 512 North Grand—*hist pl* ... TX-5
House at 514 Univ—*hist pl* ... NM-5
House at 519 Golconda—*hist pl* ... AZ-5
House at 52 Eighteenth Ave—*hist pl* ... NY-2
House at 52 Wayside Place—*hist pl* ... NJ-2
House at 521 S. Pacific—*hist pl* ... NM-5
House at 521 West Highland Blvd—*hist pl* ... TX-5
House at 523 Highland—*hist pl* ... TX-5
House at 526 Prospect Street—*hist pl* ... MA-1
House at 527 Pine—*hist pl* ... AZ-5
House at 53 Linden Street—*hist pl* ... MA-1
House at 53 Lloyd Road—*hist pl* ... NJ-2
House at 530 S. Marengo Ave—*hist pl* ... CA-9
House at 532 Harvard Street—*hist pl* ... TX-5
House at 536 Park—*hist pl* ... AZ-5
House at 54 E. 53rd Terrace—*hist pl* ... MO-7
House at 555 Deer Valley Road—*hist pl* ... UT-8
House at 5556 Flushing Road—*hist pl* ... MI-6
House at 56 Cornelia Street—*hist pl* ... NY-2
House at 5-7 Winter Street—*hist pl* ... MA-1
House at 57 Woburn Street—*hist pl* ... MA-1
House at 577 Deer Valley Road—*hist pl* ... UT-8
House at 58 Eighteenth Ave—*hist pl* ... NY-2
House at 584 Page Street—*hist pl* ... CA-9
House at 5910 Amboy Road—*hist pl* ... NY-2
House at 6 S. Marble Street—*hist pl* ... MA-1
House at 60 William Street—*hist pl* ... MA-1
House at 600 N. Washington—*hist pl* ... TX-5
House at 603 E. Thirty-first—*hist pl* ... TX-5
House at 604 East Santa Rosa—*hist pl* ... TX-5
House at 604 Elm—*hist pl* ... TX-5
House at 604 E. Twenty-seventh—*hist pl* ... TX-5
House at 609 East Live Oak—*hist pl* ... TX-5
House at 610 East Oliver—*hist pl* ... TX-5
House at 610 Tucker—*hist pl* ... TX-5
House at 611 Third Ave—*hist pl* ... AZ-5
House at 6112 Carpenter Road—*hist pl* ... MI-6
House at 613 Mora—*hist pl* ... NM-5
House at 618 Mora—*hist pl* ... NM-5
House at 618 West Janeaux—*hist pl* ... MT-8
House at 62 Daly Ave—*hist pl* ... UT-8
House at 622 Rossie Hill Drive—*hist pl* ... UT-8
House at 625 Cantrell—*hist pl* ... TX-5
House at 65 Twentieth Ave—*hist pl* ... NY-2
House at 665 Morley Ave—*hist pl* ... AZ-5
House at 67 Warren Place—*hist pl* ... NJ-2
House at 68 Eagle Rock Way—*hist pl* ... NJ-2
House at 68 Maple Street—*hist pl* ... MA-1
House at 7 South Mountain Terrace—*hist pl* ... NJ-2
House at 700 South Rogers—*hist pl* ... TX-5
House at 702 Siegfried—*hist pl* ... TX-5
House at 703 South College—*hist pl* ... TX-5
House at 704 Parker—*hist pl* ... TX-5
House at 705 3rd Street, SE—*hist pl* ... TX-5
House at 706 Siegfried—*hist pl* ... TX-5
House at 7066 Lobdell Road—*hist pl* ... MI-6
House at 708 East Brown—*hist pl* ... TX-5
House at 709 East Reynolds—*hist pl* ... TX-5
House at 712 East Marvin—*hist pl* ... TX-5
House at 714 North Tracy—*hist pl* ... MT-8
House at 7144 Madrid Ave—*hist pl* ... FL-3
House at 715 Austin—*hist pl* ... TX-5
House at 719 East Reynolds—*hist pl* ... TX-5
House at 720 Grand Canyon Ave—*hist pl* ... AZ-5
House at 7207 Ventura Ave—*hist pl* ... FL-3
House at 7217 Ventura Ave—*hist pl* ... FL-3
House at 722 West Madison—*hist pl* ... TX-5
House at 7227 San Pedro—*hist pl* ... FL-3
House at 7245 San Jose Blvd—*hist pl* ... FL-3
House at 7246 San Carlos—*hist pl* ... FL-3
House at 7246 St. Augustine Road—*hist pl* ... FL-3
House at 7249 San Pedro—*hist pl* ... FL-3
House at 7288 San Jose Blvd—*hist pl* ... FL-3
House at 729 Dedham Street—*hist pl* ... MA-1
House at 7306 St. Augustine Road—*hist pl* ... FL-3
House at 731 Preusser—*hist pl* ... TX-5
House at 7317 San Jose Blvd—*hist pl* ... FL-3
House at 733 RR—*hist pl* ... NM-5
House at 7330 Ventura Ave—*hist pl* ... FL-3
House at 7356 San Jose Blvd—*hist pl* ... FL-3
House at 736 Palisado Ave—*hist pl* ... CT-1
House at 7400 San Jose Blvd—*hist pl* ... FL-3
House at 753 East Broad Street—*hist pl* ... OH-6
House at 77 Howard Street—*hist pl* ... MA-1
House at 79-81 Salem Street—*hist pl* ... MA-1
House at 80 Lloyd Rd.—*hist pl* ... NJ-2
House at 800 Pecos—*hist pl* ... NM-5
House at 801 West—*hist pl* ... TX-5
House at 802 East Ennis—*hist pl* ... TX-5
House at 803 Cantrell—*hist pl* ... TX-5
House at 804 Siegfried—*hist pl* ... TX-5
House at 806 Jefferson—*hist pl* ... TX-5
House at 806 South Dallas—*hist pl* ... TX-5
House at 807 North Preston—*hist pl* ... TX-5
House at 809 Grand View—*hist pl* ... AZ-5
House at 810 Douglas—*hist pl* ... NM-5
House at 810 North Preston—*hist pl* ... TX-5
House at 812 Douglas—*hist pl* ... NM-5
House at 814 Douglas—*hist pl* ... NM-5
House at 815 East Campbell—*hist pl* ... TX-5
House at 816 Cantrell—*hist pl* ... TX-5
House at 816 West Water—*hist pl* ... TX-5
House at 818 Douglas—*hist pl* ... NM-5
House at 818 South Eighth—*hist pl* ... MT-8
House at 81-83 Gardner Street—*hist pl* ... MA-1
House at 821 12th—*hist pl* ... NM-5
House at 822 Douglas—*hist pl* ... NM-5
House at 823 Ohio Street—*hist pl* ... IN-6
House at 825 Heights Blvd—*hist pl* ... TX-5
House at 83 Penniman Place—*hist pl* ... MA-1
House at 844 Columbia Street—*hist pl* ... TX-5
House at 844 Courtlandt—*hist pl* ... TX-5
House at 847 Main Street, North—*hist pl* ... CT-1
House at 855-857 Oak Street—*hist pl* ... KY-4
House at 859 Oak Street—*hist pl* ... KY-4
House at 89 Rawson Road and 86 Colburne Crescent—*hist pl* ... MA-1
House at 9 Linden Street—*hist pl* ... MA-1
House at 9 Locust Place—*hist pl* ... NY-2
House at 9 North Front Street—*hist pl* ... MD-2
House at 9 Park Street—*hist pl* ... MA-1
House at 901 Cantrell—*hist pl* ... TX-5
House at 902 Selden Road—*hist pl* ... MI-6
House at 907 Pine—*hist pl* ... TX-5
House at 913 2nd—*hist pl* ... NM-5
House at 915 2nd—*hist pl* ... NM-5
House at 916 Preston Ave—*hist pl* ... MT-8
House at 917 Heights Blvd—*hist pl* ... TX-5
House at 919 Oneida Street—*hist pl* ... IA-7
House at 919 RR—*hist pl* ... NM-5
House at 919 2nd—*hist pl* ... NM-5
House at 921 Chavez—*hist pl* ... NM-5
House at 921 S. Pacific—*hist pl* ... NM-5
House at 931 Prince—*hist pl* ... NM-5
House at 933 12th—*hist pl* ... NM-5
House at 97 Warren Place—*hist pl* ... NJ-2
House Bayou—*stream* ... TX-5
Houseblock Valley—*valley* ... AK-9
House Bluff—*cliff* ... AL-4
Houseboat Creek—*stream* ... VA-3
Houseboat Cut—*channel* ... FL-3
House Bog—*swamp* ... ME-1
*House Branch* ... WV-2
House Branch—*stream* ... AR-4
House Branch—*stream* ... IN-6
House Branch—*stream* (3) ... KY-4
House Branch—*stream* ... LA-4
House Branch—*stream* (3) ... NC-3
House Branch—*stream* ... VA-3
House Branch—*stream* ... WV-2
House Brook—*stream* (2) ... ME-1
House Brook—*stream* ... MA-1
*House Butte* ... UT-8
House Butte—*summit* ... OR-9
House by the Side of the Road—*hist pl* ... NH-1
House by the "Town Gates"—*hist pl* ... MD-2
House Canyon—*valley* ... AZ-5
House Canyon—*valley* (2) ... CO-8
House Canyon—*valley* ... NV-8
House Canyon—*valley* (2) ... NM-5
House Canyon—*valley* (2) ... TX-5
House Canyon Windmill—*locale* ... TX-5
House Cave—*cave* ... TN-4
House Cem—*cemetery* ... GA-3
House Cem—*cemetery* (3) ... IL-6
House Cem—*cemetery* ... IN-6
House Cem—*cemetery* (2) ... MS-4
House Cem—*cemetery* (2) ... NM-5
House Cem—*cemetery* ... OH-6
House Cem—*cemetery* (4) ... TN-4
House Cem—*cemetery* (2) ... TX-5
House Cove—*bay* ... ME-1
House Cove—*bay* ... NC-3
House Cove Point—*cape* ... NC-3
*House Creek* ... CO-8
*House Creek* ... GA-3
*House Creek* ... LA-4
*House Creek* ... OR-9
House Creek—*bay* ... MD-2
House Creek—*gut* ... SC-3
**House Creek**—*pop pl* ... MO-7
House Creek—*stream* ... AZ-5
House Creek—*stream* ... CA-9
House Creek—*stream* (2) ... CO-8
House Creek—*stream* (3) ... GA-3
House Creek—*stream* ... ID-8
House Creek—*stream* ... LA-4
House Creek—*stream* ... MS-4
House Creek—*stream* ... MO-7
House Creek—*stream* (2) ... MT-8
House Creek—*stream* (2) ... NV-8
House Creek—*stream* (2) ... NY-2
House Creek—*stream* (2) ... NC-3
House Creek—*stream* (3) ... OK-5
House Creek—*stream* (3) ... OR-9
House Creek—*stream* ... TN-4
House Creek—*stream* (2) ... TX-5
House Creek—*stream* (2) ... WY-8
House Creek Butte—*summit* ... NV-8
House Creek Spring—*spring* ... OR-9
House Creek (Township of)—*fmr MCD* ... NC-3
House Crossing—*locale* ... TX-5
House Ditch—*canal* ... FL-3
House Ditch—*canal* ... IN-6
House Draw—*valley* ... TX-5
House Draw—*valley* ... WY-8
House Estates—*other* ... IN-6
House Fork—*stream* ... SC-3
House Fork—*stream* ... VA-3
House Fork—*stream* ... WV-2
House Fork Creek—*stream* ... KY-4
House-Forrest (CCD)—*cens area* ... NM-5
House Gap—*gap* (2) ... AR-4
*House Gulch* ... CO-8
House Gulch—*valley* ... CO-8
House Gulch—*valley* ... WY-8
House Gulch Rsvr—*reservoir* ... WY-8
House Hammock Bay—*bay* ... FL-3
House Hill—*summit* ... NY-2
House (historical)—*locale* ... AL-4
Householder, Ross E., House—*hist pl* ... AZ-5
Householder Pass—*gap* ... AZ-5
Householder Rsvr—*reservoir* ... CA-9
Household Furniture Co.—*hist pl* ... TX-5
Household No. 1 Site (36WM61)—*hist pl* ... PA-2
Household of Faith—*church* ... FL-3
House Hole—*valley* ... VA-3
House Hollow—*valley* ... KY-4
House Hollow—*valley* (2) ... MO-7
House Hollow—*valley* ... TN-4
House Hollow—*valley* (2) ... TX-5
*House Island* ... FL-3
*House Island* ... MA-1
House Island—*island* ... ME-1
House Island—*island* ... MA-1
House Island—*island* ... NC-3
House Island Light—*locale* ... ME-1
*House Key* ... FL-3
*House Lake* ... MN-6
House Lake—*lake* (2) ... MI-6
House Lake—*lake* ... NM-5
House Lake—*lake* ... WI-6
House Lake—*reservoir* ... MS-4
House Lake—*reservoir* ... NM-5
House Lake—*reservoir* ... VA-3
House Lake—*swamp* ... LA-4
House Lake Dam—*dam* ... MS-4
Houselander Mtn—*summit* ... PA-2
House Landing Strip—*airport* ... PA-2
House Ledge—*bar* ... ME-1
House Ledge—*bar* ... MA-1
Housel Gulch—*valley* ... CO-8
House Log—*locale* ... TX-5
House Log Branch—*stream* ... TX-5
Houselog Canyon—*valley* ... CO-8
House Log Canyon—*valley* ... NM-5
Houselog Creek—*stream* ... CO-8
Houselog Creek—*stream* ... OR-9
House Log Creek—*stream* ... TX-5
House Log Creek—*stream* ... WY-8
Houselog Fork—*stream* ... KY-4
House Log Gulch—*valley* ... CO-8
*House Log Run* ... PA-2
Houselog Run—*stream* ... WV-2
House Log Windmill—*locale* ... TX-5
Houseman—*locale* ... MI-6
Houseman, Peter, House—*hist pl* ... NY-2
Houseman Camp Rsvr—*reservoir* ... CA-9
Houseman Cem—*cemetery* ... VA-3
Houseman Corners—*locale* ... NY-2
Houseman Creek—*stream* ... MO-7
Houseman Field—*park* ... MI-6
Houseman Hill—*summit* ... MT-8
Houseman Hollow—*valley* ... MO-7
Houseman Lake—*lake* ... MI-6
House Meadow—*flat* ... CA-9
House Memorial African Methodist Episcopal Zion Ch—*church* ... FL-3
House Mine—*mine* (2) ... AZ-5
House Mountain—*locale* ... CA-9
House Mountain Branch—*stream* ... TX-5
House Mountain Ch—*church* ... TN-4
**House Mountain (historical)**—*pop pl* ... TN-4
House Mountain Overlook—*locale* ... VA-3
House Mountain Post Office (historical)—*building* ... TN-4
*House Mountains* ... TX-5
House Mountain Spring—*spring* ... TX-5
House Mountain Substation—*locale* ... TN-4
House Mountain Tank—*reservoir* ... AZ-5
House Mtn—*summit* ... AK-9
House Mtn—*summit* ... AZ-5
House Mtn—*summit* ... ID-8
House Mtn—*summit* (2) ... TN-4
House Mtn—*summit* (2) ... TX-5
*House Mtn Baptist Church* ... TN-4
Housen Bayou—*stream* ... TX-5
Housen Lake—*lake* ... WY-8
House of Beth-El Ministries—*church* ... FL-3
House of Calvary Hosp—*hospital* ... NY-2
House of Corrections—*building* ... MA-1
House of David—*church* ... MI-6
House Office Bldg Annex I—*building* ... DC-2
House Office Bldg Annex II—*building* ... DC-2
House Of Four Pillars—*hist pl* ... OH-6
House of God—*church* ... FL-3
House of God Ch—*church* ... AL-4
House of God Ch—*church* ... FL-3
House of God Ch—*church* ... SC-3
House of God Ch—*church* ... TN-4
House of God Saints in Christ Ch—*church* ... AL-4
House of Good Shepherd—*building* ... PA-2
House of Good Shepherd Sch—*school* ... IL-6
House of Hands—*cave* ... AZ-5
House of Happiness Cave—*cave* ... AL-4
House of Happiness Ch—*church* ... AL-4
House of Happiness Sch (historical)—*school* ... AL-4
House of History—*building* ... NY-2
House of Hope Ch—*church* ... MN-6
House of Israel Cem—*cemetery* ... OH-6
House Of Jacob Cem—*cemetery* ... OH-6
House Of Jacob Ch—*church* ... OH-6
House of Learning—*school* ... FL-3
*House of Many Hands* ... AZ-5
House of Many Windows—*locale* ... CO-8
House of Miller at Millbach—*hist pl* ... PA-2
House of Peace Synagogue—*hist pl* ... SC-3
House of Praise and Prayer—*church* ... FL-3
House of Prayer—*church* ... FL-3
House of Prayer—*church* (2) ... NC-3
House of Prayer—*church* ... OK-5
House of Prayer—*church* ... PA-2
House Of Prayer—*church* ... TN-4
House of Prayer—*church* ... TN-4
House Of Prayer—*church* (3) ... VA-3
House of Prayer Apostolic Ch—*church* ... IN-6
*House of Prayer Ch* ... AL-4
House of Prayer Ch—*church* (5) ... AL-4
House of Prayer Ch—*church* ... AR-4
House of Prayer Ch—*church* (2) ... GA-3
House of Prayer Ch—*church* (3) ... MS-4
House of Prayer Ch—*church* ... NY-2
House of Prayer Ch—*church* (3) ... NC-3
House Of Prayer Ch—*church* ... VA-3
House of Prayer Ch of God in Christ—*church* ... MS-4
*House of Prayer Church, The* ... AL-4
House of Prayer Church, The—*church* ... AL-4
House of Prayer Episcopal Church and Rectory—*hist pl* ... NJ-2
House of Prayer Mission—*church* ... PA-2
*House of Prayers Ch* ... AL-4
House of Prayer Tabernacle Ch—*church* ... MS-4
House of Providence—*hist pl* ... WA-9
House of Refuge at Gilbert's Bar—*hist pl* ... FL-3
House of Seven Gables Hist Dist—*hist pl* ... MA-1
House of Taga—*hist pl* ... MH-9
House of Taga Historical Site—*locale* ... MH-9
House of the Ghosts (historical)—*cliff* ... AZ-5
House of the Good Shepard—*church* ... MA-1
House of the Good Shepherd—*building* ... MN-6
House Of The Good Shepherd—*church* ... PA-2
House of Weller—*hist pl* ... KY-4
House of Wills—*hist pl* ... OH-6
House on Ellicott's Hill—*hist pl* ... MS-4
House on KY 1492—*hist pl* ... KY-4
House on RR Ave—*hist pl* ... MT-8
House-on-the-Hill—*building* ... CA-9
House Park—*summit* ... UT-8
House Park Butte—*summit* ... UT-8
House Pasture Spring—*spring* ... TX-5
House Pasture Tank—*reservoir* ... NM-5
House Pasture Well—*well* ... TX-5
House Pasture Windmill—*locale* (2) ... NM-5
House Peak—*summit* ... AK-9
House Place Spring—*spring* ... AZ-5
*House Point* ... NJ-2
House Point—*cape* ... AK-9
House Point—*cape* ... ME-1
House Point—*cape* ... MD-2
House Pond—*lake* ... ME-1
House Pond—*lake* (2) ... NY-2
House Pond—*lake* ... NC-3
House Pond—*lake* ... SC-3
House Pond—*reservoir* ... PA-2
House Pond—*reservoir* ... SC-3
House Pond Dam—*dam* ... PA-2
Houser—*locale* ... WA-9
Houser, David, House—*hist pl* ... SC-3
House Ranch—*locale* ... AZ-5
House Ranch—*locale* ... CA-9
House Ranch—*locale* ... WY-8
*House Range* ... UT-8
House Range—*range* ... UT-8
Houser Branch—*stream* ... TN-4
Houser Camp—*locale* ... CA-9
Houser Cave—*cave* ... TN-4
*Houser Cem* ... TN-4
Houser Cem—*cemetery* ... IA-7
Houser Cem—*cemetery* ... KY-4
Houser Cem—*cemetery* ... TN-4
*Houser Creek* ... IN-6
Houser Creek Dam—*dam* ... TN-4
Houser Creek Dam—*reservoir* ... TN-4
Houser Creek Dam Number Two—*dam* ... TN-4
Houser Dam—*dam* ... NC-3
Houser Ditch—*canal* ... IN-6
Houser Grove Ch—*church* ... KY-4
*House Ridge* ... VA-3
Houser Lake—*lake* ... MI-6
Houser Lake—*reservoir* ... NC-3
*Houser Mills* ... PA-2
House Rock—*island* ... AK-9
House Rock—*island* ... OR-9
House Rock—*locale* ... AZ-5
House Rock—*pillar* ... NC-3
House Rock—*summit* ... CO-8
House Rock—*summit* ... IN-6
House Rock—*summit* ... NC-3
House Rock—*summit* ... VA-3
House Rock—*summit* ... WA-9
House Rock, The—*pillar* ... OR-9
House Rock Branch—*stream* ... IN-6
House Rock Campground—*park* ... UT-8
House Rock Canyon—*valley* ... AZ-5
House Rock Creek—*stream* ... OR-9
*House Rock Draw* ... AZ-5
House Rock Forest Camp—*locale* ... OR-9
House Rock Mine—*mine* ... NV-8
House Rock Rapids—*rapids* ... AZ-5
House Rock Run—*stream* ... PA-2
House Rock Spring—*spring* (2) ... AZ-5
House Rock Trick Tank—*reservoir* ... AZ-5
House Rock Valley—*valley* ... AZ-5
House Rock Valley Buffalo Range—*park* ... AZ-5
House Rock Wash—*stream* ... AZ-5
Houser Peak—*summit* ... MT-8
Houser Sch (historical)—*school* ... TN-4
Housers Millpond—*lake* ... GA-3
House Rsvr—*reservoir* ... CO-8
House Run—*stream* (2) ... PA-2
**Houserville**—*pop pl* ... MI-6
**Houserville**—*pop pl* ... PA-2
Houserville Elem Sch—*school* ... PA-2
Houserville Site (36CE65)—*hist pl* ... PA-2
Houses at 120 and 122 East 92nd Street—*hist pl* ... NY-2
Houses at 146-156 East 89th Street—*hist pl* ... NY-2
Houses At 16-22 East Lee Street—*hist pl* ... MD-2
Houses at 2000-2018 Delancey Street—*hist pl* ... PA-2
Houses at 208-218 East 78th Street—*hist pl* ... NY-2
Houses at 2501-2531 Charles Street—*hist pl* ... PA-2
Houses at 26, 28 and 30 Jones Street—*hist pl* ... NY-2
Houses at 311 and 313 East 58th Street—*hist pl* ... NY-2
Houses at 326, 328 and 330 East 18th Street—*hist pl* ... NY-2
Houses at 364 and 390 Van Duzer Street—*hist pl* ... NY-2
Houses at 406 and 408 Heard—*hist pl* ... TX-5
Houses at 437-459 West 24th Street—*hist pl* ... NY-2
Houses at 647, 651-53 Fifth Ave and 4 East 52nd Street—*hist pl* ... NY-2
Houses at 703 and 704 Austin—*hist pl* ... TX-5
Houses at 76-96 Harvard Ave—*hist pl* ... MA-1
Houses at 83 and 85 Sullivan Street—*hist pl* ... NY-2
Houses at 838-862 Brightridge Street—*hist pl* ... PA-2
Houses Ch—*church* ... TN-4
Houses Chapel—*church* ... TN-4
House School (abandoned)—*locale* ... MO-7
Houses Corner—*locale* ... NJ-2
Houses Creek—*stream* ... VA-3

House Seat Branch—*stream* (2) KY-4
Houses Ferry (historical)—*locale* AL-4
Houses Island—*island* AL-4
House Site Ridge—*ridge* NC-3
Houses Lake—*reservoir* AL-4
Houses on Hunterfly Road District—*hist pl* NY-2
Houses Pond—*lake* NJ-2
Houses Pond—*reservoir* NC-3
House Spring—*spring* AZ-5
House Spring—*spring* (2) CA-9
House Spring—*spring* (3) NV-8
House Spring—*spring* NM-5
House Spring—*spring* (2) OR-9
House Spring—*spring* PA-2
House Spring—*spring* (2) TX-5
House Spring—*spring* (3) UT-8
**House Springs**—*pop pl* MO-7
House Springs—*spring* UT-8
House Square—*locale* MA-1
*Houses Spring* MO-7
*Houses Springs* MO-7
House Tank—*reservoir* (2) AZ-5
House Tank—*reservoir* (2) NM-5
House Tank—*reservoir* (6) TX-5
House Tanks—*reservoir* TX-5
House that Lives, The—*hist pl* NJ-2
House Tm-B-7—*hist pl* KY-4
House Tm-M-27—*hist pl* KY-4
House Tm-M-28—*hist pl* KY-4
Houseton Cem—*cemetery* IL-6
*Housetonnick River* MA-1
Housetop Canyon—*valley* TX-5
Housetop Mountains—*range* TX-5
Housetop Mtn—*summit* CO-8
Housetop Mtn—*summit* (3) TX-5
Housetop Mtn—*summit* WY-8
House Trap Windmill—*locale* TX-5
Houseville—*locale* PA-2
**Houseville**—*pop pl* NY-2
House Wash—*stream* AZ-5
House Water Spring—*spring* AZ-5
House Water Well—*well* CO-8
House Well—*well* (2) NM-5
House Well—*well* (4) TX-5
House Well Number Two—*well* TX-5
House Where Lincoln Died, The—*park* DC-2
House Windmill—*locale* NM-5
House Windmill—*locale* (5) TX-5
Housewright Hollow—*valley* TN-4
House 15-19 Park Street—*hist pl* MA-1
Housgen Creek—*stream* MO-7
*Houshanaden Creek* OR-9
*Houshananden Creek* OR-9
Housh Chapel—*church* AL-4
*Houshs Chapel Ch of Christ* AL-4
*Housing Bayou* TX-5
Houska Park—*park* WI-6
Housland Branch—*stream* NC-3
**Housley**—*pop pl* TN-4
**Housley Addition**—*pop pl* TN-4
Housley Cem—*cemetery* TN-4
Housley Mtn—*summit* AR-4
Housley Point Rec Area—*park* AR-4
Housman Creek—*stream* AR-4
Housman Gulch—*valley* ID-8
Housman Sch—*school* TX-5
Housman Sch (abandoned)—*school* MO-7
Housman Sch (historical)—*school* MO-7
Housmer Creek—*stream* CO-8
Housmer Park—*flat* CO-8
Housons Corners—*locale* NY-2
*Houssatonneck* MA-1
Houssiere Park—*park* LA-4
*Houstenaden Creek* OR-9
Houstenader Creek—*stream* OR-9
Housten Cem—*cemetery* TX-5
*Houston* ND-7
*Houston* OK-5
*Houston* VA-3
Houston—*locale* CO-8
Houston—*locale* DE-2
Houston—*locale* FL-3
Houston—*locale* GA-3
Houston—*locale* ID-8
Houston—*locale* NE-7
**Houston**—*pop pl* AL-4
**Houston**—*pop pl* AK-9
**Houston**—*pop pl* AR-4
**Houston**—*pop pl* DE-2
**Houston**—*pop pl* IL-6
**Houston**—*pop pl* IN-6
**Houston**—*pop pl* KY-4
**Houston**—*pop pl* MN-6
**Houston**—*pop pl* (2) MS-4
**Houston**—*pop pl* MO-7
**Houston**—*pop pl* NC-3
**Houston**—*pop pl* OH-6
**Houston**—*pop pl* PA-2
**Houston**—*pop pl* TN-4
**Houston**—*pop pl* TX-5
Houston, E. C., House—*hist pl* NE-7
Houston, George, House—*hist pl* NC-3
Houston, Governor George Smith, House—*hist pl* AL-4
Houston, Lake—*reservoir* TX-5
Houston, Mrs. Sam, House—*hist pl* TX-5
Houston, Sam, House—*hist pl* TX-5
Houston Acad—*school* AL-4
**Houston Acres**—*pop pl* KY-4
Houston and Harris County Camp—*locale* TX-5
Houston Ave—*uninc pl* GA-3
Houston Ayers Branch—*stream* TN-4
Houston Baptist Coll—*school* TX-5
Houston Borough—*civil* PA-2
Houston Boys Camp—*locale* TX-5
Houston Branch—*stream* AL-4
Houston Branch—*stream* DE-2
Houston Branch—*stream* (2) GA-3
Houston Branch—*stream* MD-2
Houston Branch—*stream* MO-7
Houston Branch—*stream* NC-3
Houston Branch—*stream* TN-4
Houston Bridge—*bridge* AL-4
Houston Brook—*stream* (4) ME-1
Houston Brook Falls—*falls* ME-1
Houston Butte—*summit* OR-9
Houston Cabin—*locale* CA-9
Houston Canyon—*valley* NM-5
Houston Carnegie Library—*hist pl* MS-4
Houston-Carr Cem—*cemetery* WV-2
Houston Cave—*cave* AL-4
Houston Cave—*cave* TN-4
Houston (CCD)—*cens area* TX-5
Houston Cem—*cemetery* (5) AL-4
Houston Cem—*cemetery* (2) AR-4
Houston Cem—*cemetery* GA-3
Houston Cem—*cemetery* ID-8
Houston Cem—*cemetery* MO-7
Houston Cem—*cemetery* NC-3
Houston Cem—*cemetery* OH-6
Houston Cem—*cemetery* OK-5
Houston Cem—*cemetery* OR-9
Houston Cem—*cemetery* (9) TN-4
Houston Cemetary—*cemetery* AR-4
*Houston Cemetery* MS-4
*Houston Ch* AL-4
Houston Ch—*church* AL-4
Houston Ch—*church* GA-3
*Houston Channel* TX-5
Houston Chapel—*church* TN-4
Houston Ch of God—*church* MS-4
Houston Ch of the Nazarene—*church* MS-4
Houston Christian Ch (historical)—*church* MS-4
*Houston City* TX-5
**Houston City**—*pop pl* PA-2
Houston City Hall—*building* MS-4
Houston Cole Library—*building* AL-4
Houston Coll (historical)—*school* TN-4
Houston Community Hosp—*hospital* MS-4
**Houston Corner**—*pop pl* AL-4
**Houston Corner**—*pop pl* ME-1
Houston Country Club—*other* TX-5
**Houston County**—*pop pl* AL-4
**Houston (County)**—*pop pl* GA-3
**Houston (County)**—*pop pl* MN-6
**Houston County**—*pop pl* TN-4
**Houston (County)**—*pop pl* TX-5
Houston County Airp—*airport* TN-4
Houston County Courthouse—*building* AL-4
Houston County Courthouse—*building* TN-4
Houston County Courthouse and Jail—*hist pl* MN-6
Houston County Health Center—*hospital* AL-4
Houston County HS—*school* AL-4
Houston County HS—*school* TN-4
Houston County Lake—*lake* TX-5
Houston County Poor Farm—*hist pl* MN-6
Houston Cove—*cape* MD-2
Houston Creek—*stream* (3) AZ-5
Houston Creek—*stream* (2) CA-9
Houston Creek—*stream* GA-3
Houston Creek—*stream* ID-8
Houston Creek—*stream* KY-4
Houston Creek—*stream* MS-4
Houston Creek—*stream* (3) OK-5
Houston Creek—*stream* TX-5
Houston Creek—*stream* WY-8
Houston Creek Sch—*school* WY-8
Houston Ditch—*canal* IN-6
Houston Draw—*valley* AZ-5
Houston Draw—*valley* MT-8
Houston Draw—*valley* WY-8
Houston Elem Sch—*school* MS-4
Houston Farris Pond Dam—*dam* MS-4
*Houston Female Academy* MS-4
Houston Female Collegiate Institute (historical)—*school* MS-4
Houston Female Seminary (historical)—*school* MS-4
Houston Fire Station No. 7—*hist pl* TX-5
Houston Fishing Club Lake—*lake* TX-5
Houston Flat—*flat* UT-8
Houston Ford—*crossing* TN-4
*Houston Fork* IN-6
Houston Gap—*gap* NC-3
Houston Gardens Park—*park* TX-5
Houston Gardens Sch—*school* TX-5
*Houston Graveyard* TN-4
Houston Grove Ch—*church* GA-3
Houston Gulch—*valley* (2) CO-8
Houston Gulch Tank—*reservoir* NM-5
**Houston Heights**—*pop pl* TX-5
Houston Heights—*uninc pl* GA-3
Houston Heights Ch—*church* GA-3
Houston Heights Fire Station—*hist pl* TX-5
**Houston Heights (subdivision)**—*pop pl* NC-3
Houston Heights Waterworks Reservoir—*hist pl* TX-5
Houston Heights Woman's Club—*hist pl* TX-5
Houston Hill—*summit* TN-4
Houston Hill JHS—*school* AL-4
Houston Hill Sch—*school* VT-1
Houston (historical)—*locale* KS-7
**Houston (historical)**—*pop pl* NC-3
Houston Hollow—*valley* (2) AL-4
Houston Hollow—*valley* AR-4
Houston Hollow—*valley* OH-6
Houston Hollow—*valley* TN-4
Houston Hollow Cave—*cave* AL-4
Houston Hollow Ch—*church* OH-6
Houston House—*hist pl* OH-6
Houston HS—*school* MS-4
**Houstonia**—*pop pl* MO-7
Houstonia Cem—*cemetery* MO-7
Houstonia Township—*civil* MO-7
Houston Intercontinental Airp—*airport* TX-5
Houston Island—*island* ME-1
Houston Jail—*hist pl* AL-4
Houston JHS—*school* NM-5
Houston Junction—*locale* PA-2
*Houston Junction Station* PA-2
Houston Knob—*summit* (2) NC-3
Houston Lake—*lake* OR-9
Houston Lake—*locale* GA-3
**Houston Lake**—*pop pl* MO-7
Houston Lake—*reservoir* GA-3
Houston Lakes—*lake* CO-8
Houston Levee Golf Course Dam—*dam* TN-4
Houston Levee Golf Course Lake—*reservoir* TN-4
Houston Library—*building* AL-4
Houston Lookout Tower—*locale* AL-4
Houston Male Acad (historical)—*school* MS-4
Houston Memorial Airp—*airport* MO-7
*Houston Memorial Library* AL-4
Houston Memorial Library—*building* AL-4
Houston Mesa—*summit* AZ-5
Houston Mesa Ruins—*hist pl* AZ-5
Houston Mine—*mine* IN-6
Houston Mission Sch—*school* KY-4
**Houston Mobile Home Park**—*pop pl* NC-3
Houston Mound—*summit* TX-5
Houston Mound Historical Marker—*park* TX-5
Houston MS—*school* MS-4
Houston Mtn—*summit* CO-8
Houston Mtn—*summit* ME-1
Houston Mtn—*summit* UT-8
Houston Municipal Airp—*airport* MS-4
Houston Negro Hosp—*hist pl* TX-5
Houston Negro Hosp Sch of Nursing Bldg—*hist pl* TX-5
Houston-Oklahoma Oil Field—*oilfield* TX-5
Houston Park—*park* IN-6
Houston Pass—*gap* AK-9
Houston Pocket—*basin* AZ-5
Houston Point—*cape* MD-2
Houston Point—*cape* MT-8
Houston Point—*cape* TX-5
*Houston Pond* ME-1
*Houston Pond* NH-1
Houston Pond—*reservoir* CO-8
Houston Post Office—*building* MS-4
Houston Post Office (historical)—*building* TN-4
Houston Presbyterian Ch—*church* MS-4
Houston Public Library—*hist pl* TX-5
Houston Ranch—*locale* AZ-5
Houston Ranch—*locale* OR-9
Houston Ranch—*locale* (2) TX-5
Houston Ridge—*ridge* NC-3
Houston Ridge—*ridge* WY-8
**Houston River**—*pop pl* LA-4
Houston River—*stream* LA-4
Houston River Canal—*canal* LA-4
Houston River Ch—*church* LA-4
Houston Run—*stream* PA-2
Houston Run—*stream* WV-2
Houston Sch—*school* CA-9
Houston Sch—*school* IL-6
Houston Sch—*school* MI-6
Houston Sch—*school* (2) MS-4
Houston Sch—*school* MO-7
Houston Sch—*school* (2) OK-5
Houston Sch—*school* PA-2
Houston Sch—*school* SD-7
Houston Sch—*school* (13) TX-5
Houston Sch—*school* VA-3
Houston Sch (abandoned)—*school* (2) MO-7
Houston Sch (historical)—*school* PA-2
Houston Sch (historical)—*school* TN-4
Houston School (Abandoned)—*locale* MO-7
Houstons Corner—*locale* VA-3
*Houstons Crossroads* AL-4
Houston Second Missionary Baptist Ch—*church* MS-4
Houston Sewage Lagoon Dam—*dam* MS-4
Houstons Fort (historical)—*locale* TN-4
*Houston Ship Canal* TX-5
Houston Ship Channel—*channel* TX-5
Houstons Island (historical)—*island* AL-4
Houstons Landing (historical)—*locale* AL-4
*Houstons Point* TX-5
Houston Spring—*spring* AL-4
Houston Spring—*spring* WY-8
Houston Spring Branch—*stream* TN-4
Houston Springs—*spring* SD-7
*Houstons Station* TN-4
*Houstons Store* AL-4
Houstons Store (historical)—*locale* AL-4
Houston Street Viaduct—*bridge* TX-5
Houston Street Viaduct—*hist pl* TX-5
Houston Strip Mine—*mine* AK-9
Houston Tank—*reservoir* AZ-5
Houston-Thorogood Ditch—*stream* DE-2
Houston Tower Site State Wildlife Area—*locale* MO-7
**Houstontown**—*pop pl* AL-4
**Houston Township**—*pop pl* KS-7
Houston (Township of)—*fmr MCD* AR-4
**Houston (Township of)**—*pop pl* IL-6
**Houston (Township of)**—*pop pl* MN-6
Houston Turn-Verein—*hist pl* TX-5
Houston Union Ch—*church* AL-4
**Houston Valley**—*pop pl* TN-4
Houston Valley—*valley* GA-3
Houston Valley—*valley* TN-4
Houston Valley Ch—*church* GA-3
Houston Valley Ch—*church* TN-4
Houston Valley Rec Area—*park* TN-4
Houston Valley Sch—*school* TN-4
Houstonville—*locale* NC-3
**Houstonville**—*pop pl* AL-4
**Houstonville (historical)**—*pop pl* NC-3
Houston Vocational Center—*school* GA-3
Houston Vocational Complex—*school* MS-4
Houston Well—*well* CO-8
Houston Whitworth Cem—*cemetery* TN-4
Houston Windmill—*locale* NM-5
Houston Yacht Club—*other* TX-5
Houston Youth Camp—*locale* GA-3
Houstown Cut—*channel* GA-3
Houstus Hill—*summit* ME-1
Houstveit Sch—*school* ND-7
**Housum**—*pop pl* PA-2
Hout Ditch—*canal* AR-4
Houte Ditch—*canal* IN-6
Houten Branch—*stream* AL-4
Houts Cem—*cemetery* MO-7
Houts Chapel—*church* MO-7
Hout Spring—*spring* CO-8
Houts Rsvr—*reservoir* CO-8
Houtz Canyon—*valley* ID-8
Houtz Cem—*cemetery* IA-7
Houtz Creek—*stream* ID-8
**Houtzdale**—*pop pl* PA-2
Houtzdale Borough—*civil* PA-2
Houtz Sch (abandoned)—*school* PA-2
Houvenkopf Mtn—*summit* NJ-2
Houx, Coulee de—*valley* LA-4
Houx Cem—*cemetery* MO-7
Houx-Hoefer-Rehkop House—*hist pl* MO-7
Houze Cem—*cemetery* TN-4
Houze Hollow—*valley* TN-4
Houze Place—*locale* CA-9
*Houzt Creek* ID-8
Hovander Homestead—*hist pl* WA-9
Hovarka Canal—*canal* UT-8
Hovater Cem—*cemetery* AL-4
Hovaters Mill (historical)—*locale* AL-4
Hovatter—*locale* WV-2
Hovda, Oliver H., House—*hist pl* MT-8
Hovde Cem—*cemetery* SD-7
Hovde Lake—*lake* MN-6
Hovel Creek—*stream* AR-4
**Hove Mobile Park**—*pop pl* ND-7
**Hoven**—*pop pl* SD-7
Hoven Country Club—*locale* SD-7
Hovenden House, Barn and Abolition Hall—*hist pl* PA-2
Hoven Municipal Airp—*airport* SD-7
Hoven Township—*civil* (2) SD-7
Hovenweep Canyon—*valley* CO-8
Hovenweep Castle (ruins)—*locale* UT-8
Hovenweep Natl Monmt—*hist pl* CO-8
Hovenweep Natl Monument—*park* CO-8
Hovenweep Natl Monument—*park* UT-8
Hovenweep Ranger Station—*locale* UT-8
Hover, George A., House—*hist pl* OR-9
Hoverhawk Ranch Airp—*airport* WA-9
H-over-H Windmill—*locale* NM-5
*Hover Lake* MI-6
Hovermale Ridge—*ridge* WY-8
Hoverrocker Ranch—*locale* AZ-5
Hoverson Rsvr—*reservoir* MT-8
Hoverstock Cem—*cemetery* IN-6
Hovet Sch—*school* ND-7
Hovey—*locale* OK-5
Hovey—*locale* TX-5
**Hovey**—*pop pl* IN-6
**Hovey**—*pop pl* MS-4
**Hovey**—*pop pl* TX-5
Hovey, Horatio N., House—*hist pl* MI-6
*Hovey Bend* TN-4
Hovey Bend—*bend* TX-5
*Hovey Branch* MS-4
Hovey Brook—*stream* ME-1
**Hovey Corner**—*pop pl* MA-1
Hovey Creek—*stream* WA-9
Hovey Dam—*dam* MA-1
Hovey Drain—*canal* MI-6
Hovey Gulch—*valley* CA-9
Hovey Gulch School—*locale* CA-9
Hovey Gully—*valley* NY-2
*Hovey Lake* MI-6
Hovey Lake—*lake* IN-6
Hovey Lake—*lake* MI-6
Hovey Lake Archaeol District—*hist pl* IN-6
Hovey Lake Fish and Wildlife Area—*park* IN-6
*Hovey Lake State Game Preserve* IN-6
Hovey Mtn—*summit* ME-1
Hovey Point—*cape* CA-9
Hovey Pond—*reservoir* MA-1
*Hoveys Beach* MI-6
Hovey Sch—*school* (2) MI-6
Hovey Sch—*school* WI-6
**Hovey's Corner**—*pop pl* MA-1
*Hoveys Lake* IN-6
*Hoveys Pond* MA-1
Hoveys Pond—*lake* MA-1
Hovey Swamp—*swamp* ME-1
**Hovey (Township of)**—*pop pl* PA-2
Hovie Island—*island* IA-7
**Hoving**—*pop pl* ND-7
**Hovious**—*pop pl* KY-4
Hovious Ridge—*ridge* KY-4
Hovis Bend—*bend* TN-4
Hovis Ranch—*locale* AZ-5
*Hovius Ridge* KY-4
**Hovland**—*pop pl* MN-6
Hovland Dam—*dam* MT-8
Hovland Lookout Tower—*locale* MN-6
Hovland State Wildlife Mngmt Area—*park* MN-6
Hovley—*locale* CA-9
Hovorka Airp—*airport* KS-7
How, Daniel, House—*hist pl* ME-1
Ho-Wah-We Boy Scout Camp (historical)—*locale* PA-2
*Howard* MN-6
*Howard* ND-7
*Howard* PA-2
HOWARD—*hist pl* MD-2
Howard—*locale* AR-4
Howard—*locale* CA-9
Howard—*locale* KY-4
Howard—*locale* LA-4
Howard—*locale* OK-5
Howard—*locale* OR-9
Howard—*locale* PA-2
Howard—*locale* RI-1
Howard—*locale* SC-3
Howard—*locale* TN-4
Howard—*locale* TX-5
Howard—*locale* WA-9
Howard—*locale* WV-2
Howard—*locale* WI-6
**Howard**—*pop pl* AL-4
**Howard**—*pop pl* CO-8
**Howard**—*pop pl* FL-3
**Howard**—*pop pl* GA-3
**Howard**—*pop pl* IN-6
**Howard**—*pop pl* KS-7
**Howard**—*pop pl* MS-4
**Howard**—*pop pl* MT-8
**Howard**—*pop pl* NY-2
**Howard**—*pop pl* OH-6
**Howard**—*pop pl* (3) PA-2
**Howard**—*pop pl* SD-7
**Howard**—*pop pl* TN-4
**Howard**—*pop pl* WI-6
Howard—*uninc pl* NY-2
Howard—*uninc pl* TX-5
Howard, Adam, House—*hist pl* OH-6
Howard, A. E., House—*hist pl* WA-9
Howard, C. R., House—*hist pl* OH-6
Howard, Frank, House—*hist pl* KS-7
Howard, Gen. Oliver Otis, House—*hist pl* DC-2
Howard, Horatio N., House—*hist pl* MI-6
Howard, Kenneth L., House—*hist pl* NC-3
Howard, Lake—*lake* (3) FL-3
Howard, Lake—*lake* WA-9
Howard, Lake—*reservoir* (2) AL-4
Howard, Lake—*reservoir* GA-3
Howard, Mount—*summit* AK-9
Howard, Mount—*summit* OR-9
Howard, Mount—*summit* WA-9
Howard, Point—*cape* AK-9
Howard Acad—*school* FL-3
**Howard Acres (subdivision)**—*pop pl* NC-3
Howard Airp—*airport* MO-7
Howard and Winslow Ditch—*canal* CO-8
Howard Ave Hist Dist—*hist pl* CT-1
*Howard Bay* ME-1
*Howard Bay* OR-9
*Howard Bay* WI-6
Howard Bay—*bay* AK-9
Howard Bay—*bay* NC-3
Howard Bay—*bay* OR-9
Howard Bay—*swamp* NC-3
**Howard Beach**—*pop pl* NY-2
Howard Bend—*bend* MO-7
Howard Block—*hist pl* MA-1
*Howard Boro* PA-2
Howard Borough—*civil* PA-2
Howard Branch—*stream* (2) AL-4
Howard Branch—*stream* AR-4
Howard Branch—*stream* (2) GA-3
Howard Branch—*stream* (7) KY-4
Howard Branch—*stream* MO-7
Howard Branch—*stream* (2) NC-3
Howard Branch—*stream* SC-3
Howard Branch—*stream* (4) TN-4
Howard Branch Sch—*school* KY-4
Howard-Breland Cem—*cemetery* MS-4
Howard Bridge—*bridge* (2) TN-4
Howard Bridge—*hist pl* CO-8
*Howard Brook* ME-1
*Howard Brook* NH-1
Howard Brook—*stream* (4) ME-1
Howard Brook—*stream* (2) MA-1
Howard Brook—*stream* NH-1
Howard Brook—*stream* VT-1
Howard Brothers' Store—*hist pl* KY-4
Howard Brown Dam—*dam* AL-4
Howard Brown Lake—*reservoir* AL-4
Howard Burks Mine—*mine* TN-4
Howard Butte—*summit* (2) OR-9
Howard Camp—*locale* ID-8
Howard Canyon—*valley* AZ-5
Howard Canyon—*valley* CA-9
Howard Canyon—*valley* CO-8
Howard Canyon—*valley* (3) OR-9
Howard Canyon—*valley* TX-5
Howard Capp Dam—*dam* (2) SD-7
Howard Career Center—*school* DE-2
*Howard Cem* TN-4
Howard Cem—*cemetery* (2) AR-4
Howard Cem—*cemetery* CO-8
Howard Cem—*cemetery* FL-3
Howard Cem—*cemetery* (2) GA-3
Howard Cem—*cemetery* (5) IL-6
Howard Cem—*cemetery* (2) IN-6
Howard Cem—*cemetery* IA-7
Howard Cem—*cemetery* (3) KS-7
Howard Cem—*cemetery* (11) KY-4
Howard Cem—*cemetery* (3) ME-1
Howard Cem—*cemetery* (2) MA-1
Howard Cem—*cemetery* (3) MI-6
Howard Cem—*cemetery* (4) MS-4
Howard Cem—*cemetery* (9) MO-7
Howard Cem—*cemetery* NE-7
Howard Cem—*cemetery* NV-8
Howard Cem—*cemetery* (4) NY-2
Howard Cem—*cemetery* (2) OH-6
Howard Cem—*cemetery* OK-5
Howard Cem—*cemetery* OR-9
Howard Cem—*cemetery* (9) TN-4
Howard Cem—*cemetery* (3) TX-5
Howard Cem—*cemetery* (2) VA-3
Howard Cemetery—*locale* TX-5
Howard Center (historical P.O.)—*locale* IA-7
Howard Center Township—*fmr MCD* IA-7
Howard Center Township Cem—*cemetery* IA-7
Howard Ch—*church* AR-4
Howard Ch—*church* (2) IL-6
Howard Ch—*church* IN-6
Howard Ch—*church* OH-6
Howard Ch—*church* SC-3
*Howard Channel* NC-3
Howard Channel—*stream* NC-3
Howard Chapel—*church* (2) AL-4
Howard Chapel—*church* GA-3
Howard Chapel—*church* IL-6
Howard Chapel—*church* IN-6
Howard Chapel—*church* MS-4
Howard Chapel—*church* MO-7
Howard Chapel—*church* (2) SC-3
Howard Chapel—*church* VA-3
**Howard Chapel**—*pop pl* TN-4
Howard Chapel Cem—*cemetery* TN-4
Howard Chapel Sch—*school* TN-4
Howard Ch (historical)—*church* TN-4
Howard Ch of Christ—*church* AL-4
Howard Cienega—*other* NM-5
*Howard City* KS-7
*Howard City* NE-7
*Howard City* SD-7
**Howard City**—*pop pl* MI-6
**Howard City**—*pop pl* NE-7
Howard City Club—*other* MI-6
Howard Coll—*school* AL-4
Howard Coll (historical)—*school* TN-4
Howard Copper Mine—*mine* AZ-5
Howard Corner—*locale* ME-1
Howard Coulee—*arroyo* MT-8
Howard Coulee—*valley* MT-8
**Howard (County)**—*pop pl* AR-4
**Howard County**—*pop pl* IN-6
**Howard (County)**—*pop pl* MD-2
**Howard County**—*pop pl* MO-7
**Howard (County)**—*pop pl* TX-5
Howard County Airp—*airport* IN-6
Howard County Courthouse—*hist pl* IA-7
Howard County Fairground—*locale* IA-7
Howard County Farm—*building* IA-7
Howard County Hosp—*hospital* IA-7
Howard County Junior Coll—*school* TX-5
Howard County Memorial Hosp—*hospital* AR-4
Howard County Museum—*locale* IA-7
Howard Cove—*bay* AK-9
Howard Cove—*bay* AR-4
Howard Cove—*bay* ME-1
*Howard Creek* AR-4
*Howard Creek* LA-4
*Howard Creek* NC-3
*Howard Creek* VA-3
*Howard Creek* WY-8
Howard Creek—*stream* (2) AL-4
Howard Creek—*stream* (2) AK-9
Howard Creek—*stream* (3) AR-4
Howard Creek—*stream* (7) CA-9
Howard Creek—*stream* (2) CO-8
Howard Creek—*stream* (4) FL-3
Howard Creek—*stream* GA-3
Howard Creek—*stream* (5) ID-8
Howard Creek—*stream* IN-6
Howard Creek—*stream* IA-7
Howard Creek—*stream* KS-7
Howard Creek—*stream* KY-4
Howard Creek—*stream* LA-4
Howard Creek—*stream* MI-6
Howard Creek—*stream* (5) MS-4
Howard Creek—*stream* (3) MO-7
Howard Creek—*stream* (2) MT-8
Howard Creek—*stream* (2) NC-3
Howard Creek—*stream* OH-6
Howard Creek—*stream* (7) OR-9
Howard Creek—*stream* SC-3
Howard Creek—*stream* TN-4
Howard Creek—*stream* (2) TX-5
Howard Creek—*stream* UT-8
Howard Creek—*stream* (4) WA-9
Howard Creek—*stream* (2) WV-2
Howard Creek—*stream* WY-8
Howard Creek Ch—*church* NC-3
Howard Creek Chute—*gut* OR-9
Howard Creek Chute—*rapids* OR-9
Howard Creek Meadows—*flat* CA-9
Howard Creek Meadows—*flat* MT-8
Howard Creek Sch—*school* CO-8
Howard Creek Trail—*trail* ID-8
Howard Creek Trail—*trail* WA-9
Howard Cutoff Trail—*trail* OR-9
Howard Dam—*dam* (2) AL-4
Howard Dam—*dam* AZ-5
Howard Dam—*dam* ND-7
Howard Dam—*dam* PA-2
Howard Dam—*dam* VT-1
Howard-Davis Cem—*cemetery* KY-4
Howard District Sch (historical)—*school* IA-7
Howard Ditch—*canal* (2) CO-8
Howard Ditch—*canal* (3) IN-6
Howard D McMillian JHS—*school* FL-3
*Howard Drain* MI-6
Howard Drain—*canal* MI-6
Howard Drain—*stream* MI-6
Howard Draw—*valley* AZ-5
Howard Draw—*valley* TX-5
Howard Draw—*valley* UT-8
Howard Drive Elem Sch—*school* FL-3
Howard Eaton Trail—*trail* WY-8
Howard Elem Sch—*school* (2) TN-4
Howard E Smith Dam—*dam* AL-4
Howard E Smith Lake—*reservoir* AL-4
**Howard Estates (subdivision)**—*pop pl* UT-8
Howard Falls—*falls* PA-2
Howard Fall Sch (abandoned)—*school* PA-2
Howard Fall Sch (historical)—*school* PA-2
**Howard Farms Beach**—*pop pl* OH-6
*Howard Female Coll* TN-4
*Howard Female Institute* TN-4
Howard Flat—*flat* CA-9
Howard Flat—*flat* ID-8
Howard Flats—*flat* CO-8
Howard Flats—*flat* WA-9
Howard Ford—*locale* TN-4
*Howard Fork* AR-4
Howard Fork—*stream* CO-8
Howard Fork—*stream* (2) KY-4
Howard Fork—*stream* WV-2
Howard Franklin Bridge—*bridge* FL-3
*Howard Furnace Gap* PA-2
Howard Gap—*gap* GA-3
Howard Gap—*gap* (2) NC-3
Howard Gap—*gap* PA-2
Howard-Gettys House—*hist pl* KY-4
Howard Glasscock Oil Field—*oilfield* TX-5
Howard Grittman Pond Dam—*dam* MS-4
Howard Grove Cem—*cemetery* IA-7
*Howard Grove Church* AL-4
*Howard Gulch* WY-8
Howard Gulch—*valley* CO-8
Howard Gulch—*valley* ID-8
Howard Hanson Rsvr—*reservoir* WA-9
Howard H Baker Sr Lake—*reservoir* TN-4
Howard Hedger Sch—*school* SD-7
**Howard Heights**—*pop pl* MD-2
**Howard Hights (subdivision)**—*pop pl* NC-3
**Howard Hill**—*pop pl* TN-4
Howard Hill—*summit* AK-9
Howard Hill—*summit* AZ-5
Howard Hill—*summit* AR-4
Howard Hill—*summit* CA-9
Howard Hill—*summit* (3) ME-1
Howard Hill—*summit* NH-1
Howard Hill—*summit* NY-2
Howard Hill—*summit* PA-2
Howard Hill—*summit* RI-1
Howard Hill—*summit* TN-4
Howard Hill—*summit* VT-1
Howard Hill—*summit* WY-8
Howard Hill Ch—*church* AR-4
Howard Hill Ch—*church* NY-2
Howard Hill Ch—*church* NC-3
Howard Hills—*other* AK-9
Howard Hill Sch—*school* AR-4
Howard Hill Sch—*school* VT-1
**Howard (historical)**—*pop pl* TN-4
Howard Hollow—*valley* (2) KY-4
Howard Hollow—*valley* (2) TN-4
Howard Hollow—*valley* TX-5
Howard Hollow—*valley* (2) UT-8
Howard Hollow—*valley* VA-3
Howard Home—*hist pl* IN-6
Howard Homestead—*hist pl* NY-2
Howard Hot Spring—*spring* NV-8
Howard HS—*hist pl* DE-2
Howard HS—*school* FL-3
Howard HS—*school* GA-3
Howard HS—*school* TN-4
Howard HS—*school* WI-6
Howard II Elem Sch—*school* MS-4
Howard Iron Works Post Office (historical)—*building* TN-4
*Howard Island* TN-4
Howard Island—*island* MA-1
Howard Island—*island* MI-6
Howard Island—*island* MO-7
Howard Island—*island* NH-1

Howard Island—*island* OH-6
Howard Island (historical)—*island* AL-4
Howard JHS—*school* FL-3
Howard J Kunstle Dam—*dam* SD-7
Howard J. Morton Memorial State Park—*locale* OR-9
Howard Johnson Ditch—*canal* IN-6
Howard Johnsons Motor Lodge Airp—*airport* PA-2
**Howard Junction (Howard)**—*pop pl* PA-2
Howard Junction Station—*locale* PA-2
Howard Knob—*summit* NC-3
Howard Knob—*summit* VA-3
*Howard Lake* KS-7
*Howard Lake* MI-6
Howard Lake—*lake* AK-9
Howard Lake—*lake* AZ-5
Howard Lake—*lake* AR-4
Howard Lake—*lake* (2) CA-9
Howard Lake—*lake* FL-3
Howard Lake—*lake* IN-6
Howard Lake—*lake* IA-7
Howard Lake—*lake* ME-1
Howard Lake—*lake* (4) MI-6
Howard Lake—*lake* (6) MN-6
Howard Lake—*lake* MS-4
Howard Lake—*lake* MT-8
Howard Lake—*lake* ND-7
Howard Lake—*lake* (2) TX-5
Howard Lake—*lake* (2) WA-9
Howard Lake—*lake* WY-8
**Howard Lake**—*pop pl* MN-6
Howard Lake—*reservoir* AL-4
Howard Lake—*reservoir* GA-3
Howard Lake—*reservoir* IN-6
Howard Lake—*reservoir* NC-3
Howard Lake City Hall—*hist pl* MN-6
Howard Lake Dam—*dam* NC-3
Howard Lake Mtn—*summit* ME-1
Howard Lake Stream—*stream* WA-9
Howard Lamar Dam—*dam* AL-4
Howard Landing—*locale* AL-4
Howard Landing—*locale* CA-9
Howard Landing—*locale* (2) NC-3
Howard Landing Ferry—*locale* CA-9
Howard Lateral—*canal* (2) CA-9
Howard L Hall Elem Sch—*school* NC-3
Howard Libbey Tree—*locale* CA-9
Howard Little Pond Dam—*dam* MS-4
**Howard Manor (subdivision)**—*pop pl* DE-2
Howard Meadow—*flat* (3) OR-9
Howard Meadows—*flat* CA-9
Howard Meadows—*flat* OR-9
Howard Meadows—*flat* WA-9
Howard Meadow Trail (jeep)—*trail* OR-9
Howard Memorial Hosp—*hospital* MS-4
Howard Memorial Tabernacle (historical)—*church* AL-4
Howard Mesa—*summit* AZ-5
Howard Miami Ch—*church* IN-6
Howard Mill—*locale* TN-4
**Howard Mills**—*pop pl* KY-4
Howard Mill Station—*locale* CA-9
*Howard Mines* AL-4
Howard Mound—*summit* AR-4
Howard Mound—*summit* FL-3
Howard MS—*school* FL-3
Howard Mtn—*summit* AZ-5
Howard Mtn—*summit* CO-8
Howard Mtn—*summit* GA-3
Howard Mtn—*summit* ID-8
Howard Mtn—*summit* (3) ME-1
Howard Mtn—*summit* (3) NY-2
Howard Municipal Airp—*airport* SD-7
Howard Nook—*ridge* KY-4
Howard No 1 Ditch—*canal* CO-8
Howard Park—*park* FL-3
Howard Park—*park* IN-6
Howard Park—*park* (2) MI-6
Howard Park—*park* MO-7
**Howard Park**—*pop pl* MD-2
Howard Parker Lake Dam—*dam* MS-4
Howard Park General Hosp—*hospital* NY-2
Howard Pass—*gap* AK-9
Howard Payne Univ—*school* TX-5
*Howard Peak* OR-9
Howard Peak—*summit* AZ-5
Howard Peak—*summit* CA-9
Howard Peak—*summit* WA-9
Howard Place—*locale* CO-8
Howard Playground—*park* MI-6
Howard Pocket—*basin* AZ-5
Howard Pocket Tank—*reservoir* AZ-5
Howard Point—*cape* (3) ME-1
Howard Point—*cape* MN-6
*Howard Pond* AZ-5
Howard Pond—*lake* (2) ME-1
Howard Pond—*lake* MA-1
Howard Pond—*lake* (2) NY-2
Howard Pond—*lake* (2) TN-4
Howard Pond—*reservoir* NC-3
Howard Pond—*reservoir* RI-1
Howard Post Office (historical)—*building* AL-4
Howard Post Office (historical)—*building* MS-4
Howard Prairie—*flat* OR-9
Howard Prairie Branch—*stream* FL-3
Howard Prairie Dam—*dam* OR-9
Howard Prairie Lake—*lake* OR-9
Howard Prairie Lake—*reservoir* (2) OR-9
*Howard Prairie Rsvr* OR-9
Howard Quarter—*locale* TN-4
Howard Quarter Ch—*church* TN-4
Howard Quarter Sch—*school* TN-4
Howard Ranch—*locale* (2) CA-9
Howard Ranch—*locale* (2) CO-8
Howard Ranch—*locale* ID-8
Howard Ranch—*locale* ND-7
Howard Ranch—*locale* OR-9
Howard Ranch—*locale* (2) TX-5
Howard Ranch—*locale* WA-9
Howard Ranch—*locale* WY-8
Howard R Driggs Sch—*school* UT-8
Howard Reed Brake—*stream* MS-4
Howard Reef—*bar* NC-3
Howard Ridge—*ridge* IN-6
Howard Ridge—*ridge* ME-1
Howard Ridge—*ridge* (2) OH-6
Howard Ridge—*ridge* TN-4
Howard Ridge Cem—*cemetery* OH-6
Howard Roosa Elementary and JHS—*school* IN-6
*Howard Roosa Sch* IN-6
Howard Roosa Sch—*school* IN-6
Howard Routh Ditch—*canal* WY-8
Howard-Royal House—*hist pl* NC-3
Howard Rsvr—*reservoir* CO-8
Howard Rsvr—*reservoir* CT-1
Howard Rsvr—*reservoir* MT-8
Howard Rsvr—*reservoir* TX-5
Howard Run—*stream* (3) OH-6
Howard Run—*stream* WV-2
*Howards* PA-2
Howards—*locale* TX-5
Howards Bar—*bar* AL-4
*Howard's Bay* ME-1
Howards Bay—*bay* IA-7
Howards Bay—*harbor* WI-6
*Howards Bluff* MS-4
Howards Bottom—*bend* KY-4
Howards Bottom Sch—*school* KY-4
*Howards Brook* MA-1
Howards Camp—*locale* MI-6
Howards Ch—*church* MO-7
Howard Sch—*school* AR-4
Howard Sch—*school* (2) CA-9
Howard Sch—*school* FL-3
Howard Sch—*school* GA-3
Howard Sch—*school* (6) IL-6
Howard Sch—*school* KS-7
Howard Sch—*school* (3) KY-4
Howard Sch—*school* MD-2
Howard Sch—*school* (2) MA-1
Howard Sch—*school* (2) MI-6
Howard Sch—*school* MO-7
Howard Sch—*school* MT-8
Howard Sch—*school* (2) NE-7
Howard Sch—*school* (2) OH-6
Howard Sch—*school* (3) OR-9
Howard Sch—*school* SC-3
Howard Sch—*school* SD-7
Howard Sch—*school* (4) TN-4
Howard Sch—*school* TX-5
Howard Sch (abandoned)—*school* PA-2
Howards Channel—*channel* NC-3
Howards Channel—*gut* NC-3
Howards Chapel—*church* (3) NC-3
Howards Chapel Baptist Ch—*church* TN-4
*Howards Chapel School* TN-4
Howard Sch (historical)—*school* (2) AL-4
Howard Schmele Dam Number 1—*dam* SD-7
Howard Schmidt Dam—*dam* OR-9
Howard Schmidt Rsvr—*reservoir* OR-9
Howard Sch Number 2—*school* LA-4
Howard School—*locale* (2) MI-6
Howards Corner—*locale* VA-3
Howards Corner—*locale* WA-9
Howard's Covered Bridge—*hist pl* GA-3
*Howards Creek* CA-9
*Howards Creek* TN-4
*Howards Creek* TX-5
**Howards Creek**—*pop pl* KY-4
Howards Creek—*stream* (3) KY-4
Howards Creek—*stream* NC-3
Howards Creek—*stream* WI-6
Howards Creek Ch—*church* KY-4
Howards Creek Mill—*locale* NC-3
Howards Creek Sch—*school* NC-3
Howards Creek (Township of)—*fmr MCD* NC-3
Howards Crossroads—*locale* SC-3
Howards Ditch—*canal* LA-4
Howard Seep—*spring* AZ-5
Howard Seep Tank—*reservoir* AZ-5
Howard Seminary—*school* MA-1
*Howards Farm* MS-4
Howard S Fernsler Academic Center—*school* PA-2
*Howards Ferry* MS-4
*Howards Fork* AR-4
*Howards Fork* CO-8
*Howard's Fork of Frog Bayou* AR-4
Howard's Gristmill—*hist pl* OR-9
**Howards Grove**—*pop pl* NH-1
**Howards Grove**—*pop pl* WI-6
Howards Grove Cem—*cemetery* KY-4
Howards Grove Ch—*church* AL-4
Howards Grove-Millersville—*post sta* WI-6
*Howards Gulch* CA-9
Howards Gulch—*valley* (2) CA-9
Howard-Shepard Cem—*cemetery* KY-4
Howard Shoals—*bar* TN-4
Howards Hollow—*valley* OH-6
**Howard Siding**—*pop pl* PA-2
Howard Silver Mine—*mine* AZ-5
*Howards Island* TN-4
Howards Knob County Park—*park* NC-3
Howards Lake—*lake* GA-3
Howards Lake—*reservoir* CO-8
*Howards Landing* AL-4
Howards Landing—*locale* (2) TN-4
Howards Landing (historical)—*locale* AL-4
Howards Lick Run—*stream* WV-2
Howard Slough—*gut* CA-9
Howard Slough—*stream* CA-9
Howard Slough—*stream* UT-8
Howard Slough Waterfowl Mngmt Area—*park* UT-8
Howards Lower Bar—*bar* AL-4
Howards Lower Forge (historical)—*locale* TN-4
Howards Mill—*locale* GA-3
**Howards Mill**—*pop pl* KY-4
Howards Mill Creek—*stream* AL-4
Howards Mill Creek—*stream* GA-3
Howards Mill Dam (historical)—*dam* TN-4
Howards Mill (historical)—*locale* (2) TN-4
Howard's Neck Plantation—*hist pl* VA-3
Howards Pit—*cave* TN-4
*Howards Pocket* WI-6
Howards Pond—*lake* SC-3
Howards Pond—*lake* UT-8
Howards Pond—*reservoir* AL-4
*Howard Spring* OR-9
Howard Spring—*spring* (2) AZ-5
Howard Spring—*spring* ID-8
Howard Spring—*spring* TN-4
Howard Spring—*spring* UT-8
Howard Spring—*spring* WY-8
Howard Springs—*locale* TN-4
**Howard Springs**—*pop pl* CA-9
Howard Springs—*spring* CA-9
Howard Springs Post Office (historical)—*building* TN-4
Howard Springs Sch (historical)—*school* TN-4
Howard Spring Wayside—*locale* ID-8
*Howards Quarter* TN-4
*Howards Quarter Missionary Baptist Church* TN-4
*Howards Quarters* TN-4
*Howards Quarters Sch* TN-4
**Howards Ridge**—*pop pl* MO-7
Howards Ridge—*ridge* MO-7
Howards Shoals—*bar* TN-4
Howards Shop Ctr—*locale* TN-4
*Howards Store* MS-4
Howards Store—*locale* MS-4
Howards Tank—*reservoir* AZ-5
Howard (State Institution)—*hospital* RI-1
Howard State Nursery—*forest* PA-2
*Howard Station* MS-4
Howardstown—*locale* KY-4
Howard Street Cem—*cemetery* MA-1
Howard Street Sch—*school* MA-1
Howard Street Sch—*school* PA-2
Howard Street Tunnel—*hist pl* MD-2
Howards Upper Forge (historical)—*locale* TN-4
Howardsville—*locale* CO-8
Howardsville—*locale* MI-6
Howardsville—*locale* (2) VA-3
**Howardsville**—*pop pl* MD-2
**Howardsville**—*pop pl* NJ-2
Howard Swamp—*lake* FL-3
Howards Well—*well* TX-5
Howards Wood Rec Area—*park* IA-7
Howard Tank—*reservoir* NM-5
Howard Tank—*reservoir* TX-5
Howard T Ennis Sch—*school* DE-2
Howard Theatre—*hist pl* DC-2
**Howardton**—*pop pl* IL-6
Howardton Cem—*cemetery* TN-4
Howardton Ch—*church* TN-4
*Howardton Missionary Baptist Ch* TN-4
Howard Tower—*pillar* LA-4
*Howardtown* PA-2
*Howard Town Baptist Church* AL-4
*Howard Town Ch* AL-4
Howardtown Ch—*church* AL-4
**Howard (Town of)**—*pop pl* NY-2
**Howard (Town of)**—*pop pl* WI-6
Howard Township—*civil* SD-7
Howard Township—*fmr MCD* (4) IA-7
**Howard Township**—*pop pl* (2) KS-7
**Howard Township**—*pop pl* (2) MO-7
**Howard Township**—*pop pl* (3) SD-7
Howard Township Hall—*building* SD-7
Howard Township (historical)—*civil* SD-7
Howard (Township of)—*fmr MCD* AR-4
**Howard (Township of)**—*pop pl* (3) IN-6
**Howard (Township of)**—*pop pl* MI-6
**Howard (Township of)**—*pop pl* OH-6
**Howard (Township of)**—*pop pl* PA-2
Howard Univ—*school* DC-2
Howard Valley—*basin* CT-1
Howard Valley—*valley* MT-8
Howard Valley—*valley* OR-9
Howard Valley Cem—*cemetery* TX-5
Howard Valley Ch—*church* CT-1
Howard View Ch—*church* TN-4
*Howardville* PA-2
Howardville—*locale* IA-7
Howardville—*locale* NY-2
Howardville—*locale* TN-4
**Howardville**—*pop pl* MD-2
**Howardville**—*pop pl* MO-7
Howardville Cem—*cemetery* IA-7
**Howardville (historical)**—*pop pl* OR-9
Howardville Post Office (historical)—*building* TN-4
Howardville Sch (historical)—*school* TN-4
*Howard Walker Dam* PA-2
Howard Walker Pond Dam—*dam* MS-4
Howard Well—*well* AZ-5
Howard Well (flowing)—*well* AZ-5
Howard White Catfish Ponds Dam—*dam* MS-4
**Howardwick**—*pop pl* TX-5
Howard Wilson Elem Sch—*school* KS-7
Howarth Park—*park* MI-6
Howarth Playground—*park* MI-6
Howarth Ranch—*locale* NE-7
Howarth Ridge—*ridge* WI-6
Howarth Sch—*school* (2) IL-6
Howarth Sch—*school* WI-6
*Howarths Village* MA-1
Howart Lakes—*lake* NE-7
*Howartown* PA-2
Howawrd Cave—*cave* TN-4
Howay-Dykstra House—*hist pl* WA-9
How-Beckman Mill—*hist pl* WI-6
How Canal—*canal* FL-3
How Cem—*cemetery* MO-7
How Come You Creek—*stream* TN-4
Howcott—*locale* LA-4
How Creek—*stream* MT-8
Howd, Eliphalet, House—*hist pl* CT-1
Howd Creek—*stream* CO-8
Howden Hall Sch—*school* VT-1
Howden Lake—*lake* MS-4
*Howdens Lake* MS-4
Howder Cem—*cemetery* IL-6
Howdeshell Cem—*cemetery* MO-7
Howd-Linsley House—*hist pl* CT-1
Howdy Ranch—*locale* NM-5
Howdy Spring—*spring* UT-8
*Howe* IL-6
*Howe* KS-7
Howe—*locale* AL-4
Howe—*locale* IA-7
**Howe**—*pop pl* ID-8
**Howe**—*pop pl* IN-6
**Howe**—*pop pl* MA-1
**Howe**—*pop pl* NE-7
**Howe**—*pop pl* OK-5
**Howe**—*pop pl* PA-2
**Howe**—*pop pl* SC-3
**Howe**—*pop pl* TX-5
Howe, C. J., Bldg—*hist pl* OR-9
Howe, Edgar W., House—*hist pl* KS-7
Howe, Edward P., Jr., House—*hist pl* CA-9
Howe, Frank M., Residence—*hist pl* MO-7
Howe, Julia Ward, Sch—*hist pl* PA-2
Howe, Mount—*summit* (2) MT-8
Howe, Richard, House—*hist pl* KS-7
Howe, Samuel Gridley and Julia Ward, House—*hist pl* MA-1
*Howe And Van Voorst Ditch* IN-6
Howe Ave Sch—*school* CA-9
Howe Branch—*stream* MO-7
*Howe Brook* MA-1
**Howe Brook**—*pop pl* ME-1
Howe Brook—*stream* (4) ME-1
Howe Brook—*stream* (2) VT-1
Howe Brook Mtn—*summit* ME-1
*Howecave* NY-2
Howe Caverns—*cave* NY-2
Howe Cem—*cemetery* CT-1
Howe Cem—*cemetery* IL-6
Howe Cem—*cemetery* KY-4
Howe Cem—*cemetery* MI-6
Howe Cem—*cemetery* SC-3
Howe Ch—*church* PA-2
*Howe Chapel* TN-4
Howe Community Park—*park* CA-9
Howe Covered Bridge—*hist pl* VT-1
Howe Creek—*stream* CA-9
Howe Creek—*stream* IL-6
Howe Creek—*stream* (2) IN-6
Howe Creek—*stream* MI-6
Howe Creek—*stream* MT-8
Howe Creek—*stream* NE-7
Howe Creek—*stream* NC-3
Howe Creek—*stream* (3) WA-9
*Howe Ditch* IN-6
Howe Drain—*canal* (2) MI-6
Howe Elem Sch—*school* PA-2
Howe Family Cem—*cemetery* AL-4
Howe Flume Hist Dist—*hist pl* UT-8
Howe Hall Sch—*school* SC-3
*Howe High School* IN-6
Howe Hill—*stream* NH-1
Howe Hill—*summit* ME-1
Howe Hill—*summit* (2) MA-1
Howe Hill—*summit* (4) NH-1
Howe Hill—*summit* VT-1
Howe Hill Cem—*cemetery* ME-1
Howe Hill Sch—*school* VT-1
**Howe (historical)**—*pop pl* OR-9
Howe Hollow—*valley* AR-4
Howe Hollow—*valley* (2) KY-4
Howe Hollow—*valley* OH-6
Howe House—*hist pl* MA-1
Howe HS—*school* MA-1
Howe Island—*island* AK-9
Howe JHS—*school* MA-1
Howe Key—*island* FL-3
Howe Key Mangrove—*island* FL-3
**Howel**—*pop pl* KY-4
Howe-Lagrange Tollgate—*locale* IN-6
Howe Lake—*lake* (4) MI-6
Howe Lake—*lake* MN-6
Howe Lake—*lake* MT-8
Howe Lake—*lake* WI-6
Howe Lake Trail—*trail* MT-8
Howe Lateral—*canal* AZ-5
*Howell* IN-6
*Howell* KY-4
Howell—*locale* GA-3
Howell—*locale* ID-8
Howell—*locale* LA-4
Howell—*locale* PA-2
Howell—*locale* WY-8
**Howell**—*pop pl* AR-4
**Howell**—*pop pl* GA-3
**Howell**—*pop pl* KS-7
**Howell**—*pop pl* MI-6
**Howell**—*pop pl* MS-4
**Howell**—*pop pl* MO-7
**Howell**—*pop pl* NJ-2
**Howell**—*pop pl* NY-2
**Howell**—*pop pl* NC-3
**Howell**—*pop pl* TN-4
**Howell**—*pop pl* UT-8
Howell, Benjamin, Homestead—*hist pl* NJ-2
Howell, F. M., and Company—*hist pl* NY-2
Howell, John W., House—*hist pl* OR-9
Howell, Lake—*lake* FL-3
Howell Airp—*airport* UT-8
Howell and Graves Sch—*school* AL-4
Howell Bluff—*cliff* FL-3
Howell Branch—*bay* SC-3
Howell Branch—*stream* AR-4
Howell Branch—*stream* FL-3
Howell Branch—*stream* GA-3
Howell Branch—*stream* LA-4
Howell Branch—*stream* NC-3
Howell Branch—*stream* SC-3
Howell Branch—*stream* (2) TN-4
Howell Branch—*stream* VA-3
Howell Branch Baptist Ch—*church* FL-3
Howell Bridge—*bridge* MS-4
Howell Bridge—*other* IL-6
*Howell Brook* CT-1
Howell-Butler House—*hist pl* NC-3
Howell Canyon—*valley* AZ-5
Howell Canyon—*valley* CA-9
Howell Canyon—*valley* (3) ID-8
Howell Canyon—*valley* NM-5
Howell Canyon—*valley* OR-9
Howell Cave—*cave* MO-7
*Howell Cem* MS-4
Howell Cem—*cemetery* (3) AL-4
Howell Cem—*cemetery* (2) AR-4
Howell Cem—*cemetery* (2) GA-3
Howell Cem—*cemetery* IN-6
Howell Cem—*cemetery* IA-7
Howell Cem—*cemetery* (4) KY-4
Howell Cem—*cemetery* LA-4
Howell Cem—*cemetery* (3) MS-4
Howell Cem—*cemetery* (6) MO-7
Howell Cem—*cemetery* NE-7
Howell Cem—*cemetery* NY-2
Howell Cem—*cemetery* (2) NC-3
Howell Cem—*cemetery* OR-9
Howell Cem—*cemetery* SD-7
Howell Cem—*cemetery* (3) TN-4
Howell Cem—*cemetery* TX-5
Howell Cem—*cemetery* WV-2
Howell Ch—*church* NC-3
Howell Cheney Regional Technical Sch—*school* CT-1
Howell Cheney Satellite Vocational Sch—*school* CT-1
Howell Club Lake—*reservoir* TX-5
**Howell County**—*pop pl* MO-7
Howell County Cem—*cemetery* MO-7
*Howell Creek* AR-4
*Howell Creek* MS-4
*Howell Creek* MO-7
*Howell Creek* NY-2
Howell Creek—*stream* AL-4
Howell Creek—*stream* AR-4
Howell Creek—*stream* CA-9
Howell Creek—*stream* FL-3
Howell Creek—*stream* GA-3
Howell Creek—*stream* (3) ID-8
Howell Creek—*stream* LA-4
Howell Creek—*stream* MN-6
Howell Creek—*stream* MO-7
Howell Creek—*stream* (2) MT-8
Howell Creek—*stream* NY-2
Howell Creek—*stream* (2) OR-9
Howell Creek—*stream* TN-4
Howell Creek—*stream* TX-5
Howell Creek—*stream* (2) VA-3
Howell Creek—*stream* WI-6
Howell Creek—*stream* WY-8
Howell Creek Spring—*spring* ID-8
Howell Dam—*dam* AL-4
Howell Ditch—*canal* IN-6
Howell Ditch—*canal* (2) OR-9
Howell Downtown Hist Dist—*hist pl* MI-6
Howell Draw—*valley* WY-8
Howell Family Cem—*cemetery* MS-4
Howell First Baptist Ch—*church* TN-4
*Howell Fork* WY-8
Howell Fork—*stream* TN-4
Howell Fork—*stream* WV-2
Howell Fork—*stream* WY-8
Howell Gap—*gap* CA-9
Howell-Garner-Monfee House—*hist pl* AR-4
**Howell Grove**—*pop pl* GA-3
Howell Gulch—*valley* ID-8
Howell Gulch—*valley* MT-8
**Howell Hill**—*pop pl* TN-4
Howell Hill—*summit* CA-9
Howell Hill—*summit* TN-4
Howell Hill Baptist Ch—*church* TN-4
Howell Hill Sch (historical)—*school* TN-4
Howell (historical)—*locale* SD-7
**Howell (historical)**—*pop pl* IA-7
**Howell (historical)**—*pop pl* MS-4
**Howell (historical)**—*pop pl* OR-9
Howell Hollow—*valley* IL-6
Howell Hollow—*valley* MO-7
Howell Hollow—*valley* (2) TN-4
Howell Hollow—*valley* TX-5
Howell Hollow—*valley* (2) WV-2
Howell Homeplace—*hist pl* NC-3
Howell House—*building* TX-5
Howell House—*hist pl* PA-2
Howell Island—*island* MO-7
Howell Key—*island* FL-3
Howell-Kohlhagen House—*hist pl* OR-9
Howell Lake—*lake* MI-6
Howell Lake—*lake* (2) OR-9
Howell Lake—*lake* (2) TX-5
Howell Lake—*lake* WA-9
Howell Lake—*lake* WI-6
Howell Lake—*lake* WY-8
Howell Lake—*reservoir* AL-4
Howell Lake—*reservoir* (2) GA-3
Howell Lake Ch—*church* FL-3
Howell Lake Dam—*dam* (4) MS-4
Howell L Watkins JHS—*school* FL-3
Howell Memorial Hosp—*hospital* GA-3
Howell Mesa—*summit* AZ-5
Howell Mill—*post sta* GA-3
Howell Mills—*locale* VA-3
Howell Missionary Baptist Ch—*church* MS-4
Howell Mountain Sch—*school* CA-9
Howell Mtn—*summit* CA-9
Howell Mtn—*summit* GA-3
Howell Mtn—*summit* SC-3
Howell Mtn—*summit* (2) TX-5
Howell Mtn—*summit* WY-8
Howell Park—*park* GA-3
Howell Park—*park* IL-6
Howell Park—*park* IN-6
Howell Park—*park* LA-4
Howell Park—*park* TN-4
**Howell Park**—*pop pl* PA-2
Howell Park Sch—*school* LA-4
Howell Peak—*summit* UT-8
Howell Place—*locale* CA-9
Howell Place—*locale* FL-3
**Howell (P.O.)**—*pop pl* NJ-2
*Howell Point* NY-2
Howell Point—*cape* (2) MD-2
Howell Point—*cape* NY-2
Howell Point—*cape* NC-3
*Howell Pond* CT-1
Howell Pond—*lake* DE-2
Howell Pond—*lake* PA-2
Howell Pond—*reservoir* AL-4
*Howell Pond Brook* CT-1
Howell Post Office (historical)—*building* TN-4
Howell Prairie—*flat* OR-9
Howell Prairie Creek—*stream* OR-9
Howell Ranch—*locale* ID-8
Howell Ranch—*locale* (2) NM-5
Howell Ranch—*locale* SD-7
Howell Ranch—*locale* WY-8
Howell Ridge—*ridge* CA-9
Howell Ridge—*ridge* OR-9
Howell Road Sch—*school* NY-2
Howell Rock—*bar* CA-9
Howell Rsvr—*reservoir* CA-9
Howell Rsvrs—*reservoir* OR-9
Howell Run—*stream* (2) WV-2
*Howells* CA-9
Howells—*locale* AL-4
Howells—*locale* SC-3
**Howells**—*pop pl* NE-7
**Howells**—*pop pl* NY-2
Howells—*post sta* CO-8
Howells, William Dean, House—*hist pl* MA-1
*Howells Branch* AL-4
Howells Brook—*stream* CT-1
Howells Camp—*locale* AL-4
Howells Cem—*cemetery* GA-3
Howell Sch—*school* AZ-5
Howell Sch—*school* IL-6
Howell Sch—*school* IN-6
Howell Sch—*school* LA-4
Howell Sch—*school* MI-6
Howell Sch—*school* MS-4
Howell Sch—*school* (2) NJ-2
Howell Sch—*school* OK-5
Howell Sch—*school* (2) SD-7
Howell Sch—*school* TN-4
Howell Sch—*school* UT-8
Howell Sch—*school* WI-6
Howell Sch (historical)—*school* AL-4
Howell Sch (historical)—*school* (2) MO-7
Howell Sch (historical)—*school* TN-4
Howell School—*locale* MI-6
Howells Corners—*locale* PA-2
**Howells Cove**—*pop pl* AL-4
Howells Cove—*valley* AL-4
*Howells Cove Church* AL-4
Howells Creek—*stream* NJ-2
Howells Creek—*stream* NY-2
*Howells Crossing* MS-4
**Howells Crossroads**—*pop pl* AL-4
**Howells Cross Roads**—*pop pl* AL-4
Howells Female Acad (historical)—*school* TN-4
*Howells Ferry* PA-2
**Howells Ferry Heights (subdivision)**—*pop pl* AL-4
Howells Ferry (historical)—*locale* MS-4
Howells Fishpond—*reservoir* GA-3
Howells Grove Sch (historical)—*school* AL-4
Howell Siding—*locale* MS-4
Howell Sinks—*basin* GA-3
*Howells Island* MO-7
*Howells Island* TN-4
Howells JHS—*school* OH-6
**Howells Junction**—*pop pl* NY-2
Howells Lake—*lake* ND-7
Howells Lake—*reservoir* TN-4
Howell Landing—*locale* CA-9
Howells Mill—*locale* VA-3
**Howells Mill**—*pop pl* WV-2
Howells Mill (historical)—*locale* AL-4
*Howells Mill Shoals* AL-4
Howell-Snowville—*cens area* UT-8
Howell-Snowville Division—*civil* UT-8
*Howell's Point* MD-2
*Howells Point* NC-3
Howells Point—*cape* NY-2
Howells Point Ridge—*ridge* CA-9
Howells Pond—*lake* NJ-2
Howells Pond—*reservoir* CT-1
Howell Spring—*spring* ID-8
Howell Spring—*spring* SD-7
**Howell Spur**—*pop pl* MS-4
Howells Ridge—*ridge* NM-5
Howells Run—*stream* PA-2
Howells Run Dam—*dam* PA-2
Howells Sch—*school* NY-2
Howell State Hosp—*hospital* MI-6
Howell Station—*locale* NJ-2
Howell Station Campground Lake Red Rock—*locale* IA-7
Howells Transfer—*uninc pl* GA-3
*Howellsville* NJ-2
Howellsville—*locale* NC-3
Howellsville—*locale* VA-3
Howellsville Branch—*stream* VA-3
Howell Swamp—*swamp* NC-3
Howell Swamp Ch—*church* NC-3
Howells Wells—*other* NM-5
Howell-Theurer House—*hist pl* UT-8
Howelltown—*locale* ID-8
Howell Township—*civil* MO-7
Howell Township—*civil* SD-7
**Howell Township**—*pop pl* ND-7
Howell (Township of)—*fmr MCD* AR-4
**Howell (Township of)**—*pop pl* MI-6
**Howell (Township of)**—*pop pl* NJ-2
Howell Tunnel—*mine* UT-8
Howell Valley—*valley* MO-7
Howell Valley Airp—*airport* MO-7
Howell Valley Ch—*church* MO-7
Howell Valley Sch—*school* MO-7
*Howellville* PA-2
Howellville—*locale* PA-2
**Howellville**—*pop pl* TX-5
Howell Well—*well* NM-5
Howell Windmill—*locale* NM-5
Howels, William Dean, House—*hist pl* ME-1
*Howels Crossroads* AL-4
Howelsen Hill—*summit* CO-8
**Howelton**—*pop pl* AL-4
Howelton Cem—*cemetery* AL-4
Howelton Ch—*church* AL-4
*Howelton Methodist Ch* AL-4
Howelton Sch (historical)—*school* AL-4
Howe Manning Sch—*school* MA-1
Howe Marsh—*swamp* NY-2
Howe Military Acad—*school* IN-6
*Howe Military Sch* IN-6
Howe Mtn—*summit* CT-1
Howe Mtn—*summit* ID-8
Howe Mtn—*summit* NY-2
*Howen Key* FL-3
Howe ( North) Peaks Trail—*trail* ME-1
*Howenstein* OH-6
**Howenstein**—*pop pl* OH-6
**Howenstine**—*pop pl* OH-6
Howenstine Sch—*school* AZ-5
Howe Park—*park* NH-1
Howe Park—*park* OR-9
Howe Peak—*summit* ME-1
Howe Peak—*summit* NH-1
Howe Peaks—*summit* ME-1
Howe Playground—*park* MA-1
Howe Point—*cape* NC-3
Howe Pond—*lake* (2) MA-1
Howe Pond—*lake* VT-1
Howe Pond—*reservoir* MA-1
Howe Pond Brook—*stream* VT-1
Howe Pond Dam—*dam* MA-1
Howe-Quimby House—*hist pl* NH-1
Howe Ranch—*locale* NM-5
Hower Coulee—*valley* MT-8
Howerdon Creek—*stream* IA-7
Howe Reservoirs—*reservoir* MA-1
Hower HS—*school* OH-6
Howe Ridge—*ridge* MT-8
Howe Ridge—*ridge* WA-9
Howe Ridge—*ridge* WI-6
Hower Lake—*lake* OH-6

Hower Mansion—*hist pl* .... OH-6
Hower Sch—*school* .... OK-5
Hower-Slote House—*hist pl* .... PA-2
*Howers Ville* .... PA-2
Howersville—*locale* .... PA-2
Howe Rsvr—*reservoir* .... NH-1
Howerter—*school* .... IL-6
*Howerton* .... PA-2
**Howerton**—*pop pl* .... PA-2
Howerton Cem—*cemetery* .... AR-4
Howerton Cem—*cemetery* .... TN-4
Howerton Ch—*church* .... VA-3
Howertons—*locale* .... VA-3
**Howertown**—*pop pl* .... PA-2
Howe Run—*stream* .... PA-2
Howery Ranch—*locale* .... WY-8
Howery Well—*well* .... NM-5
*Howes* .... MA-1
Howes—*locale* (2) .... NY-2
Howes—*locale* .... SD-7
**Howes**—*pop pl* .... MO-7
Howes, Byron, House—*hist pl* .... MN-6
Howe-Savoy Ch—*church* .... AR-4
Howes Camp—*locale* .... CA-9
*Howe's Cave* .... NY-2
**Howes Cave**—*pop pl* .... NY-2
Howes Cem—*cemetery* .... KY-4
Howes Cem—*cemetery* .... LA-4
Howes Cem—*cemetery* .... MA-1
Howes Cem—*cemetery* .... UT-8
*Howe Sch* .... PA-2
Howe Sch—*school* .... CT-1
Howe Sch—*school* .... GA-3
Howe Sch—*school* (3) .... IL-6
Howe Sch—*school* .... IA-7
Howe Sch—*school* (3) .... MA-1
Howe Sch—*school* (4) .... MI-6
Howe Sch—*school* .... MN-6
Howe Sch—*school* .... NE-7
Howe Sch—*school* .... NY-2
Howe Sch—*school* .... ND-7
Howe Sch—*school* .... OH-6
Howe Sch—*school* (2) .... PA-2
Howe Sch—*school* .... WA-9
Howe Sch—*school* (3) .... WI-6
Howe Sch (abandoned)—*school* .... PA-2
Howes Chapel—*church* .... TN-4
*Howes Chapel Baptist Ch* .... TN-4
Howe Sch (historical)—*school* .... TN-4
Howes Corner—*locale* .... ME-1
**Howes Corners**—*pop pl* (2) .... ME-1
Howes Corners Cem—*cemetery* .... WI-6
*Howes Creek* .... NC-3
Howes Ditch—*canal* .... CA-9
Howes Hollow—*valley* .... PA-2
*Howes Key* .... FL-3
*Howes Lake* .... MI-6
Howes Lake—*lake* .... MI-6
Howes Lakes—*lake* .... MT-8
Howes Landing—*locale* .... NY-2
Howes Mill—*locale* .... MO-7
*Howes Mill Post Office* .... MO-7
Howes Mill Spring—*spring* .... MO-7
Howes Mill Union Ch—*church* .... MO-7
Howes Point—*cape* .... MN-6
Howes Pond—*lake* .... MA-1
Howes Pond—*reservoir* .... MA-1
Howes Pond Dam—*dam* .... MA-1
Howe Spring—*spring* .... CA-9
Howes Rsvr—*reservoir* (2) .... MT-8
Howes Sch—*school* .... CA-9
*Howes Station* .... MA-1
Howest—*uninc pl* .... CA-9
*Howe Station* .... MA-1
Howe Station (historical)—*locale* .... TN-4
**Howes Township**—*pop pl* .... ND-7
**Howe Subdivision**—*pop pl* .... UT-8
*Howesville* .... TN-4
**Howesville**—*pop pl* .... IN-6
**Howesville**—*pop pl* .... WV-2
Howesville Ditch—*canal* .... IN-6
Howesville (historical)—*locale* .... MA-1
Howesville Negro Ch (historical)—*church* .... TN-4
*Howesville Post Office* .... TN-4
Howes Well—*well* .... OR-9
Howes Wharf (historical)—*locale* .... MA-1
Howe Tavern—*hist pl* .... OH-6
*Howetown* .... PA-2
Howe Township—*civil* .... PA-2
**Howe Township**—*pop pl* .... ND-7
**Howe (Township of)**—*pop pl* (2) .... PA-2
**Howe Valley**—*pop pl* .... KY-4
Howe Valley Ch—*church* .... KY-4
Howe Village Hist Dist—*hist pl* .... MA-1
Howe-Waffle House and Carriage House—*hist pl* .... CA-9
*Howey* .... FL-3
Howey Acad—*school* .... FL-3
Howey Height—*locale* .... FL-3
Howey House—*hist pl* .... FL-3
*Howey-In-The-Hills* .... FL-3
**Howey in the Hills**—*pop pl* .... FL-3
Howey-in-the-Hills-Okanumpka (CCD)—*cens area* .... FL-3
**Howey-in-the-Hills (RR name Howey)**—*pop pl* .... FL-3
Howey (railroad station)—*locale* .... FL-3
**Howey (RR name for Howey-In-The-Hills)**—*pop pl* .... FL-3
Howey Rsvr—*reservoir* .... CO-8
How Houses—*hist pl* .... ME-1
*Howi* .... HI-9
Howie, David W., House—*hist pl* .... WI-6
Howie Branch—*stream* .... VA-3
*Howie Cemetery* .... AL-4
Howie Ch—*church* .... NC-3
Howie Creek—*stream* .... AK-9
Howie Dam—*dam* .... SD-7
Howie Mine—*mine* .... CA-9
Howie Ranch—*locale* .... ND-7
Howie Rock—*bar* .... ME-1
Howie Sch—*school* .... MT-8
**Howie Township**—*pop pl* .... ND-7
Howinahell Canyon—*valley* .... NM-5
Howington Cem—*cemetery* .... GA-3
Howiri-ouinge—*hist pl* .... NM-5
Howison—*locale* .... MS-4
Howison Sch—*school* .... AL-4
Howison Spring—*spring* .... NV-8
Howitt, John, House—*hist pl* .... WI-6
Howitt JHS—*school* .... NY-2
*Howitt Lake* .... WI-6
Howitzer Hill—*summit* .... AL-4
Howitzer Point—*cliff* .... CA-9
Howitzer Slide—*cliff* .... NV-8
Howkan Narrows—*channel* .... AK-9
Howkan (Site)—*locale* .... AK-9
Howker Ridge—*ridge* .... NH-1
Howker Ridge Path—*trail* .... NH-1
Howkum Lake—*lake* .... OR-9
*Howlack Butte* .... OR-9
Howland—*CDP* .... ME-1
Howland—*CDP* .... OH-6
Howland—*locale* .... MO-7
Howland—*locale* .... NY-2
Howland—*locale* .... VA-3
**Howland**—*pop pl* .... TX-5
Howland, Jabez, House—*hist pl* .... MA-1
Howland Ave Sch—*school* .... MA-1
Howland (CCD)—*cens area* .... TX-5
Howland Cem—*cemetery* .... KY-4
Howland Cem—*cemetery* (2) .... MA-1
Howland Cem—*cemetery* .... NY-2
Howland Cem—*cemetery* .... OK-5
Howland Cem—*cemetery* .... VT-1
**Howland Center**—*pop pl* .... ME-1
**Howland Corners**—*pop pl* .... NY-2
**Howland Corners**—*pop pl* .... OH-6
*Howland Creek* .... WY-8
Howland Creek—*stream* .... IL-6
Howland Creek—*stream* .... MI-6
Howland Creek—*stream* .... NC-3
Howland Ditch—*canal* .... IN-6
Howland Drain—*canal* .... MI-6
**Howland Flat**—*pop pl* .... CA-9
Howland Hill—*summit* .... CA-9
Howland Hill—*summit* .... ME-1
Howland Hill—*summit* .... NH-1
Howland Hollow—*valley* .... TN-4
Howland Hook—*cape* .... NY-2
Howland Hook—*uninc pl* .... NY-2
Howland Island—*island* .... NY-2
Howland Island Game Ref—*park* .... NY-2
Howland Lake—*lake* .... MI-6
Howland Lake—*swamp* .... MI-6
Howland Ledge—*rock* .... MA-1
Howland Library—*hist pl* .... NY-2
Howland Lookout Tower—*locale* .... KY-4
Howland Mine—*mine* .... OR-9
*Howland Mt.* .... CT-1
Howland Point—*cape* .... AZ-5
Howland Point—*cape* .... NY-2
Howland Point—*cape* .... NC-3
Howland Point—*cape* .... VA-3
**Howlands**—*pop pl* .... MA-1
*Howlands Brook* .... MA-1
Howlandsburg—*locale* .... MI-6
Howlandsburg Cem—*cemetery* .... MI-6
Howlands Butte, The—*summit* .... AZ-5
Howland Sch—*school* .... IL-6
*Howlands Ferry* .... RI-1
*Howlands Glade* .... DE-2
Howlands Lake—*reservoir* .... NY-2
*Howlands Station* .... MA-1
Howland Summit—*summit* .... CA-9
**Howland (Town of)**—*pop pl* .... ME-1
**Howland (Township of)**—*pop pl* .... OH-6
Howlandville Ch—*church* .... SC-3
*How Lark Butte* .... OR-9
*Howlash Butte* .... OR-9
Howl Creek—*stream* .... ID-8
Howle Cem—*cemetery* .... MS-4
Howle Cem—*cemetery* .... SC-3
*Howle Lake* .... WI-6
Howles Grove Ch (historical)—*church* .... AL-4
Howle Site—*hist pl* .... TX-5
*Howlesville* .... VA-3
*Howlet Brook* .... MA-1
*Howlet Hill* .... NY-2
Howlett Bayou—*stream* .... MS-4
Howlett Brook—*stream* .... MA-1
Howlett Creek—*stream* .... CO-8
Howlett Creek—*stream* .... NC-3
Howlett Creek—*stream* .... WA-9
**Howlett Hill**—*pop pl* .... NY-2
Howlett Hill—*summit* .... NY-2
Howlett Ranch—*locale* .... CA-9
*Howletts Brook* .... MA-1
**Howley**—*pop pl* .... TN-4
Howley Branch—*stream* .... MO-7
Howley Sch (historical)—*school* .... TN-4
Howl Hollow—*valley* .... AR-4
Howling Dog Canyon—*valley* .... AK-9
Howling Dog Creek—*stream* .... AK-9
Howling Dog Rock—*pillar* .... AK-9
Howling Gulch—*valley* .... CA-9
Howling Valley—*valley* .... AK-9
Howling Wolf Bayou—*stream* .... MS-4
Howlis Cem—*cemetery* .... TN-4
*Howlit Hill* .... NY-2
Howl Lake—*lake* .... MN-6
Howlock Creek—*stream* .... OR-9
Howlock Mtn—*summit* .... OR-9
*Howlott Creek* .... CO-8
Howl Ranch—*locale* .... NM-5
*Howluck Butte* .... OR-9
Howluk Butte—*summit* .... OR-9
Howl Windmill—*locale* .... TX-5
How Park—*park* .... MA-1
How Point—*cape* .... NC-3
Hows Bend—*bend* .... TN-4
*Hows Cave* .... NY-2
Hows Corners—*locale* .... ME-1
**Howse**—*pop pl* .... TN-4
*Howse Baptist Church* .... TN-4
Howse Camp—*locale* .... AL-4
Howse Drain—*canal* .... MI-6
Howsel Park—*park* .... MO-7
Howse Park—*park* .... TN-4
Howser Cem—*cemetery* .... TN-4
Howser Corners—*locale* .... NY-2
Howsers Branch—*stream* .... VA-3
Howsley Creek—*stream* .... MT-8
Hows-Madden House—*hist pl* .... TN-4
Howson Cem—*cemetery* .... OH-6
Howson Creek—*stream* .... WA-9
Howson House—*hist pl* .... AR-4
Howth—*locale* .... TX-5
**Howton**—*pop pl* .... AL-4
Howton Camp—*locale* .... AL-4
Howton Cem—*cemetery* .... AR-4
*Howtons* .... AL-4
*Howtons Camp* .... AL-4
Howton Spring—*spring* .... KY-4
**Howton Subdivision (subdivision)**—*pop pl* .... AL-4
**How (Town of)**—*pop pl* .... WI-6
**Howze Beach**—*pop pl* .... LA-4
Howze Cem—*cemetery* .... LA-4
Howze Cem—*cemetery* .... SC-3
Hoxbar—*locale* .... OK-5
Hoxeng Farmstead—*hist pl* .... SD-7
Hoxey, Asa, House—*hist pl* .... TX-5
Hoxey Cem—*cemetery* .... IL-6
Hoxey Creek—*stream* .... MI-6
Hoxey Hollow—*valley* .... AR-4
Hoxey Sch—*school* .... IL-6
Hoxeyville—*locale* .... MI-6
Hoxeyville Sch—*school* .... MI-6
*Hoxie* .... RI-1
Hoxie—*locale* .... TX-5
**Hoxie**—*pop pl* .... AR-4
**Hoxie**—*pop pl* .... KS-7
Hoxie, Timothy, House—*hist pl* .... MA-1
Hoxie Ave Sch—*school* .... CA-9
Hoxie Bridge—*bridge* .... TX-5
Hoxie Brook—*stream* .... CT-1
Hoxie Brook—*stream* .... MA-1
Hoxie Brook—*stream* .... NY-2
Hoxie Cem—*cemetery* .... KS-7
Hoxie Cem—*cemetery* .... NY-2
Hoxie Chapel Cem—*cemetery* .... TX-5
Hoxie Corner—*locale* .... NY-2
*Hoxie Creek* .... MA-1
Hoxie Creek—*stream* .... OR-9
Hoxie Crossing—*locale* .... CA-9
Hoxie Drain—*canal* .... MI-6
Hoxie Drain—*stream* .... MI-6
Hoxie Elem Sch—*school* .... KS-7
Hoxie Gorge—*valley* .... NY-2
Hoxie Hill—*summit* .... NY-2
Hoxie HS—*school* .... KS-7
Hoxie Municipal Airp—*airport* .... KS-7
*Hoxie Pond* .... MA-1
Hoxie Pond—*lake* .... MA-1
Hoxie Ridge—*ridge* .... IL-6
Hoxies—*locale* .... ME-1
*Hoxies Cove* .... OR-9
Hoxsey Creek—*stream* .... MT-8
Hoxsey Creek—*stream* .... WA-9
*Hoxsie* .... RI-1
**Hoxsie**—*pop pl* .... RI-1
Hoxsie, John, House—*hist pl* .... RI-1
Hoxworth Springs—*spring* .... AZ-5
Hoy—*locale* .... MS-4
Hoy—*locale* .... WV-2
Hoy, R. E., No. 1 Oil Well—*hist pl* .... OK-5
Hoya—*locale* .... NV-8
Hoya—*post sta* .... DC-2
Hoya Cana—*basin* .... PR-3
Hoya Creek—*stream* .... AK-9
Hoyadazzithethno Creek—*stream* .... AK-9
Hoya El Ber—*valley* .... PR-3
Hoya Fria—*valley* .... PR-3
**Hoya Grande**—*pop pl* .... PR-3
Hoya Grande—*valley* .... PR-3
Hoya Hondo—*valley* .... PR-3
Hoya La Laura—*valley* .... PR-3
Hoya Las Picuas—*valley* .... PR-3
Hoya Mala (Barrio)—*fmr MCD* .... PR-3
*Hoyapi* .... AZ-5
Hoya Pozo Blanco—*valley* .... PR-3
Hoya Tank—*reservoir* .... TX-5
Hoy Canyon—*valley* .... NV-8
Hoy Cem—*cemetery* .... LA-4
Hoy Cem—*cemetery* .... OH-6
Hoy Ch—*church* .... OH-6
Hoy Chapel—*church* .... WV-2
Hoy Coulee—*valley* .... MT-8
*Hoydale* .... PA-2
Hoyden Hill—*summit* .... CT-1
Hoy Draw—*valley* .... CO-8
Hoye Bridge—*bridge* .... NV-8
Hoye Canyon—*valley* .... NV-8
Hoyem Ditch—*canal* .... MT-8
Hoyem Homestead—*locale* .... MT-8
Hoyer Coulee—*valley* .... WI-6
Hoyer Creek—*stream* .... WY-8
Hoyer Memorial Campground—*park* .... AZ-5
Hoyes—*locale* .... MD-2
*Hoye School* .... MS-4
Hoyes Field—*park* .... OH-6
Hoye Site—*hist pl* .... MD-2
**Hoyes Run**—*pop pl* .... MD-2
Hoyes Run—*stream* (2) .... MD-2
Hoyes Run—*stream* .... WV-2
Hoyes Run Sch—*school* .... WV-2
Hoye Valley—*valley* .... WI-6
Hoy Flat—*flat* .... CO-8
*Hoy Gap* .... PA-2
Hoy Gulch—*valley* .... MT-8
Hoy Hollow—*valley* .... OH-6
Hoyl Brook—*stream* .... NH-1
*Hoyle* .... MS-4
Hoyle, Lake—*lake* .... AK-9
Hoyle Bluff—*cliff* .... MO-7
Hoyle Branch—*stream* .... GA-3
Hoyle Bridge—*bridge* .... OK-5
Hoyle Canyon—*valley* .... AZ-5
Hoyle Cave—*cave* .... MO-7
Hoyle Cem—*cemetery* .... MS-4
Hoyle Cem—*cemetery* .... NC-3
Hoyle Creek—*stream* (2) .... NC-3
Hoyle Creek—*stream* .... OK-5
Hoyle D Byrd—*dam* .... MS-4
Hoyle Ditch—*canal* .... MT-8
Hoyle Memorial Ch—*church* .... NC-3
Hoyle Mtn—*summit* .... AR-4
*Hoyles Creek* .... NC-3
Hoyles Store—*locale* .... NC-3
**Hoylesville (historical)**—*pop pl* .... NC-3
Hoyle Tank—*reservoir* .... AZ-5
**Hoyleton**—*pop pl* .... IL-6
**Hoyleton (Township of)**—*pop pl* .... IL-6
Hoyle Windmill—*locale* .... TX-5
Hoy-Lo-Mae Park—*park* .... OH-6
Hoy Mtn—*summit* .... CO-8
Hoy Mtn—*summit* .... UT-8
Hoyne Playground—*park* .... IL-6
Hoyne Sch—*school* .... IL-6
**Hoyo Mulas**—*pop pl* .... PR-3
Hoyo Mulas (Barrio)—*fmr MCD* .... PR-3
*Hoyon As Lito Katan* .... MH-9
*Hoyon As Lito Lichan* .... MH-9
Hoyo Prieto—*valley* .... PR-3
Hoyos Memorial Park—*cemetery* .... NY-2
Hoy Post Office (historical)—*building* .... AL-4
Hoypus Hill—*summit* .... WA-9
Hoypus Point—*cape* .... WA-9
Hoy Ranch—*locale* .... WY-8
Hoy Run—*stream* .... PA-2
Hoy Savanna—*plain* .... NC-3
Hoy Sch (historical)—*school* .... MS-4
Hoyseth Homestead (abandoned)—*locale* .... MT-8
Hoys Fork—*stream* .... KY-4
Hoys Fork Sch—*school* .... KY-4
Hoy Spring—*spring* .... CO-8
Hoyt—*locale* .... AR-4
Hoyt—*locale* .... CO-8
Hoyt—*locale* .... FL-3
Hoyt—*locale* .... ID-8
Hoyt—*locale* .... MT-8
Hoyt—*locale* .... WV-2
Hoyt—*locale* .... WI-6
**Hoyt**—*pop pl* .... KS-7
**Hoyt**—*pop pl* .... KY-4
**Hoyt**—*pop pl* .... OK-5
**Hoyt**—*pop pl* .... WV-2
Hoyt—*uninc pl* .... TX-5
Hoyt, Benjamin, House—*hist pl* .... MA-1
Hoyt, E. S., House—*hist pl* .... MN-6
Hoyt, Samuel P., House—*hist pl* .... UT-8
Hoyt Arboretum—*park* .... OR-9
Hoyt-Barnum House—*hist pl* .... CT-1
Hoyt Bay—*bay* .... VT-1
Hoyt Block—*hist pl* .... OH-6
Hoyt Branch—*stream* .... PA-2
Hoyt Brook—*stream* (4) .... ME-1
Hoyt Brook—*stream* .... MA-1
Hoyt Brook—*stream* (5) .... NH-1
Hoyt Brook Cem—*cemetery* .... ME-1
Hoyt Canyon—*valley* .... NV-8
Hoyt Canyon—*valley* .... UT-8
Hoyt Cem—*cemetery* .... CO-8
Hoyt Cem—*cemetery* .... CT-1
Hoyt Cem—*cemetery* .... IL-6
Hoyt Cem—*cemetery* (2) .... KS-7
Hoyt Cem—*cemetery* .... NY-2
Hoyt Cem—*cemetery* .... OH-6
Hoyt Creek—*stream* .... AK-9
Hoyt Creek—*stream* .... ID-8
Hoyt Creek—*stream* .... MT-8
Hoyt Creek—*stream* .... NM-5
Hoyt Creek—*stream* .... NY-2
Hoyt Creek—*stream* (2) .... OR-9
Hoyt Creek—*stream* .... WY-8
Hoyt Crossing—*locale* .... CA-9
**Hoytdale**—*pop pl* .... PA-2
Hoyt Duvall Ranch—*locale* .... WY-8
Hoyte—*locale* .... TX-5
Hoyte Ch—*church* .... TX-5
Hoyt Elem Sch—*school* .... KS-7
Hoyt Field—*locale* .... MA-1
Hoyt Hayes Swamp—*swamp* .... CT-1
**Hoyt Heights**—*pop pl* .... SC-3
Hoyt Hill—*summit* .... ME-1
Hoyt Hill—*summit* (5) .... NH-1
Hoyt Hollow—*valley* .... NY-2
Hoyt Hollow—*valley* .... PA-2
Hoyt House—*hist pl* .... MT-8
Hoyt Island—*island* .... CT-1
Hoyt Island—*island* .... ME-1
Hoyt Island—*island* .... MN-6
Hoyt Lake—*lake* .... MI-6
**Hoyt Lakes**—*pop pl* .... MN-6
Hoyt Library—*building* .... MI-6
Hoyt Mine—*mine* .... NV-8
Hoyt Mtn—*summit* .... ID-8
Hoyt Mtn—*summit* .... ME-1
Hoyt Neck—*cape* .... ME-1
**Hoytown**—*pop pl* .... ME-1
Hoyt Park—*park* .... FL-3
Hoyt Park—*park* .... MI-6
Hoyt Park—*park* .... WI-6
Hoyt Peak—*summit* .... UT-8
Hoyt Peak—*summit* .... WY-8
Hoyt Point—*cape* .... VT-1
*Hoyt Pond* .... MA-1
Hoyt Pond—*lake* .... CT-1
Hoyt Pond—*lake* .... NH-1
Hoy Trail—*trail* .... CO-8
Hoyt Ranch—*locale* .... OR-9
**Hoyts**—*pop pl* .... NY-2
Hoyts Branch—*stream* .... IA-7
Hoyt Sch—*school* .... CT-1
Hoyt Sch—*school* .... MI-6
Hoyt Sch—*school* .... NY-2
Hoyt Sch—*school* .... WI-6
*Hoyts Corner* .... NH-1
**Hoyts Corner**—*pop pl* .... NH-1
Hoyt Shaft (historical)—*mine* .... PA-2
Hoyt-Shedd Estate—*hist pl* .... MA-1
Hoyt Shoe Factory—*hist pl* .... NH-1
Hoyts Hole—*bend* .... OR-9
Hoyts Island—*island* .... ME-1
Hoyts Pond—*lake* .... MA-1
Hoyts Swamp—*swamp* .... CT-1
**Hoytsville**—*pop pl* .... UT-8
Hoytsville Cem—*cemetery* .... UT-8
Hoyt Tank—*reservoir* .... NM-5
**Hoyttown**—*pop pl* .... ME-1
Hoyt Tunnel—*tunnel* .... PA-2
**Hoytville**—*pop pl* .... MI-6
**Hoytville**—*pop pl* .... OH-6
**Hoytville**—*pop pl* .... PA-2
Hoytville Horseback—*ridge* (2) .... ME-1
Hozannah Ch—*church* .... PA-2
Hozatka Lake—*lake* .... AK-9
Hoze Mtn—*summit* .... TN-4
Hozomeen Campground—*locale* .... WA-9
Hozomeen Creek—*stream* .... WA-9
Hozomeen Lake—*lake* .... WA-9
Hozomeen Mtn—*summit* .... WA-9
Hozomeen Ranger Station—*locale* .... WA-9
Hozzey Swamp—*swamp* .... NY-2
H P Berger Ditch—*canal* .... IN-6
H Pederson Ranch—*locale* .... ND-7
H Pierson—*locale* .... TX-5
H Pilgrim Lake Dam—*dam* .... MS-4
H Pool—*reservoir* .... MI-6
H Poole—*locale* .... TX-5
HP Tank—*reservoir* .... AZ-5
H P Tank—*reservoir* .... AZ-5
*HQ Tank* .... NM-5
H-Ranch—*locale* .... AZ-5
H Ranch—*locale* .... CA-9
H Ranch Tank—*reservoir* .... AZ-5
Hranice Cem—*cemetery* .... TX-5
H R Broadhead Pond Dam—*dam* .... MS-4
H R Carson Rsvr—*reservoir* .... CO-8
H Real Ranch—*locale* .... TX-5
H Reiser Ranch—*locale* .... NE-7
Hren Lake—*reservoir* .... IN-6
Hren Lake Dam—*dam* .... IN-6
H Reynolds Ranch—*locale* .... WY-8
H. Rivera Colon—*CDP* .... PR-3
H. Roe Bartle Scout Reservation—*locale* .... MO-7
H R Rice Sch—*school* .... SC-3
H R Sherrer Dam—*dam* .... AL-4
Hruby Conservatory of Music—*hist pl* .... OH-6
Hruska Lake—*lake* .... SD-7
H R Weisser Airp—*airport* .... IN-6
*H R Williams Landing* .... AL-4
HSA Gulf Coast Hosp—*hospital* .... FL-3
H Sanders Lake Dam—*dam* .... MS-4
H S Canyon—*valley* .... AZ-5
H Schlautmann Ranch—*locale* .... WY-8
H Schuchhardt Dam—*dam* .... SD-7
H S Dexter Grant—*civil* .... FL-3
H. S. Evans Landing (historical)—*locale* .... AL-4
*H Seven Creek* .... MT-8
H Seven Creek—*stream* .... MT-8
H Shively Ranch—*locale* .... NV-8
H Six Tank—*reservoir* .... AZ-5
H Six Well—*well* .... AZ-5
*H. S. Jewell* .... MO-7
H. S. Johnson Dam—*dam* .... OR-9
H. S. Johnson Rsvr—*reservoir* .... OR-9
H S Moody Elem Sch—*school* .... FL-3
H S Omahvndro Lake Dam—*dam* .... MS-4
H S P A Experimental Station—*locale* .... HI-9
H Spring—*spring* .... NV-8
H S Sch—*school* .... MT-8
H Stafford Cem—*cemetery* .... LA-4
H S Tank—*reservoir* .... AZ-5
H Stole Ranch—*locale* .... ND-7
H S Wedgeworth Catfish Ponds Dam—*dam* .... MS-4
H S Williams Ranch—*locale* .... NM-5
H Tank—*reservoir* .... TX-5
H Taylor Creek—*stream* .... OR-9
H Taylor Ranch—*locale* .... CO-8
*HT Butte* .... ND-7
H-T Ranch—*hist pl* .... ND-7
H T Ranch—*locale* .... ND-7
H T Ratliff Lake Dam—*dam* .... MS-4
H T Stubbs Lake Dam—*dam* .... MS-4
*Huacahella Mountains* .... AZ-5
*Huacavah* .... AZ-5
*Huacavah Mountains* .... AZ-5
*Huachuca* .... AZ-5
Huachuca Canyon—*valley* .... AZ-5
**Huachuca City**—*pop pl* .... AZ-5
**Huachuca City (Huachuca Vista)**—*pop pl* .... AZ-5
Huachuca City Sch—*school* .... AZ-5
Huachuca Mountains—*range* .... AZ-5
Huachuca Peak—*summit* .... AZ-5
Huachuca Substation—*locale* .... AZ-5
Huachuca Tank—*reservoir* .... AZ-5
**Huachuca Terrace**—*pop pl* .... AZ-5
Huachuca Terrace Post Office—*building* .... AZ-5
Huachuca Terrace Sch—*school* .... AZ-5
*Huachuca Vista* .... AZ-5
*Huaipai* .... AZ-5
*Huajatolla* .... CO-8
Huaji Cliff—*cliff* .... AK-9
Huakini Bay—*bay* .... HI-9
Hualalai—*summit* .... HI-9
*Hualalai Peak* .... HI-9
*Hualalai Volcano* .... HI-9
Hualala Rsvr—*reservoir* .... HI-9
*Hualapai* .... AZ-5
**Hualapai**—*pop pl* .... AZ-5
Hualapai Bay—*bay* .... AZ-5
Hualapai Canyon—*valley* (2) .... AZ-5
Hualapai (CCD)—*cens area* .... AZ-5
*Hualapai Falls* .... AZ-5
Hualapai Flat—*flat* .... NV-8
Hualapai Hilltop—*locale* .... AZ-5
Hualapai Indian Res—*reserve* .... AZ-5
Hualapai Indian School Res—*reserve* .... AZ-5
**Hualapai Ind Res**—*pop pl* .... AZ-5
Hualapai Interchange—*crossing* .... AZ-5
Hualapai Island—*island* .... AZ-5
*Hualapai Mountain* .... AZ-5
Hualapai Mountain County Park—*park* .... AZ-5
Hualapai Mountains—*range* .... AZ-5
Hualapai Peak—*summit* .... AZ-5
*Hualapai Reservation* .... AZ-5
Hualapai Rsvr—*reservoir* .... AZ-5
Hualapai Spring—*spring* (2) .... AZ-5
Hualapai Valley—*valley* .... AZ-5
Hualapai Valley Joshua Trees—*locale* .... AZ-5
Hualapai Wash—*stream* .... AZ-5
Hualapa Tank—*reservoir* .... AZ-5
*Hualpai* .... AZ-5
*Hualpai Bay* .... AZ-5
*Hualpai Canyon* .... AZ-5
*Hualpai Falls* .... AZ-5
*Hualpai Ind Res* .... AZ-5
*Hualpai Island* .... AZ-5
*Hualpai Mountain* .... AZ-5
*Hualpai Mountains* .... AZ-5
*Hualpai Peak* .... AZ-5
*Hualpai Reservation* .... AZ-5
*Hualpais Spring* .... AZ-5
Hualpais Spring—*spring* .... AZ-5
Hualpais Village (historical)—*locale* .... AZ-5
*Hualpai Valley* .... AZ-5
*Hualpai Wash* .... AZ-5
*Hualpi* .... AZ-5
Hualua—*civil* .... HI-9
Hualua One—*civil* .... HI-9
Hualua 2—*civil* .... HI-9
Huana Creek—*stream* .... TX-5
Huapache Canyon—*valley* .... NM-5
Huasache Tank—*reservoir* .... TX-5
Huasna—*civil* .... CA-9
Huasna—*locale* .... CA-9
Huasna Creek—*stream* .... CA-9
Huasna Peak—*summit* .... CA-9
Huasna River—*stream* .... CA-9
Huasna Sch—*school* .... CA-9
Huasna Valley—*valley* .... CA-9
Huat Oil Field—*oilfield* .... TX-5
*Huavabi Ranch* .... AZ-5
Huawai Bay—*bay* .... HI-9
Hub—*locale* (2) .... MS-4
Hub—*locale* .... TX-5
**Hub**—*pop pl* .... CA-9
Hub—*uninc pl* .... NY-2
*Hub, The* .... MS-4
Hub, The—*cape* .... DE-2
Hub, The—*island* .... ME-1
Hub, The—*summit* .... AZ-5
H U Bar Box—*basin* .... AZ-5
H U Bar Ranch—*locale* .... AZ-5
H U Bar Tank—*reservoir* .... AZ-5
Hub Attendance Center—*school* .... MS-4
**Hubball**—*pop pl* .... WV-2
*Hubbard* .... AZ-5
Hubbard—*locale* .... AL-4
Hubbard—*locale* .... AR-4
Hubbard—*locale* .... IL-6
Hubbard—*locale* .... MO-7
Hubbard—*locale* .... NV-8
Hubbard—*locale* .... NH-1
**Hubbard**—*pop pl* .... IN-6
**Hubbard**—*pop pl* .... IA-7
**Hubbard**—*pop pl* .... MD-2
**Hubbard**—*pop pl* .... MN-6
**Hubbard**—*pop pl* (2) .... MS-4
**Hubbard**—*pop pl* .... NE-7
**Hubbard**—*pop pl* .... OH-6
**Hubbard**—*pop pl* .... OR-9
**Hubbard**—*pop pl* .... TN-4
**Hubbard**—*pop pl* (2) .... TX-5
Hubbard, Col. William, House—*hist pl* .... OH-6
Hubbard, Lester, House—*hist pl* .... OH-6
Hubbard, Mount—*summit* .... AK-9
Hubbard, Nehemiah, House—*hist pl* .... CT-1
Hubbard, Renesselaer D., House—*hist pl* .... MN-6
Hubbard, S. B., House—*hist pl* .... OH-6
Hubbard, Thomas Russell, House—*hist pl* .... NH-1
Hubbard And Clampitt Drain—*canal* .... MI-6
Hubbard Basin—*basin* .... ID-8
Hubbard Basin—*basin* .... NV-8
Hubbard Brake—*lake* .... LA-4
Hubbard Brake—*swamp* .... AR-4
Hubbard Branch—*stream* .... FL-3
Hubbard Branch—*stream* (3) .... KY-4
Hubbard Branch—*stream* .... MS-4
Hubbard Branch—*stream* .... TN-4
Hubbard Branch—*stream* .... TX-5
Hubbard Branch—*stream* .... VA-3
*Hubbard Brook* .... CT-1
*Hubbard Brook* .... MA-1
Hubbard Brook—*stream* (2) .... CT-1
Hubbard Brook—*stream* .... ME-1
Hubbard Brook—*stream* .... MA-1
Hubbard Brook—*stream* (4) .... NH-1
Hubbard Brook—*stream* .... VT-1
Hubbard Brook Trail—*trail* .... NH-1
Hubbard Butte—*summit* .... NE-7
Hubbard Canyon—*valley* .... NM-5
Hubbard Canyon—*valley* .... UT-8
Hubbard Cave—*cave* .... CO-8
Hubbard (CCD)—*cens area* .... OR-9
Hubbard Cem—*cemetery* (4) .... AL-4
Hubbard Cem—*cemetery* .... AZ-5
Hubbard Cem—*cemetery* (2) .... IA-7
Hubbard Cem—*cemetery* (4) .... KY-4
Hubbard Cem—*cemetery* .... MI-6
Hubbard Cem—*cemetery* .... MN-6
Hubbard Cem—*cemetery* (3) .... MS-4
Hubbard Cem—*cemetery* .... MO-7
Hubbard Cem—*cemetery* .... NH-1
Hubbard Cem—*cemetery* (3) .... NY-2
Hubbard Cem—*cemetery* (2) .... OR-9
Hubbard Cem—*cemetery* .... SC-3
Hubbard Cem—*cemetery* (2) .... TX-5
Hubbard Cem—*cemetery* .... VA-3
Hubbard Cem—*cemetery* .... WV-2
Hubbard Chapel—*church* .... TX-5
Hubbard Chapel—*church* .... VA-3
Hubbard Chapel Sch—*school* .... MS-4
Hubbard Circle—*locale* .... MI-6
Hubbard Corner—*locale* .... NE-7
**Hubbard Corner**—*pop pl* .... MA-1
**Hubbard Corner**—*pop pl* .... VT-1
*Hubbard Corners* .... MA-1
Hubbard Corners—*locale* .... NY-2
Hubbard Coulee—*valley* .... MT-8
Hubbard Country Club—*other* .... OH-6
**Hubbard (County)**—*pop pl* .... MN-6
Hubbard County Courthouse—*hist pl* .... MN-6
Hubbard Cove—*valley* .... TN-4
*Hubbard Creek* .... AL-4
*Hubbard Creek* .... KS-7
Hubbard Creek—*locale* .... MS-4
Hubbard Creek—*stream* (2) .... AL-4
Hubbard Creek—*stream* .... AR-4
Hubbard Creek—*stream* .... CO-8
Hubbard Creek—*stream* .... FL-3
Hubbard Creek—*stream* .... GA-3
Hubbard Creek—*stream* .... KS-7
Hubbard Creek—*stream* (4) .... MS-4
Hubbard Creek—*stream* .... MT-8
Hubbard Creek—*stream* .... NY-2
Hubbard Creek—*stream* .... OH-6
Hubbard Creek—*stream* (2) .... OR-9
Hubbard Creek—*stream* .... TX-5
Hubbard Creek—*stream* .... UT-8
Hubbard Creek—*stream* .... WA-9
Hubbard Creek Lake—*lake* .... TX-5
*Hubbard Creek Reservoir* .... TX-5
Hubbard Crossing—*locale* .... NY-2
Hubbard Dam—*dam* .... AL-4
Hubbard Ditch No. 2—*canal* .... CO-8
Hubbard Ditch No. 3—*canal* .... CO-8
Hubbard Ditch No. 4—*canal* .... CO-8
Hubbard Drain—*canal* (2) .... MI-6
Hubbard Drain—*stream* .... MI-6
Hubbard Elem Sch—*school* .... AL-4
Hubbard Elem Sch—*school* .... TN-4
Hubbard Farm—*locale* .... AK-9
Hubbard Fork—*stream* (2) .... WV-2
Hubbard Gap—*gap* .... NE-7
Hubbard Glacier—*glacier* .... AK-9

Hubbard Grove—*woods* UT-8
Hubbard Gulch—*valley* (2) CA-9
Hubbard Gulch—*valley* (2) CO-8
Hubbard Gulch—*valley* ID-8
Hubbard Heights Golf Club—*other* CT-1
Hubbard Hill—*summit* CA-9
Hubbard Hill—*summit* ME-1
Hubbard Hill—*summit* MA-1
Hubbard Hill—*summit* (4) NH-1
Hubbard Hill—*summit* (2) NY-2
Hubbard Hill—*summit* OR-9
Hubbard Hill—*summit* VT-1
Hubbard Hill—*summit* VA-3
Hubbard Hill Brook—*stream* NY-2
Hubbard Hill State For—*forest* NH-1
Hubbard Hole—*bend* VA-3
Hubbard Hollow—*valley* AR-4
Hubbard Hollow—*valley* KY-4
Hubbard Hollow—*valley* PA-2
Hubbard Hosp—*hospital* MA-1
Hubbard House—*hist pl* FL-3
Hubbard House—*hist pl* IL-6
Hubbard House—*hist pl* TN-4
Hubbard HS—*school* GA-3
Hubbard Island—*island* NH-1
Hubbard JHS—*school* TX-5
**Hubbard Junction**—*pop pl* VA-3
*Hubbard Lake* AL-4
*Hubbard Lake* MI-6
Hubbard Lake—*lake* CO-8
Hubbard Lake—*lake* (2) MI-6
Hubbard Lake—*lake* (2) MN-6
Hubbard Lake—*lake* MS-4
Hubbard Lake—*lake* MO-7
Hubbard Lake—*lake* OR-9
Hubbard Lake—*lake* WA-9
**Hubbard Lake**—*pop pl* MI-6
Hubbard Lake—*reservoir* AL-4
Hubbard Lake—*swamp* AR-4
Hubbard Lakes—*reservoir* TX-5
Hubbard Landing—*locale* AL-4
Hubbard Landing (historical)—*locale* MS-4
Hubbard Lateral—*canal* ID-8
Hubbard Lodge No. 130—*hist pl* MN-6
Hubbard Lookout—*locale* MT-8
Hubbard Memorial Methodist Ch—*church* AL-4
Hubbard Mesa—*summit* CO-8
Hubbard Mine—*mine* MT-8
Hubbard Mine—*mine* WA-9
Hubbard Mineral Spring—*spring* OR-9
Hubbard Mines—*mine* CA-9
Hubbard Mine (underground)—*mine* AL-4
Hubbard Mound—*summit* OR-9
Hubbard-Mount Calm (CCD)—*cens area* TX-5
Hubbard Mtn—*summit* PA-2
Hubbard Oil Field—*oilfield* OK-5
Hubbard Park—*flat* CO-8
Hubbard Park—*park* (2) CT-1
Hubbard Park—*park* IN-6
Hubbard Park—*park* IA-7
Hubbard Park—*park* MA-1
Hubbard Park—*park* MO-7
Hubbard Park—*park* VT-1
Hubbard Park—*park* WI-6
Hubbard Park Hist Dist—*hist pl* MA-1
Hubbard Peak—*summit* AK-9
*Hubbard Plane Mill* AL-4
Hubbard Point—*cape* (2) ME-1
Hubbard Pond—*lake* CT-1
Hubbard Pond—*lake* FL-3
Hubbard Pond—*lake* ME-1
Hubbard Pond—*lake* NH-1
Hubbard Pond Dam—*dam* MS-4
Hubbard Prairie—*flat* CA-9
Hubbard Race Creek—*stream* NJ-2
Hubbard Ranch—*locale* MT-8
Hubbard Ranch—*locale* NV-8
Hubbard Ridge—*ridge* ME-1
Hubbard Ridge—*ridge* WA-9
Hubbard River—*stream* CT-1
Hubbard River—*stream* MA-1
Hubbard Road Interchange—*other* OK-5
Hubbard Rsvr—*reservoir* ID-8
Hubbard Run—*stream* OH-6
Hubbard Run—*stream* VA-3
*Hubbard-Salem Cemetery* MS-4
Hubbard Saltpeter Cave—*cave* TN-4
Hubbards Bridge—*bridge* NJ-2
Hubbards Cave—*cave* TN-4
Hubbard Sch—*school* CA-9
Hubbard Sch—*school* CT-1
Hubbard Sch—*school* (2) IL-6
Hubbard Sch—*school* (2) MI-6
Hubbard Sch—*school* MS-4
Hubbard Sch—*school* MO-7
Hubbard Sch—*school* NJ-2
Hubbard Sch—*school* NC-3
Hubbard Sch—*school* OH-6
Hubbard Sch—*school* SD-7
Hubbard Sch—*school* TX-5
Hubbard Sch—*school* WV-2
*Hubbard School* TN-4
Hubbard School—*summit* MA-1
*Hubbards Cove* TN-4
**Hubbards Cove**—*pop pl* TN-4
Hubbards Cove Baptist Ch—*church* TN-4
Hubbards Draw—*valley* OR-9
Hubbards Fork—*stream* KY-4
Hubbards Fork Ch—*church* KY-4
*Hubbards Hill* MA-1
Hubbards Lake—*lake* AL-4
Hubbards Lake Dam—*dam* AL-4
Hubbard Slough—*gut* TX-5
Hubbard Slough State Public Shooting Area—*park* SD-7
Hubbards Mill (historical)—*locale* AL-4
Hubbards Pond—*reservoir* MA-1
Hubbards Pond—*reservoir* NY-2
Hubbard Spring—*spring* CA-9
**Hubbard Springs**—*pop pl* VA-3
Hubbard Springs Ch—*church* AL-4
*Hubbard Springs Free Will Baptist Ch* AL-4
*Hubbards River* CT-1
*Hubbards River* MA-1
Hubbards Store (historical)—*locale* AL-4
Hubbard Station—*locale* CA-9
*Hubbardston* MA-1
**Hubbardston**—*pop pl* MA-1
**Hubbardston**—*pop pl* MI-6
Hubbardston Brook—*stream* MA-1
*Hubbardston Centre* MA-1
Hubbardston State For—*forest* MA-1
**Hubbardston Station**—*pop pl* MA-1
**Hubbardston (Town of)**—*pop pl* MA-1
Hubbardstown—*locale* WV-2
Hubbard Street Sch—*school* CA-9
*Hubbardsville* OH-6
**Hubbardsville**—*pop pl* NY-2
Hubbard Tank—*reservoir* (2) AZ-5
Hubbard Tank—*reservoir* TX-5
**Hubbardton**—*pop pl* VT-1
Hubbardton Battlefield—*hist pl* VT-1
Hubbardton Gulf—*valley* VT-1
Hubbardton River—*stream* VT-1
**Hubbardton (Town of)**—*pop pl* VT-1
**Hubbardtown**—*pop pl* NY-2
**Hubbard (Town of)**—*pop pl* (2) WI-6
**Hubbard (Township of)**—*pop pl* (2) MN-6
**Hubbard (Township of)**—*pop pl* OH-6
Hubbard Trail Country Club—*other* IL-6
Hubbard-Trigg House—*hist pl* TX-5
Hubbard-Upson House—*hist pl* CA-9
Hubbard Valley—*basin* CA-9
Hubbard Well—*well* NV-8
*Hubbard Woods* IL-6
**Hubbard Woods**—*pop pl* (2) IL-6
Hubbard Woods Sch—*school* IL-6
Hubbart Peak—*summit* WA-9
Hubbart Rsvr—*reservoir* MT-8
*Hubbart Swamp* MI-6
Hubbartt Ch—*church* IL-6
Hub Bayou—*stream* LA-4
Hubb Cem—*cemetery* KY-4
Hubbel Hollow—*valley* NY-2
Hubbel Island—*island* IA-7
**Hubbell**—*pop pl* IN-6
**Hubbell**—*pop pl* MI-6
**Hubbell**—*pop pl* NE-7
Hubbel Lake—*lake* OR-9
Hubbell Butte—*summit* AZ-5
Hubbell Camp—*locale* NM-5
Hubbell Canyon—*valley* NM-5
Hubbell Cem—*cemetery* KS-7
**Hubbell Corners**—*pop pl* NY-2
Hubbell Creek—*stream* MI-6
Hubbell Ditch—*canal* IN-6
Hubbell Ditch—*canal* WY-8
Hubbell Drain—*canal* MI-6
Hubbell Draw—*valley* NM-5
Hubbel Hill—*summit* AZ-5
Hubbell Hill—*summit* CT-1
Hubbell Hill Hollow—*valley* NY-2
Hubbell Lake—*lake* KS-7
*Hubbell Plateau* AZ-5
Hubbell Pond—*lake* MI-6
Hubbell Ranch—*locale* NM-5
Hubbell-Rose Creek—*fmr MCD* NE-7
Hubbells—*locale* MO-7
Hubbell Sch—*school* CT-1
Hubbell Sch—*school* IA-7
**Hubbells Corner**—*pop pl* IN-6
*Hubbells Crossroads* IN-6
Hubbell Spring—*spring* (2) NM-5
*Hubbells Station* IN-6
Hubbell Tank—*reservoir* NM-5
**Hubbellton (Hubbleton)**—*pop pl* WI-6
Hubbell Trading Post Natl Historic Site—*park* AZ-5
*Hubbellville* PA-2
Hubbel Pond—*lake* MN-6
Hubbel Pond Game Ref—*park* MN-6
Hubbel Run—*stream* PA-2
Hubbel Sch Number 1—*school* ND-7
Hubbel Sch Number 2—*school* ND-7
Hubbel Sch Number 3—*school* ND-7
Hubbels Island—*island* MI-6
Hubbel Slough—*stream* IA-7
Hubbel Well—*well* NM-5
Hubberson Gulch—*valley* CO-8
Hubbert Branch—*stream* FL-3
Hubbert Lake—*reservoir* CA-9
Hubbert Mill Creek—*stream* AL-4
**Hubbertville**—*pop pl* AL-4
Hubbertville Ch of Christ—*church* AL-4
Hubbertville Sch—*school* AL-4
**Hubble**—*pop pl* KY-4
Hubble, Edwin, House—*hist pl* CA-9
Hubble Branch—*stream* AR-4
Hubble Bridge—*bridge* AR-4
Hubble Cem—*cemetery* KY-4
Hubble Cem—*cemetery* (2) VA-3
Hubble Creek—*stream* AR-4
Hubble Creek—*stream* MI-6
Hubble Creek—*stream* (2) MO-7
Hubble Ditch—*canal* OR-9
Hubble Draw—*valley* WY-8
Hubble Gulch—*valley* MT-8
Hubble Hill—*summit* VA-3
Hubble Hollow—*valley* AR-4
Hubble Knob—*summit* KY-4
Hubbles, The—*island* NH-1
Hubble Sch—*school* (2) KY-4
**Hubbleton**—*pop pl* WI-6
Hubble Township—*civil* MO-7
**Hubbs**—*pop pl* KY-4
Hubbs Cem—*cemetery* IL-6
Hubbs Cem—*cemetery* (2) TN-4
Hubb Sch—*school* IL-6
Hubbs Creek—*stream* KY-4
Hubbs Grove Baptist Ch—*church* TN-4
Hubbs Grove Sch—*school* TN-4
Hubbs Hollow—*valley* KY-4
Hubbs House—*hist pl* AZ-5
Hubbs Miner Ditch—*canal* CA-9
Hubbs Park—*park* MO-7
Hubbs Sch—*school* NY-2
*Hubbsville* PA-2
Hubbub Lake—*lake* MN-6
Hub Butte—*summit* ID-8
Hubby Creek—*stream* NY-2
Hubby Hill—*summit* TX-5
Hub Camp—*locale* MT-8
Hub Canyon—*valley* NM-5
Hub Ch—*church* MS-4
*Hub Chapel United Methodist Church* MS-4
Hub Chute Hollow—*valley* AR-4
*Hub City* MS-4
**Hub City**—*pop pl* SD-7
**Hub City**—*pop pl* WI-6
Hub City—*uninc pl* CA-9
Hub City Hist Dist—*hist pl* MS-4
Hub Community Hall—*locale* TX-5
Hub Corn Tank—*reservoir* NM-5
Hubecky House—*hist pl* MO-7
Hube Lake—*lake* MN-6
Hubele Mounds and Village Site—*hist pl* IL-6
Hubelsville—*locale* PA-2
Hubelsville (historical)—*locale* PA-2
Huben (historical)—*locale* MO-7
Hubenstricker Drain—*canal* MI-6
Huber—*locale* MI-6
Huber—*locale* MO-7
Huber—*locale* TX-5
**Huber**—*pop pl* GA-3
**Huber**—*pop pl* IN-6
**Huber**—*pop pl* OR-9
Huber, Dr. H., Block—*hist pl* OH-6
Huber, John, House and Creamery—*hist pl* UT-8
Huber Booster Station—*other* TX-5
Huber Branch—*stream* KY-4
Huber Branch—*stream* MO-7
Huber-Briggs Cem—*cemetery* IN-6
Huber Cem—*cemetery* IN-6
Huber Cem—*cemetery* OH-6
Huber Cem—*cemetery* (2) SD-7
Huber Ch—*church* OH-6
Huber County Park—*park* OR-9
Huber Coy Cave—*cave* PA-2
Huber Creek—*stream* MI-6
Huber Ditch—*canal* OH-6
Huber Drain—*canal* MI-6
Huber Gulch—*valley* WA-9
**Huber Heights**—*pop pl* OH-6
Huber Hill—*summit* IL-6
Huber Hills—*summit* NV-8
Huber Lake—*lake* WA-9
Huber Lake—*lake* WI-6
Huber Lane Park—*park* IL-6
Huber Memorial Home—*building* IL-6
Huber Motor Sales Bldg—*hist pl* IN-6
Huber Number 1 Dam—*dam* SD-7
Huber Oil Field—*other* MI-6
Huber Park—*park* CA-9
Huber Park—*park* PA-2
Huber Park—*park* TX-5
Huber Park—*park* WY-8
**Huber Ridge**—*pop pl* OH-6
Huber Ridge—*ridge* WA-9
Huber Ridge—*ridge* WI-6
Huber Run—*stream* PA-2
**Hubers**—*pop pl* KY-4
Huber Sch—*school* (2) SD-7
Huber Sch—*school* (2) TX-5
Hubers Hollow—*valley* PA-2
Hubers Kenlite Station—*locale* KY-4
**Huber South**—*pop pl* OH-6
Huber Spring—*spring* WA-9
Hubers Run—*stream* PA-2
Huber Street Sch—*school* NJ-2
Hubert—*locale* TX-5
**Hubert**—*pop pl* GA-3
**Hubert**—*pop pl* NC-3
Hubert, Lake—*lake* MN-6
Hubert Bell Pond—*lake* FL-3
Hubert Branch—*stream* GA-3
Hubert Cem—*cemetery* TX-5
Hubert Chapel—*church* TN-4
Hubert Drain—*stream* MI-6
Hubert English Sch—*school* GA-3
Hubert Glacier—*glacier* WA-9
Hubert H Humphrey Bridge—*bridge* FL-3
Hubert Place—*locale* CA-9
Hubert Pond—*swamp* SC-3
Hubert Ridge—*ridge* TX-5
Hubert Run—*stream* PA-2
Hubert Sch—*school* MI-6
Hubert Spring Branch—*stream* TX-5
Hubert Tank—*reservoir* TX-5
**Hubertus**—*pop pl* WI-6
**Hubertville**—*pop pl* LA-4
**Hubertville**—*pop pl* TN-4
Hubertville Post Office (historical)—*building* TN-4
Huber Wash—*valley* UT-8
Huber Water Station—*other* TX-5
Hub Guard Station—*locale* UT-8
Hub Hall Cove—*bay* ME-1
Hub HIll—*summit* MS-4
Hub (historical)—*locale* AL-4
Hub (historical P.O.)—*locale* AL-4
Hub Hollow—*valley* AR-4
Hub Hollow—*valley* TN-4
Hubie Cauthen Number One Lake—*reservoir* AL-4
Hubie Cauthen Number Two Lake—*reservoir* AL-4
Hubie Cauthen Number 1 Dam—*dam* AL-4
Hubie Cauthen Number 2 Dam—*dam* AL-4
Hubie Spights Lake Dam—*dam* MS-4
*Hubigoon Lake* WI-6
Hub Island—*island* (2) NY-2
Hub Junction—*locale* GA-3
*Hub Juntion* GA-3
Hub Lake—*lake* LA-4
Hub Lake—*lake* MI-6
Hub Lake—*lake* MN-6
Hub Lake—*lake* MT-8
Hub Lake—*lake* WI-6
*Huble Creek* NC-3
*Hubler* PA-2
Hubler Cem—*cemetery* OH-6
Hubler Creek—*stream* ID-8
Hubler Gap—*gap* PA-2
Hubler Lake—*lake* MO-7
Hubler Run—*stream* PA-2
**Hublersburg**—*pop pl* PA-2
*Hublersburgh* PA-2
Hubler Sch—*school* IA-7
Hubley, Mount—*summit* AK-9
Hubley Creek—*stream* AK-9
Hubley Glacier—*glacier* AK-9
**Hubley (Township of)**—*pop pl* PA-2
Hubly—*locale* IL-6
Hubly Bridge—*other* IL-6
Hubly Sch—*school* IL-6
Hub Mine—*mine* CA-9
Hub Mine—*mine* ID-8
Hub Mine—*mine* NV-8
Hub Mine—*mine* UT-8
Hub Mine Basin—*basin* NV-8
Hub Mine (underground)—*mine* AL-4
*Hub Mountain* AK-9
Hub Neck—*cape* AL-4
*Hubner* WA-9
Hub Oil Field—*oilfield* MS-4
Hub Park—*park* IN-6
Hub Point—*summit* AZ-5
Hub Post Office (historical)—*building* MS-4
Hubquarter Creek—*stream* NC-3
Hubred Lake—*lake* MN-6
Hub Rock—*island* AK-9
Hubsch Draw—*valley* NM-5
Hub Shop Ctr—*locale* MO-7
Hubs Landing—*locale* FL-3
Hub Spring—*spring* NV-8
Hub Spring—*spring* NM-5
Hub Spring—*spring* OR-9
Hub Tank—*reservoir* NM-5
Hub Well—*well* NM-5
Hucabee Cem—*cemetery* (2) MS-4
**Hucar**—*pop pl* PR-3
**Hucares**—*pop pl* (2) PR-3
Hucares (Barrio)—*fmr MCD* PR-3
*Huchberry Spring* AZ-5
*Huching* GA-3
*Huchings* GA-3
Huchins Spring—*spring* WY-8
Huchunao—*area* GU-9
Huckabaa Pond—*lake* AL-4
Huckabaas Millpond—*reservoir* SC-3
Huckaba Branch—*stream* TN-4
Huckaba Bridge—*bridge* AL-4
**Huckabay**—*pop pl* TX-5
*Huckabee* AL-4
Huckabee Cem—*cemetery* AR-4
Huckabee Cem—*cemetery* TX-5
Huckabee Hill—*summit* TX-5
*Huckabee Lake* AL-4
*Huckabees Mill Pond* SC-3
**Huckaby**—*pop pl* MO-7
Huckaby Bridge—*bridge* AL-4
Huckaby Cem—*cemetery* OK-5
Huckaby Creek—*stream* FL-3
Huckaby Knob—*summit* TN-4
Huckaby Lake—*reservoir* TN-4
Huckaby Lake Dam—*dam* AL-4
Huckaby Lake Dam—*dam* TN-4
Huckaville—*locale* AL-4
Huckbay Canyon—*valley* NM-5
Huckbay Tank—*reservoir* NM-5
Huckberry Creek—*stream* TX-5
Huckby Cem—*cemetery* GA-3
Huckeby Branch—*stream* AL-4
Huckenberry—*locale* PA-2
Huckens Ranch (historical)—*locale* SD-7
*Huckens Rock* MA-1
Huckfeldt Draw—*valley* SD-7
Huck Finn Pond—*lake* CO-8
Huck Finn Shop Ctr—*locale* MO-7
Huckhole Swamp—*swamp* SC-3
Huckins Cem—*cemetery* MI-6
*Huckins Creek* MA-1
Huckins Island—*island* ME-1
Huckins Island—*island* MA-1
Huckins Ledge—*bar* ME-1
Huckins Neck—*cape* MA-1
*Huckins Pond* NH-1
Huckins Sch—*school* MT-8
*Huckleberry* TN-4
Huckleberry—*locale* MD-2
**Huckleberry**—*pop pl* TN-4
Huckleberry Basin—*basin* ID-8
Huckleberry Basin—*basin* WA-9
Huckleberry Bay—*bay* ID-8
Huckleberry Bay—*swamp* (3) GA-3
Huckleberry Bay—*swamp* NC-3
Huckleberry Bay—*swamp* SC-3
Huckleberry Bayou—*gut* TX-5
*Huckleberry Branch* AL-4
Huckleberry Branch—*stream* (5) AL-4
Huckleberry Branch—*stream* GA-3
Huckleberry Branch—*stream* IN-6
Huckleberry Branch—*stream* KY-4
Huckleberry Branch—*stream* MD-2
Huckleberry Branch—*stream* NC-3
Huckleberry Branch—*stream* (2) SC-3
Huckleberry Branch—*stream* (3) TN-4
Huckleberry Branch—*stream* VA-3
Huckleberry Brook—*stream* MA-1
Huckleberry Brook—*stream* NY-2
Huckleberry Butte—*summit* (2) ID-8
Huckleberry Butte—*summit* (2) OR-9
Huckleberry Butte—*summit* WA-9
Huckleberry Camp—*locale* ID-8
Huckleberry Camp—*locale* (2) NC-3
Huckleberry Camp—*locale* OR-9
*Huckleberry Campground* ID-8
Huckleberry Campground—*locale* CA-9
Huckleberry Canyon—*valley* NV-8
Huckleberry Cave—*cave* AL-4
Huckleberry Cem—*cemetery* MS-4
Huckleberry Cliff—*cliff* VA-3
**Huckleberry Corner**—*pop pl* MA-1
*Huckleberry Creek* AL-4
*Huckleberry Creek* CO-8
*Huckleberry Creek* OK-5
*Huckleberry Creek* TN-4
*Huckleberry Creek* TX-5
Huckleberry Creek—*stream* AL-4
Huckleberry Creek—*stream* (2) AR-4
Huckleberry Creek—*stream* (3) CA-9
Huckleberry Creek—*stream* CO-8
Huckleberry Creek—*stream* (2) FL-3
Huckleberry Creek—*stream* (4) ID-8
Huckleberry Creek—*stream* (2) MS-4
Huckleberry Creek—*stream* MO-7
Huckleberry Creek—*stream* (2) MT-8
Huckleberry Creek—*stream* NC-3
Huckleberry Creek—*stream* (6) OR-9
Huckleberry Creek—*stream* TN-4
Huckleberry Creek—*stream* TX-5
Huckleberry Creek—*stream* VA-3
Huckleberry Creek—*stream* (7) WA-9
Huckleberry Creek Dam—*dam* TN-4
Huckleberry Drain—*canal* (2) MI-6
Huckleberry Draw—*valley* OR-9
Huckleberry Fire Outlook—*hist pl* MT-8
Huckleberry Flat—*flat* AR-4
Huckleberry Flat—*flat* CA-9
Huckleberry Flat—*flat* ID-8
Huckleberry Flat Campground—*locale* ID-8
Huckleberry Ford Campground—*locale* WA-9
Huckleberry Forest Camp—*locale* WA-9
Huckleberry Gap—*gap* NC-3
Huckleberry Gap—*gap* OR-9
Huckleberry Gap—*gap* TN-4
Huckleberry Guard Station—*locale* OR-9
Huckleberry Gulch—*valley* MT-8
**Huckleberry Heights**—*pop pl* NC-3
**Huckleberry Hill**—*pop pl* CT-1
Huckleberry Hill—*summit* CA-9
Huckleberry Hill—*summit* (3) CT-1
Huckleberry Hill—*summit* ID-8
Huckleberry Hill—*summit* MA-1
Huckleberry Hill—*summit* (2) NH-1
Huckleberry Hill—*summit* NJ-2
Huckleberry Hill—*summit* PA-2
Huckleberry Hill—*summit* RI-1
Huckleberry Hill—*summit* VT-1
Huckleberry Hill—*summit* VA-3
Huckleberry Hill—*summit* WV-2
Huckleberry Hills—*range* NY-2
Huckleberry Hills—*summit* CO-8
Huckleberry Hills—*summit* CT-1
Huckleberry Hills Brook—*stream* CT-1
Huckleberry Hill Sch—*school* CT-1
Huckleberry Hill Sch—*school* MA-1
Huckleberry Hills Lake Dam—*dam* MS-4
Huckleberry Hollow—*valley* AR-4
Huckleberry Hollow—*valley* KY-4
Huckleberry Hollow—*valley* MO-7
Huckleberry Hollow—*valley* OK-5
Huckleberry Hot Springs—*spring* WY-8
*Huckleberry Island* NY-2
Huckleberry Island—*island* FL-3
Huckleberry Island—*island* (2) GA-3
Huckleberry Island—*island* (4) NY-2
Huckleberry Island—*island* WA-9
Huckleberry Islands—*island* FL-3
Huckleberry Knob—*summit* (3) KY-4
Huckleberry Knob—*summit* (2) NC-3
Huckleberry Knob—*summit* (2) VA-3
Huckleberry Knob—*summit* WV-2
Huckleberry Lake—*lake* (3) CA-9
Huckleberry Lake—*lake* (2) FL-3
Huckleberry Lake—*lake* (4) MI-6
Huckleberry Lake—*lake* MT-8
Huckleberry Lake—*lake* (2) NY-2
Huckleberry Lake—*lake* (2) OR-9
Huckleberry Lake—*swamp* OR-9
Huckleberry Lake Dam—*dam* MS-4
Huckleberry Landing—*locale* FL-3
Huckleberry Marsh—*swamp* NY-2
Huckleberry Marsh—*swamp* PA-2
Huckleberry Meadow—*flat* (2) CA-9
Huckleberry Meadows—*flat* CA-9
Huckleberry Mine—*mine* OR-9
Huckleberry Mountain Fire Lookout—*hist pl* WY-8
*Huckle Berry Mountains* WA-9
Huckleberry Mountain Trail—*trail* MT-8
Huckleberry Mountain Trail—*trail* OR-9
Huckleberry Mountian—*summit* WA-9
*Huckleberry Mtn* WA-9
Huckleberry Mtn—*summit* (3) AR-4
Huckleberry Mtn—*summit* (2) CA-9
Huckleberry Mtn—*summit* CO-8
Huckleberry Mtn—*summit* CT-1
Huckleberry Mtn—*summit* (4) ID-8
Huckleberry Mtn—*summit* (3) MT-8
Huckleberry Mtn—*summit* (5) NY-2
Huckleberry Mtn—*summit* (2) NC-3
Huckleberry Mtn—*summit* (8) OR-9
Huckleberry Mtn—*summit* (3) PA-2
Huckleberry Mtn—*summit* VA-3
Huckleberry Mtn—*summit* (8) WA-9
Huckleberry Mtn—*summit* WY-8
Huckleberry Park—*park* MO-7
Huckleberry Pass—*gap* CA-9
Huckleberry Pinnacle—*summit* GA-3
Huckleberry Point—*cliff* GA-3
Huckleberry Point—*summit* AR-4
Huckleberry Pond—*lake* NC-3
Huckleberry Pond—*reservoir* TN-4
Huckleberry Pond—*swamp* NC-3
Huckleberry Pond—*swamp* TN-4
Huckleberry Pond (Carolina Bay)—*swamp* NC-3
*Huckleberry Post Office* TN-4
Huckleberry Range—*range* WA-9
Huckleberry Ridge—*ridge* ID-8
Huckleberry Ridge—*ridge* IN-6
Huckleberry Ridge—*ridge* (2) KY-4
Huckleberry Ridge—*ridge* (5) NC-3
Huckleberry Ridge—*ridge* (2) PA-2
Huckleberry Ridge—*ridge* (6) TN-4
Huckleberry Ridge—*ridge* TX-5
Huckleberry Ridge—*ridge* VA-3
Huckleberry Ridge—*ridge* (3) WA-9
Huckleberry Ridge—*ridge* WV-2
Huckleberry Ridge—*ridge* WY-8
Huckleberry Ridge Mine—*mine* TN-4
Huckleberry Ridge State For—*forest* MO-7
Huckleberry River—*gut* LA-4
Huckleberry Run—*stream* WV-2
Huckleberry Sch—*school* WA-9
Huckleberry Sch (historical)—*school* MO-7
**Huckleberry Shores**—*pop pl* MA-1
**Huckleberry Spring**—*pop pl* NC-3
Huckleberry Spring—*spring* ID-8
Huckleberry Spring—*spring* (9) OR-9
Huckleberry Spring—*spring* WA-9
Huckleberry Springs—*spring* TN-4
Huckleberry Springs Branch—*stream* TN-4
Huckleberry Springs Ch—*church* TN-4
*Huckleberry Springs United Methodist Ch* TN-4
Huckleberry Stream—*stream* ME-1
*Huckleberry Swamp* NC-3
Huckleberry Swamp—*stream* NC-3
Huckleberry Swamp—*swamp* CT-1
Huckleberry Swamp—*swamp* DE-2
Huckleberry Swamp—*swamp* (4) NY-2
Huckleberry Swamp—*swamp* OH-6
Huckleberry Swamp—*swamp* PA-2
Huckleberry Swamp—*swamp* WA-9
Huckleberry Thicket—*woods* SC-3
Huckleberry Tower—*locale* KY-4
Huckleberry Trail—*trail* (2) PA-2
Huckleberry Trail—*trail* WA-9
Huckleberry Trail—*trail* WV-2
Huckleberry Trail (pack)—*trail* OR-9
*Hucklebone Lake* MI-6
Huckle Bridge—*other* MI-6
Huckleby Cem—*cemetery* OK-5
Huckle Lookout—*locale* WA-9
*Hucklerry Lake* MT-8
Huckle Run—*stream* PA-2
Hucklet Ranch—*locale* NM-5
*Huck Ovi* AZ-5
**Huck Ovi**—*pop pl* AZ-5
Hucks Field Cem—*cemetery* SC-3
Hucks Slough—*stream* TX-5
Huck Trail—*trail* PA-2
Hucmac—*locale* OK-5
Hucomer—*locale* FL-3
Hudallas Lake—*lake* MN-6
Hudd—*locale* TX-5
Huddart Park—*park* CA-9
*Huddelson Creek* ID-8
Huddelston Cem—*cemetery* TX-5
Huddens Bridge—*bridge* GA-3
Huddle—*locale* VA-3
**Huddle**—*pop pl* NY-2
Huddle Bay—*bay* NY-2
Huddle Branch—*stream* VA-3
Huddle Brook—*stream* NY-2
Huddle Creek—*stream* NY-2
Huddle Hill—*summit* NY-2
Huddle Mill—*locale* TN-4
Huddle Rocks—*island* AK-9
Huddle Sch—*school* LA-4
Huddle Sch—*school* NE-7
Huddles Hole—*basin* (2) ID-8
Huddleson Bluff—*cliff* ID-8
Huddleson Branch—*stream* TN-4
Huddleson Creek—*stream* ID-8
Huddleson Hollow—*valley* TN-4
Huddleson Sch—*school* PA-2
Huddleston—*locale* VA-3
**Huddleston**—*pop pl* AR-4
Huddleston Bridge—*bridge* TN-4
Huddleston Cem—*cemetery* (2) AR-4
Huddleston Cem—*cemetery* (2) MS-4
Huddleston Cem—*cemetery* (6) TN-4
Huddleston Cem—*cemetery* TX-5
Huddleston Ch—*church* MO-7
Huddleston Chapel (historical)—*church* MS-4
Huddleston Cove—*valley* AL-4
Huddleston Creek—*stream* AR-4
Huddleston Draw—*valley* SD-7
Huddlestone Point—*cape* MA-1
Huddleston House Tavern, The—*hist pl* IN-6
Huddleston Knob—*summit* TN-4
Huddleston Knob—*summit* WV-2
Huddleston Lake—*lake* MS-4
Huddleston Memorial Ch—*church* WV-2
Huddleston Mtn—*summit* KY-4
Huddleston Ranch—*locale* NM-5
Huddleston Rsvr—*reservoir* OR-9
Huddleston Sch (historical)—*school* MS-4
*Huddlestons Cross Roads Post Office* TN-4
Huddlestons Ford—*crossing* TN-4
Huddleston-Sills Cem—*cemetery* OH-6
Huddleston Store and McKinzie Store—*hist pl* AR-4
Huddleston Tank No 1—*reservoir* NM-5
Huddleston Tank No 2—*reservoir* NM-5
Huddleston Tank No 3—*reservoir* NM-5
Huddleston Tank No 4—*reservoir* NM-5
Huddleston Tank No 5—*reservoir* NM-5
Huddleston Well No 1—*well* NM-5
Huddleston Well No 3—*well* NM-5
Huddle Table—*summit* NE-7
Huddle Windmill—*locale* NM-5
Huddley Lakes—*lake* TX-5
Huddon Creek—*stream* AL-4
**Huddy**—*pop pl* KY-4
Huddy Gut—*gut* NC-3
Hudekoper Park—*park* PA-2
Hudelson Cem—*cemetery* IL-6
Hudeman Slough—*gut* CA-9
Hudeuc Lake—*lake* AK-9
*Hudgen Branch* TN-4
Hudgens—*locale* IL-6
Hudgens Branch—*stream* TX-5
Hudgens Bridge—*bridge* KY-4
Hudgens Cem—*cemetery* AR-4
Hudgens Cem—*cemetery* (2) MO-7
Hudgens Cem—*cemetery* (2) TN-4
Hudgens Cem—*cemetery* TX-5
Hudgens Creek—*stream* AR-4
Hudgens Creek—*stream* TN-4
Hudgens Pond—*reservoir* AL-4
Hudgens Ranch—*locale* TX-5
Hudgeon Bridge—*hist pl* KS-7
*Hudgeon Creek* AR-4
*Hudgeons Creek* IL-6
*Hudgin Creek* AR-4
Hudgins—*locale* KY-4
**Hudgins**—*pop pl* VA-3
Hudgins Branch—*stream* TX-5
Hudgins Cem—*cemetery* (2) AL-4
Hudgins Cem—*cemetery* (4) TN-4
Hudgins Cem—*cemetery* TX-5
Hudgins Creek—*stream* VA-3
*Hudgins Narrows* VA-3
Hudgins Spring Cave—*cave* AL-4
Hudgins Township—*civil* SD-7
*Hudginsville* FL-3
Hudgin (Township of)—*fmr MCD* AR-4
Hudiburg Spring—*spring* TN-4
Hudic Lake—*lake* KY-4
Hudkins Ditch—*canal* IN-6
Hudkins Draw—*valley* KS-7
Hudler Cem—*cemetery* NY-2
Hudleson Spring—*spring* OR-9
Hudlin Gap—*gap* NC-3
Hudlow Camp—*locale* ID-8
Hudlow Creek—*stream* ID-8
Hudlow Hollow—*valley* OK-5
Hudlow Mtn—*summit* ID-8
Hudlow Saddle—*gap* ID-8
Hudlow Sch—*school* AZ-5
Hudman Branch—*stream* TX-5
*Hudnall* WV-2
Hudnall—*other* WV-2
Hudnall Sch—*school* CA-9
*Hudnel Creek* KY-4
Hudnell Ditch—*canal* VA-3
Hudner—*locale* CA-9

Hunt Ditch—*canal* ID-8
Hunt Ditch—*canal* IN-6
Hunt Ditch—*canal* OR-9
Hunt Drain—*canal* (3) MI-6
Hunt Draw—*valley* UT-8
*Hunter* GA-3
*Hunter* (2) IN-6
*Hunter* MS-4
Hunter—*CDP* OH-6
Hunter—*fmr MCD* NE-7
Hunter—*locale* AK-9
Hunter—*locale* FL-3
Hunter—*locale* IL-6
Hunter—*locale* KY-4
Hunter—*locale* (2) NV-8
Hunter—*locale* PA-2
Hunter—*locale* VA-3
**Hunter**—*pop pl* AL-4
**Hunter**—*pop pl* AR-4
**Hunter**—*pop pl* KS-7
**Hunter**—*pop pl* LA-4
**Hunter**—*pop pl* MO-7
**Hunter**—*pop pl* NY-2
**Hunter**—*pop pl* ND-7
**Hunter**—*pop pl* OH-6
**Hunter**—*pop pl* OK-5
**Hunter**—*pop pl* PA-2
**Hunter**—*pop pl* (3) TN-4
**Hunter**—*pop pl* TX-5
**Hunter**—*pop pl* UT-8
**Hunter**—*pop pl* VA-3
**Hunter**—*pop pl* WV-2
Hunter, Andrew, House—*hist pl* AR-4
Hunter, Frank and Anna, House—*hist pl* WV-2
Hunter, Jacob, House—*hist pl* KY-4
Hunter, James, Stone House—*hist pl* OH-6
Hunter, John, House—*hist pl* KY-4
Hunter, John, House—*hist pl* TN-4
Hunter, John W., House—*hist pl* MI-6
Hunter, Joseph S., House—*hist pl* UT-8
Hunter, Lake—*lake* FL-3
Hunter, Mount—*summit* AK-9
Hunter, Norvall, Farm—*hist pl* OH-6
Hunter, William, House—*hist pl* OH-6
**Hunter Acres (subdivision)**—*pop pl* NC-3
Hunter Airp—*airport* TN-4
Hunter Archeol Site—*hist pl* NH-1
Hunter Army Airfield—*military* GA-3
Hunter Banks Field—*flat* NV-8
Hunter Bar—*bar* OR-9
Hunter Bay—*bay* AK-9
Hunter Bay—*bay* NY-2
Hunter Bay—*bay* WA-9
Hunter Bayou—*stream* LA-4
Hunter Bend—*bend* CA-9
Hunter Bend—*bend* TN-4
Hunter Bend—*bend* TX-5
Hunter-Best Rsvrs—*reservoir* OR-9
Hunter Bluff—*cliff* KY-4
Hunter Bluff—*cliff* TN-4
*Hunter Branch* MI-6
Hunter Branch—*stream* (4) AL-4
Hunter Branch—*stream* (2) FL-3
Hunter Branch—*stream* GA-3
Hunter Branch—*stream* IN-6
Hunter Branch—*stream* IA-7
Hunter Branch—*stream* (3) KY-4
Hunter Branch—*stream* LA-4
Hunter Branch—*stream* (2) NC-3
Hunter Branch—*stream* (3) SC-3
Hunter Branch—*stream* TN-4
Hunter Branch—*stream* TX-5
Hunter Branch—*stream* WV-2
Hunter Brook—*stream* CT-1
Hunter Brook—*stream* ME-1
Hunter Brook—*stream* (3) NY-2
Hunter Brook—*stream* VT-1
Hunter Butte—*summit* OR-9
Hunter Cabin—*locale* MT-8
Hunter Cabin—*locale* OR-9
Hunter Cabin Hollow—*valley* KY-4
Hunter Camp—*locale* CA-9
Hunter Camp—*locale* OR-9
Hunter Campground—*park* OR-9
Hunter Camp Seep—*spring* OR-9
Hunter Camp Way—*trail* OR-9
Hunter Canal—*canal* LA-4
*Hunter Canyon* CO-8
Huntor Canyon valley AZ-5
Hunter Canyon—*valley* CA-9
Hunter Canyon—*valley* (2) CO-8
Hunter Canyon—*valley* ID-8
Hunter Canyon—*valley* NM-5
Hunter Canyon—*valley* OR-9
Hunter Canyon—*valley* TX-5
Hunter Canyon—*valley* WA-9
Hunter Cem—*cemetery* (2) AR-4
Hunter Cem—*cemetery* FL-3
Hunter Cem—*cemetery* GA-3
Hunter Cem—*cemetery* (3) IL-6
Hunter Cem—*cemetery* (2) KS-7
Hunter Cem—*cemetery* (4) KY-4
Hunter Cem—*cemetery* MS-4
Hunter Cem—*cemetery* (7) MO-7
Hunter Cem—*cemetery* (6) NC-3
Hunter Cem—*cemetery* OH-6
Hunter Cem—*cemetery* (2) OK-5
Hunter Cem—*cemetery* PA-2
Hunter Cem—*cemetery* (13) TN-4
Hunter Cem—*cemetery* (2) TX-5
Hunter Cem—*cemetery* WV-2
Hunter Ch—*church* MO-7
Hunter Channel—*channel* WI-6
Hunter Chapel—*church* AL-4
Hunter Chapel—*church* AR-4
Hunter Chapel—*church* (2) MS-4
Hunter Chapel—*church* NC-3
Hunter Chapel—*church* VA-3
**Hunter Corner**—*pop pl* IN-6
*Hunter County* KS-7
*Hunter Cove* AL-4
*Hunter Cove* OR-9
Hunter Cove—*bay* AK-9
Hunter Cove—*bay* ME-1
Hunter Cove—*stream* TN-4
Hunter Cove—*valley* TN-4
Hunter Cove Cave—*cave* TN-4
Hunter Cove Cem—*cemetery* TN-4
*Hunter Creek* CA-9
*Hunter Creek* GA-3
*Hunter Creek* MI-6
*Hunter Creek* MT-8
*Hunter Creek* NE-7
*Hunter Creek* NC-3
*Hunter Creek* TN-4
**Hunter Creek**—*pop pl* OR-9
Hunter Creek—*stream* (3) AL-4
Hunter Creek—*stream* (5) AK-9
Hunter Creek—*stream* AZ-5
Hunter Creek—*stream* (5) CA-9
Hunter Creek—*stream* (2) CO-8
Hunter Creek—*stream* (4) FL-3
Hunter Creek—*stream* (3) ID-8
Hunter Creek—*stream* IN-6
Hunter Creek—*stream* (2) IA-7
Hunter Creek—*stream* KS-7
Hunter Creek—*stream* LA-4
Hunter Creek—*stream* MI-6
Hunter Creek—*stream* (3) MS-4
Hunter Creek—*stream* (2) MO-7
Hunter Creek—*stream* (3) MT-8
Hunter Creek—*stream* NV-8
Hunter Creek—*stream* NM-5
Hunter Creek—*stream* (2) NY-2
Hunter Creek—*stream* (2) NC-3
Hunter Creek—*stream* OH-6
Hunter Creek—*stream* (10) OR-9
Hunter Creek—*stream* (2) PA-2
Hunter Creek—*stream* TN-4
Hunter Creek—*stream* TX-5
Hunter Creek—*stream* (3) WA-9
Hunter Creek—*stream* (3) WY-8
Hunter Creek Camp Ground—*locale* CA-9
Hunter Creek Cem—*cemetery* NY-2
Hunter Creek Ch—*church* IN-6
Hunter Creek Ch—*church* NY-2
Hunter Creek Glacier—*glacier* AK-9
Hunter Creek Pond—*lake* IN-6
Hunter Creek Rsvr—*reservoir* MT-8
Hunter Creek Rsvr—*reservoir* NV-8
Hunter Creek Rsvr—*reservoir* OR-9
Hunter Creek Sch—*school* TX-5
*Hunter Creek Spring* OR-9
Hunter Creek Spring—*spring* MT-8
Hunter Creek Summit—*summit* ID-8
Hunter Creek Trail—*trail* OR-9
Hunter Crossing—*locale* MO-7
**Hunter Crossing (subdivision)**—*pop pl* NC-3
Hunter Cut—*canal* CA-9
**Hunterdale**—*pop pl* VA-3
Hunter Dam—*dam* ND-7
*Hunter Ditch* IN-6
Hunter Ditch—*canal* CO-8
Hunter Ditch—*canal* (3) IN-6
Hunter Ditch—*canal* OR-9
Hunter Ditch No. 2—*canal* CO-8
**Hunterdon**—*pop pl* OH-6
**Hunterdon County**—*pop pl* NJ-2
Hunterdon Med Ctr—*hospital* NJ-2
Hunter Drain—*canal* MI-6
Hunter Drain—*canal* NV-8
Hunter Drain—*stream* IN-6
Hunter Drain—*stream* MI-6
Hunter Draw—*valley* NV-8
Hunter Draw—*valley* (3) WY-8
Hunter Elem Sch—*school* TN-4
**Hunter Estates**—*pop pl* VA-3
**Hunter Farmes Subdivision**—*pop pl* UT-8
Hunterfield Brook—*stream* MA-1
Hunter Flat—*flat* AZ-5
Hunter Flat—*flat* CA-9
Hunter Flat—*flat* NV-8
Hunter Flats—*flat* CO-8
Hunter Fork—*stream* (2) WV-2
Hunter-Frost House—*hist pl* MS-4
Hunter Gap—*gap* VA-3
Hunter Gulch—*valley* CO-8
Hunter Gulch—*valley* MT-8
Hunter Gulch—*valley* OR-9
Hunter Gut—*gut* MD-2
Hunter Hall Plantation (historical)—*locale* MS-4
**Hunter Heights Subdivision**—*pop pl* UT-8
*Hunter Hill* MA-1
**Hunter Hill**—*pop pl* PA-2
Hunter Hill—*summit* FL-3
Hunter Hill—*summit* OR-9
Hunter Hill—*summit* TN-4
Hunter Hill—*summit* WV-2
**Hunter Hill Addition (subdivision)**—*pop pl* UT-8
Hunter-Hill Cem—*cemetery* AR-4
Hunter Hill Pass—*gap* OR-9
Hunter Hills—*locale* TN-4
Hunter Hill Sch (historical)—*school* MO-7
**Hunter Hills (subdivision)**—*pop pl* NC-3
**Hunter Hills (subdivision)**—*pop pl* TN-4
**Hunter Hills Subdivision**—*pop pl* UT-8
Hunter (historical)—*locale* AL-4
Hunter Hollow—*valley* AL-4
Hunter Hollow—*valley* MO-7
Hunter Hollow—*valley* (2) PA-2
Hunter Hollow—*valley* TX-5
Hunter Hollow—*valley* WI-6
Hunter Hollow Cave—*cave* AL-4
Hunter House—*hist pl* AL-4
Hunter House—*hist pl* KY-4
Hunter House—*hist pl* MI-6
Hunter House—*hist pl* RI-1
Hunter House—*hist pl* SC-3
Hunter HS—*school* MS-4
**Hunter (Hunter Station)**—*pop pl* PA-2
Hunter Interchange—*crossing* NV-8
Hunter Interchange—*locale* NV-8
*Hunter Island* OR-9
*Hunter Island* MP-9
Hunter Island—*island* AK-9
Hunter Island—*island* NY-2
Hunter Island—*island* TN-4
Hunter Island—*island* (2) WI-6
Hunter Island (historical)—*island* TN-4
*Hunter JHS* MS-4
Hunter JHS—*school* UT-8
Hunter Jim Creek—*stream* NC-3
Hunter Knob—*summit* GA-3
Hunter Knob—*summit* TN-4
*Hunter Lake* FL-3
Hunter Lake—*lake* (2) AK-9
Hunter Lake—*lake* IN-6
Hunter Lake—*lake* LA-4
Hunter Lake—*lake* MI-6
Hunter Lake—*lake* (5) MN-6
Hunter Lake—*lake* MT-8
Hunter Lake—*lake* NV-8
Hunter Lake—*lake* NY-2
Hunter Lake—*lake* OR-9
Hunter Lake—*lake* (2) WI-6
**Hunter Lake**—*pop pl* NY-2
Hunter Lake—*reservoir* OK-5
Hunter Lake—*reservoir* PA-2
Hunter Lake—*reservoir* TN-4
Hunter Lake—*swamp* LA-4
Hunter Lake Dam—*dam* PA-2
Hunter Lake Dam—*dam* TN-4
*Hunter Lakes* MI-6
Hunter Lake Sch—*school* NV-8
Hunter Landing—*locale* LA-4
Hunter Lateral—*canal* CA-9
Hunter Lateral—*canal* ID-8
Hunter-Lawrence House—*hist pl* NJ-2
Hunter Little Ranch—*locale* CA-9
Hunter Long Well—*locale* NM-5
Hunter Lookout Tower—*locale* LA-4
Hunter Lookout Tower—*locale* MO-7
Hunter Lookout Tower—*locale* VA-3
*Hunter Marsh* VA-3
Hunter Meadow—*flat* OR-9
Hunter Meadow—*flat* TN-4
Hunter Meadows—*flat* WA-9
**Hunter Meadows (subdivision)**—*pop pl* NC-3
Hunter Memorial Ch—*church* KY-4
Hunter Memorial Park—*cemetery* GA-3
Hunter Mesa—*summit* CO-8
Hunter Mesa—*summit* NM-5
Hunter Mesa—*summit* WY-8
*Hunter Mill Branch* GA-3
Hunter Mine—*mine* CA-9
Hunter Mine—*mine* CO-8
Hunter Mine—*mine* MO-7
Hunter Mining District—*civil* NV-8
*Hunter Mission Sch* AL-4
Hunter Mitthoefer Ditch—*canal* IN-6
Hunter-Morelock House—*hist pl* OR-9
Hunter Mountain Spring—*spring* OR-9
*Hunter MS* MS-4
Hunter Mtn—*summit* AR-4
Hunter Mtn—*summit* CA-9
Hunter Mtn—*summit* ME-1
Hunter Mtn—*summit* NY-2
Hunter Mtn—*summit* OR-9
Hunter Mtn—*summit* TX-5
Hunter Mtn—*summit* WA-9
Hunter Museum of Art—*building* TN-4
Hunter-Northy Ditch—*canal* MT-8
*Hunter Park* MN-6
Hunter Park—*flat* CO-8
Hunter Park—*park* CA-9
Hunter Park—*park* LA-4
Hunter Park—*park* MI-6
Hunter Park—*park* OH-6
Hunter Park—*park* OK-5
Hunter Park—*park* TX-5
**Hunter Park**—*pop pl* PA-2
Hunter Park Ch—*church* FL-3
Hunter Pass—*channel* FL-3
Hunter Peak—*summit* CO-8
Hunter Peak—*summit* ID-8
Hunter Peak—*summit* OR-9
Hunter Peak—*summit* TX-5
Hunter Peak—*summit* WY-8
Hunter Peak Campground—*locale* WY-8
Hunter Peak Ranch—*locale* WY-8
Hunter Place—*locale* CA-9
Hunter Place—*locale* NM-5
*Hunter P.O.* AL-4
Hunter Point—*cape* AL-4
Hunter Point—*cape* VA-3
Hunter Point—*cape* WA-9
Hunter Point—*cliff* MT-8
Hunter Point—*summit* (2) CA-9
Hunter Point—*summit* NV-8
Hunter Point Lookout Tower—*locale* MT-8
*Hunter Pond* NY-2
Hunter Pond—*lake* GA-3
Hunter Pond—*lake* ME-1
Hunter Pond—*lake* (2) NY-2
Hunter Post Office (historical)—*building* MS-4
Hunter Ranch—*locale* CA-9
Hunter Ranch—*locale* MT-8
Hunter Ranch—*locale* NV-8
Hunter Ranch—*locale* NM-5
Hunter Ranch—*locale* (2) OR-9
Hunter Ranch—*locale* (2) WY-8
Hunter Ranch Rsvr—*reservoir* OR-9
Hunter Ranger Station—*locale* WY-8
Hunter Ridge—*ridge* CA-9
Hunter Rock—*island* CA-9
*Hunter Rocks* PA-2
**Hunter (RR name Hunters)**—*pop pl* GA-3
*Hunter Rsvr* OR-9
Hunter Rsvr—*reservoir* CA-9
Hunter Rsvr—*reservoir* (2) CO-8
Hunter Rsvr—*reservoir* WY-8
Hunter Rsvr Dam—*dam* OR-9
Hunter Run—*stream* (3) PA-2
Hunter Run—*stream* VA-3
Hunter Run Sch (abandoned)—*school* PA-2
Hunter Run Trail—*trail* PA-2
Hunters—*locale* KY-4
Hunters—*locale* VA-3
**Hunters**—*pop pl* GA-3
**Hunters**—*pop pl* IN-6
**Hunters**—*pop pl* WA-9
*Hunters Bar* OR-9
Hunters Bay—*bay* (2) MN-6
Hunters Beach—*beach* ME-1
*Hunters Beach Brook* ME-1
*Hunters Bluff* TN-4
Hunters Bluff Post Office (historical)—*building* TN-4
Hunter's Bottom Hist Dist—*hist pl* KY-4
Hunters Brake—*swamp* AR-4
Hunters Brake—*swamp* LA-4
Hunters Branch—*stream* NC-3
Hunters Branch—*stream* (2) VA-3
Hunters Branch—*stream* WV-2
Hunters Bridge—*locale* NC-3
*Hunters' Brook* CT-1
Hunters Brook—*stream* ME-1
Hunters Brook—*stream* MI-6
Hunters Brook Bridge—*bridge* NY-2
Hunters Cabin, The—*locale* OR-9
Hunters Cabin Spring—*spring* OR-9
Hunters Camp—*locale* (3) CA-9
Hunters Camp—*locale* OR-9
Hunterscamp Branch—*stream* KY-4
Hunters Camp Windmill—*locale* TX-5
Hunters Canyon—*valley* UT-8
Hunters Cave—*locale* PA-2
Hunters Cem—*cemetery* AL-4
Hunters Cem—*cemetery* AR-4
Hunters Cem—*cemetery* MS-4
Hunters Cem—*cemetery* VA-3
Hunter Sch—*school* AL-4
Hunter Sch—*school* AK-9
Hunter Sch—*school* IL-6
Hunter Sch—*school* IN-6
Hunter Sch—*school* (4) MI-6
Hunter Sch—*school* (2) MO-7
Hunter Sch—*school* (2) NC-3
Hunter Sch—*school* (2) PA-2
Hunter Sch—*school* UT-8
Hunter Sch—*school* (2) VA-3
Hunter Sch—*school* WI-6
Hunter Sch (abandoned)—*school* (2) MO-7
Hunter Sch (abandoned)—*school* PA-2
*Hunters Chapel* AL-4
Hunters Chapel—*church* AL-4
Hunters Chapel—*church* AR-4
Hunters Chapel—*church* GA-3
Hunters Chapel—*church* LA-4
Hunters Chapel—*church* MS-4
Hunters Chapel—*church* NC-3
Hunters Chapel—*church* SC-3
Hunters Chapel AME Zion Ch—*church* AL-4
*Hunters Chapel Baptist Ch* MS-4
*Hunters Chapel Ch* AL-4
*Hunters Chapel Methodist Ch* MS-4
Hunters Chapel Sch—*school* MS-4
Hunters Chapel Sch (historical)—*school* MS-4
Hunter Sch (historical)—*school* (2) PA-2
Hunters Cove—*bay* OR-9
*Hunters Creek* MS-4
*Hunters Creek* OR-9
*Hunters Creek* PA-2
*Hunters Creek* TX-5
*Hunters Creek* WA-9
**Hunters Creek**—*pop pl* MI-6
Hunters Creek—*stream* AR-4
Hunters Creek—*stream* CA-9
Hunters Creek—*stream* CO-8
Hunters Creek—*stream* (2) GA-3
Hunters Creek—*stream* KY-4
Hunters Creek—*stream* MI-6
Hunters Creek—*stream* MO-7
Hunters Creek—*stream* (2) MT-8
Hunters Creek—*stream* NY-2
Hunters Creek—*stream* (2) NC-3
Hunters Creek—*stream* PA-2
Hunters Creek—*stream* TN-4
Hunters Creek—*stream* (2) TX-5
Hunters Creek Cem—*cemetery* MI-6
Hunters Creek Ch—*church* GA-3
Hunters Creek Drain—*canal* MI-6
**Hunters Creek (subdivision)**—*pop pl* MS-4
**Hunters Creek Village**—*pop pl* TX-5
**Hunters Creek West (subdivision)**—*pop pl* NC-3
Hunters Crossroad—*locale* GA-3
Hunters Crossroads—*locale* AL-4
Hunters Dairy Farm—*locale* NC-3
Hunters Draw—*valley* MT-8
Hunters Draw—*valley* NM-5
*Hunters Ferry* PA-2
Huntersfield Cem—*cemetery* NY-2
Huntersfield Creek—*stream* NY-2
Huntersfield Mtn—*summit* NY-2
Hunters Flat—*flat* UT-8
*Hunters Ford* IN-6
Hunters Fork Ch—*church* NC-3
**Hunters Glen (historical)**—*pop pl* AL-4
Hunters Grove Ch—*church* PA-2
Hunters Gulch—*valley* CA-9
Hunters Gulch—*valley* (2) MT-8
Hunters Hammock—*island* FL-3
*Hunters Harbor* RI-1
Hunters Harbor—*bay* MD-2
**Hunters Hill**—*pop pl* MD-2
**Hunters Hill**—*pop pl* TN-4
Hunters Hill—*summit* CA-9
Hunters Hill—*summit* CO-8
Hunters Hill—*summit* MA-1
Hunters Hill—*summit* MS-4
Hunters Hill Farm Airp—*airport* PA-2
Hunters Hole—*cave* AL-4
**Hunters Hollow**—*pop pl* KY-4
Hunters Hot Springs—*locale* MT-8
Hunters Hot Springs—*spring* OR-9
Hunters Hot Springs Canal—*canal* MT-8
Hunters Hump—*summit* WY-8
Hunter's Ironworks—*hist pl* VA-3
*Hunters Island* NY-2
Hunters Island—*bend* KS-7
Hunters Island—*flat* AR-4
Hunters Island—*island* FL-3
Hunters Island—*island* OR-9
Hunters Island Sch—*school* KS-7
Hunter Site—*hist pl* ME-1
Hunters Knob—*summit* KY-4
Hunters Lake—*lake* AK-9
Hunters Lake—*lake* CO-8
Hunters Lake—*lake* FL-3
Hunters Lake—*lake* (2) MI-6
Hunters Lake—*lake* MT-8
Hunters Lake—*lake* PA-2
Hunters Lake—*lake* (2) WI-6
Hunters Lake—*reservoir* KS-7
Hunters Lake—*reservoir* PA-2
Hunters Lake Dam—*dam* PA-2
**Huntersland**—*pop pl* NY-2
Hunter Slough—*stream* IL-6
Hunters Mill—*locale* MD-2
Hunters Mill—*locale* NJ-2
Hunters Mill (abandoned)—*locale* MO-7
Hunters Mill Branch—*stream* MD-2
Hunter's Mill Complex—*hist pl* PA-2
*Hunters Mill Creek* AL-4
Hunters Mill (historical)—*locale* MS-4
Hunters Millpond—*lake* VA-3
Hunters Millpond—*reservoir* DE-2
Hunters Millpond—*reservoir* NC-3
Hunters Mill (Township of)—*fmr MCD* NC-3
*Hunters Mtn* AR-4
Hunters Mtn—*summit* AR-4
Hunters Mtn—*summit* CT-1
*Hunters Park* MN-6
**Hunters Park**—*pop pl* MN-6
Hunters Pass—*gap* NH-1
Hunters Pass—*gap* NY-2
*Hunters Peak* CO-8
Hunters Peak—*summit* WI-6
Hunters Peak Ditch—*canal* WI-6
Hunters Peak Rsvr—*reservoir* WI-6
*Hunters Point* CA-9
*Hunters Point* TN-4
*Hunters Point* TX-5
*Hunter's Point* WA-9
Hunters Point—*cape* CA-9
Hunters Point—*cape* MI-6
Hunters Point—*cape* MN-6
Hunters Point—*cape* NY-2
Hunters Point—*cliff* AZ-5
Hunters Point—*locale* WV-2
**Hunters Point**—*pop pl* AZ-5
**Hunters Point**—*pop pl* TN-4
Hunters Point—*summit* AZ-5
Hunters Point Access Area—*park* TN-4
**Hunterspoint Ave**—*pop pl* NY-2
Hunters Point Bend—*bend* TN-4
Hunters Point Boarding Sch—*school* AZ-5
Hunters Point Campground—*park* AZ-5
Hunters Point Ferry (historical)—*crossing* TN-4
Hunters Point Golf Course—*locale* TN-4
Hunters Point Hist Dist—*hist pl* NY-2
Hunters Point Number Two—*school* CA-9
Hunters Point Pond—*reservoir* AZ-5
Hunters Point Post Office (historical)—*building* TN-4
Hunters Point Spring—*spring* AZ-5
**Hunters Point (subdivision)**—*pop pl* AL-4
Hunters Point Trading Post—*locale* AZ-5
Hunters Pond—*lake* KY-4
Hunters Prairie Sch—*school* WA-9
Hunter Spring—*spring* AZ-5
Hunter Spring—*spring* (5) CA-9
Hunter Spring—*spring* IN-6
Hunter Spring—*spring* MT-8
Hunter Spring—*spring* (10) OR-9
Hunter Spring—*spring* (3) TN-4
Hunter Spring—*spring* (2) UT-8
Hunter Spring—*spring* WA-9
Hunter Spring Run—*gut* FL-3
*Hunter Springs* OR-9
Hunter Springs—*spring* NV-8
Hunter's Ranch—*locale* MT-8
Hunters Ranch (Old Shannon Station)—*locale* NV-8
Hunters Range—*locale* PA-2
*Hunters Range Pond* PA-2
Hunters Range Sch—*school* PA-2
*Hunters Ravine* CA-9
**Hunters Ridge**—*pop pl* (2) TN-4
Hunters Ridge—*ridge* CA-9
Hunters Rock—*cliff* OH-6
Hunters Rocks—*summit* PA-2
Hunters (RR name for Hunter)—*other* GA-3
Hunters Rsvr—*reservoir* MT-8
*Hunters Run* PA-2
**Hunters Run**—*pop pl* PA-2
Hunters Run—*stream* CO-8
Hunters Run—*stream* OH-6
Hunters Run—*stream* (5) PA-2
Hunters Run—*stream* WV-2
Hunters Sch—*school* AL-4
Hunters School (abandoned)—*locale* MT-8
Hunters Shoals—*bar* TN-4
Hunters Siding—*locale* GA-3
Hunters Slough—*stream* AL-4
Hunters Slough—*stream* NE-7
*Hunters Spring* TN-4
Hunters Spring—*spring* (2) CA-9
Hunters Spring—*spring* (2) OR-9
Hunters Spring—*spring* UT-8
*Hunters Store* NC-3
**Hunters Store**—*pop pl* TN-4
Hunters Store (historical)—*locale* MS-4
**Hunters Subdivision**—*pop pl* (3) UT-8
Hunters Swamp—*stream* VA-3
**Hunter Stake Subdivision**—*pop pl* UT-8
*Hunter Station* AL-4
*Hunter Station* PA-2
*Hunter Station* TN-4
Hunter Station Baptist Ch—*church* AL-4
Hunter Station Ch of Christ—*church* AL-4
*Hunter Store* MS-4
**Hunterstown**—*pop pl* PA-2
Hunterstown Hist Dist—*hist pl* PA-2
**Hunters Trace**—*pop pl* KY-4
**Hunters Trace (subdivision)**—*pop pl* NC-3
Hunters Trail—*trail* CA-9
Hunters Trail—*trail* WA-9
Hunters Trail Shelter—*locale* WA-9
Hunter Street Baptist Ch—*church* (2) AL-4
Hunters Valley—*locale* VA-3
**Hunters Valley**—*pop pl* CA-9
Hunters Valley—*valley* CA-9
Hunters Valley—*valley* PA-2
*Huntersville* IN-6
*Huntersville* NC-3
Huntersville—*locale* KY-4
Huntersville—*locale* MN-6
Huntersville—*locale* PA-2
**Huntersville**—*pop pl* IN-6
**Huntersville**—*pop pl* MD-2
**Huntersville**—*pop pl* NC-3
**Huntersville**—*pop pl* OH-6
**Huntersville**—*pop pl* TN-4
**Huntersville**—*pop pl* (2) VA-3
**Huntersville**—*pop pl* WV-2
Huntersville Business Park—*locale* NC-3
Huntersville (CCD)—*cens area* TN-4
Huntersville Cem—*cemetery* MN-6
Huntersville Cem—*cemetery* OH-6
Huntersville Division—*civil* TN-4
Huntersville Forest Campground—*locale* MN-6
Huntersville (Magisterial District)—*fmr MCD* WV-2
Huntersville Park—*park* MN-6
Huntersville Presbyterian Church—*hist pl* WV-2
Huntersville Sch—*school* NC-3
Huntersville Sch (historical)—*school* TN-4
Huntersville State For—*forest* MN-6
Huntersville (Township of)—*civ div* MN-6
Huntersville Trinity Cem—*cemetery* PA-2
**Hunter Switch**—*pop pl* IN-6
**Hunters Woods Condo**—*pop pl* UT-8
Hunters Woods Sch—*school* VA-3
**Hunters Woods (subdivision)**—*pop pl* MS-4
Hunter Tank—*reservoir* AZ-5
Hunter Tank—*reservoir* NV-8
Hunter Tannersville Central Sch—*school* NY-2
**Hunterton**—*pop pl* KY-4
**Huntertown**—*pop pl* IN-6
**Hunter Town**—*pop pl* KY-4
**Hunter Town**—*pop pl* MS-4
Huntertown Cem—*cemetery* IN-6
Huntertown Elem Sch—*school* IN-6
**Hunter (Town of)**—*pop pl* NY-2
**Hunter (Town of)**—*pop pl* WI-6
**Hunter Township**—*pop pl* ND-7
**Hunter (Township of)**—*pop pl* IL-6
**Hunter (Township of)**—*pop pl* MN-6
Hunter Tunnel—*tunnel* CO-8
Hunter Tunnel—*tunnel* OH-6
Hunter Valley—*valley* CA-9
Hunter Valley—*valley* VA-3
Hunter Valley Mtn—*summit* CA-9
**Hunter Village Condominium**—*pop pl* UT-8
*Hunterville* VA-3
**Hunterville**—*pop pl* MO-7
Hunter Wash—*stream* CO-8
Hunter Wash—*stream* NM-5
Hunter (Watauga Valley)—*CDP* TN-4
Hunter Well—*well* NM-5
Hunter Well—*well* TX-5
Hunter Windmill—*locale* NM-5
Hunter Woods—*post sta* VA-3
Hunter Woods—*woods* WA-9
Hunt Farm—*locale* ME-1
Hunt Farmstead—*hist pl* NJ-2
Hunt Field—*park* TN-4
Hunt Fork—*stream* KY-4
Hunt Fork—*stream* WV-2
Hunt Fork John River—*stream* AK-9
Hunt Gap—*gap* TN-4
Hunt Girl Creek—*stream* ID-8
Hunt Godfrey Canal—*canal* WY-8
**Hunt (Greenville)**—*pop pl* WV-2
Hunt Gulch—*valley* CA-9
Hunt Gulch—*valley* (2) CO-8
Hunt Gulch—*valley* ID-8
Hunt Gulch—*valley* OR-9
Hunt Hill—*other* NY-2
Hunt Hill—*ridge* MA-1
Hunt Hill—*summit* (2) ME-1
Hunt Hill—*summit* (2) NY-2
Hunt Hill Point—*cape* MA-1
Hunt Hills—*summit* NY-2
Hunt (historical P.O.)—*locale* MS-4
Hunt Hollow—*locale* NY-2
**Hunt Hollow**—*pop pl* NY-2
Hunt Hollow—*valley* NY-2
Hunt Hollow—*valley* (2) OH-6
Hunt Hollow—*valley* TN-4
Hunt Hollow—*valley* TX-5
Hunt Hollow—*valley* WV-2
Hunt Hollow Cem—*cemetery* NY-2
Hunt Hot Spring—*spring* CA-9
Hunt House—*hist pl* GA-3
Hunt House—*hist pl* IL-6
Hunt House—*hist pl* NY-2
*Hunt HS* NC-3
Hunt HS—*school* MS-4
Hunt HS—*school* WA-9
Huntimer—*locale* SD-7
Huntimer Cem—*cemetery* SD-7
*Huntindon Creek* NV-8
Hunting—*locale* WI-6
*Hunting Bayou* FL-3
Hunting Bayou—*stream* TX-5
Hunting Boy Branch—*stream* NC-3
Hunting Branch—*stream* IL-6
*Hunting Brook* MA-1
**Huntingburg**—*pop pl* IN-6
Huntingburg Airp—*airport* IN-6
Huntingburg City Lake Dam—*dam* IN-6
Huntingburg Conservation Club Dam—*dam* IN-6
Huntingburg Conservation Club Lake—*reservoir* IN-6
*Huntingburgh* IN-6
Huntingburg Lake—*reservoir* IN-6
Huntingburg MS—*school* IN-6
Huntingburg Town Hall and Fire Engine House—*hist pl* IN-6
Hunting Camp Branch—*stream* TN-4
Huntingcamp Branch—*stream* WV-2
Hunting Camp Cow Camp—*locale* OR-9
Huntingcamp Creek—*stream* OH-6
Hunting Camp Creek—*stream* TN-4
Hunting Camp Creek—*stream* VA-3
Hunting Camp Ridge—*ridge* OR-9
Hunting Camp Run—*stream* WV-2
Hunting Camp Spring—*spring* TN-4
Hunting Canyon—*valley* NM-5
Hunting Club Lake Dam—*dam* MS-4
*Hunting Creek* NC-3
**Hunting Creek**—*pop pl* VA-3
Hunting Creek—*stream* CA-9
Hunting Creek—*stream* KY-4
Hunting Creek—*stream* (4) MD-2
Hunting Creek—*stream* (5) NC-3
Hunting Creek—*stream* SC-3
Hunting Creek—*stream* (3) TN-4
Hunting Creek—*stream* (6) VA-3
Hunting Creek Cem—*cemetery* NC-3
Hunting Creek Ch—*church* (2) NC-3
Hunting Creek Ch—*church* (2) VA-3
Hunting Creek Country Club—*other* KY-4
**Hunting Creek Farms**—*pop pl* TN-4
**Hunting Creek (historical)**—*pop pl* NC-3
Hunting Creek RR Bridge—*hist pl* NC-3
**Hunting Creek Subdivision**—*pop pl* UT-8
Hunting Creek Trail—*trail* VA-3
**Huntingdale**—*pop pl* MO-7
Huntingdon—*hist pl* VA-3
**Huntingdon**—*pop pl* PA-2
**Huntingdon**—*pop pl* TN-4
Huntingdon Airp—*airport* TN-4

*Hupa Mtn* CA-9
Hupa Mtn—summit CA-9
*Hupatkong Pond* NJ-2
Hupman Valley—valley VA-3
Hupmobile Tank—reservoir AZ-5
Hupobi-ouinge—hist pl NM-5
*Hupo Mtn* CA-9
**Hupp—pop pl** VA-3
Hupp Branch—stream MO-7
Hupp Cem—cemetery PA-2
Hupp Cem—cemetery WV-2
Hupp Creek—stream IA-7
Hupp Draw—valley WY-8
Hupper Island—island ME-1
Hupper Point—cape ME-1
Hupper Shoal—bar ME-1
Huppertz Sch—school TX-5
Hupp Hill—summit VA-3
Hupp Hollow—valley OH-6
Hupp Lake—lake NE-7
Hupp Ranch—locale SD-7
Hupp Run—stream WV-2
Hu-Pwi Wash—stream NV-8
Hur—locale WV-2
H U Ranch—locale WA-9
Huray Lake—lake MI-6
Hurbers Canyon—valley OR-9
Hurbert Creek—stream OR-9
*Hurbert Lake* IN-6
*Hurd (2)* NJ-2
Hurd—locale ME-1
Hurd—locale ND-7
Hurd—other NY-2
**Hurd—pop pl** LA-4
Hurd, Mary R., House—hist pl ME-1
Hurd, Mount—summit NY-2
*Hurd Brook* NJ-2
Hurd Brook—stream CT-1
Hurd Brook—stream ME-1
Hurd Brook—stream MA-1
Hurd Brook—stream NH-1
Hurd Brook—stream NY-2
Hurd Cem—cemetery KY-4
Hurd Cem—cemetery MI-6
Hurd Cem—cemetery TN-4
Hurd Cem—cemetery (2) VA-3
Hurd Cem—cemetery WV-2
Hurd Corner—locale (2) ME-1
**Hurd Corners—pop pl** NY-2
Hurd Creek—stream CO-8
Hurd Creek—stream (2) ID-8
Hurd Creek—stream MT-8
Hurd Creek—stream OK-5
Hurd Creek—stream OR-9
Hurd Creek—stream WI-6
Hurd Creek Trail—trail OK-5
Hurddles Creek—gut FL-3
Hurden-Looker Sch—school NJ-2
Hurd Gulch—valley ID-8
Hurd Hill—summit (2) ME-1
Hurd Hill—summit NH-1
Hurd Hill—summit NY-2
Hurd Hollow—valley AL-4
Hurd Hollow—valley MO-7
Hurd Hollow—valley PA-2
Hurd Hollow—valley TN-4
Hurd House-Anderson Hotel—hist pl MN-6
*Hurdister Creek* NV-8
Hurd Lake—lake CA-9
Hurd Lake Ditch—canal IL-6
**Hurdland—pop pl** MO-7
Hurdland Severs Lake—reservoir MO-7
Hurdle Field—airport NC-3
Hurdle Landing—locale NC-3
**Hurdle Mills—pop pl** NC-3
Hurdle Sch (historical)—school MS-4
Hurdlow—locale TN-4
Hurdlow Post Office (historical)—building TN-4
Hurdlow Sch (historical)—school TN-4
Hurd Marvin Drain—canal MI-6
Hurd Mtn—summit ME-1
Hurd Park—park IA-7
Hurd Peak—summit CA-9
Hurd Pond—lake (2) ME-1
Hurd Pond—lake NH-1
Hurd Pond Stream—stream ME-1
Hurd Road Sch—school MI-6
Hurd Round House—hist pl ND-7
Hurds—locale AR-4
Hurds Branch—stream VA-3
*Hurds Brook* CT-1
Hurds Brook—stream CT-1
Hurds Brook—stream NY-2
Hurd Sch—school MA-1
Hurd Sch—school MI-6
Hurd Sch—school NY-2
Hurds Chapel—church AR-4
Hurd Sch Number 1—school MI-6
Hurd Sch Number 2—school MI-6
*Hurds Corner* ME-1
Hurds Corner—locale CT-1
Hurds Corner—locale (2) ME-1
Hurd Settlement—locale NY-2
**Hurdsfield—pop pl** ND-7
Hurds Gap—gap AL-4
Hurds Gulch—valley CA-9
*Hurd Shoals Church* AL-4
Hurds Island—island IL-6
*Hurd's Lake* CT-1
Hurds Lake—reservoir CT-1
*Hurds Lake Brook* CT-1
*Hurds Pass* TX-5
*Hurds Pass Draw* TX-5
Hurds Pond—lake ME-1
Hurd Spring—spring AL-4
Hurd Spring Ridge—ridge KY-4
Hurd State Park—park CT-1
**Hurdtown—pop pl** NJ-2
**Hurdtown (Hurd)—pop pl** NJ-2
Hurdygurdy Bridge—bridge CA-9
Hurdygurdy Butte—summit CA-9
Hurdygurdy Creek—stream CA-9
Hurdygurdy Mtn—summit AK-9
*Hurey Canyon* AZ-5
**Hurffville—pop pl** NJ-2
**Hurford—pop pl** OH-6
Hurford Cem—cemetery TX-5
Hurford Run—stream OH-6
Hurger Branch—stream TX-5
Hurie Sch—school AR-4
*Hurkey Creek* CA-9
Hurlbert Camp—locale NH-1
Hurlbert Hollow—valley PA-2
Hurlbert Swamp—swamp NH-1
Hurlburt—locale WA-9
**Hurlburt—pop pl** IN-6
Hurlburt Creek—stream WY-8
**Hurlburt Field—pop pl** FL-3
Hurlburt Flats—flat OR-9
Hurlburt Highway—channel MI-6
**Hurlburt (historical)—pop pl** OR-9
*Hurlburts Brook* CT-1
Hurlbut Canyon—valley NE-7
Hurlbut Cem—cemetery CT-1
Hurlbut Glen Brook—stream NY-2
Hurlbut Memorial Gate—hist pl MI-6
Hurlbut Pond—reservoir CT-1
Hurlbut Ranch—locale NE-7
Hurlbutt Memorial Bridge—bridge CA-9
**Hurlbut (Township of)—pop pl** IL-6
Hurlbutt Ranch—locale CA-9
Hurlbutt Sch—school CT-1
Hurlbutville—locale NY-2
Hurld Sch—school MA-1
Hurleton—locale CA-9
Hurley—locale AL-4
Hurley—locale CO-8
**Hurley—pop pl** IA-7
**Hurley—pop pl** KY-4
**Hurley—pop pl** MS-4
**Hurley—pop pl** MO-7
**Hurley—pop pl** NM-5
**Hurley—pop pl** NY-2
**Hurley—pop pl** SD-7
**Hurley—pop pl** TN-4
**Hurley—pop pl** VA-3
**Hurley—pop pl** WI-6
Hurley, Lake—reservoir SD-7
**Hurley Acres—pop pl** TN-4
Hurley Bldg—hist pl AZ-5
Hurley Branch—stream (2) LA-4
Hurley Branch—stream PA-2
Hurley Branch—stream TN-4
*Hurley Brook* PA-2
Hurley Butte—summit SD-7
Hurley (CCD)—cens area NM-5
Hurley Cem—cemetery KY-4
Hurley Cem—cemetery MO-7
Hurley Cem—cemetery NM-5
Hurley Cem—cemetery NC-3
Hurley Cem—cemetery SD-7
Hurley Cem—cemetery TN-4
Hurley Cem—cemetery VA-3
Hurley Cem—cemetery WV-2
Hurley Creek—stream CA-9
Hurley Creek—stream ID-8
Hurley Creek—stream SD-7
Hurley Creek—stream (2) WA-9
Hurley Dam—dam NC-3
Hurley Dam—dam SD-7
Hurley Drain—stream DE-2
Hurley Draw—valley WY-8
*Hurley Elementary School* NC-3
Hurley Field—park KS-7
Hurley Fire Control Station—locale CA-9
Hurley Flat—flat CA-9
Hurley Flat—flat OR-9
Hurley Grove Community House—locale OK-5
**Hurley Heights (subdivision)—pop pl** DE-2
Hurley Hill—summit CT-1
Hurley Hill—summit IN-6
Hurley Hist Dist—hist pl NY-2
Hurley Hollow—valley NC-3
Hurley Hollow—valley TN-4
Hurley Hollow—valley TX-5
Hurley Hollow—valley VA-3
Hurley Hosp—hospital MI-6
Hurley Hosp—hospital OK-5
Hurley Island—island NE-7
Hurley Lake—lake (3) MN-6
Hurley Lake—lake WA-9
Hurley Lake—reservoir NC-3
Hurley Lake Dam—dam NC-3
Hurley Lookout—locale MS-4
Hurley Lookout Tower—tower MS-4
Hurley Mine—mine TN-4
Hurley Mound—hist pl OH-6
Hurley Neck—cape MD-2
Hurley Peak—summit WA-9
Hurley Point—cape ME-1
Hurley Post Office (historical)—building AL-4
Hurley Ravine—valley MN-6
Hurley Rsvr—reservoir OR-9
Hurley Sch—school CA-9
Hurley Sch—school (2) IL-6
Hurley Sch—school (2) KY-4
Hurley Sch—school NJ-2
Hurley Sch—school NC-3
Hurley Sch—school TN-4
Hurley Sch (historical)—school TN-4
Hurleys Pond—reservoir NJ-2
Hurleys Pond Dam—dam NJ-2
Hurley Spring—spring OR-9
Hurley Spring Creek—stream OR-9
*Hurleys Sch* TN-4
**Hurley (Town of)—pop pl** NY-2
Hurley Township—civil MO-7
**Hurley Township—pop pl** ND-7
**Hurley Township—pop pl** SD-7
Hurley Township (historical)—civil SD-7
Hurleyville—locale VA-3
**Hurleyville—pop pl** NY-2
Hurlingen—locale MO-7
**Hurlock—pop pl** MD-2
Hurlock Cem—cemetery IN-6
Hurlock Creek—stream MD-2
Hurlock Neck—cape MD-2
Hurl State No 1—other AK-9
**Hurlwood—pop pl** TX-5
Hurn Spring—spring AL-4
Hurn Spring Branch—stream AL-4
Hurnville—locale TX-5
Hurnville Cem—cemetery TX-5
*Hurodais-Suido* MP-9
Huron—locale MS-4
Huron—locale OR-9
Huron—locale PA-2
Huron—locale TX-5
Huron—locale WI-6
**Huron—pop pl** CA-9
**Huron—pop pl** IN-6
**Huron—pop pl** IA-7
**Huron—pop pl** KS-7
**Huron—pop pl** LA-4
**Huron—pop pl** MO-7
**Huron—pop pl** NY-2
**Huron—pop pl (2)** OH-6
**Huron—pop pl** SD-7
**Huron—pop pl** TN-4
Huron, Lake—lake MI-6
Huron, Lake—lake WI-6
Huron, Point—cape MI-6
Huron Baptist Ch—church TN-4
Huron Bay—bay (3) MI-6
Huron Beach—beach MI-6
Huron Beach—other MI-6
Huron Beach Ch—church MI-6
Huron Bldg—hist pl KS-7
Huron Bridge Park—park MI-6
Huron (CCD)—cens area CA-9
Huron Cem—cemetery IN-6
Huron Cem—cemetery MI-6
Huron Cemetery—hist pl KS-7
Huron Ch—church MI-6
Huron Ch—church MO-7
**Huron City—pop pl** MI-6
**Huron City (historical)—pop pl** ND-7
Huron Coll—school SD-7
Huron Colony—locale SD-7
**Huron Colony—pop pl** SD-7
**Huron (County)—pop pl** MI-6
**Huron (County)—pop pl** OH-6
Huron County Courthouse And
Jail—hist pl OH-6
Huron Creek—stream AK-9
Huron Creek—stream NY-2
Huron Drain—canal MI-6
Huron Elem Sch—school IN-6
Huron Evergreen Cem—cemetery NY-2
Huron Falls—falls PA-2
**Huron Gardens—pop pl** MI-6
Huron Heights—other MI-6
**Huron Heights—pop pl** MI-6
Huron (historical P.O.)—locale IA-7
Huron HS—school MI-6
**Huronia Heights—pop pl** MI-6
Huron Island*—island IA-7
Huron Islands—island MI-6
Huron Islands Lighthouse—hist pl MI-6
Huron Lake—lake MI-6
Huron (lightship)—hist pl MI-6
Huron Mall (Shop Ctr)—locale SD-7
**Huron Mountain—pop pl** MI-6
*Huron Mountains* MI-6
Huron Mountains—range MI-6
Huron Mtn—summit MI-6
Huron Natl Forest—park MI-6
Huron Natl Wildlife Ref—park MI-6
Huron No. 10 Township—civ div SD-7
**Huron Oaks—pop pl** MI-6
Huron Park—park KS-7
Huron Park—park MI-6
Huron Park Sch—school MI-6
Huron Peak—summit CO-8
Huron Point—cape MI-6
Huron Pond—lake RI-1
Huron Post Office—building TN-4
Huron Regional Airp—airport SD-7
Huron River—stream (2) MI-6
Huron River—stream OH-6
Huron River Point—cape MI-6
Huron Road Hosp—hospital OH-6
Huron Substation—other CA-9
Huron Swamp—swamp MI-6
*Hurontown* MI-6
**Hurontown—pop pl** MI-6
**Huron (Town of)—pop pl** NY-2
Huron Township—fmr MCD IA-7
**Huron Township—pop pl** ND-7
**Huron Township—pop pl** SD-7
Huron Township (historical)—civil SD-7
**Huron (Township of)—pop pl (2)** MI-6
**Huron (Township of)—pop pl** OH-6
Huron Valley Cem—cemetery MI-6
Huron Valley Ch—church MI-6
Hurraco Well—well TX-5
Hurrah Bay—swamp FL-3
Hurrah Ch—church FL-3
Hurrah Creek—stream FL-3
Hurrah Lake—lake FL-3
Hurrah Lake—lake WI-6
Hurrah Pass—gap UT-8
Hurrah Ridge—ridge NC-3
Hurrah Tower (fire tower)—tower FL-3
Hurrell Brook—stream NY-2
Hurrell Vly—swamp NY-2
Hurrican Branch—stream MS-4
*Hurricane* AL-4
*Hurricane* KY-4
*Hurricane* TN-4
*Hurricane* WV-2
Hurricane—locale AK-9
Hurricane—locale IL-6
Hurricane—locale NC-3
Hurricane—locale TN-4
Hurricane—locale VA-3
**Hurricane—pop pl** AL-4
**Hurricane—pop pl** LA-4
**Hurricane—pop pl (3)** MS-4
**Hurricane—pop pl** MO-7
**Hurricane—pop pl** NY-2
**Hurricane—pop pl** TN-4
**Hurricane—pop pl** UT-8
**Hurricane—pop pl** WV-2
**Hurricane—pop pl** WI-6
Hurricane, The—summit VT-1
Hurricane, The—valley TN-4
Hurricane Airp—airport UT-8
*Hurricane Baptist Ch* AL-4
Hurricane Baptist Ch—church AL-4
Hurricane Baptist Ch—church TN-4
*Hurricane Baptist Church* MS-4
Hurricane Basin—basin CO-8
Hurricane Bay—bay AR-4
Hurricane Bay—bay FL-3
Hurricane Bay—stream MS-4
Hurricane Bay—swamp (2) FL-3
Hurricane Bay Branch—stream MS-4
*Hurricane Bayou* AL-4
Hurricane Bayou—gut AR-4
Hurricane Bayou—stream AL-4
Hurricane Bayou—stream AR-4
Hurricane Bayou—stream (3) LA-4
Hurricane Bayou—stream MS-4
Hurricane Bayou—stream (2) TX-5
Hurricane Bend Lake—lake AR-4
Hurricane Bluff—cliff AL-4
Hurricane Bluff—cliff AR-4
Hurricane Bluff—cliff TN-4
Hurricane Bluff Waterhole—lake TX-5
*Hurricane Branch* AL-4
*Hurricane Branch* MS-4
*Hurricane Branch* TN-4
*Hurricane Branch* VA-3
Hurricane Branch—locale MS-4
Hurricane Branch—stream (12) AL-4
Hurricane Branch—stream (5) AR-4
Hurricane Branch—stream (2) FL-3
Hurricane Branch—stream (8) GA-3
Hurricane Branch—stream IN-6
Hurricane Branch—stream (22) KY-4
Hurricane Branch—stream (4) LA-4
Hurricane Branch—stream (5) MS-4
Hurricane Branch—stream (2) MO-7
Hurricane Branch—stream (4) NC-3
Hurricane Branch—stream (4) SC-3
Hurricane Branch—stream (16) TN-4
Hurricane Branch—stream TX-5
Hurricane Branch—stream (3) VA-3
Hurricane Branch—stream (12) WV-2
Hurricane Branch Ch—church GA-3
**Hurricane Branch (historical)—pop pl** TN-4
Hurricane Branch Post Office
(historical)—building TN-4
Hurricane Bridge—bridge TN-4
Hurricane Bridge—bridge VA-3
Hurricane Bridge Rec Area—park TN-4
*Hurricane Brook* NJ-2
Hurricane Brook—stream CT-1
Hurricane Brook—stream (4) ME-1
Hurricane Brook—stream (2) NH-1
Hurricane Brook—stream (2) NY-2
Hurricane Brook—stream VT-1
Hurricane Campground—locale KY-4
Hurricane Canal—canal UT-8
Hurricane Canal—hist pl UT-8
Hurricane Canyon—valley CA-9
Hurricane Cave—cave AL-4
Hurricane Cave—cave AR-4
Hurricane Cem—cemetery IL-6
Hurricane Cem—cemetery IN-6
Hurricane Cem—cemetery (2) KY-4
Hurricane Cem—cemetery MS-4
Hurricane Cem—cemetery NY-2
Hurricane Cem—cemetery (2) TN-4
Hurricane Cem—cemetery WI-6
*Hurricane Ch* AL-4
*Hurricane Ch* TN-4
Hurricane Ch—church (5) AL-4
Hurricane Ch—church (3) AR-4
Hurricane Ch—church GA-3
Hurricane Ch—church (2) IL-6
Hurricane Ch—church KY-4
Hurricane Ch—church (2) MS-4
Hurricane Ch—church MO-7
Hurricane Ch—church SC-3
Hurricane Ch—church (3) TN-4
Hurricane Ch—church (2) VA-3
Hurricane Ch—church WV-2
Hurricane Chapel—church AL-4
Hurricane Chapel—church NC-3
Hurricane Chapel—church VA-3
Hurricane City Cem—cemetery UT-8
Hurricane Cliffs—cliff AZ-5
Hurricane Cliffs—cliff UT-8
*Hurricane Cove* TN-4
Hurricane Cove—valley NC-3
Hurricane Cove—valley TN-4
Hurricane Cove Cave—cave TN-4
*Hurricane Creek* AR-4
*Hurricane Creek* GA-3
*Hurricane Creek* IN-6
*Hurricane Creek* MS-4
*Hurricane Creek* SC-3
*Hurricane Creek* TN-4
*Hurricane Creek* TX-5
Hurricane Creek—gut FL-3
Hurricane Creek—locale MS-4
**Hurricane Creek—pop pl (2)** MS-4
Hurricane Creek—stream (31) AL-4
Hurricane Creek—stream AZ-5
Hurricane Creek—stream (25) AR-4
Hurricane Creek—stream (3) FL-3
Hurricane Creek—stream (13) GA-3
Hurricane Creek—stream (9) IL-6
Hurricane Creek—stream (9) IN-6
Hurricane Creek—stream (15) KY-4
Hurricane Creek—stream (20) LA-4
Hurricane Creek—stream (35) MS-4
Hurricane Creek—stream (10) MO-7
Hurricane Creek—stream (7) NC-3
Hurricane Creek—stream OK-5
Hurricane Creek—stream OR-9
Hurricane Creek—stream (3) SC-3
Hurricane Creek—stream (31) TN-4
Hurricane Creek—stream (10) TX-5
Hurricane Creek—stream (5) VA-3
Hurricane Creek—stream (4) WV-2
*Hurricane Creek Baptist Church* MS-4
Hurricane Creek Cave—cave (2) TN-4
Hurricane Creek Cem—cemetery MS-4
*Hurricane Creek Ch* AL-4
Hurricane Creek Ch—church AL-4
Hurricane Creek Ch—church FL-3
Hurricane Creek Ch—church (2) LA-4
Hurricane Creek Ch—church MS-4
Hurricane Creek Ch—church (3) TN-4
Hurricane Creek Ditch—canal IN-6
Hurricane Creek Forest Camp—locale OR-9
Hurricane Creek Oil Field—oilfield LA-4
Hurricane Creek Pit Mine (surface)—mine AL-4
Hurricane Creek Post Office
(historical)—building MS-4
Hurricane Creek Rec Area—park TX-5
Hurricane Creek Sch (historical)—school MS-4
Hurricane Creek Sch (historical)—school TN-4
Hurricane Creek Watershed
Lake—reservoir AL-4
*Hurricane Cumberland Presbyterian Church* AL-4
Hurricane Dam—dam AZ-5
Hurricane Deck—bench CA-9
**Hurricane Deck—pop pl** MO-7
Hurricane Deck Lookout Tower—locale MO-7
Hurricane Deck Trail—trail CA-9
Hurricane Ditch—canal AR-4
Hurricane Ditch—canal OR-9
Hurricane Divide—ridge OR-9
Hurricane Division—civil UT-8
Hurricane Dock—locale TN-4
**Hurricane (Esperanza)—pop pl** MS-4
Hurricane Fault—valley UT-8
Hurricane Fields—area UT-8
*Hurricane Fork* AL-4
*Hurricane Fork* IN-6
*Hurricane Fork* TN-4
Hurricane Fork—stream (3) KY-4
Hurricane Fork—stream (3) VA-3
Hurricane Fork—stream (2) WV-2
Hurricane Fork Ch—church MO-7
Hurricane Fork Ch—church VA-3
Hurricane Gap—gap GA-3
Hurricane Gap—gap KY-4
Hurricane Gap—gap (4) NC-3
Hurricane Gap—gap TN-4
Hurricane Gap—gap VA-3
Hurricane Gap—gap WA-9
**Hurricane Gap—pop pl** KY-4
Hurricane Gap Branch—stream NC-3
Hurricane Gap Ch—church KY-4
Hurricane Gap Sch—school KY-4
**Hurricane Grange—pop pl** OR-9
Hurricane Greasy Sch—school KY-4
**Hurricane Grove—pop pl** AR-4
Hurricane Grove Cem—cemetery TN-4
*Hurricane Grove Ch* AL-4
Hurricane Grove Ch—church AL-4
Hurricane Grove Ch—church GA-3
Hurricane Grove Ch—church LA-4
Hurricane Grove Ch—church (2) TN-4
Hurricane Gulch—valley AK-9
Hurricane Gulch—valley ID-8
Hurricane Hall—hist pl KY-4
Hurricane Harbor—harbor FL-3
Hurricane Hill—locale AR-4
**Hurricane Hill—pop pl** TN-4
Hurricane Hill—summit CO-8
Hurricane Hill—summit IN-6
Hurricane Hill—summit ME-1
Hurricane Hill—summit (2) NH-1
Hurricane Hill—summit UT-8
Hurricane Hill—summit (4) VT-1
Hurricane Hill—summit WA-9
Hurricane Hill Cem—cemetery TN-4
Hurricane Hill Ch—church (2) TN-4
*Hurricane Hill Cumberland Presbyterian Ch* TN-4
**Hurricane Hills—pop pl** KY-4
Hurricane Hills Lake—lake KY-4
**Hurricane Hills (subdivision)—pop pl** AL-4
Hurricane Hill Trail—trail WA-9
Hurricane (historical)—locale AL-4
Hurricane Hole—bay VI-3
Hurricane Hollow—valley AL-4
Hurricane Hollow—valley (4) AR-4
Hurricane Hollow—valley GA-3
Hurricane Hollow—valley IL-6
Hurricane Hollow—valley (7) KY-4
Hurricane Hollow—valley (3) MO-7
Hurricane Hollow—valley (8) TN-4
Hurricane Hollow—valley UT-8
Hurricane Hollow—valley WV-2
Hurricane Hollow Creek—stream TN-4
Hurricane HS—hist pl UT-8
Hurricane HS—school UT-8
*Hurricane Island* FL-3
Hurricane Island—area MS-4
Hurricane Island—island AL-4
Hurricane Island—island IL-6
Hurricane Island—island KY-4
Hurricane Island—island (3) ME-1
Hurricane Island—island WI-6
*Hurricane Islands* ME-1
Hurricane Islands (historical)—island TN-4
Hurricane Key—island FL-3
Hurricane Knob—summit AR-4
Hurricane Knob—summit VA-3
Hurricane Lake—lake AR-4
Hurricane Lake—lake GA-3
Hurricane Lake—lake MN-6
Hurricane Lake—lake MS-4
Hurricane Lake—lake ND-7
Hurricane Lake—lake SC-3
Hurricane Lake—lake SD-7
Hurricane Lake—lake TX-5
Hurricane Lake—reservoir AZ-5
Hurricane Lake—reservoir AR-4
Hurricane Lake—reservoir FL-3
Hurricane Lake—reservoir MS-4
Hurricane Lake—reservoir NC-3
Hurricane Lake Campground—park AZ-5
Hurricane Lake Ch—church AR-4
Hurricane Lake Ch—church ND-7
Hurricane Lake Dam—dam MS-4
Hurricane Lake Natl Wildlife Ref—park ND-7
Hurricane Lake State Game Area—park AR-4
Hurricane Landing Public Use Area—park MS-4
*Hurricane Ledge* UT-8
Hurricane Ledge—bar ME-1
*Hurricane Lodge Fault* UT-8
Hurricane (Magisterial District)—fmr MCD VA-3
*Hurricane Marina* TN-4
*Hurricane Meeting House* TN-4
*Hurricane Mesa* UT-8
Hurricane Mesa—summit UT-8
Hurricane Mesa—summit WY-8
Hurricane Mesa Airp—airport UT-8
**Hurricane Mills—pop pl** TN-4
Hurricane Mills Post Office—building TN-4
Hurricane Mills Sch—school TN-4
Hurricane Mountain Mines—mine TN-4
Hurricane MS—school UT-8
*Hurricane Mtn* SC-3
Hurricane Mtn—summit AL-4
Hurricane Mtn—summit GA-3
Hurricane Mtn—summit (2) ME-1
Hurricane Mtn—summit MT-8
Hurricane Mtn—summit (2) NH-1
Hurricane Mtn—summit NY-2
Hurricane Mtn—summit (2) NC-3
Hurricane Mtn—summit SC-3
Hurricane Mtn—summit (2) TN-4
Hurricane Mtn—summit (2) VA-3
Hurricane Neck Sch—school IL-6
Hurricane On Brushy Sch—school KY-4
Hurricane Pass—channel FL-3
Hurricane Pass—gap WY-8
Hurricane Peak—summit CO-8
Hurricane Peak—summit WA-9
Hurricane Point—cape CA-9
Hurricane Point—cape FL-3
Hurricane Point—cape MS-4
Hurricane Point—cape TN-4
Hurricane Point—summit OR-9
Hurricane Pond—lake ME-1
Hurricane Pond—reservoir ME-1
*Hurricane Post Office* TN-4
Hurricane Post Office—building UT-8
Hurricane Post Office
(historical)—building MS-4
Hurricane Post Office
(historical)—building TN-4
Hurricane Rapids—rapids OR-9
*Hurricane Ridge* UT-8
Hurricane Ridge—ridge AL-4
Hurricane Ridge—ridge (3) AR-4
Hurricane Ridge—ridge GA-3
Hurricane Ridge—ridge KY-4
Hurricane Ridge—ridge ME-1
Hurricane Ridge—ridge (3) NC-3
Hurricane Ridge—ridge (6) TN-4
Hurricane Ridge—ridge VT-1
Hurricane Ridge—ridge WA-9
Hurricane Ridge—ridge (3) WV-2
*Hurricane Ridge Church* AL-4
Hurricane Ridge Church
(historical)—locale MO-7
Hurricane Ridge Site—hist pl MO-7
*Hurricane River* AL-4
*Hurricane River* TX-5
Hurricane River—stream MI-6
*Hurricane Rock* TN-4
Hurricane Rock Spring—spring TN-4
Hurricane Run—stream DE-2
Hurricane Sch—school (2) AL-4
Hurricane Sch—school KY-4
Hurricane Sch—school LA-4
Hurricane Sch—school UT-8
Hurricane Sch—school VA-3
Hurricane Sch—school WI-6
Hurricane Sch (historical)—school (2) AL-4
Hurricane Sch (historical)—school MS-4
Hurricane Sch (historical)—school (7) TN-4
Hurricane Shoal—bar GA-3
Hurricane Slough—gut AR-4
Hurricane Slough—gut LA-4
Hurricane Slough—stream (2) KY-4
Hurricane Sound—bay ME-1
Hurricane Spring—spring TN-4
Hurricane Springs Primitive Baptist
Ch—church AL-4
Hurricane State Wildlife Mngmt
Area—park MN-6
*Hurricane Store* TN-4
Hurricane Top—summit NC-3
Hurricane Township—civil MO-7
**Hurricane Township—pop pl** MO-7
Hurricane (Township of)—fmr MCD (4) AR-4
Hurricane (Township of)—fmr MCD NC-3
**Hurricane (Township of)—pop pl** IL-6
Hurricane Trail—trail AR-4
Hurricane Trail—trail NH-1
Hurricane Valley—valley GA-3
Hurricane Valley—valley TN-4
Hurricane View Cem—cemetery NC-3
Hurricane Wash—stream AZ-5
Hurricane Wash—valley (2) UT-8
Hurrich—locale CO-8
Hurried Branch—stream LA-4
Hurry—locale MD-2
Hurry Back Creek—stream ID-8
Hurryon Camp—park OR-9
Hurryon Creek—stream OR-9
Hurry Up Creek—stream ID-8
Hurry Up Creek—stream OR-9
Hurry-up Peak—summit WA-9
Hurry Up Tank—reservoir AZ-5
**Hurryville—pop pl** MO-7
Hursell Rock—rock MA-1
Hursey Cem—cemetery (2) NC-3
**Hursh—pop pl** IN-6
Hurshers Ch—church WV-2
Hursh Road Bridge (Bridge No.
38)—hist pl IN-6
*Hurshtown* IN-6
Hurshtown Bridge—bridge IN-6
**Hurshtown (Hursh)—pop pl** IN-6
Hurshtown Reservoir Dam—dam IN-6
Hurshtown Rsvr—reservoir IN-6
Hursicker Sch—school PA-2
Hursley Creek—stream MI-6
*Hurst* AL-4
*Hurst* KS-7
Hurst—locale GA-3
Hurst—locale KY-4
Hurst—locale WV-2
**Hurst—pop pl** IL-6
**Hurst—pop pl** TX-5
Hurst, Mount—summit AK-9
Hurst, William E., House—hist pl OH-6
Hurst Airp—airport PA-2
Hurst Beach—beach NC-3
**Hurstbourne—pop pl** KY-4
**Hurstbourne Acres—pop pl** KY-4
Hurst Branch—stream FL-3
Hurst Branch—stream TN-4
Hurst Branch—stream TX-5
Hurst-Bush Sch—school IL-6
Hurst Canyon—valley (2) ID-8
Hurst Cem—cemetery (3) AR-4
Hurst Cem—cemetery (2) IN-6
Hurst Cem—cemetery (3) KY-4
Hurst Cem—cemetery LA-4
Hurst Cem—cemetery (3) MO-7
Hurst Cem—cemetery OH-6
Hurst Cem—cemetery (6) TN-4
Hurst Cem—cemetery (2) VA-3
Hurst Cem—cemetery (2) WV-2
Hurst Ch—church GA-3
Hurst Ch—church WV-2
Hurst Chapel—church TN-4
*Hurst Chapel Ch* AL-4

Ilio Point—cape HI-9
Ilipog—area GU-9
Ilisong MH-9
Iliuk Arm Naknek Lake—lake AK-9
Iliuliuk Bay—bay AK-9
**Ilium**—pop pl CO-8
Ilium Bldg—hist pl NY-2
Ilium Flume—canal CO-8
Ilivit Mountains—range AK-9
Ilka Cem—cemetery TX-5
Illabe Hills Country Club—other OR-9
Illabot Creek—stream WA-9
Illabot Lake—lake WA-9
Illabot Peak WA-9
Illabot Peaks—summit WA-9
Illahaw (site)—locale FL-3
Illahe—locale OR-9
Illahe Campground—locale OR-9
Illahee UK-9
**Illahee**—pop pl (2) WA-9
Illahee Guard Station—locale OR-9
Illahee Hills OR-9
**Illahee Hills (subdivision)**—pop pl NC-3
Illahee Riffle OR-9
Illahee Rock—pillar OR-9
Illahee Spring—spring (2) OR-9
Illahee State Park—park WA-9
Illahe Hill—summit OR-9
Illahe Riffle—rapids OR-9
Illa Tank—reservoir AZ-5
Illavar Wash—stream AZ-5
Illco—locale WY-8
Ill Eagle Cave—cave AL-4
Illeginni—island MP-9
Illeginni Island MP-9
Iller Branch—stream KY-4
Iller Creek OR-9
Illgen City—locale MN-6
Illgen Falls—falls MN-6
Illges, John Paul, House—hist pl GA-3
Illges House—hist pl GA-3
Illia—locale WA-9
**Illiana**—pop pl IL-6
**Illiana Heights**—pop pl IL-6
Illiana HS—school IL-6
Illiana Racetrack—other IN-6
Illicks Mill Dam—dam PA-2
Illil—bay PW-9
Illilouette Creek—stream CA-9
Illilouette Fall—falls CA-9
Illilouette Falls CA-9
Illilouette Gorge—valley CA-9
Illilouette Ridge—ridge CA-9
Illing JHS—school CT-1
Illingsworth Creek—stream OR-9
Illini WV-2
Illini Ch—church IL-6
Illini Country Club—other IL-6
Illini State Park—park IL-6
**Illini (Township of)**—pop pl IL-6
Illiniwek Forest Preserve—park IL-6
**Illinoi**—pop pl IL-6
**Illinoi**—pop pl IN-6
Illinois, Lake—lake FL-3
Illinois And Michigan Canal—canal IL-6
Illinois and Michigan Canal—hist pl IL-6
Illinois and Mississippi Canal IL-6
Illinois and Mississippi Canal Feeder IL-6
Illinois Basin—basin WA-9
Illinois Bayou—stream AR-4
Illinois Beach State Park—park IL-6
Illinois Bend—bend TX-5
Illinois Bend—locale TX-5
Illinois Bend Ch—church MO-7
Illinois Bend Oil Field—oilfield TX-5
Illinois Bend Sch (historical)—school MO-7
Illinois Brewery—hist pl NM-5
Illinois Canyon—valley CA-9
Illinois Canyon—valley ID-8
Illinois Canyon—valley NV-8
Illinois Central Coll—school IL-6
Illinois Central Depot—hist pl MS-4
Illinois Central Lake IL-6
Illinois Central Park TN-4
Illinois Central Passenger Depot—hist pl SD-7
Illinois Central RR Depot—hist pl MS-4
Illinois Central RR Freight Depot—hist pl IN-6
Illinois Central RR Lake Dam—dam MS-4
Illinois Central RR Station and Freight Depot—hist pl KY-4
Illinois Central Rsvr—reservoir IL-6
Illinois Central Stone Arch RR Bridges—hist pl IL-6
Illinois Chapel—church AR-4
Illinois Chapel Cem—cemetery AR-4
**Illinois City**—pop pl IL-6
Illinois Creek—stream (2) AK-9
Illinois Creek—stream CA-9
Illinois Creek—stream CO-8
Illinois Creek—stream GA-3
Illinois Creek—stream (4) KS-7
Illinois Creek—stream NV-8
Illinois Creek—stream WA-9
Illinois Creek—stream WY-8
Illinois Creek Campground—locale WY-8
Illinois Department of Mines and Minerals-Springfield Mine Rescue—hist pl IL-6
Illinois Envelope Co. Bldg—hist pl MI-6
Illinois Field—other IL-6
Illinois Grove—locale IA-7
**Illinois Grove**—pop pl IA-7
Illinois Grove Cem—cemetery IA-7
Illinois Grove (historical P.O.)—locale IA-7
Illinois Gulch—valley (5) CO-8
Illinois Gulch—valley (2) ID-8
Illinois Gulch—valley (2) MT-8
Illinois Hill—summit CA-9
Illinois Industrial Sch For Boys—school IL-6
Illinois Institute of Technology—school IL-6
Illinois Iron Furnace—hist pl IL-6
**Illinois Junction**—pop pl IL-6
Illinois Lake—lake MN-6
Illinois Mine—mine (2) CO-8
Illinois Mine—mine ID-8
Illinois Mine—mine WA-9
Illinois Mine (Inactive)—mine NV-8
Illinois Mtn—summit NY-2
Illinois Natl Wild and Scenic River—park OR-9
**Illinois Park**—pop pl IL-6
Illinois Park Sch—school IL-6
Illinois Pass—gap CO-8
Illinois Peak—summit ID-8
Illinois Peak—summit MT-8
Illinois Pet Cem—cemetery IL-6
**Illinois Plant**—pop pl LA-4
Illinois Ranch—locale CO-8
Illinois Ridge—ridge CA-9
Illinois Ridge—ridge MT-8
Illinois River IN-6
Illinois River SC-3
Illinois River—stream AR-4
Illinois River—stream CO-8
Illinois River—stream IL-6
Illinois River—stream OK-5
Illinois River—stream OR-9
Illinois River Bridge—hist pl AR-4
Illinois River Ch—church OK-5
Illinois River Trail—trail CO-8
Illinois River Trail—trail OR-9
Illinois Sch—school IL-6
Illinois Slough—stream IL-6
Illinois Soldiers and Sailors Home—building IL-6
Illinois State Bank Bldg—hist pl IL-6
Illinois State Capitol—hist pl IL-6
Illinois State Penitentiary—other IL-6
Illinois State Prison (Vienna Branch)—other IL-6
Illinois Town Hall—building ND-7
Illinois Township—civil SD-7
**Illinois Township**—pop pl (4) KS-7
**Illinois Township**—pop pl ND-7
Illinois (Township of)—fmr MCD (2) AR-4
Illinois Township Sch—school SD-7
Illinoistown (Site)—locale CA-9
Illinois Traction System Mackinaw Depot—hist pl IL-6
**Illinois Valley**—pop pl OR-9
Illinois Valley—valley PA-2
Illinois Valley US Forest Service Airstrip—airport OR-9
Illinois Veterans Home IL-6
Illinois Wesleyan Univ—school IL-6
Illion (historical)—locale KS-7
Illio Point HI-9
**Illiopolis**—pop pl IL-6
**Illiopolis (Township of)**—pop pl IL-6
Illipah—locale NV-8
Illipah Creek—stream NV-8
Illipah Rsvr—reservoir NV-8
**Illmo**—pop pl MO-7
Illmo Branch—stream MO-7
Illmont Sch—school MT-8
Illmo-Scott City Sch—school MO-7
Illuk FM-9
Illumination Rock—pillar OR-9
Illusion Lake—lake TX-5
Illwill Creek—stream KY-4
Illygain MP-9
Illyria—locale IA-7
Illyria(historical P.O.)—locale IA-7
Illyria Township—fmr MCD IA-7
Ilmon—locale CA-9
Ilnik—locale AK-9
Ilnik Lake—lake AK-9
Ilnik River—stream AK-9
Ilo, Lake—reservoir ND-7
Iloli (Apana One)—civil HI-9
Iloli (Apana Two)—civil HI-9
Ilong Ch—church NC-3
Ilonia River OR-9
Ilo Ridge—ridge WY-8
Il Penseroso Acres Lake—reservoir NC-3
Il Penseroso Acres Lake Dam—dam NC-3
Il Pinole CA-9
Il Pinole Point CA-9
Ilput Island—island AK-9
I-L Ranch Airp—airport NV-8
**Ilse**—pop pl CO-8
**Ilsley**—pop pl KY-4
Ilsley Hill MA-1
Ilsley Sch—school MI-6
Ilsleys Hill MA-1
Ilsley Siding—locale KY-4
**Ilsley (sta.)**—pop pl KY-4
Ilstrup Sch—school MN-6
I L Summit—summit NV-8
Iltis Brewery and Ice House—hist pl MN-6
I L Trotter Junior Lake Dam—dam MS-4
Iluk—CDP FM-9
Ilukunboelle FM-9
Ilut Pebul PW-9
**Ilwaco**—pop pl WA-9
Ilwaco Channel—channel OR-9
Ilwaco Channel—channel WA-9
Ilyirak Creek—stream AK-9
IMA Arena—building MI-6
IMA Auditorium—building MI-6
Ima Cem—cemetery NM-5
Imacklasha MS-4
Ima Community House—locale NM-5
I Madog MH-9
**Image**—pop pl WA-9
Image Canoe Island OR-9
Image Creek—stream OR-9
Image Lake—lake MI-6
Image Lake—lake MN-6
Image Lake—lake MT-8
Image Lake—lake WA-9
Imagination Peak—summit OR-9
Imagine Lake MT-8
Ima Hogg Museum—locale TX-5
Imaiknik Lake—lake AK-9
Imakruak Lake—lake AK-9
Ima Lake—lake MN-6
Imalone—locale WI-6
Ima Mine—mine ID-8
Iman Branch—stream MO-7
Imanuel Church AL-4
I Martin Landing (historical)—locale AL-4
Ima (Site)—locale NM-5
Imbach Ditch—canal IN-6
Imbeau Bayou—gut AR-4
**Imbery**—pop pl PR-3
I & M Bldg—hist pl IN-6
**Imbler**—pop pl OR-9
Imbler Creek—stream WA-9
Imbler Drain—canal OR-9
Imbler Drain—stream ID-8
Imbler Gulch—valley OR-9
**Imboden**—pop pl AR-4
**Imboden**—pop pl VA-3
Imboden Cem—cemetery MO-7
Imboden Fork—stream MO-7
Imboden Knob—summit WV-2
Imboden Lookout Tower—locale AR-4
Imbrie Farm—hist pl OR-9
Imbs—locale IL-6
Imel Cem—cemetery PA-2
**Imelechol**—pop pl PW-9
Imelechol, Elechol Ra—beach PW-9
Imeleol PW-9
Imeliik—civil PW-9
Imelyak River—stream AK-9
**Imeong**—pop pl PW-9
Imeong, Taoch Ra—gut PW-9
Imeri Lake—lake AK-9
Imerman Memorial Park—park MI-6
Imes—locale KS-7
Imes Bridge—bridge IA-7
Imes Covered Bridge—hist pl IA-7
Imes Lake Dam—dam MS-4
Imeson Airp—airport FL-3
Imes Sch—school AZ-5
Imes Trail—trail PA-2
Imetang—cape PW-9
Imgram Branch IA-7
Imhoff Archeol Site—hist pl MO-7
Imhoff Cem—cemetery (2) IL-6
Imhoff Cem—cemetery OH-6
Imhoff Creek—stream OK-5
Imhoff House—hist pl TX-5
Imhoff Tank—reservoir ME-1
Imiaknikpak Lake—lake AK-9
Imieji Anchorage—harbor MP-9
Imieji-to MP-9
Imiet MP-9
Imik Lagoon—lake AK-9
Imikneyak Creek—stream AK-9
Imikneyak Mountains—other AK-9
Imikpuk Lake—lake AK-9
Imikrak Creek—stream AK-9
Imikruk Creek—stream AK-9
Imikruk Lagoon—lake AK-9
Imiola Church—hist pl HI-9
Imlac—locale GA-3
Imlay—locale SD-7
**Imlay**—pop pl NV-8
Imlay and Laurel Streets District—hist pl CT-1
Imlay Canyon—valley NV-8
Imlay Canyon—valley UT-8
Imlay Canyon Mine—mine NV-8
**Imlay City**—pop pl MI-6
Imlay Mine—mine NV-8
Imlay No. 24 Township—civ div SD-7
Imlay Resort Tank—reservoir AZ-5
**Imlaystown**—pop pl NJ-2
Imlaystown Hist Dist—hist pl NJ-2
Imlaystown Lake—reservoir NJ-2
Imlaystown Lake Dam—dam NJ-2
**Imlaystown (sta.) (Nelsonville)**—pop pl NJ-2
Imlay Summit—gap NV-8
Imlay Temple—summit UT-8
Imlay Township—civil SD-7
**Imlay (Township of)**—pop pl MI-6
**Imler**—pop pl PA-2
Imler Cem—cemetery OH-6
**Imlertown**—pop pl PA-2
Imlertown Run—stream PA-2
Imlos Pond—lake ME-1
**Immaculata**—pop pl PA-2
Immaculata Acad—school NY-2
Immaculata Catholic Sch—school NC-3
Immaculata Cem—cemetery PA-2
Immaculata Coll—school PA-2
Immaculata HS—hist pl IL-6
Immaculata HS—school KS-7
Immaculata HS—school MI-6
Immaculata HS—school NH-1
Immaculata Seminary—school DC-2
Immaculate Ch—church IL-6
Immaculate Conception Acad—school IA-7
Immaculate Conception Catholic Ch—church FL-3
Immaculate Conception Catholic Ch—church (4) MS-4
Immaculate Conception Catholic Ch—church (2) TN-4
Immaculate Conception Catholic Ch—church UT-8
Immaculate Conception Catholic Church and Cemetery—hist pl KY-4
Immaculate Conception Catholic Church Complex—hist pl OH-6
Immaculate Conception Catholic Sch—school AZ-5
Immaculate Conception Cem—cemetery (4) IL-6
Immaculate Conception Cem—cemetery (2) IA-7
Immaculate Conception Cem—cemetery (2) KS-7
Immaculate Conception Cem—cemetery (2) MA-1
Immaculate Conception Cem—cemetery MI-6
Immaculate Conception Cem—cemetery (3) MN-6
Immaculate Conception Cem—cemetery (3) MO-7
Immaculate Conception Cem—cemetery (4) NJ-2
Immaculate Conception Cem—cemetery (3) NY-2
Immaculate Conception Cem—cemetery ND-7
Immaculate Conception Cem—cemetery OK-5
Immaculate Conception Cem—cemetery (4) PA-2
Immaculate Conception Cem—cemetery SD-7
Immaculate Conception Cem—cemetery TX-5
Immaculate Conception Cem—cemetery WI-6
Immaculate Conception Ch—church FL-3
Immaculate Conception Ch—church (4) IA-7
Immaculate Conception Ch—church KY-4
Immaculate Conception Ch—church LA-4
Immaculate Conception Ch—church (2) MN-6
Immaculate Conception Ch—church (2) MS-4
Immaculate Conception Ch—church MO-7
Immaculate Conception Ch—church MT-8
Immaculate Conception Ch—church NE-7
Immaculate Conception Ch—church NJ-2
Immaculate Conception Ch—church NM-5
Immaculate Conception Ch—church ND-7
Immaculate Conception Ch—church (2) OH-6
Immaculate Conception Ch—church OK-5
Immaculate Conception Ch—church (2) PA-2
Immaculate Conception Ch—church SD-7
Immaculate Conception Church—hist pl AK-9
Immaculate Conception Church—hist pl KY-4
Immaculate Conception Church—hist pl OH-6
Immaculate Conception Church—hist pl OK-5
Immaculate Conception Church—hist pl TX-5
Immaculate Conception Church, School, and Rectory—hist pl OH-6
Immaculate Conception Day Care/ Kindergarten—school FL-3
Immaculate Conception Monastery—school NY-2
Immaculate Conception Novitiate—church NJ-2
Immaculate Conception Rectory at Botkins—hist pl OH-6
Immaculate Conception Sch—hist pl MO-7
Immaculate Conception Sch—school AK-9
Immaculate Conception Sch—school (2) AR-4
Immaculate Conception Sch—school (4) CA-9
Immaculate Conception Sch—school FL-3
Immaculate Conception Sch—school GA-3
Immaculate Conception Sch—school HI-9
Immaculate Conception Sch—school (5) IL-6
Immaculate Conception Sch—school IN-6
Immaculate Conception Sch—school LA-4
Immaculate Conception Sch—school (3) MA-1
Immaculate Conception Sch—school MI-6
Immaculate Conception Sch—school (2) MS-4
Immaculate Conception Sch—school (3) MO-7
Immaculate Conception Sch—school (2) NJ-2
Immaculate Conception Sch—school (9) NY-2
Immaculate Conception Sch—school (4) OH-6
Immaculate Conception Sch—school (2) OK-5
Immaculate Conception Sch—school (3) PA-2
Immaculate Conception Sch—school SD-7
Immaculate Conception Sch—school TN-4
Immaculate Conception Sch—school (3) TX-5
Immaculate Conception Sch—school (2) WI-6
Immaculate Conception Schools—school MA-1
Immaculate Conception Seminary—school NJ-2
Immaculate Conception Seminary—school NY-2
Immaculate Heart Acad—school AZ-5
Immaculate Heart Acad—school PA-2
Immaculate Heart Camp—locale MA-1
Immaculate Heart Cem—cemetery PA-2
Immaculate Heart Coll—school CA-9
Immaculate Heart Novitiate—church AZ-5
Immaculate Heart of Mary Catholic Ch—church MS-4
Immaculate Heart of Mary Cem—cemetery NM-5
Immaculate Heart of Mary Ch—church AR-4
Immaculate Heart of Mary Ch—church DE-2
Immaculate Heart of Mary Ch—church FL-3
Immaculate Heart of Mary Ch—church LA-4
Immaculate Heart of Mary Church—hist pl AR-4
Immaculate Heart of Mary Roman Catholic Ch—church IN-6
Immaculate Heart of Mary Sch—school (2) CA-9
Immaculate Heart of Mary Sch—school DE-2
Immaculate Heart of Mary Sch—school IL-6
Immaculate Heart Of Mary Sch—school KY-4
Immaculate Heart of Mary Sch—school LA-4
Immaculate Heart Of Mary Sch—school MD-2
Immaculate Heart of Mary Sch—school MI-6
Immaculate Heart of Mary Sch—school NJ-2
Immaculate Heart of Mary Sch—school NY-2
Immaculate Heart of Mary Sch—school PA-2
Immaculate Heart of Mary Sch—school WI-6
Immaculate Heart of Mary School IN-6
Immaculate Heart Of Mary Seminary—church PA-2
Immaculate Heart Retreat—locale WA-9
Immaculate Heart Sch—school IN-6
Immaculate Heart Sch—school MI-6
Immaculate Heart Seminary—school MA-1
Immaculate HS—school CT-1
Immaculate Sch—school LA-4
Immaculate School, The—school KY-4
Immanual Baptist Ch—church NC-3
Immanual Baptist Ch—church PA-2
Immanualsville PA-2
Immanualville PA-2
**Immanuel**—pop pl AR-4
Immanuel Acad—school CA-9
Immanuel Baptist Ch MS-4
Immanuel Baptist Ch TN-4
Immanuel Baptist Ch—church AL-4
Immanuel Baptist Ch—church (3) FL-3
Immanuel Baptist Ch—church KS-7
Immanuel Baptist Ch—church (4) MS-4
Immanuel Baptist Ch—church (3) TN-4
Immanuel Baptist Church—hist pl UT-8
Immanuel Camp—locale NE-7
Immanuel Cem—cemetery (3) IL-6
Immanuel Cem—cemetery (7) IA-7
Immanuel Cem—cemetery (6) KS-7
Immanuel Cem—cemetery (2) MI-6
Immanuel Cem—cemetery (18) MN-6
Immanuel Cem—cemetery MS-4
Immanuel Cem—cemetery (4) MO-7
Immanuel Cem—cemetery (14) NE-7
Immanuel Cem—cemetery (6) ND-7
Immanuel Cem—cemetery OH-6
Immanuel Cem—cemetery (2) OK-5
Immanuel Cem—cemetery PA-2
Immanuel Cem—cemetery (3) SD-7
Immanuel Cem—cemetery TX-5
Immanuel Cem—cemetery WI-6
Immanuel Ch IN-6
Immanuel Ch—church (2) AL-4
Immanuel Ch—church CO-8
Immanuel Ch—church (3) FL-3
Immanuel Ch—church (3) GA-3
Immanuel Ch—church (9) IL-6
Immanuel Ch—church (4) IN-6
Immanuel Ch—church (9) IA-7
Immanuel Ch—church (6) KS-7
Immanuel Ch—church (5) KY-4
Immanuel Ch—church LA-4
Immanuel Ch—church (2) MD-2
Immanuel Ch—church (6) MI-6
Immanuel Ch—church (25) MN-6
Immanuel Ch—church (4) MS-4
Immanuel Ch—church (5) MO-7
Immanuel Ch—church MT-8
Immanuel Ch—church (16) NE-7
Immanuel Ch—church (2) NM-5
Immanuel Ch—church (4) NY-2
Immanuel Ch—church (5) NC-3
Immanuel Ch—church (8) ND-7
Immanuel Ch—church (3) OH-6
Immanuel Ch—church (3) OK-5
Immanuel Ch—church (4) PA-2
Immanuel Ch—church (3) SC-3
Immanuel Ch—church (9) SD-7
Immanuel Ch—church (5) TN-4
Immanuel Ch—church (7) TX-5
Immanuel Ch—church (3) VA-3
Immanuel Ch—church WV-2
Immanuel Ch—church (21) WI-6
Immanuel Chapel—church TX-5
Immanuel Chapel Protestant Episcopal Church—hist pl KY-4
Immanuel Ch on the Green—church DE-2
Immanuel Christian Reformed Ch—church UT-8
Immanuel Church—hist pl TN-4
Immanuel Episcopal Ch—church TN-4
Immanuel Evangelical Lutheran Church—hist pl ID-8
Immanuel Evangelical Lutheran Church—hist pl MO-7
Immanuel Free Will Baptist Ch—church FL-3
Immanuel Hosp—hospital MN-6
Immanuel Lutheran Cem—cemetery IA-7
Immanuel Lutheran Ch—church (3) FL-3
Immanuel Lutheran Ch—church (2) IA-7
Immanuel Lutheran Ch—church KS-7
Immanuel Lutheran Ch—church NE-7
Immanuel Lutheran Church—hist pl IN-6
Immanuel Lutheran Church—hist pl MN-6
Immanuel Lutheran Church—hist pl (2) SD-7
Immanuel Lutheran Church—hist pl TX-5
Immanuel Lutheran Church—hist pl WA-9
Immanuel Lutheran Sch—school FL-3
Immanuel-Lutheran Sch—school IN-6
Immanuel Lutheran Sch—school NE-7
Immanuel Methodist Episcopal Church—hist pl ID-8
Immanuel Mission AZ-5
**Immanuel Mission**—pop pl AZ-5
Immanuel Outreach Centre—church KS-7
Immanuel Presbyterian Ch—church FL-3
Immanuel Presbyterian Church—hist pl WI-6
Immanuel Reformed Cem—cemetery IA-7
Immanuel Reformed Ch—church (2) IA-7
Immanuel Sch IN-6
Immanuels Ch—church MI-6
Immanuel Sch—school (2) CA-9
Immanuel Sch—school CT-1
Immanuel Sch—school (10) IL-6
Immanuel Sch—school IN-6
Immanuel Sch—school (4) IA-7
Immanuel Sch—school KS-7
Immanuel Sch—school (3) MI-6
Immanuel Sch—school (2) MN-6
Immanuel Sch—school (3) MO-7
Immanuel Sch—school (4) NE-7
Immanuel Sch—school ND-7
Immanuel Sch—school OK-5
Immanuel Sch—school TN-4
Immanuel Sch—school TX-5
Immanuel Sch—school VA-3
Immanuel Sch—school (6) WI-6
Immanuelsville PA-2
Immanuel Union United Methodist Ch—church DE-2
Immanuel United Methodist Ch—church DE-2
Immanuel United Methodist Ch—church IN-6
Immanue Sch—school WI-6
Immel, John, House—hist pl PA-2
Immel Dam—dam PA-2
Immells Creek MT-8
Immergrun OH-6
**Immergrun**—pop pl OH-6
**Immermere**—pop pl TX-5
Immigrant Canyon—valley (2) NV-8
Immigrant Creek—stream NV-8
Immigrant Gulch—valley OR-9
Immigrant Pass UT-8
Immigrant Spring—spring AZ-5
Immigrant Spring—spring OR-9
Immigrant Springs—spring WY-8
Immigration Wash—stream NV-8
Imm Lake—lake WI-6
**Immokalee**—pop pl FL-3
Immokalee (CCD)—cens area FL-3
Immokalee HS—school FL-3
Immokalee MS—school FL-3
Immokalee Tower—tower FL-3
Immortelle, Mount—summit NV-8
**Imnaha**—pop pl OR-9
Imnaha (CCD)—cens area OR-9
Imnaha Cem—cemetery OR-9
Imnaha Creek OR-9
Imnaha Creek—stream OR-9
Imnaha Divide—ridge OR-9
Imnaha Falls—falls OR-9
Imnaha Forest Camp—locale OR-9
Imnaha Grange—locale OR-9
Imnaha Guard Station—hist pl OR-9
Imnaha Guard Station—locale OR-9
Imnaha Rapids—rapids ID-8
Imnaha Rapids—rapids OR-9
Imnaha River—stream OR-9
Imnaitchiak Creek—stream AK-9
Imnak Bluff—cliff AK-9
Imnakpak Cliff—cliff AK-9
Imnakuk Bluff—cliff AK-9
Imnakuk Creek—stream AK-9
Imnatchiak Bluff—cliff AK-9
Imnavait Mtn—summit AK-9
Imo—locale AR-4
**Imo**—pop pl OK-5
Imoa Point—cape AS-9
Imobersteg Ditch—canal CO-8
Imo Cem—cemetery OK-5
Imocklasha MS-4
Imogene—locale SD-7
**Imogene**—pop pl IA-7
**Imogene**—pop pl MN-6
Imogene, Lake—lake MN-6
Imogene Basin—basin CO-8
Imogene Ch—church NC-3
Imogene Creek—stream CO-8
Imogene Lake—lake ID-8
Imogene Lake—lake WI-6
Imogene Mine—mine CO-8
Imogene Mine (underground)—mine AL-4
Imogene Oil Field—oilfield TX-5
Imogene Pass—gap CO-8
Imola—locale CA-9
**Imola (Napa State Hospital)**—pop pl CA-9
Imolch—other PW-9
Imolobang—building PW-9
I Molstad Dam—dam SD-7
Imong—area GU-9
Imong River—stream GU-9
Imookfau Creek AL-4
Imore—spring FM-9
Imoto Shima FM-9
Impach—locale WA-9
**Impact**—pop pl TX-5
Impaghuk Point—cape AK-9
Impaken FM-9
**Impark Township**—pop pl ND-7
Impassable Bay—swamp FL-3
Impassable Canyon—valley CO-8
Impassable Lake—lake WI-6
Impassable Marsh SD-7
Impassable Marsh (historical)—swamp IA-7
Impassable Rock—summit CA-9
Impassable Rocks—summit CA-9
Impassible Island—island AK-9
Imp Brook—stream NH-1
Imp Creek—stream ID-8
Imp Creek—stream MI-6
IM Peak—summit AZ-5
Imperial—locale WV-2
**Imperial**—pop pl CA-9
**Imperial**—pop pl GA-3
**Imperial**—pop pl IL-6
**Imperial**—pop pl MO-7
**Imperial**—pop pl NE-7
**Imperial**—pop pl PA-2
**Imperial**—pop pl TX-5
**Imperial**—pop pl VA-3
Imperial, Point—cliff AZ-5
Imperial Ave Canal—canal UT-8
**Imperial Beach**—pop pl CA-9
Imperial Beach Naval Air Station—military CA-9
Imperial Buttes Mine—mine CA-9
Imperial Canal—canal TX-5
Imperial Canal Number Five—canal TX-5
Imperial Canal Number Three—canal TX-5
Imperial Canyon UT-8
Imperial (CCD)—cens area CA-9
Imperial (CCD)—cens area TX-5
Imperial Cem—cemetery CA-9
Imperial Christina Plaza (Shop Ctr)—locale FL-3
Imperial Copper Mine—mine WA-9
**Imperial (County)**—pop pl CA-9
Imperial County Airp—airport CA-9
Imperial County Hosp—hospital CA-9
Imperial Crest—uninc pl CA-9
Imperial Dam—dam AZ-5
Imperial Dam—dam CA-9
Imperial Ditch—canal TX-5
Imperial Dunes CA-9
Imperial East—fmr MCD NE-7
Imperial-Enlow—CDP PA-2
**Imperial Estates**—pop pl FL-3
**Imperial Estates**—pop pl TN-4
Imperial Estates Elem Sch—school FL-3
Imperial Estates Park—park MN-6
**Imperial Estates (subdivision)**—pop pl NC-3
**Imperial Gardens**—pop pl IN-6
Imperial Geyser—geyser WY-8
Imperial Glass Company—hist pl OH-6
Imperial Granum-Joseph Parker Buildings—hist pl CT-1
**Imperial Group Subdivision**—pop pl TN-4
Imperial Gulch—valley ID-8
**Imperial Heights**—pop pl MI-6
Imperial Highway Monument—other CA-9
Imperial Hills IN-6
**Imperial Hills**—pop pl IN-6
Imperial Hollow—valley KY-4
Imperial Hosp—hospital CA-9
Imperial Hotel—hist pl GA-3
Imperial Hotel—hist pl OR-9
Imperial Hotel—hist pl SC-3
**Imperial (Imperial Mills)**—pop pl GA-3
Imperial Island NY-2
Imperial Isle—island NY-2
Imperialist Creek—stream TX-5
Imperialist Tank—reservoir TX-5
Imperial JHS—school CA-9
**Imperial Junction**—pop pl WV-2
Imperial Lode Mine—mine CA-9
Imperial Mall—locale FL-3
**Imperial Manor**—pop pl NJ-2
Imperial Mine—mine (3) CA-9
Imperial Mine—mine CO-8
Imperial Mine—mine NV-8
Imperial Mine—mine UT-8
Imperial Mine (historical)—mine SD-7
**Imperial Mine Junction**—pop pl MI-6
Imperial Mobile Home Park—locale AZ-5
Imperial Mtn—summit AZ-5
Imperial Natl Wildlife Ref—park AZ-5
Imperial Natl Wildlife Ref—park CA-9
Imperial Passage—channel AK-9
Imperial Pit—mine NV-8
Imperial Plaza—post sta NY-2
Imperial Plaza—post sta VA-3
**Imperial Point**—pop pl FL-3
Imperial Point Med Ctr—hospital FL-3
Imperial Point Preparatory Sch—school FL-3
Imperial PowerPlant—other NE-7
Imperial River—stream FL-3
Imperial Rsvr—reservoir AZ-5
Imperial Rsvr—reservoir CA-9
Imperial Rsvr—reservoir TX-5
Imperial Rural—fmr MCD NE-7
Imperial Sand Dunes CA-9
Imperial Sch—school (3) CA-9
Imperial School (Abandoned)—locale IL-6
Imperial Shopping Plaza—locale FL-3
Imperial Square (Shop Ctr)—locale FL-3
Imperial Square Shop Ctr—locale TN-4

Imperial Theatre—*hist pl* CA-9
Imperial Tobacco Company Bldg—*hist pl* SC-3
Imperial Valley—*valley* CA-9
Imperial Valley—*valley* UT-8
Imperial Valley Cattle Company Number One Airstrip—*airport* AZ-5
Imperial Valley Coll—*school* CA-9
Imperial Valley Sanitarium—*hospital* CA-9
Imperial Waterfowl Mngmt Area—*area* (2) CA-9
Imperial Well—*well* AZ-5
Imperial West—*fmr MCD* NE-7
Imperial Wildfowl Mngmt Area—*area* CA-9
Impet Park—*park* OH-6
Imp Face—*summit* NH-1
*Impie Creek* WA-9
Imp Lake—*lake* MI-6
Imp Lake Lookout Tower—*locale* MI-6
Imp Mtn—*summit* NH-1
Impossible Canyon—*valley* CA-9
Impossible Canyon—*valley* TX-5
Impossible Peak—*summit* UT-8
Impossible Ridge—*ridge* CA-9
Impounding Basin Number Twenty-Five—*basin* PA-2
Impounding Basin Number Twenty-Four—*basin* PA-2
Impounding Basin Number Twenty-One—*basin* PA-2
Impounding Basin Number Twenty-Two—*basin* PA-2
*Impounding Dam* PA-2
Imp Peak—*summit* MT-8
**Improve**—*pop pl* MS-4
*Improve Baptist Church* MS-4
Improve Cem—*cemetery* MS-4
Improve Ch—*church* MS-4
Improved Order of Redmen Cem—*cemetery* OR-9
Improve Lookout Tower—*locale* MS-4
Improvement Branch—*stream* DE-2
Improvement Branch—*stream* (2) KY-4
Improvement Branch—*stream* WV-2
Improvement Cove—*valley* NC-3
Improvement Creek—*stream* AR-4
Improvement Fork—*stream* KY-4
Improvement Hollow—*valley* MO-7
Improvement Lick Run—*stream* WV-2
Improve Oil Field—*oilfield* MS-4
Improve Post Office (historical)—*building* MS-4
Improve Sch—*school* MS-4
Imp Shelter—*locale* NH-1
Imp Shelter Cut Off—*trail* NH-1
Impson Church (Abandoned)—*locale* OK-5
Impson Hollow—*valley* PA-2
Impson Spring—*spring* CO-8
Impson Valley—*valley* OK-5
Imp Trail—*trail* NH-1
I M Ranch—*locale* CO-8
**Imroc**—*pop pl* FL-3
Imrodj Island—*island* MP-9
*Imruedj* MP-9
I M T Learning Center—*school* FL-3
*Imu Kalua Ua* HI-9
Imu Kalua Ua Heiau—*locale* HI-9
**Imul**—*pop pl* PW-9
*Imunooru* FM-9
*Imuroji-To* MP-9
Imuroru—*island* MP-9
*Imuroru-to* MP-9
Imuruk Basin—*lake* AK-9
Imuruk Lake—*lake* AK-9
Imusdale Cem—*cemetery* CA-9
*Imutang Point* PW-9
Imuya Bay—*bay* AK-9
Imvite Airp—*airport* NV-8
Imwen—*locale* FM-9
Imwensapw—*cape* FM-9
Imwe Takai—*unknown* FM-9
Imwin Dekehlap—*bar* FM-9
Imwindekeh Mwahu—*island* FM-9
Imwin Diadi—*locale* FM-9
Imwin Diehsou—*cape* FM-9
Imwiniak—*swamp* FM-9
Imwiniak En Dieniepw—*swamp* FM-9
Imwin Iaken Pwetik—*swamp* FM-9
Imwin Pahn Titing—*bar* FM-9
Imwin Pwet—*unknown* FM-9
Imwin Pwiki En Nahpali—*bar* FM-9
Imwin Pwokolos—*swamp* FM-9
*Imwinsapw* FM-9
Imwinsapw—*cape* FM-9
*Imwinseinpwel* FM-9
Imwinyap—*island* FM-9
*Ina* MS-4
Ina—*locale* MI-6
Ina—*other* MS-4
**Ina**—*pop pl* IL-6
Ina, Lake—*lake* FL-3
Ina, Lake—*lake* MN-6
Inabnit, Mount—*summit* MT-8
Inabnit Butte—*summit* MT-8
Inabnit Peterson Ditch—*canal* MT-8
Inaccessible House—*locale* CO-8
Inaccessible Ridge—*ridge* AK-9
Ina Coolbrith, Mount—*summit* CA-9
Inactive Cave—*cave* AL-4
**Inadale**—*pop pl* TX-5
Inadu Creek—*stream* TN-4
Inadu Knob—*summit* NC-3
Inadu Knob—*summit* TN-4
Inadu Mtn—*summit* TN-4
*Inagasa Point* MH-9
*Inagsa Point* MH-9
Ina Gulch—*valley* AK-9
Inaha—*locale* GA-3
**Ina (historical)**—*pop pl* TN-4
*Inai Fahan* MH-9
*Inai Obiam* MH-9
Ina Island—*island* AK-9
Ina Island—*island* NY-2
Inaja-Cosmit Ind Res—*17 (1980)* CA-9
Inaja Memorial Park—*park* CA-9
*Inajan* MH-9
*Ina Jima* FM-9
Inakpuk (Site)—*locale* AK-9
Inalik—*locale* AK-9
Inalik(native name for Diomede) ANV809—*reserve* AK-9
*Inama Creek* WY-8
*Inanasu* MH-9
Inanda Ch—*church* NC-3
In and Out Social Club—*hist pl* NJ-2
In And Out Tank—*reservoir* (2) TX-5
Inanudak Bay—*bay* AK-9
Ina Post Office (historical)—*building* MS-4
Ina Post Office (historical)—*building* TN-4
**Inarajan**—*pop pl* GU-9
Inarajan Bay—*bay* GU-9
Inarajan (Election District)—*fmr MCD* GU-9
Inarajan Falls—*falls* GU-9
Inarajan Ridge—*hist pl* GU-9
Inarajan River—*stream* GU-9
Inarajan Village—*hist pl* GU-9
Inari—*locale* TX-5
Ina Road Interchange—*crossing* AZ-5
Inaru River—*stream* AK-9
Ina Sch (historical)—*school* MS-4
Ina Sch (historical)—*school* TN-4
Inaso Hill—*summit* GU-9
Inaso Maso—*area* GU-9
Inati Bay—*bay* WA-9
*Inaught Slough, The* IL-6
Inavale—*locale* NY-2
**Inavale**—*pop pl* NE-7
**In-A-Vale-Estates**—*pop pl* TN-4
**Inavale (historical)**—*pop pl* OR-9
Inavale Sch—*school* NE-7
Inavale Sch—*school* OR-9
*Inawa* MP-9
Inayan—*slope* MH-9
I N Baker Ditch—*canal* KY-4
Inbe Oil Field—*other* NM-5
Inbetween Gulch—*valley* CO-8
Inbetween Spring—*spring* CO-8
Inbocht Bay—*bay* NY-2
Inbody Ch—*church* IN-6
Inborden Sch—*school* NC-3
Inca—*locale* NM-5
**Inca**—*pop pl* CA-9
Inca Cave—*cave* MO-7
Inca Draw—*valley* TX-5
Incarnate Word Acad—*school* OH-6
Incarnate Word Acad—*school* TX-5
Incarnate Word Ch—*church* MI-6
Incarnate Word Coll—*school* TX-5
Incarnate Word Convent—*church* TX-5
Incarnate Word Sch—*school* LA-4
Incarnation Camp—*locale* CT-1
Incarnation Catholic Sch—*school* FL-3
Incarnation Ch—*church* MN-6
Incarnation Sch—*school* CA-9
Incarnation Sch—*school* FL-3
Incarnation Sch—*school* OH-6
Incarnation Sch—*school* PA-2
Incendiary Creek—*stream* ID-8
Inch Branch—*stream* VA-3
Inch Brook—*stream* MA-1
Inch Ch—*church* WI-6
Inch Creek—*stream* (2) OR-9
**Inchelium**—*pop pl* WA-9
*Inch Lake* WI-6
Inch Lake—*lake* WI-6
Inch Mtn—*summit* MT-8
Inch Sch—*school* SD-7
Inchucka Landing—*locale* MS-4
Inchwagh Lake—*lake* MI-6
Incinerator Lake—*reservoir* CO-8
Incinerator Site—*hist pl* OH-6
Incision Cave—*cave* AL-4
*Incline* NV-8
**Incline**—*pop pl* AL-4
**Incline**—*pop pl* CA-9
Incline, The—*slope* CA-9
Incline Beach—*beach* NV-8
Incline Creek—*stream* NV-8
Inclined Mtn—*summit* AK-9
Incline Draw—*valley* TX-5
Inclined Temple—*summit* UT-8
Incline Gap—*gap* TN-4
Incline Golf Course—*locale* NV-8
Incline Guard Station—*locale* NV-8
Incline Hollow—*valley* (2) TN-4
Incline Hollow—*valley* (2) VA-3
Incline HS—*school* NV-8
Incline Lake—*reservoir* NV-8
Incline Landing (historical)—*locale* AL-4
Incline Lookout—*locale* WA-9
Incline Ridge—*ridge* CA-9
Incline Sch—*school* KY-4
Incline Truck Trail—*trail* WA-9
**Incline Village**—*pop pl* NV-8
Incline Village-Crystal Bay—*CDP* NV-8
Incline Village-Crystal Bay Township—*inact MCD* NV-8
Incline Windmill—*locale* TX-5
Inclose Sch—*school* IL-6
Inconsolable Range—*ridge* CA-9
*Inconstance Creek* CA-9
Inconstance Creek—*stream* CA-9
Inconstantion Creek—*stream* FL-3
**Increase**—*pop pl* MS-4
Increase Post Office (historical)—*building* MS-4
Incus Lake—*lake* MN-6
*Inda* MS-4
**Inda**—*pop pl* MS-4
Indainapolis Raceway Park—*other* IN-6
*Indain Tanks Hill* AZ-5
In-Dan-Wayne Lake—*reservoir* IL-6
Indart Ranch—*locale* CA-9
Indart Ranch—*locale* WY-8
Indecision Creek—*stream* AK-9
Indel Airpark—*airport* NJ-2
*Independence* PA-2
*Independence* SC-3
Independence—*locale* (2) CO-8
Independence—*locale* IL-6
Independence—*locale* MT-8
Independence—*locale* NY-2
Independence—*locale* (2) OK-5
Independence—*locale* PA-2
Independence—*locale* UT-8
Independence—*locale* WA-9
Independence—*locale* WV-2
**Independence**—*pop pl* AL-4
**Independence**—*pop pl* (2) CA-9
**Independence**—*pop pl* IN-6
**Independence**—*pop pl* IA-7
**Independence**—*pop pl* KS-7
**Independence**—*pop pl* KY-4
**Independence**—*pop pl* LA-4
**Independence**—*pop pl* (2) MN-6
**Independence**—*pop pl* (2) MS-4
**Independence**—*pop pl* MO-7
**Independence**—*pop pl* ND-7
**Independence**—*pop pl* (3) OH-6
**Independence**—*pop pl* OR-9
**Independence**—*pop pl* (2) PA-2
**Independence**—*pop pl* (3) TN-4
**Independence**—*pop pl* TX-5
**Independence**—*pop pl* VA-3
**Independence**—*pop pl* (2) WV-2
**Independence**—*pop pl* WI-6
Independence, Lake—*lake* (2) MN-6
Independence, Lake—*reservoir* MI-6
**Independence, Mount**—*pop pl* PA-2
Independence, Mount—*summit* ID-8
Independence, Mount—*summit* MA-1
Independence, Mount—*summit* VT-1
Independence and Independence Mill Site—*hist pl* CO-8
Independence Ave and Topping Shop Ctr—*locale* MO-7
Independence Basin—*basin* CO-8
Independence Bend—*bend* OR-9
Independence Bldg—*hist pl* NC-3
Independence Bridge—*bridge* AL-4
Independence Campground—*locale* ID-8
Independence Canyon—*valley* UT-8
Independence (CCD)—*cens area* CA-9
Independence (CCD)—*cens area* KY-4
Independence Cem—*cemetery* AL-4
Independence Cem—*cemetery* IN-6
Independence Cem—*cemetery* IA-7
Independence Cem—*cemetery* (2) KY-4
Independence Cem—*cemetery* MN-6
Independence Cem—*cemetery* MS-4
Independence Cem—*cemetery* NE-7
Independence Cem—*cemetery* OH-6
Independence Cem—*cemetery* (4) OK-5
Independence Cem—*cemetery* PA-2
Independence Cem—*cemetery* TN-4
Independence Cem—*cemetery* TX-5
Independence Cem—*cemetery* VA-3
Independence Center—*locale* MO-7
*Independence Ch* MS-4
Independence Ch—*church* AL-4
Independence Ch—*church* (2) AR-4
Independence Ch—*church* IL-6
Independence Ch—*church* (2) IN-6
Independence Ch—*church* KY-4
Independence Ch—*church* (3) MS-4
Independence Ch—*church* (6) MO-7
Independence Ch—*church* ND-7
Independence Ch—*church* (2) OK-5
Independence Ch—*church* (2) TN-4
Independence Ch—*church* (3) TX-5
Independence Ch—*church* (4) VA-3
Independence Chapel—*church* OH-6
Independence Ch (historical)—*church* AL-4
Independence Ch of Christ—*church* MS-4
Independence Church Camp—*locale* AR-4
Independence City Hall—*building* IA-7
Independence Community Coll—*school* KS-7
Independence Community Hall—*locale* MO-7
Independence Corner—*locale* NJ-2
Independence Corners Shop Ctr—*locale* MO-7
Independence Country Club—*other* KS-7
**Independence (County)**—*pop pl* AR-4
Independence County Fairgrounds—*park* AR-4
*Independence Creek* AK-9
*Independence Creek* TX-5
Independence Creek—*stream* (6) AK-9
Independence Creek—*stream* (3) CA-9
Independence Creek—*stream* (2) CO-8
Independence Creek—*stream* (2) ID-8
Independence Creek—*stream* KS-7
Independence Creek—*stream* (2) MT-8
Independence Creek—*stream* NV-8
Independence Creek—*stream* OR-9
Independence Creek—*stream* (2) TX-5
Independence Creek—*stream* WA-9
Independence Creek Ditch—*canal* OR-9
Independence Creek Natl Recreation Trail—*trail* ID-8
Independence Crossing—*locale* KS-7
Independence Ditch—*canal* CO-8
Independence Elem Sch—*school* PA-2
Independence Green Golf Course—*other* MI-6
*Independence Gulch* MT-8
Independence Gulch—*valley* AK-9
Independence Gulch—*valley* CA-9
Independence Gulch—*valley* (2) CO-8
Independence Gulch—*valley* ID-8
Independence Gulch—*valley* MT-8
Independence Hall—*building* PA-2
Independence Hall—*hist pl* CA-9
Independence Hall—*hist pl* WV-2
Independence Hall—*locale* IL-6
Independence Heights—*uninc pl* TX-5
*Independence Hill* IN-6
*Independence Hill* MA-1
**Independence Hill**—*pop pl* IN-6
Independence Hill—*summit* NV-8
Independence Hill Ch—*church* NC-3
Independence Hist Dist—*hist pl* IN-6
Independence Hist Dist—*hist pl* LA-4
Independence (historical)—*locale* NV-8
Independence (historical)—*locale* PA-2
Independence HS—*school* KS-7
Independence HS—*school* MS-4
Independence HS—*school* NC-3
Independence Interchange—*locale* NV-8
*Independence Island* ME-1
Independence Island—*island* AK-9
Independence Island—*island* PA-2
Independence JHS—*school* KS-7
Independence JHS—*school* TN-4
*Independence Lake* ID-8
Independence Lake—*lake* AK-9
Independence Lake—*lake* CA-9
Independence Lake—*lake* CO-8
Independence Lake—*lake* MI-6
Independence Lake—*lake* NY-2
Independence Lake—*lake* WA-9
Independence Lake—*reservoir* CA-9
Independence Lakes—*lake* ID-8
Independence-Liberty Bridge—*other* MO-7
Independence Lode Mine—*mine* SD-7
Independence Mall—*locale* DE-2
Independence Mall—*locale* NC-3
Independence Mall State Park—*park* PA-2
Independence Memorial Airp—*airport* MO-7
Independence Methodist Ch—*church* MS-4
Independence Methodist Church—*hist pl* IN-6
*Independence Mine* CA-9
Independence Mine—*mine* (2) AK-9
Independence Mine—*mine* AZ-5
Independence Mine—*mine* (4) CA-9
Independence Mine—*mine* CO-8
Independence Mine—*mine* (2) ID-8
Independence Mine—*mine* (2) MT-8
Independence Mine—*mine* NV-8
Independence Mine—*mine* NM-5
Independence Mine—*mine* (2) OR-9
Independence Mine—*mine* (2) UT-8
Independence Mine—*mine* (2) WA-9
Independence Mine—*mine* WY-8
Independence Mines—*hist pl* AK-9
Independence Monmt—*pillar* CO-8
*Independence Mountains* NV-8
Independence Mtn—*summit* (5) CO-8
Independence Mtn—*summit* ID-8
Independence Mtn—*summit* MT-8
Independence Mtn—*summit* NV-8
Independence Mtn—*summit* WV-2
Independence Mtns—*range* NV-8
Independence Municipal Airp—*airport* KS-7
Independence Natl Bank—*hist pl* OR-9
Independence Natl Historical Park—*park* PA-2
Independence North Shop Ctr—*locale* MO-7
Independence Number 1 Lode Mine—*mine* SD-7
Independence Park—*flat* MT-8
Independence Park—*park* IL-6
Independence Park—*park* NJ-2
Independence Park—*park* NC-3
Independence Park—*park* TX-5
Independence Pass—*gap* CO-8
Independence Pass—*gap* WA-9
Independence Peak—*summit* CA-9
Independence Peak—*summit* (2) MT-8
Independence Point—*cape* NY-2
Independence Point—*cape* ND-7
Independence Point—*cliff* CA-9
Independence Point—*ridge* CA-9
Independence Post Office (historical)—*building* TN-4
Independence Prairie—*flat* OR-9
Independence Prairie Ranger Station—*hist pl* OR-9
*Independence Presbyterian Ch* MS-4
Independence Presbyterian Church—*hist pl* OH-6
Independence Promenade—*locale* NC-3
Independence Public Carnegie Library—*hist pl* KS-7
Independence Ridge—*ridge* ID-8
Independence Ridge—*ridge* KY-4
Independence Ridge—*ridge* WA-9
*Independence River* KS-7
Independence River—*stream* NY-2
*Independence Rock* CO-8
Independence Rock—*hist pl* WY-8
Independence Rock—*pillar* OR-9
Independence Rock—*summit* WY-8
Independence Run—*stream* PA-2
*Independence Sch* PA-2
Independence Sch—*school* AR-4
Independence Sch—*school* CA-9
Independence Sch—*school* CO-8
Independence Sch—*school* (9) IL-6
Independence Sch—*school* (2) KS-7
Independence Sch—*school* (3) KY-4
Independence Sch—*school* (3) MO-7
Independence Sch—*school* OK-5
Independence Sch—*school* (2) PA-2
Independence Sch—*school* SC-3
Independence Sch—*school* SD-7
Independence Sch—*school* (2) TN-4
Independence Sch—*school* WV-2
Independence Sch (abandoned)—*school* (6) MO-7
Independence Sch (historical)—*school* MS-4
Independence Sch (historical)—*school* (5) MO-7
Independence Sch (historical)—*school* (2) PA-2
Independence Sch (historical)—*school* TN-4
Independence School—*locale* IL-6
Independence School (Abandoned)—*locale* ID-8
Independence School (Abandoned)—*locale* IL-6
Independence School (abandoned)—*locale* MO-7
Independence Shaft—*mine* UT-8
Independence Shop Ctr—*locale* NC-3
Independence Spring—*spring* TX-5
Independence Square—*locale* MO-7
Independence Square—*park* IL-6
Independence Square Festival Shop Ctr—*locale* NC-3
Independence Square Shop Ctr—*locale* TN-4
Independence State Airp—*airport* OR-9
Independence State Hosp—*hospital* IA-7
**Independence Station**—*pop pl* KY-4
**Independence (Town of)**—*pop pl* NY-2
Independence Township—*civil* (4) MO-7
Independence Township—*civil* SD-7
Independence Township—*fmr MCD* (4) IA-7
**Independence Township**—*pop pl* (4) KS-7
**Independence Township**—*pop pl* (2) SD-7
Independence (Township of)—*civ div* IL-6
Independence (Township of)—*civ div* MI-6
Independence (Township of)—*civ div* OH-6
Independence (Township of)—*fmr MCD* (3) AR-4
**Independence (Township of)**—*pop pl* NJ-2
**Independence (Township of)**—*pop pl* (2) PA-2
Independence Township Sch—*school* PA-2
Independence Valley—*basin* (2) NV-8
Independence Valley—*valley* CA-9
Independence Valley—*valley* WA-9
Independence Valley Sch—*school* KS-7
Independence Valley Well—*locale* NV-8
Independence Ward Ch—*church* ID-8
Independence Well (Dry)—*well* NV-8
**Independent**—*pop pl* FL-3
**Independent**—*pop pl* LA-4
Independent Baptist Ch—*church* IN-6
Independent Baptist Ch—*church* UT-8
Independent Bible Ch—*church* OH-6
Independent Bible Ch—*church* VA-3
Independent Bible Ch of Willow Grove—*church* PA-2
Independent Bible Fellowship Center—*church* DE-2
Independent Canal—*canal* ID-8
Independent Cem—*cemetery* (2) WI-6
Independent Ch—*church* (2) AL-4
Independent Ch—*church* AR-4
Independent Ch—*church* GA-3
Independent Ch—*church* MI-6
Independent Ch—*church* (2) MS-4
Independent Ch—*church* NC-3
Independent Ch—*church* OH-6
Independent Ch—*church* (2) OK-5
Independent Ch—*church* PA-2
Independent Ch—*church* (4) TX-5
Independent Ch—*church* (2) VA-3
Independent Ch of Christ—*church* AL-4
Independent Community Ch—*church* AL-4
Independent Congregational Church—*hist pl* PA-2
Independent Creek—*stream* WA-9
Independent Day Sch—*school* CT-1
Independent Day Sch—*school* FL-3
Independent Distict 52 Sch—*school* MT-8
Independent District of Center Sch (historical)—*school* IA-7
Independent District Pleasant Prairie Sch (historical)—*school* IA-7
Independent Ditch—*canal* CA-9
Independent Ditch—*canal* CO-8
Independent Ditch—*canal* ID-8
Independent Ditch—*canal* NM-5
Independent Ditch—*canal* WY-8
*Independent Gulch* MT-8
Independent Hill—*locale* VA-3
Independent Hill—*summit* NY-2
Independent Holiness Ch—*church* VA-3
Independent Hope Ch—*church* TX-5
Independent Lake—*lake* PA-2
Independent Methodist Ch of Tarrant—*church* AL-4
Independent Mine—*mine* CA-9
Independent Mine—*mine* OR-9
*Independent Missionary Baptist Ch* MS-4
*Independent Mountain* MT-8
Independent Mtn—*summit* WA-9
Independent Mtn—*summit* WY-8
Independent Order of Good Templars Cem—*cemetery* OR-9
Independent Order of Oddfellows, Dayton Lodge No. 273—*hist pl* OH-6
Independent Order of Odd Fellows Bldg—*hist pl* CA-9
Independent Order of Odd Fellows Hall—*hist pl* UT-8
Independent Park—*park* IL-6
Independent Pentecostal Ch of God—*church* FL-3
*Independent Pond* PA-2
Independent Ranchmen's Ditch—*canal* CO-8
Independent Ridge—*ridge* AK-9
Independent Ridge Sch (historical)—*school* MS-4
Independent RR Station—*locale* FL-3
Independent Rsvr—*reservoir* CO-8
Independents—*locale* SC-3
Independent Sch—*school* (2) CA-9
Independent Sch—*school* (2) IL-6
Independent Sch—*school* (2) IA-7
Independent Sch—*school* KS-7
Independent Sch—*school* MN-6
Independent Sch—*school* (3) TX-5
Independent Sch (abandoned)—*school* PA-2
Independent Sch District No. 2 Bldg—*hist pl* OH-6
Independent Sch (historical)—*school* MO-7
Independent Spring—*spring* AZ-5
Independent Township—*civ div* NE-7
**Independent Township**—*pop pl* KS-7
Independent Turnverein—*hist pl* IN-6
Indergard Ranch—*locale* ND-7
Inderia Fria (Barrio)—*fmr MCD* PR-3
Inderland-Ramsland Ditch—*canal* MT-8
Inderland Ranch—*locale* MT-8
Indernuhle Island—*island* WI-6
Index—*locale* AR-4
Index—*locale* NC-3
Index—*locale* VA-3
Index—*locale* WV-2
**Index**—*pop pl* KY-4
**Index**—*pop pl* NY-2
**Index**—*pop pl* WA-9
Index, Mount—*summit* WA-9
Index, The—*summit* CO-8
Index Butte—*summit* MT-8
Index Creek—*stream* (2) WA-9
Index Creek—*stream* WY-8
Index (historical)—*locale* AL-4
Index Lake—*lake* AK-9
Index Mine—*mine* CA-9
Index Mine—*mine* MT-8
*Index Mountain* WA-9
Index Mtn—*summit* AK-9
*Index Peak* WY-8
Index Peak—*summit* WY-8
Index Sch—*school* MO-7
Index Township—*civil* MO-7
Indherred Ch—*church* MN-6
India—*locale* TX-5
**India**—*pop pl* MS-4
**India**—*pop pl* PA-2
**India**—*pop pl* TN-4
India, Lake—*reservoir* GA-3
India Bay—*swamp* MS-4
*India Bench* UT-8
India Branch—*stream* IN-6
India Branch—*stream* TX-5
*India Brook* NJ-2
India Brook—*stream* NJ-2
*India Creek* TX-5
India Creek—*stream* MI-6
Indiada Cove—*bay* AK-9
Indiada Island—*island* AK-9
**Indiahoma**—*pop pl* OK-5
Indiahoma IOOF Cem—*cemetery* OK-5
Indiahoma Wye—*locale* OK-5
**India Hook**—*pop pl* SC-3
India Hook Hills—*summit* SC-3
India-Kaw Valley Elem Sch—*school* KS-7
**India Lakes (subdivision)**—*pop pl* AL-4
**Indialantic**—*pop pl* FL-3
Indialantic-Melbourne Beach (CCD)—*cens area* FL-3
Indialantic Shop Ctr—*locale* FL-3
*Indian* NC-3
Indian—*locale* AK-9
Indian—*locale* ID-8
Indian—*locale* WA-9
**Indian**—*pop pl* AR-4
**Indian**—*pop pl* VA-3
Indian—*uninc pl* WV-2
*Indian, The* WY-8
Indian, The—*locale* CA-9
**Indiana**—*pop pl* AR-4
**Indiana**—*pop pl* IA-7
**Indiana**—*pop pl* PA-2
Indiana, State of—*civil* IN-6
Indiana Acad—*school* IN-6
Indiana Area JHS—*school* PA-2
Indiana Area Senior HS—*school* PA-2
Indiana-Arizona Mine—*mine* AZ-5
*Indiana Army Ammun Plant* IN-6
Indiana Army Ammun Plant—*military* IN-6
Indiana Ave Hist Dist—*hist pl* IN-6
Indiana Baptist Ch—*church* IN-6
Indiana Basin—*basin* WA-9
**Indiana Beach**—*pop pl* IN-6
Indiana Bell Bldg—*hist pl* IN-6
Indiana Borough—*civil* PA-2
Indiana Borough 1912 Municipal Bldg—*hist pl* PA-2
Indiana Business Coll—*school* IN-6
*Indiana Central Coll* IN-6
Indiana Central Univ—*school* IN-6
Indiana Ch—*church* IN-6
Indiana Chapel—*church* IN-6
Indiana Country Club—*other* PA-2
**Indiana County**—*pop pl* PA-2
Indiana County/Jimmy Stewart Field—*airport* PA-2
Indiana Creek—*stream* CA-9
Indiana Creek—*stream* CO-8
Indiana Creek—*stream* MT-8
Indiana Creek—*stream* OR-9
Indiana Department of Natural Resources Airp—*airport* IN-6
Indiana Dunes Natl Lakeshore—*park* (2) IN-6
Indiana Dunes State Park—*park* IN-6
Indian Affairs Forestry Station—*locale* WA-9
**Indian Agency**—*pop pl* CO-8
Indian Agency HQ—*building* OR-9
Indian Agency HQ—*other* UT-8
Indian Agency Lake Dam—*dam* MS-4
Indian Agency Pond Dam—*dam* MS-4
*Indiana Girls School* (2) IN-6
*Indiana Gulch* MT-8
Indiana Gulch—*valley* CO-8
Indiana Gulch—*valley* MT-8
Indiana Gun Club—*other* IN-6
*Indiana Harbor* IN-6
Indiana Harbor—*harbor* IN-6
**Indiana Harbor**—*pop pl* IN-6
Indiana Harbor Boat Club—*locale* IN-6
Indiana Harbor Boat Club North Light—*locale* IN-6
Indiana Harbor Boat Club South Light—*locale* IN-6
Indiana Harbor Canal—*canal* IN-6
Indiana Harbor East Breakwater Light—*locale* IN-6
Indiana Harbor East Bulkhead Light—*locale* IN-6
Indiana Harbor Light 2—*locale* IN-6
Indiana Harbor Light 5—*locale* IN-6
Indiana Harbor Light 6—*locale* IN-6
Indiana Harbor Light 7—*locale* IN-6
Indiana Harbor Light 8—*locale* IN-6
Indiana Harbor North Bulkhead Light—*locale* IN-6
Indiana Harbor South Bulkhead Light—*locale* IN-6
Indiana Institute of Technology—*school* IN-6
**Indiana Junction**—*pop pl* PA-2
*Indiana Kentucky* IN-6
Indiana Lake—*lake* IN-6
Indiana Lake—*lake* MI-6
Indiana Lake—*lake* MN-6
**Indiana Lake**—*pop pl* IN-6
**Indianalo**—*pop pl* OK-5
Indiana Mall—*locale* PA-2
Indiana Michigan Electric Company—*facility* IN-6
Indiana Mine—*mine* (2) MI-6
*Indiana Mineral Springs* IN-6
**Indiana Oaks (Trailer Park)**—*pop pl* IN-6
Indiana Oxygen Company—*hist pl* IN-6
Indiana Point—*cape* MI-6
Indianapolis—*locale* IA-7
Indianapolis—*locale* OK-5
**Indianapolis**—*pop pl* IN-6
Indianapolis Bahai Assembly—*church* IN-6
Indianapolis Baptist Tabernacle—*church* IN-6
Indianapolis Baptist Temple—*church* IN-6
Indianapolis Blvd Interchange—*crossing* IN-6
Indianapolis Boys Club Camp—*park* IN-6
Indianapolis Brookside Airpark—*airport* IN-6
Indianapolis Cem—*cemetery* IA-7
Indianapolis Cem—*cemetery* KS-7
Indianapolis Ch of Jesus Christ of Latter Day Saints—*church* IN-6
Indianapolis Country Club—*other* IN-6
Indianapolis Downtown Airp—*airport* IN-6
Indianapolis First Ch of God—*church* IN-6
Indianapolis Hebrew Congregation—*church* IN-6
Indianapolis International Airp—*airport* IN-6
Indianapolis Metropolitan Airfield—*airport* IN-6
Indianapolis Motor Speedway—*hist pl* IN-6
Indianapolis Motor Speedway—*other* IN-6
Indianapolis News Bldg—*hist pl* IN-6
Indianapolis Raceway Park—*park* IN-6
Indianapolis Sailing Club—*other* IN-6
Indianapolis Sch—*school* KS-7
*Indianapolis Tabernacle* IN-6
Indianapolis Terry Airp—*airport* IN-6
Indianapolis Union RR Station—*hist pl* IN-6

**Indian Field**—pop pl VA-3
Indianfield Branch—stream VA-3
Indian Field Campgrounds—locale SC-3
Indian Field Ch—church SC-3
Indianfield Church PA-2
Indian Field Creek—stream VA-3
Indian Field Lake—lake MS-4
Indian Field Pond—lake NY-2
Indian Field Ridge—ridge CA-9
Indianfield Run—stream OH-6
Indian Fields KY-4
Indian Fields—locale KY-4
Indian Fields Branch—stream NJ-2
Indianfields Cem—cemetery MI-6
Indian Fields Cem—cemetery MI-6
Indian Fields Cem—cemetery NY-2
Indian Field Sch—school SC-3
Indian Fields Methodist Campground—hist pl SC-3
Indianfields Park—park MI-6
Indianfields (Township of)—civ div MI-6
Indian Field Swamp—stream SC-3
Indian Fishery—other CA-9
Indian Fish Weir—hist pl IA-7
Indian Flat CA-9
Indian Flat—flat (3) AZ-5
Indian Flat—flat (3) CA-9
Indian Flat—flat ID-8
Indian Flat—flat (2) OR-9
Indian Flat—flat (3) UT-8
Indian Flat—flat WY-8
Indian Flat Branch—stream TN-4
Indian Flat Campground—locale WA-9
Indian Flat Guard Station—locale CA-9
Indian Flat Ridge—ridge TN-4
Indian Flats—flat CA-9
Indian Flats—flat MT-8
Indian Flats—flat NM-5
Indian Flats—flat WY-8
Indian Flats—locale CO-8
Indian Flats Prong—stream TN-4
Indian Flats Trail TN-4
Indian Flat Tank—reservoir AZ-5
Indian Flat Tank Number Two—reservoir AZ-5
Indian Flat Trail—trail TN-4
Indian Flat Well—well AZ-5
Indian Foot—arch UT-8
Indian Foothills Park—park MO-7
Indian Foot Lake—reservoir MO-7
Indian Ford WI-6
Indian Ford—locale FL-3
Indian Ford—locale OR-9
**Indianford**—pop pl WI-6
Indian Ford Bridge—hist pl IL-6
Indian Ford Bridge—other IL-6
Indian Ford Creek—stream OR-9
Indian Ford (historical)—crossing TN-4
Indian Ford (historical)—locale MS-4
Indian Ford Lakes—locale MO-7
Indian Ford Springs—spring WA-9
**Indian Forest (subdivision)**—pop pl TN-4
Indian Fork—other TN-4
Indian Fork—stream (2) ID-8
Indian Fork—stream IN-6
Indian Fork—stream KY-4
Indian Fork—stream NC-3
Indian Fork—stream OH-6
Indian Fork—stream (2) TN-4
Indian Fork—stream (5) WV-2
Indian Fork Branch—stream AL-4
Indian Fork Ch—church KY-4
Indian Fork Ch—church (2) WV-2
Indian Fork Gap—gap TN-4
Indian Fork Poplar Creek TN-4
Indian Fort—locale OR-9
Indian Fort—other IN-6
Indian Fort Cabin—locale OR-9
Indian Fort Creek—stream OR-9
Indian Fort Earthworks (15CK7)—hist pl KY-4
Indian Fort Flat—flat OR-9
Indian Fort Hill—summit MA-1
Indian Fort Mesa—summit TX-5
Indian Fort Mountain—hist pl KY-4
Indian Fort Mtn—summit KY-4
Indian Fort Ridge—ridge OR-9
Indian Fort Road Site—hist pl NY-2
Indian Fort Rsvr—reservoir OR-9
Indian Fort Trail—trail VA-3
Indian Gap—channel NC-3
Indian Gap—gap KY-4
Indian Gap—gap NC-3
Indian Gap—gap (3) TN-4
Indian Gap—gap TX-5
Indian Gap—gap (2) VA-3
Indian Gap—gap (2) WV-2
Indian Gap—gap WY-8
**Indian Gap**—pop pl TX-5
**Indian Gap**—pop pl VA-3
Indian Gap Ch—church KY-4
Indian Gap Ch—church TN-4
Indian Gap Hill—summit KY-4
Indian Gap Island—island NC-3
Indian Gap Lake—reservoir AL-4
Indian Gap Lake Dam—dam AL-4
Indian Gap Post Office—locale VA-3
Indian Gap Run—stream VA-3
Indian Garden—flat AZ-5
Indian Garden—flat OR-9
Indian Garden Creek—stream CA-9
Indian Garden Creek—stream NV-8
Indian Garden Mtn—summit NV-8
Indian Gardens AZ-5
Indian Gardens—area AZ-5
Indian Gardens—flat AZ-5
**Indian Gardens**—pop pl AZ-5
Indian Gardens—valley UT-8
Indian Garden Spring—spring (3) NV-8
Indian Gardens Spring—spring CA-9
Indian Garden Well—well AZ-5
Indian George Creek—stream (2) WA-9
Indian George Wash—valley UT-8
Indian Girl Mine—mine (2) CA-9
Indian Glacier—glacier AK-9
Indian Glade—flat OR-9
Indian God Rock—pillar PA-2
Indian God Rock Petroglyphs Site (36VE26)—hist pl PA-2
Indian Gorge CA-9
Indian Gorge—valley CA-9
Indian Grade Spring—spring AZ-5
Indian Grade Spring—spring OR-9
Indian Grave Branch—stream (2) KY-4
Indian Grave Branch—stream NC-3
Indian Grave Branch—stream SC-3
Indian Grave Branch—stream VA-3
Indian Grave Branch—stream (2) WV-2
Indian Grave Camp—locale ID-8
Indian Grave Ch—church AL-4
Indian Grave Creek—stream AL-4
Indian Grave Creek—stream AK-9
Indian Grave Creek—stream ID-8
Indian Grave Creek—stream NC-3
Indian Grave Creek—stream OR-9
Indian Grave Creek—stream TX-5
Indian Grave Creek—stream VA-3
Indian Grave Creek—stream WI-6
Indian Grave Flat—flat WY-8
Indian Grave Flats—flat TN-4
Indian Grave Fork—stream (2) KY-4
Indian Grave Gap—gap (3) GA-3
Indian Grave Gap—gap (4) KY-4
Indian Grave Gap—gap (9) NC-3
Indian Grave Gap—gap (3) TN-4
Indian Grave Gap—gap (3) VA-3
Indian Grave Gap Branch—stream NC-3
Indian Grave Hill—summit GA-3
Indian Grave Hill—summit TN-4
Indian Grave Hollow—valley KY-4
Indian Grave Hollow—valley WV-2
Indian Grave Knob—summit GA-3
Indian Grave Lake—lake IL-6
Indian Grave Monmt—pillar KS-7
Indian Grave Mtn—summit AK-9
Indian Grave Mtn—summit GA-3
Indian Grave Mtn—summit WV-2
Indian Grave Peak—summit ID-8
Indian Grave Peak—summit UT-8
Indian Grave Point—cape MO-7
Indian Grave Point—cape TN-4
Indian Grave Point Cave—cave TN-4
Indian Grave Pond—lake AL-4
Indian Grave Ridge—ridge KY-4
Indian Grave Ridge—ridge VA-3
Indian Grave Run—stream PA-2
Indian Graves—cemetery WY-8
Indian Graves Baptist Ch (historical)—church TN-4
Indian Grave Sch—school IL-6
Indian Grave Sch—school KY-4
Indian Graves Mtn GA-3
Indian Grave Tunnel—tunnel TN-4
Indian Graveyard Basin—basin NV-8
Indian Grinding Rock—hist pl CA-9
Indian Ground Hill—summit NH-1
Indian Grove—area WY-8
Indian Grove—locale ID-8
**Indian Grove**—pop pl MI-6
**Indian Grove**—pop pl MO-7
Indian Grove Brook—stream NJ-2
Indian Grove Cem—cemetery OH-6
Indian Grove Ch—church NC-3
Indian Grove Ch—church SC-3
Indian Grove Creek NC-3
Indian Grove Creek—stream WY-8
Indian Grove Ranch—locale WY-8
Indian Grove Sch—school IL-6
Indian Grove Sch (abandoned)—school MO-7
Indian Grove Sch (historical)—school TN-4
Indian Grove (Township of)—civ div IL-6
Indian Guide—summit WY-8
Indian Guide Ranch—locale WY-8
Indian Gulch CA-9
Indian Gulch MT-8
Indian Gulch UT-8
Indian Gulch—locale CA-9
Indian Gulch—valley (7) CA-9
Indian Gulch—valley (3) CO-8
Indian Gulch—valley ID-8
Indian Gulch—valley (3) MT-8
Indian Gulch—valley (2) OR-9
Indian Gulch—valley UT-8
Indian Gulley—stream TX-5
Indian Gut—gut DE-2
Indian Guyan Creek—stream OH-6
Indian Guyandotte OH-6
Indian Hammock—island GA-3
Indian Hammock—locale MD-2
Indian Hammock Cove—bay MD-2
Indian Harbor CT-1
Indian Harbor ME-1
Indian Harbor—bay CT-1
Indian Harbor—bay NJ-2
**Indian Harbor Beach**—pop pl FL-3
**Indian Harbor Villa (subdivision)**—pop pl DE-2
**Indian Harbour Beach**—pop pl FL-3
Indian Harbour Beach Shop Ctr—locale FL-3
Indian Hatties—locale CA-9
Indian Hay Meadows—flat ID-8
Indianhead MD-2
Indian Head TX-5
Indian Head—cape AK-9
Indian Head—cliff MD-2
Indian Head—cliff NJ-2
**Indian Head**—pop pl MD-2
**Indian Head**—pop pl (2) PA-2
Indian Head—rock NH-1
Indian Head—summit (2) AZ-5
Indian Head—summit CA-9
Indianhead—summit CA-9
Indian Head—summit CA-9
Indian Head—summit (2) CO-8
Indian Head—summit CT-1
Indian Head—summit ME-1
Indian Head—summit (2) MT-8
Indian Head—summit NM-5
Indian Head—summit (2) NY-2
Indian Head—summit OR-9
Indian Head—summit TX-5
Indian Head—summit UT-8
Indian Head Acres—uninc pl FL-3
Indian Head and Trapper—pillar UT-8
Indian Head Arch—arch UT-8
Indianhead Basin—basin WA-9
Indian Head Beach—locale CA-9
Indian Head Brook—stream MA-1
Indian Head Camp—locale PA-2
Indian Head Canyon—valley ID-8
Indian Head Canyon—valley OR-9
Indian Head Dam—dam MA-1
Indian-head Hill MA-1
Indian Head Hill—summit (2) MA-1
Indian Head (historical)—locale TN-4
Indian Head Junction (White Plains) MD-2
Indianhead Lake—lake MN-6
**Indianhead Lake**—pop pl IN-6
Indianhead Lake—reservoir IN-6
**Indianhead Lake Estates**—pop pl AR-4
**Indian Head Manor**—pop pl MD-2
Indian Head Mountain MT-8
Indian Head Mtn—summit (2) AZ-5
Indian Head Mtn—summit ID-8
Indian Head Mtn—summit NY-2
Indian Head Mtn—summit TN-4
Indian Head Mtn—summit TX-5
Indian Head Naval Ordinance Station—military MD-2
Indian Head Neck—cape RI-1
**Indian Head Park**—pop pl IL-6
Indian Head Pass—gap UT-8
Indian Head Peak—summit NV-8
Indian Head Peak—summit TX-5
Indian Head Peak—summit UT-8
Indian Head Peak—summit WA-9
Indian Head Plant—CDP MD-2
**Indian Head (P.O.) (Davistown)**—pop pl PA-2
Indian Head P.O. (historical)—locale AL-4
Indian Head Point—cape TX-5
Indian-head Pond MA-1
Indian Head Pond—lake MA-1
Indian-head River MA-1
Indian Head River—stream MA-1
Indian Head River Rsvr—reservoir MA-1
Indian Head Rock—bar CA-9
Indian Head Rock—locale ID-8
Indian Head Rock—pillar MT-8
Indianhead Rock—pillar OR-9
Indian Head Rock—summit MT-8
Indian Head Rock—summit OR-9
Indian Head Rock—summit (2) WY-8
Indian Head Sch—school MD-2
Indian Head Sch—school MA-1
Indian Head Sch—school NY-2
Indian Head Shopping Mall—locale MA-1
Indian Head Spring—spring TX-5
Indian Head Swamp—swamp FL-3
Indian Head Tank—reservoir TX-5
Indianhead Technical Institute—school WI-6
Indian Health Station—locale AZ-5
Indian Heaven—basin WA-9
Indian Heaven Pond—reservoir CT-1
**Indian Heights**—pop pl IN-6
Indian Heights Park—park TX-5
Indian Henry Hollow—valley KY-4
Indian Henry Ridge—ridge ID-8
Indian Henrys Cabin—locale CO-8
Indian Henrys Hunting Ground—area WA-9
Indian Hickman—valley UT-8
Indian Hickman Canyon UT-8
Indian Hill CA-9
Indian Hill CT-1
Indian Hill FL-3
Indian Hill (2) IL-6
Indian Hill MA-1
Indian Hill—locale CA-9
Indian Hill—locale IL-6
Indian Hill—locale MS-4
Indian Hill—locale NY-2
Indian Hill—other CA-9
**Indian Hill**—pop pl AL-4
**Indian Hill**—pop pl IN-6
**Indian Hill**—pop pl (2) OH-6
**Indian Hill**—pop pl TX-5
Indian Hill—summit (3) AL-4
Indian Hill—summit (4) AZ-5
Indian Hill—summit (7) CA-9
Indian Hill—summit (2) CT-1
Indian Hill—summit (3) ID-8
Indian Hill—summit (4) IL-6
Indian Hill—summit IN-6
Indian Hill—summit (4) KY-4
Indian Hill—summit ME-1
Indian Hill—summit (6) MA-1
Indian Hill—summit MN-6
Indian Hill—summit (2) MO-7
Indian Hill—summit (3) MT-8
Indian Hill—summit (5) NE-7
Indian Hill—summit (3) NM-5
Indian Hill—summit (4) NY-2
Indian Hill—summit ND-7
Indian Hill—summit OH-6
Indian Hill—summit (3) OK-5
Indian Hill—summit OR-9
Indian Hill—summit (2) SC-3
Indian Hill—summit (5) TX-5
Indian Hill—summit UT-8
Indian Hill—summit VT-1
Indian Hill—summit (2) WA-9
Indian Hill—summit WV-2
Indian Hill—summit (3) WY-8
**Indian Hill, The Village of**—pop pl OH-6
Indian Hill Archeol District—hist pl NE-7
Indian Hill Ave Hist Dist—hist pl CT-1
Indian Hill Campground—locale MT-8
Indian Hill Cem—cemetery AL-4
Indian Hill Cem—cemetery CT-1
Indian Hill Cem—cemetery IL-6
Indian Hill Cem—cemetery KS-7
Indian Hill Cem—cemetery MS-4
Indian Hill Cem—cemetery MO-7
Indian Hill Cem (historical)—cemetery MO-7
Indian Hill Ch—church AL-4
Indian Hill Ch—church FL-3
Indian Hill Ch—church GA-3
Indian Hill Ch—church NC-3
Indian Hill Ch—church (2) SC-3
Indian Hill Ch—church TX-5
Indian Hill Ch—church (2) VA-3
Indian Hill Creek—stream ID-8
**Indian Hill Division (subdivision)**—pop pl SD-7
Indian Hill Farm Airp—airport TN-4
Indian Hill Farm (historical)—locale AL-4
Indian Hill Golf Club—other IL-6
Indian Hill HS—school NE-7
Indian Hill Island—island MO-7
Indian Hill Lake—reservoir TX-5
Indian Hill Memorial—other NY-2
Indian Hill Mine (Inactive)—mine CA-9
Indian Hill-North Village—hist pl MA-1
Indian Hill Post Office (historical)—building AL-4
Indian Hill Ridge—ridge WI-6
Indian Hills IL-6
Indian Hills—locale (2) KY-4
Indian Hills—other IL-6
**Indian Hills**—pop pl CO-8
**Indian Hills**—pop pl IN-6
**Indian Hills**—pop pl (7) KY-4
**Indian Hills**—pop pl MS-4
**Indian Hills**—pop pl NC-3
**Indian Hills**—pop pl PA-2
**Indian Hills**—pop pl TN-4
**Indian Hills**—pop pl (3) TN-4
Indian Hills—post sta FL-3
Indian Hills—range NV-8
Indian Hills—range PA-2
Indian Hills—range TX-5
Indian Hills—summit MA-1
Indian Hills—summit NM-5
Indian Hills—summit (2) OK-5
Indian Hills—summit (2) TX-5
Indian Hills—uninc pl KY-4
Indian Hills—uninc pl NM-5
Indian Hills Ch—church KY-4
Indian Hill Sch—school IL-6
Indian Hill Sch—school MI-6
Indian Hill Sch—school OH-6
**Indian Hills Cherokee Section**—pop pl KY-4
Indian Hill Sch (historical)—school MS-4
Indian Hills Ch of the Nazarene—church KS-7
Indian Hills Community Ch—church MO-7
Indian Hills Country Club—locale AL-4
Indian Hills Country Club—locale NC-3
Indian Hills Country Club—other AL-4
Indian Hills Country Club—other IL-6
Indian Hills Country Club—other KS-7
Indian Hills Country Club—other NY-2
Indian Hills Country Club—other OK-5
Indian Hills Golf and Country Club—locale FL-3
Indian Hills Golf Club—locale AL-4
Indian Hills Golf Course—other CA-9
Indian Hills Golf Course—other MI-6
Indian Hill Site—hist pl KS-7
Indian Hill Site—hist pl SC-3
Indian Hills JHS—school KS-7
Indian Hills Lake—reservoir AL-4
Indian Hills Lake—reservoir OK-5
Indian Hills Lake Dam—dam AL-4
Indian Hill Slough—stream MO-7
Indian Hills MS—school UT-8
Indian Hills Oil Field—oilfield TX-5
Indian Hills Park—park IA-7
Indian Hills Rec Area—park IA-7
Indian Hills Sch—school AR-4
Indian Hills Sch—school IL-6
Indian Hills Sch—school KY-4
Indian Hills Sch—school (2) MI-6
Indian Hills Sch—school NJ-2
Indian Hills Sch—school OH-6
Indian Hills Sch—school OR-9
Indian Hills Sch—school UT-8
Indian Hills Sch (historical)—school PA-2
Indian Hills Shop Ctr—locale (2) KS-7
Indian Hills Site—hist pl OH-6
**Indian Hills (subdivision)**—pop pl (6) AL-4
**Indian Hills (subdivision)**—pop pl (3) NC-3
**Indian Hills Subdivision**—pop pl UT-8
Indian Hills Tank—reservoir AZ-5
Indian Hills Wash—stream NV-8
Indian Hill Tank—reservoir NM-5
Indian Hill Well—locale NM-5
Indian Hill Windmill—locale TX-5
Indian Hole—locale ID-8
Indian Hole Brook—stream CT-1
Indian Hole Falls—falls OR-9
Indian Holes—basin OR-9
Indian Hollow—basin OR-9
Indian Hollow—valley AZ-5
Indian Hollow—valley IN-6
Indian Hollow—valley (2) KY-4
Indian Hollow—valley MA-1
Indian Hollow—valley NV-8
Indian Hollow—valley NM-5
Indian Hollow—valley OR-9
Indian Hollow—valley PA-2
Indian Hollow—valley (6) TX-5
Indian Hollow—valley (12) UT-8
Indian Hollow—valley VA-3
Indian Hollow—valley (2) WV-2
Indian Hollow—valley WI-6
Indian Hollow Bridge—bridge VA-3
Indian Hollow Brook—stream CT-1
Indian Hollow Campground—park AZ-5
Indian Hollow Debris Basin Rsvr—reservoir UT-8
Indian Hollow Pond—lake CT-1
Indian Hollow Run—stream PA-2
Indian Hollow Sch—school NY-2
Indian Hollow Spring—spring AZ-5
Indian Hollow Spring—spring UT-8
Indian Hollow-Thunder Springs Trail Twenty-three—trail AZ-5
Indian Hollow Trick Tank—reservoir AZ-5
Indian Home Ch—church OK-5
Indianhorse Swamp—swamp FL-3
Indian Hosp (Sells)—hospital AZ-5
Indian Hot Springs ID-8
**Indian Hot Springs**—pop pl AZ-5
**Indian Hot Springs**—pop pl TX-5
Indian Hot Springs—spring AZ-5
Indian Hot Springs—spring ID-8
Indian House Creek—stream NY-2
Indianhouse Lake—lake FL-3
Indianhouse Mtn—summit AK-9
Indian Hut Brook—stream CT-1
Indian Hut Club—other SC-3
Indian Hut Swamp—stream SC-3
Indian Ikes Point—summit NV-8
Indian Island WA-9
Indian Island—island AK-9
Indian Island—island (2) CA-9
Indian Island—island GA-3
Indian Island—island (3) IL-6
Indian Island—island (7) ME-1
Indian Island—island (2) MI-6
Indian Island—island (3) MN-6
Indian Island—island NE-7
Indian Island—island NJ-2
Indian Island—island (2) NY-2
Indian Island—island (2) NC-3
Indian Island—island OH-6
Indian Island—island (3) WA-9
Indian Island—island WY-8
**Indian Island**—pop pl ME-1
Indian Island—swamp FL-3
Indian Island Light Station—hist pl ME-1
Indian Island Slue—channel NC-3
Indian Jack Lake—lake MN-6
Indian Jack Slough—stream WA-9
Indian Jakes—locale ID-8
Indian Jim Canyon—valley ID-8
Indian Jim Place—locale ID-8
Indian Jim's Cave—hist pl VA-3
Indian Joe Canyon—valley CA-9
Indian Joe Canyon—valley NM-5
Indian Joe Cem—cemetery WA-9
Indian Joe Creek—stream CA-9
Indian Joe Island OR-9
Indian Joe Spring—spring CA-9
Indian John Hill—summit WA-9
Indian John Island—island OR-9
Indian Johnnie Creek—stream NV-8
Indian John Spring—spring CA-9
Indian Kentuck Cem—cemetery IN-6
Indian Kentuck Ch—church IN-6
Indian Kentuck Creek—stream IN-6
Indian Kentucky Creek IN-6
**Indian Kettles**—pop pl NY-2
Indian Key—hist pl FL-3
Indian Key—island (4) FL-3
Indian Key Anchorage—harbor FL-3
Indian Key Channel—channel FL-3
Indian Key Fill—island FL-3
Indian Key Pass—channel FL-3
Indian Kill—stream (3) NY-2
Indian King—locale PA-2
Indian King Tavern—hist pl NJ-2
Indian Kitchen—summit AZ-5
Indian Knob—summit AR-4
Indian Knob—summit CA-9
Indian Knob—summit (3) KY-4
Indian Knob—summit NC-3
Indian Knob—summit OH-6
Indian Knob—summit TN-4
Indian Knob—summit TX-5
Indian Knoll—hist pl KY-4
Indian Knoll—summit AZ-5
Indian Knoll—summit CA-9
Indian Knoll—summit TX-5
Indian Knoll—summit (3) UT-8
Indian Knoll Ch—church GA-3
Indian Knolls OH-6
**Indian Knolls**—pop pl OH-6
Indian Ladder—cliff NJ-2
Indian Ladder—cliff NY-2
Indian Ladder Bluff—cliff TN-4
Indian Ladder Falls—falls PA-2
Indian Lagoon—bay FL-3
Indian Lake AL-4
Indian Lake IL-6
Indian Lake IN-6
Indian Lake MA-1
Indian Lake MI-6
Indian Lake MN-6
Indian Lake MT-8
Indian Lake—lake AK-9
Indian Lake—lake (2) AZ-5
Indian Lake—lake CA-9
Indian Lake—lake CO-8
Indian Lake—lake (3) CT-1
Indian Lake—lake (5) FL-3
Indian Lake—lake (5) ID-8
Indian Lake—lake (6) IN-6
Indian Lake—lake IA-7
Indian Lake—lake (2) LA-4
Indian Lake—lake (2) ME-1
Indian Lake—lake (24) MI-6
Indian Lake—lake (12) MN-6
Indian Lake—lake MT-8
Indian Lake—lake NE-7
Indian Lake—lake (3) NM-5
Indian Lake—lake (6) NY-2
Indian Lake—lake OR-9
Indian Lake—lake (2) PA-2
Indian Lake—lake RI-1
Indian Lake—lake SC-3
Indian Lake—lake (2) TX-5
Indian Lake—lake (9) WI-6
Indian Lake—lake (2) WY-8
Indian Lake—locale KY-4
Indian Lake—locale PA-2
**Indian Lake**—pop pl (2) IN-6
**Indian Lake**—pop pl MI-6
**Indian Lake**—pop pl MO-7
**Indian Lake**—pop pl NJ-2
**Indian Lake**—pop pl NY-2
**Indian Lake**—pop pl PA-2
**Indian Lake**—pop pl TX-5
Indian Lake—reservoir (2) AL-4
Indian Lake—reservoir GA-3
Indian Lake—reservoir (3) IN-6
Indian Lake—reservoir KY-4
Indian Lake—reservoir LA-4
Indian Lake—reservoir MA-1
Indian Lake—reservoir MO-7
Indian Lake—reservoir (3) NJ-2
Indian Lake—reservoir NY-2
Indian Lake—reservoir OH-6
Indian Lake—reservoir (3) PA-2
Indian Lake—reservoir RI-1
Indian Lake—reservoir SD-7
Indian Lake—swamp MI-6
Indian Lake Airpark—airport PA-2
Indian Lake Baptist Ch—church AL-4
Indian Lake Borough—civil PA-2
Indian Lake Ch—church MN-6
Indian Lake Chapel—church NY-2
Indian Lake Country Club—other IN-6
Indian Lake Creek—stream CT-1
Indian Lake Creek—stream MI-6
Indian Lake Dam AL-4
Indian Lake Dam SD-7
Indian Lake Dam—dam (2) IN-6
Indian Lake Dam—dam (2) MA-1
Indian Lake Dam—dam (2) NJ-2
Indian Lake Dam—dam OR-9
Indian Lake Dam—dam (3) PA-2
Indian Lake Dam—dam RI-1
Indian Lake Elem Sch—school TN-4
**Indian Lake Estates**—pop pl FL-3
Indian Lake Estates Reservoir MA-1
**Indian Lake Estates (subdivision)**—pop pl AL-4
**Indian Lake Estates (subdivision)**—pop pl NC-3
**Indian Lake Farms**—pop pl TN-4
**Indian Lake Forest (subdivision)**—pop pl TN-4
Indian Lake (historical)—locale IA-7
Indian Lake Mtn—summit NY-2
Indian Lake Park—park IA-7
Indian Lake Prairie—swamp FL-3
Indian Lake Rsvr—reservoir MA-1
Indian Lake Rsvr—reservoir (2) OR-9
Indian Lakes—lake IN-6
Indian Lakes—lake (2) MI-6
Indian Lakes—lake OR-9
Indian Lake Sch—school MI-6
**Indian Lake Shores**—pop pl RI-1
Indian Lake State Park—park MI-6
**Indian Lake (subdivision)**—pop pl AL-4
Indian Lake Tank—reservoir AZ-5
Indian Lake Tower (firetower)—locale FL-3
**Indian Lake (Town of)**—pop pl NY-2
**Indian Lake (Township of)**—pop pl MN-6
Indian Lake Upper—reservoir NC-3
Indian Lake Upper Dam—dam NC-3
**Indianland**—pop pl PA-2
Indian Land Ch—church SC-3
Indian Land HS—school SC-3
Indian Landing—locale LA-4
Indian Landing—locale ME-1
Indian Landing—locale NY-2
Indian Landing—locale NC-3
**Indian Landing North (trailer park)**—pop pl DE-2
Indian Landing Sch—school NY-2
**Indian Landing (trailer park)**—pop pl DE-2
**Indian Lands**—pop pl MA-1
Indian Lane JHS (abandoned)—school PA-2
Indian Lateral—canal NM-5
Indian Lateral—canal WA-9
Indian Leap—cliff MA-1
Indian Leap Bluff—cliff MO-7
Indian Ledge—island ME-1
Indian Lick—stream MD-2
Indian Lick—stream OH-6
Indianlick Branch—stream WV-2
Indian Lick Creek—stream KY-4
Indian Lodge—locale TX-5
Indian Lodge Canyon—valley UT-8
Indian Lookout—locale PA-2
Indian Lookout—summit AZ-5
Indian Lookout Mtn—summit CO-8
Indian Lookout Tower—locale WI-6
Indian Marais—stream LA-4
Indian Mary Park—park OR-9
Indian Massacre Grave—cemetery SC-3
Indian Massacre Historical Monmt—park ID-8
Indian Meadow—flat (2) CA-9
Indian Meadow—swamp CA-9
Indian Meadow—swamp CT-1
Indian Meadow Brook—stream CT-1
Indian Meadow Creek—stream ID-8
Indian Meadow Draw WY-8
Indian Meadows—flat (2) ID-8
Indian Meadows—flat (2) MT-8
**Indian Meadows**—pop pl CO-8
**Indian Meadows**—pop pl OK-5
**Indian Meadows**—pop pl WV-2
Indian Meadows Creek—stream MT-8
Indian Meadows Guard Station—locale MT-8
Indian Meadows Spring—spring ID-8
Indian Meeting House MA-1
Indian Memorial Rec Area—park SD-7
Indian Mesa—bench NM-5
Indian Mesa—summit AZ-5
Indian Mesa—summit CO-8
Indian Mesa—summit NM-5
Indian Mesa—summit TX-5
Indian Mike Creek—stream ID-8
Indian Mike Creek—stream NV-8
Indian Mike Spring CA-9
Indian Mike Spring—spring CA-9
Indian Mike Spring—spring NV-8
Indian Mill—hist pl OH-6
Indian Mill Creek—stream ID-8
Indian Mill Creek—stream MI-6
Indian Mills—locale WV-2
**Indian Mills**—pop pl NJ-2
Indian Mills Brook—stream NJ-2
Indian Mills Dam—dam NJ-2
Indian Mills Lake—reservoir NJ-2
Indian Mills Sawmill Dam—dam NJ-2
Indian Mills Sawmill Pond—reservoir NJ-2
Indian Mission—church CA-9
Indian Mission—church ID-8
Indian Mission—church (2) MI-6
Indian Mission—church (2) OK-5
Indian Mission—hist pl MI-6
Indian Mission—locale DE-2
**Indian Mission**—pop pl CA-9
Indian Mission Boarding Sch—school AZ-5
Indian Mission Cem—cemetery SD-7
Indian Mission Ch—church DE-2
Indian Mission Ch—church MI-6
Indian Mission Ch—church OK-5
Indian Mission Church—hist pl DE-2
Indian Mission Sch—hist pl DE-2
Indian Mission Sch (historical)—school SD-7
Indian Moccasin AZ-5
**Indian Moccasin**—pop pl AZ-5
Indianmound TN-4
Indian Mound—locale LA-4
Indian Mound—locale MS-4
Indian Mound—locale TN-4
Indian Mound—other (2) IN-6
**Indian Mound**—pop pl MO-7
**Indian Mound**—pop pl TN-4
Indian Mound—summit FL-3
Indian Mound—summit (2) IL-6
Indian Mound—summit KS-7
Indian Mound—summit KY-4
Indian Mound—summit LA-4
Indian Mound—summit MI-6
Indian Mound—summit TX-5
Indian Mound Baptist Ch—church TN-4

Indian Steps Trail—*trail* ... PA-2
Indian Stone Corral—*hist pl* ... CA-9
Indian Stones—*hist pl* ... VT-1
Indians Trail—*trail* ... CA-9
Indian Stream—*stream* (8) ... ME-1
Indian Stream—*stream* ... NH-1
Indian Stream Mtn—*summit* ... ME-1
Indian Stream Sch—*school* ... NH-1
Indian Stream (Township of)—*unorg* ... ME-1
Indian Sun Dance Grounds—*locale* ... UT-8
Indian Swale—*valley* ... UT-8
Indian Swamp—*stream* ... NC-3
Indian Swamp—*stream* ... VA-3
Indian Swamp—*swamp* (3) ... GA-3
Indian Swamp—*swamp* ... NC-3
Indian Swamp—*swamp* ... PA-2
Indian Talking Rocks—*locale* ... WY-8
Indian Tank—*reservoir* (15) ... AZ-5
Indian Tank—*reservoir* (10) ... NM-5
Indian Tank—*reservoir* (2) ... TX-5
Indian Tank Hill—*summit* ... AZ-5
Indian Tanks—*reservoir* ... AZ-5
Indian Timothy Bridge—*bridge* ... WA-9
Indian Timothy Memorial Bridge—*hist pl* ... WA-9
Indian Tomb Hollow—*valley* ... AL-4
Indian Tom Creek—*stream* ... WA-9
Indian Tom Lake—*lake* ... CA-9
Indian Tom Spring—*spring* ... WA-9
Indian Top—*summit* ... NC-3
*Indian Town* ... FL-3
*Indian Town* ... MS-4
*Indiantown* ... PA-2
Indian Town—*locale* ... MD-2
Indiantown—*locale* (2) ... MD-2
Indiantown—*locale* ... MI-6
Indian Town—*locale* ... MI-6
Indiantown—*locale* (2) ... PA-2
Indian Town—*locale* ... VA-3
**Indiantown**—*pop pl* ... FL-3
**Indiantown**—*pop pl* ... MI-6
**Indian Town**—*pop pl* ... NC-3
**Indiantown**—*pop pl* ... NC-3
**Indiantown**—*pop pl* ... PA-2
**Indiantown**—*pop pl* ... SC-3
**Indiantown**—*pop pl* ... VA-3
Indian Town Bluff—*hist pl* ... TN-4
Indian Town Bridge—*bridge* ... FL-3
Indiantown Brook—*stream* ... CT-1
Indiantown (CCD)—*cens area* ... FL-3
Indian Town Cem—*cemetery* ... MI-6
Indiantown Ch—*church* ... PA-2
Indiantown Cove—*bay* ... MD-2
Indiantown Creek—*stream* ... NC-3
Indiantown Creek—*stream* ... VA-3
Indian Town Drain—*canal* ... MI-6
**Indiantown Farms (subdivision)**—*pop pl* ... DE-2
Indiantown Gap—*gap* ... PA-2
**Indiantown Gap (Lickdale)**—*pop pl* ... PA-2
Indiantown Gap Milit Reservation—*military* ... PA-2
Indiantown Gap Natl Cem—*cemetery* ... PA-2
Indiantown Gap Station—*locale* ... PA-2
Indian Town Hammock—*island* ... FL-3
Indiantown Harbor—*bay* ... CT-1
**Indiantown (historical)**—*pop pl* ... IA-7
Indiantown Island—*island* ... ME-1
Indian Town Lake—*lake* ... MI-6
Indiantown MS—*school* ... FL-3
Indiantown Neck—*cape* ... VA-3
*Indian Town Plantation* ... MA-1
Indian Town Rsvr—*reservoir* ... AZ-5
Indiantown Run—*stream* ... MD-2
Indiantown Run—*stream* ... PA-2
Indian Township—*civil* ... MO-7
Indian Township—*civil* ... SD-7
Indian Township Ind Res—*333 (1980)* ... ME-1
Indiantown Swamp—*stream* ... SC-3
Indian Town Swamp—*stream* ... VA-3
**Indiantown (Township of)**—*pop pl* ... IL-6
Indian Town Wash—*stream* ... AZ-5
Indian Trace Creek—*stream* ... IN-6
**Indian Trace (subdivision)**—*pop pl* ... AL-4
*Indian Tract* ... DE-2
**Indian Trail**—*pop pl* ... NC-3
Indian Trail—*trail* (4) ... CO-8
Indian Trail—*trail* ... GA-3
Indian Trail—*trail* ... MA-1
Indian Trail—*trail* ... MI-6
Indian Trail—*trail* ... OR-9
Indian Trail—*trail* (5) ... PA-2
Indian Trail—*trail* (2) ... UT-8
Indian Trail Bench—*bench* ... UT-8
Indian Trail Branch—*stream* ... GA-3
Indian Trail Camp—*locale* ... NY-2
Indian Trail Canyon—*valley* ... CO-8
Indian Trail Canyon—*valley* (2) ... NM-5
Indian Trail Canyon—*valley* ... OR-9
Indian Trail Creek—*stream* ... NM-5
Indian Trail Creek—*stream* ... OH-6
Indian Trail Creek—*stream* ... OR-9
Indian Trail Creek—*stream* ... TN-4
Indian Trail Draw—*valley* ... SD-7
**Indian Trail Estates**—*pop pl* ... IL-6
Indian Trail Fish Hatchery—*other* ... MO-7
Indian Trail Hollow—*valley* ... UT-8
Indian Trail Lake—*reservoir* ... NJ-2
Indian Trail Lodge—*locale* ... MT-8
Indian Trail Lookout—*locale* ... MO-7
Indian Trail Lookout Tower—*locale* ... KY-4
Indian Trail Number Three Rsvr—*reservoir* ... MA-1
Indian Trail Park—*park* ... IL-6
Indian Trail Park—*park* ... PA-2
Indian Trail Park—*park* ... WA-9
Indian Trail Pit—*basin* ... WY-8
Indian Trail Pit—*cave* ... AL-4
Indian Trail Point—*cape* ... TX-5
Indian Trail Reservoir Number 2 Dam—*dam* ... MA-1
Indian Trail Reservoir Number 3 Dam—*dam* ... MA-1
Indian Trail Ridge—*ridge* ... CO-8
Indian Trail Rsvr—*reservoir* ... MA-1
Indian Trails, The—*trail* ... OR-9
Indian Trail Sch—*school* ... IL-6
Indian Trail Sch—*school* ... KY-4
Indian Trail Sch—*school* ... MI-6
Indian Trail Sch—*school* ... NC-3
Indian Trail Sch—*school* ... WA-9
Indian Trails Country Club—*other* ... NE-7
Indian Trails Golf and Country Club—*locale* ... NC-3
Indian Trails Golf Course—*other* ... MI-6
Indian Trail Spring—*spring* ... OR-9
Indian Trails Spring—*spring* ... WY-8
Indian Trail State For—*forest* ... MO-7
*Indian Trail State Park* ... MO-7
**Indian Trail (subdivision)**—*pop pl* ... NC-3
Indian Trail Wash—*stream* ... NV-8
Indian Treaty Tree—*locale* ... WA-9
Indian Tree Golf Course—*other* ... CO-8
Indian Tree Hill—*summit* ... WY-8
Indian Trees Campground—*locale* ... MT-8
Indian Trial Canyon—*valley* ... CO-8
Indian Truck Trail—*trail* ... CA-9
Indian Tunnel—*tunnel* ... ID-8
Indian Univ of Tahlequah—*hist pl* ... OK-5
Indian Valley—*basin* (4) ... CA-9
Indian Valley—*basin* ... NE-7
Indian Valley—*flat* ... CA-9
Indian Valley—*locale* ... KY-4
**Indian Valley**—*pop pl* ... ID-8
**Indian Valley**—*pop pl* ... KS-7
**Indian Valley**—*pop pl* ... VA-3
Indian Valley—*valley* (7) ... CA-9
Indian Valley—*valley* (2) ... CO-8
Indian Valley—*valley* ... ID-8
Indian Valley—*valley* (2) ... NV-8
Indian Valley—*valley* ... OR-9
Indian Valley Branch—*stream* ... TN-4
Indian Valley Camp—*locale* ... AL-4
Indian Valley Camp Ground—*locale* ... CA-9
Indian Valley Camp Lake—*reservoir* ... AL-4
Indian Valley Camp Lake Dam—*dam* ... AL-4
Indian Valley Cem—*cemetery* ... ID-8
Indian Valley Ch—*church* ... VA-3
Indian Valley Country Club—*other* ... IL-6
Indian Valley Creek—*stream* ... CA-9
*Indian Valley Elementary School* ... AL-4
**Indian Valley Estates (subdivision)**—*pop pl* ... UT-8
Indian Valley Golf Course—*locale* ... PA-2
Indian Valley Guard Station—*locale* ... CA-9
**Indian Valley (historical)**—*pop pl* ... OR-9
Indian Valley Hot Springs—*spring* ... CA-9
Indian Valley JHS—*school* ... PA-2
Indian Valley Lake—*reservoir* (2) ... AL-4
*Indian Valley Lake Dam* ... AL-4
Indian Valley (Magisterial District)—*fmr MCD* ... VA-3
Indian Valley Mine—*mine* ... CA-9
Indian Valley Rsvr—*reservoir* ... CA-9
Indian Valley Sch—*school* ... AL-4
Indian Valley Sch—*school* (2) ... CA-9
Indian Valley Sch—*school* ... IA-7
Indian Valley Sch—*school* ... OH-6
Indian Valley Sch—*school* ... VA-3
**Indian Valley (subdivision)**—*pop pl* ... AL-4
**Indianview**—*pop pl* ... OH-6
Indian View Point—*locale* ... WA-9
Indian View Sch—*school* ... VA-3
*Indian Village* (2) ... IN-6
*Indian Village* ... MI-6
*Indian Village* ... MO-7
Indian Village—*locale* (2) ... AK-9
Indian Village—*locale* ... KS-7
Indian Village—*locale* ... NV-8
Indian Village—*locale* ... OR-9
Indian Village—*locale* ... TX-5
Indian Village—*locale* ... UT-8
**Indian Village**—*pop pl* ... CA-9
**Indian Village**—*pop pl* (4) ... IN-6
**Indian Village**—*pop pl* (3) ... LA-4
**Indian Village**—*pop pl* ... MO-7
**Indian Village**—*pop pl* ... NY-2
**Indian Village**—*pop pl* ... OK-5
**Indian Village**—*pop pl* ... OR-9
**Indian Village**—*pop pl* ... PA-2
**Indian Village**—*pop pl* ... WA-9
**Indian Village (Alcinda)**—*pop pl* ... IN-6
Indian Village Boys Camp—*locale* ... MI-6
Indian Village Camp—*locale* ... OH-6
Indian Village Cem—*cemetery* ... MI-6
Indian Village Ch—*church* ... LA-4
Indian Village Ch—*church* ... MS-4
Indian Village (Eagle Village)—*other* ... AK-9
Indian Village Elem Sch—*school* ... IN-6
Indian Village Hist Dist—*hist pl* ... MI-6
*Indian Village Lake* ... IN-6
Indian Village Landing Strip—*airport* ... SD-7
Indian Village Park—*park* ... MI-6
Indian Village Shop Ctr—*locale* ... AZ-5
Indian Village Site—*hist pl* ... IA-7
Indian Village (Site)—*locale* ... WA-9
**Indian Village South**—*pop pl* ... UT-8
Indian Village State Park—*park* ... IA-7
**Indian Village Subdivision**—*pop pl* (2) ... UT-8
Indian Village Township—*fmr MCD* ... IA-7
Indian Walk Shoals—*bar* ... TN-4
Indian Wash—*stream* ... AZ-5
Indian Wash—*stream* ... CA-9
Indian Wash—*stream* ... CO-8
Indian Wash—*valley* ... UT-8
Indian Water Canyon—*valley* ... CO-8
Indian Water Hole—*lake* (2) ... TX-5
Indian Water Hole—*reservoir* ... NM-5
Indian Waterhole Draw—*valley* ... TX-5
Indian Waterhole Windmill—*locale* ... TX-5
*Indian Water Seep* ... UT-8
Indianwater Seep—*spring* ... UT-8
Indian Well—*locale* ... CA-9
Indian Well—*locale* (3) ... NM-5
Indian Well—*well* (4) ... AZ-5
Indian Well—*well* ... CA-9
Indian Well—*well* (2) ... NV-8
Indian Well—*well* (4) ... NM-5
Indian Well—*well* (2) ... TX-5
Indian Well Bay—*swamp* ... FL-3
Indian Wells—*locale* ... AZ-5
Indian Wells—*locale* ... TX-5
**Indian Wells**—*pop pl* (2) ... CA-9
Indian Wells—*well* ... NM-5
Indian Wells Canyon—*valley* (2) ... CA-9
Indian Wells (CCD)—*cens area* ... AZ-5
*Indian Wells Creek* ... TX-5
Indian Wells Golf Course—*other* ... CA-9
**Indian Wells Subdivision**—*pop pl* ... UT-8
Indian Well State Park—*park* ... CT-1
Indian Wells Valley—*valley* ... CA-9
Indian Well Swamp—*stream* ... NC-3
Indian Well Wash—*stream* ... AZ-5
Indian Windmill—*locale* (2) ... NM-5
Indian Windmill—*locale* ... TX-5
Indian Woman Bayou—*stream* ... AR-4
Indianwood Ch—*church* ... MI-6
Indianwood Country Club—*other* ... MI-6
Indianwood Lake—*lake* ... MI-6
Indian Woods—*forest* ... CT-1
Indian Woods Ch—*church* ... NC-3
Indian Woods (Township of)—*fmr MCD* ... NC-3
Indian Writing Water Hole—*spring* ... ID-8
*India Point* ... RI-1
India Point—*cape* ... RI-1
India Post Office (historical)—*building* ... TN-4
India Sch (historical)—*school* ... TN-4
Indias Tank—*reservoir* ... TX-5
India Temple Shrine Bldg—*hist pl* ... OK-5
Indiatlantic Elem Sch—*school* ... FL-3
India Wharf—*locale* ... MA-1
Indicator Mine (Inactive)—*mine* ... NV-8
Indicator Peak—*summit* ... CA-9
Indice HS—*school* ... LA-4
Indicuts Gap—*gap* ... VA-3
**Indiera**—*pop pl* ... PR-3
**Indiera Alta**—*pop pl* ... PR-3
Indiera Alta (Barrio)—*fmr MCD* ... PR-3
Indiera Baja (Barrio)—*fmr MCD* ... PR-3
Indigo, Bayou—*stream* ... LA-4
Indigo, Lake—*lake* ... FL-3
Indigo Bay—*basin* ... SC-3
Indigo Bay—*swamp* ... SC-3
Indigo Bayou—*stream* (2) ... LA-4
Indigo Branch—*stream* ... FL-3
Indigo Branch—*stream* ... NC-3
Indigo Branch—*stream* ... SC-3
Indigo Branch—*stream* ... VA-3
Indigo Bridge—*bridge* ... SC-3
Indigo Creek—*stream* ... AL-4
Indigo Creek—*stream* ... FL-3
Indigo Creek—*stream* ... OH-6
Indigo Creek—*stream* (3) ... OR-9
Indigo Creek—*stream* ... WA-9
*Indigo Head* ... AL-4
Indigo Head—*cliff* ... FL-3
Indigo Hill—*summit* ... NH-1
Indigo Island—*island* ... NC-3
Indigo Island—*island* ... SC-3
Indigo Knob—*summit* ... AR-4
Indigo Lake—*lake* ... AK-9
Indigo Lake—*lake* ... ID-8
Indigo Lake—*lake* ... NY-2
Indigo Lake—*lake* ... OR-9
Indigo Lake—*lake* ... WA-9
Indigo Lake—*reservoir* ... VA-3
Indigo Point—*cape* ... MD-2
Indigo Pond—*lake* ... AL-4
Indigo Pond—*lake* ... CO-8
Indigo Pond—*reservoir* ... FL-3
Indigo Ponds—*lake* ... AL-4
Indigo Prairie—*flat* ... OR-9
Indigo Ridge—*ridge* ... SC-3
Indigot Creek—*stream* ... NY-2
**Indigo Terrace**—*pop pl* ... VA-3
Indigo Tunnel—*reservoir* ... MD-2
Indika—*locale* ... VA-3
Indi-Llli Park—*park* ... IN-6
Indio—*locale* ... TX-5
**Indio**—*pop pl* ... CA-9
Indio, Arroyo—*valley* ... TX-5
Indio Arroyo—*stream* ... NM-5
Indio Canyon—*valley* ... CA-9
Indio Canyon—*valley* ... NM-5
Indio Cattle Company—*locale* ... TX-5
Indio Creek—*stream* ... TX-5
Indio Hill—*summit* ... TX-5
**Indio Hills**—*pop pl* ... CA-9
Indio Hills—*range* ... CA-9
Indio (historical)—*locale* ... AL-4
Indio Lake—*lake* ... TX-5
*Indiola Landing* ... OR-9
Indio Mine (underground)—*mine* ... AL-4
Indio Mtn—*summit* ... CA-9
Indio Ranch—*locale* ... TX-5
Indio Road Tank—*reservoir* ... NM-5
Indios—*CDP* ... PR-3
Indios (Barrio)—*fmr MCD* ... PR-3
Indio Tank—*reservoir* ... AZ-5
Indio Tank—*reservoir* (2) ... TX-5
*Indipendent* ... PA-2
Inditos Camp—*locale* ... NM-5
Inditos Draw—*valley* ... NM-5
Individualized Language Acad—*school* ... FL-3
Indland Junction—*locale* ... AL-4
Indleside—*uninc pl* ... MA-1
*Indone* ... WV-2
Indonesian Embassy—*hist pl* ... DC-2
Indooli Mtn—*summit* ... AK-9
**Indore**—*pop pl* ... WV-2
Indore Chapel—*church* ... WV-2
Indo Windmill—*locale* ... NM-5
Indrio—*locale* ... FL-3
**Indrio-Saint Lucie**—*pop pl* ... FL-3
**Indus**—*pop pl* ... MN-6
Industria HS—*school* ... NY-2
*Industrial* ... ME-1
*Industrial* ... MN-6
**Industrial**—*pop pl* ... MS-4
**Industrial**—*pop pl* ... SC-3
**Industrial**—*pop pl* ... WV-2
Industrial—*uninc pl* ... AR-4
Industrial—*uninc pl* (2) ... CA-9
Industrial—*uninc pl* ... LA-4
Industrial—*uninc pl* ... TX-5
Industrial Airport—*post sta* ... KS-7
Industrial Arts Bldg—*hist pl* ... AZ-5
Industrial Arts Bldg—*hist pl* ... KY-4
Industrial Bldg—*hist pl* ... MD-2
Industrial Canal—*canal* ... TX-5
Industrial Cem—*cemetery* ... MN-6
Industrial Center Spur—*locale* ... UT-8
Industrial Ch—*church* ... MN-6
**Industrial City**—*pop pl* ... AL-4
Industrial City of Gordon/Murray/Whitfield Counties—*inactive* ... GA-3
Industrial Elem Sch (historical)—*school* ... MS-4
Industrial Farm Sch—*school* ... NY-2
**Industrial (Great Southwest Industrial Park)**—*pop pl* ... GA-3
Industrial-Hillside—*uninc pl* ... NJ-2
Industrial Hist Dist—*locale* ... TN-4
Industrial Home of the Blind—*building* ... NY-2
Industrial Home (State Training School)—*school* ... MI-6
*Industrial Institute and Coll* ... MS-4
*Industrial Island* ... MI-6
Industrial Mutual Association Auditorium—*hist pl* ... MI-6
**Industrial Park**—*pop pl* ... VA-3
Industrial Park Number 1—*locale* ... MS-4
Industrial Park Number 2—*locale* ... MS-4
**Industrial (RR name Industrial School)**—*pop pl* ... WV-2
Industrial Savings Bank Bldg—*hist pl* ... MI-6
Industrial Sch—*school* ... AL-4
Industrial Sch—*school* ... NY-2
Industrial Sch—*school* ... OK-5
Industrial School (RR name for Industrial)—*other* ... WV-2
**Industrial (Township of)**—*pop pl* ... MN-6
Industrial Trackage Subdivision—*locale* ... UT-8
*Industry* ... IN-6
Industry—*locale* ... IA-7
Industry—*locale* ... NY-2
Industry—*locale* ... PA-2
Industry—*locale* ... WV-2
**Industry**—*pop pl* ... AL-4
**Industry**—*pop pl* ... GA-3
**Industry**—*pop pl* ... IL-6
**Industry**—*pop pl* (2) ... KS-7
**Industry**—*pop pl* ... OH-6
**Industry**—*pop pl* ... PA-2
**Industry**—*pop pl* ... TX-5
**Industry (Agricultural and Industrial School)**—*pop pl* ... NY-2
Industry Borough—*civil* ... PA-2
Industry Canal—*canal* (2) ... LA-4
Industry Cem—*cemetery* ... NE-7
**Industry (City of Industry Post Office)**—*pop pl* ... CA-9
**Industry (corporate name for City of Industry)**—*pop pl* ... CA-9
Industry Creek—*stream* ... OR-9
**Industry (Frank P O)**—*pop pl* (2) ... PA-2
Industry Park—*park* ... OH-6
Industry-Rock Falls Township—*civ div* ... NE-7
Industry Sch—*school* ... AL-4
Industry Sch—*school* ... IL-6
**Industry Spur**—*pop pl* ... NM-5
**Industry (Town of)**—*pop pl* ... ME-1
Industry Township—*civil* ... PA-2
**Industry (Township of)**—*pop pl* ... IL-6
Industry Track RR Station and Siding—*building* ... AZ-5
*Ine* ... MP-9
**Ine**—*pop pl* ... MP-9
Ine Anchorage—*harbor* ... MP-9
*Ine-byochi* ... MP-9
Inedo—*area* ... GU-9
Inedral—*island* ... MP-9
*Ine Island* ... MP-9
Ine Island—*island* ... MP-9
Inemp—*island* ... FM-9
*Inenyaaru* ... MP-9
*Inenyaaru-To* ... MP-9
Inerarity Point—*cape* ... FL-3
Inerevuk Mtn—*summit* ... AK-9
Inerto Mine—*mine* ... CA-9
*Ineruri* ... MP-9
*Ineruri Island* ... MP-9
*Ineruri-To* ... MP-9
Ines, Lake—*reservoir* ... AL-4
*Ine-to* ... MP-9
*Inewa* ... MP-9
*Inewa-To* ... MP-9
*Inez* ... VA-3
Inez—*locale* ... MN-6
Inez—*locale* ... NM-5
Inez—*locale* ... NC-3
Inez—*locale* ... PA-2
Inez—*locale* ... WV-2
**Inez**—*pop pl* ... KY-4
**Inez**—*pop pl* ... TX-5
**Inez**—*pop pl* ... VA-3
Inez, Lake—*lake* ... MT-8
Inez, Lake—*reservoir* ... GA-3
Inez, Lake—*reservoir* ... NJ-2
Inez Ch—*church* ... NC-3
Inez Creek—*stream* ... MT-8
Inez Gulch—*valley* ... NV-8
Inez (historical)—*locale* ... MS-4
Inez Hotel—*hist pl* ... MS-4
Inez Lagoon—*lake* ... LA-4
Inez Park—*park* ... NM-5
Inez Point—*cape* ... MT-8
Inez (reduced usage)—*locale* ... NE-7
Inez Rock—*rock* ... MA-1
Inez Sch—*school* ... NM-5
Inez Sch—*school* ... PA-2
Inez Tank—*reservoir* ... AZ-5
Infant Buttes—*summit* ... CA-9
Infant Hill Cem—*cemetery* ... AL-4
*Infant Jesus of Prague Church* ... MS-4
Infant of Prague Brighter Day Spiritual Ch—*church* ... IN-6
Infant of Prague Sch—*school* ... NY-2
Infant of Prague Shrine—*church* ... NY-2
Infant of Prague Villa—*locale* ... OH-6
*Infantry Camp* ... AZ-5
Infantry Lake—*lake* ... LA-4
Infernal Caverns—*cave* ... CA-9
Infernal Caverns Battleground Memorial Marker—*park* ... CA-9
Inferno, The—*cliff* ... AZ-5
Inferno Canyon—*valley* ... MT-8
Inferno Cave—*cave* ... TN-4
Inferno Chasm—*valley* ... ID-8
Inferno Cone—*summit* ... ID-8
Inferno Lakes—*lake* ... CA-9
Inferno Reef—*bar* ... AK-9
Infidel Hollow—*valley* ... IL-6
Infiernillo Artesian Well—*well* ... TX-5
Infierno, Canon—*valley* ... CO-8
*Infierno Creek* ... TX-5
Infinity Archeol Site—*hist pl* ... KS-7
Infinity Rd Raw Water Reservoir Dam—*dam* ... NC-3
Infinity Rd Raw Water Rsvr—*reservoir* ... NC-3
Infirmary Cem—*cemetery* (3) ... OH-6
Infirmary Cem—*cemetery* ... WV-2
Infirmary Ditch—*canal* ... OH-6
Infirmary Run—*stream* ... OH-6
Influence, The—*hist pl* ... ME-1
*Infred Park Subdivision* ... UT-8
Inga Creek—*stream* ... MN-6
Ingakslugwat Hills—*other* ... AK-9
Inga Lake—*lake* ... MN-6
Ingall Cem—*cemetery* ... OK-5
Ingall Drain—*stream* ... MI-6
*Ingalls* ... KS-7
Ingalls—*locale* ... AR-4
Ingalls—*locale* ... ME-1
**Ingalls**—*pop pl* ... IN-6
**Ingalls**—*pop pl* ... KS-7
**Ingalls**—*pop pl* ... ME-1
**Ingalls**—*pop pl* ... MI-6
**Ingalls**—*pop pl* ... NC-3
**Ingalls**—*pop pl* ... OK-5
Ingalls, Lake—*lake* ... WA-9
Ingalls, Mount—*summit* ... CA-9
Ingalls, Mount—*summit* ... NH-1
Ingalls Ave Baptist Ch—*church* ... MS-4
Ingalls Bldg—*hist pl* ... OH-6
Ingalls Bluff—*cliff* ... CA-9
Ingalls Brook—*stream* (2) ... ME-1
Ingalls Brook—*stream* ... NH-1
Ingalls Cem—*cemetery* ... NY-2
Ingalls Creek—*stream* ... CA-9
Ingalls Creek—*stream* ... MO-7
Ingalls Creek—*stream* ... MT-8
Ingalls Creek—*stream* ... WA-9
Ingalls Crossing—*locale* ... NY-2
Ingalls Elem Sch—*school* ... KS-7
Ingalls Field (Airport)—*airport* ... VA-3
Ingalls Gulch—*valley* ... CO-8
**Ingall's Hill**—*pop pl* ... ME-1
Ingalls Hill—*summit* ... ME-1
Ingalls Hill—*summit* ... VT-1
Ingalls Hill Cem—*cemetery* ... ME-1
Ingalls House—*hist pl* ... ME-1
Ingalls House—*hist pl* ... SD-7
Ingalls Island—*island* ... ME-1
*Ingalls Landing Strip* ... KS-7
Ingalls-Logan Cem—*cemetery* ... KS-7
Ingalls Marsh—*swamp* ... NY-2
Ingalls Memorial Hosp—*hospital* ... IL-6
*Ingalls Mountain* ... NH-1
Ingalls Mtn—*summit* ... MT-8
Ingalls Municipal Airp—*airport* ... KS-7
Ingalls Park—*park* ... FL-3
**Ingalls Park**—*pop pl* ... IL-6
Ingalls Pass—*gap* ... WA-9
Ingalls Peak—*summit* ... WA-9
*Ingalls Pond* ... ME-1
Ingalls Pond—*lake* ... ME-1
Ingalls Ranch—*locale* ... CA-9
Ingalls Sch—*school* ... KS-7
Ingalls Sch—*school* ... MA-1
Ingalls Sch—*school* ... NY-2
Ingalls Siding—*locale* ... ME-1
Ingalls Station (historical)—*locale* (2) ... MA-1
Ingalls Swamp—*swamp* ... CA-9
Ingalls Swamp Ranch—*locale* ... CA-9
Ingallston—*locale* ... MI-6
**Ingallston**—*pop pl* ... IN-6
*Ingallstone* ... MI-6
**Ingallston (Township of)**—*pop pl* ... MI-6
**Ingalls Township**—*pop pl* ... KS-7
Ingalls-Wheeler-Horton Homstead Site—*hist pl* ... MA-1
Ingalsbe Slough—*stream* ... CA-9
Ingals Creek—*stream* ... ID-8
**Ingalton**—*pop pl* ... IL-6
Ingaluat Creek—*stream* ... AK-9
Ingard—*locale* ... ID-8
Ingariak Hills—*other* ... AK-9
Ingart (historical)—*locale* ... IA-7
Ingate—*locale* ... AL-4
**Ingberg Tracts (subdivision)**—*pop pl* ... SD-7
Ingeborg, Lake—*lake* ... ID-8
Ingebrand Dam—*dam* ... OR-9
Ingebrand Rsvr—*reservoir* ... OR-9
Ingebretson, Gaute, Loft House—*hist pl* ... WI-6
Ingebretson Park—*park* ... IA-7
Ingebrigtsen-Hinseth Farmstead—*hist pl* ... SD-7
Inge Cave—*cave* ... AL-4
Ingehosia Farms Lake Dam—*dam* ... MS-4
Ingelnook Sch—*school* ... SC-3
Ingelside Landing (historical)—*locale* ... MS-4
Ingels Sch—*school* ... CA-9
Ingemann Ch—*church* ... IA-7
Ingem Gut—*stream* ... MD-2
Inge Mtn—*summit* ... TX-5
Ingenio—*CDP* ... PR-3
**Ingenio**—*pop pl* ... PR-3
Ingenio Azucarero Vives—*hist pl* ... PR-3
*Ingen Lake* ... MN-6
Ingensoll Industrial Park (subdivision)—*locale* ... UT-8
**Inger**—*pop pl* ... AK-9
**Inger**—*pop pl* ... MN-6
Inge Ranch—*locale* ... CO-8
Ingerman Ditch—*canal* ... IN-6
Ingerman Lake—*lake* ... MI-6
Ingersall Branch—*stream* ... NJ-2
*Ingersall Creek* ... MT-8
Ingersol Butte—*summit* ... MT-8
Ingersol Canyon—*valley* ... NV-8
Ingersol Hill—*summit* ... PA-2
Ingersoll—*locale* ... OK-5
**Ingersoll**—*pop pl* ... WI-6
Ingersoll, Cyrus J., House—*hist pl* ... OH-6
Ingersoll, John N., House—*hist pl* ... MI-6
Ingersoll, Robert, Birthplace—*hist pl* ... NY-2
**Ingersoll Addition (subdivision)**—*pop pl* ... UT-8
Ingersoll Branch—*stream* ... ME-1
Ingersoll Cem—*cemetery* ... IL-6
Ingersoll Cem—*cemetery* ... NY-2
Ingersoll Creek—*stream* ... MT-8
Ingersoll Creek—*stream* ... OK-5
Ingersoll Dam—*dam* ... NJ-2
Ingersoll Gulch—*valley* ... OR-9
**Ingersoll (historical)**—*pop pl* ... IA-7
Ingersoll Lake—*lake* ... MI-6
Ingersoll Lake—*swamp* ... MS-4
Ingersoll Memorial Park—*park* ... IL-6
Ingersoll Mine—*mine* ... SD-7
Ingersoll Peak—*summit* ... SD-7
Ingersoll Point—*cape* ... ME-1
Ingersoll Rsvr—*reservoir* ... NJ-2
Ingersolls Branch—*stream* ... NJ-2
Ingersoll Sch—*school* (2) ... IL-6
*Ingersolls Creek* ... MT-8
Ingersolls Island—*island* ... MN-6
Ingersoll Tile Elevator—*hist pl* ... OK-5
**Ingersoll (Township of)**—*pop pl* ... MI-6
Ingersoll Wash—*valley* ... WY-8
Ingersol Memorial for Aged Men—*other* ... NY-2
Ingersol Sch—*school* ... LA-4
Ingersol Sch—*school* ... SD-7
Ingersols Landing—*locale* ... MS-4
Ingerson Cem—*cemetery* ... MI-6
Ingerson Cem—*cemetery* ... NY-2
Ingerson Lake—*lake* ... MI-6
Ingham—*locale* ... VA-3
Ingham Canyon—*valley* ... UT-8
**Ingham (County)**—*pop pl* ... MI-6
Ingham County Courthouse—*hist pl* ... MI-6
Ingham Creek Dam—*dam* ... PA-2
Ingham Hill—*summit* ... CT-1
Ingham Hill—*summit* ... ME-1
Ingham (historical P.O.)—*locale* (2) ... IA-7
Ingham Hosp—*hospital* ... MI-6
Ingham Lake—*lake* ... IA-7
**Ingham Mills**—*pop pl* ... NY-2
**Ingham Mills Station**—*pop pl* ... NY-2
Ingham Park—*park* ... MI-6
Ingham Park—*park* ... OK-5
Ingham Pass—*gap* ... UT-8
*Ingham Peak* ... UT-8
Ingham Peak—*summit* ... CA-9
Ingham Peak—*summit* ... UT-8
Ingham Ponds—*reservoir* ... CT-1
Ingham Ranch—*locale* ... TX-5
Ingham Sch (historical)—*school* ... AL-4
Ingham School (Abandoned)—*locale* ... NE-7
*Ingham Spring* ... PA-2
Ingham Stream—*stream* ... ME-1
Ingham Township—*fmr MCD* ... IA-7
**Ingham (Township of)**—*pop pl* ... MI-6
Ingham Valley—*valley* ... AL-4
Inghan Pond—*lake* ... ME-1
Inghram Branch—*stream* ... IA-7
Ingitkalik Mtn—*summit* ... AK-9
Ingle—*locale* ... CA-9
Ingle—*locale* ... FL-3
Ingle—*locale* ... KY-4
Ingle—*locale* ... WI-6
Ingle Airstrip—*airport* ... SD-7
Ingle Branch—*stream* ... NC-3
Ingleby—*locale* ... PA-2
**Ingleby**—*pop pl* ... PA-2
Ingle Cem—*cemetery* ... IL-6
Ingle Cem—*cemetery* ... OR-9
Ingle Cem—*cemetery* (4) ... TN-4
Ingle Cem—*cemetery* (2) ... VA-3
Ingle Creek—*stream* ... AK-9
Ingle Creek—*stream* ... OR-9
**Inglefield**—*pop pl* ... IN-6
*Inglefield (Ingle)* ... IN-6
*Inglehome* ... FL-3
*Ingle (Inglefield)* ... IN-6
**Ingle Mann**—*pop pl* ... OH-6
*Ingle Mills* ... AL-4
Inglemoor County Park—*park* ... WA-9
Inglemoor HS—*school* ... WA-9
Ingle Mtn—*summit* ... OR-9
Inglenook—*locale* ... PA-2
**Inglenook**—*pop pl* ... AL-4
**Inglenook**—*pop pl* ... CA-9
Inglenook Cem—*cemetery* ... CA-9
Inglenook Creek—*stream* ... CA-9
Inglenook Park—*park* ... AL-4
*Inglenook School* ... AL-4
Ingle Post Office (historical)—*building* ... AL-4
Ingle Ranch—*locale* ... CA-9
Ingle Rock—*pillar* ... OR-9
Ingle Rocks—*summit* ... TN-4
Ingles Bottom Archeol Sites—*hist pl* ... VA-3
Inglesby Rapids—*rapids* ... UT-8
Ingles Chapel—*church* ... VA-3
Ingles Coulee—*valley* ... MT-8
Ingles Creek—*stream* ... MT-8
Ingles Drain—*stream* ... MI-6
Inglesea—*locale* ... WA-9
Ingleses Windmill—*locale* (2) ... TX-5
Ingles Ferry—*hist pl* ... VA-3
Ingles Fields Gap—*gap* ... NC-3
Ingles Gap—*gap* ... NC-3
Ingleside—*building* ... TN-4
Ingleside—*CDP* ... IL-6
Ingleside—*hist pl* ... DC-2
Ingleside—*hist pl* ... NY-2
Ingleside—*hist pl* ... NC-3
Ingleside—*hist pl* ... SC-3
Ingleside—*hist pl* ... VA-3
Ingleside—*locale* ... AR-4
Ingleside—*locale* ... LA-4
Ingleside—*locale* ... MS-4
Ingleside—*locale* ... NE-7
**Ingleside**—*pop pl* ... CA-9
**Ingleside**—*pop pl* ... IL-6
**Ingleside**—*pop pl* ... KY-4
**Ingleside**—*pop pl* ... MD-2
**Ingleside**—*pop pl* ... MA-1
**Ingleside**—*pop pl* ... MI-6
**Ingleside**—*pop pl* ... NY-2
**Ingleside**—*pop pl* ... NC-3
**Ingleside**—*pop pl* ... PA-2
**Ingleside**—*pop pl* ... SC-3
**Ingleside**—*pop pl* ... TX-5
**Ingleside**—*pop pl* (2) ... VA-3
**Ingleside**—*pop pl* ... WV-2
Ingleside—*uninc pl* ... GA-3
Ingleside Cem—*cemetery* ... MS-4
Ingleside Cem—*cemetery* ... TX-5
Ingleside Ch—*church* (2) ... GA-3
Ingleside Corners—*locale* ... NY-2
Ingleside Cove—*bay* ... TX-5
*Ingleside Elementary School* ... TN-4
Ingleside Elem Sch—*school* ... AZ-5
Ingleside Golf Course—*locale* ... PA-2
**Ingleside Hill**—*pop pl* ... TN-4
*Ingleside Hills* ... TN-4
Ingleside (historical)—*locale* ... IA-7
**Ingleside on the Bay**—*pop pl* ... TX-5
Ingleside Park—*park* ... MA-1
Ingleside Park—*park* ... VA-3
*Ingleside (P.O.)* ... IL-6

Ingleside Point—cape TX-5
Ingleside Post Office (historical)—building AL-4
Ingleside Post Office (historical)—building MS-4
Ingleside Post Office (historical)—building PA-2
Ingleside Quarry—mine MT-8
Ingleside Sch—school TN-4
Ingleside Sch—school (2) VA-3
Ingleside Sch (historical)—school MS-4
**Ingleside Shore**—pop pl IL-6
**Ingleside Shores**—pop pl IL-6
Ingleside Spring—spring TN-4
**Ingleside Village (subdivision)**—pop pl AL-4
Ingles (Magisterial District)—fmr MCD VA-3
**Inglesmith**—pop pl PA-2
Ingles Mtn—summit VA-3
Ingle Terrace—hist pl IN-6
**Inglo Torrace** pop pl AL-4
Ingleton (historical)—locale AL-4
Ingleton P.O. AL-4
Ingleton Quarry—mine AL-4
Inglett Cem—cemetery GA-3
Ingleville—locale IA-7
Inglewood—hist pl VA-3
Inglewood—locale LA-4
Inglewood—locale VA-3
Inglewood—locale WA-9
**Inglewood**—pop pl CA-9
**Inglewood**—pop pl NE-7
**Inglewood**—pop pl PA-2
**Inglewood**—pop pl TN-4
Inglewood (CCD)—cens area CA-9
Inglewood Ch—church VA-3
Inglewood Country Club—other WA-9
Inglewood Elementary School PA-2
Inglewood Hills—other WA-9
Inglewood HS—school CA-9
Inglewood (Inglewood Hills)—CDP WA-9
Inglewood Junior Acad—school CA-9
Inglewood Park Cem—cemetery CA-9
Inglewood Plantation Hist Dist—hist pl LA-4
Inglewood Sch—school PA-2
Ingley Cove—bay ME-1
**Inglis**—pop pl FL-3
**Inglis**—pop pl OR-9
Inglis Branch—stream AL-4
Inglis Cem—cemetery AL-4
Inglis Hollow—valley AL-4
Inglish Ranch—locale AZ-5
Inglis Point—cape AL-4
Inglis Sch—school MO-7
Ingloothloogramiut (Summer Camp)—locale AK-9
Inguilngok Mtn—summit AK-9
Inglutalik River—stream AK-9
Ingman Ranch—locale ND-7
Ingmar Elem Sch—school PA-2
Ingmar MS—school PA-2
**Ingo**—pop pl WV-2
In God We Trust Cem—cemetery MI-6
Ingoes Creek—stream NC-3
**Ingold**—pop pl NC-3
Ingold Ch—church NC-3
Ingold Pond—lake NC-3
Ingold-Taylors Bridge Sch—school NC-3
Ingol Fork—stream KY-4
Ingomar MS-4
Ingomar—locale CA-9
**Ingomar**—pop pl MS-4
**Ingomar**—pop pl MT-8
**Ingomar**—pop pl OH-6
**Ingomar**—pop pl PA-2
Ingomar Baptist Ch—church MS-4
Ingomar Cem—cemetery MS-4
Ingomar Gun Club—other CA-9
**Ingomar (historical)**—pop pl MS-4
Ingomar Lake—lake MT-8
Ingomar Mound—hist pl MS-4
Ingomar Post Office (historical)—building MS-4
Ingomar Ranch—locale CA-9
Ingomar Sch—school MS-4
**Ingot**—pop pl CA-9
Ingot Cove—bay AK-9
Ingot Island—island AK-9
**Ingraham**—pop pl IL-6
**Ingraham**—pop pl NY-2
Ingraham, Charles H., Cottage—hist pl ME-1
Ingraham, Joseph Holt, House—hist pl ME-1
Ingraham, Lake—lake FL-3
Ingraham Bay—bay AK-9
Ingraham Brook—stream MA-1
Ingraham Cem—cemetery TN-4
Ingraham Center Sch—school IA-7
Ingraham Corners—locale NY-2
Ingraham Creek—stream AK-9
Ingraham Glacier—glacier WA-9
Ingraham Hassock—island NY-2
Ingraham Hill—summit ME-1
Ingraham Hill—summit MA-1
Ingraham Hill—summit NY-2
Ingraham Hill—summit VT-1
Ingraham Hill Cem—cemetery NY-2
Ingraham (historical)—locale (2) MS-4
Ingraham Hollow—valley AL-4
Ingraham HS—school WA-9
Ingraham Lateral—canal AZ-5
Ingraham Mtn—summit NC-3
Ingraham Plaza (Shop Ctr)—locale FL-3
Ingraham P. O. (historical)—locale AL-4
Ingraham Point—cape AK-9
Ingraham Point—cape ME-1
Ingraham Pond—lake NY-2
Ingraham Post Office (historical)—building MS-4
Ingraham Stream—stream NY-2
Ingraham Terrace—park FL-3
Ingraham Township—fmr MCD IA-7
Ingrakaklak—locale AK-9
Ingram—locale AR-4
Ingram—locale KY-4
Ingram—locale VA-3
**Ingram**—pop pl AL-4
**Ingram**—pop pl (2) NC-3
**Ingram**—pop pl PA-2
**Ingram**—pop pl TX-5
**Ingram**—pop pl WI-6
Ingram, Lake—lake FL-3
Ingram, William, House—hist pl KY-4
Ingram Arkadelphia Lake—reservoir AL-4
Ingram Baptist Church MS-4
Ingram Basin—basin CO-8
Ingram Bay—bay VA-3
Ingram Bayou—stream AL-4
**Ingram Beach**—pop pl SC-3
Ingram Bend—bend KY-4
Ingram Blvd Ch—church AR-4
Ingram Borough—civil PA-2
Ingram Branch DE-2
Ingram Branch MD-2
**Ingram Branch**—pop pl WV-2
Ingram Branch—stream AL-4
Ingram Branch—stream (2) DE-2
Ingram Branch—stream (2) KY-4
Ingram Branch—stream (2) NC-3
Ingram Branch—stream (2) TN-4
Ingram Branch Ch—church NC-3
Ingram Butte—summit OR-9
Ingram Camp—locale AL-4
Ingram Camp—locale OR-9
Ingram Canyon—valley (2) CA-9
Ingram Canyon—valley UT-8
Ingram Cave—cave TN-4
Ingram (CCD)—cens area TX-5
Ingram Cem—cemetery AL-4
Ingram Cem—cemetery AR-4
Ingram Cem—cemetery GA-3
Ingram Cem—cemetery IL-6
Ingram Cem—cemetery (3) KY-4
Ingram Cem—cemetery (3) MS-4
Ingram Cem—cemetery NM-5
Ingram Cem—cemetery (2) NC-3
Ingram Cem—cemetery (2) TN-4
Ingram Cem—cemetery (5) TX-5
Ingram Cem—cemetery WI-6
Ingram Ch—church MS-4
Ingram Ch—church WV-2
Ingram Chapel—church NC-3
Ingram Cove—bay NJ-2
Ingram Cove—bay VA-3
Ingram Creek—stream AL-4
Ingram Creek—stream AK-9
Ingram Creek—stream (4) AR-4
Ingram Creek—stream (2) CA-9
Ingram Creek—stream CO-8
Ingram Creek—stream FL-3
Ingram Creek—stream GA-3
Ingram Creek—stream KY-4
Ingram Creek—stream MO-7
Ingram Creek—stream OR-9
Ingram Creek Sch—school KY-4
Ingram Draft—valley VA-3
Ingram Falls—falls CO-8
Ingram Family Cem—cemetery AL-4
Ingram Flat—flat CA-9
Ingram Ford—locale AL-4
Ingram Guard Station—locale OR-9
Ingram Gulch—valley CO-8
**Ingram Hill**—pop pl IL-6
Ingram Hill—summit (2) TN-4
Ingram Hill Ch—church IL-6
**Ingram (historical)**—pop pl MS-4
Ingram Hollow—valley AL-4
Ingram Hollow—valley PA-2
Ingram Hollow—valley TN-4
Ingram Hollow—valley UT-8
Ingram House—hist pl OK-5
Ingram Island—island OR-9
Ingram Lake MI-6
Ingram Lake—lake AL-4
Ingram Lake—lake AR-4
Ingram Lake—lake CO-8
Ingram Lake—lake IL-6
Ingram Lake—lake MN-6
Ingram Lake—lake NM-5
Ingram Lake—reservoir (2) AL-4
Ingram Lake—reservoir TN-4
Ingram Lake Dam—dam AL-4
Ingram Mill (historical)—locale (2) AL-4
Ingram Millpond—reservoir VA-3
Ingram Mtn—summit NC-3
Ingram Park—park AL-4
Ingram Park—park FL-3
Ingram Park Mall—locale TX-5
Ingram Peak OR-9
Ingram Peak—summit CO-8
Ingram Point OR-9
Ingram Point—summit OR-9
Ingram Pond—lake DE-2
Ingram Pond—reservoir AL-4
Ingram Pond—swamp DE-2
Ingram Pond Number One AL-4
Ingram Pond Number Two—reservoir AL-4
Ingram Private Airp—airport MO-7
Ingram Ranch—locale (2) CO-8
Ingram Ridge Cem—cemetery MO-7
Ingram Ridge Ch—church MO-7
Ingrams IL-6
Ingrams MS-4
**Ingrams**—pop pl MS-4
Ingrams Branch TN-4
Ingrams Cem—cemetery MS-4
Ingram Sch—school GA-3
Ingram Sch—school MS-4
Ingram Sch—school NC-3
Ingram-Schipper Farm—hist pl MD-2
Ingram School (historical)—locale MO-7
Ingrams Crossroads AL-4
Ingram Shoals—bar KY-4
Ingram Slash—swamp MO-7
Ingram Slough—gut OR-9
Ingram Slough—stream CA-9
Ingram Slough—stream OR-9
**Ingrams Mill**—pop pl MS-4
Ingrams Mill Post Office (historical)—building MS-4
Ingram-Sowell Elementary School TN-4
Ingram-Sowell Sch—school TN-4
Ingram Spring—spring MT-8
Ingram Spring—spring (2) OR-9
Ingram Spring—spring UT-8
Ingram Spur MS-4
Ingrams Run DE-2
Ingrams Stop MS-4
Ingram State Technical Institute—school AL-4
Ingrams (Township of)—fmr MCD NC-3
Ingram Thorofare—channel NJ-2
Ingram (Township of)—fmr MCD AR-4
Ingram Wells—locale AL-4
Ingram Whitt Branch—stream KY-4
Ingri Butte—summit AK-9
Ingricherk Mtn—summit AK-9
Ingrichuak Hill—summit AK-9
**Ingrihak**—pop pl AK-9
Ingrijoak Hill—summit AK-9
Ingrijoak Hills—other AK-9
Ingrilukat Hills—other AK-9
Ingrilukat-Naskorat Hill—summit AK-9
Ingrimiut (Village Site)—locale AK-9
Ingriruk Hill—summit AK-9
Ingrisarak Mtn—summit AK-9
Ingruksukruk Creek—stream AK-9
Ingrum Ford AL-4
Ingrum Ranch—locale TX-5
**Inguadona**—pop pl MN-6
Inguadona Lake—lake MN-6
**Inguadona (Township of)**—pop pl MN-6
Inherred Ch—church ND-7
Iniakuk Lake—lake AK-9
Iniakuk River—stream AK-9
Iniam Point—cape AK-9
Inian Cove—bay AK-9
Inian Islands—area AK-9
Inian Peninsula—cape AK-9
Inians Ferry NJ-2
Inicok Creek—stream AK-9
Inigoes Creek—stream MD-2
Inikaklik Creek—stream AK-9
Inikla Island—island AK-9
I-nineteen Springs—spring AZ-5
I-nineteen Tank—reservoir AZ-5
Iniril Island (not verified)—island MP-9
**Iniskin**—pop pl AK-9
Iniskin Bay—bay AK-9
Iniskin Island—island AK-9
Iniskin Peninsula—cape AK-9
Iniskin River—stream AK-9
Iniskin Rock—bar AK-9
Iniskin Shoal—bar AK-9
Initial Point Historical Monmt—park IN-6
Initial Creek—stream CA-9
Initial Creek—stream MT-8
Initial Gulch—valley CA-9
Initial Monument—locale NY-2
Initial Monument (boundary marker)—locale NV-8
Initial Peak—summit ID-8
Initial Point—hist pl OK-5
Initial Point—locale ID-8
Initial Point—summit AZ-5
Initial Point—summit ID-8
Initial Point of Boundary Between U.S. and Mexico—hist pl CA-9
Initial Rock—hist pl ND-7
Injun Creek—stream CA-9
Injun Creek—stream MT-8
Injun Creek—stream TN-4
Injun Jim Campground—locale CA-9
Ink—locale MO-7
**Ink**—pop pl AR-4
Inkalo Creek—stream MI-6
Ink Basin—basin TX-5
Ink Bayou—gut AR-4
Ink Creek AR-4
Ink Creek—stream ID-8
Inkerman—locale WV-2
**Inkerman**—pop pl PA-2
Ink Hollow—valley MO-7
Inkhorn Brook—stream ME-1
Ink House Canyon—valley NV-8
Ink House Spring—spring NV-8
Ink Lake—lake CA-9
Inkman Spring—spring TX-5
**Inkoeya**—pop pl FM-9
**Inkom**—pop pl ID-8
Inkom Cem—cemetery ID-8
Inkom Pass—gap ID-8
In-Ko-Pah County Park—park CA-9
In-Ko-Pah Gorge—valley CA-9
In-Ko-Pah Mountains—range CA-9
Inkpot Lake—lake MI-6
Inkpot Lake—lake (3) WI-6
Ink Pots—lake NM-5
Inkpot Spring—spring WY-8
Ink Ranch—locale CA-9
Ink Rocks—pillar CA-9
Inks Creek—stream CA-9
Inks Creek Ranch—locale CA-9
Inks Dam Natl Fish Hatchery—other TX-5
Inks Lake—reservoir TX-5
Inks Lake State Park—park TX-5
**Inks Lake Village**—pop pl TX-5
Ink Spring Ranch—locale CO-8
**Inkster**—pop pl MI-6
**Inkster**—pop pl ND-7
Inkster (historical)—locale ND-7
Inkster HS—school MI-6
Inkster Lake—lake WA-9
Inkster Landing Field—airport ND-7
Inkster Town Hall—building ND-7
**Inkster Township**—pop pl ND-7
**Ink (Swander)**—pop pl OH-6
Inkwell—hist pl NC-3
Inkwell Lake—lake CO-8
Inkwell Lake—lake NM-5
Inkwell Lake—lake WI-6
Ink Wells—lake WY-8
Ink Wells Trail—trail WY-8
Inky Lake—lake MN-6
Inland AL-4
Inland MI-6
Inland—locale IA-7
Inland—locale MI-6
**Inland**—pop pl AL-4
**Inland**—pop pl NE-7
Inland Branch—stream SC-3
Inland Cem—cemetery IA-7
Inland Cem—cemetery NE-7
Inland Ch—church FL-3
Inland Corners—locale MI-6
Inland Dam AL-4
Inland Empire Electric Railway Substation—hist pl ID-8
Inland Empire Zoo—other WA-9
Inland Harbor—bay MI-6
Inland Helicoptors Heliport—airport OR-9
**Inland Junction**—pop pl AL-4
Inland Lake—dam AL-4
Inland Lake—locale AK-9
Inland Lake—lake TX-5
Inland Lake—reservoir AL-4
Inland Lake Dam AL-4
Inland Lake Dam—dam AL-4
Inland Lakes—reservoir MS-4
Inland Lakes Sch—school MI-6
Inland Manor IN-6
Inland Mine (underground)—mine AL-4
**Inland Park**—pop pl MA-1
Inland Sch—school SD-7
Inland Sea—lake IL-6
Inland Shop Ctr—other CA-9
Inland Township—fmr MCD IA-7
**Inland Township**—pop pl NE-7
**Inland (Township of)**—pop pl MI-6
Inland Valley Sch—school CA-9
Inlay Cem—cemetery MI-6
Inlet—lake NY-2
Inlet locale NY-2
Inlet—locale VA-3
**Inlet**—pop pl NY-2
**Inlet**—pop pl OH-6
**Inlet**—pop pl WI-6
Inlet—uninc pl NJ-2
Inlet—uninc pl VA-3
Inlet, The—bay MN-6
Inlet, The—channel MD-2
Inlet, The—channel MN-6
Inlet, The—lake ME-1
Inlet, The—lake NY-2
Inlet, The—stream ME-1
Inlet, The—stream OH-6
Inlet, The—stream VT-1
Inlet Bay—bay CO-8
Inlet Bay—bay MN-6
**Inlet Beach**—pop pl (2) FL-3
Inlet Brook—stream ME-1
Inlet Campground—locale ID-8
Inlet Campground—park OR-9
Inlet Canal—canal CA-9
Inlet Canal—canal SD-7
Inlet Cem—cemetery IL-6
Inlet Cem—cemetery SC-3
Inlet Cove—bay ME-1
Inlet Creek MI-6
Inlet Creek—stream FL-3
Inlet Creek—stream MI-6
Inlet Creek—stream OR-9
Inlet Creek—stream SC-3
Inlet Feeder Canal—canal TX-5
Inlet Island NC-3
Inlet Lake MN-6
Inlet of 1849 NC-3
Inlet Peninsula—cape NC-3
Inlet Point—cape (2) AK-9
Inlet Point—cape NY-2
Inlet Ridge—ridge ME-1
Inlet River OR-9
Inlet Run—stream PA-2
Inlet Sch (historical)—school PA-2
Inlet Swamp—swamp PA-2
**Inlet (Town of)**—pop pl NY-2
Inlet Valley Cem—cemetery NY-2
**Inlikita**—pop pl FL-3
Inlow Butte—summit CA-9
Inlow Cem—cemetery IN-6
Inlow Youth Camp—locale NM-5
Inmachuk River—stream AK-9
Inman—locale GA-3
Inman—locale IL-6
Inman—locale TN-4
**Inman**—pop pl KS-7
**Inman**—pop pl NE-7
**Inman**—pop pl NY-2
**Inman**—pop pl SC-3
**Inman**—pop pl VA-3
Inman, Lake—lake KS-7
Inman Airp—airport IN-6
Inman Bend—bend TN-4
Inman Bog—swamp ME-1
Inman Branch—stream GA-3
Inman Branch—stream NC-3
Inman Branch—stream (2) TN-4
Inman Brothers Dam—dam NC-3
Inman Brothers Lake—reservoir NC-3
Inman Cave—cave TN-4
Inman (CCD)—cens area SC-3
Inman Cem—cemetery AR-4
Inman Cem—cemetery GA-3
Inman Cem—cemetery MN-6
Inman Cem—cemetery MO-7
Inman Cem—cemetery NE-7
Inman Cem—cemetery (2) NC-3
Inman Cem—cemetery OH-6
Inman Cem—cemetery OR-9
Inman Cem—cemetery (3) TN-4
Inman Cem—cemetery TX-5
Inman Ch—church IN-6
Inman Ch—church NC-3
Inman Creek—stream AL-4
Inman Creek—stream AR-4
Inman Creek—stream CA-9
Inman Creek—stream (2) GA-3
Inman Creek—stream ID-8
Inman Creek—stream KS-7
Inman Creek—stream MS-4
Inman Creek—stream OR-9
Inman Creek Ch—church GA-3
Inman Drain—canal MI-6
Inman Elem Sch—school KS-7
Inmanfield—locale AL-4
Inman Ford—crossing TN-4
Inman Gulf—valley NY-2
Inman Hill—summit MA-1
**Inman (historical)**—pop pl TN-4
Inman Hollow—valley MO-7
Inman Hollow—valley (4) TN-4
Inman Hollow River Access MO-7
Inman House—hist pl SD-7
Inman HS—school KS-7
Inman Lake—lake MI-6
Inman Lake—lake WA-9
Inman Lake Dam—dam MS-4
Inman Memorial Ch—church FL-3
**Inman Mills**—pop pl SC-3
Inman Mine—mine NV-8
Inman Mine—mine OR-9
Inman Mine—mine TN-4
Inman Mine (underground)—mine AL-4
Inman North Cem—cemetery KS-7
Inman Park—hist pl GA-3
Inman Park—locale GA-3
Inman Park—park FL-3
Inman Park-Moreland Hist Dist—hist pl GA-3
Inman Pass—gap ID-8
Inman Point—cape TN-4
Inman Pond—lake NY-2
Inman Pond—lake VT-1
Inman Post Office (historical)—building TN-4
Inman Ranch—locale NM-5
Inman Ridge—ridge TN-4
Inman Rsvr—reservoir OR-9
Inmans Cave—cave TN-4
Inman Sch—school CA-9
Inman Sch—school IA-7
Inmans Lake—lake NC-3
Inman Slough—gut IL-6
Inman South Cem—cemetery KS-7
Inman Square—uninc pl MA-1
Inman Square Hist Dist—hist pl MA-1
Inman State Wildlife Mngmt Area—park MN-6
Inman Tank—reservoir NM-5
**Inman Township**—pop pl NE-7
**Inman (Township of)**—pop pl MN-6
Inman Well—well TX-5
Inman Yard—locale GA-3
In Memoriam Cem—cemetery CT-1
Inmmachuck River—stream AK-9
Inmon Creek GA-3
Inmon Ranch—locale NM-5
Inm Springs—spring NM-5
Inn at Brevard, The—locale NC-3
Inn at Brushy Creek—hist pl TX-5
Inn Brook—stream CO-8
Innem—locale FM-9
Innem, Infal—stream FM-9
Innem River—stream FM-9
Innerarity—post sta FL-3
Inner Bar—bar ME-1
Inner Bar Channel—channel TX-5
Inner Basin—basin AZ-5
Inner Basin—harbor TX-5
Inner Bay Ledges—bar ME-1
Inner Brass Island—island VI-3
Inner Breakers—bar ME-1
Inner Breakers—bar MA-1
Inner Brewster Island MA-1
Inner Church Ledge—rock MA-1
Inner Clam Bay—bay FL-3
Inner Cove Rock—island CT-1
Inner Creek—stream WA-9
Inner Dawes Ledge—bar ME-1
Inner Doctors Bay—bay FL-3
Inner Duck Rock—island ME-1
Inner Fork of the Shears, The (historical)—bar DE-2
Inner George, Lake—lake AK-9
Inner Goose Island—island ME-1
Inner Grass Lump—island NC-3
Inner Green Island—island ME-1
Inner Grindstone Ledge—bar ME-1
Inner Gut—gut MA-1
Inner Harbor—bay CA-9
Inner Harbor—bay ME-1
Inner Harbor—bay NY-2
Inner Harbor—bay GU-9
Inner Harbor—cove MA-1
Inner Harbor—harbor AK-9
Inner Harbor—harbor ME-1
Inner Harbor—harbor MA-1
Inner Harbor Basin CA-9
Inner Harbor Channel—channel FL-3
Inner Harbor Navigation Canal—canal LA-4
Inner Harbor Park—park MS-4
Inner Hardwood Island—island ME-1
Inner Heron Island ME-1
Inner Heron Island—island ME-1
Inner Heron Island Ledge—bar ME-1
Inner Hill Island—island MI-6
Inner Humpback Rock—island AK-9
Inner Iliasik Island—island AK-9
Inner Island—island ME-1
Inner Island—island MI-6
Inner Ledge—bar ME-1
Inner Mayo Ledge—rock MA-1
Inner Middle Ground—bar VA-3
Inner Minot—bar MA-1
Inner Minots MA-1
Inner Narrows—channel FL-3
Inner Passage—channel WA-9
Inner Pasture—flat CA-9
Inner Point—cape (3) AK-9
Inner Point—cape NJ-2
Inner Point Sophia AK-9
Inner Reef—bar MI-6
Inner Right Cape—cape AK-9
Inner Sand Island—island ME-1
Inners Creek—stream PA-2
Inner Seal Rock—island AK-9
Inner Seal Rock—rock MA-1
Inner Shag Ledge—bar ME-1
Inner White Top—island CT-1
Innes, Kate, House—hist pl ID-8
Innes, Thomas, House—hist pl ID-8
Innes Beaver Pond—swamp ME-1
Innes House—hist pl KY-4
Innes JHS—school OH-6
Innes Ranch—locale WY-8
Innes Rsvr—reservoir MT-8
**Inness**—pop pl SC-3
Inness, George, House—hist pl NJ-2
Inness Sch—school NJ-2
Innesvale Gulch—valley AK-9
**Innis**—pop pl LA-4
Innisbrook—locale FL-3
Innis Brook—stream ME-1
**Innisdale**—pop pl IN-6
Innisfree Lake—reservoir NC-3
Innis Riffle OR-9
Innis Street Sch—school PA-2
**Inniswold**—pop pl LA-4
Innman Cem—cemetery MO-7
Innoko River—stream AK-9
Innoko Slough—stream AK-9
Inn RV Park—park UT-8
Inns on the Natl Road—hist pl MD-2
**Innswood South (subdivision)**—pop pl MS-4
**Innswood (subdivision)**—pop pl MS-4
Ino—locale VA-3
**Ino**—pop pl AL-4
**Ino**—pop pl WI-6
Ino Baptist Church AL-4
Ino Cem—cemetery AL-4
Inoceramus Creek—stream AK-9
Ino Ch—church AL-4
Inof MH-9
Inoian Cem—cemetery AR-4
Inoino Gulch—valley HI-9
**Inola**—pop pl OK-5
Inola (CCD)—cens area OK-5
Inola Creek—stream OK-5
Inola Hill—summit OK-5
Ino Swamp—swamp WI-6
Inoul—swamp FM-9
Inoul, Dauen—gut FM-9
Inowak Creek—stream AK-9
- in part The MO 7
Imperial Gables—locale CA-9
Inroad—locale KY-4
Insalaco Shop Ctr—locale PA-2
Insall Cem—cemetery TX-5
**Insco**—pop pl KY-4
Inscription Canyon—valley AZ-5
Inscription Canyon—valley CA-9
Inscription House Airp—airport AZ-5
Inscription House Ruin—locale AZ-5
Inscription House Ruin Spring—spring AZ-5
Inscription House Trading Post—locale AZ-5
**Inscription House (Trading Post)**—pop pl AZ-5
Inscription Point—summit AZ-5
Inscription Rock—hist pl AZ-5
Inscription Rock hist pl OH-6
Inscription Rock—other NM-5
Inscription Rock—pillar AZ-5
Inscription Rock—pillar ME-1
Inscription Rock—pillar OH-6
Insel Airik MP-9
Insel Arbar MP-9
Insel Bebi MP-9
Insel Bigaritsch MP-9
Insel Bikaridj MP-9
Insel Calalin MP-9
Insel Dschokadsch FM-9
Insel Enalik MP-9
Insel Eneilik MP-9
Insel Enijun MP-9
Insel Eten FM-9
Insel Falo FM-9
Insel Fanamar FM-9
Insel Garra MP-9
Insel Gogan MP-9
Insel Igurin MP-9
Insel Jobenor MP-9
Insel Juridi MP-9
Insel Kapenor MP-9
Insel I Bogen MP-9
Insel Meidj MP-9
Insel Mummet MP-9
Inseln Enilok MP-9
Inseln Fefan FM-9
Insel Ngain MP-9
Insel Perem FM-9
Insel Pinglapp MP-9
Insel Pis FM-9
Insel Ponape FM-9
Insel Roneron MP-9
Inselruhe—hist pl OH-6
Insel Rumung FM-9
Insel Tarang MP-9
Insel Taroa MP-9
Insel Tauak FM-9
Insel Tjan MP-9
Insel Toloas FM-9
Insel Utirik MP-9
Insel Wola FM-9
Insel Yap FM-9
Inshore Channel NJ-2
**Insiaf**—pop pl (2) FM-9
Inside Creek—stream CA-9
Inside Desert—desert ID-8
Inside Lake—lake FL-3
Inside Lake—lake GA-3
Inside Lakes—lake ID-8
Inside Passage—channel AK-9
Inside Range Channel—channel OR-9
Inside Thorofare—channel NJ-2
Inskeep, P. W., House—hist pl WV-2
Inskeep Cem—cemetery IA-7
Inskeep Cem—cemetery OH-6
Inskeep Corners—locale OH-6
Inskeep Hollow—valley OH-6
Inskip—locale CA-9
**Inskip**—pop pl TN-4
Inskip Baptist Ch—church TN-4
Inskip Canyon—valley NV-8
Inskip Caves—cave CA-9
Inskip Corners OH-6
Inskip Creek CA-9
Inskip Creek—stream CA-9
Inskip Elem Sch—school TN-4
Inskip Hill—summit CA-9
Inskip Hotel—hist pl CA-9
Inskip Mine—mine NV-8
Inskip Post Office (historical)—building TN-4
Inskip Powerhouse—other CA-9
Inskip United Methodist Ch—church TN-4
**Insko (Adele)**—pop pl KY-4
Insley, Merritt, House and Outbuildings—hist pl TX-5
Insley Cove—bay MD-2
**Insmont**—pop pl CO-8
Insmont Hill—summit CO-8
Insmore—locale MS-4
Insmore Post Office (historical)—building MS-4
Inspiration WA-9
**Inspiration**—pop pl AZ-5
Inspiration Concentrator—other AZ-5
Inspiration Creek—stream MT-8
Inspiration Dam (abandoned)—dam AZ-5
Inspiration Glacier WA-9
Inspiration Glacier—glacier WA-9
Inspiration Lake—lake MD-2
Inspiration Lake—lake WA-9
Inspiration Lakes—lake MT-8
Inspiration Lodge—locale CA-9
Inspiration Main Shafts—mine AZ-5
Inspiration Mine—mine AK-9
Inspiration Pass—gap MT-8
Inspiration Peak—summit MN-6

Inspiration Peak—*summit* ... WA-9
Inspiration Peak State Wayside Park—*park* ... MN-6
*Inspiration Point* ... CA-9
*Inspiration Point* ... OR-9
Inspiration Point—*cape* ... AK-9
Inspiration Point—*cape* (7) ... CA-9
Inspiration Point—*cape* ... CO-8
Inspiration Point—*cape* ... IL-6
Inspiration Point—*cape* ... MN-6
Inspiration Point—*cape* ... MO-7
Inspiration Point—*cape* ... NY-2
Inspiration Point—*cape* ... OR-9
Inspiration Point—*cape* ... TX-5
Inspiration Point—*cape* ... UT-8
Inspiration Point—*cliff* (2) ... AZ-5
Inspiration Point—*cliff* ... AR-4
Inspiration Point—*cliff* ... CA-9
Inspiration Point—*cliff* ... TX-5
Inspiration Point—*cliff* ... UT-8
Inspiration Point—*cliff* ... WA-9
Inspiration Point—*cliff* (2) ... WY-8
Inspiration Point—*hist pl* ... CO-8
Inspiration Point—*locale* (4) ... CA-9
Inspiration Point—*locale* ... CO-8
Inspiration Point—*ridge* ... CA-9
Inspiration Point—*summit* (5) ... CA-9
Inspiration Point—*summit* ... CO-8
Inspiration Point—*summit* ... MT-8
Inspiration Point—*summit* ... OR-9
Inspiration Point Dock—*locale* ... TN-4
Inspiration Post Office—*building* ... AZ-5
Inspiration Rock—*pillar* ... AZ-5
Inspiration Sch—*school* ... AZ-5
Inspiration State Wildlife Mngmt Are—*park* ... MN-6
Inspiration Tailings Dam Number Four—*dam* ... AZ-5
Inspiration Tailings Dam Number One—*dam* ... AZ-5
Inspiration Tailings Dam Number Three—*dam* ... AZ-5
Inspiration Tailings Dam Number Two—*dam* ... AZ-5
Inspiration Tunnel—*mine* ... AZ-5
Inspired Ministries Christian Center—*church* ... FL-3
Insrefusr, Inya—*channel* ... FM-9
*Instander Creek - in part* ... PA-2
**Instanter**—*pop pl* ... PA-2
Insteness Valley—*valley* ... WI-6
**Institute**—*pop pl* ... AL-4
**Institute**—*pop pl* ... MS-4
**Institute**—*pop pl* ... NC-3
**Institute**—*pop pl* ... WV-2
**Institute**—*pop pl* ... WI-6
Institute, Mount—*summit* ... MA-1
Institute Creek—*stream* ... AL-4
Institute Creek—*stream* ... AK-9
Institute for Colored Youth—*hist pl* ... PA-2
Institute for Education of the Blind—*school* ... NY-2
Institute Hall—*hist pl* ... MS-4
Institute Hill Sch—*school* ... PA-2
Institute (historical)—*locale* ... MS-4
Institute of Contemporary Art—*building* ... MA-1
Institute of Experimental Medicine—*other* ... MN-6
Institute of Forest Genetics—*school* ... CA-9
Institute of Logopedics—*school* ... KS-7
Institute of Marine Science—*school* ... FL-3
Institute of Pennsylvania—*hospital* ... PA-2
Institute Of Textile Technology—*school* ... VA-3
Institute of the Incarnation—*school* ... MN-6
Institute of the Pennsylvania Hosp—*hist pl* ... PA-2
Institute Park—*park* ... MA-1
Institute Park—*park* ... TX-5
Institute Peak—*summit* ... AK-9
Institute Sch—*school* ... WV-2
Institute (Township of)—*fmr MCD* ... NC-3
Institutional AME Ch—*church* ... MS-4
Institutional District—*hist pl* ... MA-1
Institution Cem—*cemetery* ... OH-6
Institution Hill—*summit* ... MA-1
Instituto Loaiza Cordero—*school* ... PR-3
Instituto Psicopedagogico de Puerto Rico—*school* ... PR-3
Insula, Lake—*lake* ... MN-6
*Insular Lake* ... MN-6
Insulator Basin—*basin* ... WA-9
Insulator Creek—*stream* ... WA-9
**Insull**—*pop pl* ... KY-4
Insurance Company of North America Bldg—*hist pl* ... PA-2
Insurance Ditch—*canal* ... NC-3
Insurgence Cave—*cave* ... AL-4
Intake—*locale* ... MT-8
Intake Campground—*park* ... UT-8
Intake Creek—*stream* ... WA-9
Intake Gulch—*valley* ... SD-7
Intake Pond—*lake* ... ME-1
Intake Reservoir Dam—*dam* ... MA-1
Intake Spring—*spring* ... CA-9
Intake Trail—*trail* ... ME-1
Intake Trail—*trail* ... WA-9
Intake Trail (pack)—*trail* ... OR-9
**Intalco**—*pop pl* ... WA-9
Integral Mine—*mine* ... CA-9
Integrity Title Insurance, Trust and Safe Deposit Company—*hist pl* ... PA-2
Intelligence—*locale* ... NC-3
**Interama (subdivision)**—*pop pl* ... FL-3
Interamerican Christian Sch (1st Campus)—*school* ... FL-3
Interamerican Christian Sch (2nd Campus)—*school* ... FL-3
Interamerican Community Ch—*church* ... FL-3
Interamerican Military Acad—*school* ... FL-3
Interamerican Univ—*post sta* ... PR-3
Interamerican Univ—*school* ... PR-3
Inter American University of Puerto Rico—*facility* ... PR-3
**Interbay**—*pop pl* ... WA-9
Interbay—*uninc pl* ... FL-3
Interbay Peninsula—*cape* ... FL-3
Inter Boro HS—*school* ... PA-2
Interburan Heights—*uninc pl* ... AL-4
Interceptor Canal—*canal* ... FL-3
Intercession Ch—*church* ... SC-3
**Intercession City**—*pop pl* ... FL-3
Interchance No 32—*other* ... NY-2
Interchange—*locale* ... PA-2
Interchange—*other* ... VT-1
Interchange Eight—*crossing* (4) ... MA-1
Interchange Eighteen—*crossing* (5) ... MA-1
Interchange Eighteen and Forty—*crossing* ... MA-1
Interchange Eleven—*crossing* (5) ... MA-1
Interchange Eleven A—*crossing* ... MA-1
Interchange Eleven and Thirty-seven—*crossing* ... MA-1
Interchange Fifteen—*crossing* (5) ... MA-1
Interchange Fifty-Eight—*crossing* ... MA-1
Interchange Fifty-Five—*crossing* ... MA-1
Interchange Fifty Nine—*crossing* ... MA-1
Interchange Fifty-seven—*crossing* ... MA-1
Interchange Fifty-Six—*crossing* ... MA-1
Interchange Five—*crossing* (4) ... MA-1
Interchange Forty—*crossing* (4) ... MA-1
Interchange Forty Eight—*crossing* ... MA-1
Interchange Forty Five—*crossing* ... MA-1
Interchange Forty-Four—*crossing* ... MA-1
Interchange Forty-one—*crossing* (2) ... MA-1
Interchange Forty-One—*crossing* (2) ... MA-1
Interchange Forty Seven—*crossing* ... MA-1
Interchange Forty Six—*crossing* ... MA-1
Interchange Forty-Six—*crossing* ... MA-1
Interchange Forty-Three—*crossing* (2) ... MA-1
Interchange Forty-Two—*crossing* ... MA-1
Interchange Forty-two—*crossing* (2) ... MA-1
Interchange Four—*crossing* (4) ... MA-1
Interchange Fourteen—*crossing* ... IN-6
Interchange Fourteen—*crossing* (5) ... MA-1
Interchange Fourtyseven—*crossing* ... MA-1
Interchange M 1—*other* ... NY-2
Interchange M 10—*other* ... NY-2
Interchange M 2—*other* ... NY-2
Interchange M 3—*other* ... NY-2
Interchange M 4—*other* ... NY-2
Interchange M 5—*other* ... NY-2
Interchange M 6—*other* ... NY-2
Interchange M 7—*other* ... NY-2
Interchange M 8—*other* ... NY-2
Interchange M 9—*other* ... NY-2
Interchange Nine—*crossing* (6) ... MA-1
Interchange Nineteen—*crossing* (4) ... MA-1
Interchange No 25—*other* ... NY-2
Interchange No 28—*other* ... NY-2
Interchange No 3—*other* ... OH-6
Interchange No 40—*other* ... NY-2
Interchange No 42—*other* ... NY-2
Interchange Number 1—*crossing* ... IN-6
Interchange Oil Field—*oilfield* ... KS-7
Interchange One—*crossing* (4) ... MA-1
Interchange One Hundred Fifty—*crossing* ... AZ-5
Interchange One Hundred Fifty Four—*crossing* ... AZ-5
Interchange One Hundred Fifty One—*crossing* ... AZ-5
Interchange One Hundred Fifty Seven—*crossing* ... AZ-5
Interchange One Hundred Fifty Three—*crossing* ... AZ-5
Interchange One Hundred Fifty Two—*crossing* ... AZ-5
Interchange One Hundred Fourteen—*crossing* ... AZ-5
Interchange One Hundred Nine—*crossing* ... AZ-5
Interchange One Hundred Ninety—*crossing* ... AZ-5
Interchange One Hundred Nintyfour—*crossing* ... AZ-5
Interchange One Hundred Sixty—*crossing* ... AZ-5
Interchange One Hundred Sixty Two—*crossing* ... AZ-5
Interchange One Hundred Twelve—*crossing* ... AZ-5
Interchange One Hundred Twenty One—*crossing* ... AZ-5
Interchange Rm 1—*other* ... NY-2
Interchange Rm 2—*other* ... NY-2
Interchange Seven—*crossing* (5) ... MA-1
Interchange Seventeen—*crossing* (6) ... MA-1
Interchange Six—*crossing* (5) ... MA-1
Interchange Sixteen—*crossing* (6) ... MA-1
Interchange Sixty—*crossing* ... MA-1
Interchange Sixty-eight—*crossing* ... MA-1
Interchange Sixty-four—*crossing* ... MA-1
Interchange Sixty One—*crossing* ... MA-1
Interchange Sixty-seven—*crossing* ... MA-1
Interchange Sixty Three—*crossing* ... MA-1
Interchange Sixty Two—*crossing* ... MA-1
Interchange SM2—*other* ... NY-2
Interchange SM3—*other* ... NY-2
Interchanges 10—*other* ... NY-2
Interchange S2—*other* ... NY-2
Interchanges 20—*other* ... NY-2
Interchange S3—*other* ... NY-2
Interchange S4—*other* ... NY-2
Interchange Ten—*crossing* (6) ... MA-1
Interchange Thirteen—*crossing* (7) ... MA-1
Interchange Thirty—*crossing* (3) ... MA-1
Interchange Thirty-eight—*crossing* ... MA-1
Interchange Thirty Eight—*crossing* (3) ... MA-1
Interchange Thirty-five—*crossing* ... MA-1
Interchange Thirty Five—*crossing* ... MA-1
Interchange Thirty-five—*crossing* ... MA-1
Interchange Thirty Five—*crossing* ... MA-1
Interchange Thirty-five—*crossing* ... MA-1
Interchange Thirty-four—*crossing* (4) ... MA-1
Interchange Thirty Nine—*crossing* ... MA-1
Interchange Thirty-Nine—*crossing* ... MA-1
Interchange Thirty Nine—*crossing* ... MA-1
Interchange Thirty-Nine—*crossing* ... MA-1
Interchange Thirty-nine—*crossing* ... MA-1
Interchange Thirty-one—*crossing* ... MA-1
Interchange Thirty One—*crossing* ... MA-1
Interchange Thirty-one—*crossing* (2) ... MA-1
Interchange Thirty-seven—*crossing* ... MA-1
Interchange Thirty Seven—*crossing* (2) ... MA-1
Interchange Thirty-six—*crossing* (2) ... MA-1
Interchange Thirty Six—*crossing* (2) ... MA-1
Interchange Thirty-three—*crossing* (4) ... MA-1
Interchange Thirty Two—*crossing* ... MA-1
Interchange Thirty-two—*crossing* (2) ... MA-1
Interchange Thirty Two—*crossing* ... MA-1
Interchange Three—*crossing* (4) ... MA-1
Interchange Three and Eight A—*crossing* ... MA-1
Interchange Twelve—*crossing* (7) ... MA-1
Interchange Twenty—*crossing* (7) ... MA-1
Interchange Twenty-eight—*crossing* ... MA-1
Interchange Twenty Eight—*crossing* ... MA-1
Interchange Twenty-eight—*crossing* ... MA-1
Interchange Twenty Eight—*crossing* ... MA-1
Interchange Twenty-five—*crossing* ... MA-1
Interchange Twenty Five—*crossing* ... MA-1
Interchange Twenty-five—*crossing* ... MA-1
Interchange Twenty Five—*crossing* ... MA-1
Interchange Twenty-five and Sixty-nine—*crossing* ... MA-1
Interchange Twenty-five and Twenty-six—*crossing* ... MA-1
Interchange Twenty-four—*crossing* (3) ... MA-1
Interchange Twenty Four—*crossing* ... MA-1
Interchange Twenty-four—*crossing* ... MA-1
Interchange Twenty Four—*crossing* ... MA-1
Interchange Twenty Nine—*crossing* ... MA-1
Interchange Twenty-nine—*crossing* (3) ... MA-1
Interchange Twenty-one—*crossing* (2) ... MA-1
Interchange Twenty One—*crossing* ... MA-1
Interchange Twenty-one—*crossing* ... MA-1
Interchange Twenty-one and Sixty-six—*crossing* ... MA-1
Interchange Twenty Seven—*crossing* (3) ... MA-1
Interchange Twenty-seven—*crossing* (2) ... MA-1
Interchange Twenty Six—*crossing* ... MA-1
Interchange Twenty-Six—*crossing* ... MA-1
Interchange Twenty Six—*crossing* ... MA-1
Interchange Twenty-six—*crossing* ... MA-1
Interchange Twenty-three—*crossing* (3) ... MA-1
Interchange Twenty Three—*crossing* ... MA-1
Interchange Twenty-three—*crossing* ... MA-1
Interchange Twenty-two—*crossing* (6) ... MA-1
Interchange Two—*crossing* (3) ... MA-1
Interchange Two and Nineteen—*crossing* ... MA-1
Interchange Two Hundred Three—*crossing* ... AZ-5
Interchange W1—*other* ... NY-2
Interchange W2—*other* ... NY-2
Interchange W3—*other* ... NY-2
Interchange W4—*other* ... NY-2
Interchange W5—*other* ... NY-2
Interchange W6—*other* ... NY-2
Interchange 1—*crossing* ... FL-3
Interchange 1—*crossing* ... IN-6
Interchange 1—*crossing* (6) ... TN-4
Interchange 1—*other* ... KY-4
Interchange 1—*other* (3) ... NH-1
Interchange 1—*other* (4) ... NY-2
Interchange 1 A—*other* ... NY-2
Interchange 1C—*crossing* ... TN-4
Interchange 10—*crossing* ... FL-3
Interchange 10—*crossing* ... IN-6
Interchange 10—*crossing* ... TN-4
Interchange 10—*other* ... ME-1
Interchange 10—*other* (2) ... NH-1
Interchange 10—*other* (4) ... NY-2
Interchange 10—*other* (2) ... OH-6
Interchange 101—*crossing* ... TN-4
Interchange 104—*crossing* ... TN-4
Interchange 105—*locale* ... TN-4
Interchange 108—*crossing* (2) ... TN-4
Interchange 11—*crossing* ... IN-6
Interchange 11—*crossing* (2) ... TN-4
Interchange 11—*other* ... ME-1
Interchange 11—*other* (2) ... NY-2
Interchange 11—*other* (3) ... OH-6
Interchange 110—*crossing* ... IN-6
Interchange 110—*locale* ... TN-4
Interchange 111—*crossing* ... IN-6
Interchange 112—*crossing* ... IN-6
Interchange 112—*crossing* (2) ... TN-4
Interchange 114—*crossing* (2) ... IN-6
Interchange 114—*locale* ... TN-4
Interchange 115—*crossing* ... IN-6
Interchange 116—*crossing* ... IN-6
Interchange 116—*crossing* ... TN-4
Interchange 117—*crossing* (2) ... IN-6
Interchange 117—*crossing* (3) ... TN-4
Interchange 119—*crossing* (2) ... IN-6
Interchange 12—*crossing* ... TN-4
Interchange 12—*other* ... ME-1
Interchange 12—*other* ... NH-1
Interchange 12—*other* (2) ... NY-2
Interchange 12—*other* (2) ... OH-6
Interchange 121—*crossing* ... IN-6
Interchange 122—*crossing* ... TN-4
Interchange 124—*crossing* ... IN-6
Interchange 126—*crossing* ... TN-4
Interchange 127—*crossing* ... TN-4
Interchange 128—*crossing* ... TN-4
Interchange 129—*crossing* ... IN-6
Interchange 129—*crossing* ... TN-4
Interchange 13—*crossing* ... IN-6
Interchange 13—*crossing* ... TN-4
Interchange 13—*other* ... ME-1
Interchange 13—*other* (4) ... NY-2
Interchange 13—*other* (2) ... OH-6
Interchange 130—*crossing* ... IN-6
Interchange 133—*crossing* ... TN-4
Interchange 134—*crossing* (2) ... TN-4
Interchange 135—*crossing* ... TN-4
Interchange 137—*crossing* ... TN-4
Interchange 14—*crossing* ... IN-6
Interchange 14—*crossing* (2) ... TN-4
Interchange 14—*other* ... ME-1
Interchange 14—*other* ... NH-1
Interchange 14—*other* (3) ... NY-2
Interchange 14—*other* (2) ... OH-6
Interchange 141—*crossing* ... TN-4
Interchange 143—*crossing* (2) ... TN-4
Interchange 144—*crossing* ... TN-4
Interchange 148—*crossing* ... TN-4
Interchange 15—*crossing* (3) ... TN-4
Interchange 15—*other* ... NH-1
Interchange 15—*other* (5) ... NY-2
Interchange 15—*other* (2) ... OH-6
Interchange 152—*crossing* (2) ... TN-4
Interchange 155—*crossing* ... TN-4
Interchange 158—*crossing* ... TN-4
Interchange 16—*crossing* ... FL-3
Interchange 16—*crossing* ... IN-6
Interchange 16—*crossing* ... TN-4
Interchange 16—*other* ... NH-1
Interchange 16—*other* (3) ... NY-2
Interchange 16—*other* (2) ... OH-6
Interchange 160—*crossing* ... TN-4
Interchange 161—*crossing* ... TN-4
Interchange 17—*crossing* ... TN-4
Interchange 17—*other* (5) ... NY-2
Interchange 17—*other* ... OH-6
Interchange 174—*crossing* ... TN-4
Interchange 175—*crossing* ... TN-4
Interchange 175—*other* ... MI-6
Interchange 177—*other* ... MI-6
Interchange 178—*crossing* ... TN-4
Interchange 179—*crossing* ... TN-4
Interchange 18—*crossing* ... TN-4
Interchange 18—*other* (6) ... NY-2
Interchange 18—*other* ... OH-6
Interchange 18—*other* ... SC-3
Interchange 180—*crossing* ... TN-4
Interchange 180—*other* ... MI-6
Interchange 180A—*crossing* ... TN-4
Interchange 181—*crossing* ... TN-4
Interchange 181—*other* ... MI-6
Interchange 181A—*crossing* ... TN-4
Interchange 182—*crossing* ... TN-4
Interchange 183—*crossing* ... TN-4
Interchange 183A—*crossing* ... TN-4
Interchange 184—*crossing* ... TN-4
Interchange 184—*other* ... MI-6
Interchange 185—*other* ... MI-6
Interchange 186—*other* ... MI-6
Interchange 187—*other* ... MI-6
Interchange 188—*crossing* ... TN-4
Interchange 19—*crossing* ... TN-4
Interchange 19—*other* (4) ... NY-2
Interchange 19—*other* ... OH-6
Interchange 190—*other* ... MI-6
Interchange 192—*other* ... MI-6
Interchange 194—*other* ... SC-3
Interchange 199—*other* ... SC-3
Interchange 2—*crossing* ... FL-3
Interchange 2—*crossing* (2) ... IN-6
Interchange 2—*crossing* ... TN-4
Interchange 2—*other* ... ME-1
Interchange 2—*other* (3) ... NH-1
Interchange 2—*other* (4) ... NY-2
Interchange 2—*other* ... SC-3
Interchange 2 and 185—*crossing* ... TN-4
Interchange 20—*crossing* ... FL-3
Interchange 20—*crossing* ... IN-6
Interchange 20—*crossing* ... TN-4
Interchange 20—*other* (4) ... NY-2
Interchange 21—*crossing* ... IN-6
Interchange 21—*other* (5) ... NY-2
Interchange 22—*crossing* ... AL-4
Interchange 22—*crossing* ... TN-4
Interchange 22—*other* (5) ... NY-2
Interchange 22—*other* ... OH-6
Interchange 22—*other* ... SC-3
Interchange 226—*crossing* ... TN-4
Interchange 23—*crossing* ... IN-6
Interchange 23—*other* (5) ... NY-2
Interchange 23—*other* ... OH-6
Interchange 23—*other* ... SC-3
Interchange 232—*crossing* ... TN-4
Interchange 238—*crossing* ... TN-4
Interchange 239—*crossing* ... TN-4
Interchange 24—*crossing* ... FL-3
Interchange 24—*crossing* ... TN-4
Interchange 24—*other* (5) ... NY-2
Interchange 24—*other* ... SC-3
Interchange 245—*crossing* ... TN-4
Interchange 25—*crossing* ... IN-6
Interchange 25—*crossing* ... TN-4
Interchange 25—*other* (5) ... NY-2
Interchange 25A—*other* ... NY-2
Interchange 254—*crossing* ... TN-4
Interchange 258—*crossing* ... TN-4
Interchange 26—*other* (5) ... NY-2
Interchange 268—*crossing* ... TN-4
Interchange 27—*crossing* ... FL-3
Interchange 27—*crossing* ... IN-6
Interchange 27—*crossing* ... TN-4
Interchange 27—*other* (5) ... NY-2
Interchange 273—*crossing* ... TN-4
Interchange 276—*crossing* ... TN-4
Interchange 28—*other* (4) ... NY-2
Interchange 280—*crossing* ... TN-4
Interchange 286—*crossing* ... TN-4
Interchange 287—*crossing* ... TN-4
Interchange 288—*crossing* ... TN-4
Interchange 29—*other* (2) ... NY-2
Interchange 29 a—*other* ... NY-2
Interchange 290—*crossing* ... TN-4
Interchange 3—*crossing* ... FL-3
Interchange 3—*crossing* (2) ... IN-6
Interchange 3—*crossing* (2) ... TN-4
Interchange 3—*other* ... ME-1
Interchange 3—*other* (2) ... NH-1
Interchange 3—*other* (3) ... NY-2
Interchange 30—*crossing* ... FL-3
Interchange 30—*other* (2) ... NY-2
Interchange 300—*crossing* ... TN-4
Interchange 301—*crossing* ... TN-4
Interchange 308—*crossing* ... AL-4
Interchange 31—*crossing* ... IN-6
Interchange 31—*crossing* (2) ... TN-4
Interchange 31—*other* (3) ... NY-2
Interchange 31—*other* ... OH-6
Interchange 310—*crossing* ... AL-4
Interchange 311—*crossing* ... TN-4
Interchange 317—*crossing* ... TN-4
Interchange 318—*crossing* ... AL-4
Interchange 32—*crossing* ... AL-4
Interchange 32—*crossing* (2) ... TN-4
Interchange 32—*other* (2) ... NY-2
Interchange 32—*other* ... OH-6
Interchange 320—*crossing* ... TN-4
Interchange 322—*crossing* ... AL-4
Interchange 322—*crossing* ... TN-4
Interchange 329—*crossing* ... TN-4
Interchange 33—*crossing* ... IN-6
Interchange 33—*crossing* (2) ... TN-4
Interchange 33—*other* (4) ... NY-2
Interchange 33—*other* ... OH-6
Interchange 338—*crossing* ... TN-4
Interchange 34—*other* (3) ... NY-2
Interchange 34—*other* ... OH-6
Interchange 347—*crossing* ... TN-4
Interchange 35—*crossing* (2) ... TN-4
Interchange 35—*other* (5) ... NY-2
Interchange 350—*crossing* ... TN-4
Interchange 352—*crossing* ... TN-4
Interchange 355—*crossing* ... TN-4
Interchange 356—*crossing* ... TN-4
Interchange 36—*crossing* (2) ... TN-4
Interchange 36—*other* ... NH-1
Interchange 36—*other* (5) ... NY-2
Interchange 36—*other* ... OH-6
Interchange 36A—*other* ... NY-2
Interchange 360—*crossing* ... TN-4
Interchange 364—*crossing* ... TN-4
Interchange 368—*crossing* ... TN-4
Interchange 369—*crossing* ... TN-4
Interchange 37—*crossing* ... IN-6
Interchange 37—*other* ... NH-1
Interchange 37—*other* (5) ... NY-2
Interchange 37A—*other* ... NY-2
Interchange 373—*crossing* ... TN-4
Interchange 374—*crossing* ... TN-4
Interchange 376—*crossing* ... TN-4
Interchange 378—*crossing* ... TN-4
Interchange 379—*crossing* ... TN-4
Interchange 38—*crossing* ... AL-4
Interchange 38—*crossing* ... TN-4
Interchange 38—*other* ... NH-1
Interchange 38—*other* (5) ... NY-2
Interchange 38—*other* ... OH-6
Interchange 380—*crossing* ... TN-4
Interchange 383—*crossing* ... TN-4
Interchange 385—*crossing* ... TN-4
Interchange 386—*crossing* ... TN-4
Interchange 387—*crossing* ... TN-4
Interchange 388—*crossing* ... TN-4
Interchange 389—*crossing* ... TN-4
Interchange 39—*other* ... NH-1
Interchange 39—*other* (4) ... NY-2
Interchange 390—*crossing* ... TN-4
Interchange 392—*crossing* ... TN-4
Interchange 393—*crossing* ... TN-4
Interchange 394—*crossing* ... TN-4
Interchange 398—*crossing* ... TN-4
Interchange 4—*crossing* ... FL-3
Interchange 4—*crossing* (2) ... IN-6
Interchange 4—*crossing* (3) ... TN-4
Interchange 4—*other* ... KY-4
Interchange 4—*other* ... ME-1
Interchange 4—*other* (3) ... NH-1
Interchange 4—*other* (5) ... NY-2
Interchange 4—*other* (3) ... OH-6
Interchange 4—*other* ... SC-3
Interchange 40—*crossing* ... IN-6
Interchange 40—*other* (4) ... NY-2
Interchange 402—*crossing* ... TN-4
Interchange 41—*other* ... NH-1
Interchange 41—*other* (4) ... NY-2
Interchange 41 A—*other* ... NY-2
Interchange 412—*crossing* ... TN-4
Interchange 415—*crossing* ... TN-4
Interchange 417—*crossing* ... TN-4
Interchange 42—*crossing* ... AL-4
Interchange 42—*crossing* ... IN-6
Interchange 42—*crossing* (2) ... TN-4
Interchange 42—*other* ... NH-1
Interchange 42—*other* (4) ... NY-2
Interchange 42—*other* ... SC-3
Interchange 421—*crossing* ... TN-4
Interchange 424—*crossing* ... TN-4
Interchange 43—*other* (3) ... NY-2
Interchange 43—*other* ... SC-3
Interchange 432—*crossing* ... TN-4
Interchange 435—*crossing* ... TN-4
Interchange 44—*crossing* ... IN-6
Interchange 44—*other* (3) ... NY-2
Interchange 44—*other* ... SC-3
Interchange 440—*crossing* ... TN-4
Interchange 443—*crossing* ... TN-4
Interchange 447—*crossing* ... TN-4
Interchange 45—*crossing* ... TN-4
Interchange 45—*other* (3) ... NY-2
Interchange 45—*other* ... SC-3
Interchange 451—*crossing* ... TN-4
Interchange 46—*crossing* ... IN-6
Interchange 46—*crossing* ... TN-4
Interchange 46—*other* (2) ... NY-2
Interchange 47—*crossing* ... IN-6
Interchange 47—*crossing* ... TN-4
Interchange 48—*crossing* ... FL-3
Interchange 48—*crossing* ... TN-4
Interchange 48—*other* ... NY-2
Interchange 49—*crossing* ... IN-6
Interchange 49—*crossing* (2) ... TN-4
Interchange 49—*other* (2) ... NY-2
Interchange 5—*crossing* (2) ... FL-3
Interchange 5—*crossing* ... IN-6
Interchange 5—*crossing* ... TN-4
Interchange 5—*other* (2) ... KY-4
Interchange 5—*other* ... ME-1
Interchange 5—*other* (3) ... NH-1
Interchange 5—*other* (6) ... NY-2
Interchange 5—*other* (2) ... OH-6
Interchange 50—*crossing* ... TN-4
Interchange 50—*other* (2) ... NY-2
Interchange 51—*crossing* ... AL-4
Interchange 51—*crossing* ... TN-4
Interchange 51—*other* (2) ... NY-2
Interchange 52—*crossing* (3) ... TN-4
Interchange 52—*other* (2) ... NY-2
Interchange 52—*other* ... OH-6
Interchange 53—*other* (2) ... NY-2
Interchange 54—*crossing* ... IN-6
Interchange 54—*other* (2) ... NY-2
Interchange 54—*other* ... OH-6
Interchange 55—*crossing* ... TN-4
Interchange 55—*other* (2) ... NY-2
Interchange 56—*crossing* (2) ... TN-4
Interchange 56—*other* (2) ... NY-2
Interchange 57—*crossing* ... IN-6
Interchange 57—*crossing* (2) ... TN-4
Interchange 57—*other* (2) ... NY-2
Interchange 57—*other* ... OH-6
Interchange 58—*other* (2) ... NY-2
Interchange 59—*crossing* ... TN-4
Interchange 59—*other* ... NY-2
Interchange 59—*other* ... OH-6
Interchange 6—*crossing* (2) ... FL-3
Interchange 6—*crossing* ... IN-6
Interchange 6—*crossing* (2) ... TN-4
Interchange 6—*other* ... KY-4
Interchange 6—*other* (4) ... NH-1
Interchange 6—*other* (8) ... NY-2
Interchange 6—*other* (3) ... OH-6
Interchange 60—*crossing* (2) ... TN-4
Interchange 61—*crossing* ... TN-4
Interchange 61—*other* ... NY-2
Interchange 62—*crossing* ... TN-4
Interchange 63—*crossing* ... IN-6
Interchange 63—*crossing* ... TN-4
Interchange 63—*other* ... NY-2
Interchange 63—*other* ... OH-6
Interchange 64—*other* ... NY-2
Interchange 64—*other* ... OH-6
Interchange 66—*crossing* (2) ... TN-4
Interchange 68—*crossing* (2) ... TN-4
Interchange 68—*other* ... NY-2
Interchange 69—*crossing* ... TN-4
Interchange 69—*other* ... NY-2
Interchange 69—*other* ... OH-6
Interchange 7—*crossing* ... FL-3
Interchange 7—*crossing* (2) ... IN-6
Interchange 7—*crossing* (2) ... TN-4
Interchange 7—*other* (4) ... NH-1
Interchange 7—*other* (5) ... NY-2
Interchange 7—*other* (2) ... OH-6
Interchange 70—*other* (2) ... NY-2
Interchange 71—*other* ... NY-2
Interchange 71—*other* ... SC-3
Interchange 72—*crossing* ... TN-4
Interchange 72—*other* ... MI-6
Interchange 72—*other* ... NY-2
Interchange 72—*other* ... SC-3
Interchange 73—*other* ... SC-3
Interchange 74—*crossing* (2) ... TN-4
Interchange 74—*other* ... MI-6
Interchange 74—*other* ... OH-6
Interchange 75—*crossing* ... IN-6
Interchange 75—*other* ... MI-6
Interchange 75—*other* ... OH-6
Interchange 75—*other* ... SC-3
Interchange 76—*crossing* ... IN-6
Interchange 76—*crossing* ... TN-4
Interchange 76—*other* ... MI-6
Interchange 76—*other* (2) ... OH-6
Interchange 77—*crossing* ... IN-6
Interchange 77—*other* (2) ... OH-6
Interchange 78—*crossing* ... IN-6
Interchange 78—*other* ... MI-6
Interchange 78—*other* (2) ... OH-6
Interchange 79—*crossing* ... IN-6
Interchange 79—*crossing* ... TN-4
Interchange 79—*other* ... OH-6
Interchange 8—*crossing* (3) ... IN-6
Interchange 8—*crossing* (3) ... TN-4
Interchange 8—*other* (3) ... NH-1
Interchange 8—*other* (5) ... NY-2
Interchange 8—*other* ... OH-6
Interchange 8—*other* ... VT-1
Interchange 80—*crossing* (4) ... IN-6
Interchange 80—*crossing* ... TN-4
Interchange 80—*other* ... MI-6
Interchange 80—*other* (2) ... OH-6
Interchange 81—*crossing* ... TN-4
Interchange 81—*other* ... MI-6
Interchange 81—*other* ... OH-6
Interchange 82—*crossing* ... TN-4
Interchange 82—*other* ... NY-2
Interchange 82—*other* (2) ... OH-6
Interchange 83—*crossing* ... IN-6
Interchange 83—*other* ... NY-2
Interchange 84—*crossing* ... TN-4
Interchange 84—*other* ... NY-2
Interchange 84—*other* ... OH-6
Interchange 85—*crossing* ... IN-6
Interchange 85—*other* ... OH-6
Interchange 86—*other* ... OH-6
Interchange 87—*crossing* ... IN-6
Interchange 87—*crossing* ... TN-4
Interchange 87—*other* ... OH-6
Interchange 88—*other* ... OH-6
Interchange 89—*other* ... OH-6
Interchange 9—*crossing* (2) ... FL-3
Interchange 9—*crossing* ... IN-6
Interchange 9—*other* ... NH-1
Interchange 9—*other* (5) ... NY-2
Interchange 9—*other* (2) ... OH-6
Interchange 9—*other* ... VT-1
Interchange 90—*crossing* (2) ... IN-6
Interchange 93—*crossing* ... TN-4
Interchange 95—*crossing* ... IN-6
Interchange 96—*other* ... NY-2
Interchange 97—*locale* ... TN-4
Interchange 97—*other* ... NY-2
Interchange 98—*crossing* ... TN-4
Interchange 99—*crossing* ... IN-6
**Intercity**—*pop pl* ... WA-9
Inter-City Christian Acad—*school* ... FL-3
Intercommunity Hosp—*hospital* ... CA-9
**Intercontinental**—*pop pl* ... MO-7
Intercontinental Alloys Corporation—*facility* ... IL-6
Inter County Airp—*airport* ... PA-2
**Intercourse**—*pop pl* ... AL-4
**Intercourse**—*pop pl* ... PA-2
Intercourse Post Office (historical)—*building* ... PA-2
Intercourse Sch—*school* ... AL-4
Interdenominational Bible Way Ch—*church* ... IN-6
Interdenominational Ch—*church* ... PA-2
Interdenominational Holiness Association Campground—*locale* ... TN-4
Interfaith Christian Center—*church* ... UT-8
Interfalls Lake—*lake* ... WI-6
Inter Fork—*stream* ... WA-9
Inter Glacier—*glacier* ... WA-9
Intergreen Gorge Cem—*cemetery* ... PA-2
Interior—*locale* ... VA-3
**Interior**—*pop pl* ... SD-7
Interior County (CCD)—*cens area* ... FL-3
Interior Creek—*stream* ... MI-6
Interior Department Offices—*hist pl* ... DC-2
Interior Grain Tramway—*hist pl* ... WA-9
Interior Lake—*lake* ... MI-6
Interior Low Plateau—*plain* ... AL-4
**Interior Township**—*pop pl* ... SD-7
**Interior (Township of)**—*pop pl* ... MI-6
*Interior Valley* ... AZ-5
Interior Valley—*valley* ... AZ-5
*Interlachen* ... MN-6
**Interlachen**—*pop pl* ... FL-3
**Interlachen**—*pop pl* ... OR-9
Interlachen Community Sch—*school* ... FL-3
Interlachen Country Club—*other* ... MN-6
Interlachen-Florahome (CCD)—*cens area* ... FL-3
Interlachen HS—*school* ... FL-3
Interlachen Park—*park* ... MN-6
Interlachen Plantation—*locale* ... LA-4

Interlake Acad—school FL-3
Interlake HS—school WA-9
Interlaken MI-6
**Interlaken**—pop pl MA-1
**Interlaken**—pop pl NJ-2
**Interlaken**—pop pl NY-2
**Interlaken**—pop pl WA-9
**Interlaken Beach**—pop pl NY-2
Interlaken Dam—dam PA-2
**Interlaken Estates**—pop pl NJ-2
Interlaken Hill ME-1
**Interlaken (historical)**—pop pl ND-7
Interlaken Lake—reservoir PA-2
Interlaken Mill Bridge—hist pl RI-1
Interlaken Park—park WA-9
**Interlaken Park**—pop pl NH-1
Interlaken Resort District—hist pl CO-8
Interlaken Rsvr No. 1—reservoir CO-8
Interlake Public Sch—hist pl WA-9
**Interlochen**—pop pl MI-6
Interlochen State Park—park MI-6
Interlocking Lakes—reservoir FL-3
Intermedial Sch—school NJ-2
Intermediate Bldg—hist pl MA-1
Intermediate HS—school PA-2
Intermediate Lake—lake (2) MI-6
Intermediate River—stream (2) MI-6
Intermittent Creek—stream AK-9
Intermittent Spring—spring UT-8
Intermont—locale WV-2
Intermont Dam—dam NC-3
Intermont Girl Scout Camp—locale VA-3
Intermont Lake—reservoir NC-3
Intermountain Conservation Camp—locale CA-9
Intermountain Experimental Station—building UT-8
Intermountain Fairgrounds—locale CA-9
Intermountain Indian Sch—school UT-8
Intermountain Institute—hist pl ID-8
Intermountain Power Heliport—airport UT-8
Intermountain Speedway—locale WY-8
Intermountain Sprayers Airp—airport UT-8
Intermount Guard Station—locale WA-9
Internal Revenue Bureau DC-2
Internal Revenue Service Bldg—building DC-2
International—locale UT-8
**International**—pop pl GA-3
International—uninc pl WA-9
International Acad of Merchandising and Design—school FL-3
International Airport—other FL-3
International Airport—post sta PR-3
International Amphitheater—building IL-6
International Arena—building CA-9
International Bible Coll—school AL-4
International Bible Coll—school TX-5
**International Boundary**—pop pl MT-8
International Boundary Marker—hist pl LA-4
International Boundary Marker—hist pl TX-5
International Boundary Marker No. 1, U.S. and Mexico—hist pl NM-5
International Bridge—bridge NY-2
International Bridge—bridge (2) TX-5
International Bridge—other MI-6
International Business Park—locale NC-3
International Cem—cemetery IA-7
International City Speedway—other GA-3
International Coin Museum—building PA-2
International Community Ch—church FL-3
International Correspondence Sch—school PA-2
International Country Club—other CA-9
International Country Club—other VA-3
International Crane Foundation—other WI-6
International Creek—stream MT-8
International Creek—stream WA-9
International Falcon Reservoir TX-5
**International Falls**—pop pl MN-6
International Ferry—locale TX-5
International Fine Arts Coll—school FL-3
International Friendship Park—park MO-7
International Gardens Park—park FL-3
**International Gardens Subdivision**—pop pl UT-8
International Golf Club—locale MA-1
International & Great Northern RR Passenger Station—hist pl TX-5
International Harvester Proving Grounds AZ-5
International Harvestor Company—facility OH-6
International Hotel—hist pl CA-9
International House—hist pl AZ-5
International Institute—school CA-9
International Junction—uninc pl NY-2
International M and C Park—park FL-3
International Mine—mine NM-5
International Mine—mine NC-3
International Mineral—mine NM-5
**International Office Park**—pop pl GA-3
International Order of Oddfellows Cem—cemetery OR-9
International Order of Oddfellows Cemeteries—cemetery OR-9
International Paper Company—facility MS-4
International Paper Company—facility MO-7
International Paper Company Lake Dam—dam MS-4
International Paper Company Pond Dam—dam MS-4
International Paper Lake Dam—dam MS-4
International Peace Garden—park ND-7
International Peace Garden Airfield—airport ND-7
International Plaza Shopping Center MS-4
International Racetrack—other UT-8
International Racetrack Overrun—other UT-8
International Raceway—other CA-9
International Smelter—locale AZ-5
International Speedway—other AL-4
International Tank—reservoir NM-5
International Trade Mart—uninc pl LA-4
International Trust Company Bldg—hist pl MA-1
International Village (3) IL-6
International World Sch—school FL-3
Intern Canyon MT-8
Inter-Ocean Pass—gap CO-8
Inter-Ocean Rsvr—reservoir CO-8
Interpace Corporation—airport NJ-2
Interplanetary Airstrip—airport UT-8
Interplaza Shop Ctr—locale FL-3
Interprise Ch—church AR-4
Interrorem Guard Station—locale WA-9
Intersection—locale PA-2
Intersection Lake—lake MN-6
Inter-Southern Insurance Bldg—hist pl KY-4
Interstate—locale ID-8
Interstate—locale WV-2
**Interstate**—pop pl GA-3
Inter-state Airp—airport MO-7
Interstate Bridge—bridge MN-6
Interstate Bridge—bridge OR-9
Interstate Canal—canal NE-7
Interstate Canal—canal (2) WY-8
Interstate Ch—church MS-4
Interstate City—uninc pl MS-4
Interstate Commerce Commission Bldg DC-2
Interstate Commerce Commission Bldg (historical)—building DC-2
Interstate Ditch—canal MT-8
Interstate Ditch—canal WY-8
Interstate Fairgrounds—park WA-9
Interstate Industrial Park—locale (2) AL-4
Interstate Mall—locale (2) FL-3
Interstate North Industrial Park—locale NC-3
Interstate Number One Dam UT-8
Interstate Oil Field—oilfield CO-8
Interstate Orphanage—hist pl AR-4
Interstate Park—park IA-7
Interstate Seventy Shop Ctr—locale MO-7
Interstate State Park—park MN-6
Interstate State Park—park WI-6
Interstate Toll Bridge—bridge OR-9
Interstate West—locale TN-4
Interstate Woods—forest MS-4
Interstate Yards—locale VA-3
Interstate 108—crossing TN-4
Interurban Bridge—hist pl OH-6
**Interurban Heights**—pop pl AL-4
Intervale—hist pl VA-3
Intervale—locale ME-1
**Intervale**—pop pl NH-1
**Intervale**—pop pl VA-3
Intervale, Lake—lake NJ-2
Intervale Brook—stream (3) ME-1
Intervale Brook—stream MA-1
Intervale Cem—cemetery (2) ME-1
Intervale Country Club—other NH-1
Intervale Factory—hist pl MA-1
Intervale Pond—lake NH-1
Inter-Varsity Christian Fellowship—church FL-3
Interwald—locale WI-6
**Interwest Condominium Project Phase A**—pop pl UT-8
In The Brush, Lake—lake OR-9
In the Corner Tank—reservoir AZ-5
**Intracoastal City**—pop pl LA-4
Intracoastal Waterway—channel AL-4
Intracoastal Waterway—channel FL-3
Intracoastal Waterway—channel (2) GA-3
Intracoastal Waterway—channel LA-4
Intracoastal Waterway—channel MS-4
Intracoastal Waterway—channel NJ-2
Intracoastal Waterway—channel NC-3
Intracoastal Waterway—channel SC-3
Intracoastal Waterway—channel TX-5
Intracoastal Waterway—channel VA-3
Intracoastal Waterway (Alternate Route)—channel LA-4
**Intracostal City**—pop pl LA-4
Intreken Cave—cave AL-4
Intrenchment Creek—stream GA-3
Intrepid Rock—island CT-1
Intricate Bay—bay AK-9
Intun Cone—summit AK-9
Intungidi Hill—summit AK-9
Inuf FM-9
Inu Jima FM-9
Inuk FM-9
Inuk—civil FM-9
Inuk Kumi FM-9
Inukpak Rock—summit AK-9
Inukpasugruk Creek—stream AK-9
Inuktak Creek—stream AK-9
Inu-Shima FM-9
Inuya Creek—stream MT-8
Inuya Pass—gap MT-8
**Invale**—pop pl NY-2
Invalurak Mtn—summit AK-9
Inventory Creek—stream OR-9
Inver Grove MN-6
**Inver Grove Heights**—pop pl MN-6
Inver Grove (RR name for Inver Grove Heights)—other MN-6
Inver Grove Sch—school MN-6
**Inverlac**—pop pl ND-7
Inver Lochy Dam—dam NC-3
Inver Lochy Lake—reservoir NC-3
Invermay (historical)—locale KS-7
Inverness OH-6
Inverness—locale NY-2
Inverness—locale NC-3
**Inverness**—pop pl AL-4
**Inverness**—pop pl CA-9
**Inverness**—pop pl FL-3
**Inverness**—pop pl IL-6
**Inverness**—pop pl IN-6
**Inverness**—pop pl MD-2
**Inverness**—pop pl MS-4
**Inverness**—pop pl MT-8
Inverness Baptist Ch—church MS-4
Inverness (CCD)—cens area AL-4
Inverness (CCD)—cens area FL-3
Inverness Cem—cemetery AL-4
Inverness Cem—cemetery NY-2
Inverness Ch—church AL-4
Inverness Christian Ch—church MS-4
Inverness Division—civil AL-4
Inverness Elem Sch—school AL-4
Inverness Elem Sch—school MS-4
**Inverness Forest**—pop pl MD-2
Inverness Golf Club—other OH-6
Inverness HS (historical)—school MS-4
Inverness Independent Baptist Ch—church MS-4
Inverness Lake AL-4
Inverness MS—school FL-3
**Inverness Park**—pop pl CA-9
Inverness Plaza (Shop Ctr)—locale FL-3
Inverness Primary Sch—school FL-3
Inverness Regional Shop Ctr—locale FL-3
Inverness Ridge—ridge CA-9
Inverness Sch AL-4
Inverness Sch—school CA-9
Inverness Sch—school MD-2
**Inverness (subdivision)**—pop pl AL-4
Inverness Tower—tower FL-3
**Inverness (Township of)**—pop pl MI-6
Inverness United Methodist Ch—church MS-4
**Inverness Village**—pop pl MD-2
Inverrary—uninc pl FL-3
Inverrary Plaza (Shop Ctr)—locale FL-3
Inverrary Sch—school FL-3
**Invincible**—pop pl LA-4
Invincible Mine—mine NM-5
Invincible Rock—bar CA-9
Invisible Mtn—summit ID-8
Invitation Sch—school NC-3
Invul Mtn—summit AK-9
Inward Point—cape MA-1
In Wiyu, Foko—reef FM-9
Inwood—locale CA-9
Inwood—locale FL-3
Inwood—locale MD-2
Inwood—locale MS-4
Inwood—locale PA-2
Inwood—locale TX-5
**Inwood**—pop pl FL-3
**Inwood**—pop pl IN-6
**Inwood**—pop pl IA-7
**Inwood**—pop pl (2) NY-2
**Inwood**—pop pl WV-2
Inwood, Lake—lake FL-3
Inwood (census name for West Winter Haven)—CDP FL-3
Inwood Ch—church FL-3
Inwood Ch—church NC-3
Inwood Ch—church TX-5
Inwood Country Club—other NY-2
Inwood Creek—stream MI-6
**Inwood (East Barnet)**—pop pl VT-1
Inwood Golf Club—other IL-6
Inwood Hill Park—park NY-2
Inwood Lake—lake MI-6
Inwood Lake—lake NY-2
Inwood Lake—reservoir GA-3
Inwood L I—post sta NY-2
Inwood Park—park NY-2
Inwood Park—park OH-6
Inwood Point—cape NY-2
Inwood Sch—school CA-9
Inwood Sch—school FL-3
**Inwood (Township of)**—pop pl MI-6
Inyan Kara Cem—cemetery WY-8
Inyan Kara Creek—stream WY-8
Inyan Kara Mountain—hist pl WY-8
Inyan Kara Mtn—summit WY-8
Inyart Branch—stream KY-4
Inyo, Mount—summit (2) CA-9
**Inyo (County)**—pop pl CA-9
Inyo Crater Lakes—lake CA-9
Inyo Creek—stream CA-9
Inyo Creek—stream ID-8
Inyo (historical)—locale KS-7
**Inyokern**—pop pl CA-9
Inyo-Kern Valley CA-9
Inyo Mine—mine CA-9
Inyo Mountains—range CA-9
Inyo Natl For—forest NV-8
Inyorurak Lakes—lake AK-9
Inyorurak Pass—gap AK-9
I. N. Young Ditch—canal OR-9
Inyo Well (Dry)—well CA-9
Inyugakuligit Creek—stream AK-9
Inyuilak Creek—stream AK-9
Inyuraktoak Creek—stream AK-9
Inza MO-7
Inzer House—hist pl AL-4
Inzer Site—hist pl MS-4
Ioca Park CO-8
Iodine Creek—stream ID-8
Iodine Lake—lake WI-6
Iodine Prairie—area CA-9
Iodine Spring—spring CA-9
Iohl—locale FM-9
Ioka—locale UT-8
Ioka Cem—cemetery UT-8
Ioka Farms—locale AL-4
**Ioka (historical)**—pop pl IA-7
Iola FL-3
Iola—locale FL-3
Iola—locale KY-4
**Iola**—pop pl CO-8
**Iola**—pop pl IL-6
**Iola**—pop pl KS-7
**Iola**—pop pl PA-2
**Iola**—pop pl TX-5
**Iola**—pop pl WI-6
Iola, Lake—lake FL-3
Iola Cem—cemetery (3) KS-7
Iola Ch—church KS-7
Iola Creek NC-3
Iola Creek—stream CO-8
Iola Frans Sch—school AZ-5
Iola (historical)—locale KS-7
**Iola (historical)**—pop pl CO-8
**Iola (historical)**—pop pl IA-7
Iola (historical P.O.)—locale IA-7
Iola Hollow—valley AR-4
Iola HS—school KS-7
Iola JHS—school KS-7
Iola Lake—lake WI-6
Iola Lake—reservoir IN-6
Iola Municipal Airport KS-7
Ioland Cem—cemetery OK-5
Iolani Palace—hist pl HI-9
Iolani Palace—military HI-9
Iolani Sch—school HI-9
Iola Roberts Elementary School AL-4
Iola Run—stream IN-6
**Iola (Town of)**—pop pl WI-6
**Iola Township**—pop pl KS-7
Iole—civil HI-9
Iole—summit HI-9
Ioleau—summit HI-9
Ioleau Rsvr—reservoir HI-9
**Iolee (historical)**—pop pl FL-3
Iolehaehae—summit HI-9
Iolehaehae Camp—locale HI-9
Iolekaa Valley—valley HI-9
Ioleka Valley HI-9
Iole Mountain HI-9
Iole Stream—stream HI-9
Io Mountain HI-9
Ion MP-9
Ion—locale IA-7
Iona KS-7
Iona PA-2
Iona—locale NJ-2
Iona—locale OK-5
Iona—locale TX-5
**Iona**—pop pl FL-3
**Iona**—pop pl ID-8
**Iona**—pop pl IN-6
**Iona**—pop pl MT-8
**Iona**—pop pl PA-2
**Iona**—pop pl SD-7
Iona Cem—cemetery MO-7
Iona Cem—cemetery SD-7
Iona Ch—church MO-7
Iona Ch—church NC-3
Iona Ch—church SC-3
Iona Coll—school NY-2
Iona Cove—bay FL-3
Iona Dam—dam SD-7
**Iona Gardens**—pop pl FL-3
Iona Hills—range SD-7
Iona (historical)—locale SD-7
**Iona (Iona Lake Station)**—pop pl MN-6
Iona Island—island NY-2
Iona Lake—lake NH-1
Iona Lake—reservoir NJ-2
Iona Lake Dam—dam NJ-2
Iona Lake (RR name for Iona)—other MN-6
Iona Meetinghouse—hist pl ID-8
Iona Point—cape FL-3
Iona Pointe Shop Ctr—locale FL-3
Iona Pond NH-1
Iona Sch—school MO-7
Iona Sch—school NY-2
Iona Sch (abandoned)—school FL-3
Iona State Wildlife Mngmt Area—park MN-6
Iona Township KS-7
**Iona Township**—pop pl SD-7
Iona Township (historical)—civil SD-7
**Iona (Township of)**—pop pl (2) MN-6
Iona Wash—stream AZ-5
Ionchebi—island MP-9
Ionchebi Island MP-9
Ionchebi-to MP-9
Ione—locale CO-8
Ione—locale GA-3
**Ione**—pop pl AR-4
**Ione**—pop pl CA-9
**Ione**—pop pl NV-8
**Ione**—pop pl OR-9
**Ione**—pop pl WA-9
Ione, Lake—lake WY-8
Ione Bridge—bridge WA-9
Ione Canal—canal (2) CA-9
Ione Canyon—valley NV-8
Ione (CCD)—cens area CA-9
Ione City Centenary Church—hist pl CA-9
Ione Creek WA-9
Ione Ditch—canal WY-8
Ione Gulch—valley MT-8
Ione Hill—summit WA-9
Ione-Lexington (CCD)—cens area OR-9
Ione Marcus Gordon Memorial Park—cemetery AZ-5
Ione-Metaline Falls (CCD)—cens area WA-9
Ione Millpond—lake WA-9
Ione Mine—mine NV-8
Ione Muni Airp—airport WA-9
Ione Sch—school OK-5
Ione Spring—spring NV-8
Ione Substation—locale OR-9
Ione Summit—summit NV-8
Ione Township—inact MCD NV-8
Ione Valley—valley CA-9
Ione Valley—valley NV-8
Ione Wash—arroyo NV-8
Ionia—hist pl VA-3
Ionia—locale AR-4
**Ionia**—pop pl IA-7
**Ionia**—pop pl KS-7
**Ionia**—pop pl MI-6
**Ionia**—pop pl MO-7
**Ionia**—pop pl (2) NY-2
Ionia Cem—cemetery KS-7
Ionia Cem—cemetery NE-7
Ionia Country Club—other MI-6
**Ionia (County)**—pop pl MI-6
Ionia County Courthouse—hist pl MI-6
Ionia Downtown Commercial Hist Dist—hist pl MI-6
Ionia Hist Dist—hist pl MI-6
Ionia Lake—lake MI-6
Ionian Basin—basin CA-9
Ionia State Hosp—hospital MI-6
Ionia State Rec Area—park MI-6
Ionia State Reformatory—other MI-6
**Ionia Township**—pop pl KS-7
**Ionia (Township of)**—pop pl MI-6
Ioni Creek—stream (2) TX-5
Ioni Marsh—swamp TX-5
Ionine Creek OK-5
Ionine Creek—stream OK-5
Ionosphere Research Station—locale PA-2
Ions Creek (Township of)—fmr MCD AR-4
I'on Swamp—swamp SC-3
I.O.O.F. and Barker Buildings—hist pl IN-6
IOOF and Masonic Cem—cemetery CO-8
IOOF Bldg—hist pl AZ-5
I.O.O.F. Bldg—hist pl CA-9
I.O.O.F. Bldg—hist pl ID-8
IOOF Bldg—hist pl OR-9
I.O.O.F. Bldg of Buffalo—hist pl OK-5
I.O.O.F. Building, Mason Valley—hist pl NV-8
IOOF Camp—locale WY-8
IOOF Cem OR-9
I.O.O.F. Cem—cemetery CA-9
IOOF Cem—cemetery (2) CO-8
IOOF Cem—cemetery ID-8
IOOF Cem—cemetery (23) IN-6
IOOF Cem—cemetery (2) IA-7
IOOF Cem—cemetery MO-7
IOOF Cem—cemetery NE-7
IOOF Cem—cemetery ND-7
I.O.O.F. Cem—cemetery OR-9
IOOF Cem—cemetery OR-9
I.O.O.F. Cem—cemetery OR-9
IOOF Cem—cemetery (2) OR-9
I.O.O.F. Cem—cemetery OR-9
IOOF Cem—cemetery (2) OR-9
IOOF Cem—cemetery PA-2
Ioof Cem—cemetery PA-2
IOOF Cem—cemetery TX-5
IOOF Cem—cemetery VA-3
IOOF Cem—cemetery (4) WA-9
IOOF Fresh Air Camp—locale OH-6
I.O.O.F. Hall—hist pl CA-9
I.O.O.F. Hall—hist pl ID-8
I.O.O.F. Hall—hist pl IA-7
I.O.O.F. Hall—hist pl OK-5
IOOF Hall and Opera House—hist pl NE-7
I.O.O.F. Hebo Cem—cemetery OR-9
IOOF Home—building NY-2
IOOF Home—building OH-6
Ioof Home—building PA-2
IOOF Lodge—hist pl MT-8
I.O.O.F. Lodge—hist pl TX-5
I.O.O.F.-Mapleton Lodge 3139 Cem—cemetery OR-9
IOOF Opera House—hist pl NE-7
I.O.O.F. Organization Camp, Paulina Lake—hist pl OR-9
IOOF Relief Home—hist pl UT-8
IOOF Temple Bldg—hist pl NE-7
Iosca Creek MN-6
Iosco MI-6
Iosco, Lake—reservoir NJ-2
Iosco Cem—cemetery MN-6
**Iosco (County)**—pop pl MI-6
Iosco Creek—stream MN-6
Iosco Drain Number Three—canal MI-6
Iosco Drain Number Two—canal MI-6
**Iosco Township**—pop pl ND-7
**Iosco (Township of)**—pop pl MI-6
**Iosco (Township of)**—pop pl MN-6
**Iosepa**—pop pl UT-8
Iosepa Settlement Cemetery—hist pl UT-8
I O Smith Lake Dam—dam MS-4
**Iota**—pop pl LA-4
**Iota Flat Township**—pop pl ND-7
Iota Lake—lake MN-6
Iota Oil and Gas Field—oilfield LA-4
Iota Racetrack—locale LA-4
Iota Sch Number 1—school ND-7
Iota Sch Number 5—school ND-7
Iotla—locale NC-3
Iotla Branch—stream NC-3
Iotla Ch—church NC-3
Iotla Creek—stream NC-3
Iotla Gap—gap NC-3
Iou, Toachel—channel PW-9
Ioul Lukes—bar PW-9
Ioulomekang—island PW-9
Iouroro—summit PW-9
Iowa KS-7
**Iowa**—pop pl LA-4
Iowa, Lake—reservoir IA-7
Iowa, Sac, and Fox Presbyterian Mission—hist pl KS-7
Iowa Amphitheater—basin CO-8
Iowa Army Ammunition Plant Dam—dam IA-7
Iowa Army Ammun Plant—military IA-7
Iowa Bench—bench MT-8
Iowa Bldg—hist pl IA-7
Iowa Braille And Sightsaving Sch—school IA-7
Iowa Camp Spring—spring AZ-5
Iowa Canyon—valley CA-9
Iowa Canyon—valley NV-8
Iowa Canyon Mine—mine NV-8
Iowa Canyon Ranch—locale NV-8
Iowa Canyon Rsvr—reservoir NV-8
Iowa Canyon Sch—school NV-8
Iowa Cem—cemetery (2) KS-7
**Iowa Center**—pop pl IA-7
Iowa Center Flats—flat WY-8
Iowa Center Flats Ch—church WY-8
Iowa Central Community Coll—school (3) IA-7
Iowa Chapel Cem—cemetery OK-5
Iowa City CA-9
Iowa City—locale CA-9
**Iowa City**—pop pl FL-3
**Iowa City**—pop pl IA-7
**Iowa Colony**—pop pl TX-5
Iowa Colony Cem—cemetery TX-5
Iowa Copper Tunnel—mine UT-8
**Iowa (County)**—pop pl WI-6
Iowa County Courthouse—hist pl IA-7
Iowa County Courthouse—hist pl WI-6
Iowa County Home—building IA-7
Iowa Creek—stream (3) AK-9
Iowa Creek—stream ID-8
Iowa Creek—stream (2) KS-7
Iowa Creek—stream NV-8
Iowa Cutoff—gut IL-6
Iowa-Des Moines Natl Bank Bldg—hist pl IA-7
Iowa Ditch MO-7
Iowa Ditch—canal CA-9
Iowa Ditch—canal SD-7
Iowa Drainage Ditch—canal IA-7
Iowa Drainage Ditch—canal MO-7
**Iowa Falls**—pop pl IA-7
**Iowa Falls Junction**—pop pl IA-7
Iowa Flat—flat WA-9
Iowa Flats—flat MT-8
Iowa Flats—flat WA-9
Iowa Flats Sch—school MT-8
Iowa Gulch—valley (2) CO-8
Iowa Gulch—valley MT-8
**Iowa Hill**—pop pl CA-9
Iowa Hill—summit CA-9
Iowa Hill—summit NC-3
Iowa Hill Cem—cemetery OR-9
Iowa Hill Ditch—canal CA-9
Iowa Hill Mine—mine CA-9
Iowa Indian Cem—cemetery OK-5
**Iowa Ind Res**—pop pl KS-7
Iowa Ind Res—reserve NE-7
Iowa Island—island IL-6
Iowa Junc—locale IL-6
Iowa Junction IL-6
Iowa Junction—locale IL-6
**Iowa Junction**—pop pl LA-4
**Iowa Junction (historical)**—pop pl IA-7
Iowa Lake—lake (3) IA-7
Iowa Lake—lake (2) MN-6
Iowa Lake—lake ND-7
Iowa Lake—reservoir MN-6
Iowa Lake Dam—dam IA-7
Iowa Lake (historical)—locale IA-7
Iowa Lake (historical P.O.)—locale IA-7
Iowa Lake Marsh Public Hunting Area IA-7
Iowa Lake Marsh State Game Mngmt Area—area IA-7
Iowa Lakes Community Coll—school IA-7
Iowa Lake State Game Mngmt Area—park IA-7
Iowa Lake Township—fmr MCD IA-7
Iowa Lateral—canal WY-8
Iowa-Maple Sch—school OH-6
Iowa Masonic Library—building IA-7
Iowa Mine—mine CO-8
Iowa Mine—mine ID-8
Iowa Mine—mine WY-8
Iowa Mission Cem—cemetery OK-5
**Iowana**—pop pl IA-7
**Iowana**—pop pl MS-4
Iowana Sch—school IA-7
Iowa of Kansas Ind Res KS-7
Iowa Oil and Gas Field—oilfield LA-4
**Iowa Park**—pop pl TX-5
Iowa Park, Lake—reservoir TX-5
Iowa Park (CCD)—cens area TX-5
Iowa Peak—summit CO-8
Iowa Point—cape LA-4
**Iowa Point**—pop pl KS-7
Iowa Point Cem—cemetery KS-7
Iowa Reform Bldg—hist pl IA-7
Iowa Reservation KS-7
Iowa River IA-7
Iowa River—stream IA-7
Iowa River Cem—cemetery IA-7
Iowa River Ch—church IA-7
Iowa Sac and Fox Indian Mission—school KS-7
Iowa Sac and Fox Ind Res KS-7
Iowa Sch—school IL-6
Iowa Sch—school PA-2
Iowa Sch For The Deaf—school IA-7
Iowa Sch Number 2—school ND-7
Iowa Sch Number 3—school ND-7
Iowa Shaft—mine CO-8
Iowa Slough*—stream IA-7
Iowa Slough Lake*—lake IA-7
Iowa Soldiers Home—locale IA-7
Iowa Soldiers' Orphans' Home—hist pl IA-7
Iowa State Capitol—building IA-7
Iowa State Capitol—hist pl IA-7
Iowa State Experimental Farm—locale IA-7
Iowa State Fair and Exposition Grounds Hist Dist—hist pl IA-7
Iowa State Fair Campgrounds—locale IA-7
Iowa State Historical Bldg—hist pl IA-7
Iowa State Nursery—park IA-7
Iowa State Orphans Home—building IA-7
Iowa State Penitentiary—building IA-7
Iowa State Univ—school IA-7
Iowa State University Agronomy Farm—other IA-7
Iowa State University Geology Camp—locale WY-8
Iowa State Univ Experimental Farm—school (2) IA-7
Iowa State Univ Experimental Farm No 1—school (2) IA-7
Iowa State Univ Experimental Farms No 2—school IA-7
Iowa State Univ Experimental Station—school IA-7
Iowa State Univ Station—school IA-7
Iowa Township KS-7
Iowa Township—civil SD-7
Iowa Township—fmr MCD (10) IA-7
**Iowa Township**—pop pl (2) KS-7
**Iowa Township**—pop pl NE-7
**Iowa Township**—pop pl ND-7
**Iowa Township**—pop pl (2) SD-7
Iowa Township Cem—cemetery IA-7
Iowa Township (historical)—civil SD-7
Iowa Tunnel—mine CO-8
Iowa Union Cem—cemetery KS-7
Iowa Union College—locale IA-7
Iowa Valley Cem—cemetery NE-7
Iowa Valley Sch—school IA-7
Iowa Valley Sch—school NE-7
Iowaville Cem—cemetery IA-7
Iowaville (historical)—locale KS-7
Iowithla River—stream AK-9
Ioxikux AZ-5
Ipachol—area GU-9
**Ipapao**—pop pl GU-9
Ipar—summit FM-9
Ipar, Chuk En—summit FM-9
Ipasha Falls—falls MT-8
Ipasha Glacier—glacier MT-8
Ipasha Lake—lake MT-8
Ipasha Peak—summit MT-8
**Ipat**—pop pl FM-9
**Ipava**—pop pl IL-6
I P Bills Island—island ID-8
**Ipco**—pop pl AL-4
Ipco (railroad station)—locale FL-3
**Ipe (historical)**—pop pl TN-4
Ipei—unknown FM-9
Ipe Post Office (historical)—building TN-4
Ipewik River—stream AK-9
Iphigenia, Point—cape AK-9
Iphigenia Bay—bay AK-9
Ipiavik Lagoon—lake AK-9
Ipiga—area GU-9
Ipis—bar FM-9
Ipis—island FM-9
Ipiutak—locale AK-9
Ipiutak Archeol District—hist pl AK-9
Ipiutak Lagoon—bay AK-9
Ipiutak Site—hist pl AK-9
Iplaza—other GU-9
Ipley—locale MO-7
I P Luthold—locale TX-5
Ipnavik River—stream AK-9
Ipnek Creek—stream AK-9
Ipnek Mtn—summit AK-9
Ipnelivik River—stream AK-9
Ipock Landing—locale NC-3
I Pool—reservoir MI-6
IPP Power Plant—locale UT-8
Iprugalet Mtn—summit AK-9

**Ipsco**—*pop pl* FL-3
Ipsen Industries (Plant)—*facility* IL-6
Ipse Post Office (historical)—*building* MS-4
*Ipsom Creek* UT-8
Ipsom Ditch—*canal* KY-4
Ipson Creek—*stream* UT-8
Ipsoot Butte—*summit* OR-9
Ipsoot Creek—*stream* ID-8
Ipsoot Lake—*lake* WA-9
Ipsut Creek—*stream* WA-9
Ipsut Creek Campground—*locale* WA-9
Ipsut Creek Trail—*trail* WA-9
Ipsut Falls—*falls* WA-9
Ipsut Pass—*gap* WA-9
*Ipsut Saddle* WA-9
Ipswich—*locale* WI-6
**Ipswich**—*pop pl* MA-1
**Ipswich**—*pop pl* SD-7
*Ipswich, Town of* MA-1
Ipswich Baptist Church—*hist pl* SD-7
Ipswich Bay—*bay* MA-1
*Ipswich Beach* MA-1
Ipswich Bluff—*cape* MA-1
*Ipswich - Canada Plantation* MA-1
Ipswich (census name for Ipswich Center)—*CDP* MA-1
Ipswich Center (census name Ipswich)—*other* MA-1
*Ipswich Hamlet* MA-1
Ipswich HS—*school* MA-1
Ipswich JHS—*school* MA-1
Ipswich Light—*locale* MA-1
Ipswich Mills Dam—*dam* MA-1
*Ipswich River* MA-1
Ipswich River—*stream* MA-1
Ipswich River Dam—*dam* (2) MA-1
Ipswich River Marshes—*swamp* MA-1
Ipswich River Rsvr—*reservoir* (3) MA-1
Ipswich Sch—*school* WI-6
Ipswich State Bank—*hist pl* SD-7
**Ipswich (Town of)**—*pop pl* MA-1
**Ipswich Township**—*pop pl* SD-7
*Ipswoot Butte* OR-9
*Ipuak* FM-9
Ipuolono Rsvr—*reservoir* HI-9
Ipuu Falls—*falls* HI-9
Ipuu Ridge—*ridge* HI-9
Ipwal—*locale* FM-9
**Ipwal**—*pop pl* FM-9
Ipwek—*locale* FM-9
Ipwitek—*civil* FM-9
Ipwor—*swamp* FM-9
*Ipwupw* FM-9
Ira—*locale* OH-6
Ira—*other* PA-2
**Ira**—*pop pl* IA-7
**Ira**—*pop pl* MO-7
**Ira**—*pop pl* NY-2
**Ira**—*pop pl* TX-5
**Ira**—*pop pl* VT-1
**Ira**—*pop pl* VA-3
Ira Allen, Mount—*summit* VT-1
**Iraan**—*pop pl* TX-5
Iraan (CCD)—*cens area* TX-5
Iraan Windmill—*locale* TX-5
Irabarne Tank—*reservoir* NM-5
Ira B Jones Sch—*school* NC-3
Ira Bog—*swamp* ME-1
Ira Branch—*stream* SC-3
Ira Brook—*stream* VT-1
Ira Canyon—*valley* NM-5
Ira Cem—*cemetery* OH-6
Ira Ch—*church* MO-7
Ira Clark Park—*park* AR-4
Ira Corners—*locale* NY-2
Irad—*locale* KY-4
Irad—*locale* TN-4
**Iradale**—*pop pl* OH-6
*Iradell* NC-3
*Iradj* FM-9
Ira Gas Storage Field—*other* MI-6
Ira Hacker Ridge—*ridge* IN-6
Ira Ison Branch—*stream* KY-4
Ira J Chrisman Wind Gap Pumping Plant—*other* CA-9
Irak Creek—*stream* AK-9
*Irakong* PW-9
Ira Lump—*island* NC-3
*Iramit* AZ-5
Ira Morris Camp—*locale* NC-3
Ira Mtn—*summit* ME-1
Iran Spring—*spring* MT-8
Ira Ridge—*ridge* NM-5
**Iras**—*pop pl* FM-9
**Irasburg**—*pop pl* VT-1
**Irasburg (Town of)**—*pop pl* VT-1
Ira Sch—*school* VA-3
Ira Sch (abandoned)—*school* MO-7
Iras-Mechitiu-Mwan—*CDP* FM-9
Iras Pinnacle—*pillar* VT-1
**Ira Station**—*pop pl* NY-2
**Irasville**—*pop pl* VT-1
Ira Tank—*reservoir* NM-5
**Ira (Town of)**—*pop pl* NY-2
**Ira (Town of)**—*pop pl* VT-1
**Ira (Township of)**—*pop pl* MI-6
Iraville—*locale* VA-3
Irby—*locale* TX-5
Irby—*locale* VA-3
Irby—*locale* WA-9
Irby, Dr. William Claudius, House—*hist pl.* SC-3
Irby-Alexander Pond Dam—*dam* MS-4
Irby Bridge (historical)—*bridge* MS-4
Irby Cem—*cemetery* AL-4
Irby Cem—*cemetery* AR-4
Irby Cem—*cemetery* TX-5
Irby-Henderson-Todd House—*hist pl* SC-3
Irby Lake—*reservoir* MS-4
Irby Lake Dam—*dam* (2) MS-4
Irby Mill Creek—*stream* MS-4
Irby Post Office (historical)—*building* TN-4
Irby Ranch—*locale* NM-5
Irby Ranch—*locale* TX-5
Irby Tank—*reservoir* TX-5
IR Ditch—*canal* ID-8
*Ire* TX-5
*Iredel* NC-3
Iredell—*locale* NC-3
**Iredell**—*pop pl* TX-5
Iredell, James, House—*hist pl* NC-3
Iredell Bridge—*bridge* NC-3
Iredell Canyon—*valley* CA-9
Iredell (CCD)—*cens area* TX-5
**Iredell County**—*pop pl* NC-3
Iredell County Courthouse—*hist pl* NC-3
Iredell County Schools Special Services—*school* NC-3
Iredell House—*building* NC-3
Iredell Memorial Hosp—*hospital* NC-3
*Ireland* MA-1
Ireland—*locale* NH-1
Ireland—*locale* OH-6
**Ireland**—*pop pl* IN-6
**Ireland**—*pop pl* MS-4
**Ireland**—*pop pl* TX-5
**Ireland**—*pop pl* WA-9
**Ireland**—*pop pl* WV-2
Ireland, Charles H., House—*hist pl* NC-3
Ireland, Joseph, House—*hist pl* OH-6
Ireland, Mount—*summit* OR-9
Ireland Army Hosp—*hospital* KY-4
Ireland Brook—*stream* IN-6
Ireland Brook—*stream* NJ-2
Ireland Canyon—*valley* ID-8
Ireland Cem—*cemetery* AL-4
Ireland Ch—*church* GA-3
*Ireland Church* AL-4
**Ireland Corner**—*pop pl* ME-1
**Ireland Corners**—*pop pl* NY-2
*Ireland Creek* MD-2
Ireland Creek—*stream* CA-9
Ireland Creek—*stream* OH-6
Ireland Creek—*stream* SC-3
Ireland Elem Sch—*school* IN-6
Ireland-Gardiner Farm—*hist pl* NY-2
Ireland Grove Sch—*school* IL-6
Ireland Gulch—*valley* WA-9
**Ireland Hill**—*pop pl* AL-4
Ireland Lake—*lake* CA-9
Ireland Lake—*reservoir* IN-6
Ireland Memorial Ch—*church* AL-4
Ireland Mesa—*summit* UT-8
Ireland Mesa Canyon—*valley* UT-8
Ireland Mine—*mine* CA-9
Ireland Mine—*mine* NV-8
*Ireland Mtn* OR-9
*Ireland Parish* MA-1
*Ireland Plantation* MS-4
Ireland Point—*cape* MA-1
Ireland Pond—*lake* ME-1
Ireland Rsvr No. Five—*reservoir* CO-8
Ireland Rsvr No. Four—*reservoir* CO-8
Ireland Rsvr No. One—*reservoir* CO-8
Ireland Rsvr No. 6—*reservoir* CO-8
Ireland Sch—*school* (2) IL-6
Ireland Sch—*school* OH-6
Ireland Sch—*school* (2) TX-5
Ireland Sch (historical)—*school* MO-7
Ireland Sch (historical)—*school* PA-2
Ireland Sch Number 54 (historical)—*school* SD-7
Ireland Shaft—*mine* AZ-5
Ireland Spring—*spring* OR-9
**Ireland Springs**—*pop pl* ID-8
Ireland State Wildlife Mngmt Area—*park* MN-6
Ireland Street Cem—*cemetery* MA-1
**Irelandville**—*pop pl* NY-2
Ireland Vly—*reservoir* NY-2
Irely Creek—*stream* WA-9
Irely Lake—*lake* WA-9
Iremel—*locale* CA-9
Irem Temple Country Club—*other* PA-2
Irena—*locale* MO-7
Irena Cem—*cemetery* GA-3
Irena Lake—*reservoir* PA-2
Irendodi, Dauen—*gut* FM-9
*Irene* KS-7
*Irene* ND-7
*Irene* MP-9
Irene—*locale* LA-4
Irene—*locale* WV-2
**Irene**—*pop pl* IL-6
**Irene**—*pop pl* MS-4
**Irene**—*pop pl* SD-7
**Irene**—*pop pl* TX-5
Irene, Lake—*lake* CO-8
Irene, Lake—*lake* FL-3
Irene, Lake—*lake* (2) MN-6
Irene-Beresford Interchange—*crossing* SD-7
Irene Bridge—*bridge* SC-3
Irene Ch—*church* GA-3
Irene Creek—*stream* AK-9
Irene Creek—*stream* ID-8
Irene Creek—*stream* SC-3
Irene Creek—*stream* WA-9
Irene Creek—*stream* WY-8
Irene Glacier—*glacier* AK-9
Irene Gulch—*valley* AZ-5
Irene (historical)—*locale* AL-4
Irene (historical)—*locale* KS-7
Irene (historical P.O.)—*locale* IA-7
Irene Lake—*lake* AK-9
Irene Lake—*lake* CO-8
Irene Lake—*lake* MI-6
Irene Mill Finishing Plant—*hist pl* SC-3
Irene Mine—*mine* CO-8
Irene Mtn—*summit* WA-9
Irene No. 2 Mine—*mine* CO-8
Irene Peak—*summit* CA-9
Irene Peak—*summit* MT-8
*Irene P.O.* AL-4
Irene Post Office (historical)—*building* MS-4
Irene Ranch—*locale* (2) WY-8
Irene Sch—*school* IL-6
Irene Spring—*spring* AZ-5
Irene Spring—*spring* NV-8
**Irene Subdivision**—*pop pl* UT-8
Irene Tunnels—*mine* AZ-5
Irene Wash—*stream* AZ-5
Irene Well—*reservoir* AZ-5
*Irene Windmill* AZ-5
Irenkodi—*locale* FM-9
Ire Run—*stream* IN-6
Iresick Brook—*stream* NJ-2
Ireson Cem—*cemetery* VA-3
Ireson Hill—*summit* ME-1
*Irestown* NJ-2
Ireteba Peaks—*summit* NV-8
**Ireton**—*pop pl* IA-7
Ireton Cem—*cemetery* OK-5
Ireton Draw—*valley* WY-8
Ireton Ranch—*locale* WY-8
Irey Spring—*spring* SD-7
**Irfred Park Subdivision**—*pop pl* UT-8
*Irgen Lake* MN-6
Irgens Lake—*lake* MN-6
Irgkivik Creek—*stream* AK-9
Irgnyivik Lake—*lake* AK-9
Irgoff Hoiness Ranch—*locale* MT-8
Iric Branch—*stream* GA-3
*Iric Creek* GA-3
Irick, John, House—*hist pl* NJ-2
Iridescent Lake—*lake* CA-9
Irigaray Ranch—*locale* WY-8
Irihr—*unknown* FM-9
*Irijan* MH-9
*Irikaklik Creek* AK-9
Irikl—*bay* PW-9
Irina, Lake—*lake* AK-9
Irine, Lake—*reservoir* TX-5
Irington Branch—*stream* MS-4
**Irion (County)**—*pop pl* TX-5
Irion County Courthouse—*hist pl* TX-5
*Iriquois Point* HI-9
Iris—*locale* CA-9
Iris—*locale* CO-8
Iris—*locale* MT-8
**Iris Acres (subdivision)**—*pop pl* TN-4
*Irisado Lake* NJ-2
Irisburg—*locale* VA-3
Irisburg Sch—*school* VA-3
Iris Cem—*cemetery* CO-8
Iris Creek—*stream* MI-6
Iris Creek—*stream* OR-9
Iris Falls—*falls* WY-8
Irish, J. & O., Store—*hist pl* ME-1
Irish, Lake—*lake* FL-3
Irish, Mount—*summit* NV-8
Irish, Nathaniel, House—*hist pl* PA-2
Irish-American Canal—*canal* NV-8
Irish-American Dam—*dam* NV-8
Irish and Taylor Campground—*park* OR-9
Irish Basin—*basin* MT-8
Irish Bayou—*gut* LA-4
Irish Bayou—*stream* LA-4
Irish Bayou Canal—*canal* LA-4
Irish Bayou Lagoon—*lake* LA-4
Irish Bay Springs—*spring* ID-8
Irish Bend—*bend* OR-9
**Irish Bend**—*pop pl* LA-4
Irish Bend Bridge—*hist pl* OR-9
Irish Bend Sch—*school* OR-9
Irish Bill Creek—*stream* AR-4
Irish Bottom—*bend* KY-4
Irish Bottoms—*bend* TN-4
Irish Bottom Sch—*school* KY-4
Irish Boy Mine—*mine* MT-8
Irish Branch—*stream* MO-7
Irish Bridge—*bridge* CA-9
Irish Brook—*stream* NJ-2
Irish Brook—*stream* (2) NY-2
Irish Brook Dam—*dam* NJ-2
Irish Buffalo Creek—*stream* NC-3
Irish Butte—*summit* SD-7
Irish Camp Lake—*lake* OR-9
Irish Canyon—*valley* CA-9
Irish Canyon—*valley* CO-8
Irish Canyon—*valley* ID-8
Irish Canyon—*valley* WY-8
Irish Canyon Creek—*stream* WY-8
Irish Cem—*cemetery* (2) TN-4
Irish Channel—*channel* AK-9
Irish Channel Area Architectural District—*hist pl* LA-4
Irish Corner (Magisterial District)—*fmr MCD* WV-2
Irish Corners—*locale* NY-2
Irish Coulee—*valley* MT-8
Irish Cove—*bay* AK-9
*Irish Creek* VA-3
Irish Creek—*bay* MD-2
Irish Creek—*locale* VA-3
Irish Creek—*stream* (3) AK-9
Irish Creek—*stream* CA-9
Irish Creek—*stream* (4) ID-8
Irish Creek—*stream* (4) KS-7
Irish Creek—*stream* KY-4
Irish Creek—*stream* MD-2
Irish Creek—*stream* MI-6
Irish Creek—*stream* (2) MN-6
Irish Creek—*stream* MT-8
Irish Creek—*stream* NY-2
Irish Creek—*stream* NC-3
Irish Creek—*stream* OH-6
Irish Creek—*stream* PA-2
Irish Creek—*stream* SD-7
Irish Creek—*stream* (2) TX-5
Irish Creek—*stream* (2) VA-3
Irish Creek—*stream* WA-9
Irish Creek—*stream* WI-6
Irish Creek—*stream* WY-8
Irish Creek Cem—*cemetery* VA-3
**Irish Cut**—*pop pl* TN-4
Irish Cut Sch (historical)—*school* TN-4
Irish Ditch—*canal* MT-8
Irish Ditch—*canal* NY-2
Irish Ditch—*stream* LA-4
Irish Ditch Number One—*canal* LA-4
Irish Ditch Number Two—*canal* LA-4
Irish Drift Mine (underground)—*mine* AL-4
Irish Flats—*flat* KS-7
*Irish Fork* OH-6
Irish Gap—*gap* VA-3
Irish Glade—*flat* CA-9
Irish Green Spring—*spring* UT-8
Irish Grove Cem—*cemetery* IL-6
Irish Grove Ch—*church* (2) IL-6
Irish Grove (Election Precinct)—*fmr MCD* IL-6
Irish Grove Sch—*school* MO-7
Irish Gulch—*valley* (3) AK-9
Irish Gulch—*valley* (2) CA-9
Irish Gulch—*valley* CO-8
Irish Gulch—*valley* MT-8
Irish Gulch—*valley* OR-9
Irish Gulch—*valley* SD-7
Irish Gulch—*valley* WY-8
Irish Gulf—*valley* NY-2
*Irish Hill* DE-2
**Irish Hill**—*pop pl* WV-2
Irish Hill—*summit* (2) CA-9
Irish Hill—*summit* (2) ME-1
Irish Hill—*summit* MI-6
Irish Hill—*summit* NH-1
Irish Hill—*summit* (7) NY-2
Irish Hill—*summit* OR-9
Irish Hill—*summit* VT-1
Irish Hills—*other* CA-9
Irish Hollow—*valley* IL-6
Irish Hollow—*valley* (4) OH-6
Irish Hollow—*valley* PA-2
Irish Hollow—*valley* WI-6
Irish Hollow Cem—*cemetery* MI-6
Irish Hollow Creek—*stream* IA-7
Irish Island—*cape* MA-1
**Iris (historical)**—*pop pl* MS-4
Irish Lake—*lake* IN-6
Irish Lake—*lake* IA-7
Irish Lake—*lake* MI-6
Irish Lake—*lake* (2) MN-6
Irish Lake—*lake* (2) OR-9
Irish Lake—*lake* WY-8
Irish Lakes—*lake* AK-9
Irish Lakes—*lake* CO-8
Irish Lick Knob—*summit* WV-2
Irish Mag—*mine* AZ-5
Irishman Branch—*stream* TN-4
Irishman Coulee—*valley* MT-8
Irishman Creek—*stream* KY-4
Irishman Dam—*dam* AZ-5
Irishman Ditch—*canal* AL-4
Irishman Hill—*summit* TX-5
Irishman Run—*stream* IN-6
Irishmans Campground—*park* OR-9
Irishmans Flat—*flat* CA-9
Irishmans Hat—*cape* AK-9
*Irishmans Hill* NH-1
Irishmans Hole—*basin* MT-8
Irishmans Rock—*summit* ID-8
**Irish Meeting House**—*pop pl* PA-2
*Irishmen Gulch* OR-9
*Irish Mills* NJ-2
Irish Mtn—*summit* CA-9
Irish Mtn—*summit* (2) NY-2
Irish Mtn—*summit* OR-9
Irish Mtn—*summit* PA-2
Irish Mtn—*summit* VA-3
Irish Mtn—*summit* WA-9
Irish Mtn—*summit* (2) WV-2
Irish Point—*cape* ME-1
Irish Range, Mount—*range* NV-8
Irish Ravine—*valley* CA-9
Irish Reed Drain—*canal* MI-6
*Irish Ridge* WI-6
Irish Ridge—*ridge* CA-9
Irish Ridge—*ridge* CO-8
Irish Ridge—*ridge* ME-1
Irish Ridge—*ridge* (2) MN-6
Irish Ridge—*ridge* NY-2
Irish Ridge—*ridge* (5) OH-6
Irish Ridge—*ridge* TX-5
Irish Ridge—*ridge* (2) WV-2
Irish Ridge—*ridge* (5) WI-6
Irish Ridge Cem—*cemetery* OH-6
Irish Ridge Ch—*church* NY-2
Irish Ridge Ch—*church* OH-6
*Irish Ripple* PA-2
Irish Rock—*summit* WY-8
Irish Rose Mine—*mine* NV-8
Irish Run—*stream* (2) OH-6
Irish Run—*stream* (3) PA-2
Irish Run—*stream* (2) WV-2
Irish Sch—*school* MI-6
Irish Settlement—*locale* ME-1
Irish Settlement—*locale* (2) NY-2
Irish Settlement Brook—*stream* PA-2
Irish Settlement Cem—*cemetery* (2) NY-2
Irish Settlement Sch—*school* VT-1
Irish Settlement Trail—*trail* PA-2
Irish Slide Mine—*mine* CA-9
Irish Slough—*gut* MT-8
Irish Spring—*spring* CO-8
Irish Spring—*spring* (2) OR-9
Irishtown—*locale* NY-2
Irishtown—*locale* PA-2
**Irishtown**—*pop pl* (5) PA-2
Irishtown Ch—*church* MI-6
*Irishtown Gap* PA-2
Irishtown Gap Hollow—*valley* PA-2
Irishtown Run—*stream* (2) PA-2
**Irishtown (Township of)**—*pop pl* IL-6
Irish Valley—*valley* (3) WI-6
Irish Valley Ch—*church* PA-2
Irish Wash—*stream* CA-9
*Iris Lake* AK-9
Iris Lake—*lake* ID-8
Iris Lake—*lake* MN-6
Iris Lakes—*reservoir* GA-3
Iris Lovelady Spring—*spring* TN-4
Iris Meadows—*area* AK-9
Iris Mine—*mine* NV-8
Iris Pass—*gap* CA-9
Iris Point—*summit* MT-8
Iris Point Trail—*trail* MT-8
Iris Pond—*lake* OR-9
Iris RR Station—*locale* FL-3
Iris Sch—*school* AL-4
Iris Seep—*spring* MT-8
Iris Spring—*spring* AZ-5
Iris Tank—*reservoir* (2) AZ-5
Iris Wash—*stream* CA-9
Iriswood (Magisterial District)—*fmr MCD* VA-3
Irivik Creek—*stream* AK-9
**Irl**—*pop pl* MO-7
Irland Cem—*cemetery* MS-4
Irle Sch—*school* MT-8
Irma—*locale* AR-4
Irma—*locale* LA-4
**Irma**—*pop pl* KY-4
**Irma**—*pop pl* MO-7
**Irma**—*pop pl* WI-6
Irma, Lake—*lake* FL-3
Irma, Lake—*reservoir* GA-3
Irma Flats—*flat* WY-8
Irma Hill—*summit* WI-6
Irma (historical)—*locale* AL-4
**Irma (historical)**—*pop pl* OR-9
Irma Hotel—*hist pl* WY-8
Irma Lake—*lake* MN-6
Irma Lake—*lake* WY-8
Irma Mines—*mine* MT-8
Irma Oil Field—*oilfield* AR-4
**Irmo**—*pop pl* SC-3
Irmo (CCD)—*cens area* SC-3
Irmo HS—*school* SC-3
Irmo MS—*school* SC-3
Irmulco—*locale* CA-9
*Irodj* MP-9
Irogami Lake—*lake* WI-6
*Iroijeman Island* MP-9
*Irokois River* IN-6
*Iron* MN-6
*Iron* NC-3
*Iron* TN-4
Iron—*locale* MT-8
**Iron**—*pop pl* IL-6
*Iron, Mount* FM-9
*Irona* AL-4
Irona—*locale* NY-2
Irona—*locale* WV-2
**Irona**—*pop pl* NY-2
**Irona**—*pop pl* PA-2
Irona Ch—*church* WV-2
Iron Age Mine—*mine* CA-9
**Ironaton**—*pop pl* AL-4
Ironaton Ch of Christ—*church* AL-4
Ironaton Methodist Ch—*church* AL-4
Iron Basin—*basin* ID-8
Iron Basin—*locale* UT-8
Iron Bear Creek Trail—*trail* WA-9
Iron Beds—*cliff* CO-8
Ironbell Ch—*church* VA-3
Iron Bell Ranch—*locale* AZ-5
**Iron Belt**—*pop pl* WI-6
Iron Bend—*bend* FL-3
*Iron Berg* FM-9
Iron Block—*hist pl* WI-6
Iron Blossom Mtn—*summit* NV-8
Iron Blossom No 1—*mine* UT-8
Iron Blossom No 3—*mine* UT-8
Iron Blossom No. 3 Mine—*hist pl* UT-8
Iron Blossom Tunnel—*mine* UT-8
Iron Bluff Cem—*cemetery* TX-5
*Iron Bluffs* AL-4
Iron Bluff Sch—*school* NE-7
Iron Bog Creek—*stream* ID-8
Iron Bog Lake—*reservoir* ID-8
Iron Bog Swamp—*swamp* ID-8
Ironbound—*uninc pl* NJ-2
Iron Bound Bay—*bay* CA-9
Ironbound Island—*island* ME-1
Ironbound Mtn—*summit* ME-1
Ironbound Pond—*lake* (2) ME-1
Iron Bowl, The—*basin* UT-8
Iron Branch—*stream* DE-2
Iron Branch—*stream* LA-4
Iron Branch—*stream* NJ-2
Iron Branch—*stream* VA-3
*Iron Bridge* AL-4
Iron Bridge—*bridge* DE-2
Iron Bridge—*bridge* KY-4
Iron Bridge—*bridge* TN-4
Iron Bridge—*bridge* (2) TX-5
Iron Bridge—*bridge* VT-1
Iron Bridge—*hist pl* TX-5
Ironbridge—*locale* OK-5
Iron Bridge—*locale* PA-2
Ironbridge—*other* PA-2
**Iron Bridge**—*pop pl* PA-2
**Iron Bridge**—*pop pl* WV-2
Iron Bridge at Howard Hill Road—*hist pl* VT-1
Iron Bridge Chapel—*church* PA-2
**Iron Bridge Estates**—*pop pl* PA-2
Iron Bridge (historical)—*bridge* MS-4
Iron Bridge Landing—*locale* TN-4
Iron Bridge Park—*park* TX-5
Iron Bridge Post Office (historical)—*building* AL-4
Iron Bridge Run—*stream* WV-2
Iron Bridge Sch (historical)—*school* AL-4
Iron Bridge Sch (historical)—*school* TN-4
Iron Butte—*summit* (2) MT-8
Iron Canyon—*valley* (3) AZ-5
Iron Canyon—*valley* (7) CA-9
Iron Canyon—*valley* (2) CO-8
Iron Canyon—*valley* MT-8
Iron Canyon—*valley* NV-8
Iron Canyon—*valley* NM-5
Iron Canyon—*valley* (3) UT-8
Iron Canyon Mine—*mine* NV-8
Iron Canyon Point—*cape* UT-8
Iron Canyon Spring—*spring* AZ-5
Iron Cap Creek—*stream* MT-8
Ironcap Mine—*mine* CO-8
Iron Cap Mtn—*summit* WA-9
Iron Cap Shaft—*mine* AZ-5
Iron Center Sch—*school* MO-7
Iron Chapel—*church* OK-5
Iron Chapel Oil Field—*oilfield* OK-5
Iron Chief Mine—*mine* MT-8
*Ironcity* AL-4
*Iron City* OH-6
Iron City—*locale* CO-8
Iron City—*locale* PA-2
**Iron City**—*pop pl* AL-4
**Iron City**—*pop pl* GA-3
**Iron City**—*pop pl* PA-2
**Iron City**—*pop pl* TN-4
Iron City Baptist Ch—*church* AL-4
Iron City Baptist Ch—*church* TN-4
Iron City Freewill Baptist Ch—*church* TN-4
Iron City Islands—*island* MT-8
Iron City Methodist Ch—*church* TN-4
Iron City Mtn—*summit* AL-4
Iron City Post Office—*building* TN-4
Iron City Sch (historical)—*school* TN-4
Iron City Spring—*spring* TN-4
Iron City-St. Joseph (CCD)—*cens area* TN-4
Iron City-St Joseph Division—*civil* TN-4
Iron City United Methodist Ch—*church* AL-4
Ironclad Hill—*summit* CO-8
Ironclad Mtn—*summit* CO-8
Ironclads, The—*range* CO-8
Ironclad School (historical)—*locale* MO-7
Ironco Hollow—*valley* GA-3
Iron Corner Lake—*lake* MN-6
*Iron (corporate and RR name Iron Junction)* MN-6
Iron Corral—*locale* NV-8
Iron County—*civil* UT-8
**Iron (County)**—*pop pl* MI-6
**Iron County**—*pop pl* MO-7
**Iron (County)**—*pop pl* WI-6
Iron County Courthouse—*hist pl* MI-6
Iron County Courthouse Buildings—*hist pl* MO-7
Iron County Fair Exhibition Hall—*hist pl* MI-6
Iron County Farm—*locale* MO-7
Iron County Forest Preserve—*park* MI-6
*Iron Creek* IN-6
*Iron Creek* TX-5
*Iron Creek* WI-6
*Iron Creek* WY-8
Iron Creek—*locale* (2) AK-9
Iron Creek—*stream* (6) AK-9
Iron Creek—*stream* (7) CA-9
Iron Creek—*stream* (4) CO-8
Iron Creek—*stream* (4) ID-8
Iron Creek—*stream* IN-6
Iron Creek—*stream* (3) MI-6
Iron Creek—*stream* MN-6
Iron Creek—*stream* (5) MT-8
Iron Creek—*stream* NV-8
Iron Creek—*stream* (2) NM-5
Iron Creek—*stream* NC-3
Iron Creek—*stream* (4) OR-9
Iron Creek—*stream* (2) SD-7
Iron Creek—*stream* (3) TX-5
Iron Creek—*stream* UT-8
Iron Creek—*stream* (5) WA-9
Iron Creek—*stream* (4) WI-6
Iron Creek—*stream* (10) WY-8
Iron Creek Butte—*summit* WA-9
Iron Creek Campground—*locale* ID-8
Iron Creek Campground—*locale* WA-9
Iron Creek Cem—*cemetery* WI-6
Iron Creek Ch—*church* MI-6
Iron Creek Dam—*dam* SD-7
Iron Creek Guard Station—*locale* WA-9
Iron Creek Lake—*lake* NM-5
Iron Creek Lake—*reservoir* SD-7
Iron Creek Meadows—*swamp* WY-8
Iron Creek Mesa—*summit* NM-5
Iron Creek Oil Field—*oilfield* WY-8
Iron Creek Point—*cliff* ID-8
Iron Creek Spring—*spring* WY-8
Iron Creek Trail—*trail* SD-7
Iron Crossroads—*locale* SC-3
Iron Daisy Mine—*mine* MT-8
*Irondale* IL-6
*Irondale* IN-6
*Irondale* OH-6
Irondale—*locale* NY-2
**Irondale**—*pop pl* AL-4
**Irondale**—*pop pl* CO-8
**Irondale**—*pop pl* IN-6
**Irondale**—*pop pl* MO-7
**Irondale**—*pop pl* NY-2
**Irondale**—*pop pl* OH-6
**Irondale**—*pop pl* VA-3
**Irondale**—*pop pl* WA-9
Irondale Branch—*stream* AL-4
Irondale Bridge—*bridge* AL-4
Irondale Cem—*cemetery* MN-6
Irondale Cem—*cemetery* NY-2
Irondale Ch—*church* LA-4
Irondale Ch—*church* VA-3
Irondale City Hall—*building* AL-4
Irondale Dam—*locale* PA-2
Irondale Elem Sch—*school* AL-4
Irondale Hist Dist—*hist pl* WA-9
Irondale Jail—*hist pl* WA-9
Irondale JHS—*school* AL-4
Irondale Junction—*uninc pl* AL-4
Irondale Lake—*reservoir* MO-7
Irondale Mine—*mine* MO-7
Irondale Plaza Shop Ctr—*locale* AL-4
Irondale Sch—*school* MN-6
**Irondale (Township of)**—*pop pl* MN-6
**Irondequoit**—*pop pl* NY-2
Irondequoit Bay—*bay* (2) NY-2
Irondequoit Bay Park—*park* NY-2
Irondequoit Country Club—*other* NY-2
Irondequoit Creek—*stream* NY-2
Irondequoit HS—*school* NY-2
**Irondequoit Manor**—*pop pl* NY-2
Irondequoit Mtn—*summit* NY-2
**Irondequoit (subdivision)**—*pop pl* NY-2
**Irondequoit (Town of)**—*pop pl* NY-2
Iron Dike—*summit* AZ-5
**Iron Divide (historical)**—*pop pl* TN-4
Iron Dog Creek—*stream* SD-7
Iron Dollar Gulch—*valley* CO-8
Iron Dome—*summit* AK-9
Iron Door, The—*cape* AK-9
Iron Door Mine—*mine* OR-9
Iron Draw—*valley* CO-8
Iron Draw—*valley* SD-7
**Ironduff**—*pop pl* NC-3
**Iron Duff**—*pop pl* NC-3
Iron Duff (Township of)—*fmr MCD* NC-3
Iron Duke Mine—*mine* CA-9
Irondyke Camp—*locale* OR-9
Irondyke Creek—*stream* OR-9
Iron Dyke Mine—*mine* (2) CA-9
Iron Dyke Mine—*mine* ID-8
Ironedge Trail—*trail* CO-8
Iron Flat—*flat* AZ-5
Iron Flat Tank—*reservoir* AZ-5
Iron Fork—*stream* CA-9
Iron Fork Camp—*locale* CA-9
Iron Furnace—*locale* NY-2
Iron Gap—*gap* (2) TN-4
Iron Gate—*gap* WA-9
**Irongate**—*pop pl* NY-2
**Irongate**—*pop pl* TN-4
**Iron Gate**—*pop pl* VA-3
**Irongate**—*pop pl* VA-3
Irongate Cave—*cave* AL-4
Iron Gate Dam—*dam* CA-9
Irongate Golf Course Lake Dam—*dam* NC-3
Iron Gate Rsvr—*reservoir* CA-9
**Iron Gates**—*pop pl* DE-2
**Iron Gates**—*pop pl* MO-7
**Irongate (subdivision)**—*pop pl* (3) NC-3
*Iron God Mine* NV-8
Iron Gold Mine—*mine* NV-8
Irongrape Hammock—*island* FL-3
Iron Gulch—*valley* AK-9
Iron Gulch—*valley* CO-8

Jacoby Draw—valley ... WY-8
Jacoby Hollow—valley ... PA-2
Jacoby Mtn—summit ... OR-9
Jacoby Mtn—summit ... PA-2
Jacoby Ranch—locale ... ID-8
Jacoby Ranch—locale ... TX-5
Jacoby Sch—school ... IA-7
Jacoby Spring—spring ... CA-9
Joco Cem—cemetery ... TN-4
Jacocks—locale ... NC-3
Jacocks Creek—stream ... TN-4
Jacocks Landing—locale ... NC-3
Jacoe Store—hist pl ... CO-8
Jacolyn Park—park ... IA-7
Jacomo, Lake—reservoir ... MO-7
**Jacona**—pop pl ... NM-5
Jacona Grant—civil ... NM-5
Jacona Ranch—locale ... NM-5
Jacona Ranch Arroyo—stream ... NM-5
**Jaconita**—pop pl ... NM-5
Jacot Creek—stream ... ID-8
Jacot Park—park ... OH-6
Jacovy Creek—channel ... NJ-2
Jacoway Branch—stream ... AL-4
Jacoway Cem—cemetery ... AL-4
Jacoway Hollow—valley ... AL-4
Jaco Well—well ... AZ-5
Jacox—locale ... WV-2
Jacox JHS—school ... VA-3
Jacox Knob—summit ... WV-2
Jacox Pond—lake ... NY-2
Jacquar Field—park ... AL-4
Jacquays Run—stream ... OH-6
Jacque Creek—stream ... CO-8
*Jacqueline Lake* ... WI-6
Jacque Peak—summit ... CO-8
Jacque Ridge—ridge ... CO-8
Jacques—locale ... ID-8
Jacques, Bay—lake ... LA-4
Jacques, Bayou—gut ... LA-4
Jacques Canyon Tank No 1—reservoir ... NM-5
Jacques Canyon Tank No 2—reservoir ... NM-5
Jacques Cartier State Park—park ... NY-2
Jacques Coulee—stream ... LA-4
Jacques Coulee—valley ... MT-8
*Jacques Creek* ... OR-9
Jacques Creek—stream ... MO-7
Jacques Creek—stream ... OR-9
Jacques Dam—dam ... AZ-5
Jacques Drain—stream ... MI-6
*Jacques Gulch* ... MT-8
Jacques Gulch—valley ... CA-9
Jacques Hanlon Creek—stream ... CA-9
*Jacques Lake* ... AZ-5
Jacques Lake—lake ... WI-6
Jacques Marquette Elem Sch—school ... IN-6
Jacques Ridge—ridge ... CA-9
*Jacques River* ... ND-7
Jacques Spring—spring ... WY-8
Jacques Spur—locale ... ID-8
Jacquet Sch—school ... LA-4
Jacquez, Canada—stream ... NM-5
Jacquez, Laguna—reservoir ... NM-5
Jacquez Canyon—valley ... NM-5
Jacquinot, Point—cape ... FM-9
*Jacquinot Island* ... FM-9
Jacquish Hollow—valley ... WI-6
Jacquith Pond—lake ... NH-1
Jacquline, Lake—lake ... WY-8
Jacquot Dam—dam ... SD-7
Jac Ranch—locale ... NM-5
J A Creek—stream ... WY-8
J A Crenshaw Pond Dam—dam ... MS-4
**Jacumba**—pop pl ... CA-9
*Jacumba Hot Springs* ... CA-9
**Jacumba (Jacumba Hot Springs)**—pop pl ... CA-9
Jacumba Mountains—range ... CA-9
Jacumba Peak—summit ... CA-9
Jacumba Valley—valley ... CA-9
J A Dasher Hosp—hospital ... NC-3
**Jadden**—pop pl ... IN-6
Jade Camp—locale ... OR-9
Jade Creek—stream ... AK-9
Jade Creek—stream ... OR-9
Jade Harbor—bay ... AK-9
*Jade Lake* ... MN-6
Jade Lake—lake ... TX-5
Jade Lake—lake (2) ... WA-9
*Jade Lake Dam* ... AL-4
Jade Mine—mine ... CA-9
Jade More Branch—stream ... KY-4
Jade Mountains—other ... AK-9
Jaden Cem—cemetery ... TX-5
**Jade Park North (Trailer Park)**—pop pl ... AZ-5
Jade Prospect—mine ... WY-8
Jader Creek—stream ... WI-6
Jade Rsvr—reservoir ... OR-9
Jade Run—stream ... NJ-2
Jade Shoals—bar ... GU-9
*Jades Island* ... NC-3
Jadesville (historical)—locale ... NC-3
**Jadis (Township of)**—pop pl ... MN-6
*Jadi To* ... AZ-5
**Jadito**—pop pl ... AZ-5
*Jadito Canyon* ... AZ-5
Jadito Spring—spring ... AZ-5
*Jadito Springs* ... AZ-5
*Jadito Station* ... AZ-5
*Jadito Store* ... AZ-5
*Jadito Trading Post* ... AZ-5
Jadito Wash—stream ... AZ-5
Jadoul—locale ... MP-9
*Jadru-l* ... MP-9
Jadski Cove—bay ... AK-9
**Jadwin**—pop pl ... MO-7
Jadwin Ch—church ... MO-7
Jadwin Sch—school ... MO-7
Jady Branch—stream ... NC-3
**Jady Hill**—pop pl ... NH-1
J A Earnheart Pond Dam—dam ... MS-4
Jaeckel Hotel—hist pl ... GA-3
Jaeger Creek—stream (2) ... MO-7
Jaeger Knob—summit ... MO-7
Jaeger Lake—lake ... MN-6
Jaeger Machine Company Office Bldg—hist pl ... OH-6
Jaeger Mine—mine ... AZ-5
*Jaegers Pond* ... NJ-2

Jaeger-Witte Cem—cemetery ... TX-5
**Jaffa**—pop pl ... VA-3
**Jaffa Mosque**—pop pl ... PA-2
Jaffa Opera House—hist pl ... CO-8
*Jaffray Point* ... NH-1
*Jaffrey* ... NH-1
**Jaffrey**—pop pl ... NH-1
**Jaffrey Center**—pop pl ... NH-1
Jaffrey Center Hist Dist—hist pl ... NH-1
*Jaffrey Centre* ... NH-1
**Jaffrey Compact (census name Jaffrey)**—pop pl ... NH-1
Jaffrey Mills—hist pl ... NH-1
Jaffrey Point—cape ... NH-1
**Jaffrey (Town of)**—pop pl ... NH-1
Jaff Slough—lake ... ND-7
*Jagels Slough* ... CA-9
Jager Cem—cemetery ... NM-5
Jager Creek—stream ... MT-8
Jager Mine—mine ... MT-8
Jaggar Creek—stream ... WY-8
Jaggards Pond—reservoir ... NJ-2
Jaggards Pond Dam—dam ... NJ-2
Jaggar Peak—summit ... WY-8
Jaggars Cave (Shelter)—locale ... HI-9
Jagg Creek—stream ... WY-8
Jagged Boulder Plateau—area ... AK-9
*Jagged Island* ... WA-9
Jagged Island—island ... WA-9
*Jagged Islets* ... WA-9
Jagged Mtn—summit ... AK-9
Jagged Ridge—ridge ... WA-9
Jagged Rock—pillar ... AZ-5
Jagged Tooth Tank—reservoir ... AZ-5
**Jagger**—pop pl ... AL-4
Jagger Branch—stream ... AL-4
Jagger Cave—cave ... AL-4
Jagger-Churchill House—hist pl ... IA-7
*Jagger Creek* ... WY-8
*Jagger Creek Mine* ... AL-4
Jagger Ditch—canal ... MT-8
Jagger Hollow—valley ... AL-4
Jagger Hollow—valley ... TN-4
Jagger House—hist pl ... NY-2
Jagger Mine Number Two (underground)—mine ... AL-4
Jagger Mines (underground)—mine ... AL-4
Jagger Mine (underground)—mine (2) ... AL-4
*Jagger Number Seven Mine* ... AL-4
Jagger Pond—reservoir ... ME-1
Jaggers Cem—cemetery ... KY-4
Jagger Slope Mine (underground)—mine ... AL-4
Jaggles Canyon—valley ... ID-8
Jagiello Waterfowl Production Area—park ... MT-8
Jag Lake—lake ... WI-6
Jago—locale ... MS-4
Jago Bay—bay ... CA-9
Jago Cem—cemetery ... KY-4
*Jagoe* ... MS-4
Jagoe—locale ... TX-5
Jago Entrance—channel ... AK-9
*Jagoe Post Office* ... MS-4
Jago Lagoon—bay ... AK-9
Jago Lake—lake ... AK-9
Jago Post Office (historical)—building ... MS-4
Jago River—stream ... AK-9
Jago Spit—bar ... AK-9
Jagow Tank—reservoir ... AZ-5
Jagow Well—well ... AZ-5
J A Greco Lake Dam—dam ... MS-4
**Jagual**—pop pl ... PR-3
Jagual (Barrio)—fmr MCD (2) ... PR-3
Jagua Pasto (Barrio)—fmr MCD ... PR-3
Jaguar (Barrio)—fmr MCD ... PR-3
**Jaguas**—pop pl (2) ... PR-3
Jaguas (Barrio)—fmr MCD (4) ... PR-3
Jaguey (Barrio)—fmr MCD (2) ... PR-3
**Jagueyes**—pop pl ... PR-3
Jagueyes (Barrio)—fmr MCD ... PR-3
Jaguitas (Barrio)—fmr MCD ... PR-3
*Jagway Valley* ... AZ-5
*Jagwey Valley* ... AZ-5
Jahant Slough—stream ... CA-9
*Jahew Hollow* ... VA-3
Jahie Lake ( Salt)—lake ... NM-5
Jahile—locale ... VA-3
Jahncke Canal—canal ... LA-4
Jahnckes Ditch—canal ... LA-4
Jahn Creek—stream ... IN-6
Jahnke Creek—stream ... MT-8
Jahnke Mine—mine ... MT-8
Jahnke Sch—school ... MN-6
Jahn Rsvr—reservoir ... OR-9
Jahns Cem—cemetery ... TX-5
Jahn Sch—school ... IL-6
Jahns Valley—valley ... WI-6
*Jahuey Creek* ... TX-5
Jahu Flat—flat ... UT-8
J A Hughes Lake Number 3 Dam—dam ... AL-4
J A Hughes Number One Dam—dam ... AL-4
J A Hughes Number Two Dam—dam ... AL-4
Jail Branch—stream ... VT-1
Jail Bridge—bridge ... TN-4
Jail Brook—stream ... VT-1
Jail Canyon—valley ... CA-9
Jail Cave—cave ... AZ-5
Jail Creek—stream ... VA-3
*Jail Entrance* ... UT-8
Jail Gulch—valley ... CA-9
Jail Hill—summit ... CT-1
Jailhouse Hollow—valley ... WV-2
Jailhouse Rock—summit ... UT-8
Jailhouse Ruin—locale ... UT-8
Jailhouse Spring—spring ... UT-8
Jail Island (historical)—island ... TN-4
*Jail Lake* ... MN-6
Jail Lake—lake ... MN-6
Jail Point—cape ... VA-3
Jail Rock—pillar ... UT-8
Jail Rock—summit ... NE-7
Jail Spring—spring ... CA-9
Jaimerena Ranch—locale ... NV-8
Jain Ditch—canal ... IN-6
*Jaite* ... OH-6
**Jaite**—pop pl ... OH-6
Jaite Mill Hist Dist—hist pl ... OH-6
Jajloo—area ... GU-9
**Jajome**—pop pl ... PR-3
Jajome Alto (Barrio)—fmr MCD ... PR-3

Jajome Bajo (Barrio)—fmr MCD ... PR-3
*Jakas Gulch* ... CA-9
Jake—locale ... GA-3
Jake Allgood Gulch—valley ... CA-9
Jake and Hank Mine—mine ... CO-8
*Jake Arner Memorial Airport* ... PA-2
Jake Bay—swamp ... FL-3
Jake Best Campground—locale ... TN-4
Jake Best Creek—stream ... TN-4
Jake Branch—stream ... GA-3
Jake Branch—stream ... KS-7
Jake Branch—stream (2) ... KY-4
Jake Branch—stream (5) ... NC-3
Jake Branch—stream (3) ... TN-4
Jake Branch—stream ... VA-3
Jake Campbell Branch—stream ... KY-4
*Jake Canyon* ... ID-8
Jake Canyon—valley ... MT-8
Jake Canyon Creek stream ... MT-8
Jake Cem—cemetery ... MS-4
Jake Cem Number 2—cemetery ... MS-4
Jake Chee Windmill—locale ... NM-5
Jake Cove—valley ... NC-3
*Jake Creek* ... MO-7
*Jake Creek* ... TN-4
Jake Creek—stream (2) ... AL-4
Jake Creek—stream ... AR-4
Jake Creek—stream ... ID-8
Jake Creek—stream ... IL-6
Jake Creek—stream ... MI-6
Jake Creek—stream ... MT-8
Jake Creek—stream ... NV-8
Jake Creek—stream ... NC-3
Jake Creek—stream ... OR-9
Jake Creek—stream ... TX-5
Jake Creek—stream ... WY-8
Jake Creek Mtn—summit ... NV-8
Jake Creek Sch—school ... TX-5
Jake Deal Cove—valley ... NC-3
Jake Fork—stream (3) ... KY-4
Jake Fork Bay—bay ... KY-4
Jake Goodson Creek—stream ... GA-3
Jake Green Spring—spring ... OR-9
Jake Grove Sch (historical)—school ... MO-7
*Jake Gulch* ... ID-8
Jake Gut—stream ... MD-2
Jake Hole—basin ... FL-3
Jake Hole—bay ... FL-3
Jake Hollow—valley ... AL-4
Jake Hollow—valley ... AR-4
Jake Hollow—valley ... IN-6
Jake Hollow—valley ... KY-4
Jake Hollow—valley ... MO-7
Jake Hollow—valley ... NC-3
Jake Hollow—valley (2) ... TN-4
Jake Hollow—valley ... UT-8
*Jake Hollow - in part* ... UT-8
Jake Hughes Rsvr—reservoir ... OR-9
Jake Jones Cem—cemetery ... TN-4
Jake Kern Dam—dam ... SD-7
Jake Knob—summit ... TN-4
*Jake Lake* ... MN-6
Jake Lake—lake ... AK-9
Jake Lake—lake ... MN-6
Jakeman Creek—stream ... CO-8
Jake McCain Tank—reservoir ... AZ-5
Jake Mtn—summit ... GA-3
Jake Mtn—summit ... NC-3
Jake Prairie—locale ... MO-7
Jake Prairie Chapel—church ... MO-7
Jake Rains Windmill—locale ... TX-5
Jake Ridge—ridge ... NC-3
Jake Ridge—ridge ... TN-4
Jakeru—island ... MP-9
*Jakeru Island* ... MP-9
Jake Run—stream ... OH-6
Jake Run—stream ... PA-2
Jake Run—stream ... WV-2
*Jakeru-To* ... MP-9
Jakes Bayou—stream ... FL-3
Jakes Bayou—stream ... LA-4
*Jakes Branch* ... VA-3
*Jakes Branch* ... WV-2
Jakes Branch—stream ... IL-6
Jakes Branch—stream ... IN-6
Jakes Branch—stream (3) ... KY-4
Jakes Branch—stream ... MO-7
Jakes Branch—stream ... NJ-2
Jakes Branch—stream (2) ... WV-2
Jakes Branch Ch—church ... TN-4
Jake's Branch of Middle Creek Bridge—hist pl ... KS-7
Jakes Brook—stream ... CT-1
Jakes Butte—summit ... IN-6
Jakes Canyon—valley ... ID-8
Jakes Canyon—valley ... UT-8
Jakes Colony Ch—church ... TX-5
Jakes Corner—locale ... AZ-5
Jakes Coulee—valley ... MT-8
*Jakes Creek* ... IN-6
Jakes Creek—stream ... AR-4
Jakes Creek—stream ... CA-9
Jakes Creek—stream ... CO-8
Jakes Creek—stream ... ID-8
Jakes Creek—stream ... IN-6
Jakes Creek—stream ... KY-4
Jakes Creek—stream ... MS-4
Jakes Creek—stream ... MO-7
Jakes Creek—stream ... NE-7
Jakes Creek—stream (3) ... NV-8
Jakes Creek—stream ... NC-3
Jakes Creek—stream (4) ... TN-4
Jakes Creek—stream ... TX-5
Jakes Creek—stream ... WA-9
Jakes Creek Trail—trail ... TN-4
Jakes Draw—valley ... MT-8
Jake Seller Draw—valley ... WY-8
Jakes Fork—stream ... VA-3
Jakes Fork—stream ... WV-2
Jakes Gap—gap ... TN-4
Jakes Gulch—valley ... CA-9
Jakes Gulch—valley ... ID-8
Jake Shanty Ridge—ridge ... PA-2
Jakes Hole—bay ... TN-4
Jakes Hollow—valley ... MO-7
Jakes Hollow—valley ... TN-4
Jakes Hunting Ground—area ... CA-9
Jakes Knoll—summit ... UT-8
Jakes Knoll Rsvr—reservoir ... UT-8
Jakes Lake—lake ... MI-6

Jakes Lake—lake ... WA-9
Jakes Lower Camp—locale ... CA-9
Jakes Mine—mine ... WY-8
Jakes Mtn—summit ... TN-4
Jakes Notch—gap ... ME-1
Jakes Opening—flat ... CA-9
Jakes Peak—summit ... CA-9
Jakes Pond—lake ... MA-1
Jakes Pond—lake ... NV-8
Jakes Pond—lake ... NH-1
Jakes Pond—lake ... NY-2
Jake Spring—spring ... CA-9
Jakes Ridge—ridge ... NM-5
Jakes Rocks—cliff ... PA-2
Jakes Rocks Overlook—locale ... PA-2
Jakes Rsvr—reservoir ... MT-8
*Jakes Run* ... PA-2
**Jakes Run**—pop pl ... WV-2
Jakes Run—stream ... OH-6
Jakes Run—stream (5) ... PA-2
Jakes Run—stream (8) ... WV-2
Jakes Run Sch—school ... WV-2
Jakes Spring—spring ... NM-5
Jakes Spring—spring ... TX-5
**Jakes Tank**—pop pl ... TN-4
Jakes Tank—reservoir ... NM-5
Jakes Tank Canyon—valley ... AZ-5
*Jakes Town* ... TN-4
**Jakestown (Double Springs)**—pop pl ... TN-4
Jakes Upper Camp—locale ... CA-9
Jakes Valley—basin ... NV-8
Jakes Valley—valley ... MO-7
**Jakesville**—pop pl ... NC-3
Jakes Wash—stream ... NV-8
Jakes Wash Well—well ... NV-8
Jakes Well—well ... NV-8
Jakes Windmill—locale ... TX-5
Jake Tank—reservoir ... AZ-5
Jake Tank—reservoir ... TX-5
**Jaketown**—pop pl ... MS-4
Jaketown Creek—stream ... NY-2
Jaketown Site—hist pl ... MS-4
Jakeville—locale ... MN-6
Jake Well—well ... NM-5
Jake White Pond—lake ... FL-3
Jake Williams Lake—gut ... AR-4
Jake Windmill—locale ... NM-5
Jake Wiremen Fork—stream ... KY-4
Jakey Creek—stream ... MT-8
Jakey Ditch—canal ... CO-8
Jakey Lake—lake ... CA-9
Jakey Ridge—ridge ... OR-9
Jakeys Fork—stream ... WY-8
Jakeys Fork Trail—trail ... WY-8
Jakeys Hill—summit ... CA-9
Jakie Creek—stream ... ID-8
Jakie Creek—stream ... MT-8
Jakie Creek Trail (pack)—trail ... MT-8
Jakie Hollow—valley ... MO-7
Jakies Pass—gap ... AZ-5
Jakies Pass Spring—spring ... AZ-5
**Jakin**—pop pl ... GA-3
Jakin (CCD)—cens area ... GA-3
Jakman Hill—summit ... NY-2
Jakolof Bay—bay ... AK-9
Jakolof Bay—CDP ... AK-9
Jakolof Creek—stream ... AK-9
Jako Wash—valley ... UT-8
*Jakrou Island* ... MP-9
*Jakson Cove* ... AL-4
**Jal**—pop pl (2) ... NM-5
Jalaihai Point—summit ... GU-9
Jalama—locale ... CA-9
Jalama Beach County Park—park ... CA-9
Jalama Beach Park—park ... CA-9
Jalama Creek—stream ... CA-9
Jalama Ranch—locale ... CA-9
Jalama Sch—school ... CA-9
Jalamund Lake—lake ... AK-9
Jalangaschel—island ... FM-9
Jalangigereil—island ... FM-9
Jaloojan—area ... GU-9
Jalapa—locale ... IL-6
**Jalapa**—pop pl ... IN-6
**Jalapa**—pop pl ... SC-3
**Jalapa**—pop pl ... TN-4
Jalapa Post Office (historical)—building ... TN-4
**Jalappa**—pop pl ... PA-2
Jalappa Branch—stream ... GA-3
*Jalapuk* ... FM-9
Jal (CCD)—cens area ... NM-5
Jal Cooper Cem—cemetery ... NM-5
*Jaldonej* ... MP-9
*Jaldonet* ... MP-9
*Jale Lake* ... MN-6
*Jaliklik Islet* ... MP-9
Jalik (not verified)—island ... MP-9
Jalisco, Arroyo—stream ... CA-9
Jalisco Banco Number 67—levee ... TX-5
Jalisco Canyon—valley ... AZ-5
Jalisco Dam—dam ... AZ-5
Jalisco Ridge—ridge ... AZ-5
Jalisco Well—well ... AZ-5
Jalland Creek—stream ... OR-9
*Jallappa* ... TN-4
*Jallappa Post Office* ... TN-4
J Allison Lake Dam—dam ... MS-4
*Jaloklab* ... MP-9
Jaloklab—island ... MP-9
Jalonic Park—park ... TX-5
*Jaltoonej* ... MP-9
*Jaltuej* ... MP-9
Jaltuiej—island ... MP-9
Jaluco—locale ... SC-3
*Jaluij* ... MP-9
Jaluit Anchorage—harbor ... MP-9
Jaluit Atoll—island ... MP-9
Jaluit (County-equivalent)—civil ... MP-9
*Jaluit Harbor* ... MP-9
*Jaluit Island* ... MP-9
Jaluit Island—island ... MP-9
Jaluit Lagoon—lake ... MP-9
Jaluit Point—cape ... MP-9
Jaluit Point—ridge ... MP-9
Jam—locale ... MI-6
*Jamacao* ... CA-9
*Jamacha* ... CA-9
Jamacha—locale ... CA-9
**Jamacha Junction**—pop pl ... CA-9
Jamacha Valley—valley ... CA-9

*Jamacho* ... CA-9
Jamacho—civil ... CA-9
Jamaeson Creek—stream ... LA-4
J A Magee Lake Dam—dam ... MS-4
Jamaica—locale ... GA-3
Jamaica—locale ... NE-7
Jamaica—locale ... VA-3
**Jamaica**—pop pl ... IL-6
**Jamaica**—pop pl ... IA-7
**Jamaica**—pop pl ... NY-2
**Jamaica**—pop pl ... VT-1
Jamaica Ave Sch—school ... NY-2
Jamaica Bay—bay ... NY-2
Jamaica Bay Wildlife Ref—park ... NY-2
**Jamaica Beach**—pop pl ... TX-5
Jamaica Chamber of Commerce Bldg—hist pl ... NY-2
Jamaica Day Creek—stream ... WA-9
Jamaica Drain—canal ... AZ-5
Jamaica (historical)—civil ... DC-2
Jamaica Hosp—hospital ... NY-2
Jamaica HS—school ... IL-6
Jamaica HS—school ... NY-2
Jamaica Island—island ... ME-1
Jamaica (Magisterial District)—fmr MCD ... VA-3
*Jamaica Plains* ... MA-1
Jamaica Plain Station—locale ... MA-1
**Jamaica Plain (subdivision)**—pop pl ... MA-1
Jamaica Point—cape ... ME-1
Jamaica Point—cape ... MD-2
*Jamaica Pond* ... VT-1
Jamaica Pond—lake ... MA-1
Jamaica Savings Bank—hist pl ... NY-2
Jamaica Sch—school ... CO-8
Jamaica Square—other ... NY-2
**Jamaica (Town of)**—pop pl ... VT-1
**Jamaica (Township of)**—pop pl ... IL-6
*Jaman-Ming* ... MP-9
Jamar Cem—cemetery ... AL-4
**Jamarl Acres Subdivision**—pop pl ... UT-8
*Jamar Lake* ... MN-6
Jamback—locale ... AL-4
Jamb Creek—stream ... WY-8
Jambo Creek—stream ... WI-6
Jambo Creek Cem—cemetery ... WI-6
Jambo Creek Park—park ... WI-6
**Jamboree**—pop pl ... KY-4
Jamboree Bay—bay ... AK-9
Jam Brook—stream ... ME-1
Jam Creek—stream ... ID-8
*Jam Dam Branch* ... MI-6
Jam Dam Bridge—bridge ... MI-6
Jameison Cem—cemetery ... KY-4
Jameison Hill—summit ... KY-4
Jamenming—island ... MP-9
Jamerman Ranch—locale ... WY-8
Jamerman Rock—summit ... WY-8
*Jamerson Creek* ... MO-7
Jamerson Creek—stream ... LA-4
*Jamerson Hollow* ... TN-4
Jamerson Hollow—valley ... KY-4
*James* ... MP-9
James—locale (2) ... AL-4
James—locale ... CA-9
James—locale ... MD-2
James—locale ... NE-7
James—locale (2) ... TX-5
**James**—pop pl ... GA-3
**James**—pop pl ... IA-7
**James**—pop pl ... MS-4
**James**—pop pl ... SD-7
**James**—pop pl ... TX-5
**James**—pop pl ... VA-3
James, Capt. Benjamin, House—hist pl ... MA-1
James, Charles Worth, House—hist pl ... OH-6
James, C. N., Cabin—hist pl ... KS-7
James, Francis Wilcox, House—hist pl ... WA-9
James, Jean Butz, Museum of the Highland Park Historical Society—hist pl ... IL-6
James, Jesse, House—hist pl ... MO-7
James, Lake—lake ... IN-6
James, Lake—lake ... SC-3
James, Lake—lake ... WA-9
James, Lake—reservoir ... MI-6
James, Lake—reservoir (2) ... NC-3
James, Morgan, Homestead—hist pl ... PA-2
James, Mount—summit ... MT-8
James, T. L., House—hist pl ... LA-4
James A Allison Elem Sch—school ... IN-6
James A Carriger Sch—school ... TN-4
James A Garfield Elem Sch—school ... IN-6
James A. Garfield Natl Historic Site—hist pl ... OH-6
James A. Garfield Natl Historic Site—park ... OH-6
James A Garfield Sch—school ... CA-9
James A Garfield Statue—park ... DC-2
*James A Henry Elem Sch* ... TN-4
James A Henry Sch—school ... TN-4
James Airp—airport ... IN-6
James A Light Field—park ... AL-4
Jameson—locale ... CA-9
James and Bobby Dycus Pond Dam—dam ... MS-4
James and Dixon Canal—canal ... CA-9
James Anderson Cem—cemetery ... MS-4
James Anthony Lake—lake ... AL-4
James Archer Smith Hosp—hospital ... FL-3
James A Reed Memorial Wildlife Area—park ... MO-7
James A Shanks HS—school ... FL-3
James A Ventress Lake Dam—dam ... MS-4
James A Wheeler Lake—reservoir ... AL-4
James A Wheeler Lake Dam—dam ... AL-4
James Baird State Park—park ... NY-2
James Barnhanm Pond Dam—dam ... MS-4
James Barron Ranch—locale ... TX-5
James Bay—bay ... AZ-5
James Bay—bay ... MN-6
James Bayou—stream (2) ... LA-4
James Bayou—stream (2) ... MO-7
James Bayou—stream ... TX-5
James Bayou Township—civil ... MO-7
James B Bonham Sch—school ... TX-5
James B Davison Sch—school ... CA-9
James B Eads Elem Sch—school ... IN-6
James B. Hutton Elem Sch—school ... KS-7
James Bldg—hist pl ... TN-4
James Bluff—cliff ... AL-4
James Bradley Grant—civil ... FL-3

James Branch—stream ... DE-2
James Branch—stream ... IN-6
James Branch—stream ... KS-7
James Branch—stream ... KY-4
James Branch—stream ... LA-4
James Branch—stream (4) ... MO-7
James Branch—stream ... NJ-2
James Branch—stream (3) ... NC-3
James Branch—stream (2) ... SC-3
James Branch—stream ... TN-4
James Branch—stream ... VA-3
James Branch—stream ... WV-2
James Branch Prospect—mine ... TN-4
James Break—lake ... IL-6
James Bridger Ferry—bridge ... WY-8
James Brook—stream ... CT-1
James Brook—stream (2) ... ME-1
James Brook—stream (2) ... MA-1
James Brook—stream ... VT-1
James Brothers' House and Farm—hist pl ... MO-7
James Brothers' House and Farm (Boundary Increase)—hist pl ... MO-7
James Brothers Ranch—locale ... UT-8
James Brown Well—cave ... AL-4
James Buchanan Elem Sch—school (2) ... PA-2
James Buchanan MS—school ... PA-2
James Buchanan Parker Cem—cemetery ... MS-4
*James Buchanan Sch* ... PA-2
James Buchanan Senior HS—school ... PA-2
Jamesburg—locale ... CA-9
**Jamesburg**—pop pl ... IL-6
**Jamesburg**—pop pl ... NJ-2
Jamesburg Cem—cemetery ... KS-7
**Jamesburg Gardens**—pop pl ... NJ-2
Jamesburg Park—locale ... NJ-2
*Jamesburg Park Cemetery* ... KS-7
James Burnett Pond Dam—dam ... MS-4
James Butte—summit ... OR-9
James Bypass—canal ... CA-9
*James Cabin* ... ID-8
James Cabin—locale ... CA-9
James Cabin—locale ... NM-5
James Caldwell HS—school ... NJ-2
James Camp Branch—stream ... NC-3
*James Canal* ... CA-9
James Canal—canal ... CA-9
James Canyon—valley ... AZ-5
James Canyon—valley (3) ... CA-9
James Canyon—valley (2) ... NV-8
James Canyon—valley ... NM-5
James Canyon—valley ... OR-9
James Canyon—valley ... UT-8
James Canyon—valley ... WA-9
James Canyon Campground—locale ... NM-5
James Carr—locale ... TX-5
James Cem—cemetery (3) ... AL-4
James Cem—cemetery (4) ... AR-4
James Cem—cemetery ... GA-3
James Cem—cemetery (5) ... IN-6
James Cem—cemetery ... KY-4
James Cem—cemetery (2) ... LA-4
James Cem—cemetery ... MD-2
James Cem—cemetery ... MA-1
James Cem—cemetery (6) ... MS-4
James Cem—cemetery (3) ... MO-7
James Cem—cemetery ... NE-7
James Cem—cemetery ... NH-1
James Cem—cemetery ... NY-2
James Cem—cemetery (3) ... NC-3
James Cem—cemetery (2) ... OH-6
James Cem—cemetery ... OK-5
James Cem—cemetery ... SD-7
James Cem—cemetery (3) ... TN-4
James Cem—cemetery ... TX-5
James Cem—cemetery (2) ... VA-3
James Cem—cemetery ... WV-2
James Ch—church ... MD-2
James Ch—church (2) ... MI-6
James Ch—church ... MS-4
James Ch—church ... NC-3
James Chapel—church (2) ... AL-4
James Chapel—church ... GA-3
James Chapel—church (2) ... LA-4
James Chapel—church (2) ... MS-4
James Chapel—church ... NJ-2
James Chapel—church ... NC-3
James Chapel—church ... OK-5
James Chapel—church ... PA-2
James Chapel—church (2) ... SC-3
James Chapel—church ... TN-4
James Chapel—church (2) ... TX-5
James Chapel—church (2) ... WV-2
*James Chapel Baptist Ch* ... AL-4
James Chapel Baptist Ch—church ... AL-4
James Chapel Cem—cemetery ... LA-4
James Chapel Ch—church ... AL-4
**James City**—pop pl ... NC-3
**James City**—pop pl ... PA-2
**James City (County)**—pop pl ... VA-3
James City Lookout Tower—locale ... VA-3
James Clarke Grant—civil ... FL-3
James Corbett Byles Mine—mine ... CA-9
James County Courthouse—hist pl ... TN-4
James Court Industrial Park—locale ... DE-2
James Cove—bay ... VA-3
*James Cox Ditch* ... IN-6
James C Ratcliffe Dam—dam ... AL-4
James Cravey Dam—dam ... AL-4
*James Creek* ... AR-4
*James Creek* ... MS-4
*James Creek* ... NC-3
*James Creek* ... OK-5
*James Creek* ... PA-2
*James Creek* ... WI-6
James Creek—stream (7) ... AL-4
James Creek—stream ... AK-9
James Creek—stream (5) ... CA-9
James Creek—stream (2) ... CO-8
James Creek—stream (2) ... GA-3
James Creek—stream (3) ... ID-8
James Creek—stream ... KS-7
James Creek—stream ... MD-2
James Creek—stream (3) ... MS-4
James Creek—stream ... MO-7
James Creek—stream ... MT-8
James Creek—stream ... NV-8
James Creek—stream ... NY-2
James Creek—stream (4) ... NC-3
James Creek—stream ... OR-9

James Creek—*stream* PA-2
James Creek—*stream* SC-3
James Creek—*stream* TX-5
James Creek—*stream* WA-9
James Creek—*stream* WV-2
James Creek Acad (historical)—*school* MS-4
James Creek Access Area—*area* PA-2
*James Creek Baptist Church* MS-4
*James Creek Boat Launch* PA-2
James Creek Ch—*church* (2) MS-4
James Creek Ch—*church* PA-2
*James Creek (corporate name Marklesburg)* PA-2
James Creek No. 1 Site—*hist pl* MS-4
James Creek Point—*cape* NC-3
James Creek Rec Area—*park* MS-4
James Creek Shelter—*locale* OR-9
James Creek (Township of)—*fmr MCD* AR-4
*James Crews* MO-7
James Crooks Lake—*reservoir* AL-4
James Crooks Lake Dam—*dam* AL-4
*James Crossing* MS-4
James Crossing (historical)—*locale* KS-7
*James Crossroads* NC-3
James Crossroads—*locale* SC-3
**James Crossroads**—*pop pl* VA-3
James C Thomas Park—*park* AZ-5
James Dam—*dam* AL-4
James Dam—*dam* NC-3
James D Hoskins Bridge—*bridge* TN-4
James Dickerson Lake Dam—*dam* MS-4
James Ditch—*canal* (2) CO-8
James Ditch—*canal* (5) IN-6
James Diversion Dam—*dam* SD-7
James D McGougan Dam—*dam* NC-3
James Dobbins Lake—*reservoir* NC-3
James Dobbins Lake Dam—*dam* NC-3
James D Phelan Beach State Park—*park* CA-9
James Drain—*canal* MI-6
James Draw—*valley* CO-8
James Draw—*valley* KS-7
James Dugger Mine—*mine* TN-4
James Duncan Lake Dam—*dam* MS-4
James Dykes Memorial Park—*cemetery* GA-3
*James E Cook Church* AL-4
James Edward Burke Bridge—*bridge* TN-4
James E Holmes Regional Med Ctr—*hospital* FL-3
James E Karnes Bridge—*bridge* TN-4
James E Moss Sch—*school* UT-8
James E Roberts Special Sch—*school* IN-6
James E Stephens Elem Sch—*school* FL-3
James E Ward Agricultural and Community Center—*building* TN-4
James Farmer Lake Dam—*dam* MS-4
*James Faulkner Junior College* AL-4
James F D Lanier Memorial—*park* IN-6
*James Ferry* GA-3
James Ferry—*locale* AR-4
James Ferry (historical)—*locale* TN-4
James Flanigan Lake Dam—*dam* MS-4
James Fork—*stream* AR-4
James Fork—*stream* KY-4
James Fork—*stream* OK-5
James Fork Cem—*cemetery* AR-4
James Fork Ch—*church* AR-4
James Fowler Park—*park* AL-4
James Gap—*gap* TN-4
James Gettys Elem Sch—*school* PA-2
James Gilbert Pond Dam—*dam* MS-4
James Giles Shell Midden (15HE589)—*hist pl* KY-4
James Grantham Pond Dam—*dam* MS-4
James Griffith—*post sta* TX-5
James Grove Ch—*church* GA-3
James Hall Grant—*civil* FL-3
James-Hansford House—*hist pl* KY-4
*James Head* ME-1
James Hilbun Poultry Farm Pond Dam—*dam* MS-4
James Hill—*summit* MA-1
James Hillburn Lake Dam—*dam* MS-4
James Hill Spring—*spring* AL-4
**James Hill Township**—*pop pl* ND-7
James (historical)—*locale* AL-4
James Hodge Windmill—*locale* TX 5
James Hollow—*valley* (4) TN-4
James Hollow—*valley* (2) TX-5
James Hollow—*valley* WV-2
James Hoover Johnson Pond—*reservoir* NC-3
James Hoover Johnson Pond Dam—*dam* NC-3
James House—*hist pl* AR-4
James H Turner Dam—*dam* CA-9
James Ingram Lake Dam—*dam* AL-4
James Irvine Trail—*trail* CA-9
*James Island* FL-3
*James Island* MD-2
*James Island* WA-9
James Island—*island* AK-9
James Island—*island* (2) MD-2
James Island—*island* MI-6
James Island—*island* SC-3
James Island—*island* (2) WA-9
James Island—*island* WI-6
James Island (CCD)—*cens area* SC-3
James Island (Centerville)—*CDP* SC-3
James Island Creek—*stream* SC-3
James Island HS—*school* SC-3
*James Island Marsh* MD-2
James Island Sch—*school* SC-3
James Island State Park—*park* WA-9
James Island Yacht Club—*other* SC-3
James Jarvis Swift Creek Ditch No 3—*canal* CO-8
James Jenkins Lake Dam—*dam* MS-4
James JHS—*school* GA-3
James JHS—*school* TX-5
James Johnson Lake Dam—*dam* MS-4
James Johnston Cem—*cemetery* TN-4
James Jones Lake Dam—*dam* MS-4
James J Thomas Park—*park* OH-6
James Kenan HS—*school* NC-3
James Kenney Playground—*park* CA-9
James Kjerstad Dam—*dam* SD-7
James Knob—*summit* WV-2
James K Polk Birthplace—*locale* NC-3
James K Polk Sch—*school* VA-3
James K Shook Sch (historical)—*school* TN-4
James Lagoon—*bay* AK-9
James Laird Lake Dam—*dam* MS-4
James Lake—*lake* AK-9
James Lake—*lake* (2) FL-3
James Lake—*lake* ID-8
James Lake—*lake* IN-6
James Lake—*lake* (2) KY-4
James Lake—*lake* (2) MI-6
James Lake—*lake* (2) MN-6
James Lake—*lake* MT-8
James Lake—*lake* (2) SC-3
James Lake—*lake* TX-5
James Lake—*lake* (3) WI-6
James Lake—*lake* WY-8
James Lake—*reservoir* AL-4
James Lake—*reservoir* CO-8
James Lake—*reservoir* GA-3
James Lake—*reservoir* KS-7
James Lake—*reservoir* NC-3
James Lake—*reservoir* TN-4
James Lake—*reservoir* TX-5
James Lake Dam—*dam* MS-4
James Lake Dam—*dam* TN-4
James Lake North Canal—*canal* WY-8
James Lakes—*reservoir* GA-3
James Landing—*locale* AL-4
James Lane—*locale* WV-2
James Lateral—*canal* CO-8
James L Babson Museum—*building* MA-1
James Lee Sch—*school* (2) VA-3
James Lick JHS—*school* CA-9
James Logan HS—*school* CA-9
James-Lorah House—*hist pl* PA-2
James Love Sch—*school* NC-3
James Madison Cem—*cemetery* VA-3
James Madison Elem Sch—*school* IN-6
James Madison Elem Sch—*school* TN-4
James Madison JHS—*school* OR-9
James Madison JHS—*school* WA-9
James Madison Memorial Bldg—*building* DC-2
James Madison Memorial Bridge—*bridge* VA-3
James Madison MS—*school* FL-3
James Madison Sch—*school* CA-9
James Madison Sch—*school* IL-6
James M Anderson Elem Sch—*school* FL-3
**James Manor**—*pop pl* PA-2
James Marshall HS—*school* CA-9
James Marshall Park—*park* CA-9
James Matthews Cave—*cave* AL-4
James Maxwell Lake Dam—*dam* MS-4
James May Lake Dam—*dam* MS-4
James M Coughlin Junior Senior HS—*school* PA-2
James M. Cox Dayton International Airp—*airport* OH-6
James Meadow—*flat* OR-9
James Meadows—*civil* CA-9
James Memorial Baptist Ch—*church* AL-4
James Memorial Ch—*church* WV-2
James Memorial Library—*hist pl* ND-7
James Mill—*locale* AR-4
*James Mill Reservoir* RI-1
James Mill Spring—*spring* MO-7
James Mine—*mine* MI-6
James Mine Hist Dist—*hist pl* MI-6
James Mine (underground)—*mine* AL-4
James Mine (underground)—*mine* TN-4
James Minter Ferry (historical)—*locale* MS-4
James Monroe Elem Sch—*school* IN-6
James Monroe HS—*school* VA-3
James Monroe JHS—*school* WA-9
James Monroe Sch—*school* CA-9
James Moody—*uninc pl* TX-5
James Moore Cem—*cemetery* AL-4
James Morden Mine—*mine* CA-9
James Observatory—*building* MS-4
James O Fisher Dam—*dam* OR-9
James O Fisher Rsvr—*reservoir* OR-9
James Oil Field—*oilfield* TX-5
James O Ladner Lake Dam—*dam* MS-4
*Jameson* FL-3
*Jameson* PA-2
**Jameson**—*pop pl* MN-6
**Jameson**—*pop pl* MO-7
Jameson, George W., House—*hist pl* KY-4
Jameson, James B., House—*hist pl* TN-4
Jameson, James M., Farm—*hist pl* MI-6
Jameson Bay—*swamp* FL-3
**Jameson Beach**—*pop pl* CA-9
Jameson Bluff—*cliff* MO-7
Jameson Branch—*stream* MS-4
Jameson Canyon—*valley* CA-9
Jameson Canyon—*valley* OR-9
Jameson Cem—*cemetery* (2) AR-4
Jameson Cem—*cemetery* SC-3
Jameson Cem—*cemetery* TN-4
Jameson Cem—*cemetery* WA-9
Jameson Corners—*locale* PA-2
Jameson Cove—*bay* ME-1
Jameson Creek—*stream* CA-9
Jameson Creek—*stream* IN-6
Jameson Creek—*stream* OH-6
Jameson Creek—*stream* OR-9
Jameson Creek—*stream* TX-5
Jameson Drain—*canal* MI-6
Jameson Draw—*valley* ID-8
Jameson Fork—*stream* KY-4
Jameson Hollow—*valley* TN-4
Jameson Island—*island* MO-7
Jameson Lake—*lake* WA-9
Jameson Lake—*reservoir* CA-9
Jameson Memorial Hospital Airp—*airport* PA-2
Jameson Mtn—*summit* GA-3
Jameson Oil Field—*oilfield* TX-5
Jameson Park—*park* ND-7
Jameson Peaks—*summit* TX-5
Jameson Point—*cape* (2) ME-1
Jameson Ranch—*locale* (2) NE-7
Jameson Ranch—*locale* OR-9
Jameson Ranch—*locale* WY-8
Jameson Ridge—*summit* ME-1
Jameson Sch—*school* ME-1
Jameson Sch (abandoned)—*school* MO-7
Jameson Spring—*spring* UT-8
Jameson-Strawn Oil Field—*oilfield* TX-5
*Jameson-Walker Cem* AL-4
James O Rich Pond Dam—*dam* MS-4
James-Owens House—*hist pl* KY-4
James Park—*park* FL-3
James Park—*park* IL-6
James Park—*park* NJ-2
James Park—*park* OR-9
James Park—*park* TX-5
James Park—*park* WA-9
**James Park (subdivision)**—*pop pl* VA-3
James Path—*trail* PA-2
James Peak—*summit* CO-8
James Peak—*summit* UT-8
James Peak Lake—*lake* CO-8
*James Peters School* PA-2
James Petik Number 1 Dam—*dam* SD-7
James Petik Number 2 Dam—*dam* SD-7
James P. Harlin Museum—*building* MO-7
James Pit—*cave* AL-4
James Place—*locale* ID-8
James Plantation (historical)—*locale* MS-4
James Plummer Grant—*civil* FL-3
*James Point* FL-3
James Point—*cape* MD-2
James Point—*cliff* TN-4
James Pond—*bay* MD-2
James Pond—*lake* GA-3
James Pond—*lake* (2) ME-1
James Pond—*lake* (3) MA-1
James Pond—*lake* NH-1
James Pond—*lake* RI-1
James Pond—*reservoir* AZ-5
James Pond—*reservoir* (2) GA-3
James Pond—*reservoir* MA-1
James Pond—*reservoir* NC-3
James Pond Dam—*dam* MA-1
James Pond Dam—*dam* NC-3
James Pond Marshes—*swamp* MA-1
**Jamesport**—*pop pl* MO-7
**Jamesport**—*pop pl* NY-2
Jamesport Community Lake—*reservoir* MO-7
**Jamesport Township**—*pop pl* MO-7
James Pratt Funeral Service—*hist pl* CT-1
James Q Newton Park—*park* CO-8
James Ranch—*locale* ID-8
James Ranch—*locale* NE-7
James Ranch—*locale* (3) NM-5
James Ranch—*locale* (3) TX-5
James Ranch—*locale* UT-8
*James R. Bush (Township of)* AR-4
James Ridge—*ridge* KY-4
James Ridge—*ridge* TN-4
James Ridge—*ridge* WV-2
James Ridge Lookout—*other* NM-5
James Riley "Jim Paul" Bridge—*bridge* FL-3
*James River* MA-1
*James River* WA-9
James River—*stream* MO-7
James River*—*stream* ND-7
James River—*stream* SD-7
James River—*stream* TX-5
James River—*stream* VA-3
James River And Kanawha Canal—*canal* VA-3
James River and Kanawha Canal Hist Dist—*hist pl* VA-3
James River Bridge—*bridge* VA-3
James River Ch—*church* ND-7
James River Ch—*church* VA-3
James River Country Club—*other* VA-3
**James River Estates**—*pop pl* VA-3
James River Golf Club—*other* VA-3
James River Junction—*locale* VA-3
James River (Magisterial District)—*fmr MCD* VA-3
James River Old Channel—*channel* VA-3
James River Sch—*school* VA-3
James River Spring—*spring* TX-5
James River State Wildlife Mngmt Area—*park* VA-3
James River Valley Cem—*cemetery* ND-7
James River Valley Overlook—*locale* VA-3
**James River Valley Township**—*pop pl* ND-7
James Road and 103rd Street Shop Ctr—*locale* FL-3
James Road Park—*park* TN-4
James Road Sch—*school* OH-6
*James Rock* WA-9
James Rooney Memorial Park—*park* TX-5
James Rountree House—*building* NC-3
James Rsvr—*reservoir* AZ-5
James Rumsey Bridge—*bridge* MD-2
James Rumsey Bridge—*other* WV-2
James Run—*stream* (2) MD-2
James Sch—*school* (2) AR-4
James Sch—*school* FL-3
James Sch—*school* IL-6
James Sch—*school* (2) KS-7
James Sch—*school* MA-1
James Sch—*school* MS-4
James Sch—*school* MO-7
James Sch—*school* NC-3
James Sch—*school* SD-7
James Sch—*school* (2) TN-4
James Sch—*school* VA-3
James Sch (abandoned)—*school* PA-2
James Sch (historical)—*school* AL-4
James Sch (historical)—*school* MO-7
James Seiler Dam—*dam* SD-7
James S Hunt Elem Sch—*school* FL-3
James Slough—*lake* WI-6
*James Smalls Pond* MA-1
James Spring—*spring* AR-4
James Spring—*spring* CA-9
James Spring—*spring* MO-7
James Spring—*spring* NM-5
James Spring—*spring* OR-9
James Spring—*spring* UT-8
James Spring Cem—*cemetery* AR-4
James Square Ch—*church* VA-3
*James Station* AL-4
*James Station* MS-4
James Store—*locale* VA-3
James Street Ch—*church* TX-5
James Street Commons Hist Dist—*hist pl* NJ-2
James Street Commons Hist Dist Addendum—*hist pl* NJ-2
James Swamp—*stream* VA-3
James Switch—*locale* AR-4
James Tank—*reservoir* AZ-5
James Tank—*reservoir* NM-5
James Temple—*church* GA-3
James Temple Ch—*church* AL-4
James Templeton Cem—*cemetery* GA-3
James Templeton Sch—*school* OR-9
**James Terrace**—*pop pl* VA-3
James Thomas Park—*park* OH-6
James Thomas Pond—*lake* FL-3
James T Huff Bridge—*bridge* TN-4
James Tillman Elem Sch—*school* FL-3
Jameston Sch—*school* ID-8
*Jamestown* AL-4
*Jamestown* MD-2
*Jamestown* PA-2
Jamestown—*CDP* RI-1
Jamestown—*locale* (2) GA-3
Jamestown—*locale* IA-7
Jamestown—*locale* MS-4
Jamestown—*locale* TX-5
Jamestown—*locale* VA-3
Jamestown—*locale* WV-2
**Jamestown**—*pop pl* AL-4
**Jamestown**—*pop pl* (2) AR-4
**Jamestown**—*pop pl* CA-9
**Jamestown**—*pop pl* CO-8
**Jamestown**—*pop pl* FL-3
**Jamestown**—*pop pl* GA-3
**Jamestown**—*pop pl* ID-8
**Jamestown**—*pop pl* (2) IL-6
**Jamestown**—*pop pl* (3) IN-6
**Jamestown**—*pop pl* IA-7
**Jamestown**—*pop pl* KS-7
**Jamestown**—*pop pl* KY-4
**Jamestown**—*pop pl* LA-4
**Jamestown**—*pop pl* MI-6
**Jamestown**—*pop pl* MO-7
**Jamestown**—*pop pl* NY-2
**Jamestown**—*pop pl* NC-3
**Jamestown**—*pop pl* ND-7
**Jamestown**—*pop pl* (2) OH-6
**Jamestown**—*pop pl* OK-5
**Jamestown**—*pop pl* (3) PA-2
**Jamestown**—*pop pl* (3) SC-3
**Jamestown**—*pop pl* (2) TN-4
**Jamestown**—*pop pl* TX-5
**Jamestown**—*pop pl* WA-9
**Jamestown**—*pop pl* WI-6
**James Town**—*pop pl* WY-8
Jamestown—*uninc pl* TX-5
Jamestown Bay—*bay* AK-9
Jamestown Borough—*civil* PA-2
Jamestown Brook—*stream* RI-1
Jamestown (CCD)—*cens area* KY-4
Jamestown (CCD)—*cens area* TN-4
*Jamestown Cem* AL-4
Jamestown Cem—*cemetery* AL-4
Jamestown Cem—*cemetery* IN-6
Jamestown Cem—*cemetery* KS-7
Jamestown Cem—*cemetery* MI-6
Jamestown Cem—*cemetery* ND-7
Jamestown Cem—*cemetery* WA-9
Jamestown Cem—*cemetery* WI-6
**Jamestown Center**—*pop pl* RI-1
Jamestown Ch—*church* AL-4
Jamestown Ch—*church* AR-4
Jamestown Ch—*church* (2) VA-3
Jamestown City Cem—*cemetery* TN-4
Jamestown Coll—*school* ND-7
Jamestown Creek—*stream* AR-4
Jamestown Dam—*dam* ND-7
Jamestown Ditch—*canal* CA-9
Jamestown Division—*civil* TN-4
Jamestown Dock—*locale* KY-4
Jamestown Elem Sch—*school* NC-3
**Jamestowne (subdivision)**—*pop pl* DE-2
Jamestown Exposition Site Buildings—*hist pl* VA-3
Jamestown Falls—*falls* NY-2
**Jamestown Farms**—*pop pl* VA-3
Jamestown Festival Park—*park* VA-3
Jamestown First Baptist Ch—*church* TN-4
Jamestown Hist Dist—*hist pl* NC-3
**Jamestown (historical)**—*pop pl* OR-9
Jamestown Ice House Dam—*dam* ND-7
Jamestown Island—*island* VA-3
Jamestown Junction—*locale* ND-7
Jamestown (Magisterial District)—*fmr MCD* VA-3
Jamestown Mall—*locale* MO-7
Jamestown Mall (Shop Ctr)—*locale* MO-7
Jamestown Mall (Shop Ctr)—*locale* ND-7
Jamestown MS—*school* NC-3
Jamestown Mtn—*summit* AR-4
Jamestown Municipal Airp—*airport* ND-7
Jamestown Municipal Airp—*airport* TN-4
**Jamestown (National Historical Site)**—*pop pl* VA-3
Jamestown Natl Historic Site—*hist pl* VA-3
Jamestown Optimist Boys Camp—*locale* NY-2
**Jamestown (PA-T131/1880)**—*pop pl* PA-2
Jamestown Peak—*summit* AK-9
Jamestown Post Office—*building* TN-4
Jamestown Post Office (historical)—*building* AL-4
Jamestown Quarry Dam—*dam* NC-3
Jamestown Quarry Lake—*reservoir* NC-3
Jamestown Ranch—*locale* CO-8
*Jamestown Reservoir* ND-7
Jamestown Reservoir Dam—*dam* RI-1
Jamestown Reservoir Dam—*dam* TN-4
Jamestown Rifle Club—*other* NY-2
Jamestown Rsvr—*reservoir* ND-7
Jamestown Rsvr—*reservoir* RI-1
Jamestown Rsvr—*reservoir* TN-4
Jamestown Sch—*school* TN-4
Jamestown Sch—*school* VA-3
Jamestown Sch (historical)—*school* TN-4
James Township—*fmr MCD* IA-7
James (Township of)—*fmr MCD* AR-4
James (Township of)—*fmr MCD* MO-7
**James (Township of)**—*pop pl* MI-6
**Jamestown Shores**—*pop pl* RI-1
Jamestown (site)—*locale* NV-8
Jamestown Slough—*gut* MI-6
Jamestown Speedway—*other* NY-2
Jamestown Spring—*spring* NV-8
Jamestown State Waterfront Mngmt Area—*park* KS-7
**Jamestown Subdivision**—*pop pl* (2) UT-8
Jamestown Tabernacle Ch—*church* AL-4
*Jamestown Town Beach* RI-1
**Jamestown (Town of)**—*pop pl* RI-1
Jamestown Township—*fmr MCD* IA-7
Jamestown (Township of)—*fmr MCD* NC-3
**Jamestown (Township of)**—*pop pl* IN-6
**Jamestown (Township of)**—*pop pl* MI-6
**Jamestown (Township of)**—*pop pl* MN-6
Jamestown West (census name for West Ellicott)—*CDP* NY-2
Jamestown Windmill—*hist pl* RI-1
James T Wright Bridge—*bridge* TN-4
James Valley—*basin* NE-7
James Valley Junction—*locale* SD-7
Jamesville—*locale* AL-4
Jamesville—*locale* MO-7
Jamesville—*locale* OK-5
Jamesville—*locale* PA-2
Jamesville—*locale* SD-7
**Jamesville**—*pop pl* NY-2
**Jamesville**—*pop pl* NC-3
**Jamesville**—*pop pl* VA-3
Jamesville Beach Countt Park—*park* NY-2
Jamesville Canal—*canal* NY-2
Jamesville Ch—*church* NC-3
Jamesville-DeWitt Central Sch—*school* NY-2
Jamesville-Dewitt HS—*school* NY-2
**Jamesville (historical)**—*pop pl* MA-1
Jamesville Pond—*lake* MA-1
Jamesville Primitive Baptist Church and Cemetery—*hist pl* NC-3
Jamesville Rock Quarry—*mine* NY-2
Jamesville Rsvr—*reservoir* NY-2
Jamesville Sch—*school* WI-6
**Jamesville (subdivision)**—*pop pl* MA-1
**Jamesville Township**—*pop pl* SD-7
Jamesville (Township of)—*fmr MCD* NC-3
Jamesville Union Sch—*school* NC-3
*James V Turner Reservoir* MA-1
James V Turner Reservoir Dam—*dam* RI-1
James V Turner Rsvr—*reservoir* RI-1
James Wash—*stream* AZ-5
James Wash—*valley* AZ-5
Jamesway Huts (Abandoned)—*locale* AK-9
Jamesway Plaza—*locale* PA-2
James Well—*well* (4) AZ-5
James Wharf—*locale* VA-3
James Whitcomb Riley Elem Sch—*school* (5) IN-6
James Whitcomb Riley Monmt—*park* IN-6
James Whitcomb Riley Sch—*school* IN-6
James Whitman Landing Strip—*airport* ND-7
James Whittington Cem—*cemetery* MS-4
James Wild Horse Trap—*hist pl* NV-8
James Wilkins Grant—*civil* FL-3
James Windmill—*locale* TX-5
*James Wise Pond* AL-4
James Wise Pond—*reservoir* AL-4
James Wise Pond Dam Number 1—*dam* AL-4
James Wise Pond Dam Number 2—*dam* AL-4
James Wise Pond Number Two—*reservoir* AL-4
James W Marshall State Historical Monmt—*park* CA-9
James Wolf Canal—*canal* MS-4
James Wolf Creek—*stream* MS-4
James Wood Park—*park* OR-9
*James Wood School* AL-4
James W. Parker MS—*school* PA-2
James W Sikes Elem Sch—*school* FL-3
*James W. Trimble Dam* AR-4
James York Branch—*stream* KY-4
James York Plaza—*post sta* VA-3
Jam Hill—*summit* ME-1
Jamie, Lake—*lake* PA-2
Jamie Carlyle Hargrave Sch—*school* NC-3
**Jamieson**—*pop pl* FL-3
**Jamieson**—*pop pl* OR-9
Jamieson Cem—*cemetery* MO-7
Jamieson Ch—*church* MS-4
Jamieson Corners—*locale* NY-2
Jamieson Creek—*stream* CA-9
Jamieson Grove Ch—*church* MS-4
Jamieson Gulch—*valley* OR-9
Jamieson Hill—*summit* NY-2
Jamieson Lake—*lake* CO-8
Jamieson Lake—*reservoir* TN-4
Jamieson Lake Dam—*dam* TN-4
Jamieson Park—*locale* WA-9
Jamieson Sch—*school* IL-6
Jamieson Sch—*school* MI-6
Jamieson Tank—*reservoir* AZ-5
*Jamies Pond* ME-1
*Jamison* MO-7
Jamison—*locale* PA-2
**Jamison**—*pop pl* IA-7
**Jamison**—*pop pl* NE-7
**Jamison**—*pop pl* (3) PA-2
**Jamison**—*pop pl* SC-3
**Jamison**—*pop pl* VA-3
Jamison Branch—*stream* AL-4
Jamison Branch—*stream* DE-2
Jamison Branch—*stream* MS-4
Jamison Branch—*stream* VA-3
*Jamison Cave* TN-4
Jamison Cem—*cemetery* MS-4
Jamison Cem—*cemetery* (2) OK-5
Jamison Cem—*cemetery* TN-4
Jamison Cem—*cemetery* VA-3
**Jamison City**—*pop pl* PA-2
Jamison Corner—*locale* WA-9
*Jamison Corners* NY-2
Jamison Creek—*stream* AR-4
Jamison Creek—*stream* (2) CA-9
Jamison Creek—*stream* IL-6
Jamison Creek—*stream* OH-6
Jamison Creek—*stream* (2) VA-3
Jamison Ditch—*canal* IN-6
Jamison Full Gospel Temple—*church* MO-7
*Jamison Gap* PA-2
Jamison Gap—*gap* VA-3
Jamison Gulch—*valley* MT-8
Jamison Gulch—*valley* OR-9
Jamison Hill—*summit* AR-4
Jamison Hill Ch—*church* AR-4
Jamison Hollow—*valley* (2) TN-4
*Jamison Lake* WA-9
Jamison Lake—*lake* CA-9
Jamison Lake—*lake* IN-6
Jamison Lake—*lake* TX-5
Jamison Ledge—*bar* ME-1
Jamison Meadow—*swamp* OR-9
Jamison Mill Creek—*stream* SC-3
Jamison Mill Park Campsite—*locale* VA-3
Jamison Mine—*mine* AZ-5
Jamison Mine—*mine* CA-9
Jamison Mine No. 8—*other* WV-2
**Jamison Mine No. 9**—*pop pl* WV-2
Jamison Mtn—*summit* NC-3
Jamison Park—*park* AL-4
Jamison Pollard Oil Field—*oilfield* TX-5
Jamison Prong Wildcat Creek—*stream* WY-8
Jamison Ranch—*locale* CA-9
Jamison Ranch—*locale* OR-9
Jamison Ranch (reduced usage)—*locale* WY-8
Jamison Ravine—*valley* CA-9
Jamison Ridge—*ridge* CA-9
**Jamison Road**—*pop pl* NY-2
Jamison Rsvr—*reservoir* PA-2
Jamison Run—*stream* (4) PA-2
Jamison Run Vista—*summit* PA-2
Jamison Sch—*school* IL-6
Jamison Sch—*school* TX-5
Jamison Sch—*school* VA-3
Jamison Sch (abandoned)—*school* MO-7
Jamison Sch (historical)—*school* AL-4
Jamisons Corner—*locale* DE-2
*Jamisons Corners* PA-2
*Jamisons Mill* MS-4
Jamisons Mill Pond—*reservoir* MS-4
Jamison Spring—*spring* CA-9
Jamison Tank—*reservoir* AZ-5
Jamison Tank—*reservoir* TX-5
**Jamisonville**—*pop pl* PA-2
Jamison Water Mill (historical)—*locale* MS-4
Jamison Yard—*locale* MD-2
Jam Lake—*lake* GA-3
Jam Lake—*lake* MN-6
Jammer Lake—*lake* MN-6
Jammison Hill—*summit* KY-4
*Jamony* FL-3
*Jamony Lake* FL-3
Jam Pond—*lake* NY-2
Jamstutz Ditch—*canal* IN-6
Jamuary Rsvr—*reservoir* CO-8
Jamul—*civil* CA-9
**Jamul**—*pop pl* CA-9
Jamul Butte—*summit* CA-9
Jamul (CCD)—*cens area* CA-9
Jamul Creek—*stream* CA-9
Jamul Las Flores Sch—*school* CA-9
Jamul Mtn—*range* CA-9
Jamul Valley—*valley* CA-9
Jam Up Cave—*cave* MO-7
Jam Up Creek—*stream* MO-7
Jam Up Hollow—*valley* MO-7
*JAM-WA* MP-9
Jamwua—*island* MP-9
Janacek Springs—*spring* WI-6
Janacks Landing Shelter—*locale* NY-2
Janacks Point—*cape* NY-2
Janaf Shop Ctr—*locale* VA-3
Jana Gordo Well—*well* AZ-5
Janal Gas Field—*oilfield* TX-5
Jan Bridgmon Number Two Mine (underground)—*mine* AL-4
Jandahl Sch—*school* SD-7
Jan De Bakkers Kill—*stream* NY-2
J and E Junction—*locale* TX-5
Jandell Creek—*stream* MT-8
J and E Ormond Grant—*civil* FL-3
Janders Run—*stream* PA-2
**J and E Trailer Court (subdivision)**—*pop pl* (2) SD-7
J and J Fishing Lake—*reservoir* NC-3
J and J Trout Lake—*dam* NC-3
J and J Well—*well* NV-8
**J. And L. Ranchland**—*pop pl* TX-5
Jandls Pond—*reservoir* VA-3
J and M Trailer Park—*locale* AZ-5
Jandrew Cove—*bay* FL-3
*J Andrew Morrow Elementary School* PA-2
**J and S Subdivsion**—*pop pl* UT-8
J and W Dismal Swamp—*swamp* NC-3
*Jane* VA-3
Jane—*locale* NE-7
**Jane**—*pop pl* MO-7
Jane, Lake—*lake* FL-3
Jane, Lake—*lake* MN-6
Jane, Lake—*reservoir* (2) AL-4
Jane, Lake—*reservoir* GA-3
Jane Adams Sch—*school* IL-6
Jane Adams Sch—*school* MI-6
Jane Addams Sch—*school* (2) CA-9
Jane Addams Sch—*school* IL-6
Jane Addams Sch—*school* MI-6
Jane Addams Sch—*school* OH-6
Jane Arnett Branch—*stream* KY-4
Jane Bald—*summit* NC-3
Jane Bald—*summit* TN-4
Jane Bay—*swamp* FL-3
Jane Berrys Run—*stream* MD-2
*Jane Blackburn Subdivision* UT-8
Jane Branch—*stream* AL-4
Jane Branch—*stream* KY-4
Jane Branch—*stream* NC-3
Jane Branch—*stream* SC-3
Jane Branch—*stream* WV-2
Jane Bryan Cem—*cemetery* MO-7
*Janeburg* AL-4
*Janeburgh* AL-4
Janeburgh Post Office (historical)—*building* AL-4
Jane Cantrell Creek—*stream* NC-3
Janecek, John, House—*hist pl* NE-7
Jane Creek—*stream* AK-9
Jane Dennis Creek—*stream* OK-5
Jane Downing Island—*area* MO-7
Jane Draw—*valley* WY-8
Jane Furnace (Ruins)—*locale* VA-3
Jane Gap—*gap* KY-4
Jane Green Creek—*stream* FL-3
Jane Green Swamp—*swamp* FL-3
Jane Hills—*range* MS-4
Jane Hollow—*valley* (2) TN-4
Jane Hollow—*valley* TX-5
Jane Horton Ball Elem Sch—*school* IN-6
**Janeiro**—*pop pl* NC-3
Jane Knob—*summit* NC-3
Jane Lake—*lake* MI-6
Jane Lamb Memorial Hosp—*hospital* IA-7
**Jane Lew**—*pop pl* WV-2
Janelia—*hist pl* VA-3
Janellen Gas Field—*oilfield* TX-5
Janelle Oil Field—*oilfield* TX-5
Jane Long Sch—*school* (3) TX-5
Jane Murray Grant—*civil* FL-3
Jane Otter Branch—*stream* NC-3
Jane Phillips Sch—*school* OK-5
Jane Point—*cliff* TN-4
Jane Pond—*lake* NC-3

Jane Pond—*reservoir* FL-3
Jane Robun Branch—*stream* GA-3
Jane Robun Branch—*stream* NC-3
Jane Ridge—*ridge* (3) TN-4
*Janes* KS-7
Janes Bay—*bay* WI-6
Janes Branch Bay—*swamp* FL-3
Janes Butte—*summit* AZ-5
Janes Cem—*cemetery* (2) AR-4
Janes Cem—*cemetery* GA-3
Janes Cem—*cemetery* IN-6
Janes Cem—*cemetery* KY-4
Janes Cem—*cemetery* TN-4
Janes Cem—*cemetery* VT-1
Janes Chapel—*church* WV-2
Janes Cove—*bay* MA-1
Janes Creek—*stream* (2) AR-4
Janes Creek—*stream* CA-9
Janes Creek—*stream* (2) MO-7
Janes Creek—*stream* NC-3
Janes Creek (Township of)—*fmr MCD* AR-4
Janes Gulch—*valley* CA-9
Janes Hill—*summit* MA-1
Janes Hole—*basin* TX-5
*Jane's Island* MD-2
Janes Island—*island* MD-2
Janes Island Gut—*gut* MD-2
Janes Island State Park—*park* MD-2
Janes Meadow—*flat* WY-8
Janes Memorial Ch—*church* WV-2
Janes Mill—*locale* AL-4
Janes Place—*locale* CA-9
Janes Point—*cape* MD-2
Janes RR Station—*locale* FL-3
Janes Rsvr—*reservoir* CA-9
Janes Run—*stream* WV-2
Janes Sch—*school* CA-9
Janes Sch—*school* WI-6
Janes Spring—*spring* CO-8
Janes Tank—*spring* UT-8
**Janesville**—*pop pl* CA-9
**Janesville**—*pop pl* IL-6
**Janesville**—*pop pl* IA-7
**Janesville**—*pop pl* MN-6
**Janesville**—*pop pl* NY-2
**Janesville**—*pop pl* WI-6
Janesville Cem—*cemetery* NE-7
Janesville Cotton Mill—*hist pl* WI-6
Janesville Free Public Library—*hist pl* MN-6
Janesville Mtn—*summit* AK-9
Janesville Public Library—*hist pl* WI-6
Janesville Pumping Station—*hist pl* WI-6
Janesville Sch—*school* NE-7
**Janesville (Smithmill Post Office)**—*pop pl* PA-2
**Janesville (Town of)**—*pop pl* WI-6
**Janesville Township**—*pop pl* KS-7
**Janesville (Township of)**—*pop pl* MN-6
Janes Well—*locale* NM-5
Janes Window—*arch* TX-5
*Janet* MP-9
**Janet**—*pop pl* TX-5
Janet, Lake—*lake* MT-8
Jane Tank—*reservoir* AZ-5
Janet Mine—*mine* CA-9
Janette Lake—*lake* MN-6
Janette Lake (Unorganized Territory of)—*unorg* MN-6
Janeway Campground—*locale* CO-8
Janeway Cem—*cemetery* (2) TN-4
Jane Wayland Child Guidance Center—*school* AZ-5
Janeway Mine (underground)—*mine* AL-4
Jane Well—*well* NM-5
**Janey**—*pop pl* VA-3
Janey Branch—*stream* TN-4
*Janey Pond* MS-4
Janeys Creek—*stream* VA-3
Janeys Creek Marsh—*swamp* VA-3
Janey Tank—*reservoir* NM-5
Jangga—*area* GU-9
Jangle Ditch—*canal* CO-8
Jangle Ridge—*ridge* NV-8
Janhke Lake—*lake* MT-8
*Janiak* FM-9
*Janiak Island* FM-9
**Janice**—*pop pl* MS-4
Janice Draw—*valley* WY-8
Janice Field—*airport* ND-7
Janice Landing Recreation Site—*park* MS-4
Janice Rsvr—*reservoir* WY-8
Janice Sch—*school* MS-4
Janice Tank—*reservoir* AZ-5
Janicke House—*hist pl* NH-1
Janicke Slough—*lake* WA-9
Janie—*locale* LA-4
**Janie**—*pop pl* WV-2
Janie Bell Cem—*cemetery* TN-4
Janie Howard Wilson Elem Sch—*school* FL-3
Janies Nipples—*summit* ID-8
Janie Tank—*reservoir* AZ-5
Janikowski Ranch—*locale* ND-7
Janin Store—*hist pl* LA-4
Janis—*locale* WA-9
Janis Canyon—*valley* AZ-5
Janis Creek—*stream* SD-7
Janise—*locale* NE-7
Janis Rapids—*rapids* WA-9
Janis Spring—*spring* AZ-5
**Janke Township**—*pop pl* ND-7
Jankewitz Lake—*lake* WI-6
Jankovsky Ranch—*locale* (2) WY-8
*Jankra Brook* CT-1
Jan Lake—*lake* AK-9
Jan Mann Opportunity Center—*school* FL-3
Jan Mann Opportunity Sch—*school* FL-3
**Jan Mor Acres**—*pop pl* TN-4
Janney—*locale* FL-3
**Janney**—*pop pl* CA-9
**Janney**—*pop pl* IN-6
**Janney**—*pop pl* MT-8
**Janney**—*pop pl* PA-2
Janney Furnace—*hist pl* AL-4
Janney Gulch—*valley* MT-8
Janney Lake—*reservoir* MS-4
Janney Run—*stream* IN-6
Janney Sch—*school* DC-2
*Janneys Creek* MS-4
Jannings Hollow—*valley* MO-7
**Janni Spur**—*pop pl* WA-9
Jannone-Ballibay Airp—*airport* PA-2
*Jano* AZ-5
*Janoak* FM-9
*Janogualpa* AZ-5
Janowaik Drain—*canal* MI-6
Janowski Sch—*school* TX-5
**JanPhyl Village**—*pop pl* FL-3
**Jansen**—*pop pl* CO-8
**Jansen**—*pop pl* NE-7
Jansen, Johannes, House and Dutch Barn—*hist pl* NY-2
Jansen, Theodore, House—*hist pl* IA-7
Jansen, Thomas, House—*hist pl* NY-2
Jansen Ave Sch—*school* NY-2
*Jansen Bay* WA-9
Jansen Cem—*cemetery* CO-8
Jansen Cem—*cemetery* NE-7
Jansen Cem—*cemetery* WI-6
Jansen Creek—*stream* MI-6
Jansen Creek—*stream* WA-9
Jansen Hill—*summit* WA-9
*Jansen Kill* NY-2
Jans Herald Number 1 Dam—*dam* SD-7
Jans Hill—*summit* WA-9
Janson Brook—*stream* CT-1
Janssen, E., Bldg—*hist pl* CA-9
Janssen Oil Field—*oilfield* TX-5
Janssen Park—*hist pl* AR-4
Janssen Park—*park* AR-4
Janssen Place Hist Dist—*hist pl* MO-7
Janssen Ranch—*locale* OR-9
Janssen Sch—*school* WI-6
Janssens-Orella-Birk Bldg—*hist pl* CA-9
Janssen Spring—*spring* OR-9
Janssen Spring Creek—*stream* OR-9
Janss Site—*hist pl* NM-5
Jans 1 Dam—*dam* SD-7
*Jantucuck River* NJ-2
*Jantukuk River* NJ-2
Jantz—*locale* WA-9
Jantz Hollow—*valley* MO-7
January, Ephriam, House—*hist pl* KY-4
January, Thomas, House—*hist pl* KY-4
January Branch—*stream* AL-4
January Creek—*stream* OR-9
January Hills—*summit* MA-1
*January Island* FL-3
January Jones Mine—*mine* CA-9
January Lake—*lake* AK-9
January Mesa—*summit* CO-8
January Spring—*spring* CO-8
January Tank—*reservoir* AZ-5
January Wash—*stream* NV-8
Janum Point—*cape* GU-9
Janum Spring—*spring* GU-9
Janura Park—*park* IL-6
Janus, Lake—*lake* WA-9
Janus Butte—*ridge* OR-9
Janus Butte Trail—*trail* OR-9
*Janus Crater* AZ-5
*Janus Spring* AZ-5
Janus Spring—*spring* AZ-5
Janvier—*locale* NJ-2
Janvier Cem—*cemetery* NJ-2
Janyssek Ranch—*locale* TX-5
Janzen Rsvr—*reservoir* OR-9
JA Oelkes—*locale* TX-5
Jaotan—*locale* GU-9
Jaotan Point—*cape* GU-9
*Jao Valley* HI-9
JAO Well—*well* AZ-5
Japacha Creek—*stream* CA-9
Japacha Peak—*summit* CA-9
Japacha Spring—*spring* CA-9
Japan—*locale* MO-7
**Japan**—*pop pl* PA-2
Japanese Army Headquarters—*hist pl* FM-9
Japanese Bay—*bay* AK-9
Japanese Caves—*cave* GU-9
Japanese Cem—*cemetery* CA-9
Japanese Ch of Christ—*church* UT-8
Japanese Church of Christ—*hist pl* UT-8
Japanese Coastal Defense Gun—*hist pl* MH-9
Japanese Creek—*stream* AL-4
Japanese Creek—*stream* ID-8
Japanese Creek—*stream* (3) OR-9
Japanese Creek—*stream* UT-8
Japanese Davidson Ditch—*canal* CO-8
Japanoso Ditch—*canal* CO-8
Japanese Embassy Bldg—*hist pl* DC-2
Japanese Hill—*summit* KY-4
Japanese Hollow—*valley* OR-9
Japanese Hospital—*hist pl* (2) MH-9
Japanese House—*building* PA-2
Japanese Hydro-electric Power Plant—*hist pl* FM-9
Japanese Institute of Sawtelle—*school* CA-9
Japanese Knob—*summit* AR-4
Japanese Lake—*lake* MN-6
Japanese Lake—*lake* WA-9
Japanese Lantern—*park* DC-2
Japanese Lighthouse—*hist pl* FM-9
Japanese Lighthouse—*hist pl* MH-9
*Japanese Mandate Islands* MP-9
Japanese Meadow—*flat* OR-9
Japanesen (not verified)—*island* MP-9
Japanese Occupation Site, Kiska Island—*hist pl* AK-9
Japanese Park—*flat* WY-8
Japanese Point—*cape* CA-9
Japanese Rock—*cape* FL-3
Japanese Sch—*school* (2) HI-9
Japanese Shrine—*hist pl* FM-9
Japanese Slough—*gut* AZ-5
Japanese Spring—*spring* ID-8
Japanese Springs—*spring* OR-9
Japanese Structure—*hist pl* MH-9
Japanese Tank—*reservoir* AZ-5
Japanese Valley—*basin* UT-8
Japanese Valley—*valley* AZ-5
**Japanese Village One**—*pop pl* HI-9
Japan Hills—*other* AK-9
*Japaniizen To* MP-9
*Japaniori* MP-9
Japan Island—*island* LA-4
Japan Mine—*mine* CO-8
Japan Outside Pond—*bay* LA-4
Japan Pass—*channel* LA-4
Japan Sch—*school* MO-7
Japany Ch—*church* AR-4
J A Parsons Lake Dam—*dam* MS-4
Japatul Valley—*valley* CA-9
Japatu Station—*locale* CA-9
*Jap Bay* AK-9
*Jap Creek* AL-4
*Jap Creek* OR-9
*Jap Creek* UT-8
*Jap Davidson Ditch* CO-8
*Jap Ditch* CO-8
*Japeiroi* MP-9
Japejiroi—*island* MP-9
Japejiroi—*locale* MP-9
Japenese Artillery Road and Pohndolap Area—*hist pl* FM-9
Japenese Elementary School for Ponapean Children—*hist pl* FM-9
*Jap-Gruppe* FM-9
Japhet Brook—*stream* MA-1
Iaphet Sch—*school* TX-5
*Jap Hill* MH-9
*Jap Hollow* OR-9
*Jap-Insel* FM-9
*Jap-Inseln* FM-9
*Jap Knob* AR-4
*Jap Lake* MN-6
*Jap Lake* WA-9
Japling Run—*stream* PA-2
*Jap Meadow* OR-9
*Japonocru To* MP-9
Japonski Island—*other* AK-9
*Jappa* TN-4
**Jappa**—*pop pl* TX-5
**Jappa Oaks (subdivision)**—*pop pl* NC-3
Jappa Ridge—*ridge* KY-4
*Jap Park* WY-8
J A Price Pond Dam—*dam* MS-4
*Jap Rock* CA-9
*Jap Rock* FL-3
*Japs Lake* MI-6
*Jap Slough* AZ-5
*Jap Smith Branch* TX-5
*Jap Springs* OR-9
*Japs Valley* UT-8
*Japtan* MP-9
Japtan—*island* (2) MP-9
*Japtan Island* MP-9
Japton—*locale* AR-4
Japton (Township of)—*fmr MCD* AR-4
*Japuteikku-to* FM-9
*Japutik* FM-9
*Japuwan-to* MP-9
*Jap Valley* UT-8
Japwan—*island* MP-9
Jaqua Cem—*cemetery* KS-7
Jaqua (historical)—*locale* KS-7
Jaquar Tank—*reservoir* AZ-5
**Jaqua Township**—*pop pl* KS-7
Jaquay Lake—*reservoir* OH-6
Jaque, Bayou—*gut* LA-4
Jaque Cem—*cemetery* IN-6
Jaques—*locale* IL-6
Jaques Bridge—*locale* NJ-2
*Jaques Canyon* NM-5
*Jaques Creek* OR-9
Jaques Creek—*stream* OR-9
*Jaques Dam* AZ-5
*Jaques Gulch* MT-8
Jaques Lake—*lake* MN-6
Jaques Mtn—*summit* AZ-5
Jaques Park—*flat* CO-8
Jaques Sch—*school* ME-1
Jaques Spring—*spring* AZ-5
Jaquess Spring—*spring* AL-4
Jaques Tank—*reservoir* AZ-5
Jaquet Lake—*lake* WI-6
Jaquez Arroyo—*stream* NM-5
Jaquez Flat—*flat* NM-5
Jaquez Site Ruin—*hist pl* NM-5
Jaqui Dam—*dam* NJ-2
Jaquines Island—*island* LA-4
**Jaquins**—*pop pl* NY-2
Jaqui Pond—*reservoir* NJ-2
Jaquish Gut—*gut* ME-1
Jaquish Island—*island* ME-1
Jaquith—*locale* MS-4
Jaquith Brook—*stream* NH-1
Jaquith Park—*park* OR-9
Jaquith Pond—*lake* ME-1
*Jar* MP-9
Jar—*island* MP-9
*Jarachinal Creek* TX-5
Jaracito Canyon—*valley* NM-5
*Jaracito Park* NM-5
Jaral Canyon—*valley* NM-5
Jaral Ditch—*canal* (2) NM-5
**Jarales**—*pop pl* NM-5
Jaral Lateral No 1—*canal* NM-5
Jaral Lateral No 2—*canal* NM-5
Jaralosa Canyon—*valley* (2) NM-5
Jaralosa Creek—*stream* (2) NM-5
Jaralosa Draw—*valley* AZ-5
Jaralosa Draw—*valley* NM-5
Jaralosa Mtn—*summit* NM-5
Jaralosa Spring—*spring* NM-5
Jaralosa Windmill—*locale* NM-5
Jara Loso Spring—*spring* NM-5
Jaral Ranger Station—*locale* NM-5
Jaramie Lake—*lake* NM-5
Jaramillo, Ramon, House and Barn—*hist pl* NM-5
Jaramillo Canyon—*valley* (2) NM-5
Jaramillo Creek—*stream* NM-5
Jaramillo Overflow Ditch—*canal* CO-8
Jaramillo Ranch—*locale* NM-5
Jaramillo Spring—*spring* NM-5
Jaramosa Canyon—*valley* NM-5
J A Ranch—*hist pl* TX-5
*Jaraschanal Creek* TX-5
*Jaraschinal Creek* TX-5
**Jarbalo**—*pop pl* KS-7
Jarbalo Creek—*stream* KS-7
*Jarbeau Creek* OR-9
*Jarbeau Meadows* OR-9
**Jarbidge**—*pop pl* NV-8
Jarbidge Lake—*lake* NV-8
Jarbidge Mtns—*range* NV-8
Jarbidge Natl Forest Campground—*locale* NV-8
Jarbidge Peak—*summit* NV-8
Jarbidge Ranger District—*forest* NV-8
Jarbidge River—*stream* (2) ID-8
Jarbidge River—*stream* NV-8
Jarbidge Township—*inact MCD* NV-8
Jarbidge Wilderness—*park* NV-8
**Jarbo**—*pop pl* CA-9
Jarbo Bayou—*stream* TX-5
Jarboe Creek—*stream* OR-9
Jarboe Meadow—*flat* OR-9
*Jarboe Meadows* OR-9
*Jarboesville* MD-2
Jarboesville Run—*stream* MD-2
Jarboe Windmill—*locale* TX-5
Jarbo Gap—*gap* CA-9
*Jarbo Meadows* OR-9
Jarbo Sinks—*basin* KY-4
Jarbow Ridge—*ridge* CA-9
Jarbow Spring—*spring* CA-9
*Jarbridge* NV-8
Jarbridge Ranger District—*forest* NV-8
Jarbridge River—*stream* ID-8
Jar Brook—*stream* MA-1
Jar Butte—*summit* NM-5
Jarchow Lake—*lake* WA-9
Jardin—*locale* TX-5
Jardin Creek—*stream* TX-5
**Jardine**—*pop pl* MT-8
**Jardine**—*pop pl* WA-9
Jardine, Mount—*summit* UT-8
Jardine Bay—*swamp* GA-3
Jardine Canyon—*valley* CA-9
Jardine Ditch—*canal* MT-8
Jardine Ditch Number One—*canal* MT-8
Jardine-Hellroaring Trail—*trail* MT-8
Jardine Hot Spring—*spring* MT-8
Jardine JHS—*school* (2) KS-7
Jardine Ranch—*locale* CO-8
**Jardines de Arecibo**—*pop pl* PR-3
**Jardines de Caparra**—*pop pl* PR-3
**Jardines del Caribe**—*pop pl* PR-3
**Jardines de Monte Hatillo**—*pop pl* PR-3
**Jardines de Ponce**—*pop pl* PR-3
Jardinette Apartments—*hist pl* CA-9
Jardin Windmill—*locale* TX-5
Jardis Point—*cape* AR-4
*Jardville* NJ-2
**Jarealito**—*pop pl* PR-3
Jarebit, Lake—*reservoir* GA-3
Jared—*locale* WA-9
Jared Cem—*cemetery* (2) TN-4
Jared Hollow Cave—*cave* TN-4
Jared Sch (historical)—*school* TN-4
Jareds Fork—*stream* UT-8
Jarej-Uliga-Delap—*CDP* MP-9
Jarekit, Lake—*reservoir* GA-3
*Jarelds Creek* KY-4
Jarett Maynard Cem—*cemetery* WV-2
Jarett Place—*locale* NM-5
Jargo Sch—*school* WI-6
Jarilla Mountains—*other* NM-5
Jarillas Spring—*spring* AZ-5
Jarillas Tank—*reservoir* AZ-5
Jarilla Tank—*reservoir* TX-5
*Jariolds Creek* KY-4
Jarioso Canyon—*valley* CO-8
Jarita Canyon—*valley* NM-5
*Jarita Creek* TX-5
Jarita Creek—*stream* TX-5
Jaritas Arroyo—*stream* NM-5
Jaritas Ranch—*locale* NM-5
*Jaritto-byochi* MP-9
*Jaritto-to* MP-9
*Jarja* TX-5
*Jarkul* MP-9
Jarkwil—*island* MP-9
Jarl Number 1 Dam—*dam* SD-7
Jarl Oswarld Number 2 Dam—*dam* SD-7
Jarman, Daniel B., House and Garden—*hist pl* OR-9
Jarman Airp—*airport* PA-2
Jarman Branch—*stream* TN-4
Jarman Farm—*hist pl* TN-4
Jarman Ferry (historical)—*locale* MS-4
**Jarman Forks**—*pop pl* NC-3
Jarman Gap—*gap* VA-3
Jarman Gap—*locale* VA-3
Jarman Hollow—*valley* TN-4
Jarman House Plantation (historical)—*locale* AL-4
Jarman JHS—*school* OK-5
Jarman Landing—*locale* MS-4
*Jarmans Gap* VA-3
**Jarmantown**—*pop pl* (2) NC-3
Jarman Windmill—*locale* TX-5
Jarmany Hill Cem—*cemetery* NH-1
Jarmine Post Office (historical)—*building* TN-4
Jarmons Mine (underground)—*mine* AL-4
Jarnagan Mine—*mine* TN-4
Jarnagin Cem—*cemetery* TN-4
*Jarnagins Island* TN-4
Jarnagins Shoals—*bar* TN-4
Jarnigan Chapel—*church* TN-4
Jarnigan Knob—*summit* OH-6
Jarnigan Mtn—*summit* TN-4
Jarnigan Pond—*lake* CA-9
Jarnigan Spring—*spring* TN-4
Jarocita Park—*flat* NM-5
Jarocito Creek—*stream* CO-8
Jarocito Creek—*stream* NM-5
Jarod Cem—*cemetery* MS-4
Jarosa—*locale* NM-5
Jarosa Canyon—*valley* (2) NM-5
Jarosa Cem—*cemetery* CO-8
*Jarosa Creek* NM-5
Jarosa Creek—*stream* CO-8
Jarosa Creek—*stream* (2) NM-5
Jarosa Mesa—*summit* CO-8
Jarosa Mesa—*summit* NM-5
Jarosa Peak—*summit* CO-8
Jarosito Canyon—*valley* NM-5
**Jaroso**—*pop pl* CO-8
Jaroso Canyon—*valley* (2) NM-5
Jaroso Cem—*cemetery* CO-8
Jaroso Creek—*stream* CO-8
Jaroso Creek—*stream* NM-5
Jaroso Ditch—*canal* CO-8
*Jarosoma Mountains* AZ-5
**Jaroy**—*pop pl* GA-3
Jarrard, Levi D., House—*hist pl* NJ-2
Jarrard Creek—*stream* (2) GA-3
Jarrard Ditch—*canal* WY-8
Jarrard Gap—*gap* GA-3
Jarrard Ranch—*locale* WY-8
**Jarratt**—*pop pl* VA-3
**Jarreau**—*pop pl* LA-4
Jarre Canyon—*valley* CO-8
Jarre Creek—*stream* CO-8
Jarred Branch—*stream* TX-5
*Jarred Creek* WA-9
*Jarrej* MP-9
Jarrell—*locale* GA-3
**Jarrell**—*pop pl* TN-4
**Jarrell**—*pop pl* TX-5
*Jarrell Branch* GA-3
Jarrell Branch—*stream* KY-4
Jarrell Branch—*stream* (2) WV-2
Jarrell (CCD)—*cens area* TX-5
Jarrell Cem—*cemetery* MO-7
Jarrell Cem—*cemetery* (3) TN-4
Jarrell Cem—*cemetery* VA-3
Jarrell Cem—*cemetery* (3) WV-2
Jarrell Cove—*bay* WA-9
Jarrell Creek—*stream* MS-4
Jarrell Creek—*stream* TX-5
Jarrell Creek—*stream* WA-9
**Jarrell Farms**—*pop pl* DE-2
Jarrell Fork—*stream* KY-4
Jarrell Hollow—*valley* IN-6
Jarrell Mtn—*summit* VA-3
Jarrell Plantation—*hist pl* GA-3
Jarrell Pond—*lake* GA-3
Jarrell Ranch—*locale* NM-5
*Jarrells* WV-2
*Jarrells Branch* WV-2
Jarrells Cave—*cave* TN-4
Jarrells Cem—*cemetery* (3) WV-2
*Jarrell's Cove* WA-9
*Jarrells Creek* NC-3
Jarrells Creek—*stream* WV-2
Jarrells Flats—*flat* WV-2
Jarrell Tank No 1—*reservoir* NM-5
*Jarrel's Cove* WA-9
Jarrels Creek—*stream* KY-4
Jarrels Ferry Lake—*lake* TX-5
*Jarrets Run* NJ-2
Jarrets Summit—*summit* PA-2
Jarrett—*locale* GA-3
**Jarrett**—*pop pl* AL-4
**Jarrett**—*pop pl* KS-7
**Jarrett**—*pop pl* MN-6
Jarrett Bald—*summit* NC-3
Jarrett Bay—*bay* NC-3
Jarrett Branch—*stream* MO-7
Jarrett Branch—*stream* WV-2
Jarrett Camp Branch—*stream* NC-3
Jarrett Cem—*cemetery* AR-4
Jarrett Cem—*cemetery* GA-3
Jarrett Cem—*cemetery* NC-3
Jarrett Cem—*cemetery* TN-4
Jarrett Cem—*cemetery* TX-5
**Jarrett Cove**—*pop pl* NC-3
Jarrett Creek—*stream* MD-2
Jarrett Creek—*stream* MT-8
Jarrett Creek—*stream* (2) NC-3
Jarrett Fork—*stream* KY-4
Jarrett Hollow—*valley* NC-3
Jarrett Hollow—*valley* VA-3
Jarrett JHS—*school* MO-7
Jarrett Knob—*summit* NC-3
Jarrett Knob—*summit* TN-4
Jarrettown—*locale* PA-2
Jarrett Ranch—*locale* (2) MT-8
Jarrett Ranch—*locale* TX-5
*Jarretts* MN-6
**Jarretts**—*pop pl* IN-6
**Jarretts**—*pop pl* MN-6
Jarretts Cem—*cemetery* WV-2
Jarrett Sch—*school* HI-9
*Jarretts Creek* NC-3
Jarretts Creek—*stream* NC-3
*Jarretts Ford* MN-6
**Jarretts Ford**—*pop pl* WV-2
Jarretts Point—*cape* NC-3
**Jarrettsville**—*pop pl* MD-2
Jarrettsville Cem—*cemetery* MD-2
Jarrett Tunnel—*tunnel* NC-3
Jarris Creek—*stream* OR-9
Jarr Lake—*lake* MI-6
Jarrods Valley—*uninc pl* WV-2
*Jarroj* MP-9
*Jarrolds Creek* KY-4
*Jarrolds Creek* WV-2
**Jarrolds Valley**—*pop pl* WV-2
*Jarrolt* FL-3
Jarrot, Nicholas, House—*hist pl* IL-6
Jarrott—*locale* FL-3
Jarstad Lake—*lake* WA-9
J Arthur Duff Elem Sch—*school* PA-2
*Jarudoni-To* MP-9
*Jarutonii Island* MP-9
*Jarutoni To* MP-9
Jarvers Lake—*lake* AR-4
Jarvi, Thomas, Homestead—*hist pl* ID-8
Jarvi Creek—*stream* MI-6
Jarvies Canyon—*valley* UT-8
Jarvies Canyon Boat Camp—*locale* UT-8
*Jarvies Canyon Campground* UT-8
Jarvies Marsh Creek—*stream* WY-8
Jarvies Spring—*spring* UT-8
Jarville—*hist pl* MO-7
Jarvinen Marsh Lake—*lake* MI-6
*Jarvis* IN-6
Jarvis—*locale* TX-5
**Jarvis**—*pop pl* KY-4
**Jarvis**—*pop pl* MO-7
Jarvis, Anna, House—*hist pl* WV-2
Jarvis, Mount—*summit* (2) AK-9
Jarvis, The—*hist pl* MA-1
Jarvis, William W., House—*hist pl* IL-6
Jarvis Ave Park—*park* IL-6
Jarvis Bay—*bay* MN-6
Jarvis Bay Sch—*school* MN-6
Jarvis Branch—*stream* (2) KY-4
Jarvis Branch—*stream* NC-3
**Jarvisburg**—*pop pl* NC-3
Jarvis Canal—*canal* NC-3
Jarvis Canyon—*valley* KS-7
Jarvis Canyon—*valley* NE-7
Jarvis Cem—*cemetery* CO-8
Jarvis Cem—*cemetery* IN-6
Jarvis Cem—*cemetery* KY-4
Jarvis Cem—*cemetery* MO-7
Jarvis Cem—*cemetery* OH-6
Jarvis Cem—*cemetery* WV-2
Jarvis Ch—*church* OK-5
Jarvis Channel—*channel* NC-3
Jarvis Chapel—*church* AR-4
Jarvis College Cem—*cemetery* TX-5
Jarvis College (Jarvis Christian College)—*facility* TX-5
*Jarvis Creek* MS-4
Jarvis Creek—*stream* (3) AK-9
Jarvis Creek—*stream* KS-7
Jarvis Creek—*stream* NE-7
Jarvis Creek—*stream* NC-3
Jarvis Creek—*stream* SC-3
Jarvis Creek—*stream* TX-5
Jarvis Creek—*stream* VA-3
Jarvis Dam—*dam* AZ-5
Jarvis-Fleet House—*hist pl* NY-2
Jarvis Glacier—*glacier* AK-9
Jarvis Hill—*summit* VT-1
Jarvis Hollow—*valley* MO-7
Jarvis House—*hist pl* OH-6
Jarvis Island—*island* AK-9
Jarvis Island—*island* NH-1
*Jarvis Lake* OR-9
*Jarvis Lake* WI-6
Jarvis Lake—*lake* AR-4
Jarvis Lake—*lake* MI-6
Jarvis Lake—*lake* ND-7
Jarvis Lake—*reservoir* AZ-5
Jarvis Landing—*locale* CA-9
Jarvis Pasture—*flat* ID-8
Jarvis Pasture Rsvr No 1—*reservoir* ID-8
Jarvis Pasture Rsvr No 2—*reservoir* ID-8
Jarvis Pasture Rsvr No 3—*reservoir* ID-8
Jarvis Peak—*summit* UT-8
Jarvis Point—*cape* (2) VA-3
Jarvis Ponds—*reservoir* OR-9
Jarvis Ranch—*locale* AZ-5
Jarvis Sound—*bay* NJ-2
Jarvis Sound Thorofare—*channel* NJ-2
Jarvis Spring—*spring* (2) ID-8
Jarvis Store—*locale* KY-4
**Jarvis (Township of)**—*pop pl* IL-6
Jarvis Tunnel—*mine* CA-9
Jarvis Turn—*channel* OR-9
**Jarvisville**—*pop pl* WV-2
Jarvis Wash—*stream* AZ-5
*Jarwojion* MP-9
*Jarylies Creek* KY-4
*Ja-She Creek* CA-9
Ja She Creek—*stream* CA-9
Jaskari Lake—*lake* MN-6
Jaslowski (historical)—*locale* MT-8
Jasmer Lake—*lake* MN-6
Jasmin—*locale* CA-9
*Jasmine* MP-9
Jasmine—*locale* AR-4
*Jasmine Creek* MT-8
Jasmine Creek—*stream* MT-8
Jasmine Estates—*CDP* FL-3
**Jasmine Hill (subdivision)**—*pop pl* AL-4
Jasmine Island—*island* GA-3
Jasmine Plaza (Shop Ctr)—*locale* FL-3
Jasmin Sch—*school* CA-9
Jasna Gora Sch—*school* MA-1
Jason—*locale* (2) KY-4
**Jason**—*pop pl* NC-3
**Jason**—*pop pl* SC-3
Jason and Broadus Cem—*cemetery* IL-6
Jason Boggs Cem—*cemetery* KY-4
Jason Branch—*stream* KY-4
Jason Branch—*stream* NC-3
Jason Cabin—*locale* UT-8
Jason Cem—*cemetery* MI-6
Jason Chapel—*church* TN-4
Jason Creek—*stream* MD-2
Jason Creek—*stream* UT-8
Jason Gully—*valley* NY-2
*Jason Lake* IN-6
Jason Lake Dam—*dam* IN-6
Jason Lakes—*lake* WA-9
Jason Lee Mission Historical Marker—*other* OR-9
*Jason Niles Park* MS-4
**Jason Ridge**—*pop pl* KY-4
Jasons Branch—*stream* KY-4
Jasons Branch—*stream* NC-3
Jason Sch—*school* NC-3
Jason Sch—*school* WA-9
Jason Shoal—*bar* MA-1
Jason Spring—*spring* UT-8
Jason Tank—*reservoir* NM-5
Jasontown—*locale* MD-2
Jason (Township of)—*fmr MCD* NC-3
**Jasonville**—*pop pl* IN-6
*Jasper* KS-7
*Jasper* NV-8
*Jasper* OH-6
Jasper—*locale* OK-5
Jasper—*locale* SC-3
Jasper—*locale* VA-3
**Jasper**—*pop pl* AL-4
**Jasper**—*pop pl* AR-4
**Jasper**—*pop pl* CO-8
**Jasper**—*pop pl* FL-3
**Jasper**—*pop pl* GA-3
**Jasper**—*pop pl* IN-6
**Jasper**—*pop pl* MI-6
**Jasper**—*pop pl* MN-6
**Jasper**—*pop pl* MO-7
**Jasper**—*pop pl* NY-2
**Jasper**—*pop pl* NC-3
**Jasper**—*pop pl* OH-6
**Jasper**—*pop pl* OR-9
**Jasper**—*pop pl* TN-4
**Jasper**—*pop pl* TX-5
**Jasper**—*pop pl* VA-3
**Jasper**—*pop pl* WV-2
Jasper, Mount—*summit* NH-1
Jasper-Alamitos Union Sch—*school* CA-9
Jasper Bay—*bay* WA-9
Jasper Bend—*bend* KY-4
Jasper Brook—*stream* IN-6
Jasper Canyon—*valley* AZ-5
Jasper Canyon—*valley* NV-8
Jasper Canyon—*valley* UT-8
Jasper Canyon—*valley* WA-9
Jasper Cave—*cave* SD-7
Jasper (CCD)—*cens area* AL-4

J E Sheehan Estate Number 2 Dam—dam SD-7
J E Sheehan Estate Number 3 Dam—dam SD-7
Jeske Park—park MO-7
Jeslo Sch—school IL-6
**Jesmond Dene**—pop pl CA-9
Jeson Butte UT-8
Jespersen Spring—spring CA-9
Jesperson Sch—school CA-9
Jesrun Ch—church MS-4
**Jessama**—pop pl NC-3
Jessamine—locale FL-3
Jessamine—locale KY-4
Jessamine, Bayou—gut AL-4
Jessamine, Lake—lake FL-3
Jessamine Cem—cemetery MS-4
Jessamine Childrens Home—building KY-4
**Jessamine (County)**—pop pl KY-4
Jessamine Creek MT-8
Jessamine Creek—stream KY-4
Jessamine Lake—lake FL-3
Jessamine Ridge Ch—church MS-4
Jess Boggs Branch—stream KY-4
Jess Branch—stream (2) AL-4
Jess Branch—stream IA-7
Jess Canille Branch—stream KY-4
Jess Coulee—valley MT-8
Jess Cove—valley NC-3
Jess Creek—stream AL-4
Jess Dunn Hill—summit AL-4
Jess Dye Mine (underground)—mine AL-4
**Jesse**—pop pl OK-5
**Jesse**—pop pl WV-2
Jesse, Lake—lake LA-4
Jesse, Mount—summit NH-1
Jesse Arroyo—valley TX-5
Jesse Belle Shaft—mine CA-9
Jesse Bog—swamp ME-1
Jesse Branch—stream KY-4
Jesse Branch—stream LA-4
Jesse Branch—stream MS-4
Jesse Branch—stream NC-3
Jesse Cain Run—stream WV-2
Jesse Campground—locale CA-9
Jesse Canyon CA-9
Jesse Canyon—valley CA-9
Jesse Cole Lake—reservoir NC-3
Jesse Creek—stream AL-4
Jesse Creek—stream (2) AK-9
Jesse Creek—stream (2) ID-8
Jesse Creek—stream IL-6
Jesse Creek—stream (2) MO-7
Jesse Creek—stream TN-4
Jesse Creek—stream WA-9
Jesse Dam—dam SD-7
Jesse Davis Pond Dam—dam MS-4
Jesse Dean Smith Sch—school AL-4
Jessee Branch—stream VA-3
Jessee Cem—cemetery IL-6
Jessee Cem—cemetery KY-4
Jessee Cem—cemetery (6) VA-3
Jessee Hollow—valley VA-3
Jessee Osborne Memorial Cem—cemetery MO-7
Jessees Mill—locale VA-3
Jesse Ewing Canyon—valley UT-8
Jesse Flats—flat CO-8
Jesse Fork—stream KY-4
Jesse Fork—stream NC-3
Jesse Fork—stream WV-2
Jesse Gap—gap KY-4
Jesse Gap—gap VA-3
Jesse Gulch—valley CA-9
Jesse Gulch—valley CO-8
Jesse Hall Picnic Area—area PA-2
Jesse Hollow—valley VA-3
Jesse Holman Jones Hosp—hospital TX-5
Jesse Holmes Cem—cemetery MS-4
Jesse James Canyon—valley AZ-5
Jesse James Caves—cave TN-4
Jesse James Draw—valley TX-5
Jesse James Hill—summit OK-5
Jesse Lake ID-8
Jesse Lake MN-6
Jesse Lake WI-6
Jesse Lake WY-8
Jesse Lake—lake MN-6
Jesse Lake—lake NE-7
Jesse Lake—lake WI-6
Jesse Lake—other MN-6
Jess Elliot Cove—cove AL-4
Jesse McKesson Ditch—canal IN-6
Jesse M. Donaldson MO-7
Jesse Morrow Mtn—summit CA-9
Jesse Mound UT-8
Jesse Mtn—summit AK-9
Jessen Butte—summit UT-8
Jessen-Goodrich House—hist pl OR-9
Jessen Lake—lake UT-8
**Jessenland**—pop pl MN-6
**Jessenland (Township of)**—pop pl MN-6
Jessen Valley—valley CA-9
Jesse Owens Park—park AZ-5
Jesse Pass—gap ID-8
Jesse Pines—summit AR-4
Jesse Ridge—ridge NC-3
Jesse Run—stream (3) WV-2
Jesse Run Ch—church WV-2
Jesses Creek—stream KY-4
Jesses Creek—stream NJ-2
Jesses Creek Ch—church KY-4
Jesses High Top—summit NC-3
Jesse Shoal Point—cape NC-3
Jesses Knob—summit VA-3
Jesses Knob—summit WV-2
Jesses Knoll—summit UT-8
Jesses Point NJ-2
Jesse Spring—spring CA-9
Jesse Spring—spring OR-9
Jesse Spur—ridge KY-4
Jesse Street Minipark—park AZ-5
Jesses Well—well NV-8
Jesses Wells—well UT-8
Jesse Tank—reservoir AZ-5
**Jesseton**—pop pl AL-4
Jesseton Post Office (historical)—building AL-4
Jesse Viertel Memorial Airp—airport MO-7
Jesse Well—well NM-5
Jesse Wharton Sch—school NC-3
Jesse Windmill—locale TX-5
Jesse Yancy Memorial Library—building MS-4
Jessey Creek TN-4
Jess Fork—stream VA-3
Jess Gap—gap GA-3
Jess Heatherly Prospect—mine TN-4
Jess Hollow—valley AL-4
Jess Hollow—valley TN-4
Jess Hollow—valley VA-3
Jess Hood Creek—stream TX-5
Jessica—locale CO-8
Jessie—locale TN-4
**Jessie**—pop pl ND-7
Jessie, Lake—lake FL-3
Jessie, Lake—lake (2) MN-6
Jessie, Lake—lake ND-7
Jessie Branch—stream GA-3
Jessie Branch—stream (3) KY-4
Jessie Bruce Pond Dam—dam MS-4
Jessie-Ca Lake—lake IN-6
Jessie Cem—cemetery TX-5
Jessie C Fortenberry Cem—cemetery MS-4
Jessie Cole Lake Dam—dam NC-3
Jessie Creek TN-4
Jessie Creek—stream (2) AK-9
Jessie Creek—stream CA-9
Jessie Creek—stream ID-8
Jessie Creek—stream (2) OH-6
Jessie Creek—stream OK-5
Jessie Crowell Sch—school MI-6
Jessie Flat—flat OR-9
Jessie Forrester Dam—dam AL-4
Jessie Forrester Lake—reservoir AL-4
Jessie Gap—gap NC-3
Jessie Hill Sch—school OR-9
Jessie Hollow—valley MO-7
Jessie Island—island FL-3
Jessie James Cave—cave KY-4
Jessie Lake—lake GA-3
Jessie Lake—lake (3) MN-6
Jessie Lake—lake WI-6
Jessie Lake—lake WY-8
**Jessie Lake**—pop pl MN-6
Jessie Lake Lookout Tower—locale MN-6
Jessie Mai Aydelott Coll (historical)—school TN-4
Jessie Mine—mine MN-6
Jessie Point NJ-2
Jessie Point—cape NJ-2
Jessie Pond—lake ME-1
Jessie Post Office (historical)—building TN-4
Jessie Run—stream KY-4
Jessie Run—stream OH-6
Jessie Run—stream WV-2
Jessie Saddle—gap CA-9
Jessie Sanford Branch—stream MS-4
Jessies Branch—stream SC-3
Jessies Island—island LA-4
Jessie Slough—stream AR-4
Jessie Slough—stream WA-9
Jessies Neck—cape MA-1
Jessies Point NJ-2
Jessie Spring—spring AZ-5
Jessie Spring—spring OR-9
Jessie Street Substation—hist pl CA-9
Jessies Twist—locale UT-8
Jessie Tie Exclosure—locale UT-8
Jessie Tie Wash—valley UT-8
**Jessietown**—pop pl KY-4
Jessieville MI-6
**Jessieville**—pop pl AR-4
**Jessieville**—pop pl MI-6
Jessieville Ch—church AR-4
Jessieville (Township of)—fmr MCD AR-4
Jessie Well—well NM-5
Jessie Willies—locale FL-3
Jessie Willies Camp—locale FL-3
Jessie Willies Seminole Village—locale FL-3
Jessila Creek—stream AK-9
Jess Island—island SC-3
Jess Ivy Bay (Carolina Bay)—swamp NC-3
Jess Knob—summit NC-3
Jess Lake—lake NE-7
Jess Lake—lake WA-9
Jess Lanier HS—school AL-4
Jess Lunn—locale TX-5
Jess Maynard Hill—summit TX-5
Jess Moore Branch—stream TN-4
Jesso Creek—stream MI-6
Jesson Butte UT-8
Jesson Lake UT-8
Jesson Sch—school ND-7
Jessop—locale WV-2
Jessops Ch—church MD-2
Jessops Gulch CA-9
Jess Parrish Memorial Hosp—hospital FL-3
Jess Peak—summit AZ-5
Jess Ranch—locale CA-9
Jess Ridge TN-4
Jessum—locale CO-8
Jessup GA-3
Jessup—locale NV-8
Jessup—locale OH-6
**Jessup**—pop pl IN-6
**Jessup**—pop pl KY-4
**Jessup**—pop pl MD-2
**Jessup**—pop pl PA-2
Jessup Blair Park—park MD-2
Jessup Borough—civil PA-2
Jessup Bridge—hist pl IN-6
Jessup Canyon—valley CO-8
Jessup Cem—cemetery NC-3
Jessup Covered Bridge—bridge IN-6
**Jessup Farm Acres**—pop pl VA-3
**Jessup Farms**—pop pl VA-3
Jessup Grove Ch—church (2) NC-3
Jessup Gulch—valley CA-9
Jessup Gulch—valley CO-8
Jessup HS—school PA-2
**Jessup Mill**—pop pl NC-3
Jessup Mill Pond—reservoir MT-8
Jessup Neck—cape NY-2
Jessup Overlook—locale PA-2
Jessup Park—park CA-9
Jessup-Peckville—unnic pl PA-2
Jessup River—stream NY-2
Jessup Sch—school TX-5
Jessups Gulch—valley CA-9
**Jessups (Jessup)**—pop pl IN-6
Jessup's Landing NY-2
Jessups Landing—locale NC-3
Jessup's Mill—hist pl NC-3
Jessups Mill—locale NJ-2
Jessups Pond—reservoir NC-3
Jessups Station IN-6
**Jessup (Township of)**—pop pl PA-2
Jess Valley—valley CA-9
Jess Well—locale NM-5
Jess Windmill—locale TX-5
Jess Yancey Lake Dam—dam MS-4
Jester—locale AL-4
Jester—locale OK-5
**Jester**—pop pl TX-5
Jester Branch—stream SC-3
Jester Cem—cemetery OK-5
Jester Creek KS-7
Jester Creek—stream GA-3
Jester Creek—stream KS-7
Jester Crossroads DE-2
**Jester Gardens**—pop pl VA-3
Jester Hill—summit OH-6
Jester Park—park IA-7
Jester Park—park TX-5
Jester Post Office (historical)—building TN-4
Jester Village Shop Ctr—locale TX-5
Jesterville DE-2
**Jesterville**—pop pl MD-2
Jestes Cem—cemetery NC-3
Jestice Creek—stream AR-4
Jest Island—island FL-3
Jestlamb Sch—school FL-3
Jesuit Bend—locale LA-4
Jesuit Cem—cemetery MI-6
Jesuit Church PA-2
Jesuit College PA-2
Jesuit Draw—valley TX-5
Jesuit Hill—summit AZ-5
Jesuit HS—school CA-9
Jesuit HS—school FL-3
Jesuit HS—school OR-9
Jesuit HS—school TX-5
Jesuit Retreat—church WI-6
Jesuit Seminary—school MN-6
JE Sulphur Spring—spring WY-8
**Jesup**—pop pl AR-4
**Jesup**—pop pl GA-3
**Jesup**—pop pl IA-7
Jesup, Lake—lake FL-3
Jesup (CCD)—cens area GA-3
Jesup (Township of)—fmr MCD AR-4
Jesus, Mount—summit KS-7
Jesus Canyon—valley (2) AZ-5
Jesus Canyon—valley (2) CA-9
Jesus Canyon—valley CO-8
Jesus Canyon—valley (2) NM-5
Jesus Canyon—valley (2) TX-5
Jesus Canyon Wash—stream AZ-5
Jesus Cem—cemetery GA-3
Jesus Ch—church (3) GA-3
Jesus Ch—church MS-4
Jesus Ch—church TN-4
Jesus Christ Ch—church (2) AL-4
Jesus Draw—valley TX-5
Jesus Goudy Ridge Trail Two hundred ninety eight—trail AZ-5
Jesus Grove OR-9
Jesusita Trail—trail CA-9
Jesus Maria—civil CA-9
Jesus Maria—locale CA-9
Jesus Maria Creek CA-9
Jesus Maria Creek—stream CA-9
Jesus Maria River CA-9
Jesus Maria Windmill—locale TX-5
Jesus Marie Convent—hist pl MA-1
Jesus Mesa—summit CO-8
Jesus Mesa—summit (2) NM-5
Jesus Name Apostolic Ch—church AL-4
Jesus Name Ch—church (2) AL-4
Jesus Name Ch—church (2) AR-4
Jesus Name Ch—church KY-4
Jesus Name Ch—church (2) LA-4
Jesus Name Ch—church MI-6
Jesus Name Ch—church (7) MS-4
Jesus Name Ch—church OK-5
Jesus Name Ch of Charity Chapel AL-4
Jesus Name Church, The—church AL-4
Jesus Name Tabernacle—church (2) MS-4
Jesus of Prague Ch—church MS-4
Jesus Only Holiness Ch—church AL-4
Jesus Saves Baptist Ch—church FL-3
Jesus Spring—spring AZ-5
Jesus Spring—spring CA-9
Jesus Tank—reservoir (3) AZ-5
Jesus Tank—reservoir NM-5
Jesus Water AZ-5
Jet—locale AL-4
Jet—locale CA-9
**Jet**—pop pl OK-5
Jet Basin—basin UT-8
Jet Branch—stream SC-3
Jet Brook—stream PA-2
Jet Creek—stream WA-9
Jeter, Gov. Thomas B., House—hist pl SC-3
Jeter Branch TN-4
Jeter Branch—stream AL-4
Jeter Branch—stream ID-8
Jeter Cem—cemetery MS-4
Jeter Cem—cemetery MO-7
Jeter Cem—cemetery SC-3
Jeter Ch—church SC-3
Jeter Chapel—church SC-3
Jeter Chapel—church VA-3
Jeter Creek—stream GA-3
Jeter Creek—stream TN-4
Jeter Hill—summit TN-4
Jeter Island PA-2
Jeter Landing—locale TN-4
**Jeter Mountain Terrace**—pop pl NC-3
Jeter Mtn—summit NC-3
J E Terry Elem Sch—school AL-4
Jeter Sch—school AL-4
Jeter Sch—school TN-4
Jeter Sch—school VA-3
Jeters Chapel—church VA-3
Jeters Lake—lake NM-5
**Jetersville**—pop pl VA-3
Jeter Towhead—island TN-4
Jeterville—locale GA-3
Jet Fox Rsvr—reservoir UT-8
Jethro OH-6
Jethro—locale AR-4
Jethro Ch—church AR-4
Jethroe Run—stream OH-6
**Jethro Park (subdivision)**—pop pl NC-3
Jet Lake—lake CO-8
Jet Mine—mine NV-8
**Jetmore**—pop pl KS-7
Jetmore East Oil Field—oilfield KS-7
Jetmore Elem Sch—school KS-7
Jetmore HS—school KS-7
Jetmore Municipal Airp—airport KS-7
Jetmore Oil Field—oilfield KS-7
Jeto Lake—reservoir IN-6
Jetport Municipal Golf Course—locale AL-4
Jet Propulsion Laboratory (NASA/Cal. Tech.)—building CA-9
Jet Run—stream IN-6
Jets Creek VA-3
Jets Hollow—valley WV-2
Jetson—locale KY-4
Jetson (CCD)—cens area KY-4
**Jetson (historical)**—pop pl OR-9
**Jetson (Whittinghill)**—pop pl KY-4
Jet Spring—spring NV-8
Jet Stadium—locale FL-3
Jetsville—locale WV-2
Jett—locale VA-3
**Jett**—pop pl KY-4
Jett Arch—arch AZ-5
Jett Bridge—bridge TN-4
Jett Canyon—valley NV-8
Jett Cem—cemetery IL-6
Jett Cem—cemetery TN-4
Jett Cem—cemetery TX-5
Jett Cem—cemetery VA-3
Jett Cem—cemetery WV-2
Jett Creek VA-3
Jett Creek—stream AK-9
Jett Creek—stream OR-9
Jett Drift Mine (underground)—mine AL-4
Jette, Mount—summit AK-9
Jetteau Point—cape ME-1
Jette Lake—lake MT-8
Jett Ford—locale VA-3
Jett Gap—gap VA-3
Jett (historical)—locale AL-4
**Jett (historical)**—pop pl OR-9
Jett Hollow—valley MO-7
Jetties Beach—beach MA-1
Jett Mine (underground)—mine AL-4
Jett Mtn—summit AL-4
Jetton Cem—cemetery AL-4
Jetton Cem—cemetery KY-4
Jetton JHS—school KY-4
Jetton Ranch—locale TX-5
Jetto-to Spring AZ-5
**Jett (Patterson)**—pop pl VA-3
**Jetts**—pop pl MS-4
Jett Sch—school MS-4
Jetts Creek—locale KY-4
Jetts Creek—stream KY-4
Jetts Creek—stream VA-3
Jett Sinkhole Cave—cave AL-4
Jett Spring—spring OR-9
Jetty Channel—channel TX-5
Jetty Creek—stream OR-9
Jetty Island—island WA-9
Jetty Lagoon—lake OR-9
Jetty Lake—lake AK-9
Jetty Park—park FL-3
Jetty Sands—bar OR-9
Jettyto Spring AZ-5
Jetzers Lake—lake WI-6
Jeudevine Mtn—summit VT-1
J E Upton Junior Catfish Pond Dam—dam MS-4
Jevnaker Cem—cemetery MN-6
Jevnaker Ch—church MN-6
**Jevne (Township of)**—pop pl MN-6
J E Walker Lake—reservoir TN-4
J E Walker Lake Dam—dam TN-4
Jew Branch—stream MS-4
Jew Creek—stream AR-4
Jew Creek—stream MT-8
Jewel TN-4
Jewel, Lake—lake (2) FL-3
Jewel Basin—basin MT-8
Jewel Box—other MO-7
Jewel Branch—stream TN-4
Jewel Brook—stream MA-1
Jewel Cave—cave SD-7
Jewel Cave—cave TN-4
Jewel Cave Natl Monmt—park SD-7
Jewel Cem—cemetery ME-1
Jewel Cem—cemetery TX-5
Jewel Ch—church MO-7
Jewel City—locale KY-4
Jewel Corners—locale PA-2
Jewel Creek TX-5
Jewel Creek—stream MI-6
Jewel Creek—stream OR-9
Jewel Draw—valley WY-8
Jewelers' Bldg—hist pl IL-6
Jewel Fire Tower—tower FL-3
Jewel Gap—gap TN-4
Jewel Gulch ID-8
Jewel Hill—summit KY-4
Jewel Hole—valley VA-3
Jewel Hollow—valley TN-4
Jewel Island NY-2
Jewell AL-4
Jewell—locale AR-4
Jewell—locale CA-9
Jewell—locale IA-7
Jewell—locale MD-2
Jewell—locale PA-2
Jewell—locale TX-5
Jewell—locale WV-2
**Jewell**—pop pl (2) GA-3
**Jewell**—pop pl IA-7
**Jewell**—pop pl KS-7
**Jewell**—pop pl NY-2
**Jewell**—pop pl OH-6
**Jewell**—pop pl OR-9
**Jewell**—pop pl TN-4
Jewell, Bradbury, House—hist pl NH-1
**Jewella (historical)**—pop pl LA-4
Jewel Lake—lake AK-9
Jewel Lake—lake (3) CA-9
Jewel Lake—lake (2) CO-8
Jewel Lake—lake FL-3
Jewel Lake—lake ID-8
Jewel Lake—lake MT-8
Jewel Lake—lake TX-5
Jewel Lake—lake UT-8
Jewel Lake—lake WA-9
Jewel Lake—reservoir CA-9
Jewel Lakes—lake WA-9
Jewel Lake Windmill—locale TX-5
Jewell Apartments—hist pl IA-7
Jewell Bldg—hist pl NE-7
Jewell Bluff—cliff TN-4
Jewell Branch—stream SC-3
Jewell Branch—stream VA-3
Jewell Brook—stream VT-1
Jewell Camp Chapel—church VA-3
Jewell Canyon—valley WY-8
Jewell (CCD)—cens area OR-9
Jewell Cem—cemetery KS-7
Jewell Cem—cemetery (2) KY-4
Jewell Cem—cemetery MO-7
Jewell Cem—cemetery NE-7
Jewell Cem—cemetery ND-7
Jewell Centre KS-7
Jewell Chapel—church VA-3
Jewell City KS-7
**Jewell City**—pop pl KY-4
Jewell Corner—locale NY-2
Jewell County—civil KS-7
Jewell County Dam—dam KS-7
Jewell County Lake—reservoir KS-7
Jewell County State Lake—reservoir KS-7
Jewell County State Lake Dam—dam KS-7
Jewell County State Park—park KS-7
Jewell Creek TX-5
Jewell Draw—valley WY-8
Jewell Elem Sch—school KS-7
Jewell Fulton Canal—canal TX-5
Jewell Gulch—valley CA-9
Jewell Gulch—valley ID-8
Jewell Hall—hist pl MO-7
Jewell Hill—summit AZ-5
Jewell Hill—summit ME-1
Jewell Hill—summit MA-1
Jewell Hill—summit (2) NH-1
Jewell Hill Brook—stream NH-1
Jewell Hist Dist—hist pl GA-3
**Jewell Hollow**—pop pl VA-3
Jewell Hollow—valley VA-3
Jewell Hollow Overlook—locale VA-3
Jewell HS—school KS-7
Jewell Island NY-2
Jewell Island—area AK-9
Jewell Island—island ME-1
Jewell Junction—locale OR-9
**Jewell Junction**—pop pl IA-7
Jewell Key—island FL-3
Jewell Lake—lake ME-1
Jewell Lake—lake MI-6
Jewell Lake—lake MN-6
Jewell Lake—lake MT-8
Jewell Mtn—summit GA-3
Jewell Park AZ-5
Jewell Park—park NE-7
Jewell Park—park WI-6
Jewell Point—cape NC-3
Jewell Post Office (historical)—building TN-4
Jewell Prospect—mine TN-4
Jewell Ridge—other KY-4
**Jewell Ridge**—pop pl VA-3
**Jewell Ridge (RR name Jewell)**—pop pl VA-3
**Jewell Road**—pop pl IL-6
Jewell (RR name for Jewell Ridge)—other VA-3
Jewell Rsvr—reservoir OR-9
Jewells CA-9
Jewell Sch—school NE-7
Jewell Sch—school WV-2
Jewells Corner—locale ME-1
**Jewells Hill (historical)**—pop pl MS-4
Jewells Pond—lake MA-1
Jewell Spring CA-9
Jewell Town District—hist pl NH-1
Jewell (Township of)—fmr MCD AR-4
Jewell Trail—trail NH-1
Jewell Valley—locale VA-3
Jewell Valley—valley CA-9
Jewell Valley Sch—school VA-3
**Jewell Village**—pop pl IN-6
Jewell Well—well AZ-5
**Jewell (West Vienna)**—pop pl NY-2
**Jewel Manor**—pop pl NY-2
Jewel Mine—mine AZ-5
Jewel Mine—mine CA-9
Jewel Mtn—summit AK-9
Jewel Post Office (historical)—building AL-4
Jewelry Lake—lake CA-9
Jewels Camp—locale TX-5
Jewel Spring—spring AZ-5
Jewel Spring—spring CA-9
Jewel Springs—spring WY-8
Jewel Valley CA-9
Jewelville—locale GA-3
Jewess Mine—mine CA-9
Jewett—locale MO-7
Jewett—locale TN-4
Jewett—locale WI-6
**Jewett**—pop pl CA-9
**Jewett**—pop pl IL-6
**Jewett**—pop pl ME-1
**Jewett**—pop pl NY-2
**Jewett**—pop pl OH-6
**Jewett**—pop pl TX-5
Jewett, Frank, House—hist pl OH-6
Jewett, Lake—lake MN-6
Jewett, Sarah Orne, House—hist pl ME-1
Jewett Allot Well—well WY-8
Jewett Ave Park—park OH-6
Jewett Branch—stream TN-4
Jewett Brook—stream ME-1
Jewett Brook—stream NH-1
Jewett Brook—stream (3) VT-1
Jewett Cave—cave TN-4
Jewett Cem—cemetery ME-1
Jewett Cem—cemetery MI-6
Jewett Cem—cemetery (2) MO-7
Jewett Cem—cemetery OH-6
Jewett Cem—cemetery TN-4
Jewett Cem—cemetery TX-5
Jewett Center—locale NY-2
Jewett Ch (historical)—church TN-4
**Jewett City**—pop pl CT-1
Jewett Cove—bay (2) ME-1
Jewett Creek KY-4
Jewett Creek TN-4
Jewett Creek—stream (3) CA-9
Jewett Creek—stream MI-6
Jewett Creek—stream MN-6
Jewett Creek—stream NE-7
Jewett Creek—stream NY-2
Jewett Creek—stream OR-9
Jewett Creek—stream SD-7
Jewett Creek—stream (2) WA-9
Jewett Dam SD-7
Jewett Drain—canal MI-6
Jewett-Eastman House—hist pl ME-1
Jewette Cem—cemetery TN-4
Jewette Creek NY-2
Jewett Gap Canyon—valley NM-5
Jewett Hill NH-1
Jewett Hill—summit ME-1
Jewett Hill—summit MA-1
Jewett Hill—summit NY-2
Jewett HS—school FL-3
Jewett Lake—lake (2) MI-6
Jewett Lake—lake OR-9
Jewett-Marquez (CCD)—cens area TX-5
Jewett Park—park IL-6
Jewett Point—cape ME-1
Jewett Pond—lake (2) ME-1
Jewett Pond—lake VT-1
Jewett Presbyterian Church TN-4
Jewett Red Flat Rsvr—reservoir WY-8
Jewett Ridge—ridge CA-9
Jewett Rock—pillar CA-9
Jewett Run OH-6
Jewett Sch—school CA-9
Jewett Sch—school FL-3
Jewett Sch—school KS-7
Jewett Sch—school (2) MI-6
Jewett Sch—school NH-1
Jewett Sch (historical)—school TN-4
Jewetts Hill MA-1
Jewetts Hill NH-1
Jewett Site—hist pl OK-5
Jewetts Landing AL-4
Jewett Stream—stream ME-1
Jewett Street Sch—school NH-1
Jewett-Thompson House—hist pl FL-3
**Jewett (Town of)**—pop pl NY-2
**Jewett Township**—pop pl SD-7
Jewett (Unorganized Territory of)—unorg MN-6
Jewett Valley—area NM-5
Jewett Valley—valley CA-9
Jewett Valley Cem—cemetery NM-5
Jewett Valley Ditch—canal NM-5
Jewett Valley Sch—school MN-6
Jewettville—locale NY-2
**Jewettville**—pop pl NY-2
Jewett Work Center—locale NM-5
Jewfish Basin—bay FL-3
Jewfish Bush Banks—bar FL-3
Jewfish Channel—channel FL-3
Jewfish Creek—gut (2) FL-3
Jewfish Hole—bay FL-3
Jewfish Key FL-3
Jewfish Key—island FL-3
Jewfish Point—cape CA-9
Jew Hill—summit PA-2
Jewish Cem—cemetery AL-4
Jewish Cem—cemetery MA-1
Jewish Cem—cemetery MN-6
Jewish Cem—cemetery (3) MS-4
Jewish Cem—cemetery (2) OH-6
Jewish Cemeteries—cemetery IL-6
Jewish Cemetery—hist pl MS-4
Jewish Community Center—building NV-8
Jewish Community Center—locale OH-6
Jewish Community Center—school DE-2
Jewish Community Center Preschool—school FL-3
Jewish Community Day Sch Palm Beach County—school FL-3
Jewish Consumptives Relief Sanatorium CO-8
Jewish Consuptives' Relief Society—hist pl CO-8
Jewish Hosp—hospital MO-7
Jewish Hosp—hospital NY-2
Jewish Hosp—hospital OH-6
Jewish Hosp for Chronic Diseases—hospital NY-2
Jewish HS of South Florida—school FL-3
Jewish Natl Home for Asthmatic Children—other CO-8
Jewish People's Institute—hist pl IL-6
Jewish Quarter Island NC-3
Jewish Rest Cem—cemetery AR-4
Jewish Sch—school IL-6
Jewish Shelter Home—hist pl OR-9
Jewish Young Men's and Women's Association—hist pl NY-2
Jewit Lake—lake OR-9
Jewitt Creek—stream MI-6
Jewitt Hill NY-2
Jewitt Lake—lake MN-6
Jewitt Pond—reservoir SD-7
Jewitts Creek MN-6
Jewkes Canyon—valley UT-8
Jewkes Hollow—valley UT-8
Jewkes Mine—mine UT-8
Jewkes Place—locale NM-5
Jew Lake—swamp IL-6
Jew Mtn—summit MT-8
Jewn River—stream AK-9
Jew Peak—summit MT-8
Jew Point—cape FL-3
Jew Pond—lake NH-1
Jews Creek—stream LA-4
Jews Creek—stream MS-4
Jewsharp Bend—bend KY-4
Jews-harp Lake—lake LA-4
Jews Hollow—valley PA-2
Jews Quarter Island NC-3
Jews Run—stream PA-2
Jews Run Jeep Trail—trail PA-2
**Jewtown**—pop pl GA-3
**Jewtown**—pop pl PA-2
Jezebel Lake—reservoir OR-9

Jim Thorpe Tomb—cemetery PA-2
Jimtown DE-2
Jimtown IN-6
Jimtown TN-4
Jimtown WV-2
Jimtown—locale DE-2
Jimtown—locale IL-6
Jimtown—locale KY-4
Jimtown—locale MD-2
Jimtown—locale MT-8
Jimtown—locale OH-6
Jimtown—locale OK-5
Jimtown—locale PA-2
Jimtown—locale WV-2
Jimtown—locale WI-6
**Jimtown**—pop pl CA-9
**Jimtown**—pop pl IL-6
**Jimtown**—pop pl (2) IN-6
**Jimtown**—pop pl (2) KY-4
**Jimtown**—pop pl OH-6
**Jimtown**—pop pl OR-9
**Jimtown**—pop pl PA-2
**Jimtown**—pop pl TN-4
**Jimtown**—pop pl (2) WV-2
Jimtown Branch—stream IL-6
Jimtown Branch—stream WI-6
Jimtown Cem—cemetery MO-7
Jimtown (historical)—locale KS-7
**Jimtown (historical)**—pop pl TN-4
Jimtown Hollow—valley OH-6
Jimtown Hollow—valley (2) TN-4
Jimtown Sch—school IL-6
Jimtown Sch (historical)—school MO-7
Jimtown Site (15OH19)—hist pl KY-4
Jim Trail—trail PA-2
Jim Turner Mine (underground)—mine AL-4
Jim Ute Branch—stream NC-3
Jim Ute Ridge—ridge NC-3
Jim Walker Cem—cemetery TN-4
Jim Warren Park—park TN-4
Jim Washum Spring—spring WY-8
Jim Watkins Windmill—locale CO-8
Jim Watson Creek—stream WA-9
Jim Wayne Canyon—valley WY-8
Jim Wayne Spring—spring WY-8
Jim Well—well NM-5
**Jim Wells (County)**—pop pl TX-5
Jim Wells Creek—stream MT-8
Jim White Hollow—valley TX-5
Jim White Hollow—valley WV-2
Jim White Ridge—ridge AR-4
Jim White Ridge—ridge OR-9
Jim Williams Canal—canal LA-4
Jim Wills Canyon—valley UT-8
Jim Wilson Canyon—valley SD-7
Jim Wilson Rsvr—reservoir UT-8
Jim Windmill—locale TX-5
*Jim Wolf Creek* MS-4
*Jim Wolfe Baptist Church* MS-4
Jim Wood Ridge—ridge ME-1
Jim Woodruff Dam—dam FL-3
Jim Woodruff Dam—dam GA-3
*Jim Woodruff Reservoir* FL-3
*Jim Woodruff Reservoir* GA-3
Jim Wright Branch—stream TN-4
Jim Wright Lake—lake TX-5
Jim Yarbro Slough—stream TN-4
Jimy Creek—stream AL-4
Jim York Pond Dam—dam MS-4
Jim Young Chute—stream IL-6
Jim Young Fork—stream WV-2
Jim Young Island—island IL-6
Jim Young Lake—swamp LA-4
Jim Youngs Landing (historical)—locale MS-4
*Jin* FM-9
Jinago—ridge GU-9
Jinago, Mount—summit GU-9
Jinapsan Beach—beach GU-9
Jinapsan Point—summit GU-9
Jinapsan Site—hist pl GU-9
Jinbol—island MP-9
Jinco Lake—reservoir GA-3
Jinedrol—island MP-9
*Jinero* MP-9
Jingeeruk Point—cape AK-9
Jingle Hole—cave TN-4
Jingle Lake—lake MI-6
Jingling Hole Knob—summit KY-4
Jingling Rocks—summit VA-3
Jingo—locale KY-4
Jingo—other TN-4
**Jingo**—pop pl KS-7
Jingo Cem—cemetery KS-7
Jingo Lake—lake MN-6
*Jingo Post Office* TN-4
Jingwak Lake—lake MI-6
Jingwak Lake—lake WI-6
Jinimi—island MP-9
Jinkerson Branch—stream VA-3
Jinkerson Cem—cemetery MO-7
*Jinkes Slough* FL-3
Jink (historical)—locale AL-4
*Jinkins Chapel* AL-4
Jinkins-Sheron Cem—cemetery TN-4
Jinks—locale GA-3
Jinks—locale KY-4
Jinks Branch—locale TX-5
Jinks Branch—stream TX-5
Jinks Creek—gut NC-3
Jinks Creek—stream CO-8
Jinks Creek—stream OR-9
Jinks Creek—stream WA-9
Jinks Gulch—valley ID-8
Jinks Hollow—valley IL-6
Jinks Hollow—valley MO-7
Jinks JHS—school FL-3
Jinks Lake—lake MN-6
Jinks Lodge—locale NC-3
Jinks Pond—lake TX-5
Jinks Well—well NM-5
*Jinme* MP-9
Jinnie Gap Run—stream PA-2
*Jinns Run* OH-6
Jinny Hill—summit CT-1
Jinnys Branch—locale NC-3
Jinnys Branch—stream NC-3
Jinnys Branch Ch—church NC-3
Jinwrights Gin (historical)—locale AL-4
Jinx Lake—lake MN-6
Jinx Lateral—canal ID-8
Jinx Well—well TX-5
Jipson Slough—gut MN-6
*Jiquibo* AZ-5
J I Ranch—locale AZ-5
J Ira Valley—valley CO-8
Jirdon Park—flat WY-8
Jireh Cem—cemetery WY-8
Jirka Sch—school IL-6
*Jiroi* MP-9
Jiron Canyon—valley NM-5
*Jirongkan Island* MP-9
Jirup Island—island FM-9
Jischke's Meat Market—hist pl WI-6
Jisco Lake—reservoir OH-6
*Jisini Lake* MN-6
Jiskooksnuk Hill—summit AK-9
J Issacs Dam—dam SD-7
*Jitokeon* MP-9
Jitney Gulch—valley ID-8
*Jitney Mary Creek* OR-9
Jitni—island MP-9
*Jitoeon* MP-9
Jitroken (not verified)—locale MP-9
Jitterbug Lake—lake MN-6
Jittoen—CDP MP-9
Jivaro, Lake—reservoir KS-7
*Jivers Creek* NE-7
Jividen Ranch—locale NE-7
*Jiyabo* MP-9
Jiyabo—island MP-9
*Jiyabo-To* MP-9
J J Draw—valley WY-8
J. J. H. Heliport—airport WA-9
J J J Ranch—locale ND-7
J J Kelly Sch—school VA-3
J J Madison Dam—dam TN-4
J J Madison Lake—reservoir TN-4
*J J McClain High School* MS-4
JJ Mowels—locale TX-5
J Joe Curve—locale CA-9
J Jones—locale TX-5
J Jones Grant—civil FL-3
JJ & PK Airp—airport PA-2
**J J R Spur**—pop pl AR-4
J J Rsvr—reservoir UT-8
J.J. Tank—reservoir AZ-5
J J Waterhouse Claim—civil MS-4
J J Water Spring—spring CO-8
J J Windmill—locale CO-8
J K Butte—summit SD-7
J K Creek—stream WY-8
J K D Farms Airp—airport WA-9
J Kern Ditch—canal MT-8
J K Gulch—valley SD-7
J K Hurdle Lake Dam—dam MS-4
J K Mtn—summit AZ-5
J K Ridge—ridge CO-8
J K Simpson Lake—dam MS-4
JK Tank—reservoir AZ-5
J K Well—well AZ-5
J Kykendall Ranch—locale ND-7
J Lake—lake MT-8
J Lake—reservoir IN-6
J Lateral—canal CA-9
J Lazy H Mesa—bench NM-5
J Lazy H Tank—reservoir NM-5
J L Bar Spring—spring AZ-5
J L Crenshaw Lake Number One—reservoir AL-4
J L Crenshaw Number 1 Dam—dam AL-4
J L Crenshaw Number 2 Dam—dam AL-4
**J L Durgins Subdivision**—pop pl UT-8
J L Eason Junior Pond Dam—dam MS-4
J L Eddy—rapids UT-8
J Lee Ranch—locale NE-7
J Line Pond—lake WA-9
J L Morrison Dam Number 1—dam AL-4
J L Morrison Dam Number 2—dam AL-4
J L Morrison Lake Number One—reservoir AL-4
J L Morrison Lake Number Two—reservoir AL-4
J L Ranch—locale CO-8
J L Sanchez and Others Grant—civil FL-3
J L Spring—spring OR-9
J L Sullivan Playground—locale MA-1
J Lutz—airport NJ-2
*J Madlen Ditch* IN-6
J Main Drain—canal ID-8
J Mangin Dam—dam SD-7
J M A Ranch—locale TX-5
J Martin Landing (historical)—locale AL-4
J Maxwell Pond—reservoir IN-6
J Maxwell Pond Dam—dam IN-6
J M Canyon—valley TX-5
JM Cathings—locale TX-5
J McCormick Ranch—locale MT-8
J McDougal Ranch—locale CA-9
J McGowan—locale TX-5
J M Creek—stream WY-8
J M Dean Pond—dam MS-4
J M Elliott Junior Sch—school AL-4
J M Fourmile Well—well NM-5
*J M Frost Lake* TX-5
J M Gaston Number One Lake—reservoir AL-4
J M Gaston Number Two Lake—reservoir AL-4
J M Gaston Number 1 Dam—dam AL-4
J M Gaston Number 2 Dam—dam AL-4
J M Gentry Dam—dam AL-4
J M Granger Dam—dam AL-4
J M Hanson Grant—civil FL-3
J M Hill Elem Sch—school PA-2
J Miller Ranch—locale NE-7
J M Johnson Pond Dam—dam MS-4
J M Junction—locale PA-2
J. M. Junction—other PA-2
J M Lewis Ranch—locale NM-5
J M McKnight Ranch—locale NM-5
J Moeller Dam—dam SD-7
J M Prunty Ranch—locale NV-8
*J M Quarles Elementary School* MS-4
J M Rault Lake Dam—dam MS-4
J M Robbins Ditch—canal IN-6
J M Roberts Pond—reservoir AL-4
J M Roberts Pond Dam—dam AL-4
J M Rsvr—reservoir CO-8
J M Sanchez Grant—civil FL-3
J M Savory Lake Dam—dam MS-4
J. M. S. Bldg—hist pl IN-6
J M Sessions Lake Dam—dam MS-4
J M Spring—spring AZ-5
J M Sykes Landing—locale NC-3
J M Tank—reservoir NM-5
J & M Trading Post—hist pl OH-6
J & M Trading Post - Annex—hist pl OH-6
J M Williams Pond Dam—dam MS-4
J M Wise Pond—lake FL-3
J Myer—locale TX-5
J N Bishop Spring—spring OR-9
J N Brown Lake Dam—dam MS-4
J N Camp—locale TX-5
J-N Creek—stream OK-5
J N (Ding) Darling Natl Wildlife Ref—park FL-3
J N Siding—locale TX-5
Jo, Lake—reservoir NC-3
Jo, Mount—summit NY-2
Joa—other GU-9
Jo Ab Branch—stream NC-3
Joachim Bridge—bridge NY-2
Joachim Cem—cemetery MO-7
Joachim Cem—cemetery SD-7
Joachim Creek—stream MO-7
Joachim Park—park MO-7
Joachim Township—civil MO-7
Joads Spring—spring UT-8
**Joan**—pop pl AR-4
**Joan**—pop pl KY-4
Joan, Lake—reservoir AL-4
Joan Branch—stream GA-3
Joan Creek—stream ID-8
Joan Creek—stream MT-8
Joan Creek Pass—gap MT-8
*Joanesburg* WI-6
Joanette Tank—reservoir AZ-5
Joan Gulch—valley ID-8
Joan Lake—lake AK-9
Joan Lake—lake UT-8
Joan Lake—lake WA-9
Joan Lake—reservoir MO-7
Joan Lake Airp—airport MO-7
Joan Mine—mine MN-6
Jo Ann, Lake—lake FL-3
Jo-ann, Lake—reservoir PA-2
Joanna—locale MO-7
**Joanna**—pop pl PA-2
**Joanna**—pop pl SC-3
Joanna, Lake—lake FL-3
*Joanna Bald* NC-3
Joanna (CCD)—cens area SC-3
Jo Anna Cem—cemetery AL-4
Jo Anna Ch—church AL-4
Joanna Creek—stream AK-9
Joanna Furnace—locale PA-2
Joanna Furnace Complex—hist pl PA-2
**Joanna Heights**—pop pl PA-2
Joanna Mine—mine NV-8
Joanna Mtn—summit NC-3
*Jo Ann Creek* OR-9
JoAnn Creek—stream OR-9
Joanne, Lake—lake FL-3
Joanne Creek—stream WY-8
Joannes Park—park WI-6
Joanne Tank—reservoir AZ-5
Joann Lake—lake MI-6
Jo Ann Lake—lake WI-6
Jo-Anns Lakes—lake GA-3
Joann Spring—spring UT-8
Joan of Arc Sch—school MA-1
Joan of Arc Sch—school SD-7
Joan Park—park OH-6
Joan Society Cem—cemetery GA-3
Joan Society Hall—building GA-3
*Joans River* NC-3
Joans Windmill—locale TX-5
**Joaquin**—pop pl TX-5
Joaquin, Mount—summit AK-9
Joaquin Barella Grant—civil FL-3
Joaquin Brook—stream ME-1
Joaquin Canyon—valley AZ-5
Joaquin Canyon—valley (2) CA-9
Joaquin Canyon—valley (2) NM-5
Joaquin Creek—stream AZ-5
Joaquin Creek—stream GA-3
Joaquin Flat—flat (2) CA-9
Joaquin Gulch—valley CA-9
Joaquin Mesa—summit NM-5
Joaquin Miller Campground—park OR-9
Joaquin Miller JHS—school (2) CA-9
Joaquin Miller Park—park CA-9
Joaquin Miller Trail (pack)—trail OR-9
Joaquin Miller Wayside—locale OR-9
Joaquin Mill (Site)—locale CA-9
Joaquin Peak—summit CA-9
Joaquin Ridge—ridge CA-9
Joaquin Rocks—pillar CA-9
Joaquin Rsvr—reservoir OR-9
Joaquin Sch—school UT-8
Joaquin Spring—spring CA-9
Joaquin Springs—spring TX-5
Joash (historical)—locale KS-7
Job—locale KY-4
**Job**—pop pl WV-2
Jo Bar Ranch—locale NM-5
Jobbers Brook—stream NH-1
Jobbers' Canyon Hist Dist—hist pl NE-7
Jobbers Mtn—summit VA-3
Jobbers Park—park IL-6
Jobbes Fork—stream KY-4
*Job Canyon* NV-8
Job Cem—cemetery NV-8
*Job Cemetery* AL-4
Job Chapel—church NC-3
Job Corps Conservation Center—locale MO-7
Job Corps Pond—reservoir UT-8
Job Creek—stream ID-8
Job Creek—stream NJ-2
Job Creek—stream OR-9
Job Creek—stream PA-2
Job Creek—stream SC-3
Jobe—locale MO-7
Jobe, Phillip W., House—hist pl TX-5
Jobe Branch—stream (2) KY-4
Jobe Canyon—valley OR-9
Jobe Cem—cemetery AL-4
Jobe Cem—cemetery MO-7
Jobe Cem—cemetery TN-4
Jobe Chapel—church GA-3
Jobe Creek—stream ID-8
Jobe Creek—stream MT-8
**Jobee Acres (subdivision)**—pop pl SD-7
**Jobe (historical)**—pop pl TN-4
Jobe Hollow—valley MS-4
Jobeik—island MP-9
Jobenor—island MP-9
*Jobenor Channel Reiher Durchfahrt* MP-9
Jobenor Island—island MP-9
Jobes—locale MS-4
Jobes—locale OK-5
Jobes Branch—stream VA-3
Jobes Chapel—church GA-3
Jobes Creek—stream MS-4
Jobes Dam—dam WI-6
Jobes Ditch—stream MD-2
Jobes Hill—summit GA-3
Jobes Hollow—valley WV-2
Jobes Island—island VA-3
Jobe Skis Mont 1 Heliport—airport WA-9
Jobes Lake—lake MS-4
Jobes Run—stream PA-2
*Jobes Station* MS-4
Jobe Township—civil MO-7
Jobe Windmill—locale TX-5
Jobgen Sch—school SD-7
*Job Hill* MA-1
Job Hill—summit MA-1
Job Hollow—valley (2) MO-7
Jobildunk Ravine—basin NH-1
Job Island—island ME-1
Job Island—island MA-1
Job Knob—summit (2) WV-2
Job Knob Branch—stream WV-2
*Jobler Creek* GA-3
*Jobley Creek* GA-3
Job Mtn—summit VT-1
*Jobna* MP-9
*Job Neck* MA-1
*Jobancillos Creek* TX-5
**Jobos**—pop pl (2) PR-3
Jobos, Bahia de—bay PR-3
Jobos (Barrio)—fmr MCD (2) PR-3
Jobos Saltillo—falls PR-3
Job Peak—summit NV-8
Job Place Sch—school WI-6
Job Point—cape NJ-2
*Job Pond* MA-1
J O Brady Lake Dam—dam MS-4
Job Run—stream OH-6
Job Run—stream (2) WV-2
Jobs—locale OH-6
Jobs Branch—stream GA-3
Jobs Cabin (Township of)—fmr MCD NC-3
Jobs Canyon—valley CA-9
Jobs Canyon—valley NV-8
Jobs Cem—cemetery OH-6
Jobs Cem—cemetery TN-4
Jobs Chapel—church NC-3
Jobs Corner—locale NY-2
**Jobs Corners**—pop pl PA-2
Jobs Creek—bay NH-1
Jobs Creek—stream GA-3
Jobs Creek—stream IL-6
Jobs Creek—stream MO-7
Jobs Creek—stream NJ-2
Jobs Creek—stream NC-3
Jobs Ditch—canal MD-2
Jobs Ditch—stream DE-2
Jobs Garden—locale OR-9
Jobs Head—summit UT-8
Jobs Hill—summit MA-1
Jobs Hill—summit RI-1
Jobs Hollow—valley OH-6
*Jobs Island* TN-4
*Jobs Island* VA-3
Jobs Knob—summit OH-6
Jobs Mtn—summit ME-1
Jobs Neck—cape MA-1
Jobs Neck—isthmus MA-1
Jobs Neck Cove—bay MA-1
Jobs Neck Pond—lake MA-1
Jobson Hollow Cove—bay MO-7
Jobs Peak—summit (2) CA-9
Jobs Peak—summit NC-3
*Jobs Pond* MA-1
Jobs Pond—lake CT-1
Jobs Pond—lake VT-1
Jobs Run—stream WV-2
Jobs Sister—summit CA-9
Jobs Spring Ch—church GA-3
Jobs Temple—church WV-2
Job's Temple—hist pl WV-2
**Jobstown**—pop pl NJ-2
Job Swale Creek—stream OR-9
*Jobtan* MP-9
**Joburn**—pop pl OK-5
Job Wiggins Grant—civil FL-3
Jobwno—island MP-9
*Jobwro* MP-9
Joby Creek—stream NY-2
Joby Hollow—valley TN-4
Jo-Byrns HS—school TN-4
*Jo Byrns Sch* TN-4
*Jocasse* SC-3
Jocassee—locale SC-3
Jocelyn Creek—stream KS-7
Jocelyn Hill—summit MA-1
Jocelyn Hollow Branch—stream TN-4
Jocelyn Mine (historical)—mine PA-2
Jocelyn Ridge—ridge OK-5
*Jocinah Creek* IN-6
Jocinah Creek—stream IN-6
**Jock**—pop pl KY-4
Jock Ch—church KY-4
Jock Coulee—valley MT-8
Jock Creek—stream AL-4
Jock Draw—valley WY-8
Jocker Point—cape MI-6
Jockey—locale TN-4
**Jockey**—pop pl IN-6
Jockey Branch—stream NC-3
Jockeybush Lake—lake NY-2
Jockeybush Outlet—stream NY-2
**Jockeycamp Run**—pop pl WV-2
Jockeycamp Run—stream WV-2
Jockey Cap—island OR-9
Jockey Cap—summit ME-1
Jockey Cap Island—island NH-1
Jockey City Corners—locale MO-7
Jockey Creek—stream NY-2
Jockey Creek—stream TN-4
Jockey Hill—locale NH-1
Jockey Hill—locale NY-2
Jockey Hill—summit NY-2
Jockey Hill—summit VT-1
Jockey Hollow—valley KY-4
Jockey Hollow—valley WI-6
Jockey Hollow Run—stream OH-6
Jockey Knob—summit PA-2
Jockey Post Office (historical)—building TN-4
Jockey Ridge—ridge NC-3
Jockeys Canyon—valley UT-8
Jockey Spring—spring UT-8
Jock Falls—falls KY-4
*Jock Minivah* ME-1
Jock Mock Bay—bay MN-6
Jock Mock Lake—lake MN-6
Jock Mock Point—cape MN-6
Jocko Creek—stream GA-3
Jocko Creek—stream MI-6
Jocko Creek—stream MT-8
Jocko Lake—lake WI-6
Jocko Lookout—locale MT-8
*Jocko Peak* MT-8
Jocko Pond—lake MI-6
*Jocko Rapids* UT-8
Jocko River—stream MT-8
Jock Page Hill—summit NH-1
Jock Pond—lake FL-3
Jock Pond—lake NY-2
Jocks Brook—stream NY-2
Jocks Canyon—valley UT-8
Jocks Creek—stream TX-5
Jocks Lake Dam—dam MS-4
Jocks Narrows—gut MN-6
Jocks Pond—lake NY-2
Jocks Pond Outlet—stream NY-2
Jock Stream—stream ME-1
Jockys Branch—stream KY-4
Jocobs Cem—cemetery TN-4
Jo Co Creek—gut NY-2
Jo Co Marsh—swamp NY-2
J O Connell Ranch—locale ND-7
Jocqueway Creek—stream OH-6
J O Creek—stream MT-8
*Jo Dandy Mine* MT-8
J O Dandy Mine—mine AZ-5
**Jo Daviess (County)**—pop pl IL-6
**Jo Daviess (Township of)**—pop pl MN-6
*Jod Creek* WA-9
Jodeco, Lake—reservoir GA-3
Jode Hollow—valley KY-4
**Jo Dell (subdivision)**—pop pl AL-4
Joder—locale NE-7
Jodes Flat—flat UT-8
Jodes Hollow—valley UT-8
Jo-Dey Estate—locale MI-6
Jodey Point—cape UT-8
**Jodie**—pop pl WV-2
Jodie B Cove—valley NC-3
Jodie Lake—lake UT-8
**Jodie (RR name Bryce)**—pop pl WV-2
Jo Drain—stream MI-6
J O D Ranch—locale CO-8
Jodrie Brook—stream NH-1
Jodrie Hill—summit NH-1
Jody Branch—stream KY-4
Jody Creek—stream (3) OR-9
Jody Hollow—valley AR-4
Jodys Knoll—summit UT-8
Jodys Lake—lake AZ-5
Joe—locale TX-5
**Joe**—pop pl OK-5
Joe, Lake—lake FL-3
Joe Allen Lake Dam—dam MS-4
Joe and Ben Creek—gut SC-3
Joe and Dans Pit—cave AL-4
Joe and His Dog—summit UT-8
Joe Aucoin Bayou—gut LA-4
Joe Baca Draw—valley AZ-5
Joe Baden Cem—cemetery MS-4
Joe Bailey Windmill—locale TX-5
Joe Baker Canyon—valley CO-8
Joe Baker Canyon—valley NM-5
Joe Baker Sag—summit NY-2
*Joe Bakers Shoal* NJ-2
Joe Bald Park—park MO-7
Joe Bar—locale CA-9
Joe Barber Hollow—valley TN-4
Joe Barnes Vocational Technical Center—school MS-4
Joe Basin—basin CA-9
Joe Basin—bay TN-4
Joe Bay—bay (2) FL-3
Joe Bay—swamp SC-3
Joe Bayou—gut AL-4
Joe Bayou—stream MS-4
Joe Bayou Boeuf River—gut LA-4
Joe Beach Ledge—rock MA-1
Joe Becker Memorial Stadium—other MO-7
Joe Beck Plantation—locale AR-4
Joe Beck Spring—spring MO-7
Joe Begant Draw—valley WY-8
Joe Bell Coulee—valley MT-8
Joe Bell Mtn—summit TX-5
Joe Berta Bullock Sch—school FL-3
Joe Best Spring—spring AZ-5
*Joe B. Hogsett Reservoir* TX-5
Joe Billy Basin—basin NV-8
Joe B Johnson Dam—dam AL-4
Joe Black Coulee—valley MT-8
Joe Blackmon Pond Dam—dam MS-4
Joe Black Spring—spring TX-5
Joe Blake Hill—summit AZ-5
Joe Boggio Ranch—locale MT-8
Joe Bowen Canyon—valley CA-9
Joe Bowers—mine UT-8
Joe Bowers Creek—stream MT-8
*Joe Boyle Brook* NH-1
*Joe Branch* WV-2
Joe Branch—locale WV-2
Joe Branch—stream AL-4
Joe Branch—stream AR-4
Joe Branch—stream IL-6
Joe Branch—stream (5) KY-4
Joe Branch—stream LA-4
Joe Branch—stream MD-2
Joe Branch—stream MS-4
Joe Branch—stream MO-7
Joe Branch—stream (3) NC-3
Joe Branch—stream OK-5
Joe Branch—stream SC-3
Joe Branch—stream (6) TN-4
Joe Branch—stream TX-5
Joe Branch—stream VA-3
Joe Branch—stream (2) WV-2
Joe Brigance Memorial Park—park MS-4
*Joe Brights Lighthouse Camp* AL-4
Joe Brook—stream ME-1
Joe Brook—stream NY-2
Joe Brook—stream VT-1
Joe Brown Canal—canal LA-4
Joe Brown Creek—stream MT-8
Joe Brown Fork—stream KY-4
Joe Brown Lake—lake TX-5
Joe Brown Pond—bay LA-4
*Joe Brown Spit* WA-9
*Joe Browns Pond* LA-4
Joe B Shirley Lookout Tower—tower AL-4
Joe Budd Supply Ditch—canal WY-8
Joe Budd Wildlife Mngmt Area—park FL-3
Joe Burleson (Township of)—fmr MCD AR-4
Joe Burris Ledge—rock MA-1
Joe Bush Creek—stream AK-9
Joe Bush Creek—stream ND-7
Joe Bush Creek—stream SD-7
Joe Bush Fisherman Parking—locale UT-8
Joe Bush Gulch—valley CO-8
Joe Bush Mtn—summit CO-8
Joe Cabin Arroyo—stream NM-5
Joe Cards Airpark—airport OR-9
Joe Carillo Canyon—valley NM-5
Joe Carlson Sch—school AZ-5
Joe Carrol Cabin—locale AK-9
*Joe Carrollo Canyon* NM-5
Joe Cauthen Lake Dam—dam (2) MS-4
Joe Clark Brook—stream CT-1
Joe Cone Landing—locale GA-3
*Joe Cook School* MS-4
Joe Cooley Bay—bay LA-4
Joe Coro Brook—stream ME-1
Joe Cottons Lake—reservoir TN-4
Joe Cottons Lake Dam—dam TN-4
Joe Coulee Creek—stream WI-6
Joe Cove—basin GA-3
Joe Cove—valley (2) NC-3
Joe Covington Pond Dam—dam MS-4
Joe Cox Creek—stream OR-9
Joe Crane Lake—lake CA-9
*Joe Creek* TN-4
*Joe Creek* WA-9
Joe Creek—stream (4) AK-9
Joe Creek—stream AR-4
Joe Creek—stream CA-9
Joe Creek—stream CO-8
Joe Creek—stream (2) GA-3
Joe Creek—stream (2) ID-8
Joe Creek—stream KS-7
Joe Creek—stream MI-6
Joe Creek—stream MT-8
Joe Creek—stream NY-2
Joe Creek—stream (2) NC-3
Joe Creek—stream OK-5
Joe Creek—stream (4) OR-9
Joe Creek—stream SD-7
Joe Creek—stream TN-4
Joe Creek—stream TX-5
Joe Creek—stream (2) VA-3
Joe Creek—stream (8) WA-9
Joe Creek—stream WI-6
Joe Creek—stream (3) WY-8
Joe Creek Rec Area—park SD-7
Joe Creek (RR name for Comfort)—other WV-2
Joe C Reese Lake Dam—dam MS-4
Joe Crow Dam—dam OR-9
Joe Crow Rsvr—reservoir OR-9
Joe Curtis Point—cape TN-4
Joe Dahar Creek—stream UT-8
Joe D Airp—airport PA-2
Joe Daley Creek—stream ID-8
Joe Daly—mine UT-8
Joe Dandy Mine—mine (2) CO-8
Joe Dave Branch—stream NC-3
Joe David Landing—locale LA-4
Joe Davis Canyon—valley CO-8
Joe Davis Hill—summit CO-8
Joe Davis Stadium—park AL-4
Joe Day Branch—stream KY-4
Joe Day Creek—stream OR-9
Joe Day Lake—lake IA-7
Joe Days Bay—bay SD-7
Joe Days Creek—stream SD-7
Joe Day Tank—reservoir (2) NM-5
Joe Dennis Pond—bay LA-4
Joe Devel Peak—summit CA-9
Joe Devlin Island—island AK-9
Joe Ditch—canal WY-8
Joe Ditch—stream GA-3
Joe D Lewis Airp—airport MO-7
Joe Dollar Gulch—valley SD-7
*Joe Dollar Mine* SD-7
Joe Dollar Mine—mine SD-7
*Joe Dorr Creek* UT-8
Joe Doss Hollow—valley VA-3
Joe Dozier Dam—dam AL-4
Joe Dozier Lake—reservoir AL-4
Joe Drain—stream MI-6
Joe Draw—valley (2) WY-8
Joe Dubay Brook—stream ME-1
Joe Durrant Hollow—valley UT-8
Joe Dyer Butte—summit OR-9
*Joe Dyer Point* ME-1
*Joe Dyers Point* ME-1
Joe Eason Mtn—summit NV-8
Joe E Brown Park—park OH-6
Joe Eckles Towhead—flat TN-4
Joe Ed Creek—stream LA-4
Joe Edwards Creek—stream LA-4
Joe Elliot Tree Memorial—other CA-9
Joe Ellis Island (historical)—island SD-7
Joe Ellis Park—flat CO-8
Joe Emge Creek—stream WY-8
Joe English Brook—stream NH-1
Joe English Hill—summit NH-1
Joe English Pond—lake NH-1
Joe Entz Tank—reservoir AZ-5
Joe Fell Lake—lake MN-6
Joe Fisher Rsvr—reservoir OR-9
Joe Flogger Shoal—bar DE-2
Joe Fork—stream KY-4
Joe Fork—stream WV-2

John West Vly—lake NY-2
John W Fisher Bridge—bridge TN-4
John W Flannagan Rsvr—reservoir VA-3
John W Gattman Park—park AL-4
John W Haraton Regional Med Ctr TN-4
John W Harton Memorial Hosp—hospital TN-4
John W Harton Regional Med Ctr TN-4
John White Enlargement Ditch—canal WY-8
John White Gap—gap AR-4
John White Island—island ME-1
John White Ranch—locale NM-5
JOHN W. HUBBARD (sternwheeler)—hist pl KY-4
John Wiggins Bayou—gut TX-5
John Will Hollow—valley KY-4
John Williams Canyon—valley UT-8
John Williams Cave—cave TN-4
John Williams Ranch—locale NM-5
John Willis Chapel—church MS-4
John Wills Bench—bench UT-8
John Wilson Sch—school KY-4
John Windmill—locale NM-5
John Winthrop Sch—school CT-1
John W Kendall Elem Sch—school IN-6
John W Kyle State Park—park MS-4
John W. McCormack—post sta MA-1
John Wood Elem Sch—school IN-6
John Woodnam Higgins Armory—building MA-1
John Woosley Creek—stream KY-4
John W Overton Bridge AL-4
John Wright Rsvr—reservoir NV-8
John W Starr Memorial Forest MS-4
John W Tank—reservoir TX-5
John Wyleys Landing (historical)—locale TN-4
John Yarbro Branch—stream TN-4
Johny Branch—stream VA-3
Johny Creek—stream (2) MT-8
Johny Creek—stream ND-7
John Yeates HS—school VA-3
Johny Gulch—valley MT-8
John Young Branch—stream KY-4
John Young Gully—valley TX-5
John Young Lake Dam—dam MS-4
John Young Meadows—flat OR-9
Johny Slough—gut AK-9
Johnywady Creek—stream AL-4
John Z Canyon—valley OR-9
Joho Canyon—valley TX-5
Johonnett Brook—stream ME-1
Joho Spring—spring TX-5
Joho Tank—reservoir TX-5
Johua Hall Grain Mill—building TX-5
Johua Hall Sawmill—building TX-5
Joice—pop pl IA-7
Joice Creek MA-1
Joice Creek—stream MT-8
Joice Island—island CA-9
Joice Island Club—other CA-9
Joices Island CA-9
Joice Spring—spring OR-9
Joiner—locale TX-5
Joiner—pop pl AR-4
Joiner Bank—bar SC-3
Joiner Bay—swamp SC-3
Joiner Branch—stream (2) AL-4
Joiner Branch—stream KY-4
Joiner Branch—stream TX-5
Joiner Brook—stream VT-1
Joiner Camp—locale AZ-5
Joiner Cem—cemetery AL-4
Joiner Cem—cemetery GA-3
Joiner Cem—cemetery IL-6
Joiner Cem—cemetery LA-4
Joiner Cem—cemetery MO-7
Joiner Cem—cemetery SC-3
Joiner Cem—cemetery TN-4
Joiner Creek—stream GA-3
Joiner Creek—stream LA-4
Joiner Dam—dam AL-4
Joiner Elementary School MS-4
Joiner Hollow—valley (2) TN-4
Joiner Hollow Church TN-4
Joiner Lake—lake FL-3
Joiner Lake—reservoir AL-4
Joiner Lake Dam—dam MS-4
Joiner Pond—lake GA-3
Joiner Post Office (historical)—building MS-4
Joiner Rsvr—reservoir CA-9
Joiners Branch TN-4
Joiners Branch—stream GA-3
Joiners Bridge—bridge AL-4
Joiners Campground TN-4
Joiner Sch—school IL-6
Joiners Cove—bay MD-2
Joiners Store (historical)—locale AL-4
Joiner Swamp—swamp SC-3
Joiner Swamp Sch—school SC-3
Joinertown—pop pl AL-4
Joinerville—locale TX-5
Joines Cem—cemetery TN-4
Joines Ch—church KY-4
Joines-Shrader Cem TN-4
Joint Cave—cave AL-4
Joint Crack Creek—stream VA-3
Joint Creek OR-9
Joint Drainage Ditch 16—canal IA-7
Joint Drainage Ditch 9-13—canal IA-7
Jointer Creek—channel GA-3
Jointer Creek—stream OK-5
Jointer Island—island GA-3
Jointers Island GA-3
Jointer Windmill—locale NM-5
Jointgrass Brook MA-1
Joint Grass Brook—stream MA-1
Joint HS—school PA-2
Joint Knob—summit KY-4
Joint Lake—lake AK-9
Joint Ridge—ridge TN-4
Joint Sch—school NE-7
Joint Sch—school ND-7
Joint Sch (historical)—school PA-2
Joint Trail—trail UT-8
Joint Union HS—school (3) CA-9
Joint Union Sch—school CA-9
Joint Well—well (2) TX-5
Jo Island ME-1
Jo Jan Van Camp—locale TX-5
Jo Jo—pop pl PA-2
Jojoba Wash—stream CA-9
Jojo Creek—stream WY-8
Jojo Draw—valley MT-8
Jo Jo Junction—pop pl PA-2
Jo Jo Lake—lake OR-9
Jojo Lake—lake WY-8
Jojo Mtn—summit WY-8
Jojo To MP-9
J O Junction—locale WY-8
Jokaj FM-9
Jokaj Harbor FM-9
Jokaji FM-9
Jokaji Ko FM-9
Jokaj Island FM-9
Jokaji to FM-9
Jokaj Passage FM-9
Jokake AZ-5
Jokaki—locale AZ-5
Jokelu Lake—lake MN-6
Joker TX-5
Joker—locale WV-2
Joker Marchant Stadium—locale FL-3
Joker Mine—mine AZ-5
Joker Mine—mine NV-8
Joker Mtn—summit WA-9
Joker Peak—summit ID-8
Jokes Gulch ID-8
Joki Creek—stream MN-6
Jokinaugh Island—island AK-9
Jokodowski Creek—stream CO-8
Jokoei Lake—lake AK-9
JOK Rsvr No 1—reservoir CO-8
Jokse Cem—cemetery TX-5
Jolanda, Lake—reservoir WA-9
Joleena Farm—locale AZ-5
Jo Leighton Ground—bar ME-1
Jolen—island MP-9
Jolene Mine—mine AZ-5
Joleo Mine—mine AZ-5
Joler—pop pl OR-9
Jolertown Ridge—ridge KY-4
Jolesch House—hist pl TX-5
Joles Creek—stream IA-7
Joley Cem—cemetery AL-4
Jolie Hollow—valley UT-8
Joliet—pop pl IL-6
Joliet—pop pl MT-8
Joliet—pop pl TX-5
Joliet Army Ammun Plant—military IL-6
Joliet Bridge—hist pl MT-8
Joliet Cem—cemetery MT-8
Joliet Country Club—other IL-6
Joliet Ditch—canal MT-8
Joliet East Side Hist Dist—hist pl IL-6
Joliet Hollow—valley IL-6
Joliet HS—hist pl MT-8
Joliet Junior Coll—school IL-6
Joliet Municipal Airport—hist pl IL-6
Joliet Municipal Stadium—other IL-6
Joliet Residential Hist Dist—hist pl MT-8
Joliett—pop pl PA-2
Joliett Ch—church PA-2
Joliette—pop pl ND-7
Joliette (historical)—locale ND-7
Joliette Interchange—crossing ND-7
Joliette Township—pop pl ND-7
Joliet Township—pop pl NE-7
Joliet Township HS—hist pl IL-6
Joliet (Township of)—pop pl IL-6
Jolietville—pop pl IN-6
Joliff—uninc pl VA-3
Joliff Inlet Public Use Area—park OK-5
Jolin Dam—dam ND-7
Jolivue—pop pl VA-3
Jolla Canyon, La—valley AZ-5
Jolla Peak, La—summit AZ-5
Jolla Tank—reservoir NM-5
Jolla Tank, La—reservoir AZ-5
Jolla Vieja Canyon—valley CA-9
Joller—pop pl PA-2
Jollet, Bayou—gut (2) LA-4
Jollett—locale VA-3
Jolley—locale ID-8
Jolley—pop pl IA-7
Jolley, Francis Marion, House—hist pl UT-8
Jolley Cem—cemetery TN-4
Jolley Creek—stream CO-8
Jolley Creek—stream SD-7
Jolley Creek—stream WA-9
Jolley Flat—flat ID-8
Jolley Gulch—valley UT-8
Jolley Hollow—valley PA-2
Jolley Hollow—valley UT-8
Jolley Ranch—locale CO-8
Jolley Rsvr—reservoir WY-8
Jolleys Chapel—church AR-4
Jolleys Hole—basin UT-8
Jolleys Lake—reservoir SC-3
Jolleys Neck—cape VA-3
Jolley Spring—spring CA-9
Jolley Springs Baptist Church TN-4
Jolley Springs Ch—church TN-4
Jolley Subdivision—pop pl UT-8
Jolleyville—pop pl IN-6
Jolliet Run—stream WV-2
Jolliff—locale VA-3
Jolliff Cem—cemetery IL-6
Jolliffee Cem—cemetery (2) WV-2
Jolliff Rocks—summit IN-6
Jolliff Sch (historical)—school MO-7
Jolliff Spring—spring MO-7
Jolliff Spring Branch—stream MO-7
Jolliff Store—locale AR-4
Jollity Ch—church IN-6
Jollo Creek—stream CA-9
Jolloru, Canada Del —valley CA-9
Jolls Cem—cemetery NY-2
Jolly—locale GA-3
Jolly—locale KY-4
Jolly—locale MO-7
Jolly—locale SD-7
Jolly—pop pl IA-7
Jolly—pop pl MS-4
Jolly—pop pl TX-5
Jolly Acres Summer Camp—locale MD-2
Jolly Ann Lake—lake MN-6
Jolly Bay—bay FL-3
Jolly Branch—stream (2) NC-3
Jolly Brook—stream IN-6
Jolly Brook—stream ME-1
Jolly Cave—cave MO-7
Jolly Cem—cemetery KY-4
Jolly Cem—cemetery MO-7
Jolly Cem—cemetery NC-3
Jolly Cem—cemetery PA-2
Jolly Ch—church MS-4
Jolly Corner—pop pl FL-3
Jolly Creek AR-4
Jolly Creek—stream AL-4
Jolly Creek—stream AR-4
Jolly Creek—stream MS-4
Jolly Creek—stream MO-7
Jolly Creek—stream OR-9
Jolly Creek—stream TN-4
Jolly Creek—stream WA-9
Jolly Draw—valley WY-8
Jolly Dump—locale SD-7
Jolly Flats—flat SD-7
Jolly Gap—gap NC-3
Jolly Giant Creek—stream CA-9
Jolly Gulch—valley AK-9
Jolly Hill—locale VI-3
Jolly Hollow Branch—stream VA-3
Jolly Holly Branch VA-3
Jolly Island TN-4
Jolly Island—island NH-1
Jolly Island—island NY-2
Jolly Lake—lake TX-5
Jolly Lake—reservoir TN-4
Jolly Lake Dam—dam MS-4
Jolly Lake Dam—dam TN-4
Jollyman Sch—school CA-9
Jolly Mill—hist pl MO-7
Jolly Mill Hollow—valley UT-8
Jolly Mill Point—cape UT-8
Jolly Mine—mine SD-7
Jolly Mountain Lookout Trail—trail WA-9
Jolly Mtn—summit NC-3
Jolly Mtn—summit VT-1
Jolly Mtn—summit WA-9
Jolly Place Tank—reservoir AZ-5
Jolly Pond—reservoir GA-3
Jolly Pond—reservoir VA-3
Jolly Post Office (historical)—building MS-4
Jolly Ranch—locale UT-8
Jolly Ridge—ridge KY-4
Jolly River—stream FL-3
Jolly Rsvr—reservoir WY-8
Jolly Sailor Gulch—valley ID-8
Jollys Cabin—locale AK-9
Jolly Sch—school KY-4
Jolly Sch—school SD-7
Jollys Chapel Missionary Baptist Church MS-4
Jollys Creek NY-2
Jolly Sink—basin AZ-5
Jollys Island TN-4
Jollys Island Sch (historical)—school TN-4
Jollys Lake—lake WA-9
Jollys Old Field Landing—locale NC-3
Jollys Pond—lake WA-9
Jolly Spring—spring AL-4
Jolly Spring—spring UT-8
Jolly Springs Baptist Church TN-4
Jolly Springs Cem—cemetery TN-4
Jollys Rock—cape TN-4
Jollystreet—locale SC-3
Jolly Tank—reservoir AZ-5
Jollytown—pop pl PA-2
Jollyville—pop pl OK-5
Jollyville—pop pl (2) TX-5
Jollyville Cem—cemetery TX-5
Jollyville Hill—summit IA-7
Jollyville (historical P.O.)—pop pl IA-7
Jollyville Plateau—plain TX-5
Jolly Well—well CO-8
Jollywell Branch—stream AL-4
Jolman Sch—school MI-6
Jolo—pop pl WV-2
Jolon—pop pl CA-9
Jolon Creek—stream CA-9
Jolon Valley—valley CA-9
Jolo Sch—school WV-2
Jolty KY-4
Jo Lu Subdivision—pop pl UT-8
Jo Lynn Subdivision—pop pl UT-8
Jomaha Creek—stream MT-8
Jomar Lake—reservoir MS-4
Jo-mary Island—island ME-1
Jo-Mary Lake—lake ME-1
Jo-Mary Mtn—summit ME-1
Jo-Mary Pond—lake ME-1
Jo-Mary Trail—trail ME-1
Jo Mill Oil Field—oilfield TX-5
Jon—pop pl AL-4
Jonadab Creek—stream NJ-2
Jonah—locale OK-5
Jonah—pop pl TX-5
Jonah Bay—bay AK-9
Jonah Coulee WI-6
Jonah Creek TN-4
Jonah Creek—stream KS-7
Jonah Creek—stream TX-5
Jonah Drain—stream ID-8
Jonah Gulch—valley WY-8
Jonah Lake AR-4
Jonah Lake—lake AR-4
Jonah Lake—lake CO-8
Jonah Rsvr—reservoir WY-8
Jonahs Coulee—valley WI-6
Jonahs Run—stream OH-6
Jonahs Run Ch—church OH-6
Jonah Tank—reservoir NM-5
Jonahville Cem—cemetery NC-3
Jonahville Ch—church NC-3
Jonah Well—well TX-5
Jonancy—locale KY-4
Jonancy—pop pl WV-2
Jonaquin Creek—stream NC-3
Jonas—pop pl PA-2
Jonas, Bayou—stream AL-4
Jonas, Bayou—stream LA-4
Jonas, Charles R., Federal Bldg—hist pl NC-3
Jonas, Karel, House—hist pl WI-6
Jonas Brown Drain—stream MI-6
Jonas Cem—cemetery (2) TX-5
Jonas Cem—cemetery WV-2
Jonas Chapel—church MS-4
Jonas Chapel Sch—school MS-4
Jonas Coulee WI-6
Jonas Creek—gut NY-2
Jonas Creek—stream NC-3
Jonas Creek—stream (2) OR-9
Jonas Creek—stream PA-2
Jonas Cutting-Edward Kent House—hist pl ME-1
Jonas Draft—valley VA-3
Jonas E Salk JHS—school WA-9
Jonas Fields—summit NC-3
Jonas Flat—flat OR-9
Jonas Green State Park—park MD-2
Jonas Hill—summit WA-9
Jonas Hollow—valley WV-2
Jonas Island—island NJ-2
Jonas Johnson Island—island IL-6
Jonas Lobe Cem—cemetery GA-3
Jonas Mtn—summit GA-3
Jonas Mtn—summit OR-9
Jonason Lake—lake MN-6
Jonas Phillips Mine (underground)—mine TN-4
Jonas Ridge—pop pl NC-3
Jonas Ridge—ridge NC-3
Jonas Ridge Sch Building—school NC-3
Jonas Ridge (Township of)—fmr MCD NC-3
Jonas Run—stream VA-3
Jonatham Creek OH-6
Jonathan MN-6
Jonathan—locale ID-8
Jonathan—locale MS-4
Jonathan—pop pl NC-3
Jonathan, Mount—summit WA-9
Jonathan Alder HS—school OH-6
Jonathan Bourne Library—building MA-1
Jonathan Branch—stream IL-6
Jonathan Branch—stream VA-3
Jonathan Creek NC-3
Jonathan Creek—stream CA-9
Jonathan Creek—stream (2) IL-6
Jonathan Creek—stream IN-6
Jonathan Creek—stream IA-7
Jonathan Creek—stream KY-4
Jonathan Creek—stream OH-6
Jonathan Creek—stream TN-4
Jonathan Creek—stream WA-9
Jonathan Creek Cabin Area—park KY-4
Jonathan Creek Ch—church IL-6
Jonathan Creek Overlook—locale NC-3
Jonathan Creek (Township of)—civ div IL-6
Jonathan Crossroads—locale NC-3
Jonathan Day Cem—cemetery MS-4
Jonathan Dickinson State Park—park FL-3
Jonathan Fisher Memorial—hist pl ME-1
Jonathan Fork—stream KY-4
Jonathan Island—island RI-1
Jonathan Jennings Elem Sch—school IN-6
Jonathan Knob—summit WV-2
Jonathan Mine—mine CO-8
Jonathan Pond MA-1
Jonathan Pond—lake NH-1
Jonathan Run—stream (2) PA-2
Jonathan Run—stream (2) WV-2
Jonathan Run Falls—falls PA-2
Jonathans Bluff—cliff MS-4
Jonathan Sch—school (2) KY-4
Jonathans Creek—stream TN-4
Jonathans Creek (Township of)—fmr MCD NC-3
Jonathans Island RI-1
Jonathans Pond MA-1
Jonathans Pond (historical)—lake MA-1
Jonathans Run PA-2
Jonathan (sta.)—pop pl MN-6
Jonathan Thorofare—channel NJ-2
Jonathan Watson Grant—civil FL-3
Jonay Pond—reservoir IN-6
Jonay Pond Dam—dam IN-6
Jonben—pop pl WV-2
Jon B Richard Grant—civil FL-3
Jonca Creek—stream MO-7
Jonce Canyon—valley NM-5
Jonce Tank—reservoir NM-5
Jondan Creek NE-7
Jondik Creek—stream AK-9
Jones CA-9
Jones MS-4
Jones NC-3
Jones SD-7
Jones WI-6
Jones—locale IL-6
Jones—locale MD-2
Jones—locale OH-6
Jones—locale TX-5
Jones—locale VA-3
Jones—locale WV-2
Jones—pop pl AL-4
Jones—pop pl GA-3
Jones—pop pl (2) KY-4
Jones—pop pl LA-4
Jones—pop pl MD-2
Jones—pop pl MI-6
Jones—pop pl MN-6
Jones—pop pl NC-3
Jones—pop pl OK-5
Jones—pop pl TN-4
Jones, Abel, House—hist pl ME-1
Jones, Abraham, House—hist pl MD-2
Jones, A. C., House—hist pl SC-3
Jones, A.D. (Boss), House—hist pl NY-2
Jones, Alpheus, House—hist pl NC-3
Jones, Arthur J., House—hist pl AR-4
Jones, Bayou—gut LA-4
Jones, Benjamin, House—hist pl NJ-2
Jones, B. F., Memorial Library—hist pl PA-2
Jones, Charles William, House—hist pl FL-3
Jones, Col. William, House—hist pl IN-6
Jones, Crabtree, House—hist pl NC-3
Jones, David, House—hist pl TN-4
Jones, David H., House—hist pl UT-8
Jones, Dr. Beverly, House—hist pl NC-3
Jones, Dr. Noble Wiley, House—hist pl OR-9
Jones, Dudley, House—hist pl MS-4
Jones, Eli and Sybil, House—hist pl ME-1
Jones, Elijah Pelton, House—hist pl OH-6
Jones, Elizabeth M., House—hist pl UT-8
Jones, Enoch, House—hist pl DE-2
Jones, Fred B., Estate—hist pl WI-6
Jones, George Washington, House—hist pl TX-5
Jones, Gov. Thomas G., House—hist pl AL-4
Jones, Granville D., House—hist pl WI-6
Jones, Harry W., House—hist pl MN-6
Jones, Huff, House—hist pl WI-6
Jones, Jedd, House—hist pl ID-8
Jones, Jesse Fuller, House—hist pl NC-3
Jones, J. M., House—hist pl TX-5
Jones, John, House—hist pl MA-1
Jones, John J., House—hist pl OH-6
Jones, John James, House—hist pl GA-3
Jones, John Paul, House—hist pl NH-1
Jones, John Paul, JHS—hist pl PA-2
Jones, J. W., Bldg—hist pl ID-8
Jones, Lake—lake MA-1
Jones, Lake—lake MN-6
Jones, Lewis, House—hist pl IN-6
Jones, Margaret and George Riley, House—hist pl IN-6
Jones, Matthew, House—hist pl VA-3
Jones, Merritt, Tavern—hist pl KY-4
Jones, Morgan, 1677 Pottery Kiln—hist pl VA-3
Jones, Moses, House—hist pl KY-4
Jones, Nancy, House—hist pl NC-3
Jones, Oliver P., House—hist pl TX-5
Jones, Pearl J., House—hist pl GA-3
Jones, Point—summit AL-4
Jones, Robert O., House—hist pl WI-6
Jones, Sam, Memorial United Methodist Church—hist pl GA-3
Jones, Samuel S., Cobblestone House—hist pl WI-6
Jones, Tavy, House—hist pl KS-7
Jones, Thomas, House—hist pl UT-8
Jones, Thomas W., House—hist pl MA-1
Jones, T. J., Apartments—hist pl ID-8
Jones, Wade H., Sr., House—hist pl LA-4
Jones, W. H., Mansion—hist pl OH-6
Jones, William C., House—hist pl AL-4
Jones, William R., House—hist pl MA-1
Jones Acad—school OK-5
Jones Acres—pop pl GA-3
Jones African Methodist Episcopal Tabernacle—church IN-6
Jones Airp—airport PA-2
Jones and Ausmus Flat—flat OR-9
Jones and Read Mine (underground)—mine AL-4
Jones and Voyles Mine (historical)—mine PA-2
Jones Arroyo—stream (3) NM-5
Jones Arroyo—valley CO-8
Jones Bailey Cem—cemetery AL-4
Jones Balsam NC-3
Jones-Banks-Leigh House—hist pl MS-4
Jones Bar—bar AL-4
Jones Bar—bar CA-9
Jones Bar—bar ID-8
Jones Basin—basin UT-8
Jones Bay NY-2
Jones Bay—bay CA-9
Jones Bay—bay NC-3
Jones Bay—bay TN-4
Jones Bay—bay TX-5
Jones Bay—bay WA-9
Jones Bay—swamp GA-3
Jones-Bayless Cem—cemetery TN-4
Jones Bayou TN-4
Jones Bayou—bay (2) FL-3
Jones Bayou—gut (2) LA-4
Jones Bayou—gut TX-5
Jones Bayou—stream (4) LA-4
Jones Bayou—stream (3) MS-4
Jones Bayou Baptist Church MS-4
Jones Bayou Church MS-4
Jones Beach MH-9
Jones Beach—beach (2) NY-2
Jones Beach—beach GU-9
Jones Beach—pop pl (2) NY-2
Jones Beach State Park—park NY-2
Jones Bed Mine (underground)—mine AL-4
Jones Bench—bench UT-8
Jones Bend TN-4
Jones Bend—bend GA-3
Jones Bend—bend (4) TN-4
Jones Bend Blount County Park—park TN-4
Jones Bend Creek—stream TN-4
Jones Bend Lake—reservoir TN-4
Jones Big Swamp—stream SC-3
Jones Big Swamp—swamp SC-3
Jones Block—hist pl MA-1
Jones Blue Eye Lake—reservoir AL-4
Jones Bluff AL-4
Jones Bluff—cliff (2) AL-4
Jones Bluff—cliff WA-9
Jones Bluff Dam—pop pl AL-4
Jones Bluff Lake AL-4
Jones Bluff Lock and Dam AL-4
Jones Bluff Park AL-4
Jones Bluff Shoals—bar AL-4
Jones Bog—swamp ME-1
Jonesboro AL-4
Jonesboro IN-6
Jonesboro MS-4
Jonesboro NC-3
Jonesboro TN-4
Jonesboro—locale ME-1
Jonesboro—locale FL-3
Jonesboro—locale OH-6
Jonesboro—locale OR-9
Jonesboro—locale VA-3
Jonesboro—pop pl (2) AL-4
Jonesboro—pop pl AR-4
Jonesboro—pop pl GA-3
Jonesboro—pop pl IL-6
Jonesboro—pop pl IN-6
Jonesboro—pop pl LA-4
Jonesboro—pop pl ME-1
Jonesboro—pop pl OH-6
Jonesboro—pop pl OR-9
Jonesboro—pop pl TX-5
Jonesboro—pop pl VA-3
Jonesboro Baptist Church AL-4
Jonesboro Bridge—bridge VA-3
Jonesboro Canal—canal OR-9
Jonesboro (CCD)—cens area GA-3
Jonesboro (CCD)—cens area TN-4
Jonesboro Cem—cemetery AL-4
Jonesboro Ch—church AL-4
Jonesboro Ch—church NC-3
Jonesboro Ch—church VA-3
Jonesboro Church MS-4
Jonesboro Community Center—building AL-4
Jonesboro Creek—stream MS-4
Jonesboro Crossing—locale NC-3
Jonesboro District No. 1 (Election Precinct)—fmr MCD IL-6
Jonesboro District No. 2 (Election Precinct)—fmr MCD IL-6
Jonesboro Division—civil TN-4
Jonesboro Elem Sch—school AL-4
Jonesboro Elem Sch—school NC-3
Jonesboro Heights—pop pl NC-3
Jonesboro Heights (RR name Jonesboro)—uninc pl NC-3
Jonesboro High School TN-4
Jonesboro Hist Dist—hist pl GA-3
Jonesboro Hist Dist—hist pl NC-3
Jonesboro Hist Dist—hist pl TN-4
Jonesboro Hollow—valley TN-4
Jonesboro Post Office TN-4
Jonesboro Presbyterian Ch—church TN-4
Jonesboro (RR name for Jonesboro Heights)—other NC-3
Jonesboro Sch—school IL-6
Jonesboro Sch—school NC-3
Jonesboro Sch—school TN-4
Jonesboro Sch—school VA-3
Jonesboro Sch (historical)—school AL-4
Jonesboro Station—locale ME-1
Jonesboro (Town of)—pop pl ME-1
Jonesboro (Township of)—fmr MCD AR-4
Jonesborough AL-4
Jonesborough IN-6
Jonesborough NC-3
Jonesborough—pop pl TN-4
Jonesborough Ch of Christ—church TN-4
Jonesborough City Hall—building TN-4
Jonesborough Elem Sch—school TN-4
Jonesborough (historical)—locale MS-4
Jonesborough (Jonesboro)—pop pl TN-4
Jonesborough MS—school TN-4
Jonesborough Post Office—building TN-4
Jonesboro United Methodist Ch—church TN-4
Jones Bottom—bend AR-4
Jones Bottom Cem—cemetery AR-4
Jones-Bowman House—hist pl OH-6
Jones Brake—swamp LA-4
Jones Branch DE-2
Jones Branch TN-4
Jones Branch WV-2
Jones Branch—stream (12) AL-4
Jones Branch—stream (3) AR-4
Jones Branch—stream DE-2
Jones Branch—stream FL-3
Jones Branch—stream (5) GA-3
Jones Branch—stream IL-6
Jones Branch—stream (2) IN-6
Jones Branch—stream IA-7
Jones Branch—stream (19) KY-4
Jones Branch—stream (3) LA-4
Jones Branch—stream (3) MS-4
Jones Branch—stream (10) MO-7
Jones Branch—stream (11) NC-3
Jones Branch—stream SC-3
Jones Branch—stream (22) TN-4
Jones Branch—stream (12) TX-5
Jones Branch—stream (8) VA-3
Jones Branch—stream (3) WV-2
Jones Branch—stream WI-6
Jones Branch Ditch—canal IN-6
Jones Branch Sch (historical)—school MO-7
Jones Bridge TN-4
Jones Bridge—bridge ME-1
Jones Bridge—bridge SC-3
Jones Bridge—bridge TN-4
Jones Bridge—bridge TX-5
Jones Brook VT-1
Jones Brook—stream (9) ME-1
Jones Brook—stream (2) MA-1
Jones Brook—stream NH-1
Jones Brook—stream (5) NY-2
Jones Brook—stream (8) VT-1
Jonesburg—locale KY-4
Jonesburg—locale LA-4
Jonesburg—pop pl MO-7
Jones Butte CA-9
Jones Butte—summit ID-8
Jones Butte—summit (2) OR-9
Jones Cabin Creek—stream UT-8
Jones Cabin Run—stream WV-2
Jones Camp NE-7
Jones Camp—locale ME-1
Jones Camp—locale NM-5
Jones Camp Creek—stream CA-9
Jones Camp Creek—stream MI-6
Jones Camp Ground AL-4
Jones Canal—canal LA-4
Jones Canal—canal OR-9
Jones Canyon OR-9
Jones Canyon—stream OR-9
Jones Canyon—valley (5) AZ-5
Jones Canyon—valley (2) CA-9
Jones Canyon—valley (2) CO-8
Jones Canyon—valley (2) ID-8
Jones Canyon—valley KS-7
Jones Canyon—valley (3) NE-7
Jones Canyon—valley (5) NV-8
Jones Canyon—valley (10) NM-5
Jones Canyon—valley (7) OR-9
Jones Canyon—valley (4) TX-5
Jones Canyon—valley (2) UT-8
Jones Canyon—valley WA-9
Jones Canyon Creek—stream KS-7
Jones Cave MA-1
Jones Cave—cave MO-7
Jones Cave—cave TN-4
Jones Cem MS-4
Jones Cem TN-4
Jones Cem—cemetery (23) AL-4
Jones Cem—cemetery (21) AR-4
Jones Cem—cemetery FL-3
Jones Cem—cemetery (14) GA-3
Jones Cem—cemetery (11) IL-6
Jones Cem—cemetery (10) IN-6
Jones Cem—cemetery IA-7
Jones Cem—cemetery (2) KS-7
Jones Cem—cemetery (27) KY-4
Jones Cem—cemetery (2) LA-4
Jones Cem—cemetery ME-1
Jones Cem—cemetery MA-1
Jones Cem—cemetery (3) MI-6
Jones Cem—cemetery (21) MS-4
Jones Cem—cemetery (14) MO-7
Jones Cem—cemetery (3) NY-2

Jones Cem—*cemetery* (13) ... NC-3
Jones Cem—*cemetery* (5) ... OH-6
Jones Cem—*cemetery* (4) ... OK-5
Jones Cem—*cemetery* ... OR-9
Jones Cem—*cemetery* (6) ... SC-3
Jones Cem—*cemetery* (55) ... TN-4
Jones Cem—*cemetery* (12) ... TX-5
Jones Cem—*cemetery* (12) ... VA-3
Jones Cem—*cemetery* (6) ... WV-2
Jones Cem—*cemetery* ... WI-6
Jones Cemeteries—*cemetery* ... TX-5
Jones Cemeteries—*cemetery* ... WV-2
*Jones Ch* ... MS-4
Jones Ch—*church* ... AL-4
Jones Ch—*church* ... IA-7
Jones Ch—*church* ... KY-4
Jones Ch—*church* ... MS-4
Jones Ch—*church* ... NC-3
Jones Ch—*church* ... TN-4
Jones Ch—*church* ... VA-3
*Jones Chapel* ... AL-4
*Jones Chapel* ... MS-4
Jones Chapel—*church* (10) ... AL-4
Jones Chapel—*church* ... FL-3
Jones Chapel—*church* (6) ... GA-3
Jones Chapel—*church* (2) ... IN-6
Jones Chapel—*church* (3) ... KY-4
Jones Chapel—*church* ... MD-2
Jones Chapel—*church* (17) ... MS-4
Jones Chapel—*church* ... MO-7
Jones Chapel—*church* (13) ... NC-3
Jones Chapel—*church* (4) ... SC-3
Jones Chapel—*church* (12) ... TN-4
Jones Chapel—*church* (3) ... TX-5
Jones Chapel—*church* (3) ... VA-3
**Jones Chapel**—*pop pl* ... AL-4
**Jones Chapel**—*pop pl* ... MS-4
**Jones Chapel**—*pop pl* ... TN-4
*Jones Chapel Baptist Church* ... MS-4
*Jones Chapel Baptist Church* ... TN-4
Jones Chapel (CCD)—*cens area* ... AL-4
Jones Chapel Cem—*cemetery* ... IN-6
Jones Chapel Cem—*cemetery* (2) ... MS-4
Jones Chapel Cem—*cemetery* ... TN-4
Jones Chapel Cem—*cemetery* ... TX-5
*Jones Chapel Ch* ... AL-4
Jones Chapel Ch—*church* (3) ... AL-4
*Jones Chapel Ch of Christ* ... AL-4
*Jones Chapel Church of God* ... MS-4
Jones Chapel Division—*civil* ... AL-4
Jones Chapel (historical)—*church* ... MS-4
Jones Chapel (historical)—*church* ... TN-4
**Jones Chapel (historical)**—*pop pl* ... TN-4
Jones Chapel Methodist Ch—*church* ... AL-4
Jones Chapel Missionary Baptist Ch—*church* ... MS-4
Jones Chapel Post Office (historical)—*building* ... AL-4
Jones Chapel Sch—*school* ... AL-4
Jones Chapel Sch—*school* ... KY-4
Jones Chapel Sch—*school* ... TN-4
Jones Chapel Sch (historical)—*school* ... AL-4
Jones Chapel Sch (historical)—*school* ... MS-4
Jones Ch (historical)—*church* ... AL-4
Jones Ch (historical)—*church* ... TN-4
**Jones City**—*pop pl* ... NM-5
**Jones City**—*pop pl* ... OH-6
Jones Clark Ditch—*canal* ... IN-6
Jones Clark Island (historical)—*island* ... TN-4
Jonesco, Lake—*reservoir* ... GA-3
Jones Coll—*school* ... FL-3
Jones Coll for Females (historical)—*school* ... AL-4
Jones Colony Ch—*church* ... TX-5
Jones Community Ch—*church* ... AR-4
Jones Cone—*pillar* ... MT-8
*Jones Corner* ... VA-3
Jones Corner—*locale* (2) ... ME-1
Jones Corner—*locale* ... NH-1
Jones Corner—*locale* ... OH-6
Jones Corner—*locale* (2) ... VA-3
**Jones Corner**—*pop pl* ... CA-9
**Jones Corner**—*pop pl* ... FL-3
**Jones Corner**—*pop pl* ... NC-3
**Jones Corner**—*pop pl* ... VA-3
Jones Corners—*locale* (4) ... NY-2
Jones Corners—*locale* ... VA-3
**Jones Corners**—*pop pl* ... NY-2
Jones Corral Draw—*valley* ... UT-8
*Jones Corral Forest Service Station* ... UT-8
Jones Corral Guard Station—*locale* ... UT-8
Jones Corral Rsvr—*reservoir* ... UT-8
*Jones Corral Spring* ... UT-8
*Jones Coulee* ... MT-8
*Jones Coulee* ... WI-6
Jones Coulee—*stream* ... MT-8
Jones Coulee—*valley* ... MT-8
*Jones County* ... AL-4
Jones County—*civil* ... SD-7
**Jones (County)**—*pop pl* ... GA-3
**Jones County**—*pop pl* ... MS-4
**Jones County**—*pop pl* ... NC-3
**Jones (County)**—*pop pl* ... TX-5
*Jones County Agricultural High School* ... MS-4
Jones County Community Hosp—*hospital* ... MS-4
Jones County Courthouse—*building* (2) ... MS-4
Jones County Courthouse—*hist pl* ... GA-3
Jones County Home—*building* ... MS-4
Jones County Junior Coll—*school* ... MS-4
Jones County Lake—*reservoir* ... MS-4
Jones County Lake Dam—*dam* ... MS-4
Jones County Training Sch (historical)—*school* ... MS-4
*Jones Cove* ... ME-1
*Jones Cove* ... MA-1
Jones Cove—*bay* ... FL-3
Jones Cove—*bay* (3) ... ME-1
Jones Cove—*bay* ... VA-3
**Jones Cove**—*pop pl* ... TN-4
Jones Cove—*valley* (3) ... AL-4
Jones Cove—*valley* (4) ... NC-3
Jones Cove—*valley* ... TN-4
Jones Cove Branch—*stream* ... NC-3
Jones Cow Camp—*locale* ... TX-5
*Jones Creek* ... AR-4
*Jones Creek* ... CA-9
*Jones Creek* ... DE-2
*Jones Creek* ... GA-3
*Jones Creek* ... ID-8
*Jones Creek* ... IN-6
*Jones Creek* ... IA-7
*Jones Creek* ... MD-2
*Jones Creek* ... MT-8
*Jones Creek* ... NC-3
*Jones Creek* ... OK-5
*Jones Creek* ... TN-4
*Jones Creek* ... TX-5
*Jones Creek* ... VA-3
*Jones Creek* ... WI-6
Jones Creek—*bay* ... FL-3
Jones Creek—*bay* (2) ... MD-2
Jones Creek—*gut* ... SC-3
Jones Creek—*locale* ... GA-3
Jones Creek—*locale* ... TX-5
**Jones Creek**—*pop pl* ... LA-4
**Jones Creek**—*pop pl* ... TX-5
**Jones Creek**—*pop pl* ... VA-3
Jones Creek—*stream* (13) ... AL-4
Jones Creek—*stream* (2) ... AK-9
Jones Creek—*stream* (4) ... AR-4
Jones Creek—*stream* (6) ... CA-9
Jones Creek—*stream* (5) ... CO-8
Jones Creek—*stream* (2) ... FL-3
Jones Creek—*stream* (12) ... GA-3
Jones Creek—*stream* (6) ... ID-8
Jones Creek—*stream* ... IN-6
Jones Creek—*stream* (3) ... IA-7
Jones Creek—*stream* (2) ... KS-7
Jones Creek—*stream* (8) ... KY-4
Jones Creek—*stream* (5) ... LA-4
Jones Creek—*stream* ... ME-1
Jones Creek—*stream* (4) ... MD-2
Jones Creek—*stream* (2) ... MI-6
Jones Creek—*stream* (16) ... MS-4
Jones Creek—*stream* (5) ... MO-7
Jones Creek—*stream* (10) ... MT-8
Jones Creek—*stream* (2) ... NE-7
Jones Creek—*stream* (2) ... NV-8
Jones Creek—*stream* ... NJ-2
Jones Creek—*stream* (3) ... NY-2
Jones Creek—*stream* (12) ... NC-3
Jones Creek—*stream* ... ND-7
Jones Creek—*stream* (3) ... OK-5
Jones Creek—*stream* (13) ... OR-9
Jones Creek—*stream* (2) ... PA-2
Jones Creek—*stream* (2) ... SC-3
Jones Creek—*stream* (2) ... SD-7
Jones Creek—*stream* (11) ... TN-4
Jones Creek—*stream* (17) ... TX-5
Jones Creek—*stream* ... UT-8
Jones Creek—*stream* (12) ... VA-3
Jones Creek—*stream* (9) ... WA-9
Jones Creek—*stream* ... WV-2
Jones Creek—*stream* (5) ... WI-6
Jones Creek—*stream* (5) ... WY-8
Jones Creek—*swamp* ... SC-3
Jones Creek Bar—*bar* ... AL-4
Jones Creek Canyon—*valley* ... WY-8
Jones Creek Ch—*church* ... AL-4
Jones Creek Ch—*church* ... GA-3
Jones Creek Ch—*church* ... KY-4
Jones Creek Ch—*church* ... LA-4
Jones Creek Ch (historical)—*church* ... AL-4
Jones Creek Day Use Area—*locale* ... KY-4
Jones Creek Forge (40DS30)—*hist pl* ... TN-4
Jones Creek (historical)—*locale* ... MS-4
**Jones Creek (historical)**—*pop pl* ... NC-3
Jones Creek Lake—*reservoir* ... TN-4
Jones Creek Sch—*school* ... KY-4
Jones Creek Sch—*school* ... LA-4
Jones Creek Sch (historical)—*school* ... AL-4
Jones Creek Spring—*spring* ... SD-7
Jones Creek Swamp—*swamp* ... GA-3
Jones Creek 101-102-0 Dam—*dam* ... TN-4
*Jones Crossing* ... TN-4
Jones Crossing—*locale* ... AZ-5
Jones Crossing—*locale* ... GA-3
Jones Crossing—*locale* ... ID-8
Jones Crossing—*locale* ... MS-4
Jones Crossing—*locale* ... WV-2
**Jones Crossing**—*pop pl* ... NY-2
*Jones Crossroads* ... AL-4
Jones Crossroads—*locale* ... AL-4
Jones Crossroads—*locale* ... DE-2
Jones Crossroads—*locale* (2) ... GA-3
Jones Crossroads—*locale* (3) ... SC-3
**Jones Crossroads**—*pop pl* ... AL-4
**Jones Crossroads**—*pop pl* ... GA-3
**Jones Crossroads**—*pop pl* (2) ... SC-3
Jones-Cutler House—*hist pl* ... OH-6
Jones Cut-Off—*bend* ... AR-4
Jones Dairy Farm—*hist pl* ... WI-6
Jonesdale—*locale* ... WI-6
**Jonesdale Subdivision**—*pop pl* ... UT-8
Jones Dam—*dam* (2) ... AL-4
Jones Dam—*dam* ... OR-9
Jones Dam—*dam* ... SD-7
Jones Dam—*dam* ... TN-4
Jones Dam—*dam* ... UT-8
Jones Dam Hollow—*valley* ... WV-2
Jones Defeat Hollow—*valley* ... IN-6
*Jones Ditch* ... IN-6
Jones Ditch—*canal* ... AZ-5
Jones Ditch—*canal* (2) ... CO-8
Jones Ditch—*canal* ... ID-8
Jones Ditch—*canal* ... IL-6
Jones Ditch—*canal* (7) ... IN-6
Jones Ditch—*canal* ... MD-2
Jones Ditch—*canal* (2) ... MT-8
Jones Ditch—*canal* (2) ... OH-6
Jones Ditch—*canal* ... OR-9
Jones Ditch—*canal* ... UT-8
Jones Ditch Number 2—*canal* ... OH-6
Jones Dock—*locale* ... VT-1
Jones-Donnell Cem—*cemetery* ... AL-4
Jones Drain—*canal* (2) ... MI-6
Jones Drain—*canal* ... WY-8
Jones Drain—*stream* ... CA-9
Jones Draw—*valley* (2) ... CO-8
Jones Draw—*valley* (2) ... TX-5
Jones Draw—*valley* (7) ... WY-8
Jones Draw Tank—*reservoir* ... NM-5
Jones Dugout Spring—*spring* ... NV-8
Jones East Sch (historical)—*school* ... MO-7
*Jones Elementary School* ... NC-3
*Jones Elementary School* ... TN-4
Jones-Erwin Cem—*cemetery* ... NY-2
Jones Estate—*hist pl* ... KY-4
Jones Eugene Number 1 Dam—*dam* ... SD-7
Jones Falls—*falls* ... TN-4
Jones Falls—*stream* ... MD-2
*Jones Falls Branch* ... TN-4
Jones Falls Run—*stream* ... VA-3
**Jones Farm**—*pop pl* ... OH-6
Jones Farm Dam—*dam* ... TN-4
Jones Farm Lake—*reservoir* ... TN-4
Jones Farm Tank—*reservoir* ... NM-5
Jones Ferry—*locale* ... NC-3
Jones Ferry (historical)—*locale* ... NC-3
Jones Field—*island* ... AL-4
Jones Field—*park* ... TN-4
**Jonesfield (Township of)**—*pop pl* ... MI-6
Jones Flat—*flat* (2) ... CA-9
Jones Flat—*flat* ... CO-8
Jones Flat—*flat* (2) ... NV-8
Jones-Florence Plantation—*hist pl* ... GA-3
*Jones Folly* ... NC-3
Jones Ford—*locale* ... AL-4
Jones Ford—*locale* ... MS-4
Jones Ford—*locale* (2) ... TN-4
Jones Ford (historical)—*crossing* (2) ... TN-4
*Jones Fork* ... CA-9
Jones Fork—*stream* ... AR-4
Jones Fork—*stream* (5) ... KY-4
Jones Fork—*stream* ... TN-4
Jones Fork—*stream* ... VA-3
*Jones Fork Creek* ... AR-4
Jones Fork Creek—*stream* ... ID-8
Jones Fork Silver Creek—*stream* ... CA-9
Jones Gap—*gap* (4) ... GA-3
Jones Gap—*gap* ... KY-4
Jones Gap—*gap* (2) ... NC-3
Jones Gap—*gap* ... SC-3
Jones Gap—*gap* (2) ... TN-4
Jones Gap—*gap* ... VA-3
Jones Gap Ch—*church* ... NC-3
Jones Garden Island—*island* ... ME-1
Jones Grove Cem—*cemetery* ... IL-6
Jones Grove Cem—*cemetery* ... MS-4
Jones Grove Ch—*church* (3) ... GA-3
Jones Grove Ch—*church* (2) ... MS-4
Jones Grove Ch—*church* (2) ... NC-3
Jones Grove Ch—*church* ... TN-4
Jones Grove Ch—*church* ... VA-3
Jones Grove Sch—*school* ... TN-4
Jones Gulch—*valley* ... AZ-5
Jones Gulch—*valley* (4) ... CA-9
Jones Gulch—*valley* (5) ... CO-8
Jones Gulch—*valley* ... ID-8
Jones Gulch—*valley* ... OR-9
Jones Gulch—*valley* ... WY-8
Jones Gully—*valley* ... FL-3
Jones Gully—*valley* ... TX-5
Jones Gut—*gut* ... AL-4
Jones Hall—*hist pl* ... NH-1
Jones Hall, Youngstown State Univ—*hist pl* ... OH-6
Jones Hammock—*island* ... FL-3
Jones Hammock Creek—*stream* ... GA-3
*Jones-Haynes Cemetery* ... TN-4
*Jones Hill* ... MA-1
Jones Hill—*ridge* ... NH-1
Jones Hill—*summit* (2) ... AL-4
Jones Hill—*summit* (2) ... AZ-5
Jones Hill—*summit* ... CA-9
Jones Hill—*summit* ... CO-8
Jones Hill—*summit* ... KY-4
Jones Hill—*summit* (3) ... ME-1
Jones Hill—*summit* ... MA-1
Jones Hill—*summit* (2) ... MT-8
Jones Hill—*summit* (4) ... NH-1
Jones Hill—*summit* (6) ... NY-2
Jones Hill—*summit* ... OH-6
Jones Hill—*summit* ... OR-9
Jones Hill—*summit* ... PA-2
Jones Hill—*summit* ... SC-3
Jones Hill—*summit* (2) ... TN-4
Jones Hill—*summit* ... UT-8
Jones Hill—*summit* (2) ... VT-1
*Jones-Hill Baptist Church* ... AL-4
Jones Hill Cem—*cemetery* ... AL-4
Jones Hill Ch—*church* (2) ... NC-3
Jones Hill Ch—*church* ... SC-3
Jones Hill Sch—*school* ... NH-1
Jones (historical)—*locale* ... MS-4
**Jones (historical)**—*pop pl* ... NC-3
Jones Hole—*valley* ... UT-8
Jones Hole Creek—*stream* ... UT-8
Jones Hole Fish Hatchery—*locale* ... UT-8
*Jones Hole Natl Fish Hatchery* ... UT-8
Jones Hole Ranger Station—*locale* ... UT-8
Jones Hole Springs—*spring* ... UT-8
Jones Hole Swamp—*stream* ... VA-3
Jones Hole Trail—*trail* ... UT-8
*Jones Hollow* ... TN-4
Jones Hollow—*valley* (6) ... AL-4
Jones Hollow—*valley* ... AZ-5
Jones Hollow—*valley* (4) ... AR-4
Jones Hollow—*valley* ... ID-8
Jones Hollow—*valley* ... IL-6
Jones Hollow—*valley* (5) ... KY-4
Jones Hollow—*valley* ... MS-4
Jones Hollow—*valley* (4) ... MO-7
Jones Hollow—*valley* (2) ... NY-2
Jones Hollow—*valley* ... OH-6
Jones Hollow—*valley* (15) ... TN-4
Jones Hollow—*valley* (3) ... TX-5
Jones Hollow—*valley* (5) ... UT-8
Jones Hollow—*valley* (6) ... VA-3
Jones Hollow—*valley* ... WV-2
Jones Hollow Camp Area—*locale* ... KY-4
Jones Hollow Rsvr—*reservoir* ... UT-8
Jones Homestead—*locale* ... CO-8
Jones Horse Camp—*locale* ... OR-9
Jones Hosp—*hospital* ... TX-5
Jones House—*hist pl* ... AR-4
Jones House—*hist pl* ... IL-6
Jones House—*hist pl* ... KY-4
Jones House—*hist pl* ... LA-4
Jones House—*hist pl* ... NC-3
Jones House—*hist pl* ... TX-5
Jones HS—*school* ... AL-4
Jones HS—*school* ... FL-3
Jones HS—*school* ... IL-6
Jones HS—*school* ... NC-3
Jones HS—*school* (3) ... TX-5
Jones-Hunt House—*hist pl* ... TX-5
Jones Hunting and Fishing Club—*locale* ... AL-4
Jones Inlet—*channel* ... NY-2
*Jones Island* ... AL-4
Jones Island—*cape* ... WI-6
Jones Island—*island* ... FL-3
Jones Island—*island* (2) ... GA-3
Jones Island—*island* ... LA-4
Jones Island—*island* ... MI-6
Jones Island—*island* ... MO-7
Jones Island—*island* ... MT-8
Jones Island—*island* ... NJ-2
Jones Island—*island* (3) ... NY-2
Jones Island—*island* ... NC-3
Jones Island—*island* ... SC-3
Jones Island—*island* ... SD-7
Jones Island—*island* (4) ... TN-4
Jones Island—*island* ... WA-9
**Jones Island**—*pop pl* ... NJ-2
Jones Island—*uninc pl* ... WI-6
Jones Island (historical)—*island* (2) ... TN-4
Jones Islands—*area* ... AK-9
*Jones Island Shoals* ... TN-4
Jones-Jarvis House—*hist pl* ... NC-3
Jones JHS—*school* ... MS-4
Jones JHS—*school* ... NC-3
Jones JHS—*school* ... OH-6
Jones JHS—*school* ... PA-2
Jones-Keeney Wildlife Mngmt Area—*park* ... KY-4
Jones-Kime-Brown Property Cem—*cemetery* ... OR-9
*Jones Knob* ... NC-3
Jones Knob—*summit* ... GA-3
Jones Knob—*summit* (2) ... KY-4
Jones Knob—*summit* (5) ... NC-3
Jones Knob—*summit* ... OH-6
Jones Knob—*summit* ... TN-4
Jones Knob—*summit* (2) ... VA-3
Jones Knoll—*summit* ... MA-1
Jones Lagoon—*lagoon* ... FL-3
Jones Lagoon—*lake* ... FL-3
*Jones Lake* ... AL-4
*Jones Lake* ... AR-4
*Jones Lake* ... MI-6
*Jones Lake* ... OR-9
*Jones Lake* ... PA-2
*Jones Lake* ... TN-4
*Jones Lake* ... TX-5
Jones Lake—*lake* (2) ... AR-4
Jones Lake—*lake* ... CA-9
Jones Lake—*lake* ... CO-8
Jones Lake—*lake* (2) ... FL-3
Jones Lake—*lake* ... GA-3
Jones Lake—*lake* ... IL-6
Jones Lake—*lake* ... IN-6
Jones Lake—*lake* (3) ... LA-4
Jones Lake—*lake* (7) ... MI-6
Jones Lake—*lake* (6) ... MN-6
Jones Lake—*lake* ... MS-4
Jones Lake—*lake* ... MO-7
Jones Lake—*lake* ... MT-8
Jones Lake—*lake* (2) ... NE-7
Jones Lake—*lake* ... NJ-2
Jones Lake—*lake* (2) ... NY-2
Jones Lake—*lake* ... NC-3
Jones Lake—*lake* (4) ... ND-7
Jones Lake—*lake* ... PA-2
Jones Lake—*lake* ... SC-3
Jones Lake—*lake* (4) ... TX-5
Jones Lake—*lake* ... WA-9
Jones Lake—*lake* (3) ... WI-6
Jones Lake—*lake* ... WY-8
Jones Lake—*reservoir* (5) ... AL-4
Jones Lake—*reservoir* ... GA-3
Jones Lake—*reservoir* ... MS-4
Jones Lake—*reservoir* ... NM-5
Jones Lake—*reservoir* (2) ... NC-3
Jones Lake—*reservoir* ... OH-6
Jones Lake—*reservoir* ... SC-3
Jones Lake—*reservoir* (2) ... SD-7
Jones Lake—*reservoir* ... TN-4
Jones Lake—*reservoir* (2) ... TX-5
Jones Lake—*reservoir* ... VA-3
Jones Lake—*swamp* ... LA-4
Jones Lake—*swamp* ... MN-6
Jones Lake Bay—*swamp* ... NC-3
Jones Lake Canyon—*valley* ... CO-8
Jones Lake Dam—*dam* (6) ... MS-4
Jones Lake Dam—*dam* (2) ... NC-3
Jones Lake Dam—*dam* (2) ... SD-7
Jones Lake Lookout Tower—*locale* ... NC-3
Jones Lakes—*reservoir* ... GA-3
Jones Lake Spring—*spring* ... CO-8
Jones Lake State Park—*park* ... NC-3
*Jones Land* ... DE-2
*Jones Landing* ... AL-4
*Jones Landing* ... MS-4
Jones Landing—*locale* ... LA-4
Jones Landing—*locale* ... MD-2
Jones Landing—*locale* ... NC-3
Jones Landing—*locale* (2) ... VA-3
**Jones Landing**—*pop pl* ... FL-3
Jones Lane Branch—*stream* ... KY-4
Jones Lateral—*canal* ... CO-8
Jones Lateral—*canal* ... ID-8
Jones Lateral—*canal* ... NM-5
Jones & Laughlin Steel Corporation—*facility* ... IL-6
Jones Lava—*lava* ... OR-9
Jones Law Sch—*school* ... AL-4
Jones Ledge—*bar* ... ME-1
Jones Ledge—*bench* ... RI-1
Jones-Lee House—*building* ... NC-3
Jones-Lee House—*hist pl* ... NC-3
Jones Marsh—*swamp* ... ME-1
Jones Meadow—*flat* ... CA-9
Jones Meadow—*flat* ... MT-8
Jones Meadow—*flat* ... NC-3
Jones Meadow—*flat* ... TN-4
*Jones Meadows* ... CA-9
Jones Memorial African Methodist Episcopal Zion Ch—*church* ... TN-4
Jones Memorial Cem—*cemetery* ... MS-4
Jones Memorial Ch—*church* ... AL-4
Jones Memorial Ch—*church* (2) ... GA-3
Jones Memorial Ch—*church* ... TN-4
Jones Memorial Chapel—*church* ... FL-3
Jones Memorial Library—*hist pl* ... VA-3
Jones Memorial Park—*cemetery* ... MS-4
Jones Memorial Park—*park* ... IA-7
Jones Memorial Presbyterian Ch—*church* ... MS-4
Jones Memorial United Methodist Ch—*church* ... TN-4
Jones Mesa—*summit* ... AZ-5
*Jones Mill* ... AL-4
*Jones Mill* ... AR-4
*Jones Mill* ... NC-3
*Jones Mill* ... TN-4
Jones Mill—*locale* ... AL-4
Jones Mill—*locale* ... KY-4
Jones Mill—*locale* (2) ... ME-1
Jones Mill—*locale* (2) ... NJ-2
Jones Mill—*locale* ... NC-3
Jones Mill—*locale* ... VA-3
**Jones Mill**—*pop pl* ... ME-1
**Jones Mill**—*pop pl* ... MS-4
**Jones Mill**—*pop pl* ... TN-4
Jones Mill Branch—*stream* ... DE-2
Jones Mill Cem—*cemetery* ... GA-3
Jones Mill Creek—*stream* ... FL-3
Jones Mill (historical)—*locale* (2) ... AL-4
Jones Mill (historical)—*locale* (2) ... GA-3
Jones Mill (historical)—*locale* (3) ... MS-4
Jones Mill (historical)—*locale* ... NC-3
Jones Mill (historical)—*locale* ... PA-2
Jones Mill (historical)—*locale* ... TN-4
*Jones Mill (Jones Mills)* ... AR-4
Jones Millpond—*lake* ... PA-2
Jones Mill Pond—*lake* ... VT-1
Jones Millpond—*lake* ... VA-3
Jones Millpond—*locale* ... GA-3
Jones Millpond—*reservoir* ... GA-3
Jones Millpond—*reservoir* ... NC-3
Jones Millpond—*reservoir* ... VA-3
Jones Mill Post Office (historical)—*building* ... TN-4
Jones Mill Run—*stream* ... PA-2
Jones Mill Run Hist Dist—*hist pl* ... WV-2
*Jones Mills* ... TN-4
**Jones Mills**—*pop pl* ... AR-4
**Jones Mills**—*pop pl* ... PA-2
Jones Mills (historical)—*locale* ... MS-4
Jones Mill Site (3HS28)—*hist pl* ... AR-4
**Jones Mills (Jones Mill)**—*pop pl* ... AR-4
*Jones Mills Post Office* ... TN-4
Jones Mine—*mine* ... CA-9
Jones Mine—*mine* ... CO-8
Jones Mine—*mine* (2) ... NM-5
Jones Mine—*mine* (2) ... TN-4
Jones Mine—*mine* ... UT-8
Jones Mine (underground)—*mine* ... AL-4
Jones Mound—*summit* ... AK-9
Jones Mound—*summit* ... TX-5
Jones Mountain Tank—*reservoir* ... AZ-5
Jones Mountain Trail—*trail* ... VA-3
Jones MS—*school* ... TX-5
*Jones Mtn* ... GA-3
*Jones Mtn* ... MA-1
Jones Mtn—*summit* ... AL-4
Jones Mtn—*summit* (3) ... AZ-5
Jones Mtn—*summit* (3) ... AR-4
Jones Mtn—*summit* ... CA-9
Jones Mtn—*summit* (2) ... CO-8
Jones Mtn—*summit* ... CT-1
Jones Mtn—*summit* (2) ... GA-3
Jones Mtn—*summit* ... MT-8
Jones Mtn—*summit* (3) ... NY-2
Jones Mtn—*summit* (3) ... NC-3
Jones Mtn—*summit* ... PA-2
Jones Mtn—*summit* (2) ... TN-4
Jones Mtn—*summit* ... TX-5
Jones Mtn—*summit* ... VT-1
Jones Mtn—*summit* (3) ... VA-3
Jones Mtn—*summit* ... WV-2
Jones Narrows—*stream* ... GA-3
*Jone's Neck* ... ME-1
Jones Neck—*cape* ... ME-1
Jones Neck—*cape* ... VA-3
Jones Neck Cutoff—*bend* ... VA-3
*Jones New Church* ... TN-4
Jones North Ditch—*canal* ... WY-8
Jones North Well—*well* ... NM-5
Jones Nose—*cliff* ... MA-1
Jones Number 2 Pump—*other* ... OR-9
Jones Old River—*lake* ... LA-4
Jones Park—*flat* ... AZ-5
Jones Park—*flat* (2) ... CO-8
Jones Park—*park* ... AZ-5
Jones Park—*park* ... CA-9
Jones Park—*park* (2) ... IL-6
Jones Park—*park* (2) ... MA-1
Jones Park—*park* ... MI-6
Jones Park—*park* ... NC-3
Jones Park—*park* ... OH-6
Jones Park—*park* ... TX-5
Jones Park—*park* (2) ... WI-6
Jones Park—*uninc pl* ... LA-4
Jones Pass—*gap* ... AK-9
Jones Pass—*gap* ... CO-8
Jones Pass—*gap* ... WY-8
Jones Pass Trail—*trail* ... WY-8
*Jones Pass Tunnel* ... CO-8
Jones Peak—*summit* ... AZ-5
Jones Peak—*summit* ... CO-8
Jones Peak—*summit* ... KY-4
Jones Peak—*summit* ... NM-5
Jones Peak—*summit* ... TX-5
Jones Pit—*basin* ... WA-9
Jones Place—*locale* ... CA-9
Jones Playground—*park* ... OH-6
Jones Pocosin—*swamp* ... NC-3
*Jonespoint* ... NY-2
*Jone's Point* ... VA-3
Jones Point—*cape* ... AK-9
Jones Point—*cape* ... AR-4
Jones Point—*cape* ... CA-9
Jones Point—*cape* (3) ... FL-3
Jones Point—*cape* ... LA-4
Jones Point—*cape* (2) ... ME-1
Jones Point—*cape* ... MD-2
Jones Point—*cape* ... NE-7
Jones Point—*cape* ... NJ-2
Jones Point—*cape* (2) ... NY-2
Jones Point—*cape* ... TN-4
Jones Point—*cape* (3) ... VA-3
Jones Point—*cape* ... WI-6
Jones Point—*cliff* ... AZ-5
**Jones Point**—*pop pl* (2) ... NY-2
Jones Point Lighthouse and District of Columbia South Cornerstone—*hist pl* ... VA-3
Jones Point Lookout—*locale* ... CA-9
*Jones Pond* ... MA-1
*Jones Pond* ... NH-1
*Jones Pond* ... PA-2
*Jones Pond* ... SC-3
*Jones Pond* ... VA-3
Jones Pond—*lake* ... CT-1
Jones Pond—*lake* ... DE-2
Jones Pond—*lake* (3) ... FL-3
Jones Pond—*lake* (4) ... GA-3
Jones Pond—*lake* (5) ... ME-1
Jones Pond—*lake* (3) ... MA-1
Jones Pond—*lake* ... MI-6
Jones Pond—*lake* (5) ... NY-2
Jones Pond—*lake* ... OR-9
Jones Pond—*lake* ... TN-4
Jones Pond—*lake* ... VT-1
Jones Pond—*lake* (2) ... VA-3
Jones Pond—*reservoir* ... AL-4
Jones Pond—*reservoir* ... AZ-5
Jones Pond—*reservoir* ... MA-1
Jones Pond—*reservoir* (4) ... NC-3
Jones Pond—*reservoir* (2) ... SC-3
Jones Pond—*reservoir* ... VA-3
Jones Pond Dam—*dam* ... MA-1
Jones Pond Dam—*dam* (3) ... NC-3
**Jonesport**—*pop pl* ... ME-1
Jones Portal—*mine* ... PA-2
Jonesport Center (census name Jonesport)—*other* ... ME-1
**Jonesport (Town of)**—*pop pl* ... ME-1
Jones Post Office (historical)—*building* ... TN-4
Jones Prairie—*flat* ... CA-9
Jones Prairie—*flat* ... TX-5
Jones Prairie—*locale* ... TX-5
Jones Prairie Sch—*school* ... CA-9
Jones-Price Cem—*cemetery* ... NC-3
Jones Prospect—*mine* ... TN-4
Jones Pup Creek—*stream* ... AK-9
Jones Quarry—*mine* ... AZ-5
Jones Quarry—*mine* ... TN-4
Jones Quarry Creek—*stream* ... IL-6
Jones Ranch—*locale* (2) ... AZ-5
Jones Ranch—*locale* ... CA-9
Jones Ranch—*locale* (2) ... CO-8
Jones Ranch—*locale* ... ID-8
Jones Ranch—*locale* ... MT-8
Jones Ranch—*locale* (4) ... NM-5
Jones Ranch—*locale* ... OR-9
Jones Ranch—*locale* ... SD-7
Jones Ranch—*locale* (5) ... TX-5
Jones Ranch—*locale* (3) ... WY-8
Jones Ranch Creek—*stream* ... UT-8
Jones Ranch HQ—*locale* ... NM-5
Jones Ranch Sch—*school* ... NM-5
Jones Ravine—*valley* ... CA-9
Jones-Read-Touvelle House—*hist pl* ... OH-6
Jones Rice Mill Branch—*stream* ... FL-3
*Jones Ridge* ... OR-9
**Jones Ridge**—*pop pl* ... IL-6
Jones Ridge—*ridge* ... AL-4
Jones Ridge—*ridge* ... AK-9
Jones Ridge—*ridge* ... AZ-5
Jones Ridge—*ridge* (2) ... AR-4
Jones Ridge—*ridge* (2) ... CA-9
Jones Ridge—*ridge* (3) ... KY-4
Jones Ridge—*ridge* ... OK-5
Jones Ridge—*ridge* (5) ... TN-4
Jones Ridge—*ridge* ... UT-8
Jones Ridge—*ridge* ... VA-3
Jones Ridge—*ridge* (2) ... WA-9
Jones Ridge—*ridge* ... WV-2
Jones Ridge Cem—*cemetery* ... AR-4
Jones Ridge Sch—*school* ... KY-4
*Jones' River* ... MA-1
Jones River—*stream* ... AK-9
Jones River—*stream* (2) ... MA-1
*Jones River Brook* ... MA-1
Jones River Brook—*stream* ... MA-1
Jones River Marshes—*swamp* (2) ... MA-1
*Jones-river Pond* ... MA-1
Jones River Rsvr—*reservoir* ... MA-1
Jones River Shipyard—*locale* ... MA-1
Jones River Wapping Road Dam—*dam* ... MA-1
Jones Road Ch—*church* ... FL-3
Jones Road Ch—*church* ... TN-4
Jones Road Hist Dist—*hist pl* ... NY-2
Jones-Roberts Farmstead—*hist pl* ... MN-6
Jones Rock—*bar* ... VT-1
Jones Rock—*bar* ... WA-9
Jones Rocks—*island* ... CT-1
Jones Rsvr—*reservoir* ... ID-8
Jones Rsvr—*reservoir* (3) ... MT-8
Jones Rsvr—*reservoir* ... OR-9
Jones Rsvr—*reservoir* ... TX-5
Jones Rsvr—*reservoir* ... UT-8
Jones Rsvr—*reservoir* (2) ... WY-8
Jones Rsvr Number One—*reservoir* ... OR-9
Jones Ruby Mine—*mine* ... NC-3
*Jones Run* ... PA-2
Jones Run—*stream* ... IN-6
Jones Run—*stream* ... NE-7
Jones Run—*stream* ... OH-6
Jones Run—*stream* (6) ... PA-2
Jones Run—*stream* (4) ... VA-3
Jones Run—*stream* (3) ... WV-2
Jones Sch—*hist pl* ... AR-4
Jones Sch—*school* ... AL-4
Jones Sch—*school* ... AR-4
Jones Sch—*school* ... CA-9
Jones Sch—*school* ... CT-1
Jones Sch—*school* ... DE-2
Jones Sch—*school* ... FL-3
Jones Sch—*school* (3) ... GA-3
Jones Sch—*school* (8) ... IL-6
Jones Sch—*school* ... IA-7
Jones Sch—*school* (3) ... KY-4
Jones Sch—*school* (2) ... LA-4
Jones Sch—*school* (2) ... MA-1
Jones Sch—*school* (6) ... MI-6
Jones Sch—*school* (5) ... MS-4
Jones Sch—*school* ... MO-7
Jones Sch—*school* (2) ... NC-3
Jones Sch—*school* (2) ... OH-6
Jones Sch—*school* ... OK-5
Jones Sch—*school* ... OR-9
Jones Sch—*school* ... PA-2
Jones Sch—*school* (2) ... SC-3
Jones Sch—*school* (2) ... SD-7
Jones Sch—*school* (2) ... TN-4
Jones Sch—*school* (6) ... TX-5
Jones Sch—*school* (3) ... VA-3
Jones Sch—*school* ... WV-2

Jones Sch—school (2) WI-6
Jones Sch (abandoned)—school MO-7
Jones Sch (historical)—school (8) AL-4
Jones Sch (historical)—school (2) MS-4
Jones Sch (historical)—school MO-7
Jones Sch (historical)—school PA-2
Jones Sch (historical)—school (8) TN-4
Jones School IN-6
Jones School KS-7
Joness Creek DE-2
Jones Seep Well—well AZ-5
Jones Settlement—locale GA-3
Jones Shaft—mine UT-8
Jones Shed Ch—church TN-4
Jones-Sherman House—hist pl OR-9
Jones Shoals—bar (2) TN-4
Jones Shop Ctr—locale MS-4
Jones Siding—locale NJ-2
Jones Siding—pop pl IA-7
Joness Land DE-2
Jones Slough—gut (2) WI-6
Jones Slough—stream AL-4
Jones Slough—stream TN-4
Jones South Ditch—canal WY-8
Jones Spring KS-7
Jones Spring—spring AZ-5
Jones Spring—spring GA-3
Jones Spring—spring ID-8
Jones Spring—spring (3) MO-7
Jones Spring—spring (2) NV-8
Jones Spring—spring (2) OR-9
Jones Spring—spring SD-7
Jones Spring—spring (3) TN-4
Jones Spring—spring TX-5
Jones Spring—spring UT-8
Jones Spring—spring WI-6
Jones Spring—spring WY-8
Jones Spring Draw—valley NM-5
Jones Spring Impoundment—reservoir WI-6
Jones Spring Point—summit NV-8
Jones Spring Ranch—locale NM-5
**Jones Springs**—pop pl WV-2
Jones Springs—spring AZ-5
Jones Springs—spring NV-8
Jones Springs—spring OR-9
Jones Springs—spring WY-8
Jones Springs (historical)—locale NC-3
Jones Spring Wash—stream NV-8
Jones Spur—ridge KY-4
Jones Square—park NY-2
Jones State For—forest VT-1
Jones Station GA-3
Jones Station IN-6
Jones Station TN-4
Jones Station—other TN-4
Jones Station (historical)—locale PA-2
Jones Station Post Office TN-4
Jones Store—locale (2) VA-3
**Jones Store**—pop pl VA-3
Jones Store (historical)—locale AL-4
Jones Store (historical)—locale (2) TN-4
Jones Street Cem—cemetery CT-1
Jones Street JHS—school LA-4
Jones Street Pond—lake CT-1
Jones Street Residential Hist
Dist—hist pl GA-3
Jones Street Sch—school GA-3
**Jones Subdivision**—pop pl MS-4
**Jones Subdivision**—pop pl (3) UT-8
Jones Summit—summit CO-8
Jones Swamp NC-3
Jones Swamp VA-3
Jones Swamp—stream NC-3
Jones Swamp—stream (2) SC-3
Jones Swamp—stream (2) VA-3
Jones Swamp—swamp FL-3
Jones Switch AL-4
Jones Tabernacle—church NC-3
Jonestand Ditch—canal KY-4
Jones Tank—reservoir (9) AZ-5
Jones Tank—reservoir (6) NM-5
Jones Tank—reservoir (5) TX-5
Jones Tanks—reservoir NM-5
Jones Tanks—reservoir TX-5
Jones Tavern—hist pl MA-1
Jones Temple—church GA-3
Jones Temple—church NC-3
**Jones Terrace**—pop pl PA-2
Jones Top Creek—stream VA-3
Jonestown MS-4
Jonestown—locale KY-4
Jonestown—locale MD-2
Jonestown—locale (2) OH-6
Jonestown—locale TN-4
Jonestown—locale VA-3
**Jonestown**—pop pl IN-6
**Jonestown**—pop pl (2) MD-2
**Jonestown**—pop pl (4) MS-4
**Jonestown**—pop pl (2) NC-3
**Jonestown**—pop pl (4) PA-2
**Jonestown**—pop pl SC-3
**Jonestown**—pop pl TX-5
Jonestown Borough—civil PA-2
Jonestown Cem—cemetery TN-4
Jonestown Cem—cemetery TX-5
Jonestown Cut-Off—channel MS-4
Jonestown Elem Sch—school PA-2
**Jonestown (historical)**—pop pl TN-4
Jonestown MS—school MS-4
Jonestown Post Office
(historical)—building TN-4
Jones Township—civil KS-7
Jones Township—fmr MCD IA-7
**Jones Township**—pop pl SD-7
Jones (Township of)—fmr MCD (4) AR-4
**Jones (Township of)**—pop pl MN-6
**Jones (Township of)**—pop pl PA-2
**Jonestown (sta.) (West
Jonestown)**—pop pl PA-2
Jones Trail—trail PA-2
Jones Trail—trail VA-3
Jones Training Sch—school TN-4
Jones Troughs—spring OR-9
Jones Twist—stream CO-8
Jones Valley—basin (2) CA-9
Jones Valley—basin NE-7
Jones Valley—bend TX-5
**Jones Valley**—pop pl AL-4
**Jones Valley**—pop pl TN-4
Jones Valley—valley (4) AL-4
Jones Valley—valley AR-4
Jones Valley—valley (3) CA-9
Jones Valley—valley TX-5
Jones Valley—valley (4) WI-6
Jones Valley Campground—locale CA-9
Jones Valley Cem—cemetery TN-4
Jones Valley Ch—church NC-3
Jones Valley Ch—church TX-5
Jones Valley Elementary School AL-4
**Jones Valley Estates**—pop pl AL-4
Jones Valley HS—school AL-4
Jones Valley Post Office
(historical)—building TN-4
Jones Valley Recreation Center—park AL-4
Jones Valley Sch—school AL-4
Jones Vane Creek—stream AL-4
**Jonesview**—pop pl AL-4
Jones View Ch—church NC-3
Jonesview Elementary School AL-4
Jones View Sch—school AL-4
Jonesville AL-4
Jonesville AZ-5
Jonesville—locale AL-4
Jonesville—locale FL-3
Jonesville—locale GA-3
Jonesville—locale MD-2
Jonesville—locale PA-2
Jonesville—locale (2) TN-4
Jonesville—locale TX-5
**Jonesville**—pop pl AK-9
**Jonesville**—pop pl AR-4
**Jonesville**—pop pl CA-9
**Jonesville**—pop pl IL-6
**Jonesville**—pop pl IN-6
**Jonesville**—pop pl (2) KY-4
**Jonesville**—pop pl LA-4
**Jonesville**—pop pl (2) MI-6
**Jonesville**—pop pl NY-2
**Jonesville**—pop pl NC-3
**Jonesville**—pop pl (2) SC-3
**Jonesville**—pop pl VT-1
**Jonesville**—pop pl VA-3
Jonesville Acad—hist pl VT-1
Jonesville Baptist Ch—church FL-3
Jonesville Bridge—other MI-6
**Jonesville Camp Ground**—pop pl VA-3
Jonesville (CCD)—cens area SC-3
Jonesville Cem—cemetery KY-4
Jonesville Cem—cemetery TX-5
Jonesville Ch—church FL-3
Jonesville Ch—church SC-3
Jonesville Creek—stream NC-3
Jonesville Elem Sch—school NC-3
Jonesville Golf Course Lake—reservoir NC-3
Jonesville Golf Course Lake Dam—dam NC-3
Jonesville (historical)—locale AL-4
Jonesville (Magisterial District)—fmr MCD VA-3
Jonesville Methodist
Campground—hist pl VA-3
Jonesville Park—park VA-3
Jonesville Post Office TN-4
Jonesville Sch—school KY-4
Jonesville Sch—school TX-5
Jonesville Sch—school WI-6
Jonesville School (Abandoned)—locale IL-6
**Jonesville (subdivision)**—pop pl AL-4
Jonesville Zion Ch—church NC-3
Jones Warehouses—hist pl RI-1
Jones Wash—arroyo AZ-5
Jones Water Campground—park AZ-5
Jones Water Spring—spring AZ-5
Jones Well—locale (4) NM-5
Jones Well—well (3) AZ-5
Jones Well—well (5) NM-5
Jones Well—well OR-9
Jones Well—well (2) TX-5
Jones Well—well UT-8
Jones Well Guard Station—locale OR-9
Jones Wendell Well—well ID-8
Jones West Central Sch—school SD-7
Jones Wharf—locale ME-1
Jones Wheat Sch—school GA-3
Jones-Willis House—hist pl KY-4
Jones Windmill—locale (3) NM-5
Jones Windmill—locale TX-5
Jones Wood Sch (historical)—school AL-4
Jones Gulch—valley CO-8
Joney Branch—stream KY-4
Jongejeugd Sch (historical)—school SD-7
Jon Gulch—valley MT-8
Jon Hill—ridge CA-9
Jonhs Creek SC-3
Jonica Gap—gap GA-3
**Jonican**—pop pl KY-4
Jonican Bayou—stream MS-4
Jonican Branch—stream KY-4
Jonive Sch—school CA-9
Jonkin Knob TN-4
Jonnican Branch—stream VA-3
Jonnies Branch—stream WV-2
Jonnies Well—well NM-5
Jonnie Tank—reservoir NM-5
Jonnie Tanks—reservoir NM-5
Jonnikin Creek—stream VA-3
Jonnum Mines—mine MO-7
Jonny Hollow—valley KY-4
Jonny Mine—mine NV-8
**Jonny Smith Subdivision**—pop pl AL-4
Jonquil—locale AR-4
**Jonsee**—pop pl KY-4
Jon S Flat—flat NM-5
Jon S Mountain Tank—reservoir NM-5
Jon S Mtn—summit NM-5
Jon S Tank—reservoir NM-5
Jon Tank—reservoir NM-5
Jont Creek—stream OR-9
Jont Stream—stream ME-1
Jonvick Creek—stream MN-6
Jonys Valley—valley WI-6
J.O. Pass—gap CA-9
Jopic Sch—school TN-4
Joplin—locale AR-4
Joplin—locale TX-5
Joplin—locale VA-3
**Joplin**—pop pl MO-7
**Joplin**—pop pl MT-8
**Joplin**—pop pl WV-2
Joplin, Scott, House—hist pl MO-7
Joplin Branch—stream SC-3
Joplin Branch—stream WV-2
Joplin Carnegie Library—hist pl MO-7
Joplin Cem—cemetery IL-6
Joplin Cem—cemetery MO-7
Joplin Connor Hotel—hist pl MO-7
Joplin Creek—stream MO-7
Jopling Cemetery TN-4
Jopling Mine—mine MI-6
**Joplin (historical)**—pop pl MS-4
Joplin Hole—bend TX-5
Joplin Hollow—valley TN-4
Joplin Junior Coll—school MO-7
Joplin Mill Branch—stream SC-3
Joplin Mine—mine AZ-5
Joplin Municipal Airp—airport (2) MO-7
Joplin Rec Area—park AR-4
Joplin Ridge—ridge NM-5
Joplin Sch (historical)—school MS-4
Joplins Mill (historical)—locale MS-4
Joplin Township—civil MO-7
Joplin Trail—trail CA-9
Joplin Truck Trail—trail CA-9
Joplin Union Depot—hist pl MO-7
Joplor—locale NC-3
Joppa AZ-5
Joppa—locale KY-4
Joppa—locale MT-8
Joppa—locale TN-4
Joppa—locale TX-5
Joppa—locale WV-2
**Joppa**—pop pl AL-4
**Joppa**—pop pl IL-6
**Joppa**—pop pl IN-6
**Joppa**—pop pl MD-2
**Joppa**—pop pl MI-6
**Joppa**—pop pl NC-3
**Joppa**—pop pl OH-6
**Joppa**—pop pl TN-4
Joppa Cem—cemetery FL-3
Joppa Cem—cemetery TN-4
Joppa (census name
Joppatowne)—uninc pl MD-2
Joppa Ch—church AL-4
Joppa Ch—church FL-3
Joppa Ch—church (2) KY-4
Joppa Ch—church VA-3
Joppa Creek—stream AL-4
Joppa Elem Sch—school TN-4
Joppa Flats—flat MA-1
**Joppa Heights**—pop pl MD-2
Joppa Hill—summit NH-1
Joppa JHS—school AL-4
Joppa Junction—locale IL-6
Joppa Lake—lake FL-3
**Joppa Manor**—pop pl MD-2
Joppa Mill—locale VA-3
Joppa Post Office—building AL-4
Joppa Post Office (historical)—building TN-4
Joppa Ridge—ridge KY-4
Joppa Sch—school TN-4
**Joppa Springs**—pop pl MD-2
**Joppa (subdivision)**—pop pl MA-1
**Joppatowne**—pop pl MD-2
Joppatowne (census name for
Joppa)—CDP MD-2
Joppa United Mthodist Ch—church TN-4
Joppa Village MA-1
Jopp Bridge—other MI-6
Jopp Cem—cemetery NE-7
Jopp Lake—lake MN-6
Jops Harbor—bay AZ-5
Jops Landing AZ-5
Jops Landing—locale AZ-5
Jopuna MP-9
Jopuna—island MP-9
Jopuna Island MP-9
Joque Sch—school MI-6
**Joquin**—pop pl (2) AL-4
Joquin Ch—church AL-4
Joquin Sch (historical)—school AL-4
J O Ranch—locale WY-8
Jordan AL-4
Jordan IN-6
Jordan MS-4
Jordan PA-2
Jordan WI-6
Jordan—locale AR-4
Jordan—locale GA-3
Jordan—locale KY-4
Jordan—locale MI-6
Jordan—locale MN-6
Jordan—locale MO-7
Jordan—locale NM-5
Jordan—locale NC-3
Jordan—locale (2) OR-9
Jordan—locale TX-5
Jordan—locale WA-9
Jordan—locale WV-2
Jordan—locale WI-6
**Jordan**—pop pl (3) AL-4
**Jordan**—pop pl ID-8
**Jordan**—pop pl (2) IN-6
**Jordan**—pop pl IA-7
**Jordan**—pop pl MN-6
**Jordan**—pop pl MT-8
**Jordan**—pop pl NY-2
**Jordan**—pop pl NC-3
**Jordan**—pop pl (2) SC-3
**Jordan**—pop pl UT-8
Jordan, Arthur, Memorial Hall—hist pl IN-6
Jordan, Charles A., House—hist pl ME-1
Jordan, Joseph, House—hist pl VA-3
Jordan, Lake—lake FL-3
Jordan, Marion Jasper, Farm—hist pl NC-3
Jordan, Mount—summit CA-9
Jordan, Mount—summit ID-8
Jordan, Newton, House—hist pl TN-4
Jordan, Orin, House—hist pl CA-9
Jordan, Thomas, Polygonal Barn—hist pl IA-7
Jordan Acres Sch—school ME-1
**Jordan Addition (vacated)**—pop pl UT-8
Jordan and Salt Lake City Canal—canal UT-8
Jordan Area Park—park MN-6
Jordan Artesian Well—well AL-4
Jordan Bailey Cem—cemetery MS-4
Jordan Bank Hopewell Elem Sch—school PA-2
Jordan Basin—basin WA-9
Jordan Bay—bay ME-1
Jordan Bay—bay VT-1
Jordan Bay—swamp FL-3
Jordan Bay—swamp GA-3
Jordan Bayou—gut LA-4
Jordan Bayou—stream MS-4
Jordan Beach—beach ME-1
Jordan-Bellew House—hist pl GA-3
Jordan Branch AL-4
Jordan Branch IN-6
Jordan Branch MS-4
Jordan Branch NC-3
Jordan Branch—stream (4) AL-4
Jordan Branch—stream (2) AR-4
Jordan Branch—stream DE-2
Jordan Branch—stream (3) GA-3
Jordan Branch—stream IN-6
Jordan Branch—stream KS-7
Jordan Branch—stream (3) KY-4
Jordan Branch—stream LA-4
Jordan Branch—stream (8) MO-7
Jordan Branch—stream (2) NC-3
Jordan Branch—stream (2) SC-3
Jordan Branch—stream (3) TN-4
Jordan Branch—stream TX-5
Jordan Branch—stream VA-3
Jordan Brewery Ruins—hist pl MN-6
Jordan Bridge—locale PA-2
Jordan Bridge (Toll)—bridge VA-3
Jordan Brook VA-3
Jordan Brook—stream (3) CT-1
Jordan Brook—stream (4) ME-1
Jordan Brook—stream NH-1
Jordan Brook—stream NJ-2
Jordan Butte—summit (2) OR-9
Jordan Canal—canal MS-4
Jordan Canyon—valley AZ-5
Jordan Canyon—valley (3) NM-5
Jordan Canyon—valley (2) OR-9
Jordan Canyon—valley UT-8
Jordan Canyon—valley WY-8
Jordan Cove—cave (2) AL-4
Jordan (CCD)—cens area OR-9
Jordan Cem MS-4
Jordan Cem—cemetery (8) AL-4
Jordan Cem—cemetery (3) AR-4
Jordan Cem—cemetery CT-1
Jordan Cem—cemetery FL-3
Jordan Cem—cemetery GA-3
Jordan Cem—cemetery (2) IL-6
Jordan Cem—cemetery (3) IN-6
Jordan Cem—cemetery (2) IA-7
Jordan Cem—cemetery KS-7
Jordan Cem—cemetery (2) KY-4
Jordan Cem—cemetery LA-4
Jordan Cem—cemetery (2) ME-1
Jordan Cem—cemetery (5) MS-4
Jordan Cem—cemetery NE-7
Jordan Cem—cemetery OK-5
Jordan Cem—cemetery PA-2
Jordan Cem—cemetery (3) TN-4
Jordan Cem—cemetery (2) TX-5
Jordan Cem—cemetery WV-2
Jordan Center—locale IL-6
Jordan Center—locale WI-6
Jordan Ch AL-4
Jordan Ch—church (2) AL-4
Jordan Ch—church (3) GA-3
Jordan Ch—church IL-6
Jordan Ch—church IN-6
Jordan Ch—church MS-4
Jordan Ch—church PA-2
Jordan Ch—church (5) SC-3
Jordan Ch—church VA-3
Jordan Ch—church WV-2
Jordan Ch—church WI-6
Jordan Chapel—church AL-4
Jordan Chapel—church FL-3
Jordan Chapel—church (2) GA-3
Jordan Chapel—church IL-6
Jordan Chapel—church WV-2
Jordan Chapel Cem—cemetery IL-6
Jordan Chapel Ch AL-4
Jordan Chapel Church MS-4
Jordan City—uninc pl GA-3
Jordan Coulee—valley MT-8
Jordan Cove—bay CT-1
Jordan Cove—bay OR-9
Jordan Craters—crater OR-9
Jordan Creek IL-6
Jordan Creek MT-8
Jordan Creek TX-5
Jordan Creek WI-6
**Jordan Creek**—pop pl OR-9
Jordan Creek—stream (3) AL-4
Jordan Creek—stream (2) AK-9
Jordan Creek—stream (4) AR-4
Jordan Creek—stream (6) CA-9
Jordan Creek—stream GA-3
Jordan Creek—stream (4) ID-8
Jordan Creek—stream (8) IL-6
Jordan Creek—stream (8) IN-6
Jordan Creek—stream (9) IA-7
Jordan Creek—stream (3) KS-7
Jordan Creek—stream (2) LA-4
Jordan Creek—stream MI-6
Jordan Creek—stream MN-6
Jordan Creek—stream (4) MS-4
Jordan Creek—stream (7) MO-7
Jordan Creek—stream MT-8
Jordan Creek—stream (4) NE-7
Jordan Creek—stream (5) NC-3
Jordan Creek—stream (2) OH-6
Jordan Creek—stream (11) OR-9
Jordan Creek—stream PA-2
Jordan Creek—stream (5) SC-3
Jordan Creek—stream TN-4
Jordan Creek—stream (5) TX-5
Jordan Creek—stream VA-3
Jordan Creek—stream (6) WA-9
Jordan Creek—stream WV-2
Jordan Creek—stream (2) WI-6
Jordan Creek—stream (3) WY-8
Jordan Creek Campground—locale ID-8
Jordan Creek Canyon—valley OR-9
Jordan Creek Cem—cemetery IL-6
Jordan Creek Ch—church KS-7
Jordan Creek Trail—trail WA-9
Jordan Crossing—locale MT-8
Jordan Cutoff Trail—trail OR-9
Jordan Dam—dam AL-4
Jordan Ditch—canal AL-4
Jordan Ditch—canal CO-8
Jordan Ditch—canal (2) IN-6
Jordan Drain MI-6
Jordan Drain—canal MI-6
Jordan Drain—canal OR-9
Jordan Drane Church MS-4
Jordan Draw—valley CO-8
Jordan Draw—valley WY-8
**Jordanelle**—pop pl UT-8
Jordan Ferry—locale LA-4
Jordan Flat—flat (4) CA-9
Jordan Fork—stream (2) KY-4
Jordan Fork—stream WV-2
Jordan Gap—gap (2) AL-4
Jordan Gap—gap TX-5
**Jordan Green Subdivision**—pop pl UT-8
Jordan Grove Baptist Ch MS-4
Jordan Grove Baptist Ch—church MS-4
Jordan Grove Cem—cemetery IL-6
Jordan Grove Cem—cemetery MS-4
Jordan Grove Ch—church AL-4
Jordan Grove Ch—church (3) GA-3
Jordan Grove Ch—church (2) MS-4
Jordan Grove Ch—church NC-3
Jordan Guard Station—locale OR-9
Jordan Gulch—valley CO-8
Jordan Gully—valley TX-5
Jordan Harbor—bay ME-1
Jordan-Hare Stadium—park AL-4
Jordan Heights NY-2
Jordan Hill WA-9
**Jordan Hill**—pop pl LA-4
Jordan Hill—summit AL-4
Jordan Hill—summit CA-9
Jordan Hill—summit GA-3
Jordan Hill—summit IL-6
Jordan Hill—summit LA-4
Jordan Hill—summit (2) NH-1
Jordan Hill—summit NY-2
Jordan Hill Cem—cemetery MS-4
Jordan Hill Ch—church GA-3
Jordan Hill Ch—church (2) MS-4
Jordan Hill Ch—church NC-3
**Jordan Hills Estates
Subdivision**—pop pl UT-8
Jordan Hist Dist—hist pl MN-6
Jordan Hollow—other PA-2
Jordan Hollow—valley (2) MO-7
Jordan Hollow—valley (5) PA-2
Jordan Hollow—valley (4) TN-4
Jordan Hollow—valley TX-5
Jordan Hollow—valley (3) VA-3
Jordan Hollow Trail—trail PA-2
Jordan Hosp—hospital MA-1
Jordan Hot Springs—spring CA-9
Jordan House—hist pl IA-7
Jordan House—hist pl MS-4
Jordan House—hist pl NC-3
Jordan HS—hist pl UT-8
Jordan HS—school (2) CA-9
Jordan HS—school GA-3
Jordan HS—school MS-4
Jordan HS—school UT-8
Jordania SC-3
**Jordania**—pop pl SC-3
Jordan Island—island (2) ME-1
Jordan Island—island NC-3
Jordan JHS—school (2) CA-9
Jordan JHS—school MN-6
Jordan JHS—school UT-8
**Jordan Junction**—pop pl SD-7
Jordan Knob PA-2
Jordan Knob—summit TN-4
Jordan-Koch House—hist pl TX-5
Jordan Lake—lake AK-9
Jordan Lake—lake FL-3
Jordan Lake—lake LA-4
Jordan Lake—lake MI-6
Jordan Lake—lake MN-6
Jordan Lake—lake (2) MS-4
Jordan Lake—lake MT-8
Jordan Lake—lake NE-7
Jordan Lake—lake NY-2
Jordan Lake—lake OR-9
Jordan Lake—lake (3) SC-3
Jordan Lake—lake UT-8
Jordan Lake—lake (2) WI-6
Jordan Lake—reservoir (3) AL-4
Jordan Lake—reservoir MS-4
Jordan Lake Diversion—reservoir AL-4
Jordan Landing—locale AR-4
Jordan Lateral—canal AZ-5
Jordan Ledge—bench ME-1
Jordan Light Ch—church WV-2
Jordan Lookout Tower—locale AL-4
Jordan Lookout Tower—locale MI-6
Jordan-Matthews HS—school NC-3
Jordan Meadow—flat NV-8
Jordan Meadow Creek—stream NV-8
Jordan Meadow Flat—flat NV-8
Jordan Meadow Mtn—summit NV-8
Jordan Meadows Flat NV-8
**Jordan Meadows (subdivision)**—pop pl
(2) AZ-5
Jordan Mesa Tank—reservoir NM-5
Jordan Mill—locale SC-3
Jordan Millpond—lake GA-3
Jordan Millpond NC-3
Jordan Millpond—reservoir GA-3
**Jordan Mills**—pop pl ME-1
Jordan Mine—mine AZ-5
**Jordan Mines**—pop pl VA-3
Jordan Mtn—summit LA-4
Jordan Mtn—summit ME-1
Jordan Mtn—summit MT-8
Jordan Mtn—summit NC-3
Jordan Mtn—summit TX-5
Jordan Mundil Dam—dam SD-7
Jordan Narrows—gap UT-8
Jordan Number Four Mine—mine TN-4
**Jordan Oak (subdivision)**—pop pl NC-3
Jordan Outlet—channel NY-2
Jordan Park—park IN-6
Jordan Park—park PA-2
Jordan Park—park UT-8
**Jordan Park Apartments**—pop pl PA-2
Jordan Park Ch—church AL-4
Jordan Park Ch of Christ AL-4
**Jordan Park Subdivision**—pop pl UT-8
Jordan Pass—gap MT-8
Jordan Peak—summit CA-9
Jordan Pines Recreation Site—locale UT-8
Jordan Place—locale GA-3
**Jordan Place Subdivision**—pop pl UT-8
**Jordan (Pleasant Corners)**—pop pl PA-2
Jordan Point OR-9
Jordan Point—cape AL-4
Jordan Point—cape (3) ME-1
Jordan Point—cape OR-9
Jordan Point—cape VT-1
Jordan Point—cape VA-3
Jordan Point Country Club—other VA-3
**Jordan Point Subdivision**—pop pl UT-8
Jordan Pond—lake ME-1
Jordan Pond—lake MA-1
Jordan Pond—lake NY-2
Jordan Pond—lake SC-3
Jordan Pond—reservoir NC-3
Jordan Pond—reservoir WI-6
Jordan Pond Dam—dam NC-3
Jordan Ponds—lake WA-9
Jordan Private Cemetery AL-4
Jordan Ranch—locale AZ-5
Jordan Ranch—locale CA-9
Jordan Ranch—locale MT-8
Jordan Ranch—locale OR-9
Jordan Ranch—locale SD-7
Jordan Ranch—locale (2) WY-8
Jordan Recreation Center—other PA-2
Jordan Reef—bar ME-1
Jordan Reservoir AL-4
Jordan Ridge—ridge ME-1
Jordan Ridge—ridge NV-8
Jordan Ridge—ridge TN-4
Jordan Ridge Sch—school UT-8
Jordan River OR-9
Jordan River PA-2
Jordan River—stream ME-1
Jordan River—stream (2) MI-6
Jordan River—stream NY-2
Jordan River—stream UT-8
Jordan River—stream VA-3
Jordan River State Park—park UT-8
Jordan Rock House—pillar TN-4
Jordan Rsvr—reservoir MT-8
Jordan Rsvr—reservoir OR-9
Jordan Run—locale WV-2
Jordan Run—stream OH-6
Jordan Run—stream (3) PA-2
Jordan Run—stream (2) VA-3
Jordan Run—stream (2) WV-2
Jordans Bay AL-4
Jordans Branch—stream VA-3
Jordans Branch—stream WV-2
Jordans Cem—cemetery MS-4
Jordans Ch—church NC-3
Jordan Sch—hist pl ME-1
Jordan Sch—school (4) CA-9
Jordan Sch—school FL-3
Jordan Sch—school (3) IL-6
Jordan Sch—school IN-6
Jordan Sch—school (2) MI-6
Jordan Sch—school NE-7
Jordan Sch—school PA-2
Jordan Sch (abandoned)—school PA-2
Jordans Chapel—church VA-3
Jordan's Chapel—hist pl WV-2
Jordan Sch District Administration
Bldg—hist pl UT-8
Jordan Sch (historical)—school PA-2
Jordans Creek IL-6
Jordans Creek MS-4
Jordans Creek NC-3
Jordans Creek TX-5
Jordans Creek—stream IN-6
Jordans Creek—stream TX-5
Jordans Delight—island ME-1
Jordans Delight Ledge—bar ME-1
Jordan Seminary—school MI-6
Jordans Grove—locale IA-7
Jordans Siding—locale TN-4
Jordans Knob—summit PA-2
Jordans Lake—lake WI-6
Jordans Lake—reservoir NC-3
Jordans Lakes—reservoir GA-3
Jordans Landing—locale NC-3
Jordan Slough—gut FL-3
Jordan Slough—gut IL-6
Jordan Slough—stream IL-6
Jordans Mill—locale AL-4
Jordans Millpond—reservoir NC-3
Jordans Point OR-9
Jordan's Point VA-3
Jordan Spring—spring ID-8
Jordan Spring—spring (3) OR-9
Jordan Spring—spring (2) TN-4
Jordan Spring Branch—stream AL-4
Jordan Spring Branch—stream TN-4
Jordan Springs—locale VA-3
Jordan Springs Cem—cemetery TX-5
**Jordan Springs (historical)**—pop pl TN-4
Jordan Springs Post Office TN-4
Jordans Springs TN-4
Jordans Springs Post Office
(historical)—building TN-4
Jordans Store—locale NC-3
Jordans Store—locale TX-5
Jordans Store—locale VA-3
Jordans Store Post Office
(historical)—building TN-4
Jordans Swamp NC-3
Jordan Station Ch—church GA-3
Jordan Stream—stream ME-1
Jordan Street Assembly of God
Ch—church FL-3
Jordan Street Ch—church SC-3
Jordansville MA-1
Jordansville—locale MA-1
Jordan Swamp—stream NC-3
Jordan Swamp—swamp MD-2
Jordan Swamp—swamp WI-6
Jordan Tank—reservoir (2) NM-5
Jordan Tank—reservoir TX-5
Jordan Temple Ch—church LA-4
Jordan Top—summit VA-3
**Jordantown**—pop pl NJ-2
Jordantown Cem—cemetery NJ-2
**Jordan (Town of)**—pop pl WI-6
Jordan Township—civil (2) MO-7
Jordan Township—civil PA-2
Jordan Township—fmr MCD IA-7
Jordan Township—obs name ND-7

**Jordan Township**—pop pl .... SD-7
**Jordan (Township of)**—pop pl .... IL-6
**Jordan (Township of)**—pop pl (2) .... IN-6
**Jordan (Township of)**—pop pl .... MI-6
**Jordan (Township of)**—pop pl .... MN-6
**Jordan (Township of)**—pop pl (3) .... PA-2
Jordan Trail—trail .... PA-2
Jordan Valley .... UT-8
Jordan Valley—locale .... PA-2
**Jordan Valley**—pop pl .... OR-9
Jordan Valley—valley (2) .... OR-9
Jordan Valley Baptist Ch—church .... UT-8
Jordan Valley Canal .... OR-9
Jordan Valley Memorial Park—cemetery .... TX-5
Jordan Valley Water Purification Dam—dam .... UT-8
Jordan Valley Water Purification Rsvr—reservoir .... UT-8
**Jordan View Estates Subdivision**—pop pl .... UT-8
Jordan Village .... IN-6
**Jordan Village**—pop pl .... CT-1
Jordan Village Hist Dist—hist pl .... NY-2
**Jordan Village Subdivision**—pop pl .... UT-8
Jordanville .... MA-1
**Jordanville**—pop pl .... NY-2
**Jordanville**—pop pl .... OH-6
**Jordanville**—pop pl .... SC-3
Jordanville Ch—church .... SC-3
Jordanville (historical P.O.)—locale .... IN-6
Jordanville Public Library—hist pl .... NY-2
Jordanville Sch—school .... IL-6
**Jordanville (subdivision)**—pop pl .... AL-4
Jordan Wash—stream .... AZ-5
**Jordan (Waterford Po)**—pop pl .... CT-1
Jordan Waterhole Rsvr—reservoir .... OR-9
Jordan W Chambers .... MO-7
Jordan Well—well .... AZ-5
Jordan-Williams House—hist pl .... TN-4
Jorden .... WA-9
**Jorden**—pop pl .... WA-9
Jorden Branch—stream (2) .... NC-3
Jorden Cem—cemetery .... MS-4
Jorden Creek .... TX-5
Jorden Creek .... WA-9
Jorden Hill—summit .... WA-9
Jorden Lake—lake .... MT-8
Jordens Chapel—church .... NC-3
Jordens Store .... TX-5
Jordon .... GA-3
**Jordon**—pop pl .... IN-6
Jordon, Col, Meltiah, House—hist pl .... ME-1
Jordon Bay .... ME-1
Jordon Branch—stream .... AR-4
Jordon Branch—stream .... VA-3
Jordon Cem—cemetery (2) .... IN-6
Jordon Core .... OR-9
Jordon Creek .... IL-6
Jordon Creek .... MS-4
Jordon Creek .... TX-5
Jordon Creek .... WA-9
Jordon Creek—stream .... AR-4
Jordon Creek—stream (2) .... IN-6
Jordon Creek—stream .... MI-6
Jordon Creek—stream .... OH-6
Jordon Creek—stream .... OR-9
Jordon Drain—canal .... MI-6
Jordon Drain—stream .... MI-6
Jordon Ferry—locale .... LA-4
Jordon Ferry Bridge—bridge .... LA-4
Jordon Gully—valley .... TX-5
Jordon Hill .... LA-4
Jordon Hill Cem—cemetery .... LA-4
Jordon Hollow .... PA-2
Jordon Hollow—valley .... MO-7
Jordon Hollow—valley .... TN-4
Jordon Hosp—hospital .... MA-1
**Jordonia**—pop pl .... TN-4
Jordon Lake .... AL-4
Jordon Lake—reservoir .... VA-3
Jordon Pond .... MA-1
Jordon Run .... WV-2
Jordons Cem—cemetery .... MS-4
Jordons Ch—church .... MS-4
Jordon Sch—school .... IL-6
Jordon School .... MS-4
Jordon Springs (historical)—locale .... KS-7
Jordons Springs .... AL-4
Jordon Stream Ch—church (2) .... GA-3
Jordontown Ch—church .... VA-3
Jordson Coulee—valley .... WI-6
Joree Millpond—lake .... GA-3
Jorgen Lake .... MN-6
Jorgensen Coulee—valley .... MT-8
Jorgensen Hollow—valley .... UT-8
Jorgensen Lake—lake .... WA-9
Jorgensen Point—summit .... CA-9
Jorgensen Pond—lake .... UT-8
Jorgens Lake—lake .... MN-6
Jorgenson, Chris, Studio—hist pl .... CA-9
Jorgenson Creek—stream .... UT-8
Jorgenson Ditch—canal (2) .... MT-8
Jorgenson Flat—flat .... UT-8
Jorgenson Hill—summit .... WA-9
Jorgenson Lake—lake (2) .... MN-6
Jorgenson Ranch—locale .... MT-8
Jorgenson River—stream .... SD-7
Jorgeson Flat .... UT-8
Jornada—locale .... NM-5
Jornada Del Muerto—area .... NM-5
Jornada Dikes—levee .... NM-5
Jornada Draw—valley .... NM-5
Jornada Lakes—lake .... NM-5
Jornada Sch—school .... NM-5
Jornado Lateral—canal .... TX-5
Jorn Lake—lake .... OR-9
Jorosa Creek—stream .... AK-9
Jorsell Park—park .... MN-6
Jorstad Cabin—locale .... CA-9
Jorstad Spring—spring .... SD-7
Jorstadt Island—island .... NY-2
Jorsted Creek—stream .... WA-9
Jory Basin—basin .... OR-9
Jory Blocks .... PA-2
Jory Canyon—valley .... OR-9
Jory Cem—cemetery .... OR-9
Jory Creek—stream .... OR-9
Jory Hill—ridge .... OR-9
Jory Hill—summit .... WY-8
Jory Ranch—locale .... NV-8
Jorytown .... PA-2
Joryville County Park—park .... OR-9
Joscelyn—locale .... NY-2
Jose, Bayou—gut .... LA-4
Jose Antonio Canyon—valley .... NM-5
Jose Basin—basin .... CA-9
Jose Bay—bay .... MS-4
Jose Bayou—gut .... MS-4
Jose Butte—summit .... NM-5
Jose Canyon—valley .... NM-5
Jose Chapel—church .... AR-4
Joseco—locale .... NV-8
Jose Creb Bayou—gut .... AL-4
Jose Creek—stream .... CA-9
Jose Creek—stream .... ID-8
Jose Creek—stream .... IN-6
Jose Creek—stream .... MI-6
Jose de la Maza Arrendondo Grant—civil .... FL-3
Jose del Valle Park—park .... CA-9
Josefa—locale (2) .... PR-3
**Josefa**—pop pl (3) .... PR-3
Josefina Artesian Well—well .... TX-5
Josefina Windmill—locale .... TX-5
Jose Gabriel Tank—reservoir .... NM-5
Jose Ignacio Canyon—valley .... NM-5
Jose Ignacio Spring—spring .... NM-5
Jose Juan Tank—reservoir .... AZ-5
Jose Lake—lake .... MI-6
Joselino Tank—reservoir .... NM-5
Jose Manuel Sanchez Baca—civil .... NM-5
Jose Maria Canyon—valley (2) .... NM-5
Jose Maria Spring—spring .... NM-5
Jose Maria Spring—spring .... TX-5
Jose Maria Well—well .... NM-5
Jose Marie Windmill—locale .... NM-5
Jose Marti Riverfront Park—park .... FL-3
Jose Marti Sch—school .... FL-3
**Jose Mercado**—pop pl (2) .... PR-3
Jose Miguel Creek—stream .... NM-5
Josendal Springs—spring .... WY-8
**Josenhans**—pop pl .... MD-2
Jose Opening—flat .... CA-9
Jose Perea—civil .... NM-5
Joseph—locale .... AK-9
Joseph—locale .... ID-8
**Joseph**—pop pl .... MS-4
**Joseph**—pop pl .... OR-9
**Joseph**—pop pl .... UT-8
Joseph, Beth, Synagogue—hist pl .... NY-2
Joseph, Joseph, House—hist pl .... MI-6
Joseph, Lyman C., House—hist pl .... RI-1
Joseph Adit—mine .... UT-8
Joseph Allred Dam—dam .... NC-3
Joseph Allred Lake—reservoir .... NC-3
Joseph and Mary—pillar .... UT-8
Josepha Pol Grant—civil .... FL-3
Joseph Bayou—gut .... LA-4
Joseph Bonelly Grant—civil .... FL-3
Joseph Branch—stream .... KY-4
Joseph Branch—stream .... LA-4
Joseph Branch Ch—church .... NC-3
Joseph Brumfield Cemetery .... MS-4
Joseph Byran Park—park .... VA-3
Joseph Caldwells Tavern .... DE-2
Joseph Canyon—valley .... CA-9
Joseph Canyon—valley .... OR-9
Joseph Canyon—valley .... UT-8
Joseph Canyon—valley .... WA-9
Joseph Canyon Viewpoint—locale .... OR-9
Joseph (CCD)—cens area .... OR-9
Joseph Cem—cemetery .... AL-4
Joseph Cem—cemetery .... ID-8
Joseph Cem—cemetery .... LA-4
Joseph Cem—cemetery .... OR-9
Joseph Cem—cemetery .... UT-8
Joseph Chapel—church .... KY-4
Joseph Chapel—church .... MS-4
Joseph Chapel—church .... MO-7
Joseph Chapel—church (2) .... TN-4
Joseph Chapel—church .... WV-2
Joseph-Cherrington House—hist pl .... OH-6
**Joseph City**—pop pl .... AZ-5
Joseph City Elem Sch—school .... AZ-5
Joseph City HS—school .... AZ-5
Joseph City Post Office—building .... AZ-5
Joseph City Spring—spring .... AZ-5
Joseph City Tank—reservoir .... AZ-5
Joseph City Wash—stream .... AZ-5
Joseph Cook Library—building .... MS-4
Joseph Creek—stream .... AL-4
Joseph Creek—stream (2) .... AK-9
Joseph Creek—stream (3) .... CA-9
Joseph Creek—stream .... MT-8
Joseph Creek—stream .... OR-9
Joseph Creek—stream .... WA-9
Joseph Creek—stream .... WI-6
Joseph Creek Basin—basin .... CA-9
Joseph Creek Ranch—locale .... CA-9
Joseph Cruzat and Francisco De Viller Grant—civil .... FL-3
Joseph Cruzat Grant—civil .... FL-3
Joseph Delespine Grant—civil .... FL-3
Joseph Eckels Bar .... TN-4
Joseph E Smith Elem Sch—school .... TN-4
Joseph Fenwick Grant—civil .... FL-3
Joseph Finegan Elem Sch—school .... FL-3
Joseph Flats—flat .... UT-8
Joseph F Tuttle JHS—school .... IN-6
Joseph Gale Sch—school .... OR-9
Joseph Gaunt Grant—civil .... FL-3
Joseph G. Wilson Elem Sch—school .... OR-9
Joseph Harbor Bayou—stream .... LA-4
Joseph H. Douglass Sch—school .... DE-2
Joseph H Hilshorn Museum and Sculpture Gardens—building .... DC-2
Joseph Hollow—valley .... MO-7
Joseph House—hist pl .... GA-3
Josephine—locale .... KY-4
**Josephine**—pop pl .... AL-4
**Josephine**—pop pl .... ND-7
**Josephine**—pop pl .... PA-2
**Josephine**—pop pl .... TX-5
**Josephine**—pop pl .... VA-3
**Josephine**—pop pl .... WV-2
Josephine, Lake—lake .... AK-9
Josephine, Lake—lake .... CA-9
Josephine, Lake—lake (3) .... FL-3
Josephine, Lake—lake (2) .... MN-6
Josephine, Lake—lake .... MT-8
Josephine, Lake—lake .... ND-7
Josephine, Lake—lake .... SC-3
Josephine, Mount—summit .... MN-6
Josephine, Mount—summit .... WA-9
Josephine Canyon—valley .... AZ-5
Josephine Canyon—valley .... CA-9
Josephine Canyon Trail Number 133—trail .... AZ-5
Josephine Cave—cave .... PA-2
Josephine Cem—cemetery .... TX-5
Josephine Ch—church .... AL-4
**Josephine County**—pop pl .... OR-9
Josephine County-Grants Pass Airp—airport .... OR-9
Josephine Crag—pillar .... WA-9
Josephine Creek—stream .... CA-9
Josephine Creek—stream .... FL-3
Josephine Creek—stream (2) .... ID-8
Josephine Creek—stream .... MT-8
Josephine Creek—stream .... OR-9
Josephine Creek—stream .... WA-9
Josephine Creek Trail—trail .... MT-8
Josephine Ditch—canal .... WY-8
Josephine Goldwater Hosp—hospital .... AZ-5
Josephine Gulch—valley .... AK-9
**Josephine (historical)**—pop pl .... TN-4
Josephine Hollow—valley .... UT-8
Josephine Island—island .... TX-5
Josephine Lake—lake (3) .... CA-9
Josephine Lake—lake .... CO-8
Josephine Lake—lake .... ID-8
Josephine Lake—lake .... MN-6
Josephine Lake—lake .... MT-8
Josephine Lake—lake .... OR-9
Josephine Lake—lake .... SD-7
Josephine Lake—lake (2) .... WA-9
Josephine Lakes—lake .... WA-9
Josephine Lkae—lake .... CO-8
Josephine Memorial Hospital Emergency Heliport—airport .... OR-9
Josephine Mine—mine (3) .... CA-9
Josephine Mine—mine .... CO-8
Josephine Mine—mine (2) .... MT-8
Josephine Mine—mine .... WA-9
Josephine Motte—summit .... TX-5
Josephine Mountain .... CA-9
Josephine Mtn—summit .... OR-9
Josephine Park—park .... MT-8
Josephine Peak—summit .... AZ-5
Josephine Peak—summit .... CA-9
Josephine Peak—summit .... MT-8
Josephine Post Office (historical)—building .... TN-4
Josephine Reef—bar .... TX-5
Josephine Rsvr—reservoir .... NV-8
Josephine Saddle—gap .... AZ-5
Josephine Saddle—gap .... CA-9
Josephine Saddle Madera Trail Number 134—trail .... AZ-5
Josephine Sch—school .... MT-8
Josephine Shaft—mine .... NV-8
Josephine Spring—spring (2) .... NV-8
Josephine Tank—reservoir .... AZ-5
Josephine Tunnel—tunnel .... AZ-5
Josephine Young Memorial Park—cemetery .... OR-9
Josephite Point—summit .... UT-8
Josephium Coll—school .... OH-6
Joseph J Baum Memorial Park—park .... IA-7
Joseph J Bingham Elem Sch—school .... IN-6
Joseph Jones Memorial Park .... MS-4
Joseph Lake—lake .... MN-6
Joseph Lane JHS—school .... OR-9
Joseph L Block JHS—school .... IN-6
Joseph L Meek Land Claim Historical Marker—other .... OR-9
Joseph Lowrey Grant—civil .... FL-3
Joseph Ludlow Ditch—canal .... IN-6
Joseph Martin Golf Course—locale .... PA-2
Joseph M Farley Nuclear Power Plant—building .... AL-4
Joseph M Hernandez Grant—civil .... FL-3
Joseph Mine—mine .... NM-5
Joseph M. McVey Elem Sch—school .... DE-2
Joseph Mountain Mines—mine .... OR-9
Joseph Mtn—summit .... AL-4
Joseph Mtn—summit .... NY-2
Joseph Neylans Spring—spring .... MS-4
Joseph Noriega Grant—civil .... FL-3
Joseph Peak—summit .... UT-8
Joseph Peak—summit .... WY-8
Joseph Peavett (Heirs) Grant—civil .... FL-3
Joseph Phillips Grant—civil .... FL-3
Joseph Plains—flat .... ID-8
Joseph Pond .... MA-1
Joseph Post Office (historical)—building .... MS-4
Joseph Priestly School .... PA-2
Joseph Rain and William Bailey Grant—civil .... FL-3
Joseph R Brown Wayside Park—park .... MN-6
Joseph Reed Park—park .... AZ-5
Joseph Rogers Dam—dam .... OR-9
Joseph Rogers Rsvr—reservoir .... OR-9
Josephs Airp—airport .... DE-2
Joseph Salrin Arm—canal .... IN-6
Joseph Salrin Arm of Zick Lateral .... IN-6
Josephs Bay—swamp .... MS-4
Josephs Beach—beach .... MA-1
Josephs Cem—cemetery .... OH-6
Joseph Sch (historical)—school .... MS-4
Josephs Coat Springs—spring .... WY-8
Josephs Fork—stream .... WV-2
Josephs Mills—locale .... WV-2
Joseph Smith Monmt—pillar .... VT-1
Joseph Smith Spring—spring .... UT-8
Joseph Smyth Dam—dam .... PA-2
Joseph Smyth Pond—reservoir .... PA-2
Joseph S Neidig Elem Sch—school .... PA-2
Josephson—locale .... ID-8
Josephs Pond—lake .... MA-1
Joseph Spring—spring .... AZ-5
**Joseph Springs**—pop pl .... AL-4
Joseph Springs—spring .... AL-4
Joseph Springs Cemetery .... AL-4
Josephs Sch—school .... FL-3
Joseph State Airp—airport .... OR-9
Joseph Stilwell JHS—school .... FL-3
Josephs Town .... GA-3
Joseph Summeral Grant—civil .... FL-3
Joseph Summerland Grant—civil .... FL-3
Joseph Swamp .... VA-3
Joseph Swamp—stream .... VA-3
Joseph Sylvia State Beach Park—park .... MA-1
Josephtown—locale .... PA-2
Josephtown Station—locale .... PA-2
Joseph Tunnel Mountain .... OR-9
Josephus Lake—lake .... ID-8
**Josephville**—pop pl .... MO-7
Joseph Wales Grant—civil .... FL-3
Joseph Warm Spring—spring .... OR-9
Joseph Zito Sch—school .... AZ-5
Jose Placencia Canyon—valley .... NM-5
Jose Pond—lake .... ME-1
Jose Ranch—locale .... NV-8
Jose Sanchez Grant—civil .... FL-3
Joses Bayou .... MS-4
Jose Sch—school .... MI-6
Jose Second Canyon—valley .... NM-5
Jose Second Dam No 1—dam .... NM-5
Jose Second Dam No 2—dam .... NM-5
Jose Second Dam No 3—dam .... NM-5
Joses Hollow .... CA-9
Joses Meadow—swamp .... MA-1
Jose Tank—reservoir (2) .... TX-5
Jose Vigil Lake—lake .... NM-5
Jose Well—well .... NM-5
Josey Acad—school .... GA-3
Josey Branch—stream .... FL-3
Josey Cem—cemetery .... LA-4
Josey Ch—church .... GA-3
Josey Creek—stream .... MS-4
Josey Creek Baptist Church .... MS-4
Josey Creek Cem—cemetery .... MS-4
Josey Creek Ch—church .... MS-4
Josh, Mount—summit .... AZ-5
Josh Ames Ditch—canal .... CO-8
Josh Branch—stream .... MS-4
Josh Branch—stream .... VA-3
Josh Branch—stream .... WV-2
Josh Brook—stream .... NH-1
Josh Canyon—valley .... WY-8
Josh Creek—stream .... NJ-2
Josh Creek—stream .... OR-9
Josh Creek—stream .... TN-4
Josh Creek—stream .... WY-8
Josh Hollow—valley .... KY-4
Josh Hollow—valley .... TN-4
Josh Hollow—valley .... UT-8
Josh Hollow—valley .... WV-2
Joshia Cove—bay .... DE-2
Joshia Prong—bay .... DE-2
Joshlin Creek .... MI-6
Joshling Creek—stream .... AR-4
Josh Point—cape .... MD-2
Josh Pond—lake .... ME-1
Josh Spring—spring .... AZ-5
Joshua—locale .... CA-9
**Joshua**—pop pl .... FL-3
**Joshua**—pop pl .... NY-2
**Joshua**—pop pl .... SC-3
**Joshua**—pop pl .... TX-5
Joshua Branch .... NC-3
Joshua Branch—stream .... KY-4
Joshua Branch—stream .... NJ-2
Joshua Branch—stream (2) .... NC-3
Joshua Branch—stream .... TN-4
Joshua Butte—summit .... SD-7
Joshua Canyon—valley .... NM-5
Joshua Cem—cemetery .... AL-4
Joshua Cem—cemetery .... TX-5
Joshua Chapel A.M.E. Church—hist pl .... TX-5
Joshua Cove—bay .... CT-1
Joshua Cove—valley .... CA-9
Joshua Creek—stream .... CA-9
Joshua Creek—stream .... CT-1
Joshua Creek—stream (2) .... FL-3
Joshua Creek—stream (2) .... NC-3
Joshua Creek—stream .... TX-5
Joshua Creek—stream (2) .... VA-3
Joshua Creek Cem—cemetery .... FL-3
Joshua Crosby Dam—dam .... AZ-5
Joshua Falls—locale .... VA-3
Joshua Flat—flat .... CA-9
Joshua Flats—flat .... CA-9
Joshua Green River—stream .... AK-9
Joshua Hennington Cem—cemetery .... MS-4
Joshua Hill—summit .... CT-1
Joshua Hill—summit .... MA-1
Joshua Hill Hollow—valley .... MO-7
Joshua Hollow—valley .... NV-8
Joshua Memorial Park—cemetery .... CA-9
Joshua Mountain .... NV-8
Joshua Mtn .... MA-1
Joshua Mtn—summit .... CA-9
Joshua Mtn—summit (2) .... NC-3
Joshua Point .... NY-2
Joshua Point—cape .... CT-1
Joshua Pond—lake .... MA-1
Joshua Post Office (historical)—building .... TN-4
Joshua Ridge—ridge .... NC-3
Joshua Rock—pillar .... CT-1
Joshua Rock—summit .... NY-2
Joshuas Branch—stream .... SC-3
Joshua Sch—school (2) .... CA-9
Joshua Sch—school .... KY-4
Joshua Sch—school .... SC-3
Joshua's Meadows—hist pl .... MD-2
Joshuas Run—stream .... WV-2
Joshua Tank—reservoir .... NM-5
**Joshua (Township of)**—pop pl .... IL-6
**Joshua Tree**—pop pl .... CA-9
Joshua Tree Forest-Bureau of Land Mngmt .... UT-8
Joshua Tree Natl Monmt—park .... CA-9
Joshua Tree Natl Monument HQ—locale .... CA-9
Joshua Tree Natural Area—reserve .... UT-8
Joshus Fork—stream .... WV-2
Josiah Bassetts Pond .... MA-1
Josiah Brook—stream .... ME-1
Josiah Creek—stream .... TN-4
Josiah Hess Covered Bridge No. 122—hist pl .... PA-2
Josiah Hester Lake Dam—dam .... MS-4
Josiah Nelson House Site—locale .... MA-1
Josiah Powell Cem—cemetery .... MS-4
Josiah Quincy House Museum—building .... MA-1
Josiah River .... ME-1
Josiahs Cove—bay .... ME-1
Josiah Springs—spring .... UT-8
Josiah Trail—trail .... TN-4
Josias Brook—stream .... ME-1
Josias River—stream .... ME-1
**Josie**—pop pl .... AL-4
Josie Bassett Morris Cabin .... UT-8
Josie Bayou—stream .... TX-5
Josie Branch—stream .... KY-4
Josie Creek—stream .... AK-9
Josie Creek—stream .... ID-8
Josie Creek—stream .... OR-9
Josie Creek—stream .... WI-6
Josie Creek County Park—park .... WI-6
Josie Harry Towhead—flat .... TN-4
Josie Hollow—valley .... MO-7
Josie Lake—lake .... TX-5
Josie Lake—lake .... WI-6
Josie Leg Creek—stream .... AL-4
Josie Mine—mine .... SD-7
Josie Morris Ranch .... UT-8
Josie Pearl Spring—spring .... NV-8
Josies Brook—stream .... ME-1
Josie Spring—spring .... ID-8
**Josie Township**—pop pl .... NE-7
Josius River .... ME-1
**Joslin**—pop pl .... IL-6
**Joslin**—pop pl .... NH-1
Joslin, Falcon, House—hist pl .... AK-9
Joslin Basin—basin .... MT-8
Joslin Branch—stream .... MO-7
Joslin Branch—stream .... TN-4
Joslin Brook—stream .... MA-1
Joslin Cem—cemetery .... NH-1
Joslin Creek—stream .... MI-6
Joslin Creek—stream .... MT-8
Joslin Farm—hist pl .... VT-1
Joslin Hill—summit (2) .... NH-1
Joslin Hill—summit .... NY-2
Joslin Lake—lake (2) .... MI-6
Joslin Park—park .... TX-5
Joslin Sch—school .... IL-6
Joslin Sch—school .... MA-1
Joslin Sch—school .... TX-5
Joslin Slough—stream .... IL-6
Joslin Turn—locale .... VT-1
Joslyn, George A., Mansion—hist pl .... NE-7
Joslyn Cem—cemetery (2) .... NY-2
Joslyn Drain—stream .... MI-6
Joslyn Park—park .... CA-9
Joslyn Pond—lake .... PA-2
**Joslyn Trace (subdivision)**—pop pl .... NC-3
Jo Snow Creek .... WI-6
Joso—locale .... WA-9
Joso Meadow—flat .... OR-9
Josper Flats—flat .... ID-8
J O Spring—spring .... MT-8
Jo Spring—spring .... TX-5
J O Spring—spring .... WY-8
Jossart Island—island .... WI-6
Josselet—locale .... TX-5
Josselyn—locale .... NE-7
Josserand—locale .... TX-5
Josserand Cem—cemetery .... TX-5
Josseyln—locale .... NE-7
Jossie Gut Hist Dist—hist pl .... VI-3
Josslyn Island—island .... FL-3
Josslyn Island Site—hist pl .... FL-3
**Jossman Acres**—pop pl .... MI-6
Jostad Coulee—valley .... WI-6
Jost Creek—stream (2) .... ID-8
Jost Creek—stream .... WY-8
J O Stuart Pond Dam—dam .... MS-4
Josy Creek .... MS-4
Jot .... FM-9
Jotank Creek .... VA-3
Jotan Lake—lake .... MN-6
Jot Em Down—locale .... TX-5
**Jot 'Em Down**—pop pl .... TX-5
Jot'Em Down Store—locale .... GA-3
**Jot Em Down Store**—pop pl .... GA-3
Jotner Pond .... GA-3
Joubert—locale .... SD-7
Joubert and White Bldg—hist pl .... NY-2
Joubert Cem—cemetery .... IL-6
Joubert Diggings—locale .... CA-9
Joubert Lake—lake .... SD-7
Joubert Post Office (historical)—building .... SD-7
**Joubert Township**—pop pl .... SD-7
Jouett, Capt. Jack, House—hist pl .... KY-4
Jouett Creek—stream .... KY-4
Jouett Creek—stream .... TN-4
Jouett Sch—school .... VA-3
Jouett's Creek .... KY-4
Jougelard Ranch—locale .... ID-8
Joughin Cove—bay .... CA-9
Joughin Ranch—locale .... CA-9
Joula Creek—stream .... MN-6
Joulious Creek—stream .... UT-8
Joulious Park—park .... UT-8
Joulters Creek—stream .... IL-6
Jountin .... FM-9
Jourda Canal—canal .... LA-4
Jourdain Creek—stream .... MT-8
Jourdan Creek—stream .... MS-4
Jourdan Dam .... AL-4
Jourdan Hollow—valley .... MO-7
Jourdan Pond .... MA-1
Jourdan River—stream .... MS-4
Jourdans Chapel .... MS-4
**Jourdanton**—pop pl .... TX-5
Jourdanton (CCD)—cens area .... TX-5
Jourdanton Oil Field—oilfield .... TX-5
Jourden Creek—stream .... AL-4
Jourdens Mill (historical)—locale .... TN-4
Jourdens Shoals—bar .... TN-4
Journagans and McLeans Steam Mill (historical)—locale .... AL-4
Journal Bldg—hist pl .... ME-1
Journal-Gazette Bldg—hist pl .... IN-6
Journal Island—island .... OH-6
Journal Square—locale .... NJ-2
Journal Square Station—locale .... NJ-2
Journey Cake .... KS-7
Journey Cem—cemetery .... IL-6
Journey Cem—cemetery .... MO-7
Journey Hill—summit .... GA-3
Journey Hollow—valley .... TN-4
Journey's End—hist pl .... FL-3
Journeys End Camp—locale .... VT-1
Journeys End Lake—lake .... NY-2
Journigan Creek .... TX-5
Journigan Mine—mine .... AZ-5
Journigan Spring—spring .... AZ-5
Jove Creek—channel .... GA-3
Jove Lake—lake .... WA-9
Jove Peak—summit .... WA-9
J Oviatt Bowers Park—park .... AL-4
Jovista—locale .... CA-9
Jovita .... FL-3
**Jovita**—pop pl .... WA-9
Jowell Center (reduced usage)—locale .... TX-5
Jowell Creek—stream .... TX-5
Jowell Sch—school .... TX-5
Jower Cem—cemetery .... TN-4
Jowers Branch—stream .... NC-3
Jowers Cem—cemetery .... AL-4
Jowers Cem—cemetery .... SC-3
Jowers Cem—cemetery .... TN-4
Jowers Chapel—church .... GA-3
Jowers Creek—stream .... LA-4
Jowler Creek—stream .... MO-7
Joy—locale .... KS-7
Joy—locale .... MO-7
Joy—locale .... NC-3
Joy—locale .... OH-6
Joy—locale .... UT-8
Joy—locale .... WV-2
**Joy**—pop pl .... AL-4
**Joy**—pop pl .... AR-4
**Joy**—pop pl .... IL-6
**Joy**—pop pl (2) .... KY-4
**Joy**—pop pl .... NY-2
**Joy**—pop pl .... OK-5
**Joy**—pop pl (2) .... TX-5
**Joy**—pop pl .... WA-9
Joy, Lake—lake .... GA-3
Joy, Lake—lake .... WA-9
Joy, Lake—reservoir (2) .... AL-4
Joy, Lake—reservoir .... IL-6
**Joy, Mount**—pop pl .... OH-6
**Joy, Mount**—pop pl (2) .... PA-2
Joy, Mount—summit .... PA-2
**Joya de los Santos**—pop pl .... PR-3
Joy Baptist Ch—church .... FL-3
Joy Bay—bay .... ME-1
Joy Brook—stream .... NY-2
Joy Brook—stream .... VT-1
Joy Cabin—locale .... AZ-5
Joy Canyon—valley .... NM-5
Joyce—locale .... NE-7
Joyce—locale .... OH-6
Joyce—locale .... WA-9
**Joyce**—pop pl .... LA-4
**Joyce**—pop pl .... MD-2
**Joyce**—pop pl .... PA-2
**Joyce**—pop pl .... TX-5
Joyce, Jacob O., House—hist pl .... OH-6
Joyce, Lake—lake .... FL-3
Joyce, Lake—reservoir .... AL-4
Joyce, Lake—reservoir .... IN-6
Joyce, Lake—reservoir .... VA-3
Joyce Airp—airport .... IN-6
Joyce Beach—beach .... ME-1
Joyce Branch—stream .... FL-3
Joyce Branch—stream .... SC-3
Joyce Cem—cemetery .... AR-4
Joyce Cem—cemetery .... IL-6
Joyce Cem—cemetery .... IN-6
Joyce Cem—cemetery .... KY-4
Joyce Cem—cemetery .... MA-1
Joyce Cem—cemetery .... NC-3
Joyce Cem—cemetery .... TN-4
Joyce Chapel—church .... NC-3
Joyce City—locale .... AR-4
Joyce Creek—stream .... MO-7
Joyce Creek—stream .... NC-3
Joyce Creek—stream (2) .... OR-9
Joyce Creek—stream .... WY-8
Joyce Dam—dam .... AL-4
Joyce Dam—dam .... NC-3
Joyce Dam—dam .... UT-8
Joyce Elem Sch—school .... KS-7
Joyce Fork—stream .... KY-4
**Joyce Heights**—pop pl .... VA-3
Joyce Hill Lookout Tower .... AL-4
Joyce Hollow—valley .... KY-4
Joyce Island .... CA-9
Joyce Island .... ME-1
Joyce Island—island .... KY-4
Joyce Kilmer Elem Sch—school .... IN-6
Joyce Kilmer Memorial—park .... NC-3
Joyce Kilmer Monmt—park .... PA-2
Joyce Kilmer Park—park .... MA-1
Joyce Kilmer-Slickrock Wilderness Area—park .... NC-3
Joyce Kilmer Trail—trail .... PA-2
Joyce Lake—lake .... GA-3
Joyce Lake—lake .... MI-6
Joyce Lake—lake .... OR-9
Joyce Lake—lake .... UT-8
Joyce Lake—lake (2) .... WI-6
Joyce Lake—reservoir .... NC-3
**Joyce Lane**—pop pl .... MD-2
Joy Cem—cemetery .... ME-1
Joy Cem—cemetery .... OH-6
Joy Cem—cemetery .... VT-1
Joyce M Bullock Elem Sch—school .... FL-3
Joyce Memorial JHS—school .... MA-1
Joyce Methodist Episcopal Ch—church .... AL-4
Joyce Mill—locale .... NC-3
Joyce Park—park .... AZ-5
Joyce Park—park .... IA-7
Joyce Point—cape .... ME-1
Joyce Ranch—locale .... NM-5
Joyce Ridge—ridge .... KY-4
Joyce-Road Sch—school .... NY-2
Joyce Rsvr—reservoir .... OR-9
Joyce Rsvr—reservoir .... UT-8
Joyce Sch—school .... MI-6
Joyces Creek .... MA-1
**Joyceton**—pop pl .... NC-3
Joyceville—locale .... VA-3
**Joyceville**—pop pl .... CT-1
Joy Ch—church .... GA-3
Joy Ch—church .... MO-7
Joy Ch—church .... TX-5
Joy Chapel Cem—cemetery .... MD-2
Joy Cove—bay .... ME-1
Joy Creek .... CO-8
Joy Creek—stream .... ID-8
Joy Creek—stream .... IA-7
Joy Creek—stream (2) .... KS-7
Joy Creek—stream .... OR-9
Joy Creek—stream .... TN-4

**Judson**—*pop pl* ND-7
**Judson**—*pop pl* SC-3
Judson, Capt. David, House—*hist pl* CT-1
Judson, Lake—*lake* AL-4
Judson, The—*hist pl* IL-6
Judson Baptist Ch—*church* IN-6
Judson Bldg—*hist pl* IN-6
Judson Brook—*stream* NY-2
Judson-Bulloch Cem—*cemetery* GA-3
Judson Cem—*cemetery* (2) AL-4
Judson Cem—*cemetery* GA-3
Judson Cem—*cemetery* SC-3
Judson Cem—*cemetery* TX-5
Judson Ch—*church* (3) AL-4
Judson Ch—*church* AR-4
Judson Ch—*church* LA-4
Judson Ch—*church* MI-6
Judson Ch—*church* MO-7
Judson Ch—*church* NC-3
Judson Ch—*church* TN-4
Judson Ch—*church* TX-5
Judson Ch—*church* WV-2
Judson Coll—*school* AL-4
Judson Coll—*school* OR-9
Judson Creek—*stream* OR-9
Judson Falls—*falls* MI-6
*Judson Female Institute* AL-4
Judson Hill—*summit* PA-2
Judson Hill Cem—*cemetery* PA-2
Judson Hills—*summit* CO-8
Judson (historical)—*locale* KS-7
Judson Hollow—*valley* PA-2
Judson HS—*school* TX-5
**Judsonia**—*pop pl* AR-4
Judson Institute (historical)—*school* MS-4
Judson JHS—*school* OR-9
*Judson Lake* MN-6
Judson Lake—*lake* (2) WA-9
Judson Landing—*locale* OR-9
Judson Memorial Ch—*church* AR-4
Judson Memorial Ch—*church* WI-6
Judson Memorial Church, Campanile, and Judson Hall—*hist pl* NY-2
Judson Mine—*mine* MN-6
*Judson Missionary Baptist Ch* TN-4
*Judson Missionary Baptist Church* AL-4
**Judson No. 02**—*pop pl* SC-3
**Judson Park (subdivision)**—*pop pl* AL-4
Judson Point—*cape* NY-2
Judson Pond—*lake* NH-1
Judson Rock—*pillar* OR-9
Judson Rock Creek—*stream* OR-9
Judson Rocks—*cliff* OR-9
Judson Sch—*school* AZ-5
Judson Sch—*school* IL-6
Judson Sch—*school* TN-4
*Judsons Church* TN-4
Judson-Taft House—*hist pl* MA-1
**Judson Township**—*pop pl* ND-7
**Judson (Township of)**—*pop pl* MN-6
*Judy* IN-6
**Judy**—*pop pl* KY-4
Judy, Lake—*reservoir* GA-3
Judy Ann Branch—*stream* KY-4
Judy Bayou—*stream* MS-4
*Judy Branch* IN-6
Judy Branch—*stream* MO-7
Judy Branch—*stream* NC-3
Judy Branch—*stream* TN-4
Judy Branch Sch (historical)—*school* TN-4
Judy Byrd Mtn—*summit* VA-3
Judy Canyon—*valley* NM-5
Judy Cem—*cemetery* KS-7
Judy Cem—*cemetery* MO-7
Judy Creek—*stream* AL-4
Judy Creek—*stream* AK-9
Judy Creek—*stream* IN-6
Judy Creek—*stream* KY-4
Judy Creek—*stream* LA-4
Judy Creek—*stream* MT-8
Judy Creek—*stream* OR-9
Judy Creek—*stream* VA-3
Judy Creek—*stream* WA-9
*Judy Ditch* IN-6
Judy Gap—*gap* WV-2
Judy Gap—*locale* WV-2
Judy Hill—*summit* AK-9
Judy Hill—*summit* OK-5
Judy Island—*island* MA-1
Judy Lake—*lake* FL-3
Judy Lake—*lake* MI-6
Judy Lake—*lake* SC-3
Judy Lake—*lake* WA-9
Judy Lake Drain—*stream* MI-6
Judy Mtn—*summit* GA-3
Judy North Highline Ditch—*canal* CO-8
Judy Ridge—*ridge* WV-2
Judy Rocks—*summit* WV-2
Judy Run—*stream* PA-2
Judy Run—*stream* WV-2
Judys Branch—*stream* IL-6
Judy Sch—*school* KS-7
Judy Sch—*school* MO-7
Judy Sch (historical)—*school* MO-7
Judy Slough—*gut* LA-4
Judy Spring—*spring* OR-9
Judy Spring—*spring* WV-2
Judy Springs Campground—*locale* WV-2
Judys Slough—*gut* AL-4
Judy Swamp—*stream* VA-3
Judy Tank—*reservoir* (2) AZ-5
Judytown Branch—*stream* KY-4
**Judyville**—*pop pl* IN-6
**Judyville**—*pop pl* KY-4
Judy Wash—*arroyo* AZ-5
*Judy Wash Dam* AZ-5
Judy Wash Retarding Dam—*dam* AZ-5
*Juel Creek* ND-7
Juel Creek—*stream* WY-8
Juel Ranch—*locale* WY-8
Juel Rsvr—*reservoir* WY-8
Juergens Lake—*lake* MN-6
Jueschke Well—*well* NM-5
Jug, The—*cliff* AZ-5
Jug, The—*island* WV-2
*Jugaji to* MP-9
*Jugan-to* MP-9
Jug Bay—*bay* MD-2
Jug Bayou—*stream* LA-4
Jug Bend (historical)—*bend* SD-7
Jug Branch—*stream* AL-4
Jug Brook—*stream* VT-1
Jug Buttes (historical)—*summit* SD-7
Jug Canyon—*valley* NM-5
*Jug Creek* CO-8
*Jug Creek* SD-7
Jug Creek—*gut* FL-3
Jug Creek—*stream* AR-4
Jug Creek—*stream* GA-3
Jug Creek—*stream* (3) ID-8
Jug Creek—*stream* MI-6
Jug Creek—*stream* MT-8
Jug Creek—*stream* NJ-2
Jug Creek—*stream* OR-9
Jug Creek—*stream* SD-7
Jug Creek—*stream* TN-4
Jug Creek—*stream* WA-9
Jug Creek—*stream* WI-6
Jug Creek Point—*cape* FL-3
Jug Creek Point Shoal—*bar* FL-3
Jug Creek Shoal—*bar* FL-3
Jug Creek Swamp—*swamp* FL-3
Jug End—*cliff* MA-1
**Jug Fork**—*pop pl* MS-4
Juggernaut Pond—*lake* NH-1
Juggernaut Trail—*trail* VT-1
Juggler Lake—*lake* (2) MN-6
Juggling Creek—*gut* MD-2
Juggs Gap—*gap* VA-3
Jug Gulch—*valley* CO-8
*Jug Handle, The* UT-8
Jug Handle, The—*arch* UT-8
Jug Handle Creek—*stream* CA-9
Jughandle Hollow—*valley* AL-4
Jughandle Mtn—*summit* ID-8
*Jug Handle Natural Arch* UT-8
Jug Handle Run—*stream* PA-2
*Jug Handles, The* UT-8
Jug Harris Towhead—*island* AR-4
Jug Hill—*summit* ME-1
Jug Hill—*summit* NH-1
Jug Hill Camp—*locale* NY-2
Jug (historical)—*locale* AL-4
Jug Hole—*lake* TX-5
Jug Hollow—*valley* (2) PA-2
Jug Hollow Lake—*reservoir* AL-4
Jug House—*locale* CO-8
Jug Island—*island* (2) AK-9
Jug Island—*island* FL-3
Jug Island—*island* (2) MN-6
Jug Island—*island* NY-2
Jug Island—*locale* FL-3
Jug Lake—*lake* FL-3
Jug Lake—*lake* GA-3
Jug Lake—*lake* LA-4
Jug Lake—*lake* MN-6
Jug Lake—*lake* MS-4
Jug Lake—*lake* (2) WA-9
Jug Lake—*lake* WI-6
Jug Lake Trail—*trail* WA-9
Jug Meadows—*flat* ID-8
Jug Motte Creek—*stream* KS-7
*Jug Mtn* OR-9
Jug Mtn—*summit* (2) NY-2
Jug Mtn—*summit* (2) OR-9
Jugornot Hollow—*valley* KY-4
Jugow Creek—*stream* OR-9
Jug Pond—*lake* NY-2
Jug Post Office (historical)—*building* AL-4
Jug Prairie Cem—*cemetery* WI-6
*Jug Rock* IN-6
Jug Rock—*pillar* CA-9
Jug Rock—*rock* MA-1
Jug Rock—*summit* ID-8
Jug Rock—*summit* UT-8
Jug Rock Flat—*flat* UT-8
**Jug Run**—*pop pl* OH-6
Jug Run—*stream* IL-6
Jug Run—*stream* MO-7
Jug Run—*stream* (3) OH-6
Jug Run—*stream* WV-2
Jug Run Sch—*school* IL-6
**Jugs Corners**—*pop pl* OH-6
Jugs Creek—*stream* VA-3
Jug Spring—*spring* AR-4
Jug Spring—*spring* CA-9
Jug Spring—*spring* CO-8
Jug Spring—*spring* ID-8
Jug Spring—*spring* OR-9
Jugs Tank—*reservoir* NM-5
Jug Stream—*stream* ME-1
Jug Tank—*reservoir* (3) NM-5
Jug Tank—*reservoir* (5) TX-5
*Jug Tavern* GA-3
Jug Tavern—*hist pl* NY-2
*Jugtown* PA-2
Jugtown—*locale* PA-2
**Jugtown**—*pop pl* MD-2
**Jugtown**—*pop pl* (2) NC-3
**Jugtown**—*pop pl* (2) PA-2
**Jug Town**—*pop pl* TN-4
Jugtown Hist Dist—*hist pl* NJ-2
Jugtown (historical)—*locale* AL-4
Jugtown Hollow—*valley* MO-7
Jugtown Mountain—*airport* NJ-2
Jugtown Plains—*flat* ME-1
Jugtown Sch—*school* PA-2
Jug Trail—*trail* CO-8
Jugville—*locale* KY-4
**Jugville**—*pop pl* (2) MI-6
Jug Well—*well* TX-5
Jug Windmill—*locale* TX-5
Juhala Hill—*summit* SD-7
Juhaze Prairie—*flat* CA-9
Juhl—*locale* MI-6
Juhl Cem—*cemetery* MI-6
Juhle, Mount—*summit* AK-9
Juhl Natl Wildlife Mngmt Area—*park* ND-7
Ju Hollow Trail—*trail* PA-2
Juice Creek—*stream* WA-9
Juido Windmill—*locale* TX-5
Juilliard—*locale* TX-5
Jukebox Cave—*cave* UT-8
*Jukes Butte* UT-8
Jukes Cem—*cemetery* MO-7
Juknen—*locale* MP-9
Jukola Boardinghouse—*hist pl* MN-6
Jule Allen Branch—*stream* NC-3
Juleane Rsvr—*reservoir* WI-6
Jule Creek—*stream* MT-8
*Jule Fork* WV-2
*Jule LakA VAR Gail Lake* MN-6
*Jule Lake* MN-6
Jule Lake—*lake* MI-6
Julep Bend—*bend* WV-2
Jule Pond—*lake* NY-2
Jules—*locale* IL-6
Jules, Lake—*reservoir* AL-4
Jules Bowl—*basin* WY-8
**Julesburg**—*pop pl* CO-8
**Julesburg**—*pop pl* MO-7
Julesburg Cem—*cemetery* CO-8
Julesburg Rsvr—*reservoir* CO-8
Julesburg Water Works—*other* CO-8
Jules Cem—*cemetery* LA-4
Jules Creek—*stream* MO-7
Jules Creek—*stream* ND-7
Jules Creek—*stream* VA-3
Jules Cutoff—*gut* LA-4
Jules Island—*island* MA-1
*Jule Webb Fork* WV-2
*Julia* GA-3
Julia—*locale* WV-2
Julia—*other* GA-3
**Julia**—*pop pl* (2) PR-3
Julia, Bayou—*gut* LA-4
Julia, Lake—*lake* FL-3
Julia, Lake—*lake* (2) MN-6
Julia, Lake—*lake* WA-9
Julia, Lake—*lake* (3) WI-6
Julia, Lake—*lake* WY-8
Julia, Lake—*reservoir* GA-3
Julia, Lake—*reservoir* NY-2
Julia, Mount—*summit* WI-6
Julia, Point—*cape* WA-9
*Julia Ann Furnace* PA-2
Julia-Ann Square Hist Dist—*hist pl* WV-2
*Julia Armstrong School* MS-4
Julia Artesian Well—*well* TX-5
Julia Bow Hollow—*valley* KY-4
Julia Cove—*bay* ME-1
Julia Creek—*stream* AK-9
Julia Creek—*stream* IN-6
Julia Creek—*stream* WI-6
Julia Davis Park—*park* ID-8
Julia Dean Creek—*stream* AR-4
Julia E Test JHS—*school* IN-6
**Juliaetta**—*pop pl* ID-8
Juliaetta Cem—*cemetery* ID-8
Julia Fiske Mine—*mine* CO-8
Julia Glover Flat—*flat* CA-9
Julia Hollow—*valley* MO-7
*Julia Island* FL-3
*Julia Lake* MI-6
Julia Lake—*lake* FL-3
Julia Lake—*lake* GA-3
Julia Lake—*lake* MN-6
Julia Lake—*lake* TX-5
Julia Lake—*lake* WI-6
Julia Lake—*reservoir* CA-9
*Julia L Armstrong Elementary School* MS-4
Julia Lee Mine—*mine* MT-8
Julia Mine—*mine* MT-8
Julia Mine—*mine* NV-8
Julian—*locale* KS-7
Julian—*locale* TX-5
**Julian**—*pop pl* CA-9
**Julian**—*pop pl* NE-7
**Julian**—*pop pl* NC-3
**Julian**—*pop pl* PA-2
**Julian**—*pop pl* WV-2
Julian, Lake—*reservoir* NC-3
Julian, Mount—*summit* CO-8
Juliana, Lake—*lake* FL-3
Juliana Drift Mine (underground)—*mine* AL-4
*Juliana Furnace* PA-2
Julian Artesian Well—*well* TX-5
Juliana Sch—*school* MI-6
Julian Bayou—*stream* LA-4
Julian Branch—*stream* MO-7
Julian Canyon—*valley* NM-5
Julian Cem—*cemetery* CA-9
Julian Cem—*cemetery* MO-7
Julian Cem—*cemetery* OH-6
Julian Cem—*cemetery* TN-4
Julian Chapel (historical)—*church* TN-4
Julian Cheney Dam—*dam* SD-7
Julian-Clark House—*hist pl* IN-6
Julian Creek—*stream* AK-9
Julian Creek—*stream* NV-8
Julian Creek—*stream* OK-5
Julian Creek—*stream* SC-3
Julian Creek—*stream* TX-5
Juliand Hill—*summit* NY-2
Julian Ditch Camp—*locale* CO-8
Julian D Parker Elem Sch—*school* FL-3
Julian Farm—*hist pl* KY-4
*Julian Furnace* PA-2
Julian Greggs Dam—*dam* OH-6
Julian Grist Mill (historical)—*building* TX-5
Julian Gulch—*valley* OR-9
Julian Hill—*summit* NM-5
Julian Hill Ch—*church* NC-3
**Julian (historical)**—*pop pl* SD-7
Julian Hotel—*hist pl* OR-9
Julian Lake—*lake* CO-8
Julian Lane Park—*park* NY-2
Julian Lookout Tower—*locale* MO-7
Julian Mill Creek—*stream* FL-3
Julian Mine—*mine* AZ-5
Julian Nance Island—*island* TN-4
Julianne, Lake—*lake* GA-3
Julian Newman Elem Sch—*school* AL-4
Julian Oil Field—*oilfield* TX-5
Julian Pasture—*flat* TX-5
Julian Place—*locale* NM-5
Julian Post Office (historical)—*building* TX-5
Julian Price Lake Dam—*dam* NC-3
Julian Price Memorial Park—*park* NC-3
Julian Ranch—*locale* MT-8
Julian Rocks—*summit* CA-9
Julian Sch—*school* AZ-5
Julian Sch—*school* IL-6
Julian Sch—*school* LA-4
*Julians Chapel* TN-4
*Julian Sch Number 57* IN-6
Julians Hole—*spring* NV-8
Julians Lake—*reservoir* NC-3
Julians Lake Dam—*dam* NC-3
Julians Rock—*summit* TN-4
Julian Station—*locale* NJ-2
Julian Tanks—*reservoir* NM-5
Julian Valley—*basin* NE-7
Julian Wash—*stream* AZ-5
Julian Wash—*stream* CA-9
*Julian Waters Lake* AL-4
Julian Waters Lake Dam—*dam* AL-4
Julian Well—*well* NV-8
Julian Well—*well* NM-5
Julian Well (Windmill)—*locale* TX-5
Julian Windmill—*locale* NM-5
Julian Windmill—*locale* TX-5
Julia Post Office (historical)—*building* AL-4
Julia Randall Sch—*school* AZ-5
Julias Creek—*stream* CA-9
Julia Street Methodist Ch—*church* AL-4
Julia Street Row—*hist pl* LA-4
Julia Tank—*reservoir* AZ-5
Julie Branch—*stream* NC-3
Julie Cove—*valley* NC-3
Julie Creek—*stream* AK-9
Julie Creek—*stream* ID-8
Julie Creek—*stream* MS-4
Julie Creek—*stream* OR-9
Julie Creek—*stream* TX-5
**Julie Estates Subdivision**—*pop pl* UT-8
Julie High Top—*summit* NC-3
Julie Knob—*summit* NC-3
Julien—*locale* IA-7
Julien—*locale* KY-4
**Julien**—*pop pl* LA-4
Julien, Bayou—*stream* LA-4
Julien, Denis, Inscription—*hist pl* CO-8
Julien Creek—*stream* CA-9
Julien Ditch—*canal* IN-6
Julien Dubuque Bridge—*bridge* IA-7
Julien Dubuque Bridge—*other* IL-6
Julien Dubuque Monmt—*park* IA-7
**Julien Hill**—*pop pl* IL-6
Julien Incription Panel—*hist pl* UT-8
Julien Inscription—*hist pl* UT-8
Julienne HS—*school* OH-6
Julien Sch—*school* CA-9
Julienton—*locale* GA-3
*Julienton Plantation* GA-3
Julienton River—*stream* GA-3
Julie Pond—*lake* MD-2
Julie Pond—*reservoir* GA-3
Julie Ridge—*ridge* (2) NC-3
Julie Sch—*school* MA-1
Julies Fork—*stream* SC-3
Julies Island—*island* FL-3
Juliet, Lake—*reservoir* NJ-2
Julie Tank—*reservoir* NM-5
Juliet Cem—*cemetery* IN-6
Juliet Creek—*stream* MT-8
*Juliet Lake* MI-6
Juliet Lake—*lake* MI-6
Juliet Post Office, Mount—*building* TN-4
*Juliett* IN-6
**Julietta**—*pop pl* IN-6
**Juliette**—*pop pl* FL-3
**Juliette**—*pop pl* GA-3
Juliette Basin—*basin* ID-8
Juliette Creek—*stream* ID-8
Juliette Low Sch—*school* GA-3
Juliett Sch (historical)—*school* MS-4
Juliff—*locale* TX-5
Julington Cem—*cemetery* FL-3
Julington Ch—*church* FL-3
Julington Creek—*stream* FL-3
Julington Creek Elem Sch—*school* FL-3
Julington Creek Sch—*school* FL-3
Julio Creek—*stream* TX-5
Julio Draw—*valley* TX-5
Julio Draw—*valley* WY-8
Julio Juan Canyon—*valley* NM-5
Julion Cem—*cemetery* OH-6
Julios Shop Ctr—*locale* MA-1
*Julious* AR-4
Julip—*locale* KY-4
Julip Run—*stream* PA-2
Julius—*locale* AK-9
**Julius**—*pop pl* AR-4
Julius, Lake—*lake* WA-9
Julius Bacot Sibley Cem—*cemetery* MS-4
Julius Branch—*stream* (2) KY-4
Julius Caesar, Mount—*summit* CA-9
Julius Cem—*cemetery* OK-5
*Julius Cesar* CA-9
Julius Creek—*stream* AK-9
Julius Creek—*stream* SD-7
Julius Flat Dam—*dam* UT-8
Julius Flat Rsvr—*reservoir* UT-8
Julius Gulch—*valley* MT-8
Julius Hollow—*valley* MO-7
Julius Knob—*summit* NC-3
Julius Melcher—*post sta* TX-5
Julius Park—*flat* UT-8
Julius Park Dam—*dam* UT-8
Julius Park Rsvr—*reservoir* UT-8
Julius Parks—*flat* CO-8
Julius Pasture—*flat* UT-8
Julius Peak—*summit* NV-8
Julius Pond Branch—*stream* TN-4
Julius Reef—*bar* AK-9
Julius Sch (abandoned)—*school* PA-2
**Juliustown**—*pop pl* NJ-2
Julius T Wright Sch—*school* AL-4
*Julliard* TX-5
**Julliard**—*pop pl* TX-5
Julliard Park—*park* CA-9
Julliard Sch—*school* NY-2
Jullien Cem—*cemetery* TN-4
Jullsburg Municipal Airp—*airport* CO-8
**Julog**—*pop pl* GU-9
Julson Cem—*cemetery* WI-6
*Jults Island* NY-2
Ju-Lu, Lake—*lake* LA-4
July Creek—*stream* (2) AK-9
July Creek—*stream* ID-8
July Creek—*stream* MT-8
July Creek—*stream* (3) WA-9
July Creek Campground—*locale* WA-9
July Cut—*channel* GA-3
July Fourth Mtn—*summit* AK-9
July Lake—*lake* FL-3
July Lake—*lake* MS-4
July Lake—*lake* WI-6
July Mtn—*summit* AL-4
July Pit—*cave* AL-4
July Point—*cape* NC-3
July Ridge—*ridge* WA-9
July Run—*stream* WV-2
July Spring—*spring* FL-3
July Spring—*spring* OK-5
July Spring—*spring* OR-9
*Julytown* NJ-2
*July 4 Butte* AZ-5
Jumanes Knob—*summit* NM-5
Juma Reef—*bar* AK-9
Jumbers Point—*cape* UT-8
Jumbie Bay—*bay* VI-3
Jumbile Cove—*gut* TX-5
Jumbled Hills—*summit* NV-8
Jumbled Mtn—*summit* NV-8
Jumbled Rock Gulch—*valley* NV-8
Jumble Lake—*lake* CA-9
Jumbo—*locale* AL-4
Jumbo—*locale* NJ-2
Jumbo—*locale* OK-5
Jumbo—*locale* TX-5
**Jumbo**—*pop pl* AR-4
**Jumbo**—*pop pl* KY-4
**Jumbo**—*pop pl* OH-6
**Jumbo**—*pop pl* TN-4
**Jumbo**—*pop pl* WV-2
Jumbo, Mount—*summit* AK-9
Jumbo, Mount—*summit* MT-8
Jumbo Basin—*basin* AK-9
Jumbo Basin—*basin* ID-8
Jumbo Basin—*basin* NV-8
Jumbo Camp (Site)—*locale* ID-8
Jumbo Canyon—*valley* ID-8
Jumbo Canyon—*valley* UT-8
*Jumbo Creek* WI-6
Jumbo Creek—*stream* (3) AK-9
Jumbo Creek—*stream* (3) ID-8
Jumbo Creek—*stream* MT-8
Jumbo Creek—*stream* OR-9
Jumbo Creek—*stream* (2) WA-9
Jumbo Dome—*summit* AK-9
Jumbo Falls—*falls* NV-8
Jumbo Hill—*summit* TX-5
Jumbo Hill Windmill—*locale* TX-5
Jumbo Island—*island* AK-9
Jumbo Lake—*lake* (2) MT-8
*Jumbo Lakes* MI-6
Jumbo Landing—*locale* ME-1
Jumbo Lode Mine—*mine* SD-7
Jumbo Lookout Trail (pack)—*trail* MT-8
Jumbo Mine—*mine* AK-9
Jumbo Mine—*mine* (2) CA-9
Jumbo Mine—*mine* (2) CO-8
Jumbo Mine—*mine* ID-8
Jumbo Mine—*mine* (3) MT-8
Jumbo Mine—*mine* (3) NV-8
Jumbo Mine—*mine* UT-8
Jumbo Mtn—*summit* (2) CO-8
Jumbo Mtn—*summit* ID-8
Jumbo Mtn—*summit* (3) MT-8
Jumbo Mtn—*summit* (2) WA-9
Jumbo Pass—*gap* NV-8
Jumbo Pasture—*flat* AZ-5
Jumbo Peak—*summit* AK-9
Jumbo Peak—*summit* MT-8
Jumbo Peak—*summit* (2) NV-8
Jumbo Peak—*summit* WA-9
*Jumbo Reservoir* CO-8
Jumbo Reservoir Campground—*locale* CO-8
Jumbo Ridge—*ridge* OR-9
Jumbo River—*stream* MI-6
Jumbo Rock—*bar* AK-9
Jumbo Rocks—*locale* CA-9
Jumbo Rocks Campground—*locale* CA-9
Jumbo Rsvr—*reservoir* CO-8
Jumbo Sch—*school* WV-2
Jumbo (Site)—*locale* NV-8
Jumbo Spring—*spring* CA-9
Jumbo Spring—*spring* MO-7
Jumbo Spring—*spring* (2) NV-8
Jumbo Springs—*spring* OR-9
Jumbo Table—*summit* WY-8
Jumbo Tank—*reservoir* (2) AZ-5
Jumbo Tank—*reservoir* TX-5
Jumbo Wash—*stream* NV-8
Jumbo Wash—*valley* AZ-5
**Jumeau**—*pop pl* FL-3
Jumel Terrace Hist Dist—*hist pl* NY-2
**Jumonville**—*pop pl* PA-2
Jumonville Cave—*cave* PA-2
Jumonville Rocks—*cliff* PA-2
**Jump**—*pop pl* OH-6
Jump, Dr. Samuel Vaughn, House—*hist pl* IN-6
Jump, The—*gap* LA-4
*Jump and Run* NC-3
Jump And Run Branch—*stream* AL-4
Jump and Run Branch—*stream* (2) NC-3
Jump-And Run Branch—*stream* NC-3
Jump and Run Creek—*stream* NC-3
Jump Branch—*stream* MS-4
Jump Branch—*stream* WV-2
Jump Brook—*stream* NY-2
Jump Canyon—*valley* AZ-5
Jump Canyon—*valley* WA-9
Jump Corners—*locale* NY-2
Jump Cove—*valley* NC-3
Jump Creek—*stream* AL-4
Jump Creek—*stream* AK-9
Jump Creek—*stream* FL-3
Jump Creek—*stream* ID-8
Jump Creek—*stream* MS-4
Jump Creek—*stream* (2) OR-9
Jump Creek—*stream* (2) UT-8
Jump Creek Canyon—*valley* ID-8
Jump Creek Falls—*falls* ID-8
Jumper, Lake—*lake* FL-3
Jumper Cem—*cemetery* OK-5
Jumper Creek—*stream* AR-4
Jumper Creek—*stream* CO-8
Jumper Creek—*stream* FL-3
Jumper Creek—*stream* (2) OK-5
Jumper Creek Canal—*canal* FL-3
Jumper Creek Swamp—*swamp* FL-3
Jumper Drift (historical)—*mine* PA-2
Jumper Island—*island* FL-3
Jumper Lake—*lake* CO-8
Jumper Lake—*lake* FL-3
Jumper Ledge—*bar* ME-1
Jumper Sch (historical)—*school* MS-4
Jumpers Ponds—*reservoir* SC-3
*Jumpers Spring* AL-4
Jumpers Spring Branch—*stream* AL-4
Jumper Tank—*reservoir* TX-5
**Jumpertown**—*pop pl* MS-4
Jumpertown Attendance Center—*school* MS-4
Jumpertown Cem—*cemetery* MS-4
Jumpertown Ch—*church* MS-4
Jumpertown Ch of Christ—*church* MS-4
Jumpertown Consolidated Sch (historical)—*school* MS-4
*Jumpertown Methodist Church* MS-4
Jump Hill—*summit* NY-2
Jump Hill—*summit* TN-4
Jumpin Branch—*stream* VA-3
Jumping Bayou—*gut* LA-4
Jumping Bayou—*stream* LA-4
**Jumping Branch**—*pop pl* WV-2
Jumping Branch—*stream* MO-7
Jumping Branch—*stream* (2) NC-3
Jumping Branch—*stream* (2) SC-3
Jumping Branch—*stream* TN-4
Jumping Branch—*stream* (5) VA-3
Jumping Branch—*stream* WV-2
Jumping Branch Creek—*stream* TX-5
Jumping Brook—*stream* NH-1
Jumping Brook—*stream* (2) NJ-2
Jumping Brook Country Club—*other* NJ-2
Jumping Brook Dam—*dam* NJ-2
Jumping Brook Rsvr—*reservoir* NJ-2
Jumping Creek—*stream* (2) MS-4
Jumping Creek—*stream* MT-8
Jumping Creek—*stream* NC-3
Jumping Creek—*stream* VA-3
Jumping Creek Campground—*locale* MT-8
Jumping Divide—*other* NM-5
Jumping Gully—*canal* SC-3
Jumping Gully—*stream* FL-3
Jumping Gully—*stream* LA-4
Jumping Gully—*stream* SC-3
Jumping Gully—*valley* AL-4
Jumping Gully—*valley* FL-3
Jumping Gully Branch—*stream* FL-3
Jumping Gully Creek—*stream* FL-3
Jumping Gully Creek—*stream* (2) GA-3
Jumping Gully Creek—*stream* LA-4
*Jumping Gut* WV-2
Jumping Gut Creek—*stream* SC-3
Jumping Gut Run—*stream* WV-2
Jumping Hill—*summit* RI-1
Jumping Hills—*summit* SC-3
Jumping Horse Stock Ranch—*locale* MT-8
Jumping Juniper Branch—*stream* NC-3
Jumping Moses School—*rapids* TN-4
Jumping-off Draw—*valley* WY-8
Jumping Off Point—*summit* UT-8
Jumpingqbranch—*stream* AR-4
Jumping Rock—*pillar* OR-9
*Jumping Run* NC-3
Jumping Run—*stream* GA-3
Jumping Run—*stream* (12) NC-3
Jumping Run—*stream* OH-6
Jumping Run—*stream* SC-3
Jumping Run—*stream* VA-3
Jumping Run Branch—*stream* NC-3
Jumping Run Ch—*church* (2) NC-3
*Jumping Run Creek* NC-3
Jumping Run Creek—*stream* (3) NC-3
Jumping Run Creek—*stream* (2) SC-3
Jumping Run Creek—*stream* VA-3
Jumping Spring—*spring* AZ-5
Jumping Spring—*spring* NM-5
Jumpin In Creek—*stream* GA-3
Jumpinoff Rock Overlook—*locale* NC-3
Jump Lake—*lake* (2) MN-6
Jump Log Bayou—*gut* LA-4
Jump Mtn—*summit* VA-3
Jumpoff—*ridge* CA-9
Jump Off—*summit* NC-3
Jumpoff, The—*cliff* AZ-5
Jumpoff, The—*cliff* NY-2
Jumpoff, The—*cliff* OR-9
Jumpoff, The—*cliff* SD-7
Jumpoff, The—*cliff* TN-4
Jumpoff, The—*cliff* UT-8
Jumpoff, The—*cliff* WY-8
Jumpoff, The—*summit* CA-9
Jumpoff, The—*summit* UT-8
Jump-Off Canyon—*valley* AZ-5
Jumpoff Canyon—*valley* AZ-5
Jump Off Canyon—*valley* ID-8
Jumpoff Canyon—*valley* ID-8
Jumpoff Canyon—*valley* OR-9
Jumpoff Canyon—*valley* (2) UT-8
**Jumpoff Canyon Subdivision**—*pop pl* UT-8
Jumpoff Cem—*cemetery* TN-4
Jumpoff Ch—*church* TN-4
*Jumpoff Cove* TN-4
Jumpoff Cove—*valley* TN-4
Jumpoff Cove Branch—*stream* TN-4
Jumpoff Creek—*stream* AK-9
Jumpoff Creek—*stream* (2) CA-9
Jumpoff Creek—*stream* MS-4
Jump Off Creek—*stream* MO-7
Jumpoff Creek—*stream* TN-4
Jumpoff Divide—*gap* SD-7
Jumpoff Falls—*falls* TN-4
Jump Off Gap—*gap* NC-3
Jumpoff Gap—*gap* NC-3
*Jumpoff Hill* AZ-5
Jumpoff Hill—*summit* ID-8
Jumpoff Hollow—*valley* MO-7
Jumpoff Hollow—*valley* UT-8
Jumpoff Icefall—*falls* AK-9
Jumpoff Joe—*cliff* OR-9
Jumpoff Joe—*cliff* WA-9
Jumpoff Joe—*locale* OR-9
Jump Off Joe—*summit* WA-9
Jumpoff Joe Bluff—*cliff* WA-9
Jumpoff Joe Camp—*locale* OR-9
Jump Off Joe Canyon—*valley* OR-9
Jumpoff Joe Creek—*stream* OR-9
Jumpoff Joe Creek—*stream* (2) WA-9
Jumpoff Joe Curve—*locale* CA-9
Jumpoff Joe Lake—*lake* OR-9
Jumpoff Joe Lake—*lake* WA-9
Jump-off Joe Mtn—*summit* OR-9
Jumpoff Joe Mtn—*summit* OR-9
Jumpoff Joe Mtn—*summit* WA-9
Jumpoff Joe Peak—*summit* OR-9

Jump Off Joe Point—cliff WA-9
Jumpoff Joe Trail—trail OR-9
Jumpoff Lake WA-9
Jumpoff Meadows—flat WA-9
Jumpoff Mountain WA-9
Jump-Off Mountain Dam—dam NC-3
Jump-Off Mountain Lake—reservoir NC-3
Jumpoff Mtn—summit NC-3
Jumpoff Peak—summit ID-8
Jump Off Peak—summit MT-8
Jumpoff Ridge—ridge AZ-5
Jump-off Ridge—ridge GA-3
Jumpoff Ridge—ridge (2) WA-9
Jumpoff Rock—cliff NC-3
Jump-Off Rock—summit AL-4
Jumpoff Sch (historical)—school TN-4
Jumpoff Spring—spring AZ-5
Jump-Off Spring—spring AZ-5
Jump-off Spring—spring AZ-5
Jumpoff Spring—spring SD-7
Jumpoff Spring—spring UT-8
Jumpoff Tank—reservoir AZ-5
Jumpover Creek—stream NC-3
Jump Pass—channel FL-3
Jump Pond—lake ME-1
**Jump River**—pop pl WI-6
Jump River—stream WI-6
Jump River Fire Tower—locale WI-6
Jump River Town Hall—hist pl WI-6
**Jump River (Town of)**—pop pl WI-6
Jump Rock—summit VA-3
Jump Rock Run—stream WV-2
Jump Run—bay NC-3
Jumps, The—summit VA-3
Jumps Cem—cemetery GA-3
Jump Station—locale KY-4
Jumptown—locale MD-2
Jump-up—cliff UT-8
Jump-up, The—cliff NC-3
Jumpup Canyon—valley AZ-5
Jump-Up Canyon—valley UT-8
Jumpup Divide—summit AZ-5
Jumpup Point—cliff AZ-5
Jumpup Ridge—ridge NC-3
Jumpup Spring—spring AZ-5
Jumpup Spring—spring UT-8
Jumpup Tank—reservoir AZ-5
Jump Up Tank—reservoir AZ-5
Jumpup Trick Tank—reservoir AZ-5
Jumukahi, Cape—cape HI-9
Jumullong Manglo, Mount—summit GU-9
Junaluska NC-3
Junaluska, Lake—reservoir NC-3
Junaluska Ch—church NC-3
Junaluska City Park—park NC-3
Junaluska Creek—stream NC-3
Junaluska Elem Sch—school NC-3
Junaluska Gap—gap NC-3
Junaluska Mountain NC-3
Junaluska Ridge NC-3
Juncal CA-9
Juncal (Barrio)—fmr MCD PR-3
Juncal Campground—locale CA-9
Juncal Canyon—valley CA-9
Juncal Dam—dam CA-9
Juncob Lake—lake MI-6
Junco Creek—stream AK-9
Junco Creek—stream MN-6
Junco Creek—stream OR-9
Junco Lake—lake CO-8
Junco Lake—lake MN-6
Junco Lake—lake OR-9
Junco Lake—lake WY-8
**Juncos**—pop pl PR-3
Juncos (Municipio)—civil PR-3
Juncos (Pueblo)—fmr MCD PR-3
Junction AL-4
Junction CA-9
Junction IN-6
Junction KS-7
Junction KY-4
Junction ND-7
Junction—locale NY-2
Junction—locale NC-3
Junction—locale TN-4
Junction—locale WA-9
Junction—locale WV-2
Junction—locale WI-6
**Junction**—pop pl IL-6
**Junction**—pop pl LA-4
**Junction**—pop pl OH-6
**Junction**—pop pl TX-5
**Junction**—pop pl UT-8
Junction, Bayou—stream LA-4
Junction, Lake—reservoir TX-5
Junction, The MS-4
Junction, The MO-7
Junction Airp—airport UT-8
Junction Ave Sch—school CA-9
Junction Bar ID-8
Junction Bar—bar CA-9
Junction Bay—bay MN-6
Junction Bear Run Branch Station—locale PA-2
Junction Bluffs—cliff CA-9
Junction Blvd—uninc pl NY-2
Junction Bostonia Branch Station—locale PA-2
Junction Branch—stream MO-7
Junction Burn—area OR-9
Junction Butte—summit CA-9
Junction Butte—summit CO-8
Junction Butte—summit UT-8
Junction Butte—summit WY-8
Junction Camp—locale (2) CA-9
Junction Campground—locale CA-9
Junction Canyon—valley UT-8
Junction Captina Spur OH-6
Junction Cem—cemetery ID-8
Junction Cem—cemetery UT-8
Junction City—locale MS-4
Junction City—locale SD-7
**Junction City**—pop pl AR-4
**Junction City**—pop pl CA-9
**Junction City**—pop pl GA-3
**Junction City**—pop pl KS-7
**Junction City**—pop pl KY-4
**Junction City**—pop pl LA-4
**Junction City**—pop pl MO-7
**Junction City**—pop pl OH-6
**Junction City**—pop pl OR-9
**Junction City**—pop pl WA-9
**Junction City**—pop pl WI-6
Junction City (CCD)—cens area GA-3
Junction City (CCD)—cens area KY-4
Junction City (CCD)—cens area OR-9
**Junction City (Glen Ridge Station)**—pop pl IL-6
Junction City HS—school KS-7
Junction City Municipal Airp—airport KS-7
Junction City Oil Field—oilfield MS-4
Junction City Rsvr—reservoir KS-7
Junction City Substation—locale OR-9
Junction Cove UT-8
Junction Crater—crater AZ-5
Junction Creek MT-8
Junction Creek—stream (2) AK-9
Junction Creek—stream CA-9
Junction Creek—stream CO-8
Junction Creek—stream (3) ID-8
Junction Creek—stream MN-6
Junction Creek—stream MT-8
Junction Creek—stream (2) OR-9
Junction Creek—stream (2) UT-8
Junction Creek—stream (2) WA-9
Junction Elem Sch—school KS-7
Junction Ferry—locale MO-7
Junction Hill—summit KY-4
Junction Hill—summit NY-2
Junction Hill Cem—cemetery UT-8
Junction Hills—summit UT-8
**Junction (historical)**—pop pl IA-7
Junction House—locale CA-9
Junction House (Site)—locale CA-9
Junction Interstate Nineteen Interchange—crossing AZ-5
Junction Island—island (3) AK-9
Junction Lake—flat OR-9
Junction Lake—lake CA-9
Junction Lake—lake (2) OR-9
Junction Lake—lake (2) WA-9
Junction Lake—lake WI-6
Junction Lake—lake (2) WY-8
Junction Light—locale AK-9
Junction Lookout (historical)—locale MO-7
Junction Lower Cem—cemetery UT-8
Junction Meadow CA-9
Junction Meadow—flat (3) CA-9
Junction Mine—mine CA-9
Junction Mine—mine NM-5
Junction Mtn—summit MT-8
Junction Mtn—summit WA-9
Junction Northwest (CCD)—cens area TX-5
Junction Overlook—locale AZ-5
Junction Pass—gap CA-9
Junction Peak—summit CA-9
Junction Peak—summit (2) ID-8
Junction Plaza (Shop Ctr)—locale NC-3
Junction Pond OR-9
Junction Post Office—building UT-8
Junction Pumping Station—other CA-9
Junction Ranch—locale CA-9
Junction Ranger Station—locale SD-7
Junction Ridge—ridge CA-9
Junction Ridge—ridge ID-8
Junction Ridge—ridge LA-4
Junction RR Depot—hist pl IN-6
Junction Rsvr—reservoir CA-9
Junction Rsvr—reservoir ID-8
Junction Rsvr—reservoir OR-9
Junction Rsvr—reservoir WY-8
Junction Ruin—locale UT-8
Junction Saddle—gap AZ-5
Junction Sch—school (3) CA-9
Junction Sch—school CO-8
Junction Sch—school IL-6
Junction Sch—school IA-7
Junction Sch—school UT-8
Junction Shop and Herman Street District—hist pl MA-1
Junction Southeast (CCD)—cens area TX-5
Junction Spring—spring CA-9
Junction Spring—spring (2) ID-8
Junction Spring—spring (2) OR-9
Junction Spring—spring UT-8
Junction State Route Eightfour Interchange—crossing AZ-5
Junction Station—uninc pl CA-9
**Junction Switch**—pop pl IA-7
Junction Tank—reservoir (4) AZ-5
Junction Tank Number One—reservoir AZ-5
Junction Tanks—reservoir AZ-5
Junction. The—locale AL-4
Junction Township—fmr MCD IA-7
**Junction Township**—pop pl KS-7
Junction Valley CA-9
Junction Valley—basin UT-8
Junction Valley—valley ID-8
Junction Waterhole—reservoir OR-9
Junction Well—well NV-8
Junction Whitehall Station—building PA-2
Junction Windmill—locale TX-5
Juncture Peak—summit AK-9
Juncus Lake—lake MT-8
Jund Dam—dam ND-7
June, Bayou—stream LA-4
June, Lake—lake AR-4
June, Lake—reservoir (2) TX-5
June, Lewis, House—hist pl CT-1
June, Mount—summit OR-9
Juneau—locale PA-2
**Juneau**—pop pl AK-9
**Juneau**—pop pl NC-3
**Juneau**—pop pl WI-6
Juneau—uninc pl WI-6
Juneau, Mount—summit AK-9
Juneau (Borough) AK-9
Juneau (Census Subarea)—cens area AK-9
**Juneau (County)**—pop pl WI-6
Juneau County Courthouse—hist pl WI-6
Juneau County Ditch—canal WI-6
Juneau Creek—stream (2) AK-9
Juneau HS—school WI-6
Juneau International Airp—airport AK-9
Juneau Island—island AK-9
Juneau Lake—lake AK-9
Juneau Lake—lake ND-7
Juneau Park—park WI-6
Juneau Spur—locale AR-4
Juneautown WI-6
Juneberry Cem—cemetery MN-6
Juneberry Ridge—ridge MN-6
Juneberry Trail—trail PA-2
June Branch—stream SC-3
June Branch—stream TN-4
Junebug Branch—stream TN-4
June Bug Campground—locale NM-5
Junebug Creek TN-4
Junebug Creek—stream TN-4
June Bug (historical)—locale AL-4
June Bug Hollow—valley TN-4
June Bug Mine—mine NV-8
Juneburn Branch—stream SC-3
June Canyon—valley NV-8
June Carter Hollow—valley AR-4
June Cem—cemetery (2) NY-2
June Cem—cemetery VT-1
June Creek—stream (3) AK-9
June Creek—stream (3) CO-8
June Creek—stream (3) ID-8
June Creek—stream WA-9
June Creek—stream (3) WY-8
June Creek Ditch—canal CO-8
**Junedale**—pop pl PA-2
**Junedale (RR name Leviston)**—pop pl PA-2
June Day Mine—mine ID-8
June Draw—valley WY-8
June Ellen Mine—mine NV-8
June Grass Table—summit ID-8
June Heaton Tank—reservoir AZ-5
**June (historical)**—pop pl OR-9
June Hollow—valley PA-2
June House—hist pl LA-4
June In Winter, Lake—lake FL-3
Junekaket Creek—stream AK-9
Junekaket Slough—stream AK-9
Juneks Point—cape WI-6
June Lake WI-6
June Lake—lake CA-9
June Lake—lake MI-6
June Lake—lake (2) MN-6
June Lake—lake OR-9
June Lake—lake (2) WA-9
June Lake—lake (3) WI-6
**June Lake**—pop pl CA-9
June Lake—reservoir AR-4
June Lake Flow WA-9
June Lake Junction—locale CA-9
**June Meadows**—pop pl PA-2
June Mtn—summit MA-1
June Mtn—summit WA-9
**June Park**—pop pl FL-3
June Pond—lake FL-3
June Pond—lake MA-1
June Pond Strand—stream SC-3
June Rose Ch—church OK-5
June Rsvr—reservoir OR-9
Junes Bottom—bend UT-8
June Sch—school MI-6
June Spring AZ-5
June Spring—spring OR-9
June Spring—spring UT-8
**June Street (subdivision)**—pop pl MA-1
Junet—locale MI-6
June Tank—reservoir AZ-5
June Tank—reservoir NM-5
"June Tolliver" House—hist pl VA-3
Junetta Creek—stream OR-9
June Wash—stream CA-9
Juneway Terrace Park—park IL-6
**Junewood**—pop pl PA-2
Juney Whank Branch—stream NC-3
Jung, Alf, House—hist pl TX-5
Jung, Joe, House—hist pl TX-5
Jungbluth Ditch—canal OH-6
Jung Carriage Factory—hist pl WI-6
Jungclause Airp—airport IN-6
Jung Creek—stream TX-5
Jung Dam—dam ND-7
Junge Park—park IA-7
Jungfrau—summit TX-5
Jungfrau Lake—lake WA-9
Jung Hotel—hist pl LA-4
Jungjuk Creek—stream AK-9
Jung Lake—reservoir ND-7
Jungle—uninc pl FL-3
**Jungle, The**—pop pl FL-3
Jungle Basin—basin NV-8
Jungle Bay—bay FL-3
Jungle Butte—summit WA-9
Jungle Canyon—valley CO-8
Jungle Creek—stream AK-9
Jungle Creek—stream (7) ID-8
Jungle Creek—stream MI-6
Jungle Creek—stream (4) MT-8
Jungle Creek—stream (4) OR-9
Jungle Creek—stream (5) WA-9
Jungle Creek Campground—locale WA-9
Jungle Creek Trail—trail ID-8
Jungle Dam—dam AZ-5
Jungle Ditch IN-6
Jungle Gardens—locale LA-4
Jungle Gulch—valley ID-8
Jungle Hill—summit WA-9
Jungle Island SD-7
Jungle Lake—lake ID-8
Jungle Lake—lake WI-6
Jungle Park—park IN-6
Jungle Point—cliff ID-8
Jungle Point—summit (2) ID-8
Jungle Ridge—ridge TN-4
Jungles, The—other NM-5
Jungles Ditch—canal IN-6
Jungles Gate—other NM-5
Jungle Spring—spring CA-9
Jungle Spring—spring CO-8
Jungle Spring—spring (3) OR-9
Jungle Spring—spring WA-9
Jungman Lake—reservoir TX-5
Jungmann Hall—locale NE-7
Jungmann Sch—school NE-7
Jungman Sch—school IL-6
**Jungo**—pop pl NV-8
Jungo Flat—flat NV-8
Jungo Hills—summit NV-8
Jungo Stadium—other MO-7
Jung Ranch—locale TX-5
Jung Storage Bldg—hist pl TX-5
Juniata PA-2
Juniata—locale IA-7
Juniata—locale KS-7
Juniata—locale PA-2
**Juniata**—pop pl MI-6
**Juniata**—pop pl NE-7
**Juniata**—pop pl (2) PA-2
Juniata, Lake—lake FL-3
Juniata Bridge—locale PA-2
Juniata Cem—cemetery NE-7
Juniata Coll—school PA-2
**Juniata County**—pop pl PA-2
Juniata Crossing—locale PA-2
Juniata Elem Sch—school PA-2
Juniata Furnace—locale PA-2
**Juniata Gap**—pop pl PA-2
Juniata (historical)—locale AL-4
Juniata (historical)—locale (2) KS-7
Juniata Lake—lake PA-2
Juniata Memorial Cem—cemetery PA-2
Juniata Natl Wildlife Ref—park ND-7
Juniata Ovens PA-2
Juniata Park—park PA-2
Juniata P.O. AL-4
Juniata River Overlook—locale PA-2
Juniata Rsvr—reservoir CO-8
Juniata Run—stream PA-2
Juniata School PA-2
**Juniata Terrace**—pop pl PA-2
Juniata Terrace Borough—civil PA-2
**Juniata Township**—pop pl NE-7
**Juniata (Township of)**—pop pl MI-6
**Juniata (Township of)**—pop pl (4) PA-2
Juniata Valley Ch—church PA-2
Juniata Valley Elem Sch—school PA-2
Juniata Valley HS—school PA-2
Juniataville PA-2
Juniata Woolen Mill and Newry Manor—hist pl PA-2
Juni Lake—lake MN-6
Juningguira Mtn—summit AK-9
Junio—locale PR-3
Junior—locale LA-4
**Junior**—pop pl (2) WV-2
Junior, Lake—lake TN-4
Junior Acad—school FL-3
Junior Acad—school GA-3
Junior Acad—school MO-7
Junior Acad—school NY-2
Junior Acad—school VA-3
**Junior Acres (subdivision)**—pop pl AL-4
Junior Bay—bay ME-1
Junior Branch—stream LA-4
Junior College—other TN-4
Junior College Lake—reservoir AL-4
Junior Creek—stream WA-9
Junior Furnace—locale OH-6
Junior Hall Sch—school IL-6
Junior HS—school FL-3
Junior HS—school (2) MA-1
Junior HS—school NY-2
Junior HS—school WI-6
Junior HS East—school MI-6
Junior HS North—school IN-6
Junior HS No 172—school NY-2
Junior HS Number 1—school NJ-2
Junior HS Number 3—school NJ-2
Junior HS Number 5—school NJ-2
Junior HS South—school IN-6
Junior HS 10—school NY-2
Junior HS 101—school (2) NY-2
Junior HS 111—school NY-2
Junior HS 115—school (2) NY-2
Junior HS 117—school NY-2
Junior HS 118—school (2) NY-2
Junior HS 12—school NY-2
Junior HS 120—school (2) NY-2
Junior HS 123—school NY-2
Junior HS 125—school NY-2
Junior HS 126—school (2) NY-2
Junior HS 127—school NY-2
Junior HS 128—school NY-2
Junior HS 135—school NY-2
Junior HS 136—school (3) NY-2
Junior HS 139—school NY-2
Junior HS 141—school (2) NY-2
Junior HS 142—school (2) NY-2
Junior HS 143—school NY-2
Junior HS 145—school (2) NY-2
Junior HS 148—school NY-2
Junior HS 149—school (2) NY-2
Junior HS 155—school NY-2
Junior HS 157—school NY-2
Junior HS 158—school NY-2
Junior HS 16—school NY-2
Junior HS 162—school NY-2
Junior HS 164—school NY-2
Junior HS 166—school NY-2
Junior HS 167—school NY-2
Junior HS 168—school NY-2
Junior HS 171—school NY-2
Junior HS 178—school NY-2
Junior HS 180—school NY-2
Junior HS 185—school NY-2
Junior HS 188—school NY-2
Junior HS 189—school NY-2
Junior HS 190—school NY-2
Junior HS 194—school NY-2
Junior HS 198—school NY-2
Junior HS 202—school NY-2
Junior HS 210—school (2) NY-2
Junior HS 211—school NY-2
Junior HS 217—school NY-2
Junior HS 218—school NY-2
Junior HS 22—school NY-2
Junior HS 220—school NY-2
Junior HS 223—school NY-2
Junior HS 227—school NY-2
Junior HS 228—school NY-2
Junior HS 231—school NY-2
Junior HS 232—school NY-2
Junior HS 234—school NY-2
Junior HS 240—school NY-2
Junior HS 258—school NY-2
Junior HS 259—school NY-2
Junior HS 263—school NY-2
Junior HS 265—school NY-2
Junior HS 275—school NY-2
Junior HS 278—school NY-2
Junior HS 285—school NY-2
Junior HS 29—school NY-2
Junior HS 292—school NY-2
Junior HS 296—school NY-2
Junior HS 3—school NY-2
Junior HS 30—school NY-2
Junior HS 33—school NY-2
Junior HS 35—school NY-2
Junior HS 37—school NY-2
Junior HS 40—school NY-2
Junior HS 43—school (2) NY-2
Junior HS 44—school NY-2
Junior HS 45—school (2) NY-2
Junior HS 49—school NY-2
Junior HS 50—school NY-2
Junior HS 51—school (3) NY-2
Junior HS 52—school (2) NY-2
Junior HS 54—school NY-2
Junior HS 55—school (2) NY-2
Junior HS 57—school NY-2
Junior HS 59—school NY-2
Junior HS 6—school NY-2
Junior HS 60—school (2) NY-2
Junior HS 61—school (2) NY-2
Junior HS 64—school NY-2
Junior HS 65—school NY-2
Junior HS 68—school NY-2
Junior HS 72—school NY-2
Junior HS 73—school (2) NY-2
Junior HS 74—school NY-2
Junior HS 78—school NY-2
Junior HS 8—school NY-2
Junior HS 81—school NY-2
Junior HS 82—school NY-2
Junior HS 83—school NY-2
Junior HS 96—school NY-2
Junior HS 98—school NY-2
Junior HS 99—school NY-2
Junior Hyalite Camp—locale MT-8
Junior Island—island MN-6
Junior Lake—lake FL-3
Junior Lake—lake ME-1
Junior Mtn—summit ME-1
Junior Museum—building CA-9
Junior Order United American Mechanics Natl Orphans Home—hist pl NC-3
Junior Point—summit WA-9
Junior Schmidt Number 1 Dam—dam SD-7
Juniors Hill Ch—church FL-3
Junior Stream—stream ME-1
Junior Tank—reservoir NM-5
Junior Women Club Park—park NC-3
Junipe Creek NC-3
Junipen Gap—gap OR-9
Juniper AZ-5
Juniper—locale CA-9
Juniper—locale FL-3
Juniper—locale GA-3
Juniper—locale ID-8
Juniper—locale MI-6
Juniper—locale NC-3
Juniper—locale OR-9
**Juniper**—pop pl OR-9
Juniper Air Park—airport OR-9
Juniper Bark Canyon—valley AZ-5
Juniper Basin—basin AZ-5
Juniper Basin—basin ID-8
Juniper Basin—basin NV-8
Juniper Basin—basin NM-5
Juniper Basin—basin OR-9
Juniper Basin Creek—stream OR-9
Juniper Basin Ranch—locale ID-8
Juniper Basin Rsvr—reservoir (2) ID-8
Juniper Basin Rsvr—reservoir OR-9
Juniper Basin Spring—spring OR-9
Juniper Bay—bay NC-3
Juniper Bay—locale SC-3
Juniper Bay—stream SC-3
Juniper Bay—swamp FL-3
Juniper Bay—swamp (2) MS-4
Juniper Bay—swamp (5) NC-3
Juniper Bay—swamp (2) SC-3
Juniper Bay (Carolina Bay)—swamp NC-3
Juniper Bay Creek—stream NC-3
Juniper Bay Point—cape NC-3
Juniper Beach—locale WA-9
**Juniper Beach**—pop pl KY-4
Juniper Bed Grounds—flat OR-9
Juniper Bog—swamp ME-1
Juniper Bowl—basin CA-9
Juniper Branch ME-1
Juniper Branch NC-3
Juniper Branch—stream (2) FL-3
Juniper Branch—stream (2) GA-3
Juniper Branch—stream (9) NC-3
Juniper Branch—stream SC-3
Juniper Brook—stream (2) ME-1
Juniper Butte—locale OR-9
Juniper Butte—summit CA-9
Juniper Butte—summit ID-8
Juniper Butte—summit (3) OR-9
Juniper Butte—summit WY-8
Juniper Camp—locale CA-9
Juniper Camp—locale OR-9
Juniper Canal—canal NC-3
Juniper Canyon WA-9
Juniper Canyon—valley AZ-5
Juniper Canyon—valley CO-8
Juniper Canyon—valley NV-8
Juniper Canyon—valley (2) NM-5
Juniper Canyon—valley (14) OR-9
Juniper Canyon—valley TX-5
Juniper Canyon—valley (2) WA-9
Juniper Canyon Rsvr—reservoir OR-9
Juniper Cem—cemetery FL-3
Juniper Cem—cemetery ME-1
Juniper Ch—church FL-3
Juniper Ch—church NC-3
Juniper Chapel—church NC-3
Juniper Chapel—church OH-6
**Juniper Circle**—pop pl PA-2
Juniper Cove—cove MA-1
Juniper Cove Park—park TX-5
Juniper Creek CA-9
Juniper Creek FL-3
Juniper Creek GA-3
Juniper Creek OR-9
Juniper Creek VA-3
Juniper Creek—bay NC-3
Juniper Creek—stream (4) AL-4
Juniper Creek—stream (2) AK-9
Juniper Creek—stream (2) CA-9
Juniper Creek—stream (11) FL-3
Juniper Creek—stream (3) GA-3
Juniper Creek—stream (4) ID-8
Juniper Creek—stream (2) MS-4
Juniper Creek—stream NV-8
Juniper Creek—stream (9) NC-3
Juniper Creek—stream (15) OR-9
Juniper Creek—stream (2) SC-3
Juniper Creek—stream TX-5
Juniper Creek—stream VA-3
Juniper Creek—stream WA-9
Juniper Creek—stream (2) WY-8
Juniper Creek—swamp FL-3
Juniper Creek Islands—island FL-3
Juniper Creek Point—cape NC-3
Juniper Creek Rsvr—reservoir OR-9
Juniper Dam—dam AZ-5
Juniper Dam—dam MT-8
Juniper Draw—valley (2) ID-8
Juniper Draw—valley NM-5
Juniper Draw—valley TX-5
Juniper Draw—valley WY-8
Juniper Dump—locale NV-8
Juniper Flat AZ-5
Juniper Flat—flat (4) AZ-5
Juniper Flat—flat (4) CA-9
Juniper Flat—flat NV-8
Juniper Flat—flat NM-5
Juniper Flat—flat (4) OR-9
Juniper Flats—flat AZ-5
Juniper Flats—flat (2) CA-9
Juniper Flat Spring—spring OR-9
Juniper Flat Tank—reservoir (2) AZ-5
Juniper Flat Tanks—reservoir NM-5
Juniper For Survival Training Site—area WA-9
Juniper Gas Field—oilfield TX-5
Juniper Glade—flat OR-9
Juniper Glade Pond—lake OR-9
Juniper Golf Course—other OR-9
Juniper Grade—locale OR-9
**Juniper Grove**—pop pl MS-4
Juniper Grove Baptist Church MS-4
Juniper Grove Ch—church MS-4
Juniper Grove Wash—valley AZ-5
Juniper Gulch AZ-5
Juniper Gulch—valley (3) CA-9
Juniper Gulch—valley ID-8
Juniper Gulch—valley (5) OR-9
Juniper Haven Cem—cemetery OR-9
**Juniper Heights**—pop pl AZ-5
Juniper Hill—summit AZ-5
Juniper Hill—summit CA-9
Juniper Hill—summit (3) MA-1
Juniper Hill—summit NM-5
Juniper Hill—summit NY-2
Juniper Hill—summit RI-1
Juniper Hill Country Club—locale MA-1
Juniper Hill Farm-Maxwell Evarts House—hist pl VT-1
Juniper Hill Municipal Park—park KY-4
**Juniper Hills**—pop pl CA-9
Juniper Hill Sch—school MA-1
Juniper Hill Sch—school NY-2
Juniper Hill Spring—spring OR-9
**Juniper (historical)**—pop pl (2) OR-9
**Juniper Hot Springs**—pop pl CO-8
Juniper Island—island MN-6
Juniper Island—island NY-2
Juniper Island—island VT-1
Juniper Island—summit AK-9
Juniper Jim Spring—spring CA-9
Juniper Knee Bog—swamp ME-1
Juniper Knee Pond—lake ME-1
Juniper Knoll—summit CA-9
Juniper Lake OR-9
Juniper Lake—lake (2) CA-9
Juniper Lake—lake ID-8
Juniper Lake—lake MN-6
Juniper Lake—lake NM-5
Juniper Lake—lake (2) OR-9
Juniper Lake—reservoir FL-3
Juniper Lake—reservoir GA-3
**Juniper Lake Resort**—pop pl CA-9
Juniper Ledge—bar VT-1
Juniper Level Ch—church NC-3
Juniper Mesa—summit AZ-5
Juniper Mesa Tank—reservoir (2) AZ-5
Juniper Mine—mine AZ-5
Juniper Mine—mine CA-9
Juniper Mine—mine NV-8
Juniper Mine—mine SD-7
Juniper Mountain Ranch—locale OR-9
Juniper Mountains—range AZ-5
Juniper Mountain Waterhole—well OR-9
Juniper Mountain Waterhole Number Two—lake OR-9
Juniper Mtn OR-9
Juniper Mtn—summit AZ-5
Juniper Mtn—summit CA-9
Juniper Mtn—summit CO-8
Juniper Mtn—summit ID-8
Juniper Mtn—summit NV-8
Juniper Mtn—summit (5) OR-9
Junipero Serra HS—school CA-9
Junipero Serra Peak—summit CA-9
Juniper Park—park OR-9
Juniper Park Campground—park UT-8
Juniper Park Ranch—locale OR-9
**Juniper Park Resort**—pop pl UT-8
Juniper Pass—gap CO-8
Juniper Pass—gap (2) NV-8
Juniper Pass—gap UT-8
Juniper Peak—summit NV-8
Juniper Peak—summit (2) NM-5
Juniper Peak—summit TX-5
Juniper Peak—summit WA-9
Juniper Point—cape CA-9
Juniper Point—cape CT-1
Juniper Point—cape ME-1
Juniper Point—cape (2) MA-1
Juniper Point—cape OR-9
Juniper Point—cape WA-9
Juniper Point—summit AZ-5
Juniper Point—summit OR-9
Juniper Point Light—locale MA-1
Juniper Point Rec Area—park OK-5
Juniper Point Rsvr—reservoir OR-9
Juniper Pond—lake MA-1
Juniper Pond—lake NY-2
Juniper Pond—swamp NC-3
Juniper Prairie—flat FL-3
Juniper Ranch Rsvr—reservoir OR-9
Juniper Ridge—ridge (3) AZ-5

Juniper Ridge—*ridge* (3) CA-9
Juniper Ridge—*ridge* NV-8
Juniper Ridge—*ridge* NM-5
Juniper Ridge—*ridge* (7) OR-9
Juniper Ridge—*ridge* WA-9
Juniper Ridge Lookout Tower—*tower* AZ-5
Juniper Ridge Spring—*spring* CA-9
Juniper Ridge Tank—*reservoir* NM-5
Juniper Rsvr—*reservoir* (3) OR-9
Juniper Rsvr—*reservoir* WY-8
Juniper Run—*Swamp* SC-3
*Junipers, The* ID-8
Junipers, The—*woods* AZ-5
Juniper Sch—*school* (2) CA-9
Juniper Sch—*school* NV-8
Juniper Serra Museum—*building* CA-9
Juniper Serra Sch—*school* CA-9
Juniper Spring—*spring* (14) AZ-5
Juniper Spring—*spring* (8) CA-9
Juniper Spring—*spring* (2) ID-8
Juniper Spring—*spring* (3) NV-8
Juniper Spring—*spring* (3) NM-5
Juniper Spring—*spring* (12) OR-9
Juniper Spring—*spring* TX-5
Juniper Spring Campground—*locale* ID-8
Juniper Spring Creek Rsvr—*reservoir* OR-9
Juniper Spring Draw—*valley* OR-9
Juniper Spring Rsvr—*reservoir* OR-9
*Juniper Springs* CO-8
**Juniper Springs**—*pop pl* CA-9
Juniper Springs—*spring* FL-3
Juniper Springs—*spring* NV-8
Juniper Springs—*spring* WA-9
Juniper Springs Ch—*church* NC-3
Juniper Springs Rec Area—*park* FL-3
Juniper Spur—*summit* ND-7
Juniper Station—*locale* GA-3
Juniper Station—*locale* ID-8
**Juniper Subdivision**—*pop pl* UT-8
Juniper Swamp—*stream* (4) NC-3
Juniper Swamp—*stream* SC-3
Juniper Swamp—*swamp* AL-4
Juniper Swamp—*swamp* FL-3
Juniper Swamp—*swamp* (2) NC-3
Juniper Swamp Brook—*stream* ME-1
Juniper Swamp Brook—*stream* NY-2
Juniper Swamp Point—*cape* NC-3
Juniper Tank—*reservoir* (18) AZ-5
Juniper Tank—*reservoir* (5) NM-5
Juniper Tank Dam—*dam* AZ-5
Juniper Trail—*trail* OR-9
Juniper Tree Draw—*valley* ID-8
Juniper Tree Rsvr—*reservoir* (2) OR-9
Juniper Tree Tank—*reservoir* AZ-5
Juniper Trick Tank—*reservoir* (2) AZ-5
Juniper Valley—*valley* ID-8
Juniper Valley Park—*park* NY-2
Juniper Waterhole—*reservoir* OR-9
Juniper Well—*well* (2) AZ-5
Juniper Well—*well* (2) NM-5
Juniper Windmill—*locale* NM-5
**Junius**—*pop pl* SD-7
Junius Ch—*church* NY-2
Junius Ponds—*lake* NY-2
Junius Ridge—*ridge* LA-4
**Junius (Town of)**—*pop pl* NY-2
Junjik River—*stream* AK-9
Junk Cem—*cemetery* PA-2
Junk Creek—*stream* WY-8
Junk Ditch—*canal* IN-6
Junk Draw—*valley* WY-8
Junken Ledge—*bar* ME-1
Junkens Creek—*stream* OR-9
*Junker* ND-7
Junker—*locale* NC-3
Junker, Jens N. and Anna, Farmstead—*hist pl* SD-7
Junker Sch—*school* TX-5
Junker Sch (abandoned)—*school* SD-7
*Junket Hill* MA-1
Junk Hill—*summit* WY-8
Junkie Creek—*stream* TX-5
Junkin Gravel Company Lake Dam—*dam* MS-4
Junkins Brook—*stream* ME-1
Junkins Camp—*locale* ME-1
Junkins Cem—*cemetery* OR-9
Junkins Island—*island* ME-1
Junkins Lake—*lake* MN-6
Junkins Lake—*lake* MS-4
Junkins Park—*basin* CO-8
Junkins Park Creek—*stream* CO-8
Junkins Park Sch—*school* CO-8
Junkins Point—*cape* ME-1
Junkins Run—*stream* KY-4
Junkins Sch—*school* IL-6
Junk of Pork—*bar* ME-1
Junk of Pork Island—*island* ME-1
Junkpile Spring—*spring* OR-9
*Junks Bayou* LA-4
*Junks Creek* MI-6
*Junks Lake* MI-6
Junkston Post Office (historical)—*building* TN-4
Junk Windmill—*locale* NM-5
Junkyard Bay—*swamp* SC-3
Junkyard Creek—*stream* NM-5
Junkyard Creek—*stream* TX-5
**Junland**—*pop pl* MO-7
Junnie, Lake—*lake* WI-6
Junniper Springs Two hundred ninety five Trail—*trail* AZ-5
Juno—*locale* GA-3
Juno—*locale* ND-7
Juno—*locale* TX-5
Juno—*locale* WA-9
**Juno**—*pop pl* NC-3
**Juno**—*pop pl* OR-9
**Juno**—*pop pl* TN-4
**Juno Beach**—*pop pl* FL-3
Juno Beach Ocean Park—*park* FL-3
Juno Beach United Methodist Ch—*church* FL-3
Juno (CCD)—*cens area* GA-3
Juno Cem—*cemetery* TX-5
Juno Ch—*church* TN-4
*Juno Ch of Christ* TN-4
**Junod**—*pop pl* IL-6
Juno-Echo Mine—*mine* WA-9
Juno Gulch—*valley* MT-8
**Juno Isles (subdivision)**—*pop pl* FL-3
Juno Lake—*lake* MI-6
Juno Lake—*lake* MN-6
Juno Mine—*mine* AZ-5
Juno Mine (historical)—*mine* SD-7
Juno Mtn—*summit* AK-9
Junop, Bay—*lake* LA-4
Juno Park—*park* FL-3
Juno Post Office (historical)—*building* TN-4
Junor Hollow—*valley* TX-5
Juno (RR name for Caretta)—*other* WV-2
Juno Sch (historical)—*school* TN-4
Juno Temple—*summit* AZ-5
**Junta**—*pop pl* GA-3
**Junta**—*pop pl* NM-5
Junta Creek—*stream* ID-8
Junte—*locale* KY-4
Juntunen Site—*hist pl* MI-6
**Juntura**—*pop pl* OR-9
Juntura Airstrip—*airport* OR-9
Juntura (CCD)—*cens area* OR-9
Juntura Cem—*cemetery* OR-9
Juntura Investment Company Canal—*canal* OR-9
Juntura Valley—*valley* OR-9
Ju Ot Te Park —*park* AZ-5
Jupa Lake—*lake* WI-6
**Jupe**—*pop pl* TX-5
*Jupiter* AL-4
Jupiter—*lake* AK-9
Jupiter—*locale* CA-9
**Jupiter**—*pop pl* FL-3
**Jupiter**—*pop pl* NC-3
Jupiter—*summit* OR-9
Jupiter, Mount—*summit* WA-9
Jupiter Canyon—*valley* AZ-5
Jupiter (CCD)—*cens area* FL-3
Jupiter Cem—*cemetery* FL-3
Jupiter Cem—*cemetery* MN-6
Jupiter Ch—*church* MS-4
Jupiter Creek—*stream* ID-8
Jupiter Ditch—*canal* CA-9
Jupiter Federal Bridge—*bridge* FL-3
Jupiter Hill—*summit* UT-8
*Jupiter Inlet* FL-3
Jupiter Inlet—*gut* FL-3
**Jupiter Inlet Beach Colony**—*pop pl* FL-3
**Jupiter Inlet Colony**—*pop pl* FL-3
Jupiter Inlet Historic and Archeol Site—*hist pl* FL-3
Jupiter Inlet Lighthouse—*hist pl* FL-3
Jupiter Island—*island* FL-3
**Jupiter Island**—*pop pl* FL-3
Jupiter Island Country Club—*locale* FL-3
Jupiter Island Park—*park* FL-3
Jupiter Lake—*lake* MN-6
Jupiter Lakes—*lake* WA-9
Jupiter Mall—*locale* FL-3
Jupiter Mine—*mine* (4) AZ-5
Jupiter Mine—*mine* (2) CA-9
Jupiter Mine—*mine* UT-8
Jupiter Mine (historical)—*mine* SD-7
Jupiter Mission Cem—*cemetery* MN-6
Jupiter Mountain—*ridge* CA-9
Jupiter MS—*school* FL-3
Jupiter Mtn—*summit* CO-8
Jupiter Pharmacy—*uninc pl* TX-5
*Jupiter Point* AZ-5
Jupiter Point—*cape* CT-1
Jupiter Ridge—*ridge* MA-1
Jupiter Ridge—*ridge* NV-8
*Jupiter River* FL-3
Jupiter Sch—*school* (2) FL-3
Jupiter Sound—*bay* FL-3
Jupiter Spring—*spring* AZ-5
Jupiter Temple—*summit* AZ-5
**Jupiter (Township of)**—*pop pl* MN-6
Jura, Mount—*summit* CA-9
*Juracka Brook* CT-1
Jura Knob—*summit* CO-8
Jurdan Creek—*stream* IA-7
**Jurden (Penjur)**—*pop pl* AR-4
Jurden Sch—*school* MO-7
Jurdon Creek—*stream* LA-4
Jureano Mtn—*summit* ID-8
Jureano Placer Diggings—*mine* ID-8
Jureczki House—*hist pl* TX-5
Juret Branch—*stream* TX-5
Jurett (historical)—*locale* KS-7
Jurgenson—*locale* MN-6
Jurica Sch—*school* MT-8
Juridi—*island* MP-9
*Juridi Island* MP-9
*Jurijer* MP-9
Jurista—*civil* CA-9
Jurjevich Canal—*canal* LA-4
Jurko Ranch—*locale* AZ-5
Jurn Drain—*canal* MI-6
*Jurney Creek* NC-3
Jurnigan Draw—*valley* NM-5
Jurnigan Spring—*spring* NM-5
Jurries Springs—*spring* OR-9
Jurry Spring—*spring* UT-8
*Jurupa* CA-9
Jurupa, Mount—*summit* CA-9
Jurupa (CCD)—*cens area* CA-9
Jurupa Cultural Center—*building* CA-9
Jurupa Ditch—*canal* CA-9
Jurupa Hills Country Club—*other* CA-9
Jurupa Hills Sch—*school* CA-9
Jurupa JHS—*school* CA-9
Jurupa Mountains—*range* CA-9
Jurupa (Rubidoux)—*civil* CA-9
Jurupa (Stearns)—*civil* CA-9
**Jurutungo**—*pop pl* PR-3
**Jury**—*pop pl* MO-7
**Jury**—*pop pl* TX-5
Jury Drain—*canal* MI-6
*Jury Hill* RI-1
Jury Hollow—*valley* MO-7
Jury Ridge—*ridge* TN-4
Juse (historical)—*locale* KS-7
Juso Ranch—*locale* SD-7
J U Spring—*spring* AZ-5
Jus Rsvr—*reservoir* ID-8
Jusserand Memorial—*park* DC-2
**Just**—*pop pl* NC-3
Justa Farm—*locale* PA-2
**Just A Farm**—*pop pl* PA-2
**Just-A-Mere Landing (subdivision)**—*pop pl* NC-3
Just Canal—*canal* ID-8
Just Crossroads—*locale* NC-3
Just Elem Sch—*school* FL-3
**Justell**—*pop pl* KY-4
Justensen Flats—*flat* UT-8
Just for Kids Acad—*school* FL-3
Justice—*locale* KY-4
**Justice**—*pop pl* IL-6
**Justice**—*pop pl* NC-3
**Justice**—*pop pl* WV-2
Justice, Mount—*summit* CO-8
**Justice Addition**—*pop pl* WV-2
Justice Bay—*bay* WI-6
Justice Bldg—*building* FL-3
Justice Branch—*stream* KY-4
*Justice Brook* MA-1
Justice Brook—*stream* MA-1
Justiceburg—*locale* TX-5
Justiceburg Lake—*reservoir* TX-5
Justiceburg Oil Field—*oilfield* TX-5
Justice Cem—*cemetery* NC-3
Justice Cem—*cemetery* OH-6
Justice Cem—*cemetery* VA-3
Justice Cem—*cemetery* (4) WV-2
Justice Ch—*church* KY-4
Justice Chapel—*church* LA-4
Justice Creek—*stream* (2) AK-9
Justice Creek—*stream* NC-3
**Justice Heights (subdivision)**—*pop pl* NC-3
Justice Heights United Methodist Ch—*church* MS-4
Justice Hill—*summit* CO-8
Justice Hill—*summit* MA-1
Justice Hollow—*valley* OH-6
Justice Hollow—*valley* TN-4
Justice Mill Creek—*stream* AL-4
Justice Mine—*mine* MT-8
Justice Mtn—*summit* TN-4
*Justice Neck* MA-1
Justice Ridge—*ridge* NC-3
Justice Run—*stream* PA-2
Justice Sch—*school* IL-6
Justice Sch—*school* OK-5
Justice Sch (historical)—*school* TN-4
Justice Shaft—*mine* NV-8
*Justices Mill* TN-4
**Justiceville**—*pop pl* KY-4
**Justin**—*pop pl* TX-5
Justina—*locale* LA-4
Justina Road Sch—*school* FL-3
Justin Canal—*canal* CA-9
Justine Spitalny Sch—*school* AZ-5
Justin Lake—*reservoir* PA-2
Justin McCarthy Ranch—*locale* WY-8
Justin N Study Elem Sch—*school* IN-6
Justin-Roanoke (CCD)—*cens area* TX-5
Justins Bay—*lake* AL-4
Justins Creek—*stream* IA-7
Justins Windmill—*well* AZ-5
Justis Cem—*cemetery* TN-4
Justis Cem—*cemetery* TX-5
Justis Dam—*dam* TN-4
Justis Gut—*gut* VA-3
Justis Lake—*reservoir* TN-4
Just Island—*island* AK-9
Justiss Cem—*cemetery* TX-5
Justiss Creek—*stream* TX-5
Justisson Ditch—*canal* MT-8
**Justisville**—*pop pl* VA-3
Just-It, Lake—*reservoir* NJ-2
Just Lake—*lake* MI-6
Justo Tank—*reservoir* NM-5
Justover Field Airp—*airport* NV-8
Justo Windmill—*locale* TX-5
**Justus**—*pop pl* OH-6
**Justus**—*pop pl* PA-2
Justus Cem—*cemetery* IN-6
Justus Cem—*cemetery* NC-3
Justus Cove—*valley* NC-3
Justus Creek—*stream* GA-3
Justus Ditch—*canal* ID-8
Justus Gap—*gap* GA-3
Justus Mtn—*summit* GA-3
Justus Sch—*school* OK-5
Justus Spring—*spring* OR-9
Jute Bay—*bay* AK-9
Jute Creek—*stream* AK-9
Jute Island—*island* AK-9
*Jute Lake* MN-6
Jute Lake—*lake* WI-6
Jute Lake Lookout Tower—*locale* WI-6
Juten Valley—*basin* NE-7
Jute Peak—*summit* AK-9
Juterboch Farm Cem—*cemetery* OH-6
Jut Lake—*lake* MN-6
**Jutland**—*pop pl* NJ-2
Jutland Creek—*bay* MD-2
Jutland Dam—*dam* NJ-2
Jutland Lake—*reservoir* NJ-2
Jutland Neck—*cape* MD-2
Juts Creek—*stream* NC-3
Jutten Cabin—*locale* CO-8
Jutten Camp—*locale* CO-8
Jutten Lakes—*lake* CO-8
Jutte Run—*stream* IN-6
Juttner Point—*cape* MI-6
Jutts Gap—*gap* NC-3
Juvenile Hall—*locale* CA-9
Juvenile Services Program—*school* FL-3
Juvigny Valley—*basin* MI-6
Jux Canyon—*valley* UT-8
J Vanham—*locale* TX-5
J V Blalock Lake Dam—*dam* MS-4
J V Gulch—*valley* CO-8
J V Ranch Airp—*airport* KS-7
J Wahus Ranch—*locale* ND-7
J Walker Ranch—*locale* ND-7
J Walter Becker Memorial Park—*cemetery* IL-6
J Walz Ranch—*locale* NE-7
Jwa Qwaw Gwa Spring—*spring* AZ-5
*J.W. Barney Rsvr* OR-9
J W Braswell Pond Dam—*dam* MS-4
J W Coon Elem Sch—*school* NC-3
J W Corbett Wildlife Mngmt Area—*park* FL-3
*JW Dismal Swamp* NC-3
J W Floyd Ditch—*canal* CO-8
J W Hartfield Lake Dam—*dam* MS-4
J Willey Dam—*dam* SD-7
J Will Taylor Bridge—*bridge* TN-4
**J. W. Johnson**—*pop pl* NY-2
J W Jones Sch—*school* TX-5
J W Lackey Dam—*dam* NC-3
J & W Landing Strip—*airport* PA-2
J W Marshall Shop—*other* CA-9
J W Mayhall Lake Dam—*dam* AL-4
JW Powell Sch—*school* AL-4
J W Poynter JHS—*school* OR-9
*J W Price Elementary School* PA-2
J W Ranch—*locale* NV-8
J W Spendlove Rsvr—*reservoir* AZ-5
JW Stone Airp—*airport* NC-3
J W Stoner Pond Dam—*dam* MS-4
J W Stowe Lake—*reservoir* NC-3
J W Stowe Lake Dam—*dam* NC-3
J W Sutton Ditch—*canal* CO-8
J W Sutton Ditch No 2—*canal* CO-8
J W Tank—*reservoir* AZ-5
J W Thornton Landing (historical)—*locale* AL-4
*J W Thorntons Landing* AL-4
J W Turlington Elem Sch—*school* NC-3
J W Vinson Lake Dam—*dam* MS-4
J W Wells State Park—*park* MI-6
J W Wilson Pond Dam—*dam* MS-4
J X Ranch—*locale* NM-5
J Yates Ranch—*locale* NM-5
*Jykill Sound* GA-3
J Y Monk Park—*park* NC-3
J Y Ranch—*locale* TX-5
J Y Ranch—*locale* WY-8
J Y Ranch South Camp—*locale* TX-5
J Y Ranch West Camp—*locale* TX-5
J-z Airp—*airport* WA-9
*J Z George Attendance Center* MS-4
*J Z George High School* MS-4
J Z George Sch—*school* MS-4
J Z Rogers Spring—*spring* AZ-5
J-1 Canal—*canal* OR-9
J-2 Creek—*stream* TX-5
J-2 Windmill—*locale* TX-5

# K

K, Ditch—*canal* MS-4
K, Lateral—*canal* (2) MT-8
K, Tank—*reservoir* AZ-5
*Ku* IN-6
Ka—*locale* VA-3
Kaa—*cape* HI-9
Kaa—*civil* HI-9
Kaa—*locale* FM-9
Kaa—*summit* HI-9
Kaa, Infal—*stream* FM-9
KAAA-AM (Kingman)—*tower* AZ-5
Kaalahina Ridge—*ridge* HI-9
Kaaawa—*civil* HI-9
**Kaaawa**—*pop pl* HI-9
Kaaawa Beach Park—*park* HI-9
Kaaawa Point—*cape* HI-9
Kaaawa Stream—*stream* HI-9
*Kaaba Mine* AZ-5
*Kaaben To* MP-9
*Kaacooe Hill* NY-2
Kaaealii—*summit* HI-9
Kaa Fishpond—*reservoir* HI-9
Kaa Gulch—*valley* (2) HI-9
Kaaha—*cape* HI-9
Kaaha—*summit* HI-9
Kaahakini Stream—*stream* HI-9
Kaaha Point—*cape* HI-9
Kaaheiki Stream—*stream* HI-9
Kaahina Stream—*stream* HI-9
Kaahole Valley—*valley* HI-9
*Kaahua* HI-9
Kaahue—*bay* HI-9
*Kaahukuula* HI-9
Kaahumanu Church—*hist pl* HI-9
Kaahumanu Sch—*school* HI-9
Kaaiea Gulch—*valley* HI-9
Kaaikahi Spring—*spring* HI-9
Kaaikukai Gulch—*valley* HI-9
Kaailana Valley—*valley* HI-9
Kaakaaniu—*civil* HI-9
*Kaakaanui* HI-9
Kaakaulua Gulch—*valley* HI-9
*Kaakcoot Hill* NY-2
*Kaakeoote Hill* NY-2
*Kaakeoot Hill* NY-2
*Kaakepa* HI-9
Kaakepa—*civil* HI-9
Kaakepa—*summit* HI-9
*Kaakepa Hill* HI-9
Kaala—*cape* HI-9
Kaala—*civil* HI-9
Kaala—*summit* (3) HI-9
Kaalaala—*civil* HI-9
Kaalaala Gulch—*valley* HI-9
Kaalaala Makai—*civil* HI-9
*Kaalaala Makakupu* HI-9
Kaalaea—*cape* HI-9
Kaalaea—*civil* HI-9
Kaalaea Stream—*stream* HI-9
Kaalaiki—*civil* HI-9
Kaalaiki—*summit* HI-9
Kaalaina Gulch—*valley* HI-9
Kaalakei Valley—*valley* HI-9
*Kaala Mountain* HI-9
*Kaala Peak* HI-9
Kaala Stream—*stream* HI-9
Kaalau Stream—*stream* HI-9
**Kaalawai**—*pop pl* HI-9
Kaalela—*cape* HI-9
Kaali—*cliff* HI-9
Kaaliali—*summit* HI-9
Kaalialinui Valley—*valley* HI-9
Kaaliali Trail—*trail* HI-9
*Kaali Cliff* HI-9
Kaalo—*bay* HI-9
Kaaloa—*cliff* HI-9
*Kaaluala Bay* HI-9
Kaalualu—*locale* HI-9
Kaalualu Bay—*bay* HI-9
Kaalula Stream—*stream* HI-9
Kaamola—*civil* HI-9
*Kaan* MH-9
Ka'an—*slope* MH-9
Kaana—*locale* HI-9
Kaana—*summit* HI-9
Kaanakeakua—*summit* HI-9
Kaanamahuna Valley—*valley* HI-9
KAAN-AM (Bethany)—*tower* MO-7
**Kaanapali**—*pop pl* HI-9
KAAN-FM (Bethany)—*tower* MO-7
Kaao—*civil* (2) HI-9
Kaaoao Gulch—*valley* HI-9
Kaao Homesteads—*civil* HI-9
Kaapahu—*civil* (3) HI-9
Kaapahu—*summit* (3) HI-9
Kaapahu Gulch—*valley* HI-9
Kaapahu Homesteads—*civil* HI-9
Kaapahu Ridge—*ridge* HI-9
Kaapahu Stream—*stream* HI-9
Kaapipa Point—*cape* HI-9
Kaapoko—*civil* HI-9
Kaapoko Homesteads—*civil* HI-9
Kaapoko Stream—*stream* (2) HI-9
Kaapoo Lake—*lake* MN-6
Kaapuna—*cape* HI-9
Kaapuna—*civil* HI-9
Kaapuna Lava Flow Of 1950—*lava* HI-9
*Kaari Creek* WI-6
*Kaaruka* MP-9
*Kaarukai Island* MP-9
*Kaarukai-to* MP-9
Kaaruk Lake—*lake* AK-9
Kaase Cem—*cemetery* TX-5
*Kaaterskill* NY-2
Kaaterskill Clove—*valley* NY-2
Kaaterskill Creek—*stream* NY-2
Kaaterskill Falls—*falls* NY-2
Kaatz Icehouse—*hist pl* CT-1
Kaatz Pond—*lake* CT-1
Kaau—*locale* HI-9
Kaauau Point—*cape* HI-9
Kaau Crater—*crater* HI-9
Kaauhuhu—*civil* HI-9
Kaauhuhu Homesteads—*civil* (2) HI-9
*Kaaulamapoko Point* HI-9
*Kaaumakua Peak* HI-9
*Kaawa* HI-9
Kaawalii Stream—*stream* HI-9
Kaawaloa—*civil* HI-9
Kaawaloa—*locale* HI-9
Kaawaloa Valley—*valley* HI-9
Kaawaloho Gulch—*valley* HI-9
**Kaawanui**—*pop pl* HI-9
Kaawanui Gulch—*valley* HI-9
Kaawanui Rsvr—*reservoir* HI-9
**Kaawanui Village**—*pop pl* HI-9
*Kaawaroa* HI-9
Kaaweiki Ridge—*ridge* HI-9
Kaaweiki Valley—*valley* HI-9
Kaawikiwiki—*civil* HI-9
Kaawikiwiki Gulch—*valley* HI-9
*Kabahaia Inseln* MP-9
*Kabahala* MP-9
Kabau, Lake—*reservoir* NY-2
Kabba Mine—*mine* AZ-5
Kabba Texas Mine—*mine* WA-9
Kabba Wash—*stream* AZ-5
Kabben—*island* MP-9
*Kabbenbock-Insel* MP-9
Kabbenbock Island—*island* MP-9
*Kabbenbokku To* MP-9
*Kabben Island* MP-9
Kabben Island—*island* MP-9
*Kabben-to* MP-9
*Kabbo Island* MP-9
Kabbo Island—*island* MP-9
*Kabbok Island* MP-9
*Kabbuk* MP-9
Kabbwok—*island* MP-9
*Kabecona Lake* MN-6
KABE-FM (Orem)—*tower* (2) UT-8
Kabekel—*stream* PW-9
Kabekona Bay—*bay* MN-6
**Kabekona Corner**—*pop pl* MN-6
Kabekona Lake—*lake* MN-6
Kabekona Lookout Tower—*locale* MN-6
Kabekona River—*stream* (2) MN-6
*Kabelabelagen* MP-9
*Kabelbelkan Island* MP-9
Kabell Creek—*stream* UT-8
*Kabelle* MP-9
Kabelle Island—*island* MP-9
Kabell Hollow—*valley* UT-8
*Kabell Lake* UT-8
Kabell Lakes—*lake* UT-8
*Kabell Meadow* UT-8
Kabell Meadows—*flat* UT-8
Kabell Ridge—*ridge* UT-8
Kabell Spring—*spring* UT-8
Kabelmacher Cem—*cemetery* TX-5
*Kaben* MP-9
*Kabenbok* MP-9
Kaben Island—*island* (?) MP-9
*Kaben-to* MP-9
*Kabenuuwaru* MP-9
*Kabenuuwaru-To* MP-9
*Kabenwor* MP-9
*Kabere To* MP-9
*Kaberuberukan* MP-9
Kaberuberukan—*island* MP-9
*Kaberuberukan-To* MP-9
**Kabetogama**—*pop pl* MN-6
Kabetogama Ch—*church* MN-6
Kabetogama Lake—*lake* MN-6
Kabetogama Lookout Tower—*locale* MN-6
Kabetogama State For—*forest* MN-6
KABI-AM (Abilene)—*tower* KS-7
KABI-FM (Abilene)—*tower* KS-7
*Kabinbok* MP-9
*Kabinbwokw* MP-9
*Kabinwod* MP-9
*Kabinwor Island* MP-9
*Kabir Creek* OR-9
*Kabir Rsvr* OR-9
**Kabis and Myers Subdivision**—*pop pl* UT-8
*Kabito* AZ-5
*Kabito Creek* AZ-5
*Kabito Plateau* AZ-5
*Kabito Spring* AZ-5
Kable House—*hist pl* VA-3
Kabler, John, House—*hist pl* MI-6
**Kabletown**—*pop pl* WV-2
Kabletown (Magisterial
District)—*fmr MCD* WV-2
Kabletown Sch—*school* WV-2
Kabob—*locale* NY-2
*Kabokel River* PW-9
Kabol Lake—*lake* WI-6
Kabo Sch—*school* MT-8
Kabuch Point—*cape* AK-9
*Kabueie Creek* WA-9
K'abul—*summit* FM-9
Kabusie Creek—*stream* WA-9
Kabustasa Lake—*lake* MN-6
Kabwolbwolkan—*island* MP-9
Kabyai Creek—*stream* CA-9
Kachauik, Mount—*summit* AK-9
Kachauik River—*stream* AK-9
Kachele Cem—*cemetery* TX-5
Kachele Pond—*lake* CT-1
Kachelmacher Park—*park* OH-6
Kachelman Cem—*cemetery* AL-4
Kachemach Mound—*summit* AK-9
Kachemach River—*stream* AK-9
*Kachemak* AK-9
**Kachemak**—*pop pl* AK-9
Kachemak Bay—*bay* AK-9
Kachemak Bay State Park—*park* AK-9
Kachemak Bay State Wilderness
Park—*park* AK-9
**Kachemak City**—*pop pl* AK-9
Kachemak Creek—*stream* AK-9
Kachemak Glacier—*glacier* AK-9
**Kachemak Silo**—*pop pl* AK-9
*Ka-ches Lake* WA-9
*Ka-ches River* WA-9
Kachess Dam—*dam* WA-9
Kachess Guard Station—*locale* WA-9
Kachess Lake—*reservoir* WA-9
Kachess Ridge—*ridge* WA-9
Kachess Ridge Trail—*trail* WA-9
Kachess River—*stream* WA-9
*Kachess Rsvr* WA-9
Kachiksuk Bluffs—*cliff* AK-9
*Kachina Bridge* UT-8
Kachina Bridge—*other* UT-8
Kachina Point—*cliff* AZ-5
Kachina Points—*summit* AZ-5
Kachina Sch—*school* AZ-5
Kachwona Creek—*stream* AK-9
KACI-AM—*tower* OR-9
**Kackley**—*pop pl* KS-7
Kackley Spring—*spring* ID-8
Kacrowtuk Lake—*lake* AK-9
Kacy Tank—*reservoir* NM-5
Kadaay—*locale* FM-9
Kadachan Glacier—*glacier* AK-9
Kadachrome Flat—*flat* UT-8
Kadake Bay—*bay* AK-9
Kadake Creek—*stream* AK-9
Kadakina Creek—*stream* AK-9
Kadakina Lake—*lake* AK-9
**Kadane Corner**—*pop pl* TX-5
Kadane Oil Field—*oilfield* TX-5
**Kadashan**—*pop pl* OK-5
Kadashan Bay—*bay* AK-9
Kadashan Bottom—*bend* OK-5
Kadashan River—*stream* AK-9
*Kaday* FM-9
Kade Creek—*stream* MT-8
Kaders Eddy—*bay* NC-3
Kade Run—*stream* WV-2
*Kades Cove Methodist Church* TN-4
Kadesh—*locale* LA-4
Kadesh Branch—*stream* LA-4
Kadesh Ch—*church* NC-3
Kadesh Chapel—*church* WV-2
Kadet Country Club—*locale* TN-4
KADI-AM (Camdenton)—*tower* MO-7
Kadijah, Lake—*lake* IL-6
Kading Creek—*stream* MI-6
Kading Ranger Station—*locale* MT-8
Kadin Island—*island* AK-9
Kadin Lake—*lake* AK-9
*Kadjangle* PW-9
Kadleroshilik River—*stream* AK-9
Kadletz Creek—*stream* (2) ID-8
*Kado Island* PW-9
**Kadoka**—*pop pl* SD-7
**Kadoka Junction**—*pop pl* SD-7
Kadoka Lake—*reservoir* SD-7
Kadoka Lake Dam—*dam* SD-7
*Kadoka Landing Strip* SD-7
Kadoka Municipal Airp—*airport* SD-7
Kadoka Township—*civil* SD-7
Kadok Landing—*locale* AK-9
Kadota—*locale* CA-9
*Kado To* PW-9
Kadruakvik Creek—*stream* AK-9
Kadunce River—*stream* MN-6
Kadunce River State Park—*park* MN-6
Kadwell Field Airp—*airport* WA-9
*Kady Creek* AL-4
Kady Gulch—*valley* MT-8
*Kaeakakurao To* PW-9
Kaea Point—*cape* HI-9
*Kaechele Pond* CT-1
*Kaede* FM-9
Kaehler-Rector House—*hist pl* CA-9
Kaehoeho—*civil* HI-9
*Kaeide* FM-9
*Kaeide Jima* FM-9
Kaelekii Point—*cape* HI-9
Kaeleku—*civil* HI-9
**Kaeleku**—*pop pl* HI-9
*Kaelepului Pond* HI-9
Kaelepulu Playground—*park* HI-9
Kaelepulu Pond—*lake* HI-9
Kaelhuk Pass—*gut* AK-9
Kaelopuli—*area* HI-9
Kaelua—*island* HI-9
**Kaemesang**—*pop pl* PW-9
Kaemi—*cape* HI-9
Kaena—*civil* HI-9
Kaena—*summit* HI-9
Kaenaiki—*cape* HI-9
Kaena Milit Reservation—*military* HI-9
Kaena Point—*cape* (4) HI-9
Kaena Point Facility—*military* HI-9
Kaenta Spring—*spring* OR-9
Kaeo—*civil* HI-9
Kaeo—*summit* (2) HI-9
*Kaeo Cone* HI-9
*Kaeo Mtn* HI-9
*Kaeo Peak* HI-9
*Kaeo Puu* HI-9
Kaercher Creek Dam—*dam* PA-2
*Kaeroga* MP-9
*Kaeroga Island* MP-9
Kaeroga Pass—*channel* MP-9
*Kaeroga-suido* MP-9
*Kaeroga-to* MP-9
Kaese Mill—*hist pl* MD-2
Kaese Mill—*locale* MD-2
KAET-TV (Phoenix)—*tower* AZ-5
Kaewai Sch—*school* HI-9
Kaffee Slough—*stream* WA-9
*Kaffetalya* MS-4
KAFF-FM (Flagstaff)—*tower* AZ-5
Kaffie Ranch—*locale* TX-5
Kaffir—*locale* TX-5
*Kafi Talaia* MS-4
Kaflia Bay—*bay* AK-9
Kafounchu—*bar* FM-9
Kagalaska Island—*island* AK-9
Kagalaska Strait—*channel* AK-9
Kagaluk Lake—*lake* AK-9
Kagalurpak Lake—*lake* AK-9
*Kagaman* MH-9
Kagamil Island—*island* AK-9
Kagamil Pass—*channel* AK-9
Kagamil Volcano—*summit* AK-9
Kagankaguti Lake—*lake* AK-9
Kagan Lake—*lake* AK-9
Kaga Point—*cape* AK-9
Kagati Lake—*lake* AK-9
Kagayan Flats—*flat* AK-9
Kageet Point—*cape* AK-9
**Kagel Canyon**—*pop pl* CA-9
Kagel Canyon—*valley* CA-9
Kagel Divide—*gap* CA-9
Kagel Mtn—*summit* CA-9
Kagel Sch—*school* WI-6
Kagel Shelter—*locale* NY-2
Kagerise Store and House—*hist pl* PA-2
*Kager Island* AL-4
Kagevah, Lake—*lake* WY-8
Kagevah Pass—*gap* WY-8
Kagevah Peak—*summit* WY-8
Kaghasuk Lake—*lake* AK-9
Kaghkusalik Point—*cape* AK-9
Kaghoopalik Point—*cape* AK-9
KAGI-AM—*tower* OR-9
Kagiluak Bight—*bay* AK-9
Kagiluak Creek—*stream* AK-9
Kaginen Island—*island* MP-9
Kagle Branch—*stream* AR-4
Kagle Branch—*stream* NC-3
Kagle Mtn—*summit* NC-3
Kaglers Bridge (historical)—*bridge* MS-4
Kagley Cem—*cemetery* TN-4
Kagley Chapel—*church* TN-4
Kagley Dam—*dam* TN-4
Kagley Hollow—*valley* KY-4
Kagley Lake—*reservoir* IN-4
*Kagley Methodist Church* TN-4
*Kagleys Chapel Baptist Church* TN-4
Kagleys Chapel Cem—*cemetery* TN-4
Kaglor Branch—*stream* NC-3
*Kagman* MH-9
*Kagman Point* MH-9
KAGO-AM—*tower* OR-9
KAGO-FM—*tower* OR-9
Kaguerk Creek—*stream* AK-9
Kagueruh Creek—*stream* AK-9
Kaguk Cove—*bay* AK-9
Kaguyak—*locale* (2) AK-9
Kaguyak ANV812—*reserve* AK-9
Kaguyak Bay—*bay* AK-9
Kaguyak Crater—*crater* AK-9
Kaguyak Village Site—*hist pl* AK-9
Kagvik Creek—*stream* AK-9
Kagy Cem—*cemetery* OH-6
Kagy Ditch—*canal* OH-6
Kahaakea Gulch—*valley* HI-9
*Kahaapilani* HI-9
Kahachi Miliuk—*locale* AZ-5
Kahaea—*area* HI-9
Kahaiawa—*cape* HI-9
Kahaino—*area* HI-9
Kahakaaulana Island—*island* HI-9
Kahakahakea—*cape* HI-9
Kahakahakea Trail—*trail* HI-9
Kahakapao Gulch—*valley* HI-9
*Kahaka Point* HI-9
Kahakuloa—*civil* HI-9
**Kahakuloa**—*pop pl* HI-9
Kahakuloa Bay—*bay* HI-9
Kahakuloa Head—*cape* HI-9
Kahakuloa Homesteads—*civil* HI-9
*Kahakuloa Point* HI-9
Kahakuloa Stream—*stream* HI-9
**Kahala**—*pop pl* HI-9
Kahala, Lae o—*cape* HI-9
Kahala Beach—*beach* HI-9
Kahala Point—*cape* HI-9
Kahala Sch—*school* HI-9
Kahalau—*island* HI-9
*Kahalawe Gulch* HI-9
*Kahalawe Stream* HI-9
Kahaleaimakani Gulch—*valley* HI-9
Kahalelani—*summit* HI-9
*Ka Halepalaoa* HI-9
Kahalepohaku—*cape* HI-9
Kahalii—*civil* HI-9
Kahal Kadosh Beth Elohim
Synagogue—*hist pl* SC-3
Kahalulu Gulch—*valley* HI-9
Kahaluu—*civil* (2) HI-9
**Kahaluu**—*pop pl* (2) HI-9
Kahaluu Bay—*bay* HI-9
Kahaluu County Park—*park* HI-9
Kahaluu Fish Pond—*hist pl* HI-9
Kahaluu For Res—*forest* HI-9
Kahaluu Hist Dist—*hist pl* HI-9
Kahaluu (Libbyville)—*CDP* HI-9
Kahaluu Pond—*lake* HI-9
Kahaluu Sch—*school* HI-9
Kahaluu Stream—*stream* HI-9
Kahaluu Taro Lo'i—*hist pl* HI-9
Kahana—*civil* (2) HI-9
**Kahana**—*pop pl* (2) HI-9
Kahana Bay—*bay* HI-9
Kahana Bay Beach Park—*park* HI-9
*Kahana Camp* HI-9
Kahanahaiki—*civil* HI-9
Kahanaiki Gulch—*valley* HI-9
Kahanaiki Stream—*stream* HI-9
Kahananui—*civil* HI-9
Kahananui Gulch—*valley* HI-9
Kahana Point—*cape* HI-9
Kahana Stream—*stream* (2) HI-9
Kahana Valley—*valley* HI-9
Kahana Valley State Park—*park* HI-9
Kahanui—*civil* HI-9
Kahanui (Apana One)—*civil* HI-9
Kahanui (Apana Three)—*civil* HI-9
Kahapapa Fishpond—*lake* HI-9
**Kahatchee**—*pop pl* AL-4
Kahatchee Cem—*cemetery* AL-4
Kahatchee Creek—*stream* AL-4
*Kahatchee Hills* AL-4
Kahatchee Lookout Tower—*locale* AL-4
Kahatchee Mtn—*summit* AL-4
*Kahatchie* AL-4
Kahaualea—*civil* HI-9
Kahau Gulch—*valley* HI-9
Kahauiki—*civil* HI-9
Kahauiki Gulch—*valley* HI-9
Kahauiki Stream—*stream* HI-9
Kahaukea—*crater* HI-9
*Kahaula Cone* HI-9
Kahauloa—*bay* HI-9
Kahauloa—*crater* HI-9
Kahauloa One—*civil* HI-9
Kahauloa Two—*civil* HI-9
Kahaumanu—*area* HI-9
*Kahaupu Gulch* HI-9
Kahaupu Gulch—*valley* HI-9
Kahawaihapapa—*cape* HI-9
Kahawaihapapa Gulch—*valley* HI-9
Kahawaiiki Gulch—*valley* HI-9
Kahawaiiki Stream—*stream* HI-9
Kahawai Kolono—*stream* HI-9
Kahawailiilii Gulch—*valley* HI-9
*Kahawainai Gulch* HI-9
Kahawainui Gulch—*valley* HI-9
Kahawainui Stream—*stream* HI-9
*Ka hawys afse Creek* SD-7
Kahbakong Cem—*cemetery* MN-6
*Kahe* HI-9
Kahea—*beach* HI-9
Kahea Gulch—*valley* HI-9
Kaheaka Rsvr—*reservoir* HI-9
Kaheawai—*area* HI-9
Kahe Beach Park—*park* HI-9
Kaheeia Bay—*bay* HI-9
*Ka Heiau o Kalalea* HI-9
*Ka Heiau o Molilele* HI-9
Kahei Four—*civil* HI-9
Kahei Homesteads—*civil* HI-9
Kahei One—*civil* HI-9
Kahei One-Four—*civil* HI-9
Kahei Point—*cape* HI-9
Kahei Three—*civil* HI-9
Kahei Two—*civil* HI-9
*Kaheka* HI-9
Kaheka—*bay* HI-9
Kahekapoeleele Valley—*valley* HI-9
**Kaheka Village**—*pop pl* HI-9
Kahekili Leap—*cliff* HI-9
*Kahekilis Leap* HI-9
Kahele—*valley* HI-9
Kahelepo House—*locale* HI-9
Kahelunui Valley—*valley* HI-9
Kahelu Ridge—*ridge* HI-9
Kahemano—*well* HI-9
*Kahena Ditch* HI-9
Kahenawai—*summit* HI-9
Kaheo Point—*cape* HI-9
Kahe Point—*cape* HI-9
Kahet—*slope* MH-9
Kaheu Gulch—*valley* HI-9
*Kahewaku* HI-9
Kahgeatak Creek—*stream* AK-9
*Kahiawai* HI-9
Kahikinui—*civil* HI-9
Kahikinui For Res—*forest* HI-9
Kahikinui House—*locale* HI-9
Kahikolu Church—*hist pl* HI-9
Kahili—*beach* HI-9
Kahili—*summit* (2) HI-9
Kahili Falls—*falls* HI-9
Kahiliholo Stream—*stream* HI-9
Kahililoa—*cape* HI-9
Kahililoa—*summit* HI-9
Kahilipali Kahaea—*civil* HI-9
Kahilipali Nui—*civil* HI-9
Kahilipali Point—*cape* HI-9
Kahili Quarry—*mine* HI-9
KA Hill—*summit* AZ-5
Kahill Fire Tower—*tower* PA-2
Kahiltna Dome—*summit* AK-9
Kahiltna Glacier—*glacier* AK-9
Kahiltna Notch—*gap* AK-9
Kahiltna Pass—*gap* AK-9
Kahiltna Peaks—*summit* AK-9
Kahiltna River—*stream* AK-9
Kahinaakalani—*cape* HI-9
Kahinahina Forest Cabin—*locale* HI-9
Kahinahina Ridge—*ridge* HI-9
Kahinahina Trail—*trail* HI-9
Kahinano—*civil* HI-9
*Kahinaokalani* HI-9
Kahinapohaku—*cape* HI-9
Kahinawai Gulch—*valley* HI-9
Kahinihiniula—*cape* HI-9
Kahiola—*civil* HI-9
Kahio (Site)—*locale* HI-9
Kahipa—*summit* HI-9
Kahiu Point—*cape* HI-9
Kahiwa Falls—*falls* HI-9
Kahiwa Gulch—*valley* HI-9
*Kahiwamoku Island* HI-9
Kahk, Dolen—*summit* FM-9
Kahkatak Creek—*stream* AK-9
**Kahkhout Mountain**—*pop pl* PA-2
Kahkhout Mtn—*summit* PA-2
Kah Kwa Country Club—*other* PA-2
Kahkwa Creek—*stream* WA-9
Kahl, Henry, House—*hist pl* IA-7
Kahl Bldg—*hist pl* IA-7
*Kahle* PA-2
Kahle Cem—*cemetery* MO-7
Kahle Lake—*reservoir* PA-2
Kahle Lake Dam—*dam* PA-2
Kahle Park—*locale* MI-6
Kahler—*locale* CO-8
Kahler Basin—*basin* OR-9
Kahler Bluff—*cliff* MO-7
Kahler Butte—*summit* OR-9
Kahler Creek—*stream* OR-9
Kahler Creek—*stream* WA-9
Kahler MS—*school* IN-6
Kahler Sch (abandoned)—*school* PA-2
Kahlert Mercantile Store—*hist pl* MN-6
Kahle Run—*stream* PA-2
Kahle Sch—*school* IL-6
Kahle Sch—*school* PA-2
**Kahle Siding**—*pop pl* PA-2
Kahles Pond—*lake* WI-6
Kahle Tower—*tower* PA-2
Kahletown—*locale* PA-2
Kahletown Hill—*summit* PA-2
*Kahl Gap* PA-2
Kahl Montgomery Jewish Temple
(historical)—*church* AL-4
Kah Lookout—*locale* MT-8
**Kahlotus**—*pop pl* WA-9
Kahlotus, Lake—*lake* WA-9
Kahlotus (CCD)—*cens area* WA-9
Kahlstorf Lake—*lake* MN-6
*Kahly Run* PA-2
Kahm—*locale* IL-6
Kah Mah Singh Ridge—*ridge* WA-9
Kahmar—*civil* FM-9
Kahmar, Dolen—*summit* FM-9
KAHM-FM (Prescott)—*tower* AZ-5
Kah Mtn—*summit* MT-8
Kahn, Albert, House—*hist pl* MI-6
Kahn, Emanuel, House—*hist pl* UT-8
*Kahnah Creek* CO-8
Kahn Brook—*stream* CT-1
**Kahneeta Hot Springs**—*pop pl* OR-9
Kahneska Branch—*stream* NC-3
Kahnirukmiut (Summer Camp)—*locale* AK-9
Kahniruk River—*stream* AK-9
Kahn Lake—*reservoir* IN-6
Kahn Lake Dam—*dam* IN-6
Kahn Playground—*park* CA-9
Kahn Ponds—*lake* CT-1
**Kahns**—*pop pl* LA-4
**Kahn's Spur**—*pop pl* SC-3
Ka-Ho, Lake—*reservoir* IL-6
Kahoaea—*summit* HI-9
Kahoahuna Homesteads—*civil* HI-9
Kahoaloha Valley—*valley* HI-9
Kahoama Stream—*stream* HI-9
Kahoana Valley—*valley* HI-9
Kahoano—*summit* HI-9
**Kahoga**—*pop pl* OK-5
Kahoiawa Bay—*bay* HI-9
Kahoiawa Point—*cape* HI-9
**Kahoka**—*pop pl* AR-4
**Kahoka**—*pop pl* MO-7
Kahoka Municipal Airp—*airport* MO-7

Kahokunui—*beach* HI-9
Kahola, Lake—*reservoir* KS-7
Kahola Creek—*stream* KS-7
Kaholaiki Bay—*bay* HI-9
*Kaholalele* HI-9
Kaholalele Falls—*falls* HI-9
Kahol Cem—*cemetery* OH-6
Kaholo, Pali—*cliff* HI-9
Kaholoapele—*summit* HI-9
Kaholo Gulch—*valley* HI-9
*Kahololoa* HI-9
Kaholo Pali—*cliff* HI-9
Kaholopoo Gulch—*valley* HI-9
Kaholopoohina—*summit* HI-9
Kaholuamano—*area* HI-9
*Kaholuamanu* HI-9
Kaholua o Kahawali Crater—*crater* HI-9
Kahoma Shaft Pump—*other* HI-9
Kahoma Stream—*stream* HI-9
Kahoma Tunnel—*tunnel* HI-9
Kahonohono—*summit* HI-9
Kahonua—*beach* HI-9
Kahookamakea Gulch—*valley* HI-9
*Kahookee Creek* NC-3
Kahoolawe—*island* HI-9
Kaho'olawe Island Archeol District—*hist pl* HI-9
Kahoolewa Ridge—*ridge* HI-9
Kahoopulu—*summit* HI-9
Kahoopulu Stream—*stream* HI-9
Kahoopuu Stream—*stream* HI-9
Kahre Lake Dam—*dam* IN-6
Kahring Lake—*lake* MN-6
Kahr Lake—*reservoir* IN-6
Kah Shakes Cove—*bay* AK-9
Kah Shakes Lake—*lake* AK-9
Kah Shakes Point—*cape* AK-9
Kah Sheets Bay—*bay* AK-9
Kah Sheets Creek—*stream* AK-9
Kah Sheets Island—*island* AK-9
Kah Sheets Lake—*lake* AK-9
Kah-Tan-Da, Lake—*reservoir* MO-7
Kahtava Lake—*lake* MN-6
*Kahua* HI-9
Kahua—*civil* (3) HI-9
Kahua—*summit* HI-9
Kahuaawi Gulch—*valley* HI-9
Kahua Gulch—*valley* HI-9
Kahuai—*civil* HI-9
Kahualau Gulch—*valley* HI-9
Kahualelepulu—*area* HI-9
Kahuamaa Flat—*flat* HI-9
Kahuamoa—*summit* HI-9
Kahua Olohu—*summit* HI-9
Kahua One—*civil* HI-9
Kahua Ranch—*locale* HI-9
Kahua Two—*civil* HI-9
*Kahuauli Peak* HI-9
Kahuawai Spring—*spring* HI-9
Kahue—*civil* HI-9
Kahue—*well* HI-9
Kahuenaha—*area* HI-9
Kahue Point—*cape* HI-9
Kahuku—*cape* HI-9
Kahuku—*civil* (3) HI-9
**Kahuku**—*pop pl* HI-9
Kahuku For Res—*forest* HI-9
Kahuku Habitation Area—*hist pl* HI-9
Kahuku Homesteads—*civil* HI-9
**Kahuku (Kahuku Ranch)**—*pop pl* HI-9
*Kahukuoo* HI-9
Kahuku Point—*cape* HI-9
Kahukupoko—*cape* (2) HI-9
Kahuku Ranch—*locale* HI-9
*Kahulawe* HI-9
Kahulialii—*area* HI-9
Kahului—*bay* HI-9
Kahului—*civil* HI-9
**Kahului**—*pop pl* HI-9
Kahului Airp—*airport* HI-9
Kahului Bay—*bay* (2) HI-9
Kahului (CCD)—*cens area* HI-9
Kahului Harbor—*harbor* HI-9
Kahului One-Two—*civil* HI-9
Kahuna, Lae o—*cape* HI-9
Kahuna Falls—*falls* HI-9
Kahunalii Valley—*valley* HI-9
Kahuntla, Lake—*lake* AK-9
Kahuuwai Gulch—*valley* HI-9
Kahuwai—*civil* HI-9
Kahuwai Bay—*bay* HI-9
Kahuwai Crater—*crater* HI-9
*Kahuwai Gulch* HI-9
Kah-Wah-C Golf Course—*other* OK-5
*Kah-wi-chi* WA-9
*Kah-wi-chi Creek* WA-9
Kaiaakea—*civil* HI-9
Kaiaakea Point—*cape* HI-9
*Ka lae o Kaiwa* HI-9
Kaiahi Gulch—*valley* HI-9
Kaiaka Bay—*bay* HI-9
*Kaiaka Hill* HI-9
Kaiaka Point—*cape* HI-9
Kaiakekua—*cape* HI-9
Kaiak Lake—*lake* MN-6
Kaiamiki—*civil* HI-9
Kaiapaokailio—*summit* HI-9
Kaia Point—*cape* HI-9
**Kaibab**—*pop pl* AZ-5
**Kaibab**—*pop pl* CO-8
Kaibab (CCD)—*cens area* AZ-5
Kaibab Dam—*dam* AZ-5
Kaibab Elem Sch—*school* AZ-5
*Kaibab Gulch* UT-8
Kaibab Ind Res—*93 (1980)* AZ-5
Kaibab Lake—*reservoir* AZ-5
Kaibab Lake Recreation Site Kaibab Lake Campground—*park* AZ-5
Kaibab Lodge—*locale* AZ-5
*Kaibab Mountain* UT-8
*Kaibab Mountains* AZ-5
Kaibab Natl For—*forest* AZ-5
*Kaibab Paiute Reservation* AZ-5
Kaibab Plateau—*plain* AZ-5
Kaibab Plateau—*plain* UT-8
*Kaibab Spring* AZ-5
*Kaibab Trail* AZ-5
Kaibab Wash—*stream* AZ-5
*Kaibakku* PW-9
*Kaibakku Island* PW-9
*Kaibeto* AZ-5
*K'ai' Bii' To* AZ-5
*Kaibito* AZ-5
**Kaibito**—*pop pl* AZ-5
Kaibito Airp—*airport* AZ-5
Kaibito Boarding Sch—*school* AZ-5
Kaibito Creek—*stream* AZ-5
**Kaibito (Lower Kaibito)**—*pop pl* AZ-5
*K-ai Bito Plateau* AZ-5
Kaibito Plateau—*plain* AZ-5
*K-ai Bito Spring* AZ-5
Kaibito Spring—*spring* AZ-5
*Kaibito Springs* AZ-5
*Kaibito Wash* AZ-5
*Kaide-Jima* FM-9
Kaidera Camp—*locale* WA-9
*Kaiders Camp* WA-9
*Kaido Shima* FM-9
*Kaido To* FM-9
*Kaiehu* HI-9
Kaiehu Point—*cape* HI-9
Kaieie—*civil* HI-9
Kaieie Heiau—*locale* HI-9
Kaieie Homesteads—*civil* HI-9
Kaieie Stream—*stream* HI-9
*Kaieie Waho Channel* HI-9
*Kaieiwaho Channel* HI-9
Kaier Sch—*school* MI-6
*Kaiewaho-canal* HI-9
Kaifer Sch—*school* IL-6
Kaigani—*locale* AK-9
Kaigani Strait—*channel* AK-9
Kaigan Point—*cape* AK-9
*Kaighn Ave Dam* NJ-2
Kaighn Point—*cape* NJ-2
*Kaighns Point* NJ-2
Kaighns Point—*uninc pl* NJ-2
Kaigler Cem—*cemetery* (2) MS-4
Kaigler Cem—*cemetery* SC-3
Kaigler Creek—*stream* MS-4
Kaihalulu Bay—*bay* HI-9
*Kaihiopuaa* HI-9
Kaiholena—*civil* HI-9
Kaiholena—*summit* (2) HI-9
Kaiholena Gulch—*valley* HI-9
**Kaihon Kug**—*pop pl* AZ-5
Kaihooa—*civil* HI-9
Kaihuakala—*summit* HI-9
Kaihuiki—*civil* HI-9
Kaihukiako—*summit* HI-9
Kaihuokapuaa—*cape* HI-9
*Kaihuopuaa* HI-9
*Kai Ieiewaho* HI-9
*Kai it tu* KS-7
*Kaijen* MP-9
*Kaijen-to* MP-9
*Kaijien To* MP-9
Kaikaina—*summit* HI-9
*Kai Kaiwi* HI-9
Kaikena—*cape* HI-9
Kaikipauula—*summit* HI-9
Kaikli Cove—*bay* AK-9
Kaikout Kill—*stream* NY-2
Kaikshak Hill—*summit* AK-9
Kailaidshi (historical)—*locale* AL-4
*Kailau* HI-9
Kail Cem—*cemetery* TN-4
Kailcheebito Spring—*spring* AZ-5
Kail Creek—*stream* TN-4
Kailiili—*cape* HI-9
Kailiili—*locale* HI-9
Kailiiliahinale—*summit* HI-9
Kailiili Ridge—*ridge* HI-9
Kailiili Stream—*stream* HI-9
Kailikaula Stream—*stream* HI-9
Kailikii (Site)—*locale* HI-9
*Kaillil* HI-9
*Kailio* HI-9
*Kailio Peak* HI-9
Kailio Point—*cape* HI-9
*Kaili Point* HI-9
Kailiu, Lae o—*cape* HI-9
*Kailiu Cape* HI-9
Kailiula—*civil* (2) HI-9
Kailiula Gulch—*valley* HI-9
Kailiu Point—*cape* HI-9
Kailua—*civil* (2) HI-9
**Kailua**—*pop pl* (3) HI-9
Kailua—*summit* HI-9
Kailua Bay—*bay* (3) HI-9
Kailua Beach—*beach* HI-9
Kailua Beach Park—*park* HI-9
Kailua (census name for Kailua Kona)—*CDP* HI-9
Kailua Ditch—*canal* HI-9
Kailua Field—*park* HI-9
Kailua Gulch—*valley* HI-9
Kailua HS—*school* HI-9
*Kailua Kona* HI-9
Kailua Kona (census name Kailua)—*CDP* HI-9
Kailuapuhi Waikalua Homesteads—*civil* HI-9
*Kailua Stream* HI-9
Kailua Stream—*stream* HI-9
**Kailua Village**—*pop pl* HI-9
**Kai Malino (Kealia)**—*pop pl* HI-9
Kaimaloo—*summit* HI-9
Kaime Ranch—*locale* (2) NM-5
Kaimu—*civil* HI-9
**Kaimu**—*pop pl* HI-9
Kaimu Beach—*beach* HI-9
**Kaimu (Black Sand Beach)**—*pop pl* HI-9
Kaimukanaka Falls—*falls* HI-9
**Kaimuki**—*pop pl* HI-9
Kaimuki Fire Station—*hist pl* HI-9
Kaimuki HS—*school* HI-9
Kaimuki Playground—*park* HI-9
Kaimuki Sch—*school* HI-9
*Kaimulgee AL-T17 (p.80)* AL-4
Kaimu-Makena Homesteads—*civil* HI-9
Kaimumano—*summit* HI-9
Kaimuokanaka—*basin* HI-9
Kaimu Park—*park* HI-9
Kaimu Stream—*stream* HI-9
Kaimuuwala—*cape* HI-9
Kaimwaimw—*cape* FM-9
Kaina Creek—*stream* AK-9
Kaina Creek—*stream* MT-8
Kaina Lake—*lake* AK-9
Kaina Lake—*lake* MT-8
Kainalimu Bay—*bay* HI-9
**Kainaliu**—*pop pl* HI-9
Kainalu—*civil* HI-9
Kainalu Gulch—*valley* HI-9
Kainalu Sch—*school* HI-9
Kainamanu—*summit* (2) HI-9
Kaina Mtn—*summit* MT-8
Kainaohe Fishpond—*lake* HI-9
Kainapahoa Gulch—*valley* HI-9
*Kainapuaa* HI-9
*Kainapuaa Peak* HI-9
*Kainawaauika* HI-9
Kainawaaunui—*summit* HI-9
Kain Bridge—*bridge* ND-7
Kaincaid Mtn—*summit* KY-4
Kain Cove—*bay* TX-5
Kainehe—*civil* HI-9
Kainehe Gulch—*valley* HI-9
Kainehe Homesteads—*civil* HI-9
Kaine Lake—*lake* WI-6
Kain Run—*stream* OH-6
Kains Sch (historical)—*school* AL-4
Kains Siding—*locale* IA-7
*Kaintuck* AL-4
Kaintuck Cem—*cemetery* MO-7
Kaintuck Ch—*church* MO-7
Kaintuck Chute—*channel* AL-4
Kaintuck Hollow—*valley* MO-7
Kaintuck Sch—*school* MO-7
Kaio—*area* HI-9
*Kai o Aleuuihaha* HI-9
*Kaiokalohi* HI-9
*Kai o Kalohi Channel* HI-9
Kaiole Bay—*bay* HI-9
Kaiolohia Bay—*bay* HI-9
Kaiona Beach Park—*park* HI-9
Kaiopae Gulch—*valley* HI-9
Kaiopae Point—*cape* HI-9
*Kai o Pailolo* HI-9
*Kai Pailolo* HI-9
*Kaipapau Gulch* HI-9
Kaipapau Hill—*summit* HI-9
Kaipapau Point—*cape* HI-9
Kaipapau Stream—*stream* HI-9
Kaiparowits Plateau—*range* UT-8
Kaiparowitz Peak—*summit* UT-8
*Kaiparowitz Plateau* UT-8
*Kai Peto Plateau* AZ-5
*Kaipeto Spring* AZ-5
Kaipoioi Gulch—*valley* HI-9
Kaipuhaa—*civil* HI-9
Kaipukaihina—*beach* HI-9
Kaipukaulua Gulch—*valley* HI-9
KAIR-AM (Tucson)—*tower* AZ-5
*Kairua* HI-9
Kaise Lake—*lake* WI-6
Kaisen Gulch—*valley* CA-9
Kaiser—*locale* CA-9
**Kaiser**—*pop pl* MO-7
**Kaiser**—*pop pl* WI-6
Kaiser ALuminum & Chemical Corporation—*facility* OH-6
Kaiser Bay—*swamp* GA-3
Kaiser Bottom—*swamp* AL-4
Kaiser Bottom Mine (surface)—*mine* AL-4
Kaiser Branch—*stream* AL-4
Kaiser Butte—*summit* WA-9
Kaiser Butte Guard Station—*locale* WA-9
Kaiser Canyon—*valley* LA-9
Kaiser Canyon—*valley* WA-9
Kaiser-Carlton Lake Dam—*dam* MS-4
Kaiser Cem—*cemetery* AL-4
Kaiser Cem—*cemetery* MO-7
Kaiser Cem—*cemetery* TX-5
Kaiser Cem—*cemetery* VA-3
Kaiser Center—*uninc pl* CA-9
*Kaiser Creek* NC-3
Kaiser Creek—*stream* (2) CA-9
Kaiser Creek—*stream* MT-8
Kaiser Creek—*stream* OR-9
Kaiser Creek—*stream* SD-7
Kaiser Creek—*stream* (2) TX-5
*Kaiser Crest* CA-9
Kaiser Diggings Guard Station—*locale* CA-9
Kaiser Ditch—*canal* (2) IN-6
Kaiser Ditch—*canal* NE-7
Kaiser Divide—*ridge* WY-8
Kaiser Drain—*canal* MI-6
*Kaiser Draw* CO-8
Kaiser Flat—*flat* TX-5
Kaiser Hill—*summit* MO-7
Kaiser Hollow—*valley* KY-4
Kaiser Hollow—*valley* OH-6
Kaiser Hollow—*valley* PA-2
Kaiser Hollow—*valley* TN-4
Kaiser Hosp—*hospital* (4) CA-9
Kaiser Lake—*lake* FL-3
Kaiser Lake—*lake* MI-6
Kaiser Lake—*lake* MT-8
Kaiser Lake—*lake* PA-2
Kaiser Lake—*reservoir* NC-3
Kaiser Lake (Dry)—*lake* NM-5
Kaiser Lookout Tower—*locale* MO-7
Kaiser Lumber Company Office—*hist pl* WI-6
Kaiser Meadow—*flat* CA-9
Kaiser Mine—*mine* NV-8
Kaiser Number 1 Dam—*dam* SD-7
Kaiser Park—*park* (2) CA-9
Kaiser Park—*park* IN-6
Kaiser Pass—*gap* CA-9
Kaiser Pass Meadow—*flat* CA-9
Kaiser Peak—*summit* TX-5
Kaiser Peak Meadows—*flat* CA-9
*Kaiser Pond* FL-3
Kaiser Ranch—*locale* TX-5
Kaiser Ridge—*ridge* CA-9
Kaiser's—*hist pl* WI-6
Kaiser Sch—*school* (2) CA-9
Kaiser Sch—*school* (2) MI-6
Kaiser Sch—*school* OK-5
**Kaiser's Eagle Mountain (Iron Chief Mine)**—*pop pl* CA-9
Kaiser's Ice Cream Parlour—*hist pl* OK-5
Kaiser-Sievers Ditch—*canal* CO-8
Kaiser Spring—*spring* AZ-5
Kaiser Spring—*spring* CO-8
Kaiser Spring—*spring* NV-8
Kaiser Spring—*spring* WY-8
Kaiser Spring Canyon—*valley* AZ-5
Kaiser Spring Wash—*arroyo* AZ-5
Kaisertown—*locale* NY-2
*Kaiserville* OR-9
**Kaiserville**—*pop pl* MI-6
**Kaiserville**—*pop pl* PA-2
Kaiser Wash—*stream* AZ-5
Kaiser Wash Spring—*spring* AZ-5
Kaiser Waterhole—*spring* AZ-5
Kaiser Well—*well* NV-8
Kaiser Well Number Two—*well* NV-8
Kaishin—*island* MP-9
*Kaishin Island* MP-9
Kaishi Point—*cape* AK-9
Kai Si Caude Well—*well* AZ-5
Kai-Si-Kaid Well Number One—*well* AZ-5
Kai-Si-Kaid Well Number Two—*well* AZ-5
Kai Si Kato—*spring* (2) AZ-5
*Ka Island* MP-9
Kaisoots Mtn—*summit* WA-9
*Kaitjimok* AZ-5
Kaiuchali Island—*island* AK-9
Kaiugnak Bay—*bay* AK-9
Kaiulani Sch—*school* HI-9
*Ka-i-urs-kuta* KS-7
*Kaiwainui Stream* HI-9
Kaiwaloa Heiau—*summit* HI-9
Kaiwa Stream—*stream* HI-9
Kaiwhat Pass—*gap* WA-9
Kaiwi Channel—*channel* HI-9
*Kaiwiiwi* HI-9
Kaiwiki—*civil* (3) HI-9
Kaiwiki Gulch—*valley* HI-9
Kaiwiki Homesteads One-Two—*civil* HI-9
Kaiwiki Homesteads Three—*civil* HI-9
Kaiwiki Stream—*stream* HI-9
Kaiwikoele Stream—*stream* HI-9
Kaiwilahilahi—*civil* HI-9
Kaiwilahilahi Stream—*stream* HI-9
Ka Iwi o Pele—*summit* HI-9
Kaiwi Point—*cape* (2) HI-9
Kaiyak, Lake—*lake* AK-9
Kaiyuh Mountains—*other* AK-9
Kaiyuh Slough—*stream* AK-9
*Kajamble* PW-9
*Kajangeru* PW-9
*Kajangeru To* PW-9
*Kajangle* PW-9
*Kajangle Durchfahrt* PW-9
*Kajangle Inseln* PW-9
*Kajangle Islands* PW-9
*Kajangle Passage* PW-9
*Kajanguru Shoto* PW-9
*Kajanguru Suido* PW-9
*Kajanguru To* PW-9
Kajer, Wencl, Farmstead—*hist pl* MN-6
KAJO-AM—*tower* OR-9
Kajutakrok Creek—*stream* AK-9
**Kaka**—*pop pl* AZ-5
Kaka, Lae o—*cape* HI-9
Kakaako Fire Station—*hist pl* HI-9
Kakaako Gulch—*valley* HI-9
Kakaako Pumping Station—*hist pl* HI-9
Kakaalani—*summit* HI-9
Kakaauki Stream—*stream* HI-9
Kakaaukuu Gulch—*valley* HI-9
Kakabika Falls—*falls* MI-6
*Kakagan River* WI-6
Kakagon River—*stream* WI-6
Kakagon Slough—*gut* WI-6
Kakagrak Hills—*summit* AK-9
Kakahaia Fishpond—*lake* HI-9
Kakahkituli Pass—*gut* AK-9
Kakaik State Wildlife Mngmt Area—*park* MN-6
Kakakawawai—*summit* HI-9
Kakalahale—*summit* HI-9
Kakalehale—*civil* HI-9
Kakamut—*locale* AK-9
Kakanee, Lake—*reservoir* WA-9
Kakanoni Point—*cape* HI-9
Kakapa Bay—*bay* HI-9
*Kaka Point* HI-9
Kakashe Mtn—*summit* MT-8
Kaka Valley—*valley* AZ-5
Kaka Wash—*stream* AZ-5
**Kake**—*pop pl* AK-9
Kake Cove—*bay* AK-9
Kakeha Falls—*falls* HI-9
*Kakehapoileele Valley* HI-9
Kake Helistop—*airport* KS-7
*Kakekapoeleele Valley* HI-9
Kakeout Dam—*dam* NJ-2
Kakeout Rsvr—*reservoir* NJ-2
KAKE-TV (Wichita)—*tower* KS-7
Kak Hollow—*valley* IN-6
Kakhonak—*locale* AK-9
Kakhonak Bay—*bay* AK-9
Kakhonak Bay—*locale* AK-9
Kakhonak (Kokhanok)—*other* AK-9
Kakhonak Lake—*lake* AK-9
Kakhonak River—*stream* AK-9
Kakiagun Lake—*lake* AK-9
*Kakiat* NY-2
Kakiat Trail—*trail* NY-2
*Kakigo Lake* MN-6
Kakiiwai—*cape* HI-9
Kakio—*area* HI-9
Kakio—*civil* HI-9
**Kakio**—*pop pl* HI-9
Kakio Point—*cape* HI-9
Kakipi Gulch—*valley* HI-9
Kak Island—*island* AK-9
Kakitos Mtn—*summit* MT-8
Kakivilak Creek—*stream* AK-9
*Kakiwai* HI-9
Kakiweka—*civil* HI-9
Kakiweka Gulch—*valley* HI-9
Kaklan Cem—*cemetery* TN-4
Kaklik Naitka Creek—*stream* AK-9
Kaklongegek Creek—*stream* AK-9
Kaknau Creek—*stream* AK-9
Kaknu Lake—*lake* AK-9
Kako Creek—*stream* AK-9
Ka Kohl Hill—*summit* AZ-5
Kako Lake—*lake* AK-9
**Kako Landing**—*pop pl* AK-9
Kako Mine—*mine* AK-9
Kakoni—*civil* HI-9
*Kakooa* HI-9
Kakoon Lake—*lake* AK-9
Ka Kotk Mtn—*summit* AZ-5
Kakovo Island—*island* AK-9
Kakpeyak River—*stream* AK-9
Kaksajookalik Island—*island* AK-9
Kaks Lake—*lake* MI-6
Kaksu River—*stream* AK-9
Kaksurok Mtn—*summit* AK-9
**Kaktovik**—*pop pl* AK-9
Kaktovik Lagoon—*bay* AK-9
Kaktus Korner—*locale* CA-9
*Kaku Cape* MP-9
Kakuhalahala—*civil* HI-9
Kakuhan Range—*range* AK-9
Kakuktahuk Pass—*gut* AK-9
Kakuktukruich Bluff—*cliff* AK-9
Kakukturat Mtn—*summit* AK-9
Kakul, Point—*cape* AK-9
Kakul Narrows—*channel* AK-9
Kakul Rock—*other* AK-9
*Kakut Mountain* PA-2
Kakvuiyat Bend—*bend* AK-9
Kakwan Point—*cape* AK-9
KAKZ-AM (Wichita)—*tower* KS-7
*Kala* HI-9
Kalaalaau Valley—*valley* HI-9
*Kalaanui* HI-9
Kalaau o Kalakani—*cape* HI-9
Kalabera—*slope* MH-9
Kalaberan Kattan, Laderan—*cliff* MH-9
*Kalaberan Lichan* MH-9
Kalaberan Lichan, Laderan—*cliff* MH-9
Kalabera Pass—*gap* MH-9
Kala Ch—*church* VA-3
Kala Creek—*stream* AK-9
Ka Lae—*cape* HI-9
**Kalae**—*pop pl* HI-9
Ka Laea—*cape* HI-9
Kalaeahole—*cape* HI-9
Ka Lae Amana—*cape* HI-9
*Ka Lae a Puki* HI-9
Ka Lae Apuki—*cape* HI-9
*Kalaeeha* HI-9
*Ka Lae Hala* HI-9
Kalaehiamoe—*cape* HI-9
*Ka Lae Honono* HI-9
*Kalaehonu* HI-9
Kalaekapu—*cape* HI-9
Ka Lae Kiki—*cape* HI-9
Ka Lae Kiloia—*cape* HI-9
*Ka Lae Kupapau* HI-9
*Kalaeloa* HI-9
Kalaeloa—*cape* HI-9
Kalaeloa Harbor—*bay* HI-9
Kalaeloa Rsvr—*reservoir* HI-9
Ka Lae Mamane—*cape* HI-9
Kalaemamo—*island* HI-9
Ka Lae Mau—*cape* HI-9
*Kalaemilo* HI-9
Kalaemilo—*cape* HI-9
*Ka Lae Noio* HI-9
Ka Lae o Hoaiku—*cape* HI-9
Kalae Oio Beach Park—*park* HI-9
*Kalaeokaea* HI-9
*Kalaeokaea Point* HI-9
Kalaeokahano—*cape* HI-9
*Kalaeokahano Point* HI-9
Kalaeokahipa Gulch—*valley* HI-9
*Ka Lae o Kahoni* HI-9
Ka Lae o Kahonu—*ridge* HI-9
*Ka Lae o Kailio* HI-9
Ka Lae o Kaiwa—*cape* HI-9
*Kalaeokalaau* HI-9
*Ka Lae o Kallio* HI-9
*Ka Lae o Kawai* HI-9
Ka Lae o Kowali—*cape* HI-9
Kalaeola—*cape* HI-9
*Ka Lae o Malae* HI-9
Ka Lae Paakai—*cape* HI-9
Kalae Paakai—*cape* HI-9
Ka Lae Paakai—*cape* HI-9
*Ka Lae Paoo* HI-9
Kalaepohaku—*island* HI-9
Kalaepohaku Playground—*park* HI-9
Kalaepohaku Ridge—*ridge* HI-9
KALA-FM (Davenport)—*tower* IA-7
Kalagvik, Mount—*summit* AK-9
Kalahaku—*summit* HI-9
Kalahaku Overlook—*locale* HI-9
Kalahaku Pali—*cliff* HI-9
*Kalahao Valley* HI-9
Kalaheo—*civil* HI-9
**Kalaheo**—*pop pl* HI-9
Kalaheo Filtration Plant—*other* HI-9
Kalaheo Gulch—*valley* HI-9
Kalaheo (Homestead)—*CDP* HI-9
Kalaheo Homesteads—*civil* HI-9
Kalaheo Intermediate Sch—*school* HI-9
Kalaheo Playground—*park* HI-9
Kalaheo Sch—*school* HI-9
Kalahiki—*civil* HI-9
Kalahiki Beach—*beach* HI-9
Kalahiki Cem—*cemetery* HI-9
Kalahopele Gulch—*valley* HI-9
Kalahu—*summit* HI-9
Kalahuapueo—*summit* HI-9
*Kalahuipuaa* HI-9
Kalahu Point—*cape* HI-9
Kalaieha—*summit* HI-9
Kalaina—*cliff* HI-9
Kalaipaloa Point—*cape* HI-9
Kalai Stream—*stream* HI-9
Kalakaket Creek—*stream* AK-9
Kalakaket Creek Radio Relay Site—*other* AK-9
Kalakala—*beach* HI-9
Kalakalaula—*civil* HI-9
Kalakaoo Stream—*stream* HI-9
Kalakaua Golf Course—*other* HI-9
Kalakaua Park—*park* HI-9
Kalakaua Sch—*school* HI-9
Kalakohi Gulch—*valley* HI-9
Kalala—*civil* HI-9
Kalalae Point—*cape* HI-9
Kalala Two—*civil* HI-9
Kalalau—*civil* (2) HI-9
Kalalau Beach—*beach* HI-9
Kalalau Lookout—*locale* HI-9
Kalalau Stream—*stream* HI-9
Kalalau Trail—*trail* HI-9
Kalalau Valley—*valley* HI-9
Kalala 1—*civil* HI-9
*Kalalea* HI-9
Kalalea—*summit* HI-9
Kalalea, Heiau o—*locale* HI-9
Kalaloa Point—*cape* HI-9
Kalaloch—*locale* WA-9
Kalaloch Campground—*locale* WA-9
Kalaloch Creek—*stream* WA-9
Kalaloch Rocks—*summit* WA-9
*Kalalock Creek* WA-9
Kalalua—*crater* HI-9
*Kalalua Crater* HI-9
*Kalaluanahelehela* HI-9
Kalaluanahelehele—*summit* HI-9
Kalaluapuu—*summit* HI-9
Kalalula Stream—*stream* HI-9
*Kalalunahelehela* HI-9
Kalama—*bay* HI-9
Kalama—*cape* HI-9
**Kalama**—*pop pl* WA-9
Kalama (CCD)—*cens area* WA-9
Kalama Falls—*falls* WA-9
Kalamaiki Gulch—*valley* HI-9
Kalamakapala—*civil* HI-9
Kalamakowali Homesteads—*civil* HI-9
Kalamakumu—*civil* HI-9
Kalama Lower Range—*channel* OR-9
Kalama Lower Range—*channel* WA-9
Kalamalu—*summit* HI-9
Kalamanu—*bay* HI-9
Kalamanui Gulch—*valley* HI-9
Kalama Park—*park* HI-9
*Kalama Point* HI-9
Kalama Ranger Station—*locale* WA-9
Kalama River—*stream* WA-9
Kalama Stream—*stream* HI-9
Kalamath Mine—*mine* CA-9
Kalamau—*civil* HI-9
**Kalamaula**—*pop pl* HI-9
Kalamaumi—*civil* HI-9
Kalama Upper Range—*channel* OR-9
Kalama Upper Range—*channel* WA-9
Kalama Valley—*valley* HI-9
Kalamawaiawaawa—*civil* HI-9
*Kalamazoo* KS-7
Kalamazoo—*fmr MCD* NE-7
Kalamazoo—*locale* AR-4
Kalamazoo—*locale* FL-3
Kalamazoo—*locale* WV-2
**Kalamazoo**—*pop pl* MI-6
Kalamazoo Cem—*cemetery* NE-7
Kalamazoo Ch—*church* NC-3
Kalamazoo Christian Sch—*school* MI-6
Kalamazoo Coll—*school* MI-6
Kalamazoo Country Club—*other* MI-6
**Kalamazoo (County)**—*pop pl* MI-6
*Kalamazoo Creek* NV-8
Kalamazoo Creek—*stream* NV-8
Kalamazoo (historical)—*locale* KS-7
Kalamazoo Lake—*lake* MI-6
Kalamazoo Municipal Airp—*airport* MI-6
Kalamazoo Nature Center—*park* MI-6
Kalamazoo River—*stream* MI-6
Kalamazoo Speedway—*other* MI-6
Kalamazoo State Hosp—*hospital* MI-6
Kalamazoo State Hosp Water Tower—*hist pl* MI-6
Kalamazoo Summit—*gap* NV-8
**Kalamazoo (Township of)**—*pop pl* MI-6
Kalamazoo-Valley Community Coll—*school* MI-6
Kalamink Creek—*stream* MI-6
**Kalamo**—*pop pl* MI-6
**Kalamo (Township of)**—*pop pl* MI-6
Kalanaanaole Colony—*civil* HI-9
Kalanai Point—*cape* HI-9
Kalanaokuaiki Pali—*cliff* HI-9
Kalani—*cape* HI-9
Kalanianaole Beach Park—*park* HI-9
Kalanianaole Colony—*other* HI-9
Kalanianaole Sch—*school* HI-9
Kalani HS—*school* HI-9
*Kalanikaula* HI-9
Kalanikaula—*summit* HI-9
Kalanipuao Rock—*island* HI-9
Kalanipuu—*summit* HI-9
Kalaniwahine Gulch—*valley* HI-9
Kalanu Prong—*stream* TN-4
Kalaoa—*civil* HI-9
**Kalaoa**—*pop pl* HI-9
Kalaoa Five—*civil* HI-9
Kalaoa Four—*civil* HI-9
Kalaoa Homesteads—*civil* HI-9
Kalaoa One-Four—*civil* HI-9
Kalaoa One-Two—*civil* HI-9
Kalaoa-Ooma Homesteads—*civil* HI-9
Kalaoa Sch—*school* HI-9
Kalaoa Stream—*stream* HI-9
Kalaoa Three—*civil* HI-9
Kalaoa Three-Four—*civil* HI-9
Kalaoa Valley—*valley* HI-9
*Kalap* FM-9
Kalapa—*summit* HI-9
Kalapahapuu Gulch—*valley* HI-9
*Kalapa Hill* HI-9
Kalapaki—*civil* HI-9
Kalapaki Beach—*beach* HI-9
Kalapa Konomanu—*ridge* HI-9
Kalapamoa Ridge—*ridge* HI-9
Kalapana—*civil* HI-9
**Kalapana**—*pop pl* HI-9
Kalapana Trail—*trail* HI-9
*Kalapanu* HI-9
Kalapawale Gulch—*valley* HI-9
Kalapawili Ridge—*ridge* HI-9
Kalapili—*cape* HI-9
Kala Point—*cape* WA-9
Kalarama—*locale* NJ-2
Kalarvik Point—*cape* AK-9
Kalasik Creek—*stream* AK-9
Kalasik Lake—*lake* AK-9
Kala Slough—*stream* AK-9
Kalauao—*civil* HI-9
**Kalauao**—*pop pl* HI-9
*Kalauao Creek* HI-9
*Kalauao Gulch* HI-9
Kalauao Spring—*spring* HI-9
*Kalauao Station* HI-9
Kalauao Stream—*stream* HI-9
*Kalauau River* HI-9
Ka Laulau—*cape* HI-9
*Kalaulea* HI-9
Kalauonakukui Heiau—*locale* HI-9
Kalaupapa—*civil* HI-9

**Kalaupapa**—*pop pl* HI-9
*Kalaupapa Leper Settlement* HI-9
**Kalaupapa (Leprosy Colony)**—*pop pl* HI-9
Kalaupapa Natl Historic Park—*park* HI-9
Kalawao—*civil* HI-9
**Kalawao**—*pop pl* HI-9
Kalawao (CCD)—*cens area* HI-9
*Kalawao (County)* HI-9
Kalawao Park—*park* HI-9
*Kalawokailo* HI-9
**Kalber**—*pop pl* WA-9
Kalberer Quarry—*mine* KY-4
Kalbito Springs—*spring* AZ-5
Kalbough Cem—*cemetery* WV-2
Kalbwok—*island* MP-9
Kal Creek—*stream* AK-9
Kaldachabuna Lake—*lake* AK-9
Kaldolyeit Lake—*lake* AK-9
Kale—*locale* WV-2
Kalea—*cape* HI-9
*Kalea Park* AL-4
Ka-Lea Park—*park* AL-4
*Kale Branch* VA-3
Kale Branch—*stream* LA-4
Kale Branch—*stream* VA-3
Kale Creek—*stream* ID-8
Kale Creek—*stream* OH-6
Kale Creek—*stream* OR-9
Kale Dick Hollow—*valley* OK-5
Kaleetan Butte—*summit* OR-9
Kaleetan Creek—*stream* WA-9
Kaleetan Lake—*lake* WA-9
Kaleetan Peak—*summit* WA-9
Kale Gap—*gap* NC-3
Kale Gap—*gap* TN-4
Kaleg Cem—*cemetery* IN-6
Kale Hollow—*valley* WV-2
*Kalehu* HI-9
Kalehua Gulch—*valley* HI-9
*Ka Lehua Hakihaki* HI-9
Kalehuahakihaki—*summit* HI-9
*Kalehuahakihaki Peak* HI-9
KaLehua (Site)—*locale* HI-9
*Kalehu Point* HI-9
Kaleia—*beach* HI-9
Kaleib Spring—*spring* OR-9
Kaleinamanu Ridge—*ridge* HI-9
Kale Island—*island* IN-6
Kalekta Bay—*bay* AK-9
Kale Lake—*lake* IN-6
Kale Lake—*lake* MN-6
Kalele—*cape* HI-9
Kalele—*summit* HI-9
Kalele Gulch—*valley* HI-9
Kaleleiki Stream—*stream* HI-9
**Kalem**—*pop pl* MS-4
*Kalem Church* MS-4
Kalena—*civil* HI-9
Kalena Gulch—*valley* HI-9
Kalena Stream—*stream* HI-9
Kalengawar—*locale* FM-9
Kalentine Hole—*lake* TX-5
Kaleolehuula—*summit* HI-9
Kalepa—*civil* HI-9
Kalepa—*summit (2)* HI-9
Kalepa For Res—*forest* HI-9
Kalepa Gulch—*valley (2)* HI-9
Kalepalehua Gulch—*valley* HI-9
Kalepa Point—*cape (2)* HI-9
Kalepa Ridge—*ridge (2)* HI-9
*Kalepa Stream* HI-9
Kalepa Well—*well* HI-9
Kalepe a Moa—*civil* HI-9
Kalepeamoa—*summit* HI-9
Kalepolepo—*locale* HI-9
Kalepp Lake—*reservoir* WI-6
**Kaler**—*pop pl* KY-4
Kaler Branch—*stream* IN-6
Kaler Hollow—*valley* UT-8
Kaler Hollow Campground—*park* UT-8
Kaler Sch—*school* ME-1
**Kalers Corner**—*pop pl* ME-1
Kalers Pond—*lake* ME-1
Kales Branch—*stream* KY-4
*Kale School* IN-6
Kale Slough—*stream* LA-4
*Kaleuluges Reef* PW-9
**Kaleva**—*pop pl* MI-6
Kaleva Bay—*bay* MN-6
*Kaleva Creek* MI-6
Kalevala Sch—*school* MN-6
**Kalevala (Township of)**—*pop pl* MN-6
Kaleva Temple—*hist pl* MI-6
Kaley Ford—*locale* MO-7
Kaley Sch—*school* FL-3
Kaley Sch—*school* IN-6
Kalgary—*locale* TX-5
Kalgin Island—*island* AK-9
Kalhabuk Creek—*stream* AK-9
Kalhabuk Mtn—*summit* AK-9
Kalhagen Cem—*cemetery* ND-7
Kalhagu Cove—*bay* AK-9
Kali, Taoch Ra—*channel* PW-9
Kaliae—*civil* HI-9
Kaliakh River—*stream* AK-9
*Kaliali* HI-9
Kalialinui—*civil* HI-9
Kalialinui Gulch—*valley* HI-9
*Kalida* KS-7
Kalida—*locale* TN-4
**Kalida**—*pop pl* OH-6
Kalida Cem—*cemetery* KS-7
*Kalifonski* AK-9
*Kalifonsky* AK-9
Kalifonsky—*CDP* AK-9
*Kalifonsky Beach* AK-9
**Kalifornsky**—*pop pl* AK-9
Kalifornsky Beach—*beach* AK-9
Kaligagan Island—*island* AK-9
Kaliguricheark River—*stream* AK-9
Kalihi—*civil (3)* HI-9
**Kalihi**—*pop pl* HI-9
Kalihi Channel—*channel* HI-9
Kalihi Fire Station—*hist pl* HI-9
Kalihikai—*civil* HI-9
**Kalihi Kai**—*pop pl* HI-9
Kalihikai Beach—*beach* HI-9
Kalihikai Park—*park* HI-9
Kalihi Kai Sch—*school* HI-9
Kalihi Point—*cape* HI-9
Kalihi Sch—*school* HI-9
Kalihi Stream—*stream* HI-9
Kalihi Uka Sch—*school* HI-9
Kalihi Valley—*valley* HI-9
Kalihi Valley Field—*park* HI-9
Kalihi Waena Sch—*school* HI-9
Kalihiwai—*civil* HI-9
**Kalihiwai**—*pop pl* HI-9
Kalihiwai Bay—*bay* HI-9
*Kalihiwai Landing* HI-9
Kalihiwai River—*stream* HI-9
Kalihiwai Rsvr—*reservoir* HI-9
*Kalihiwa River* HI-9
Kaliipaa—*area* HI-9
*Kaliiwaa* HI-9
Kaliko—*summit* HI-9
Kalikpik River—*stream* AK-9
Kalik River—*stream* AK-9
Kaliksneethnook River—*stream* AK-9
*Kali Mtn* HI-9
Kalina—*locale* CA-9
Kalina Dam—*dam* ND-7
Kalina Lake—*reservoir* ND-7
Kalinin Bay—*bay* AK-9
Kalinin Point—*cape* AK-9
Kalinke—*locale* WI-6
**Kali-Oka Springs (subdivision)**—*pop pl* AL-4
Kaliopi—*locale* KY-4
Kalipoa—*area* HI-9
*Kalispel* MT-8
*Kalispel Bay* ID-8
*Kalispel Creek* ID-8
*Kalispel Creek* WA-9
**Kalispel Ind Res**—*pop pl* WA-9
*Kalispel Island* ID-8
**Kalispell**—*pop pl* MT-8
Kalispell Air Force Station—*military* MT-8
Kalispell Bay—*bay* ID-8
Kalispell Bay—*bay* MT-8
*Kalispell Creek* WA-9
Kalispell Creek—*stream* ID-8
Kalispell Creek—*stream* WA-9
Kalispell Falls—*falls* WA-9
Kalispell Island—*island* ID-8
*Kalispell Lake* WA-9
Kalispell Northwest—*cens area* MT-8
Kalispell Rock—*summit* WA-9
Kalispell Southwest—*cens area* MT-8
Kalitan Creek—*stream* OR-9
*Kaliu Hill* HI-9
*Kaliuwaa* HI-9
Kalka Island—*island* AK-9
**Kalkaska**—*pop pl* MI-6
**Kalkaska (County)**—*pop pl* MI-6
Kalkaska State For—*forest* MI-6
**Kalkaska (Township of)**—*pop pl* MI-6
Kalkberg—*ridge* NY-2
Kalkenbrenner Lake—*lake* MN-6
Kalkun Cay—*island* VI-3
Kalla—*locale* AK-9
Kallager Ditch—*canal* OH-6
Kalla Lake—*lake* MN-6
Kallam Grove Ch—*church* NC-3
KALL-AM (Salt Lake City)—*tower* UT-8
*Kallamuchee River* MS-4
Kallander Creek—*stream* MI-6
Kallands—*locale* AK-9
Kallan Sch—*school* WI-6
Kallarichuk Hills—*other* AK-9
Kallarichuk River—*stream* AK-9
Kalleva Island—*island* MN-6
KALL-FM (Salt Lake City)—*tower* UT-8
Kallio, Mount—*summit* MI-6
Kallio Lake—*lake* MN-6
Kallis Creek—*stream* MT-8
Kallison Park—*park* TX-5
Kallison Ranch—*locale* TX-5
Kallman Home for Children—*building* NY-2
Kallmeyers Bluff—*cliff* MO-7
Kallmeyier Cem—*cemetery* MO-7
Kalloch (historical)—*locale* KS-7
*Kallock* ME-1
Kallock Cem—*cemetery* KS-7
**Kallops Corners**—*pop pl* NY-2
*Kallus* ME-1
KALM AM (Thayer)—*tower* MO-7
**Kalmar (Township of)**—*pop pl* MN-6
Kalmback Lake—*lake* AK-9
**Kalmia**—*pop pl* MD-2
**Kalmia**—*pop pl* NC-3
Kalmia Gardens—*park* SC-3
Kalmia (historical)—*locale* AL-4
Kalmia Lake—*lake (2)* CA-9
Kalmiopsis Wilderness Area—*reserve* OR-9
Kalmus Park Beach—*beach* MA-1
Kalmus Park Beach—*park* MA-1
**Kalo**—*pop pl* IA-7
Kaloaloa—*summit* HI-9
Kalohewahewa Stream—*stream* HI-9
Kalohi Channel—*channel* HI-9
Kaloi—*civil* HI-9
Kaloi Gulch—*valley* HI-9
*Kalo Island* MP-9
Kalo Island—*island* MP-9
Kaloko—*cape* HI-9
Kaloko—*civil* HI-9
Ka Loko Ditch—*canal* HI-9
Kalokoeli Fishpond—*lake* HI-9
Kaloko Fishpond—*reservoir* HI-9
Kaloko-Honokohau Natl Historic Site—*park* HI-9
Kaloko Point—*cape* HI-9
*Kaloko Rsvr* HI-9
Ka Loko Rsvr—*reservoir* HI-9
Kalokut Creek—*stream* AK-9
Kaloli Point—*cape* HI-9
Kalolo—*bay* HI-9
*Kaloloch* WA-9
**Kalon**—*pop pl* FL-3
Kalona—*locale* AL-4
**Kalona**—*pop pl* IA-7
Kalona Gulch—*valley* HI-9
Kalone Cem—*cemetery* LA-4
Kalopa—*civil* HI-9
Kalopa Gulch—*valley* HI-9
Kalopa Homesteads—*civil* HI-9
**Kalopa Mauka (Kalopa)**—*pop pl* HI-9
Kalop Branch—*stream* SC-3
Kalorama—*post sta* DC-2
Kalorama Circle—*locale* DC-2
Kalorama Park—*park* DC-2
**Kalorama Park**—*pop pl* IN-6
Kalorama Sch—*school* IA-7
Kalorama Triangle Hist Dist—*hist pl* DC-2
Kalou Marsh—*swamp* HI-9
*Kalou Pond* HI-9
**Kalreda Woods**—*pop pl* PA-2
Kalset Point—*cape* WA-9
Kalsin Bay—*bay* AK-9
Kalsin Creek—*stream* AK-9
Kalsin Island—*island* AK-9
Kalsin Pond—*lake* AK-9
Kalsin Reef—*bar* AK-9
**Kalskag**—*pop pl* AK-9
Kalskag(native name for Upper Kalskag) ANV815—*Reserve* AK-9
Kalsow State Prairie—*park* IA-7
Kalsta Ditch—*canal* MT-8
Kalstad Sch—*school* MN-6
Kalsta Ranch—*locale* MT-8
**Kaltag**—*pop pl* AK-9
Kaltag Mountains—*other* AK-9
Kaltag Portage—*trail* AK-9
Kaltag River—*stream* AK-9
Kalte Canyon—*valley* CA-9
**Kalten Acres**—*pop pl* MD-2
Kalua—*civil* HI-9
Kaluaaha—*civil* HI-9
**Kaluaaha**—*pop pl* HI-9
Kaluaaha—*summit* HI-9
Kaluaaha Gulch—*valley* HI-9
Kaluaahole—*cape* HI-9
Kaluapuhi Fishpond—*lake* HI-9
*Kaluapuhi Pond* HI-9
*Kaluapuni Pond* HI-9
Kaluaa Stream—*stream* HI-9
Kalua Awa—*summit* HI-9
Kaluahaulu Ridge—*ridge* HI-9
Kaluahauoni—*summit* HI-9
Kaluahee Rock—*island* HI-9
Kaluahine Falls—*falls* HI-9
*Kaluahohe* HI-9
Kaluahonu—*crater* HI-9
Kaluaihakoko—*cape* HI-9
Kaluaiki—*crater* HI-9
Kaluakailio—*civil* HI-9
Kaluakanaka—*summit* HI-9
Kaluakau—*summit* HI-9
Kaluakauila Gulch—*valley* HI-9
Kaluakauila Stream—*stream* HI-9
Kaluakoi—*civil* HI-9
*Kaluakoi Gulch* HI-9
Kaluakoi Valley—*valley* HI-9
Kaluaieo—*summit* HI-9
Kaluaolohe Gulch—*valley* HI-9
Kaluamakani—*crater* HI-9
Kaluamakua Stream—*stream* HI-9
*Kaluamoa* HI-9
Kaluanamaulu Valley—*valley* HI-9
Kaluanui—*cape* HI-9
Kaluanui—*civil* HI-9
Kaluanui—*crater* HI-9
Kaluanui Flats—*flat* HI-9
Kaluanui Heiau—*locale* HI-9
Kaluanui Ridge—*ridge* HI-9
Kaluanui Stream—*stream* HI-9
Kaluaohonu—*cape* HI-9
Kaluaokalani—*cape* HI-9
Kaluaokalani Valley—*valley* HI-9
Kaluaokapioho Heiau—*locale* HI-9
Kaluaokawahine—*summit* HI-9
Kalua o Lapa—*summit* HI-9
Kaluaolohe—*summit* HI-9
Kaluapeelua Gulch—*valley* HI-9
Kaluapepeiao Gulch—*valley* HI-9
*Kaluapuhi* HI-9
Kaluapuhi—*cape* HI-9
Kaluapuhi—*summit* HI-9
Kaluapuhi Pond—*lake* HI-9
Kaluapulani Gulch—*valley* HI-9
Kalubik Creek—*stream* AK-9
Kaluchagun—*locale* AK-9
Kaluchagun Slough—*gut* AK-9
Kalue—*cape* HI-9
Kaluich Creek—*stream* AK-9
Kaluiiki Branch—*stream* HI-9
Kalukalu One-Two—*civil* HI-9
Kalukna River—*stream* AK-9
Kalukruatchiak Point—*cape* AK-9
Kaluktavik River—*stream* AK-9
*Kalula* KS-7
Kalulu—*cape* HI-9
Kalulu—*civil* HI-9
Kalulu—*summit* HI-9
Kaluluktok Creek—*stream* AK-9
*Kalulu Point* HI-9
Kaluna Cliff—*cliff* CA-9
Kalunawaikaala Stream—*stream* HI-9
*Kalunawaikaale Stream* HI-9
**Kalunite**—*pop pl* UT-8
Kalun Lake—*lake* AK-9
*Kaluokalani Valley* HI-9
**Kalurah**—*pop pl* NY-2
Kalurivik Creek—*stream* AK-9
Kalusuk Creek—*stream* AK-9
Kalutna River—*stream* AK-9
Kaluu o ka Oo—*crater* HI-9
Kaluvarawluk Mtn—*summit* AK-9
Kaluyut Mountains—*other* AK-9
Kalvelage, Joseph B., House—*hist pl* WI-6
Kalves Creek—*stream* GA-3
**Kalvesta**—*pop pl* KS-7
*Kama* FM-9
Kama, Lae o—*cape* HI-9
*Kamaal Creek* OR-9
Kamaee—*civil* HI-9
Kamaee Homesteads—*civil* HI-9
Kamaee Stream—*stream* HI-9
Kamahale—*summit* HI-9
Kamahuehue Fishpond—*lake* HI-9
Kamahuna—*summit* HI-9
*Kamaike Point* HI-9
Kamaiki Point—*cape* HI-9
Kamaile Heiau—*summit* HI-9
Kamaileunu Ridge—*ridge* HI-9
Kamaili—*civil* HI-9
Kamaili—*locale* HI-9
Kamaili Homesteads—*civil* HI-9
*Kamaio* HI-9
Kamakahi Gulch—*valley* HI-9
Kamakahonu, Residence Of King Kamehameha I—*hist pl* HI-9
Kamakaia Hills—*summit* HI-9
Kamakaia Lava Flow—*lava* HI-9
Kamakaiauka—*summit* HI-9
Kamakaiawaena—*summit* HI-9
Kamakaipo—*locale* HI-9
Kamakaipo Gulch—*valley* HI-9
Kamakalepo—*lava* HI-9
*Kamakalino* HI-9
Kamakamaka Point—*cape* HI-9
Kamakapaa—*summit* HI-9
Kamakeanu—*summit* HI-9
*Kamakmaka Point* HI-9
Kamakoa Gulch—*valley* HI-9
Kamakou—*summit* HI-9
*Kamakou Peak* HI-9
*Kamala* HI-9
*Kamalalaea Bay* HI-9
Kamala Point—*cape* HI-9
Kamalii Ridge—*ridge* HI-9
**Kamalino**—*pop pl* HI-9
Kamalino Bay—*bay* HI-9
Kamalo—*civil* HI-9
**Kamalo**—*pop pl* HI-9
Kamalo Gulch—*valley* HI-9
Kamalo Harbor—*bay* HI-9
*Kamalomalo* HI-9
Kamalomaloo—*civil* HI-9
Kamalomaloo Stream—*stream* HI-9
*Kamalomalo Stream* HI-9
*Kamamaloo* HI-9
*Kamamaloo* HI-9
*Kamamaloo Stream* HI-9
Kamanaiki Stream—*stream* HI-9
Kamanakai Gulch—*valley* HI-9
Kamanamana—*cape* HI-9
*Kamana Mountain* HI-9
Kamananui—*civil* HI-9
Kamananui Ditch Tunnel—*tunnel* HI-9
Kamananui Stream—*stream* HI-9
*Kamana Peak* HI-9
*Kamanawa* HI-9
Kamanawa Bay—*bay* HI-9
Kamanawai Gulch—*valley* HI-9
Kamanawa Point—*cape* HI-9
Kamane—*cape* HI-9
Kamanele Square—*locale* HI-9
Kamani—*summit* HI-9
Kamankeag Brook—*stream* ME-1
Kamankeag (historical)—*locale* ME-1
Kamankeag Pond—*lake* ME-1
Kamano—*civil* HI-9
Kamanoni—*civil* HI-9
Kamanu—*summit* HI-9
*Kamanu Mtn* HI-9
Kamao—*civil* HI-9
*Kamaoa* HI-9
Kamaoa Homesteads—*civil* HI-9
Kamaoa Pueo—*civil* HI-9
Kamaohanui—*summit* HI-9
*Kamaohanui Peak* HI-9
Kamaohe Bay—*bay* HI-9
Kamaohi Gulch—*valley* HI-9
Kamaole—*beach* HI-9
Kamaole—*civil* HI-9
Kamaole Beach Park—*park* HI-9
Kamaole Homesteads—*civil* HI-9
Kamaolii—*summit* HI-9
Kamar Oil Field—*oilfield* TX-5
**Kamas**—*pop pl* UT-8
Kamas Cem—*cemetery* UT-8
Kamas Division—*civil* UT-8
Kamas Fish Hatchery—*locale* UT-8
Kamas Lake—*reservoir* UT-8
Kamas Lake Dam—*dam* UT-8
Kamas Post Office—*building* UT-8
*Kamas Prarie* UT-8
Kamas Valley—*valley* UT-8
Kamas Wildlife Mngmt Area—*park* UT-8
*Kamatuck* AZ-5
Kamaui—*civil* HI-9
Kamaulele—*summit* HI-9
*Kamaulele Peak* HI-9
Kamawai—*area* HI-9
**Kamay**—*pop pl* TX-5
*Kambek* PW-9
Kambich Ranch—*locale* MT-8
Kambich Springs—*spring* MT-8
*Kambitch Reservoir* AZ-5
*Kambitch Tank* AZ-5
Kambitch Tank—*reservoir* AZ-5
*Kambitsch Tank* AZ-5
Kambitsch Tank—*reservoir* AZ-5
*Kamehameha Cocoanut Grove* HI-9
Kamehameha Coconut Grove—*locale* HI-9
Kamehameha Field—*park* HI-9
**Kamehameha Heights**—*pop pl* HI-9
Kamehameha I Birthplace—*locale* HI-9
Kamehameha III's Birthplace—*hist pl* HI-9
Kamehameha III Sch—*school* HI-9
Kamehameha Park—*park* HI-9
Kamehameha Sch—*school* HI-9
Kamehameha V Post Office—*hist pl* HI-9
Kamehameha V Wall, Archeol Site (T-20 and T-42-3) 50-60-04-706—*hist pl* HI-9
Kamehame Hill—*summit* HI-9
Kamehameiki—*civil* HI-9
Kamehamenui—*civil* HI-9
Kamehame Ridge—*ridge* HI-9
**Kamela**—*pop pl* OR-9
Kamennoi Island—*island* AK-9
Kamenoi Point—*cape* AK-9
*Kamenoko-Sho* MH-9
*Kameoko Sho* MH-9
Kamerchiluk Slough—*gut* AK-9
Kameron—*locale* ID-8
**Kamesang**—*pop pl* PW-9
Kame Stream—*stream* AK-9
Kametolook River—*stream* AK-9
**Kamey**—*pop pl* TX-5
Kamey Island—*island* TX-5
Kamey-Six Mile (CCD)—*cens area* TX-5
Kamiache Creek—*stream* WA-9
**Kamiah**—*pop pl* ID-8
Kamiah Gulch—*valley* ID-8
Kamiakan Butte—*summit* WA-9
Kamiak Butte—*summit* WA-9
Kamiak Butte State Park—*park* WA-9
*Kamiakin Butte* WA-9
*Kamiakin Mountain* WA-9
Kamiakin's Gardens—*hist pl* WA-9
*Kamiak Mountain* WA-9
Kamiki Ridge—*ridge* HI-9
Kamiktungitak Creek—*stream* AK-9
**Kamilche**—*pop pl* WA-9
Kamilche (CCD)—*cens area* WA-9
Kamilche Point—*cape* WA-9
Kamilche Valley—*valley* WA-9
*Kamilianlul Mountain* PW-9
*Kamilo* HI-9
Kamilo Gulch—*valley* HI-9
Kamiloiki Valley—*valley* HI-9
*Kamilolo* HI-9
Kamiloloa—*civil* HI-9
**Kamiloloa**—*pop pl* HI-9
Kamiloloa Gulch—*valley* HI-9
Kamilonui Valley—*valley* HI-9
Kamilo Pae Alii—*cape* HI-9
Kamilo Pae Kanaka—*cape* HI-9
Kamilo Point—*cape (3)* HI-9
Kamimela Lake—*lake* MN-6
Kamimi, Lae o—*cape* HI-9
Kaminer, John J., House—*hist pl* SC-3
Kaminski Creek—*stream* WI-6
Kaminski Hill—*summit* MT-8
Kaminski Spring—*spring* MT-8
Kaminsky Lake—*lake* MI-6
Kamishak Bay—*bay* AK-9
Kamishak River—*stream* AK-9
*Kamiyangaru* PW-9
*Kamiyangaur* PW-9
Kamkaun Spring—*spring* OR-9
Kam Lake—*lake* IL-6
Kamloop Cove—*bay* CO-8
Kamloops—*hist pl* MI-6
Kamloops Island—*island* MI-6
Kamloops Island—*island* WA-9
Kamloops Point—*cape* MI-6
**Kamm**—*pop pl* MT-8
Kamm, Jacob, House—*hist pl* OR-9
Kamma Mtns—*summit* NV-8
Kamm and Schellinger Brewery—*hist pl* IN-6
Kamm Ditch—*canal* WA-9
Kammel Coulee—*valley* WI-6
Kammer Beach—*beach* MH-9
Kammerdiner Cross Line Trail—*trail* PA-2
**Kammerer**—*pop pl* PA-2
Kammerer Tanks—*reservoir* NM-5
Kammerzell Lake—*reservoir* CO-8
**Kammeyer Addition (subdivision)**—*pop pl* UT-8
Kamm Island Park—*park* IN-6
Kamms—*post sta* OH-6
Kamms Corner—*locale* WY-8
**Kamms Corner**—*pop pl* OH-6
*Kamoa* HI-9
*Kamoalii Stream* HI-9
Kamoamoa—*civil* HI-9
Kamoamoa (Site)—*locale* HI-9
Ka Moa o Pele—*summit* HI-9
Kamoa Point—*cape* HI-9
Kamoa Point Complex—*hist pl* HI-9
Kamoauau—*civil* HI-9
Kamohio Bay—*bay* HI-9
*Kamohoalii Lava Flow* HI-9
*Kamoi* MH-9
Kamoi Point—*cape* HI-9
Kamokala Ridge—*ridge* HI-9
Kamoku—*civil* HI-9
Kamoku—*summit* HI-9
Kamoku Flats—*flat* HI-9
*Kamoku Hill* HI-9
Kamokuna—*beach* HI-9
*Kamokuna Point* HI-9
Kamole—*summit* HI-9
Kamole Gulch—*valley* HI-9
Kamole Weir—*dam* HI-9
Kamoloumi Stream—*stream* HI-9
*Kamome Island* MP-9
Kamome Island—*island* MP-9
*Kamomoa* HI-9
Kamona Sch—*school* MI-6
*Kamondorski (census name Komandorski Village)* CA-9
*Kamone Island* MP-9
*Kamooalii Lava Flow* HI-9
Kamooalii Lava Flow—*lava* HI-9
Kamooalii Stream—*stream* HI-9
Kamoohoopulu Ridge—*ridge* HI-9
Kamookoa Ridge—*ridge* HI-9
Kamoo Koleaka—*summit* HI-9
**Kamooloa**—*pop pl* HI-9
Kamooloa Stream—*stream* HI-9
*Kamoouau* HI-9
*Kamori* PW-9
*Kamori Island* PW-9
*Kamori To* PW-9
Kampark Campground—*park* UT-8
**Kampe**—*pop pl* NJ-2
Kampel Airp—*airport* PA-2
Kamper Park—*park* MS-4
**Kampeska**—*pop pl* SD-7
Kampeska, Lake—*lake* SD-7
Kampeska Cem—*cemetery* SD-7
**Kampeska Township**—*pop pl* SD-7
Kampfe, Lake—*reservoir* NJ-2
Kampfe Lake—*uninc pl* NJ-2
Kamph Memorial Park—*park* CA-9
Kamp Kalmia—*locale* NJ-2
Kamp Kentwood—*locale* VA-3
Kamp Kewanee—*locale* PA-2
Kamp Kill Kare—*locale* NY-2
**Kamp Klamath**—*pop pl* CA-9
Kamp Koinonia—*locale* TX-5
Kampmeyer Cem—*cemetery* IL-6
Kamp Mound Site—*hist pl* IL-6
Kampong—*hist pl* FL-3
Kampoosa Brook—*stream* MA-1
**Kampos**—*pop pl* NV-8
Kamppinen Ranch—*locale* MT-8
Kamp Ranch—*locale* WY-8
Kampschroeder Bend—*bend* MO-7
Kamps-Stiens Island—*island* IL-6
**Kampsville**—*pop pl* IL-6
Kampsville Hollow—*valley* IL-6
**Kampville**—*pop pl* MO-7
**Kampville Beach**—*pop pl* MO-7
**Kampville Court**—*pop pl* MO-7
Kampville Sch—*school* MO-7
Kamp Washington—*locale* VA-3
Kamradt Draw—*valley* NM-5
Kamradt Ranch—*locale* NM-5
**Kamrar**—*pop pl* IA-7
Kamrath Site—*hist pl* WI-6
*Kamuela* HI-9
**Kamuela (census name Waimea)**—*pop pl* HI-9
Kamuliwai—*bay* HI-9
Kam Wah Chung Company Bldg—*hist pl* OR-9
**Kamwele**—*pop pl* FM-9
Kamweng—*locale* FM-9
Kamwome—*island* MP-9
*Kan* FM-9
*Ka'na* CO-8
*Kana-a* AZ-5
*Kana-a Creek* AZ-5
*Kana-a Valley* AZ-5
Kanaa Valley—*valley* AZ-5
*Kana-a Wash* AZ-5
Kanaa Wash—*arroyo* AZ-5
**Kanab**—*pop pl* UT-8
Kanab Canyon—*valley* AZ-5
Kanab City Cem—*cemetery* UT-8
Kanab Creek—*stream* AZ-5
Kanab Creek—*stream* UT-8
Kanab Division—*civil* UT-8
**Kanabec (County)**—*pop pl* MN-6
Kanabec County Courthouse—*hist pl* MN-6
**Kanabec (Township of)**—*pop pl* MN-6
*Kanab Elementary School* UT-8
Kanab HS—*school* UT-8
Kanabilay—*cape* FM-9
*Kanab Mountains* AZ-5
*Kanab Mountains* UT-8
Kanab Municipal Airp—*airport* UT-8
Kanabownits Canyon—*valley* AZ-5
Kanabownits Lookout Tower—*tower* AZ-5
Kanabownits Spring—*spring* AZ-5
Kanab Plateau—*plain* AZ-5
Kanab Plateau—*plain* UT-8
Kanab Point—*cliff* AZ-5
Kanab Post Office—*building* UT-8
Kanab Rapids—*rapids* AZ-5
Kanab Sch—*school* UT-8
Kan-ac-to, Lake—*lake* NY-2
Kanady Cem—*cemetery* IL-6
Kanady Creek—*stream* AL-4
Kanady Creek—*stream* GA-3
Kanady Hollow—*valley* OH-6
Kanaej—*island* MP-9
Kanaele—*well* HI-9
Kanaele Swamp—*swamp* HI-9
Kanaenae—*ridge* HI-9
Kanaga Bay—*bay* AK-9
Kanaga Island—*island* AK-9
Kanaga Pass—*channel* AK-9
Kanaga Sound—*bay* AK-9
Kanaga Volcano—*summit* AK-9
Kanagtatlek Creek—*stream* AK-9
Kanagunut Island—*island* AK-9
*Kanaha* HI-9
Kanaha—*cape* HI-9
Kanahaha—*area* HI-9
*Kanaha Island* HI-9
*Kanaha Peak* HI-9
Kanaha Pond—*lake* HI-9
Kanaha Pond Waterfowl Ref—*park* HI-9
*Kanahappa Ridge* OR-9
Kanaha Rock—*summit* HI-9
Kanaha Stream—*stream (2)* HI-9
Kanahau—*summit* HI-9
Kanaha Valley—*valley* HI-9
*Kanahena* HI-9
Kanahena—*civil* HI-9
Kanahena—*locale* HI-9
*Kanahena Point* HI-9
Kanahena Point—*cape* HI-9
Kanahonua—*civil* HI-9
Kanahualii Falls—*falls* HI-9
Kanaic—*cape* HI-9
Kanaio—*civil* HI-9
Kanaio Ch—*church* HI-9
Kanaio Homesteads—*other* HI-9
Kanaio Prison Camp (Abandoned)—*locale* HI-9
*Kanaka Bar* CA-9
Kanaka Bar—*bar* CA-9
Kanaka Bay—*bay* WA-9
Kanaka Creek—*stream (6)* CA-9
Kanaka Creek—*stream* WA-9
Kanaka Cutoff—*canal* CA-9
Kanaka Flat—*flat* CA-9
Kanaka Glade—*flat* CA-9
Kanaka Gulch—*valley (3)* CA-9
Kanaka Gulch—*valley* OR-9
Kanaka Lake—*reservoir* UT-8
*Kanakaleonui* HI-9
Kanakaleonui Ranger Station—*locale* HI-9
Kanakaloloa—*area* HI-9
Kanakaloloa—*summit* HI-9
Kanakamilae—*area* HI-9
Kanaka Mine—*mine* CA-9
Kanakanak (U S Government Hospital)—*hospital* AK-9
Kanaka Peak—*summit (2)* CA-9
*Kanaka Point* HI-9
Kanaka Rapids—*rapids* ID-8
Kanakau One-Two—*civil* HI-9
*Kanakea Bay* HI-9
Kanakea Pond—*bay* HI-9
Kanak Island—*island* AK-9
Kanaknoll Point—*cape* AK-9
Kanakou—*summit* HI-9
*Kanakti Mtn* CA-9
Kanaktok Creek—*stream* AK-9
Kanaktok Mtn—*summit* AK-9
Kanakuk-Kanakomo Church Camp—*locale* MO-7
Kanalku Bay—*bay* AK-9
Kanalku Lake—*lake* AK-9
Kanalku Mtn—*summit* AK-9
Kanaloa—*cape* HI-9
Kanaloa Gulch—*valley* HI-9
Kanaloiki Valley—*valley* HI-9
Kanalo Valley—*valley* HI-9
Kanalukaha—*cape* HI-9
*Kanal Von Kossol* PW-9
Kanaly Sch—*school* SD-7
*Kanamaka* MA-1
Kananaka—*area* HI-9

Kanapaha—*hist pl* FL-3
Kanapaha—*locale* FL-3
Kanapaha, Lake—*reservoir* FL-3
Kanapaha Cem—*cemetery* FL-3
Kanapaha Ch—*church* FL-3
Kanapaha Prairie—*flat* FL-3
Kanapak—*locale* AK-9
Kanapalu Gulch—*valley* HI-9
*Kanapa Prairie* FL-3
Kana Park—*park* AZ-5
Kanape Brook—*stream* NY-2
Kanape Jeep Trail—*trail* NY-2
*Kanapolis* KS-7
Kanapou Bay—*bay* HI-9
*Kanapu* HI-9
*Kanara* UT-8
*Kanara Creek* UT-8
**Kanaranzi**—*pop pl* MN-6
Kanaranzi Creek—*stream* MN-6
**Kanaranzi (Township of)**—*pop pl* MN-6
*Kanaraville* UT-8
*Ka'na River* WY-8
*Kanarra* UT-8
*Kanarra Creek* UT-8
Kanarra Creek—*stream* UT-8
Kanarra Mtn—*summit* UT-8
**Kanarraville**—*pop pl* UT-8
Kanarraville Cem—*cemetery* UT-8
Kanasatka, Lake—*lake* NH-1
Kanaskat—*locale* WA-9
Kanaskat Junction—*locale* WA-9
Kanatak—*locale* AK-9
Kanatak Creek—*stream* AK-9
Kanatak Lagoon—*bay* AK-9
Kanatak Lake—*lake* AK-9
Kanatak Pass—*gap* AK-9
**Kanata Manayunk**—*pop pl* IN-6
*Kanat As Frailan* MH-9
*Kanat Fahang Katan* MH-9
*Kanat Fahang Lichan* MH-9
*Kanat Falipe* MH-9
*Kanat Fanaganam Katan* MH-9
*Kanat Fanaganam Lichan* MH-9
*Kanat Fanhang Katan* MH-9
*Kanat Fanunchuluyan* MH-9
*Kanat Felipe* MH-9
*Kanat Halaihai* MH-9
*Kanat I Apicot* MH-9
*Kanat I Daog* MH-9
*Kanat I Eddot* MH-9
Kanati Fork—*stream* NC-3
*Kanati Fork Bald* NC-3
*Kanat I Hasngot* MH-9
*Kanat Inanaso* MH-9
*Kanat I Pitot* MH-9
*Kanat Laremies* MH-9
*Kanat Laulau* MH-9
*Kanat Magpi* MH-9
*Kanat Nanasu* MH-9
Kanaton Ridge—*ridge* AK-9
*Kanat Papau* MH-9
*Kanat Papua* MH-9
*Kanat Rapugau* MH-9
*Kanat Rueda* MH-9
*Kanat Tablan Katan* MH-9
*Kanat Iablan Lichan* MH-9
*Kanat Tadung* MH-9
*Kanat Tadung Laulau* MH-9
*Kanat Tadung Mahetog* MH-9
*Kanat Tadung Rapugau* MH-9
*Kanat Tapblan Katan* MH-9
*Kanat Unai Fahang* MH-9
*Kanat Unai Nanasu* MH-9
Kanaueue One-Two—*civil* HI-9
**Kanauga**—*pop pl* OH-6
Kanauga Sch—*school* OH-6
Kanaugh Lake—*lake* WY-8
Kanauguk River—*stream* AK-9
*Kanaun* FM-9
Kanause Drain—*canal* MI-6
Kanause Lake—*lake* MI-6
Kanause Lake Drain—*canal* MI-6
Kanawauke, Lake—*reservoir* NY-2
Kanawauke Circle—*locale* NY-2
**Kanawha**—*pop pl* IA-7
**Kanawha**—*pop pl* TX-5
**Kanawha**—*pop pl* WV-2
Kanawha Airp—*airport* WV-2
*Kanawha Branch* WV-2
Kanawha Branch—*stream* WV-2
Kanawha Chapel—*church* WV-2
Kanawha Chapel—*locale* WV-2
Kanawha Chapel Ch—*church* WV-2
*Kanawha City* WV-2
**Kanawha City**—*pop pl* WV-2
Kanawha City (RR name Owens)—*uninc pl* WV-2
Kanawha City Sch—*school* WV-2
**Kanawha (County)**—*pop pl* WV-2
Kanawha County Courthouse—*hist pl* WV-2
**Kanawha Drive**—*pop pl* WV-2
**Kanawha Drive (Revel)**—*pop pl* WV-2
**Kanawha Estates**—*pop pl* WV-2
**Kanawha Falls**—*pop pl* WV-2
Kanawha Fork—*stream* WV-2
Kanawha Fork Ch—*church* WV-2
**Kanawha Head**—*pop pl* WV-2
Kanawha Hotel—*hist pl* WV-2
*Kanawha River* NC-3
*Kanawha River* VA-3
*Kanawha River* WV-2
Kanawha River—*stream* WV-2
Kanawha Run—*stream (2)* WV-2
Kanawha Run Camping Area—*locale* WV-2
Kanawha Run Ch—*church* WV-2
Kanawha Sch—*school* CA-9
Kanawha Sch—*school* WV-2
Kanawha Spring—*spring* MD-2
Kanawha State For—*forest* WV-2
Kanawha Station—*locale* WV-2
Kanawyer Gap—*gap* CA-9
Kanawyers—*locale* CA-9
Kanayat Creek—*stream* AK-9
Kanayut Bluff—*cliff* AK-9
Kanayut River—*stream* AK-9
Kanbrick—*locale* KS-7
Kancamagus, Mount—*summit* NH-1
Kancamagus Brook—*stream* NH-1
*Kancamagus Notch* NH-1
Kancamagus Pass—*gap* NH-1
Kanco—*locale* KS-7
Kanda—*locale* WY-8
K And D Mine—*mine* AK-9
Kandik River (Charley Creek)—*stream* AK-9
*Kandiota Lake* ND-7
Kandiota Post Office (historical)—*building* ND-7
Kandiotta Lake—*lake* ND-7
Kandivoh Township—*civ div* ND-7
**Kandiyohi**—*pop pl* MN-6
**Kandiyohi (County)**—*pop pl* MN-6
*Kandiyohi Lake* MN-6
**Kandiyohi (Township of)**—*pop pl* MN-6
K-and-K Resort—*locale* SD-7
K and L Canyon—*valley* UT-8
Kandle Lake—*reservoir* NJ-2
**K And M Junction**—*pop pl* WV-2
Kandolph Coulee—*valley* ND-7
Kandota Cem—*cemetery* MN-6
**Kandota (Township of)**—*pop pl* MN-6
Kandra—*locale* CA-9
K and R Mine—*mine* IL-6
K And R Rsvr—*reservoir* NM-5
K and R Well—*well* NM-5
K and R Well—*well* SD-7
Kandt Lake—*lake* ND-7
K and T Memorial Gardens—*cemetery* KY-4
K and W Lake—*reservoir* NC-3
K and W Lake Dam—*dam* NC-3
Kandy Kane Park—*park* WI-6
*Kane* AZ-5
Kane—*locale* TX-5
Kane—*locale* WY-8
**Kane**—*pop pl* IL-6
**Kane**—*pop pl* KY-4
**Kane**—*pop pl* PA-2
Kane, E. C., House—*hist pl* OR-9
Kane, John, House—*hist pl* NY-2
Kane, John P., Mansion—*hist pl* NY-2
Kane, Thomas L., Memorial Chapel—*hist pl* PA-2
*Kaneaimoa* HI-9
Kaneaimoa Point—*cape* HI-9
Kaneaki Heiau—*locale* HI-9
Kanealole Stream—*stream* HI-9
Kaneana Cave—*cave* HI-9
Kaneapua—*island* HI-9
Kane Area HS—*school* PA-2
Kane Area MS—*school* PA-2
Kanearok Creek—*stream* AK-9
Kaneaukai—*cape* HI-9
**Kaneb**—*pop pl* KY-4
**Kaneb**—*pop pl* NE-7
Kane Borough—*civil* PA-2
Kane Branch—*stream* KY-4
*Kane Cairn* AZ-5
*Kane Canyon* AZ-5
Kane Canyon—*valley* ID-8
Kane Canyon—*valley* NV-8
Kane Canyon—*valley* UT-8
Kane Cem—*cemetery* MO-7
Kane Cem—*cemetery* VA-3
Kane Cem—*cemetery* WY-8
Kane Corral—*locale* AZ-5
Kane County—*civil* UT-8
**Kane (County)**—*pop pl* IL-6
Kane County Hosp—*hospital* UT-8
Kane Cow Camp—*locale* WY-8
*Kane Creek* ID-8
*Kane Creek* IN-6
*Kane Creek* OR-9
*Kane Creek* VA-3
*Kane Creek* WY-8
Kane Creek—*stream* ID-8
Kane Creek—*stream* NE-7
Kane Creek—*stream (3)* OR-9
Kane Creek—*stream* PA-2
Kane Crossroads—*locale* MD-2
Kane-David Cem—*cemetery* TN-4
Kane Ditch—*canal* IN-6
Kane Draw—*valley (2)* WY-8
*Kane Dry Lake* CA-9
*Kanee Creek* AL-4
*Kanee Creek* MS-4
Kaneeleele Heiau—*locale* HI-9
Kaneetaksmiut (Summer Camp)—*locale* AK-9
Kane Experimental For HQ—*forest* PA-2
Kane Falls—*falls* NY-2
Kane Gap—*gap* VA-3
Kane Gap—*gap* WV-2
Kane Gulch—*valley* ID-8
Kane Gulch—*valley* OR-9
Kane Gulch—*valley* UT-8
Kane Gulch Ranger Station—*locale* UT-8
Kane Gulch Trailhead—*locale* UT-8
Kaneha Ditch—*canal* HI-9
Kaneha Reservoirs—*reservoir* HI-9
*Kane Hill* HI-9
Kanehinke Ditch—*canal* OR-9
*Kanehoa* HI-9
*Kanehoalani* HI-9
*Kanehoalani Hill* HI-9
*Kanehoa Peak* HI-9
Kanehoe Naval Air Station—*hist pl* HI-9
Kanehoe Ranch Bldg—*hist pl* HI-9
Kane Hollow—*valley (2)* UT-8
Kanehu—*area* HI-9
Kanehu Rsvr Number One—*reservoir* HI-9
Kanehu Rsvr Number Three—*reservoir* HI-9
Kanehu Rsvr Number Two—*reservoir* HI-9
*Kaneiho Point* HI-9
*Kaneilio* HI-9
Kaneilio Point—*cape* HI-9
Kane Islands—*area* AK-9
Kanekanaka Point—*cape* HI-9
Kanekauila Heiau—*civil* HI-9
Kanekaukii Point—*cape* HI-9
Kanekii—*area* HI-9
Kanekiki—*civil* HI-9
Kanektok River—*stream* AK-9
Kanekula—*summit* HI-9
*Kane Lake* CA-9
Kane Lake—*lake (2)* MN-6
Kane Lake—*reservoir* ID-8
Kaneland Sch—*school* IL-6
Kanelik—*locale* AK-9
Kanelik Pass—*gut* AK-9
*Kaneloa Gulch* HI-9
Kane Memorial Hosp—*hospital* PA-2
Kanemoeala Gulch—*valley* HI-9
Kane Mountains—*summit* NY-2
Kanem Point—*cape* WA-9
Kanenelu—*bay* HI-9
Kanenelu Flat—*flat* HI-9
Kane Nui o Hamo—*crater* HI-9
Kaneohe—*civil* HI-9
**Kaneohe**—*pop pl* HI-9
Kaneohe Bay—*bay* HI-9
Kaneohe Bay Marine Corps Air Station—*military* HI-9
Kaneohe Beach Park—*park* HI-9
Kaneohe (census name for Mokapu)—*CDP* HI-9
Kaneohe Fishing Pier—*locale* HI-9
Kaneohe For Res—*forest* HI-9
*Kaneohe Harbor* HI-9
Kaneohe Marine Corps Air Station—*military* HI-9
Kaneohe Sch—*school* HI-9
*Kaneohe Stream* HI-9
Kaneohe Stream—*stream* HI-9
Kaneohe Yacht Club—*other* HI-9
*Kaneoko-Sho* MH-9
Kane Opening—*flat* CA-9
Kane Peak—*summit* AK-9
*Kane Point* MD-2
*Kane Point* UT-8
Kane Point—*cape (2)* UT-8
Kanepuu—*summit* HI-9
Kane Ranch—*locale* AZ-5
Kane Ranch—*locale* CO-8
Kaner Flat—*flat* WA-9
Kaner Flat Trail—*trail* WA-9
*Kane Ridge* AZ-5
*Kane Ridge* IN-6
Kane Ridge—*ridge* ME-1
Kane Run—*stream (2)* PA-2
Kane Run—*stream* WV-2
Kane Sch—*school* MA-1
Kane Sch—*school* PA-2
Kane Sch (historical)—*school* PA-2
**Kanes Creek**—*pop pl* WV-2
Kanes Creek—*stream* VA-3
Kanes Creek—*stream* WV-2
Kanesholm—*locale* PA-2
Kanes Lake—*lake* NE-7
Kanes Open Camp (BSA)—*locale* NY-2
*Kane's Point* MD-2
*Kane Spring* AZ-5
Kane Spring—*locale* CA-9
Kane Spring—*locale* UT-8
Kane Spring—*spring (5)* AZ-5
Kane Spring—*spring (2)* ID-8
Kane Spring—*spring (6)* UT-8
Kane Spring Canyon—*valley* AZ-5
Kane Spring Draw—*valley* UT-8
Kane Spring Gulch—*valley* OR-9
Kane Spring Mtn—*summit (2)* AZ-5
Kane Spring Rsvr—*reservoir* OR-9
*Kane Springs* AZ-5
*Kane Springs* CA-9
Kane Springs—*spring* AZ-5
Kane Springs—*spring* CA-9
Kane Springs—*spring* NV-8
Kane Springs—*spring (2)* OR-9
Kane Springs—*spring* UT-8
*Kane Springs Canyon* AZ-5
Kane Springs Canyon—*valley* UT-8
Kane Springs Creek—*stream* UT-8
Kane Springs Picnic Area—*park* UT-8
Kane Springs Valley—*valley* NV-8
*Kane Springs Wash* AZ-5
Kane Springs Wash—*stream* NV-8
Kane Spring Wash—*valley* UT-8
Kanes Spring—*spring* AZ-5
*Kanesville* IL-6
**Kanesville**—*pop pl* UT-8
Kanesville Sch—*school* UT-8
Kanetown—*locale* WV-2
Kane Township—*fmr MCD (2)* IA-7
**Kane Township**—*pop pl* ND-7
Kane Township (historical)—*civil* ND-7
**Kane (Township of)**—*pop pl* IL-6
Kane Trail—*trail* AZ-5
Kanetuche Ch—*church* AL-4
Kanetuche Creek—*stream* AL-4
*Kane Valley* UT-8
**Kaneville**—*pop pl* IL-6
**Kaneville**—*pop pl* PA-2
**Kaneville (Township of)**—*pop pl* IL-6
Kanewaa Point—*cape* HI-9
*Kanewai* HI-9
Kanewai Field—*park* HI-9
Kanewai Stream—*stream* HI-9
Kane Wash—*stream* CA-9
Kane Wash—*valley* UT-8
Kaney Bayou—*gut* AR-4
Kaney Chapel—*church* OK-5
Kaney Creek—*stream* AR-4
Kaney Head Creek—*stream* GA-3
Kaney Ridge—*ridge* AR-4
*Kang* FM-9
Kanga Bay—*bay* AK-9
Kanga Island—*island* AK-9
Kangaroo Basin—*valley* OR-9
*Kangaroo Cave* TN-4
Kangaroo Creek—*stream* CA-9
Kangaroo Gulch—*valley* CO-8
Kangaroo Headland—*cliff* AZ-5
Kangaroo Lake—*lake* CA-9
Kangaroo Lake—*lake* WI-6
Kangaroo Mtn—*summit* CA-9
Kangaroo Point—*cliff* AR-4
Kangaroo Point Upper Bar—*bar* MS-4
Kangaroo Ridge—*ridge* WA-9
Kangaroo Stadium—*other* TX-5
Kangas Bay—*bay* MN-6
Kangas Creek—*stream* MN-6
Kangas Lake—*lake (2)* MN-6
Kangee Camp—*locale* AK-9
Kangeeghuk Bay—*bay* AK-9
Kangeekiksatharuk Cove—*bay* AK-9
Kangeekiktharuk Cove—*bay* AK-9
Kangighsak Point—*cape* AK-9
Kangik (Abandoned)—*locale* AK-9
Kangik River—*stream* AK-9
Kangiktoolikmiut (Summer Camp)—*locale* AK-9
Kangilipak, Lake—*lake* AK-9
Kangirlvar Bay—*bay* AK-9
Kangley—*locale* WA-9
**Kangley**—*pop pl* IL-6
**Kangly**—*pop pl* IL-6
Kangnaksnak Point—*cape* AK-9
Kangokakli Pass—*gut* AK-9
Kangukhsam Mtn—*summit* AK-9
Kaniahiku—*civil* HI-9
Kaniahiku Homesteads—*civil* HI-9
**Kaniahiku Village**—*pop pl* HI-9
*kaniah Mountains* WA-9
Kaniakapupu—*hist pl* HI-9
*Kanif* FM-9
**Kanif**—*pop pl* FM-9
Kanifaay—*civil* FM-9
*Kanifay* FM-9
Kanifay (Municipality)—*civ div* FM-9
*Kaniff* FM-9
*Kanifu* FM-9
Kanik Creek—*stream* AK-9
Kanik River—*stream* AK-9
*Kanikso Lake* ID-8
Kaniksrak, Lake—*lake* AK-9
Kaniksu Mtn—*summit* ID-8
Kaniksu Ranch—*locale* WA-9
Kanikula Glacier—*glacier* AK-9
Kaniku Lava Flow—*lava* HI-9
Kanikyakstalikmiut—*locale* AK-9
Kanim, Lake—*lake* WA-9
Kanima Sch—*school* OK-5
Kanine Ridge—*ridge* OR-9
Kanisakrok Lake—*lake* AK-9
Kanis Park—*park* AR-4
Kanitch—*hist pl* AK-9
*Kaniyohi Township* ND-7
*Kankakee* IN-6
**Kankakee**—*pop pl* IL-6
**Kankakee**—*pop pl* IN-6
Kankakee Bluffs—*cliff* IL-6
**Kankakee (County)**—*pop pl* IL-6
Kankakee Cut-Off—*stream* IL-6
Kankakee Drainage Ditch—*canal* IL-6
Kankakee Hill—*summit* CO-8
Kankakee Memorial Gardens—*cemetery* IL-6
Kankakee River—*stream* IL-6
Kankakee River—*stream* IN-6
*Kankakee River State Park* IN-6
Kankakee River State Park—*park* IL-6
*Kankakee State Game Preserve* IN-6
Kankakee State Hosp—*hospital* IL-6
**Kankakee (Township of)**—*pop pl* IL-6
**Kankakee (Township of)**—*pop pl (2)* IN-6
**Kankakee Valley**—*pop pl* IL-6
Kankapot Creek—*stream* WI-6
Kankone Peak—*summit* AK-9
Kanloyak—*locale* AK-9
Kannah—*locale* CO-8
Kannah Creek—*stream* CO-8
Kannah Creek Extension Ditch or Whitewater Ditch No 2—*canal* CO-8
Kannah Creek Flow Line—*canal* CO-8
Kannah Creek Highline Ditch—*canal* CO-8
Kannally Ranch—*locale* AZ-5
Kannally Wash—*stream* AZ-5
KANN-AM (Ogden)—*tower* UT-8
**Kannapolis**—*pop pl* NC-3
Kannapolis Golf Course—*locale* NC-3
Kannapolis Lake—*reservoir* NC-3
*Kannatagan* MP-9
*Kannatagan-To* MP-9
Kannat Tapbla—*slope* MH-9
*Kanniatobbee Creek* OK-5
*Kannie Creek* AL-4
*Kannie Creek* MS-4
Kanoa—*summit* HI-9
**Kanoa, Chalan**—*pop pl* MH-9
Kanoa, Lagunan Chalan—*bay* MH-9
Kanoa, Unai Chalan—*beach* MH-9
Kanoa Fishpond—*lake* HI-9
Kanoa Ridge—*ridge* HI-9
Kanodes Mill—*locale* VA-3
Kanohuluiwi Homesteads—*civil* HI-9
Kanokolus Bog—*swamp* ME-1
*Kanokti Mtn* CA-9
Kanola—*summit* HI-9
Kanola Creek—*stream* OK-5
Kanoma Gulch—*valley* AK-9
*Kanomaka* MA-1
*Kanomika* MA-1
Kanomika Neck—*cape* MA-1
**Kanona**—*pop pl* KS-7
**Kanona**—*pop pl* NY-2
Kanona Cem—*cemetery* KS-7
Kanongiksuk Creek—*stream* AK-9
*Kanoniaha* MA-1
Kanoni Point—*cape* HI-9
*Kanon Island* MP-9
Kanon Island—*island* MP-9
Kanonone Waterhole—*lake* HI-9
*Kanoon* FM-9
**Kanopolis**—*pop pl* KS-7
Kanopolis Cem—*cemetery* KS-7
Kanopolis Dam—*dam* KS-7
Kanopolis Lake—*reservoir* KS-7
*Kanopolis Land Field* KS-7
Kanopolis MS—*school* KS-7
*Kanopolis Reservoir* KS-7
Kanopolis State Park—*park* KS-7
Kanopolis State Park Airp—*airport* KS-7
**Kanorado**—*pop pl* KS-7
**Kanosh**—*pop pl* UT-8
*Kanosh Butte* UT-8
Kanosh Canyon—*valley* UT-8
Kanosh Cem—*cemetery* UT-8
*Kanosh Creek* UT-8
Kanosh Indian Village—*locale* UT-8
Kanosh Ind Res—*reserve* UT-8
Kanosh Tithing Office—*hist pl* UT-8
Kanosh Wildlife Mngmt Area—*park* UT-8
Kano Stream—*stream* HI-9
Kanouli Valley—*valley* HI-9
*Kanounou* HI-9
Kanounou Point—*cape* HI-9
*Kanouse Brook* NJ-2
Kanouse Brook—*stream* NJ-2
Kanouse Mtn—*summit* NJ-2
Kansada (historical)—*locale* KS-7
KANS-AM (Larned)—*tower* KS-7
*Kansapolis* KS-7
*Kansas* PA-2
Kansas—*locale* AR-4
Kansas—*locale* GA-3
Kansas—*locale* KY-4
Kansas—*locale (2)* TN-4
**Kansas**—*pop pl* AL-4
**Kansas**—*pop pl* IL-6
**Kansas**—*pop pl* IN-6
**Kansas**—*pop pl* OH-6
**Kansas**—*pop pl* OK-5
**Kansas**—*pop pl* VT-1
Kansas, State of—*civil* KS-7
Kansas Army Ammun Plant—*military* KS-7
Kansas Ave Sch—*school* KS-7
Kansas Ave United Methodist Ch—*church* KS-7
Kansas Baptist Ch—*church* AL-4
Kansas Branch—*stream* KY-4
Kansas Branch—*stream* NC-3
Kansas Branch—*stream* PA-2
Kansas (CCD)—*cens area* OK-5
Kansas Cem—*cemetery* AR-4
Kansas Cem—*cemetery* IN-6
Kansas Cem—*cemetery* OK-5
Kansas Center Cem—*cemetery* KS-7
*Kansas Centre* KS-7
Kansas Centre (historical)—*locale* KS-7
Kansas Ch—*church* IN-6
Kansas Ch—*church* OK-5
Kansas City—*locale* OR-9
Kansas City—*locale* TN-4
**Kansas City**—*pop pl* KS-7
**Kansas City**—*pop pl* MO-7
Kansas City, Kansas City Hall and Fire HQ—*hist pl* KS-7
Kansas City Area Vocational-Technical Sch—*school* KS-7
Kansas City Athenaeum—*hist pl* MO-7
*Kansas City Bible College* KS-7
Kansas City Coll and Bible Sch—*school* KS-7
Kansas City Country Club—*other* KS-7
Kansas City Downtown Airp—*airport* MO-7
Kansas City International Airp—*airport (2)* MO-7
Kansas City International Drag Strip—*other* MO-7
Kansas City Kansas Community Coll—*school* KS-7
Kansas City Live Stock Exchange—*hist pl* MO-7
Kansas City Masonic Temple—*hist pl* MO-7
Kansas City Metropolitan Junior Coll—*school (2)* MO-7
Kansas City Mine—*mine* CO-8
Kansas City Public Library—*hist pl* MO-7
Kansas City Royals Ball Park—*locale* FL-3
Kansas City Slope Mine (underground)—*mine* AL-4
Kansas City Southern Depot—*hist pl (2)* LA-4
Kansas City Suburban Airpark—*airport* KS-7
Kansas City Waterworks—*other* MO-7
Kansas Corners—*locale* OH-6
Kansas Creek—*stream* AK-9
Kansas Creek—*stream* OK-5
Kansas Creek—*stream (2)* OR-9
Kansas Falls—*falls* KS-7
Kansas Falls—*locale* KS-7
*Kansas Falls Station* KS-7
Kansas First Territorial Capitol—*building* KS-7
Kansas Flat Sch—*school* SD-7
Kansas Hill—*summit* TN-4
Kansas (historical)—*locale* AL-4
Kansas Hollow—*valley* NY-2
Kansas Hollow—*valley* TN-4
Kansas Lake—*lake* AR-4
Kansas Lake—*lake* MN-6
Kansas Lake Ch—*church* MN-6
Kansas Landing—*locale* MS-4
Kansas Mesa—*summit* CO-8
Kansas Mine—*mine* AZ-5
Kansas Natl Guard—*military* KS-7
Kansas Neurological Institute—*hospital* KS-7
*Kansas Ordinance Plant* KS-7
Kansas Post Office (historical)—*building* TN-4
Kansas Prairie—*flat* WA-9
Kansas Prairie Cem—*cemetery* WA-9
Kansas Prairie Siphon—*other* WA-9
Kansas Ridge—*ridge* PA-2
Kansas Ridge—*ridge* WV-2
Kansas River—*stream* KS-7
Kansas Sch—*school* TN-4
Kansas Sch (historical)—*school* TN-4
Kansas Settlement—*locale* AZ-5
Kansas State Capitol—*hist pl* KS-7
*Kansas State College* KS-7
Kansas State College Experiment Station—*locale* KS-7
*Kansas State College of Pittsburg* KS-7
Kansas State Horticulture Farm—*locale* KS-7
Kansas State Sch for the Deaf—*school* KS-7
Kansas State Sch for the Visually Handicapped—*school* KS-7
Kansas State Teachers Coll—*school* KS-7
Kansas State Univ Experimental Farm—*school* KS-7
Kansas Street Sch—*school* TN-4
Kansas Substation—*locale* AZ-5
Kansas Sugar Refining Company Mill—*hist pl* KS-7
Kansas Sweetwater Canal—*canal* FL-3
Kansas Technical Institute—*school* KS-7
**Kansas (Township of)**—*pop pl (2)* IL-6
Kansas Valley—*valley* NM-5
Kansas Valley—*valley* PA-2
Kansas Valley Park Area—*park* PA-2
Kansas Valley Run—*stream* PA-2
Kansas Velley Lake—*basin* NM-5
**Kansasville**—*pop pl* WI-6
Kansas Wesleyan Univ—*school* KS-7
KANS-FM (Larned)—*tower* KS-7
Kanson Draw—*valley* WY-8
Kanson Ranch—*locale* WY-8
*Kansopolis* KS-7
**Kansota**—*pop pl* MN-6
Kansteiner Cem—*cemetery* TX-5
Kantangnak Creek—*stream* AK-9
*Kantatinchunk* PA-2
Kant Hotel—*hist pl* SD-7
Kantishna—*locale* AK-9
Kantishna Hills—*range* AK-9
Kantishna River—*stream* AK-9
**Kantner**—*pop pl* PA-2
**Kantner (RR name Stoyestown (sta.))**—*pop pl* PA-2
Kantner Sch—*school* MI-6
Kants Mill (historical)—*locale* AL-4
**Kanty**—*pop pl* PA-2
**Kantz**—*pop pl* PA-2
**Kantz Corners**—*pop pl* PA-2
Kantz House—*hist pl* AR-4
KANU-FM (Lawrence)—*tower* KS-7
Kanuga Lake—*reservoir* NC-3
Kanuga Lake Lower Dam—*dam* NC-3
**Kanuga Park (subdivision)**—*pop pl* NC-3
**Kanuga Pines**—*pop pl* NC-3
**Kanuga Ridge (subdivision)**—*pop pl* NC-3
Kanu Island—*island* AK-9
Kanuktik Creek—*stream* AK-9
Kanuktik Lake—*lake* AK-9
Kanukuawa Fishpond—*lake* HI-9
Kanunuk Slough—*stream* AK-9
Kanupa—*summit* HI-9
Kanutchan Creek—*stream* OR-9
Kanuti Canyon—*valley* AK-9
Kanuti Chalatna Creek—*stream* AK-9
Kanuti Flats—*flat* AK-9
Kanuti Kilolitna River—*stream* AK-9
Kanuti Lake—*lake* AK-9
Kanuti River—*stream* AK-9
*Kan Van Vugarfy* NH-1
Kanview—*uninc pl* KS-7
Kanwaka—*locale* KS-7
Kanwaka Sch—*school* KS-7
**Kanwaka Township**—*pop pl* KS-7
Kanyak River—*stream* AK-9
Kanza Cem—*cemetery* CO-8
*Kanzas* KS-7
*Kanzas River* KS-7
Kanz Cem—*cemetery* TX-5
KANZ-FM (Garden City)—*tower* KS-7
Kanzigg Hill—*summit* OH-6
Kaoaini Fishpond—*lake* HI-9
*Kaoaini Pond* HI-9
Kaohai—*civil* HI-9
Kaohaoha Gulch—*valley* HI-9
Kaohe—*civil (2)* HI-9
Kaoheanu Stream—*stream* HI-9
Kaohe Five—*civil* HI-9
Kaohe Four—*civil* HI-9
Kaohe Game Mngmt Area—*park* HI-9
Kaohe Homesteads—*civil* HI-9
Kaohe One-Three—*civil* HI-9
Kaohe Ranch—*locale* HI-9
Kaohe Six—*civil* HI-9
Kaohe Three—*civil* HI-9
Kaohe Two—*civil (2)* HI-9
Kaohe Valley—*valley* HI-9
Kaohikaipu Island (State Bird Refuge)—*island* HI-9
*Kaoiki* HI-9
Kaoiki Pali—*cliff* HI-9
*Ka Oio Point* HI-9
Kaoio Point—*cape* HI-9
Kaokao Ridge—*ridge* HI-9
Kaolak River—*stream* AK-9
KAOL-AM (Carrollton)—*tower* MO-7
Kaoledoly Slough—*gut* AK-9
Kaolin—*locale* AL-4
Kaolin—*locale* GA-3
Kaolin—*locale* IL-6
Kaolin—*locale* PA-2
**Kaolin**—*pop pl* AL-4
Kaolin Creek—*stream* MO-7
Kaolin Hollow—*valley* TX-5
Kaolin Mine—*mine* TX-5
Kaolin Township—*civil* MO-7
Kaolin Wash—*stream* NV-8
Kaoma—*civil* HI-9
Kaoma Point—*cape* HI-9
Kaonihu—*cape* HI-9
Kaonohi, Lae o—*cape* HI-9
Kaonohiokala Ridge—*ridge* HI-9
Kaonohua—*summit* HI-9
Kaonohua Gulch—*valley* HI-9
Kaonoulu—*civil* HI-9
**Kaonoulu**—*pop pl* HI-9
*Kaonoulu Gulch* HI-9
Kaonoulu Gulch—*valley* HI-9
Kaooa—*summit* HI-9
Kaopala—*beach* HI-9
Kaopala Gulch—*valley* HI-9
Kaopapa—*area* HI-9
Kaopapa—*island* HI-9
Kaopapawai Waterhole—*lake* HI-9
Kaopeahina Fishpond—*lake* HI-9
Kaou—*summit* HI-9
*Kaowahi* HI-9
Kapaa—*civil* HI-9
**Kapaa**—*pop pl* HI-9
Kapaa Beach Park—*park* HI-9
Kapaa (CCD)—*cens area* HI-9
Kapaa Homesteads—*civil* HI-9
Kapaa HS—*school* HI-9
Kapaahu—*civil* HI-9
**Kapaahu**—*pop pl* HI-9
Kapaaiki Point—*cape* HI-9
Kapaakea—*civil* HI-9
Kapaakea—*summit* HI-9
Kapaakea Gulch—*valley* HI-9
*Kapaalalaea Stream* HI-9
Kapaanui—*civil* HI-9
Kapaa One-Two—*civil* HI-9
Kapaa Park—*park* HI-9
Kapaa Quarry—*mine* HI-9
*Kapaa River* HI-9
*Kapaa Stream* HI-9
Kapaa Stream—*stream* HI-9
Kapaau—*civil* HI-9
**Kapaau**—*pop pl* HI-9
Kapaau Gulch—*valley* HI-9
Kapaau (Kohala)—*CDP* HI-9
Kapache Coulee—*valley* MT-8
Kapae Gulch—*valley* HI-9
*Kapaeokahi Bay* HI-9
*Kap Agingan* MH-9
*Kapaha Mountain* HI-9
*Kapaheehee Stream* HI-9
**Kapahi**—*pop pl* HI-9
Kapahi Ditch—*canal* HI-9
Kapahili Gulch—*valley* HI-9
Kapahi Park—*park* HI-9
Kapahi Stream—*stream* HI-9
Kapahukapu—*civil* HI-9
**Kapahulu**—*pop pl* HI-9

Katalla Oil Field (Inactive)—*other* AK-9
Katalla River—*stream* AK-9
Katalla Slough—*gut* AK-9
Katalo Butte—*summit* OR-9
Katalsta Ridge—*ridge* NC-3
Katalysine Spring—*spring* PA-2
**Katama**—*pop pl* MA-1
Katama—*summit* NM-5
Katama Bay—*bay* MA-1
Katama Bay Marshes—*swamp* MA-1
Katama Neck—*cape* MA-1
Katama Point—*cape* MA-1
Katama Wharf—*locale* MA-1
*Katamiwick* MA-1
*Katana Creek* TX-5
*Katapan Mene Shoska* KS-7
Katasa Creek—*stream* WA-9
*Katayma* MA-1
*Katayma Bay* MA-1
*Katayma Point* MA-1
*Kataymuck* MA-1
*Katchamadrogga Creek* AL-4
Katchanapee, Lake—*reservoir* GA-3
*Katchass Lake* WA-9
*Katchass River* WA-9
*Katchi* MP-9
Katchii—*island* MP-9
*Katchii Island* MP-9
*Katchii-to* MP-9
Katchin Creek—*stream* AK-9
*Kate* TN-4
*Kate* MP-9
**Kate**—*pop pl* AR-4
Kate, Mount—*summit* AK-9
Kate Adams Chute—*channel* MS-4
Kate Adams Lake—*lake* AR-4
Kate Aubrey Dikes—*levee* TN-4
Kate Aubrey Towhead—*flat* TN-4
Kate Aubrey Towhead Bar—*bar* TN-4
Kate Branch—*stream* (2) KY-4
Kate Branch—*stream* NC-3
Kate Branch—*stream* TN-4
Kate Brook—*stream* VT-1
Kate Campbell Anderson Memorial Park—*park* TN-4
*Kate Campbell Robertson Park* TN-4
Kate Camp Branch—*stream* KY-4
*Katechay Island* MI-6
*Kate Creek* TX-5
Kate Creek—*stream* ID-8
Kate Creek—*stream* (2) MT-8
Kate Creek—*stream* OR-9
*Kate Duncan Smith D A R School* AL-4
Kateekuk Island—*island* AK-9
Kateel River—*stream* AK-9
Kate Fork—*stream* KY-4
Kate Fowler Branch—*stream* SC-3
*Kate Griffin Junior High School* MS-4
Kate Hardy Mine—*mine* CA-9
Kate Hill—*summit* NY-2
Kate Hollow—*valley* TN-4
Kate Hollow—*valley* UT-8
Kate Hollow—*valley* VT-1
Kate Hollow—*valley* (2) WV-2
Kate Kennedy Sch—*school* CA-9
Kate Knob—*summit* NC-3
Kate Knob—*summit* WV-2
*Kate Lake* MI-6
Kateland—*hist pl* LA-4
**Kateland**—*pop pl* LA-4
Katella Hosp—*hospital* CA-9
Katella Sch—*school* (2) CA-9
Katell Branch—*stream* MO-7
Katellen—*locale* PA-2
Kate Lodge—*locale* AR-4
Katemcy—*locale* TX-5
Katemcy Creek—*stream* TX-5
Katemcy Rocks—*summit* TX-5
Kate M Smith Elem Sch—*school* FL-3
Kate Mtn—*summit* NY-2
Katenai Hill—*summit* AK-9
Katen Cem—*cemetery* NE-7
Katen Corner—*locale* ME-1
Kate O Sessions Memorial Park—*park* CA-9
Kate Peak—*summit* NV-8
Kate Pier Creek—*stream* WI-6
Kate Pier Lake—*lake* WI-6
*Kater Crossing* TN-4
Kate Run—*stream* WV-2
Kates Basin—*basin* WY-8
Kates Bay—*bay* MI-6
Kates Bay Cem—*cemetery* MI-6
*Kates Branch* VA-3
*Kates Branch* WV-2
Kates Branch—*stream* AL-4
Kates Branch—*stream* KY-4
Kates Branch—*stream* (2) WV-2
Kates Chapel—*church* NC-3
Kates Chapel—*church* WV-2
Kates Cow Camp—*locale* CA-9
Kates Creek—*stream* AL-4
Kates Creek—*stream* AR-4
Kates Creek—*stream* NC-3
Kates Creek—*stream* TX-5
Kates Creek—*stream* VA-3
Kates Creek—*stream* WV-2
Kates Creek Meadow—*lake* NJ-2
Kates Dairy—*flat* OR-9
Kates Hole—*basin* TX-5
Kates Hollow—*valley* MO-7
Kates Hollow—*valley* PA-2
Kates Lake—*lake* IN-6
Kates Lake—*lake* MI-6
Kates Lake—*lake* MS-4
Kates Lake—*lake* OH-6
Kates Mountain Overlook—*locale* WV-2
Kates Mtn—*summit* WV-2
Kates Needle—*summit* AK-9
Kates Point—*cape* UT-8
*Kates Pond* IN-6
Kates Pond—*lake* MS-4
Kate Spring—*spring* (2) NV-8
Kate Spring—*spring* OR-9
*Kate Springs* NV-8
Kates Sch (historical)—*school* MS-4
**Katesville**—*pop pl* NC-3
Kate Sweeney Bend (historical)—*bend* SD-7
Kate Tank—*reservoir* AZ-5
Katete River—*stream* AK-9
Kathakne Village—*locale* AK-9
Kathaleen Island—*island* AK-9
Kathan Creek—*stream* WI-6
Kathan Lake—*lake* WI-6
Kathan Meadows—*flat* VT-1
*Katharine Atoll* MP-9
Katharine Branson Sch—*school* CA-9
*Katharine Island* MP-9
Katharyn—*locale* KY-4
*Katheren Lake* MI-6
Katherina Cem—*cemetery* WI-6
**Katherine**—*pop pl* AZ-5
Katherine, Lake—*lake* CA-9
Katherine, Lake—*lake* CO-8
Katherine, Lake—*lake* FL-3
Katherine, Lake—*lake* NH-1
Katherine, Lake—*reservoir* OH-6
Katherine, Lake—*reservoir* SC-3
Katherine, Mount—*summit* NH-1
Katherine Allison Dam—*dam* AL-4
Katherine Allison Lake—*reservoir* AL-4
Katherine Extension Mine—*mine* AZ-5
Katherine Finchy Sch—*school* CA-9
Katherine Island—*island* MN-6
*Katherine Lake* MI-6
Katherine Lake—*lake* MI-6
Katherine Lake—*lake* MN-6
Katherine Lake—*lake* NM-5
Katherine Lake—*lake* WI-6
*Katherine Landing* AZ-5
Katherine Mine—*mine* AZ-5
KATHERINE M. LEE (Schooner)—*hist pl* DE-2
Katherine Ranger Station—*locale* AZ-5
Katherine Sch—*school* CA-9
Katherine Street Lake Dam—*dam* MS-4
Katherine Wash—*stream* AZ-5
Kathio Site—*hist pl* MN-6
**Kathio (Township of)**—*pop pl* MN-6
**Kathleen**—*pop pl* FL-3
**Kathleen**—*pop pl* GA-3
Kathleen, Lake—*lake* AK-9
Kathleen, Lake—*lake* MT-8
Kathleen, Lake—*lake* WA-9
Kathleen, Lake—*lake* WI-6
Kathleen, Lake—*reservoir* NC-3
Kathleen Baptist Ch—*church* FL-3
Kathleen Ch—*church* GA-3
Kathleen Creek—*stream* AK-9
Kathleen Elem Sch—*school* FL-3
*Kathleen Grammar Sch* FL-3
*Kathleen HS* FL-3
Kathleen HS—*school* FL-3
Kathleen JHS—*school* FL-3
*Kathleen Lake* WI-6
Kathleen Lake—*lake* CO-8
Kathleen Lookout Tower—*locale* GA-3
Kathleen Siding—*locale* AR-4
Kathleen Valley—*valley* CA-9
Kathmoor—*locale* VA-3
*Kathrina Lake* MN-6
*Kathrine Pond Swamp* PA-2
KATHRYN—*hist pl* MD-2
Kathryn—*locale* CA-9
**Kathryn**—*pop pl* ND-7
Kathryn, Lake—*lake* (2) FL-3
Kathryn, Lake—*lake* ID-8
Kathryn, Lake—*lake* NJ-2
Kathryn, Mount—*summit* AK-9
Kathryn Dam—*dam* ND-7
Kathryne Jane Islands—*island* NC-3
Kathryn Lake—*lake* WI-6
Kathryn Park—*park* MI-6
Kathul Mtn—*summit* AK-9
Kathwood—*locale* SC-3
**Kathwood**—*pop pl* SC-3
Kathwood Lakes—*lake* SC-3
Kathy, Lake—*reservoir* GA-3
Kathy Ball Park—*park* TX-5
Kathy Creek—*stream* TX-5
**Kathy Hills**—*pop pl* TN-4
Kathys Canyon—*valley* UT-8
Kathys Patch Airp—*airport* MO-7
Kathy Tank—*reservoir* AZ-5
**Katie**—*pop pl* OK-5
Katie, Lake—*lake* MN-6
Katie Branch—*stream* NC-3
Katie Branch—*stream* VA-3
Katie Brown Canyon—*valley* WY-8
Katie Creek—*stream* AK-9
Katie Creek—*stream* NC-3
Katie Fleck Spring—*spring* WA-9
Katie (historical P.O.)—*locale* MS-4
Katie Island—*island* MD-2
Katie Knob—*summit* AR-4
Katie Lake—*lake* AK-9
Katie Lake—*lake* MI-6
Katie Meadow Slough—*stream* KY-4
Katie Post Office (historical)—*building* AL-4
Katies Creek—*stream* KY-4
Katies Gourd—*lake* TN-4
Katies Place—*locale* ID-8
**Katies Place Subdivision**—*pop pl* UT-8
Katiktak Mtn—*summit* AK-9
Kating Lake—*lake* WI-6
Katinka Lake—*lake* WI-6
Katka—*locale* ID-8
Katka Creek—*stream* ID-8
Katka Pass—*gap* ID-8
Katka Peak—*summit* ID-8
Katka Peak Trail—*trail* ID-8
Katley Brook—*stream* MA-1
Katley Hill—*summit* MA-1
Katlian, Mount—*summit* AK-9
Katlian Bay—*bay* AK-9
Katlian River—*stream* AK-9
Katlitna River—*stream* AK-9
Katmai, Mount—*summit* AK-9
Katmai Bay—*bay* AK-9
Katmai Canyon—*valley* AK-9
Katmai Lakes—*lake* AK-9
Katmai Natl Park—*park* AK-9
Katmai Pass—*gap* AK-9
Katmai Reef—*bar* AK-9
Katmai River—*stream* AK-9
Katmai Rock—*island* AK-9
Katmai Village Site—*locale* AK-9
Kato—*locale* PA-2
KATO-AM (Safford)—*tower* AZ-5
Kato Bay—*swamp* SC-3
Katolinat, Mount—*summit* AK-9
Katoma Branch—*stream* SC-3
**Katonah**—*pop pl* NY-2
Katonah, Lake—*reservoir* NY-2
Katonah Village Hist Dist—*hist pl* NY-2
*Katota tokah River* SD-7
Katotawa Creek—*stream* OH-6
Katoya Lake—*lake* MT-8
Katrikiorak Creek—*stream* AK-9
Katrina Falls—*falls* NY-2
Katrina Lake—*lake* MN-6
Katrine—*locale* VA-3
Katrine, Lake—*lake* NY-2
Katrine, Loch—*lake* WA-9
Katrine Creek—*stream* AK-9
Katron Cem—*cemetery* VA-3
Katron Sediment Basin Dam Number One—*dam* TN-4
Katron Sediment Basin Number One Rsvr—*reservoir* TN-4
**Katsbaan**—*pop pl* NY-2
Katsbaan Ch—*church* NY-2
*Katsel Lake* MN-6
Katskill Hill—*summit* CA-9
*Katsuben To* MP-9
*Katsuck Butte* OR-9
Katsuck Creek—*stream* ID-8
Katsuk Butte—*summit* (2) OR-9
Katsuk Glacier—*glacier* WA-9
Katsuk Peak—*summit* WA-9
Kattej—*island* MP-9
Kattell Creek—*stream* NY-2
**Kattellville**—*pop pl* NY-2
Kattellville Cem—*cemetery* NY-2
*Kattelville* NY-2
**Kattelville**—*pop pl* NY-2
Kattenbracher House—*hist pl* IA-7
Kattenburg Canyon—*valley* CA-9
Kattenhorn Mine—*mine* NV-8
Katterman Ch—*church* OH-6
*Katterueru Mtn* PW-9
*Katterueru San* PW-9
*Katteruueru San* PW-9
Kattle Cem—*cemetery* VT-1
Kattskill Bay—*bay* NY-2
**Kattskill Bay**—*pop pl* NY-2
Katula Creek—*stream* WA-9
KATU-TV—*tower* OR-9
*Katvine* VA-3
**Katy**—*pop pl* LA-4
**Katy**—*pop pl* TX-5
**Katy**—*pop pl* WV-2
Katy Allen Lake—*reservoir* MO-7
Katy Bess Well—*well* NM-5
Katy Branch—*stream* AR-4
Katy Branch—*stream* KY-4
Katy Branch—*stream* (2) TN-4
Katy Bridge—*bridge* TX-5
Katy Cem—*cemetery* AR-4
Katy Ch—*church* WV-2
Katy Cooper Branch—*stream* KY-4
Katy Creek—*stream* NC-3
Katy Creek—*stream* OR-9
Katy Creek—*stream* WA-9
Katy Creek—*stream* WY-8
Katydid Colliery (historical)—*mine* PA-2
Katydid Lake—*lake* MN-6
Katydid Ranch—*locale* OR-9
Katydid Slough—*gut* IL-6
Katydid Slough—*swamp* IL-6
Katydid Trail—*trail* VA-3
Katy Hollow—*valley* TN-4
Katy Hosp—*hospital* KS-7
Katy Knob—*summit* GA-3
Katy Lake—*lake* MT-8
Katy Lake—*lake* OK-5
Katy Lake—*reservoir* KS-7
Katy Lake—*reservoir* MO-7
Katy Lake—*reservoir* OK-5
Katy Lake—*reservoir* (3) TX-5
Katy Lake Dam—*dam* KS-7
**Katy Lick**—*pop pl* WV-2
Katy Lick Run—*stream* WV-2
*Katy Mountain* NY-2
Katy Mtn—*summit* AR-4
Katy Mtn—*summit* OR-9
Katy Pace Valley—*basin* KY-4
Katy Park—*park* KS-7
Katy Park—*park* TX-5
Katy Reed Shop Ctr—*locale* TX-5
Katy Reid Hollow—*valley* IL-6
Katy Rsvr—*reservoir* OK-5
Katy Run—*stream* (2) WV-2
*Katys Lick* WV-2
*Katys Lick Creek* WV-2
Katys Nipple—*cliff* CO-8
Katys Nipple—*summit* WY-8
*Katys Pond* MA-1
Katy Young Branch—*stream* VA-3
KATZ-AM (St Louis)—*tower* MO-7
Katz and Leavitt Apartment House—*hist pl* MA-1
Katz Corner Sch—*school* IL-6
Katz Dam—*dam* ND-7
Katzehin River—*stream* AK-9
Katzenjammer Kids—*pillar* UT-8
**Katzenmeyer**—*pop pl* MS-4
Katzenstein House—*hist pl* AR-4
Katzer Drain Branch—*canal* WY-8
Katzer Drain Branch A—*canal* WY-8
Katzer Drain Branch B—*canal* WY-8
Katzer Drain Branch C—*canal* WY-8
Katzer Drain Branch D—*canal* WY-8
Katzer Main Drain—*canal* WY-8
Katz Island—*island* AK-9
Katz Oil Field—*oilfield* TX-5
Katz Park—*park* IL-6
Katz Pond—*lake* NY-2
Kau—*civil* HI-9
Kau, Moku o—*island* HI-9
Kauaea—*civil* HI-9
Kauai—*island* HI-9
Kauai Channel—*channel* HI-9
**Kauai (County)**—*pop pl* HI-9
Kauai HS—*school* HI-9
*Kauaikanae River* HI-9
*Kauaikanana Stream* HI-9
*Kauaikanane Stream* HI-9
Kauaikinana Stream—*stream* HI-9
Kauai Technical Sch—*school* HI-9
Kauakaiakaola Heiau—*locale* HI-9
Kauakio Bay—*bay* HI-9
Kauakiu Point—*cape* HI-9
Kauamanu—*civil* HI-9
*Kauao Peak* HI-9
Kauaopuu—*summit* HI-9
Kauaopuu Stream—*stream* HI-9
Kauapea Beach—*beach* HI-9
*Kaua Peak* HI-9
Kauaula—*civil* HI-9
Kauaula Rsvr—*reservoir* HI-9
Kauaula Stream—*stream* HI-9
Kauaula Tunnel—*tunnel* HI-9
Kaubashine Creek—*stream* WI-6
Ka-U Bay—*bay* HI-9
Kaub Cem—*cemetery* KS-7
Kauber, Warren F., Funeral Home—*hist pl* OH-6
Kau (CCD)—*cens area* HI-9
Kauda Point—*cape* AK-9
Kauder Creek—*stream* ID-8
Kau Desert—*plain* HI-9
Kau Desert Trail—*trail* HI-9
Kaueleau—*civil* HI-9
**Kaueleau**—*pop pl* HI-9
Kauer Rsvr—*reservoir* OR-9
Kauer Spring—*spring* CO-8
*Kauffman* PA-2
**Kauffman**—*pop pl* PA-2
Kauffman, Linus B., House—*hist pl* OH-6
Kauffman, William, House—*hist pl* CO-8
Kauffman Bay—*bay* MI-6
Kauffman Cem—*cemetery* PA-2
Kauffman Ch—*church* PA-2
Kauffman Creek—*stream* CO-8
Kauffman Creek—*stream* MT-8
Kauffman Dam—*dam* PA-2
Kauffman Ditch—*canal* IN-6
Kauffman (historical)—*locale* AL-4
Kauffman House—*hist pl* CO-8
**Kauffman (Kauffman's Station)**—*pop pl* PA-2
Kauffman Park—*park* OH-6
Kauffman Park—*park* PA-2
*Kauffman Reservoir* PA-2
Kauffman Saddle—*gap* ID-8
Kauffmans Ch—*church* PA-2
Kauffman Sch—*school* IL-6
Kauffmans Island—*island* FL-3
Kauffman Spring—*spring* CA-9
*Kauffmans Run Dam* PA-2
Kauffman Tank—*reservoir* NM-5
*Kauffmar Branch* AL-4
Kaufman—*locale* IL-6
**Kaufman**—*pop pl* TX-5
Kaufman, E. C., House—*hist pl* TX-5
Kaufman, Frank J., House—*hist pl* OH-6
Kaufman, H. L., House—*hist pl* OK-5
Kaufman, Sam, Site—*hist pl* TX-5
Kaufman Branch—*stream* AL-4
Kaufman Branch—*stream* TX-5
Kaufman Branch—*stream* WV-2
Kaufman Campground—*locale* NY-2
Kaufman Campgrounds—*locale* NY-2
Kaufman Canyon—*valley* WA-9
Kaufman (CCD)—*cens area* TX-5
Kaufman Cem—*cemetery* IL-6
Kaufman Cem—*cemetery* IN-6
Kaufman Cem—*cemetery* OH-6
Kaufman Cem—*cemetery* PA-2
Kaufman Ch—*church* PA-2
Kaufman City Lakes—*reservoir* TX-5
**Kaufman (County)**—*pop pl* TX-5
Kaufman Creek—*stream* AK-9
Kaufman Creek—*stream* CO-8
Kaufman Ditch—*canal* (2) IN-6
Kaufman Drain—*canal* MI-6
Kaufman Drain—*stream* MI-6
Kaufman Draw—*valley* TX-5
Kaufman Draw—*valley* WY-8
Kaufman Guard Station—*locale* ID-8
Kaufman Gulch—*valley* AK-9
Kaufman Gulch—*valley* ID-8
Kaufman Hollow—*valley* TN-4
Kaufman Lake—*lake* MT-8
Kaufman Lake—*reservoir* TX-5
Kaufmann—*locale* PA-2
Kaufman Pass—*gap* AK-9
Kaufman Pasture—*flat* CO-8
Kaufman Pond (historical)—*reservoir* IN-6
Kaufman Ranch—*locale* (2) NM-5
Kaufman Resort—*locale* SD-7
Kaufman Ridge—*ridge* CA-9
Kaufman Ridge—*ridge* (2) CO-8
Kaufman Rsvr—*reservoir* PA-2
Kaufman Run—*stream* PA-2
Kaufman Sch—*school* MI-6
Kaufman Sch (historical)—*school* PA-2
Kaufman's Distillery Covered Bridge—*hist pl* PA-2
Kaufman Seep—*spring* UT-8
*Kaufmans Island* FL-3
Kaufmans Lake—*lake* MT-8
Kaufman Slough—*gut* IL-6
Kaufman Slough—*gut* SD-7
Kaufman Spring—*spring* AZ-5
Kaufman Springs—*spring* WA-9
Kaufman-Straus Bldg—*hist pl* KY-4
Kaufman Tanks—*reservoir* AZ-5
Kau Gulch—*valley* HI-9
*Kauhako* HI-9
Kauhako—*civil* HI-9
Kauhako Bay—*bay* HI-9
Kauhako Crater—*crater* HI-9
*Kauhaku* HI-9
Kauhao Pali—*cliff* HI-9
Kauhao Ridge—*ridge* HI-9
Kauhao Valley—*valley* HI-9
*Kauhaupa Gulch* HI-9
Kauhaupa Gulch—*valley* HI-9
Kauhi—*summit* HI-9
Kauhikoa—*canal* HI-9
Kauhikoa—*summit* HI-9
Kauhikoa Ditch—*canal* HI-9
Kauhioaiakini Pond—*lake* HI-9
Kauhiuhi—*area* HI-9
Kauhiula—*civil* HI-9
Kauhola Point—*cape* HI-9
Kauhola Point Light—*locale* HI-9
Kau HS—*school* HI-9
Kauhuhuula—*civil* HI-9
Kauhuhuula Gulch—*valley* HI-9
Kauhuhuula Iki—*civil* HI-9
*Kauhuuhuula* HI-9
*Kauhuuhuula Gulch* HI-9
*Kauhuuhuulu* HI-9
Kauhuula—*island* HI-9
Kauhuula—*summit* HI-9
Kauiaha Gulch—*valley* HI-9
*Kauichungak Creek* AK-9
*Kauiki* HI-9
Kauiki—*summit* HI-9
Kauiki Head—*summit* HI-9
Kauilii Point—*cape* HI-9
Kaujema Island—*island* FM-9
Kaukahoku Trail—*trail* HI-9
Kauka Homesteads—*civil* HI-9
Kaukakee State Fish and Wildlife Area—*park* IN-6
Kaukalaelae Point—*cape* HI-9
Kaukamoku Gulch—*valley* HI-9
Kaukaopua—*summit* HI-9
Kaukauai Gulch—*valley* HI-9
**Kaukauna**—*pop pl* WI-6
**Kaukauna (Town of)**—*pop pl* WI-6
Kauke—*locale* OH-6
Kaukelei—*summit* HI-9
Kaukini Ridge—*ridge* HI-9
Kaukiuki Falls—*falls* HI-9
Kaukohoku—*locale* HI-9
*Kaukonahua River* HI-9
Kaukonahua Stream—*stream* HI-9
Kauk River—*stream* AK-9
Kauku—*summit* HI-9
*Kauku Crater* HI-9
*Kaukuhoku* HI-9
*Kaukulaelae Point* HI-9
Kaukulau—*civil* HI-9
Kaula—*island* HI-9
Kaula Bay—*bay* HI-9
Kaula Gulch—*valley* HI-9
Kaulahuki—*summit* HI-9
*Kaulainaiwi* HI-9
Kaulainaiwi Island—*island* HI-9
Kaulakahi Channel—*channel* HI-9
*Kaulaka Passage* HI-9
*Kaulala* HI-9
Kaulala Point—*cape* HI-9
Kaulalewelewe—*summit* HI-9
Kaulana—*civil* HI-9
Kaulana Bay—*bay* HI-9
Kaulana Gulch—*valley* HI-9
Kaulanamauna—*bay* HI-9
Kaulanamauna—*civil* HI-9
*Kaulana Point* HI-9
Kaulani—*cape* HI-9
Kaulaula Valley—*valley* HI-9
*Ka Ule Cape* HI-9
Kauleoli One-Two—*civil* HI-9
Kaulitski Rsvr—*reservoir* MT-8
Kaul Memorial Hosp—*hospital* PA-2
**Kaulmont**—*pop pl* PA-2
Kaulolo—*summit* HI-9
Kauls Lake—*reservoir* AL-4
Kaulton—*uninc pl* AL-4
Kaulton Field—*park* AL-4
*Kaulton Park* AL-4
Kaultui Mtn—*summit* AK-9
Kaultuinjek Creek—*stream* AK-9
Ka Ulu a Paoa Heiau—*locale* HI-9
Kauluoa Point—*cape* HI-9
Kaulu Pali—*cliff* HI-9
Kaulupo—*cape* HI-9
Kaulu Stream—*stream* (2) HI-9
Kauluwai—*summit* HI-9
Kauluwela Sch—*school* HI-9
Kaumahaloa—*summit* HI-9
Kaumaikeohu—*summit* HI-9
Kaumakani—*civil* HI-9
**Kaumakani**—*pop pl* HI-9
Kaumakani—*summit* HI-9
Kaumakani-Hanapepe (CCD)—*cens area* HI-9
Kaumakani Point—*cape* HI-9
**Kaumalapau**—*pop pl* HI-9
Kaumalapau Gulch—*valley* HI-9
Kaumalapau Harbor—*bay* HI-9
*Kaumalapu Harbor* HI-9
Kaumala Ridge—*ridge* HI-9
Kaumalumalu—*civil* HI-9
Kaumana—*civil* HI-9
**Kaumana**—*pop pl* HI-9
Kaumana Cave—*cave* HI-9
Kaumana Cem—*cemetery* HI-9
Kaumana Homesteads—*civil* HI-9
Kaumanalehua—*summit* HI-9
*Kaumanamana* HI-9
Kaumanamana Point—*cape* HI-9
Kaumana Sch—*school* HI-9
Kaumana Springs—*spring* HI-9
Kaumoali—*civil* HI-9
Kaumoali Gulch—*valley* HI-9
Kaumoku Stream—*stream* HI-9
Kaump Cem—*cemetery* WI-6
Kaumuhonu Valley—*valley* HI-9
Kaumuki—*summit* HI-9
Kaumu o Kaleihoohie—*summit* HI-9
*Kaunakaka* HI-9
Kaunakakai—*civil* HI-9
**Kaunakakai**—*pop pl* HI-9
Kaunakakai Gulch—*valley* HI-9
Kaunakakai Harbor—*bay* HI-9
Kaunala—*civil* HI-9
Kaunala Bay—*bay* HI-9
Kaunala Gulch—*valley* (2) HI-9
Kaunalewa—*locale* HI-9
Kaunalewa Ridge—*ridge* HI-9
Kaunalewa Shaft—*reservoir* HI-9
Kaunaloa—*civil* HI-9
*Kaunalu Bay* HI-9
*Kaunalu Gulch* HI-9
Kaunamano—*civil* (2) HI-9
Kaunamano Gulch—*valley* HI-9
Kaunamano Homesteads—*civil* (2) HI-9
*Kaunameek* MA-1
Kaunaoa Beach—*beach* HI-9
Kaunaoa Point—*cape* HI-9
*Kaunapahu* HI-9
Kauna Point—*cape* HI-9
Kaunauhane—*civil* HI-9
Kaunene—*locale* HI-9
**Kauneonga**—*pop pl* NY-2
**Kauneonga Lake**—*pop pl* NY-2
Kaune Sch—*school* NM-5
Kaunewinne, Lake—*reservoir* WI-6
Kauniho—*civil* (2) HI-9
Kaunoahua Ridge—*ridge* HI-9
Kaunoa Sch—*school* HI-9
Kaunolu—*civil* HI-9
Kaunolu Bay—*bay* HI-9
Kaunolu Village Site—*hist pl* HI-9
Kaunonen Lake—*lake* MN-6
*Kaunuahane* HI-9
Kaununui—*cape* HI-9
*Kaununui Point* HI-9
*Kaunuohoa Ridge* HI-9
Kaunuohua—*summit* HI-9
Kaunuohua Ridge—*ridge* HI-9
*Kaunu o Kaleioohie* HI-9
Kaunuopou—*cape* HI-9
*Kaunuopou Point* HI-9
Kaunupahu—*summit* HI-9
*Kaup* AL-4
*Kaupakalua* HI-9
Kaupakuea—*civil* HI-9
Kaupakuea Homesteads—*civil* HI-9
*Kaupakuhale* HI-9
Kaupakuhale—*summit* HI-9
*Kaupakuhale Mtn* HI-9
**Kaupakulua**—*pop pl* HI-9
*Kaupakulua Gulch* HI-9
Kaupakulua Gulch—*valley* HI-9
Kaupakulua Rsvr—*reservoir* HI-9
Kaupalaoa—*civil* HI-9
Kaupale Rsvr—*reservoir* HI-9
Kaupans Point—*cape* MN-6
Kaupikiawa—*cape* HI-9
**Kaupo**—*pop pl* HI-9
*Kaupoa Hill* HI-9
Kaupo Bay—*bay* HI-9
Kaupo Beach Park—*park* HI-9
Kaupo Gap—*slope* HI-9
Kaupo Homesteads—*other* HI-9
*Kaupo Landing* HI-9
Kaupo Trail—*trail* HI-9
Kaupp Hereford Ranch Number 1 Dam—*dam* SD-7
Kaupp Hereford Ranch Number 2 Dam—*dam* SD-7
Kauppi Lake—*lake* MN-6
*Kaupps Lake* MN-6
Kaupps Mill (historical)—*locale* AL-4
Kaupuaa—*bay* HI-9
Kaupuaa—*summit* HI-9
*Kaupulehu* HI-9
Kaupulehu—*civil* HI-9
Kaupulehu—*locale* HI-9
Kaupulehu Crater—*crater* HI-9
Kaupulehu For Res—*forest* HI-9
Kaupulehu Lava Flow—*lava* HI-9
Kaupuni Stream—*stream* HI-9
KAUR-FM (Sioux Falls)—*tower* SD-7
Kausen Creek—*stream* OR-9
Kauslers Island—*island* MI-6
Kausooth—*locale* WV-2
*Kautatunchunk* PA-2
Kau Trail—*trail* HI-9
Kautsch Branch—*stream* MO-7
*Kautz* IN-6
Kautz Cleaver—*ridge* WA-9
Kautz Creek—*stream* OR-9
Kautz Creek—*stream* WA-9
*Kautz Fork* WA-9
Kautz Glacier—*glacier* WA-9
Kauunuoku—*summit* HI-9
*Kauuwaa* HI-9
*Kauwaloa* HI-9
Kauwalu—*island* HI-9
Kauwalu Gulch—*valley* HI-9
Kauwehu Falls—*falls* HI-9
Kavachurak Creek—*stream* AK-9
Kavaksurak Mtn—*summit* AK-9
Kavalga Island—*island* AK-9
Kavalghak Bay—*bay* AK-9
Kavalla Creek—*stream* MT-8
Kaval Lake Rec Area—*park* CO-8
Kavan—*other* KY-4
Kavanagh Bay—*bay* WI-6
Kavanaugh—*locale* KY-4
Kavanaugh, Gov. Edward, House—*hist pl* ME-1
Kavanaugh Acad—*hist pl* KY-4
Kavanaugh and Shea Bldg—*hist pl* OK-5
Kavanaugh Branch—*stream* PA-2
Kavanaugh Camp—*locale* KY-4
Kavanaugh Cem—*cemetery* IL-6
Kavanaugh Creek—*stream* CA-9
Kavanaugh Creek—*stream* ID-8
Kavanaugh Creek—*stream* MT-8
Kavanaugh Hill—*summit* CT-1
Kavanaugh Hills—*spring* MT-8
Kavanaugh Hollow—*valley* PA-2
Kavanaugh Ridge—*ridge* CA-9
*Kavanaugh Run* PA-2
Kavanaugh Sch—*school* CA-9
Kavanaugh Sch (abandoned)—*school* MO-7
Kavearak Point—*cape* AK-9
*Kaven Atoll* MP-9
Kavenaugh Post Office (historical)—*building* TN-4
Kaven Island—*island* MP-9
Kaver Rsvr—*reservoir* OR-9
Kavet Creek—*stream* AK-9
Kaviak Creek—*stream* AK-9
Kavik River—*stream* AK-9
Kaviktit Mtn—*summit* AK-9
Kaviruk River—*stream* AK-9
**Kavito**—*pop pl* KY-4
Kavolik—*summit* AZ-5
Kavrorak Hill—*summit* AK-9
Kavrorak Lagoon—*lake* AK-9
Kavrorak Springs—*spring* AK-9
*Kavul* FM-9
*Kavvaxiak* AZ-5
KAVV-FM (Sierra Vista)—*tower* (2) AZ-5
*Kaw* OK-5
Kaw—*locale* NV-8
*Kawaa Bay* HI-9
Kawaaloa—*bay* HI-9
Kawa Bay—*bay* HI-9
Kawaewae—*summit* HI-9
Kawaewae Heiau—*hist pl* HI-9
Kawaguesaga Lake—*lake* WI-6
Kawahae Puu Hue Trail—*trail* HI-9

*Kawahiau* ... HI-9
Kawahine Ridge—*ridge* ... HI-9
Kawahna, Lake—*reservoir* ... NC-3
Kawahuna—*area* ... HI-9
*Kawai* ... HI-9
Kawaiahao Church and Mission Houses—*hist pl* ... HI-9
**Kawaihae**—*pop pl* ... HI-9
Kawaihae Bay—*bay* ... HI-9
*Kawaihae Harbor* ... HI-9
Kawaihae Hoepa Trail—*trail* ... HI-9
Kawaihae-Kahua Trail—*trail* ... HI-9
Kawaihae - Kawaihae Uka Trail—*trail* ... HI-9
Kawaihae One—*civil* ... HI-9
Kawaihae Pier—*locale* ... HI-9
Kawaihae-Puu Hue Trail—*trail* ... HI-9
Kawaihae Two—*civil* ... HI-9
Kawaihae Uka (Site)—*locale* ... HI-9
*Kawailuku Gulch* ... HI-9
Kawaihapai—*civil* ... HI-9
Kawaihapai Rsvr—*reservoir* ... HI-9
Kawaihau—*bay* ... HI-9
**Kawaihau**—*pop pl* ... HI-9
*Kawaihoa* ... HI-9
Kawaihoa—*cape* ... HI-9
*Kawaihoa Cape* ... HI-9
*Kawaihoa Point* ... HI-9
Kawaihoa Point—*cape* ... HI-9
Kawaiholehole Gulch—*valley* ... HI-9
**Kawaihua**—*pop pl* ... HI-9
Kawaiiki Ditch Tunnel—*tunnel* ... HI-9
Kawaiiki Ridge—*ridge* ... HI-9
Kawaiiki Stream—*stream* (2) ... HI-9
Kawaiiki Valley—*valley* ... HI-9
*Kawaiili Stream* ... HI-9
Kawaika-A—*locale* ... AZ-5
Kawaikalia Gulch—*valley* ... HI-9
Kawaikapu—*civil* ... HI-9
Kawaikapu—*summit* ... HI-9
Kawaikapu Gulch—*valley* ... HI-9
Kawaikini—*summit* ... HI-9
*Kawaikini Peak* ... HI-9
Kawaiki Stream—*stream* ... HI-9
*Kawaikoi River* ... HI-9
Kawaikoi Stream—*stream* ... HI-9
Kawailena Stream—*stream* ... HI-9
Kawailewa—*summit* ... HI-9
Kawaili Gulch—*valley* ... HI-9
*Kawailiilii Gulch* ... HI-9
*Kawailioa Point* ... HI-9
*Kawaili Stream* ... HI-9
Kawailiula—*locale* ... HI-9
*Kawailoa* ... HI-9
Kawailoa—*area* ... HI-9
Kawailoa—*civil* ... HI-9
Kawailoa Bay—*bay* ... HI-9
Kawailoa Beach—*beach* ... HI-9
**Kawailoa Beach**—*pop pl* ... HI-9
Kawailoa Camp—*locale* ... HI-9
Kawailoa For Res—*forest* ... HI-9
Kawailoa Girls Home—*building* ... HI-9
Kawailoa Gulch—*valley* ... HI-9
**Kawailoa (Kawailoa Camp)**—*pop pl* ... HI-9
Kawailoa Ryusenji Temple—*hist pl* ... HI-9
Kawailoa Soto Mission—*church* ... HI-9
Kawailoa Soto Sch—*school* ... HI-9
Kawailoa Trail—*trail* ... HI-9
Kawaimanu—*summit* ... HI-9
*Kawainiu* ... HI-9
Kawainui—*civil* ... HI-9
**Kawainui**—*pop pl* ... HI-9
Kawainui Bay—*bay* ... HI-9
Kawainui Canal—*canal* ... HI-9
Kawainui Marsh—*swamp* ... HI-9
Kawainui Stream—*stream* (5) ... HI-9
*Kawai Nui Swamp* ... HI-9
*Kawaipaka Stream* ... HI-9
Kawaipapa—*civil* ... HI-9
Kawaipapa Gulch—*valley* (2) ... HI-9
Kawaipapa Valley—*valley* ... HI-9
Kawai Point—*cape* ... HI-9
Kawaipoko Stream—*stream* ... HI-9
*Kawaipuiia Stream* ... HI-9
Kawaipuua Stream—*stream* ... HI-9
Kawaiu Gulch—*valley* ... HI-9
Kawaiula Valley—*valley* ... HI-9
Kawaiuliuli—*summit* ... HI-9
Kawaiumakua—*summit* ... HI-9
Kawaiu Valley—*valley* ... HI-9
*Kawaiwai* ... HI-9
Kawak Butte—*summit* ... OR-9
Kawakiu Gulch—*valley* ... HI-9
*Kawakiu Hill* ... HI-9
Kawakiuiki—*bay* ... HI-9
Kawakiunui—*bay* ... HI-9
Kawakoe Gulch—*valley* ... HI-9
Kawala—*civil* ... HI-9
*Kawalii Stream* ... HI-9
Kawalski Drain—*stream* ... MI-6
Kawalski Lake—*lake* ... WI-6
Kawameeh Park—*park* ... NJ-2
Kawana—*locale* ... NC-3
Kawana Bay—*bay* ... NY-2
**Kawan Acres (subdivision)**—*pop pl* ... DE-2
Kawanak Channel—*channel* ... AK-9
Kawanak Pass—*stream* ... AK-9
Kawananakoa Sch—*school* ... HI-9
Kawana Sch—*school* ... CA-9
Kawana Springs—*spring* ... CA-9
Kawano Ditch—*canal* ... HI-9
**Kawanui (Honalo)**—*pop pl* ... HI-9
Kawanui One-Two—*civil* ... HI-9
*Kawaquesaga Lake* ... WI-6
Kaw Area Vocational-Technical Sch—*school* ... KS-7
Kawasachong Lake—*lake* ... MN-6
*Kawasak Passage* ... PW-9
Kawa Springs—*spring* ... HI-9
*Kawassak* ... PW-9
Kawa Stream—*stream* (2) ... HI-9
Kawawia Island—*island* ... MN-6
Kawbawgam, Lake—*lake* ... MI-6
*Kaw City* ... KS-7
**Kaw City**—*pop pl* ... OK-5
Kaw City (CCD)—*cens area* ... OK-5
**Kaw City (corporate name for Kaw)**—*pop pl* ... OK-5
Kaw City Depot—*hist pl* ... OK-5
*Kaw (corporate name Kaw City)* ... OK-5
**Kaweah**—*pop pl* ... CA-9

Kaweah, Lake—*reservoir* ... CA-9
Kaweah, Mount—*summit* ... CA-9
Kaweah Basin—*basin* ... CA-9
Kaweah Camp—*locale* ... CA-9
Kaweah Canal—*canal* ... CA-9
Kaweah Gap—*gap* ... CA-9
Kaweah Peaks Ridge—*ridge* ... CA-9
Kaweah Queen—*summit* ... CA-9
*Kaweah River* ... CA-9
Kaweah River—*stream* ... CA-9
Kaweah Sch—*school* ... CA-9
Kaweck Drain—*canal* ... MI-6
Kaweea—*summit* ... HI-9
Kaweehnali Slough—*stream* ... AK-9
Kawee Point—*cape* ... HI-9
*Kawela* ... HI-9
Kawela—*civil* (5) ... HI-9
**Kawela**—*pop pl* (2) ... HI-9
Kawela, Mount—*summit* ... HI-9
*Kawela Bay* ... HI-9
Kawela Bay—*bay* ... HI-9
Kawela Camp—*locale* ... HI-9
Kawela Gulch—*valley* (3) ... HI-9
Kawela Intake—*other* ... HI-9
**Kawela (Kawela Bay)**—*pop pl* ... HI-9
Kawela Loa—*summit* ... HI-9
*Kawela Mtn* ... HI-9
*Kawela Station* ... HI-9
Kawela Stream—*stream* ... HI-9
*Kawelikoa* ... HI-9
Kawelikoa Point—*cape* ... HI-9
Kawelohea—*island* ... HI-9
*Kawen* ... MP-9
*Kawen Island* ... MP-9
*Kaweonui* ... HI-9
Kaweonui Point—*cape* ... HI-9
*Kaweshka River* ... MN-6
*Kawia* ... CA-9
Kawiakpak Creek—*stream* ... AK-9
Kawialik Lake—*lake* ... AK-9
Kawich Canyon—*valley* ... NV-8
Kawichiark River—*stream* ... AK-9
Kawich Peak—*summit* ... NV-8
Kawich Range—*range* ... NV-8
Kawich Valley—*basin* ... NV-8
*Kawick Peak* ... NV-8
Kawiele Pumping Station—*other* ... HI-9
Kawikohale Point—*cape* ... HI-9
Kawili Point—*cape* ... HI-9
Kaw Indian Agency—*hist pl* ... OK-5
*Kawio Fishpond* ... HI-9
Kawishiwi Lake—*lake* ... MN-6
Kawishiwi Lake Campground—*locale* ... MN-6
Kawishiwi River—*stream* ... MN-6
Kawi Stream—*stream* ... HI-9
Kawita Talahassi (historical)—*locale* ... AL-4
Kawiu Fishpond—*lake* ... HI-9
*Kawiwi* ... HI-9
Kawiwi Stream—*stream* ... HI-9
Kaw Junction—*uninc pl* ... KS-7
Kawkawak, Lake—*lake* ... WA-9
**Kawkawlin**—*pop pl* ... MI-6
Kawkawlin Creek—*stream* ... MI-6
Kawkawlin Creek Flooding—*reservoir* ... MI-6
Kawkawlin Oil Field—*other* ... MI-6
*Kawkawlin River* ... MI-6
Kawkawlin River—*stream* ... MI-6
Kawkawlin River Ch—*church* ... MI-6
**Kawkawlin (Township of)**—*pop pl* ... MI-6
Kawkawlin Village Sch—*school* ... MI-6
Kaw Lake—*reservoir* ... OK-5
Kawmuhonu Bay—*bay* ... HI-9
Kawneer Company Plant—*facility* ... GA-3
Kaw Oil Field—*oilfield* (2) ... OK-5
Kawokhawik Island—*island* ... AK-9
Kawokhawik Pass—*channel* ... AK-9
Kawokhawik Slough—*gut* ... AK-9
*Kaw Reservoir* ... OK-5
*Kaw River* ... KS-7
Kaw Township—*civil* ... MO-7
**Kaw Township**—*pop pl* (2) ... KS-7
Kawuneeche Valley—*valley* ... CO-8
Kaw Valley Sch—*school* ... KS-7
Kaw Wildlife Area—*park* ... KS-7
Kaxa (historical)—*locale* ... AL-4
Kay—*locale* (2) ... AR-4
**Kay**—*pop pl* ... KY-4
Kay, Lake—*reservoir* ... AR-4
Kay, Thomas, Woolen Mill—*hist pl* ... OR-9
Kayaderosseras Creek—*stream* (2) ... NY-2
Kayaderosseras Range—*range* ... NY-2
*Kayakakoua* ... HI-9
Kayak Cape—*cape* ... AK-9
Kayak Creek—*stream* ... AK-9
Kayak Entrance—*channel* ... AK-9
Kayak Island—*island* (2) ... AK-9
Kayak Lake—*lake* ... AK-9
Kayak Mtn—*summit* ... AK-9
Kayak Point—*cape* ... WA-9
Kayaksak Mtn—*summit* ... AK-9
Kayak (Site)—*locale* ... AK-9
Kayan—*locale* ... VA-3
Kayandee—*locale* ... CA-9
*Kayangel* ... PW-9
*Kayangel Atoll* ... PW-9
Kayangel (County-equivalent)—*civil* ... PW-9
Kayangel Islands—*island* ... PW-9
*Kayangel Municipality* ... PW-9
*Kayangel Passage* ... PW-9
*Kayangle* ... PW-9
Kayare—*uninc pl* ... TX-5
*Kayatana Creek* ... TX-5
Kay Ave Sch—*school* ... CT-1
Kay Ave Sch—*school* ... OH-6
Kay Bar Ranch—*locale* ... NM-5
Kay Bayou—*gut* ... MS-4
**Kay Bee Heights**—*pop pl* ... TX-5
Kay-Bee Mobile Villa—*locale* ... AZ-5
Kay Blockhouse—*locale* ... NV-8
Kay Bottom—*bend* ... IN-6
Kay Branch—*stream* ... AL-4
Kay Branch—*stream* ... KY-4
Kay Branch—*stream* ... MO-7
Kay Branch—*stream* ... NJ-2
Kay Branch—*stream* ... TX-5
**Kaycee**—*pop pl* ... WY-8
Kaycee Cem—*cemetery* ... WY-8
Kaycee Lagoon—*lake* ... WY-8
Kay Cem—*cemetery* ... GA-3
Kay Cem—*cemetery* ... LA-4

Kay Cem—*cemetery* ... TX-5
Kay Cem—*cemetery* ... VA-3
Kay Chee Draw—*valley* ... NM-5
Kay Coulee—*valley* ... MT-8
**Kay (County)**—*pop pl* ... OK-5
Kay County Courthouse—*hist pl* ... OK-5
*Kay Creek* ... OR-9
Kay Creek—*stream* (2) ... AK-9
Kay Creek—*stream* (2) ... ID-8
Kay Creek—*stream* ... MT-8
Kay Creek—*stream* ... OR-9
Kay Creek—*stream* ... TX-5
Kay Creek—*stream* ... WA-9
Kay Creek—*stream* ... WI-6
Kay Creek—*stream* ... WY-8
Kay Dam—*dam* ... OR-9
Kaydeross Park—*park* ... NY-2
Kay-El-Bar Ranch—*hist pl* ... AZ-5
**Kayem**—*pop pl* ... IL-6
*Kayenta* ... AZ-5
**Kayenta**—*pop pl* ... AZ-5
Kayenta Airp—*airport* ... AZ-5
Kayenta Boarding Sch—*school* ... AZ-5
*Kayenta Creek* ... AZ-5
Kayenta Elem Sch—*school* ... AZ-5
Kayenta Post Office—*building* ... AZ-5
Kayenta Preschool—*school* ... AZ-5
Kaye Oil Field—*oilfield* ... WY-8
Kaye Sch—*school* ... MO-7
*Kayes Pass* ... MP-9
Kaye Thompson Dam—*dam* ... NC-3
Kaye Thompson Lake—*reservoir* ... NC-3
Kay Ferry (historical)—*locale* ... AL-4
**Kayford**—*pop pl* ... WV-2
Kayford Mtn—*summit* ... WV-2
Kay Fork—*stream* ... KY-4
Kay Fork—*stream* ... PA-2
**Kayfour**—*pop pl* ... AZ-5
Kayfour RR Station—*building* ... AZ-5
**Kay Gardens**—*pop pl* ... NJ-2
Kay Hill—*summit* ... OR-9
Kay Hill—*summit* ... WA-9
Kay Hollow—*valley* ... WV-2
Kayigyalik Lake—*lake* ... AK-9
*Kay-i-you River* ... MT-8
**Kayjay**—*pop pl* ... KY-4
*Kaylen Lake* ... NJ-2
Kayler Butte—*summit* ... AZ-5
Kayler Spring—*spring* ... AZ-5
KAYL-FM (Storm Lake)—*tower* ... IA-7
Kaylo Creek—*stream* ... AR-4
Kaylor—*locale* ... PA-2
**Kaylor**—*pop pl* ... AL-4
**Kaylor**—*pop pl* ... PA-2
**Kaylor**—*pop pl* ... SD-7
Kaylor Branch—*stream* ... MO-7
Kaylor Bridge—*bridge* ... PA-2
Kaylor Brook—*stream* ... ME-1
Kaylor Hollow—*valley* ... PA-2
Kaylor Knob—*summit* ... NC-3
Kaylor Knob—*summit* ... VA-3
Kaylor Mtn—*summit* ... NM-5
Kaylor Ridge—*ridge* ... OH-6
Kaylor Ridge Cem—*cemetery* ... OH-6
*Kaylors* ... PA-2
*Kaylors Knob* ... NC-3
Kaylor Spring—*spring* ... OR-9
Kaylor Tank—*reservoir* ... NM-5
**Kaylor Township**—*pop pl* ... SD-7
**Kay Lyn Manor Subdivision**—*pop pl* ... UT-8
*Kay Lynn Manor Subdivision* ... UT-8
Kay Mine—*mine* ... AZ-5
Kay Mine—*mine* ... NV-8
Kaymoor—*locale* ... WV-2
**Kaymoor No 1**—*pop pl* ... WV-2
Kay Mtn—*summit* ... TX-5
KAYN-FM (Nogales)—*tower* ... AZ-5
Kaynor Technical Sch—*school* ... CT-1
Kayoskh Lake—*lake* ... MN-6
Kayostia Beach—*beach* ... WA-9
*Kayo To* ... FM-9
*Kayo Tuna* ... FL-3
Kayouche Coulee—*stream* ... LA-4
Kayouche Coulee Golf Course—*other* ... LA-4
Kayoulah—*locale* ... VA-3
Kay Park—*park* ... IL-6
Kay Peak—*summit* ... WA-9
Kay Peninsula—*cape* ... WA-9
Kaypod Airp—*airport* ... KS-7
*Kaypod Landing Field* ... KS-7
Kay Pond—*lake* ... NJ-2
KAYQ-FM (Warsaw)—*tower* ... MO-7
Kay Rodgers Park—*park* ... AR-4
Kay Rsvr—*reservoir* ... OR-9
*Kay Run* ... VA-3
KAYS-AM (Hays)—*tower* ... KS-7
Kays Branch—*stream* ... KY-4
Kay Sch—*school* ... TX-5
Kays Chapel—*church* ... IN-6
Kays Chapel—*church* ... TN-4
*Kays Creek* ... UT-8
Kays Creek—*stream* ... UT-8
Kays Creek Fort (historical)—*locale* ... UT-8
**Kays Creek Subdivision**—*pop pl* ... UT-8
Kayser, Adolph H., House—*hist pl* ... WI-6
Kayser, George R., House—*hist pl* ... AZ-5
Kayser Cem—*cemetery* ... TX-5
Kayser Mill Trail—*trail* ... NM-5
Kayser Mutual Ditch—*canal* ... CO-8
Kayser Spring—*spring* ... CO-8
*Kays Ferry* ... AL-4
Kays Hill—*summit* ... NY-2
Kaysinger Bluff—*cliff* ... MO-7
Kaysinger Bluff Public Use Area—*park* ... MO-7
*Kaysinger Bluff Reservoir* ... MO-7
Kays Lake—*reservoir* ... IL-6
Kays Landing (historical)—*locale* ... TN-4
Kays Meadow—*flat* ... UT-8
Kays Point—*cape* ... MO-7
*Kays Run* ... VA-3
Kays Tank—*reservoir* ... AZ-5
Kay Street-Catherine Street-Old Beach Road Hist Dist—*hist pl* ... RI-1
KAYS-TV (Hays)—*tower* ... KS-7
**Kay Subdivision**—*pop pl* ... OH-6
**Kaysville**—*pop pl* ... UT-8
Kaysville and Layton Memorial Cem—*cemetery* ... UT-8
Kaysville Bible Ch—*church* ... UT-8
*Kaysville City Cemetery* ... UT-8

**Kaysville Heights Subdivision**—*pop pl* ... UT-8
Kaysville JHS—*school* ... UT-8
Kaysville Post Office—*building* ... UT-8
Kaysville Sch—*school* ... UT-8
Kay Tank—*reservoir* (2) ... AZ-5
Kay Tank—*reservoir* ... TX-5
Kaytoggie Diversion Dam—*dam* ... AZ-5
*Kayungur* ... PW-9
Kayuta—*other* ... NY-2
Kayuta Lake—*reservoir* ... NY-2
**Kayuta Lake (Kayuta)**—*pop pl* ... NY-2
*Kaywae Island* ... SC-3
*Kaywae River* ... SC-3
**Kaywin (P.O.)**—*pop pl* ... PA-2
**Kaywin (subdivision)**—*pop pl* ... PA-2
**Kaywood**—*pop pl* ... TN-4
**Kaywood Gardens**—*pop pl* ... MD-2
Kaywood Plantation—*locale* ... MS-4
Kaywood Plantation Airp—*airport* ... MS-4
Kaywood Plantation Lake Dam—*dam* ... MS-4
Kaywood Point—*cape* ... MD-2
Kaywood Wash—*stream* ... AZ-5
Kazakof Bay—*bay* ... AK-9
Kazen MS—*school* ... TX-5
Kazens Pond—*lake* ... NY-2
Kazer Point—*cape* ... NC-3
Kazhutak—*locale* ... AK-9
Kazik Hill—*summit* ... AK-9
KAZM-AM (Sedona)—*tower* ... AZ-5
Kazmier Lake—*lake* ... WI-6
*Kazyanguru Guido* ... PW-9
K Bar Creek—*stream* ... MT-8
K Bar Creek—*stream* ... SD-7
K Bar Draw—*valley* ... WY-8
K Bar K Ranch—*locale* ... AZ-5
K Bar Ranch—*locale* ... TX-5
K Bar Z Ranch—*locale* ... WY-8
KBAS-AM (Bullhead City)—*tower* ... AZ-5
KBBC-FM (Lake Havasu City)—*tower* (2) ... AZ-5
KBBD-FM (Beaver)—*tower* ... UT-8
KBBG-FM (Waterloo)—*tower* ... IA-7
KBBR-AM—*tower* ... OR-9
KBBX-AM (Centerville)—*tower* ... UT-8
KBCC-AM (Cuba)—*tower* ... MO-7
KBCH-AM—*tower* ... OR-9
KBCM-FM (Sioux City)—*tower* ... IA-7
KBCT-FM (Fairfield)—*tower* ... IA-7
KBDF-AM—*tower* ... OR-9
KBDY-FM (St Louis)—*tower* ... MO-7
KBEA-AM (Mission)—*tower* ... KS-7
KBEQ-FM (Kansas City)—*tower* ... MO-7
KBFL-FM (Buffalo)—*tower* ... MO-7
KBFS-AM (Belle Fourche)—*tower* ... SD-7
KBHB-AM (Sturgis)—*tower* ... SD-7
KBIA-FM (Columbia)—*tower* ... MO-7
KBJC-FM (Great Bend)—*tower* ... KS-7
KBJM-AM (Lemmon)—*tower* ... SD-7
KBKB-FM (Fort Madison)—*tower* ... IA-7
KBKN-FM—*tower* ... OR-9
KBKR-AM—*tower* ... OR-9
KBKR-FM—*tower* ... OR-9
KBLQ-AM (Logan)—*tower* ... UT-8
KBLQ-FM (Logan)—*tower* ... UT-8
KBLT-FM (Baxter Springs)—*tower* ... KS-7
KBLU-AM (Yuma)—*tower* ... AZ-5
KBMC-FM—*tower* ... OR-9
KBME-TV (Bismarck)—*tower* ... ND-7
K B Mitchell Pond Dam—*dam* ... MS-4
KBMR-AM (Bismarck)—*tower* (2) ... ND-7
KBMV-AM (Birch Tree)—*tower* ... MO-7
KBMV-FM (Birch Tree)—*tower* ... MO-7
KBND-AM—*tower* (2) ... OR-9
KBOA-AM (Kennett)—*tower* ... MO-7
KBOO-FM—*tower* ... OR-9
KBOY-AM—*tower* ... OR-9
KBOY-FM—*tower* ... OR-9
KBPS-AM—*tower* ... OR-9
KBRA-FM (Wichita)—*tower* ... KS-7
KBRE-AM (Cedar City)—*tower* ... UT-8
KBRE-FM (Cedar City)—*tower* ... UT-8
K Briggs Ranch—*locale* ... SD-7
KBRK-AM (Brookings)—*tower* ... SD-7
K Brown Ranch—*locale* ... WY-8
KBSI-TV (Cape Girardeau)—*tower* ... MO-7
KBSK Mtn—*summit* ... NV-8
K B Spring—*spring* ... OR-9
KBTC-AM (Houston)—*tower* ... MO-7
KBTN-AM (Neosho)—*tower* ... MO-7
KBTO-FM (Bottineau)—*tower* ... ND-7
KBUF-FM (Garden City)—*tower* ... KS-7
KBUH-AM (Brigham City)—*tower* ... UT-8
KBUH-FM (Brigham City)—*tower* ... UT-8
KBUZ-FM (Arkansas City)—*tower* ... KS-7
KBVR-FM—*tower* ... OR-9
KBWA-AM (Williams)—*tower* ... AZ-5
KBXN-AM (Tremonton)—*tower* ... UT-8
KBYU-FM (Provo)—*tower* ... UT-8
KBYU-TV (Provo)—*tower* ... UT-8
KBZB-AM (Bisbee)—*tower* ... AZ-5
KBZY-AM—*tower* ... OR-9
KCAC-FM (Lexington)—*tower* (2) ... MO-7
K Camp—*locale* ... TX-5
K Canal—*canal* ... ID-8
K Canal—*canal* (2) ... MT-8
K Cat Corners—*locale* ... NY-2
K Cave—*cave* ... AL-4
KCBW-FM (Sedalia)—*tower* ... MO-7
KCBY-TV—*tower* ... OR-9
KCCA-TV (Sierra Vista)—*tower* ... AZ-5
KCCK-FM (Cedar Rapids)—*tower* ... IA-7
KCCQ-FM (Ames)—*tower* ... IA-7
KCCR-AM (Pierre)—*tower* ... SD-7
K C Creek—*stream* (2) ... WI-6
KCCS-AM—*tower* ... OR-9
KCCU-FM (Columbus)—*tower* ... KS-7
KCCV-AM (Independence)—*tower* ... MO-7
KCEE-AM (Tucson)—*tower* ... AZ-5
KCEL-FM—*tower* ... OR-9
KCFS-FM (Sioux Falls)—*tower* ... SD-7
KCFV-FM (Ferguson)—*tower* ... MO-7
KCFX-FM (Harrisonville)—*tower* (2) ... MO-7
KCGB-FM—*tower* ... OR-9
KCGL-FM (Centerville)—*tower* ... UT-8
KCGQ-FM (Gordonville)—*tower* ... MO-7
KCHA-FM (Charles City)—*tower* ... IA-7
KCHC-FM—*tower* ... OR-9
KCHE-FM (Cherokee)—*tower* ... IA-7
KCHI-AM (Chillicothe)—*tower* ... MO-7
KCHI-FM (Chillicothe)—*tower* ... MO-7
KCHR-AM (Charleston)—*tower* ... MO-7

KCII-FM (Washington)—*tower* ... IA-7
KCJB-AM (Minot)—*tower* ... ND-7
KCJB-FM (Minot)—*tower* ... ND-7
Kckel Spring—*spring* ... AZ-5
KCKS-FM (Concordia)—*tower* ... KS-7
KCKY-AM (Coolidge)—*tower* ... AZ-5
K C Lake—*lake* ... NE-7
KCLC-FM (St Charles)—*tower* ... MO-7
KCLG-AM (Washington)—*tower* ... UT-8
KCLO-AM (Leavenworth)—*tower* ... KS-7
KCLS-AM (Flagstaff)—*tower* ... AZ-5
KCLU-FM (Rolla)—*tower* ... MO-7
KCLY-FM (Clay Center)—*tower* ... KS-7
K C Mine—*mine* ... CA-9
K C Mine Camp—*locale* ... CA-9
KCMO-AM (Kansas City)—*tower* ... MO-7
KCMQ-FM (Columbia)—*tower* ... MO-7
KCMW-FM (Warrensburg)—*tower* ... MO-7
KCMX-AM—*tower* ... OR-9
KCMX-FM—*tower* (2) ... OR-9
KCNB-FM (Waterloo)—*tower* ... IA-7
KCND-FM (Bismarck)—*tower* ... ND-7
KCNR-AM—*tower* ... OR-9
KCNR-FM—*tower* ... OR-9
KCNW-AM (Fairway)—*tower* ... KS-7
KCOM-KOHC Heliport—*airport* ... MO-7
KCOU-FM (Columbia)—*tower* ... MO-7
KCPT-TV (Kansas City)—*tower* ... MO-7
KCPW-FM (Kansas City)—*tower* ... MO-7
KCPX-AM (Salt Lake City)—*tower* ... UT-8
KCPX-FM (Salt Lake City)—*tower* ... UT-8
KC Ranch—*locale* ... TX-5
K C Ranch—*locale* ... TX-5
K Creek—*stream* ... CO-8
K Creek—*stream* ... ID-8
K Creek—*stream* ... OR-9
K Creek—*stream* ... UT-8
KCRF-FM—*tower* ... OR-9
KCRJ-FM (Cottonwood)—*tower* ... AZ-5
KCRV-AM (Caruthersville)—*tower* ... MO-7
KCTV-TV (Kansas City)—*tower* ... MO-7
KCUB-FM (Tuscon)—*tower* ... AZ-5
KCUR-FM (Kansas City)—*tower* ... MO-7
KCUZ-AM (Clifton)—*tower* ... AZ-5
K C Valley—*basin* ... NE-7
KCVO-FM (Camdenton)—*tower* ... MO-7
KCWA-FM (Arnold)—*tower* ... MO-7
KCXL-AM (Liberty)—*tower* ... MO-7
KCYX-AM—*tower* ... OR-9
KDAB-FM (Ogden)—*tower* (2) ... UT-8
KDAK-AM (Carrington)—*tower* ... ND-7
KDAM-FM (Monroe City)—*tower* ... MO-7
KDAP-AM (Douglas)—*tower* ... AZ-5
K Darland Dam—*dam* ... SD-7
K Davis Hill—*summit* ... OR-9
KDBX-FM (Boonville)—*tower* ... MO-7
KDCK-FM (Dodge City)—*tower* ... KS-7
KDDR-AM (Oakes)—*tower* ... ND-7
KDEB-TV (Springfield)—*tower* ... MO-7
KDEX-AM (Dexter)—*tower* ... MO-7
KDEX-FM (Dexter)—*tower* ... MO-7
KDFN-AM (Doniphan)—*tower* ... MO-7
KDHX-FM (St Louis)—*tower* ... MO-7
KDIC-FM (Grinnell)—*tower* ... IA-7
K Ditch—*canal* ... MT-8
KDIX-AM (Dickinson)—*tower* ... ND-7
KDIX-TV (Dickinson)—*tower* ... ND-7
KDJI-AM (Holbrook)—*tower* ... AZ-5
KDJQ-AM (Mesa)—*tower* ... AZ-5
KDKA-AM (Pittsburgh)—*tower* ... PA-2
KDKA-TV (Pittsburgh)—*tower* ... PA-2
KDKB-FM (Mesa)—*tower* ... AZ-5
KDKD-AM (Clinton)—*tower* ... MO-7
KDKD-FM (Clinton)—*tower* ... MO-7
KDLO-FM (Watertown)—*tower* ... SD-7
KDLR-AM (Devils Lake)—*tower* ... ND-7
*K D McKellar Elementary School* ... TN-4
KDMI-FM (Des Moines)—*tower* ... IA-7
KDMO-AM (Carthage)—*tower* ... MO-7
KDNL-TV (St Louis)—*tower* ... MO-7
K Dorsey Number 1 Dam—*dam* ... SD-7
K Dorsey Number 2 Dam—*dam* ... SD-7
KDOT-AM (Provo)—*tower* ... UT-8
KDOV-AM—*tower* ... OR-9
KDPS-FM (Des Moines)—*tower* ... IA-7
K Drain—*canal* ... CA-9
KDRO-AM (Sedalia)—*tower* ... MO-7
KDSE-TV (Dickinson)—*tower* ... ND-7
KDSJ-AM (Deadwood)—*tower* ... SD-7
KDSN-FM (Denison)—*tower* ... IA-7
KDSU-FM (Fargo)—*tower* (2) ... ND-7
KDUN-AM—*tower* ... OR-9
KDVL-FM (Devils Lake)—*tower* ... ND-7
KDVV-FM (Topeka)—*tower* ... KS-7
KDWD-FM (Burlington)—*tower* ... IA-7
KDXU-AM (Saint George)—*tower* (2) ... UT-8
KDYL-AM (Salt Lake City)—*tower* ... UT-8
*Ke* ... LA-4
*Kea* ... HI-9
Kea, Mauna—*summit* (2) ... HI-9
Keaa—*civil* ... HI-9
Keaa Beach—*beach* ... HI-9
Keaahala Spring—*spring* ... HI-9
Keaahala Stream—*stream* ... HI-9
Keaaiki Gulch—*valley* ... HI-9
Keaakaukau Gulch—*valley* ... HI-9
Keaaku Gulch—*valley* ... HI-9
Keaalau—*civil* ... HI-9
**Keaalu**—*pop pl* ... HI-9
*Keaau* ... HI-9
Keaau—*civil* (2) ... HI-9
**Keaau**—*pop pl* ... HI-9
Keaau Beach Park—*park* ... HI-9
Keaau Camp—*locale* ... HI-9
Keaau Homesteads—*civil* ... HI-9
Keaaulu Gulch—*valley* ... HI-9
*Keaau Makua Forest Reserve* ... HI-9
Keaau-Mountain View (CCD)—*cens area* ... HI-9
Keaau (Olaa)—*CDP* ... HI-9
Keaau Orchard—*other* ... HI-9
*Keaau Peak* ... HI-9
Keaau Ranch—*locale* ... HI-9
Kea'au Talus Sites Archeol District—*hist pl* ... HI-9
Kea Cem—*cemetery* ... TN-4
Kea Chapel—*church* ... MS-4
Keach Brook—*stream* ... CT-1
Keach Brook—*stream* ... RI-1
**Keaches Corners**—*pop pl* ... NY-2
Keachi Baptist Church—*hist pl* ... LA-4

Keachi Presbyterian Church—*hist pl* ... LA-4
Keachi Store—*hist pl* ... LA-4
Keachi United Methodist Church—*hist pl* ... LA-4
*Keach Pond* ... CT-1
*Keach Pond* ... RI-1
Keach Pond—*lake* ... CT-1
Keach Sch—*school* ... IL-6
Keadle Bridge—*bridge* ... SC-3
Keady Point—*cape* ... NY-2
Keafaber Ditch—*canal* ... IN-6
Keafer Sch (abandoned)—*school* (2) ... PA-2
*Keag* ... ME-1
Keag—*other* ... ME-1
*Keagitic River* ... NJ-2
*Keag River* ... ME-1
Keagy Cem—*cemetery* ... PA-2
Keagy Dam—*dam* ... PA-2
Keagy Hill—*summit* ... PA-2
Keahakea—*civil* ... HI-9
*Keahalaka* ... HI-9
*Keahi* ... HI-9
*Keahiakahoe* ... HI-9
*Keahiakahoe Peak* ... HI-9
Keahiakalio—*summit* ... HI-9
Keahialaka—*civil* ... HI-9
Keahialoa—*summit* ... HI-9
*Keahialoa Peak* ... HI-9
Keahikano—*summit* ... HI-9
*Keahikauo* ... HI-9
Keahikauo—*summit* ... HI-9
Keahi Point—*cape* ... HI-9
Ke-ahole Airp—*airport* ... HI-9
Keahole Point—*cape* ... HI-9
Keahua—*civil* ... HI-9
**Keahua**—*pop pl* ... HI-9
Keahua—*summit* ... HI-9
Keahuaiwi Gulch—*valley* ... HI-9
Keahua One—*civil* ... HI-9
Keahua Stream—*stream* ... HI-9
Keahua Two—*civil* ... HI-9
Keahuoku—*summit* ... HI-9
Keahuolu—*civil* ... HI-9
Keahuolu Point—*cape* ... HI-9
Keaina—*bay* ... HI-9
Keaina Gulch—*valley* ... HI-9
Keaiwa—*civil* ... HI-9
Keaiwa Gulch—*valley* ... HI-9
Keaiwa Heiau—*hist pl* ... HI-9
Keaiwa Heiau—*locale* ... HI-9
Keaiwa Lava Flow Of 1823—*lava* ... HI-9
Keaiwa Rsvr—*reservoir* ... HI-9
Keakaamanu—*summit* ... HI-9
Keakapulu Flat—*flat* ... HI-9
*Keakea* ... HI-9
Keakealani Sch—*school* ... HI-9
Keakuaumi—*cape* ... HI-9
Keaku Cave—*cave* ... HI-9
Keaku Falls—*falls* ... HI-9
*Keakulikuli* ... HI-9
Keakulikuli Point—*cape* ... HI-9
Keaku Valley—*basin* ... HI-9
Kealaalea Hills—*summit* ... HI-9
Kealahewa—*civil* ... HI-9
**Kealahou**—*pop pl* ... HI-9
Kealahou Homesteads One-Two—*civil* ... HI-9
Kealahou One-Two—*civil* ... HI-9
Kealahou Sch—*school* ... HI-9
Kealahou Three-Four—*civil* ... HI-9
Kealaikahiki, Lae o—*cape* ... HI-9
Kealaikahiki Channel—*channel* ... HI-9
*Kealaikahiki Point* ... HI-9
Kealakaha—*civil* ... HI-9
Kealakaha Stream—*stream* ... HI-9
*Kealakeakua* ... HI-9
*Kealakeakua Bay* ... HI-9
Kealakehe Homesteads—*civil* ... HI-9
Kealakehe Mauka Tract—*civil* ... HI-9
*Kealakekua* ... HI-9
Kealakekua—*civil* ... HI-9
**Kealakekua**—*pop pl* ... HI-9
Kealakekua Bay—*bay* ... HI-9
Kealakekua Bay Historical District—*hist pl* ... HI-9
Kealakio—*bay* ... HI-9
Kealakomo—*civil* ... HI-9
Kealakomo—*locale* ... HI-9
Kealaloloa Ridge—*ridge* ... HI-9
Kealapuali—*locale* ... HI-9
Kealapupuakiha—*beach* ... HI-9
Kealavik River—*stream* ... AK-9
Kealawela—*summit* ... HI-9
Kealber Cem—*cemetery* ... IN-6
Kealea—*bay* ... HI-9
**Kealey**—*pop pl* ... MI-6
Kealia—*civil* (2) ... HI-9
**Kealia**—*pop pl* (2) ... HI-9
Kealia Aupuni—*civil* ... HI-9
Kealia Beach—*beach* ... HI-9
Kealia Ditch—*canal* ... HI-9
Kealia For Res—*forest* ... HI-9
Kealiakapu—*civil* ... HI-9
*Kealialalo* ... HI-9
Kealialalo, Lua—*crater* ... HI-9
*Kealialalo Crater* ... HI-9
*Kealialuna* ... HI-9
Kealialuna, Lua—*crater* ... HI-9
*Kealialuna Crater* ... HI-9
Kealia One—*civil* ... HI-9
Kealia Pond—*lake* ... HI-9
*Kealia River* ... HI-9
Kealia Stream—*stream* ... HI-9
Kealia Trail—*trail* ... HI-9
Kealia Two—*civil* ... HI-9
Kealii Gulch—*valley* ... HI-9
Kealii Iki—*civil* ... HI-9
Kealii Nui—*civil* ... HI-9
Kealii Point—*cape* ... HI-9
Kealii Stream—*stream* ... HI-9
Kealing JHS—*school* ... TX-5
Kealing Sch—*school* ... KS-7
Kealohi, Lae o—*cape* ... HI-9
Kealok Creek—*stream* ... AK-9
*Kealo Valley* ... MO-7
Keal Run—*locale* ... PA-2
Kealy Sch—*school* ... NJ-2
*Keam* ... AZ-5
*Keamaku* ... HI-9
*Keam Canyon* ... AZ-5
*Keamoku* ... HI-9
Keamoku Lava Flow—*lava* ... HI-9
*Keams Canon* ... AZ-5

**Keams Canyon**—*pop pl* AZ-5
Keams Canyon—*valley* AZ-5
Keams Canyon Boarding Sch—*school* AZ-5
Keams Canyon Campground—*park* AZ-5
Keams Canyon Community Park—*park* AZ-5
Keams Canyon Day Sch—*school* AZ-5
Keams Canyon Post Office—*building* AZ-5
Keams Canyon Road Interchange—*crossing* AZ-5
Keams Canyon Wash—*stream* AZ-5
Keam Spring—*spring* AZ-5
**Keamuku**—*pop pl* HI-9
Keamuku Lava Flow—*lava* HI-9
Kean, The—*hist pl* MI-6
Keana—*civil* HI-9
*Keanaakaluapaaa* HI-9
Keanaawi Ridge—*ridge* HI-9
Keana Bihopa—*summit* HI-9
Keanae—*civil* HI-9
**Keanae**—*pop pl* HI-9
Keanae Point—*cape* HI-9
Keanae Sch—*school* HI-9
Keanae Valley—*valley* HI-9
Keanae Valley Lookout Park—*park* HI-9
*Keanahaki Bay* HI-9
Keanahalululu Gulch—*valley* HI-9
Keanaihiihi—*summit* HI-9
Keanakaiole Gulch—*valley* HI-9
Keanakakoi (Ancient Quarry)—*mine* HI-9
Keanakakoi Crater—*crater* HI-9
Keanakaluapuaa—*bay* HI-9
Keanakapua—*cape* HI-9
Keanakoholua Ridge—*ridge* HI-9
Ke Ana Kolea—*area* HI-9
**Keanakolu**—*pop pl* HI-9
Keanakua—*beach* HI-9
Keanalele Waterhole—*lake* HI-9
Keananuionaha Point—*cape* HI-9
Keanapaakai—*area* (2) HI-9
Keanapaakai—*locale* HI-9
Keanapahu—*summit* HI-9
Keanapakulua Falls—*falls* HI-9
Keanapapa Point—*cape* HI-9
Keanapou Fishpond—*lake* HI-9
Keanapuka—*summit* HI-9
Keanapuka Cave—*cave* HI-9
Keanapukalua—*cape* HI-9
Keanapuka (Wanapuka)—*cape* HI-9
Keanauhi Valley—*valley* HI-9
*Kean Creek* OR-9
*Keane* HI-9
**Keane**—*pop pl* NC-3
*Keane Creek* IN-6
*Keane Creek* OR-9
Keaneeqey—*cape* FM-9
Keanes Creek—*stream* OR-9
Keane Spring—*spring* CA-9
Keane Wonder Mill—*mine* CA-9
Keane Wonder Mine—*mine* CA-9
Keane Wonder Springs—*spring* CA-9
Keaney Swamp—*swamp* NY-2
Keans Bay—*bay* IN-6
**Keansburg**—*pop pl* NJ-2
Keans Creek—*stream* IN-6
Keans Neck—*cape* SC-3
Keanua Gulch—*valley* HI-9
Keanuiomano—*civil* HI-9
Keanuiomano Stream—*stream* HI-9
Keany Pass—*gap* CA-9
Keaoi—*island* HI-9
Keaoopu Stream—*stream* HI-9
Ke A Pele o Iki—*lava* HI-9
Ke A Pohina—*lava* HI-9
Ke A Poomoku Lava Flow—*lava* HI-9
Keapua—*summit* HI-9
Keapuka—*cape* HI-9
Keapuna—*summit* HI-9
Kearbey Cem—*cemetery* MO-7
Kear Branch—*stream* TN-4
Kearchoffer Flat—*flat* CA-9
Kearfott-Bane House—*hist pl* WV-2
Kearins Playground—*park* MA-1
Kearkan—*island* MP-9
Kearl Canyon—*valley* UT-8
Kearleys Bridge (historical)—*bridge* AL-4
Kearl Pond—*reservoir* UT-8
Kearl Ranch—*locale* UT-8
Kearl Rsvr—*reservoir* UT-8
Kearl Spring—*spring* (2) UT-8
Kearnens Bend—*bend* AL-4
Kearnery Gulch—*valley* WA-9
*Kearney* NJ-2
Kearney—*locale* AR-4
Kearney—*locale* MD-2
Kearney—*locale* MS-4
Kearney—*locale* NM-5
**Kearney**—*pop pl* MO-7
**Kearney**—*pop pl* NE-7
**Kearney**—*pop pl* NC-3
**Kearney**—*pop pl* PA-2
**Kearney**—*pop pl* SC-3
Kearney, Edward S., House—*hist pl* NJ-2
Kearney, Lake—*reservoir* NE-7
Kearney, M. Theo, Park and Mansion—*hist pl* CA-9
Kearney, Shemuel, House—*hist pl* NC-3
Kearney Beach—*beach* AK-9
Kearney Branch—*stream* KS-7
Kearney Brook—*stream* MA-1
Kearney Canal—*canal* ID-8
Kearney Canal—*canal* NE-7
Kearney Cem—*cemetery* IL-6
Kearney Cem—*cemetery* KY-4
Kearney Cem—*cemetery* MO-7
*Kearney Creek* WY-8
Kearney Creek—*stream* NC-3
Kearney Creek—*stream* WA-9
Kearney Gulch—*valley* CO-8
*Kearney Hills* KS-7
Kearney (historical)—*locale* AL-4
Kearney (historical)—*locale* KS-7
Kearney JHS—*school* CO-8
*Kearney Lake* NE-7
*Kearney Lake* WY-8
Kearney Lake—*lake* MT-8
*Kearney Lake Reservoir* WY-8
Kearney Lateral—*canal* CA-9
*Kearney Mesa* CA-9
Kearney Mine (Active)—*mine* NM-5
Kearney Municipal Airp—*airport* NE-7
Kearney Park—*flat* CO-8
**Kearney Park**—*pop pl* MS-4
Kearney Park (County Park)—*park* CA-9
Kearney Park Industrial Area—*locale* MS-4
Kearney Park Lake—*reservoir* MS-4
Kearney Park Lake Dam—*dam* MS-4
*Kearney P.O.* AL-4
Kearney Pond—*lake* MN-6
Kearney Post Office (historical)—*building* MS-4
Kearney Sch—*school* NM-5
Kearney Sch (historical)—*school* PA-2
Kearneys Creek Dam—*dam* NC-3
Kearney Square—*uninc pl* MA-1
Kearney Substation—*other* CA-9
**Kearneysville**—*pop pl* WV-2
Kearney Township—*civil* MO-7
**Kearney (Township of)**—*pop pl* MI-6
Kearney (Washington)—*other* CA-9
Kearn Lake—*lake* AZ-5
Kearns—*locale* AL-4
**Kearns**—*pop pl* UT-8
Kearns, George and Edward, Houses—*hist pl* OH-6
Kearns, Thomas, Mansion and Carriage House—*hist pl* UT-8
Kearns Basin—*basin* MT-8
Kearns Bldg—*hist pl* UT-8
Kearns Branch Post Office—*building* UT-8
Kearns Canyon—*valley* CO-8
Kearns Creek—*stream* (2) MT-8
Kearns Ditch—*canal* WY-8
Kearns Gap—*gap* PA-2
Kearns HS—*school* UT-8
Kearns JHS—*school* UT-8
Kearns (reduced usage)—*locale* CO-8
Kearns Rsvr—*reservoir* OR-9
Kearns Shop Ctr—*locale* UT-8
Kearns Siding—*locale* UT-8
Kearns Spring—*spring* NV-8
Kearns-St. Ann's Orphanage—*hist pl* UT-8
Kearns Well—*well* NV-8
Kearny—*locale* TX-5
Kearny—*locale* WY-8
**Kearny**—*pop pl* AZ-5
**Kearny**—*pop pl* NJ-2
Kearny, Lawrence, House—*hist pl* NJ-2
Kearny Airp—*airport* AZ-5
Kearny Campsite and Trail—*hist pl* AZ-5
Kearny County—*civil* KS-7
Kearny Creek—*stream* WY-8
Kearny Helistop—*airport* NJ-2
Kearny HS—*school* CA-9
Kearny HS—*school* NJ-2
Kearny Junction—*uninc pl* NJ-2
Kearny Lake Rsvr—*reservoir* WY-8
*Kearny Lakes* WY-8
Kearny Mesa—*summit* CA-9
Kearny Mesa Park—*park* CA-9
Kearny Municipal Pool—*other* AZ-5
**Kearny Park (subdivision)**—*pop pl* NC-3
Kearny Point—*cape* NJ-2
Kearny Point Reach—*channel* NJ-2
Kearny Reach—*channel* NJ-2
Kearny Sch—*school* PA-2
Kearsage Mine—*mine* MT-8
Kearsarge—*locale* CA-9
**Kearsarge**—*pop pl* MI-6
**Kearsarge**—*pop pl* NH-1
**Kearsarge**—*pop pl* PA-2
Kearsarge, Mount—*summit* NH-1
Kearsarge Brook—*stream* NH-1
Kearsarge Group—*mine* CA-9
Kearsarge North—*summit* NH-1
Kearsarge Pass—*gap* CA-9
Kearsarge Peak—*summit* CA-9
Kearsarge Pinnacles—*pillar* CA-9
Kearsarge Trail—*trail* NH-1
Kearsarge Valley Golf Course—*other* NH-1
Kearse Chapel—*church* SC-3
Kearse Theater—*hist pl* WV-2
*Kearsley* MI-6
Kearsley Canal—*canal* ID-8
Kearsley Creek—*stream* MI-6
Kearsley HS—*school* MI-6
Kearsley Park—*park* MI-6
Kearsley Rsvr—*reservoir* MI-6
Kearsley Sch—*school* OH-6
*Keary* KY-4
**Keasbey**—*pop pl* NJ-2
*Keasbey Creek* NJ-2
**Keasbey Heights**—*pop pl* NJ-2
**Keasbey (Keasbeys)**—*pop pl* NJ-2
*Keasbeys* NJ-2
Keasbeys Creek—*stream* NJ-2
*Keasbeys (Keasbey)* NJ-2
Keas Bridge (historical)—*bridge* MS-4
*Keasby* NJ-2
Keasby Reach—*channel* NJ-2
*Keasbys Creek* NJ-2
Keas Canyon—*valley* NV-8
Keas Cem—*cemetery* TN-4
Keas Ch—*church* GA-3
Keasey—*locale* OR-9
*Keasey Run* PA-2
Keasey Run—*stream* PA-2
Keasler Branch—*stream* NC-3
Keasler Cem—*cemetery* IL-6
Keasler Lake—*reservoir* NC-3
Keasler Lake Dam—*dam* NC-3
Keasley Sch (historical)—*school* AL-4
Keas Old Millpond—*reservoir* GA-3
Keas Peak—*summit* NV-8
KEAS Tabernacle Christian Methodist Episcopal Church—*hist pl* KY-4
Keaster Creek—*stream* MT-8
**Keatchie**—*pop pl* LA-4
Keatchie Bayou—*stream* LA-4
Keater Hill—*summit* NY-2
Keathley Branch—*stream* KY-4
*Keathley Cem* TN-4
Keathley Draw—*valley* WY-8
Keathley Pond—*lake* AR-4
Keaths Creek—*stream* MS-4
Keathy Cem—*cemetery* TN-4
Keating—*locale* OR-9
**Keating**—*pop pl* PA-2
Keating, Clarence, House—*hist pl* ID-8
Keating, Jeffery and Mary, House—*hist pl* CO-8
Keating Creek—*stream* AK-9
Keating Creek—*stream* AZ-5
Keating Creek—*stream* OR-9
Keating Gulch—*valley* MT-8
Keating Hollow—*valley* TN-4
Keating JHS—*school* CO-8
**Keating Junction**—*pop pl* PA-2
Keating Mines—*mine* MT-8
Keating Pond—*lake* CT-1
Keating Pond Brook—*stream* CT-1
Keating Range—*summit* AK-9
Keating Ridge—*ridge* AZ-5
Keating Ridge—*ridge* ID-8
Keating Sch—*school* CA-9
Keating Sch—*school* MI-6
**Keating Summit**—*pop pl* PA-2
**Keating (Township of)**—*pop pl* (2) PA-2
Keating Windmill—*locale* NE-7
Keatley Springs Ch—*church* WV-2
*Keaton* SD-7
**Keaton**—*pop pl* KY-4
Keaton Beach—*locale* FL-3
Keaton Branch—*stream* VA-3
Keaton Branch—*stream* WV-2
Keaton Cem—*cemetery* NC-3
Keaton Cem—*cemetery* TN-4
Keaton Creek—*stream* GA-3
Keaton Ditch—*canal* IN-6
*Keaton Ferry* MS-4
Keaton Fork—*stream* KY-4
Keaton Gap—*gap* TN-4
Keaton Grove Ch—*church* NC-3
Keaton Hollow—*valley* AL-4
Keaton Hollow—*valley* (2) TN-4
Keaton Lake—*lake* AL-4
Keatons Campsite—*locale* MO-7
*Keaton Springs* TN-4
Keaton Springs Branch—*stream* TX-5
Keaton Springs Mine—*mine* TN-4
Keatons Run—*stream* VA-3
Keaton (Township of)—*fmr MCD* AR-4
Keats—*locale* VA-3
**Keats**—*pop pl* KS-7
Keats Branch—*stream* NC-3
Keats Branch—*stream* VA-3
**Keats Crossing (subdivision)**—*pop pl* (2) AZ-5
Keats Hollow—*valley* TN-4
Keats Sch—*school* PA-2
Keatts Cem—*cemetery* TN-4
Keaty Branch—*stream* AL-4
Keau—*summit* HI-9
*Keauakaluapaaa* HI-9
*Keauhoa* HI-9
Keauhou—*area* HI-9
Keauhou—*bay* HI-9
Keauhou—*civil* (2) HI-9
**Keauhou**—*pop pl* HI-9
Keauhou Bay—*bay* HI-9
Keauhou Holua Slide—*hist pl* HI-9
Keauhou Landing (Site)—*locale* HI-9
Keauhou One—*civil* HI-9
Keauhou Point—*cape* HI-9
Keauhou Ranch—*locale* HI-9
Keauhou Sch—*school* HI-9
Keauhou Two—*civil* HI-9
*Keauhua* HI-9
**Keaukaha**—*pop pl* HI-9
Keauohana—*civil* HI-9
Keauohana For Res—*forest* HI-9
Keauohana-Kehena-Keekee Homesteads—*civil* HI-9
*Ke Au o Kanewaa* HI-9
*Keauouana* HI-9
Keavy—*locale* KY-4
Keavy (CCD)—*cens area* KY-4
Keawa Bay—*bay* HI-9
Keawaeli Bay—*bay* HI-9
Keawaiki—*bay* HI-9
Keawaiki—*beach* HI-9
**Keawaiki**—*pop pl* HI-9
Keawaiki Bay—*bay* (2) HI-9
Keawakalani—*cape* HI-9
Keawakapu—*locale* HI-9
Keawalai Ch—*church* HI-9
Keawalua—*beach* HI-9
Keawanui—*bay* HI-9
Keawanui—*cape* HI-9
Keawanui—*civil* (2) HI-9
Keawanui—*locale* HI-9
Keawanui Bay—*bay* (2) HI-9
Keawanui Fishpond—*lake* HI-9
Keawanui Gulch—*valley* HI-9
Keawaula—*civil* HI-9
Keawehala Point—*cape* HI-9
Keaweiki—*cape* HI-9
Keawekaheka Bay—*bay* HI-9
Keawekaheka Point—*cape* HI-9
Keaweula Bay—*bay* HI-9
Keawewai Camp—*locale* HI-9
Keawewai Gulch—*valley* HI-9
Keawewai Springs—*spring* HI-9
Keawewai Stream—*stream* HI-9
Keay Brook—*stream* ME-1
*Keays Place* OH-6
Keays Tank—*reservoir* AZ-5
Keazer Mtn—*summit* NH-1
Keazy Branch—*stream* TN-4
*Kebara To* FM-9
Kebar (historical)—*locale* KS-7
Kebbe Creek—*stream* OR-9
**Keb (historical)**—*pop pl* IA-7
Kebjeltak—*civil* MP-9
*KEB-JELTOK* MP-9
Kebler Mine—*mine* CO-8
Kebler Pass—*gap* CO-8
Kebler Run—*stream* OH-6
Kebo Mtn—*summit* ME-1
Kebort Sch (historical)—*school* PA-2
**Keborts Corners**—*pop pl* PA-2
KE Bullock Waterfowl Mngmt Area—*park* UT-8
*Kebumkewis* ME-1
K E Canyon—*valley* AZ-5
*Kechaien Island* MP-9
Kechaien Island—*island* MP-9
*Kechairukku Island* MP-9
Kechairukku Island—*island* MP-9
*Kechaujautsuku* MP-9
*Kechautsu* MP-9
Kechautsu—*island* MP-9
*Kechautsu Island* MP-9
*Kechautsu-to* MP-9
*Kechceachy River* NH-1
*Kecheachy iver* NH-1
Keche Mtn—*summit* AK-9
*Kechetotawnon Point* MI-6
*Kechewaishke Lake* WI-6
**Kechi**—*pop pl* KS-7
Kechi Cem—*cemetery* KS-7
Kechi Center Sch—*school* KS-7
*Kechi City* KS-7
Kechi Sch—*school* OK-5
**Kechi Township**—*pop pl* KS-7
KECH-TV—*tower* OR-9
Kechumstuk—*locale* AK-9
Kechumstuk Creek—*stream* AK-9
Kechumstuk Mtn—*summit* AK-9
Keck—*locale* KY-4
**Keck**—*pop pl* WA-9
Keck, Joseph, House—*hist pl* IA-7
Keck Canyon—*valley* OR-9
Keck Cem—*cemetery* (4) TN-4
Keck Cem—*cemetery* TX-5
Keck Cem—*cemetery* WV-2
Keck Ditch—*canal* IN-6
Keck Hollow—*valley* AR-4
Keck Hollow—*valley* PA-2
Keck Hollow—*valley* TN-4
Keck Knob—*summit* AR-4
Keckley Run—*stream* VA-3
Keckolie Cem—*cemetery* IL-6
Keck Park—*park* PA-2
Keck Ridge—*ridge* OH-6
Kecks Airp—*airport* NC-3
Kecks Bridge—*bridge* PA-2
**Kecksburg**—*pop pl* PA-2
**Kecks Center**—*pop pl* NY-2
Kecks Center Cem—*cemetery* NY-2
Kecks Center Creek—*stream* NY-2
Keck Sch—*school* MO-7
Keck Sch—*school* SD-7
Kecks Chapel Post Office (historical)—*building* TN-4
Kecks Corner—*locale* CA-9
*Kecks Corners* CA-9
Kecks Creek—*stream* AR-4
*Kecks Hollow* TN-4
Keck Slough—*stream* OR-9
Kecks Point—*cape* MN-6
Kecks Rsvr—*reservoir* ID-8
Kecks Store (historical)—*locale* TN-4
*Kecksville* IN-6
*Keckyate* NY-2
**Kecoughtan**—*pop pl* VA-3
*Kecoughtan Creek* VA-3
Kecoughtan HS—*school* VA-3
Kecoughtan (Veterans Administration Center)—*hospital* VA-3
Kedar Brook—*stream* ME-1
KEDD-AM (Dodge City)—*tower* KS-7
**Keddie**—*pop pl* CA-9
Keddie Peak—*summit* CA-9
Keddie Point—*cape* CA-9
Keddie Ridge—*ridge* CA-9
Keddy Field—*flat* OR-9
Keddy Ranch—*locale* NV-8
Kedears Hill—*summit* ME-1
Kedebel Taoch—*gut* PW-9
Kedeliel—*unknown* FM-9
Kedeu, Ngcheludel—*bar* PW-9
Kedges Straits—*channel* MD-2
*Kedge Straits* MD-2
Kedinker Island—*island* RI-1
Kedira—*locale* FM-9
Kedjebe—*island* MP-9
*Kedjin* MP-9
Ked Ra Ngchemiangel—*hist pl* PW-9
*Ked Ra Tund* PW-9
Kedron—*locale* (2) IL-6
Kedron—*locale* NC-3
Kedron—*locale* WV-2
**Kedron**—*pop pl* AR-4
**Kedron**—*pop pl* LA-4
**Kedron**—*pop pl* (2) TN-4
Kedron Brook—*stream* NH-1
Kedron Brook—*stream* NY-2
Kedron Brook—*stream* VT-1
Kedron Cem—*cemetery* TN-4
Kedron Ch—*church* AR-4
Kedron Ch—*church* (2) KY-4
Kedron Ch—*church* LA-4
Kedron Ch—*church* PA-2
Kedron Ch—*church* SC-3
Kedron Ch—*church* (2) TN-4
Kedron Ch—*church* VA-3
*Kedron Creek* TX-5
Kedron Creek—*stream* MN-6
Kedron Drain—*stream* MI-6
Kedron (historical)—*locale* KS-7
**Kedron Park**—*pop pl* PA-2
Kedron Sch (abandoned)—*school* PA-2
Kedron Sch (historical)—*school* MS-4
Kedron School—*locale* IL-6
Kedron Township—*fmr MCD* IA-7
Kedvale Playground—*park* IL-6
*Kedzie* IL-6
Kedzie Creek—*stream* MT-8
*Kedzie Grace* IL-6
*Kee* HI-9
*Kee* MA-1
Kee, Sam, Laundry Bldg—*hist pl* CA-9
*Keeau Makua Forest Reserve* HI-9
**Keeaumoku**—*pop pl* HI-9
Keebaugh Cem—*cemetery* OH-6
Kee Beach—*beach* HI-9
Keeble Chapel—*church* TN-4
*Keebler* TN-4
Keebler Branch—*stream* TN-4
Keebler Cem—*cemetery* (2) TN-4
*Keebler Crossroad* TN-4
Keebler Crossroads—*locale* TN-4
Keebler Institute (historical)—*school* TN-4
*Keeblers Cross Road* TN-4
*Keeblers Cross Roads* TN-4
Keeblers Cross Roads Post Office (historical)—*building* TN-4
*Keebles Chapel Baptist Church* TN-4
Keebles Chapel Cem—*cemetery* TN-4
Kee Branch—*stream* TX-5
**Keech**—*pop pl* PA-2
Keech Airp—*airport* NC-3
*Keech Brook* CT-1
*Keech Brook* RI-1
Keechelus Dam—*dam* WA-9
Keechelus Lake—*reservoir* WA-9
Keechelus Ridge—*ridge* WA-9
*Keechelus Rsvr* WA-9
*Keechey Creek* TX-5
Keech Hill—*summit* RI-1
Keechi—*locale* TX-5
Keechi Cem—*cemetery* TX-5
*Keechi Creek* TX-5
Keechi Creek—*stream* OK-5
Keechi Creek—*stream* (2) TX-5
*Keechie Creek* TX-5
Keechie Creek—*stream* TX-5
Keechi Lake—*reservoir* TX-5
Keech Pond—*reservoir* (2) RI-1
Keech Pond Dam—*dam* RI-1
*Keechs Island* RI-1
KEED-AM—*tower* OR-9
Keedley Swamp—*swamp* SC-3
Keedy Cove—*valley* TN-4
Keedy Hill—*summit* WA-9
Keedy House—*hist pl* MD-2
**Keedysville**—*pop pl* MD-2
Keefauver Cem—*cemetery* TN-4
Keefauver Elem Sch—*school* PA-2
**Keefe**—*pop pl* TN-4
Keefe Ave Sch—*school* WI-6
Keefe Camp—*locale* ME-1
Keefe Canyon—*valley* KS-7
Keefe Cem—*cemetery* TN-4
Keefe Ch—*church* TN-4
*Keefe Creek* MT-8
Keefe Ditch—*canal* IN-6
Keefe (historical)—*locale* MS-4
Keefe Lake—*lake* WA-9
*Keefe Mountain* CO-8
Keefe No 2 Camp—*locale* ME-1
*Keefe Peak* CO-8
Keefe Peak—*summit* CO-8
Keefe Post Offfice (historical)—*building* TN-4
*Keefer* PA-2
Keefer—*locale* KY-4
Keefer—*locale* TX-5
Keefer Branch—*stream* IL-6
Keefer Cave—*cave* PA-2
Keefer Cem—*cemetery* MI-6
Keefer Cem—*cemetery* TX-5
Keefer Ch (abandoned)—*church* PA-2
*Keefer Church* PA-2
Keefer Covered Bridge No. 7—*hist pl* PA-2
Keefer Creek—*stream* (2) AK-9
Keefer Cutoff—*stream* AK-9
Keefer-Evans Ditch—*canal* IN-6
Keefer Gap—*gap* PA-2
Keefer Hill—*summit* AZ-5
Keefer Mill—*locale* PA-2
Keefer Mtn—*summit* AR-4
Keefer Mtn—*summit* PA-2
Keefe Row—*hist pl* WY-8
Keefer Pond—*swamp* TX-5
Keefer Ranch—*locale* CA-9
Keefer Ridge—*ridge* (2) CA-9
Keefers—*locale* PA-2
**Keefers**—*pop pl* PA-2
Keefers Corners—*locale* NY-2
Keefers Field—*airport* PA-2
*Keefers Island* PA-2
Keefer Slough—*stream* CA-9
Keefer Spring—*spring* MT-8
Keefer Station Covered Bridge—*hist pl* PA-2
*Keefer Valley* MN-6
Keefe Sch—*school* CT-1
Keefe Sch—*school* MA-1
Keefe Sch—*school* MN-6
Keefe Sch (historical)—*school* TN-4
*Keefeton* OK-5
**Keefeton**—*pop pl* OK-5
Keef-Filley Bldg—*hist pl* TX-5
Kee Flats—*flat* WV-2
Keefover Cem—*cemetery* KS-7
Keef Spring—*spring* TN-4
**Keefton**—*pop pl* OK-5
**Keefton (historical)**—*pop pl* SD-7
**Keegan**—*pop pl* ME-1
Keegan Bayou—*stream* MS-4
Keegan Creek—*stream* NE-7
Keegan Hill—*summit* NY-2
*Keegan Lake* MN-6
*Keegan Lake* SD-7
Keegan Peak—*summit* MT-8
Keegans Bayou—*stream* TX-5
*Keegans Lake* MN-6
**Keego**—*pop pl* AL-4
Keego, Lake—*lake* AL-4
**Keego Harbor**—*pop pl* MI-6
Keego Lake—*lake* WI-6
Keehia—*civil* HI-9
Keehia Gulch—*valley* HI-9
Keehi Lagoon—*lake* HI-9
Keehi Lagoon Beach—*beach* HI-9
Keehi Lagoon Beach Park—*park* HI-9
Kee Hollow—*valley* WV-2
Kee House—*hist pl* CA-9
**Keei**—*pop pl* HI-9
*Keei Beach* HI-9
Keei Beach—*beach* HI-9
*Keei Landing* HI-9
Keei One—*civil* HI-9
Keei One-Two—*civil* HI-9
Keei Two—*civil* HI-9
Keekee—*civil* HI-9
Keekee Gulch—*valley* HI-9
Keekeehia—*cemetery* HI-9
Keekee One-Two—*civil* HI-9
Keeku Heiau—*locale* HI-9
Keekwulee Falls—*falls* WA-9
Keel—*locale* MS-4
Keela—*locale* FL-3
Kee Lake—*lake* ND-7
Keeland Creek—*stream* AR-4
Keeland Lake—*lake* AR-4
Keeland Slough—*gut* AR-4
Keelans Corner—*locale* MI-6
Keel Bluff—*cliff* MO-7
*Keel Boat* MS-4
Keelboat Pass—*channel* (2) LA-4
Keel Branch—*stream* TN-4
Keel Branch—*stream* VA-3
Keel Cave—*cave* AL-4
Keel Cave—*cave* (2) TN-4
Keel Cem—*cemetery* AL-4
Keel Cem—*cemetery* MS-4
Keel Cem—*cemetery* OK-5
Keel Cem—*cemetery* (2) TN-4
Keel Creek—*stream* GA-3
Keel Creek—*stream* NC-3
Keel Creek—*stream* (2) OK-5
Keel Creek—*stream* TX-5
Keele Cem—*cemetery* MO-7
Keele Cem—*cemetery* (2) TN-4
Keele Hollow—*valley* AR-4
Keele Hollow—*valley* TN-4
Keelen Cem—*cemetery* AL-4
Keeler—*locale* ID-8
Keeler—*locale* KS-7
Keeler—*locale* TX-5
**Keeler**—*pop pl* CA-9
**Keeler**—*pop pl* MI-6
Keeler, Diadatus, House—*hist pl* OH-6
Keeler Bay—*bay* VT-1
**Keeler Bay**—*pop pl* VT-1
Keeler Brook—*stream* VT-1
Keeler Corner—*locale* AR-4
Keeler Cove—*bay* CT-1
Keeler Creek—*stream* CA-9
Keeler Creek—*stream* ID-8
Keeler Creek—*stream* MT-8
Keeler Creek—*stream* OK-5
Keeler Creek—*stream* (2) OR-9
Keeler Creek—*stream* PA-2
Keeler Flats—*flat* CA-9
Keeler Glade—*locale* MD-2
Keeler Glade—*locale* WV-2
*Keeler Kreek* ID-8
Keeler Lake—*lake* MI-6
Keeler Mine—*mine* CA-9
Keeler Mtn—*summit* AL-4
Keeler Mtn—*summit* MT-8
Keeler Needle—*pillar* CA-9
Keeler Park—*park* OK-5
Keeler Park—*park* TX-5
*Keeler Peak* MT-8
*Keeler Pond* VT-1
Keeler Pond—*lake* MA-1
Keeler Pond—*lake* VT-1
Keeler Rock—*bar* ME-1
Keelers Brook—*stream* CT-1
Keelersburg—*locale* PA-2
*Keelersburgh* PA-2
Keeler Sch—*school* MI-6
Keeler's Korner—*hist pl* WA-9
Keelers Post Office (historical)—*building* TN-4
**Keelersville**—*pop pl* PA-2
**Keelersville**—*pop pl* TX-5
Keeler Tavern—*hist pl* CT-1
**Keeler (Township of)**—*pop pl* MI-6
Keeler Tunnel—*mine* UT-8
Keeler Well—*well* NM-5
Keele Spring—*spring* AR-4
*Keeley Branch* MO-7
Keeley Canyon—*valley* UT-8
Keeley Cem—*cemetery* TN-4
Keeley Creek—*stream* MN-6
Keeley Farm—*locale* ME-1
Keeley Island—*Island* MN-6
Keeley Knob—*summit* WV-2
Keeley Lake—*lake* ME-1
Keeley Sch—*school* IL-6
Keel Ford (historical)—*locale* TN-4
Keel Fork—*stream* KY-4
Keel Hill—*summit* KY-4
Keel (historical)—*locale* AL-4
Keel Hollow—*valley* AL-4
Keel Hollow—*valley* (2) TN-4
*Keelinawi* HI-9
**Keelinawi**—*pop pl* HI-9
Keelinawili—*locale* HI-9
Keeline—*locale* WY-8
Keeline Ranch—*locale* WY-8
Keeling—*locale* VA-3
**Keeling**—*pop pl* (2) TN-4
**Keeling**—*pop pl* VA-3
Keeling Bend—*bend* AL-4
Keeling Branch—*stream* (2) TN-4
Keeling Cem—*cemetery* (3) TN-4
Keeling Chapel—*church* MS-4
Keeling Cove—*bay* VA-3
Keeling Drain—*gut* VA-3
Keeling Hill—*summit* IL-6
Keeling Hill—*summit* KY-4
Keeling Hollow—*valley* MO-7
Keeling Hollow—*valley* TN-4
Keeling House—*hist pl* VA-3
Keeling Island—*island* AL-4
Keeling Post Office (historical)—*building* TN-4
Keeling Sch—*school* IL-6
Keeling Sch (historical)—*school* TN-4
Keel Lookout Tower—*locale* VA-3
Keel Mtn—*summit* AL-4
Keel Mtn—*summit* OR-9
Keelo Creek—*stream* MI-6
Keelors Union Ch—*church* PA-2
Keelough Pond—*reservoir* AL-4
Keelough Pond Dam—*dam* AL-4
Keel Pit—*cave* AL-4
Keel Post Office (historical)—*building* MS-4
Keel Ridge—*ridge* PA-2
Keel Ridge Mine—*mine* MI-6
Keel Rock—*rock* MA-1
Keel Sandy Creek—*stream* OK-5
Keels Cem—*cemetery* SC-3
Keel Sch—*school* TN-4
Keels Creek—*stream* AR-4
Keel Sinks—*basin* AL-4
*Keels Mountain* AL-4
Keel Spring—*spring* NV-8
Keel Spring—*spring* UT-8
Keels Sch—*school* SC-3
Keelstone Branch—*stream* MO-7
Keelstone Sch (abandoned)—*school* MO-7
Keelville—*locale* KS-7
Keely Ch—*church* PA-2
Keely Draw—*valley* WY-8
Keelys Church Cem—*cemetery* PA-2
*Keen* NE-7
**Keen**—*pop pl* PA-2
Keenam Brook—*lake* VT-1
Keenan—*locale* MN-6

Keith Memorial Methodist Ch—church .... TN-4
Keith Mill Branch—stream .... AL-4
Keith Mountain .... MA-1
Keith Mtn—summit .... MT-8
Keith-O'Brien Bldg—hist pl .... UT-8
Keith Park—park .... TX-5
Keith Peak—summit .... AZ-5
Keith Press Bldg—hist pl .... MS-4
Keith Quarter—locale .... SC-3
Keith Ranch—locale .... AZ-5
Keith Ranch—locale (2) .... TX-5
Keith Ranch—locale .... WY-8
Keith Ridge—ridge .... IN-6
Keith Rsvr—reservoir (2) .... ID-8
Keith Rsvr—reservoir (2) .... WY-8
Keith Rsvr No 2—reservoir .... WY-8
Keith Run—stream .... WV-2
Keithsburg—locale .... GA-3
**Keithsburg**—pop pl .... IL-6
Keithsburg Hist Dist—hist pl .... IL-6
**Keithsburg (Township of)**—pop pl .... IL-6
Keith Sch—school .... GA-3
Keith Sch—school .... IL-6
Keith Sch—school .... KY-4
Keith Sch—school .... MA-1
Keith Sch—school .... MI-6
Keith Sch—school .... MO-7
Keith Sch (historical)—school .... AL-4
Keiths Creek .... IL-6
Keith's Creek .... VA-3
Keiths Cross Roads .... DE-2
Keiths Dome—summit .... CA-9
Keith Sebelius Lake—reservoir .... KS-7
Keiths Gin Landing (historical)—locale .... AL-4
Keiths Mill—locale .... GA-3
Keith Spring—spring .... PA-2
Keith Spring—spring (2) .... TN-4
Keith Spring Cem—cemetery .... TN-4
Keith Spring Ch—church .... TN-4
Keith Spring Hollow—valley .... TN-4
**Keith Springs**—pop pl .... TN-4
Keith Springs—spring .... MO-7
Keith Springs Baptist Church .... TN-4
Keith Springs Cemetery .... TN-4
Keith Spring School .... TN-4
Keith Springs Picnic Area—locale .... MO-7
Keith Springs Sch (historical)—school .... TN-4
Keiths Ranch—locale .... NM-5
Keith Station .... ND-7
Keith Tank—reservoir .... AZ-5
Keithton—locale .... TX-5
**Keith (Township of)**—pop pl .... IL-6
Keith Trail—trail .... PA-2
Keith Valley MS—school .... PA-2
**Keithville**—pop pl .... LA-4
Keithville Sch—school .... LA-4
**Keith W Fullmer Subdivision**—pop pl .... UT-8
Keitts Bridge—bridge .... SC-3
**Keitts Crossroads**—pop pl .... SC-3
Keitzman Slough—lake .... MN-6
Keivling Creek—stream .... SC-3
Keiwa Ridge—ridge .... HI-9
**Keizer**—pop pl .... OR-9
Keizer Bottom—bend .... OR-9
Keizer Rapids—rapids .... OR-9
Kejaeon .... MP 9
Kejaiing—island .... MP-9
Kejairik—island .... MP-9
Kejarak .... MP-9
Kejawij .... MP-9
Kejbwe .... MP-9
Kejen .... MP-9
Kejiboi—island .... MP-9
Kejiboi Island .... MP-9
Kejibo Island .... MP-9
Kejien .... MP-9
Kejien—island .... MP-9
Kejikabowa—island .... MP-9
KEJO-FM—tower .... OR-9
Kejr Oil Field—oilfield .... CO-8
Kejulik Pass—gap .... AK-9
Kejulik River—stream .... AK-9
Kekaalaau—summit .... HI-9
Kekaa Point—cape (2) .... HI-9
Kekachtauanim .... PA-2
Kekaghtenemin Mountain .... PA-2
**Kekaha**—pop pl .... HI-9
Kekaha Beach Park—park .... HI-9
Kekaha Ditch—canal .... HI-9
Kekaha Milit Reservation—military .... HI-9
Kekaha Sch—school .... HI-9
Kekaha Shaft—reservoir .... HI-9
Kekaha-Waimea (CCD)—cens area .... HI-9
Kekaloa Heiau—locale .... HI-9
Kekawaka—locale .... CA-9
Kekawaka Creek—stream .... CA-9
Kekegam Lake—lake .... WI-6
Kekekabic Lake—lake .... MN-6
Kekekabic Lookout Tower—locale .... MN-6
Kekekabic Ponds—lake .... MN-6
Kekekakabic Lake .... MN-6
Kekepa .... HI-9
Kekepa Island (State Bird Refuge)—island .... HI-9
Kekepanagliesek .... ME-1
Kekereiel Dormechol—island .... PW-9
Kekerei El Toi .... PW-9
Kekereiel Toi—channel .... PW-9
Kekerel Debochel—channel .... PW-9
Kekerel Euchel—channel .... PW-9
Kekerel Toi .... PW-9
Kekerel Toi Passage .... PW-9
Kekeron (not verified)—island .... MP-9
Kekiktuk River—stream .... AK-9
Kekingo Shores Lake—reservoir .... IN-6
Kekionga .... IN-6
Kekionga Lake Dam—dam .... IN-6
Kekionga Mine—mine .... CO-8
Kekionga MS—school .... IN-6
Kekiwi Point—cape .... HI-9
Kek Lake—lake .... MN-6
Kekoalele Ridge—ridge .... HI-9
Keko Canyon—valley .... NM-5
Keko Canyon Tank No 1—reservoir .... NM-5
Keko Canyon Tank No 2—reservoir .... NM-5
Kekoiki—summit .... HI-9
Keko Island .... MP-9
**Kekoskee**—pop pl .... WI-6
Kekuaaiopihi—cape .... HI-9
Kekualele—civil .... HI-9
Kekualele Gulch—valley .... HI-9
Kekuapawela—civil .... HI-9
Kekuapoowai Falls—falls .... HI-9
Kekuawahaulaula—summit .... HI-9
Keku Creek—stream .... AK-9
Keku Islands—area .... AK-9
Keku Islets—area .... AK-9
Kekupua Valley—valley .... HI-9
Kekur Island—island .... AK-9
Kekur Peninsula—cape .... AK-9
Kekur Point—cape (2) .... AK-9
Keku Strait—channel .... AK-9
**Kelat**—pop pl .... KY-4
**Kelawea**—pop pl .... HI-9
Kelawea Camp .... HI-9
**Kelayres**—pop pl .... PA-2
Kelball Run—stream .... WV-2
Kelcema Lake—lake .... WA-9
Kelchner Drain—stream .... MI-6
Kelden—locale .... MI-6
Kelder Hill—summit .... PA-2
Keldron—locale .... SD-7
KELE-FM (Aurora)—tower .... MO-7
Keley Pond—lake .... CT-1
Kelez, Mount—summit .... AK-9
**Kelford**—pop pl .... NC-3
Kelgaya Bay—bay .... AK-9
Kelgaya Point—cape .... AK-9
Kelham, Edward, House—hist pl .... IN-6
Kelhi Corners—locale .... NY-2
Kelhnne Tank—reservoir .... NM-5
Kelier Butte—summit .... SD-7
**Kelim**—pop pl .... CO-8
Kelinger Branch—stream .... TN-4
Keliuli Bay—bay .... HI-9
Kelkeny .... MN-6
Kelker—locale .... CO-8
**Kell**—pop pl .... IL-6
Kell, Frank, House—hist pl .... TX-5
Kell, Lake—lake .... FL-3
Kell, William H., House—hist pl .... WI-6
Kellacey—locale .... KY-4
**Kellam Place (subdivision)**—pop pl .... NC-3
Kellams Bridge—bridge .... NY-2
Kellams Bridge—bridge .... PA-2
Kellams Cem—cemetery .... GA-3
Kellams Creek—stream .... GA-3
Kellam Spring .... AZ-5
Kellams Sch (abandoned)—school .... PA-2
Kellam Tank—reservoir .... AZ-5
Kellan Creek .... AL-4
Kellancy .... KY-4
Kelland .... OK-5
Kelland Drain—canal .... MI-6
**Kelland Heights**—pop pl .... TX-5
Kellands Pond—reservoir .... AZ-5
**Kellar**—pop pl .... WV-2
Kellar, Abraham, House—hist pl .... KY-4
Kellar And Riga Drain—canal .... MI-6
Kellar Branch—stream .... TN-4
Kellar Creek—stream .... OR-9
Kellar Ditch—canal .... IN-6
Kellar Drain—canal .... MI-6
Kellar Lake—lake .... NM-5
Kellar Park—park .... MI-6
Kollar Quarry Landing—locale .... Al -4
Kellar Ranch—locale .... AZ-5
Kellar Run—stream .... WV-2
Kellar Sch—school (2) .... IL-6
Kellars Corners—locale .... MI-6
Kellars Gap .... PA-2
Kellars Gap Hollow—valley .... PA-2
Kellarville .... TX-5
Kellas Creek—stream .... NY-2
Kellas Sch—school .... KS-7
Kell Bay—bay .... AK-9
Kell Branch—stream .... KY-4
Kell Branch—stream .... TN-4
Kell Cem—cemetery .... AL-4
Kell Cem—cemetery .... GA-3
Kell Cem—cemetery .... KY-4
Kell Cem—cemetery .... MS-4
Kell Cem—cemetery .... VA-3
Kell Ditch—canal (2) .... IN-6
Kelle .... MP-9
Kellehan Creek—stream .... WY-8
**Kellehan Crossroads**—pop pl .... SC-3
Kelleher Dam—dam .... MA-1
Kelleher Field—park .... NY-2
Kelleher Mesa—summit .... NM-5
Kellem Hill Creek—stream .... AL-4
Kellen Pond—reservoir .... DE-2
Keller—locale .... CO-8
Keller—locale .... GA-3
Keller—locale .... IL-6
Keller—locale .... MD-2
Keller—locale .... WA-9
**Keller**—pop pl .... IN-6
**Keller**—pop pl .... IA-7
**Keller**—pop pl .... LA-4
**Keller**—pop pl .... TX-5
**Keller**—pop pl .... VA-3
Keller, Jacob, Farm—hist pl .... PA-2
Keller Arm—canal (2) .... IN-6
Keller Bay .... NY-2
Keller Bay—bay .... TX-5
Keller Bayou—stream .... LA-4
Keller Bend—bend .... TN-4
Keller Bend Cave—cave .... TN-4
Keller Bend Park—park .... TN-4
Keller Bluff—cliff .... TN-4
Keller Branch—stream .... AL-4
Keller Branch—stream .... IN-6
Keller Branch—stream (2) .... MO-7
Keller Branch—stream .... NC-3
Keller Branch—stream .... SC-3
Keller Branch—stream (2) .... TX-5
Keller Bridge—bridge .... OR-9
Keller Brothers Airp—airport .... PA-2
Keller Brothers Landing Strip—airport .... KS-7
Keller Butte—summit .... WA-9
Kellerby Cem—cemetery .... OK-5
Keller Cabin Spring—spring .... OR-9
Keller Campgrounds—locale .... VA-3
Keller Canyon .... AZ-5
Keller Canyon—valley .... AZ-5
Keller Canyon—valley .... NM-5
Keller Canyon—valley .... UT-8
Keller Cem—cemetery .... IL-6
Keller Cem—cemetery .... IN-6
Keller Cem—cemetery .... IA-7
Keller Cem—cemetery (3) .... LA-4
Keller Cem—cemetery (3) .... MO-7
Keller Cem—cemetery (2) .... OH-6
Keller Cem—cemetery .... OK-5
Keller Cem—cemetery .... TN-4
Keller Cem—cemetery (2) .... VA-3
Keller Cem—cemetery .... WV-2
Keller Ch—church .... NC-3
Keller Ch—church .... PA-2
Keller Ch—church (2) .... WV-2
Keller Chapel—church .... PA-2
Keller Cliffs—cliff .... CA-9
**Keller Corner**—pop pl .... TX-5
Keller Cove—valley .... NC-3
Keller Creek—stream .... AL-4
Keller Creek—stream .... CA-9
Keller Creek—stream .... ID-8
Keller Creek—stream .... IA-7
Keller Creek—stream .... MT-8
Keller Creek—stream (2) .... OR-9
Keller Creek—stream .... TN-4
Keller Creek—stream .... TX-5
Keller Creek—stream .... WA-9
Keller Creek—stream .... WI-6
Keller Creek Campground—park .... OR-9
Keller Dam—dam .... UT-8
Keller Ditch .... IN-6
Keller Ditch—canal .... CO-8
Keller Ditch—canal (2) .... IN-6
Keller Ditch—canal .... KY-4
Keller Drain—canal .... MI-6
Keller Draw—valley .... NM-5
Keller Elem Sch—school .... AZ-5
Keller Esparza-Vera Bend—bend .... TX-5
Keller Field Camp—locale .... TX-5
Keller Gap—gap .... NC-3
Keller Gap—gap .... TN-4
Keller Golf Course—other .... MN-6
Keller-Grunder House—hist pl .... TX-5
Keller Hill—summit .... IN-6
Keller Hill—summit .... NY-2
Keller Hill—summit .... PA-2
Keller Hollow—valley .... MO-7
Keller Hollow—valley (2) .... TN-4
Keller House—hist pl .... TX-5
Keller House—hist pl .... WA-9
Keller House and Derick—hist pl .... ID-8
Keller HS—school .... FL-3
Keller Island—island .... OH-6
Keller Island—island .... WI-6
Keller Knob—summit .... NC-3
Keller Knoll—summit .... UT-8
Keller Lake—lake .... AR-4
Keller Lake—lake .... CA-9
Keller Lake—lake .... LA-4
Keller Lake—lake (3) .... MN-6
Keller Lake—lake (2) .... NE-7
Keller Lake—reservoir .... AR-4
Keller Lake—reservoir .... WI-6
Keller Lake—swamp (2) .... MN-6
Keller Lake Dam—dam .... MS-4
**Kellerman**—pop pl .... AL-4
Kellerman Cem—cemetery .... TX-5
Kellerman Gulch—valley .... WY-8
Kellerman Leaming Ditch—canal .... IN-6
Kellerman Mine (underground)—mine .... AL-4
Kellerman Number 1 Mine (surface)—mine .... AL-4
Kellerman Number 2 Mine (surface)—mine .... AL-4
Kellerman Number 6 Mine (underground)—mine .... AL-4
Keller Meadows—swamp .... CA-9
Keller Memorial Bridge—bridge .... AL-4
Keller Memorial Hosp—hospital .... AL-4
Keller Mtn—summit .... CO-8
Keller Park—park .... IN-6
Keller Park—park (2) .... MN-6
Keller Peak—summit .... CA-9
Keller Place—locale .... CA-9
Keller Point—cape .... ME-1
Keller Pond—reservoir .... AZ-5
Keller Pond—reservoir .... NJ-2
Keller Pond Dam—dam .... NJ-2
Keller Pumping Station—other .... TX-5
Keller Quarry—mine .... AL-4
Keller Quarry Cave—cave .... AL-4
Keller Quarry Landing .... AL-4
Keller Ranch—locale .... AZ-5
Keller Ranch—locale .... CA-9
Keller Ranch—locale .... MT-8
Keller Ranch—locale (3) .... NE-7
Keller Reservoir Dam—dam .... PA-2
Keller Ridge—ridge .... CA-9
Keller Rsvr—reservoir (2) .... PA-2
Keller Rsvr—reservoir .... UT-8
Keller Run .... PA-2
Keller Run—stream .... PA-2
Keller Run—stream .... WV-2
Kellers .... TN-4
Kellers Bay .... NY-2
Kellers Bay—bay .... NY-2
Kellers Bayou—stream .... LA-4
Kellers Branch .... IN-6
**Kellersburg**—pop pl .... PA-2
Kellers Cabin—locale .... OR-9
Kellers Ch—church .... PA-2
Keller Sch—school .... CO-8
Keller Sch—school (3) .... IL-6
Keller Sch—school .... NE-7
Keller Sch—school .... OH-6
Keller Sch—school .... PA-2
Keller Sch—school .... SD-7
Keller Sch (historical)—school .... MS-4
Keller Sch (historical)—school .... MO-7
**Kellers Church**—pop pl .... PA-2
Keller's Covered Bridge—hist pl .... PA-2
Kellers Dam .... SD-7
Kellers Dam—dam .... SD-7
Keller Shelter—bay .... CA-9
Kellers Hollow .... TN-4
Kellers Island—island .... ID-8
Keller Site—hist pl .... AR-4
Keller Site—hist pl .... SC-3
Kellers Lake—lake .... LA-4
Kellers Landing .... AL-4
Kellers Landing Strip—airport .... PA-2
Kellers Mill .... PA-2
Kellers Mill—other .... PA-2
Keller Spring—spring .... NV-8
Keller Spring—spring .... NM-5
Keller Spring—spring .... OR-9
Kellers Ranch—locale .... CA-9
Kellers Run—stream .... OH-6
Kellers Slough—gut .... LA-4
Keller State Wildlife Mngmt Area—park .... MN-6
**Kellersville**—pop pl .... NC-3
**Kellersville**—pop pl .... PA-2
Kellersville Esker—ridge .... PA-2
Keller Tank—reservoir .... NM-5
**Kellerton**—pop pl .... IA-7
Kellerton (historical)—locale .... SD-7
Kellertown—locale .... TN-4
**Keller Township**—pop pl .... ND-7
Keller Valley—valley .... CA-9
Kellerville .... TX-5
Kellerville—locale .... MO-7
Kellerville—locale .... NC-3
**Kellerville**—pop pl .... IL-6
**Kellerville**—pop pl .... IN-6
**Kellerville**—pop pl .... PA-2
**Kellerville**—pop pl .... TX-5
Keller Well—well .... UT-8
Kelleter Lookout Tower—locale .... MO-7
Kellet Mine—mine .... CA-9
Kellett Bluff—cliff .... WA-9
Kellett Cem—cemetery .... AR-4
Kellett Ledge—bar .... WA-9
Kellett Sch—school .... SD-7
Kelletts Lake—reservoir .... SC-3
**Kellettville**—pop pl .... PA-2
Kelley .... IN-6
Kelley .... KS-7
Kelley .... ND-7
Kelley .... WI-6
Kelley—locale .... MT-8
Kelley—other .... PA-2
Kelley—other .... WI-6
**Kelley**—pop pl .... IA-7
Kelley—uninc pl .... PA-2
Kelley, Barney, House—hist pl .... OH-6
Kelley, Isaac, Site (23CT111 and 23CT1)—hist pl .... MO-7
Kelley, Jacob, House—hist pl .... SC-3
Kelley, James, House—hist pl .... KY-4
Kelley, Mancel, House—hist pl .... WA-9
Kelley, Marion and Julia, House—hist pl .... ID-8
Kelley, Mount—summit .... AK-9
Kelley, Oliver H., Homestead—hist pl .... MN-6
Kelley Bar .... WA-9
Kelley Bay .... MA-1
Kelley Bay—swamp .... MO-7
Kelley Bayou—stream .... IN-6
Kelley Bayou—stream (2) .... LA-4
Kelley Bluff—cliff .... MO-7
Kelley Branch—stream .... AL-4
Kelley Branch—stream (2) .... FL-3
Kelley Branch—stream .... GA-3
Kelley Branch—stream (3) .... KY-4
Kelley Branch—stream .... MS-4
Kelley Branch—stream (4) .... MO-7
Kelley Branch—stream .... NC-3
Kelley Branch—stream .... OH-6
Kelley Branch—stream (3) .... TN-4
Kelley Bridge—other .... MO-7
**Kelley Brook**—pop pl .... WI-6
Kelley Brook—stream .... NH-1
Kelley Brook—stream .... NY-2
Kelley Brook—stream .... RI-1
Kelley Brook—stream .... VT-1
Kelley Cabin—locale .... MT-8
Kelley Canal—canal .... LA-4
Kelley Canyon—valley .... UT-8
Kelley Cem—cemetery .... AL-4
Kelley Cem—cemetery .... AR-4
Kelley Cem—cemetery .... GA-3
Kelley Cem—cemetery .... IL-6
Kelley Cem—cemetery (2) .... IN-6
Kelley Cem—cemetery .... KY-4
Kelley Cem—cemetery .... LA-4
Kelley Cem—cemetery (3) .... MO-7
Kelley Cem—cemetery .... NY-2
Kelley Cem—cemetery .... NC-3
Kelley Cem—cemetery .... OH-6
Kelley Cem—cemetery .... OK-5
Kelley Cem—cemetery (6) .... TN-4
Kelley Cem—cemetery .... WV-2
Kelley Ch—church .... TX-5
Kelley Chapel—church .... GA-3
Kelley Chapel—church .... TN-4
Kelley Chapel—church .... WV-2
Kelley Chapel Cem—cemetery .... GA-3
Kelley Community Center—locale .... CO-8
Kelley Coulee—valley .... MT-8
Kelley Cove—bay .... NC-3
Kelley Cove—valley .... NC-3
Kelley Cove—valley .... TN-4
Kelley Creek .... AL-4
Kelley Creek .... MS-4
Kelley Creek .... MO-7
Kelley Creek .... NV-8
Kelley Creek .... WV-2
Kelley Creek .... WY-8
Kelley Creek—stream .... AL-4
Kelley Creek—stream .... AR-4
Kelley Creek—stream (2) .... CA-9
Kelley Creek—stream .... GA-3
Kelley Creek—stream .... MI-6
Kelley Creek—stream (3) .... MT-8
Kelley Creek—stream .... NV-8
Kelley Creek—stream .... NC-3
Kelley Creek—stream (2) .... OR-9
Kelley Creek—stream (4) .... TN-4
Kelley Creek—stream (3) .... TX-5
Kelley Creek—stream (2) .... WA-9
Kelley Creek—stream .... WI-6
Kelley Creek—stream .... WY-8
Kelley Ditch—canal .... CO-8
Kelley Drain—canal .... IN-6
Kelley Drain—canal (3) .... MI-6
Kelley Draw—valley .... WY-8
Kelley Falls .... OR-9
Kelley Field—park .... OR-9
Kelley Flats—flat .... CO-8
Kelley Fork .... KY-4
Kelley-Fredrickson House and Office Bldg—hist pl .... IN-6
Kelley Grade—slope .... CA-9
Kelley Guard Station—locale .... WY-8
Kelley Gulch .... MT-8
Kelley Gulch—valley .... MT-8
Kelley Highline and Kermode Ditch No. 2—canal .... CO-8
**Kelley Hill**—pop pl .... GA-3
Kelley Hill—summit .... IN-6
Kelley Hill—summit .... ME-1
Kelley Hill—summit .... MS-4
Kelley Hollow .... MO-7
Kelley Hollow—valley (2) .... MO-7
Kelley Hollow—valley .... PA-2
Kelley Hollow—valley .... TN-4
Kelley Hollow—valley .... WA-9
Kelley House—hist pl .... IA-7
Kelley House—hist pl .... TN-4
**Kelley Kay Acres Subdivision**—pop pl .... UT-8
Kelley Knob—summit .... WV-2
Kelley Lake .... AL-4
Kelley Lake .... CA-9
Kelley Lake .... MI-6
Kelley Lake—reservoir .... GA-3
Kelley Lake—swamp .... MN-6
**Kelleyland**—pop pl .... ME-1
Kelley-Leonard Mine (underground)—mine .... AL-4
Kelley Mill Branch—stream .... GA-3
Kelley Mine—mine .... KY-4
Kelley Mine—mine .... MT-8
Kelley Mine (underground)—mine .... TN-4
Kelley Mountain—ridge .... GA-3
Kelley Mtn—summit .... AL-4
Kelley Mtn—summit .... GA-3
Kelley Mtn—summit .... MO-7
Kelley Mtn—summit .... NC-3
Kelley Mtn—summit .... TN-4
Kelley Mtn—summit .... VA-3
Kelley Mtn—summit .... WV-2
Kelley Park—locale .... NE-7
Kelley Park—park .... CA-9
Kelley Park—park .... OH-6
Kelley Peak—summit .... TX-5
Kelley Playground—park .... MI-6
Kelley Point—cape .... ME-1
Kelley Point—cape .... OR-9
Kelley Pond .... MA-1
Kelley Pond—lake .... NY-2
Kelley Pond—reservoir .... AL-4
Kelley Pond—reservoir .... CT-1
Kelley Ranch—locale .... NE-7
Kelley Ranch—locale (2) .... TX-5
Kelley Ridge—ridge .... AL-4
Kelley Ridge—ridge .... IN-6
Kelley Ridge—ridge .... TN-4
Kelley Rsvr—reservoir .... CA-9
Kelley Rsvr—reservoir .... MT-8
Kelley Run—stream .... PA-2
Kelley Run—stream .... WV-2
Kelley Run Prairie Creek .... IN-6
Kelley's .... OH-6
Kelleys—locale .... LA-4
Kelleys—locale .... NY-2
Kelleys Bay—bay .... MA-1
Kelleys Brook .... RI-1
Kelleys Camp—locale .... AZ-5
Kelley Sch—school (2) .... CA-9
Kelley Sch—school .... IL-6
Kelley Sch—school .... ME-1
Kelley Sch—school .... NY-2
Kelley Sch—school .... PA-2
Kelley Sch—school .... SC-3
Kelleys Chapel—church .... GA-3
Kelleys Chapel—church .... TN-4
Kelleys Corner—locale .... NH-1
**Kelleys Corner**—pop pl .... NH-1
Kelleys Creek .... TN-4
Kelleys Creek—stream .... LA-4
Kelley's Crossing—locale .... MS-4
Kelleys Crossing Public Use Area—park .... MS-4
Kelleys Ferry .... TN-4
Kelleys Island .... DE-2
Kelleys Island .... TN-4
Kelleys Island—island .... OH-6
**Kelleys Island**—pop pl .... OH-6
Kelleys Island Hist Dist (Boundary Increase)—hist pl .... OH-6
Kelleys Island South Shore District—hist pl .... OH-6
Kelleys Island State Park—park .... OH-6
Kelleys Island (Township of)—other .... OH-6
Kelleys Korner—locale .... OR-9
Kelleys Lake .... AL-4
Kelleys Lake—lake .... WI-6
Kelleys Mill (historical)—locale .... AL-4
Kelleys Mill (historical)—locale .... TN-4
Kelleys Place—area .... UT-8
Kelleys Point—cape .... TN-4
Kelleys Pond .... MA-1
Kelleys Pond—lake .... MA-1
Kelley Spring—spring .... CA-9
Kelley Spring—spring .... NM-5
Kelley Spring—spring .... PA-2
**Kelley Springs**—pop pl .... MO-7
Kelleys Run .... PA-2
Kelleys Shoals .... TN-4
Kelleys Sough .... ND-7
Kelley Stand—locale .... VT-1
Kelley Street Incinerator—other .... TX-5
Kelleys Well—well .... CA-9
Kelley Tank—reservoir .... AZ-5
Kelleytown—locale .... GA-3
**Kelley Town**—pop pl .... TN-4
Kelley Township—civil .... MO-7
Kelley (Township of)—other .... IL-6
Kelley Trail—trail .... NH-1
Kelley Valley—valley .... MO-7
**Kelley View**—pop pl .... VA-3
Kelleyville (2) .... IL-6
Kelleyville .... OK-5
Kelleyville .... PA-2
Kelleyville—locale .... PA-2
**Kelleyville**—pop pl .... NH-1
Kelley Well—well (2) .... TX-5
Kelley Windmill—locale .... TX-5
**Kellgreen Acres Subdivision**—pop pl .... UT-8
Kell Hollow—valley .... MO-7
Kell House—hist pl .... LA-4
Kellie Creek—stream .... MI-6
**Kelliher**—pop pl .... MN-6
**Kelliher (Township of)**—pop pl .... MN-6
Kellinbach Lake—lake .... WI-6
Kellings Lakes—lake .... WI-6
Kellion Cem—cemetery .... MO-7
Kellison Cem—cemetery .... WV-2
Kellison Hollow—valley .... VA-3
Kellison Ridge—ridge .... VA-3
Kellisons Creek—stream .... TX-5
Kellis Park—park .... TX-5
Kellis Pond—lake .... NY-2
Kellis Store—locale .... MS-4
Kellis Store Post Office (historical)—building .... MS-4
**Kellner**—pop pl .... WI-6
Kellner Campground—park .... AZ-5
Kellner Canyon—valley .... AZ-5
Kellner Canyon Spring—spring .... AZ-5
Kellner Cem—cemetery .... NE-7
Kellner Cem—cemetery .... TX-5
Kellner Creek—stream .... TX-5
**Kellners Corners**—pop pl .... WI-6
Kellners Lake—lake .... WI-6
Kellners Pond—lake .... CT-1
**Kellnersville**—pop pl .... WI-6
Kelln Oil Field—oilfield .... TX-5
Kello Blancett Ditch—canal .... NM-5
Kelloch Mtn—summit .... ME-1
Kellock Run—stream .... PA-2
Kellog .... IA-7
Kellog .... MN-6
**Kellog**—pop pl .... CA-9
**Kellog**—pop pl .... IL-6
Kellog, Ethol, House—hist pl .... OH-6
Kellog Bay .... VT-1
Kellog Branch—stream .... MO-7
Kellog Brook—stream .... MA-1
Kellog Canyon—valley .... NM-5
Kellog (C&O RR name for Kellogg)—other .... WV-2
Kellogg—locale .... CA-9
Kellogg—locale .... IL-6
Kellogg—locale .... KS-7
Kellogg—locale .... MO-7
Kellogg—locale .... NY-2
Kellogg—locale .... ND-7
Kellogg—locale .... OR-9
Kellogg—locale .... PA-2
Kellogg—locale .... TX-5
**Kellogg**—pop pl .... ID-8
**Kellogg**—pop pl .... IA-7
**Kellogg**—pop pl .... MI-6
**Kellogg**—pop pl .... MN-6
**Kellogg**—pop pl .... NY-2
Kellogg, Elijah, Church—hist pl .... ME-1
Kellogg, Elijah, House—hist pl .... ME-1
Kellogg, Frank B., House—hist pl .... MN-6
Kellogg, Gen. Martin, House—hist pl .... CT-1
Kellogg, John, House and Barn—hist pl .... OH-6
Kellogg, W.K., House—hist pl .... MI-6
Kellogg Bay .... VT-1
Kellogg Biological Preserve—park .... MI-6
Kellogg Branch .... MD-2
Kellogg Branch—stream .... MD-2
Kellogg Brook .... MA-1
Kellogg Brook—stream .... ME-1
Kellogg Canyon—valley .... TX-5
Kellogg Cem—cemetery (2) .... MO-7
Kellogg Cem—cemetery .... OH-6
Kellogg Cem—cemetery .... OR-9
Kellogg Cem—cemetery .... PA-2
Kellogg Community Coll—school .... MI-6
Kellogg Corners—locale .... CT-1
Kellogg Corners—locale (2) .... NY-2
Kellogg Corners—locale .... OH-6
Kellogg (C&O RR name Kellog)—uninc pl .... WV-2
Kellogg Creek—stream .... AR-4
Kellogg Creek—stream (2) .... CA-9
Kellogg Creek—stream .... GA-3
Kellogg Creek—stream .... OH-6
Kellogg Creek—stream .... OR-9
Kellogg Creek—stream .... TX-5
Kellogg Creek—stream (2) .... WA-9
Kellogg Drain—canal .... MI-6
Kellogg Field—other .... MI-6
Kellogg Golf Club—other .... ID-8
Kellogg Golf Course—other .... IL-6
Kellogg Grange—locale .... OR-9
Kellogg Gulch—valley .... CA-9
Kellogg House—hist pl .... OH-6
Kellogg HS—school .... ID-8
Kellogg Island—island .... VT-1
Kellogg JHS—school .... MI-6
Kellogg JHS—school .... MN-6
Kellogg Lake—lake .... CA-9
Kellogg Lake—lake (3) .... MI-6
Kellogg Lake—reservoir .... MO-7
Kellogg Lake—reservoir .... OR-9
Kellogg Lake—swamp .... MI-6
Kellogg Lake Dam—dam (2) .... MS-4
Kellogg Lake Park—park .... MO-7
Kellogg Lookout Tower—locale .... MI-6
**Kellogg Marsh**—pop pl .... WA-9
Kellogg Marsh Grange—locale .... WA-9
Kellogg Mine—mine .... AZ-5
Kellogg Mine—mine .... CA-9
Kellogg Mine—mine .... MT-8
Kellogg Mountain Lookout Tower—tower .... PA-2
Kellogg Mtn—summit .... AZ-5
Kellogg Mtn—summit .... CA-9
Kellogg Mtn—summit .... NY-2
Kellogg Mtn—summit .... PA-2
Kellogg Park—park (2) .... CA-9
Kellogg Park—park .... MI-6
Kellogg Park—park .... NJ-2
Kellogg Peak—summit .... ID-8
Kellogg Point—cape .... AK-9
Kellogg Pond—lake (2) .... CT-1
Kellogg Pond—lake .... NY-2
Kellogg Public Library and Neville Public Museum—hist pl .... WI-6
Kellogg Ranch—locale .... AZ-5
Kellogg Ranch—locale .... MT-8
Kellogg Ranch—locale .... NE-7
Kellogg Ranch—locale (2) .... ND-7
Kellogg Ranch—locale .... OR-9
Kellogg Ravine—valley .... CA-9
Kellogg Ravine—valley .... IL-6
Kellogg Rsvr—reservoir .... NY-2
Kellogg Saddle—gap .... ID-8
Kelloggs Bridge—other .... MI-6
Kellogg Sch—school (2) .... CA-9
Kellogg Sch—school (2) .... IL-6

Kenneth Anderson Dam—*dam* UT-8
Kenneth Anderson Rsvr—*reservoir* UT-8
Kenneth Ave Sch—*school* CA-9
Kenneth Branch—*stream* KY-4
Kenneth Cabin—*locale* CA-9
Kenneth Cem—*cemetery* MN-6
**Kenneth City**—*pop pl* FL-3
Kenneth Creek—*stream* NC-3
Kenneth Jenkins Pond Dam—*dam* MS-4
Kenneth Lake—*lake* CA-9
Kenneth Lake—*lake* ID-8
Kenneth Love Lake Dam—*dam* MS-4
Kenneth Raymer Lake—*reservoir* NC-3
Kenneth Raymer Lake Dam—*dam* NC-3
Kenneth Sch—*hist pl* MN-6
Kenneth Spring—*spring* OR-9
Kenneth Tank—*reservoir* AZ-5
**Kenneth Township**—*pop pl* KS-7
Kenneth Walker Elem Sch—*school* IN-6
Kenneth Wright Dam—*dam* AL-4
Kennet Mine—*mine* MT-8
*Kenneto Creek* NY-2
*Kennett* VA-3
**Kennett**—*pop pl* MO-7
Kennett Archeol Site—*hist pl* MO-7
Kennett Cem—*cemetery* VA-3
Kennett City Hall and Masonic Lodge—*hist pl* MO-7
Kennett Consolidated Sch—*school* PA-2
Kennett Hollow—*valley* KY-4
*Kennett HS* PA-2
Kennett Memorial Airp—*airport* MO-7
Kennett MS—*school* PA-2
**Kennett Square**—*pop pl* PA-2
Kennett Square Borough—*civil* PA-2
Kennett Square Country Club—*other* PA-2
Kennett Square Rsvr—*reservoir* PA-2
**Kennett (Township of)**—*pop pl* PA-2
**Kennewick**—*pop pl* WA-9
Kennewick Game Farm—*park* WA-9
Kennewick General Hospital Heliport—*airport* WA-9
Kennewick Main Canal—*canal* WA-9
**Kenney**—*pop pl* IL-6
**Kenney**—*pop pl* TX-5
Kenney, David, House—*hist pl* MA-1
Kenney Branch—*stream* AL-4
Kenney Brook—*stream* MN-6
Kenney Brook—*stream* NH-1
Kenney Brook—*stream* (2) NY-2
Kenney Camp—*locale* CO-8
Kenney Cem—*cemetery* (2) MO-7
Kenney Coulee—*valley* MT-8
*Kenney Creek* ID-8
*Kenney Creek* WY-8
Kenney Creek—*stream* AR-4
Kenney Creek—*stream* CO-8
Kenney Creek—*stream* ID-8
Kenney Creek—*stream* KS-7
Kenney Creek—*stream* UT-8
Kenney Creek—*stream* VA-3
Kenney Creek—*stream* WA-9
Kenney Creek Rsvr—*reservoir* CO-8
Kenney Ditch—*canal* CA-9
Kenney Ditch—*canal* CO-8
Kenney Drain—*canal* MI 6
Kenney Flats—*flat* CO-8
Kenney Grove—*woods* CA-9
Kenney Hill Ch—*church* AL-4
Kenney Lake—*lake* AK-9
Kenney Lake—*lake* (3) MN-6
Kenney Mtn—*summit* AR-4
Kenney-New-Wehdem Sch—*school* TX-5
*Kenney Rim* WY-8
**Kenneys**—*pop pl* PA-2
Kenney Sch—*school* IA-7
Kenneys Creek—*stream* CO-8
Kenney's Fort Site (41WM465)—*hist pl* TX-5
*Kenneys Pond* MA-1
Kenneys Road Beach—*beach* NY-2
Kenneytown—*locale* TN-4
Kenney (Township of)—*fmr MCD* AR-4
**Kennicott**—*pop pl* AK-9
Kennicott Glacier—*glacier* AK-9
Kennicott River—*stream* AK-9
Kennicott's Grove—*hist pl* IL-6
Kennicott Slough Rsvr—*reservoir* CO-8
*Kennidale* AL-4
*Kennilworth* LA-4
*Kennilworth Canal* LA-4
Kennimer Branch—*stream* AR-4
Kennison—*locale* WV-2
Kennison Bay—*bay* NY-2
Kennison Cabin—*locale* WY-8
Kennison Creek—*stream* MS-4
Kennison Hill—*summit* ME-1
Kennison Mountains—*ridge* WV-2
Kennison Mountain Trail—*trail* WV-2
Kennison Mtn—*summit* (2) WV-2
Kennison Rock—*summit* TX-5
Kennison Rsvr—*reservoir* OR-9
Kennison Run—*stream* WV-2
Kennison Spring—*spring* MT-8
Kennison Spring—*spring* NV-8
**Kennison Township**—*pop pl* ND-7
Kenniston Hill—*summit* (2) ME-1
*Kenniwood Park* WY-8
**Kennolia**—*pop pl* MS-4
Kennolyn Camp—*locale* CA-9
Kennon, Mount—*summit* MT-8
Kennon Brook—*stream* NY-2
Kennon Cem—*cemetery* KY-4
Kennon Cem—*cemetery* MO-7
Kennon Cow Camp—*locale* CO-8
*Kennon Creek* GA-3
Kennon Creek—*stream* VA-3
Kennon Island—*island* AK-9
Kennon Marsh—*swamp* VA-3
**Kennonsburg**—*pop pl* OH-6
Kennoys Islands—*island* AK-9
**Kennvale**—*pop pl* OH-6
*Kenny* IL-6
Kenny—*locale* CA-9
Kenny—*locale* FL-3
**Kenny**—*pop pl* PA-2
Kenny, Coulee—*stream* LA-4
Kenny Barger Ditch—*canal* CO-8
Kenny Branch—*stream* LA-4
Kenny Branch—*stream* MO-7
Kenny Branch Sch—*school* SC-3
*Kenny Brook* ME-1
Kenny Brook—*stream* MA-1
Kenny Brook—*stream* NY-2
**Kenny Brook (subdivision)**—*pop pl* TN-4
Kenny Camp—*locale* FL-3
Kenny Cem—*cemetery* IN-6
Kenny Cove—*bay* AK-9
*Kenny Creek* CO-8
*Kenny Creek* MO-7
Kenny Creek—*stream* AK-9
Kenny Creek—*stream* CA-9
Kenny Creek—*stream* MS-4
Kenny Creek—*stream* NV-8
Kenny Creek—*stream* OK-5
Kenny Creek—*stream* WA-9
*Kenny Creek Reservoir* CO-8
**Kennydale**—*pop pl* WA-9
Kenny Ditch—*canal* IN-6
Kenny Draw—*valley* WY-8
Kennyetto Creek—*stream* NY-2
*Kennyetto Reservoir* NY-2
Kenny Flats—*flat* NY-2
Kenny Gulch—*valley* OR-9
Kenny Hill Sch (historical)—*school* AL-4
**Kenny (historical)**—*pop pl* OR-9
Kenny Hollow—*valley* MO-7
*Kenny Lake* WY-8
Kenny Lake—*lake* MN-6
Kenny Lake—*lake* WI-6
Kenny Lake—*lake* WY-8
Kenny Marsh—*swamp* MD-2
Kenny Mine—*mine* CA-9
Kenny Moore Rsvr—*reservoir* CO-8
Kenny Mtn—*summit* CO-8
Kenny Park—*park* MN-6
Kenny Point—*cape* NJ-2
Kenny Pond—*lake* VT-1
Kenny Prairie—*flat* OR-9
Kenny Rehabilitation Institute—*hospital* MN-6
Kenny Ridge—*ridge* CA-9
**Kenny Row**—*pop pl* PA-2
Kennys Bend—*bend* TN-4
Kennys Cem—*cemetery* TN-4
Kenny Sch—*school* MN-6
Kenny School—*locale* MI-6
*Kennys Creek* MN-6
Kenny Spring—*spring* (3) OR-9
Kenny Tank—*reservoir* AZ-5
Kennyville Sch—*school* MN-6
Kenny Well—*well* AZ-5
Kenny Well—*well* NM-5
Kennywood—*uninc pl* PA-2
*Kennywood Park* WY-8
Kennywood Park—*hist pl* PA-2
Kennywood Park—*park* PA-2
Keno—*locale* KY-4
Keno—*locale* MI-6
Keno—*locale* OH-6
**Keno**—*pop pl* OR-9
**Keno**—*pop pl* TX-5
Keno Air Force Station—*military* OR-9
Kenobo Lake—*lake* MI-6
Keno Bridge—*bridge* OR-9
Keno Camp—*locale* CA-9
Keno (CCD)—*cens area* OR-9
Keno Cem—*cemetery* OH-6
Keno Cem—*cemetery* OR-9
Kenockee Cem—*cemetery* MI-6
**Kenockee (Township of)**—*pop pl* MI-6
Keno Creek—*stream* AK-9
Keno Creek—*stream* ID-8
Keno Creek—*stream* KS-7
Keno Creek—*stream* MT-8
Keno Creek—*stream* OK-5
Keno Creek—*stream* WY-8
Keno Dam—*dam* (2) OR-9
Kenogama Lake—*lake* MN-6
Keno Guard Station—*locale* OR-9
Keno Gulch—*valley* CO-8
Keno Gulch—*valley* OR-9
**Keno (historical)**—*pop pl* MS-4
*Keno Lake* MN-6
**Kenoma**—*pop pl* MO-7
Kenoma Creek—*stream* KS-7
Kenomene—*bay* HI-9
Keno Mtn—*summit* MT-8
Keno Post Office (historical)—*building* MS-4
Keno Rsvr—*reservoir* OR-9
**Kenosha**—*pop pl* WI-6
Kenosha Cem—*cemetery* NE-7
Kenosha Country Club—*other* WI-6
**Kenosha (County)**—*pop pl* WI-6
Kenosha County Courthouse and Jail—*hist pl* WI-6
Kenosha Creek—*stream* CO-8
Kenosha Creek—*stream* NE-7
Kenosha Gulch—*valley* CO-8
*Kenosha Lake* CT-1
Kenosha Lake—*lake* MI-6
*Kenosha Mountain* CO-8
Kenosha Mtns—*summit* CO-8
Ken-O-Sha Park—*park* MI-6
Kenosha Park—*park* WI-6
Ken-O-Sha Park Sch—*school* MI-6
Kenosha Pass—*gap* CO-8
Kenosha Sch—*school* NE-7
Kenosha Spur—*locale* CA-9
Kenosia, Lake—*lake* CT-1
*Kenosia Lake* CT-1
Keno Spring—*spring* OR-9
Keno Springs Ranch—*locale* OR-9
Kenova—*locale* WA-9
**Kenova**—*pop pl* AR-4
**Kenova**—*pop pl* WV-2
Kenowa Hills HS—*school* MI-6
Kenoza Ave Pond Dam—*dam* MA-1
**Kenoza Lake**—*pop pl* NY-2
Kenoza Lake—*reservoir* MA-1
Kenoza Lake—*reservoir* NY-2
Kenoza Lake Dam—*dam* MA-1
Kenozia Lake—*lake* NY-2
Ken-Ray Lake—*reservoir* IN-6
Ken-Ray Lake Dam—*dam* IN-6
Kenrick Park—*park* MA-1
Kenrick Seminary—*school* MO-7
**Kenricksville**—*pop pl* OH-6
*Kenridge* OH-6
**Kenridge**—*pop pl* OH-6
Kenridge Lake—*lake* OH-6
Kenrock—*locale* PA-2
**Ken Rock**—*pop pl* IL-6
**Kenroy**—*pop pl* WA-9
Kenroy Park—*park* WA-9
Kenroy Sch—*school* WA-9
**Kensal**—*pop pl* ND-7
**Kensal Township**—*pop pl* ND-7
Kens Cave—*cave* PA-2
Kens Creek—*stream* WV-2
**Kensee**—*pop pl* KY-4
Kensee Ch—*church* KY-4
Kensee Hollow—*valley* KY-4
Kensely, J., House—*hist pl* MA-1
Kenser Creek—*stream* MO-7
*Kenser Valley Run* PA-2
**Kensett**—*pop pl* AR-4
**Kensett**—*pop pl* IA-7
Kensett Cem—*cemetery* IA-7
Kensett Township—*fmr MCD* IA-7
Kensett (Township of)—*fmr MCD* AR-4
*Kensey Cemetery* MO-7
Kensfather Ranch—*locale* MT-8
Kensico Cem—*cemetery* NY-2
**Kensico Cemetery**—*pop pl* NY-2
Kensico Dam—*dam* NY-2
Kensico Dam Plaza—*locale* NY-2
Kensico Lake—*lake* NY-2
Kensico Rsvr—*reservoir* NY-2
Ken Sidey Nature Area—*park* IA-7
*Kensie Beach* CT-1
Kensie Creek—*stream* LA-4
Kensie Point—*cape* CT-1
Kensing—*locale* TX-5
Kensing—*school* MA-1
Kensing Cem—*cemetery* (2) TX-5
Kensinger Cem—*cemetery* PA-2
*Kensington* IL-6
*Kensington* MI-6
*Kensington* ND-7
Kensington—*locale* IL-6
Kensington—*locale* KY-4
Kensington—*locale* SC-3
**Kensington**—*pop pl* CA-9
**Kensington**—*pop pl* CT-1
**Kensington**—*pop pl* GA-3
**Kensington**—*pop pl* KS-7
**Kensington**—*pop pl* MD-2
**Kensington**—*pop pl* MN-6
**Kensington**—*pop pl* NH-1
**Kensington**—*pop pl* (2) NY-2
**Kensington**—*pop pl* OH-6
**Kensington**—*pop pl* PA-2
**Kensington**—*pop pl* SC-3
**Kensington**—*pop pl* TN-4
**Kensington**—*pop pl* VA-3
Kensington—*uninc pl* NY-2
Kensington (CCD)—*cens area* GA-3
Kensington Cem—*cemetery* ND-7
Kensington Ch—*church* TN-4
**Kensington Estates**—*pop pl* MD-2
**Kensington Heights**—*pop pl* MD-2
**Kensington Heights**—*pop pl* PA-2
Kensington Hist Dist—*hist pl* MD-2
Kensington (historical)—*locale* ND-7
Kensington HS—*school* NY-2
Kensington HS for Girls—*hist pl* PA-2
Kensington JHS—*school* MD-2
Kensington-Johnson Sch—*school* NY-2
*Kensington Junction* IL-6
**Kensington Knolls**—*pop pl* MD-2
Kensington Metropolitan Park—*park* MI-6
Kensington Mine—*mine* AK-9
Kensington Park—*CDP* FL-3
Kensington Park—*park* CA-9
Kensington Park—*park* IL-6
Kensington Park—*park* KS-7
Kensington Park—*park* MI-6
**Kensington Park**—*pop pl* GA-3
Kensington Park Baptist Ch—*church* FL-3
Kensington Park Hist Dist—*hist pl* MA-1
Kensington Park Sch—*school* FL-3
Kensington Plantation—*locale* SC-3
Kensington Plantation House—*hist pl* SC-3
Kensington Sch—*school* CT-1
Kensington Sch—*school* IL-6
Kensington Sch—*school* MD-2
Kensington Sch—*school* MI-6
Kensington Sch—*school* MO-7
Kensington Sch—*school* OH-6
Kensington State Wildlife Mngmt Area—*park* MN-6
**Kensington (subdivision)**—*pop pl* (2) AZ-5
**Kensington (Town of)**—*pop pl* NH-1
**Kensington Township**—*pop pl* ND-7
**Kensington Trace (subdivision)**—*pop pl* NC-3
**Kensington View**—*pop pl* MD-2
**Kensington Woods (subdivision)**—*pop pl* MS-4
Kens Lake—*reservoir* UT-8
Kens Lake Dam—*dam* UT-8
Kensler Cem—*cemetery* IA-7
Kensler Elem Sch—*school* KS-7
Kenslers Bend (historical)—*bend* SD-7
Kens Plaza Shop Ctr—*locale* TN-4
Ken Spring—*spring* WA-9
Kenspur—*locale* MT-8
**Kens Subdivision**—*pop pl* UT-8
Kens Tank—*reservoir* (2) AZ-5
Kenstin Manor Airp—*airport* IN-6
Kenston HS—*school* OH-6
Kenston Lake—*lake* OH-6
*Kent* IN-6
*Kent* PA-2
*Kent* VT-1
*Kent* VA-3
Kent—*fmr MCD* NE-7
Kent—*locale* AL-4
Kent—*locale* AR-4
Kent—*locale* FL-3
Kent—*locale* OK-5
Kent—*locale* SC-3
Kent—*locale* VA-3
**Kent**—*pop pl* AL-4
**Kent**—*pop pl* CT-1
**Kent**—*pop pl* DC-2
**Kent**—*pop pl* IL-6
**Kent**—*pop pl* IN-6
**Kent**—*pop pl* (2) IA-7
**Kent**—*pop pl* KY-4
**Kent**—*pop pl* MN-6
**Kent**—*pop pl* OH-6
**Kent**—*pop pl* OR-9
**Kent**—*pop pl* TX-5
**Kent**—*pop pl* VA-3
**Kent**—*pop pl* WA-9
**Kent**—*pop pl* WV-2
Kent, Charles Adolph, Sr., House—*hist pl* LA-4
Kent, Charles House—*hist pl* OH-6
Kent, J., Residence—*hist pl* OH-6
Kent, Jerry, House—*hist pl* AZ-5
Kent, Moses, House—*hist pl* NH-1
Kent, Mount—*summit* NH-1
Kent, Mount—*summit* WA-9
Kent, Mount—*summit* WY-8
Kent, Sydney, House—*hist pl* IL-6
Kent, Zeno, House—*hist pl* OH-6
Kenta Canal—*canal* LA-4
**Kent Acres**—*pop pl* DE-2
**Kent Acres-south Dover Manor**—*pop pl* DE-2
KENT-AM (Prescott)—*tower* AZ-5
Kent and Fishkills Ch—*church* NY-2
*Kentawah Canal* MS-4
Kentawka, Bogue—*stream* MS-4
Kentawka Canal—*canal* MS-4
Kent Bayou—*stream* LA-4
Kent Bayou Oil and Gas Field—*oilfield* LA-4
Kent Benaroya Heliport—*airport* WA-9
*Kent Branch* VA-3
Kent Branch—*stream* IL-6
Kent Branch—*stream* (2) LA-4
Kent Branch—*stream* TX-5
Kent Branch—*stream* (2) VA-3
**Kent (Brice Station)**—*pop pl* NY-2
Kent Bridge (historical)—*bridge* AL-4
Kent Brook—*stream* NY-2
Kent Brook—*stream* RI-1
Kent Brook—*stream* VT-1
*Kent Canyon* CA-9
Kent Canyon—*valley* CA-9
Kent Canyon—*valley* ID-8
Kent Canyon—*valley* NV-8
Kent Canyon—*valley* UT-8
Kent Cem—*cemetery* (3) FL-3
Kent Cem—*cemetery* IL-6
Kent Cem—*cemetery* IN-6
Kent Cem—*cemetery* LA-4
Kent Cem—*cemetery* ME-1
Kent Cem—*cemetery* MS-4
Kent Cem—*cemetery* MO-7
Kent Cem—*cemetery* MT-8
Kent Cem—*cemetery* NE-7
Kent Cem—*cemetery* OH-6
Kent Cem—*cemetery* TN-4
Kent Cem—*cemetery* VT-1
Kent Center Vocational Technical HS—*school* DE-2
Kent Chapel—*church* IA-7
Kent Chapel—*church* MO-7
Kent Christian Acad—*school* DE-2
**Kent City**—*pop pl* MI-6
**Kent Cliffs**—*pop pl* NY-2
Kent Community Center—*building* AL-4
Kent Compressor Station—*other* OR-9
*Kent Corner* MI-6
*Kent Corner* RI-1
**Kent Corner**—*pop pl* MA-1
**Kent Corner**—*pop pl* RI-1
Kent Corners—*locale* MI-6
**Kent Corners**—*pop pl* NY-2
*Kent (corporate name Jacksonville)* PA-2
*Kent Corr* MI-6
Kent Country Club—*other* MI-6
**Kent County**—*pop pl* DE-2
**Kent (County)**—*pop pl* MD-2
**Kent (County)**—*pop pl* MI-6
**Kent County**—*pop pl* RI-1
**Kent (County)**—*pop pl* TX-5
Kent County Courthouse—*hist pl* RI-1
Kent County International Airp—*airport* MI-6
Kent County Orthopedic Sch—*school* DE-2
Kent County Sewer Treatment Plant—*locale* DE-2
Kent County Vocational Sch—*school* MI-6
*Kent County Vocational Technical Center* DE-2
Kent Cove—*bay* (2) ME-1
Kent-Crane Shell Midden—*hist pl* TX-5
*Kent Creek* IN-6
*Kent Creek* TX-5
Kent Creek—*stream* AK-9
Kent Creek—*stream* CA-9
Kent Creek—*stream* ID-8
Kent Creek—*stream* IL-6
Kent Creek—*stream* KS-7
Kent Creek—*stream* MT-8
Kent Creek—*stream* OR-9
Kent Creek—*stream* (2) TX-5
Kent Creek—*stream* WA-9
Kent Creek—*stream* WI-6
Kent-Delord House—*hist pl* NY-2
Kent Ditch—*canal* (2) IN-6
Kent Ditch—*canal* MT-8
Kent Ditch—*canal* OH-6
Kent Ditch—*canal* WY-8
Kent Drain—*canal* NV-8
Kent Draw—*valley* TX-5
Kent Elem Sch—*school* IN-6
**Kentenia**—*pop pl* KY-4
Kentenia State For—*forest* KY-4
Kenter Canyon—*valley* CA-9
Kenter Canyon Sch—*school* CA-9
**Kent Estates Subdivision**—*pop pl* UT-8
Kent Falls—*falls* NY-2
Kent Falls Brook—*stream* CT-1
Kent Falls State Park—*park* CT-1
Kent Farms Airp—*airport* WA-9
**Kentfield**—*pop pl* CA-9
Kent Furnace—*locale* CT-1
**Kent Gardens**—*pop pl* VA-3
**Kent Gardens (subdivision)**—*pop pl* PA-2
**Kent Garden (subdivision)**—*pop pl* NC-3
Kent Grove—*woods* CA-9
*Kent Heights* RI-1
Kent Hill—*summit* NH-1
Kent Hill—*summit* TX-5
Kent Hill—*summit* VT-1
Kent Hills—*locale* NY-2
Kent Hill Sch (historical)—*school* AL-4
Kent Hills Sch—*school* MI-6
Kent (historical)—*locale* KS-7
**Kent (historical)**—*pop pl* RI-1
**Kent (historical)**—*pop pl* TN-4
Kent Hollow—*valley* AL-4
Kent Hollow—*valley* CT-1
Kent Hollow—*valley* NC-3
Kent Hollow—*valley* PA-2
Kent Hollow—*valley* (2) TN-4
Kent Hollow—*valley* VT-1
Kent Hollow Cem—*cemetery* CT-1
Kent Hollow Dam—*dam* CT-1
Kent House and Hitchens House—*hist pl* IN-6
Kent HS—*school* WA-9
Kent Industrial Center—*locale* MI-6
Kent Industrial District—*hist pl* OH-6
Kent Iron Furnace—*hist pl* CT-1
Kent Island—*island* CA-9
Kent Island—*island* DE-2
Kent Island—*island* MD-2
Kent Island—*island* NH-1
**Kent Island Estates**—*pop pl* MD-2
Kent Island Narrows—*channel* MD-2
Kent Jail—*hist pl* OH-6
Kent JHS—*school* MD-2
Kent JHS—*school* OH-6
Kent Junction—*locale* VA-3
Kent Lake—*lake* ID-8
Kent Lake—*lake* MN-6
Kent Lake—*lake* (2) MT-8
Kent Lake—*lake* WA-9
Kent Lake—*lake* WI-6
Kent Lake—*reservoir* CA-9
Kent Lake—*reservoir* MI-6
Kent Lake—*reservoir* VA-3
Kent Lake Drain—*canal* NV-8
Kent Lake Sch—*school* MT-8
Kentland—*locale* IL-6
**Kentland**—*pop pl* IN-6
**Kentland**—*pop pl* MD-2
Kentland Elem Sch—*school* IN-6
**Kentland Farms**—*pop pl* VA-3
Kentland Municipal Airp—*airport* IN-6
Kentland Park—*park* MD-2
Kentland Sch—*school* MD-2
Kent LaRoco Canal—*canal* ID-8
Kent La Roco Canal—*canal* ID-8
Kent Lateral—*canal* AZ-5
Kent Lookout Tower—*locale* WI-6
Kent Meadows—*flat* WY-8
*Kent Meadows Lake* WA-9
Kent Memorial Ch—*church* MO-7
Kent Memorial Gardens (Cemetery)—*cemetery* MI-6
Kentmere—*locale* DE-2
Kent Mill—*locale* FL-3
Kent Mill Cem—*cemetery* NY-2
Kent Mill Lake—*reservoir* FL-3
*Kent Mill Pond* FL-3
Kent Mine—*mine* MT-8
Kent Mine—*mine* WY-8
**Kentmore Park**—*pop pl* MD-2
**Kentmorr**—*pop pl* MD-2
Kent Mtn—*summit* AL-4
Kent Mtn—*summit* AR-4
Kent Mtn—*summit* CT-1
Kent Mtn—*summit* TX-5
*Kent Narrows* MD-2
Kent Neighborhood Hist Dist—*hist pl* VT 1
**Kentner**—*pop pl* IA-7
Kentner Creek—*stream* IN-6
Kentner Spring—*spring* TX-5
**Kentner Township**—*pop pl* ND-7
Kent North Vocational Technical HS—*school* DE-2
Kent Oaks Hosp—*hospital* MI-6
Kento-Boo Ch—*church* KY-4
*Kenton* IL-6
**Kenton**—*pop pl* DE-2
**Kenton**—*pop pl* KY-4
**Kenton**—*pop pl* MI-6
**Kenton**—*pop pl* OH-6
**Kenton**—*pop pl* OK-5
**Kenton**—*pop pl* OR-9
**Kenton**—*pop pl* TN-4
Kenton (CCD)—*cens area* DE-2
Kenton Cem—*cemetery* MI-6
Kenton Cem—*cemetery* OK-5
Kenton Ch—*church* DE-2
Kenton Ch—*church* OH-6
Kenton Ch of Christ—*church* TN-4
Kenton City Hall—*building* TN-4
Kenton City Park—*park* TN-4
**Kenton (County)**—*pop pl* KY-4
Kenton County Library—*hist pl* KY-4
Kenton Courthouse Square Hist Dist—*hist pl* OH-6
Kenton Creek—*stream* OH-6
Kenton Cumberland Presbyterian Ch—*church* TN-4
Kenton Elem Sch—*school* TN-4
Kenton-Furnace Sch—*school* KY-4
**Kenton Hills**—*pop pl* KY-4
Kenton Hist Dist—*hist pl* DE-2
Kenton HS—*school* KY-4
Kenton HS—*school* TN-4
Kenton Hundred—*civil* DE-2
Kenton-Hunt Farm—*hist pl* OH-6
Kenton-Mason Hall (CCD)—*cens area* TN-4
Kenton-Mason Hall Division—*civil* TN-4
Kenton Methodist Ch—*church* TN-4
Kenton Mill—*locale* CA-9
Kenton Mine—*mine* CA-9
Kenton Park—*park* OR-9
Kenton Post Office—*building* TN-4
Kenton Post Office—*hist pl* DE-2
Kenton Public Library—*hist pl* OH-6
Kenton Sch—*school* CO-8
Kenton Sch—*school* IL-6
Kenton Sch—*school* OH-6
Kenton Sch—*school* OR-9
Kentons Mill (historical)—*locale* AL-4
**Kentontown**—*pop pl* KY-4
Kenton United Methodist Ch—*church* DE-2
**Kenton Vale**—*pop pl* KY-4
Kenton Yard—*locale* OR-9
Kent Park—*park* PA-2
**Kent Park**—*pop pl* MA-1
Kent Park—*uninc pl* VA-3
Kent Peak—*locale* OR-9
Kent Peak—*summit* (2) ID-8
Kent Peak—*summit* MT-8
Kent Place Sch—*school* NJ-2
Kent Plantation House—*hist pl* LA-4
Kent Point—*cape* MD-2
Kent Point—*cape* VA-3
*Kent Pond* MA-1
Kent Pond—*lake* NH-1
Kent Pond—*lake* VT-1
Kent Ranch—*locale* AZ-5
Kent Ranch—*locale* MT-8
Kent Ranch—*locale* WA-9
*Kent Ridge* VA-3
Kent Rocks—*summit* MA-1
*Kent Rsvr* OR-9
Kent Rsvr—*reservoir* NY-2
Kent Rsvr—*reservoir* OR-9
Kent Run—*stream* (2) OH-6
Kent Run—*stream* (2) PA-2
Kentry Ridge—*ridge* WA-9
Kents Canyon—*valley* ID-8
Kent Sch—*school* CO-8
Kent Sch—*school* MT-8
Kent Sch—*school* NE-7
Kent Sch—*school* NY-2
Kent Sch—*school* OH-6
Kent Sch—*school* WA-9
Kent Sch—*school* WV-2
Kents Chapel—*church* PA-2
Kent's Corner Hist Dist—*hist pl* VT-1
**Kents Corners**—*pop pl* NY-2
**Kents Corners**—*pop pl* VT-1
Kents Creek—*stream* NY-2
Kents Creek—*stream* VA-3
Kents Gulch—*valley* MT-8
**Kents Hill**—*pop pl* ME-1
Kent's Hill Sch Hist Dist—*hist pl* ME-1
Kent Simmons Hollow—*valley* VA-3
*Kent's Island* MD-2
*Kents Island* MS-4
Kents Island—*island* MA-1
Kents Lake—*lake* UT-8
Kents Lake—*reservoir* GA-3
Kents Lake Campground—*locale* UT-8
Kents Lake Number One (Upper)—*reservoir* UT-8
Kents Lake Number One Upper Dam—*dam* UT-8
Kents Lake Number Two (Middle)—*dam* UT-8
Kents Lake Number Two (Middle)—*reservoir* UT-8
Kents Landing—*locale* GA-3
Kents Ledge—*bench* VT-1
Kents Millpond—*reservoir* GA-3
Kents Peak—*summit* ID-8
*Kent's Point* MD-2
Kents Pond—*lake* CT-1
Kent Spring—*spring* AZ-5
Kent Spring—*spring* NV-8
Kent Spring—*spring* OR-9
Kent Spring—*spring* UT-8
Kent Spring Trail 156—*trail* AZ-5
Kents Ridge—*ridge* VA-3
*Kents Rocks* MA-1
Kents Run—*stream* PA-2
Kents Spring—*spring* UT-8
*Kent's Store* VA-3
**Kents Store**—*pop pl* VA-3
Kent State Univ—*school* (2) OH-6
Kent-Stein Park—*park* IA-7
Kent-Sussex Line Branch—*stream* DE-2
Kent Swim Club—*other* DE-2
Kent Tank—*reservoir* NM-5
**Kent (Town of)**—*pop pl* CT-1
**Kent (Town of)**—*pop pl* NY-2
**Kent Township**—*pop pl* ND-7
**Kent Township**—*pop pl* SD-7
**Kent (Township of)**—*pop pl* IL-6
**Kent (Township of)**—*pop pl* IN-6
**Kent Trailer Park**—*pop pl* OH-6
*Kentuck* AL-4
Kentuck—*locale* AL-4
Kentuck—*locale* VA-3
Kentuck—*locale* WV-2
**Kentuck**—*pop pl* VA-3
*Kentuck Branch* AL-4
Kentuck Ch—*church* VA-3
Kentuck Corners—*locale* PA-2
Kentuck Country Club—*other* OR-9
*Kentuck Creek* KS-7
Kentuck Creek—*stream* OR-9
Kentuck Creek—*stream* TX-5
Kentuck Creek—*stream* WI-6
Kentuck Fork—*stream* WV-2
Kentuck Fork Sch—*school* WV-2
Kentuck Gulch—*valley* CA-9
Kentuck Inlet—*bay* OR-9
Kentuck Island—*island* NC-3
Kentuck Knob—*summit* PA-2
*Kentuck Lake* WI-6
Kentuck Lake—*lake* WI-6
Kentuck Ledges—*bench* CT-1
Kentuck Mine—*mine* (2) CA-9
Kentuck Mine—*mine* ID-8
Kentuck Mountain—*ridge* AL-4
Kentuck Mtn—*summit* AZ-5
Kentuck Museum—*building* AL-4
Kentuck Park—*park* AL-4
Kentuck Pond—*lake* NY-2
Kentuck Ranger Station—*locale* AL-4
Kentuck Run—*stream* WV-2
Kentucks Cabin—*locale* AZ-5
*Kentuck School* PA-2
Kentucks Grave—*cemetery* AZ-5
Kentuck Slough—*stream* OR-9
Kentuck Spring—*spring* AZ-5
Kentuck Spring Campground—*park* AZ-5
Kentuck Swamp—*swamp* MD-2
Kentuck Union Ch—*church* PA-2
Kentucky—*locale* MI-6
**Kentucky**—*pop pl* AR-4
**Kentucky**—*pop pl* IL-6
Kentucky Air Natl Guard and Archeol Site—*hist pl* KY-4
Kentucky and Indiana Bank—*hist pl* KY-4
Kentucky Bend—*bend* MS-4
Kentucky Bend Bar—*bar* AR-4
Kentucky Bend Bar—*bar* MS-4
Kentucky Bend Revetment—*levee* MS-4
Kentucky Bldg—*hist pl* KY-4
Kentucky Branch—*stream* FL-3
Kentucky Branch—*stream* KY-4

Kentucky Branch—*stream* TX-5
Kentucky Butte—*summit* OR-9
*Kentucky Canyon* NM-5
Kentucky Canyon—*valley* OR-9
Kentucky Ch—*church* AR-4
Kentucky Christian Coll—*school* KY-4
*Kentucky Creek* IN-6
Kentucky Creek—*stream* (2) AK-9
Kentucky Creek—*stream* CA-9
Kentucky Creek—*stream* ID-8
Kentucky Creek—*stream* IL-6
Kentucky Creek—*stream* KS-7
Kentucky Creek—*stream* NC-3
Kentucky Creek—*stream* OK-5
Kentucky Creek—*stream* OR-9
Kentucky Creek—*stream* WI-6
Kentucky Dam—*dam* KY-4
Kentucky Dam Boat Basin—*harbor* KY-4
Kentucky Dam Marina—*harbor* KY-4
Kentucky Dam Tree Nursery—*other* KY-4
**Kentucky Dam Village**—*pop pl* KY-4
Kentucky Dam Village State Park—*park* KY-4
Kentucky Distillery (Plant)—*facility* KY-4
Kentucky Fair And Exposition Center—*locale* KY-4
**Kentucky Farms**—*pop pl* VA-3
Kentucky Flat—*flat* CA-9
Kentucky Flat—*flat* OR-9
**Kentucky Fried Chicken Subdivision**—*pop pl* UT-8
Kentucky Gap—*gap* KY-4
Kentucky Governor's Mansion—*hist pl* KY-4
Kentucky Gulch—*valley* AZ-5
Kentucky Gulch—*valley* (2) CO-8
Kentucky Gulch—*valley* MT-8
Kentucky Gulch—*valley* OR-9
**Kentucky Heights**—*pop pl* TN-4
Kentucky Heights Ch—*church* KY-4
Kentucky Hill—*summit* VA-3
Kentucky Hollow—*valley* MO-7
Kentucky Hollow Sch (historical)—*school* MO-7
Kentucky Hotel—*hist pl* VA-3
Kentucky House—*locale* CA-9
Kentucky Island—*island* GA-3
Kentucky Knoll Cem—*cemetery* WV-2
Kentucky Lake—*lake* MI-6
Kentucky Lake—*reservoir* (2) KY-4
Kentucky Lake—*reservoir* TN-4
Kentucky Landing—*locale* FL-3
Kentucky Landing—*locale* MS-4
Kentucky (Magisterial District)—*fmr MCD* WV-2
Kentucky Military Institute—*school* KY-4
Kentucky Mine—*mine* (2) NV-8
Kentucky Mine Group—*mine* CA-9
*Kentucky Mountain* AZ-5
Kentucky Mountain Bible Institute—*school* KY-4
Kentucky Mtn—*summit* VA-3
Kentucky Mutt Creek—*stream* TX-5
Kentucky Natl Bank—*hist pl* KY-4
Kentucky Park—*flat* NM-5
Kentucky Point—*cape* KY-4
Kentucky Point Bar—*bar* KY-4
Kentucky Raceway—*other* KY-4
Kentucky Ranch—*locale* CA-9
Kentucky Ravine—*valley* CA-9
*Kentucky Reservoir* KY-4
Kentucky Ridge—*ridge* CA-9
Kentucky Ridge—*ridge* (2) KY-4
Kentucky Ridge—*ridge* OR-9
Kentucky Ridge (CCD)—*cens area* KY-4
Kentucky Ridge Ch—*church* IN-6
Kentucky Ridge Lookout Tower—*locale* KY-4
Kentucky Ridge Mine—*mine* CA-9
Kentucky Ridge State For—*forest* KY-4
Kentucky River—*stream* KY-4
*Kentucky Rsvr* TN-4
Kentucky Sch—*school* OH-6
Kentucky Slough—*stream* MO-7
Kentucky Southern Campus Univ of Louisville—*school* KY-4
Kentucky Spring—*spring* TN-4
Kentucky Springs—*spring* CA-9
Kentucky Springs Canyon—*valley* CA-9
Kentucky State Arsenal—*hist pl* KY-4
Kentucky State Capitol—*hist pl* KY-4
Kentucky State Coll—*school* KY-4
Kentucky State Penitentiary Farm—*other* KY-4
Kentucky Street Sch—*hist pl* KY-4
Kentucky-Tennessee Spur—*locale* TN-4
*Kentuckytown* TX-5
Kentucky Town—*locale* TX-5
**Kentuckytown**—*pop pl* TX-5
*Kentuckytown Community* TX-5
**Kentucky Township**—*pop pl* KS-7
Kentucky (Township of)—*fmr MCD* (4) AR-4
Kentucky Village—*school* KY-4
Kentucky Wagon Works—*hist pl* KY-4
Kentucky Wesleyan Coll—*school* KY-4
Kentucky Woodlands Natl Wildlife Ref—*park* KY-4
Kentucky 30 Interchange—*other* KY-4
Kentucky 7 Interchange—*other* KY-4
*Kentuctah Creek* MS-4
Kentuctah Creek—*stream* MS-4
Kent-Valentine House—*hist pl* VA-3
**Kent Village**—*pop pl* MD-2
*Kentville* TN-4
Kentville Sch—*school* IL-6
*Kentwood* IN-6
**Kentwood**—*pop pl* IN-6
**Kentwood**—*pop pl* LA-4
**Kentwood**—*pop pl* MI-6
**Kentwood Condominium**—*pop pl* UT-8
**Kentwood Estates (subdivision)**—*pop pl* UT-8
Kentwood HS—*school* MI-6
**Kentwood-In-The-Pines**—*pop pl* CA-9
**Kent Woodlands**—*pop pl* CA-9
**Kentwood Manor**—*pop pl* TX-5
Kentwood Park—*park* NC-3
Kentwood Sch—*school* CA-9
Kentwood Sch—*school* MI-6
**Kentwood (subdivision)**—*pop pl* MS-4
**Kentwood (subdivision)**—*pop pl* NC-3
Kenty Creek—*stream* AK-9
Kenty Creek—*stream* MS-4
Kentyre Ch—*church* SC-3
Kenucane Sch—*school* WI-6
*Kenuckpacook* MA-1

Kenu Lake—*lake* WI-6
Kenunga Creek—*stream* AK-9
Kenusky Creek—*stream* OR-9
Kenutchen Creek—*stream* OR-9
**Kenvil**—*pop pl* NJ-2
**Kenvir**—*pop pl* KY-4
Ken-Warren Playground—*park* LA-4
Ken-Well Park—*park* IL-6
Kenwells—*locale* NY-2
*Kenwetah Creek* MS-4
Kenwick—*uninc pl* KY-4
**Kenwick Village**—*pop pl* PA-2
Kenwill Apartments—*hist pl* AZ-5
Ken Wolfe Lake—*reservoir* IA-7
*Kenwood* (2) IL-6
*Kenwood* (2) MN-6
*Kenwood* MS-4
*Kenwood* OH-6
Kenwood—*locale* AR-4
Kenwood—*locale* GA-3
Kenwood—*locale* IA-7
Kenwood—*locale* MO-7
Kenwood—*locale* NY-2
Kenwood—*locale* OK-5
Kenwood—*locale* VA-3
**Kenwood**—*pop pl* AL-4
**Kenwood**—*pop pl* CA-9
**Kenwood**—*pop pl* IL-6
**Kenwood**—*pop pl* IN-6
**Kenwood**—*pop pl* KY-4
**Kenwood**—*pop pl* (3) MD-2
**Kenwood**—*pop pl* MA-1
**Kenwood**—*pop pl* NJ-2
**Kenwood**—*pop pl* NY-2
**Kenwood**—*pop pl* OH-6
**Kenwood**—*pop pl* (3) PA-2
**Kenwood**—*pop pl* TN-4
**Kenwood**—*pop pl* TX-5
**Kenwood**—*pop pl* (2) VA-3
Kenwood—*uninc pl* GA-3
Kenwood—*uninc pl* KY-4
**Kenwood Acres (subdivision)**—*pop pl* NC-3
Kenwood Baptist Ch—*church* TN-4
**Kenwood Beach**—*pop pl* MD-2
Kenwood Ch—*church* KY-4
Kenwood Ch—*church* TX-5
Kenwood Ch—*church* VA-3
Kenwood Country Club—*other* MD-2
Kenwood Country Club—*other* OH-6
Kenwood Creek—*stream* AK-9
Kenwood Elem Sch—*school* FL-3
Kenwood Elem Sch—*school* IN-6
**Kenwood Estates**—*pop pl* NY-2
*Kenwood Gardens* OH-6
Kenwood Hill—*summit* KY-4
**Kenwood Hills**—*pop pl* OH-6
Kenwood HS—*school* MD-2
**Kenwood Knolls**—*pop pl* OH-6
**Kenwood Knolls (subdivision)**—*pop pl* NC-3
**Kenwood (local name Kenwood Station)**—*pop pl* OH-6
Kenwood Park—*park* IA-7
Kenwood Park—*park* KS-7
Kenwood Park—*park* MI-6
Kenwood Park—*park* MN-6
Kenwood Park—*park* NC-3
Kenwood Park—*park* OK-5
Kenwood Park—*park* TX-5
**Kenwood Park**—*pop pl* MD-2
**Kenwood Place**—*pop pl* TX-5
Kenwood Post Office (historical)—*building* MS-4
Kenwood Sch—*school* FL-3
Kenwood Sch—*school* ID-8
Kenwood Sch—*school* (2) IL-6
Kenwood Sch—*school* IA-7
Kenwood Sch—*school* KY-4
Kenwood Sch—*school* MI-6
Kenwood Sch—*school* (2) MN-6
Kenwood Sch—*school* NE-7
Kenwood Sch—*school* (3) OH-6
Kenwood Sch—*school* OR-9
Kenwood Sch—*school* PA-2
Kenwood Sch—*school* TX-5
Kenwood Station (local name for Kenwood)—*other* OH-6
**Kenwood Villa Subdivision**—*pop pl* UT-8
Kenworth Hist Dist—*hist pl* NC-3
Kenworth Sch—*school* NC-3
Kenworthy Gap—*gap* VA-3
Kenworthy Lake—*lake* WA-9
Kenworthy Ranch—*locale* AZ-5
Ken Wortity Station—*locale* CA-9
Ken Wye—*locale* KY-4
*Kenyon* KS-7
Kenyon—*locale* ID-8
Kenyon—*locale* VA-3
**Kenyon**—*pop pl* AR-4
**Kenyon**—*pop pl* MN-6
**Kenyon**—*pop pl* RI-1
Kenyon, A. L., House—*hist pl* WI-6
Kenyon Bay—*bay* MI-6
Kenyon Bay—*bay* NC-3
Kenyon Bayou—*stream* LA-4
Kenyon Bridge—*hist pl* NH-1
Kenyon Cem—*cemetery* (2) KS-7
Kenyon Cem—*cemetery* MO-7
Kenyon Ch—*church* AL-4
Kenyon Ch—*church* OK-5
Kenyon Coll—*school* OH-6
Kenyon College—*hist pl* OH-6
Kenyon Corner—*locale* CO-8
Kenyon Corners—*locale* NY-2
Kenyon Cove—*valley* CA-9
Kenyon Creek—*stream* GA-3
Kenyon Creek—*stream* MT-8
Kenyon Creek—*stream* OK-5
Kenyon Creek—*stream* (2) WI-6
Kenyon Creek—*stream* WY-8
Kenyon Hill—*summit* ME-1
Kenyon Hill—*summit* (3) NH-1
Kenyon Hill—*summit* NY-2
Kenyon Hill—*summit* RI-1
*Kenyon Hollow* PA-2
Kenyon Hollow—*valley* MO-7
Kenyon Hollow—*valley* PA-2
Kenyon Island—*island* TX-5
Kenyon Islands—*island* NY-2
*Kenyon Lake* NY-2
Kenyon Lake—*lake* MI-6

Kenyon Lake—*swamp* MI-6
Kenyon Lodge—*locale* AR-4
*Kenyon Mills* RI-1
Kenyon Mtn—*summit* NY-2
Kenyon Mtn—*summit* OR-9
Kenyon Opera House—*hist pl* MN-6
Kenyon Park—*flat* WY-8
Kenyon Ranch—*locale* AZ-5
*Kenyons* RI-1
Kenyon Sch—*school* AR-4
Kenyon Sch (abandoned)—*school* PA-2
Kenyon Scudder Boys Camp—*locale* CA-9
*Kenyon's (Kenyon)* RI-1
Kenyon Springs—*spring* WI-6
Kenyon Station—*locale* AZ-5
Kenyon Substation Well—*well* ID-8
Kenyon Tank—*reservoir* AZ-5
Kenyontown Creek—*stream* NY-2
**Kenyon (Township of)**—*pop pl* MN-6
*Kenyonville* RI-1
Kenyonville—*locale* CT-1
**Kenyonville**—*pop pl* NY-2
**Kenzie**—*pop pl* GA-3
Kenzie Chapel—*church* AL-4
Kenzie Ravine—*valley* CA-9
**Kenzin**—*pop pl* NM-5
**Keo**—*pop pl* AR-4
*Keoaenelu* HI-9
Keo Cem—*cemetery* AR-4
**Keogh**—*pop pl* ID-8
Keogh Creek—*stream* ID-8
Keogh Lake—*lake* WA-9
Keogh Landing Strip—*airport* ND-7
Keogh Ranch—*locale* MT-8
Keogh Ranch—*locale* NE-7
Keohler Rsvr—*reservoir* OR-9
Keoka Lake—*lake* ME-1
Keokea—*civil* (3) HI-9
**Keokea**—*pop pl* (2) HI-9
Keokea Bay—*bay* HI-9
*Keokea Harbor* HI-9
Keokea Point—*cape* HI-9
**Keokee**—*pop pl* VA-3
Keokee Ch—*church* PA-2
Keokee Creek—*stream* ID-8
Keokee Lake—*lake* ID-8
Keokee Lake—*reservoir* VA-3
Keokee Mtn—*summit* ID-8
Keokirk Mine—*mine* MT-8
Keokirk Mtn—*summit* MT-8
Keoklevik River—*stream* AK-9
Keokuk—*locale* (2) TX-5
**Keokuk**—*pop pl* IA-7
Keokuk, Lake—*lake* IL-6
Keokuk, Moses, House—*hist pl* OK-5
Keokuk Cem—*cemetery* OK-5
Keokuk County Courthouse—*hist pl* IA-7
Keokuk County Farm—*building* IA-7
Keokuk Dam—*dam* IL-6
Keokuk Falls—*locale* OK-5
Keokuk Lake—*lake* IA-7
Keokuk Lock and Dam—*hist pl* IA-7
Keokuk Mine—*mine* CA-9
Keokuk Oil Field—*oilfield* OK-5
Keokuk Substation—*other* WA-9
Keokuk Township—*fmr MCD* IA-7
Keolewa—*summit* HI-9
KEOL-FM—*tower* OR-9
**Keolu Hills**—*pop pl* HI-9
**Keomah**—*pop pl* IA-7
Keomah, Lake—*reservoir* IA-7
Keomah Dam—*dam* IA-7
Keomo Point—*cape* HI-9
Keomuku—*beach* HI-9
**Keomuku**—*pop pl* HI-9
*Keonapoko* HI-9
Keone Bay—*bay* HI-9
Keoneeleele Flat—*flat* HI-9
Keonehanau—*cape* HI-9
Keoneheehee—*lava* HI-9
Keoneheehee—*ridge* HI-9
*Keonehehee* HI-9
Keonehehee—*area* HI-9
Keonehelelee—*beach* HI-9
Keonehunehune—*summit* HI-9
Keonenelu—*summit* HI-9
Keonenui—*cape* HI-9
Keoneoio—*locale* HI-9
*Keoneoio Bay* HI-9
Keoneoio Gulch—*valley* HI-9
Keoneokanuku—*bay* HI-9
Keonepoko—*cape* HI-9
Keonepoko Homesteads—*civil* HI-9
Keonepoko Iki—*civil* HI-9
Keonepoko Nui—*civil* HI-9
*Keonepoku Iki* HI-9
*Keonepoku Nui* HI-9
Keoneuli—*bay* HI-9
Keoniki—*civil* HI-9
Keoniloa Bay—*bay* HI-9
**Keono (historical)**—*pop pl* OR-9
Keonokuino—*civil* HI-9
Keon Sch—*school* NY-2
Keopaweo—*summit* HI-9
Keopfgen Lake—*lake* MI-6
*Ke-opke* AZ-5
Keo Point—*cape* AK-9
Keopu Cem—*cemetery* HI-9
*Keopuka* HI-9
*Keopuka Island* HI-9
Keopukaloa—*civil* HI-9
Keopuka One-Two—*civil* HI-9
Keopuka Rock—*island* HI-9
Keopukauuku—*civil* HI-9
Keopu One-Three—*civil* HI-9
**Keosauqua**—*pop pl* IA-7
Keo Springs Sch—*school* WI-6
Keota—*locale* NM-5
**Keota**—*pop pl* CO-8
**Keota**—*pop pl* IA-7
**Keota**—*pop pl* MO-7
**Keota**—*pop pl* OK-5
Keota (CCD)—*cens area* OK-5
Keota Cem—*cemetery* OK-5
Keota Oil Field—*oilfield* CO-8
Keota Sch—*school* NE-7
Keota Stone Circles Archeol District—*hist pl* CO-8
Keough—*locale* ME-1
Keough Draw—*valley* SD-7

**Keough Hot Springs**—*pop pl* CA-9
Keough Lake—*lake* WI-6
Keough Ranch—*locale* NV-8
Keough Spring—*spring* (2) NV-8
Keoulu Hills Sch—*school* HI-9
Keoun Creek—*stream* AR-4
**Keowee**—*pop pl* (2) SC-3
Keowee Ch—*church* SC-3
Keowee HS—*school* SC-3
*Keowee River* NC-3
*Keowee River* SC-3
Keowee River—*stream* SC-3
Keown—*locale* PA-2
Keown Falls—*falls* GA-3
Keown Falls Rec Area—*locale* GA-3
Keowns—*locale* WI-6
**Keown Station**—*pop pl* PA-2
**Keownville**—*pop pl* MS-4
Keownville Baptist Ch—*church* MS-4
Keownville Post Office (historical)—*building* MS-4
Kepani Rsvr—*reservoir* HI-9
Kepaniwai Park—*park* HI-9
Kepapa Spring—*spring* HI-9
*Kepara* FM-9
*Kepara Inseln* FM-9
Kepara Island—*island* FM-9
*Kepara Islands* FM-9
*Kepar Inseln* FM-9
*Kepar Islands* FM-9
Kepehs—*locale* FM-9
Kephart—*locale* CA-9
Kephart, Mount—*summit* TN-4
*Kephart Corners* PA-2
Kephart Dam—*dam* PA-2
Kephart Hollow—*valley* PA-2
Kephart Prong—*stream* NC-3
Kephart Run—*stream* VA-3
KEPH-FM (Ephraim)—*tower* UT-8
Kepidau Deleur—*channel* FM-9
Kepidauen Nahkapw—*channel* FM-9
Kepi Gulch—*valley* HI-9
Kepin Awak—*locale* FM-9
Kepin Awak, Pilen—*stream* FM-9
**Kepindau**—*pop pl* FM-9
Kepindau—*unknown* FM-9
Kepindeweiso—*bay* FM-9
Kepin Keileng—*locale* FM-9
Kepin Lahpar—*unknown* FM-9
Kepinlahpar, Dauen—*gut* FM-9
Kepin Lahpar, Pillap En—*stream* FM-9
**Kepinleh**—*pop pl* FM-9
Kepin Mahu—*valley* FM-9
Kepin Mweli—*locale* FM-9
Kepinne—*civil* FM-9
Kepinne—*valley* FM-9
Kepin Pehs—*unknown* FM-9
Kepin Pilen Luhke—*bay* FM-9
Kepin Rohi—*locale* FM-9
Kepin Semwei—*valley* FM-9
Kepin Souna—*unknown* FM-9
Kepin Uh—*unknown* FM-9
Kepinwou—*locale* FM-9
Kepio—*civil* HI-9
Kepio Point—*cape* HI-9
Kepira—*cape* FM-9
Kepirar—*bay* FM-9
Kepkep—*locale* FM-9
*Keplar* TN-4
Keplar Baptist Ch—*church* TN-4
Kepler—*locale* KY-4
Kepler—*locale* TN-4
Kepler Branch—*stream* WI-6
Kepler Cascades—*falls* WY-8
Kepler Coulee—*valley* MN-6
Kepler Creek—*stream* LA-4
Kepler Creek Lake—*reservoir* LA-4
Kepler Elem Sch—*school* TN-4
Kepler Lake—*lake* AK-9
Kepler Lake—*lake* MI-6
Keplers—*other* PA-2
**Keplers Mill**—*pop pl* PA-2
*Keplers Mills* PA-2
Keplers Mill Station—*building* PA-2
Kepler Trail—*trail* PA-2
Kepley Oil Field—*oilfield* KS-7
Keplinger, Harry A., House—*hist pl* IN-6
Keplinger Cave—*cave* TN-4
Keplinger Cem—*cemetery* IL-6
Keplinger Cem—*cemetery* TN-4
Keplinger Creek—*stream* TN-4
Keplinger Hollow—*valley* WV-2
Keplinger Lake—*lake* CO-8
Kepner—*locale* PA-2
Kepner Cem—*cemetery* MO-7
Kepner JHS—*school* CO-8
Kepner Knob—*summit* PA-2
Kepner Pond—*lake* FL-3
*Kepners Knob* PA-2
KEPO-FM—*tower* OR-9
Kepono—*cape* HI-9
Kepookoholua—*summit* HI-9
Keppel HS—*school* CA-9
Keppel Sch—*school* (2) CA-9
Keppen Sch—*school* MI-6
Kepper Cem—*cemetery* OH-6
Kepper Lake—*lake* MN-6
Kepple Bottoms—*bend* MT-8
Kepple Creek—*stream* AL-4
Kepple Creek—*stream* IL-6
**Kepple Hill**—*pop pl* PA-2
**Kepple Hill (Pleasant View)**—*pop pl* PA-2
Kepple Lake—*lake* MN-6
Kepple Lake—*lake* WA-9
Keppler Creek—*stream* LA-4
Keppler Ditch—*canal* OH-6
Kepples—*locale* PA-2
**Kepples Corner**—*pop pl* PA-2
**Kepples Corners**—*pop pl* PA-2
Kepples Ranch—*locale* MT-8
Keprohi—*civil* FM-9
Kepros Mtn—*summit* ID-8
**Keptown**—*pop pl* IL-6
*Kepuhi* HI-9
Kepuhi—*cape* (2) HI-9
Kepuhi—*locale* HI-9
Kepuhi O Kahio Point—*cape* HI-9
Kepuhi Point—*cape* (4) HI-9
Kepulauan Mapia—*island* FM-9
Kepuna Gulch—*valley* HI-9

Kepuni Gulch—*valley* HI-9
*Kequaseganset Pond* MA-1
Kera Lakes—*reservoir* WV-2
**Kera Landing**—*pop pl* WV-2
Keraland Rec Area—*park* WV-2
Keranen Creek—*stream* MI-6
Kerber Creek—*stream* CO-8
Kerberg Dam—*dam* SD-7
Kerber's Marine Grocery—*hist pl* OH-6
Kerbs Hosp—*hospital* VT-1
Kerbs Lake—*lake* MN-6
**Kerby**—*pop pl* MI-6
**Kerby**—*pop pl* OR-9
Kerby Brook—*stream* MA-1
Kerby Cem—*cemetery* AR-4
Kerby Cem—*cemetery* IA-7
Kerby Creek—*stream* OR-9
Kerby Ditch—*canal* OR-9
Kerby Field—*park* MI-6
Kerby Flat—*flat* OR-9
**Kerby Hill**—*pop pl* MD-2
Kerby Hill—*summit* OR-9
**Kerby Hills**—*pop pl* MD-2
Kerby Knob—*locale* KY-4
Kerby Mtn—*summit* OR-9
Kerby Peak—*summit* OR-9
Kerby Peak Trail—*trail* OR-9
Kerby Point—*cape* NY-2
Kerby Ridge—*ridge* OR-9
*Kerbys Bridge* AL-4
Kerby Slough—*stream* OR-9
Kerby Tank—*reservoir* TX-5
*Kerbyville* OR-9
Kerce Cem—*cemetery* FL-3
Kerch Canal—*canal* AR-4
Kerch Community Chapel—*church* MN-6
Kerch Ditch—*canal* IN-6
*Kercheval* MI-6
**Kercheval**—*pop pl* IN-6
Kercheval Ranch—*locale* WA-9
Kerchimbo Bay—*bay* LA-4
Kerchoff Powerhouse—*other* CA-9
Kerchurak Creek—*stream* AK-9
Kerckhoff Dam—*dam* CA-9
Kerckhoff Dome—*summit* CA-9
Kerckhoff Lake—*reservoir* CA-9
*Kere* MP-9
Kere—*island* MP-9
*Kerenegan* MP-9
Kerenegan—*island* MP-9
*Keren Neff Ditch* IN-6
Kerens—*locale* CA-9
**Kerens**—*pop pl* TX-5
**Kerens**—*pop pl* WV-2
Kerens (CCD)—*cens area* TX-5
Kerens Cem—*cemetery* TX-5
Kerens City Lake—*reservoir* TX-5
*Kere-To* MP-9
Kerf Creek—*stream* ID-8
Kerfoot—*locale* VA-3
Kerfoot Creek—*stream* WY-8
Kerfoot House—*hist pl* OK-5
Kerfoot Lakes—*lake* MN-6
Kergerson Lake—*lake* CA-9
**Kerhonkson**—*pop pl* NY-2
Kerhonkson Rsvr—*reservoir* NY-2
Keri—*locale* FL-3
Keril Canyon—*valley* CA-9
Keri Lookout Tower—*tower* FL-3
**Kerin**—*pop pl* MS-4
Kerir, Pilen—*stream* FM-9
*Kerkhoff Dome* CA-9
**Kerkhoven**—*pop pl* MN-6
**Kerkhoven (Township of)**—*pop pl* MN-6
Kerkoff Canyon—*valley* CA-9
Kerlagon Cem—*cemetery* MO-7
Kerlee Creek—*stream* ID-8
Kerlee Creek—*stream* MT-8
Kerlee Lake—*lake* MT-8
Kerlee Ridge—*ridge* ID-8
Kerless Knob—*summit* WV-2
Kerley Cem—*cemetery* AL-4
Kerley Cem—*cemetery* IL-6
Kerley Cem—*cemetery* TN-4
Kerley Hollow—*valley* TN-4
Kerley Post Office (historical)—*building* TN-4
Kerley Sch—*school* SD-7
**Kerleys Corners**—*pop pl* NY-2
Kerley Spring—*spring* AL-4
Kerley Valley—*valley* AZ-5
Kerlin—*locale* AR-4
Kerlin Cem—*cemetery* MO-7
Kerlin Creek—*stream* CA-9
**Kerlinger**—*pop pl* CA-9
Kerlin Hill—*summit* NM-5
Kerloo Creek—*stream* NE-7
*Kerl Station* FL-3
Kermac Mine No 22—*mine* NM-5
Kermac Mine No 30—*mine* NM-5
Kermac No 10 Mine—*mine* NM-5
Kermac Nuclear Fuels Processing Plant—*locale* NM-5
Ker Magee Lake Dam—*dam* MS-4
**Kerman**—*pop pl* CA-9
Kerman (CCD)—*cens area* CA-9
Kerman Spring—*spring* OR-9
Kerman Substation—*other* CA-9
Kerman Union HS—*school* CA-9
Kermit—*locale* NM-5
Kermit—*locale* ND-7
Kermit—*locale* VA-3
**Kermit**—*pop pl* TX-5
**Kermit**—*pop pl* WV-2
Kermit (CCD)—*cens area* TX-5
Kermit Daughterly Lake Dam—*dam* MS-4
Kermit-Johnson-Number 1 Dam—*dam* SD-7
Kermit (Magisterial District)—*fmr MCD* WV-2
Kermit Sand Hills—*other* TX-5
Kermit Windmill—*locale* TX-5
Kermode Ditch—*canal* CO-8
Kermon Gulch—*valley* AK-9
Kermsuh Lake—*lake* UT-8
*Kern* CA-9
*Kern* IN-6
Kern—*locale* AK-9
Kern—*locale* FL-3
Kern—*locale* MO-7
Kern, Rufus A., House—*hist pl* OH-6
Kernachan Cem—*cemetery* AL-4
Kernachan Plantation (historical)—*locale* AL-4

**Kernan**—*pop pl* IL-6
**Kernan**—*pop pl* LA-4
Kernan—*uninc pl* NY-2
Kernan, James Lawrence, Hosp—*hist pl* MD-2
Kernan Canyon—*valley* CO-8
**Kernan Corner**—*pop pl* NJ-2
Kernan Hosp—*hospital* MD-2
Kernan Lagoon—*lake* NE-7
Kernan Point—*cape* OR-9
Kernan Pond—*lake* NY-2
Kernan Sch—*school* NY-2
Kernan Spring—*spring* OR-9
Kern Basin—*basin* (2) OR-9
*Kern Bluff Oil Field* CA-9
Kern Branch—*stream* TN-4
Kern Branch—*stream* WV-2
Kern Branch, Beale Memorial Library—*hist pl* CA-9
Kern Bridge—*hist pl* MN-6
Kern Brothers Dam—*dam* OR-9
Kern Canyon—*valley* (2) CA-9
Kern Canyon—*valley* UT-8
Kern Canyon Ranger Station—*locale* CA-9
Kern Cem—*cemetery* IN-6
Kern Cem—*cemetery* MI-6
Kern Cem—*cemetery* OH-6
Kern Cem—*cemetery* VA-3
**Kern City**—*pop pl* CA-9
Kern City Golf Course—*other* CA-9
**Kern (County)**—*pop pl* CA-9
Kern County Industrial Farm—*locale* CA-9
Kern County Land Company Ranch—*locale* CA-9
Kern County Park—*park* CA-9
Kern County Regional Park—*park* CA-9
Kern Creek—*stream* (2) AK-9
Kern Creek—*stream* OR-9
Kern Creek—*stream* WI-6
Kern Creek Rsvr—*reservoir* OR-9
Kern Creek Spring—*spring* OR-9
Kern Ditch County Drain—*canal* CA-9
Kerndt, G., & Brothers Office Block—*hist pl* IA-7
Kerndt G., and Brothers Elevator and Warehouses, No. 11, No.12 and No.13—*hist pl* IA-7
Kerne Chapel—*church* NC-3
Kern Effigy (33WA372)—*hist pl* OH-6
Kernell—*locale* CA-9
Kerner Brook—*stream* NY-2
*Kerners Crossroads* NC-3
*Kerners Mill Creek* NC-3
Kerners Mill Creek—*stream* NC-3
**Kernersville**—*pop pl* NC-3
Kernersville Ch—*church* NC-3
Kernersville City Lake—*reservoir* NC-3
Kernersville Depot—*hist pl* NC-3
Kernersville Elem Sch—*school* NC-3
Kernersville Lake—*reservoir* NC-3
Kernersville Memorial Gardens—*cemetery* NC-3
Kernersville (Township of)—*fmr MCD* NC-3
Kernersville Water Supply Dam—*dam* NC-3
Kerner Village Shop Ctr—*locale* NC-3
Kerney Branch Sch—*school* SC-3
Kern Flat—*flat* CA-9
*Kern Front Oil Field* CA-9
Kern Glen—*basin* PA-2
Kern Glen Creek—*stream* PA-2
Kern Hollow—*valley* WV-2
**Kern Homes**—*pop pl* CA-9
Kernick Mine—*mine* NV-8
Kernie—*locale* KY-4
Kern Island Canal—*canal* CA-9
Kern Island Drain—*canal* CA-9
Kern Junction (Kern)—*uninc pl* CA-9
Kern Junior Acad—*school* CA-9
Kern-Kaweah River—*stream* CA-9
Kern Lake—*lake* CA-9
Kern Lake—*lake* NE-7
Kern Lake—*lake* WI-6
**Kern Lake**—*pop pl* CA-9
Kern Lake Bed—*flat* CA-9
Kern Memorial United Methodist Ch—*church* TN-4
Kern Mine—*mine* NM-5
Kern Mtns—*range* NV-8
Kern Neff Ditch—*canal* IN-6
Kernodle-Pickett House—*hist pl* NC-3
Kernoodle Lake—*reservoir* MO-7
**Kern Orchard**—*pop pl* KY-4
Kern Park—*park* TX-5
Kern Park—*park* WI-6
Kern Peak—*summit* CA-9
Kern Peak Stringer—*stream* CA-9
Kern Playground—*park* MI-6
Kern Point—*summit* (2) CA-9
Kern Ranch—*locale* WY-8
Kern Ridge—*ridge* (2) CA-9
*Kern River* CA-9
Kern River—*stream* CA-9
Kern River Channel—*stream* CA-9
Kern River Flood Canal—*canal* CA-9
Kern River Number One Flow Line—*canal* CA-9
*Kern River Oil Field* CA-9
Kern River State Park—*park* CA-9
Kern River Valley Cem—*cemetery* CA-9
Kern Rsvr—*reservoir* OR-9
Kern Run—*stream* PA-2
*Kerns* VA-3
Kerns—*locale* MN-6
Kerns—*locale* MT-8
Kerns—*locale* VA-3
**Kerns**—*pop pl* CO-8
Kern Saint Sch—*school* NC-3
Kerns Branch—*stream* TN-4
Kerns Cem—*cemetery* KS-7
Kerns Cem—*cemetery* OK-5
Kerns Cem—*cemetery* WV-2
Kern Sch—*school* MI-6
Kerns Chapel—*church* IL-6
Kerns Chapel—*church* MO-7
**Kerns Corner**—*pop pl* MI-6
Kerns Dam—*dam* PA-2
Kerns Hollow—*valley* OH-6
Kerns Hollow—*valley* VA-3
Kerns Hollow—*valley* WV-2
Kerns Lake—*lake* MT-8
Kerns Memorial Ch—*church* VA-3
*Kerns Mill* PA-2
Kerns Mtn—*summit* VA-3

Kerns Pond—*reservoir* GA-3
Kern Springs—*locale* VA-3
Kerns Quarry—*mine* TN-4
Kerns Ridge—*ridge* VA-3
Kerns Run—*stream* PA-2
Kerns Sch—*school* (2) IL-6
Kerns Sch—*school* OR-9
Kernstown—*locale* VA-3
*Kernsville* PA-2
**Kernsville**—*pop pl* PA-2
Kernsville Elem Sch—*school* PA-2
Kerns Waterhole—*lake* OR-9
**Kern Township**—*pop pl* ND-7
*Kernvale* CA-9
**Kernvale**—*pop pl* CA-9
Kern Valley HS—*school* CA-9
*Kernville* PA-2
**Kernville**—*pop pl* CA-9
**Kernville**—*pop pl* OR-9
**Kernville**—*pop pl* PA-2
Kernwood Park—*park* MA-1
Kerny Mine (underground)—*mine* AL-4
*Kerods Run* PA-2
*Keroke* MP-9
Keroma Community Hall—*building* KS-7
Keroma (historical)—*locale* KS-7
*Keroo Wharf* MD-2
Kerosene Cave—*cave* PA-2
Kerosene Lake—*lake* ID-8
Kerosene Pond—*lake* ME-1
Kerper City—*locale* CO-8
Kerr—*locale* AR-4
Kerr—*locale* (2) OH-6
Kerr—*locale* PA-2
**Kerr**—*pop pl* MN-6
**Kerr**—*pop pl* MS-4
**Kerr**—*pop pl* MO-7
**Kerr**—*pop pl* NC-3
**Kerr**—*pop pl* PA-2
**Kerr**—*pop pl* TX-5
Kerr, Albertina, Nursery—*hist pl* OR-9
Kerr, Andrew, House—*hist pl* DE-2
Kerr, Benjamin F., House—*hist pl* OH-6
Kerr, Beverly and Lula, House—*hist pl* TX-5
Kerr, Gen. William, House—*hist pl* NC-3
Kerr, James, House—*hist pl* NC-3
Kerr, John G., Company—*hist pl* IN-6
Kerr, Lake—*lake* FL-3
*Kerr Addition* PA-2
Kerr Ave Sch—*school* CA-9
Kerr-Boyd Cem—*cemetery* OH-6
Kerr Branch—*stream* AL-4
Kerr Branch—*stream* NC-3
Kerr Branch—*stream* TN-4
Kerr Branch—*stream* TX-5
Kerr Bridge—*bridge* MT-8
Kerr Brothers South Ranch—*locale* NM-5
Kerr Campground—*locale* WA-9
Kerr Canyon—*valley* ID-8
Kerr Canyon—*valley* (3) NM-5
Kerr Canyon—*valley* OR-9
Kerr Cave—*cave* AL-4
Kerr Cem—*cemetery* IN-6
Kerr Cem—*cemetery* (2) KY-4
Kerr Cem—*cemetery* MI-6
Kerr Cem—*cemetery* (2) MO-7
Kerr Cem—*cemetery* NC-3
Kerr Cem—*cemetery* OH-6
Kerr Cem—*cemetery* TN-4
Kerr Cem—*cemetery* TX-5
Kerr Chapel—*church* TX-5
**Kerr City**—*pop pl* FL-3
Kerr Community Center—*hist pl* TX-5
Kerr Corner—*locale* OH-6
Kerr Coulee—*valley* MT-8
**Kerr (County)**—*pop pl* TX-5
*Kerr Creek* SC-3
*Kerr Creek* VA-3
Kerr Creek—*stream* CA-9
Kerr Creek—*stream* (2) ID-8
Kerr Creek—*stream* IN-6
Kerr Creek—*stream* MI-6
Kerr Creek—*stream* NC-3
Kerr Creek—*stream* OR-9
Kerr Creek—*stream* SC-3
Kerr Creek—*stream* (2) TX-5
Kerr Creek—*stream* WA-9
Kerr Creek—*stream* WY-8
Kerr Dam—*dam* MT-8
Kerr Elem Sch—*school* PA-2
Kerr Gulch—*valley* (2) CO-8
*Kerr Hill* PA-2
Kerr Hill—*locale* MI-6
Kerr Hill—*summit* OK-5
Kerr Hill Ch—*church* PA-2
Kerrick—*locale* IL-6
**Kerrick**—*pop pl* MN-6
**Kerrick**—*pop pl* TX-5
Kerrick, W. T., House—*hist pl* KY-4
Kerrick Bridge—*bridge* VA-3
Kerrick Canyon—*valley* CA-9
Kerrick Gulch—*valley* CA-9
Kerrick Meadow—*flat* CA-9
Kerrick Sch—*school* KY-4
Kerrick Swamp—*swamp* MD-2
**Kerrick (Township of)**—*pop pl* MN-6
*Kerrigan Peak* AZ-5
Kerri Hills Sch—*school* CA-9
Kerrington Draw—*valley* SD-7
Kerr Island—*flat* IL-6
Kerr Island—*island* FL-3
Kerr Island—*island* IN-6
Kerriston—*locale* WA-9
Kerr JHS—*school* CA-9
Kerr JHS—*school* OK-5
Kerr Lake—*lake* CA-9
Kerr Lake—*lake* CO-8
Kerr Lake—*lake* (2) ID-8
Kerr Lake—*lake* MI-6
Kerr Lake—*lake* MN-6
Kerr Marsh—*swamp* NC-3
Kerr Mill—*hist pl* NC-3
Kerr Mill Park—*park* NC-3
Kerr Mine—*mine* MN-6
**Kerrmoor**—*pop pl* PA-2
Kerr Mtn—*summit* MT-8
Kerr Notch—*gap* OR-9
Kerr Park—*park* CA-9
Kerr Park—*park* OH-6
Kerr Park—*park* TX-5

Kerr-Patton House—*hist pl* NC-3
Kerr Peak—*summit* CA-9
Kerr Place—*hist pl* VA-3
Kerr Pond—*lake* ME-1
Kerr Ranch—*locale* NV-8
Kerr Ranch—*locale* (2) NM-5
Kerr Ranch—*locale* (2) TX-5
Kerr Research Center—*other* OK-5
*Kerr Reservoir* NC-3
*Kerr Reservoir* VA-3
Kerr Run—*stream* (3) OH-6
Kerrs Cem—*cemetery* OH-6
Kerr Sch—*school* LA-4
Kerr Sch—*school* OK-5
Kerr Sch—*school* (2) PA-2
Kerr Sch—*school* VA-3
Kerr Sch—*school* WV-2
Kerr Sch (abandoned)—*school* (2) PA-2
Kerrs Chapel—*church* NC-3
Kerrs Corners—*locale* NJ-2
**Kerrs Corners**—*pop pl* (2) PA-2
**Kerrs Creek**—*pop pl* (2) VA-3
Kerrs Creek—*stream* NY-2
Kerrs Creek—*stream* VA-3
Kerrs Creek Ch—*church* VA-3
Kerrs Creek (Magisterial District)—*fmr MCD* VA-3
Kerr Spring—*spring* CA-9
Kerr Spring—*spring* GA-3
Kerr Spring—*spring* NM-5
Kerr Spring—*spring* PA-2
Kerr Spring—*spring* TN-4
Kerrs Rapids—*rapids* ID-8
Kerrs Rapids—*rapids* OR-9
Kerrs (RR name for Kerr)—*other* OH-6
Kerrsville—*locale* PA-2
Kerr Tank—*lake* NM-5
Kerr Tank—*reservoir* (2) NM-5
**Kerrtown**—*pop pl* PA-2
Kerrtown Elem Sch—*school* PA-2
Kerrtown Sch (historical)—*school* PA-2
**Kerr (Township of)**—*pop pl* IL-6
Kerruish Park—*park* OH-6
Kerr Valley—*valley* OR-9
Kerrville—*locale* MO-7
**Kerrville**—*pop pl* TN-4
**Kerrville**—*pop pl* TX-5
Kerrville (CCD)—*cens area* TX-5
Kerrville Ch—*church* TN-4
Kerrville State Park—*park* TX-5
Kerrville Windmill—*locale* TX-5
Kerr Well—*well* NM-5
Kerr Well No 1—*locale* NM-5
Kerr Well No 2—*locale* NM-5
Kerr Wildlife Mngmt Area—*park* TX-5
Kerry—*locale* ND-7
**Kerry**—*pop pl* OR-9
Kerry, William, House—*hist pl* IN-6
Kerry Canyon—*valley* CA-9
Kerry Canyon Campground—*locale* CA-9
Kerry Canyon Trail—*trail* CA-9
Kerry Creek—*stream* WA-9
**Kerry Estates (subdivision)**—*pop pl* MS-4
Kerry Island—*island* OR-9
Kerry Lake—*lake* MN-6
**Kerry Siding**—*pop pl* NY-2
Kerryville—*locale* NY-2
Kerscoha Lake—*reservoir* AL-4
*Kersen Creek* WA-9
**Kersey**—*pop pl* CO-8
**Kersey**—*pop pl* IN-6
**Kersey**—*pop pl* PA-2
Kersey Branch—*stream* FL-3
Kersey Branch—*stream* NC-3
Kersey Cem—*cemetery* AR-4
Kersey Cem—*cemetery* GA-3
Kersey Cem—*cemetery* TX-5
*Kersey Coates* MO-7
Kersey Creek—*stream* IL-6
Kersey Creek—*stream* VA-3
Kersey Creek Canal—*canal* UT-8
Kersey Finney Ditch—*canal* IN-6
Kersey-Gill—*cens area* CO-8
Kersey Lake—*lake* GA-3
Kersey Lake—*lake* MT-8
Kersey Pond—*reservoir* AL-4
*Kersey Run* PA-2
Kersey Run—*stream* PA-2
**Kerseys Evergreen Acres**—*pop pl* DE-2
Kersha Bench—*bench* UT-8
Kersha Creek—*stream* UT-8
*Kershaw* NC-3
Kershaw—*locale* AL-4
Kershaw—*locale* MT-8
**Kershaw**—*pop pl* NC-3
**Kershaw**—*pop pl* SC-3
**Kershaw Acres (subdivision)**—*pop pl* DE-2
Kershaw Airp—*airport* AL-4
*Kershaw Branch* VA-3
Kershaw Canyon—*valley* NV-8
Kershaw (CCD)—*cens area* SC-3
**Kershaw (County)**—*pop pl* SC-3
Kershaw Creek—*stream* NC-3
Kershaw Ditch—*canal* CO-8
Kershaw Hollow—*valley* AL-4
Kershaw Lake—*lake* OR-9
Kershaw Mtn—*summit* MT-8
Kershaw-Ryan State Park—*park* NV-8
Kershaw Sch—*school* IL-6
Kershaw Sch—*school* NJ-2
**Kershaws Subdivision**—*pop pl* UT-8
Kershener Hill—*summit* NY-2
Kershner Bridge—*bridge* PA-2
Kershner Cem—*cemetery* MO-7
Kershner Ditch—*canal* WY-8
Kersky, Lake—*lake* FL-3
Kersten Creek—*stream* WI-6
Kersten Lake—*lake* WI-6
*Kerster Lake* WI-6
Kerstetter Path—*trail* PA-2
Kerstiens Dam—*dam* SD-7
Kersting Hosp—*hospital* TX-5
Kersting Lake—*lake* MN-6
**Kerston**—*pop pl* MI-6
Kerston Station—*locale* MI-6
Kerswill Acad—*school* SC-3
Kerswill Lake—*lake* MI-6
*Kerthaus* PA-2
Kerth Cem—*cemetery* WI-6
*Kertley Mountain* VA-3

Kerton Creek—*stream* IL-6
**Kerton (Township of)**—*pop pl* IL-6
Kerton Valley Sch—*school* IL-6
Kertsonville (Township of)—*civ div* MN-6
Keruluk Creek—*stream* AK-9
*Kerville* PA-2
Kervin Branch—*stream* LA-4
Kervin Cem—*cemetery* AL-4
Kerwin Brook—*stream* ME-1
Kerwin Lake—*lake* WA-9
*Kerwin Neck* MD-2
*Kerwin Poin* MD-2
*Kerwo* AZ-5
**Kerwo**—*pop pl* AZ-5
Kerwo Day Sch—*school* AZ-5
Kerwo Well—*well* AZ-5
Kerz—*locale* KY-4
*Kesagagan Lake* MN-6
Kesagiagan Lake—*lake* MN-6
*Kesagiagon Lake* MN-6
*Kesauaol* PW-9
Kescayo Gansett Pond—*lake* MA-1
KESD-FM (Brookings)—*tower* SD-7
*Keseayogansett Pond* MA-1
Kesebekuu, Toachel Ra—*channel* PW-9
Keseberg Canyon—*valley* OR-9
Keseha Ranch—*locale* AZ-5
Kesena Dam—*dam* AZ-5
Kesh Creek—*stream* ID-8
**Keshena**—*pop pl* WI-6
**Keshena Falls**—*pop pl* WI-6
Keshena Lake—*lake* WI-6
Keshena Sch—*school* WI-6
Keshequa Creek—*stream* NY-2
*Kesill Island* PW-9
Keski Island—*island* AK-9
Keskinen Airp—*airport* RI-1
Kesler Bridge—*bridge* GA-3
Kesler Covered Bridge—*hist pl* GA-3
Kesler Ditch—*canal* IN-6
Kesler Field Airp—*airport* IN-6
**Kesler Hills**—*pop pl* TN-4
Kesler Lake—*lake* MI-6
Kesler Manufacturing Co.-Cannon Mills Co. Plant No. 7 Hist Dist—*hist pl* NC-3
Kesler Ridge Sch—*school* KY-4
*Keslers* PA-2
Kesler Sch (historical)—*school* PA-2
*Keslers Crosslanes* WV-2
**Keslers Cross Lanes**—*pop pl* WV-2
Keslers Memorial Ch—*church* WV-2
Keslers Mill—*locale* VA-3
Keslerson Branch—*stream* VA-3
Kesler Tunnel—*tunnel* MD-2
*Keslerville* PA-2
**Kesley**—*pop pl* IA-7
Kesling JHS—*school* IN-6
Kesling Mill—*locale* WV-2
Kesling Sch—*school* WV-2
KESM-FM (Eldorado Springs)—*tower* MO-7
Kesner Cove—*valley* VA-3
*Kesoboku Einfahrt* PW-9
Kessay Spring—*spring* AZ-5
Kess Creek—*stream* KY-4
Kesse Cem—*cemetery* SC-3
Kessel—*locale* WV-2
Kessel Creek—*stream* WA-9
Kesseler Trail—*trail* PA-2
*Kessel Hill* PA-2
Kessel Ranch—*locale* ND-7
Kesselring Run—*stream* OH-6
Kessel Run—*stream* WV-2
Kessi Ditch—*canal* IN-6
*Kessing Creek* CA-9
Kessing Creek—*stream* CA-9
Kessinger—*locale* KY-4
Kessinger Ditch—*canal* IN-6
**Kessington**—*pop pl* MI-6
Kessiso Rocks—*bar* WA-9
Kessler—*locale* LA-4
**Kessler**—*pop pl* OH-6
**Kessler**—*pop pl* WV-2
Kessler Canyon—*valley* UT-8
Kessler Canyon—*valley* WY-8
Kessler Cem—*cemetery* ID-8
Kessler Cem—*cemetery* KY-4
Kessler Cem—*cemetery* (2) MO-7
Kessler Creek—*stream* ID-8
Kessler Creek—*stream* MO-7
Kessler Creek—*stream* OR-9
Kessler Creek Spring—*spring* ID-8
Kessler Ditch—*canal* WY-8
Kessler Flat—*flat* CA-9
Kessler Flats—*flat* MT-8
Kessler Gap—*gap* WY-8
Kessler Institute—*school* NJ-2
Kessler Krest Independent Baptist Ch—*church* IN-6
Kessler Lake—*lake* MI-6
*Kessler Mill* VA-3
Kessler Mtn—*summit* AR-4
Kessler Park—*uninc pl* TX-5
Kessler Peak—*summit* (2) CA-9
Kessler Peak—*summit* (2) UT-8
Kessler Run—*stream* OH-6
*Kesslers* PA-2
**Kesslers**—*pop pl* MT-8
Kessler Sch—*school* IL-6
Kessler Sch—*school* MT-8
Kessler Sch—*school* WA-9
*Kesslers Mill* VA-3
**Kesslers Mill**—*pop pl* VA-3
Kessler Spring—*spring* CA-9
Kessler Spring—*spring* UT-8
Kesslers Ranch—*locale* WA-9
Kesslers Sch (abandoned)—*school* PA-2
**Kesslersville**—*pop pl* PA-2
Kessler Tank—*reservoir* AZ-5
Kessler Tank—*reservoir* NM-5
*Kesslerville* PA-2
Kesslerville—*locale* PA-2
**Kesslerville**—*pop pl* PA-2
Kessner Bridge—*bridge* IN-6
Kessner Run—*stream* WV-2
Kesson Bayou—*bay* FL-3
**Kester**—*pop pl* CA-9
Kester Ave Sch—*school* CA-9
Kester Cem—*cemetery* (2) IN-6
Kester Creek—*stream* PA-2
Kester Ditch—*canal* CO-8

Kester Drain—*stream* MI-6
Kester Draw—*valley* WA-9
Kester Fly Inn Airp—*airport* IN-6
Kester Mine—*mine* OR-9
Kester Mtn—*summit* OK-5
Kester Pond—*reservoir* OR-9
Kesters Camp—*locale* CA-9
Kester Sch—*school* MT-8
Kestersen Lake—*reservoir* MO-7
Kesterson Cem—*cemetery* AR-4
Kesterson Cem—*cemetery* KY-4
Kesterson Cem—*cemetery* (3) TN-4
Kesterson Ditch—*canal* CA-9
Kesterson Mill—*locale* VA-3
Kesterson Ranch—*locale* MT-8
Kesterson Sch—*school* NE-7
Kesterson-Watkins House—*hist pl* TN-4
**Kester Subdivision**—*pop pl* UT-8
Kester Sweet Ditch—*canal* CO-8
Kestler Bldg—*hist pl* OH-6
Kestler Field—*park* FL-3
*Kestler Mountain* AR-4
Kestner Creek—*gut* FL-3
Kestner Creek—*stream* WA-9
Kestrel Island—*island* AK-9
KESTREL (steam yacht)—*hist pl* NJ-2
Keswick—*hist pl* VA-3
Keswick—*locale* VA-3
**Keswick**—*pop pl* CA-9
**Keswick**—*pop pl* IA-7
**Keswick**—*pop pl* KY-4
**Keswick**—*pop pl* MI-6
Keswick Christian Sch—*school* FL-3
Keswick Dam—*dam* CA-9
Keswick Ditch—*canal* CA-9
**Keswick Grove**—*pop pl* NJ-2
**Keswick Grove (Conference Grounds)**—*pop pl* NJ-2
Keswick Lake—*lake* NJ-2
**Keswick (subdivision)**—*pop pl* NC-3
Keswick Theatre—*hist pl* PA-2
Ketah Center (Shop Ctr)—*locale* FL-3
*Ketankin Creek* VA-3
Keta River—*stream* AK-9
*Ketavie Point* AK-9
**Ketchall (historical)**—*pop pl* TN-4
Ketchall Post Office (historical)—*building* TN-4
Ketchall Quarry—*mine* TN-4
Ketchalls Ford—*locale* TN-4
Ketcham—*locale* PA-2
Ketcham Bog—*swamp* ME-1
Ketcham Ditch—*canal* OH-6
Ketcham Drain—*stream* MI-6
Ketcham Lake—*lake* WI-6
Ketcham Sch—*school* DC-2
Ketcham Sch (historical)—*school* AL-4
Ketcham Slough—*stream* CA-9
*Ketch Brook* CT-1
Ketch Brook—*stream* CT-1
Ketch Creek—*stream* OK-5
*Ketchebedokee Creek* AL-4
*Ketchells Pond* PA-2
Ketchel Mtn—*summit* AR-4
Ketchem Cem—*cemetery* IN-6
Ketchem Creek—*stream* AK-9
Ketchem Dome—*summit* AK-9
Ketchem Sch (historical)—*school* MO-7
Ketchen—*locale* TN-4
Ketchen Cem—*cemetery* KY-4
*Ketchens Creek* TN-4
Ketchepedrakee Creek—*stream* AL-4
Ketchepedrakee Watershed Dam Number 15—*dam* AL-4
Ketcher Cem—*cemetery* OK-5
Ketcherside Dam—*dam* AZ-5
Ketcherside Fire Tower—*locale* AR-4
Ketcherside Gap—*gap* MO-7
*Ketcherside Mountain* TN-4
Ketcherside Mtn—*summit* MO-7
Ketchersid Mtn—*summit* TN-4
Ketcher Spring—*spring* OK-5
Ketch Hill—*summit* OK-5
Ketch Hollow—*valley* WV-2
*Ketch Hollow Brook* CT-1
**Ketchikan**—*pop pl* AK-9
Ketchikan (Census Subarea)—*cens area* AK-9
Ketchikan Coast Guard Base—*military* AK-9
Ketchikan Creek—*stream* AK-9
Ketchikan Creek—*stream* MT-8
Ketchikan East—*CDP* AK-9
**Ketchikan Gateway (Borough)**—*pop pl* AK-9
Ketchikan Harbor—*harbor* AK-9
Ketchikan International Airp—*airport* AK-9
Ketchikan Ranger House—*hist pl* AK-9
Ketchikan Rifle Range—*other* AK-9
Ketchin Bldg—*hist pl* SC-3
Ketchin Butte—*summit* OR-9
Ketchketch Butte—*summit* OR-9
Ketch Lake—*reservoir* OK-5
*Ketch Mills* CT-1
Ketch Point—*cape* VA-3
Ketch Pond—*lake* ME-1
Ketch Ranch—*locale* OK-5
Ketchum—*locale* ME-1
**Ketchum**—*pop pl* ID-8
**Ketchum**—*pop pl* OK-5
Ketchum, B., House—*hist pl* NY-2
Ketchum, Lake—*lake* WA-9
Ketchum Branch—*stream* GA-3
Ketchum Branch—*stream* VA-3
Ketchum Brook—*stream* VT-1
Ketchum Buttes—*summit* WY-8
Ketchum Cem—*cemetery* TN-4
Ketchum Cem—*cemetery* VA-3
Ketchum Corners—*locale* NY-2
Ketchum Creek—*stream* MI-6
Ketchum Creek—*stream* WI-6
Ketchum Dam—*dam* OR-9
Ketchum Ditch—*canal* CA-9
Ketchum Gulch—*valley* CA-9
Ketchum Hollow—*valley* MO-7
Ketchum Island—*island* WI-6
Ketchum Lake—*lake* ME-1
Ketchum Lake—*lake* MI-6
Ketchum Lake—*lake* MN-6
Ketchum Lake—*lake* SD-7
Ketchum Lake—*lake* WI-6
Ketchum Lake State Public Shooting Area—*park* SD-7

Ketchum Mine—*mine* UT-8
Ketchum Mtn—*summit* TX-5
Ketchum Oil Field—*oilfield* TX-5
Ketchum Park—*park* MI-6
Ketchum Pond—*lake* NC-3
Ketchum Pond—*lake* OR-9
Ketchum Rsvr—*reservoir* OR-9
Ketchum Run—*stream* PA-2
**Ketchums Corner**—*pop pl* NY-2
Ketchum Spring—*spring* TX-5
**Ketchum Subdivision**—*pop pl* UT-8
Ketchumup Stock Trail—*trail* CO-8
**Ketchumville**—*pop pl* NY-2
Ketchumville Branch—*stream* NY-2
Ketchumville State For—*forest* NY-2
Ketchum Well—*well* SD-7
**Ketchuptown**—*pop pl* SC-3
KETC-TV (St Louis)—*tower* MO-7
**Keteban Switch (historical)**—*pop pl* IA-7
Ket Hing Society Bldg—*hist pl* HI-9
Ketik River—*stream* AK-9
Ketili Creek—*gut* AK-9
Ketili River—*gut* AK-9
Ketler Sch—*school* NJ-2
Ketlkede Creek—*stream* AK-9
Ketlkede Mtn—*summit* AK-9
*Ketman Ditch* IN-6
Ketnel Park—*park* SD-7
Ketner—*locale* PA-2
Ketner Branch—*stream* GA-3
Ketner Chapel—*church* NC-3
Ketner Cove Lake—*reservoir* TN-4
Ketner Cove Lake Dam—*dam* TN-4
Ketner Gap—*gap* TN-4
**Ketner Heights (subdivision)**—*pop pl* NC-3
Ketner Mill—*locale* TN-4
Ketner Rsvr—*reservoir* CO-8
Ketner's Mill and Bridge—*hist pl* TN-4
Ketners Point—*cape* WA-9
Ketoctin Cem—*cemetery* VA-3
Ketoctin Ch—*church* VA-3
Ketok Mtn—*summit* AK-9
**Ketona**—*pop pl* AL-4
Ketona Bridge Cave—*cave* AL-4
*Ketona Cave* AL-4
Ketona JHS—*school* AL-4
Ketona Lakes—*lake* AL-4
Ketowke Mtn—*summit* MT-8
Ketron—*locale* VA-3
Ketron—*locale* WA-9
Ketron Branch—*stream* VA-3
Ketron Camp Branch—*stream* NC-3
Ketron Cem—*cemetery* TX-5
Ketron Cem—*cemetery* VA-3
Ketron Ch—*church* WV-2
Ketron Chapel—*church* VA-3
Ketron HS—*school* TN-4
Ketron Island—*island* WA-9
*Ketron MS* TN-4
**Ketrontown**—*pop pl* VA-3
Ketscher Ranch—*locale* CA-9
Kett—*locale* CA-9
*Kettellville* NY-2
*Kettem Hill Creek* AL-4
Kettenbach, Henry C., House—*hist pl* ID-8
Ketten Lake—*lake* MN-6
Kettenpom—*locale* CA-9
Kettenpom Creek—*stream* CA-9
Kettenpom Peak—*summit* CA-9
Kettenpom Valley—*valley* CA-9
Ketter, Frederick, Warehouse—*hist pl* WI-6
Ketterer, Emil, House—*hist pl* MT-8
Ketterer Ditch—*canal* MT-8
Ketter Hollow—*valley* IN-6
Ketterina Branch—*stream* IL-6
Kettering—*CDP* MD-2
**Kettering**—*pop pl* OH-6
Kettering, Charles F., House—*hist pl* OH-6
Kettering, William, Homestead—*hist pl* OH-6
Kettering Field—*park* OH-6
**Kettering (historical)**—*pop pl* OR-9
Kettering HS—*school* MI-6
Kettering Memorial Hosp—*hospital* OH-6
Kettering Sch—*school* CA-9
Kettering Sch—*school* MI-6
Kettering Sch—*school* OH-6
Ketterlinc Cem—*cemetery* SD-7
Ketterlinus JHS—*school* FL-3
Ketterman—*locale* WV-2
Ketterman Knob—*summit* WV-2
*Kettintelbe* CA-9
Kettle—*locale* KY-4
Kettle—*locale* WV-2
Kettle, The—*basin* AZ-5
Kettle, The—*basin* TX-5
Kettle, The—*basin* VA-3
Kettle, The—*locale* PA-2
Kettle, The—*other* PA-2
Kettle, The—*valley* TN-4
Kettle Beaver—*swamp* NY-2
Kettle Belly Glade—*flat* OR-9
Kettlebelly Ridge—*ridge* CA-9
Kettlebottom—*bar* MA-1
Kettlebottom—*basin* ME-1
Kettle Bottom Rock—*pillar* RI-1
Kettle Branch—*stream* AL-4
Kettle Branch—*stream* GA-3
Kettle Branch—*stream* SC-3
Kettle Branch—*stream* (2) TN-4
*Kettle Brook* CT-1
Kettle Brook—*stream* (2) CT-1
Kettle Brook—*stream* MA-1
Kettle Brook—*stream* VT-1
Kettle Brook Reservoir Number 1 Dam—*dam* MA-1
Kettle Brook Reservoir Number 2 Dam—*dam* MA-1
Kettle Brook Reservoir Number 3 Dam—*dam* MA-1
Kettle Brook Reservoir Number 4 Dam—*dam* MA-1
Kettle Brook Rsvr Number Four—*reservoir* MA-1
Kettle Brook Rsvr Number One—*reservoir* MA-1
Kettle Brook Rsvr Number Three—*reservoir* MA-1
Kettle Brook Rsvr Number Two—*reservoir* MA-1
Kettle Butte—*summit* ID-8

Kettle Butte Drain—*stream* ID-8
Kettle Camp—*locale* CO-8
Kettlecamp Branch—*stream* KY-4
Kettlecamp Cem—*cemetery* IL-6
Kettlecamp Ch—*church* KY-4
Kettle Canyon—*valley* VA-3
Kettle Cape—*cape* AK-9
Kettle Ch—*church* TN-4
*Kettle Corner* RI-1
Kettle Corner—*locale* RI-1
Kettle Cove—*bay* ME-1
Kettle Cove—*cove* (2) MA-1
**Kettle Cove Village**—*pop pl* MA-1
*Kettle Creek* ID-8
*Kettle Creek* NJ-2
*Kettle Creek* OR-9
*Kettle Creek* UT-8
Kettle Creek—*stream* AR-4
Kettle Creek—*stream* CO-8
Kettle Creek—*stream* CT-1
Kettle Creek—*stream* FL-3
Kettle Creek—*stream* (2) GA-3
Kettle Creek—*stream* (2) ID-8
Kettle Creek—*stream* IN-6
Kettle Creek—*stream* IA-7
Kettle Creek—*stream* (2) KY-4
Kettle Creek—*stream* MS-4
Kettle Creek—*stream* MO-7
Kettle Creek—*stream* NJ-2
Kettle Creek—*stream* (4) OR-9
Kettle Creek—*stream* (4) PA-2
Kettle Creek—*stream* TN-4
Kettle Creek—*stream* UT-8
Kettle Creek—*stream* WA-9
Kettle Creek—*stream* WV-2
Kettle Creek—*stream* WY-8
Kettle Creek—*swamp* FL-3
Kettle Creek Battlefield—*hist pl* GA-3
Kettle Creek Ch—*church* GA-3
Kettle Creek Gorge—*valley* PA-2
Kettle Creek Gorge Natural Area—*area* PA-2
Kettle Creek Lake—*reservoir* PA-2
Kettle Creek Lake Dam—*dam* PA-2
Kettle Creek Sch—*school* (2) KY-4
Kettle Creek State Park—*park* PA-2
Kettle Creek Trail—*trail* OR-9
Kettle Dome—*pillar* CA-9
Kettle Dome—*summit* AK-9
Kettle Falls—*locale* MN-6
**Kettle Falls**—*pop pl* WA-9
Kettle Falls (CCD)—*cens area* WA-9
Kettle Falls Dam—*dam* MN-6
Kettle Falls District—*hist pl* WA-9
Kettle Falls Hist Dist—*hist pl* MN-6
Kettle Falls Hotel—*hist pl* MN-6
Kettlefield Knob—*summit* WV-2
*Kettle Foot Lookout Tower* TN-4
Kettlefoot Lookout Tower—*locale* TN-4
Kettlefoot Wildlife Mngmt Area—*park* TN-4
Kettle Gap—*gap* KY-4
Kettle Gap—*gap* PA-2
Kettle Gap—*gap* TN-4
Kettle Gulch—*valley* CO-8
Kettle Gulch—*valley* WY-8
Kettle Hammock—*island* FL-3
Kettle Harbor—*harbor* FL-3
Kettle Hill—*summit* NY-2
Kettle Hill—*summit* PA-2
Kettle Hole—*basin* PA-2
Kettle Hole—*bend* PA-2
Kettle Hole Pond—*lake* RI-1
Kettle Hole Trail—*trail* PA-2
Kettle Hollow—*valley* (2) AR-4
Kettle Hollow—*valley* MO-7
Kettle Hollow—*valley* MT-8
Kettle Hollow—*valley* (2) TN-4
Kettle Hollow—*valley* TX-5
Kettle Hollow—*valley* (3) VA-3
Kettle Hollow—*valley* WI-6
Kettle Hollow Sch—*school* TN-4
Kettle Island—*island* FL-3
Kettle Island—*island* MA-1
**Kettle Island**—*pop pl* KY-4
Kettle Island Branch—*stream* KY-4
Kettle Island Cem—*cemetery* KY-4
Kettle Island Ledge—*rock* MA-1
Kettle-Jens House—*hist pl* CO-8
*Kettle Lake* MI-6
*Kettle Lake* WI-6
Kettle Lake—*lake* ID-8
Kettle Lake—*lake* (2) MI-6
Kettle Lake—*lake* (4) MN-6
Kettle Lake—*lake* NY-2
Kettle Lake—*lake* ND-7
Kettle Lake—*lake* OR-9
Kettle Lake—*lake* SD-7
Kettle Lake—*lake* WA-9
Kettle Lake—*lake* (3) WI-6
Kettle Lake—*reservoir* MS-4
Kettle Lake Sch—*school* MI-6
Kettle Lake Swamp—*swamp* MI-6
Kettleman—*locale* CA-9
Kettleman Cem—*cemetery* MS-4
**Kettleman City**—*pop pl* CA-9
Kettleman Compressor Station—*other* CA-9
Kettleman Hills—*other* CA-9
Kettleman Hills Compressor Station—*other* CA-9
Kettleman Plain—*plain* CA-9
Kettleman Station—*other* CA-9
**Kettleman Station**—*pop pl* CA-9
**Kettle Mills**—*pop pl* TN-4
Kettle Moraine Lake—*lake* WI-6
Kettle Moraine State Correctional Institute—*other* WI-6
Kettle Moraine State For—*forest* WI-6
Kettle Moraine Youth Camp—*locale* WI-6
Kettle Mtn—*summit* CA-9
Kettle Mtn—*summit* (2) NY-2
Kettle Mtn—*summit* VT-1
Kettle Peak—*summit* (2) CA-9
Kettle Point—*cape* RI-1
Kettle Pond—*lake* CT-1
Kettle Pond—*lake* (2) NY-2
Kettle Pond—*lake* VT-1
Kettle Pond—*reservoir* VA-3
Kettler Cem—*cemetery* AL-4
Kettle Ridge—*ridge* CA-9
**Kettle River**—*pop pl* MN-6
Kettle River—*stream* (2) MN-6

Kettle River—stream ... WA-9
Kettle River Arm—bay ... WA-9
Kettle River Campground—locale ... WA-9
Kettle River Mine—mine ... WA-9
Kettle River Slough—gut ... MN-6
Kettle River (Township of)—civ div ... MN-6
Kettle Rock—pillar ... OR-9
Kettle Rock—summit ... CA-9
Kettle Rock—summit ... NC-3
Kettle Rock Lake—lake ... CA-9
Kettle Rock Spring—spring ... CA-9
Kettler Park—park ... IN-6
**Kettlersville**—pop pl ... OH-6
Kettle Rsvr—reservoir ... PA-2
*Kettle Run* ... PA-2
Kettle Run—stream (2) ... NJ-2
Kettle Run—stream (2) ... OH-6
Kettle Run—stream (3) ... PA-2
Kettle Run—stream (2) ... VA-3
Kettle Run—stream (3) ... WV-2
*Kettle Run Gap* ... PA-2
Kettles, The—basin ... ID-8
Kettles Creek—stream ... VA-3
Kettleson Meadow—flat ... OR-9
Kettle Spring—spring ... ID-8
Kettle Spring Run—stream ... PA-2
Kettle Springs Mtn—summit ... PA-2
Kettlestick Branch—stream ... VA-3
Kettlesticks Creek—stream ... VA-3
Kettle Top Butte—summit ... NM-5
Kettle Top Butte Site (LA48995)—hist pl ... NM-5
Kettletown Brook—stream ... CT-1
Kettletown State Park—park ... CT-1
Kettle Trail—trail (2) ... PA-2
Kettling Creek—stream ... WA-9
Kettling Lake—lake ... WA-9
Kettner Canyon—valley ... NM-5
Ketton Cem—cemetery ... TN-4
Ketty Gulch—valley ... CA-9
Ketund, Rois—summit ... PW-9
*Ketzel Island* ... OH-6
Keuffel and Esser Manufacturing Complex—hist pl ... NJ-2
Keuffel Cem—cemetery ... TX-5
Keughen Ditch—canal ... MT-8
**Keuka**—pop pl ... FL-3
**Keuka**—pop pl ... NY-2
Keuka, Lake—lake ... FL-3
Keuka Coll—school ... NY-2
Keuka Inlet—stream ... NY-2
Keuka Lake—lake ... NY-2
Keuka Lake Ch—church ... NY-2
Keuka Lake Outlet—stream ... NY-2
**Keuka Park**—pop pl ... NY-2
Keuning Sch (historical)—school ... SD-7
Keuny Cabin (ruins)—locale ... OR-9
**Keuterville**—pop pl ... ID-8
Kevan Mtn—summit ... MT-8
Kevet—locale ... CA-9
**Kevil**—pop pl ... KY-4
Keviles Hill—summit ... NY-2
Kevin—locale ... MN-6
**Kevin**—pop pl ... MT-8
Kevin Depot—hist pl ... MT-8
Kevinjik Creek—stream ... AK-9
Kevin Lake—lake ... WY-8
Kevin Mine—mine ... MN-6
Kevin Sunburst Oil Field—oilfield ... MT-8
**Kevin (Williams)**—pop pl ... TX-5
**Kevinwood Estates Subdivision**—pop pl ... UT-8
Kevuk Creek—stream ... AK-9
Kew—locale ... IA-7
**Kew**—pop pl ... MI-6
Kewa—locale ... WA-9
Kewa Cem—cemetery ... WA-9
*Kewadin* ... ME-1
*Kewadin* ... MI-6
*Kewadin* ... MN-6
*Kewadin* ... PA-2
**Kewadin**—pop pl ... MI-6
Ke-wag-a-wan Lake—lake ... MI-6
Kewagek Creek—stream ... AK-9
*Kewahatchee* ... AL-4
Kewahatchie—locale ... AL-4
Kewahatchie Spring—spring ... AL-4
Kewalo Basin—harbor ... HI-9
Kewanee—locale ... GA-3
Kewanee—locale ... KY-4
Kewanee—locale ... MS-4
**Kewanee**—pop pl ... IL-6
**Kewanee**—pop pl ... MO-7
Kewanee, Lake—reservoir ... PA-2
Kewanee Post Office (historical)—building ... MS-4
**Kewanee (Township of)**—pop pl ... IL-6
**Kewanna**—pop pl ... IN-6
Kewanna Elem Sch—school ... IN-6
Kewa Sch—school ... WA-9
**Kewaskum**—pop pl ... WI-6
**Kewaskum (Town of)**—pop pl ... WI-6
Kewaskum Union Cem—cemetery ... WI-6
*Kewasokogan Lake* ... WI-6
**Kewaunee**—pop pl ... WI-6
**Kewaunee (County)**—pop pl ... WI-6
Kewaunee Nuclear Powerplant—other ... WI-6
Kewaunee River—stream ... WI-6
Kewaunee River State Public Fishery Area—park ... WI-6
Kewaunee State Public Hunting Grounds—park ... WI-6
Kewawenon Mission—hist pl ... MI-6
Kewee Creek—stream ... WV-2
Keweenaw Bay—bay ... MI-6
**Keweenaw Bay**—pop pl ... MI-6
Keweenaw Bay Cem—cemetery ... MI-6
**Keweenaw (County)**—pop pl ... MI-6
Keweenaw County Park—park ... MI-6
Keweenaw Mountain Lodge and Golf Course Complex—hist pl ... MI-6
Keweenaw Peninsula—cape ... MI-6
Keweenaw Point—cape ... MI-6
Kewee Ridge—ridge ... WV-2
Kew-Forest Sch—school ... NY-2
**Kew Gardens**—pop pl ... NY-2
Kew Hill—summit ... VT-1
Kewin Park—park ... CA-9
Kewley Ranch—locale ... SD-7
Kew Sch—school ... CA-9

KEX-AM—tower ... OR-9
KEXS-AM (Excelsior Springs)—tower ... MO-7
Key—locale ... IA-7
Key—locale ... TN-4
Key—locale ... TX-5
**Key**—pop pl ... AL-4
**Key**—pop pl ... OH-6
**Key**—pop pl ... SC-3
**Key**—pop pl ... WV-2
Key, Francis Scott, Sch—hist pl ... PA-2
Key, George, Ranch—hist pl ... CA-9
Key Acres Dam—dam ... TN-4
Key Acres Lake—reservoir ... TN-4
KEYA-FM (Belcourt)—tower ... ND-7
Key Allegro (Frandolig Island)—island ... TX-5
Keyaluvik—locale ... AK-9
Keya Paha—fmr MCD ... NE-7
Keyapaha—locale ... SD-7
Keya Paha County HS—hist pl ... NE-7
*Keyapaha River* ... SD-7
Keya Paha River—stream ... NE-7
Keya Paha River—stream ... SD-7
**Keyapaha Township**—pop pl ... SD-7
Key Basin—basin ... AL-4
*Key Bay* ... MI-6
Key Bay—bay ... SC-3
**Key Biscayne**—pop pl ... FL-3
*Key Biscayne Bay* ... FL-3
Key Biscayne (CCD)—cens area ... FL-3
Key Biscayne Elem Sch—school ... FL-3
Key Biscayne Shop Ctr—locale ... FL-3
Keyboard of the Winds—pillar ... CO-8
Keyboard Pond—lake ... CT-1
*Key Branch* ... LA-4
*Key Branch* ... NJ-2
Key Branch—stream (2) ... AL-4
Key Branch—stream ... AR-4
Key Branch—stream ... LA-4
Key Branch—stream ... MS-4
Key Branch—stream ... NC-3
Key Branch—stream ... SC-3
Key Branch—stream ... TN-4
Key Bridge—bridge ... DC-2
Key Bridge—bridge ... SC-3
Key Cabin Tank—reservoir ... TX-5
Key Camp—locale ... AL-4
Key Cave—cave ... AL-4
Key Cem—cemetery (6) ... AL-4
Key Cem—cemetery ... AR-4
Key Cem—cemetery ... GA-3
Key Cem—cemetery ... KY-4
Key Cem—cemetery ... LA-4
Key Cem—cemetery ... OR-9
Key Cem—cemetery (4) ... TN-4
Key Center—locale ... WA-9
Key Ch—church ... TN-4
**Key Colony Beach**—pop pl ... FL-3
Key Colony Beach Shop Ctr—locale ... FL-3
Key Corner—locale ... TN-4
*Key Creek* ... AL-4
Key Creek—gut ... SC-3
Key Creek—stream ... AK-9
Key Creek—stream ... CO-8
Key Creek—stream ... GA-3
Key Creek—stream ... ID-8
Key Creek—stream ... KY-4
Key Creek—stream ... MO-7
Key Creek—stream ... TX-5
*Key East* ... NJ-2
*Key Elementary School* ... MS-4
*Key Elm Sch* ... PA-2
Keyer Brook—stream ... VT-1
*Keyes* ... SD-7
**Keyes**—pop pl ... CA-9
**Keyes**—pop pl ... OK-5
Keyes Branch—stream ... MO-7
*Keyes Branch Creek* ... MO-7
*Keyes Brook* ... MA-1
Keyes Brook—stream ... ME-1
Keyes Brook—stream (2) ... MA-1
Keyes Brook—stream ... NY-2
Keyes Bungalow—hist pl ... CA-9
Keyes Canyon—valley ... CA-9
Keyes (CCD)—cens area ... OK-5
Keyes Cem—cemetery ... IN-6
Keyes Cem—cemetery ... TX-5
Keyes Corner—locale ... ME-1
*Keyes Creek* ... CA-9
*Keyes Creek* ... OR-9
Keyes Creek—stream ... OR-9
Keyes Creek—stream ... WI-6
Keyes Dam—dam ... AL-4
Keyes Draw—valley ... WY-8
**Keyeser**—pop pl ... WI-6
*Keyes Gap* ... VA-3
*Keyes Gap* ... WV-2
Keyes Helium Plant—other ... OK-5
Keyes Hollow—locale ... NH-1
*Keyes Lake* ... ND-7
Keyes Lake—lake ... MN-6
Keyes Lake—lake (2) ... WI-6
Keyes Lake—reservoir ... AL-4
Keyes Memorial Beach—beach ... MA-1
Keyes Mine—mine ... CA-9
*Keyes Mtn* ... OR-9
Keyes Mtn—summit ... OR-9
Keyes Mtn—summit ... VT-1
Keyes Peak—summit ... CA-9
Keyes Point—cape ... AK-9
Keyes Point—cape ... TN-4
Keyes Point—locale ... TN-4
Keyes Point Dikes—levee ... TN-4
Keyes Point Landing—locale ... TN-4
*Keyes Point Revetment* ... TN-4
*Keyes Pond* ... ME-1
Keyes Pond—lake ... MA-1
**Keyesport**—pop pl ... IL-6
Keyesport Access Area—locale ... IL-6
Keyesport Landing—locale ... IL-6
Keyesport Oil Field—other ... IL-6
Keyes Sch—school ... TX-5
Keyes Sch (historical)—school ... MO-7
**Keyes Summit**—pop pl ... MO-7
Keyes Swamp—swamp ... MA-1
Key Estero Island Shops—locale ... FL-3
Keyesville—locale ... CA-9
**Keyesville**—pop pl ... WI-6
Keyes Well—well ... NM-5
Key Field (airport)—airport ... MS-4
Key Field (Airport)—airport ... MS-4

Key Flower Mine—mine ... NV-8
Key Ford—locale ... TN-4
Keyger Mtn—summit ... MO-7
Key Gully—valley ... TX-5
*Keyhatchie* ... AL-4
Key Haven—other ... FL-3
*Key Hill* ... NY-2
**Key Hill**—pop pl ... AL-4
Key Hill Ch—church ... AL-4
Key Hill Lookout Tower—locale ... AR-4
Keyhold Cave—cave ... TN-4
Keyhole—locale ... CO-8
Keyhole, The—arch ... CO-8
Keyhole, The—gap ... CA-9
Keyhole, The—gap ... CO-8
**Keyhole, The**—pop pl ... FL-3
Keyhole, The—summit ... CO-8
Keyhole Arch—arch ... UT-8
*Keyhole Bridge* ... AZ-5
Keyhole Canyon—valley ... NV-8
Keyhole Canyon Archeol Site—locale ... NV-8
Keyhole Cave—cave ... MT-8
Keyhole Cave—cave ... TN-4
Keyhole Dam—dam ... AZ-5
Keyhole Dam—dam ... WY-8
Keyhole House—hist pl ... MS-4
Keyhole Natural Bridge—arch ... AZ-5
Keyhole Ranch—locale ... WY-8
Keyhole Rsvr—reservoir ... WY-8
*Keyhole Ruin* ... UT-8
Keyhole Ruins—locale ... UT-8
Keyhole Windmill—locale ... NM-5
Key Hollow—valley ... AL-4
Key Hollow—valley (2) ... TN-4
Key Inlet—gut ... SC-3
Key Lake—lake ... WI-6
**Key Largo**—pop pl ... FL-3
Key Largo Anglers Club Pier Light—locale ... FL-3
Key Largo Baptist Temple—church ... FL-3
Key Largo Beacon Number 22—locale ... FL-3
Key Largo Beacon Number 29—locale ... FL-3
Key Largo Beacon Number 33—locale ... FL-3
Key Largo Christian Acad—school ... FL-3
Key Largo Club—locale ... FL-3
Key Largo Elem Sch—school ... FL-3
Key Largo Hammocks State Botanical Site—park ... FL-3
Key Largo Natl Marine Sanctuary—park ... FL-3
**Key Largo Park (subdivision)**—pop pl ... FL-3
**Key Largo Village**—pop pl ... FL-3
*Key Largo Waterway* ... FL-3
Keylon Hollow—valley ... TN-4
Keylon Springs—spring ... TN-4
**Keymar**—pop pl ... MD-2
Key Memorial Chapel—hist pl ... NC-3
*Keymes Beach* ... WA-9
**Keymes Beach**—pop pl ... WA-9
*Key Mill* ... AL-4
Key Mill Branch—stream ... AL-4
Key Mine—mine ... AZ-5
Key Mtn—summit ... AR-4
KEYN-FM (Wichita)—tower ... KS-7
**Keyno**—pop pl ... AL-4
Keynot Canyon—valley ... CA-9
*Keynote Peak* ... CA-9
Keynot Peak—summit ... CA-9
*Key Paha River* ... NE-7
*Key Paha River* ... SD-7
Key Park—park ... MN-6
Key Peninsula—cape ... WA-9
Key Pittman Wildlife Mngmt Area—park ... NV-8
Key Plantation (historical)—locale ... AL-4
Key Plaza (Shop Ctr)—locale ... FL-3
Key Plaza Shop Ctr—locale ... FL-3
Key Point—cape ... FL-3
*Key Pond* ... MA-1
Key Pond—lake ... FL-3
**Keyport**—pop pl ... NJ-2
**Keyport**—pop pl ... WA-9
**Keyport**—pop pl ... WV-2
Keyport Harbor—bay ... NJ-2
Keyport Naval Torpedo Station—other ... WA-9
Key Post Office (historical)—building ... AL-4
Key Post Office (historical)—building ... TN-4
Key Ranch—locale ... MT-8
Key Ranch—locale (2) ... NM-5
Key Reed Gap—gap ... TN-4
Key Reef—bar ... AK-9
Key Reef Rock—other ... AK-9
Key Ridge—ridge ... OH-6
Key Ridge Sch—school ... OH-6
*Key Rock* ... WV-2
**Keyrock**—pop pl ... WV-2
Keyrock Ch—church ... WV-2
*Key Royale* ... FL-3
Key Run—stream ... VA-3
*Keys* ... NJ-2
Keys—locale ... IL-6
**Keys**—pop pl ... FL-3
**Keys**—pop pl ... OK-5
**Keys**—pop pl ... PA-2
Keys, Thomas Isaac, House—hist pl ... MS-4
Keysacker Cem—cemetery ... IN-6
*Keys Branch* ... NJ-2
Keys Branch—stream ... GA-3
Keys Branch—stream ... TN-4
Keys Branch—stream (2) ... TX-5
Keys Brook—stream ... ME-1
Keys Brothers Ranch—locale ... MT-8
**Keysburg**—pop pl ... AL-4
**Keysburg**—pop pl ... KY-4
*Keysburgh* ... AL-4
Keys Camp—locale ... TX-5
Keys Canal—canal ... NC-3
Keys Canyon—valley ... CA-9
Keys Cem—cemetery ... AL-4
Keys Cem—cemetery ... MS-4
Keys Cem—cemetery ... OH-6
Keys Cem—cemetery ... OK-5
Keys Cem—cemetery ... WV-2
Keys Ch—church ... MS-4
Key Sch—school ... CA-9
Key Sch—school ... DC-2
Key Sch—school ... GA-3
Key Sch—school ... IL-6
Key Sch—school ... MI-6
Key Sch—school ... MS-4
Key Sch—school ... OK-5
Key Sch—school ... PA-2
Keys Chapel—church ... MS-4

**Keys Chapel**—pop pl ... TN-4
Keys Chapel (historical)—church ... AL-4
*Key School Number 103* ... IN-6
*Keys Creek* ... CA-9
Keys Creek—stream (2) ... CA-9
Keys Creek—stream ... KS-7
Keys Creek—stream ... KY-4
Keys Creek—stream ... MS-4
Keys Creek—stream ... OR-9
Keys Creek—stream (2) ... TX-5
Keys Crossing—locale ... TX-5
Keys Crossroads—locale ... NC-3
Keys Deadening—locale ... MS-4
Keys Desert Queen Ranch—hist pl ... CA-9
*Keyser* ... AL-4
*Keyser* ... WI-6
**Keyser**—pop pl ... WV-2
**Keyser**—pop pl ... WI-6
Keyser Airp—airport ... KS-7
Keyser Brook—stream ... ME-1
Keyser Brook—stream ... NH-1
Keyser Brook—stream ... NY-2
Keyser Brown Lake—lake ... MT-8
Keyser Cem—cemetery ... NY-2
Keyser Cem—cemetery ... TX-5
Keyser Creek—stream ... CA-9
Keyser Creek—stream (2) ... CO-8
Keyser Creek—stream ... MT-8
Keyser Creek—stream ... PA-2
Keyser Creek—stream ... TX-5
Keyser Creek—stream ... WY-8
Keyser Creek Sch—school ... MT-8
Keyser Divide Trail—trail ... CO-8
Keyser Hill—summit ... NH-1
Keyser Hollow—valley (2) ... KY-4
Keyser Hollow—valley ... VA-3
Keyser Industrial Park—locale ... PA-2
*Keyser Island* ... CT-1
Keyser Kill—stream ... NY-2
*Keyser Mtn* ... NH-1
Keyser Mtn—summit ... VA-3
Keyser Oak Shop Ctr—locale ... PA-2
Keyser Path—trail ... VA-3
Keyser Point—cape ... CT-1
Keyser Point—cape ... MD-2
Keyser Pond—lake ... NH-1
Keyser Rsvr—reservoir ... OR-9
Keyser Rsvr—reservoir ... WV-2
Keyser Run—stream ... VA-3
Keyser Run—stream ... WV-2
Keyser Sch—school ... OH-6
Keysers Ridge—locale ... MD-2
Keysers Run—stream ... MD-2
**Keyser (Township of)**—pop pl ... IN-6
Keyser Township Sch 8—hist pl ... IN-6
**Keyser Valley**—pop pl ... PA-2
**Keys Field**—pop pl ... SC-3
Keys Gap—gap ... AR-4
Keys Gap—gap ... VA-3
Keys Gap—gap ... WV-2
Keys Gap Lean-to—building ... WV-2
Keys Grove Ch—church ... GA-3
Keys Hill Hist Dist—hist pl ... MS-4
Keys Hollow—valley ... AR-4
Keys Hollow—valley ... TX-5
*Keys Lake* ... WI-6
Keys Lake—lake ... LA-4
Keys Lake—lake ... MS-4
Keys Lake—lake ... NE-7
Keys Mill—locale ... AL-4
Keys Mill—locale ... TN-4
Keys Mill Creek—stream ... MS-4
Keys Mill Dam—dam ... VA-3
*Keysmills* ... AL-4
Keysmills Post Office (historical)—building ... AL-4
Keys Mission Ch—church ... OK-5
*Keys Mtn* ... OR-9
Keys Mtn—summit ... CA-9
Keys Mtn—summit ... OR-9
*Keysor Creek* ... NE-7
Keysor Sch—school ... MO-7
Keys Park—park ... IL-6
*Keys Point* ... TN-4
Keys Pond—lake ... ME-1
Keys Pond—reservoir ... GA-3
Key Spring—spring (2) ... AL-4
Key Spring—spring ... TN-4
Keys Ranch—locale ... CA-9
Keys Ranch—locale ... MT-8
Keys Ranch—locale ... NE-7
Keys RR Station—locale ... FL-3
Keys Rsvr—reservoir ... OR-9
Keys Run—stream ... PA-2
Keys Run—stream ... VA-3
Keys Spring—spring ... OK-5
Key Station—locale ... TN-4
Key Station Post Office (historical)—building ... TN-4
Keyster Cem—cemetery ... WV-2
Keyston Creek—stream ... CA-9
*Keystone* ... KS-7
*Keystone* ... NE-7
Keystone—locale ... CA-9
Keystone—locale (3) ... CO-8
Keystone—locale ... LA-4
Keystone—locale ... MT-8
Keystone—locale (2) ... NV-8
Keystone—locale (2) ... OH-6
Keystone—locale ... WA-9
Keystone—locale ... WV-2
**Keystone**—pop pl ... AL-4
**Keystone**—pop pl ... CA-9
**Keystone**—pop pl ... DE-2
**Keystone**—pop pl ... IN-6
**Keystone**—pop pl ... IA-7
**Keystone**—pop pl ... LA-4
**Keystone**—pop pl ... MI-6
**Keystone**—pop pl ... NE-7
**Keystone**—pop pl ... ND-7
**Keystone**—pop pl (5) ... PA-2
**Keystone**—pop pl ... SD-7
**Keystone**—pop pl ... TN-4
**Keystone**—pop pl ... WV-2
**Keystone**—pop pl ... WI-6
**Keystone**—pop pl ... WY-8
**Keystone Acres (subdivision)**—pop pl ... UT-8
Keystone Arch—arch ... UT-8
Keystone at the Crossing Shop Ctr—locale ... IN-6

*Keystone Basin* ... CO-8
Keystone Bay—bay ... MI-6
Keystone Bldg—hist pl ... IL-6
Keystone Bldg—hist pl ... MN-6
Keystone Bldg—hist pl ... PA-2
Keystone Camp—locale ... NC-3
Keystone Camp—locale ... OK-5
Keystone Camp (historical)—locale ... PA-2
Keystone Canyon—valley ... AK-9
Keystone Canyon—valley ... AZ-5
Keystone Canyon—valley ... CA-9
Keystone Canyon—valley ... CO-8
Keystone Canyon—valley ... NV-8
Keystone Canyon—valley ... WA-9
Keystone Cem—cemetery ... IL-6
Keystone Cem—cemetery ... IA-7
Keystone Cem—cemetery (2) ... KS-7
Keystone Cem—cemetery ... OH-6
Keystone Cem—cemetery ... SD-7
Keystone Ch—church (3) ... FL-3
Keystone Ch—church ... IN-6
Keystone Ch—church ... MO-7
Keystone Ch—church ... WI-6
Keystone Coll—school ... PA-2
Keystone Colliery—building ... PA-2
Keystone Colliery (historical)—mine ... PA-2
Keystone Community Church—hist pl ... NE-7
Keystone Corners—locale ... WA-9
*Keystone Creek* ... WY-8
Keystone Creek—stream (3) ... AK-9
Keystone Creek—stream ... CA-9
Keystone Creek—stream ... MT-8
Keystone Creek—stream ... OR-9
Keystone Creek—stream ... WY-8
Keystone Dam—dam ... CO-8
Keystone Dam—dam ... OK-5
Keystone Dam—dam ... PA-2
Keystone Ditch—canal ... LA-4
Keystone Ditch—canal ... WY-8
Keystone Diversion Dam—dam ... NE-7
Keystone Drift Fence—other ... MT-8
Keystone Dump—locale ... NV-8
Keystone Elem Sch—school ... PA-2
Keystone Elem Sch—school ... TN-4
Keystone Extension Mine—mine ... AZ-5
Keystone Ferry Landing—locale ... WA-9
Keystone Field—park ... IL-6
Keystone Flat—flat ... CA-9
Keystone Furnace—hist pl ... OH-6
Keystone Guard Station—locale ... WY-8
Keystone Gulch—valley (2) ... CO-8
Keystone Gulch—valley (4) ... ID-8
Keystone Gulch—valley (2) ... MT-8
Keystone Gulch—valley ... OR-9
Keystone Gulch—valley ... UT-8
Keystone Harbor—bay ... WA-9
**Keystone Heights**—pop pl ... FL-3
Keystone Heights (CCD)—cens area ... FL-3
Keystone Heights Elem Sch—school ... FL-3
Keystone Heights Junior/Senior HS—school ... FL-3
Keystone Helicopter Corp/Toll Brothers Airp—airport ... PA-2
*Keystone Heliport* ... PA-2
Keystone Hill—summit ... NV-8
Keystone (historical)—locale ... FL-3
Keystone (historical)—locale ... KS-7
**Keystone (historical)**—pop pl ... MO-7
**Keystone (historical)**—pop pl ... ND-7
Keystone Hollow—valley ... AR-4
Keystone Hook and Ladder Company—hist pl ... PA-2
Keystone Hotel—hist pl ... PA-2
Keystone Industrial Park—locale ... PA-2
**Keystone Islands**—pop pl ... FL-3
Keystone Job Corp Center—building ... PA-2
*Keystone Junction* ... PA-2
Keystone Junction—locale ... NV-8
*Keystone Junior College* ... PA-2
Keystone Junior-Senior HS—school ... PA-2
Keystone Lake—lake (2) ... FL-3
Keystone Lake—reservoir ... AL-4
Keystone Lake—reservoir ... OK-5
Keystone Lake—reservoir (2) ... PA-2
Keystone Lake (CCD)—cens area ... OK-5
Keystone Lock and Dam—dam ... LA-4
Keystone Lode Mine—mine ... SD-7
Keystone Lookout Tower—locale ... OH-6
**Keystone Manor**—pop pl ... IN-6
Keystone Meadows—area ... CA-9
Keystone Meadows—flat ... ID-8
Keystone Mine—mine (4) ... AZ-5
Keystone Mine—mine (5) ... CA-9
Keystone Mine—mine (2) ... CO-8
Keystone Mine—mine ... ID-8
Keystone Mine—mine ... MT-8
Keystone Mine—mine (3) ... NV-8
Keystone Mine—mine ... OK-5
Keystone Mine—mine (2) ... OR-9
Keystone Mine—mine ... SD-7
Keystone Mine—mine (3) ... WA-9
Keystone Mine—mine ... WY-8
Keystone Mine And Fluorite Floatation Mill—mine ... KY-4
Keystone Mine (historical)—mine ... PA-2
Keystone Mtn—summit ... CA-9
Keystone Mtn—summit ... CO-8
Keystone Mtn—summit ... ID-8
Keystone Mtn—summit ... MT-8
Keystone Oaks HS—school ... PA-2
Keystone Park—park ... FL-3
Keystone Park Airp—airport ... PA-2
Keystone Park Dam—dam ... PA-2
Keystone Peak—summit ... AZ-5
Keystone Peak—summit ... MT-8
Keystone Pilot Mine—mine ... CA-9
Keystone Pocket—bay ... TN-4
Keystone Point—cape ... MI-6
Keystone Point—summit ... WA-9
Keystone Point Park—park ... FL-3
Keystone Point Shop Ctr—locale ... FL-3
Keystone Pond—lake ... MI-6
Keystone Presbyterian Ch—church ... TN-4
Keystone Quarry—mine ... SC-3
Keystone Quarry Cave—cave ... PA-2
Keystone Ranch—locale ... CA-9
Keystone Ranch—locale ... CO-8
Keystone Ranch—locale ... OR-9
Keystone Ranch—locale ... TX-5
Keystone Range—channel ... NJ-2

Keystone Range—channel ... PA-2
Keystone Ranger Station—locale ... WY-8
Keystone Ravine—valley (2) ... CA-9
*Keystone Reservoir* ... OK-5
*Keystone Reservoir* ... PA-2
Keystone Ridge—ridge ... AZ-5
Keystone Ridge—ridge ... UT-8
Keystone Rock—summit ... WI-6
Keystone Rsvr—reservoir ... MT-8
Keystone Run—stream ... PA-2
Keystone Sch—hist pl ... SD-7
Keystone Sch—school ... MO-7
Keystone Sch—school (2) ... PA-2
Keystone Sch—school ... TN-4
Keystone Sch—school ... WA-9
Keystone Sch (historical)—school ... PA-2
Keystone Shaft—mine ... NV-8
Keystone Shaft—mine ... NM-5
Keystone Ski Area—other ... CO-8
Keystone Southeast Oil Field—oilfield ... TX-5
Keystone Spring—spring ... CA-9
Keystone Spring—spring ... CO-8
Keystone Spring—spring ... MT-8
Keystone Spring—spring ... NV-8
Keystone Springs—spring ... UT-8
Keystone State Park—park ... OK-5
Keystone State Park—park ... PA-2
Keystone Station—locale ... NE-7
Keystone Station Dam—dam ... PA-2
**Keystone Switch**—pop pl ... IL-6
Keystone Tank—reservoir (2) ... AZ-5
**Keystone (Town of)**—pop pl ... WI-6
**Keystone Township**—pop pl ... KS-7
**Keystone Township**—pop pl ... ND-7
Keystone Township (historical)—civil ... ND-7
**Keystone (Township of)**—pop pl ... MN-6
Keystone Trading Company Store—hist pl ... SD-7
Keystone United Methodist Ch—church ... FL-3
Keystone Wash—stream ... NV-8
Keystone Well—well ... AZ-5
Keystone Well—well ... NV-8
Keystone Yacht Club—other ... NY-2
Keys Troughs—spring ... OR-9
Keys View—summit ... CA-9
*Keysville* ... CA-9
*Keysville* ... FL-3
*Keysville* ... KS-7
Keysville—locale ... WI-6
**Keysville**—pop pl ... FL-3
**Keysville**—pop pl ... GA-3
**Keysville**—pop pl ... MD-2
**Keysville**—pop pl ... MO-7
**Keysville**—pop pl ... VA-3
Keysville (CCD)—cens area ... GA-3
Keysville Ch—church ... NC-3
Keysville Lookout Tower—locale ... MO-7
Keysville Rsvr—reservoir ... VA-3
**Keysville Township**—pop pl ... KS-7
Keyt, Gideon, House—hist pl ... OH-6
Key Tank—reservoir ... NM-5
Keyte Creek—stream ... OR-9
**Keytesville**—pop pl ... MO-7
**Keytesville (sta.)**—pop pl ... MO-7
Keytesville ( Station)—locale ... MO-7
**Keytesville Township**—pop pl ... MO-7
*Keyton* ... AL-4
**Keyton**—pop pl ... AL-4
Keyton Branch—stream ... AL-4
Keyton Cem—cemetery ... AL-4
Keyton Ch—church ... AL-4
Keyton Creek—stream ... WY-8
**Keytons**—pop pl ... AL-4
Keyton Sch (historical)—school ... AL-4
**Keytsville**—pop pl ... IN-6
*Key Underwood Coondog Memorial Park* ... AL-4
Keyup Brook—stream ... MA-1
Key Vaca Cut—channel ... FL-3
*Key Vacas* ... FL-3
*Keyville* ... MD-2
*Keywadin* ... ME-1
*Keywadin* ... MI-6
*Keywadin* ... PA-2
Key Way Airp—airport ... WA-9
Keyway Park—park ... KS-7
Key Well—well ... AZ-5
*Key West* ... IL-6
Key West—locale ... MN-6
**Key West**—pop pl ... FL-3
**Key West**—pop pl ... IA-7
**Key West**—pop pl ... VA-3
Key West Baptist Temple—church ... FL-3
Key West Bight—bay ... FL-3
Key West (CCD)—cens area ... FL-3
Key West Cem—cemetery ... KS-7
Key West Cem—cemetery ... OK-5
Key West Country Club—locale ... FL-3
Key West Hist Dist—hist pl ... FL-3
Key West Hist Dist (Boundary Increase)—hist pl ... FL-3
Key West HS—school ... FL-3
Key West International Airp—airport ... FL-3
Key West Mine—mine ... NV-8
Key West Natl Wildlife Ref—park ... FL-3
Key West Naval Air Station—military ... FL-3
Key West Naval Hospital—military ... FL-3
Key West Skill Center—school ... FL-3
**Key West Township**—pop pl ... KS-7
Keywood—locale ... VA-3
Keywood Branch—stream ... VA-3
Keywood Hollow—valley ... VA-3
KEYY-AM (Provo)—tower ... UT-8
KEYZ-AM (Williston)—tower (2) ... ND-7
Kezan Creek—stream ... NE-7
Kezar Basin—basin ... CO-8
Kezar Brook—stream ... ME-1
Kezar Cem—cemetery ... ME-1
*Kezar Creek* ... NE-7
Kezar Falls—falls ... ME-1
**Kezar Falls**—pop pl ... ME-1
Kezar Falls Hill—summit ... ME-1
Kezar Hill—summit (2) ... ME-1
Kezar Hill—summit ... MA-1
Kezar Lake—lake ... NH-1
Kezar Lake—reservoir ... ME-1
Kezar Lake Camp—locale ... ME-1
Kezar Outlet—stream ... ME-1
Kezar Pond—lake (2) ... ME-1
Kezar River—stream ... ME-1
Kezar Stadium—other ... CA-9

Kiger Creek KS-7
Kiger Creek—stream (2) OR-9
Kiger Cutoff—bend OR-9
Kiger Gorge—valley OR-9
Kiger Hill—summit VA-3
Kiger Island—island OR-9
Kigezruk Creek—stream AK-9
Kiggin—locale CO-8
Kiggins Bowl—basin WA-9
**Kight**—pop pl WV-2
Kight Cem—cemetery GA-3
Kight Cem—cemetery WV-2
Kight Ch—church OK-5
Kight Hollow—valley AL-4
Kight Sch—school GA-3
Kigigak Island—island AK-9
Kigiktowk Creek—stream AK-9
Kigin Ditch—canal IN-6
Kiglapak Mountains—summit AK-9
Kigluaik Mountains—other AK-9
Kigoumiut (Summer Camp)—locale AK-9
Kigtsugtag Mtn—summit AK-9
Kigul Island—island AK-9
Kigun Bay—bay AK-9
Kihaapilani—summit HI-9
Kihaapilani Hill HI-9
Kihalani—civil HI-9
**Kihalani Homestead**—pop pl HI-9
Kihalani Homesteads—civil HI-9
Kihalani Stream—stream HI-9
Kihaloko Fishpond—lake HI-9
Kihapuhala—civil HI-9
Kihe HI-9
**Kihei**—pop pl HI-9
Kihei (CCD)—cens area HI-9
Kihei Pier—locale HI-9
Ki-He-Kah Ranch—locale AZ-5
Kiheki—locale OK-5
Kihewamoko Island HI-9
Kihewamoku (Bird Refuge)—island HI-9
Kihewamoku Island HI-9
Kihewamoku Islet HI-9
Ki Hill HI-9
Kihlid, Pilen—stream FM-9
**Kiholo**—pop pl HI-9
Kiholo Bay—bay HI-9
Kiholo-Puako Trail—trail HI-9
Kihouna—cape HI-9
KIHR-AM—tower OR-9
Kii—bay HI-9
Kii—cape HI-9
Kii—locale HI-9
Kii—swamp HI-9
Kiialaa Valley—valley HI-9
Kiikan—island MP-9
Kiikan Island MP-9
Kiikan-To MP-9
KIIK-FM (Davenport)—tower IA-7
Kiikolu—summit HI-9
Kiilae—civil HI-9
Kiilae Bay—bay HI-9
Kiilae Watercourse—stream HI-9
Kiilai HI-9
Kii Landing HI-9
Kii Lava Flow Of 1955—lava HI-9
Kiingyak Lake—lake AK-9
Kiinohu Gulch—valley HI-9
Kiiokalani—civil HI-9
Kii Petroglyphs—hist pl HI-9
Kii Point—cape (2) HI-9
Kiisanat FM-9
Kiiyo MP-9
Kiiyo-suido MP-9
Kiiyo-to MP-9
Kijbwa MP-9
Kijbwe MP-9
Kijen—island MP-9
Kijik—locale AK-9
Kijik Hist Dist—hist pl AK-9
Kijik Lake—lake AK-9
Kijik Mtn—summit AK-9
Kijik River—stream AK-9
Kijin-bwi IslanA STATUS BGN MP-9
Kijjen—island MP-9
KIJK-FM—tower OR-9
Kijk-Uit Mtn—summit NY-2
KIJV-AM (Huron)—tower SD-7
Kikahe River—stream AK-9
Kikak Creek—stream AK-9
Kikakpak Bluff—cliff AK-9
Kikala—civil (2) HI-9
Kikala-Keokea Homesteads—civil HI-9
Kikalrodik Hill—summit AK-9
Kikapoo Creek KS-7
Kikartamjingia Point—cape AK-9
Kikartik Rock—island AK-9
Kikaua Point—cape HI-9
Kikdooli Butte—summit AK-9
Kikegtek Island—island AK-9
Kikeout Mtn—summit NJ-2
Kikepa Point—cape HI-9
**Kiker**—pop pl GA-3
Kiker Lake—reservoir TX-5
Kiker Lake Dam—dam MS-4
**Kikers**—pop pl NC-3
Kikertalik Lake—lake AK-9
Kiket Bay—bay WA-9
Kiket Island—island WA-9
Kikewamoku Island HI-9
Kikiaeae—area HI-9
Kikiakala—summit HI-9
Kikiakrorak River—stream AK-9
Kikiaola—hist pl HI-9
Kikiaola Harbor—harbor HI-9
Kikikausgruak Island—island AK-9
Kikiktak Islands—area AK-9
Kikiktalik Rock—island AK-9
Kikiktat Mtn—summit AK-9
Kikikyak Hill—summit AK-9
Kikipua Point—cape HI-9
Kikitaliorak Lake—lake AK-9
Kikkatuck Airp—airport PA-2
Kikku Creek—stream AK-9
Kiklukh River—stream AK-9
Kiklupiklak Hills—other AK-9
Kikmiksot Mtn—summit AK-9
Kikmiktalikamiut—locale AK-9
Kikneak River—stream AK-9
Kiknik Creek—stream AK-9
KIKO-AM (Miami)—tower AZ-5
Kikoa Point—cape HI-9
KIKO-FM (Globe)—tower AZ-5
Kikoligarak Creek—stream AK-9
Kikolik Creek—stream AK-9
Kikoo—civil HI-9
Kikoo—summit HI-9
Kikoojit Rocks—island AK-9
Kikoo Peak HI-9
Kikoula Gulch—valley HI-9
Kikpyat Creek—stream AK-9
KIKS-AM (Iola)—tower KS-7
Kiktak Island—island AK-9
Kiktoya Creek—stream AK-9
Kikuktok Mtn—summit AK-9
Kiku Shima FM-9
Kiku To FM-9
KIKX-AM (Tucson)—tower AZ-5
**Kila**—pop pl MT-8
Kila—summit HI-9
Kilachee Creek AL-4
Kilaga Springs—locale CA-9
Kilagen Island—island MP-9
Kilamer MP-9
Kilan Branch—stream KY-4
Ki Landing HI-9
Kilane MP-9
Kilange MP-9
Kilangnak Bluff—cliff AK-9
Kilarc Powerhouse—other CA-9
Kilarc Rsvr—reservoir CA-9
**Kilarm Junction (Killarm)**—pop pl WV-2
Kilarney GA-3
Kilarney Shores—uninc pl FL-3
**Kilarney Woods (subdivision)**—pop pl NC-3
Kilau—civil HI-9
Kilauea HI-9
Kilauea—civil HI-9
**Kilauea**—pop pl HI-9
Kilauea Bay—bay HI-9
Kilauea Caldera HI-9
Kilauea Camp HI-9
Kilauea Crater—crater HI-9
Kilauea Crater—hist pl HI-9
Kilauea For Res—forest HI-9
Kilauea Gulch—valley HI-9
Kilauea Iki HI-9
Kilauea Iki Crater—crater HI-9
Kilauea Milit Camp—military HI-9
Kilauea Milit Camp (U.S. Army)—military HI-9
Kilauea Park—park HI-9
Kilauea Point—cape HI-9
Kilauea Point Lighthouse—hist pl HI-9
Kilauea Sch—hist pl HI-9
Kilauea Sch—school HI-9
**Kilauea Settlement**—pop pl HI-9
Kilauea Settlement Lots—civil HI-9
Kilauea Stream—stream HI-9
Kilau Stream—stream HI-9
Kilawe MP-9
Kilback Pond—lake NH-1
Kilbaine Lateral—canal ID-8
Kilbart Creek NC-3
Kilbart Slough—stream NC-3
Kilbeck Hills—range CA-9
Kilberg Canyon AZ-5
Kilberg Creek AZ-5
Kilberg Peak AZ-5
Kilborn Ch (historical)—church MO-7
Kilborn Creek—stream WA-9
Kilborne District Park—park NC-3
Kilborne Lake—lake MI-6
Kilborn Gulch—valley MT-8
Kilborn Lake—lake CA-9
Kilborn Post Office (historical)—building SD-7
Kilborn Ranch—locale TX-5
Kilborn School—locale MI-6
Kilborn Spring—spring CO-8
Kilborn Spring—spring WA-9
**Kilborn Township**—pop pl SD-7
Kilborn Tunnel—mine NV-8
Kilbourn WI-6
**Kilbourn**—pop pl IA-7
Kilbourn Ave Row House Hist Dist—hist pl WI-6
Kilbourn Cem—cemetery VA-3
**Kilbourne**—pop pl IL-6
**Kilbourne**—pop pl LA-4
**Kilbourne**—pop pl OH-6
Kilbourne Hole—basin NM-5
Kilbourne Hollow—valley PA-2
Kilbourne House—hist pl OH-6
Kilbourne Park Ch—church SC-3
**Kilbourne (Township of)**—pop pl IL-6
Kilbourn Masonic Temple—hist pl WI-6
Kilbourn Park—park IL-6
Kilbourn Park—park WI-6
Kilbourn Park—uninc pl SC-3
Kilbourn Public Library—hist pl WI-6
Kilbourn Road Ditch—canal WI-6
Kilbourn Sch—school WI-6
Kilbourns Corner—locale KS-7
Kilbourn Street Park—park WI-6
Kilbourntown WI-6
**Kilbournville**—pop pl WI-6
Kilbrennan Creek—stream MT-8
Kilbrennan Lake—lake MT-8
Kilbride, Dr. E. A., Clinic—hist pl MN-6
Kilbride, Lake—lake TX-5
Kilbridge Post Office (historical)—building TN-4
Kilbuck—uninc pl PA-2
Kilbuck Bluffs For Preserve—forest IL-6
Kilbuck Creek IN-6
Kilbuck Creek OH-6
Kilbuck Mountains—range AK-9
Kilbuck Run—stream PA-2
Kilbuck Township—CDP PA-2
**Kilbuck (Township of)**—pop pl PA-2
Kilburn, Mount—summit NH-1
Kilburn Branch—stream MO-7
Kilburn Branch—stream TN-4
Kilburn Brook—stream MA-1
Kilburn Brook—stream NH-1
Kilburn Brook—stream VT-1
Kilburn Cem—cemetery AR-4
Kilburn Cem—cemetery TN-4
Kilburn Ch—church AL-4
Kilburn Ch of Christ AL-4
Kilburn Fork—stream KY-4
Kilburn Hills—summit NM-5
Kilburn (historical)—locale AL-4
Kilburn Hollow—valley TN-4
Kilburnie—hist pl SC-3
Kilburn Mtn—summit NY-2
Kilburn Pond—lake NH-1
Kilburn Sch—school MO-7
Kilburn Sch (historical)—school AL-4
Kilby CT-1
Kilby—locale AL-4
Kilby—locale NC-3
Kilby—locale VA-3
Kilby, Lake—reservoir VA-3
Kilby Branch—stream GA-3
Kilby Branch—stream (3) NC-3
Kilby Cem—cemetery VA-3
Kilby Ch—church MO-7
Kilby Corner—locale MD-2
Kilby Correctional Facility—building AL-4
Kilby Cove—valley NC-3
Kilby Creek—stream CA-9
Kilby Creek—stream (2) NC-3
Kilby Gap—gap (2) NC-3
Kilby Hotel—hist pl NC-3
Kilby House—hist pl AL-4
Kilby Island—island NC-3
Kilby Lake VA-3
Kilby Lake—lake WI-6
Kilby Mill—locale GA-3
Kilby Prison (historical)—building AL-4
Kilbys Creek—stream VA-3
Kilby Shores—uninc pl VA-3
Kilby Spring—spring WI-6
Kilchis Falls—falls OR-9
Kilchis Flat—bar OR-9
Kilchis Lookout—locale OR-9
Kilchis River—stream OR-9
Kilchis River County Park OR-9
Kilchis River Rec Area—park OR-9
Kilchlis Meadow—island MN-6
Kilcoin Pond—lake NY-2
Kilcoyne Cem—cemetery WV-2
Kilcrease Cem—cemetery OK-5
Kildaire Country Club—other OH-6
**Kildaire Farms (subdivision)**—pop pl NC-3
Kildare—locale NY-2
**Kildare**—pop pl GA-3
**Kildare**—pop pl OK-5
**Kildare**—pop pl TX-5
**Kildare Annex**—pop pl VA-3
Kildare Junction—locale TX-5
Kildare Lake—lake WI-6
Kildare-McCormick House—hist pl AL-4
Kildare Oil Field—oilfield TX-5
Kildare Outlet—stream NY-2
Kildare Pond—lake NY-2
**Kildare (Town of)**—pop pl WI-6
**Kildare (Township of)**—pop pl MN-6
**Kildav**—pop pl KY-4
Kilday KY-4
Kildee Point—cape DE-2
**Kildeer**—pop pl IL-6
Kildeer Creek CO-8
Kildeer Lake MN-6
Kildeer Mtn—summit NC-3
Kildeer Point—cape ME-1
Kildeer Sch—school IL-6
Kildee Wesleyan Ch—church NC-3
Kildee Windmill—locale TX-5
**Kildere Estates (subdivision)**—pop pl AL-4
Kildoo Bridge—bridge PA-2
Kildoogan Creek—stream TX-5
Kildow Cem—cemetery OH-6
Kildugan Creek—stream TX-5
Kildugan Tank—reservoir TX-5
Kildugan Well—well TX-5
Kile MP-9
Kile—island MP-9
Kilea—summit HI-9
Kile Branch—stream TX-5
Kile Cem—cemetery LA-4
Kile Cem—cemetery OH-6
Kile Creek—stream MO-7
Kile Ditch—canal OH-6
**Kile (Kileville)**—pop pl OH-6
Kile Knob—summit WV-2
Kile Lake—reservoir TN-4
Kileman MP-9
Kilemar MP-9
Kileu—summit (2) HI-9
Kiler Canyon—valley CA-9
Kiler Creek—stream CA-9
Kile Run—stream WV-2
Kile Springs—spring TN-4
**Kileville**—pop pl OH-6
**Kiley**—pop pl IN-6
Kiley Hollow—valley TN-4
Kiley Sch—school MA-1
Kiley Sch—school WI-6
Kilfoil Draw—valley TX-5
**Kilfoil Township**—pop pl NE-7
Kilfore Creek UT-8
Kilgallon Gulch—valley MT-8
Kilgo Ch (historical)—church MS-4
Kilgoe Mtn—summit AL-4
Kilgo Post Office (historical)—building AL-4
Kilgore—locale TX-5
**Kilgore**—pop pl AL-4
**Kilgore**—pop pl ID-8
**Kilgore**—pop pl KY-4
**Kilgore**—pop pl NE-7
**Kilgore**—pop pl OH-6
**Kilgore**—pop pl (2) PA-2
**Kilgore**—pop pl SC-3
**Kilgore**—pop pl TX-5
Kilgore, Josiah, House—hist pl SC-3
Kilgore Basin—basin NV-8
Kilgore Basin—basin UT-8
Kilgore Branch—stream AL-4
Kilgore Branch—stream AR-4
Kilgore Branch—stream TN-4
Kilgore Branch—stream TX-5
Kilgore Bridge—bridge SC-3
Kilgore Canyon—valley WA-9
Kilgore Cave—cave TN-4
Kilgore (CCD)—cens area (2) TX-5
Kilgore Cem TX-5
Kilgore Cem—cemetery (2) AR-4
Kilgore Cem—cemetery (2) GA-3
Kilgore Cem—cemetery ID-8
Kilgore Cem—cemetery IN-6
Kilgore Cem—cemetery KY-4
Kilgore Cem—cemetery OH-6
Kilgore Cem—cemetery TN-4
Kilgore Cem—cemetery TX-5
Kilgore Cem—cemetery (4) VA-3
Kilgore Ch—church AL-4
Kilgore College Demonstration Farm—locale TX-5
Kilgore Creek TX-5
Kilgore Creek—stream IA-7
Kilgore Creek—stream NE-7
Kilgore Creek—stream NC-3
Kilgore Creek—stream TX-5
Kilgore Creek—stream VA-3
Kilgore Creek—stream WV-2
Kilgore Creek—stream WY-8
Kilgore Dam—dam OR-9
Kilgore Gap—gap AR-4
Kilgore Gulch—valley CO-8
Kilgore Gulch—valley OR-9
Kilgore Heights Sch—school TX-5
Kilgore (historical)—locale (2) MS-4
Kilgore Lake—lake ND-7
Kilgore Lake—lake OH-6
Kilgore Lateral—canal NM-5
Kilgore Lodge—locale AR-4
Kilgore Lodge Ch—church AR-4
Kilgore Mill Covered Bridge and Mill Site—hist pl GA-3
Kilgore Mine (underground)—mine AL-4
Kilgore Mtn—summit AR-4
**Kilgore Plantation**—pop pl LA-4
Kilgore Pond—lake ME-1
Kilgore Post Office (historical)—building MS-4
Kilgore Ridge—ridge (2) CA-9
Kilgore Ridge—ridge UT-8
Kilgore RR Station—locale FL-3
Kilgore Rsvr OR-9
Kilgore Rsvr—reservoir OR-9
Kilgore Sch—school ME-1
Kilgore Sch (historical)—school TN-4
Kilgore Slough—gut LA-4
Kilgore Spring—spring (2) OR-9
Kilgore Spring—spring TN-4
Kilgore Spring—spring UT-8
Kilgores Rocks—summit MD-2
Kilgore Station—locale TN-4
**Kilgore Subdivision**—pop pl TN-4
Kilgore Tank—reservoir AZ-5
Kilgore Tank—reservoir TX-5
Kilgore (Township of)—fmr MCD AR-4
Kilgo United Methodist Ch—church NC-3
Kilgour Branch—stream MD-2
Kilgour Ch—church OH-6
Kilgour Sch—school OH-6
Kilgour Spur—locale NY-2
**Kilgravel**—pop pl NE-7
Kilgus Branch—stream MI-6
Kilham Creek—stream TN-4
Kili—island MP-9
Kilian Cave—cave AL-4
Kilian Ranch—locale MT-8
Kilich Point—cape AK-9
Kili (County-equivalent)—civil MP-9
KILI-FM (Porcupine)—tower SD-7
Kiliga AL-4
Kiligmak Inlet—gut AK-9
Kiliguak Creek—stream AK-9
Kiligwa River—stream AK-9
Kili Hill—summit AK-9
Kili Island MP-9
Kilik—island MP-9
Kilikmak Creek—stream AK-9
Kilikralik Creek—stream AK-9
Kilikralik Point—cape AK-9
Kiliktagik Island—island AK-9
Kiliovilik Creek—stream AK-9
Kiliovilik Range—range AK-9
Kilisut Harbor—bay WA-9
Kiliuda Bay—bay AK-9
Kiliuda Rock—bar AK-9
Kilkare Marsh—swamp WI-6
**Kilkare Woods**—pop pl CA-9
Kilkelly Creek—stream WA-9
Kilkenny—hist pl GA-3
Kilkenny—locale NC-3
Kilkenny—other GA-3
**Kilkenny**—pop pl MN-6
Kilkenny Club GA-3
Kilkenny Cove—bay ME-1
Kilkenny Creek—stream GA-3
Kilkenny Fork—stream OR-9
Kilkenny Hill—summit NY-2
Kilkenny Landing—locale NC-3
Kilkenny Landing—other NC-3
Kilkenny Stream—stream ME-1
Kilkenny (Township of)—fmr MCD NH-1
**Kilkenny (Township of)**—pop pl MN-6
Killak River—stream AK-9
Killamacue Creek—stream OR-9
Killamacue Dam—dam OR-9
Killamacue Lake—lake OR-9
Killam Creek—stream OR-9
Killam Fawcett Rsvr—reservoir OR-9
Killam Oil Field—oilfield TX-5
Killam Ranch—locale TX-5
Killam Sch—school IL-6
Killam Siding—locale TX-5
Killams Pond—lake PA-2
Killan Creek—stream LA-4
Killanger Peak—summit CA-9
**Killarm**—pop pl WV-2
Killarney WV-2
Killarney—locale FL-3
Killarney—locale GA-3
**Killarney**—pop pl GA-3
**Killarney**—pop pl WV-2
Killarney, Lake—lake AK-9
Killarney, Lake—lake (2) FL-3
Killarney, Lake—lake IL-6
Killarney, Lake—lake LA-4
Killarney, Lake—lake WA-9
Killarney, Lake—reservoir MO-7
Killarney Baptist Ch—church FL-3
**Killarney Beach**—pop pl MI-6
Killarney Creek—stream AK-9
Killarney Creek—stream ID-8
Killarney Lake—lake ID-8
Killarney Lake—lake MI-6
Killarney Lake—reservoir WI-6
Killarney Mtn—summit ID-8
Killarney Park—locale PA-2
Killarney Point—cape MI-6
Killarney Rsvr—reservoir CO-8
Killarney Sch—school FL-3
**Killarney Shores**—pop pl MO-7
**Killarney Shores (subdivision)**—pop pl FL-3
**Killawog**—pop pl NY-2
Killbuck NY-2
**Kill Buck**—pop pl NY-2
**Killbuck**—pop pl OH-6
Killbuck Cem—cemetery IL-6
Killbuck Creek—stream IL-6
Killbuck Creek—stream IN-6
Killbuck Creek—stream OH-6
Killbuck Ditch—canal OH-6
Kill Buck Knob—summit TN-4
Killbuck Run OH-6
Killbuck Run PA-2
Killbuck Run—stream PA-2
Killbucks Creek OH-6
Killbuck (Township of)—other OH-6
**Killbuck (Township of)**—pop pl OH-6
Killburn Hollow—valley TN-4
Killcohook Natl Wildlife Ref—park DE-2
Killcohook Natl Wildlife Ref—park NJ-2
Killcreas Lake—lake AL-4
Kill Creek KS-7
Kill Creek—stream IN-6
Kill Creek—stream (2) KS-7
Kill Creek Ch—church KS-7
**Kill Creek Township**—pop pl KS-7
Kill Dead Creek—stream AR-4
Kill Dee Branch—stream TN-4
**Killdeer**—pop pl ND-7
Killdeer Cem—cemetery ND-7
Killdeer Creek—stream CO-8
Killdeer Draw—valley SD-7
Killdeer Island—cape MA-1
Killdeer Lake MN-6
Killdeer Lake—lake AK-9
Killdeer Lake—lake MI-6
Killdeer Lake—lake MN-6
Killdeer Mountains—range ND-7
Killdeer Mountain State Game Mngmt Area—park ND-7
Killdeer Plains Wildlife Area—park OH-6
Killdeer Well—well NM-5
Killdergen Creek—stream MO-7
Killdevil Hill—summit NC-3
Kill Devil Hill Monument Natl Memorial NC-3
**Kill Devil Hills**—pop pl NC-3
Kill Devil Hills Water Tank—tower NC-3
Kill Dry Creek—stream CA-9
Kill Dry Ridge—ridge CA-9
**Killduff**—pop pl IA-7
Killeak Lakes—lake AK-9
Killean TX-5
Killearn—CDP FL-3
Killearn Center (Shop Ctr)—locale FL-3
**Killearn Estates**—pop pl FL-3
Killearn Gardens State Park—park FL-3
Killearn Lakes Elem Sch—school FL-3
Killearn United Methodist Ch—church FL-3
Killearn United Methodist Preschool/ Kindergarten—school FL-3
Killebrew Cave—cave TN-4
Killebrew Cem—cemetery GA-3
Killebrew Cem—cemetery TX-5
Killebrew Lake—lake WA-9
Killed Woman Creek MT-8
Killeegko AL-4
**Killeen**—pop pl TX-5
**Killeen Base**—pop pl TX-5
Killeen (CCD)—cens area TX-5
Killeen Memorial Park (Cemetery)—cemetery TX-5
Killefer Sch—school CA-9
Killem Horse Creek—stream MT-8
Kille Mine—mine NV-8
Killem Quick Creek—stream MT-8
Killem Swamp—stream NC-3
**Killen**—pop pl AL-4
Killenbeck Drain—canal MI-6
Killenbeck Rsvr—reservoir MT-8
Killen Branch—stream VA-3
Killenbuck Drain MI-6
Killen (CCD)—cens area AL-4
Killen Cem—cemetery MS-4
Killen Creek—stream WA-9
Killen Creek Campground—locale WA-9
Killen Division—civil AL-4
Killen Hollow—valley VA-3
Killen Park—park AL-4
Killen Pond—reservoir DE-2
Killen Pond Dam—dam DE-2
Killen Pond State Park—park DE-2
**Killens Addition (subdivision)**—pop pl DE-2
Killens Ferry Gas Field—oilfield LA-4
Killens Hill—summit NC-3
Killens Pond State Park DE-2
Killen Stadium—locale LA-4
Killen Woods State Park—park MN-6
Killer Bay—bay AK-9
Killer Cem—cemetery OK-5
Killer Chasm Cave—cave AL-4
Killer Creek GA-3
Killer Mtn—summit OK-5
Killets Creek—stream NC-3
Killett, Marcheston, Farm—hist pl NC-3
Killey Cem—cemetery MO-7
Killey Glacier—glacier AK-9
Killey River—stream AK-9
Killfillian Hollow—valley KY-4
Killfoil Creek—stream UT-8
Killfore Creek UT-8
**Killgo**—pop pl SC-3
Killgore Cem—cemetery OK-5
Killgore Fort House—hist pl VA-3
Killgore House—hist pl LA-4
Killgore Island—island NE-7
Kill Hollow—valley OK-5
Killi MP-9
**Killian**—pop pl LA-4
**Killian**—pop pl SC-3
Killian Bayou—stream LA-4
Killian Branch—stream LA-4
Killian Canal IN-6
Killian Cem—cemetery AL-4
Killian Cem—cemetery AR-4
Killian Cem—cemetery KY-4
Killian Cem—cemetery NE-7
Killian Ch—church (2) LA-4
Killian Ch—church SC-3
Killian Coulee—valley ND-7
Killian Creek—stream AK-9
Killian Creek—stream NC-3
Killian Crossrads NC-3
**Killian Crossroads**—pop pl NC-3
Killian Ditch—canal IN-6
Killian Gap—gap TN-4
Killian Hollow—valley UT-8
Killian Knob—summit NC-3
Killian Mill—locale AL-4
Killian Mtn—summit NC-3
Killian Pines Ch—church FL-3
Killians Chapel—church TN-4
**Killians Chapel**—pop pl TN-4
Killian Sch (historical)—school MO-7
Killian Sch (historical)—school TN-4
Killians Gap TN-4
Killians Mountains NC-3
Killian Spring—spring UT-8
Killian Springs—spring UT-8
Killian State Wildlife Mngmt Area—park MN-6
Killick Pond—lake ME-1
Killick Stone Island—island ME-1
Killico Branch—stream GA-3
Killi Creek—stream AK-9
Killik Bend—bend AK-9
Killikrankia Plantation (historical)—locale MS-4
Killik River—stream AK-9
Killin—locale AR-4
Killing Branch—stream TX-5
**Killinger**—pop pl PA-2
Killinger Creek—stream PA-2
Killinger Creek—stream VA-3
**Killingly Center**—pop pl CT-1
Killingly HS—school CT-1
Killingly Memorial Sch—school CT-1
Killingly Pond—reservoir CT-1
Killingly Pond—reservoir RI-1
**Killingly (Town of)**—pop pl CT-1
Killings Cem—cemetery AR-4
Killings Creek NC-3
Killingsworth Ch—church AL-4
Killingsworth Cove—valley AL-4
Killingsworth Cove Branch—stream AL-4
Killingsworth Crossroads—locale FL-3
Killingsworth Farm—hist pl GA-3
Killingsworth Lake—reservoir AL-4
Killingsworth Lake Dam—dam AL-4
Killingsworth Sch—school CA-9
Killingsworth Sch (historical)—school AL-4
Killington Peak—summit VT-1
**Killington (Sherburne Center)**—pop pl VT-1
Killington Ski Area—area VT-1
**Killingworth**—pop pl CT-1
Killingworth Branch—stream TX-5
Killingworth Rsvr—reservoir CT-1
**Killingworth (Town of)**—pop pl CT-1
Killinupak Mtn—summit AK-9
Killion Canal—canal IN-6
Killion Canal Ditch IN-6
Killion Cem—cemetery IN-6
Killion Ridge—ridge TN-4
Killisnoo Harbor—bay AK-9
Killisnoo Island—island AK-9
Killisnoo (ruins)—locale AK-9
Killjordan Creek—stream IL-6
Killkelly Creek WA-9
Killkelly Sch for Girls (historical)—school MS-4
Killkenny Rocks—summit CT-1
Killman Hollow—valley MO-7
Killman Pond—lake ME-1
**Killmaster**—pop pl MI-6
Killmon Cove—bay VA-3
Killmore IN-6
Killmore Creek IN-6
Killneck Creek—stream VA-3
Killommwar—island MP-9
**Killona**—pop pl LA-4
Killough Cem—cemetery TX-5
Killough Creek—stream TX-5
Killough Dam—dam AL-4
Killough Lake—reservoir AL-4
Killough Ranch—locale NM-5
Killough Sch (historical) school MS-4
Killough Spring—spring AL-4
**Killough Springs**—pop pl AL-4
Killo Windmill—locale NM-5
Killpack Canyon—valley UT-8
Killpack Mine—mine UT-8
Killpatrick Creek—stream AL-4
Killpatrick Drain—canal MI-6
Killpeck Creek—stream MD-2
Killpecker Creek—stream CO-8
Killpecker Creek—stream (2) WY-8
Killpecker Ridge—ridge NC-3
Kill Pond Bar—bar MA-1
Killrell Sch (historical)—school TN-4
Killroy Lake—lake MN-6
Killsnake River—stream WI-6
Killsnake State Wildlife Area—park WI-6
Killsnight Creek—stream MT-8
Killsnight Spring—spring MT-8
Kill Swamp—stream NC-3
Kill Van Coll NJ-2
Kill Van Kuhl NJ-2
Kill Van Kull—stream NJ-2
Kill Van Kull—stream NY-2
Kill Von Kull NY-2
Kill Wash—stream NV-8
Killwell Run—stream OH-6
Kill Woman Creek—stream MT-8
Killy Brook RI-1
Killy Brook—stream RI-1
Killybrooke Sch—school CA-9
Killycassida Creek AL-4
Killycassidda Creek AL-4
Killy Draw WY-8
Killyon Canyon—valley UT-8
**Killyons Subdivision**—pop pl UT-8
Killys Brook RI-1
**Kilmanagh**—pop pl MI-6
Kilmanagh Ch—church MI-6
Kilman Hosp—hospital TX-5
Kilmantavi (Abandoned)—locale AK-9
**Kilmarnock**—pop pl VA-3
Kilmarnock Landing VA-3
Kilmarnock Wharf—locale VA-3

*Kinakappu* ... FM-9
Kinakapw—*civil* ... FM-9
Kinak Bay—*bay* (2) ... AK-9
Kinak River—*stream* ... AK-9
Kinak (Site)—*locale* ... AK-9
Kina Lake—*lake* ... AK-9
*Kinard* ... SC-3
Kinard—*locale* ... AR-4
Kinard—*locale* ... FL-3
**Kinard**—*pop pl* ... FL-3
Kinard Cem—*cemetery* ... AL-4
Kinard Cem—*cemetery* ... MS-4
Kinard Cem—*cemetery* ... TX-5
Kinard Chapel—*church* ... SC-3
**Kinard Estates**—*pop pl* ... TX-5
Kinard Lake Dam—*dam* ... MS-4
**Kinards**—*pop pl* ... SC-3
Kinards Creek—*stream* ... SC-3
Kinaruk Lake—*lake* ... AK-9
Kinaruk River—*stream* ... AK-9
Kinau, Cape—*cape* ... HI-9
Kinau Street Sch—*school* ... HI-9
Kinawa Sch—*school* ... MI-6
*Kinazen* ... MP-9
*Kinazen To* ... MP-9
Kinbal Sch—*school* ... IL-6
Kinbawn—*hist pl* ... PA-2
**Kinbrae**—*pop pl* ... MN-6
Kinbrae Cem—*cemetery* ... MN-6
Kinbrae Lake—*lake* ... MN-6
Kinbrae Slough—*lake* ... MN-6
*Kincade* ... KS-7
*Kincade Creek* ... AL-4
*Kincade Creek* ... MS-4
Kincade Hill—*summit* ... TN-4
Kincade Ridge—*ridge* ... KY-4
Kincades Landing—*locale* ... MS-4
*Kincaid* ... GA-3
*Kincaid* ... ND-7
Kincaid—*fmr MCD* ... NE-7
Kincaid—*locale* ... CA-9
Kincaid—*locale* ... MS-4
Kincaid—*locale* ... ND-7
Kincaid—*locale* ... TN-4
Kincaid—*locale* ... VA-3
**Kincaid**—*pop pl* ... IL-6
**Kincaid**—*pop pl* ... KS-7
**Kincaid**—*pop pl* ... WV-2
Kincaid-Anderson House—*hist pl* ... SC-3
Kincaid-Ausmus House—*hist pl* ... TN-4
Kincaid Bayou—*stream* ... LA-4
Kincaid Branch—*stream* (2) ... KY-4
Kincaid Branch—*stream* ... TN-4
Kincaid Bridge—*bridge* ... LA-4
Kincaid Canyon—*valley* ... OR-9
Kincaid Canyon—*valley* ... TX-5
Kincaid Cem—*cemetery* ... AL-4
Kincaid Cem—*cemetery* ... KS-7
Kincaid Cem—*cemetery* ... MO-7
Kincaid Cem—*cemetery* (2) ... TN-4
Kincaid Cem—*cemetery* ... VA-3
Kincaid Cem—*cemetery* ... WV-2
Kincaid Ch—*church* ... TN-4
Kincaid Creek—*stream* ... KY-4
Kincaid Creek—*stream* ... OH-6
Kincaid Creek—*stream* ... TX-5
Kincaid Ditch—*canal* ... WY-8
Kincaid Draw—*valley* ... WY-8
Kincaide Cem—*cemetery* ... MS-4
Kincaide Creek—*stream* ... AL-4
Kincaide Creek—*stream* ... MS-4
Kincaide Park—*park* ... MA-1
**Kincaid Hills**—*pop pl* ... FL-3
Kincaid Historical Monmt—*park* ... TN-4
Kincaid Hollow—*valley* ... GA-3
Kincaid House—*hist pl* ... TN-4
Kincaid-Howard House—*hist pl* ... TN-4
Kincaid Knob—*summit* ... WV-2
Kincaid Lake—*lake* ... WA-9
Kincaid Lake—*reservoir* ... NJ-2
Kincaid Lake Dam—*dam* ... NJ-2
Kincaid Mine (underground)—*mine* ... AL-4
Kincaid Mounds—*summit* ... IL-6
Kincaid Mtn—*summit* ... GA-3
Kincaid Park—*park* ... OR-9
Kincaid Point—*cape* ... MT-8
Kincaid Post Office (historical)—*building* ... MS-4
Kincaid Post Office (historical)—*building* ... TN-4
Kincaid Ranch—*locale* ... CA-9
Kincaid Ranch—*locale* ... NM-5
Kincaid Ranch—*locale* ... TX-5
Kincaid Rsvr—*reservoir* ... ID-8
Kincaid Rsvr—*reservoir* ... LA-4
Kincaid Run—*stream* ... WV-2
Kincaid Sch—*school* ... GA-3
Kincaid Sch (historical)—*school* ... MO-7
*Kincaids Forge* ... TN-4
Kincaid Site—*hist pl* ... IL-6
Kincaid Slough—*stream* ... AR-4
Kincaid Spring—*spring* ... TN-4
Kincaid Spring—*spring* ... TX-5
**Kincaid Springs**—*pop pl* ... OH-6
Kincaid Springs State Fish Hatchery—*other* ... OH-6
Kincaid Stream—*stream* ... ME-1
Kincaid Trail—*trail* ... TX-5
Kincaid Trail—*trail* ... WA-9
*Kincaid United Methodist Church* ... TN-4
Kincannon Canyon—*valley* ... CA-9
Kincannon Ferry (historical)—*locale* ... TN-4
*Kincannon Mtn* ... AR-4
Kincannon Mtn—*summit* ... AR-4
*Kincannons Ferry* ... TN-4
Kincannons Ferry Post Office (historical)—*building* ... TN-4
Kincannons Ford (historical)—*locale* ... TN-4
Kincer Mill—*locale* ... VA-3
Kinchafoonee Ch—*church* ... GA-3
Kinchafoonee Creek—*stream* ... GA-3
*Kinchafoonee River* ... GA-3
*Kinchatoonee Creek* ... GA-3
Kinch Canyon—*valley* ... CA-9
*Kinchefoonee Creek* ... GA-3
Kinchelo Creek—*stream* ... TX-5
Kinchelo Creek—*stream* ... WA-9
Kincheloe—*other* ... MI-6
**Kincheloe**—*pop pl* ... WV-2
Kincheloe AFB—*military* ... MI-6
Kincheloe Camp—*locale* ... MT-8
Kincheloe Cem—*cemetery* ... IL-6
Kincheloe Cem—*cemetery* ... TN-4
Kincheloe-Cox Cem—*cemetery* ... TN-4
Kincheloe Creek—*stream* ... WV-2
**Kincheloe (historical)**—*pop pl* ... TN-4
Kincheloe Homestead—*locale* ... NM-5
Kincheloe Mill—*locale* ... TN-4
Kincheloe Point—*cape* ... OR-9
Kincheloe Post Office (historical)—*building* ... TN-4
Kincheloe Ranch—*locale* ... MT-8
Kincheloe Spring—*spring* ... TN-4
*Kinchelo Peak* ... TX-5
Kinchen Cem—*cemetery* ... LA-4
Kincheon—*locale* ... AL-4
Kincheon Creek—*stream* ... AL-4
**Kincheonville**—*pop pl* ... TX-5
Kinches Chapel—*church* ... NC-3
Kinch Farms Airp—*airport* ... WA-9
**Kinchloes Bluff**—*pop pl* ... KY-4
Kinchlow Hollow—*valley* ... MO-7
Kinchlow Hollow Cove—*bay* ... MO-7
Kinch McKinney Hill—*locale* ... WY-8
Kinch McKinney Spring—*spring* ... WY-8
Kinch Sch (historical)—*school* ... PA-2
*Kinchy Creek* ... OR-9
Kindaid-Taylor Ranch (reduced usage)—*locale* ... TX-5
**Kindall**—*pop pl* ... AR-4
Kindall Island—*island* ... NE-7
KIND-AM (Independence)—*tower* ... KS-7
Kindanina Lake—*lake* ... AK-9
**Kinde**—*pop pl* ... MI-6
*Kindelberger Landing Area* ... PA-2
Kindelberger Landing Strip—*airport* ... PA-2
Kindel Cem—*cemetery* ... KS-7
Kindell Drain—*stream* ... MI-6
*Kinder* ... IN-6
**Kinder**—*pop pl* ... IN-6
**Kinder**—*pop pl* ... LA-4
**Kinder**—*pop pl* ... MO-7
**Kinder**—*pop pl* ... WV-2
Kinder Branch—*stream* ... KY-4
Kinder Branch—*stream* ... VA-3
Kinder Canal—*canal* ... LA-4
Kinder Care—*school* ... FL-3
Kinder Care Childrens Center—*school* ... FL-3
Kinder Care Learning Center—*school* (6) ... FL-3
Kinder Cem—*cemetery* ... IL-6
Kinder Cem—*cemetery* ... LA-4
Kinder Cem—*cemetery* (3) ... MO-7
Kinder Cem—*cemetery* ... OR-9
Kinder Cem—*cemetery* ... WV-2
Kinder Ch—*church* ... IN-6
Kinder Chapel—*church* ... MO-7
Kinder Chapel (abandoned)—*church* ... MO-7
Kinder Chapel Cem—*cemetery* ... MO-7
Kinder Creek—*stream* ... NC-3
Kinder Crossing—*locale* ... AZ-5
Kinder Crossing Trail—*trail* ... AZ-5
Kinder Ditch—*canal* ... LA-4
Kinder Draw—*valley* ... AZ-5
Kinder Ford—*locale* ... MO-7
Kindergarden Center Sch—*school* ... FL-3
Kindergarten Bay—*bay* ... AK-9
Kindergarten Elem Sch—*school* ... KS-7
Kinderhook—*locale* ... OH-6
Kinderhook—*locale* ... PA-2
Kinderhook—*locale* ... TN-4
Kinderhook—*locale* ... VA-3
**Kinderhook**—*pop pl* ... IL-6
**Kinderhook**—*pop pl* ... MI-6
**Kinderhook**—*pop pl* ... NY-2
**Kinderhook**—*pop pl* ... VA-3
Kinderhook Branch—*stream* ... TN-4
*Kinderhook Brook* ... MA-1
*Kinderhook Brook* ... NY-2
Kinderhook Cem—*cemetery* ... OH-6
Kinderhook Cem—*cemetery* ... TN-4
*Kinderhook Creek* ... NY-2
Kinderhook Creek—*stream* ... MA-1
Kinderhook Creek—*stream* ... NY-2
Kinderhook Lake—*reservoir* ... IN-6
Kinderhook Lake—*reservoir* ... NY-2
Kinderhook Sch—*school* ... IL-6
**Kinderhook (Town of)**—*pop pl* ... NY-2
**Kinderhook (Township of)**—*pop pl* ... IL-6
**Kinderhook (Township of)**—*pop pl* ... MI-6
Kinderhook Village District hist pl ... NY-2
*Kinder Irrigation Canal* ... LA-4
Kinder Lake—*lake* ... WI-6
Kinderland Preparatory Sch—*school* ... FL-3
Kinderlou—*locale* ... GA-3
Kinderogen Lake—*reservoir* ... NY-2
Kinder Oil Field—*oilfield* ... LA-4
Kinderpost—*locale* ... MO-7
Kinder Run—*stream* ... IN-6
Kinder Slough—*stream* ... AR-4
Kinder's Mill—*hist pl* ... PA-2
Kinder Spring—*spring* ... AZ-5
Kinder Tank—*reservoir* ... AZ-5
Kinder Township—*civil* ... MO-7
Kinder Valley—*basin* ... VA-3
KIND-FM (Independence)—*tower* ... KS-7
**Kindful Acres (subdivision)**—*pop pl* ... NC-3
Kindig Camp—*locale* ... CA-9
Kindla Spring—*spring* ... TX-5
Kindleberger, Frederick, Stone House and Barn—*hist pl* ... OH-6
Kindleberger Park—*park* ... MI-6
Kindle Lake—*lake* ... MN-6
Kindler, Paul, House—*hist pl* ... CA-9
Kindle Sch—*school* ... NJ-2
Kindlespire County Park—*park* ... IA-7
Kindley Cem—*cemetery* ... AR-4
Kindley House—*hist pl* ... AR-4
Kindling Altar Cem—*cemetery* ... MS-4
Kindling Altar Ch—*church* (2) ... MS-4
Kindling Star Baptist Ch—*church* ... MS-4
Kindness Sch—*school* ... KY-4
Kind Providence Cem—*cemetery* ... MS-4
Kind Providence Ch—*church* ... MS-4
Kindra, W. H., Apartments—*hist pl* ... OH-6
**Kindred**—*pop pl* ... ND-7
Kindred Cem—*cemetery* ... MS-4
Kindred Island—*island* ... WA-9
Kindred Sch—*school* ... TX-5
Kindred Slough—*gut* ... WA-9
Kindred Slough—*stream* ... WA-9
*Kindrew Corners* ... NY-2
*Kindrews Corners* ... NY-2
*Kindrick* ... VA-3
**Kindrick**—*pop pl* ... VA-3
Kindrick Branch—*stream* ... MO-7
Kindrick Cem—*cemetery* ... TN-4
*Kindrick Creek* ... GA-3
Kindrick Mtn—*summit* ... VA-3
*Kindrick Pond* ... FL-3
Kindrick School (Abandoned)—*locale* ... MO-7
Kindschi Lake—*lake* ... ND-7
Kindschis Spring—*spring* ... WI-6
Kindt Ranch—*locale* ... WY-8
Kindts Corner—*locale* ... PA-2
Kindy Creek—*stream* ... WA-9
**Kindy Forest**—*pop pl* ... NC-3
Kineberger Lake—*lake* ... MO-7
*Kinebeto (Kimbeto)* ... NM-5
Kineeghit Point—*cape* ... AK-9
Kinegnak—*locale* ... AK-9
Kinegnak River—*stream* ... AK-9
*Kinegon* ... MP-9
*Kinejon* ... MP-9
*Kineman Creek* ... ND-7
Kineo, Mount—*ridge* ... NH-1
Kineo, Mount—*summit* ... ME-1
Kineo Cove—*bay* ... ME-1
Kineo Mtn—*summit* ... CO-8
Kineo Quarry—*mine* ... ME-1
Kineo (Township of)—*unorg* ... ME-1
Kinepoway Lookout Tower—*locale* ... WI-6
Kiner Hollow—*valley* ... TN-4
Kiner Hollow—*valley* ... WV-2
Kinesava, Mount—*summit* ... UT-8
*Kiney Hollow* ... TN-4
KINF-FM (Dodge City)—*tower* ... KS-7
**Kinfield Village (subdivision)**—*pop pl* ... NC-3
*Kinfolk Ridge* ... MO-7
**Kinfolk Ridge**—*pop pl* ... MO-7
**Kinfolks Ridge**—*pop pl* ... MO-7
*Kinfs Pass* ... TX-5
*King* ... CA-9
*King* ... SD-7
King—*fmr MCD* ... NE-7
King—*locale* (2) ... AR-4
King—*locale* ... IL-6
King—*locale* ... LA-4
King—*locale* ... MS-4
King—*locale* (2) ... TX-5
King—*locale* ... WV-2
**King**—*pop pl* ... ID-8
**King**—*pop pl* ... IN-6
**King**—*pop pl* ... IA-7
**King**—*pop pl* ... KY-4
**King**—*pop pl* ... NC-3
**King**—*pop pl* ... PA-2
**King**—*pop pl* ... TN-4
**King**—*pop pl* ... TX-5
**King**—*pop pl* ... WV-2
**King**—*pop pl* ... WI-6
King—*uninc pl* ... CA-9
King, Alexander, House—*hist pl* ... CT-1
King, Dr., House—*hist pl* ... OH-6
King, Dr. Alexander T., House and Carriage House—*hist pl* ... CO-8
King, Dr. Franklin, House-Idlewild—*hist pl* ... NC-3
King, Edward, House—*hist pl* ... RI-1
King, E. L., House—*hist pl* ... MN-6
King, Gov. William, House—*hist pl* ... ME-1
King, Henrietta M., HS—*hist pl* ... TX-5
King, Isaac, House and Barn—*hist pl* ... OR-9
King, L. B. and Co. Bldg—*hist pl* ... MI-6
King, Martin Luther, Jr., Hist Dist—*hist pl* ... GA-3
King, Martin Luther, Jr., Natl Historic Site and Preservation—*hist pl* ... GA-3
King, Martin Luther, Jr., Park—*hist pl* ... NY-2
King, M. J., House—*hist pl* ... KY-4
King, M. L., Blvd Hist Dist—*hist pl* ... TN-4
King, Mrs. J. C., House—*hist pl* ... TX-5
King, Patrick J., House—*hist pl* ... IL-6
King, Polaski, House—*hist pl* ... NY-2
King, Samuel W., House—*hist pl* ... OR-9
King, Tandy, House—*hist pl* ... GA-3
King, Thomas, Inscription—*hist pl* ... ME-1
King, William, House—*hist pl* ... TN-4
Kingaglia Lake—*lake* ... AK-9
King Airfield Hanger—*hist pl* ... MA-1
King Airp—*airport* ... TN-4
Kingak Cliff—*cliff* ... AK-9
Kingak Hill—*summit* ... AK-9
Kingak Mtn—*summit* ... AK-9
Kingaktakamiut (Summer Camp)—*locale* ... AK-9
**King And Anderson**—*pop pl* ... MS-4
King and Anderson Lake Dam—*dam* ... MS-4
King And Anderson Ranch—*locale* ... MS-4
*King and Andersons* ... MS-4
King and Bartlett Camps—*locale* ... ME-1
King and Bartlett Lake—*lake* ... ME-1
King and Bartlett Mtn—*summit* ... ME-1
*King And Queen* ... VA-3
**King and Queen (County)**—*pop pl* ... VA-3
**King And Queen Court House**—*pop pl* ... VA-3
King and Queen Hill—*summit* ... MT-8
King and Queens Bluff—*cliff* ... TN-4
King And Queen Sch—*school* ... VA-3
King And Queen Swamp—*stream* ... VA-3
King and Smith Cem—*cemetery* ... TX-5
King Arroyo—*stream* ... CO-8
King Arroyo—*stream* ... NM-5
King Arthur Castle—*summit* ... AZ-5
**King Arthur Court**—*pop pl* ... TN-4
*Kingas Bay* ... MN-6
Kingasivik Mountains—*other* ... AK-9
*Kingas Lake* ... MN-6
*King Atendance Center* ... MS-4
Kingaviksak Mtn—*summit* ... AK-9
King Banco Number 48—*levee* ... TX-5
King Bar—*bar* ... AL-4
King & Bartlett (Township of)—*unorg* ... ME-1
*King Bay* ... FL-3
*King Bay* ... GA-3
*King Bay* ... LA-4
King Bay—*bay* ... MN-6
King Bay—*bay* ... NY-2
*King Bayou* ... AR-4
King Bayou—*gut* (2) ... LA-4
King Bayou—*stream* ... AR-4
King Bay State Wetland Game Mngmt Area—*park* ... NY-2
Kingbee—*locale* ... KY-4
King Bee Bayou—*gut* ... LA-4
Kingbee Ch—*church* ... KY-4
Kingbee Ridge—*ridge* ... KY-4
King Bee Spring—*spring* ... MO-7
King Bench—*bench* (3) ... UT-8
*King Bend* ... AL-4
King Bend—*bend* ... IL-6
King Benjamin Mine—*mine* (2) ... AZ-5
King Block—*hist pl* ... NJ-2
King Bluff—*cliff* ... MS-4
King Bluff—*cliff* ... MO-7
King Bluff—*cliff* ... WI-6
Kingbolt Spring—*spring* (2) ... OR-9
Kingborough MS—*school* ... TX-5
King Bottom Spring—*spring* ... UT-8
*King Branch* ... WV-2
King Branch—*stream* (4) ... AL-4
King Branch—*stream* ... AR-4
King Branch—*stream* ... FL-3
King Branch—*stream* (2) ... GA-3
King Branch—*stream* (2) ... IN-6
King Branch—*stream* (3) ... KY-4
King Branch—*stream* (5) ... MS-4
King Branch—*stream* (3) ... MO-7
King Branch—*stream* ... NC-3
King Branch—*stream* ... PA-2
King Branch—*stream* (2) ... SC-3
King Branch—*stream* (10) ... TN-4
King Branch—*stream* (3) ... TX-5
King Branch Ch—*church* ... SC-3
*King Bridge* ... PA-2
King Bridge—*bridge* ... AL-4
*King Brook* ... MA-1
King Brook—*stream* (2) ... ME-1
King Brook—*stream* (2) ... MA-1
King Brook—*stream* (2) ... NY-2
King Brook—*stream* (2) ... VT-1
King Brook Island—*island* ... ME-1
King Bros Ranch—*locale* ... NM-5
King Brothers Ranch—*locale* ... WY-8
King Brown Cabin (ruins)—*locale* ... OR-9
Kingburg Lake—*lake* ... MN-6
King Cabin Canyon—*valley* ... OR-9
King Caesar House—*building* ... MA-1
King Caesar House—*hist pl* ... MA-1
King Camp—*locale* ... NM-5
King Camp—*locale* ... OR-9
King Camp Branch—*stream* (2) ... KY-4
King Canal—*canal* ... FL-3
King Canal—*canal* ... LA-4
King Canal—*canal* ... MS-4
*King Canyon* ... AZ-5
*King Canyon* ... UT-8
King Canyon—*valley* (2) ... AZ-5
King Canyon—*valley* (3) ... CA-9
King Canyon—*valley* ... ID-8
King Canyon—*valley* ... MT-8
King Canyon—*valley* (3) ... OR-9
King Canyon—*valley* (2) ... WA-9
King-Casper-Ward-Bazemore House—*hist pl* ... NC-3
King Cave—*cave* (2) ... AL-4
*King Cem* ... MS-4
King Cem—*cemetery* (10) ... AL-4
King Cem—*cemetery* (6) ... AR-4
King Cem—*cemetery* ... FL-3
King Cem—*cemetery* (6) ... GA-3
King Cem—*cemetery* (5) ... IL-6
King Cem—*cemetery* (3) ... IN-6
King Cem—*cemetery* (3) ... IA-7
King Cem—*cemetery* (9) ... KY-4
King Cem—*cemetery* (3) ... LA-4
King Cem—*cemetery* ... MD-2
King Cem—*cemetery* ... MI-6
King Cem—*cemetery* (2) ... MN-6
King Cem—*cemetery* (10) ... MS-4
King Cem—*cemetery* (5) ... MO-7
King Cem—*cemetery* ... NM-5
King Cem—*cemetery* (2) ... NY-2
King Cem—*cemetery* (4) ... NC-3
King Cem—*cemetery* (4) ... OH-6
King Cem—*cemetery* (2) ... OK-5
King Cem—*cemetery* (21) ... TN-4
King Cem—*cemetery* (9) ... TX-5
King Cem—*cemetery* ... VT-1
King Cem—*cemetery* (2) ... VA-3
King Cem—*cemetery* (3) ... WV-2
King Center—*locale* ... CO-8
King Ch—*church* ... LA-4
King Ch—*church* (2) ... OH-6
*King Chapel* ... AL-4
King Chapel—*church* ... FL-3
King Chapel—*church* (2) ... GA-3
King Chapel—*church* ... MS-4
King Chapel Cem—*cemetery* ... AL-4
King Chapel Cem—*cemetery* ... GA-3
*King Chapel Church* ... AL-4
King Charles—*uninc pl* ... NC-3
**King Charles Commons**—*pop pl* ... MD-2
**King Circle**—*pop pl* ... SC-3
*King City* ... KS-7
King City—*locale* ... AK-9
**King City**—*pop pl* ... CA-9
**King City**—*pop pl* ... MO-7
**King City**—*pop pl* ... OR-9
**King City**—*pop pl* ... TX-5
King City (CCD)—*cens area* ... CA-9
**King City Township**—*pop pl* ... KS-7
**King Clarion Hills Subdivision**—*pop pl* ... UT-8
King Coal Mine—*mine* ... CO-8
King Cole—*locale* ... OR-9
**King Cole**—*pop pl* ... VA-3
King Coll—*school* ... TN-4
King Colony Ranch—*locale* ... MT-8
King Consolidated Ditch—*canal* ... CO-8
Kingcopsico Point—*cape* ... VA-3
King Corner—*locale* ... WA-9
**King Corner**—*pop pl* ... MA-1
King Corners—*locale* ... NY-2
**King Corners**—*pop pl* ... OH-6
King Corner Sch—*school* ... WI-6
King Coulee—*valley* ... MN-6
King Coulee—*valley* (4) ... MT-8
**King (County)**—*pop pl* ... TX-5
**King County**—*pop pl* ... WA-9
King County Creek—*stream* ... AK-9
King County Enumclaw Park—*park* ... WA-9
King County Park—*park* ... WA-9
*King Cove* ... MA-1
*King Cove* ... TN-4
King Cove—*bay* (2) ... AK-9
King Cove—*bay* ... NJ-2
**King Cove**—*pop pl* ... AK-9
King Cove—*valley* (2) ... AL-4
King Cove—*valley* ... GA-3
King Cove—*valley* ... UT-8
King Cove Cem—*cemetery* ... AL-4
King Cove Lagoon—*bay* ... AK-9
King Covered Bridge—*hist pl* ... PA-2
King Cove Sch (historical)—*school* ... AL-4
King Crab Landing—*locale* ... NJ-2
*King Creek* ... IL-6
*King Creek* ... MD-2
*King Creek* ... NC-3
*King Creek* ... OH-6
*King Creek* ... OR-9
*King Creek* ... SC-3
*King Creek* ... TN-4
*King Creek* ... TX-5
*King Creek* ... VA-3
*King Creek* ... WA-9
*King Creek* ... WV-2
King Creek—*stream* ... AL-4
King Creek—*stream* (5) ... AK-9
King Creek—*stream* ... AZ-5
King Creek—*stream* (3) ... CA-9
King Creek—*stream* (3) ... CO-8
King Creek—*stream* ... FL-3
King Creek—*stream* ... GA-3
King Creek—*stream* (6) ... ID-8
King Creek—*stream* (2) ... IL-6
King Creek—*stream* ... IN-6
King Creek—*stream* ... IA-7
King Creek—*stream* (2) ... KY-4
King Creek—*stream* (2) ... MI-6
King Creek—*stream* (2) ... MN-6
King Creek—*stream* (5) ... MS-4
King Creek—*stream* (4) ... MT-8
King Creek—*stream* ... NY-2
King Creek—*stream* (6) ... NC-3
King Creek—*stream* ... OK-5
King Creek—*stream* (10) ... OR-9
King Creek—*stream* ... PA-2
King Creek—*stream* (2) ... SC-3
King Creek—*stream* (4) ... TN-4
King Creek—*stream* (4) ... TX-5
King Creek—*stream* ... UT-8
King Creek—*stream* (3) ... VA-3
King Creek—*stream* (8) ... WA-9
King Creek—*stream* (3) ... WI-6
King Creek—*stream* (3) ... WY-8
King Creek Bottoms—*flat* ... MS-4
King Creek Camp—*locale* ... KY-4
King Creek Campground—*locale* ... UT-8
**King Creek (historical)**—*pop pl* ... TN-4
King Creek Landing—*locale* ... SC-3
King Creek Rsvr—*reservoir* ... MT-8
King Creek Sch—*school* ... WV-2
King Creek Spring—*spring* ... ID-8
King Creek Spring—*spring* ... MT-8
King Creek Well Number One—*well* ... MT-8
King Creek Well Number Two—*well* ... MT-8
King Crest—*summit* ... AZ-5
King Crest Trail—*trail* ... CA-9
**Kingdale**—*pop pl* ... NC-3
King Dam—*dam* ... OR-9
King Dam—*dam* ... SD-7
King Dam—*dam* ... TN-4
King Dam—*reservoir* ... TN-4
King Dam Rsvr—*reservoir* ... SD-7
King David Cem—*cemetery* ... NY-2
King David Cem—*cemetery* ... PA-2
King David Ch—*church* (3) ... MS-4
King David Ch—*church* ... SC-3
*King David Christian Church* ... MS-4
King David Hill—*summit* ... ME-1
King David Lodge Hall—*building* ... VA-3
*King David Mine* ... UT-8
King David Mine—*mine* ... CA-9
King David Sch—*school* ... MS-4
King David Spring—*spring* ... CA-9
King Davis Ch—*church* ... MS-4
King Ditch—*canal* ... AL-4
King Ditch—*canal* ... CA-9
King Ditch—*canal* (2) ... IN-6
King Ditch—*canal* ... LA-4
King Ditch—*canal* ... OH-6
King Ditch—*canal* ... UT-8
King Ditch—*canal* (2) ... WY-8
King Ditch No 1—*canal* ... WY-8
King Ditch No 2—*canal* ... WY-8
*Kingdom* ... MO-7
**Kingdom**—*pop pl* ... IL-6
**Kingdom**—*pop pl* ... NY-2
Kingdom, The—*locale* ... ME-1
Kingdom, The—*summit* ... NY-2
Kingdom Bog—*lake* ... ME-1
Kingdom Bridge—*bridge* ... NY-2
Kingdom Brook—*stream* ... VT-1
Kingdom Cem—*cemetery* ... IA-7
Kingdom Cem—*cemetery* ... MS-4
Kingdom Cem—*cemetery* (3) ... NY-2
Kingdom Ch—*church* (2) ... AL-4
Kingdom Ch—*church* ... IL-6
Kingdom Ch—*church* ... MO-7
Kingdom Ch—*church* ... OK-5
Kingdom Ch—*church* ... PA-2
Kingdom Ch—*church* ... TN-4
**Kingdom City**—*pop pl* ... MO-7
Kingdom Come Creek—*stream* ... KY-4
Kingdom Come Creek Sch—*hist pl* ... KY-4
Kingdom Come Creek Sch—*school* ... KY-4
Kingdom Come Sch—*school* ... KY-4
Kingdom Crossroads—*locale* ... AL-4
*Kingdom Cumberland Presbyterian Ch* ... TN-4
*Kingdom Hall* ... UT-8
Kingdom Hall—*building* ... MI-6
Kingdom Hall—*church* ... AR-4
Kingdom Hall—*church* ... FL-3
Kingdom Hall—*church* (4) ... GA-3
Kingdom Hall—*church* ... IN-6
Kingdom Hall—*church* (4) ... IA-7
Kingdom Hall—*church* ... MD-2
Kingdom Hall—*church* ... MA-1
Kingdom Hall—*church* (3) ... MI-6
Kingdom Hall—*church* (3) ... MS-4
Kingdom Hall—*church* (2) ... MO-7
Kingdom Hall—*church* (2) ... NY-2
Kingdom Hall—*church* (2) ... NC-3
Kingdom Hall—*church* ... OH-6
Kingdom Hall—*church* ... PA-2
Kingdom Hall—*church* ... TN-4
Kingdom Hall—*church* (4) ... WI-6
**Kingdom Hall**—*pop pl* ... MA-1
Kingdom Hall Ch—*church* (4) ... AL-4
Kingdom Hall Ch—*church* ... FL-3
Kingdom Hall Ch—*church* ... GA-3
Kingdom Hall Ch—*church* ... IN-6
Kingdom Hall Ch—*church* ... IA-7
Kingdom Hall Ch—*church* ... MS-4
Kingdom Hall Ch—*church* (2) ... NY-2
Kingdom Hall Ch—*church* ... NC-3
Kingdom Hall Ch—*church* (3) ... OH-6
Kingdom Hall Ch—*church* (3) ... PA-2
Kingdom Hall Ch—*church* ... SC-3
Kingdom Hall Ch—*church* ... WV-2
Kingdom Hall Ch—*church* ... WI-6
Kingdom Hall Jehovahs Witnesses—*church* ... FL-3
*Kingdom Hall North Unit* ... IN-6
Kingdom Hall of Jehonvahs Witnesses—*church* ... MS-4
Kingdom Hall of Jehovahs Witnesses—*church* (22) ... AL-4
Kingdom Hall of Jehovahs Witnesses—*church* (2) ... FL-3
Kingdom Hall of Jehovahs Witnesses—*church* (12) ... MS-4
Kingdom Hall of Jehovahs Witnesses—*church* (3) ... TN-4
Kingdom Hall of Jehovahs Witnesses (American Fork)—*church* ... UT-8
Kingdom Hall of Jehovahs Witnesses Ch—*church* ... AL-4
Kingdom Hall of Jehovahs Witnesses (Provo-Orem)—*church* ... UT-8
Kingdom Hall of Jehovahs Witnesses—*church* ... AL-4
Kingdom Hall of Jehovahs Witnesses (South and Central)—*church* ... FL-3
Kingdom Hall of Jehovah Witnesses—*church* ... MS-4
Kingdom Hall of Jehova's Witnesses—*church* (2) ... MT-8
Kingdom Hall Sebastian Congregation—*church* ... FL-3
Kingdom Hollow—*valley* ... VA-3
Kingdom Island—*island* ... IN-6
Kingdom of God in Christ Ch—*church* ... MS-4
Kingdom of Heaven Ch—*church* ... OH-6
Kingdom Sch—*school* ... AL-4
Kingdom Sch—*school* (2) ... IL-6
Kingdom Valley—*valley* ... VT-1
Kingdon—*locale* ... CA-9
*Kingdon Church* ... AL-4
Kingdoodle Creek—*stream* ... AR-4
Kingdoodle Knob—*summit* ... AR-4
King Drain—*canal* (3) ... MI-6
King Drain—*canal* ... OR-9
King Drain—*stream* (2) ... MI-6
King Draw—*valley* ... MT-8
King Draw—*valley* ... NM-5
King Draw—*valley* ... OK-5
King Draw—*valley* (3) ... WY-8
**Kingegan**—*pop pl* ... AK-9
*King Elementary School* ... PA-2
King Elem Sch—*school* ... NC-3
Kingelm Lake—*lake* ... WI-6
King Emmanuel Ch—*church* ... SC-3
Kingen Gun Club—*other* ... IN-6
Kingen Hotel—*hist pl* ... CA-9
Kingerly Summit—*gap* ... NV-8
Kingery Cem—*cemetery* ... IL-6
Kingery Cem—*cemetery* ... IN-6
Kingery Cem—*cemetery* ... NE-7
Kingery Cem—*cemetery* ... OH-6
Kingery Cem—*cemetery* ... VA-3
Kingery Hill—*summit* ... VA-3
Kingery Sch—*school* ... IL-6
**Kingery Township**—*pop pl* ... KS-7
King Estate JHS—*school* ... CA-9
**King Farm Estates Subdivision**—*pop pl* ... UT-8
**King Farms**—*pop pl* ... CA-9
**King Ferry**—*pop pl* ... NY-2
**King Ferry Station**—*pop pl* ... NY-2
**Kingfield**—*pop pl* ... ME-1
**Kingfield**—*pop pl* ... TN-4
**Kingfield (Town of)**—*pop pl* ... ME-1
Kingfish Camp—*locale* ... KY-4
Kingfish Creek—*stream* ... WA-9
**Kingfisher**—*pop pl* ... OK-5
Kingfisher Bluff—*cliff* ... TX-5
Kingfisher Camp—*locale* ... OR-9
Kingfisher Canyon—*valley* ... UT-8
Kingfisher (CCD)—*cens area* ... OK-5
Kingfisher Cem—*cemetery* ... OK-5
Kingfisher College Site—*hist pl* ... OK-5
**Kingfisher (County)**—*pop pl* ... OK-5
**Kingfisher Cove**—*pop pl* ... NJ-2
Kingfisher Creek—*stream* ... AK-9
Kingfisher Creek—*stream* ... NJ-2
Kingfisher Creek—*stream* ... OK-5
Kingfisher Creek—*stream* ... TN-4
Kingfisher Creek—*stream* ... UT-8
Kingfisher Creek—*stream* ... WV-2
Kingfisher Hill—*summit* ... IL-6
Kingfisher Hollow—*valley* ... MO-7
Kingfisher Hollow—*valley* ... OK-5
Kingfisher Island—*island* ... UT-8
Kingfisher Island Campground—*park* ... UT-8
*Kingfisher Lake* ... MN-6
Kingfisher Lake—*lake* ... MN-6
Kingfisher Lake—*reservoir* ... AR-4
Kingfisher Lakes—*lake* ... KY-4
Kingfisher Park—*locale* ... UT-8
Kingfisher Peak—*summit* ... WY-8
Kingfisher Point—*cape* ... AK-9
Kingfisher Point—*cape* ... CA-9
Kingfisher Pond—*lake* ... MA-1
Kingfisher Post Office—*hist pl* ... OK-5
Kingfisher Ridge—*ridge* ... CA-9
Kingfisher Stringer—*stream* ... CA-9
Kingfisher Tower—*locale* ... NY-2
Kingfisher Waterhole—*lake* ... TX-5
Kingfish Lodge—*locale* ... AL-4
*King Fish Shoal* ... NC-3
Kingfish Shoal—*bar* ... NC-3
Kingfish Shoals—*bar* ... FL-3
King Flat—*flat* ... CA-9

King Flats Creek—*stream* SC-3
King-Flowers-Keaton House—*hist pl* NC-3
King Forest Camp—*locale* OR-9
King-Freeman-Speight House—*hist pl* NC-3
King Gap—*gap* (2) AL-4
King Gap—*gap* TN-4
**King George**—*pop pl* VA-3
King George Bay—*bay* AK-9
King George Bayou—*stream* LA-4
**King George (County)**—*pop pl* VA-3
King George HS—*school* VA-3
King George Island—*island* LA-4
King George Lookout Tower—*locale* VA-3
King George Mtn—*summit* VA-3
King George Peak—*summit* CA-9
*King George Point* VA-3
King George Point—*cape* VA-3
King George Ridge—*ridge* CA-9
King Gulch—*valley* AZ-5
King Gulch—*valley* (4) CO-8
King Gulch—*valley* OR-9
Kingham Creek—*stream* TX-5
King Harbor—*locale* CA-9
*King Heijahs Town* FL-3
*King Helahs Town* FL-3
King Hill—*locale* WA-9
**King Hill**—*pop pl* ID-8
**King Hill**—*pop pl* LA-4
King Hill—*summit* AL-4
King Hill—*summit* CT-1
King Hill—*summit* (2) ID-8
King Hill—*summit* KS-7
King Hill—*summit* ME-1
King Hill—*summit* MA-1
King Hill—*summit* (2) MO-7
King Hill—*summit* (2) NE-7
King Hill—*summit* NH-1
King Hill—*summit* (3) NY-2
King Hill—*summit* PA-2
King Hill—*summit* VT-1
King Hill—*summit* WA-9
King Hill—*summit* VI-3
King Hill Baptist Ch—*church* AL-4
King Hill Cem—*cemetery* NY-2
King Hill Cem—*cemetery* PA-2
King Hill Ch—*church* AL-4
King Hill Ch of Christ—*church* AL-4
King Hill Creek—*stream* (2) ID-8
King Hill Ditch—*canal* ID-8
King Hill Main Canal—*canal* ID-8
King Hill Park—*park* AL-4
King Hill Quarry—*other* NE-7
King Hill Sch—*school* IL-6
King Hill Sch—*school* PA-2
**King Hill (subdivision)**—*pop pl* AL-4
King Hill Winter Sports Area—*locale* MT-8
King (historical)—*locale* AL-4
**King (historical)**—*pop pl* OR-9
*King Hollow* PA-2
King Hollow—*valley* (3) AL-4
King Hollow—*valley* (5) AR-4
King Hollow—*valley* KY-4
King Hollow—*valley* MS-4
King Hollow—*valley* (3) MO-7
King Hollow—*valley* NY-2
King Hollow—*valley* OH-6
King Hollow—*valley* OK-5
King Hollow—*valley* (7) TN-4
King Hollow—*valley* TX-5
King Hollow Branch—*stream* TN-4
King Hollow Spring—*spring* TN-4
King Hollow Trail—*trail* OH-6
King Hollow Trail—*trail* PA-2
King Homestead—*hist pl* TN-4
King Homestead—*locale* CO-8
Kinghorn Two Top Ranch—*locale* SD-7
King House—*hist pl* AL-4
King House—*hist pl* MA-1
King House—*hist pl* NC-3
King HS—*school* FL-3
King HS—*school* OH-6
King HS—*school* (2) TX-5
King HS—*school* WI-6
*Kinght Canyon* AZ-5
Kinghthouse Hollow—*valley* TN-4
**Kinghurst Park (subdivision)**—*pop pl* NC-3
**Kinghurst (Township of)**—*pop pl* MN-6
King II Archeol Site—*hist pl* MO-7
Kingins Cem—*cemetery* TN-4
King Intermediate Sch—*school* NC-3
*King Island* AL-4
King Island—*island* (2) AK-9
King Island—*island* CA-9
King Island—*island* IL-6
King Island—*island* (2) ME-1
King Island—*island* MT-8
King Island—*island* (2) PA-2
King Island (Ukivok)—*other* AK-9
King James Ch—*church* NC-3
King JHS—*school* CA-9
King JHS—*school* ME-1
King Johnson Sch—*school* VA-3
King Knob—*summit* PA-2
King Knob—*summit* (2) WV-2
King Knob Cem—*cemetery* WV-2
King Knob Ch—*church* WV-2
King Knob Run—*stream* WV-2
King-Knowles-Gheesling House—*hist pl* GA-3
*King Lake* MN-6
King Lake—*lake* AL-4
King Lake—*lake* AK-9
King Lake—*lake* CO-8
King Lake—*lake* (5) FL-3
King Lake—*lake* (2) IN-6
King Lake—*lake* (2) LA-4
King Lake—*lake* (6) MI-6
King Lake—*lake* (3) MN-6
King Lake—*lake* MO-7
King Lake—*lake* NM-5
King Lake—*lake* OR-9
King Lake—*lake* (2) TX-5
King Lake—*lake* (3) WA-9
King Lake—*lake* (3) WI-6
**King Lake**—*pop pl* NE-7
King Lake—*reservoir* CO-8
King Lake—*reservoir* CT-1
King Lake—*reservoir* NC-3
King Lake Cem—*cemetery* MI-6
King Lake Dam—*dam* (3) MS-4
King Lake Dam—*dam* NC-3
King Lakes—*lake* ID-8
King Lake Trail—*trail* CO-8
Kingland Cem—*cemetery* IA-7
King Lateral—*canal* CA-9
King Lear Peak—*summit* NV-8
*Kingler Spring* AZ-5
Kinglet Creek—*stream* MI-6
Kinglet Lake—*lake* OR-9
Kinglet Spring—*spring* AZ-5
Kinglewood Airp—*airport* MO-7
Kingley—*locale* MT-8
Kingley Creek—*stream* IN-6
King Lithia Prospect Mine—*mine* SD-7
King Lookout Tower—*locale* MI-6
King Lumber Company
Warehouse—*hist pl* VA-3
Kingman—*locale* OR-9
Kingman—*locale* VA-3
**Kingman**—*pop pl* AZ-5
**Kingman**—*pop pl* IL-6
**Kingman**—*pop pl* IN-6
**Kingman**—*pop pl* KS-7
**Kingman**—*pop pl* ME-1
**Kingman**—*pop pl* OH-6
Kingman, Gardner J., House—*hist pl* MA-1
Kingman, Lake—*lake* VA-3
Kingman, Romanzo, House—*hist pl* ME-1
Kingman Airfield—*airport* AZ-5
Kingman Airp—*airport* AZ-5
Kingman Brook—*stream* (2) ME-1
Kingman Carnegie Library—*hist pl* KS-7
Kingman City Bldg—*hist pl* KS-7
Kingman City Hall—*building* AZ-5
Kingman Commercial Hist Dist—*hist pl* AZ-5
Kingman Country Club—*other* KS-7
*Kingman Country Club and Golf Course* AZ-5
Kingman County—*civil* KS-7
Kingman County Courthouse—*hist pl* KS-7
*Kingman County State Game Mngmt Area* KS-7
Kingman County State Lake—*reservoir* KS-7
Kingman County State Lake Dam—*dam* KS-7
Kingman Ditch—*canal* WY-8
Kingman Drain—*canal* OR-9
Kingman Grammar Sch—*hist pl* AZ-5
Kingman Gulch—*valley* ID-8
Kingman (historical)—*locale* AL-4
Kingman HS—*school* AZ-5
Kingman HS—*school* KS-7
Kingman JHS—*school* AZ-5
Kingman Kolony—*locale* OR-9
Kingman Lake—*lake* DC-2
Kingman Lateral—*canal* OR-9
Kingman-More Bldg—*hist pl* OK-5
Kingman Municipal Airp—*airport* KS-7
Kingman Municipal Golf Course—*other* AZ-5
Kingman Museum—*building* MI-6
Kingman North (CCD)—*cens area* AZ-5
King Manor—*hist pl* NY-2
Kingman Park—*park* NY-2
Kingman Pass—*gap* WY-8
*Kingman P.O.* AL-4
Kingman Pond—*lake* MA-1
Kingman Post Office—*building* AZ-5
Kingman RR Station—*building* AZ-5
Kingman Sch—*school* IL-6
Kingman Sch—*school* NJ-2
Kingman South (CCD)—*cens area* AZ-5
Kingman State Fishing Lake and Wildlife
Area—*park* KS-7
Kingman Tavern Museum—*building* MA-1
**Kingman Township**—*pop pl* KS-7
**Kingman (Township of)**—*pop pl* MN-6
Kingman (Township of)—*unorg* ME-1
*Kingman Union High School* AZ-5
Kingman (Unorganized Territory
of)—*unorg* ME-1
Kingman Wash—*valley* AZ-5
King-McNeil Cem—*cemetery* IL-6
King Meadow—*flat* WA-9
King Meadows—*flat* NC-3
King Memorial Cem—*cemetery* VA-3
King Memorial Center—*locale* AZ-5
King Memorial Ch—*church* VA-3
King Memorial Chapel—*church* TX-5
King Memorial Chapel—*hist pl* IA-7
King Memorial Hosp—*hospital* AL-4
King Merritt Ranch—*locale* WY-8
King Mesa—*summit* UT-8
Kingmetolik Creek—*stream* AK-9
King Mica Mine—*mine* SD-7
King Mill Branch—*stream* AL-4
King Millpond—*reservoir* SC-3
King Mills—*locale* KY-4
**King Mills**—*pop pl* AR-4
King Mine—*mine* CA-9
King Mine—*mine* (2) CO-8
King Mine—*mine* MN-6
King Mine—*mine* MT-8
King Mine—*mine* NV-8
King Mine—*mine* (2) TN-4
King Mine—*mine* (2) UT-8
King Mine (Inactive)—*mine* KY-4
**King Mines**—*pop pl* OH-6
King Mine (underground)—*mine* (2) AL-4
**Kingmont**—*pop pl* WV-2
Kingmont Siding—*locale* MT-8
*King Mountain* AL-4
King Mountain Fish Hatchery—*other* GA-3
King Mountain Oil Field—*oilfield* TX-5
King Mountain Sch—*school* TN-4
King Mountain Sch (historical)—*school* MO-7
King Mountain Truck Trail—*trail* OR-9
King MS—*school* FL-3
*King Mtn* NC-3
King Mtn—*summit* (2) AK-9
King Mtn—*summit* (2) CA-9
King Mtn—*summit* CO-8
King Mtn—*summit* (2) ID-8
King Mtn—*summit* (2) KY-4
King Mtn—*summit* ME-1
King Mtn—*summit* MO-7
King Mtn—*summit* (3) MT-8
King Mtn—*summit* (3) NC-3
King Mtn—*summit* (2) OK-5
King Mtn—*summit* (3) OR-9
King Mtn—*summit* (2) TN-4
King Mtn—*summit* (2) TX-5
King Mtn—*summit* (3) WA-9
King Mtn—*summit* WY-8
King Museum—*building* PA-2
King Noahs Branch—*stream* VA-3
King No 2 Well—*well* WY-8
King No 4 Well—*well* WY-8
King Number 1 Dam—*dam* SD-7
King Oak Hill—*summit* MA-1
Kingo Cem—*cemetery* MN-6
King of Arizona Mine—*mine* AZ-5
King of Glory Ch—*church* FL-3
King Of Glory Ch—*church* OH-6
King of Glory Ch—*church* TX-5
King of Kings Ch—*church* MI-6
King of Kings Ch—*church* NY-2
King of Kings Lutheran Ch
(WELS)—*church* FL-3
King of Kings Lutheran Elem Sch—*school* FL-3
King of Lead Mine—*mine* AZ-5
King of Peace Cem—*cemetery* OR-9
**King of Prussia**—*pop pl* PA-2
King of Prussia Industrial Park—*locale* PA-2
King of Prussia Inn—*hist pl* PA-2
King of Prussia Plaza—*locale* PA-2
King of Prussia Station—*locale* PA-2
King Of The West Creek—*stream* ID-8
King Of The West Mine—*mine* ID-8
King of the West Mine—*mine* SD-7
King Oil Field—*oilfield* OK-5
King Oil Field—*other* IL-6
King Oil Field—*other* NM-5
Kingokakthluk Lake—*lake* AK-9
**Kingola**—*pop pl* TX-5
*King On His Throne* UT-8
King-on-his-Throne—*summit* UT-8
King Opening—*cave* VT-1
King Oscar's Settlement—*hist pl* MN-6
King Park—*park* NY-2
King Park—*park* WI-6
King Peak—*summit* AZ-5
King Peak—*summit* CA-9
King Peak—*summit* NV-8
King Philip Brook—*stream* MA-1
King Philip Mills—*hist pl* MA-1
King Philips Chair—*summit* RI-1
King Philip's Hill—*hist pl* MA-1
KING PHILIP (ship) and REPORTER (schooner)
Shipwreck Site—*hist pl* CA-9
King Philip Spring—*spring* MA-1
King Philips Rock—*summit* MA-1
King Phillip Brook—*stream* CT-1
King Phillip Cave—*cave* CT-1
King Phillip Guzzler—*reservoir* AZ-5
King Phillip HS—*school* MA-1
King Phillip Mtn—*summit* CT-1
King Phillip Sch—*school* CT-1
King-Phillips-Deibel House—*hist pl* OH-6
King Phillips Lookout—*cliff* MA-1
King Phillips Swamp—*swamp* MA-1
King Place—*locale* NM-5
**King Place Subdivision**—*pop pl* UT-8
King Point—*cape* MA-1
King Point—*cape* NC-3
King Point—*cape* TN-4
King Point—*cape* VA-3
King Point Marsh—*swamp* NC-3
*King Pond* MA-1
King Pond—*lake* (2) FL-3
King Pond—*lake* (2) ME-1
King Pond—*lake* MI-6
King Pond—*lake* NJ-2
King Pond—*lake* RI-1
King Pond—*reservoir* NC-3
King Pond—*swamp* TN-4
King Pond Dam—*dam* NC-3
King Ponds—*lake* VT-1
King Post Office (historical)—*building* MS-4
King Prospect—*mine* (2) TN-4
*King & Queen Church* VA-3
King Ranch—*hist pl* TX-5
King Ranch—*locale* (2) CO-8
King Ranch—*locale* (2) NM-5
King Ranch—*locale* (2) OR-9
King Ranch—*locale* SD-7
King Ranch—*locale* (2) TX-5
King Ranch—*locale* (2) UT-8
King Ranch Airp—*airport* KS-7
King Ranch Borregos Oil Field—*oilfield* TX-5
King Ranch Windmill—*locale* TX-5
King Range—*range* CA-9
King Ravine—*valley* NH-1
Kingree Chapel—*church* AR-4
King-Reed Cem—*cemetery* TN-4
Kingree Lake—*reservoir* TN-4
Kingrey Cem—*cemetery* LA-4
Kingrey Cem—*cemetery* (2) OH-6
Kingrey Place—*locale* MT-8
*King Ride* AZ-5
King Rider Sch—*school* AR-4
King Ridge—*ridge* AZ-5
King Ridge—*ridge* (2) TN-4
King Ridge—*ridge* TX-5
King Ridge—*ridge* VA-3
King Ridge Tank—*reservoir* AZ-5
*King River* CA-9
King River—*stream* AK-9
King Rocks—*summit* WV-2
King Rough Hollow—*stream* WV-2
*King Row* UT-8
King Row Shop Ctr—*locale* FL-3
King Rsvr—*reservoir* (3) CO-8
King Rsvr—*reservoir* MT-8
King Rsvr—*reservoir* OR-9
King Rsvr—*reservoir* (2) WY-8
King Rsvr No 1—*reservoir* WY-8
*King Run* PA-2
King Run—*stream* OH-6
King Run—*stream* PA-2
King Run—*stream* WV-2
King-Runkle House—*hist pl* VA-3
Kingry Marsh—*swamp* OR-9
*Kings* AL-4
*Kings* IN-6
*Kings* MS-4
*Kings* NC-3
Kings—*locale* IL-6
Kings—*locale* NY-2
**Kings**—*pop pl* AL-4
**Kings**—*pop pl* IL-6
**Kings**—*pop pl* MS-4
**Kings**—*pop pl* WI-6
Kings Acad—*school* FL-3
**Kings Acres (subdivision)**—*pop pl* AL-4
**Kings Addition (subdivision)**—*pop pl* UT-8
Kings Airfield—*airport* PA-2
*Kings Airp* PA-2
Kings Airp—*airport* PA-2
Kings Airstrip—*airport* OR-9
Kingsale Swamp—*swamp* VA-3
**King Salmon**—*pop pl* AK-9
**King Salmon**—*pop pl* CA-9
King Salmon Airport—*mil airp* AK-9
King Salmon Bay—*bay* AK-9
King Salmon Creek—*stream* (2) AK-9
King Salmon Island—*island* AK-9
King Salmon River—*stream* (3) AK-9
Kings Apostle Ch—*church* MD-2
Kings Assembly of God Ch—*church* DE-2
*Kings Bald* NC-3
Kings Bar—*bar* TN-4
Kings Battery—*locale* AL-4
*Kings Bay* FL-3
*King's Bay* GA-3
*Kings Bay* MN-6
*Kings Bay* NY-2
Kings Bay—*bay* AK-9
Kings Bay—*bay* GA-3
Kings Bay—*bay* VT-1
Kings Bay—*lake* FL-3
**Kings Bay**—*pop pl* FL-3
Kings Bay—*post sta* GA-3
Kings Bay—*swamp* GA-3
Kings Bay—*swamp* NC-3
Kings Bay (Carolina Bay)—*swamp* NC-3
Kings Bay Country Club—*locale* FL-3
Kings Bayou—*gut* MS-4
Kings Bayou—*stream* AR-4
Kings Bayou—*stream* LA-4
Kings Bay Plaza (Shop Ctr)—*locale* FL-3
Kings Beach—*beach* MA-1
**Kings Beach**—*pop pl* CA-9
*Kings Bench* UT-8
Kings Bend—*bend* (2) AL-4
Kings Bend—*bend* TN-4
Kings Bend—*cape* AL-4
Kings Bend Cave—*cave* TN-4
Kings Bend Cem—*cemetery* AL-4
Kings Bend Mine (underground)—*mine* TN-4
Kingsberry—*locale* VA-3
Kingsberry Gulch—*valley* MT-8
Kingsberry Park—*park* OH-6
Kingsberry Sch—*school* GA-3
Kings Bluff—*cliff* AL-4
Kings Bluff—*cliff* MN-6
Kings Bluff—*cliff* NC-3
Kings Bluff—*summit* NJ-2
Kings Bluff Aqueduct—*canal* NC-3
Kings Bluff State Wildlife Area—*park* MO-7
Kings Boat Landing—*locale* GA-3
Kingsboro—*locale* GA-3
**Kingsboro**—*pop pl* NY-2
**Kingsboro**—*pop pl* NC-3
**Kingsboro Estates
(subdivision)**—*pop pl* NC-3
Kingsboro Hist Dist—*hist pl* NY-2
*Kingsborough* CO-8
Kingsborough Ch—*church* TX-5
Kingsborough Community Coll—*school* NY-2
Kingsborough Park—*park* TX-5
Kingsborough Sch—*school* TX-5
*Kingsborough South* CO-8
Kings Bottom—*bend* UT-8
*Kings Bottoms* AL-4
Kings Bowl—*basin* ID-8
*Kings Branch* MS-4
*Kings Branch* TN-4
Kings Branch—*stream* AL-4
Kings Branch—*stream* (2) AR-4
Kings Branch—*stream* (2) GA-3
Kings Branch—*stream* KY-4
Kings Branch—*stream* (2) MD-2
Kings Branch—*stream* MO-7
Kings Branch—*stream* (3) NC-3
Kings Branch—*stream* OK-5
Kings Branch—*stream* TN-4
Kings Branch—*stream* (5) TX-5
Kings Branch—*stream* VA-3
Kings Branch—*stream* WV-2
Kings Branch Cem—*cemetery* KY-4
Kings Branch Ch—*church* GA-3
*Kings Branch Creek* TX-5
*Kings Bridge* AL-4
Kings Bridge—*bridge* NC-3
King's Bridge—*hist pl* PA-2
Kings Bridge—*locale* (2) PA-2
Kingsbridge—*locale* WI-6
**Kings Bridge**—*pop pl* NY-2
**Kings Bridge Heights**—*pop pl* NY-2
*Kings Brook* MA-1
Kings Brook—*stream* MA-1
Kings Brook—*stream* NH-1
Kings Brook—*stream* NY-2
Kingsburg—*fmr MCD* NE-7
Kingsburg—*locale* SD-7
**Kingsburg**—*pop pl* CA-9
**Kingsburg**—*pop pl* SC-3
Kingsburg Branch—*canal* CA-9
Kingsburg (CCD)—*cens area* CA-9
Kingsburg Cem—*cemetery* CA-9
Kingsbury—*CDP* NV-8
Kingsbury—*locale* ME-1
Kingsbury—*locale* OH-6
**Kingsbury**—*pop pl* IN-6
**Kingsbury**—*pop pl* NY-2
**Kingsbury**—*pop pl* TX-5
**Kingsbury Beach**—*pop pl* MA-1
Kingsbury Branch—*stream* IL-6
Kingsbury Branch—*stream* VT-1
Kingsbury Brook—*stream* PA-2
Kingsbury Brook—*stream* VT-1
Kingsbury Canyon—*valley* WA-9
Kingsbury Cem—*cemetery* IL-6
Kingsbury Cem—*cemetery* NE-7
Kingsbury Cem—*cemetery* (2) TX-5
Kingsbury Cem—*cemetery* VT-1
Kingsbury Community Ch (United Church of
Christ)—*church* UT-8
Kingsbury County—*civil* SD-7
Kingsbury County Courthouse—*hist pl* SD-7
Kingsbury Covered Bridge—*hist pl* VT-1
Kingsbury Creek—*stream* IL-6
Kingsbury Creek—*stream* IN-6
Kingsbury Creek—*stream* MI-6
Kingsbury Creek—*stream* MN-6
Kingsbury Creek—*stream* NC-3
Kingsbury Creek—*stream* OH-6
Kingsbury Creek—*stream* WY-8
Kingsbury Ditch—*canal* MT-8
Kingsbury Elem Sch—*school* IN-6
*Kingsbury Gulch* MT-8
Kingsbury Gulch—*valley* CA-9
Kingsbury Gulch—*valley* OR-9
Kingsbury Hill—*summit* (3) NH-1
Kingsbury Hill—*summit* PA-2
Kingsbury Hill Cem—*cemetery* PA-2
Kingsbury Hill Ch (historical)—*church* PA-2
Kingsbury House—*hist pl* MA-1
Kingsbury HS—*school* MA-1
Kingsbury HS—*school* TN-4
Kingsbury Industrial Park—*locale* IN-6
Kingsbury Lake—*lake* MT-8
**Kingsbury Manor**—*pop pl* VA-3
Kingsbury Mtn—*summit* AZ-5
Kingsbury Mtn—*summit* MA-1
Kingsbury Oil Field—*oilfield* WY-8
Kingsbury (Plantation of)—*civ div* ME-1
Kingsbury Pond—*lake* CT-1
Kingsbury Pond—*lake* MA-1
Kingsbury Pond—*reservoir* ME-1
Kingsbury Pond—*reservoir* MA-1
Kingsbury Pond Dam—*dam* MA-1
Kingsbury Pond (historical)—*lake* MA-1
Kingsbury Ranch—*locale* ID-8
Kingsbury Ranch—*locale* NE-7
Kingsbury Ravine—*valley* CA-9
Kingsbury Ridge—*ridge* WY-8
Kingsbury Run—*stream* OH-6
Kingsbury Run Park—*park* OH-6
Kingsbury Sch—*school* CA-9
Kingsbury Sch—*school* IL-6
Kingsbury Sch—*school* MA-1
Kingsbury Sch—*school* MI-6
Kingsbury Sch—*school* OH-6
Kingsbury Sch—*school* TN-4
*Kingsbury's Pond* MA-1
Kingsburys Pond—*lake* MA-1
Kingsbury Spring—*spring* AZ-5
*Kingsbury State Fish and Game Area* IN-6
Kingsbury State Fish And Game
Area—*park* IN-6
*Kingsbury State Fish and Wildlife Area* IN-6
Kingsbury State Fish and Wildlife
Area—*park* IN-6
Kingsbury Stream—*stream* ME-1
**Kingsbury (subdivision)**—*pop pl* TN-4
**Kingsbury (Town of)**—*pop pl* NY-2
Kings Cabin—*locale* OR-9
Kings Campground—*locale* CA-9
Kings Canal—*canal* LA-4
**Kings Canon**—*pop pl* CO-8
Kings Canyon—*locale* CO-8
Kings Canyon—*valley* AZ-5
Kings Canyon—*valley* (2) CA-9
Kings Canyon—*valley* (2) CO-8
Kings Canyon—*valley* NE-7
Kings Canyon—*valley* NV-8
Kings Canyon—*valley* (2) UT-8
Kings Canyon—*valley* WA-9
Kings Canyon Bottom—*bend* UT-8
Kings Canyon Creek—*stream* NV-8
Kings Canyon JHS—*school* CA-9
Kings Canyon Mine—*mine* CO-8
Kings Canyon Natl Park—*park* CA-9
Kings Canyon Overlook—*locale* CA-9
King's Canyon Petroglyphs—*hist pl* AR-4
Kings Canyon Ranch—*locale* CA-9
Kings Castle—*summit* CA-9
Kings Causeway Branch—*stream* DE-2
Kings Cave—*cave* IN-6
Kings Cave—*cave* PA-2
**Kings Cave**—*pop pl* IN-6
Kings Cem—*cemetery* AL-4
Kings Cem—*cemetery* (2) AR-4
Kings Cem—*cemetery* KY-4
Kings Cem—*cemetery* MT-8
Kings Cem—*cemetery* NY-2
Kings Cem—*cemetery* OH-6
Kings Cem—*cemetery* WV-2
*King Sch* AL-4
*King Sch* OR-9
*King Sch* TN-4
Kings Ch—*church* AL-4
Kings Ch—*church* DE-2
Kings Ch—*church* IA-7
Kings Ch—*church* KY-4
Kings Ch—*church* (2) NC-3
King Sch—*school* AL-4
King Sch—*school* (3) CA-9
King Sch—*school* HI-9
King Sch—*school* (5) IL-6
King Sch—*school* IA-7
King Sch—*school* MA-1
King Sch—*school* (5) MI-6
King Sch—*school* MN-6
King Sch—*school* MS-4
King Sch—*school* MO-7
King Sch—*school* MT-8
King Sch—*school* NE-7
King Sch—*school* NH-1
King Sch—*school* NM-5
King Sch—*school* OH-6
King Sch—*school* OR-9
King Sch—*school* SC-3
King Sch—*school* SD-7
King Sch—*school* TN-4
King Sch—*school* (2) TX-5
King Sch—*school* UT-8
King Sch—*school* VT-1
King Sch—*school* WV-2
King Sch (abandoned)—*school* MO-7
King Sch (abandoned)—*school* (2) PA-2
Kings Channel—*channel* (2) NC-3
Kings Chapel—*church* (4) AL-4
Kings Chapel—*church* (4) GA-3
Kings Chapel—*church* IL-6
Kings Chapel—*church* IN-6
Kings Chapel—*church* KY-4
Kings Chapel—*church* MA-1
Kings Chapel—*church* MS-4
Kings Chapel—*church* (2) MO-7
Kings Chapel—*church* NC-3
Kings Chapel—*church* OH-6
Kings Chapel—*church* (2) SC-3
Kings Chapel—*church* TN-4
Kings Chapel—*church* (2) VA-3
Kings Chapel—*church* WV-2
King's Chapel—*hist pl* MA-1
Kings Chapel—*locale* PA-2
**Kings Chapel**—*pop pl* AL-4
*Kings Chapel AME Church* AL-4
Kings Chapel Burying Ground—*cemetery* MA-1
Kings Chapel Ch of Christ—*church* AL-4
*Kings Chapel Church* AL-4
Kings Chapel (historical)—*church* MS-4
Kings Chapel Sch—*school* AL-4
Kings Chapel Sch—*school* GA-3
Kings Chapel Sch (abandoned)—*school* MO-7
King Sch (historical)—*school* AL-4
King Sch (historical)—*school* MS-4
King Sch (historical)—*school* MO-7
King Sch Number 37 (historical)—*school* SD-7
King School Cave—*cave* AL-4
Kings Christian Sch—*school* FL-3
**Kings Cliff (trailer park)**—*pop pl* DE-2
Kings Coll—*school* NY-2
Kings Coll—*school* NC-3
**Kings (Cora)**—*pop pl* GA-3
*Kings Corner* MA-1
Kings Corner—*locale* ID-8
Kings Corner—*locale* MS-4
Kings Corner—*locale* OR-9
Kings Corner—*locale* VA-3
Kings Corner—*other* MI-6
**Kings Corner**—*pop pl* CO-8
**Kings Corner**—*pop pl* CT-1
**Kings Corner**—*pop pl* MI-6
Kings Corner Cem—*cemetery* IN-6
Kings Corner Ch—*church* LA-4
Kings Corners—*locale* MI-6
Kings Corners—*locale* (2) NY-2
Kings Corners—*locale* PA-2
**Kings Corners**—*pop pl* (2) OH-6
Kingscote—*hist pl* RI-1
Kingscote Creek—*stream* VA-3
**King Scott Siding**—*pop pl* NC-3
Kings Coulee—*valley* MT-8
*Kings (County)* NY-2
**Kings (County)**—*pop pl* CA-9
**Kings County**—*pop pl* MD-2
**Kings County**—*pop pl* NY-2
Kings County Country Club—*other* CA-9
Kings County Courthouse—*hist pl* CA-9
Kings County General Hosp—*hospital* CA-9
Kings County Hosp—*hospital* NY-2
Kings County Savings Bank—*hist pl* NY-2
*Kings Cove* IL-6
Kings Cove—*cove* MA-1
*King's Creek* MD-2
*Kings Creek* MS-4
*Kings Creek* OH-6
*Kings Creek* TN-4
Kings Creek—*channel* NC-3
Kings Creek—*cove* MD-2
Kings Creek—*gut* NC-3
Kings Creek—*locale* KY-4
Kings Creek—*locale* MD-2
**Kings Creek**—*pop pl* NC-3
**Kings Creek**—*pop pl* OH-6
**Kingscreek**—*pop pl* OH-6
**Kings Creek**—*pop pl* SC-3
Kings Creek—*stream* AK-9
Kings Creek—*stream* (2) AR-4
Kings Creek—*stream* (2) CA-9
Kings Creek—*stream* FL-3
Kings Creek—*stream* GA-3
Kings Creek—*stream* KS-7
Kings Creek—*stream* KY-4
Kings Creek—*stream* (6) MD-2
Kings Creek—*stream* MI-6
Kings Creek—*stream* (3) MS-4
Kings Creek—*stream* MT-8
Kings Creek—*stream* NJ-2
Kings Creek—*stream* (7) NC-3
Kings Creek—*stream* OH-6
Kings Creek—*stream* OK-5
Kings Creek—*stream* (2) PA-2
Kings Creek—*stream* (2) SC-3
Kings Creek—*stream* (2) TN-4
Kings Creek—*stream* (2) TX-5
Kings Creek—*stream* (3) VA-3
Kings Creek—*stream* WA-9
Kings Creek—*stream* WV-2
Kings Creek Campground—*locale* CA-9
Kingscreek Cem—*cemetery* OH-6
Kings Creek Cem—*cemetery* SC-3
Kings Creek Ch—*church* SC-3
Kings Creek Chapel—*church* WV-2
Kings Creek Falls—*falls* CA-9
King's Creek Furnace Site
(38CK71)—*hist pl* SC-3
Kings Creek Post Office
(historical)—*building* TN-4
Kings Creek Sch—*school* NC-3
Kings Creek (Township of)—*fmr MCD* NC-3
Kings Creek Watershed Site Number
Sixtyone—*reservoir* TX-5
**Kings Croft (subdivision)**—*pop pl* DE-2
*Kings Crossing* MS-4
Kings Crossing—*locale* VA-3
Kings Crossroads—*locale* DE-2
Kings Crossroads—*locale* (2) VA-3
**Kings Crossroads**—*pop pl* (2) NC-3
Kings Crown—*summit* ID-8
Kings Crown—*summit* NM-5
Kings Crown—*summit* UT-8
Kings Crown Peak—*summit* AZ-5
*Kings Cuttoff* AL-4
**Kingsdale**—*pop pl* MN-6
**Kingsdale**—*pop pl* PA-2
**Kingsdale**—*pop pl* VA-3
Kingsdale Air Park—*airport* PA-2
Kings Dam—*dam* WI-6
Kings Daughter Hosp—*hospital* (2) MS-4
Kings Daughters Hosp—*hospital* MS-4
Kings Daughters Memorial—*park* MS-4
**Kingsdown**—*pop pl* KS-7
Kings Eddy—*locale* VA-3
Kings Eddy Bar—*bar* TN-4
Kingsessing—*uninc pl* PA-2
Kingsessing Park—*park* PA-2
Kings Falls—*falls* NY-2
*King's Farm* MH-9
*King's Farm Hill* MH-9

Kings Ferry ... MS-4
Kings Ferry—locale ... IL-6
Kings Ferry—locale ... MS-4
**Kings Ferry**—pop pl ... FL-3
**Kings Ferry**—pop pl ... NY-2
Kings Ferry Bridge—bridge ... GA-3
Kings Ferry (historical)—locale ... AL-4
Kings Ferry Landing (historical)—locale ... AL-4
King's Field House—hist pl ... CT-1
Kingsfield Landing (historical)—locale ... TN-4
Kingsfield Plantation ... MA-1
Kings Flat—flat ... CO-8
Kings Flow—lake ... NY-2
Kings Ford—locale ... TN-4
**Kingsford**—pop pl ... FL-3
**Kingsford**—pop pl ... MI-6
Kingsford Elem Sch—school ... FL-3
**Kingsford Heights**—pop pl ... IN-6
Kingsford Heights Elem Sch—school ... IN-6
Kingsford Heights Sch—school ... MI-6
Kingsford Park Sch—school ... NY-2
Kingsford-Quinnesec Cem—cemetery ... MI-6
**Kingsford (subdivision)**—pop pl ... NC-3
Kings Forest ... NC-3
**Kings Forest**—pop pl ... MA-1
Kings Forge (historical)—locale ... TN-4
Kings Fork—locale ... VA-3
Kings Fork—stream ... KY-4
Kings Gap ... PA-2
Kings Gap—gap ... GA-3
Kings Gap—gap ... VA-3
Kings Gap Hollow—valley ... PA-2
Kings Gap Hollow Trail—trail ... PA-2
Kings Gap Spring—spring ... OR-9
Kings Gap State Park—park ... PA-2
Kings Garden—park ... WA-9
**Kings Gardens**—pop pl ... KS-7
Kingsgate—CDP ... WA-9
**Kingsgate**—pop pl ... OH-6
Kingsgate Mall—locale ... MA-1
**Kingsgate (subdivision)**—pop pl (2) ... AZ-5
**Kingsgate (subdivision)**—pop pl ... TN-4
**Kingsgate Subdivision**—pop pl ... UT-8
Kings Giant Plaza Shop Ctr—locale ... TN-4
Kings Glacier—glacier ... AK-9
**Kings Grant**—pop pl ... ME-1
**Kings Grant**—pop pl ... VA-3
Kings Grant Park—park ... FL-3
**Kings Grant (subdivision)**—pop pl ... DE-2
**Kings Grant (subdivision)**—pop pl ... NC-3
**Kings Grove**—pop pl ... MD-2
Kings Grove Cem—cemetery ... ME-1
Kings Grove Ch—church (2) ... SC-3
Kings Grove Ch—church ... VA-3
Kings Grove Sch—school ... MO-7
**Kings Heights**—pop pl ... OR-9
**Kings Heights (subdivision)**—pop pl ... MS-4
Kings Highway—locale ... TX-5
Kings Highway Bridge—bridge ... VA-3
Kings Highway Cem—cemetery ... CT-1
Kings Highway Ch—church ... NC-3
Kings Highway District—hist pl ... NJ-2
Kings Highway Elem Sch—school ... PA-2
Kings Highway Hosp—hospital ... NY-2
Kings Highway Sch ... PA-2
Kings Highway Sch—school ... FL-3
**Kings Hill**—pop pl ... NJ-2
**Kings Hill**—pop pl ... VA-3
**Kingshill**—pop pl ... VI-3
Kings Hill—summit ... CA-9
Kings Hill—summit ... MA-1
Kings Hill—summit ... MT-8
Kings Hill—summit ... NE-7
Kings Hill—summit ... NH-1
Kings Hill—summit ... TX-5
King's Hill Archeol Site—hist pl ... MO-7
Kings Hill Brook—stream ... VT-1
Kings Hill Camp—locale ... MT-8
Kings Hill Campground—locale ... MT-8
Kings Hill Cem—cemetery ... AR-4
Kings Hill Ch—church ... AR-4
Kings Hill (historical)—locale ... AL-4
Kings Hill Missionary Baptist Church ... TN-4
Kings Hill Mtn—summit ... VT-1
Kings Hill Pass—gap ... MT-8
Kings Hill Point—summit ... CA-9
Kings Hill Pond—lake ... VT-1
Kings Hill Post Office (historical)—building ... AL-4
Kings Hills—range ... TX-5
Kingshill Sch—school ... VI-3
Kings Hill Sch (historical)—school ... MS-4
Kings (historical)—locale ... AL-4
King Shoal Branch—stream ... WV-2
King Shoals Run—stream ... WV-2
Kings Hole ... OR-9
Kings Hole—basin ... KY-4
Kings Hole—lake ... TN-4
Kings Hole Rsvr—reservoir ... OR-9
Kings Hollow—valley ... KY-4
Kings Hollow—valley ... MO-7
Kings Hollow—valley ... PA-2
King Shop Ctr ... AL-4
Kings House of Retreats Chapel—church ... IL-6
King Sink—basin ... MO-7
King Sink Pit—cave ... AL-4
Kings Island ... CA-9
Kings Island ... IL-6
Kings Island ... ME-1
Kings Island ... SC-3
Kings Island ... TN-4
Kings Island—island ... CA-9
Kings Island—island ... CT-1
Kings Island—island ... GA-3
Kings Island—island ... MN-6
Kings Island—island ... NC-3
**Kings Island**—pop pl ... IL-6
Kings Island—post sta ... OH-6
Kings Island (historical)—island ... AL-4
Kings-Kaweah Divide—ridge ... CA-9
Kings Kern Divide—ridge ... CA-9
**Kings (King)**—pop pl ... AR-4
Kings Knob ... PA-2
Kings Knob—summit ... WV-2
Kings Lake—lake ... AK-9
Kings Lake—lake ... GA-3
Kings Lake—lake (2) ... MN-6
Kings Lake—lake ... MO-7
Kings Lake—lake ... NE-7
Kings Lake—lake ... OH-6
Kings Lake—lake ... SD-7
Kings Lake—lake ... UT-8
Kings Lake—lake (2) ... WA-9
Kings Lake—locale ... MO-7
Kings Lake—reservoir ... FL-3
Kings Lake—reservoir (3) ... GA-3
Kings Lake—reservoir ... MO-7
Kingsland—CDP ... TX-5
Kingsland—hist pl ... VA-3
Kingsland—locale ... MI-6
**Kingsland**—pop pl ... AR-4
**Kingsland**—pop pl ... FL-3
**Kingsland**—pop pl ... GA-3
**Kingsland**—pop pl ... IN-6
**Kingsland**—pop pl ... NJ-2
**Kingsland**—pop pl ... TX-5
**Kingsland**—pop pl ... VA-3
Kingsland Bay—bay ... VT-1
Kingsland (CCD)—cens area ... GA-3
Kingsland Cem—cemetery ... AR-4
Kingsland Cem—cemetery ... GA-3
Kingsland Cem—cemetery ... TX-5
Kingsland Creek—stream ... NJ-2
Kingsland Creek—stream ... VA-3
Kingsland Homestead—hist pl ... NY-2
**Kings Landing**—pop pl ... AL-4
**Kings Landing**—pop pl ... MA-1
**Kings Landing**—pop pl ... MI-6
**Kings Landing**—pop pl ... NC-3
Kings Landing Cem—cemetery ... NY-2
Kings Landing (historical)—locale ... MS-4
**Kings Landing (historical)**—pop pl ... OR-9
Kings Landing Public Use Area—park ... AL-4
Kingsland Lake—lake ... NJ-2
Kingsland Lake—reservoir ... TX-5
Kingsland Landing—locale ... AR-4
Kingsland Manor—hist pl ... NJ-2
Kingsland Park—park ... NJ-2
Kingsland Point—cape ... NY-2
Kingsland Point County Park—park ... NY-2
Kingsland Sch—school ... VA-3
Kingsland's Point ... NY-2
Kingsland Station—locale ... NJ-2
Kingsland (Township of)—fmr MCD ... AR-4
Kings Lane Sch—school ... TN-4
Kingsley ... FL-3
Kingsley—locale ... AL-4
Kingsley—locale ... MD-2
Kingsley—locale ... MI-6
Kingsley—locale ... OR-9
**Kingsley**—pop pl ... FL-3
**Kingsley**—pop pl ... IA-7
**Kingsley**—pop pl ... KY-4
**Kingsley**—pop pl ... MI-6
**Kingsley**—pop pl ... PA-2
Kingsley—uninc pl ... TN-4
Kingsley—uninc pl ... TX-5
Kingsley, Chester, House—hist pl ... MA-1
Kingsley Airfield ... OR-9
Kingsley Ave Ch—church ... TN-4
Kingsley Ave Freewill Baptist Ch ... TN-4
**Kingsley Beach**—pop pl ... FL-3
Kingsley Bog—lake ... ME-1
Kingsley Brook—stream ... NY-2
Kingsley Campground—park ... OR-9
Kingsley Cave—cave ... CA-9
Kingsley Cem—cemetery ... IA-7
Kingsley Cem—cemetery ... OR-9
Kingsley Cem—cemetery ... VT-1
Kingsley Cem—cemetery (2) ... WI-6
Kingsley Ch—church (2) ... IN-6
Kingsley Ch—church ... MD-2
Kingsley Ch—church ... OH-6
Kingsley Chapel Baptist Ch—church ... MS-4
Kingsley Ch (historical)—church ... TN-4
Kingsley Corner—locale ... MN-6
Kingsley Cove—valley ... CA-9
Kingsley Covered Bridge—hist pl ... VT-1
Kingsley Creek—gut ... FL-3
Kingsley Creek—stream ... AK-9
Kingsley Creek—stream ... CA-9
Kingsley Creek—stream ... FL-3
Kingsley Creek—stream ... ID-8
Kingsley Creek—stream ... MT-8
Kingsley Creek—stream ... OR-9
Kingsley Crossing—locale ... AR-4
Kingsley Dam—dam ... NE-7
Kingsley Draw ... NV-8
Kingsley Elem Sch—school ... TN-4
Kingsley Falls—falls ... NY-2
Kingsley Field (airport)—airport ... OR-9
Kingsley Flowage—swamp ... ME-1
Kingsley Glade—flat ... CA-9
Kingsley Glades—flat ... CA-9
Kingsley Gulch—valley ... CA-9
**Kingsley Hills**—pop pl ... TN-4
Kingsley House—hist pl ... MA-1
Kingsley Knoll—summit ... NY-2
Kingsley Lake ... FL-3
Kingsley Lake—lake ... CA-9
Kingsley Lake—lake ... FL-3
Kingsley Lake—lake ... MN-6
**Kingsley Lake**—pop pl ... FL-3
Kingsley Lookout Tower—locale ... MI-6
Kingsley Mine—mine ... UT-8
Kingsley Mountains ... NV-8
Kingsley Park—park ... MA-1
Kingsley Park—park ... OR-9
Kingsley Plantation—hist pl ... FL-3
Kingsley Plantation State Historical Site—park ... FL-3
Kingsley Point—ridge ... NV-8
Kingsley Reservoir ... NE-7
Kingsley Rsvr ... OR-9
Kingsley Run—stream ... PA-2
Kingsley Sch—school (2) ... CA-9
Kingsley Sch—school ... IA-7
Kingsley Sch—school ... TN-4
Kingsleys Pothole—lake ... MN-6
Kingsley Square (Shop Ctr)—locale ... FL-3
**Kingsley Station**—pop pl ... TN-4
Kingsley Town Hall—building ... ND-7
**Kingsley Township**—pop pl ... ND-7
**Kingsley (Township of)**—pop pl ... PA-2
**Kingsley Village**—pop pl ... FL-3
Kings Log Landing—locale ... AL-4
Kings Lookout—locale ... MO-7
King Slough ... AK-9
King Slough—gut ... AR-4
King Slough—gut ... MO-7
King Slough—stream ... CA-9
King Slough—stream ... OR-9
**Kings Manor**—pop pl ... PA-2
**Kings Manor**—pop pl ... VA-3
**Kings Manor (Kings Manor South)**—pop pl ... MD-2
Kings Manor South—other ... MD-2
Kingsman Sch—school ... DC-2
Kings Marina Camp—locale ... AL-4
Kings Marsh—lake ... MI-6
Kings Meadow—flat ... CA-9
Kings Meadow—flat ... UT-8
Kings Meadow Canyon—valley ... UT-8
Kings Meadow Park—park ... FL-3
Kings Memorial Ch—church ... AL-4
Kings Mill—locale ... AL-4
Kings Mill—locale ... MI-6
**Kings Mill**—pop pl ... MI-6
**Kings Mill**—pop pl ... TX-5
Kings Mill Bridge—hist pl ... TN-4
**Kingsmill Camp**—pop pl ... TX-5
Kings Mill Creek ... VA-3
Kings Mill Creek—stream ... GA-3
Kings Mill Creek—stream ... IL-6
Kingsmill Creek—stream ... VA-3
Kings Mill Creek—stream ... VA-3
Kings Mill (historical)—locale ... PA-2
Kings Mill (historical)—locale ... TN-4
Kingsmill Neck—cape ... VA-3
Kingsmill Plantation—hist pl ... VA-3
Kingsmill Point—cape ... AK-9
Kings Millpond—reservoir ... GA-3
Kings Mill Pond—reservoir ... GA-3
Kingsmill Pond—reservoir ... VA-3
Kings Millpond—reservoir ... VA-3
**Kings Mills**—pop pl ... OH-6
Kings Mill (Site)—locale ... CA-9
Kings Mine—mine ... CA-9
**Kings Mine**—pop pl ... OH-6
King Smith Hollow—valley ... PA-2
Kings Mound Cemetery ... MS-4
Kings Mount ... NC-3
**Kings Mountain**—pop pl ... KY-4
**Kings Mountain**—pop pl ... NC-3
Kings Mountain—ridge ... NC-3
Kings Mountain Bar—bar ... AL-4
Kings Mountain Camp—locale ... NC-3
Kings Mountain City Lake Number Two—dam ... NC-3
Kings Mountain City Lake Number Two—reservoir ... NC-3
Kings Mountain Country Club—other ... PA-2
Kings Mountain HS—school ... NC-3
Kings Mountain JHS—school ... NC-3
Kings Mountain Mica Company Dam—dam ... NC-3
Kings Mountain Mica Company Lake—reservoir ... NC-3
Kings Mountain Natl Military Park—hist pl ... SC-3
Kings Mountain Number One Dam—dam ... NC-3
Kings Mountain Number One Lake—reservoir ... NC-3
Kings Mountain Pinnacle ... NC-3
Kings Mountain Resort - golf course ... PA-2
Kings Mountain Rsvr—reservoir ... NC-3
Kings Mountain Sch—school ... CA-9
Kings Mountain Sch—school ... TN-4
Kings Mountain Sch—school ... VA-3
Kings Mountain State Park—park ... SC-3
Kings Mountain View Ch—church ... NC-3
Kings Mtn ... OR-9
Kings Mtn—summit ... AL-4
Kings Mtn—summit ... AK-9
Kings Mtn—summit ... GA-3
Kings Mtn—summit ... ME-1
Kings Mtn—summit ... MA-1
Kings Mtn—summit ... NY-2
Kings Mtn—summit (2) ... NC-3
Kings Mtn—summit ... OR-9
Kings Mtn—summit ... SC-3
Kings Mtn—summit ... TN-4
Kings Mtn—summit ... TX-5
Kings Mtn—summit ... WA-9
Kings Mtn Reservoir ... NC-3
Kingsoliver Ditch—canal ... IN-6
King Soloman Creek ... CO-8
King Solomon Baptist Ch—church (3) ... MS-4
King Solomon Camp—locale ... KS-7
King Solomon Cem—cemetery ... AR-4
King Solomon Cem—cemetery ... LA-4
King Solomon Ch ... MS-4
King Solomon Ch—church ... IN-6
King Solomon Ch—church (4) ... LA-4
King Solomon Ch—church (6) ... MS-4
King Solomon Ch (historical)—church ... MS-4
King Solomon Creek—stream ... AK-9
King Solomon Creek—stream ... CO-8
King Solomon Gulch—valley ... AZ-5
King Solomon Gulch—valley ... CO-8
King Solomon Memorial Park (Cemetery)—cemetery ... NJ-2
King Solomon Mine—mine ... AZ-5
King Solomon Mine—mine (3) ... CA-9
King Solomon Mine—mine ... CO-8
King Solomon Mine—mine ... NV-8
King Solomon Mine—mine ... WA-9
King Solomon Mine—mine ... WY-8
King Solomon Mtn—summit ... CO-8
King Solomon Sch (historical)—school (2) ... MS-4
King Solomons Mine—mine ... CA-9
King Solomons Ridge—ridge ... CA-9
Kingsolver Sch—school ... KY-4
Kings Park ... IL-6
Kings Park—locale ... MN-6
Kings Park—park ... FL-3
**Kings Park**—pop pl ... CA-9
**Kings Park**—pop pl ... NY-2
**Kings Park**—pop pl ... VA-3
Kings Park HS—school ... NY-2
Kings Park Sch—school ... VA-3
Kings Park State Hosp—hospital ... NY-2
**Kings Park West**—pop pl ... VA-3
Kings Pass—channel ... TX-5
Kings Pass—gap ... ID-8
Kings Pass—gap ... UT-8
Kings Pasture—flat ... UT-8
Kings Pasture Rsvr—reservoir ... UT-8
Kings Peak ... CA-9
Kings Peak ... UT-8
Kings Peak—summit ... ID-8
Kings Peak—summit ... UT-8
Kings Peaks ... UT-8
Kings Pillars—pillar ... HI-9
King Spit—bar ... WA-9
Kings Plaza—locale ... MA-1
Kings Plaza—locale (2) ... PA-2
Kings Plaza (Shop Ctr)—locale ... MA-1
Kings Point ... MD-2
Kings Point—cape ... AK-9
Kings Point—cape ... LA-4
Kings Point—cape ... ME-1
Kings Point—cape ... MI-6
Kings Point—cape (2) ... MN-6
Kings Point—cape ... MS-4
Kings Point—cape ... MT-8
Kings Point—cape ... NC-3
Kings Point—cape ... VA-3
Kings Point—cape ... WA-9
Kings Point—CDP ... FL-3
**Kings Point**—pop pl ... MO-7
**Kings Point**—pop pl ... NY-2
**Kings Point**—pop pl ... TN-4
**Kings Point**—pop pl ... VA-3
Kings Point—summit ... UT-8
Kings Point Baptist Church ... TN-4
Kings Point Cem—cemetery ... TN-4
Kings Point Ch—church ... TN-4
Kings Point Lake ... LA-4
Kings Point Lake—lake ... LA-4
Kings Point Marina—locale ... NC-3
Kings Point Park—park ... NY-2
Kings Point Post Office (historical)—building ... TN-4
Kings Point Sch (abandoned)—school ... MO-7
Kings Point Sch (historical)—school ... TN-4
Kings Pond—lake (3) ... MA-1
Kings Pond—lake ... MI-6
Kings Pond—lake ... NY-2
Kings Pond—lake (2) ... VT-1
Kings Pond—reservoir (2) ... GA-3
Kings Pond—reservoir ... NJ-2
Kings Pond—reservoir (2) ... NC-3
Kings Pond—reservoir ... SC-3
Kings Pond—reservoir ... VA-3
Kings Pond Dam—dam ... MA-1
Kings Pond Dam—dam (2) ... NC-3
Kings Ponds—lake ... MI-6
Kings Pool—area ... MA-1
**Kingsport**—pop pl ... TN-4
Kingsport Airp—airport ... MO-7
Kingsport (CCD)—cens area ... TN-4
Kingsport Cemetery ... TN-4
Kingsport City Hall—building ... TN-4
Kingsport Division—civil ... TN-4
Kingsport Health Center—hospital ... TN-4
Kingsport Mall Shop Ctr—locale ... TN-4
**Kingsport North**—pop pl ... TN-4
Kingsport Post Office—building ... TN-4
Kingsport Rifle Range—locale ... TN-4
Kingsport Rsvr—reservoir ... TN-4
Kingsport Univ Center—school ... TN-4
Kings Prairie—flat ... AR-4
Kings Prairie Ch—church ... MO-7
Kings Prairie Sch—school ... MO-7
Kings Prairie Township—civil ... MO-7
Kings Preparatory HS—school ... NY-2
King Spring—spring ... AL-4
King Spring—spring ... AZ-5
King Spring—spring ... CA-9
King Spring—spring ... ID-8
King Spring—spring ... KY-4
King Spring—spring ... MO-7
King Spring—spring (2) ... MT-8
King Spring—spring (6) ... OR-9
King Spring—spring (2) ... TN-4
King Spring—spring ... UT-8
King Spring Branch—stream ... AL-4
King Spring Cave—cave ... TN-4
**King Springs**—pop pl ... TN-4
King Springs Elementary School ... TN-4
King Springs Sch—school ... TN-4
King Springs Shop Ctr—locale ... TN-4
Kings Private Sch—school ... FL-3
King Spruce Camp—locale ... OR-9
King Spruce Trail—trail ... OR-9
King Spur—ridge ... CA-9
Kings Purity Supreme Plaza—locale ... MA-1
Kings Ranch—locale ... AZ-5
Kings Range ... CA-9
Kings Rest—area ... NM-5
King's Rest Hotel Motor Court—hist pl ... AZ-5
Kingsridge ... TN-4
**Kings Ridge**—pop pl ... MD-2
**Kings Ridge**—pop pl ... TN-4
Kings Ridge—ridge ... CA-9
Kings Ridge—ridge (2) ... KY-4
Kings Ridge—ridge ... LA-4
Kings Ridge—ridge ... WV-2
Kings Ridge Shop Ctr—locale ... MO-7
**Kings Ridge (subdivision)**—pop pl ... DE-2
Kings River—stream (2) ... AK-9
Kings River—stream ... AR-4
Kings River—stream (2) ... CA-9
Kings River—stream ... MO-7
Kings River—stream ... NV-8
Kings River—stream ... OR-9
Kings River Access ... MO-7
Kings River Canyon ... CA-9
Kings River Cem—cemetery ... CA-9
Kings River Public Use Area—locale ... MO-7
Kings River Ranch—locale ... NV-8
Kings River Range ... NV-8
Kings River Range ... OR-9
Kings River Sch—school (2) ... CA-9
Kings River Sch—school ... NV-8
Kings River (Township of)—fmr MCD (2) ... AR-4
Kings River Trail—trail ... CA-9
Kings River Valley—valley ... NV-8
Kings Road—locale ... FL-3
Kings Road Sch—school ... IL-6
Kings Road Sch—school ... SC-3
Kings Rock ... MA-1
Kings Rock—bar ... CA-9
**Kings Row Manor Condominium**—pop pl ... UT-8
**Kings Row Subdivision**—pop pl ... UT-8
Kings Run—stream ... OH-6
Kings Run—stream (4) ... PA-2
Kings Run—stream ... VA-3
Kings Run—stream (2) ... WV-2
Kings Saddle—gap ... OR-9
Kings Sch—school ... CA-9
Kings Sch—school ... FL-3
Kings Sch—school ... IL-6
Kings Sch—school ... MS-4
Kings Sch—school ... WV-2
Kings Sch (historical)—school (3) ... AL-4
Kings Sch (historical)—school (3) ... MS-4
Kings Sch (historical)—school ... PA-2
Kings Sch (historical)—school (2) ... TN-4
Kings School ... TN-4
Kings School Corner—locale ... NY-2
**Kings Second Addition (subdivision)**—pop pl ... DE-2
Kings Settlement—locale ... NY-2
Kings Shoal Ford (historical)—locale ... TN-4
Kings Shoals ... TN-4
Kings Shoals—bar ... TN-4
Kings Shop Ctr—locale (2) ... MA-1
Kings Shopping Plaza—locale ... MA-1
Kings Signal ... MS-4
Kings Slough ... OR-9
Kings Slough—lake ... MN-6
Kings Slough—stream ... AK-9
Kings Slough Island—island ... AK-9
Kings Slough Village—locale ... AK-9
Kings Spring—spring (2) ... AL-4
Kings Station ... AL-4
Kings Station ... IN-6
**Kings Station**—pop pl ... NY-2
Kings Store ... AL-4
Kings Store—locale ... VA-3
**Kings Store**—pop pl ... IN-6
Kings Table, The ... HI-9
King Stadium—other ... NM-5
King's Tavern—hist pl ... MS-4
Kings Tavern (historical)—locale ... MS-4
Kings Temple Missionary Baptist Ch—church ... MS-4
Kingston ... AL-4
Kingston ... MD-2
Kingston ... MO-7
Kingston ... OH-6
Kingston ... PA-2
Kingston ... VT-1
Kingston—hist pl ... MD-2
Kingston—locale ... AR-4
Kingston—locale ... LA-4
Kingston—locale ... MT-8
Kingston—locale ... OR-9
**Kingston**—pop pl (2) ... AL-4
**Kingston**—pop pl ... AR-4
**Kingston**—pop pl ... FL-3
**Kingston**—pop pl ... GA-3
**Kingston**—pop pl ... ID-8
**Kingston**—pop pl (2) ... IL-6
**Kingston**—pop pl ... IN-6
**Kingston**—pop pl (2) ... IA-7
**Kingston**—pop pl (2) ... KY-4
**Kingston**—pop pl ... MD-2
**Kingston**—pop pl ... MA-1
**Kingston**—pop pl ... MI-6
**Kingston**—pop pl ... MN-6
**Kingston**—pop pl ... MS-4
**Kingston**—pop pl ... MO-7
**Kingston**—pop pl ... NV-8
**Kingston**—pop pl ... NH-1
**Kingston**—pop pl ... NJ-2
**Kingston**—pop pl ... NM-5
**Kingston**—pop pl ... NY-2
**Kingston**—pop pl ... OH-6
**Kingston**—pop pl ... OK-5
**Kingston**—pop pl (2) ... PA-2
**Kingston**—pop pl ... RI-1
**Kingston**—pop pl ... TN-4
**Kingston**—pop pl ... TX-5
**Kingston**—pop pl ... UT-8
**Kingston**—pop pl (2) ... VA-3
**Kingston**—pop pl ... WA-9
**Kingston**—pop pl ... WV-2
**Kingston**—pop pl ... WI-6
Kingston Airpark—airport ... OR-9
Kingston Ave Hosp—hospital ... NY-2
Kingston Baptist Ch—church ... AL-4
Kingston Bay—bay ... MA-1
Kingston Bay Marshes—swamp ... MA-1
Kingston Borough—civil ... PA-2
Kingston Branch—stream ... AR-4
Kingston Brook—stream ... NY-2
Kingston Campground—locale ... NV-8
Kingston Canal—canal ... UT-8
Kingston Canyon—valley ... NM-5
Kingston Canyon—valley ... UT-8
Kingston Cave—cave ... PA-2
Kingston (CCD)—cens area ... GA-3
Kingston (CCD)—cens area ... TN-4
Kingston (CCD)—cens area ... WA-9
Kingston Cem—cemetery ... AR-4
Kingston Cem—cemetery (2) ... IL-6
Kingston Cem—cemetery ... MI-6
Kingston Cem—cemetery ... MS-4
Kingston Cem—cemetery ... NV-8
Kingston Cem—cemetery ... TX-5
Kingston Cem—cemetery ... UT-8
Kingston Cem—cemetery ... WI-6
Kingston Cemeteries—cemetery ... WV-2
Kingston (census name for Kingston Center)—CDP ... MA-1
Kingston Center (census name Kingston)—other ... MA-1
Kingston Ch—church ... AL-4
Kingston Ch—church ... MD-2
Kingston Ch—church ... MS-4
Kingston Ch—church ... OH-6
Kingston Ch of Christ—church ... TN-4
Kingston City Hall—hist pl ... NY-2
Kingston City Park—park ... TN-4
Kingston Creek—stream ... CA-9
Kingston Creek—stream ... MD-2
Kingston Creek—stream ... NV-8
Kingston Creek—stream ... OR-9
Kingston Dam—dam ... NH-1
Kingston Division—civil ... TN-4
Kingstone Creek—stream ... WI-6
Kingston Elem Sch—school ... TN-4
Kingstone Lisle—building ... TN-4
**Kingston Estates**—pop pl ... NJ-2
Kingston First Baptist Ch—church ... TN-4
Kingston Flowage—reservoir ... WI-6
Kingston Fort (historical)—locale ... UT-8
Kingston-Forty Fort—uninc pl ... PA-2
Kingston Grange—locale ... WA-9
Kingston Hall—hist pl ... MD-2
**Kingston Heights**—pop pl ... TN-4
**Kingston Heights Addition (subdivision)**—pop pl ... UT-8
**Kingston Heights Annexes (subdivision)**—pop pl ... UT-8
Kingston Hill—summit ... RI-1
**Kingston Hills**—pop pl ... TN-4
Kingston (historical)—locale ... KS-7
Kingston Historical Marker—park ... CA-9
Kingston (historical P.O.)—locale ... MA-1
Kingston Hollow—valley ... VA-3
Kingston House—hist pl ... PA-2
Kingston JHS—school ... TN-4
Kingston Key—island ... FL-3
**Kingston Knolls Terrace**—pop pl ... AZ-5
Kingston Lake—lake ... IL-6
Kingston Lake—lake ... MI-6
Kingston Lake—stream ... SC-3
Kingston Lake Swamp ... SC-3
Kingston Landing—locale ... MD-2
Kingston Memorial Gardens—cemetery ... TN-4
Kingston Methodist Church—hist pl ... MS-4
Kingston Methodist Protestant Ch—church ... AL-4
Kingston Mill Hist Dist—hist pl ... NJ-2
Kingston Mine—mine ... MT-8
**Kingston Mines**—pop pl ... IL-6
Kingston Mountains ... CA-9
Kingston Mtn—summit ... WV-2
Kingston Oil Field—oilfield ... MS-4
Kingston Peak—summit ... CA-9
Kingston Peak—summit ... CO-8
Kingston Pike Ch—church ... TN-4
Kingston Pike Shop Ctr—locale ... TN-4
Kingston Plains—flat ... MI-6
Kingston Plantation (historical)—locale ... AL-4
Kingston Point—cape ... NY-2
Kingston Pond—lake ... MI-6
Kingston-Port Ewen Suspension Bridge—hist pl ... NY-2
Kingston Post Office—building ... TN-4
Kingston Presbyterian Church Cemetery—hist pl ... SC-3
Kingston Ranch ... NV-8
Kingston Ranch (historical)—locale ... NV-8
Kingston Range—range ... CA-9
Kingston Ranger Station—locale ... NV-8
Kingston Ranger Station—locale ... NM-5
Kingston-Rhinecliff Bridge—bridge ... NY-2
Kingston Ridge—ridge ... ID-8
Kingston River Terminal—locale ... IL-6
Kingston/Rondout 2 Lighthouse—hist pl ... NY-2
Kingston RR Station—hist pl ... RI-1
Kingston Rsvr Number Four—reservoir ... NY-2
Kingston Rsvr Number One—reservoir ... NY-2
Kingston Rsvr Number Two—reservoir ... NY-2
Kingston Sch—school ... AL-4
Kingston Sch—school ... CA-9
Kingston Sch—school ... MA-1
Kingston Sch—school ... MO-7
Kingston Sch—school ... NJ-2
Kingston Sch—school ... OH-6
Kingston Sch—school ... OR-9
Kingston Sch (historical)—school ... MO-7
**Kingston Shores**—pop pl ... MA-1
Kingston Spring—spring ... CA-9
Kingston Spring—spring ... TN-4
**Kingston Springs**—pop pl ... TN-4
Kingston Springs (CCD)—cens area ... TN-4
Kingston Springs Division—civil ... TN-4
Kingston Springs Elem Sch—school ... TN-4
Kingston Springs Hotel and Buildings—hist pl ... TN-4
Kingston Springs Post Office—building ... TN-4
Kingston Stadium—other ... IA-7
Kingston State Park—park ... NH-1
Kingston Station—locale ... LA-4
**Kingston Station**—pop pl ... RI-1
Kingston (sta.) (West Kingston) ... RI-1
Kingston Steam Plant—building ... TN-4
Kingston Stockade District—hist pl ... NY-2
**Kingston (subdivision)**—pop pl ... MA-1
Kingston Summit—gap ... NV-8
**Kingston (Town of)**—pop pl ... MA-1
**Kingston (Town of)**—pop pl ... NH-1
**Kingston (Town of)**—pop pl ... NY-2
**Kingston (Town of)**—pop pl (2) ... WI-6
Kingston Township—civil ... MO-7
**Kingston Township**—pop pl ... MO-7
**Kingston Township**—pop pl ... ND-7
Kingston Township (historical)—civil ... ND-7
**Kingston (Township of)**—pop pl ... IL-6
**Kingston (Township of)**—pop pl ... MI-6
**Kingston (Township of)**—pop pl ... MN-6
**Kingston (Township of)**—pop pl ... OH-6
**Kingston (Township of)**—pop pl ... PA-2
Kingston United Methodist Ch—church ... TN-4
Kingston Village Hist Dist—hist pl ... RI-1
Kingston Wash—stream ... CA-9
Kingston Waterfront Park—park ... TN-4
**Kingston (Westmoore)**—pop pl ... PA-2
Kingston Wildlife Mngmt Area and Refuge—park ... TN-4
**Kingston Woods**—pop pl ... TN-4
Kingstown ... NJ-2
**Kingstown**—pop pl ... MD-2
**Kingstown**—pop pl ... NY-2
**Kingstown**—pop pl ... VA-3
**Kingstown**—pop pl ... WV-2
Kings Town Hill ... RI-1
Kings Trail—trail ... PA-2
**Kingstree**—pop pl ... SC-3
Kingstree (CCD)—cens area ... SC-3
Kingstree Golf Course—other ... SC-3
Kingstree Hist Dist—hist pl ... SC-3
Kingstree Swamp Canal—canal ... SC-3
King Street Cem—cemetery ... CT-1
King Street Cem—cemetery ... NY-2
King Street Cem—cemetery ... OH-6
King Street Ch—church ... CT-1
King Street Elem Sch—school ... PA-2
King Street Hist Dist—hist pl ... AL-4
King Street Sch—school ... NY-2
King Street Station—hist pl ... WA-9
King Street Station—locale ... WA-9
Kings Turquoise Mines—mine ... CO-8

**King Subdivision**—pop pl UT-8
Kings Valley—basin OR-9
Kings Valley—locale MD-2
**Kings Valley**—pop pl OR-9
**Kings Valley**—pop pl TN-4
Kings Valley—valley CA-9
Kings Valley—valley MO-7
Kings Valley—valley UT-8
Kings Valley Cem—cemetery OR-9
Kings Valley Sch (abandoned)—school MO-7
Kingsview PA-2
Kings View Hosp—hospital CA-9
**Kings Village**—pop pl TX-5
Kingsville AL-4
Kingsville KS-7
Kingsville—locale CA-9
Kingsville—locale WV-2
**Kingsville**—pop pl LA-4
**Kingsville**—pop pl MD-2
**Kingsville**—pop pl MO-7
**Kingsville**—pop pl OH-6
**Kingsville**—pop pl PA-2
**Kingsville**—pop pl TX-5
**Kingsville**—pop pl VA-3
Kingsville (CCD)—cens area TX-5
Kingsville Ch—church AL-4
Kingsville Ch—church SC-3
Kingsville Junction—locale UT-8
Kingsville Naval Air Station—military TX-5
Kingsville On-the-Lake OH-6
**Kingsville On-the-Lake**—pop pl OH-6
Kingsville (sta.) (RR name for North Kingsville)—other OH-6
Kingsville Township—civil MO-7
**Kingsville (Township of)**—pop pl OH-6
King Swamp GA-3
King Swamp—swamp GA-3
King Swamp—swamp NC-3
Kingsway—locale OH-6
Kingsway—uninc pl NY-2
Kings Way Ch—church GA-3
Kingsway Ch—church MO-7
Kingsway HS—school NJ-2
Kingsway Mall—locale MO-7
Kingsway Plaza Shop Ctr—locale NC-3
**Kingsway Terrace**—pop pl AL-4
**Kingsway Village**—pop pl NJ-2
Kings Well—well (2) AZ-5
Kings Well—well UT-8
Kings Wharf—locale VI-3
Kingswood—locale VA-3
**Kings Wood**—pop pl GA-3
**King's Wood**—pop pl GA-3
**Kingswood**—pop pl KY-4
**Kingswood**—pop pl NJ-2
**Kingswood**—pop pl TN-4
**Kingswood**—pop pl TX-5
**Kingswood**—pop pl VA-3
Kings Wood—uninc pl GA-3
Kingswood—uninc pl NM-5
Kingswood Camp—locale MN-6
Kingswood Camp—locale NY-2
Kingswood Ch—church VA-3
**Kingswood Court**—pop pl VA-3
Kingswood Elem Sch—school FL-3
**Kingswood Estates**—pop pl PA-2
Kingswood Lake—lake NH-1
**Kingswood Manor**—pop pl FL-3
Kingswood Methodist Ch—church DE-2
Kingswood Montessori Sch—school FL-3
**Kingswood Park**—pop pl PA-2
**Kings Woods**—pop pl NJ-2
Kingswood Sch—school CA-9
Kingswood Sch—school CT-1
Kingswood Sch—school MI-6
Kingswood Sch—school NC-3
Kingswood Sch—school OH-6
Kingswood Shop Ctr—locale AL-4
**Kingswood (subdivision)**—pop pl AL-4
**Kingswood (subdivision)**—pop pl (3) NC-3
**Kingswood Terra**—pop pl IN-6
King Tabernacle—church KY-4
King Tank—reservoir (2) AZ-5
King Tank—reservoir (3) NM-5
King Tank Number Three—reservoir AZ-5
King Tom Pond—lake RI-1
Kington, W. W., House—hist pl KY-4
Kington Lake—lake KY-4
Kington Lake—reservoir SC-3
King Tonopah—mine NV-8
King Top—summit UT-8
**Kingtown**—pop pl AL-4
**Kingtown**—pop pl AR-4
**Kingtown**—pop pl NJ-2
**Kingtown**—pop pl PA-2
**Kingtown**—pop pl VA-3
Kingtown Branch—stream GA-3
**King (Town of)**—pop pl WI-6
King Township—civil MO-7
King Township—fmr MCD IA-7
**King Township**—pop pl SD-7
King (Township of)—fmr MCD AR-4
**King (Township of)**—pop pl IL-6
**King (Township of)**—pop pl MN-6
**King (Township of)**—pop pl PA-2
King Trail PA-2
King Trail—trail MT-8
King Trail—trail PA-2
King Trunk Factory and Showroom—hist pl FL-3
King-Tune Drift Mine AL-4
King Tut Mine—mine SD-7
King Tut Placer Mine—mine AZ-5
King Tutt Mesa (historical)—summit AZ-5
**Kingvale**—pop pl CA-9
King Valley—valley AZ-5
King Valley Ch—church WI-6
**King Valley Subdivision**—pop pl UT-8
**Kingview**—pop pl PA-2
Kingville—locale AL-4
**Kingville**—pop pl SC-3
Kingville Ch—church AL-4
Kingville (historical)—locale KS-7
Kingville Post Office (historical)—building AL-4
King Vly—swamp NY-2
King Vly Creek—stream NY-2
King Vly Mtn—summit NY-2
King-Walker Place—hist pl TN-4
King Waterhole—lake TX-5
King Well—locale NM-5
King Well—well (3) AZ-5
King Well—well CO-8
King Well—well OR-9
King-Whatley Bldg—hist pl AR-4
**King Whites Fork**—pop pl NC-3
**King William**—pop pl VA-3
**King William (County)**—pop pl VA-3
King William County Courthouse—hist pl VA-3
King William Hist Dist—hist pl TX-5
King William HS—school VA-3
King Williams Narrows—channel MN-6
King-Wilson Oil Field—oilfield TX-5
King Windmill—locale NM-5
Kingwood—locale NJ-2
**Kingwood**—pop pl AR-4
**Kingwood**—pop pl PA-2
**Kingwood**—pop pl WV-2
Kingwood—uninc pl GA-3
Kingwood—uninc pl OR-9
Kingwood Cem—cemetery WV-2
Kingwood Center—hist pl OH-6
Kingwood Ch—church NJ-2
Kingwood Ch—church WV-2
**Kingwood Estates**—pop pl TN-4
**Kingwood Forest (subdivision)**—pop pl NC-3
**Kingwood (historical)**—pop pl NC-3
**Kingwood Junction**—pop pl WV-2
Kingwood (Magisterial District)—fmr MCD WV-2
Kingwood Methodist Ch—church AL-4
Kingwood Sch—school PA-2
Kingwood Station—locale NJ-2
**Kingwood (subdivision)**—pop pl AL-4
**Kingwood (subdivision)**—pop pl PA-2
**Kingwood (subdivision)**—pop pl TX-5
**Kingwood (Township of)**—pop pl NJ-2
King Woolford Mill Site—mine CA-9
Kinhaw AL-4
Kinhaway R WV-2
Kinhaw Post Office AL-4
Kin Hubbard Ridge—ridge IN-6
Kinia River—stream AK-9
Kinicom Pond MA-1
Kinihapai Stream—stream HI-9
Kinikin Heights—summit CO-8
Kinikinik—locale CO-8
Kiniklik—locale AK-9
Kiniklik Island—island AK-9
Kinion Cem—cemetery MO-7
Kinion Lake—reservoir AR-4
Kinipaghulghat Mountains—other AK-9
Kinishba Ruins—hist pl AZ-5
Kinishba Ruins—locale AZ-5
Kinishba Tank—reservoir AZ-5
Kinishba Well—well AZ-5
Kinjockity Ranch—locale AZ-5
Kink, The—bend AK-9
Kink, The—cliff FL-3
Kink, The—hist pl AK-9
Kinkade, John W., Farmstead—hist pl WA-9
Kinkade Cem—cemetery IL-6
Kinkade Creek OR-9
Kinkade Sch—school IL-6
Kinkaid—fmr MCD (3) NE-7
Kinkaid—locale NV-8
Kinkaid, Mount—summit AK-9
Kinkaid Cabin—locale CA-9
Kinkaid Cem—cemetery MN-6
Kinkaid Creek—stream AK-9
Kinkaid Creek—stream IL-6
Kinkaid Creek—stream WA-9
**Kinkaid Estates**—pop pl TN-4
**Kinkaid (historical)**—pop pl TN-4
Kinkaid Hollow—valley TN-4
Kinkaid Lake—reservoir IL-6
Kinkaid Microwave Station—tower NV-8
Kinkaid Sch—school NE-7
Kinkaid Sch—school TX-5
**Kinkaid (Township of)**—pop pl IL-6
Kinkale Creek OR-9
Kink Creek—stream (3) OR-9
Kinkead, Henry P., House—hist pl KY-4
Kinkead Cem—cemetery MO-7
Kinkead Cem—cemetery TN-4
Kinkead House—hist pl KY-4
Kinkeads Landing MS-4
Kinkead Spring—spring NV-8
Kinkel Point—cape WI-6
Kinker Sch (historical)—school SD-7
KINK-FM—tower OR-9
Kinkhead, George, Barn—hist pl KS-7
Kinkheads Forge (historical)—locale TN-4
Kinkler—locale TX-5
**Kinkler (New Kinkler)**—pop pl TX-5
Kinkle Sch—school MO-7
Kin Kletso Ruins—locale NM-5
Kin Klizhin Ruins—locale NM-5
Kin Klizhin Wash—stream NM-5
**Kinkora**—pop pl NJ-2
**Kinkora Heights**—pop pl PA-2
Kinkora Range—channel NJ-2
Kinkora Range—channel PA-2
Kinks Creek—stream AR-4
Kinky Branch—stream TX-5
Kinky Creek—stream WY-8
Kinky Island—island AK-9
Kin Lani AZ-5
Kinlaw—locale GA-3
Kinlaw Cem—cemetery NC-3
Kinley Cemetery MS-4
Kinley Creek—stream AR-4
Kinley Creek—stream CA-9
Kinley Creek—stream SC-3
Kinley Mtn—summit NC-3
Kinley Plateau—plain ND-7
Kin-li-Chee AZ-5
**Kinlichee**—pop pl AZ-5
Kinlichee Chapter House—locale AZ-5
Kin-Li-Chee Creek AZ-5
Kinlichee Creek—stream AZ-5
**Kinlichee (Kin-li-chee)**—pop pl AZ-5
Kinlichee Sch—school AZ-5
Kinlichee Tribal Park—park AZ-5
Kinloch MS-4
**Kinloch**—pop pl MO-7
Kinloch Creek—stream SC-3
Kinloch Island—island SC-3
Kinloch Park—park FL-3
Kinloch Park Elem Sch—school FL-3
Kinloch Park JHS—school FL-3
Kinloch Plantation MS-4
Kinloch Plantation—locale SC-3
Kinloch Sch—school FL-3
Kinloch Sch—school MI-6
Kinlock—hist pl KY-4
Kinlock—locale MS-4
**Kinlock**—pop pl PA-2
Kinlock Church AL-4
**Kinlock (historical)**—pop pl AL-4
Kinlock Knob—summit AL-4
Kinlock Knob Lookout Tower AL-4
Kinlock Lookout Tower—locale AL-4
Kinlock Point—cape NY-2
Kinlock Post Office (historical)—building AL-4
Kinlock Sch (historical)—school MS-4
Kinlock Spring—spring AL-4
**Kinloss Township**—pop pl ND-7
Kinman Knob—summit MO-7
Kinman Pond—lake CA-9
**Kinmount**—pop pl MN-6
Kinmount Creek—stream MN-6
**Kinmount (sta.)**—pop pl MN-6
**Kinmundy**—pop pl IL-6
**Kinmundy (Township of)**—pop pl IL-6
Kin Naa daa (Maize House) (LA 1872)—hist pl NM-5
Kinnacum Pond—lake MA-1
Kin Nahasbas Ruins—locale NM-5
Kin Nahzin Ruins—locale NM-5
**Kinnaird (historical)**—pop pl MS-4
Kinnaird Point—cape MD-2
Kinnairds Point MD-2
Kinnakeet NC-3
Kinnaman Ranch—locale WY-8
Kinnamon Cem—cemetery IL-6
Kinnamon Ridge—ridge WI-6
Kinnan Dam—dam OR-9
Kinnan Rsvr—reservoir OR-9
Kinnan Sch—school IL-6
Kinnard, Claiborne, House—hist pl TN-4
Kinnard Cem—cemetery KY-4
Kinnard Cem—cemetery TN-4
Kinnard Creek GA-3
Kinnard Creek—stream GA-3
Kinnard Hollow—valley MO-7
Kinnard Spring—spring TN-4
Kinnatkan—island MP-9
Kinnazzi Spring—spring AZ-5
**Kinnear**—pop pl WY-8
Kinnear Brook—stream MA-1
Kinnear Cem—cemetery IN-6
Kinnear Mine—mine WY-8
Kinnear Valley—valley WY-8
Kinne Brook—stream MA-1
Kinne Brook—stream NY-2
Kinne Cem—cemetery CT-1
Kinne Cem—cemetery IN-6
Kinne Corners—locale NY-2
Kinne Drain—canal MI-6
Kinneg Lake WI-6
Kinneloa Ranch—locale CA-9
**Kinnelon**—pop pl NJ-2
Kinnelon Dam—dam NJ-2
Kinnelon Sch—school NJ-2
Kinnelworth Cem—cemetery OK-5
Kinneman Creek—stream ND-7
Kinneman Lake—lake IL-6
Kinnemore Slough—stream MO-7
Kinnemore Slough Ditch—canal AR-4
Kinner, John, House—hist pl CO-8
Kinner Cem—cemetery KY-4
Kinner Falls—falls CA-9
Kinner Gully—stream LA-4
Kinner Hill—summit NY-2
Kinnerly Peak—summit MT-8
Kinners Branch—stream TN-4
Kinners Knob—summit NY-2
Kinners Old Stand TN-4
Kinnet Branch—stream IN-6
Kinnett Dam—dam AL-4
Kinnett Lake—reservoir AL-4
**Kinneville**—pop pl MI-6
Kinney MI-6
Kinney TX-5
Kinney—locale NM-5
**Kinney**—pop pl MI-6
**Kinney**—pop pl MN-6
**Kinney**—pop pl PA-2
Kinney, Aaron, House—hist pl OH-6
Kinney, Eli, House—hist pl OH-6
Kinney, Joseph, Mausoleum—hist pl ID-8
**Kinney and Gourlays Improved City Plat**—pop pl UT-8
Kinney Bayou—stream TX-5
Kinney Branch—stream IL-6
Kinney Branch—stream (2) KY-4
Kinney Branch—stream SC-3
Kinney Brook MA-1
Kinney Cameron Lake—reservoir NC-3
Kinney Cameron Lake Dam—dam NC-3
Kinney Camp Hollow—valley KY-4
Kinney Canyon—valley OR-9
Kinney Canyon—valley SD-7
Kinney Canyon—valley WY-8
Kinney Cem—cemetery MI-6
Kinney Cem—cemetery OH-6
Kinney Cem—cemetery TN-4
Kinney Cem—cemetery WI-6
Kinney Corners PA-2
Kinney Corners—locale NY-2
Kinney Coulee—valley WI-6
**Kinney (County)**—pop pl TX-5
Kinney Cove—bay (2) ME-1
**Kinney Cove**—pop pl ME-1
Kinney Creek CO-8
Kinney Creek MI-6
Kinney Creek MO-7
Kinney Creek MT-8
Kinney Creek WY-8
Kinney Creek—stream CA-9
Kinney Creek—stream (2) CO-8
Kinney Creek—stream (4) ID-8
Kinney Creek—stream (3) MI-6
Kinney Creek—stream (2) MN-6
Kinney Creek—stream MS-4
Kinney Creek—stream MO-7
Kinney Creek—stream MT-8
Kinney Creek—stream NY-2
Kinney Creek—stream (3) OR-9
Kinney Creek—stream (2) WA-9
Kinney Creek—stream (3) WY-8
Kinney Creek Trail—trail CO-8
Kinney Ditch—canal IN-6
Kinney Divide—ridge WY-8
Kinney Drain MI-6
Kinney Drain—canal (2) MI-6
Kinney Draw—valley (2) WY-8
**Kinney Estates**—pop pl UT-8
Kinney Farmstead-Tay-e-he-Dah Site—hist pl WI-6
Kinney Flat—flat AZ-5
Kinney Grove Ch—church AL-4
Kinney Grove Missionary Baptist Ch AL-4
Kinney Gulch—valley MT-8
Kinney Gulf—valley NY-2
Kinney Heights—uninc pl KS-7
Kinney Hill—summit ME-1
Kinney Hill—summit NH-1
Kinney Hill—summit NY-2
Kinney (historical)—locale KS-7
Kinney Hollow—valley KY-4
Kinney Hollow—valley OH-6
Kinney Hollow—valley PA-2
Kinney Hollow Trail—trail PA-2
Kinney Island—island PA-2
Kinney Johnson Sch (abandoned)—school PA-2
Kinney Junction—locale AZ-5
Kinney Lake WI-6
Kinney Lake—lake MI-6
Kinney Lake—lake (2) MN-6
Kinney Lake—lake NE-7
Kinney Lake—lake OR-9
Kinney Lake—lake SC-3
Kinney Lake—lake WI-6
Kinney Lake—reservoir CO-8
Kinney Lake—reservoir WI-6
Kinney Lookout—tower AZ-5
Kinney Mtn—summit AL-4
Kinney Mtn—summit AZ-5
Kinney Mtn—summit OR-9
Kinney Nation—locale ME-1
Kinney Octagon Barn—hist pl IA-7
Kinney Park—park OR-9
Kinney Peak—summit CO-8
Kinney Point—cape ID-8
Kinney Point—cape WA-9
Kinney Point—cliff ID-8
Kinney Point—summit AZ-5
Kinney Pond—reservoir CT-1
Kinney Public Camp—locale CA-9
Kinney Ranch—locale SD-7
Kinney Ridge—ridge OR-9
Kinney Ridge—ridge PA-2
Kinney Rim—cliff WY-8
Kinney Rsvr—reservoir CA-9
Kinney Rsvr—reservoir WY-8
Kinneys—locale TN-4
Kinney Sch—school (4) MI-6
Kinney Sch—school MN-6
Kinney Sch (abandoned)—school PA-2
Kinney Sch (historical)—school MO-7
Kinney Sch (historical)—school TN-4
**Kinneys Copper Plant (subdivision)**—pop pl UT-8
Kinneys Corners—locale CT-1
Kinneys Head—summit ME-1
Kinney Shores ME-1
**Kinney Shores**—pop pl ME-1
Kinneys Meadow—flat UT-8
Kinneys Meadows UT-8
Kinneys Peak—summit UT-8
Kinneys Pond PA-2
Kinney Spring—spring SD-7
Kinney Spring—spring UT-8
Kinney Spring—spring WY-8
Kinney Station KS-7
Kinney Swamp—swamp PA-2
Kinney Tank—reservoir AZ-5
Kinneytown Brook—stream CT-1
Kinney Trail—trail (2) PA-2
Kinney Valley—valley WI-6
Kinneyville Creek—stream PA-2
Kinneyville Pond—lake PA-2
Kinneyville Pond Dam—dam PA-2
Kinney Well—well AZ-5
Kinney Wells—locale NM-5
Kinney Wood Park—flat WY-8
Kinnick Cem—cemetery TN-4
Kinnickinick Creek OH-6
KinnickinnicA VAR Kinnickinick Creek OH-6
Kinnickinnic Cem—cemetery WI-6
Kinnickinnic Creek OH-6
Kinnickinnic Creek—stream MI-6
Kinnickinnick Creek OH-6
**Kinnickinnick (Kinnikinnick)**—pop pl OH-6
Kinnickinnic River—stream (2) WI-6
Kinnickinnic River Parkway—park WI-6
Kinnickinnic River State Fishery Area—park WI-6
Kinnickinnic Sandbar—bar WI-6
Kinnickinnic State Park—park WI-6
**Kinnickinnic (Town of)**—pop pl WI-6
**Kinniconick**—pop pl KY-4
Kinniconick Creek—stream KY-4
Kinniconick Sch—school KY-4
Kinnicum Pond—lake NH-1
Kinniken Evans Ditch—canal DE-2
Kinnikinic Creek OH-6
Kinnikinic Creek—stream ID-8
Kinnikinick CO-8
Kinnikinick Campground—park AZ-5
Kinnikinick Canyon—valley AZ-5
Kinnikinick Dam—dam AZ-5
Kinnikinick Lake—reservoir AZ-5
Kinnikinick Spring—spring AZ-5
Kinnikinick Spring—spring UT-8
Kinnikinic Lake WY-8
Kinnikinnick Branch—stream KY-4
Kinnikinnick Creek—stream ID-8
Kinnikinnick Creek—stream OH-6
Kinnikinnick Spring—spring UT-8
Kinnikinnic Lake—lake OR-9
Kinnikum Pond NH-1
Kinnimiki Creek—stream MT-8
Kinnin Cave—cave KY-4
Kinningham Branch—stream KY-4
Kinnischtzke Airfield—airport ND-7
Kinnison Wash—arroyo AZ-5
Kin ni taahll Well—well AZ-5
Kinnlen Star Ch—church AR-4
Kinnley Chapel Cem—cemetery KY-4
Kinnon Creek—stream TX-5
Kinnorutin Creek—stream AK-9
Kinnorutin Pass—gap AK-9
Kinny Lake—lake WI-6
Kino—locale AZ-5
Kino—locale KY-4
Kino—locale VA-3
KINO-AM (Winslow)—tower AZ-5
Kino Community Hospital Heliport—airport AZ-5
Kinodjeng MP-9
Kinogami Lake—lake MN-6
**Kino Heights Subdivision**—pop pl UT-8
Kino JHS—school AZ-5
Kino Park—park AZ-5
Kino Peak—summit AZ-5
Kino Plaza North Shop Ctr—locale AZ-5
Kino Post Office—building AZ-5
Kino RR Station—building AZ-5
Kino Spring—spring AZ-5
**Kino Springs**—pop pl AZ-5
Kino Springs—spring AZ-5
Kino Springs Dam—dam AZ-5
Kino Springs Lake—reservoir AZ-5
**Kino (sta.)**—pop pl AZ-5
Kinouna HI-9
Kinport—locale ID-8
**Kinport**—pop pl PA-2
Kinport Peak—summit ID-8
Kinreed Coulee—valley MT-8
**Kinross**—pop pl IA-7
**Kinross**—pop pl MI-6
Kinross Lake—lake MI-6
Kinross Tower—locale MI-6
**Kinross (Township of)**—pop pl MI-6
**Kinsale**—pop pl VA-3
Kinsale Branch—stream VA-3
Kinsanl Sch (historical)—school AL-4
Kinsaul Sch AL-4
Kins Creek WV-2
Kinsella Sch—school CT-1
Kinsell Draw—valley NM-5
Kinsell Ranch—locale NM-5
Kinser Branch—stream TN-4
Kinser Bridge—other MO-7
Kinser Cem—cemetery IN-6
Kinser Cem—cemetery KY-4
Kinser Cem—cemetery WV-2
Kinser Ch—church (2) TN-4
Kinser Chapel—church MO-7
Kinser Ch of God TN-4
Kinser Creek—stream IA-7
Kinser Creek—stream TN-4
Kinser Creek—stream VA-3
Kinser Heights—summit PA-2
Kinser Pond—lake TN-4
Kinsers Tabernacle TN-4
Kinser Tabernacle TN-4
Kinsey—locale FL-3
Kinsey—locale MO-7
**Kinsey**—pop pl AL-4
**Kinsey**—pop pl IN-6
**Kinsey**—pop pl MT-8
**Kinsey**—pop pl OH-6
Kinsey, John L., Sch—hist pl PA-2
Kinsey Baptist Ch—church AL-4
Kinsey Bayou—bay AL-4
Kinsey Branch—stream GA-3
Kinsey Canyon—valley NV-8
Kinsey Cem—cemetery AR-4
Kinsey Cem—cemetery (2) FL-3
Kinsey Cem—cemetery IN-6
Kinsey Cem—cemetery IA-7
Kinsey Cem—cemetery MO-7
Kinsey Creek CA-9
Kinsey Creek—stream AR-4
Kinsey Creek—stream (2) CA-9
Kinsey Creek—stream ID-8
Kinsey Creek—stream MO-7
Kinsey Creek—stream OR-9
Kinsey Highline Canal—canal MT-8
Kinsey Hill—summit PA-2
Kinsey Jones Pond—reservoir NC-3
Kinsey Lake—lake MI-6
Kinsey Lower Canal—canal MT-8
Kinsey Main Canal—canal (2) MT-8
Kinsey Marsh—swamp WA-9
Kinsey Middle Canal—canal MT-8
Kinsey Mtn—summit AR-4
Kinsey Number 2 Pumping Station—other MT-8
Kinsey Post Office (historical)—building AL-4
Kinsey Ranch—locale CA-9
Kinsey Ridge—ridge (2) CA-9
Kinsey Rsvr—reservoir (2) OR-9
Kinsey Run—stream IN-6
Kinsey Run—stream VA-3
Kinsey Sch—school AZ-5
Kinsey Sch—school IA-7
Kinsey Sch—school (2) PA-2
Kinseys Pond—harbor NJ-2
Kinseytown—locale GA-3
Kinshan Cove—bay AK-9
Kinshan Cove—locale AK-9
Kinshuda Hill—summit AK-9
Kinsinger Run—stream WV-2
Kins Island—island MT-8
**Kinsler**—pop pl SC-3
Kinsler Cem—cemetery TN-4
**Kinsley**—pop pl KS-7
Kinsley, Martin, House—hist pl ME-1
Kinsley Corners—locale PA-2
Kinsley Creek KS-7
Kinsley Draw—valley NV-8
Kinsley Guard Station—locale CA-9
Kinsley (historical)—locale NV-8
Kinsley HS—school KS-7
Kinsley Mtns—summit NV-8
Kinsley Municipal Airp—airport KS-7
Kinsley Point—cape FL-3
Kinsley Ranch (2) AZ-5
Kinsley Spring—spring NV-8
Kinsley Tank—reservoir AZ-5
Kinsley Township—civil KS-7
**Kinsley Township**—pop pl KS-7
Kinsloe—locale TX-5
Kinslow Cem—cemetery AR-4
Kinslow Cem—cemetery KY-4
Kinslow Hollow—valley MO-7
**Kinsman**—pop pl IL-6
**Kinsman**—pop pl (2) OH-6
Kinsman Brook—stream MA-1
Kinsman Cabin—locale NH-1
Kinsman Cem—cemetery ME-1
Kinsman Cem—cemetery NH-1
**Kinsman Corner**—pop pl MA-1
Kinsman Creek—stream CA-9
Kinsman Drain—canal MI-6
Kinsman Flat—flat CA-9
Kinsman Lake—reservoir NC-3
Kinsman Lake—reservoir OH-6
Kinsman Mountain—ridge NH-1
Kinsman Notch—gap NH-1
Kinsman Pond—lake NH-1
Kinsman Pond Trail—trail NH-1
Kinsman Ridge Trail—trail NH-1
Kinsman Sch—school OH-6
**Kinsman (Township of)**—pop pl OH-6
Kinson Creek MS-4
Kins Run WV-2
Kinster Branch—stream KY-4
**Kinston**—pop pl AL-4
**Kinston**—pop pl NC-3
**Kinston Acres (subdivision)**—pop pl DE-2
Kinston (CCD)—cens area AL-4
Kinston Cem—cemetery AL-4
Kinston Clinic—hospital NC-3
Kinston Country Club & Gulf Course—locale NC-3
Kinston Division—civil AL-4
Kinston Drag Strip—locale NC-3
Kinston First Baptist Ch—church AL-4
Kinston HS—school AL-4
Kinston HS—school NC-3
**Kinstonian Hights (subdivision)**—pop pl NC-3
Kinston JHS—school NC-3
Kinston Lookout Tower—locale NC-3
Kinston Plaza Shop Ctr—locale NC-3
Kinston Square—locale NC-3
Kinston (Township of)—fmr MCD NC-3
**Kinta**—pop pl OK-5
Kintabush Creek AL-4
Kinta HS—hist pl OK-5
Kinta Lake—reservoir OK-5
Kintanga Bay—bay AK-9
Kintanga Point—cape AK-9
Kintayakni (historical)—locale AL-4
Kint Cem—cemetery IA-7
Kintchloe Branch—stream TX-5
Kinter—locale AZ-5
**Kinter**—pop pl PA-2
Kinterbish—locale AL-4
Kinterbish Creek—stream AL-4
Kinterbish Creek—stream MS-4
Kinterbish JHS—school AL-4
Kinterbish Sch AL-4
Kinterbish State Wildlife Mngmt Area—park AL-4
Kinter Crossing—locale PA-2
Kinter Hill—summit PA-2
Kinter Hill Sch (abandoned)—school PA-2
**Kintersburg**—pop pl PA-2
Kintersburg Bridge—bridge PA-2
Kintersburg Covered Bridge—hist pl PA-2
Kin Tiel—hist pl AZ-5
Kintigh Sch—school SD-7
**Kintire (Township of)**—pop pl MN-6
Kintla Creek—stream MT-8
Kintla Glacier—glacier MT-8
Kintla Lake—lake MT-8
Kintla Lake Campground—locale MT-8
Kintla Lake Ranger Station—hist pl MT-8
Kintla Peak—summit MT-8
Kintla Well—well MT-8
Kintner Hill—summit PA-2
Kintner House Hotel—hist pl IN-6
Kintner-McGrain House—hist pl IN-6
Kintners Tavern PA-2
**Kintnersville**—pop pl PA-2
Kintnerville PA-2
Kintner-Withers House—hist pl IN-6
**Kinton**—pop pl AR-4
**Kinton**—pop pl OR-9
**Kinton Fork**—pop pl NC-3
Kinton Forks NC-3
Kinton Knob—summit PA-2
Kinton Knob Fire Tower—tower PA-2
Kinton Point—cape CA-9
**Kintons Cross Road**—pop pl NC-3
Kintons Mill AL-4
Kintown Hill—summit IL-6
Kintown Hollow—valley IL-6
Kintyre—locale MT-8
**Kintyre**—pop pl ND-7
Kintyre Creek—stream MT-8
Kintz Cem—cemetery IA-7
Kintz Cem—cemetery WY-8
Kintz Creek—stream MI-6
Kintz Creek—stream PA-2
Kintz Creek—stream WY-8
Kintz Creek Dam—dam PA-2
Kintz Creek Lake—reservoir PA-2
Kintzele Ditch—canal IN-6
Kintz Swamp—swamp PA-2
Kinuk Island—island AK-9
Kinusta Mesa—summit AZ-5
Kinwamakwad Lake—lake MI-6
**Kinwood**—pop pl TX-5
Kinwood Cem—cemetery WI-6
Kinworthy Rsvr—reservoir OR-9
Kin Ya-ah (Ruin)—locale NM-5
Kinyo FM-9
**Kinyon**—pop pl CA-9
Kinyon Cem—cemetery IL-6
Kinyon Cem—cemetery MI-6
Kinyon Cem—cemetery MT-8
Kinyon Coulee—valley MT-8
Kinyon Creek—stream WA-9
Kinyon Lake—lake MI-6
Kinyon Sch—school MO-7
Kinyon Station AZ-5
**Kinyon Township**—pop pl ND-7
Kinyo To FM-9
Kinzalow Spring—spring TN-4
Kinza Memorial Ch—church NC-3
Kinzarof Lagoon—bay AK-9
Kinzel Branch—stream TN-4

Kirkman Cem—*cemetery* TN-4
Kirkman Ch—*church* PA-2
**Kirkman Crossroad**—*pop pl* NC-3
Kirkman Hill—*summit* CA-9
Kirkman (historical)—*locale* MS-4
Kirkman Hollow—*valley* UT-8
Kirkman House—*hist pl* WA-9
Kirkman Landing—*locale* MS-4
Kirkman Road United Methodist Ch—*church* FL-3
*Kirkmans Creek* NE-7
**Kirkmansville**—*pop pl* KY-4
Kirkmansville (CCD)—*cens area* KY-4
Kirkman Technical HS—*school* TN-4
*Kirkman Vocational and Technical Sch* TN-4
Kirk-McRoberts Cem—*cemetery* IN-6
Kirkmere Sch—*school* OH-6
Kirk O'Cliff Ch—*church* VA-3
Kirkofer Lake—*reservoir* IN-6
Kirkofer Lake Dam—*dam* IN-6
Kirk of Our Savior—*church* MI-6
Kirk of the Lake Presbyterian Ch—*church* FL-3
Kirkos Creek—*stream* AR-4
Kirk Park—*park* IL-6
Kirk Park—*park* NY-2
**Kirkpatrick**—*pop pl* IN-6
**Kirkpatrick**—*pop pl* OH-6
**Kirkpatrick**—*pop pl* OR-9
Kirkpatrick, E. W., House and Barn—*hist pl* TX-5
**Kirkpatrick Addition**—*pop pl* TX-5
Kirkpatrick Cem—*cemetery* AL-4
Kirkpatrick Cem—*cemetery* AR-4
Kirkpatrick Cem—*cemetery* KY-4
Kirkpatrick Cem—*cemetery* OH-6
Kirkpatrick Cem—*cemetery* WV-2
Kirkpatrick Cem—*cemetery* WI-6
Kirkpatrick Creek—*stream* CA-9
Kirkpatrick Ditch—*canal* (2) IN-6
Kirkpatrick Draw—*valley* MT-8
*Kirkpatrick Elementary School* MS-4
Kirkpatrick Hill—*summit* MT-8
Kirkpatrick House—*hist pl* AL-4
Kirkpatrick JHS—*school* TX-5
Kirkpatrick Lake—*reservoir* GA-3
Kirkpatrick Lake (historical)—*lake* TN-4
Kirkpatrick Landing—*locale* AL-4
Kirkpatrick Marsh—*swamp* MD-2
Kirkpatrick Park—*park* TN-4
Kirkpatrick Ranch—*locale* NE-7
Kirkpatrick Ranch—*locale* TX-5
Kirkpatrick Rsvr—*reservoir* OR-9
Kirkpatrick Sch—*school* MS-4
*Kirkpatricks Island* TN-4
Kirkpatricks Shoals—*bar* AL-4
Kirkpatrick Valley—*basin* NE-7
Kirk Peak—*summit* NM-5
*Kirk P.O.* AL-4
Kirk Point—*cape* AK-9
Kirk Point—*cape* NC-3
Kirk Point—*cape* VA-3
Kirk Pond—*reservoir* AZ-5
Kirk Ranch—*locale* WY-8
Kirk Ridge—*ridge* KY-4
Kirk Ridge—*ridge* WV-2
Kirkridge Ch—*church* MI-6
Kirk Ridge Ch—*church* WV-2
Kirk Road Sch—*school* NY-2
Kirk Rock—*summit* WA-9
Kirks Basin—*basin* UT-8
*Kirks Branch* DE-2
Kirks Bridge—*locale* PA-2
Kirk's Cabin Complex—*hist pl* UT-8
Kirks Camp—*locale* TN-4
Kirks Cave—*cave* TN-4
Kirk Sch—*school* (2) CA-9
Kirk Sch—*school* MN-6
Kirk Sch (abandoned)—*school* MO-7
Kirk Sch (historical)—*school* AL-4
Kirk Sch (historical)—*school* TN-4
Kirks Creek—*stream* NC-3
Kirksey—*locale* SC-3
**Kirksey**—*pop pl* KY-4
Kirksey (CCD)—*cens area* KY-4
Kirksey (CCD)—*cens area* SC-3
Kirksey Cem—*cemetery* AL-4
Kirksey Cem—*cemetery* TN-4
Kirksey Creek—*stream* MS-4
Kirksey Dam—*dam* AL-4
Kirksey HS—*school* AL-4
Kirksey Lake—*reservoir* AL-4
Kirksey Mtn—*summit* SC-3
Kirksey Park—*park* AR-4
*Kirksey P. O.* MS-4
Kirkseys Bend—*bend* AL-4
*Kirkseys Mill* AL-4
Kirks Fork—*stream* ID-8
Kirks Gap—*gap* AL-4
Kirks Gin (historical)—*locale* MS-4
**Kirks Grove**—*pop pl* AL-4
Kirks Grove Post Office (historical)—*building* AL-4
*Kirks Homestead Knoll* UT-8
**Kirkside**—*pop pl* VA-3
Kirks Landing—*locale* LA-4
Kirks Landing (historical)—*locale* AL-4
*Kirks Mill* NC-3
Kirks Mill Creek—*stream* NC-3
Kirks Mills—*locale* PA-2
Kirks Mills Hist Dist—*hist pl* PA-2
Kirks Mills Post Office (historical)—*building* PA-2
**Kirks Mine No 3**—*pop pl* KY-4
Kirks Plantation—*locale* MS-4
Kirk Spring—*spring* TN-4
Kirk Spring—*spring* UT-8
Kirk Springs—*spring* OK-5
Kirk Springs Hollow—*valley* OK-5
Kirks Run—*stream* PA-2
Kirkstall—*locale* TN-4
Kirkstone Lake—*reservoir* TN-4
Kirkstone Lake Dam—*dam* TN-4
Kirk Street Agents House—*building* MT-8
*Kirksville* IN-6
**Kirksville**—*pop pl* IL-6
**Kirksville**—*pop pl* IN-6
**Kirksville**—*pop pl* KY-4
**Kirksville**—*pop pl* MO-7
Kirksville Coll of Osteopathic Medicine—*school* MO-7
Kirksville Country Club—*other* MO-7
Kirksville Municipal Airp—*airport* MO-7
Kirksville Pumping Station (historical)—*building* MO-7
Kirksville Sch—*school* KY-4
Kirk Swamp—*swamp* SC-3
Kirk Tank—*reservoir* AZ-5
*Kirk Town* AL-4
Kirktown Creek—*stream* MI-6
*Kirkville* IN-6
*Kirkville* KS-7
Kirkville—*locale* KY-4
Kirkville—*locale* MS-4
**Kirkville**—*pop pl* CA-9
**Kirkville**—*pop pl* IA-7
**Kirkville**—*pop pl* MS-4
**Kirkville**—*pop pl* NY-2
Kirkville Baptist Ch—*church* MS-4
Kirkville Cem—*cemetery* MS-4
Kirkville Post Office (historical)—*building* MS-4
Kirkville Station—*locale* IA-7
**Kirkville (Wheeling)**—*pop pl* IN-6
*Kirkwood* IN-6
Kirkwood—*fmr MCD* NE-7
Kirkwood—*hist pl* AL-4
Kirkwood—*locale* CA-9
Kirkwood—*locale* DE-2
Kirkwood—*locale* FL-3
Kirkwood—*locale* GA-3
Kirkwood—*locale* KS-7
Kirkwood—*locale* KY-4
Kirkwood—*locale* NY-2
Kirkwood—*locale* PA-2
Kirkwood—*locale* WV-2
**Kirkwood**—*pop pl* (2) CA-9
**Kirkwood**—*pop pl* IL-6
**Kirkwood**—*pop pl* MD-2
**Kirkwood**—*pop pl* MO-7
**Kirkwood**—*pop pl* NJ-2
**Kirkwood**—*pop pl* NY-2
**Kirkwood**—*pop pl* NC-3
**Kirkwood**—*pop pl* OH-6
**Kirkwood**—*pop pl* SC-3
**Kirkwood**—*pop pl* TN-4
**Kirkwood**—*pop pl* WI-6
Kirkwood, Joseph, House—*hist pl* OH-6
Kirkwood Baptist Ch—*church* TN-4
Kirkwood Bar—*bar* ID-8
Kirkwood Branch—*stream* TX-5
Kirkwood Cem—*cemetery* CA-9
Kirkwood Cem—*cemetery* MO-7
Kirkwood Cem—*cemetery* NE-7
Kirkwood Cem—*cemetery* OH-6
**Kirkwood Center**—*pop pl* NY-2
Kirkwood Ch—*church* KY-4
Kirkwood Ch—*church* NE-7
Kirkwood Corrals—*locale* ID-8
Kirkwood Cow Camp—*locale* ID-8
Kirkwood Creek—*stream* (2) CA-9
Kirkwood Creek—*stream* ID-8
Kirkwood Creek—*stream* MT-8
Kirkwood Creek—*stream* NY-2
Kirkwood Ferry (historical)—*locale* MS-4
**Kirkwood Gardens**—*pop pl* DE-2
*Kirkwood Gas Field* CA-9
**Kirkwood Heights**—*pop pl* OH-6
Kirkwood (historical)—*locale* IA-7
Kirkwood (historical)—*locale* MS-4
Kirkwood (historical)—*locale* SD-7
Kirkwood (historical P.O.)—*locale* IA-7
Kirkwood House—*hist pl* IA-7
Kirkwood Lake—*lake* (2) CA-9
Kirkwood Lake—*lake* MI-6
Kirkwood Lake—*lake* MS-4
Kirkwood Lake—*reservoir* KY-4
Kirkwood Lake—*reservoir* NJ-2
Kirkwood Lake Dam—*dam* NJ-2
Kirkwood Methodist Ch—*church* DE-2
Kirkwood Mine (underground)—*mine* AL-4
Kirkwood Missouri Pacific Depot—*hist pl* MO-7
Kirkwood Number One Mine (underground)—*mine* TN-4
Kirkwood Park—*park* DE-2
**Kirkwood Park (subdivision)**—*pop pl* MS-4
Kirkwood Plaza Shop Ctr—*locale* ND-7
Kirkwood Post Office (historical)—*building* AL-4
Kirkwood Post Office (historical)—*building* PA-2
Kirkwood Ridge—*ridge* CA-9
Kirkwood Ridge—*ridge* MT-8
Kirkwood Sch—*school* (2) IA-7
Kirkwood Sch—*school* MI-6
Kirkwood Sch—*school* MS-4
Kirkwood Sch—*school* SD-7
Kirkwood Sch (historical)—*school* TN-4
Kirkwoods Mine (underground)—*mine* AL-4
Kirkwood Spring—*spring* CA-9
Kirkwood Spring—*spring* OR-9
Kirkwood Springs—*locale* KY-4
Kirkwood Springs Gas Field—*oilfield* KY-4
**Kirkwood (subdivision)**—*pop pl* NC-3
**Kirkwood (Town of)**—*pop pl* NY-2
**Kirkwood (Township of)**—*pop pl* OH-6
Kirkwood Trail—*trail* MT-8
KIRL-AM (St Charles)—*tower* MO-7
Kirland Cem—*cemetery* MS-4
Kirley—*locale* SD-7
Kirley Draw—*valley* SD-7
Kirley Gulch—*valley* WY-8
Kirley (historical)—*locale* (2) SD-7
Kirman Lake—*lake* CA-9
Kirns Ranch—*locale* MT-8
**Kiro**—*pop pl* KS-7
**Kiroli Woods**—*pop pl* LA-4
*Kiromo* MP-9
*Kiromon Island* MP-9
Kiromon Island—*island* MP-9
*Kiromon-To* MP-9
**Kiron**—*pop pl* IA-7
Kiron Cem—*cemetery* IA-7
Kirpens Island—*island* NY-2
Kirscher Ranch—*locale* MT-8
*Kirschner* MO-7
**Kirschner**—*pop pl* MO-7
Kirschner Lake—*lake* AK-9
**Kirschnerville**—*pop pl* NY-2
**Kirschs Corner**—*pop pl* IN-6
Kirstein Bldg—*hist pl* NY-2
**Kirt**—*pop pl* WV-2
*Kirtak* AZ-5
**Kirtland**—*pop pl* NM-5
**Kirtland**—*pop pl* OH-6
Kirtland, Jared P., House—*hist pl* OH-6
**Kirtland Addition**—*pop pl* NM-5
Kirtland Air Force Base—*military* NM-5
Kirtland Cem—*cemetery* NM-5
Kirtland Cem—*cemetery* OH-6
Kirtland Country Club—*other* OH-6
**Kirtland Hills**—*pop pl* OH-6
Kirtland Hills—*summit* OH-6
Kirtland Hills (Township of)—*other* OH-6
Kirtland Park—*park* OH-6
Kirtland Sch—*school* MA-1
Kirtland Temple—*hist pl* OH-6
Kirtland (Township of)—*other* OH-6
Kirtley—*locale* KY-4
Kirtley—*locale* WY-8
**Kirtley**—*pop pl* TX-5
Kirtley Cem—*cemetery* KY-4
Kirtley Creek—*stream* ID-8
Kirtley Marine Camp—*locale* AL-4
Kirtley Mine—*mine* CO-8
Kirtley Mtn—*summit* VA-3
Kirton Cem—*cemetery* SC-3
Kirts Butte—*summit* MT-8
Kirtsis Park—*park* OR-9
Kirtwright Sch—*school* IL-6
Kirtz Ditch—*canal* CO-8
Kirtz Hollow—*valley* VA-3
*Kiruau* MH-9
Kiruktagiak River—*stream* AK-9
Kirunu—*island* MP-9
Kirushkin Island—*island* AK-9
*Kirusu* MH-9
*Kirusu-San* MH-9
*Kiruusu* MH-9
*Kiruusu San* MH-9
Kirven, J. D., House—*hist pl* TX-5
Kirven (historical)—*locale* AL-4
**Kirvin**—*pop pl* TX-5
Kirwan Creek—*bay* MD-2
**Kirwan Heights**—*pop pl* PA-2
Kirwan Neck—*cape* MD-2
Kirwan Point—*cape* MD-2
Kirwin—*locale* WY-8
**Kirwin**—*pop pl* KS-7
Kirwin Cem—*cemetery* KS-7
Kirwin Dam—*dam* KS-7
Kirwin Encampment (historical)—*locale* KS-7
**Kirwin Heights**—*pop pl* PA-2
Kirwin Main Canal—*canal* KS-7
Kirwin Natl Wildlife Ref—*park* KS-7
*Kirwin Neck* MD-2
Kirwin Rsvr—*reservoir* KS-7
**Kirwin Township**—*pop pl* KS-7
Kirwin Wildlife Area—*park* KS-7
KIRX-AM (Kirksville)—*tower* MO-7
**Kiryas Joel**—*pop pl* NY-2
*Kisamore Knob* WV-2
*Kisano* PW-9
Kisaralik Lake—*lake* AK-9
Kisaralik River—*stream* AK-9
Kisatchie—*forest* LA-4
**Kisatchie**—*pop pl* LA-4
Kisatchie Bayou—*stream* LA-4
Kisatchie Lookout Tower—*locale* LA-4
Kisatcie Guard Station—*locale* LA-4
K. I. Sawyer AFB—*military* MI-6
Kisaymaruktuk Mtn—*summit* AK-9
Kisch—*locale* IL-6
**Kisco Park**—*pop pl* NY-2
Kisco River—*stream* NY-2
KISD-AM—*tower* OR-9
Kise—*locale* KY-4
Kise Cem—*cemetery* VA-3
Kise Creek—*stream* TN-4
Kise Crossing—*locale* IL-6
Kisemaruktuk Mtn—*summit* AK-9
Kise Mill Bridge—*hist pl* PA-2
Kise Mill Bridge Hist Dist—*hist pl* PA-2
Kisenmacher Cem—*cemetery* IA-7
Kiser—*locale* TN-4
Kiser Bend—*bend* VA-3
Kiser Branch—*stream* FL-3
Kiser Branch—*stream* (2) KY-4
*Kiser Cem* TN-4
Kiser Cem—*cemetery* IA-7
Kiser Cem—*cemetery* KY-4
Kiser Cem—*cemetery* TN-4
Kiser Cem—*cemetery* (6) VA-3
Kiser Cem—*cemetery* WV-2
Kiser Chapel—*church* TN-4
**Kiser Corners**—*pop pl* PA-2
Kiser Creek CO-8
Kiser Creek—*stream* CO-8
Kiser Creek—*stream* GA-3
Kiser Creek—*stream* IL-6
Kiser Creek—*stream* OR-9
Kiser Creek Campground—*locale* CO-8
Kiser Creek Diversion Ditch—*canal* IL-6
Kiser Dam—*dam* NC-3
Kiser Ditch—*canal* (2) OH-6
Kiser Gap—*gap* VA-3
Kiser Hill—*summit* VA-3
Kiser Hill Cem—*cemetery* VA-3
*Kiser Hill Church* MS-4
Kiser Hollow—*valley* KY-4
Kiser Hollow—*valley* VA-3
Kiser Hollow—*valley* WV-2
Kiser HS—*school* OH-6
Kiser JHS—*school* NC-3
Kiser Lake—*lake* IN-6
Kiser Lake—*reservoir* NC-3
Kiser Lake—*reservoir* OH-6
Kiser Mill Creek—*stream* AL-4
Kiser Ridge—*ridge* VA-3
Kiser Ridge—*ridge* WV-2
Kiser Rsvr—*reservoir* CO-8
Kiser Run—*stream* OH-6
Kiser Sch—*school* NM-5
Kiser Sch—*school* NC-3
Kiser Sch—*school* PA-2
Kiser Slough Rsvr—*reservoir* CO-8
*Kiser Station* TN-4
Kiser Station—*hist pl* KY-4
Kiserton—*locale* KY-4
Kiser Township (historical)—*civil* SD-7
**Kise Spur**—*pop pl* IL-6
**Kishacoquillas**—*pop pl* PA-2
*Kishacoquillas Creek* PA-2
Kishacoquillas Creek—*stream* PA-2
Kishacoquillas HS—*school* PA-2
*Kishacoquillas Junior Senior HS* PA-2
Kishacoquillas Sch—*school* PA-2
Kishacoquillas Valley—*valley* PA-2
Kisha Farm Cem—*cemetery* OH-6
*Kishaqua Creek* NY-2
Kishbrock Island—*island* AK-9
*Kish-e-neh-na Creek* MT-8
Kishenehn Creek—*stream* MT-8
Kishenehn Patrol Cabin—*locale* MT-8
Kishenehn Ranger Station Hist Dist—*hist pl* MT-8
*Kish-e-nehu Creek* MT-8
*Kishinehn Creek* MT-8
*Kishinena Creek* MT-8
Kishketon Lake—*lake* OK-5
*Kishlen* DE-2
Kishpaugh Lake—*lake* ND-7
Kishpaugh Mines—*mine* NJ-2
Kishwalks—*locale* OR-9
Kishwaukee—*locale* IL-6
Kishwaukee Cem—*cemetery* IL-6
Kishwaukee Coll—*school* IL-6
Kishwaukee For Preserve—*forest* IL-6
**Kishwaukee Glen**—*pop pl* IL-6
Kishwaukee Glen—*valley* IL-6
*Kishwaukee River* IL-6
Kishwaukee River—*stream* IL-6
Kishwaukee Sch—*school* (2) IL-6
Kish Zhini Tank—*reservoir* AZ-5
Kish Zhini Wash—*stream* AZ-5
Kisimigiuktuk Hill—*summit* AK-9
Kisimilat Creek—*stream* AK-9
Kisimilok Creek—*stream* AK-9
Kisimilok Mtn—*summit* AK-9
Kisimilot Mountains—*range* AK-9
Kisinger Lakes—*lake* WY-8
Kisinger Lakes Trail—*trail* WY-8
Kisinger Mtn—*summit* TX-5
Kisiwa Creek—*stream* KS-7
Kiska—*locale* CA-9
Kiskadinna Lake—*lake* MN-6
Kiska Harbor—*bay* AK-9
Kiska Island—*island* AK-9
**Kiska Island**—*pop pl* AK-9
*Kiskakon* IN-6
**Kiskatom**—*pop pl* NY-2
Kiskatom Brook—*stream* NY-2
Kiskatom Ch—*church* NY-2
Kiskatom Flats—*flat* NY-2
Kiska Volcano—*summit* AK-9
Kiskiack—*hist pl* VA-3
Kiski Airp—*airport* PA-2
**Kiskimere**—*pop pl* PA-2
Kiskiminetas Junction—*locale* PA-2
Kiskiminetas River—*stream* PA-2
Kiskiminetas Spring Sch (abandoned)—*school* PA-2
**Kiskiminetas (Township of)**—*pop pl* PA-2
*Kiskiminitas* PA-2
Kiskiminitas—*locale* PA-2
*Kiskiminitas River* PA-2
*Kiskimintas River* PA-2
*Kiski Valley Airport* PA-2
Kisler Ranch—*locale* WY-8
Kisling Cem—*cemetery* IA-7
Kisling Creek—*stream* IN-6
Kislowrut Hills—*summit* AK-9
**Kis-Lyn**—*pop pl* PA-2
**Kis-Lyn (Keystone Job Corps Center)**—*pop pl* PA-2
Kismaliuk Bay—*bay* AK-9
*Kismet* TN-4
Kismet—*locale* CA-9
**Kismet**—*pop pl* KS-7
**Kismet**—*pop pl* NY-2
Kismet Creek—*stream* MT-8
Kismet Elem Sch—*school* KS-7
Kismet Mine—*mine* CA-9
Kismet Peak—*summit* WY-8
*Kismet Post Office* TN-4
Kismuth Mine—*mine* CO-8
Kisner Slough—*stream* AL-4
KISN-FM (Salt Lake City)—*tower* UT-8
*Kisnop Brook* MA-1
Kisogle Mtn—*summit* AK-9
Kissack Bay—*bay* CA-9
Kissack Cove—*bay* CA-9
Kissacook Hill—*summit* MA-1
Kissawaug Swamp—*swamp* CT-1
*Kiss Creek* MT-8
Kissee Cem—*cemetery* AR-4
Kissee Cem—*cemetery* MO-7
Kissee Creek—*stream* AR-4
**Kissee Mills**—*pop pl* MO-7
Kissee Mills Cem—*cemetery* MO-7
Kissee Mills Ch—*church* MO-7
Kissee Mills Public Use Area—*locale* MO-7
Kissel, George A., House—*hist pl* WI-6
Kissel, Louis, House—*hist pl* WI-6
Kissel, William L., House—*hist pl* WI-6
*Kissel Hill* PA-2
**Kissel Hill**—*pop pl* PA-2
Kissel Hill Elem Sch—*school* PA-2
**Kissell Hill**—*pop pl* PA-2
Kissel Point—*cape* ME-1
Kissel Run—*stream* WV-2
Kissel's Addition Hist Dist—*hist pl* WI-6
Kissel's Wheelock Addition Hist Dist—*hist pl* WI-6
Kissel Trail—*trail* PA-2
Kissel Valley—*valley* WI-6
Kissem Run—*stream* PA-2
Kissena Corridor—*park* NY-2
Kissena Lake—*lake* NY-2
Kissena Park—*park* NY-2
Kissen Brook—*stream* CT-1
Kissenger—*locale* MO-7
Kissenger Hill—*summit* MO-7
Kisser Branch—*stream* KY-4
Kisseten Bay—*bay* AK-9
Kissey Branch—*stream* KY-4
*Kisshcoquillas Valley* PA-2
Kissick—*locale* MO-7
Kissick Canyon—*valley* MT-8
Kissick Swamp—*swamp* WI-6
Kissick Swamp State Wildlife Mngmt Area—*park* WI-6
*Kissima* PA-2
*Kissime* PA-2
*Kissimmee* FL-3
**Kissimmee**—*pop pl* FL-3
**Kissimmee**—*pop pl* PA-2
Kissimmee, Lake—*lake* FL-3
Kissimmee Billy Strand—*swamp* FL-3
Kissimmee (CCD)—*cens area* FL-3
Kissimmee Hosp—*hospital* FL-3
Kissimmee Korners Shop Ctr—*locale* FL-3
*Kissimmee Lake* FL-3
Kissimmee Memorial Hosp—*hospital* FL-3
Kissimmee Park—*locale* FL-3
Kissimmee River—*stream* FL-3
Kissimmee River Camp—*locale* FL-3
Kissing Bower Lake—*reservoir* GA-3
Kissing Bridge—*bridge* KY-4
Kissing Camels Country Club—*other* CO-8
Kissing Couple—*pillar* CO-8
*Kissinger* KY-4
Kissinger Creek—*stream* MI-6
Kissinger Gulch—*valley* CO-8
Kissinger Hollow—*valley* KY-4
*Kissinger Mills* PA-2
Kissinger Run—*stream* WV-2
**Kissingers Mill**—*pop pl* PA-2
Kissingers Sch (abandoned)—*school* PA-2
Kissinger Union Ch—*church* PA-2
**Kissipee**—*pop pl* MI-6
Kiss Lake—*lake* (2) WI-6
**Kisslers Corner**—*pop pl* MI-6
Kissler Springs—*spring* NV-8
**Kissling Crossing**—*pop pl* TN-4
Kissock Block Bldg—*hist pl* CO-8
Kissock Cem—*cemetery* MO-7
Kissock Creek—*stream* MO-7
**Kissock Subdivision**—*pop pl* UT-8
Kist Creek—*stream* OR-9
*Kister* WV-2
Kister—*locale* CA-9
Kister Mill—*hist pl* OH-6
**Kist (historical)**—*pop pl* OR-9
*Kistler* WV-2
**Kistler**—*pop pl* (2) PA-2
**Kistler**—*pop pl* WV-2
Kistler Borough—*civil* PA-2
Kistler Cem—*cemetery* MO-7
Kistler Creek—*stream* PA-2
Kistler Elem Sch—*school* KS-7
Kistler House—*hist pl* MA-1
Kistler Ledge—*bench* PA-2
Kistler-Longacre Sch—*school* PA-2
Kistler Ranch—*locale* CA-9
Kistler-Rodriguez House—*hist pl* CO-8
Kistler Run—*stream* PA-2
Kistlers Chapel—*church* NC-3
*Kistlers Creek* PA-2
Kistler Spring—*spring* OR-9
Kistler Swamp—*swamp* PA-2
Kistler Union Ch—*church* NC-3
Kistler Valley—*valley* PA-2
Kistner, Dr. Frank B., House—*hist pl* OR-9
Kistner Hardy Dam—*dam* MT-8
Kist Windmill—*locale* NM-5
*Kita* MH-9
*Kita* MP-9
*Kita* PW-9
Kita Island—*island* AK-9
*Kita Jima* FM-9
Kitalitna Creek—*stream* AK-9
Kitalou—*locale* TX-5
*Kita Misaki* FM-9
**Kitamw**—*pop pl* FM-9
Kitamw, Pilen—*stream* FM-9
*Kita Shima* FM-9
*Kita Suido* FM-9
*Kita-suido* MP-9
*Kita To* MH-9
Kit Bluff—*cliff* TN-4
Kit Bottom—*bend* TN-4
Kit Branch—*stream* VA-3
Kit Canyon—*valley* OR-9
Kit Canyon Waterhole—*reservoir* OR-9
Kit Carson—*pillar* CA-9
**Kit Carson**—*pop pl* CA-9
**Kit Carson**—*pop pl* CO-8
Kit Carson, Mount—*summit* WA-9
Kit Carson Bay—*bay* UT-8
Kit Carson Campground—*locale* CA-9
Kit Carson Cem—*cemetery* CO-8
Kit Carson Cem—*cemetery* NM-5
Kit Carson Gulch—*valley* MT-8
Kit Carson Gulch Creek—*stream* MT-8
*Kit Carson Inscription* AZ-5
Kit Carson Inscription—*locale* AZ-5
Kit Carson JHS—*school* CA-9
Kit Carson Mesa—*summit* NM-5
Kit Carson Mtn—*summit* AZ-5
Kit Carson Mtn—*summit* CO-8
Kit Carson Museum—*locale* NM-5
Kit Carson Park—*park* CO-8
Kit Carson Park—*park* NM-5
Kit Carson Ridge—*ridge* TN-4
Kit Carson Round-Up Park—*park* CO-8
Kit Carsons Cave—*cave* NM-5
Kit Carson Sch—*school* (3) CA-9
Kit Carson Sch—*school* KY-4
Kit Carson Sch—*school* NV-8
Kit Carson Sch—*school* NM-5
Kit Carson Sch (historical)—*school* TN-4
Kit Carson Trail—*trail* NM-5
Kitchal Bay—*bay* NY-2
Kitchamakin Hill—*summit* MA-1
**Kitchawan**—*pop pl* NY-2
Kitchawan, Lake—*lake* NY-2
**Kitchel**—*pop pl* IN-6
Kitchel Branch—*stream* MO-7
Kitchel Creek—*stream* IN-6
Kitchel Key—*island* FL-3
*Kitchell* IN-6
Kitchell—*locale* NJ-2
Kitchel Lake—*reservoir* CO-8
Kitchell Cem—*cemetery* MO-7
*Kitchell Creek* IN-6
Kitchell Hill—*summit* MO-7
**Kitchell (Kitchel)**—*pop pl* IN-6
Kitchell Lake—*reservoir* NJ-2
Kitchell Lake Dam—*dam* NJ-2
*Kitch-e-lus Lake* WA-9
Kitchen—*locale* OH-6
**Kitchen**—*pop pl* WV-2
Kitchen, Pete, Ranch—*hist pl* AZ-5
*Kitchen, The* MA-1
Kitchen, The—*basin* (2) UT-8
Kitchen, The—*bay* FL-3
Kitchen, The—*channel* FL-3
Kitchen, The—*other* AK-9
Kitchen, Van, House—*hist pl* KY-4
Kitchen, William, House—*hist pl* PA-2
Kitchen Anchorage—*bay* AK-9
Kitchen Bayou—*swamp* AR-4
Kitchen Branch—*stream* AR-4
Kitchen Branch—*stream* FL-3
Kitchen Branch—*stream* KY-4
Kitchen Branch—*stream* (2) NC-3
Kitchen Branch—*stream* TX-5
Kitchen Brook—*stream* MA-1
Kitchen Canyon—*valley* UT-8
Kitchen Cem—*cemetery* GA-3
Kitchen Cem—*cemetery* KY-4
Kitchen Cem—*cemetery* (3) MO-7
Kitchen Cem—*cemetery* TX-5
Kitchen Corral Point—*cape* UT-8
Kitchen Corral Spring—*spring* UT-8
Kitchen Corral Wash—*valley* UT-8
Kitchen Cove—*area* NM-5
Kitchen Cove—*bay* FL-3
Kitchen Cove—*bay* ME-1
Kitchen Cove—*valley* NC-3
Kitchen Cove Point—*cape* ME-1
Kitchen Cow House Pond—*lake* FL-3
*Kitchen Creek* FL-3
*Kitchen Creek* ID-8
*Kitchen Creek* MT-8
Kitchen Creek—*stream* CA-9
Kitchen Creek—*stream* CO-8
Kitchen Creek—*stream* (2) ID-8
Kitchen Creek—*stream* IN-6
Kitchen Creek—*stream* (2) LA-4
Kitchen Creek—*stream* OR-9
Kitchen Creek—*stream* PA-2
Kitchen Creek—*stream* TX-5
Kitchen Creek—*stream* (2) WV-2
Kitchen Creek Ch—*church* LA-4
Kitchen Creek Falls—*falls* PA-2
Kitchen Creek Gorge—*valley* PA-2
Kitchener—*locale* MS-4
Kitchen Fork—*stream* KY-4
Kitchen Gap—*gap* GA-3
Kitchen Gulch—*valley* MT-8
Kitchen Gulch—*valley* OR-9
Kitchen Hollow—*valley* AR-4
Kitchen Hollow—*valley* (2) TN-4
*Kitchen Key* FL-3
Kitchen Key—*island* FL-3
Kitchen Lake—*reservoir* OK-5
Kitchen Meadow—*flat* NV-8
Kitchen Mtn—*summit* MS-4
Kitchen Neck—*bay* GA-3
*Kitchen Ranch* AZ-5
Kitchen Ranch—*locale* NM-5
Kitchen Rsvr—*reservoir* WY-8
Kitchen Run—*stream* OH-6
Kitchens—*locale* TN-4
Kitchens, Richard L., Post No. 41—*hist pl* AR-4
Kitchens Branch—*stream* MO-7
Kitchens Branch—*stream* NC-3
Kitchens Cem—*cemetery* AL-4
Kitchens Cem—*cemetery* TN-4
Kitchens Cem (historical)—*cemetery* TN-4
Kitchen Sch (abandoned)—*school* PA-2
Kitchens Creek—*stream* MI-6
Kitchens Creek—*stream* TN-4
Kitchens Knob—*summit* (2) NC-3
Kitchens Landing—*locale* GA-3
**Kitchens Mill**—*pop pl* AL-4
Kitchens Mtn—*summit* GA-3
Kitchens of Sara Lee—*facility* IL-6
Kitchen Spring—*spring* AZ-5
Kitchens Sch (historical)—*school* TN-4
Kitchens Tank—*reservoir* AZ-5
Kitchen Valley—*valley* CA-9
**Kitchenville**—*pop pl* TX-5
Kitchen Well—*locale* NM-5
*Kitchepedrache Creek* AL-4
*Kitches Corners* PA-2
Kitches Corners—*locale* PA-2
Kitchi Creek—*stream* MN-6
Kitchie Cem—*cemetery* MI-6
Kitchi Gammi Club—*hist pl* MN-6
Kitchi Gammi Park—*park* MN-6
Kitchi Lake—*lake* MN-6
Kitching Cove—*bay* FL-3
Kitching Creek—*stream* FL-3
Kitching Peak—*summit* CA-9
Kitching Peak Trail (Pack)—*trail* CA-9
Kitchings Lake Dam—*dam* MS-4
**Kitchings Mill**—*pop pl* SC-3
*Kitchinibui-to* MP-9
Kitchins Siding (historical)—*locale* NC-3
Kitchi Pines Ch—*church* MN-6
Kitchners Lake—*lake* MI-6
Kitch Spring—*spring* CO-8
Kit Creek—*stream* MN-6
Kit Creek—*stream* NC-3
Kite—*locale* KY-4
Kite—*locale* TN-4
**Kite**—*pop pl* FL-3
**Kite**—*pop pl* (2) GA-3
*Kite Branch* TX-5
Kite Branch—*stream* TN-4
Kite Canyon—*valley* ID-8
Kite (CCD)—*cens area* GA-3
Kite Cem—*cemetery* MO-7
Kite Cem—*cemetery* NE-7
Kite Cem—*cemetery* (2) TN-4
Kite Creek—*stream* TN-4
Kite Creek—*stream* TX-5
Kite Hollow—*valley* VA-3
Kite Island—*island* AK-9
Kite Island—*island* SD-7
Kite Knob—*summit* WV-2
Kitel—*unknown* FM-9
Kitel, Dauen—*gut* FM-9
Kite Lake—*lake* (2) CO-8
Kitemaug—*locale* CT-1
Kite Mountain—*ridge* TN-4
Kite Pens—*locale* TX-5
Kite Ranch—*locale* WY-8
Kiter Creek—*stream* OR-9

Kiters Sch—school PA-2
Kite Sch—school AL-4
Kite School—locale KY-4
*Kites Creek* TN-4
Kites Lake—lake GA-3
Kites Pond—reservoir AL-4
Kite Spring—spring WY-8
Kites Run—stream WV-2
Kite Windmill—locale NM-5
Kite Windmill—locale (2) TX-5
Kitfield Ledge—rock MA-1
*Kit-Hanne* DE-2
*Kit Hanne* PA-2
Kithcart Ditch—canal IN-6
*Kithol* FM-9
Kit Hole—bay FL-3
Kithool—summit FM-9
Kiti—civil FM-9
Kiti, Pillapen—stream FM-9
Kitialap—locale FM-9
Kiti Epwur—swamp FM-9
Kitietik—locale FM-9
Kitigan Lake—lake MN-6
*Kiti Harbor* FM-9
*Kitihi Lake* MN-6
Kitingirak Gap—gap AK-9
Kitiram Ipitanga Hills—range AK-9
*Kiti River* FM-9
Kit Island—island AK-9
Kitkonak Hill—summit AK-9
Kitkum Bay—bay AK-9
Kit Lake—lake AK-9
Kit Lake—lake WY-8
Kitley Cem—cemetery IN-6
Kitlik River—stream AK-9
Kitling Creek—stream WA-9
Kitling Lake—lake WA-9
Kitling Peak—summit WA-9
Kit Love Branch—stream KY-4
Kitluk River—stream AK-9
Kit Mtn—summit TX-5
Kitnagak Bay—bay AK-9
Kitnagak Point—cape AK-9
Kitnarrow Branch—stream KY-4
Kitnepaluk—locale AK-9
Kitnepaluk Creek—stream AK-9
Kitnik Mtn—summit AK-9
Kitnik River—stream AK-9
Kitoi Bay—bay AK-9
Kitovi Point—cape AK-9
Kit Point—summit KY-4
Kit Price Prairie—flat ID-8
Kitrell Creek Reservoir Dam—dam MS-4
KITR-FM (Creston)—tower IA-7
Kitsap—other WA-9
**Kitsap County**—pop pl WA-9
Kitsap Creek—stream WA-9
Kitsap Golf—other WA-9
Kitsap Lake—lake WA-9
**Kitsap Lake**—pop pl WA-9
Kitsap Lake Community Club—building WA-9
Kitsap Memorial State Park—park WA-9
*Kits Corner* WA-9
Kits Creek—stream MI-6
Kits Creek—stream (2) VA-3
Kitsee Inlet—bay TX-5
*Kits Hammocks* DE-2
Kits Hollow—valley TX-5
*Kit siel* AZ-5
*Kits-il* AZ-5
Kit Sili Wash—stream AZ-5
Kitsillie Chapter House—locale AZ-5
*Kits Kait* KS-7
Kits Knob—summit NC-3
*Kitson* GA-3
Kitson (historical)—locale AL-4
**Kitson Hot Springs**—pop pl OR-9
*Kitson P.O.* AL-4
Kitson Ridge—ridge OR-9
Kitson Ridge Trail—trail OR-9
Kitson Rsvr—reservoir CO-8
**Kitsonville**—pop pl WV-2
Kitson Woolen Mill—hist pl PA-2
*Kits Peak* AZ-5
Kits Peak—summit NV-8
Kits Point—cape MD-2
Kit Spring Branch—stream NC-3
Kitsuma Peak—summit NC-3
Kit Swamp—stream NC-3
Kit Swamp—swamp GA-3
Kit Swamp Ch—church NC-3
**Kitt**—pop pl IN-6
Kittahutty Creek—stream MS-4
**Kittanning**—pop pl PA-2
Kittanning Borough—civil PA-2
*Kittanning Campus* PA-2
Kittanning Country Club—other PA-2
*Kittanning Gap* PA-2
**Kittanning Heights**—pop pl PA-2
Kittanning JHS—school PA-2
Kittanning Point—cliff PA-2
Kittanning Rsvr—reservoir PA-2
Kittanning Run—stream PA-2
Kittanning Senior HS—school PA-2
Kittanning (sta.)—uninc pl PA-2
Kittanning State For—forest PA-2
Kittanning Township Elem Sch—school PA-2
**Kittanning (Township of)**—pop pl PA-2
Kittanset Golf Club—locale MA-1
*Kittatinhy Mountain* PA-2
Kittatinny—locale PA-2
Kittatinny Camp—locale NJ-2
Kittatinny Camp Lake—reservoir NJ-2
Kittatinny Camp Lake Dam—dam NJ-2
Kittatinny Creek—stream NJ-2
**Kittatinny Lake**—pop pl NJ-2
Kittatinny Lake—reservoir NJ-2
Kittatinny Lake Dam—dam NJ-2
*Kittatinny Mountains* NJ-2
*Kittatinny Mountains* PA-2
*Kittatinny Mtn* PA-2
Kittatinny Mtn—range (2) PA-2
Kittatinny Mtn—summit NJ-2
Kittatinny Mtn—summit PA-2
*Kittatinny Mtn Range* NJ-2
*Kittatinny Mtn Range* PA-2
Kittatinny Sch (historical)—school PA-2
Kittatinny Tunnel—tunnel PA-2
*Kittaton Creek* VA-3
Kitt Brook—stream CT-1

*Kitteaumut* MA-1
Kittelson Slough—lake ND-7
Kitten Canyon—valley NM-5
Kitten Canyon—valley OR-9
Kitten Canyon Rsvr—reservoir OR-9
Kitten Canyon Spring—spring OR-9
Kitten Creek—stream ID-8
Kitten Creek—stream KS-7
Kitten Creek—stream MN-6
Kitten Creek—stream MO-7
Kitten Creek—stream NC-3
Kitten Creek—stream OR-9
Kitten Creek—stream WA-9
Kitten Creek—stream WY-8
Kittenger Cem—cemetery MO-7
Kittenger Hollow—valley VA-3
*Kitten Key* FL-3
Kitten Lake—lake MI-6
Kitten Pass—channel AK-9
Kitten Rock—pillar OR-9
Kitten Run—stream OH-6
Kittens, The—area AK-9
Kitten Springs—spring NV-8
Kitten Springs Canyon—valley NV-8
Kitter Canyon—valley CA-9
Kitteredge Brook—stream ME-1
Kittering Creek—stream MS-4
Kitterlin Bay—bay LA-4
Kitterlin Creek—stream LA-4
*Kitterlins Creek* LA-4
*Kitterlins Lake* LA-4
Kitterman, Nola, House—hist pl MO-7
**Kitterman Corners**—pop pl IN-6
Kitterman Sch—school IL-6
Kitterville Cem—cemetery KS-7
Kitterville Community Hall—building KS-7
**Kittery**—pop pl ME-1
Kittery Center (census name Kitterey)—other ME-1
**Kittery Foreside**—pop pl ME-1
Kittery Island—island ME-1
Kittery Point—cape ME-1
**Kittery Point**—pop pl ME-1
**Kittery (Town of)**—pop pl ME-1
Kittewan Creek—stream VA-3
*Kitthantemessink* DE-2
*Kitti* FM-9
*Kittiakaska Branch* AL-4
*Kitticaska Branch* AL-4
*Kitticaski Creek* AL-4
*Kitticaski School* AL-4
Kittiewan—hist pl VA-3
Kittilngook Bay—bay AK-9
Kitti Mack Mine—mine CO-8
Kitti (Municipality)—civ div FM-9
Kittinger, David, Residence—hist pl OH-6
Kittinger Cem—cemetery VA-3
Kittingers Chapel—church VA-3
**Kittitas**—pop pl WA-9
Kittitas Canyon—valley WA-9
Kittitas (CCD)—cens area WA-9
**Kittitas County**—pop pl WA-9
Kittitas Micro-Wave Station—other WA-9
Kittitas Valley—basin WA-9
Kittiwake Head—cape AK-9
Kittiwake Pond—lake AK-9
Kittle—locale AR-4
Kittle Cem—cemetery (2) MI-6
Kittle Creek—stream WV-2
Kittle Lake—lake MI-6
Kittlelick Ridge—ridge WV-2
*Kittleman* CA-9
Kittle Post Office (historical)—building TN-4
Kittlers—locale AR-4
Kittle Run—stream KY-4
Kittle Run—stream WV-2
Kittles Landing—locale GA-3
Kittleson Creek—stream MN-6
Kittleson House—hist pl WI-6
Kittleson Lake—lake (2) MN-6
Kittleson Place—locale OR-9
Kittleson Valley—valley WI-6
*Kittleson Valley Creek* WI-6
Kittner Hollow—valley AR-4
*Kittoctan Creek* VA-3
Kitt Peak—summit AZ-5
Kitt Peak Natl Observatory—building AZ-5
Kitt Point—cape MD-2
Kittredge—locale IL-6
**Kittredge**—pop pl CO-8
**Kittredge**—pop pl SC-3
Kittredge, Alvah, House—hist pl MA-1
Kittredge Bldg—hist pl CO-8
Kittredge Brook—stream ME-1
Kittredge Canal—canal OR-9
Kittredge Dam—dam MA-1
Kittredge Dam Rsvr—reservoir MA-1
Kittredge Hill—summit NH-1
Kittredge Hills—summit VT-1
Kittredge Mansion—hist pl MA-1
Kittredge Park—park MA-1
Kittredge Ranch—locale OR-9
Kittrell—locale (2) MS-4
**Kittrell**—pop pl NC-3
**Kittrell**—pop pl TN-4
**Kittrell**—pop pl TX-5
Kittrell Branch—stream TN-4
Kittrell (CCD)—cens area TN-4
Kittrell Cem—cemetery MS-4
Kittrell Cem—cemetery (4) TN-4
Kittrell Ch—church MS-4
*Kittrell Creek* MS-4
Kittrell Creek—stream GA-3
Kittrell Division—civil TN-4
Kittrell Hill—summit TN-4
**Kittrell Hill (subdivision)**—pop pl NC-3
Kittrell Hollow—valley (2) TN-4
Kittrell House—hist pl AR-4
Kittrell Junior Coll—school NC-3
Kittrell Landing—locale TN-4
Kittrell Mill Creek—stream MS-4
Kittrell Ridge—ridge (2) TN-4
*Kittrells Landing* TN-4
Kittrell (Township of)—fmr MCD NC-3
Kittrel Sch—school IA-7
Kittridge Cem—cemetery MI-6
Kittridge Creek—stream NV-8
Kittridge Ranch—locale NV-8
Kittridge Springs—spring NV-8
Kittridge Street Sch—school CA-9

**Kitts**—pop pl KY-4
Kitts Branch—stream MD-2
Kitts Cem—cemetery (3) TN-4
Kitts Corner—locale RI-1
Kitts Corner—locale WA-9
Kitts Creek—stream KY-4
Kitts Creek—stream VA-3
**Kitts Hill**—pop pl MD-2
**Kitts Hill**—pop pl OH-6
Kitts Hollow—valley TN-4
**Kitts Hummock**—pop pl DE-2
Kitts Hummock—summit DE-2
Kitts Island—island CT-1
Kitts Knob—summit KY-4
Kitts Mill (site)—locale OR-9
**Kittson (County)**—pop pl MN-6
Kittson Coulee—valley MT-8
Kittson Memorial Ch—church VA-3
*Kitts Peak* AZ-5
Kitts Point—cape MD-2
Kitts Point—cliff TN-4
*Kitts Pond* RI-1
Kitts Rocks—bar ME-1
Kitts Thorofare—channel NJ-2
**Kittville**—pop pl MA-1
Kitty, Lake—lake FL-3
Kitty Ann Creek—stream MI-6
Kitty Branch—stream AL-4
Kitty Burton Mine—mine ID-8
Kitty Clyde Mine—mine CO-8
Kitty Cobble—summit NY-2
Kitty Creek—stream (3) CO-8
Kitty Creek—stream IN-6
Kitty Creek—stream IA-7
Kitty Creek—stream KS-7
Kitty Creek—stream MT-8
Kitty Creek—stream NC-3
Kitty Creek—stream OH-6
Kitty Creek—stream OR-9
Kitty Creek—stream WI-6
Kitty Creek—stream WY-8
**Kitty Fork**—pop pl NC-3
*Kitty Gulch* CO-8
Kitty Gulch—valley ID-8
**Kitty Hawk**—pop pl NC-3
Kitty Hawk Bay—bay NC-3
**Kitty Hawk Beach**—pop pl NC-3
Kitty Hawk Estates Airp—airport MO-7
*Kitty Hawk Fishing Pier* NC-3
Kitty Hawk Life-Saving Station—hist pl NC-3
Kitty Hawk Pier—locale NC-3
Kitty Hawk Sch—school CA-9
Kitty Hawk Sch—school OH-6
Kitty Hollow—valley TN-4
Kitty Joe Canyon—valley AZ-5
Kitty Joe Canyon Spring—spring AZ-5
Kitty Joe Spring—spring AZ-5
Kitty Lake—lake AK-9
Kitty Oil And Gas Field—oilfield WY-8
Kitty Pan Tank—reservoir AZ-5
*Kitty Point* MD-2
Kitty Ray Mtn—summit TN-4
Kitty Ridge—ridge CA-9
Kitty Ridge—ridge NC-3
Kitty Run—stream IN-6
Kittys Corner—locale MD-2
Kitty Spring—spring ID-8
Kitty Spring—spring NM-5
Kitty Spring—spring OR-9
Kitty Spring Creek—stream MT-8
Kitty Springs—lake WI-6
Kitty Sweeten Cem—cemetery IL-6
**Kittyton (historical)**—pop pl TN-4
Kittyton Post Office (historical)—building TN-4
Kitty Wheelin Ford—locale MO-7
Kitwin HS—school TX-5
Kitzman Ditch—canal OH-6
Kitzmeyer Furniture Factory—hist pl NV-8
Kitzmiller—locale WA-9
**Kitzmiller**—pop pl MD-2
Kitzmiller, Martin, House—hist pl TN-4
Kitzmiller Cem—cemetery WV-2
*Kitzmiller (corporate name Kitzmillerville)* MD-2
**Kitzmiller (historical)**—pop pl TN-4
*Kitzmillersville* MD-2
**Kitzmillerville (corporate name for Kitzmiller)**—pop pl MD-2
*Kitzville* MN-6
**Kitzville**—pop pl MN-6
Kiuchman Rock—other AK-9
Kiugtlugtulit Mtn—summit AK-9
Kiuka Cem—cemetery TN-4
Kiuka Sch (historical)—school TN-4
Kiukpalik Island—island AK-9
Kiul—island FM-9
Kiul, Foko—reef FM-9
KIUL-AM (Garden City)—tower KS-7
*Kiunk Ditch* DE-2
Kiup Spring—spring NV-8
Kiutuestia Creek—stream GA-3
Kiva—locale MI-6
Kiva Beach—locale CA-9
Kivalik Inlet—gut AK-9
**Kivalina**—pop pl AK-9
Kivalina Lagoon—lake AK-9
Kivalina River—stream AK-9
Kivandeba Lake—lake MN-6
Kivaniva Lake—lake MN-6
Kiva Point—cliff CO-8
Kiva Sch—school AZ-5
*Kivdera Lake* MI-6
Kiveepuk Bay—bay AK-9
Kiver Branch—stream TN-4
Kivett Cem—cemetery IA-7
Kivett Dam Number 3—dam OR-9
Kivett Lake—reservoir IN-6
Kivett Lake—reservoir NC-3
Kivett Lake Dam Number One—dam NC-3
Kivett Lake Number One—reservoir NC-3
Kivett Rsvr Number 1—reservoir OR-9
Kivett Rsvr Number 2—reservoir OR-9
Kivett Rsvr Number 3—reservoir OR-9
*Kivey Branch* TN-4
*Kividera Lake* MI-6
Kividlo—locale AK-9
Kivikangas Ditch—canal MT-8
Kivisto Cem—cemetery MS-4
Kivivik Creek—stream AK-9
Kivliktort Mtn—summit AK-9
KIVR-AM—tower OR-9

Kiwa, Lake—lake OR-9
Kiwa Butte—summit OR-9
Kiwa Ditch—canal CO-8
KIWA-FM (Sheldon)—tower IA-7
Kiwah Creek—stream ID-8
Kiwah Creek—stream MT-8
Kiwah Meadow—flat ID-8
**Kiwalik**—pop pl AK-9
Kiwalik Lagoon—bay AK-9
Kiwalik Mtn—summit AK-9
Kiwalik River—stream AK-9
**Kiwana Subdivision**—pop pl UT-8
Kiwanda, Cape—cape OR-9
Kiwanda Beach—beach OR-9
**Kiwanda Beach**—pop pl OR-9
Kiwanda Creek—stream OR-9
Kiwani Cabin—locale NM-5
Kiwanis Camp—locale MA-1
Kiwanis Camp—locale MT-8
Kiwanis Camp—locale OR-9
Kiwanis Camp—locale TX-5
*Kiwanis Dam* ND-7
Kiwanis Field—park IL-6
Kiwanis Field—park TX-5
Kiwanis-Hobart Park—park FL-3
Kiwanis Island—island FL-3
Kiwanis Lake—lake OH-6
Kiwanis Lake—lake WY-8
**Kiwanis Lake**—pop pl OH-6
Kiwanis Lake—reservoir PA-2
Kiwanis Lake Park—park VA-3
*Kiwanis Park* TN-4
Kiwanis Park—park AK-9
Kiwanis Park—park AZ-5
Kiwanis Park—park AR-4
Kiwanis Park—park FL-3
Kiwanis Park—park ID-8
Kiwanis Park—park (2) IL-6
Kiwanis Park—park IA-7
Kiwanis Park—park (3) MI-6
Kiwanis Park—park MO-7
Kiwanis Park—park MT-8
Kiwanis Park—park NY-2
Kiwanis Park—park ND-7
Kiwanis Park—park OR-9
Kiwanis Park—park PA-2
Kiwanis Park—park TX-5
Kiwanis Park—park WI-6
Kiwanis Youth Camp—locale CO-8
Kiwanis Youth Camp—locale OK-5
Kiwanivista Park—park WV-2
Kiwa Springs—spring OR-9
Kiwassa Lake—lake NY-2
Kiwi Mesa—summit NV-8
Kiwook Pass—gap AK-9
Kixmiller's Store—hist pl IN-6
Kixmiller Summit—gap NV-8
KIXQ-FM (Webb City)—tower MO-7
KIXX-FM (Watertown)—tower SD-7
**Kiya, Chalan**—pop pl MH-9
Kiya, Unai Chalan—beach MH-9
Kiyak Creek—stream AK-9
Kiyokyaliksamiut River—stream AK-9
Kiyokyaliksamiut (Summer Camp)—locale AK-9
Kiyi Spring—spring ID-8
Kiyo Crag—summit MT-8
Kiyo Crag Lake—lake MT-8
*Kizer* TN-4
Kizer—locale AR-4
Kizer Cem—cemetery (2) TN-4
Kizer Cem—cemetery TX-5
*Kizer Corners* PA-2
Kizer Creek—stream OK-5
Kizer Creek—stream OR-9
Kizer Elem Sch—school NC-3
*Kizer Lake* PA-2
Kizer Pond—reservoir PA-2
Kizer Pond Dam—dam PA-2
Kizer Post Office (historical)—building TN-4
Kizer Ranch—locale OR-9
Kizer Ridge—ridge TN-4
Kizer Sch—school TN-4
Kizer Sch (historical)—school PA-2
*Kizers Corners* PA-2
Kizer Slough—stream OR-9
*Kizers Pond* PA-2
Kizhuchia Creek—stream AK-9
Kizhuyak Bay—bay AK-9
KIZZ-FM (Minot)—tower ND-7
Kizziah Spring Branch—stream AL-4
Kizzia Trail—trail AR-4
Kizzie Run—stream OH-6
Kizzort Branch—stream AL-4
KJAB-FM (Mexico)—tower MO-7
KJAM-AM (Madison)—tower SD-7
KJAM-FM (Madison)—tower SD-7
KJAN-FM (Atlantic)—tower IA-7
Kjar Coulee—valley MT-8
Kjaringa Kjeft—bay MI-6
KJCF-AM (Festus)—tower MO-7
KJCK-AM (Junction City)*—tower KS-7
KJCK-FM (Junction City)—tower KS-7
K J Clark JHS—school AL-4
KJDY-AM—tower OR-9
KJEL-AM (Lebanon)—tower MO-7
**Kjellberg Park**—pop pl MN-6
KJEM-FM (Seligman)—tower (2) MO-7
Kjemhus Hill—summit ND-7
KJEZ-FM (Poplar Bluff)—tower MO-7
KJFM-FM (Louisiana)—tower MO-7
KJHK-FM (Lawrence)—tower KS-7
KJIB-FM—tower OR-9
**KJirksey**—pop pl MS-4
KJJJ-AM (Phoenix)—tower AZ-5
KJJJ-FM (Glendale)—tower AZ-5
KJJQ-AM (Volga)—tower SD-7
KJJY-FM (Ankeny)—tower IA-7
KJKJ-AM (Flagstaff)—tower AZ-5
KJLA-AM (Kansas City)—tower MO-7
KJLR-FM (Sparta)—tower MO-7
KJLS-FM (Hays)—tower KS-7
KJMO-FM (Jefferson City)—tower MO-7
KJOK-FM (Yuma)—tower AZ-5
Kjostad Lake—lake MN-6
KJPW-AM (Waynesville)—tower MO-7
KJPW-FM (Waynesville)—tower MO-7
KJQN-AM (Ogden)—tower UT-8
KJRG-AM (Newton)—tower KS-7
KJSN-FM—tower OR-9

K Junction—locale OR-9
KJYK-FM (Tucson)—tower AZ-5
KKAA-AM (Aberdeen)—tower SD-7
KKAF-FM (Eloy)—tower (2) AZ-5
KKAN-AM (Phillipsburg)—tower KS-7
KKAT-FM (Lyons)—tower KS-7
KKBL-FM (Monett)—tower MO-7
KKCA-FM (Fulton)—tower MO-7
KKDY-FM (West Plains)—tower MO-7
*KK Eeke* FM-9
K Kelly Ranch—locale NM-5
KKEZ-FM (Fort Dodge)—tower IA-7
KKFI-FM (Kansas City)—tower MO-7
KKHJ-FM (Rapid City)—tower SD-7
K King Ranch—locale NE-7
KKJC-AM (Blue Springs)—tower MO-7
KKJO-AM (St Joseph)—tower MO-7
KKKX-FM (Ottawa)—tower KS-7
KKLL-AM (Webb City)—tower MO-7
KKLS-AM (Rapid City)—tower SD-7
KKLT-FM (Phoenix)—tower AZ-5
KKLX-FM (Moab)—tower UT-8
K K Mines—mine KY-4
KKMO-FM (Eldon)—tower MO-7
KKOA-AM (Minot)—tower ND-7
KKOW-AM (Pittsburg)—tower KS-7
KKOY-AM (Chanute)—tower KS-7
KKOZ-AM (Ava)—tower MO-7
KKQQ-FM (Volga)—tower SD-7
KKRC-FM (Sioux Falls)—tower SD-7
KKRD-FM (Wichita)—tower KS-7
KKRK-FM (Douglas)—tower AZ-5
KKRL-FM (Carroll)—tower IA-7
KKRQ-FM (Iowa City)—tower (2) IA-7
**Kkrval**—pop pl CO-8
KKSD-FM (Gregory)—tower SD-7
KKUZ-FM (Joplin)—tower MO-7
KKWZ-FM (Richfield)—tower UT-8
**Klaasville**—pop pl IN-6
Klaber—locale WA-9
Klaber Branch—stream KY-4
*Klabneh Creek* WA-9
*Klachemin Island* WA-9
Klachopis Point—cape WA-9
Klacking Creek—stream MI-6
**Klacking (Township of)**—pop pl MI-6
Klacks Island Park—park IA-7
KLAD-AM—tower (2) OR-9
Kladder Station—locale PA-2
Klag Bay—bay AK-9
Klager, Hulda, Lilac Gardens—hist pl WA-9
Klages State Wildlife Mngmt Areas—park MN-6
**Klagetoh**—pop pl AZ-5
Klagetoh—well AZ-5
Klagetoh Trading Post—locale AZ-5
Klag Island—island AK-9
Klag Mine—mine CO-8
Klahanie—locale WA-9
Klahhane Ridge—ridge WA-9
Klahini River—stream AK-9
*Klahostah Rock* WA-9
Klahowya Creek—stream WA-9
**Klahr**—pop pl PA-2
Klaibudech—island PW-9
**Klair Estate**—pop pl DE-2
Klakas Inlet—bay AK-9
Klakas Island—island AK-9
Klakas Lake—lake AK-9
Klak Butte—summit OR-9
Klak Creek—stream AK-9
*K Lake* MO-7
Klak Lake—lake AK-9
Klalbaimunket Lake—lake AK-9
Klaluthyiit Bluff—cliff AK-9
Klama Ranch—locale CO-8
*Klamas Creek* OR-9
Klamath—locale CA-9
**Klamath Agency**—pop pl OR-9
Klamath Air Force Station—military CA-9
Klamath Canyon—valley OR-9
Klamath (CCD)—cens area CA-9
**Klamath County**—pop pl OR-9
Klamath Creek—stream OR-9
**Klamath Falls**—pop pl OR-9
Klamath Falls (CCD)—cens area OR-9
*Klamath Falls - Lakeview Wayside* OR-9
**Klamath Falls Southeast**—pop pl OR-9
**Klamath Falls Yard**—pop pl OR-9
Klamath Forest Natl Wildlife Ref—reserve OR-9
Klamath Game Mngmt Area—park OR-9
**Klamath Glen**—pop pl CA-9
Klamath Hills—summit OR-9
**Klamath Junction**—pop pl OR-9
Klamath Marsh—swamp OR-9
Klamath Memorial Park—cemetery OR-9
Klamath Mountains—range (2) OR-9
Klamath Natl For—forest CA-9
Klamathon—locale CA-9
Klamathon Spring—spring CA-9
Klamath Point—cape OR-9
Klamath Ridge—ridge OR-9
*Klamath River* CA-9
**Klamath River**—pop pl CA-9
Klamath River—stream CA-9
Klamath River—stream OR-9
Klamath River Post Office—locale CA-9
Klamath River Recreation Site—park OR-9
Klamath River Sch—school CA-9
Klamath Strait—channel OR-9
Klamath Strait Drain Outlet—canal CA-9
Klamath Strait Drain Outlet—canal OR-9
*Klamath Straits* OR-9
Klam Creek—stream AK-9
Klamm Park—park KS-7
Klandi Ranch—locale ND-7
Klandl Spring—spring ND-7
K-Land Park—park FL-3
Klanelneechena Creek—stream AK-9
Klang Memorial Park—park MN-6
Klan Hill—summit AK-9
Klapatche Park—park WA-9
Klapatche Point—cliff WA-9
Klapatche Ridge—ridge WA-9
Klapot Point—cape WA-9
**Klapperthall Junction**—pop pl PA-2
Klara Ch—church ND-7
*Klara Peak* AZ-5
Klare Spring—spring CA-9
Klase Ditch—canal OH-6

Klasey Park—park NE-7
Klasi Cem—cemetery SD-7
Klasing Sch—school IL-6
*Klaskain* OR-9
*Klaskain Creek* OR-9
*Klaskania* OR-9
*Klaskania Creek* OR-9
Klaskanine Fish Hatchery—other OR-9
*Klaskanine River* OR-9
Klaskanine River—stream OR-9
Klaskanine Summit—summit OR-9
*Klaskonine* OR-9
*Klaskonine Creek* OR-9
Klason State Wildlife Mngmt Area—park MN-6
Klas Rock—bar WA-9
Klatakhna Creek—stream AK-9
Klatawa Lake—lake MT-8
K Lateral—canal CA-9
Klatsuta River—stream AK-9
Klatt Camp—locale WA-9
Klatt Mine—mine CA-9
Klatt Ranch—locale MT-8
**Klatt Road**—pop pl AK-9
Klatzer Dam—dam SD-7
Klau—locale CA-9
Klaudt Sch—school SD-7
Klau Mine—mine CA-9
Klaus Block—hist pl OH-6
Klaus Lake—lake WA-9
Klaus Lake—lake WI-6
Klauson Pasture—flat CO-8
Klaus Park—park MO-7
Klaus Park—park ND-7
Klaus Ranch—locale OR-9
Klauss Drain—canal MI-6
Klavano Bridge—bridge WA-9
Klawa Creek—stream ID-8
Klawak (Klawock)—other AK-9
Klawak Lake—lake AK-9
Klawak River—stream AK-9
Klawasi River—stream AK-9
Klawatti Creek—stream WA-9
*Klawatti Glacier* WA-9
Klawatti Glacier—glacier WA-9
Klawatti Lake—lake WA-9
Klawatti Peak—summit WA-9
Klawhop Butte—summit OR-9
Klawitter Creek—stream WI-6
**Klawock**—pop pl AK-9
Klawock Harbor—bay AK-9
Klawock Inlet—bay AK-9
Klawock Island—island AK-9
Klawock Lake—lake AK-9
Klawock Reef—bar AK-9
Klawock River—stream AK-9
K Lazy K Ranch Dam—dam SD-7
K Lazy S Ranch—locale WY-8
Klbael—summit PW-9
KLBM-AM—tower OR-9
KLBM-FM—tower OR-9
K L Carver Sch—school CA-9
KLCC-FM—tower OR-9
KLCD-FM (Decorah)—tower IA-7
KLCF-AM (Clifton)—tower AZ-5
K L Creek—stream AZ-5
KLDN-FM (Eldon)—tower MO-7
Kleaver Lake—lake CA-9
Kleban Lake Dam—dam (2) MS-4
**Klebeang**—pop pl PW-9
Klebeang, Taoch Ra—gut PW-9
Klebe Lake—lake ND-7
Kleber Dam—dam MI-6
**Kleberg**—pop pl TX-5
**Kleberg (County)**—pop pl TX-5
Kleberg Park—park TX-5
Kleberg Point—cape TX-5
*Klebiate Spring Mountain* AL-4
Kleburg Sch—school TX-5
Kleburne—locale TN-4
*Kleckers Ville* PA-2
*Kleckner Creek* NV-8
Kleckner Creek—stream NV-8
Kleckner Ranch—locale CO-8
*Klecknersville* PA-2
**Klecknersville**—pop pl PA-2
*Klee* OH-6
*Klee Fahrwasser* MP-9
Klee Mill—locale MD-2
Kleenburn—locale WY-8
Kleenman Community Center—building TN-4
Klee Pass—channel MP-9
*Klee Passage* MP-9
Klees Cem—cemetery MI-6
Klees Creek—stream OR-9
Klees Pond—lake MI-6
Kleffman Lake—lake MN-6
Kleg (historical)—locale AL-4
Klegstads Slough—gut MI-6
Klehini River—stream AK-9
Kleimann Lake—lake TX-5
*Kleimrong* MP-9
Klein—locale AL-4
Klein—locale TX-5
**Klein**—pop pl MS-4
**Klein**—pop pl MT-8
Klein, Stephen, House—hist pl TX-5
*Klein Acres* IL-6
Klein Airp—airport IN-6
Klein and Sutmar Block—hist pl ND-7
Kleinart Drain—canal MI-6
Klein Bay—bay VI-3
Klein Branch—stream MO-7
Klein Branch—stream TX-5
Klein Bridge—other IL-6
Klein Cem—cemetery OH-6
Klein Cem—cemetery TX-5
Klein Ch—church AL-4
Klein Ch—church TX-5
Klein Coulee—valley MT-8
Klein Creek—stream AK-9
Klein Creek—stream WA-9
Klein Creek—stream WI-6
Klein Dairy Farmhouse—hist pl WI-6
*Klein Dam* SD-7
Kleindorfer Hollow—valley IN-6
Kleine Canyon—valley CA-9
Kleine Kill—stream NY-2
*Kleine Kill Lake* NY-2
Kleine Lake—reservoir NC-3
Kleiner Creek—stream OR-9

Knob Hill—*summit* (2) ... IN-6
Knob Hill—*summit* ... NV-8
Knob Hill—*summit* (2) ... OR-9
Knob Hill—*summit* ... VT-1
Knob Hill—*summit* ... VA-3
Knob Hill—*summit* ... WA-9
*Knob Hill Administrative Site* ... AZ-5
Knob Hill Campground—*locale* ... MN-6
Knobhill Cem—*cemetery* ... MI-6
Knob Hill Cem—*cemetery* ... NE-7
Knob Hill Cem—*cemetery* ... TX-5
Knobhill Grange—*locale* ... WA-9
Knob Hill Mine—*mine* ... WA-9
Knob Hill Pond—*lake* ... VT-1
Knob Hill Ranger Station—*locale* ... AZ-5
Knob Hill Sch (abandoned)—*school* ... MO-7
**Knob Hill (subdivision)**—*pop pl* ... NC-3
Knob Hill Windmill—*locale* ... TX-5
Knob Hollow—*valley* ... KY-4
Knob Island—*island* ... AK-9
Knob Island—*island* ... NY-2
Knobit, The—*summit* ... NY-2
*Knob Lake* ... WY-8
Knob Lake—*lake* ... AK-9
Knob Lake—*lake* ... CA-9
Knob Lake—*lake* ... MI-6
Knob Lake—*reservoir* ... IN-6
Knob Lakes—*lake* ... WY-8
Knob Lake Saw-Mill Hollow Dam—*dam* ... IN-6
Knoblaugh Ditch—*canal* ... IN-6
Knoblaw—*locale* ... TX-5
Knoble, Joseph, Brewery—*hist pl* ... AR-4
*Knoble Lake* ... MN-6
*Knobley Mountain* ... WV-2
Knob Lick—*locale* ... KY-4
**Knob Lick**—*pop pl* ... MO-7
Knoblick Branch—*stream* ... GA-3
Knob Lick Branch—*stream* (2) ... KY-4
Knoblick Branch—*stream* ... KY-4
Knob Lick Branch—*stream* ... KY-4
Knob Lick Cem—*cemetery* ... KY-4
*Knoblick Creek* ... KY-4
Knoblick Creek—*stream* (3) ... KY-4
Knob Lick Creek—*stream* ... KY-4
Knob Lick Hill—*summit* ... KY-4
Knoblick Knob—*summit* ... IN-6
Knob Lick Lookout—*locale* ... MO-7
Knob Lick Mtn—*summit* ... MO-7
Knob Lick Sch—*school* (2) ... KY-4
Knoblock Cabin—*locale* ... CA-9
Knob Lock Mtn—*summit* ... NY-2
Knoblock Windmill—*locale* ... NM-5
Knobly Ch—*church* ... WV-2
Knobly Mtn—*range* ... WV-2
Knobly Tunnel—*tunnel* (2) ... WV-2
Knob Mine Number 2 (surface)—*mine* ... AL-4
Knob Mine (surface)—*mine* ... AL-4
Knob Mine (underground)—*mine* (2) ... AL-4
Knob Mountain Trail—*trail* ... VA-3
Knob Mtn—*summit* ... AZ-5
Knob Mtn—*summit* ... ID-8
Knob Mtn—*summit* ... MT-8
Knob Mtn—*summit* ... NY-2
Knob Mtn—*summit* (2) ... PA-2
Knob Mtn—*summit* ... UT-8
Knob Mtn—*summit* (3) ... VA-3
**Knob Noster**—*pop pl* ... MO-7
Knob Noster State Park—*park* ... MO-7
Knob Oaks—*uninc pl* ... TX-5
Knob Of Rocks—*summit* ... VA-3
Knob Peak—*summit* ... CA-9
Knob Peak—*summit* ... OR-9
Knob Point—*cape* ... AK-9
Knob Point—*summit* ... CA-9
Knob Point—*summit* ... OR-9
**Knob Point (subdivision)**—*pop pl* ... PA-2
Knob Pond—*lake* ... NY-2
Knob Prairie Cem—*cemetery* ... IL-6
Knob Prairie Ch—*church* ... IL-6
Knob Prairie Ch—*church* ... OH-6
Knob Prairie Creek—*stream* ... IL-6
Knob Ridge—*ridge* ... AK-9
Knob Ridge—*ridge* ... PA-2
Knob Ridge—*ridge* ... WV-2
**Knob Ridge (subdivision)**—*pop pl* ... NC-3
Knob Rock—*pillar* ... OR-9
Knob Rock Creek—*stream* ... OR-9
Knob Rock Dam—*dam* ... NM-5
Knob Rsvr—*reservoir* ... OR-9
Knob Rsvr—*reservoir* (2) ... WY-8
Knob Run—*stream* (2) ... PA-2
Knob Run—*stream* ... WV-2
Knobs—*locale* ... WV-2
*Knobs, The* ... IN-6
*Knobs, The* ... TX-5
Knobs, The—*range* ... VA-3
Knobs, The—*ridge* ... KY-4
Knobs, The—*ridge* (2) ... TN-4
Knobs, The—*summit* ... IN-6
Knobs, The—*summit* ... KY-4
Knobs, The—*summit* ... OR-9
Knobs, The—*summit* (2) ... PA-2
Knobs, The—*summit* (2) ... TN-4
Knobs Ch—*church* ... IL-6
Knobs Ch—*church* ... NC-3
Knob Sch—*school* ... AR-4
Knob Sch—*school* ... WV-2
Knob Sch (abandoned)—*school* (2) ... MO-7
Knob Sch (historical)—*school* ... MO-7
*Knobs Creek* ... TX-5
Knobs Creek Ch (historical)—*church* ... TN-4
Knobs Fire Tower, The—*tower* ... PA-2
Knobs Hill—*locale* ... AL-4
Knobs Overlook—*locale* ... IN-6
Knob Spring—*spring* ... MT-8
*Knob Spring Baptist Ch* ... TN-4
Knob Spring Ch—*church* ... TN-4
Knob Springs—*spring* ... PA-2
Knobs Sch—*school* ... IL-6
Knobs Sheep Camp—*locale* ... OR-9
Knobs (Township of)—*other* ... NC-3
Knob Sublateral—*canal* ... ID-8
**Knobsville**—*pop pl* ... PA-2
Knob Tank—*reservoir* (4) ... AZ-5
Knobton Post Office (historical)—*building* ... TN-4
Knobtop Mtn—*summit* ... CO-8
*Knobtown* ... MO-7
Knobtown—*locale* ... MS-4
**Knobtown**—*pop pl* ... MO-7
Knob (Township of)—*fmr MCD* ... AR-4

*Knob Valhermoso* ... AL-4
Knob View Sch—*school* ... MO-7
Knobview Township—*civil* ... MO-7
**Knobville**—*pop pl* ... PA-2
Knoby Mine—*mine* ... MT-8
Knoby Park—*flat* ... MT-8
Knoby Spring—*spring* ... MT-8
Knoche Oil Field—*other* ... MO-7
*Knoches Reservoir* ... CA-9
Knoch Junior Senior HS—*school* ... PA-2
Knoch Rsvr—*reservoir* ... CA-9
*Knochs Rsvr* ... CA-9
Knockanat Lake—*lake* ... LA-4
Knockemdown Key—*island* ... FL-3
**Knockemstiff**—*pop pl* ... OH-6
Knocker Creek—*stream* ... SD-7
Knocker Ponds—*lake* ... MO-7
Knockers Hole—*bend* ... NH-1
Knockhock—*locale* ... AK-9
Knocking Cave Creek—*stream* ... KY-4
Knocking Run—*stream* ... WV-2
Knock Knees Gut—*gut* ... VA-3
Knockout Creek—*stream* ... WA-9
Knocks Folly—*hist pl* ... MD-2
Knocks Sch (historical)—*school* ... MS-4
Knodel Cem—*cemetery* ... SD-7
Knodel Sch—*school* ... SD-7
Knodenfeldt Cem—*cemetery* ... SD-7
KNOD-FM (Harlan)—*tower* ... IA-7
**Knoebel**—*pop pl* ... MD-2
Knoebel, Lawrence L., Covered Bridge—*hist pl* ... PA-2
**Knoebels Corner**—*pop pl* ... MD-2
**Knoebel's Grove**—*pop pl* ... PA-2
**Knoebels Grove**—*pop pl* ... PA-2
Knoeber Landing Strip—*airport* ... KS-7
Knoell, Christopher, Farmstead—*hist pl* ... NE-7
**Knoell East (subdivision)**—*pop pl* (2) ... AZ-5
**Knoell Mesa (subdivision)**—*pop pl* (2) ... AZ-5
Knoff Bend Ch—*church* ... IL-6
*Knoff Dam* ... AL-4
Knoff Lake—*reservoir* ... AL-4
Knoff Spring—*spring* ... WY-8
Knoil (historical)—*locale* ... SD-7
**Knoke**—*pop pl* ... IA-7
Knoke Sch—*school* ... ND-7
Knokes Creek—*stream* ... AL-4
Knoke Spring—*spring* ... WI-6
Knoles Cem—*cemetery* ... OK-5
Knoles Hole Spring—*spring* ... AZ-5
*Knoll* ... SD-7
Knoll—*locale* ... VA-3
Knoll, The—*bar* ... MS-4
Knoll, The—*island* ... UT-8
Knoll, The—*summit* ... NH-1
Knoll, The—*summit* ... NC-3
Knoll, The—*summit* (4) ... UT-8
Knoll Bay—*bay* ... AK-9
Knoll Branch—*stream* ... TX-5
Knoll Brook—*stream* ... OH-6
Knoll Cedars—*summit* ... NC-3
Knoll Cem—*cemetery* ... IA-7
Knoll Cem—*cemetery* ... MN-6
*Knoll Creek* ... TN-4
Knoll Creek—*stream* ... ID-8
Knoll Creek—*stream* ... NV-8
Knoll Creek—*stream* ... NC-3
Knoll Creek Experimental Station - University of Nevada—*locale* ... NV-8
Knoll Creek Springs—*spring* ... NV-8
*Knollcrest* (2) ... IL-6
**Knollcrest**—*pop pl* ... CT-1
Knoll Crest Cem—*cemetery* ... NE-7
Knollcroft—*hist pl* ... NY-2
Knoll Dam—*dam* ... AZ-5
Knoll Ditch—*canal* ... UT-8
**Knolle**—*pop pl* ... TX-5
Knoll East Subdivision Mini Park—*park* ... AZ-5
Knoll East Subdivision Water Retention Basin—*reservoir* ... AZ-5
Knolle Cem—*cemetery* ... TX-5
Knolle Hill—*summit* ... IL-6
Knollenberg Ditch—*canal* ... IN-6
Knoll Head—*cape* ... AK-9
Knoll Hill—*summit* ... UT-8
Knoll Hollow—*valley* (2) ... UT-8
Knoll House Creek—*stream* ... NC-3
Knolling Knob—*summit* ... TN-4
*Knollis Church* ... TN-4
Knoll Island—*island* ... NC-3
Knoll I-80 Heliport—*airport* ... UT-8
Knollkreg Cem—*cemetery* ... VA-3
*Knoll Lake* ... WY-8
Knoll Lake—*reservoir* ... AZ-5
Knoll Lake Campground—*park* ... AZ-5
**Knollmere**—*pop pl* ... MA-1
Knoll Mtn—*summit* ... NV-8
Knoll Park—*park* ... AL-4
Knoll Point—*cape* ... AK-9
Knoll Pond—*lake* ... NJ-2
Knoll Pond Rsvr—*reservoir* ... NV-8
Knoll Ponds—*lake* ... TX-5
Knoll Ranch—*locale* ... NE-7
Knoll Ridge—*ridge* ... AZ-5
Knoll Run—*stream* ... IN-6
Knolls—*locale* ... UT-8
**Knolls, The**—*pop pl* ... VA-3
Knolls, The—*range* ... CT-1
Knolls, The—*summit* ... ID-8
Knolls, The—*summit* ... NV-8
Knolls, The—*summit* (2) ... UT-8
Knolls Association Dam—*dam* ... NC-3
Knolls Association Lake—*reservoir* ... NC-3
Knoll Sch—*school* ... MI-6
*Knolls Lake* ... AZ-5
Knoll Spring—*spring* ... NV-8
Knoll Spring—*spring* ... UT-8
Knoll Springs—*spring* ... UT-8
*Knolls Ridge* ... AZ-5
Knolls Rsvr—*reservoir* ... CO-8
Knolls Sch—*school* (2) ... CA-9
Knolls Vista Sch—*school* ... WA-9
Knolls Windmill—*locale* ... NM-5
Knoll Tank—*reservoir* (2) ... AZ-5
**Knollton Heights**—*pop pl* ... IN-6
**Knollview**—*pop pl* ... MD-2
Knollville Sch—*school* ... IA-7
*Knollwood* ... IL-6
Knollwood—*hist pl* ... MA-1
Knollwood—*hist pl* ... NH-1

Knollwood—*hist pl* ... TN-4
Knollwood—*locale* ... MD-2
**Knollwood**—*pop pl* ... CT-1
**Knollwood**—*pop pl* (3) ... IL-6
**Knollwood**—*pop pl* (2) ... MD-2
**Knollwood**—*pop pl* (2) ... NJ-2
**Knollwood**—*pop pl* ... NC-3
**Knollwood**—*pop pl* ... OH-6
**Knollwood**—*pop pl* ... TN-4
**Knollwood**—*pop pl* ... TX-5
**Knollwood**—*pop pl* ... WV-2
**Knollwood Acres (subdivision)**—*pop pl* ... NC-3
Knollwood Cem—*cemetery* ... MN-6
Knollwood Cem—*cemetery* ... NC-3
Knollwood Cem—*cemetery* ... OH-6
**Knollwood Condominium**—*pop pl* ... UT-8
Knollwood Country Club—*other* ... MI-6
Knollwood Country Club—*other* ... NY-2
Knollwood Elem Sch—*school* ... NC-3
**Knollwood Estates Plat One (subdivision)**—*pop pl* ... UT-8
Knollwood Field—*airport* ... NC-3
Knollwood Golf Course—*other* ... CA-9
Knollwood Hosp—*hospital* ... CA-9
Knollwood Memorial Gardens Cem—*cemetery* ... WI-6
Knollwood Memorial Park—*cemetery* ... MA-1
Knollwood Park—*park* ... DE-2
Knollwood Park—*park* ... MI-6
**Knollwood Park**—*pop pl* ... MI-6
Knollwood Park Cem—*cemetery* ... NY-2
Knollwood Sch—*school* ... CA-9
Knollwood Sch—*school* ... OH-6
Knollwood Sch—*school* ... SD-7
Knollwood Shop Ctr—*locale* ... NC-3
**Knollwood (subdivision)**—*pop pl* (2) ... AL-4
**Knollwood (subdivision)**—*pop pl* (5) ... NC-3
**Knollwood (subdivision)**—*pop pl* ... TN-4
**Knollwood Subdivision**—*pop pl* ... UT-8
Knollwood Village—*locale* ... OH-6
Knolly Flats—*flat* ... UT-8
Knoop Cem—*cemetery* ... OH-6
Knoops Sch—*school* ... KY-4
Knopf Cem—*cemetery* ... IL-6
**Knopp**—*pop pl* ... KY-4
Knopp Branch—*stream* ... TX-5
Knopp Cem—*cemetery* ... TX-5
Knopp Creek—*stream* ... GA-3
*Knop Pond* ... MA-1
Knopp Run—*stream* ... IN-6
Knops Pond—*lake* ... MA-1
*Knops PondfMountain Lake* ... MA-1
Knopti Creek—*stream* ... CA-9
Knore Cem—*cemetery* ... OH-6
Knorpp—*locale* ... MO-7
Knorr Creek—*stream* ... WA-9
KNOS-FM (Marshall)—*tower* ... MO-7
Knot—*locale* ... GA-3
KNOT-AM (Prescott)—*tower* ... AZ-5
*Knot Creek* ... NV-8
KNOT-FM (Prescott)—*tower* ... AZ-5
Knotgrass Ridge—*ridge* ... WA-9
Knothead Hill—*summit* ... MO-7
Knothe Spring—*spring* ... AZ-5
Knot Hollow—*valley* ... TN-4
Knot Hollow—*valley* ... VA-3
Knoth Rsvr—*reservoir* ... CO-8
*Knot Island* ... NC-3
*Knot Isle* ... NC-3
Knotmaul Run—*stream* ... VA-3
Knot Mole Branch—*stream* ... VA-3
Knot Point—*cape* ... AK-9
Knot Point—*cape* ... MD-2
**Knot Point**—*pop pl* ... LA-4
*Knots Island* ... NC-3
Knots Pond—*reservoir* ... SC-3
**Knott**—*pop pl* ... FL-3
**Knott**—*pop pl* ... GA-3
**Knott**—*pop pl* ... TX-5
Knot Tableland—*plain* ... OR-9
Knott Branch—*stream* ... TX-5
Knott Cem—*cemetery* ... MS-4
Knott Cem—*cemetery* (3) ... TN-4
Knott Cem—*cemetery* ... TX-5
**Knott (County)**—*pop pl* ... KY-4
Knott Creek—*stream* ... NV-8
Knott Creek Channel—*canal* ... NV-8
Knott Creek Ranch—*locale* ... NV-8
Knott Creek Rsvr—*reservoir* ... NV-8
Knott Hill—*summit* ... IN-6
Knott Hill Sch—*school* ... SC-3
Knott Hollow—*valley* ... KY-4
Knotting, Lake—*lake* ... WI-6
*Knottingham* ... IL-6
Knottingham Butte—*summit* ... OR-9
Knottingham Rsvr—*reservoir* ... OR-9
Knott Island—*island* ... MD-2
Knottly Hollow—*valley* ... KY-4
Knott Post Office (historical)—*building* ... TN-4
Knott Ranch—*locale* ... CO-8
Knott RR Station—*locale* ... FL-3
Knott Run—*stream* ... PA-2
*Knotts* ... FL-3
Knotts, Nellie and Thomas, House—*hist pl* ... IA-7
*Knotts Bay* ... MN-6
Knotts Berry Farm—*locale* ... CA-9
Knotts Branch—*stream* ... AR-4
Knotts Cem—*cemetery* ... WV-2
Knotts Ch—*church* ... WV-2
Knott Sch—*school* ... CA-9
Knott School (Abandoned)—*locale* ... WI-6
*Knotts Creek* ... OR-9
Knotts Creek—*stream* ... AR-4
Knotts Creek—*stream* ... OR-9
Knotts Creek—*stream* ... VA-3
Knotts Crossing—*locale* ... MD-2
Knotts Crossroads—*locale* ... NC-3
Knotts Grove Ch—*church* ... NC-3
Knotts Hollow—*valley* ... WV-2
Knotts Island—*island* ... MN-6
Knotts Island—*island* ... NC-3
**Knotts Island**—*pop pl* ... NC-3
Knotts Island Bay—*bay* ... NC-3
Knotts Island Ch—*church* ... NC-3
Knotts Island Channel—*channel* ... NC-3
Knotts Island Elem Sch—*school* ... NC-3
*Knotts Landing* ... TN-4
Knotts Landing—*locale* ... NC-3
Knotts Neck—*cape* ... VA-3

Knotts Pond—*reservoir* ... SC-3
Knott Spring—*spring* ... OR-9
Knotts Ridge—*ridge* ... WV-2
Knotts Sch—*school* ... MO-7
Knott Street Sch—*school* ... OR-9
**Knottsville**—*pop pl* ... KY-4
**Knottsville**—*pop pl* ... WV-2
Knottsville-Wesleyan Ch—*church* ... WV-2
**Knotty Branch**—*pop pl* ... SC-3
Knotty Branch—*stream* ... SC-3
Knotty Creek—*stream* ... IA-7
Knottyhead Cave—*cave* ... TN-4
Knotty Hollow—*valley* ... TN-4
Knotty Poplar Fork—*stream* ... KY-4
Knotty Poplar Fork—*stream* ... VA-3
Knotvold Branch—*stream* ... MN-6
Knotwell Lookout Tower (historical)—*locale* ... MO-7
Knotz, John, House—*hist pl* ... MN-6
*Knoulton's Gore* ... VT-1
**Knousetown**—*pop pl* ... PA-2
Knowd—*locale* ... TX-5
Knowelhurst—*locale* ... NY-2
Knowels Pond Dam—*dam* ... AL-4
Knower House—*hist pl* ... NY-2
Knowl—*summit* ... AK-9
Knowland Brook—*stream* ... ME-1
Knowland Lake—*lake* ... MI-6
Knowland Rsvr—*reservoir* ... WY-8
Knowland Slough—*reservoir* ... OR-9
Knowland State Arboretum And Park—*park* ... CA-9
Knowledge Hill Sch—*school* ... KS-7
Knowler Park—*park* ... MD-2
*Knowles* ... DE-2
Knowles—*fmr MCD* ... NE-7
Knowles—*locale* ... CA-9
Knowles—*locale* ... MT-8
**Knowles**—*pop pl* ... MS-4
**Knowles**—*pop pl* ... NM-5
**Knowles**—*pop pl* ... OK-5
**Knowles**—*pop pl* ... WI-6
Knowles, Lake—*lake* ... FL-3
Knowles, Lucius, House—*hist pl* ... MA-1
Knowles Bay—*bay* ... AK-9
Knowles Bldg—*hist pl* ... MT-8
Knowles Branch—*stream* ... GA-3
Knowles Brook—*stream* (2) ... ME-1
Knowles Brook—*stream* ... NY-2
Knowles Brook—*stream* ... RI-1
Knowles Canyon—*valley* ... CO-8
Knowles Canyon—*valley* ... UT-8
Knowles Cem—*cemetery* ... IL-6
Knowles Cem—*cemetery* ... IN-6
Knowles Cem—*cemetery* ... NM-5
Knowles Cem—*cemetery* ... OH-6
Knowles Cem—*cemetery* (2) ... OK-5
*Knowles Cemetery* ... AL-4
Knowles Chapel—*church* ... GA-3
Knowles Corner—*locale* ... ME-1
**Knowles Corner**—*pop pl* ... CA-9
*Knowles Creek* ... PA-2
Knowles Creek—*stream* ... CO-8
Knowles Creek—*stream* ... MN-6
Knowles Creek—*stream* ... MT-8
Knowles Creek—*stream* ... OR-9
Knowles Creek—*stream* ... WI-6
Knowles Crossroads—*locale* ... DE-2
Knowles Drain—*canal* ... MI-6
Knowles Drain—*swamp* ... FL-3
Knowles Falls—*falls* ... MT-8
Knowles Grain Elevator—*hist pl* ... OK-5
Knowles Gulch—*valley* ... CA-9
Knowles Head—*cape* ... AK-9
Knowles Hill—*summit* ... ME-1
Knowles Hill—*summit* ... MA-1
Knowles Hill—*summit* ... WA-9
Knowles Hollow—*valley* ... TN-4
Knowles Island—*island* ... AL-4
Knowles Island—*island* ... NH-1
Knowles Junction—*locale* ... CA-9
*Knowles Lake* ... MI-6
Knowles Lake—*lake* ... IN-6
Knowles Lake—*lake* ... MT-8
Knowles Lode Claim Mine—*mine* ... SD-7
Knowles Marshes—*swamp* ... MD-2
Knowles Oil and Gas Field—*oilfield* ... LA-4
Knowles Peak—*summit* ... MT-8
Knowles Place—*locale* ... NM-5
Knowles Point—*cape* ... RI-1
Knowles Pond—*lake* ... FL-3
Knowles Pond—*lake* (2) ... NH-1
Knowles Ranch—*locale* ... UT-8
Knowles Ridge—*ridge* ... TN-4
Knowles Ridge Cave—*cave* ... TN-4
Knowles Rocks—*bar* ... ME-1
Knowles Sch—*school* ... CA-9
Knowles Sch—*school* ... NM-5
**Knowlesville**—*pop pl* ... NY-2
**Knowlesville Station**—*pop pl* ... NY-2
Knowles Well—*well* (2) ... NM-5
Knowles Windmill—*locale* ... NM-5
Knowles Windmill—*locale* ... TX-5
Knowlton—*hist pl* ... PA-2
Knowlton—*locale* ... IA-7
Knowlton—*locale* ... KY-4
Knowlton—*locale* ... MT-8
Knowlton—*locale* ... PA-2
**Knowlton**—*pop pl* ... AR-4
**Knowlton**—*pop pl* ... NJ-2
**Knowlton**—*pop pl* ... PA-2
**Knowlton**—*pop pl* ... WI-6
Knowlton, Dr. William A., House—*hist pl* ... OH-6
Knowlton, Jabez, Store—*hist pl* ... ME-1
*Knowlton Bayou* ... AR-4
Knowlton Bayou—*gut* ... AR-4
*Knowlton Branch* ... CT-1
Knowlton Brook—*stream* (2) ... CT-1
Knowlton Cem—*cemetery* ... ME-1
Knowlton Cem—*cemetery* ... MT-8
Knowlton Cem—*cemetery* ... NH-1
Knowlton Cem—*cemetery* (2) ... OH-6
Knowlton Cem—*cemetery* ... WI-6
Knowlton Corner—*locale* ... ME-1
Knowlton Covered Bridge—*hist pl* ... OH-6
Knowlton Creek—*stream* ... MN-6
Knowlton Creek—*stream* ... MT-8
Knowlton Creek—*stream* ... WA-9
Knowlton Crevasse (1916)—*bay* ... AR-4
Knowlton Frame Cem—*cemetery* ... NJ-2

Knowlton Hat Factory—*hist pl* ... MA-1
Knowlton Heights—*locale* ... ID-8
Knowlton Hill—*summit* ... CT-1
Knowlton Hill—*summit* ... ME-1
Knowlton Hill—*summit* ... NH-1
Knowlton Hollow—*valley* ... PA-2
Knowlton Knob—*summit* ... WA-9
Knowlton Lake—*lake* ... MI-6
Knowlton Point—*cape* ... MS-4
Knowlton Pond—*reservoir* ... CT-1
Knowlton Ranch—*locale* ... CO-8
Knowlton Ranch—*locale* ... MT-8
Knowlton Revetment—*levee* ... AR-4
Knowlton Ridge—*ridge* ... WI-6
Knowlton Sch—*school* ... ME-1
Knowlton Sch—*school* ... MA-1
Knowlton Sch—*school* ... UT-8
Knowlton Sch—*school* ... WI-6
Knowltons Corner—*locale* ... ME-1
Knowltons Fork—*valley* ... UT-8
Knowlton Station—*building* ... PA-2
Knowlton Tank—*reservoir* ... NM-5
**Knowlton (Town of)**—*pop pl* ... WI-6
**Knowlton (Township of)**—*pop pl* ... NJ-2
**Knowltonwood**—*pop pl* ... PA-2
Knownothing Cove—*bay* ... ME-1
Knownothing Creek—*stream* ... CA-9
Know-nothing Creek—*stream* ... CA-9
Knownothing Lake—*lake* ... CA-9
Knownothing Mine—*mine* ... CA-9
Know River—*stream* ... NH-1
*Knowsville* ... NY-2
Knowsville—*uninc pl* ... NY-2
Knox—*locale* ... IL-6
Knox—*locale* ... MO-7
Knox—*locale* ... MT-8
Knox—*locale* ... NE-7
Knox—*locale* ... OH-6
Knox—*locale* ... SC-3
**Knox**—*pop pl* ... GA-3
**Knox**—*pop pl* (2) ... IN-6
**Knox**—*pop pl* ... MS-4
**Knox**—*pop pl* ... NY-2
**Knox**—*pop pl* ... ND-7
**Knox**—*pop pl* ... OH-6
**Knox**—*pop pl* (2) ... PA-2
Knox, Abner, Farm—*hist pl* ... KY-4
Knox, Fort—*other* ... KY-4
Knox, James W., House—*hist pl* ... TX-5
Knox, Point—*cape* ... CA-9
Knox, R. M., House—*hist pl* ... AR-4
*Knox Academy* ... AL-4
KNOX-AM (Grand Forks)—*tower* ... ND-7
**Knox Area**—*pop pl* ... NC-3
Knox Atoll—*island* ... MP-9
Knox Bayou—*stream* ... MS-4
Knox Bldg—*hist pl* ... NY-2
**Knoxboro**—*pop pl* ... NY-2
Knoxboro-Augusta Cem—*cemetery* ... NY-2
Knoxboro Creek—*stream* ... GA-3
Knox Borough—*civil* ... PA-2
*Knoxborough Creek* ... GA-3
Knox Bottoms—*bend* ... MT-8
Knox Branch—*stream* (3) ... AL-4
Knox Branch—*stream* ... GA-3
Knox Branch—*stream* ... LA-4
Knox Branch—*stream* (3) ... MO-7
Knox Branch—*stream* (2) ... TX-5
Knox Bridge—*bridge* ... GA-3
Knox Brook—*stream* ... NH-1
*Knoxbrough Creek* ... GA-3
Knox Butte—*summit* ... OR-9
Knox Butte Cem—*cemetery* ... OR-9
Knox Butte Sch—*school* ... OR-9
Knox Canyon—*valley* ... ID-8
Knox Canyon—*valley* ... OR-9
Knox Canyon—*valley* ... TX-5
Knox Cem—*cemetery* ... AR-4
Knox Cem—*cemetery* (3) ... GA-3
Knox Cem—*cemetery* ... KY-4
Knox Cem—*cemetery* ... LA-4
Knox Cem—*cemetery* ... MS-4
Knox Cem—*cemetery* ... MO-7
Knox Cem—*cemetery* ... NY-2
Knox Cem—*cemetery* ... ND-7
Knox Cem—*cemetery* ... OH-6
Knox Cem—*cemetery* ... OR-9
Knox Cem—*cemetery* (2) ... TN-4
Knox Cem—*cemetery* (2) ... TX-5
Knox Cem—*cemetery* ... WI-6
Knox Center—*locale* ... ME-1
Knox Ch—*church* ... MO-7
Knox Ch—*church* ... NY-2
Knox Chapel—*church* ... GA-3
Knox Chapel—*church* ... IN-6
Knox Chapel—*church* ... NC-3
Knox Chapel—*church* ... OH-6
Knox Chapel—*church* ... PA-2
**Knox City**—*pop pl* ... TX-5
Knox City (CCD)—*cens area* ... TX-5
Knox City Cem—*cemetery* ... MO-7
Knox City Cem—*cemetery* ... TX-5
Knox City Country Club—*other* ... TX-5
**Knox City (Knox Station)**—*pop pl* ... MO-7
Knox Community HS—*school* ... IN-6
Knox Community JHS—*school* ... IN-6
Knox Corner—*locale* ... ME-1
Knox Corner Ch—*church* ... ME-1
**Knox (County)**—*pop pl* ... IL-6
**Knox County**—*pop pl* ... IN-6
**Knox (County)**—*pop pl* ... KY-4
**Knox (County)**—*pop pl* ... ME-1
**Knox County**—*pop pl* ... MO-7
**Knox (County)**—*pop pl* ... OH-6
**Knox County**—*pop pl* ... TN-4
**Knox (County)**—*pop pl* ... TX-5
Knox County Country Club—*other* ... IL-6
Knox County Courthouse—*building* ... TN-4
Knox County Courthouse—*hist pl* ... ME-1
Knox County Courthouse—*hist pl* ... OH-6
Knox County Courthouse—*hist pl* ... TN-4
Knox County Farm (historical)—*locale* ... TN-4
Knox County Health Center—*hospital* ... TN-4
*Knox County Hosp* ... TN-4
Knox County HS—*school* ... MO-7
*Knox County Industrial School* ... TN-4
Knox County Infirmary—*hist pl* ... OH-6
Knox County Penal Farm—*locale* ... TN-4
Knox County Prison Farm (historical)—*locale* ... TN-4

*Knox County Workhouse* ... TN-4
*Knox Creek* ... IA-7
*Knox Creek* ... MO-7
Knox Creek—*stream* ... AL-4
Knox Creek—*stream* ... GA-3
Knox Creek—*stream* (3) ... ID-8
Knox Creek—*stream* (2) ... KY-4
Knox Creek—*stream* ... MI-6
Knox Creek—*stream* ... MT-8
Knox Creek—*stream* ... NV-8
Knox Creek—*stream* ... NC-3
Knox Creek—*stream* (2) ... SC-3
Knox Creek—*stream* ... VA-3
Knox Creek—*stream* ... WA-9
Knox Creek—*stream* ... WI-6
Knox Creek Ch—*church* ... KY-4
*Knoxdale* ... PA-2
Knoxdale—*locale* ... OH-6
**Knox Dale**—*pop pl* ... PA-2
Knoxdale (RR name for Knox Dale)—*other* ... PA-2
**Knox Dale (RR name Knoxdale)**—*pop pl* ... PA-2
Knox-Doss JHS—*school* ... TN-4
Knox Draw—*valley* ... TX-5
**Knox (Edenburg)**—*pop pl* ... PA-2
Knoxe Grove—*woods* ... IL-6
*Knox Elementary School* ... AL-4
Knox Elem Sch—*school* ... AZ-5
Knox Farm Hist Dist—*hist pl* ... NC-3
Knox Flat—*flat* ... CA-9
Knox Ford Bridge—*other* ... MO-7
**Knoxfork**—*pop pl* ... KY-4
Knox Fork—*stream* ... KY-4
Knox Gap—*gap* ... TN-4
*Knox Group* ... MP-9
Knox Grove Ch—*church* ... NC-3
Knox Gulch—*valley* ... CA-9
**Knoxhill**—*pop pl* ... FL-3
Knox Hill—*summit* ... FL-3
Knox Hill—*summit* ... ME-1
Knox Hill Branch—*stream* ... KY-4
Knox Hill Cem—*cemetery* ... KY-4
Knox Hill Ch—*church* ... FL-3
Knox Hill Corner—*locale* ... ME-1
**Knox Hill Dwellings**—*pop pl* ... DC-2
Knox Hill Sch—*school* ... FL-3
Knox (historical)—*locale* ... KS-7
Knox Hollow—*valley* (2) ... TN-4
Knox HQ—*building* ... NY-2
Knox HQ—*hist pl* ... NY-2
Knox HS—*school* ... MS-4
*Knox-Insel* ... MP-9
*Knox Inseln* ... MP-9
*Knox Island* ... MN-6
Knox Island—*island* ... MP-9
Knox JHS—*school* ... NC-3
Knox Knob—*summit* ... KY-4
*Knox Lake* ... MS-4
*Knox Lake* ... MT-8
Knox Lake—*lake* ... ID-8
Knox Lake—*lake* ... ME-1
Knox Lake—*lake* ... MI-6
Knox Lake—*lake* ... NE-7
Knox Lake—*lake* ... TX-5
Knox Lake—*lake* ... WA-9
Knox Lake—*reservoir* ... OH-6
Knox Ledge Corner—*locale* ... ME-1
Knox Lee Powerplant—*other* ... TX-5
Knox Lick Draft—*valley* ... VA-3
Knox (Locality)—*locale* ... IA-7
Knoxlyn—*locale* ... PA-2
Knox (Magisterial District)—*fmr MCD* ... VA-3
Knox Marsh—*swamp* ... MD-2
Knox Marsh Brook—*stream* ... NH-1
Knox Meadow—*flat* ... OR-9
Knox Memorial Bridge—*bridge* ... FL-3
Knox Mill (historical)—*locale* ... MS-4
**Knox Mills**—*pop pl* ... WI-6
Knox Mine—*mine* ... MN-6
Knox Mine (underground)—*mine* ... AL-4
Knox Mtn—*summit* ... CA-9
Knox Mtn—*summit* (2) ... ME-1
Knox Mtn—*summit* ... NH-1
Knox Mtn—*summit* ... OR-9
Knox Mtn—*summit* ... VT-1
Knox Number 1 Dam—*dam* ... SD-7
Knox Number 2 Dam—*dam* ... SD-7
Knoxo—*locale* ... MS-4
Knoxo Cem—*cemetery* ... MS-4
Knoxo Ch—*church* ... MS-4
Knox Oil Field—*oilfield* ... TX-5
Knoxo Oil Field—*oilfield* ... MS-4
Knoxo Post Office (historical)—*building* ... MS-4
Knox Park—*park* ... WA-9
**Knox Park**—*pop pl* ... TN-4
Knox Pass—*gap* ... MT-8
Knox Peak—*summit* ... AK-9
Knox Plaza Shop Ctr—*locale* ... TN-4
*Knox Point* ... CA-9
Knox Point—*cape* ... MA-1
Knox Point—*cape* ... MN-6
Knox Pond—*lake* ... MA-1
Knox Pond—*reservoir* ... OR-9
Knox Ranch—*locale* ... MT-8
Knox Ranch—*locale* ... OR-9
Knox Ridge—*ridge* ... ME-1
Knox Ridge—*ridge* ... MT-8
Knox Rsvr—*reservoir* ... CO-8
**Knox Run**—*pop pl* ... PA-2
Knox Run—*stream* ... IN-6
Knox Run—*stream* ... PA-2
Knox Sch—*school* ... AL-4
Knox Sch—*school* ... CA-9
Knox Sch—*school* ... IL-6
Knox Sch—*school* ... MN-6
Knox Sch—*school* (2) ... NY-2
Knox Sch—*school* ... OH-6
Knox Sch—*school* ... TX-5
Knox Sch (abandoned)—*school* ... PA-2
Knox Sch (historical)—*school* ... MS-4
Knox Sch (historical)—*school* ... TN-4
Knox (Site)—*locale* ... ID-8
Knoxs Landing—*locale* ... AL-4
Knox Slough State Game Mngmt Area—*park* ... ND-7
Knox Spring—*spring* ... CA-9
Knox Spring—*spring* ... GA-3
Knox Spring—*spring* ... MT-8
Knox Spring—*spring* ... OR-9

Knoxs Private Airstrip—*airport* OR-9
**Knox Spur**—*pop pl* MT-8
Knox Spur Station—*locale* PA-2
**Knox (sta.)**—*pop pl* ME-1
**Knox (sta.)**—*pop pl* PA-2
Knox Station—*locale* ME-1
Knox Store—*locale* SC-3
Knox Street Ch—*church* TX-5
Knox Suck—*swamp* GA-3
Knox Surratt Dam—*dam* NC-3
Knox Surratt Lake—*reservoir* NC-3
Knox Swamp—*swamp* MI-6
Knox Temple—*church* AL-4
**Knox (Town of)**—*pop pl* ME-1
**Knox (Town of)**—*pop pl* NY-2
**Knox (Town of)**—*pop pl* WI-6
Knox Township—*fmr MCD* (2) IA-7
**Knox Township**—*pop pl* ND-7
**Knox (Township of)**—*pop pl* IL-6
**Knox (Township of)**—*pop pl* IN-6
**Knox (Township of)**—*pop pl* (5) OH-6
**Knox (Township of)**—*pop pl* (3) PA-2
**Knox Trailer Park (subdivision)**—*pop pl* NC-3
Knox Valley—*valley* TN-4
Knox Vernon Speedway—*other* OH-6
*Knoxville* IN-6
*Knoxville* PA-2
Knoxville—*locale* AL-4
Knoxville—*locale* NE-7
**Knoxville**—*pop pl* AL-4
**Knoxville**—*pop pl* (2) AR-4
**Knoxville**—*pop pl* CA-9
**Knoxville**—*pop pl* GA-3
**Knoxville**—*pop pl* IL-6
**Knoxville**—*pop pl* IA-7
**Knoxville**—*pop pl* KY-4
**Knoxville**—*pop pl* MD-2
**Knoxville**—*pop pl* MS-4
**Knoxville**—*pop pl* MO-7
**Knoxville**—*pop pl* OH-6
**Knoxville**—*pop pl* OR-9
**Knoxville**—*pop pl* (3) PA-2
**Knoxville**—*pop pl* TN-4
**Knoxville**—*pop pl* TX-5
**Knoxville**—*pop pl* WV-2
Knoxville Baptist Tabernacle Ch—*church* TN-4
Knoxville Boat Club Dock—*locale* TN-4
Knoxville Borough—*civil* PA-2
Knoxville Business College—*hist pl* TN-4
Knoxville Catholic HS—*school* TN-4
Knoxville (CCD)—*cens area* TN-4
Knoxville Cem—*cemetery* AL-4
Knoxville Cem—*cemetery* AR-4
Knoxville Cem—*cemetery* MS-4
Knoxville Cem—*cemetery* PA-2
Knoxville Cem—*cemetery* TX-5
Knoxville City Hall—*building* TN-4
Knoxville Civic Auditorium—*building* TN-4
Knoxville Coll—*school* TN-4
Knoxville College Hist Dist—*hist pl* TN-4
Knoxville Council Girl Scout Camp—*locale* TN-4
Knoxville Creek—*stream* CA-9
Knoxville Division—*civil* TN-4
Knoxville Downtown Island Airp—*airport* TN-4
Knoxville Iron Foundry Complex-Nail Factory and Warehouse—*hist pl* TN-4
Knoxville JHS—*hist pl* PA-2
*Knoxville Junction* TN-4
Knoxville Junction—*locale* AR-4
Knoxville Lake—*lake* AK-9
Knoxville Memorial Park—*cemetery* TN-4
Knoxville Methodist Ch—*church* MS-4
Knoxville Mine—*mine* IL-6
Knoxville Mine—*mine* TN-4
Knoxville MS—*school* PA-2
*Knoxville Municipal Airport* TN-4
Knoxville Municipal Stadium—*park* TN-4
Knoxville News-Sentinel Airp—*airport* TN-4
Knoxville Oil Field—*oilfield* MS-4
Knoxville Plantation (historical)—*locale* AL-4
Knoxville Pond—*reservoir* IA-7
Knoxville Pond Dam—*dam* IA-7
Knoxville Post Office—*building* TN-4
Knoxville Post Office—*hist pl* TN-4
Knoxville Post Office (historical)—*building* MS-4
*Knoxville Presbyterian Church* AL-4
Knoxville Rsvr—*reservoir* PA-2
Knoxville Sch—*school* ME-1
Knoxville Sch—*school* NE-7
Knoxville Tower Oil Field—*oilfield* MS-4
Knoxville Township—*civil* MO-7
Knoxville Township—*fmr MCD* IA-7
Knoxville YMCA Bldg—*hist pl* TN-4
Knoxville YMCA Camp—*locale* TN-4
Knoxville Zoological Park—*park* TN-4
Knoxway Bay—*bay* WA-9
Knoxway Canyon—*valley* WA-9
**Knoxwood**—*pop pl* AL-4
KNPT-AM—*tower* (2) OR-9
KNPT-FM—*tower* OR-9
KNST-AM (Tucson)—*tower* (2) AZ-5
KNSX-FM (Steelville)—*tower* MO-7
KNTL-FM—*tower* OR-9
Knubble—*summit* ME-1
*Knubble, The* MA-1
Knubble, The—*cape* MA-1
Knubble Bay—*bay* ME-1
Knubble Ledge—*bar* ME-1
Knub Hill—*summit* AK-9
Knuckey Lake—*lake* MN-6
Knucklebone Rsvr—*reservoir* OR-9
Knuckle Cem—*cemetery* KY-4
Knuckle Ch—*church* KY-4
Knuckles Branch—*stream* KY-4
Knuckles Chapel—*church* SC-3
Knuckles Rsvr—*reservoir* CO-8
Knuckles Well—*well* NM-5
Knuckup Hill—*summit* MA-1
Knudsen Bar—*bar* CA-9
**Knudsen Corner**—*pop pl* UT-8
Knudsen Gap—*gap* HI-9
Knudsen JHS—*school* MI-6
Knudsen Ranch—*locale* CA-9
Knudsen Ranch—*locale* ID-8
Knudsen Ranch—*locale* NE-7
**Knudsens Corner**—*pop pl* UT-8
Knudson, Christen and Johanne, Farm—*hist pl* TX-5
Knudson Branch—*stream* TX-5
Knudson Branch—*stream* WI-6
Knudson Coulee—*valley* MT-8
Knudson Coulee—*valley* WI-6
Knudson Cove—*bay* AK-9
**Knudson Cove (Clover Pass)**—*pop pl* AK-9
*Knudson Creek* WI-6
Knudson Dam—*dam* SD-7
Knudson Ditch—*canal* MT-8
**Knudson (historical)**—*pop pl* OR-9
Knudson JHS—*school* NV-8
*Knudson Lake* WI-6
Knudson Lake—*lake* MN-6
Knudson Lateral—*canal* ID-8
Knudson Ranch—*locale* NV-8
Knudson Rsvr—*reservoir* MT-8
Knudson Slough—*lake* ND-7
Knudson Spring—*spring* MT-8
Knudson Spring Number Two—*spring* MT-8
Knudsvig Lake—*lake* ND-7
Knuedler Lake—*lake* CA-9
Knuepper Cem—*cemetery* TX-5
Knugormiut Summer Camp—*locale* AK-9
Knull—*locale* ID-8
Knull Grange—*locale* ID-8
Knulthkarm Creek—*stream* CA-9
Knupp Creek—*stream* OR-9
Knuppenburg, James, House—*hist pl* WA-9
Knuppenburg Lake—*lake* WA-9
Knuppe Sch—*school* SD-7
Knupple Cem—*cemetery* TX-5
Knupp Sch (historical)—*school* PA-2
Knurr Log House—*hist pl* PA-2
Knust Drain—*stream* MI-6
Knust Draw—*valley* TX-5
Knute Creek—*stream* ID-8
Knute Creek—*stream* MI-6
Knute Draw—*valley* TX-5
Knute Lake—*lake* MN-6
Knute Rockne Memorial Monmt—*pillar* KS-7
Knutes Creek—*stream* WI-6
Knuteson Creek—*stream* WI-6
Knuteson Lake—*lake* WI-6
Knuteson Spring—*spring* WI-6
**Knute (Township of)**—*pop pl* MN-6
Knuth Ditch—*canal* WY-8
Knutruin Rock—*bar* AK-9
Knutsen Lake—*lake* MI-6
Knutsen Lake—*lake* MN-6
Knutsen Spring—*spring* SD-7
Knutson Airp—*airport* ND-7
Knutson Bay—*bay* AK-9
Knutson Cem—*cemetery* SD-7
Knutson Creek—*stream* AK-9
Knutson Creek—*stream* MI-6
Knutson Creek—*stream* ND-7
Knutson Dam—*dam* MN-6
Knutson Lake—*lake* AK-9
Knutson Lake—*lake* (2) MN-6
Knutson Lake—*lake* WI-6
Knutson Mtn—*summit* AK-9
Knutson Ranch—*locale* SD-7
Knutson Saddle—*gap* OR-9
Knutson Sch Number 2 (historical)—*school* SD-7
Knuts Spring—*spring* CA-9
Knutz Creek—*stream* CA-9
KNWC-AM (Sioux Falls)—*tower* SD-7
KNWC-FM (Sioux Falls)—*tower* (2) SD-7
KNXV-TV (Phoenix)—*tower* AZ-5
Knyvet Square—*park* MA-1
KNZA-FM (Hiawatha)—*tower* KS-7
KOAC-AM—*tower* OR-9
KOA Campground—*park* (2) UT-8
KOAC-TV—*tower* OR-9
K O A Dam—*dam* NC-3
Koae—*locale* HI-9
Koaeae—*civil* HI-9
*Koae Cone* HI-9
Koaekea—*summit* HI-9
Koai—*summit* HI-9
Koaie—*civil* HI-9
*Koaie River* HI-9
Koaie Stream—*stream* HI-9
*Koai Hill* HI-9
Koakanini Falls—*falls* HI-9
Koakapar—*unknown* FM-9
KOAK-FM (Red Oak)—*tower* IA-7
Koala Gulch—*valley* HI-9
KOAL-AM (Price)—*tower* (2) UT-8
Koalensa Plantation (historical)—*locale* MS-4
Koale Stream—*stream* HI-9
Koali—*civil* HI-9
**Koali**—*pop pl* HI-9
Koali—*summit* HI-9
Koalii—*summit* HI-9
*Koali Mtn* HI-9
Koalusha Landing—*locale* MS-4
Koa Mill—*locale* HI-9
Koamoahd, Pilen—*stream* FM-9
KOA Monticello—*park* UT-8
KOAM-TV (Pittsburg)—*tower* KS-7
Koa Nui—*area* HI-9
KOAP-FM—*tower* OR-9
KOAP-TV—*tower* OR-9
*Koar Creek* PA-2
Koasati (historical)—*locale* AL-4
Koasr—*locale* FM-9
Kobakof Bay—*bay* AK-9
Kobasang Harbor—*harbor* PW-9
*Kobasang Island* PW-9
Kobbe Sch—*school* MN-6
*Kobb Hill* IN-6
KOBC-FM (Joplin)—*tower* MO-7
*Kob Creek* IN-6
Kobe—*locale* CO-8
Kobeh Valley—*basin* NV-8
Kobe Lake—*lake* MN-6
Koberg Beach—*beach* OR-9
Koberg Beach Wayside—*locale* OR-9
Koberg Slough—*lake* OR-9
**Koberman**—*pop pl* MO-7
Kobey Park—*flat* CO-8
KOBH-AM (Hot Springs)—*tower* SD-7
KOBH-FM (Hot Springs)—*tower* SD-7
KOBI-TV—*tower* OR-9
Koblegard Sch—*school* WV-2
*Kobler* MH-9
*Kobler Airfield* MH-9
Kobler Field—*airport* MH-9
Kobler Park—*park* TX-5
Kobolunuk—*locale* AK-9
Kobrock Lake Dam—*dam* MS-4
**Kobuk**—*pop pl* AK-9
*Kobuk (Census Area)* AK-9
*Kobuk (Census Subarea)* AK-9
Kobuk Creek—*stream* AK-9
Kobuk Lake—*lake* AK-9
Kobuk River—*stream* AK-9
Kobuk River Delta—*area* AK-9
Kobuk Valley Natl Park—*park* AK-9
Kobus Lake—*lake* WI-6
**Kobuta**—*pop pl* PA-2
Kobuta Station—*locale* PA-2
K O Butte—*summit* OR-9
Kocacho Creek—*stream* AK-9
Kocer Ranch—*locale* SD-7
Koch—*locale* MS-4
**Koch**—*pop pl* MO-7
**Koch**—*pop pl* TX-5
Koch, Carl, Block—*hist pl* WI-6
Koch, I. B., House—*hist pl* AZ-5
Koch, John E., Jr., House—*hist pl* OH-6
Koch, Robert, Hosp—*hist pl* MO-7
Koch Branch—*stream* TX-5
Koch Butte—*summit* OR-9
Koch Cem—*cemetery* NE-7
Koch Cem—*cemetery* OH-6
Koch Cem—*cemetery* (2) TX-5
Koch Creek—*stream* ID-8
Koch Creek—*stream* OR-9
Koch Creek—*stream* WY-8
Koch Ditch—*canal* NV-8
Koch Drug Store—*hist pl* IA-7
Kochendefer Covered Bridge—*hist pl* PA-2
Kochenderfers Ch—*church* PA-2
*Kocher Airport* PA-2
Kocher Cem—*cemetery* PA-2
*Kocher Creek* MI-6
Kocher Hollow—*valley* PA-2
Kocher Mtn—*summit* PA-2
Kochers Field—*airport* PA-2
Koch Hosp—*hospital* MO-7
Kochilagok Hill—*summit* AK-9
Kochis Arroyo—*stream* NM-5
*Koch Island* MI-6
Koch Island—*island* (2) WI-6
Kochluk Pass—*stream* AK-9
Koch Mountain Trail—*trail* OR-9
Koch Mtn—*summit* MT-8
Koch Mtn—*summit* OR-9
Kochners Corners—*locale* PA-2
Koch Peak—*summit* MT-8
Koch Ranch—*locale* WY-8
Koch Ridge—*locale* AR-4
Koch Ridge—*ridge* PA-2
Koch Sch—*school* IL-6
Koch Sch—*school* SD-7
Kochs Creek—*stream* MO-7
Koch Spring Branch Brush Creek—*stream* CO-8
Koch Springs—*spring* CO-8
Kochs Ridge—*ridge* LA-4
Kochtitzky Ditch No 1—*canal* (2) AR-4
Kochu Island—*island* AK-9
**Kochville**—*pop pl* MI-6
Kochville and Branches Drain—*canal* MI-6
Kochville and Frankenlust Drain—*stream* MI-6
Kochville Ch—*church* MI-6
Kochville Drain—*canal* MI-6
**Kochville (Township of)**—*pop pl* MI-6
Koch Warner Drain—*stream* MI-6
Koch Windmill—*locale* NM-5
Kock Lake—*lake* MT-8
Kock Park—*park* MO-7
Kodachrome Basin Campground—*park* UT-8
Kodachrome Basin State Park—*park* UT-8
*Kodachrome Basin State Reserve* UT-8
Kodak—*locale* NV-8
**Kodak**—*pop pl* KY-4
**Kodak**—*pop pl* TN-4
Kodak Gulch—*valley* ID-8
Kodak House—*locale* CO-8
Kodak Peak—*summit* WA-9
Kodak Point—*cliff* SD-7
Kodak (Post Office)—*locale* TN-4
Kodak Sch—*school* TN-4
Kodan—*locale* WI-6
Kodan Sch—*school* WI-6
*Koddo Island* MP-9
Koddo Island—*island* MP-9
*Koddo-to* MP-9
Kodels Canyon—*valley* CO-8
KODE-TV (Joplin)—*tower* MO-7
Kodiak—*locale* MO-7
**Kodiak**—*pop pl* AK-9
Kodiak Airp—*airport* AK-9
Kodiak (Coast Guard) Station—*military* AK-9
Kodiak Creek—*stream* ID-8
Kodiak Fisheries Cannery—*locale* AK-9
Kodiak Island—*island* AK-9
**Kodiak Island (Borough)**—*pop pl* AK-9
**Kodiak Island (Census Subarea)**—*pop pl* AK-9
Kodiak Naval Operating Base and Forts Greely and Abercrombie—*hist pl* AK-9
Kodiak Pond—*reservoir* OR-9
Kodiak Rock—*bar* AK-9
*Kodiak Station (Census Subarea)* AK-9
Kodiak 011 Site—*hist pl* AK-9
KODL-AM—*tower* OR-9
**Kodol**—*pop pl* WV-2
*Kodonce River* MN-6
Kodosin Minnkohwin Lake—*lake* AK-9
Kodosin Nolitna Creek—*stream* AK-9
*Kodu* MP-9
Koduit Lake—*lake* AK-9
KOD-171 Site—*hist pl* AK-9
KOD-233 Site—*hist pl* AK-9
Koea—*civil* HI-9
KOEA-FM (Doniphan)—*tower* MO-7
Koebel Sch—*school* OH-6
Koegel Hills—*range* NV-8
Koeglar Hill—*summit* TX-5
Koeglar Hill Cem—*cemetery* TX-5
*Koe Hadjos Town* FL-3
*Koehenderfers Church* PA-2
Koehenderfers Sch—*school* PA-2
Koehier Cem—*cemetery* ND-7
Koehler—*locale* NM-5
**Koehler**—*pop pl* VA-3
Koehler, Frank, House and Office—*hist pl* WI-6
Koehler, Jackson, Eagle Brewery—*hist pl* PA-2
Koehler Cem—*cemetery* MI-6
Koehler Cem—*cemetery* ND-7
Koehler Ditch—*canal* IN-6
Koehler Draw—*valley* WY-8
Koehler Ford—*locale* WI-6
Koehler Fortified Archeol Site—*hist pl* MO-7
Koehler Hill—*summit* OK-5
Koehler Lake—*lake* WI-6
Koehler Lake—*reservoir* NM-5
Koehler Mine—*mine* NM-5
**Koehler (Township of)**—*pop pl* MI-6
Koehler Tunnel—*mine* CO-8
Koehn Cem—*cemetery* IL-6
*Koehn Dry Lake* CA-9
Koehne-Poast Farm—*hist pl* OH-6
Koehnke Rsvr—*reservoir* OR-9
Koehn Lake—*flat* CA-9
**Koele**—*pop pl* HI-9
Koele Keomuku Trail—*trail* HI-9
Koeller Cem—*cemetery* MO-7
Koelling Islands—*island* MO-7
**Koeltztown**—*pop pl* MO-7
Koen—*locale* CO-8
Koen Burn (historical)—*locale* AL-4
Koen Canal—*canal* KS-7
Koen Creek—*stream* MO-7
Koen Creek—*stream* TX-5
Koeneman, Lake—*lake* WA-9
Koenig—*locale* CO-8
**Koenig**—*pop pl* MO-7
Koenig Bldg—*hist pl* IA-7
Koenig Cem—*cemetery* MO-7
Koenig Creek—*stream* TX-5
Koenig Lake—*lake* CA-9
Koenig Park—*park* TX-5
Koenig Point—*cape* NY-2
Koenig Ranch—*locale* CO-8
Koenig Ranch—*locale* MT-8
Koenig Ranch—*locale* TX-5
Koenig Rsvr—*reservoir* CO-8
Koenig Sch Number 1—*school* ND-7
Koenig Sch Number 3—*school* ND-7
Koenig Sch Number 4—*school* ND-7
Koenigs Creek—*stream* PA-2
Koenigs Creek Dam—*dam* PA-2
**Koenig's Point (Conklin Cove)**—*pop pl* NY-2
Koenig Spring—*spring* NV-8
Koenig State Public Shooting Area—*park* SD-7
Koening Park—*park* OH-6
Koening Sch—*school* WI-6
Koennecke Ranch—*locale* TX-5
**Koenton**—*pop pl* AL-4
Koepenick—*locale* WI-6
*Koepenick Station* WI-6
Koepke Canyon—*valley* WA-9
Koepke Coulee—*valley* MT-8
Koepke Ditch—*canal* IN-6
Koepke Slough—*stream* AK-9
Koepke Slough—*stream* OR-9
Koepmier Lake—*lake* WI-6
Koeppe Sch—*school* OH-6
Koepsel House—*hist pl* WI-6
Koepter Ditch—*canal* OH-6
**Koerber**—*pop pl* FL-3
Koerner Cem—*cemetery* IL-6
Koerth—*locale* TX-5
Koessler Lake—*lake* MT-8
Koester—*locale* MO-7
Koester, Charles, House—*hist pl* KS-7
Koester, Nicholas, Bldg—*hist pl* IA-7
Koester Block Hist Dist—*hist pl* KS-7
Koester Ditch—*canal* IN-6
Koester Lakes—*lake* MI-6
Koester/Patburg House—*hist pl* IN-6
Koester Ranch—*locale* CA-9
Koetter Hollow—*valley* IN-6
Koetter Lake—*lake* MN-6
KOEZ-FM (Newton)—*tower* KS-7
Kofa—*locale* AZ-5
Kofa Butte—*summit* AZ-5
Kofa Cabin—*building* AZ-5
Kofa Dam—*dam* AZ-5
Kofa Dam Wash—*stream* AZ-5
Kofa Deep Well—*well* AZ-5
Kofa Game Range—*park* AZ-5
Kofa HS—*school* AZ-5
Kofa Manganese Mine—*mine* AZ-5
Kofa Monument—*locale* AZ-5
Kofa Mountains—*summit* AZ-5
Kofa Queen Canyon—*valley* AZ-5
Kofa Queen Mine—*mine* AZ-5
*Kofa Range* AZ-5
**Kofa (sta.)**—*pop pl* AZ-5
*Kofa Station* AZ-5
Kofferls Pond—*reservoir* NJ-2
Kofferls Pond Dam—*dam* NJ-2
Koff Lateral—*canal* CA-9
Kofford Creek—*stream* UT-8
Kofford Ridge—*ridge* MT-8
KOFO-AM (Ottawa)—*tower* KS-7
K Of P Cem—*cemetery* KY-4
K Of P Cem—*cemetery* WV-2
Kof Point—*cape* AK-9
Kofu Park—*park* CA-9
Kogan Place—*locale* NV-8
*Kogars Island* AL-4
Koger, William, House—*hist pl* AL-4
Koger, William, House—*hist pl* TX-5
Koger Branch—*stream* AR-4
Koger Branch—*stream* MO-7
Koger Cem—*cemetery* KS-7
Koger Cem—*cemetery* KY-4
Koger Cem—*cemetery* (2) MO-7
Koger Cem—*cemetery* TX-5
Koger Creek—*stream* AL-4
Koger Creek—*stream* (2) KY-4
Koger Creek—*stream* VA-3
Koger Executive Park—*locale* NC-3
Koger Fork—*stream* KY-4
Koger Hollow—*valley* OH-6
Koger Ranch—*locale* NM-5
Koger Sch—*school* SC-3
Koger Sch (abandoned)—*school* MO-7
Kogers Island—*island* AL-4
Koger Spring—*spring* KY-4
Kogers Rock (historical)—*island* AL-4
Koger Tank—*reservoir* AZ-5
Koggiling Creek—*stream* AK-9
**Koggiung**—*pop pl* AK-9
Kogisn Mtn—*summit* AK-9
**K O G Junction**—*pop pl* MO-7
Kogok River—*stream* AK-9
Kogoluktuk River—*stream* AK-9
Kogosukruk River—*stream* AK-9
Kogotpak River—*stream* AK-9
Kogoyuk Creek—*stream* AK-9
Kogruk Creek—*stream* AK-9
Kogrukluk River—*stream* AK-9
Kogru River—*stream* AK-9
Kohaahu—*cape* HI-9
*Kohai-hai* HI-9
Kohakohau Stream—*stream* HI-9
*Kohala* (2) HI-9
Kohala District Courthouse—*hist pl* HI-9
Kohala Ditch—*canal* HI-9
Kohala Hosp—*hospital* HI-9
*Kohala Mill* (2) HI-9
Kohala Mountains—*summit* HI-9
Kohalapilau—*area* HI-9
Kohala Schools—*school* HI-9
*Kohanaike* HI-9
*Kohanaike Homesteads* HI-9
Kohanaiki—*civil* HI-9
Kohanaiki Homesteads—*civil* HI-9
*Kohansick* NJ-2
Kohanza Brook—*stream* CT-1
**Kohatk**—*pop pl* AZ-5
Kohatk Valley—*valley* AZ-5
Kohatk Wash—*stream* AZ-5
Kohatk Well—*well* AZ-5
*Kohelepelepe Hill* HI-9
Kohelepelepe (Puu Mai)—*summit* HI-9
Kohen Ranch—*locale* AZ-5
Kohen Windmill—*locale* TX-5
Koheo—*locale* HI-9
*Koheo Hala* HI-9
Kohe o Hala—*cape* HI-9
Koheo One-Two—*civil* HI-9
Koheo Point—*cape* HI-9
KOHI-AM—*tower* OR-9
Kohi Island—*island* AK-9
*Kohi Kug* AZ-5
Kohi Kug (site)—*locale* AZ-5
Kohinoor Junction—*uninc pl* PA-2
Kohinoor Mine (Inactive)—*mine* NV-8
*Kohinoor Spring* AZ-5
Kohinoor Spring—*spring* AZ-5
Kohl, Ernst Martin, Bldg—*hist pl* TX-5
Kohl, W. S., Barn—*hist pl* ID-8
**Kohlberg**—*pop pl* WI-6
Kohlberg—*summit* PA-2
Kohlbush Cem—*cemetery* MO-7
**Kohl City**—*pop pl* MO-7
Kohl Creek—*stream* CA-9
Kohler—*locale* KY-4
**Kohler**—*pop pl* (2) WI-6
Kohler—*uninc pl* CA-9
Kohler, John Michael, House—*hist pl* WI-6
Kohler Bay—*bay* MN-6
Kohler Bridge—*bridge* MO-7
Kohler Canyon—*valley* CA-9
Kohler Cem—*cemetery* WI-6
**Kohler city**—*pop pl* MO-7
Kohler Company (Warehouse)—*facility* WI-6
Kohler Ditch—*canal* CA-9
Kohler Ditch—*canal* IN-6
Kohler Hill—*summit* MO-7
Kohler Hollow—*valley* (2) PA-2
Kohler Lake—*lake* MT-8
Kohler-McPhaul House—*hist pl* TX-5
Kohler Mtn—*summit* PA-2
Kohler Rsvr—*reservoir* CO-8
Kohler Sch—*school* CA-9
Kohler Sch—*school* PA-2
Kohlers Gap—*gap* PA-2
Kohlers Old River—*gut* SC-3
Kohlers Pond—*lake* NJ-2
Kohler Spring—*spring* WA-9
**Kohlertown**—*pop pl* NY-2
Kohler Valley—*valley* PA-2
*Kohley Creek* WA-9
Kohlhoff Lake—*lake* WI-6
Kohlman Cem—*cemetery* WI-6
Kohlman Lake—*lake* MN-6
Kohlmann, Friederich, House—*hist pl* WI-6
Kohl Mansion—*hist pl* CA-9
**Kohlmeier Township**—*pop pl* ND-7
Kohl Memorial Park—*park* PA-2
Kohlmeyer Corner—*locale* PA-2
Kohlmeyer Private Airstrip—*airport* OR-9
Kohlmyre Sch (abandoned)—*school* MO-7
**Kohlsaat**—*pop pl* WV-2
Kohlsaat Peak—*summit* AK-9
Kohl Sch—*school* CO-8
Kohls Creek—*stream* KS-7
**Kohls Ranch**—*pop pl* AZ-5
**Kohlsville**—*pop pl* WI-6
Kohlsville River—*stream* WI-6
Kohlsville Sch—*school* WI-6
Kohms Cave—*cave* MO-7
*Kohn Dam* AL-4
Kohne Number One Ditch—*canal* IN-6
Kohne Number Two Ditch—*canal* IN-6
Kohn Hill—*summit* MN-6
Kohn JHS—*school* LA-4
Kohn Lake—*lake* MN-6
Kohnoosky Creek—*stream* OK-5
Kohn Sch—*school* IL-6
Kohokachalla Mtn—*summit* AK-9
*Koholaleie Landing* HI-9
Koholalele—*civil* HI-9
Koholalele Gulch—*valley* HI-9
Koholalele Landing—*locale* HI-9
Kohola Point—*cape* HI-9
Koholoina Stream—*stream* HI-9
Kohones Ranch—*locale* MT-8
Kohout Lake—*reservoir* NJ-2
Kohout Lake Dam—*dam* NJ-2
**Kohr**—*pop pl* MT-8
*Kohring Lake* MN-6
Kohr Island—*island* PA-2
**Kohrs**—*pop pl* MT-8
Kohrs, William K., Free Memorial Library—*hist pl* MT-8
Kohrs and Bielenberg Ditch—*canal* MT-8
Kohrville—*locale* TX-5
KOHS-FM (Orem)—*tower* UT-8
Koht Kohl Hill—*summit* AZ-5
KOHU-AM—*tower* OR-9
Kohua Ridge—*ridge* HI-9
KOHU-FM—*tower* OR-9
Kohute Gulch—*valley* CA-9
Koi—*bar* FM-9
*Koiahi Gulch* HI-9
Koianglas (Site)—*locale* AK-9
Koiawe Stream—*stream* HI-9
*Koijaka* DE-2
*Koilbah Creek* AL-4
*Koilbah Creek* MS-4
K Oil Field—*oilfield* TX-5
Koili Point—*cape* HI-9
Koinenia, Lake—*reservoir* OR-9
Koinonia Retreat Ch—*church* MN-6
Koinonia Southern Baptist Ch—*church* IN-6
Koins Bluff—*cliff* LA-4
KOIN-TV—*tower* OR-9
**Koinzan Ranch**—*pop pl* NE-7
Koio, Dolen—*summit* FM-9
Koiohi—*summit* HI-9
Koip Crest—*ridge* CA-9
Koip Peak—*summit* CA-9
Koip Peak Pass—*gap* CA-9
Koistenen Brook—*stream* CT-1
Koitlah Point—*cape* WA-9
*Ko-it Peak* CA-9
*Ko-it Ridge* CA-9
Koivisto Sch—*school* MN-6
Koiyaktot Mtn—*summit* AK-9
KOJC-FM (Cedar Rapids)—*tower* IA-7
*Kojjen Island* MP-9
Kojjouj—*island* MP-9
K O Junction—*locale* PA-2
**K.o. Junction**—*pop pl* PA-2
*KO Junction Station* PA-2
**Kokadjo**—*pop pl* ME-1
*Kokadjo Lake* ME-1
*Kokadjo River* ME-1
Koka Island—*island* AK-9
Koka Island Passage—*channel* AK-9
Kokanee Cove—*bay* CO-8
Kokechik Bay—*bay* AK-9
Kokechik River—*stream* AK-9
Kokee Air Force Station—*military* HI-9
Kokee Ditch—*canal* HI-9
Kokee Instrumentation Station—*locale* HI-9
**Kokee (Kokee Lodge)**—*pop pl* HI-9
Kokee Lodge—*building* HI-9
Kokeene Hollow—*valley* OH-6
Kokee State Park—*park* HI-9
Kokee Stream—*stream* HI-9
**Kokel Corner**—*pop pl* OR-9
*Kokelekele Stream* HI-9
Koker Creek—*stream* IA-7
Koker Knob—*summit* TN-4
Kokernot—*locale* TX-5
Kokernot Branch—*stream* TX-5
Kokernot Creek—*stream* TX-5
Kokernot Mun Park—*park* TX-5
Kokernot Ranch—*locale* TX-5
*Kokesburg* NJ-2
Kokesh County Rec Area—*locale* IA-7
Kokhanok ANV831—*reserve* AK-9
Kokhila Hills—*other* AK-9
*Koki* HI-9
Koki—*beach* HI-9
*Kokial Islands* PW-9
Kokii—*summit* HI-9
Kokinhenik Bar—*bar* AK-9
Kokinhenik Branch—*channel* AK-9
Kokinhenik Island—*island* AK-9
Kokio—*civil* HI-9
Koki Point—*cape* HI-9
Kokirat Creek—*stream* AK-9
KOKK-AM (Huron)—*tower* SD-7
Kokko—*tunnel* FM-9
Koklong Creek—*stream* AK-9
Koknuk Flats—*other* AK-9
*Koko* HI-9
*Koko* TN-4
**Ko Ko**—*pop pl* TN-4
**Koko**—*pop pl* TN-4
KOKO-AM (Warrensburg)—*tower* MO-7
Koko Crater—*crater* HI-9
**Kokohahi**—*pop pl* HI-9
Koko Head—*summit* HI-9
Koko Head Natural Park—*park* HI-9
Koko Head Sch—*school* HI-9
Kokoiki—*civil* HI-9
**Kokokahi**—*pop pl* HI-9
Koko Lake—*lake* OR-9
Kokole Point—*cape* HI-9
Kokolik Lake—*lake* AK-9
Kokolik River—*stream* AK-9
Kokoloe Lake—*reservoir* GA-3
Kokololio Gulch—*valley* HI-9
Kokomis Ferry—*locale* FL-3
Kokomo—*locale* CO-8
Kokomo—*locale* TX-5
**Kokomo**—*pop pl* AR-4
**Kokomo**—*pop pl* HI-9
**Kokomo**—*pop pl* IN-6
**Kokomo**—*pop pl* MS-4
Kokomo—*summit* HI-9
Kokomo Cem—*cemetery* MS-4
Kokomo Ch—*church* AL-4
Kokomo City Bldg—*hist pl* IN-6
Kokomo Corners—*locale* NY-2
Kokomo Creek—*stream* AK-9
Kokomo Creek—*stream* AR-4
Kokomo Creek—*stream* IN-6
Kokomo Gulch—*valley* CO-8
Kokomo Hosp—*hospital* IN-6
Kokomo HS—*school* IN-6
Kokomo Mall—*locale* IN-6
Kokomo Municipal Airp—*airport* IN-6
Kokomo Pass—*gap* CO-8
*Kokomo Reservoir* IN-6
Kokomo Rsvr Number One—*reservoir* IN-6
Kokomo Sch—*school* MS-4
Kokomo Waterworks Dam Number 2—*dam* IN-6
Kokomo Waterworks Rsvr Number Two—*reservoir* IN-6
Kokomo Zion Ch—*church* IN-6
Kokoolau—*summit* HI-9
*Kokoolau Crater* HI-9
Kokoolau Crater—*crater* HI-9
Kokopnyama—*locale* AZ-5

Kokopuk Creek—stream AK-9
Koko Reef Lake—reservoir MS-4
Kokoroche MH-9
Kokorocnito MH-9
Kokoshing OH-6
Kokosing House—hist pl OH-6
Kokosing River—stream OH-6
Kokots Creek—stream WI-6
Kokoweef Peak—summit CA-9
Kok Ranch—locale NM-5
**Kokrines**—pop pl AK-9
Kokrines Hills—range AK-9
Kokruagarok—locale AK-9
Koksetna River—stream AK-9
KOKS-FM (Poplar Bluff)—tower MO-7
Koksh Ranch—locale WY-8
Koksumok AZ-5
Koktuli River—stream AK-9
Kokuli AZ-5
Kokumpat Creek—stream AK-9
Kokuso, Oror En—locale FM-9
Kokwok River—stream AK-9
Kola—locale MS-4
Kola Cem—cemetery MS-4
Kola Ch (historical)—church MS-4
Kolacny Canyon—valley KS-7
Kolalen MP-9
Kolalen—locale MP-9
Kolaloa Gulch—valley HI-9
Kolana Rock—summit CA-9
Kola Post Office (historical)—building MS-4
Kola Sch (historical)—school (2) MS-4
Kolash Island—island AK-9
Kolavinarak River—stream AK-9
**Kolb**—pop pl WI-6
Kolb, Dielman, Homestead—hist pl PA-2
Kolb Airp—airport PA-2
Kolb Arch—arch AZ-5
Kolb Branch—stream MO-7
Kolb Bridge AZ-5
Kolb Brothers "Cat Camp"
Inscription—hist pl UT-8
Kolb Cem—cemetery AL-4
Kolb Cem—cemetery OK-5
Kolb Creek—stream CA-9
Kolb Creek—stream IN-6
Kolb Creek—stream OH-6
Kolb Ditch—canal IN-6
Kolb Drain—canal MI-6
**Kolbe**—pop pl IL-6
Kolbe HS—school CT-1
**Kolberg**—pop pl WI-6
Kolberg Ranch—locale MT-8
Kolbes Corner—locale MD-2
Kolb Inscription-1911—other UT-8
Kolb JHS—school CA-9
Kolb Lake—reservoir TX-5
Kolble House—hist pl MT-8
Kolb Park—park FL-3
Kolb Park—park KY-4
Kolb Park—park MI-6
Kolb Quarry—mine KY-4
Kolb Rock—island MA-1
Kolb Rsvr—reservoir OR-9
Kolb Sch—school MI-6
Kolbs Ferry (historical)—locale MS-4
Kolburne Sch—school CT-1
Kolburne Sch—school MA-1
Kolbusz Park—park WI-6
Kolcheck Basin—basin NV-8
Kolcheck Mine—mine NV-8
Kolcheck Springs—spring NV-8
Kolchicher Mtn—summit AK-9
Kolda (historical)—locale SD-7
Kolda Sch—school SD-7
Koldok—locale ND-7
Koldok State Game Mngmt Area—park ND-7
KOLD-TV (Tucson)—tower AZ-5
Kole HI-9
Kolea—civil HI-9
Kolealiilii—summit HI-9
Kolealiilii Stream—stream HI-9
Kolea Powerhouse—other HI-9
Kolea Rsvr—reservoir HI-9
Kolea Stream—stream HI-9
Koleebue Creek—stream AK-9
**Koleen**—pop pl IN-6
Kole Island MP-9
Kolekfikpuk Lake—lake AK-9
Kole Kill Island—island ME-1
Kolekl PW-9
Kolekole—summit HI-9
Kolekole Gulch HI-9
Kolekole Mtn HI-9
Kolekole Park—park HI-9
Kolekole Pass—gap HI-9
Kolekole Peak HI-9
Kolekole Stream—stream HI-9
Kolelemook Lake—lake NH-1
**Kolewood (subdivision)**—pop pl NC-3
Kolezal John Number 8 Dam—dam SD-7
**Koliganek**—pop pl AK-9
Koliganek ANV832—reserve AK-9
Kolin—locale LA-4
Kolin—locale MT-8
Kolin Creek—stream WI-6
Kolingo Creek—stream CA-9
Kolipatvooka AZ-5
Kolipsun Creek—stream AK-9
Kolke Creek—stream MI-6
Kolker House—hist pl IA-7
Kolkman Basin—basin CO-8
Kollatschny Cem—cemetery TX-5
Koll Coulee—valley WI-6
Koll Ditch No. 1—canal CO-8
Koll Drain—canal MI-6
Kolle Creek—stream WA-9
Kollehner Cem—cemetery IL-6
Kollen Park—park MI-6
Kollen Sch—school MI-6
Koller—locale NE-7
Kolling Creek—stream MN-6
Kolling Elem Sch—school IN-6
Kollioksak Lake—lake AK-9
Kollioksak River—stream AK-9
Kollman Branch—stream IN-6
Kollmeyer Cem—cemetery MO-7
Kollock Cem—cemetery GA-3
Kollocks Sch—school SC-3
Kolloen, Mount—summit AK-9
Koll Ranch—locale NM-5
Kolls (historical)—locale SD-7
Kolls Lake—lake TX-5
**Kolls Township**—pop pl SD-7
Kollutarak Creek—stream AK-9
Kollutuk Creek—stream AK-9
Kollutuk Mtn—summit AK-9
Kolmakof Lake—lake AK-9
Kolmakof River—stream AK-9
Kolmakof (Site)—locale AK-9
Kolmakov Redoubt Site—hist pl AK-9
Kolmar Park—park IL-6
Kolmer Cem—cemetery IL-6
Kolmer Gulch—valley CA-9
Kolmer Site—hist pl IL-6
Kolmetz Pond FL-3
Kolmetz Pond—lake (2) FL-3
**Kolmont**—pop pl OH-6
Kolo—civil HI-9
Koloa—civil HI-9
**Koloa**—pop pl HI-9
Koloa Beach—beach HI-9
Koloa Cem—cemetery HI-9
Koloa Ditch—canal HI-9
Koloa Gulch—valley HI-9
Koloaha—civil HI-9
Koloakapohu—summit HI-9
Koloa Landing—locale HI-9
**Koloa Mill**—pop pl HI-9
Koloa-Poipu (CCD)—cens area HI-9
Koloa Reservoir HI-9
Koloa River HI-9
Koloa Stream HI-9
Kolob Arch—arch UT-8
Kolob Arch Trail—trail UT-8
Kolob Basin—basin UT-8
Kolob Basin Overlook—locale UT-8
Kolob Campground—locale UT-8
Kolob Canyon Road Terminus
Campground—park UT-8
Kolob Canyons Viewpoint—locale UT-8
Kolob Canyons Visitor Center—locale UT-8
Kolob Creek—stream UT-8
Kolob Creek Dam—dam UT-8
Kolob Creek Rsvr—reservoir UT-8
Kolob Peak—summit UT-8
Kolob Plateau UT-8
Kolob Rsvr—reservoir UT-8
Kolob Terrace—bench UT-8
Kolob Visitor Center UT-8
Kolo Gulch—valley HI-9
Kolokaw (historical)—locale KS-7
Kolokea Valley—valley HI-9
**Kolokee**—pop pl FL-3
Koloko (historical)—locale KS-7
Kolokole HI-9
Kolokolo HI-9
Kolokolo Cave—cave HI-9
Kolokolo Point—cape HI-9
**Kolola Springs**—pop pl MS-4
Kolola Springs Baptist Ch—church MS-4
Kolol'-en' MP-9
Kolomak River—stream AK-9
Kolomin Lake—lake AK-9
Kolomoki GA-3
Kolomoki, Lake—reservoir GA-3
Kolomoki Creek GA-3
Kolomoki Creek—stream GA-3
Kolomoki Mounds—hist pl GA-3
Kolomoki Mounds State Park—park GA-3
**Kolonia**—pop pl FM-9
Kolonia (Municipality)—civ div FM-9
Kolonie FM-9
Kolopa—cape HI-9
Kolopua—summit HI-9
Kolo Ridge—ridge (2) HI-9
Kolostick Butte—summit OR-9
Kolotuk Creek—stream AK-9
Kolovik (abandoned)—locale AK-9
Kolo Wharf—locale HI-9
Kolpack Lake—lake WI-6
Kolpack Lookout Tower—locale WI-6
Kolping Park—park MI-6
Kolpin Mtn—summit OK-5
KOLR-TV (Springfield)—tower MO-7
KOLS-FM (De Soto)—tower MO-7
Kolsta Coulee—valley MT-8
Kolstad Coulee—valley MT-8
Kolstad Lake—lake MN-6
Kolsta Sch—school WI-6
**Kolter**—pop pl LA-4
Kolter Sch—school TX-5
Koluktak Lakes—lake AK-9
KOLY-AM (Mobridge)—tower SD-7
KOLY-FM (Mobridge)—tower SD-7
Komakok Creek—stream AK-9
Komakan Reef PW-9
Komakawai—locale HI-9
Komakawai Waterholes—lake HI-9
Komaktjiuurt AZ-5
Komaktjuert AZ-5
Komak Wuacho—locale AZ-5
Koma Lake—lake MN-6
Komalik AZ-5
Komalty—locale OK-5
**Komandorski Village**—pop pl CA-9
**Komandorski Village (census name for Kamondorski)**—pop pl CA-9
Komarek East Sch—school IL-6
Komarek West Sch—school IL-6
**Komar Park**—pop pl NY-2
Komatke AZ-5
**Komatke**—pop pl AZ-5
Kombaxia AZ-5
KOMB-FM (Fort Scott)—tower KS-7
KOMC-AM (Branson)—tower MO-7
Komebail Lagoon PW-9
Komelih AZ-5
Komelik AZ-5
**Komelik**—pop pl AZ-5
Komelik Mtn—summit AZ-5
Komelik Pass—gap AZ-5
Komensky—locale MN-6
**Komensky**—pop pl TX-5
Komensky Cem—cemetery WI-6
Komensky Sch—school (2) IL-6
Komensky Sch—school NE-7
Komensky Station—locale WI-6
**Komensky (Town of)**—pop pl WI-6
Komich Gulch—valley MT-8
Komire MP-9
Komire-to MP-9
Komite Lake MI-6
Komkomlap MP-9
Kom Kug—locale AZ-5
Kom Kug Windmill—well AZ-5
Komle Island MP-9
Komliangl PW-9
Komlih AZ-5
Komoiarak Slough—stream AK-9
Komo Kulshan Guard Station—locale WA-9
Komolokl PW-9
Komolokl Island PW-9
Komooloa Stream HI-9
Komo Point—cliff AZ-5
Komo Tv Heliport—airport WA-9
Komo Vaya AZ-5
Komp Lake Dam—dam MS-4
KOMR-FM (St Louis)—tower MO-7
Komstad Ch—church SD-7
Komstad Covenent Church SD-7
**Komstad (historical)**—pop pl SD-7
Komstad Sch Number 46
(historical)—school SD-7
Komtie Lake MI-6
Komukomurapu MP-9
Komukomurapu-to MP-9
KOMU-TV (Columbia)—tower MO-7
Kom Vaya AZ-5
**Kom Vo**—pop pl AZ-5
Kom Vo Valley—valley AZ-5
**Komwonlaid**—pop pl FM-9
Komwon Takaitol—bar FM-9
Kona—locale KY-4
**Kona**—pop pl NC-3
Kona (Airline name for Kailua Kona) HI-9
Kona Branch Univ of Hawaii Agricultural
Experiment Station—school HI-9
Kona Ch—church NC-3
Kona Hills—summit MI-6
Kona Hosp—hospital HI-9
Konahuanui—summit HI-9
**Kona (Mater)**—pop pl KY-4
Konanae HI-9
Konangokuo MH-9
Konantz Cem—cemetery CO-8
Konanui Gulch—valley HI-9
Konarut Mtn—summit AK-9
**Konawa**—pop pl OK-5
Konawa (CCD)—cens area OK-5
Konawa Cem—cemetery OK-5
Konawaena Sch—school HI-9
Konawaugus Valley—gap NY-2
Konchanee Lake—lake AK-9
Konde Branch—stream TX-5
Ko-ne-cau River AL-4
Ko-ne-cau River FL-3
Kone-Cliett House—hist pl TX-5
Konedsin Minnkohwin Lake—lake AK-9
Konejokenen MP-9
Koners Grove Ch—church NC-3
Koneruk Creek—stream AK-9
Kones Corner—locale SD-7
Koness River—stream AK-9
Konets Head—summit AK-9
Kongakut River—stream AK-9
Kongakut River Delta—area AK-9
Kongamak Lakes MA-1
Konga Mtn OR-9
Konganevik Point—cape AK-9
Kongauru PW-9
Kongauru Island PW-9
Kongauru-To PW-9
Kongeruk River—stream AK-9
Kongiganak—locale AK-9
Kongiganak ANV833—reserve AK-9
Kongishluk Bay—bay AK-9
Kongkok Basin—basin AK-9
Kongkok Bay—bay AK-9
Kongnignanohk River—stream AK-9
**Kongo**—pop pl MS-4
Kongoru Island PW-9
Kongoru To PW-9
Kongouru PW-9
**Kongsberg**—pop pl ND-7
Kongsberg Cem—cemetery MN-6
Kongsberg (historical)—locale ND-7
Kongscut Mtn—summit CT-1
Kongsvinger Ch—church (2) MN-6
Kongumavik Creek—stream AK-9
Koniag Glacier—glacier AK-9
Koniag Peak—summit AK-9
KONI-AM (Spanish Fork)—tower UT-8
**Konig**—pop pl SC-3
**Konigsmark**—pop pl IA-7
Konik, Oror En—locale FM-9
Konink Point—cape VI-3
Koniska Cem—cemetery MN-6
Konitz Airp—airport KS-7
Koniuji Island—island (2) AK-9
Koniuji Strait—channel AK-9
**Konkapot**—pop pl MA-1
Konkapot Brook CT-1
Konkapot Brook—stream MA-1
Konkapot Col—gap MA-1
Konkapot Creek MA-1
Konkapot River—stream CT-1
Konkapot River—stream MA-1
Konkel Lake MI-6
Konkel Sch—school CA-9
Konklin Run PA-2
Konklin Sch—school OK-5
**Konkolville**—pop pl ID-8
Konlei PW-9
Konlei Head PW-9
**Konnarock**—pop pl VA-3
Konnarock Cem—cemetery VA-3
Konnidale AL-4
Konnoak Elem Sch—school NC-3
Konochti Mountain CA-9
Konockti Mountain CA-9
Konocti, Mount—summit CA-9
Konocti Bay—bay CA-9
Konohasset Harbor MA-1
Konohasset Harbour MA-1
Konohasset Rocks MA-1
Konohiki Stream—stream HI-9
Konokti Bay CA-9
Konokti Mountain CA-9
Konolds Pond—lake CT-1
Konold Spring—spring UT-8
Konomac Lake—swamp FL-3
Konomoc, Lake—reservoir CT-1
Konomoc Hill—summit CT-1
Konon MP-9
Konoon—island MP-9
Konopik Rsvr—reservoir CO-8
Konopot Brook MA-1
Kono Tayee Point—cape CA-9
Konova Lake—lake AK-9
Konrad Creek—stream ID-8
Konrad Kjerstad Dam—dam SD-7
Konrei PW-9
Konrei Point PW-9
Konsas Valley Picnic Area PA-2
Konsin Beach—locale WI-6
Konteka Creek—stream MI-6
Kon Tiki Mobile Home Park—locale AZ-5
Kontio Lake—lake MI-6
Kontrashibuna Lake—lake AK-9
Konvicka Cem—cemetery TX-5
Konwakiton Glacier—glacier CA-9
Konwon Island MP-9
Konzas KS-7
Konzas River KS-7
Koobs House—hist pl SD-7
Koobuk Creek—stream AK-9
Koocanusa, Lake—lake MT-8
**Koochiching (County)**—pop pl MN-6
Koochiching County Courthouse—hist pl MN-6
Koochiching State For—forest MN-6
Koochogey Corners—locale PA-2
Koocks Branch—stream TX-5
Koockville—locale TX-5
KOOD-TV (Hays)—tower KS-7
Koogle Cem—cemetery OH-6
Koogle Creek—stream TX-5
Koogle Jump-Off—cliff TX-5
Koogler JHS—school NM-5
Kooher Park—park PA-2
Kooka—civil HI-9
Kookatsh AZ-5
Kook Creek—stream AK-9
Kooke Mountain WA-9
Kooken Field Stadium—other TX-5
Kooken Sch—school TX-5
Kooker Cem—cemetery PA-2
Kooker Park—park FL-3
Kookjilik Point—cape AK-9
Kook Lake—lake AK-9
Koo Koo Creek—stream MT-8
Kookoolau HI-9
Kookooligit Mountains—other AK-9
Kookoolik Cape—cape AK-9
Kookoolik Hill—summit AK-9
Kookoolik (Old Village Site)—locale AK-9
Kookooliktook River—stream AK-9
Kookoosh Lake—lake MN-6
Kookoosint Ridge—ridge MT-8
Kookooskie Resort WA-9
Kooku Beach—beach AK-9
Kookukluk Creek—stream AK-9
Kool-Aid Lake—lake WA-9
Koolan Range HI-9
Koolau HI-9
Koolau Boys Home—building HI-9
Koolau Ditch—canal (3) HI-9
Koolau Ditch Tunnel—tunnel HI-9
Koolau Gap—slope HI-9
Koolaukani Valley—valley HI-9
Koolauloa (CCD)—cens area HI-9
Koolaupapa HI-9
Koolaupoko (CCD)—cens area HI-9
Koolau Range—range HI-9
Koolau Rsvr—reservoir HI-9
Kool Cem—cemetery IL-6
Kool Corner—locale AZ-5
Kool Creek—stream MT-8
Koole Lake—lake AK-9
KOOL-FM (Phoenix)—tower AZ-5
KOOL Heliport—airport AZ-5
Kool Lake—lake OH-6
Koo-loo- moo-kee Creek GA-3
Koolside Park—park TX-5
Kool Spring—spring OR-9
Koomer Branch—stream KY-4
Koomer Ridge—ridge KY-4
Koomer Ridge Camping and Picnic
Area—locale KY-4
Koomer Ridge Trail—trail KY-4
Koomlangeelkuk Bay—bay AK-9
**Koon**—pop pl KY-4
Koon, John Jacob Calhoun,
Farmstead—hist pl SC-3
Koon, Lake—reservoir PA-2
Koon, Thomas, House—hist pl MD-2
Koon Branch—stream AL-4
Koon Branch—stream NC-3
Koon Branch—stream SC-3
Koonce—locale SC-3
Koonce Bldg—hist pl AR-4
Koonce Cem—cemetery IL-6
Koonce Creek—stream LA-4
Koonce Creek—stream TX-5
Koon Cem—cemetery KS-7
Ko-o-ne-cuh River AL-4
Ko-o-ne-cuh River FL-3
Koone Hollow—valley AR-4
Kooney Spring—spring OR-9
Koong Hill—summit NY-2
Koon Hill—summit TX-5
Koon Kreek Klub—locale TX-5
Koon Lake PA-2
Koon Lake—lake WI-6
Koonoe Creek TX-5
Koons Cem—cemetery KY-4
Koons Cem—cemetery PA-2
Koon Sch—school MI-6
Koons Creek—stream PA-2
Koons Dam PA-2
Koons Dam—locale PA-2
Koonsen Cem—cemetery TX-5
Koons House—hist pl AR-4
Koons Memorial Park—cemetery PA-2
Koons Pond—reservoir SC-3
Koons Site—hist pl TX-5
**Koonsville**—pop pl PA-2
Koonts, Capt. John, Jr., Farm—hist pl NC-3
**Koontz**—pop pl WV-2
Koontz and Davis Creek—stream OR-9
Koontz Bayou—stream TX-5
Koontz Bayou Drain—canal TX-5
Koontz Bend—bend WV-2
Koontz Cem—cemetery IL-6
Koontz Cem—cemetery IN-6
Koontz Cem—cemetery OH-6
Koontz Cem—cemetery VA-3
Koontz Ch—church OH-6
Koontz Ch—church PA-2
Koontz Church Cem—cemetery MD-2
Koontz Creek OR-9
Koontz Creek—stream (2) OR-9
Koontz Creek—stream TN-4
Koontz Ditch—canal (2) IN-6
Koontze Creek TN-4
Koontz Hollow—valley AR-4
Koontz Hollow—valley VA-3
Koontz Hollow—valley WV-2
Koontz Homestead—locale OR-9
Koontz House—hist pl MS-4
**Koontz Lake**—pop pl IN-6
Koontz Lake—reservoir IN-6
Koontz Lake Dam—dam IN-6
Koontz Ranch—locale NM-5
Koontz Run—stream MD-2
Koontz Sch—school IL-6
Koontz Spring—spring PA-2
Koontzville—locale WA-9
**Koontzville**—pop pl NC-3
**Koontzville**—pop pl PA-2
Koonze Creek TN-4
Koopee Creek—stream MT-8
Kooper Ranch—locale NE-7
Ko-opke AZ-5
Koop Lake—lake MN-6
Koopman Canyon—valley CA-9
Koopman Gas Field—oilfield TX-5
Koops Creek—stream MI-6
Koops Island—island IL-6
Koosah Falls—falls OR-9
Koosah Mtn—summit OR-9
Koosah River AL-4
Koos Bay OR-9
Koos Ditch—canal IN-6
Koosel Lake WI-6
Kooser Firetower—tower PA-2
Kooser Lake—reservoir PA-2
Kooser Run—stream PA-2
Kooser Run Dam—dam PA-2
Kooser Spring—spring PA-2
Kooser State Park—park PA-2
Kooser State Park Family Cabin
District—hist pl PA-2
KOOS-FM—tower OR-9
**Koosharem**—pop pl UT-8
Koosharem Campground—park UT-8
Koosharem Canal—canal UT-8
Koosharem Cem—cemetery UT-8
Koosharem Creek—stream UT-8
Koosharem Dam—dam UT-8
Koosharem Guard Station—locale UT-8
Koosharem Pasture Spring—spring UT-8
Koosharem Reservoir Recreation
Site—park UT-8
Koosharem Rsvr—reservoir UT-8
Koosharem Sch—school UT-8
**Kooskia**—pop pl ID-8
Kooskia Natl Fish Hatchery—other ID-8
Kooskooskia Meadows—flat ID-8
**Kooskooskie**—pop pl WA-9
Koosle Lake WI-6
Koosmus Creek WA-9
Koos River OR-9
Kooste Lake WI-6
Kootah Creek—stream MT-8
Kootanie River MT-8
Kootenai ID-8
**Kootenai**—pop pl ID-8
Kootenai Bay—bay ID-8
Kootenai Camp—locale MT-8
Kootenai County Courthouse—hist pl ID-8
Kootenai Creek—stream (4) MT-8
Kootenai Falls—falls MT-8
Kootenai Falls—locale MT-8
Kootenai Flats—flat MT-8
Kootenai HS—school ID-8
**Kootenai Ind Res**—pop pl ID-8
Kootenai Inn—hist pl ID-8
Kootenai Lakes—lake MT-8
Kootenai Lodge Hist Dist—hist pl MT-8
Kootenai Mountain ID-8
Kootenai Mountain MT-8
Kootenai Mtn—summit MT-8
Kootenai Narrows—gap MT-8
Kootenai Natl Wildlife Ref—park ID-8
Kootenai Orchard—flat ID-8
Kootenai Pass—gap MT-8
Kootenai Peak—summit ID-8
Kootenai Peak—summit MT-8
Kootenai Point—cape ID-8
Kootenai Point—summit ID-8
Kootenai Range MT-8
Kootenai River—stream ID-8
Kootenai River—stream MT-8
Kootenay ID-8
Kootenay River MT-8
Kootenia Natl For—forest MT-8
Kootenie River MT-8
Kootienay River MT-8
Koots Fork—stream IN-6
Kootznahoo Head—summit AK-9
Kootznahoo Inlet—bay AK-9
Kootznahoo Roads—bay AK-9
Kootzville WA-9
Koovukseluk Point—cape AK-9
Koozata Lagoon—bay AK-9
Koozata River—stream AK-9
Koozers Run PA-2
KOPA-AM (Scottsdale)—tower AZ-5
Kopac Camp—locale MT-8
Kopachuck State Park—park WA-9
Kopakaka Ridge—ridge HI-9
Kopala—summit HI-9
Kope Cem—cemetery IN-6
Kopeegon Point MA-1
Kope Gulch—valley HI-9
Kope Hollow—valley OH-6
Kope Kon Point—cape MI-6
**Kopernik Shores**—pop pl TX-5
Kopiah—locale WA-9
Kopil, Dauen—gut FM-9
Kopiliula Falls—falls HI-9
Kopiliula Stream HI-9
Kopiliula Stream—stream HI-9
Koping Ditch—canal CO-8
Kopman Bayou—gut LA-4
Kopman Cem—cemetery IL-6
KOPN-FM (Columbia)—tower MO-7
KOPO-FM (Marana)—tower (2) AZ-5
Kopoho HI-9
Kopp—locale VA-3
**Kopp**—pop pl VA-3
Kopp Creek—stream IL-6
Kopp Creek—stream OH-6
Kopp Creek—stream OR-9
Koppe—locale TX-5
**Koppel**—pop pl PA-2
Koppel Borough—civil PA-2
Koppen Creek—stream AK-9
Koppenhafer Rsvr—reservoir CO-8
Koppenhoffer Sch—school PA-2
Koppen Mtn—summit WA-9
**Kopperl**—pop pl TX-5
**Koppers**—pop pl AL-4
**Kopperston**—pop pl WV-2
Kopperston Ch—church WV-2
Kopperstone WV-2
Kopperston Mtn—summit WV-2
Koppers Wildlife Mngmt Area—park TN-4
Kopperud Cem—cemetery MN-6
Kopperud Lake—lake MN-6
**Kopper View Mobile Home Park Subdivision**—pop pl UT-8
Koppes Creek—stream ID-8
Koppes No 1 Well—well WY-8
Koppes No 2 Well—well WY-8
Koppes No 3 Well—well WY-8
Koppes No 4 Well—well WY-8
Koppick Knob—summit TN-4
Kopplein—locale OR-9
Kopplein Creek—stream OR-9
Kopp Sch—school MI-6
Koprian Ranch—locale NM-5
Koprian Springs—spring NM-5
Kopshesut Creek—stream AK-9
Kopsi Creek—stream MT-8
Kopta Slough—stream CA-9
Kopwungupwung—stream FM-9
Kora AL-4
Kora MP-9
Kora, Lake—reservoir NY-2
Korack PW-9
Korah—uninc pl VA-3
Korak PW-9
**Koran**—pop pl LA-4
Kora Post Office (historical)—building AL-4
Kora Temple—hist pl ME-1
Koratenlap MP-9
Korb Creek—stream KS-7
**Korbel**—pop pl (2) CA-9
Korb Lake—lake MN-6
Korblex—locale CA-9
Korb River—stream MN-6
Korb Run—stream PA-2
Korby Lake—lake NY-2
Kordick Lake—lake WI-6
Kordilsau PW-9
Kordonowy Dam—dam ND-7
Kordonowy Ranch—locale ND-7
Kordon Ranch—locale ND-7
Kordzik Hills—summit TX-5
Korea—locale KY-4
Korea—locale VA-3
**Korea**—pop pl PR-3
KORE-AM—tower OR-9
Korean Baptist Ch—church FL-3
Korean Cem—cemetery LA-4
Korean Central Baptist Ch of
Orlando—church FL-3
Korean Ch of Utah—church UT-8
Korean Methodist Ch—church DE-2
Korean Presbyterian Ch—church FL-3
Korean Tunnel—tunnel HI-9
Korell Cabin—locale MT-8
Koren—locale WA-9
Koren Library—hist pl IA-7
Koreor PW-9
Koreor Island PW-9
Koreshan State Park—park FL-3
Koreshan Unity Cem—cemetery FL-3
Koreshan Unity Settlement Hist
Dist—hist pl FL-3
**Korf**—pop pl TX-5
Korga Island—island AK-9
Koridot, I—slope MH-9
Koriga Point—cape AK-9
Korijlang—island MP-9
Korizek Mine—mine MT-8
Korman Gap—gap PA-2
KORN-AM (Mitchell)—tower SD-7
Kornbow Lake—reservoir NC-3
Kornbow Lake Dam—dam NC-3
**Kornbow (subdivision)**—pop pl NC-3
Korn Canyon—valley AZ-5
Korn Coulee—valley WI-6
Kornegay—locale NC-3
Kornegay, Marshall, House and
Cemetery—hist pl NC-3
Kornegay Bar—bar AL-4
Kornegay Homestead—locale WY-8
Kornegay Lake—reservoir AL-4
Kornegay Lake Dam—dam AL-4
Kornegay Ranch—locale NM-5
Korner Sch (abandoned)—school PA-2
Korner's Folly—hist pl NC-3
**Korn Krest**—pop pl PA-2
**Kornman**—pop pl CO-8
Korns Cem—cemetery IA-7
Korn Sch—school CT-1
Korns Sch (historical)—school PA-2
Kornthal Ch—church IL-6
Kornui Lake—lake AK-9
**Koro**—pop pl WI-6
Koro Ch—church IN-6
Koroll Valley AZ-5
Koron MP-9
**Korona**—pop pl FL-3
Korong—island MP-9
Korongdik—island MP-9
Koroni FM-9

Kucks Cabin—locale ... CA-9
Kuckup Park—flat ... OR-9
Kuckup Spring—spring ... OR-9
**Kuckville**—pop pl ... NY-2
K U Creek—stream ... TX-5
Kucu ... FM-9
Kucuwa ... FM-9
Kuder Creek—stream ... IA-7
Kuder Creek—stream ... OR-9
**Kuderna Acres (subdivision)**—pop pl ... AL-4
Kuderna Lake—reservoir ... AL-4
Kudge Bay—swamp ... SC-3
Kudiakof Islands—island ... AK-9
KUDL-FM (Kansas City)—tower ... KS-7
Kudner Tank—reservoir ... NM-5
Kudobin Islands—island ... AK-9
Kudzu Cave ... AL-4
Kuebelar Ditch—canal ... OH-6
Kuebeler, August, House—hist pl ... OH-6
Kuebeler-Stang Block—hist pl ... OH-6
Kuebler-Artes Bldg—hist pl ... IN-6
Kuebler Ranch—locale ... CA-9
Kuebler Sch—school ... KY-4
KUED-TV (Salt Lake City)—tower ... UT-8
Kuee Ruins ... HI-9
Kuee (Ruins)—locale ... HI-9
Kueffer Rsvr—reservoir ... MT-8
**Kuehn**—pop pl ... MT-8
Kuehn, Andrew, Warehouse—hist pl ... SD-7
Kuehn, August, House—hist pl ... IN-6
Kuehn Blacksmith Shop-Hardware Store—hist pl ... WI-6
Kuehn Ditch—canal ... IN-6
Kuehne Dam—dam ... OR-9
Kuehners Pond—lake ... PA-2
Kuehne Rsvr—reservoir ... OR-9
Kuehn House—hist pl ... MO-7
Kuehn Lake—lake ... WI-6
Kuehns Creek—stream ... TX-5
Kuehns Park—park ... IA-7
Kuehn Well—well ... AZ-5
Kuejeirin To ... MP-9
Kuejerin-to ... MP-9
Kuejierin ... MP-9
Kueka ... FL-3
Kuenster Creek—stream ... WI-6
Kueny Canyon—valley ... OR-9
Kueny Ditch—canal ... OR-9
Kueny Ranch—locale ... OR-9
Kuenzer, Joseph II, House—hist pl ... OH-6
Kuenzi Rsvr—reservoir ... OR-9
Kuenzli Cem—cemetery ... KS-7
Kuenzli Creek—stream ... KS-7
KUER-FM (Salt Lake City)—tower ... UT-8
Kueshner Branch—stream ... KY-4
Kuester Lake—reservoir ... MT-8
**Kuesters Lake**—pop pl ... NE-7
Kuezyerin-To ... MP-9
Kuffel Canyon—valley ... CA-9
Kuffies Point—cape ... MA-1
Kuffner Creek ... WI-6
Kufner Creek—stream ... WI-6
Kugachevik Creek—stream ... AK-9
Kugachiak Creek—stream ... AK-9
Kugarak River—stream ... AK-9
Kugejagaen ... MP-9
Kugejapaen ... MP-9
Kugel Creek—stream ... AK-9
Kugel Creek—stream ... WA-9
Kugel Lake—lake ... AK-9
Kugirarok Creek—stream ... AK-9
Kugkpaga River—stream ... AK-9
Kugle Oil Field—oilfield ... TX-5
Kugler Field—school ... NC-3
Kugler Mine—mine ... ND-7
Kugler Ranch—locale ... NE-7
**Kugler (Township of)**—pop pl ... MN-6
KUGN-AM—tower ... OR-9
KUGN-FM—tower ... OR-9
Kugrak River—stream ... AK-9
Kugrua Bay—bay ... AK-9
Kugrua River—stream ... AK-9
Kugruk Lagoon—bay ... AK-9
Kugruk River—stream ... AK-9
Kugrupaga Inlet—bay ... AK-9
Kugrupaga River—stream ... AK-9
KUGT-AM (Jackson)—tower ... MO-7
Kuguklik River—stream ... AK-9
Kugukpak Creek—stream ... AK-9
Ku Gulch—valley ... CO-8
Kugun Point—cape ... AK-9
Kugururok River—stream ... AK-9
Kuguyuk Lake—lake ... AK-9
Kuhar Park—park ... MN-6
Kuheeia—locale ... HI-9
Kuheia ... HI-9
Kuheia Bay ... HI-9
Kuhio Bay—bay ... HI-9
Kuhio Monument—other ... HI-9
Kuhio Sch—school ... HI-9
**Kuhio Village**—pop pl ... HI-9
Kuhiwa Gulch—valley ... HI-9
Kuhiwa Valley—basin ... HI-9
**Kuhl**—pop pl ... PA-2
Kuhl, Christina, House—hist pl ... WI-6
Kuhl Dock—locale ... FL-3
Kuhl Gun Club—other ... CA-9
Kuhl Lake—lake ... MN-6
Kuhlman—locale ... FL-3
Kuhlman Cem—cemetery ... OK-5
Kuhlman Creek—stream ... TX-5
Kuhlman Gully—valley ... TX-5
Kuhlmann Bayou—stream ... LA-4
**Kuhlmann Heights**—pop pl (2) ... CO-8
Kuhlmann Landing Field—airport ... KS-7
Kuhlman Oil Field—oilfield ... TX-5
Kuhlman Rsvr—reservoir ... CO-8
Kuhl Ridge—ridge ... WA-9
Kuhl Road Speedway—other ... PA-2
Kuhl Sch—school ... NE-7
Kuhn ... IL-6
**Kuhn**—pop pl ... IL-6
Kuhn Barnett Sch—school ... VA-3
Kuhn Bayou—stream ... AR-4
Kuhn Branch—stream ... TX-5
Kuhn Branch—stream ... WV-2
Kuhn Canyon—valley ... OR-9
Kuhn Cem—cemetery ... OK-5
Kuhn Creek—stream ... KY-4
Kuhn Creek—stream ... MO-7
Kuhn Ditch—canal (4) ... IN-6
Kuhn Drain—canal ... CA-9
Kuhne Hill—summit ... AZ-5
Kuhn Emergency Airstrip—airport ... OR-9
Kuhnen, Nicholas J., House—hist pl ... IA-7
Kuhner JHS—school ... IN-6
Kuhnert Quarry—mine ... OR-9
Kuhnes Ranch—locale ... MT-8
Kuhn Glades—flat ... WV-2
Kuhnhausen Spring—spring ... WA-9
Kuhn Hill—summit ... MI-6
Kuhn Hill—summit ... TX-5
Kuhn Hollow—valley ... WV-2
Kuhn Hosp—hospital ... MS-4
Kuhn Lake ... IN-6
Kuhn Lake—lake ... IN-6
Kuhn Lake—lake (2) ... MI-6
Kuhn Memorial State Hosp ... MS-4
Kuhn Mill (historical)—locale ... TN-4
Kuhn Ranch—locale ... CA-9
Kuhn Ridge—ridge ... OR-9
Kuhn Ridge—ridge ... WV-2
Kuhns ... IL-6
**Kuhns**—pop pl ... NC-3
Kuhns, Benjamin F., Bldg—hist pl ... OH-6
Kuhns Crossing—locale ... CO-8
Kuhns Lake—lake ... IN-6
Kuhns Mill—locale ... PA-2
Kuhn Spit—bar ... WA-9
Kuhn Spit Archeol Site—hist pl ... WA-9
Kuhn Station—locale ... IL-6
Kuhn Station Site—hist pl ... IL-6
**Kuhnsville**—pop pl ... PA-2
Kuhntown—locale ... PA-2
Kuhn Trail—trail ... PA-2
Kuholilea—civil ... HI-9
Kuhr Coulee—valley ... MT-8
Kuhre, William D., House—hist pl ... UT-8
Kuhsuman Creek—stream ... AK-9
Kuhua—civil (2) ... HI-9
Kuhua Bay—bay ... HI-9
Kuhulu Rock—island ... HI-9
Kuhumu Rsvr—reservoir ... HI-9
Kui—cape ... HI-9
Kuia—civil ... HI-9
Kuiaha ... HI-9
Kuiaha—civil ... HI-9
Kuiaha Gulch ... HI-9
Kuiaha - Pauwela - Kapukalua Homesteads—civil ... HI-9
Kuiaha Point—cape ... HI-9
Kuiak River—stream ... AK-9
Kuia Stream—stream ... HI-9
Kuia Valley—valley ... HI-9
Kui Channel—channel ... HI-9
KUIK-AM—tower (2) ... OR-9
Kuikcherk River—stream ... AK-9
Kuikchungnak Creek—stream ... AK-9
Kuiki—summit ... HI-9
Kuikui, Lae o—cape ... HI-9
Kuikuipapa Gulch ... HI-9
Kuikuipapa Gulch—valley ... HI-9
Kuikui Point ... HI-9
Kui-la-tsu-ko ... WA-9
Kuilau Ridge—ridge ... HI-9
Kuilei Cliffs—cliff ... HI-9
Kuilei Gulch—valley ... HI-9
Kuilei One—civil ... HI-9
Kuilei One-Two—civil ... HI-9
Kuili—summit ... HI-9
Kuili Hill ... HI-9
Kuilioloa Heiau (Site)—locale ... HI-9
Kuiman Creek—stream ... OR-9
Kuinanaho Gulch—valley ... HI-9
KUIN-FM (Vernal)—tower ... UT-8
Kuinihu—summit ... HI-9
Kuiper Draw—valley ... WY-8
Kuiper Ranch—locale ... WY-8
Kuirzinjik Lake (Lobo Lake)—lake ... AK-9
Kuitan Lake—lake ... OR-9
Kui Tatk—locale ... AZ-5
Kuit Vaya ... AZ-5
Kuit Vaya—locale ... AZ-5
Kuit Vaya Well—well ... AZ-5
Kuiu Island—island ... AK-9
Kuiukta Bay—bay ... AK-9
Kuiuktulik River—stream ... AK-9
Kujus Lake—lake ... MN-6
Kujawa or Burg Lake—lake ... MI-6
Kujowski Central Ditch—canal ... OH-6
Kujulik Bay—bay ... AK-9
K. U. Junction ... KY-4
Kuka Creek—stream ... AK-9
Kuka Crossing—locale ... MT-8
Kukaeiole Valley—valley ... HI-9
Kukahaula ... HI-9
Kuka (historical)—locale ... KS-7
Kukaiau—civil ... HI-9
**Kukaiau**—pop pl ... HI-9
Kukaiau Gulch—valley ... HI-9
Kukaiau Ranch ... HI-9
Kukai Hill ... HI-9
Kukailimoku Point—cape ... HI-9
Kukaimanini Island—island ... HI-9
Kukaipaa ... HI-9
Kukaipaa Point ... HI-9
Kukaiwaa Point—cape ... HI-9
Kukak—locale ... AK-9
Kukak Bay—bay ... AK-9
Kukak Creek—stream ... AK-9
Kukaki Stream—stream ... HI-9
Kukaklek Lake—lake ... AK-9
Kukaklik Lake—lake ... AK-9
Kukak Point—cape ... AK-9
Kukaktlik River—stream ... AK-9
Kukaktlim Lake—lake ... AK-9
Kukak Village Site—hist pl ... AK-9
Kukak Volcano—summit ... AK-9
Kukalauula Pali—cliff ... HI-9
Kukamahu Gulch—valley ... HI-9
Kukaniloko Birthstones—hist pl ... HI-9
**Kukanono**—pop pl ... HI-9
Kuka Ranch—locale ... MT-8
Kuke Chehedagi Tank—reservoir ... AZ-5
Kukiat ... NY-2
Kukiawaa Point ... HI-9
Kukihihi—cape ... HI-9
Kukii—summit ... HI-9
Kukii Heiau—locale ... HI-9
Kukii Point—cape ... HI-9
Kukio—locale ... HI-9
Kukio Bay—bay ... HI-9
Kukio One—civil ... HI-9
Kukio Two—civil ... HI-9
Kukkan Bay—bay ... AK-9
Kukkan Passage—channel ... AK-9
Kukku ... FM-9
Kukku Village ... FM-9
**Kukkuwu**—pop pl ... FM-9
Kukkuwu, Oror En—locale ... FM-9
Kukomalik ... AZ-5
Kukop ... FM-9
Kukpowruk Pass—channel ... AK-9
Kukpowruk River—stream ... AK-9
Kukpuk—locale ... AK-9
Kukpuk River—stream ... AK-9
KUKQ-AM (Tempe)—tower ... AZ-5
Kuk River—stream ... AK-9
Kukruk Creek—stream ... AK-9
Kuks Canyon—valley ... OR-9
Kukthluk River—stream ... AK-9
KUKU-AM (Willow Springs)—tower ... MO-7
Kukuau First ... HI-9
Kukuau One—civil ... HI-9
Kukuau Second ... HI-9
Kukuau Two—civil ... HI-9
Kuku Cape ... MP-9
Kukue ... FM-9
KUKU-FM (Willow Springs)—tower ... MO-7
**Kukui**—pop pl ... HI-9
Kukui—summit (2) ... HI-9
Kukuiaonanipahu Gulch—valley ... HI-9
Kukui Bay—bay ... HI-9
Kukuihae—area ... HI-9
Kukuihaele—civil ... HI-9
**Kukuihaele**—pop pl ... HI-9
Kukuihaele Landing—locale ... HI-9
Kukuihala—civil ... HI-9
Kukui Heiau—hist pl ... HI-9
Kukui Heiau—locale ... HI-9
Kukuihoolua (Bird Refuge)—island ... HI-9
Kukuihoolua Island ... HI-9
Kukuihoolua Islet ... HI-9
Kukuikea—civil ... HI-9
Kukuilamalamahii Gulch—valley ... HI-9
Kukuinui Ridge—ridge ... HI-9
Kukuiokahoalii—summit ... HI-9
Kukuiokanaloa—cliff ... HI-9
Kukuioli ... HI-9
Kukuiolono Park—park ... HI-9
Kukuiopae—civil ... HI-9
Kukuiopae Homesteads—civil ... HI-9
Kukuipahu—civil ... HI-9
Kukuipalaoa Island—island ... HI-9
Kukuipilau Heiau—hist pl ... HI-9
Kukui Point—cape (3) ... HI-9
Kukuipuha Valley—valley ... HI-9
Kukui Stream—stream ... HI-9
Kukui Trail—trail ... HI-9
Kukuiula—civil ... HI-9
**Kukuiula**—pop pl ... HI-9
Kukuiula Bay—bay ... HI-9
Kukuiula Gulch—valley ... HI-9
Kukuiulaiki—civil ... HI-9
**Kukui Village**—pop pl ... HI-9
Kukuiwaluhia—civil ... HI-9
Kukuk Drain—stream ... MI-6
Kukukpilak Creek—stream ... AK-9
Kukuku Gulch—valley ... HI-9
Kukumamalu Gulch—valley ... HI-9
Kuku Point—cape ... HI-9
Kuku Point—RIDGE ... MP-9
Kukura Creek—stream ... MI-6
Kukuwu ... FM-9
Kukwe ... FM-9
Kula ... HI-9
Kula—civil ... HI-9
Kulaalamihi Fishpond—lake ... HI-9
Kula (CCD)—cens area ... HI-9
Kula For Res—forest ... HI-9
Kulaikahonu—civil ... HI-9
Kulaimano Homesteads—civil ... HI-9
Kula Kala Point ... WA-9
Kulakala Point—cape ... WA-9
Kulakaoo Stream ... HI-9
Kulak Point—cape ... AK-9
Kulakula Point ... WA-9
Kulanaililia—summit ... HI-9
Kulanakii—civil ... HI-9
Kulanakii Stream—stream ... HI-9
Kulanapahu—summit ... HI-9
Kulani—summit ... HI-9
Kulani, Pali o—cliff ... HI-9
Kulaniapia Falls—falls ... HI-9
Kulani Cone ... HI-9
Kulanihakoi Gulch ... HI-9
Kulanihakoi Gulch—valley ... HI-9
Kulani Project—area ... HI-9
Kulani Project—locale ... HI-9
Kulani Project (Penal Institution)—building ... HI-9
Kulaokaea—summit ... HI-9
Kula o Kalalaoloa—bench ... HI-9
Kula Pipe Line—other ... HI-9
Kula Pipeline—other ... HI-9
Kulas, E. J., Estate Hist Dist—hist pl ... OH-6
Kula Sanatorium—hospital ... HI-9
**Kula (Waiakoa)**—pop pl ... HI-9
Kulepeamoa Point—cape ... HI-9
Kulepiamoa Ridge—ridge ... HI-9
Kulgurak Island—island ... AK-9
Kuli ... FM-9
Kuliak Bay—bay ... AK-9
Kulichito Ch—church ... OK-5
Kulichkof Island—island (2) ... AK-9
Kulichkof Rock—island ... AK-9
Kulihai—civil ... HI-9
Kulihaili Stream—stream ... HI-9
Kuli Inla ... OK-5
Kulik, Lake—lake ... AK-9
Kulik Lake—lake (2) ... AK-9
Kulikoa Point—cape ... HI-9
Kuliliak Bay—bay ... AK-9
Kuliouou—civil ... HI-9
**Kuliouou**—pop pl ... HI-9
Kuliouou Beach Park—park ... HI-9
Kuliouou For Res—forest ... HI-9
Kuliouou Gulch ... HI-9
Kuliouou Homesteads—civil ... HI-9
Kuliouou Valley—valley ... HI-9
Kulla Kulla, Lake—lake ... WA-9
Kulla Kulla Creek—stream ... WA-9
Kullerstrand Sch—school ... CO-8
KULL-FM (Scott City)—tower ... KS-7
Kullgren House—hist pl ... CO-8
Kulli ... OK-5
Kulliinla ... OK-5
**Kulli (Kullituklo)**—pop pl ... OK-5
**Kullituklo**—pop pl ... OK-5
Kullituklo Ch—church ... OK-5
Kullituklo Sch—school ... OK-5
**Kulm**—pop pl ... ND-7
Kulm Cem—cemetery ... SD-7
Kulm-Edgeley Dam—dam ... ND-7
Kulmogon Slough—gut ... AK-9
Kulm Sch—school ... SD-7
**Kulm Township**—pop pl ... SD-7
Kuloa ... HI-9
Kuloa Point—cape (2) ... HI-9
Kulo-Kala Point ... WA-9
Kuloli—summit ... HI-9
Kuloli Hill ... HI-9
Kulosville ... PA-2
Kulotauk ... PW-9
**Kulp**—pop pl ... PA-2
Kulp Ch—church ... PA-2
**Kulpmont**—pop pl ... PA-2
Kulpmont Borough—civil ... PA-2
**Kulps**—pop pl ... PA-2
Kulps Corner—locale ... PA-2
**Kulpsville**—pop pl ... PA-2
**Kulptown**—pop pl ... PA-2
Kulshan Cabin—locale ... WA-9
Kulshan Cem—cemetery ... WA-9
Kulshan Creek—stream ... WA-9
Kulshan Ridge—ridge ... WA-9
Kult Ditch—canal ... IN-6
Kulthieth Mtn—summit ... AK-9
Kulthieth River—stream ... AK-9
Kultus Lake ... OR-9
Kulua ... HI-9
Kulua Cones ... HI-9
Kulua Gulch—valley ... HI-9
Kulua Hill ... HI-9
Kulua Mountain ... HI-9
Kulugra Ridge—ridge ... AK-9
Kului Gulch—valley ... HI-9
Kulukak—locale ... AK-9
Kulukak Bay—bay ... AK-9
Kulukak Point—cape ... AK-9
Kulukak River—stream ... AK-9
Kuluk Bay—bay ... AK-9
Kulukbuk Hills—other ... AK-9
Kuluk Shoal—bar ... AK-9
Kuluruak (Site)—locale ... AK-9
Kulvagavik—locale ... AK-9
KULY-AM (Ulysses)—tower ... KS-7
**Kulzers Spur**—pop pl ... WA-9
Kum, Unun En—bar ... FM-9
KUMA-AM—tower ... OR-9
KUMA-FM—tower ... OR-9
Kumaipo Stream—stream ... HI-9
Kumakalii ... HI-9
Kumakalii Peak ... HI-9
Kumakaula Heiau—locale ... HI-9
Kumakkui ... MP-9
Kumakua Gulch—valley ... HI-9
Kumano Rsvr—reservoir ... HI-9
Kumanumanu—summit ... HI-9
Kumaru Island ... MP-9
Kumaru Island—island ... MP-9
Kumaru-to ... MP-9
Kum Ba Yah Camp—locale ... ID-8
Kumbrabow State For—forest ... WV-2
Kumekumeyel River ... PW-9
Kumelos Drain—canal ... WY-8
Kumimi—cape ... HI-9
Kumimi—civil ... HI-9
**Kumis**—pop pl ... VA-3
Kumiva Peak—summit ... NV-8
Kumkachutz Wawasit ... AZ-5
Kumler—locale ... IL-6
Kumler, Elias, House—hist pl ... OH-6
Kumler Hall—hist pl ... SC-3
Kumlik Island—island ... AK-9
**Kum-Li Meadows Subdivision**—pop pl ... UT-8
Kumliun Creek—stream ... AK-9
Kumlunak Peninsula—cape ... AK-9
Kummel Creek—stream ... WI-6
Kummer—locale ... WA-9
Kummer Draw—valley ... WA-9
Kummerfeld Oil Field—oilfield ... WY-8
Kummer Junction—other ... WA-9
Kummer Ridge—ridge ... ND-7
Kumoa Gulch ... HI-9
Kumor Draw—valley ... WY-8
Kumo Valley—valley ... UT-8
Kump, Gov. H. Guy, House—hist pl ... WV-2
Kumpf Sch—school ... MO-7
Kumph Pond—lake ... NY-2
Kumpohui Creek—stream ... CA-9
**Kump Station**—pop pl ... MD-2
Kumpula Point—cape ... MN-6
KUMR-FM (Rolla)—tower ... MO-7
Kumu—civil ... HI-9
Kumuawane Stream—stream ... HI-9
Kumueli—civil ... HI-9
Kumueli Gulch—valley ... HI-9
Kumuiilahi—summit ... HI-9
Kumukahi ... HI-9
Kumukahi, Cape—cape ... HI-9
Kumukahi Cap ... HI-9
Kumukahi Channel ... HI-9
Kumukahi Point ... HI-9
Kumukaumaha—crater ... HI-9
Kumukehi Point ... HI-9
Kumukehu Point—cape ... HI-9
Kumukou—crater ... HI-9
**Kumukumu**—pop pl ... HI-9
Kumukumu Stream—stream ... HI-9
Kumumau ... HI-9
Kumumau Point—cape ... HI-9
Kumuweia Ridge ... HI-9
Kumuwela Ridge—ridge ... HI-9
Kumuwela Trail—trail ... HI-9
KUMV-TV (Williston)—tower ... ND-7
**Kuna**—pop pl ... ID-8
Kuna Butte—summit ... ID-8
Kuna Canal—canal ... ID-8
Kuna Cave—cave ... ID-8
Kuna Creek—stream ... CA-9
Kuna Crest—ridge ... CA-9
Kunaghak Creek—stream ... AK-9
Kunaka—cape ... HI-9
Kuna Lake—lake ... CA-9
Kunalele Valley—valley ... HI-9
Kunamakst Creek—stream ... WA-9
Kuna Peak—summit ... CA-9
Kunarak Creek—stream ... AK-9
Kuna River—stream ... AK-9
Kunath ... VA-3
**Kunath**—pop pl ... VA-3
Kunath Ranch—locale ... WY-8
Kunath Store—locale ... VA-3
Kunawai Spring—spring ... HI-9
Kunayosh Creek ... AK-9
Kunayosh Creek—stream ... AK-9
Kuncanowet Hills—summit ... NH-1
Kunce Cem—cemetery ... IN-6
Kunckle Reservoir ... CA-9
Kunda Airp—airport ... PA-2
Kunde Knoll—summit ... AZ-5
Kunde Mtn—summit ... AZ-5
Kundert Rsvr—reservoir ... OR-9
Kunde Tank—reservoir ... AZ-5
Kunefke Sch (historical)—school ... SD-7
Kune Oil Field—oilfield ... KS-7
Kuner—locale ... CO-8
Kuner Sch—school ... CO-8
Kunes Creek—stream ... WI-6
**Kunesh**—pop pl ... WI-6
Kuney Canyon ... OR-9
Kuneytown—locale ... NY-2
Kungealarook Creek—stream ... AK-9
Kungealoruk Creek—stream ... AK-9
Kungeekan Island—island ... MP-9
Kungeekan-To ... MP-9
Kungiakrok Creek—stream ... AK-9
Kungok River—stream ... AK-9
Kungsboro—locale ... NC-3
Kungsugrug River—stream ... AK-9
Kunhardt, George, Estate—hist pl ... MA-1
Kunia ... HI-9
**Kunia Camp (Kunia Post Office)**—pop pl ... HI-9
**Kunia (Kunia Camp)**—pop pl ... HI-9
KUNI-FM (Cedar Falls)—tower ... IA-7
Kunini Gulch—valley ... HI-9
Kunjamuc river ... NY-2
Kunjamuk Bay—bay ... NY-2
Kunjamuk Cave—cave ... NY-2
Kunjamuk Mtn—summit ... NY-2
Kunjamuk River—stream ... NY-2
Kunjwan ... MH-9
Kunk Creek—stream ... AK-9
Kunkel Bldg—hist pl ... PA-2
Kunkel Cem—cemetery ... TN-4
Kunkel Cem—cemetery ... TX-5
Kunkel Lake—lake ... IN-6
Kunkel Lake—lake ... ND-7
Kunkel Point—cape ... NY-2
Kunkel Sch—school ... PA-2
Kunkel State Wildlife Mngmt Area—park ... MN-6
Kunkers Run—stream ... OH-6
Kunk Lake—lake ... AK-9
**Kunkle**—pop pl ... OH-6
**Kunkle**—pop pl ... PA-2
Kunkle Cem—cemetery ... OH-6
Kunkle Cem—cemetery ... PA-2
Kunkle Flat—flat ... SD-7
Kunkle Hill—summit ... PA-2
Kunkle Log House—hist pl ... OH-6
Kunkle Rsvr—reservoir ... CA-9
Kunkle Sch—school ... MO-7
Kunkles Dam—dam ... PA-2
Kunkles Dam—reservoir ... PA-2
Kunkles Gap ... PA-2
**Kunkletown**—pop pl (2) ... PA-2
Kunkleville ... PA-2
Kunk-pa-pa CreeK (historical)—stream ... SD-7
Kunoa Gulch—valley ... HI-9
KUNQ-FM (Houston)—tower ... MO-7
Kun River—stream ... AK-9
Kuns Branch—stream ... WV-2
Kunschke Lake—lake ... MI-6
Kunsch Lake ... MI-6
Kuns Ditch—canal ... IN-6
Kunselman Creek—stream ... MT-8
Kunshi ... PA-2
Kunsiniali Point—cape ... AK-9
Kunski ... PA-2
Kunsmans Corner ... PA-2
Kunsmans Crossing ... PA-2
Kunsmiller JHS—school ... CO-8
Kuns Park—park ... CA-9
Kunta Sch—school ... OK-5
Kunto Shoto ... FM-9
Kuntz Branch—stream ... KS-7
Kuntz Canyon—valley ... CA-9
Kuntz Cem—cemetery ... OH-6
Kuntz Creek—stream ... CA-9
Kuntz Creek—stream ... CO-8
Kuntz Creek—stream ... ID-8
Kuntz Creek—stream ... MN-6
Kuntz Draw ... TX-5
Kuntz Flat—flat ... UT-8
Kuntzford ... PA-2
Kuntz Gulch—valley ... CO-8
Kuntz Hollow—valley ... UT-8
Kuntz Lake—lake ... MN-6
Kuntz Ridge—ridge ... IN-6
Kuntzsford ... PA-2
Kunu—island ... FM-9
Kunuk Creek—stream ... AK-9
Kunyanak Creek—stream ... AK-9
Kuny Elem Sch—school ... IN-6
Kunzas Island ... MN-6
Kunz Creek ... TX-5
Kunze, Gustave, Barn—hist pl ... ID-8
Kunze, Rudolf, Barn—hist pl ... ID-8
Kunze Cem—cemetery ... IN-6
Kunze Cem—cemetery ... KS-7
Kunze Creek—stream ... MI-6
Kunze Lake—lake ... MI-6
**Kunze Township**—pop pl ... ND-7
Kunz Island—island ... WI-6
Kunzlers Ranch—locale ... UT-8
Kunz Ranch—locale ... NV-8
Kunz Rsvr—reservoir ... OR-9
Kuoben Island ... MP-9
Kuoben-To ... MP-9
Kuobuen Island—island ... MP-9
Kuoitak ... AZ-5
Kuooteppu ... MP-9
Kuooteppu To ... MP-9
Kuop Atoll ... FM-9
Kuop To ... FM-9
Kuo Stream—stream ... HI-9
Kuoteppu ... MP-9
Kuoteppu-to ... MP-9
Kuotoppu-To ... MP-9
Kuou Stream—stream ... HI-9
Kupaa Gulch—valley ... HI-9
Kupaahu ... HI-9
Kupahua—civil ... HI-9
Kupahua Homesteads—civil ... HI-9
Kupaia—summit ... HI-9
Kupaia Gulch—valley ... HI-9
Kupaianaha—summit ... HI-9
Kupanaha, Puu—summit ... HI-9
Kupapau Hill—summit ... HI-9
Kupapaulua Gulch—valley ... HI-9
Kupapau Point—cape ... HI-9
Kuparuk River—stream ... AK-9
Kuparuk River Delta—area ... AK-9
Kuparuk State No 1—well ... AK-9
Kupaua Valley—valley ... HI-9
KUPD-FM (Tempe)—tower ... AZ-5
K U Peak—summit ... TX-5
Kupeke—civil ... HI-9
Kupeke Fishpond—lake ... HI-9
Kupeke Gulch—valley ... HI-9
Kupenau—summit ... HI-9
Kuper Well—well ... NM-5
Kupfer Spring—spring ... WA-9
Kupigruak Channel—channel ... AK-9
Kupikipikio Point—cape ... HI-9
Kupk ... AZ-5
Kupk—locale ... AZ-5
Kupke ... AZ-5
Kupk Hills—range ... AZ-5
KUPK-TV (Garden City)—tower ... KS-7
KUPL-AM—tower ... OR-9
KUPL-FM—tower ... OR-9
Kuplie Lake—lake ... WI-6
Kuplu, Inlulu—lagoon ... FM-9
Kuplu, Inya—channel ... FM-9
Kupluruak Point—cape ... AK-9
Kuplu Te—locale ... FM-9
Kuplu Wan—locale ... FM-9
**Kupolo**—pop pl ... HI-9
Kuponop—well ... FM-9
Kupopolo Heiau—hist pl ... HI-9
Kupp Atoll ... FM-9
Kupper—airport ... NJ-2
**Kupreanof**—pop pl ... AK-9
Kupreanof Harbor—bay ... AK-9
Kupreanof Island—island ... AK-9
Kupreanof Mtn—summit (2) ... AK-9
Kupreanof Peninsula—cape (2) ... AK-9
Kupreanof Point—cape ... AK-9
Kupreanof Strait—channel ... AK-9
Kup River State No 1—well ... AK-9
Kupuk Creek—stream ... AK-9
Kupunkamint Mtn—summit ... MT-8
Kupupolo Heiau—locale ... HI-9
Kupwuriso—summit ... FM-9
KURA-AM (Moab)—tower ... UT-8
Kurakon-to ... MP-9
Kurakonto To ... MP-9
Kuramadaoru Passage ... PW-9
Kuramadaoru Suido ... PW-9
Kurass Lake—lake ... MN-6
Kurby Hollow—valley ... WI-6
Kurby Windmill—locale ... TX-5
**Kurdo**—pop pl ... AR-4
Kure Atoll—island ... HI-9
**Kure Beach**—pop pl ... NC-3
Kure Island ... HI-9
Kure Island—island ... HI-9
Kurgorak Bay—bay ... AK-9
Kurikka Creek—stream ... WI-6
Kuriko Lake—lake ... MN-6
Kurisumasu-Ko ... MP-9
Kurk Creek—stream ... KY-4
Kurkindoll Creek—stream ... TX-5
Kurn Hattin Home—locale ... VI-1
KURO-FM (Huron)—tower ... SD-7
**Kuroki**—pop pl ... ND-7
Kuropak Creek—stream ... AK-9
Kuror Island ... MP-9
Kuroru-to ... MP-9
Kurotaoko ... PW-9
Kurre Cem—cemetery ... MO-7
**Kurreville**—pop pl ... MO-7
Kurru ... FM-9
Kurry Creek—stream ... ID-8
Kurt Creek—stream ... WI-6
**Kurten**—pop pl ... TX-5
Kurten Cem—cemetery ... TX-5
Kurten Sch—school ... TX-5
**Kurth**—pop pl ... WI-6
Kurth, J. H., House—hist pl ... TX-5
Kurth Coulee—valley ... MT-8
Kurth Draw—valley ... CO-8
Kurth-Glover House—hist pl ... TX-5
Kurt Hollow—valley ... WV-2
Kurth Sch—school ... SD-7
Kurths Island—island ... FL-3
**Kurthwood**—pop pl ... LA-4
Kurthwood Ch—church ... LA-4
Kurthwood Fire Tower—locale ... LA-4
**Kurtistown**—pop pl ... HI-9
Kurtistown Sch—school ... HI-9
Kurtley Draw—valley ... WY-8
Kurtluk River—stream ... AK-9
Kurt Peak—summit ... MT-8
Kurtz ... MN-6
Kurtz—locale ... MI-6
**Kurtz**—pop pl ... IN-6
Kurtz, Adam, House—hist pl ... VA-3
Kurtz, J., and Sons Store Bldg—hist pl ... NY-2
Kurtz, T. M., House—hist pl ... PA-2
Kurtz Airp—airport ... PA-2
Kurtz Cem—cemetery ... OH-6
Kurtz Creek—stream ... MI-6
Kurtz Creek—stream ... MT-8
Kurtz Creek—stream ... ND-7
Kurtz Dam—dam ... PA-2
Kurtz Ditch—canal ... IN-6

# L

*L* FL-3
L—*mine* ID-8
L, Lateral—*canal* MT-8
L, Mount—*island* MA-1
L, Tank—*reservoir* AZ-5
*La* UT-8
*La Abra* AZ-5
*La Abra Plain* AZ-5
**La Abras**—*pop pl* PR-3
La Abra Valley—*valley* AZ-5
**Laager**—*pop pl* TN-4
Laager Congregational Methodist
Ch—*church* TN-4
Laager Post Office (historical)—*building* TN-4
Laager Sch (historical)—*school* TN-4
Laahana—*island* HI-9
L A Ainger JHS—*school* FL-3
Laak—*island* MP-9
Laakso Lake—*lake* MI-6
*Laalaau* HI-9
**La Aldea**—*pop pl* (2) PR-3
La Aleta—*ridge* CA-9
**La Alhambra**—*pop pl* PR-3
**La Alianza**—*pop pl* PR-3
Laaloa One-Two—*civil* HI-9
**La Anna**—*pop pl* PA-2
*La Arana Creek* TX-5
Laarbab—*island* MP-9
La Arena—*flat* CA-9
**La Arena**—*pop pl* PR-3
Laark—*locale* LA-4
La Atravezada—*summit* TX-5
Laauhihaihai—*summit* HI-9
Laaumama—*civil* HI-9
Laauokala Point—*cape* HI-9
Laau Point—*cape* HI-9
La Aura Crossing—*locale* TX-5
Laau Ridge—*ridge* HI-9
Laay—*locale* FM-9
La Baca Canyon—*valley* NM-5
La Baca Lake—*lake* NM-5
Labach Woods—*woods* IL-6
*Labaddie Creek* MO-7
La Badia del Divisadero—*lake* TX-5
La Badia de Pitoso—*lake* TX-5
**Labadie**—*pop pl* MO-7
Labadie Bottoms—*bend* MO-7
Labadie Creek—*stream* MO-7
Labadie Drain—*canal* MI-6
Labadie Powerplant Water Tanks—*other* MO-7
Labadie Sch—*school* MI-6
**Labadieville**—*pop pl* LA-4
**Labadieville** (sta.)—*pop pl* LA-4
*La Badilla Grande* TX-5
La Bahia—*locale* TX-5
La Baig Spring—*spring* CA-9
La Bajada—*locale* NM-5
La Bajada—*slope* CA-9
La Bajada Hill—*ridge* NM-5
La Bajada Mesa—*bench* NM-5
La Bajada Mesa Agricultural
Site—*hist pl* NM-5
La Bajada Mine—*mine* NM-5
**La Balear**—*pop pl* PR-3
La Ballona—*uninc pl* CA-9
La Ballona Sch—*school* CA-9
Laban—*locale* TX-5
Laban—*locale* VA-3
Labana Ch—*church* AR-4
Laban Bayou—*stream* MS-4
La Bandera Ranch—*locale* TX-5
Labandera Rock—*other* AK-9
La Bandera Tank—*reservoir* TX-5
**Laban (historical)**—*pop pl* TN-4
Labanon Ch—*church* AR-4
Laban Post Office (historical)—*building* TN-4
Laban Sch—*school* KS-7
Laban Sharp Cem—*cemetery* TN-4
Labans Pond—*lake* MA-1
La Barbe, Point—*cape* MI-6
LaBare Creek—*stream* OR-9
Labaredj—*island* MP-9
*Labaredj Island* MP-9
Labaree Creek—*stream* AK-9
La Barenda Windmill—*locale* TX-5
La Barge—*other* OK-5
**Labarge**—*pop pl* MI-6
**La Barge**—*pop pl* WY-8
LaBarge, Lake—*lake* MI-6
La Barge Canyon—*valley* AZ-5
*La Barge Creek* ND-7
La Barge Creek—*stream* AZ-5
La Barge Creek—*stream* WY-8
La Barge Gas And Oil Field—*oilfield* WY-8
LaBarge Guard Station—*locale* WY-8
*Labarge Lake* MN-6
La Barge Lake—*lake* MI-6
La Barge Lake—*lake* WA-9
LaBarge Meadows—*flat* WY-8
La Barge Mtn—*summit* (2) AZ-5
LaBarge Rock—*pillar* MT-8
LaBarge Spring—*spring* AZ-5
Labarge Spring Number Two—*spring* AZ-5
Labar Island—*island* NJ-2
*Labarit* MP-9
Labar Lake—*lake* TX-5
*LaBaron Creek* UT-8
La Baron Creek—*stream* UT-8
Labaron Dam—*dam* UT-8
*La Baron Lake* UT-8
LaBaron Meadows—*flat* UT-8
*La Baron Reservoir* UT-8
Labaron Rsvr—*reservoir* UT-8
*Labarque Creek* MO-7
La Barque Creek—*stream* MO-7
La Barr, Lake—*lake* NY-2
**La Barra**—*pop pl* PR-3
La Barranca Colorada—*civil* CA-9
**La Barranca Subdivision**—*pop pl* UT-8
La Barre—*other* LA-4
**Labarre**—*pop pl* LA-4
**Labarre (La Barre)**—*pop pl* LA-4
Labarre Sch—*school* LA-4
**La Barr Meadows**—*pop pl* CA-9
LaBarry Ranch—*locale* NV-8
*Labars Island* PA-2
*Labarsville* PA-2
Labascus—*locale* KY-4
**Labatt**—*pop pl* TX-5
LaBaum Creek—*stream* AR-4
Labauve, Bayou—*stream* LA-4
Labauve, Felix, House—*hist pl* MS-4
*La Bauve Bayou* LA-4
*Labavedj Island* MP-9
Labavedj Island—*island* MP-9
**La Bayamonesa**—*pop pl* PR-3
Labbe Brook—*stream* ME-1
Labbe Camp—*locale* ME-1
Labbee Fld Airp—*airport* WA-9
Labbe Mine—*mine* NV-8
Labbe Oil Field—*oilfield* TX-5
Labbe Pond—*lake* ME-1
Labbe Rsvr—*reservoir* CO-8
Labbide Mill Creek—*stream* MD-2
Labby—*locale* ME-1
*Labeasche River* OR-9
Labeau Gulch—*valley* CO-8
La Becerra Windmill—*locale* TX-5
Labell Ditch—*stream* MT-8
*Labelle* OH-6
LaBelle—*locale* MN-6
Labelle—*other* OH-6
**La Belle**—*pop pl* FL-3
**Labelle**—*pop pl* ID-8
**LaBelle**—*pop pl* MO-7
**La Belle**—*pop pl* MO-7
**La Belle**—*pop pl* PA-2
**La Belle**—*pop pl* TX-5
La Belle, Lac—*lake* MI-6
La Belle, Lac—*lake* MN-6
La Belle, Lac—*lake* WI-6
LaBelle Bayou—*gut* AR-4
La Belle Bridge—*bridge* FL-3
La Belle (CCD)—*cens area* FL-3
Labelle (CCD)—*cens area* TX-5
LaBelle Cem—*cemetery* MO-7
La Belle Cem—*cemetery* WI-6
LaBelle Community Sch—*school* FL-3
La Belle Creek—*stream* NM-5
La Belle Creek—*stream* ND-7
LaBelle Creek—*stream* SD-7
LaBelle Elem Sch—*school* FL-3
**Labelle Estates (subdivision)**—*pop pl* MS-4
La Belle Gulch—*valley* MT-8
Labelle Haven Ch—*church* TN-4
LaBelle HS—*school* FL-3
LaBelle Intermediate Sch—*school* FL-3
LaBelle Lake—*lake* MN-6
La Belle Lake—*lake* WI-6
La Belle Lodge—*locale* NM-5
La Belle Lookout Tower—*locale* WI-6
La Belle Mine—*mine* CO-8
LaBelle MS—*school* FL-3
La Belle Oil Field—*oilfield* TX-5
La Belle Park—*park* MN-6
Labelle Place Ch—*church* TN-4
LaBelle Plaza (Shop Ctr)—*locale* FL-3
LaBelle Sch—*school* NE-7
LaBelle Sch (abandoned)—*school* MO-7
LaBelle Slough—*lake* SD-7
Labelle Slurry Pond Three Dam—*dam* PA-2
La Belle Tour—*hist pl* CA-9
La Belle Township—*civil* MO-7
Labelle Township—*civil* SD-7
**La Belle Township**—*pop pl* SD-7
*La Belle View* OH-6
Labellevue Mine—*mine* OR-9
Labell Run—*stream* WV-2
Label Reef—*bar* AK-9
Labens Point—*cape* DE-2
La Bentolera—*ridge* NM-5
Labera, Lake—*reservoir* GA-3
Laberdie Creek—*stream* KS-7
*La Bete Creek* KS-7
La Bethel Methodist Ch—*church* MS-4
**Labette**—*pop pl* KS-7
Labette Cem—*cemetery* KS-7
Labette Community Coll—*school* KS-7
*Labette Community Junior College* KS-7
Labette County—*civil* KS-7
Labette County Fairgrounds—*locale* KS-7
Labette Creek—*stream* KS-7
*Labette Creek Dam* KS-7
Labette Creek Tributary Bridge—*hist pl* KS-7
**Labette Township**—*pop pl* KS-7
**Labish**—*pop pl* OR-9
**Labish Center**—*pop pl* OR-9
Labish Center Sch—*school* OR-9
*Labish Ditch* OR-9
**Labish Village**—*pop pl* OR-9
Labitt Creek—*stream* TX-5
**La Blanca**—*pop pl* TX-5
La Blanca Artesian Well—*well* TX-5
La Blanca Gas Field—*oilfield* TX-5
La Blanca Windmill—*locale* (2) TX-5
LaBlanc Field—*park* MI-6
*La Blanche* KS-7
La Blanche Apartments—*hist pl* PA-2
Lablanche (historical)—*locale* KS-7
La Blanquilla—*island* PR-3
LaBleu Cem—*cemetery* LA-4
La Bleu Sch—*school* OR-9
Labo—*island* MP-9
La Boca—*locale* CO-8
**La Boca**—*pop pl* PR-3
La Boca Canyon—*valley* CO-8
La Boca Cem—*cemetery* CO-8
La Boca De Las Canada Del Pinole
—*civil* CA-9
La Boca Ditch—*canal* CO-8
Labo Del Rio Bridge—*hist pl* CO-8
*LaBohn Gap* WA-9
La Bohn Gap—*gap* WA-9
La Bohn Lakes—*lake* WA-9
*Labo Island* MP-9
La Boiteaux Woods—*park* OH-6
Labold Field—*park* OH-6
Labold House and Gardens—*hist pl* OH-6
LaBold Lake Dam—*dam* SD-7
La Bolsa—*area* NM-5
La Bolsa—*locale* NM-5
La Bolsa Banco Number 27—*levee* TX-5
La Bolsa Bend—*bend* TX-5
La Bolsa Chica—*civil* CA-9
*La Bolt* SD-7
**LaBolt**—*pop pl* SD-7
**La Bolt**—*pop pl* SD-7
LaBolt Cem—*cemetery* SD-7
LaBolt Lake—*lake* SD-7
Labon Bacot Cem—*cemetery* MS-4
La Bonita Park—*park* CA-9
La Bonitas Banco Number 37—*levee* TX-5
Labonte Brook—*stream* CT-1
La Bonte Canyon—*valley* WY-8
La Bonte Creek—*stream* WY-8
La Bonte Ranch—*locale* WY-8
La Bontys Point—*cape* MN-6
**Laboon**—*pop pl* GA-3
La Boon Cem—*cemetery* GA-3
La Boquilla—*valley* TX-5
**Laboratory**—*pop pl* NC-3
**Laboratory**—*pop pl* PA-2
Laboratory Dam—*dam* MO-7
**Laboratory (Daniel-Rhyne
Mill)**—*pop pl* NC-3
Laboratory HS—*school* IA-7
Laboratory of Anthropology—*building* NM-5
Laboratory of Anthropology—*hist pl* NM-5
Labor Bank Bldg—*hist pl* NJ-2
*La Borcita* NM-5
**La Borcita**—*pop pl* NM-5
**Laborcita**—*pop pl* NM-5
Laborcita Canyon—*valley* NM-5
Laborcitas Creek—*stream* TX-5
Laborcitas Windmill—*locale* TX-5
*Laborda Canyon* CA-9
**Laborde**—*pop pl* PA-2
Laborde Branch—*stream* PA-2
Laborde Canyon—*valley* CA-9
La Borde Cem—*cemetery* NE-7
LaBorde House, Store and Hotel—*hist pl* TX-5
Labor del Llano Windmill—*locale* TX-5
Laborde Sch (abandoned)—*school* PA-2
Laborde Well—*well* NV-8
Labores Well—*well* TX-5
Labor Field—*park* CT-1
Laboring Backbone—*ridge* TN-4
Laboring Bay—*gut* AR-4
Laboring Society Cem—*cemetery* LA-4
*Labor in Vain Brook* MA-1
*Labor in Vain Creek* MA-1
Labor In Vain Creek—*stream* MA-1
Labor in Vain Creek—*stream* MA-1
Labors Cem—*cemetery* OK-5
La Bota Ranch—*locale* TX-5
La Botella—*flat* NM-5
La Botella Chiquita—*cape* NM-5
*Labott* PA-2
**La Bott**—*pop pl* PA-2
**Labott**—*pop pl* PA-2
Labouchere Bay—*bay* AK-9
Labouchere Island—*island* AK-9
Labou Flat—*flat* NV-8
Labourne Bayou—*stream* LA-4
*Labouve Bayou* LA-4
Labozinski Drain—*stream* MI-6
Labrador Brook—*stream* NH-1
Labrador Creek—*stream* NY-2
Labrador Creek—*stream* OR-9
Labrador Gulch—*valley* SD-7
Labrador Hill—*summit* NY-2
*Labrador Lake* NY-2
Labrador Meadow—*swamp* ME-1
Labrador Pond—*lake* ME-1
Labrador Pond—*lake* MN-6
Labrador Pond—*lake* NH-1
Labrador Pond—*lake* NY-2
*Labranch* LA-4
*La Branch* MI-6
**La Branch**—*pop pl* LA-4
**La Branch**—*pop pl* MI-6
La Branche—*locale* LA-4
LaBranche—*locale* MI-6
Labranche Canal—*canal* (2) LA-4
LaBranche Plantation
Dependency—*hist pl* LA-4
**Labranza**—*pop pl* CA-9
Labras Lake—*swamp* IL-6
*La Brea* CA-9
La Brea—*civil* CA-9
*La Brea Canyon* CA-9
*La Brea Creek* CA-9
La Brea Creek—*stream* CA-9
La Brea Fossil Pits—*mine* CA-9
La Brecha—*gap* CA-9
Labrecque Dam—*dam* SD-7
Labre Creek—*gut* MI-6
*Labrero Island* TX-5
*La Brie Lake* MN-6
La Brie Lake—*lake* OR-9
*Labrinth Canyon* UT-8
La Brisa Ranch—*locale* TX-5
La Broche Canyon—*valley* CA-9
Labron Hollow—*valley* MO-7
La-Brooklyn Ch—*church* AL-4
Labrosse Creek—*stream* CA-9
Labruyere Park—*park* MO-7
Labuco—*locale* AL-4
Labuco Drift Mine (underground)—*mine* AL-4
LaBudde Creek—*stream* WI-6
La Budde Creek State Wildlife
Area—*area* WI-6
LaBuena—*locale* FL-3
*La Bum Creek* AR-4
*Labung* FM-9
**Laburnum Manor**—*pop pl* VA-3
Laburnum Sch—*school* VA-3
La Burrita Creek—*stream* TX-5
La Butte—*summit* OR-9
*Labuyere Park* MO-7
Labwlo—*island* MP-9
Labyche-Estorge House—*hist pl* LA-4
Labyrinth—*pillar* PA-2
Labyrinth Bay—*bay* AZ-5
Labyrinth Bay—*bay* UT-8
*Labyrinth Canyon* NV-8
Labyrinth Canyon—*valley* (2) UT-8
Labyrinth Mtn—*summit* WA-9
Labyrinths—*area* UT-8
Labyrinth State Memorial, The—*park* IN-6
*Lac* MN-6
Lac—*civil* CA-9
Lac, Bayou du—*channel* LA-4
Lac, Bayou du—*stream* LA-4
La Cabrada Tank—*reservoir* TX-5
La Cabra Mesa—*summit* NM-5
Laca Camp—*locale* NV-8
La Cache, Bayou—*stream* LA-4
La Cache JHS—*school* LA-4
Laca Creek—*stream* NV-8
Lacact Ch—*church* GA-3
*Lac a Cyprents* LA-4
La Cadena Windmill—*locale* TX-5
*Lac a Deux Boutes* LA-4
La Caida—*reservoir* NM-5
La Caja—*valley* NM-5
La Cal Basin—*basin* NM-5
La Caldera—*basin* CA-9
La Calichera Windmill—*locale* TX-5
Lacamas—*locale* WA-9
Lacamas Campground—*locale* WA-9
*Lacamas Creek* WA-9
Lacamas Creek—*stream* (4) WA-9
Lacamas Lake—*lake* WA-9
Lacamas Prairie—*flat* WA-9
Lacamas Sch—*school* WA-9
*La Camp* LA-4
Lacamp—*locale* LA-4
Lacamp Ch—*church* LA-4
*La Canada* CA-9
La Canada —*civil* CA-9
La Canada—*stream* (2) NM-5
La Canada—*uninc pl* CA-9
La Canada Bonita—*valley* NM-5
La Canada Country Club—*other* CA-9
La Canada de la Lena—*stream* NM-5
La Canada de la Lena—*valley* NM-5
La Canada del Almagre—*stream* NM-5
La Canada de la Loma de
Arena—*stream* NM-5
La Canada del Alto de la
Reunion—*stream* NM-5
La Canada de las Gallinas—*stream* NM-5
La Canada del Carro—*stream* NM-5
La Canada del Cerro—*stream* NM-5
La Canada del Guajalote—*stream* NM-5
La Canada de los Maes—*stream* NM-5
La Canada del Salado—*valley* NM-5
La Canada Ditch—*canal* NM-5
La Canada El Salado—*other* NM-5
**La Canada-Flintridge**—*pop pl* CA-9
**La Canada Flintridge** —*pop pl* CA-9
La Canada Honda—*stream* NM-5
La Canada HS—*school* CA-9
La Canada Ranch —*locale* AZ-5
La Canada Santiago—*stream* NM-5
La Canada Santiago—*valley* NM-5
La Canada Sch —*school* CA-9
La Canada Simada —*valley* CA-9
La Canada Verde Creek —*stream* CA-9
La Canada Windmill—*locale* NM-5
La Canasta Banco No 4—*levee* TX-5
La Capilla de Don Silverio
(Chapel)—*church* NM-5
**La Capital**—*pop pl* PR-3
La Carbonera—*civil* CA-9
**La Careda**—*pop pl* NM-5
**Lacarne**—*pop pl* OH-6
*La Carne Creek* OH-6
La Carne (RR name for Lacarne—*other* OH-6
Lac-a-Roy Lake—*lake* MN-6
La Carpa Potreros—*locale* CA-9
La Carpa Spring—*spring* CA-9
La Carpe, Bayou—*stream* LA-4
*La Carpe Creek* OH-6
Lacarpe Creek—*stream* OH-6
La Casa—*locale* TX-5
La Casa Alvarado—*hist pl* CA-9
La Casa Blanca—*building* PR-3
**La Casa de Piedra**—*pop pl* PR-3
La Casa Primera de Rancho San
Jose—*hist pl* CA-9
La Casa Trail Mobile Villa—*locale* AZ-5
La Casa Valley Boys Ranch—*locale* TX-5
La Case Solariega de Jose De
Diego—*hist pl* PR-3
**La Casita**—*pop pl* TX-5
La Casita del Arroyo—*locale* CA-9
La Casita Mobile Park—*locale* AZ-5
Lac A'Sostien—*lake* LA-4
La Casse Camp—*locale* MT-8
**Lacassine**—*pop pl* LA-4
Lacassine, Bayou—*stream* LA-4
Lacassine Natl Wildlife Ref—*park* LA-4
Lacassine Point—*cape* LA-4
Lacata Bridge—*bridge* FL-3
**La Catalana**—*pop pl* PR-3
*Lac aux Mortes Reservoir* ND-7
Lac aux Outlet Works Dam (non-
functional)—*dam* ND-7
*Lac aux Siene* LA-4
Lacawac—*hist pl* PA-2
Lacawac, Lake—*reservoir* PA-2
Lacawanna, Lake—*reservoir* MO-7
*Lac Bayou des Sot* LA-4
Lac Blanc Oil and Gas Field—*oilfield* LA-4
**Lac Courte Oreilles Ind Res**—*pop pl* WI-6
Lac Courte Oreilles State Wildlife Mngmt
Area—*park* WI-6
*Lac Court Oreilles* WI-6
*Lac du Flambeau* WI-6
**Lac du Flambeau**—*pop pl* WI-6
**Lac du Flambeau Ind Res**—*pop pl* WI-6
Lac du Flambeau (Station)—*locale* WI-6
**Lac du Flambeau (Town of)**—*pop pl* WI-6
*Lac du Verde* WI-6
**Lace**—*pop pl* IL-6
La Cebadilla Lake—*reservoir* AZ-5
La Cebolla—*summit* NM-5
La Cebolla Valley—*valley* NM-5
Lace Camp—*locale* OR-9
Lacefield Cem—*cemetery* TN-4
Lace House—*hist pl* NY-2
Lace House—*hist pl* SC-3
La Ceja—*ridge* CA-9
La Ceja—*ridge* NM-5
La Cejita—*ridge* NM-5
Lace Lake—*lake* MN-6
Lace Lake—*lake* MT-8
**Lacelle**—*pop pl* IA-7
**La Center**—*pop pl* KY-4
**La Center**—*pop pl* WA-9
La Center (CCD)—*cens area* KY-4
La Center (CCD)—*cens area* WA-9
La Center View-air Airp—*airport* WA-9
Laceola—*locale* TX-5
La Ceramica—*building* PR-3
**La Ceramica**—*pop pl* PR-3
La Cerda—*locale* TX-5
Lace River—*stream* AK-9
LaCerte Lake—*lake* WI-6
Lace Sch—*school* IL-6
*Lacey* MS-4
*Lacey* NC-3
Lacey—*locale* KY-4
Lacey—*locale* NJ-2
Lacey—*locale* OK-5
**Lacey**—*pop pl* AR-4
**Lacey**—*pop pl* IA-7
**Lacey**—*pop pl* MI-6
**Lacey**—*pop pl* WA-9
Lacey, Gen. John, Homestead—*hist pl* PA-2
*Lacey Branch* LA-4
Lacey Branch—*stream* AL-4
Lacey Branch—*stream* (2) MO-7
Lacey Branch—*stream* NC-3
Lacey Branch—*stream* TN-4
Lacey Branch—*stream* TX-5
Lacey Branch—*stream* WV-2
Lacey Bridge—*bridge* TX-5
Lacey Cem—*cemetery* AL-4
Lacey Cem—*cemetery* AR-4
Lacey Cem—*cemetery* IA-7
Lacey Cem—*cemetery* TN-4
Lacey Creek—*stream* IL-6
Lacey Creek—*stream* KY-4
Lacey Creek—*stream* MI-6
Lacey Creek—*stream* MT-8
Lacey Creek—*stream* VA-3
Lacey Flat—*flat* ID-8
**Lacey Forest**—*pop pl* VA-3
*Lacey Fork of Cedar Creek* TX-5
Lacey Forks Canyon—*valley* AZ-5
Lacey Gulch—*valley* MT-8
Lacey Island—*island* AK-9
Lacey-Keosauqua State Park—*park* IA-7
**Lacey (Lacey Forest)**—*pop pl* VA-3
Lacey Lake—*lake* IL-6
Lacey Lake—*lake* MI-6
Lacey Lake—*lake* MN-6
Lacey Lake Number 2—*reservoir* AL-4
Lacey Landing—*locale* VA-3
**Lacey Park**—*pop pl* PA-2
Lacey Point—*cliff* AZ-5
Lacey Ranch—*locale* NM-5
*Lacey Run* PA-2
Lacey Run—*stream* PA-2
Lacey Sch—*school* (3) IL-6
**Laceys Chapel**—*pop pl* AL-4
Laceys Chapel Elem Sch
(historical)—*school* AL-4
Laceys Lake Number One—*reservoir* AL-4
**Lacey Spring**—*pop pl* VA-3
Lacey Spring Ch—*church* AL-4
Lacey Spring Recreation Center—*park* AL-4
**Laceys Spring**—*pop pl* AL-4
Laceys Spring—*spring* AL-4
Laceys Spring (CCD)—*cens area* AL-4
Laceys Spring Cem—*cemetery* AL-4
Laceys Spring Ch—*church* AL-4
Laceys Spring Division—*civil* AL-4
Laceys Springs Elem Sch—*school* AL-4
Laceys Springs Post Office—*building* AL-4
Lacey Street Cem—*cemetery* PA-2
**Lacey Township**—*pop pl* KS-7
Lacey Township Cem—*cemetery* KS-7
**Lacey (Township of)**—*pop pl* NJ-2
Lacey Tunnel Number 3—*tunnel* MT-8
Lacey Valley—*valley* CA-9
**Laceyville**—*pop pl* PA-2
Laceyville Borough—*civil* PA-2
Lacey V. Murrow Floating
Bridge—*hist pl* WA-9
Lac Frontiere—*locale* ME-1
La Chamisalosa Canyon—*valley* NM-5
**La Changa**—*pop pl* PR-3
La Chanza Windmill—*locale* TX-5
*Lachapella Creek* WY-8
LaChapelle Creek—*stream* UT-8
LaChapelle Creek—*stream* WY-8
La Chapelle Place—*locale* MT-8
La Chapena Banco Number 99—*levee* TX-5
**La Charbonniere (historical)**—*pop pl* MO-7
LaChard, Lake—*lake* FL-3
La Charrette Bottom—*bend* MO-7
Lachary Pond (historical)—*lake* MA-1
La Chata Crater—*summit* NM-5
La Chata Ranch—*locale* TX-5
La Chaussee Spit—*bar* AK-9
Lachbuna Lake—*lake* AK-9
Lacher Ford—*locale* TN-4
La Chicharra Banco Number 94—*levee* TX-5
Lachicotte Creek—*stream* SC-3
**Lachine**—*pop pl* MI-6
Lachman Club—*other* CA-9
Lachman Sch—*school* MI-6
**Lachmund (historical)**—*pop pl* OR-9
La Cholla Airpark—*airport* AZ-5
La Cholla Wash—*arroyo* AZ-5
La Chorrera—*valley* PR-3
La Chuacha—*summit* NM-5
La Chuachia—*locale* NM-5
Lachusa Canyon—*valley* CA-9
Lachusa Fire Patrol Station—*locale* CA-9
LaChusa Hill—*summit* TX-5
LaChusa Ranch—*locale* TX-5
Lachute—*locale* LA-4
**La Chute**—*pop pl* LA-4
Lachute, Bayou—*gut* LA-4
Lachute Lake—*lake* LA-4
Lacie—*locale* KY-4
La Cienaga—*flat* NM-5
**La Cienaga**—*pop pl* NM-5
La Cienaga—*spring* CA-9
*La Cienega* CA-9
La Cienega—*locale* NM-5
La Cienega—*stream* TX-5
La Cienega—*swamp* TX-5
La Cienega Mission—*church* NM-5
La Cienega Park—*park* CA-9
La Cienega Spring—*spring* CA-9
La Cima—*summit* CA-9
La Cinta Canyon—*valley* NM-5
La Cinta Cem—*cemetery* NM-5
La Cinta Creek—*stream* NM-5
La Cinta Creek Windmill—*locale* NM-5
La Cinta Mesa—*summit* NM-5
La Cinta Ranch—*locale* NM-5
La Cinta Tank—*reservoir* NM-5
Lacire, Bayou—*gut* LA-4
Lacjac—*locale* CA-9
*Lackamas Creek* WA-9
Lackamas Creek—*stream* WA-9
Lackamas Sch—*school* WA-9
Lackard Park—*park* PA-2
**Lackawack**—*pop pl* NY-2
*Lackawana Canal* NY-2
*Lackawanna* PA-2
**Lackawanna**—*pop pl* FL-3
**Lackawanna**—*pop pl* NY-2
Lackawanna, Lake—*reservoir* NJ-2
*Lackawanna and Bloomsburg Junction* PA-2
Lackawanna Ave Commerical Hist
Dist—*hist pl* PA-2
Lackawanna Canal—*canal* NY-2
Lackawanna County—*civil* PA-2

**Lackawanna (County)**—*pop pl* PA-2
Lackawanna Dam—*dam* PA-2
Lackawanna Gulch—*valley* CO-8
Lackawanna HS—*school* NY-2
Lackawanna Lake—*lake* WI-6
Lackawanna Lake—*reservoir* PA-2
Lackawanna Mill—*locale* CO-8
Lackawanna Mine—*mine* CO-8
Lackawanna Mtn—*summit* PA-2
Lackawanna Park—*park* FL-3
Lackawanna River—*stream* PA-2
Lackawanna Sch—*school* FL-3
Lackawanna Springs—*spring* NV-8
Lackawanna Station—*locale* PA-2
Lackawannock Airp—*airport* PA-2
Lackawannock Creek—*stream* PA-2
**Lackawannock (Township of)**—*pop pl* PA-2
**Lackawaxen**—*pop pl* PA-2
*Lackawaxen Creek* PA-2
Lackawaxen Lake—*lake* UT-8
*Lackawaxen River* PA-2
Lackawaxen River—*stream* PA-2
**Lackawaxen (Township of)**—*pop pl* PA-2
Lack Branch—*stream* MO-7
*Lack Creek* NC-3
Lack Creek—*stream* CA-9
Lackens Branch—*stream* KY-4
Lackerman Airstrip—*airport* NV-8
*Lackerman Ranch Airport* NV-8
Lackey—*fmr MCD* NE-7
**Lackey**—*pop pl* KY-4
**Lackey**—*pop pl* MS-4
**Lackey**—*pop pl* VA-3
Lackey, John Alexander, House—*hist pl* NC-3
Lackey Basin—*valley* UT-8
Lackey Bluff—*cliff* AR-4
Lackey Branch—*stream* (2) KY-4
Lackey Bridge—*bridge* AL-4
Lackey Bridge—*other* IL-6
Lackey Cave—*cave* TN-4
Lackey Cem—*cemetery* AL-4
Lackey Cem—*cemetery* GA-3
Lackey Cem—*cemetery* (2) IL-6
Lackey Cem—*cemetery* KY-4
Lackey Cem—*cemetery* MS-4
Lackey Cem—*cemetery* OH-6
Lackey Cem—*cemetery* PA-2
Lackey Cem—*cemetery* WV-2
Lackey Cove—*valley* AL-4
Lackey Creek—*stream* KY-4
Lackey Creek—*stream* OR-9
Lackey Creek—*stream* (2) TN-4
Lackey Creek—*stream* TX-5
Lackey Dam—*dam* MA-1
Lackey Draw—*valley* WY-8
Lackey Gap—*gap* (2) AL-4
Lackey General Merchandise and Warehouse—*hist pl* AR-4
**Lackey Hill**—*pop pl* NC-3
Lackey HS—*school* MD-2
**Lackey (Lackie)**—*pop pl* MS-4
Lackey Mtn—*summit* NC-3
Lackey-Overbeck House—*hist pl* IN-6
Lackey Place—*locale* CA-9
Lackey Pond—*reservoir* MA-1
Lackey Post Office (historical)—*building* MS-4
Lackey Ranch—*locale* NM-5
Lackey Ridge—*ridge* OH-6
Lackeys Bay—*bay* MA-1
Lackeys Cabin—*park* CA-9
Lackeys Cave—*cave* AL-4
Lackey Sch—*school* SD-7
*Lackeys Creek* TN-4
Lackeys Ferry (historical)—*locale* MS-4
Lackeys Hole—*bend* OR-9
Lackeys Lake—*lake* OR-9
Lackeys Mill (historical)—*locale* AL-4
Lackeys Sch (abandoned)—*school* PA-2
**Lackey Store**—*pop pl* NC-3
**Lackey Town**—*pop pl* NC-3
Lackey Windmill—*locale* NM-5
Lackie—*other* MS-4
Lackie Cem—*cemetery* AR-4
Lackie Gulch—*valley* AK-9
*Lackies Ferry* MS-4
Lackland—*other* TX-5
**Lackland**—*pop pl* MO-7
Lackland AFB Training Annex—*military* TX-5
Lackland Air Force Base—*military* TX-5
**Lackland City**—*pop pl* TX-5
**Lackland Heights**—*pop pl* TX-5
**Lackland Hospital**—*pop pl* TX-5
Lackland HS—*school* TX-5
**Lackland Terrace**—*pop pl* TX-5
Lackland Terrace Park—*park* TX-5
**Lackland Training Annex**—*pop pl* TX-5
Lack Lateral—*canal* CA-9
Lackmans—*locale* KS-7
Lackner Pond—*lake* OR-9
Lackner's Tavern—*hist pl* CO-8
*Lack Run* PA-2
Lacks Chapel—*church* MS-4
Lacks Creek—*stream* CA-9
**Lack (Township of)**—*pop pl* PA-2
*Lac la Belle* MI-6
**Lac La Belle**—*pop pl* MI-6
**Lac La Belle**—*pop pl* WI-6
Lac La Buche—*bay* MS-4
Lac La Croix—*lake* MN-6
Laclair Drain—*canal* WA-9
La Clair Spring—*spring* OR-9
*Lac La Joie* TN-4
Lac Lake—*lake* (2) MN-6
*Lac La Mar* MN-6
La Clavijo—*summit* CA-9
Laclede—*locale* KS-7
Laclede—*mine* UT-8
**Laclede**—*pop pl* ID-8
**La Clede**—*pop pl* IL-6
**Laclede**—*pop pl* MO-7
Laclede Cem—*cemetery* KS-7
Laclede Cem—*cemetery* NE-7
**Laclede County**—*pop pl* MO-7
Laclede County Camp—*locale* MO-7
Laclede County Jail—*hist pl* MO-7
*Laclede Creek* WY-8
Laclede Park—*park* MO-7
Laclede (RR name for La Clede)—*other* IL-6
Laclede Sch—*school* MO-7
Laclede's Landing—*hist pl* MO-7
LaClede Stage Station—*locale* WY-8
Laclede Station Ruin—*hist pl* WY-8
**La Clede (Township of)**—*pop pl* IL-6
*Lac Leven Lakes* CA-9
La Clocha (Site)—*locale* TX-5
Lac Long—*stream* LA-4
Lac Louette—*lake* IL-6
*Lac Masse* MS-4
*Lac Niquisipique* NH-1
La Cochera Windmill—*locale* TX-5
Lacock Run—*stream* PA-2
Lacock Sch—*school* PA-2
Lacock Spring—*spring* PA-2
La Colcha Windmill—*locale* TX-5
La Colectiva Tabacalera—*hist pl* PR-3
La Colima Sch—*school* CA-9
La Colina JHS—*school* CA-9
La Colorado Mine—*mine* CA-9
**Lacoma**—*pop pl* TX-5
**Lacoma**—*pop pl* WV-2
Lacoma, Lake—*lake* NY-2
La Coma Ranch—*locale* (2) TX-5
*Lacomas Creek* WA-9
La Coma Tallac—*summit* CA-9
La Coma Windmill—*locale* (2) TX-5
**Lacomb**—*pop pl* OR-9
Lacomb Bay—*bay* MI-6
Lacomb Cem—*cemetery* OR-9
**Lacombe**—*pop pl* LA-4
Lacombe, Bayou—*stream* LA-4
Lacombe Bayou—*stream* LA-4
Lacomb Irrigation Canal—*canal* OR-9
Lacomb Siding—*locale* MT-8
*Lacompton* KS-7
Lacon—*locale* KY-4
**Lacon**—*pop pl* AL-4
**Lacon**—*pop pl* IL-6
**Lacona**—*pop pl* IA-7
**Lacona**—*pop pl* NY-2
Lacona Clock Tower—*hist pl* NY-2
La Concepcion Ranch—*locale* TX-5
**La Concordia**—*pop pl* PR-3
Lacon Country Club—*other* IL-6
La Conejo Windmill—*locale* TX-5
Laconia—*locale* IA-7
**Laconia**—*pop pl* AR-4
**Laconia**—*pop pl* IN-6
**Laconia**—*pop pl* NH-1
**Laconia**—*pop pl* TN-4
Laconia Circle—*area* AR-4
Laconia Circle Levee—*levee* AR-4
Laconia Crevasse—*bay* AR-4
Laconia District Court—*hist pl* NH-1
Laconia Elem Sch—*school* IN-6
Laconia Landing—*locale* AR-4
Laconia Passenger Station—*hist pl* NH-1
Laconia Post Office—*building* TN-4
Laconia State Sch—*school* NH-1
Lacon Mountain—*ridge* AL-4
Lacon Mountain Ch—*church* AL-4
*Laconner* WA-9
**La Conner**—*pop pl* WA-9
La Conner (CCD)—*cens area* WA-9
La Conner Hist Dist—*hist pl* WA-9
Lacon Post Office (historical)—*building* AL-4
**La Constancia**—*pop pl* NM-5
La Constancia Ditch—*canal* NM-5
La Constancia Lateral—*canal* NM-5
Laconte—*locale* GA-3
*La Conte Crater* OR-9
**Lacon (Township of)**—*pop pl* IL-6
**Lacoochee**—*pop pl* FL-3
Lacoochee (CCD)—*cens area* FL-3
Lacoochee Elem Sch—*school* FL-3
Lacoosa Marina—*locale* AL-4
LaCopita Dam—*dam* NM-5
La Copita Pasture—*flat* TX-5
La Copita Windmill—*locale* TX-5
La Cordillera—*island* PR-3
Lacore Lake—*lake* MI-6
La Corona—*summit* CA-9
Lacosca Creek—*stream* (2) CA-9
**La Costa**—*pop pl* CA-9
La Costa Beach—*beach* CA-9
La Costa Country Club—*other* CA-9
*La Costa Creek* CA-9
La Costa Creek—*stream* CA-9
LaCosta Test Pile South Light—*locale* FL-3
La Costa Valley—*valley* CA-9
*Lacoste* TX-5
**La Coste**—*pop pl* TX-5
Lacoste (RR name for La Coste)—*other* TX-5
**La Coste (RR name Lacoste)**—*pop pl* TX-5
Lacoste Sch—*school* LA-4
Lacota—*locale* FL-3
**Lacota**—*pop pl* MI-6
*La Coulee A Elphage* LA-4
La Counts Creek—*stream* GA-3
LaCoup Bridge—*bridge* LA-4
**Lacour**—*pop pl* LA-4
**La Cour**—*pop pl* TX-5
LaCour, Ovide, Store—*hist pl* LA-4
Lacour Cem—*cemetery* LA-4
LaCourse Pond—*reservoir* CT-1
Lacourse Pond—*reservoir* OH-6
Lacour's Fish and Ice Company Bldg—*hist pl* LA-4
Lacours Island—*island* IL-6
Lacour Spur—*locale* LA-4
LaCoute Lake—*lake* ME-1
LaCoute Point—*cape* ME-1
La Covana—*valley* PR-3
*Lac Qui Parle* MN-6
**Lac qui Parle**—*pop pl* MN-6
Lac qui Parle Cem—*cemetery* MN-6
Lac qui Parle Ch—*church* MN-6
**Lac qui Parle (County)**—*pop pl* MN-6
Lac qui Parle County Courthouse—*hist pl* MN-6
Lac qui Parle Dam—*dam* MN-6
*Lac qui Parle Lake* MN-6
Lac qui Parle Mission Park—*park* MN-6
Lac qui Parle Mission Site—*hist pl* MN-6
Lac qui Parle Park—*park* MN-6
*Lac qui Parle Reservoir* MN-6
Lac qui Parle River—*stream* MN-6
Lac Qui Parle State Wildlife Mngmt Area—*park* MN-6
Lac qui Parle (Township of)—*civ div* MN-6
*La Creek* SD-7
LaCreek (historical)—*locale* SD-7
Lacreek Natl Wildlife Ref—*park* SD-7
La Creole JHS—*school* OR-9
*La Creole River* OR-9
**LaCrescent**—*pop pl* MN-6
**La Crescent**—*pop pl* MN-6
**La Crescenta**—*pop pl* CA-9
La Crescenta-Montrose—*CDP* CA-9
La Crescenta Sch—*school* CA-9
**La Crescent (Township of)**—*pop pl* MN-6
**La Cresta**—*pop pl* (2) CA-9
**La Cresta Park Subdivision**—*pop pl* UT-8
**La Crew**—*pop pl* IA-7
La Cristianita Historic Site—*park* CA-9
**La Croft**—*pop pl* OH-6
Lacroix, Bayou—*stream* MS-4
Lacroix Bay—*gut* LA-4
Lacroix Creek—*stream* LA-4
La Croix Depot—*locale* ME-1
LaCroix Lake—*lake* MN-6
La Croix Sch—*school* MN-6
La Crone Playground—*park* MI-6
*Lacross* KS-7
*LaCross* MS-4
*LaCrosse* IN-6
*La Crosse* MO-7
*Lacrosse* WA-9
*Lacrosse* WI-6
La Crosse—*locale* GA-3
La Crosse—*locale* IL-6
**LaCrosse**—*pop pl* AR-4
**La Crosse**—*pop pl* FL-3
**LaCrosse**—*pop pl* FL-3
**La Crosse**—*pop pl* IN-6
**La Crosse**—*pop pl* KS-7
**La Crosse**—*pop pl* VA-3
**La Crosse**—*pop pl* WA-9
**La Crosse**—*pop pl* WI-6
LaCrosse, Lake—*lake* WA-9
LaCrosse, Mount—*summit* WA-9
La Crosse-Brookdale Township—*civil* KS-7
La Crosse (CCD)—*cens area* WA-9
La Crosse Cem—*cemetery* KS-7
La Crosse Cem—*cemetery* VA-3
**La Crosse (corporate and RR name for Lacrosse)**—*pop pl* WA-9
Lacrosse (corporate and RR name La Crosse)—*post sta* WA-9
**La Crosse (County)**—*pop pl* WI-6
La Crosse County Sch of Agriculture and Domestic Economy—*hist pl* WI-6
La Crosse Elementary and HS—*school* IN-6
Lacrosse Grange—*locale* WA-9
La Crosse Hosp—*hospital* WI-6
LaCrosse HS—*school* KS-7
LaCrosse Lake—*lake* MI-6
LaCrosse Lookout Tower—*tower* FL-3
La Crosse (Magisterial District)—*fmr MCD* VA-3
Lacrosse Muni Airp—*airport* WA-9
La Crosse Municipal Airp—*airport* WI-6
La Crosse Post Office (historical)—*building* MO-7
La Crosse Ridge—*ridge* WI-6
La Crosse River—*stream* WI-6
Lacrosse (Township of)—*fmr MCD* AR-4
**La Crosse (Township of)**—*pop pl* MN-6
LaCrosse Valley Sch—*school* WI-6
La Cross Sch—*school* NE-7
La Cruz Ditch—*canal* NM-5
La Cruz Peak—*summit* NM-5
*La Cruz Resaca* TX-5
La Cruz Resaca—*lake* TX-5
La Cruz Rock—*island* CA-9
Lacs Des Atlemands Gas Field—*oilfield* LA-4
*Lac Superieur* MN-6
Lac tete de Bouef—*lake* LA-4
Lactona Corporation Airp—*airport* PA-2
La Cuba—*summit* CA-9
La Cuchilla—*area* NM-5
La Cuchilla—*ridge* NM-5
La Cuchilla—*ridge* PR-3
La Cuchilla de la Monjonera—*cliff* NM-5
La Cuerva Park—*flat* NM-5
**La Cuesta**—*pop pl* NM-5
**La Cuesta**—*pop pl* PR-3
La Cuesta—*summit* CA-9
**La Cuestecita**—*pop pl* NM-5
La Cueva—*locale* NM-5
**La Cueva**—*pop pl* NM-5
La Cueva Camp—*locale* NM-5
La Cueva Campground—*locale* NM-5
La Cueva Canal—*canal* NM-5
La Cueva Canyon—*valley* (4) NM-5
La Cueva Cem—*cemetery* NM-5
La Cueva Guard Station—*locale* NM-5
La Cueva Hist Dist—*hist pl* NM-5
La Cueva Lake—*lake* (2) NM-5
La Cueva Peak—*summit* NM-5
La Cueva Rec Area—*locale* NM-5
La Cueva Ridge—*ridge* NM-5
La Cueva Spring—*spring* NM-5
La Cueva Tank—*reservoir* NM-5
La Cueva Windmill—*locale* NM-5
La Cuidad de Mexico Grocery—*hist pl* AZ-5
**La Cumbre**—*pop pl* PR-3
La Cumbre—*summit* CA-9
La Cumbre JHS—*school* CA-9
La Cumbre Peak—*summit* CA-9
La Cuna—*other* CA-9
Lacuna Glacier—*glacier* AK-9
La Curena—*summit* PR-3
Lacure Sch—*school* MI-6
*Lacy* AL-4
Lacy—*locale* CO-8
Lacy—*locale* SD-7
**Lacy**—*pop pl* IN-6
**Lacy**—*pop pl* KS-7
**Lacy**—*pop pl* TN-4
**Lacy**—*pop pl* TX-5
Lacy Airp—*airport* AZ-5
*Lacy Branch* TN-4
Lacy Branch—*stream* IN-6
Lacy Branch—*stream* (2) KY-4
Lacy Branch—*stream* LA-4
Lacy Branch—*stream* TN-4
Lacy Branch—*stream* VA-3
Lacy Buke Furnace (historical)—*locale* AL-4
Lacy Cem—*cemetery* IA-7
Lacy Cem—*cemetery* KY-4
Lacy Cem—*cemetery* MS-4
Lacy Cem—*cemetery* (2) TN-4
Lacy Cem—*cemetery* (2) TX-5
Lacy Cem—*cemetery* WV-2
Lacy Ch—*church* AL-4
**Lacy Corners**—*pop pl* NY-2
Lacy Cove—*bay* AK-9
Lacy Creek—*stream* GA-3
Lacy Creek—*stream* ID-8
Lacy Creek—*stream* (2) KY-4
Lacy Creek—*stream* MS-4
Lacy Creek—*stream* MT-8
Lacy Creek—*stream* NY-2
Lacy Creek—*stream* OK-5
Lacy Creek—*stream* TN-4
Lacy Creek—*stream* (3) TX-5
Lacy Creek Ch—*church* KY-4
Lacy Drain—*stream* IN-6
Lacy Draw—*valley* (2) TX-5
*Lacy Fork* TX-5
Lacy Fork—*stream* KY-4
Lacy Fork—*stream* TX-5
*Lacy Fork Cedar Creek* TX-5
*Lacygne* KS-7
**La Cygne**—*pop pl* KS-7
La Cygne Corner—*locale* KS-7
*La Cygne Lake* KS-7
La Cygnes Lake—*reservoir* KS-7
La Cygne State Fishing Lake and Wildlife Area—*park* KS-7
**Lacy Hill**—*pop pl* AR-4
Lacy Hill—*summit* CA-9
Lacy (historical)—*locale* AL-4
**Lacy (historical)**—*pop pl* OR-9
Lacy Hollow—*valley* AL-4
Lacy Hollow—*valley* TN-4
Lacy Islands—*island* TN-4
**Lacy (Lacy Hill)**—*pop pl* AR-4
Lacy Lake—*lake* MI-6
Lacy Lake—*reservoir* OK-5
**Lacy-Lakeview**—*pop pl* TX-5
Lacy Lookout Tower—*locale* MS-4
**Lacymark**—*pop pl* FL-3
*Lacy Memorial Church* TN-4
Lacy-Mercedes Gas Field—*oilfield* TX-5
Lacy Millpond—*lake* VA-3
Lacy Mtn—*summit* AR-4
Lacy Mtn—*summit* WY-8
Lacy Oil Seep—*spring* WA-9
Lacy Park—*park* (2) CA-9
Lacy Place—*locale* NM-5
Lacy Reservation—*park* AL-4
*Lacy Run* PA-2
Lacy Run—*stream* MD-2
Lacy Sch—*school* KY-4
Lacy Sch—*school* MO-7
Lacy Sch—*school* NC-3
Lacy Sch—*school* TX-5
*Lacy's Creek* TX-5
Lacys Creek—*stream* NC-3
Lacy Security Facility—*other* CA-9
Lacys Ford (historical)—*locale* AL-4
*Lacys Fork* TX-5
*Lacys Fork of Cedar Creek* TX-5
Lacy Spring—*spring* TN-4
*Lacys Spring* AL-4
**Lacy Subdivision**—*pop pl* MS-4
Lacy Tank—*reservoir* NM-5
Lacy Trap Branch—*stream* TN-4
Lacy Trap Ridge—*ridge* TN-4
Lacy-Van Vleet House—*hist pl* NY-2
Lacyville—*locale* MO-7
Lacyville—*locale* TX-5
Lacy Well—*well* NM-5
Lacy Windmill—*locale* NM-5
Lad, Lake—*reservoir* TN-4
Lada—*area* GU-9
Ladae—*summit* GU-9
Ladai—*area* GU-9
Ladanan Creek—*stream* AK-9
Lad Cem—*cemetery* MS-4
Ladd—*locale* AK-9
Ladd—*locale* OR-9
**Ladd**—*pop pl* AR-4
**Ladd**—*pop pl* IL-6
**Ladd**—*pop pl* OH-6
**Ladd**—*pop pl* TX-5
**Ladd**—*pop pl* VA-3
Ladd Acres Sch—*school* OR-9
Ladd Arboretum—*park* IL-6
Ladd Arroyo—*stream* NM-5
Ladd Bay—*bay* VT-1
Ladd Branch—*stream* AR-4
Ladd Branch—*stream* NC-3
Ladd Brook—*stream* ME-1
Ladd Brook—*stream* VT-1
Ladd Canal—*canal* AR-4
Ladd Canyon—*valley* CA-9
Ladd Canyon—*valley* NV-8
Ladd Canyon—*valley* OR-9
Ladd Canyon Pond—*lake* OR-9
Ladd Canyon Spring—*spring* CA-9
Ladd Carriage House—*hist pl* OR-9
*Ladd Cem* TN-4
Ladd Cem—*cemetery* KS-7
Ladd Cem—*cemetery* (2) KY-4
Ladd Cem—*cemetery* ME-1
Ladd Cem—*cemetery* MO-7
Ladd Cem—*cemetery* NH-1
Ladd Cem—*cemetery* NY-2
Ladd Cem—*cemetery* OH-6
Ladd Cem—*cemetery* (6) TN-4
Ladd Center Sch—*school* MI-6
Ladd Chapel—*church* MO-7
*Ladd Cove* TN-4
Ladd Cove—*valley* TN-4
*Ladd Creek* OR-9
Ladd Creek—*stream* AL-4
Ladd Creek—*stream* CA-9
Ladd Creek—*stream* (2) OR-9
Ladd Creek—*stream* TN-4
Ladd Creek—*stream* WI-6
Ladd Creek Campground—*park* OR-9
Ladd Creek Lookout Tower—*locale* WI-6
Ladd Creek Pickup Ditch—*canal* OR-9
Ladden Branch—*stream* MO-7
Ladder Butte—*summit* CA-9
*Ladder Canyon* CO-8
Ladder Canyon—*valley* CO-8
Ladder Canyon—*valley* ID-8
Ladder Canyon—*valley* UT-8
Ladder Cave—*cave* AL-4
*Ladder Creek* CO-8
*Ladder Creek* KS-7
Ladder Creek—*stream* (2) CO-8
Ladder Creek—*stream* (3) ID-8
Ladder Creek—*stream* KS-7
Ladder Creek—*stream* WA-9
*Ladder Creek Canyon* CO-8
Ladder Creek Oil Field—*oilfield* CO-8
Ladder Draw—*valley* NM-5
Ladder Hill—*summit* NH-1
Ladder Island—*island* AK-9
Ladder Lake—*lake* CA-9
Ladder Mtn—*summit* NY-2
Ladder Ranch—*locale* NM-5
Ladder Ridge—*ridge* CA-9
Ladder Rock—*pillar* CA-9
Ladder Rsvr—*reservoir* AZ-5
Ladders Park—*park* SD-7
*Ladder Spring* WY-8
Ladder Tank—*reservoir* (2) AZ-5
Ladder Tank—*reservoir* NM-5
Ladder Tank—*reservoir* TX-5
Ladder Trail—*trail* TN-4
Ladder Windmill—*locale* TX-5
**Ladd Estates**—*pop pl* TN-4
Ladd Farmhouse—*hist pl* NY-2
Ladd Field—*hist pl* AK-9
Ladd-Gilman House—*hist pl* NH-1
Ladd Glacier—*glacier* OR-9
**Ladd Hill**—*pop pl* OR-9
Ladd Hill—*summit* CT-1
Ladd Hill—*summit* IN-6
Ladd Hill—*summit* ME-1
Laddie Creek—*stream* WA-9
Laddie Creek—*stream* WY-8
Laddie Lake—*lake* MN-6
Laddie Park—*flat* CO-8
Laddies Cove—*basin* CA-9
**Laddie Village**—*pop pl* TN-4
Laddis Pit—*cave* AL-4
*Ladd Junction* IL-6
Ladd Lake—*lake* NM-5
Ladd Lake—*lake* OH-6
Ladd Lookout—*locale* WA-9
Ladd Marsh—*swamp* OR-9
Ladd Marsh Game Mngmt Area—*park* OR-9
Ladd-Mattoon House—*hist pl* OH-6
Ladd Memorial Cem—*cemetery* AR-4
*Ladd Memorial Stadium* AL-4
Ladd Mine—*mine* (2) CA-9
Ladd Mine—*mine* NV-8
Ladd Mtn—*summit* NV-8
Ladd Mtn—*summit* NH-1
Ladd Mtn—*summit* WA-9
Laddon Ch—*church* AL-4
Laddon Creek—*stream* AL-4
**Laddonia**—*pop pl* MO-7
Ladd Peak—*summit* WY-8
Ladd Point—*cape* VT-1
Ladd Pond—*lake* ME-1
Ladd Ridge—*ridge* OH-6
Ladds—*locale* GA-3
**Ladds**—*pop pl* TN-4
Ladd's Addition Hist Dist—*hist pl* OR-9
Ladds Branch—*stream* MS-4
Ladds Branch—*stream* NC-3
Laddsburg—*locale* PA-2
Ladd's Castle—*hist pl* NJ-2
*Ladds Cave* TN-4
Ladds Cem—*cemetery* TN-4
Ladd Sch—*school* CA-9
Ladd Sch—*school* MI-6
Ladd Sch—*school* MO-7
Ladd Sch—*school* VA-3
Ladd Sch—*school* WI-6
Ladd Sch No 2—*school* AR-4
Ladds Circle—*locale* OR-9
*Ladds Cove* TN-4
Ladds Creek—*stream* AR-4
Ladds Creek—*stream* CA-9
Ladds Creek—*stream* ID-8
Ladds Creek—*stream* PA-2
Ladds Creek—*stream* WA-9
Ladds Point—*cape* TN-4
Ladd Springs Ch—*church* TN-4
*Ladd Springs Ch of God* TN-4
Ladds Shoals—*bar* TN-4
Ladd Stadium—*other* AL-4
Ladd's Tavern—*hist pl* OH-6
Ladd Street Cem—*cemetery* NH-1
Ladd Street Ch—*church* GA-3
Ladd Tank—*reservoir* AZ-5
**Ladd Township**—*pop pl* ND-7
*Laded* AL-4
**La Delfina**—*pop pl* PR-3
LaDelle—*locale* SD-7
**Ladelle**—*pop pl* AR-4
LaDelle (historical)—*locale* SD-7
LaDelle Township (historical)—*civil* SD-7
Ladell (historical)—*locale* AL-4
**La Delta**—*pop pl* CA-9
Ladely Ranch—*locale* NE-7
**Lademisang**—*pop pl* PW-9
Laden—*locale* KY-4
Ladendorf Park—*park* IL-6
**Ladentown**—*pop pl* NY-2
Ladentown Mtn—*summit* NY-2
*Ladeoan Lasso* MH-9
Ladera—*other* GU-9
**Ladera**—*pop pl* CA-9
Ladera del Norte Sch—*school* NM-5
Ladera Heights—*CDP* CA-9
*Laderan Achugau* MH-9
*Laderan Adelug* MH-9
*Laderan As Mahalang* MH-9
*Laderan Banadero* MH-9
*Laderan Carolinas San Hilo* MH-9
*Laderan Carolinas San Papa* MH-9
*Laderan Chiguet* MH-9
*Laderan Dago* MH-9
*Laderan Gonna* MH-9
*Laderan Hagman* MH-9
*Laderan I Agag* MH-9
*Laderan I Daog* MH-9
*Laderan I Madog* MH-9
*Laderan kalaberan Kanat* MH-9
*Laderan Kalaberan Katan* MH-9
*Laderan Kalaberan Lichen* MH-9
*Laderan Lagua* MH-9
*Laderan Lasso* MH-9
*Laderan Laulau* MH-9
*Laderan Machegit* MH-9
*Laderan Magpi* MH-9
*Laderan Obyan* MH-9
*Laderan Papau* MH-9
*Laderan Papua* MH-9
*Laderan Tagpochau* MH-9
*Laderan Takpochau* MH-9
*Laderan Tanke* MH-9
*Laderan Unai Lagua* MH-9
Ladera Palma Sch—*school* CA-9
Ladera Park—*park* CA-9
Ladera Sch—*school* (2) CA-9
Ladera Vista JHS—*school* CA-9
*Laderon Dago* MH-9
Lader Point—*cape* NY-2
Lade Run—*stream* WV-2
Ladessa Cem—*cemetery* OK-5
Ladeux Meadow—*flat* CA-9
Ladew Topiary Gardens and House—*hist pl* MD-2
La Dicha Well—*well* TX-5
Ladies Acad (historical)—*school* TN-4
*Ladies Bluff* TN-4
Ladies Branch—*stream* MO-7
**Ladiesburg**—*pop pl* MD-2
*Ladies Canyon* CA-9
Ladies Canyon—*valley* (2) CA-9
Ladies Cem—*cemetery* GA-3
Ladies Chapel—*church* (2) KY-4
Ladies Creek—*stream* OR-9
Ladies Delight Hill—*summit* ME-1
Ladies Evergreen Cem—*cemetery* NE-7
Ladies Island—*island* SC-3
Ladies Island Ch—*church* SC-3
Ladies Library Association Bldg—*hist pl* MI-6
Ladies' Literary Club—*hist pl* MI-6
Ladies' Literary Club Bldg—*hist pl* MI-6
Ladies Literary Club Clubhouse—*hist pl* UT-8
Ladies of the Maccabees Bldg—*hist pl* MI-6
Ladies Pass—*gap* TX-5
Ladies Pass—*gap* WA-9
Ladies Spring—*spring* WA-9
Ladieu Hill—*summit* NH-1
**Ladiga**—*pop pl* AL-4
Ladiga Cem—*cemetery* AL-4
Ladiga Creek—*stream* AL-4
*Ladiga Mountain* AL-4
Ladiga Sch (historical)—*school* AL-4
Ladig Ditch—*canal* IN-6
Ladins Landing—*locale* TN-4
Ladio, Arroyo el—*valley* TX-5
La Divina Providencia, Episcopal Church Sch—*school* FL-3
Lad Lake—*reservoir* TN-4
Lad Lake Dam—*dam* TN-4
Ladle, The—*island* ME-1
Ladless Hill—*hist pl* KY-4
Ladleton—*locale* NY-2
*Ladley Run* PA-2
*Ladley Run* WV-2
*Ladmisang* PW-9
Ladner—*locale* SD-7
*Ladner Cem* MS-4
Ladner Cem—*cemetery* MI-6
Ladner Cem—*cemetery* (3) MS-4
Ladner Cem—*cemetery* SD-7
Ladner Creek—*stream* MI-6
Ladner Lake Dam—*dam* MS-4
Ladner Sch—*school* ME-1
Ladnier Hill—*summit* MS-4
Lad 'n' Lass Sch—*school* FL-3
Lado, Rio—*stream* CO-8
*Ladoc Tasis* MH-9
*Ladoga* AL-4
Ladoga—*locale* IA-7
Ladoga—*locale* MI-6
Ladoga—*locale* ND-7
**Ladoga**—*pop pl* IN-6
**Ladoga**—*pop pl* WI-6
Ladoga Cem—*cemetery* IA-7
Ladoga Rest Park—*park* IN-6
*Ladogar Flats* WY-8
Lado Island—*island* MP-9
**La Dolores**—*pop pl* PR-3
Ladona—*uninc pl* PA-2
*Ladonia* FL-3
Ladonia—*locale* NC-3
**Ladonia**—*pop pl* AL-4
**Ladonia**—*pop pl* TX-5
Ladonia Baptist Ch—*church* AL-4
Ladonia (CCD)—*cens area* TX-5
Ladonia (RR Name For Holder)—*other* FL-3
*Ladonia Station* FL-3
**LaDonna Mesa Subdivision**—*pop pl* UT-8
La Doo Creek—*stream* CA-9
**Ladora**—*pop pl* CO-8
**Ladora**—*pop pl* IA-7
Ladora Cem—*cemetery* IA-7
*Ladore Canyon* CO-8
Ladore Cem—*cemetery* KS-7
Ladore Creek—*stream* OR-9
Ladore (historical)—*locale* KS-7
**La Dore Subdivision**—*pop pl* UT-8
**Ladore Township**—*pop pl* KS-7
Ladow—*locale* WA-9
Ladow Butte—*summit* WA-9
Ladow Millpond—*reservoir* NJ-2
Ladow Yeshiva Sch—*school* FL-3
LA Draw—*valley* NM-5
*Ladron Canyon* NM-5
*Ladrone Gulch* NM-5
*Ladrone Islands* MH-9
Ladrones, Canada De Los —*valley* CA-9
*Ladrones Islands* MH-9
Ladrones Islands—*area* AK-9
Ladrones Tank—*reservoir* NM-5
Ladrone Tank—*reservoir* AZ-5
Ladron Gulch—*valley* NM-5
Ladron Peak—*summit* NM-5
Ladron Spring—*spring* AZ-5
**Ladson**—*pop pl* GA-3
**Ladson**—*pop pl* SC-3
La Ducet Creek—*stream* MT-8
La Duc Lake—*lake* MN-6
**La Due**—*pop pl* MO-7
**Ladue**—*pop pl* MO-7
La Due Cem—*cemetery* WI-6
Ladue Chapel—*church* MO-7

Lagoda Elem Sch—*school* IN-6
Lago de Cidra—*reservoir* PR-3
Lago de Guajataco—*reservoir* PR-3
Lago del Bosque—*reservoir* TX-5
Lago de Matrullas—*reservoir* PR-3
*Lago de San Jose* TX-5
Lago Dos Bocas—*reservoir* PR-3
Lago El Guineo—*reservoir* PR-3
Lago Garzas—*reservoir* PR-3
Lago Gely—*lake* PR-3
Lago Giles—*lake* PR-3
Lago Guayabal—*reservoir* PR-3
Lago Guayo—*reservoir* PR-3
Lago Jordan—*reservoir* PR-3
Lagol—*locale* CA-9
Lago La Torre—*reservoir* PR-3
La Goleta—*civil* CA-9
Lago Lindo—*lake* FL-3
Lago Loiza—*reservoir* PR-3
Lago Lucchetti—*reservoir* PR-3
Lagoma Bay—*bay* AK-9
Lago Maggiore—*lake* FL-3
Lago Managua—*lake* PR-3
Lagomarsino Canyon—*valley* NV-8
Lagomarsino Petroglyph Site—*hist pl* NV-8
Lago Melania—*reservoir* PR-3
Lago Minore—*lake* FL-3
Lago Moline—*reservoir* PR-3
Lago Monaco—*lake* FL-3
*Lagona* CA-9
*Lagonda* OH-6
*La Gonda* PA-2
Lagonda—*lake* PA-2
Lagonda—*locale* LA-4
**Lagonda**—*pop pl* MO-7
**La Gonda**—*pop pl* PA-2
Lagonda, Lake—*lake* FL-3
Lagonda Club Bldg—*hist pl* OH-6
Lagonda Field—*park* OH-6
*Lagonda Plantation* LA-4
Lagonda (RR name for Bayou Vista)—*other* LA-4
Lagonda Sch—*school* OH-6
Lagonegro Sch—*school* NY-2
Lagoni Lake—*lake* MT-8
Lago Numero Five—*reservoir* PR-3
Lago Numero Four—*reservoir* PR-3
Lago Numero One—*reservoir* PR-3
Lago Numero Three—*reservoir* PR-3
Lago Numero Two—*reservoir* PR-3
**La Gonzalez**—*pop pl* (2) PR-3
Lagoo—*park* UT-8
Lagoo Creek—*stream* WI-6
Lagoon—*lake* CA-9
Lagoon—*locale* AK-9
**Lagoon**—*pop pl* NC-3
Lagoon—*valley* UT-8
*Lagoon, The* CT-1
*Lagoon, The* OR-9
Lagoon, The—*bay* AK-9
Lagoon, The—*bay* FL-3
Lagoon, The—*bay* MS-4
Lagoon, The—*bay* NJ-2
Lagoon, The—*bay* NY-2
Lagoon, The—*bay* NC-3
Lagoon, The—*bend* CA-9
Lagoon, The—*harbor* NY-2
Lagoon, The—*lake* CA-9
Lagoon, The—*lake* FL-3
Lagoon, The—*lake* GA-3
Lagoon, The—*lake* MO-7
Lagoon, The—*lake* TX-5
Lagoon, The—*lake* (2) WA-9
Lagoon, The—*stream* AZ-5
Lagoon, The—*stream* TN-4
Lagoon, The—*swamp* IN-6
Lagoon A—*reservoir* NC-3
*Lagoona Beach* MI-6
**Lagoona Beach**—*pop pl* MN-6
Lagoon A Dam—*dam* NC-3
*Lagoona Mayax* FL-3
*Lagoona Mayux* FL-3
**Lagoon Beach**—*pop pl* MI-6
Lagoon Brady—*lake* LA-4
Lagoon Branch—*stream* (2) TN-4
Lagoon Brook—*stream* ME-1
Lagoon Camp—*locale* OR-9
Lagoon Canyon—*valley* UT-8
Lagoon Ch—*church* AL-4
Lagoon Creek—*gut* SC-3
Lagoon Creek—*stream* (2) AK-9
Lagoon Creek—*stream* CA-9
Lagoon Creek—*stream* IN-6
Lagoon Creek—*stream* NC-3
Lagoon Creek—*stream* OK-5
Lagoon Creek—*stream* TN-4
Lagoon D—*reservoir* NC-3
Lagoon D Dam—*dam* NC-3
*Lagoon Fork* AZ-5
Lagoon Giraud—*lake* LA-4
**Lagoon Heights**—*pop pl* MA-1
Lagoon Island—*island* AK-9
*Lagoon Lake* CO-8
Lagoon Lake—*lake* (2) CA-9
Lagoon Lake—*lake* FL-3
Lagoon Lake—*lake* MT-8
*Lagoon Lake, The* FL-3
Lagoon Maxent—*gut* LA-4
*Lagoon Palo Verde* CA-9
Lagoon Park—*park* (2) MN-6
Lagoon Park—*post sta* AL-4
Lagoon Point—*cape* (2) AK-9
Lagoon Point—*cape* WA-9
Lagoon Point—*cape* VI-3
**Lagoon Point**—*pop pl* WA-9
Lagoon Pond—*lake* MA-1
*Lagoons, The* OR-9
Lagoon Tank—*reservoir* AZ-5
Lagoon Trail—*trail* CA-9
Lagoon Trail—*trail* VA-3
Lagoon Valley—*valley* CA-9
Lago Patillas—*reservoir* PR-3
Lago Pellejas—*reservoir* PR-3
Lago Poncena—*lake* PR-3
La Gorce, Mount—*summit* AK-9
La Gorce Arch—*arch* UT-8
La Gorce Country Club—*locale* FL-3
LaGorce Glacier—*glacier* AK-9
La Gorce Island—*island* FL-3
La Gorce Island—*uninc pl* FL-3
*La Gorda* LA-4
Lagorin Slough—*lake* ND-7
**Lagos del Sol (subdivision)**—*pop pl* AL-4
Lagoshen Ch—*church* TN-4
Lago Spring—*spring* AS-9
La Gotera—*locale* NM-5
La Gotera Well—*well* NM-5
**Lago Vista**—*pop pl* TX-5
Lago Vista Alegre—*lake* PR-3
**Lago Vista Circle Subdivision**—*pop pl* UT-8
Lago Vista Sch—*school* TX-5
Lago Vivi—*reservoir* PR-3
Lagow Cem—*cemetery* IL-6
LaGrace Cem—*cemetery* SD-7
LaGrace (historical)—*locale* SD-7
LaGrace Township—*civil* SD-7
La Graisse, Lake—*lake* LA-4
*Lagrallal Lake* CO-8
La Granada Mtn—*summit* CA-9
*La Grand* KS-7
La Granda Sch—*school* CA-9
**La Grande**—*pop pl* OR-9
**La Grande**—*pop pl* WA-9
**LaGrande**—*pop pl* WA-9
La Grande Aqueduct—*canal* OR-9
La Grande (CCD)—*cens area* OR-9
La Grande Country Club—*other* OR-9
LA Grande Dam—*dam* OR-9
LaGrande Dam—*dam* WA-9
La-Grande Island—*island* ME-1
La Grande Municipal Airp—*airport* OR-9
La Grande Neighborhood Club—*hist pl* OR-9
**La Grande Princesse**—*pop pl* VI-3
La Grande Princesse Sch—*hist pl* VI-3
La Grande Rsvr—*reservoir* OR-9
LaGrande Rsvr—*reservoir* WA-9
La Grande Watershed—*other* OR-9
Lagrand Hollow—*valley* TX-5
LaGrand State Wildlife Mngmt Area—*park* MN-6
**La Grand (Township of)**—*pop pl* MN-6
*La Grange* IN-6
*La Grange* KS-7
*La Grange* ME-1
La Grange—*hist pl* DE-2
La Grange—*hist pl* MD-2
LaGrange—*hist pl* MD-2
LaGrange—*hist pl* NC-3
La Grange—*locale* AL-4
Lagrange—*locale* NY-2
LaGrange—*locale* OH-6
La Grange—*locale* VA-3
Lagrange—*locale* VA-3
**La Grange**—*pop pl* AR-4
**LaGrange**—*pop pl* AR-4
**La Grange**—*pop pl* CA-9
**La Grange**—*pop pl* FL-3
**La Grange**—*pop pl* GA-3
**La Grange**—*pop pl* (2) IL-6
**Lagrange**—*pop pl* IN-6
**La Grange**—*pop pl* KY-4
**Lagrange**—*pop pl* ME-1
**La Grange**—*pop pl* MI-6
**La Grange**—*pop pl* MO-7
**Lagrange**—*pop pl* NY-2
**La Grange**—*pop pl* NC-3
**La Grange**—*pop pl* OH-6
**Lagrange**—*pop pl* OH-6
**Lagrange**—*pop pl* PA-2
**LaGrange**—*pop pl* TN-4
**La Grange**—*pop pl* TN-4
**La Grange**—*pop pl* TX-5
**La Grange**—*pop pl* WI-6
**LaGrange**—*pop pl* WY-8
**La Grange**—*pop pl* VI-3
La Grange, Lake—*reservoir* WI-6
LaGrange Bayou—*bay* FL-3
La Grange (CCD)—*cens area* GA-3
La Grange (CCD)—*cens area* KY-4
La Grange (CCD)—*cens area* TX-5
*Lagrange Cem* TN-4
LaGrange Cem—*cemetery* AL-4
LaGrange Cem—*cemetery* IN-6
La Grange Cem—*cemetery* MS-4
LaGrange Cem—*cemetery* NY-2
LaGrange Cem—*cemetery* TN-4
LaGrange Cem—*cemetery* WI-6
LaGrange Cem—*cemetery* WY-8
LaGrange Ch—*church* AL-4
LaGrange Ch—*church* MS-4
La Grange Ch—*church* MS-4
LaGrange Ch—*church* OH-6
La Grange Coll—*school* GA-3
LaGrange College Monument—*other* AL-4
La Grange Coll (historical)—*school* AL-4
Lagrange Community Hall—*building* KS-7
La Grange Country Club—*other* IL-6
**Lagrange County**—*pop pl* IN-6
La Grange County Courthouse—*hist pl* IN-6
LaGrange Creek—*stream* MT-8
Lagrange Creek—*stream* VA-3
LaGrange Crevasse—*lake* MS-4
La Grange Dam—*dam* CA-9
La Grange Ditch—*canal* CA-9
La Grange Elem Sch—*school* NC-3
La Grange Elem Sch—*school* TN-4
LaGrange Furnace (historical)—*locale* TN-4
LaGrange Furnace (40SW214)—*hist pl* TN-4
**La Grange Highlands**—*pop pl* IL-6
La Grange Hist Dist—*hist pl* TN-4
La Grange (historical)—*locale* AL-4
Lagrange (historical)—*locale* KS-7
La Grange (historical)—*locale* MS-4
LaGrange (historical)—*locale* SD-7
La Grange HS—*school* LA-4
La Grange Island—*island* (2) IL-6
La Grange Island—*island* PA-2
La Grange JHS—*school* LA-4
*La Grange (Lagrange)* IN-6
La Grange Lake—*lake* MI-6
LaGrange Landing (historical)—*locale* TN-4
La Grange Locks—*dam* IL-6
La Grange Magnetic Station—*other* TX-5
La Grange Methodist Ch—*church* TN-4
*La Grange Military Academy* AL-4
La Grange Mine—*mine* CA-9
LaGrange Mtn—*summit* AL-4
Lagrange Oil Field—*oilfield* MS-4
**La Grange Park**—*pop pl* IL-6
**La Grange Park**—*pop pl* MI-6
**La Grange Park Subdivision**—*pop pl* UT-8
La Grange Park Woods—*woods* IL-6
*La Grange P.O.* AL-4
*La Grange Point* FL-3
**La Grange Point**—*pop pl* FL-3
*La Grange Polytechnic Institute* AL-4
*Lagrange Post Office* TN-4
La Grange Post Office—*building* TN-4
LaGrange Presbyterian Church—*hist pl* NC-3
*La Grange Road* IL-6
La Grange Rock Shelter—*hist pl* AL-4
Lagrange (RR Name For La Grange)—*other* FL-3
**La Grange (RR name Lagrange)**—*pop pl* FL-3
La Grange Rsvr—*reservoir* CA-9
*La Grange Sch* PA-2
La Grange Sch—*school* AL-4
La Grange Sch—*school* CO-8
La Grange Sch—*school* IL-6
LaGrange Sch—*school* IA-7
La Grange Sch—*school* KS-7
LaGrange Sch—*school* MS-4
La Grange Sch—*school* MO-7
LaGrange Sch—*school* NY-2
Lagrange Sch—*school* OH-6
Lagrange Sch—*school* PA-2
LaGrange Terrace—*hist pl* NY-2
La Grange Towhead—*island* MS-4
La Grange Town Hall—*building* NC-3
**Lagrange (Town of)**—*pop pl* ME-1
**La Grange (Town of)**—*pop pl* NY-2
**La Grange (Town of)**—*pop pl* (2) WI-6
La Grange Township—*fmr MCD* IA-7
La Grange (Township of)—*fmr MCD* AR-4
**Lagrange (Township of)**—*pop pl* IL-6
**La Grange (Township of)**—*pop pl* MI-6
**Lagrange (Township of)**—*pop pl* OH-6
La Grange Village Hist Dist—*hist pl* IL-6
**Lagrangeville**—*pop pl* NY-2
**Lagrangeville (La Grange)**—*pop pl* NY-2
La Grange Waterworks—*other* GA-3
La Grange West (CCD)—*cens area* TX-5
**La Granja**—*pop pl* PR-3
*La Grasse River* NY-2
La Grava Artesian Well—*well* TX-5
L A Green Dam—*dam* TN-4
L A Green Lake—*reservoir* TN-4
**Lagro**—*pop pl* IN-6
Lagro Creek—*stream* IN-6
La Grones Ch—*church* TX-5
**Lagro (Township of)**—*pop pl* IN-6
Lagroulle Creek—*stream* TX-5
La Grove Sch—*school* IL-6
Lag Rsvr—*reservoir* WY-8
*Lagrue Bayou* AR-4
La Grue Bayou—*stream* AR-4
La Grue Lake—*lake* AR-4
La Grues Lake—*swamp* AR-4
LaGrue Springs—*locale* AR-4
La Grue (Township of)—*fmr MCD* AR-4
La Grulla Artesian Well—*well* TX-5
La Grulla (CCD)—*cens area* TX-5
La Grulla Cow Camp—*locale* NM-5
**La Grulla (Grulla PO)**—*pop pl* TX-5
La Grulla Lake—*lake* CO-8
La Grulla Lake—*lake* NM-5
La Grulla Plateau—*area* NM-5
La Grulla Ranch—*locale* NM-5
La Grulla Ridge—*ridge* NM-5
La Grulla Well—*well* TX-5
Lags Landing—*airport* NJ-2
La Guaba—*locale* PR-3
*Lagua Beach* MH-9
*Lagua Cliffs* MH-9
Laguana del Gallego—*lake* NM-5
Laguan River—*stream* GU-9
*La Guarde Creek* CO-8
La Guardia Airp—*airport* NY-2
**Laguardo**—*pop pl* TN-4
**La Guardo**—*pop pl* TN-4
Laguardo HS (historical)—*school* TN-4
Laguardo Post Office (historical)—*building* TN-4
Laguardo Rec Area—*park* TN-4
Laguas River—*stream* GU-9
Lagua Tank—*reservoir* TX-5
Lague Ditch—*canal* IN-6
Laguina—*area* GU-9
**La Guinea**—*pop pl* PR-3
**La Guitarra**—*pop pl* PR-3
*Lagulus* FM-9
*Laguna* AZ-5
*Laguna* CA-9
Laguna—*civil* CA-9
Laguna—*locale* AZ-5
Laguna—*locale* TX-5
Laguna—*locale* UT-8
**Laguna**—*pop pl* AZ-5
**Laguna**—*pop pl* CA-9
**Laguna**—*pop pl* NM-5
**La Guna**—*pop pl* TX-5
Laguna—*post sta* PR-3
Laguna—*stream* CA-9
Laguna, Arroyo—*stream* CA-9
Laguna, Canada De La —*valley* CA-9
Laguna, Mount—*summit* CA-9
*Laguna, The* CA-9
Laguna Abeyta—*reservoir* NM-5
Laguna Aguas Prietas—*lake* PR-3
Laguna Alamo—*reservoir* NM-5
Laguna Algodones—*lake* PR-3
Laguna Americana—*lake* NM-5
Laguna Anaconda—*reservoir* NM-5
Laguna Anones—*lake* PR-3
Laguna Arenas—*lake* PR-3
Laguna Army Airfield—*military* AZ-5
Laguna Atascosa Natl Wildlife Ref—*park* TX-5
Laguna Atolladero—*lake* PR-3
Laguna Bandeja—*lake* NM-5
*Laguna Beach* MO-7
**Laguna Beach**—*pop pl* CA-9
**Laguna Beach**—*pop pl* FL-3
**Laguna Beach**—*pop pl* MO-7
Laguna Beach Country Club—*other* CA-9
Laguna Blanca—*lake* (3) NM-5
Laguna Blanca Sch—*school* CA-9
Laguna Blanquita—*reservoir* NM-5
Laguna Bocanasilla—*lake* PR-3
Laguna Bonita—*lake* (3) NM-5
Laguna Bonita—*reservoir* NM-5
Laguna Borregos—*reservoir* NM-5
Laguna Brillante—*lake* NM-5
*Laguna Campground* AZ-5
Laguna Campground—*locale* CA-9
Laguna Canal—*canal* CA-9
Laguna Canoneros—*reservoir* NM-5
*Laguna Canyon* AZ-5
Laguna Canyon—*valley* (3) CA-9
Laguna Cartagena—*lake* PR-3
Laguna Castillo—*lake* NM-5
Laguna (CCD)—*cens area* NM-5
Laguna Cem—*cemetery* AZ-5
Laguna Cem—*cemetery* CO-8
Laguna Cerro Negro—*lake* NM-5
Laguna Chico—*lake* NM-5
Laguna Chute—*lake* NM-5
Laguna Colorada—*lake* NM-5
*Laguna Colorado* NM-5
Laguna Colorado—*reservoir* NM-5
Laguna Compressor Station—*other* NM-5
Laguna Concho—*lake* NM-5
*Laguna Creek* CA-9
**Laguna Creek**—*pop pl* CA-9
Laguna Creek—*stream* AZ-5
Laguna Creek—*stream* (7) CA-9
Laguna Creek—*stream* ID-8
Laguna Cruz—*lake* NM-5
Laguna Cuarenta—*lake* NM-5
Laguna Cuates—*reservoir* NM-5
Laguna Dam—*dam* AZ-5
**Laguna Dam**—*pop pl* CA-9
Laguna de Agua—*lake* NM-5
Laguna de Alejandro—*lake* NM-5
Laguna de Baca—*reservoir* NM-5
Laguna de Cornelio—*lake* PR-3
Laguna de Cosme—*lake* NM-5
Laguna de Damacio—*lake* NM-5
Laguna de Frances—*reservoir* NM-5
Laguna de la Choza—*lake* NM-5
Laguna de la Grulla—*swamp* NM-5
Laguna de la Lena—*reservoir* NM-5
*Laguna De La Merced* CA-9
Laguna De La Merced—*civil* CA-9
Laguna de la Punta de la Sierra—*lake* NM-5
Laguna del Arabe—*lake* NM-5
Laguna de las Bacas—*reservoir* NM-5
Laguna De Las Calabasas—*civil* CA-9
Laguna de las Ranas—*lake* NM-5
Laguna de las Salinas—*lake* PR-3
Laguna del Cerro—*lake* NM-5
Laguna del Cerro Rojo—*lake* NM-5
Laguna del Chical—*lake* NM-5
Laguna del Condado—*lake* PR-3
Laguna del Desaque—*lake* NM-5
Laguna del Flamenco—*lake* PR-3
*Laguna Del Madre* TX-5
Laguna del Monte—*lake* NM-5
Laguna de los Encuerados—*swamp* TX-5
*Laguna de los Olmos* TX-5
Laguna De Los Olmos—*bay* TX-5
Laguna De Los Palos Colorados—*civil* CA-9
Laguna De Los Palos Colorados (Tract No. 2)—*civil* CA-9
Laguna de los Pinos—*lake* NM-5
Laguna de los Terreros—*lake* NM-5
Laguna del Padre—*lake* NM-5
Laguna Del Perro—*lake* NM-5
*Laguna del Rio Sabinas* TX-5
Laguna del Sauino—*reservoir* NM-5
Laguna del Tul—*lake* NM-5
Laguna del Tuloso—*lake* NM-5
Laguna del Vino—*reservoir* NM-5
Laguna de Molino—*lake* PR-3
Laguna de Pinones—*lake* PR-3
Laguna de Puerto Nuevo—*lake* PR-3
Laguna De San Antonio—*civil* CA-9
Laguna de Santa Rosa—*stream* CA-9
Laguna De Tache—*civil* CA-9
Laguna Eagle Tail Lateral—*canal* NM-5
Laguna Eduardo—*reservoir* NM-5
Laguna Elefante—*reservoir* NM-5
Laguna El Pobre—*lake* PR-3
Laguna Encina—*lake* NM-5
Laguna Escondido—*reservoir* NM-5
Laguna Flora—*lake* NM-5
Laguna Fria—*lake* NM-5
Laguna Gatuna—*lake* NM-5
Laguna Gloria—*hist pl* TX-5
Laguna Grande—*lake* NM-5
Laguna Grande—*lake* PR-3
Laguna Guaniquilla—*lake* PR-3
Laguna Gurule—*reservoir* NM-5
Laguna Harbor—*bay* CA-9
**Laguna Heights**—*pop pl* TX-5
Laguna Hilda—*lake* CO-8
**Laguna Hills**—*pop pl* CA-9
Laguna Hills (Leisure World)—*CDP* CA-9
Laguna Honda—*lake* CA-9
Laguna Honda—*lake* NM-5
Laguna Honda Home—*building* CA-9
Laguna Honda Sch—*school* CA-9
Laguna Huerfana—*lake* NM-5
Laguna Huero—*reservoir* NM-5
Laguna Ind Res—*reserve* CA-9
*Laguna Jaquez* NM-5
Laguna Joyuda—*lake* PR-3
Laguna Juan Garcia—*lake* NM-5
**Laguna Junction**—*pop pl* CA-9
Laguna Kiani—*lake* PR-3
Laguna Lake—*lake* AZ-5
Laguna Lake—*lake* (3) CA-9
Laguna Lake—*reservoir* CA-9
Laguna Lake—*uninc pl* CA-9
*Laguna Lakes* CA-9
Laguna La monia—*lake* NM-5
Laguna La Plata—*lake* PR-3
Laguna Larga—*lake* (3) NM-5
Laguna Larga Pasture—*flat* TX-5
Laguna Larga Well—*well* TX-5
Laguna Largo—*lake* NM-5
Laguna Lateral—*canal* NM-5
Laguna La Torrecilla—*lake* PR-3
Laguna Leon—*reservoir* NM-5
Laguna Lorenza—*reservoir* NM-5
Laguna Los Corozos—*lake* PR-3
Laguna Macho—*lake* NM-5
Laguna Madre—*reservoir* NM-5
Laguna Madrid—*lake* NM-5
Laguna Mason—*lake* NM-5
Laguna Mata Redonda—*lake* PR-3
Laguna Matias—*lake* PR-3
Laguna Meadow—*flat* CA-9
Laguna Meadow—*flat* TX-5
Laguna Monte Largo—*lake* PR-3
Laguna Mountains—*range* CA-9
Laguna Mountains—*summit* AZ-5
Laguna Mtn—*summit* CA-9
Laguna Negra—*lake* CO-8
Laguna Nieve—*lake* NM-5
**Laguna Niguel**—*pop pl* CA-9
*Lagunan Tanapag* MH-9
*Laguna Olmos* TX-5
Laguna Ortiz—*reservoir* NM-5
Laguna Palma—*reservoir* MO-7
Laguna Panda Windmill—*locale* TX-5
Laguna Park—*park* CA-9
Laguna Park—*park* (3) TX-5
**Laguna Park**—*pop pl* TX-5
Laguna Peak—*summit* CA-9
Laguna Peak—*summit* NM-5
Laguna Piedra—*lake* NM-5
Laguna Piedra—*reservoir* (2) NM-5
Laguna Pinabete Mocho—*lake* NM-5
Laguna-Pine Valley (CCD)—*cens area* CA-9
Laguna Pino—*lake* NM-5
Laguna Plata—*lake* NM-5
Laguna Playa Grande—*lake* PR-3
Laguna Point—*cape* (2) CA-9
Laguna Polvadera—*reservoir* NM-5
Laguna Pueblo—*hist pl* NM-5
**Laguna Pueblo**—*pop pl* NM-5
Laguna Pueblo (Indian Reservation)—*reserve* NM-5
Laguna Puerto Diablo—*lake* PR-3
Laguna Quates—*reservoir* NM-5
Laguna Quebrada—*reservoir* NM-5
Laguna Ranch—*locale* (4) CA-9
Laguna Rec Area—*park* CA-9
Laguna Recreation Site One Hundred Fifty—*park* AZ-5
Laguna Redonda—*lake* NM-5
Laguna Reyes—*lake* NM-5
Laguna Rica—*lake* PR-3
Laguna Ridge—*ridge* CA-9
Laguna Road Sch—*school* CA-9
Laguna Rsvr—*reservoir* AZ-5
Laguna Rsvr—*reservoir* CA-9
Laguna Ruybal—*lake* CO-8
Lagunas—*lake* CA-9
Lagunas—*locale* NM-5
*Laguna Sabina* TX-5
*Laguna Salada* TX-5
Laguna Salada—*lake* CA-9
Laguna Salada—*lake* NM-5
Laguna Salada Mesa—*summit* NM-5
Laguna Salada Spring—*spring* AZ-5
*Laguna Salado* TX-5
*Laguna Saladoj* TX-5
Laguna San Jose—*lake* PR-3
Laguna Santiago—*lake* NM-5
Lagunas (Barrio)—*fmr MCD* PR-3
Laguna Sch—*school* AZ-5
Laguna Sch—*school* (3) CA-9
Lagunas Cuatas—*summit* NM-5
Laguna Seca—*civil* CA-9
Laguna Seca—*flat* NM-5
Laguna Seca—*lake* (5) NM-5
Laguna Seca—*locale* TX-5
Laguna Seca—*reservoir* NM-5
Laguna Seca—*swamp* CA-9
Laguna Seca, Canada —*valley* CA-9
Laguna Seca Creek—*stream* CA-9
Laguna Seca Draw—*valley* NM-5
Laguna Seca Mesa—*summit* (2) NM-5
Laguna Seca Race Track—*other* CA-9
Laguna Seca Racetrack—*other* CA-9
Laguna Seca Ranch—*locale* CA-9
Laguna Seca Ranger Station—*locale* CA-9
**Laguna Shores**—*pop pl* TX-5
Laguna Simon—*reservoir* NM-5
Lagunas Negras—*stream* TX-5
Laguna Spring—*spring* AZ-5
Laguna (sta.) (New Laguna)—*other* NM-5
Laguna Tank—*reservoir* (3) TX-5
Laguna Techillas—*reservoir* NM-5
Laguna Telesfor—*lake* NM-5
Laguna Tierra Amatosa—*lake* NM-5
Laguna Tonto—*lake* NM-5
Laguna Torrito—*lake* NM-5
Laguna Tortuguero—*lake* PR-3
Laguna Toston—*basin* NM-5
Laguna Trujillo—*reservoir* NM-5
Laguna Valley—*valley* AZ-5
Laguna Vieja—*lake* NM-5
**Laguna Vista**—*pop pl* TX-5
*Laguna wash* AZ-5
Laguna Windmill—*locale* (2) TX-5
**Laguna Woods**—*pop pl* IL-6
Laguna Yanuel—*lake* PR-3
Laguna Yeso—*lake* NM-5
Laguna Zoni—*lake* PR-3
Lagune, Bayou la—*gut* LA-4
Lagunillas Creek—*stream* TX-5
*Lagunita* CA-9
Lagunita—*lake* CA-9
**Lagunita**—*pop pl* CA-9
**Lagunita**—*pop pl* NM-5
Lagunita—*reservoir* NM-5
Lagunita Canyon—*valley* NM-5
Lagunita Lake—*lake* CA-9
Lagunitas—*locale* NM-5
**Lagunitas**—*pop pl* CA-9
Lagunitas, Lake—*reservoir* CA-9
Lagunita Saddle—*gap* NM-5
Lagunita Sch—*school* CA-9
Lagunitas Country Club—*other* CA-9
Lagunitas Creek—*stream* CA-9
Lagunitas Creek—*stream* NM-5
Lagunitas District Sch—*school* CA-9
Lagunitas-Forest Knolls—*CDP* CA-9
Lagunitas Fork—*stream* NM-5
Lagunitas Guard Station—*locale* NM-5
Lagunita Spring—*spring* NM-5
Lagunita Springs—*spring* NM-5
Lagunitas Well—*well* NM-5
Lagunitas Windmill—*locale* TX-5
Lagunita Tank—*reservoir* AZ-5
Lagunita Tank—*reservoir* NM-5
La Guzpa Canyon—*valley* NM-5
La Habra—*civil* CA-9
**La Habra**—*pop pl* CA-9
**La Habra Heights**—*pop pl* CA-9
La Habra HS—*school* CA-9
La Hacienda—*hist pl* CO-8
La Hae Spring—*spring* MO-7
**Lahaina**—*pop pl* HI-9
Lahaina (CCD)—*cens area* HI-9
Lahaina Hist Dist—*hist pl* HI-9
*Lahainaluna* HI-9
**Lahainaluna**—*pop pl* HI-9
Lahainaluna Ditch—*canal* HI-9
*Lahainaluna Stream* HI-9
Lahaina Pump Ditch One—*canal* HI-9
Lahaina Pump Ditch Two—*canal* HI-9
La Hamaca—*area* PR-3
Lahar Lookout—*summit* WA-9
*La Harp* KS-7
*Laharpe* KS-7
**La Harpe**—*pop pl* IL-6
**La Harpe**—*pop pl* KS-7
La Harpe Cem—*cemetery* KS-7
La Harpe Creek—*stream* IL-6
La Harpe Elem Sch—*school* KS-7
LaHarpe Hist Dist—*hist pl* IL-6
**La Harpe (Township of)**—*pop pl* IL-6
*LaHart Public Hunting Area* IA-7
La Hart State Public Hunting Area—*area* IA-7
La Hart State Public Hunting Area—*park* IA-7
Lahaska—*locale* PA-2
Lahaska Creek—*stream* PA-2
Lahaska Junction—*other* PA-2
Lahaska Station (Lahaska Junction)—*locale* PA-2
Lahaway Creek—*stream* NJ-2
Lahaway Plantation Dam—*dam* NJ-2
Lahaye Lake—*reservoir* LA-4
*LaHayn* IN-6
La Hedionda Lake—*lake* TX-5
Laher Lake—*lake* WI-6
La Hermosa Assembly—*church* UT-8
Lahey—*locale* TX-5
Lahey Creek—*stream* TX-5
Lahey Sch—*school* IA-7
Lahiamanu Gulch—*valley* HI-9
**Lahiere**—*pop pl* NJ-2
Lahikiola—*summit* HI-9
Lahilahi Point—*cape* HI-9
Lahkir—*locale* FM-9
*Lahler Lake* WI-6
Lahlum, A. H., House—*hist pl* TX-5
*Lahman Lake* OH-6
**Lahmansville**—*pop pl* WV-2
Lahmeyer Creek—*stream* MO-7
Lah Mine—*mine* ND-7
Laho—*locale* UT-8
**LaHogue**—*pop pl* IL-6
**La Hogue**—*pop pl* IL-6
**Lahoma**—*pop pl* OK-5
Lahomene Falls—*falls* HI-9
**La Honda**—*pop pl* CA-9
La Honda Canyon—*valley* CA-9
La Honda Creek—*stream* CA-9
**La Honda Park**—*pop pl* CA-9
La Honda Spring—*spring* CA-9
La Honda Well—*well* CA-9
Lahontan Dam—*dam* NV-8
Lahontan Dam and Power Station—*hist pl* NV-8
Lahontan Mtns—*summit* NV-8
Lahontan Natl Fish Hatchery—*locale* NV-8
Lahontan Rsvr—*reservoir* NV-8
Lahontan Valley—*basin* NV-8
Lahontan Well—*well* NV-8
**La Hood Park**—*pop pl* MT-8
Lahoole—*cape* HI-9
Lahore—*locale* VA-3
La Hoya Creek—*stream* CA-9
Lahr Farm—*hist pl* PA-2
Lahrity Lake—*lake* MT-8
Lahr Lake Dam—*dam* IN-6
Lahser HS—*school* MI-6
Lahti Butte—*summit* SD-7
Lahti Creek—*stream* MI-6
Lahti Creek—*stream* MN-6
Lahtinen Spring Rsvr—*reservoir* ID-8
*Lahtl Creek* MI-6
Lahue Cem—*cemetery* KY-4
**La Huerta**—*pop pl* NM-5
La Huerta Windmill—*locale* TX-5
La Huida Canyon—*valley* NM-5
Lahuipuaa—*civil* HI-9
Lahuipuaa—*locale* HI-9
Lahusage, Lake—*reservoir* AL-4
Lahusage Dam—*dam* AL-4
*Lahy* FM-9
*Lai* FM-9
Laiap—*island* FM-9
*Laiap Island* FM-9
Laida Slough—*gut* AK-9
Laida Spit—*bar* AK-9
Laidig—*locale* PA-2
Laidig Spring Trail—*trail* PA-2
Laidlaw—*locale* NY-2
Laidlaw Butte—*summit* ID-8
Laidlaw Butte—*summit* OR-9
Laidlaw Cem—*cemetery* MI-6
Laidlaw Corrals—*locale* ID-8
Laidlaw Creek—*stream* ID-8
Laidlaw Hill—*summit* NY-2
Laidlaw Island—*island* WA-9
Laidlaw Lake—*lake* ID-8
Laidlaw Park—*park* IL-6
Laidlaw Park Holding Corral—*locale* ID-8
Laidlaw Sch—*school* IL-6
Laidlaws Pond—*lake* NJ-2
Laidley Field—*park* WV-2
Laidley Run—*stream* PA-2
Laidley Run—*stream* WV-2
Laidley-Summers-Quarrier House—*hist pl* WV-2
Laidlow Creek—*stream* ID-8
*Laie* MP-9
Laie—*beach* HI-9
Laie—*civil* HI-9
**Laie**—*pop pl* HI-9
Laie Bay—*bay* HI-9
Laie Cave—*cave* HI-9
*Laie Point* HI-9
Laie Point—*cape* HI-9

Laie Puu—*summit* HI-9
Laie Temple—*church* HI-9
L'Aigle Creek—*stream* AR-4
La Iglesia de Santa Cruz and Site of the Plaza of Santa Cruz de la Canada—*hist pl* NM-5
La Iglesia Metodista Mexicana, El Divino Redentor—*hist pl* AZ-5
*Lai Islands* MP-9
Lail Cave—*cave* TN-4
*Lailly Run* WV-2
Laimi—*civil* HI-9
Laimmersville Sch—*school* CA-9
*Laina* HI-9
*Laina Hill* HI-9
Lainamaia Point—*cape* HI-9
Lain Cem—*cemetery* OK-5
Lain Cem—*cemetery* TN-4
Lain Creek—*stream* TX-5
La India—*locale* TX-5
La India Windmill—*locale* TX-5
Laine, James H., Barn—*hist pl* ID-8
Laine Cem—*cemetery* (2) TN-4
Lain-Estburg House—*hist pl* WI-6
Laing—*locale* MI-6
Laing—*locale* WA-9
Laing—*locale* WV-2
*Laing Creek* WI-6
Laing House of Plainfield Plantation—*hist pl* NJ-2
Laing HS—*school* SC-3
Laingkat—*locale* GA-3
*La Inglesa Pajaros* MH-9
Laing Park—*park* IN-6
Laing Ranch—*locale* NV-8
**Laings**—*pop pl* OH-6
**Laingsburg**—*pop pl* MI-6
Laing Sch—*school* IA-7
Laing Sch—*school* MI-6
Laing Sch—*school* SC-3
**Laings Garden**—*pop pl* PA-2
*Laing Station* WA-9
*Laing Township* KS-7
Lainhart Cem—*cemetery* NY-2
Lain Lake—*lake* OK-5
Lainsville—*locale* IA-7
Lain Technical Institute—*school* IN-6
**Lair**—*pop pl* KY-4
Lair, John, House—*hist pl* KY-4
Lair Cem—*cemetery* OH-6
Lair Cem—*cemetery* TX-5
*Laird* MS-4
Laird—*fmr MCD* NE-7
Laird—*locale* FL-3
Laird—*locale* KS-7
Laird—*locale* WY-8
Laird—*other* MS-4
**Laird**—*pop pl* CO-8
**Laird**—*pop pl* PA-2
Laird, Hugh, House—*hist pl* AZ-5
Laird, Mount—*summit* UT-8
Laird Ave Sch—*school* OH-6
Laird Bayou—*bay* FL-3
Laird Bluff—*cliff* MO-7
Laird Branch—*stream* LA-4
Laird Branch—*stream* MS-4
Laird Canal—*canal* CO-8
Laird Canyon—*valley* NM-5
Laird Cem—*cemetery* IL-6
Laird Cem—*cemetery* MI-6
Laird Cem—*cemetery* PA-2
Laird Ch—*church* IL-6
Laird Corners—*locale* NY-2
Laird Creek—*stream* MI-6
Laird Creek—*stream* MN-6
Laird Creek—*stream* (2) MT-8
Laird Creek—*stream* OR-9
**Laird Crossing**—*pop pl* PA-2
Laird Dam—*dam* OR-9
Laird Gulch—*valley* WA-9
Laird Hall—*hist pl* OH-6
**Laird Hill**—*pop pl* TX-5
Laird Hosp—*hospital* MS-4
Laird Lake—*lake* CA-9
Laird Lake—*lake* MI-6
Laird Lake—*lake* MT-8
Laird Lake—*lake* ND-7
Laird Lake—*lake* OR-9
Laird Lake Dam—*dam* MS-4
Laird Landing—*locale* CA-9
Laird Meadow—*flat* CA-9
Laird Memorial Hosp—*hospital* TX-5
Laird Mill Creek—*stream* FL-3
Lairdon Gulch—*valley* MT-8
Laird Park—*park* CA-9
Laird Park—*park* ID-8
Laird Park—*park* UT-8
Laird Point—*cape* FL-3
Laird Pond—*reservoir* VT-1
Laird Ranch—*locale* MT-8
Laird Rsvr—*reservoir* OR-9
Lairds—*locale* WA-9
Lairds Airp—*airport* PA-2
Lairds Camp—*locale* CA-9
Laird Sch—*school* AZ-5
Laird Sch—*school* IL-6
Laird Sch—*school* MT-8
Laird Sch—*school* PA-2
Lairds Corner—*locale* CA-9
Lairds Creek—*stream* KS-7
Lairds Knob—*summit* VA-3
Lairds Lake—*reservoir* MS-4
Lairds Landing—*locale* CA-9
Laird Slough—*gut* CA-9
Laird Spring—*spring* NV-8
Laird Spring—*spring* UT-8
Laird Station—*locale* PA-2
**Lairdsville**—*pop pl* NY-2
**Lairdsville**—*pop pl* PA-2
Lairdsville Covered Bridge—*hist pl* PA-2
Lairds Well—*well* CA-9
**Laird Township**—*pop pl* NE-7
**Laird (Township of)**—*pop pl* MI-6
*Lairey Island* ME-1
*Laireys Island* ME-1
*Laireys Ledge* ME-1
*Laireys Narrows* ME-1
Lair Hill—*summit* OH-6
Lair Lake—*lake* MN-6
Lair Mtn—*summit* MA-1
Lair Park—*park* PA-2
**Lairport**—*pop pl* CA-9
Lair Ranch—*locale* NE-7
*Lair Reservoir* NY-2
*Lairson Creek* OR-9
*Lairson Rock* OR-9
Lairs Run—*stream* VA-3
Lais, Charles, House—*hist pl* CA-9
Laisdell Hill—*summit* VT-1
La Isla—*inactive* TX-5
**La Isolina**—*pop pl* PR-3
*Laitimer Lake* MN-6
Laituri, Gust, Homestead—*hist pl* ID-8
Laiva Windmill—*locale* TX-5
La Jaca Well No 1—*well* NM-5
La Jamaica Windmill—*locale* TX-5
La Jara—*locale* NM-5
**La Jara**—*pop pl* CO-8
**La Jara**—*pop pl* NM-5
La Jara Arroyo—*stream* CO-8
La Jara Canyon—*valley* CO-8
La Jara Canyon—*valley* (7) NM-5
La Jara Canyon Tank—*reservoir* NM-5
La Jara Cem—*cemetery* CO-8
La Jara Creek—*stream* CO-8
La Jara Creek—*stream* (4) NM-5
La Jara Depot—*hist pl* CO-8
La Jara Hogback Well—*well* NM-5
La Jara Lake—*reservoir* (2) NM-5
La Jaral Ranch—*locale* NM-5
La Jara Meadows—*flat* CO-8
La Jara Mesa—*summit* (2) NM-5
La Jara Peak—*summit* NM-5
La Jara Rsvr—*reservoir* CO-8
La Jara Sch—*school* NM-5
La Jara Spring—*spring* (2) NM-5
La Jara Tank—*reservoir* NM-5
La Jara Well—*well* NM-5
La Jara Well No 2—*well* NM-5
La Jara Well No 3—*well* NM-5
La Jarita Cem—*cemetery* TX-5
La Jarita Creek—*stream* TX-5
La Jarita Ranch—*locale* TX-5
La Jarita Ranches—*locale* NM-5
**Lajas**—*pop pl* PR-3
**Lajas Arriba**—*pop pl* PR-3
Lajas Arriba (Barrio)—*fmr MCD* PR-3
Lajas (Municipio)—*civil* PR-3
Lajas (Pueblo)—*fmr MCD* PR-3
La Javalina Windmill—*locale* TX-5
La Jencia Creek—*stream* NM-5
La Jencia Ranch—*locale* NM-5
Lajeunesse Creek—*stream* OR-9
Lajinjaj—*locale* MP-9
La Jita Camp—*locale* TX-5
**Lajitas**—*pop pl* TX-5
Lajitas Boat Crossing—*locale* TX-5
Lajitas Mesa—*summit* TX-5
Lajitas Vehicle Crossing—*locale* TX-5
Lajoie, Lake—*reservoir* TN-4
Lajoie, Lake—*reservoir* TN-4
**La Jolla**—*pop pl* (2) CA-9
La Jolla Alfalfa—*flat* NM-5
La Jolla Amago—*locale* CA-9
La Jolla Basin—*basin* CA-9
La Jolla Bay—*bay* CA-9
La Jolla Canyon—*valley* AZ-5
La Jolla Canyon—*valley* (2) CA-9
La Jolla Canyon—*valley* NM-5
La Jolla Caves—*cave* CA-9
La Jolla Country Club—*other* CA-9
La Jolla Creek—*stream* CA-9
La Jolla de Santa Rosa—*flat* NM-5
La Jolla Heights Park—*park* CA-9
La Jolla Hermosa Park—*park* CA-9
La Jolla HS—*school* CA-9
**La Jolla Ind Res**—*pop pl* CA-9
**La Jolla Mesa**—*pop pl* CA-9
La Jolla Mesa—*summit* CA-9
La Jolla Park—*park* CA-9
La Jolla Peak—*summit* CA-9
LaJolla Ranch—*locale* AZ-5
**La jolla Ranch**—*pop pl* CA-9
La Jolla Sch—*school* (2) CA-9
La Jolla Shores Beach—*beach* CA-9
La Jolla Spring—*spring* (2) CA-9
La Jolla Spring—*spring* MO-7
La Jolla Strand Park—*park* CA-9
La Jolla Valley—*basin* CA-9
La Jolla Valley—*valley* CA-9
La Jolla Wash—*stream* AZ-5
La Jolla Women's Club—*hist pl* CA-9
*La Jora Creek* CO-8
*La Jose* PA-2
LaJose Cem—*cemetery* PA-2
*La Jose (corporate name Newburg)* PA-2
LaJose Junction Station—*locale* PA-2
La Jose Station—*locale* PA-2
La Jota—*civil* CA-9
*La Joya* NM-5
**Lajoya**—*pop pl* NM-5
**La Joya**—*pop pl* (2) NM-5
**La Joya**—*pop pl* TX-5
**La Joya**—*pop pl* PR-3
La Joya Cem—*cemetery* NM-5
La Joya Creek—*stream* TX-5
La Joya del Pedregal—*bench* NM-5
La Joya Ditch—*canal* NM-5
La Joya Flats—*flat* NM-5
La Joya Goodwin Pump—*other* TX-5
**La Joya Heights Subdivision**—*pop pl* UT-8
La Joya Lake—*reservoir* TX-5
*La Joya Peak* CA-9
La Joya Quicksilver Mine—*mine* CA-9
La Joya Sch—*school* CA-9
La Joya (Siding)—*locale* NM-5
**La Joya (sta.)**—*pop pl* NM-5
La Joya Tio Gregorio—*valley* NM-5
La Joya Windmill—*locale* NM-5
**La Juanita**—*pop pl* PR-3
La Juita Canyon—*valley* NM-5
*La Junta* CO-8
La Junta—*locale* TX-5
**La Junta**—*pop pl* CO-8
**La Junta**—*pop pl* NM-5
**La Junta**—*pop pl* TX-5
La Junta Basin—*basin* CO-8
La Junta Bomb Score Site—*military* CO-8
La Junta Campground—*locale* NM-5
La Junta Canyon—*valley* NM-5
La Junta Creek—*stream* NM-5
La Junta de los Rios Archeol District—*hist pl* TX-5
**La Junta Gardens**—*pop pl* CO-8
La Junta Mine—*mine* CO-8
La Junta Municipal Airp—*airport* CO-8
La Junta Peak—*summit* CO-8
**La Junta Village**—*pop pl* CO-8
**La Jurado**—*pop pl* PR-3
*Lajurnak* MP-9
Lak-A-Ana Lake—*lake* FL-3
*Lakalaho Creek* MT-8
Lakanardia, Lake—*lake* LA-4
**Lakato Estates Subdivision**—*pop pl* UT-8
*Lakatoh Canal* NE-7
*Lakatoh Ditch* NE-7
L A K Draw—*valley* WY-8
*Lake* AL-4
*Lake* CA-9
*Lake* FL-3
*Lake* GA-3
*Lake* IN-6
*Lake* KS-7
*Lake* ME-1
*Lake* MA-1
*Lake* MN-6
*Lake* MS-4
*Lake* OH-6
*Lake* PA-2
*Lake* UT-8
Lake—*fmr MCD* NE-7
Lake—*lake* MS-4
Lake—*lake* WY-8
Lake—*locale* CO-8
Lake—*locale* KY-4
Lake—*locale* NY-2
Lake—*locale* VT-1
Lake—*locale* VA-3
Lake—*locale* WI-6
Lake—*locale* WY-8
Lake—*other* NY-2
**Lake**—*pop pl* GA-3
**Lake**—*pop pl* ID-8
**Lake**—*pop pl* LA-4
**Lake**—*pop pl* MD-2
**Lake**—*pop pl* MI-6
**Lake**—*pop pl* MS-4
**Lake**—*pop pl* MO-7
**Lake**—*pop pl* NJ-2
**Lake**—*pop pl* OK-5
**Lake**—*pop pl* PA-2
**Lake**—*pop pl* TX-5
**Lake**—*pop pl* VA-3
**Lake**—*pop pl* WV-2
**Lake**—*pop pl* WY-8
Lake—*uninc pl* WI-6
Lake, Bay—*lake* (2) MI-6
Lake, Ditch—*lake* (2) AR-4
Lake, Jack—*lake* AK-9
Lake, Shrode—*lake* AK-9
Lake, Tank—*reservoir* NM-5
Lake, The—*lake* (2) CO-8
Lake, The—*lake* (4) NM-5
Lake, The—*lake* NY-2
Lake, The—*lake* WA-9
Lake, The—*lake* WY-8
Lake, The—*reservoir* (2) AZ-5
Lake, The—*reservoir* (2) TX-5
Lake, The—*swamp* NC-3
Lake, The (stock tank)—*reservoir* AZ-5
Lake, Van—*lake* NM-5
*Lake Abanakee* NY-2
Lake Abilene Filter Plant—*other* TX-5
*Lake Absarraca* WY-8
Lake Absegami Dam—*dam* NJ-2
Lake Abundance Creek—*stream* MT-8
Lake Accotink Park—*park* VA-3
*Lake Adair* WA-9
*Lake Adam* MT-8
*Lake Adda* MN-6
**Lake Adelle**—*pop pl* MO-7
Lake Advance Dam—*dam* MS-4
Lake Afton Boys Ranch—*locale* KS-7
Lake Afton County Park—*park* KS-7
Lake Afton Dam*—*dam* KS-7
Lake Agape Dam—*dam* TN-4
Lake Agassiz Sch—*school* ND-7
*Lake Agawam* MA-1
*Lake Agusta* MI-6
Lake Ahquabi State Park—*park* IA-7
Lake-Air Airp—*airport* UT-8
Lakeaires Sch—*school* MN-6
*Lake Alaska* TX-5
**Lake Alaska**—*pop pl* TX-5
Lake Albert Dam—*dam* NJ-2
Lake Aleeda—*reservoir* PA-2
Lake Aleeda Dam—*dam* PA-2
Lake Alexander Dam Number One—*dam* AL-4
**Lake Alfred**—*pop pl* FL-3
Lake Alfred Elem Sch—*school* FL-3
*Lake Alice* WA-9
*Lake Alice* WI-6
**Lake Alice**—*pop pl* WA-9
Lake Alice Cem—*cemetery* MN-6
*Lake Alice Clarissa* WA-9
Lake Alice Creek—*stream* MN-6
*Lake Alice Dam* ND-7
Lake Alice Dam—*dam* TN-4
Lake Alice Natl Wildlife Ref—*park* ND-7
Lake Alice Park—*park* MN-6
Lake Alice State Game Mngmt Area—*park* NY-2
**Lake Alice (Township of)**—*pop pl* MN-6
Lake Allie Park—*park* MN-6
*Lake Alloway* NJ-2
Lake Almanor Country Club—*other* CA-9
Lake Alma State Res—*park* OH-6
**Lake Alpine**—*pop pl* CA-9
*Lake Althea* MA-1
*Lake Altho* FL-3
Lake Altoona Dam—*dam* PA-2
Lake Alturas Lodge—*locale* ID-8
*Lake Altyn* MT-8
**Lake Aluma**—*pop pl* OK-5
Lake Alva Campground—*locale* MT-8
Lake Alvin State Rec Area—*park* SD-7
*Lake Ambrose* LA-4
Lake Amelia Cem—*cemetery* MN-6
Lake Ames Dam—*dam* NJ-2
*Lake Amherst* VT-1
*Lake Amy Belle* WI-6
**Lake Andes**—*pop pl* SD-7
Lake Andes Municipal Airp—*airport* SD-7
Lake Andes Natl Wildlife Ref—*park* SD-7
Lake and Forest Club Dam—*dam* IN-6
*Lake Andrew* MN-6
Lake Andrew Acres Dam—*dam* NC-3
**Lake Andrew (Township of)**—*pop pl* MN-6
Lake Anedna Dam—*dam* AL-4
*Lake Angeline* MI-6
**Lake Angeline**—*pop pl* MI-6
**Lake Angelus**—*pop pl* MI-6
Lake Anita State Park—*park* IA-7
**Lake Ann**—*pop pl* MI-6
*Lake Annalaide* MN-6
Lake Ann Cem—*cemetery* MN-6
Lake Ann Dam—*dam* TN-4
Lake Anne—*post sta* VA-3
Lake Anne Dam—*dam* NC-3
**Lake Anne (subdivision)**—*pop pl* NC-3
**Lake Annette Village**—*pop pl* MO-7
Lake Annie Mtn—*summit* CA-9
Lake Ann Sch—*school* FL-3
*Lake Anthony* MA-1
Lake Antietam Dam—*dam* PA-2
Lake Antoine Park—*park* MI-6
**Lake Apopka**—*pop pl* FL-3
Lake Apopka Lock and Dam—*dam* FL-3
*Lake Apopke* FL-3
**Lake Appaloosa Estates**—*pop pl* MS-4
*Lake Apthorp* FL-3
*Lake Apthrope* FL-3
Lake Aquillo—*other* OH-6
*Lake Arcadia* NJ-2
Lake Ardoch Dam—*dam* ND-7
*Lake Aretta* FL-3
*Lake Aricara* SD-7
**Lake Ariel**—*pop pl* PA-2
**Lake Ariel (Ariel)**—*pop pl* PA-2
Lake Ariel Dam—*dam* PA-2
Lake Arm—*canal* IN-6
*Lake Arnedra Dam* AL-4
**Lake Arrowhead**—*pop pl* CA-9
**Lake Arrowhead**—*pop pl* GA-3
**Lake Arrowhead**—*pop pl* MO-7
**Lake Arrowhead**—*pop pl* NJ-2
Lake Arrowhead—*uninc pl* GA-3
Lake Arrowhead Sch—*school* CA-9
Lake Arrowhead Scout Camps—*locale* CA-9
*Lake Arthur* PA-2
**Lake Arthur**—*pop pl* LA-4
**Lake Arthur**—*pop pl* NM-5
Lake Arthur Cem—*cemetery* NM-5
Lake Arthur Country Club—*other* PA-2
*Lake Arthur Golf Course* PA-2
Lake Arthur Oil Field—*oilfield* LA-4
*Lake Arville* MN-6
Lake Ashby Canal—*canal* FL-3
Lake Ashby Creek—*stream* FL-3
Lake Ashby Shores—*locale* FL-3
Lake Ashnoca Dam—*dam* NC-3
Lake Ashroe Dam—*dam* NJ-2
Lake Ashtabula Dam—*dam* ND-7
*Lake Atlanta* AR-4
Lake Attendance Center—*school* MS-4
Lake Attitash Dam—*dam* MA-1
*Lake Atwood Creek* UT-8
*Lake Aubrey* GA-3
*Lake Auburn* AL-4
Lake Auburn Ch—*church* MN-6
Lake Augusta—*reservoir* PA-2
*Lake Augusta Dam* PA-2
*Lake Austin* VT-1
Lake Austin Metropolitan—*park* TX-5
Lake Austin Pond Dam—*dam* NC-3
Lake Ave Cem—*cemetery* CT-1
Lake Averic Dam—*dam* MA-1
Lake Ave Woods East—*woods* IL-6
Lake Ave Woods West—*woods* IL-6
*Lake Avoca* MN-6
Lake Avolley—*swamp* LA-4
**Lake-A-Wana**—*pop pl* TN-4
Lake-A-Way Dam—*dam* MS-4
*Lake Azwell* WA-9
*Lake Ballinger* TX-5
*Lake Bamba* NJ-2
*Lake Bancroft* SD-7
Lake Bank Cem—*cemetery* IL-6
*Lake Barbara* TX-5
**Lake Barbara**—*pop pl* TX-5
Lake Barcroft—*CDP* VA-3
*Lake Bardwell* TX-5
Lake Barkley State Park—*park* KY-4
Lake Barnegat Dam—*dam* NJ-2
*Lake Barnes* MI-6
Lake Barre Oil Field—*oilfield* LA-4
*Lake Barre Pass* LA-4
**Lake Barrington**—*pop pl* IL-6
*Lake Bar's Leak* MI-6
*Lake Barton* KS-7
Lake Barton Shop Ctr—*locale* FL-3
**Lake Bashan**—*pop pl* CT-1
Lake Basin—*basin* CA-9
Lake Basin—*basin* ID-8
Lake Basin—*basin* MT-8
Lake Basin—*basin* (2) OR-9
Lake Basin—*basin* UT-8
Lake Basin—*basin* WA-9
Lake Basin—*basin* WY-8
Lake Basin Creek—*stream* OR-9
Lake Bassola Dam—*dam* KS-7
*Lake Bay* NJ-2
Lake Bay—*bay* (3) AK-9
**Lakebay**—*pop pl* WA-9
Lake Bay Creek—*stream* AK-9
*Lake Bayou* LA-4
Lake Bayou—*gut* AR-4
Lake Bayou—*gut* LA-4
Lake Bayou—*gut* TX-5
Lake Bayou—*stream* MS-4
Lake Bayou—*stream* TX-5
*Lake Bayou des Sot* LA-4
Lakebay Sch—*school* WA-9
Lake Bear Gulch—*valley* CA-9
*Lake Beashear* KY-4
Lake Beaver Dam—*dam* MS-4
*Lake Beceros* LA-4
Lake Bed, The—*lake* WY-8
Lake Bed Draw—*valley* WY-8
Lake Bedford Camp—*locale* FL-3
Lake Bed Rsvr—*reservoir* WY-8
Lakebed Waterhole—*lake* (2) OR-9
Lake Bed Waterhole—*lake* OR-9
Lake Bed Waterhole—*reservoir* OR-9
**Lake Bel Air**—*pop pl* RI-1
Lake-Bell House—*hist pl* AR-4
*Lake Bellows* MI-6
*Lake Bells* WI-6
Lake Belt Cem—*cemetery* MN-6
**Lake Belt (Township of)**—*pop pl* MN-6
Lake Bemidji State Park—*park* MN-6
*Lake Benbow* CA-9
Lake Ben Cem—*cemetery* MN-6
Lake Bench—*bench* CO-8
Lake Bend Landing—*locale* AL-4
*Lake Ben Morrow* OR-9
*Lake Benson* AR-4
Lake Benson Dam—*dam* NC-3
Lake Benton—*other* IL-6
**Lake Benton**—*pop pl* MN-6
Lake Benton Camp—*locale* IL-6
Lake Benton Opera House—*hist pl* MN-6
Lake Benton Opera House and Kimball Bldg (Boundary Increase)—*hist pl* MN-6
**Lake Benton (Township of)**—*pop pl* MN-6
Lake Berryessa Park HQ—*locale* CA-9
**Lake Beseck**—*pop pl* CT-1
*Lake Beth* WA-9
Lake Bethel Cem—*cemetery* IN-6
Lake Bethesda Park—*park* FL-3
*Lake Betty* MN-6
**Lake Beulah**—*pop pl* WI-6
Lake Bickerstaff Dam—*dam* AL-4
*Lake Bigler* CA-9
*Lake Bigler* NV-8
Lake Billy Chinook State Airp—*airport* OR-9
**Lake Biltmore Estates (subdivision)**—*pop pl* (2) AZ-5
*Lake Bimini Dam* PA-2
Lake Binder—*reservoir* IA-7
Lake Bird—*locale* FL-3
Lake Bistineau Gas Field—*oilfield* LA-4
Lake Bistineau State Park—*park* LA-4
*Lake Bitz* ND-7
Lake Blaine Sch—*school* MT-8
*Lake Bluestem* KS-7
Lake Bluff—*cliff* GA-3
**Lake Bluff**—*pop pl* IL-6
**Lake Bluff**—*pop pl* NY-2
Lake Bluff Sch—*school* WI-6
Lake Blytheburn Dam—*dam* PA-2
Lake Bodana Dam—*dam* IN-6
**Lake Bodona**—*pop pl* IN-6
Lake Boeuf Gas Field—*oilfield* LA-4
Lake Bogue Homo Dam—*dam* MS-4
*Lake Bogue Homo State Fishing Lake* MS-4
*Lake Bois Sec* LA-4
*Lake Boltz* KY-4
Lake Bomoseen—*other* VT-1
*Lake Bonair Brook* CT-1
**Lake Bonaparte**—*pop pl* NY-2
**Lake Bonaparte (Bonaparte)**—*pop pl* NY-2
Lake Bonneville—*reservoir* OR-9
*Lake Borgne Canal* LA-4
**Lakeborough**—*pop pl* CO-8
*Lake Bottom* UT-8
Lake Bottom—*bend* (2) UT-8
Lake Bottom—*bend* WV-2
Lake Bottom Canal—*canal* UT-8
*Lake Boulevard Addition* IL-6
*Lake Boullar* FL-3
*Lake Bourem* UT-8
*Lake Bowden* FL-3
**Lake Bracken**—*pop pl* IL-6
**Lake Bradford**—*pop pl* FL-3
Lake Bradford Baptist Ch—*church* FL-3
*Lake Branch* AR-4
Lake Branch—*stream* CO-8
Lake Branch—*stream* FL-3
Lake Branch—*stream* IL-6
Lake Branch—*stream* (3) IN-6
Lake Branch—*stream* KY-4
Lake Branch—*stream* (2) MO-7
Lake Branch—*stream* OR-9
Lake Branch—*stream* (3) TX-5
Lake Branch—*stream* (2) WV-2
Lake Branch Cem—*cemetery* IL-6
Lake Brandt Ch—*church* NC-3
Lake Brandt Dam—*dam* NC-3
**Lake Brantley**—*pop pl* FL-3
Lake Brantley Community United Brethren Church, The—*church* FL-3
Lake Brantley HS—*school* FL-3
Lake Bray Dam—*dam* MA-1
Lake Breeze Ch—*church* OH-6
Lake Breeze Ski Lodge—*locale* TX-5
*Lake Brennan* CO-8
**Lake Briarwood**—*pop pl* IL-6
Lake Bridenthal House—*hist pl* NE-7
Lake Bridge—*locale* LA-4
**Lake Bridgeport**—*pop pl* TX-5
Lake Bridgeport Youth Camp—*locale* TX-5
*Lake Bright* FL-3
*Lake Bristow* OK-5
Lake Britton Archeol District—*hist pl* CA-9
**Lake Bronson**—*pop pl* MN-6
Lake Bronson Site—*hist pl* MN-6
Lake Bronson State Park—*park* MN-6
Lakebrook—*locale* OR-9
Lake Brook—*stream* (2) ME-1
Lake Brook—*stream* (3) NY-2
Lake Brook—*stream* VT-1
Lake Brooks Dam—*dam* NC-3
**Lake Brownwood**—*pop pl* TX-5
Lake Brownwood State Park—*park* TX-5
*Lake Bruce* AL-4
**Lake Bruce**—*pop pl* IN-6
**Lake Bruin**—*pop pl* LA-4
Lake Bruin State Park—*park* LA-4
*Lake Bryan* NE-7
*Lake Bryce Dam* AL-4
*Lake Brynhild* WA-9
**Lake Buena Vista**—*pop pl* FL-3
Lake Buffum Ch—*church* FL-3
Lake Bully Camp—*lake* LA-4
*Lake Burien* WA-9
Lake Burien Heights—*other* WA-9
*Lake Burlington* NC-3
Lake Burlington Sediment Pool—*reservoir* NC-3
Lake Burlington Sediment Pool Number Two—*reservoir* NC-3
Lake Burlington Sed Pool Number One Dam—*dam* NC-3
Lake Burlington Sed Pool Number Two Dam—*dam* NC-3
Lake Burton Game Mngmt Area (historical)—*park* GA-3
*Lake Buskey* WI-6
*Lake Butler* FL-3
**Lake Butler**—*pop pl* FL-3
Lake Butler (CCD)—*cens area* FL-3
Lake Butler Creek—*stream* FL-3
Lake Butler Elem Sch—*school* FL-3
Lake Butler Hosp and Hand Surgery—*hospital* FL-3
Lake Butler MS—*school* FL-3
Lake Butler Wildlife Mngmt Area—*park* FL-3
Lake Butler Wildlife Mngmt Area Raiford Tract—*park* FL-3
Lake Butner Water Supply Dam—*dam* NC-3
*Lake Buttahatchee Dam* AL-4
*Lake Butte* WY-8
Lake Butte—*summit* OR-9
Lake Butte—*summit* WY-8
**Lake Butte des Morts**—*pop pl* WI-6
Lake Byllesby County Park—*park* MN-6
*Lake Byran* FL-3
Lake Byron Sch—*school* SD-7
**Lake Byron Township**—*pop pl* SD-7
**Lake Cable**—*pop pl* OH-6
Lake Cable Sch—*school* OH-6
**Lake Cain Hills**—*pop pl* FL-3
*Lake Calahan* LA-4
*Lake Caldwell* AL-4
*Lake Calebasse* LA-4
Lake Calebasse—*bay* LA-4
*Lake Caloosa* FL-3
*Lake Calugi* WI-6
**Lake Camelot**—*pop pl* IL-6
Lake Camille Shop Ctr—*locale* FL-3
Lake Cammack Dam—*dam* NC-3
Lake Camp—*locale* WA-9
*Lake Campaguas* TX-5
Lake Camp Baldwin—*reservoir* OR-9
Lake Campbell—*locale* SD-7
**Lake Campbell**—*pop pl* SD-7
Lake Campbell Cem—*cemetery* SD-7
Lake Campbell Ch—*church* SD-7
Lake Campbell Dam—*dam* SD-7
Lake Campbell Outlet—*stream* SD-7
Lake Campbell Resort—*locale* SD-7
Lake Campground—*locale* CA-9
Lake Camp Gulch—*valley* OR-9
Lakecamp Lake—*lake* CA-9
Lake Campo Gas Field—*oilfield* LA-4
Lake Campo Pass—*channel* LA-4
Lake Camp Spring—*spring* OR-9
Lake Camp Springs—*spring* OR-9
Lake Canadohta—*civil* PA-2
Lake Canal—*canal* (2) CO-8
Lake Canal—*canal* (2) UT-8
Lake Canal Rsvr No. 1—*reservoir* CO-8
**Lake Canyada**—*pop pl* IA-7
*Lake Canyon* UT-8
Lake Canyon—*valley* (4) CA-9
Lake Canyon—*valley* (2) CO-8
Lake Canyon—*valley* ID-8
Lake Canyon—*valley* MT-8
Lake Canyon—*valley* NE-7
Lake Canyon—*valley* NM-5
Lake Canyon—*valley* (7) UT-8
Lake Canyon Spring—*spring* MT-8
Lake Canyon Spring—*spring* UT-8
Lake Canyon Wildlife Mngmt Area—*park* UT-8
**Lake Capri**—*pop pl* GA-3
*Lake Caracaljo* NJ-2
Lake Carasaljo Dam—*dam* NJ-2
*Lake Carasaljo* NJ-2
*Lake Carde Dam* PA-2
**Lake Carey**—*pop pl* PA-2
Lake Carey Dam—*dam* PA-2
**Lake Carlinville**—*pop pl* IL-6
Lake Carlos State Park—*park* MN-6
*Lake Carl Pleasant* AZ-5
Lake Carl Pleasant—*locale* AZ-5
**Lake Carmel**—*pop pl* NY-2
*Lake Carnac* MS-4
Lake Carobeth—*reservoir* PA-2
Lake Caroline Dam—*dam* PA-2
*Lake Carolyn Dam* AL-4
Lake Carrier (historical)—*locale* MS-4
Lake Carrier Sch—*school* MS-4
Lake Carroll—*CDP* FL-3
**Lake Carroll**—*pop pl* IL-6
Lake Carroll Baptist Ch—*church* FL-3
Lake Carroll Cem—*cemetery* FL-3
Lake Carroll RR Station—*locale* FL-3
Lake Carrona Number 1 Dam—*dam* AL-4
Lake Carrona Number 2 Dam—*dam* AL-4
*Lake Carson* PA-2
Lake Castle Dam—*dam* MS-4
Lake Catalpa—*reservoir* PA-2
Lake Catalpa Dam—*dam* PA-2
*Lake Catawba* NC-3
*Lake Catherine* AR-4
*Lake Catherine* MI-6
*Lake Catherine* MS-4
*Lake Catherine* TN-4
Lake Catherine—*CDP* IL-6
**Lake Catherine**—*pop pl* AR-4
**Lake Catherine**—*pop pl* LA-4
Lake Catherine Dam—*dam* MS-4
Lake Catherine Quarry—*hist pl* AR-4
Lake Catherine State Park—*park* AR-4
Lake Catoma Dam—*dam* AL-4
Lake Cavalier Dam—*dam* MS-4
*Lake Cavanaugh* WA-9
Lake Cayuga—*reservoir* PA-2
*Lake Cecilia* MI-6
Lake Cem—*cemetery* AL-4
Lake Cem—*cemetery* AR-4
Lake Cem—*cemetery* KS-7
Lake Cem—*cemetery* ME-1
Lake Cem—*cemetery* (2) MI-6
Lake Cem—*cemetery* (3) MS-4
Lake Cem—*cemetery* MO-7
Lake Cem—*cemetery* (2) OH-6
Lake Cem—*cemetery* OK-5
Lake Cem—*cemetery* SD-7
Lake Cem—*cemetery* WA-9
Lake Cem—*cemetery* WV-2

Lake Center—locale IA-7
**Lake Center**—pop pl MN-6
**Lake Center**—pop pl MS-4
Lake Center Cem—cemetery IA-7
Lake Center Ch—church MI-6
Lake Center Dam—dam MS-4
Lake Center Lodge—locale CA-9
Lake Center Mall (Shop Ctr)—locale IA-7
Lake Center Sch—school CA-9
Lake Center Sch—school MI-6
Lake Center Township (historical)—civil SD-7
**Lake Centralia**—pop pl IL-6
Lake Ch—church GA-3
Lake Ch—church (2) MS-4
Lake Ch—church WV-2
Lake Chabot Municipal Golf Course—other CA-9
Lake Chadokee NY-2
Lake Chambers WA-9
Lake Champlain Toll Bridge—bridge NY-2
Lake Champlain Toll Bridge—bridge VT-1
Lake Channelqcanyon—valley ID-8
Lake Chaparral Dam—dam KS-7
Lake Chapel—church GA-3
Lake Chapel—church (2) IN-6
Lake Chapel—church NC-3
Lake Chapel—church SC-3
Lake Chaplion Ch—church MS-4
Lake Chapman PA-2
Lake Chapot Park—park CA-9
Lake Chargoggaggmanchaugaggchabunagungamaug MA-1
Lake Char-gogg-a-gogg-man-chogg-a-gogg MA-1
**Lake Charles**—pop pl LA-4
**Lake Charles**—pop pl NY-2
Lake Charles—swamp MS-4
Lake Charles Air Force Station—military LA-4
Lake Charles Cem—cemetery MO-7
Lake Charles Country Club—other LA-4
Lake Charles Dam—dam AL-4
Lake Charles Dam—dam (2) NC-3
Lake Charles Hosp—hospital LA-4
Lake Charles Landing—locale MS-4
Lake Charles Municipal Airp—airport LA-4
Lake Charles Northeast—other LA-4
Lake Charles Radio Range Station—locale LA-4
**Lake Charleston**—pop pl IL-6
Lake Charles Trail—trail CO-8
Lake Charley Cem—cemetery MN-6
**Lake Charlotte**—pop pl IL-6
**Lake Charm**—pop pl FL-3
Lake Chatuge NC-3
Lake Chatuge Rec Area—park GA-3
Lake Chaugunagungamaug Dam—dam MA-1
Lake Chautauga Dam—dam MS-4
Lake Cheeseman CO-8
Lake cheesman CO-8
Lake Chelan—lake WA-9
Lake Chelan Golf and Country Club—other WA-9
Lake Chelan Hydroelectric Power Plant—hist pl WA-9
Lake Chelan Natl Rec Area—park WA-9
Lake Chelan State Park—park WA-9
**Lake Cherokee**—pop pl TX-5
Lake Chetak WI-6
Lake Ch (historical)—church MO-7
Lake Chickasaw OK-5
Lake Chicot LA-4
Lake Chicot Oil and Gas Field—oilfield LA-4
Lake Chicot State Park—park AR-4
Lake Chien—bay LA-4
Lake Childs FL-3
Lake Chittenden MI-6
Lake Choctaw—reservoir PA-2
Lake Choctaw Dam—dam PA-2
Lake Choupique LA-4
Lake Chriner OK-5
Lake Christian Preschool and Kindergarten—school FL-3
Lake Chub NC-3
Lake Chulavista Dam—dam AL-4
**Lake Church**—pop pl WI-6
Lake Church Cem—cemetery IA-7
**Lake Cicott**—pop pl IN-6
**Lake Cindy**—pop pl GA-3
Lake City AL-4
Lake City—locale CA-9
Lake City—locale KY-4
**Lake City**—pop pl AR-4
**Lake City**—pop pl CA-9
**Lake City**—pop pl CO-8
**Lake City**—pop pl FL-3
**Lake City**—pop pl GA-3
**Lake City**—pop pl IL-6
**Lake City**—pop pl IA-7
**Lake City**—pop pl KS-7
**Lake City**—pop pl ME-1
**Lake City**—pop pl MI-6
**Lake City**—pop pl MN-6
**Lake City**—pop pl (3) MS-4
**Lake City**—pop pl MO-7
**Lake City**—pop pl (2) PA-2
**Lake City**—pop pl SC-3
**Lake City**—pop pl SD-7
**Lake City**—pop pl TN-4
**Lake City**—pop pl TX-5
**Lake City**—pop pl (2) WA-9
Lake City Army Ammunition Plant—other MO-7
Lake City Borough—civil PA-2
Lake City Canyon—valley CA-9
Lake City (CCD)—cens area FL-3
Lake City Cem—cemetery IA-7
Lake City Cem—cemetery MI-6
Lake City Cem—cemetery SD-7
Lake City Ch (historical)—church MS-4
Lake City City Hall—hist pl MN-6
Lake City (Collier County) Public Library—building FL-3
Lake City Country Club—locale FL-3
Lake City Country Club—other MN-6
Lake City East (CCD)—cens area TN-4
Lake City East Division—civil TN-4
Lake City Elem Sch—school TN-4
Lake City Hist Dist—hist pl CO-8
Lake City (historical)—locale SD-7
Lake City HS TN-4
Lake City JHS—school FL-3
Lake City Junior Coll—school FL-3
Lake City Lakes—lake WA-9
Lake City Med Ctr—hospital FL-3
Lake City MS—school TN-4
**Lake City (North Girard)**—pop pl PA-2
Lake City Post Office—building TN-4
Lake City Run—stream PA-2
Lake City Sch—school PA-2
Lake City-Scranton (CCD)—cens area SC-3
Lake City (Site)—locale CA-9
**Lake City Township**—pop pl KS-7
Lake City Township (historical)—civil SD-7
Lake City (Township of)—fmr MCD AR-4
Lake City West (CCD)—cens area TN-4
Lake City West Division—civil TN-4
Lake Claiborne LA-4
Lake Claiborne Dam—dam MS-4
Lake Claire LA-4
Lake Claire—reservoir CO-8
Lake Clark TX-5
**Lake Clarke Shores**—pop pl FL-3
Lake Clark Natl Monmt—park AK-9
Lake Clark Natl Park—park AK-9
Lake Clark Pass—gap AK-9
**Lake Clear**—pop pl NY-2
Lake Clear Ch—church NY-2
Lake Clear Outlet—stream NY-2
Lake Clearwater NJ-2
Lake Cleburne Dam—dam AL-4
Lake Cle Elum WA-9
Lake Clementine CA-9
Lake Cliff Park—park TX-5
Lake Cloverdale CA-9
Lake Club NC-3
**Lake Club**—pop pl NJ-2
**Lake Club Estates (subdivision)**—pop pl TN-4
Lake Clydia Rsvr—reservoir CO-8
Lake Cochichewick Outlet Dam—dam MA-1
Lake Cochise AZ-5
Lake Cochituate Dam—dam MA-1
Lake Cockran—swamp FL-3
Lake Coffee Mill TX-5
**Lake Colby**—pop pl NY-2
Lake Coldwater Dam—dam KS-7
Lake Cole Dam—dam MS-4
Lake Collinwood MN-6
**Lake Colonial Estates**—pop pl TN-4
Lake Colonial Estates Dam—dam TN-4
Lake Columbia Dam—dam MS-4
Lake Comfort—locale NC-3
Lake Community Hosp—hospital FL-3
Lake Como—locale MS-4
Lake Como—other WI-6
**Lake Como**—pop pl FL-3
**Lake Como**—pop pl NJ-2
**Lake Como**—pop pl NY-2
**Lake Como**—pop pl PA-2
Lake Como Acad (historical)—school MS-4
Lake Como Baptist Ch—church MS-4
**Lake Como Beach**—pop pl WI-6
Lake Como Cem—cemetery MS-4
Lake Como Cem—cemetery TX-5
Lake Como (Como)—uninc pl NJ-2
Lake Como Dam—dam DE-2
Lake Como Dam—dam PA-2
Lake Como Outlet—stream NY-2
Lake Como Park—park TX-5
Lake Como Post Office (historical)—building MS-4
Lake Como Sch—school FL-3
Lake Compounce Carousel—hist pl CT-1
Lake Concord Dam—dam NC-3
**Lake Contrary**—pop pl MO-7
Lake Conway Woods Shop Ctr—locale FL-3
Lake Cooper IL-6
Lake Copiah Dam—dam MS-4
Lake Cora—other MI-6
Lake Corasljo NJ-2
Lake Cormoran Bayou MS-4
**Lake Cormorant**—pop pl MS-4
Lake Cormorant Bayou—stream MS-4
Lake Cormorant Post Office—building MS-4
Lake Cornelia Park—park MN-6
Lake Cornelia State Game Mngmt Area—park IA-7
Lake Corner—locale IL-6
Lake Corpus Christi State Park—park TX-5
Lake Corrier Dam—dam NC-3
Lake Corriher Dam—dam NC-3
Lake Corsicana—uninc pl TX-5
Lake Coulee Creek WI-6
Lake Country Cem—cemetery IN-6
Lake Country Village Shop Ctr—locale AZ-5
Lake County—civil SD-7
**Lake (County)**—pop pl CA-9
**Lake County**—pop pl FL-3
**Lake (County)**—pop pl IL-6
**Lake County**—pop pl IN-6
**Lake (County)**—pop pl MI-6
**Lake (County)**—pop pl MN-6
**Lake (County)**—pop pl OH-6
**Lake County**—pop pl OR-9
**Lake County**—pop pl TN-4
Lake County Area Vocational-Technical Center—school FL-3
Lake County Courthouse—building TN-4
Lake County Courthouse—hist pl CA-9
Lake County Courthouse—hist pl IN-6
Lake County Courthouse and Sheriff's Residence—hist pl MN-6
Lake County HS—school TN-4
Lake County-Lakeview Airp—airport OR-9
Lake County Park—park WI-6
Lake County Recreational Park—park TN-4
Lake County Shop Ctr—locale TN-4
Lake County Tower—locale FL-3
Lake County Township Hall—building SD-7
**Lake Cove**—pop pl LA-4
**Lake Coves**—pop pl AL-4
**Lake Cove (subdivision)**—pop pl AL-4
Lake Cowdry MN-6
Lake Crane Island—island LA-4
Lake Crawford—reservoir PA-2
Lake Crawford Dam—dam PA-2
Lake Creek CO-8
Lake Creek GA-3
Lake Creek ID-8
Lake Creek MO-7
Lake Creek MT-8
Lake Creek OR-9
Lake Creek TX-5
Lake Creek UT-8
Lake Creek WA-9
Lake Creek WY-8
Lake Creek—CDP SD-7
Lake Creek—gut SC-3
Lake Creek—locale GA-3
Lake Creek—locale IL-6
Lake Creek—locale OK-5
Lake Creek—locale TX-5
**Lake Creek**—pop pl ID-8
**Lake Creek**—pop pl MO-7
**Lakecreek**—pop pl OR-9
**Lake Creek**—pop pl TX-5
Lake Creek—stream (2) AL-4
Lake Creek—stream (7) AK-9
Lake Creek—stream (2) CA-9
Lake Creek—stream (10) CO-8
Lake Creek—stream (2) GA-3
Lake Creek—stream (32) ID-8
Lake Creek—stream (2) IL-6
Lake Creek—stream (2) IA-7
Lake Creek—stream (3) KS-7
Lake Creek—stream (2) KY-4
Lake Creek—stream LA-4
Lake Creek—stream (2) MS-4
Lake Creek—stream (4) MO-7
Lake Creek—stream (19) MT-8
Lake Creek—stream (2) NE-7
Lake Creek—stream (2) NV-8
Lake Creek—stream NY-2
Lake Creek—stream NC-3
Lake Creek—stream (4) OK-5
Lake Creek—stream (31) OR-9
Lake Creek—stream (2) PA-2
Lake Creek—stream (3) SD-7
Lake Creek—stream TN-4
Lake Creek—stream (12) TX-5
Lake Creek—stream (7) UT-8
Lake Creek—stream (18) WA-9
Lake Creek—stream WI-6
Lake Creek—stream (20) WY-8
Lake Creek Basin—basin WA-9
Lake Creek Bridge—hist pl OR-9
Lake Creek Campground—locale MT-8
Lake Creek Campground—locale (2) WA-9
Lake Creek Campground—locale (2) WY-8
Lake Creek Cem—cemetery IA-7
Lake Creek Cem—cemetery KS-7
Lake Creek Cem—cemetery MO-7
Lake Creek Cem—cemetery OR-9
Lake Creek Cem—cemetery TX-5
Lake Creek Ch—church GA-3
Lake Creek Ch—church IL-6
Lake Creek Ch—church MO-7
Lake Creek Ch—church (2) TX-5
Lake Creek Community House—locale NC-3
Lakecreek Dam—dam OR-9
Lake Creek Ditch—canal CO-8
Lake Creek Ditch—canal WY-8
Lake Creek Divide—ridge WY-8
Lake Creek (Election Precinct)—fmr MCD IL-6
Lake Creek Flat—flat MT-8
Lake Creek Flats—flat OR-9
Lake Creek Flats—flat WY-8
Lake Creek Forest Camp—locale (2) OR-9
Lake Creek Guard Station—locale OR-9
Lake Creek Lake—lake WY-8
Lake Creek Lake—reservoir TX-5
**Lakecreek (Lake Creek)**—pop pl OR-9
Lake Creek Lakes—lake (2) ID-8
Lake Creek Oil Field—oilfield KS-7
Lake Creek Oil Field—oilfield TX-5
Lake Creek Oil Field—oilfield WY-8
Lake Creek Picnic Ground OR-9
Lake Creek Point—cliff ID-8
Lake Creek Post Office (historical)—building TN-4
Lake Creek Ranch—locale ID-8
Lake Creek Rec Area—park OR-9
Lake Creek Reservoir TX-5
Lake Creek Resort—locale WY-8
Lake Creek Rsvr—reservoir NV-8
Lakecreek Rsvr—reservoir OR-9
Lake Creek Sch—school CO-8
Lake Creek Sch—school GA-3
Lake Creek Sch—school OR-9
Lake Creek Township—civil MO-7
Lake Creek Township—civil SD-7
Lake Creek Township—fmr MCD IA-7
Lake Creek (Township of)—fmr MCD NC-3
Lake Creek Trail—trail CO-8
Lake Creek Trail—trail (2) MT-8
Lake Creek Trail—trail OR-9
Lake Creek Trail—trail WA-9
Lake Creek Well (Dry)—well NV-8
**Lake Crescent**—pop pl WA-9
**Lakecrest**—pop pl IL-6
**Lake Crest**—pop pl IL-6
**Lakecrest**—pop pl IN-6
**Lake Crest**—pop pl (2) TN-4
Lake Crest Ch—church MI-6
**Lake Crest Estates**—pop pl TX-5
**Lakecrest (subdivision)**—pop pl NC-3
Lake Creswell (historical)—locale MS-4
**Lakecroft II (subdivision)**—pop pl DE-2
**Lake Crystal**—pop pl MN-6
**Lake Crystal Farms**—pop pl VA-3
Lake Cumberland Boys Camp—locale KY-4
Lake Cumberland State Park—park KY-4
Lake Cushman Reservoir WA-9
Lake C.w. Mccanaughy NE-7
Lake C.w. mcconaughy NE-7
**Lake Cypress**—pop pl TX-5
Lake Da Ko Tah Dam—dam SD-7
**Lakedale**—pop pl NC-3
**Lakedale**—pop pl WA-9
Lake Dale Branch—stream FL-3
**Lake Dalecarlia**—pop pl IN-6
Lake Dalecarlia Dam East—dam IN-6
Lake Dalecarlia Dam West—dam IN-6
Lake Dale Ch—church FL-3
Lakedale Resort WA-9
Lake Dallas TX-5
**Lake Dallas**—pop pl TX-5
Lake Dallas Dam TX-5
Lake Dalrymple Dam—dam PA-2
Lake Dam FL-3
Lake Dam—dam MS-4
Lake Damon MA-1
Lake Damon MI-6
**Lake Daniel**—pop pl NC-3
Lake Daniels TX-5
Lake D'Arbonne State Park—park LA-4
Lake Darby—CDP OH-6
Lake Darling State Park—park IA-7
Lake Daroma—swamp MS-4
Lake Darrynane Dam—dam KS-7
Lake Daugherty FL-3
Lake Davey Crockett TX-5
Lake David Crockett TX-5
Lake David D Terry AR-4
Lake David Interchange—other AR-4
Lake David Park—park FL-3
Lake Davis FL-3
Lake Davy Crockett TN-4
Lake Dawson TX-5
Lake Dean FL-3
Lake Decade LA-4
Lake Decatur GA-3
Lake DeForest Dam—dam TN-4
Lake De Lago Dam—dam KS-7
Lake Delancy Rec Area—park FL-3
Lake de la Valle—gut LA-4
Lake Delaware—locale NY-2
Lake Delevan MI-6
Lake Delmont—reservoir PA-2
**Lake Delta**—pop pl NY-2
**Lake Delton**—pop pl WI-6
**Lake Denise**—pop pl PA-2
**Lake Denmark**—pop pl NJ-2
Lake Denmark Dam—dam NJ-2
Lake Dennison MA-1
Lake Denoon Sch—school WI-6
Lake Derrick OR-9
Lake DeSmet Canal—canal WY-8
Lake Desmond Dam—dam NC-3
**Lake Desolation**—pop pl NY-2
Lake Desolation Trail—trail UT-8
Lake Desor Campground—locale MI-6
Lake Devin Dam—dam NC-3
Lake De Weese CO-8
Lake DeWeese Lodge—locale CO-8
Lake Diane AR-4
Lake Dick—hist pl AR-4
**Lake Dick**—pop pl AR-4
Lake Dick Dam—dam MS-4
Lake Dickey WA-9
Lake Dick Landing—locale MS-4
Lake Didier LA-4
**Lake Dilldear**—pop pl IN-6
Lake Dilldear Dam—dam IN-6
Lake Dillon CT-1
Lake District Sch (historical)—school IA-7
Lake Ditch IN-6
Lake Ditch—canal AR-4
Lake Ditch—canal (2) CO-8
Lake Ditch—canal IN-6
Lake Ditch—canal MO-7
Lake Ditch—canal (2) NV-8
Lake Dixie Dam—dam AL-4
Lake Dockery Dam—dam MS-4
**Lake Dolloff**—pop pl WA-9
Lake Dom—reservoir PA-2
Lake Don Pedro CA-9
Lake Dorr Rec Area—park FL-3
Lake Doster Golf Club—other MI-6
Lake Dozier Dam AL-4
Lake Drain IN-6
Lake Drain—canal NM-5
Lake Drain—stream (2) FL-3
Lake Drain—stream IN-6
Lake Drain Branch—stream TX-5
Lake Drain Creek—stream TX-5
Lake Drain Sink—basin FL-3
Lake Drain Slough—stream LA-4
Lake Draw—valley CO-8
Lake Draw—valley (2) UT-8
Lake Draw—valley (4) WY-8
**Lake Dreamland**—pop pl KY-4
Lake Drive—locale TN-4
**Lake Drive**—pop pl TN-4
Lake Drive Baptist Ch—church TN-4
Lake Drive Cem—cemetery TN-4
Lake Drive Cem—cemetery WI-6
**Lake Drive Estates**—pop pl AL-4
Lake Drive Sch—school WI-6
Lake Druid Dam—dam MS-4
Lake Drummond Ch—church VA-3
Lake Duck MN-6
Lake du Diable—channel LA-4
Lake Duesch MN-6
Lake Duke AL-4
Lake Duke Dam Lower—dam AL-4
**Lake Dunmore**—pop pl VT-1
Lake Dunmore Sch—school VT-1
Lake Durant Camp—locale NY-2
Lake Duroy WI-6
**Lake Dweller**—pop pl TN-4
Lake Eanes Park—park TX-5
Lake Easton State Park—park WA-9
Lake Eaton State Camp—locale NY-2
**Lake Eau Claire**—pop pl WI-6
Lake Eau Claire County Park—park WI-6
Lake Echee SC-3
Lake Echo Dam—dam TN-4
Lake Eden MI-6
**Lake Edgewood**—pop pl IN-6
Lake Edgewood Dam—dam IN-6
Lake Edina Park—park MN-6
Lake Edith WI-6
Lake Edmonston CA-9
Lake Edna Dam—dam OR-9
Lake Edson CA-9
Lake Edward Cem—cemetery MN-6
Lake Edward Dam—dam IN-6
Lake Edwards Dam—dam MS-4
Lake Edwards (Township of)—civ div MN-6
Lake Elam Baptist Ch—church AL-4
Lake El Dorado KS-7
Lake Eldora Ski Area—other CO-8
Lake Eleanor MI-6
Lake Eleanor Creek—stream CA-9
Lake Eleanor Dam—dam IA-7
Lake Eleanor Ranger Station—locale CA-9
Lake Eleanor Reservoir CA-9
Lake Elem Sch MS-4
Lake Elem Sch—school MS-4
**Lake Eliza**—pop pl IN-6
Lake Elizabeth WI-6
Lake Elizabeth Ch—church MN-6
Lake Elizabeth (Township of)—civ div MN-6
Lake Elledge Dam AL-4
Lake Ellen MN-6
**Lake Ellen**—pop pl NC-3
Lake Ellen Baptist Ch—church FL-3
Lake Ellen Ch—church FL-3
Lake Ellen Dam—dam TN-4
Lake Ellenor Village (Shop Ctr)—locale FL-3
Lake Elliot AL-4
Lake Ellis Dam—dam MA-1
Lake Ellyn PA-2
Lake Ellyn Dam—dam PA-2
**Lake Elmdale**—pop pl AR-4
**Lake Elmo**—pop pl MN-6
**Lake Elmore**—pop pl VT-1
Lake Elmsmere OH-6
Lake Eloi Light 1—locale LA-4
Lake Elsie Natl Wildlife Ref—park ND-7
**Lake Elsinore**—pop pl CA-9
Lake Elton Dam—dam NC-3
**Lake Elysian**—pop pl MN-6
Lake Emelene MI-6
Lake Emeline MI-6
**Lake Emily**—pop pl WI-6
Lake Emily Cem—cemetery MN-6
Lake Emily Cem—cemetery WI-6
Lake Emily Sch—school WI-6
Lake Emma Cem—cemetery MN-6
Lake Emma Lookout Tower—locale MI-6
**Lake Emma (Township of)**—pop pl MN-6
Lake Emmeline MI-6
Lake Emory Dam—dam NC-3
**Lake End**—pop pl LA-4
Lake End Oil Field—oilfield LA-4
Lake End Park—park LA-4
Lake Englesby MI-6
Lake Enno NJ-2
**Lake Erie Beach**—pop pl NY-2
Lake Erie Beagle Club—other NY-2
Lake Erie Coll—school OH-6
Lake Erie Community Park—park PA-2
Lake Erie State Park—park NY-2
Lake Erskine Dam—dam NJ-2
Lake Eshquaguma MN-6
**Lake Estates**—pop pl IL-6
**Lake Estates**—pop pl TX-5
Lake Estline NJ-2
Lake Ethel Trail—trail WY-8
Lake Eton FL-3
Lake Eufaula GA-3
Lake Eunice—locale MN-6
Lake Eunice Cem—cemetery MN-6
Lake Eunice Ch—church MN-6
**Lake Eunice (Township of)**—pop pl MN-6
Lake Euphemia NC-3
Lake Eureka KS-7
Lake Evens WA-9
**Lake Everett**—pop pl IN-6
Lake Excelsior FL-3
Lake Fairfax County Park—park VA-3
**Lake Fairlee**—pop pl VT-1
Lake Falmouth Dam—dam NC-3
Lake Fanganiszky DE-2
Lake Farley Park—park SD-7
**Lake Farm**—pop pl AR-4
Lake Farms Archeol District—hist pl WI-6
Lake Fausse Point LA-4
Lake Faussepointe LA-4
Lake Fausse Pointe Cut—canal LA-4
Lake Fayette TX-5
Lake Fegan State Park KS-7
Lake Feldtman MI-6
Lake Feldtmann MI-6
Lake Felicity—bay LA-4
Lake Fenton—CDP MI-6
Lake Fenton Sch—school MI-6
Lake Fern—locale FL-3
Lake Fernald MN-6
Lake Fernell MN-6
Lake Ferrell Oil Field—area TX-5
Lake Feusse Point LA-4
Lakefield—locale LA-4
Lakefield—locale MI-6
**Lakefield**—pop pl MN-6
**Lakefield**—pop pl WI-6
Lakefield Cem—cemetery (2) MI-6
Lakefield Ch—church MI-6
**Lakefield (Township of)**—pop pl (2) MI-6
Lake Fifteen WI-6
Lake Fifteen Creek WI-6
Lake Fin-Feather—reservoir IA-7
Lake Fin-Feather Dam—dam IA-7
Lake Fisher Dam—dam NC-3
Lake Fish Hatchery Hist Dist—hist pl WY-8
Lake Five MI-6
Lake Five MN-6
**Lake Five**—pop pl WI-6
Lake Five Creek MI-6
Lake Five Sch—school WI-6
**Lake Five State Wildlife Mngmt Area**—pop pl MN-6
Lake Flambeau WI-6
Lake Flat—flat AZ-5
Lake Flat—flat UT-8
Lake Flat No. 8 Township—civ div SD-7
Lake Flat Township—civil SD-7
Lake Fleury MI-6
Lake Florence WA-9
Lake Florence—lake OR-9
Lake Florence Dam—dam PA-2
Lake Florida Ch—church MN-6
**Lake Floyd**—pop pl WV-2
Lake Fluety MI-6
Lake Ford—locale MD-2
Lake Ford (historical)—locale MO-7
Lake Foreen Dam—dam AL-4
Lake Forest KS-7
Lake Forest—CDP AL-4
**Lake Forest**—pop pl CA-9
**Lake Forest**—pop pl (2) FL-3
**Lake Forest**—pop pl (2) IL-6
**Lake Forest**—pop pl NJ-2
**Lake Forest**—pop pl SC-3
**Lake Forest**—pop pl TN-4
**Lake Forest**—pop pl TX-5
**Lake Forest**—pop pl WA-9
Lake Forest—uninc pl LA-4
Lake Forest—uninc pl TX-5
Lake Forest Acad—school IL-6
Lake Forest Baptist Ch—church FL-3
Lake Forest Cem—cemetery IL-6
Lake Forest Cem—cemetery MI-6
Lake Forest Coll—school IL-6
Lake Forest Country Club—other OH-6
Lake Forest Creek—stream IN-6
Lake Forest Dam—dam AL-4
Lake Forest Dam—dam MS-4
Lake Forest East Elem Sch—school DE-2
Lake Forest Estates IL-6
**Lake Forest Estates**—pop pl NE-7
**Lake Forest Estates**—pop pl TN-4
Lake Forest Estates—post sta MO-7
**Lake Forest Estates (subdivision)**—pop pl AL-4
**Lake Forest Estates (subdivision)**—pop pl NC-3
Lake Forest Golf Course—locale AL-4
**Lake Forest Hills**—pop pl FL-3
**Lake Forest Hills (subdivision)**—pop pl FL-3
Lake Forest Hist Dist—hist pl IL-6
Lake Forest HS—school DE-2
**Lake Forest Manor**—pop pl FL-3
**Lake Forest Mobile Home Est**—pop pl DE-2
Lake Forest North—CDP WA-9
Lake Forest North Elem Sch—school DE-2
Lake Forest Park—park PA-2
Lake Forest Park—park (2) TX-5
**Lake Forest Park**—pop pl WA-9
**Lake Forest Park (subdivision)**—pop pl MA-1
Lake Forest Presbyterian Ch—church TN-4
Lake Forest Ranch Camp—locale MS-4
Lake Forest Sch—school (3) FL-3
Lake Forest Sch—school NC-3
Lake Forest Shop Ctr—locale FL-3
Lake Forest South Elem Sch—school DE-2
**Lake Forest (subdivision)**—pop pl AL-4
**Lake Forest (subdivision)**—pop pl MS-4
**Lake Forest (subdivision)**—pop pl (2) NC-3
Lake Fork CO-8
Lake Fork ID-8
Lake Fork UT-8
**Lake Fork**—pop pl ID-8
**Lake Fork**—pop pl IL-6
**Lake Fork**—pop pl MO-7
**Lake Fork**—pop pl OH-6
Lake Fork—stream (9) CO-8
Lake Fork—stream (4) ID-8
Lake Fork—stream (5) IL-6
Lake Fork—stream MT-8
Lake Fork—stream (2) NM-5
Lake Fork—stream OR-9
Lake Fork—stream (5) UT-8
Lake Fork—valley CO-8
Lake Fork Bighorn Creek—stream MT-8
Lake Fork Bridge Creek MT-8
Lake Fork Campground—locale CO-8
Lake Fork Campground—park OR-9
Lake Fork Canal—canal UT-8
Lake Fork Canyon—valley NM-5
Lake Fork Ch—church IL-6
Lake Fork Ch—church OH-6
Lake Fork Cochetopa Creek—stream CO-8
Lake Fork Corral—locale UT-8
Lake Fork Creek ID-8
Lake Fork Creek MT-8
Lake Fork Creek UT-8
Lake Fork Creek—stream OR-9
Lake Fork Creek—stream TX-5
Lake Fork Creek—stream UT-8
Lake Fork Creek—stream WY-8
Lake Fork Crescent River—stream AK-9
Lake Fork Extension Canal—canal UT-8
Lake Fork Falls—falls WY-8
Lake Fork Forest Service Station UT-8
Lake Fork Forest Service Station—locale ID-8
Lake Fork Forest Service Station—locale UT-8
Lake Fork Guard Station—locale UT-8
Lake Fork Gunnison CO-8
Lake Fork - in part UT-8
Lake Fork Knik River—stream AK-9
Lake Fork Licking River—stream OH-6
Lake Fork Mesa—bench NM-5
Lake Fork Minnesota Creek—stream CO-8
Lake Fork Mohican River—stream OH-6
Lakefork Mountain UT-8
Lake Fork Mtn—summit UT-8
Lake Fork North Crestone Creek—stream CO-8
Lake Fork Paint River—stream AK-9
Lake Fork Peak—summit NM-5
Lake Fork Ranch—locale CO-8
Lake Fork Reservoir ID-8
Lakefork River UT-8
Lake Fork River—stream UT-8
Lake Fork Rsvr—reservoir (2) TX-5
Lakefork Sch—hist pl OH-6
Lake Fork Special Ditch—stream IL-6
Lake Fork Spring—spring ID-8
**Lake Fork (Township of)**—pop pl IL-6
Lake Fork Trail—trail CO-8
Lake Fork Western Canal—canal UT-8
Lake Fork Wildlife Mngmt Area—park UT-8
Lakeformer Creek MS-4
Lake Forrest Dam—dam MS-4
Lake Fort Scott—reservoir KS-7
Lake Fort Smith State Park—park AR-4
Lake Fortuna—bay LA-4
Lake Fountain Head Dam—dam AL-4
Lake Fourteen WI-6
Lake Fox Dam—dam AL-4
Lake Frances—locale AR-4
Lake Frances—uninc pl FL-3
Lake Frances Dam—dam MT-8
Lake Francis AR-4
Lake Francis MT-8
Lake Francis OK-5
Lake Francis Sch—school MN-6
Lake Francis State Public Shooting Area—park SD-7
Lake Francos LA-4
Lake Frank MD-2
Lake Franklin Pierce NH-1
Lake Frazier Swamp—swamp LA-4
**Lake Fremont**—pop pl MN-6
Lake Fremont Cem—cemetery MN-6
Lake Fremont (Township of)—civ div MN-6
Lake Freya WA-9

Lake Frierson Dam ... AL-4
Lake Front ... IN-6
Lakefront Dock—locale ... TN-4
Lake Front Duck Club—other ... UT-8
Lakefront Estates ... AL-4
**Lakefront Lodge**—pop pl ... TX-5
Lake Front Park—park ... IL-6
Lakefront Park—park ... IN-6
Lake Front Park—park ... WI-6
**Lake Front Village (subdivision)**—pop pl ... AL-4
Lake Fualkton State Game Ref—park ... SD-7
Lake Furnal ... MN-6
Lake Gage Cem—cemetery ... IN-6
Lake Galena ... PA-2
Lake Galena—reservoir ... PA-2
Lake Galilee Dam—dam ... TN-4
Lake Galoria Dam—dam ... AL-4
Lake Garda Sch—school ... CT-1
**Lake Garda ( within MSA's 1170 and 3280 )**—pop pl ... CT-1
**Lake Gardens**—pop pl ... NY-2
Lake Gardner ... KS-7
Lake Gardner Dam—dam ... MA-1
**Lake Garfield**—pop pl ... FL-3
Lake Garfield Dam—dam ... MA-1
Lake Garnett Park—park ... KS-7
Lake Gary Dam—dam ... AL-4
Lake Genele Dam—dam ... NC-3
**Lake Genesis Country (subdivision)**—pop pl ... TN-4
Lake Geneva ... PA-2
**Lake Geneva**—pop pl ... FL-3
**Lake Geneva**—pop pl ... IN-6
**Lake Geneva**—pop pl ... WI-6
Lake Geneva Camp—locale ... MN-6
Lake Geneva Campground—locale ... WY-8
Lake Geneva Dam—dam ... IN-6
Lake George ... TX-5
**Lake George**—pop pl ... CO-8
**Lake George**—pop pl ... MI-6
**Lake George**—pop pl ... MN-6
**Lake George**—pop pl ... NY-2
**Lake George**—pop pl (2) ... WI-6
Lake George—reservoir ... PA-2
Lake George Battlefield Park—park ... NY-2
Lake George Beach State Park—park ... NY-2
Lake George Canal—canal ... IN-6
Lake George Cem—cemetery ... CO-8
Lake George Cem—cemetery ... SD-7
Lake George County Park—park ... MN-6
Lake George Dam—dam (2) ... AL-4
Lake George Dam—dam (2) ... IN-6
Lake George Dam—dam ... MA-1
Lake George Dam—dam ... NJ-2
Lake George Dam—dam ... PA-2
Lake George Dam North Unit—dam ... ND-7
Lake George Drainage Ditch—canal ... MS-4
Lake George Glacier—glacier ... AK-9
Lake George Landing—locale ... MS-4
Lake George Natl Wildlife Ref—park ... ND-7
Lake George Point—cape ... FL-3
Lake George Sch—school ... SD-7
Lake George State Public Shooting Area—park ... SD-7
**Lake George (Town of)**—pop pl ... NY-2
**Lake George Township**—pop pl ... ND-7
**Lake George Township**—pop pl ... SD-7
**Lake George (Township of)**—pop pl (2) ... MN-6
**Lake Gerald**—pop pl ... MI-6
Lake Gerard Dam—dam ... NJ-2
Lake Gertrude ... FL-3
Lake Gibbon ... MI-6
Lake Gibson Ch—church ... FL-3
Lake Gibson Conservation Dam—dam ... IN-6
Lake Gibson JHS—school ... FL-3
Lake Gibson Senior HS—school ... FL-3
Lake Gibson United Methodist Ch—church ... FL-3
Lake Giles Dam—dam ... PA-2
Lake Girard ... NJ-2
Lake Girard Park—park ... MN-6
Lake Gitchagumee ... MI-6
**Lake Glenwood (subdivision)**—pop pl ... NC-3
Lake Glesbiski ... WI-6
Lake Gloria—reservoir ... PA-2
Lake Gloria Dam—dam ... AL-4
**Lake Gogebic**—pop pl ... MI-6
Lake Gordon Dam—dam ... PA-2
Lake Grace Dam—dam ... AL-4
Lake Gracie ... LA-4
Lake Grampus—swamp ... AR-4
Lake Grand Bayou ... LA-4
Lake Grand Ecaille—bay ... LA-4
**Lake Grange**—pop pl ... IN-6
Lake Grassy ... FL-3
Lake Graveline ... MS-4
Lake Gray ... MI-6
Lake Green Countrie—reservoir ... PA-2
Lake Greenville Dam—dam ... AL-4
Lake Greenwood ... IN-6
Lake Griffin Dam—dam ... AL-4
Lake Griffin State Park—park ... FL-3
**Lake Grinnell**—pop pl ... NJ-2
Lake Grinnell Dam—dam ... NJ-2
Lake Groundhog Campsite—locale ... PA-2
**Lake Grove**—pop pl ... NY-2
Lake Grove—uninc pl ... OR-9
Lake Grove Cem—cemetery ... AR-4
Lake Grove Cem—cemetery ... MA-1
Lake Grove Cem—cemetery ... TX-5
Lake Grove Ch—church (4) ... AR-4
Lake Grove Ch—church ... KY-4
Lake Grove Ch—church ... MN-6
Lake Grove Ch—church ... MS-4
Lake Grove Ch—church ... TN-4
Lake Grove Park—park ... OR-9
Lake Grove Sch—school ... AR-4
Lake Grove Sch—school ... IL-6
Lake Grove Sch—school ... MS-4
Lake Grove Sch—school ... OR-9
**Lake Grove (Township of)**—pop pl ... MN-6
Lake Guard Station—locale ... UT-8
Lake Gulch—valley (2) ... CA-9
Lake Gulch—valley (3) ... CO-8
Lake Gulch—valley ... ID-8
Lake Gulch—valley ... MT-8
Lake Gulch—valley ... OR-9
Lake Gulch—valley ... WY-8
Lake Guntersville State Park—park ... AL-4
Lake Habert ... TX-5
Lake Haik Pochee ... FL-3
Lake Halbert—uninc pl ... TX-5
Lake Hall ... FL-3
Lakehall—locale ... AR-4
Lake Hallala ... AL-4
**Lake Hallie**—pop pl ... WI-6
Lake Hallie Ch—church ... WI-6
Lake Hamburg—lake ... FL-3
Lake Hamilton ... AR-4
**Lake Hamilton**—pop pl ... AR-4
**Lake Hamilton**—pop pl ... FL-3
Lake Hamilton—reservoir ... PA-2
Lake Hamilton Ch—church ... AR-4
Lake Hamilton Dam—dam ... NC-3
Lake Hamilton Dam—dam ... PA-2
Lake Hamilton Dam—hist pl ... OH-6
Lake Hamilton (Township of)—fmr MCD ... AR-4
Lake Hamlin ... FL-3
Lake Hamlin ... MI-6
Lake Hammal ... MN-6
Lake Hammil ... WI-6
Lake Hamolton Dam ... PA-2
Lake Hamsen ... SD-7
Lake Hancock Target Range—other ... WA-9
Lake Hanska Cem—cemetery ... MN-6
Lake Hanska Ch—church ... MN-6
**Lake Hanska (Township of)**—pop pl ... MN-6
Lake Harasu Golf Course—other ... AZ-5
Lake Harbor ... MI-6
Lakeharbor—locale ... TN-4
**Lake Harbor**—pop pl ... FL-3
Lake Harbor Ch—church ... MS-4
Lake Harbor Estates ... MI-6
**Lake Harbor Estates**—pop pl ... TN-4
Lake Harbor Hills ... MI-6
Lake Harbor Point ... MI-6
Lake Hardeman Dam—dam ... TN-4
Lake Harden ... MN-6
Lake Hardesty ... OK-5
Lake Hardin ... MN-6
Lake Hardy Dam—dam ... IN-6
Lake Hargis Dam—dam ... AL-4
Lake Harmon ... IA-7
**Lake Harmony**—pop pl ... PA-2
Lake Harney ... OR-9
Lake Harriet ... WI-6
Lake Harriet Camp—locale ... OR-9
Lake Harriet Dam—dam ... OR-9
Lake Harriet Sch—school ... MN-6
Lake Harrington ... MO-7
Lake Harris ... MT-8
Lake Harris—lake ... FL-3
Lake Harris Dam—dam ... AL-4
Lake Harrison ... MS-4
**Lake Hart**—pop pl ... IN-6
Lake Hastings Park—park ... NE-7
Lake Hatch Oil and Gas Field—oilfield ... LA-4
Lake Hathcock ... AL-4
Lake Hattie Canal—canal ... WY-8
Lake Hattie Rsvr—reservoir ... WY-8
Lake Hattie Supply Canal—canal ... WY-8
Lake Hattie Supply Ditch No 2—canal ... WY-8
**Lake Hattie (Township of)**—pop pl ... MN-6
Lake Hauto ... PA-2
Lake Hauto—locale ... PA-2
Lake Hauto Dam—dam ... PA-2
**Lake Havasu City**—pop pl ... AZ-5
Lake Havasu City Airp—airport ... AZ-5
Lake Havasu City HS—school ... AZ-5
Lake Havasu City Post Office—building ... AZ-5
Lake Havasu JHS—school ... AZ-5
Lake Havasu State Park—park ... AZ-5
Lake Haven Dam—dam ... IN-6
**Lake Haven (subdivision)**—pop pl ... NC-3
Lake Hawaco ... IN-6
Lake Hawthorn ... FL-3
Lake Hayes—locale ... LA-4
**Lake Hayward**—pop pl ... CT-1
Lake Hayward Brook—stream ... CT-1
Lake Hazel Dam—dam ... MS-4
Lake Hazel Dam—dam ... NC-3
Lake Hazel Sch—school ... ID-8
Lakehead—locale ... CA-9
Lake Hebgen Lodge—locale ... MT-8
Lake Hefner Golf Course—other ... OK-5
Lake Hefner Park—park ... OK-5
**Lake Heights**—pop pl ... WA-9
Lake Heights Sch—school ... WA-9
**Lake Helen**—pop pl ... FL-3
Lake Helen—reservoir ... AL-4
Lake Helen-Cassadaga Cem—cemetery ... FL-3
Lake Helen Dam ... AL-4
Lake Helen Dam—dam ... MS-4
Lake Helfner ... OK-5
Lake Helmerich Dam—dam ... IN-6
Lake Hemet Main Canal—canal ... CA-9
Lake Hendricks Dam—dam ... IA-7
Lake Hendricks State Rec Area—park ... SD-7
**Lake Hendricks Township**—pop pl ... SD-7
Lake Henry—lake ... OR-9
**Lake Henry**—pop pl ... MN-6
Lake Henry—reservoir ... PA-2
Lake Henry Ch—church ... MS-4
Lake Henry Dam—dam ... MS-4
Lake Henry Dam—dam (2) ... PA-2
Lake Henry Inlet—gut ... CO-8
**Lake Henry (Township of)**—pop pl ... MN-6
Lake Henshaw (Recreation Area)—park ... CA-9
Lake Heritage—reservoir ... PA-2
Lake Heritage Dam—dam ... PA-2
Lake Herman Dam—dam ... NC-3
Lake Herman State Park—park ... SD-7
Lake Hermitage ... LA-4
Lake Hermitage—other ... LA-4
Lake Hermitage Oil and Gas Field—oilfield ... LA-4
Lake Hessler ... WA-9
**Lake Hester Township**—pop pl ... ND-7
Lake Heyburn ... OK-5
Lake Heyburn State Park—park ... OK-5
Lake Hiawassa ... FL-3
Lake Hiawatha ... MI-6
**Lake Hiawatha**—pop pl ... MA-1
**Lake Hiawatha**—pop pl ... NJ-2
Lake Hiawatha Dam—dam ... MA-1
Lake Hickory Country Club—locale ... NC-3
Lake Hico Dam—dam ... MS-4
Lake Hiddenwood Dam—dam ... SD-7
Lake Hiddewood State Park—park ... SD-7
Lake Hideaway Dam—dam ... IN-6
Lake Higgins Dam—dam ... NC-3
Lake Highland Baptist Ch—church ... AL-4
Lake Highland Ch—church ... TX-5
Lake Highland Preparatory Sch—school ... FL-3
**Lake Highlands**—pop pl ... AL-4
Lake Highlands—uninc pl ... TX-5
Lake Highlands Sch—school ... TX-5
Lake Hilbert ... WI-6
Lake Hilda ... WI-6
Lake Hill ... PA-2
**Lake Hill**—pop pl ... NY-2
Lake Hill—summit ... AK-9
Lake Hill—summit ... CA-9
Lake Hill—summit (2) ... CO-8
Lake Hill—summit ... WA-9
Lake Hill—summit ... WY-8
Lakehill Airp—airport ... PA-2
Lake Hill Campground—locale ... UT-8
Lake Hill Cem—cemetery ... NY-2
Lake Hill Cem—cemetery ... UT-8
Lake Hill Ch—church ... AL-4
Lake Hill Dam—dam ... TN-4
**Lake Hill Estates (subdivision)**—pop pl ... AL-4
Lakehill Landing Area ... PA-2
Lake Hill Marina—locale ... AL-4
Lake Hill Memorial Garden—cemetery ... TN-4
Lake Hill No. 5 Township—civ div ... SD-7
Lakehills—locale ... GA-3
**Lake Hills**—pop pl ... IN-6
**Lake Hills**—pop pl (2) ... TN-4
**Lake Hills**—pop pl ... TX-5
**Lake Hills**—pop pl ... VA-3
**Lake Hills**—pop pl ... WA-9
Lake Hills Ch—church (2) ... TN-4
Lake Hill Sch—school ... IL-6
Lake Hill Sch—school ... MO-7
Lake Hills Ch of Christ ... TN-4
Lake Hills Club Dam—dam ... NC-3
Lake Hills Country Club—other ... IN-6
**Lake Hills Estates**—pop pl ... CA-9
Lakehill Shop Ctr—locale ... AR-4
Lake Hills Memorial Cemetery ... UT-8
Lake Hills Memorial Gardens—cemetery ... GA-3
Lake Hills Memorial Park ... UT-8
**Lakehills (North Lake)**—pop pl ... TX-5
**Lake Hills North (subdivision)**—pop pl ... AL-4
Lake Hills Plaza (Shop Ctr)—locale ... FL-3
Lake Hills Presbyterian Ch ... TN-4
Lake Hills Sch—school ... FL-3
Lake Hills Sch—school ... MI-6
Lake Hills Sch—school ... WA-9
Lake Hills Sewage Disposal—other ... WA-9
Lake Hills Shop Ctr—locale ... TN-4
**Lake Hills Subdivision**—pop pl ... UT-8
Lake Hill Township—civil ... SD-7
**Lake (historical)**—pop pl ... OR-9
**Lake Hiwasse**—pop pl ... OK-5
**Lake Hiwassee**—pop pl ... OK-5
Lake Hobbie—lake ... KS-7
Lake Hodgsons ... OH-6
Lake Hogan Dam—dam ... NC-3
Lake Holbrook Dam—dam ... MA-1
Lake Holcombe ... WI-6
**Lake Holcombe (Town of)**—pop pl ... WI-6
Lakehole in the Ground Waterhole—reservoir ... OR-9
Lake Holes Branch—stream ... FL-3
Lake Holiday Hide-Away Dam—dam ... IN-6
**Lake Holiday (Holiday Lake)**—pop pl ... IL-6
Lake Holiness Ch—church ... MS-4
Lake Holliday ... IN-6
Lake Hollow—valley ... AR-4
Lake Hollow—valley ... ID-8
Lake Hollow—valley ... OH-6
Lake Hollow—valley ... TN-4
Lake Hollow—valley ... TX-5
Lake Hollow—valley (3) ... UT-8
Lake Holloway (census name Crystal Lake)—other ... FL-3
Lake Holly Dam—dam ... IN-6
Lake Holmes ... ND-7
Lakehoma Ch—church ... OK-5
Lake Hooker ... WA-9
Lake Hook Sch—school ... MN-6
Lake Hopatcong ... NJ-2
**Lake Hopatcong**—pop pl ... NJ-2
Lake Hopatcong (census name Espanong) ... NJ-2
Lake Hopatcong Dam—dam ... NJ-2
Lake Hopatcong (sta.) (Landing) ... NJ-2
Lake Hopewell ... CT-1
Lake Horace ... NH-1
Lake Horseshoe ... MN-6
**Lake Hortonia**—pop pl ... VT-1
Lake Hosea Dam—dam ... NC-3
Lake Hoskins Dam—dam ... ND-7
Lake Hosp—hospital ... MS-4
Lake Hosp of the Palm Beaches—hospital ... FL-3
Lake Hotel—locale ... WY-8
Lake House Meadow—flat ... MT-8
Lake Houser—reservoir ... NC-3
Lake Howard ... AL-4
Lake Howard—locale ... AL-4
**Lake Howard**—pop pl ... GA-3
Lake Howell Bible Chapel—church ... FL-3
Lake Howell HS—school ... FL-3
Lake HS—school ... OH-6
Lake Hubbard ... TX-5
**Lake Hubert**—pop pl ... MN-6
**Lake Hughes**—pop pl ... CA-9
Lake Hughes Dam—dam ... NC-3
Lake Hughes Truck Trail—trail ... CA-9
Lake Humphreys ... CT-1
**Lake Humphreys**—pop pl ... OK-5
Lake Hunice—lake ... OR-9
Lake Hunt Dam—dam ... NC-3
**Lake Huntington**—pop pl ... NY-2
Lake Huntington Cem—cemetery ... NY-2
**Lake Huron Beach**—pop pl ... MI-6
Lake Huron Camp—locale ... MI-6
**Lakehurst**—pop pl ... NJ-2
**Lakehurst**—pop pl ... NY-2
Lakehurst Air Engineering Center—military ... NJ-2
Lakehurst NAS—post sta ... NJ-2
Lakehurst Naval Air Station—military ... NJ-2
**Lakehurst Station**—pop pl ... NJ-2
**Lake Ibsen Township**—pop pl ... ND-7
Lake Icaria—reservoir ... IA-7
Lake Icaria Dam—dam ... IA-7
Lake Ida Canal—canal ... FL-3
Lake Ida Cem—cemetery ... MN-6
**Lake Ida Heights (subdivision)**—pop pl ... AL-4
Lake Ida Sch—school ... MN-6
**Lake Ida (Township of)**—pop pl ... MN-6
Lake Idlewild ... KS-7
Lake Idlewild ... MI-6
Lake IHM—lake ... MI-6
**Lake Iliff**—pop pl ... NJ-2
Lake Ilo Dam—dam ... ND-7
Lake Ilo Natl Wildlife Ref—park ... ND-7
Lake Imperial ... TX-5
Lake Inez ... AL-4
Lake Inez—lake ... MI-6
Lake Inez Campground—locale ... MT-8
Lake Inez Dam—dam ... NJ-2
Lake Interlocken ... FL-3
**Lake Intervale**—pop pl ... NJ-2
**Lake In The Clouds**—pop pl ... PA-2
Lake in the Clouds—reservoir ... PA-2
Lake-In-The-Clouds Dam—dam ... PA-2
**Lake in the Hills**—pop pl ... IL-6
Lake in the Hills—reservoir ... IL-6
Lake In The Ledges, The—lake ... NY-2
Lake in the Sky Dam—dam ... TN-4
**Lake in the Woods**—pop pl ... IL-6
Lake in the Woods Campground—park ... OR-9
Lake In The Woods Dam—dam ... AL-4
Lake in the Woods Dam—dam ... IN-6
Lake Inwater ... TN-4
Lake Ioscoe ... NJ-2
Lake Iowa County Rec Area—park ... IA-7
Lake Irena ... MT-8
Lake Irena—reservoir ... PA-2
Lake Irena Dam—dam ... PA-2
Lake Irene ... MT-8
**Lake Iroquois**—pop pl ... IL-6
Lake Iroquois Sch—school ... VT-1
Lake Irrigation District Canal—canal ... ID-8
Lake Isabel Inlet Ditch—canal ... NM-5
Lake Isabella ... CA-9
Lake Isabella ... MN-6
**Lake Isabella**—pop pl ... CA-9
Lake Isabella (CCD)—cens area ... CA-9
Lake Isabella (Isabella)—CDP ... CA-9
Lake Ishkote ... MI-6
Lake Isom—swamp ... TN-4
Lake Isom Natl Wildlife Ref—park ... TN-4
Lake Issaquenna ... SC-3
Lake Issqueena ... SC-3
Lake Issue—lake ... FL-3
Lake Istokpoga ... FL-3
Lake Istopoga ... FL-3
**Lake Itasca**—pop pl ... MN-6
Lake Itawamba Dam—dam ... MS-4
Lake Iveen ... OR-9
Lake Ivis ... FL-3
Lake Jackson—locale ... FL-3
**Lake Jackson**—pop pl ... TX-5
**Lake Jackson**—pop pl ... VA-3
Lake Jackson Ch—church ... FL-3
Lake Jackson Christian Acad—school ... FL-3
**Lake Jackson Farms**—pop pl ... TX-5
Lake Jackson Free Will Baptist Ch—church ... FL-3
Lake Jackson Mounds—hist pl ... FL-3
Lake Jackson United Methodist Ch—church ... FL-3
**Lake James**—pop pl ... IN-6
Lake James Ch—church ... NC-3
Lake James Dam—dam ... NC-3
Lake James Golf Course—other ... IN-6
Lake James Park—park ... NE-7
Lake James Patrol Cabin—locale ... WA-9
Lake Jamie—reservoir ... PA-2
Lake Jamie Dam—dam ... PA-2
Lake Jane Dam ... AL-4
Lake Jason ... IN-6
Lake Jason ... WA-9
Lake Jean—reservoir ... PA-2
Lake Jean Dam—dam ... PA-2
Lake Jeanette Campground—locale ... MN-6
Lake Jeanette Dam—dam ... NC-3
Lake Jeffrie ... FL-3
Lake Joggord ... FL-3
**Lake Jem**—pop pl ... FL-3
Lake Jennings Park—park ... CA-9
**Lake Jessie**—pop pl ... ND-7
**Lake Jessie (Township of)**—pop pl ... MN-6
Lake Jessup ... FL-3
Lake JHS—school ... CO-8
Lake Joann ... MI-6
Lake Jo-Ann—reservoir ... PA-2
**Lake Joanna**—pop pl ... FL-3
Lake Jo-Ann Dam—dam ... PA-2
Lake Johanna Cem—cemetery ... MN-6
Lake Johanna (Township of)—civ div ... MN-6
Lake John ... SD-7
Lake John—reservoir ... PA-2
Lake John Dam—dam ... PA-2
Lake John Paul Dam—dam ... AL-4
Lake Johnson ... FL-3
Lake Johnson ... MI-6
Lake Johnson Dam—dam ... NC-3
Lake Johnson Nature Park—park ... NC-3
Lake Johnston—reservoir ... PA-2
Lake Jordan ... AL-4
Lake Jourdan ... AL-4
**Lake Jovita**—pop pl ... FL-3
**Lake Joy**—pop pl ... AL-4
**Lake Joy**—pop pl ... WA-9
Lake Juanita ... FL-3
Lake Juanita Outlet Control Dam—dam ... ND-7
**Lake Judge Perez**—pop pl ... LA-4
**Lake Judge Perez (Lake Hermitage)**—pop pl ... LA-4
Lake Judson Dam—dam ... AL-4
Lake Jules Dam—dam ... AL-4
Lake Juliet Dam—dam ... NJ-2
**Lake Junaluska**—pop pl ... NC-3
Lake Junaluska Dam—dam ... NC-3
Lake Junction ... MO-7
Lake Junction—locale ... NJ-2
Lake Junction—locale ... WY-8
**Lake Junction**—pop pl ... MO-7
Lake June—uninc pl ... TX-5
Lake June Ch—church ... TX-5
**Lake Juniata**—pop pl ... FL-3
Lake Juvet ... NY-2
Lake Kabetogama—other ... MN-6
Lake Kachess ... WA-9
Lake Kalmia Dam—dam ... NJ-2
Lake Kampeska ... SD-7
Lake Kanikan ... ID-8
Lake Kannapolis Dam—dam ... NC-3
Lake Kanosha ... CT-1
**Lake Kapowsin**—pop pl ... WA-9
Lake Katherine Shop Ctr—locale ... FL-3
**Lake Kathryn Estates (Trailer Park)**—pop pl ... FL-3
**Lake Kathryn Heights**—pop pl ... FL-3
Lake Kathryn Village—uninc pl ... FL-3
Lake Kathyrn Dam—dam ... NJ-2
**Lake Katonah**—pop pl ... NY-2
**Lake Katrine**—pop pl ... NY-2
Lake Kawbawgan ... MI-6
Lake Kechewaishke ... WI-6
Lake Keechelus ... WA-9
**Lake Keesus**—pop pl ... WI-6
Lake Kenilworth Dam—dam ... NC-3
Lake Kennedy ... MI-6
Lake Kennedy ... UT-8
Lake Kennedy ... WY-8
Lake Kenosha ... CT-1
Lake Keomah State Park—park ... IA-7
Lake Ker ... FL-3
Lake Kerr ... FL-3
Lake Kerr Key—island ... FL-3
Lake Kewaguesaga ... WI-6
Lake Key—island ... FL-3
Lake Key Pass—channel ... FL-3
Lake Kichapoo ... TX-5
**Lake Killarney**—pop pl ... IL-6
Lake Kimberly Dam—dam ... PA-2
**Lake Kiowa**—pop pl ... TX-5
Lake Kippax ... ND-7
**Lake Kirkwood**—pop pl ... CA-9
Lake Kissimmee State Park—park ... FL-3
**Lake Kitchawan**—pop pl ... NY-2
Lake Kitchigamin ... WI-6
Lake Kiwa ... OR-9
Lake Knob—summit ... PA-2
**Lake Kohola**—pop pl ... KS-7
lake Koosel ... WI-6
Lake Koronis Assembly Ground—locale ... MN-6
Lakekta Point—cape ... AK-9
Lake Kurtz—reservoir ... PA-2
Lake Kushaqua ... NY-2
Lake Kvidera ... MI-6
Lake La Bell ... WI-6
Lake Labish—flat ... OR-9
Lake Labish Ditch—canal ... OR-9
Lake Labish Sch—school ... OR-9
Lake La Butte ... MS-4
**Lake Lackawanna**—pop pl ... NJ-2
Lake Lackawanna Dam—dam ... NJ-2
Lake Lackawanna Golf Course—other ... NJ-2
Lake La Crosse ... WA-9
Lake Ladore—reservoir ... PA-2
Lake Ladore Dam—dam ... PA-2
Lake LaFaye ... WI-6
Lake La Fortuna ... LA-4
Lake La Joie ... TN-4
Lake Lajoie Dam—dam ... TN-4
Lake La Joye ... TN-4
Lake Lamar Bruce Dam—dam ... MS-4
Lake Lamar Dam—dam ... NC-3
**Lake Lancelot**—pop pl ... IL-6
Lakeland ... IN-6
Lakeland ... MS-4
Lakeland—locale ... MD-2
Lakeland—locale ... NJ-2
**Lakeland**—pop pl ... FL-3
**Lakeland**—pop pl ... GA-3
**Lakeland**—pop pl ... KY-4
**Lakeland**—pop pl ... LA-4
**Lakeland**—pop pl ... MD-2
**Lakeland**—pop pl ... MI-6
**Lakeland**—pop pl ... MN-6
**Lakeland**—pop pl ... MS-4
**Lakeland**—pop pl ... MO-7
**Lakeland**—pop pl (2) ... NY-2
**Lakeland**—pop pl (2) ... OH-6
**Lakeland**—pop pl ... IN-4
**Lakeland**—pop pl (2) ... TX-5
**Lakeland**—pop pl ... VA-3
Lakeland—uninc pl ... MD-2
Lakeland Baptist Temple—church ... FL-3
**Lakeland Beach**—pop pl ... OH-6
**Lakeland (Camden County Institutions)**—pop pl ... NJ-2
Lakeland Canal—canal ... CA-9
Lakeland (CCD)—cens area ... FL-3
Lakeland (CCD)—cens area ... GA-3
Lakeland Cem—cemetery ... NJ-2
Lakeland Ch—church (2) ... IL-6
Lakeland Ch—church (2) ... MI-6
Lakeland Ch—church ... MS-4
Lakeland Ch—church ... MO-7
Lakeland Christian Ch—church ... FL-3
**Lakeland College**—pop pl ... WI-6
Lakeland Coll of Business—school ... FL-3
Lakeland Dam—dam ... TN-4
Lakeland Farm—locale ... TX-5
Lakeland Farm Lake—reservoir ... LA-4
Lakeland Farms—locale ... AL-4
Lakeland Farms Dam Number Eight—dam ... AL-4
Lakeland Farms Dam Number Eighteen—dam ... AL-4
Lakeland Farms Dam Number Eleven—dam ... AL-4
Lakeland Farms Dam Number Fifteen—dam ... AL-4
Lakeland Farms Dam Number Five—dam ... AL-4
Lakeland Farms Dam Number Four—dam ... AL-4
Lakeland Farms Dam Number Fourteen—dam ... AL-4
Lakeland Farms Dam Number Nine—dam ... AL-4
Lakeland Farms Dam Number Nineteen—dam ... AL-4
Lakeland Farms Dam Number One—dam ... AL-4
Lakeland Farms Dam Number Seven—dam ... AL-4
Lakeland Farms Dam Number Seventeen—dam ... AL-4
Lakeland Farms Dam Number Six—dam ... AL-4
Lakeland Farms Dam Number Sixteen—dam ... AL-4
Lakeland Farms Dam Number Ten—dam ... AL-4
Lakeland Farms Dam Number Thirteen—dam ... AL-4
Lakeland Farms Dam Number Three—dam ... AL-4
Lakeland Farms Dam Number Twelve—dam ... AL-4
Lakeland Farms Dam Number Two—dam ... AL-4
Lakeland Farms Lake Number Eight—reservoir ... AL-4
Lakeland Farms Lake Number Eleven ... AL-4
Lakeland Farms Lake Number Five ... AL-4
Lakeland Farms Lake Number Four ... AL-4
Lakeland Farms Lake Number Nine ... AL-4
Lakeland Farms Lake Number Seven—reservoir ... AL-4
Lakeland Farms Lake Number Six—reservoir ... AL-4
Lakeland Farms Lake Number Ten ... AL-4
Lakeland Farms Lake Number Three ... AL-4
Lakeland Farms Pond Number Eight ... AL-4
Lakeland Farms Pond Number Fifteen—reservoir ... AL-4
Lakeland Farms Pond Number Fourteen—reservoir ... AL-4
Lakeland Farms Pond Number Nineteen—reservoir ... AL-4
Lakeland Farms Pond Number One ... AL-4
Lakeland Farms Pond Number Seventeen ... AL-4
Lakeland Farms Pond Number Sixteen—reservoir ... AL-4
Lakeland Farms Pond Number Twelve ... AL-4
Lakeland Farms Pond Number Two ... AL-4
Lakeland Farms 12 Acre Lake—reservoir ... AL-4
Lakeland Farms 12 Acre Lake Dam—dam ... AL-4
**Lakeland Forest (subdivision)**—pop pl ... AL-4
Lakeland Golf Course—locale ... PA-2
Lake Land Gun Club—other ... CA-9
**Lakeland Heights**—pop pl ... TX-5
Lakeland Highlands—CDP ... FL-3
Lakeland Highlands—ridge ... FL-3
Lakeland Highlands JHS—school ... FL-3
**Lakeland Hills**—pop pl ... IL-6
**Lakeland Hills**—pop pl ... TX-5
Lakeland Hills Country Club—other ... WI-6
Lake Land Hills Golf Club—other ... MI-6
**Lakeland Hills (subdivision)**—pop pl ... NC-3
Lakeland (historical)—locale ... KS-7
**Lakeland (historical)**—pop pl ... IN-6
**Lakeland Homes**—pop pl ... VA-3
Lakeland Hosp—hospital ... WI-6
Lakeland HS—school ... IN-6
Lakeland HS—school ... NY-2
**Lake Landing**—pop pl ... NC-3
Lake Landing Hist Dist—hist pl ... NC-3
Lake Landing (Township of)—fmr MCD ... NC-3
Lakeland JHS—school ... IN-6
**Lakeland Junction**—pop pl ... MN-6
Lakeland Lake—lake ... TX-5
Lakeland Lake—reservoir ... TN-4
Lakeland Lake—reservoir ... VA-3
Lakeland Mall—locale ... FL-3
Lakeland Manor Lake Dam—dam ... IN-6
Lakeland Memorial Gardens—cemetery ... FL-3
Lakeland Memorial Park—cemetery ... NC-3
Lakeland Memorial Park Cemetary—cemetery ... NC-3
Lakeland Memory Gardens Cem—cemetery ... IA-7
Lakeland Municipal Airp—airport ... FL-3
Lakeland North—CDP ... WA-9
Lake Landon ... MN-6
Lakeland Park ... IL-6
Lakeland Park—park (2) ... TX-5
**Lakeland Park**—pop pl ... TN-4
Lakeland Public Library—building ... FL-3
Lakeland Regional Med Ctr—hospital ... FL-3
**Lakeland (River Region Hospital)**—pop pl ... KY-4
Lakeland Sch—school ... CA-9
Lakeland Sch—school ... IL-6
Lakeland Sch—school ... MD-2
Lakeland Sch—school ... MI-6
Lakeland Sch—school ... OH-6
Lakeland Sch—school ... TX-5
Lakeland Sch—school ... WA-9
Lakeland Sch—school ... WI-6
Lakeland Senior HS—school ... FL-3
Lakeland Sewage Pond—reservoir ... TN-4
Lakeland Sewage Pond Dam—dam ... TN-4
Lakeland Shop Ctr—locale ... OK-5
**Lakeland Shores**—pop pl ... MN-6
Lakeland South—CDP ... WA-9
Lakeland South Center (Shop Ctr)—locale ... FL-3
Lakeland Square Mall—locale ... FL-3
**Lakeland Subdivision**—pop pl ... TN-4
**Lakeland Subdivision**—pop pl ... UT-8
Lakeland Tower (fire tower)—tower ... FL-3
**Lakeland (Town of)**—pop pl ... WI-6
**Lakeland Village**—pop pl ... CA-9
**Lakeland Village**—pop pl ... WA-9
Lake Langhofer—lake ... AR-4
Lake Langley ... LA-4
Lake Lanier ... GA-3
**Lake Lanier**—pop pl ... SC-3
Lake Lanier Sailing Club—other ... GA-3
**Lake Lansing**—pop pl ... MI-6
Lake Lansing Ch—church ... MI-6
Lake Lapourde ... LA-4
Lake Largo Dam—dam ... NC-3
Lake La Rose Gas Field—oilfield ... LA-4
Lake Larrabee ... KS-7
Lake Larto ... LA-4
Lake Larue ... MS-4
Lake Larue ... TX-5
Lake LaRue Dam—dam ... MS-4
Lake Lasalle Dam—dam ... IN-6
Lake Lashaway Dam—dam ... MA-1
Lake Lateral—canal ... NM-5
Lake Lathrop ... MO-7
Lake Latimore Dam—dam ... PA-2
Lake Latonka ... IN-6
**Lake Latonka**—pop pl ... IN-6
Lake Latonka—reservoir ... PA-2
Lake Latonka Dam—dam ... IN-6
Lake Latonka Dam—dam ... PA-2
Lake Lauderdale Dam—dam ... NC-3

Lake Laura ... MN-6
Lake Laura Dam—dam ... PA-2
Lake Laura Dam—dam ... TN-4
Lake Laurance Dam—dam ... OR-9
Lake Laura Ridge—ridge ... PA-2
Lake Laura Trail—trail ... PA-2
Lake Laurel Dam—dam ... NC-3
Lake Lavela ... AL-4
**Lake Lawn**—pop pl ... WI-6
Lakelawn Memorial Park—cemetery ... PA-2
Lakelawn Park Golf Course—locale ... PA-2
**Lake Lawrence**—pop pl ... IL-6
Lake Le-Aqua-Na State Park—park ... IL-6
Lake Leavitt Inlet Canal—canal ... CA-9
Lake le Bleu ... LA-4
Lake Lee ... FL-3
Lake Lee Dam—dam ... NC-3
**Lake Leelanau**—pop pl ... MI-6
Lake Lefferts Dam—dam ... NJ-2
Lake Legler ... MN-6
Lake Lehigh—reservoir ... PA-2
Lake Lehigh Dam—dam ... PA-2
Lake Lehman—reservoir ... PA-2
Lake Lehman Dam—dam ... PA-2
Lake Leland ... WA-9
**Lake Lenape**—pop pl ... NJ-2
Lake Lenape—reservoir ... PA-2
Lake Lenape Cave Shelter—locale ... PA-2
Lake Lenape Dam—dam (2) ... NJ-2
Lake Lenape Dam—dam (2) ... PA-2
Lake Lenora ... AL-4
Lake Lenora Dam ... AL-4
Lake Lenora Dam—dam ... AL-4
**Lake Leota**—pop pl ... WA-9
Lake Lepace—reservoir ... MS-4
Lake Lesage ... MI-6
Lake Letterkenny—reservoir ... PA-2
Lake Letterkenny Dam—dam ... PA-2
Lake Leven Cem—cemetery ... MN-6
Lake Lewis Burtschi ... OK-5
Lake Lewis Smith ... AL-4
Lakel Flat—flat ... AZ-5
Lake Liberty ... NY-2
Lake Lida Cem—cemetery ... MN-6
Lake Lillian ... WI-6
**Lake Lillian**—pop pl ... MN-6
Lake Lillian Ch—church ... MN-6
Lake Lillian (Township of)—civ div ... MN-6
Lake Lillie ... CO-8
Lake Lilly Ch—church ... LA-4
Lake Lilyan ... MI-6
**Lake Lincoln**—pop pl ... IN-6
**Lake Lincolndale**—pop pl ... NY-2
**Lake Linden**—pop pl ... MI-6
Lake Linden Village Hall and Fire Station—hist pl ... MI-6
**Lake Lindsey**—pop pl ... FL-3
**Lakeline**—pop pl ... OH-6
Lakeline (Township of)—other ... OH-6
**Lake Linganore**—pop pl ... MD-2
Lake Link ... MN-6
Lake-Little House—hist pl ... WA-9
Lake Lizzy ... WI-6
Lake Llewellyn ... NJ-2
Lake Llewelyn ... NJ-2
Lake Loda ... MI-6
Lake Lodge—locale ... WY-8
Lake Logan Dam—dam ... NC-3
Lake Logan Dam—dam ... TN-4
Lake Lombard ... GA-3
Lake Lona Sch—school ... FL-3
Lake Long ... LA-4
Lake Long ... TX-5
Lake Long Bayou—stream ... LA-4
Lake Long Interlaken ... WI-6
Lake Long Jim ... WA-9
Lake Long Oil and Gas Field—oilfield ... LA-4
Lake Lookout Dam—dam ... MA-1
Lake Lookout Dam—dam ... TN-4
**Lake Lookover**—pop pl ... NJ-2
Lake Loomis ... OH-6
Lake Loraine ... WI-6
Lake Loramie State Park—park ... OH-6
Lake Lorene Lake Dam—dam ... AL-4
Lake Loretta ... WI-6
Lake Lorman Dam—dam ... MS-4
Lake Lorraine ... MA-1
Lake Lorraine—CDP ... FL-3
Lake Lorraine Point—cape ... WA-9
**Lake Los Angeles**—pop pl ... CA-9
**Lake Lotawana**—pop pl ... MO-7
Lake Louis ... LA-4
Lake Louis Burtschi State Game Reservation—park ... OK-5
Lake Louis Burtseki ... OK-5
Lake Louise ... MI-6
Lake Louise ... MT-8
**Lake Louise**—pop pl ... WA-9
Lake Louise—reservoir ... PA-2
Lake Louise Ch—church ... MI-6
Lake Louise Dam—dam (2) ... AL-4
Lake Louise Dam—dam ... IN-6
Lake Louise Dam—dam ... PA-2
Lake Louise Rec AreaAnd Wildlife Ref—park ... SD-7
Lake Louise Sch—school ... MN-6
**Lake Louisvilla**—pop pl ... KY-4
Lake Louisvilla Ch—church ... KY-4
Lake Lowell Sch—school ... ID-8
Lake Lowery ... MS-4
Lake Lowndes State Park—park ... MS-4
Lake Lucas ... NC-3
**Lake Lucerne**—pop pl ... FL-3
**Lake Lucerne**—pop pl ... GA-3
**Lake Lucerne**—pop pl ... OH-6
Lake Lucerne Park—park ... FL-3
Lake Luciana Shop Ctr—locale ... FL-3
Lake Lucile—swamp ... MS-4
**Lake Lucille**—pop pl ... NY-2
Lake Lucille Dam—dam ... MS-4
Lake Lucille Oil Field—oilfield ... MS-4
Lake Lucille Park—park ... FL-3
Lake Lucina—uninc pl ... FL-3
Lake Lucina Sch—school ... FL-3
Lake L U Dam—dam ... AL-4
Lake Luisa Dam—dam ... MA-1
Lake Luisa Rsvr—reservoir ... MA-1
**Lake Lure**—pop pl : ... NC-3
Lake Lure Dam—dam ... NC-3
Lake Lurleen Dam—dam ... AL-4
Lake Lurleen State Park—park ... AL-4
Lake Luther Dam—dam ... MS-4
**Lake Luzerne**—pop pl ... NY-2
Lake Luzerne-Hadley—CDP ... NY-2
**Lake Luzerne (Town of)**—pop pl ... NY-2
Lake Lynda Dam—dam ... MS-4
**Lake Lynn (Cheat Haven)**—pop pl ... PA-2
Lake Lynn Dam ... NC-3
Lake Lynn Dam—dam (2) ... NC-3
**Lake Lynn (subdivision)**—pop pl ... NC-3
Lake Lynwood ... IL-6
Lake Macaco ... FL-3
Lake Macbride State Park—park ... IA-7
Lake Machias—bay ... LA-4
**Lake Mack Park**—pop pl ... FL-3
Lake Madam Lee ... LA-4
Lake Madison Ch—church ... SD-7
Lake Madison Lutheran Church ... SD-7
Lake Magadalene United Methodist Kindergarten—school ... FL-3
Lake Magdalene—CDP ... FL-3
Lake Magdalene Ch—church ... FL-3
Lake Magdalene Elem Sch—school ... FL-3
Lake Magdolene ... FL-3
Lake Maggiore Baptist Ch—church ... FL-3
Lake Magnor ... WI-6
Lake Maharry Dam—dam ... IA-7
Lake Mahkennac ... MA-1
Lake Mahoney ... GA-3
Lake Mahopac ... NY-2
**Lake Mahopac**—pop pl ... NY-2
Lake Mahopac Ridge—ridge ... NY-2
Lake Maini ... FL-3
Lake Maitland ... FL-3
Lake Maitland—other ... FL-3
Lake Majaco ... FL-3
**Lake Majella**—pop pl ... CA-9
Lake Majesty ... OR-9
Lake Major ... FL-3
Lake Makawhee ... IA-7
Lake Makhpiahlutah ... WY-8
Lake Mallalieu ... WI-6
Lake Malley ... LA-4
Lake Malone ... TX-5
Lake Malone State Park—park ... KY-4
Lake Mamie ... WI-6
Lake Manatee State Park—park ... FL-3
Lake Manatu ... IN-6
Lake Manawa ... IA-7
Lake Manawa State Park—park ... IA-7
Lakeman Harbor—bay ... ME-1
Lakeman Island—island ... ME-1
Lake Manitou ... MI-6
**Lake Manitou**—pop pl ... IN-6
Lake Manitu ... IN-6
Lake Manjo—reservoir ... PA-2
Lake Manjo Dam—dam ... PA-2
Lakeman Lakes—lake ... CO-8
Lakeman Point—cape ... ME-1
Lake Mansion—hist pl ... NV-8
Lake Manzanedo—reservoir ... PA-2
Lake Maononona ... MA-1
Lake Marburg Dam—dam ... PA-2
Lake Marcia Dam—dam ... NJ-2
Lake Maree Dam—dam ... NC-3
Lake Margaret ... AL-4
Lake Margaret ... WI-6
Lake Margaret Dam—dam ... ND-7
Lake Margarethe ... MI-6
**Lake Margrethe**—pop pl ... MI-6
Lake Margus—reservoir ... PA-2
Lake Maria Cem—cemetery ... WI-6
Lake Mariana ... FL-3
**Lake Marian Highlands**—pop pl ... FL-3
Lake Marie ... MN-6
Lake Marie ... WI-6
**Lake Marie**—pop pl ... IL-6
Lake Marie Dam ... AL-4
Lake Marie Sch—school ... CA-9
Lake Marinda ... MN-6
Lake Marion ... NV-8
**Lake Marion**—pop pl ... IL-6
Lake Marion Creek—stream ... FL-3
Lake Markham ... FL-3
Lake Marl Bea ... MI-6
Lake Marna ... LA-4
Lake Marshall (Township of)—civ div ... MN-6
Lake Martha ... WI-6
Lake Martha—reservoir ... MS-4
Lake Martha Dam—dam ... MS-4
Lake Martin Dam—dam ... AL-4
Lake Mary ... AZ-5
Lake Mary ... GA-3
**Lake Mary**—pop pl ... AZ-5
**Lake Mary**—pop pl ... CA-9
**Lake Mary**—pop pl ... FL-3
Lake Mary Boating Site—locale ... AZ-5
Lake Mary Cem—cemetery ... MN-6
Lake Mary Crawford State Fishing Lake ... MS-4
Lake Mary Dam—dam ... UT-8
Lake Maryland ... MN-6
Lake Mary Meadows—flat ... AZ-5
Lake Mary Oil Field—oilfield ... MS-4
Lake Mary-Phoebe ... UT-8
Lake Mary-Phoebe Dam ... UT-8
Lake Mary Plantation (historical)—locale ... MS-4
**Lake Mary Ronan**—pop pl ... MT-8
Lake Mary Sch—school ... FL-3
Lake Mary Tank ... AZ-5
**Lake Mary (Township of)**—pop pl ... MN-6
Lake Mary Valley—valley ... AZ-5
Lake Mason ... WI-6
Lake Mason Natl Wildlife Ref—park ... MT-8
Lake Massabesic ... NH-1
Lake Masse ... MS-4
Lake Massesna ... OK-5
Lake Mathews (CCD)—cens area ... CA-9
Lake Mattamuskeet Pump Station—hist pl ... NC-3
Lake Mattamuskeet (Unorganized Territory of)—unorg ... NC-3
**Lake Mattawa**—pop pl ... MA-1
Lake Mattawanakee ... MA-1
Lake Mattawa North Outlet Dam—dam ... MA-1
Lake Mattawa South Outlet Dam—dam ... MA-1
Lake Mattie Marsh—swamp ... FL-3
Lake Matton ... IL-6
Lake Maude—uninc pl ... FL-3
Lake Maurepas Oil Field—oilfield ... LA-4
Lake Mauwehoo ... CT-1
Lake Mavaco ... FL-3
**Lake Maxine**—pop pl ... IN-6
Lake Maxler Dam ... IN-6
Lake May ... MA-1
Lake Mayaimi ... FL-3
Lake Maymi ... FL-3
Lake McArthur ... ND-7
Lake McBride ... KS-7
**Lake McCoy**—pop pl ... IN-6
**Lake McDonald**—pop pl ... MT-8
Lake McDonald Lodge—hist pl ... MT-8
Lake McKenzie—locale ... FL-3
Lake McKenzie Dam—dam ... NC-3
Lake Mclain ... WY-8
Lake McPhaul Dam—dam ... NC-3
Lake Meade—reservoir ... PA-2
Lake Meade Dam—dam ... PA-2
Lake Mead Lodge—building ... NV-8
Lake Mead Marina—harbor ... NV-8
Lake Mead Natl Rec Area—park ... AZ-5
Lake Mead Natl Rec Area—park ... NV-8
Lake Mead Natl Rec Area(Also NV)—park. AZ-5
Lake Mead Natl Recreation Area—park ... NV-8
Lake Meadow Pond ... PA-2
**Lake Mead Rancheros (Antares)**—pop pl ... AZ-5
Lake Meadwood Dam ... AL-4
**Lake Medina Highlands**—pop pl ... TX-5
Lake Melaken Dam—dam ... AL-4
**Lake Mendelin Estates**—pop pl ... FL-3
Lake Menomonie ... WI-6
Lake Merced Country Club—other ... CA-9
Lake Meredith Inlet—canal ... CO-8
Lake Meredith Natl Rec Area—park ... TX-5
Lake Meredith Outlet—canal ... CO-8
Lake Meredith Reservoir ... CO-8
Lake Meredith Reservoir Inlet ... CO-8
Lake Meredith Reservoir Outlet ... CO-8
Lake Meridian—other ... WA-9
Lake Merriam Ditch—canal ... CO-8
Lake Merritt Wild Duck Refuge—hist pl ... CA-9
Lake Metacomet ... MA-1
Lake Metan ... WA-9
Lake Metigoshe ... ND-7
**Lake Metigoshe**—pop pl ... ND-7
Lake Metigoshe Dam—dam ... ND-7
Lake Metigoshe State Park—park ... ND-7
Lake Meyer—reservoir ... IA-7
Lake Meyer County Park—park ... IA-7
Lake Meyer Dam—dam ... IA-7
Lake Miakka ... FL-3
Lake Miami Dam—dam ... IA-7
Lake Miccosukee ... FL-3
Lake Michael ... WI-6
Lake Michael Dam—dam ... NC-3
Lake Michael Trail—trail ... WA-9
Lake Michie Dam—dam ... NC-3
**Lake Michigan Beach**—pop pl ... MI-6
Lake Michigan Campground—locale ... MI-6
Lake Michigan Coll—school ... MI-6
Lake Michigan Estates ... MI-6
**Lake Michigan Estates**—pop pl ... WI-6
Lake Michigan Ship Canal ... WI-6
Lake Mildred Warner ... AL-4
**Lake Mill**—pop pl ... IN-6
**Lake Mills**—pop pl ... IA-7
**Lake Mills**—pop pl ... WI-6
**Lake Mills (Town of)**—pop pl ... WI-6
**Lake Milton**—pop pl ... OH-6
Lake Milton Temple—church ... OH-6
Lake Minadoka ... ID-8
Lake Minatare Sch—school ... NE-7
Lake Minausin—reservoir ... PA-2
Lake Minausin Dam—dam ... PA-2
**Lake Minchumina**—pop pl ... AK-9
Lake Mine—mine ... AZ-5
Lake Mine—mine ... MI-6
Lake Mine—mine ... SD-7
**Lake Mine**—pop pl ... MI-6
Lake Minneola ... PA-2
**Lake Minnewaska**—pop pl ... NY-2
Lake Minnewaska Cliffhouse—locale ... NY-2
Lake Minnie ... FL-3
Lake Minnie ... WI-6
Lake Minniehana—lake ... FL-3
Lake Minsi ... PA-2
Lake Miomi ... FL-3
Lake Miranda ... MN-6
Lake Miriam Dam—dam ... AL-4
Lake Miriam Square (Shop Ctr)—locale ... FL-3
Lake Mirimichi Dam—dam ... MA-1
Lake Mirror Promenade—hist pl ... FL-3
Lake Mishawum ... MA-1
Lake Mishnock—lake ... RI-1
**Lake Mishnock**—pop pl ... RI-1
Lake Mitchell ... VT-1
Lake Mocoma ... PA-2
**Lake Mohave**—pop pl ... AZ-5
Lake Mohave Ranchos Airp—airport ... AZ-5
Lake Mohave Recreation Site Kathrine Landing—locale ... AZ-5
Lake Mohave Resort—locale ... AZ-5
Lake Mohawk (census name for Sparta)—CDP ... NJ-2
Lake Mohawk Dam—dam ... MS-4
Lake Mohawk Dam—dam ... NJ-2
Lake Mohawk Golf Club—other ... NJ-2
**Lake Mohee**—pop pl ... IN-6
Lake Mohee Dam—dam ... IN-6
Lake Mohonk Mountain House Complex—hist pl ... NY-2
Lake Mokoma ... PA-2
Lake Mokoma Dam—dam ... PA-2
Lake Molly Dam—dam ... IN-6
Lake Mongoulois Oil and Gas Field—oilfield ... LA-4
Lake Monomona ... NH-1
Lake Monomonac Dam—dam ... MA-1
Lake Monomonack ... NH-1
Lake Monroe ... GA-3
**Lake Monroe**—pop pl ... FL-3
Lake Monroe Airp—airport ... IN-6
Lake Monroe Dam—dam ... MS-4
Lake Monroe Dam—dam ... NC-3
**Lake Monroe East Subdivision**—pop pl ... MS-4
**Lake Monroe West Subdivision**—pop pl ... MS-4
Lakemont—locale ... FL-3
Lakemont—locale ... GA-3
**Lakemont**—pop pl ... GA-3
**Lakemont**—pop pl ... NY-2
**Lakemont**—pop pl ... PA-2
**Lakemont**—pop pl ... SC-3
**Lakemont**—pop pl ... TN-4
Lakemont Acad—school ... NY-2
Lake Montauk Harbor ... NY-2
**Lakemont Cabin Area**—pop pl ... TN-4
Lakemont Cem—cemetery ... NY-2
Lakemont Ch—church ... AL-4
Lakemont Ch—church ... GA-3
Lakemont Ch—church ... TN-4
Lakemont Dam ... PA-2
Lakemont Dam—dam ... NC-3
**Lake Montezuma**—pop pl ... AZ-5
Lake Montezuma Post Office—building ... AZ-5
Lake Montgomery ... FL-3
**Lakemont Heights**—pop pl ... TN-4
Lakemont Lake—lake ... MS-4
Lakemont Lake Dam—dam ... MS-4
**Lakemont Landing**—pop pl ... OH-6
Lake Montonia Dam—dam ... NC-3
Lakemont Park—park ... PA-2
Lakemont Park Dam—dam ... PA-2
Lakemont Park Lake ... PA-2
Lake Montrose Dam—dam ... PA-2
Lake Montrose Plaza—area ... PA-2
Lakemont Rsvr—reservoir ... PA-2
Lakemont Sch—school ... FL-3
Lakemont Sch—school ... GA-3
Lakemont Sch—school ... PA-2
**Lakemont (subdivision)**—pop pl ... NC-3
Lakemont Terrace—uninc pl ... PA-2
Lakemoor ... TN-4
**Lakemoor**—pop pl ... IL-6
**Lakemoor**—pop pl ... TN-4
Lake Moore ... MA-1
**Lakemoore**—pop pl ... TN-4
**Lakemoor Hills**—pop pl ... TN-4
**Lake Moraine**—pop pl ... NY-2
**Lakemore**—pop pl ... OH-6
**Lakemore Hills**—pop pl ... TN-4
**Lake Morena Village**—pop pl ... CA-9
Lakemore (Township of)—other ... OH-6
**Lake Morey**—pop pl ... VT-1
Lake Moses ... MN-6
Lake Moss ... MI-6
Lake Mound Cem—cemetery ... IL-6
Lake Mount ... PA-2
Lake Mountain Community Hall—locale ... CA-9
Lake Mountain Creek—stream ... WY-8
Lake Mountain Lookout Complex—hist pl. AZ-5
Lake Mountain Ranch—locale (2) ... CA-9
Lake Mountain Tank—reservoir ... AZ-5
Lake Mountain Trail—trail ... OR-9
Lake Mountanis ... WI-6
Lake Mount Union Dam—dam ... PA-2
Lake Mount Zion ... IN-6
Lake Moxie ... ME-1
**Lake Moxie**—pop pl ... ME-1
Lake Mtn—summit (2) ... AZ-5
Lake Mtn—summit (2) ... CA-9
Lake Mtn—summit ... CO-8
Lake Mtn—summit (3) ... ID-8
Lake Mtn—summit (2) ... ME-1
Lake Mtn—summit (3) ... MT-8
Lake Mtn—summit ... NV-8
Lake Mtn—summit (2) ... NM-5
Lake Mtn—summit ... OR-9
Lake Mtn—summit ... PA-2
Lake Mtn—summit (2) ... UT-8
Lake Mtn—summit ... VT-1
Lake Mtn—summit ... WA-9
Lake Mtn—summit (3) ... WY-8
Lake Mtns—summit ... UT-8
Lake Munuscong ... MI-6
Lake Murphysboro State Park—park ... IL-6
Lake Murray Chapel—church ... OK-5
Lake Murray Fire Tower—locale ... SC-3
Lake Murray Park—park ... CA-9
**Lake Murray Shores**—pop pl ... SC-3
Lake Murray State Park—park ... OK-5
Lake Murtaugh ... ID-8
Lake Musconetcong Dam—dam ... NJ-2
Lakemwei—valley ... FM-9
Lake Myacco ... FL-3
**Lake Mykee Town**—pop pl ... MO-7
Lake Myola Dam—dam ... MA-1
Lake Myra Dam—dam ... NC-3
Lake Myrtle—reservoir ... GA-3
Lake Myrtle Elem Sch—school ... FL-3
Lake Nacoochee ... GA-3
Lake Naha ... WA-9
Lake Nahwatel ... WA-9
**Lakenan**—pop pl ... MO-7
Lake Nancy ... WI-6
Lake Nancy Flowage ... WI-6
Lake Nanita Trail—trail ... CO-8
Lake Naomi Dam—dam ... PA-2
**Lake Naomi Estates**—pop pl ... PA-2
Lake Naraticion ... NJ-2
Lake Naraticon ... NJ-2
Lake Natasha ... OR-9
Lake Natchez Pass—channel ... LA-4
Lake Natoma Trail—trail ... CA-9
Lake Naubesatuck ... CT-1
Lake Nawatzel ... WA-9
**Lake Nebagamon**—pop pl ... WI-6
Lake Nebagamon Auditorium—hist pl ... WI-6
Lake Nebagamon Ch—church ... WI-6
Lake Nebo ... IN-6
Lake Neepaulin Dam—dam ... NJ-2
Lake Neighborhood—locale ... NC-3
**Lake Nelson**—pop pl ... NJ-2
Lake Nelson Dam—dam ... NJ-2
Lake Nelson Memorial Cem—cemetery ... NJ-2
Lake Nemaha ... KS-7
Lake Neoma Dam—dam ... MS-4
**Lake Nepessing**—pop pl ... MI-6
Lake Neponset ... UT-8
Lake Neshaminy—reservoir ... PA-2
Lake Neskowin—lake ... OR-9
Lake Nessmuk—reservoir ... PA-2
Lake Nessmuk Dam—dam ... PA-2
Lake Netta ... MN-6
**Lake Netta**—pop pl ... MN-6
Lake Nettie Natl Wildlife Ref—park ... ND-7
Lake Newnan ... FL-3
Lakengren, Lake—reservoir ... OH-6
Lakenham Cem—cemetery ... MA-1
**Lake Nichols**—pop pl ... MN-6
Lake Nicholson Cem—cemetery ... SD-7
Lake Nicol Dam—dam ... AL-4
Lake Niconzah Dam ... IN-6
Lake Nilson ... SD-7
Lake Nina ... CA-9
Lake Nina ... WA-9
Lake Ninevah ... VT-1
Lake Nissaki ... CT-1
Lake Nockamixon—reservoir ... PA-2
**Lake Noji**—pop pl ... IN-6
Lake Nokomis ... WI-6
Lake Nokomis Flowage ... WI-6
Lake Nokomis Park—park ... MN-6
**Lake Nokopen**—pop pl ... CA-9
Lake Nokwe Bay ... WI-6
Lake Nolin Dam—dam ... AL-4
Lakenon—locale ... TX-5
Lake Noquebay Wildlife Area—park ... WI-6
Lake Norbeck ... MD-2
**Lake Norden**—pop pl ... SD-7
Lake Norfork ... AR-4
Lake Norfork ... MO-7
Lake Norfork Ch—church ... AR-4
Lake Norman Airp—airport ... NC-3
Lake Norman Aviation ... NC-3
**Lake Normandy Estates**—pop pl ... MD-2
Lake North Bass ... WI-6
Lake Norwood ... NC-3
Lake No-Se-Um—lake ... OR-9
Lake Nothing ... WI-6
Lake Nowatzel ... WA-9
Lake No 1—lake ... AK-9
Lake No 11—lake ... NM-5
Lake No 12—reservoir ... NM-5
Lake No 13—reservoir ... NM-5
Lake No 14—reservoir ... NM-5
Lake No. 2 ... PA-2
Lake No 20—reservoir ... NM-5
Lake No 3—lake ... AK-9
Lake Number Five ... WI-6
Lake Number Four ... MN-6
Lake Number Nine ... WI-6
Lake Number One ... MN-6
Lake Number One Dam—dam ... MN-6
Lake Number Seven—reservoir ... AL-4
Lake Number Seven Dam—dam ... AL-4
Lake Number Ten—lake ... MI-6
Lake Number Three ... MN-6
Lake Number Two ... AL-4
Lake Number Two ... MN-6
Lake Number Two Dam—dam ... MN-6
Lake Number Two Hundred Twenty Six ... WI-6
Lake Number 2 ... PA-2
Lake Number 5—lake ... FL-3
Lake Oaks Park—park ... LA-4
Lake Ocquittunk Dam—dam ... NJ-2
Lake Octanatchee ... FL-3
**Lake Odessa**—pop pl ... MI-6
Lake Odessa Public Hunting Area—area ... IA-7
Lake O'Donnell Dam—dam ... TN-4
**Lake of Hills**—pop pl ... MS-4
Lake of Isles—island ... MN-6
Lake Of Isles Brook—stream ... CT-1
Lake of Pines Dam—dam ... MS-4
Lake Of Second Trees—bay ... LA-4
Lake Of The Blessed Sacrament ... NY-2
Lake of The Cherokees ... OK-5
Lake of the Clouds Trail—trail ... CO-8
Lake of the Cross ... LA-4
Lake of the Falls County Park—park ... WI-6
Lake of the Forest—locale ... KS-7
Lake of the Forest Dam—dam ... KS-7
Lake of the Forest (RR name Forest Lake)—uninc pl ... KS-7
Lake Of The Four Seasons—reservoir ... PA-2
Lake Of The Four Seasons Dam—dam ... PA-2
Lake of the Hills ... IL-6
**Lake of the Hills**—pop pl ... FL-3
Lake of the Island—island ... CA-9
Lake of the Island Creek—stream ... CA-9
Lake Of The Lillies ... NJ-2
Lake of the Ozarks Recreational Demonstration Area Barn/Garage in—hist pl ... MO-7
Lake of the Ozarks Recreational Demonstration Area Rising Sun She—hist pl ... MO-7
Lake of the Ozarks Recreational Demonstration Area Shelter at McC—hist pl ... MO-7
Lake of the Ozarks State Park—park ... MO-7
Lake of the Ozarks State Park Camp Clover Point Recreation Hall—hist pl ... MO-7
Lake of the Ozarks State Park Camp Rising Sun Recreation Hall—hist pl ... MO-7
Lake of the Ozarks State Park Highway 134 Hist Dist—hist pl ... MO-7
Lake of the Red Cedars, The ... IN-6
Lake of the Sun ... WA-9
Lake of the Sun Island ... WA-9
Lake Of The Sun River ... WA-9
Lake of the Three Fires Dam—dam ... IA-7
Lake of the Winds ... IL-6
Lake of the Winds—lake ... OR-9
Lake of the Woods ... MI-6
Lake of the Woods ... MO-7
Lake of the Woods—lake ... OR-9
Lake of the Woods—locale ... CA-9
Lake of the Woods—locale ... OR-9
**Lake of the Woods**—pop pl ... AZ-5
**Lake Of The Woods**—pop pl ... CA-9
**Lake of the Woods**—pop pl ... IL-6
**Lake of the Woods**—pop pl ... IN-6
**Lake of the Woods**—pop pl ... MI-6
**Lake-of-the-Woods**—pop pl ... MO-7
Lake Of The Woods Bible Camp—locale ... MN-6
Lake of the Woods (County)—civil ... MN-6
Lake of the Woods Dam—dam ... AZ-5
Lake of the Woods Dam—dam ... IN-6
**Lake Of The Woods (Lake O'woods)**—pop pl ... OR-9
Lake of the Woods Mtn—summit ... OR-9
Lake Of The Woods Park—park ... IL-6
Lake of the Woods Ranger Station-Work Center—hist pl ... OR-9
Lake of the Woods Tank'—reservoir ... AZ-5
Lake Of The Woods Trail—trail ... WY-8
Lake of Three Fires State Park—park ... IA-7
Lake of Tte Woods—lake ... MI-6
Lake Ogallala Dam—dam ... TN-4
Lake Ogallala State Rec Area—park ... NE-7
Lake Ogemaga ... WI-6
Lake Ogletree Number One Dam—dam ... AL-4
Lake Okemah ... OK-5
Lake Oklawaha ... FL-3
Lake Okoboji Seaplane Base—other ... IA-7
**Lake Ola**—pop pl ... FL-3
Lake Ola Chapel—church ... FL-3
Lake Ola Dam—dam ... AL-4
Lake Olathe ... KS-7
Lake Olson ... MN-6
Lake O'Mahoney ... WY-8
Lake Ondawa Dam—dam ... PA-2
Lake Oneida Dam—dam ... PA-2
Lake Oneonta ... WI-6
Lake Onota ... MA-1
Lake Ontelaunee Dam—dam ... PA-2
Lake on the Hill ... MI-6
Lake Oowah Dam—dam ... UT-8
Lake Opechee ... NH-1
Lake Openaki ... NJ-2
Lake Ophelia ... LA-4
Lake Orange Dam—dam ... NC-3
Lake Ordings ... WI-6
Lake Orienta Elem Sch—school ... FL-3
**Lake Orion**—pop pl ... MI-6
**Lake Orion Heights**—pop pl ... MI-6
Lake Orion HS—school ... MI-6
Lake Oroville State Rec Area—park ... CA-9
Lake Osceola ... NC-3
**Lake Osceola**—pop pl ... NY-2
**Lake Osiris Colony**—pop pl ... NY-2
Lake Osoyoos State Park—park ... WA-9
**Lake O'Springs**—pop pl ... OH-6
Lake Ostokpoga ... FL-3
**Lake Oswego**—pop pl ... OR-9
Lake Oswego Country Club—other ... OR-9
Lake Oswego Dam—dam ... OR-9
Lake Oswego HS—school ... OR-9
Lake Oswego Hunt Club Ensemble—hist pl ... OR-9
Lake Oswego JHS—school ... OR-9
Lake Oswego Odd Fellows Hall—hist pl ... OR-9
**Lake Oswego (Oswego)**—pop pl ... OR-9
Lake Otatsy Trail—trail ... MT-8
Lake o' the Forest ... WI-6
Lake O' the Hills Dam—dam ... MS-4
Lake Ouachita State Park—park ... AR-4
Lake Ouatche ... LA-4
Lake Outlet—channel ... NY-2
Lakeover Ch of God—church ... MS-4
**Lakeover Estates (subdivision)**—pop pl ... MS-4
**Lakeover (subdivision)**—pop pl ... MS-4
Lake Owasippe ... MI-6
**Lake Owassa**—pop pl ... NJ-2
Lake Owassa Dam—dam ... NJ-2
Lake Owasso Sch—school ... MN-6
Lake Owen Creek—stream ... WY-8
Lake O Woods ... OR-9
Lake O'Woods—hist pl ... NC-3
**Lake O'woods**—pop pl ... OR-9
Lake o' Woods Mountain ... OR-9
Lake Owyhee State Park—park ... OR-9
Lake Oxford ... NC-3
**Lake Ozark**—pop pl ... MO-7
Lake Ozonia Outlet—stream ... NY-2
Lake Pagie ... LA-4
Lake Pagie Gas Field—oilfield ... LA-4
Lake Pahagaco—reservoir ... PA-2
Lake Pahagaco Dam—dam ... PA-2
Lake Palakka ... FL-3
Lake Palourd ... LA-4
Lake Palourde ... LA-4
Lake Palourde Gas Field—oilfield ... LA-4
**Lake Pana**—pop pl ... IL-6
**Lake Panamoka**—pop pl ... NY-2
**Lake Panasoffkee**—pop pl ... FL-3
Lake Panasoffkee (RR name Panasoffkee)—CDP ... FL-3
Lake Panorama Dam—dam ... IA-7
Lake Paradise Dam ... AL-4
Lake Park ... WA-9
Lake Park—flat (2) ... CO-8
Lake Park—flat ... UT-8
Lake Park—locale ... PA-2
Lake Park—other ... WA-9
Lake Park—park (2) ... IL-6
Lake Park—park ... MA-1
Lake Park—park (3) ... MN-6
Lake Park—park ... NV-8
Lake Park—park (2) ... OH-6
Lake Park—park (3) ... WI-6
**Lake Park**—pop pl ... FL-3
**Lake Park**—pop pl ... GA-3
**Lake Park**—pop pl ... IN-6
**Lake Park**—pop pl ... IA-7
**Lake Park**—pop pl ... MN-6
**Lake Park**—pop pl (3) ... TN-4
**Lake Park**—pop pl ... VT-1
Lake Park—post sta ... IL-6
Lake Park (CCD)—cens area ... GA-3
Lake Park Cem—cemetery ... GA-3
Lake Park Cem—cemetery ... MN-6
Lake Park Cem—cemetery ... NJ-2
Lake Park Cem—cemetery ... OH-6
Lake Park Cem—cemetery ... SD-7
Lake Park Ch—church ... GA-3
Lake Park Ch—church ... PA-2
Lake Park Dam—dam ... MS-4
Lake Park Developmental Center—school ... FL-3
Lake Park Elem Sch—school ... FL-3
Lake Parker ... SD-7
**Lake Park Estates**—pop pl ... FL-3
**Lake Park Estates**—pop pl ... IL-6
**Lake Park Forest**—pop pl ... IL-6
Lake Park HS—school ... IL-6
Lake Park Public Library—building ... FL-3
Lake Park Sch—school ... FL-3
**Lake Park (subdivision)**—pop pl ... MS-4
**Lake Park (subdivision)**—pop pl (2) ... NC-3
**Lake Park Subdivision**—pop pl ... UT-8
**Lake Park (Township of)**—pop pl ... MN-6
Lake Park Wild Rice Sch—school ... MN-6
**Lake Parlin (historical)**—pop pl ... ME-1
Lake Parsippany—locale ... NJ-2
Lake Parsippany Dam—dam ... NJ-2
Lake Parsippany Dyke Number One—dam ... NJ-2
Lake Parsons Dam—dam ... KS-7
**Lake Pasadena Heights**—pop pl ... FL-3
Lake Pass—channel ... TX-5

Lake Pass—gap CO-8
Lake Pass Bayou—stream LA-4
Lake Pasture—flat CO-8
Lake Pasture—flat UT-8
Lake Pasture Oil Field—oilfield TX-5
Lake Pasture Windmill—locale TX-5
Lake Patasa LA-4
Lake Patricia Dam—dam ND-7
Lake Paugus NH-1
Lake Pauline VT-1
Lake Pauline Powerplant—other TX-5
Lake Paupackan PA-2
Lake Paupackan Dam—dam PA-2
Lake Payne AL-4
Lake Payne Ch—church AL-4
Lake Peak—summit CA-9
Lake Peak—summit NV-8
Lake Peak—summit NM-5
Lake Peak—summit OR-9
Lake Peak—summit UT-8
Lake Pearl LA-4
**Lake Pearl**—pop pl MA-1
**Lake Peekskill**—pop pl NY-2
Lake Peignuer LA-4
Lake Pelican AR-4
Lake Pelto Oil Field—oilfield LA-4
Lake Penelope NY-2
Lake Penland Dam—dam OR-9
Lake Peosta Channel—channel IA-7
Lake Perry FL-3
Lake Perry Dam—dam IN-6
Lake Perry Dam—dam MS-4
Lake Perry State Fishing Lake MS-4
Lake Peter MI-6
**Lake Petersburg**—pop pl IL-6
Lake-Peterson House—hist pl IL-6
Lake Petit LA-4
Lake Phipps CT-1
**Lake Piasa**—pop pl IL-6
**Lake Pickett**—pop pl FL-3
Lake Piegneur LA-4
Lake Pillsbury Ranch—locale CA-9
**Lake Pine**—pop pl NJ-2
Lake Pinecrest—reservoir PA-2
Lake Pinecrest Dam—dam PA-2
**Lake Pines**—pop pl DE-2
**Lake Pines Apartment Condominium**—pop pl UT-8
Lake Piomingo Dam—dam MS-4
**Lake Piomingo (subdivision)**—pop pl MS-4
Lake Pit—basin OR-9
Lake Pitman AL-4
Lake Place MS-4
Lake Place (historical)—locale SD-7
**Lake Placid**—pop pl FL-3
**Lake Placid**—pop pl NY-2
**Lake Placid**—pop pl TX-5
Lake Placid Camp—locale TN-4
Lake Placid (CCD)—cens area FL-3
**Lake Placid (Chickasaw Park)**—pop pl TN-4
Lake Placid Club—uninc pl NY-2
Lake Placid Dam—dam TN-4
Lake Placid Elem Sch—school FL-3
Lake Placid MS—school FL-3
Lake Placid Senior HS—school FL-3
Lake Placid Shop Ctr—locale FL-3
Lake Plateau—plain MT-8
**Lake Platte View**—pop pl NE-7
**Lake Pleasant**—pop pl MA-1
**Lake Pleasant**—pop pl MI-6
**Lake Pleasant**—pop pl NY-2
**Lake Pleasant**—pop pl PA-2
Lake Pleasant Airp—airport PA-2
Lake Pleasant Ch—church GA-3
Lake Pleasant Corners—locale PA-2
Lake Pleasant (historical)—locale AZ-5
Lake Pleasant Inn—locale AZ-5
Lake Pleasant Landing Field—airport AZ-5
Lake Pleasant Outlet—stream PA-2
Lake Pleasant Regional Park—park AZ-5
**Lake Pleasant (Town of)**—pop pl NY-2
Lake Pleasant (Township of)—civ div MN-6
Lake Plymouth Dam—dam NJ-2
Lake Pocassee SD-7
Lake Pochung Dam—dam NJ-2
Lake Pocket—basin AZ-5
Lake Pocket—valley WY-8
Lake Pocotopaug—CDP CT-1
Lake Point ME-1
Lake Point WY-8
Lake Point—cape AK-9
Lake Point—cape AR-4
Lake Point—cape LA-4
Lake Point—cape NC-3
Lake Point—cape OR-9
Lake Point—cape UT-8
**Lakepoint**—pop pl UT-8
**Lake Point**—pop pl UT-8
Lake Point Bayou—stream LA-4
Lake Point Campground—locale WY-8
Lake Point Cem—cemetery UT-8
Lakepoint Cemetery UT-8
Lake Point Interchange—other UT-8
Lake Point Junction—locale UT-8
Lake Pokahsee SD-7
Lake Polourd LA-4
Lake Pomeroy Dam—dam TN-4
**Lake Pomeroy (subdivision)**—pop pl TN-4
Lake Ponca OK-5
Lake Ponca Park—park OK-5
Lake Pond—bay LA-4
Lake Ponderosa Dam—dam IA-7
Lake Pons Dam—dam OR-9
Lake Pontchartrain Causeway—bridge LA-4
Lake Ponte Vedra FL-3
Lake Pool Ch—church TX-5
Lake Poponoming PA-2
Lakeport NH-1
Lakeport—locale AR-4
Lakeport—locale WI-6
**Lakeport**—pop pl CA-9
**Lakeport**—pop pl FL-3
**Lakeport**—pop pl MI-6
**Lakeport**—pop pl NH-1
**Lakeport**—pop pl NY-2
**Lakeport**—pop pl SD-7
**Lakeport**—pop pl TX-5
Lakeport Bay—bay NY-2
Lakeport (CCD)—cens area CA-9
Lakeport Cem—cemetery AR-4
Lake Port Cem—cemetery SD-7
Lakeport Ch—church AR-4
Lakeport Ch—church FL-3
Lakeport Chapel—church NY-2
Lakeport (historical)—locale SD-7
**Lakeport (historical)**—pop pl OR-9
Lakeport Lake AR-4
Lakeport Peak—summit CA-9
Lakeport Plantation—hist pl AR-4
Lakeport State Park—park MI-6
Lake Port Township—civil SD-7
Lakeport Township—fmr MCD IA-7
**Lakeport (Township of)**—pop pl MN-6
Lake Potter FL-3
Lake Poulton TX-5
Lake Powell FL-3
Lake Powell Island AZ-5
Lake Powell Island UT-8
Lake Powell Navajo Tribal Park—park AZ-5
Lake Powell Overlook—locale UT-8
Lake Powhatan Dam—dam NC-3
Lake Powhatan Recreation Site NC-3
Lake Prairie Ch—church IN-6
Lake Prairie Creek—stream CA-9
Lake Prairie Elem Sch—school IN-6
Lake Prairie Township—fmr MCD IA-7
Lake Prairie (Township of)—civ div MN-6
Lake Prairir—area CA-9
**Lake Preston**—pop pl SD-7
Lake Preston Cem—cemetery SD-7
Lake Preston Lakebed—flat SD-7
Lake Preston Municipal Airp—airport SD-7
**Lake Primrose**—pop pl IN-6
Lake Property Lake—reservoir NC-3
Lake Property Lake Dam—dam NC-3
**Lake Providence**—pop pl LA-4
Lake Providence Ch—church TX-5
Lake Providence Hist Dist—hist pl LA-4
Lake Providence Methodist Ch (historical)—church MS-4
Lake Providence Port—locale LA-4
Lake Providence Reach—channel MS-4
Lake Providence Residential Street Hist Dist—hist pl LA-4
Lake Providence Sch—school LA-4
Lake Punderson OH-6
Lake Purdy AL-4
**Lake Purdy**—pop pl NY-2
Lake Purdy Cave—cave AL-4
Lake Purdy Dam—dam AL-4
Lake Pyoca Dam—dam IN-6
Lake Quannapowitt Dam—dam MA-1
Lake Quigsigamond Dam—dam MA-1
Lake Quinapoxet MA-1
Lake Quinault (CCD)—cens area WA-9
Lake Quinn Dam—dam PA-2
Lake Quivira KS-7
**Lake Quivira**—pop pl KS-7
Lake Raccourci LA-4
Lake Raccourci—bay LA-4
Lake Raleigh Dam—dam NC-3
Lake Ranch—locale CA-9
Lake Ranch—locale NE-7
Lake Ranch—locale NV-8
Lake Ranch—locale TX-5
Lake Ranch Rsvr—reservoir CA-9
Lake Ranch Sch—school WY-8
Lake Range NV-8
Lake Range—range NV-8
Lake Ranger Station—locale WY-8
Lake Ransom Canyon TX-5
**Lake Ransom Canyon**—pop pl TX-5
Lake Ransome Canyon Village TX-5
**Lake Raponda**—pop pl VT-1
Lake Raven MN-6
Lake Rayponda VT-1
Lake Raystown PA-2
Lake Raytown Resort Rothrock Marina—locale PA-2
Lake Reams—lake FL-3
Lake Rebecca Park—park MN-6
Lake Redbud KS-7
Lake Redding Park—park CA-9
Lake Redman—reservoir PA-2
Lake Redstone County Park—park WI-6
Lake Reed FL-3
Lake Refuge NC-3
Lake Region Ch—church MN-6
Lake Region Golf Club—locale FL-3
Lake Region Hosp—hospital MN-6
Lake Rene PA-2
Lake Rene—reservoir PA-2
Lake Rene Dam—dam PA-2
Lake Renee—reservoir PA-2
Lake Renee Dam—dam PA-2
Lake Reno Cem—cemetery MN-6
Lake Reno Ch—church MN-6
Lake Reno Sch—school MN-6
Lake Repose NY-2
**Lake Rescue**—pop pl VT-1
Lake Resort Marina TN-4
Lake Retreat WA-9
**Lake Retreat**—pop pl WA-9
Lake Retreat Dam—dam AL-4
Lake Richie Trail—trail MI-6
Lake Richland Boat Dock—locale TN-4
Lake Ridge—CDP VA-3
Lake Ridge—locale AR-4
Lake Ridge—locale KS-7
**Lakeridge**—pop pl NV-8
**Lake Ridge**—pop pl NJ-2
**Lake Ridge**—pop pl NY-2
**Lakeridge**—pop pl WA-9
**Lake Ridge**—pop pl WA-9
**Lake Ridge**—pop pl WV-2
Lake Ridge—ridge AZ-5
Lake Ridge—ridge (3) CA-9
Lake Ridge—ridge CO-8
Lake Ridge—ridge ID-8
Lake Ridge—ridge LA-4
Lake Ridge—ridge MT-8
Lake Ridge—ridge OH-6
Lake Ridge—ridge (2) OR-9
Lake Ridge—ridge (4) UT-8
Lake Ridge—ridge WA-9
Lake Ridge—ridge WI-6
Lake Ridge—ridge (2) WY-8
Lakeridge Campground—locale MA-1
Lake Ridge Cem—cemetery MI-6
Lake Ridge Ch—church TX-5
Lakeridge Golf Course—locale NV-8
Lakeridge Heights CT-1
Lake Ridge Island—island OH-6
Lake Ridge Island Mounds—hist pl OH-6
Lakeridge JHS—school UT-8
**Lake Ridgelea Subdivision**—pop pl MS-4
Lake Ridge Point—cape NY-2
Lake Ridge Rsvr—reservoir OR-9
Lake Ridge Sch—school UT-8
Lakeridge Sch—school WA-9
Lake Ridge Spring—spring OR-9
**Lakeridge (subdivision)**—pop pl AL-4
**Lakeridge (subdivision)**—pop pl MS-4
**Lake Ridge Subdivision**—pop pl UT-8
Lake Ridge Tank—reservoir AZ-5
Lake Ridge Trail (Jeep)—trail CA-9
Lake Rillard WA-9
Lake Rim Dam—dam NC-3
Lake Ripple Dam 47—dam MA-1
Lake Rips—rapids ME-1
Lake River CA-9
Lake River—stream WA-9
**Lake Riviera**—pop pl NJ-2
**Laker Lane Condominium**—pop pl UT-8
Lake Road Cem—cemetery OH-6
Lake Road Ch—church VA-3
Lakeroad Chapel—church MN-6
Lake Road Sch—school MO-7
Lake Road Sch—school NY-2
**Lake Road (subdivision)**—pop pl TN-4
Lake Robert Rooke Dam—dam NJ-2
Lake Roberts Campground—locale NM-5
Lake Robin Dam—dam AL-4
Lake Rock—summit ID-8
Lake Rock Lake—lake ID-8
Lake Rogerine NJ-2
Lake Rogers Dam—dam NC-3
**Lake Rogers Isle**—pop pl FL-3
Lake Rohunta Dam—dam MA-1
**Lake Roland**—pop pl MD-2
**Lake Roland**—pop pl MI-6
Lake Roland Park—park MD-2
**Lake Ron**—pop pl WV-2
**Lake Ronkonkoma**—pop pl NY-2
Lake Ronkonkoma Cem—cemetery NY-2
**Lake Ronkonkoma Heights**—pop pl NY-2
Lake Roothaan ID-8
Lake Rosa L MS-4
Lake Roseau LA-4
Lake Roslyn—reservoir OR-9
Lake Roslyn Dam—dam OR-9
Lake Ross Barnett State Fishing Lake MS-4
Lake Rowena Recreation Dam—dam PA-2
Lake Royale Dam—dam NC-3
Laker Point—cape ME-1
Lake RR Station—hist pl MS-4
Lakers Creek—gut NC-3
**Laker Subdivision**—pop pl UT-8
Lake Rsvr—reservoir MT-8
Lake Ruden—lake OR-9
Lake Ruff WY-8
Lake Rugby Dam—dam NC-3
**Lake Rugby (subdivision)**—pop pl NC-3
Lake Run PA-2
**Lake Run**—pop pl PA-2
Lake Run—stream IL-6
Lake Run—stream IN-6
Lake Run—stream NC-3
Lake Run—stream OH-6
Lake Run—stream (3) PA-2
Lake Russell Dam—dam PA-2
Lake Ruth—lake FL-3
Lakes, The—lake CA-9
Lakes, The—lake NV-8
Lakes, The—lake PA-2
Lakes, The—lake UT-8
Lakes, The—lake WY-8
Lakes, The—other NM-5
**Lakes, The**—pop pl AZ-5
**Lakes, The**—pop pl NV-8
Lake Sabethan KS-7
Lake Sabula—reservoir PA-2
Lake Sabula Dam—dam PA-2
Lake Sacajawea Park—hist pl WA-9
Lake Sagamore NC-3
Lake Saginaw Dam—dam NJ-2
Lake Saint Catherine State Park—park VT-1
**Lake Saint Croix Beach**—pop pl MN-6
Lake Saint George State Park—park ME-1
Lake Saint John CO-8
Lake Saint John Crevasse LA-4
Lake Saint John Oil and Gas Field—oilfield LA-4
Lake Saint Marys OH-6
Lake Saint Peter Canal—canal LA-4
Lake Saint Sophia NH-1
Lake Sakakawea State Park—park ND-7
Lake Salikwa ID-8
Lake Saltonstall Outlet Dam—dam MA-1
Lake Salvadore LA-4
Lake Salvador Oil Field—oilfield LA-4
Lake Samoset Dam—dam MA-1
Lake Sanatoga—reservoir PA-2
Lake Sand Gas Field—oilfield LA-4
**Lake San Marcos**—pop pl CA-9
Lake Santa Rosa FL-3
Lake Santee Dam—dam IN-6
Lake Sarah MN-6
**Lake Sarah**—pop pl MN-6
Lake Sarah Ch—church MN-6
**Lake Sarah (Township of)**—pop pl MN-6
**Lake Saunders Trailer Park**—pop pl FL-3
**Lake Sawyer**—pop pl WA-9
Lake Saxony—reservoir PA-2
Lake Saxony Dam—dam PA-2
Lakes Basin—basin CA-9
Lakes Basin Campground—locale CA-9
Lakes Basin Guard Station—locale CA-9
Lakes Basin Petroglyphs—hist pl CA-9
Lakes Bay—bay NJ-2
Lakes Branch—stream KY-4
Lake Sch—school (4) CA-9
Lake Sch—school IL-6
Lake Sch—school KY-4
Lake Sch—school ME-1
Lake Sch—school (5) MI-6
Lake Sch—school (3) MS-4
Lake Sch—school MO-7
Lake Sch—school MT-8
Lake Sch—school NE-7
Lake Sch—school NV-8
Lake Sch—school NJ-2
Lake Sch—school (3) OH-6
Lake Sch—school OK-5
Lake Sch—school VT-1
Lake Sch—school WA-9
Lake Sch—school (2) WI-6
Lakes Channel—channel NJ-2
Lakes Chapel Cem—cemetery TX-5
Lake Sch (historical)—school (2) MS-4
Lake Sch (historical)—school MO-7
Lake Schneider MI-6
Lake School—locale NE-7
Lake Schultz State Park—park OK-5
Lake Scott State Park—park KS-7
Lakes Coulee—valley WI-6
Lakes Coulee Creek—stream WI-6
Lakes Coulee State Public Hunting Grounds—park WI-6
Lakes Cove—bay MD-2
Lake Scranton Dam—dam PA-2
Lakes Creek MT-8
Lakes Creek—stream NJ-2
Lakes Creek—stream NC-3
Lakes District (census name for Lakewood Center)—CDP WA-9
Lakes East Golf Course—other AZ-5
Lake Sebois ME-1
**Lake Secor**—pop pl NY-2
Lake Section Community Sch—school MI-6
Lake Sega NC-3
**Lake Sega (subdivision)**—pop pl NC-3
Lake Seguano FL-3
Lake Seguano GA-3
Lake Seguin PA-2
Lake Selmac Dam—dam OR-9
Lake Seminole Ch—church FL-3
Lake Seminole Hosp—hospital FL-3
Lake Seminole Park—park FL-3
Lakes End Forest Camp—locale OR-9
Lake Sequilla WI-6
Lake Serene Dam—dam MS-4
Lake Serene East Dam—dam MS-4
Lake Serene North Dam—dam MS-4
**Lake Serene North (subdivision)**—pop pl MS-4
Lake Serene South Dam—dam MS-4
Lake Serene Southeast Dam—dam MS-4
**Lake Serene South (subdivision)**—pop pl MS-4
Lake Seventeen MI-6
Lake Sewall MT-8
Lake Sewell MT-8
Lake Sexton Airp—airport MO-7
Lakes Fishpond UT-8
**Lake Shadow**—pop pl TN-4
Lake Shafer IN-6
Lake Shannoo WI-6
Lake Shaokotan MN-6
Lake Sharpe—lake FL-3
**Lake Shawnee**—pop pl NJ-2
Lake Shawnee Dam—dam NJ-2
Lake Shechi AL-4
Lake Shehawken—reservoir PA-2
Lake Shelby MS-4
Lake Shelby Dam—dam MS-4
Lake Shelia Dam—dam NC-3
Lake Shellrock Rsvr OR-9
Lake Shenandoah Dam—dam NJ-2
Lake Shenorock NY-2
Lake Shenorock—other NY-2
Lake Shenrock NY-2
Lake Sheppard TX-5
**Lake Sheridan**—pop pl PA-2
Lake Sheridan Dam—dam PA-2
Lake Sheridan Hill—summit PA-2
**Lake Sherwood**—pop pl MI-6
**Lake Sherwood**—pop pl MO-7
Lake Sherwood Dam—dam AL-4
Lake Sherwood Presbyterian Ch—church FL-3
Lake Sherwood Rec Area—park WV-2
Lake Sherwood Trail—trail WV-2
Lake Shetek State Park—park MN-6
Lake Shipp Elem Sch—school FL-3
**Lake Shipp Heights (subdivision)**—pop pl FL-3
Lake Shipshewana IN-6
**Lakeshire**—pop pl MO-7
Lake Shirley ND-7
Lake Shirley Dam—dam MA-1
Lake Shirley Improvement Corp Dam MA-1
Lake Shmidell CA-9
Lake Shop Ctr—locale AL-4
Lakeshore CA-9
Lake Shore IN-6
Lake Shore—locale KS-7
Lakeshore—locale KY-4
**Lakeshore**—pop pl (2) CA-9
**Lake Shore**—pop pl FL-3
**Lake Shore**—pop pl KS-7
**Lakeshore**—pop pl KS-7
**Lakeshore**—pop pl LA-4
**Lake Shore**—pop pl MD-2
**Lake Shore**—pop pl MI-6
**Lake Shore**—pop pl MN-6
**Lakeshore**—pop pl MS-4
**Lake Shore**—pop pl TN-4
**Lake Shore**—pop pl TX-5
**Lake Shore**—pop pl UT-8
**Lake Shore**—pop pl WA-9
Lakeshore—uninc pl WI-6
Lake Shore And Michigan Southern Passenger Depot—hist pl OH-6
Lake Shore And Michigan Southern RR Depot—hist pl OH-6
Lake Shore and Michigan Southern RR Depot and Freight House—hist pl OH-6
Lake Shore Apartments—hist pl IL-6
Lake Shore Baptist Ch—church FL-3
Lakeshore Baptist Ch—church MS-4
Lakeshore Basin—basin UT-8
Lake Shore Bayou—gut LA-4
Lakeshore Campground—locale CA-9
Lake Shore Canal—canal (2) LA-4
Lake Shore Cem—cemetery (2) MI-6
Lake Shore Central HS—school NY-2
Lakeshore Ch—church AR-4
Lake Shore Ch—church GA-3
Lake Shore Ch—church LA-4
Lakeshore Ch—church (2) MI-6
Lake Shore Ch—church OH-6
Lake Shore Ch—church TN-4
Lakeshore Ch—church TX-5
Lake Shore Community Hall—locale MO-7
Lake Shore Country Club—other IL-6
Lake Shore Country Club—other OH-6
Lake Shore Dam—dam NC-3
Lakeshore Ditch—canal NV-8
Lakeshore Dock—locale TN-4
Lake Shore Drive Cabin Site Area—locale (2) AL-4
**Lake Shore Drive Subdivision (subdivision)**—pop pl AL-4
**Lake Shore Estates**—pop pl AL-4
**Lakeshore Estates**—pop pl GA-3
**Lakeshore Estates**—pop pl (2) TN-4
**Lake Shore Estates**—pop pl TX-5
**Lake Shore Estates (subdivision)**—pop pl FL-3
**Lakeshore Gardens**—pop pl TN-4
**Lakeshore Gardens**—pop pl TX-5
Lakeshore Hosp—hospital AL-4
Lake Shore Hosp—hospital FL-3
Lake Shore House—hist pl NV-8
Lake Shore HS—school FL-3
Lakeshore HS—school MI-6
Lake Shore HS—school MI-6
Lake Shore JHS—school FL-3
Lake Shore JHS—school LA-4
Lakeshore JHS—school MI-6
Lake Shore Lodge—building MT-8
Lakeshore (marina)—harbor TN-4
Lakeshore Marina—locale AL-4
Lake Shore & Michigan Southern Freight Depot—hist pl NY-2
Lake Shore & Michigan Southern RR Station—hist pl NY-2
Lake Shore & Michigan Southern RR Station—hist pl OH-6
Lake Shore Mine—mine AZ-5
Lakeshore Mine—mine MT-8
Lakeshore Mine—mine NV-8
Lakeshore Mtn—summit MT-8
Lakeshore Nature Trail—trail TN-4
Lake Shore Park MN-6
Lakeshore Park MS-4
Lake Shore Park—park IL-6
Lakeshore Park—park LA-4
Lakeshore Park—park MN-6
Lake Shore Park—park NY-2
Lake Shore Park—park OH-6
Lakeshore Park—park WA-9
Lake Shore Park—park WI-6
**Lake Shore Park**—pop pl MN-6
**Lake Shore Park**—pop pl NH-1
Lakeshore Plaza Shop Ctr—locale GA-3
Lake Shore Private Sch—school FL-3
Lakeshore Ranch—locale CA-9
Lakeshore Ranch—locale TX-5
Lakeshore Rec Area—park MS-4
Lake Shore Road Sch—school NY-2
Lakeshore Rsvr—reservoir CA-9
Lake Shore Run—stream IN-6
Lake Shores IN-6
**Lake Shores**—pop pl DE-2
**Lake Shores**—pop pl IN-6
**Lake Shores**—pop pl SC-3
**Lake Shores**—pop pl VA-3
Lakeshore Sch—school (2) CA-9
Lake Shore Sch—school FL-3
Lake Shore Sch—school (2) IL-6
Lakeshore Sch—school LA-4
Lake Shore Sch—school (2) MI-6
Lakeshore Sch—school NY-2
Lake Shore Sch—school WA-9
Lake Shore Sch—school WI-6
Lake Shores Country Club—locale WI-6
**Lake & Shores Estates (subdivision)**—pop pl NC-3
Lake Shore Ski Club—other MI-6
Lake Shores Lake Dam—dam MS-4
**Lake Shores (subdivision)**—pop pl NC-3
**Lake Shore (subdivision)**—pop pl AL-4
**Lakeshore (subdivision)**—pop pl MS-4
**Lake Shore (Township of)**—pop pl MN-6
**Lakeshor Manor**—pop pl TN-4
Lake Showlow AZ-5
Lakeside CA-9
Lakeside CO-8
Lakeside (2) MI-6
Lakeside MN-6
Lakeside MO-7
Lakeside NV-8
Lakeside NC-3
Lakeside OH-6
Lakeside TN-4
Lakeside—CDP FL-3
Lakeside—hist pl LA-4
Lakeside—locale AR-4
Lakeside—locale CO-8
Lakeside—locale MI-6
Lakeside—locale MS-4
Lakeside—locale (2) MT-8
Lakeside—locale NH-1
Lakeside—locale OK-5
Lakeside—locale TN-4
Lakeside—locale TX-5
Lakeside—locale UT-8
Lakeside—locale VT-1
**Lakeside**—pop pl (2) AZ-5
**Lakeside**—pop pl (2) AR-4
**Lakeside**—pop pl CA-9
**Lakeside**—pop pl CO-8
**Lakeside**—pop pl (2) CT-1
**Lakeside**—pop pl FL-3
**Lakeside**—pop pl GA-3
**Lakeside**—pop pl (3) IN-6
**Lakeside**—pop pl IA-7
**Lakeside**—pop pl (2) LA-4
**Lakeside**—pop pl (2) MA-1
**Lakeside**—pop pl (2) MI-6
**Lakeside**—pop pl MN-6
**Lakeside**—pop pl (2) MO-7
**Lakeside**—pop pl MT-8
**Lakeside**—pop pl NE-7
**Lakeside**—pop pl NJ-2
**Lakeside**—pop pl (3) NY-2
**Lakeside**—pop pl NC-3
**Lakeside**—pop pl (3) OH-6
**Lakeside**—pop pl OK-5
**Lakeside**—pop pl OR-9
**Lakeside**—pop pl (2) PA-2
**Lakeside**—pop pl SC-3
**Lake Side**—pop pl TN-4
**Lakeside**—pop pl TN-4
**Lakeside**—pop pl (4) TX-5
**Lakeside**—pop pl VA-3
**Lakeside**—pop pl WA-9
**Lakeside**—pop pl WI-6
Lakeside—uninc pl AR-4
Lakeside—uninc pl (2) VA-3
**Lakeside Acres**—pop pl AL-4
**Lakeside Acres**—pop pl KS-7
**Lakeside Acres Addition**—pop pl KS-7
**Lakeside Acres Subdivision**—pop pl UT-8
Lakeside Airp—airport AL-4
Lakeside Airp—airport KS-7
Lakeside AME Ch (historical)—church AL-4
Lakeside Amusement Park—park VA-3
Lakeside Baptist Ch—church FL-3
Lakeside Baptist Church TN-4
Lakeside Bays—bay NV-8
Lakeside Beach—beach IA-7
Lakeside Beach State Park—park NY-2
Lakeside Bridge—other IL-6
Lakeside Butte—summit UT-8
Lakeside Camp—locale MI-6
Lakeside Campground UT-8
Lakeside Campground—locale CA-9
Lakeside Campground—locale CO-8
Lakeside Campground—park AZ-5
Lakeside Campground—park UT-8
Lakeside Cem—cemetery (2) AR-4
Lakeside Cem—cemetery CA-9
Lakeside Cem—cemetery (2) CO-8
Lakeside Cem—cemetery DE-2
Lakeside Cem—cemetery FL-3
Lakeside Cem—cemetery (2) IL-6
Lakeside Cem—cemetery (3) IN-6
Lakeside Cem—cemetery (3) ME-1
Lakeside Cem—cemetery (3) MA-1
Lakeside Cem—cemetery (11) MI-6
Lakeside Cem—cemetery (16) MN-6
Lakeside Cem—cemetery MO-7
Lakeside Cem—cemetery NH-1
Lakeside Cem—cemetery (2) NY-2
Lakeside Cem—cemetery ND-7
Lakeside Cem—cemetery OH-6
Lakeside Cem—cemetery PA-2
Lakeside Cem—cemetery SD-7
Lakeside Cem—cemetery TX-5
Lakeside Cem—cemetery (7) WI-6
Lakeside Ch—church AL-4
Lakeside Ch—church (3) FL-3
Lakeside Ch—church GA-3
Lake Side Ch—church GA-3
Lakeside Ch—church GA-3
Lake Side Ch—church IA-7
Lakeside Ch—church LA-4
Lakeside Ch—church (2) MI-6
Lakeside Ch—church (2) MS-4
Lakeside Ch—church MO-7
Lakeside Ch—church NC-3
Lakeside Ch—church OH-6
Lakeside Ch—church (2) SC-3
Lakeside Ch—church SD-7
Lakeside Ch—church TN-4
Lakeside Chapel—church AR-4
Lakeside Chapel—church IN-6
Lakeside Chapel—church MI-6
Lakeside Chapel—church MT-8
Lakeside Children Home—building MI-6
Lakeside Ch of Tarrant City—church AL-4
Lakeside Ch of the Nazarene—church FL-3
Lakeside Christian Sch—school FL-3
**Lakeside City**—pop pl TX-5
Lakeside Community Chapel—church FL-3
Lakeside Country Club AL-4
Lakeside Country Club—other (2) MN-6
Lakeside Country Club—other SC-3
Lakeside Country Club—other (2) TX-5
Lakeside Country Club—other VA-3
Lakeside Court Park—park MN-6
Lakeside Dam—dam AZ-5
Lakeside Dam—dam PA-2
Lakeside Development—hist pl VT-1
Lakeside Ditch—canal CA-9
Lakeside Dock—locale TN-4
Lakeside Elementary School TN-4
Lakeside Elem Sch—school FL-3
Lakeside Elem Sch—school KS-7
**Lakeside Estates**—pop pl TN-4
Lakeside Estates Dam AL-4
Lakeside Estates Dam—dam AL-4
Lakeside Estates Lake AL-4
**Lakeside Estates (subdivision)**—pop pl MS-4
**Lakeside Estates (subdivision)**—pop pl TN-4
**Lakeside Estates (trailer park)**—pop pl DE-2
**Lakeside Farms**—pop pl CA-9
Lakeside Farms Sch—school CA-9
Lakeside Ferry (historical)—locale MS-4
Lakeside Golf Club—other CA-9
Lakeside Golf Club—other MO-7
Lakeside Golf Course—locale TN-4
Lakeside Golf Course—other CA-9
Lakeside Golf Course—other OK-5
Lakeside Grange—locale WA-9
Lakeside Hall—locale CO-8
**Lakeside Heights**—pop pl TX-5
Lakeside Heliport—airport UT-8
**Lakeside Highlands**—pop pl AL-4
**Lakeside Hills**—pop pl VA-3
Lakeside Hills—uninc pl GA-3
Lakeside Hist Dist—hist pl OH-6
Lake Side (historical)—locale KS-7
**Lakeside Homes**—pop pl VA-3
Lakeside Hosp—hospital CA-9
Lakeside Hosp—hospital MI-6
Lakeside Hosp—hospital MO-7
Lakeside Hotel—hist pl AR-4
Lakeside HS—school OR-9
Lakeside Inn—hist pl FL-3
**Lakeside Knolls**—pop pl IL-6
Lakeside Lake CO-8
Lakeside Lake—lake NM-5
Lakeside Lake—lake WI-6
Lakeside Lake—reservoir SC-3

Lakeside Lake—*reservoir* ..... TX-5
Lakeside Landing—*locale* ..... ME-1
Lakeside Lateral—*canal* ..... CO-8
Lakeside Lodge—*locale* ..... TN-4
**Lakeside Manor**—*pop pl* ..... DE-2
**Lakeside Manor**—*pop pl* ..... MD-2
*Lakeside-Marblehead* ..... OH-6
Lakeside Marina—*locale* ..... MS-4
Lakeside Memorial Gardens—*cemetery* ..... NC-3
Lakeside Memorial Gardens (Cemetery)—*cemetery* ..... KY-4
Lakeside Memorial Hosp—*hospital* ..... NY-2
Lakeside Memorial Lawn (Cemetery)—*cemetery* ..... CA-9
Lakeside Memorial Park—*cemetery* (2) ..... FL-3
Lakeside Memorial Park—*cemetery* ..... NY-2
Lakeside Memory Gardens—*cemetery* ..... FL-3
Lakeside Methodist Camp—*locale* ..... TN-4
Lakeside Methodist Ch—*church* ..... AL-4
Lakeside Mills Hist Dist—*hist pl* ..... NC-3
*Lakeside Mine* ..... SD-7
Lakeside Mine—*mine* ..... NV-8
Lakeside MS—*school* ..... FL-3
Lakeside MS—*school* ..... IN-6
Lakeside Mtns—*range* ..... UT-8
Lakeside Park—*locale* ..... FL-3
Lakeside Park—*locale* ..... MI-6
Lakeside Park—*park* ..... AZ-5
Lakeside Park—*park* (2) ..... CA-9
Lakeside Park—*park* ..... CO-8
Lakeside Park—*park* ..... FL-3
Lakeside Park—*park* ..... IL-6
Lakeside Park—*park* (3) ..... KS-7
Lakeside Park—*park* ..... LA-4
Lakeside Park—*park* (2) ..... MI-6
Lakeside Park—*park* (2) ..... MN-6
Lakeside Park—*park* ..... MS-4
Lakeside Park—*park* ..... NY-2
Lakeside Park—*park* ..... OH-6
Lakeside Park—*park* ..... PA-2
Lakeside Park—*park* (2) ..... TX-5
Lakeside Park—*park* ..... VA-3
Lakeside Park—*park* (2) ..... WI-6
**Lakeside Park**—*pop pl* ..... CA-9
**Lakeside Park**—*pop pl* ..... GA-3
**Lakeside Park**—*pop pl* ..... IN-6
**Lakeside Park**—*pop pl* ..... KY-4
**Lakeside Park**—*pop pl* ..... NJ-2
**Lakeside Park**—*pop pl* (4) ..... NY-2
**Lakeside Park**—*pop pl* ..... TN-4
**Lakeside Park**—*pop pl* ..... TX-5
Lakeside Park Country Club—*other* ..... TX-5
Lakeside Park Dam—*dam* ..... AZ-5
*Lakeside Park Elementary School* ..... TN-4
Lakeside Park Rsvr—*reservoir* ..... PA-2
Lakeside Park Sch—*school* ..... TN-4
**Lakeside Park (subdivision)**—*pop pl* ..... TN-4
**Lakeside Park Subdivision**—*pop pl* ..... UT-8
Lakeside Plantation (historical)—*locale* ..... MS-4
Lakeside Plaza (Shop Ctr)—*locale* ..... FL-3
Lakeside Point—*cape* ..... AK-9
Lakeside Pond—*lake* ..... PA-2
Lakeside Pond Dam—*dam* ..... PA-2
Lakeside Pool—*lake* ..... KY-4
*Lakeside Presbyterian Church* ..... MS-4
Lakeside Press Bldg—*hist pl* ..... IL-6
Lakeside Ranch—*locale* ..... CO-8
*Lakeside Range* ..... UT-8
Lakeside Ranger Station—*locale* ..... AZ-5
*Lakeside Reservoir* ..... AZ-5
**Lakeside Resort**—*pop pl* ..... UT-8
*Lakeside Sch* ..... IN-6
Lakeside Sch—*school* ..... AR-4
Lake Side Sch—*school* ..... AR-4
Lakeside Sch—*school* ..... AR-4
Lakeside Sch—*school* (3) ..... CA-9
Lakeside Sch—*school* (2) ..... CO-8
Lake Side Sch—*school* ..... IL-6
Lakeside Sch—*school* (2) ..... IL-6
Lakeside Sch—*school* ..... IN-6
Lakeside Sch—*school* ..... KS-7
Lakeside Sch—*school* ..... KY-4
Lakeside Sch—*school* ..... LA-4
Lakeside Sch—*school* ..... MA-1
Lakeside Sch—*school* (3) ..... MI-6
Lakeside Sch—*school* ..... MN-6
Lakeside Sch—*school* ..... NE-7
Lakeside Sch—*school* (3) ..... NY-2
Lakeside Sch—*school* ..... NC-3
Lakeside Sch—*school* ..... OH-6
Lakeside Sch—*school* ..... PA-2
Lake Side Sch—*school* ..... SD-7
Lakeside Sch—*school* ..... TN-4
Lakeside Sch—*school* ..... TX-5
Lakeside Sch—*school* ..... VA-3
Lakeside Sch—*school* (5) ..... WI-6
Lakeside Sch (historical)—*school* ..... TN-4
Lakeside Sch Number 2—*school* ..... ND-7
Lakeside School—*locale* ..... MI-6
Lakeside Shoppes—*locale* ..... FL-3
Lakeside Speedway—*other* ..... NJ-2
Lakeside Square (Shop Ctr)—*locale* ..... UT-8
Lakeside State Airp—*airport* ..... OR-9
**Lakeside (subdivision)**—*pop pl* ..... MS-4
**Lakeside (subdivision)**—*pop pl* (2) ..... NC-3
**Lakeside Subdivision**—*pop pl* ..... UT-8
Lake-Side Terrace Apartments—*hist pl* ..... IL-6
**Lakeside (Town of)**—*pop pl* ..... WI-6
**Lakeside Township**—*pop pl* ..... SD-7
**Lakeside (Township of)**—*pop pl* (2) ..... MN-6
Lakeside Trail—*trail* ..... OR-9
Lakeside Trail—*trail* ..... PA-2
Lakeside Trail—*trail* ..... WY-8
**Lakeside (Trailer Park)**—*pop pl* ..... NY-2
Lakeside Union Sch—*school* (2) ..... CA-9
Lakeside-United States Air Force Heliport—*airport* ..... UT-8
Lakeside Valley—*basin* ..... UT-8
Lakeside Village—*locale* ..... KS-7
**Lakeside Village**—*pop pl* ..... NC-3
**Lakeside Village**—*pop pl* ..... OK-5
**Lakeside Village**—*pop pl* ..... TX-5
**Lakeside Village**—*pop pl* ..... VA-3
*Lakeside Villas* ..... IL-6
**Lakeside Vista**—*pop pl* ..... MD-2
**Lake Siding**—*pop pl* ..... SC-3
Lake Sidney—*swamp* ..... FL-3
*Lake Sidney Lanier* ..... TN-4
Lake Silver Sch—*school* ..... FL-3
**Lake Sinai Township**—*pop pl* ..... SD-7
Lake Sinca—*reservoir* ..... PA-2
*Lake Sinca Dam* ..... PA-2
*Lake Siseebakwet* ..... MN-6
*Lakes Island* ..... NY-2
Lakes Island—*island* ..... MA-1
**Lakesite**—*pop pl* ..... TN-4
Lakesite Marina—*locale* ..... TN-4
Lake Site Number Three Dam—*dam* ..... TN-4
*Lake Sixteen* ..... MI-6
Lake Sixteen State Public Shooting Area—*park* ..... SD-7
Lake Sixteen State Wildlife Mngmt Area—*park* ..... MN-6
Lakes Kill—*stream* ..... NY-2
*Lake Skimmerhorn* ..... MN-6
**Lake Slagle**—*pop pl* ..... OH-6
Lakes Lake—*reservoir* ..... CO-8
Lakes Landing (historical)—*locale* ..... MS-4
Lakes Lookout, The—*summit* ..... OR-9
Lakes Lookout Spring, The—*spring* ..... OR-9
Lake Slough—*gut* ..... AL-4
Lake Slough—*gut* ..... KY-4
Lake Slough—*gut* ..... LA-4
Lake Slough—*gut* ..... OR-9
Lake Slough—*stream* ..... AR-4
Lake Slough—*stream* ..... FL-3
Lake Slough—*stream* ..... MO-7
Lake Slough—*stream* ..... TX-5
Lakes (Magisterial District)—*fmr MCD* ..... VA-3
Lakes Mall—*locale* ..... FL-3
Lakes Memorial Cem—*cemetery* ..... WA-9
Lakes Mills Bridge—*locale* ..... NY-2
**Lake Smith**—*pop pl* ..... VA-3
Lake Smith Dam—*dam* ..... IA-7
Lake Smith Park—*park* ..... IA-7
**Lakesmith Terrace**—*pop pl* ..... VA-3
Lake Socapatoy Dam—*dam* ..... AL-4
*Lakes Of Bayou Marion* ..... LA-4
**Lakes of the Four Seasons**—*pop pl* ..... IN-6
Lakes of the Rough—*lake* ..... WY-8
Lake Solitude Dam—*dam* ..... NJ-2
Lake Solitude Trail—*trail* ..... WY-8
*Lake Somerset Dam* ..... PA-2
Lake Sonoma Dam—*dam* ..... NJ-2
*Lake Sonona* ..... NJ-2
*Lake Sooey* ..... NJ-2
Lake Sophia Dam—*dam* ..... PA-2
*Lake Soule* ..... FL-3
Lakes Passage—*gut* ..... FL-3
*Lake Spaulding Reservoir* ..... CA-9
*Lake Splendor* ..... SD-7
Lakes Pocosin—*swamp* ..... NC-3
*Lake's Pond Brook* ..... CT-1
Lakes Pond Brook—*stream* ..... CT-1
Lakes Pond Ch—*church* ..... CT-1
**Lake Spring**—*pop pl* ..... MO-7
Lake Spring—*spring* ..... CA-9
Lake Spring—*spring* (2) ..... NV-8
Lake Spring—*spring* ..... NM-5
Lake Spring—*spring* (3) ..... OR-9
Lake Spring—*spring* (2) ..... UT-8
Lake Spring—*spring* (2) ..... WY-8
Lake Spring Ch—*church* ..... KY-4
Lake Spring Creek—*stream* ..... GA-3
Lake Springs Valley—*basin* ..... NE-7
Lake Square Mall—*locale* ..... FL-3
Lakes Sch—*school* ..... MI-6
**Lakes (subdivision), The**—*pop pl* ..... NC-3
*Lake Stafford* ..... OH-6
**Lake Stafford**—*pop pl* ..... FL-3
Lake Stamford Park—*park* ..... TX-5
*Lake Stampede* ..... OR-9
*Lake Stamper* ..... FL-3
Lake Stanley Ch—*church* ..... FL-3
Lake Stanmor—*reservoir* ..... PA-2
*Lake Stanmor Dam* ..... PA-2
*Lake Station* ..... SD-7
**Lake Station**—*pop pl* ..... IN-6
**Lake Station**—*pop pl* ..... NY-2
**Lake Station**—*pop pl* ..... OK-5
Lake Station Sch—*school* ..... MO-7
**Lake Stay (Township of)**—*pop pl* ..... MN-6
**Lake St. Catherine**—*pop pl* ..... VT-1
**Lake St. Croix Beach**—*pop pl* ..... MN-6
*Lake Stearns* ..... FL-3
Lake Stephenson Oil Field—*oilfield* ..... TX-5
Lake Steven Elem Sch—*school* ..... FL-3
Lake Steven JHS—*school* ..... FL-3
**Lake Stevens**—*pop pl* ..... WA-9
Lake Stevens (CCD)—*cens area* ..... WA-9
Lake Stevens Elem Sch—*school* ..... FL-3
Lake Stevens MS—*school* ..... FL-3
*Lake Stewart* ..... NC-3
Lake Stickney—*CDP* ..... WA-9
**Lake St. Louis**—*pop pl* ..... MO-7
**Lake Stockholm**—*pop pl* ..... NJ-2
Lake Stockholm Dam—*dam* ..... NJ-2
*Lake Stockton* ..... NJ-2
Lake Stomar Rsvr—*reservoir* ..... OR-9
**Lakestone (subdivision)**—*pop pl* ..... NC-3
Lake Stonycreek Dam—*dam* ..... PA-2
Lake Strauss Dam—*dam* ..... PA-2
Lake Stream—*stream* ..... UT-8
*Lake Street* ..... MN-6
**Lake Street**—*pop pl* ..... MA-1
Lake Street Fire Station—*hist pl* ..... MA-1
Lake Street Hist Dist—*hist pl* ..... NY-2
*Lake Street Junior High School* ..... AL-4
Lake Street Memorial Park—*cemetery* ..... IL-6
Lake Street Sch—*school* ..... AL-4
Lake Street Sch—*school* ..... CT-1
Lake Street Sch—*school* ..... ME-1
Lake Street Sch—*school* ..... MA-1
Lake Street Sch—*school* ..... NY-2
Lake Stuart Trail—*trail* ..... WA-9
Lake Substation—*other* ..... ID-8
**Lake Success**—*pop pl* ..... NY-2
Lake Success Dam—*dam* ..... NJ-2
Lake Sueann Dam—*dam* ..... AL-4
**Lake Sullivan**—*pop pl* ..... IN-6
**Lake Summerset**—*pop pl* ..... IL-6
Lake Summit Dam—*dam* ..... NC-3
Lake/Sumter Community Mental Health—*hospital* ..... FL-3
Lake Sumter Junior Coll—*school* ..... FL-3
Lake Sunapee Golf Course—*other* ..... NH-1
Lake Sundown—*reservoir* ..... IA-7
Lake Sundown Dam—*dam* ..... IA-7
**Lake Sunnyside**—*pop pl* ..... NY-2
Lake Superior Campground—*locale* ..... MI-6
Lake Superior Park—*park* ..... MI-6
Lake Superior State For—*forest* ..... MI-6
Lake Surf Dam—*dam* ..... NC-3
Lake Susie Dam—*dam* ..... ND-7
Lake Susie Natl Wildlife Ref—*park* ..... ND-7
Lake Susquehanna—*reservoir* ..... PA-2
*Lake Susquehanna Dam* ..... NJ-2
Lake Susquehanna Dam—*dam* ..... PA-2
*Lake Susupe* ..... MH-9
Lake Sutton State Public Shooting Areas—*park* ..... SD-7
Lakesville—*locale* ..... MD-2
Lake Swamp—*stream* (2) ..... SC-3
Lake Swamp—*swamp* ..... NC-3
Lake Swamp—*swamp* ..... SC-3
Lake Swamp (CCD)—*cens area* ..... SC-3
Lake Swamp Sch—*school* ..... SC-3
Lake Swan Camp—*locale* ..... FL-3
**Lake Swannanoa (Swannanoa)**—*pop pl* ..... NJ-2
*Lake Swanson* ..... AL-4
Lakes West Golf Course—*other* ..... AZ-5
Lake Swiftwater Dam—*dam* ..... PA-2
Lake Sybelia Elem Sch—*school* ..... FL-3
*Lake Sycamore* ..... NJ-2
**Lake Sylvan**—*pop pl* ..... OH-6
Lake Taal Dam—*dam* ..... TN-4
*Lake Table Rock Reservoir* ..... AR-4
*Lake Table Rock Reservoir* ..... MO-7
**Lake Tacoma**—*pop pl* ..... IL-6
Lake Taghkanic State Park—*park* ..... NY-2
Lake Tahoe Airp—*airport* ..... CA-9
Lake Tahoe (CCD)—*cens area* ..... CA-9
Lake Tahoe Dam—*hist pl* ..... CA-9
Lake Tahoe Golf Course—*other* ..... CA-9
Lake Tahoma Dam—*dam* ..... NC-3
*Lake Take Tie* ..... WA-9
**Lake Talmadge**—*pop pl* ..... GA-3
Lake Talquin Baptist Ch—*church* ..... FL-3
Lake Talquin State Rec Area—*park* ..... FL-3
**Lake Tamarack**—*pop pl* ..... NJ-2
Lake Tamarack Dam—*dam* ..... NJ-2
**Lake Tamarisk**—*pop pl* ..... CA-9
*Lake Tampaguas* ..... TX-5
Lake Tangipahoa Dam—*dam* ..... MS-4
**Lake Tanglewood**—*pop pl* ..... TX-5
Lake Tank—*lake* ..... TX-5
Lake Tank—*reservoir* (4) ..... AZ-5
Lake Tank—*reservoir* (15) ..... NM-5
Lake Tank—*reservoir* (4) ..... TX-5
Lake Tank, The—*reservoir* ..... AZ-5
*Lake Tannamus* ..... WA-9
*Lake Tanner* ..... LA-4
Lake Tanner Dam—*dam* ..... AL-4
**Lake Tansi**—*pop pl* ..... TN-4
**Lake Tansi Village**—*pop pl* ..... TN-4
**Lake Tapawingo**—*pop pl* ..... MO-7
Lake Tappan Dam—*dam* ..... NJ-2
**Lake Tara**—*pop pl* ..... GA-3
**Lake Taro**—*pop pl* ..... SC-3
Lake Tarpon—*lake* ..... FL-3
**Lake Tarpon**—*pop pl* ..... FL-3
Lake Tarpon Canal—*canal* ..... FL-3
Lake Tarpon Ch—*church* ..... FL-3
Lake Tarpon Chapel—*church* ..... FL-3
**Lake Tarpon Mobile Homes**—*pop pl* ..... FL-3
*Lake Tartarus* ..... CA-9
Lake Tarzian Dam—*dam* ..... IN-6
Lake Tashmoo East Jetty Light—*locale* ..... MA-1
*Lake Tasse* ..... LA-4
Lake Taylor JHS—*school* ..... VA-3
*Lake Tecomseh* ..... VA-3
*Lake Tefft* ..... RI-1
**Lake Tekakwitha**—*pop pl* ..... MO-7
**Lake Telemark**—*pop pl* ..... NJ-2
Lake Telemark Dam—*dam* ..... NJ-2
Lake Temescal Regional Park—*park* ..... CA-9
*Lake Terra Alta* ..... WV-2
**Lake Terrace**—*pop pl* ..... VA-3
Lake Terrace Park—*park* ..... LA-4
*Lake Terrell* ..... OK-5
Lake Terrell State Game Ref—*park* ..... WA-9
*Lake Terry* ..... WY-8
Lake Texoma State Park—*park* ..... OK-5
Lake Theis Windmill—*locale* ..... TX-5
Lake Thel Dam—*dam* ..... AL-4
Lake Theo Folsom Site Complex—*hist pl* ..... TX-5
Lake Thibadeau Natl Wildlife Ref—*park* ..... MT-8
*Lake Thirteen* ..... MI-6
*Lake Thirty* ..... MI-6
*Lake Thirty-five* ..... MI-6
*Lake Thirty Three* ..... MI-6
*Lake Thirty-three Creek* ..... MI-6
*Lake Thirty Two* ..... MI-6
Lake Thisted Cem—*cemetery* ..... SD-7
Lake Tholloco Dam—*dam* ..... AL-4
*Lake Thomas* ..... TX-5
*Lake Thomas* ..... WA-9
*Lake Thomas* ..... WI-6
**Lake Thomas**—*pop pl* ..... TX-5
Lake Thomas Dam—*dam* ..... MS-4
*Lake Thompson* ..... ME-1
*Lake Thompson* ..... MA-1
*Lake Thompson* ..... ND-7
*Lake Thorpe* ..... NC-3
**Lake Thunderbird**—*pop pl* ..... IL-6
Lake Tia Khata Dam—*dam* ..... TN-4
*Lake Tiak-O'Kata* ..... MS-4
Lake Tiak-O-Kata Dam—*dam* ..... MS-4
Lake Tiaroga Dam—*dam* ..... NC-3
*Lake Tillery Dam* ..... NC-3
Lake Timberline—*reservoir* ..... PA-2
Lake Timberline Dam—*dam* ..... PA-2
Lake Tina Dam—*dam* ..... AL-4
Lake Tiorati Brook—*stream* ..... NY-2
*Lake Tippecanoe* ..... IN-6
*Lake Titus Stream* ..... NY-2
*Lake Toccoa* ..... GA-3
Lake Toc-O-Leen Dam—*dam* ..... MS-4
*Lake Toke-Tie* ..... WA-9
Lake Toketie—*lake* ..... WA-9
**Lake Tomahawk**—*pop pl* ..... WI-6
Lake Tomahawk Dam—*dam* ..... NC-3
Lake Tomahawk Lookout Tower—*locale* ..... WI-6
**Lake Tomahawk (Town of)**—*pop pl* ..... WI-6
Lake Tom-A-Lex Dam—*dam* ..... NC-3
Laketon—*locale* ..... KY-4
Laketon—*locale* ..... MI-6
Laketon—*locale* ..... TX-5
**Laketon**—*pop pl* ..... IN-6
**Laketon**—*pop pl* ..... NE-7
**Laketon**—*pop pl* ..... PA-2
**Laketon**—*pop pl* ..... SC-3
Laketon Cem—*cemetery* ..... IN-6
Laketon Cem—*cemetery* ..... MI-6
Laketon Elem Sch—*school* ..... IN-6
**Laketon Heights**—*pop pl* ..... PA-2
Laketon (historical)—*locale* ..... SD-7
Laketon Schools—*school* ..... MI-6
Laketon Slough—*stream* ..... MI-6
**Laketon Township**—*pop pl* ..... SD-7
**Laketon (Township of)**—*pop pl* ..... MI-6
Lake Topanemus Dam—*dam* ..... NJ-2
*Lake Topenemus* ..... NJ-2
Lake Towhee—*reservoir* ..... PA-2
Lake Towhee Dam—*dam* ..... PA-2
Lake Towhee Park—*park* ..... PA-2
*Lake Town* ..... LA-4
**Laketown**—*pop pl* ..... UT-8
*Lake Town Canyon* ..... UT-8
Laketown Canyon—*valley* ..... UT-8
Laketown Cem—*cemetery* ..... UT-8
Laketown Ch—*church* ..... WI-6
Laketown Moravian Brethren's Church—*hist pl* ..... MN-6
**Lake (Town of)**—*pop pl* (2) ..... WI-6
Laketown Sch—*school* ..... IL-6
Laketown Sch—*school* ..... ND-7
*Lake Townsend* ..... MT-8
*Lake Township* ..... KS-7
Lake Township—*civil* ..... KS-7
Lake Township—*civil* ..... MO-7
Lake Township—*civil* (2) ..... SD-7
Lake Township—*fmr MCD* (8) ..... IA-7
Lake Township—*inact MCD* ..... NV-8
**Lake Township**—*pop pl* ..... KS-7
**Lake Township**—*pop pl* ..... MO-7
**Lake Township**—*pop pl* (3) ..... NE-7
**Lake Township**—*pop pl* ..... ND-7
**Lake Township**—*pop pl* (8) ..... SD-7
Lake Township Hall—*building* ..... SD-7
Lake Township (historical)—*civil* ..... ND-7
Lake Township (historical)—*civil* ..... SD-7
Lake (Township of)—*fmr MCD* (3) ..... AR-4
Lake (Township of)—*other* ..... OH-6
**Lake (Township of)**—*pop pl* ..... IL-6
**Lake (Township of)**—*pop pl* (3) ..... IN-6
**Lake (Township of)**—*pop pl* (8) ..... MI-6
**Lake (Township of)**—*pop pl* (2) ..... MN-6
**Lake (Township of)**—*pop pl* (4) ..... OH-6
**Lake (Township of)**—*pop pl* (3) ..... PA-2
Lake Township Sch—*hist pl* ..... OH-6
*Laketown (Southlawn)* ..... IL-6
Lake Town Townhall—*building* ..... ND-7
**Laketown (Town of)**—*pop pl* ..... WI-6
Lake Town Township—*civil* ..... ND-7
**Laketown (Township of)**—*pop pl* ..... MI-6
**Laketown (Township of)**—*pop pl* ..... MN-6
**Lake Toxaway**—*pop pl* ..... NC-3
Lake Toxaway Ch—*church* (2) ..... NC-3
Lake Trace Dam—*dam* ..... NC-3
Lake Tract Sch—*school* ..... NJ-2
Lake Trafford Elem Sch—*school* ..... FL-3
Lake Trail—*trail* ..... ME-1
Lake Trail—*trail* ..... PA-2
Lake Trails Church Camp—*locale* ..... MN-6
Lake Trammell Oil Field—*oilfield* ..... TX-5
*Lake Tranquility* ..... AL-4
Lake Trap Windmill—*locale* ..... TX-5
*Lake Traverse* ..... SD-7
Lake Traverse Presbyterian Ch—*church* ..... SD-7
Lake Trenton Pumping Station—*locale* ..... ND-7
*Lake Trinidad* ..... TX-5
Lake Trois Jeans—*bay* ..... LA-4
*Lake Tucker* ..... WA-9
Lake Tullahoma Dam—*dam* ..... TN-4
**Lake Tullahoma Estates**—*pop pl* ..... TN-4
Lake Tunnel—*tunnel* ..... VA-3
Lake Tu Peek—*reservoir* ..... PA-2
Lake Tuscaloosa Dam—*dam* ..... AL-4
Lake Tuscoba Dam—*dam* ..... AL-4
*Lake Twenty Four* ..... MI-6
*Lake Twenty Three* ..... LA-4
*Lake Twenty-Two* ..... MI-6
*Lake Twiddy* ..... NC-3
*Lake Umbarger* ..... TX-5
*Lake Underbell* ..... FL-3
Lake Underwood—*reservoir* ..... PA-2
Lake Underwood Dam—*dam* ..... PA-2
*Lake Undine* ..... MA-1
Lake Union Air Service Seaplane Base—*airport* ..... WA-9
Lake Union Cem—*cemetery* ..... MN-6
Lake Union Ch—*church* ..... MN-6
Lake Union Ch—*church* ..... PA-2
Lake Union Chrysler Air Seaplane Base—*airport* ..... WA-9
Lake Union Heliport—*airport* ..... WA-9
Lake Union Sch—*school* ..... IL-6
Lake Unity Dam—*dam* ..... NC-3
Lake Vale Cem—*cemetery* ..... MA-1
*Lake Valerie* ..... LA-4
Lake Valhalla Dam—*dam* ..... NJ-2
Lake Valley—*basin* ..... AZ-5
Lake Valley—*basin* ..... CA-9
Lake Valley—*basin* ..... OR-9
Lake Valley—*flat* ..... CA-9
Lake Valley—*locale* ..... OK-5
**Lake Valley**—*pop pl* ..... CA-9
**Lake Valley**—*pop pl* (2) ..... NM-5
**Lake Valley**—*pop pl* ..... TN-4
Lake Valley—*valley* ..... CA-9
Lake Valley Boarding Sch—*school* ..... NM-5
Lake Valley Cem—*cemetery* ..... TX-5
Lake Valley Ch—*church* ..... KY-4
Lake Valley Chapter House—*locale* ..... NM-5
Lake Valley Country Club—*locale* ..... MO-7
Lake Valley (depression)—*valley* ..... NV-8
Lake Valley Landing Strip—*airport* ..... NV-8
Lake Valley Sch—*school* ..... AZ-5
Lake Valley Sch—*school* ..... NE-7
**Lake Valley (subdivision)**—*pop pl* ..... NC-3
Lake Valley Summit—*gap* ..... NV-8
Lake Valley Summit Spring—*spring* ..... NV-8
**Lake Valley (Township of)**—*pop pl* ..... MN-6
**Lake Vanare**—*pop pl* ..... NY-2
Lake Vance Dam—*dam* ..... NC-3
Lake Vann Dam—*dam* ..... AL-4
Lake Van Rod—*other* ..... NM-5
Lake Van Vac—*bay* ..... FL-3
*Lake Varret* ..... LA-4
*Lake Veil* ..... WI-6
*Lake Veret* ..... LA-4
*Lake Vermilion* ..... MN-6
Lake Vermilion (Unorganized Territory of)—*unorg* ..... MN-6
**Lake Victor**—*pop pl* ..... TX-5
*Lake Victoria* ..... IN-6
*Lake View* ..... AL-4
*Lakeview* ..... AZ-5
*Lakeview* (2) ..... IL-6
*Lake View* ..... LA-4
*Lakeview* ..... ME-1
*Lake View* ..... MA-1
*Lakeview* ..... MS-4
*Lakeview* ..... NY-2
*Lakeview* ..... SC-3
*Lake View* ..... UT-8
Lakeview—*locale* ..... AL-4
Lakeview—*locale* ..... AK-9
Lakeview—*locale* ..... AR-4
Lakeview—*locale* ..... FL-3
Lakeview—*locale* ..... GA-3
Lakeview—*locale* ..... IL-6
Lake View—*locale* ..... KS-7
Lake View—*locale* ..... MS-4
Lakeview—*locale* (2) ..... MT-8
Lakeview—*locale* ..... NV-8
Lakeview—*locale* ..... OK-5
Lakeview—*locale* ..... PA-2
Lakeview—*locale* ..... SD-7
Lakeview—*locale* (2) ..... TN-4
Lakeview—*locale* (3) ..... TX-5
Lakeview—*other* ..... NY-2
**Lakeview**—*pop pl* (3) ..... AL-4
**Lakeview**—*pop pl* ..... AK-9
**Lakeview**—*pop pl* ..... AZ-5
**Lakeview**—*pop pl* ..... AR-4
**Lake View**—*pop pl* (2) ..... AR-4
**Lakeview**—*pop pl* (3) ..... CA-9
**Lake View**—*pop pl* ..... CO-8
**Lake View**—*pop pl* ..... FL-3
**Lakeview**—*pop pl* (3) ..... GA-3
**Lakeview**—*pop pl* ..... ID-8
**Lakeview**—*pop pl* ..... IN-6
**Lake View**—*pop pl* (2) ..... IN-6
**Lakeview**—*pop pl* ..... IN-6
**Lakeview**—*pop pl* ..... IA-7
**Lakeview**—*pop pl* ..... KY-4
**Lakeview**—*pop pl* (2) ..... LA-4
**Lake View**—*pop pl* ..... ME-1
**Lakeview**—*pop pl* (2) ..... MD-2
**Lakeview**—*pop pl* (3) ..... MI-6
**Lakeview**—*pop pl* (2) ..... MO-7
**Lake View**—*pop pl* ..... NJ-2
**Lakeview**—*pop pl* ..... NJ-2
**Lake View**—*pop pl* ..... NY-2
**Lakeview**—*pop pl* (3) ..... NY-2
**Lakeview**—*pop pl* (3) ..... NC-3
**Lakeview**—*pop pl* (2) ..... OH-6
**Lake View**—*pop pl* ..... OH-6
**Lakeview**—*pop pl* ..... OH-6
**Lakeview**—*pop pl* ..... OR-9
**Lake View**—*pop pl* ..... SC-3
**Lakeview**—*pop pl* (4) ..... TN-4
**Lake View**—*pop pl* ..... TX-5
**Lakeview**—*pop pl* (5) ..... TX-5
**Lake View**—*pop pl* ..... TX-5
**Lakeview**—*pop pl* ..... TX-5
**Lakeview**—*pop pl* ..... UT-8
**Lakeview**—*pop pl* ..... VA-3
**Lakeview**—*pop pl* ..... WA-9
**Lakeview**—*pop pl* ..... WI-6
**Lake View**—*pop pl* ..... WI-6
Lakeview—*uninc pl* ..... LA-4
Lake View—*uninc pl* ..... MA-1
Lakeview—*uninc pl* ..... NJ-2
Lakeview—*uninc pl* ..... TX-5
Lake View—*uninc pl* ..... WI-6
**Lakeview Acres**—*pop pl* ..... IL-6
**Lakeview Acres**—*pop pl* ..... KY-4
**Lakeview Acres (subdivision)**—*pop pl* ..... NC-3
**Lake View Addition (subdivision)**—*pop pl* ..... UT-8
Lake View Airp—*airport* ..... TN-4
**Lakeview Assembly**—*pop pl* ..... TX-5
Lakeview Assembly of God Evangel Christian Sch—*school* ..... AL-4
*Lakeview Baptist Ch* ..... AL-4
*Lakeview Baptist Ch* ..... MS-4
Lakeview Baptist Ch—*church* (2) ..... AL-4
Lakeview Baptist Ch—*church* (3) ..... FL-3
Lakeview Baptist Ch—*church* ..... MS-4
*Lakeview Baptist Church* ..... TN-4
Lakeview Baptist Kindergarten—*school* ..... FL-3
**Lakeview Beach (subdivision)**—*pop pl* ..... AL-4
Lake View Camp—*locale* ..... TN-4
Lakeview Camp—*locale* ..... UT-8
Lake View Campground—*locale* ..... CO-8
Lakeview Campground—*locale* ..... CO-8
Lake View Campground—*locale* ..... ID-8
Lakeview Campground—*locale* ..... MT-8
Lake View Campground—*locale* ..... WY-8
Lake View Campground—*park* ..... AZ-5
Lakeview Canyon—*valley* ..... CA-9
Lakeview Cave—*cave* ..... AL-4
Lakeview (CCD)—*cens area* ..... OR-9
Lake View (CCD)—*cens area* ..... SC-3
Lakeview (CCD)—*cens area* ..... TX-5
Lakeview Cem—*cemetery* (2) ..... AL-4
Lakeview Cem—*cemetery* ..... CA-9
Lakeview Cem—*cemetery* (2) ..... CO-8
Lakeview Cem—*cemetery* (3) ..... CT-1
Lakeview Cem—*cemetery* ..... FL-3
Lakeview Cem—*cemetery* ..... ID-8
Lakeview Cem—*cemetery* (3) ..... IL-6
Lakeview Cem—*cemetery* (2) ..... IN-6
Lake View Cem—*cemetery* ..... IA-7
Lakeview Cem—*cemetery* (2) ..... KS-7
Lakeview Cem—*cemetery* ..... KY-4
Lakeview Cem—*cemetery* (5) ..... ME-1
Lake View Cem—*cemetery* ..... ME-1
Lakeview Cem—*cemetery* (3) ..... ME-1
Lakeview Cem—*cemetery* (3) ..... MA-1
Lakeview Cem—*cemetery* (2) ..... MI-6
Lake View Cem—*cemetery* (4) ..... MI-6
Lakeview Cem—*cemetery* (9) ..... MI-6
Lake View Cem—*cemetery* ..... MI-6
Lakeview Cem—*cemetery* (3) ..... MI-6
Lakeview Cem—*cemetery* (4) ..... MN-6
Lake View Cem—*cemetery* ..... MN-6
Lakeview Cem—*cemetery* (3) ..... MN-6
Lake View Cem—*cemetery* ..... MN-6
Lakeview Cem—*cemetery* (2) ..... MN-6
Lake View Cem—*cemetery* ..... MN-6
Lakeview Cem—*cemetery* ..... MN-6
Lake View Cem—*cemetery* ..... MN-6
Lakeview Cem—*cemetery* (5) ..... MN-6
Lakeview Cem—*cemetery* (2) ..... MT-8
Lake View Cem—*cemetery* ..... NE-7
Lakeview Cem—*cemetery* (4) ..... NH-1
Lakeview Cem—*cemetery* (4) ..... NY-2
Lake View Cem—*cemetery* ..... NY-2
Lakeview Cem—*cemetery* (6) ..... NY-2
Lake View Cem—*cemetery* (2) ..... NY-2
Lake View Cem—*cemetery* (2) ..... ND-7
Lakeview Cem—*cemetery* ..... ND-7
Lake View Cem—*cemetery* ..... ND-7
Lake View Cem—*cemetery* ..... OH-6
Lakeview Cem—*cemetery* ..... OH-6
Lakeview Cem—*cemetery* ..... OK-5
Lakeview Cem—*cemetery* ..... PA-2
Lake View Cem—*cemetery* ..... PA-2
Lakeview Cem—*cemetery* ..... PA-2
Lake View Cem—*cemetery* ..... SC-3
Lake View Cem—*cemetery* ..... SD-7
Lakeview Cem—*cemetery* ..... SD-7
Lake View Cem—*cemetery* (2) ..... SD-7
Lakeview Cem—*cemetery* ..... SD-7
Lakeview Cem—*cemetery* (2) ..... TN-4
Lakeview Cem—*cemetery* (3) ..... TX-5
Lakeview Cem—*cemetery* (2) ..... UT-8
Lake View Cem—*cemetery* ..... UT-8
Lakeview Cem—*cemetery* (5) ..... VT-1
Lakeview Cem—*cemetery* (2) ..... VA-3
Lakeview Cem—*cemetery* ..... WA-9
Lake View Cem—*cemetery* ..... WA-9
Lakeview Cem—*cemetery* (2) ..... WI-6
Lake View Cem—*cemetery* ..... WI-6
Lakeview Cem—*cemetery* ..... WI-6
Lake View Cem—*cemetery* ..... WI-6
Lakeview Cem—*cemetery* (7) ..... WI-6
Lakeview Cem—*cemetery* ..... WY-8
Lake View Cem—*cemetery* ..... WY-8
Lakeview Center—*school* ..... FL-3
Lakeview Ch—*church* (5) ..... AL-4
Lakeview Ch—*church* ..... AR-4
Lake View Ch—*church* ..... AR-4
Lake View Ch—*church* ..... FL-3
Lakeview Ch—*church* ..... FL-3
Lakeview Ch—*church* (2) ..... GA-3
Lake View Ch—*church* ..... GA-3
Lakeview Ch—*church* (5) ..... GA-3
Lakeview Ch—*church* ..... IL-6
Lake View Ch—*church* (2) ..... IN-6
Lake View Ch—*church* ..... KY-4
Lakeview Ch—*church* (2) ..... KY-4
Lakeview Ch—*church* ..... MN-6
Lakeview Ch—*church* (2) ..... MS-4
Lake View Ch—*church* ..... MS-4
Lakeview Ch—*church* ..... MS-4
Lakeview Ch—*church* ..... NC-3
Lake View Ch—*church* ..... NC-3
Lakeview Ch—*church* ..... NC-3
Lake View Ch—*church* ..... NC-3
Lakeview Ch—*church* ..... NC-3
Lakeview Ch—*church* ..... OH-6
Lakeview Ch—*church* (2) ..... SC-3
Lakeview Ch—*church* (4) ..... TN-4
Lake View Ch—*church* ..... TN-4
Lakeview Ch—*church* ..... TN-4
Lakeview Ch—*church* (9) ..... TX-5
Lakeview Ch—*church* ..... VA-3
Lake View Ch—*church* ..... WV-2
Lakeview Chapel—*church* ..... GA-3
Lakeview Chapel—*church* ..... MN-6
Lakeview Chapel—*church* ..... WA-9
Lakeview Ch (historical)—*church* ..... AL-4
Lakeview Ch of the Nazarene—*church* ..... KS-7
Lakeview Community Cem—*cemetery* ..... TX-5
Lakeview Community Ch—*church* ..... NY-2
Lakeview Community Hall—*locale* ..... TX-5
**Lakeview Condominium**—*pop pl* ..... UT-8
**Lakeview Condominiums of Bountiful**—*pop pl* ..... UT-8
Lakeview Consolidated HS—*school* ..... PA-2
**Lake View (corporate name for Lakeview)**—*pop pl* ..... SC-3
*Lakeview (corporate name Lake View)* ..... SC-3
Lakeview Country Club—*locale* ..... MO-7
Lakeview Country Club—*other* ..... AL-4
Lakeview Country Club—*other* ..... KS-7
Lake View Country Club—*other* ..... PA-2
Lakeview Country Club—*other* ..... WA-9
Lakeview Country Club—*other* ..... WV-2
Lakeview Country Club (historical)—*locale* ..... GA-3
Lake View Country Club Lake—*reservoir* ..... AL-4
Lakeview County Home—*locale* ..... IN-6
Lake View Dam—*dam* ..... AL-4
Lake View Dam—*dam* ..... IN-6
Lake View Dam—*dam* ..... MS-4
Lake View Dam—*dam* ..... NC-3
Lakeview Ditch—*canal* ..... WY-8
Lakeview Dock—*locale* ..... AL-4
Lakeview Dock—*locale* (2) ..... TN-4
Lakeview Duck Club—*other* ..... CA-9
*Lakeview Elem Sch* ..... PA-2
Lakeview Elem Sch—*school* ..... AL-4
Lake View Elem Sch—*school* ..... PA-2
Lakeview Elem Sch—*school* (2) ..... TN-4
**Lakeview Equestrian Park (subdivision)**—*pop pl* ..... UT-8
**Lakeview Estates**—*pop pl* ..... AL-4
**Lakeview Estates**—*pop pl* ..... GA-3
**Lakeview Estates**—*pop pl* ..... IN-6
**Lakeview Estates**—*pop pl* (2) ..... NC-3
**Lakeview Estates**—*pop pl* ..... TN-4
**Lakeview Estates**—*pop pl* ..... TX-5
Lakeview Estates Dam—*dam* ..... TN-4
Lakeview Estates Lake—*reservoir* ..... IN-6
Lakeview Estates Lake—*reservoir* ..... TN-4
Lakeview Estates Lake Dam—*dam* ..... IN-6
Lake View Estates Lakes—*reservoir* ..... AL-4
**Lake View Estates (Lakeview Farm Estates)**—*pop pl* ..... IL-6
Lake View Estates Pond—*reservoir* ..... NC-3
Lake View Estates Pond Dam—*dam* ..... NC-3
**Lakeview Estates (subdivision)**—*pop pl* (2) ..... AL-4

Lake Yale Baptist Assembly—*church* ... FL-3
Lake Yard—*locale* ... OR-9
Lakey Branch—*stream* ... KY-4
Lakey Canyon—*valley* ... CO-8
Lakey Cem—*cemetery* ... MO-7
Lakey Cem—*cemetery* ... NC-3
Lakey Cem—*cemetery* ... TX-5
*Lakey Cemetery* ... TN-4
Lakey Creek—*stream* ... ID-8
LaKey Creek—*stream* ... IL-6
Lakey Creek—*stream* ... NC-3
Lake Yenruogis County Park—*park* ... IA-7
Lakey Gap—*gap* ... NC-3
Lakey Gap Chapel—*church* ... NC-3
Lakey Knob—*summit* ... NC-3
Lakey Ranch—*locale* (2) ... MT-8
Lakey Rsvr—*reservoir* ... ID-8
Lakeys Branch—*stream* ... IN-6
Lakey Woods Knob—*summit* ... TN-4
Lake Zahl Dam—*dam* ... ND-7
Lake Zahl Natl Wildlife Ref—*park* ... ND-7
*Lake Zamora* ... AL-4
*Lake Zem* ... FL-3
Lake Zion Ch—*church* ... LA-4
**Lake Zurich**—*pop pl* ... IL-6
Lake Zurich Cem—*cemetery* ... IL-6
Lake 16 Dam—*dam* ... SD-7
*Lake 22* ... MI-6
*Lake 27* ... MI-6
*Lake 35* ... MI-6
*Lakin* ... KS-7
Lakin—*locale* ... CA-9
Lakin—*locale* ... WV-2
**Lakin**—*pop pl* ... KS-7
Lakina Glacier—*glacier* ... AK-9
Lakina Lake—*lake* ... AK-9
Lakina River—*stream* ... AK-9
Lakin Brook—*stream* ... NY-2
Lakin Cem—*cemetery* ... KS-7
Lakin Cem—*cemetery* ... WV-2
Lakin Ch—*church* ... MN-6
Lakin Chapel—*church* ... OH-6
Lakin Dam—*dam* ... CA-9
Lakin Draw—*valley* ... KS-7
Lakin Elem Sch—*school* ... KS-7
Lakin Hill—*summit* ... ME-1
Lakin HS—*school* ... KS-7
*Lakin Lake* ... MI-6
**Lakin (Lakin State Hospital)**—*pop pl* ... WV-2
Lakin Landing Field—*airport* ... KS-7
Lakin Place—*locale* ... OR-9
*Lakin Pond* ... NH-1
Lakins Island—*island* ... NY-2
Lakin Slough State Game Mngmt
Area—*park* ... IA-7
*Lakins Pond* ... NH-1
Lakin State Hosp—*hospital* ... WV-2
**Lakin Township**—*pop pl* (3) ... KS-7
**Lakin (Township of)**—*pop pl* ... MN-6
*Laki Peak* ... OR-9
Lakley Sch (abandoned)—*school* ... MO-7
Lakloey Hill—*summit* ... AK-9
*Lakne* ... MP-9
Lakner Dam—*dam* ... SD-7
*Lakola* ... IA-7
Lakolaho Creek—*stream* ... MT-8
Lakonta(Truax)—*locale* ... IA-7
Lakota—*locale* ... UT-8
Lakota—*locale* ... VA-3
Lakota—*locale* ... WA-9
Lakota—*other* ... TX-5
**Lakota**—*pop pl* ... IA-7
**Lakota**—*pop pl* ... ND-7
Lakota Dam—*dam* ... SD-7
Lakotah Canal—*canal* ... NE-7
**Lakota Homes (subdivision)**—*pop pl* ... SD-7
Lakota HS—*school* (2) ... OH-6
Lakota Juior HS—*school* ... WA-9
Lakota Lake—*reservoir* ... SD-7
Lakota Lake—*reservoir* ... VT-1
Lakota Municipal Airp—*airport* ... ND-7
Lakota Peak—*summit* ... SD-7
*Lakota Resort* ... UT-8
**Lakota Township**—*pop pl* ... ND-7
L A K Ranch—*locale* ... WY-8
L A K Rsvr—*reservoir* ... WY-8
*Laksapur Creek* ... MS-4
Lakso Slough—*stream* ... AK-9
La Labor Windmill—*locale* (2) ... TX-5
La Ladera—*locale* ... NM-5
**La Ladera**—*pop pl* ... NM-5
*La Ladera del Bosquesito* ... NM-5
La Laguna—*lake* ... NM-5
La Laguna (Gutierrez)—*civil* ... CA-9
La Laguna Seca—*civil* ... CA-9
La Laguna (Stearns)—*civil* ... CA-9
La Laguna Windmill—*locale* ... TX-5
Lalahala—*bay* ... HI-9
Lala Hill Ch—*church* ... TX-5
La Lake—*lake* ... MN-6
Lalakea—*civil* ... HI-9
Lalakea Ditch—*canal* ... HI-9
Lalakea Fishpond—*lake* ... HI-9
Lalakea Rsvr—*reservoir* ... HI-9
Lalakea Stream—*stream* ... HI-9
**Lalakoa**—*pop pl* ... HI-9
*Lalamilo* (2) ... HI-9
Lalamilo—*civil* ... HI-9
La Lande—*locale* ... NM-5
La Lande Cem—*cemetery* ... NM-5
Lalang—*island* ... FM-9
LaLanne, Dominique, House and
Store—*hist pl* ... LA-4
Lalapo—*area* ... GU-9
Lalas Rock—*island* ... GU-9
*Lalaupapa* ... HI-9
*Lalayag* ... MH-9
Lalayak—*slope* ... MH-9
*Lalayas* ... MH-9
La Lechusa Tank—*reservoir* ... NM-5
Lalen, Lake—*lake* ... AK-9
La Leona—*locale* ... TX-5
La Leona Cem—*cemetery* ... TX-5
La Leona Ranch—*locale* ... TX-5
Lale Pond Number 2 Dam—*dam* ... SD-7
LaLera, Lake—*reservoir* ... GA-3
*LaLesna* ... AZ-5
Laliberte Camp—*locale* ... ME-1
Lalich Field—*airport* ... PA-2
La Liebre—*civil* ... CA-9
La Liebre Ranch—*locale* ... CA-9
La Liendre—*locale* ... NM-5
**Lalimere**—*pop pl* ... IN-6
La Linea Windmill—*locale* ... TX-5
Lallah Branch—*stream* ... TX-5
La Llanura—*flat* ... CA-9
Lallie—*locale* ... ND-7
Lallie North—*unorg reg* ... ND-7
**Lallie Township**—*pop pl* ... ND-7
Lally Creek—*stream* ... OR-9
**Lalo**—*pop pl* ... GU-9
Laloafu Stream—*stream* ... AS-9
La Loba—*ridge* ... CA-9
La Loba Windmill—*locale* ... TX-5
Lalo Canyon—*valley* ... NM-5
Lalofutu Point—*cape* ... AS-9
Laloi Stream—*stream* ... AS-9
Lalolamauta Stream—*stream* ... AS-9
La Loma—*locale* ... NM-5
La Loma—*uninc pl* ... CA-9
La Loma Alta—*summit* ... NM-5
*La Loma Azul* ... KS-7
LaLoma Cem—*cemetery* ... NM-5
La Loma de Arena—*summit* ... NM-5
La Loma del Mudo—*summit* ... NM-5
La Loma Hills—*range* ... CA-9
La Loma JHS—*school* ... CA-9
**La Loma (Llano Viejo)**—*pop pl* ... NM-5
La Loma Park—*park* ... CA-9
La Loma Plaza Hist Dist—*hist pl* ... NM-5
**LaLoma Ranch**—*pop pl* ... AZ-5
**La Loma Subdivision**—*pop pl* ... UT-8
La Loma Windmill—*locale* ... TX-5
La Lomera—*ridge* ... CA-9
La Lomica—*summit* ... CA-9
La Lomita Hist Dist—*hist pl* ... TX-5
La Lomita Mission—*church* ... TX-5
**Lalomoana**—*pop pl* ... AS-9
*Lalone Island* ... NY-2
Laloniu Cove—*bay* ... AS-9
Lalopapa Marsh—*swamp* ... AS-9
Lalo Peak—*summit* ... AZ-5
*Lalo Point* ... MH-9
**Lalopua**—*pop pl* ... AS-9
Lalor Sch—*school* ... NJ-2
Laloulu Ridge—*ridge* ... AS-9
La Luisa—*CDP* ... PR-3
**La Luisa**—*pop pl* ... PR-3
**Lalumiere (Parochial School)**—*pop pl* ... IN-6
**La Luna**—*pop pl* ... PR-3
La Luneta—*summit* ... CA-9
**La Luz**—*pop pl* ... NM-5
La Luz Canyon—*valley* ... NM-5
La Luz Hist Dist—*hist pl* ... NM-5
La Luz Mine—*mine* ... NM-5
La Luz Pottery Factory—*hist pl* ... NM-5
La Luz Sch—*school* ... FL-3
La Luz Sch—*school* ... NM-5
La Luz Trail (Foot)—*trail* ... NM-5
La Luz Well—*well* ... TX-5
Lam—*island* ... FM-9
Lam—*island* ... MP-9
**Lama**—*pop pl* ... NM-5
Lama Airfield—*airport* ... CO-8
Lama Canyon—*valley* ... NM-5
La Madera—*locale* ... NM-5
**La Madera**—*pop pl* ... NM-5
La Madera Arroyo—*stream* ... NM-5
La Madera Canyon—*valley* ... NM-5
La Madera Cem—*cemetery* ... NM-5
La Madera Mountains—*other* ... NM-5
LaMadera Park—*park* ... AZ-5
La Madera Ski Area—*locale* ... NM-5
La Madre Mtn—*summit* ... NV-8
LaMadre Spring—*spring* ... NV-8
La Madrilena—*hist pl* ... TX-5
La Magada Windmill—*locale* ... TX-5
Lamahni—*cape* ... FM-9
La Majada Grant—*civil* ... NM-5
La Majada Mesa—*bench* ... NM-5
Lamalees Creek—*stream* ... IA-7
*Lamaloa* ... HI-9
Lamaloa Gulch—*valley* (2) ... HI-9
Lamaloa Head—*summit* ... HI-9
Lamaloloa—*civil* ... HI-9
Lamalone Lodge—*locale* ... NM-5
*Laman* ... MH-9
Laman—*locale* ... TX-5
*La Mance Creek* ... NC-3
Lamance Creek—*stream* ... NV-8
Lamance Creek—*stream* ... NC-3
**Lamanda Park**—*pop pl* ... CA-9
*Lama Negra* ... AZ-5
La Manga—*locale* ... NM-5
La Manga Camp—*locale* ... NM-5
La Manga Canyon—*valley* ... NM-5
La Manga Cow Camp—*locale* ... CO-8
La Manga Creek—*stream* ... CO-8
La Manga Creek—*stream* ... NM-5
La Manga Pass—*gap* ... CO-8
La Manga Stock Driveway—*trail* ... CO-8
La Manga Summer Home Group—*locale* ... CO-8
La Manga Tank—*reservoir* ... NM-5
Lamanibot—*slope* ... MH-9
Lamanibot Sampapa', Puntan—*cape* ... MH-9
Lamanibot Sanhilo, Puntan—*cape* ... MH-9
Lamanite Arch—*arch* ... UT-8
LaMaquina Creek—*stream* ... NM-5
*Lamar* ... MI-6
*Lamar* ... FM-9
Lamar—*locale* ... AL-4
Lamar—*locale* ... GA-3
Lamar—*locale* ... KS-7
Lamar—*locale* ... PA-2
Lamar—*locale* ... TX-5
Lamar—*locale* ... WI-6
**Lamar**—*pop pl* ... AR-4
**Lamar**—*pop pl* ... CO-8
**Lamar**—*pop pl* ... IN-6
**Lamar**—*pop pl* ... LA-4
**Lamar**—*pop pl* ... MS-4
**Lamar**—*pop pl* ... MO-7
**Lamar**—*pop pl* ... NE-7
**Lamar**—*pop pl* ... OK-5
**Lamar**—*pop pl* ... SC-3
**Lamar**—*pop pl* ... TX-5
**Lamar**—*pop pl* ... WA-9
**Lamar**—*pop pl* ... WV-2
Lamar—*uninc pl* ... TN-4
Lamar, Lake—*reservoir* ... NC-3
Lamar, Lake—*reservoir* ... TN-4
Lamar, Lucius Quintus Cincinnatus,
House—*hist pl* ... MS-4
Lamar Acad—*school* ... SC-3
**Lamara Heights**—*pop pl* ... GA-3
La Mar Artesian Well—*well* ... TX-5
Lamar-Blanchard House—*hist pl* ... GA-3
Lamar Bldg—*hist pl* ... GA-3
Lamar Branch—*stream* ... GA-3
Lamar Branch—*stream* ... TX-5
Lamar Bridge—*bridge* ... AL-4
Lamar Bruce, Lake—*reservoir* ... MS-4
Lamar Buffalo Ranch—*hist pl* ... WY-8
Lamar Camp—*locale* ... PA-2
Lamar Canal—*canal* ... CO-8
Lamar Canal Diversion Dam—*dam* ... CO-8
Lamar Canyon—*valley* ... TX-5
Lamar Canyon—*valley* ... WY-8
Lamar (CCD)—*cens area* ... SC-3
Lamar Cem—*cemetery* ... AL-4
Lamar Cem—*cemetery* ... GA-3
Lamar Cem—*cemetery* ... KY-4
Lamar Cem—*cemetery* ... MO-7
Lamar Cem—*cemetery* ... OK-5
Lamar Cem—*cemetery* ... TX-5
Lamar Ch—*church* ... GA-3
Lamar Ch—*church* ... LA-4
La Marche Creek—*stream* (2) ... MT-8
La Marche Creek Ranch—*locale* ... MT-8
Lamarche Game Trap—*hist pl* ... MT-8
LaMarche Gulch—*valley* ... MT-8
La Marche Gulch—*valley* ... MT-8
LaMarche Lake—*lake* ... MT-8
Lamarck, Mount—*summit* ... CA-9
Lamarck Col—*gap* ... CA-9
Lamarck Creek—*stream* ... CA-9
Lamar Communications Facility
Annex—*military* ... CO-8
Lamar Community Center—*hist pl* ... WI-6
Lamar Consolidated HS—*school* ... TX-5
Lamar Country Club—*other* ... MO-7
**Lamar County**—*pop pl* ... AL-4
**Lamar (County)**—*pop pl* ... GA-3
**Lamar County**—*pop pl* ... MS-4
**Lamar (County)**—*pop pl* ... TX-5
Lamar County Airp—*airport* ... AL-4
Lamar County Courthouse—*building* ... AL-4
Lamar County Courthouse—*hist pl* ... GA-3
*Lamar County General Hospital* ... AL-4
Lamar County Hosp—*hist pl* ... TX-5
*Lamar County Lake* ... AL-4
Lamar County Med Ctr—*hospital* ... AL-4
Lamar County Public Lake Dam—*dam* ... AL-4
Lamar County Training Sch—*school* ... AL-4
Lamar Creek—*stream* ... GA-3
Lamar Creek—*stream* ... ID-8
Lamar Creek—*stream* ... IN-6
**Lamard (Township of)**—*pop pl* ... IL-6
Lamareau Ranch—*locale* ... UT-8
*Lamareau Tank* ... UT-8
Lamareaux Tank—*reservoir* ... UT-8
*Lamar Elementary School* ... MS-4
*Lamar Elementary School* ... TN-4
La Mar Flat—*flat* ... CA-9
*Lamar Foundation Elementary School* ... MS-4
*Lamar Foundation Middle-High School* ... MS-4
LaMar Heights—*other* ... OH-6
**Lamar Heights**—*pop pl* ... MO-7
**La Mar Heights**—*pop pl* ... OH-6
*Lamar High School* ... TN-4
Lamar Hotel—*hist pl* ... MS-4
Lamar House Hotel—*hist pl* ... TN-4
Lamar HS—*school* ... PA-2
Lamar HS—*school* ... TX-5
**La Marina**—*pop pl* (2) ... PR-3
La Marina Sch—*school* ... CA-9
La Marion Sch (historical)—*school* ... MS-4
Lamarion Wildlife Mngmt Area—*park* ... AL-4
Lamar JHS—*school* (6) ... TX-5
Lamar Lake—*lake* ... FL-3
Lamar Lake—*lake* ... WA-9
Lamar Lake—*reservoir* ... MO-7
Lamar Lake—*reservoir* ... TX-5
LaMarla Lake—*lake* ... UT-8
Lamar Lookout Tower—*locale* ... MS-4
Lamar Memory Gardens—*cemetery* ... AL-4
Lamar Mill Creek—*stream* ... AL-4
La Marmita—*basin* ... CA-9
Lamar Mounds—*summit* ... GA-3
Lamar Mtn—*summit* ... OK-5
Lamar Mtn—*summit* ... WY-8
Lamar Municipal Airp—*airport* ... CO-8
Lamar Municipal Airp—*airport* ... MO-7
Lamar Natl Fish Hatchery—*locale* ... PA-2
Lamar Oil—*oilfield* ... LA-4
Lamar Park—*park* ... MI-6
Lamar Park—*park* ... TX-5
La Mar Park—*park* ... WI-6
**Lamar Park**—*pop pl* ... MS-4
Lamar Park Post Office—*building* ... TX-5
Lamar Peninsula—*cape* ... TX-5
Lamar Plaza Shop Ctr—*locale* ... TX-5
Lamar-Porter Field—*park* ... AR-4
Lamar Puckett Lake Dam—*dam* ... MS-4
**La Marque**—*pop pl* ... TX-5
La Marque-Hitchcock (CCD)—*cens area* ... TX-5
Lamar Ranger Station—*locale* ... WY-8
Lamar Reservoirs—*reservoir* ... CO-8
La Marr Gulch—*valley* ... OR-9
Lamar River—*stream* ... WY-8
Lamar River Trail—*trail* ... WY-8
Lamar Rsvr—*reservoir* ... AZ-5
**La Mars**—*pop pl* ... ND-7
Lamars Box (historical)—*locale* ... MS-4
Lamar Sch—*school* ... GA-3
La Mar Sch—*school* ... IA-7
Lamar Sch—*school* (2) ... MS-4
Lamar Sch—*school* ... PA-2
Lamar Sch—*school* ... TN-4
Lamar Sch—*school* (3) ... TX-5
La Mar Sch—*school* ... TX-5
Lamar Sch—*school* (18) ... TX-5
Lamar Sch (historical)—*school* (2) ... MS-4
Lamar School (historical)—*locale* ... MO-7
Lamars Creek—*stream* ... GA-3
Lamarsh Ch—*church* ... IL-6
Lamarsh Creek—*stream* ... IL-6
La Marsh Creek—*stream* ... WY-8
LaMarsh Ranch—*locale* ... WY-8
Lamar Slough—*gut* ... TX-5
Lamarsons Plantation (historical)—*locale* ... TN-4
Lamar Spring—*spring* ... AR-4
Lamar Spring—*spring* ... PA-2
La Mars Town Hall—*building* ... ND-7
**La Mars Township**—*pop pl* ... ND-7
Lamar Street Viaduct—*bridge* ... TX-5
Lamar Tech (Lamar State Coll of
Technology)—*school* ... TX-5
**Lamar Terrace**—*pop pl* ... TX-5
Lamartina Bldg—*hist pl* ... LA-4
*Lamartine* ... OH-6
Lamartine—*locale* ... AR-4
Lamartine—*locale* ... CO-8
Lamartine—*other* ... OH-6
**Lamartine**—*pop pl* ... PA-2
**Lamartine**—*pop pl* ... WI-6
**Lamartine (Town of)**—*pop pl* ... WI-6
Lamartine Tunnel—*mine* ... CO-8
**Lamar Township**—*pop pl* ... MO-7
Lamar (Township of)—*fmr MCD* (2) ... AR-4
**Lamar (Township of)**—*pop pl* ... PA-2
Lamar University—*post sta* ... TX-5
**Lamarville**—*pop pl* ... GA-3
Lamar Waterworks—*other* ... CO-8
Lamar Windmill—*locale* ... TX-5
Lamas Branch—*stream* ... OK-5
**Lamasco**—*pop pl* ... KY-4
**Lamasco**—*pop pl* ... TX-5
Lamasco Park—*park* ... IN-6
Lamastus Cem—*cemetery* ... TN-4
Lamata Creek—*stream* ... WA-9
La Mata Lake—*reservoir* ... TX-5
**Lamatan**—*pop pl* ... DE-2
**Lamatan I**—*pop pl* ... DE-2
**Lamatan II**—*pop pl* ... DE-2
La Matansa Windmill—*locale* ... TX-5
*Lamatol Bay* ... FM-9
Lamaux Ranch—*locale* ... LA-4
*Lamay Island* ... UT-8
*La Mayita* ... CO-8
*Lamays Landing* ... TN-4
La May Tank—*reservoir* ... NM-5
*Lamb* ... MI-6
*Lamb* ... MS-4
*Lamb* ... TX-5
Lamb—*locale* ... CO-8
Lamb—*locale* (2) ... KY-4
**Lamb**—*pop pl* ... IL-6
**Lamb**—*pop pl* ... IN-6
**Lamb**—*pop pl* ... MI-6
Lamb, James H., House—*hist pl* ... NC-3
Lamb, Lafayette, House—*hist pl* ... IA-7
Lamb, Thomas, Farm—*hist pl* ... DE-2
Lamb, Thomas, House—*hist pl* ... DE-2
Lamb and Smith Ditch—*canal* ... CO-8
*Lambard School* ... AL-4
Lamb Bayou—*stream* ... AR-4
Lamb Bldg—*hist pl* ... WI-6
Lamb Bottoms—*basin* ... TN-4
Lamb Branch—*stream* ... AL-4
Lamb Branch—*stream* (2) ... NC-3
Lamb Brook—*stream* ... ME-1
Lamb Brook—*stream* ... VT-1
Lamb Butte—*summit* ... OR-9
Lamb Butte—*summit* ... WA-9
Lamb Camp—*locale* ... AZ-5
Lamb Camp—*locale* ... CA-9
Lamb Canal—*canal* ... LA-4
Lamb Canyon—*valley* ... CA-9
Lamb Canyon—*valley* ... NV-8
Lamb Canyon—*valley* ... UT-8
Lamb Canyon Spring—*spring* ... UT-8
Lamb Cave—*cave* ... AL-4
Lamb Cem—*cemetery* (2) ... AL-4
Lamb Cem—*cemetery* ... AR-4
Lamb Cem—*cemetery* ... CO-8
Lamb Cem—*cemetery* ... IL-6
Lamb Cem—*cemetery* (2) ... IN-6
Lamb Cem—*cemetery* ... KS-7
Lamb Cem—*cemetery* (3) ... KY-4
Lamb Cem—*cemetery* ... MO-7
Lamb Cem—*cemetery* ... NY-2
Lamb Cem—*cemetery* ... NC-3
Lamb Cem—*cemetery* ... PA-2
Lamb Cem—*cemetery* (4) ... TN-4
Lamb Cem—*cemetery* ... TX-5
Lamb Cem—*cemetery* ... WV-2
Lamb City Brook—*stream* ... MA-1
**Lamb Corners**—*pop pl* ... OH-6
**Lamb (County)**—*pop pl* ... TX-5
Lamb Cove—*bay* (2) ... ME-1
Lamb Cove—*valley* ... AR-4
*Lamb Creek* ... TX-5
*Lamb Creek* ... VA-3
*Lamb Creek* ... WA-9
*Lamb Creek* ... WI-6
Lamb Creek—*locale* ... ID-8
Lamb Creek—*stream* ... AK-9
Lamb Creek—*stream* ... AR-4
Lamb Creek—*stream* ... CA-9
Lamb Creek—*stream* ... GA-3
Lamb Creek—*stream* (4) ... ID-8
Lamb Creek—*stream* ... IN-6
Lamb Creek—*stream* ... MI-6
Lamb Creek—*stream* (2) ... MT-8
Lamb Creek—*stream* ... NE-7
Lamb Creek—*stream* ... NV-8
Lamb Creek—*stream* ... NC-3
Lamb Creek—*stream* (3) ... OR-9
Lamb Creek—*stream* ... TN-4
Lamb Creek—*stream* (3) ... WA-9
Lamb Creek—*stream* ... WY-8
Lamb Creek Campground—*locale* ... MT-8
Lambda Chi Site, RI-704—*hist pl* ... RI-1
Lambda Rock—*island* ... AK-9
Lambdin Branch—*stream* ... TN-4
Lambdin Cem—*cemetery* ... OK-5
Lamb Ditch—*canal* ... CO-8
Lamb Ditch—*canal* ... IN-6
Lamb Draw—*valley* ... WY-8
Lambeau Field—*other* ... WI-6
Lambe Ditch No 1—*canal* ... WY-8
*Lamber* ... AR-4
*Lamber* ... OK-5
Lamberjack Lake—*reservoir* ... OH-6
Lamberson—*locale* ... OK-5
Lamberson, Jack, House—*hist pl* ... IA-7
Lamberson and Riggs Ranch—*locale* ... AZ-5
Lamberson Branch—*stream* ... PA-2
Lamberson Butte—*summit* ... OR-9
Lamberson Butte Spur Trail—*trail* ... OR-9
Lamberson Canyon—*valley* ... NV-8
Lamberson Canyon—*valley* ... OR-9
Lamberson Ditch—*canal* ... CA-9
Lamberson Ditch—*canal* ... IN-6
Lamberson-Markley Houses—*hist pl* ... OH-6
Lamberson Ranch—*locale* ... AZ-5
*Lambert* ... MI-6
Lambert—*inactive* ... MO-7
Lambert—*locale* ... MI-6
Lambert—*locale* ... TN-4
Lambert—*locale* ... WY-8
**Lambert**—*pop pl* ... AL-4
**Lambert**—*pop pl* ... AR-4
**Lambert**—*pop pl* (2) ... CA-9
**Lambert**—*pop pl* ... KY-4
**Lambert**—*pop pl* ... MS-4
**Lambert**—*pop pl* ... MT-8
**Lambert**—*pop pl* ... NC-3
**Lambert**—*pop pl* ... OK-5
**Lambert**—*pop pl* ... PA-2
**Lambert**—*pop pl* ... SC-3
Lambert, J. C., Site—*hist pl* ... TX-5
Lambert Acres Golf Course—*locale* ... TN-4
Lambert Bama Ranch Dam—*dam* ... AL-4
Lambert Bama Ranch Lake—*reservoir* ... AL-4
Lambert Bayou—*gut* ... AR-4
Lambert Bayou—*stream* ... LA-4
Lambert Bend—*bend* ... OR-9
Lambert Bldg—*hist pl* ... MO-7
Lambert Branch—*stream* ... AL-4
Lambert Branch—*stream* ... GA-3
Lambert Branch—*stream* (2) ... KY-4
Lambert Branch—*stream* ... MS-4
Lambert Branch—*stream* ... NC-3
Lambert Branch—*stream* (2) ... TX-5
Lambert Branch—*stream* (4) ... WV-2
Lambert Brook—*stream* ... ME-1
Lambert Cem—*cemetery* (2) ... AL-4
Lambert Cem—*cemetery* (2) ... GA-3
Lambert Cem—*cemetery* ... IL-6
Lambert Cem—*cemetery* ... IN-6
Lambert Cem—*cemetery* ... KY-4
Lambert Cem—*cemetery* (2) ... LA-4
Lambert Cem—*cemetery* ... MS-4
Lambert Cem—*cemetery* ... MO-7
Lambert Cem—*cemetery* ... NE-7
Lambert Cem—*cemetery* ... NC-3
Lambert Cem—*cemetery* ... PA-2
Lambert Cem—*cemetery* ... SC-3
Lambert Cem—*cemetery* (3) ... TN-4
Lambert Cem—*cemetery* ... TX-5
Lambert Cem—*cemetery* (3) ... VA-3
Lambert Cem—*cemetery* (5) ... WV-2
*Lambert Ch* ... AL-4
Lambert Ch—*church* ... WV-2
Lambert Chapel—*church* ... AL-4
Lambert Chapel—*church* (2) ... MS-4
Lambert Chapel—*church* ... TX-5
Lambert Chapel—*church* ... WV-2
Lambert Chapel Sch—*school* ... MS-4
*Lambert Cove* ... MA-1
Lambert Cove—*valley* ... NC-3
Lambert Creek—*stream* ... CA-9
Lambert Creek—*stream* ... MI-6
Lambert Creek—*stream* ... MT-8
Lambert Creek—*stream* (2) ... NC-3
Lambert Creek—*stream* (2) ... WA-9
Lambert Creek (historical)—*stream* ... VA-3
Lambert Dam—*dam* ... NC-3
Lambert Dam—*dam* ... TN-4
Lambert-Deacon-Hull Printing Company
Bldg—*hist pl* ... MO-7
Lambert Ditch—*canal* ... AR-4
Lambert Ditch—*canal* (2) ... IN-6
*Lambert Dome* ... CA-9
Lambert Drain—*canal* ... MI-6
Lambert Drain—*stream* ... MI-6
Lambert Farm Site, RI-269—*hist pl* ... RI-1
Lambert Field—*park* ... GA-3
Lambert Flats—*flat* ... CA-9
*Lambert Fork* ... VA-3
Lambert Fork—*stream* ... NC-3
Lambert Gap—*gap* ... WV-2
Lambert Gardens—*locale* ... OR-9
**Lambert Grove**—*pop pl* ... AL-4
Lambert Grove Ch—*church* ... AL-4
Lambert Hill—*summit* ... CA-9
Lambert Hill—*summit* ... GA-3
Lambert Hill—*summit* ... IN-6
Lambert Hill—*summit* (2) ... MA-1
Lambert Hill—*summit* ... PA-2
Lambert Hill—*summit* ... WA-9
Lamberth Memorial Ch—*church* ... NC-3
Lambert Hollow—*valley* ... KY-4
Lambert Hollow—*valley* (2) ... MO-7
Lambert Hollow—*valley* ... OH-6
Lambert Hollow—*valley* (2) ... TN-4
Lambert Hollow—*valley* ... UT-8
Lambert Hollow—*valley* ... VA-3
Lambert Hollow—*valley* (2) ... WV-2
Lambert House—*hist pl* ... AR-4
Lambert HS—*school* ... MS-4
Lamberths Mound—*summit* ... AL-4
**Lamberti**—*pop pl* ... PR-3
Lambert Island—*island* ... ME-1
*Lambert Islands* ... MP-9
Lambert Lake—*lake* ... LA-4
Lambert Lake—*lake* ... ME-1
Lambert Lake—*lake* ... MI-6
Lambert Lake—*lake* ... MN-6
Lambert Lake—*lake* ... SD-7
Lambert Lake—*lake* ... UT-8
**Lambert Lake**—*pop pl* ... ME-1
Lambert Lake—*reservoir* ... IN-6
Lambert Lake—*reservoir* ... NC-3
Lambert Lake—*reservoir* ... TN-4
Lambert Lake (Township of)—*unorg* ... ME-1
Lambert Landing—*locale* ... AL-4
Lambert Lateral—*canal* ... IN-6
**Lambert (Marcus)**—*pop pl* ... AR-4
Lambert Meadow—*flat* (2) ... UT-8
Lambert Mill Dam—*dam* ... NC-3
Lambert Mill Dam—*reservoir* ... NC-3
Lambert Mill (historical)—*locale* ... MS-4
Lambert Mine—*mine* ... CA-9
Lambert Mine Camp Site—*locale* ... NM-5
Lambert Mtn—*summit* ... NC-3
Lambert Mtn—*summit* ... WA-9
*Lamberton* ... NJ-2
**Lamberton**—*pop pl* ... MN-6
**Lamberton**—*pop pl* ... NY-2
**Lamberton**—*pop pl* (2) ... PA-2
**Lamberton**—*pop pl* ... WV-2
Lamberton Brook—*stream* ... MA-1
Lamberton Brook Dam—*dam* ... MA-1
Lamberton Brook Rsvr—*reservoir* ... MA-1
Lamberton Cabin—*hist pl* ... AR-4
Lamberton Cem—*cemetery* ... MN-6
Lamberton Creek—*stream* ... MI-6
Lamberton Farmers Elevator—*hist pl* ... MN-6
Lamberton HS (abandoned)—*school* ... PA-2
Lamberton Lake—*lake* ... MI-6
**Lamberton (Lambert Works)**—*pop pl* ... PA-2
Lamberton Mine—*mine* ... MN-6
Lamberton MS—*school* ... PA-2
Lamberton Rsvr—*reservoir* ... ID-8
Lamberton Sch—*school* ... NY-2
Lamberton Sch—*school* (2) ... PA-2
Lamberton Sch—*school* ... WI-6
Lamberton State Wildlife Mngmt
Area—*park* ... MN-6
**Lamberton (Township of)**—*pop pl* ... MN-6
Lamberton West Side Canal—*canal* ... ID-8
Lambert-Parent House—*hist pl* ... OH-6
Lambert Park—*park* ... CA-9
Lambert Park—*park* ... MN-6
Lambert Park—*uninc pl* ... LA-4
Lambert Place—*locale* ... CO-8
*Lambert Point* ... VA-3
Lambert Point—*cape* ... ME-1
Lambert Point—*cape* ... NC-3
Lambert Point—*summit* ... OR-9
Lambert Post Office (historical)—*building* ... TN-4
Lambert Ranch—*locale* ... NE-7
Lambert Ranch—*locale* ... NM-5
Lambert Ranch—*locale* ... TX-5
Lambert Ranch—*locale* ... UT-8
Lambert Ridge—*ridge* ... CA-9
Lambert Ridge—*ridge* ... LA-4
Lambert Ridge—*ridge* ... NH-1
Lambert Ridge—*ridge* ... TN-4
Lambert Rocks—*lava* ... OR-9
Lambert Rsvr—*reservoir* ... CA-9
Lambert Rsvr—*reservoir* (2) ... CO-8
Lambert Run—*stream* (2) ... WV-2
Lambert Run Ch—*church* ... WV-2
*Lamberts* ... AL-4
**Lambert (Sag)**—*pop pl* ... IL-6
Lambert Saint Louis International
Airp—*airport* ... MO-7
Lamberts Bay—*swamp* ... NC-3
*Lamberts Bayou* ... MS-4
Lambert Sch—*school* ... AL-4
Lambert Sch—*school* ... CA-9
Lambert Sch—*school* ... IL-6
Lambert Sch—*school* ... IA-7
Lambert Sch—*school* ... KY-4
Lambert Sch—*school* ... MI-6
Lamberts Chapel—*church* ... VA-3
Lambert Sch (historical)—*school* ... TN-4
*Lambert School* ... MS-4
Lambert School—*locale* ... WA-9
Lamberts Corner—*locale* ... WA-9
Lamberts Cove—*cove* ... MA-1
Lamberts Cove Cem—*cemetery* ... MA-1
Lamberts Cove Ch—*church* ... MA-1
Lambertsen Ranch—*locale* ... WY-8
Lamberts Gin (historical)—*locale* ... AL-4
Lamberts Lake—*lake* ... GA-3
Lamberts Landing (historical)—*locale* ... MS-4
Lambert Slough—*stream* ... OR-9
Lambertson Cem—*cemetery* ... KS-7
Lambertson Lake—*lake* ... ID-8
*Lambert's Point* ... VA-3
Lamberts Point—*cape* ... VA-3
**Lamberts Point**—*pop pl* ... VA-3
Lamberts Point Terminal—*locale* ... VA-3
Lambert Spring—*spring* ... CO-8
*Lambert Springs* ... WI-6
Lamberts Run—*stream* ... PA-2
**Lamberts Store**—*pop pl* ... MS-4
Lambert Station—*locale* ... KY-4
Lambert-St. Louis Int. Airp—*airport* ... MO-7
*Lambertsville* ... NJ-2
**Lambertsville**—*pop pl* ... PA-2
Lambert Table—*summit* ... ID-8
**Lambert (Township of)**—*pop pl* ... MN-6
**Lambertville**—*pop pl* ... MI-6
**Lambertville**—*pop pl* ... NJ-2
Lambertville Hist Dist—*hist pl* ... NJ-2
Lambertville House—*hist pl* ... NJ-2
Lambert Well—*well* ... NM-5
Lambert Windmill—*locale* ... NM-5
Lambert Works—*other* ... PA-2
Lambeth, Shadrach, House—*hist pl* ... NC-3
Lambeth-Boutwell Cem—*cemetery* ... AL-4
Lambeth Bridge—*other* ... MO-7
Lambeth Cem—*cemetery* ... MO-7
Lambeth Ch—*church* ... AL-4
*Lambeth Ch Cemetery* ... AL-4
Lambeth Field—*other* ... VA-3
*Lambeth Free Holiness Ch* ... AL-4
Lambeth Inn—*hist pl* ... NC-3
**Lambeth (Lambeth's Siding)**—*pop pl* ... NC-3
Lambeth Mtn—*summit* ... NC-3
**Lambeth Riding**—*pop pl* ... DE-2
Lambeth Sch (abandoned)—*school* ... MO-7
Lambeth's Siding—*other* ... NC-3
Lambethville—*locale* ... AR-4
Lamb-Ferebee House—*hist pl* ... NC-3
Lamb-Fish Bridge—*hist pl* ... MS-4
*Lamb Fork* ... TN-4
Lamb Fork Creek—*stream* ... TN-4
Lamb Gap—*gap* ... CA-9
Lamb Glacier—*glacier* ... AK-9
Lamb Gulch—*valley* ... UT-8
Lamb Gulf—*valley* (2) ... TN-4
Lamb Hill—*summit* ... CA-9
Lamb Hill—*summit* ... MA-1
Lamb Hill—*summit* ... MI-6
Lamb Hill—*summit* ... NY-2
Lamb Hill Cem—*cemetery* ... NY-2
Lamb Hollow—*valley* ... PA-2
Lamb Hollow—*valley* (2) ... TN-4
Lamb Homestead—*locale* ... NM-5
Lamb Hotel—*building* ... AZ-5
Lambie Ranch—*locale* ... CA-9
Lambiers Dock—*locale* ... NJ-2
Lambing Camp Canyon—*valley* ... OR-9

**Lanare**—*pop pl* CA-9
*Lanare Oil Field* CA-9
Lanarine Windmill—*locale* TX-5
*Lanark* FL-3
Lanark—*locale* AR-4
Lanark—*locale* ID-8
Lanark—*locale* MT-8
Lanark—*locale* TX-5
**Lanark**—*pop pl* IL-6
**Lanark**—*pop pl* NM-5
**Lanark**—*pop pl* PA-2
**Lanark**—*pop pl* WV-2
Lanark Cem—*cemetery* ID-8
Lanark (historical)—*locale* KS-7
**Lanark (Town of)**—*pop pl* WI-6
*Lanark Township* KS-7
Lanark Village—*locale* FL-3
**Lanatana Estates**—*pop pl* TN-4
La Natividad—*civil* CA-9
Lanaux Canal—*canal* LA-4
Lanaux Island—*island* LA-4
Lanbaugh No 4 Draw—*valley* WY-8
**Lancashire**—*pop pl* DE-2
Lancashire Rocks—*bar* AK-9
Lancassange Creek—*stream* IN-6
*Lancaster* AL-4
*Lancaster* IN-6
*Lancaster* OR-9
Lancaster—*building* NE-7
Lancaster—*locale* AZ-5
Lancaster—*locale* FL-3
Lancaster—*locale* IL-6
Lancaster—*locale* IA-7
Lancaster—*locale* WA-9
**Lancaster**—*pop pl* CA-9
**Lancaster**—*pop pl* IL-6
**Lancaster**—*pop pl* (3) IN-6
**Lancaster**—*pop pl* KS-7
**Lancaster**—*pop pl* KY-4
**Lancaster**—*pop pl* MA-1
**Lancaster**—*pop pl* MN-6
**Lancaster**—*pop pl* MO-7
**Lancaster**—*pop pl* NH-1
**Lancaster**—*pop pl* NY-2
**Lancaster**—*pop pl* NC-3
**Lancaster**—*pop pl* OH-6
**Lancaster**—*pop pl* (2) OR-9
**Lancaster**—*pop pl* PA-2
**Lancaster**—*pop pl* SC-3
**Lancaster**—*pop pl* TN-4
**Lancaster**—*pop pl* TX-5
**Lancaster**—*pop pl* VA-3
**Lancaster**—*pop pl* WI-6
Lancaster, Fred, Barn—*hist pl* AR-4
Lancaster, James A., Site—*hist pl* CO-8
Lancaster, John, House—*hist pl* KY-4
Lancaster, John L., House—*hist pl* AR-4
Lancaster, Judge Columbia, House—*hist pl* WA-9
Lancaster, Lake—*lake* FL-3
Lancaster Airp—*airport* PA-2
Lancaster Ave—*uninc pl* PA-2
Lancaster Ave Sch—*school* WI-6
Lancaster Baptist Ch—*church* TN-4
Lancaster Block—*hist pl* ME-1
Lancaster Branch—*stream* KY-4
Lancaster Branch—*stream* MS-4
Lancaster Branch—*stream* SC-3
Lancaster Brook—*stream* (2) ME-1
Lancaster Cave—*cave* MO-7
Lancaster Cave—*cave* TN-4
Lancaster Cave Number Four—*cave* TN-4
Lancaster Cave Number One—*cave* TN-4
Lancaster Cave Number Three—*cave* TN-4
Lancaster Cave Number Two—*cave* TN-4
Lancaster (CCD)—*cens area* KY-4
Lancaster (CCD)—*cens area* SC-3
*Lancaster Cem* MS-4
Lancaster Cem—*cemetery* AL-4
Lancaster Cem—*cemetery* AR-4
Lancaster Cem—*cemetery* GA-3
Lancaster Cem—*cemetery* (2) IL-6
Lancaster Cem—*cemetery* (2) KY-4
Lancaster Cem—*cemetery* (2) MS-4
Lancaster Cem—*cemetery* MO-7
Lancaster Cem—*cemetery* PA-2
Lancaster Cem—*cemetery* SC-3
Lancaster Cem—*cemetery* (2) TN-4
Lancaster Cem—*cemetery* TX-5
Lancaster Cem—*cemetery* VA-3
Lancaster Cemetery—*hist pl* KY-4
*Lancaster Center* MA-1
Lancaster Center—*other* MA-1
Lancaster Central Sch—*school* IN-6
*Lancaster Centre* MA-1
Lancaster Ch—*church* IN-6
Lancaster Chapel—*church* IN-6
Lancaster Chapel—*church* OH-6
Lancaster Christian JHS—*school* PA-2
Lancaster City—*civil* PA-2
**Lancaster City (historical)**—*pop pl* SD-7
Lancaster Club Lake—*reservoir* TX-5
Lancaster Commercial Hist Dist—*hist pl* KY-4
Lancaster Compact (census name Lancaster)—*other* NH-1
**Lancaster Corner**—*pop pl* MD-2
Lancaster Country Club—*other* OH-6
Lancaster Country Club—*other* PA-2
Lancaster Country Day Sch—*school* PA-2
**Lancaster County**—*pop pl* PA-2
**Lancaster (County)**—*pop pl* SC-3
**Lancaster (County)**—*pop pl* VA-3
Lancaster County Courthouse—*hist pl* PA-2
Lancaster County Courthouse—*hist pl* SC-3
Lancaster County House of Employment—*hist pl* PA-2
Lancaster County Jail—*hist pl* SC-3
Lancaster County Park—*park* PA-2
*Lancaster County Vocational Technical School* PA-2
Lancaster Court—*locale* DE-2
Lancaster Court House Hist Dist—*hist pl* VA-3
Lancaster Cove—*bay* AK-9
Lancaster Creek—*stream* AK-9
Lancaster Creek—*stream* AZ-5
Lancaster Creek—*stream* ID-8
Lancaster Creek—*stream* MI-6
Lancaster Creek—*stream* OR-9
Lancaster Creek—*stream* TX-5
Lancaster Creek—*stream* VA-3
Lancaster Crematorium—*hist pl* PA-2
**Lancaster Crossroads**—*pop pl* NC-3
Lancaster Downtown Hist Dist—*hist pl* SC-3
Lancaster Drain—*canal* MI-6
Lancaster East Sch—*school* IL-6
Lancaster (Election Precinct)—*fmr MCD* IL-6
Lancaster Elem Sch—*school* FL-3
Lancaster Falls—*falls* OR-9
Lancaster Gap—*gap* VA-3
Lancaster General Hosp—*hospital* PA-2
Lancaster General Hospital Airp—*airport* PA-2
Lancaster Golf and Country Club—*other* NY-2
**Lancaster Hill**—*pop pl* TN-4
Lancaster Hill—*summit* TX-5
Lancaster Hill Ch—*church* TN-4
Lancaster Hist Dist—*hist pl* OH-6
Lancaster Hist Dist—*hist pl* PA-2
Lancaster Hist Dist (Boundary Increase)—*hist pl* PA-2
Lancaster Hist Dist (Boundary Increase II)—*hist pl* PA-2
Lancaster (historical)—*locale* MS-4
Lancaster Hollow—*valley* AR-4
Lancaster Hollow—*valley* OK-5
Lancaster Hollow—*valley* TN-4
Lancaster Industrial Sch for Girls—*hist pl* MA-1
Lancaster Jaycee Park—*park* PA-2
Lancaster Junction—*locale* WI-6
**Lancaster Junction**—*pop pl* PA-2
Lancaster Lake—*lake* IN-6
Lancaster Lake—*lake* MI-6
Lancaster Lake—*lake* WA-9
**Lancaster (Lancaster Center)**—*pop pl* MA-1
Lancaster Memorial Sch—*school* MA-1
Lancaster Memorial Sch—*school* NH-1
Lancaster Methodist Episcopal Camp Ground Hist Dist—*hist pl* OH-6
*Lancaster Mill Pond* MA-1
Lancaster Millpond—*reservoir* MA-1
Lancaster Mills—*CDP* SC-3
Lancaster MS—*school* MA-1
Lancaster Mtn—*summit* CA-9
Lancaster Municipal Bldg—*hist pl* WI-6
Lancaster Municipal Park—*park* PA-2
*Lancaster New Grant* MA-1
Lancaster Osteopathic Hosp—*hospital* PA-2
Lancaster Park—*park* TX-5
**Lancaster Park**—*pop pl* IN-6
Lancaster Plaza—*locale* PA-2
*Lancaster Point* FL-3
Lancaster Post Office—*building* TN-4
Lancaster Presbyterian Church—*hist pl* SC-3
Lancaster Road Sch—*school* CT-1
Lancaster Rsvr—*reservoir* SC-3
Lancaster Run—*stream* MD-2
Lancaster Rural Memorial Park—*park* NY-2
Lancaster Sch—*hist pl* IA-7
Lancaster Sch—*school* PA-2
Lancaster Sch—*school* (2) TN-4
Lancaster Shop Ctr—*locale* PA-2
Lancaster Speedway—*other* NY-2
Lancaster Speedway—*other* PA-2
Lancaster Speedway—*other* SC-3
Lancaster Spring—*spring* NM-5
Lancaster Spring—*spring* TN-4
Lancaster Square—*locale* PA-2
Lancaster Square (Shop Ctr)—*locale* FL-3
Lancaster State For—*forest* MA-1
Lancaster State Forest—*park* MA-1
*Lancaster Station* OR-9
*Lancaster Terrace* ID-8
Lancaster Theological Seminary—*school* PA-2
**Lancaster (Town of)**—*pop pl* MA-1
**Lancaster (Town of)**—*pop pl* NH-1
**Lancaster (Town of)**—*pop pl* NY-2
**Lancaster Township**—*pop pl* KS-7
*Lancaster Township Junior High School* PA-2
Lancaster (Township of)—*fmr MCD* AR-4
Lancaster (Township of)—*other* OH-6
**Lancaster (Township of)**—*pop pl* IL-6
**Lancaster (Township of)**—*pop pl* (3) IN-6
**Lancaster (Township of)**—*pop pl* (2) PA-2
Lancaster Trust Company—*hist pl* PA-2
*Lancaster Valley* CA-9
*Lancaster Valley* PA-2
Lancaster Valley—*valley* CA-9
**Lancaster Village**—*pop pl* DE-2
**Lancasterville**—*pop pl* PA-2
Lancaster Watch Company—*hist pl* PA-2
Lancaster West Main Street Hist Dist—*hist pl* OH-6
Lancaster Yards—*locale* TX-5
Lancaster-Young Cem—*cemetery* OR-9
Lance—*airport* NJ-2
Lance Airp—*airport* PA-2
Lance Branch—*stream* (3) GA-3
Lance Canyon—*valley* UT-8
Lance Cem—*cemetery* MO-7
Lance Cem—*cemetery* SC-3
Lance Cem—*cemetery* (2) TN-4
Lance Cove—*valley* NC-3
**Lance Creek**—*pop pl* WY-8
Lance Creek—*stream* (2) GA-3
Lance Creek—*stream* NC-3
Lance Creek—*stream* SD-7
Lance Creek—*stream* WY-8
Lance Creek Community Ch—*church* WY-8
Lance Creek Elem Sch—*school* WY-8
Lance Creek Oil Field—*oilfield* WY-8
Lanceford Creek—*stream* FL-3
Lance Gulch—*valley* CA-9
Lance Hill Cem—*cemetery* WA-9
Lance Hills—*range* WA-9
Lance House—*hist pl* MO-7
Lance Lake—*lake* MI-6
Lancel Creek—*stream* CA-9
Lancelot, Lake—*lake* IL-6
**Lancelot Acres**—*pop pl* TN-4
Lancelot Lake—*lake* OR-9
Lancelot Point—*cliff* AZ-5
Lance Lumpkin Stadium—*park* MS-4
Lance Mill—*locale* GA-3
Lance Mtn—*summit* GA-3
Lance Mtn—*summit* NC-3
Lance Point—*cape* (2) AK-9
Lance Pond—*lake* PA-2
**Lancer**—*pop pl* KY-4
**Lancer Acres Subdivision**—*pop pl* UT-8
Lances, Bayou des—*stream* LA-4
Lanceville—*locale* TN-4
*Lancey* KY-4
Lancey Creek—*stream* MT-8
Lancha Plana—*locale* CA-9
Lanchbury Ranch—*locale* WY-8
*Lanchport* WV-2
**Lancing**—*pop pl* TN-4
Lancing (CCD)—*cens area* TN-4
Lancing Division—*civil* TN-4
Lancing Elem Sch—*school* TN-4
Lancing Post Office—*building* TN-4
Lancy Brook—*stream* NH-1
*Land* VA-3
Land—*locale* AZ-5
**Land**—*pop pl* AL-4
**Land**—*pop pl* SC-3
Land, Francis, House—*hist pl* VA-3
Land, Lake—*lake* OR-9
**Landa**—*pop pl* ND-7
Landa Cem—*cemetery* ND-7
Landacre Hollow—*valley* WV-2
*Landaff* NH-1
Landaff—*locale* MD-2
**Landaff Center**—*pop pl* NH-1
**Landaff (Town of)**—*pop pl* NH-1
Landa Gas Field—*oilfield* TX-5
Landa Home Ranch—*locale* NV-8
Landaker Cem—*cemetery* OH-6
Landam Branch—*stream* SC-3
Landa Park—*park* TX-5
**Landa Park Highlands**—*pop pl* TX-5
Land Archeol Site—*hist pl* MO-7
Landavaso Rsvr—*reservoir* NM-5
**Landax**—*pop pl* OR-9
Landax Landing Park—*park* OR-9
**Landay Gautreaux Subdivision**—*pop pl* LA-4
Land Bank Bldg—*hist pl* MO-7
Land Bay—*swamp* FL-3
Landberg Lake—*lake* WI-6
Land Between The Lakes—*area* KY-4
Land Between The Lakes—*park* TN-4
Land Branch—*stream* GA-3
Land Branch—*stream* KY-4
Land Branch—*stream* TN-4
Land Bridge—*bridge* SC-3
Land Cem—*cemetery* FL-3
Land Cem—*cemetery* GA-3
Land Cem—*cemetery* IL-6
Land Cem—*cemetery* (2) IN-6
Land Cem—*cemetery* MN-6
Land Cem—*cemetery* (3) TN-4
Land Cem—*cemetery* TX-5
Land Ch—*church* AL-4
Landco—*locale* CA-9
Land Company Spring—*spring* CA-9
*Land Creek* ID-8
Land Creek—*stream* (2) ID-8
Land Creek—*stream* MS-4
Land Creek—*stream* TX-5
Land Cut—*channel* TX-5
Land Drain—*stream* IN-6
**Landeck**—*pop pl* OH-6
Landecker Ch—*church* MO-7
Landecker Sch—*school* MO-7
Landels Sch—*school* CA-9
**Landenberg**—*pop pl* PA-2
Landenberger, C. A., House—*hist pl* OR-9
Landenberg Junction—*locale* DE-2
*Landenburg* PA-2
Landen Mounds I and II—*hist pl* OH-6
Landen (Township of)—*civ div* OH-6
Lander—*locale* MD-2
**Lander**—*pop pl* PA-2
**Lander**—*pop pl* WY-8
Lander, Mount—*summit* WY-8
Lander Cem—*cemetery* KY-4
Lander Cem—*cemetery* TN-4
Lander Coll—*school* SC-3
Lander College Old Main Bldg—*hist pl* SC-3
Lander County—*civil* NV-8
Lander County Airp—*airport* NV-8
*Lander Creek* WY-8
Lander Creek—*stream* ID-8
Lander Creek—*stream* (3) WY-8
Lander Crossing—*locale* CA-9
Lander Crossing—*locale* MT-8
Lander Cut-off Rsvr—*reservoir* WY-8
**Landerdale**—*pop pl* IN-6
Lander Downtown Hist Dist—*hist pl* WY-8
Lander Extension Ditch—*canal* CO-8
Landergin—*locale* TX-5
Landergin-Harrington House—*hist pl* TX-5
Landergin (historical)—*locale* KS-7
Landergin Mesa—*hist pl* TX-5
Landergrin Sch—*school* TX-5
Lander Haven Country Club—*locale* OH-6
Lander Hill—*summit* (2) WY-8
**Lander (historical)**—*pop pl* OR-9
Lander-Hopkins House—*hist pl* TX-5
Lander Hudson Oil Field—*oilfield* WY-8
Lander Park Carousel—*hist pl* KS-7
Lander Peak—*summit* WY-8
Lander Road—*hist pl* ID-8
*Landers* CT-1
*Landers* IL-6
Landers—*locale* AR-4
**Landers**—*pop pl* AR-4
**Landers**—*pop pl* CA-9
Landers Branch—*stream* TX-5
Landers Canyon—*valley* OR-9
Landers Cave—*cave* AL-4
Landers Cem—*cemetery* AL-4
Landers Cem—*cemetery* AR-4
Landers Cem—*cemetery* MO-7
Landers Cem—*cemetery* TN-4
Landers Chapel—*church* NC-3
Landers Corners—*locale* NY-2
*Landers Creek* MO-7
*Landers Creek* MT-8
Landers Creek—*stream* (2) CA-9
Landers Creek—*stream* KS-7
Landers Creek—*stream* KY-4
Landers Creek—*stream* (2) NY-2
Landers Creek—*stream* TX-5
Landers Creek—*stream* WA-9
Landers Creek—*stream* WV-2
Landers Creek Bridge—*hist pl* KS-7
**Landersdale**—*pop pl* IN-6
Landers Ditch—*canal* AR-4
Landers Fork—*stream* MT-8
*Landers Fork Blackfoot River* MT-8
Landers Fork Trail—*trail* MT-8
Landers Hollow—*valley* MO-7
Landers Island—*island* AR-4
Lander (Site)—*locale* NV-8
Landers Lake—*lake* CA-9
Landers Lake—*reservoir* TX-5
Landers Landing Public Access—*park* MS-4
Landers Meadow—*flat* CA-9
Landers Meadow Guard Station—*locale* CA-9
L Anderson Ranch—*locale* ND-7
**Landers Park**—*pop pl* DE-2
Lander Spring—*spring* AZ-5
Lander Spring—*spring* SD-7
Landers Ranch—*locale* SD-7
Landers Sch (historical)—*school* AL-4
**Landers (subdivision)**—*pop pl* MS-4
Landers Theater—*hist pl* MO-7
**Landersville**—*pop pl* AL-4
Landersville Elem Sch (historical)—*school* AL-4
Landerth Mine—*mine* CO-8
Lander Valley Rsvr—*reservoir* WY-8
Lander Well—*well* NV-8
Lander Well Number One—*well* NV-8
Landes—*locale* IL-6
Landes—*locale* WV-2
Landes, Samuel, House—*hist pl* OH-6
Landes Cem—*cemetery* IN-6
Landes Cem—*cemetery* VA-3
Landes Creek—*stream* OR-9
*Landes Hollow* VA-3
Landes Hollow—*valley* VA-3
Landes Hollow—*valley* WV-2
Landes Park—*park* CA-9
**Landess**—*pop pl* IN-6
Landess Cem—*cemetery* IN-6
*Landesville* IN-6
*Landex* OR-9
Landfair Ch—*church* OH-6
**Landfall**—*pop pl* MN-6
Landford Cem—*cemetery* MD-2
**Landgraff**—*pop pl* WV-2
Landgren Dam A—*dam* ND-7
Landgren Dam B—*dam* ND-7
Landgren Lake—*lake* MN-6
**Landgrove**—*pop pl* VT-1
Landgrove Sch—*school* VT-1
**Landgrove (Town of)**—*pop pl* VT-1
*Landham Brook* MA-1
Landham Brook—*stream* MA-1
Land Harbors Lake—*reservoir* NC-3
Land Harbors Lake Dam—*dam* NC-3
Land Hill—*summit* UT-8
L and H Spring—*spring* OR-9
**Landia**—*pop pl* NY-2
*Landin Branch* TN-4
Landin Cove—*valley* TN-4
**Landing**—*pop pl* NJ-2
**Landing, Lake**—*pop pl* NC-3
Landing, The—*locale* AK-9
Landing, The—*locale* DE-2
Landing, The—*locale* ME-1
Landing, The—*locale* MO-7
**Landing, The**—*pop pl* NY-2
Landing, The (Shop Ctr)—*locale* FL-3
Landing Bay—*bay* NY-2
Landing Beaches, Aslito-Isley Field, and Marpi Point—*hist pl* MH-9
Landing Brook—*stream* NH-1
Landing Cem—*cemetery* NY-2
**Landing (census: Shore Hills (Lake Hopatcong(sta.))**—*0pop pl* NJ-2
Landing Cove—*bay* VA-3
Landing Creek—*stream* ID-8
Landing Creek—*stream* KY-4
Landing Creek—*stream* MO-7
Landing Creek—*stream* (2) NJ-2
Landing Creek—*stream* OR-9
Landing Creek—*stream* SD-7
Landing Creek Spring—*spring* OR-9
**Landing Creek Township**—*pop pl* SD-7
Landing Field—*airport* SD-7
Landing Gut—*gut* MD-2
Landingham Hill—*summit* WA-9
Landing Hill—*summit* CA-9
Landing Hill—*summit* CT-1
Landing Hill—*summit* NY-2
Landing Lake—*lake* WI-6
Landing Neck Ch—*church* MD-2
*Landing Number Two* GA-3
Landing Ridge—*ridge* KY-4
Landing Ridge—*ridge* NC-3
Landing Run—*stream* IN-6
Landing Run—*stream* (2) KY-4
**Landings, The**—*pop pl* GA-3
Landings, The—*uninc pl* FL-3
**Landings at Riverbend Subdivision**—*pop pl* UT-8
Landing Sch—*school* (2) NY-2
**Landings (subdivision), The**—*pop pl* (2) AZ-5
Landing Strip Draw—*valley* WY-8
Landing Strip Tank—*reservoir* (2) AZ-5
**Landingville**—*pop pl* PA-2
Landingville Borough—*civil* PA-2
Landin Lake—*lake* MI-6
Landin Park—*park* AZ-5
**Landin Park**—*pop pl* OH-6
**Landis**—*pop pl* AR-4
**Landis**—*pop pl* NC-3
**Landis**—*pop pl* OH-6
Landis, Absalom Lowe, House—*hist pl* TN-4
**Landisburg**—*pop pl* PA-2
**Landisburg**—*pop pl* WV-2
Landisburg Borough—*civil* PA-2
Landisburg Cave—*cave* PA-2
Landisburg Cem—*cemetery* PA-2
*Landis Cem* TN-4
Landis Cem—*cemetery* AR-4
Landis Cem—*cemetery* OH-6
Landis Cem—*cemetery* TN-4
Landis Creek—*stream* CO-8
Landis Creek—*stream* PA-2
Landis Creek—*stream* WY-8
Landis Dam—*dam* SD-7
Landis Dam—*dam* TN-4
Landis Ditch—*canal* IN-6
Landis Draw—*valley* WY-8
Landis Elem Sch—*school* NC-3
Landis Farm—*locale* PA-2
**Landis Farms**—*pop pl* PA-2
Landis Gulch—*valley* CA-9
Landis Homestead—*hist pl* PA-2
Landis JHS—*school* NJ-2
Landis Lake—*lake* IN-6
Landis Lake—*lake* MN-6
Landis Lake—*reservoir* TN-4
Landis Mill Covered Bridge—*hist pl* PA-2
*Landis Mill Pond* IN-6
**Landis Northeast**—*pop pl* NC-3
Landis Park—*park* NJ-2
*Landis Pond* IN-6
Landis Quarry Cave—*cave* PA-2
Landis Ranch—*locale* CO-8
Landis Ranch—*locale* NE-7
Landis Run—*stream* PA-2
Landis Sch—*school* CA-9
Landis Sch—*school* OH-6
Landis Shoe Company Bldg—*hist pl* PA-2
Landis Spring Branch—*stream* MD-2
**Landis Store**—*pop pl* PA-2
**Landis Valley**—*pop pl* PA-2
*Landis Valley Museum* PA-2
Landisville—*locale* PA-2
**Landisville**—*pop pl* NJ-2
**Landisville**—*pop pl* PA-2
*Landisville Elementary School* PA-2
Landisville Post Office (historical)—*building* PA-2
Landis Water Reservoir Dam—*dam* NC-3
Landis Water Rsvr Lake—*reservoir* NC-3
Landis Well Sch—*school* PA-2
L and J RV Park—*park* UT-8
Land Lake—*lake* WI-6
Land Lake Dam—*dam* MS-4
Landlith—*locale* DE-2
Landlocked Bay—*bay* AK-9
Landlocked Creek—*stream* AK-9
Landlookers Creek—*stream* MI-6
Landlord Fowler Tavern—*hist pl* MA-1
Landman Creek—*stream* TX-5
**Landmark**—*pop pl* AL-4
**Landmark**—*pop pl* ID-8
**Landmark**—*pop pl* TN-4
Landmark, The—*summit* AZ-5
Landmark, The—*summit* WY-8
Landmark Assembly Ch—*church* KY-4
Landmark Baptist Acad—*school* AR-4
*Landmark Baptist Ch* MS-4
Landmark Baptist Ch—*church* AR-4
Landmark Baptist Ch—*church* FL-3
Landmark Baptist Ch—*church* MS-4
Landmark Baptist Tabernacle—*church* DE-2
Landmark Baptist Temple—*church* AL-4
Landmark Bayou—*stream* MS-4
Landmark Branch—*stream* AR-4
Landmark Cem—*cemetery* (2) AR-4
*Landmark Ch* AL-4
Landmark Ch—*church* (2) AL-4
Landmark Ch—*church* (4) AR-4
Land Mark Ch—*church* FL-3
Land Mark Ch—*church* GA-3
Landmark Ch—*church* IN-6
Landmark Ch—*church* (3) NC-3
Landmark Ch—*church* OH-6
Land Mark Ch—*church* OK-5
Landmark Ch—*church* OK-5
Landmark Ch—*church* TN-4
Landmark Ch of Christ—*church* AL-4
Landmark Christian Sch—*school* FL-3
Landmark Creek—*stream* ID-8
**Landmark Estates (subdivision)**—*pop pl* TN-4
Landmark Gap—*gap* AK-9
Landmark Gap Lake—*lake* AK-9
Landmark Helispot—*airport* NV-8
Landmark Inn Complex—*hist pl* TX-5
Landmark Learning Center—*school* FL-3
Landmark Letter—*locale* NV-8
Landmark Letter—*other* CA-9
Landmark Letter—*other* ID-8
Landmark Letter—*pillar* AZ-5
Landmark Letter—*pillar* (2) NV-8
Landmark Letter—*reservoir* NV-8
Landmark Letters—*locale* CA-9
Landmark Letters Branch—*park* UT-8
Landmark Missionary Baptist Ch (ABA)—*church* FL-3
Landmark Missionary Cem—*cemetery* MS-4
Landmark Mtn—*summit* AZ-5
Landmark Park—*park* AL-4
Landmark Peak—*summit* ID-8
Landmark Plaza (Shop Ctr)—*locale* FL-3
Landmark Rock—*pillar* ID-8
Landmark Rock—*pillar* NV-8
Landmark Rsvr—*reservoir* ID-8
Landmark Sch—*school* AR-4
Landmark Shop Ctr—*locale* VA-3
Landmark Square—*uninc pl* VA-3
**Landmarks (subdivision)**—*pop pl* AL-4
**Land Mark (subdivision)**—*pop pl* TN-4
Landmark Tank—*reservoir* AZ-5
Landmark Tavern—*hist pl* OH-6
Landmark Village Shop Ctr—*locale* TN-4
Landmark Wash—*valley* AZ-5
L and M Dam—*dam* AL-4
L and M Elementary and HS—*school* IN-6
*Land Methodist Protestant Church* AL-4
Land M Lake—*reservoir* AL-4
Land Mtn—*summit* WY-8
L and N Lake—*reservoir* KY-4
L And N Reservoir Dam—*dam* TN-4
L And N Rsvr—*reservoir* TN-4
**Lando**—*pop pl* SC-3
Land Office—*hist pl* NY-2
Land of Lakes Catfish Farm Dam—*dam* TN-4
Land of Lakes Catfish Farm Lake—*reservoir* TN-4
Land of Nod—*locale* ME-1
**Land of Pines**—*pop pl* NJ-2
**Land of Pleasant Living (subdivision)**—*pop pl* DE-2
Land of Promise—*locale* VA-3
Land of Rest Cem—*cemetery* ME-1
*Land of Standing Rock* UT-8
Land of Standing Rocks—*area* UT-8
*Land of the Never Sweats* CA-9
*Land of Time and Room Enough, The* AZ-5
Land O Lakes—*CDP* FL-3
Land O' Lakes—*lake* WI-6
**Land Olakes**—*pop pl* MN-6
**Land O'Lakes**—*pop pl* WI-6
Land O'Lakes Cem—*cemetery* WI-6
Land O Lakes Dam—*dam* MS-4
Land O' Lakes HS—*school* FL-3
Land O'Lakes State For—*forest* MN-6
**Land O'Lakes (Town of)**—*pop pl* WI-6
**Lando Mines**—*pop pl* WV-2
**Landon**—*pop pl* MS-4
Landon Branch—*stream* (2) MO-7
Landon Branch—*stream* TX-5
Landon Brook—*stream* NY-2
Landon Camp—*locale* MT-8
Landon Cem—*cemetery* IL-6
Landon Cem—*cemetery* IN-6
Landon Cem—*cemetery* TN-4
Landon Creek—*stream* KS-7
Landon Creek—*stream* WY-8
Landon Ditch—*canal* IN-6
Landon Draw—*valley* KS-7
Landon HS—*school* FL-3
Landon JHS—*school* KS-7
Landon Lake—*lake* MI-6
Landon Oil Field—*oilfield* TX-5
Landon Ranch—*locale* MT-8
Landon Ridge—*ridge* MT-8
Landon Sch—*school* MD-2
Landon Sch—*school* MI-6
Landon Sch—*school* OH-6
Landon Spring—*spring* AZ-5
**Landon Station**—*pop pl* PA-2
**Landon Village**—*pop pl* MD-2
**Landon Village Subdivision**—*pop pl* UT-8
Landonville—*locale* MD-2
Landon Windmill—*locale* NM-5
**Landon Woods**—*pop pl* MD-2
**Land O'Pines**—*pop pl* VA-3
Landora Bridge—*bridge* VA-3
Landora Lake—*reservoir* CO-8
Landore—*locale* ID-8
Lando Sch—*school* SC-3
**Landover**—*pop pl* MD-2
**Landover Estates**—*pop pl* MD-2
**Landover Hills**—*pop pl* MD-2
**Landover Knolls**—*pop pl* MD-2
**Landover Park**—*pop pl* MD-2
Landowner Creek—*stream* MT-8
Landowner Mtn—*summit* MT-8
Land Park—*uninc pl* CA-9
Landphere Creek—*stream* IA-7
Land Pond—*reservoir* NC-3
Landram Ridge—*ridge* IN-6
Land Ranch—*locale* NE-7
Land Ranch Spring—*spring* ID-8
Landrein Tank—*reservoir* TX-5
Landreth, David, Sch—*hist pl* PA-2
Landreth Cem—*cemetery* NC-3
Landreth Cem—*cemetery* TX-5
Landreth Ch—*church* MO-7
Landreth Channel—*channel* NJ-2
Landreth Channel—*channel* PA-2
Landreth Draw—*valley* TX-5
Landreth Hollow—*valley* IN-6
**Landreth Manor**—*pop pl* PA-2
Landreth Park—*park* MO-7
Landreth Sch—*school* (2) IL-6
Landreth Sch—*school* PA-2
Landrith Bridge—*bridge* OR-9
Landro Canyon—*valley* NM-5
Landrock—*summit* UT-8
Landrom Mtn—*summit* TN-4
Land RR Station—*building* AZ-5
Landrum—*hist pl* KY-4
Landrum—*locale* FL-3
Landrum—*locale* GA-3
**Landrum**—*pop pl* FL-3
**Landrum**—*pop pl* SC-3
**Landrum**—*pop pl* TX-5
Landrum, Andrew J., House—*hist pl* CA-9
Landrum Branch—*stream* MO-7
Landrum (CCD)—*cens area* SC-3
Landrum Cem—*cemetery* (3) KY-4
Landrum Cem—*cemetery* MS-4
Landrum Cem—*cemetery* MO-7
Landrum Cem—*cemetery* OH-6
Landrum Cem—*cemetery* OK-5
Landrum Cem—*cemetery* TX-5
Landrum Creek—*stream* AL-4
Landrum Creek—*stream* MS-4
Landrum Creek—*stream* NC-3
Landrum Creek—*stream* (2) TX-5
Landrum Field—*park* MS-4
Landrum Hollow—*valley* AL-4
Landrum Sch—*school* TX-5
Landrum Sch (historical)—*school* MS-4
Landrums Creek—*stream* AL-4
Landrums Fort (historical)—*military* AL-4
Land Run—*stream* IN-6
Landrus—*locale* PA-2
Landry—*locale* LA-4
Landry Bay—*bay* LA-4
Landry Canal—*canal* LA-4
Landry Cem—*cemetery* (2) LA-4
Landry HS—*school* (2) LA-4
Landry Tomb—*hist pl* LA-4
Landsaw—*locale* KY-4
Landsaw Branch—*stream* KY-4
Landsaw Ch—*church* KY-4
Landsaw Creek—*stream* KY-4
Landsberry Cem—*cemetery* MO-7
Lands Branch—*stream* IL-6
Lands Branch—*stream* NJ-2
Landsburg—*locale* WA-9
Landsburg Ch—*church* GA-3
Landscape—*uninc pl* CA-9
Landscape Arch—*arch* UT-8
Lands Cem—*cemetery* TN-4
Lands Ch—*church* MN-6
Land Sch—*school* MO-7
Land Sch (abandoned)—*school* MO-7
*Lands Chapel* TN-4
Lands Chapel—*church* KY-4
Lands Chapel—*church* VA-3
Lands Chapel Cem—*cemetery* TN-4
Lands Chapel Sch (historical)—*school* TN-4
*Lands Creek* KS-7
Lands Creek—*stream* NC-3
Lands Crossroads—*locale* GA-3
**Lands Crossroads**—*pop pl* AL-4
*Landsdale Sch* TN-4

Landsdell Cave—*cave* ... AL-4
*Landsdown* ... NJ-2
**Landsdown**—*pop pl* ... NJ-2
**Landsdowne (subdivision)**—*pop pl* ... NC-3
**Landsdown (subdivision)**—*pop pl* ... NC-3
*Lands End* ... CA-9
*Lands End* ... VA-3
Lands End—*cape* ... CA-9
Lands End—*cape* ... FL-3
Lands End—*cape* ... MA-1
Lands End—*cape* ... RI-1
Lands End—*cliff* ... CO-8
Land's End—*hist pl* ... NC-3
Lands End—*hist pl* ... VA-3
Lands End—*locale* ... CT-1
Lands End—*other* ... CA-9
**Lands End**—*pop pl* ... MD-2
**Lands End**—*pop pl* ... MA-1
**Lands End**—*pop pl* ... SC-3
Lands End—*summit* ... UT-8
Lands End Cem—*cemetery* ... CT-1
Lands End Highway—*channel* ... MI-6
Lands End Overlook Picnic Ground—*locale* ... CO-8
Landsend Peak—*summit* ... CO-8
Land's End Plantation—*hist pl* ... LA-4
Lands End Plantation—*locale* ... LA-4
**Lands End Ranch**—*pop pl* ... FL-3
Lands End Ridge—*ridge* ... TN-4
Lands End Road Tabby Ruins—*hist pl* ... SC-3
**Lands End (subdivision)**—*pop pl* ... NC-3
*Landsford* ... ND-7
Landsford—*locale* ... SC-3
Landsford Canal—*hist pl* ... SC-3
Landsford (CCD)—*cens area* ... SC-3
Landsford Plantation House—*hist pl* ... SC-3
Lands Island—*island* ... CA-9
Landslide Butte—*summit* ... MT-8
Landslide Creek—*stream* ... AK-9
Landslide Creek—*stream* ... CA-9
Landslide Creek—*stream* ... ID-8
Landslide Creek—*stream* ... MI-6
Landslide Creek—*stream* ... MT-8
Landslide Dam—*dam* ... WY-8
Landslide Grove—*woods* ... CA-9
Landslide Peak—*summit* ... CO-8
Landslide Spring—*spring* ... CA-9
Landslip Mtn—*summit* ... CO-8
*Land Slough* ... CA-9
Landsman Camp—*locale* ... AZ-5
Landsman Creek—*stream* ... CO-8
Landsman Hill—*summit* ... CO-8
Landsman Kill—*stream* ... NY-2
Landsman Spring—*spring* ... AZ-5
Lands of Mission Santa Barbara—*civil* ... CA-9
Landsome Branch—*stream* ... KY-4
Lands Pond—*reservoir* ... NC-3
Lands Pond Dam—*dam* ... NC-3
Land Spring—*spring* ... ID-8
Land Spring—*spring* ... MO-7
Lands Run—*stream* ... VA-3
Lands Run Gap—*gap* ... VA-3
**Landstad**—*pop pl* ... WI-6
Landstad Cem—*cemetery* (2) ... MN-6
Landstad Cem—*cemetery* ... ND-7
Landstad Ch—*church* ... MN-6
Landston Cem—*cemetery* ... AL-4
**Landstreet**—*pop pl* ... PA-2
Landsverk Cem—*cemetery* ... MN-6
Land Tank—*reservoir* ... AZ-5
Landt Bldg—*hist pl* ... OH-6
Land Title Bldg—*hist pl* ... PA-2
Landtown—*locale* ... VA-3
**Land Township**—*pop pl* ... ND-7
**Land (Township of)**—*pop pl* ... MN-6
**Landusky**—*pop pl* ... MT-8
Landusky Cem—*cemetery* ... MT-8
**Landville**—*pop pl* ... WV-2
Landville Elem Sch—*school* ... PA-2
Landward House—*hist pl* ... KY-4
L and W Catfish Ponds Dam—*dam* (2) ... MS-4
Landwehr Creek—*stream* ... WI-6
Landwood Ch—*church* ... NC-3
L and W Ranch—*locale* ... TX-5
Landy Lake—*lake* ... FL-3
Lane—*locale* ... AL-4
Lane—*locale* ... AK-9
Lane—*locale* ... CA-9
Lane—*locale* ... NE-7
Lane—*locale* ... TX-5
**Lane**—*pop pl* ... ID-8
**Lane**—*pop pl* ... IL-6
**Lane**—*pop pl* ... KS-7
**Lane**—*pop pl* ... NV-8
**Lane**—*pop pl* ... NC-3
**Lane**—*pop pl* ... OH-6
**Lane**—*pop pl* ... OK-5
**Lane**—*pop pl* ... SC-3
**Lane**—*pop pl* ... SD-7
**Lane**—*pop pl* ... TN-4
**Lane**—*pop pl* ... TX-5
**Lane**—*pop pl* ... WV-2
Lane—*post sta* ... NY-2
Lane—*uninc pl* ... FL-3
Lane—*uninc pl* ... OK-5
Lane, Anthony, House—*hist pl* ... MA-1
Lane, David, House—*hist pl* ... MA-1
Lane, Deacon Samuel and Jabez, Homestead—*hist pl* ... NH-1
Lane, Ebenezer, House—*hist pl* ... OH-6
Lane, Edward H., House—*hist pl* ... NH-1
Lane, Fitz Hugh, House—*hist pl* ... MA-1
Lane, Henry S., House—*hist pl* ... IN-6
Lane, Job, House—*hist pl* ... MA-1
Lane, Joel, House—*hist pl* ... NC-3
Lane, John, House—*hist pl* ... MS-4
Lane Allen Sch—*school* ... KY-4
Lane and Shipley Mine (underground)—*mine* ... TN-4
Lanear Creek—*stream* ... TN-4
*L'Aneau Island* ... LA-4
Lane Bay—*bay* ... FL-3
Lane Bayou—*stream* ... MS-4
**Lane Beach**—*pop pl* ... MD-2
Lane Bend—*bend* ... AR-4
Lane-Bennett House—*hist pl* ... NC-3
Lane Branch—*stream* (2) ... AL-4
Lane Branch—*stream* ... KS-7
Lane Branch—*stream* (9) ... KY-4
Lane Branch—*stream* (2) ... MO-7
Lane Branch—*stream* (3) ... NC-3
Lane Branch—*stream* (3) ... TN-4
Lane Branch—*stream* ... VA-3
Lane Branch—*stream* ... WV-2
Lane Brook—*stream* (3) ... ME-1
Lane Brook Hills—*summit* ... ME-1
Lane Brook Meadows—*swamp* ... ME-1
Lane Brook Pond—*lake* ... ME-1
*Lane Brothers Bar* ... AL-4
**Laneburg**—*pop pl* ... AR-4
Laneburg Cem—*cemetery* ... AR-4
Laneburg HS—*school* ... AR-4
Lane Cabbage Camp—*locale* ... FL-3
Lane Cabin—*hist pl* ... OK-5
Lane Camp Branch—*stream* ... VA-3
Lane Canyon—*valley* ... OK-5
Lane Canyon—*valley* ... SD-7
Lane Canyon—*valley* ... WY-8
Lane (CCD)—*cens area* ... SC-3
Lane Cem—*cemetery* ... AL-4
Lane Cem—*cemetery* ... AR-4
Lane Cem—*cemetery* (5) ... GA-3
Lane Cem—*cemetery* (2) ... IL-6
Lane Cem—*cemetery* (2) ... IN-6
Lane Cem—*cemetery* ... KS-7
Lane Cem—*cemetery* (2) ... KY-4
Lane Cem—*cemetery* ... LA-4
Lane Cem—*cemetery* (2) ... ME-1
Lane Cem—*cemetery* ... MI-6
Lane Cem—*cemetery* ... MS-4
Lane Cem—*cemetery* (3) ... MO-7
Lane Cem—*cemetery* ... NY-2
Lane Cem—*cemetery* ... OK-5
Lane Cem—*cemetery* (2) ... SC-3
Lane Cem—*cemetery* (10) ... TN-4
Lane Cem—*cemetery* (2) ... TX-5
Lane Cem—*cemetery* (3) ... VA-3
Lane Cem—*cemetery* ... WI-6
**Lane Cemetery**—*pop pl* ... ID-8
Lane Center (Shop Ctr)—*locale* ... FL-3
*Lane Ch* ... AL-4
Lane Ch—*church* ... WV-2
*Lane Chapel* ... TN-4
Lane Chapel—*church* (2) ... AL-4
Lane Chapel—*church* (2) ... GA-3
Lane Chapel—*church* ... SC-3
Lane Chapel—*church* ... TN-4
Lane Chapel Cem—*cemetery* ... TN-4
Lane Chapel Ch—*church* ... AL-4
Lane Chapel Christian Methodist Episcopal Ch—*church* ... KS-7
Lane Chapel CME Ch—*church* ... MS-4
*Lane Chool* ... FM-9
**Lane City**—*pop pl* ... NV-8
**Lane City**—*pop pl* ... TX-5
Lane Coll—*school* ... OR-9
Lane Coll—*school* ... TN-4
Lane College Hist Dist—*hist pl* ... MS-4
Lane Community Ch—*church* ... MO-7
Lane Community Coll—*school* (2) ... OR-9
Lane County—*civil* ... KS-7
**Lane County**—*pop pl* ... OR-9
Lane County Clerk's Bldg—*hist pl* ... OR-9
Lane County State Lake—*reservoir* ... KS-7
Lane County State Lake Dam—*dam* ... KS-7
Lane Cove—*bay* ... FL-3
Lane Cove—*bay* ... MI-6
Lane Cove—*valley* ... TN-4
Lane Cove Trail—*trail* ... MI-6
*Lane Creek* ... MD-2
*Lane Creek* ... OR-9
*Lane Creek* ... TN-4
Lane Creek—*stream* (2) ... AK-9
Lane Creek—*stream* ... CO-8
Lane Creek—*stream* (2) ... GA-3
Lane Creek—*stream* (2) ... ID-8
Lane Creek—*stream* (9) ... OR-9
Lane Creek—*stream* ... TX-5
Lane Creek—*stream* (2) ... WA-9
Lane Creek—*stream* ... WI-6
Lane Creek—*stream* ... WY-8
Lane Creek Campground—*park* ... OR-9
Lanedale—*building* ... IA-7
Lane Dam—*dam* ... AL-4
Lane District Cem—*cemetery* ... CT-1
Lane Ditch—*canal* ... IN-6
Lane Drain—*stream* ... MI-6
Lane Farm—*hist pl* ... KY-4
Lane Fire Tower—*locale* ... SC-3
*Lane Fork* ... MO-7
Lane Fork—*stream* ... KY-4
Lane Fork—*stream* ... VA-3
Lane Fort Ch—*church* ... AR-4
Lane Gap—*gap* ... TN-4
Lane Grove—*woods* ... CA-9
Lane Grove Ch—*church* ... GA-3
Lane Gulch—*valley* ... CO-8
*Lanehart* ... MS-4
Laneheart—*locale* ... MS-4
Lane Heights Cem—*cemetery* ... MI-6
Lane Hill—*summit* ... CA-9
Lane Hill—*summit* ... CT-1
Lane Hill—*summit* ... ME-1
Lane Hill—*summit* (2) ... NY-2
Lane Hill Sch—*school* ... TN-4
*Lane Hollow* ... TN-4
Lane Hollow—*valley* ... KS-7
Lane Hollow—*valley* ... MO-7
Lane Hollow—*valley* ... OK-5
Lane Hollow—*valley* ... TN-4
Lane Hollow—*valley* ... TX-5
Lane Hollow—*valley* (2) ... VA-3
Lane Hollow Branch—*stream* ... TN-4
Lane Homestead—*locale* ... WY-8
Lane-Hoovan House—*hist pl* ... OH-6
Lane Hotel—*hist pl* ... AR-4
Lane House—*hist pl* ... GA-3
Lane House—*hist pl* ... PA-2
Lane HS—*school* ... VA-3
*Lane Institute* ... TN-4
*Laneir* ... NC-3
*Lane Island* ... ME-1
Lane Island—*island* ... AK-9
Lane Island—*island* ... ME-1
Lane-Kendrick-Sherling House—*hist pl* ... AL-4
*Lane Lake* ... WI-6
Lane Lake—*lake* ... CA-9
Lane Lake—*lake* ... IN-6
Lane Lake—*lake* ... MI-6
Lane Lake—*lake* ... NE-7
Lane Landing—*locale* ... FL-3
Lane Landing—*locale* ... GA-3
Lane Landing—*locale* ... NC-3
Lane Landing (historical)—*locale* ... MS-4
Lane (Laneville)—*uninc pl* ... PA-2
Lanelang—*cape* ... FM-9
Lane-Lenoir Cem—*cemetery* ... MS-4
Lanel Substation—*locale* ... OR-9
Lanely—*locale* ... TX-5
Lane Manor Recreation Center—*park* ... MD-2
Lanemaut—*cape* ... FM-9
Lane Meadow Creek—*stream* ... WY-8
Lane Memorial Cem—*cemetery* ... TX-5
Lane Memorial Gardens (cemetery)—*cemetery* ... OR-9
Lane Memorial Hosp—*hospital* ... LA-4
*Lane Mesa* ... OR-9
Lane Mill—*locale* ... CA-9
Lane Mountain Trail—*trail* ... AZ-5
Lane Mtn—*summit* ... AZ-5
Lane Mtn—*summit* ... CA-9
Lane Mtn—*summit* ... OR-9
Lane Mtn—*summit* ... WA-9
*Lanengulu* ... FM-9
*Lanenguluu* ... FM-9
Lane Number 1 Mine (underground)—*mine* ... TN-4
Lane Number 2 Mine (underground)—*mine* ... TN-4
Lane Number 3 Mine (underground)—*mine* ... TN-4
Lane Park—*park* ... AL-4
**Lane Park**—*pop pl* ... FL-3
Lane Park Cem—*cemetery* ... FL-3
Lane Pasture Windmill—*locale* ... NM-5
Lane Peak—*summit* ... WA-9
Lane Pinnacle—*summit* ... NC-3
Lane Plateau—*plain* ... OR-9
Lane Plaza Shop Ctr—*locale* ... AL-4
Lane Pond—*lake* ... CT-1
Lane Pond—*lake* (2) ... FL-3
Lane Pond—*lake* ... ME-1
Lane Pond—*lake* ... MD-2
Lane Pond—*lake* ... MA-1
Lane Pool Creek—*stream* ... TX-5
Laneport—*locale* ... TX-5
Lane Post Office (historical)—*building* ... TN-4
**Lane Prairie**—*pop pl* ... TX-5
Lane Prairie Ch—*church* ... TX-5
Lane Prospect—*mine* ... AK-9
*Laner* ... FM-9
Lane Ranch—*locale* ... CA-9
Lane Ranch—*locale* (2) ... MT-8
Lane Ranch—*locale* (2) ... NM-5
Lane Ranch—*locale* (2) ... OR-9
Lane Ridge—*ridge* ... VA-3
Laneri HS—*school* ... TX-5
Lane-Riley House—*hist pl* ... TX-5
Lane River—*stream* ... AK-9
Lane River—*stream* ... FL-3
Lane River—*stream* ... NH-1
Lane Rsvr—*reservoir* ... CA-9
Lane Rsvr—*reservoir* ... CO-8
Lane Rsvr Number Four—*reservoir* ... OR-9
Lane Rsvr Number One—*reservoir* ... OR-9
Lanes—*church* ... NC-3
Lanes—*locale* ... CA-9
**Lanes**—*pop pl* ... OH-6
Lane Salt Lake—*lake* ... NM-5
*Lanes Bayou* ... MS-4
Lanes Bluff—*cliff* ... OK-5
*Lanes Bogue* ... MS-4
*Lanesboro* ... MA-1
**Lanesboro**—*pop pl* ... IA-7
**Lanesboro**—*pop pl* ... MN-6
**Lanesboro**—*pop pl* ... PA-2
**Lanesboro**—*pop pl* ... VT-1
Lanesboro Borough—*civil* ... PA-2
Lanesboro Cem—*cemetery* ... IA-7
Lanesboro Cem—*cemetery* ... MN-6
Lanesboro Hist Dist—*hist pl* ... MN-6
Lanesboro Sch—*school* ... SD-7
**Lanesboro (Town name Lanesborough)**—*pop pl* ... MA-1
Lanesboro Township—*civil* ... SD-7
Lanesboro (Township of)—*fmr MCD* ... NC-3
**Lanesborough**—*pop pl* ... MA-1
Lanesborough Center Cem—*cemetery* ... MA-1
*Lanesborough Pond* ... MA-1
**Lanesborough (Town of)**—*pop pl* ... MA-1
*Lanes Bottom* ... WV-2
Lanes Branch—*stream* (2) ... IL-6
Lanes Branch—*stream* ... OH-6
Lanes Branch—*stream* ... WV-2
Lanes Bridge—*bridge* ... CA-9
Lanes Brook—*stream* ... ME-1
Lanes Brook—*stream* ... VT-1
*Lanesburg* ... AR-4
**Lanesburgh (Township of)**—*pop pl* ... MN-6
Lanes Cem—*cemetery* ... MS-4
Lanes Ch—*church* ... GA-3
Lanes Ch—*church* ... TX-5
Lane Sch—*school* ... AL-4
Lane Sch—*school* (2) ... CA-9
Lane Sch—*school* (2) ... IL-6
Lane Sch—*school* ... LA-4
Lane Sch—*school* ... ME-1
Lane Sch—*school* ... MA-1
Lane Sch—*school* ... MI-6
Lane Sch—*school* ... MT-8
Lane Sch—*school* ... NE-7
Lane Sch—*school* ... NY-2
Lane Sch—*school* (2) ... OH-6
Lane Sch—*school* ... OR-9
Lane Sch—*school* ... TX-5
Lane Sch—*school* ... VA-3
Lane Sch—*school* ... WV-2
Lane Sch—*school* ... WI-6
Lanes Chapel—*church* ... AL-4
Lanes Chapel—*church* ... IN-6
Lanes Chapel—*church* ... KY-4
Lanes Chapel—*church* ... MS-4
Lanes Chapel—*church* ... NC-3
Lanes Chapel—*church* ... TX-5
Lanes Chapel Cem—*cemetery* ... TN-4
Lanes Chapel Ch—*church* ... AL-4
Lanes Chapel Ch—*church* ... TN-4
Lanes Chapel Sch—*school* ... TX-5
Lane's Chapel Site—*hist pl* ... MS-4
Lane Sch (historical)—*school* ... AL-4
Lane Sch II—*hist pl* ... ID-8
Lane School (Abandoned)—*locale* ... NE-7
Lanes Corner—*locale* (2) ... VA-3
Lanes Cove—*cove* ... MA-1
Lanes Creek—*locale* ... SC-3
Lanes Creek—*stream* ... GA-3
Lanes Creek—*stream* ... ID-8
Lanes Creek—*stream* ... NC-3
Lanes Creek—*stream* ... SC-3
Lanes Creek—*stream* ... VA-3
Lanes Creek Ch—*church* ... NC-3
Lanes Creek (Township of)—*fmr MCD* ... NC-3
*Lanes Crossroads Church* ... AL-4
Lanesdale Sch—*school* ... WI-6
Lanes Ferry Ch—*church* ... LA-4
Lanes Ferry Park—*park* ... NC-3
*Lanesfield* ... KS-7
Lanesfield Sch—*hist pl* ... KS-7
Lanesfield Sch—*school* ... KS-7
Lanes Ford—*locale* ... MO-7
Lanes Ford—*locale* ... VA-3
*Lanes Fork* ... MO-7
Lanes Fork—*stream* ... MO-7
Lanes Grave Cem—*cemetery* ... ID-8
*Lanes Grove* ... PA-2
Lanes Gulch—*valley* ... ID-8
**Lane Siding**—*pop pl* ... KY-4
*Lane Sigow* ... FM-9
Lanes Island—*island* ... ME-1
Lanes Island—*island* ... NY-2
*Lanes Lake* ... MN-6
Lanes Lake—*lake* ... IL-6
Lanes Lake—*lake* ... MI-6
Lanes Lake—*reservoir* ... AL-4
Lane Slough—*stream* ... CA-9
Lanes Mill—*locale* ... KY-4
Lanes Mill Creek—*stream* ... GA-3
Lane's Mill Historic Buildings—*hist pl* ... OH-6
*Lanes Mill Pond* ... NJ-2
**Lanes Mills**—*pop pl* ... NJ-2
**Lanes Mills**—*pop pl* ... PA-2
*Lane Spit* ... WA-9
*Lane's Pond* ... ME-1
*Lanes Pond* ... NJ-2
Lanes Pond—*lake* ... GA-3
Lanes Pond—*lake* ... NY-2
Lanes Pond—*reservoir* ... AL-4
Lanesport—*locale* ... AR-4
Lanes Post Office (historical)—*building* ... AL-4
Lanes Prairie—*locale* ... MO-7
Lane Spring—*spring* ... AL-4
Lane Spring—*spring* (2) ... AZ-5
Lane Spring—*spring* ... CA-9
Lane Spring—*spring* (3) ... MO-7
Lane Spring—*spring* ... NM-5
Lane Spring—*spring* ... OR-9
Lane Spring—*spring* ... TN-4
Lane Spring—*spring* ... WA-9
Lane Spring Campground—*locale* ... MO-7
**Lane Springs**—*pop pl* ... AL-4
Lane Springs Sch (historical)—*school* ... AL-4
Lanes Ranch—*locale* ... NM-5
Lanes Run—*stream* ... KY-4
Lanes Run—*stream* ... MD-2
Lane's Run Hist Dist—*hist pl* ... KY-4
*La Ness* ... KS-7
Laness (historical)—*locale* ... KS-7
Lanes Store—*locale* ... NC-3
Lane Stadium—*other* ... VA-3
**Lane Station**—*pop pl* ... OH-6
Lane Street Ch—*church* ... NC-3
*Lanesugow* ... FM-9
Lanes Valley—*valley* ... OH-6
*Lanesville* ... MA-1
Lanesville—*locale* ... NY-2
Lanesville—*locale* ... VA-3
**Lanesville**—*pop pl* ... CT-1
**Lanesville**—*pop pl* ... IL-6
**Lanesville**—*pop pl* ... IN-6
**Lanesville**—*pop pl* ... MA-1
Lanesville Cem—*cemetery* ... IN-6
Lanesville Reservoir Dam—*dam* ... IN-6
Lanesville Skyways Airp—*airport* ... IN-6
**Lanesville (Township of)**—*pop pl* ... IL-6
Lane Swamp—*stream* ... NC-3
Lane Tank—*reservoir* (3) ... AZ-5
Lane-Tarkington House—*hist pl* ... TX-5
Lane Technical HS—*school* ... IL-6
Lane-Towers House—*hist pl* ... FL-3
Lanetown Ch—*church* ... TN-4
Lanetown Ch—*church* ... TX-5
Lanetown Hollow—*valley* ... MO-7
Lane Town Sch (historical)—*school* ... TN-4
**Lane Township**—*pop pl* (2) ... KS-7
**Lane (Township of)**—*pop pl* ... IN-6
Lanetown Spring—*spring* ... MO-7
Lane Tree (Camp Site)—*locale* ... UT-8
Lane Troughs Windmill—*locale* ... TX-5
**Lanett**—*pop pl* ... AL-4
Lanett (CCD)—*cens area* ... AL-4
*Lanett Cemetery* ... AL-4
Lanett Division—*civil* ... AL-4
Lanett Municipal Airp—*airport* ... AL-4
Lane Univ—*hist pl* ... KS-7
Lane Valley—*valley* ... CA-9
Lane Valley—*valley* ... MN-6
Lane Valley—*valley* ... NV-8
**Laneview**—*pop pl* ... TN-4
**Laneview**—*pop pl* ... VA-3
*Laneview Academy* ... TN-4
*Laneview Baptist Ch* ... TN-4
Laneview Baptist Ch—*church* ... TN-4
Laneview Ch—*church* ... TN-4
Laneview Coll (historical)—*school* ... TN-4
Laneview Post Office (historical)—*building* ... TN-4
Laneview Sch—*school* ... CA-9
Laneview Sch (historical)—*school* ... TN-4
**Lane Village**—*pop pl* ... MA-1
**Lane Village Subdivision**—*pop pl* ... UT-8
Laneville—*locale* ... AL-4
Laneville—*locale* ... KS-7
**Laneville**—*pop pl* ... AL-4
**Laneville**—*pop pl* ... PA-2
**Laneville**—*pop pl* ... TX-5
**Laneville**—*pop pl* ... WV-2
Laneville (CCD)—*cens area* ... TX-5
Laneville Ch—*church* ... TX-5
Laneville Sch—*school* ... MI-6
Lane Vly—*swamp* ... NY-2
Lane Waterhole Number Eleven—*reservoir* ... OR-9
Lane Waterhole Number Twelve—*reservoir* ... OR-9
*Laneway Farm Dam* ... MA-1
Lane Well—*well* ... CA-9
Lane Well—*well* ... MT-8
Lane Well—*well* ... OR-9
Lane Wildlife Area—*park* ... KS-7
Lane Windmill—*locale* ... TX-5
**Lanewood**—*pop pl* ... MI-6
Lanexa—*locale* ... VA-3
Laney—*locale* ... AL-4
**Laney**—*pop pl* ... AL-4
**Laney**—*pop pl* ... GA-3
**Laney**—*pop pl* ... SC-3
**Laney**—*pop pl* ... WI-6
Laney, J. D., House—*hist pl* ... OK-5
*Lane Yaboch* ... FM-9
*Laney Branch* ... TN-4
Laney Branch—*stream* ... AL-4
Laney Canyon—*valley* ... WY-8
Laney Cem—*cemetery* ... MO-7
Laney Cem—*cemetery* ... NC-3
Laney Cem—*cemetery* (3) ... VA-3
Laney Creek—*stream* ... AL-4
Laney Creek—*stream* ... MT-8
Laney Hall—*building* ... NC-3
Laney Hollow—*valley* ... KY-4
Laney Hollow—*valley* ... WV-2
Laney HS—*school* ... GA-3
Laney Landing Strip—*airport* ... ND-7
Laney P.O. (historical)—*building* ... AL-4
Laney Ranch—*locale* ... NM-5
*Laney Rim* ... WY-8
Laney Rim—*cliff* ... WY-8
Laneys Airp—*airport* ... NC-3
Laney Sch—*school* ... GA-3
Laney Spring—*spring* ... NM-5
Laney Spring—*spring* ... WY-8
Laney Tank—*reservoir* ... NM-5
Laney-Walker North Hist Dist—*hist pl* ... GA-3
Laney Wash—*valley* ... WY-8
Laney Well—*well* ... NM-5
Lanfair—*locale* ... CA-9
Lanfair Buttes—*summit* ... CA-9
*Lanfair Corner* ... CA-9
*Lanfair Junction* ... CA-9
*Lanfair Site* ... CA-9
Lanfair Valley—*valley* ... CA-9
Lanfear Sch—*school* ... MI-6
Lanfield Hollow—*valley* ... NY-2
**Lanford**—*pop pl* ... SC-3
Lanford Grove Ch—*church* ... SC-3
*Lanford Station* ... SC-3
*Lang* ... OH-6
*Lang* ... FM-9
Lang—*locale* ... CA-9
Lang—*locale* ... KS-7
Lang, William, Townhouse—*hist pl* ... CO-8
*Lang Air Park* ... NC-3
Langan Ball Park—*park* ... AL-4
Langan Creek—*stream* ... IL-6
Langan Creek—*stream* ... PA-2
Langan Swamp—*swamp* ... PA-2
*Langar* ... FM-9
*L'angar* ... MP-9
*Langar Island* ... FM-9
Langarow—*bay* ... FM-9
Lang Bay—*bay* ... WA-9
Lang Bayou—*gut* ... MS-4
Langbehn Sch—*school* ... IA-7
Langberg Sch—*school* ... ND-7
**Langberg Township**—*pop pl* ... ND-7
Lang Branch—*stream* ... FL-3
Lang Branch—*stream* ... NC-3
Lang Branch—*stream* ... SC-3
Lang Brook—*stream* ... VT-1
Lang Canyon—*valley* ... AZ-5
Lang Canyon—*valley* (3) ... CA-9
Lang Canyon—*valley* ... OR-9
Lang Cem—*cemetery* ... MO-7
Lang Cem—*cemetery* ... TN-4
Lang Chapel—*church* ... TX-5
*Lang Chapel African Methodist Episcopal Zion Church* ... AL-4
*Lang Creek* ... MI-6
*Lang Creek* ... MS-4
*Lang Creek* ... MT-8
Lang Creek—*stream* ... AZ-5
Lang Creek—*stream* ... GA-3
Lang Creek—*stream* (2) ... MT-8
Lang Creek—*stream* ... OH-6
Lang Creek—*stream* (2) ... TX-5
Langdale (CCD)—*cens area* ... AL-4
Langdale Cem—*cemetery* ... AL-4
Langdale Division—*civil* ... AL-4
Langdales Pond—*lake* ... GA-3
**Langdale (subdivision)**—*pop pl* ... AL-4
Langdale Yard—*locale* ... GA-3
Langdeau Site—*hist pl* ... SD-7
Langdom Mine—*mine* ... MN-6
*Langdon* ... MN-6
Langdon—*locale* ... GA-3
Langdon—*locale* ... KS-7
Langdon—*locale* ... MO-7
Langdon—*locale* ... OR-9
Langdon—*locale* (2) ... PA-2
**Langdon**—*pop pl* ... DC-2
**Langdon**—*pop pl* ... IA-7
**Langdon**—*pop pl* ... KS-7
**Langdon**—*pop pl* ... MN-6
**Langdon**—*pop pl* ... NH-1
**Langdon**—*pop pl* ... NY-2
**Langdon**—*pop pl* ... ND-7
**Langdon**—*pop pl* ... PA-2
**Langdon**—*pop pl* ... WA-9
Langdon—*summit* ... UT-8
Langdon, Gov. John, Mansion—*hist pl* ... NH-1
Langdon, Mount—*summit* ... NH-1
Langdon Ave Sch—*school* ... CA-9
Langdon Bend Public Access—*locale* ... MO-7
Langdon Branch—*stream* ... AL-4
Langdon Branch—*stream* ... KY-4
Langdon Brook—*stream* ... ME-1
Langdon Brook—*stream* ... NH-1
Langdon Cem—*cemetery* (2) ... KS-7
Langdon Cem—*cemetery* ... MO-7
Langdon Cem—*cemetery* ... NY-2
Langdon Cem—*cemetery* ... NC-3
Langdon Cem—*cemetery* ... OH-6
Langdon Ch—*church* ... AL-4
*Langdon City* ... AL-4
Langdon City Post Office (historical)—*building* ... AL-4
Langdon Corners—*locale* ... NY-2
Langdon Creek—*stream* ... OR-9
Langdon Creek—*stream* ... UT-8
Langdon Creek—*stream* ... WA-9
*Langdon Creek- in part* ... UT-8
**Langdondale**—*pop pl* ... PA-2
Langdon Glacier—*glacier* ... AK-9
Langdon Gulch—*valley* ... CA-9
Langdon Gulch—*valley* ... ID-8
Langdon Hill—*summit* ... NY-2
Langdon (historical)—*locale* (2) ... AL-4
Langdon Hollow—*valley* ... KY-4
Langdon House—*hist pl* ... OH-6
Langdonia Post Office (historical)—*building* ... TN-4
Langdon Knob—*summit* ... KY-4
Langdon Lake—*lake* ... MN-6
Langdon Lake—*reservoir* ... OR-9
Langdon Lake Dam—*dam* ... OR-9
Langdon Lateral—*canal* ... ID-8
Langdon Lookout Tower—*tower* ... AL-4
*Langdon Mountains* ... UT-8
Langdon Mtn—*summit* ... UT-8
Langdon Municipal Airp—*airport* ... ND-7
Langdon Park—*park* ... DC-2
**Langdon Place**—*pop pl* ... KY-4
Langdon Point—*summit* ... ID-8
Langdon Pond—*reservoir* ... NC-3
Langdon Rsvr—*reservoir* ... ND-7
Langdon Sch—*hist pl* ... SD-7
Langdon Sch—*school* ... DC-2
Langdon Sch—*school* ... IL-6
Langdon Sch—*school* ... SD-7
Langdon Site—*hist pl* ... MO-7
Langdons Pond Number One Dam—*dam* ... NC-3
Langdons Pond Number Two Dam—*dam* ... NC-3
Langdon Street Hist Dist—*hist pl* ... WI-6
**Langdon (Town of)**—*pop pl* ... NH-1
**Langdon Township**—*pop pl* ... KS-7
**Langdon Township**—*pop pl* ... ND-7
Lang Drain—*canal* ... MI-6
Langeba Island—*island* ... MP-9
Lange-Calahan Cem—*cemetery* ... LA-4
Lange Canyon—*valley* ... CO-8
Lange Cem—*cemetery* (2) ... MO-7
Lange Cem—*cemetery* ... TX-5
Lange Creek—*stream* ... IA-7
Lange Creek—*stream* ... MT-8
Langedahl Cem—*cemetery* ... ND-7
Lange Island—*island* ... AK-9
Langejammer Creek—*stream* ... MO-7
Lange Lagoon Natl Wildlife Mgt Area—*park* ... NE-7
Lange Lake—*lake* ... TX-5
Langel Creek—*stream* ... OR-9
Langell Canyon—*valley* ... ID-8
Langell (CCD)—*cens area* ... OR-9
Langellier Sch—*school* ... IL-6
Langell Ridge—*ridge* ... OR-9
*Langells Valley* ... OR-9
Langell Valley—*locale* ... OR-9
Langell Valley—*valley* ... OR-9
**Langeloth**—*pop pl* ... PA-2
Langeloth Elem Sch—*school* ... PA-2
Langely Ranch—*locale* ... NM-5
Langemo Pioneer Cem—*cemetery* ... ND-7
Langenbaum Lake—*lake* ... IN-6
**Langenbaum Lake**—*pop pl* ... IN-6
Langenberger Cem—*cemetery* ... IN-6
*Langenderfer* ... OH-6
Langenderfer Ditch—*canal* ... OH-6
Langendoerfer Cem—*cemetery* ... MO-7
Langen Rsvr—*reservoir* ... MT-8
*Lange Plain* ... WA-9
Lange Pond—*lake* ... IL-6
*Langer* ... FM-9
Lange Rack—*channel* ... NY-2
*Lange Ranch* ... ND-7
Lange Ravine—*valley* ... TX-5
Langer Lake—*lake* ... ID-8
Langer Lake—*lake* ... WI-6
Langer Monmt—*park* ... ID-8
Langer Peak—*summit* ... ID-8
Langer Ranch—*locale* ... CA-9
Langers Pond—*lake* ... CT-1
*Langes* ... WI-6
Langes Bay—*bay* ... MI-6
Lange Sch—*school* ... AR-4
Lange Sch—*school* ... IN-6
*Langes Corner* ... WI-6
**Langes Corner**—*pop pl* ... WI-6
*Lange's Corners* ... WI-6
**Langes Corners**—*pop pl* ... WI-6
Langes Crest—*area* ... WA-9
Langes Ferry (historical)—*locale* ... IA-7
*Langes Run* ... AZ-5
Langes Run—*stream* ... OH-6
Lange State Wildlife Mngmt Area—*park* ... MN-6
*Langes Wash* ... AZ-5
Langewald Pond—*reservoir* ... MA-1
Langfield Falls—*falls* ... WA-9
Langfitt Run—*stream* ... WV-2
**Langford**—*pop pl* ... AR-4
**Langford**—*pop pl* ... MD-2
**Langford**—*pop pl* ... MS-4
**Langford**—*pop pl* ... NY-2
**Langford**—*pop pl* ... SD-7
**Langford**—*pop pl* ... VA-3
Langford, Mount—*summit* ... WY-8
*Langford Academy* ... TN-4
*Langford Bay* ... MD-2
*Langford Branch* ... TX-5
Langford Branch—*stream* ... NC-3
Langford Branch—*stream* ... TN-4
Langford Branch—*stream* (3) ... TX-5
Langford Cairn—*locale* ... WY-8
Langford Cairn—*summit* ... WY-8
Langford Cem—*cemetery* (2) ... AR-4
Langford Cem—*cemetery* ... GA-3
Langford Cem—*cemetery* ... OK-5
Langford Cem—*cemetery* ... TN-4
Langford Cem—*cemetery* (2) ... TX-5
*Langford Corners* ... MD-2
Langford Cove—*bay* ... TN-4
**Langford Cove**—*pop pl* ... TN-4

Lantz Cem—*cemetery* (3) PA-2
**Lantz Corners**—*pop pl* PA-2
**Lantz (Deerfield)**—*pop pl* MD-2
Lantz (Deerfield Station)—*locale* MD-2
Lantz Hill—*summit* WV-2
Lantz Mills—*locale* VA-3
Lantz Mtn—*summit* VA-3
Lantz Pond—*lake* WI-6
Lantz Rapids—*rapids* ID-8
Lantz Ridge—*ridge* CA-9
Lantz Ridge—*ridge* WV-2
La Nueva Libertad—*hist pl* TX-5
Lanvale—*locale* NC-3
*Lanvalle* NC-3
Lanway Drain—*canal* MI-6
*Lanx Run* PA-2
Lanyon Trail (pack)—*trail* CA-9
**Lanyon**—*pop pl* IA-7
Lanyon Park *park* CO 8
Lanzie Spring—*spring* WA-9
Lanzl, Haerman, House—*hist pl* IL-6
Lanz Lake—*lake* NE-7
*Lanz Run* PA-2
*Laodicea Cem* MS-4
Laodicea Cem—*cemetery* MS-4
Laodicea Ch—*church* AL-4
*Laodicea Primitive Baptist Church* MS-4
*Laokatong Creek* NJ-2
Laolao—*slope* MH-9
Laolao—*summit* GU-9
Laolao, Bahia—*bay* MH-9
**Laolao, Chalan**—*pop pl* MH-9
Laolao, Kannat—*stream* MH-9
Laolao, Kannat Taddong—*stream* MH-9
Laolao, Laderan—*cliff* MH-9
Laolao, Okso'—*summit* MH-9
Laolao, Sabanan—*slope* MH-9
Laolao, Unai—*beach* MH-9
Laolao Kattan—*slope* MH-9
Laolao Kattan, Puntan—*cape* MH-9
Laolao Kattan, Unai—*beach* MH-9
Laolao River—*stream* GU-9
Laolao Stream—*stream* AS-9
La Olla—*valley* CA-9
La Olla de los Encinos—*other* NM-5
**Laona**—*pop pl* NY-2
**Laona**—*pop pl* WI-6
Laona Cem—*cemetery* IL-6
Laona Cem—*cemetery* WI-6
Laona Heights For Preserve—*forest* IL-6
Laona Junction—*locale* WI-6
Laona Lookout Tower—*locale* WI-6
**Laona (Town of)**—*pop pl* WI-6
**Laona (Township of)**—*pop pl* IL-6
**Laona (Township of)**—*pop pl* MN-6
*Laopi* MN-6
La Osa Ranch—*locale* AZ-5
Lao Sch—*school* MN-6
La Otra Sch—*school* AZ-5
**Laotto**—*pop pl* IN-6
Laotto Elem Sch—*school* IN-6
La Otto (Laotto)—*other* IN-6
Laoulu Stream—*stream* AS-9
La Oveja—*summit* CA-9
La Oveja Well (Windmill)—*locale* TX-5
*Lap* FM-9
Lap—*locale* MD-2
Lapa (Barrio)—*fmr MCD* (2) PR-3
*Lapagao* MH-9
Lapaiki—*area* HI-9
Lapaiki Gulch—*valley* HI-9
Lapakahi—*civil* HI-9
Lapakahi Complex—*hist pl* HI-9
Lapakohana—*summit* HI-9
**Lapala**—*pop pl* NY-2
*Lapalapa* HI-9
*La Palisade River* MS-4
Lapalli Creek—*stream* WY-8
**La Palma**—*pop pl* AZ-5
**La Palma**—*pop pl* CA-9
LaPalma Corral—*locale* AZ-5
La Palma JHS—*school* CA-9
La Palma Park—*park* CA-9
La Palmas JHS—*school* CA-9
**La Paloma**—*pop pl* CA-9
**La Paloma**—*pop pl* TX-5
La Paloma Canyon—*valley* NM-5
La Paloma Cow Camp—*locale* TX-5
La Paloma Flat—*flat* CA-9
La Paloma HS—*school* CA-9
LaPaloma Mine—*mine* NM-5
La Paloma Ranch—*locale* CA-9
La Paloma Ranch—*locale* TX-5
La Paloma Tank—*reservoir* NM-5
La Palomera—*summit* CA-9
*Lapan Creek* TX-5
Lapan Drain—*canal* MI-6
Lapanocia, Lake—*lake* FL-3
*La Pansa* CA-9
Lapans Bay—*bay* VT-1
La Panta Mine—*mine* NV-8
La Panta (site)—*locale* NV-8
La Panza—*locale* CA-9
La Panza Campground—*locale* CA-9
La Panza Canyon—*valley* CA-9
La Panza Ranch—*locale* CA-9
La Panza Range—*range* CA-9
La Panza Summit—*gap* CA-9
La Par, Point—*cape* MI-6
La Para—*locale* TX-5
La Para Creek—*stream* TX-5
**La Parada**—*pop pl* PR-3
*Lapardes Cove* GA-3
La Pareia—*other* NM-5
La Parguera—*CDP* PR-3
La Parida Banco Number 144—*levee* TX-5
Lapa Ridge—*ridge* HI-9
La Paries Ch—*church* LA-4
La Parita—*locale* TX-5
La Parita Canyon—*valley* NM-5
La Parita Creek—*stream* TX-5
**Lapark**—*pop pl* PA-2
La Parra Landing—*locale* TX-5
La Parra Ranch—*locale* TX-5
La Parra Well—*well* TX-5
La Particion Ranch—*locale* TX-5
Lapata—*locale* TN-4
La Patera—*locale* CA-9
La Patera Sch—*school* CA-9
La Patrona Windmill—*locale* TX-5

Lapaulala Gulch—*valley* HI-9
La Pawac Brook—*stream* VT-1
Lapawai Bay—*bay* HI-9
*Lapaynor School* TX-5
*La Paz* AZ-5
*Lapaz* IN-6
**La Paz**—*pop pl* IN-6
La Paz Acad—*school* FL-3
La Paz Arroyo—*valley* AZ-5
La Paz Canyon—*valley* CA-9
La Paz Cem—*cemetery* TX-5
*Lapaz (corporate and RR name La Paz)* IN-6
**La Paz County**—*pop pl* AZ-5
La Paz County Courthouse—*building* AZ-5
Lapaz Elem Sch—*school* IN-6
*La Paz Ferry* AZ-5
*Lapaz Junction* IN-6
**La Paz Junction**—*pop pl* IN-6
*La Paz Mountains* AZ-5
La Paz Mtn—*summit* AZ-5
La Paz Sch—*school* CA-9
**La Paz Valley (subdivision)**—*pop pl* AZ-5
La Paz Wash—*stream* AZ-5
La Paz Well—*well* AZ-5
Lap Circle Ranch—*locale* SD-7
**Lap Corner**—*pop pl* IN-6
Lap Creek—*stream* MT-8
La Peans Canal—*canal* LA-4
La Pear Pond—*reservoir* CO-8
**Lapeer**—*pop pl* MI-6
Lapeer, Lake—*reservoir* MI-6
Lapeer and Sanilac Drain—*canal* MI-6
Lapeer Camp—*locale* MI-6
Lapeer Ch—*church* NY-2
Lapeer Country Club—*other* MI-6
**Lapeer (County)**—*pop pl* MI-6
Lapeer County Courthouse—*hist pl* MI-6
*Lapeer Heights* MI-6
**Lapeer Heights**—*pop pl* MI-6
Lapeer (historical)—*locale* KS-7
*Lapeer Junction* MI-6
Lapeer Park—*park* MI-6
Lapeer State Game Area—*park* MI-6
Lapeer State Home—*building* MI-6
**Lapeer (Town of)**—*pop pl* NY-2
**Lapeer (Township of)**—*pop pl* MI-6
*Lapehu* HI-9
Lapehu Point—*cape* HI-9
**Lapel**—*pop pl* IN-6
La Pela Windmill—*locale* TX-5
Lapel Elementary and HS—*school* IN-6
*Lapell* IN-6
Lapell Cem—*cemetery* VT-1
**La Penusca** —*pop pl* TX-5
La Peregrina—*summit* PR-3
Laperell Creek—*stream* MI-6
La Perouse, Mount—*summit* AK-9
La Perouse Bay (Keoneoio Bay)—*bay* HI-9
La Perouse Glacier—*glacier* AK-9
LaPet Creek—*stream* LA-4
La Petite Acad—*school* (4) FL-3
La Petite Child Care Center—*school* FL-3
La Petra—*locale* NM-5
**Lapeyrouse**—*pop pl* LA-4
Lapeyrouse Canal—*canal* (2) LA-4
Lapeyrouse Oil and Gas Field—*oilfield* LA-4
Lapham—*locale* AZ-5
**Lapham**—*pop pl* TX-5
Lapham Bay—*bay* VT-1
**Lapham Bay**—*pop pl* VT-1
Lapham Branch—*stream* MI-6
Lapham Brook—*stream* (2) ME-1
Lapham Canyon—*valley* CO-8
Lapham Creek—*stream* OR-9
Lapham Creek—*stream* WA-9
Lapham Dam—*dam* OR-9
Lapham Hill—*summit* WI-6
Lapham Island—*island* VT-1
Lapham Junction—*locale* WI-6
Lapham-Patterson House—*hist pl* GA-3
Lapham Pond—*lake* RI-1
Lapham Ranch—*locale* OR-9
Lapham Rsvr—*reservoir* OR-9
Lapham Sch—*school* IL-6
Lapham Sch—*school* (2) MI-6
Lapham Sch—*school* WI-6
Laphams Mills—*locale* (2) NY-2
Lapham Tank—*reservoir* AZ-5
Laphan Ditch—*canal* MT-8
**La Pica**—*pop pl* (3) PR-3
Lapice Oil Field—*oilfield* LA-4
Lapidea—*locale* PA-2
**Lapidea**—*pop pl* PA-2
**Lapidea Hills**—*pop pl* PA-2
**Lapidum**—*pop pl* MD-2
La Piedad Cem—*cemetery* TX-5
La Piedad Cementerio Numero Dos—*cemetery* TX-5
La Piedad Cementerio Numero Uno—*cemetery* TX-5
La Piedra—*summit* PR-3
La Piedra Well—*well* TX-5
La Pierre Coulee—*valley* MT-8
Lapile—*locale* AR-4
Lapile Cem—*cemetery* AR-4
*Lapile Creek* AR-4
Lapile (Township of)—*fmr MCD* AR-4
Lapin Creek—*stream* CO-8
*La Pine* AL-4
*Lapine* OR-9
**Lapine**—*pop pl* (2) AL-4
**Lapine**—*pop pl* LA-4
**La Pine**—*pop pl* OR-9
Lapine, Bayou—*stream* LA-4
Lapine Brake—*swamp* LA-4
LaPine Ch—*church* AL-4
Lapine Ch—*church* LA-4
*Lapine Creek* LA-4
La Pine Sch—*school* OR-9
Lapine Sch (historical)—*school* AL-4
La Pine Siding—*locale* OR-9
Lapine State Rec Area—*area* OR-9
La Pine State Rec Area—*park* OR-9
Lapington Store (historical)—*locale* AL-4
**Lapis**—*pop pl* CA-9
Lapis Canyon—*valley* NM-5
*Lap Island* FM-9
Lapis Point—*summit* NM-5
Lapis Siding—*locale* CA-9
Lapis Valley—*valley* NM-5

La Pita Well—*well* TX-5
Lapka Cem—*cemetery* MO-7
*La Place* LA-4
*Laplace* MN-6
**La Place**—*pop pl* AL-4
**La Place**—*pop pl* IL-6
**LaPlace**—*pop pl* IL-6
**La Place**—*pop pl* LA-4
**Laplace**—*pop pl* LA-4
LaPlace Cem—*cemetery* IL-6
La Place Ch—*church* AL-4
Laplace Oil and Gas Field—*oilfield* LA-4
La Place Post Office (historical)—*building* AL-4
**La Placita**—*pop pl* NM-5
**La Placita**—*pop pl* PR-3
La Placita De Abajo District—*hist pl* NM-5
*La Placita Shopping Center* AZ-5
La Placita Village Shop Ctr—*locale* AZ-5
La Plaisance Bay—*bay* MI-6
La Plaisance Creek—*stream* MI-6
Laplan Canyon—*valley* UT-8
Lapland—*area* KY-4
**Lapland**—*pop pl* IN-6
**Lapland**—*pop pl* KS-7
Lapland Pond—*lake* NY-2
Lapland Sch—*school* VT-1
**La Plant**—*pop pl* SD-7
**LaPlant**—*pop pl* SD-7
La Plant Archeol Site—*hist pl* MO-7
*La Plant Corners* NY-2
La Plante Coulee—*valley* MT-8
*La Plants Corners* NY-2
*Laplap Passage* MP-9
*Laplata* TN-4
**La Plata**—*pop pl* CO-8
**La Plata**—*pop pl* MD-2
**LaPlata**—*pop pl* MD-2
**La Plata**—*pop pl* MO-7
**LaPlata**—*pop pl* MO-7
**LaPlata**—*pop pl* NM-5
**La Plata**—*pop pl* PR-3
La Plata Basin—*basin* CO-8
La Plata Canyon—*valley* NV-8
La Plata Canyon—*valley* UT-8
LaPlata Cem—*cemetery* NM-5
La Plata Gulch—*valley* CO-8
La Plata Indian Ditch—*canal* NM-5
La Plata JHS—*school* TX-5
**La Plata (Laplata)**—*pop pl* NM-5
La Plata Mine—*mine* UT-8
La Plata Mtns—*range* CO-8
La Plata Peak—*summit* CO-8
Laplata PO—*locale* NM-5
La Plata Powerplant—*other* CO-8
La Plata River—*stream* CO-8
La Plata River—*stream* NM-5
La Plata River and Cherry Creek Ditch—*canal* CO-8
La Plata (ruins)—*locale* UT-8
La Plata (site)—*locale* NV-8
La Plata Spring—*spring* NV-8
La Plata Township—*civil* MO-7
La Platte—*fmr MCD* NE-7
**LaPlatte**—*pop pl* NE-7
LaPlatte Cem—*cemetery* NE-7
La Platte River—*stream* VT-1
*La Platt River* VT-1
La Playa—*CDP* PR-3
**La Playa**—*pop pl* CA-9
**La Playa**—*pop pl* PR-3
La Plaza—*locale* FL-3
La Plaza—*locale* NM-5
**La Plaza**—*pop pl* PR-3
La Plaza Ditch—*canal* NM-5
La Plaz Coulee—*valley* MT-8
**La Plena**—*pop pl* PR-3
Lapley Hollow—*valley* WV-2
*Laplop River* VT-1
*Laplotte River* VT-1
*La Pluie* MN-6
La Pluma Sch—*school* CA-9
*Laplume* PA-2
**La Plume**—*pop pl* PA-2
La Plume Slough—*gut* WI-6
La Plume Station—*locale* PA-2
**La Plume (Township of)**—*pop pl* PA-2
Lapoel Creek—*stream* WA-9
Lapoel Point—*cape* WA-9
Lapoile Creek—*stream* AR-4
**Lapoint**—*pop pl* UT-8
Lapoint Cem—*cemetery* UT-8
**La Pointe**—*pop pl* WI-6
La Pointe Brook—*stream* VT-1
La Pointe Cem—*cemetery* WI-6
La Pointe Indian Cemetery—*hist pl* WI-6
La Pointe Island—*island* MI-6
LaPointe Light—*locale* WI-6
La Pointe Light Station—*hist pl* WI-6
LaPointe Park—*park* NJ-2
La Pointe Park—*park* WI-6
**La Pointe (Town of)**—*pop pl* WI-6
LaPoint Sch—*school* UT-8
Lapolds Ford (historical)—*locale* PA-2
La Polka—*civil* CA-9
La Polvadera Canyon—*valley* NM-5
LaPomkeag Lake—*lake* ME-1
LaPomkeag Stream—*stream* ME-1
La Pompa Draw—*valley* NM-5
Lapon Canyon—*valley* NV-8
Lapond Lake—*lake* MN-6
Lapon Meadows—*flat* NV-8
*Laport* KS-7
*La Porte* CO-8
*Laporte* IA-7
**La Porte**—*pop pl* CA-9
**Laporte**—*pop pl* CO-8
**LaPorte**—*pop pl* IN-6
**La Porte**—*pop pl* IN-6
**Laporte**—*pop pl* MI-6
**Laporte**—*pop pl* MN-6
**Laporte**—*pop pl* (2) OH-6
**Laporte**—*pop pl* PA-2
**La Porte**—*pop pl* TX-5
Laporte, Bayou—*stream* MS-4
La Porte Air Natl Guard Station—*building* TX-5
La Porte Ave Sch—*school* CO-8
La Porte Bald Mtn—*summit* CA-9
Laporte Borough—*civil* PA-2
Laporte Cem—*cemetery* MI-6
LaPorte Cem—*cemetery* NE-7

La Porte Cem—*cemetery* TX-5
La Porte Cem—*cemetery* VT-1
Laporte Cemetary—*cemetery* CO-8
**La Porte City**—*pop pl* IA-7
La Porte City Station—*hist pl* IA-7
LaPorte City Town Hall and Fire Station—*hist pl* IA-7
LaPorte Coulee—*valley* ND-7
**La Porte County**—*pop pl* IN-6
LaPorte Creek—*stream* MI-6
Laporte Fair Grounds—*locale* IN-6
La Porte Hollow—*valley* PA-2
La Porte HS—*school* IN-6
La Porte Municipal Airp—*airport* IN-6
La Porteria —*locale* CA-9
Laportes Pond—*reservoir* RI-1
**Laporte (Township of)**—*pop pl* PA-2
La Posa Long-Term Visitor Area—*park* AZ-5
La Posa Plain—*plain* AZ-5
La Posita Windmill—*locale* TX-5
**La Posta**—*pop pl* CO-8
La Posta Canyon—*valley* CO-8
La Posta Creek—*stream* CA-9
La Posta Ind Res—*reserve* CA-9
La Posta Quemada Ranch—*locale* AZ-5
*La Posta Quemado Canyon* AZ-5
La Posta Ranch—*locale* CA-9
La Posta Service—*locale* CA-9
La Posta Valley—*valley* CA-9
La Poudre Pass—*gap* CO-8
La Poudre Pass Creek—*stream* CO-8
La Poudre Pass Ranger Station—*locale* CO-8
La Poudre Pass Trail—*trail* CO-8
Lapover Lake—*lake* OR-9
Lapover Meadows—*flat* OR-9
Lapover Ranch—*locale* OR-9
La Poynor Sch—*school* TX-5
**Lappans**—*pop pl* MD-2
Lappatatong Creek—*stream* NJ-2
Lappatubby Creek—*stream* MS-4
*Lappatuppy Creek* MS-4
Lapp Ditch—*canal* OH-6
Lapperell—*locale* OH-6
Lapperell Ch—*church* OH-6
Lapperell Hollow—*valley* OH-6
Lappi Lake—*lake* MT-8
*Lappin* KS-7
Lappin, Lake—*lake* FL-3
Lappin Cem—*cemetery* IL-6
Lappin Cem—*cemetery* TN-4
Lapping Memorial Park—*park* IN-6
Lappin-Hayes Block—*hist pl* WI-6
*Lappin Lake* MI-6
Lappin Run—*stream* PA-2
Lapp Log House—*hist pl* PA-2
*Lapp Pond* NY-2
Lapps—*locale* PA-2
Lapps Cem—*cemetery* PA-2
Lapp Spring—*spring* MO-7
**La Pradera**—*pop pl* PR-3
*La Pradera Park* AZ-5
Laprades Mill—*locale* VA-3
LaPraire Township—*civil* SD-7
**La Prairie**—*pop pl* IL-6
**La Prairie**—*pop pl* MN-6
La Prairie Center—*locale* IL-6
**Laprairie Center**—*pop pl* IL-6
LaPrairie Grange Hall No. 79—*hist pl* WI-6
LaPrairie Park—*park* WI-6
**La Prairie (Town of)**—*pop pl* WI-6
**La Prairie Township**—*pop pl* SD-7
**La Prairie (Township of)**—*pop pl* IL-6
**La Prairie (Township of)**—*pop pl* MN-6
La Precita Windmill—*locale* TX-5
Lap Reef—*bar* TX-5
Lap Reef Bank—*bar* TX-5
*La Prel Creek* WY-8
**Laprele**—*pop pl* WY-8
La Prele Creek—*stream* WY-8
La Prele Gorge—*valley* WY-8
La Prele Main Canal—*canal* WY-8
LaPrele Ranger Station—*locale* WY-8
La Prele Rsvr—*reservoir* WY-8
LaPrele Sch—*school* WY-8
**La Presa**—*pop pl* CA-9
La Presa Azul—*reservoir* TX-5
La Presa Crossing—*locale* TX-5
La Presa Grande—*reservoir* TX-5
La Presita Windmill—*locale* TX-5
Laprey Valley—*locale* VI-3
La Preza Windmill—*locale* TX-5
La Primaria Sch—*school* CA-9
La Prudera Park—*park* AZ-5
**La Pryor**—*pop pl* TX-5
La Pryor (CCD)—*cens area* TX-5
La Pryor Cem—*cemetery* TX-5
Lapsley Run—*stream* VA-3
Lapsley Run Ch—*church* VA-3
Lapstone Ledge—*bar* ME-1
Lapstone Point—*cape* NY-2
**La Puebla**—*pop pl* NM-5
La Puente—*civil* CA-9
**La Puente**—*pop pl* CA-9
**La Puente**—*pop pl* NM-5
**La Puente**—*pop pl* PR-3
La Puente Community Ditch—*hist pl* NM-5
La Puente Hist Dist—*hist pl* NM-5
La Puente HS—*school* CA-9
**La Puerta**—*pop pl* TX-5
La Puerta Grande—*valley* NM-5
*La Puerta Limita* AZ-5
La Puerta Springs—*spring* CA-9
Lapula Rsvr—*reservoir* WY-8
La Punta Larga—*island* TX-5
La Punta Windmill—*locale* TX-5
La Puntilla—*cape* PR-3
La Pureta Windmill—*locale* TX-5
La Purisema Ch—*church* NM-5
*La Purisima Concepcion* AZ-5
*La Purisima Concepcion* TX-5
La Purisima Concepcion—*civil* CA-9
La Purisima Mission—*hist pl* CA-9
La Purisima Mission State Historical Monument—*park* CA-9
La Purisima Windmill—*locale* TX-5
La Purisma Windmill—*locale* TX-5
*La Purissima Concepcion* CA-9
**La Push**—*pop pl* WA-9
**Lapwai**—*pop pl* ID-8
Lapwai Creek—*stream* ID-8

Lapwai Lake—*lake* ID-8
Lapwai State Game Farm—*park* ID-8
Lapwai Valley—*valley* ID-8
Lapworth Creek—*stream* IA-7
Lapwusi—*locale* FM-9
Laqua Buttes—*summit* CA-9
Laque Hollow—*valley* WI-6
La Questa de Trujillo—*summit* NM-5
**Laquey**—*pop pl* MO-7
Laquey Hollow—*valley* MO-7
Laquey Sch—*school* MO-7
Laquey School (abandoned)—*locale* MO-7
Laquin—*locale* PA-2
LaQuinta—*hist pl* OK-5
**La Quinta**—*pop pl* CA-9
**La Quinta**—*pop pl* PR-3
La Quinta Channel—*channel* TX-5
La Quinta HS—*school* CA-9
La Quinta Island—*island* TX-5
La Quinta Ranch—*locale* CA-9
La Quinta Turning Basin—*harbor* TX-5
*La Quitani Valley* AZ-5
*La Quituni* AZ-5
Laquna del Padre—*reservoir* NM-5
Laqunita Tank—*reservoir* NM-5
Lara—*locale* VA-3
Larabee—*locale* CA-9
**Larabee**—*pop pl* PA-2
Larabee Buttes—*summit* CA-9
Larabee Creek—*stream* CA-9
Larabee Gulch—*valley* MT-8
Larabee Lake—*lake* MI-6
Larabee Meadows—*flat* ID-8
**Larabee Ranch**—*pop pl* CA-9
Larabee Sch—*school* IL-6
Larabee Valley—*valley* CA-9
Laraby Creek—*stream* MI-6
Lara Cem—*cemetery* TX-5
Laradon Hall—*school* CO-8
**La Rae Estates Subdivision**—*pop pl* UT-8
*Laragon Lake* WI-6
Lara Kendall Elem Sch—*school* TN-4
La Rambla—*flat* CA-9
**La Rambla**—*pop pl* PR-3
**Laramie**—*pop pl* WY-8
Laramie, Marcus, House—*hist pl* MO-7
Laramie Country Club—*locale* WY-8
*Laramie Creek* WY-8
Laramie Creek—*stream* WA-9
Laramie Downtown Hist Dist—*hist pl* WY-8
Laramie Lake—*lake* CO-8
Laramie Mtns—*range* WY-8
Laramie Park—*park* IL-6
Laramie Peak—*summit* WY-8
Laramie Poudre Tunnel—*tunnel* CO-8
*Laramie Range* WY-8
*Laramie Reservoir* OH-6
Laramie River—*stream* CO-8
Laramie River—*stream* WY-8
Laramie River Ditch No 1—*canal* WY-8
Laramie Sch—*school* IL-6
*Laramore* KS-7
Laramore Ditch—*canal* IN-6
Laramore Mtn—*summit* NY-2
**La Rampla**—*pop pl* PR-3
Laran—*locale* LA-4
Laran Cem—*cemetery* LA-4
Larand—*locale* CO-8
Larand School—*locale* CO-8
**La Ratina**—*pop pl* PR-3
Lara Tower—*summit* MA-1
Laraway Gulch—*valley* ID-8
Laraway Lake—*lake* MI-6
Laraway Mtn—*summit* VT-1
Larb Creek—*stream* MT-8
Larb Hills—*spring* (3) MT-8
Larb Hollow—*valley* UT-8
Larc Camp—*locale* OH-6
**Larch**—*pop pl* MI-6
Larch Ave Sch—*school* CA-9
Larch Bay—*bay* AK-9
Larch Butte—*summit* ID-8
Larch Clover Park—*park* CA-9
*Larch Creek* MT-8
*Larch Creek* OR-9
Larch Creek—*stream* (4) ID-8
Larch Creek—*stream* MN-6
Larch Creek—*stream* (2) MT 8
Larch Creek—*stream* (3) OR-9
Larch Creek—*stream* WA-9
Larch Cristensen Spring—*spring* UT-8
Larches, The—*hist pl* MA-1
Larch Hill—*summit* MT-8
Larch Hill Pass—*gap* MT-8
Larch Hill Trail—*trail* MT-8
**Larch (historical)**—*pop pl* OR-9
*L'Archipel de Saint Lazare* MH-9
Larch Lake—*lake* MN-6
Larch Lake—*lake* (2) WA-9
Larch Lakes—*lake* WA-9
Larch Lakes Creek—*stream* WA-9
**Larchland**—*pop pl* IL-6
Larchmiller Park—*park* OK-5
Larchmont—*hist pl* MA-1
**Larchmont**—*pop pl* DE-2
**Larchmont**—*pop pl* NY-2
**Larchmont**—*pop pl* PA-2
**Larchmont**—*pop pl* (2) VA-3
**Larchmont**—*pop pl* WA-9
Larchmont Gardens—*uninc pl* NY-2
Larchmont Gardens Park—*park* FL-3
Larchmont Harbor—*bay* NY-2
**Larchmont Knolls**—*pop pl* MD-2
*Larchmont Lake* CT-1
Larchmont Manor—*uninc pl* NY-2
**Larchmont North**—*pop pl* NY-2
**Larchmont Riviera**—*pop pl* CA-9
Larchmont Sch—*school* CA-9
Larchmont Sch—*school* MD-2
Larchmont Sch—*school* OH-6
Larchmont Sch—*school* VA-3
Larchmont Sch—*school* WA-9
**Larchmont Square**—*pop pl* PA-2
**Larchmont Terrace**—*pop pl* VA-3
Larchmound—*hist pl* IL-6
Larch Mountain Trail—*trail* ID-8
Larch Mtn—*summit* (2) ID-8
Larch Mtn—*summit* (2) OR-9
Larch Mtn—*summit* (2) WA-9
Larch Park—*park* MI-6

Larch Pass—*gap* WA-9
Larch Point—*summit* MT-8
Larch Summit—*summit* OR-9
**Larchwood**—*pop pl* IA-7
**Larchwood**—*pop pl* MT-8
Larchwood Cem—*cemetery* IA-7
Larchwood Cem—*cemetery* MT-8
Larchwood Township—*fmr MCD* IA-7
Larc Lane Sch—*school* OH-6
Larcom Oil Field—*oilfield* KS-7
Lard, Lake—*lake* PA-2
Lard Branch—*stream* MS-4
Lard Branch—*stream* TX-5
Lard Brook—*stream* ME-1
Lard Camp Trail—*trail* ME-1
Lard Can Slough—*swamp* FL-3
Lard Creek—*stream* AL-4
*Lardecia Church* AL-4
**Lardent**—*pop pl* AL-4
*Lard Hollow* MS-4
**Lardin**—*pop pl* PA-2
**Lardintown**—*pop pl* PA-2
Lardintown Run—*stream* PA-2
Lard Lake—*lake* MI-6
Lard Lake—*lake* OR-9
Lard Lake (historical)—*lake* IA-7
Lardner, Ring, House—*hist pl* MI-6
**Lardo**—*pop pl* ID-8
Lard Pond—*lake* (3) ME-1
*Lards Creek* KS-7
Lards Ranch—*locale* NM-5
Lard Tank—*reservoir* NM-5
*Lard Town* PA-2
Lardy State Public Shooting Area—*park* SD-7
Laredo—*locale* MT-8
**Laredo**—*pop pl* MO-7
**Laredo**—*pop pl* TX-5
Laredo AFB—*military* TX-5
Laredo Air Force Station—*military* TX-5
Laredo (CCD)—*cens area* TX-5
Laredo Flats—*flat* MT-8
Laredo International Airp—*airport* TX-5
Laredo Junior Coll—*school* TX-5
La Redonda Lake—*lake* TX-5
Laredo Sch—*school* CO-8
*Lareent L'Argent Landing* MS-4
**La Reforma**—*pop pl* TX-5
La Reforma Oil And Gas Field—*oilfield* TX-5
Lare Glacier—*glacier* AK-9
La Reine—*locale* VI-3
Lareine HS—*school* MD-2
**Lar-Eli-Do (subdivision)**—*pop pl* MS-4
Laremies, Kannat—*stream* MH-9
*Laremies Ravine* MH-9
**Larence Cordrey Subdivision**—*pop pl* DE-2
Larence Swamp—*swamp* MA-1
La Rendija—*other* NM-5
**Lares**—*pop pl* PR-3
Lares (Barrio)—*fmr MCD* PR-3
Lares (Municipio)—*civil* PR-3
Lares (Pueblo)—*fmr MCD* PR-3
La Retama Windmill—*locale* TX-5
Laretta, Lake—*lake* ND-7
**La Reusitte**—*pop pl* LA-4
Larey Draw—*valley* WY-8
Larga, Canada —*valley* CA-9
Larga, Laguna—*lake* (2) TX-5
Larga, Sierra—*summit* TX-5
**Largain**—*pop pl* GA-3
Larg Branch—*stream* MS-4
Large—*locale* PA-2
Large, Bayou du—*stream* LA-4
*Large Agingan Beach* MH-9
*Large Bayou* FL-3
Large Branch—*stream* NC-3
Large Branch—*stream* TN-4
Large Brown Rock—*island* OR-9
Large Cem—*cemetery* (2) VA-3
Large Creek—*stream* MT-8
Large Drain—*stream* IN-6
Large Green Island—*island* ME-1
Large Henry Lake—*lake* MN-6
Large Island—*island* TN-4
Large Lake—*lake* OR-9
*Large Marpo* MH-9
Large Meadow—*flat* CA-9
Largen Cem—*cemetery* VA-3
**Largent** *pop pl* (2) WV-2
Largent Cem—*cemetery* (2) TN-4
Largent Cem—*cemetery* TX-5
Largent Creek—*stream* IL-6
Largent Creek—*stream* TX-5
Largent Hollow—*valley* TN-4
Largent Pond—*lake* OR-9
Largent Sch—*school* MT-8
Largent Spring—*spring* TN-4
Largent Windmill—*locale* TX-5
Large Park—*park* CA-9
*Large Pigeon Lake* WI-6
*Larger Church* MS-4
Larger Creek—*stream* WA-9
*Larger Cross Roads* NJ-2
*Larger Horton Pond* NC-3
*Large Run* PA-2
Larges Ch—*church* TN-4
Large Sch—*school* VA-3
*Larges Chapel United Methodist Church* TN-4
Large Station—*building* PA-2
Large Whiskers Tank—*reservoir* AZ-5
Large Williams Spring—*spring* NV-8
*Large wWest Bay* FM-9
Largilliere Creek—*stream* ID-8
*Largin Lake* WI-6
Largis Dam—*dam* SD-7
Largo—*locale* CA-9
Largo—*locale* MN-6
Largo—*locale* (2) NM-5
**Largo**—*pop pl* FL-3
**Largo**—*pop pl* MD-2
**Largo**—*pop pl* TN-4
Largo, Arroyo—*stream* CA-9
Largo, Key—*island* FL-3
Largo, Lake—*reservoir* NC-3
Largo Canyon—*valley* CO-8
Largo Canyon—*valley* (4) NM-5
Largo Central Elem Sch—*school* FL-3
Largo Ch of the Nazarene—*church* FL-3
*Largo Creek* AZ-5
Largo Creek—*stream* AK-9
Largo Creek—*stream* AZ-5

Las Vegas HS Academic Bldg and Gymnasium—*hist pl* NV-8
Las Vegas Iron Works—*hist pl* NM-5
Las Vegas Mormon Fort—*hist pl* NV-8
Las Vegas Mormon Fort (Boundary Increase)—*hist pl* NV-8
Las Vegas Natl Wildlife Ref—*park* NM-5
Las Vegas Plaza—*hist pl* NM-5
Las Vegas Ranch—*locale* AZ-5
Las Vegas Range—*range* NV-8
Las Vegas Ranger District—*forest* NV-8
Las Vegas RR and Power Company Bldg—*hist pl* NM-5
Las Vegas Springs—*hist pl* NV-8
*Las Vegas Square* NV-8
Las Vegas (town)—*uninc pl* NM-5
Las Vegas Township—*inact MCD* NV-8
**Las Vegas Town (West Las Vegas Post Office)**—*pop pl* NM-5
Las Vegas Valley—*valley* NV-8
Las Vegas Valley Lateral—*canal* NV-8
*Las Vegas Wash* NV-8
Las Vegas Wash—*stream* NV-8
Las Vegitas Spring—*spring* NM-5
Las Ventanas—*area* NM-5
Las Ventanas Ridge—*ridge* NM-5
Las Ventanas Windmill—*locale* NM-5
Las Viboras Windmill—*locale* TX-5
Las Vigas Creek—*stream* CO-8
**Las Villas (subdivision)**—*pop pl* (2) AZ-5
**Las Vinas**—*pop pl* CA-9
Las Virgenes—*civil* CA-9
Las Virgenes Canyon—*valley* CA-9
Las Virgenes Creek—*stream* CA-9
Las Virgenes School (abandoend)—*locale* CA-9
**Las Viudas**—*pop pl* PR-3
Laswell—*locale* VA-3
Laswell Branch—*stream* IL-6
Laswell Tank—*reservoir* NM-5
Las Yeguas Canyon—*valley* NM-5
Las Yeguas Ranch—*locale* CA-9
**Las Yescas**—*pop pl* TX-5
La Taca Windmill—*locale* TX-5
**Latah**—*pop pl* WA-9
Latah Cem—*cemetery* WA-9
*Latah Creek* ID-8
*Latah Creek* WA-9
Lataiuer Post Office (historical)—*building* MS-4
Lata Mtn—*summit* AS-9
Latan Bend—*bend* MO-7
Latanes—*locale* VA-3
Latania, Bayou—*stream* LA-4
Latania Bayou—*stream* LA-4
Latania Hill—*summit* LA-4
Latania Lake—*lake* LA-4
Latanier—*locale* LA-4
Latanier, Bayou—*stream* LA-4
Latanier Bayou—*stream* LA-4
Latanier Ch—*church* LA-4
Latanier Ditch—*canal* LA-4
Latanier Island—*island* LA-4
LaTart Sch—*school* WI-6
Latax Rocks—*bar* AK-9
La Taza Windmill—*locale* TX-5
Latch—*locale* TX-5
**Latcha**—*pop pl* OH-6
Latchaw Creek—*stream* NY-2
Latchaw Creek—*stream* PA-2
Latchaw Mine—*mine* CO-8
*Latchaw Run* PA-2
Latchel Branch—*stream* MO-7
Latch Hollow—*valley* AR-4
**Latchie**—*pop pl* OH-6
Latchie Branch—*stream* AL-4
Latchum Creek—*stream* MD-2
Latchum Sch—*school* IN-6
Latch Valley—*valley* WI-6
Late Creek—*stream* MT-8
Lateer Cem—*cemetery* PA-2
Late Lake—*lake* MT-8
Lately Prairie—*flat* OR-9
La Tembladera, Charca—*basin* PR-3
Latenache, Bayou—*stream* LA-4
Latenache Drainage Canal, Bayou—*canal* LA-4
Late Point—*cape* AK-9
Late Point—*cape* GU-9
Lateral—*canal* (2) CA-9
Lateral, A—*canal* AZ-5
Lateral A—*canal* (4) CA-9
Lateral A—*canal* ID-8
Lateral A—*canal* WA-9
Lateral A—*canal* WY-8
Lateral A Canal—*canal* NC-3
Lateral A-six—*canal* CA-9
Lateral B—*canal* (4) CA-9
Lateral B—*canal* CO-8
Lateral B—*canal* OR-9
Lateral B—*canal* WA-9
Lateral B—*canal* WY-8
Lateral B 1—*canal* ID-8
Lateral B-2—*canal* AZ-5
Lateral B-2—*canal* ID-8
Lateral C—*canal* CA-9
Lateral C—*canal* CO-8
Lateral C—*canal* (2) ID-8
Lateral C—*canal* OR-9
Lateral C—*canal* WA-9
Lateral C—*canal* WY-8
Lateral Canal D—*canal* NC-3
Lateral Canal E—*canal* NC-3
Lateral Canal F—*canal* NC-3
Lateral Canal G—*canal* NC-3
Lateral Canal H—*canal* NC-3
*Lateral Canal No. 2* AR-4
Lateral Canyon—*valley* ID-8
Lateral Creek—*stream* (2) MI-6
Lateral C 1—*canal* ID-8
Lateral C 5—*canal* ID-8
Lateral C 6—*canal* ID-8
Lateral D—*canal* (2) ID-8
Lateral D—*canal* WY-8
Lateral Ditch No 1—*canal* IA-7
Lateral Ditch No 2—*canal* MO-7
Lateral Ditch No 3—*canal* MO-7
Lateral Ditch Number Three—*canal* MO-7
Lateral D 1—*canal* ID-8
Lateral D-23—*canal* WY-8
Lateral D-56—*canal* WY-8
Lateral E—*canal* ID-8
Lateral E—*canal* WA-9
Lateral East—*canal* CA-9
Lateral East-Seven—*canal* CA-9
Lateral Eight—*canal* (4) CA-9
Lateral Eight-A—*canal* CA-9
Lateral Eighteen—*canal* CA-9
Lateral Eleven—*canal* CA-9
Lateral E Pilot Butte Canal—*canal* OR-9
Lateral E 1—*canal* ID-8
Lateral E-65—*canal* NE-7
Lateral F—*canal* (2) CA-9
Lateral F—*canal* ID-8
Lateral F—*canal* OR-9
Lateral F—*canal* WA-9
Lateral Five—*canal* (3) CA-9
Lateral Five A—*canal* CA-9
Lateral Five B—*canal* (2) CA-9
Lateral Five East—*canal* CA-9
Lateral Five North—*canal* CA-9
Lateral Five South—*canal* CA-9
Lateral Five West—*canal* CA-9
Lateral Fortyseven—*canal* CO-8
Lateral Fortythree—*canal* CA-9
Lateral Four—*canal* (3) CA-9
Lateral Four A—*canal* CA-9
Lateral Four North—*canal* (2) CA-9
Lateral Four South—*canal* CA-9
Lateral Fourteen—*canal* CA-9
Lateral Four West—*canal* CA-9
Lateral F 1—*canal* ID-8
Lateral G—*canal* CA-9
Lateral G—*canal* WA-9
Lateral Glacier—*glacier* AK-9
Lateral H—*canal* (2) CA-9
Lateral H—*canal* ID-8
Lateral H—*canal* ND-7
Lateral H—*canal* OR-9
Lateral H-Three—*canal* CA-9
Lateral H-103—*canal* WY-8
Lateral H-105—*canal* WY-8
Lateral H-141—*canal* WY-8
Lateral H-65—*canal* WY-8
Lateral H-71—*canal* WY-8
Lateral H-79—*canal* WY-8
Lateral H-89—*canal* WY-8
Lateral I—*canal* ID-8
Lateral Ironstone Canal—*canal* CO-8
Lateral J—*canal* CA-9
Lateral J—*canal* ID-8
Lateral J—*canal* WA-9
Lateral J Pilot Butte Canal—*canal* OR-9
*Lateral K* MT-8
Lateral K—*canal* CA-9
Lateral K—*canal* ID-8
Lateral K—*canal* ND-7
Lateral K—*canal* WA-9
Lateral L—*canal* ND-7
Lateral L—*canal* WA-9
Lateral Lateral Number Five And One Half—*canal* CA-9
Lateral M—*canal* CA-9
Lateral M—*canal* NM-5
Lateral M—*canal* ND-7
Lateral N—*canal* ID-8
Lateral N—*canal* ND-7
Lateral N—*canal* WA-9
Lateral Nine—*canal* (4) CA-9
Lateral No 1—*canal* (4) AR-4
Lateral No 1—*canal* ID-8
Lateral No 1—*canal* (2) IA-7
Lateral No 1—*canal* (7) MO-7
Lateral No 1—*canal* NE-7
Lateral No 1—*canal* (2) UT-8
Lateral No 1—*canal* WY-8
Lateral No 1 (historical)—*canal* MO-7
Lateral No 10—*canal* AR-4
Lateral No 10—*canal* IA-7
Lateral No 10—*canal* MO-7
Lateral No 10—*canal* NE-7
Lateral No 11—*canal* AR-4
Lateral No 12—*canal* AR-4
Lateral No 13—*canal* AR-4
Lateral No 13—*canal* NE-7
*Lateral No. 15* ID-8
Lateral No 15—*canal* AR-4
Lateral No 15—*canal* ID-8
Lateral No 16—*canal* AR-4
Lateral No 17—*canal* ID-8
Lateral No 18—*canal* MO-7
Lateral No 18—*canal* NE-7
Lateral No 1.8—*canal* WA-9
Lateral No 19—*canal* MO-7
Lateral No 2—*canal* (3) AR-4
Lateral No 2—*canal* IA-7
Lateral No 2—*canal* (6) MO-7
Lateral No 2—*canal* (2) NE-7
Lateral No 2—*canal* (2) UT-8
Lateral No 2—*canal* WY-8
Lateral No 2 Moores Ditch—*canal* AR-4
Lateral No 20—*canal* NE-7
Lateral No 21—*canal* ID-8
Lateral No 2 1/2—*canal* UT-8
Lateral No 27—*canal* MO-7
*Lateral No. 3* AR-4
Lateral No 3—*canal* (4) AR-4
Lateral No 3—*canal* (3) MO-7
Lateral No 3—*canal* NE-7
Lateral No 3—*canal* (2) UT-8
Lateral No 4—*canal* (2) AR-4
Lateral No 4—*canal* (2) MO-7
Lateral No 4—*canal* NE-7
Lateral No 4—*canal* UT-8
*Lateral No. 5* AR-4
Lateral No 5—*canal* (2) AR-4
Lateral No 5—*canal* (2) UT-8
*Lateral No. 6* AR-4
Lateral No 6—*canal* AR-4
Lateral No 6—*canal* MO-7
Lateral No 6—*canal* NE-7
Lateral No 7—*canal* AR-4
Lateral No 7—*canal* MO-7
Lateral No 8—*canal* AR-4
Lateral No 8—*canal* CA-9
Lateral No 8—*canal* IA-7
Lateral No 8—*canal* NE-7
Lateral No 9—*canal* AR-4
Lateral No 9—*canal* NE-7
Lateral Number Eight—*canal* CA-9
Lateral Number Eleven—*canal* CA-9
Lateral Number Fifteen Ditch—*canal* IN-6
Lateral Number Five—*canal* CA-9
Lateral Number Five—*canal* IN-6
Lateral Number Five Ditch—*canal* IN-6
Lateral Number Four—*canal* CA-9
Lateral Number Four—*canal* IN-6
Lateral Number Four And One Half—*canal* CA-9
Lateral Number Nine—*canal* CA-9
Lateral Number One—*canal* (3) CA-9
Lateral Number Seven—*canal* (2) CA-9
Lateral Number Seventy-seven—*canal* IN-6
Lateral Number Six—*canal* (2) CA-9
Lateral Number Three—*canal* (2) CA-9
Lateral Number Three-B—*canal* CA-9
Lateral Number Twelve—*canal* CA-9
*Lateral Number Two* MO-7
Lateral Number Two—*canal* CA-9
*Lateral Number 1* IN-6
*Lateral Number 2* MO-7
Lateral O—*canal* ID-8
Lateral One—*canal* (4) CA-9
Lateral P—*canal* WA-9
Lateral P-27.0- A—*canal* WY-8
Lateral P-27.0- B—*canal* WY-8
Lateral P-27.0- C—*canal* WY-8
Lateral P-27.0- D—*canal* WY-8
Lateral P-28.2—*canal* WY-8
Lateral P-31.7—*canal* WY-8
Lateral P-31.7- B—*canal* WY-8
Lateral P-32.8—*canal* WY-8
Lateral P-34.0—*canal* WY-8
Lateral P-34.9—*canal* WY-8
Lateral R—*canal* WA-9
Lateral R—*canal* WY-8
Lateral R Canal—*canal* TX-5
Lateral R-9 N—*canal* WY-8
Lateral S—*canal* WA-9
Lateral S—*canal* WY-8
Lateral Sch (historical)—*school* MO-7
Lateral Seven—*canal* CA-9
Lateral Seven-A—*canal* CA-9
Lateral Site Number Eight—*reservoir* TX-5
Lateral Site Number Eleven—*reservoir* TX-5
Lateral Site Number Four—*reservoir* TX-5
Lateral Site Number Nine—*reservoir* TX-5
Lateral Site Number Seven—*reservoir* TX-5
Lateral Site Number Six—*reservoir* TX-5
Lateral Site Number Ten—*reservoir* TX-5
Lateral Site Number Three—*reservoir* TX-5
Lateral Site Number Twelve—*reservoir* TX-5
Lateral Site Number Two—*reservoir* (2) TX-5
Lateral Six A—*canal* CA-9
Lateral Six East—*canal* CA-9
Lateral Sixe B—*canal* (2) CA-9
Lateral Six North—*canal* CA-9
Lateral Six South—*canal* CA-9
Lateral Sixteen—*canal* CA-9
Lateral Six (upper)—*canal* CA-9
Lateral S-2—*canal* ID-8
Lateral T—*canal* ID-8
Lateral T—*canal* WA-9
Lateral T—*canal* WY-8
Lateral T Canal—*canal* TX-5
Lateral Thirteen—*canal* CA-9
Lateral Three—*canal* (4) CA-9
Lateral Three North—*canal* CA-9
Lateral Three South—*canal* CA-9
Lateral Three West—*canal* CA-9
Lateral Twelve—*canal* CA-9
Lateral Two—*canal* (4) CA-9
Lateral Two-A—*canal* CA-9
Lateral Two A—*canal* CA-9
Lateral Two South—*canal* CA-9
Lateral U—*canal* WY-8
Lateral U Canal—*canal* TX-5
Lateral V—*canal* ID-8
Lateral V—*canal* WY-8
Lateral V 1—*canal* ID-8
Lateral V-2—*canal* ID-8
Lateral V-3—*canal* ID-8
Lateral W—*canal* WY-8
Lateral W 113—*canal* WY-8
Lateral W 135—*canal* WY-8
Lateral W-9—*canal* ID-8
Lateral X—*canal* ID-8
Lateral X-1—*canal* ID-8
Lateral X-4—*canal* ID-8
Lateral Y—*canal* ID-8
Lateral Y-1—*canal* ID-8
Lateral Y-2—*canal* ID-8
Lateral Y-3—*canal* ID-8
Lateral Z—*canal* ID-8
Lateral 1—*canal* WA-9
Lateral 10—*canal* CA-9
Lateral 10 Main—*canal* NE-7
Lateral 11 Main—*canal* NE-7
Lateral 12 Main—*canal* NE-7
Lateral 13 Main—*canal* NE-7
Lateral 14 Main—*canal* NE-7
Lateral 1465—*canal* ID-8
*Lateral 15 of Leman-Birk-Newcomer Ditch* IN-6
Lateral 197—*canal* OR-9
Lateral 2—*canal* WA-9
Lateral 2 A—*canal* ID-8
Lateral 2 B—*canal* ID-8
Lateral 21 Main—*canal* NE-7
Lateral 213—*canal* ID-8
Lateral 24—*canal* NE-7
Lateral 3—*canal* WA-9
Lateral 4—*canal* WA-9
Lateral 4A—*canal* AR-4
Lateral 6 A—*canal* AR-4
Lateral 6 B—*canal* AR-4
Lateral 614—*canal* ID-8
Lateral 7 Main—*canal* NE-7
Lateral 702—*canal* ID-8
Lateral 702-A—*canal* ID-8
**La Terraza (subdivision)**—*pop pl* (2) AZ-5
La Terrera—*ridge* NM-5
*Lates Run* PA-2
Latest Out Mine—*mine* ID-8
La Tete Bay—*bay* LA-4
La Tetita Peak—*summit* NM-5
*La Tex* TX-5
Latex—*locale* LA-4
**Latex**—*pop pl* TX-5
**Latexo**—*pop pl* TX-5
Latexo Cem—*cemetery* TX-5
Latexo Community Center—*building* TX-5
Latexo Sch—*school* TX-5
Latham—*locale* AL-4
Latham—*locale* IA-7
Latham—*locale* NC-3
Latham—*locale* OK-5
Latham—*locale* WY-8
**Latham**—*pop pl* IL-6
**Latham**—*pop pl* KS-7
**Latham**—*pop pl* KY-4
**Latham**—*pop pl* MO-7
**Latham**—*pop pl* NY-2
**Latham**—*pop pl* OH-6
**Latham**—*pop pl* OR-9
**Latham**—*pop pl* TN-4
Latham-Baker House—*hist pl* NC-3
Latham Bog—*swamp* CT-1
Latham Branch—*stream* AL-4
Latham Branch—*stream* KY-4
Latham Brook—*stream* RI-1
Latham Bungalow—*hist pl* ID-8
Latham Canyon—*valley* NM-5
Latham Cave—*cave* AL-4
Latham Cem—*cemetery* (2) AL-4
Latham Cem—*cemetery* KS-7
Latham Cem—*cemetery* MS-4
Latham Cem—*cemetery* MO-7
Latham Cem—*cemetery* NY-2
Latham Cem—*cemetery* TN-4
Latham Cem—*cemetery* TX-5
Latham Ch—*church* AL-4
Latham Chapel—*church* TN-4
**Latham Corners**—*pop pl* NY-2
*Latham Creek* AL-4
Latham Creek—*stream* GA-3
Latham Creek—*stream* NV-8
Latham Creek—*stream* NC-3
Latham Creek—*stream* TX-5
Latham Creek—*stream* WY-8
Latham Dam—*dam* SD-7
Latham Ditch—*canal* CO-8
Latham Draw—*valley* WY-8
Latham Elem Sch—*school* NC-3
Latham Gap Tank—*reservoir* NM-5
Latham Gulch—*valley* MT-8
Latham Hollow—*valley* ID-8
Latham House—*hist pl* NC-3
Latham Island—*island* FL-3
Latham Lake—*lake* NC-3
Latham Lake—*reservoir* SD-7
Latham Lake Dam—*dam* MS-4
Latham Memorial Ch—*church* AL-4
Latham Mill—*locale* MO-7
Latham Narrows—*gap* AL-4
Latham Oil Field—*oilfield* KS-7
Latham Park—*park* IA-7
**Latham Park**—*pop pl* IL-6
**Latham Park**—*pop pl* NC-3
Latham Pass—*gap* WY-8
Latham Playground—*park* MI-6
Latham Pond—*lake* NY-2
Latham Pond Dam—*dam* MS-4
Latham Ranch—*locale* NM-5
Latham Ranch—*locale* SD-7
Latham River—*stream* GA-3
Latham Sch—*school* NY-2
Latham Sch—*school* OR-9
Latham Sch—*school* SD-7
*Lathams Chapel Baptist Ch* TN-4
**Lathams Corners**—*pop pl* NY-2
Latham Slough—*gut* CA-9
Latham Spring—*spring* ID-8
Latham Spring—*spring* NV-8
Latham Spring—*spring* WY-8
Latham Springs Bible Camp—*locale* TX-5
**Latham Town**—*pop pl* NC-3
Latham Township—*civil* SD-7
Latham United Methodist Church—*hist pl* AL-4
**Lathamville**—*pop pl* AL-4
*Lathan* AL-4
Lathan Ranch—*locale* NM-5
Lathan Spring—*spring* TN-4
Lathan Spring Branch—*stream* TN-4
Lath Branch—*stream* KS-7
Lath Branch Cem—*cemetery* KS-7
Lath Branch Sch—*school* KS-7
Lathea Ch—*church* NC-3
Lathe Branch—*stream* LA-4
**Lathem**—*pop pl* SC-3
Lathem Cem—*cemetery* SC-3
*Lathem Methodist Church* AL-4
Lathem Ridge—*ridge* WV-2
Lathem Ridge Cem—*cemetery* WV-2
**Lathemtown**—*pop pl* GA-3
Lathemtown (CCD)—*cens area* GA-3
Lathen Hill—*summit* TN-4
Latheran Creek—*stream* OK-5
Lather Branch—*stream* NC-3
Lather Mtn—*summit* OR-9
Lathers Sch—*school* MI-6
Lathert Canyon—*valley* NM-5
Lathin Cem—*cemetery* TN-4
Lathley Hollow—*valley* OH-6
L A Thompson Pond Dam—*dam* MS-4
Lathram Chapel—*church* FL-3
*Lathram River* GA-3
*Lathrop* PA-2
Lathrop—*locale* MI-6
Lathrop—*locale* OH-6
**Lathrop**—*pop pl* AL-4
**Lathrop**—*pop pl* CA-9
**Lathrop**—*pop pl* MO-7
Lathrop, Bryan, House—*hist pl* IL-6
Lathrop, Dr. Daniel, Sch—*hist pl* CT-1
Lathrop, Dr. Joshua, House—*hist pl* CT-1
Lathrop, J. V., House—*hist pl* CO-8
Lathrop, Mount—*summit* AK-9
*Lathrop Academy* MO-7
Lathrop Bayou—*bay* FL-3
Lathrop Brook—*stream* CT-1
Lathrop Canyon—*valley* UT-8
Lathrop Creek—*stream* OR-9
Lathrope Sch (historical)—*school* MO-7
Lathrop Family Practice Heliport—*airport* MO-7
Lathrop Glacier—*glacier* OR-9
Lathrop Gulch—*valley* WA-9
Lathrop Hall—*hist pl* WI-6
Lathrop Heath—*swamp* ME-1
Lathrop House—*hist pl* CA-9
Lathrop HS—*school* AK-9
Lathrop JHS—*school* CA-9
Lathrop Lookout Tower—*locale* AL-4
Lathrop-Mathewson-Ross House—*hist pl* CT-1
Lathrop-Munn Cobblestone House—*hist pl* WI-6
Lathrop Point—*cape* FL-3
Lathrop Sch—*school* IL-6
Lathrop Sch—*school* (2) OH-6
Lathrop State Park—*park* CO-8
Lathrop Street Elem Sch—*school* PA-2
*Lathrops Well* NV-8
*Lathrops Wells* NV-8
Lathrop Township—*civil* MO-7
**Lathrop (Township of)**—*pop pl* PA-2
*Lathrop Wells* (2) NV-8
Lathrop Wells Cone—*summit* NV-8
*Lathrum Spring* WY-8
*Lathrup* MI-6
Lathrup Gulf—*valley* NY-2
Lathrup Sch—*school* MI-6
**Lathrup Village**—*pop pl* MI-6
Laths Pond—*lake* NY-2
La Tice Branch—*stream* LA-4
La Tierra Amarilla—*area* NM-5
Latigo Canyon—*valley* (2) CA-9
*Latigo Creek* OR-9
Latigo Creek—*stream* OR-9
Latigo Lake—*lake* OR-9
Latigo Ranch—*locale* NM-5
Latigo Tank—*reservoir* TX-5
La Tijera—*uninc pl* CA-9
La Tijera Sch—*school* CA-9
**La Tijera (Scissors)**—*pop pl* TX-5
Latimer—*locale* IA-7
Latimer—*locale* OH-6
Latimer—*locale* SC-3
Latimer—*locale* UT-8
**Latimer**—*pop pl* IA-7
**Latimer**—*pop pl* KS-7
**Latimer**—*pop pl* MS-4
Latimer, William and Etta, House—*hist pl* TX-5
Latimer Brook—*stream* CT-1
Latimer Cem—*cemetery* KS-7
Latimer Cem—*cemetery* OH-6
Latimer Cem—*cemetery* (2) TN-4
Latimer Ch—*church* MS-4
**Latimer (County)**—*pop pl* OK-5
Latimer Creek—*stream* IL-6
**Latimer Estates**—*pop pl* DE-2
Latimer Ford—*locale* MS-4
Latimer Gulch—*valley* CA-9
Latimer Hill—*summit* CT-1
Latimer Hill—*summit* MA-1
Latimer JHS—*school* PA-2
Latimer-Johnson Cem—*cemetery* TN-4
Latimer Lake—*lake* MN-6
Latimer Lookout Tower—*locale* MS-4
Latimer Park—*park* WI-6
Latimer Playground—*park* OK-5
Latimer Sch—*hist pl* PA-2
Latimer Sch—*school* CA-9
Latimer Shoal—*bar* VA-3
Latimer Siding—*locale* VA-3
Latimer Springs—*spring* TN-4
**Latimore**—*pop pl* PA-2
Latimore Branch—*stream* MS-4
Latimore Ch—*church* PA-2
Latimore Creek—*stream* IL-6
Latimore Creek—*stream* PA-2
Latimore Sch (historical)—*school* MO-7
Latimore Tank—*reservoir* AZ-5
**Latimore (Township of)**—*pop pl* PA-2
Latin—*uninc pl* CA-9
Latin America Bible Institute—*school* CA-9
Latin American Assembly of God Ch—*church* UT-8
Latin American Bible Institute—*school* TX-5
*La Tinaoca* AZ-5
La Tina Ranch—*locale* TX-5
Latin Bay—*bay* SD-7
Latino Americano Park—*park* AZ-5
Latin Sch—*school* IN-6
La Tinta Basin—*basin* CA-9
La Tinta Hill—*summit* CA-9
Latiolais, Alexandre, House—*hist pl* LA-4
Latir Cem—*cemetery* NM-5
Latir Creek—*stream* (2) NM-5
Latir Lakes—*lake* NM-5
Latir Mesa—*summit* NM-5
Latir Peak—*summit* NM-5
*Latis Langua* TX-5
*Latis Lengua* TX-5
*Latis Lingo* TX-5
*Latis Lingua* TX-5
Latite Ridge—*ridge* UT-8
Latium—*locale* TX-5
Latium Cem—*cemetery* TX-5
Latlrop Cem—*cemetery* OK-5
Latman Lake—*lake* CO-8
Latner Branch—*stream* (2) AL-4
Latner Cem—*cemetery* GA-3
*Lato* MP-9
Lato—*locale* AL-4
Latoback Island—*island* MP-9
Latoka, Lake—*lake* MN-6
*Latoka Lake* MN-6
La Toma Crosscut Canal (historical)—*canal* AZ-5
Laton—*locale* KS-7
**Laton**—*pop pl* CA-9
*Latona* AL-4
*Latona* CA-9
Latona—*locale* IL-6
Latona Ave Sch—*school* CA-9
Latona Town Hall—*building* ND-7
**Latona Township**—*pop pl* ND-7
Laton (CCD)—*cens area* CA-9
**Laton Hill**—*pop pl* AL-4
*Laton Hill Baptist Church* AL-4
Laton Hill Cem—*cemetery* AL-4
Laton Hill Ch—*church* AL-4
Latonia—*locale* WV-2
**Latonia**—*pop pl* KY-4
**Latonia**—*pop pl* MS-4
**Latonia Lakes**—*pop pl* KY-4
Latonia Post Office (historical)—*building* MS-4
Latonia Racetrack—*other* KY-4
Laton Mine—*mine* CA-9
Laton Point—*summit* OR-9
Laton Swamp—*stream* VA-3
Latopie Lake—*lake* CA-9
La Tordilla Windmill—*locale* TX-5
**La Torre**—*pop pl* PR-3
La Torre (Barrio)—*fmr MCD* PR-3
La Torrecilla—*summit* PR-3
La Torre Well—*well* TX-5
**La Tosca**—*pop pl* PR-3
Latouche (Aban'd)—*locale* AK-9
*La Touche de la Cote Bucanieus* KS-7
Latouche Glacier—*glacier* AK-9
Latouche Island—*island* AK-9
Latouche Passage—*channel* AK-9
Latouche Peak—*summit* AK-9
**Latour**—*pop pl* AR-4
**Latour**—*pop pl* MO-7
LaTour, Alexis, House—*hist pl* LA-4
Latour Baldy—*summit* ID-8
Latour Butte—*summit* CA-9
*La Tour (corporate name Latour)* MO-7
Latour Creek—*stream* ID-8
**Latourell**—*pop pl* OR-9
Latourell Creek—*stream* OR-9
*Latourelle Creek* OR-9
*Latourelle Falls* OR-9
*Latourelle Falls Creek* OR-9
*Latourelle Prairie* OR-9
Latourell Falls—*falls* OR-9
**Latourell Falls**—*pop pl* OR-9
Latourell Prairie—*flat* OR-9
Latourette, Charles David, House—*hist pl* (2) OR-9
LaTourette House—*hist pl* NY-2
La Tourette Park—*park* NY-2
Latour Fire Station—*locale* CA-9
**Latour Junction**—*pop pl* AR-4
Latour Peak—*summit* ID-8
Latour State For—*forest* CA-9
Latour Trail—*trail* CA-9
La Toutena Mary Creek—*stream* OR-9
La Toutena Mary Spring—*spring* OR-9
**La Trappe**—*pop pl* PA-2
La Trappe Creek—*stream* MD-2
La Trenca Windmill—*locale* TX-5
La Trinidad Mine—*mine* CA-9
La Trinidad Well—*well* TX-5
Latrobe—*locale* WV-2
**Latrobe**—*pop pl* CA-9
**Latrobe**—*pop pl* PA-2
Latrobe Airp—*airport* PA-2
Latrobe Borough—*civil* PA-2
Latrobe Country Club—*locale* PA-2
Latrobe Creek—*stream* CA-9
Latrobe Elem Sch—*school* PA-2
Latrobe Hosp—*hospital* PA-2
*Latrobe HS* PA-2
Latrobe JHS—*school* PA-2
Latrobe Park—*park* MD-2
Latrobe Reservoir Dam—*dam* PA-2
Latrobe Rsvr—*reservoir* PA-2
**La Trocha**—*pop pl* PR-3
Latshaw Cem—*cemetery* IN-6
**Latta**—*pop pl* IN-6
**Latta**—*pop pl* OK-5
**Latta**—*pop pl* SC-3
Latta Arcade—*hist pl* NC-3
Latta Brook—*stream* NY-2
Latta (CCD)—*cens area* SC-3
**Latta Grove**—*pop pl* PA-2
Latta Grove Ch—*church* PA-2
Latta Grove Sch (abandoned)—*school* PA-2
Latta Hist Dist No. 1—*hist pl* SC-3
Latta Hist Dist No. 2—*hist pl* SC-3
Latta House—*hist pl* NC-3
Latta House—*hist pl* TN-4
Latta Lake—*lake* IN-6
Latta Landing Strip—*airport* KS-7
Latta Lookout Tower—*locale* SC-3
Latta Northwest Oil Field—*oilfield* KS-7
Latta Oil Field—*oilfield* KS-7
Latta Park—*park* NC-3
Latta Run—*stream* PA-2
**Lattasburg**—*pop pl* OH-6
Lattas Cem—*cemetery* TX-5
Latta Sch—*school* IL-6
Latta Sch—*school* OK-5
Lattas Creek—*stream* IN-6
Lattas Creek—*stream* TX-5
Lattas Ranch Trail—*trail* WY-8
**Lattasville**—*pop pl* OH-6
Latta Tank—*reservoir* AZ-5
Latta Tanks—*reservoir* NM-5
Lattaville—*locale* OH-6
Lattawanna, Lake—*reservoir* OK-5
**Latta Yard**—*pop pl* IN-6
Latte Heights—*CDP* GU-9
Latter Creek—*stream* MI-6
*Latter Day Saint Baptist Ch* AL-4
Latter Day Saint Hosp—*hospital* ID-8
Latter Day Saints Cem—*cemetery* IA-7
Latter Day Saints Cem—*cemetery* NE-7
Latter-Day Saints Ch—*church* IL-6
Latter Day Saints Ch—*church* IN-6
Latter Day Saints Ch—*church* (3) MS-4
Latter-Day Saints Ch—*church* MO-7
Latter Day Saints Ch—*church* MO-7
Latterday Saints Ch—*church* TN-4
Latter Day Saints Ch—*church* WY-8
**Latterday Saints Church**—*pop pl* NC-3
Latter Day Saints Church Records Storage Area—*locale* UT-8
Latter Day Saints Hosp—*hospital* UT-8
Latter Day Saints Temple—*church* AZ-5
Lattery Canal—*canal* LA-4
Latte Stone—*other* GU-9
Latte Stone Park—*park* GU-9
Lattice Bridge—*bridge* WI-6
Lattice Cottage—*hist pl* NH-1
Lattie Coor Sch—*school* AZ-5
Lattimer—*locale* WV-2
**Lattimer**—*pop pl* PA-2
Lattimer Hill—*summit* NY-2
**Lattimer Mines**—*pop pl* PA-2
Lattimer Sch—*school* SC-3
**Lattimore**—*pop pl* NC-3
Lattimore, John, House—*hist pl* NC-3
Lattimore Cem—*cemetery* NC-3
Lattimore Sch—*school* NC-3
Lattin-Crandall Octagon Barn—*hist pl* NY-2
**Lattingtown**—*pop pl* NY-2
Lattin Hill—*summit* CT-1
*Lattins Landing* CT-1
Lattins Landing—*locale* CT-1

Laurel Grove Cem—cemetery ... WA-9
Laurel Grove Ch—church ... NC-3
Laurel Grove Ch—church ... SC-3
Laurel Grove Ch—church ... TN-4
Laurel Grove Ch—church (3) ... VA-3
Laurel Grove Ch—church (2) ... WV-2
Laurel Grove Creek—stream ... GA-3
**Laurel Grove Estates**—pop pl ... VA-3
Laurel Grove (historical)—locale ... AL-4
Laurel Grove Lookout Tower—locale ... TN-4
Laurel Grove-North Cemetery—hist pl ... GA-3
**Laurel Grove Plantation**—pop pl ... LA-4
Laurel Grove Sch—school ... MI-6
Laurel Grove Sch—school (2) ... PA-2
Laurel Grove Sch—school ... TN-4
Laurel Grove Sch (abandoned)—school ... PA-2
Laurel Grove Sch (historical)—school ... TN-4
Laurel Grove-South Cemetery—hist pl ... GA-3
Laurel Gulch ... TN-4
Laurel Gulch—valley (2) ... CA-9
Laurel Gully Brook—stream ... NJ-2
Laurel Hall—hist pl ... MA-1
Laurel Hall Sch—school ... CA-9
**Laurel Harbor**—pop pl ... NJ-2
Laurel Harness Racing Track—other ... MD-2
Laurel Heights ... MO-7
**Laurel Heights**—pop pl ... VA-3
Laurel Heights—uninc pl ... TX-5
Laurel Heights—uninc pl ... WA-9
Laurel Heights Sch (historical)—school ... TN-4
Laurel Heights State Sanitarium—hospital ... CT-1
Laurel Hill ... CT-1
Laurel Hill ... MA-1
Laurelhill ... MS-4
Laurel Hill ... PA-2
Laurel Hill ... RI-1
Laurel Hill ... SC-3
Laurelhill ... TN-4
Laurel Hill—hist pl ... LA-4
Laurel Hill—hist pl ... SC-3
Laurel Hill—locale ... SC-3
Laurel Hill—locale (3) ... TN-4
Laurel Hill—locale ... TX-5
**Laurel Hill**—pop pl ... FL-3
**Laurel Hill**—pop pl ... LA-4
**Laurelhill**—pop pl ... MS-4
**Laurel Hill**—pop pl ... MS-4
**Laurel Hill**—pop pl (3) ... NC-3
**Laurel Hill**—pop pl (3) ... PA-2
**Laurel Hill**—pop pl ... RI-1
**Laurel Hill**—pop pl (2) ... VA-3
Laurel Hill—range ... PA-2
Laurel Hill—ridge ... OR-9
Laurel Hill—summit ... CA-9
Laurel Hill—summit (2) ... CT-1
Laurel Hill—summit ... FL-3
Laurel Hill—summit (2) ... KY-4
Laurel Hill—summit ... MD-2
Laurel Hill—summit ... MA-1
Laurel Hill—summit ... NH-1
Laurel Hill—summit (2) ... NJ-2
Laurel Hill—summit (2) ... NY-2
Laurel Hill—summit ... NC-3
Laurel Hill—summit (4) ... PA-2
Laurel Hill—summit ... RI-1
Laurel Hill—summit (2) ... SC-3
Laurel Hill—summit ... VA-3
Laurel Hill—summit (2) ... WA-9
Laurel Hill—uninc pl ... NY-2
Laurel Hill—uninc pl ... PA-2
Laurel Hill Baptist Ch—church ... FL-3
Laurel Hill (CCD)—cens area ... FL-3
Laurel Hill Cem—cemetery ... AL-4
Laurel Hill Cem—cemetery ... CT-1
Laurel Hill Cem—cemetery ... DE-2
Laurel Hill Cem—cemetery ... FL-3
Laurel Hill Cem—cemetery (3) ... GA-3
Laurel Hill Cem—cemetery ... IL-6
Laurel Hill Cem—cemetery ... IN-6
Laurel Hill Cem—cemetery (2) ... IA-7
Laurel Hill Cem—cemetery ... KS-7
Laurel Hill Cem—cemetery ... KY-4
Laurel Hill Cem—cemetery ... ME-1
Laurel Hill Cem—cemetery (3) ... MA-1
Laurel Hill Cem—cemetery (2) ... MS-4
Laurel Hill Cem—cemetery ... MO-7
Laurel Hill Cem—cemetery (2) ... NE-7
Laurel Hill Cem—cemetery ... NH-1
Laurel Hill Cem—cemetery (2) ... NJ-2
Laurel Hill Cem—cemetery (2) ... NY-2
Laurel Hill Cem—cemetery ... OR-9
Laurel Hill Cem—cemetery (6) ... PA-2
Laurel Hill Cem—cemetery (2) ... SC-3
Laurel Hill Cem—cemetery ... TN-4
Laurel Hill Cem—cemetery (2) ... TX-5
Laurel Hill Cem—cemetery ... WV-2
Laurel Hill Cemeteries—cemetery ... PA-2
Laurel Hill Cemetery—hist pl ... PA-2
Laurel Hill Ch—church ... GA-3
Laurel Hill Ch—church (2) ... LA-4
Laurel Hill Ch—church (2) ... MS-4
Laurel Hill Ch—church (6) ... NC-3
Laurel Hill Ch—church ... OH-6
Laurel Hill Ch—church ... PA-2
Laurel Hill Ch—church (2) ... SC-3
Laurel Hill Ch—church ... TX-5
Laurel Hill Ch—church (8) ... VA-3
Laurel Hill Ch—church ... WV-2
Laurel Hill Creek—stream ... PA-2
Laurel Hill Creek Dam—dam ... PA-2
Laurel Hill Creek Rsvr—reservoir ... PA-2
Laurel Hill Dam ... NC-3
Laurel Hill Dam—dam ... NC-3
Laurel Hill Elem Sch—school ... NC-3
Laurel Hill Fire Tower—tower ... PA-2
Laurel Hill Furnace ... PA-2
Laurel Hill Furnace—hist pl ... PA-2
Laurel Hill Hist Dist—hist pl ... CT-1
Laurel Hill Lake—reservoir ... PA-2
Laurel Hill Lake—reservoir ... TN-4
Laurel Hill Lake Dam—dam ... PA-2
Laurel Hill Lake Dam—dam ... TN-4
Laurel Hill (Magisterial District)—fmr MCD ... WV-2
Laurel Hill Oil Field—oilfield ... MS-4
Laurel Hill Park—park ... MA-1
Laurel Hill Park—park ... OR-9
Laurel Hill Plantation—hist pl ... MS-4
Laurel Hill Plantation—locale ... LA-4
**Laurel Hill Plantation**—pop pl ... SC-3
Laurel Hill Plantation (historical)—locale ... MS-4
Laurel Hill Plantation (historical)—locale ... TN-4
Laurel Hill Point—cape ... SC-3
Laurel Hill Post Office ... TN-4
Laurelhill Post Office (historical)—building ... MS-4
Laurel Hill Presbyterian Church—hist pl ... NC-3
Laurel Hill RDA—hist pl ... PA-2
Laurel Hills ... WV-2
Laurel Hills—locale ... GA-3
**Laurel Hills**—pop pl ... NC-3
Laurel Hill Sch—school ... FL-3
Laurel Hill Sch—school ... IA-7
Laurel Hill Sch—school ... NJ-2
Laurel Hill Sch—school ... OR-9
Laurel Hill Sch—school ... SC-3
Laurel Hill Sch—school ... TN-4
Laurel Hill Sch—school ... WV-2
Laurel Hills Sch—school ... MO-7
**Laurel Hills (subdivision)**—pop pl ... AL-4
Laurel Hill State Park—park (2) ... PA-2
Laurel Hill Tabernacle—church ... PA-2
Laurel Hill (Township of)—fmr MCD ... NC-3
Laurel Hill Tunnel—tunnel ... PA-2
Laurel Hill United Pentecostal Church ... TN-4
Laurel Hill Village—locale ... PA-2
Laurel Hill Wildlife Mngmt Area—park ... TN-4
Laurel Hist Dist—hist pl ... DE-2
Laurel (historical)—locale ... KS-7
Laurel Hole Spring—spring ... AZ-5
Laurel Hollow ... AR-4
**Laurel Hollow**—pop pl ... NY-2
Laurel Hollow—valley ... KY-4
Laurel Hollow—valley ... OR-9
Laurel Hollow—valley (2) ... TN-4
Laurel Hollow—valley (4) ... VA-3
Laurel Hollow—valley (3) ... WV-2
**Laurel Homes**—pop pl ... NJ-2
Laurel Homes Hist Dist—hist pl ... OH-6
Laurel Hosp—hospital ... CA-9
Laurel HS—hist pl ... MD-2
Laurel HS—school ... MD-2
**Laurelhurst**—pop pl ... NJ-2
**Laurelhurst**—pop pl ... OR-9
**Laurelhurst**—pop pl ... WA-9
Laurelhurst Park—park ... OR-9
Laurelhurst Park—park ... WA-9
Laurelhurst Sch—school ... OR-9
Laurel Industrial Sch Hist Dist—hist pl ... VA-3
**Laurel Iron Works**—pop pl ... WV-2
Laurel Island—island ... GA-3
Laurel Island—island ... NH-1
Laurel-Jones County Library—building ... MS-4
Laurel Junction—locale ... PA-2
Laurel Junior Senior High School ... PA-2
Laurel Knob—summit (4) ... NC-3
Laurel Knob—summit ... WV-2
Laurel Knob Ch—church ... NC-3
Laurel Knob Gap—gap ... NC-3
Laurel Knob Mtn—summit ... NC-3
Laurel Knoll—summit ... SC-3
Laurella—locale ... PA-2
Laurel Lagoon Dam—dam ... MS-4
Laurel Lake ... CT-1
Laurel Lake ... MA-1
Laurel Lake ... MN-6
Laurel Lake ... NJ-2
Laurel Lake ... PA-2
Laurel Lake—lake (2) ... CA-9
Laurel Lake—lake (2) ... CT-1
Laurel Lake—lake ... MD-2
Laurel Lake—lake ... MI-6
Laurel Lake—lake ... MN-6
Laurel Lake—lake ... NH-1
Laurel Lake—lake (3) ... NJ-2
Laurel Lake—lake (3) ... NY-2
Laurel Lake—lake ... OR-9
Laurel Lake—lake ... PA-2
Laurel Lake—lake ... TX-5
Laurel Lake—lake ... VT-1
Laurel Lake—lake ... VA-3
Laurel Lake—lake ... WI-6
Laurel Lake—lake ... WY-8
**Laurel Lake**—pop pl ... NH-1
**Laurel Lake**—pop pl ... NJ-2
**Laurel Lake**—pop pl ... PA-2
Laurel Lake—reservoir ... GA-3
Laurel Lake—reservoir (2) ... MA-1
Laurel Lake—reservoir (3) ... NJ-2
Laurel Lake—reservoir (4) ... NC-3
Laurel Lake—reservoir (4) ... PA-2
Laurel Lake—reservoir (3) ... TN-4
Laurel Lake—reservoir ... WV-2
Laurel Lake Creek—stream ... PA-2
Laurel Lake Dam—dam (2) ... MA-1
Laurel Lake Dam—dam ... NJ-2
Laurel Lake Dam—dam (2) ... NC-3
Laurel Lake Dam—dam (2) ... TN-4
**Laurel Lake Estates (subdivision)**—pop pl ... NC-3
Laurel Lakes—lake ... CA-9
Laurel Lakes—lake ... KY-4
Laurel Lake Sch—school ... MA-1
Laurel Land Memorial Park (Cemetery)—cemetery (2) ... TX-5
Laurel Lane Sch—school ... NY-2
Laurella Sch (abandoned)—school ... PA-2
Laurel Lawn Cem—cemetery ... NJ-2
**Laurel Lea**—pop pl ... LA-4
Laurel Lea Ch—church ... LA-4
**Laurel Lea Subdivision**—pop pl ... UT-8
Laurel Ledge Sch—school ... CT-1
Laurel Lick—stream (2) ... WV-2
Laurel Lick Branch—stream ... KY-4
Laurel Lick Branch—stream ... TN-4
Laurel Lick Branch—stream ... WV-2
Laurel Lick Cem—cemetery ... WV-2
Laurel Lick Ch—church ... WV-2
Laurel Lick Run—stream ... OH-6
Laurel Lick Run—stream ... PA-2
Laurel Lick Run—stream (2) ... WV-2
Laurel Lick Run Trail—trail ... WV-2
Laurel Lick Trail—trail ... WV-2
Laurel Log Branch—stream ... NC-3
Laurelly Branch—stream (2) ... WV-2
Laurelly Fork—stream ... PA-2
Laurelly Hill Trail—trail ... PA-2
**Laurel Manor**—pop pl ... NJ-2
**Laurel Manor**—pop pl ... VA-3
Laurel Manor—uninc pl ... NJ-2
Laurel Marsh—swamp ... MI-6
Laurel Memorial Cem—cemetery ... NJ-2
Laurel Mill and Col. Jordan Jones House—hist pl ... NC-3
Laurel Mills—locale ... VA-3
Laurel Mine—mine ... CA-9
**Laurel Mobile Home Park (trailer park)**—pop pl ... DE-2
Laurel Mounds—hist pl ... MN-6
**Laurel Mountain**—pop pl ... PA-2
Laurel Mountain—ridge ... WV-2
Laurel Mountain Branch—stream ... NC-3
Laurel Mountain Cave—cave ... TN-4
Laurel Mountain Ch—church ... WV-2
Laurel Mountain Dam—dam ... TN-4
Laurel Mountain Lake—reservoir ... TN-4
Laurel Mountain Park—park ... PA-2
Laurel Mountain Ski Resort—locale ... PA-2
Laurel Mountain State Park—park ... PA-2
Laurel Mountain Trail—trail ... NC-3
**Laurel Mountain Village**—pop pl ... PA-2
Laurel Mount Boro—inactive ... PA-2
Laurel Mount Chapel—church ... PA-2
Laurel Mtn—summit (2) ... CA-9
Laurel Mtn—summit (4) ... NC-3
Laurel Mtn—summit ... OR-9
Laurel Mtn—summit ... PA-2
Laurel Mtn—summit (3) ... TN-4
Laurel Mtn—summit ... VA-3
Laurel Oak Cem—cemetery ... MO-7
Laurel Oak Country Club—other ... NJ-2
Laurel Park—park ... GA-3
Laurel Park—park ... OH-6
Laurel Park—park ... OR-9
Laurel Park—park ... VA-3
Laurel Park—park ... WV-2
**Laurel Park**—pop pl ... FL-3
**Laurel Park**—pop pl ... MA-1
**Laurel Park**—pop pl ... NJ-2
**Laurel Park**—pop pl (3) ... NC-3
**Laurel Park**—pop pl ... PA-2
**Laurel Park**—pop pl ... RI-1
**Laurel Park**—pop pl ... VA-3
Laurel Park Ch—church ... VA-3
Laurel Park Ch—church ... WV-2
Laurel Park Hill—summit ... CT-1
Laurel Park Lake—reservoir ... NC-3
Laurel Park Lake Dam—dam ... NC-3
**Laurel Park (Rutherton)**—pop pl ... PA-2
**Laurel Park (subdivision)**—pop pl ... TN-4
Laurel Park Village ... NC-3
**Laurel Park Villas (subdivision)**—pop pl ... NC-3
Laurel Patch Bald—summit ... NC-3
Laurelpatch Branch—stream ... KY-4
Laurelpatch Run—stream ... WV-2
Laurel-Petersville (CCD)—cens area ... KY-4
Laurel Pines Ch—church ... NC-3
Laurel Pines Country Club—other ... MD-2
Laurel Plains Sch—school ... NY-2
Laurel Point—cape ... NC-3
Laurel Point—cape ... SC-3
Laurel Point—cape ... VA-3
Laurel Point—cliff ... AL-4
**Laurel Point**—pop pl ... WV-2
Laurel Point Cem—cemetery ... PA-2
Laurel Point Cem—cemetery ... WV-2
Laurel Point Ch—church ... KY-4
Laurel Point Ch—church ... WV-2
Laurel Point Light House—tower ... NC-3
Laurel Point Sch—school ... PA-2
Laurel Pond—lake ... NJ-2
Laurel Post Office (historical)—building ... SD-7
Laurel Post Office (historical)—building ... TN-4
Laurel Prong—stream ... VA-3
Laurel Prong Trail—trail ... VA-3
Laurel Quarry—mine ... OR-9
Laurel Racetrack—other ... MD-2
Laurel-Rex Fire Company House—hist pl ... PA-2
Laurel Ridge ... WV-2
**Laurel Ridge**—pop pl ... LA-4
**Laurel Ridge**—pop pl ... OH-6
**Laurel Ridge**—pop pl ... TN-4
Laurel Ridge—ridge (3) ... KY-4
Laurel Ridge—ridge ... LA-4
Laurel Ridge—ridge (5) ... NC-3
Laurel Ridge—ridge ... OH-6
Laurel Ridge—ridge ... OR-9
Laurel Ridge—ridge (5) ... PA-2
Laurel Ridge—ridge ... SC-3
Laurel Ridge—ridge (3) ... TN-4
Laurel Ridge—ridge ... VA-3
Laurel Ridge—ridge ... WV-2
Laurel Ridge Camp—locale ... KY-4
Laurel Ridge Canal—canal ... LA-4
Laurel Ridge Ch—church ... PA-2
Laurel Ridge Dam—dam ... PA-2
Laurel Ridge Lake ... PA-2
Laurelridge Lake—reservoir ... PA-2
Laurel Ridge Oil and Gas Field—oilfield ... LA-4
**Laurel Ridge Plantation**—pop pl ... LA-4
Laurel Ridge Sch (abandoned)—school ... PA-2
Laurel Ridge Sch (historical)—school ... PA-2
Laurel Ridge Sports Lake ... PA-2
**Laurel Ridge Subdivision**—pop pl ... UT-8
Laurel Ridge Trail—trail ... PA-2
Laurel River ... DE-2
Laurel River—stream ... KY-4
Laurel River Ch—church ... KY-4
Laurel River Lake—reservoir ... KY-4
Laurel River Rsvr ... KY-4
Laurel River Sch—school ... KY-4
**Laurel Rock Acres**—pop pl ... NC-3
Laurel RR Station—hist pl ... MD-2
Laurel Ruff Center—school ... CA-9
Laurel Run ... OH-6
Laurel Run ... PA-2
Laurel Run ... TN-4
Laurel Run ... WV-2
**Laurel Run**—pop pl ... PA-2
**Laurel Run**—pop pl ... WV-2
Laurel Run—stream ... IN-6
Laurel Run—stream ... KY-4
Laurel Run—stream (8) ... MD-2
Laurel Run—stream (2) ... NJ-2
Laurel Run—stream (6) ... OH-6
Laurel Run—stream (62) ... PA-2
Laurel Run—stream ... TN-4
Laurel Run—stream (11) ... VA-3
Laurel Run—stream (71) ... WV-2
Laurel Run Borough—civil ... PA-2
Laurel Run Branch—stream ... PA-2
Laurel Run Cem—cemetery ... PA-2
Laurel Run Ch—church (3) ... PA-2
Laurel Run Cliffs—cliff ... TN-4
Laurel Run Creek ... TN-4
Laurel Run Dam—dam (2) ... PA-2
Laurel Run Hollow ... OH-6
Laurel Run Lake—lake ... PA-2
Laurel Run North Branch ... PA-2
Laurel Run Number Two Dam—dam ... PA-2
Laurel Run & Olivers Mills Stations—locale ... PA-2
Laurel Run Rsvr—reservoir (4) ... PA-2
Laurel Run Sch—school ... WV-2
Laurel Run Sch (abandoned)—school ... PA-2
Laurel Run Sch (historical)—school ... PA-2
Laurel Run Trail—trail (2) ... WV-2
Laurels, The—basin ... VA-3
Laurel Sch—school ... AL-4
Laurel Sch—school (10) ... CA-9
Laurel Sch—school ... CO-8
Laurel Sch—school ... CT-1
Laurel Sch—school ... IA-7
Laurel Sch—school (3) ... KY-4
Laurel Sch—school ... LA-4
Laurel Sch—school ... MI-6
Laurel Sch—school ... NY-2
Laurel Sch—school ... NC-3
Laurel Sch—school ... OH-6
Laurel Sch—school ... OR-9
Laurel Sch—school (2) ... PA-2
Laurel Sch—school (2) ... SD-7
Laurel Sch—school ... TN-4
Laurel Sch—school (2) ... VA-3
Laurel Sch—school ... WV-2
Laurel Sch Hist Dist—hist pl ... CO-8
Laurel Sch (historical)—school (2) ... PA-2
Laurel Sch (historical)—school ... TN-4
Laurel Senior HS—school ... DE-2
Laurel Shanty Landing—locale ... AL-4
Laurel Shoal ... WV-2
Laurel Shoal Run—stream ... WV-2
Laurel-Snow Trail—trail ... TN-4
Laurels Pine Well Cabins—locale ... MI-6
Laurel Spring—spring (4) ... AZ-5
Laurel Spring—spring (3) ... CA-9
Laurel Spring Ch—church ... NC-3
Laurel Spring Ch—church ... SC-3
Laurel Spring Ch—church ... TN-4
Laurel Springs—locale ... NC-3
**Laurel Springs**—pop pl ... NJ-2
**Laurel Springs**—pop pl ... TN-4
Laurel Springs—spring ... CA-9
Laurel Springs—spring ... GA-3
Laurel Springs Branch—stream ... VA-3
Laurel Springs Ch—church (3) ... NC-3
Laurel Springs Ch—church ... TN-4
Laurel Springs Ch—church ... VA-3
Laurel Springs Club—other ... CA-9
Laurel Springs Creek—stream ... VA 3
Laurel Springs Crossroads—locale ... VA-3
Laurel Springs Dam—dam ... NJ-2
Laurel Springs Gap—gap ... VA-3
Laurel Springs Sch—school ... NC-3
Laurel Springs Sch (historical)—school ... TN-4
**Laurel Springs (subdivision)**—pop pl ... NC-3
Laurel Spur—ridge ... TN-4
Laurel Spur Ridge—ridge ... NC-3
Laurel Stockyards—locale ... MT-8
Laurel Street Sch—school ... CA-9
Laurel Street Sch—school ... CT-1
Laurel Street Sch—school ... MA-1
Laurel Street Sch—school ... NY-2
Laurel Sudduth Bluff Cem—cemetery ... TX-5
Laurel Summit—locale ... PA-2
Laurel Summit Picnic Area—area ... PA-2
Laurel Summit State Park—park ... PA-2
Laurel Swamp—swamp ... PA-2
Laurel Swamp—swamp ... SC-3
Laurel Swamp Draft—valley ... PA-2
Laurel Swamp (historical)—swamp ... PA-2
Laurel Swamp Run—stream ... PA-2
Laurel Swamp Trail—trail ... PA-2
Laurel Swamp Union Ch—church ... PA-2
Laurelton ... NY-2
**Laurelton**—pop pl ... NJ-2
**Laurelton**—pop pl (2) ... NY-2
**Laurelton**—pop pl ... PA-2
**Laurelton Acres**—pop pl ... NJ-2
Laurelton Chapel—church ... NC-3
**Laurelton Heights**—pop pl ... NJ-2
Laurelton (local name for Brick Town)—other ... NJ-2
**Laurelton Park**—pop pl ... NJ-2
Laurelton State Village—locale ... PA-2
Laurelton State Village Farms—locale ... PA-2
Laurelton State Village Proper ... PA-2
Laurelton Yacht Basin—harbor ... NJ-2
Laurel Top—summit (2) ... NC-3
Laurel Top—summit (2) ... TN-4
Laurel Town ... DE-2
Laurel (Township of)—fmr MCD ... NC-3
**Laurel (Township of)**—pop pl ... IN-6
**Laurel (Township of)**—pop pl ... OH-6
Laurel Trail—trail ... WV-2
**Laurel Valley**—pop pl ... TN-4
Laurel Valley Canal—canal ... LA-4
Laurel Valley Ch—church ... VA-3
Laurel Valley Golf Club—other ... PA-2
Laurel Valley Golf Course—locale ... TN-4
Laurel Valley HS—school ... PA-2
Laurel Valley Mine—mine ... NC-3
**Laurel Valley Plantation**—pop pl ... LA-4
Laurel Valley Sugar Plantation—hist pl ... LA-4
Laurel View Ch—church ... TN-4
Laurel View River—stream ... GA-3
**Laurel Villa**—pop pl ... FL-3
Laurelville ... PA-2
**Laurelville**—pop pl ... OH-6
**Laurelville**—pop pl (3) ... PA-2
**Laurel Walk**—pop pl ... MD-2
Laurelwood ... TN-4
Laurelwood—hist pl ... SC-3
**Laurelwood**—pop pl ... OR-9
Laurelwood Acad—school ... OR-9
Laurelwood Cem—cemetery ... PA-2
Laurelwood Cem—cemetery ... SC-3
**Laurel Wood Estates (subdivision)**—pop pl ... TN-4
**Laurel Wood Hills (subdivision)**—pop pl ... NC-3
**Laurelwood Hills (subdivision)**—pop pl ... NC-3
**Laurel Wood Mobile Home Park**—pop pl ... PA-2
Laurelwood Municipal Golf Course—other ... OR-9
Laurelwood Park—park ... NV-8
Laurelwood Rsvr—reservoir ... OR-9
Laurel Woods—locale ... NC-3
Laurelwood Sch—school ... CA-9
**Laurel Woods (subdivision)**—pop pl ... PA-2
Laurel Yacht Club Boat Dock—locale ... TN-4
Laurely Fork—stream ... PA-2
Lauren ... ND-7
Lauren—locale ... MN-6
Laurence Branch—stream ... IN-6
Laurence Brook ... MA-1
Laurence Brook ... NH-1
Laurence Creek—stream ... CO-8
Laurence East, Lake—reservoir ... FL-3
Laurence G. Hanscom Field—other ... MA-1
**Laurence Harbor**—pop pl ... NJ-2
Laurence Knob—summit ... NC-3
Laurence Manning Acad—school ... SC-3
Laurence Pond—bay ... LA-4
Laurence Staff Pond—lake ... FL-3
Laurence West, Lake—lake ... FL-3
**Laurendine**—pop pl ... AL-4
**Lauren Farms**—pop pl ... DE-2
**Laurens**—pop pl ... IA-7
**Laurens**—pop pl ... NY-2
**Laurens**—pop pl ... SC-3
Laurens Academy ... TN-4
Laurens (CCD)—cens area ... SC-3
Laurens Cem—cemetery ... IA-7
**Laurens (County)**—pop pl ... GA-3
**Laurens (County)**—pop pl ... SC-3
Laurens County Courthouse—hist pl ... SC-3
**Laurens Hill**—pop pl ... GA-3
Laurens Hill Ch—church ... GA-3
Laurens Hist Dist—hist pl ... SC-3
Laurens Hist Dist (Boundary Increase)—hist pl ... SC-3
Laurens HS—school ... GA-3
Laurens Memorial Gardens—cemetery ... GA-3
Laurens Memorial Hosp—hospital ... GA-3
Laurens Public Library—hist pl ... IA-7
Laurens Road Ch—church ... SC-3
**Laurens (Town of)**—pop pl ... NY-2
Laurent Ditch—canal ... CO-8
Laurentian Divide—ridge ... MN-6
Laurent Lake—lake ... TX-5
Laurent Mine—mine ... NV-8
Laurents Point—cape ... LA-4
Laureola Sch—school ... CA-9
Lauretta Mine—mine ... NM-5
Laurette—locale ... IL-6
**Laurie**—pop pl ... MO-7
Laurie Cem—cemetery ... MO-7
Laurio Draw—valloy ... WY-8
Laurie Hollow—valley ... MO-7
Laurie Lakes—lake ... MI-6
Laurie Park—park ... IN-6
Laurier—locale ... WA-9
Laurier, Bayou—gut ... LA-4
Laurier, Lake—lake (2) ... LA-4
Laurier Bay—lake ... LA-4
Laurier Bayou—gut ... LA-4
Lauries Landing Airp—airport ... MO-7
Laurie Tank—reservoir ... NM-5
Laurietta—hist pl ... MS-4
**Laurin**—pop pl ... MT-8
**Laurinburg**—pop pl ... NC-3
Laurinburg-Maxton Airp—airport ... NC-3
**Laurinburg West**—pop pl ... NC-3
Laurin Canyon—valley ... MT-8
Laurin Cem—cemetery ... MT-8
Laurin Creek—stream ... MI-6
Laurin Hill—summit ... TX-5
**Laurin Lake (subdivision)**—pop pl ... NC-3
Lauritsen Cabin—hist pl ... AK-9
Lauritzen Canal—canal ... CA-9
**Laurium**—pop pl ... MI-6
Lauro Canyon—valley ... CA-9
Lauro Canyon Dam ... CA-9
Lauro Dam—dam ... CA-9
Lauronzon Canyon—valley ... OR-9
Laur Sch (historical)—school ... PA-2
Laurs Lake—reservoir ... MN-6
Laurs Lake State Wildlife Mngmt Area—park ... MN-6
Laurys ... PA-2
**Laurys Station**—pop pl ... PA-2
**Laurys Station (Laurys)**—pop pl ... PA-2
Lausaa Stream—stream ... AS-9
Lausanne Sch—school ... TN-4
**Lausanne (Township of)**—pop pl ... PA-2
Lausen Ranch—locale ... TX-5
Lauserica Camp—locale ... OR-9
Lausmann State Park—park ... OR-9
La Utah—summit ... NM-5
Lautaw Creek ... ID-8
Lautaw Creek ... WA-9
Lautenschlager Drain ... MI-6
Lauterman Creek—stream ... OR-9
Lauterman Creek—stream ... WI-6
Lauterman Lake—lake ... WI-6
Lauterwasser Creek—stream ... CA-9
Lauther Cem—cemetery ... LA-4
Lauthner Branch—stream ... TN-4
Lautner School—locale ... MI-6
Lautz—locale ... TX-5
Lautz Bay—bay ... WI-6
Lautzenhiser Airpark—airport ... IN-6
Lautzenhizer Ditch—canal ... IN-6
Lauulu—cape ... HI-9
Lauulu—summit ... HI-9
Lauulu Trail—trail ... HI-9
Lauvergne Island ... FM-9
Lauvers Ch—church ... PA-2
Lauvertown ... PA-2
Lauxman Farms—locale ... PA-2
Lauxmont Farms—locale ... PA-2
Lauzer Fish Pond Rsvr—reservoir ... WY-8
Lauzers Lake—lake ... MN-6
Lauzon Gulch—valley ... SD-7
Lauzon (historical)—locale ... SD-7
Lauzon Ranch—locale ... SD-7
Lauzon Sch—school ... SD-7
Lauzon Tank—reservoir ... AZ-5
Lava—locale (2) ... NM-5
Lava—locale ... NY-2
Lava—locale ... OR-9
Lava, Point—cape ... AK-9
Lava Bed Mountains—range ... CA-9
Lava Beds, The—lava ... NV-8
Lava Beds Camp—locale ... NV-8
Lava Beds Creek—stream ... NV-8
Lava Beds Natl Monmt—park ... CA-9
Lava Bed Spring ... OR-9
Lava Boulder Creek—stream ... CO-8
Lava Bridge—arch ... WA-9
Lava Butte ... AZ-5
Lava Butte—summit ... AZ-5
Lava Butte—summit ... CA-9
Lava Butte—summit (2) ... ID-8
Lava Butte—summit ... MT-8
Lava Butte—summit ... NV-8
Lava Butte—summit ... NM-5
Lava Butte—summit (2) ... OR-9
Lava Butte—summit ... WA-9
Lava Butte Geological Area—area ... OR-9
Lava Butte Lakes—lake ... ID-8
Lava Butte Trail—trail ... ID-8
Lava Butte Trail—trail ... WA-9
Lava Butte Wash—stream ... NV-8
**Lavaca**—pop pl ... AL-4
**Lavaca**—pop pl ... AR-4
Lavaca Bay—bay ... TX-5
Lavaca Bridge—bridge ... NE-7
Lavaca Cem—cemetery ... NE-7
**Lavaca (County)**—pop pl ... TX-5
Lavaca County Courthouse—hist pl ... TX-5
Lavaca Creek—stream ... TX-5
Lavaca Flats—flat ... NE-7
Lava Camp—locale ... CA-9
Lava Campground—park ... OR-9
Lava Camp Lake—lake ... OR-9
Lava Canyon—valley ... AZ-5
Lava Canyon—valley ... ID-8
Lava Canyon—valley ... TX-5
Lava Canyon Rapids—rapids ... AZ-5
Lava Cap Mine—mine ... CA-9
Lava Cap Rsvr—reservoir ... CA-9
Lavaca River—stream ... TX-5
Lava Cascades—lava ... ID-8
Lavaca Slough ... TX-5
Lava Cast For—forest ... OR-9
Lava Cast Forest—lava ... OR-9
Lava Cast Forest Campground—park ... OR-9
Lava Caves—cave ... WA-9
Lava Cem—cemetery ... NY-2
Lavacicle Cave—cave ... OR-9
Lavacicle Cave Geological Area ... OR-9
Lava Cliff—cliff ... AZ-5
Lava Cliff Rapids—rapids ... AZ-5
Lava Cove—bay ... AK-9
Lava Crater—summit ... NM-5
Lava Creek ... ID-8
Lava Creek—stream (4) ... AK-9
Lava Creek—stream ... AZ-5
Lava Creek—stream (2) ... CA-9
Lava Creek—stream (2) ... CO-8
Lava Creek—stream (5) ... ID-8
Lava Creek—stream (2) ... OR-9
Lava Creek—stream (2) ... WA-9
Lava Creek—stream (3) ... WY-8
Lava Creek Campground—locale ... WY-8
Lava Creek Campgrounds—locale ... WY-8
Lava Creek Canyon—valley ... WY-8
Lava Creek Ranch—locale ... WY-8
Lava Creek Spring—spring ... CA-9
Lava Creek Trail—trail ... WY-8
Lavada ... WV-2
Lava Dam—cliff ... UT-8
Lavade Draw—valley ... NM-5
Lavade Lake—lake ... NM-5
**Lavadero**—pop pl ... PR-3
Lavadero (Barrio)—fmr MCD ... PR-3
Lava Desert—plain ... UT-8
Lava Divide—ridge ... WA-9
Lava Dome—lava ... WA-9
Lavadoure Cem—cemetery ... OR-9
Lavadoure Community Hall—locale ... OR-9
Lavadoure Creek—stream ... OR-9
**Lavadoure (historical)**—pop pl ... OR-9
Lava Escondido Spring—spring ... TX-5
Lava Falls—cliff ... AZ-5
Lava Falls Airp—airport ... AZ-5
Lava Falls Rapids—falls ... AZ-5
Lava Flat—flat ... ID-8
Lava Flat—flat ... OR-9
Lava Flow Of 1750—lava ... HI-9
Lava Flow Of 1801—lava ... HI-9
Lava Flow Of 1840—lava (2) ... HI-9
Lava Flow Of 1843—lava ... HI-9
Lava Flow Of 1851—lava ... HI-9
Lava Flow Of 1852—lava ... HI-9
Lava Flow Of 1855—lava ... HI-9
Lava Flow Of 1859—lava ... HI-9
Lava Flow Of 1868—lava ... HI-9
Lava Flow Of 1880—lava ... HI-9
Lava Flow Of 1881—lava ... HI-9
Lava Flow Of 1887—lava ... HI-9
Lava Flow Of 1899—lava ... HI-9
Lava Flow Of 1907—lava ... HI-9
Lava Flow Of 1916—lava ... HI-9
Lava Flow Of 1919—lava ... HI-9
Lava Flow Of 1920—lava ... HI-9
Lava Flow Of 1921—lava ... HI-9
Lava Flow of 1922—lava ... HI-9
Lava Flow of 1923—lava ... HI-9
Lava Flow Of 1926—lava ... HI-9
Lava Flow Of 1935—lava ... HI-9
Lava Flow Of 1942—lava ... HI-9
Lava Flow Of 1949—lava ... HI-9
Lava Flow Of 1950—lava ... HI-9
Lava Flow Of 1954—lava ... HI-9
Lava Flow Of 1955—lava ... HI-9
Lava Flow of 1959—lava ... HI-9
Lava Flow Of 1961—lava ... HI-9
Lava Flow Of 1962—lava ... HI-9
Lava Flow of 1963—lava ... HI-9
Lava Flow Of 1963—lava ... HI-9
Lava Flow Of 1965—lava ... HI-9
Lava Flow Wash—stream ... CA-9
Lava Fork—stream ... AK-9
Lava Gate—area ... NM-5
Lava Glacier—glacier ... WA-9

Lava Gulch—valley ... ID-8
Lava Hills—lava ... CA-9
**Lava (historical)**—pop pl ... OR-9
**Lava Hot Springs**—pop pl ... ID-8
Lava Hot Springs Cem—cemetery ... ID-8
Lava Island—island ... AK-9
Lava Island—island ... OR-9
Lava Island Campground—park ... OR-9
Lava Island Falls—falls ... OR-9
Lava Lake—lake ... AK-9
Lava Lake—lake ... CA-9
Lava Lake—lake ... CO-8
Lava Lake—lake ... ID-8
Lava Lake—lake ... MT-8
Lava Lake—lake ... OR-9
Lava Lake—lake ... UT-8
Lava Lake Rsvr—reservoir ... ID-8
Lavaland Sch—school ... NM-5
**LaVale** pop pl ... MD-2
La Vale—uninc pl ... MD-2
La Vale-Narrows Park—CDP ... MD-2
La Vale Tollgate House—hist pl ... MD-2
**Lavalette**—pop pl ... WV-2
Laval Lake—lake ... OR-9
Lavalle ... WI-6
LaValle—locale ... MO-7
**La Valle**—pop pl ... MO-7
**La Valle**—pop pl ... WI-6
La Valle Creek—stream ... MT-8
**La Vallee**—pop pl ... VI-3
Lavalle House—hist pl ... FL-3
LaValle Mill Pond—reservoir ... WI-6
**La Valle (Town of)**—pop pl ... WI-6
**Lavallette**—pop pl ... NJ-2
Lavalley ... CO-8
**La Valley**—pop pl ... CO-8
LaValley Sch—school ... SD-7
LaValley Township—civil ... SD-7
**La Valley Township**—pop pl ... SD-7
Lava Manos Well—well ... TX-5
Lava Mountains—other ... CA-9
Lava Mtn—summit ... AK-9
Lava Mtn—summit ... ID-8
Lava Mtn—summit (3) ... MT-8
Lava Mtn—summit ... WY-8
Lava Narrows ... UT-8
Lavania Cove—bay ... AS-9
**Lavansville**—pop pl ... PA-2
Lava Pass—gap ... OR-9
Lava Peak—summit (2) ... CA-9
Lava Peak—summit ... MT-8
Lava Pinnacle—pillar ... AZ-5
Lava Plastered Cones—summit ... HI-9
Lava Point—beach ... ID-8
Lava Point—cape ... AK-9
Lava Point—cape ... UT-8
Lava Point—summit ... AZ-5
Lava Point Campground—park ... UT-8
Lava Point Trail—trail ... UT-8
LaVarder Lakes ... UT-8
LA VAR Eshquagama Lake ... MN-6
Lava Ridge—ridge (2) ... ID-8
Lava Ridge—ridge ... NV-8
Lava Ridge—ridge (2) ... UT-8
Lava River Cave—cave ... AZ-5
Lava River Cave—cave ... ID-8
Lava River Caves State Park—flat ... OR-9
Lava Rock Rsvr—reservoir ... CA-9
Lava Rock Sch—school ... OR-9
Lava Rsvr—reservoir ... OR-9
Lavaside Sch—school ... ID-8
Lava Sinks Rsvr—reservoir ... OR-9
Lava Slides—slope ... CA-9
Lava Spring—spring ... CA-9
Lava Spring—spring ... ID-8
Lava Spring—spring ... NM-5
Lava Spring—spring (4) ... OR-9
Lava Spring—spring ... UT-8
Lava Springs—spring ... CA-9
Lava Springs—spring ... OR-9
LaVasseur Park—park ... IL-6
Lavassi Creek—stream ... CA-9
Lava Tank—reservoir (2) ... AZ-5
Lava Top—lava ... CA-9
Lava Top Butte—summit ... OR-9
Lava Trail—trail ... OR-9
Lava Tree State Park—park ... HI-9
Lava Wash—stream ... AZ-5
Lava Well—well ... OR-9
Lava Well Ranch—locale ... NM-5
Laveaga Peak—summit ... CA-9
Laveck Creek—stream ... MT-8
Lave Creek—stream ... AR-4
Lave Creek (Township of)—fmr MCD ... AR-4
Laveel Branch—stream ... MD-2
**Laveen**—pop pl ... AZ-5
Laveen, Canal (historical)—canal ... AZ-5
Laveen Childrens Home—building ... AZ-5
Laveen Post Office—building ... AZ-5
Laveen Sch—school ... AZ-5
Laveen South Branch, Canal (historical)—canal ... AZ-5
La Vega—flat ... CA-9
La Vega—flat ... NM-5
**La Vega**—pop pl (4) ... PR-3
La Vega HS—school ... TX-5
La Vega Ranch—locale ... CO-8
La Vega Redonda—flat ... CO-8
La Veille—hist pl ... MD-2
Lavell Drain—canal ... MI-6
**Lavelle**—pop pl ... PA-2
Lavelle Sch for the Blind—school ... NY-2
Lavelle Site—hist pl ... MS-4
**Lavelle Woods (subdivision)**—pop pl ... AL-4
**Lavell Subdivision**—pop pl ... UT-8
**Lavell (Township of)**—pop pl ... MN-6
Lavelock Cem—cemetery ... MO-7
Lavels Lake—lake ... ME-1
La Venada Well—well ... TX-5
Lavena Hollow—valley ... TX-5
Lavender ... MP-9
Lavender—locale ... GA-3
Lavender—locale ... TX-5
**Lavender**—pop pl ... TN-4
**Lavender**—pop pl ... VA-3
Lavender, Bryan, House—hist pl ... NC-3
**Lavender Acres (subdivision)**—pop pl ... AL-4
Lavender Branch—stream ... AR-4
Lavender Branch—stream ... TN-4
Lavender Branch—stream ... TX-5
Lavender Bridge—bridge ... OH-6
Lavender Bridge—bridge ... TN-4
Lavender Canal—canal ... CA-9
Lavender Canyon ... UT-8
Lavender Canyon—valley ... UT-8
Lavender Cem—cemetery (2) ... TN-4
**Lavender Corner**—pop pl ... MI-6
Lavender Creek—stream ... GA-3
Lavender Creek—stream ... UT-8
Lavender Fork—stream ... WV-2
Lavender Hill—summit ... IL-6
Lavender Hills—range ... WY-8
Lavender Knob—summit ... TN-4
Lavender Lake—lake ... MI-6
Lavender Mtn—summit ... GA-3
Lavender Open Pit Mine—mine ... AZ-5
Lavender Point—cliff ... CO-8
Lavender Point—cliff ... UT-8
Lavender Post Office (historical)—building ... TN-4
Lavender Run—stream ... IN-6
Lavender Sch—school ... CO-8
Lavender Well—well ... NM-5
Lavene Creek—stream ... MT-8
Lavenia Bilingual Sch—school ... FL-3
La Ventana ... AZ-5
La Ventana—gap ... NM-5
LaVentana—locale ... NM-5
La Ventana Mesa—summit ... NM-5
**La Vera (subdivision)**—pop pl ... AL-4
Laver Ditch—canal ... OH-6
La Verendrye Site—hist pl ... SD-7
LaVergne ... IL-6
LaVergne ... TN-4
**La Vergne**—pop pl ... TN-4
**La Vergne (corporate and RR name for Lavergne)**—pop pl ... TN-4
Lavergne (corporate name La Vergne) ... TN-4
La Vergne Sch—school ... IL-6
**La Verkin**—pop pl ... UT-8
Laverkin Canal ... UT-8
La Verkin Canal—canal ... UT-8
La Verkin Cem—cemetery ... UT-8
La Verkin Creek—stream ... UT-8
La Verkin Creek Trail—trail ... UT-8
La Verkin Post Office—building ... UT-8
La Verkin Sch—school ... UT-8
Lavern ... WV-2
Lavern—locale ... WV-2
**La Verne**—pop pl ... CA-9
**Laverne**—pop pl ... OK-5
LaVerne, Lake—reservoir ... WI-6
Laverne (CCD)—cens area ... OK-5
La Verne Coll—school ... CA-9
Laverne County Park—park ... OR-9
Laverne Creek—stream ... ID-8
LaVerne Dilweg—uninc pl ... WI-6
Laverne Falls—falls ... OR-9
La Verne Heights Sch—school ... CA-9
Laverne Lake—lake ... IA-7
LaVerne Lake—lake ... WI-6
Laverne Memorial Cem—cemetery ... OK-5
Laverne's North Main Street District—hist pl ... OK-5
Lavernia—other ... TX-5
**La Vernia**—pop pl ... TX-5
La Vernia (CCD)—cens area ... TX-5
La Vernia Cem—cemetery ... TX-5
**La Vernia (Lavernia)**—pop pl ... TX-5
La Vernia Oil Field—oilfield ... TX-5
Lavernia Sch—school ... FL-3
**Laverock**—pop pl ... PA-2
Laverty—locale ... OK-5
Laverty Cem—cemetery ... IA-7
Laverty Cem—cemetery ... OK-5
Laverty Ch—church ... OK-5
Laverty Lakes—lake ... OR-9
Laverty-Martindale House—hist pl ... WI-6
**Lavery**—pop pl ... PA-2
Lavery Brook—stream ... VT-1
Laverys Corner—locale ... NY-2
**La Veta**—pop pl ... CO-8
La Veta Cem—cemetery ... CO-8
La Veta Landing Field—airport ... CO-8
La Veta Pass ... CO-8
**La Veta Pass**—pop pl ... CO-8
La Veta Pass Narrow Gauge RR Depot—hist pl ... CO-8
La Veta Peak ... CO-8
La Veta Sch—school ... CA-9
Lavezzola Creek—stream ... CA-9
Lavezzola Ranch—locale ... CA-9
Lavic—locale ... CA-9
Lavic Dry Lake ... CA-9
Lavicie Meadow Barren—flat ... PA-2
Lavic Lake—flat ... CA-9
Lavic Mountain Mine—mine ... CA-9
La Vida Mineral Springs—locale ... CA-9
La Vida Mission—school ... NM-5
La Viejo—pillar ... NM-5
Lavigia Hill—summit ... CA-9
**La Villa**—pop pl ... TX-5
**Lavilla**—pop pl ... WA-9
Laville High School ... IN-6
Laville Junior-Senior HS—school ... IN-6
**La Villita**—pop pl ... NM-5
La Villita Hist Dist—hist pl ... TX-5
Lavina ... TN-4
**La Vina**—pop pl ... CA-9
**Lavina**—pop pl ... MT-8
Lavina, Lake—lake ... WI-6
Lavina Creek—stream ... MT-8
Lavina Creek—stream ... UT-8
La Vina Hosp and Sanitorium—hospital ... CA-9
Lavina Mine—mine ... NV-8
La Vina Sch—school ... CA-9
La Vinateria Campground—locale ... NM-5
Lavina Water Users Association Ditch—canal ... MT-8
Lavin Creek—stream ... ID-8
Lavine, Lake—lake ... MI-6
Lavine Creek—stream ... ID-8
LaVine Sch—school ... MN-6
Lavinghouse Cem—cemetery ... LA-4
Lavinia—locale (2) ... MN-6
**Lavinia**—pop pl ... IA-7
**Lavinia**—pop pl ... TN-4
Lavinia Baptist Ch—church ... TN-4
Lavinia Causeway—bridge ... DE-2
Lavinia Ch (historical)—church ... AL-4
Lavinia Fork—stream ... WV-2
Lavinia Park—park ... MO-7
Lavinia Post Office—building ... TN-4
**Lavin Spur**—pop pl ... MT-8
Lavin Tank—reservoir ... AZ-5
Lavisa Fork ... KY-4
Lavisa Fork ... VA-3
Lavise Cem—cemetery ... WI-6
La Visnaga Windmill—locale ... TX-5
Lavista—locale ... WA-9
**La Vista**—pop pl ... GA-3
**La Vista**—pop pl ... NE-7
Lavista, Point—cape ... FL-3
La Vista Cem—cemetery ... CA-9
Lavista Lake—lake ... WA-9
**LaVista Park Subdivision**—pop pl ... UT-8
La Vista Ranch—locale ... TX-5
La Vista Sch—school ... CA-9
La Viuda—summit ... TX-5
La Viva Plaza (Shop Ctr)—locale ... FL-3
Lavley Creek ... OR-9
LaVoice Lake—lake ... AR-4
Lavoie Brook—stream ... ME-1
Lavoie Creek—stream ... ID-8
La Voie Sch—school ... MA-1
Lavoi State Wildlife Mngmt Area—park ... MN-6
La Volanta Windmill—locale ... TX-5
Lavold Ranch—locale ... MT-8
Lavold Rsvr—reservoir ... MT-8
Lavon—locale ... NV-8
**Lavon**—pop pl ... MT-8
**Lavon**—pop pl ... TX-5
**Lavon Beach Estates**—pop pl ... TX-5
Lavon Dam—dam ... TX-5
**Lavonia**—pop pl ... GA-3
Lavonia Carnegie Library—hist pl ... GA-3
Lavonia (CCD)—cens area ... GA-3
Lavonia Ch—church ... NC-3
Lavonia Commercial Hist Dist—hist pl ... GA-3
Lavonia Cotton Mill—hist pl ... GA-3
Lavonia Park—park ... TX-5
Lavonia Roller Mill—hist pl ... GA-3
Lavon Lake—lake ... MT-8
Lavon Lake—reservoir ... TX-5
Lavon Lake Encampment—locale ... TX-5
**Lavon Lake Lodges**—pop pl ... TX-5
Lavon Reservoir ... TX-5
Lavon Shearer Dam—dam (2) ... SD-7
**Lavon Shores Estates**—pop pl ... TX-5
Lavorcita ... NM-5
Lavor Windmill—locale ... TX-5
**Lavoy**—pop pl ... WV-2
Lavoy Exceptional Center—school ... FL-3
La Voy Lakes—flat ... OR-9
La Voy Tables—plain ... OR-9
Lavrock Canyon—valley ... CA-9
Lavs Lake—lake ... WI-6
Law—locale ... TX-5
**Law**—pop pl ... TN-4
Law, Bay—bay ... LA-4
Law, Bayou—gut ... LA-4
Law, Mount—summit ... CO-8
Law, Oren, House and Outbuildings—hist pl ... ID-8
Law, Thomas, House—hist pl ... DC-2
Lawai—civil ... HI-9
**Lawai**—pop pl ... HI-9
Lawai Bay—bay ... HI-9
Lawai Pump—other ... HI-9
Lawai Stream—stream ... HI-9
Lawalts ... PA-2
Lawango Run—stream ... PA-2
**La Ward**—pop pl ... TX-5
La Ward-Lolita (CCD)—cens area ... TX-5
Laward (RR name for La Ward)—other ... TX-5
**La Ward (RR name Laward)**—pop pl ... TX-5
**Lawarence Hights (subdivision)**—pop pl ... NC-3
Law Branch—stream ... KY-4
Law Branch—stream (2) ... TN-4
Law Cem—cemetery ... GA-3
Law Cem—cemetery ... SC-3
Law Chapel—church ... WV-2
**Law Chapel**—pop pl ... TN-4
Law Chapel Sch (historical)—school ... TN-4
Lawco—locale ... OH-6
**Lawco**—pop pl ... OH-6
Lawco Lake—reservoir ... OH-6
Law Creek—stream ... GA-3
Law Creek—stream ... MI-6
Law Creek—stream ... MT-8
Law Creek—stream ... TX-5
Lawdon ... CA-9
Lawen—locale ... OR-9
Law Enforcement Center Airp—airport (2) ... NC-3
Lawerance Windmill—locale ... TX-5
Lawer Rsvr—reservoir ... CA-9
Lawes Cabins—locale ... MI-6
Lawes Ditch—stream ... MD-2
Lawford—locale ... VA-3
Lawford—locale ... WV-2
Lawground Branch—stream ... GA-3
Law Ground Creek—stream ... GA-3
Law Grounds—locale ... GA-3
Lawhead Canyon—valley ... CA-9
Lawhead Creek—stream ... CA-9
Lawhead Creek—stream ... OR-9
Lawhead Gulch—valley ... CO-8
Lawhead Hollow—valley ... OK-5
Lawhead Lake—lake ... MI-6
Lawhead Trail—trail ... PA-2
Law Hill—summit ... NY-2
**Lawhon**—pop pl ... LA-4
Lawhon Cemetery ... AL-4
Lawhon JHS ... MS-4
Lawhon Post Office (historical)—building ... AL-4
Lawhon Sch—school ... MS-4
Lawhon Shop Ctr—locale ... FL-3
Lawhons Mill—locale ... FL-3
Lawhon Springs Cem—cemetery ... TX-5
Lawhon Springs Sch—school ... TX-5
Lawhorn, Buford, House—hist pl ... MO-7
Lawhorn Canyon ... NM-5
Lawhorn Canyon—valley ... NM-5
Lawhorn Cem—cemetery ... AL-4
Lawhorn Cem—cemetery ... KY-4
Lawhorn Cem—cemetery ... VA-3
Lawhorn Creek—stream ... IL-6
Lawhorne Creek—stream ... OR-9
**Lawhorn Hill**—pop pl ... KY-4
Lawhorn Hollow—valley ... KY-4
Lawhorn Hollow—valley ... OH-6
Lawhorns Ranch—locale ... NM-5
Lawhorn Woods—woods ... TX-5
Law HS—school ... CT-1
**Lawing**—pop pl ... AK-9
Lawing Cem—cemetery ... NC-3
Lawings Chapel—church ... NC-3
Law Island—island ... VT-1
La Wis Wis Campground—locale ... WA-9
La Wis Wis Guard Station No. 1165—hist pl ... WA-9
Lawitzke Drain—canal ... MI-6
Law Lake—lake ... NM-5
Law Lake—lake ... WA-9
Law Landing (historical)—locale ... AL-4
Lawler—locale ... IL-6
**Lawler**—pop pl ... IA-7
**Lawler**—pop pl ... MN-6
Lawler, W. T., House—hist pl ... TN-4
Lawler Bend—bend ... KY-4
Lawler Branch—stream ... TX-5
Lawler Canyon—valley ... OR-9
Lawler Cem—cemetery (5) ... AL-4
Lawler Cem—cemetery (2) ... IL-6
Lawler Cem—cemetery ... IN-6
Lawler Cem—cemetery ... MI-6
Lawler Ch—church (2) ... AL-4
Lawler Ch—church ... TX-5
Lawler Ch—church ... WV-2
Lawler Creek—stream ... AZ-5
Lawler Ditch—canal ... IL-6
Lawler Ditch—canal (2) ... IN-6
Lawler-Hetherington Double House—hist pl ... AZ-5
Lawler Lake—lake ... MI-6
Lawler Lake—lake ... WI-6
Lawler Lateral—canal ... AZ-5
Lawler Lookout Tower—locale ... MN-6
Lawler Mill Branch—stream ... AL-4
Lawler Park—park ... IL-6
Lawler Peak—summit ... AZ-5
Lawler Place Plantation (historical)—locale ... AL-4
Lawler Ranch—locale ... NE-7
Lawler Ridge—ridge ... ME-1
Lawler Spring—spring ... AZ-5
Lawler-Whiting House—hist pl ... AL-4
Lawless Cem—cemetery ... KY-4
Lawless Creek—stream ... VA-3
Lawless Ditch—canal ... IN-6
Lawless JHS—school ... LA-4
Lawless Lake—lake ... MN-6
Lawless Point—cape ... VA-3
Lawless Ranch—locale ... CA-9
Lawless Sch—school ... IL-6
Lawless Sch—school ... LA-4
Lawless Tank—reservoir ... AZ-5
Lawley—locale ... AL-4
**Lawley**—pop pl ... AL-4
Lawleys Chapel Cem—cemetery ... AL-4
Lawlin Pond—lake ... NJ-2
Lawlins Pond ... NJ-2
Lawlor, Mount—summit ... CA-9
Lawlor Bay—swamp ... FL-3
Lawlor Ravine—valley ... CA-9
Lawlor Sch—school ... MA-1
Lawman Ford—locale ... ID-8
Law Mtn—summit ... ME-1
Lawn—fmr MCD ... NE-7
**Lawn**—pop pl ... PA-2
**Lawn**—pop pl ... TX-5
**Lawn**—pop pl ... WV-2
Lawn, The—hist pl ... MD-2
Lawnbird Cem—cemetery ... AR-4
Lawn Cem—cemetery ... CT-1
Lawn Cem—cemetery ... IA-7
Lawn Cem—cemetery ... NJ-2
Lawn Creek ... VA-3
Lawn Creek—stream ... WY-8
Lawn Creek Point ... VA-3
Lawn Crest Memorial Cem—cemetery ... CA-9
Lawn Crest Recreation Center—building ... PA-2
Lawncroft Cem—cemetery ... CT-1
Lawn Croft Cem—cemetery ... PA-2
Lawndale ... OH-6
Lawndale ... PA-2
Lawndale—locale ... CA-9
Lawndale—locale ... MD-2
Lawndale—locale (2) ... MI-6
Lawndale—locale ... PA-2
**Lawndale**—pop pl ... CA-9
**Lawndale**—pop pl ... DE-2
**Lawndale**—pop pl ... IL-6
**Lawndale**—pop pl ... MN-6
**Lawndale**—pop pl ... NC-3
**Lawndale**—pop pl ... OH-6
**Lawndale**—pop pl ... PA-2
Lawndale—post sta ... IN-6
Lawndale—uninc pl ... NC-3
**Lawndale Addition (subdivision)**—pop pl ... UT-8
Lawndale Army Missile Plant—military ... CA-9
Lawndale Cem—cemetery ... IL-6
Lawn Dale Cem—cemetery ... IN-6
Lawndale Ch—church ... MI-6
Lawn Dale Ch—church ... SC-3
Lawndale Farm Complex—hist pl ... OH-6
**Lawndale Farms**—pop pl ... VA-3
**Lawndale Homes (subdivision)**—pop pl ... NC-3
Lawndale HS—school ... CA-9
**Lawndale Junction**—pop pl ... NC-3
Lawndale Park—park ... IL-6
Lawndale Presbyterian Ch—church ... MS-4
Lawndale Sch—hist pl ... PA-2
Lawndale Sch—school ... IL-6
Lawndale Sch—school ... OH-6
Lawndale Shop Ctr—other ... IN-6
Lawndale Station—building ... PA-2
Lawndale Swamp—swamp ... MN-6
**Lawndale (Township of)**—pop pl ... IL-6
Lawne Lake—lake ... FL-3
Lawnel Subdivision ... MI-6
Lawnes Creek—stream ... VA-3
Lawnes Neck—cape ... VA-3
Lawnes Point—cape ... VA-3
**Lawnford Acres (subdivision)**—pop pl ... PA-2
Lawngate—locale ... AL-4
Lawn Haven Baptist Ch ... MS-4
Lawn Haven Cem—cemetery ... NM-5
Lawnhaven Cem—cemetery ... PA-2
Lawn Haven Ch—church ... MS-4
Lawnhaven Memorial Gardens (Cemetery)—cemetery ... TX-5
**Lawnhurst**—pop pl ... PA-2
Lawn Hill—locale ... IA-7
Lawn Hill Cem—cemetery ... IA-7
Lawn Hill Cem—cemetery ... MO-7
Lawn Hill Sch—school ... IA-7
Lawn Knob—summit ... WV-2
Lawn Lake—lake ... MT-8
Lawn Lake—reservoir ... CO-8
Lawn Lake Trail—trail ... CO-8
Lawn Manor Sch—school ... IL-6
Lawn Pond—reservoir ... SC-3
Lawn Ridge ... KS-7
Lawn Ridge—locale ... IL-6
Lawnridge Cem—cemetery ... IL-6
Lawn Ridge Cem—cemetery ... IL-6
Lawn Ridge Cem—cemetery ... KS-7
Lawn Ridge Ch—church ... MO-7
Lawnridge (historical)—locale ... KS-7
Lawn Ridge Township ... KS-7
Lawn Ridge Township—civ div ... KS-7
Lawn Run—stream ... IN-6
Lawn Sch—school ... OH-6
Lawn Sch—school ... PA-2
Lawns Creek ... VA-3
Lawns Creek Point ... VA-3
Lawnsdale Sch—school ... WI-6
**Lawnside**—pop pl ... NJ-2
Lawnside Cem—cemetery ... NJ-2
Lawnside Sch—school ... NJ-2
Lawnside Station—locale ... NJ-2
**Lawnton**—pop pl ... PA-2
Lawn Township ... KS-7
**Lawn View**—pop pl ... PA-2
Lawnview Cem—cemetery ... OK-5
Lawnview Memorial Park—cemetery ... PA-2
Lawn View Sch—school ... OH-6
Lawnville—locale ... TN-4
**Lawnville Meadows (subdivision)**—pop pl ... TN-4
Lawnwood Cem—cemetery ... GA-3
Lawnwood Cem—cemetery ... WV-2
Lawnwood Elem Sch—school ... FL-3
Lawnwood Med Ctr—hospital ... FL-3
Lawnwood Memorial Park—cemetery ... GA-3
Law Park—park ... TX-5
Law Park—park ... WI-6
Law Ponds—lake ... CO-8
Law Post Office (historical)—building ... TN-4
Lawrence—cemetery ... TN-4
Lawrence—hist pl ... DE-2
Lawrence—locale ... CA-9
Lawrence—locale ... MN-6
Lawrence—locale ... NJ-2
Lawrence—locale ... UT-8
Lawrence—locale ... WA-9
**Lawrence**—pop pl ... AL-4
**Lawrence**—pop pl (2) ... IL-6
**Lawrence**—pop pl ... IN-6
**Lawrence**—pop pl ... KS-7
**Lawrence**—pop pl ... MA-1
**Lawrence**—pop pl ... MI-6
**Lawrence**—pop pl ... MS-4
**Lawrence**—pop pl ... NE-7
**Lawrence**—pop pl ... NY-2
**Lawrence**—pop pl ... NC-3
**Lawrence**—pop pl ... OH-6
**Lawrence**—pop pl ... OK-5
**Lawrence**—pop pl ... PA-2
**Lawrence**—pop pl ... TN-4
**Lawrence**—pop pl ... TX-5
**Lawrence**—pop pl ... WI-6
Lawrence—post sta ... WA-9
Lawrence, Amos, House—hist pl ... VT-1
Lawrence, City of—civil ... MA-1
Lawrence, G. E., House—hist pl ... TX-5
Lawrence, Isaac, House—hist pl ... CT-1
Lawrence, John P., Plantation—hist pl ... NC-3
Lawrence, Lake—lake ... IL-6
Lawrence, Lake—lake ... WA-9
Lawrence, Phineas, House—hist pl ... MA-1
Lawrence, William, House—hist pl ... MA-1
Lawrence, William, House—hist pl ... OH-6
Lawrence Acad—school ... MA-1
Lawrence Airp—airport ... PA-2
Lawrence and Chapin Bldg—hist pl ... MI-6
Lawrence Armstrong Lake Dam—dam ... MS-4
Lawrence Arroyo—stream ... NM-5
Lawrence Ave Sch—school ... NY-2
Lawrence Baker Sheppard Dam—dam ... PA-2
Lawrence Baker Sheppard Rsvr—reservoir ... PA-2
Lawrence Basin—basin ... CA-9
Lawrence Beach—uninc pl ... NY-2
Lawrence Branch—stream (2) ... AR-4
Lawrence Branch—stream ... GA-3
Lawrence Branch—stream (2) ... KY-4
Lawrence Branch—stream ... LA-4
Lawrence Branch—stream (2) ... TN-4
Lawrence Branch—stream (2) ... TX-5
Lawrence Bridge—bridge ... SC-3
**Lawrence Brook**—pop pl ... NJ-2
Lawrence Brook—stream (2) ... MA-1
Lawrence Brook—stream ... NH-1
Lawrence Brook—stream ... NJ-2
Lawrence Brook—stream ... NY-2
Lawrence Brook—stream ... VT-1
Lawrence Brook Cem—cemetery ... MA-1
**Lawrence Brook Manor**—pop pl ... NJ-2
**Lawrenceburg**—pop pl ... IN-6
**Lawrenceburg**—pop pl ... IA-7
**Lawrenceburg**—pop pl (2) ... KY-4
**Lawrenceburg**—pop pl ... MO-7
**Lawrenceburg**—pop pl ... PA-2
**Lawrenceburg**—pop pl ... TN-4
Lawrenceburg (CCD)—cens area ... KY-4
Lawrenceburg (CCD)—cens area ... TN-4
Lawrenceburg Ch of the Nazarene—church ... TN-4
Lawrenceburg City Cem—cemetery ... TN-4
Lawrenceburg City Hall—building ... TN-4
Lawrenceburg Cumberland Presbyterian Ch—church ... TN-4
Lawrenceburg Division—civil ... TN-4
Lawrenceburg Elementary School ... TN-4
Lawrenceburg Golf and Country Club—locale ... TN-4
Lawrenceburgh ... IN-6
Lawrenceburgh ... PA-2
Lawrenceburgh ... TN-4
Lawrenceburg (historical P.O.)—locale ... IA-7
Lawrenceburgh Post Office ... TN-4
**Lawrenceburg Junction**—pop pl ... IN-6
Lawrenceburg Municipal Airp—airport ... TN-4
Lawrenceburg Plaza Shop Ctr—locale ... TN-4
Lawrenceburg Post Office—building ... TN-4
Lawrenceburg Power Plant—building ... TN-4
Lawrenceburg Sanitarium and Hosp—hospital ... TN-4
Lawrenceburg Sch (historical)—school ... TN-4
Lawrenceburg Shopping Plaza Shop Ctr—locale ... TN-4
Lawrenceburg Speedway and Dragstrip—locale ... TN-4
Lawrenceburg Township ... KS-7
Lawrenceburg (Township of)—civ div ... IN-6
Lawrenceburg United Pentecostal Ch—church ... TN-4
Lawrence Canal—canal ... LA-4
Lawrence Canyon—valley ... CA-9
Lawrence Cave—cave ... WV-2
Lawrence Cem—cemetery ... AL-4
Lawrence Cem—cemetery ... AR-4
Lawrence Cem—cemetery (4) ... GA-3
Lawrence Cem—cemetery ... IN-6
Lawrence Cem—cemetery (2) ... KY-4
Lawrence Cem—cemetery ... MI-6
Lawrence Cem—cemetery ... MS-4
Lawrence Cem—cemetery (2) ... MO-7
Lawrence Cem—cemetery (2) ... NY-2
Lawrence Cem—cemetery ... NC-3
Lawrence Cem—cemetery ... OH-6
Lawrence Cem—cemetery (4) ... TN-4
Lawrence Cem—cemetery (4) ... TX-5
Lawrence Cem—cemetery ... UT-8
Lawrence Cem—cemetery (2) ... VA-3
Lawrence Cem—cemetery ... WV-2
Lawrence Cem—cemetery ... WI-6
Lawrence Center Ch—church ... GA-3
Lawrence Center Sch—school ... AL-4
Lawrence Central HS—school ... MA-1
Lawrence Ch—church ... GA-3
Lawrence Ch—church ... LA-4
Lawrence Ch—church ... MN-6
Lawrence Ch—church ... NC-3
Lawrence Ch—church ... OH-6
Lawrence Chapel ... AL-4
Lawrence Chapel—church ... KY-4
Lawrence Chapel—church ... OH-6
Lawrence Chapel—church ... SC-3
Lawrence Chapel—church ... TN-4
Lawrence Chapel—church ... WV-2
Lawrence Chapel Cem—cemetery ... AL-4
Lawrence Chapel Methodist Episcopal Ch (historical)—church ... AL-4
Lawrence Chapel School ... AL-4
Lawrence Ch of God—church ... IN-6
Lawrence City Hall—building ... MA-1
Lawrence Coll—school ... WI-6
Lawrence Corner—locale ... NJ-2
**Lawrence Corner**—pop pl ... NH-1
**Lawrence Corners**—pop pl ... PA-2
Lawrence Country Club—other ... KS-7
Lawrence Country Club—other ... NE-7
Lawrence County—civil ... SD-7
**Lawrence County**—pop pl ... AL-4
**Lawrence (County)**—pop pl ... AR-4
**Lawrence (County)**—pop pl ... IL-6
**Lawrence County**—pop pl ... IN-6
**Lawrence (County)**—pop pl ... KY-4
**Lawrence County**—pop pl ... MS-4
**Lawrence County**—pop pl ... MO-7
**Lawrence (County)**—pop pl ... OH-6
**Lawrence County**—pop pl ... PA-2
**Lawrence County**—pop pl ... TN-4
Lawrence County Area Vocational Technical Sch—school ... PA-2
Lawrence County Associaton Church Camp—locale ... AL-4
Lawrence County Christian Sch—school ... AL-4
Lawrence County Courthouse—building ... AL-4
Lawrence County Courthouse—building ... TN-4
Lawrence County Courthouse—hist pl ... MO-7
Lawrence County Courthouse—hist pl ... PA-2
Lawrence County Farm (historical)—locale ... TN-4
Lawrence County Home (historical)—building ... TN-4
Lawrence County Hosp—hospital ... AL-4
Lawrence County Hosp—hospital ... MS-4
Lawrence County Hosp—hospital ... TN-4
Lawrence County HS—school ... AL-4
Lawrence County HS—school ... TN-4
Lawrence County Jail—hist pl ... TN-4
Lawrence County Memorial Gardens—cemetery ... TN-4
Lawrence County Park—park ... AL-4
Lawrence County Public Library—building ... TN-4
Lawrence County Vocational Center—school ... TN-4
Lawrence Cove—bay ... ME-1
Lawrence Cove—bay ... VA-3
**Lawrence Cove**—pop pl ... AL-4
Lawrence Cove—valley ... AL-4
Lawrence Cove Baptist Church ... AL-4
Lawrence Cove Cem—cemetery ... AL-4
Lawrence Cove Ch—church ... AL-4
Lawrence Cove Post Office (historical)—building ... AL-4
Lawrence Cove Sch—school ... AL-4
Lawrence Creek ... AL-4
Lawrence Creek ... NE-7
**Lawrence Creek**—pop pl ... OK-5
Lawrence Creek—stream ... AL-4
Lawrence Creek—stream (2) ... AK-9
Lawrence Creek—stream ... AZ-5
Lawrence Creek—stream ... CA-9
Lawrence Creek—stream (2) ... CO-8
Lawrence Creek—stream ... GA-3
Lawrence Creek—stream (2) ... ID-8
Lawrence Creek—stream ... IL-6
Lawrence Creek—stream ... IN-6
Lawrence Creek—stream ... IA-7
Lawrence Creek—stream ... KS-7
Lawrence Creek—stream (2) ... KY-4

Lawrence Creek—*stream* LA-4
Lawrence Creek—*stream* MI-6
Lawrence Creek—*stream* MN-6
Lawrence Creek—*stream* MS-4
Lawrence Creek—*stream* MT-8
Lawrence Creek—*stream* (2) NY-2
Lawrence Creek—*stream* (3) OR-9
Lawrence Creek—*stream* (2) TN-4
Lawrence Creek—*stream* (2) TX-5
Lawrence Creek—*stream* (2) WI-6
Lawrence Creek—*stream* WY-8
Lawrence Creek Ch—*church* KS-7
Lawrence Creek Ch—*church* KY-4
Lawrence Creek Ch—*church* LA-4
Lawrence Creek State Wildlife Area—*park* WI-6
Lawrence Crossing—*locale* AZ-5
*Lawrence Dam* MA-1
Lawrence Dam—*dam* NJ-2
Lawrence Ditch—*canal* CO-8
Lawrence Ditch—*canal* HI-9
Lawrence Ditch—*canal* WY-8
Lawrence Donelan Dam—*dam* SD-7
Lawrence Drain—*canal* MI-6
Lawrence Draw—*valley* CO-8
Lawrence Draw—*valley* TX-5
Lawrence Draw—*valley* WY-8
Lawrence Elem Sch—*school* KS-7
**Lawrence Estates Subdivision**—*pop pl* UT-8
**Lawrence Farms**—*pop pl* NY-2
Lawrence Ferry (historical)—*locale* AL-4
Lawrence Field—*island* FL-3
Lawrence Field—*park* KS-7
Lawrencefield Chapel—*church* WV-2
Lawrence Flick State Hosp—*hospital* PA-2
Lawrence Fork—*stream* NE-7
Lawrence Four Corners—*locale* VT-1
Lawrence Full Gospel Tabernacle—*church* IN-6
Lawrence Furnace—*locale* OH-6
Lawrence Glacier—*glacier* AK-9
*Lawrence Grove Baptist Church* TN-4
Lawrence Grove Ch—*church* TN-4
Lawrence Gulch—*valley* MT-8
Lawrence Gulf—*valley* GA-3
Lawrence Hall Orphanage—*building* IL-6
Lawrence Hill—*summit* WI-6
*Lawrence Hills* PA-2
Lawrence (historical)—*locale* AL-4
**Lawrence (historical)**—*pop pl* MS-4
Lawrence Hollow—*valley* AR-4
Lawrence Hollow—*valley* IN-6
Lawrence Hollow—*valley* (4) MO-7
Lawrence Hollow—*valley* NY-2
Lawrence Hollow—*valley* TN-4
Lawrence Hollow—*valley* TX-5
Lawrence Hollow—*valley* WV-2
Lawrence House—*hist pl* TX-5
Lawrence HS—*school* KS-7
Lawrence HS—*school* (2) MA-1
Lawrence Independent Baptist Ch—*church* IN-6
Lawrence Institute (historical)—*school* MS-4
Lawrence Institute of Technology—*school* MI-6
*Lawrence Island* NY-2
Lawrence Island—*cape* MA-1
Lawrence Island—*island* TX-5
Lawrence JHS—*school* CA-9
Lawrence JHS—*school* MA-1
Lawrence JHS—*school* NJ-2
Lawrence JHS—*school* NY-2
Lawrence Junction—*locale* KS-7
Lawrence Junction—*locale* PA-2
Lawrence Kennedy Canal—*canal* ID-8
Lawrence Key—*locale* TX-5
Lawrence Key Cem—*cemetery* TX-5
Lawrence Knob—*summit* TN-4
*Lawrence Lake* MI-6
*Lawrence Lake* MN-6
Lawrence Lake—*lake* CA-9
Lawrence Lake—*lake* IN-6
Lawrence Lake—*lake* (5) MI-6
Lawrence Lake—*lake* (6) MN-6
Lawrence Lake—*lake* NY-2
Lawrence Lake—*lake* WI-6
Lawrence Lake—*reservoir* AL-4
Lawrence Lake—*reservoir* GA-3
Lawrence Lake—*reservoir* NJ-2
Lawrence Lake—*reservoir* WI-6
Lawrence Lakes—*lake* TX-5
Lawrence Landing—*locale* NC-3
Lawrence Library—*hist pl* ME-1
Lawrence Light Guard Armory—*hist pl* MA-1
Lawrence Lookout Tower—*locale* AL-4
Lawrence Lookout Tower—*locale* WI-6
Lawrence Mansion—*hist pl* NJ-2
Lawrence Marsh—*swamp* NY-2
Lawrence Memorial Bridge—*bridge* KY-4
Lawrence Memorial Ch—*church* VA-3
Lawrence Memorial Chapel—*church* NY-2
Lawrence Memorial Gardens—*cemetery* AR-4
Lawrence Memorial Hosp—*hospital* AR-4
Lawrence Memorial Hosp—*hospital* CT-1
Lawrence Memorial Hosp—*hospital* MA-1
Lawrence Mill—*locale* MA-1
Lawrence Mill (historical)—*locale* AL-4
Lawrence Mill (historical)—*locale* TN-4
Lawrence Mills—*locale* PA-2
Lawrence Mill (Site)—*locale* CA-9
Lawrence Mine—*mine* ID-8
Lawrence Model Lodging Houses—*hist pl* MA-1
Lawrence Moro Creek—*stream* AR-4
*Lawrence Mountain* AL-4
Lawrence Mtn—*summit* ME-1
Lawrence Mtn—*summit* MT-8
Lawrence Municipal Airp—*airport* KS-7
Lawrence No 1 Ditch—*canal* CO-8
Lawrence Number Two (historical)—*locale* KS-7
Lawrence Oil And Gas Field—*other* IL-6
Lawrence Opera House—*hist pl* NE-7
Lawrence Park—*park* AZ-5
Lawrence Park—*park* IL-6
Lawrence Park—*park* IN-6
Lawrence Park—*park* LA-4
Lawrence Park—*park* MT-8
Lawrence Park—*park* PA-2
Lawrence Park—*park* TX-5
**Lawrence Park**—*pop pl* NY-2
**Lawrence Park**—*pop pl* PA-2
Lawrence Park—*uninc pl* TX-5
Lawrence Park Golf Club—*locale* PA-2
*Lawrence Park Golf Course* PA-2
Lawrence Park Hist Dist—*hist pl* NY-2
**Lawrence Park (subdivision)**—*pop pl* PA-2
**Lawrence Park (Township of)**—*pop pl* PA-2
Lawrence Playground—*park* CA-9
Lawrence Playground—*park* OH-6
Lawrence Point—*cape* MN-6
Lawrence Point—*cape* NY-2
Lawrence Point—*cape* WA-9
Lawrence Police Station—*building* MA-1
Lawrence Pond—*lake* MA-1
Lawrence Pond—*reservoir* (2) AL-4
Lawrence Pontius Ditch—*canal* IN-6
**Lawrenceport**—*pop pl* IN-6
Lawrence Post Office (historical)—*building* AL-4
Lawrence Post Office (historical)—*building* PA-2
Lawrence Public Sch—*hist pl* PA-2
Lawrence Radiation Laboratory—*school* CA-9
Lawrence Ranch—*locale* NM-5
Lawrence Ranch—*locale* OR-9
Lawrence Ranch—*locale* WY-8
Lawrence Reservoir Dam—*dam* MA-1
Lawrence Road JHS—*school* NY-2
**Lawrence (RR name Hills)**—*pop pl* PA-2
Lawrence Rsvr—*reservoir* MA-1
Lawrence Run—*stream* NC-3
Lawrence Run—*stream* PA-2
Lawrence Saint Sch—*school* OH-6
*Lawrences Branch* NJ-2
Lawrence Sch—*school* AL-4
Lawrence Sch—*school* AZ-5
Lawrence Sch—*school* (3) CA-9
Lawrence Sch—*school* CO-8
Lawrence Sch—*school* IL-6
Lawrence Sch—*school* (2) IN-6
Lawrence Sch—*school* (2) MA-1
Lawrence Sch—*school* NJ-2
Lawrence Sch—*school* NY-2
Lawrence Sch—*school* OH-6
Lawrence Sch—*school* (2) SD-7
Lawrence Sch—*school* TX-5
Lawrence Sch—*school* WI-6
Lawrence Sch (abandoned)—*school* MO-7
Lawrence Sch (historical)—*school* PA-2
Lawrence Sch (historical)—*school* TN-4
*Lawrences Deadening* MS-4
*Lawrences Hill* AL-4
Lawrences Mill—*locale* GA-3
Lawrences Mills—*locale* PA-2
Lawrence Smith Memorial Airp—*airport* MO-7
*Lawrences Neck* MA-1
Lawrences Neck—*cape* MA-1
*Lawrence's Point* NY-2
Lawrence Spring—*spring* AZ-5
Lawrence Spring—*spring* TN-4
Lawrence Springs—*locale* TX-5
**Lawrence Spur**—*pop pl* SD-7
Lawrence State Wildlife Mngmt Area—*park* MN-6
Lawrence Street Cemetery—*hist pl* MA-1
Lawrence Street Sch—*school* MA-1
*Lawrence Swamp* MA-1
Lawrence Swamp—*stream* VA-3
**Lawrenceton**—*pop pl* MO-7
**Lawrence (Town of)**—*pop pl* NY-2
**Lawrence (Town of)**—*pop pl* (2) WI-6
Lawrence Township—*civil* KS-7
**Lawrence Township**—*pop pl* (2) KS-7
**Lawrence Township**—*pop pl* (2) SD-7
Lawrence Township Hist Dist—*hist pl* NJ-2
Lawrence (Township of)—*fmr MCD* AR-4
**Lawrence (Township of)**—*pop pl* IL-6
**Lawrence (Township of)**—*pop pl* IN-6
**Lawrence (Township of)**—*pop pl* MI-6
**Lawrence (Township of)**—*pop pl* (2) MN-6
**Lawrence (Township of)**—*pop pl* (2) NJ-2
**Lawrence (Township of)**—*pop pl* (4) OH-6
**Lawrence (Township of)**—*pop pl* (2) PA-2
Lawrence Trail—*trail* NH-1
Lawrence United Methodist Ch—*church* IN-6
Lawrence Valley—*valley* AK-9
*Lawrenceville* IL-6
*Lawrenceville* PA-2
**Lawrenceville**—*pop pl* AL-4
**Lawrenceville**—*pop pl* AR-4
**Lawrenceville**—*pop pl* GA-3
**Lawrenceville**—*pop pl* IL-6
**Lawrenceville**—*pop pl* IN-6
**Lawrenceville**—*pop pl* KY-4
**Lawrenceville**—*pop pl* NJ-2
**Lawrenceville**—*pop pl* (4) NY-2
**Lawrenceville**—*pop pl* OH-6
**Lawrenceville**—*pop pl* (3) PA-2
**Lawrenceville**—*pop pl* VA-3
**Lawrenceville**—*pop pl* WV-2
Lawrenceville Borough—*civil* PA-2
Lawrenceville Campground—*locale* GA-3
Lawrenceville (CCD)—*cens area* GA-3
Lawrenceville Cem—*cemetery* AL-4
Lawrenceville Cem—*cemetery* IL-6
Lawrenceville Cem—*cemetery* NJ-2
Lawrenceville Cem—*cemetery* PA-2
Lawrenceville Cem—*cemetery* VA-3
Lawrenceville Ch—*church* AR-4
Lawrenceville Ch—*church* VA-3
**Lawrenceville Hills**—*pop pl* VA-3
Lawrenceville (historical)—*locale* NC-3
Lawrenceville Male and Female Acad (historical)—*school* AL-4
Lawrenceville Missionary Baptist Ch—*church* AL-4
Lawrenceville Municipal Airp—*airport* IL-6
Lawrenceville Post Office (historical)—*building* AL-4
Lawrenceville Sch—*hist pl* NJ-2
Lawrenceville Sch—*school* NJ-2
**Lawrenceville (sta.)**—*pop pl* NY-2
Lawrence Vocational Technical Sch—*school* MA-1
Lawrence Wasteway—*canal* MA-1
Lawrence Well—*well* NM-5
*Lawreneville* KY-4
Lawrens Acad (historical)—*school* TN-4
Lawrens Branch—*stream* NJ-2
Lawrie—*locale* OK-5
Lawrie Cem—*cemetery* OK-5
Lawrie Creek—*stream* OK-5
Lawrie Gulch—*valley* MT-8
Lawron Chapel—*church* MN-6
Law Rsvr—*reservoir* CO-8
Law Run—*stream* WV-2
**Lawry**—*pop pl* ME-1
Lawry Branch—*stream* SC-3
Lawry Pond—*lake* ME-1
Lawrys Island—*island* ME-1
Lawrys Ledge—*island* ME-1
Lawrys Narrows—*gut* ME-1
Laws—*fmr MCD* NE-7
Laws—*locale* NC-3
Laws—*locale* TN-4
**Laws**—*pop pl* CA-9
Laws, Alexander, House—*hist pl* DE-2
Laws Branch—*stream* SC-3
Laws Brook—*stream* MA-1
*Lawsburg* IN-6
Laws Camp—*locale* CA-9
Laws Cem—*cemetery* NC-3
Laws Cem—*cemetery* (2) TN-4
Law Sch—*school* IL-6
Law Sch—*school* KY-4
Law Sch—*school* (2) MI-6
Laws Chapel—*church* TN-4
Laws Chapel—*church* TX-5
*Laws Chapel Baptist Ch* TN-4
Laws Chapel Cem—*cemetery* TN-4
*Laws Chapel Church* TN-4
Law Sch (historical)—*school* SD-7
*Laws Church* DE-2
**Laws Corner**—*pop pl* WA-9
Laws Cove—*bay* MD-2
*Laws Creek* TN-4
Laws Creek—*stream* IL-6
Laws Creek—*stream* MA-1
Laws Creek—*stream* OR-9
*Laws Cross Road* SC-3
Laws Gut—*gut* MD-2
Law Shaft (historical)—*mine* PA-2
**Lawshe**—*pop pl* OH-6
Lawshe, George, Well House—*hist pl* ID-8
Lawshe Run—*stream* PA-2
*Lawshill* MS-4
**Laws Hill**—*pop pl* MS-4
**Laws Hill**—*pop pl* TN-4
Laws Hill—*summit* AZ-5
*Laws Hill Cemetery* TN-4
Lawshill Post Office (historical)—*building* MS-4
Laws Hill Sch (historical)—*school* MS-4
Laws Hill Trick Tank—*reservoir* AZ-5
*Laws Lake* MN-6
Laws Mennonite Ch—*church* DE-2
Laws Narrow Gauge RR Hist Dist—*hist pl* CA-9
Laws Natural Tank—*reservoir* AZ-5
Lawson—*locale* KY-4
Lawson—*locale* MI-6
Lawson—*locale* SC-3
Lawson—*locale* TX-5
**Lawson**—*pop pl* AL-4
**Lawson**—*pop pl* AR-4
**Lawson** *pop pl* CO-8
**Lawson**—*pop pl* MO-7
**Lawson**—*pop pl* VA-3
Lawson, Lake—*reservoir* VA-3
Lawson, Mount—*summit* WA-9
Lawson, Thomas, House—*hist pl* KY-4
Lawsona, Lake—*lake* FL-3
Lawson Airpark Airp—*airport* WA-9
Lawson Bay—*bay* LA-4
Lawson Bend—*bend* TN-4
Lawson Bluff—*cliff* WA-9
Lawson Bottom—*bend* KY-4
*Lawson Branch* MO-7
*Lawson Branch* TN-4
Lawson Branch—*stream* AL-4
Lawson Branch—*stream* GA-3
Lawson Branch—*stream* (3) KY-4
Lawson Branch—*stream* LA-4
Lawson Branch—*stream* MS-4
Lawson Branch—*stream* MO-7
Lawson Branch—*stream* (3) TN-4
Lawson Branch—*stream* WV-2
Lawson Butte—*summit* OR-9
Lawson Canal—*canal* TX-5
Lawson Canyon—*valley* AZ-5
Lawson Canyon—*valley* (2) CA-9
*Lawson Cem* AL-4
Lawson Cem—*cemetery* AL-4
Lawson Cem—*cemetery* (2) AR-4
Lawson Cem—*cemetery* (3) KY-4
Lawson Cem—*cemetery* (2) MS-4
Lawson Cem—*cemetery* MO-7
Lawson Cem—*cemetery* NY-2
Lawson Cem—*cemetery* (3) NC-3
Lawson Cem—*cemetery* OK-5
Lawson Cem—*cemetery* (9) TN-4
Lawson Cem—*cemetery* (2) TX-5
Lawson Cem—*cemetery* (6) VA-3
Lawson Cem—*cemetery* WV-2
Lawson Cem—*cemetery* WI-6
Lawson Ch—*church* AR-4
Lawson Ch—*church* WV-2
*Lawson Chapel* AL-4
Lawson Chapel—*church* KY-4
Lawson Chapel—*church* LA-4
Lawson Chapel—*church* MS-4
Lawson Chapel—*church* (2) NC-3
Lawson Chapel—*church* TN-4
Lawson Chapel—*church* VA-3
Lawson Chapel Cem—*cemetery* TN-4
*Lawson Chapel Ch of Christ* MS-4
*Lawson Chapel United Methodist Church* TN-4
Lawson Coulee—*valley* ND-7
Lawson Cove—*valley* UT-8
Lawson Cove Canyon—*valley* UT-8
Lawson Cove Rsvr—*reservoir* UT-8
*Lawson Creek* OR-9
Lawson Creek—*stream* (2) AK-9
Lawson Creek—*stream* AR-4
Lawson Creek—*stream* CA-9
Lawson Creek—*stream* CO-8
Lawson Creek—*stream* GA-3
Lawson Creek—*stream* ID-8
Lawson Creek—*stream* IL-6
Lawson Creek—*stream* KY-4
Lawson Creek—*stream* NC-3
Lawson Creek—*stream* (4) OR-9
Lawson Creek—*stream* VA-3
Lawson Crossing—*locale* TX-5
**Lawson Crossroad**—*pop pl* TN-4
Lawson Drain—*canal* (2) MI-6
Lawson Drain—*stream* (2) MI-6
Lawson Field—*airport* GA-3
Lawson Ford—*locale* AL-4
Lawson Ford—*locale* TN-4
**Lawson Forest**—*pop pl* VA-3
*Lawson Fork* SC-3
*Lawson Fork Creek* SC-3
Lawson Gant Lot—*ridge* NC-3
Lawson Gant Lot—*summit* TN-4
Lawson Gant Lot Branch—*stream* NC-3
Lawson Gap—*gap* AL-4
Lawson Gap—*gap* TN-4
Lawson Glade—*stream* NM-5
Lawson Grove Ch—*church* SC-3
Lawson Gulch—*valley* CA-9
**Lawsonham**—*pop pl* PA-2
**Lawson Heights**—*pop pl* PA-2
Lawson High Top—*summit* KY-4
Lawson Hill—*summit* AL-4
Lawson Hill—*summit* CA-9
**Lawson (historical)**—*pop pl* TN-4
Lawson Hollow—*valley* (2) AR-4
Lawson Hollow—*valley* (2) KY-4
Lawson Hollow—*valley* PA-2
Lawson Hollow—*valley* (2) TN-4
Lawson Hollow—*valley* TX-5
Lawson Hollow—*valley* VA-3
**Lawsonia**—*pop pl* MD-2
Lawson Lake—*lake* NY-2
Lawson Lake—*lake* TX-5
Lawson Lake—*lake* WA-9
Lawson Lake—*reservoir* GA-3
Lawson Lake Number 1—*reservoir* AL-4
Lawson Lake Number 1 Dam—*dam* AL-4
Lawson Lake Number 2—*reservoir* AL-4
Lawson Lake Number 2 Dam—*dam* AL-4
Lawson Lakes—*reservoir* AL-4
Lawson Marsh—*swamp* MD-2
Lawson Mill—*locale* (2) TN-4
Lawson Mine—*mine* AZ-5
*Lawson Mountain* AL-4
Lawson Mtn—*summit* GA-3
Lawson Mtn—*summit* KY-4
Lawson Mtn—*summit* OR-9
Lawson Mtn—*summit* TN-4
Lawson Neck—*cape* VA-3
Lawson Oil Field—*oilfield* TX-5
Lawson Park—*park* KY-4
Lawson Park—*park* MI-6
Lawson Park—*park* TX-5
Lawson Peak—*summit* CA-9
Lawson Point—*cape* MD-2
Lawson Point—*cliff* TX-5
Lawson Pond—*lake* GA-3
Lawson Pond—*lake* NY-2
Lawson Pond—*lake* SC-3
Lawson Post Office (historical)—*building* TN-4
Lawson Reef—*bar* WA-9
Lawson Ridge—*ridge* CO-8
Lawson Rock—*bar* WA-9
Lawson Rsvr—*reservoir* CO-8
*Lawsons* AL-4
Lawsons Bridge (historical)—*bridge* AL-4
Lawson Sch—*school* AR-4
Lawson Sch—*school* IL-6
Lawson Sch—*school* MI-6
Lawson Sch—*school* (2) TN-4
Lawson Sch—*school* VA-3
Lawsons Chapel—*church* KY-4
Lawsons Chapel—*church* VA-3
Lawson Sch (historical)—*school* MO-7
Lawson Sch (historical)—*school* TN-4
*Lawsons Creek* MS-4
Lawsons Creek—*stream* (2) VA-3
Lawsons Fork Creek—*stream* SC-3
*Lawsons Fork Of The Pacolet River* SC-3
Lawson Shore—*beach* NC-3
Lawson Site—*hist pl* MS-4
*Lawsons Lake* NY-2
Lawsons Lake—*reservoir* IN-6
Lawsons Lake Dam—*dam* IN-6
Lawsons Marsh—*swamp* MD-2
Lawsons Mill—*locale* NC-3
Lawson's Pond Plantation—*hist pl* SC-3
Lawson Spring—*spring* (2) CA-9
*Lawsons Run* FL-3
*Lawsons Store* AL-4
Lawsons Store—*locale* VA-3
**Lawsons Store (Spanish Grove)**—*pop pl* VA-3
Lawson State Coll—*school* AL-4
Lawson Street Sch—*school* WV-2
Lawson Temple—*church* SC-3
Lawson Top—*summit* NY-2
Lawson Tower—*hist pl* MA-1
Lawson Tower—*tower* MA-1
*Lawson Town* AL-4
Lawsontown—*locale* AL-4
Lawson Valley—*valley* CA-9
Lawsonville—*locale* TX-5
**Lawsonville**—*pop pl* (2) NC-3
Lawsonville Ave Sch—*school* NC-3
Lawsonville Ch—*church* NC-3
Lawsonville Elem Sch—*school* NC-3
Lawsonville Road Ch—*church* NC-3
Lawson Williams Cem—*cemetery* OK-5
Laws Point—*cape* DE-2
Laws Point—*cape* MA-1
Laws Pond—*reservoir* NC-3
Laws Pond Dam—*dam* NC-3
Laws Ridge—*ridge* VT-1
Laws Sch—*school* TN-4
Laws Sch (historical)—*school* TN-4
Laws Spring—*hist pl* AZ-5
Laws Swamp—*stream* SC-3
Laws Swamp Ch—*church* SC-3
Laws Thorofare—*channel* MD-2
*Lawstown* IN-6
Laws Trail—*trail* WA-9
**Lawsville Center**—*pop pl* PA-2
**Lawtell**—*pop pl* LA-4
Lawtell Sch—*school* LA-4
**Lawtey**—*pop pl* FL-3
Lawtey (CCD)—*cens area* FL-3
Lawtey Cem—*cemetery* FL-3
Lawtey Elem Sch—*school* FL-3
*Lawther* ND-7
Lawther, James L., House—*hist pl* MN-6
Lawthorne Mill—*locale* VA-3
*Lawton* PA-2
Lawton—*locale* GA-3
Lawton—*locale* KY-4
Lawton—*locale* PA-2
Lawton—*locale* SC-3
Lawton—*locale* WI-6
**Lawton**—*pop pl* IN-6
**Lawton**—*pop pl* IA-7
**Lawton**—*pop pl* KS-7
**Lawton**—*pop pl* (2) MI-6
**Lawton**—*pop pl* NV-8
**Lawton**—*pop pl* ND-7
**Lawton**—*pop pl* OK-5
Lawton, Chauncey N., House—*hist pl* IN-6
Lawton, George H., House—*hist pl* NY-2
Lawton-Almy-Hall Farm—*hist pl* RI-1
Lawton Branch—*stream* FL-3
Lawton Canyon—*valley* AZ-5
Lawton (CCD)—*cens area* OK-5
Lawton Cem—*cemetery* IN-6
Lawton Cem—*cemetery* MA-1
Lawton Cem—*cemetery* ND-7
Lawton Cem—*cemetery* SC-3
Lawton Cem—*cemetery* TX-5
Lawton City Dump—*other* OK-5
Lawton Country Club and Golf Course—*other* OK-5
Lawton Creek—*stream* CA-9
Lawton Creek—*stream* SC-3
Lawton Creek—*stream* WA-9
Lawton Dam—*dam* OK-5
Lawton Drain—*stream* MI-6
Lawton Elem Sch—*school* FL-3
**Lawton Gardens (subdivision)**—*pop pl* PA-2
Lawton Grove Ch—*church* GA-3
Lawton Hill—*summit* NY-2
Lawton Hill—*summit* RI-1
**Lawton (historical)**—*pop pl* OR-9
Lawtonka, Lake—*reservoir* OK-5
*Lawton Lake* NY-2
Lawton Lake—*lake* MI-6
Lawton Meadow—*flat* CA-9
Lawton Mounds—*hist pl* SC-3
Lawton Municipal Airp—*airport* OK-5
**Lawton (New Lawton)**—*pop pl* TN-4
Lawton Park—*park* IN-6
Lawton Park—*park* NY-2
Lawton Park—*park* SC-3
Lawton Point—*cape* NC-3
Lawton Pond—*lake* GA-3
Lawton Ranch—*locale* MT-8
Lawton Road Ch—*church* FL-3
**Lawton (RR name Brownwood)**—*pop pl* WV-2
**Lawtons**—*pop pl* NY-2
**Lawtons**—*pop pl* RI-1
Lawton Sch—*school* CA-9
Lawton Sch—*school* LA-4
Lawton Sch—*school* MI-6
Lawton Sch—*school* PA-2
Lawton Sch—*school* WA-9
Lawton Sch (historical)—*school* TN-4
Lawtons Corner (historical)—*locale* MA-1
Lawton Shaft—*mine* NV-8
Lawton's Mill—*hist pl* RI-1
*Lawton Station* NY-2
*Lawtons Valley* RI-1
**Lawton Township**—*pop pl* ND-7
Lawton Valley—*valley* RI-1
Lawton Valley Reservoir—*lake* RI-1
Lawton Valley Reservoir Dam—*dam* RI-1
Lawton Valley Rsvr—*reservoir* RI-1
Lawtonville Cem—*cemetery* GA-3
Lawtonville Crossroads—*locale* SC-3
*Lawurell* MS-4
Lawvers Ch—*church* PA-2
Law Well—*well* NM-5
Law Windmill—*locale* NM-5
*Lawyer* VA-3
Lawyer Canyon—*valley* NM-5
Lawyer Cem—*cemetery* NY-2
Lawyer Cow Camp—*locale* CA-9
Lawyer Creek—*stream* (2) ID-8
**Lawyerdale Estates**—*pop pl* OH-6
Lawyer Gap—*gap* AR-4
**Lawyer Heights**—*pop pl* MD-2
Lawyer Hollow—*valley* AR-4
Lawyer Lake—*lake* NE-7
Lawyer Mtn—*summit* NY-2
Lawyers—*locale* VA-3
Lawyers Bldg—*hist pl* MI-6
Lawyers Cove—*bay* MD-2
Lawyers Hill—*summit* MD-2
Lawyers Square Shop Ctr—*locale* NC-3
**Lawyers Station (subdivision)**—*pop pl* NC-3
**Lawyersville**—*pop pl* NY-2
Lawyer Trail—*trail* CA-9
**Lax**—*pop pl* GA-3
Laxague Spring—*spring* (2) NV-8
Laxaque Spring—*spring* NV-8
*Laxaretta Creek* VA-3
*Laxaretto Creek* VA-3
Lax Cem—*cemetery* TN-4
Lax Chapel—*church* WI-6
Lax Creek—*stream* KY-4
*Laxerette Creek* VA-3
Laxey Cem—*cemetery* WI-6
Laxey Mine—*mine* ID-8
Laxion Lake—*reservoir* TN-4
Lax Lake—*lake* MN-6
**Lax Lake**—*pop pl* MN-6
**Laxon**—*pop pl* NC-3
Laxon Cem—*cemetery* TN-4
Laxon Creek—*stream* NC-3
Laxon Lake—*lake* MN-6
*Laxon Park* OR-9
*Laxourell Creek* OR-9
Lax (RR name for Crown)—*other* WV-2
Laxson Creek—*stream* TX-5
Laxson Park—*park* OR-9
Laxstrom Gulch—*valley* OR-9
Laxton Cave—*cave* MO-7
Laxton Cem—*cemetery* MO-7
Laxton Hollow—*valley* MO-7
Laxton Hollow—*valley* TN-4
Laxton Lake—*reservoir* TN-4
Laxton Lake Dam—*dam* TN-4
Laxton Spring—*spring* MO-7
*Lay* AL-4
*Lay* KS-7
*Lay* MS-4
*Lay* TN-4
*Lay* FM-9
Lay—*fmr MCD* NE-7
**Lay**—*pop pl* CO-8
Lay, Samuel, House—*hist pl* OH-6
Lay Bend—*cape* AL-4
Lay-Bozka House—*hist pl* TX-5
Lay Branch—*stream* AR-4
Lay Branch—*stream* KY-4
*Lay Cem* TN-4
Lay Cem—*cemetery* FL-3
Lay Cem—*cemetery* (2) KY-4
Lay Cem—*cemetery* MS-4
Lay Cem—*cemetery* (2) MO-7
Lay Cem—*cemetery* OH-6
Lay Cem—*cemetery* (8) TN-4
Laycock Creek—*stream* (2) OR-9
Laycock Long Ditch—*canal* OR-9
Laycock Sch—*school* IL-6
Laycock Shearing Pens—*locale* WY-8
Laycock Spring—*spring* WY-8
Laycock Well—*well* NM-5
Lay Creek—*stream* AR-4
Lay Creek—*stream* CO-8
Lay Creek—*stream* (2) MT-8
Lay Dam—*dam* (2) AL-4
Layer Cem—*cemetery* TX-5
Lay Falls—*falls* AR-4
Layfayette Pass—*gap* WI-6
Layfield—*locale* IL-6
Layfield—*locale* PA-2
Layfield Hollow—*valley* PA-2
Layfield Pond—*lake* GA-3
Layfields Cem—*cemetery* WV-2
Layfields Run—*stream* WV-2
Lay Gap—*gap* TN-4
Layhigh—*locale* OH-6
**Layhill**—*pop pl* MD-2
**Layhill Gardens**—*pop pl* MD-2
**Layhill South**—*pop pl* MD-2
**Layhill Village**—*pop pl* MD-2
Lay Hollow—*valley* (2) TN-4
Lay Hollow Branch—*stream* TN-4
Lay Inlet—*bay* WA-9
Lay Lake—*reservoir* AL-4
Laylan Coulee—*valley* MT-8
Layland—*locale* WV-2
**Layland**—*pop pl* OH-6
Layland Canyon—*valley* WY-8
Layland Ch—*church* WV-2
**Layland Heights**—*pop pl* WV-2
*Layman* OK-5
Layman—*locale* OH-6
**Layman**—*pop pl* KY-4
**Layman**—*pop pl* VA-3
Layman, Christopher C., Law Office—*hist pl* OH-6
Layman Area—*area* CA-9
Layman Bar—*bar* CA-9
Layman Cem—*cemetery* IN-6
Layman Cem—*cemetery* KY-4
Layman Creek—*stream* WI-6
Layman Drain—*canal* MI-6
Layman Gulch—*valley* OR-9
Layman Knob—*summit* KY-4
Layman Mine—*mine* CA-9
Laymans Ch—*church* NC-3
Layman Sch—*school* IL-6
Layman Sch—*school* WV-2
*Laymans Creek* WI-6
Laymans Creek—*stream* WI-6
Laymans Pond—*reservoir* AL-4
Laymantown Cem—*cemetery* VA-3
Laymantown Community Ch—*church* VA-3
Laymantown Creek—*stream* VA-3
Laymens Retreat—*church* PA-2
Laymens Retreat House—*building* CA-9
*Laymensville* WV-2
Laymon Ch—*church* IN-6
Lay Mtn—*summit* KY-4
**Layne**—*pop pl* AR-4
Layne Branch—*stream* TN-4
Layne Cem—*cemetery* NH-1
Layne Cem—*cemetery* (3) TN-4
Layne Cem—*cemetery* WV-2
Layne Chapel—*church* TN-4
Layne Cove—*valley* TN-4
Layne Cove Ch—*church* TN-4
Layne Creek—*stream* OR-9
*Laynecrest* IN-6
Layne Hill—*summit* NH-1
Layne Park—*park* CA-9
Layne Sch—*school* TX-5
*Laynes Chapel* TN-4
Laynes Chapel Cem—*cemetery* TN-4
**Laynesville**—*pop pl* KY-4
Laynesville Post Office (historical)—*building* TN-4
Layneville—*locale* MO-7
*Layng Creek* OR-9
Layng Creek—*stream* OR-9
Layng Creek Ranger Station—*locale* OR-9
Layon—*summit* GU-9
*Layopolis* WV-2
*Layopolis (corporate name Sand Fork)* WV-2
Layout Camp—*locale* WA-9
Layout Canyon—*valley* UT-8
Layout Creek—*stream* MT-8
Layout Creek—*stream* WA-9
Layout Tunnel—*canal* UT-8
Lay Peak—*summit* CO-8
Lay Post Office (historical)—*building* AL-4
Lay-Pritchett House—*hist pl* CT-1
**Layrelwood Estates Subdivision**—*pop pl* UT-8
Lay Ridge—*ridge* TN-4
*Laysan* HI-9
Laysan Island—*island* (2) HI-9
Lays Bayou—*stream* LA-4
Lays Cem—*cemetery* TN-4
Lay Sch—*school* TN-4
Lays Dam—*dam* TN-4
*Laysen* HI-9
*Lays Ferry* AL-4
Lays Gap—*gap* SC-3
*Lays Hollow* TN-4
Lays Lake—*reservoir* AL-4
Lays Lake—*reservoir* TN-4
*Layson* HI-9

Layson Creek—*stream* NV-8
Laysons Branch—*stream* KY-4
Lay Spring—*spring (2)* TN-4
Lay Spring Caves—*cave* TN-4
Lay Springs—*locale* AL-4
*Lays Ridge* TN-4
Lays Ridge—*ridge* PA-2
*Lays School* TN-4
**Laysville**—*pop pl* CT-1
*Laysville Brook* CT-1
*Layton* AZ-5
Layton—*locale* KS-7
Layton—*locale* NJ-2
Layton—*locale* VA-3
**Layton**—*pop pl* FL-3
**Layton**—*pop pl* IL-6
**Layton**—*pop pl* IN-6
**Layton**—*pop pl* PA-2
**Layton**—*pop pl* UT-8
Layton, George W., House—*hist pl* UT-8
Layton, John Henry, House—*hist pl* UT-8
Layton, Richard, House—*hist pl* NJ-2
**Laytona**—*pop pl* UT-8
Layton Bldg—*hist pl* AR-4
Layton Branch—*stream* TN-4
Layton Bridge—*hist pl* PA-2
Layton Canyon—*valley* CA-9
Layton Canyon—*valley* NM-5
Layton Canyon—*valley* OK-5
Layton Canyon—*valley* SD-7
Layton Cem—*cemetery* AR-4
Layton Cem—*cemetery (2)* IN-6
Layton Cem—*cemetery* NY-2
Layton Cem—*cemetery* TN-4
Layton Chapel—*church* KY-4
Layton Chapel—*church* NC-3
*Layton City Cemetery* UT-8
Layton Community Ch—*church* UT-8
Layton Corners—*locale* DE-2
**Layton Corners**—*pop pl* MI-6
**Layton (corporate name for Long Key)**—*pop pl* FL-3
Layton Coulee—*valley* MT-8
Layton Creek—*stream* UT-8
Layton Creek—*stream* VA-3
Layton Dam No. 2—*dam* OR-9
*Layton Ditch* DE-2
Layton Ditch—*canal* OH-6
Layton Draft—*valley* PA-2
Layton Drain—*canal* WY-8
Layton Drain Branch A—*canal* WY-8
*Layton Elementary School* UT-8
Layton Field—*flat (2)* NV-8
Layton Gulch—*valley* CO-8
Layton Hall Sch—*school* VA-3
Layton Hill—*summit* PA-2
Layton Hill—*summit* WA-9
Layton Hills Baptist Ch—*church* UT-8
Layton Hills Mall Convenience Center (shopping)—*locale* UT-8
Layton Hollow—*valley* MO-7
Layton Hollow—*valley* PA-2
Layton House—*hist pl* MD-2
Layton HS—*school* UT-8
**Laytonia**—*pop pl* MD-2
Layton Industrial Park Subdivision—*locale* UT-8
Layton Lake—*lake* AR-4
Layton Lake—*lake* ME-1
Layton Lateral Ditch—*canal* CO-8
**Layton Meadows Condominium**—*pop pl* UT-8
*Layton Mills* IN-6
Layton Mine—*mine* OR-9
Layton Mine (underground)—*mine* AL-4
Layton Park—*park* MI-6
Layton Park—*uninc pl* WI-6
**Layton Park Plaza Condominium**—*pop pl* UT-8
**Layton Park Subdivision**—*pop pl* UT-8
Layton Pass—*gap* CA-9
Layton Post Office—*building* UT-8
Layton Prairie—*flat* WA-9
Layton Prairie School—*locale* WA-9
Layton Ranch—*locale* WY-8
Layton Rsvr Number 2—*reservoir* OR-9
*Laytons* VA-3
Laytons Branch—*stream (2)* VA-3
Layton Sch—*school* MO-7
Layton Sch—*school* OH-6
Layton Sch—*school* UT-8
Layton Sch (abandoned)—*school* MO-7
Layton Sch (historical)—*school* MS-4
*Laytons Corner* DE-2
Laytons Lake—*reservoir* NJ-2
*Laytons Landing* VA-3
Layton Spring—*spring (2)* CA-9
Layton Spring—*spring* ID-8
Layton Spring—*spring (2)* NV-8
Laytons Store (historical)—*locale* AL-4
Layton Station—*locale* UT-8
**Layton Subdivision**—*pop pl* UT-8
**Laytonsville**—*pop pl* MD-2
Laytonsville Sch—*school* KY-4
*Laytons Wharf* VA-3
Layton Tank—*reservoir (2)* AZ-5
Layton Township—*fmr MCD* IA-7
**Layton Township**—*pop pl* ND-7
Layton-Vaughn Ditch—*stream* DE-2
**Laytonville**—*pop pl* CA-9
Laytonville Cem—*cemetery* CA-9
Laytonville-Leggett (CCD)—*cens area* CA-9
**Laytonville Rancheria (Indian Reservation)**—*pop pl* CA-9
Layton Wash—*stream* CO-8
Layton Well—*well* AZ-5
Layton Well—*well* CA-9
**Laytown**—*pop pl* NC-3
Laytown Creek—*stream* NC-3
**Layville**—*pop pl* WV-2
Lay Ward Ditch—*canal* MT-8
Lay Waterhole—*spring* NV-8
Layway Swamp—*swamp* GA-3
Laywell Branch—*stream* WV-2
Laywell Ch—*church* WV-2
La Zaca—*civil* CA-9
*La Zaca Creek* CA-9
*La Zaca Rancho* CA-9
La Zanja—*locale* PR-3
La Zanja—*valley* CA-9
La Zanja Canyon—*valley* CA-9
Lazare—*locale* TX-5
Lazaref Peak—*summit* AK-9
Lazaref Reef—*bar* AK-9
Lazaref River—*stream* AK-9
Lazaretto, The—*hist pl* PA-2
Lazaretto Creek—*channel* GA-3
Lazaretto Creek—*stream* VA-3
Lazaretto Point—*cape* MD-2
Lazaro, Mount—*summit* AK-9
Lazaro Canyon—*valley* CA-9
Lazarus Branch—*stream* VA-3
Lazarus Ch—*church* MD-2
*Lazarus Creek* MN-6
Lazarus Creek—*stream* MN-6
Lazarus Creek—*stream* SD-7
Lazarus Hill—*summit* NY-2
Lazarus Island—*island* OR-9
Lazarus Tanks—*reservoir* AZ-5
Lazarus Windmill—*locale* TX-5
**Lazbuddie**—*pop pl* TX-5
Lazbuddie Cem—*cemetery* TX-5
**Lazear**—*pop pl* CO-8
Lazear Cem—*cemetery* PA-2
Lazeart Mine—*mine* WY-8
Lazell Drain—*canal* MI-6
Lazenby Cem—*cemetery* GA-3
Lazenby Lake—*reservoir* AL-4
Lazer Creek—*stream* GA-3
*Lazette* KS-7
Lazier, Mount—*summit* AK-9
Lazier Creek—*stream* MT-8
Lazinka Sch—*school* OR-9
Lazona Trailer Court—*locale* AZ-5
La Z Tank—*reservoir* TX-5
**Lazy Acre**—*pop pl* CA-9
**Lazy Acres**—*pop pl* LA-4
**Lazy Acres**—*pop pl* TN-4
Lazy Acres Camp—*locale* CO-8
Lazy Acres Pond—*lake* NJ-2
**Lazy Bar Subdivision**—*pop pl* UT-8
Lazy Bay—*bay* AK-9
Lazy Bay—*bay* MT-8
Lazy Bend—*bend* TX-5
Lazy Bend Forest Camp—*locale* OR-9
Lazy B Oil Field—*oilfield* TX-5
Lazy Boy Mine—*mine* AZ-5
Lazy Branch—*stream* KY-4
Lazy Branch—*stream (2)* MO-7
Lazy Branch—*stream (2)* TN-4
Lazy B Ranch Airstrip—*airport* AZ-5
Lazy Brook Country Club—*other* IA-7
Lazy Campground—*locale* CA-9
Lazy C Bar J Ranch—*locale* NM-5
Lazy C J Jack Creek Ranch—*locale* WY-8
Lazy C Ranch—*locale* CA-9
Lazy C Ranch Lake Dam—*dam* MS-4
*Lazy Creek* AR-4
Lazy Creek—*stream* AL-4
Lazy Creek—*stream* AR-4
Lazy Creek—*stream* CA-9
Lazy Creek—*stream* ID-8
Lazy Creek—*stream (2)* IN-6
Lazy Creek—*stream* KS-7
Lazy Creek—*stream (2)* MS-4
Lazy Creek—*stream* MO-7
Lazy Creek—*stream* MT-8
Lazy Creek—*stream (3)* OR-9
Lazy Creek—*stream* WI-6
Lazy Creek Meadow—*flat* MT-8
Lazy C-Z Rsvr—*reservoir* TX-5
Lazy Day Ranch—*locale* WY-8
Lazy Daze Mobile Home Park—*locale* AZ-5
Lazy Dollar Ranch—*locale* ND-7
Lazy D Ranch—*locale* CO-8
Lazy D Trailer Ranch—*locale* AZ-5
Lazy E Ranch—*locale* NM-5
Lazy F C Ranch—*locale* ID-8
Lazy F Ranch—*locale* TX-5
Lazy Grove—*area* ID-8
Lazy Gulch—*valley* CO-8
Lazygut Island—*island* ME-1
Lazygut Ledge—*bar* ME-1
Lazy Heart 9 Ranch—*locale* WY-8
Lazy Hill—*summit* MA-1
Lazy Hill—*summit* NY-2
Lazy Hills Ranch—*locale* TX-5
Lazy Hollow—*valley* NE-7
Lazy Hollow Sch—*school* NE-7
Lazy Island—*island* FL-3
Lazy Island Lake—*lake* WI-6
Lazy J Oil Field—*other* NM-5
Lazy J Ranch—*locale* AZ-5
Lazy J Trailer Lodge—*locale* AZ-5
Lazy K Airport, The—*airport* IN-6
Lazy KJ Ranch—*locale* AZ-5
Lazy K Lake—*reservoir* MS-4
Lazy K Ranch—*locale* TX-5
Lazy K Slash Well—*well* NM-5
Lazy K T Ranch—*locale* MT-8
Lazy Lady Island—*island* VT-1
**Lazy Lagoon (trailer park)**—*pop pl* DE-2
Lazy Lake—*lake* AK-9
Lazy Lake—*lake* FL-3
**Lazy Lake**—*pop pl* FL-3
Lazy Lake—*reservoir* IN-6
Lazy Lake—*reservoir* WI-6
Lazy Lake Dam—*dam* IN-6
**Lazy Lake (subdivision)**—*pop pl* DE-2
Lazy Lane Ranch—*locale* TX-5
**Lazy L Estates Subdivision**—*pop pl* UT-8
**Lazy Living Acres**—*pop pl* AL-4
Lazyman Butte—*summit* CA-9
Lazyman Camp—*locale* CA-9
Lazy Man Creek—*stream* MT-8
Lazyman Creek—*stream* MT-8
Lazyman Flat—*flat* CA-9
Lazyman Gulch—*valley* MT-8
Lazyman Hill—*summit* MT-8
Lazy Man Mine—*mine* NV-8
Lazyman Ridge—*ridge* CA-9
Lazy Man Rsvr—*reservoir* OR-9
Lazy Moon Ranch—*locale* CA-9
Lazy Mtn—*summit* AK-9
Lazy Oak Corner—*locale* VA-3
Lazy Open A—*locale* WY-8
Lazy Point—*cape* NY-2
Lazy Point Canal—*canal (2)* LA-4
Lazy P Ranch—*locale* MT-8
*Lazy Ridge* CO-8
Lazy River M Ranch—*locale* WY-8
Lazy River Ranch—*locale* CO-8
Lazy Rocks—*bar* MA-1
Lazy RR Ranch—*locale* AZ-5
Lazy Run—*stream* IN-6
Lazy Run—*stream* WV-2
Lazy S Ranch—*locale* TX-5
Lazy S Windmill—*locale* TX-5
Lazy Tank—*reservoir* AZ-5
Lazy Tom Pond—*lake* ME-1
Lazy Tom Stream—*stream* ME-1
Lazy T Ranch—*locale* CA-9
Lazy T Ranch—*locale* MT-8
Lazy T-seven Ranch—*locale* AZ-5
Lazy T 4 Ranch—*locale* MT-8
Lazy U Club Lake Dam—*dam* MS-4
Lazy U Lake—*lake* MS-4
Lazy U Ranch—*locale* TX-5
Lazy Valley—*valley* TX-5
Lazy V Bar Ranch—*locale* NM-5
Lazy V Lake—*reservoir* AL-4
**Lazy V Lake Acres**—*pop pl* AL-4
Lazy V Ranch Dam—*dam* AL-4
Lazy Water Lake—*reservoir* SC-3
Lazy W Farms Airp—*airport* MO-7
Lazy W J Ranch—*locale* CO-8
Lazy X Ranch—*locale* TX-5
Lazy Y Cow Camp—*locale* CO-8
Lazy Y Point—*cliff* CO-8
Lazy Y Ranch—*locale* AZ-5
Lazy Y Summer Camp—*locale* CO-8
Lazzard Ch—*church* LA-4
*Lazzaretto* PA-2
Lazzell Cem—*cemetery* WV-2
*Lazzeretta Creek* VA-3
L Bachand Dam—*dam* SD-7
L Barnica Dam—*dam* SD-7
L Barnum Ranch—*locale* NE-7
L Bar Ranch—*locale* WY-8
L Bass Lake—*lake* WI-6
L Bayou Mc Cutchen—*gut* LA-4
Lbex Peak—*summit* ID-8
L B Hayes Dam—*dam* AL-4
LBJ Pit—*cave* AL-4
LBJ Ranch—*locale* TX-5
L B Morris Elem Sch—*school* PA-2
L Boisdore Claim—*civil* MS-4
L Bowden Creek—*stream* FL-3
LB Tank—*reservoir* NM-5
LB Wells—*well* NM-5
L Canal—*canal* ID-8
L Canal—*canal* MT-8
L Canal—*canal* NV-8
L Canal—*canal* OR-9
L C Canyon—*valley* NM-5
L C Gallett Lake Dam—*dam* MS-4
L C Hardy Dams—*dam* AL-4
L C Land Incorporated Airp—*airport* KS-7
**Lc&n Junction**—*pop pl* LA-4
L Connell Ranch—*locale* ND-7
LC Page—*uninc pl* VA-3
L C Ranch—*locale* NM-5
L-C Ranch—*locale* UT-8
L. C. Ranch HQ—*hist pl* NM-5
*L Creek* NV-8
L Davidson Branch—*stream* NC-3
L D Emmons Pond Dam—*dam* MS-4
L D F Community Sch—*school* IA-7
L D Hill Sch—*school* GA-3
L-Diamond Ranch—*locale* MT-8
L D McArthur Elem Sch—*school* FL-3
*L & D Mountain* NV-8
L-D Pond—*lake* NY-2
L-D Pond Outlet—*stream* NY-2
L Drain—*canal* CA-9
L Drain—*canal* NV-8
L D Ranch—*locale* WY-8
L D Ranch Airp—*airport* UT-8
LDS Academy Park Wards 1,2—*church* UT-8
LDS Alpine Wards 1,2—*church* UT-8
LDS Alpine Wards 3,5—*church* UT-8
LDS Alpine Wards 4,6—*church* UT-8
LDS Altamont Wards 1,2, Bluebell Ward—*church* UT-8
LDS Alton Ward—*church* UT-8
LDS Amalga Ward—*church* UT-8
LDS American Fork Training School Ward—*church* UT-8
LDS American Fork Wards 1,5,18—*church* UT-8
LDS American Fork Wards 10, 23—*church* UT-8
LDS American Fork Wards 11, 17—*church* UT-8
LDS American Fork Wards 12,22—*church* UT-8
LDS American Fork Wards 13, 26—*church* UT-8
LDS American Fork Wards 14, 20—*church* UT-8
LDS American Fork Wards 2,29—*church* UT-8
LDS American Fork Wards 3,27—*church* UT-8
LDS American Fork Wards 4,15, 25—*church* UT-8
LDS American Fork Wards 6,8,24, 28—*church* UT-8
LDS American Fork Wards 7,16—*church* UT-8
LDS American Fork Wards 9,21, 30—*church* UT-8
LDS American Fork Ward 19—*church* UT-8
LDS Annabella, Central Wards—*church* UT-8
LDS Antimony Ward—*church* UT-8
LDS Ashley Wards 1,2, Maeser Ward 3—*church* UT-8
LDS Aurora Wards 1,2—*church* UT-8
LDS Axtell Ward—*church* UT-8
LDS Ballard, Ballard North Wards—*church* UT-8
LDS Bear Lake Ward—*church* UT-8
LDS Beaver Wards 1,2,5—*church* UT-8
LDS Beaver Wards 3,4—*church* UT-8
LDS Bell Ward, Granite Wards 3, 17—*church* UT-8
LDS Belmont Wards 1,2, Beaver Ward—*church* UT-8
LDS Belvedere Ward—*church* UT-8
LDS Benjamin Wards 1,2—*church* UT-8
LDS Bennion Care Center Ward—*church* UT-8
LDS Bennion Wards 1,8,11,21—*church* UT-8
LDS Bennion Wards 12,14,15,19, Granger Ward 4—*church* UT-8
LDS Bennion Wards 18,20, Willow Bay Ward—*church* UT-8
LDS Bennion Wards 2,4—*church* UT-8
LDS Bennion Wards 3,5,6—*church* UT-8
LDS Bennion Wards 7,10,17—*church* UT-8
LDS Bennion Wards 9,16,22—*church* UT-8
LDS Bennion Ward 13—*church* UT-8
LDS Benson Ward—*church* UT-8
LDS Birdseye Ward—*church* UT-8
LDS Blanding Wards 1,5,8—*church* UT-8
LDS Blanding Wards 2,3,7—*church* UT-8
LDS Blanding Wards 4,6—*church* UT-8
LDS Bloomington Hills Wards 1,2,3, 4—*church* UT-8
LDS Bloomington Wards 1,2,5—*church* UT-8
LDS Bloomington Wards 3,4,6—*church* UT-8
LDS Bluffdale Wards 1,2—*church* UT-8
LDS Bluffdale Ward 3, Riverton Ward 18—*church* UT-8
LDS Bluff Ward—*church* UT-8
LDS Bonneville Ward (Salt Lake City)—*church* UT-8
LDS Bonneville Wards 1,2 (Provo), Provo Wards 15,22—*church* UT-8
LDS Boulder Ward—*church* UT-8
LDS Bountiful Wards 1,3—*church* UT-8
LDS Bountiful Wards 10,27—*church* UT-8
LDS Bountiful Wards 11,45,55—*church* UT-8
LDS Bountiful Wards 12,22—*church* UT-8
LDS Bountiful Wards 13,53—*church* UT-8
LDS Bountiful Wards 14, 25, 39—*church* UT-8
LDS Bountiful Wards 14,37—*church* UT-8
LDS Bountiful Wards 16,24,33—*church* UT-8
LDS Bountiful Wards 17,23,30—*church* UT-8
LDS Bountiful Wards 18,41—*church* UT-8
LDS Bountiful Wards 2,21—*church* UT-8
LDS Bountiful Wards 26,58—*church* UT-8
LDS Bountiful Wards 29,44—*church* UT-8
LDS Bountiful Wards 32,42,51—*church* UT-8
LDS Bountiful Wards 34,54—*church* UT-8
LDS Bountiful Wards 35,47—*church* UT-8
LDS Bountiful Wards 4,20,36—*church* UT-8
LDS Bountiful Wards 46,48—*church* UT-8
LDS Bountiful Wards 49,52,59—*church* UT-8
LDS Bountiful Wards 5,43—*church* UT-8
LDS Bountiful Wards 7,15,57—*church* UT-8
LDS Bountiful Wards 8,40—*church* UT-8
LDS Bountiful Wards 9,31—*church* UT-8
LDS Bountiful Ward 28, Val Verda Ward 8—*church* UT-8
LDS Bridgeland Ward—*church* UT-8
LDS Brigham City Wards 1,25—*church* UT-8
LDS Brigham City Wards 12,17, 23—*church* UT-8
LDS Brigham City Wards 3,8,11, 15—*church* UT-8
LDS Brigham City Wards 4,22—*church* UT-8
LDS Brigham City Wards 5,14, 20—*church* UT-8
LDS Brigham City Wards 6, Garland Wards 1, 2—*church* UT-8
LDS Brigham City Wards 6,9—*church* UT-8
LDS Brigham City Wards 7, 13—*church* UT-8
LDS Brigham City Ward 18—*church* UT-8
LDS Brigham City Ward 2, Mantua Ward—*church* UT-8
LDS Brigham City Ward 24, Elwood Ward—*church* UT-8
LDS Brighton, Edison, Poplar Wards—*church* UT-8
LDS Brighton Ward—*church* UT-8
LDS Bryan Ward—*church* UT-8
LDS Burch Creek Ward, Ogden Wards 74, 77—*church* UT-8
LDS Butler Wards 1,8,12—*church* UT-8
LDS Butler Wards 11,27,33—*church* UT-8
LDS Butler Wards 14, 22—*church* UT-8
LDS Butler Wards 16,19,35—*church* UT-8
LDS Butler Wards 17,29—*church* UT-8
LDS Butler Wards 23,24,36—*church* UT-8
LDS Butler Wards 25,37—*church* UT-8
LDS Butler Wards 28,34—*church* UT-8
LDS Butler Wards 3,26,31—*church* UT-8
LDS Butler Wards 30, 32—*church* UT-8
LDS Butler Wards 4,10,18—*church* UT-8
LDS Butler Wards 6,13,15—*church* UT-8
LDS Butler Wards 7,20,38—*church* UT-8
LDS Butler Wards 9,21—*church* UT-8
LDS Butler Ward 2—*church* UT-8
LDS BYU Asian Ward, Provo Ward 9—*church* UT-8
LDS BYU Wards 10,23,24,31,32,38,71,92,144, Lamanite 159—*church* UT-8
LDS BYU Wards 11,49,51,66,74,108, 154—*church* UT-8
LDS BYU Wards 115,143, Orem Wards 14, 15—*church* UT-8
LDS BYU Wards 13,21,28,96, 138—*church* UT-8
LDS BYU Wards 157,158, Orem Wards 19, 38—*church* UT-8
LDS BYU Wards 16,36,41,42,45,48,72,91,122, 123—*church* UT-8
LDS BYU Wards 17,27,43,86, 113—*church* UT-8
LDS BYU Wards 18,33,140—*church* UT-8
LDS BYU Wards 2,12,15,82,98,104,147,150, 151,152,153—*church* UT-8
LDS BYU Wards 20,30,46,64,68,82,118, 120—*church* UT-8
LDS BYU Wards 25,85—*church* UT-8
LDS BYU Wards 26,73—*church* UT-8
LDS BYU Wards 3,6,22,32,39,40,61,63,78, 119—*church* UT-8
LDS BYU Wards 34,44, Oak Hills Wards 5, 6—*church* UT-8
LDS BYU Wards 35,69,100,112,117, 170—*church* UT-8
LDS BYU Wards 37,60,87,102—*church* UT-8
LDS BYU Wards 4,14,19,47,65,67,81, 94—*church* UT-8
LDS BYU Wards 5,59,139—*church* UT-8
LDS BYU Wards 56,77,130,134,135,136, 137—*church* UT-8
LDS BYU Wards 58,70, Orem Wards 5, 60—*church* UT-8
LDS BYU Wards 7,8,106,111—*church* UT-8
LDS BYU Wards 75,97,114,145 (Lamanite)—*church* UT-8
LDS BYU Ward 1, Edgemont Ward 19, Provo Ward 19—*church* UT-8
LDS BYU Ward 103, Lakeview Wards 1,3, 4—*church* UT-8
LDS BYU Ward 109—*church* UT-8
LDS BYU Ward 133, Orem Wards 45, 52—*church* UT-8
LDS BYU Ward 141—*church* UT-8
LDS BYU Ward 146, Orem Wards 46, 78—*church* UT-8
LDS BYU Ward 154—*church* UT-8
LDS BYU Ward 156, Provo Wards 10, 16—*church* UT-8
LDS BYU Ward 29, Provo Wards 5, 8—*church* UT-8
LDS BYU Ward 53, Lakeview Wards 6, 7—*church* UT-8
LDS BYU Ward 54, Park Ward, Provo Ward 4—*church* UT-8
LDS BYU Ward 62, Orem Wards 50, 86—*church* UT-8
LDS BYU Ward 76—*church* UT-8
LDS BYU Ward 79—*church* UT-8
LDS BYU Ward 84—*church* UT-8
LDS BYU Ward 89, Provo Wards 27, 31—*church* UT-8
LDS BYU Ward 9, Provo Wards 28, 32—*church* UT-8
LDS BYU Ward 98, Orem Ward 76—*church* UT-8
LDS Cache Ward 1—*church* UT-8
LDS Cache Ward 2—*church* UT-8
LDS Callao Ward—*church* UT-8
LDS Cambodian Ward, Granger South Ward 3, Granger West Ward 4—*church* UT-8
LDS Cannonville Ward—*church* UT-8
LDS Cannon Wards 1,2 (Tongan)—*church* UT-8
LDS Cannon Wards 2,8—*church* UT-8
LDS Cannon Wards 3,4—*church* UT-8
LDS Cannon Wards 5,9—*church* UT-8
LDS Cannon Wards 6,7—*church* UT-8
LDS Canyon Rim Wards 1,2—*church* UT-8
LDS Canyon Rim Wards 3,4—*church* UT-8
LDS Canyon Rim Ward 5, Rosecrest Wards 1, 2—*church* UT-8
LDS Canyon Ward, Spanish Fork Wards 14, 21—*church* UT-8
LDS Capitol Hill Wards 1,2—*church* UT-8
LDS Capitol Hill Ward 3, Ensign Peak, Monte de Sion Ward—*church* UT-8
LDS Carbonville Wards 1,2—*church* UT-8
LDS Castle Dale Wards 1,2—*church* UT-8
LDS Castle Dale Ward 3, Orangeville Ward 3—*church* UT-8
LDS Castle Valley Ward—*church* UT-8
LDS Cedar Hills Ward, Manila Wards 1, 3—*church* UT-8
LDS Cedar Valley Ward—*church* UT-8
LDS Cedar Wards 1,12,14—*church* UT-8
LDS Cedar Wards 13,17—*church* UT-8
LDS Cedar Wards 2,8—*church* UT-8
LDS Cedar Wards 3,18, Enoch Ward 5—*church* UT-8
LDS Cedar Wards 4,6,11,15—*church* UT-8
LDS Cedar Wards 5,10,19—*church* UT-8
LDS Cedar Wards 7,9,16—*church* UT-8
LDS Center, Daniel, Mill Road Wards—*church* UT-8
LDS Centerfield Wards 1,2—*church* UT-8
LDS Centerville Wards 1,11—*church* UT-8
LDS Centerville Wards 10,15,22—*church* UT-8
LDS Centerville Wards 14,20—*church* UT-8
LDS Centerville Wards 2,9,21—*church* UT-8
LDS Centerville Wards 3,6,19—*church* UT-8
LDS Centerville Wards 4,12,13—*church* UT-8
LDS Centerville Wards 5,7,18—*church* UT-8
LDS Centerville Wards 8,16—*church* UT-8
LDS Center Wards 2,3, Meadow Ward—*church* UT-8
LDS Central Park, Madison Wards—*church* UT-8
LDS Charleston Ward—*church* UT-8
LDS Circleville Wards 1,2—*church* UT-8
LDS Clarkston Ward—*church* UT-8
LDS Clark Ward, Grantsville Ward 8—*church* UT-8
LDS Clearfield Wards 1,5,19—*church* UT-8
LDS Clearfield Wards 12,13,15, 17—*church* UT-8
LDS Clearfield Wards 2,11,16—*church* UT-8
LDS Clearfield Wards 3,7,18—*church* UT-8
LDS Clearfield Wards 4,9,14,20—*church* UT-8
LDS Clearfield Wards 6,8,10—*church* UT-8
LDS Cleveland Wards 1,2—*church* UT-8
LDS Clinton Wards 1,8,10—*church* UT-8
LDS Clinton Wards 2,9—*church* UT-8
LDS Clinton Wards 3,4,6—*church* UT-8
LDS Clinton Wards 5,7,11—*church* UT-8
LDS Coalville Wards 1,2—*church* UT-8
LDS College of Eastern Utah Ward—*church* UT-8
LDS College Wards 1,2,3—*church* UT-8
LDS College Ward (Wellsville)—*church* UT-8
LDS College Ward 5, Lakeview Wards 2, 5—*church* UT-8
LDS College Ward 6, Vineyard Ward—*church* UT-8
LDS Colonial Hills Wards 1,2—*church* UT-8
LDS Copperton Ward—*church* UT-8
LDS Corinne Ward 2, Bear River Ward 1—*church* UT-8
LDS Cornish Ward—*church* UT-8
LDS Cottonwood Wards 1,9—*church* UT-8
LDS Cottonwood Wards 11,13, 15—*church* UT-8
LDS Cottonwood Wards 12,16—*church* UT-8
LDS Cottonwood Wards 2,14,17—*church* UT-8
LDS Cottonwood Wards 3,5,8—*church* UT-8
LDS Cottonwood Wards 4,7—*church* UT-8
LDS Cottonwood Wards 6,10—*church* UT-8
LDS Cottonwood Wards 9,14—*church* UT-8
LDS Country Meadow Nursing Home Ward—*church* UT-8
LDS Cove Point Ward—*church* UT-8
LDS Cove Ward—*church* UT-8
LDS Crescent Wards 1,24,30—*church* UT-8
LDS Crescent Wards 11,12,27,28, 31—*church* UT-8
LDS Crescent Wards 13,18, Dimple Dell Ward—*church* UT-8
LDS Crescent Wards 14,16—*church* UT-8
LDS Crescent Wards 15,20,26—*church* UT-8
LDS Crescent Wards 2,17,25—*church* UT-8
LDS Crescent Wards 3,4,7—*church* UT-8
LDS Crescent Wards 5,19,29—*church* UT-8
LDS Crescent Wards 6,9,23—*church* UT-8
LDS Crescent Wards 8,21, Granite Ward 4, Pinecrest Ward—*church* UT-8
LDS Crescent Ward 10, Crescent View Ward—*church* UT-8
LDS Crystal Heights Wards 1,2—*church* UT-8
LDS Curlew Ward—*church* UT-8
LDS Dai-Ichi (Japanese), Fairmont Wards—*church* UT-8
LDS Daniels, Liberty, Liberty Park Wards—*church* UT-8
LDS Davis Wards 1,4—*church* UT-8
LDS Davis Wards 2,3—*church* UT-8
LDS Decker Lake, Granger Wards 9, 15—*church* UT-8
LDS Delta Wards 1,4—*church* UT-8
LDS Delta Wards 2,5,6,7—*church* UT-8
LDS Delta Ward 9—*church* UT-8
LDS Deseret Ward, Oasis Ward—*church* UT-8
LDS Dixie College Wards 1,2,3,4,5,6,7, 8—*church* UT-8
LDS Douglas Ward—*church* UT-8
LDS Draper Wards 1,9—*church* UT-8
LDS Draper Wards 2,6,10—*church* UT-8
LDS Draper Wards 3,15,16—*church* UT-8
LDS Draper Wards 4,5,13—*church* UT-8
LDS Draper Wards 7,12—*church* UT-8
LDS Draper Wards 8,11,14—*church* UT-8
LDS Duchesne Wards 1,3—*church* UT-8
LDS Duchesne Wards 2,4—*church* UT-8
LDS Dugway Ward—*church* UT-8
LDS Dutch John Ward—*church* UT-8
LDS Eagle Gate Ward 1, Salt Lake Ward 20—*church* UT-8
LDS Eagle Gate Ward 7—*church* UT-8
LDS Eagle Gate Ward 8—*church* UT-8
LDS East Carbon, Sunnyside Wards—*church* UT-8
LDS Eastland Ward—*church* UT-8
LDS East Mill Creek Wards 1,11, 12—*church* UT-8
LDS East Mill Creek Wards 3,7, 16—*church* UT-8
LDS East Mill Creek Wards 3,9, 15—*church* UT-8
LDS East Mill Creek Wards 4,6—*church* UT-8
LDS East Mill Creek Wards 5,10, 13—*church* UT-8
LDS East Mill Creek Wards 8,14—*church* UT-8
LDS East Mill Creek Ward 19—*church* UT-8
LDS Eden Ward, Huntsville Ward 3—*church* UT-8
LDS Edgehill Wards 1,2—*church* UT-8
LDS Edgemont Wards 13,15—*church* UT-8
LDS Edgemont Wards 2,7,17—*church* UT-8
LDS Edgemont Wards 4,6,10,16—*church* UT-8
LDS Edgemont Wards 5,8,11—*church* UT-8
LDS Edgemont Wards 9,18,20—*church* UT-8
LDS Edgemont Ward 12—*church* UT-8
LDS Edgemont Ward 14—*church* UT-8
LDS Elberta Ward—*church* UT-8
LDS Eldredge, Lee, Miller Wards—*church* UT-8
LDS Elkridge Wards 1,2—*church* UT-8
LDS Elmo Ward—*church* UT-8
LDS Elsinore Wards 1,2, Joseph Ward—*church* UT-8
LDS Emerson, Samoan Wards—*church* UT-8
LDS Emery Ward—*church* UT-8
LDS Emigration Ward 1—*church* UT-8
LDS Enoch Wards 1,2,3,4—*church* UT-8
LDS Ensign Waeds 1,2—*church* UT-8
LDS Ensign Wards 3,4—*church* UT-8
LDS Ensign Wards 5,6—*church* UT-8
LDS Enterprise Wards 1,2,3—*church* UT-8
LDS Ephraim Wards 1,5—*church* UT-8
LDS Ephraim Ward 2, Snow College Wards 1,2, 5—*church* UT-8
LDS Ephraim Ward 3,4—*church* UT-8
LDS Erda Wards 1,2—*church* UT-8
LDS Escalante, Eva Dawn Wards, Rose Park Wards 5,6,7,8—*church* UT-8
LDS Escalante Ward—*church* UT-8
LDS Eureka Ward—*church* UT-8
LDS Fairview Wards 2,3—*church* UT-8
LDS Fairview Ward 1—*church* UT-8
LDS Farmington Wards 1,3,13—*church* UT-8
LDS Farmington Wards 12,17—*church* UT-8
LDS Farmington Wards 2,9,14—*church* UT-8
LDS Farmington Wards 4,11—*church* UT-8
LDS Farmington Wards 6,10,16—*church* UT-8
LDS Farmington Wards 7,8,15—*church* UT-8
LDS Farr West Wards 1,3,4—*church* UT-8
LDS Farr West Ward 2—*church* UT-8
LDS Fayette Ward—*church* UT-8
LDS Ferron Wards 1,2—*church* UT-8
LDS Ferron Wards 3,4,5—*church* UT-8
LDS Fiddlers Canyon Ward—*church* UT-8
LDS Fielding Ward—*church* UT-8
LDS Fillmore Wards 1,4—*church* UT-8
LDS Fillmore Wards 2,3—*church* UT-8
LDS Flowell Ward—*church* UT-8
LDS Forest Dale Ward—*church* UT-8
LDS Fort Douglas Post Chapel—*church* UT-8
LDS Fountain Green Wards 1,2—*church* UT-8
LDS Francis Ward—*church* UT-8
LDS Fremont Ward—*church* UT-8
LDS Fruit Heights Wards 1,2—*church* UT-8
LDS Fruit Heights Wards 3,6—*church* UT-8
LDS Fruit Heights Wards 4,5—*church* UT-8
LDS Fruitland Ward—*church* UT-8
LDS Garden Heights, Garden Heights North, Garden Heights South—*church* UT-8
LDS Garden Park Wards 1,2—*church* UT-8
LDS Garland Ward 3—*church* UT-8
LDS Garrison Ward—*church* UT-8
LDS Genola Ward—*church* UT-8
LDS Glendale Ward—*church* UT-8
LDS Glenwood Wards 1,2—*church* UT-8
LDS Glines Wards 1,5—*church* UT-8
LDS Glines Wards 2,4—*church* UT-8
LDS Glines Ward 3, Vernal Ward 3—*church* UT-8
LDS Golden Living Center Ward—*church* UT-8
LDS Goshen Ward—*church* UT-8
LDS Grandview Wards 1,2—*church* UT-8
LDS Granger So. Wards 1,2, Granger W. Ward 1, Jordan No. Ward 9—*church* UT-8

LDS Tooele Wards 1,6—*church* UT-8
LDS Tooele Wards 11,15—*church* UT-8
LDS Tooele Wards 12,16—*church* UT-8
LDS Tooele Wards 2,3,10—*church* UT-8
LDS Tooele Wards 4,14—*church* UT-8
LDS Tooele Wards 5,8—*church* UT-8
LDS Tooele Wards 7,18—*church* UT-8
LDS Tooele Ward 13—*church* UT-8
LDS Tooele Ward 17—*church* UT-8
LDS Torrey Ward—*church* UT-8
LDS Tremonton Ward 5, Thatcher Penrose Ward 1—*church* UT-8
LDS Tremonton Ward 6, Willard Wards 1, 2—*church* UT-8
LDS Tremonton Ward 7—*church* UT-8
LDS Tremonton Ward 9—*church* UT-8
LDS Trenton Ward—*church* UT-8
LDS Tridell Ward—*church* UT-8
LDS Tropic Ward—*church* UT-8
LDS Uintah Wards 1,2,5—*church* UT-8
LDS Uintah Wards 3,4,6,7—*church* UT-8
LDS Union Wards 1,13—*church* UT-8
LDS Union Wards 11,20,27—*church* UT-8
LDS Union Wards 12,14,31—*church* UT-8
LDS Union Wards 18,19,23—*church* UT-8
LDS Union Wards 2,29—*church* UT-8
LDS Union Wards 3,22,34—*church* UT-8
LDS Union Wards 4,16,35—*church* UT-8
LDS Union Wards 5,17,21—*church* UT-8
LDS Union Wards 6,25,26—*church* UT-8
LDS Union Wards 7,10,30—*church* UT-8
LDS Union Wards 8,28—*church* UT-8
LDS Union Wards 9,15,24,33—*church* UT-8
LDS University Wards 4,8,9,12,20, 21—*church* UT-8
LDS Upton Ward—*church* UT-8
LDS Utah State Prison Ward—*church* UT-8
LDS Valley View Wards 1,10—*church* UT-8
LDS Valley View Wards 3,9—*church* UT-8
LDS Valley View Wards 4,5,12—*church* UT-8
LDS Valley View Wards 6,7—*church* UT-8
LDS Val Verda Wards 2,6—*church* UT-8
LDS Val Verda Wards 3,4—*church* UT-8
LDS Venice Ward—*church* UT-8
LDS Vernal Wards 1,5,9—*church* UT-8
LDS Vernal Wards 2,4—*church* UT-8
LDS Vernal Wards 6,7—*church* UT-8
LDS Vernon Ward—*church* UT-8
LDS Veyo Ward—*church* UT-8
LDS Virgin Ward—*church* UT-8
LDS Wales Ward—*church* UT-8
LDS Wallsburg Ward—*church* UT-8
LDS Wanship Ward—*church* UT-8
LDS Warren, West Warren Wards—*church* UT-8
LDS Wasatch Canyon Hospital Ward—*church* UT-8
LDS Wasatch Ward 1—*church* UT-8
LDS Washington Terrace Wards 1, 4—*church* UT-8
LDS Washington Terrace Wards 2,7, 11—*church* UT-8
LDS Washington Terrace Wards 3, 6—*church* UT-8
LDS Washington Terrace Wards 5,8, 12—*church* UT-8
LDS Washington Terrace Wards 9, 10—*church* UT-8
LDS Washington Wards 1,3,4,7, 10—*church* UT-8
LDS Weber State College Wards 3,4,5, 7—*church* UT-8
LDS Wellington Wards 1,4—*church* UT-8
LDS Wellington Wards 2,3—*church* UT-8
LDS Wellsville Ward 3, Logan Wards 30, 39—*church* UT-8
LDS Wellsville Ward 4, Logan Univ Wards 7,8, 13,14,15,17,23,26—*church* UT-8
LDS Wellsville Ward 5—*church* UT-8
LDS Wells Ward—*church* UT-8
LDS Wendover Ward—*church* UT-8
LDS West Bountiful Wards 1,7,8—*church* UT-8
LDS West Bountiful Wards 2,3,5—*church* UT-8
LDS West Bountiful Wards 4,6,9—*church* UT-8
LDS West Jordan Wards 1,5—*church* UT-8
LDS West Jordan Wards 11,23—*church* UT-8
LDS West Jordan Wards 12,35, 69—*church* UT-8
LDS West Jordan Wards 13,25—*church* UT-8
LDS West Jordan Wards 16,63—*church* UT-8
LDS West Jordan Wards 19,28, 57—*church* UT-8
LDS West Jordan Wards 2,48—*church* UT-8
LDS West Jordan Wards 20,36—*church* UT-8
LDS West Jordan Wards 22,51, 70—*church* UT-8
LDS West Jordan Wards 26,31, 50—*church* UT-8
LDS West Jordan Wards 29,43—*church* UT-8
LDS West Jordan Wards 3,15,47—*church* UT-8
LDS West Jordan Wards 30,54,58, 61—*church* UT-8
LDS West Jordan Wards 34,42, 65—*church* UT-8
LDS West Jordan Wards 37,39,45, 60—*church* UT-8
LDS West Jordan Wards 4,44—*church* UT-8
LDS West Jordan Wards 40,52,64, 67—*church* UT-8
LDS West Jordan Wards 41,55, 56—*church* UT-8
LDS West Jordan Wards 49,59, 62—*church* UT-8
LDS West Jordan Wards 6,14,21—*church* UT-8
LDS West Jordan Wards 7,17—*church* UT-8
LDS West Jordan Wards 8,27,66—*church* UT-8
LDS West Jordan Wards 9,32,46—*church* UT-8
LDS West Jordan Ward 38, Winder Ward 15—*church* UT-8
LDS West Jordan Ward 53—*church* UT-8
LDS West Jordan Ward 71, City Center Ward—*church* UT-8
LDS West Point Wards 1,3,5—*church* UT-8
LDS West Point Wards 2,4,6,7—*church* UT-8
LDS West Weber Wards 1,2—*church* UT-8
LDS White Mesa Ward—*church* UT-8
LDS Whiterocks Ward—*church* UT-8
LDS Whittier Ward—*church* UT-8
LDS Wilford Wards 1,2—*church* UT-8
LDS Willard Ward 3, Brigham City Ward 10—*church* UT-8
LDS Wilson Wards 1,2—*church* UT-8
LDS Winder Wards 2,5,10—*church* UT-8
LDS Winder Wards 3,13—*church* UT-8
LDS Winder Wards 4,11,12—*church* UT-8
LDS Winder Wards 6,8—*church* UT-8
LDS Winder Wards 7,14—*church* UT-8
LDS Winder Wards 9,16—*church* UT-8
LDS Woodland Wards—*church* UT-8
LDS Woodruff Ward—*church* UT-8
LDS Woods Cross Wards 2,6,9—*church* UT-8
LDS Woods Cross Wards 3,4,8—*church* UT-8
LDS Woods Cross Ward 1,5,7—*church* UT-8
LDS Yalecrest Wards 1,2—*church* UT-8
LDS Yale Wards 1,2—*church* UT-8
LDS Young Ward—*church* UT-8
L D Thaggard Dam—*dam* AL-4
*L D Thaggard Pond* AL-4
L D Whitehead Ranch—*locale* TX-5
*Lea* OK-5
Lea—*locale* NM-5
Lea, Hampton, House—*hist pl* MS-4
Lea, Henry C., Sch of Practice—*hist pl* PA-2
Lea Allison Ranch—*locale* TX-5
Lea Bethel Ch—*church* NC-3
Lea Block—*hist pl* OH-6
*Leabon* FM-9
Leabow Cem—*cemetery* TN-4
Leabow Hollow—*valley* TN-4
Lea Branch—*stream* TN-4
**Leaburg**—*pop pl* OR-9
Leaburg Dam—*dam* OR-9
Leaburg Power Plant—*other* OR-9
Leaburg Rsvr—*reservoir* OR-9
Lea Cem—*cemetery* AR-4
Lea Cem—*cemetery* LA-4
Lea Cem—*cemetery* (4) MS-4
*Leach* IN-6
Leach—*locale* OK-5
**Leach**—*pop pl* KY-4
**Leach**—*pop pl* TN-4
Leach, Philip, House—*hist pl* ME-1
Leach Airp—*airport* CO-8
*Lea Chapel* AL-4
Lea Chapel—*church* AL-4
Leach Branch—*stream* KY-4
Leach Branch—*stream* NE-7
Leach Bridge (historical)—*bridge* TN-4
Leach Brook—*stream* MA-1
Leach Camp Trail—*trail* OR-9
*Leach Canyon* NV-8
Leach Canyon—*valley* CA-9
Leach Canyon—*valley* NV-8
Leach Canyon—*valley* UT-8
Leach Cem—*cemetery* AL-4
Leach Cem—*cemetery* AR-4
Leach Cem—*cemetery* IN-6
Leach Cem—*cemetery* (2) KY-4
Leach Cem—*cemetery* ME-1
Leach Cem—*cemetery* MA-1
Leach Cem—*cemetery* (2) MO-7
Leach Cem—*cemetery* NC-3
Leach Cem—*cemetery* OH-6
Leach Cem—*cemetery* PA-2
Leach Cem—*cemetery* (4) TN-4
Leach Cem—*cemetery* TX-5
Leach Cem—*cemetery* VT-1
Leach Cemetary—*cemetery* AR-4
Leach Chapel—*church* KY-4
Leach Coulee—*valley* MT-8
Leach Creek—*stream* (2) CO-8
Leach Creek—*stream* MO-7
Leach Creek—*stream* NV-8
Leach Creek—*stream* PA-2
Leach Creek—*stream* TN-4
Leach Creek—*stream* (2) VT-1
Leach Creek—*stream* (2) WA-9
Leach Creek Ch—*church* NC-3
*Leach Ditch* IN-6
Leach Draw—*valley* WY-8
Leach Elementary and JHS—*school* IN-6
*Leaches Lake* VT-1
*Leaches Pond* MA-1
*Leaches Stream* MA-1
Leach Gap—*gap* TN-4
Leach Hill—*summit* ME-1
Leach Hill—*summit* NY-2
Leach Hill—*summit* (2) VT-1
Leach Hollow—*valley* TN-4
Leach Hot Springs—*spring* NV-8
Leach Lake—*flat* CA-9
Leach Lake—*lake* AK-9
Leach Lake—*lake* (2) MI-6
Leach Lake—*lake* NE-7
Leach Lake—*lake* (2) WI-6
Leach Lake—*reservoir* NY-2
Leachman Draw—*valley* NM-5
Leach Mtn—*summit* TN-4
Leach Pine Brook—*stream* NY-2
Leach Point—*cape* ME-1
*Leach Pond* VT-1
Leach Pond—*lake* (2) MA-1
Leach Post Office—*building* TN-4
Leach Ranch—*locale* (2) NE-7
Leach Ranch—*locale* NV-8
Leach Ranch Landing Strip—*airport* ND-7
Leach Rock—*bar* ME-1
Leach Run—*stream* VA-3
Leach Run—*stream* WV-2
*Leach Sch* IN-6
Leach Sch—*school* MN-6
Leach Sch—*school* OK-5
*Leach Sch Number 68* IN-6
Leachs Island—*island* NH-1
Leachs Mill (historical)—*locale* MS-4
*Leach's Point* ME-1
*Leachs Pond* MA-1
Leach Spring—*spring* CA-9
Leach Spring Ch—*church* NC-3
*Leachs Stream* MA-1
Leach Store (historical)—*locale* MS-4
**Leachtown**—*pop pl* WV-2
Leachtown Schools—*school* WV-2
Leach Trail—*trail* NY-2
*Leachville* NC-3
**Leachville**—*pop pl* AR-4
Leachville Cem—*cemetery* AR-4
**Leachville Junction**—*pop pl* MO-7
Leach Windmill—*locale* NM-5
**Leacock**—*pop pl* PA-2
Leacock Ch—*church* PA-2
Leacock Elem Sch—*school* PA-2
Leacock Point—*ridge* ID-8
Leacock Ranch—*locale* ID-8
**Leacock (Township of)**—*pop pl* PA-2
**Lea (County)**—*pop pl* NM-5
Lea County Courthouse—*hist pl* NM-5
Lea County Hobbs Airp—*airport* NM-5
Lea Cove—*bay* MI-6
Lea Creek—*stream* MS-4
Lea Creek—*stream* TN-4
Leacy Spring—*spring* OR-9
**Lead**—*pop pl* SD-7
Lea-Davis Cem—*cemetery* MS-4
Leaday—*locale* TX-5
Leaday Cem—*cemetery* TX-5
Lead Bayou—*stream* MS-4
Leadbelt Creek—*stream* ID-8
Lead Belt Technical Sch—*school* MO-7
*Leadbetter Branch* NC-3
Leadbetter Brook—*stream* ME-1
*Leadbetter Creek* NC-3
Leadbetter Creek—*stream* LA-4
Leadbetter Island—*island* ME-1
*Leadbetter Lake* WA-9
*Leadbetter Landing* TN-4
Leadbetter Narrows—*channel* ME-1
Leadbetter Point—*cape* WA-9
Leadbetter Pond—*lake* (2) ME-1
Leadbetter Ridge—*ridge* TN-4
Leadbetter Spring—*spring* AR-4
Lead Branch—*stream* KY-4
Lead Branch—*stream* TN-4
Lead Branch Junction—*locale* MO-7
Lead Camp Canyon—*valley* NM-5
Lead Canyon—*valley* CA-9
Lead Canyon—*valley* NM-5
*Lead City* SD-7
*Lead Creek* WY-8
Lead Creek—*stream* ID-8
Lead Creek—*stream* IN-6
Lead Creek—*stream* KY-4
Lead Creek—*stream* MO-7
Lead Creek—*stream* WA-9
Lead Creek—*stream* WI-6
Lead Creek—*stream* WY-8
Lead Creek Hollow—*valley* TN-4
Lead-Dike Mine—*mine* AZ-5
Lead Draw—*valley* ID-8
Lead Draw—*valley* SD-7
Lead Drift Mine—*mine* AR-4
Leadenhall Street Baptist Church—*hist pl* MD-2
Leadenham Creek—*stream* MD-2
*Leaden Peak* AZ-5
Leadenwah Creek—*stream* SC-3
Leader—*locale* CO-8
Leader—*locale* OK-5
**Leader**—*pop pl* MN-6
Leader Bldg—*hist pl* WA-9
Leader Community Hall—*building* MN-6
Leader Creek—*stream* (2) OK-5
Leader Hollow—*valley* AR-4
Leader Island—*island* AK-9
Leader Lake—*lake* WI-6
Leader Lake—*reservoir* WA-9
Leader Mine (Inactive)—*mine* UT-8
Leader Mtn—*summit* AR-4
Leader Mtn—*summit* NV-8
Leader Mtn—*summit* WA-9
Leader Nursing Rehabilation Center—*building* PA-2
Leader Sch—*school* CO-8
Leader Sch—*school* NE-7
**Leaders Heights**—*pop pl* PA-2
Leaders Heights Elem Sch—*school* PA-2
Leader Well—*well* TX-5
Leadfield—*hist pl* CA-9
Leadfield—*locale* CA-9
Lead Fork—*stream* AR-4
Lead Gulch—*valley* CA-9
Lead Gulch—*valley* (2) MT-8
**Lead Hill**—*pop pl* AR-4
Lead Hill—*summit* (2) AR-4
Lead Hill—*summit* (2) MO-7
Lead Hill—*summit* NY-2
Lead Hill—*summit* WA-9
Lead Hill Ch—*church* MO-7
Lead Hill Mine—*mine* WA-9
Lead Hill Public Use Area—*park* AR-4
Lead Hill Sch—*school* AR-4
Lead Hill Sch (historical)—*school* MO-7
Lead Hill Township—*civil* MO-7
Lead Hist Dist—*hist pl* SD-7
Lead Hollow—*valley* AL-4
Lead Hollow—*valley* AR-4
Lead Hollow—*valley* IL-6
Leading Bayou—*gut* LA-4
*Leading Creek* TN-4
Leading Creek—*stream* OH-6
Leading Creek—*stream* (3) WV-2
Leading Creek Ch—*church* WV-2
Leadingham Branch—*stream* KY-4
Leading Point—*cape* AK-9
Leading Point—*cape* MD-2
Leading Point—*uninc pl* MD-2
*Leading Ridge* PA-2
*Leading Ridge* TN-4
Leading Ridge—*ridge* GA-3
Leading Ridge—*ridge* PA-2
Leading Ridge—*ridge* (2) TN-4
Leading Ridge—*ridge* (3) VA-3
Leading Ridge—*ridge* (3) WV-2
Leading Ridge Trail—*trail* VA-3
**Leadington**—*pop pl* MO-7
Lead Island—*island* IA-7
Lead Island Chute—*stream* IA-7
Lea Ditch—*canal* WY-8
**Lead Junction**—*pop pl* MO-7
Lead King Basin—*basin* CO-8
Lead King Hills—*range* WA-9
Lead King Mine—*mine* UT-8
Lead King Mine—*mine* WA-9
Lead Lake—*lake* NV-8
Lead Lake Canal—*canal* NV-8
Lead Lily Shaft—*mine* AZ-5
Lead Lode Mine—*mine* OR-9
Leadman Cem—*cemetery* KY-4
*Leadmine* WV-2
**Lead Mine**—*pop pl* MO-7
**Leadmine**—*pop pl* MO-7
**Lead Mine**—*pop pl* WV-2
**Lead Mine**—*pop pl* WI-6
**Leadmine**—*pop pl* WI-6
*Lead Mine Bend* TN-4
Leadmine Bend—*bend* TN-4
Leadmine Bend Creek—*stream* TN-4
Leadmine Branch—*stream* GA-3
Leadmine Branch—*stream* KY-4
*Lead Mine Brook* MA-1
Leadmine Brook—*stream* CT-1
Lead Mine Brook—*stream* CT-1
Leadmine Brook—*stream* CT-1
Leadmine Brook—*stream* MA-1
Leadmine Brook—*stream* NH-1
Lead Mine Canyon—*valley* NV-8
Lead Mine Canyon—*valley* NM-5
Lead Mine Ch—*church* WI-6
Lead Mine Creek—*stream* (2) AR-4
Lead Mine Gap—*gap* NC-3
Lead Mine Hill—*summit* CT-1
Lead Mine Hills—*summit* NV-8
Lead Mine Hollow—*valley* AR-4
Lead Mine Hollow—*valley* MO-7
Lead Mine Hollow—*valley* OK-5
Leadmine Ledge—*summit* NH-1
*Lead-mine Mtn* MA-1
Leadmine Mtn—*summit* MA-1
Lead Mine Mtn—*summit* VT-1
*Lead-mine Pond* MA-1
Leadmine Pond—*lake* MA-1
Leadmine Ridge—*ridge* NC-3
Leadmine Ridge—*ridge* TN-4
Lead Mine Ridge—*ridge* TN-4
*Lead Mine Run* WV-2
Leadmine Run—*stream* WV-2
*Lead Mines, The* PA-2
Lead Mines Cem—*cemetery* AL-4
Lead Mine Sch—*school* WI-6
Leadmine Sch (abandoned)—*school* MO-7
Lead Mines (Magisterial District)—*fmr MCD* VA-3
Lead Mine State For—*forest* MO-7
Leadmine State For—*forest* NH-1
Lead Mine Valley—*valley* TN-4
Lead Mtn—*summit* (2) CA-9
Lead Mtn—*summit* (2) CO-8
Lead Mtn—*summit* ME-1
Lead Mtn—*summit* NV-8
Lead Mtn—*summit* NM-5
Lead Mtn—*summit* UT-8
Lead-Off Ridge—*ridge* VA-3
**Leadore**—*pop pl* ID-8
Leadore Hill—*summit* ID-8
Leadore Ranger Station—*locale* ID-8
Lead Pencil Mtn—*summit* WA-9
Lead Pencil Spring—*spring* WA-9
Lead Pill Mine—*mine* AZ-5
Lead Pipe Spring—*spring* CA-9
Leadpoint—*locale* WA-9
Leadpole Mtn—*summit* GA-3
Lead Pond—*lake* FL-3
Lead Pond—*lake* NY-2
Lead Queen Mine—*mine* AZ-5
Lead Run—*stream* OH-6
Lead Run—*stream* PA-2
Leads Cem—*cemetery* CT-1
*Leads Creek* WY-8
*Leadstone Creek* MT-8
**Leadsville**—*pop pl* WV-2
Leadsville (Magisterial District)—*fmr MCD* WV-2
Lead Trust Mine—*mine* WA-9
*Leadurny Point* ME-1
Leadus Chapel—*church* AL-4
Leadus Sch—*school* AL-4
Leadvale—*locale* (2) TN-4
*Leadvale Baptist Church* TN-4
Leadvale Ch—*church* TN-4
Leadvale Creek—*stream* TN-4
Leadvale Post Office (historical)—*building* TN-4
*Lead Vein* TN-4
Leadville—*locale* ID-8
Leadville—*locale* MT-8
**Leadville**—*pop pl* CO-8
Leadville Canyon—*valley* NV-8
Leadville Hist Dist—*hist pl* CO-8
Leadville Hollow—*valley* MO-7
Leadville Hollow—*valley* PA-2
Leadville Junction—*locale* CO-8
Leadville Mine—*mine* (2) ID-8
Leadville Mine—*mine* WA-9
Leadville Mtn—*summit* AK-9
Leadville Mtn—*summit* NV-8
Leadville Natl Fish Hatchery—*hist pl* CO-8
Leadville Natl Fish Hatchery—*park* CO-8
Leadville North—*cens area* CO-8
Leadville (Site)—*locale* NV-8
Leadville Troughs—*spring* NV-8
Lead Well—*well* AZ-5
**Leadwood**—*pop pl* MO-7
Leadwood Cem—*cemetery* MO-7
Leadys Sch (historical)—*school* AL-4
Lea Elem Sch—*school* PA-2
Leaeno Mtn—*summit* AS-9
*Leaf* MS-4
Leaf—*locale* CA-9
Leaf—*locale* GA-3
**Leaf**—*pop pl* MS-4
Lea Farm Plantation (historical)—*locale* TN-4
Leafbank Run—*stream* WV-2
Leaf Branch—*stream* IN-6
Leaf Camp—*locale* CA-9
Leaf Cem—*cemetery* MS-4
Leaf Ch—*church* MS-4
Leafdale—*locale* KY-4
Lea Female Coll (historical)—*school* MS-4
*Leaf Fire Tower* MS-4
Leaf Hill—*summit* AZ-5
Leaf Lake—*lake* (3) AK-9
Leaf Lake—*lake* MI-6
Leaf Lake—*lake* (3) MN-6
**Leaf Lake**—*pop pl* MN-6
Leaf Lake—*reservoir* TN-4
Leaf Lake Cem—*cemetery* (2) MN-6
Leaf Lake Ch—*church* MN-6
Leaf Lake Dam—*dam* TN-4
**Leaf Lake (Township of)**—*pop pl* MN-6
Leaflet Ch—*church* NC-3
Leaf Lookout Tower—*locale* MS-4
Lea Flowage—*reservoir* WI-6
Leaf Mountain Ch—*church* MN-6
**Leaf Mountain Township**—*pop pl* ND-7
Leaf Mountain (Township of)—*civ div* MN-6
Leaf-On Hill—*summit* ND-7
Leaf On The Hill Creek—*stream* ND-7
**Leaf Park**—*pop pl* PA-2
Leaf Pond—*reservoir* MS-4
Leaf River—*locale* MN-6
**Leaf River**—*pop pl* IL-6
**Leaf River**—*pop pl* MN-6
**Leaf River**—*pop pl* MS-4
Leaf River—*stream* IL-6
Leaf River—*stream* MN-6
Leaf River—*stream* MS-4
*Leaf River Baptist Church* MS-4
*Leaf River Bridge* MS-4
Leaf River Bridge—*hist pl* MS-4
Leaf River Cem—*cemetery* MN-6
Leaf River Cem—*cemetery* MS-4
Leaf River Ch—*church* MN-6
Leaf River Ch—*church* (2) MS-4
*Leaf River Game Mngmt Area* MS-4
*Leaf River Game Refuge* MS-4
Leaf River P.O. (historical)—*building* MS-4
Leaf River Sch (historical)—*school* MS-4
Leaf River State Wildlife Mngmt Area—*park* MS-4
**Leaf River (Township of)**—*pop pl* IL-6
**Leaf River (Township of)**—*pop pl* MN-6
Leaf Rock Creek—*stream* MT-8
Leaf Run—*stream* IN-6
Leaf Sch—*school* IL-6
Leaf Spring—*spring* CA-9
Leafu Stream—*stream* AS-9
Leaf Valley—*locale* MN-6
**Leaf Valley (Township of)**—*pop pl* MN-6
Leaf Water Pueblo(LA 300)—*hist pl* NM-5
Leafy Bower Sch—*school* IL-6
**Leafydale Terrace**—*pop pl* PA-2
League—*locale* WV-2
League Chapel—*church* MS-4
League Chapel Sch (historical)—*school* TN-4
**League City**—*pop pl* TX-5
League City Oil Field—*oilfield* TX-5
League Creek—*stream* MS-4
League Island—*flat* PA-2
League Island—*other* PA-2
*League Island Navy Yard* PA-2
League Lake—*lake* WI-6
League Park—*hist pl* OH-6
League Ponds—*swamp* TX-5
League Ranch—*locale* (2) TX-5
League Rock—*pillar* RI-1
League Sch—*school* MA-1
Leagueville—*locale* TX-5
*Leah* WY-8
Leah—*locale* GA-3
Lea Harris Cem—*cemetery* TN-4
*Leahi* HI-9
Leahi—*cape* HI-9
**Leahi**—*pop pl* HI-9
Leahigh—*locale* MD-2
Leahi Hosp—*hospital* HI-9
*Leahi Point* HI-9
Leah Lake—*lake* MN-6
Leah Rsvr—*reservoir* WY-8
Leahs Chapel—*church* NC-3
Leahy—*locale* WA-9
Leahy Field—*park* GU-9
Leahy Hill—*summit* IL-6
Leahy Hollow—*valley* NY-2
Leahy Place—*locale* WY-8
Leahy Sch—*school* MA-1
Leahy Spring—*spring* ID-8
Leahy Upper Reservoir Dam—*dam* MA-1
Leaird Cem—*cemetery* IN-6
Leak Branch—*stream* NC-3
Leak Canyon—*valley* NM-5
Leak Cem—*cemetery* GA-3
Leak Cem—*cemetery* MS-4
*Leak Creek* TX-5
Leak Creek—*stream* AL-4
Leak Creek—*stream* NC-3
Leak Ditch—*canal* IN-6
Leake, Will and Mary, House—*hist pl* TX-5
Leake Acad—*school* MS-4
**Leake County**—*pop pl* MS-4
Leake County Agricultural HS (historical)—*school* MS-4
Leake County Memorial Hosp—*hospital* MS-4
Leake Creek—*stream* MS-4
Leake-Ingham Bldg—*hist pl* AR-4
Leake Lake—*lake* IL-6
Leake Lake Dam—*dam* MS-4
Leake Park—*park* MI-6
Leakes Sch—*school* NC-3
*Leakes Switch* MS-4
**Leakesville**—*pop pl* MS-4
Leakesville Attendance Center—*school* MS-4
*Leakesville HS* MS-4
**Leakesville Junction**—*pop pl* VA-3
Leakesville Methodist Ch—*church* MS-4
Leake (Township of)—*fmr MCD* AR-4
**Leakey**—*pop pl* TX-5
Leakey Springs—*spring* TX-5
Leak Fork—*stream* NC-3
*Leakille* MS-4
Leakin Park—*park* MD-2
Leak Island—*island* NC-3
Leak Lake—*lake* AR-4
Leak Memorial Ch—*church* NC-3
Leak Quarry—*mine* AL-4
**Leak Run**—*pop pl* PA-2
Leak Run—*stream* PA-2
Leaks Chapel—*church* VA-3
Leaks Grove Ch—*church* NC-3
Leaks Mill (historical)—*locale* AL-4
Leak Spring—*spring* NM-5
Leak Street Elem Sch—*school* NC-3
*Leaksville* NC-3
Leaksville—*locale* VA-3
**Leaksville**—*pop pl* NC-3
Leaksville Commercial Hist Dist—*hist pl* NC-3
Leaksville JHS—*school* NC-3
Leaksville Junction—*locale* VA-3
Leaksville Lagoon Dam—*dam* MS-4
Leaksville (Township of)—*fmr MCD* NC-3
Leak Well—*locale* NM-5
Leaky Mtn—*summit* WY-8
Leaky Rsvr—*reservoir* OR-9
Leaky Tank—*reservoir* AZ-5
Leaky Well—*well* NM-5
Leal—*locale* CO-8
Leal—*locale* TX-5
**Leal**—*pop pl* ND-7
Lea Laboratory—*hist pl* NC-3
Lealaeli Hill—*summit* AS-9
Lealafaalava Mtn—*summit* AS-9
Leala JHS—*school* AS-9
Lea Lake—*lake* NM-5
Lea Lake—*reservoir* TN-4
Lea Lake Dam—*dam* TN-4
Leala Point—*cape* AS-9
Lealataua (County of)—*civ div* AS-9
Leal Canyon—*valley* NM-5
Leal Cem—*cemetery* TX-5
Lealman Ave Sch—*school* FL-3
Lealman JHS—*school* FL-3
Lealman (Lellman)—*CDP* FL-3
**Lealman (Lellman Station)**—*pop pl* FL-3
Leal Sch—*school* IL-6
**Lealtad**—*pop pl* PR-3
*Lealu* HI-9
Lea Lumber Company Airp—*airport* NC-3
**Leama**—*pop pl* TN-4
*Leaman* PA-2
**Leaman**—*pop pl* NC-3
**Leaman**—*pop pl* TN-4
Leaman Cave—*cave* PA-2
Leaman Lake—*lake* WI-6
**Leaman Place**—*pop pl* PA-2
Leaman Place Covered Bridge—*hist pl* PA-2
Leaman Place Junction(STRA RR name for Leaman Place)—*other* PA-2
**Leaman Place (STRA name Leaman Place Junction)**—*pop pl* PA-2
Leamans Store (historical)—*locale* AL-4
Leamens Post Office (historical)—*building* TN-4
**Leamersville**—*pop pl* PA-2
Leamex Oil Field—*other* NM-5
Leaming Canyon—*valley* CA-9
*Leaming Creek* NJ-2
*Leaming Ditch* IN-6
Leaming Field Airp—*airport* MO-7
*Leaming Mills* NJ-2
Leamings Mill—*locale* NJ-2
Leamington—*locale* IL-6
**Leamington**—*pop pl* UT-8
Leamington Canal—*canal* UT-8
Leamington Canyon—*valley* UT-8
Leamington Cem—*cemetery* UT-8
Leamington Pass—*gap* UT-8
Leamon Cem—*cemetery* IL-6
Leamon Hollow—*valley* KY-4
Leanamanu Point—*cape* AS-9
Leanaopou Point—*cape* AS-9
Leanaosaualii Point—*cape* AS-9
Lean Creek—*stream* CO-8
Lean Creek—*stream* ID-8
Leander—*locale* KY-4
Leander—*locale* LA-4
Leander—*locale* MN-6
Leander—*locale* NC-3
Leander—*locale* WV-2
**Leander**—*pop pl* OK-5
**Leander**—*pop pl* TX-5
Leander, Lake—*lake* MN-6
Leander Boyer Ditch—*canal* IN-6
Leander Ch—*church* AL-4
Leander Ch—*church* LA-4
Leander Creek—*stream* MN-6
Leander Creek—*stream* NE-7
**Leander (historical)**—*pop pl* OR-9
Leander Mtn—*summit* TN-4
Leander Pond—*lake* CT-1
Leander Post Office (historical)—*building* AL-4
**Leander Spur**—*pop pl* MN-6
**Leando**—*pop pl* IA-7
Leando Cem—*cemetery* IA-7
Leandro Canyon—*valley* CO-8
Leandro Canyon—*valley* NM-5
Leandro Creek—*stream* NM-5
Leandro Lake—*lake* CO-8
Leandro Ranch—*church* NM-5
Leandro Tank—*reservoir* NM-5
*Leane Spring* AZ-5
Leang—*locale* FM-9
Leanhart Canyon—*valley* UT-8
Leaning Oak Golf Course—*other* AL-4
Leaning Pine Run—*stream* PA-2
Leaning Rock—*island* OR-9
Leaning Tower—*cliff* CA-9
Leaning Tower Windmill—*locale* TX-5
Leaning Tree Creek—*stream* WY-8
Leaning Windmill—*locale* NM-5
*Lean Lake* WI-6
Lean Lake—*lake* MN-6
Lean Mine Hollow—*valley* AR-4
Leann—*locale* MO-7
Le Ann, Lake—*lake* MI-6
Leanna—*locale* KS-7
**Leanna**—*pop pl* TN-4
Leanne Lake—*lake* AK-9
Leanora Mine (underground)—*mine* AL-4
Lean Sch—*school* MI-6
Lean-To Canyon—*valley* UT-8
Lean-to Creek—*stream* WY-8
Lean-To Point—*cape* UT-8
Lean-to Point—*summit* ID-8
Lean-To Ridge—*ridge* ID-8
Le-An-Wa Lake—*lake* IN-6
Leaoao Peak—*summit* AS-9
Lea Oil Field—*oilfield* TX-5
Lea Oil Field—*other* NM-5
*Leaone Lake* WI-6
**Leap**—*pop pl* FM-9
Leap Airp—*airport* PA-2
Lea Park—*park* IL-6
Leap Creek—*stream* UT-8
Leap Creek—*stream* WA-9
Leaper—*locale* OH-6
Leaper Creek—*stream* OK-5
Leaper Lake—*lake* MI-6
Leapers—*locale* MI-6
*Leapers Creek* NC-3
Leapfrog Creek—*stream* OR-9
**Leap (historical)**—*pop pl* OR-9
*Leaping Arch* UT-8
*Leaping Brook* CO-8
Leaping Well Brook—*stream* MA-1

*Leed* ... MA-1
Leedale—*locale* ... TX-5
**Leedale (Gindale)**—*pop pl* ... TX-5
**Lee Dale Shores**—*pop pl* ... VA-3
Lee Dam—*dam* ... AL-4
Lee Dam—*dam* (2) ... AZ-5
Lee Dam—*dam* ... SD-7
Lee Daniel Creek—*stream* ... GA-3
Lee Davis Drain—*canal* ... MI-6
Lee-Davis HS—*school* ... VA-3
Leed Canyon—*valley* ... TX-5
*Leed Creek* ... MD-2
*Leed Creek* ... WY-8
Leeder Bluff—*cliff* ... MO-7
**Leedey**—*pop pl* ... OK-5
Leedey Lake—*reservoir* ... OK-5
*Leed Gap* ... AL-4
Lee Ditch—*canal* (2) ... IN-6
Lee Ditch—*canal* (2) ... UT-8
Lee Ditch—*canal* (2) ... WY-8
Lee Ditch—*stream* ... NC-3
Leedle Mill Truss Bridge—*hist pl* ... WI-6
**Leedo (historical)**—*pop pl* ... MS-4
Leedom, David, Farm—*hist pl* ... PA-2
Leedom Elem Sch—*school* ... PA-2
**Leedom Estates**—*pop pl* ... PA-2
**Leedom (historical)**—*pop pl* ... TN-4
*Leedom School* ... PA-2
**Lee Donald**—*pop pl* ... MS-4
**Leedon Estates**—*pop pl* ... DE-2
**Leedon Estates**—*pop pl* ... PA-2
**Leedon Gardens**—*pop pl* ... PA-2
**Leedot Heights Subdivision**—*pop pl* ... UT-8
Lee Drainage Canal—*canal* ... CA-9
Lee Draw—*valley* ... CO-8
Lee Draw—*valley* ... NM-5
Lee Draw—*valley* ... WY-8
*Leeds* ... IL-6
*Leeds* ... MO-7
*Leeds* ... NJ-2
*Leeds* ... TN-4
Leeds—*locale* ... IL-6
**Leeds**—*pop pl* ... AL-4
**Leeds**—*pop pl* ... IA-7
**Leeds**—*pop pl* ... ME-1
**Leeds**—*pop pl* ... MD-2
**Leeds**—*pop pl* ... MA-1
**Leeds**—*pop pl* ... MO-7
**Leeds**—*pop pl* ... NY-2
**Leeds**—*pop pl* ... ND-7
**Leeds**—*pop pl* ... SC-3
**Leeds**—*pop pl* ... UT-8
**Leeds**—*pop pl* ... WI-6
Leeds—*post sta* ... ME-1
Leeds and Northrup Company
Airp—*airport* ... PA-2
Leeds Ave Sch—*school* ... NJ-2
Leeds Campground—*locale* ... SC-3
Leeds (CCD)—*cens area* ... AL-4
Leeds Cem—*cemetery* ... MD-2
Leeds Cem—*cemetery* ... ND-7
Leeds Cem—*cemetery* ... UT-8
Leeds Cem—*cemetery* ... WI-6
Leeds Center—*locale* ... WI-6
**Leeds Center (Town name Leeds)**
**(Centraltown)**—*pop pl* ... ME-1
Leeds Ch—*church* ... VA-3
Leeds City Park—*park* ... AL-4
Leeds Civic Center—*building* ... AL-4
Leeds Creek—*bay* ... MD-2
Leeds Creek—*stream* ... UT-8
Leeds Creek—*stream* (2) ... WY-8
Leeds Ditch—*canal* ... UT-8
Leeds Division—*civil* ... AL-4
Leeds Draw—*valley* ... KS-7
Leeds Elem Sch—*school* ... AL-4
Leeds Flat—*flat* ... NY-2
Leeds Hill—*summit* ... NH-1
Leeds (historical)—*locale* ... KS-7
Leeds Hollow—*valley* ... PA-2
Leeds HS—*school* ... AL-4
Leeds Iron Foundry—*hist pl* ... LA-4
Leeds Island—*island* ... OR-9
*Leeds JHS* ... AL-4
Leeds JHS—*school* ... PA-2
*Leeds Junction* ... MO-7
Leeds Junction—*locale* ... ME-1
Leeds Lookout Tower—*locale* ... SC-3
Leeds Mineral Spring—*spring* ... AL-4
Leeds Mineral Well—*locale* ... AL-4
Leeds Municipal Airp—*airport* ... ND-7
Leeds Plain Cem—*cemetery* ... ME-1
**Leeds Point**—*pop pl* ... NJ-2
Leeds Pond—*lake* ... NY-2
Leeds Presbyterian Ch—*church* ... AL-4
Leeds Ranch—*locale* ... NE-7
Leeds Reef—*ridge* ... UT-8
Leeds Sch—*school* ... LA-4
Leeds Sch (historical)—*school* ... MO-7
Leeds State Wildlife Mngmt Area—*park* ... MN-6
Leeds Tithing Office—*hist pl* ... UT-8
Leedstown—*locale* ... VA-3
**Leeds (Town of)**—*pop pl* ... WI-6
**Leeds Township**—*pop pl* ... ND-7
**Leeds (Township of)**—*pop pl* ... MN-6
*Leeds Village* ... MA-1
*Leedsville* ... KS-7
*Leedsville* ... NJ-2
Leedsville—*locale* ... NY-2
Leed Tank—*reservoir* ... TX-5
Lee-Dubard House—*hist pl* ... MS-4
**Leedy**—*pop pl* ... MS-4
Leedy Cem—*cemetery* ... IN-6
Leedy Ditch—*canal* (3) ... IN-6
**Leedys Gardens**—*pop pl* ... MI-6
Lee Edwards Sch—*school* ... NC-3
*Lee Elementary School* ... MS-4
Lee Elem Sch—*school* ... KS-7
**Lee Estates**—*pop pl* ... TN-4
Lee Experimental For—*forest* ... VA-3
**Leef**—*pop pl* ... WI-6
Lee Falls—*falls* ... OR-9
Lee Falls—*falls* ... PA-2
Lee Farm, The—*hist pl* ... VT-1
**Lee Farms (subdivision)**—*pop pl* ... AL-4
Leef Cem—*cemetery* ... WI-6
**Leefe**—*pop pl* ... WY-8
Lee-Fendall House—*hist pl* ... VA-3
*Lee Ferry* ... AZ-5
**Leefield**—*pop pl* ... GA-3
Lee Fields Cem—*cemetery* ... NC-3
Lee Fire Tower—*locale* ... PA-2
**Lee Five Corners**—*pop pl* ... NH-1
Leef Knob—*summit* ... WV-2
Lee Flat—*flat* ... CA-9
Lee Flat—*flat* ... ID-8
Lee Flats—*flat* ... NE-7
Lee Ford—*crossing* ... TN-4
Lee Ford Bridge—*bridge* ... TN-4
Lee Ford (historical)—*locale* ... TN-4
**Lee Forest**—*pop pl* ... VA-3
Lee Forest Service Station—*locale* ... NV-8
Lee Fork—*stream* ... WV-2
Lee Frice Camp—*locale* ... CA-9
**Leef (Township of)**—*pop pl* ... IL-6
Leegan Cem—*cemetery* ... TN-4
Lee Gap—*gap* (2) ... AL-4
Lee Gap—*gap* ... KY-4
Lee Gap—*gap* ... NC-3
Lee Gap—*gap* ... TX-5
Lee-Goldwell Cem—*cemetery* ... KY-4
Lee Greer Shop Ctr—*locale* ... TN-4
Lee Grove Ch—*church* ... GA-3
Lee Guard Cabin—*locale* ... MT-8
*Lee Guard Station* ... NV-8
Lee Guard Station—*locale* ... WY-8
Lee Gulch—*valley* ... AK-9
Lee Gulch—*valley* (3) ... CO-8
Lee Gulch—*valley* ... MT-8
Lee Gulch—*valley* ... OR-9
Lee Gully—*valley* ... TX-5
*Leehafen* ... FM-9
Lee Hall—*hist pl* ... VA-3
**Lee Hall**—*pop pl* ... VA-3
Lee Hall Ch—*church* ... VA-3
Lee Haney Windmill—*locale* ... NM-5
Lee Hart Dam—*dam* ... AL-4
*Lee Hart Lake* ... AL-4
**Lee Heights**—*pop pl* ... LA-4
**Lee Heights**—*pop pl* ... VA-3
*Lee Heights Baptist Church* ... TN-4
Lee Heights Ch—*church* ... AL-4
Lee Heights Ch—*church* ... TN-4
Lee Henry Branch—*stream* ... GA-3
Lee Highway Cave—*cave* ... TN-4
Lee Highway Ch of God—*church* ... TN-4
Lee Highway Christian Academy—*church* ... TN-4
Lee Hill—*ridge* ... CA-9
Lee Hill—*summit* ... CO-8
Lee Hill—*summit* ... GA-3
Lee Hill—*summit* ... MS-4
Lee Hill—*summit* ... NM-5
Lee Hill—*summit* ... PA-2
Lee Hill—*summit* ... VT-1
Lee Hill—*summit* ... VI-3
Lee Hill (Magisterial District)—*fmr MCD* ... VA-3
Lee (historical)—*locale* ... KS-7
Lee (historical)—*locale* ... ND-7
**Lee (historical)**—*pop pl* ... IA-7
**Lee (historical)**—*pop pl* ... TN-4
**Lee-Hi Village**—*pop pl* ... VA-3
Leehmann Ranch—*locale* ... OR-9
Lee Hollow—*valley* ... AL-4
Lee Hollow—*valley* (2) ... AR-4
Lee Hollow—*valley* (2) ... KY-4
Lee Hollow—*valley* (4) ... MO-7
Lee Hollow—*valley* (5) ... TN-4
Lee Hollow—*valley* ... TX-5
Lee Hollow—*valley* ... UT-8
Lee Hollow—*valley* (2) ... VA-3
Lee Hollow—*valley* ... WV-2
Lee Hollow Mines—*mine* ... TN-4
Lee Hollow Trail—*trail* ... PA-2
Lee Homestead—*hist pl* ... MT-8
Lee Hosp—*hospital* ... NY-2
Lee Hotel—*hist pl* ... AZ-5
Lee Hot Springs—*spring* ... NV-8
Lee House—*hist pl* ... KY-4
Lee House—*hist pl* ... MS-4
Lee Howard Spring—*spring* ... AZ-5
Lee HS—*school* (2) ... AL-4
Lee HS—*school* ... CT-1
Lee HS—*school* (2) ... FL-3
Lee HS—*school* ... MA-1
Lee HS—*school* ... MI-6
Lee HS—*school* ... MS-4
Lee HS—*school* (2) ... TX-5
Lee HS—*school* ... VA-3
Lee Hugh Bay—*swamp* ... NC-3
Lee Island—*island* ... ME-1
Lee-Jackson Sch—*school* ... VA-3
Lee-Jeffers Sch—*school* ... NC-3
Lee JHS—*school* (2) ... FL-3
Lee JHS—*school* ... TX-5
Lee JHS—*school* ... VA-3
Lee JHS—*school* ... WA-9
Lee Jiggs Campground—*locale* ... NV-8
Lee Johnson Spring—*spring* ... AZ-5
Lee Jones Creek—*stream* ... VA-3
Lee Joseph Creek—*stream* ... DE-2
*Leek* ... MS-4
Leek, Clyde, Round Barn—*hist pl* ... IL-6
Leek Cave—*cave* ... TN-4
Leek Cem—*cemetery* ... AR-4
Leek Cem—*cemetery* ... MI-6
*Leek Creek* ... AL-4
Leek Creek—*stream* ... TX-5
Leeke Lake—*lake* ... MI-6
Leek Island—*island* ... PA-2
*Leek Lake* ... MN-6
Leek Lake—*lake* ... MN-6
Leek-McKeen Cem—*cemetery* ... NJ-2
Lee Knob—*summit* (2) ... TN-4
Lee Knob—*summit* ... WV-2
*Leek Post Office* ... MS-4
Leek Ranch—*locale* ... SD-7
*Leek Run* ... PA-2
Leeks Canyon—*valley* ... WY-8
Leeks Lake—*lake* ... MI-6
Leek's Lodge—*hist pl* ... WY-8
Leeks Lodge—*locale* ... WY-8
Leek Spring Hill—*summit* ... CA-9
Leek Spring Valley—*valley* ... CA-9
**Leektown**—*pop pl* ... NJ-2
Leek Valley—*valley* ... WI-6
*Lee Lake* ... MT-8
*Lee Lake* ... WI-6
Lee Lake—*lake* (3) ... CA-9
Lee Lake—*lake* (2) ... FL-3
Lee Lake—*lake* ... ID-8
Lee Lake—*lake* ... IN-6
Lee Lake—*lake* ... LA-4
Lee Lake—*lake* (2) ... MI-6
Lee Lake—*lake* (8) ... MN-6
Lee Lake—*lake* ... ND-7
Lee Lake—*lake* ... OR-9
Lee Lake—*lake* (2) ... SD-7
Lee Lake—*lake* (2) ... TX-5
Lee Lake—*lake* ... WA-9
Lee Lake—*lake* (3) ... WI-6
Lee Lake—*lake* ... WY-8
Lee Lake—*reservoir* ... CO-8
Lee Lake—*reservoir* ... MS-4
Lee Lake—*reservoir* ... MO-7
Lee Lake—*reservoir* ... NC-3
Lee Lake—*reservoir* ... PA-2
Lee Lake—*reservoir* ... VA-3
Lee Lake—*reservoir* (2) ... WI-6
Lee Lake—*stream* ... MS-4
Lee Lake—*swamp* ... LA-4
Lee Lake—*swamp* ... NC-3
Lee Lake Dam—*dam* (2) ... MS-4
Lee Lake Dam—*dam* ... NC-3
Leelanau, Lake—*lake* ... MI-6
**Leelanau (County)**—*pop pl* ... MI-6
Leelanau Peninsula—*cape* ... MI-6
**Leelanau Schools**—*pop pl* ... MI-6
**Leelanau Shores**—*pop pl* ... MI-6
**Leelanau (Township of)**—*pop pl* ... MI-6
*Leeland* ... GA-3
Leeland—*locale* ... MD-2
Leeland—*locale* ... NV-8
Leeland—*locale* ... VA-3
*Leeland Golf Course* ... PA-2
*Leeland Heights* ... FL-3
*Lee Landing* ... AL-4
*Lee Landing* ... LA-4
Leeland (Magisterial District)—*fmr MCD* ... VA-3
Lee Lateral—*canal* ... CA-9
Lee Lateral—*canal* ... CO-8
Lee L Caldwell Elem Sch—*school* ... IN-6
Lee L Driver JHS—*school* ... IN-6
Lee Ledford Branch—*stream* ... GA-3
Lee Ledford Branch—*stream* ... NC-3
Leelee Point—*cape* ... AS-9
**Lee (Lees Station)**—*pop pl* ... TN-4
Leele Mtn—*summit* ... AS-9
Leele Stream—*stream* ... AS-9
Lee Lodge—*locale* ... SC-3
Lee Logan Camp—*locale* ... CA-9
Lee Long Bridge—*bridge* ... AL-4
Lee-Longsworth House—*hist pl* ... WV-2
Lee Lookout Tower—*locale* (2) ... MS-4
Lee (Magisterial District)—*fmr MCD* (4) ... VA-3
Lee (Magisterial District)—*fmr MCD* (2) ... WV-2
Leeman—*locale* ... WI-6
Leeman Brook—*stream* ... ME-1
Leeman Gulch—*valley* ... CO-8
Leeman Lake—*lake* ... MN-6
Leeman Lakes—*lake* ... CO-8
**Lee Manor**—*pop pl* ... VA-3
Leemans Brook—*stream* ... NH-1
Leemans Corner—*locale* ... TN-4
Leemans Corner Sch—*school* ... TN-4
*Leemans Ferry* ... AL-4
Lee March Gulch—*valley* ... CA-9
Lee Marsh—*swamp* ... VA-3
Leemaster—*locale* ... VA-3
**Lee Meadows**—*pop pl* ... VA-3
Lee Meadows—*swamp* ... NJ-2
Lee Memorial Free Will Baptist
Ch—*church* ... MS-4
Lee Memorial Garden Cem—*cemetery* ... FL-3
Lee Memorial Hosp—*hospital* ... FL-3
Lee Memorial Park—*cemetery* ... MS-4
Lee Memorial Park—*park* ... VA-3
Lee Memorial United Methodist
Ch—*church* ... FL-3
Lee Memory Gardens—*cemetery* ... NC-3
Lee Merkle Field (airport)—*airport* ... AL-4
Lee Merriweather Dam—*dam* ... AL-4
**Lee Mesa Subdivision**—*pop pl* ... UT-8
*Lee Millpond* ... SC-3
*Leemine* ... PA-2
Lee Mine—*mine* ... IL-6
Lee Mine—*mine* ... PA-2
**Lee Mine**—*pop pl* ... PA-2
Lee Mines—*mine* ... CA-9
Lee Mission Cemetery—*hist pl* ... OR-9
Lee-Mitts House—*hist pl* ... MS-4
**Leemon**—*pop pl* ... MO-7
Leemon Cem—*cemetery* ... AL-4
Leemon Sch—*school* ... IL-6
Leemon Slough—*bay* ... AL-4
**Lee Mont**—*pop pl* ... VA-3
Lee Mont Branch—*stream* ... VA-3
Leemont Cem—*cemetery* ... VA-3
Lee Moore Intercepting Drain—*canal* ... TX-5
Leemo Ridge—*ridge* ... AS-9
Lee Morris Spring—*spring* ... OR-9
Lee Mountain Cem—*cemetery* ... AR-4
Lee Mountain Spring—*spring* ... AZ-5
Lee Mountain Tanks—*reservoir* ... AZ-5
Lee MS—*school* ... FL-3
Lee Mtn—*summit* (3) ... AZ-5
Lee Mtn—*summit* (3) ... AR-4
Lee Mtn—*summit* ... GA-3
Lee Mtn—*summit* ... MO-7
Lee Mtn—*summit* ... MT-8
Lee Mtn—*summit* ... NM-5
Lee Mtn—*summit* ... NC-3
Lee Mtn—*summit* ... PA-2
Lee Mullins Lake Dam—*dam* ... MS-4
*Leen* ... MP-9
Lee Norse Number Five Airp—*airport* ... PA-2
Lee Norse Number One Airp—*airport* ... PA-2
Leenthrop Memorial Cem—*cemetery* ... MN-6
**Leenthrop (Township of)**—*pop pl* ... MN-6
Lee Number Two Ditch—*canal* ... IN-6
Lee Oil Field—*oilfield* ... KS-7
*Lee Park* ... AZ-5
Lee Park—*basin* ... NE-7
Lee Park—*park* ... FL-3
Lee Park—*park* ... IA-7
Lee Park—*park* ... MS-4
Lee Park—*park* ... OK-5
Lee Park—*park* ... OR-9
Lee Park—*park* (2) ... PA-2
Lee Park—*park* ... SD-7
Lee Park—*park* ... TN-4
Lee Park—*park* ... TX-5
**Lee Park**—*pop pl* ... PA-2
**Lee Park**—*pop pl* ... VA-3
Lee Park Cem—*cemetery* ... NE-7
Lee Pass—*gap* ... UT-8
Leep Creek—*stream* ... OR-9
Lee Peak—*summit* ... ID-8
Lee Peak—*summit* (2) ... NV-8
Lee Peak—*summit* ... NM-5
Lee Peak—*summit* ... OR-9
Lee Peer Station—*locale* ... AL-4
**Leeper**—*pop pl* ... MO-7
**Leeper**—*pop pl* ... PA-2
Leeper, Mount—*summit* ... AK-9
Leeper, Samuel, Jr., House—*hist pl* ... IN-6
Leeper Bluff—*cliff* ... TN-4
Leeper Bottom—*bend* ... TN-4
Leeper Branch—*stream* (2) ... MO-7
Leeper Branch (historical)—*stream* ... TN-4
Leeper Bridge—*bridge* ... KS-7
Leeper Cem—*cemetery* (2) ... KY-4
Leeper Cem—*cemetery* (2) ... MO-7
Leeper Cem—*cemetery* (2) ... TN-4
Leeper Ch—*church* ... IL-6
Leeper Creek—*stream* ... AK-9
Leeper Creek—*stream* ... MS-4
Leeper Creek—*stream* ... TX-5
Leeper Glacier—*glacier* ... AK-9
Leeper Gulch—*valley* ... MT-8
Leeper Hill—*summit* ... KY-4
Leeper Lake—*lake* ... IL-6
Leeper Lake—*lake* ... MN-6
Leeper Lake—*lake* ... OK-5
Leeper Park—*park* ... IN-6
Leeper Pond—*lake* ... NJ-2
**Leeper (RR name Tylersburg**
**(sta.))**—*pop pl* ... PA-2
Leeper Run—*stream* ... PA-2
Leeper Sch—*school* ... OH-6
*Leepers Creek* ... NC-3
Leepers Creek—*stream* ... NC-3
Leepers Ferry (historical)—*locale* ... TN-4
Leeper Spring—*spring* ... MO-7
Leeper Spring—*spring* ... TN-4
Leeper Stadium—*other* ... TX-5
**Leepertown (Township of)**—*pop pl* ... IL-6
*Leep Hollow Run* ... PA-2
Lee Place Ch (historical)—*church* ... AL-4
Lee Plaza East Shop Ctr—*locale* ... TN-4
Lee Plaza Hotel—*hist pl* ... MI-6
Lee Point—*cape* ... MI-6
Lee Point—*cliff* ... UT-8
Lee Pond—*lake* ... GA-3
Lee Pond—*lake* (2) ... MA-1
Lee Pond—*reservoir* ... AL-4
Lee Pond—*reservoir* ... CT-1
Lee Pond—*reservoir* ... MA-1
Lee Pond—*reservoir* ... NC-3
Lee Pond—*reservoir* ... VA-3
Lee Pond—*swamp* ... GA-3
Lee Pond Brook—*stream* ... MA-1
Lee Pond Brook Rsvr—*reservoir* ... MA-1
Lee Pond Ch—*church* ... AL-4
Lee Pond Dam—*dam* ... MA-1
Lee Pond Dam—*dam* ... MS-4
Lee Pope—*locale* ... GA-3
Leeport Ridge—*ridge* ... KY-4
Lee Prairie—*flat* ... OR-9
Lee Promontory—*cliff* ... WA-9
Lee Pump—*well* ... CA-9
Leepy Mtns—*range* ... UT-8
Leer—*locale* ... MI-6
Lee Ranch—*locale* ... MT-8
Lee Ranch—*locale* (2) ... NM-5
Lee Ranch—*locale* ... WY-8
*Lee Ranger Station* ... NV-8
Leer Ch—*church* ... MI-6
Leer Creek—*stream* ... WI-6
Lee Recreation Center—*building* ... TN-4
Lee Reservoir Dam—*dam* ... MA-1
Lee Reservoirs—*reservoir* ... CO-8
Lee Ridge—*ridge* ... MT-8
Lee Ridge—*ridge* ... TN-4
Lee Ridge Ch—*church* ... AR-4
Lee Ridge Mines—*mine* ... TN-4
Lee Ridge Trail—*trail* ... MT-8
*Lee-rite Creek* ... LA-4
Lee River—*bay* ... MA-1
Lee River—*stream* ... VT-1
*Lee Road* ... OH-6
Lee Road Ch—*church* ... LA-4
Lee Road Sch—*school* ... LA-4
Lee Road Sch—*school* ... NY-2
Lee Road Shop Ctr—*locale* ... FL-3
Lee Rowe Ditch—*canal* ... MO-7
Leers Canyon—*valley* ... UT-8
Lee Rsvr—*reservoir* ... MA-1
Lee Run—*stream* ... VA-3
Lee Run—*stream* (3) ... WV-2
Lee Russell Canyon—*valley* ... NM-5
Lee Russell Spring—*spring* ... NM-5
Lee Russell Tank—*reservoir* ... NM-5
*Lees* ... SC-3
*Lees* ... TN-4
Lees—*locale* ... TX-5
**Lees**—*pop pl* ... PA-2
**Lees**—*pop pl* ... SC-3
Lees, Point—*cape* ... AK-9
Lee Sanders Ditch—*canal* ... NV-8
Lees Bar (historical)—*bar* ... AL-4
Lees Bay—*stream* ... GA-3
*Lees Branch* ... MS-4
Lees Branch—*stream* ... GA-3
Lees Branch—*stream* (2) ... NC-3
Lees Branch—*stream* ... SC-3
Lees Branch—*stream* ... TX-5
Lees Branch—*stream* ... VA-3
Lees Bridge—*bridge* ... KY-4
Lees Bridge—*locale* ... PA-2
*Leesburg* ... KS-7
*Leesburg* ... MS-4
*Leesburg* ... NC-3
*Leesburg* ... PA-2
Leesburg—*hist pl* ... ID-8
Leesburg—*locale* ... ID-8
**Leesburg**—*pop pl* ... AL-4
**Leesburg**—*pop pl* ... FL-3
**Leesburg**—*pop pl* ... GA-3
**Leesburg**—*pop pl* ... IL-6
**Leesburg**—*pop pl* (2) ... IN-6
**Leesburg**—*pop pl* ... KY-4
**Leesburg**—*pop pl* ... MS-4
**Leesburg**—*pop pl* ... NJ-2
**Leesburg**—*pop pl* ... OH-6
**Leesburg**—*pop pl* ... PA-2
**Leesburg**—*pop pl* ... SC-3
**Leesburg**—*pop pl* ... TN-4
**Leesburg**—*pop pl* ... TX-5
**Leesburg**—*pop pl* ... VA-3
Leesburg Baptist Ch—*church* ... MS-4
Leesburg Branch—*stream* ... SC-3
Leesburg Branch—*stream* ... TN-4
Leesburg (CCD)—*cens area* ... AL-4
Leesburg (CCD)—*cens area* ... FL-3
Leesburg (CCD)—*cens area* ... GA-3
Leesburg Cem—*cemetery* ... GA-3
Leesburg Cem—*cemetery* ... KS-7
Leesburg Cem—*cemetery* ... MS-4
Leesburg Cem—*cemetery* ... TN-4
Leesburg Ch—*church* ... SC-3
Leesburg Ch—*church* ... TN-4
Leesburg Division—*civil* ... AL-4
Leesburg East (CCD)—*cens area* ... FL-3
Leesburg Elem Sch—*school* ... IN-6
*Leesburgh* ... AL-4
*Leesburgh* ... OH-6
*Leesburgh* ... TN-4
Leesburgh (historical)—*locale* ... KS-7
Leesburg Hist Dist—*hist pl* ... VA-3
Leesburgh Post Office
(historical)—*building* ... TN-4
Leesburg HS—*school* ... FL-3
Leesburg Industrial Park—*locale* ... AL-4
Leesburg JHS—*school* ... FL-3
Leesburg (Magisterial District)—*fmr MCD* ... VA-3
Leesburg Montessori Sch—*school* ... FL-3
Leesburg-Newsome (CCD)—*cens area* ... TX-5
Leesburg Park—*park* ... AL-4
Leesburg Post Office—*building* ... AL-4
Leesburg Post Office
(historical)—*building* ... MS-4
Leesburg Prairie—*flat* ... MS-4
Leesburg Presbyterian Ch—*church* ... TN-4
Leesburg Regional Med Ctr—*hospital* ... FL-3
Leesburg Sch—*school* ... NJ-2
**Leesburg Station**—*pop pl* ... PA-2
**Leesburg (Township of)**—*pop pl* ... OH-6
Lees Camp—*locale* ... AK-9
Lees Camp—*locale* ... CA-9
Lees Camp—*locale* ... OR-9
**Lee's Camp**—*pop pl* ... OR-9
*Lees Cemetery* ... TN-4
*Lees Ch* ... DE-2
*Lees Ch* ... TN-4
Lees Ch—*church* (2) ... NC-3
Lee Sch—*school* ... AL-4
Lee Sch—*school* (3) ... AR-4
Lee Sch—*school* (4) ... CA-9
Lee Sch—*school* (5) ... FL-3
Lee Sch—*school* (2) ... GA-3
Lee Sch—*school* (4) ... IL-6
Lee Sch—*school* ... IA-7
Lee Sch—*school* (3) ... KY-4
Lee Sch—*school* ... MA-1
Lee Sch—*school* (5) ... MI-6
Lee Sch—*school* (3) ... MN-6
Lee Sch—*school* ... MO-7
Lee Sch—*school* (6) ... OK-5
Lee Sch—*school* (2) ... OR-9
Lee Sch—*school* ... SC-3
Lee Sch—*school* (4) ... TX-5
Lee Sch—*school* (3) ... VA-3
Lee Sch—*school* ... WA-9
Lee Sch—*school* ... WI-6
Lees Chapel—*church* (3) ... AL-4
Lees Chapel—*church* ... DE-2
Lees Chapel—*church* (3) ... GA-3
Lees Chapel—*church* (3) ... MS-4
Lees Chapel—*church* (4) ... NC-3
Lees Chapel—*church* ... TN-4
Lees Chapel—*church* ... TX-5
Lees Chapel—*church* ... VA-3
Lees Chapel—*locale* ... OK-5
Lees Chapel Baptist Ch—*church* ... MS-4
Lees Chapel Cem—*cemetery* ... OK-5
*Lees Chapel Ch* ... AL-4
Lee Sch (historical)—*school* (4) ... MS-4
Lee Sch (historical)—*school* ... MO-7
*Lee School* ... TN-4
Leesch Sch—*school* ... SD-7
Lees Corner—*locale* ... SD-7
Lees Corner—*locale* ... TN-4
Lees Corner—*locale* ... VA-3
Lees Cove—*bay* ... VA-3
Lees Cove P.O. (historical)—*locale* ... AL-4
*Lees Creek* ... MD-2
*Lees Creek* ... MS-4
*Lee's Creek* ... MT-8
**Lees Creek**—*pop pl* ... LA-4
**Lees Creek**—*pop pl* ... OH-6
Lees Creek—*stream* ... AR-4
Lees Creek—*stream* ... GA-3
Lees Creek—*stream* (2) ... KY-4
Lees Creek—*stream* ... LA-4
Lees Creek—*stream* ... NY-2
Lees Creek—*stream* ... NC-3
Lees Creek—*stream* ... OH-6
Lees Creek—*stream* ... OR-9
Lees Creek—*stream* ... PA-2
Lees Creek—*stream* ... TN-4
Lees Creek—*stream* (2) ... VA-3
Lees Creek—*stream* ... WA-9
Lees Creek Branch—*stream* ... OH-6
Lee's Creek Ceremonial Center Site (Boundary
Increase)—*hist pl* ... OK-5
Lee's Creek Ceremonial Site—*hist pl* ... OK-5
Lee's Creek Covered Bridge—*hist pl* ... KY-4
Lees Creek Dam—*dam* ... PA-2
Lees Creek (historical)—*stream* ... PA-2
Lees Creek (Township of)—*fmr MCD* (2) ... AR-4
*Lees Crossing* ... PA-2
**Lees Crossing**—*pop pl* ... GA-3
Lees Crossroad Ch—*church* ... NC-3
*Lees Crossroads* ... SC-3
Lees Crossroads—*locale* (2) ... SC-3
**Lees Crossroads**—*pop pl* ... PA-2
**Lees Cross Roads**—*pop pl* ... PA-2
Lees Cut—*channel* ... NC-3
Leesdale—*locale* ... CA-9
Leesdale—*locale* ... MS-4
**Leesdale**—*pop pl* ... AL-4
Leesdale Lookout Tower—*locale* ... MS-4
Leesdale Post Office (historical)—*building* ... AL-4
Lees Ditch—*canal* ... DE-2
Lee Seminary—*church* ... TN-4
*Lees Ferry* ... AL-4
*Lees Ferry* ... AZ-5
Lees Ferry—*hist pl* ... AZ-5
Lees Ferry—*locale* ... AZ-5
Lees Ferry (historical)—*locale* (2) ... AL-4
Lees Ferry (historical)—*locale* ... TN-4
Lees Field (airport)—*airport* ... MS-4
Lees Flat—*flat* ... NV-8
Lees Flat—*locale* ... MS-4
Lees Ford—*crossing* ... TN-4
Lees Ford Camp—*locale* ... VA-3
Lees Ford Dock—*locale* ... KY-4
Lees Ford (historical)—*crossing* ... TN-4
Lees Gap—*gap* ... PA-2
Lees Gap—*gap* ... VA-3
Lees Grove Ch—*church* ... NC-3
Lees Gulch—*valley* ... ID-8
Lees Gulf—*valley* ... TN-4
Lee Shaft—*mine* ... AZ-5
*Lees Hill* ... MA-1
Lees Hill—*summit* ... VT-1
Lees Hill—*summit* ... VA-3
Lee Shoals Ch—*church* ... SC-3
Lees Hollow—*valley* ... NY-2
Lees Hollow—*valley* ... UT-8
**Leeside**—*pop pl* ... NY-2
Lee Siding—*locale* ... MO-7
Lee Sink—*basin* ... FL-3
Lees Island—*island* ... NY-2
Lee Site (16 EBR 51)—*hist pl* ... LA-4
*Lees Lake* ... AL-4
Lees Lake—*lake* ... MT-8
Lees Lake—*lake* ... WI-6
Lees Lake—*reservoir* (3) ... AL-4
Lees Lake—*reservoir* ... CA-9
Lees Lake—*reservoir* ... GA-3
Lees Lake Cem—*cemetery* ... TN-4
Lees Lake Drain—*canal* ... MI-6
*Lees Landing* ... MS-4
Lees Landing—*locale* ... NC-3
**Lees Landing**—*pop pl* ... LA-4
Lees Landing (historical)—*locale* ... AL-4
Lees Landing (historical)—*locale* ... TN-4
**Lees Lick**—*pop pl* ... KY-4
Lees Lodge—*locale* ... CA-9
Lees-McRae Coll—*school* ... NC-3
Lees Meadow—*flat* ... CA-9
Lee Smelter Gulch—*valley* ... CO-8
*Lees Mill* ... TN-4
Lees Mill—*locale* (2) ... MD-2
Lees Mill—*locale* ... NH-1
Lee's Mill—*locale* ... NC-3
Lees Mill—*locale* ... PA-2
Lees Mill—*locale* (2) ... VA-3
**Lees Mill**—*pop pl* ... GA-3
Lees Mill (historical)—*locale* ... MS-4
*Lees Mill Pond* ... SC-3
Lees Mill Pond—*reservoir* ... NC-3
Lees Millpond—*reservoir* (2) ... VA-3
Lees Mill Pond Dam—*dam* ... NC-3
*Lees Mills* ... NC-3
Lees Mills (Township of)—*fmr MCD* ... NC-3
Lees Mine—*mine* ... AZ-5
**Lee's (Mobile Home Park)**—*pop pl* ... NH-1
Leesoffskaia Bay—*bay* ... AK-9
Leesome Lake—*lake* ... WI-6
*Leeson* ... KS-7
Leeson Brook—*stream* ... RI-1
Leeson Canyon—*valley* ... NM-5
Leeson Park—*park* ... WI-6
Leeson Ranch—*locale* ... NM-5
Lee Spalding Sch—*school* ... MI-6
**Lees Park**—*pop pl* ... AL-4
Lees Peak—*summit* ... OR-9
*Leespeer* ... AL-4
**Leespeer**—*pop pl* ... AL-4
*Leespeer Station* ... AL-4
Lees Point—*cape* ... ID-8
Lees Point Landing—*locale* ... TN-4
*Lees Pond* ... AL-4
Lees Pond—*lake* ... AL-4
Lees Pond—*lake* ... CT-1
Lees Pond—*lake* ... NH-1
Lees Pond—*lake* ... NY-2
Lees Pond—*reservoir* ... NC-3
Lees Pond Brook—*stream* ... CT-1
**Leesport**—*pop pl* ... PA-2
Leesport Borough—*civil* ... PA-2
Leesport Lock House—*hist pl* ... PA-2
Lee Spring—*locale* ... TX-5
Lee Spring—*spring* ... AL-4
Lee Spring—*spring* (3) ... AZ-5
Lee Spring—*spring* ... KS-7
Lee Spring—*spring* ... MO-7
Lee Spring—*spring* (2) ... NV-8
Lee Spring—*spring* ... NM-5
Lee Spring—*spring* ... OR-9
Lee Spring—*spring* (5) ... TN-4
Lee Spring Canyon—*valley* ... NV-8
Lee Spring Ch—*church* (2) ... TX-5
Lee Spring Hollow—*valley* ... TN-4
Lee Springs—*spring* ... TX-5
*Lees Ranch* ... SD-7
Lees Ranch—*locale* ... UT-8
*Lees River* ... MA-1
Lees Run—*stream* ... OH-6
Lees Run Cem—*cemetery* ... OH-6
Lees Sch (historical)—*school* ... AL-4
Lees Sch (historical)—*school* ... TN-4
Lees Shoals—*bar* ... TN-4
Lees Spring—*spring* ... CO-8
Lees Spring—*spring* ... UT-8
Lees Spring Branch—*stream* ... TN-4
Lees Spring Wash—*valley* ... UT-8
**Lees Station**—*pop pl* ... TN-4
Lees Station Ch—*church* ... TN-4
Lees Store (historical)—*locale* ... AL-4
**Lee's Summit**—*pop pl* ... MO-7
**Lees Summit**—*pop pl* ... MO-7
Lees Summit Ch—*church* ... MO-7
Lees Summit Heliport—*airport* ... MO-7
Lee State Park—*park* ... SC-3
*Lee Station* ... AL-4
Lee Station (historical)—*locale* ... AL-4
Lee Stewart and Eskin Ditch—*canal* ... CO-8

*Lee-Stokes Cemetery* TN-4
Lee Store (historical)—*locale* AL-4
**Leestown**—*pop pl* KY-4
Leestown Sch—*school* KY-4
**Lees Township**—*pop pl* KS-7
Lees Township (historical)—*civil* ND-7
Lees (Township of)—*fmr MCD* NC-3
Leestown Terrace—*uninc pl* KY-4
Lee Street Field—*park* MS-4
Lee Street Playground—*park* WI-6
Lee Street Sch—*school* GA-3
Lee Street Sch—*school* MA-1
Lee Summit—*summit* CA-9
*Leesville* NJ-2
Leesville—*locale* CA-9
Leesville—*locale* CT-1
Leesville—*locale* NJ-2
Leesville—*locale* VA-3
**Leesville**—*pop pl* IL-6
**Leesville**—*pop pl* IN-6
**Leesville**—*pop pl* LA-4
**Leesville**—*pop pl* MO-7
**Leesville**—*pop pl* NY-2
**Leesville**—*pop pl* NC-3
**Leesville**—*pop pl* (2) OH-6
**Leesville**—*pop pl* SC-3
**Leesville**—*pop pl* TX-5
Leesville Cem—*cemetery* KY-4
Leesville Cem—*cemetery* NY-2
Leesville Cem—*cemetery* TX-5
Leesville Ch—*church* SC-3
Leesville Ch—*church* (2) TX-5
Leesville College Hist Dist—*hist pl* SC-3
*Leesville Cross Road* OH-6
**Leesville Cross Roads (Leesville)**—*pop pl* OH-6
Leesville Dam—*dam* VA-3
Leesville Gap—*gap* CA-9
Leesville Lake—*reservoir* OH-6
Leesville Lake—*reservoir* VA-3
Leesville Lookout Tower—*locale* LA-4
Leesville Pond—*reservoir* MA-1
Leesville Pond Dam—*dam* MA-1
Leesville Road Ch—*church* VA-3
*Leesville Rsvr* OH-6
Leesville Schoolhouse—*hist pl* TX-5
Leesville State Wildlife Mngmt Area—*park* MO-7
Leesville Temple—*church* VA-3
Leesville Town Hall—*hist pl* OH-6
**Leesville Township**—*pop pl* MO-7
Leesville (Township of)—*fmr MCD* NC-3
Leesville Wildlife Area—*park* OH-6
*Lee Swamp* VA-3
Lee Swamp—*stream* NC-3
Lee Swamp—*stream* SC-3
Lees Windmill—*locale* CO-8
**Lees Woods**—*pop pl* MD-2
Leesylvania Archeol Site (44PW7)—*hist pl* VA-3
Leet—*locale* WV-2
Lee Tabernacle—*church* SC-3
Lee Tank—*reservoir* (5) AZ-5
Lee Tank—*reservoir* (2) NM-5
Leet Cem—*cemetery* NY-2
Leete, Pelatiah, House—*hist pl* CT-1
*Leete Island* CT-1
*Leete Island* NY-2
Lee Terminal—*building* KY-4
Leete Sch—*school* CT-1
Leetes Island—*cape* CT-1
**Leetes Island**—*pop pl* CT-1
Leeth Creek—*stream* AL-4
Leeth Creek—*stream* OH-6
Leeth Creek Cem—*cemetery* OH-6
Leeth Hill—*summit* AL-4
Leet (historical)—*locale* SD-7
Lee Thomas Campground—*park* OR-9
Lee Thomas Crossing—*locale* OR-9
Lee Thomas Meadow—*summit* OR-9
Leeth Spring—*spring* AL-4
Lee Tire and Rubber Company—*hist pl* PA-2
Leeton—*locale* UT-8
**Leeton**—*pop pl* MO-7
**Leetonia**—*pop pl* MN-6
**Leetonia**—*pop pl* OH-6
**Leetonia**—*pop pl* PA-2
Leet Oro Bad Pond *lake* MA-1
Lee Towhead—*island* MO-7
Lee Towhead Revetment—*levee* TN-4
Leetown—*locale* KY-4
Leetown—*locale* VA-3
**Leetown**—*pop pl* MS-4
**Lee Town**—*pop pl* VA-3
**Leetown**—*pop pl* WV-2
Leetown Brook—*stream* NY-2
Lee Town Ch—*church* MS-4
**Lee (Town of)**—*pop pl* ME-1
**Lee (Town of)**—*pop pl* MA-1
**Lee (Town of)**—*pop pl* NH-1
**Lee (Town of)**—*pop pl* NY-2
Leetown Sch—*school* MS-4
Lee Township—*civil* MO-7
Lee Township—*fmr MCD* (5) IA-7
**Lee Township**—*pop pl* ND-7
**Lee Township**—*pop pl* SD-7
Lee Township Hall—*building* SD-7
Lee (Township of)—*fmr MCD* (4) AR-4
**Lee (Township of)**—*pop pl* (2) IL-6
**Lee (Township of)**—*pop pl* (3) MI-6
**Lee (Township of)**—*pop pl* MN-6
**Lee (Township of)**—*pop pl* (3) OH-6
Lee Travis Well—*well* NV-8
Leet Ridge—*ridge* OH-6
**Leets**—*pop pl* VA-3
Leet Sch—*school* WV-2
**Leetsdale**—*pop pl* PA-2
Leetsdale Borough—*civil* PA-2
Leet Spring—*spring* GA-3
**Leetsville**—*pop pl* MI-6
Leet Township—*CDP* PA-2
**Leet (Township of)**—*pop pl* PA-2
Leet Weidner Drain—*stream* MI-6
**Leevale**—*pop pl* WV-2
Lee Valley—*locale* TN-4
**Lee Valley**—*pop pl* NE-7
Lee Valley—*valley* CA-9
Lee Valley—*valley* OR-9
Lee Valley—*valley* (2) TN-4
Lee Valley—*valley* UT-8
Lee Valley—*valley* (3) WI-6
Lee Valley Cem—*cemetery* TN-4
Lee Valley Ch—*church* LA-4
Lee Valley Ch—*church* NY-2
Lee Valley Ch (historical)—*church* TN-4
Lee Valley Dam—*dam* AZ-5
Lee Valley Post Office (historical)—*building* TN-4
Lee Valley Rsvr—*reservoir* AZ-5
Lee Valley Sch (historical)—*school* (2) TN-4
**Leevan**—*pop pl* TX-5
Leeville—*locale* MS-4
**Leeville**—*pop pl* LA-4
**Leeville**—*pop pl* TN-4
Leeville (historical)—*locale* SD-7
Leeville HS (historical)—*school* TN-4
Leeville Post Office (historical)—*building* TN-4
*Leevinging* CA-9
**Lee Vining**—*pop pl* CA-9
Lee Vining Canyon—*valley* CA-9
Lee Vining Creek—*stream* CA-9
*Leevining Peak* CA-9
Lee Vining Peak—*summit* CA-9
Lee Vining Ranger Station—*locale* CA-9
Leevy Cem—*cemetery* SC-3
**Lee Walker Heights (subdivision)**—*pop pl* NC-3
**Lee-Wamba Subdivision**—*pop pl* MS-4
*Leeward Islands* HI-9
Leeward Oahu Community Coll—*school* HI-9
Leeward Passage—*channel* VI-3
Lee Ward Sch—*school* WV-2
Leeward Seine Beach—*locale* NC-3
Lee Wash—*stream* CA-9
Lee Well—*well* AZ-5
Lee Well—*well* (2) NM-5
Lee Well—*well* TX-5
Lee Wildlife Mngmt Area—*park* FL-3
Lee Windmill—*locale* NV-8
Lee Windmill—*locale* NM-5
Lee Windmill—*locale* (2) TX-5
**Leewood**—*pop pl* VA-3
**Leewood**—*pop pl* WV-2
Leewood—*uninc pl* TN-4
Leewood Camp—*locale* OR-9
Leewood Elem Sch—*school* FL-3
Lee Wooden County Park—*park* OR-9
Leewood Golf Club—*other* NY-2
Lee Wood Picnic Area—*locale* CO-8
Lee Woods Spring—*spring* OR-9
**Lee Wood (subdivision)**—*pop pl* NC-3
Leewood Yards—*locale* TN-4
*Lee Wright Creek* LA-4
Lee Wright Ranch—*locale* WY-8
Lee Wright Well—*well* NM-5
Leezer Cem—*cemetery* WV-2
Lefao Ridge—*ridge* AS-9
Le Fay Lake—*lake* WA-9
**Lefeber**—*pop pl* OK-5
LeFeber, Charles, House—*hist pl* NM-5
*Lefebre* PA-2
*Lefebre Canyon* AZ-5
*Lefebres* PA-2
LeFebres Canyon—*valley* NM-5
*LeFebres Creek* PA-2
LeFebres Creek—*stream* NM-5
LeFebres Mesa—*summit* NM-5
Le Ferre Lake—*lake* MI-6
Lefever Cem—*cemetery* NY-2
Lefever Cem—*cemetery* OH-6
*Le Fever Creek* UT-8
Lefever Creek—*stream* AR-4
Lefever Creek—*stream* CA-9
Lefever Falls—*locale* NY-2
Lefever House—*hist pl* AZ-5
Lefever Sch—*school* IL-6
Lefevre—*locale* PA-2
LeFevre, Owen E., House—*hist pl* CO-8
Le Fevre Canyon—*valley* AZ-5
Le Fevre Creek—*stream* UT-8
Lefevre Prairie—*flat* OR-9
Lefevre Ridge—*ridge* AZ-5
Lefevre Sch (abandoned)—*school* PA-2
LeFevre Spring—*spring* WV-2
*Leff* ND-7
Leffcoots Millpond—*reservoir* SC-3
Leffel Cem—*cemetery* (2) VA-3
*Lefferson Lake* AR-4
Leffert Ditch—*canal* IN-6
Lefferts—*uninc pl* NY-2
Lefferts, Lake—*reservoir* NJ-2
Lefferts Homestead—*building* NY-2
Lefferts-Laidlaw House—*hist pl* NY-2
Lefferts Mill—*locale* NY-2
Lefferts Pond—*lake* VT-1
Leffew Branch—*stream* KY-4
Leffew Mine—*mine* TN-4
Leffew Mine (surface)—*mine* TN-4
Leffew Store (historical)—*locale* TN-4
**Leffingwell**—*pop pl* CT-1
Leffingwell—*uninc pl* CA-9
Leffingwell Camp Site—*hist pl* AK-9
Leffingwell Country Club—*other* OH-6
Leffingwell Creek—*stream* (2) CA-9
Leffingwell Hill—*summit* MA-1
Leffingwell Inn—*hist pl* CT-1
Leffingwell Point—*cape* MI-6
Leffingwell Sch—*school* CA-9
Leffingwell Sch—*school* CT-1
Leffis Key—*island* FL-3
Leffler Cem—*cemetery* IN-6
Leffler Creek—*stream* MT-8
**Leffler (historical)**—*pop pl* OR-9
Lefford Branch—*stream* VA-3
**Lefgren Subdivision**—*pop pl* UT-8
Le Fils Slough—*gut* FL-3
*Lefin* FM-9
Lefler Cem—*cemetery* IN-6
Lefler Cem—*cemetery* MO-7
Lefler Creek—*stream* AK-9
Lefler Sch—*school* MO-7
Lefler Sch—*school* NE-7
Le Fleur Bluff—*cliff* MS-4
**Lefleurs**—*pop pl* LA-4
*Le Fleurs Bluff* MS-4
LeFleurs Bluff Tourist Center—*building* MS-4
Leflora Cem—*cemetery* MS-4
*Le Flore* MS-4
*Le Flore* OK-5
**Le Flore**—*pop pl* MS-4
**Leflore**—*pop pl* MS-4
**Leflore**—*pop pl* OK-5
LeFlore, Capt. Charles, House—*hist pl* OK-5
**Leflore County**—*pop pl* MS-4
**Le Flore (County)**—*pop pl* OK-5
Leflore County Country Club—*locale* MS-4
Leflore County Courthouse—*building* MS-4
LeFlore County Courthouse—*hist pl* OK-5
Leflore County HS—*school* MS-4
Leflore County Penal Farm—*locale* MS-4
Leflore County Vocational Technical Center—*school* MS-4
*Leflore Creek* OK-5
Leflore Creek—*stream* MS-4
Leflore Creek—*stream* OK-5
Le Flore HS—*school* AL-4
Lefman—*locale* TX-5
**Lefor**—*pop pl* ND-7
**Lefors**—*pop pl* TX-5
Lefrak City—*uninc pl* NY-2
*Le Framboise Island* SD-7
Le Framboise Island Rec Area—*park* SD-7
*Left Allen Creek* UT-8
Left Asaph Run—*stream* PA-2
Left Bear Creek—*stream* TX-5
Left Beaver Ch—*church* KY-4
*Left Branch Banner Hollow* WV-2
*Left Branch Barkshanty Hollow* PA-2
Left Branch Bark Shanty Hollow—*valley* PA-2
Left Branch Big Nelson Run—*stream* PA-2
Left Branch Blue Lick Creek—*stream* IN-6
Left Branch Boiler Run—*stream* PA-2
*Left Branch Cape Creek* NC-3
Left Branch Cooks Run—*stream* PA-2
Left Branch Fourmile Run—*stream* PA-2
Left Branch Gnatty Creek—*stream* WV-2
Left Branch Half Mile Run—*stream* PA-2
Left Branch Hyner Run—*stream* PA-2
Left Branch Lieb Run—*stream* PA-2
Left Branch Long Hollow—*valley* AZ-5
Left Branch Lushbaugh Run—*stream* PA-2
*Left Branch Mile Run* PA-2
Left Branch Mill Run—*stream* WV-2
*Left Branch Miracle Run* WV-2
Left Branch Montour Run—*stream* PA-2
Left Branch Moose Creek—*stream* PA-2
Left Branch Nanny Branch—*stream* VA-3
Left Branch North Fork Cherry River—*stream* WV-2
Left Branch Powder Creek—*stream* OR-9
Left Branch Puncheon Run—*stream* PA-2
*Left Branch Straight Run* PA-2
Left Branch Trail—*trail* PA-2
Left Branch Young Womans Creek—*stream* PA-2
Left Buckhorn Creek—*stream* TX-5
Left Buffalo Run—*stream* WV-2
Left Cape—*cape* AK-9
Left Coulee—*valley* MT-8
Left Cove—*bay* AK-9
Left Creek—*stream* WY-8
Left Drain—*stream* IN-6
Left Dry Creek Sch—*school* KY-4
Left Elk Creek—*stream* AK-9
Left Foot Creek—*stream* WI-6
Left Foot Lake—*lake* WI-6
*Left Fork* KY-4
*Left Fork* NC-3
*Left Fork* TN-4
*Left Fork* VA-3
*Left Fork* WV-2
Left Fork—*stream* ID-8
Left Fork—*stream* KY-4
Left Fork—*stream* WA-9
Left Fork—*stream* WV-2
Left Fork Abner Branch—*stream* VA-3
Left Fork A Canyon—*valley* UT-8
Left Fork Acord Branch—*stream* WV-2
Left Fork Ages Creek—*stream* KY-4
Left Fork Alexander Canyon—*valley* UT-8
Left Fork Allen Creek—*stream* WV-2
Left Fork Alum Creek—*stream* WV-2
Left Fork Andy Trent Branch—*stream* KY-4
Left Fork Andy Trent Branch—*valley* VA-3
Left Fork Antelope Canyon—*valley* UT-8
Left Fork Antone Creek—*stream* UT-8
Left Fork Apache Canyon—*valley* CO-8
Left Fork Apple Creek—*stream* IL-6
Left Fork Armstrong Creek—*stream* WV-2
Left Fork Arnett Branch—*stream* KY-4
Left Fork Arnold Creek—*stream* WV-2
Left Fork Ash Branch—*stream* WV-2
Left Fork Ashers Fork—*stream* KY-4
Left Fork Ballard Fork—*stream* WV-2
Left Fork Barnes Run—*stream* WV-2
Left Fork Barrel Spring Creek—*stream* CO-8
Left Fork Bates Fork—*stream* KY-4
Left Fork Beans Creek—*stream* NC-3
Left Fork Bear Branch—*stream* KY-4
Left Fork Bear Creek—*stream* ID-8
Left Fork Bear Creek—*stream* KY-4
Left Fork Bear Creek—*stream* OH-6
Left Fork Bearfield Run—*stream* PA-2
Left Fork Bearpen Creek—*stream* VA-3
Left Fork Beaver Canyon—*valley* UT-8
Left Fork Beaver Creek—*stream* (2) KY-4
Left Fork Beaver Creek—*stream* UT-8
Left Fork Beaver Creek—*stream* WV-2
Left Fork Beaverdam Run—*stream* PA-2
Left Fork Beech Creek—*stream* WV-2
Left Fork Beechy Creek—*stream* KY-4
Left Fork Beehive Branch—*stream* KY-4
Left Fork Beetree Branch—*stream* KY-4
Left Fork Beetree Creek—*stream* NC-3
Left Fork Ben Creek—*stream* WV-2
Left Fork Betty Creek—*stream* WY-8
Left Fork Bias Branch—*stream* WV-2
Left Fork Big Asphalt Canyon—*valley* UT-8
Left Fork Big Beaver Creek—*stream* WV-2
Left Fork Big Branch—*stream* KY-4
Left Fork Big Branch—*stream* VA-3
Left Fork Big Branch—*stream* WV-2
Left Fork Big Creek—*stream* AR-4
Left Fork Big Creek—*stream* WV-2
Left Fork Big Double Creek—*stream* KY-4
Left Fork Big Elk Creek—*stream* KY-4
Left Fork Big Elk Creek—*stream* WV-2
Left Fork Big Log Gulch—*valley* MT-8
Left Fork Big Run—*stream* WV-2
*Left Fork Big Sandy Creek* WV-2
Left Fork Bill Branch—*stream* KY-4
Left Fork Bird Creek—*stream* CA-9
Left Fork Birdseye—*stream* OR-9
Left Fork Blackberry Creek—*stream* KY-4
Left Fork Black Brook—*stream* ME-1
Left Fork Black Canyon Creek—*stream* WA-9
*Left Fork Blacksmith Fork Canyon* UT-8
Left Fork Blacktail Creek—*stream* WY-8
Left Fork Blaine Creek—*stream* KY-4
*Left Fork Blubber Creek* UT-8
Left Fork Blubber Creek—*stream* UT-8
Left Fork Blue Fly Creek—*stream* UT-8
Left Fork Blue Hole Creek—*stream* KY-4
Left Fork Bone Creek—*stream* WV-2
Left Fork Brier Creek—*stream* WV-2
Left Fork Brimstone Creek—*stream* TN-4
Left Fork Broad Branch—*stream* WV-2
Left Fork Brooks Run—*stream* PA-2
Left Fork Brush Canyon—*valley* ID-8
Left Fork Brushy Creek—*stream* KY-4
Left Fork Brushy Fork—*stream* KY-4
Left Fork Buckhannon River—*stream* WV-2
*Left Fork Buffalo Creek* WY-8
Left Fork Buffalo Creek—*stream* KY-4
Left Fork Buffalo Creek—*stream* MT-8
Left Fork Bull Creek—*stream* (2) WV-2
Left Fork Bull Run—*stream* WV-2
Left Fork Bunker Creek—*stream* UT-8
Left Fork Bushy Fork—*stream* KY-4
Left Fork Cache Creek—*stream* AK-9
Left Fork Cains Creek—*stream* KY-4
Left Fork Campbell Creek—*stream* KY-4
Left Fork Campbell Run—*stream* WV-2
Left Fork Camp Creek—*stream* KY-4
Left Fork Camp Creek—*stream* VA-3
Left Fork Camp Creek—*stream* WV-2
*Left Fork Canaan Gulch* CA-9
Left Fork Cane Creek—*stream* NC-3
Left Fork Cane Creek—*stream* VA-3
Left Fork Caney Creek—*stream* (3) KY-4
Left Fork Canoe Run—*stream* PA-2
Left Fork Carcass Wash—*valley* UT-8
Left Fork Carr Gulch—*valley* CO-8
Left Fork Cavenders Creek—*stream* GA-3
Left Fork Cedar Creek—*stream* UT-8
Left Fork Ch—*church* WV-2
*Left Fork Chasm Prong* NC-3
Left Fork Chenoweth Creek—*stream* WV-2
Left Fork Cherry Creek—*stream* (2) ID-8
Left Fork Chicosa Canyon—*valley* CO-8
Left Fork Chynoweth Canyon—*valley* UT-8
Left Fork Claylick Run—*stream* WV-2
Left Fork Clear Creek—*stream* UT-8
Left Fork Clendenin Creek—*stream* WV-2
Left Fork Cloverlick Creek—*stream* KY-4
Left Fork Clover Run—*stream* WV-2
*Left Fork Coal Creek* UT-8
Left Fork Coal Creek—*stream* VA-3
Left Fork Copeland Creek—*stream* TN-4
Left Fork Cotton Creek—*stream* UT-8
Left Fork Cottonwood Canyon—*valley* (2) UT-8
Left Fork Coulter Branch—*stream* GA-3
Left Fork Cove Canyon—*valley* UT-8
Left Fork Cow Canyon—*valley* CO-8
Left Fork Cow Creek—*stream* KY-4
Left Fork Cow Creek—*stream* WV-2
Left Fork Cow Run—*stream* WV-2
Left Fork Crab Creek—*stream* UT-8
Left Fork Crane Creek—*stream* WV-2
Left Fork Cranks Creek—*stream* KY-4
*Left Fork Creek* UT-8
Left Fork Creek—*stream* ID-8
Left Fork Crooked Creek—*stream* OH-6
Left Fork Currant Creek—*stream* UT-8
Left Fork Dan Branch—*stream* WV-2
Left Fork Daniels Creek—*stream* KY-4
Left Fork Daniels Run—*stream* WV-2
Left Fork Danskin Creek—*stream* ID-8
Left Fork Davis Creek—*stream* WV-2
Left Fork Davy Branch—*stream* WV-2
Left Fork Days Canyon—*valley* UT-8
Left Fork Deadhorse Creek—*stream* MT-8
Left Fork Deadman Creek—*stream* UT-8
Left Fork Death Canyon—*valley* ID-8
Left Fork Deep Creek—*stream* NC-3
Left Fork Deep Creek—*stream* UT-8
Left Fork Dial Branch—*stream* KY-4
Left Fork Divide Creek—*stream* ID-8
Left Fork Dixfork—*stream* KY-4
Left Fork Dry Branch—*stream* TN-4
Left Fork Dry Canyon—*valley* ID-8
Left Fork Dry Creek—*stream* ID-8
Left Fork Dry Creek—*stream* (2) KY-4
Left Fork Dry Creek—*stream* UT-8
Left Fork Dry Hollow—*valley* ID-8
Left Fork Dry Pine Canyon—*valley* ID-8
Left Fork Durbin Creek—*stream* KY-4
Left Fork Dutchman Run—*stream* WV-2
Left Fork Dutchmans Canyon—*valley* UT-8
Left Fork East Fork Canyon—*valley* ID-8
Left Fork East Fourmile Draw—*valley* CO-8
Left Fork Eightmile Canyon—*valley* ID-8
Left Fork Elisha Creek—*stream* KY-4
*Left Fork Elk Creek* KY-4
Left Fork Elk Creek—*stream* WV-2
Left Fork Elk Fork—*stream* KY-4
Left Fork Elk Fork—*stream* WV-2
Left Fork Elkhorn Creek—*stream* KY-4
Left Fork Enoch Canyon—*valley* UT-8
*Left Fork Ethel Hollow* WV-2
Left Fork Fall Creek—*stream* (2) ID-8
Left Fork Falls Run—*stream* WV-2
Left Fork Farmington Creek—*stream* UT-8
Left Fork Farrar Brook—*stream* ME-1
Left Fork Fielder Creek—*stream* OR-9
Left Fork Files Creek—*stream* WV-2
Left Fork Fish Creek—*stream* UT-8
Left Fork Fish Haven Canyon—*valley* ID-8
Left Fork Fish Haven Spring—*spring* ID-8
Left Fork Five And Twenty Mile Creek—*stream* WV-2
Left Fork Flatrock Creek—*stream* WV-2
Left Fork Flick Gulch—*valley* CO-8
Left Fork Foots Creek—*stream* OR-9
Left Fork Fortymile Gulch—*valley* UT-8
Left Fork Fourmile Creek—*stream* UT-8
Left Fork Fox Creek—*stream* VA-3
Left Fork Frasure Branch—*stream* KY-4
Left Fork Freemans Creek—*stream* WV-2
Left Fork French Creek—*stream* (2) WV-2
Left Fork Frozencamp Creek—*stream* WV-2
Left Fork Frozen Creek—*stream* OR-9
Left Fork Fugitt Creek—*stream* KY-4
Left Fork Funston Run—*stream* PA-2
Left Fork Georges Creek—*stream* KY-4
*Left Fork Georgetown Canyon* ID-8
Left Fork Gilbert Creek—*stream* WV-2
Left Fork Goose Creek—*stream* AK-9
Left Fork Grapevine Creek—*stream* KY-4
Left Fork Grassy Creek—*stream* KY-4
Left Fork Greasy Creek—*stream* KY-4
Left Fork Green Branch—*stream* PA-2
Left Fork Greenbrier Creek—*stream* WV-2
Left Fork Green Creek—*stream* WV-2
Left Fork Greenhow Branch—*stream* KY-4
Left Fork Griffin Creek—*stream* KY-4
Left Fork Grove Run—*stream* PA-2
Left Fork Guess Fork—*stream* VA-3
Left Fork Guilder Sleeve Canyon—*valley* UT-8
Left Fork Hammond Creek—*stream* KY-4
Left Fork Harris Creek—*stream* AK-9
Left Fork Hauser Creek—*stream* ID-8
Left Fork Haycock Creek—*stream* UT-8
Left Fork Heiners Creek—*stream* UT-8
*Left Fork Heines Creek* UT-8
Left Fork Hevner Run—*stream* PA-2
Left Fork Hipple Fork Little Sandy River—*stream* KY-4
*Left Fork Hobble Creek* UT-8
Left Fork Hobble Creek—*stream* UT-8
Left Fork Holloway Draft—*valley* VA-3
Left Fork Holly Bush Creek—*stream* KY-4
Left Fork Holly River—*stream* WV-2
Left Fork Hollywood Run—*stream* WV-2
Left Fork Holty Branch—*stream* KY-4
Left Fork Home Branch—*stream* KY-4
Left Fork Home Creek—*stream* VA-3
Left Fork Honeysuckle Spring—*spring* AZ-5
Left Fork Hoods Fork—*stream* KY-4
Left Fork Horner Hollow—*valley* TN-4
Left Fork Howards Creek—*stream* KY-4
Left Fork Hunter Creek—*stream* AK-9
Left Fork Huntington Creek—*stream* UT-8
Left Fork Hurley Branch—*stream* TN-4
Left Fork Hurricane Creek—*stream* VA-3
Left Fork Hurricane Creek—*stream* WV-2
Left Fork Indian Canyon—*valley* UT-8
Left Fork Indian Creek—*stream* VA-3
Left Fork Indian Grave Branch—*stream* KY-4
Left Fork Iron Bog Creek—*stream* ID-8
Left Fork Island Creek—*stream* (2) KY-4
Left Fork Ivy Creek—*stream* KY-4
Left Fork Jesse Run—*stream* WV-2
Left Fork Joes Creek—*stream* WV-2
Left Fork Joes Run—*stream* WV-2
Left Fork John Henry Canyon—*valley* UT-8
Left Fork Kane Wash—*valley* UT-8
Left Fork Kelly Branch—*stream* KY-4
Left Fork Kellys Creek—*stream* WV-2
Left Fork Kidney Gulch—*stream* OR-9
Left Fork Kites Run—*stream* WV-2
Left Fork Knawl Creek—*stream* WV-2
Left Fork Knox Canyon—*valley* ID-8
Left Fork Kougarok River—*stream* AK-9
Left Fork Koyle Branch—*stream* KY-4
Left Fork Lacy Creek—*stream* KY-4
Left Fork Lake Canyon—*valley* UT-8
Left Fork Lake Creek—*stream* CO-8
Left Fork Lake Fork—*stream* UT-8
Left Fork Laurel Branch—*stream* VA-3
*Left Fork Laurel Creek* WV-2
Left Fork Laurel Creek—*stream* KY-4
Left Fork Laurel Creek—*stream* WV-2
Left Fork Laurel Fork—*stream* KY-4
Left Fork Laurel Fork—*stream* (3) WV-2
Left Fork Leatherwood Creek—*stream* WV-2
Left Fork Lens Creek—*stream* WV-2
Left Fork Leonard Slough—*stream* MT-8
Left Fork Leviso Fork—*stream* KY-4
Left Fork Lewis Creek—*stream* KY-4
Left Fork Lick Branch—*stream* (2) KY-4
Left Fork Lick Creek—*stream* (2) VA-3
Left Fork Lick Creek—*stream* (2) WV-2
Left Fork Lick Fork—*stream* VA-3
Left Fork Lick Gulch—*valley* OR-9
Left Fork Licking River—*stream* KY-4
Left Fork Linn Camp Branch—*stream* VA-3
Left Fork Little Basin Creek—*stream* MT-8
Left Fork Little Bear Creek—*stream* MT-8
Left Fork Little Blaine Creek—*stream* KY-4
Left Fork Little Boulder Creek—*stream* WA-9
Left Fork Little Cove Creek—*stream* TN-4
Left Fork Little Dutch Hollow—*valley* UT-8
Left Fork Little Garden Creek—*stream* VA-3
Left Fork Little Hobble Creek—*stream* UT-8
Left Fork Little Point Creek—*stream* KY-4
Left Fork Little Red Creek—*stream* UT-8
Left Fork Little Sand Run—*stream* WV-2
Left Fork Little Sandy Creek—*stream* WV-2
Left Fork Little Spring Creek—*stream* WV-2
Left Fork Loafer Canyon—*valley* UT-8
Left Fork Log Hollow—*valley* UT-8
Left Fork Longbottom Creek—*stream* WV-2
Left Fork Long Branch—*stream* VA-3
Left Fork Long Branch—*stream* WV-2
Left Fork Long Fork—*stream* KY-4
Left Fork Looney Creek—*stream* VA-3
Left Fork Lower Creek—*stream* WV-2
Left Fork Lower Pigeon Branch—*stream* KY-4
Left Fork Lydias Canyon—*valley* UT-8
Left Fork Lynn Creek—*stream* WV-2
Left Fork Maces Creek—*stream* KY-4
Left Fork Macfarlan Creek—*stream* WV-2
Left Fork Maggoty Run—*stream* WV-2
Left Fork Malachi Branch—*stream* KY-4
Left Fork Maple Canyon—*valley* ID-8
Left Fork Maple Canyon—*valley* (2) UT-8
Left Fork Maple Creek—*stream* ID-8
Left Fork Markham Creek—*stream* AZ-5
*Left Fork Markham Wash* AZ-5
Left Fork Marrowbone Creek—*stream* KY-4
Left Fork Marrowbone Creek—*stream* WV-2
Left Fork Martins Fork Cumberland River—*stream* KY-4
Left Fork Middle Creek Levisa Fork—*stream* KY-4
Left Fork Middle Fork Ogden River—*stream* UT-8
Left Fork Middle Fork Spruce Pine Creek—*stream* VA-3
Left Fork Mill Canyon—*valley* ID-8
Left Fork Mill Creek—*stream* KY-4
Left Fork Mill Creek—*stream* PA-2
Left Fork Mill Creek—*stream* TN-4
Left Fork Mill Creek—*stream* (3) WV-2
Left Fork Miller Creek—*stream* UT-8
Left Fork Miller Creek—*stream* WV-2
Left Fork Miller Run—*stream* (2) PA-2
Left Fork Millers Fork—*stream* WV-2
Left Fork Mill Fork—*stream* UT-8
Left Fork Mill Run—*stream* PA-2
Left Fork Millstone Creek—*stream* KY-4
Left Fork Moore Creek—*stream* KY-4
Left Fork Morgan Fork—*stream* OH-6
Left Fork Mount Sterling Branch—*stream* KY-4
Left Fork Mud Lick—*stream* KY-4
Left Fork Mudlick Run—*stream* WV-2
Left Fork Mud River—*stream* WV-2
Left Fork Mud Run—*stream* WV-2
Left Fork Mulberry Creek—*stream* NC-3
Left Fork Nats Creek—*stream* KY-4
Left Fork Naylon Canyon—*valley* UT-8
Left Fork Neals Creek—*stream* MO-7
Left Fork Neely Branch—*stream* WV-2
Left Fork North Creek—*stream* UT-8
Left Fork North Fork Cranberry River—*stream* WV-2
Left Fork North Hornet Creek—*stream* ID-8
Left Fork Nottely River—*stream* GA-3
Left Fork Oak Creek—*stream* UT-8
*Left Fork Of South Fork* UT-8
Left Fork Old Canyon—*valley* UT-8
Left Fork Old Field Fork—*stream* WV-2
Left Fork Openmouth Branch—*stream* WV-2
Left Fork Otter Creek—*stream* (2) KY-4
Left Fork Otter Run—*stream* PA-2
Left Fork Owens Creek—*stream* WA-9
Left Fork Painted Rock Canyon—*valley* UT-8
*Left Fork Parchment Creek* WV-2
Left Fork Parker Branch—*stream* WV-2
Left Fork Partridge Creek—*stream* NC-3
Left Fork Pawpaw Creek—*stream* VA-3
Left Fork Pennington Branch—*stream* TN-4
Left Fork Pete Nelson Hollow—*valley* UT-8
Left Fork Petercave Fork—*stream* KY-4
Left Fork Peter Creek—*stream* KY-4
Left Fork Peterson Creek—*stream* ID-8
Left Fork Philadelphia Creek—*stream* CO-8
Left Fork Pine Creek—*stream* WV-2
Left Fork Placer Creek—*stream* ID-8
*Left Fork Pocatalico River* WV-2
Left Fork Pole Canyon—*valley* UT-8
Left Fork Pole Creek—*stream* UT-8
Left Fork Poplar Creek—*stream* WV-2
Left Fork Proctor Canyon—*valley* UT-8
Left Fork Proctor Creek—*stream* WV-2
Left Fork Puncheon Creek—*stream* KY-4
Left Fork Queen Shoals Creek—*stream* WV-2
Left Fork Race Fork—*stream* VA-3
Left Fork Rockcastle Creek—*stream* KY-4
Left Fork Raimie Creek—*stream* WA-9
Left Fork Ranch Canyon—*valley* UT-8
Left Fork Raven Fork—*stream* NC-3
Left Fork Red Creek—*stream* WV-2
Left Fork Redman Creek—*stream* NC-3
Left Fork Red Rock Canyon—*valley* CO-8
*Left Fork Redwine Creek* KY-4
Left Fork Reedy Creek—*stream* WV-2
Left Fork Reuben Branch—*stream* KY-4
*Left Fork Rhodes Canyon* UT-8
Left Fork Rich Creek—*stream* (2) WV-2
Left Fork Riffe Branch—*stream* WV-2
Left Fork Right Fork—*stream* UT-8
Left Fork Right Fork Buckhannon River—*stream* WV-2
*Left Fork Right Fork Haycock Creek* UT-8
Left Fork Right Fork Little Kanawha River—*stream* WV-2
Left Fork Right Fork Trace Fork—*stream* WV-2
Left Fork Rilda Canyon—*valley* UT-8
Left Fork Rileys Canyon—*valley* UT-8
*Left Fork Road Canyon* NM-5
Left Fork Rock Canyon—*valley* ID-8
Left Fork Rock Canyon—*valley* UT-8
Left Fork Rockcastle Creek—*stream* WV-2
Left Fork Rock Creek—*stream* KY-4
Left Fork Rock Creek—*stream* TN-4
Left Fork Rock Creek—*stream* UT-8
Left Fork Rock Creek—*stream* WV-2
Left Fork Rockhouse Creek—*stream* (2) KY-4
Left Fork Rockhouse Fork—*stream* WV-2
Left Fork Rocky Branch—*stream* KY-4
Left Fork Rocky Canyon—*valley* ID-8
Left Fork Rocky Point Draw—*valley* CO-8
Left Fork Roe Creek—*stream* KY-4
Left Fork Rush Creek—*stream* VA-3
Left Fork Rush Run—*stream* WV-2
Left Fork Sacaton Draw—*valley* NM-5
Left Fork Salt Creek—*stream* UT-8
*Left Fork Sam Stover Canyon* UT-8
Left Fork Sam Stowe Canyon—*valley* UT-8
Left Fork Sam Stowe Creek—*stream* UT-8
Left Fork Sand Hollow—*valley* ID-8
Left Fork Sandlick Creek—*stream* WV-2
Left Fork Sand Run—*stream* WV-2
Left Fork Sandy Creek—*stream* UT-8
Left Fork Sandy Creek—*stream* (2) WV-2
Left Fork Sanford Creek—*stream* UT-8
*Left Fork Santaciara River* UT-8
Left Fork Santa Clara River—*stream* UT-8
Left Fork Sardine Creek—*stream* OR-9
Left Fork Sawmill Canyon—*valley* UT-8
Left Fork Scheidler Run—*stream* WV-2
Left Fork Scotty Creek—*stream* OR-9
Left Fork Scrabble Creek—*stream* WV-2
Left Fork Scriver Creek—*stream* ID-8
Left Fork Seedtick Branch—*stream* KY-4
Left Fork Shannon Branch—*stream* KY-4
Left Fork Shingle Mill Creek—*stream* UT-8
Left Fork Shurtz Canyon—*valley* UT-8
Left Fork Silver Creek—*stream* NV-8
Left Fork Skamokawa Creek—*stream* WA-9
Left Fork Skin Fork—*stream* WV-2
Left Fork Slab Creek—*stream* UT-8
Left Fork Slab Creek—*stream* WV-2
Left Fork Slate Creek—*stream* UT-8
Left Fork Slate Creek—*stream* VA-3
Left Fork Slate Creek—*stream* WV-2
Left Fork Slaughter Creek—*stream* ID-8
Left Fork Smith Branch—*stream* KY-4

Left Fork Smith Run—*stream* PA-2
Left Fork Soap Gulch—*valley* MT-8
Left Fork Soldier Creek—*stream* CO-8
Left Fork South Fork Ogden River—*stream* UT-8
Left Fork South Fork Provo River—*stream* UT-8
Left Fork South Oak Brush Canyon—*valley* UT-8
Left Fork Spence Branch—*stream* KY-4
Left Fork Spencer Canyon—*valley* UT-8
Left Fork Spring Branch—*stream* KY-4
Left Fork Spring Canyon—*valley* UT-8
Left Fork Spring Creek—*gut* UT-8
Left Fork Spring Creek—*stream* WV-2
Left Fork Spring Fork—*stream* (2) WV-2
Left Fork Spruce Branch—*stream* KY-4
Left Fork Spruce Creek—*stream* WV-2
Left Fork Spruce Fork—*stream* (2) WV-2
Left Fork Sprulock Creek—*stream* WV-2
Left Fork Stake Springs Draw—*valley* CO-8
Left Fork State Bridge Draw—*valley* CO-8
Left Fork Steer Creek—*stream* WV-2
Left Fork Stillwell Creek—*stream* WV-2
Left Fork Stink Hollow—*valley* PA-2
Left Fork Stone Creek—*stream* MT-8
Left Fork Straight Creek—*stream* KY-4
Left Fork Straight Creek—*stream* WV-2
Left Fork Sucker Creek—*stream* OR-9
Left Fork Sullivan Canyon—*valley* UT-8
Left Fork Summerville Wash—*valley* UT-8
Left Fork Summit Creek—*stream* UT-8
Left Fork Swamp Creek—*stream* MT-8
Left Fork Swannanor River—*stream* NC-3
Left Fork Sycamore Branch—*stream* WV-2
Left Fork Sycamore Creek—*stream* KY-4
Left Fork Sycamore Creek—*stream* (2) WV-2
Left Fork Sycamore Fork—*stream* WV-2
Left Fork Tallowbox Creek—*stream* OR-9
Left Fork Tally Creek—*stream* ID-8
Left Fork Taylor Hollow—*valley* UT-8
*Left Fork Threemile Creek* UT-8
Left Fork Timber Canyon—*valley* UT-8
Left Fork Tims Draft—*valley* VA-3
*Left Fork Tinker Fork* KY-4
Left Fork Toler Creek—*stream* KY-4
Left Fork Tommys Draw—*valley* CO-8
Left Fork Trace Branch—*stream* KY-4
Left Fork Trace Creek—*stream* KY-4
Left Fork Trace Fork—*stream* (2) KY-4
Left Fork Trail—*trail* PA-2
Left Fork Trap Branch—*stream* KY-4
Left Fork Trap Fork—*stream* WV-2
*Left Fork Triplett Run* WV-2
Left Fork Troublesome Creek—*stream* KY-4
Left Fork Turkey Branch—*stream* WV-2
Left Fork Turners Creek—*stream* KY-4
Left Fork Turtle Creek—*stream* KY-4
Left Fork Twentymile Brook—*stream* ME-1
*Left Fork Twin Creek* ID-8
Left Fork Twomile Creek—*stream* KY-4
Left Fork Twomile Creek—*stream* WV-2
Left Fork Ulysses Creek—*stream* KY-4
Left Fork U M Creek—*stream* UT-8
Left Fork Upper Bear Creek—*stream* KY-4
Left Fork Upper Burning Creek—*stream* WV-2
Left Fork Upper Devil Creek—*stream* KY-4
Left Fork Upper Kanab Creek—*stream* UT-8
Left Fork Upper Second Creek—*stream* KY-4
Left Fork Upper Twin Branch—*stream* VA-3
Left Fork Vinson Branch—*stream* KY-4
Left Fork Vock Canyon—*valley* AZ-5
Left Fork Waddoups Canyon—*valley* ID-8
Left Fork Wagstaff Hollow—*valley* UT-8
Left Fork Walker Hollow—*valley* UT-8
Left Fork Water Canyon—*valley* UT-8
Left Fork Webb Creek—*stream* NC-3
Left Fork West Canyon—*valley* UT-8
*Left Fork West Fork* CA-9
*Left Fork West Fork Creek* CA-9
Left Fork West Fork Little Kanawha River—*stream* WV-2
Left Fork West Glacier Creek—*stream* AK-9
Left Fork White Oak Creek—*stream* (2) KY-4
Left Fork White Oak Creek—*stream* (3) WV-2
Left Fork White River—*stream* UT-8
Left Fork Whites Creek—*stream* TN-4
Left Fork Whitman Creek—*stream* WV-2
Left Fork Whitmore Canyon—*valley* UT-8
Left Fork Wildhorse Canyon—*valley* UT-8
Left Fork Wildhorse Creek—*stream* ID-8
Left Fork Williams Branch—*stream* KY-4
Left Fork Willow Creek—*stream* UT-8
Left Fork Wilson Creek—*stream* WV-2
Left Fork Windy Creek—*stream* AK-9
Left Fork Winn Branch—*stream* KY-4
Left Fork Witcher Creek—*stream* WV-2
Left Fork Wolf Creek—*stream* ID-8
Left Fork Wolf Creek—*stream* WV-2
Left Fork Wolfpit Branch—*stream* KY-4
Left Fork Wolf Run—*stream* WV-2
Left Fork York Canyon—*valley* NM-5
Left Frying Pan Trail—*trail* PA-2
Left Hand—*locale* WV-2
Left Hand Allen Creek—*stream* UT-8
Left Hand Barret Creek—*stream* CO-8
Lefthand Bay—*bay* AK-9
Left Hand Bear Creek—*stream* SD-7
*Left Hand Branch Mill Creek* CA-9
Left Hand Bull Canyon—*valley* UT-8
Left Hand Canyon—*valley* AZ-5
Lefthand Canyon—*valley* (2) AZ-5
Left Hand Canyon—*valley* CA-9
Lefthand Canyon—*valley* CO-8
Left Hand Canyon—*valley* CO-8
Left Hand Canyon—*valley* NV-8
Lefthand Canyon—*valley* NM-5
Left Hand Canyon—*valley* NM-5
Left Hand Canyon—*valley* OR-9
Left Hand Canyon—*valley* UT-8
Left-hand Canyon—*valley* UT-8
Left Hand Chute of Little River—*stream* AR-4
Left Hand Collet Canyon—*valley* UT-8
*Left Hand Collet Wash* UT-8
Left Hand Corral Creek—*stream* CO-8
*Lefthand Creek* WV-2
Left Hand Creek—*stream* (2) CO-8
Left Hand Creek—*stream* OR-9
Left Hand Creek—*stream* TX-5
Lefthand Creek—*stream* WV-2
Left Hand Creek—*stream* WV-2
Left Hand Creek—*stream* WY-8
Left Hand Dawson Creek—*stream* CO-8
Lefthand Ditch—*canal* NM-5
Lefthand Ditch (Wind River B Canal)—*canal* WY-8
Lefthand Draw—*valley* (2) CO-8
Left Hand Draw—*valley* TX-5
Left Hand Duncan Creek—*stream* TX-5
Left Hand Falls Canyon—*valley* TX-5
Left Hand Fish Creek—*stream* UT-8
*Lefthand Fork* OH-6
*Left Hand Fork* UT-8
*Lefthand Fork* WV-2
Lefthand Fork—*stream* KY-4
Left Hand Fork—*stream* VA-3
Lefthand Fork—*stream* (2) WV-2
*Left Hand Fork Alexander Canyon* UT-8
Left Hand Fork Arthurs Creek—*stream* UT-8
Left Hand Fork Axhandle Canyon—*valley* UT-8
Lefthand Fork Bearhole Fork—*stream* WV-2
Left Hand Fork Beaverdam Creek—*stream* ID-8
Left Hand Fork Blacksmith Fork Canyon—*valley* UT-8
Lefthand Fork Bluff Fork—*stream* WV-2
Left Hand Fork Brush Creek—*stream* OR-9
Left Hand Fork Butterfield Canyon—*valley* UT-8
Left Hand Fork Coon Canyon—*valley* UT-8
Lefthand Fork Cooper Creek—*stream* WV-2
Left Hand Fork Cottonwood Gulch—*valley* MT-8
Left Hand Fork Dalton Creek—*stream* UT-8
Left Hand Fork Deadman Creek—*stream* MT-8
Left Hand Fork Dove Creek—*stream* UT-8
Left Hand Fork Dry Gulch—*valley* MT-8
Left Hand Fork Dude Canyon—*valley* CO-8
Left Hand Fork Dunn Canyon—*valley* UT-8
Left Hand Fork East Fork Bear River—*stream* UT-8
Left Hand Fork Georgetown Canyon—*valley* ID-8
Left Hand Fork Government Canyon—*valley* UT-8
Left Hand Fork Harrys Branch—*stream* WV-2
Left Hand Fork Hoover Fork—*stream* WV-2
*Left Hand Fork Jellico Creek* TN-4
Left Hand Fork Johnson Creek—*stream* UT-8
Left Hand Fork Kelsey Canyon—*valley* UT-8
Left Hand Fork Logging Canyon—*valley* CO-8
Left Hand Fork Lone Pine Canyon—*valley* UT-8
Left Hand Fork Marsh Creek—*stream* ID-8
Left Hand Fork Martinez Canyon—*valley* CO-8
Lefthand Fork Meadow Creek—*stream* WV-2
Left Hand Fork Middle Canyon—*valley* UT-8
Lefthand Fork North Creek—*stream* CO-8
*Left Hand Fork of Donkey Creek* UT-8
Left Hand Fork of Donkey Creek Dam—*dam* UT-8
Lefthand Fork Old Buck Creek—*stream* KY-4
Left Hand Fork Old Laketown Canyon—*valley* UT-8
Left Hand Fork Oso Canyon—*valley* CO-8
Lefthand Fork Paint Creek—*stream* WV-2
*Lefthand Fork Parowan Creek* UT-8
Left Hand Fork Peterson Creek—*stream* UT-8
Left Hand Fork Pine Creek—*stream* UT-8
Lefthand Fork Rock Creek—*stream* WA-9
Left Hand Fork Settlement Canyon—*valley* UT-8
Left Hand Fork Soldier Canyon—*valley* UT-8
Left Hand Fork Specimen Creek—*stream* CA-9
Lefthand Fork Stackpole Run—*stream* WV-2
Lefthand Fork Tommy Creek—*stream* WV-2
*Lefthand Fork Triplett Run* WV-2
Lefthand Fork Turkey Creek—*stream* WV-2
Left Hand Fork Uncles Creek—*stream* CA-9
Left Hand Fork White Gulch—*valley* MT-8
Lefthand Fork Widemouth Creek—*stream* WV-2
Left Hand Hollow—*valley* MO-7
Lefthand Hollow—*valley* VA-3
Left Hand Horse Creek—*stream* TX-5
Left Hand Inskip Canyon—*valley* NV-8
Lefthand Left Fork Ben Creek—*stream* WV-2
Lefthand Luman Creek—*stream* WY-8
Left Hand Meadow Creek—*stream* CO-8
Left Hand Moss Wash—*stream* AZ-5
Left Hand Nash Wash—*valley* UT-8
Left Hand Needle Creek—*stream* CO-8
*Left Hand Parrish Creek* OR-9
*Lefthand Prong* AR-4
Left Hand Prong—*stream* AR-4
Left Hand Prong Little Canoe Creek—*stream* AL-4
*Lefthand Prong North Fork Illinois Bayou* AR-4
Left Hand Prong Turkey Creek—*stream* TX-5
Left Hand Rsvr—*reservoir* CO-8
Left Hand Rsvr—*reservoir* UT-8
*Lefthand Run* WV-2
Left Hand Run—*stream* (3) WV-2
Lefthand Sch—*school* WV-2
Lefthand Shutup—*valley* TX-5
*Left Hand Silver Falls Canyon* UT-8
Left Hand South Fork North Eden Canyon—*valley* UT-8
Left Hand Spring—*spring* (3) AZ-5
Left Hand Spring—*spring* OK-5
Left Hand Stump Fork—*valley* UT-8
Lefthand Tank—*reservoir* AZ-5
Left Hand Tank—*reservoir* AZ-5
Lefthand Tank—*reservoir* AZ-5
Left Hand Threeforks Floy Canyon—*valley* UT-8
Left Hand Turner River—*stream* FL-3
Left Hand Tusher Canyon—*valley* UT-8
Left Hand Valley Rsvr—*reservoir* CO-8
Left Head Port Moller—*bay* AK-9
Lefthead River—*stream* AK-9
Lefthook Canyon—*valley* NM-5
*Left Hurricane Fork* VA-3
*Left Mill Run Trail* PA-2
**Lefton**—*pop pl* IL-6
*Left Prong* NC-3
Left Prong Anglin Branch—*stream* KY-4
Left Prong Anthony Creek—*stream* TN-4
Left Prong Bear Creek—*stream* AR-4
Left Prong Benson Run—*stream* VA-3
Left Prong Bent Creek—*stream* NC-3
Left Prong Big Creek—*stream* TN-4
Left Prong Brasstown Creek—*stream* GA-3
Left Prong Burningtown Creek—*stream* NC-3
Left Prong Caney Creek—*stream* TN-4
Left Prong Catawba River—*stream* NC-3
Left Prong Clear Creek—*stream* NC-3
Left Prong Dix Creek—*stream* AZ-5
Left Prong Fourmile Canyon—*valley* AZ-5
Left Prong Galford Run—*stream* WV-2
Left Prong Hampton Creek—*stream* TN-4
Left Prong Hiwassee River—*stream* TN-4
Left Prong Hodge Branch—*stream* TN-4
Left Prong Johnson Creek—*stream* NC-3
Left Prong Mill Creek—*stream* NC-3
Left Prong Molasses Bayou—*gut* TX-5
*Left Prong Mountain Creek* AR-4
Left Prong Mountain Creek—*stream* AR-4
Left Prong Newberry Creek—*stream* NC-3
Left Prong New Creek—*stream* WV-2
Left Prong Pegamore Creek—*stream* GA-3
Left Prong Ramseys Draft—*valley* VA-3
Left Prong Ray Branch—*stream* NC-3
Left Prong Rich Fork—*stream* OH-6
Left Prong Rough Fork—*stream* NC-3
Left Prong Skelton Run—*stream* WV-2
Left Prong Smith Branch—*stream* TN-4
Left Prong South Toe River—*stream* NC-3
Left Prong Still Fork Creek—*stream* NC-3
Left Prong Stony Fork—*stream* NC-3
Left Prong Three Forks Run—*stream* MD-2
*Left Prong Tims Draft* VA-3
Left Prong Upper Prong Sinkhole Creek—*stream* TN-4
*Left Prong Williams Creek* TN-4
Left Prong Wilson Creek—*stream* VA-3
Left Quichapa Canyon—*valley* UT-8
Left Redwood Creek—*stream* OR-9
Left Riemer Creek—*stream* TX-5
Left Roberts Canyon—*valley* CO-8
Lefts Point—*cape* MI-6
Left Steele Run Trail—*trail* PA-2
Left Stony Hollow—*valley* PA-2
Left Straight Run—*stream* PA-2
*Left Strait Run* PA-2
Left Strait Run Trail—*trail* PA-2
Left Stringer—*stream* CA-9
Leftt Hand Fork Government Canyon—*valley* UT-8
Left Trail—*trail* MD-2
Left Turkeytoe Branch—*stream* KY-4
Leftwich—*locale* TN-4
**Leftwich**—*pop pl* VA-3
*Leftwich Branch* WV-2
Leftwich Cem—*cemetery* TN-4
Leftwich Cem—*cemetery* VA-3
*Leftwich Community Club* MS-4
Leftwich Hollow—*valley* TN-4
Leftwich Hollow Branch—*stream* TN-4
Leftwich House—*hist pl* OH-6
Leftwich Rsvr—*reservoir* CO-8
Leftwich Sch—*school* MS-4
Lefty Creek—*stream* OR-9
Lefutu Ridge—*ridge* AS-9
Legal Cem—*cemetery* AL-4
Legal Ch—*church* OK-5
Legal Corner Sch—*school* IL-6
Legall Spring—*spring* WA-9
Legal Mine (underground)—*mine* AL-4
Legal Tender Ditch—*canal* CO-8
Legal Tender Mine—*mine* (2) CO-8
Legal Tender Mine—*mine* MT-8
Legal Tender Mine—*mine* SD-7
Legan—*island* MP-9
Leganger Cem—*cemetery* SD-7
*Legan Island* MP-9
*Legan Islands* MP-9
**Legante Paseo (subdivision)**—*pop pl* (2) AZ-5
Legaotaema Point—*cape* AS-9
Legare Anchorage—*harbor* FL-3
Legare-Morgan House—*hist pl* SC-3
**Legareville**—*pop pl* SC-3
Legas Lake—*lake* OK-5
Legat Cem—*cemetery* PA-2
Legat Creek—*stream* MN-6
**Legate**—*pop pl* TN-4
Legate Cem—*cemetery* AR-4
Legate Cem—*cemetery* OK-5
Legate Cem—*cemetery* TN-4
*Le'Gate Hill* MA-1
Legate Hill—*summit* (2) MA-1
Legate Hill Brook—*stream* MA-1
Legate Lake—*lake* AR-4
Legate Post Office (historical)—*building* TN-4
Le Gates Cove—*bay* MD-2
Legation of the Union of South Africa Bldg—*building* DC-2
Legat Lake—*lake* MN-6
Legato—*locale* VA-3
Legault Mtn—*summit* CO-8
Leg Branch—*stream* MO-7
Leg Church Sch—*school* MO-7
Leg Creek—*stream* ID-8
Leg Creek—*stream* IN-6
*Legendary Hills* IN-6
**Legendary Hills**—*pop pl* IN-6
Legend City Amusement Park—*park* AZ-5
Legend Creek—*stream* ID-8
Legend Creek—*stream* MN-6
**Legend Estates (subdivision)**—*pop pl* (2) AZ-5
**Legend Hills (subdivision)**—*pop pl* NC-3
*Legend Lake* MS-4
*Legend Lake* MT-8
Legend Lake—*lake* ID-8
Legend Lake—*lake* MN-6
Legendre Canal—*canal* LA-4
Legend Rock Petroglyph Site—*hist pl* WY-8
Legend Rocks—*cliff* WY-8
Legend (Township of)—*other* OH-6
Leger Badlands Dam—*dam* SD-7
Leger Cem—*cemetery* (2) LA-4
Leger Dam—*reservoir* SD-7
Leger East Dam—*dam* SD-7
Leger Fork—*stream* KY-4
Leger Irrigation Dam—*dam* SD-7
Leger Lake—*reservoir* LA-4
**Legerwood**—*pop pl* NC-3
*Leges Point* MD-2
Legett Cem—*cemetery* MS-4
Legette Sch—*school* CA-9
*Legg* AL-4
Legg, Harry F., House—*hist pl* MN-6
Legg, John, House—*hist pl* MA-1
Leggat Creek—*stream* MT-8
Leggat Mtn—*summit* MT-8
Legg Branch—*stream* AL-4
Legg Bridge—*bridge* AL-4
Legg Bridge—*bridge* GA-3
Legg Bridge—*bridge* ND-7
Legg Cem—*cemetery* (2) AL-4
Legg Chapel Cem—*cemetery* MS-4
Legg Creek—*stream* TN-4
Legg Creek—*stream* TX-5
Legg Creek—*stream* WY-8
Legg Ditch—*canal* IN-6
Legge Cem—*cemetery* MA-1
Legge Lake—*lake* NE-7
Legget Creek—*stream* PA-2
Legget Hill—*summit* MT-8
**Legget (historical)**—*pop pl* TN-4
*Legget Mountain* MT-8
Leggets Branch—*stream* TX-5
*Leggetsville* NC-3
Leggett—*locale* MS-4
**Leggett**—*pop pl* CA-9
**Leggett**—*pop pl* NC-3
**Leggett**—*pop pl* TX-5
Leggett, Thomas H., House—*hist pl* CA-9
*Leggett Branch* TN-4
Leggett Branch—*stream* NC-3
Leggett Branch—*stream* TN-4
Leggett Cabin Spring—*spring* NM-5
Leggett Canal—*canal* NC-3
Leggett Canyon—*valley* NM-5
Leggett Cem—*cemetery* AR-4
Leggett Cem—*cemetery* MS-4
Leggett Cem—*cemetery* NC-3
Leggett Cem—*cemetery* (2) TN-4
Leggett Creek—*stream* (2) CA-9
Leggett Creek—*stream* ID-8
Leggett Creek—*stream* WI-6
**Leggett Crossroads**—*pop pl* NC-3
Leggett Gulch—*valley* OR-9
*Leggett Hill* MA-1
Leggett House—*hist pl* CA-9
Leggett House Cem—*cemetery* NC-3
Leggett Lake—*lake* MI-6
Leggett Lake—*reservoir* NC-3
Leggett Lake Dam—*dam* NC-3
Leggett Landing—*locale* AL-4
Leggett Memorial Hosp—*hospital* TX-5
Leggett Mill Pond—*reservoir* SC-3
*Leggett Mountain* MT-8
**Leggett Park (subdivision)**—*pop pl* NC-3
Leggett Pasture Tank—*reservoir* NM-5
Leggett Peak—*summit* NM-5
Leggett Placer Mine—*mine* ID-8
Leggett Pond—*reservoir* NC-3
Leggett Pond Dam—*dam* NC-3
Leggett Post Office (historical)—*building* MS-4
Leggett Rsvr—*reservoir* CO-8
Leggett Sch—*school* (2) MI-6
Leggett Sch—*school* OH-6
Leggett Sch (historical)—*school* MS-4
Leggetts Creek—*stream* PA-2
Leggetts Creek Shaft—*mine* PA-2
Leggetts Crossroads—*locale* NC-3
Leggett Valley—*basin* CA-9
Legg Fork Tupper Creek—*stream* WV-2
Legg Hill—*summit* MA-1
Leggins Spring—*spring* OR-9
Leggit Creek—*stream* CA-9
Leggit Creek—*stream* ID-8
Leggit Lake—*lake* ID-8
*Leggits Creek* PA-2
Leggitt Cem—*cemetery* MS-4
Legg Lake—*lake* CA-9
Leggo (historical)—*locale* MS-4
Leggo Sch (historical)—*school* MS-4
Leggottville Sch—*school* IL-6
Legg Post Office (historical)—*building* AL-4
Legg Sch—*school* WV-2
Leggs Memorial Chruch—*church* WV-2
Leggs Mill (historical)—*locale* TN-4
Leggtown—*locale* AL-4
Leggtown Cem—*cemetery* IL-6
Leggtown Ch—*church* AL-4
**Leggtown (Legg)**—*pop pl* AL-4
*Leghorn* KS-7
Leghorn Mine—*mine* AZ-5
*Legiep Islands* MP-9
Le Gier-Lovellette Cem—*cemetery* IL-6
*Legilim Berg* FM-9
*Leginiau* FM-9
Legin Mines—*mine* CO-8
**Legion**—*pop pl* TX-5
Legion Ave—*post sta* MD-2
*Legion Beach* NC-3
Legion County Park—*park* MI-6
*Legion Creek* TX-5
Legion Creek—*stream* TX-5
Legion Eyer Park—*park* NY-2
Legion Field—*locale* MA-1
Legion Field—*park* AL-4
Legion Field—*park* FL-3
Legion Field—*park* IN-6
Legion Field—*park* (2) MS-4
Legion-Kenner Park—*park* PA-2
*Legion Lake* MS-4
Legion Lake—*lake* IL-6
Legion Lake—*lake* MI-6
Legion Lake—*lake* MS-4
Legion Lake—*lake* SC-3
Legion Lake—*lake* WY-8
Legion Lake—*reservoir* (2) GA-3
Legion Lake—*reservoir* (2) MS-4
Legion Lake—*reservoir* (2) NC-3
Legion Lake—*reservoir* SC-3
Legion Lake—*reservoir* SD-7
Legion Lake—*swamp* MN-6
Legion Lake Dam—*dam* (3) MS-4
Legion Lake Dam—*dam* SD-7
Legion Memorial Ch—*church* VA-3
Legion Memorial Park—*park* IA-7
Legion Park—*park* CA-9
Legion Park—*park* FL-3
Legion Park—*park* (2) IL-6
Legion Park—*park* IN-6
Legion Park—*park* (3) IA-7
Legion Park—*park* (2) KY-4
Legion Park—*park* LA-4
Legion Park—*park* MA-1
Legion Park—*park* MN-6
Legion Park—*park* (3) NE-7
Legion Park—*park* NM-5
Legion Park—*park* OK-5
Legion Park—*park* OR-9
Legion Park—*park* PA-2
Legion Park—*park* (2) WI-6
Legion Park—*park* WY-8
**Legion Park**—*pop pl* NC-3
Legion Park Bowl—*hist pl* AL-4
Legion Park Campground—*locale* UT-8
Legion Park Golf Course—*other* CO-8
Legion Park No 2—*park* IL-6
Legion Park Sch—*school* LA-4
Legion Picnic Islands—*park* FL-3
*Legion Pond* NC-3
Legion Sch—*school* OK-5
Legion Shop Ctr—*locale* MA-1
Legions Lake Dam—*dam* MS-4
Legion Stadium—*locale* NC-3
Legion (V.A. Hospital)—*uninc pl* TX-5
*Legionville* PA-2
Legionville—*hist pl* PA-2
**Legionville**—*pop pl* MN-6
Legionville Run—*stream* PA-2
Leg Lake—*lake* (2) MI-6
Leg Lake—*lake* MN-6
Leg Lake—*lake* WY-8
**Legler**—*pop pl* NJ-2
Legler, Henry E., Regional Branch of the Chicago Public Library—*hist pl* IL-6
Legler Lake—*lake* MN-6
Legler School Branch—*stream* WI-6
L'eglise de Deju—*church* LA-4
L'Eglise du Precieux Sang—*hist pl* RI-1
Legman Island—*island* AK-9
Legness Drain—*stream* MI-6
Lego—*locale* WV-2
Legoe Bay—*bay* WA-9
**Lego (historical)**—*pop pl* TN-4
Lego Landing—*locale* TN-4
*Legonda* KS-7
**Legonier**—*pop pl* LA-4
Legoo Lake—*lake* WI-6
Lego Point—*cape* MD-2
Lego Post Office (historical)—*building* TN-4
**Le Gore**—*pop pl* MD-2
Le Gore Bridge—*bridge* MD-2
LeGore Bridge—*hist pl* MD-2
Legore Lake—*lake* OR-9
Legore Mine—*mine* OR-9
Le Gore Sch—*school* CA-9
Lego Sch—*school* TN-4
Legoys Bay—*bay* NY-2
*Legrand* AL-4
Legrand—*locale* MI-6
**Le Grand**—*pop pl* AL-4
**Le Grand**—*pop pl* CA-9
**Le Grand**—*pop pl* IA-7
**Legrand**—*pop pl* KY-4
Legrand Ave Ch of Christ—*church* AL-4
Le Grand Canal—*canal* (2) CA-9
Legrand Cem—*cemetery* NC-3
*Le Grand dall de la Columbia* OR-9
LeGrande—*locale* KY-4
Le Grande Cem—*cemetery* AR-4
*Le Grande Dalle de Columbia* OR-9
*Le Grande Riviere* KS-7
Le Grand Sewage Disposal—*other* CA-9
Le Grand Township—*fmr MCD* IA-7
*LeGraph* MI-6
Legreid Lake—*lake* ND-7
*Legroom Creek* AL-4
*LeGros* IN-6
*Le Groupe* PW-9
LeGrow—*locale* WA-9
Legs, The—*summit* AZ-5
Legs Landing—*locale* TN-4
Legue Coulee—*valley* WI-6
Leguino Tank—*reservoir* NM-5
Leguisamo (Barrio)—*fmr MCD* PR-3
Legunita Wash—*stream* AZ-5
Lehak—*cape* FM-9
Lehamite Creek—*stream* CA-9
Le Hardy Rapids—*rapids* WY-8
*Le Hardys Rapids* WY-8
Lehdau, Pilen—*stream* FM-9
*Leheigh Hills* PA-2
Leher Canal—*canal* TX-5
LeHeup Hill—*summit* FL-3
Lehew—*locale* NM-5
**Lehew**—*pop pl* WV-2
Lehew Cem—*cemetery* NC-3
Lehew Ranch—*locale* NM-5
*Lehey Creek* TX-5
**Lehi**—*pop pl* AZ-5
**Lehi**—*pop pl* AR-4
**Lehi**—*pop pl* UT-8
Lehi Airp—*airport* UT-8
Lehiak—*locale* FM-9
Lehia Park—*park* HI-9
Lehi Canyon—*valley* UT-8
Lehi Cem—*cemetery* UT-8
*Lehi City* UT-8
Lehi City Hall—*hist pl* UT-8
*Lehi Creek* PA-2
Lehi Division—*civil* UT-8
Lehi Elem Sch—*school* AZ-5
*Lehigh* FL-3
*Lehigh* PA-2
Lehigh—*locale* GA-3
Lehigh—*locale* IL-6
Lehigh—*locale* MT-8
Lehigh—*locale* WI-6
**Lehigh**—*pop pl* AL-4
**Lehigh**—*pop pl* FL-3
**Lehigh**—*pop pl* IA-7
**Lehigh**—*pop pl* KS-7
**Lehigh**—*pop pl* NY-2
**Lehigh**—*pop pl* ND-7
**Lehigh**—*pop pl* OK-5
**Lehigh**—*pop pl* PA-2
**Lehigh Acres**—*pop pl* FL-3
Lehigh Acres (CCD)—*cens area* FL-3
Lehigh Acres Christian Acad—*school* FL-3
Lehigh Acres MS—*school* FL-3
Lehigh Canal—*canal* PA-2
Lehigh Canal—*hist pl* (2) PA-2
Lehigh Canal; Allentown to Hopeville Section—*hist pl* PA-2
Lehigh Canal: Eastern Section Glendon and Abbott Street Industrial Sites—*hist pl* PA-2
Lehigh Cem—*cemetery* (2) KS-7
Lehigh Cem—*cemetery* MT-8
Lehigh Cem—*cemetery* OK-5
Lehigh Cement Company Lake—*lake* FL-3
*Lehigh Centre* PA-2
*Lehigh Ch* PA-2
Lehigh Ch—*church* PA-2
Lehigh Channel—*channel* NJ-2
Lehigh Channel—*channel* PA-2
Lehigh Coal And Navigation Canal—*canal* PA-2
Lehigh Country Club—*other* PA-2
**Lehigh County**—*pop pl* PA-2
Lehigh County Community Coll—*school* PA-2
*Lehigh County Home* PA-2
Lehigh County Prison—*hist pl* PA-2
Lehigh Creek—*stream* MI-6
Lehigh Elem Sch—*school* FL-3
*Lehigh Falls* PA-2
**Lehigh Furnace**—*pop pl* PA-2
Lehigh Furnace Gap—*gap* PA-2
Lehigh Gap—*gap* PA-2
**Lehigh Gap**—*pop pl* (2) PA-2
Lehigh Gap Sch (abandoned)—*school* (2) PA-2
Lehigh Gap Station—*locale* PA-2
Lehigh Gorge—*valley* PA-2
Lehigh Gorge State Park—*park* PA-2
Lehigh Gulch—*valley* CO-8
*Lehigh Hill* PA-2
Lehigh Hill—*summit* RI-1
*Lehigh Hills* PA-2
Lehigh Lake—*lake* FL-3
Lehigh Memorial Park—*cemetery* FL-3
Lehigh Memorial Park—*park* IL-6
*Lehigh Mtn* PA-2
Lehigh Mtn—*summit* PA-2
*Lehigh Park Eleme ntary School* PA-2
Lehigh Park Spring—*spring* PA-2
**Le High Park (subdivision)**—*pop pl* PA-2
Lehigh Parkway Elem Sch—*school* PA-2
*Lehigh Parkway Sch* PA-2
Lehigh Pond—*lake* PA-2
Lehigh Raymond Run—*stream* IL-6
Lehigh River—*stream* PA-2
Lehigh RR Station—*locale* FL-3
*Lehigh Run* PA-2
Lehighs Canal—*canal* FL-3
**Lehigh Spur**—*pop pl* IN-6
Lehigh Strip Mine—*mine* OK-5
*Lehigh Tannery* PA-2
Lehigh Tannery—*other* PA-2
**Lehighton**—*pop pl* PA-2
Lehighton Airp (historical)—*airport* PA-2
Lehighton Area HS—*school* PA-2
Lehighton Area JHS—*school* PA-2
Lehighton Borough—*civil* PA-2
Lehighton Reservoirs—*reservoir* PA-2
Lehighton Rsvr—*reservoir* PA-2
**Lehigh Township**—*pop pl* KS-7
Lehigh Township Elem Sch—*school* PA-2
**Lehigh (Township of)**—*pop pl* (4) PA-2
Lehigh Univ—*school* PA-2
Lehigh Unversity Athletic Field—*park* PA-2
**Lehigh Valley**—*pop pl* PA-2
Lehigh Valley Facility—*post sta* PA-2
Lehigh Valley Industrial Park—*locale* PA-2
*Lehigh Valley Interchange* PA-2
Lehigh Valley Junction—*locale* NY-2
Lehigh Valley Mall—*locale* PA-2
Lehigh Valley Post Office—*building* PA-2
Lehigh Valley RR HQ Bldg—*hist pl* PA-2
Lehigh Valley RR Station—*hist pl* (2) NY-2
Lehigh Valley Tunnel—*tunnel* PA-2
*Lehighville* PA-2
*Lehigh Water Gap* PA-2
Lehi HS—*school* UT-8
Lehi JHS—*school* UT-8
*Lehi Junction* UT-8
**LeHillier**—*pop pl* MN-6
Lehi Post Office—*building* UT-8
Lehi Sch—*school* AR-4
Lehi Sch—*school* UT-8
Lehi South Branch, Canal (historical)—*canal* AZ-5
Lehi Substation—*locale* AZ-5
Lehi Tintic—*mine* UT-8
**Lehle Mwahu**—*pop pl* FM-9
Lehmam Creek—*stream* OR-9
*Lehman* KS-7
*Lehman* MS-4
*Lehman* OR-9
Lehman—*locale* TX-5
**Lehman**—*pop pl* (2) PA-2
**Lehman**—*pop pl* TX-5
Lehman, Lake—*lake* FL-3
*Lehman Academy* TN-4
Lehman Airp—*airport* PA-2
Lehman Basin—*basin* ID-8
Lehman Butte—*summit* ID-8
Lehman Caves Natl Monument—*park* NV-8
Lehman Cem—*cemetery* OH-6
Lehman Cem—*cemetery* WI-6
Lehman Creek—*stream* ID-8
Lehman Creek—*stream* NV-8
Lehman Creek—*stream* OR-9
Lehman Creek Forest Service Recreation Site—*locale* NV-8
Lehman Dam—*dam* AL-4
Lehman Ditch—*canal* CO-8
Lehman Ditch—*canal* (2) IN-6
Lehman Drain—*canal* MI-6
Lehman Gasoline Plant—*oilfield* TX-5
Lehman Gulch—*valley* CO-8
Lehman Hollow—*valley* PA-2
*Lehman Hot Springs* OR-9
**Lehman Hot Springs**—*pop pl* OR-9
Lehman HS—*school* OH-6
Lehman Island—*island* ME-1
*Lehman Lake* TX-5
Lehman Lake—*lake* LA-4
Lehman Lake—*lake* MI-6
Lehman Lake—*lake* MN-6
Lehman Lake—*lake* NE-7
Lehman Lake—*lake* WI-6
Lehman Lake—*reservoir* AL-4
Lehman Lake—*reservoir* PA-2

Lehman Lake Dam—*dam* PA-2
Lehman Meadow—*flat* OR-9
Lehman Memorial Ch—*church* PA-2
Lehman Mill—*locale* AZ-5
Lehman Mtn—*summit* AZ-5
Lehmann Cem—*cemetery* MS-4
Lehmann Cem—*cemetery* TX-5
Lehmann Creek—*stream* MS-4
Lehmann Mtn—*summit* TX-5
Lehman Orchard and Aqueduct—*hist pl* NV-8
Lehman Park—*park* IN-6
Lehman Point—*summit* AL-4
Lehman Run—*stream* (3) PA-2
Lehman's, Port Royal Covered Bridge—*hist pl* PA-2
Lehmans Bluff—*cliff* AL-4
Lehman Sch—*school* KS-7
Lehmans Mill—*locale* MD-2
**Lehman Springs**—*pop pl* OR-9
**Lehman Subdivision**—*pop pl* UT-8
*Lehmansville* WV-2
**Lehman (Township of)**—*pop pl* (2) PA-2
Lehman Trail—*trail* PA-2
Lehman Trailer Forest Service Recreation Site—*locale* NV-8
Lehman-Tunnell Mansion—*hist pl* WY-8
Lehman Windmill—*locale* (2) TX-5
*Lehmasters* PA-2
Lehmasters (RR name for Lemasters)—*other* PA-2
Lehmasters Station—*locale* PA-2
Lehmback, Charles, Farmstead—*hist pl* IN-6
Lehmberg, Dr. H. B., House—*hist pl* AZ-5
Lehmer Ditch—*canal* WY-8
**Lehmkuhl Landing**—*pop pl* OH-6
Lehmquen—*building* MS-4
Lehn-Apco North Oil Field—*oilfield* TX-5
Lehn-Apco Oil Field—*oilfield* TX-5
Lehn Diadi—*stream* FM-9
Lehn Diepei—*stream* FM-9
Lehne Ranch—*locale* TX-5
Lehner Coulee—*valley* MT-8
*Lehner Lake* PA-2
Lehner Lakes—*reservoir* PA-2
Lehner Lateral—*canal* CA-9
Lehner Mammoth-Kill Site—*hist pl* AZ-5
Lehner Spring—*spring* WY-8
Lehn Keseurek—*locale* FM-9
Lehn Mesi—*stream* FM-9
*Lehn Mwatatar* FM-9
*Lehn Mwesei* FM-9
Le Homme Dieu, Lake—*lake* MN-6
Lehoula Beach—*beach* HI-9
Lehoullier Bldg—*hist pl* NH-1
*Lehperei* FM-9
Lehpwel—*swamp* FM-9
Lehpwelen Kulu—*swamp* FM-9
Lehpwelen Takai—*swamp* FM-9
Lehpwelen Tomwara—*swamp* FM-9
**Lehpweltik**—*pop pl* FM-9
Lehr—*locale* MS-4
**Lehr**—*pop pl* ND-7
**Lehr**—*pop pl* TX-5
Lehr-Beglad-Henne Fish Dam—*dam* ND-7
*Lehr Ditch* IN-6
Lehr Lake—*lake* MI-6
Lehrman Day Sch of Temple Emanu-el—*school* FL-3
Lehrman Slough—*lake* SD-7
Lehrman Slough State Public Shooting Area—*park* SD-7
Lehrton Cem—*cemetery* MS-4
*Lehrton Church* MS-4
**Lehrton (historical)**—*pop pl* MS-4
LeHS—*school* CA-9
LeHS—*school* IL-6
LeHS (abandoned)—*school* PA-2
Lehsou Ditch—*canal* MT-8
Lehtinen Creek—*stream* MN-6
Lehtoantoal—*stream* FM-9
Lehto Lake—*lake* WI-6
Leh-tso-bii-to Wash—*stream* NM-5
*Lehu* HI-9
Lehua—*island* HI-9
*Lehuahaki Mountain* HI-9
*Lehua Island* HI-9
Lehua Landing—*locale* HI-9
*Lehuawehe Bay* HI-9
Lehuawehi Point—*cape* HI-9
*Lehunt* KS-7
Le Hunt—*locale* KS-7
**Lehunt**—*pop pl* KS-7
Lehunua Island—*island* AK-9
Lehuula—*summit* HI-9
Lehuula Mauka Tract—*civil* HI-9
Lehuula One-Two—*civil* HI-9
Lehy Chapel—*church* LA-4
*Lei* FM-9
Leib Carriage House—*hist pl* CA-9
Leib Cem—*cemetery* KS-7
Leiberg Coulee—*valley* MT-8
Leiberg Creek—*stream* ID-8
Leiberg Peak—*summit* ID-8
*Leiberg Point* ID-8
Leiberg Saddle—*gap* ID-8
Leibert Creek—*stream* PA-2
*Leiberts Creek* PA-2
Leiberts Gap—*gap* PA-2
Leiberts Sch—*school* PA-2
Leibeyville—*locale* PA-2
**Leibhardt**—*pop pl* NY-2
Leibhart, Oscar, Site (36YO9)—*hist pl* PA-2
Leibhart Dam—*dam* NC-3
Leibhart Lake—*reservoir* NC-3
Leibharts Corner—*locale* PA-2
Leibig—*locale* MO-7
Leiblig Cem—*cemetery* OH-6
Leib Run Trail—*trail* PA-2
Leibs Creek—*stream* PA-2
*Leibysville* PA-2
**Leicester**—*pop pl* MA-1
**Leicester**—*pop pl* NY-2
**Leicester**—*pop pl* NC-3
**Leicester**—*pop pl* VT-1
**Leicester (census name Leicester Center)**—*pop pl* MA-1
*Leicester Center* MA-1
Leicester Center (census name Leicester)—*other* MA-1
*Leicester Corners* VT-1
Leicester Corners—*other* VT-1
*Leicester Four Corners* VT-1
Leicester Hill—*summit* MA-1
Leicester Hollow Brook—*stream* VT-1
Leicester HS—*school* MA-1
**Leicester Junction**—*pop pl* VT-1
Leicester Junior Coll—*school* MA-1
Leicester Meeting House—*hist pl* VT-1
Leicester River—*stream* VT-1
Leicester (RR name for Leicester Junction)—*other* VT-1
Leicester Sch—*school* NC-3
**Leicester (Town of)**—*pop pl* MA-1
**Leicester (Town of)**—*pop pl* NY-2
**Leicester (Town of)**—*pop pl* VT-1
**Leicester Township**—*pop pl* NE-7
Leicester (Township of)—*fmr MCD* NC-3
Leich, Charles, and Company—*hist pl* IN-6
Leich Ford—*locale* MO-7
Leichner Spring—*spring* IN-6
*Leichti Pond Number 4* OR-9
Leichty Ditch—*canal* IN-6
Leickhart Post Office (historical)—*building* TN-4
Leick House—*hist pl* KY-4
Leidendecker Ditch—*canal* IN-6
Leidermann Ridge—*ridge* GA-3
Leidermann Ridge—*ridge* TN-4
Leidigh Mill Creek—*stream* OH-6
Leidighs—*locale* PA-2
Leidig Meadow—*flat* CA-9
Leiding Cem—*cemetery* MN-6
**Leiding (Township of)**—*pop pl* MN-6
Leidy—*locale* PA-2
Leidy, Dr. Joseph, House—*hist pl* PA-2
Leidy, Mount—*summit* WY-8
Leidy Creek—*stream* CA-9
Leidy Creek—*stream* NV-8
Leidy Creek—*stream* WY-8
Leidy Elem Sch—*school* PA-2
Leidy Lake—*lake* MI-6
Leidy Lake—*lake* WY-8
Leidy Lake Game Area—*park* MI-6
Leidy Peak—*summit* UT-8
*Leidys Creek* PA-2
*Leidystown* PA-2
Leidytown—*locale* PA-2
**Leidy (Township of)**—*pop pl* PA-2
Leif Erickson Park—*park* IA-7
Leif Ericson Park—*park* IA-7
Leif Ericson Sch—*school* IL-6
Leiferman Memorial Sch—*school* MN-6
Leifeste Cem—*cemetery* TX-5
Leiffer House—*hist pl* CO-8
*Leige Creek* WY-8
**Leigh**—*pop pl* NE-7
**Leigh**—*pop pl* TX-5
Leigh, Benjamin Watkins, House—*hist pl* VA-3
Leigh, Ichabod, House—*hist pl* NJ-2
Leigh, Lake—*lake* AK-9
Leigh, Lake—*swamp* PA-2
Leigh Arroyo—*valley* TX-5
Leigh Canyon—*valley* (2) WY-8
Leigh Cem—*cemetery* AL-4
Leigh Cem—*cemetery* NE-7
*Leigh Chapel* TN-4
Leigh Chapel Post Office (historical)—*building* TN-4
Leigh Creek—*stream* MT-8
Leigh Creek—*stream* VA-3
Leigh Creek—*stream* WY-8
Leigh Creek Campground—*locale* WY-8
Leigh Creek Vee—*flat* WY-8
Leighcrest—*building* MS-4
Leighdon Bluff Ferry (historical)—*locale* MS-4
Leigh Farm—*hist pl* NC-3
Leigh Farm—*locale* UT-8
Leigh Flowage—*lake* WI-6
Leighfs Pond—*lake* NY-2
Leigh HS—*school* CA-9
Leigh Lake—*lake* MT-8
Leigh Lake—*lake* WY-8
Leigh (Magisterial District)—*fmr MCD* (2) VA-3
Leigh Mall Shop Ctr—*locale* MS-4
**Leigh Mill**—*pop pl* VA-3
Leigh Monmt—*pillar* WY-8
Leigh Mtn—*summit* VA-3
*Leigh Nixon Crossroads* NC-3
*Leigh Nixons Crossroads* NC-3
Leigh Pond—*reservoir* VA-3
Leigh Ranch—*locale* CA-9
Leighs—*locale* VA-3
**Leighs**—*pop pl* TN-4
Leighs Camp—*locale* AL-4
Leigh Sch—*school* (2) IL-6
Leighs Chapel—*church* TN-4
**Leighs Chapel**—*pop pl* TN-4
Leighs Corner—*other* VA-3
*Leighs Landing* MS-4
*Leighs Landing P.O.* MS-4
Leighs Landing Sch (historical)—*school* MS-4
Leighs Mill Pond—*lake* ME-1
Leighs Temple—*church* NC-3
Leigh Street Baptist Church—*hist pl* VA-3
*Leighton* MS-4
Leighton—*locale* KY-4
Leighton—*locale* MN-6
**Leighton**—*pop pl* AL-4
**Leighton**—*pop pl* IA-7
**Leighton**—*pop pl* LA-4
**Leighton**—*pop pl* TN-4
Leighton, Adam P., House—*hist pl* ME-1
Leighton Brook—*stream* ME-1
Leighton Brook—*stream* MN-6
Leighton Brook—*stream* (2) NH-1
Leighton (CCD)—*cens area* AL-4
Leighton Cem—*cemetery* ME-1
Leighton Ch—*church* MI-6
Leighton Corners—*locale* NH-1
**Leighton Corners**—*pop pl* NH-1
*Leighton Cove* ME-1
Leighton Cove—*bay* ME-1
Leighton Division—*civil* AL-4
Leighton Elem Sch—*school* AL-4
Leighton Gap—*gap* AL-4
Leighton Hill—*summit* ME-1
Leighton Hill—*summit* VT-1
Leighton (historical)—*locale* MS-4
Leighton Lake—*lake* CA-9
Leighton Lake—*lake* MN-6
Leighton Ledges—*bar* ME-1
Leighton Ledges—*summit* ME-1
Leighton MS—*school* AL-4
Leighton Neck—*cape* ME-1
Leighton Park—*park* FL-3
Leighton Point—*cape* (2) ME-1
Leighton Rock—*island* ME-1
**Leightons Corner**—*pop pl* MA-1
**Leighton (Township of)**—*pop pl* MI-6
**Leigh (Township of)**—*pop pl* MN-6
Leighty Camp—*locale* WA-9
Leighty Hollow—*valley* PA-2
Leighty Lake—*reservoir* OH-6
Leigh Well—*well* UT-8
Leila, Mary, Cotton Mill and Village—*hist pl* GA-3
Leila Arboretum—*park* MI-6
Leila Ch—*church* GA-3
Leila Hosp—*hospital* MI-6
Leila Leeds Memorial Chapel—*church* NY-2
Leila Mtn—*summit* AS-9
Leila Store—*locale* MO-7
Leilehua Golf Course—*other* HI-9
Leilehua HS—*school* HI-9
Leileia Mtn—*summit* AS-9
*Leilono* HI-9
*Leilono Crater* HI-9
Leiman Cem—*cemetery* MO-7
Leiman House—*hist pl* FL-3
Leimback Ditch—*canal* MT-8
Leimert Park—*park* CA-9
Leinakekua Point—*cape* HI-9
*Leinaopapio* HI-9
Leinaopapio Point—*cape* HI-9
*Leina Park* MA-1
**Leinart**—*pop pl* TN-4
**Leinarts**—*pop pl* TN-4
Leinarts Post Office (historical)—*building* TN-4
Leinbachs—*locale* PA-2
Leinedecker Ranch—*locale* AZ-5
Leineke Branch—*stream* IL-6
Leinenweber Lake—*lake* OR-9
*Leinenwerder Lake* OR-9
Leinhardt, Albert and Kate, House—*hist pl* TX-5
**Leininger Acres**—*pop pl* IN-6
Leininger Camp—*locale* CA-9
Leininger Cem—*cemetery* IA-7
Leininger Lake—*lake* IN-6
Leiningers Ch—*church* PA-2
Leiningers Run—*stream* PA-2
Leinkauf Hist Dist—*hist pl* AL-4
Leinkauf Sch—*school* AL-4
*Leinohaunui Pali* HI-9
Leinohaunui Point—*cape* HI-9
Leinokano Point—*cape* HI-9
**Leino Park**—*pop pl* MA-1
Leins Ditch—*canal* IN-6
Leinster Bay—*bay* VI-3
Leinster Bay—*locale* VI-3
Leinster Hill—*summit* VI-3
Leinster Point—*cape* VI-3
**Lein Township**—*pop pl* ND-7
Leinukalahua—*summit* HI-9
Leinweber Sch—*school* IL-6
Leip—*island* MP-9
Leiper, Thomas, Estate—*hist pl* PA-2
Leiper Ch—*church* PA-2
Leiper-Scott House—*hist pl* AR-4
*Leipers Creek* NC-3
Leipers Creek—*stream* TN-4
**Leipers Fork**—*pop pl* TN-4
Leipers Fork—*stream* TN-4
Leipers Fork Ch—*church* TN-4
**Leipers Fork (Hillsboro)**—*pop pl* TN-4
Leipers Fork Post Office (historical)—*building* TN-4
*Leiperts Gap* PA-2
Leiperville—*locale* PA-2
Leiperville Sch (abandoned)—*school* PA-2
Leiphart Mill—*locale* PA-2
Leiphart Sch—*school* MI-6
**Leipsic**—*pop pl* DE-2
**Leipsic**—*pop pl* IN-6
**Leipsic**—*pop pl* OH-6
Leipsic Bridge—*bridge* DE-2
Leipsic City Hall—*hist pl* OH-6
*Leipsic Creek* DE-2
*Leipsic Junction* OH-6
Leipsic Junction—*locale* OH-6
Leipsic River—*stream* DE-2
Leipsic River Range Lights—*other* DE-2
*Leipsic Station* DE-2
Leipsig—*locale* WI-6
Leipsig Sch—*school* WI-6
**Leipzig Township**—*pop pl* ND-7
*Leirelom* FM-9
Leir (historical)—*locale* SD-7
Lei Rsvr—*reservoir* MT-8
**Leisenring**—*pop pl* PA-2
Leisenring No. 3—*other* PA-2
Leiser Ray Mine—*mine* CA-9
Leiser Run—*stream* PA-2
Leiseth Farms Landing Strip—*airport* ND-7
Leisher Mill—*locale* NY-2
Leishman Point—*cape* NY-2
Leiskau Cem—*cemetery* WI-6
Leisner Cabin—*locale* WY-8
Leisner Creek—*stream* MI-6
Leison Pit—*cave* AL-4
Leissner Cem—*cemetery* TX-5
Leist A Site (22Sh520;22N1)—*hist pl* MS-4
Leister Valley—*valley* PA-2
Leistikow Memorial Park—*park* ND-7
Leistville—*locale* OH-6
Leisure—*locale* KY-4
**Leisure**—*pop pl* IN-6
**Leisure**—*pop pl* MI-6
Leisure Canyon—*valley* AZ-5
**Leisure City**—*pop pl* FL-3
**Leisure City**—*pop pl* IL-6
Leisure City Ch—*church* FL-3
Leisure City Elem Sch—*school* FL-3
Leisure City Park—*park* FL-3
Leisure Creek—*stream* IA-7
Leisure Ditch—*canal* IN-6
Leisure Lake—*lake* MI-6
Leisure Lake—*lake* MO-7
Leisure Lake—*lake* NE-7
Leisure Lake—*lake* PA-2
Leisure Lake—*lake* WI-6
Leisure Lake—*reservoir* AL-4
Leisure Lake—*reservoir* IA-7
Leisure Lake—*reservoir* MO-7
Leisure Lake—*reservoir* PA-2
Leisure Lake Park—*park* FL-3
Leisure Lakes—*lake* MI-6
Leisure Lakes—*reservoir* PA-2
Leisureland Airpark Airp—*airport* WA-9
**Leisure Living**—*pop pl* CO-8
Leisure Park—*park* FL-3
Leisure Plaza (Shop Ctr)—*locale* FL-3
**Leisure Point (trailer park)**—*pop pl* DE-2
Leisure Run—*stream* (2) PA-2
Leisure Spring—*spring* AZ-5
Leisure Square—*post sta* OK-5
Leisure Time Mobile Park—*locale* AZ-5
**Leisure Town**—*pop pl* CA-9
**Leisuretowne**—*pop pl* NJ-2
*Leisure Village* IL-6
**Leisure Village**—*pop pl* NJ-2
*Leisure World* CA-9
**Leisure World**—*pop pl* MD-2
**Leisure World**—*pop pl* NJ-2
Leisure World—*uninc pl* (2) CA-9
Leisure World Golf Club—*other* CA-9
**Leisure World (subivision)**—*pop pl* AZ-5
**Leisure World (Trailer Park)**—*pop pl* AZ-5
*Leisy Creek* NE-7
Leisy Sch (abandoned)—*school* OR-9
**Leitch**—*pop pl* MD-2
Leitch, William T., House—*hist pl* WI-6
Leitch Bayou—*swamp* MI-6
*Leitch Branch* MS-4
Leitch Creek—*stream* ID-8
*Leitches Wharf* MD-2
**Leitchfield**—*pop pl* KY-4
Leitchfield (CCD)—*cens area* KY-4
Leitchfield Crossing—*locale* KY-4
Leitch Hollow—*valley* KY-4
Leitch Lateral—*canal* CA-9
Leitch Mill Branch—*stream* MS-4
Leitch Rsvr—*reservoir* WY-8
*Leitchs* MD-2
Leitch Sch—*school* CA-9
Leitch Sch—*school* IL-6
*Leitchs Wharf* MD-2
Leitch Wharf—*locale* MD-2
Leitel Creek—*stream* OR-9
Leitendorf Hills—*other* NM-5
Leitensdorfer Arroyo—*stream* CO-8
Leiter—*locale* WY-8
Leiter Ditch—*canal* WY-8
Leiter II Bldg—*hist pl* IL-6
**Leitersburg**—*pop pl* MD-2
**Leiters Ford**—*pop pl* IN-6
*Leiters (Leiters Ford)* IN-6
Leiterville—*locale* MT-8
Leith—*locale* OH-6
**Leith**—*pop pl* ND-7
**Leith**—*pop pl* PA-2
Leitha Creek—*stream* WA-9
Leith Cem—*cemetery* IL-6
Leith Cem—*cemetery* IA-7
Leith Creek—*stream* NC-3
Leith Creek—*stream* SC-3
Leitheiser Lake—*lake* MN-6
Leith-Hatfield—*CDP* PA-2
Leith Lake—*lake* MI-6
Leith Lake—*lake* WI-6
Leith Mtn—*summit* WV-2
Leith Pond—*lake* ME-1
Leith Post Office (historical)—*building* AL-4
Leith Run—*stream* OH-6
Leith (siding)—*locale* NV-8
Leith Slope Mine (underground)—*mine* AL-4
Leith Spring—*spring* MO-7
**Leithsville**—*pop pl* PA-2
*Leithsville P. O.* PA-2
**Leithton**—*pop pl* IL-6
**Leithton**—*pop pl* VA-3
Leithtown—*locale* VA-3
Leith Walk Sch—*school* MD-2
**Leitner**—*pop pl* AR-4
Leitner Cem—*cemetery* GA-3
Leitner Creek—*stream* FL-3
Leitner Hollow—*valley* WI-6
Leitner Pond—*reservoir* GA-3
Leitners Branch—*stream* GA-3
Leitt Cem—*cemetery* NY-2
*Leitz Spring* GA-3
Leivas Ranch—*locale* AZ-5
**Leivasy**—*pop pl* WV-2
**Leivasy Junction**—*pop pl* WV-2
Leizes Bridge (historical)—*bridge* PA-2
Lejemwa—*island* MP-9
*Lejeune* FM-9
**Lejeune**—*pop pl* LA-4
Lejeune, Point—*cape* FM-9
*LeJeune Golf Course* FL-3
LeJeune House—*hist pl* LA-4
Lejeune HS—*school* NC-3
**Le Jeune Spur**—*pop pl* LA-4
Lejkibwa—*island* MP-9
*L. E. Junction* KY-4
L & E Junction—*locale* KY-4
**Lejunior (Shields)**—*pop pl* KY-4
Lekau, Lake—*reservoir* NJ-2
Leke Run—*stream* WV-2
Lekwa Marsh—*swamp* IA-7
Lekwa Marsh Public Hunting Area—*park* IA-7
Lela—*locale* GA-3
Lela—*locale* LA-4
Lela—*locale* OK-5
**Lela**—*pop pl* TX-5
*Le Lac Due Saint Sacrement* NY-2
Lela Cem—*cemetery* OK-5
Lela Courthouse—*building* GA-3
Lelaen—*locale* MP-9
Lelafield Sch—*school* KY-4
Le La Mine—*mine* AZ-5
*Leland* AL-4
*Leland* KS-7
Leland—*locale* AR-4
Leland—*locale* FL-3
Leland—*locale* GA-3
Leland—*locale* LA-4
Leland—*locale* UT-8
Leland—*locale* WA-9
**Leland**—*pop pl* ID-8
**Leland**—*pop pl* IL-6
**Leland**—*pop pl* IA-7
**Leland**—*pop pl* MI-6
**Leland**—*pop pl* MS-4
**Leland**—*pop pl* NC-3
**Leland**—*pop pl* OR-9
**Leland**—*pop pl* WI-6
Leland, Deacon William, House—*hist pl* MA-1
Leland, Lake—*lake* WA-9
Leland, Mount—*summit* AK-9
Leland, Muret N., House—*hist pl* MN-6
Leland Bar—*bar* AR-4
Leland Bench—*bench* UT-8
Leland Bowman Lock—*dam* LA-4
Leland Brook—*stream* RI-1
Leland Butte—*summit* AZ-5
Leland Castle—*hist pl* NY-2
Leland Cem—*cemetery* ID-8
Leland Cem—*cemetery* KS-7
Leland Cem—*cemetery* ME-1
Leland Cem—*cemetery* MI-6
Leland Cem—*cemetery* NE-7
*Leland Cemetery* TN-4
Leland Ch—*church* KS-7
Leland Chute—*lake* AR-4
Leland Coll—*school* LA-4
Leland College—*hist pl* LA-4
Leland Creek—*stream* CA-9
Leland Creek—*stream* CO-8
Leland Creek—*stream* (2) WA-9
Leland Cutoff—*bend* AR-4
Leland Dam—*dam* ND-7
Leland Edwards Dam—*dam* (2) SD-7
Leland Elem Sch—*school* MS-4
**Leland Grove**—*pop pl* IL-6
Leland Grove Ch—*church* SC-3
Leland Gulch—*valley* CA-9
Leland Hill—*summit* MA-1
Leland Hill—*summit* NY-2
Leland Hill—*summit* VT-1
Leland Hist Dist—*hist pl* MI-6
Leland Hotel—*hist pl* IN-6
Leland HS—*school* CA-9
Leland HS—*school* MS-4
Leland Islands—*island* AK-9
Leland JHS—*school* MD-2
Leland Lagoon Dam—*dam* MS-4
Leland Lake—*lake* TX-5
Leland Lake—*lake* WA-9
Leland Lakes—*lake* CA-9
Leland McInnis Castfish Pond Dam—*dam* MS-4
Leland Memorial Hosp—*hospital* MD-2
Leland Millpond—*reservoir* MA-1
Leland Millpond—*reservoir* WI-6
Leland Mill Race—*canal* UT-8
Leland Mine (underground)—*mine* AL-4
Leland MS—*school* MS-4
Leland Neck—*cape* AR-4
Leland Park—*park* CA-9
Leland Park Station—*locale* IL-6
Leland Point—*cape* ME-1
Leland Pond—*lake* NY-2
Leland Post Office (historical)—*building* AL-4
Leland Presbyterian Ch—*church* MS-4
Leland Ranch—*locale* ND-7
Leland River—*stream* MI-6
Leland Rsvr—*reservoir* (2) CA-9
Leland Sch—*school* ND-7
Leland Sch—*school* WI-6
**Lelands Corner**—*pop pl* MD-2
Leland Shop Ctr—*locale* AL-4
*Lelands Pond* MA-1
Leland Street Sch—*school* CA-9
*Lelandsville* MA-1
**Leland (Township of)**—*pop pl* MI-6
Leland United Methodist Ch—*church* MS-4
**Lelan (Genntown)**—*pop pl* OH-6
Lelavale—*locale* TX-5
Lele—*locale* FM-9
Leleahina Heiau—*hist pl* HI-9
*Leled Lane* AL-4
Lele Harbor—*harbor* FM-9
Lele Island—*island* FM-9
*Leleiwi* HI-9
Leleiwi—*summit* (2) HI-9
Leleiwi Pali—*cliff* HI-9
Leleiwi Park—*park* HI-9
Leleiwi Point—*cape* HI-9
Lelekaae Falls—*falls* HI-9
Lelekea Bay—*bay* HI-9
*Lelekeanu Stream* HI-9
Lelekea Stream—*stream* HI-9
Lelekoae—*cape* HI-9
Lelemako Gulch—*valley* HI-9
Lele o Kalihipaa, Pali—*cliff* HI-9
Lele Point—*cape* FM-9
Lelet, Bayou—*gut* LA-4
Leleux—*locale* LA-4
**Leleux**—*pop pl* LA-4
L-Eleven Spring—*spring* AZ-5
Lelia, Lake—*lake* FL-3
Leliaetta—*locale* OK-5
Lelia Lake—*lake* TX-5
**Lelia Lake**—*pop pl* TX-5
Lelia Lake Creek—*stream* TX-5
Lelia Myers Dam—*dam* AL-4
Lelia Myers Lake—*reservoir* AL-4
**Leliaton**—*pop pl* GA-3
Lelieux Oil and Gas Field—*oilfield* LA-4
Lelig Coulee—*valley* MT-8
**Lella (historical)**—*pop pl* TN-4
Lella Post Office (historical)—*building* TN-4
Lelliot Spring—*spring* OR-9
*Lellman* FL-3
Lellman—*other* FL-3
**Leloaloa**—*pop pl* AS-9
*Leloup* KS-7
**Le Loup**—*pop pl* KS-7
**Leloup**—*pop pl* KS-7
*Lelow Basin* MT-8
Lelow Basin Spring Number Two—*spring* MT-8
Lelsey Drain—*stream* MI-6
Lelu, Molsron—*harbor* FM-9
Leluh Ruins—*hist pl* FM-9
Lelu Island—*island* FM-9
Lelu (Municipality)—*civ div* FM-9
Lely—*CDP* FL-3
**Lely Golf Estates**—*pop pl* FL-3
Lely HS—*school* FL-3
**Lelyland**—*pop pl* FL-3
Lely Presbyterian Ch—*church* FL-3
**Lely Tropical Estates**—*pop pl* FL-3
*Lema* NY-2
Lemafa Ridge—*ridge* AS-9
Lemafa Saddle—*gap* AS-9
*Lemah Creek* ID-8
Lemah Creek—*stream* ID-8
Lemah Creek—*stream* WA-9
Lemah Mountian—*summit* WA-9
Le Maire Cem—*cemetery* LA-4
Lemalsamac Ch—*church* TN-4
Lemanasky Lake—*lake* WA-9
Lemanasky Mtn—*summit* WA-9
Leman Birk Newcomer Ditch—*canal* IN-6
*Leman Creek* NC-3
*Leman Ditch* IN-6
Leman Ferry (historical)—*locale* AL-4
Lemon Gap—*gap* NC-3
Leman Hollow—*valley* PA-2
Leman Lake—*lake* MN-6
Leman Lake—*reservoir* TX-5
Lemann Store—*hist pl* LA-4
**Lemannville**—*pop pl* LA-4
*Leman Siding* UT-8
*Lemansky Lake* WA-9
**Lemans Subdivision**—*pop pl* UT-8
*Leman Station* MO-7
LeMar, Lake—*reservoir* NC-3
**Le Mar Addition (subdivision)**—*pop pl* UT-8
*Le Marais du Cygne River* KS-7
*Le Marne* OK-5
*Le Marne* TX-5
Lemarr Cem—*cemetery* (2) TN-4
**Le Mars**—*pop pl* IA-7
Le Mars Municipal Park—*park* IA-7
Le Mars Public Library—*hist pl* IA-7
*Lemaster* PA-2
Lemaster Field—*airport* KS-7
**Lemasters**—*pop pl* PA-2
**Lemasters (RR name Lehmasters)**—*pop pl* PA-2
Lemasul—*island* FM-9
*Le May* MO-7
**Lemay**—*pop pl* MO-7
**Lemay**—*pop pl* UT-8
Lemay Island—*summit* UT-8
*Lemay Lake* MN-6
Lemay Lake—*lake* MN-6
Lemay (Luxemburg)—*CDP* MO-7
**Le Mayne**—*pop pl* AL-4
Lemay Siding—*locale* UT-8
**Lemay (sta.)**—*pop pl* MO-7
Lemay Street Sch—*school* CA-9
Lemay Township—*civil* MO-7
Lemay Wash—*stream* CO-8
Lembcke Ranch—*locale* WY-8
Lembeck and Betz Eagle Brewing Company District—*hist pl* NJ-2
Lembeck Lake—*reservoir* MO-7
Lemberg Lateral—*canal* ID-8
Lembert Dome—*summit* CA-9
Lembke House—*hist pl* NM-5
Lembke Lake—*lake* MN-6
Lembke Landing—*locale* NE-7
Lembo—*airport* NJ-2
Lemcke Spring—*spring* OR-9
Lemeh-va—*spring* AZ-5
Lemei Lake—*lake* WA-9
Lemei Rock—*summit* WA-9
*Lemeis* FM-9
*Lemen* MO-7
Lemen Branch—*stream* IL-6
Lemen Cem—*cemetery* KY-4
Lemen Lake—*lake* OH-6
Lemen Landing—*locale* KY-4
**Lementon**—*pop pl* IL-6
*Lemenville* MO-7
Lemer, Lake—*lake* ND-7
Lemer-Berger Ditch—*canal* IN-6
Lemert—*locale* ND-7
**Lemert**—*pop pl* OH-6
Lemert Airp—*airport* IN-6
Lemert Bridge—*bridge* TN-4
Lemert Creek—*stream* GA-3
Lemert Ditch—*canal* IN-6
Lemes Canyon—*valley* NM-5
Lemesurier Island—*island* AK-9
Lemesurier Light—*locale* AK-9
Lemesurier Point—*cape* (2) AK-9
**Lemeta**—*pop pl* AK-9
Lemeuse Creek—*stream* LA-4
Lem Fork—*stream* WV-2
**Lemhi**—*pop pl* ID-8
Lemhi Bar—*bar* ID-8
Lemhi County Courthouse—*hist pl* ID-8
Lemhi Creek—*stream* ID-8
Lemhi Lake—*lake* ID-8
Lemhi Pass—*gap* (2) ID-8
Lemhi Pass—*gap* MT-8
Lemhi Pass—*hist pl* ID-8
Lemhi Point—*summit* ID-8
*Lemhi Range* ID-8
*Lemhi Range* MT-8
Lemhi Range—*locale* ID-8
Lemhi Range—*range* ID-8
Lemhi Ridge—*ridge* ID-8
Lemhi River—*stream* ID-8
Lemhi Union Gulch—*valley* ID-8
Lemhi Valley—*valley* ID-8
**Leming**—*pop pl* TX-5
Leming Cem—*cemetery* TN-4
**Leming Subdivision**—*pop pl* TN-4
Lemington—*locale* WI-6
**Lemington**—*pop pl* VT-1
Lemington Elem Sch—*hist pl* PA-2
Lemington Elem Sch—*school* PA-2
*Lemington Sch* PA-2
**Lemington (Town of)**—*pop pl* VT-1
Lemira Sch—*school* SC-3
Lemish Butte—*summit* OR-9
Lemish Lake—*lake* OR-9
*le Missoui* KS-7
*Le Missouri* KS-7
**Lemitar**—*pop pl* NM-5
Lemitar Ditch—*canal* NM-5
Lemitar Ditch Lateral—*canal* NM-5
Lemitar Riverside Drain—*canal* NM-5
Lemitar Waste Lateral—*canal* NM-5
Lemiti Butte—*summit* OR-9
Lemiti Campground—*park* OR-9

Lent Lateral—*canal* AZ-5
**Lentner**—*pop pl* MO-7
Lentner Township—*civil* MO-7
Lento—*locale* CA-9
Lento—*locale* KS-7
Lenton Flat—*flat* WA-9
**Lenton Township**—*pop pl* ND-7
**Lents**—*pop pl* OR-9
Lents Cove—*bay* NY-2
**Lents Junction**—*pop pl* OR-9
Lents Park—*park* OR-9
Lents Sch—*school* OR-9
**Lentsville**—*pop pl* NY-2
**Lent (Township of)**—*pop pl* MN-6
Lentz, John A., House—*hist pl* NC-3
Lentz Branch—*stream* TX-5
Lentz Cem—*cemetery* IA-7
Lentz Cem—*cemetery* MS-4
Lentz Cem—*cemetery* (2) OH-6
Lentz Cem—*cemetery* TN-4
Lentz Cem—*cemetery* TX-5
Lentz Chapel—*church* TN-4
Lentz Creek—*stream* WA-9
Lentz Creek—*stream* (2) WI-6
Lentz Field—*park* CA-9
Lentz Hotel—*hist pl* NC-3
Lentz House (Hotel Sheller)—*hist pl* IN-6
Lentzier Creek—*stream* IN-6
Lentz Peak—*summit* MT-8
Lentz Point—*cape* MT-8
Lentz Sch—*school* WI-6
Lentz Sch (abandoned)—*school* PA-2
Lentz Spring—*spring* MO-7
Lentzton—*locale* NC-3
Lentzville—*locale* AL-4
Lentzville Branch—*stream* AL-4
Lentzville Cem—*cemetery* AL-4
Lentzville Ch (historical)—*church* AL-4
Lentzville Post Office (historical)—*building* AL-4
Lentzville Sch (historical)—*school* AL-4
Lentz-Williams Cem—*cemetery* TN-4
*Lenua* HI-9
*Lenua Ferry* SC-3
*Lenuds Ferry* SC-3
Lenwil—*locale* LA-4
**Lenwood**—*pop pl* CA-9
Lenwood, Lake—*lake* WI-6
Lenwood Ch—*church* GA-3
Lenwood Ch—*church* LA-4
**Lenwood Heights**—*pop pl* PA-2
Lenwood Park—*park* CA-9
Lenwood Sch—*school* CA-9
Lenwot, Infal—*stream* FM-9
Lenz—*locale* OR-9
Lenz—*locale* TX-5
**Lenz**—*pop pl* OR-9
**Lenzburg**—*pop pl* IL-6
**Lenzburg (Township of)**—*pop pl* IL-6
Lenz Cem—*cemetery* IA-7
Lenz Creek—*stream* ID-8
Lenz Creek—*stream* OR-9
Lenzen Ranch—*locale* WY-8
Lenzie Ranch—*locale* WA-9
Lenz Lake—*lake* WA-9
Lenz Lateral—*canal* OR-9
Lenz Ranch—*locale* OR-9
Lenz Sch—*school* IL-6
*Lenzton* NC-3
Leo—*locale* GA-3
Leo—*locale* MN-6
Leo—*locale* SC-3
Leo—*locale* TX-5
**Leo**—*pop pl* IN-6
**Leo**—*pop pl* MI-6
**Leo**—*pop pl* OH-6
**Leo**—*pop pl* TX-5
**Leo**—*pop pl* WY-8
Leo, Lake—*gut* SD-7
Leo, Lake—*lake* AK-9
Leo, Lake—*lake* MN-6
Leo, Lake—*lake* WA-9
Leo, Point—*cape* AK-9
Leo Anchorage—*bay* AK-9
Leo Berens Dam—*dam* SD-7
Leo Canyon—*valley* AZ-5
Leo Canyon—*valley* NM-5
Leo Canyon Tank—*reservoir* AZ-5
Leo Carrillo State Beach—*park* CA-9
Leo Creek—*stream* MI-6
Leo Creek—*stream* WI-6
Leo Harrolds Lake Dam—*dam* MS-4
Leohmans Plaza—*locale* PA-2
Leo HS—*school* IL-6
Leo Island—*island* AK-9
LeoJoerg Lake—*lake* WI-6
Leo Junior/Senior HS—*school* IN-6
**Leola**—*pop pl* AR-4
**Leola**—*pop pl* PA-2
**Leola**—*pop pl* SD-7
Leola, Lake—*reservoir* AL-4
Leola Cem—*cemetery* SD-7
Leola Community Park—*park* PA-2
Leola Country Club—*locale* SD-7
Leola Creek—*stream* WA-9
Leola Dam—*dam* SD-7
Leola Ditch—*canal* WI-6
Leola Elem Sch—*school* PA-2
Leola (historical)—*locale* AL-4
*Leo Lake* MN-6
Leo Lake—*lake* ID-8
Leo Lake—*lake* (2) MN-6
Leo Lake—*reservoir* CO-8
*Leola Lake* WI-6
Leola Peak—*summit* WA-9
Leola Post Office (historical)—*building* AL-4
**Leola (Town of)**—*pop pl* WI-6
Leola Township—*civil* SD-7
**Leola Township**—*pop pl* SD-7
Leolo Ridge—*ridge* AS-9
Leolyn—*locale* PA-2
**Leolyn**—*pop pl* PA-2
**Leoma**—*pop pl* TN-4
Leoma Baptist Ch—*church* TN-4
Leoma (CCD)—*cens area* TN-4
Leoma Cem—*cemetery* TN-4
Leoma Ch of Christ—*church* TN-4
Leoma Division—*civil* TN-4
Leoma Elem Sch—*school* TN-4
Leoma Lakes—*lake* CA-9
Leoma Methodist Ch—*church* TN-4
Leoman Spring—*spring* NV-8
Leoma Post Office—*building* TN-4
**Leominster**—*pop pl* MA-1
Leominster, City of—*civil* MA-1
*Leominster Centre* MA-1
Leominster Corner—*locale* NH-1
Leominster HS—*school* MA-1
*Leominster Reservoir* MA-1
Leominster State For—*forest* MA-1
*Leon* KS-7
Leon—*locale* AL-4
Leon—*locale* CA-9
Leon—*locale* CO-8
Leon—*locale* ID-8
Leon—*locale* KY-4
Leon—*locale* MD-2
Leon—*locale* NM-5
Leon—*locale* OH-6
Leon—*locale* VA-3
Leon—*locale* WA-9
**Leon**—*pop pl* IA-7
**Leon**—*pop pl* KS-7
**Leon**—*pop pl* NY-2
**Leon**—*pop pl* NC-3
**Leon**—*pop pl* OK-5
**Leon**—*pop pl* VA-3
**Leon**—*pop pl* WV-2
**Leon**—*pop pl* WI-6
Leon—*uninc pl* FL-3
Leon, Arroyo—*stream* CA-9
Leon, Arroyo—*valley* TX-5
Leon, Bayou—*stream* LA-4
Leon, Canada Del —*valley* CA-9
Leon, Lake—*reservoir* (3) TX-5
Leona—*locale* OR-9
Leona—*locale* PA-2
**Leona**—*pop pl* KS-7
**Leona**—*pop pl* TX-5
Leona, Arroyo—*stream* CA-9
Leona, Mount—*summit* WA-9
Leona Branch—*stream* MS-4
Leona Branch—*stream* TX-5
Leona Burk Ch—*church* WV-2
Leona B Warren Sch—*school* AL-4
Leona Cem—*cemetery* PA-2
Leona Ch—*church* FL-3
Leona Creek—*stream* TX-5
Leona Creek—*stream* UT-8
Leona Draw—*valley* TX-5
Leona Heights Park—*park* CA-9
*Leonai* ID-8
Leona Lake—*lake* AK-9
Leona Lake—*reservoir* IN-6
Leona Lake Dam—*dam* IN-6
**Leona Mines**—*pop pl* VA-3
Leona Park—*park* TX-5
*Leonard* FL-3
*Leonard* KS-7
*Leonard* TN-4
Leonard—*fmr MCD* NE-7
Leonard—*locale* AL-4
Leonard—*locale* CO-8
Leonard—*locale* IL-6
Leonard—*locale* VA-3
Leonard—*locale* WV-2
**Leonard**—*pop pl* AR-4
**Leonard**—*pop pl* MI-6
**Leonard**—*pop pl* MN-6
**Leonard**—*pop pl* MO-7
**Leonard**—*pop pl* ND-7
**Leonard**—*pop pl* OK-5
**Leonard**—*pop pl* PA-2
**Leonard**—*pop pl* (2) TN-4
**Leonard**—*pop pl* TX-5
Leonard, Capt. Charles, House—*hist pl* MA-1
Leonard, James, House—*hist pl* MA-1
Leonard, T. A., Barn—*hist pl* WA-9
Leonard Bay—*bay* VT-1
Leonard Bluff—*cliff* TN-4
*Leonard Branch* AL-4
Leonard Branch—*stream* LA-4
Leonard Branch—*stream* NC-3
Leonard Branch—*stream* (2) TN-4
Leonard Brook—*stream* NH-1
Leonard Brook—*stream* (2) NY-2
Leonard-Burt Mine—*mine* MN-6
Leonard Camp Windmill—*locale* TX-5
*Leonard Canyon* AZ-5
Leonard Canyon—*valley* AZ-5
Leonard Canyon—*valley* OR-9
Leonard Cave—*cave* TN-4
Leonard (CCD)—*cens area* TX-5
Leonard Cem—*cemetery* AL-4
Leonard Cem—*cemetery* AR-4
Leonard Cem—*cemetery* CT-1
Leonard Cem—*cemetery* (2) IL-6
Leonard Cem—*cemetery* KY-4
Leonard Cem—*cemetery* ME-1
Leonard Cem—*cemetery* MN-6
Leonard Cem—*cemetery* (2) NE-7
Leonard Cem—*cemetery* NC-3
Leonard Cem—*cemetery* ND-7
Leonard Cem—*cemetery* PA-2
Leonard Cem—*cemetery* (4) TN-4
Leonard Cem—*cemetery* VA-3
Leonard Ch—*church* AR-4
Leonard Ch—*church* (2) TN-4
Leonard Ch—*church* VA-3
Leonard Chapel—*church* AL-4
Leonard Chapel—*church* (2) LA-4
*Leonard Ch of Christ* TN-4
**Leonard Corner**—*pop pl* RI-1
Leonard Cove—*bay* MD-2
Leonard Creek—*stream* AL-4
Leonard Creek—*stream* MI-6
Leonard Creek—*stream* MT-8
Leonard Creek—*stream* NV-8
Leonard Creek—*stream* (2) NC-3
Leonard Creek—*stream* (2) OR-9
Leonard Creek—*stream* (2) PA-2
Leonard Creek Basin—*basin* NV-8
Leonard Creek Lake—*lake* NV-8
Leonard Creek Meadows—*flat* NV-8
Leonard Creek Ranch—*locale* NV-8
Leonard Creek Slough—*stream* NV-8
Leonard Creek Well—*well* NV-8
*Leonard Daniel Cemetery* AL-4
Leonard Draw—*valley* NM-5
Leonard Elem Sch—*school* PA-2
*Leonard Estates* AL-4
Leonard Fork—*stream* NC-3
Leonard Hall Sch—*school* MD-2
Leonard Harrison State Park—*park* PA-2
Leonard Heights—*post sta* MI-6
Leonard Hill—*summit* NY-2
Leonard Hollow—*valley* MO-7
Leonard Hollow—*valley* TN-4
Leonard Hollow—*valley* VA-3
*Leonard Hollow Creek* PA-2
Leonard Horn Ditch No. 1—*canal* CO-8
Leonard Hosp—*hospital* TN-4
Leonard House—*hist pl* MD-2
Leonardi—*locale* CA-9
Leonard Island—*island* AK-9
Leonardi Spring—*spring* CA-9
Leonard JHS—*school* NY-2
Leonard Kjerstad Number 2 Dam—*dam* SD-7
Leonard Kjerstad Number 3 Dam—*dam* SD-7
Leonard Lake—*lake* MI-6
Leonard Lake—*lake* WI-6
Leonard Lake—*reservoir* CA-9
Leonard Lateral—*canal* ID-8
Leonard Mine—*mine* MT-8
Leonard Mine (underground)—*mine* TN-4
Leonard Mtn—*summit* TX-5
Leonard Municipal Airp—*airport* ND-7
Leonard Nixon Springs—*lake* WI-6
Leonardo—*hist pl* MO-7
**Leonardo**—*pop pl* NJ-2
Leonard Oak Sch—*school* KY-4
Leonardo Harbor—*bay* NJ-2
**Leonardo Store**—*pop pl* VA-3
Leonard Park—*park* CA-9
Leonard Park—*park* IN-6
Leonard Park—*park* MO-7
Leonard Park—*park* NY-2
Leonard Park—*park* TX-5
Leonard Phillips Dam—*dam* NC-3
Leonard Phillips Lake—*reservoir* NC-3
Leonard Place—*locale* (2) MT-8
Leonard P. O. (historical)—*building* PA-2
Leonard Point—*cliff* AZ-5
*Leonard Pond* MA-1
Leonard Pond—*lake* CT-1
Leonard Pond—*lake* ME-1
Leonard Pond—*lake* MD-2
Leonard Pond—*lake* MA-1
Leonard Pond—*lake* NH-1
Leonard Pond—*lake* NY-2
Leonard Pond Run—*stream* MD-2
Leonard Post Office (historical)—*building* AL-4
Leonard Ranch—*locale* FL-3
Leonard Ranch—*locale* WY-8
Leonard Rock Shelter—*hist pl* NV-8
*Leonard Run* PA-2
Leonard Run—*stream* NY-2
Leonard Run—*stream* PA-2
Leonard Run—*stream* WV-2
Leonards—*locale* FL-3
Leonards—*locale* NJ-2
**Leonards**—*pop pl* (2) WI-6
Leonards Basin—*basin* CO-8
Leonards Bridge—*bridge* CT-1
**Leonardsburg**—*pop pl* OH-6
Leonards Canyon—*valley* UT-8
Leonard Sch—*hist pl* MA-1
Leonard Sch—*school* AR-4
Leonard Sch—*school* (2) MA-1
Leonard Sch—*school* (2) MI-6
Leonard Sch—*school* OH-6
Leonard Sch—*school* OK-5
Leonard Sch (abandoned)—*school* MO-7
Leonards Chapel—*church* OH-6
Leonards Chapel—*church* TN-4
*Leonards Chapel Church* AL-4
Leonard Sch (historical)—*school* (2) TN-4
*Leonard School* PA-2
*Leonards Creek* NC-3
*Leonards Creek* PA-2
Leonards Crossroads—*other* NC-3
Leonards Fork Ch—*church* NC-3
Leonards Hot Springs—*spring* CA-9
Leonard Siding—*locale* FL-3
Leonard Siding—*uninc pl* MD-2
Leonards Lake—*lake* KS-7
Leonards Lake—*lake* MO-7
Leonards Lakes—*lake* WI-6
Leonard Slough—*stream* MT-8
Leonard Slough—*stream* OR-9
Leonardson Cem—*cemetery* MI-6
Leonards Point—*cape* NC-3
**Leonards Point**—*pop pl* WI-6
*Leonards Pond* MA-1
Leonards Pond—*lake* (2) MA-1
Leonards Pond Dam—*dam* MA-1
Leonard Spring—*spring* CA-9
Leonard Spring—*spring* WA-9
Leonard Spring Hollow—*valley* WV-2
**Leonard Springs**—*pop pl* IN-6
Leonards Ridge—*ridge* CO-8
Leonards Ridge—*ridge* WA-9
*Leonards Thorofare* NJ-2
Leonard Street Sch—*school* NC-3
**Leonardsville**—*pop pl* NY-2
**Leonardsville**—*pop pl* PA-2
Leonardsville (Township of)—*civ div* MN-6
Leonardt, Emil, House—*hist pl* TX-5
Leonard Taylor Pond Dam—*dam* MS-4
Leonard Thorofare—*channel* NJ-2
**Leonardtown**—*pop pl* MD-2
**Leonardtown**—*pop pl* TN-4
**Leonard Township**—*pop pl* (2) ND-7
**Leonardville**—*pop pl* KS-7
**Leonardville**—*pop pl* NJ-2
Leonardville Cem—*cemetery* KS-7
Leonard Wenck Dam—*dam* SD-7
**Leonard (Wolfrun)**—*pop pl* VA-3
Leonard Ziesier Number 1 Dam—*dam* SD-7
Leonard Ziesler Number 2 Dam—*dam* SD-7
Leona River—*stream* TX-5
Leona River Archeol Site—*hist pl* TX-5
Leona Siphon—*canal* CA-9
Leona Spring—*spring* UT-8
Leona Tank—*reservoir* (4) TX-5
**Leona Valley**—*pop pl* CA-9
Leona Valley—*valley* CA-9
Leona Valley Ranch—*locale* CA-9
Leon Baird Peak—*summit* WY-8
Leon Bay—*bay* AK-9
*Leon Branch* NC-3
Leon Brooks Hines Lake—*reservoir* AL-4
Leon Burris Lake Dam—*dam* MS-4
Leon Canyon—*valley* AZ-5
Leon Canyon—*valley* (2) CA-9
Leon Canyon—*valley* CO-8
Leon Canyon—*valley* NV-8
Leon Cem—*cemetery* KS-7
Leoncita Creek—*stream* TX-5
Leoncita Ranch—*locale* TX-5
*Leoncitas Creek* TX-5
Leoncita Spring—*spring* TX-5
Leoncitas Windmill—*locale* TX-5
Leoncito—*locale* NM-5
Leoncito Draw—*valley* NM-5
Leoncitos Well—*well* TX-5
Leoncitos Windmill—*locale* (2) TX-5
Leon Cito Windmill—*locale* TX-5
Leon Community Center—*building* MT-8
**Leon Corners**—*pop pl* IL-6
**Leon County**—*pop pl* FL-3
**Leon (County)**—*pop pl* TX-5
Leon County Courthouse and Jails—*hist pl* TX-5
Leon Cow Camp—*locale* CO-8
*Leon Creek* TX-5
Leon Creek—*stream* CO-8
Leon Creek—*stream* NM-5
Leon Creek—*stream* (5) TX-5
Leon Creek Powerplant—*other* TX-5
Leonda Cem—*cemetery* IN-6
Leon Daiches Sch—*school* TX-5
Leon Draw—*valley* WY-8
Leone—*locale* ID-8
**Leone**—*pop pl* AS-9
Leone, Florentine, and Carpathia Apartment Buildings—*hist pl* NE-7
Leone, Lake—*lake* AK-9
Leone Bay—*bay* AS-9
*Leone Canyon* AZ-5
Leone Creek—*stream* OR-9
Leonedas Draw—*valley* TX-5
*Leoneitas Creek* TX-5
Leone Lake—*lake* OR-9
Leon Elem Sch—*school* KS-7
Leone Mine—*mine* CO-8
Leon Eubanks Pond Dam—*dam* MS-4
Leoney Cem—*cemetery* TN-4
Leon Hamilton Place—*locale* FL-3
Leonhard Sch—*school* MI-6
Leonhart Dam—*dam* NC-3
Leonhart Lake—*reservoir* NC-3
Leon Heights Sch—*school* TX-5
*Leon H. Garvin Dam* PA-2
*Leon H. Gavin Dam* NY-2
Leon Hill—*summit* TX-5
Leon Hollow—*valley* AR-4
Leon HS—*school* FL-3
Leoni—*locale* TN-4
**Leoni**—*pop pl* MI-6
*Leonia* MS-4
Leonia—*locale* ID-8
**Leonia**—*pop pl* FL-3
**Leonia**—*pop pl* NJ-2
Leonia Knob—*summit* ID-8
Leonia Post Office (historical)—*building* MS-4
Leonia Trail—*trail* ID-8
Leonidas—*locale* TX-5
**Leonidas**—*pop pl* MI-6
**Leonidas**—*pop pl* MN-6
Leonidas Mine—*mine* MN-6
Leonidas Polk Memorial Ch—*church* LA-4
Leonidas Sch—*school* MI-6
**Leonidas (Township of)**—*pop pl* MI-6
Leoni Fire Tank—*reservoir* CA-9
Leoni Meadow—*flat* CA-9
Leoni Millpond—*lake* MI-6
Leoni Post Office (historical)—*building* TN-4
Leonis Adobe—*hist pl* CA-9
*Leoni School* TN-4
*Leonis Valley* CA-9
**Leoni (Township of)**—*pop pl* MI-6
**Leon Junction**—*pop pl* TX-5
Leon Junction Sch—*school* TX-5
Leon Lake—*lake* MN-6
Leon Lake—*lake* MT-8
Leon Lake—*reservoir* CO-8
Leon Manuel Cem—*cemetery* LA-4
Leon Memorial Tabernacle—*church* WV-2
Leon Mercer Jordan—*post sta* MO-7
Leon Mine—*mine* CA-9
Leon Mine (underground)—*mine* AL-4
Leon Mtn—*summit* TX-5
Leon Oil Field—*oilfield* KS-7
**Leonor**—*pop pl* PR-3
Leonora Creek—*stream* AK-9
Leonora Mine—*mine* UT-8
Leonor Canyon—*valley* CO-8
**Leonore**—*pop pl* IL-6
Leonore, Lake—*lake* FL-3
Leonor Hamble JHS—*school* AZ-5
Leon Park Rsvr—*reservoir* CO-8
Leon Peak—*summit* CO-8
Leon Peak Rsvr—*reservoir* CO-8
Leon P. O. (historical)—*locale* AL-4
Leon Powerplant—*other* TX-5
*Leon Reservoir* TX-5
Leon River—*stream* TX-5
Leon Sch—*school* IL-6
Leon Sch—*school* WV-2
Leons Pass—*gut* LA-4
Leon Spring—*spring* AZ-5
Leon Spring—*spring* TX-5
Leon Spring Canyon—*valley* TX-5
**Leon Springs**—*pop pl* TX-5
Leon Springs Ch—*church* TX-5
*Leon Springs Reservoir* TX-5
**Leonta**—*pop pl* NY-2
**Leonton**—*pop pl* FL-3
**Leon (Town of)**—*pop pl* NY-2
**Leon (Town of)**—*pop pl* (2) WI-6
**Leon (Township of)**—*pop pl* (2) MN-6
Leon Tunnel—*tunnel* CO-8
*Leon Valley* WI-6
**Leon Valley**—*pop pl* TX-5
Leon Valley—*valley* WI-6
Leon Valley Golf Course—*other* TX-5
Leon Valley Oil And Gas Field—*oilfield* TX-5
Leon Valley Sch—*school* WI-6
*Leonville* KS-7
**Leonville**—*pop pl* LA-4
Leonville Sch—*school* LA-4
Leon Windmill—*locale* NM-5
Leoo Ridge—*ridge* AS-9
**Leopard**—*pop pl* PA-2
Leopard Bayou—*stream* LA-4
Leopard Branch—*stream* TX-5
Leopard Creek—*stream* AR-4
Leopard Creek—*stream* (2) CO-8
Leopard Creek—*stream* (3) TX-5
Leopard Creek Canyon—*valley* CO-8
**Leopard Lakes**—*pop pl* PA-2
Leopard Point—*cape* LA-4
Leopard Point—*cape* AS-9
Leopard Run—*stream* WV-2
Leopard Spring—*spring* CA-9
Leo Park—*park* GA-3
Leo Petroglyph—*hist pl* OH-6
Leo Petroglyph State Memorial—*park* OH-6
**Leopold**—*pop pl* IN-6
**Leopold**—*pop pl* MO-7
**Leopold**—*pop pl* WV-2
Leopold, Aldo, Shack—*hist pl* WI-6
Leopold Creek—*stream* ID-8
Leopold Creek—*stream* OR-9
Leopold Hotel—*hist pl* WA-9
Leopold Island—*island* IL-6
Leopold Lake—*lake* CA-9
Leopoldo Diversion Dam—*dam* NM-5
Leopold Street Shule—*hist pl* NY-2
**Leopold (Township of)**—*pop pl* IN-6
Leopold Vista (Historical Monument)—*other* NM-5
**Leopolis**—*pop pl* WI-6
**Leora**—*pop pl* MO-7
Leora Lake—*lake* MN-6
Leo Reef Light—*locale* WA-9
Leo Ritter Dam—*dam* SD-7
Leo Rogers Well—*well* ID-8
Leo Ruona Pond Number 1 Dam—*dam* SD-7
Leos Angus Ranch Airp—*airport* MO-7
Leo Sch—*school* SC-3
Leos Pond—*reservoir* IA-7
Leo Spring—*spring* NV-8
Leo Spring—*spring* UT-8
*Leot* FM-9
Leota—*locale* MI-6
Leota—*locale* UT-8
**Leota**—*pop pl* IN-6
**Leota**—*pop pl* MN-6
**Leota**—*pop pl* MS-4
**Leota**—*pop pl* MO-7
Leota, Lake—*lake* WA-9
Leota, Lake—*reservoir* WI-6
Leota Bottom—*bend* UT-8
Leota Cem—*cemetery* MN-6
Leota Landing—*locale* MS-4
Leota Park—*flat* MT-8
Leota Peak—*summit* MT-8
Leota Shoals (inundated)—*bar* AL-4
*Leota Township* KS-7
**Leota (Township of)**—*pop pl* MN-6
**Leoti**—*pop pl* KS-7
Leotie Post Office (historical)—*building* TN-4
**Leotis**—*pop pl* MS-4
Leotis Post Office (historical)—*building* MS-4
Leoti Township—*civil* KS-7
Leo Turner Pond Dam—*dam* MS-4
Leo Valley Sch—*school* NE-7
**Leoville**—*pop pl* KS-7
Leoville (historical)—*locale* KS-7
Leoville Oil Field—*oilfield* KS-7
Leo V Mine—*mine* WI-6
Leo Williams—*dam* AL-4
Leo Williams Dam—*reservoir* AL-4
**Lep**—*pop pl* OK-5
Lepage Creek—*stream* WI-6
Le Page Park—*flat* OR-9
Lepage Run—*stream* OH-6
**LePageville**—*pop pl* GA-3
Le Pageville—*uninc pl* GA-3
**Lepanto**—*pop pl* AR-4
**Lepanto Junction**—*pop pl* AR-4
*LePanto (Lepanto)* AR-4
**Lepanto (LePanto)**—*pop pl* AR-4
Lepa Stream—*stream* AS-9
*Lepau* HI-9
Le Paul Slough—*reservoir* ND-7
Lepau Point—*cape* HI-9
*Lepeamoa* HI-9
Lepeamoa Rock—*island* HI-9
*Lepeampa Rock* HI-9
Lepelepe—*summit* HI-9
Lepen, Dolen—*summit* FM-9
*Lepeomoa Rock* HI-9
Le Perron Flat—*flat* CA-9
Le Perron Peak—*summit* CA-9
LePerron Peak Spring—*spring* CA-9
*Le Petite Prairie Bend* TN-4
Le Petit Pass—*channel* LA-4
Le Petit Pass Island—*island* LA-4
Le Petit Trianon—*hist pl* CA-9
Lepeuli—*civil* HI-9
Lepine—*locale* AS-9
Lepisi—*locale* AS-9
Lepisi Cove—*bay* AS-9
Lepisi Point—*cape* AS-9
*Lep Island* MP-9
Lepiwei—*cape* FM-9
Lepley County Park—*park* IA-7
Lepley Creek—*stream* MT-8
Lepley Lake—*lake* MI-6
Lepley Run—*stream* OH-6
Lepleys Creek—*stream* MT-8
Le Poidevin Dam—*dam* MT-8
Lepoil Rock—*island* CA-9
Lepoloa—*civil* HI-9
Lepoloa-Kauniho Homesteads—*civil* HI-9
Leport-Toupin House—*hist pl* NV-8
*Leppe Island* NY-2
Leppert, C., Barn—*hist pl* OH-6
Leppert, C., Cabin—*hist pl* OH-6
Leppert, C., Farm—*hist pl* OH-6
Lepp Hollow—*valley* MO-7
Leppi Tank—*reservoir* AZ-5
Leppleman Drain—*stream* MI-6
Leppy Hills—*summit* NV-8
Leppy Pass—*gap* UT-8
Leppy Peak—*summit* NV-8
*Leppy Range* UT-8
Leppy Rsvr—*reservoir* NV-8
Leppy Rsvr—*reservoir* OR-9
Leppy Spring—*spring* CA-9
Leprechaun Lake—*lake* WA-9
**Leprocomio**—*pop pl* PR-3
Leprohi—*summit* FM-9
*Lepros* FM-9
Lepton Ch—*church* KY-4
**Leptondale**—*pop pl* NY-2
Lepua—*locale* AS-9
Lepua Point—*cape* AS-9
Lepue Crater—*crater* AS-9
Lepul, Lake—*lake* WA-9
Lepula—*locale* AS-9
Lequerica Trap—*basin* OR-9
**Lequire**—*pop pl* OK-5
**L'Erable**—*pop pl* IL-6
L'Erable Bridge—*other* IL-6
Lerado—*locale* KS-7
**Lerado**—*pop pl* OH-6
Lerado Cem—*cemetery* KS-7
L-E Ranch—*locale* NM-5
LeRay, Vincent, House—*hist pl* NY-2
LeRay Hotel—*hist pl* NY-2
LeRay Mansion—*hist pl* NY-2
**LeRaysville**—*pop pl* PA-2
**Le Raysville**—*pop pl* PA-2
Le Raysville Borough—*civil* PA-2
**Le Ray (Town of)**—*pop pl* NY-2
**Le Ray (Township of)**—*pop pl* MN-6
Lerblance Cem—*cemetery* OK-5
Lerch—*locale* AR-4
Lerch, Gustov C., House—*hist pl* IA-7
Lerch Creek—*bay* MD-2
Lerch Creek Marsh—*swamp* MD-2
Lerche Lake—*lake* WI-6
Lerchs—*locale* PA-2
*Lerchs Creek* MD-2
Lerch Tavern—*hist pl* PA-2
Lerch Trail—*trail* PA-2
**Lerdal**—*pop pl* MN-6
Lerdal Sch—*school* MN-6
Lerdo—*locale* CA-9
Lerdo Canal—*canal* CA-9
Lerdo Sch—*school* CA-9
*Le Reax Springs* AZ-5
**Lereley**—*pop pl* MD-2
*Le Rete Creek* KS-7
*Le Riviere des Missouri* KS-7
*Le Riviere des Osages* KS-7
Lerkenlund—*locale* VI-3
Lerkenlund Bay—*bay* VI-3
Lerla, Lake—*lake* FL-3
Lerman Spring—*spring* AL-4
Lermeny Ranch—*locale* SD-7
Lermond Cove—*bay* ME-1
Lermond Mill—*hist pl* ME-1
Lermond Pond—*lake* ME-1
**Lerna**—*pop pl* IL-6
Lerner Spring—*spring* AL-4
Lerner Theatre—*hist pl* IN-6
**Lernerville**—*pop pl* PA-2
Le Roi Mine—*mine* CA-9
Lerona—*locale* CA-9
**Lerona**—*pop pl* WV-2
Lerona Fire Lane—*other* CA-9
Lerose—*locale* KY-4
Lerose Cem—*cemetery* KY-4
Le Rosen Sch—*school* LA-4
Lerose Sch—*school* KY-4
*Le Rouge* AR-4
*Le Rous Spring* AZ-5
Lerous Substation (electric substation)—*locale* AZ-5
*Le Roux* AZ-5
Leroux Creek—*stream* CO-8
Leroux Creek—*stream* ID-8
*Leroux Fork* AZ-5
*Leroux Prairie* AZ-5
*Leroux Spring* AZ-5
Leroux Spring—*spring* AZ-5
*Le Roux Wash* AZ-5
Leroux Wash—*stream* AZ-5
*LeRoux Wash Valley* AZ-5
*Leroy* GA-3
*Leroy* KS-7
*Leroy* OH-6
*Leroy* MP-9
Leroy—*fmr MCD* NE-7
Leroy—*locale* AL-4
Leroy—*locale* CO-8
Leroy—*locale* FL-3
Leroy—*locale* MT-8
Leroy—*locale* PA-2
Leroy—*other* IL-6
Leroy—*other* OH-6
**Le Roy**—*pop pl* (2) IL-6
**Leroy**—*pop pl* IN-6
**LeRoy**—*pop pl* IA-7
**Le Roy**—*pop pl* IA-7
**Le Roy**—*pop pl* KS-7
**Leroy**—*pop pl* LA-4
**Leroy**—*pop pl* MI-6
**Le Roy**—*pop pl* MI-6
**Le Roy**—*pop pl* MN-6
**Leroy**—*pop pl* MO-7
**Le Roy**—*pop pl* NY-2
**Leroy**—*pop pl* ND-7
**Leroy**—*pop pl* OK-5
**Le Roy**—*pop pl* PA-2
**Leroy**—*pop pl* TX-5
**Le Roy**—*pop pl* WV-2
**LeRoy**—*pop pl* WV-2
**LeRoy**—*pop pl* WI-6
**Le Roy**—*pop pl* WY-8
LeRoy, Daniel, House—*hist pl* NY-2
Le Roy, Lake—*reservoir* NY-2
Leroy Airp—*airport* KS-7
Le Roy Boys Home—*building* CA-9
Leroy Bridge—*locale* WY-8
Leroy Cave—*cave* IN-6
Leroy Cave—*cave* MO-7
Leroy Cem—*cemetery* CO-8
Le Roy Cem—*cemetery* KS-7
Le Roy Cem—*cemetery* MN-6
Leroy Cem—*cemetery* MO-7
Leroy Cem—*cemetery* OK-5
Leroy Center—*locale* OH-6
LeRoy Country Club—*other* NY-2
*Leroy Creek* WI-6

Leroy Creek—stream AK-9
Leroy Creek—stream NC-3
Leroy Creek—stream (2) WA-9
LeRoy Creek—stream WI-6
Leroy D Fienburg Elem Sch—school FL-3
Leroy Drive Sch—school CO-8
LeRoy Elem Sch—school KS-7
Leroy George Lake Dam—dam (2) MS-4
*Leroy High School* AL-4
*Leroy Hollow* MO-7
LeRoy HS—school KS-7
Le Roy Island—island NY-2
**Le Roy Island**—pop pl NY-2
LeRoy Lake—reservoir NC-3
*Le Roy (Leroy)* IN-6
LeRoy McKnight Ranch—locale NM-5
*Leroy Mine* SD-7
Leroy Mine—mine (2) AZ-5
Le Roy Mine—mine CA-9
Leroy Mtn—summit NY-2
Le Roy Park—park CA-9
Leroy Peak—summit ME-1
Leroy Percy Game Mngmt Area—park MS-4
Leroy Percy State Park—park MS-4
Leroy Ponds—lake FL-3
LeRoy Public Library—hist pl MN-6
Leroy (RR name for Le Roy)—other MI-6
Le Roy Rsvr—reservoir NY-2
Leroy Sch—school AL-4
Leroy Sch—school KY-4
Le Roy School—locale IL-6
*Le Roys Corners* NY-2
*Leroys Mills* NY-2
*Leroy Smith Lake* IN-6
Leroy Smith Lake Dam—dam IN-6
Leroys Point—cape WI-6
Leroy Spring—spring CO-8
Leroys Sch—school KY-4
Leroy Theatre—hist pl RI-1
**Le Roy (Town of)**—pop pl NY-2
LeRoy Township—civil SD-7
Leroy Township—fmr MCD IA-7
Le Roy Township—fmr MCD IA-7
Leroy Township—fmr MCD IA-7
**Le Roy Township**—pop pl KS-7
**Leroy Township**—pop pl MO-7
**Le Roy Township**—pop pl SD-7
Le Roy (Township of)—civ div MI-6
**Le Roy (Township of)**—pop pl IL-6
**Leroy (Township of)**—pop pl MI-6
**Le Roy (Township of)**—pop pl MI-6
**Le Roy (Township of)**—pop pl MN-6
**Leroy (Township of)**—pop pl OH-6
**Leroy (Township of)**—pop pl PA-2
**Leroy (Township of)**—pop pl WI-6
Leroy Wood Sch—school MA-1
Lersch, John, House—hist pl OH-6
Lerton Cem—cemetery NE-7
Lertora Lake—lake CA-9
Lerty—locale VA-3
Lery, Bayou—gut LA-4
Lery, Lake—lake LA-4
**Lesage**—pop pl WV-2
Lesage, Lake—cemetery MI-6
LeSage Lake—lake MI-6
Lesaire, Bayou de—gut LA-4
Leson—locale IA-7
Leson-Gould Bldg—hist pl MO-7
*Lesarau* FM-9
**Le Sauk (Township of)**—pop pl MN-6
Lesbas—locale KY-4
*Les Belle Pierres Hills* ND-7
Lesbia—locale NM-5
Lesbia Post Office (historical)—building TN-4
Lescaze House—hist pl NY-2
*Les Chenaux Islands* MI-6
Les Cheneaux Channel—channel MI-6
**Les Cheneaux Club**—pop pl MI-6
Les Cheneaux Islands—island MI-6
Leschi Glacier—glacier WA-9
*Les Coquins* OR-9
Les Draw—valley WY-8
Lesea Stream—stream AS-9
Leseburg Ditch—canal WY-8
Les George Point—cape UT-8
*Les Grandes Isles* MS-4
*Les Grandes Sables* MI-6
*Lesha Peak* AZ-5
**Leshara**—pop pl NE-7
Leshara Site—hist pl NE-7
**Leshara Township**—pop pl NE-7
Lesh Ditch—canal IN-6
Lesh Ditch—canal WA-9
Lesher, Frank, House—hist pl MI-6
Lesher Cem—cemetery PA-2
Lesher Ditch—canal IN-6
Lesher JHS—school CO-8
Lesher Lake—lake NE-7
Lesher Run—stream PA-2
Le Sieur Cem—cemetery MO-7
Le Sieur Township—civil MO-7
Lesina Stream—stream AS-9
*Les Isles Marianes* MH-9
*Les Isles Uracas* MH-9
Lesje Ch—church ND-7
Leske Bar—hist pl TX-5
Leskine, Bayou—stream LA-4
Leskinen Creek—stream MN-6
Leskinen Lake—lake MN-6
L E Skipper Pond—reservoir AL-4
L E Skipper Pond Dam—dam AL-4
Leslee Lake—lake FL-3
Lesle Run—stream PA-2
**Lesley**—pop pl TX-5
Lesley Coll—school MA-1
Lesley Lake—lake TX-5
Lesley Run—stream OH-6
Lesley Temple CME Ch—church AL-4
Lesley-Travers Mansion—hist pl DE-2
*Leslie* AL-4
*Leslie* KS-7
*Leslie* SC-3
Leslie—fmr MCD NE-7
Leslie—locale KY-4
Leslie—locale LA-4
Leslie—locale MD-2
Leslie—locale VA-3
Leslie—locale WI-6
**Leslie**—pop pl AR-4
**Leslie**—pop pl GA-3
**Leslie**—pop pl ID-8
**Leslie**—pop pl IA-7
**Leslie**—pop pl MI-6
**Leslie**—pop pl MO-7
**Leslie**—pop pl WV-2
Leslie Branch—stream AL-4
Leslie Branch—stream KY-4
Leslie Branch—stream WV-2
Leslie Butte—summit ID-8
Leslie Caldwell Dam—dam SD-7
Leslie Canyon—valley AZ-5
Leslie Cem—cemetery AR-4
Leslie Cem—cemetery IN-6
Leslie Cem—cemetery KY-4
Leslie Cem—cemetery PA-2
Leslie Cem—cemetery WI-6
Leslie Ch—church MN-6
Leslie Ch—church NC-3
Leslie Chamberlain Lake—reservoir NC-3
Leslie Chamberlain Lake Dam—dam NC-3
**Leslie (County)**—pop pl KY-4
*Leslie Creek* PA-2
Leslie Creek—stream AZ-5
Leslie Creek—stream MT-8
Leslie Creek—stream PA-2
Leslie Creek—stream WA-9
*Leslie Creek - in part* PA-2
Leslie-De Soto (CCD)—cens area GA-3
Leslie-DeSoto (RR name for Leslie)—other GA-3
Leslie Golf Course—other MI-6
Leslie Gulch—valley OR-9
Leslie Gulch Camp—locale OR-9
Leslie (historical)—locale SD-7
Leslie Homestead—locale CO-8
Leslie JHS—school OR-9
Leslie Lake—lake MT-8
*Leslie Lick Hollow* VA-3
Leslie Lick Hollow—valley VA-3
Leslie Mine—mine PA-2
Leslie Point—cape MT-8
Leslie Recreation Center—park PA-2
**Leslie (Riderville)**—pop pl AL-4
Leslie Ridge—ridge AL-4
**Leslie (RR name Leslie-DeSoto)**—pop pl GA-3
Leslie Run—locale PA-2
Leslie Run—stream OH-6
Leslie Run—stream PA-2
Leslie Run Station—locale PA-2
Leslie Sch—school KY-4
Leslie Sch—school MI-6
Leslie Sch—school WI-6
Leslies Landing—locale MS-4
Leslie Slough—gut MS-4
Leslie Spring—spring MT-8
Leslie Spring—spring NM-5
Leslie Springs—spring ID-8
Leslie Street Park—park TN-4
Leslie Tank—reservoir AZ-5
Leslie Tank Number Two—reservoir AZ-5
**Leslie Township**—pop pl MO-7
**Leslie (Township of)**—pop pl MI-6
**Leslie (Township of)**—pop pl MN-6
*Leslieville* NC-3
Leslie Windmill—locale NM-5
Leslin Lake—lake MN-6
Lesmalinston—locale WV-2
L Esmay Slough—stream IA-7
Lesmeister Lake—lake ND-7
Lesmil—locale OH-6
Les Myers Community Park—park NC-3
Lesna Mountains, La—range AZ-5
Lesna Peak—summit AZ-5
Lesna Peak, La—summit AZ-5
Lesna Spring—spring AZ-5
Lesner Bridge—bridge VA-3
Lesnini Creek—stream CA-9
Lesnini Lateral—canal CA-9
Lesofski Homestead—locale MT-8
Lesoine Sch—school PA-2
Lesolo Ridge—ridge AS-9
**Le Sourdsville**—pop pl OH-6
*Les Palos* PW-9
**Lespedeza**—pop pl MS-4
*Lespedeza P.O.* MS-4
L'Esperance—locale VI-3
L'Esperance Hist Dist—hist pl VI-3
Lesperance Mtn—summit NY-2
Les Petites Lacs a Blakewood—lake LA-4
Lespideza Point—cape MS-4
Lespideza Point Public Use Area—park MS-4
Les Rsvr—reservoir WY-8
*Less Creek* VA-3
Lessels Shop (historical)—locale MS-4
Lessenbery Cem—cemetery AR-4
Lessenger JHS—school MI-6
Lessenger Sch—school (2) MI-6
*Lesser* MS-4
Lesser Cherry Portage—trail MN-6
*Lesser Crossroads* NJ-2
Lessering Draw—valley SD-7
Lessering Ranch—locale SD-7
Lessie—locale FL-3
Lessig Canyon—valley NE-7
Lessing Cem—cemetery TX-5
**Lessley**—pop pl MS-4
Lessley Cem—cemetery AR-4
Lessley Cem—cemetery IL-6
Lessley Cem—cemetery MO-7
Lessley Cem—cemetery OK-5
Lessley Post Office (historical)—building MS-4
Lesslie—CDP SC-3
Lesslie Tank—reservoir AZ-5
Lesson, Point—cape FM-9
Lessor Cem—cemetery WI-6
Lessor State Wildlife Mngmt Area—park MN-6
**Lessor (Town of)**—pop pl WI-6
**Lessor (Township of)**—pop pl MN-6
*Les Taskaque* AL-4
Lester—locale AR-4
Lester—locale CO-8
Lester—locale GA-3
Lester—locale IL-6
Lester—locale NY-2
Lester—locale OH-6
**Lester**—pop pl (2) AL-4
**Lester**—pop pl AR-4
**Lester**—pop pl IA-7
**Lester**—pop pl NE-7
**Lester**—pop pl PA-2
**Lester**—pop pl SC-3
**Lester**—pop pl WA-9
**Lester**—pop pl WV-2
Lester, L. T., House—hist pl TX-5
Lester, Mount—summit WY-8
Lester, Nathan, House—hist pl CT-1
Lester And Haltom No. 1 Well Site—hist pl AR-4
Lester Branch—stream AL-4
Lester Branch—stream (2) KY-4
Lester Branch—stream VA-3
*Lester Canyon* CO-8
Lester Cem—cemetery AL-4
Lester Cem—cemetery AR-4
Lester Cem—cemetery CT-1
Lester Cem—cemetery FL-3
Lester Cem—cemetery (2) GA-3
Lester Cem—cemetery IA-7
Lester Cem—cemetery LA-4
Lester Cem—cemetery MI-6
Lester Cem—cemetery (2) MS-4
Lester Cem—cemetery (2) MO-7
Lester Cem—cemetery (3) TN-4
Lester Cem—cemetery (7) VA-3
Lester Cem—cemetery (2) WV-2
Lester Cemeteries—cemetery WV-2
*Lester Chapel* AL-4
Lester Chapel—church KY-4
Lester Chapel—church TN-4
Lester Chapel Sch—school TN-4
Lester Creek—stream CO-8
Lester Creek—stream (2) ID-8
Lester Creek—stream KY-4
Lester Creek—stream OR-9
Lester Creek—stream SC-3
Lester Creek—stream (2) WA-9
Lester Creek Forest Service Station—locale ID-8
*Lester Creek Reservoir* CO-8
Lester Creek Springs—spring ID-8
Lester Dam—dam NY-2
Lester Depot—hist pl WA-9
Lester Ditch—canal MS-4
Lester Draw—valley WY-8
Lester E Cox Med Ctr North Heliport—airport MO-7
Lester E Cox Med Ctr South Heliport—airport MO-7
*Lester Elementary School* MS-4
Lester Field (airport)—airport MS-4
Lester Flow—reservoir NY-2
Lester Fork—stream VA-3
Lester Hetzel Dam—dam SD-7
Lester Hill Sch—school MS-4
Lester (historical P.O.)—locale IA-7
Lester Hollow—valley AL-4
Lester HS—school TN-4
Lester Island—island AK-9
Lester Island—island FL-3
Lester Jackson Dam—dam TN-4
Lester Jackson Lake—reservoir TN-4
Lester James Dam—dam OR-9
Lester James Dam No. 3—dam OR-9
Lester James Rsvr—reservoir OR-9
Lester James Rsvr Number 3—reservoir OR-9
Lesterjet Tank—reservoir TX-5
Lester Junction—locale AR-4
Lester Junction—locale NE-7
Lester Lake—lake FL-3
Lester Lake—lake (2) MI-6
Lester Lake—lake MN-6
Lester Lake—lake WI-6
Lester Lake—lake WY-8
Lester Manor—locale VA-3
Lester May Lake Dam—dam MS-4
Lester Memorial Ch—church KY-4
Lester Memorial Methodist Ch—church AL-4
Lester Mtn—summit CO-8
*Lester Park* MN-6
Lester Park—park MN-6
Lester Park—park UT-8
**Lester Park**—pop pl MN-6
Lester Park Sch—school MN-6
Lester Pass—gap WY-8
Lester Pond—swamp GA-3
Lester Post Office—building AL-4
**Lester Prairie**—pop pl MN-6
Lester Prong—stream TN-4
Lester R. Davis Memorial State For—forest MO-7
Lester Ridge—ridge IN-6
Lester River—stream MN-6
Lesters—locale TN-4
Lester S—uninc pl NC-3
Lesters Cem—cemetery MS-4
Lester Sch—school IL-6
Lester Sch—school MS-4
Lester Sch—school TN-4
Lester Sch—school WV-2
Lester Sch (abandoned)—school (2) PA-2
Lesters Chapel—church AL-4
*Lesters Chapel Ch* AL-4
Lester Sch (historical)—school MS-4
*Lesters Grove Sch* TN-4
*Lestershire* NY-2
*Lesters Hollow* TN-4
Lesters Hollow—valley TN-4
Lesters Lake—reservoir TN-4
Lesters Post Office (historical)—building TN-4
Lester Spring—spring KY-4
Lester Square Memorial Park—park IN-6
Lester State Airp—airport WA-9
Lester Street Chapel—church AL-4
**Lester Subdivision**—pop pl UT-8
Lester Township—fmr MCD IA-7
Lester Township Cem—cemetery IA-7
Lester (Township of)—fmr MCD AR-4
Lester Trail—trail PA-2
Lester Trail—trail WA-9
Lesterville—locale MI-6
**Lesterville**—pop pl AR-4
**Lesterville**—pop pl MO-7
**Lesterville**—pop pl SD-7
Lesterville Rec Area—park SD-7
Lesterville Township—civil MO-7
Lesterville Township—civil SD-7
Lester Well—well MT-8
Les Trois Island—island ME-1
Le Sueur—locale MN-6
LeSueur—locale VA-3
**Le Sueur**—pop pl MN-6
LeSueur Cem—cemetery SD-7
*Le Sueur Center* MN-6
Le Sueur Country Club—other MN-6
**Le Sueur (County)**—pop pl MN-6
Le Sueur County Courthouse and Jail—hist pl MN-6
Le Sueur Creek—stream MN-6
Le Sueur Park—park MN-6
Le Sueur River—stream MN-6
Le Sueur River Ch—church MN-6
LeSueur Township—civil SD-7
**Le Sueur Township**—pop pl SD-7
Lesui Ridge—ridge AS-9
LeSure Cem—cemetery MS-4
Lesure Heath Lake—lake MN-6
*Let* TN-4
Let, The—bay MA-1
Leta—locale MO-7
*Letakroki* MP-9
Let Alone Creek—stream VA-3
Letal Sch—school IA-7
Letan—locale NE-7
Letan Sch—school NE-7
**Letart**—pop pl WV-2
**Letart Falls**—pop pl OH-6
Letart Island—island WV-2
**Letart (Township of)**—pop pl OH-6
Letbetter Lake—reservoir TX-5
Letch—locale WV-2
**Letcher**—pop pl AL-4
**Letcher**—pop pl KY-4
**Letcher**—pop pl MO-7
**Letcher**—pop pl SD-7
*Letcher Catholic Church* SD-7
*Letcher Cemetery* SD-7
Letcher Ch—church AL-4
**Letcher (County)**—pop pl KY-4
Letcher Creek—stream CO-8
Letcher (historical)—locale AL-4
Letcher Lake—lake SD-7
Letcher Ridge—ridge TN-4
**Letchers**—pop pl AL-4
**Letcher Township**—pop pl SD-7
Letchworth—locale AR-4
Letchworth Cem—cemetery LA-4
Letchworth Central HS—school NY-2
Letchworth Sch (abandoned)—school MO-7
Letchworth State Park—park NY-2
Letchworth Village State Mental Institution—hospital NY-2
Let Dyer Branch—stream KY-4
Letepwel—plain FM-9
Let-Er Buck Meadow—flat CA-9
Leter Ranch—locale NV-8
Leter Rsvr—reservoir NV-8
Letford—locale GA-3
Letha—locale ID-8
Letha Bridge—bridge ID-8
Letha Ponds—lake MD-2
Lethas Spring—spring OR-9
Lethco Ranch—locale (2) TX-5
Lethe Lake—lake MN-6
**Letherbark**—pop pl WV-2
Letherby Falls—falls MI-6
Lethermans Well—well NM-5
Leth Sch—school NE-7
Letica Corporation—facility MI-6
Leti Point—cape AS-9
Let Island—island AK-9
Letitia—locale KS-7
Letitia—locale KY-4
Letitia—locale OK-5
**Letitia**—pop pl NC-3
Letitia Cem—cemetery OR-9
Letitia Creek—stream OR-9
Letitia Lake—lake CO-8
Letjegol—island FM-9
Letney Cem—cemetery TX-5
Letnikof Cove—bay AK-9
Leto (census name for Pine Crest)—CDP FL-3
Leto Comprehensive HS—school FL-3
**Letohatchee**—pop pl AL-4
Letohatchee Ch—church AL-4
**Letohatchee (RR name Letohatchie)**—pop pl AL-4
*Letohatchie Creek* AL-4
Letohatchie (RR name for Letohatchee)—other AL-4
**Leton**—pop pl LA-4
**Letona**—pop pl AR-4
Leto Point—cape AK-9
Letort—locale PA-2
Letort Ch—church PA-2
*Letort Elem Sch* PA-2
Letort Elem Sch—school PA-2
Letort Park—park PA-2
Letort Spring—spring PA-2
Letort Spring Run—stream PA-2
Letot Cem—cemetery TX-5
**Le Tourneau**—pop pl MS-4
Le Tourneau—uninc pl GA-3
Le Tourneau Creek—stream WI-6
Le Tourneau Lake—lake WI-6
Le Tourneau Lake—reservoir GA-3
Letourneau Lake Dam—dam MS-4
Letourneau Sch—school MA-1
Le Tourneau Technical Institute—school TX-5
Letovsky-Rohret House—hist pl IA-7
Let Post Office (historical)—building TN-4
L E Traver Ranch—locale CA-9
*Le Trinass* LA-4
*Let Run* WV-2
Letsch Cem—cemetery TX-5
Letsche Elem Sch—hist pl PA-2
Letsinger Branch—stream IN-6
Letsinger Ditch—canal IN-6
Letson Point—cape AL-4
Letson Settlement—locale AL-4
Letta, Lake—lake FL-3
Lett Cem—cemetery MI-6
Lett Cem—cemetery TN-4
Letteau Canyon—valley CA-9
Lette Cem—cemetery IL-6
Letteken Ponds (duck ponds)—reservoir OR-9
Letter Box—locale CA-9
Letterbox Canyon—valley (2) CA-9
Letterbox Creek—stream CA-9
Letterbox Hill—summit CA-9
Letter Cove—bay MD-2
Letter Creek—stream MD-2
Letter D—pillar NV-8
Lettered Rock Ch—church KY-4
Lettered Rock Ridge—ridge KY-4
Lettered Rock Ridge—ridge NC-3
Lettered Rocks—summit KY-4
Letter Gap—locale WV-2
Letter Gulch—valley MT-8
Letterkenny Army Depot—military PA-2
Letterkenny Rsvr—reservoir PA-2
**Letterkenny (Township of)**—pop pl PA-2
Letterman—post sta CA-9
Letterman Army Med Ctr—uninc pl CA-9
Letterman Cem—cemetery MO-7
Letterman General Hosp—hospital CA-9
Letter M Ranch—locale TX-5
Letterrock Mtn—summit NY-2
LETTIE G. HOWARD-MYSTIC C (schooner)—hist pl NY-2
Lettie M Cook Memorial For—forest NY-2
Lettie Shaffer Hollow—valley PA-2
Lettingham Hollow—valley KY-4
Lettis Creek—stream FL-3
Lettis Grove Ch—church NC-3
Letton Canyon—valley NM-5
Letton Cem—cemetery KY-4
**Letts**—pop pl IN-6
**Letts**—pop pl IA-7
Letts Cem—cemetery MI-6
**Letts Corner**—pop pl IN-6
Letts Creek—stream CA-9
Letts Creek—stream MI-6
Letts Lakes—reservoir AL-4
Letts Ridge—ridge CA-9
Letts Sch—school IN-6
*Lettsville* IA-7
**Lettsville**—pop pl IN-6
*Lettsworth* LA-4
**Lettsworth**—pop pl LA-4
Lettsworth, Bayou—stream LA-4
Lettuce Branch—stream NC-3
Lettuce Creek—stream FL-3
Lettuce Hollow Ch—church NC-3
Lettuce Lake—lake CA-9
Lettuce Lake—lake (2) FL-3
Lettuce Lake—swamp FL-3
Lettuce Lake Cutoff—gut FL-3
Lettuce Patch Springs—spring CO-8
Letula—locale AS-9
Le Tulle, Lake—lake TX-5
Le Tulle Park—park TX-5
Letz Creek—stream OR-9
Letzen Gulch—valley MT-8
Letz Lake—lake MT-8
Letz Oil Field—oilfield TX-5
Leua Stream—stream AS-9
**Leucadia**—pop pl CA-9
Leucadia Park—park CA-9
Leucite Hills—range WY-8
Leuck Ditch—canal IN-6
Leuen Anchorage—harbor MP-9
Leuenberger Ranch—locale WY-8
Leuen Island—island MP-9
Leuetik Peilong—unknown FM-9
Leuhman Ridge—ridge CA-9
Leuins Point Cem—cemetery IA-7
Leuizenger Creek—stream OR-9
Leuns Holes—basin NV-8
*Leuot* FM-9
**Leupp**—pop pl AZ-5
Leupp Boarding Sch—school AZ-5
Leupp Corner—locale AZ-5
**Leupp Corner (Trading Post)**—pop pl AZ-5
Leupp Lateral—canal AZ-5
**Leupp (Old Leupp)**—pop pl AZ-5
Leupp Post Office—building AZ-5
Leupp Sch—school AZ-5
Leupp Traffic Interchange—crossing AZ-5
Leurahn—locale FM-9
Leuren Kill—stream NY-2
**Leusoalii**—pop pl AS-9
Leuthey Lake—lake WI-6
Leuth Flying Service Airp—airport MS-4
Leuthold, Jacob, Jr., House—hist pl MN-6
Leuthold Couloir—valley OR-9
Leuthold Sch—school MT-8
Leutu Point—cape AS-9
Leuty, Isaac, House—hist pl MI-6
Leuty Cem—cemetery (2) TN-4
Leuty Creek—stream ID-8
Leuzinger HS—school CA-9
Levaga Ridge—ridge AS-9
Levage Creek—stream OR-9
Levagood Park—park MI-6
Levais Wash—arroyo AZ-5
Levale, Lake—lake MT-8
Levalley Creek—stream MT-8
Leval Town Hall—building ND-7
**Leval Township**—pop pl ND-7
**Levan**—pop pl UT-8
*Levan Bay* AL-4
Levan Cem—cemetery UT-8
Levan Farm—hist pl PA-2
Le Vanger Lakes—lake UT-8
Levanger Well—locale OR-9
**Levanna**—pop pl NY-2
**Levanna**—pop pl OH-6
Levanna Branch—stream OH-6
Levan Number 2 Mine (underground)—mine AL-4
Levan Peak—summit UT-8
Levan Ridge—slope UT-8
Levansaller Hill—summit ME-1
*Levans Bay* AL-4
**Levant**—pop pl KS-7
**Levant**—pop pl ME-1
**Levant**—pop pl NY-2
Levant Cem—cemetery NY-2
**Levan (Township of)**—pop pl IL-6
Levant Sch—school NY-2
**Levant (Town of)**—pop pl ME-1
**Levant Township**—pop pl ND-7
Levan Wildlife Mngmt Area—park UT-8
Leva Point—cape AS-9
LeVasseur, Lake—lake MI-6
LeVasseur Creek—stream MI-6
Le Vasseur Falls—falls WY-8
Le Vasseur Ranch—locale WY-8
**Levasy**—pop pl MO-7
Levasy Cem—cemetery MO-7
Leveaux Creek—stream MN-6
Leveaux Mtn—summit MN-6
Levee—locale KY-4
**Levee**—pop pl CA-9
Levee Bridge—bridge MS-4
Levee Cem—cemetery LA-4
Levee Drain—canal CA-9
Levee Lake—lake LA-4
Levee Number One Canal—canal CA-9
Levee Number 33—levee FL-3
Levee Number 35—canal FL-3
Levee Number 35A—canal FL-3
Levee Number 36—levee FL-3
Levee Number 37—levee FL-3
Levee Number 40—levee FL-3
Levee Number 68A—levee FL-3
Levee Pond Ch—church IL-6
Levees Creek—stream MS-4
*Levees Creek Oil Field* MS-4
**Levee Siding**—pop pl IL-6
Levees Oil Field—oilfield MS-4
Levee Spur—locale CA-9
**Levee (Township of)**—pop pl IL-6
Levee 15—levee FL-3
Levee 18—levee FL-3
Levee 19—levee FL-3
Levee 23—levee FL-3
Levee 28—levee (2) FL-3
Levee 28 Tieback—levee FL-3
Levee 3—levee FL-3
Levee 30—levee FL-3
Levee 38E—levee FL-3
Levee 38W—levee FL-3
Levee 39—levee FL-3
Levee 4—levee FL-3
Levee 5—levee FL-3
Levee 6—levee FL-3
Levee 60—levee FL-3
Levee 67—levee FL-3
Levee 67A—levee FL-3
Levee 67C—levee FL-3
Levee 7—levee FL-3
Level—locale NE-7
**Level**—pop pl MD-2
Level, The—flat GA-3
Level Acres Farm Airp—airport PA-2
Level Bench—bench UT-8
Level Branch—stream KY-4
Level Branch—stream PA-2
Level Club—hist pl NY-2
Level Corner—locale PA-2
Level Corner Sch (abandoned)—school PA-2
Level Creek—stream GA-3
Level Creek—stream KS-7
Level Creek Ch—church GA-3
**Level Cross**—pop pl (2) NC-3
Level Cross (Township of)—fmr MCD NC-3
Leveldale Cem—cemetery IL-6
Level Green—locale KY-4
**Level Green**—pop pl PA-2
Level Green Ch—church KY-4
Level Green Ch—church (2) SC-3
Level Green Ch—church VA-3
Level Green Sch—school KY-4
Level Green Sch (abandoned)—school PA-2
Level Grove Ch—church GA-3
Level Hill—summit ME-1
Level Hill Cem—cemetery IL-6
Level Hill Ch—church GA-3
Level Islands—area AK-9
**Level Land**—pop pl SC-3
**Levelland**—pop pl TX-5
Levelland And Slaughter Oil And Gas Field—oilfield TX-5
Levelland (CCD)—cens area TX-5
Levelland Country Club—other TX-5
Levelland Cove—bay GA-3
Levelland Mtn—summit GA-3
Level Meadows Creek—stream WY-8
Level Mtn—summit AK-9
**Levelock**—pop pl AK-9
Levelock ANV843—reserve AK-9
Levelock Creek—stream AK-9
*Level Park* MI-6
**Level Park**—pop pl MI-6
**Level Plains**—pop pl AL-4
**Level Plains Crossroads**—pop pl AL-4
Level Pond—lake VA-3
Level Road—locale AL-4
**Levelroad**—pop pl AL-4
Level Run—locale VA-3
Level Run Ch—church VA-3
Levels—locale NC-3
**Levels**—pop pl WV-2
Levels, The—ridge TN-4
Levels Ch—church SC-3
Levels Ch—church WV-2
Levels Hollow—valley TX-5
**Level Siding**—pop pl SD-7
Level Tank—reservoir TX-5
Levelton Chapel—church NC-3
Levelwood Ch—church KY-4
Levelwood Sch—school KY-4
*Level Woods Park* MS-4
Leven, Loch—lake FL-3
Levengood Gulch—valley MT-8
Leven Lake—lake MN-6
Levensaler Brook—stream ME-1
*Levens Chapel* AL-4
*Levens Church* AL-4
Levenseller Mtn—summit ME-1
Levenseller Pond—lake ME-1
*Levens Gulch* MT-8
Levens Gulch—valley OR-9
Levens Ledge Mine—mine OR-9
**Leven (Township of)**—pop pl MN-6
Leveque Creek—stream MI-6
Lever Bldg—hist pl SC-3
Lever Chapel—church SC-3
Levere Ditch—canal CO-8
*Leverentz* MI-6
Leverentz Lake—lake MI-6
Leverenz Rsvr—reservoir OR-9
*Leverett* GA-3
Leverett—locale AL-4
Leverett—locale GA-3
Leverett—locale IL-6
Leverett—locale IA-7
**Leverett**—pop pl MA-1

**Leverett**—pop pl ... MS-4
Leverett, William J., House—hist pl ... NM-5
Leverett Cem—cemetery ... GA-3
Leverett Cem—cemetery ... SC-3
Leverett Center ... MA-1
Leverett Centre ... MA-1
Leverette Cem—cemetery ... GA-3
Leverette Neck—bay ... GA-3
Leverett Pond—lake (2) ... MA-1
Leverett Pond—reservoir ... MA-1
Leverett Pond Dam—dam ... MA-1
Leverett Post Office (historical)—building ... MS-4
Leveretts—locale ... GA-3
Leverett Sch—school ... AR-4
Leveretts Chapel—locale ... TX-5
Leveretts Station ... GA-3
**Leverett (sta.)**—pop pl ... MA-1
Leverett State For—forest ... MA-1
**Leverett Station**—pop pl ... MA-1
**Leverett (Town of)**—pop pl ... MA-1
Lever House—hist pl ... NY-2
Leverich—locale ... ND-7
Leverich Creek—stream ... MT-8
Leverich Drain—canal ... MI-6
Leverich Park—park ... WA-9
Leverich Sch—school ... MT-8
Leveridge Ditch ... MI-6
Levering—locale ... WA-9
**Levering**—pop pl ... MI-6
Levering, William, Sch—hist pl ... PA-2
Levering Creek—bay ... MD-2
Levering Hall—hist pl ... OH-6
Levering Mission—hist pl ... OK-5
Levering Run—stream ... OH-6
Levering Sch—school ... PA-2
Leverington Cem—cemetery ... PA-2
Le Verken Creek ... UT-8
Le Verkin Creek ... UT-8
Lever Lake—reservoir ... TN-4
Lever Lake Dam—dam ... TN-4
Leverney (Township of)—fmr MCD ... AR-4
Le Vert ... AL-4
Levert—locale ... AL-4
Levert—locale ... LA-4
**Levert**—pop pl ... IN-6
Le Verte—locale ... TX-5
LeVert Hist Dist—hist pl ... GA-3
Le Vert Post Office (historical)—building ... AL-4
Levert Sch (historical)—school ... AL-4
**Levert (St. John)**—pop pl ... LA-4
**Levesque**—pop pl ... AR-4
Levesque Island—island ... ME-1
Levesque Spring—spring ... WI-6
Leveston Bluff—cliff ... SC-3
Levett Gardens Cem—cemetery ... GA-3
Levey—locale ... WA-9
**Levey**—pop pl ... IA-7
**Levey**—pop pl ... WA-9
Levey, Louis, Mansion—hist pl ... IN-6
Levey Ditch Camp—locale ... CA-9
Levey JHS—school ... MI-6
Levey Landing Park—park ... WA-9
Levey School (historical)—locale ... MO-7
Levey Township—fmr MCD ... IA-7
Le Vezu Ranch—locale ... CA-9
Levi ... SC-3
**Levi**—pop pl (2) ... KY-4
**Levi**—pop pl ... TX-5
**Levi**—pop pl ... VA-3
Levi, Cape—cape ... ME-1
Levi And Esther Fuller Forest Preserve—park ... IL-6
**Levias**—pop pl ... KY-4
Leviathan Canyon—valley ... CA-9
Leviathan Canyon—valley ... NV-8
Leviathan Creek—stream ... CA-9
Leviathan Creek—stream ... CO-8
Leviathan Gulch—valley ... ID-8
Leviathan Lake—lake ... CO-8
Leviathan Mine—mine (2) ... AZ-5
Leviathan Mine—mine ... CA-9
Leviathan Peak—summit ... CA-9
Leviathan Peak—summit ... CO-8
Levi Branch—stream ... AR-4
Levi Branch—stream ... KY-4
Levi Branch—stream ... NC-3
Levi Brook—stream ... VT-1
Levi Carter Park—park ... NE-7
Levi Cave—cave ... TN-4
Levi Cem—cemetery ... TN-4
Levi Ch—church ... VA-3
Levi Ch—church ... WV-2
Levick Mill—locale ... MO-7
Levi Coffin House—building ... IN-6
Levi Creek—stream ... MT-8
Levi Dunn Branch—stream ... TX-5
Levi Gap—gap ... TN-4
Levi Hill—summit ... AR-4
Levi Hill—summit ... KY-4
Levi Hill—summit ... NH-1
Levi Hollow—valley ... AR-4
Levi Hollow—valley ... MO-7
Levi Hollow—valley ... TN-4
Levi Hollow—valley ... UT-8
Levi Jackson Wilderness Road State Park—park ... KY-4
Levi Lake—lake ... LA-4
Levi Lake—swamp ... LA-4
Levi Lewis Branch—stream ... KY-4
Levi Memorial Hosp—hospital ... AR-4
Levi Mtn—summit ... OK-5
Levinau ... FM-9
Levindale Home—locale ... MD-2
Levindusky Lake—lake ... MN-6
Levine, Louis, House—hist pl ... MI-6
Levine Ranch—locale ... MT-8
Leviner Cem—cemetery ... NC-3
Leving Peak ... CA-9
**Levings**—pop pl ... IL-6
Levings Gulch—valley ... MT-8
Levings Park—park ... IL-6
Levining Creek ... CA-9
Levin Post Office (historical)—building ... AL-4
**Levins**—pop pl ... LA-4
Levins Chapel—church ... AL-4
Levinski Creek—stream ... MT-8
Levinski Ridge—ridge ... MT-8
Levinsky, Lake—lake ... MT-8
Levinson—locale ... TX-5
Levinson Rsvr—reservoir ... TX-5
Levins Store (historical)—locale ... AL-4
Levi Pond—lake ... VT-1
Levi Rock Shelter—hist pl ... TX-5
Levi Rouch Ditch—canal ... IN-6
Levis—locale ... CA-9
Levis—locale (2) ... WI-6
**Levisa**—pop pl ... VA-3
Levisa Fork—stream ... KY-4
Levisa Fork—stream ... VA-3
Levisa Junction—locale ... KY-4
Levis Branch ... TN-4
Levis Branch—stream ... KY-4
Levis Cem—cemetery ... WI-6
Levi Sch—school ... TN-4
Levis Creek—stream ... WI-6
Levisee Creek—stream ... WV-2
Levis Falls ... PA-2
Levis Mound—summit ... WI-6
Levison Camp—locale ... CO-8
Levi Sparkman Grant—civil ... FL-3
Levi Spring—spring ... OR-9
Levis Temple Church of God in Christ ... MS-4
Leviston ... CA-9
Leviston ... PA-2
**Leviston**—pop pl ... PA-2
Leviston (RR name for Junedale)—other ... PA-2
**Levis (Town of)**—pop pl ... WI-6
Levisy Flat—flat ... AR-4
Levisy Flat Cem—cemetery ... AR-4
**Levita**—pop pl ... TX-5
Levi Temple—church ... MS-4
Levitt Creek—stream (2) ... WI-6
Levitt Creek Cem—cemetery ... WI-6
Levitte Cem—cemetery ... IL-6
Levittown (2) ... NJ-2
**Levittown**—pop pl ... NY-2
**Levittown**—pop pl ... PA-2
**Levittown**—pop pl ... PR-3
Levittown Baptist Ch—church ... PA-2
Levittown Plaza—locale ... PA-2
**Levittown-Tullytown**—pop pl ... PA-2
Levitt Sch—school ... WI-6
Levitt Spring ... ID-8
Levitt Tank—reservoir ... AZ-5
Leviture Creek—stream ... MI-6
Levi-Welder House—hist pl ... TX-5
Levi Well—well ... UT-8
Levi White Sch—school ... GA-3
Lev Olds Cem—cemetery ... TX-5
Levosel ... FM-9
Levsa Canyon—valley ... CO-8
Levy ... KS-7
Levy—locale ... NM-5
Levy—locale ... VA-3
**Levy**—pop pl ... AR-4
**Levy**—pop pl ... SC-3
Levy, Henry, House—hist pl ... AZ-5
Levy, Soloman, House—hist pl ... OH-6
Levy Bay—bay ... FL-3
Levy Bay—swamp ... SC-3
Levy Bldg—hist pl ... AZ-5
Levy Brothers Bldg—hist pl ... KY-4
**Levy County**—pop pl ... FL-3
Levy Creek—stream ... KY-4
Levy Hollow—valley ... MO-7
Levy House—hist pl ... NV-8
Levy Lake—lake ... FL-3
Levy Park—park ... FL-3
Levy Park—park ... TX-5
Levys ... SC-3
Levy Sch—school ... LA-4
Levy Sch—school ... NY-2
Levy Slough—stream ... IN-6
Levy Special Education Elem Sch—school ... KS-7
Levys Prairie—swamp ... FL-3
Levy Station ... SC-3
Levyville Cem—cemetery ... FL-3
Lewallen Branch—stream ... MS-4
Lewallen Cem—cemetery ... AL-4
Lewallen Cem—cemetery ... MO-7
Lewallen Cem—cemetery (2) ... TN-4
Lewallen Mtn—summit ... AR-4
**Lewarae**—pop pl ... NC-3
**Leware (Midway)**—pop pl ... NC-3
Lewarks Hill ... NC-3
Lewarton Coulee—valley ... MT-8
**Lewbeach**—pop pl ... NY-2
Lewden, John, House—hist pl ... DE-2
Lewden Green Park—park ... DE-2
Lewellan Engelhardt Dam—dam ... SD-7
**Lewellen**—pop pl ... NE-7
Lewellen Branch—stream ... KY-4
Lewellen Branch—stream ... MO-7
Lewellen Cem—cemetery ... MO-7
Lewellen Creek—stream ... ID-8
Lewellen Graveyard ... MS-4
Lewellen House—hist pl ... NM-5
Lewellen Ranch—locale ... WY-8
Lewellen Sch—school ... MO-7
Lewellien Cem—cemetery ... MS-4
Lewelling, Henderson, House—hist pl ... IA-7
Lewelling Creek—stream ... ID-8
Lewelling Mc Cormick Ditch—canal ... CO-8
Lewelling Sch—school ... CA-9
Lewelling Sch—school ... OR-9
Lewellyn, John T., House—hist pl ... UT-8
Lewellyn Branch—stream ... NC-3
Lewellyn Cove—valley ... NC-3
Lewellyn Creek—stream ... TX-5
Lewellyn Park Township—civil ... SD-7
**Lewer Pewabic**—pop pl ... MI-6
Lewers Brook ... CT-1
Lewers Cem—cemetery ... MS-4
Lewers Chapel Cem—cemetery ... MS-4
Lewers Chapel Ch—church ... MS-4
Lewers Chapel Sch—school ... MS-4
Lewers Creek—stream ... NV-8
**Lewes**—pop pl ... DE-2
Lewes and Rehoboth Canal—canal ... DE-2
Lewes and Rehoboth Hundred—civil ... DE-2
**Lewes Beach**—pop pl ... DE-2
Lewes-Cape May Ferry—locale ... DE-2
Lewes (CCD)—cens area ... DE-2
Lewes Creek ... DE-2
Lewes Creek ... FL-3
Lewes Creek—stream ... DE-2
Lewes Hist Dist—hist pl ... DE-2
Lewes JHS—school ... DE-2
Lewes Naval Facility—military ... DE-2
Lewes Presbyterian Ch—church ... DE-2
Lewes Presbyterian Church—hist pl ... DE-2
Lewes River ... DE-2
Lewes Sound ... DE-2
Lewes Town ... DE-2
Lewetik—civil ... FM-9
Lewetik Peiei—unknown ... FM-9
Lewey Brook ... ME-1
Lewey Cove ... ME-1
Lewey Lake ... ME-1
Lewey Lake—lake ... NY-2
Lewey Mtn—summit ... NY-2
Leweys Lake ... ME-1
Lewey's Ocve ... ME-1
Lew Galbraith Golf Course—other ... CA-9
Lew Hand Meadow—flat ... ID-8
Lewi—civil ... FM-9
Lewi, Dauen—gut ... FM-9
Lewi, Dolen—summit ... FM-9
Lewi, Pilen—stream ... FM-9
Lewin Brook—stream ... MA-1
Lewin Brook Pond—reservoir ... MA-1
Lewin Brook Pond Upper Dam—dam ... MA-1
Lewing Cem—cemetery ... LA-4
Lewing Chapel—church (2) ... LA-4
Lewing Creek—stream ... LA-4
Lewin Hill—summit ... VA-3
Lewin (historical)—locale ... AL-4
Lewin Pond—lake ... VT-1
Lewinsville—locale ... VA-3
**Lewinsville Heights**—pop pl ... VA-3
Lewinsville Sch—school ... VA-3
Lewi River ... FM-9
Lewis ... DE-2
Lewis—locale (2) ... AR-4
Lewis—locale ... FL-3
Lewis—locale ... GA-3
Lewis—locale ... NV-8
Lewis—locale ... OR-9
Lewis—locale ... UT-8
Lewis—park ... WA-9
**Lewis**—pop pl (2) ... AL-4
**Lewis**—pop pl ... CO-8
**Lewis**—pop pl ... IN-6
**Lewis**—pop pl ... IA-7
**Lewis**—pop pl ... KS-7
**Lewis**—pop pl ... KY-4
**Lewis**—pop pl ... MO-7
**Lewis**—pop pl ... NY-2
**Lewis**—pop pl ... NC-3
**Lewis**—pop pl ... SC-3
**Lewis**—pop pl ... WV-2
**Lewis**—pop pl ... WI-6
Lewis—school ... MO-7
Lewis, A. J., House—hist pl ... MS-4
Lewis, Alpheus, House—hist pl ... KY-4
Lewis, Canal (historical)—canal ... AZ-5
Lewis, Charles D., House—hist pl ... MA-1
Lewis, Charles W. Bldg—hist pl ... NM-5
Lewis, Col. Alfred E., House—hist pl ... MS-4
Lewis, Col. James, House—hist pl ... TN-4
Lewis, Deacon Willard, House—hist pl ... MA-1
Lewis, Dr. A. C., House—hist pl ... OH-6
Lewis, Dr. John, House—hist pl ... KY-4
Lewis, Edward Simon, House—hist pl ... DC-2
Lewis, E. H., House—hist pl ... MN-6
Lewis, Evan, House—hist pl ... PA-2
Lewis, Fred, Cottage—hist pl ... ID-8
Lewis, Gov. James T., House—hist pl ... WI-6
Lewis, Inez Johnson, Sch—hist pl ... CO-8
Lewis, Iva, House—hist pl ... MO-7
Lewis, J. A., House—hist pl ... GA-3
Lewis, Jefferson, House—hist pl ... DE-2
Lewis, John L., House—hist pl ... IL-6
Lewis, John W., House—hist pl ... IL-6
Lewis, Joshua, House—hist pl ... MA-1
Lewis, Lake—reservoir ... AL-4
Lewis, Lake—reservoir ... GA-3
Lewis, L'Dora, Mound (22SI512)—hist pl ... MS-4
Lewis, Lloyd, House—hist pl ... IL-6
Lewis, Mount—summit (4) ... CA-9
Lewis, Mount—summit ... MT-8
Lewis, Mount—summit ... NV-8
Lewis, Mount—summit ... NY-2
Lewis, Mount Cass—summit ... AK-9
Lewis, Point—cape ... MI-6
Lewis, Samuel, House—hist pl ... OH-6
Lewis, Sinclair, Boyhood Home—hist pl ... MN-6
Lewis, William, House—hist pl ... TX-5
Lewis, Woodson, House—hist pl ... KY-4
Lewisa, Mount—summit ... WY-8
Lewis Adair Creek ... MI-6
**Lewis Addition**—pop pl ... OH-6
Lewis Airp—airport ... KS-7
Lewis Airp—airport ... MS-4
Lewis and Clark Camp at Slaughter River—hist pl ... MT-8
Lewis and Clark Camp Site-1804 Number Two—locale ... IA-7
Lewis and Clark Cavern State Park—park ... MT-8
Lewis and Clark Center (Shop Ctr)—locale ... MO-7
Lewis and Clark Ch—church ... MO-7
Lewis and Clark Coll—school ... OR-9
Lewis and Clark Community Coll—school ... IL-6
Lewis and Clark Hotel—hist pl ... ND-7
Lewis and Clark HS—school ... MT-8
Lewis and Clark HS—school ... WA-9
Lewis and Clark JHS—school ... OK-5
Lewis And Clark Lake—lake ... MO-7
Lewis And Clark Lake—reservoir ... NE-7
Lewis and Clark Lake—reservoir ... SD-7
Lewis and Clark Memorial Bridge—bridge ... SD-7
Lewis and Clark Memorial Gardens—cemetery ... ID-8
Lewis and Clark Natl For—forest ... MT-8
Lewis and Clark Natl Wildlife Ref—park ... OR-9
Lewis and Clark Park—park ... MT-8
Lewis and Clark Park—park ... WA-9
Lewis and Clark Pass ... ID-8
Lewis and Clark Pass ... MT-8
Lewis and Clark Pass—gap ... MT-8
Lewis and Clark Picnic Area—locale ... MT-8
Lewis and Clark Range—range ... MT-8
Lewis and Clark Rec Area—park ... ND-7
Lewis and Clark River—stream ... OR-9
Lewis and Clark Salt Cairn Historic Monument—other ... OR-9
Lewis and Clark Sch—school ... ID-8
Lewis and Clark Sch—school (2) ... MT-8
Lewis and Clark Sch—school (4) ... ND-7
Lewis and Clark Sch—school ... OR-9
Lewis and Clark Sch—school (2) ... WA-9
Lewis and Clark's Pass ... MT-8
Lewis And Clark State Memorial Park—park ... IL-6
Lewis And Clark State Park—park ... IA-7
Lewis And Clark State Park—park ... MO-7
Lewis and Clark State Park—park ... ND-7
Lewis and Clark State Park—park ... OR-9
Lewis and Clark State Park—park ... WA-9
Lewis And Clark Township—civil ... MO-7
Lewis and Clark Trail—trail ... MT-8
Lewis and Clark Trail—trail ... ND-7
Lewis And Clark Trail—trail ... WY-8
Lewis and Clark Trail Museum—building ... ND-7
Lewis and Clark Trail State Park—park ... WA-9
Lewis and Clark Trail-Travois Road—hist pl ... WA-9
Lewis and Clark Viaduct—canal ... KS-7
**Lewis and Clark Village**—pop pl ... MO-7
Lewis and Killian Lake—reservoir ... LA-4
Lewis and Pranty Creek ... AZ-5
Lewis and Pranty Creek—stream ... AZ-5
Lewis and Pranty Creek Bridge—hist pl ... AZ-5
LEWIS ARK (Houseboat)—hist pl ... CA-9
Lewis Atwood Brook—stream ... CT-1
Lewis Ave Sch—school ... CA-9
Lewis Ave Sch—school ... MT-8
Lewis Bar—bar ... AL-4
Lewis Barker Mine (underground)—mine ... TN-4
Lewis Barn—hist pl ... ID-8
Lewis Bay—bay ... MA-1
Lewis Bayou ... AR-4
Lewis Bayou—gut ... LA-4
Lewis Bayou—stream ... AR-4
Lewis B Bowen Pond ... MA-1
**Lewisberry**—pop pl ... PA-2
Lewisberry Borough—civil ... PA-2
Lewis Bluff—cliff ... FL-3
Lewis Bluff Landing ... AL-4
**Lewisboro**—pop pl ... NY-2
**Lewisboro (Town of)**—pop pl ... NY-2
Lewis Bottoms—bend ... IA-7
Lewis Bottoms Access County Park—park ... IA-7
Lewis Branch ... TN-4
**Lewis Branch**—pop pl ... TN-4
Lewis Branch—stream (4) ... AL-4
Lewis Branch—stream (2) ... FL-3
Lewis Branch—stream ... GA-3
Lewis Branch—stream (2) ... IN-6
Lewis Branch—stream (8) ... KY-4
Lewis Branch—stream ... MS-4
Lewis Branch—stream (4) ... NC-3
Lewis Branch—stream ... OR-9
Lewis Branch—stream (7) ... TN-4
Lewis Branch—stream (2) ... TX-5
Lewis Branch—stream ... VA-3
Lewis Branch Adair Creek—stream ... MI-6
Lewis Branch Ch—church ... TN-4
Lewis Bridge ... TN-4
Lewis Bridge—bridge ... NC-3
Lewis Bridge—bridge ... WA-9
Lewis Bridge—other ... MI-6
Lewis Brook ... CT-1
Lewis Brook—stream ... CT-1
Lewis Brook—stream ... ME-1
Lewis Brook—stream ... NH-1
Lewis Brook—stream ... NJ-2
Lewis Brook—stream (2) ... NY-2
Lewis Brook—stream ... PA-2
Lewis Brook—stream ... VT-1
Lewis Brothers Bldg—hist pl ... AR-4
Lewis Buff—cliff ... AL-4
Lewis Bungalow—hist pl ... ID-8
Lewisburg ... IN-6
Lewisburg—locale ... NJ-2
Lewisburg—locale ... NY-2
Lewisburg—locale ... NC-3
**Lewisburg**—pop pl ... AL-4
**Lewisburg**—pop pl ... AR-4
**Lewisburg**—pop pl ... IL-6
**Lewisburg**—pop pl ... IN-6
**Lewisburg**—pop pl (2) ... KY-4
**Lewisburg**—pop pl (2) ... LA-4
**Lewisburg**—pop pl ... MS-4
**Lewisburg**—pop pl ... OH-6
**Lewisburg**—pop pl ... OR-9
**Lewisburg**—pop pl ... PA-2
**Lewisburg**—pop pl ... TN-4
**Lewisburg**—pop pl ... WV-2
Lewisburg Airp (historical)—airport ... TN-4
Lewisburg Area HS—school ... PA-2
Lewisburg Area MS—school ... PA-2
Lewisburg Ave Hist Dist—hist pl ... TN-4
Lewisburg Borough—civil ... PA-2
Lewisburg Branch—stream ... AR-4
Lewisburg (CCD)—cens area ... KY-4
Lewisburg (CCD)—cens area ... TN-4
Lewisburg Cem—cemetery ... AR-4
Lewisburg Cem—cemetery ... IA-7
Lewisburg Cem—cemetery ... KY-4
Lewisburg City Hall—building ... TN-4
Lewisburg Community Hosp—hospital ... TN-4
Lewisburg Corners—locale ... NY-2
Lewisburg Cumberland Presbyterian Ch—church ... TN-4
Lewisburg Division—civil ... TN-4
Lewisburg First Baptist Ch—church ... TN-4
Lewisburgh ... TN-4
Lewisburgh—locale ... IA-7
Lewisburg Hist Dist—hist pl ... WV-2
**Lewisburg (historical)**—pop pl ... OR-9
Lewisburg HS—school ... KY-4
Lewisburg Industrial Park—locale ... TN-4
Lewisburg JHS—school ... AL-4
Lewisburg (Magisterial District)—fmr MCD ... WV-2
Lewisburg Mine (underground)—mine ... AL-4
Lewisburg Oil and Gas Field—oilfield ... LA-4
Lewisburg Penitentiary ... PA-2
Lewisburg Post Office—building ... TN-4
Lewisburg Post Office (historical)—building ... MS-4
Lewisburg Pumping Station—building ... TN-4
Lewisburg Reservoir Dam—dam ... TN-4
Lewisburg Ridge—ridge ... AR-4
Lewisburg Rsvr—reservoir ... TN-4
Lewisburg United Methodist Homes—building ... PA-2
Lewis Butte—summit ... OR-9
Lewis Butte—summit ... WA-9
Lewis B Wilson Airp—airport ... GA-3
Lewis Camp—locale ... PA-2
Lewis Camp—park ... OR-9
Lewis Campground—locale ... CA-9
Lewis Canal—canal (2) ... NC-3
Lewis Canyon—valley ... AZ-5
Lewis Canyon—valley ... CA-9
Lewis Canyon—valley ... ID-8
Lewis Canyon—valley ... NV-8
Lewis Canyon—valley (4) ... NM-5
Lewis Canyon—valley (2) ... TX-5
Lewis Canyon—valley (3) ... UT-8
Lewis Canyon—valley ... WY-8
Lewis Canyon Campground—park ... AZ-5
Lewis Canyons—area ... CO-8
Lewis-Capehart-Roseberry House—hist pl ... WV-2
Lewis Carroll Elem Sch—school ... FL-3
Lewis Cass Junior-Senior HS—school ... IN-6
Lewis Cass Sch—school ... MI-6
Lewis Cave—cave ... MO-7
Lewis Cem ... AL-4
Lewis Cem—cemetery (3) ... AL-4
Lewis Cem—cemetery (3) ... AR-4
Lewis Cem—cemetery ... CO-8
Lewis Cem—cemetery (3) ... GA-3
Lewis Cem—cemetery (4) ... IL-6
Lewis Cem—cemetery ... IN-6
Lewis Cem—cemetery (2) ... IA-7
Lewis Cem—cemetery ... KS-7
Lewis Cem—cemetery (10) ... KY-4
Lewis Cem—cemetery ... ME-1
Lewis Cem—cemetery ... MI-6
Lewis Cem—cemetery ... MN-6
Lewis Cem—cemetery (6) ... MS-4
Lewis Cem—cemetery (8) ... MO-7
Lewis Cem—cemetery ... NM-5
Lewis Cem—cemetery (4) ... NY-2
Lewis Cem—cemetery (9) ... NC-3
Lewis Cem—cemetery (5) ... OH-6
Lewis Cem—cemetery (2) ... OK-5
Lewis Cem—cemetery (3) ... OR-9
Lewis Cem—cemetery (4) ... PA-2
Lewis Cem—cemetery (12) ... TN-4
Lewis Cem—cemetery (7) ... TX-5
Lewis Cem—cemetery (5) ... VA-3
Lewis Cem—cemetery (2) ... WV-2
Lewis Cem—cemetery (2) ... WI-6
Lewis Cem - in part ... MS-4
**Lewis Center**—pop pl ... OH-6
Lewis Ch—church (2) ... AL-4
Lewis Ch—church ... AR-4
Lewis Ch—church ... LA-4
Lewis Ch—church ... MS-4
Lewis Ch—church ... NC-3
Lewis Ch—church ... VA-3
Lewis Chapel—church (2) ... AL-4
Lewis Chapel—church ... KY-4
Lewis Chapel—church ... LA-4
Lewis Chapel—church ... MS-4
Lewis Chapel—church ... NC-3
Lewis Chapel—church (3) ... TN-4
Lewis Chapel—church (3) ... TX-5
Lewis Chapel—locale ... TN-4
Lewis Chapel Baptist Ch ... AL-4
Lewis Chapel Cem—cemetery ... MS-4
Lewis Chapel Ch ... AL-4
Lewis Chapel (historical)—church ... TN-4
Lewis Chapel Sch—school ... NC-3
Lewis Chapel Sch—school ... TN-4
Lewis Chapel Sch (historical)—school ... MS-4
Lewis Ch (historical)—church ... PA-2
Lewis-Clark Canoe Camp State Park—park ... ID-8
Lewis & Clark Cem—cemetery ... OR-9
Lewis Clark Sch—school ... NE-7
Lewis-Clark State Coll—school ... ID-8
Lewis Coll—school ... IL-6
Lewis Community Hospital ... TN-4
Lewis Corner—locale ... GA-3
Lewis Corner—locale ... IL-6
Lewis Corner—locale ... MD-2
Lewis Corner—locale ... PA-2
Lewis Corners—locale ... NY-2
**Lewis Corners**—pop pl ... NY-2
**Lewis Corners**—pop pl ... PA-2
Lewis Coulee—valley ... MT-8
**Lewis (County)**—pop pl ... KY-4
**Lewis County**—pop pl ... MO-7
**Lewis (County)**—pop pl ... NY-2
**Lewis County**—pop pl ... TN-4
**Lewis County**—pop pl ... WA-9
**Lewis (County)**—pop pl ... WV-2
Lewis County Courthouse—building ... TN-4
Lewis County Elem Sch—school ... TN-4
Lewis County Hosp—hospital ... TN-4
Lewis County HS—school ... TN-4
Lewis County Infirmary—hospital ... KY-4
Lewis County Library—building ... TN-4
Lewis County MS—school ... TN-4
Lewis County Nursing Home—building ... TN-4
Lewis Cove—bay (2) ... ME-1
Lewis Cove—cove ... MA-1
Lewis Cove—valley ... NC-3
Lewis Creek ... AL-4
Lewis Creek ... CA-9
Lewis Creek ... DE-2
Lewis Creek ... NV-8
Lewis Creek ... UT-8
Lewis Creek ... WA-9
Lewis Creek—bay ... MD-2
Lewis Creek—bay ... NC-3
Lewis Creek—channel ... FL-3
Lewis Creek—gut ... NC-3
Lewis Creek—locale ... KY-4
**Lewis Creek**—pop pl ... IN-6
Lewis Creek—stream (3) ... AL-4
Lewis Creek—stream ... AZ-5
Lewis Creek—stream (2) ... AR-4
Lewis Creek—stream (8) ... CA-9
Lewis Creek—stream (5) ... CO-8
Lewis Creek—stream (2) ... GA-3
Lewis Creek—stream (4) ... ID-8
Lewis Creek—stream (2) ... IL-6
Lewis Creek—stream (2) ... IN-6
Lewis Creek—stream (5) ... KY-4
Lewis Creek—stream (2) ... LA-4
Lewis Creek—stream (2) ... MS-4
Lewis Creek—stream (2) ... MO-7
Lewis Creek—stream (5) ... MT-8
Lewis Creek—stream ... NV-8
Lewis Creek—stream ... NY-2
Lewis Creek—stream (6) ... NC-3
Lewis Creek—stream ... OK-5
Lewis Creek—stream (9) ... OR-9
Lewis Creek—stream (2) ... PA-2
Lewis Creek—stream ... SD-7
Lewis Creek—stream (4) ... TN-4
Lewis Creek—stream (7) ... TX-5
Lewis Creek—stream ... VT-1
Lewis Creek—stream (3) ... VA-3
Lewis Creek—stream (3) ... WA-9
Lewis Creek—stream ... WY-8
Lewis Creek Ch—church ... IN-6
Lewis Creek County Park—park ... OR-9
Lewis Creek Drainage Ditch—canal ... TN-4
Lewis Creek Rsvr—reservoir ... TX-5
Lewis Creek Sch—school (2) ... KY-4
Lewis Creek Tributary Lake Site 60-11 Dam—dam ... TN-4
Lewis Creek Tributary Lake 60-11—reservoir ... TN-4
Lewis Crossing—locale ... PA-2
Lewis Cross Roads ... DE-2
Lewis Crossroads—locale ... NC-3
**Lewis Cross Roads**—pop pl ... SC-3
Lewis Cut—gut ... FL-3
**Lewisdale**—pop pl ... KY-4
**Lewisdale**—pop pl (2) ... MD-2
Lewisdale Sch—school ... MD-2
Lewis Dam—dam ... AL-4
Lewis Dam—dam ... PA-2
Lewis Dam—dam ... SD-7
Lewis Dam—dam ... TN-4
Lewis Ditch—canal ... CA-9
Lewis Ditch—canal ... MI-6
Lewis Ditch—canal ... MT-8
Lewis Ditch—canal ... OR-9
Lewis Ditch—canal ... WY-8
Lewis Ditch—gut ... DE-2
Lewis Drain—canal (2) ... MI-6
Lewis Drain—stream ... MI-6
Lewis Draw—valley ... TX-5
Lewis Draw—valley (3) ... WY-8
Lewis Draw No 2—valley ... WY-8
Lewis Draw No 3—valley ... WY-8
Lewis Draw No 4—valley ... WY-8
Lewis Draw No 5—valley ... WY-8
Lewis Draw No 6—valley ... WY-8
Lewis Elem Sch—school ... FL-3
Lewis Elem Sch—school ... NC-3
**Lewis Estates Subdivision**—pop pl ... UT-8
**Lewis Estates (subdivision)**—pop pl ... UT-8
**Lewisetta**—pop pl ... VA-3
Lewisette ... VA-3
Lewis Eure Lake Dam—dam ... MS-4
**Lewis Evans Subdivision (subdivision)**—pop pl ... AL-4
Lewis Falls ... ME-1
Lewis Falls—falls ... PA-2
Lewis Falls—falls (2) ... WY-8
Lewis Family Tenant Agricultural Complex—hist pl ... DE-2
Lewis Farm—hist pl ... VA-3
Lewis Farm Cem—cemetery ... OH-6
Lewis Farmhouse—hist pl ... WI-6
Lewis Ferry (historical)—locale ... AL-4
Lewisfield Plantation—hist pl ... SC-3
Lewis Flat—flat (3) ... CA-9
Lewis Flat—flat ... WY-8
Lewis Flats—flat ... NM-5
Lewis Flats Ch—church ... NM-5
Lewis Flats Sch—school ... NM-5
Lewis Ford (historical)—locale ... MO-7
Lewis Fork ... ID-8
Lewis Fork ... NC-3
Lewis Fork ... OR-9
Lewis Fork ... WA-9
Lewis Fork ... WY-8
Lewis Fork—stream ... CA-9
Lewis Fork—stream (2) ... KY-4
Lewis Fork—stream ... NC-3
Lewis Fork—stream (2) ... VA-3
Lewis Fork—stream ... WV-2
Lewis Fork Ch—church ... KY-4
Lewis Fork Ch—church ... NC-3
Lewis Fork Creek ... NC-3
Lewis Fork Overlook—locale ... NC-3
Lewis Fork (Township of)—fmr MCD ... NC-3
Lewis Gale Hosp—hospital ... VA-3
Lewis Gap—gap ... NC-3
Lewis Gap—gap ... TN-4
**Lewis Gardens**—pop pl ... VA-3
Lewis Glacier—glacier ... OR-9
Lewis Glacier—glacier ... WA-9
Lewis Glacier Hotel—hist pl ... MT-8
Lewis Gulch—valley ... AK-9
Lewis Gulch—valley (3) ... CA-9
Lewis Gulch—valley ... CO-8
Lewis Gulch—valley ... MT-8
Lewis Gully—valley ... TX-5
Lewis Gut—gut ... CT-1
Lewis Gut—stream ... NC-3
**Lewis Heights**—pop pl ... MD-2
Lewis Hill—ridge ... CA-9
Lewis Hill—summit ... CT-1
Lewis Hill—summit ... KY-4
Lewis Hill—summit ... ME-1
Lewis Hill—summit ... MA-1
Lewis Hill—summit ... MO-7
Lewis Hill—summit ... NH-1
Lewis Hill—summit ... SD-7
Lewis Hill—summit ... TX-5
Lewis Hill Cem—cemetery ... PA-2
Lewis (historical)—locale ... AL-4
Lewis (historical)—locale ... KS-7
Lewis Hollow ... MO-7
Lewis Hollow—valley (2) ... AL-4
Lewis Hollow—valley (2) ... AR-4
Lewis Hollow—valley ... KY-4
Lewis Hollow—valley ... MS-4
Lewis Hollow—valley (6) ... MO-7
Lewis Hollow—valley (2) ... NY-2
Lewis Hollow—valley ... PA-2
Lewis Hollow—valley (4) ... TN-4
Lewis Hollow—valley ... UT-8
Lewis Hollow—valley ... VA-3

*L'Homme Dieu Shoal* ... MA-1
L'Hommedieu Shoal—*bar* ... MA-1
L'Homme Pond—*bay* ... LA-4
L Horseshoe Lake—*lake* ... WI-6
L Hoyt Ranch—*locale* ... NE-7
L H Ranch—*locale* ... NM-5
*L H Williams Cemetery* ... MS-4
Liahona Camp—*locale* ... CA-9
L I and M Canal—*canal* ... LA-4
Liano Windmill—*locale* ... TX-5
Liar Lake—*lake* ... GA-3
*Liar Mountain* ... MA-1
Liar Rocks—*area* ... AK-9
Liars Corner—*locale* ... OH-6
Liars Lake—*reservoir* ... AL-4
*Liars Lake Dam* ... AL-4
Liars Peak—*summit* ... ID-8
Liars Prairie—*flat* ... WA-9
Lias Creek—*stream* ... AL-4
Lib—*island* ... MP-9
*Liball Island* ... FM-9
Libanon Hill—*locale* ... VI-3
Libbey—*locale* ... OK-5
Libbey, Edward D., House—*hist pl* ... OH-6
Libbey Glacier—*glacier* ... AK-9
*Libbey Islands* ... ME-1
Libbie Edward Sch—*school* ... UT-8
Libbs Canyon—*valley* ... UT-8
Libbs Lake—*lake* ... MN-6
Libbs Park—*park* ... NE-7
Libbs Spring—*spring* ... UT-8
Libb Wallace Ranch—*locale* ... TX-5
**Libby**—*pop pl* ... KY-4
**Libby**—*pop pl* ... MN-6
**Libby**—*pop pl* ... MT-8
**Libby**—*pop pl* ... OR-9
**Libby**—*pop pl* ... TX-5
Libby, Charles, House—*hist pl* ... CA-9
Libby Arm—*bay* ... OR-9
Libby Army Airfield/Sierra Vista Muncipal Airp—*airport* ... AZ-5
Libby Bluff—*cliff* ... AR-4
Libby Bog—*swamp* ... ME-1
Libby Branch—*stream* ... MN-6
Libby Brook—*stream* (9) ... ME-1
Libby Camp—*locale* (2) ... ME-1
Libby Cem—*cemetery* (5) ... ME-1
Libby Ch—*church* ... TX-5
Libby Corner—*locale* ... ME-1
Libby Cove—*bay* ... ME-1
Libby Cove—*bay* ... MO-7
*Libby Creek* ... OR-9
Libby Creek—*stream* ... AK-9
Libby Creek—*stream* ... ME-1
Libby Creek—*stream* (2) ... MT-8
Libby Creek—*stream* ... OR-9
Libby Creek—*stream* ... WA-9
Libby Creek—*stream* ... WI-6
Libby Creek—*stream* (2) ... WY-8
Libby Creek Campground—*locale* ... MT-8
Libby Creek Picnic Ground—*locale* ... WY-8
Libby Divide Trail—*trail* ... MT-8
Libby Field—*locale* ... MA-1
Libby Fisheries Station—*other* ... MT-8
Libby Flats—*flat* ... WY-8
Libby Head—*summit* ... ME-1
Libby Heights—*uninc pl* ... FL-3
*Libby Hill* ... ME-1
**Libby Hill**—*pop pl* ... ME-1
Libby Hill—*summit* (5) ... ME-1
Libby Hill—*summit* ... VT-1
Libby-Hill Block—*hist pl* ... ME-1
Libby Hills—*spring* ... MT-8
Libby Hollow—*valley* ... MO-7
Libby HS—*school* ... MT-8
Libby HS—*school* ... OH-6
Libby Island—*island* ... AK-9
Libby Island—*island* ... ME-1
Libby Island Light Station—*hist pl* ... ME-1
Libby Islands—*island* ... ME-1
Libby JHS—*school* ... WA-9
*Libby Lake* ... MT-8
Libby Lake—*lake* (2) ... MN-6
Libby Lake—*lake* ... WA-9
Libby Lake—*lake* ... WY-8
Libby Lakes—*lake* ... MT-8
Libby Lodge—*hist pl* ... WY-8
Libby-MacArthur House—*hist pl* ... ME-1
Libby McNeil and Libby Fruit and Vegetable Cannery—*hist pl* ... CA-9
Libby Mine—*mine* ... OR-9
Libby Mtn—*summit* ... ME-1
Libby Mtn—*summit* ... NH-1
Libby Pinnacle—*summit* ... ME-1
Libby Pit—*locale* ... ME-1
Libby Point—*cape* ... ME-1
Libby Point—*cape* ... NY-2
Libby Point—*cape* ... WI-6
Libby Point Light—*locale* ... WA-9
Libby River—*stream* ... AK-9
Libby River—*stream* ... ME-1
Libby Run—*stream* ... PA-2
Libby Sch—*school* ... CA-9
Libby Sch—*school* ... IL-6
Libby Sch—*school* ... ME-1
Libbyshears—*bar* ... ME-1
**Libbys Pit**—*pop pl* ... ME-1
Libbys Point—*cape* ... ME-1
Libby Spring—*spring* ... NM-5
Libby Terrace Park—*park* ... VA-3
**Libbytown**—*pop pl* ... ME-1
**Libby (Township of)**—*pop pl* ... MN-6
Libby-Tozier Sch—*school* ... ME-1
Libby Trail—*trail* ... PA-2
*Libbyville* (2) ... HI-9
Libbyville—*locale* ... AK-9
*Libby-Waipio* ... HI-9
Lib Corners—*locale* ... NY-2
Lib (County-equivalent)—*civil* ... MP-9
Lib Cross Island—*island* ... WI-6
*Libeij-en'* ... MP-9
**Liber**—*pop pl* ... IN-6
**Liberal**—*pop pl* ... IN-6
**Liberal**—*pop pl* ... KS-7
**Liberal**—*pop pl* ... MO-7
**Liberal**—*pop pl* ... OR-9
Liberal Cem—*cemetery* ... MO-7
Liberal Creek—*stream* ... ID-8
Liberal HS—*school* ... KS-7
Liberality Ch—*church* ... TN-4
Liberality Sch (historical)—*school* ... TN-4
Liberal Memorial Cem—*cemetery* ... KS-7
Liberal Mtn—*summit* ... ID-8
Liberal Municipal Airp—*airport* ... KS-7
Liberal Township—*fmr MCD* ... IA-7
**Liberal Township**—*pop pl* ... KS-7
Liberal Trinity Ch of God in Christ—*church* ... MS-4
Liberal Union Hall—*hist pl* ... MN-6
Liberator Creek—*stream* ... AK-9
Liberator Lake—*lake* ... AK-9
Liberator Ridge—*ridge* ... AK-9
Liber Cem—*cemetery* ... IN-6
Liberia—*hist pl* ... VA-3
**Liberia**—*pop pl* ... NC-3
Liberia Ch—*church* ... MD-2
Liberia Park—*park* ... TX-5
Liberia Woods—*uninc pl* ... VA-3
*Liberon* ... MP-9
Libertad Windmill—*locale* ... TX-5
*Liberty* ... AL-4
*Liberty* ... IL-6
*Liberty* ... OH-6
*Liberty* ... TX-5
Liberty—*fmr MCD* (4) ... NE-7
Liberty—*locale* ... AL-4
Liberty—*locale* ... AK-9
Liberty—*locale* (5) ... AR-4
Liberty—*locale* ... CA-9
Liberty—*locale* (3) ... CO-8
Liberty—*locale* ... DE-2
Liberty—*locale* (2) ... FL-3
Liberty—*locale* ... GA-3
Liberty—*locale* ... ID-8
Liberty—*locale* (2) ... KY-4
Liberty—*locale* ... LA-4
Liberty—*locale* ... MS-4
Liberty—*locale* ... MO-7
Liberty—*locale* (2) ... OK-5
Liberty—*locale* ... PA-2
Liberty—*locale* ... RI-1
Liberty—*locale* (6) ... TN-4
Liberty—*locale* (7) ... TX-5
Liberty—*locale* (4) ... VA-3
Liberty—*locale* ... WA-9
Liberty—*locale* ... WI-6
Liberty—*other* ... IL-6
Liberty—*other* ... TX-5
**Liberty**—*pop pl* (5) ... AL-4
**Liberty**—*pop pl* ... AZ-5
**Liberty**—*pop pl* ... ID-8
**Liberty**—*pop pl* (2) ... IL-6
**Liberty**—*pop pl* ... IN-6
**Liberty**—*pop pl* ... IA-7
**Liberty**—*pop pl* ... KS-7
**Liberty**—*pop pl* (3) ... KY-4
**Liberty**—*pop pl* ... ME-1
**Liberty**—*pop pl* ... MI-6
**Liberty**—*pop pl* (4) ... MS-4
**Liberty**—*pop pl* (2) ... MO-7
**Liberty**—*pop pl* ... NE-7
**Liberty**—*pop pl* ... NY-2
**Liberty**—*pop pl* (3) ... NC-3
**Liberty**—*pop pl* ... OH-6
**Liberty**—*pop pl* (3) ... OK-5
**Liberty**—*pop pl* (2) ... OR-9
**Liberty**—*pop pl* (3) ... PA-2
**Liberty**—*pop pl* ... SC-3
**Liberty**—*pop pl* (10) ... TN-4
**Liberty**—*pop pl* (3) ... TX-5
**Liberty**—*pop pl* ... UT-8
**Liberty**—*pop pl* ... WA-9
**Liberty**—*pop pl* (2) ... WV-2
Liberty—*post sta* ... MI-6
Liberty, Lake—*reservoir* ... TX-5
Liberty, Mount—*summit* ... NH-1
Liberty Acad (historical)—*school* ... TN-4
**Liberty Acres**—*pop pl* ... CA-9
**Liberty Acres**—*pop pl* ... IL-6
**Liberty Acres Subdivision**—*pop pl* ... UT-8
Liberty Airp—*airport* ... MO-7
Liberty All Ch—*church* ... TN-4
Liberty Apostolic Pentecostsal Ch—*church* ... TN-4
*Liberty Baptist Ch* ... AL-4
*Liberty Baptist Ch* ... MS-4
*Liberty Baptist Ch* ... TN-4
Liberty Baptist Ch—*church* ... AL-4
Liberty Baptist Ch—*church* (4) ... FL-3
Liberty Baptist Ch—*church* (4) ... MS-4
Liberty Baptist Ch—*church* ... TN-4
Liberty Baptist Ch (historical)—*church* ... MS-4
Liberty Baptist Christian Sch—*school* ... FL-3
Liberty Baptist Church—*hist pl* ... IN-6
Liberty Baptist Church—*hist pl* ... ND-7
Liberty Bay—*bay* ... WA-9
Liberty Bayou—*stream* ... LA-4
**Liberty Bell**—*pop pl* ... CO-8
Liberty Bell Cem—*cemetery* ... OK-5
*Liberty Bell Ch* ... AL-4
Liberty Bell Ch—*church* ... GA-3
Liberty Bell Community Center—*locale* ... AR-4
Liberty Bell Complex—*locale* ... TN-4
Liberty Bell Elem Sch—*school* ... PA-2
Liberty Bell Flats—*flat* ... CO-8
*Liberty Bell Junior High School* ... TN-4
*Liberty Bell Mine* ... SD-7
Liberty Bell Mine—*mine* ... AK-9
Liberty Bell Mine—*mine* ... CO-8
Liberty Bell Mine—*mine* ... NM-5
Liberty Bell Mtn—*summit* ... WA-9
Liberty Bell No 2 Mine—*mine* ... CO-8
Liberty Bell Park—*park* ... PA-2
Liberty Bell Pavilion—*building* ... PA-2
**Liberty Bell Ranchettes Subdivision**—*pop pl* ... UT-8
Liberty Bell Sch—*school* (2) ... WI-6
Liberty Bell Sch (abandoned)—*school* ... MO-7
*Liberty Bell School* ... PA-2
**Liberty Bell Village**—*pop pl* ... CO-8
Liberty Bend Bridge—*other* ... MO-7
Liberty Bible Ch—*church* ... AL-4
Liberty Bible Ch—*church* ... VA-3
Liberty Bible Fellowship Ch—*church* ... AL-4
Liberty Bldg—*hist pl* ... OR-9
Liberty Blvd Sch—*school* ... CA-9
Liberty Borough—*civil* (2) ... PA-2
Liberty Bottom—*bend* ... OR-9
Libertybowl Branch—*stream* ... WV-2
Liberty Branch—*stream* ... IN-6
Liberty Branch—*stream* ... MS-4
Liberty Branch—*stream* (4) ... TN-4
Liberty Branch—*stream* ... VA-3
Liberty Bridge—*bridge* ... PA-2
Liberty Bridge—*hist pl* ... PA-2
Liberty Butte—*summit* (2) ... ID-8
*Liberty Canal* ... LA-4
Liberty Canyon—*valley* ... CA-9
Liberty Canyon—*valley* ... WA-9
*Liberty Cap* ... ME-1
Liberty Cap—*pillar* ... CO-8
Liberty Cap—*summit* ... CA-9
Liberty Cap—*summit* (2) ... WA-9
Liberty Cap Trail—*trail* ... CO-8
Liberty Castle—*cliff* ... UT-8
Liberty (CCD)—*cens area* ... KY-4
Liberty (CCD)—*cens area* ... SC-3
*Liberty Cem* ... AL-4
*Liberty Cem* ... MS-4
Liberty Cem—*cemetery* (19) ... AL-4
Liberty Cem—*cemetery* ... AZ-5
Liberty Cem—*cemetery* (18) ... AR-4
Liberty Cem—*cemetery* (2) ... CA-9
Liberty Cem—*cemetery* (2) ... CO-8
Liberty Cem—*cemetery* (2) ... GA-3
Liberty Cem—*cemetery* ... ID-8
Liberty Cem—*cemetery* (10) ... IL-6
Liberty Cem—*cemetery* (4) ... IN-6
Liberty Cem—*cemetery* (9) ... IA-7
Liberty Cem—*cemetery* (4) ... KS-7
Liberty Cem—*cemetery* (8) ... KY-4
Liberty Cem—*cemetery* ... LA-4
Liberty Cem—*cemetery* (2) ... MI-6
Liberty Cem—*cemetery* (18) ... MS-4
Liberty Cem—*cemetery* (13) ... MO-7
Liberty Cem—*cemetery* (3) ... NE-7
Liberty Cem—*cemetery* ... NY-2
Liberty Cem—*cemetery* (2) ... NC-3
Liberty Cem—*cemetery* (2) ... ND-7
Liberty Cem—*cemetery* (3) ... OH-6
Liberty Cem—*cemetery* (7) ... OK-5
Liberty Cem—*cemetery* ... OR-9
Liberty Cem—*cemetery* (19) ... TN-4
Liberty Cem—*cemetery* (16) ... TX-5
Liberty Cem—*cemetery* ... UT-8
Liberty Cem—*cemetery* (3) ... VA-3
Liberty Cem—*cemetery* ... WV-2
Liberty Cem—*cemetery* (2) ... WI-6
*Liberty Cemetery* ... KS-7
**Liberty Center**—*pop pl* ... IN-6
**Liberty Center**—*pop pl* ... IA-7
**Liberty Center**—*pop pl* ... OH-6
Liberty Center Cem—*cemetery* ... AR-4
Liberty Center Cem—*cemetery* ... IA-7
Liberty Center Ch—*church* ... OK-5
*Liberty Center High School* ... IN-6
Liberty Center Sch—*school* (2) ... IA-7
*Liberty Ch* ... AL-4
*Liberty Ch* ... MO-7
*Liberty Ch* ... TN-4
Liberty Ch—*church* (64) ... AL-4
Liberty Ch—*church* (20) ... AR-4
Liberty Ch—*church* (2) ... FL-3
Liberty Ch—*church* (32) ... GA-3
Liberty Ch—*church* (13) ... IL-6
Liberty Ch—*church* (17) ... IN-6
Liberty Ch—*church* ... IA-7
Liberty Ch—*church* (26) ... KY-4
Liberty Ch—*church* (6) ... LA-4
Liberty Ch—*church* ... MI-6
Liberty Ch—*church* (25) ... MS-4
Liberty Ch—*church* (21) ... MO-7
Liberty Ch—*church* (22) ... NC-3
Liberty Ch—*church* (8) ... OH-6
Liberty Ch—*church* (5) ... OK-5
Liberty Ch—*church* (3) ... PA-2
Liberty Ch—*church* (7) ... SC-3
Liberty Ch—*church* (37) ... TN-4
Liberty Ch—*church* (15) ... TX-5
Liberty Ch—*church* (24) ... VA-3
Liberty Ch—*church* (9) ... WV-2
Liberty Ch (abandoned)—*church* (2) ... MO-7
Liberty Chapel—*church* (2) ... GA-3
Liberty Chapel—*church* (4) ... IN-6
Liberty Chapel—*church* ... LA-4
Liberty Chapel—*church* ... MS-4
Liberty Chapel—*church* ... NE-7
Liberty Chapel—*church* (11) ... OH-6
Liberty Chapel—*church* ... TN-4
Liberty Chapel—*church* (2) ... TX-5
Liberty Chapel—*church* ... VA-3
**Liberty Chapel**—*pop pl* ... MS-4
*Liberty Chapel Cem* ... MS-4
Liberty Chapel Cem—*cemetery* ... MS-4
Liberty Chapel Cem—*cemetery* ... TX-5
*Liberty Chapel Methodist Episcopal Church* ... MS-4
Liberty Chapel Public Sch (historical)—*school* ... MS-4
Liberty Chapel Sch—*school* ... TX-5
Liberty Ch (historical)—*church* (5) ... AL-4
Liberty Ch (historical)—*church* (2) ... MS-4
Liberty Ch (historical)—*church* ... MO-7
Liberty Ch (historical)—*church* (3) ... TN-4
*Liberty Ch of Christ* ... AL-4
*Liberty Ch of Christ* ... MS-4
Liberty Ch of Christ (historical)—*church* ... TN-4
Liberty Ch of Mer—*church* ... MS-4
*Liberty Ch of the Brethern* ... TN-4
*Liberty Christian Church* ... MS-4
Liberty Church—*locale* ... AR-4
Liberty Church Cem—*cemetery* ... NC-3
Liberty Church (historical)—*locale* (2) ... MO-7
Liberty Church Spring—*spring* ... AL-4
**Liberty City**—*pop pl* ... AL-4
**Liberty City**—*pop pl* ... GA-3
**Liberty City**—*pop pl* ... TX-5
Liberty City Sch—*school* ... FL-3
Liberty Colored Sch (historical)—*school* ... TN-4
Liberty Commons—*locale* ... MO-7
Liberty Community Center—*locale* ... CO-8
Liberty Community Hall—*locale* ... MO-7
Liberty Community Hall—*locale* ... TN-4
Liberty Community Hall—*locale* ... TX-5
*Liberty Congregational Methodist Church* ... AL-4
Liberty Consolidated Sch (historical)—*school* ... MS-4
*Liberty Coosa Church* ... AL-4
Liberty Corner—*locale* ... ME-1
**Liberty Corner**—*pop pl* ... NJ-2
*Liberty Corners* ... NJ-2
Liberty Corners—*locale* (2) ... NY-2
Liberty Corners—*locale* ... PA-2
**Liberty Corners**—*pop pl* ... IN-6
**Liberty Corners**—*pop pl* ... MI-6
**Liberty Corners**—*pop pl* ... WI-6
**Liberty County**—*pop pl* ... FL-3
**Liberty (County)**—*pop pl* ... GA-3
**Liberty (County)**—*pop pl* ... TX-5
Liberty County Courthouse—*hist pl* ... GA-3
Liberty County HS—*school* ... GA-3
*Liberty Creek* ... ID-8
Liberty Creek—*stream* ... AL-4
Liberty Creek—*stream* (2) ... AK-9
Liberty Creek—*stream* ... AR-4
Liberty Creek—*stream* ... GA-3
Liberty Creek—*stream* (3) ... ID-8
Liberty Creek—*stream* ... IL-6
Liberty Creek—*stream* ... KS-7
Liberty Creek—*stream* ... KY-4
Liberty Creek—*stream* (2) ... LA-4
Liberty Creek—*stream* ... MT-8
Liberty Creek—*stream* ... NE-7
Liberty Creek—*stream* ... TN-4
Liberty Creek—*stream* (2) ... TX-5
Liberty Creek—*stream* ... VA-3
Liberty Creek—*stream* ... WA-9
Liberty Creek—*stream* ... WI-6
Liberty Creek Cem—*cemetery* ... NE-7
Liberty Crossroads—*locale* ... AL-4
Liberty Cumberland Ch—*church* ... GA-3
Liberty-Cumberland Ch—*church* ... KY-4
Liberty Cumberland Presbyterian Ch (historical)—*church* ... MS-4
*Liberty Cumberland Presbyterian Church* ... TN-4
Liberty-Curtin Sch—*school* ... PA-2
Liberty Cut—*canal* ... CA-9
Liberty Dam—*dam* ... MD-2
Liberty-Dayton (CCD)—*cens area* ... TX-5
Liberty Ditch—*canal* ... CA-9
Liberty Drain Sch—*school* ... NC-3
Liberty Eagle Sch (abandoned)—*school* ... MO-7
Liberty East Ch—*church* ... AL-4
Liberty Elem Sch—*school* ... AZ-5
Liberty Elem Sch—*school* (3) ... IN-6
Liberty Elem Sch—*school* ... KS-7
Liberty Elem Sch—*school* ... MS-4
Liberty Elem Sch—*school* ... NC-3
Liberty Elem Sch—*school* ... PA-2
Liberty Elem Sch—*school* ... TN-4
Liberty Falls—*falls* ... AK-9
Liberty Farm—*hist pl* ... MA-1
Liberty Farm—*locale* ... CA-9
Liberty Farms—*locale* ... CA-9
Liberty Farms East Canal—*canal* ... CA-9
Liberty Farms South Canal—*canal* ... CA-9
Liberty Fire Company No. 5—*hist pl* ... PA-2
Liberty Fork—*locale* ... VA-3
Liberty Fork O'Brien Creek—*stream* ... AK-9
*Liberty Freewill Baptist Ch* ... AL-4
Liberty Freewill Baptist Ch—*church* ... TN-4
Liberty Furnace—*locale* ... VA-3
Liberty Gap—*gap* ... TN-4
Liberty Gap—*gap* ... WV-2
Liberty Gap Glacier—*glacier* ... WA-9
**Liberty Gardens**—*pop pl* ... NY-2
Liberty Gem Mine—*mine* ... ID-8
Liberty Grace Ch—*church* ... AL-4
Liberty Grange—*locale* ... OR-9
Liberty Grove—*locale* ... TN-4
Liberty Grove—*locale* (2) ... TX-5
**Liberty Grove**—*pop pl* ... AL-4
**Liberty Grove**—*pop pl* ... MD-2
*Liberty Grove Baptist Church* ... AL-4
*Liberty Grove Baptist Church* ... TN-4
Liberty Grove Cem—*cemetery* ... AL-4
Liberty Grove Cem—*cemetery* ... MS-4
Liberty Grove Cem—*cemetery* ... TN-4
Liberty Grove Cem—*cemetery* ... TX-5
Liberty Grove Cem—*cemetery* ... WI-6
*Liberty Grove Ch* ... AL-4
Liberty Grove Ch—*church* (3) ... AL-4
Liberty Grove Ch—*church* (2) ... GA-3
Liberty Grove Ch—*church* ... KY-4
Liberty Grove Ch—*church* ... LA-4
Liberty Grove Ch—*church* (2) ... MS-4
Liberty Grove Ch—*church* (5) ... NC-3
Liberty Grove Ch—*church* (2) ... TN-4
Liberty Grove Sch—*school* (2) ... TN-4
Liberty Grove Sch (abandoned)—*school* ... MO-7
**Liberty Grove (Town of)**—*pop pl* ... WI-6
**Liberty Grove Township**—*pop pl* ... ND-7
Liberty Guard Station—*locale* ... WA-9
Liberty Guinn Sch—*school* ... GA-3
Liberty Gulch—*valley* (2) ... CA-9
Liberty Gulch—*valley* (2) ... ID-8
*Liberty Hall* ... PA-2
Liberty Hall—*airport* ... NJ-2
Liberty Hall—*hist pl* ... AL-4
Liberty Hall—*hist pl* (2) ... GA-3
Liberty Hall—*hist pl* ... IA-7
Liberty Hall—*hist pl* ... KY-4
Liberty Hall—*hist pl* ... ME-1
Liberty Hall—*hist pl* ... MD-2
Liberty Hall—*hist pl* ... MA-1
Liberty Hall—*hist pl* ... NJ-2
Liberty Hall—*hist pl* ... NC-3
Liberty Hall—*hist pl* ... PA-2
Liberty Hall—*locale* ... AR-4
Liberty Hall—*locale* ... MO-7
Liberty Hall—*locale* ... PA-2
Liberty Hall—*locale* ... VA-3
**Liberty Hall**—*pop pl* ... TN-4
Liberty Hall Cem—*cemetery* ... VA-3
*Liberty Hall Church* ... TN-4
Liberty Hall Sch—*school* ... MO-7
Liberty Hall Sch—*school* ... PA-2
Liberty Hall Sch—*school* ... VA-3
Liberty Hall Sch (abandoned)—*school* ... MO-7
Liberty Hall Sch (historical)—*school* ... AL-4
Liberty Hall Site—*hist pl* ... VA-3
Liberty Harbor—*bay* ... NJ-2
**Liberty Heights**—*pop pl* ... KY-4
**Liberty Heights (subdivision)**—*pop pl* ... MA-1
**Liberty Heights (subdivision)**—*pop pl* ... TN-4
**Liberty Highlands**—*pop pl* ... AL-4
*Liberty High School* ... MS-4
*Liberty Hill* ... MA-1
*Libertyhill* ... TN-4
Liberty Hill—*hist pl* ... GA-3
Liberty Hill—*locale* (2) ... AL-4
Liberty Hill—*locale* (2) ... GA-3
Liberty Hill—*locale* ... SC-3
Liberty Hill—*locale* (7) ... TN-4
Liberty Hill—*locale* (3) ... TX-5
Liberty Hill—*locale* ... VA-3
Liberty Hill—*locale* ... WV-2
**Liberty Hill**—*pop pl* (3) ... AL-4
**Liberty Hill**—*pop pl* ... CT-1
**Libertyhill**—*pop pl* ... GA-3
**Liberty Hill**—*pop pl* ... LA-4
**Liberty Hill**—*pop pl* ... NC-3
**Liberty Hill**—*pop pl* ... SC-3
**Liberty Hill**—*pop pl* (3) ... TN-4
**Liberty Hill**—*pop pl* (2) ... TX-5
Liberty Hill—*summit* ... AL-4
Liberty Hill—*summit* ... AR-4
Liberty Hill—*summit* ... CA-9
Liberty Hill—*summit* ... MA-1
Liberty Hill—*summit* ... MS-4
Liberty Hill—*summit* ... NH-1
Liberty Hill—*summit* ... TX-5
Liberty Hill—*summit* ... VT-1
Liberty Hill—*uninc pl* ... SC-3
*Liberty Hill Baptist Ch* ... AL-4
*Liberty Hill Baptist Ch* ... TN-4
Liberty Hill Baptist Ch—*church* (2) ... AL-4
Liberty Hill Baptist Ch—*church* (2) ... TN-4
*Liberty Hill Baptist Church* ... MS-4
Liberty Hill-Cedar Park (CCD)—*cens area* ... TX-5
Liberty Hill Cem—*cemetery* (8) ... AL-4
Liberty Hill Cem—*cemetery* ... AR-4
Liberty Hill Cem—*cemetery* ... CT-1
Liberty Hill Cem—*cemetery* (3) ... GA-3
Liberty Hill Cem—*cemetery* (2) ... LA-4
Liberty Hill Cem—*cemetery* (6) ... MS-4
Liberty Hill Cem—*cemetery* (2) ... MO-7
Liberty Hill Cem—*cemetery* ... NC-3
Liberty Hill Cem—*cemetery* ... OH-6
Liberty Hill Cem—*cemetery* ... SC-3
Liberty Hill Cem—*cemetery* (2) ... TN-4
Liberty Hill Cem—*cemetery* (6) ... TX-5
Liberty Hill Cem—*cemetery* ... VA-3
*Liberty Hill Ch* ... AL-4
*Liberty Hill Ch* ... TN-4
Liberty Hill Ch—*church* (17) ... AL-4
Liberty Hill Ch—*church* (8) ... AR-4
Liberty Hill Ch—*church* ... FL-3
Liberty Hill Ch—*church* (14) ... GA-3
Liberty Hill Ch—*church* ... KY-4
Liberty Hill Ch—*church* (3) ... LA-4
Liberty Hill Ch—*church* (9) ... MS-4
Liberty Hill Ch—*church* ... MO-7
Liberty Hill Ch—*church* (8) ... NC-3
Liberty Hill Ch—*church* (3) ... OH-6
Liberty Hill Ch—*church* ... OK-5
Liberty Hill Ch—*church* (8) ... SC-3
Liberty Hill Ch—*church* (5) ... TN-4
Liberty Hill Ch—*church* (4) ... TX-5
Liberty Hill Ch—*church* (2) ... VA-3
Liberty Hill Chapel—*church* ... MS-4
Liberty Hill Ch (historical)—*church* ... MS-4
Liberty Hill Ch (historical)—*church* ... TN-4
Liberty Hill Ch of Christ—*church* ... TN-4
Liberty Hill Diggings—*mine* ... CA-9
Liberty Hill Hist Dist—*hist pl* ... SC-3
Liberty Hill (historical)—*locale* ... AL-4
Liberty Hill (historical)—*locale* ... MS-4
**Liberty Hill (historical)**—*pop pl* ... MS-4
**Liberty Hill (historical)**—*pop pl* ... NC-3
Liberty Hill Lookout—*locale* ... TX-5
Liberty Hill Lookout Tower—*locale* ... SC-3
*Liberty Hill Methodist Church* ... MS-4
*Liberty Hill Methodist Protestant Ch* ... TN-4
Liberty Hill Number 3 Mine (surface)—*mine* ... AL-4
**Liberty Hill Park (subdivision)**—*pop pl* ... NC-3
*Liberty Hill Post Office* ... TN-4
Libertyhill Post Office (historical)—*building* ... TN-4
*Liberty Hill Primitive Baptist Church* ... AL-4
**Liberty Hills**—*pop pl* ... IN-6
*Liberty Hill Sch* ... TN-4
Liberty Hill Sch—*hist pl* ... TN-4
Liberty Hill Sch—*school* ... AR-4
Liberty Hill Sch—*school* ... FL-3
Liberty Hill Sch—*school* ... IL-6
Liberty Hill Sch—*school* (3) ... LA-4
Liberty Hill Sch—*school* ... MS-4
Liberty Hill Sch—*school* (3) ... SC-3
Liberty Hill Sch—*school* (3) ... TN-4
Liberty Hill Sch—*school* ... TX-5
Liberty Hill Sch—*school* ... VA-3
Liberty Hill Sch (historical)—*school* (5) ... AL-4
Liberty Hill Sch (historical)—*school* (3) ... MS-4
Liberty Hill Sch (historical)—*school* (3) ... TN-4
Liberty HIll Sch (historical)—*school* ... TN-4
Liberty Hill Sch (historical)—*school* (3) ... TN-4
Liberty Hill Sch (historical)—*school* ... TX-5
Libertyhill Hills Country Club—*other* ... MO-7
*Liberty Hill United Methodist Ch* ... TN-4
Liberty Hill United Methodist Ch—*church* ... TN-4
*Liberty Hill United Methodist Church* ... MS-4
Liberty Hist Dist—*hist pl* ... TN-4
Liberty Hist Dist—*hist pl* ... WA-9
Liberty (historical)—*locale* ... AL-4
Liberty (historical)—*locale* ... KS-7
**Liberty (historical)**—*pop pl* ... OR-9
Liberty Hollow—*valley* ... MO-7
Liberty Hollow—*valley* (2) ... TN-4
Liberty Home Ch—*church* ... AL-4
Liberty HS—*school* ... AL-4
Liberty HS—*school* ... MO-7
Liberty HS—*school* ... PA-2
Liberty HS—*school* ... VA-3
Liberty HS (historical)—*school* ... TN-4
Liberty Intermediate Sch—*school* ... KS-7
*Liberty Island* ... IL-6
Liberty Island—*island* ... CA-9
Liberty Island—*island* ... NJ-2
Liberty Island Ferry—*locale* ... CA-9
*Liberty Island Gas Field* ... CA-9
Liberty JHS—*school* ... FL-3
Liberty JHS—*school* ... IN-6
Liberty JHS—*school* ... NC-3
Liberty Knoll Sch—*school* ... NE-7
*Liberty Lake* ... IL-6
Liberty Lake—*lake* ... IL-6
Liberty Lake—*lake* ... NV-8
Liberty Lake—*lake* ... TN-4
Liberty Lake—*lake* ... WA-9
**Liberty Lake**—*pop pl* ... WA-9
Liberty Lake—*reservoir* ... MD-2
Liberty Lake—*reservoir* ... OH-6
Liberty Lake—*reservoir* ... OK-5
Liberty Lake (CCD)—*cens area* ... WA-9
Liberty Lake Regional Park—*park* ... WA-9
Liberty Lakes—*lake* ... ID-8
Liberty Lakes—*lake* ... KS-7
Liberty Lake (Siding)—*locale* ... WA-9
**Liberty Lake (sta.)**—*pop pl* ... WA-9
Libertyland Grand Carousel—*hist pl* ... TN-4
Liberty Landing—*locale* ... AL-4
Liberty Landing Airp—*airport* ... MO-7
Liberty Landing Shop Ctr—*locale* ... MO-7
Liberty Lateral—*canal* ... NM-5
Liberty Lawn Cem—*cemetery* ... IL-6
Liberty Loan Sch—*school* ... IL-6
*Liberty Lookout Tower* ... MS-4
Liberty Lookout Tower—*locale* ... GA-3
Liberty-Loomis Hosp—*hospital* ... NY-2
Liberty Magee Cem—*cemetery* ... MS-4
**Liberty Manor**—*pop pl* ... MD-2
Liberty Masonic Acad (historical)—*school* ... TN-4
Liberty Meadows—*flat* ... MT-8
**Liberty Meadows Subdivision**—*pop pl* ... UT-8
Liberty Memorial—*other* ... MO-7
Liberty Mesa—*summit* ... NM-5
*Liberty Methodist Ch* ... MS-4
*Liberty Methodist Ch* ... TN-4
Liberty Methodist Ch—*church* ... MS-4
Liberty Methodist Ch—*church* ... TN-4
*Liberty Methodist Church* ... AL-4
Liberty Methodist Episcopal Ch (historical)—*church* ... AL-4
*Liberty Mill* ... VA-3
Liberty Millrace—*canal* ... CA-9
Liberty Millrace Canal—*canal* ... CA-9
*Liberty Mills* ... PA-2
Liberty Mills—*locale* ... VA-3
**Liberty Mills**—*pop pl* ... IN-6
Liberty Mine—*mine* (2) ... AZ-5
Liberty Mine—*mine* (2) ... CA-9
Liberty Mine—*mine* (2) ... CO-8
Liberty Mine—*mine* ... ID-8
Liberty Mine—*mine* ... MT-8
Liberty Mine—*mine* ... NV-8
Liberty Mine—*mine* ... WA-9
Liberty Mine—*mine* ... WI-6
Liberty Mine (underground)—*mine* ... AL-4
*Liberty Missionary Baptist Ch* ... TN-4
Liberty Missionary Baptist Ch—*church* ... AL-4
Liberty Missionary Ch—*church* ... TX-5
Liberty Mobile Home Park—*locale* ... AZ-5
Liberty Mound—*summit* ... WI-6
*Liberty Mountain* ... VA-3
Liberty MS—*school* ... IN-6
Liberty Mtn—*summit* ... WA-9
Liberty Municipal Airp—*airport* ... TX-5
Liberty Municipal Park—*park* ... NY-2
Liberty Oil Field—*oilfield* ... MS-4
Liberty Park—*hist pl* ... UT-8
Liberty Park—*park* ... IL-6
Liberty Park—*park* ... IN-6
Liberty Park—*park* ... IA-7
Liberty Park—*park* ... MO-7
Liberty Park—*park* ... NJ-2
Liberty Park—*park* (2) ... NY-2
Liberty Park—*park* ... PA-2
Liberty Park—*park* ... TX-5
Liberty Park—*park* (3) ... UT-8
**Liberty Park**—*pop pl* ... IL-6
**Liberty Park**—*pop pl* ... IN-6
**Liberty Park**—*pop pl* ... VA-3
Liberty Park—*post sta* ... WA-9
Liberty Park—*uninc pl* ... CA-9
Liberty Park Baptist Ch—*church* ... AL-4
Liberty Park Canal—*canal* ... ID-8
Liberty Park Cem—*cemetery* ... NY-2
Liberty Park Lake—*lake* ... OH-6
Liberty Park (PM)—*post sta* ... WA-9
Liberty Park Sch—*school* ... VA-3
Liberty Pass—*gap* ... NV-8
Liberty Pilgrim Cem—*cemetery* ... OH-6
Liberty Pit—*mine* ... NV-8
*Liberty Pit Copper Mine* ... NV-8
Liberty Plain—*plain* ... MA-1
**Liberty Plain**—*pop pl* ... MA-1
Liberty Plaza—*locale* ... PA-2
Liberty Plaza Shop Ctr—*locale* ... TN-4
Liberty Point—*cape* ... ME-1
Liberty Point—*locale* ... FL-3
Liberty Point Cem—*cemetery* ... KY-4
Liberty Point Ch—*church* ... KY-4
Liberty Point Number Two (railroad siding)—*locale* ... FL-3
Libertypole—*locale* ... NY-2
**Liberty Pole**—*pop pl* ... WI-6
*Liberty Pole Creek* ... ID-8
Liberty Pole Hill—*summit* ... MA-1
Liberty Pole Hill—*summit* ... WI-6
Liberty Post Office (historical)—*building* ... TN-4
Liberty Prairie Cem—*cemetery* ... IL-6
Liberty Prairie Cem—*cemetery* ... WI-6
Liberty Prairie Sch—*school* ... IL-6
Liberty Presbyterian Church—*hist pl* ... MS-4
*Liberty Primitive Baptist Ch* ... AL-4
Liberty Ridge—*ridge* ... KY-4
Liberty Ridge—*ridge* ... WA-9
Liberty Ridge—*ridge* ... WI-6
Liberty Ridge Cem—*cemetery* ... IL-6
*Liberty River Ch* ... AL-4
Liberty Road—*locale* ... KY-4
Liberty Row—*hist pl* ... NC-3
Liberty Run—*stream* ... WV-2
*Liberty Sch* ... AL-4
*Liberty Sch* ... MO-7
*Liberty Sch* ... TN-4
Liberty Sch—*hist pl* ... TN-4
Liberty Sch—*school* (2) ... AL-4
Liberty Sch—*school* ... AZ-5
Liberty Sch—*school* (2) ... AR-4
Liberty Sch—*school* (3) ... CA-9
Liberty Sch—*school* (4) ... CO-8
Liberty Sch—*school* (2) ... GA-3
Liberty Sch—*school* (23) ... IL-6
Liberty Sch—*school* (2) ... IN-6
Liberty Sch—*school* (5) ... IA-7
Liberty Sch—*school* (3) ... KS-7
Liberty Sch—*school* (3) ... KY-4
Liberty Sch—*school* (2) ... MA-1

Liberty Sch—*school* MI-6
Liberty Sch—*school* MN-6
Liberty Sch—*school* MS-4
Liberty Sch—*school* (10) MO-7
Liberty Sch—*school* MT-8
Liberty Sch—*school* (3) NE-7
Liberty Sch—*school* (2) NJ-2
Liberty Sch—*school* (2) NM-5
Liberty Sch—*school* (3) ND-7
Liberty Sch—*school* (3) OH-6
Liberty Sch—*school* (7) OK-5
Liberty Sch—*school* (3) OR-9
Liberty Sch—*school* (4) PA-2
Liberty Sch—*school* SC-3
Liberty Sch—*school* (2) SD-7
Liberty Sch—*school* TN-4
Liberty Sch—*school* (3) TX-5
Liberty Sch—*school* UT-8
Liberty Sch—*school* WA-9
Liberty Sch—*school* (2) WV-2
Liberty Sch—*school* (4) WI-6
Liberty Sch (abandoned)—*school* (11) MO-7
Liberty Sch (historical)—*school* (6) AL-4
Liberty Sch (historical)—*school* IA-7
Liberty Sch (historical)—*school* (4) MS-4
Liberty Sch (historical)—*school* (7) MO-7
Liberty Sch (historical)—*school* (2) PA-2
Liberty Sch (historical)—*school* (16) TN-4
Liberty Sch No 1—*school* MO-7
Liberty Sch No. 4, Friendship Bldg—*hist pl* PA-2
Liberty Sch Number 1—*school* ND-7
Liberty Sch Number 13 (historical)—*school* TN-4
*Liberty School* UT-8
Liberty School—*locale* NE-7
Liberty School—*locale* TX-5
Liberty School (Abandoned)—*locale* IL-6
Liberty School (abandoned)—*locale* MO-7
Liberty School (Abandoned)—*locale* MO-7
Liberty School (historical)—*locale* (4) MO-7
Liberty Sewage Lagoon Dam—*dam* MS-4
Liberty Shelter—*locale* NH-1
Liberty Shop Ctr—*locale* MS-4
*Liberty Shopping Center* PA-2
Liberty (siding)—*locale* AZ-5
Liberty (site)—*locale* OR-9
Liberty Spring—*spring* MT-8
Liberty Spring Cem—*cemetery* SC-3
Liberty Spring Ch—*church* GA-3
Liberty Spring Ch—*church* SC-3
Liberty Spring Ch—*church* VA-3
Liberty Spring Creek—*stream* UT-8
Liberty Springs—*spring* NV-8
Liberty Springs Ch—*church* AR-4
Liberty Springs Ch—*church* TX-5
Liberty Spring Trail—*trail* NH-1
*Liberty Square* AZ-5
Liberty Square—*locale* MA-1
Liberty Square—*locale* PA-2
Liberty Square—*park* CA-9
**Liberty Square**—*pop pl* FL-3
**Liberty Square**—*pop pl* NJ-2
Liberty Square Community Center—*locale* FL-3
Liberty Square Post Office (historical)—*building* PA-2
Liberty Square Shop Ctr—*locale* VA-3
**Liberty (sta.)**—*pop pl* AZ-5
**Liberty (Stanhope)**—*pop pl* KY-4
Liberty Street Hist Dist—*hist pl* CA-9
Liberty Street Hist Dist—*hist pl* NY-2
Liberty Street Sch—*school* KY-4
Liberty Street Sch—*school* (2) NY-2
Liberty Street Sch—*school* SC-3
**Liberty Subdivision**—*pop pl* UT-8
Liberty Substation—*locale* AZ-5
Liberty Temple—*church* AL-4
Liberty Temple—*church* AR-4
Liberty Temple—*church* SC-3
Liberty Temple Christian Mission Apostolic Ch—*church* FL-3
Liberty Theater—*hist pl* GA-3
Liberty Theatre—*hist pl* LA-4
Liberty Theatre—*hist pl* OH-6
Liberty Thorofare—*channel* NJ-2
Liberty Tower—*hist pl* NY-2
**Libertytown**—*pop pl* (2) MD-2
Libertytown Branch—*stream* MD-2
Liberty Town Hall—*building* ND-7
**Liberty (Town of)**—*pop pl* ME-1
**Liberty (Town of)**—*pop pl* NY-2
**Liberty (Town of)**—*pop pl* (4) WI-6
*Liberty Township* KS-7
Liberty Township—*civ div* NE-7
Liberty Township—*civil* (4) KS-7
Liberty Township—*civil* (20) MO-7
Liberty Township—*civil* (2) SD-7
Liberty Township—*fmr MCD* (21) IA-7
**Liberty Township**—*pop pl* (15) KS-7
**Liberty Township**—*pop pl* (5) MO-7
**Liberty Township**—*pop pl* (3) NE-7
**Liberty Township**—*pop pl* (2) ND-7
**Liberty Township**—*pop pl* (7) SD-7
Liberty Township Cem—*cemetery* IA-7
Liberty (Township of)—*fmr MCD* (11) AR-4
Liberty (Township of)—*fmr MCD* NC-3
Liberty (Township of)—*other* NC-3
**Liberty (Township of)**—*pop pl* (2) IL-6
**Liberty (Township of)**—*pop pl* (18) IN-6
**Liberty (Township of)**—*pop pl* (2) MI-6
**Liberty (Township of)**—*pop pl* (3) MN-6
**Liberty (Township of)**—*pop pl* NJ-2
**Liberty (Township of)**—*pop pl* (25) OH-6
**Liberty (Township of)**—*pop pl* (8) PA-2
Liberty Trail—*trail* NH-1
Liberty Tree District—*hist pl* MA-1
Liberty Tree Mall—*locale* MA-1
Liberty Triadelphia (Magisterial District)—*fmr MCD* WV-2
Liberty Tunnel—*tunnel* PA-2
Liberty Union Ch—*church* IA-7
Liberty Union Ch—*church* (2) MO-7
Liberty Union HS—*school* CA-9
Liberty Union Sch—*school* IA-7
Liberty Union Sch—*school* OH-6
Liberty Union Tabernacle—*church* KY-4
Liberty United Ch—*church* MO-7
Liberty United Methodist Ch—*church* AL-4
*Liberty United Methodist Church* MS-4
Liberty Universal Ch—*church* SC-3
*Liberty Universalist Church* MS-4
Liberty Universalist Church and Feasterville Acad Hist Dist—*hist pl* SC-3
**Liberty Valley**—*pop pl* AR-4
Liberty Valley—*valley* NM-5
Liberty Valley—*valley* PA-2
Liberty Valley—*valley* TN-4
Liberty Valley Ch—*church* AR-4
Liberty Valley Ch—*church* TN-4
*Liberty Valley Ch of Christ* TN-4
Liberty Valley Sch—*school* PA-2
Liberty View Ch—*church* GA-3
Liberty View Ch—*church* IN-6
Liberty Village Hist Dist—*hist pl* NY-2
**Liberty Village (subdivision)**—*pop pl* (2) AZ-5
*Libertyville* PA-2
Libertyville—*locale* NJ-2
**Libertyville**—*pop pl* AL-4
**Libertyville**—*pop pl* IL-6
**Libertyville**—*pop pl* (2) IN-6
**Libertyville**—*pop pl* IA-7
**Libertyville**—*pop pl* MO-7
**Libertyville**—*pop pl* NY-2
Libertyville Estates—*other* IL-6
Libertyville Sch—*school* IL-6
Libertyville (Township of)—*civ div* IL-6
Liberty Vista Point—*locale* CA-9
Liberty Warehouse—*hist pl* SC-3
Liberty Wesleyan Ch—*church* NC-3
Liberty Wildlife Area—*park* OH-6
Libfarm—*locale* CA-9
Libhart Creek—*stream* MI-6
*Lib Insel* MP-9
*Libiron* MP-9
Libiron—*island* MP-9
*Lib Island* MP-9
*Liboan Island* FM-9
Libolt Rsvr—*reservoir* OR-9
Libolt Sch—*school* IL-6
Liborio Negron Torres—*CDP* PR-3
*Library* PA-2
Library—*hist pl* NE-7
**Library**—*pop pl* PA-2
Library East—*hist pl* FL-3
Library Elem Sch—*school* PA-2
Library Hall—*building* PA-2
Library Hall—*hist pl* IL-6
Library Junction—*locale* PA-2
Library of Congress—*building* DC-2
*Library of Congress Annex* DC-2
Library Park—*hist pl* WI-6
Library Park—*park* (2) AZ-5
Library Park Hist Dist—*hist pl* NM-5
Library Park Hist Dist—*hist pl* NY-2
Library Park Hist Dist—*hist pl* WI-6
Libre Park—*park* AZ-5
Libre Windmill—*locale* TX-5
Libscomb Pond Dam—*dam* MS-4
Libson Sch—*school* IL-6
**Libuse**—*pop pl* LA-4
Libuse Czech Cem—*cemetery* LA-4
Libuse Lookout Tower—*locale* LA-4
Lib Windmill—*locale* NM-5
Li Calzi—*airport* NJ-2
Lice Hill—*summit* AZ-5
Lice Island—*island* FL-3
Lices Lake—*lake* MS-4
Lichau Creek—*stream* CA-9
Lichee Sinil Spring—*spring* AZ-5
Lichen Creek—*stream* CA-9
Lichen Lake—*lake* MN-6
Lichen Sch—*school* CA-9
*Lichfield* KS-7
Lichliter Mound And Village Site—*hist pl* OH-6
Lichte Branch—*stream* MO-7
Lichte Creek—*stream* MI-6
Lichtenberg Mtn—*summit* WA-9
*Lichtenhahn Caves* UT-8
Lichtenstein, S. Julius, House—*hist pl* TX-5
Lichtenthaler Spring—*spring* OR-9
Lichtenwasser Lake—*lake* WA-9
Lichte Ranch—*locale* MT-8
Lichte Ruby Creek Ditch—*canal* MT-8
Lichtman Camp No 1—*locale* VA-3
Lichtstern House—*hist pl* IL-6
Lichty—*locale* WA-9
Lichty Cabin—*locale* WY-8
Lichty Cem—*cemetery* (2) PA-2
Lichty Ch—*church* PA-2
Lichty Sch (abandoned)—*school* PA-2
Lick—*locale* CA-9
Lick—*locale* MO-7
**Lick**—*pop pl* IL-6
**Lick**—*pop pl* WV-2
Lick, James, Mill—*hist pl* CA-9
Lick Bayou—*gut* LA-4
Lick Bayou—*stream* (2) LA-4
Lick Block Run—*stream* VA-3
Lick Bottom—*bend* KY-4
Lick Bottom Hollow—*valley* VA-3
*Lick Branch* AL-4
*Lick Branch* IN-6
*Lick Branch* TN-4
*Lick Branch* TX-5
*Lick Branch* VA-3
*Lick Branch* WV-2
Lick Branch—*locale* AR-4
**Lick Branch**—*pop pl* KY-4
Lick Branch—*stream* (13) AL-4
Lick Branch—*stream* (17) AR-4
Lick Branch—*stream* GA-3
Lick Branch—*stream* (6) IL-6
Lick Branch—*stream* (3) IN-6
Lick Branch—*stream* IA-7
Lick Branch—*stream* (74) KY-4
Lick Branch—*stream* (8) LA-4
Lick Branch—*stream* (5) MS-4
Lick Branch—*stream* (14) MO-7
Lick Branch—*stream* (10) NC-3
Lick Branch—*stream* OH-6
Lick Branch—*stream* OK-5
Lick Branch—*stream* (2) PA-2
Lick Branch—*stream* SC-3
Lick Branch—*stream* (40) TN-4
Lick Branch—*stream* (13) TX-5
Lick Branch—*stream* (27) VA-3
Lick Branch—*stream* (42) WV-2
Lick Branch Ch—*church* IN-6
Lick Branch Ch—*church* KY-4
Lick Branch Ch—*church* MS-4
Lick Branch Ch—*church* TN-4
Lick Branch Community Ch—*church* KY-4
Lick Branch Cove—*bay* MO-7
Lick Branch Creek—*stream* MS-4
Lick Branch Hurricane Creek—*stream* LA-4
Lick Branch (RR name for Switchback)—*other* WV-2
Lick Branch Sch—*school* (3) KY-4
Lick Branch Sch—*school* MS-4
Lick Branch Sch (historical)—*school* TN-4
Lick Branch Trail—*trail* WV-2
Lick Brook—*stream* NY-2
Lickburg—*locale* KY-4
Lick Canyon—*valley* CA-9
Lick Canyon—*valley* NM-5
Lick Ch—*church* KY-4
Lick Cove—*valley* TN-4
*Lick Creek* AR-4
*Lick Creek* ID-8
*Lick Creek* IN-6
*Lick Creek* KY-4
*Lick Creek* LA-4
*Lick Creek* MO-7
*Lick Creek* MT-8
*Lick Creek* NC-3
*Lick Creek* OH-6
*Lick Creek* TN-4
*Lick Creek* TX-5
*Lick Creek* VA-3
*Lick Creek* WV-2
*Lick Creek* WY-8
Lick Creek—*locale* KY-4
Lick Creek—*locale* WV-2
Lick Creek—*other* WV-2
**Lick Creek**—*pop pl* IL-6
**Lick Creek**—*pop pl* (2) TN-4
Lick Creek—*stream* (12) AL-4
Lick Creek—*stream* AK-9
Lick Creek—*stream* (20) AR-4
Lick Creek—*stream* (7) CA-9
Lick Creek—*stream* (2) CO-8
Lick Creek—*stream* (5) GA-3
Lick Creek—*stream* (13) ID-8
Lick Creek—*stream* (12) IL-6
Lick Creek—*stream* (19) IN-6
Lick Creek—*stream* (3) IA-7
Lick Creek—*stream* (29) KY-4
Lick Creek—*stream* (6) LA-4
Lick Creek—*stream* (9) MS-4
Lick Creek—*stream* (17) MO-7
Lick Creek—*stream* (8) MT-8
Lick Creek—*stream* (9) NC-3
Lick Creek—*stream* (3) OH-6
Lick Creek—*stream* (4) OK-5
Lick Creek—*stream* (16) OR-9
Lick Creek—*stream* (4) PA-2
Lick Creek—*stream* (6) SC-3
Lick Creek—*stream* (29) TN-4
Lick Creek—*stream* (13) TX-5
Lick Creek—*stream* UT-8
Lick Creek—*stream* (6) VA-3
Lick Creek—*stream* WA-9
Lick Creek—*stream* (9) WV-2
Lick Creek—*stream* (2) WY-8
*Lick Creek Baptist Church* TN-4
Lick Creek Cem—*cemetery* (2) MO-7
Lick Creek Cem—*cemetery* OH-6
Lick Creek Cem—*cemetery* TN-4
*Lick Creek Ch* TN-4
Lick Creek Ch—*church* (2) IL-6
Lick Creek Ch—*church* IN-6
Lick Creek Ch—*church* (2) MO-7
Lick Creek Ch—*church* NC-3
Lick Creek Ch—*church* OH-6
Lick Creek Ch—*church* (2) TN-4
Lick Creek Ch—*church* (2) VA-3
Lick Creek Ch—*church* (2) WV-2
Lick Creek Ch (historical)—*church* (2) TN-4
Lick Creek Dam—*dam* AL-4
Lick Creek Ditch—*canal* MO-7
Lick Creek Drain—*canal* IL-6
Lick Creek (Election Precinct)—*fmr MCD* IL-6
Lick Creek Falls—*falls* OK-5
Lick Creek Guard Station—*hist pl* OR-9
**Lick Creek (historical)**—*pop pl* TN-4
*Lick Creek - in part* TN-4
Lick Creek Landing—*locale* (2) TN-4
Lick Creek Lateral—*canal* IL-6
Lick Creek Lookout—*locale* ID-8
Lick Creek Methodist Ch—*church* TN-4
Lick Creek Mill—*locale* TN-4
Lick Creek Mtn—*summit* TN-4
Lick Creek Point—*summit* ID-8
Lick Creek Pond—*reservoir* AL-4
Lick Creek Post Office (historical)—*building* TN-4
Lick Creek Ranger Station—*locale* OR-9
Lick Creek Rec Area—*locale* AR-4
Lick Creek Rec Area—*park* TN-4
Lick Creek Sch—*school* (2) AR-4
Lick Creek Sch—*school* IL-6
Lick Creek Sch—*school* MO-7
Lick Creek Sch—*school* WV-2
Lick Creek Sch (historical)—*school* TN-4
Lick Creek Spring—*spring* KY-4
Lick Creek Station—*locale* KY-4
Lick Creek Summit—*gap* ID-8
Lick Creek Township—*civil* MO-7
Lick Creek Township—*fmr MCD* (2) IA-7
Lick Creek (Township of)—*fmr MCD* AR-4
Lick Creek Trail—*trail* MO-7
Lick Creek Trail—*trail* OR-9
Lick Creek Trail (historical)—*trail* OR-9
Lickdab Creek—*stream* CO-8
**Lickdale**—*pop pl* PA-2
Lickdale Sch—*school* PA-2
Lick Draft—*valley* PA-2
Lick Draft—*valley* (2) VA-3
Lick Drain—*stream* WV-2
*Lickenhole* VA-3
Licket Creek—*stream* NE-7
Lick Falls—*falls* KY-4
Lick Flat—*flat* TX-5
Lickfold Lake Dam—*dam* MS-4
Lick Ford—*locale* AR-4
*Lick Fork* AR-4
*Lick Fork* KY-4
*Lick Fork* WV-2
Lick Fork—*locale* KY-4
**Lick Fork**—*pop pl* VA-3
**Lick Fork**—*pop pl* WV-2
Lick Fork—*stream* AL-4
Lick Fork—*stream* (3) AR-4
Lick Fork—*stream* IN-6
Lick Fork—*stream* (29) KY-4
Lick Fork—*stream* (4) MO-7
Lick Fork—*stream* (3) NC-3
Lick Fork—*stream* (3) OH-6
Lick Fork—*stream* SC-3
Lick Fork—*stream* TN-4
Lick Fork—*stream* (3) VA-3
Lick Fork—*stream* (12) WV-2
Lick Fork Branch—*stream* SC-3
Lick Fork Cave—*cave* AL-4
Lick Fork Cedar Creek—*stream* VA-3
Lick Fork Ch—*church* (2) KY-4
Lick Fork Ch—*church* NC-3
Lick Fork Ch—*church* OH-6
Lick Fork Ch—*church* VA-3
*Lick Fork Creek* IN-6
*Lick Fork Creek* NC-3
Lick Fork Creek—*stream* AR-4
Lickfork Creek—*stream* TN-4
Lick Fork Freewill Ch—*church* WV-2
Lick Fork Lake—*reservoir* SC-3
Lick Fork Ridge—*ridge* WV-2
Lick Fork Sch—*school* (3) KY-4
Lick Fork Sch—*school* TN-4
**Lick Fork Spur Junction**—*pop pl* WV-2
Lick Fork State Rec Area—*park* IN-6
Lickfort Creek—*stream* VA-3
Lick Gap—*gap* PA-2
Lick Gap Trail—*trail* PA-2
Lick Gulch—*valley* (2) CA-9
Lick Gulch—*valley* ID-8
Lick Gulch—*valley* MT-8
Lick Gulch—*valley* OR-9
Lick Hill—*summit* MO-7
Lick Hill Sch (historical)—*school* MO-7
*Lick Hollow* OH-6
Lick Hollow—*valley* AL-4
Lick Hollow—*valley* (9) AR-4
Lick Hollow—*valley* IL-6
Lick Hollow—*valley* (3) MO-7
Lick Hollow—*valley* (5) PA-2
Lick Hollow—*valley* (12) TN-4
Lick Hollow—*valley* TX-5
Lick Hollow—*valley* (2) WV-2
Lick Hollow Branch—*stream* TN-4
*Lick Hollow Mountain* PA-2
Lick Hollow Picnic Area—*locale* PA-2
Lick Hollow Trail—*trail* PA-2
Lick HS—*school* CA-9
**Licking**—*pop pl* MO-7
*Licking Branch* AL-4
Licking Branch—*stream* KY-4
Licking Branch—*stream* NC-3
Licking Ch—*church* OH-6
Licking Ch—*church* PA-2
**Licking (County)**—*pop pl* OH-6
Licking County Courthouse—*hist pl* OH-6
*Licking Creek* IN-6
*Licking Creek* PA-2
Licking Creek—*stream* AK-9
Licking Creek—*stream* (2) IN-6
Licking Creek—*stream* MD-2
Licking Creek—*stream* NV-8
Licking Creek—*stream* (6) PA-2
Licking Creek—*stream* (2) VA-3
Licking Creek—*stream* WV-2
Licking Creek Dam—*dam* PA-2
Licking Creek Fishing Club—*other* VA-3
Licking Creek Sch—*school* WV-2
**Licking Creek (Township of)**—*pop pl* PA-2
Licking Fork—*stream* CA-9
Licking Fork—*stream* (2) KY-4
Licking Gorge—*valley* OH-6
Licking Heights HS—*school* OH-6
Lickinghole Creek—*stream* (3) VA-3
Lickinghole (Magisterial District)—*fmr MCD* VA-3
Licking (Magisterial District)—*fmr MCD* WV-2
Licking Ranch—*locale* NV-8
**Licking River**—*pop pl* KY-4
Licking River—*stream* KY-4
Licking River—*stream* OH-6
Licking River Sch—*school* KY-4
Licking Riverside Hist Dist—*hist pl* KY-4
Licking Rock Branch—*stream* KY-4
Licking Rockhouse Branch—*stream* KY-4
Licking Run—*stream* PA-2
Licking Run—*stream* VA-3
Licking Sch—*school* NE-7
Licking Springs—*spring* OH-6
Licking State Forest Nursery—*locale* MO-7
**Licking (Township of)**—*pop pl* IL-6
**Licking (Township of)**—*pop pl* IN-6
**Licking (Township of)**—*pop pl* (2) OH-6
**Licking (Township of)**—*pop pl* PA-2
Licking Valley HS—*school* OH-6
**Licking View**—*pop pl* OH-6
**Lickingville**—*pop pl* PA-2
Lickin Hollow—*valley* AR-4
Lick Island Run—*stream* PA-2
*Lick Knob* AR-4
Lick Knob—*summit* (2) WV-2
Lick Lake—*lake* ID-8
Lick Lake—*lake* (2) MT-8
Licklider Cem—*cemetery* MO-7
Licklider Dam—*dam* OR-9
Licklider Rsvr—*reservoir* OR-9
Licklo Fork—*stream* KY-4
Licklog—*locale* TN-4
*Licklog Branch* AL-4
*Licklog Branch* NC-3
Licklog Branch—*stream* AL-4
Lick Log Branch—*stream* AR-4
Licklog Branch—*stream* (2) KY-4
Licklog Branch—*stream* (3) NC-3
Licklog Branch—*stream* (5) TN-4
Licklog Branch—*stream* (2) VA-3
Lick Log Branch—*stream* VA-3
Lick Log Branch—*stream* WV-2
Licklog Branch—*stream* WV-2
Lick Log Creek—*stream* (3) GA-3
Licklog Creek—*stream* GA-3
Lick Log Creek—*stream* GA-3
Lick Log Creek—*stream* MO-7
Licklog Creek—*stream* (4) NC-3
Lick Log Creek—*stream* SC-3
Lick Log Fork—*stream* KY-4
Licklog Fork—*stream* KY-4
Lick Log Fork—*stream* KY-4
Lick Log Gap—*gap* NC-3
Licklog Gap—*gap* (7) NC-3
*Lick Log Hollow* TN-4
Lick Log Hollow—*valley* (2) MO-7
Licklog Hollow—*valley* (2) TN-4
Lick Log Hollow—*valley* WV-2
Licklog Knob—*summit* (2) NC-3
Licklog Mtn—*summit* GA-3
Licklog Mtn—*summit* (2) NC-3
Licklog Mtn—*summit* SC-3
*Licklog Ridge* NC-3
Licklog Ridge—*ridge* TN-4
Licklog Ridge Trail—*trail* TN-4
Lick Log Shaft Mine—*mine* TN-4
Licklog Springs Gap—*gap* VA-3
Licklog Tank—*reservoir* AZ-5
Licklog Top—*summit* TN-4
*Licklog Trail* TN-4
**Lickly Corners**—*pop pl* MI-6
Lickly Corners Cem—*cemetery* MI-6
*Lick Mountain* AR-4
*Lick Mountain* PA-2
**Lick Mountain**—*pop pl* AR-4
Lick Mountain Ch—*church* VA-3
Lick Mountain (Township of)—*fmr MCD* AR-4
Lick Mtn—*summit* (3) AR-4
Lick Mtn—*summit* CA-9
Lick Mtn—*summit* (2) MT-8
Lick Mtn—*summit* (2) NC-3
Lick Mtn—*summit* OK-5
Lick Mtn—*summit* (5) VA-3
Lick Observatory (University of California)—*school* CA-9
*Lickowens Mtn* AR-4
Lick Owens Mtn—*summit* AR-4
Lick Park—*flat* CO-8
*Lick Point* ID-8
Lick Point—*cape* TN-4
Lick Point—*summit* ID-8
Lick Points—*ridge* VA-3
Lick Pond—*swamp* IL-6
*Lick Pond Ditch* AR-4
Lick Pond Slough—*stream* AR-4
*Lick Pond Slough Ditch* AR-4
Lick Prairie Cem—*cemetery* IL-6
Lick Prairie Ch—*church* IL-6
Lick Prairie Community Hall—*locale* MO-7
Lick Prairie (Election Precinct)—*fmr MCD* IL-6
Lick Prong Run—*stream* OH-6
Lick Ridge—*ridge* NM-5
Lick Ridge—*ridge* NC-3
Lick Ridge—*ridge* (2) PA-2
Lick Ridge—*ridge* (5) TN-4
Lick Ridge—*ridge* (4) VA-3
Lick Ridge Trail—*trail* PA-2
Lick Rock—*summit* NC-3
Lick Rock—*summit* OR-9
Lick Rock—*summit* TN-4
*Lick Run* AL-4
*Lick Run* IN-6
*Lick Run* OH-6
*Lick Run* PA-2
*Lick Run* TN-4
*Lick Run* VA-3
*Lick Run* WV-2
Lick Run—*locale* (2) PA-2
Lick Run—*locale* VA-3
Lick Run—*stream* IL-6
Lick Run—*stream* (3) IN-6
Lick Run—*stream* (6) KY-4
Lick Run—*stream* MD-2
Lick Run—*stream* (2) NC-3
Lick Run—*stream* (19) OH-6
Lick Run—*stream* (28) PA-2
Lick Run—*stream* SC-3
Lick Run—*stream* TN-4
Lick Run—*stream* (13) VA-3
Lick Run—*stream* (46) WV-2
*Lick Run Creek* NC-3
*Lick Run Gap* PA-2
Lick Run Hill—*summit* PA-2
**Lick Run Junction**—*pop pl* WV-2
Lick Run Knob—*summit* WV-2
Lick Run Lick Run—*stream* OH-6
Lick Run Plantation—*hist pl* WV-2
Lick Run Sch—*school* KY-4
Lick Run Sch—*school* WV-2
Lick Run Sch (historical)—*school* PA-2
Lick Run Trail—*trail* (3) PA-2
Lick Run Trail—*trail* WV-2
Lick Run Tunnel—*tunnel* VA-3
*Licksburg* KY-4
Licks Cem—*cemetery* OH-6
Lick Sch—*school* OH-6
Lick Sch (historical)—*school* TN-4
Lick School (historical)—*locale* MO-7
Licks Creek—*stream* MI-6
Lick Shoals Run—*stream* WV-2
*Lickskillet* AL-4
*Lickskillet* IN-6
*Lickskillet* KS-7
*Lick Skillet* MS-4
Lickskillet—*basin* AL-4
Lickskillet—*locale* (2) KY-4
Lickskillet—*locale* (2) NC-3
Lickskillet—*locale* OH-6
Lickskillet—*locale* TN-4
**Lickskillet**—*pop pl* AL-4
**Lickskillet**—*pop pl* GA-3
**Lick Skillet**—*pop pl* KY-4
**Lickskillet**—*pop pl* MO-7
**Lick Skillet**—*pop pl* TN-4
**Lick Skillet**—*pop pl* VA-3
Lick Skillet Acad (historical)—*school* MS-4
Lickskillet Branch—*stream* KY-4
Lickskillet Branch—*stream* (2) NC-3
Lickskillet Branch—*stream* OH-6
Lickskillet Branch—*stream* (2) TN-4
Lickskillet Branch—*stream* VA-3
Lickskillet Creek—*stream* AL-4
Lickskillet Creek—*stream* KY-4
Lick Skillet Creek—*stream* MS-4
Lick-Skillet Cut-Off—*bend* TX-5
Lick Skillet Gulch—*valley* CO-8
Lick Skillet (historical)—*locale* (2) AL-4
Lick Skillet Hollow—*valley* IN-6
Lickskillet Hollow—*valley* TN-4
Lickskillet Hollow—*valley* VA-3
Lick Skillet Hollow—*valley* VA-3
Lick Skillet Knob—*summit* KY-4
Lick-Skillet Lake—*lake* OK-5
Lickskillet Run—*stream* OH-6
Lickskillet Sch—*school* KS-7
Lick Slough—*gut* TX-5
Lick Slough—*stream* TN-4
Lick Spring—*spring* MO-7
Lick Spring—*spring* (3) OR-9
Lick Spring Ch—*church* IN-6
Lick Springs—*locale* NY-2
Lickstone Bald—*summit* NC-3
Lickstone Overlook—*locale* NC-3
Lickstone Ridge—*ridge* (2) NC-3
Lickstone Tunnel—*tunnel* NC-3
Lick Tank—*reservoir* NM-5
**Lickton**—*pop pl* TN-4
Lickton Field—*park* FL-3
**Lick (Township of)**—*pop pl* OH-6
Lickup Creek—*stream* MS-4
*Lick Valley* PA-2
Lick Valley Sch (abandoned)—*school* MO-7
**Lickville**—*pop pl* SC-3
Lickville Cem—*cemetery* NY-2
Lickville Ch—*church* SC-3
Lick Wash—*valley* UT-8
Licky Branch—*stream* VA-3
**Lico**—*pop pl* WV-2
Lida—*locale* KY-4
**Lida**—*pop pl* NV-8
Lida, Lake—*lake* MN-6
Lida Canyon—*valley* NV-8
*Lida Creek* AZ-5
Lida Island—*island* AK-9
*Lida Junction Airport* NV-8
Lida Junction Airstrip—*airport* NV-8
Lida Summit—*gap* NV-8
**Lida (Township of)**—*pop pl* MN-6
Lida Valley—*valley* NV-8
Lida Wash—*stream* NV-8
Lid Creek—*stream* MT-8
**Liddell**—*pop pl* NC-3
Liddell Archeol Site—*hist pl* AL-4
*Liddell Attendance Center* MS-4
Liddell Cem—*cemetery* MS-4
Liddell Creek—*stream* CA-9
Liddell Elem Sch—*school* MS-4
Liddell HS—*school* MS-4
Liddell-McNinch House—*hist pl* NC-3
**Liddell (Old Anson)**—*pop pl* WI-6
Liddell (Township of)—*fmr MCD* AR-4
Liddenfield—*locale* PA-2
**Lidderdale**—*pop pl* IA-7
**Liddieville**—*pop pl* LA-4
Liddle, Alexander, Farmhouse—*hist pl* NY-2
Liddle, Robert, Farmhouse—*hist pl* NY-2
Liddle, Thomas, Farm Complex—*hist pl* NY-2
Liddle Brook—*stream* NY-2
Liddle Ditch—*canal* CO-8
Liddon Lake—*reservoir* MS-4
Liddy Creek—*stream* AR-4
Liddy Hollow—*valley* OH-6
Lide, Evan J., House—*hist pl* SC-3
Lide, John W., House—*hist pl* SC-3
Lideen Hill—*summit* MT-8
*Lidel Creek* TX-5
*Lidel Gap* TX-5
**Lidell Corners**—*pop pl* NY-2
Lidell Creek—*stream* NY-2
Lider—*locale* TX-5
Lider Lake—*lake* WA-9
**Lidgerwood**—*pop pl* ND-7
Lidgerwood Park—*park* NJ-2
Lidgerwood Sch—*school* WA-9
*Lidice* IL-6
**Lidice**—*pop pl* IL-6
*Lidilbut* MP-9
Lidilbut—*island* MP-9
Lidios Windmill—*locale* TX-5
Lid Kay Camp—*locale* WA-9
Lidke Hill—*summit* NY-2
**Lidke's Corners**—*pop pl* MI-6
*Lido, The* FL-3
Lido Beach—*beach* FL-3
Lido Beach—*beach* NY-2
**Lido Beach**—*pop pl* NY-2
Lido Beach—*uninc pl* FL-3
**Lido Isle**—*pop pl* CA-9
Lido Isle Reach—*channel* CA-9
Lido Key—*island* FL-3
Lido Key—*uninc pl* FL-3
Lids Pocket—*bay* TN-4
Lidstone Hill—*summit* MT-8
Lidtke Mill—*locale* IA-7
Lidy Creek—*stream* PA-2
Lidyhites Hill—*summit* CT-1
Lidyhites Pond—*lake* CT-1
**Lidy Hot Springs**—*pop pl* ID-8
Lidy Hot Springs—*spring* ID-8
Lidy S Lake—*reservoir* AL-4
*Lidy S Lake Dam* AL-4
Lie, Aslak, Cabin—*hist pl* WI-6
Lieb Cem—*cemetery* TX-5
Liebe Canyon—*valley* CA-9
Liebel Peak—*summit* CA-9
Liebel Ranch—*locale* CA-9
Liebelt Sch—*school* SD-7
*Liebentahl* KS-7
**Liebenthal**—*pop pl* KS-7
Lieberg Lake—*lake* MN-6
Lieberman Canyon—*valley* CA-9
*Lieber Reservoir* IN-6
*Lieber State Park* IN-6
Liebes Cove—*bay* AK-9
Liebey Park—*flat* CO-8
Liebhardt—*locale* NY-2
Liebhardt Sch—*school* NY-2
Liebhart Cem—*cemetery* IL-6
Liebig, Mount—*summit* MT-8
Lieblein House—*hist pl* MI-6
Liebold Lake—*reservoir* IA-7
Liebold Mtn—*summit* TX-5
*Lie Branch* AL-4
Lieb-Rawls House—*hist pl* MS-4
*Liebre Creek* OR-9
Liebre Gulch—*valley* CA-9
*Liebre Mountains* CA-9
Liebre Mtn—*summit* CA-9

Liebres Tank—*reservoir* AZ-5
Liebre Twins—*summit* CA-9
Liebre Windmill—*locale* TX-5
Liebrook Hill—*summit* OH-6
Lieb Run—*stream* PA-2
Lieb Sch—*school* IL-6
Liebs Island—*island* OH-6
**Liebs Island**—*pop pl* OH-6
**Liebys Trailer Park**—*pop pl* PA-2
Liechti Pond—*lake* OR-9
Liechti Pond Number One—*lake* OR-9
Liechti Pond Number Two—*lake* OR-9
Liechty Cem—*cemetery* IN-6
Liechty Hill—*summit* TN-4
Liederkranz—*hist pl* NE-7
Lief Cove—*bay* AK-9
*Lie Festa Creek* TX-5
*Lief Lake* MN-6
*Lieq* FM-9
*Liege* MO-7
*Liege - in part* MO-7
Liege Lake—*lake* WI-6
Liehue Gut—*gut* NC-3
Liem Primary Sch—*school* AZ-5
**Lien**—*pop pl* SD-7
Lien Airfield—*airport* SD-7
*Lienbergers Lake* WI-6
Lienche Cem—*cemetery* IL-6
Liendo Plantation—*hist pl* TX-5
Lien Draw—*valley* NV-8
Lien Gulch—*valley* MT-8
Lienhart Mine—*mine* CO-8
Lien Park—*park* SD-7
Lien Ranch—*locale* MT-8
Liens Creek—*stream* MI-6
Liens Dams—*dam* ND-7
**Lien Township**—*pop pl* SD-7
**Lien (Township of)**—*pop pl* MN-6
Lieppe Bank—*bar* FM-9
Liere—*unknown* FM-9
Lierle Creek—*stream* IL-6
Lies Branch—*stream* TX-5
Liesburg Homestead—*locale* CO-8
Liese Field—*park* TX-5
Lieser Sch—*school* WA-9
Lieskof, Cape—*cape* AK-9
Liesnoi Island—*island* (3) AK-9
Liesnol Shoal—*bay* AK-9
Lietner Ranch—*locale* SD-7
Lietnik—*locale* AK-9
Lietpas—*locale* FM-9
Lietz Sch—*school* CA-9
Lieuallen, Almon Asbury, House—*hist pl* ID-8
Lieu Hollow—*valley* WV-2
Lieuna Lake—*lake* MN-6
*Lieung Lake* MN-6
Lieurance Cem—*cemetery* OH-6
*Lieure Brook* CT-1
*Lieutenant Creek* VA-3
Lieutenant Creek—*stream* CO-8
Lieutenant Creek—*stream* OR-9
Lieutenant Draw—*valley* MT-8
*Lieutenant Duddy Elementary School* PA-2
Lieutenant Island—*island* MA-1
Lieutenant Island Bar—*bar* MA-1
Lieutenant River—*stream* CT-1
Lieutenant River III Site—*hist pl* CT-1
Lieutenant River IV Site—*hist pl* CT-1
Lieutenant River No. 2—*hist pl* CT-1
Lieutenant Run—*stream* VA-3
*Lieutenants Island* MA-1
Lieuy Lake—*lake* AK-9
Lievan Sch—*school* IL-6
Lieva Springs—*spring* CA-9
Liever Marches Bay Hist Dist—*hist pl* VI-3
Lievre Brook—*stream* CT-1
Lievres Tank—*reservoir* AZ-5
**Liewellyn Corners**—*pop pl* PA-2
Lifalifa Point—*cape* AS-9
**Life**—*pop pl* TN-4
Life and Praise Fellowship Ch—*church* FL-3
Lifeboat United Methodist Ch—*church* MS-4
Life Cem—*cemetery* KS-7
Life Cem—*cemetery* WV-2
Lifegate Ch—*church* AL-4
Lifeland Branch—*stream* SC-3
Lifeland Cem—*cemetery* SC-3
Life Line Ch—*church* AR-4
Life Line Ch—*church* TX-5
**Lifenite**—*pop pl* LA-4
Life Post Office (historical)—*building* TN-4
Life Raft Lake—*lake* MN-6
Lifers Landing—*locale* IL-6
Life Savers Bldg—*hist pl* NY-2
Lifesaving Creek—*stream* OR-9
Life Saving Service Station (historical)—*building* NC-3
Life Sch—*school* TN-4
Lifes Run—*stream* WV-2
**Lifestyle**—*pop pl* VA-3
Life Tabernacle—*church* (2) FL-3
Life Tabernacle—*church* IN-6
Life Temple Ch—*church* NC-3
Liffy Island—*island* NJ-2
Liford Cem—*cemetery* TN-4
**Lifsey**—*pop pl* GA-3
Lifter Lake—*lake* MI-6
Lifting Rock Branch—*stream* NC-3
Lift Lock (historical)—*dam* AL-4
Lifton—*locale* ID-8
**Liftwood**—*pop pl* DE-2
*Ligatapar* FM-9
*Ligatapar Island* FM-9
Lige—*locale* OK-5
Lige Branch—*stream* AR-4
Lige Branch—*stream* (2) MS-4
Lige Branch—*stream* NC-3
Lige Grimm Hollow—*valley* KY-4
Lige Hays Branch—*stream* KY-4
Lige Hollow—*valley* TN-4
Lige Lake—*lake* GA-3
Lige Lick Branch—*stream* KY-4
Liges Branch—*stream* KY-4
Ligett Cem—*cemetery* OH-6
Ligett Creek—*stream* MO-7
Lige Warren Hollow—*valley* TN-4
Liggans Corner—*locale* VA-3
Ligget, J., Residence—*hist pl* OH-6
Ligget Creek—*stream* ID-8
Liggett—*locale* CO-8
**Liggett**—*pop pl* CO-8
**Liggett**—*pop pl* IN-6
**Liggett**—*pop pl* KY-4
Liggett—*uninc pl* TX-5
Liggett and Myers (Rice-Stix) Bldg—*hist pl* MO-7
*Liggett-Andrews Cemetery* TN-4
Liggett Branch—*stream* TN-4
Liggett Cem—*cemetery* TN-4
Liggett Crossing—*locale* OH-6
Liggett Ditch—*canal* CO-8
Liggett & Myers Tobacco Co. Bldg—*hist pl* MO-7
Liggett Sch—*school* MI-6
Liggett Sch (historical)—*school* MO-7
*Liggett's Grove* IL-6
Liggett Station—*locale* PA-2
Liggett Street Sch—*school* CA-9
Liggitt Ditch—*canal* OH-6
Lighah Fork—*valley* UT-8
Light—*locale* AL-4
Light—*locale* AZ-5
Light—*locale* MO-7
Light—*locale* TX-5
**Light**—*pop pl* AR-4
**Light**—*pop pl* NC-3
**Light**—*pop pl* WV-2
Light and Life Chapel—*church* CO-8
Light and Life Free Methodist Chapel—*church* IN-6
Light and Life Sch—*school* CA-9
Light Bay—*swamp* (2) GA-3
Light Branch—*stream* IN-6
Lightburn—*locale* WV-2
Lightburn Lateral—*canal* CO-8
Light Canyon—*valley* (2) CA-9
Lightcap Sch—*school* SD-7
Light Cem—*cemetery* AZ-5
Light Cem—*cemetery* (2) IN-6
Light Cem—*cemetery* MO-7
Light Cem—*cemetery* NY-2
Light Cem—*cemetery* (2) TN-4
Light Chapel—*locale* TX-5
Light Chapel Ch—*church* TX-5
Light Chute—*stream* IL-6
Light Coulee—*valley* MT-8
Light Creek—*stream* OH-6
Light Creek—*stream* TN-4
Light Creek—*stream* TX-5
Lighted Top—*summit* VA-3
Light Eightynine—*locale* TX-5
Lightening Basin—*valley* CO-8
Lightening Gulch—*valley* CO-8
Lighter Bay—*bay* FL-3
Lighter Bayou—*lake* FL-3
Lighter Creek—*stream* AK-9
Lighter Knot Creek—*stream* FL-3
Lighter Knot Swamp—*stream* NC-3
Lighter Knott Creek—*stream* AL-4
Lighter Log Pond—*lake* FL-3
Lighter Snag Creek—*stream* AL-4
Lighter Snag Creek—*stream* FL-3
Lighter-than-Air Ship Hangars—*hist pl* CA-9
Lighterwood Bayou—*stream* AR-4
Light Fiftynine—*locale* TX-5
*Lightfoot* AL-4
Lightfoot—*locale* VA-3
**Lightfoot**—*pop pl* GA-3
**Lightfoot**—*pop pl* TN-4
Lightfoot Bar—*bar* ID-8
Lightfoot Bay—*bay* MI-6
Lightfoot Branch—*stream* AL-4
Lightfoot Cem—*cemetery* AL-4
Lightfoot Cem—*cemetery* (2) TX-5
Lightfoot Creek—*stream* CA-9
Lightfoot Creek—*stream* TX-5
Lightfoot Creek—*stream* VA-3
Lightfoot Dam—*dam* AL-4
Lightfoot Fork—*stream* KY-4
Lightfoot Hollow—*valley* WI-6
Lightfoot Hot Springs—*spring* ID-8
Light Foot Lake—*lake* MN-6
Lightfoot Lake—*reservoir* AL-4
Lightfoot Mill—*hist pl* PA-2
Lightfoot Pit—*mine* CA-9
Lightfoot Post Office (historical)—*building* TN-4
Lightfoot Public Use Area—*park* MO-7
Lightfoot Ridge—*ridge* WI-6
Lightfoot Sch—*school* VA-3
Lightfoots Furnace—*locale* DE-2
Lightfoot Tunnel—*mine* CA-9
Lightfoot Well—*locale* NM-5
Lightfoot Windmill—*locale* NM-5
Light Ford—*locale* AL-4
Light Fourteen—*tower* NC-3
Lightfritz Ridge—*ridge* OH-6
Light Gap—*gap* AL-4
Light Gap—*gap* NC-3
Light Ground Pocosin—*swamp* NC-3
Light Gulch—*valley* CO-8
Light Hall—*hist pl* NM-5
Light Hall Well—*well* AZ-5
Light Hill—*summit* TX-5
Lighthipe Substation—*other* CA-9
**Light (historical)**—*pop pl* TN-4
Light Hollow—*valley* TN-4
*Lighthouse* FL-3
Lighthouse—*hist pl* NY-2
Lighthouse—*post sta* OK-5
Lighthouse Assembly of God—*church* FL-3
Lighthouse Baptist Ch—*church* FL-3
Lighthouse Baptist Ch—*church* TN-4
*Lighthouse Bay* FL-3
Lighthouse Bay—*bay* (2) NC-3
Lighthouse Bay—*bay* WI-6
Lighthouse Bayou—*bay* FL-3
Lighthouse Bayou—*gut* LA-4
Lighthouse Bayou—*gut* MS-4
Lighthouse Bayou—*stream* LA-4
Lighthouse Beach—*beach* OR-9
**Lighthouse Beach**—*pop pl* NY-2
Light House Camp—*locale* AL-4
Light House Camp—*locale* MI-6
Lighthouse Canyon—*valley* UT-8
*Lighthouse Ch* AL-4
Lighthouse Ch—*church* (3) AL-4
Light House Ch—*church* AL-4
Lighthouse Ch—*church* (2) AL-4
Lighthouse Ch—*church* FL-3
Lighthouse Ch—*church* (2) LA-4
Lighthouse Ch—*church* MI-6
Lighthouse Ch—*church* (2) MS-4
Lighthouse Ch—*church* (2) NC-3
Light House Ch—*church* OK-5
Light House Ch—*church* TN-4
Lighthouse Channel—*channel* NC-3
Lighthouse Church, The—*church* MO-7
Lighthouse Community Ch—*church* AL-4
Lighthouse County Park—*park* MI-6
Lighthouse Cove—*bay* DE-2
Lighthouse Cove—*bay* RI-1
Lighthouse Cove—*bay* TX-5
Lighthouse Cove—*cove* MA-1
*Lighthouse Creek* AR-4
*Lighthouse Creek* NC-3
*Lighthouse Creek* SC-3
Lighthouse Creek—*bay* NC-3
Lighthouse Creek—*stream* AR-4
Lighthouse Creek—*stream* GA-3
Lighthouse Creek—*stream* SC-3
Lighthouse Ditch—*canal* AR-4
Lighthouse Field—*building* PA-2
Lighthouse First Pentecostal Ch—*church* MS-4
Lighthouse For God Ch—*church* OH-6
Lighthouse Hill—*summit* CT-1
Lighthouse Hill—*summit* MA-1
Lighthouse Hill—*summit* NY-2
Lighthouse Hill—*summit* VT-1
Lighthouse Inlet—*bay* SC-3
*Lighthouse Island* FL-3
*Light-house Island* MA-1
*Light House Island* NY-2
Lighthouse Island—*island* MI-6
Lighthouse Island—*island* SC-3
Lighthouse Lake—*lake* KY-4
Lighthouse Landing—*locale* SC-3
Lighthouse Marina and Campground—*locale* IA-7
Lighthouse Marsh—*swamp* MA-1
Lighthouse Mission of Orlando—*church* FL-3
Lighthouse Missions Outreach—*church* FL-3
Lighthouse One Hundred Nineteen—*locale* SC-3
Lighthouse One Hundred Seventeen—*locale* SC-3
Lighthouse One Hundred Sixteen—*locale* SC-3
Lighthouse Park—*park* PA-2
*Lighthouse Pass* TX-5
Lighthouse Peak—*summit* TX-5
Lighthouse Plaza (Shop Ctr)—*locale* FL-3
*Light House Point* MA-1
*Lighthouse Point* MI-6
Lighthouse Point—*cape* AK-9
Lighthouse Point—*cape* CT-1
Lighthouse Point—*cape* FL-3
Lighthouse Point—*cape* LA-4
Lighthouse Point—*cape* MA-1
Lighthouse Point—*cape* (5) MI-6
Lighthouse Point—*cape* MS-4
Lighthouse Point—*cape* NY-2
Lighthouse Point—*cape* SC-3
Lighthouse Point—*cape* WA-9
**Lighthouse Point**—*pop pl* (2) FL-3
Lighthouse Point Carousel—*hist pl* CT-1
Lighthouse Point Gas Field—*oilfield* LA-4
Lighthouse Point Park—*park* CT-1
Lighthouse Pond—*lake* NJ-2
Lighthouse Pool—*lake* FL-3
Lighthouse Reef—*bar* WI-6
*Light-House Rock* AZ-5
Lighthouse Rock—*pillar* AZ-5
Lighthouse Rock—*pillar* OR-9
Lighthouse Rock—*pillar* (2) WI-6
Lighthouse Sch—*school* CA-9
Lighthouse Sch—*school* IL-6
Lighthouse Six—*locale* SC-3
Lighthouse Tabernacle—*church* IN-6
Lighthouse Tabernacle—*church* (2) MI-6
Lighthouse Tabernacle—*church* TN-4
Lighthouse Tabernacle—*church* WV-2
Lighthouse Temple—*church* OK-5
Lighthouse Thirty-three—*locale* SC-3
Lighthouse Twelve—*locale* SC-3
Lighthouse Twenty-three—*locale* SC-3
Lighting Bayou—*stream* LA-4
Lighting Camp—*locale* CA-9
Lighting Camp Ridge—*ridge* CA-9
Lighting Canyon—*valley* AZ-5
Lighting Creek—*stream* IA-7
Lighting Creek—*stream* ND-7
Lighting Creek Campground—*locale* WA-9
*Lighting Crow Creek* SD-7
Lighting Knot Cove—*bay* MD-2
*Lighting Lake* WY-8
Lighting Mtn—*summit* CA-9
Lighting Ridge—*ridge* NM-5
Lighting Ridge—*ridge* WY-8
*Lighting Rock* UT-8
Lighting Tree Point—*cape* CA-9
Light JHS—*school* OH-6
Lightkeeper's House—*hist pl* MN-6
Light Lake—*lake* MI-6
Lightle Flat—*flat* OR-9
Lightle House—*hist pl* AR-4
Lightline Lake—*lake* MS-4
*Lightmile Creek* UT-8
Light Mill—*locale* TN-4
Light Model Tank No. 95—*hist pl* GU-9
Lightner—*locale* TX-5
**Lightner**—*pop pl* PA-2
Lightner, Isaac, House—*hist pl* PA-2
Lightner Cem—*cemetery* MO-7
Lightner Cem—*cemetery* OH-6
Lightner Cem—*cemetery* VA-3
*Lightner Creek* IA-7
Lightner Creek—*stream* CO-8
Lightner Draw—*valley* ID-8
Lightner Hosp—*hospital* IL-6
Lightner Mine—*mine* (2) CA-9
Lightner Peak—*summit* (2) CA-9
Lightner Ranch—*locale* WY-8
Lightner Run—*stream* (2) PA-2
Lightner Run—*stream* VA-3
Lightners Elem Sch (abandoned)—*school* PA-2
Lightners Flat—*flat* CA-9
*Lightners Run* PA-2
*Lightners Sch* PA-2
**Lightners Tract**—*pop pl* PA-2
Lightner Trail—*trail* PA-2
Lightning Brook—*stream* VT-1
*Lightning Bug Center* TN-4
Lightning Bug Hollow—*valley* TX-5
Lightning Bug Spring—*spring* TX-5
Lightning Camp Ridge—*ridge* CA-9
Lightning Canyon—*valley* CA-9
Lightning Corral—*locale* CA-9
Lightning C Ranch—*locale* TX-5
*Lightning Creek* ID-8
*Lightning Creek* MT-8
*Lightning Creek* OR-9
Lightning Creek—*stream* AK-9
Lightning Creek—*stream* CA-9
Lightning Creek—*stream* (14) ID-8
Lightning Creek—*stream* KS-7
Lightning Creek—*stream* (3) MT-8
Lightning Creek—*stream* ND-7
Lightning Creek—*stream* (2) OK-5
Lightning Creek—*stream* (5) OR-9
Lightning Creek—*stream* (2) SD-7
Lightning Creek—*stream* (6) WA-9
Lightning Creek—*stream* WI-6
Lightning Creek—*stream* (2) WY-8
Lightning Creek Ch—*church* OK-5
Lightning Creek Oil Field—*oilfield* WY-8
Lightning Creek Placers—*mine* OR-9
Lightning Creek Ridge—*ridge* WA-9
Lightning Creek Rocks—*summit* ID-8
Lightning Creek Saddle—*gap* ID-8
Lightning Creek State Wildlife Area—*park* WI-6
**Lightning Creek Township**—*pop pl* ND-7
Lightning Creek Trail—*trail* MT-8
Lightning Creek Trail (historical)—*trail* ID-8
Lightning Delivery Co. Warehouse—*hist pl* AZ-5
Lightning Dike—*dam* WY-8
Lightning Dock Mtn—*summit* NM-5
Lightning Draw—*valley* (2) UT-8
Lightning Flat—*flat* TX-5
Lightning Flat—*flat* UT-8
Lightning Fork Little Elk Creek—*stream* ID-8
Lightning Gulch—*valley* (3) CA-9
Lightning Gulch—*valley* (2) OR-9
Lightning Hill—*summit* NH-1
Lightning Hill—*summit* NY-2
Lightning Hills—*summit* TX-5
**Lightning (historical)**—*pop pl* OR-9
Lightning Hollow—*valley* TN-4
Lightning Hollow—*valley* UT-8
Lightning Killed Bull Spring—*spring* UT-8
Lightning Lake—*lake* ID-8
Lightning Lake—*lake* MN-6
Lightning Lake—*lake* MT-8
Lightning Lake—*lake* NM-5
Lightning Lake—*lake* (2) UT-8
Lightning Lake—*lake* WA-9
Lightning Lakes—*lake* WY-8
Lightning Ledge—*bench* ME-1
Lightning Mesa—*bench* NM-5
Lightning Mesa—*summit* AZ-5
Lightning Mesa Tank—*reservoir* NM-5
*Lightning Mountain* MT-8
Lightning Mtn—*summit* ID-8
Lightning Mtn—*summit* NH-1
Lightning Park—*area* UT-8
Lightning Park—*flat* AZ-5
Lightning Park—*flat* UT-8
*Lightning Peak* ID-8
Lightning Peak—*summit* (2) ID-8
Lightning Peak—*summit* (2) MT-8
Lightning Peak—*summit* UT-8
Lightning Peak—*summit* WA-9
*Lightning Point* ID-8
Lightning Point—*cape* NY-2
Lightning Point—*cliff* ID-8
Lightning Point—*summit* TX-5
*Lightning Point Creek* ID-8
Lightning Points—*summit* ID-8
Lightning Ranch Airstrip—*airport* AZ-5
Lightning Ridge—*ridge* CA-9
Lightning Ridge—*ridge* CO-8
Lightning Ridge—*ridge* (4) ID-8
Lightning Ridge—*ridge* (2) UT-8
Lightning Ridge Ch—*church* OK-5
Lightning Rock—*pillar* UT-8
Lightning R Ranch—*locale* AZ-5
*Lightning Run* PA-2
Lightning Run—*stream* PA-2
Lightning Spring—*spring* (2) CA-9
Lightning Spring—*spring* MT-8
Lightning Spring—*spring* NM-5
Lightning Spring—*spring* (2) OR-9
Lightning Spring—*spring* UT-8
Lightning Spring—*spring* WA-9
Lightning Spring (39HN204)—*hist pl* SD-7
Lightning Trail—*trail* CA-9
Lightning Valley—*basin* NE-7
Lightning Windmill—*locale* NM-5
Light Nixon Fork—*locale* NC-3
Light Oak Ch—*church* NC-3
Light of Christ Catholic Ch—*church* FL-3
Light of Hope Chapel—*church* MI-6
Light of Liberty Ch—*church* VA-3
Light of the Word Ch—*church* AL-4
Light of the World Ch—*church* AL-4
Light of the World Holy Ch of God—*church* FL-3
Light of the World Temple—*church* AL-4
Light One Hundred Fifty-four Little River Winyah Bay—*locale* SC-3
Light Park—*park* KS-7
Light Peak—*summit* OR-9
Light Pink Ch—*church* TN-4
Light Pink Quarry—*mine* TN-4
Light Point—*cape* AK-9
Light Post Office (historical)—*building* TN-4
Light Ridge—*ridge* OR-9
Light Run—*stream* IN-6
Light Run—*stream* OH-6
Light Run—*stream* (2) WV-2
*Lights Chapel* TN-4
*Lights Chapel Baptist Church* TN-4
Lights Chapel Cem—*cemetery* TN-4
Light Sch (historical)—*school* AL-4
Light Sch (historical)—*school* MO-7
Lights Creek—*stream* CA-9
Lights Dam—*dam* PA-2
Light Seventynine—*locale* TX-5
Lightsey—*locale* MS-4
Lightsey Bay—*bay* GA-3
Lightsey Hammock—*island* GA-3
*Lightseys Mill Pond* AL-4
Lightseys Mill Pond Dam—*dam* AL-4
Lightseys Pond—*reservoir* AL-4
Lights Ford Bridge—*other* WV-2
**Lights (historical)**—*pop pl* OR-9
Light Sixtynine—*locale* TX-5
Light Spring—*spring* ID-8
Light Spring—*spring* NM-5
*Lightstreet* PA-2
**Light Street**—*pop pl* PA-2
**Lightsville**—*pop pl* IL-6
**Lightsville**—*pop pl* OH-6
Light Swamp—*swamp* NC-3
Light Trout Club Lake—*reservoir* VT-1
Light Twentyone—*locale* TX-5
Light Twenty-seven Winyah Bay Western Channel—*locale* SC-3
**Lightville (historical)**—*pop pl* MS-4
**Lightwood**—*pop pl* AL-4
Lightwood Knot Branch—*stream* AL-4
Lightwood Knot Branch—*stream* (2) SC-3
*Lightwood Knot Creek* NC-3
*Lightwood Knot Creek* SC-3
Lightwood Knot Creek—*stream* AL-4
Lightwood Knot Creek—*stream* FL-3
Lightwood Knot Creek—*stream* NC-3
Lightwood Knot Creek—*stream* (2) SC-3
Lightwood Knox Canal—*canal* FL-3
Lightwood Log Branch—*stream* SC-3
Lightwood Log Creek—*stream* GA-3
Lightwood Mtn—*summit* NC-3
Lightwood Pond—*lake* NC-3
Lightwood Sch—*school* AL-4
Lightwood Snag Bay—*bay* NC-3
Lightwood Swamp—*swamp* VA-3
Ligias Fork—*stream* TN-4
*Ligias Fork Creek* TN-4
*Ligias Post Office* TN-4
Ligias Ridge—*ridge* TN-4
*Ligieb* MP-9
*Ligiep* MP-9
Ligif—*cape* FM-9
*Lignite* ND-7
Lignite—*locale* AK-9
Lignite—*locale* AR-4
Lignite—*locale* VA-3
**Lignite**—*pop pl* ND-7
*Lignite Canyon* UT-8
Lignite Creek—*stream* (2) AK-9
Lignite Creek—*stream* MT-8
**Lignite Junction**—*pop pl* ND-7
Lignite Mine—*mine* ND-7
Lignite Sch Number 3—*school* ND-7
Lignite Spring—*spring* MS-4
Lignum—*locale* VA-3
Lignumvitae Basin—*bay* FL-3
Lignumvitae Channel—*channel* FL-3
*Lignum Vitae Key* FL-3
Lignumvitae Key—*island* FL-3
Lignumvitae Key Aquatic Preserve—*park* FL-3
Lignumvitae Key Bank—*bar* FL-3
Ligon—*locale* KY-4
Ligon Cem—*cemetery* (2) AL-4
Ligon Cem—*cemetery* MS-4
Ligon Cem—*cemetery* TN-4
*Ligon Creek* AL-4
Ligon Creek—*stream* AL-4
Ligon Creek—*stream* AR-4
Ligonee Brook—*stream* NY-2
Ligon HS—*school* NC-3
**Ligonia**—*pop pl* ME-1
**Ligonier**—*pop pl* IN-6
**Ligonier**—*pop pl* PA-2
Ligonier Airp—*airport* IN-6
Ligonier Borough—*civil* PA-2
Ligonier Country Club—*other* PA-2
Ligonier Dam—*dam* PA-2
*Ligonier Golf Club* PA-2
Ligonier Hist Dist—*hist pl* IN-6
Ligonier Point—*cape* NY-2
Ligonier Rsvr—*reservoir* PA-2
**Ligonier (Township of)**—*pop pl* PA-2
Ligonier Township Rsvr—*reservoir* PA-2
Ligonier Valley HS—*school* PA-2
Ligon Oil Field—*oilfield* TX-5
Ligon Ranch—*locale* (3) TX-5
Ligon Slough—*gut* MO-7
Ligon Springs—*locale* AL-4
Ligon Springs Ch—*church* AL-4
*Ligon Springs Ch of Christ* AL-4
Ligon Springs Sch (historical)—*school* AL-4
Ligon Windmill—*locale* TX-5
Ligo Sch—*school* (2) PA-2
Ligs Spring—*spring* CA-9
Liguan—*area* GU-9
Liguan Point—*cape* GU-9
**Liguori**—*pop pl* MO-7
Ligurta—*locale* AZ-5
Lihau—*summit* HI-9
Lihiwai—*hist pl* HI-9
Lihiwai (Boundary Increase)—*hist pl* HI-9
Liholiho Sch—*school* HI-9
**Lihue**—*pop pl* HI-9
Lihue Airp—*airport* HI-9
Lihue (CCD)—*cens area* HI-9
Lihue Cem—*cemetery* HI-9
Lihue Civic Center Hist Dist—*hist pl* HI-9
Lihue Hongwanji Mission—*hist pl* HI-9
Lihue Knob—*summit* NC-3
Lihue-Koloa For Res—*forest* HI-9
Lihue Park—*park* HI-9
Liichliter Gulch—*valley* CO-8
Lii Haaditiih Hill—*summit* AZ-5
Lii Haditiih Tank—*reservoir* AZ-5
Liil—*locale* FM-9
Liilioholo—*cape* HI-9
Lijeron—*island* MP-9
*Lijeron Island* MP-9
Lijibworo—*island* MP-9
Lik, Foko—*reef* FM-9
Lik'aay—*cape* FM-9
*Likaman* MP-9
*Lik'ay* FM-9
*Likeley Hollow* AL-4
Likelike Sch—*school* HI-9
**Likely**—*pop pl* CA-9
**Likely**—*pop pl* FL-3
Likely Gulch—*valley* CO-8
Likely Mtn—*summit* CA-9
Likely Rancheria (Indian Reservation)—*reserve* CA-9
Likens Cem—*cemetery* OH-6
Likens Ch—*church* OH-6
Likens Run—*stream* PA-2
*Likenwise Dam* SD-7
Likes—*summit* FM-9
Likes Creek—*stream* AK-9
Likes Lake—*reservoir* NV-8
*Likieb* MP-9
*Likieb Inseln* MP-9
*Likieb Islands* MP-9
Likiej—*island* MP-9
Likiep Atoll—*island* (2) MP-9
Likiep (County-equivalent)—*civil* MP-9
Likiep Island—*island* MP-9
Likiep Island Anchorage—*harbor* MP-9
Likiep Lagoon (not verified)—*lake* MP-9
**Likiep (not verified)**—*pop pl* MP-9
Likin Kotokot—*unknown* FM-9
Likinloang—*unknown* FM-9
Likin Mweli, Dauen—*gut* FM-9
Likin Nahri—*bar* FM-9
Likin Peilam—*bar* FM-9
Likin Peinko—*locale* FM-9
Likins Rsvr—*reservoir* WY-8
**Likkie**—*pop pl* FM-9
*Likkijjine Island* MP-9
Likleb—*island* MP-9
Liksuklo Creek—*stream* OK-5
*Lil* FM-9
Lila—*locale* NY-2
**Lila**—*pop pl* WV-2
Lila, Lake—*lake* GA-3
Lila, Lake—*lake* NY-2
*Lilac* MP-9
Lilac—*locale* CA-9
Lilac—*locale* KY-4
Lilac—*locale* MS-4
**Lilac**—*pop pl* TX-5
Lila Canyon—*valley* UT-8
Lilac Canal—*canal* CA-9
Lilac Ch—*church* TX-5
*Lilac Circle Homes* IL-6
Lilac Drain—*canal* CA-9
Lilac Golf Club—*other* MI-6
**Lilac (historical)**—*pop pl* TN-4
Lila C Mine—*mine* CA-9
Lilac Park—*park* OK-5
Lilac Plaza (Shop Ctr)—*locale* IA-7
Lilac Post Office (historical)—*building* MS-4
Lilac Tunnel—*tunnel* CA-9
Lilak Creek—*stream* MI-6
Lila Lake—*lake* AK-9
Lila Lake—*lake* WA-9
Lila Point—*cliff* UT-8
Lila Rebecca Webster Lake—*reservoir* AL-4
Lila Rebecca Webster Lake Dam—*dam* AL-4
**Lilbert**—*pop pl* TX-5
**Lilbourn**—*pop pl* MO-7
Lilbourn Fortified Village Archeol Site—*hist pl* MO-7
**Lilburn**—*pop pl* GA-3
Lilburn (CCD)—*cens area* GA-3
Lilburn Post Office (historical)—*building* TN-4
Lil Creek—*stream* AK-9
Lild—*island* PW-9
Lile—*locale* WV-2
*Lile Academy* AL-4
*Lileb* MP-9
Lile Cem—*cemetery* (2) AL-4
**Liledoun**—*pop pl* NC-3
**Liledown**—*pop pl* NC-3
Lile Post Office (historical)—*building* AL-4
**Liles Addition (subdivision)**—*pop pl* TN-4
Liles Airp—*airport* TN-4
Liles Brake—*swamp* AR-4
Liles Branch—*stream* AL-4
Liles Cem—*cemetery* AL-4
Liles Cem—*cemetery* OR-9
Liles Cem—*cemetery* TN-4
*Liles Creek* NC-3
Liles Ditch—*canal* OH-6
Liles Hollow—*valley* MO-7
Liles Hollow—*valley* TN-4
Liles Lake—*reservoir* AL-4
Liles Lookout Tower—*locale* NC-3
**Lilesville**—*pop pl* NC-3
Lilesville Sch—*school* NC-3
Lilesville (Township of)—*fmr MCD* NC-3
Liletown—*locale* KY-4
Liletown Cem—*cemetery* KY-4
*Lilian* MS-4
Lilian—*locale* VA-3
Lili Creek—*stream* AK-9
Lilienfeld, David, House—*hist pl* MI-6
Lilienthal Bldg—*hist pl* OH-6
Lilienthal Mtn—*summit* WA-9
Lilies, Lake of the—*reservoir* NJ-2
Liliko Gulch—*valley* HI-9
Lili Lake—*lake* AK-9
Lililoa—*cape* HI-9
*Lilinoe* HI-9
*Lilipond* GA-3
Liliput Creek—*stream* NC-3
Lilita—*locale* AL-4
Liliuokalani Gardens—*cape* HI-9
Liliuokalani Sch—*school* HI-9
*Lilius Lake* MI-6
Lilja Sch—*school* MA-1
Liljegren Passage—*channel* AK-9
Lillabridge Lake (historical)—*lake* MO-7
Lilla Ch—*church* GA-3
**Lillamay**—*pop pl* TN-4
Lillamay Post Office (historical)—*building* TN-4
Lillamay Sch (historical)—*school* TN-4
Lillan Post Office (historical)—*building* TN-4
**Lillard**—*pop pl* TX-5
Lillard Bluff—*cliff* TN-4
Lillard Branch—*stream* TN-4
Lillard Cem—*cemetery* MO-7
Lillard Cem—*cemetery* OK-5
Lillard Cem—*cemetery* TN-4
Lillard Chapel—*church* TN-4
Lillard Creek—*stream* OK-5
Lillard Dam—*dam* OR-9
Lillard Ditch—*canal* IN-6
Lillard Ditch—*canal* OR-9
Lillard Gap—*gap* TN-4
Lillard Hill—*cape* WA-9

Lillard Lake—*lake* OR-9
Lillard Mill—*locale* TN-4
Lillard Mill Power Plant
(historical)—*building* TN-4
**Lillard Park**—*pop pl* OK-5
Lillard Rsvr—*reservoir* OR-9
Lillard Sch—*school* MO-7
*Lillards Mills* TN-4
Lillards Mills Post Office
(historical)—*building* TN-4
Lillard-Sprague House—*hist pl* AR-4
*Lillard Waterhole* OR-9
**Lille**—*pop pl* ME-1
Lilleas—*locale* OR-9
**Lilleas (historical)**—*pop pl* OR-9
*Lillefalskijlen* DE-2
**Lillehoff Township**—*pop pl* ND-7
Liller Run—*stream* WV-2
*Lilley* MI-6
Lilley—*locale* MI-6
Lilley, Robert D., House—*hist pl* OH-6
Lilley Canyon—*valley* NM-5
Lilley Creek—*stream* LA-4
Lilley Grave Cem—*cemetery* CA-9
Lilley Gulch—*valley* CO-8
Lilley Hill—*summit* OH-6
*Lilley Lake* MI-6
Lilley Lake—*lake* MI-6
Lilley Mtn—*summit* CA-9
Lilley Park—*flat* NM-5
Lilley Park Spring—*spring* NM-5
Lilley Run—*stream* PA-2
Lilley Sch—*school* NE-7
Lilleys Island—*island* MO-7
Lilleys Neck—*cape* VA-3
**Lilley (Township of)**—*pop pl* MI-6
*Lillian* SD-7
**Lillian**—*pop pl* AL-4
**Lillian**—*pop pl* MS-4
**Lillian**—*pop pl* NE-7
**Lillian**—*pop pl* TX-5
**Lillian**—*pop pl* WV-2
Lillian, Lake—*lake* FL-3
Lillian, Lake—*lake* MN-6
Lillian, Lake—*lake* (2) WA-9
Lillian, Lake—*reservoir* UT-8
Lillian, Mount—*summit* WA-9
Lillian A Pedigo Sch—*school* TN-4
Lillian Bridge—*bridge* AL-4
Lillian Bridge—*other* FL-3
Lillian Brook—*stream* NY-2
Lillian Ch—*church* AL-4
Lillian Creek—*stream* (2) AK-9
Lillian Creek—*stream* MN-6
Lillian Creek—*stream* NE-7
Lillian Creek—*stream* OR-9
Lillian Creek—*stream* WA-9
Lillian Dabney Sch (historical)—*school* AL-4
Lillian Dickson Sch—*school* NY-2
*Lillian Dunge Sch* AL-4
Lillian Elem Sch (historical)—*school* AL-4
Lillian Emery Elem Sch—*school* IN-6
Lillian Falls—*falls* OR-9
Lillian Fountain Sch (historical)—*school* TN-4
Lillian Glacier—*glacier* WA-9
Lillian Hill—*summit* CA-9
Lillian Home Heart House—*building* PA-2
Lillian Jensen Ranch—*locale* WY-8
Lillian Lake—*lake* CA-9
Lillian Lake—*lake* FL-3
Lillian Lake—*lake* (3) MN-6
Lillian Lake—*lake* (2) MT-8
Lillian Metz Ditch—*canal* IN-6
Lillian M Reiffel Elem Sch—*school* IN-6
Lillian Park—*park* CA-9
Lillian River—*stream* WA-9
Lillian River Trail—*trail* WA-9
Lillian Schmitt Elem Sch—*school* IN-6
Lillian Shelter—*locale* WA-9
Lillian Street Sch—*school* CA-9
Lillian Swamp—*swamp* AL-4
**Lillian Township**—*pop pl* NE-7
Lillian Valley—*valley* NE-7
Lillian Wald—*uninc pl* NY-2
Lilliard Sch (historical)—*school* TN-4
**Lillibridge**—*pop pl* FL-3
Lillibridge, Simon, Farm—*hist pl* RI-1
Lillibridge Creek—*stream* IA-7
Lillibridge Creek—*stream* NY-2
Lillibridge Creek—*stream* PA-2
Lillibridge Pond—*lake* RI-1
Lillibridge Ranch—*locale* ND-7
Lillibridge Sch—*school* IL-6
Lillibridge Sch—*school* MI-6
*Lillie* CO-8
**Lillie**—*pop pl* LA-4
Lillie, Frank R., House—*hist pl* IL-6
*Lillie Burney Junior High School* MS-4
Lillie Ch—*church* LA-4
Lillie Cooper Sch—*school* GA-3
Lillie Creek—*stream* AK-9
Lillie Ditch—*canal* CO-8
Lillie Flat—*flat* OR-9
Lillie Grove Ch—*church* AL-4
Lillie Hill—*summit* NY-2
Lillie Hill Baptist Ch—*church* AL-4
Lillie Lake—*lake* MI-6
Lillie Lake—*lake* WI-6
Lillie Lake—*reservoir* CO-8
*Lillie Mountain* CO-8
Lilliendahl—*locale* VI-3
Lillie Rsvr—*reservoir* CO-8
Lillies Branch—*stream* VA-3
Lillies Ch—*church* AL-4
Lillie Sch—*school* MI-6
*Lillies Chapel* AL-4
Lillies Chapel Sch (historical)—*school* AL-4
Lillies Pinnacle—*summit* NY-2
**Lilliesville**—*pop pl* VT-1
Lilliesville Brook—*stream* VT-1
*Lillieville* VT-1
**Lillieville**—*pop pl* VT-1
*Lillieville Brook* VT-1
Lillie Walker Irrigation Pond—*reservoir* OR-9
Lillie Walker Irrigation Pond Dam—*dam* OR-9
**Lillington**—*pop pl* NC-3
Lillington Creek—*stream* NC-3
Lillington MS—*school* NC-3
Lillington (Township of)—*fmr MCD* NC-3
Lillinonah, Lake—*reservoir* CT-1
*Lillinonah Lake* CT-1
Lilli Pond—*lake* NY-2
*Lilliput Creek* NC-3
Lilliput Glacier—*glacier* CA-9
**Lilliput Landing (subdivision)**—*pop pl* NC-3
Lilliput Trail—*trail* CA-9
**Lillis**—*pop pl* KS-7
Lillis Albina Park—*park* OR-9
Lillis HS—*school* MO-7
Lillis Lake—*lake* MT-8
Lillis Ranch—*locale* CA-9
*Lillius Lake* MI-6
**Lilliwaup**—*pop pl* WA-9
Lilliwaup Bay—*bay* WA-9
Lilliwaup Creek—*stream* WA-9
Lilliwaup Falls—*falls* WA-9
Lilliwaup Swamp—*swamp* WA-9
Lilliwig Creek—*stream* AK-9
Lillus Creek—*stream* TX-5
*Lilluwaup* WA-9
*Lilly* FL-3
*Lilly* OH-6
*Lilly* TN-4
Lilly—*locale* IL-6
Lilly—*locale* MO-7
Lilly—*locale* VA-3
**Lilly**—*pop pl* GA-3
**Lilly**—*pop pl* NC-3
**Lilly**—*pop pl* PA-2
**Lilly**—*pop pl* TX-5
Lilly, Augustus, House—*hist pl* MI-6
*Lilly Addition* WV-2
Lillybanks—*hist pl* OH-6
*Lilly Baptist Ch* AL-4
Lilly Bay—*bay* WI-6
Lilly Bay—*swamp* SC-3
Lilly Bay Creek—*stream* WI-6
Lilly Bayou—*stream* LA-4
Lilly Biological Laboratories—*hist pl* IN-6
Lilly Borough—*civil* PA-2
Lilly Branch—*stream* GA-3
Lilly Branch—*stream* IL-6
Lilly Branch—*stream* MO-7
Lilly Branch—*stream* VT-1
Lilly Branch—*stream* WV-2
Lilly Bridge—*bridge* TN-4
Lilly Bridge—*hist pl* PA-2
Lillybrook—*locale* WV-2
Lilly Brook—*stream* MA-1
*Lilly Cache Creek* IL-6
Lilly Canyon—*valley* CA-9
*Lilly Cem* MS-4
Lilly Cem—*cemetery* MS-4
Lilly Cem—*cemetery* MO-7
Lilly Cem—*cemetery* NY-2
Lilly Cem—*cemetery* TN-4
Lilly Cem—*cemetery* WV-2
Lilly Ch—*church* (2) AL-4
Lilly Chapel—*church* AL-4
**Lilly Chapel**—*pop pl* OH-6
Lilly Chapel Cem—*cemetery* AL-4
*Lilly Creek* MN-6
*Lilly Creek* TX-5
*Lilly Creek* WV-2
Lilly Creek—*stream* AK-9
Lilly Creek—*stream* CA-9
Lilly Creek—*stream* FL-3
Lilly Creek—*stream* GA-3
Lilly Creek—*stream* (2) IN-6
Lilly Creek—*stream* MN-6
Lilly Creek—*stream* MS-4
Lilly Creek—*stream* OK-5
Lilly Creek—*stream* OR-9
Lilly Creek—*stream* SD-7
Lilly Creek—*stream* TX-5
Lilly Creek—*stream* VA-3
Lilly Creek Ch—*church* IN-6
*Lilly Dale* IN-6
*Lilly Dale* NY-2
Lillydale—*locale* WV-2
**Lilly Dale**—*pop pl* IN-6
**Lillydale**—*pop pl* TN-4
**Lillydale**—*pop pl* WV-2
*Lillydale Assembly* NY-2
Lilly Dale Cem—*cemetery* ND-7
Lillydale Cem—*cemetery* PA-2
Lilly Dale Ch—*church* IN-6
**Lillydale (historical)**—*pop pl* TN-4
*Lillydale Landing* TN-4
Lillydale Post Office (historical)—*building* TN-4
Lillydale Rec Area—*park* TN-4
Lillydale Sch (historical)—*school* TN-4
Lilly Dam—*dam* NC-3
Lilly Fork—*stream* WV-2
*Lilly Grove* TN-4
**Lilly Grove**—*pop pl* WV-2
Lilly Grove Ch—*church* AL-4
Lilly Grove Ch (historical)—*church* AL-4
Lilly Grove Sch (historical)—*school* AL-4
**Lillyhaven**—*pop pl* WV-2
Lilly Heights Sch—*school* WV-2
*Lillyhill Ch* AL-4
Lilly Hill Ch—*church* (2) AL-4
Lilly Hill Ch (historical)—*church* AL-4
Lilly Hollow—*valley* MO-7
*Lilly Lake* MT-8
*Lilly Lake* NJ-2
*Lilly Lake* NY-2
*Lilly Lake* OR-9
Lilly Lake—*lake* (3) AK-9
Lilly Lake—*lake* (2) MI-6
Lilly Lake—*lake* MN-6
Lilly Lake—*lake* MT-8
Lilly Lake—*lake* PA-2
Lilly Lake—*lake* (2) TX-5
Lilly Lake—*lake* UT-8
Lilly Lake—*lake* (2) WA-9
Lilly Lake—*lake* (4) WI-6
**Lilly Lake**—*pop pl* WI-6
Lilly Lake—*reservoir* NC-3
Lilly Lake—*reservoir* TX-5
Lilly Lake Campground—*locale* UT-8
Lilly Lake Cem—*cemetery* MI-6
Lilly Lake County Park—*park* WI-6
Lillylands Canal—*canal* CO-8
Lillylands Intake—*canal* CO-8
Lilly Lookout Tower—*tower* IN-6
*Lilly Mann Ditch* IN-6
Lilly Meadows—*flat* CA-9
Lilly Memorial Ch (historical)—*church* TN-4
Lilly Mine—*mine* CA-9
Lilly Mtn—*summit* CA-9
Lilly Mtn—*summit* WV-2
Lilly No 11 Sch—*school* WV-2
Lilly Number Two Rsvr—*reservoir* PA-2
Lilly-of-the-Valley Ch—*church* TX-5
Lillypad Pond—*lake* NY-2
Lilly Pad Tank—*reservoir* TX-5
Lilly Park—*flat* CO-8
**Lilly Park**—*pop pl* WV-2
Lilly Point—*cape* VA-3
Lilly Point Marsh—*swamp* VA-3
*Lillypond* GA-3
*Lilly Pond* MA-1
*Lilly Pond* NJ-2
Lilly Pond—*lake* CO-8
Lilly Pond—*lake* CT-1
Lilly Pond—*lake* (2) ME-1
Lilly Pond—*lake* (2) MA-1
Lilly Pond—*lake* (2) NY-2
Lilly Pond—*lake* OR-9
**Lillypond**—*pop pl* GA-3
Lilly Pond—*swamp* MA-1
Lilly Pond Creek—*stream* NC-3
Lilly Pump—*other* OR-9
Lilly Quick Creek—*stream* SC-3
Lilly Rapids—*rapids* TN-4
Lilly Reservoirs—*reservoir* PA-2
Lilly Ridge—*ridge* WI-6
Lilly Roadside Park—*park* TX-5
*Lilly Rock* CA-9
Lilly Run—*stream* IN-6
Lilly Run—*stream* (2) PA-2
**Lilly Run Junction**—*pop pl* PA-2
Lillys Cem—*cemetery* TN-4
Lilly Sch—*school* (2) IL-6
*Lillys Chapel* AL-4
*Lillys Chapel* TN-4
Lillys Chapel Cem—*cemetery* NC-3
Lillys Chapel Sch—*school* NC-3
Lilly Sch Number 53—*school* IN-6
Lillys Cove—*bay* ME-1
*Lillys Creek* TX-5
Lilly Shoals—*rapids* AL-4
Lillys Millpond—*reservoir* NC-3
Lilly Spring—*spring* FL-3
Lilly Spring—*spring* ID-8
Lilly Spring—*spring* OK-5
Lilly Station—*locale* PA-2
Lilly Tank—*reservoir* AZ-5
*Lilly Valley Church* MS-4
Lilly Valley Sch—*school* AL-4
Lilly Valley Sch (historical)—*school* MS-4
*Lillyville* PA-2
Lillyville—*locale* IL-6
**Lillyville**—*pop pl* PA-2
Lillyville Forest Camp—*locale* OR-9
Lilly Well—*well* NM-5
**Lilmay**—*pop pl* KY-4
Liloe Spring—*spring* HI-9
*Liluis Lake* MI-6
Liluis Lake—*lake* MI-6
*Lily* MO-7
*Lily* OH-6
Lily—*locale* FL-3
**Lily**—*pop pl* KY-4
**Lily**—*pop pl* SD-7
**Lily**—*pop pl* WI-6
Lily, Lake—*lake* (3) FL-3
Lily, Lake—*lake* NJ-2
Lily, Mount—*summit* MT-8
Lilyama Mine—*mine* CA-9
Lily Baptist Ch—*church* (3) AL-4
Lily Basin—*basin* WA-9
Lily Basin Trail—*trail* WA-9
*Lily-bass Lake* WI-6
Lily Bass Lake—*lake* WI-6
*Lily Bay* WI-6
Lily Bay—*bay* ME-1
Lily Bay—*lake* ME-1
Lily Bay Brook—*stream* ME-1
*Lily Bay Mountains* ME-1
Lily Bay Mtn—*summit* ME-1
Lily Bay State Park—*park* ME-1
Lily Bay (Township of)—*unorg* ME-1
Lily B Creek—*stream* OR-9
Lily Belle Mine—*mine* CO-8
Lily Bog—*swamp* ME-1
Lily Boom Cutoff—*channel* LA-4
Lily Branch—*stream* GA-3
Lily Branch—*stream* NC-3
Lily Branch—*stream* WV-2
Lily Branch Ch—*church* NC-3
Lily Bridge—*bridge* NC-3
Lily Brook—*stream* CT-1
Lily Brook—*stream* MA-1
Lily Brook—*stream* NY-2
Lily Brook—*stream* VT-1
**Lily Cache**—*pop pl* IL-6
**Lily Cache Acres**—*pop pl* IL-6
Lily Cache Creek—*stream* IL-6
Lily Camp—*locale* OR-9
Lily Canyon—*valley* NM-5
Lily Cem—*cemetery* WV-2
Lily Cem—*cemetery* WI-6
*Lily Ch* AL-4
Lily Ch—*church* (2) AL-4
Lily Ch—*church* FL-3
Lily Chapel—*church* NC-3
Lily Chapel—*church* OH-6
Lily Coulee—*valley* MT-8
Lily Cove—*bay* ME-1
Lily Cove Branch—*stream* VA-3
Lily Creek—*stream* AK-9
Lily Creek—*stream* (2) CA-9
Lily Creek—*stream* IL-6
Lily Creek—*stream* KS-7
Lily Creek—*stream* KY-4
Lily Creek—*stream* MI-6
Lily Creek—*stream* MN-6
Lily Creek—*stream* MT-8
Lily Creek—*stream* (2) WA-9
Lily Cup—*locale* CA-9
*Lilydale* NY-2
**Lilydale**—*pop pl* MN-6
**Lily Dale**—*pop pl* NY-2
Lily Dale Sch—*school* KS-7
Lily Ditch—*canal* WY-8
Lily Farm—*locale* MO-7
**Lily Flag**—*pop pl* AL-4
**Lily Flagg**—*pop pl* AL-4
Lily Flagg Club—*locale* AL-4
Lily Gap—*gap* CA-9
Lily Gardens Park—*park* IL-6
**Lilyglen (historical)**—*pop pl* OR-9
*Lilygreen Ch* AL-4
Lily Green Ch—*church* AL-4
Lily Grove—*locale* TN-4
**Lily Grove**—*pop pl* AL-4
Lily Grove Baptist Ch—*church* MS-4
Lily Grove Ch—*church* AL-4
Lily Grove Ch—*church* MO-7
Lily Grove Ch—*church* TX-5
Lily Grove Ch (reduced usage)—*church* TX-5
Lily Grove Missionary Baptist Ch—*church* AL-4
Lily Grove Missionary Baptist Ch—*church* TN-4
Lily Grove Sch (historical)—*school* TN-4
Lily Gulch—*valley* CA-9
Lily Hill—*summit* VT-1
Lily Hill Cem—*cemetery* TX-5
*Lily Hill Ch* AL-4
Lily Hill Ch—*church* (2) AL-4
Lily Hill Ch—*church* TN-4
Lily Hill Ch—*church* TX-5
Lily (historical)—*locale* AL-4
**Lily (historical)**—*pop pl* SD-7
Lily Hole—*lake* MA-1
Lily Hole Spring—*spring* AZ-5
Lily Hollow—*valley* WY-8
Lily Island—*locale* TX-5
Lily Island Cem—*cemetery* TX-5
Lily Lagoon—*lake* LA-4
*Lily Lake* AK-9
*Lily Lake* CA-9
*Lily Lake* MI-6
*Lily Lake* NJ-2
*Lily Lake* PA-2
*Lily Lake* UT-8
*Lily Lake* WI-6
Lily Lake—*lake* AL-4
Lily Lake—*lake* (5) AK-9
Lily Lake—*lake* (11) CA-9
Lily Lake—*lake* (6) CO-8
Lily Lake—*lake* (2) FL-3
Lily Lake—*lake* (2) ID-8
Lily Lake—*lake* (3) IL-6
Lily Lake—*lake* IN-6
Lily Lake—*lake* IA-7
Lily Lake—*lake* (4) ME-1
Lily Lake—*lake* (7) MI-6
Lily Lake—*lake* (14) MN-6
Lily Lake—*lake* (2) MT-8
Lily Lake—*lake* NE-7
Lily Lake—*lake* NH-1
Lily Lake—*lake* (4) NY-2
Lily Lake—*lake* (5) OR-9
Lily Lake—*lake* (3) UT-8
Lily Lake—*lake* (5) WA-9
Lily Lake—*lake* (10) WI-6
Lily Lake—*lake* (4) WY-8
**Lily Lake**—*pop pl* IL-6
Lily Lake—*reservoir* (2) CO-8
Lily Lake—*reservoir* MO-7
Lily Lake—*reservoir* NJ-2
Lily Lake—*reservoir* PA-2
Lily Lake—*swamp* IL-6
Lily Lake—*swamp* NY-2
Lily Lake—*swamp* TN-4
Lily Lake Cem—*cemetery* IL-6
Lily Lake Ch—*church* IL-6
Lily Lake Creek—*stream* UT-8
Lily Lake Dam—*dam* NJ-2
Lily Lake Dam—*dam* PA-2
Lily Lake Drain—*canal* IL-6
Lily Lakes—*lake* UT-8
Lily Lake Sch—*school* KS-7
Lily Lake Sch—*school* MN-6
Lilylands Canal—*canal* CO-8
Lilylands Rsvr—*reservoir* CO-8
Lily Mae Cem—*cemetery* MS-4
Lily Marsh—*swamp* NY-2
Lily Mere—*lake* MA-1
Lily Miller Branch—*stream* FL-3
Lily Mine—*mine* CA-9
Lily Mine—*mine* CO-8
Lily Mine (underground)—*mine* AL-4
**Lilymoor**—*pop pl* IL-6
Lily Mountain Trail—*trail* CO-8
Lily Mtn—*summit* CO-8
Lily Mtn—*summit* KY-4
Lily Number One Rsvr—*reservoir* PA-2
Lily of the Valley Ch—*church* FL-3
Lily of The Valley Ch—*church* MO-7
Lily of the Valley Ch—*church* NC-3
Lily of the Valley Ch—*church* VA-3
Lily of the Valley Ch—*church* WV-2
Lily of the West Gulch—*valley* MT-8
Lily Orchard Ch—*church* MS-4
Lily-Orphan Boy Mine—*mine* MT-8
Lily Pad Brook—*stream* NY-2
*Lily Pad Creek* WI-6
Lily Pad Creek—*stream* CO-8
Lilypad Creek—*stream* NY-2
Lilypad Creek—*stream* WI-6
*Lily Pad Lake* UT-8
Lily Pad Lake—*lake* (4) CA-9
Lilypad Lake—*lake* CA-9
Lily Pad Lake—*lake* (2) CO-8
Lily Pad Lake—*lake* ID-8
Lilypad Lake—*lake* MI-6
Lily Pad Lake—*lake* MN-6
Lilypad Lake—*lake* MN-6
Lilypad Lake—*lake* MT-8
Lily Pad Lake—*lake* MT-8
Lilypad Lake—*lake* OR-9
Lily Pad Lake—*lake* OR-9
Lily Pad Lake—*lake* (4) UT-8
Lilypad Lake—*lake* WA-9
Lilypad Lake—*lake* WI-6
Lilypad Lake—*lake* WY-8
Lily Pad Lake—*reservoir* OK-5
Lily Pad Lakes—*lake* UT-8
*Lilypad Pond* NY-2
Lily Pad Pond—*lake* ME-1
Lilypad Pond—*lake* (4) NY-2
Lily Pad Pond—*lake* NY-2
Lilypad Pond—*lake* (2) NY-2
Lily Pad Pond—*lake* VT-1
Lilypad Pond—*lake* WY-8
Lilypad Ponds—*lake* NY-2
Lily Pad Rsvr—*reservoir* CO-8
Lily Park—*flat* CO-8
Lily Patch Tank—*reservoir* NM-5
Lily Plummer Cem—*cemetery* AL-4
Lily Pod Pond—*lake* NY-2
*Lily Pond* GA-3
*Lily Pond* MA-1
*Lily Pond* NJ-2
*Lily Pond* VA-3
Lily Pond—*bay* WI-6
Lily Pond—*lake* AL-4
Lily Pond—*lake* (3) CA-9
Lily Pond—*lake* (3) CO-8
Lily Pond—*lake* (4) CT-1
Lily Pond—*lake* FL-3
Lily Pond—*lake* ID-8
Lily Pond—*lake* IL-6
Lily Pond—*lake* (2) IA-7
Lily Pond—*lake* (21) ME-1
Lily Pond—*lake* (11) MA-1
Lily Pond—*lake* (3) MI-6
Lily Pond—*lake* MN-6
Lily Pond—*lake* MS-4
Lily Pond—*lake* MO-7
Lily Pond—*lake* (11) NH-1
Lily Pond—*lake* (8) NY-2
Lily Pond—*lake* OH-6
Lily Pond—*lake* OR-9
Lily Pond—*lake* (2) RI-1
Lily Pond—*lake* (6) VT-1
Lilypond—*locale* GA-3
Lily Pond—*reservoir* CO-8
Lily Pond—*reservoir* CT-1
Lily Pond—*reservoir* (2) MA-1
Lily Pond—*reservoir* NY-2
Lily Pond—*reservoir* PA-2
Lily Pond—*reservoir* WY-8
Lily Pond—*swamp* ME-1
Lily Pond—*swamp* MI-6
*Lily Pond, The* ME-1
*Lily Pond Beach* RI-1
Lily Pond Bog—*swamp* MA-1
Lily Pond Brook—*stream* NH-1
Lily Pond Brook—*stream* NY-2
Lily Pond Creek—*stream* OK-5
Lily Pond Dam—*dam* MA-1
Lily Pond Hill—*summit* NY-2
Lily Pond (historical)—*lake* (2) MA-1
Lily Pond (historical)—*swamp* MA-1
Lily Pond Lake—*lake* CO-8
Lily Pond Lake—*lake* WA-9
Lily Pond Lake—*lake* WY-8
Lily Pond Outlet Dam—*dam* MA-1
Lily Pond Park—*flat* CO-8
Lily Ponds—*lake* MA-1
Lily Pond Spring—*spring* CO-8
Lilypons—*locale* MD-2
Lilypons Bridge—*bridge* MD-2
Lily Post Office (historical)—*building* MS-4
Lily Ridge—*ridge* MO-7
Lily Ridge Ch—*church* MO-7
Lily River—*stream* WI-6
Lily Rock—*summit* CA-9
Lily Rose Ch—*church* MS-4
*Lily Run* PA-2
Lily Sch—*school* AL-4
Lilys Chapel—*church* TN-4
Lily Spring—*spring* CA-9
Lily Springs—*springs* WI-6
Lily Springs State Fishery Area—*park* WI-6
Lily State Public Shooting Area—*park* SD-7
Lily Swamp Post Office
(historical)—*building* TN-4
Lily Valley—*flat* CA-9
Lily Valley—*valley* PA-2
Lily Valley Ch—*church* NC-3
Lily White Guard Station—*locale* OR-9
*Lima* IN-6
*Lima* MI-6
Lima—*locale* IA-7
Lima—*locale* NC-3
Lima—*locale* OH-6
**Lima**—*pop pl* IL-6
**Lima**—*pop pl* MT-8
**Lima**—*pop pl* NY-2
**Lima**—*pop pl* OH-6
**Lima**—*pop pl* OK-5
**Lima**—*pop pl* PA-2
**Lima**—*pop pl* SC-3
**Lima**—*pop pl* VA-3
**Lima**—*pop pl* WV-2
Lima Army Tank Center—*military* OH-6
Lima Branch—*stream* TX-5
**Limaburg**—*pop pl* KY-4
Lima Cem—*cemetery* MI-6
Lima Cem—*cemetery* MN-6
Lima Cem—*cemetery* OH-6
Lima-Centennial Valley—*cens area* MT-8
**Lima Center**—*pop pl* MI-6
**Lima Center**—*pop pl* WI-6
Lima Center Cem—*cemetery* WI-6
Lima Center Sch—*school* WI-6
Lima Ch—*church* IN-6
Lima Ch—*church* OH-6
Lima Cleaning and Pressing
Company—*hist pl* OH-6
Lima Dam—*dam* MT-8
Limadbwobw—*island* MP-9
Lima Elem Sch—*school* IN-6
Lima Highway Ch—*church* OK-5
Lima (historical)—*locale* KS-7
Limahuli Falls—*falls* HI-9
Limahuli Stream—*stream* HI-9
*Limahuli Valley* HI-9
Lima Lake—*lake* MN-6
Limaloa Gulch—*valley* HI-9
*Limaluli* HI-9
Lima Memorial Hall—*hist pl* OH-6
Lima Mtn—*summit* MN-6
Limani (Barrio)—*fmr MCD* PR-3
Limantour, Estero De—*bay* CA-9
Limantour Spit—*bar* CA-9
Liman Windmill—*locale* NM-5
Lima Ordnance Modification
Center—*military* OH-6
Lima Peaks—*summit* MT-8
Lima Rsvr—*reservoir* MT-8
**Limas**—*pop pl* PR-3
Lima Sch—*school* MO-7
Lima State Hosp—*hospital* OH-6
**Lima (Town of)**—*pop pl* NY-2
**Lima (Town of)**—*pop pl* (4) WI-6
**Lima (Township of)**—*pop pl* (2) IL-6
**Lima (Township of)**—*pop pl* IN-6
**Lima (Township of)**—*pop pl* MI-6
**Lima (Township of)**—*pop pl* MN-6
**Lima (Township of)**—*pop pl* OH-6
Lima-Union Ch—*church* WI-6
Lima Village Hist Dist—*hist pl* NY-2
**Limaville**—*pop pl* OH-6
Limb, Lester, House—*hist pl* UT-8
Limbarg Drain—*canal* MI-6
Limbaugh, Lake—*reservoir* AL-4
Limbaugh Canyon—*valley* CO-8
Limbaugh Cem—*cemetery* MO-7
Limbaugh Cem—*cemetery* TN-4
Limbaugh Dam—*dam* AL-4
Limb Branch—*stream* IL-6
Limb Camp Creek—*stream* CA-9
*Limb Creek* AL-4
Limber Camp (historical)—*locale* OR-9
Limber Camp Spring—*spring* OR-9
Limber Creek—*stream* CO-8
Limber Creek—*stream* OR-9
Limber Flag—*summit* UT-8
Limberger Ridge—*ridge* OH-6
Limbergh Spring—*spring* AZ-5
Limber Jim Creek—*stream* OR-9
Limber Jim Meadow—*flat* OR-9
Limber Jim Ridge—*ridge* OR-9
Limber Jim Trail (jeep)—*trail* OR-9
Limber Lake—*lake* ID-8
*Limberloss Creek* IN-6
*Limberlost* IN-6
Limberlost—*locale* MO-7
Limberlost Ch—*church* IN-6
*Limber Lost Creek* IN-6
Limberlost Creek—*stream* IN-6
Limberlost Creek—*stream* OH-6
Limberlost Forest Camp—*locale* OR-9
**Limberlost Hills**—*pop pl* IN-6
Limberlost State Game Res—*park* IN-6
Limberlost State Memorial—*park* IN-6
Limberlost Trail—*trail* VA-3
Limber Luke Creek—*stream* ID-8
Limber Pine Bench—*bench* CA-9
Limber Pine Springs—*spring* CA-9
Limber Pine Trail—*trail* UT-8
Limber Pine Trail Head—*locale* UT-8
Limber Point—*cape* RI-1
Limber Pole Creek—*stream* SC-3
Limber Pole Mtn—*summit* SC-3
Limber Ridge—*ridge* WV-2
Limbert—*uninc pl* MS-4
Limb Island—*island* AK-9
Limbo, Mount—*summit* NV-8
Limbocker Creek—*stream* MI-6
Limbocker Drain—*canal* MI-6
Limbo Creek—*stream* OK-5
Limbo Sch—*school* IL-6
Limbough Branch—*stream* MO-7
Limbrick Branch—*stream* SC-3
Limb Run—*stream* IN-6
**Limbs**—*pop pl* TN-4
Limbs Store (historical)—*locale* TN-4
Limburger Cabin—*locale* OR-9
Limburger Spring—*spring* WY-8
**Limco (Limoneira)**—*pop pl* CA-9
Lime—*locale* AL-4
Lime—*locale* (2) CO-8
Lime—*locale* OR-9
Lime, Lake—*lake* WI-6
Lime Barrel Shoal—*bar* NY-2
Lime Bluff—*locale* PA-2
*Lime Branch* GA-3
Lime Branch—*stream* (5) AL-4
Lime Branch—*stream* (2) GA-3
Lime Branch—*stream* KY-4
Lime Branch—*stream* LA-4
Lime Branch—*stream* (3) TX-5
Lime Branch Cem—*cemetery* GA-3
Lime Branch Ch—*church* GA-3
Lime Branch Sch (historical)—*school* AL-4
Lime Butte—*summit* AK-9
Lime Butte—*summit* MT-8
Lime Buttes—*summit* WY-8
Lime Camp—*locale* AZ-5
Lime Canyon—*valley* (3) CA-9
Lime Canyon—*valley* CO-8
Lime Canyon—*valley* NV-8
Lime Canyon—*valley* NM-5
Lime Canyon—*valley* (2) UT-8
Lime Cave—*cave* AL-4
Lime Cave Peak—*summit* MT-8
Lime City—*locale* IA-7
Lime City—*locale* TX-5
**Lime City**—*pop pl* OH-6
Lime City Sch—*school* IA-7
Lime Cove—*bay* NV-8
*Lime Creek* CO-8
*Lime Creek* ID-8
*Lime Creek* IA-7
*Lime Creek* KS-7
*Lime Creek* MT-8
*Lime Creek* WA-9
Lime Creek—*locale* MI-6
Lime Creek—*locale* MN-6
Lime Creek—*stream* (2) AK-9
Lime Creek—*stream* AZ-5
Lime Creek—*stream* CA-9
Lime Creek—*stream* (6) CO-8
Lime Creek—*stream* (2) GA-3
Lime Creek—*stream* (9) ID-8
Lime Creek—*stream* IL-6
Lime Creek—*stream* (4) IA-7
Lime Creek—*stream* KS-7
Lime Creek—*stream* LA-4
Lime Creek—*stream* (2) MI-6
Lime Creek—*stream* (2) MN-6
Lime Creek—*stream* (8) MT-8
Lime Creek—*stream* (2) NE-7
Lime Creek—*stream* (3) NV-8
Lime Creek—*stream* OK-5
Lime Creek—*stream* (2) OR-9
Lime Creek—*stream* TX-5
Lime Creek—*stream* UT-8
Lime Creek—*stream* (8) WA-9
Lime Creek—*stream* (2) WY-8
Lime Creek Basin—*basin* NV-8
Lime Creek Campground—*locale* CO-8

Lime Creek Canyon—*valley* CO-8
Lime Creek Cem—*cemetery* MI-6
Lime Creek Cem—*cemetery* MN-6
Lime Creek Cem—*cemetery* NE-7
Lime Creek Ch—*church* IA-7
Lime Creek Ch—*church* MN-6
Lime Creek County Park—*park* IA-7
Lime Creek Mtn—*summit* WA-9
Lime Creek Spring—*spring* AZ-5
Lime Creek Stock Driveway—*trail* CO-8
Lime Creek Township—*fmr MCD* (2) IA-7
**Lime Crest**—*pop pl* NJ-2
**Limecrest**—*pop pl* OH-6
**Limedale**—*pop pl* AR-4
**Limedale**—*pop pl* IN-6
Limedale Junction—*locale* AR-4
Lime-Dixie Cem—*cemetery* OR-9
Lime Dyke—*other* CA-9
Limedyke Mtn—*summit* CA-9
Lime Glacier—*glacier* AK-9
Lime Grove—*locale* NE-7
Lime Gulch—*stream* OR-9
Lime Gulch—*valley* AK-9
Lime Gulch—*valley* (3) CA-9
Lime Gulch—*valley* (5) MT-8
Lime Gulch—*valley* (3) OR-9
*Lime Hill* AL-4
Limehill—*locale* PA-2
Lime Hill—*locale* VA-3
Lime Hill—*summit* AZ-5
Lime Hill—*summit* CA-9
Lime Hill—*summit* NV-8
Lime Hill—*summit* TX-5
Lime Hill—*summit* WA-9
Lime Hills—*other* AK-9
Lime Hills—*range* ND-7
Lime Hills—*ridge* AZ-5
Lime Hollow—*valley* PA-2
Lime Hollow—*valley* TX-5
Lime Hollow Run—*stream* WV-2
**Limehouse**—*pop pl* (2) SC-3
Limehouse Branch—*stream* SC-3
Limehouse Bridge—*bridge* SC-3
*Limehouse Corners* SC-3
Limehouse Cove—*bay* MD-2
**Limehouse Station**—*pop pl* SC-3
Limehurst Pond—*lake* VT-1
Lime Island—*island* ME-1
Lime Island—*island* MI-6
**Lime Island**—*pop pl* MI-6
*Limeki Branch* WV-2
*Limekill Creek* WY-8
Lime Kill Hollow—*valley* UT-8
**Lime Kiln**—*pop pl* AL-4
**Lime Kiln**—*pop pl* MD-2
**Limekiln**—*pop pl* PA-2
Lime Kiln, The—*rock* CT-1
**Limekiln Acres (subdivision)**—*pop pl* PA-2
Limekiln Bayou—*stream* LA-4
Lime Kiln Branch—*stream* AL-4
Limekiln Branch—*stream* GA-3
Limekiln Branch—*stream* MD-2
Limekiln Branch—*stream* NC-3
Limekiln Branch—*stream* TX-5
Limekiln Branch—*stream* WV-2
Limekiln Bridge—*bridge* VA-3
Limekiln Bridge—*other* MO-7
Limekiln Brook—*stream* CT-1
Limekiln Brook—*stream* NY-2
*Limekiln Canyon* UT-8
Lime Kiln Canyon—*valley* AZ-5
Limekiln Canyon—*valley* (4) CA-9
Limekiln Canyon—*valley* (4) ID-8
Limekiln Canyon—*valley* (3) MT-8
Lime Kiln Canycn—*valley* NV-8
Limekiln Canyon—*valley* NM-5
Lime Kiln Canyon—*valley* TX-5
Limekiln Canyon—*valley* (4) UT-8
Limekiln Canyon Wash—*stream* CA-9
Lime Kiln Cave—*cave* TN-4
Limekiln Ch—*church* LA-4
Limekiln Coulee—*valley* MT-8
*Limekiln Creek* CA-9
*Lime Kiln Creek* MS-4
Lime Kiln Creek—*stream* AL-4
Limekiln Creek—*stream* (2) CA-9
Limekiln Creek—*stream* CO-8
Limekiln Creek—*stream* ID-8
Limekiln Creek—*stream* IL-6
Limekiln Creek—*stream* MS-4
Lime Kiln Creek—*stream* MT-8
Limekiln Creek—*stream* (2) MT-8
Limekiln Creek*—*stream* NE-7
Lime Kiln Creek—*stream* NY-2
Limekiln Creek—*stream* (2) NY-2
Limekiln Creek—*stream* NC-3
Limekiln Creek—*stream* OR-9
Limekiln Creek—*stream* PA-2
Limekiln Creek—*stream* SD-7
Limekiln Creek—*stream* (2) TX-5
Limekiln Creek—*stream* UT-8
Limekiln Creek—*stream* WY-8
Limekiln Creek (historical)—*locale* SD-7
Limekiln Draw—*valley* (2) UT-8
Limekiln Falls—*falls* NY-2
Limekiln Ford (historical)—*locale* MO-7
Limekiln Fork—*stream* ID-8
Lime Kiln Fork—*stream* KY-4
*Limekiln Golf Course* PA-2
*Lime Kiln Gulch* CO-8
Limekiln Gulch—*valley* CA-9
Limekiln Gulch—*valley* CO-8
Lime Kiln Gulch—*valley* CO-8
Limekiln Gulch—*valley* CO-8
Limekiln Gulch—*valley* ID-8
Limekiln Gulch—*valley* MT-8
Limekiln Gulch—*valley* UT-8
Limekiln Gulch—*valley* WY-8
Lime Kiln Gulch—*valley* WY-8
Limekiln Hill—*summit* CA-9
Lime Kiln Hill—*summit* KY-4
Limekiln Hill—*summit* MT-8
Limekiln Hill—*summit* WA-9
Limekiln Hill—*summit* WI-6
*Lime Kiln Hollow* TN-4
Lime Kiln Hollow—*valley* AL-4
Limekiln Hollow—*valley* AR-4
Lime Kiln Hollow—*valley* AR-4
Limekiln Hollow—*valley* KY-4
Limekiln Hollow—*valley* MO-7
Lime Kiln Hollow—*valley* (3) MO-7
Limekiln Hollow—*valley* (2) MO-7
Lime Kiln Hollow—*valley* (4) MO-7
Limekiln Hollow—*valley* PA-2
Limekiln Hollow—*valley* (9) TN-4
Limekiln Hollow—*valley* (3) UT-8
Limekiln Hollow—*valley* VA-3
Limekiln Knob—*summit* KY-4
Limekiln Knoll—*summit* UT-8
*Lime Kiln Lake* IN-6
Limekiln Lake—*lake* ID-8
Limekiln Lake—*lake* IN-6
Limekiln Lake—*lake* (2) MI-6
Limekiln Lake—*lake* NY-2
Lime Kiln Lake—*lake* OH-6
*Limekiln Lakes* MI-6
Lime Kiln Landing—*locale* TN-4
Lime Kiln Lighthouse—*locale* WA-9
*Limekiln Methodist Episcopal Church* AL-4
Lime Kiln Mine—*mine* AZ-5
Lime Kiln Mtn—*summit* MO-7
Limekiln Mtn—*summit* MT-8
Limekiln Mtn—*summit* (3) NY-2
Lime Kiln Park—*flat* WY-8
Lime Kiln Point—*cape* MI-6
Limekiln Point—*cape* VT-1
Limekiln Point—*cape* WA-9
Limekiln Post Office—*building* PA-2
*Lime Kiln Rapids* ID-8
Limekiln Rapids—*rapids* ID-8
Limekiln Rapids—*rapids* WA-9
Limekiln Ridge—*ridge* IN-6
Lime Kiln Ridge—*ridge* KY-4
Limekiln Ridge—*ridge* WV-2
Limekiln Run—*stream* VA-3
Limekiln Run—*stream* (2) WV-2
*Lime Kilns* NY-2
Lime Kilns—*hist pl* RI-1
Lime Kilns—*hist pl* UT-8
Limekiln Sch—*school* CA-9
Limekiln Sch—*school* TX-5
Limekiln Sch (abandoned)—*school* PA-2
Limekiln Slough—*stream* IL-6
Limekiln Spring—*spring* CA-9
Limekiln Spring—*spring* CO-8
Limekiln Spring—*spring* MO-7
Limekiln Spring—*spring* MT-8
Lime Kiln Spring—*spring* NV-8
Limekiln Spring—*spring* (2) UT-8
Limekiln Swamp—*swamp* NY-2
Limekiln Valley—*valley* CO-8
*Limekiln Wash* UT-8
Limekiln Wash—*stream* AZ-5
Limekiln Wash—*valley* UT-8
Limekiln Waterhole—*lake* TX-5
Limekin Gulch—*valley* CO-8
Limekin Tank—*reservoir* TX-5
Limeklin Gulch—*valley* CA-9
*Lime Lake* MI-6
Lime Lake—*lake* (2) IN-6
Lime Lake—*lake* (9) MI-6
Lime Lake—*lake* (2) MN-6
Lime Lake—*lake* (2) WA-9
**Lime Lake**—*pop pl* NY-2
Lime Lake—*reservoir* MI-6
Lime Lake—*reservoir* NY-2
Lime Lakebed—*basin* MN-6
Lime Lake Inlet—*stream* MI-6
Lime Lake-Machias—*CDP* NY-2
Lime Lake Outlet—*stream* NY-2
Lime Lakes—*lake* MI-6
**Lime Lake (Township of)**—*pop pl* MN-6
Lime Ledges—*bench* NY-2
Limeless Lake—*lake* LA-4
Lime Mesa—*summit* CO-8
Lime Mountain Mine—*mine* NV-8
Lime Mountain Spring—*spring* AZ-5
*Lime Mtn* AZ-5
Lime Mtn—*summit* (2) AZ-5
Lime Mtn—*summit* CA-9
Lime Mtn—*summit* ID-8
Lime Mtn—*summit* (3) NV-8
Lime Mtn—*summit* (2) UT-8
Lime Mtn—*summit* WA-9
Lime Park—*flat* CO-8
*Lime Peak* AK-9
*Lime Peak* AZ-5
Lime Peak—*summit* AK-9
Lime Peak—*summit* AZ-5
Lime Peak—*summit* TX-5
Lime Peak—*summit* UT-8
Lime Plant Hollow—*valley* KY-4
Lime Plant Sch—*school* WV-2
Lime Point—*cape* AK-9
Lime Point—*cape* (2) CA-9
Lime Point—*cliff* UT-8
Limepoint Creek—*stream* ID-8
Lime Pond—*lake* NH-1
**Limeport**—*pop pl* PA-2
Limeport Hill—*summit* PA-2
Lime Quarry Mine—*mine* UT-8
Limerick—*locale* IL-6
Limerick—*locale* MS-4
Limerick—*locale* NY-2
Limerick—*locale* OH-6
Limerick—*locale* SC-3
**Limerick**—*pop pl* GA-3
**Limerick**—*pop pl* ME-1
**Limerick**—*pop pl* PA-2
Limerick Basin—*basin* NV-8
Limerick Basin Mine—*mine* NV-8
Limerick Canyon—*valley* NV-8
Limerick Cem—*cemetery* IL-6
Limerick Center—*locale* PA-2
Limerick Country Club—*locale* PA-2
*Limerick Elementary School* PA-2
Limerick Hist Dist—*hist pl* KY-4
Limerick Hist Dist (Boundary
Increase)—*hist pl* KY-4
Limerick (historical)—*locale* MO-7
**Limerick Mills**—*pop pl* ME-1
Limerick Nuclear Power Plant—*building* PA-2
Limerick Sch—*school* PA-2
*Limerick Siding* GA-3
Limericks Landing—*locale* MS-4
**Limerick (Town of)**—*pop pl* ME-1
**Limerick (Township of)**—*pop pl* PA-2
Limerick Upper Village Hist Dist—*hist pl* ME-1
*Limeridge* WI-6
Lime Ridge—*locale* PA-2
**Lime Ridge**—*pop pl* PA-2
**Lime Ridge**—*pop pl* WI-6
Lime Ridge—*ridge* CA-9
Lime Ridge—*ridge* CO-8
Lime Ridge—*ridge* MT-8
Lime Ridge—*ridge* NV-8
Lime Ridge—*ridge* PA-2
Lime Ridge—*ridge* UT-8
Lime Ridge—*ridge* WA-9
Lime Ridge—*ridge* WY-8
*Limeridge (corporate name Lime Ridge)* WI-6
Lime Ridge Sch (abandoned)—*school* PA-2
*Lime Rock* AL-4
*Lime Rock* PA-2
*Lime Rock* RI-1
Lime Rock—*bar* ME-1
Lime Rock—*locale* AL-4
Limerock—*locale* PA-2
Lime Rock—*pillar* CA-9
Lime Rock—*pillar* GA-3
Lime Rock—*pillar* OR-9
**Lime Rock**—*pop pl* (2) CT-1
**Lime Rock**—*pop pl* NY-2
**Lime Rock**—*pop pl* PA-2
**Lime Rock**—*pop pl* RI-1
**Lime Rock**—*pop pl* WV-2
Limerock Canyon—*valley* CA-9
Limerock Canyon—*valley* UT-8
Lime Rock Ch—*church* AL-4
Limerock Gulch—*valley* CA-9
Lime Rock Hill—*summit* AR-4
Lime Rock Hist Dist—*hist pl* CT-1
Lime Rock Light—*locale* RI-1
*Limerock Mill* PA-2
Limerock Mill—*locale* PA-2
Limerock Mtn—*summit* ID-8
Lime Rock Mtn—*summit* TX-5
Limerock Peak—*summit* CA-9
Lime Rock Point—*cape* VT-1
Lime Rock Sch—*school* AL-4
Lime Rock Spring—*spring* CA-9
Limerock Spring—*spring* (2) NV-8
Limerock Spring—*spring* UT-8
Limerock Trail—*trail* WV-2
Limerock Village Hist Dist—*hist pl* RI-1
Lime Rock Well (Flowing)—*well* NV-8
Lime Run—*stream* IN-6
Limery Coulee—*valley* WI-6
Limery Ridge—*ridge* WI-6
Lime Saddle—*gap* CA-9
Lime Saddle Memorial Park—*park* CA-9
Lime Saddle Powerhouse—*other* CA-9
Lime Saint Sch—*school* FL-3
Lime Siding—*locale* MN-6
Lime Sink—*basin* FL-3
Lime Sink—*locale* AL-4
Lime Sink (CCD)—*cens area* GA-3
Lime Sink Creek—*stream* (2) GA-3
Limesink Pond—*lake* AL-4
Lime Sinks Cave—*cave* PA-2
Lime Sink Sch—*school* FL-3
Lime Slough—*gut* FL-3
*Lime Spring* IA-7
Lime Spring—*spring* (3) AZ-5
Lime Spring—*spring* (2) ID-8
Lime Spring—*spring* (2) NV-8
Lime Spring—*spring* (3) UT-8
Lime Spring Branch—*stream* AL-4
Lime Spring Branch—*stream* GA-3
Lime Spring Camp—*locale* PA-2
*Limesprings* IA-7
**Lime Springs**—*pop pl* IA-7
Lime Springs—*spring* AZ-5
Lime Springs Ch—*church* (2) AL-4
Lime Springs Creek—*stream* AK-9
Lime Springs Lake—*reservoir* AL-4
Lime Springs Mill Complex—*hist pl* IA-7
*Lime Spring Tank* AZ-5
**Lime Spur**—*pop pl* CA-9
Limestack Mtn—*summit* AK-9
*Lime Station* AL-4
*Limestone* IL-6
Limestone—*locale* AL-4
Limestone—*locale* AR-4
Limestone—*locale* FL-3
Limestone—*locale* KY-4
Limestone—*locale* MT-8
Limestone—*locale* SC-3
Limestone—*locale* TX-5
**Limestone**—*pop pl* FL-3
**Limestone**—*pop pl* GA-3
**Limestone**—*pop pl* ME-1
**Limestone**—*pop pl* MI-6
**Limestone**—*pop pl* NY-2
**Limestone**—*pop pl* OH-6
**Limestone**—*pop pl* OK-5
**Limestone**—*pop pl* PA-2
**Limestone**—*pop pl* TN-4
**Limestone**—*pop pl* TX-5
**Limestone**—*pop pl* (3) WV-2
Limestone, The—*summit* WY-8
**Limestone Acres**—*pop pl* DE-2
*Limestone Baptist Youth Camp* AL-4
Limestone Bar (historical)—*bar* AL-4
Limestone Bay—*bay* VI-3
Limestone Bench—*bench* UT-8
Limestone Bluffs—*cliff* CA-9
Limestone Bluffs State Public Hunting
Area—*park* NE-7
Limestone Branch—*stream* (2) AL-4
Limestone Branch—*stream* (2) FL-3
Limestone Branch—*stream* GA-3
Limestone Branch—*stream* IN-6
Limestone Branch—*stream* (3) KY-4
Limestone Branch—*stream* TN-4
Limestone Branch—*stream* VA-3
Limestone Branch—*stream* (2) WV-2
Limestone Brook—*stream* ME-1
Limestone Brook—*stream* NY-2
Limestone Butte—*summit* (2) MT-8
Limestone Butte—*summit* OR-9
Limestone Butte—*summit* SD-7
Limestone Butte Dam—*dam* SD-7
Limestone Butte Rsvr—*reservoir* SD-7
*Limestone Canyon* AZ-5
Limestone Canyon—*valley* (5) AZ-5
Limestone Canyon—*valley* CA-9
Limestone Canyon—*valley* (4) MT-8
Limestone Canyon—*valley* NM-5
Limestone Canyon—*valley* SD-7
Limestone Cave—*cave* MT-8
Limestone Cave—*cave* UT-8
Limestone Caves—*cave* CA-9
Limestone Cem—*cemetery* (2) AL-4
Limestone Cem—*cemetery* (2) FL-3
Limestone Cem—*cemetery* IL-6
Limestone Cem—*cemetery* SC-3
Limestone Cem—*cemetery* TN-4
Limestone Center (census name
Limestone)—*other* ME-1
Limestone Ch—*church* AL-4
Limestone Ch—*church* FL-3
Limestone Ch—*church* (3) GA-3
Limestone Ch—*church* IL-6
Limestone Ch—*church* MS-4
Limestone Ch—*church* OK-5
Limestone Ch—*church* PA-2
Limestone Ch—*church* (2) SC-3
Limestone Ch—*church* TN-4
Limestone Ch—*church* (3) WV-2
Limestone Channel—*channel* NJ-2
Limestone Ch (historical)—*church* MS-4
*Limestone Ch of God in Christ* MS-4
*Limestone Ch of the Brethern* TN-4
**Limestone City**—*pop pl* OH-6
Limestone Cliff Campground—*locale* CA-9
Limestone Cliffs—*cliff* AK-9
Limestone Cliffs—*cliff* UT-8
Limestone Coll—*school* SC-3
Limestone Correctional Facility—*building* AL-4
**Limestone County**—*pop pl* AL-4
**Limestone (County)**—*pop pl* TX-5
Limestone County Area Vocational Technical
Center—*school* AL-4
Limestone County Courthouse—*building* AL-4
Limestone County Fairground—*locale* AL-4
Limestone County Park—*park* AL-4
Limestone Cove—*locale* TN-4
Limestone Cove Ch—*church* TN-4
Limestone Cove Post Office
(historical)—*building* TN-4
Limestone Cove Rec Area—*park* TN-4
Limestone Cove Sch (historical)—*school* TN-4
Limestone Cove Trail—*trail* TN-4
*Limestone Creek* AL-4
*Limestone Creek* UT-8
Limestone Creek—*stream* (6) AL-4
Limestone Creek—*stream* (4) AK-9
Limestone Creek—*stream* CA-9
Limestone Creek—*stream* CO-8
Limestone Creek—*stream* (3) FL-3
Limestone Creek—*stream* (9) GA-3
Limestone Creek—*stream* (3) IL-6
Limestone Creek—*stream* (2) IN-6
Limestone Creek—*stream* IA-7
Limestone Creek—*stream* (4) KS-7
Limestone Creek—*stream* KY-4
Limestone Creek—*stream* (2) MS-4
Limestone Creek—*stream* (2) MO-7
Limestone Creek—*stream* (7) MT-8
Limestone Creek—*stream* (3) NY-2
Limestone Creek—*stream* NC-3
Limestone Creek—*stream* OH-6
Limestone Creek—*stream* (3) OK-5
Limestone Creek—*stream* (2) OR-9
Limestone Creek—*stream* (4) SC-3
Limestone Creek—*stream* (2) TN-4
Limestone Creek—*stream* (2) UT-8
Limestone Creek—*stream* (2) VA-3
Limestone Creek—*stream* WA-9
Limestone Creek—*stream* WI-6
Limestone Creek Bar—*bar* AL-4
Limestone Creek Sewage Treatment
Plant—*locale* AL-4
Limestone Draw—*valley* CO-8
Limestone Draw—*valley* OK-5
Limestone Fire Station—*building* AZ-5
Limestone Gap—*gap* AK-9
Limestone Gap—*gap* CO-8
Limestone Gap—*gap* KY-4
Limestone gap—*gap* TX-5
Limestone Gap—*locale* OK-5
**Limestone Gap**—*pop pl* DE-2
**Limestone Gardene**—*pop pl* DE-2
**Limestone Gardens**—*pop pl* DE-2
Limestone Gulch—*valley* (2) AK-9
Limestone Gulch—*valley* AZ-5
Limestone Gulch—*valley* (2) CA-9
Limestone Gulch—*valley* (3) ID-8
Limestone Hill—*locale* WV-2
Limestone Hill—*summit* CO-8
Limestone Hill—*summit* ME-1
Limestone Hill—*summit* (2) OK-5
Limestone Hill—*summit* WA-9
Limestone Hill—*summit* WY-8
Limestone Hills—*other* AK-9
**Limestone Hills**—*pop pl* DE-2
Limestone Hills—*spring* MT-8
Limestone Hills—*summit* AZ-5
Limestone Hills—*summit* NV-8
Limestone Hills Park—*park* DE-2
Limestone (historical)—*locale* AL-4
Limestone (historical)—*locale* MS-4
Limestone Hogback—*ridge* AK-9
Limestone Hollow—*valley* OH-6
Limestone Hollow—*valley* OK-5
Limestone Hollow—*valley* PA-2
Limestone Hollow—*valley* TN-4
Limestone Hollow—*valley* VA-3
Limestone HS—*school* IL-6
Limestone Inlet—*bay* AK-9
Limestone Island—*island* NY-2
*Limestone Islands* PW-9
Limestone Junction—*locale* WA-9
Limestone Knob—*summit* KY-4
Limestone Lake—*lake* KY-4
Limestone Lake—*lake* MN-6
Limestone Lakes—*reservoir* AL-4
Limestone Lakes Dam Number 1—*dam* AL-4
Limestone Lakes Dam Number 2—*dam* AL-4
Limestone Landing (historical)—*locale* AL-4
Limestone Ledge—*ridge* NY-2
Limestone Memorial Gardens
(cemetery)—*cemetery* GA-3
Limestone Mine Cave—*cave* TN-4
*Limestone Missionary Baptist Church* TN-4
*Limestone Mountains* AZ-5
*Limestone Mountains* MI-6
Limestone Mtn—*summit* AK-9
Limestone Mtn—*summit* (2) AZ-5
Limestone Mtn—*summit* MI-6
Limestone Mtn—*summit* MT-8
Limestone Mtn—*summit* UT-8
Limestone Mtn—*summit* WV-2
Limestone Mtn—*summit* WY-8
Limestone Palisades—*cliff* MT-8
Limestone Pass—*gap* MT-8
Limestone Pass Trail—*trail* MT-8
Limestone Pasture—*flat* AZ-5
Limestone Peak—*summit* AZ-5
Limestone Peak—*summit* MT-8
Limestone Peak—*summit* NV-8
Limestone Peak—*summit* UT-8
Limestone Plateau—*area* SD-7
Limestone Pocket—*basin* AZ-5
Limestone Point—*cape* AK-9
Limestone Point—*cape* ME-1
Limestone Point—*cape* UT-8
Limestone Point—*cape* WA-9
Limestone Point—*cliff* CA-9
Limestone Point—*cliff* ID-8
Limestone Post Office—*building* TN-4
Limestone Post Office
(historical)—*building* AL-4
Limestone Post Office
(historical)—*building* PA-2
Limestone Pothole—*basin* UT-8
Limestone Pot Holes—*basin* UT-8
Limestone Quarry—*mine* AZ-5
Limestone Quarry—*mine* UT-8
Limestone Ranch—*locale* AZ-5
*Limestone Ridge* PA-2
*Limestone Ridge* PW-9
Limestone Ridge—*ridge* AK-9
Limestone Ridge—*ridge* (2) AZ-5
Limestone Ridge—*ridge* (2) CA-9
Limestone Ridge—*ridge* CO-8
Limestone Ridge—*ridge* MO-7
Limestone Ridge—*ridge* (3) MT-8
Limestone Ridge—*ridge* NV-8
Limestone Ridge—*ridge* (2) OK-5
Limestone Ridge—*ridge* (5) PA-2
Limestone Ridge—*ridge* TN-4
Limestone Ridge—*ridge* VA-3
Limestone Ridge—*ridge* WV-2
Limestone Ridge Tank Number
One—*reservoir* AZ-5
Limestone Ridge Tank Number
Two—*reservoir* AZ-5
Limestone Rim—*summit* WY-8
Limestone Rsvr—*reservoir* AZ-5
Limestone Rsvr—*reservoir* UT-8
Limestone Run—*stream* OH-6
Limestone Run—*stream* (6) PA-2
Limestone Run—*stream* (5) WV-2
Limestones, The—*hist pl* IL-6
Limestone Sch—*school* IL-6
Limestone Sch—*school* MT-8
Limestone Sch—*school* OK-5
Limestone Sch—*school* (3) WV-2
Limestone Sch (historical)—*school* MO-7
Limestone Sch (historical)—*school* (2) TN-4
Limestone Slough—*stream* AL-4
*Limestone Spring* UT-8
Limestone Spring—*spring* (7) AZ-5
Limestone Spring—*spring* CO-8
Limestone Spring—*spring* NV-8
Limestone Spring—*spring* SC-3
Limestone Spring—*spring* SD-7
Limestone Spring—*spring* (5) UT-8
Limestone Spring—*spring* WA-9
Limestone Spring Branch—*stream* AL-4
Limestone Springs—*locale* KY-4
**Limestone Springs**—*pop pl* TN-4
Limestone Springs Ch—*church* SC-3
Limestone Springs Hist Dist—*hist pl* SC-3
Limestone Springs Post Office
(historical)—*building* TN-4
Limestone Stream—*stream* ME-1
Limestone Tank—*reservoir* (15) AZ-5
Limestone Tanks—*reservoir* AZ-5
**Limestone (Town of)**—*pop pl* ME-1
Limestone Township—*civil* PA-2
Limestone Township—*civil* SD-7
**Limestone Township**—*pop pl* KS-7
Limestone (Township of)—*fmr MCD* AR-4
Limestone (Township of)—*fmr MCD* (2) NC-3
**Limestone (Township of)**—*pop pl* (2) IL-6
**Limestone (Township of)**—*pop pl* MI-6
**Limestone (Township of)**—*pop pl* MN-6
**Limestone (Township of)**—*pop pl* (5) PA-2
Limestone Trail—*trail* OR-9
Limestone Vale—*hist pl* OH-6
**Limestoneville**—*pop pl* PA-2
Limestone Wall—*cliff* MT-8
Limestone Well—*well* (2) AZ-5
Limestown (Township of)—*other* PA-2
**Limestreet**—*pop pl* NY-2
Limestreet Cem—*cemetery* NY-2
Lime Tank—*reservoir* (2) AZ-5
**Limeton**—*pop pl* VA-3
*Limetown* PA-2
**Lime (Township of)**—*pop pl* MN-6
Limetree—*locale* VI-3
Limetree Bay—*bay* VI-3
Limetree Cove—*bay* VI-3
Lime Tree Hammock—*island* FL-3
Lime Valley—*locale* PA-2
Lime Valley Covered Bridge—*hist pl* PA-2
**Lime Village**—*pop pl* AK-9
Lime Village ANV845—*reserve* AK-9
Limeville—*locale* KY-4
**Limeville**—*pop pl* PA-2
Limeville Branch—*stream* KY-4
**Limeville (Tongs)**—*pop pl* KY-4
Lime Wash—*stream* NV-8
Limewood Beach—*beach* CT-1
**Liminga**—*pop pl* MI-6
Liming Cem—*cemetery* MS-4
Liming Cem—*cemetery* WV-2
Liming Park—*park* OH-6
Liming Ridge Ch—*church* WV-2
Liming Rsvr—*reservoir* MT-8
**Limington**—*pop pl* ME-1
Limington Acad—*hist pl* ME-1
**Limington (Town of)**—*pop pl* ME-1
Limitar—*locale* NM-5
Limit Brook—*stream* NH-1
Limit Creek—*stream* AK-9
Limit Creek—*stream* MT-8
Limit Gun Club—*other* CA-9
Limit Island—*island* AK-9
Limit Run—*stream* IN-6
Lim Lake—*lake* MI-6
Limnological Research Station—*hist pl* MN-6
Limon—*locale* CA-9
**Limon**—*pop pl* CO-8
**Limon**—*pop pl* (4) PR-3
**Limona**—*pop pl* FL-3
Limona Elem Sch—*school* FL-3
Limon (Barrio)—*fmr MCD* (2) PR-3
Limon Country Club—*other* CO-8
**Limoneira**—*pop pl* CA-9
Limones—*locale* PR-3
**Limones**—*pop pl* PR-3
Limones (Barrio)—*fmr MCD* PR-3
Limonite Ore Bank Mine—*mine* TN-4
Limonite Post Office (historical)—*building* TN-4
**Limon Junction**—*pop pl* CO-8
Limon Pond—*lake* CT-1
Limp—*locale* KY-4
Limp—*locale* SC-3
*Limpanai* MH-9
*Limpani* MH-9
Limpet Creek—*stream* AK-9
Limpia Canyon—*valley* TX-5
*Limpia Canyon Creek* TX-5
Limpia Creek—*stream* TX-5
Limpia Mtn—*summit* TX-5
Limpia Spring—*spring* TX-5
Limpia Windmill—*locale* TX-5
*Limpid Creek* WA-9
Limpios Tank—*reservoir* AZ-5
Limpp Community State Lake—*reservoir* MO-7
Limpy Creek—*stream* MN-6
Limpy Creek—*stream* (2) OR-9
Limpy Mtn—*summit* OR-9
Limpy Prairie—*flat* (2) OR-9
Limpy Rock—*pillar* OR-9
**Lim Rock**—*pop pl* AL-4
*Limrock Blowing Cave* AL-4
Lim Rock Sch—*school* AL-4
Limstrong—*locale* VA-3
Limukoko Point—*cape* (2) HI-9
*Limwo'* FM-9
*Limwoq* FM-9
**Linadale**—*pop pl* FL-3
*Linaman Lake* CA-9
*Linam Cemetery* TN-4
Linam Ranch—*locale* NM-5
**Linan**—*pop pl* WV-2
*Linananimis River* WA-9
Lin and Randys Pit—*cave* AL-4
Linapuni Sch—*school* HI-9
Linard Creek—*stream* VA-3
*Linaria* TN-4
*Linaria Post Office* TN-4
Lina Rocks—*summit* VA-3
Linary—*cemetery* TN-4
Linary—*locale* TN-4
Linary Ch of Christ—*church* TN-4
Linary Post Office (historical)—*building* TN-4
Linary Sch (historical)—*school* TN-4
Linaweaver, Dr. Albert, House—*hist pl* OH-6
Lina Windmill—*locale* TX-5
Linberg, Eric and Martha, Farm—*hist pl* TX-5
*Linbergh* AL-4
**Linberry**—*pop pl* NC-3
Linbom Lake—*lake* MN-6
Linbom Lake State Wildlife Mngmt
Area—*park* MN-6
Lin Branch—*stream* IL-6
Lin Branch—*stream* TN-4
Linbrook—*uninc pl* CA-9
Linburg Cem—*cemetery* NE-7
**Linby**—*pop pl* IA-7
Lincamp Branch—*stream* WV-2
Lincecum—*locale* LA-4
Lincecum Bayou—*stream* LA-4
Lincecums Mill (historical)—*locale* MS-4
Lincecums Shoals (historical)—*bar* MS-4
**Linch**—*pop pl* WY-8
Linchberg Mine—*mine* NM-5
Linch Branch—*stream* GA-3
*Linchburg* TN-4
**Linchester**—*pop pl* MD-2
Linch Landing Strip—*airport* KS-7
Linch Ranch—*locale* WY-8
*Linchs Creek* NC-3
**Linck and Griffins Addition
Subdivision**—*pop pl* UT-8
Linck Cem—*cemetery* KY-4
Linck Creek—*stream* KS-7
**Lincklaen**—*pop pl* NY-2
**Lincklaen Center**—*pop pl* NY-2
**Lincklaen (Town of)**—*pop pl* NY-2
Lincliff—*hist pl* KY-4
Linclon County Hosp—*hospital* NC-3
**Linco**—*pop pl* GA-3
*Lincoln* AZ-5
*Lincoln* GA-3
*Lincoln* IN-6
*Lincoln* MS-4
*Lincoln* NJ-2
*Lincoln* ND-7
*Lincoln* OR-9
Lincoln—*fmr MCD* (6) NE-7
Lincoln—*locale* CO-8
Lincoln—*locale* KY-4
Lincoln—*locale* NJ-2
Lincoln—*locale* OK-5
Lincoln—*locale* WA-9
**Lincoln**—*pop pl* (3) AL-4
**Lincoln**—*pop pl* AR-4
**Lincoln**—*pop pl* CA-9
**Lincoln**—*pop pl* DE-2
**Lincoln**—*pop pl* FL-3
**Lincoln**—*pop pl* ID-8
**Lincoln**—*pop pl* IL-6
**Lincoln**—*pop pl* IN-6
**Lincoln**—*pop pl* (2) IA-7
**Lincoln**—*pop pl* KS-7
**Lincoln**—*pop pl* ME-1
**Lincoln**—*pop pl* MD-2
**Lincoln**—*pop pl* MA-1
**Lincoln**—*pop pl* (3) MI-6
**Lincoln**—*pop pl* (2) MN-6
**Lincoln**—*pop pl* MO-7
**Lincoln**—*pop pl* MT-8
**Lincoln**—*pop pl* NE-7

**Lincoln**—*pop pl* NH-1
**Lincoln**—*pop pl* NM-5
**Lincoln**—*pop pl* (2) NY-2
**Lincoln**—*pop pl* ND-7
**Lincoln**—*pop pl* OH-6
**Lincoln**—*pop pl* (3) OR-9
**Lincoln**—*pop pl* (2) PA-2
**Lincoln**—*pop pl* TN-4
**Lincoln**—*pop pl* TX-5
**Lincoln**—*pop pl* (2) UT-8
**Lincoln**—*pop pl* VT-1
**Lincoln**—*pop pl* VA-3
**Lincoln**—*pop pl* WA-9
**Lincoln**—*pop pl* WV-2
**Lincoln**—*pop pl* WI-6
Lincoln, Ambrose, Jr., House—*hist pl* MA-1
Lincoln, Anselm, House—*hist pl* NY-2
Lincoln, Asa, House—*hist pl* MA-1
Lincoln, Gen. Benjamin, House—*hist pl* MA-1
Lincoln, Gen. Thomas, House—*hist pl* MA-1
Lincoln, Gov. Levi, House—*hist pl* MA-1
Lincoln, Lake—*lake* FL-3
Lincoln, Lake—*reservoir* IN-6
Lincoln, Lake—*reservoir* MO-7
Lincoln, Mary Todd, House—*hist pl* KY-4
Lincoln, Mordecai, House—*hist pl* KY-4
Lincoln, Mordecai, House—*hist pl* PA-2
Lincoln, Mount—*summit* CA-9
Lincoln, Mount—*summit* (2) CO-8
Lincoln, Mount—*summit* MA-1
Lincoln, Mount—*summit* NV-8
Lincoln, Mount—*summit* NH-1
Lincoln, Mount—*summit* WA-9
Lincoln Achievement Center—*school* IN-6
**Lincoln Acres**—*pop pl* CA-9
**Lincoln Acres**—*pop pl* PA-2
*Lincoln Addition* IL-6
**Lincoln Addition Subdivision**—*pop pl* UT-8
*Lincoln Airfield* KS-7
Lincoln Airp—*airport* NC-3
*Lincoln Alternative School* PA-2
Lincoln Amish Sch Number Two—*school* IN-6
Lincoln Amphitheatre—*basin* CO-8
Lincoln Anchorage—*bay* AK-9
**Lincoln Ave**—*pop pl* MD-2
Lincoln Ave Baptist Ch—*church* TN-4
Lincoln Ave Sch—*school* FL-3
Lincoln Ave Sch—*school* MI-6
Lincoln Ave Sch—*school* WI-6
Lincoln Back Branch—*stream* IN-6
Lincoln Baptist Ch—*church* AL-4
Lincoln Baptist Ch—*church* TN-4
Lincoln Bar—*bar* OR-9
Lincoln Bay—*bay* MI-6
**Lincoln Beach**—*pop pl* MO-7
**Lincoln Beach**—*pop pl* OR-9
Lincoln Beach Wayside—*park* OR-9
Lincoln Bench—*bench* OR-9
Lincoln Bench Rsvr—*reservoir* OR-9
Lincoln Bight—*bay* AK-9
Lincoln Bldg—*hist pl* NY-2
Lincoln Bldg—*hist pl* ND-7
Lincoln Bluff—*cliff* CA-9
Lincoln Borough—*civil* PA-2
Lincoln Boyhood Home—*hist pl* KY-4
Lincoln Boyhood Natl Memorial—*hist pl* IN-6
Lincoln Boyhood Natl Memorial—*park* IN-6
Lincoln Branch—*stream* AL-4
Lincoln Branch—*stream* KY-4
*Lincoln Brook* MA-1
Lincoln Brook—*stream* ME-1
Lincoln Brook—*stream* NH-1
Lincoln Brook—*stream* NY-2
Lincoln Brook—*stream* VT-1
Lincoln Brook Trail—*trail* NH-1
**Lincoln (Br. P.O.)**—*pop pl* RI-1
Lincoln Butte—*summit* WA-9
Lincoln Bypass Canal—*canal* ID-8
Lincoln Cabin Site—*park* IN-6
Lincoln Canal—*canal* CA-9
Lincoln Canyon—*valley* AZ-5
Lincoln Canyon—*valley* CO-8
Lincoln Canyon—*valley* NV-8
Lincoln Canyon—*valley* (5) NM-5
Lincoln Canyon—*valley* OR-9
Lincoln Carnegie Library—*hist pl* KS-7
Lincoln Caverns—*cave* PA-2
Lincoln (CCD)—*cens area* KY-4
Lincoln Cem—*cemetery* (3) AL-4
Lincoln Cem—*cemetery* FL-3
Lincoln Cem—*cemetery* GA-3
Lincoln Cem—*cemetery* ID-8
Lincoln Cem—*cemetery* (4) IL-6
Lincoln Cem—*cemetery* (11) IA-7
Lincoln Cem—*cemetery* (3) KS-7
Lincoln Cem—*cemetery* (3) ME-1
Lincoln Cem—*cemetery* (3) MA-1
Lincoln Cem—*cemetery* (2) MI-6
Lincoln Cem—*cemetery* MN-6
Lincoln Cem—*cemetery* MS-4
Lincoln Cem—*cemetery* (4) MO-7
Lincoln Cem—*cemetery* OH-6
Lincoln Cem—*cemetery* (2) OK-5
Lincoln Cem—*cemetery* PA-2
Lincoln Cem—*cemetery* VA-3
Lincoln Cem—*cemetery* (5) WI-6
*Lincoln Center* KS-7
*Lincoln Center* MA-1
Lincoln Center—*building* MD-2
Lincoln Center—*building* (2) NY-2
Lincoln Center—*locale* IA-7
**Lincoln Center**—*pop pl* KS-7
**Lincoln Center**—*pop pl* ME-1
**Lincoln Center**—*pop pl* MA-1
Lincoln Center Cem—*cemetery* (2) IA-7
Lincoln Center Cem—*cemetery* ME-1
Lincoln Center Cem—*cemetery* MO-7
*Lincoln Center City* KS-7
Lincoln Center Hist Dist—*hist pl* MA-1
Lincoln Center HS—*school* FL-3
Lincoln Center Sch—*school* IA-7
Lincoln Center Sch—*school* SD-7
Lincoln Center School (Abandoned)—*locale* OK-5
*Lincoln Centre* KS-7
*Lincoln Centre* MA-1
Lincoln Centre (historical)—*locale* SD-7
Lincoln Centre (historical P.O.)—*locale* IA-7
Lincoln Ch—*church* IL-6
Lincoln Ch—*church* IN-6
Lincoln Ch—*church* IA-7
Lincoln Ch—*church* (3) MN-6
Lincoln Ch—*church* PA-2
Lincoln Ch—*church* TX-5
Lincoln Channel—*channel* AK-9
Lincoln Chapel—*church* WI-6
*Lincoln City* DE-2
**Lincoln City**—*pop pl* IN-6
**Lincoln City**—*pop pl* OR-9
Lincoln City—*uninc pl* FL-3
Lincoln City—*uninc pl* TX-5
*Lincoln City (Lincoln)* DE-2
**Lincoln City (Oceanlake)**—*pop pl* OR-9
Lincoln City Park Number 1—*park* FL-3
Lincoln City Park Number 2—*park* FL-3
Lincoln Club—*hist pl* NY-2
**Lincoln Colliery**—*pop pl* PA-2
Lincoln Community Center—*locale* AL-4
Lincoln Community Hall—*building* KS-7
Lincoln Community Hall—*hist pl* MT-8
Lincoln Community Sch—*school* VT-1
Lincoln Compact (census name Lincoln)—*other* ME-1
Lincoln Consolidated Shool—*school* MS-4
Lincoln Corral Canyon—*valley* ID-8
Lincoln Country Club—*other* MI-6
Lincoln Country Club—*other* NE-7
Lincoln Country Club Lake—*reservoir* IN-6
Lincoln Country Club Lake Dam—*dam* IN-6
*Lincoln County* NC-3
Lincoln County—*civil* KS-7
Lincoln County—*civil* NV-8
Lincoln County—*civil* SD-7
**Lincoln (County)**—*pop pl* AR-4
**Lincoln (County)**—*pop pl* GA-3
**Lincoln (County)**—*pop pl* KY-4
**Lincoln (County)**—*pop pl* ME-1
**Lincoln (County)**—*pop pl* MN-6
**Lincoln County**—*pop pl* MS-4
**Lincoln County**—*pop pl* MO-7
**Lincoln (County)**—*pop pl* NM-5
**Lincoln County**—*pop pl* NC-3
**Lincoln (County)**—*pop pl* OK-5
**Lincoln County**—*pop pl* OR-9
**Lincoln County**—*pop pl* TN-4
**Lincoln County**—*pop pl* WA-9
**Lincoln (County)**—*pop pl* WV-2
**Lincoln (County)**—*pop pl* WI-6
Lincoln County Airp—*airport* NV-8
Lincoln County Airp—*airport* NC-3
Lincoln County Courthouse—*building* MS-4
Lincoln County Courthouse—*building* TN-4
Lincoln County Courthouse—*hist pl* GA-3
Lincoln County Courthouse—*hist pl* KS-7
Lincoln County Courthouse—*hist pl* KY-4
Lincoln County Courthouse—*hist pl* NV-8
Lincoln County Courthouse—*hist pl* NC-3
Lincoln County Courthouse—*hist pl* WI-6
Lincoln County Courthouse—*hist pl* WY-8
Lincoln County Courthouse and Jail—*hist pl* MN-6
Lincoln County Fairgrounds—*hist pl* MN-6
Lincoln County Fairgrounds—*locale* ID-8
Lincoln County Fairgrounds—*locale* TN-4
Lincoln County Fair Grounds—*locale* WY-8
Lincoln County Farm (historical)—*locale* TN-4
Lincoln County Health Center—*hospital* MS-4
Lincoln County Hosp—*hospital* TN-4
Lincoln County Hosp—*hospital* WA-9
Lincoln County HS—*school* TN-4
Lincoln County Poor House Farm—*hist pl* TN-4
**Lincoln Court Condominium**—*pop pl* UT-8
Lincoln Courthouse Square Hist Dist—*hist pl* IL-6
Lincoln Cove—*bay* (2) ME-1
Lincoln Covered Bridge—*hist pl* VT-1
*Lincoln Creek* UT-8
Lincoln Creek—*stream* (3) AK-9
Lincoln Creek—*stream* CA-9
Lincoln Creek—*stream* CO-8
Lincoln Creek—*stream* GA-3
Lincoln Creek—*stream* (3) ID-8
Lincoln Creek—*stream* IN-6
Lincoln Creek—*stream* KS-7
Lincoln Creek—*stream* KY-4
Lincoln Creek—*stream* MI-6
Lincoln Creek—*stream* MO-7
Lincoln Creek—*stream* MT-8
Lincoln Creek—*stream* NE-7
Lincoln Creek—*stream* NV-8
Lincoln Creek—*stream* OR-9
Lincoln Creek—*stream* (3) WA-9
Lincoln Creek—*stream* WI-6
Lincoln Creek—*stream* WY-8
Lincoln Creek Campground—*locale* CA-9
Lincoln Creek Cem—*cemetery* NE-7
Lincoln Creek Grange—*locale* WA-9
Lincoln Creek Pathway—*park* WI-6
Lincoln Creek Valley—*valley* ID-8
Lincoln Crest—*locale* CA-9
**Lincolndale**—*pop pl* NY-2
Lincolndale, Lake—*lake* NY-2
**Lincoln Dale Township**—*pop pl* ND-7
Lincoln-Dime Box (CCD)—*cens area* TX-5
Lincoln Ditch—*canal* IN-6
Lincoln Ditch—*canal* MT-8
Lincoln Drain—*canal* MI-6
Lincoln Early Childhood Center—*school* PA-2
Lincoln-Eastaboga (CCD)—*cens area* AL-4
Lincoln-Eastaboga Division—*civil* AL-4
Lincoln (Election Precinct)—*fmr MCD* IL-6
Lincoln Elementary and JHS—*school* IN-6
*Lincoln Elem Sch* PA-2
*Lincoln Elem Sch* TN-4
Lincoln Elem Sch—*hist pl* PA-2
Lincoln Elem Sch—*school* AL-4
Lincoln Elem Sch—*school* (2) AZ-5
Lincoln Elem Sch—*school* FL-3
Lincoln Elem Sch—*school* (12) IN-6
Lincoln Elem Sch—*school* (28) KS-7
Lincoln Elem Sch—*school* (8) PA-2
Lincoln Elem Sch—*school* TN-4
Lincoln Eliot Sch—*school* MA-1
Lincoln Estate-Elm Park Hist Dist—*hist pl* MA-1
*Lincoln Estates* MI-6
**Lincoln Estates**—*pop pl* FL-3
**Lincoln Estates**—*pop pl* IL-6
Lincoln Estates Park—*park* FL-3
Lincoln Evergreen Memorial Park—*cemetery* FL-3
*Lincoln Falls* MT-8
Lincoln Falls—*falls* PA-2
**Lincoln Falls**—*pop pl* PA-2
Lincoln Farm Lake—*lake* NY-2
Lincolnfellow Hill—*locale* KY-4
Lincoln Field—*park* FL-3
Lincoln Field—*park* MN-6
Lincoln Fields—*park* IL-6
Lincoln Fields Station—*locale* IL-6
Lincoln Flat—*flat* NV-8
**Lincoln Forest (subdivision)**—*pop pl* NC-3
Lincoln Gap—*gap* VT-1
*Lincoln Gardens* IL-6
Lincoln Gardens Park—*park* FL-3
**Lincoln Gardens Subdivision**—*pop pl* UT-8
*Lincoln Garfield Elementary School* PA-2
Lincoln Glen Sch—*school* CA-9
Lincoln Grade Sch—*school* KS-7
Lincoln Grange—*locale* OR-9
Lincoln Grange Hall—*locale* PA-2
Lincoln Greens Golf Course—*other* IL-6
Lincoln Grove Ch—*church* NC-3
Lincoln Grove Sch—*school* NE-7
Lincoln Guard Station—*locale* WA-9
Lincoln Gulch—*valley* (2) CO-8
Lincoln Gulch—*valley* (3) MT-8
Lincoln Gulch—*valley* UT-8
Lincoln Gulch—*valley* (2) WY-8
Lincoln Gulch Campground—*locale* CO-8
Lincoln Gulch Connection Canal—*canal* CO-8
Lincoln Hall—*building* NY-2
Lincoln Hall—*hist pl* KY-4
*Lincoln Heights* OH-6
**Lincoln Heights**—*pop pl* CA-9
**Lincoln Heights**—*pop pl* (2) IN-6
**Lincoln Heights**—*pop pl* NC-3
**Lincoln Heights**—*pop pl* (3) OH-6
**Lincoln Heights**—*pop pl* PA-2
Lincoln Heights—*uninc pl* MD-2
Lincoln Heights—*uninc pl* PA-2
*Lincoln Heights Baptist Church* TN-4
Lincoln Heights Branch—*hist pl* CA-9
Lincoln Heights Ch—*church* TN-4
Lincoln Height Sch—*school* NC-3
Lincoln Heights Park—*park* NE-7
Lincoln Heights Sch—*school* MI-6
Lincoln Heights Sch—*school* (2) NC-3
Lincoln Heights Sch—*school* TN-4
Lincoln Heights Sch—*school* WA-9
**Lincoln Heights (subdivision)**—*pop pl* FL-3
**Lincoln Heights (subdivision)**—*pop pl* MA-1
**Lincoln Heights (subdivision)**—*pop pl* (3) NC-3
Lincoln Heights (Township of)—*other* OH-6
Lincoln Heights Village Shop Ctr—*locale* KS-7
Lincoln Heritage House—*hist pl* KY-4
Lincoln Heritage Trail—*trail* IL-6
Lincoln Highway—*hist pl* NE-7
Lincoln Highway Bridge—*hist pl* IA-7
Lincoln Highway Bridge—*hist pl* UT-8
*Lincoln Highway (Two Hundred and Eleventh Street)* IL-6
**Lincoln Hill**—*pop pl* PA-2
Lincoln Hill—*summit* CA-9
Lincoln Hill—*summit* IN-6
Lincoln Hill—*summit* MA-1
Lincoln Hill—*summit* NV-8
Lincoln Hill—*summit* NH-1
Lincoln Hill—*summit* NY-2
Lincoln Hill—*summit* (2) VT-1
Lincoln Hill—*summit* VA-3
Lincoln Hill Camp—*locale* MA-1
Lincoln Hill Mine—*mine* NV-8
**Lincoln Hills**—*pop pl* CO-8
**Lincoln Hills**—*pop pl* GA-3
**Lincoln Hills**—*pop pl* IL-6
**Lincoln Hills**—*pop pl* IN-6
Lincoln Hills Golf Course—*other* MI-6
Lincoln Hills Sch—*school* MN-6
Lincoln Hist Dist—*hist pl* NM-5
Lincoln Hollow—*valley* MO-7
Lincoln Hollow—*valley* NC-3
Lincoln Hollow—*valley* VT-1
Lincoln Home Natl Historic Site—*hist pl* IL-6
Lincoln Home Natl Historic Site—*park* IL-6
Lincoln Homestead and Cemetery—*hist pl* VA-3
Lincoln Homestead Memorial Park—*park* IL-6
Lincoln Homestead State Park—*park* KY-4
Lincoln Hosp—*hospital* AZ-5
Lincoln Hosp—*hospital* FL-3
Lincoln Hosp—*hospital* NY-2
Lincoln House—*hist pl* ME-1
Lincoln House Club—*hist pl* MA-1
Lincoln House Point—*cape* MA-1
Lincoln HS—*hist pl* WI-6
Lincoln HS—*school* AL-4
Lincoln HS—*school* (2) AR-4
Lincoln HS—*school* (4) CA-9
Lincoln HS—*school* (2) FL-3
Lincoln HS—*school* IL-6
Lincoln HS—*school* (2) IN-6
Lincoln HS—*school* (3) IA-7
Lincoln HS—*school* KS-7
Lincoln HS—*school* KY-4
Lincoln HS—*school* LA-4
Lincoln HS—*school* (3) MI-6
Lincoln HS—*school* (2) MN-6
Lincoln HS—*school* MO-7
Lincoln HS—*school* NJ-2
Lincoln HS—*school* NY-2
Lincoln HS—*school* NC-3
Lincoln HS—*school* OH-6
Lincoln HS—*school* OR-9
Lincoln HS—*school* (2) PA-2
Lincoln HS—*school* SC-3
Lincoln HS—*school* SD-7
Lincoln HS—*school* (4) TX-5
Lincoln HS—*school* UT-8
Lincoln HS—*school* (3) WA-9
Lincoln HS—*school* (3) WI-6
Lincoln HS—*school* WY-8
Lincoln HS (historical)—*school* MS-4
Lincoln Hy-Chicago Heights Interchange—*other* IL-6
Lincolnia—*CDP* VA-3
**Lincolnia**—*pop pl* VA-3
**Lincolnia Heights**—*pop pl* VA-3
**Lincolnia Park**—*pop pl* VA-3
Lincolnia Sch—*school* VA-3
Lincoln Independence Sch—*school* PA-2
Lincoln Institute—*school* KY-4
Lincoln Institute Complex—*hist pl* KY-4
Lincoln Interchange—*crossing* ND-7
Lincoln-Irving Sch—*school* IL-6
Lincoln Island—*island* (2) AK-9
Lincoln Island—*island* MN-6
Lincoln Island—*island* NH-1
Lincoln Jackson Elem Sch—*school* PA-2
Lincoln JHS—*school* (3) CA-9
Lincoln JHS—*school* CO-8
Lincoln JHS—*school* CT-1
Lincoln JHS—*school* IL-6
Lincoln JHS—*school* (3) IN-6
Lincoln JHS—*school* ME-1
Lincoln JHS—*school* MA-1
Lincoln JHS—*school* (2) MI-6
Lincoln JHS—*school* (2) MN-6
Lincoln JHS—*school* MO-7
Lincoln JHS—*school* MT-8
Lincoln JHS—*school* NJ-2
Lincoln JHS—*school* NM-5
Lincoln JHS—*school* (2) NY-2
Lincoln JHS—*school* (2) NC-3
Lincoln JHS—*school* (2) PA-2
Lincoln JHS—*school* TN-4
Lincoln JHS—*school* TX-5
Lincoln JHS—*school* UT-8
Lincoln JHS—*school* (2) WA-9
Lincoln JHS—*school* (3) WI-6
Lincoln Junction—*locale* MI-6
**Lincoln Junction**—*pop pl* ID-8
Lincoln Junior High—*school* OR-9
*Lincoln Knolls Plaza* OH-6
Lincoln Knolls Plaza Shop Ctr—*locale* OH-6
*Lincoln Lake* CO-8
*Lincoln Lake* MI-6
Lincoln Lake—*lake* CO-8
Lincoln Lake—*lake* (4) MI-6
Lincoln Lake—*lake* (2) MN-6
Lincoln Lake—*lake* MT-8
Lincoln Lake—*lake* (3) WI-6
Lincoln Lake—*reservoir* AR-4
Lincoln Lake—*reservoir* TN-4
Lincoln Lake Dam—*dam* TN-4
Lincoln Lake Trail—*trail* MT-8
Lincoln Landing—*locale* GA-3
Lincoln Land Junior Coll—*school* IL-6
Lincoln Ledge—*bar* ME-1
Lincoln Liberty Life Insurance Bldg—*hist pl* NE-7
**Lincoln (Lincoln City)**—*pop pl* DE-2
Lincoln Lodge—*hist pl* MT-8
Lincoln Log Cabin State Historic Site—*park* IL-6
*Lincoln Log Cabin State Park* IL-6
Lincoln Lookout Tower—*locale* MS-4
Lincoln Lookout Tower—*locale* MO-7
Lincoln Lookout Tower (historical)—*locale* MI-6
Lincoln (Magisterial District)—*fmr MCD* (3) WV-2
**Lincoln Manor Condominium**—*pop pl* UT-8
Lincoln Manor Park—*park* MI-6
Lincoln-Marti Day Care Center—*school* FL-3
Lincoln-Marti Nursery Sch—*school* FL-3
Lincoln-McKinley Sch—*school* MT-8
*Lincoln Meadows* MI-6
Lincoln Memorial—*hist pl* DC-2
Lincoln Memorial Baptist Ch—*church* AL-4
Lincoln Memorial Bridge—*bridge* IN-6
Lincoln Memorial Bridge—*other* IL-6
Lincoln Memorial Cem—*cemetery* FL-3
Lincoln Memorial Cem—*cemetery* GA-3
Lincoln Memorial Cem—*cemetery* IL-6
Lincoln Memorial Cem—*cemetery* KY-4
Lincoln Memorial Cem—*cemetery* MD-2
Lincoln Memorial Cem—*cemetery* ND-7
Lincoln Memorial Cem—*cemetery* OR-9
Lincoln Memorial Cem—*cemetery* (2) SC-3
Lincoln Memorial Cem—*cemetery* VA-3
Lincoln Memorial Cem—*cemetery* WV-2
Lincoln Memorial Ch—*church* KY-4
Lincoln Memorial Gardens—*cemetery* FL-3
Lincoln Memorial Gardens of Ocala—*cemetery* FL-3
Lincoln Memorial Hosp—*hospital* OH-6
Lincoln Memorial Natl Historic Park—*park* KY-4
Lincoln Memorial Park—*cemetery* FL-3
Lincoln Memorial Park—*cemetery* IL-6
Lincoln Memorial Park—*cemetery* LA-4
Lincoln Memorial Park—*cemetery* MI-6
Lincoln Memorial Park—*cemetery* NE-7
Lincoln Memorial Park—*cemetery* NJ-2
Lincoln Memorial Park (Cemetery)—*cemetery* CA-9
Lincoln Memorial Park (Cemetery)—*cemetery* TX-5
Lincoln Memorial Sch—*school* FL-3
Lincoln Memorial Univ—*school* TN-4
Lincoln Memory Gardens Cem—*cemetery* IN-6
Lincoln Mid Sch—*school* IL-6
*Lincoln Mill* WA-9
Lincoln Mills—*locale* ME-1
Lincoln Mine—*mine* AZ-5
Lincoln Mine—*mine* CA-9
Lincoln Mine—*mine* (2) CO-8
Lincoln Mine—*mine* ID-8
Lincoln Mine—*mine* (3) NV-8
Lincoln Mine(Old Rollins Mine 1857)—*mine* UT-8
Lincoln Mine Pibal Station—*locale* NV-8
Lincoln Motor Company Plant—*hist pl* MI-6
*Lincoln Mountain* WA-9
Lincoln Mountains—*summit* AK-9
Lincoln MS—*school* PA-2
Lincoln Mtn—*summit* (2) CO-8
Lincoln Mtn—*summit* MT-8
Lincoln Mtn—*summit* NY-2
Lincoln Mtn—*summit* VT-1
Lincoln Municipal Airp—*airport* KS-7
Lincoln Municipal Airp—*airport* MO-7
Lincoln Municipal Airp—*airport* NE-7
Lincoln Museum—*building* DC-2
Lincoln Normal Sch (historical)—*school* AL-4
**Lincoln Parish**—*pop pl* LA-4
*Lincoln Park* IL-6
*Lincoln Park* MI-6
*Lincoln Park* RI-1
Lincoln Park—*airport* NJ-2
Lincoln Park—*flat* CO-8
Lincoln Park—*flat* MT-8
Lincoln Park—*park* (9) CA-9
Lincoln Park—*park* (3) CO-8
Lincoln Park—*park* DC-2
Lincoln Park—*park* (2) FL-3
Lincoln Park—*park* HI-9
Lincoln Park—*park* (11) IL-6
Lincoln Park—*park* (3) IN-6
Lincoln Park—*park* (3) KS-7
Lincoln Park—*park* LA-4
Lincoln Park—*park* MD-2
Lincoln Park—*park* (2) MA-1
Lincoln Park—*park* (3) MI-6
Lincoln Park—*park* (3) MN-6
Lincoln Park—*park* MO-7
Lincoln Park—*park* MT-8
Lincoln Park—*park* (3) NE-7
Lincoln Park—*park* (2) NJ-2
Lincoln Park—*park* (4) NY-2
Lincoln Park—*park* NC-3
Lincoln Park—*park* ND-7
Lincoln Park—*park* (8) OH-6
Lincoln Park—*park* (5) OK-5
Lincoln Park—*park* PA-2
Lincoln Park—*park* SD-7
Lincoln Park—*park* (2) TN-4
Lincoln Park—*park* (7) TX-5
Lincoln Park—*park* VA-3
Lincoln Park—*park* (7) WA-9
Lincoln Park—*park* (5) WI-6
**Lincoln Park**—*pop pl* CO-8
**Lincoln Park**—*pop pl* FL-3
**Lincoln Park**—*pop pl* GA-3
**Lincoln Park**—*pop pl* IN-6
**Lincoln Park**—*pop pl* MI-6
**Lincoln Park**—*pop pl* NV-8
**Lincoln Park**—*pop pl* NH-1
**Lincoln Park**—*pop pl* (3) NJ-2
**Lincoln Park**—*pop pl* (2) NY-2
**Lincoln Park**—*pop pl* (3) NC-3
**Lincoln Park**—*pop pl* (3) PA-2
**Lincoln Park**—*pop pl* RI-1
**Lincoln Park**—*pop pl* (2) TN-4
**Lincoln Park**—*pop pl* TX-5
**Lincoln Park**—*pop pl* (2) VA-3
Lincoln Park, South Pond Refectory—*hist pl* IL-6
Lincoln Park Baptist Ch—*church* TN-4
Lincoln Park Cem—*cemetery* FL-3
Lincoln Park Cem—*cemetery* WV-2
Lincoln Park Ch—*church* AL-4
Lincoln Park Ch—*church* VA-3
*Lincoln Park Elementary School* TN-4
Lincoln Park Elem Sch—*school* FL-3
Lincoln Park Elem Sch—*school* IN-6
Lincoln Park Elem Sch—*school* PA-2
Lincoln Park Hist Dist—*hist pl* NJ-2
Lincoln Park Hist Dist—*hist pl* NM-5
Lincoln Park Hist Dist (Boundary Increase)—*hist pl* NM-5
Lincoln Park HS—*school* MI-6
Lincoln Park MS—*school* FL-3
Lincoln Park Sch—*school* FL-3
Lincoln Park Sch—*school* IL-6
Lincoln Park Sch—*school* MI-6
Lincoln Park Sch—*school* NV-8
Lincoln Park Sch—*school* OH-6
Lincoln Park Sch—*school* OR-9
Lincoln Park Sch—*school* PA-2
Lincoln Park Sch—*school* TN-4
Lincoln Park (Shop Ctr)—*locale* FL-3
**Lincoln Park (subdivision)**—*pop pl* AL-4
**Lincoln Park (subdivision)**—*pop pl* NC-3
**Lincoln Park (subdivision)**—*pop pl* PA-2
**Lincoln Park Subdivision**—*pop pl* UT-8
Lincoln Park United Methodist Ch—*church* TN-4
Lincoln Park (Valley Junction)—*uninc pl* CA-9
*Lincoln Pass* MT-8
Lincoln Pass—*gap* MT-8
Lincoln Peak—*summit* AK-9
Lincoln Peak—*summit* ID-8
Lincoln Peak—*summit* MT-8
Lincoln Peak—*summit* NV-8
Lincoln Peak—*summit* VT-1
Lincoln Peak—*summit* WA-9
**Lincoln Pioneer Village**—*pop pl* IN-6
Lincoln Place—*uninc pl* PA-2
**Lincoln Plantation**—*pop pl* ME-1
Lincoln (Plantation of)—*civ div* ME-1
Lincoln Plateau—*plain* WA-9
Lincoln Playground—*locale* MA-1
Lincoln Playground—*park* NY-2
Lincoln Plaza—*locale* MA-1
Lincoln Plaza Shop Ctr—*locale* AZ-5
Lincoln Plaza Shop Ctr—*locale* MS-4
Lincoln Point—*cape* UT-8
Lincoln Point—*cliff* WY-8
Lincoln Pond—*lake* (2) ME-1
Lincoln Pond—*lake* MA-1
Lincoln Pond—*lake* NH-1
Lincoln Pond—*reservoir* NY-2
Lincoln Post Office (historical)—*building* PA-2
Lincoln Post Office (historical)—*building* TN-4
Lincoln Public Library—*hist pl* IL-6
Lincoln Ranch—*locale* AZ-5
Lincoln Ranch—*locale* CO-8
Lincoln Ranch—*locale* WY-8
Lincoln Ranger Station—*locale* MT-8
*Lincoln Regional Hospital* TN-4
Lincoln Regional Park—*park* AZ-5
**Lincoln Ridge**—*pop pl* KY-4
Lincoln Ridge—*ridge* CA-9
Lincoln Ridge—*ridge* ME-1
**Lincoln Ridge (Whitney Young Jr. Memorial School)**—*pop pl* KY-4
Lincoln River—*stream* MI-6
Lincoln River Sch—*school* MI-6
Lincoln Road—*post sta* FL-3
Lincoln Road Mall—*locale* FL-3
Lincoln Road Sch Number 1—*school* LA-4
Lincoln Road Sch Number 2—*school* LA-4
Lincoln Road Shop Ctr—*locale* MS-4
Lincoln Rock—*island* AK-9
Lincoln Rock—*pillar* CA-9
Lincoln Rock—*summit* WA-9
Lincoln Rocks—*bar* OR-9
Lincoln Rodeo Grounds—*locale* CA-9
Lincoln Rsvr—*reservoir* CO-8
Lincoln Rsvr—*reservoir* ID-8
Lincoln Rsvr—*reservoir* MA-1
Lincoln Rsvr—*reservoir* NH-1
Lincoln Run—*stream* KY-4
Lincoln Savage MS—*school* OR-9
*Lincoln Sch* IN-6
*Lincoln Sch* PA-2
*Lincoln Sch* TN-4
Lincoln Sch—*hist pl* AL-4
Lincoln Sch—*hist pl* (2) CO-8
Lincoln Sch—*hist pl* IL-6
Lincoln Sch—*hist pl* IA-7
Lincoln Sch—*hist pl* KY-4
Lincoln Sch—*hist pl* MI-6
Lincoln Sch—*hist pl* MO-7
Lincoln Sch—*hist pl* WI-6
Lincoln Sch—*school* AL-4
Lincoln Sch—*school* (4) AZ-5
Lincoln Sch—*school* AR-4
Lincoln Sch—*school* (58) CA-9
Lincoln Sch—*school* (11) CO-8
Lincoln Sch—*school* (5) CT-1
Lincoln Sch—*school* (2) FL-3
Lincoln Sch—*school* HI-9
Lincoln Sch—*school* (9) ID-8
Lincoln Sch—*school* (68) IL-6
Lincoln Sch—*school* (9) IN-6
Lincoln Sch—*school* (35) IA-7
Lincoln Sch—*school* (3) KS-7
Lincoln Sch—*school* (4) KY-4
Lincoln Sch—*school* LA-4
Lincoln Sch—*school* (12) ME-1
Lincoln Sch—*school* (2) MD-2
Lincoln Sch—*school* (14) MA-1
Lincoln Sch—*school* (27) MI-6
Lincoln Sch—*school* (25) MN-6
Lincoln Sch—*school* (10) MO-7
Lincoln Sch—*school* (6) MT-8
Lincoln Sch—*school* (8) NE-7
Lincoln Sch—*school* NV-8
Lincoln Sch—*school* NH-1
Lincoln Sch—*school* (18) NJ-2
Lincoln Sch—*school* NM-5
Lincoln Sch—*school* (12) NY-2
Lincoln Sch—*school* (4) NC-3
Lincoln Sch—*school* (7) ND-7
Lincoln Sch—*school* (35) OH-6
Lincoln Sch—*school* (20) OK-5
Lincoln Sch—*school* (6) OR-9
Lincoln Sch—*school* (23) PA-2
Lincoln Sch—*school* (2) SC-3
Lincoln Sch—*school* (15) SD-7
Lincoln Sch—*school* (4) TN-4
Lincoln Sch—*school* (9) TX-5
Lincoln Sch—*school* (6) UT-8
Lincoln Sch—*school* VT-1
Lincoln Sch—*school* VA-3
Lincoln Sch—*school* (11) WA-9
Lincoln Sch—*school* (6) WV-2
Lincoln Sch—*school* (36) WI-6
Lincoln Sch—*school* (2) WY-8
Lincoln Sch (abandoned)—*school* (2) PA-2
Lincoln Sch (abandoned)—*school* SD-7
Lincoln Sch Bldg—*hist pl* MN-6
Lincoln Sch (Faulkner)—*school* MA-1
Lincoln Sch (historical)—*school* IA-7
Lincoln Sch (historical)—*school* (3) MO-7
Lincoln Sch (historical)—*school* (2) PA-2
Lincoln Sch (historical)—*school* TN-4
Lincoln Sch Number 1—*school* (4) ND-7
Lincoln Sch Number 1—*school* OH-6
*Lincoln Sch Number 18* IN-6
Lincoln Sch Number 2—*school* (3) ND-7
Lincoln Sch Number 2—*school* OH-6
Lincoln Sch Number 2 (abandoned)—*school* ND-7
Lincoln Sch Number 3—*school* ND-7
Lincoln Sch Number 3 (abandoned)—*school* ND-7
Lincoln Sch Number 4—*school* ND-7
Lincoln School—*locale* MI-6
Lincoln School—*locale* MN-6
Lincoln School (abandoned)—*locale* CA-9
Lincoln School (historical)—*locale* MO-7
Lincoln Schools—*school* OH-6
Lincoln Sch (Revere)—*school* MA-1
Lincoln Sch (Wyoming)—*school* MA-1
*Lincolnshire* IL-6
*Lincolnshire* (4) IN-6
**Lincolnshire**—*pop pl* IL-6
**Lincolnshire**—*pop pl* IN-6
**Lincolnshire**—*pop pl* KY-4
**Lincoln Shire**—*pop pl* SC-3
Lincolnshire, The—*hist pl* MA-1
Lincolnshire Branch—*stream* VA-3
Lincolnshire Country Club—*other* IL-6
Lincolnshire Fields Golf Course—*other* IL-6
Lincolnshire Sch—*school* OH-6
Lincolns Home—*building* IL-6
Lincoln Shop Ctr—*other* CO-8
*Lincoln Shopping Center* PA-2
Lincoln Siding Station—*locale* PA-2
Lincoln Slough—*stream* MT-8
**Lincolns Mills**—*pop pl* ME-1
Lincoln's New Salem State Park—*park* IL-6
Lincolns New Salem State Park—*park* IL-6
Lincoln's New Salem Village—*hist pl* IL-6
Lincoln Speedway—*other* PA-2
Lincoln Spring—*spring* AZ-5
Lincoln Springs Ch—*church* TX-5
Lincoln Square—*locale* MA-1
Lincoln Square—*park* IL-6
**Lincoln (sta.)**—*pop pl* KY-4
Lincoln Star Mine—*mine* WY-8
Lincoln State Hosp—*hospital* NE-7
Lincoln State Park—*park* GA-3
Lincoln State Park—*park* IN-6
Lincoln Statue—*park* DC-2
Lincoln Street Hist Dist—*hist pl* ME-1
Lincoln Street Sch—*school* CA-9
Lincoln Street Sch—*school* IL-6
Lincoln Street Sch—*school* (2) MA-1
Lincoln-Sudbury Regional HS—*school* MA-1
Lincoln Tank—*reservoir* AZ-5
Lincoln Tank—*reservoir* NM-5
Lincoln Tank—*reservoir* TX-5
**Lincoln Terrace**—*pop pl* PA-2
Lincoln Terrace Park—*park* NY-2
Lincoln Terrace Sch—*school* VA-3

**Lindsey**—*pop pl* ... AL-4
**Lindsey**—*pop pl* ... KS-7
**Lindsey**—*pop pl* ... OH-6
**Lindsey**—*pop pl* ... WI-6
Lindsey—*uninc pl* ... PA-2
Lindsey, Lake—*lake* ... FL-3
Lindsey, Lake—*locale* ... FL-3
Lindsey, Mount—*summit* ... CO-8
Lindsey, Samuel, House—*hist pl* ... DE-2
Lindsey, William, House—*hist pl* ... MA-1
Lindsey, William, House—*hist pl* ... WA-9
Lindsey Bay—*bay* ... FL-3
Lindsey Bldg—*hist pl* ... OH-6
Lindsey Bluff—*cliff* ... TX-5
Lindsey Bluffs—*ridge* ... WI-6
Lindsey Bog—*swamp* ... ME-1
Lindsey Branch—*stream* (4) ... AL-4
Lindsey Branch—*stream* ... AR-4
Lindsey Branch—*stream* (2) ... GA-3
Lindsey Branch—*stream* ... LA-4
Lindsey Branch—*stream* ... NC-3
Lindsey Branch—*stream* ... TX-5
Lindsey Branch—*stream* ... WV-2
Lindsey Bridge—*bridge* ... IA-7
Lindsey Bridge—*bridge* ... MS-4
Lindsey Bridge—*bridge* ... TN-4
Lindsey Bridge—*other* ... IL-6
Lindsey Brook—*stream* (2) ... ME-1
Lindsey Brook—*stream* ... NY-2
Lindsey Canal—*canal* ... VA-3
Lindsey Canyon—*valley* ... AZ-5
Lindsey Canyon—*valley* ... CO-8
*Lindsey Cem* ... TN-4
Lindsey Cem—*cemetery* (8) ... AL-4
Lindsey Cem—*cemetery* (2) ... AR-4
Lindsey Cem—*cemetery* ... GA-3
Lindsey Cem—*cemetery* (2) ... IL-6
Lindsey Cem—*cemetery* ... LA-4
Lindsey Cem—*cemetery* (4) ... MS-4
Lindsey Cem—*cemetery* ... MO-7
Lindsey Cem—*cemetery* (5) ... TN-4
Lindsey Cem—*cemetery* ... TX-5
Lindsey Cem—*cemetery* ... WI-6
Lindsey Ch—*church* ... AL-4
Lindsey Ch—*church* ... TN-4
Lindsey Chapel—*church* ... IN-6
Lindsey Chapel—*church* ... KY-4
Lindsey Chapel—*church* ... OK-5
Lindsey Ch (historical)—*church* ... TN-4
**Lindsey Circle Condominium**—*pop pl* ... UT-8
Lindsey Cove—*bay* ... CT-1
Lindsey Cove—*bay* ... ME-1
*Lindsey Creek* ... AR-4
*Lindsey Creek* ... CA-9
Lindsey Creek—*stream* (4) ... AL-4
Lindsey Creek—*stream* ... CA-9
Lindsey Creek—*stream* ... CO-8
Lindsey Creek—*stream* ... FL-3
Lindsey Creek—*stream* ... GA-3
Lindsey Creek—*stream* (2) ... ID-8
Lindsey Creek—*stream* (2) ... IA-7
Lindsey Creek—*stream* ... KS-7
Lindsey Creek—*stream* ... KY-4
Lindsey Creek—*stream* ... MI-6
Lindsey Creek—*stream* ... MS-4
Lindsey Creek—*stream* ... MT-8
Lindsey Creek—*stream* ... NY-2
Lindsey Creek—*stream* ... OH-6
Lindsey Creek—*stream* ... OR-9
Lindsey Creek—*stream* ... SC-3
Lindsey Creek—*stream* ... TN-4
Lindsey Creek—*stream* (2) ... TX-5
Lindsey Creek—*stream* (2) ... WY-8
Lindsey Creek—*uninc pl* ... GA-3
Lindsey Creek State Park—*park* ... OR-9
Lindsey Drain—*canal* ... MI-6
Lindsey Drainage Ditch—*canal* ... AR-4
Lindsey Draw—*valley* ... SD-7
*Lindsey Ford* ... MS-4
Lindsey Gardens—*park* ... UT-8
Lindsey Grave—*cemetery* ... AZ-5
Lindsey Grove Cem—*cemetery* ... TN-4
Lindsey Grove Ch—*church* ... TN-4
Lindsey Hall Ch—*church* ... AL-4
Lindsey Harris Lake Dam—*dam* ... MS-4
**Lindsey (historical)**—*pop pl* ... OR-9
*Lindsey Hollow* ... TN-4
Lindsey Hollow—*valley* ... AL-4
Lindsey Hollow—*valley* ... PA-2
Lindsey Hollow—*valley* (3) ... TN-4
Lindsey-Honeycomb Creek Wild Area—*park* ... AL-4
Lindsey Hopkins Technical Education Center—*school* ... FL-3
*Lindsey Lake* ... MI-6
Lindsey Lake—*lake* ... FL-3
Lindsey Lake—*lake* ... IN-6
Lindsey Lake—*lake* ... LA-4
Lindsey Lake—*lake* ... MN-6
Lindsey Lake—*lake* ... MS-4
Lindsey Lake—*lake* ... NM-5
Lindsey Lake—*reservoir* ... MS-4
Lindsey Lake Dam—*dam* (2) ... MS-4
Lindsey Lakes—*lake* ... CA-9
Lindsey Lateral—*canal* ... ID-8
Lindsey Memorial Ch—*church* ... GA-3
Lindsey Mill Branch—*stream* ... AL-4
Lindsey Mine—*mine* ... MO-7
Lindsey Mine—*mine* ... NV-8
Lindsey Mtn—*summit* ... ID-8
Lindsey Mtn—*summit* ... MS-4
Lindsey Mtn—*summit* ... MO-7
Lindsey Pond—*reservoir* ... OR-9
Lindsey Pond Dam—*dam* ... MS-4
Lindsey Ponds Dam—*dam* ... MS-4
*Lindsey Private Cemetery* ... AL-4
Lindsey Ranch—*locale* ... AZ-5
Lindsey Ranch—*locale* ... TX-5
Lindsey Ranch—*locale* ... WY-8
*Lindsey Reservoir* ... CO-8
Lindsey Ridge—*ridge* ... TN-4
Lindsey Sch—*school* ... IL-6
Lindsey Sch—*school* ... MN-6
Lindsey Sch—*school* ... NM-5
Lindsey Sch—*school* ... NY-2
Lindsey Sch—*school* ... OK-5
Lindsey Sch (abandoned)—*school* ... MO-7
Lindsey Sch (abandoned)—*school* (2) ... PA-2
*Lindseys Chapel Church* ... AL-4
*Lindseys Chapel Freewill Baptist Church of God* ... AL-4
Lindsey Sch (historical)—*school* (2) ... MS-4
Lindsey Sch (historical)—*school* ... SD-7
Lindseys Creek—*stream* ... AR-4
Lindseys Crossing—*locale* ... AL-4
Lindseys Ferry (historical)—*locale* ... AL-4
Lindseys Lake—*reservoir* ... SC-3
Lindsey Slough—*gut* ... TX-5
Lindsey Slough—*stream* ... CA-9
*Lindsey Slough Gas Field* ... CA-9
Lindsey Spring—*spring* ... CO-8
Lindsey Spring—*spring* ... WY-8
Lindsey Spring Cave—*cave* ... AL-4
Lindsey Spring Ch—*church* ... MS-4
Lindseys Ranch (historical)—*locale* ... SD-7
*Lindseys Slough* ... AR-4
Lindsey Tank—*reservoir* ... AZ-5
Lindsey Township—*civil* ... MO-7
**Lindseyville**—*pop pl* ... KY-4
Lindsey Wilson Coll—*school* ... KY-4
**Lindside**—*pop pl* ... WV-2
Lindside Ch—*church* ... WV-2
Lindsley Ave Church of Christ—*hist pl* ... TN-4
Lindsley Bend—*bend* ... TN-4
Lindsley Brook—*stream* ... CT-1
Lindsley Canyon—*valley* ... SD-7
**Lindsley Corners**—*pop pl* ... NY-2
Lindsley Creek—*stream* (2) ... OR-9
Lindsley Ditch—*canal* ... OH-6
Lindsley Hill—*summit* ... CT-1
**Lindsley (historical)**—*pop pl* ... TN-4
Lindsley Hollow—*valley* ... NY-2
Lindsley House—*hist pl* ... FL-3
Lindsley Islands (historical)—*island* ... TN-4
Lindsley Lake—*lake* ... MI-6
Lindsley Park—*uninc pl* ... GA-3
*Lindsley Pond* ... CT-1
Lindsley Prairie—*flat* ... AR-4
Lindsley Sch—*school* ... MI-6
Lind Spring—*spring* ... UT-8
Lindstrand Ditch—*canal* ... IN-6
Lindstrew Ford—*locale* ... MO-7
**Lindstrom**—*pop pl* ... MN-6
Lindstrom Bayou—*stream* ... LA-4
Lindstrom Creek—*stream* ... ND-7
Lindstrom Peak—*summit* ... ID-8
Lindstrom Sch—*school* ... CA-9
Lindstrom Sch—*school* ... MN-6
Lind Town Hall—*building* ... ND-7
**Lind (Town of)**—*pop pl* ... WI-6
**Lind Township**—*pop pl* ... ND-7
**Lind (Township of)**—*pop pl* ... MN-6
Lindvig Ridge—*ridge* ... WI-6
Lind-Washtucna (CCD)—*cens area* ... WA-9
Lindwerm—*uninc pl* ... WI-6
Lindwood Cem—*cemetery* ... MA-1
Lindwood Cem—*cemetery* ... MI-6
**Lindy**—*pop pl* ... NE-7
Lindy Ann Mine—*mine* ... NM-5
Lindy Branch—*stream* ... KY-4
Lindy Camp Branch—*stream* ... TN-4
Lindy Creek—*stream* ... KY-4
Lindy Creek—*stream* ... PA-2
Lindy Lake—*lake* ... MI-6
Lindy Lake—*lake* ... WI-6
**Lindy Lake**—*pop pl* ... NJ-2
Lindy Lake—*reservoir* ... NJ-2
Lindy Peak—*summit* (2) ... MT-8
Lindy Run—*stream* ... WV-2
Lindy Run Trail—*trail* ... WV-2
*Lindys Lake* ... NJ-2
*Lindy Town* ... WV-2
**Lindytown**—*pop pl* ... WV-2
Lindzy Cem—*cemetery* ... AR-4
Line—*locale* ... AR-4
Line Acad—*school* ... GA-3
Linear Lake—*lake* ... UT-8
Line Ave Sch—*hist pl* ... LA-4
Line Ave Sch—*school* ... LA-4
**Lineback (historical)**—*pop pl* ... TN-4
Linebarge Cem—*cemetery* ... AL-4
Linebarger Branch—*stream* ... AL-4
Linebarger Branch—*stream* ... MS-4
Linebarger Chapel—*church* ... IN-6
Linebarger House—*hist pl* ... AR-4
Linebarier Chapel—*church* ... AR-4
Linebarker Cem—*cemetery* ... GA-3
Linebaugh Bend—*bend* ... TN-4
Linebaugh Ranch—*locale* ... OR-9
**Lineberger Acres (subdivision)**—*pop pl* ... NC-3
*Lineberger Park* ... NC-3
**Lineberry**—*pop pl* ... NC-3
Lineberry Cem—*cemetery* ... TN-4
Lineberry Ch—*church* ... NC-3
Lineberry Creek—*stream* ... NC-3
Lineberry Fork—*stream* ... TN-4
Lineberry Hollow—*valley* ... TN-4
Lineberry Lake—*reservoir* ... NC-3
Lineberry Lake Dam—*dam* ... NC-3
Lineberry Windmill—*locale* ... TX-5
Line Bluff—*summit* ... OR-9
**Lineboro**—*pop pl* ... MD-2
Line Boy Mine—*mine* ... AZ-5
Line Boy Spring—*spring* ... AZ-5
Line Branch—*stream* ... AL-4
Line Branch—*stream* ... FL-3
Line Branch—*stream* (3) ... KY-4
Line Branch—*stream* ... NC-3
Line Branch—*stream* ... OK-5
Line Branch—*stream* (2) ... TX-5
Line Branch Hollow—*valley* ... VA-3
Line Bridge—*bridge* ... GA-3
*Line Brook* ... MA-1
**Linebrook**—*pop pl* ... MA-1
Line Brook—*stream* ... IN-6
Line Brook—*stream* ... NH-1
Line Brook—*stream* ... NY-2
Line Brook—*stream* (2) ... VT-1
Linebrook Sch—*school* ... MA-1
Lineburg—*locale* ... WV-2
Lineburger Park—*park* ... NC-3
Line Butte—*summit* ... OR-9
Line Camp—*locale* ... SD-7
Linecamp Branch—*stream* ... KY-4
Line Camp Creek—*stream* ... MT-8
Line Camp Spring—*spring* ... AZ-5
Line Canal—*canal* ... NC-3
*Line Canyon* ... CO-8
Line Canyon—*valley* (2) ... CO-8
Line Canyon—*valley* ... ID-8
Line Canyon—*valley* ... NM-5
Line Canyon—*valley* ... OR-9
Line Canyon—*valley* (2) ... UT-8
Line C Ditch—*canal* ... IL-6
Line Cem—*cemetery* (2) ... KS-7
Line Cem—*cemetery* ... MO-7
*Line Cemetery* ... AL-4
Line Ch—*church* ... DE-2
Line Ch—*church* ... NH-1
Line Church, The—*church* ... GA-3
*Line City* ... AZ-5
*Line Consolidated School* ... MS-4
Line Coulee—*valley* ... MT-8
Line Cove—*bay* ... AZ-5
*Line Creek* ... AR-4
*Line Creek* ... CO-8
*Line Creek* ... GA-3
*Line Creek* ... MS-4
Line Creek—*stream* (3) ... AL-4
Line Creek—*stream* ... AR-4
Line Creek—*stream* ... CA-9
Line Creek—*stream* ... CO-8
Line Creek—*stream* (3) ... GA-3
Line Creek—*stream* (5) ... ID-8
Line Creek—*stream* (4) ... KY-4
Line Creek—*stream* ... LA-4
Line Creek—*stream* ... MD-2
Line Creek—*stream* (4) ... MS-4
Line Creek—*stream* ... MO-7
Line Creek—*stream* (7) ... MT-8
Line Creek—*stream* (2) ... NY-2
Line Creek—*stream* (2) ... NC-3
Line Creek—*stream* (3) ... OK-5
Line Creek—*stream* (6) ... OR-9
Line Creek—*stream* ... SD-7
Line Creek—*stream* ... TN-4
Line Creek—*stream* (2) ... TX-5
Line Creek—*stream* ... UT-8
Line Creek—*stream* ... VA-3
Line Creek—*stream* ... WA-9
Line Creek—*stream* ... WV-2
Line Creek—*stream* (5) ... WY-8
*Line Creek Baptist Church* ... MS-4
Line Creek Cem—*cemetery* ... MS-4
Line Creek Ch—*church* ... GA-3
Line Creek Ch—*church* ... KY-4
Line Creek Ch—*church* ... LA-4
Line Creek Ch—*church* ... MS-4
Line Creek Ch (historical)—*church* ... AL-4
Line Creek Guard Station—*locale* ... MT-8
Line Creek (historical)—*locale* ... MS-4
Line Creek Lake—*lake* ... CA-9
Line Creek Lake Number Three B—*reservoir* ... TN-4
Line Creek Park—*park* ... MO-7
Line Creek Plateau—*plain* ... MT-8
Line Creek P.O. (historical)—*locale* ... AL-4
Line Creek Post Office (historical)—*building* ... MS-4
Line Creek Watershed Dam Number Three B—*dam* ... TN-4
Line Ditch—*canal* ... DE-2
Line Ditch—*canal* ... KY-4
Line Ditch—*canal* ... MT-8
Line Draw—*valley* ... WY-8
Lined Trees Windmill—*well* ... AZ-5
Linefork—*locale* ... KY-4
Line Fork—*stream* (2) ... KY-4
Line Fork—*stream* ... TN-4
Line Fork Sch—*school* ... KY-4
*Line Gap Tank* ... NM-5
Line Gulch—*valley* (3) ... CA-9
Line Gulch—*valley* (2) ... ID-8
Line Gut—*gut* ... VA-3
Lineham Springs—*spring* ... ID-8
Linehan Flat—*flat* ... ID-8
Line Hill—*summit* ... NH-1
Line Hill—*summit* ... PA-2
Line Hollow—*valley* (2) ... TN-4
Line Island—*other* ... AK-9
**Linekin**—*pop pl* ... ME-1
Linekin Bay—*bay* ... ME-1
Linekin Neck—*cape* ... ME-1
Linekona Sch—*hist pl* ... HI-9
Linekon Sch—*school* ... HI-9
*Line Lake* ... WI-6
Line Lake—*lake* ... GA-3
Line Lake—*lake* ... ID-8
Line Lake—*lake* (2) ... MI-6
Line Lake—*lake* (2) ... MN-6
Line Lake—*lake* ... ND-7
Line Lake—*lake* (2) ... WI-6
Line Laurel Creek—*stream* ... WV-2
**Line Lexington**—*pop pl* ... PA-2
*Lineman Lake* ... CA-9
Line Mountain—*locale* ... PA-2
Line Mountain HS—*school* ... PA-2
Line Mtn—*range* ... PA-2
*Linen Bar* ... VA-3
Linen Mill Wharf (historical)—*locale* ... MA-1
Line Oak Slough—*stream* ... TX-5
Line Park—*park* ... MO-7
Line Point—*summit* ... ID-8
Line Pond—*lake* (2) ... ME-1
Line Pond—*lake* ... NH-1
Line Pond—*lake* (3) ... NY-2
Line Pond—*lake* (3) ... VT-1
Line Pond—*swamp* ... TX-5
Line Pond Mtn—*summit* ... ME-1
Lineport Post Office (historical)—*building* ... TN-4
Line Prairie—*flat* ... MS-4
Line Prairie Ch—*church* ... MS-4
Line Prairie Sch—*school* ... MS-4
Line Ranch Tank—*reservoir* ... NM-5
Liner Cem—*cemetery* ... GA-3
Liner Cove—*valley* (2) ... NC-3
Liner Creek—*stream* ... MO-7
Liner Creek—*stream* ... NC-3
Line Rider Creek—*stream* ... MT-8
Line Ridge—*ridge* ... TN-4
Liner Island—*island* ... AK-9
Line Rock Gap—*gap* ... NC-3
Line Rock Gap—*gap* ... SC-3
Liners—*locale* ... TN-4
Liners Chapel Sch (historical)—*school* ... TN-4
*Liners Sch* ... TN-4
Line Run—*stream* ... MD-2
Line Run—*stream* ... OH-6
Line Run—*stream* ... PA-2
Line Run—*stream* ... VA-3
Line Runner Ridge—*ridge* ... NC-3
**Line Runner Ridge (subdivision)**—*pop pl* ... NC-3
**Lines**—*pop pl* ... MS-4
Lines, Samuel Shepard, House—*hist pl* ... GA-3
Lines Canyon—*valley* ... AZ-5
Line Sch—*school* ... KY-4
Lines Creek—*stream* ... ID-8
Lines Island—*island* ... ME-1
*Lines Island Channel* ... ME-1
Lines Mill—*locale* ... KY-4
*Lines Mills* ... NY-2
Line Spring—*locale* ... TN-4
Line Spring—*spring* ... CA-9
Line Spring—*spring* ... CO-8
Line Spring—*spring* (2) ... ID-8
Line Spring—*spring* ... MT-8
Lines Sch—*school* ... PA-2
Lines Sch (historical)—*school* ... PA-2
Lines Tank—*reservoir* ... AZ-5
*Linestone Creek* ... MT-8
*Linestone Ridge* ... WV-2
Line Street HS (historical)—*school* ... MS-4
Linesville—*locale* ... GA-3
**Linesville**—*pop pl* ... PA-2
Linesville Borough—*civil* ... PA-2
Linesville Branch—*stream* ... GA-3
Linesville Conneaut Summit HS—*school* ... PA-2
Linesville Creek—*stream* (2) ... PA-2
Line Swamp—*swamp* ... NH-1
Line Tank—*reservoir* (3) ... AZ-5
Line Tank—*reservoir* (4) ... NM-5
Line Tank—*reservoir* ... TX-5
Linetree Hollow—*valley* ... OH-6
Line Tunnel—*tunnel* ... KY-4
Line V Canal—*canal* ... TX-5
*Lineville* ... MO-7
**Lineville**—*pop pl* ... AL-4
**Lineville**—*pop pl* ... IA-7
Lineville Baptist Ch—*church* ... AL-4
Lineville (CCD)—*cens area* ... AL-4
Lineville Club Lake—*reservoir* ... AL-4
Lineville Dam—*dam* ... AL-4
Lineville Division—*civil* ... AL-4
Lineville Elem Sch—*school* ... AL-4
Lineville HS—*school* ... AL-4
Lineville Lake—*reservoir* ... AL-4
Line V Seven Ranch—*locale* ... AZ-5
Lineweaver Cem—*cemetery* ... OH-6
Lineweaver Sch—*school* ... AZ-5
Line Well—*well* (4) ... NM-5
Line Well—*well* (3) ... TX-5
Line Windmill—*locale* ... NM-5
Line Windmill—*locale* (4) ... TX-5
Liney Hollow—*valley* ... KY-4
**Linfield**—*pop pl* ... PA-2
Linfield Coll—*school* ... OR-9
Linfield Sch—*school* ... WI-6
Linfor—*locale* ... ID-8
**Linford Acres Subdivision**—*pop pl* ... UT-8
Linfor Hill—*summit* ... ID-8
**Lingae**—*pop pl* ... GU-9
L Ingalls Number 1 Dam—*dam* ... SD-7
L Ingalls Number 2 Dam—*dam* ... SD-7
Linganore—*locale* ... MD-2
Linganore Creek—*stream* ... MD-2
**Lingard**—*pop pl* ... CA-9
Lingard Lateral—*canal* ... CA-9
Ling Branch—*stream* ... NC-3
Ling Canyon—*valley* ... NV-8
Lingebaugh Mtn—*summit* ... AR-4
*Lingelbach Creek* ... OR-9
Lingemann Sch—*school* (2) ... MI-6
Lingenfelter Cem—*cemetery* ... KY-4
Lingeo, Bayou—*gut* ... LA-4
Lingerfeldt Elem Sch—*school* ... NC-3
Lingerfelt Island—*island* ... GA-3
**Linger Lake**—*pop pl* ... TN-4
Linger Lake—*reservoir* ... TN-4
Linger Lake Dam—*dam* ... TN-4
Linger Longer Lake—*reservoir* ... IN-6
Linger Longer Prairie—*flat* ... OR-9
**Lingerlost (subdivision)**—*pop pl* ... AL-4
Linger Point—*cape* ... NJ-2
Linger Ranch—*locale* ... CO-8
*Linger Run* ... WV-2
Linger Run—*stream* ... WV-2
*Lingertot Pond* ... PA-2
Lingertots Dam—*dam* ... PA-2
Lingertots Pond—*reservoir* ... PA-2
Lingerts Pond—*reservoir* ... NJ-2
Lingiy—*summit* ... FM-9
Lingle—*locale* ... MS-4
**Lingle**—*pop pl* ... WY-8
*Linglebach Creek* ... OR-9
Linglebeck Creek—*stream* ... OR-9
Lingle Cem—*cemetery* ... IN-6
Lingle Cem—*cemetery* ... MS-4
Lingle Cem—*cemetery* ... WY-8
Lingle Creek—*stream* ... IL-6
Lingle Creek—*stream* ... IA-7
Lingle Creek—*stream* ... PA-2
Lingle Drain—*stream* ... MI-6
Lingle Island—*island* ... PA-2
Lingle Lake—*reservoir* ... NC-3
Lingle Lake Dam—*dam* ... MS-4
Lingle Lake Dam—*dam* ... NC-3
Lingle Post Office (historical)—*building* ... MS-4
Lingle Sch—*school* ... IL-6
**Lingles Crossroads**—*pop pl* ... SC-3
Lingles Sch and Educational Clinic—*school* ... FL-3
**Linglestown**—*pop pl* ... PA-2
Linglestown Elem Sch—*school* ... PA-2
Linglestown JHS—*school* ... PA-2
Lingle Stream—*stream* ... PA-2
*Lingletown* ... PA-2
Lingle Trail—*trail* ... PA-2
*Lingle Valley* ... PA-2
Lingle Valley Trail—*trail* ... PA-2
**Lingleville**—*pop pl* ... TX-5
Lingner Ranch—*locale* ... NE-7
Lingo—*locale* ... NM-5
**Lingo**—*pop pl* ... MO-7
Lingo, Lake—*lake* ... AR-4
Lingo Canyon—*valley* ... CA-9
Lingo Cem—*cemetery* ... MO-7
Lingo Cem—*cemetery* ... TN-4
Lingo Cove—*bay* ... DE-2
Lingo Creek—*stream* ... DE-2
Lingo Creek—*stream* ... MO-7
**Lingo Estate (trailer park)**—*pop pl* ... DE-2
*Lingohocken* ... PA-2
*Lingohocking* ... PA-2
Lingo Lake—*lake* ... TX-5
Lingo Landing—*locale* ... DE-2
Lingo Mtn—*summit* ... AL-4
Lingo Point—*cape* ... DE-2
Lingo Pond—*reservoir* ... AL-4
*Lingos Creek* ... DE-2
Lingos Falls—*falls* ... TX-5
Lingos Landing—*locale* ... CA-9
*Lingos Point* ... DE-2
Lingo Township—*civil* ... MO-7
Lingroth Lake—*lake* ... MN-6
Lingrove Ch—*church* ... LA-4
Lingshire—*locale* ... MT-8
*Linguist Creek* ... TX-5
Lingum Lake—*lake* ... MS-4
**Linhart**—*pop pl* ... PA-2
Linheart Ch—*church* ... MO-7
**Linhigh**—*pop pl* ... MD-2
Lin Hollow—*valley* ... KY-4
Lin Hollow—*valley* (2) ... TX-5
Linholm Cem—*cemetery* ... AL-4
Liniar Bay—*bay* ... NC-3
Linie Lac—*lake* ... WI-6
Lininger Ditch—*canal* ... CO-8
Lininger Lake—*reservoir* ... CO-8
Lininger Mtn—*summit* ... CO-8
Link—*locale* ... OR-9
Link—*locale* ... TN-4
Link—*locale* ... WV-2
**Link**—*pop pl* ... LA-4
Link, Lake—*lake* ... FL-3
Link, The—*trail* ... NH-1
Link, Theodore, Historic Buildings—*hist pl* ... MO-7
Linka, Lake—*lake* ... MN-6
Linka Creek—*stream* ... NV-8
Linka Mine—*mine* ... NV-8
Linkay Creek—*gut* ... SC-3
Link Bar Spring—*spring* ... OR-9
**Link Belt**—*pop pl* ... PA-2
Link Branch—*stream* ... IL-6
Link Branch—*stream* ... TN-4
Link Bridge—*bridge* ... TN-4
Link Canyon—*valley* ... UT-8
Link Canyon Mine—*mine* ... UT-8
Link Canyon Wash—*stream* ... UT-8
Link Cem—*cemetery* (3) ... MO-7
Link Cem—*cemetery* ... NY-2
Link Cem—*cemetery* ... ND-7
Link Cem—*cemetery* (3) ... TN-4
Link Ch—*church* ... MO-7
*Link Creek* ... CO-8
*Link Creek* ... UT-8
Link Creek—*stream* (2) ... CO-8
Link Creek—*stream* ... MO-7
Link Creek—*stream* ... NC-3
Link Creek—*stream* ... OR-9
Link Creek—*stream* ... WI-6
Link Creek Recreation Site—*park* ... OR-9
Link Dart Tank—*reservoir* ... AZ-5
Link Ditch—*canal* ... CO-8
Link Ditch No. 1—*canal* ... CO-8
Linke, William L., House—*hist pl* ... CT-1
Linke Lake—*lake* ... NE-7
Linkenhoker Cem—*cemetery* ... VA-3
Linker Cem—*cemetery* ... AR-4
Linker Creek—*stream* ... AR-4
Linker Dam—*dam* ... SD-7
Linker Dam Rsvr—*reservoir* ... SD-7
Linker Mtn—*summit* ... AR-4
Linkers Mill (historical)—*locale* ... MS-4
Link Farm Site—*hist pl* ... TN-4
Link Five—*locale* ... TX-5
Link Flat Natural Area—*area* ... UT-8
Link Flats—*flat* ... UT-8
Link HIlls Country Club—*locale* ... TN-4
Link Hollow—*valley* ... IN-6
Link Hollow—*valley* ... MO-7
**Linkhorn**—*pop pl* ... VA-3
Linkhorn Bay—*bay* ... VA-3
**Linkhorn Estates**—*pop pl* ... VA-3
**Linkhorn Park**—*pop pl* ... VA-3
Linkhorn Park Sch—*school* ... VA-3
Linkhorn Point—*cape* ... VA-3
**Linkhorn Shores**—*pop pl* ... VA-3
Link House—*hist pl* ... TX-5
Linkins Lake—*lake* ... CO-8
Link Island—*island* ... AK-9
*Link Lake* ... MN-6
Link Lake—*lake* ... AK-9
Link Lake—*lake* (2) ... MN-6
Link Lake—*lake* ... MT-8
Link Lake—*lake* ... OR-9
Link Lake Lookout Tower—*locale* ... MN-6
Link Lake Trail—*trail* ... MN-6
Linklater, Zula, House—*hist pl* ... OR-9
Linklater Lake—*lake* ... MI-6
*Link Log Creek* ... GA-3
Link Mine—*mine* ... NV-8
Link Mountain—*ridge* ... AR-4
Link Mtn—*summit* ... MT-8
Linkous Chapel—*church* ... VA-3
Linkous Sch—*school* ... VA-3
Link Park—*flat* ... MT-8
Link Phillips Cem—*cemetery* ... TN-4
Link Point—*summit* ... AZ-5
Link Ranch—*locale* ... NM-5
*Link River* ... OR-9
Link River—*stream* ... OR-9
Link River Dam—*dam* ... OR-9
Link Sch (abandoned)—*school* ... MO-7
Link Sch (historical)—*school* ... PA-2
Link Sch (historical)—*school* ... TN-4
Link Shaft—*mine* ... NM-5
Links Landing Heliport—*airport* ... MO-7
Links Landing Seaplane Base—*airport* ... MO-7
**Links Point (subdivision)**—*pop pl* (2) ... AZ-5
Links Pond—*lake* ... NY-2
Link Spring—*spring* ... AZ-5
Link Spring—*spring* ... CO-8
Link Spring—*spring* ... OR-9
Link Spring—*spring* ... TN-4
Link Spring Ridge—*ridge* ... CO-8
*Linksville* ... IN-6
Linkswiler Branch—*stream* ... VA-3
Link Trail—*trail* ... CO-8
Link Trail—*trail* ... MA-1
Linkum Creek—*stream* ... AK-9
*Linkville* ... IN-6
*Linkville* ... MO-7
**Linkville**—*pop pl* ... IN-6
**Linkville**—*pop pl* ... MI-6
**Linkville**—*pop pl* ... MO-7
Linkville Cem—*cemetery* ... MI-6
Linkville Cem—*cemetery* ... OR-9
**Linkwood**—*pop pl* ... MD-2
**Linkwood Estates**—*pop pl* ... TX-5
Linkwood Park—*park* ... TX-5
Linlawn Sch—*school* ... IN-6
Linlee Sch—*school* ... KY-4
Linley Hollow—*valley* ... UT-8
Linley Ridge—*ridge* ... AR-4
Linlier—*locale* ... VA-3
**Linlithgo**—*pop pl* ... NY-2
Linlithgo Mills—*locale* ... NY-2
Linlog Branch—*stream* ... TN-4
Lin Luce Branch—*stream* ... TX-5
Linly Cem—*cemetery* ... KY-4
Linlyco Lake—*lake* ... NY-2
Linmea Park—*park* ... KS-7
*Linn* ... AL-4
*Linn* ... IL-6
Linn—*locale* ... OK-5
Linn—*locale* ... TX-5
Linn—*locale* ... WV-2
**Linn**—*pop pl* ... KS-7
**Linn**—*pop pl* ... MS-4
**Linn**—*pop pl* ... MO-7
**Linn**—*pop pl* ... PA-2
Linn, Alexander and James, Homestead—*hist pl* ... NJ-2
Linn, Mount—*summit* ... CA-9
Linn, R. N., House—*hist pl* ... HI-9
Linn, Will, House—*hist pl* ... KY-4
Linnaeus, Mount—*summit* ... UT-8
Linnard Well—*well* ... CO-8
Linn Ave Ch—*church* ... OK-5
Linn Baptist Ch—*church* ... MS-4
Linn Barker Mtn—*summit* ... AR-4
Linnbeck Lake—*lake* ... MI-6
Linn-Benton Community Coll—*school* (2) ... OR-9
*Linn Branch* ... PA-2
*Linn Branch* ... WV-2
Linn Branch—*stream* ... KY-4
Linn Branch—*stream* (3) ... MO-7
Linn Branch—*stream* ... TX-5
Linn Branch—*stream* ... VA-3
Linn Branch—*stream* ... WV-2
Linn Branch Bridge—*other* ... MO-7
Linn Brook—*stream* ... PA-2
Linn Camp Branch—*stream* ... VA-3
*Linn Camp Creek* ... VA-3
Linn Cem—*cemetery* ... AL-4
Linn Cem—*cemetery* ... IN-6
Linn Cem—*cemetery* ... LA-4
Linn Cem—*cemetery* (2) ... MO-7
Linn Cem—*cemetery* ... OK-5
Linn Cem—*cemetery* ... TX-5
Linn Cem—*cemetery* ... WV-2
Linn Center Sch (abandoned)—*school* ... MO-7
Linn County—*civil* ... KS-7
**Linn County**—*pop pl* ... MO-7
**Linn County**—*pop pl* ... OR-9
Linn County Courthouse—*hist pl* ... KS-7
Linn County Fairgrounds—*park* ... KS-7
Linn County Home—*building* ... IA-7
Linn Cove—*valley* ... NC-3
Linn Cove Branch—*stream* ... NC-3
*Linn Creek* ... MO-7
**Linn Creek**—*pop pl* ... MO-7
Linn Creek—*stream* (2) ... AR-4
Linn Creek—*stream* ... IL-6
Linn Creek—*stream* ... IN-6
Linn Creek—*stream* ... IA-7
Linn Creek—*stream* (4) ... MO-7
Linn Creek—*stream* (2) ... TX-5
Linn Creek Bend—*bend* ... MO-7
Linn Creek Ch—*church* ... MO-7
Linn Creek-Grand Glaize Memorial Airp—*airport* ... MO-7
Linn Creek (Township of)—*fmr MCD* ... AR-4
**Linn Crossing**—*pop pl* ... AL-4
**Linndale**—*pop pl* ... OH-6
Linn Draw—*valley* ... WY-8
**Linne**—*pop pl* ... CA-9
Linnea Hall—*hist pl* ... OR-9
Linne Cem—*cemetery* ... TX-5
Linnehan Branch—*stream* ... TX-5
Linnehan Valley—*valley* ... WI-6
Linnel Cem—*cemetery* ... MN-6
Linn Elem Sch—*school* (2) ... KS-7
**Linnell (Labor Camp)**—*pop pl* ... CA-9
Linnell Post Office—*building* ... CA-9
Linneman Bldg—*hist pl* ... OH-6
Linneman Lake—*lake* ... MN-6
**Linnemann**—*pop pl* ... OR-9
*Linnemann Junction* ... OR-9
**Linnemann Junction**—*pop pl* ... OR-9
Linne Oil Field—*oilfield* ... TX-5
Linne Sch—*school* ... IL-6
**Linneus**—*pop pl* ... ME-1
**LinNeus**—*pop pl* ... MO-7
**Linneus (Town of)**—*pop pl* ... ME-1
Linnewebber Ditch—*canal* ... IN-6
Linne Woods—*woods* ... IL-6
Linney Branch—*stream* ... KY-4
Linney Butte—*summit* ... OR-9
Linney Cem—*cemetery* ... TX-5
Linney Corners—*locale* ... VA-3
Linney Creek—*stream* ... OR-9
Linney Creek—*stream* ... TX-5
Linney Creek Campground—*park* ... OR-9
Linney Hollow—*valley* ... AL-4
Linney Mtn—*summit* ... NC-3
Linneys Grove Ch—*church* ... NC-3
Linney Tanks—*reservoir* ... TX-5
*Linnez* ... MP-9
Linn Flat—*locale* ... TX-5
Linn Flat Cem—*cemetery* ... TX-5
Linn Glacier—*glacier* ... OR-9
*Linngrove* ... IN-6
**Linn Grove**—*pop pl* ... IN-6
**Linn Grove**—*pop pl* ... IA-7
Linn Grove Cem—*cemetery* ... CO-8

**Lisbon**—*pop pl* IL-6
**Lisbon**—*pop pl* IN-6
**Lisbon**—*pop pl* IA-7
**Lisbon**—*pop pl* LA-4
**Lisbon**—*pop pl* ME-1
**Lisbon**—*pop pl* MD-2
**Lisbon**—*pop pl* MI-6
**Lisbon**—*pop pl* NH-1
**Lisbon**—*pop pl* NY-2
**Lisbon**—*pop pl* NC-3
**Lisbon**—*pop pl* ND-7
**Lisbon**—*pop pl* (2) OH-6
**Lisbon**—*pop pl* PA-2
**Lisbon**—*pop pl* TN-4
Lisbon—*uninc pl* TX-5
Lisbon Brook—*stream* CT-1
Lisbon Canyon—*valley* UT-8
Lisbon Cem—*cemetery* MI-6
Lisbon Cem—*cemetery* NY-2
Lisbon Cem—*cemetery* (2) OH-6
Lisbon Cem—*cemetery* TX-5
*Lisbon Center* ME-1
**Lisbon Center**—*pop pl* IL-6
**Lisbon Center**—*pop pl* ME-1
Lisbon Central Sch—*school* NY-2
Lisbon Ch—*church* GA-3
Lisbon Ch—*church* IL-6
Lisbon Ch—*church* SC-3
Lisbon Ch—*church* WI-6
**Lisbon Compact (census name Lisbon)**—*pop pl* NH-1
Lisbon Country Club—*other* CT-1
Lisbon Creek—*stream* IL-6
Lisbon Creek—*stream* NY-2
Lisbon Dam—*dam* NJ-2
Lisbon Dam—*dam* ND-7
**Lisbon Falls**—*pop pl* ME-1
Lisbon Fork—*stream* OH-6
Lisbon Gap—*gap* UT-8
Lisbon Hist Dist—*hist pl* OH-6
Lisbon Inn—*hist pl* NH-1
Lisbon Landing (historical)—*locale* AL-4
Lisbon Mine—*mine* UT-8
Lisbon Mines—*mine* WY-8
Lisbon Municipal Airp—*airport* ND-7
Lisbon Oil And Gas Field—*oilfield* (2) AR-4
Lisbon Oil Field—*oilfield* (2) LA-4
Lisbon Oil Field—*oilfield* UT-8
Lisbon Opera House—*hist pl* ND-7
Lisbon P.O. (historical)—*building* AL-4
Lisbon Post Office (historical)—*building* TN-4
Lisbon Ridge—*locale* ME-1
Lisbon Ridge—*ridge* ME-1
Lisbon Sch—*school* CT-1
Lisbon Sch—*school* MI-6
Lisbon Sch—*school* TX-5
Lisbon Sch (historical)—*school* TN-4
Lisbon Spring—*spring* UT-8
Lisbon Town Hall—*hist pl* NY-2
**Lisbon (Town of)**—*pop pl* CT-1
**Lisbon (Town of)**—*pop pl* ME-1
**Lisbon (Town of)**—*pop pl* NH-1
**Lisbon (Town of)**—*pop pl* NY-2
**Lisbon (Town of)**—*pop pl* (2) WI-6
**Lisbon Township**—*pop pl* SD-7
Lisbon (Township of)—*fmr MCD* NC-3
**Lisbon (Township of)**—*pop pl* IL-6
**Lisbon (Township of)**—*pop pl* MN-6
Lisbon Valley—*valley* UT-8
Lisbon Winery—*hist pl* CA-9
*Lisburg* PA-2
Lisburg Field—*airport* ND-7
**Lisburn**—*pop pl* PA-2
Lisburn Cave—*cave* PA-2
Lisburne Hills—*other* AK-9
Lisburne Hills—*summit* AK-9
Lisburne Ridge—*ridge* AK-9
Lisburn Plantation House—*hist pl* LA-4
Lischy Ch—*church* PA-2
**Lisco**—*pop pl* NE-7
Lisco Canal*—*canal* NE-7
Lisco Canal—*canal* NE-7
*Lisco Creek* AL-4
**Liscomb**—*pop pl* IA-7
Liscomb Brook—*stream* NH-1
Liscomb Brook—*stream* NY-2
Liscomb Township—*fmr MCD* IA-7
Liscom Butte—*summit* MT-8
Liscom Butte Spring—*spring* MT-8
Liscom Creek—*stream* MT-8
Liscome Bay—*bay* AK-9
Lisco Memorial Cem—*cemetery* NE-7
Liscome Point—*cape* AK-9
Liscom Hill—*summit* CA-9
Liscom Mountain Spring—*spring* MT-8
Liscom Slough—*stream* CA-9
Liscon Creek—*stream* MI-6
Liscum—*locale* AZ-5
Liscum Cem—*cemetery* KS-7
Liscum Hill—*summit* TX-5
Liscum Slough—*stream* AK-9
Lisemby Cem—*cemetery* IL-6
Lisenbee Branch—*stream* NC-3
Lisenbee Ridge—*ridge* NC-3
Lisenberry Mtn—*summit* (2) NC-3
*Lisenby* AL-4
Lisenby Cem—*cemetery* GA-3
Lisenby Creek—*stream* WY-8
Lisenby Hosp—*hospital* FL-3
Lisenlund Hill—*summit* VI-3
Lisez Run—*stream* WV-2
**Lisha Kill**—*pop pl* NY-2
Lisha Kill—*stream* NY-2
Lish Branch—*stream* KY-4
Lish Cem—*cemetery* MD-2
Lisher Cem—*cemetery* IN-6
Lish Homestead Cem—*cemetery* NY-2
Lish Lake—*lake* OR-9
Lishman Bldg—*hist pl* HI-9
Lisianski Inlet—*bay* AK-9
Lisianski Island—*island* HI-9
Lisianski Peninsula—*cape* AK-9
Lisianski Point—*cape* AK-9
Lisianski River—*stream* AK-9
Lisianski Strait—*channel* AK-9
**Lisitzky Subdivision**—*pop pl* AZ-5
Lisk Creek—*stream* (2) MT-8
Lisk Creek Dam—*dam* MT-8
**Liske**—*pop pl* MI-6
Liskey—*locale* CA-9
Lisko—*locale* CA-9
Liskow Sch—*school* MI-6
Lisk Point—*cape* FL-3
*Lisla* MS-4
*Lisla Post Office* MS-4
*Lisle* MS-4
**Lisle**—*pop pl* IL-6
**Lisle**—*pop pl* MO-7
**Lisle**—*pop pl* NY-2
L'isle a Pete, Lake—*lake* LA-4
*L'Isle au Chevereuil* MS-4
*L'Isle aux Vaisseaux* MS-4
Lisle Branch—*stream* WV-2
L'Isle Chaude—*island* MS-4
L'Isle Chaude Bay—*gut* MS-4
*Lisle Post Office* MS-4
Lisle-Shields Town House—*hist pl* MS-4
*Lislesville* NC-3
**Lisletown**—*pop pl* KY-4
**Lisle (Town of)**—*pop pl* NY-2
**Lisle (Township of)**—*pop pl* IL-6
**Lisman**—*pop pl* AL-4
**Lisman**—*pop pl* KY-4
**Lisman**—*pop pl* OH-6
Lisman (CCD)—*cens area* AL-4
Lisman Cem—*cemetery* KY-4
Lisman Division—*civil* AL-4
Lisman JHS—*school* AL-4
Lismore—*locale* LA-4
**Lismore**—*pop pl* MN-6
Lismore Cem—*cemetery* LA-4
Lismore Cem—*cemetery* MN-6
Lismore Ch—*church* LA-4
Lismore Landing Oil Field—*oilfield* LA-4
**Lismore (Township of)**—*pop pl* MN-6
Lisner Home—*locale* DC-2
*Lisong* MH-9
Lisong, I—*slope* MH-9
Lisor Cem—*cemetery* IA-7
Lispenard-Rodman-Davenport House—*hist pl* NY-2
Lisque Creek—*stream* CA-9
Liss Gap—*gap* GA-3
**Lissie**—*pop pl* TX-5
Lissie, Lake—*reservoir* GA-3
*Lissie Melton Hollow* TN-4
Lissie Milton Hollow—*valley* TN-4
Lissie Oil Field—*oilfield* TX-5
List—*locale* CA-9
List, Henry K., House—*hist pl* WV-2
List Drain—*canal* MI-6
Listenberger Ditch—*canal* IN-6
Listening Hill—*summit* NY-2
Listening Rock—*locale* NC-3
Listening Top—*summit* TN-4
Listen Key—*island* FL-3
*Lister* AL-4
Lister Bldg—*hist pl* MO-7
Lister Camp—*locale* FL-3
Lister Cem—*cemetery* GA-3
Lister Cem—*cemetery* IA-7
Lister Community Ch—*church* ME-1
*Lister Ferry* AL-4
Listerhill—*locale* AL-4
Lister Hill—*summit* WA-9
Lister Landing—*locale* FL-3
Lister Memorial Ch—*church* AL-4
Lister Park—*park* NY-2
Lister Sch—*school* WA-9
Listers Corner—*locale* NC-3
Listers Ferry (historical)—*locale* AL-4
Lister Spring—*spring* (2) UT-8
**Listie**—*pop pl* PA-2
Listie Cem—*cemetery* PA-2
List Lake—*lake* MI-6
Listle Creek—*stream* MT-8
**Listonburg**—*pop pl* PA-2
Liston Cem—*cemetery* NM-5
Liston Creek—*stream* IN-6
Liston Creek—*stream* MI-6
Liston Flat—*flat* UT-8
Liston Hollow—*valley* WV-2
Liston House—*hist pl* DE-2
Listonia—*locale* GA-3
Liston Lake Mine—*mine* OR-9
Liston Point—*cape* DE-2
Liston Range—*channel* DE-2
Liston Range—*channel* NJ-2
Liston Ranger Rear Light Station—*hist pl* DE-2
Liston Run—*stream* OH-6
Liston Sch (historical)—*school* PA-2
Liston Seep—*spring* UT-8
*Listons Point* DE-2
Liston Township—*fmr MCD* IA-7
*Listonville* PA-2
List Ranch—*locale* TX-5
List Sch—*school* MI-6
Listwood Sch—*school* NY-2
Liswell Hill—*summit* MA-1
Litaker (Township of)—*fmr MCD* NC-3
*Lit Branch* AL-4
Litch Branch—*stream* KY-4
Litche Education Center—*school* PA-2
*Litchfield* AZ-5
Litchfield—*locale* AZ-5
Litchfield—*locale* CA-9
Litchfield—*locale* KS-7
Litchfield—*locale* PA-2
**Litchfield**—*pop pl* CT-1
**Litchfield**—*pop pl* (2) IL-6
**Litchfield**—*pop pl* MI-6
**Litchfield**—*pop pl* MN-6
**Litchfield**—*pop pl* NE-7
**Litchfield**—*pop pl* NH-1
**Litchfield**—*pop pl* NY-2
**Litchfield**—*pop pl* OH-6
Litchfield, James, House—*hist pl* MI-6
Litchfield Airp—*airport* AZ-5
**Litchfield Beach**—*pop pl* SC-3
Litchfield Branch—*stream* TN-4
Litchfield Cem—*cemetery* AZ-5
Litchfield Cem—*cemetery* CT-1
Litchfield Cem—*cemetery* MO-7
Litchfield Cem—*cemetery* NE-7
Litchfield Cem—*cemetery* NY-2
Litchfield Central Sch—*school* ME-1
Litchfield Ch—*church* VA-3
**Litchfield Corners**—*pop pl* ME-1
**Litchfield County (in (P)MSA 1170,1930, 3280,8880)**—*pop pl* CT-1
**Litchfield (Goodyear)**—*pop pl* AZ-5
*Litchfield High School* AL-4
Litchfield Hill—*summit* VT-1
Litchfield Hist Dist—*hist pl* CT-1
Litchfield (historical)—*locale* MS-4
Litchfield JHS—*school* AL-4
Litchfield JHS—*school* OH-6
Litchfield Junction—*locale* AZ-5
Litchfield Lake—*reservoir* IL-6
Litchfield Ledge—*cliff* NY-2
Litchfield Mansion—*building* NY-2
Litchfield Opera House—*hist pl* MN-6
**Litchfield Park**—*pop pl* AZ-5
Litchfield Park Dam—*dam* AZ-5
Litchfield Park Elem Sch—*school* AZ-5
Litchfield Park Post Office—*building* AZ-5
Litchfield Plains—*locale* ME-1
**Litchfield (Purgatory)**—*pop pl* ME-1
Litchfield Recreation Grounds—*park* NE-7
Litchfield RR Station—*building* AZ-5
Litchfield Rsvr—*reservoir* CT-1
Litchfield Sch—*school* NH-1
Litchfield Sch—*school* SD-7
Litchfield Sch For Boys—*school* CT-1
*Litchfield Siding* AZ-5
Litchfields Sch—*school* ME-1
Litchfield State For—*forest* NH-1
Litchfield Substation—*locale* AZ-5
**Litchfield (Town of)**—*pop pl* CT-1
**Litchfield (Town of)**—*pop pl* ME-1
**Litchfield (Town of)**—*pop pl* NH-1
**Litchfield (Town of)**—*pop pl* NY-2
**Litchfield (Township of)**—*pop pl* MI-6
**Litchfield (Township of)**—*pop pl* MN-6
**Litchfield (Township of)**—*pop pl* OH-6
**Litchfield (Township of)**—*pop pl* PA-2
Litchfield Villa—*hist pl* NY-2
Litchford Cem—*cemetery* TN-4
**Litchford Forest (subdivision)**—*pop pl* NC-3
Litchford Hollow—*valley* WV-2
Litch Meadow—*flat* OR-9
Litch Ranch—*locale* OR-9
*Litchton* AZ-5
**Litchville**—*pop pl* ND-7
Litchville Town Hall—*building* ND-7
**Litchville Township**—*pop pl* ND-7
Litchy Creek—*stream* WA-9
Lit Creek—*stream* TX-5
Litening Gas—*hist pl* MT-8
Literary Hall—*hist pl* WV-2
**Literberry**—*pop pl* IL-6
Literberry (Election Precinct)—*fmr MCD* IL-6
*Lithan Falls* OR-9
Lithan Falls—*falls* OR-9
Lithco Creek—*stream* AL-4
**Lithgow**—*pop pl* NY-2
Lithgow Creek—*stream* OR-9
Lithgow Hill—*summit* ME-1
Lithgow House—*hist pl* ME-1
Lithgow Library—*hist pl* ME-1
Lithgow Rock—*bar* ME-1
Lithgow Spring—*spring* OR-9
Lithgrove—*locale* IA-7
*Lithia* FL-3
Lithia—*locale* IL-6
Lithia—*locale* ND-7
**Lithia**—*pop pl* FL-3
**Lithia**—*pop pl* MA-1
**Lithia**—*pop pl* VA-3
Lithia Branch—*stream* NC-3
Lithia Cem—*cemetery* FL-3
*Lithia Church* FL-3
Lithia Creek—*stream* AR-4
Lithia (historical)—*locale* SD-7
Lithia Park—*hist pl* OR-9
Lithia Park—*park* OR-9
Lithia Post Office (historical)—*building* SD-7
Lithia Sch—*school* SD-7
**Lithia Spring**—*pop pl* PA-2
Lithia Spring—*spring* CA-9
Lithia Spring—*spring* OR-9
Lithia Spring—*spring* TN-4
*Lithia Springs* IL-6
*Lithia Springs* TN-4
**Lithia Springs**—*pop pl* GA-3
**Lithia Springs**—*pop pl* NC-3
**Lithia Springs**—*pop pl* PA-2
Lithia Springs—*spring* FL-3
Lithia Springs Creek—*stream* IL-6
Lithia Springs Creek—*stream* PA-2
Lithia Springs-Douglasville (CCD)—*cens area* GA-3
Lithia Springs Reservoir Dam—*dam* MA-1
Lithia Springs Rsvr—*reservoir* MA-1
Lithia Square—*post sta* FL-3
Lithia (Station)—*locale* FL-3
Lithia Township (historical)—*civil* SD-7
Lithia Valley—*uninc pl* PA-2
Lithia Valley—*valley* PA-2
Lithic Ridge—*ridge* NV-8
**Lithium**—*pop pl* MO-7
Lithium (historical)—*locale* KS-7
Lithkealik River—*stream* AK-9
*Lithodendron Creek* AZ-5
Lithodendron Wash—*stream* AZ-5
Lithodendron Wash Bridge—*hist pl* AZ-5
Lithograph Canyon—*valley* SD-7
Lithograph Fork—*stream* UT-8
Lithograph Spring—*spring* AZ-5
Lithograph Spring—*spring* SD-7
**Lithonia**—*pop pl* GA-3
Lithonia (CCD)—*cens area* GA-3
Lithonia Ch—*church* GA-3
Lithonia Country Club—*other* GA-3
**Lithopolis**—*pop pl* OH-6
Lithuanian Cem—*cemetery* CT-1
Lithuanian Cem—*cemetery* (4) IL-6
Lithuanian Cem—*cemetery* (2) MA-1
Lithuanian Cem—*cemetery* NH-1
Lithuanian Legation Bldg—*building* DC-2
Lithuanian Sch—*school* IL-6
Litigation Hill—*ridge* NV-8
**Lititz**—*pop pl* PA-2
Lititz Borough—*civil* PA-2
Lititz Elem Sch—*school* PA-2
Lititz Moravian Hist Dist—*hist pl* PA-2
Lititz Post Office (historical)—*building* PA-2
*Lititz Run* PA-2
Lititz Run—*stream* PA-2
Lititz Spring—*spring* PA-2
Lititz Springs Cave—*cave* PA-2
Lititz Springs Park—*park* PA-2
Litka Park—*park* IA-7
Litle Cedar Creek—*stream* NE-7
Litle Cedar Mountain Cave—*cave* TN-4
Litle Crow Butte—*summit* NE-7
Litle Flat—*flat* OR-9
*Litlejohn Creek* CA-9
Litler Landing—*locale* TN-4
Litman Run—*stream* OH-6
Litner Point—*cape* MN-6
Litnik Mtn—*summit* AK-9
*Litnikoff Cave* AL-4
Lito, As—*plain* MH-9
Lito'Kattan, Hoyon As—*basin* MH-9
Litomysl—*locale* MN-6
Liton Branch—*stream* LA-4
*Lito Place* MH-9
Litroe—*locale* LA-4
Litschel Lake—*reservoir* MO-7
Litschke Lake—*lake* WA-9
Lits Department Store—*hist pl* PA-2
Litsey—*locale* KY-4
Litsey Cem—*cemetery* IA-7
Litsitz Memorial Playground—*park* MI-6
**Litson Subdivision**—*pop pl* UT-8
Littauer Hosp—*hospital* NY-2
Littcarr—*locale* KY-4
**Littell**—*pop pl* WA-9
Littell, David, House—*hist pl* PA-2
Littell Cem—*cemetery* KS-7
Littell Number One Lake—*reservoir* TN-4
Littell Number One Lake Dam—*dam* TN-4
Littel-Lord Farmstead—*hist pl* NJ-2
Littens Branch—*stream* IN-6
*Littens Creek* NC-3
Litte Park—*flat* ID-8
Litteral Fork—*stream* KY-4
Litteral (Township of)—*fmr MCD* AR-4
Litter Creek—*stream* WA-9
Litterer Laboratory—*hist pl* TN-4
**Littig**—*pop pl* TX-5
Littig, John, House—*hist pl* IA-7
Littig Brothers/Mengel & Klindt/Eagle Brewery—*hist pl* IA-7
Littl Blue Mtn—*summit* NY-2
Little—*locale* KY-4
Little—*locale* OK-5
**Little**—*pop pl* IN-6
**Little**—*pop pl* WV-2
Little, Arthur D., Inc., Bldg—*hist pl* MA-1
Little, Edward, House—*hist pl* ME-1
Little, John Phillips, House—*hist pl* NC-3
Little, Lake—*reservoir* MS-4
Little, Russell M., House—*hist pl* NY-2
Little, Thomas K., House—*hist pl* ID-8
Little, W. J., House—*hist pl* NC-3
Little AAA Tank—*reservoir* NM-5
Little Abbie Creek—*stream* AL-4
Little Abbott Brook—*stream* ME-1
Little Abercorn Creek—*stream* GA-3
Little Abiqua Creek—*stream* OR-9
Little Abraham Canal—*canal* UT-8
Little Abraham River—*stream* AK-9
*Little Abrams Creek* GA-3
Little Abrams Creek—*stream* GA-3
Little Abrams Gap—*gap* NC-3
Little Abrams Gap—*gap* TN-4
Little Acorn Creek—*stream* AL-4
**Little Acre**—*pop pl* IN-6
**Little Acres**—*pop pl* AZ-5
**Little Acres**—*pop pl* IN-6
**Little Acres**—*pop pl* MA-1
**Little Acres (subdivision)**—*pop pl* DE-2
**Little Acres Subdivision**—*pop pl* UT-8
Little Ada Lake—*lake* MN-6
Little Adam Lake—*lake* MS-4
Little Adams Cem—*cemetery* SC-3
Little Adams Cross Bayou—*stream* LA-4
Little Adobe Flat—*flat* NV-8
Little Africa—*locale* SC-3
Little African Lake—*lake* MI-6
Little Agate Creek—*stream* CO-8
Little Agency Plains—*flat* OR-9
*Little Agingan Beach* MH-9
Little Agnes Mtn—*summit* CO-8
Little Aguja Canyon—*valley* TX-5
Little Aguja Mtn—*summit* TX-5
Little Aide Sch—*school* VA-3
Little Aitken Cave—*cave* PA-2
Little Ajo Mountains—*summit* AZ-5
*Little Akapilco Creek* GA-3
Little Alabama Bayou—*stream* LA-4
Little Alafia Cem—*cemetery* FL-3
*Little Alamance Creek* NC-3
Little Alamance Creek—*stream* (2) NC-3
Little Alamo Tank—*reservoir* AZ-5
Little Alamo Tank—*reservoir* TX-5
Little Alamuchee Creek—*stream* MS-4
Little Alapaha River—*stream* FL-3
Little Alapaha River—*stream* GA-3
Little Alaqua Creek—*stream* FL-3
Little Alarka Creek—*stream* NC-3
**Little Albany**—*pop pl* OR-9
Little Albert Creek—*stream* AK-9
Little Alden Lake—*lake* MN-6
Little Alderbed Mtn—*summit* NY-2
Little Alder Brook—*stream* ME-1
Little Alder Creek—*stream* CO-8
Little Alder Creek—*stream* ID-8
Little Alder Creek—*stream* MO-7
Little Alder Creek—*stream* (2) NV-8
Little Alder Creek—*stream* NY-2
Little Alder Creek—*stream* (2) OR-9
Little Alder Creek—*stream* TX-5
Little Alder Stream—*stream* ME-1
Little Aldrich Mtn—*summit* OR-9
Little Aleck Lake—*lake* MI-6
Little Alinchak Bay—*bay* AK-9
Little Alinchak Creek—*stream* AK-9
Little Alkali Canyon—*valley* CO-8
*Little Alkali Creek* WA-9
Little Alkali Creek—*stream* CO-8
Little Alkali Creek—*stream* (2) WY-8
Little Alkali Flat Creek—*stream* WA-9
*Little Alkali Lake* NE-7
Little Alkali Lake—*lake* CA-9
Little Alkali Lake—*lake* NE-7
Little Alkali Lake—*lake* NV-8
Little Alkali Spring—*spring* NV-8
Little Alkali Spring—*spring* OR-9
Little Allagash Falls—*falls* ME-1
Little Allan Mtn—*summit* ME-1
Little Allatoona Creek—*stream* GA-3
*Little Allegheny Mountains* PA-2
Little Allegheny Mountain Trail—*trail* WV-2
Little Allegheny Mtn—*summit* MD-2
Little Allegheny Mtn—*summit* PA-2
Little Allegheny Mtn—*summit* WV-2
Little Allegheny Trail—*trail* WV-2
Little Allen Creek—*stream* TX-5
Little Allens Creek—*stream* TN-4
Little Alligator Creek—*gut* FL-3
Little Alligator Creek—*stream* FL-3
Little Alligator Creek—*stream* (3) GA-3
Little Alligator Creek—*stream* SC-3
Little Alligator River—*stream* NC-3
Little Alligator Swamp—*swamp* NC-3
Little Allison Creek—*stream* SC-3
Little Almosa Canyon—*valley* CO-8
Little Almota Creek—*stream* WA-9
*Little Alps* AZ-5
Little Alps—*locale* OR-9
*Little Alstrom Point* UT-8
Little Alstrom Point—*cape* UT-8
Little Alum Creek—*stream* (3) TX-5
Little Alum Creek—*stream* WV-2
Little Alum Fork—*stream* AR-4
Little Alum Pond—*lake* MA-1
Little Alva Ch—*church* IN-6
Little Alvord Creek—*stream* OR-9
Little Alvord Well—*well* OR-9
Little Amador Mine—*mine* CA-9
Little Ambejackmockamus Falls—*falls* ME-1
**Little America**—*pop pl* IL-6
**Little America**—*pop pl* NY-2
**Little America**—*pop pl* WY-8
*Little American Creek* SD-7
Little American Creek—*stream* MT-8
Little American Falls—*falls* MN-6
Little American Island—*island* MN-6
Little American Mine—*hist pl* MN-6
Little America Well—*well* WY-8
Little Amicalola Creek—*stream* GA-3
*Little Amicolola* GA-3
*Little Amite River* LA-4
Little Amnicon River—*stream* WI-6
Little Amos Creek—*stream* KY-4
Little Ampersand Pond—*lake* NY-2
*Little Ance Creek* MO-7
*Little Anderson Bar* UT-8
Little Anderson Creek—*stream* ID-8
Little Anderson Creek—*stream* PA-2
Little Anderson Gulch—*valley* CO-8
Little Anderson Lake—*lake* WA-9
*Little Anderson Run* PA-2
Little Andrew Lake—*lake* MN-6
Little Andrews Creek—*stream* WA-9
Little Androscoggin River—*stream* ME-1
Little and Stuckys Lake—*reservoir* AL-4
Little Andy Creek—*stream* NC-3
Little Andy Mtn—*summit* GA-3
Little Angel Canyon—*valley* NM-5
Little Angelfish Creek—*gut* FL-3
Little Angry Creek—*stream* CO-8
Little Anna Bar (inundated)—*bar* UT-8
Little Anna Lake—*lake* MN-6
Little Anna Mine—*mine* CA-9
Little Annapurna—*summit* WA-9
Little Annapurna Peak—*summit* WA-9
Little Anneewakee Creek—*stream* GA-3
Little Annemessex River—*stream* MD-2
*Little Annemessic River* MD-2
Little Annie Mine—*mine* AK-9
Little Annie Mine—*mine* (2) CO-8
Little Ann River—*stream* MN-6
*Little Antelope Creek* NV-8
Little Antelope Creek—*stream* (2) CA-9
Little Antelope Creek—*stream* (2) CO-8
Little Antelope Creek—*stream* MT-8
Little Antelope Creek—*stream* NE-7
Little Antelope Creek—*stream* ND-7
Little Antelope Creek—*stream* OK-5
Little Antelope Creek—*stream* WY-8
Little Antelope Draw—*valley* WY-8
Little Antelope Flat—*flat* ID-8
Little Antelope Flat—*flat* OR-9
Little Antelope Grade—*locale* CA-9
Little Antelope Interchange—*crossing* AZ-5
Little Antelope Rsvr—*reservoir* OR-9
Little Antelope Spring—*spring* (5) NV-8
Little Antelope Summit—*gap* NV-8
Little Antelope Tank—*reservoir* (2) AZ-5
Little Antelope Tank—*reservoir* NM-5
Little Antelope Valley—*flat* CA-9
Little Antelope Valley—*valley* (2) CA-9
Little Antelope Valley—*valley* UT-8
Little Antelope Well—*well* CA-9
*Little Antietam Creek* PA-2
Little Antietam Creek—*stream* (2) MD-2
Little Antioch Cem—*cemetery* MS-4
*Little Antioch Church* MS-4
Little Antire Creek—*stream* MO-7
*Little Antler Lake* MN-6
Little Antler Lake—*lake* MN-6
Little Antoine Creek—*stream* (3) AR-4
Little Antone Creek—*stream* OR-9
*Little Ants Creek* MO-7
Little Apache Canyon—*valley* NM-5
Little Apache Hill—*summit* TX-5
Little Aparejo Creek—*stream* ID-8
Little Apex Mtn—*summit* MT-8
Little Apookta Creek—*stream* MS-4
Little Apoon Pass—*gut* AK-9
Little Apple Creek—*stream* IL-6
Little Apple Creek—*stream* MO-7
Little Apple Creek—*stream* (2) OH-6
Little Apple Creek Sch—*school* IL-6
Little Applegate Butte—*summit* OR-9
Little Applegate Recreation Site—*park* OR-9
Little Applegate River—*stream* OR-9
Little Apple Mountain—*ridge* VA-3
Little Appleton Lake—*lake* MI-6
Little Aquavitae—*bar* MA-1
Little Aquilla Creek—*stream* TX-5
Little Arbor Vitae Lake—*lake* WI-6
Little Arch Canyon—*valley* UT-8
*Little Arch Creek* FL-3
Little Arch Creek—*gut* FL-3
Little Archibald Lake—*lake* WI-6
*Little Aremacolola* GA-3
Little Arizona Spring—*spring* AZ-5
Little Arkansas Canyon—*valley* ID-8
Little Arkansas Creek—*stream* KS-7
Little Arkansas Creek—*stream* TX-5
*Little Arkansas River* KS-7
Little Arkansas River—*stream* KS-7
**Little Arkansaw**—*pop pl* AR-4
Little Arkansaw Creek—*stream* WI-6
Little Ark Ch—*church* VA-3
Little Arlington Cem—*cemetery* IN-6
Little Arlington Cem—*cemetery* WV-2
Little Armidge Creek—*stream* TX-5
Little Arm Lake—*lake* MN-6
Little Armuchee Creek—*stream* GA-3
Little Arnot Run—*stream* PA-2
Little Arsenic Springs Campground—*locale* NM-5
Little Artesian Well—*well* AZ-5
Little Arthur Creek—*stream* CA-9
*Little Asaph Run* PA-2
Little Ascutney Mtn—*summit* VT-1
Little Ashbough Canyon—*valley* MT-8
Little Ashcake Creek—*stream* VA-3
Little Ash Creek—*stream* (2) AZ-5
Little Ash Creek—*stream* WY-8
Little Asher Branch—*stream* KY-4
*Little Asher Creek* IA-7
Little Asher Creek—*stream* IA-7
Little Ashes Lake—*lake* WA-9
*Little As-na-con-comic Pond* MA-1
Little Asnebumskit Hill—*summit* MA-1
Little Aso Tank—*reservoir* AZ-5
*Little Asparos Canyon* NM-5
Little Aspen Butte—*summit* OR-9
Little Asphalt Canyon—*valley* UT-8
Little Asphalt Ridge—*ridge* UT-8
*Little Assawaman Bay* DE-2
Little Assawoman Bay—*bay* DE-2
Little Atchafalaya Bayou—*gut* MS-4
Little Atchafalaya Bayou—*stream* MS-4
Little Atchafalaya River—*stream* LA-4
Little Atkinson Mesa—*summit* CO-8
Little Atlantic Gulch—*valley* WY-8
Little Atoy Creek—*stream* TX-5
Little Attapulgus Creek—*stream* GA-3
Little Attitash Mtn—*summit* NH-1
Little Aucilla River—*stream* FL-3
Little Aughwick Creek—*stream* PA-2
Little Auglaize River—*stream* OH-6
Little Aunts Creek—*stream* MO-7
*Little Au Sable Creek* MI-6
Little Au Sable Lake—*lake* MI-6
Little Ausable River—*stream* NY-2
*Little Austin Creek* CA-9
Little Austin Pond—*lake* ME-1
*Little Auxvasse Creek* MO-7
Little Avenal Creek—*stream* CA-9
Little Averill Lake—*lake* VT-1
Little Avery Creek—*stream* IA-7
Little Axe—*locale* OK-5
Little Axel Land Island—*island* AK-9
Little Babb Windmill—*locale* TX-5
Little Baboosic Lake—*lake* NH-1
Little Babson Island—*island* ME-1
Little Bachelor Creek—*stream* KS-7
Little Backbone Creek—*stream* CA-9
Little Back Creek—*stream* (3) VA-3
Little Back River—*stream* GA-3
Little Back River—*stream* SC-3
Little Back Swamp—*stream* NC-3
Little Bacon Creek—*stream* TN-4
Little Bacon Island—*island* DE-2
Little Badger Campground—*park* OR-9
*Little Badger Creek* MT-8
Little Badger Creek—*stream* CO-8
Little Badger Creek—*stream* MN-6
Little Badger Creek—*stream* (2) MT-8
Little Badger Creek—*stream* OR-9
Little Badger Creek—*stream* WY-8
Little Badger Creek Trail—*trail* OR-9
Little Badger Spring—*spring* MT-8
Little Badlands—*area* ND-7
Little Badlands—*area* SD-7
Little Badwater Lake—*lake* MI-6
Little Bagley Mtn—*summit* CA-9
*Little Bahala Baptist Church* MS-4
Little Bahala Cem—*cemetery* MS-4
Little Bahala Ch—*church* MS-4
Little Bahala Creek—*stream* MS-4
Little Baht Harbor—*bay* AK-9
Little Bailey Run—*stream* (2) PA-2
Little Baird Creek—*stream* WA-9
Little Baker Brook—*stream* ME-1
Little Baker Brook—*stream* NY-2
*Little Baker Creek* MS-4
Little Baker Creek—*stream* TN-4
*Little Baker Dry Creek* WY-8
Little Baker Gulch—*valley* CO-8
Little Bakers Creek—*stream* MS-4
*Little Bald* GA-3
*Little Bald* NC-3
*Little Bald* TN-4
Little Bald—*summit* GA-3
Little Bald—*summit* (7) NC-3
Little Bald—*summit* (3) TN-4
Little Bald Branch—*stream* (2) NC-3
Little Bald Cove—*valley* GA-3
Little Bald Creek—*stream* TN-4
Little Bald Hill—*summit* CA-9
Little Bald Hill—*summit* PA-2
Little Bald Hill—*summit* UT-8
Little Bald Knob—*summit* GA-3
Little Bald Knob—*summit* (2) NC-3
Little Bald Knob—*summit* TN-4
Little Bald Knob—*summit* VA-3
*Little Bald Mountain* CO-8
Little Bald Mountain Prairie—*flat* OR-9
Little Bald Mountain Spring—*spring* WA-9
*Little Bald Mtn* NC-3
*Little Bald Mtn* WA-9
Little Bald Mtn—*summit* (2) CA-9
Little Bald Mtn—*summit* CO-8
Little Bald Mtn—*summit* (3) GA-3
Little Bald Mtn—*summit* ID-8
Little Bald Mtn—*summit* NV-8
Little Bald Mtn—*summit* (2) NC-3
Little Bald Mtn—*summit* (2) OR-9
Little Bald Mtn—*summit* TN-4
Little Bald Mtn—*summit* UT-8

Little Bald Mtn—summit WA-9
Little Bald Mtn—summit WY-8
Little Baldpate Mtn—summit ME-1
Little Bald Ridge—ridge WY-8
Little Bald Ridge Creek—stream MO-7
Little Bald Rock—summit CA-9
Little Bald Rock Mtn—summit NC-3
Little Baldwin Creek—stream OR-9
Little Baldy—summit (7) CA-9
Little Baldy—summit (3) CO-8
Little Baldy—summit (2) ID-8
Little Baldy—summit MT-8
Little Baldy—summit OK-5
Little Baldy—summit (4) OR-9
Little Baldy—summit TN-4
Little Baldy—summit (2) UT-8
Little Baldy—summit (3) WA-9
Little Baldy Canyon—valley ID-8
Little Baldy Creek—stream ID-8
Little Baldy Creek—stream OR-9
Little Baldy Mountain ID-8
Little Baldy Mtn—summit CA-9
Little Baldy Mtn—summit (4) CO-8
Little Baldy Mtn—summit ID-8
Little Baldy Mtn—summit OR-9
Little Baldy Mtn—summit UT-8
Little Baldy Peak—summit WA-9
Little Baldy Ridge—ridge CA-9
Little Baldy Saddle—gap CA-9
Little Baldy Tank—reservoir AZ-5
Little Baldy Trail—trail WA-9
Little Baldy Trail (historical)—trail OR-9
Little Ballard Creek—stream UT-8
Little Ball Bluff Lake—lake MN-6
Little Ball Club Lake—lake MN-6
Little Ball Island—island VA-3
Little Ball Lake IN-6
Little Ballplay Creek—stream AL-4
Little Bally—summit (2) CA-9
Little Balsam Creek—stream WI-6
Little Balsam Ridge NC-3
Little Baltimore—locale VA-3
**Little Baltimore**—pop pl DE-2
Little Banana Island—island WI-6
Little Banana Lake—lake FL-3
Little Banana Patch—locale FL-3
Little Bang Branch—stream MS-4
Little Bangs Island ME-1
Little Bankiter Well—well CO-8
Little Banks Island—island ID-8
Little Bankson Lake—lake MI-6
Little Bannock Shoals Run—stream WV-2
Little Baptize Lake—lake AR-4
Little Bar—bar OR-9
Little Bar—bar TX-5
Little Baraboo River WI-6
Little Baraboo River—stream WI-6
Little Barbee Lake—lake IN-6
Little Barbour Creek—stream AL-4
Little Bare Beach—locale FL-3
Little Bark Creek—stream OH-6
Little Barker Arroyo—stream CO-8
Little Barker Arroyo—stream (2) NM-5
Little Barker Arroyo—valley CO-8
Little Barker Creek—stream CA-9
Little Barker Dam UT-8
Little Barker Reservoir UT-8
Little Barkhouse Gulch—valley CA-9
Little Bark Shanty Creek—stream CA-9
Little Barnard Pond—lake ME-1
Little Barn Creek—stream AR-4
Little Barndoor Island—island NH-1
Little Barnes Creek—stream LA-4
Little Barnes Ditch—canal CO-8
Little Barnes Hollow—valley TX-5
Little Barnett Lake—lake SC-3
Little Barn Island NY-2
Little Barn Knob—summit KY-4
Little Barnwell Island—hist pl SC-3
Little Barnwell Island—island SC-3
Little Baron Lake—lake ID-8
Little Bar Rapids—rapids OR-9
Little Barren—locale KY-4
Little Barren—locale TN-4
**Little Barren**—pop pl TN-4
Little Barren Ch—church KY-4
Little Barren Ch—church TN-4
Little Barren Creek—stream MO-7
Little Barren Creek—stream TN-4
Little Barren Missionary Baptist Church TN-4
Little Barren Post Office (historical)—building (2) TN-4
Little Barren River—stream KY-4
Little Barren Sch—school KY-4
Little Barrenshe Run—stream WV-2
Little Barrett Hollow—valley TN-4
Little Bartlett Mtn—summit CO-8
Little Bartley Pond—lake ME-1
Little Barton Creek—stream (2) TX-5
Little Bartons Creek—stream TN-4
Little Bar X Draw—valley WY-8
Little Base Lake—lake WI-6
Little Basin—basin CA-9
Little Basin—basin CO-8
Little Basin—basin FL-3
Little Basin—basin (3) ID-8
Little Basin—basin KS-7
Little Basin—basin MS-4
Little Basin—basin (3) UT-8
Little Basin—basin (2) WY-8
Little Basin Canyon—valley MT-8
Little Basin Creek—stream CA-9
Little Basin Creek—stream FL-3
Little Basin Creek—stream ID-8
Little Basin Creek—stream (3) MT-8
Little Basin Creek—stream (2) OR-9
Little Basin Creek—stream WY-8
Little Basin Hollow—valley PA-2
Little Basin Ranch—locale (2) WY-8
Little Basket Bay—bay AK-9
Little Basket Springs—spring UT-8
Little Bason Island (historical)—island ND-7
Little Bass Creek—stream MI-6
Little Bassett Creek—stream AL-4
Little Bassetts Creek AL-4
Little Bassetts Creek—stream AL-4
Little Bass Lake MI-6
Little Bass Lake WI-6
Little Bass Lake—lake FL-3
Little Bass Lake—lake (7) MI-6
Little Bass Lake—lake (15) MN-6
Little Bass Lake—lake (14) WI-6
Little Basswood Island—island NY-2
Little Basswood Lake—lake MN-6
Little Bat Cave—cave TN-4
Little Bateau Bay—lake AL-4
Little Bateau Lake MI-6
Little Bateau Lake—lake WI-6
Little Bates Creek—stream WY-8
Little Battle Brook—stream ME-1
Little Battle Creek—stream IN-6
Little Battle Creek—stream MT-8
Little Battleground Creek—stream GA-3
Little Battlement Lake—reservoir CO-8
Little Battle Mtn—summit OR-9
Little Battle Mtn—summit VA-3
Little Battle Run—stream (2) WV-2
Little Bauer Rsvr—reservoir CO-8
Little Baugh Creek—stream ID-8
Little Baullie Mesa—summit UT-8
Little Bause Lake—reservoir IN-6
Little Baxter Swamp—stream SC-3
Little Bay AR-4
Little Bay—bay AL-4
Little Bay—bay (3) AK-9
Little Bay—bay AR-4
Little Bay—bay DE-2
Little Bay—bay FL-3
Little Bay—bay (2) LA-4
Little Bay—bay ME-1
Little Bay—bay MA-1
Little Bay—bay (2) MS-4
Little Bay—bay NH-1
Little Bay—bay NJ-2
Little Bay—bay (4) NY-2
Little Bay—bay TX-5
Little Bay—bay VA-3
Little Bay—locale AR-4
Little Bay—stream LA-4
Little Bay Branch—stream SC-3
Little Bay Cem—cemetery AR-4
Little Bay Creek—stream IL-6
Little Bay Creek—stream MS-4
Little Bay Creek—stream NY-2
Little Bay d Enoc MI-6
Little Bay De Noc—bay MI-6
Little Bay de Noque MI-6
Little Bay d'Enoquet MI-6
little Bay des Noquet MI-6
Little Bay Ditch—canal AR-4
Little Bay Ditch—canal DE-2
Little Bay Hammock—island GA-3
Little Bayhorse Lake—lake ID-8
Little Bay Island—island AL-4
Little Bay John—gut AL-4
Little Bay Jose—lake LA-4
Little Bay Lake—lake AR-4
Little Bay Lake—lake FL-3
Little Bayou AR-4
Little Bayou FL-3
Little Bayou LA-4
Little Bayou—bay (2) FL-3
Little Bayou—gut AL-4
Little Bayou—stream (2) AR-4
Little Bayou—stream (3) LA-4
Little Bayou—stream (2) TX-5
Little Bayou Black—stream (2) LA-4
Little Bayou Boeuf LA-4
Little Bayou Boeuf—stream LA-4
Little Bayou Bonne Idee—stream LA-4
Little Bayou Brison—stream LA-4
Little Bayou Canot—stream AL-4
Little Bayou Castine—stream LA-4
Little Bayou Chene—stream (2) LA-4
Little Bayou Chene Blanc—stream LA-4
Little Bayou Chevreau—gut LA-4
Little Bayou Clear—stream LA-4
Little Bayou Creek—stream KY-4
Little Bayou de Chien—stream KY-4
Little Bayou de Large LA-4
Little Bayou De Loutre—stream AR-4
Little Bayou de Loutre—stream LA-4
Little Bayou De Plomb—stream LA-4
Little Bayou Des Ourses—stream LA-4
Little Bayou d'Inde—stream LA-4
Little Bayou du Chien KY-4
Little Bayou False River LA-4
Little Bayou Frelon—stream LA-4
Little Bayou Galion—stream LA-4
Little Bayou Gravenburg—stream LA-4
Little Bayou Jessamine—gut AL-4
Little Bayou Jessie—stream LA-4
Little Bayou Jose—gut LA-4
Little Bayou Loco—stream TX-5
Little Bayou Long—stream (2) LA-4
Little Bayou Macon—gut AR-4
Little Bayou Mallet—stream LA-4
Little Bayou Meto—stream AR-4
Little Bayou Na Benchasse—gut LA-4
Little Bayou Na Bonchassee LA-4
Little Bayou Penchant—gut LA-4
Little Bayou Pierre—gut LA-4
Little Bayou Pierre—stream (2) LA-4
Little Bayou Pierre—stream MS-4
Little Bayou Pigeon—stream LA-4
Little Bayou Platte—gut LA-4
Little Bayou San Miguel LA-4
Little Bayou Sara—stream LA-4
Little Bayou Sara—stream MS-4
Little Bayou Sorrel—stream LA-4
Little Bay Pomme d'Or—lake LA-4
Little Bazile Creek—stream NE-7
Little Beach NJ-2
Little Beach NC-3
Little Beach—bar MA-1
Little Beach—beach ME-1
Little Beach—beach MA-1
Little Beach—beach NJ-2
Little Beach—island VA-3
Little Beach Bayou LA-4
Little Beach Bayou—gut LA-4
Little Beach Cove—bay VA-3
Little Beach Creek—stream MS-4
Little Beach Hill—summit MA-1
Little Beach Hollow—valley AR-4
Little Beach Pond—lake PA-2
Little Bean Brook—stream WI-6
Little Bean Canyon—valley CO-8
Little Bean Lake—lake MO-7
Little Beans Creek—stream TX-5
**Little Bear**—pop pl WY-8
Little Bear Basin—basin CA-9
Little Bear Bay—bay NY-2
Little Bear Bay—bay UT-8
Little Bear Bay—swamp FL-3
Little Bear Bayou—stream MS-4
Little Bear Branch—stream AL-4
Little Bear Branch—stream IL-6
Little Bear Branch—stream NC-3
Little Bear Brook—stream (3) NH-1
Little Bear Brook—stream NJ-2
Little Bear Brook Pond—lake NH-1
Little Bear Camp—locale OR-9
Little Bear Canyon—valley (2) CA-9
Little Bear Canyon—valley ID-8
Little Bear Canyon—valley (4) NM-5
Little Bear Canyon—valley (2) UT-8
Little Bear Canyon—valley WY-8
Little Bear Cave—cave AL-4
Little Bear Cave—cave AR-4
Little Bear Cave—cave MO-7
Little Bear Cave Hollow—valley AR-4
Little Bear Cem—cemetery WY-8
Little Bear Creek AL-4
Little Bear Creek CO-8
Little Bear Creek GA-3
Little Bear Creek ID-8
Little Bear Creek IN-6
Little Bear Creek KS-7
Little Bear Creek MI-6
Little Bear Creek MS-4
Little Bear Creek OH-6
Little Bear Creek TN-4
Little Bear Creek WA-9
Little Bear Creek WI-6
**Little Bear Creek**—pop pl KY-4
Little Bear Creek—stream (6) AL-4
Little Bear Creek—stream (2) AK-9
Little Bear Creek—stream (4) AR-4
Little Bear Creek—stream (5) CA-9
Little Bear Creek—stream (5) CO-8
Little Bear Creek—stream (3) FL-3
Little Bear Creek—stream (6) GA-3
Little Bear Creek—stream (7) ID-8
Little Bear Creek—stream (2) IL-6
Little Bear Creek—stream (2) IN-6
Little Bear Creek—stream (4) IA-7
Little Bear Creek—stream (2) KS-7
Little Bear Creek—stream (2) KY-4
Little Bear Creek—stream (2) LA-4
Little Bear Creek—stream MD-2
Little Bear Creek—stream (4) MI-6
Little Bear Creek—stream (2) MN-6
Little Bear Creek—stream (2) MS-4
Little Bear Creek—stream (5) MO-7
Little Bear Creek—stream (6) MT-8
Little Bear Creek—stream NM-5
Little Bear Creek—stream (5) NC-3
Little Bear Creek—stream (3) OH-6
Little Bear Creek—stream (11) OR-9
Little Bear Creek—stream (3) PA-2
Little Bear Creek—stream SC-3
Little Bear Creek—stream SD-7
Little Bear Creek—stream (6) TX-5
Little Bear Creek—stream (3) UT-8
Little Bear Creek—stream (2) VA-3
Little Bear Creek—stream (5) WI-6
Little Bear Creek—stream (6) WY-8
Little Bear Creek Cabin Area KY-4
Little Bear Creek Church AL-4
Little Bear Creek Dam—dam AL-4
Little Bear Creek Meadow—flat OR-9
Little Bear Creek Rsvr—reservoir AL-4
Little Bear Creek Spring—spring MT-8
Little Bear Creek Tank—reservoir TX-5
Little Bear Dam AZ-5
Little Bear Ditch—canal CO-8
Little Bear Draw—valley MT-8
Little Beards Creek—stream NY-2
Little Beards Creek—stream VA-3
Little Bear Flat—flat CA-9
Little Bear Flowage—reservoir WI-6
Little Bear Fork—stream (2) WV-2
Little Bear Gap PA-2
Little Bear Gap Run—stream PA-2
Little Bear Gulch—valley (3) CA-9
Little Bear Gulch—valley CO-8
Little Bear Gulch—valley (2) MI-8
Little Bear Haven Creek—stream CA-9
Little Bear Hill—summit MA-1
Little Bearhole Pond—lake MA-1
Little Bear Hollow—valley MO-7
Little Bear Hollow—valley UT-8
Little Bear Hollow—valley VA-3
Little Bearhouse Creek—stream AR-4
Little Bear Island—island (2) FL-3
Little Bear Island—island MN-6
Little Bear Island—island NH-1
Little Bear Island (historical)—island ND-7
Little Bear Lake CA-9
Little Bear Lake MI-6
Little Bear Lake WI-6
Little Bear Lake—lake AK-9
Little Bear Lake—lake AR-4
Little Bear Lake—lake (5) CA-9
Little Bear Lake—lake (2) CO-8
Little Bear Lake—lake (2) FL-3
Little Bear Lake—lake ID-8
Little Bear Lake—lake LA-4
Little Bear Lake—lake (5) MI-6
Little Bear Lake—lake (4) MN-6
Little Bear Lake—lake (2) MT-8
Little Bear Lake—lake (4) WI-6
Little Bear Lake—lake WY-8
Little Bear Lake Drain—stream MI-6
Little Bear Mound—summit KS-7
Little Bear Mtn—summit CO-8
Little Bear Mtn—summit (3) ME-1
Little Bear Mtn—summit NM-5
Little Bear Number Two Cave—cave AL-4
Little Bear Park—flat CO-8
Little Bear Park—park CA-9
Little Bear Paw Fork—stream WY-8
Little Bearpaw Meadow—flat CA-9
Little Bear Peak—summit CA-9
Little Bear Peak—summit CO-8
Little Bear Peak—summit MT-8
Little Bearpen Gap—gap NC-3
Little Bearpen Mtn—summit NC-3
Little Bear Point—cape MI-6
Little Bear Pond—lake ME-1
Little Bear Pond—lake UT-8
Little Bear Reservior—reservoir NM-5
Little Bear Ridge—ridge ID-8
Little Bear Ridge Cem—cemetery ID-8
Little Bear River—stream CA-9
Little Bear River—stream UT-8
Little Bear Rock—summit CA-9
Little Bear Rock Branch—stream VA-3
Little Bear Rough—stream IL-6
Little Bear Run—stream (3) PA-2
Little Bear Run—stream SD-7
Little Bear Run—stream WY-8
Little Bear Sch—hist pl MT-8
Little Bear Sch—school MT-8
Little Bearskin Creek—stream VA-3
Little Bearskin Lake—lake WI-6
Little Bearskin Mtn—summit UT-8
Little Bear Skull Creek—stream MT-8
Little Bear Spring—spring CA-9
Little Bear Spring—spring (3) NM-5
Little Bear Spring—spring (2) OR-9
Little Bear Spring—spring (2) UT-8
Little Bear Springs—spring NM-5
Little Bear Station—locale MT-8
Little Bear Swamp MA-1
Little Bear Swamp—stream NC-3
Little Bear Swamp—swamp MA-1
Little Bear Swamp—swamp NY-2
Little Bear Swamp—swamp PA-2
Little Beartail Creek—stream MS-4
Little Bear Tank—reservoir NM-5
Little Beartown Branch—stream VA-3
Little Beartrack Lake—lake MN-6
Little Beartrack Lakes—lake CO-8
Little Bear Trail—trail CO-8
Little Bear Trail—trail PA-2
Little Bear Trap—gap CA-9
Little Beartrap Branch—stream NC-3
Little Beartrap Creek—stream WI-6
Little Beartrap Ridge—ridge NC-3
Little Bear Valley—valley CA-9
Little Bear Valley Creek—stream CA-9
Little Bear Wallow Creek—stream (2) CA-9
Little Bearwallow Creek—stream NC-3
Little Bear Wallow Meadow—flat CA-9
Little Bearwallow Mtn—summit NC-3
Little Bear Willow Spring—spring WA-9
Little Beason Run—stream WV-2
Little Beatons Lake—lake MI-6
Little Beaty Canyon—valley CO-8
Little Beaty Dam—dam CO-8
Little Beaucoup Creek—stream (2) IL-6
Little Beauty Creek—stream AK-9
Little Beaver Brook—stream ME-1
Little Beaver Camp—locale PA-2
Little Beaver Campground—locale WA-9
Little Beaver Canyon—valley CA-9
Little Beaver Cave—cave MO-7
Little Beaver Cem—cemetery PA-2
Little Beaver Creek CA-9
Little Beaver Creek KS-7
Little Beaver Creek MS-4
Little Beaver Creek ND-7
Little Beaver Creek OH-6
Little Beaver Creek OR-9
Little Beaver Creek PA-2
Little Beaver Creek SD-7
Little Beaver Creek—stream (2) AL-4
Little Beaver Creek—stream AR-4
Little Beaver Creek—stream CA-9
Little Beaver Creek—stream (7) CO-8
Little Beaver Creek—stream (6) ID-8
Little Beaver Creek—stream (2) IL-6
Little Beaver Creek—stream (5) IA-7
Little Beaver Creek—stream (2) KS-7
Little Beaver Creek—stream (4) KY-4
Little Beaver Creek—stream MD-2
Little Beaver Creek—stream (5) MI-6
Little Beaver Creek—stream MN-6
Little Beaver Creek—stream (3) MS-4
Little Beaver Creek—stream (2) MO-7
Little Beaver Creek—stream (7) MT-8
Little Beaver Creek—stream (2) NE-7
Little Beaver Creek—stream NV-8
Little Beaver Creek—stream (2) NC-3
Little Beaver Creek—stream (3) ND-7
Little Beaver Creek—stream (6) OH-6
Little Beaver Creek—stream (3) OK-5
Little Beaver Creek—stream (5) OR-9
Little Beaver Creek—stream (2) PA-2
Little Beaver Creek—stream (3) SC-3
Little Beaver Creek—stream SD-7
Little Beaver Creek—stream (2) TN-4
Little Beaver Creek—stream (2) TX-5
Little Beaver Creek—stream (2) VA-3
Little Beaver Creek—stream WA-9
Little Beaver Creek—stream (2) WV-2
Little Beaver Creek—stream WI-6
Little Beaver Creek—stream (8) WY-8
Little Beaver Creek Canal—canal TN-4
Little Beaver Creek Trail—trail ID-8
Little Beaverdam Branch—stream SC-3
Little Beaverdam Ch—church SC-3
Little Beaverdam Creek ID-8
Little Beaverdam Creek MS-4
Little Beaverdam Creek—stream AL-4
Little Beaver Dam Creek—stream CO-8
Little Beaverdam Creek—stream (5) GA-3
Little Beaverdam Creek—stream KY-4
Little Beaver Dam Creek—stream LA-4
Little Beaverdam Creek—stream MS-4
Little Beaverdam Creek—stream (4) NC-3
Little Beaverdam Creek—stream PA-2
Little Beaverdam Creek—stream (3) SC-3
Little Beaverdam Creek—stream TN-4
Little Beaverdam Swamp NC-3
Little Beaver Hollow—valley OK-5
Little Beaver Island Creek—stream NC-3
Little Beaver Kill—stream (2) NY-2
Little Beaver Lake MI-6
Little Beaver Lake—lake (3) AK-9
Little Beaver Lake—lake MI-6
Little Beaver Lake—lake MN-6
Little Beaver Lake—lake MT-8
Little Beaver Lake—lake PA-2
Little Beaver Lake—reservoir WV-2
Little Beaver Mine—mine UT-8
Little Beaver Mtn—summit NY-2
Little Beaver Oil Field—oilfield CO-8
Little Beaver Pond—lake (4) ME-1
Little Beaver Pond Creek—stream VA-3
Little Beaver Ridge—ridge OR-9
Little Beaver Rsvr—reservoir CO-8
Little Beaver Run—stream PA-2
Little Beaver Slough—stream AR-4
Little Beaver Spring—spring WY-8
Little Beaver State Park—park WV-2
**Little Beaver (Township of)**—pop pl PA-2
Little Bed Tick Creek—stream WY-8
Little Bee Bayou—gut AR-4
Little Bee Branch—stream TN-4
Little Beech Bayou—stream LA-4
Little Beech Branch—stream AR-4
Little Beech Branch—stream KY-4
Little Beech Branch—stream VA-3
Little Beech Creek—stream GA-3
Little Beech Creek—stream (3) KY-4
Little Beech Creek—stream OH-6
Little Beech Creek—stream (2) OR-9
Little Beech Creek—stream TN-4
Little Beech Creek—stream TX-5
Little Beech Fork—stream (2) KY-4
Little Beech Hill—summit ME-1
Little Beech Knob—summit WV-2
Little Beech Mtn—summit WV-2
Little Beech Sch—school TN-4
Little Beechy Creek—stream WV-2
Little Beechy Run—stream WV-2
Little Bee Creek—stream KY-4
Little Bee Creek—stream TX-5
Little Beef Creek—stream WA-9
Little Beef Harbor—bay WA-9
Little Beef Meadows—flat UT-8
Little Beef Tank—reservoir TX-5
Little Bee Mtn—summit GA-3
Little Bee Mtn—summit TX-5
Little Bee Run—stream WV-2
Little Bees Creek—stream SC-3
Little Beeswax Creek—stream AL-4
Little Beggar Trail—trail HI-9
Little Beicegel Creek—stream ND-7
Little Belknap—summit OR-9
Little Bell Ch—church LA-4
Little Bell Creek—stream NE-7
Little Bell Flat—flat NV-8
Little Bell Island—island NC-3
Little Bell Lake—lake AR-4
Little Bellows Bay—bay NC-3
Little Bellrose Creek—gut TX-5
Little Bell Shaft—mine UT-8
Little Bellville Creek—stream AR-4
Little Belmont Creek—stream MT-8
Little Belmont Point—summit MT-8
Little Belt Creek—stream MT-8
Little Belt Mtns—range MT-8
Little Belt Sch (reduced usage)—school MT-8
Little Bemidji Lake—reservoir MN-6
Little Bench Ditch—canal UT-8
Little Bend—bay MS-4
Little Bend—bend AZ-5
Little Bend—bend FL-3
Little Bend—bend (3) KY-4
Little Bend—bend LA-4
Little Bend—bend (2) SD-7
Little Bend—bend (2) TN-4
Little Bend Creek—stream OR-9
Little Bend (historical)—island SD-7
Little Bend (historical)—locale SD-7
Little Bend Mine AL-4
Little Bend Park—park OR-9
Little Bend Post Office (historical)—building SD-7
Little Bend Rec Area—park SD-7
Little Bend Ridge—ridge KY-4
Little Bend Township—civil SD-7
Little Bend Tunnel—tunnel WV-2
Little Ben Mine—mine MT-8
Little Bennett Brook—stream ME-1
Little Bennett Creek—stream CO-8
Little Bennett Creek—stream MD-2
Little Bennett Pond—lake ME-1
Little Ben Port Lake—lake SC-3
Little Bens Lake—lake LA-4
Little Benson Creek—stream KY-4
Little Benson Pond—lake ME-1
Little Bent Creek—stream TN-4
Little Bent Creek—stream VA-3
Little Berg Creek—stream ID-8
Little Berger Cem—cemetery MO-7
Little Berger Creek—stream MO-7
Little Bergess Lake—lake MI-6
Little Bernal Branch—stream NC-3
Little Bernard Creek—stream TX-5
Little Bernard River TX-5
Little Berry Canyon—valley UT-8
Little Berry Pond—lake (2) ME-1
Little Bertram Lake—lake WI-6
Little Bessie Creek—stream IL-6
Little Bethany Ch—church LA-4
Little Bethany Ch—church MN-6
Little Bethany Creek—stream TN-4
Little Bethel Baptist Ch—church IN-6
Little Bethel Baptist Church AL-4
Little Bethel Bayou—stream LA-4
Little Bethel Cem—cemetery TX-5
Little Bethel Ch AL-4
Little Bethel Ch—church (2) AL-4
Little Bethel Ch—church AR-4
Little Bethel Ch—church (7) GA-3
Little Bethel Ch—church (2) KY-4
Little Bethel Ch—church MS-4
Little Bethel Ch—church MO-7
Little Bethel Ch—church (4) SC-3
Little Bethel Ch—church (5) TN-4
Little Bethel Ch—church TX-5
Little Bethel Ch—church (6) VA-3
Little Bethel Ch—church (2) WV-2
Little Bethel Church Cem—cemetery VA-3
Little Bethlehem Cem—cemetery AR-4
Little Bethlehem Ch—church AR-4
Little Bethlehem Ch—church NC-3
Little Bethlehem Ch—church TX-5
Little Betsie River—stream MI-6
Little Betsy River—stream MI-6
Little Beulah Baptist Ch (historical)—church AL-4
Little Bidden Creek—stream CA-9
Little Big Bend, The—bend TX-5
Little Bigby Creek—stream TN-4
Little Big Cave—cave AL-4
Little Big Creek—stream TX-5
Little Big Creek—stream WA-9
Little Bigelow Mtn—summit ME-1
Little Bigger Creek—stream AR-4
Little Big Hole Tank—reservoir AZ-5
Little Big Horn Peak AZ-5
Little Bighorn Peak—summit AZ-5
Little Big Horn River WY-8
Little Bighorn River—stream MT-8
Little Bighorn River—stream WY-8
Little Big Horn Well—well AZ-5
Little Big Lake—lake MS-4
Little Biglow Lake—lake PA-2
Little Big Mtn—summit NV-8
Little Big Tank—reservoir TX-5
Little Big Wood Pond—lake ME-1
Little Bill Chain Branch—stream KY-4
Little Bill Mine—mine CA-9
Little Bills Cave—cave AL-4
Little Bill Slaven Knob—summit TN-4
Little Bill Spring—spring CO-8
Little Bill Tank—reservoir AZ-5
Little Biloxi Creek MS-4
Little Biloxi Game Mngmt Area MS-4
Little Biloxi River—stream MS-4
Little Biloxi State Wildlife Mngmt Area—park MS-4
Little Bingamon Creek—stream WV-2
Little Bingham Canyon—valley CO-8
Little Bingo Creek—canal IN-6
Little Biorka Island—island AK-9
**Little Birch**—pop pl WV-2
Little Birch Creek—stream IN-6
Little Birch Creek—stream (2) MT-8
Little Birch Creek—stream (2) UT-8
Little Birch Island—island (3) ME-1
Little Birch Island—island NH-1
Little Birch Island—island NY-2
Little Birch Island Run—stream PA-2
Little Birch Lake—lake (3) MN-6
Little Birch Lake—lake WI-6
Little Birch Mtn—summit WV-2
Little Birch Pond—lake NY-2
Little Birch River—stream WV-2
Little Birch Stream—stream ME-1
Little Bird Branch—stream TN-4
Little Bird Creek—stream MT-8
Little Bird Island LA-4
Little Bird Island—island FL-3
Little Bird Island—island MA-1
Little Bird Island—island TX-5
Little Bird Key FL-3
Little Bird Key—island (3) FL-3
Little Bird Kindergarten and Day Care—school FL-3
Little Bird Lake—lake MN-6
Little Bird Sch (historical)—school SD-7
Little Birdsong Creek—stream TN-4
Little Bishop Creek—stream IL-6
Little Bit Pit—cave AL-4
Little Bitter Creek WY-8
Little Bitter Creek—stream TX-5
Little Bitter Creek—stream WY-8
Little Bitterroot Lake—lake MT-8
Little Bitterroot River—stream MT-8
Little Bitterwater Canyon—valley CA-9
Little Bitterwater Spring—spring CA-9
Little Bivens Bayou—stream AR-4
**Little Black**—pop pl WI-6
Little Black Bayou—stream MS-4
Little Blackberry Creek—stream WV-2
Little Blackbird Reef—bar WI-6
Little Black Branch—stream FL-3
Little Black Branch—stream VT-1
Little Black Brook—stream ME-1
Little Black Brook—stream NY-2
Little Black Brook—stream PA-2
Little Black Brook Lake—lake ME-1
Little Black Butte—summit OR-9
Little Black Butte—summit WY-8
Little Black Canyon—valley OR-9
Little Black Cap Mtn—summit ME-1
Little Black Cem—cemetery WI-6
Little Black Creek GA-3
Little Black Creek—stream AL-4
Little Black Creek—stream AK-9
Little Black Creek—stream (2) FL-3
Little Black Creek—stream (3) GA-3
Little Black Creek—stream IN-6
Little Black Creek—stream (3) MI-6
Little Black Creek—stream (4) MS-4
Little Black Creek—stream (2) NY-2
Little Black Creek—stream NC-3
Little Black Creek—stream OH-6
Little Black Creek—stream PA-2
Little Black Creek—stream (3) SC-3
Little Black Creek—stream TX-5
Little Black Creek Cem—cemetery MS-4
Little Black Creek Ch—church MS-4
Little Black Creek Water Park—park MS-4
Little Blackfish Lake—lake AR-4
Little Blackfoot River—stream ID-8
Little Blackfoot River—stream MT-8
Little Blackford Creek—stream KY-4
Little Black Fork MS-4
Little Black Fork—stream WV-2
Little Black Fork Trail—trail WV-2
Little Black Fox Mtn—summit CA-9
Little Blackgum Branch—stream NC-3
Little Blackhawk Canal—canal UT-8
Little Blackhawk Creek—stream CA-9
Little Black Hills—summit AZ-5
Little Black Hill Tank—reservoir (3) AZ-5
Little Black (historical)—locale MS-4
Little Blackhoof Lake—lake MN-6
Little Black Island—island ME-1
Little Blackjack Branch—stream OH-6
Little Blackjack Pond—lake TX-5
Little Black Knob—summit NV-8
Little Black Lake—lake MI-6
Little Black Lake—lake NY-2
Little Black Lake—lake WA-9
Little Black Lake—swamp LA-4
Little Black Ledge—bar ME-1
Little Blacklog Fork—stream KY-4
Little Black Lookout Tower—locale KY-4
Little Black Mesa—summit (2) AZ-5
Little Black Mesa—summit CO-8
Little Black Mesa—summit UT-8

*Little Black Moshannon Creek* PA-2
*Little Black Mountains* VA-3
*Little Black Mtn* KY-4
Little Black Mtn—*range* VA-3
Little Black Mtn—*summit (2)* AZ-5
Little Black Mtn—*summit (2)* CA-9
Little Black Mtn—*summit* KY-4
Little Black Mtn—*summit* NH-1
Little Black Mtn—*summit (2)* NM-5
Little Black Mtn—*summit* UT-8
Little Black Mtns—*summit* NV-8
Little Black Peak—*summit* NV-8
Little Black Peak—*summit* NM-5
Little Black Pine Rough—*ridge* NC-3
Little Black Point—*cliff* CO-8
Little Black Ponds—*lake* ME-1
*Little Black River* MS-4
Little Black River—*stream* AK-9
Little Black River—*stream* AR-4
Little Black River—*stream* ME-1
Little Black River—*stream (2)* MI-6
Little Black River—*stream* MO-7
Little Black River—*stream* WI-6
Little Black River Archeol District—*hist pl* MO-7
Little Black Rock—*bar* MA-1
Little Black Rock—*pillar* CA-9
Little Black Rock—*pillar* OR-9
Little Black Rock—*rock* MA-1
Little Black Rock—*summit* CA-9
Little Black Rock—*summit* OR-9
Little Blackrock Spring—*spring* CA-9
*Little Blacks Creek* GA-3
Little Blacks Fork—*stream* WY-8
Little Black Slough—*swamp* IL-6
Little Blacksmith Lake—*lake* WI-6
Little Black Spot Mtn—*summit* AZ-5
Little Black State For—*forest* MO-7
*Little Blackstone River* MA-1
Little Black Stump Gulch—*valley* OR-9
Little Blacktail Creek—*stream* CO-8
Little Blacktail Creek—*stream (2)* MT-8
Little Blacktail Mtn—*summit* ID-8
**Little Black (Town of)**—*pop pl* WI-6
Little Black (Township of)—*fmr MCD* AR-4
Little Blackwater Ch—*church* AR-4
Little Blackwater Creek—*stream* AL-4
Little Blackwater Creek—*stream* KY-4
Little Blackwater Creek—*stream* MO-7
Little Blackwater Mine (surface)—*mine* AL-4
Little Blackwater River—*stream* MD-2
Little Blackwater River—*stream* WV-2
Little Blackwater Sound—*bay* FL-3
Little Blackwood Creek—*stream* AL-4
Little Blackwood Creek—*stream* NE-7
Little Blade Hollow—*valley* AR-4
Little Blaine Creek—*stream* KY-4
Little Blair Creek—*stream* MO-7
Little Blair Valley—*basin* CA-9
Little Blake Lake—*lake* WI-6
Little Blakely Creek—*stream* AR-4
Little Blakey Creek—*stream* AR-4
*Little Blalock Island* WA-9
Little Blalock Island—*island* WA-9
*Little Blanca Mountains* TX-5
Little Blanca Mtn—*summit* TX-5
*Little Blanca Peak* TX-5
Little Blanche Creek—*stream* AK-9
Little Blanco Canyon—*valley* NM-5
Little Blanco Creek—*stream* TX-5
*Little Blanco River* CO-8
*Little Blanco River* TX-5
Little Blanco River—*stream* TX-5
Little Blanco Trail—*trail* CO-8
Little Blanket Shelter—*locale* OR-9
Little Blind Bull Creek—*stream* WY-8
Little Blind Canyon—*valley* ID-8
Little Blind Ditch—*canal* IN-6
Little Blind Spring—*spring* OR-9
Little Blitzen River—*stream* OR-9
Little Blizzard Run—*stream* WV-2
Little Blocker Creek—*stream* AR-4
Little Blodgett Lake—*lake* MI-6
Little Bloody Creek—*stream* KS-7
Little Bloody Creek—*stream* KY-4
Little Bloom Creek—*stream* MO-7
Little Blooming Grove Creek—*stream* PA-2
Little Blount Lake—*reservoir* MS-4
Little Blowout Creek—*stream* ID-8
*Little Blue* MO-7
**Little Blue**—*pop pl* MO-7
Little Blue—*summit* ME-1
Little Blue Box—*basin* AZ-5
Little Blue Branch—*stream* MO-7
Little Blue Ch—*church* SC-3
*Little Blue Creek* CO-8
*Little Blue Creek* IN-6
*Little Blue Creek* TX-5
Little Blue Creek—*stream (3)* AL-4
Little Blue Creek—*stream* AZ-5
Little Blue Creek—*stream* CA-9
Little Blue Creek—*stream* CO-8
Little Blue Creek—*stream* ID-8
Little Blue Creek—*stream* IL-6
Little Blue Creek—*stream (2)* IN-6
Little Blue Creek—*stream* MT-8
Little Blue Creek—*stream* NM-5
Little Blue Creek—*stream* OK-5
Little Blue Creek—*stream* TN-4
Little Blue Creek—*stream (2)* TX-5
Little Blue Creek—*stream* WA-9
Little Blue Creek—*stream* WV-2
Little Blue Creek Ch—*church* WV-2
Little Blue Creek Forty-one Trail—*trail* AZ-5
Little Blue Creek Rsvr—*reservoir* ID-8
Little Blue Dome—*summit* CA-9
Little Blue Gainey Points—*area* TX-5
Little Blue Grouse Mtn—*summit* WA-9
Little Bluegut Creek—*stream* AL-4
Little Blue Hill—*summit* MA-1
Little Blue Hole—*lake* AR-4
Little Blue Hole—*lake* MS-4
Little Blue Hole—*lake (2)* TX-5
Little Bluejay Creek—*stream* CO-8
Little Blue Joint Creek—*stream* MT-8
Little Blue Knob—*summit* GA-3
Little Blue Lake—*lake* FL-3
Little Blue Lake—*lake (2)* MI-6
Little Blue Lake—*lake (2)* WA-9
Little Blue Mesa—*summit* NM-5
Little Blue Mine—*mine* OR-9
Little Blue Mine—*mine* SD-7
Little Blue Mtn—*summit* NY-2
Little Blue Pond—*lake* FL-3
Little Blue Pond—*lake* NY-2
Little Blue Pond—*lake* UT-8
Little Blue Ridge—*ridge* CA-9
*Little Blue River* IN-6
*Little Blue River* MO-7
*Little Blue RIVER* NE-7
Little Blue River—*stream (3)* IN-6
Little Blue River—*stream* KS-7
Little Blue River—*stream* MO-7
Little Blue River*—*stream* NE-7
Little Blue River—*stream* OK-5
Little Blue River Ch—*church (3)* IN-6
Little Blue River Lakes—*reservoir* MO-7
Little Blue Rock Creek—*stream* OH-6
Little Blue Run—*stream* PA-2
Little Blue Run Dam—*dam* PA-2
Little Blue Sch—*school* NE-7
Little Blue Spring—*spring* AL-4
Little Blue Spring—*spring* FL-3
Little Blue Spring Branch—*stream* KY-4
Little Blue Spring Ch—*church* KY-4
Little Bluestem—*locale* MO-7
*Little Bluestone Creek* GA-3
Little Bluestone Creek—*stream* VA-3
Little Bluestone River—*stream* WV-2
Little Blue Table—*summit* ID-8
Little Blue Table Rsvr—*reservoir* ID-8
**Little Blue Township**—*pop pl* KS-7
**Little Blue Township**—*pop pl* NE-7
Little Blue Water Creek—*stream* AL-4
Little Bluewater Creek—*stream* AL-4
Little Bluewater Creek—*stream* TN-4
Little Blue Well—*well* NM-5
Little Bluewing Creek—*stream* VA-3
Little Bluff—*cliff* VT-1
Little Bluff Creek—*stream* IA-7
Little Bluff Creek—*stream* MS-4
Little Bluff Creek—*stream* TN-4
Little Bluff Creek—*stream* TX-5
Little Bluffer Brook—*stream* ME-1
Little Bluffer Pond—*lake* ME-1
Little Bluff Lake—*lake* FL-3
Little Bluff Lake—*reservoir* KY-4
Little Bluff Mtn—*summit* NY-2
*Little Bluff Point* VT-1
Little Bluff Swamp—*swamp* NC-3
Little Bly Tank—*reservoir* AZ-5
Little Boardman Mtn—*summit* ME-1
**Little Boars Head**—*pop pl* NH-1
Little Boat Harbor—*bay* MI-6
Little Bobcat Creek—*stream* MT-8
Little Bobcat Creek—*stream* NM-5
Little Bob Lake—*lake* WY-8
Little Bobs Creek—*stream* TX-5
Little Bobs Lake—*lake* MI-6
Little Bobs Park—*park* MN-6
*Little Bocilla Bay* FL-3
*Little Bocilla Island* FL-3
Little Bodcau Creek—*stream (2)* AR-4
*Little Bodcaw Creek* AR-4
Little Bodie Mine—*mine* CA-9
Little Boeuf Creek—*stream* MO-7
Little Bog—*swamp* ME-1
*Little Bogasha River* MS-4
Little Bog Branch—*stream* TX-5
Little Bog Brook—*stream* ME-1
Little Bog Creek—*stream* AZ-5
*Little Boggs Creek* IN-6
Little Boggy Bayou—*gut* AR-4
Little Boggy Branch—*stream* AL-4
Little Boggy Branch—*stream* GA-3
*Little Boggy Creek* WY-8
Little Boggy Creek—*stream* FL-3
Little Boggy Creek—*stream (2)* TX-5
Little Boggy Creek—*stream* WY-8
Little Boggy Swamp—*stream* SC-3
Little Boggy Swamp—*swamp* FL-3
Little Bog Pond—*lake* NH-1
Little Bog River—*stream* ME-1
Little Bogue—*stream* MS-4
*Little Bogue Creek* MS-4
Little Bogue Desha—*stream* MS-4
Little Bogue Falaya—*stream* LA-4
*Little Bogue Falaya River* LA-4
Little Bogue Hollow—*valley* MO-7
Little Bogue Homo—*stream* MS-4
*Little Bogue Homo Creek* MS-4
Little Bogus Creek—*gut* AK-9
Little Bogus Creek—*stream* CA-9
Little Bohemia Creek—*stream* MD-2
Little Bohinkleman Creek—*stream* WA-9
Little Boiling Creek—*stream* FL-3
Little Boiling Spring—*spring* AZ-5
Little Bois Brule River—*stream* WI-6
Little Bois Bubert Harbor—*bay* ME-1
Little Bois Bubert Island—*island* ME-1
Little Bokeelia Bay—*bay* FL-3
Little Bokeelia Island—*island* FL-3
Little Bollibokka Creek—*stream* CA-9
Little Bombay Hook—*cape* DE-2
Little Bonable Lake—*lake* FL-3
**Little Bonanza**—*pop pl* UT-8
Little Bonanza Creek—*stream (2)* AK-9
Little Bonanza Mill—*locale* CO-8
Little Bonaparte Creek—*stream* WA-9
Little Bonaparte Mtn—*summit* WA-9
Little Bone Run—*stream* NY-2
Little Boney Windmill—*locale* NM-5
Little Bonito Creek—*stream* NM-5
Little Bonito Creek—*stream* AZ-5
Little Bonne Femme Ch—*church* MO-7
Little Bonne Femme Creek—*stream* MO-7
Little Bonnet Lake—*lake* FL-3
Little Bonpas Creek—*stream* IL-6
*Little Book Cliffs* UT-8
Little Booming Shoal Hollow—*valley* MO-7
Little Boom Island—*island* WI-6
Little Boone Creek—*stream* ID-8
Little Boone Creek—*stream* MO-7
Little Bootjack Lake—*lake* MT-8
Little Boot Lake—*lake* MI-6
Little Boot Lake—*lake* MN-6
Little Boot Lake—*lake* WI-6
Little Borax Lake—*lake* CA-9
*Little Bordeaux Creek* NE-7
Little Bordeaux Creek—*stream* NE-7
Little Borego (Site)—*locale* CA-9
*Little Borough Church* AL-4
Little Borrego Tank—*reservoir* TX-5
*Little Bosque Creek* TX-5
Little Boston—*locale* WA-9
**Little Boston (Boston)**—*pop pl* CT-1
Little Bostwick Lake—*lake* MI-6
Little Bottom Branch—*stream* MS-4
Little Bottom Branch—*stream* NC-3
Little Bottom Cliff—*cliff* KY-4
Little Bottom Creek—*stream* MO-7
Little Bottom Creek—*stream* OR-9
Little Bottoms Trail—*trail* TN-4
Little Bougher Run—*stream* PA-2
Little Boulder Basin—*basin* NV-8
Little Boulder Canyon—*valley* AZ-5
*Little Boulder Creek* OR-9
Little Boulder Creek—*stream (3)* AK-9
Little Boulder Creek—*stream (4)* CA-9
Little Boulder Creek—*stream (4)* ID-8
Little Boulder Creek—*stream* MT-8
Little Boulder Creek—*stream (5)* OR-9
Little Boulder Creek—*stream (4)* WA-9
Little Boulder Creek—*stream* WY-8
Little Boulder Dam—*reservoir* UT-8
Little Boulder Grove—*woods* CA-9
Little Boulder Lake—*lake* CA-9
Little Boulder Lake—*lake* OR-9
Little Boulder Park—*flat* MT-8
Little Boulder Pond—*lake* AZ-5
Little Boulder River—*stream* MT-8
Little Boulder Spring—*spring* NV-8
Little Boulder Way Trail—*trail* OR-9
Little Boulin Tank—*reservoir* AZ-5
Little Bourbeuse River—*stream* MO-7
Little Bow—*locale* NY-2
*Little Bow Bench* UT-8
Little Bowen Creek—*stream* MO-7
Little Bower Lake—*lake* IN-6
Little Bowerman Lake—*lake* OR-9
Little Bowker Lake—*lake* WI-6
Little Bowlin Brook—*stream* ME-1
Little Bowlin Pond—*lake* ME-1
Little Bowman Pond—*lake* NY-2
Little Bow Mtn—*summit* OK-5
Little Bown Bench—*bench* UT-8
*Little Bowns Bench* UT-8
Little Bow Pond—*reservoir* NH-1
Little Bowstring Lake—*lake* MN-6
Little Box, The—*gap* TX-5
Little Box Campground—*locale* CO-8
Little Box Canyon—*valley* CO-8
Little Box Canyon—*valley (2)* ID-8
Little Box Canyon—*valley* NV-8
Little Box Canyon—*valley* NM-5
Little Box Canyon Dam—*dam* AZ-5
Little Box Creek—*stream* MS-4
Little Box Elder Cave—*cave* WY-8
*Little Box Elder Coulee* MT-8
Little Box Elder Coulee—*valley* MT-8
Little Box Elder Creek—*stream* MT-8
Little Boxelder Creek—*stream* MT-8
Little Box Elder Creek—*stream* WY-8
Little Box Lake—*reservoir* AZ-5
Little Box Windmill—*locale* NM-5
*Little Boy Creek* AZ-5
Little Boyd Lake—*lake* TX-5
Little Boyer Lake—*lake* MN-6
Little Boyer Mill Trail—*trail* PA-2
Little Boyer Trail—*trail* PA-2
Little Boy Falls—*falls* ME-1
Little Boykin Bar—*bar* SC-3
Little Boy Lake—*lake (2)* MN-6
Little Boynton Cutoff—*channel* FL-3
*Little Boy River* MN-6
Little Bracken Creek—*stream* KY-4
Little Bradford Bayou—*stream* MS-4
Little Bradford Island—*island* FL-3
Little Bradford Lake—*lake* MI-6
Little Bradshaw Basin—*basin* ID-8
Little Bradshaw Creek—*stream* MT-8
Little Bradshaw Creek—*stream (2)* TN-4
Little Brady Creek—*stream* TX-5
Little Bragg Canyon—*valley* NM-5
Little Brake—*flat* LA-4
Little Brake—*swamp* LA-4
*Little Branch* WV-2
Little Branch—*stream (5)* AL-4
Little Branch—*stream* AR-4
Little Branch—*stream* FL-3
Little Branch—*stream (4)* GA-3
Little Branch—*stream (8)* KY-4
Little Branch—*stream (3)* MO-7
Little Branch—*stream (4)* NC-3
Little Branch—*stream* SC-3
Little Branch—*stream (3)* TN-4
Little Branch—*stream* VA-3
Little Branch—*stream (2)* WV-2
Little Branch Bay—*bay* AK-9
Little Branch Beaver Creek—*stream* FL-3
Little Branch Cem—*cemetery (2)* AL-4
Little Branch Ch—*church (2)* AL-4
Little Branch Primitive Baptist Ch—*church* AL-4
Little Branch Sch—*school* SC-3
Little Brandywine Creek—*stream* IN-6
Little Brannan Creek—*stream* CA-9
Little Brasstown Ch—*church* NC-3
Little Brasstown Creek—*stream* NC-3
Little Brasstown Creek—*stream* SC-3
Little Brasstown Gap—*gap* GA-3
Little Brassua Lake—*lake* ME-1
Little Brawn—*summit* ME-1
Little Brazil Creek—*stream* MO-7
Little Brazil Creek—*stream* MT-8
Little Brazos River—*stream* TX-5
Little Brazos River Diversion Channel—*channel* TX-5
Little Break—*channel* DE-2
Little Break Hollow—*valley* PA-2
Little Breaking Ledge—*bar* ME-1
Little Bream Lake—*lake* FL-3
Little Breed Creek—*stream* MT-8
Little Bremen Creek—*stream* MN-6
Little Bremner River—*stream* AK-9
Little Brevoort Lake—*lake* MI-6
Little Brevoort Lake Campground—*locale* MI-6
Little Brevoort River—*stream* MI-6
*Little Brevort Lake* MI-6
Little Brewer Canyon—*valley* UT-8
Little Brewington Creek—*stream* TX-5
*Little Brewster Island* MA-1
Little Brewster Island—*island* MA-1
Little Brewster Spring—*spring* AZ-5
Little Brian Spring—*spring* MT-8
*Little Briar Creek* GA-3
*Little Briar Creek* PA-2
Little Briar Creek—*stream* AL-4
Little Briar Creek—*stream* MS-4
Little Briches Spring—*spring* OR-9
Little Brick Cem—*cemetery* KY-4
Little Brick Church—*hist pl* WV-2
Little Brick House—*hist pl* IL-6
Little Brick Island—*island* MN-6
Little Brick Sch—*school (6)* IL-6
Little Brick Sch—*school* IA-7
Little Brick Sch—*school* MI-6
Little Brick Sch—*school* MO-7
Little Brick Sch—*school* NE-7
*Little Bridge* UT-8
Little Bridge—*arch* UT-8
Little Bridge—*other* MI-6
**Little Bridge**—*pop pl* MA-1
Little Bridge Branch—*stream* NC-3
Little Bridge Canyon—*valley* MT-8
Little Bridge Canyon—*valley* UT-8
*Little Bridge Creek* AL-4
Little Bridge Creek—*stream* MO-7
Little Bridge Creek—*stream (2)* OR-9
Little Bridge Creek—*stream* WA-9
*Little Bridger Creek* WY-8
Little Bridger Creek—*stream* MT-8
Little Bridge Run—*stream* AL-4
Little Briens Lake—*lake* WI-6
*Little Brier Creek* SC-3
Little Brier Creek—*stream* GA-3
Little Brier Creek—*stream* NC-3
Little Brier Creek—*stream* SC-3
Little Brier Creek—*stream* WV-2
Little Brier Creek Ch—*church* GA-3
Little Brier Gap—*gap* TN-4
Little Brierpatch Lake—*lake* GA-3
Little Brier Run—*stream* PA-2
Little Briery Creek—*stream* NC-3
Little Briery Creek—*stream* VA-3
Little Briggs Creek—*stream* CA-9
Little Brimmer Lake—*lake* MI-6
Little Brimstone Creek—*stream (2)* TN-4
Little Brimstone Island—*island* ME-1
Little Brindle Canyon—*valley* TX-5
Little Bristo Creek—*stream* OR-9
**Little Britain**—*pop pl* NY-2
**Little Britain**—*pop pl* PA-2
Little Britain Airp—*airport* PA-2
Little Britain Ch—*church* PA-2
*Little Britain Island* SC-3
Little Britain Post Office (historical)—*building* PA-2
Little Britain Sch—*school* NY-2
**Little Britain (Township of)**—*pop pl* PA-2
Little Britan Elem Sch—*school* PA-2
Little Britches Rsvr—*reservoir* MT-8
Little British Creek—*stream* CO-8
Little Britt Creek—*stream* FL-3
Little Britton Island—*island* SC-3
Little Broadaxe Bayou—*stream* LA-4
*Little Broad Creek* WV-2
Little Broad Creek—*stream* NC-3
Little Broad Run—*stream* WV-2
Little Brokenstraw Creek—*stream* NY-2
Little Brokenstraw Creek—*stream* PA-2
Little Broken Valley—*valley* TN-4
Little Brook—*locale* NJ-2
**Littlebrook**—*pop pl* TN-4
Little Brook—*stream (4)* CT-1
Little Brook—*stream (2)* ME-1
Little Brook—*stream* MA-1
Little Brook—*stream* MI-6
Little Brook—*stream (4)* NH-1
Little Brook—*stream* NJ-2
Little Brook—*stream* NY-2
Little Brook—*stream* VT-1
Little Brook—*stream* WI-6
*Little Brook Creek* MI-6
Littlebrook Industrial Park—*locale* TN-4
Little Brooklyn Lake—*lake* WY-8
Little Brook Sch (historical)—*school* SD-7
Little Brother—*summit* OR-9
Little Brother Lake—*lake* MT-8
Little Brothers Slough—*gut* FL-3
Little Broughton Island—*island* GA-3
Little Brower Lake—*lake* MI-6
Little Brown Bear Creek—*stream* CA-9
*Little Brown Bench* UT-8
Little Brown Branch—*stream* MO-7
Little Brown Cem—*cemetery* MS-4
Little Brown Ch—*church* AR-4
Little Brown Ch—*church* KY-4
Little Brown Ch—*church* MS-4
Little Brown Ch—*church (2)* MO-7
Little Brown Ch—*church* MT-8
Little Brown Ch—*church* SD-7
Little Brown Ch in—*church* IA-7
Little Brown Creek—*stream* MS-4
Little Brown Creek—*stream (2)* NC-3
Little Brown Creek—*stream* TX-5
Little Brown Creek Freewill Baptist Ch—*church* MS-4
Little Brown Lake—*lake* CO-8
Little Brown Lake—*lake* SC-3
*Little Brown Methodist Church* SD-7
*Little Brown Missionary Baptist Ch* MS-4
Little Brown Point—*cliff* WY-8
Little Brown Sch—*school* IL-6
*Little Browns Creek* MS-4
*Little Browns Creek* NC-3
Little Browns Creek—*stream* CA-9
Little Browns Creek—*stream* CO-8
Little Browns Creek—*stream* ID-8
Little Browns Creek—*stream* MS-4
Little Browns Creek—*stream* SC-3
*Little Browns Hole* CO-8
*Little Brown's Mountain* ME-1
Little Brownson Bay—*bay* AK-9
*Little Brubaker Creek* PA-2
Little Brubaker Run—*stream* PA-2
Little Bruce Ridge—*ridge* TN-4
Little Brumley Creek—*stream* VA-3
Little Brundrett Lake—*lake* TX-5
*Little Brush Creek* TN-4
Little Brush Creek—*stream* AL-4
Little Brush Creek—*stream (3)* KY-4
Little Brush Creek—*stream* MI-6
Little Brush Creek—*stream* MS-4
Little Brush Creek—*stream (3)* MO-7
Little Brush Creek—*stream (2)* NC-3
Little Brush Creek—*stream (2)* PA-2
Little Brush Creek—*stream (2)* TN-4
Little Brush Creek—*stream* UT-8
Little Brush Creek—*stream (3)* VA-3
Little Brush Creek—*stream* WV-2
Little Brush Creek—*stream* WY-8
Little Brush Creek Cave—*cave* UT-8
Little Brush Creek Ditch—*canal* WY-8
Little Brush Creek Knob—*summit* UT-8
Little Brush Creek Petroglyphs—*hist pl* UT-8
*Little Brush Creek Reservoir* UT-8
Little Brush Lake—*lake* MI-6
Little Brushman—*summit* AK-9
*Little Brush Mtn* VA-3
Little Brush Mtn—*summit* NC-3
Little Brush Mtn—*summit* VA-3
Little Brush Run—*stream* WV-2
Little Brushy—*summit* AZ-5
Little Brushy Branch—*stream* LA-4
Little Brushy Canyon—*valley* NM-5
Little Brushy Ch—*church* MO-7
*Little Brushy Creek* MO-7
*Little Brushy Creek* SC-3
*Little Brushy Creek* TX-5
Little Brushy Creek—*stream (7)* AR-4
Little Brushy Creek—*stream (2)* GA-3
Little Brushy Creek—*stream (2)* KY-4
Little Brushy Creek—*stream (2)* LA-4
Little Brushy Creek—*stream* MS-4
Little Brushy Creek—*stream (3)* MO-7
Little Brushy Creek—*stream* NM-5
Little Brushy Creek—*stream* SC-3
Little Brushy Creek—*stream (6)* TX-5
Little Brushy Creek—*stream* WA-9
Little Brushy Fork—*stream* IN-6
Little Brushy Fork—*stream* NC-3
Little Brushy Lake—*lake (2)* AR-4
Little Brushy Lake—*lake (3)* TX-5
*Little Brushy Mtn* VA-3
Little Brushy Mtn—*range* VA-3
Little Brushy Mtn—*summit* AZ-5
Little Brushy Mtn—*summit* TN-4
Little Brushy Mtn—*summit (4)* VA-3
Little Brushy Pond—*lake* FL-3
Little Brushy Pond—*lake* KY-4
Little Brushy Ridge—*ridge* VA-3
*Little Brushy Spring* AZ-5
Little Brushy Tank—*reservoir* AZ-5
*Little Brushy Waterhole* AZ-5
*Little Brusters Island* MA-1
Little Bryant Creek—*stream* AL-4
Little Bubbler, The—*spring* PA-2
*Little Buckatabon Lake* WI-6
Little Buck Basin—*valley* UT-8
Little Buck Canyon—*valley* CO-8
Little Buck Canyon—*valley* OR-9
Little Buck Canyon—*valley* UT-8
*Little Buck Creek* IN-6
*Little Buck Creek* NC-3
*Little Buck Creek* SC-3
Little Buck Creek—*stream* AL-4
Little Buck Creek—*stream* AR-4
Little Buck Creek—*stream (2)* GA-3
Little Buck Creek—*stream* ID-8
Little Buck Creek—*stream (2)* IN-6
Little Buck Creek—*stream* KS-7
Little Buck Creek—*stream* KY-4
Little Buck Creek—*stream* MO-7
Little Buck Creek—*stream (3)* NC-3
Little Buck Creek—*stream (2)* OR-9
Little Buck Creek—*stream* SC-3
Little Buck Creek—*stream* TN-4
Little Buck Creek—*stream* TX-5
Little Buck Creek—*stream* WA-9
Little Buck Creek—*stream* WY-8
Little Buck Creek Ch—*church* NC-3
Little Buckeye Cove—*valley* NC-3
Little Buckeye Creek—*stream (2)* CA-9
Little Buckeye Creek—*stream* GA-3
Little Buckeye Lake—*lake* MI-6
Little Buckhead Cem—*cemetery* GA-3
Little Buckhead Creek—*stream* GA-3
Little Buckhead Creek—*stream* OK-5
Little Buck Hill—*summit* NC-3
Little Buckhorn Creek—*stream* AL-4
Little Buckhorn Creek—*stream* AZ-5
Little Buckhorn Creek—*stream* ID-8
Little Buckhorn Hollow—*valley* PA-2
Little Buckhorn Mine—*mine* CO-8
Little Buckhorn Ranch—*locale* CA-9
Little Buckhorn Tank—*reservoir (2)* AZ-5
Little Buckhorn Tank—*reservoir* NM-5
Little Buckhorn Trail—*trail* PA-2
Little Buckingham Mtn—*summit* PA-2
Little Buck Island (historical)—*island* AL-4
Little Buck Knob—*summit* OH-6
*Little Buck Lake* WI-6
Little Buck Lake—*lake* AR-4
Little Buck Lake—*lake* MN-6
Little Buck Lake—*lake* WI-6
Little Bucklick Creek—*stream* OH-6
Little Bucklick Run—*stream* WV-2
Little Buck Mine—*mine* NV-8
Little Buck Mountain Pond—*lake* NY-2
Little Buck Mtn—*summit* CA-9
Little Buck Mtn—*summit* CO-8
Little Buck Mtn—*summit (2)* NY-2
Little Buck Mtn—*summit* WA-9
Little Buck Pond—*swamp* TX-5
Little Buck Public Hunting Area—*area* IA-7
Little Buck Ridge—*ridge* CA-9
Little Buck Rock—*summit* CA-9
Little Buck Rsvr—*reservoir* CO-8
Little Buck Run—*stream* WV-2
Little Buck Shoals—*bar* AL-4
Little Buckskin Mountains—*summit* AZ-5
Little Buckskin Tank—*reservoir* AZ-5
Little Bucktail Creek—*stream* CO-8
Little Buffalo Basin—*basin* WY-8
*Little Buffalo Bayou* AR-4
Little Buffalo Ch—*church* GA-3
Little Buffalo Ch—*church* MO-7
*Little Buffalo Creek* OH-6
Little Buffalo Creek—*stream (2)* AR-4
Little Buffalo Creek—*stream* CO-8
Little Buffalo Creek—*stream (3)* GA-3
Little Buffalo Creek—*stream* IA-7
Little Buffalo Creek—*stream* MN-6
Little Buffalo Creek—*stream (2)* MO-7
Little Buffalo Creek—*stream* NY-2
Little Buffalo Creek—*stream (7)* NC-3
Little Buffalo Creek—*stream* OH-6
Little Buffalo Creek—*stream* OK-5
Little Buffalo Creek—*stream (3)* PA-2
Little Buffalo Creek—*stream* SC-3
Little Buffalo Creek—*stream* SD-7
Little Buffalo Creek—*stream (4)* TX-5
Little Buffalo Creek—*stream (4)* VA-3
Little Buffalo Creek—*stream (5)* WV-2
Little Buffalo Creek—*stream (2)* WY-8
Little Buffalo Creek Dam—*dam* PA-2
Little Buffalo Gulch—*valley* MT-8
Little Buffalo Hill—*summit* MT-8
Little Buffalo Hist Dist—*hist pl* PA-2
Little Buffalo Lake—*lake* MT-8
Little Buffalo Lake—*reservoir* PA-2
*Little Buffalo Mountain* PA-2
Little Buffalo Ranch—*locale* WY-8
Little Buffalo River—*stream* AR-4
Little Buffalo River—*stream* MS-4
Little Buffalo River—*stream* TN-4
Little Buffalo Run—*stream* MD-2
Little Buffalo Run—*stream* PA-2
Little Buffalo Run—*stream* WV-2
Little Buffalo Slough—*stream* WI-6
Little Buffalo State Park—*park* PA-2
Little Buffalo Stream—*stream* ME-1
Little Buffalo Swamp—*stream* GA-3
**Little Buffalo Township**—*pop pl* SD-7
Little Buffalo Well—*well* NV-8
*Little Buffer Creek* OR-9
Little Bugaboo Creek—*stream* NC-3
Little Bugaboo Creek—*stream* OK-5
Little Bugg Mill Hollow—*valley* AL-4
Little Bulge—*swamp* GA-3
Little Bull Bayou—*stream* LA-4
Little Bull Branch—*stream* NC-3
Little Bull Camp Creek—*stream* NV-8
Little Bull Canyon—*valley* AZ-5
Little Bull Canyon—*valley* UT-8
Little Bull Cedar Creek—*stream* WY-8
**Little Bull Creek**—*pop pl* KY-4
Little Bull Creek—*stream* AR-4
Little Bull Creek—*stream* CO-8
Little Bull Creek—*stream* GA-3
Little Bull Creek—*stream* IN-6
Little Bull Creek—*stream* KS-7
Little Bull Creek—*stream (2)* KY-4
Little Bull Creek—*stream* NJ-2
Little Bull Creek—*stream* OH-6
Little Bull Creek—*stream* PA-2
Little Bull Creek—*stream (2)* SC-3
Little Bull Creek—*stream* TN-4
Little Bull Creek—*stream (2)* TX-5
Little Bull Creek—*stream* WY-8
Little Bull Creek Rsvr—*reservoir* OR-9
Little Bull Diversion Canal—*canal* MI-6
*Little Bulldog Creek* ID-8
Little Bulldog Creek—*stream* ID-8
Little Bull Draw—*valley* CO-8
Little Bull Elk Canyon—*valley* MT-8
Little Bull Elk Creek—*stream* MT-8
Little Bull Elk Ridge—*ridge* MT-8
Little Bull Falls—*falls (2)* WI-6
Little Bullfrog Creek—*stream* FL-3
Little Bullfrog Creek—*stream* TX-5
Little Bull Gulch—*valley* CO-8
Little Bullhead Lake—*lake* MI-6
Little Bull Hill—*summit* ME-1
Little Bull Island—*island* MT-8
Little Bull Junior Creek—*stream* WI-6
Little Bull Ledge—*island* ME-1
Little Bull Mtn—*summit* TN-4
Little Bull Rapids—*rapids* MI-6
Little Bull Run—*stream* OR-9
Little Bull Run—*stream (2)* VA-3
Little Bull Run—*stream* WV-2
Little Bullskin Creek—*stream (2)* KY-4
Little Bullskin Creek—*stream* OH-6
Little Bullskin Sch—*school* KY-4
Little Bull Swamp—*swamp* SC-3
Little Bull Swamp Creek—*stream* SC-3
Little Bull Tank—*reservoir* AZ-5
Little Bull Tank—*reservoir* TX-5
Little Bull Tank Number Two—*reservoir* AZ-5
Little Bull Tunnel—*tunnel* VA-3
Little Bull Valley—*valley* CA-9
Little Bull Valley—*valley* UT-8
Little Bull Valley Wash—*valley* UT-8
*Little Bullwhacker Coulee* MT-8
Little Bullwhacker Creek—*stream* MT-8
Little Bullwhacker Creek—*stream* WY-8
Little Bumblebee Creek—*stream* ID-8
Little Bumblebee Island—*island* FL-3
Little Bunches Creek—*stream* KY-4
Little Bunchgrass Lookout—*locale* OR-9
Little Bunch Grass Meadow—*flat* CA-9
Little Bundy Creek—*stream* VA-3
Little Bunk Robinson Spring—*spring* NM-5
Little Bunny Creek—*stream* AL-4
Little Burbank Canyon—*valley* NV-8
Little Burdick Hollow—*valley* PA-2
Littleburg—*locale* SD-7
Little Burgaw Creek—*stream* NC-3
Little Burgess Island—*island* NY-2
Littleburg Mason Grant—*civil* FL-3
Little Burnett Canyon—*valley* ID-8
Little Burnett Creek—*stream* CA-9
Little Burn Mtn—*summit* NY-2
Little Burns Canyon—*valley* ID-8
Little Burns Mtn—*summit* MO-7
Little Burnt Branch—*stream* MD-2
Little Burnt Creek—*stream* ID-8
Little Burnt Fork—*stream* MT-8
Little Burnt Fork Lakes—*lake* MT-8
Little Burnt Island—*island* ME-1
Little Burnt Land Stream—*stream* ME-1
Little Burnt Peak—*summit* CA-9
Little Burnt Pond—*lake (2)* ME-1
Little Burnt Shanty Lake—*lake* MN-6
*Little Burnt Ship Creek* NY-2
Little Burnt Swamp—*stream* NC-3
Little Burr Creek—*stream* CA-9
Little Burro Bay—*bay* NV-8
Little Burro Mountains—*other* NM-5

Little Cold Water Creek—stream NC-3
Little Coldwater Creek—stream VA-3
Little Cold Water River MS-4
Little Coleman Canyon—valley NV-8
Little Coleman Creek—stream VA-3
Little Coleman Lake—lake NE-7
Little Cole Mtn—summit NC-3
Little Colewa Bayou LA-4
Little Colewa Bayou—stream LA-4
Little Colewa Creek—stream LA-4
Little College Pond—lake MA-1
Little Collins Draw—valley NM-5
Little Collis Creek—stream GA-3
Little Collom Gulch—valley CO-8
Little Colly Bay—swamp NC-3
Little Colly Ch—church KY-4
Little Colly Creek NC-3
Little Colly Creek—stream KY-4
Little Colly Creek—stream NC-3
Little Colorado (CCD)—cens area AZ-5
Little Colorado Desert—area WY-8
Little Colorado Plateau AZ-5
Little Colorado River—stream AZ-5
Little Colorado River Bridge—bridge AZ-5
Little Colorado River Gorge—valley AZ-5
Little Colorado River Navajo Tribal Park—park AZ-5
Little Colorado Spring—spring CO-8
Little Colorado Tank—reservoir TX-5
Little Colorado Well No 1—well WY-8
Little Colorado Well No 10—well WY-8
Little Colorado Well No 11—well WY-8
Little Colorado Well No 12—well WY-8
Little Colorado Well No 13—well WY-8
Little Colorado Well No 2—well WY-8
Little Colorado Well No 3—well WY-8
Little Colorado Well No 4—well WY-8
Little Colorado Well No 5—well WY-8
Little Colorado Well No 6—well WY-8
Little Colorado Well No 8—well WY-8
Little Colorado Well No 9—well WY-8
Little Columbine Creek—stream CO-8
Little Colvin Creek—stream LA-4
Little Colvin Lake—lake KY-4
Little Colyell Creek—stream LA-4
Little Comanche Creek—stream CO-8
Little Comanche Creek—stream TX-5
Little Come And See Ch—church MS-4
Little Come And See Ch Number 2—church MS-4
Little Comfort MA-1
Little Comfort Island—island RI-1
Little Comfort Lake—lake MN-6
Little Comite Creek—stream LA-4
Little Comite Creek—stream MS-4
Little Commissary Brook—stream VT-1
Little Commissioner Creek—stream GA-3
Little Company Of Mary Hosp—hospital IN-6
Little Competine Creek—stream IA-7
**Little Compton**—pop pl RI-1
Little Compton Common Hist Dist—hist pl RI-1
Little Compton Commons RI-1
**Little Compton (Town of)**—pop pl RI-1
Little Concho Creek—stream TX-5
Little Conch Reef—bar FL-3
Little Concord Pond—lake ME-1
Little Cone—summit CO-8
Little Conecuh River—stream AL-4
Little Conehoma Creek—stream MS-4
Little Conejo Creek—stream NM-5
Little Conemaugh River—stream PA-2
Little Cones—summit NV-8
Little Conestoga—stream PA-2
Little Conestoga Creek—stream PA-2
Little Conesus Creek—stream NY-2
Little Conewago PA-2
Little Conewago Creek—stream (2) PA-2
Little Conewango Creek—stream NY-2
Little Conger Creek—stream IN-6
Little Congregational Cem—cemetery KS-7
Little Conneautte Creek PA-2
Little Conneauttee Creek—stream PA-2
Little Connection Slough—gut CA-9
Little Connoquenessing Creek—stream PA-2
Little Connors Creek—stream WI-6
Little Conns Creek—stream IN-6
Little Conococheague Creek—stream MD-2
Little Conococheague Creek—stream PA-2
Little Conowago Creek PA-2
Little Conowingo Creek—stream PA-2
Little Conrad Gulch—valley CA-9
Little Constance Bayou—stream LA-4
Little Constance Lake—lake LA-4
Little Constance Lake—lake MN-6
Little Contentnea Creek—stream NC-3
Little Cook Island—island IA-7
Little Cool Creek—stream IN-6
**Little Cooley**—pop pl PA-2
Little Coolidge Mountain—ridge NH-1
Little Coon Branch—stream NC-3
Little Coon Creek PA-2
Little Coon Creek—stream AL-4
Little Coon Creek—stream AR-4
Little Coon Creek—stream IA-7
Little Coon Creek—stream KS-7
Little Coon Creek—stream (3) MO-7
Little Coon Creek—stream NV-8
Little Coon Creek—stream PA-2
Little Coon Creek—stream TN-4
Little Coonewah Creek—stream MS-4
Little Coonewar Creek MS-4
Little Coon Gap—gut FL-3
Little Coon Lake—lake (2) MN-6
Little Coon Mtn—summit AL-4
Little Coon Never Hole—cave AL-4
Little Coon Run—stream PA-2
Little Coon Valley—valley AL-4
Little Co-op Creek—stream UT-8
Little Cooper Creek—stream TX-5
Little Cooper Lake—lake IL-6
Little Coopers Creek—stream WV-2
Little Cooter Lake—lake GA-3
Little Coot Island ME-1
Little Copiah Creek—stream MS-4
Little Copperas Creek—stream TX-5
Little Copperas Mtn—summit OH-6
Little Copper Butte—summit ID-8
Little Copper Creek ID-8
Little Copper Creek—stream AZ-5
Little Copper Creek—stream (2) ID-8
Little Copper Creek—stream VA-3
Little Copper Lake—lake MN-6
Little Copper Mountain Tank—reservoir AZ-5
Little Copper Spring AZ-5
Little Coquille Bay—bay LA-4
Little Corazones Spring—spring TX-5
Little Corkscrew Island—island FL-3
Little Cormorant Lake—lake MN-6
Little Corners PA-2
**Little Corners**—pop pl PA-2
Little Corney Bayou AR-4
Little Corney Bayou LA-4
Little Corney Bayou—stream LA-4
Little Corney Creek—stream LA-4
Little Cornhouse Reach—channel GA-3
Little Cornhouse Reach—channel SC-3
Little Cornie Bayou LA-4
Little Cornie Bayou—stream (3) AR-4
Little Cornie Creek AR-4
Little Cornie Creek LA-4
Little Cornish Creek—stream GA-3
Little Corn Lake—lake WI-6
Little Corral Creek—stream (2) MT-8
Little Corral Creek—stream WY-8
Little Corral Draw—valley SD-7
Little Corral Gulch—valley CO-8
Little Corral Gulch—valley MT-8
Little Corral Gulch Spring—spring CO-8
Little Cossatot River—stream AR-4
Little Costas Lake Dam—dam MS-4
Little Costilla Creek—stream NM-5
Little Costilla Peak—summit NM-5
Little Cotaco Creek AL-4
Little Cotaco Creek—stream AL-4
Little Coteau, Bayou—stream LA-4
Little Cotton Indian Creek GA-3
Little Cotton Indian Creek—stream GA-3
Little Cotton Lake—lake AR-4
Little Cotton Lake—lake MN-6
Little Cottonwood UT-8
Little Cottonwood Bay—bay ID-8
Little Cottonwood Campground—park UT-8
Little Cottonwood Canyon AZ-5
Little Cottonwood Canyon UT-8
Little Cottonwood Canyon—valley (2) AZ-5
Little Cottonwood Canyon—valley CA-9
Little Cottonwood Canyon—valley (4) NV-8
Little Cottonwood Canyon—valley (2) UT-8
Little Cottonwood Creek MT-8
Little Cottonwood Creek NV-8
Little Cottonwood Creek WY-8
Little Cottonwood Creek—stream AK-9
Little Cottonwood Creek—stream (3) CA-9
Little Cottonwood Creek—stream (5) CO-8
Little Cottonwood Creek—stream (5) ID-8
Little Cottonwood Creek—stream (10) MT-8
Little Cottonwood Creek—stream (2) NE-7
Little Cottonwood Creek—stream (5) NV-8
Little Cottonwood Creek—stream (3) OR-9
Little Cottonwood Creek—stream (2) SD-7
Little Cottonwood Creek—stream (3) TX-5
Little Cottonwood Creek—stream (4) UT-8
Little Cottonwood Creek—stream WA-9
Little Cottonwood Creek—stream (8) WY-8
Little Cottonwood Draw—valley MT-8
Little Cottonwood Draw—valley (2) WY-8
**Little Cottonwood East Subdivision**—pop pl UT-8
Little Cottonwood Lake SD-7
Little Cottonwood Lake—lake MN-6
Little Cottonwood Lake—lake NV-8
Little Cottonwood Lake—lake SD-7
Little Cottonwood Lake—reservoir OK-5
Little Cottonwood Peak—summit CA-9
Little Cottonwood River—stream MN-6
Little Cottonwood Rsvr—reservoir CO-8
Little Cottonwood Rsvr—reservoir ID-8
Little Cottonwood Sch—school NE-7
Little Cottonwood Spring—spring AZ-5
Little Cottonwood Spring—spring CA-9
Little Cottonwood Spring—spring ID-8
Little Cottonwood Spring—spring (2) NV-8
Little Cottonwood Spring—spring UT-8
Little Cottonwood Springs—spring ID-8
**Little Cottonwood Subdivision**—pop pl UT-8
Little Cottonwood Tank—reservoir AZ-5
**Little Cottonwood Valley Subdivision**—pop pl UT-8
Little Cottonwood Windmill—locale NM-5
Little Cougar Canyon—valley AZ-5
Little Cougar Creek—stream ID-8
Little Cougar Creek—stream OR-9
Little Cougar Lake—lake WA-9
Little Coulee—valley ND-7
Little Country Ch—church AL-4
Little Country Ch—church FL-3
Little Country Ch—church OH-6
Little Country Ch—church VA-3
Little Country Ch—church WV-2
Little Country Church, The—church NC-3
Little Courtney Canyon—valley OR-9
Little Courtois Creek—stream MO-7
Little Court Oreilles Lake WI-6
Little Cove NC-3
Little Cove—basin OR-9
Little Cove—bay ME-1
Little Cove—locale TN-4
Little Cove—valley (2) AL-4
Little Cove—valley (2) ID-8
Little Cove—valley NC-3
Little Cove—valley (3) TN-4
Little Cove—valley UT-8
Little Cove Branch—stream (2) TN-4
Little Cove Canyon—valley WA-9
Little Cove Ch—church PA-2
Little Cove Creek AL-4
Little Cove Creek—stream (2) AL-4
Little Cove Creek—stream AR-4
Little Cove Creek—stream ID-8
Little Cove Creek—stream MT-8
Little Cove Creek—stream (2) NC-3
Little Cove Creek—stream OR-9
Little Cove Creek—stream PA-2
Little Cove Creek—stream (3) TN-4
Little Cove Creek—stream (2) VA-3
Little Cove Creek—stream WV-2
Little Cove Creek Baptist Church TN-4
Little Cove Creek Ch—church TN-4
Little Cove Gap—gap TN-4
Little Cove Mountain—ridge VA-3
Little Cove Mtn—summit WV-2
Little Cove Point—cape MD-2
Little Cove Run—stream WV-2
Little Cove Valley—valley PA-2
Little Cow—summit WA-9
Little Cowan Creek—stream KY-4
Little Cowans Dead River—lake MS-4
Little Cowboy Creek—stream SD-7
Little Cowboy Draw—valley NM-5
Little Cowboy Windmill—locale AZ-5
Little Cow Canyon—valley CO-8
Little Cow Canyon—valley NV-8
Little Cow Canyon Spring—spring NV-8
Little Cow Creek KS-7
Little Cow Creek TN-4
Little Cow Creek—stream AR-4
Little Cow Creek—stream CA-9
Little Cow Creek—stream FL-3
Little Cow Creek—stream ID-8
Little Cow Creek—stream KS-7
Little Cow Creek—stream LA-4
Little Cow Creek—stream MO-7
Little Cow Creek—stream (2) OK-5
Little Cow Creek—stream (2) OR-9
Little Cow Creek—stream TN-4
Little Cow Creek—stream (2) TX-5
Little Cow Creek—stream UT-8
Little Cow Creek—stream (2) WY-8
Little Coweta Ch—church OK-5
Little Cow Fork—stream KY-4
Little Cow Gulch—valley (2) CA-9
Little Cowhead Creek—stream SC-3
Little Cowhole Mtn—summit CA-9
Little Cow Horn Lake—lake MN-6
Little Cowhorn Mtn—summit OR-9
Little Cowhorn Valley—flat CA-9
Little Cowhouse Cem—cemetery TX-5
Little Cowhouse Creek—stream TX-5
Little Cowikee Creek—stream AL-4
Little Cow Knob—summit WV-2
Little Cow Lake—lake LA-4
Little Cow Lake—stream AR-4
Little Cow Mtn—summit CA-9
Little Cow Mtn—summit NC-3
Little Cow Mtn—summit OK-5
Little Cowpen Branch—stream NC-3
Little Cowpen Creek—stream AL-4
Little Cowpen Creek—stream GA-3
Little Cowpen Creek—stream OK-5
Little Cow Pond—lake AR-4
Little Cox Head—cape ME-1
Little Coyote Canyon—valley (2) AZ-5
Little Coyote Canyon—valley OR-9
Little Coyote Coulee—valley MT-8
Little Coyote Creek—stream CA-9
Little Coyote Creek—stream NV-8
Little Coyote Creek—stream NM-5
Little Coyote Creek—stream TX-5
Little Coyote Lake—lake MN-6
Little Coyote Mtn—summit WA-9
Little Coyote Point—cape CA-9
Littlecrab TN-4
**Littlecrab**—pop pl TN-4
**Little Crab**—pop pl TN-4
Little Crabb Creek KS-7
Little Crabb Creek—stream KS-7
Little Crab Creek KS-7
Little Crab Creek—stream TN-4
Little Crab Lake MN-6
Little Crab Lake—lake MN-6
Little Crab Lake—lake WI-6
Little Crab Orchard Creek—stream (2) IL-6
Little Crab Post Office TN-4
Littlecrab Post Office (historical)—building TN-4
Little Crab Sch (historical)—school TN-4
Little Crabtree Creek—stream NC-3
Little Crabtree Creek—stream PA-2
Little Cracker Box Creek MT-8
Little Cracker Creek—stream OR-9
Little Craggy Creek—stream OR-9
Little Craggy Knob—summit NC-3
Little Craggy Peak—summit OR-9
Little Crampton Mtn—summit CO-8
Little Cranberry Creek—stream OH-6
Little Cranberry Creek—stream VA-3
Little Cranberry Island—island ME-1
Little Cranberry Lake MI-6
Little Cranberry Lake—lake MI-6
Little Cranberry Lake—lake (2) MN-6
Little Cranberry Lake—lake WI-6
Little Cranberry Pond—lake MA-1
Little Cranberry River—stream MI-6
Little Crane Campground—park OR-9
Little Crane Creek—stream (2) CA-9
Little Crane Creek—stream MO-7
Little Crane Creek—stream NC-3
Little Crane Creek—stream OH-6
Little Crane Creek—stream (2) OR-9
Little Crane Creek Rsvr—reservoir ID-8
Little Crane Key FL-3
Little Crane Key—island FL-3
Little Crane Pond—lake MA-1
Little Crane Pond Ditch—canal IN-6
Little Crane Swamp—swamp MA-1
Little Crane Valley—valley MO-7
Little Crapo Lake—lake MI-6
Little Crasco Creek—stream TX-5
Little Crater—cliff CA-9
Little Crater—summit ID-8
Little Crater Creek—stream OR-9
Little Crater Lake—lake CA-9
Little Crater Lake—lake OR-9
Little Crater Meadow—swamp OR-9
Little Crater Rsvr—reservoir OR-9
Little Crawford Creek UT-8
Little Crawford Creek—stream GA-3
Little Crawford Spring—spring UT-8
Little Crawling Stone Lake—lake WI-6
Little Crawl Key—island FL-3
Little Crazy Mountains—other AK-9
Little Crease Mtn—summit VA-3
Little Creek AL-4
Little Creek AR-4
Little Creek DE-2
Little Creek GA-3
Little Creek ID-8
Little Creek IL-6
Little Creek IN-6
Little Creek IA-7
Little Creek KY-4
Little Creek MD-2
Little Creek MA-1
Little Creek MS-4
Little Creek MT-8
Little Creek NC-3
Little Creek PA-2
Little Creek SC-3
Little Creek TN-4
Little Creek TX-5
Little Creek WA-9
Little Creek WV-2
Little Creek—bay MD-2
Little Creek—bay NC-3
Little Creek—locale NC-3
Little Creek—locale (2) TN-4
**Little Creek**—pop pl DE-2
**Little Creek**—pop pl KY-4
**Little Creek**—pop pl LA-4
**Little Creek**—pop pl MS-4
**Little Creek**—pop pl TN-4
**Little Creek**—pop pl VA-3
Little Creek—stream (33) AL-4
Little Creek—stream (6) AK-9
Little Creek—stream AZ-5
Little Creek—stream (22) AR-4
Little Creek—stream (8) CA-9
Little Creek—stream (5) CO-8
Little Creek—stream DE-2
Little Creek—stream (10) FL-3
Little Creek—stream (49) GA-3
Little Creek—stream (11) ID-8
Little Creek—stream (15) IL-6
Little Creek—stream (12) IN-6
Little Creek—stream (5) IA-7
Little Creek—stream (2) KS-7
Little Creek—stream (12) KY-4
Little Creek—stream (17) LA-4
Little Creek—stream (6) MD-2
Little Creek—stream MA-1
Little Creek—stream MI-6
Little Creek—stream (33) MS-4
Little Creek—stream (23) MO-7
Little Creek—stream (5) MT-8
Little Creek—stream (2) NE-7
Little Creek—stream (2) NV-8
Little Creek—stream (2) NJ-2
Little Creek—stream (2) NM-5
Little Creek—stream (4) NY-2
Little Creek—stream (52) NC-3
Little Creek—stream (3) OH-6
Little Creek—stream (2) OK-5
Little Creek—stream (13) OR-9
Little Creek—stream PA-2
Little Creek—stream RI-1
Little Creek—stream (7) SC-3
Little Creek—stream SD-7
Little Creek—stream (21) TN-4
Little Creek—stream (23) TX-5
Little Creek—stream (10) UT-8
Little Creek—stream (22) VA-3
Little Creek—stream (7) WA-9
Little Creek—stream (11) WV-2
Little Creek—stream (2) WI-6
Little Creek—stream (5) WY-8
Little Creek—swamp FL-3
Little Creek Access Area—area NC-3
Little Creek Airpark Airp—airport TN-4
Little Creek Amphibious Base—military VA-3
Little Creek Baptist Ch—church TN-4
Little Creek Basin Trail—trail WA-9
Little Creek Bridge—bridge DE-2
Little Creek Campground—park UT-8
Little Creek Cave—cave AL-4
Little Creek Cem—cemetery (2) GA-3
Little Creek Cem—cemetery (2) IN-6
Little Creek Cem—cemetery MO-7
Little Creek Cem—cemetery WI-6
Little Creek Ch TN-4
Little Creek Ch—church AR-4
Little Creek Ch—church DE-2
Little Creek Ch—church (4) GA-3
Little Creek Ch—church KY-4
Little Creek Ch—church (2) LA-4
Little Creek Ch—church (2) MS-4
Little Creek Ch—church MO-7
Little Creek Ch—church (3) NC-3
Little Creek Ch—church OK-5
Little Creek Ch—church (6) WV-2
Little Creek Channel—channel VA-3
Little Creek Cove—bay VA-3
Little Creek Dam—dam VA-3
Little Creek Eagle Creek KY-4
Little Creek East Shop Ctr—locale VA-3
Little Creek Falls—falls NC-3
Little Creek Gap—gap NC-3
Little Creek Golf Course—locale PA-2
Little Creek Guard Station—locale ID-8
Little Creek Hollow—valley TN-4
Little Creek Hundred—civil (2) DE-2
Little Creek Hundred Rural Hist Dist—hist pl DE-2
Little Creek Impoundment Dams—dam AL-4
Little Creek - in part MS-4
Little Creek Knoll UT-8
Little Creek Lake—reservoir VA-3
Little Creek Landing DE-2
Little Creek Landing—locale DE-2
Little Creek Marsh—swamp MD-2
Little Creek Methodist Church—hist pl DE-2
Little Creek Mine Lake—reservoir AL-4
Little Creek Mtn—summit UT-8
Little Creek Naval Amphibious Base—military VA-3
**Little Creek (Norfolk Yard)**—pop pl VA-3
Little Creek Oil Field—oilfield LA-4
Little Creek Oil Field—oilfield MS-4
Little Creek Peak—summit (2) UT-8
Little Creek Pond MA-1
Little Creek Ridge—ridge UT-8
Little Creek Rsvr—reservoir UT-8
Little Creek Rsvr—reservoir VA-3
Little Creek Sanitorium—hospital TN-4
Little Creek Sch—school CO-8
Little Creek Sch—school (2) KY-4
Little Creek Sch—school MO-7
Little Creek Sch—school VA-3
Little Creek Sch—school WV-2
Little Creek Sch—school WI-6
Little Creek Sch (historical)—school TN-4
Little Creek School—church NC-3
Little Creek School—locale MO-7
Little Creek Sinks—basin UT-8
Little Creek Site (31 DH 351)—hist pl NC-3
Little Creek Spring—spring MO-7
Little Creek Spring—spring NV-8
Little Creek Spring—spring NM-5
Little Creek Spring—spring (2) OR-9
Little Creek Swamp—stream NC-3
Little Creek Trail (Pack)—trail NM-5
Little Creek Union Ch—church WV-2
Little Creek Valley—basin UT-8
Little Creek Valley—valley UT-8
Little Creek Wildlife Area—park DE-2
Little Creek Wildlife Area Logan Tract—park DE-2
Little Creek Wood Bench—bench UT-8
Little Crenshaw Tank—reservoir TX-5
Little Crevasse—gut LA-4
Little Cribs Creek—stream NC-3
Little Cripple Deer Creek—stream MS-4
Little Crispen Island—island GA-3
Little Crockett Tank—reservoir NM-5
Little Crody Lake—lake MN-6
Little Crooked Branch—stream KY-4
Little Crooked Creek—stream AL-4
Little Crooked Creek—stream AR-4
Little Crooked Creek—stream FL-3
Little Crooked Creek—stream GA-3
Little Crooked Creek—stream (2) IL-6
Little Crooked Creek—stream IN-6
Little Crooked Creek—stream LA-4
Little Crooked Creek—stream (2) MO-7
Little Crooked Creek—stream MT-8
Little Crooked Creek—stream (2) NC-3
Little Crooked Creek—stream (2) TN-4
Little Crooked Creek Landing—locale TN-4
Little Crooked Creek School (abandoned)—locale MT-8
Little Crooked Lake MI-6
Little Crooked Lake WI-6
Little Crooked Lake—lake IN-6
Little Crooked Lake—lake NY-2
Little Crooked Lake—lake WI-6
Little Crooked Ravine—valley ID-8
Little Crooked Run—stream PA-2
Little Crooked Run—stream VA-3
Little Crooked Run—stream WV-2
Little Crooked Thorofare—channel NJ-2
Little Cross Creek—stream AR-4
Little Cross Creek—stream KS-7
Little Cross Creek—stream NC-3
Little Cross L Spring—spring WY-8
Little Cross Meadows—flat WY-8
Little Crotched Lake—lake MI-6
Little Croton Creek—stream (2) TX-5
Little Croton Windmill—locale TX-5
Little Crow Basin—basin WA-9
Little Crow Canyon—valley NM-5
Little Crow Creek—stream AL-4
Little Crow Creek—stream AR-4
Little Crow Creek—stream CO-8
Little Crow Creek—stream SC-3
Little Crow Creek—stream TN-4
Little Crow Creek Cove—cave TN-4
Little Crow Hills—other AK-9
Little Crow Island—island SC-3
Little Crow Lake—lake MN-6
Little Crowley Creek—stream OR-9
Little Crowley Springs—spring OR-9
Little Crow Mtn—summit NY-2
Little Crown Butte—summit MT-8
Little Crownest Creek TX-5
Little Crow Peak—summit SD-7
Little Crow Run—stream PA-2
Little Crow Run—stream VA-3
Little Crows Nest Creek—stream TX-5
Little Cruises Creek—stream KY-4
Little Crumbly Knob—summit GA-3
Little Crum Creek—stream PA-2
Little Crystal Lake MI-6
Little Crystal Lake—lake CO-8
Little Crystal Lake—lake (2) MI-6
Little Cuba Landing—locale MS-4
Little Cub Branch—stream WV-2
Little Cub Creek—stream CO-8
Little Cub Creek—stream KY-4
Little Cub Creek—stream NC-3
Little Cub Creek—stream (2) TN-4
Little Cub Creek—stream VA-3
Little Cub Creek—stream WA-9
Little Cub Creek—stream (2) WV-2
Little Cub Lake—lake WI-6
Little Cub Lake—reservoir IN-6
Little Cub Pond—lake NH-1
Little Cuervo Creek—stream NM-5
Little Cuevo Canyon—valley NM-5
Little Cuevo Well—well NM-5
Little Cultus Campground—park OR-9
Little Cultus Lake—lake OR-9
Little Cumberland Island—island GA-3
Little Cumberland Island Lighthouse—locale GA-3
Little Cumberland Mountain—ridge TN-4
Little Cumberland Mtn—summit AL-4
Little Cumberland Mtn—summit TN-4
Little Cummins Creek—stream OR-9
Little Cunningham Tank—reservoir TX-5
Little Curltail Creek—stream SC-3
Little Currant Creek NV-8
Little Currant Hollow—valley ID-8
Little Curry Creek—stream GA-3
Little Cussetah Cem—cemetery OK-5
Little Cussetah Ch—church (2) OK-5
Little Cut—channel TX-5
Little Cut—gut WI-6
Little Cut Bank Creek AL-4
Little Cut Foot Sioux Lake—lake MN-6
Little Cutoff—stream LA-4
Little Cutoff Bayou—stream LA-4
Little Cutoff Creek—stream AR-4
Little Cut River—stream MI-6
Little Cut Rsvr—reservoir OR-9
Little Cut Spring—spring NV-8
Little Cuyahoga River—stream OH-6
Little Cypress—locale KY-4
**Little Cypress**—pop pl TX-5
Little Cypress Bay—basin SC-3
Little Cypress Bayou LA-4
Little Cypress Bayou—stream (2) AR-4
Little Cypress Bayou—stream LA-4
Little Cypress Bayou—stream (3) TX-5
Little Cypress Bend—bend TN-4
Little Cypress Creek—stream AL-4
Little Cypress Creek—stream AZ-5
Little Cypress Creek—stream (6) AR-4
Little Cypress Creek—stream (2) FL-3
Little Cypress Creek—stream (2) GA-3
Little Cypress Creek—stream (5) KY-4
Little Cypress Creek—stream LA-4
Little Cypress Creek—stream MO-7
Little Cypress Creek—stream (2) TN-4
Little Cypress Creek—stream (7) TX-5
Little Cypress Creek Canal—canal TN-4
Little Cypress Ditch—canal AR-4
Little Cypress Ditch—canal IL-6
Little Cypress Grove Lake—lake LA-4
Little Cypress Lake LA-4
Little Cypress Lake—lake AR-4
Little Cypress Pond—swamp TX-5
Little Cypress Sch—school TX-5
Little Cypress Slough—gut TN-4
Little Cypress Slough—stream KY-4
Little Cypress Swamp—swamp FL-3
Little Dad Lake—lake NE-7
Little Dads Creek—stream OR-9
Little Dagger Hill—summit TX-5
Little Dailey Bayou—gut MI-6
Little Daisy Creek—stream AK-9
Little Daisy Mine—mine AZ-5
Little Daisy Mine—mine MT-8
Little Daisy Tank—reservoir AZ-5
Little Daley—valley UT-8
Little Dalles—gap WA-9
Little Dall River—stream AK-9
Littledals Ferry Site (historical)—locale NC-3
Little Dalton Canyon—valley CA-9
Little Dalton Picnic Area—locale CA-9
Little Dalton Wash—stream CA-9
Little Dam—dam NM-5
Little Dam—dam NC-3
**Little Dam**—pop pl CO-8
Little Dam Branch—stream NC-3
Little Dam Branch—stream TN-4
Little Dam Draw—valley SD-7
Little Dam Lake—lake NY-2
Little Dam North Tank—reservoir AZ-5
Little Dam Tavern Brook—stream CT-1
Little Danceyard Creek—stream MO-7
Little Dancing Creek—stream VA-3
Little Dan Creek CA-9
Little Dandy Mine—mine MT-8
Little Dandy Windmill—locale CO-8
Little Dane Coulee—valley MT-8
Little Dan Hole Pond—lake NH-1
Little Daniels Run—stream PA-2
Little Dann Creek—stream CA-9
Little Dan River—stream NC-3
Little Dan River—stream VA-3
Little Darb Branch—stream NC-3
Little Darbonne Bayou LA-4
Little Darbonne Bayou—stream LA-4
Little Darby Creek—stream OH-6
Little Darby Creek—stream PA-2
Little Darby Peak—summit CA-9
Little Dardenne Creek—stream MO-7
Little Dardis Lake—lake WI-6
Little Dark Canyon—valley OR-9
Little Dark Canyon Trail—trail OR-9
Little Dark Hollow—valley TN-4
Little Dark Hollow—valley WV-2
Little Dark Hollow Trail—trail TN-4
Little Dark Run—stream VA-3
Little Dark Shade Creek—stream PA-2
Little Darling Mine—mine CO-8
Little Daugherty Run—stream PA-2
Little Dauphin Island—island AL-4
Little Daveggio Creek—stream ID-8
Little Davenport Creek—stream OK-5
Little Davenport Creek—stream UT-8
Little Davenport Wildlife Mngmt Area—park UT-8
Little David Mountain NC-3
Little Davis Creek—stream CA-9
Little Davis Gulch—valley MT-8
Little Davis Key—island FL-3
Little Davis Mtn—summit NC-3
Little Davis Mtn—summit UT-8
Little Dawson Creek—stream MI-6
Little Daycamp Branch—stream WV-2
Little Daykoo Harbor—bay AK-9
Little Day Tank—reservoir NM-5
Little Deacon Creek—stream OR-9
Little Dead Creek—gut FL-3
Little Dead Diamond River—stream NH-1
Little Dead Dog Canyon—valley OR-9
Little Deadening Creek—stream WV-2
Little Dead Horse Lake—lake MN-6
Little Dead Key—island FL-3
Little Deadman Creek—stream CO-8
Little Deadman Creek—stream MT-8
Little Deadman Island—island WA-9
Little Dead River—stream MI-6
Little Deadwood Gulch—valley CO-8
Little Deal Island—island MD-2
Little Deals Island MD-2
Little Dean Creek—stream OR-9
Little Deceiper Creek—stream AR-4
Little Deception Rock—pillar OR-9
Little Decker Branch—stream MO-7
Little Dee Creek—stream WY-8
Little Deedie Lake—lake LA-4
Little Deep Branch—stream FL-3
Little Deep Cem—cemetery ND-7
Little Deep Creek NC-3
Little Deep Creek WA-9
Little Deep Creek—stream (2) CA-9
Little Deep Creek—stream (2) ID-8
Little Deep Creek—stream MT-8
Little Deep Creek—stream NM-5
Little Deep Creek—stream NC-3
Little Deep Creek—stream (2) ND-7
Little Deep Creek—stream OK-5
Little Deep Creek—stream OR-9
Little Deep Creek—stream WA-9
Little Deep Creek—stream WY-8
Little Deep Fork Creek—stream OK-5
Little Deep Fork River OK-5
Little Deep Gap—gap NC-3

Little Deep Lake—lake (2) MN-6
Little Deep Lake—lake WI-6
Little Deep Marsh Island—island NC-3
Little Deep Red Creek—stream OK-5
**Little Deep Township**—pop pl ND-7
Little Deer Canyon—valley CA-9
Little Deer Creek OR-9
Little Deer Creek—stream (6) CA-9
Little Deer Creek—stream CO-8
Little Deer Creek—stream GA-3
Little Deer Creek—stream (3) ID-8
Little Deer Creek—stream (5) IN-6
Little Deer Creek—stream KS-7
Little Deer Creek—stream (2) MD-2
Little Deer Creek—stream MI-6
Little Deer Creek—stream (2) MO-7
Little Deer Creek—stream NY-2
Little Deer Creek—stream OH-6
Little Deer Creek—stream OK-5
Little Deer Creek—stream (3) OR-9
Little Deer Creek—stream (5) PA-2
Little Deer Creek—stream TX-5
Little Deer Creek—stream UT-8
Little Deer Creek—stream (2) WA-9
Little Deer Creek—stream (2) WY-8
Little Deer Creek Cem—cemetery IN-6
Little Deer Creek Ch—church TX-5
Little Deer Creek Landing (historical)—locale MS-4
Little Deer Creek Ridge—ridge ID-8
Little Deerfield Mtn—summit NY-2
Little Deer Hill—summit ME-1
Little Deer Hollow—valley UT-8
Little Deer Isle—island ME-1
**Little Deer Isle**—pop pl ME-1
Little Deer Lake—lake CA-9
Little Deer Lake—lake FL-3
Little Deer Lake—lake MN-6
Little Deer Lake—lake (2) NY-2
Little Deer Lakes—lake ID-8
Little Deer Lakes—reservoir AL-4
Little Deerlick Creek—stream NY-2
Little Deer Mtn—summit CA-9
Little Deer Mtn—summit VT-1
Little Deer Peak—summit UT-8
Little Deer Peak—summit WA-9
Little Deer Point—cape ID-8
Little Deer Pond NY-2
Little Deer Pond—lake PA-2
Little Deer Site—hist pl OK-5
Little Deerskin Creek WI-6
Little Deerskin River—stream WI-6
Little Deer Valley—valley AZ-5
Little De Gray Creek—stream AR-4
Little Deils Island MD-2
Little Delaware Creek KS-7
Little Delaware Creek—stream (2) OK-5
Little Delaware River—stream KS-7
Little Delaware River—stream NY-2
Little Delight Island—island NY-2
Little Dell Lake UT-8
Little Dells—bend WI-6
Little Dell Station—hist pl UT-8
Little Delta River—stream AK-9
Little Democracy Sch—school IL-6
Little Den—basin NV-8
Little Den Creek—stream NV-8
Little Denham Bayou—stream FL-3
Little Denmark Cem—cemetery MI-6
Little Dent Run—stream PA-2
Little Dents Run PA-2
Little Dents Run—stream PA-2
Little Dents Run—stream WV-2
Little Denver Creek—stream AK-9
Little Denver Jake Draw—valley WY-8
Little Depoe Creek OR-9
Little Depot Creek—stream OR-9
Little Derby Creek—stream AK-9
Little Derrick Lake—lake WA-9
Little Derrieusseaux Creek—stream AR-4
Little Deschutes Campground—park OR-9
Little Deschutes River—stream OR-9
Little Deschutes River—stream WA-9
Little Desert—flat UT-8
Little Desert—plain CA-9
Little Desert—plain UT-8
Little Devil Bayou—bay TX-5
Little Devil Creek IA-7
Little Devil Creek—stream CO-8
Little Devil Creek—stream MI-6
Little Devil Creek—stream WV-2
Little Devil Cut—canal LA-4
Little Devilhole Creek—stream WV-2
Little Devil Hole Run—stream WV-2
Little Devil Lake—lake AK-9
Little Devil Lake—lake WI-6
Little Devil Peak—summit NV-8
Little Devil Peak—summit WA-9
Little Devils Basin Creek WY-8
Little Devils Basin Creek—stream WY-8
Little Devils Canyon—valley CA-9
Little Devils Canyon—valley OR-9
Little Devils Garden—swamp FL-3
Little Devils Hole—basin UT-8
Little Devils Hollow—valley TX-5
Little Devil's Island MD-2
Little Devils Lake WI-6
Little Devils Lake—lake MN-6
Little Devils Mtn—summit CA-9
Little Devils River—stream TX-5
Little Devils Stairs—valley VA-3
Little Devils Stairs Trail—trail VA-3
Little Devils Table—summit NV-8
Little Devil Stairs VA-3
Little Devils Teeth Rapids—rapids ID-8
Little Devils Tower—pillar SD-7
Little Devils Track River MN-6
Little Devil Track River—stream MN-6
Little Devil Wash—stream CA-9
Little Dew Lake—lake MN-6
Little Diameter—summit NY-2
Little Diamond Bar Lake—lake NE-7
Little Diamond Brook—stream NJ-2
Little Diamond Creek—stream AZ-5
Little Diamond Creek—stream UT-8
Little Diamond Fork UT-8
Little Diamond Island ME-1
Little Diamond Island—island ME-1
Little Diamond Island Landing—locale ME-1
Little Diamond Lake—lake MN-6
Little Diamond Pond—lake NH-1
Little Diamond Pond—lake NY-2
Little Diamond Rim—ridge AZ-5
Little Diamond Windmill—locale TX-5
Little Diana Slough—stream GA-3
Little Diann Lake—lake MN-6
Little Dice Branch—stream AL-4
Little Dickey Creek—stream AL-4
Little Dickinson Creek—stream WY-8
Little Dick Lake—lake MN-6
Little Dick Lake—lake WA-9
Little Dick Mine—mine CO-8
Little Dicks Bottom—bend UT-8
Little Dick Windmill—locale TX-5
Little Difficult Creek—stream KY-4
Little Difficult Run—stream VA-3
Little Digger Mtn—summit OR-9
Little Dimmick Pond—lake ME-1
Little Dinah Pond—swamp TX-5
Little Dingley Pond—lake ME-1
Little Dinner Lake—lake MN-6
Little Diomede (Diomede)—other AK-9
Little Diomede Island—island AK-9
Little Dismal Creek—stream AL-4
Little Dismal Creek—stream TN-4
Little Dismal Swamp—swamp NC-3
Little Dispatch Creek—gut FL-3
Little Ditch—canal (3) IN-6
Little Ditch—canal UT-8
Little Ditch—channel DE-2
Little Ditch Creek—stream ID-8
Little Ditch Lake—lake KY-4
Little Ditch No 3—canal AR-4
Little Ditch Pond—lake FL-3
Little Ditney Hill—summit IN-6
Little Divide Lake—lake WY-8
Little Dividing Ridge—ridge TN-4
**Little Dixi**—pop pl KY-4
**Little Dixie**—pop pl (2) AR-4
**Little Dixie**—pop pl KY-4
Little Dixie Creek—stream AK-9
Little Dixie Lake—reservoir MO-7
Little Dixie State Wildlife Area MO-7
Little Dixie State Wildlife Mngmt Area—park MO-7
Little Dixie Wash—stream CA-9
Little Dixon Creek—stream AL-4
Little Dixon Lake—lake AR-4
Little Dixon Lake—lake MN-6
Little Dix Windmill—locale NM-5
Little Dochet Island—island ME-1
Little Doctor Creek—stream GA-3
Little Doctors Bayou—stream LA-4
Little Doctor Seminole Village—locale FL-3
Little Dodd Spring—spring CA-9
Little Dodge Pond—lake CT-1
Little Dodling Hill—summit ME-1
Little Doe—locale TN-4
Little Doe Baptist Church TN-4
Little Doe Campground—locale CA-9
Little Doe Ch—church TN-4
Little Doe Creek—stream KY-4
Little Doe Creek—stream NC-3
Little Doe Creek—stream OR-9
Little Doe Hill—summit VA-3
Little Doe Mine—mine OR-9
Little Doe Post Office (historical)—building TN-4
Little Doe Ridge—ridge CA-9
Little Doe River—stream TN-4
Little Doe River Ch—church TN-4
Little Doerr Lake—lake MI-6
Little Doe Run—stream IN-6
Little Doe Run—stream VA-3
Little Dog Branch—stream KY-4
Little Dog Canyon—valley (2) NM-5
Little Dog Canyon—valley UT-8
Little Dog Cem—cemetery SD-7
Little Dog Creek—stream CA-9
Little Dog Creek—stream KY-4
Little Dog Creek—stream MT-8
Little Dog Creek—stream OK-5
Little Dog Creek—stream OR-9
Little Dog Creek—stream SD-7
Little Dog Creek—stream WY-8
Little Dog Dam—dam SD-7
Little Dog Draw—valley SD-7
Little Doggie Canyon—valley UT-8
Little Doggie Spring—spring UT-8
Little Dogie Canyon UT-8
Little Dogie Tank—reservoir AZ-5
Little Dog Lake—lake UT-8
Little Dog Mtn—summit MT-8
Little Dog Run—stream PA-2
Little Dog Run—stream WV-2
Little Dog Slaughter Creek—stream KY-4
Little Dog Spring—spring OR-9
Little Dog Spring Creek—stream SD-7
Little Dog Valley—valley (2) UT-8
Little Dog Valley Peak—summit UT-8
Little Dogwood Lake—reservoir MO-7
Little Dogwood Run—stream PA-2
Little Dollar Creek—stream AK-9
Little Dollar Hide Creek—stream IN-6
Little Dollar Lake MI-6
Little Dollar Lake—lake MI-6
Little Dollie Tunnel—mine UT-8
Little Dolly Bay—bay FL-3
Little Dolores River CO-8
Little Dolores River—stream CO-8
Little Dolores River—stream UT-8
Little Dome—other AK-9
Little Dome—summit CO-8
Little Dome—summit MA-1
Little Dome—summit WY-8
Little Dome Creek—stream (2) AK-9
Little Dome Rock—pillar OR-9
Little Dominguez Creek—stream CO-8
Little Donahue Creek—stream MT-8
Little Donahue Lake—lake (2) WI-6
Little Doney Hollow—valley OH-6
Little Don Island—island GA-3
Little Donkey Flat—flat UT-8
Little Dooley Creek—stream CA-9
Little Door Creek—stream WI-6
Little Doris Lake—lake CA-9
Little Dorrell Creek—stream VA-3
Little Dosier Creek—stream TX-5
Little Dosier Slough—bay TX-5
Little Doty Branch—stream KY-4
Little Double—summit TN-4
Little Double Branch—stream SC-3
Little Double Branch—stream TN-4
Little Double Branch—stream VA-3
Little Double Bridges Creek—stream AL-4
Little Double Creek—stream AL-4
Little Double Creek—stream KY-4
Little Double Creek—stream MS-4
Little Double Island WA-9
Little Double Lakes—lake GA-3
Little Doubles—summit VA-3
Little Doubles Branch—stream KY-4
Little Doubtful Canyon—valley AZ-5
Little Doubtful Canyon—valley NM-5
Little Dove Ch—church (3) KY-4
Little Dove Ch—church VA-3
Little Dove Ch—church WV-2
Little Dove Creek—stream GA-3
Little Dragon—ridge AZ-5
Little Dragon Mountains—summit AZ-5
Little Dragoons AZ-5
Little Dram Branch—stream FL-3
Little Dram Island—island ME-1
Little Draw MT-8
Little Draw—valley OR-9
Little Draw—valley TX-5
Little Draw—valley (2) WY-8
Little Draw Rsvr—reservoir ID-8
Little Draw Tank—reservoir AZ-5
Little Dresden Island—island IL-6
Little Driftwood Creek—stream KS-7
Little Driftwood Creek—stream OK-5
Little Dripping Spring—spring CO-8
Little Drisko Island—island ME-1
Little Drum Creek—bay NC-3
Little Drum Creek—stream AL-4
Little Drum Creek—stream OK-5
Little Drum Lake—lake MN-6
Little Drum Mtns—range UT-8
Little Drum Pass—gap UT-8
Little Drum Rsvr—reservoir UT-8
Little Drum Spring—spring UT-8
Little Drum Well—well UT-8
Little Dry Branch—stream TN-4
Little Dry Branch—stream TX-5
Little Dry Brushy Creek—stream TX-5
Little Dry Canyon—valley AZ-5
Little Dry Canyon—valley ID-8
Little Dry Canyon—valley (2) NV-8
Little Dry Cove—valley VA-3
Little Dry Creek OR-9
Little Dry Creek WY-8
Little Dry Creek—stream (4) AL-4
Little Dry Creek—stream AR-4
Little Dry Creek—stream (9) CA-9
Little Dry Creek—stream (5) CO-8
Little Dry Creek—stream FL-3
Little Dry Creek—stream (2) GA-3
Little Dry Creek—stream ID-8
Little Dry Creek—stream (3) LA-4
Little Dry Creek—stream (3) MS-4
Little Dry Creek—stream (2) MO-7
Little Dry Creek—stream (2) MT-8
Little Dry Creek—stream NM-5
Little Dry Creek—stream NC-3
Little Dry Creek—stream (2) OK-5
Little Dry Creek—stream (3) OR-9
Little Dry Creek—stream (4) TN-4
Little Dry Creek—stream (4) TX-5
Little Dry Creek—stream (8) WY-8
Little Dry Elk Creek—stream TN-4
Little Dry Fork—stream (2) IL-6
Little Dry Fork—stream KY-4
Little Dry Fork—stream (2) MO-7
Little Dry Frio Creek—stream TX-5
Little Dry Gulch—valley CO-8
Little Dry Gulch—valley (3) ID-8
Little Dry Hollow—valley PA-2
Little Dry Hollow—valley UT-8
Little Dry Island—island AK-9
Little Dry Lake—lake AZ-5
Little Dry Lake—lake CA-9
Little Dry Lake—lake CO-8
Little Dry Lake—lake MN-6
Little Dry Lake—lake UT-8
Little Dry Meadow—flat (2) CA-9
Little Dry Mesa—summit UT-8
Little Dry Muddy Spring—spring WY-8
Little Dry Prairie—area FL-3
Little Dry River—stream VA-3
Little Dry Run—stream TN-4
Little Dry Run—stream (2) VA-3
Little Dry Run Mtn—summit TN-4
Little Dry Run Valley—valley TN-4
Little Dry Valley—valley TX-5
Little Dry Valley—valley UT-8
Little Dry Vee Slope—flat WY-8
Little Dry Water Users Association Canal—canal MT-8
Little Dry Wood Creek—stream MO-7
Little Drywood Creek—stream WI-6
Little Duck—locale VA-3
Little Duck Branch—stream SC-3
Little Duck Branch—stream VA-3
Little Duck Cove—bay ME-1
Little Duck Creek AL-4
Little Duck Creek DE-2
Little Duck Creek—stream AL-4
Little Duck Creek—stream CO-8
Little Duck Creek—stream (2) IN-6
Little Duck Creek—stream KS-7
Little Duck Creek—stream MI-6
Little Duck Creek—stream NC-3
Little Duck Creek—stream OH-6
Little Duck Creek—stream SC-3
Little Duck Creek—stream (2) TX-5
Little Duck Island—island ME-1
Little Duck Key FL-3
Little Duck Key—island FL-3
Little Duck Lake MI-6
Little Duck Lake—lake CA-9
Little Duck Lake—lake MI-6
Little Duck Pond—lake (3) ME-1
Little Duck Pond—lake MA-1
Little Duck Pond—lake (2) NY-2
Little Duck River—stream TN-4
Little Duck Roost—swamp AL-4
Little Duck Slough CA-9
Little Duck Well—well TX-5
Little Dudley Creek—stream TN-4
Little Duffau Creek—stream TX-5
Little Duffy Lake—lake OR-9
Little Dugan Lake—lake WI-6
Little Dugdemona Creek LA-4
Little Dugdemona River—stream LA-4
Little Dugger Creek—stream NC-3
Little Dugger Mtn—summit NC-3
Little Dugout Creek—stream IL-6
Little Duke Creek—stream MD-2
Little Dukes Pond—lake GA-3
Little Dumb Brook—stream ME-1
Little Dummy Lake—lake WI-6
Little Dump Ch (abandoned)—church MO-7
Little Duncan Bay—bay AK-9
Little Duncan Canyon—valley CA-9
Little Duncan Draw—valley TX-5
Little Duncan Mtn—summit UT-8
Little Duncan Ridge—ridge GA-3
Little Duncan Run—stream OH-6
Little Dung Thorofare—channel NJ-2
Little Dunham Lake—lake WI-6
Little Dunkard Mill Run—stream WV-2
Little Dunn Ch—church TX-5
Little Dunn Creek—stream FL-3
Little Dunns Lake—lake GA-3
Little Durbin Creek—stream SC-3
Little Dutch KS-7
Little Dutch Canyon—valley OR-9
Little Dutch Creek—stream CO-8
Little Dutch Creek—stream KS-7
Little Dutch Hollow—valley UT-8
Little Dutchman Creek—stream KY-4
Little Dutchman Creek—stream SC-3
Little Dutton Pond—lake ME-1
Little Dutton Spring—spring CO-8
Little Dwarf Lake MI-6
Little Dyer Mtn—summit CA-9
Little Dyer Pond—lake ME-1
Little Dyke Creek—stream CO-8
**Little Eagle**—pop pl SD-7
Little Eagle Branch IN-6
Little Eagle Campsite—locale ME-1
Little Eagle Ch—church KS-7
Little Eagle Chief Creek—stream OK-5
Little Eagle Creek KY-4
Little Eagle Creek OR-9
Little Eagle Creek—stream IL-6
Little Eagle Creek—stream (2) IN-6
Little Eagle Creek—stream IA-7
Little Eagle Creek—stream KY-4
Little Eagle Creek—stream MI-6
Little Eagle Creek—stream MT-8
Little Eagle Creek—stream OK-5
Little Eagle Creek—stream (2) OR-9
Little Eagle Creek—stream (2) TN-4
Little Eagle Creek—stream WI-6
Little Eagle Creek—stream WY-8
Little Eagle Creek Ch—church IN-6
Little Eagle Lake—lake AR-4
Little Eagle Lake—lake WA-9
Little Eagle Rock—pillar NM-5
Little Eagle Springs—spring WY-8
Little Eagleton Run—stream PA-2
Little Eagle Trail—trail OK-5
Little Ear Mtn—summit NM-5
**Little Earren**—pop pl TN-4
Little Ease NJ-2
Little Ease Creek—stream NC-3
Little Ease Run—stream NJ-2
**Little Easonburg**—pop pl NC-3
Little Eastanollee Creek—stream GA-3
Little Eastatoe Creek—stream SC-3
Little East Blue Creek OK-5
Little East Branch Cupsuptic River—stream ME-1
Little East Branch Huron River—stream MI-6
Little East Canyon Creek UT-8
Little East Creek—stream MN-6
Little Easter Marsh—swamp VA-3
Little East Fork OH-6
Little East Fork—stream AK-9
Little East Fork—stream (2) KY-4
Little East Fork—stream TN-4
Little East Fork—stream UT-8
Little East Fork Canyon Creek—stream CA-9
Little East Fork Elk Creek—stream ID-8
Little East Fork Emerald Creek—stream ID-8
Little East Fork Ohio Brush Creek—stream OH-6
Little East Fork Pigeon River—stream NC-3
Little East Fork Sch—school TN-4
Little East Fork Spring—spring AZ-5
Little East Fork Steamboat Creek—stream ID-8
Little East Fork Todds Fork OH-6
Little East Lake—lake ME-1
Little East Lake—lake MN-6
Little East Locust Creek—stream MO-7
Little East Neck—cape NY-2
Little East Pasture Well—well NM-5
Little East Pond—lake NH-1
Little East Pond Brook—stream NH-1
Little East Pond Trail—trail NH-1
Little East Sandy Creek—stream PA-2
Little East Tank—reservoir NM-5
Little Eaton Island—island ME-1
**Little Eau Claire**—pop pl WI-6
Little Eau Claire River—stream WI-6
Little Eau Plaine River WI-6
Little Eau Pleine Flowage—lake WI-6
Little Eau Pleine River—stream WI-6
Little Ebenezer Ch—church GA-3
Little Ebenezer Creek—stream GA-3
Little Eberling Tank—reservoir AZ-5
Little Ebhorse Stream—stream ME-1
Little Eccles Canyon—valley UT-8
Little Echeconnee Creek—stream GA-3
Little Echo Canyon—valley NV-8
Little Echo Creek—stream CO-8
Little Echo Lake—lake CO-8
Little Echo Lake—lake ME-1
Little Econlockhatchee River—stream FL-3
Little Eddy—lake TX-5
Little Eddy Lake—lake LA-4
Little Eddy Lake—lake MS-4
Little Eden Brook—stream NY-2
Little Edge Mountain VA-3
Little Edisto—locale SC-3
Little Edisto Island—island SC-3
Little Edson Butte—summit OR-9
Little Egg Creek—stream TX-5
Little Egg Harbor—bay NJ-2
Little Egg Harbor Bay NJ-2
Little Egg Harbor (Township of)—civ div NJ-2
Little Egg Harbour NJ-2
Little Egging Beach—beach MD-2
Little Egg Inlet—bay NJ-2
Little Egg Island—island AK-9
Little Egg Island—island GA-3
Little Egg Island—island MA-1
Little Egg Lake—lake CA-9
Little Egg Marsh—swamp NY-2
Little Egg Rock MA-1
Little Egg Rock—island ME-1
Little Egg Rock—rock MA-1
Little Egg Rock Shoals—bar ME-1
Little Egypt—flat UT-8
Little Egypt—locale NC-3
**Little Egypt**—pop pl MA-1
Little Egypt Baptist Ch—church IN-6
Little Egypt Creek—stream PA-2
Little Egypt Geologic Site—locale UT-8
Little Egypt Rsvr—reservoir MA-1
Little Egypt Valley—valley WA-9
Little Egypt Youth Camp—locale IL-6
Little Eightmile Canyon—valley ID-8
Little Eightmile Creek—stream ID-8
Little Eightmile Creek—stream OH-6
Little Eightmile Island—island AK-9
Little Eightmile Lake—lake WA-9
Little Elam Ch AL-4
Little Elam Ch—church AL-4
Little Elam Ch—church VA-3
Little Elam Lake—lake AR-4
Little Elbow Creek—stream MN-6
Little Elbow Lake—lake (2) MN-6
Little Elbow Lake State Park—park MN-6
Little Elbow Pond—reservoir TX-5
Little Elbow Run—stream WV-2
Little Elden Mtn—summit AZ-5
Little Elden Spring—spring AZ-5
Little Elder Creek—gut NJ-2
Little Elder Creek—stream OR-9
Little Elder Pond—lake MA-1
Little Eldorado Creek—stream (3) AK-9
Little Eldred Lake—lake MI-6
Little Electric Well—well AZ-5
Little Eligo Pond VT-1
Little Elizabeth River MA-1
**Little Elk**—pop pl PA-2
Little Elk Basin—basin CO-8
Little Elk Branch—stream KY-4
Little Elk Canyon—valley SD-7
Little Elk Ch—church AL-4
Little Elk Ch—church NC-3
Little Elk Ch—church TN-4
Little Elk Ch—church WV-2
Little Elk Chapel—church PA-2
Little Elk Corners PA-2
Little Elk Creek MT-8
Little Elk Creek TN-4
Little Elk Creek—stream (3) CO-8
Little Elk Creek—stream (5) ID-8
Little Elk Creek—stream IA-7
Little Elk Creek—stream KS-7
Little Elk Creek—stream KY-4
Little Elk Creek—stream MD-2
Little Elk Creek—stream MT-8
Little Elk Creek—stream NY-2
Little Elk Creek—stream (2) NC-3
Little Elk Creek—stream OK-5
Little Elk Creek—stream (3) OR-9
Little Elk Creek—stream (3) PA-2
Little Elk Creek—stream SD-7
Little Elk Creek—stream (2) TN-4
Little Elk Creek—stream UT-8
Little Elk Creek—stream WA-9
Little Elk Creek—stream (3) WV-2
Little Elk Creek—stream WI-6
Little Elk Creek—stream WY-8
Little Elk Creek Cem—cemetery WI-6
Little Elk Creek Ch—church WI-6
Little Elk Creek Sch—school WI-6
Little Elk Farm—hist pl MD-2
Little Elk Fork Creek TN-4
Little Elk Gulch—valley MT-8
Little Elkhart Creek—stream IN-6
Little Elkhart Creek—stream TX-5
Little Elkhart Lake—lake WI-6
Little Elkhart Lake Sch—school WI-6
Little Elkhart River IN-6
Little Elkhart River—stream IN-6
Little Elkhart River Ditch IN-6
Little Elkhart River Ditch—canal IN-6
Little elkhart River Dredge Ditch IN-6
Little Elkhead Creek CO-8
Little Elkhorn—locale WA-9
Little Elkhorn Bar—bar ID-8
Little Elkhorn Creek OR-9
Little Elkhorn Creek—stream ID-8
Little Elkhorn Creek—stream IA-7
Little Elkhorn Creek—stream KY-4
Little Elkhorn Creek—stream MO-7
Little Elkin Ch—church NC-3
Little Elkin Creek—stream NC-3
Little Elkin River NC-3
Little Elk Knob—summit NC-3
Little Elk Lake—lake CA-9
Little Elk Lake—lake MN-6
Little Elk Lake—lake (2) UT-8
Little Elk Lake—reservoir PA-2
Little Elk Lake Creek CA-9
Little Elk Lake Creek—stream CA-9
Little Elk Mtn—summit ID-8
Little Elk Mtn—summit NC-3
Little Elk Mtn—summit OR-9
Little Elk Park CO-8
Little Elk Park—flat CO-8
Little Elk Prairie—flat OR-9
Little Elk Ridge—ridge NC-3
Little Elk River MD-2
Little Elk River MN-6
Little Elk River PA-2
Little Elk River—stream MN-6
Little Elk River—stream MT-8
Little Elk River—stream WI-6
Little Elk Run—stream (2) PA-2
Little Elk Sch—school AL-4
Little Elk Sch—school TN-4
Little Elk Spring—spring KY-4
**Little Elk (Township of)**—pop pl MN-6
Little Ella Ch—church KY-4
Little Ellejoy Creek—stream TN-4
Little Ellen Hill—summit CO-8
Little Ellen Lake—lake FL-3
Little Ellie Creek—stream VA-3
Little Elligo Pond—lake VT-1
Little Elliott Mesa—summit UT-8
Little Elliott Ridge—ridge WV-2
Little Ellis Creek—stream WV-2
Little Ellis Mtn—summit NY-2
Little Ellis Pond—lake ME-1
Little Elm—locale TX-5
**Little Elm**—pop pl TX-5
Little Elm Cem—cemetery (2) TX-5
Little Elm Ch—church AR-4
Little Elm Creek SD-7
Little Elm Creek—stream KS-7
Little Elm Creek—stream OK-5
Little Elm Creek—stream (8) TX-5
Little Elmgrove Bayou—bay TX-5
Little Elm Lateral—canal IL-6
Little Elmore Pond—lake VT-1
Little Elm Pond—lake ME-1
Little Elm River—stream MI-6
Little Elsie Mine—mine CA-9
Little Emanuel Creek—stream SD-7
Little Embarras River—stream IL-6
Little Emerald Lake—lake CO-8
Little Emigrant Canyon—valley AZ-5
Little Emigrant Creek—stream OR-9
Little Emigrant Spring—spring OR-9
Little Emigration Canyon—valley UT-8
Little Emil Spring—swamp WI-6
Little Emily Creek—stream OR-9
**Little Emory**—pop pl TN-4
Little Emory Creek TN-4
Little Emory River—stream TN-4
Little Emorys River TN-4
Little Emuckfaw Creek—stream AL-4
Little Enchanted Pond—lake ME-1
Little Endicott Creek—stream NC-3
Little England—hist pl VA-3
Little England Chapel—hist pl VA-3
Little English Gulch—valley CO-8
Little Equinox—summit VT-1
Little Equinunk Creek—stream PA-2
Little Escambia Baptist Church AL-4
Little Escambia Cem—cemetery AL-4
Little Escambia Ch—church AL-4
Little Escambia Creek—stream AL-4
Little Escambia Creek—stream FL-3
Little Escutarsis Pond ME-1
Little Escutasis Pond ME-1
Little Escutassis Pond ME-1
Little Eshquagama Lake MN-6
Little Eskquagama Lake MN-6
Little Eskutarsis Pond ME-1
Little Eskutassis Pond—lake ME-1
Little Esquagamah Lake MN-6
Little Esquagama Lake—lake MN-6
Little E Tank—reservoir AZ-5
Little Ethel Ch—church KY-4
Little Ettie Ch—church OH-6
Little Euchre Creek OR-9
Little Euchre Mtn—summit OR-9
Little Eucutta Creek—stream MS-4
Little Eureka Spring—spring AZ-5
Little Eva Mine—mine UT-8
Little Evans Gulch—valley CO-8
Little Eve Creek—bay NC-3
Little Everglades—swamp FL-3
Little Ezekial Church AL-4
Little Ezion Ch—church LA-4
Little Fabius River—stream MO-7
Little Fabuler Creek AR-4
Little Fabuler Creek LA-4
Little Fabuler Slough AR-4
Little Fabuler Slough LA-4
Little Factory Creek—stream OH-6
Little Fairmont Island—island AK-9
Little Fair River—stream MS-4
Little Fall Branch—stream NC-3
Little Fall Branch—stream TN-4
Little Fall Creek—stream (3) ID-8
Little Fall Creek—stream NC-3
Little Fall Creek—stream (2) OR-9
Little Fall Creek—stream PA-2
Little Fall Creek—stream TX-5
Little Fall Creek—stream VA-3
Little Fall Creek—stream (2) WY-8
Little Falling Creek—stream GA-3
Little Falling River VA-3
Little Falling River—stream VA-3
Little Falling Rock Branch—stream KY-4
Little Falling Water Creek—stream TN-4
Little Falling Waters Creek TN-4
Little Fall Rock Branch—stream TN-4
Little Falls ME-1
Little Falls MN-6
Littlefalls NY-2
Little Falls WI-6
Little Falls—falls (2) AL-4
Little Falls—falls DC-2
Little Falls—falls ID-8
Little Falls—falls (5) ME-1
Little Falls—falls NV-8
Little Falls—falls (3) NC-3
Little Falls—falls (2) OR-9
Little Falls—falls PA-2
Little Falls—falls TN-4
Little Falls—falls TX-5
Little Falls—falls (2) WI-6
Little Falls—locale WA-9
**Little Falls**—pop pl ME-1
**Little Falls**—pop pl MN-6
**Little Falls**—pop pl NJ-2
**Little Falls**—pop pl NY-2
**Little Falls**—pop pl VA-3
**Little Falls**—pop pl WV-2
**Little Falls**—pop pl WI-6
Little Falls—stream MD-2
Little Falls—stream PA-2
Little Falls Branch—stream MD-2
Little Falls Brook MA-1
Little Falls Brook—stream ME-1
Little Falls Carnegie Library—hist pl MN-6
Little Falls Cem—cemetery WA-9
Little Falls Creek—stream AK-9
Little Falls Creek—stream CA-9
Little Falls Creek—stream PA-2

Little Falls Creek—stream (2) ... SC-3
Little Falls Creek—stream ... WA-9
Little Falls Dam—dam ... MD-2
Little Falls Flowage ... WI-6
Little Falls Hydroelectric Power Plant—hist pl ... WA-9
Little Falls Lake—reservoir ... WI-6
Little Falls Light—locale ... WV-2
Little Falls Meetinghouse—hist pl ... MD-2
Little Falls Park—park ... MD-2
Little Falls Pond ... WI-6
Little Falls Pond—lake ... ME-1
Little Falls River ... ME-1
Little Falls Run—stream ... VA-3
Little Falls Spring—spring ... CA-9
Little Falls (sta.)—uninc pl ... NJ-2
Little Falls Stream ... ME-1
**Little Falls (Town of)**—pop pl ... NY-2
**Little Falls (Town of)**—pop pl ... WI-6
Little Falls (Township of)—civ div ... MN-6
**Little Falls (Township of)**—pop pl ... NJ-2
**Little Falls (Trailer Park)**—pop pl ... NY-2
Little False Bayou ... LA-4
Little False River—gut ... LA-4
Little Family Cem—cemetery ... TX-5
Little Family Church, The—church ... OH-6
Little Fandango—ridge ... NV-8
Little Fannegusha Creek—stream ... MS-4
Little Fanney Mine—mine ... CO-8
Little Fannie Mine—mine ... NM-5
Little Faras Run—stream ... AR-4
Little Fargo Cem—cemetery ... ND-7
Little Farm Creek Canal—canal ... UT-8
Little Farm Pond—lake ... MA-1
**Little Farms**—pop pl ... LA-4
**Little Farms**—pop pl ... OH-6
Little Farms (census name River Ridge)—other ... LA-4
Little Far Mtn—summit ... NY-2
Little Farnsworth Peak Heliport—airport ... UT-8
Littlefatche (historical)—locale ... AL-4
Little Fat Creek—stream ... WV-2
Little Faun—bar ... MA-1
Little Fawn Canyon—valley ... CA-9
Little Fawn Picnic Area—park ... OR-9
Little Fawn River ... IN-6
Little Fawn River ... MI-6
Little Fawn River—stream ... IN-6
Little Fawn Spring—spring ... OR-9
Little Fay Mtn—summit ... NY-2
Little Federal Run—stream ... PA-2
Little Feeding Ground Lake—lake ... MI-6
Little Felix Canyon—valley ... NM-5
Little Felix Tank—reservoir ... NM-5
Little Female Pond—lake ... ME-1
Little Femme Osage Creek—stream ... MO-7
Little Ferguson Brook—stream ... ME-1
Little Ferguson Creek—stream ... SC-3
Little Fern Cave—cave ... AL-4
Little Ferris Creek—stream ... OR-9
Little Ferry—airport ... NJ-2
**Little Ferry**—pop pl ... NJ-2
Little Ferry Canyon—valley ... OR-9
Little Ferry Creek—stream ... CA-9
Little Ferry Junction—uninc pl ... NJ-2
Little Ferry Landing—locale ... VA-3
Little Ferry (sta.)—uninc pl ... NJ-2
Little Fiddle Creek—stream ... CA-9
Little Fiddler—summit ... ID-8
Little Fiddler Creek—stream ... ID-8
Little Fiddler Flat—flat ... ID-8
Little Fiddlers Island—island ... GA-3
Littlefield ... AZ-5
Littlefield ... ME-1
Littlefield—locale ... NC-3
**Littlefield**—pop pl ... AZ-5
**Littlefield**—pop pl ... NH-1
**Littlefield**—pop pl ... TX-5
Littlefield, Inez and Davis, Bea, House—hist pl ... AZ-5
Littlefield Bend—bend ... TX-5
Littlefield Branch—stream ... KY-4
Littlefield Branch—stream ... TN-4
Littlefield Brook—stream (2) ... ME-1
Littlefield Brook—stream ... NH-1
Littlefield (CCD)—cens area ... TX-5
Littlefield Cem—cemetery ... IL-6
Littlefield Cem—cemetery (2) ... ME-1
Littlefield Cem—cemetery ... NE-7
Little Field Cem—cemetery ... NC-3
Littlefield Cem—cemetery ... OR-9
Littlefield Cem—cemetery ... TX-5
Littlefield Ch—church ... MI-6
Little Field Ch—church ... NC-3
Littlefield-Chase Farmstead—hist pl ... ME-1
Littlefield Corner ... ME-1
**Littlefield Corner**—pop pl ... ME-1
Littlefield Country Club—other ... TX-5
Littlefield Cove—bay ... ME-1
Little Field Creek ... MI-6
Littlefield Creek—stream (2) ... CA-9
Littlefield Creek—stream ... WY-8
Littlefield Ditch—canal ... OR-9
Little Field Draw—valley ... CO-8
Littlefield-Dustin Farm—hist pl ... ME-1
Little Fielder Draw—valley ... TX-5
Littlefield Hill—summit ... NH-1
Little Field Hollow—valley ... MO-7
Littlefield Homestead—hist pl ... ME-1
Littlefield House—hist pl ... TX-5
Littlefield HS—school ... NC-3
Little Field Island ... AZ-5
Littlefield-Keeping House—hist pl ... ME-1
Littlefield Lake—lake (2) ... MI-6
Littlefield Mills ... ME-1
Littlefield Pond—lake (2) ... ME-1
Littlefield Ridge—ridge ... VA-3
Littlefield River—stream ... ME-1
Littlefield-Roberts House—hist pl ... MA-1
Littlefield Rsvr—reservoir ... CA-9
Littlefield Rsvr—reservoir ... OR-9
Littlefield Sch—school ... IL-6
Littlefield (Site)—locale ... ID-8
Littlefields Pond—lake ... MA-1
Littlefield Spring—spring ... NV-8
Littlefield Spring—spring ... OR-9
Little Field Tank—reservoir ... NM-5
Littlefield Tavern—hist pl ... ME-1
**Littlefield (Township of)**—pop pl ... MI-6
Little Field Windmill—locale ... TX-5

Little Fiery Gizzard Creek—stream ... TN-4
Little Fightingtown Creek—stream ... GA-3
Little Fill Hollow—valley ... PA-2
Little Fine Gold Creek—stream ... CA-9
Little Finger—summit ... CO-8
Little Finger Lake ... MI-6
Little Finger Lake—lake ... OR-9
Little Finger Ridge—ridge ... MT-8
Little Finley Creek—stream ... CA-9
Little Finley Creek—stream ... MO-7
Little Fir Cem—cemetery (2) ... AR-4
Little Fir Creek—stream ... ID-8
Little Fir Creek—stream ... OR-9
Little Firecoal Branch—stream ... KY-4
Little Firehole Canyon—valley ... WY-8
Little Firehole Meadows—flat ... WY-8
Little Firehole River—stream ... WY-8
Little Firescald Knob—summit ... NC-3
Little Firescald Knob—summit ... TN-4
Little Fires Creek—stream ... NC-3
Little Fir Landing—locale ... AR-4
Little First Broad River—stream ... NC-3
Little Fish Canyon—valley ... AZ-5
Little Fish Creek ... NY-2
Little Fish Creek—stream ... AK-9
Little Fish Creek—stream ... CO-8
Little Fish Creek—stream (2) ... ID-8
Little Fish Creek—stream (2) ... MT-8
Little Fish Creek—stream ... NY-2
Little Fish Creek—stream ... OR-9
Little Fish Creek—stream ... WY-8
Little Fish Creek Ditch—canal ... CO-8
Little Fish Creek Pond—lake ... NY-2
Little Fishdam River—stream ... MI-6
Little Fisher Highway—channel ... MI-6
Little Fisher Pond—lake ... ME-1
Little Fisher River—stream ... NC-3
Little Fishers Peak Mesa—summit ... CO-8
Little Fishhawk Creek—stream ... FL-3
Little Fishhawk Creek—stream ... OR-9
Little Fishhawk Mtn—summit ... NC-3
Little Fishing Bay—bay ... NC-3
Little Fishing Creek—stream ... GA-3
Little Fishing Creek—stream ... MD-2
Little Fishing Creek—stream ... NC-3
Little Fishing Creek—stream (2) ... PA-2
Little Fishing Creek—stream ... WV-2
Little Fishing Point—cape ... NC-3
Little Fishing Rock—bar ... ME-1
Little Fish Lake ... NV-8
Little Fish Lake—lake ... FL-3
Little Fish Lake—lake ... MI-6
Little Fish Lake—lake ... MT-8
Little Fish Lake—lake ... NV-8
Little Fish Lake—lake ... OR-9
Little Fish Lake—lake (2) ... WA-9
Little Fish Lake Ranch—locale ... NV-8
Little Fish Lake Valley—valley ... NV-8
Little Fish Pond—lake (2) ... ME-1
Little Fish Pond—lake (2) ... NY-2
Little Fish Ponds—lake ... ME-1
Little Fish River ... NC-3
Little Fish Shelter—locale ... WA-9
Little Fishtrap—bay ... WA-9
Little Fish Trap Branch—stream ... KY-4
Little Fishtrap Creek—stream ... OR-9
Little Fish Trap Lake—lake ... MN-6
Little Fishweir Creek—stream ... FL-3
Little Five—lake ... NY-2
Little Five Lakes—lake ... CA-9
Little Five Mile Creek ... NV-8
Little Fivemile Creek—stream ... ID-8
Little Fivemile Creek—stream ... OK-5
Little Fivemile Creek—stream ... TX-5
Little Fivemile Creek—stream ... WV-2
Little Five Mile Pond ... MA-1
Little Five Mile Pond—lake ... MA-1
Little Five Points—locale ... GA-3
Little Flag Lake—lake ... LA-4
Little Flag Lake—lake ... OK-5
Little Flanders Field Cem—cemetery ... AL-4
Little Flat—flat ... ID-8
Little Flat—flat ... PA-2
Little Flat—flat ... SD-7
Little Flat—flat ... UT-8
Little Flat Branch—stream ... AR-4
Littleflat Branch—stream ... NC-3
Little Flat Branch—stream ... TX-5
Little Flat Brook—stream ... NJ-2
Little Flat Camp Branch—stream ... GA-3
Little Flat Canyon—valley ... ID-8
Little Flat Coulee—valley ... MT-8
Little Flat Creek ... AL-4
Little Flat Creek ... TN-4
Little Flat Creek—stream ... AR-4
Little Flat Creek—stream ... GA-3
Little Flat Creek—stream ... ID-8
Little Flat Creek—stream ... IN-6
Little Flat Creek—stream (3) ... KY-4
Little Flat Creek—stream ... MO-7
Little Flat Creek—stream ... NC-3
Little Flat Creek—stream (3) ... TN-4
Little Flat Creek Baptist Church ... TN-4
Little Flat Creek Ch—church ... TN-4
Little Flat Fire Tower—tower ... PA-2
Little Flat Lake—lake ... IL-6
Little Flat Lake—lake ... MN-6
Little Flat Lake—lake ... MS-4
Little Flat Lake Lookout Tower—locale ... MN-6
Little Flat Mtn—summit ... VA-3
Little Flat Pond ... MA-1
Little Flat River—stream ... LA-4
Little Flatrock Branch—stream ... TX-5
Little Flatrock Ch—church ... IN-6
Little Flat Rock Creek ... TX-5
Little Flatrock Creek—stream ... OH-6
Little Flat Rock Creek—stream ... SC-3
Little Flatrock Creek—stream ... TX-5
Little Flat Rock River ... IN-6
Little Flatrock River—stream ... IN-6
Little Flat Rsvr—reservoir ... OR-9
Little Flats—flat ... SD-7
Little Flat Top ... VA-3
Little Flattop—summit ... TX-5
Little Flat Top—summit (2) ... UT-8
Little Flattop—summit ... WY-8
Little Flattop Mountain ... WY-8
Little Flat Top Mtn ... VA-3
Little Flattop Mtn—summit ... TX-5
Little Flattop Mtn—summit ... WY-8

Little Flat Tops—summit ... CO-8
Little Flatty Creek—stream ... NC-3
Little Fletchers Lake—lake ... LA-4
Little Flint Branch—stream ... AL-4
Little Flint Creek—stream ... AR-4
Little Flint Creek—stream ... IN-6
Little Flint Creek—stream ... IA-7
Little Flint Mill Branch—stream ... TN-4
Little Flint Run—stream ... WV-2
Little Flock—locale (2) ... TX-5
**Little Flock**—pop pl ... AR-4
Little Flock Cem—cemetery (2) ... AL-4
Little Flock Cem—cemetery (2) ... AR-4
Little Flock Cem—cemetery ... GA-3
Little Flock Cem—cemetery ... IN-6
Little Flock Cem—cemetery ... MS-4
Little Flock Cem—cemetery ... TX-5
Little Flock Ch—church (2) ... AR-4
Little Flock Ch—church (2) ... FL-3
Little Flock Ch—church (2) ... GA-3
Little Flock Ch—church (2) ... IL-6
Little Flock Ch—church (2) ... IN-6
Little Flock Ch—church (6) ... KY-4
Little Flock Ch—church (2) ... LA-4
Little Flock Ch—church ... MS-4
Little Flock Ch—church ... MO-7
Little Flock Ch—church (2) ... OK-5
Little Flock Ch—church (7) ... TX-5
Little Flock Ch—church ... VA-3
Little Flock Ch—church ... WV-2
Little Flock Chapel—church ... IA-7
Little Flock Creek—stream ... TX-5
Little Flock Sch (abandoned)—school ... MO-7
Little Flock Sch (reduced usage)—school ... TX-5
Little Flora Creek—stream ... MO-7
Little Florida Mountains—other ... NM-5
Little Flounder Creek—gut ... FL-3
Little Flower Catholic Ch—church ... FL-3
Little Flower Cem—cemetery ... NE-7
Little Flower Cem—cemetery ... ND-7
Little Flower Ch—church ... IN-6
Little Flower Creek ... MS-4
Little Flower HS—school ... PA-2
Little Flower Manor—school ... PA-2
Little Flower Mission—church ... MN-6
Little Flower Sch—school ... AL-4
Little Flower Sch—school ... FL-3
Little Flower Sch—school ... IL-6
Little Flower Sch—school ... LA-4
Little Flower Sch—school (3) ... MD-2
Little Flower Sch—school ... NV-8
Little Flower Sch—school ... ND-7
Little Flower Sch—school ... OH-6
Little Flower Sch—school ... OK-5
Little Flower Sch—school ... TN-4
Little Flower Sch—school (2) ... TX-5
Little Floyd Lake—lake ... MN-6
Little Floyd River—stream ... IA-7
Little Floyd Sch—school ... MN-6
Little Flume Gulch—valley ... MT-8
Little Fluty Branch—stream ... KY-4
Little Fly Creek—stream ... KS-7
Little Fly Creek—stream ... MO-7
Little Fly Creek—stream ... OR-9
Little Fly Creek—stream ... WA-9
Little Flying H Lake—lake ... NM-5
Little Flying Point—cape ... ME-1
Little Flys Creek ... PA-2
Little Fodder Stack ... TN-4
Little Fodderstack—summit (2) ... TN-4
Little Fodderstack Mtn—summit ... NC-3
Little Foley Pond—lake ... ME-1
Little Folks Sch—school ... TX-5
Little Folland Creek—stream ... OR-9
Little Folly Creek ... VA-3
Little Fool Creek—stream ... AR-4
Little Forbush Creek—stream ... NC-3
Little Fordoche Bayou—stream ... LA-4
Little Fordoche Creek—stream ... LA-4
Little Fordway Mtn—summit ... NY-2
Little Forest Ch—church ... VA-3
Little Forest Creek—stream ... UT-8
Little Forest Park—park ... DC-2
Little Fork ... NC-3
Little Fork ... OR-9
Little Fork ... TN-4
Little Fork ... WV-2
Little Fork—gut ... DE-2
**Little Fork**—pop pl ... KY-4
**Littlefork**—pop pl ... MN-6
Little Fork—stream (5) ... KY-4
Little Fork—stream (4) ... NC-3
Little Fork—stream ... VA-3
Little Fork—stream (5) ... WV-2
Little Fork Bayou—gut ... LA-4
Little Fork Big Creek ... UT-8
Little Fork Canoe Creek—stream ... KY-4
Littlefork Cem—cemetery ... MN-6
Little Fork Ch—church ... KY-4
Little Fork Ch—church ... MN-6
Little Fork Ch—church (2) ... VA-3
Little Fork Church—hist pl ... VA-3
Little Fork Creek ... IN-6
Little Fork Creek—stream ... NC-3
Little Fork Creek—stream ... SC-3
Little Fork Draft—valley ... PA-2
Little Fork Duck River ... TN-4
Little Forked Lake—lake ... NY-2
Little Forked Run—stream ... OH-6
Little Forker Tank—reservoir ... TX-5
Little Fork Flat Fork ... TN-4
Little Fork Hill—summit ... PA-2
Little Fork Lake—lake ... WI-6
Little Fork Lick Creek—stream ... KY-4
Little Fork Little Chilliwack River—stream ... WA-9
Little Fork Little Sandy River—stream ... KY-4
Little Fork Mtn—summit ... NC-3
Little Fork Mtn—summit (3) ... TN-4
Little Fork Of Rainy River ... MN-6
Little Fork Owyhee River ... ID-8
Little Fork Owyhee River ... NV-8
Little Fork Ridge ... NC-3
Little Fork Ridge—ridge ... KY-4
Little Fork Ridge—ridge (2) ... NC-3
Little Fork Ridge—ridge ... VA-3
Little Fork River ... MN-6
Little Fork River—stream ... MN-6
Little Fork Sch—school ... KY-4
little Fork South Fork Owyhee River ... ID-8

Little Fork South Fork Owyhee River ... NV-8
Little Fork Spring—spring ... ID-8
Little Fork Third Fork Rock Creek—stream ... ID-8
Little Fork Trail—trail ... WV-2
Little Fork Willow Creek—stream ... NV-8
Little Fort Crawford Creek—stream ... FL-3
Little Fort Hill—summit ... NY-2
Little Fort Island—island ... AK-9
Little Fort Island—island ... ME-1
Little Fort Rec Area—park ... VA-3
Little Fort Sch—school ... IL-6
Little Fort Trail—trail ... VA-3
Little Fort Valley—basin ... VA-3
Little Fort Valley—valley ... VA-3
Little Fortyeight Creek—stream ... TN-4
Little Fortyfour Spring—spring ... AZ-5
Little Fossil Creek—stream ... TX-5
Little Foster Creek—stream ... NC-3
Little Foundation Creek—stream ... CO-8
Little Fountain—locale ... VI-3
Little Fountain Creek—stream ... CO-8
Little Fourche a Renault—stream ... MO-7
Little Fourche Creek—stream ... AR-4
Little Fourche Maline—stream ... OK-5
Little Four Mile Creek ... IN-6
Little Four Mile Creek ... OH-6
Little Fourmile Creek—stream ... CO-8
Little Four Mile Creek—stream ... IN-6
Little Fourmile Creek—stream ... IA-7
Little Four Mile Creek—stream (2) ... OH-6
Little Fourmile Creek—stream ... TN-4
Little Fourmile Draw—valley ... CO-8
Little Fourmile Run—stream ... PA-2
Little Fourteen, Lake—lake ... MN-6
Little Fourth Of July Creek—stream ... ID-8
Little Fourty Creek—stream ... AL-4
Little Fowler Lake—lake ... MN-6
Little Fowler Pond—lake (2) ... ME-1
Little Fox Creek—stream ... AK-9
Little Fox Creek—stream ... IL-6
Little Fox Creek—stream ... MO-7
Little Fox Creek—stream ... NY-2
Little Fox Creek—stream (2) ... VA-3
Little Fox Island—island ... IL-6
Little Fox Island—island ... VA-3
Little Fox Islands ... VA-3
Little Fox Lake—lake ... FL-3
Little Fox Lake—reservoir ... IN-6
Little Fox Lake—reservoir ... OH-6
Little Fox Lake Dam—dam ... IN-6
Little Fox River—stream ... IL-6
Little Fox River*—stream ... IA-7
Little Fox River—stream ... MI-6
Little Fox River—stream ... MO-7
Little Fox Sch—school ... MO-7
Little Fox Sch—school (2) ... VA-3
**Little France**—pop pl ... NY-2
Little France Cem—cemetery ... NY-2
Little Franklin Creek—stream ... OR-9
Little Franklin Ledge—bar ... ME-1
Little Franks—locale ... AZ-5
Little Franks Well—well ... AZ-5
Little Frazier Bayou—stream ... MS-4
Little Frazier Lake—lake ... OR-9
Little Fred Burr Lake—lake ... MT-8
Little Fred Hills ... MT-8
Little Fredonyer—summit (2) ... CA-9
Little Freeborn Lake—lake ... MN-6
Little Freeman Tank—reservoir ... AZ-5
Little Freezeout—gap ... ID-8
Little French Creek—stream ... CA-9
Little French Creek—stream (2) ... ID-8
Little French Creek—stream ... WA-9
Little French Gulch—valley (2) ... CO-8
Little French Island—island ... ME-1
Little Frenchman Coulee—valley ... MT-8
Little Fresh Creek ... MD-2
Little Fresh Kills—stream ... NY-2
Little Fresh Pond—lake ... NY-2
Little Fresh Water Branch—stream ... NC-3
Little Freshwater Creek—stream ... CA-9
Little Frey Creek—stream ... CA-9
Little Friar—summit ... VA-3
Little Friess Lake—lake ... WI-6
Little Frisco Mtns—summit ... UT-8
Little Frog Ague Creek—stream ... AL-4
Little Frog Bayou—stream ... AR-4
Little Frog Creek—stream ... WI-6
Little Frog Lake—lake ... ID-8
Little Frog Lake—lake ... WI-6
Little Frog Mtn—summit ... TN-4
Little Frost Lake—lake ... MI-6
Little Frost Pond—lake ... ME-1
Little Froze Creek—stream ... CO-8
Little Frozen Creek—stream ... KY-4
Little Frozen Knob—summit ... GA-3
Little Fruin Creek—stream ... OR-9
Little Fryingpan Canyon—valley ... CA-9
Little Fryingpan Valley—basin ... TX-5
Little Fudges Creek—stream ... WV-2
Little Fuller Brook—stream ... NY-2
Little Fumee Lake—lake ... MI-6
Little Gabbro Lake—reservoir ... MN-6
Little Gadwell Windmill—locale ... AZ-5
Little Gaines Creek—stream ... MS-4
Little Galena Gulch—valley ... MT-8
Little Galilee Ch—church ... IL-6
Little Gallagher Creek—stream ... ID-8
Little Gallberry Bay—swamp ... NC-3
Little Gallberry Bay (Carolina Bay)—swamp ... NC-3
Little Gallilee Pond—reservoir ... MA-1
Little Gallinas Canyon—valley ... NM-5
Little Galloo Island—island ... NY-2
Little Galum Creek—stream ... IL-6
Little Gamble Creek ... TX-5
Little Gamble Gully—valley ... TX-5
Little Gambler Creek—stream ... CA-9
Little Gandia Slough—gut ... TX-5
Little Gant Lake—lake ... FL-3
Little Ganz Lake—lake ... MN-6
Little Gap ... PA-2
Little Gap—gap (3) ... PA-2
Little Gap—gap ... TN-4
Little Gap—gap ... UT-8
Little Gap—gap ... VA-3
**Little Gap**—pop pl ... PA-2
Little Gap, The—gap ... NM-5
Little Gap Channel—channel ... VA-3
Little Gap Covered Bridge—hist pl ... PA-2

Little Gap Creek ... TN-4
Little Gap Creek—stream ... CA-9
Little Gap Creek—stream ... ID-8
Little Gap Creek—stream ... NC-3
Little Gap Creek—stream ... TN-4
Little Gap Run—stream ... PA-2
Little Gap (ski area)—locale ... PA-2
Little Gap Trail—trail (2) ... PA-2
Little Gap Well—well ... NM-5
Little Garcia Park—flat ... NM-5
Little Garden Creek—stream ... VA-3
Little Garfield Creek—stream ... AK-9
Little Gar Lake—lake ... FL-3
Little Garlic River—stream ... MI-6
Little Garner Creek—stream ... KY-4
Little Garnett—locale ... AR-4
Little Garrett Creek—stream ... MS-4
Little Garrison Hammock—summit ... FL-3
Little Garvan Creek ... SC-3
Little Garvin Creek—stream ... SC-3
Little Gasparilla Island—island ... FL-3
Little Gasparilla Pass—gut ... FL-3
Little Gassaway Creek—stream ... TN-4
Little Gassoway Lake—lake ... LA-4
Little Gate Branch—stream ... VA-3
Little Gator Creek—gut ... FL-3
Little Gator Point—cape ... FL-3
Little Gavanski Island—island ... AK-9
Little Gayland Creek—stream ... GA-3
Little Gelatt Lake—lake ... WY-8
Little Gem Cave ... MO-7
Little Gem Lake—lake ... CO-8
Little Gem Mine—mine ... CO-8
Little Gem Mine—mine ... NV-8
Little Gem Rsvr—reservoir ... CO-8
Little Gem Sch—school ... NE-7
Little Generostee Creek—stream ... SC-3
**Little Genesee**—pop pl ... NY-2
Little Genesee Cem—cemetery ... NY-2
Little Genesee Creek—stream ... NY-2
Little Genesee Creek—stream ... PA-2
Little Geneva Ch—church ... GA-3
Little Genito Creek—stream ... VA-3
Little George, Lake—lake ... MI-6
Little George Creek—stream ... VA-3
Little George Creek—stream ... WI-6
Little George Head Island—island ... ME-1
Little George Park—park ... IA-7
Little George Pond—lake ... AZ-5
Little George Rsvr—reservoir ... AZ-5
Little Georges Canyon—valley ... NV-8
Little Georges Creek—stream ... AR-4
Little Georges Creek—stream ... SC-3
Little Georgetown—locale ... MD-2
**Little Georgetown**—pop pl ... KY-4
**Little Georgetown**—pop pl ... WV-2
Little Georgia ... MS-4
Little Georgia Creek—stream ... VA-3
Little German Creek—stream ... AL-4
**Little Germany**—pop pl ... PA-2
Little Germany Creek—stream ... GA-3
Little Gerstle River—stream ... AK-9
Little Getaway Canyon—valley ... TX-5
Little Geyser Spring—spring ... NV-8
Little Giant Bar ... UT-8
Little Giant Basin—basin ... CO-8
Little Giant Creek—stream ... MI-6
Little Giant Creek—stream ... WA-9
Little Giant Mine—mine ... AZ-5
Little Giant Mine—mine ... NV-8
Little Giant Mine—mine ... UT-8
Little Giant Pass—gap ... WA-9
Little Giant Peak—summit ... CO-8
Little Giant Rsvr No. 1—reservoir ... CO-8
Little Giant Rsvr No. 2—reservoir ... CO-8
Little Giant Spring—spring ... AZ-5
Little Gibraltar—island ... CA-9
Little Gibson Lake—lake ... WI-6
Little Gila Canal—canal ... AZ-5
Little Gila River—stream ... AZ-5
Little Gilbert Brook—stream ... ME-1
Little Gilbert Creek—stream ... UT-8
Little Gilbert Creek—stream ... WY-8
Little Gilbertsons Slough—gut ... MN-6
Little Gilder Creek—stream ... SC-3
Little Gilkey Lake—lake ... MI-6
Little Gillam Draw—valley ... CO-8
Little Gillespie Brook—stream ... ME-1
Little Gillett Lake—lake ... WI-6
Little Gilmore Creek—stream ... TX-5
Little Gilsen Butte ... UT-8
Little Gilson Butte—summit ... UT-8
Little Gilstad Lake—lake ... MN-6
Little Gimlet Creek—stream ... KY-4
Little Gingerbread House Day Sch—school ... FL-3
Little Gin Lake—lake ... LA-4
Little Girl Point ... MI-6
Little Girls Point—cape ... MI-6
Little Gists Creek—stream ... TN-4
Little Gizzard Creek—stream ... TN-4
Little Glacier Slough—gut ... AK-9
Little Gladden Creek—stream ... MO-7
Little Glade Ch—church ... NC-3
Little Glade Ch—church ... WV-2
Little Glade Creek—stream ... LA-4
Little Glade Creek—stream ... NC-3
Little Glade Creek—stream ... WV-2
Little Glade Millpond—lake ... NC-3
Little Glade Run—stream ... PA-2
Little Glade Run—stream ... WV-2
Little Gladesville Creek—stream ... GA-3
Little Glady Creek—stream ... GA-3
Little Glady Run—stream ... WV-2
Little Glasses Bay—bay ... OK-5
Little Glasses Creek—stream ... OK-5
Little Glass Mtn—summit ... CA-9
Little Glazer Ridge ... CA-9
Little Glazer Ridge—ridge ... CA-9
Little Glazypeau Creek—stream ... AR-4
Little Gleason Forestry Plantation—forest ... CA-9
Little Gnat Lake—lake ... MN-6
Little Goat Canyon—valley ... AZ-5
Little Goat Creek—stream ... WA-9
Little Goat Island—island ... AR-4
Little Goat Island—island ... SC-3
Little Goat Island—island ... TN-4
Little Goat Lake—lake ... AK-9
Little Goat Lake—lake ... MT-8
Little Goat Mountain ... ID-8
Little Goat Mtn—summit ... WA-9

Little Goat Mtns—range ... ID-8
Little Gobbler—valley ... TX-5
Little Goblintown Creek—stream ... VA-3
Little Goddard Brook—stream ... ME-1
Little Goddard Ridge—ridge ... ME-1
Little Goddel Bayou—stream ... LA-4
Little God Keys Pass—channel ... MS-4
Little Goff Creek—stream ... OK-5
Little Gold Creek—stream (2) ... AK-9
Little Gold Creek—stream ... MT-8
Little Gold Creek—stream ... OR-9
Little Golden Gate Bridge—bridge ... CA-9
Little Golden Prospect—mine ... AZ-5
Little Gold Gulch—valley ... AZ-5
Little Gold Hill—summit ... CA-9
Little Gold Lake—lake ... CA-9
Little Goldmine Hill—summit ... NY-2
Little Goldstream Creek—stream ... AK-9
Little Golf Pond—lake ... FL-3
Little Gonsoulin Bayou—stream ... LA-4
Little Good Creek—stream ... TX-5
Little Good Harbor—bay ... ME-1
Little Good Harbor—bay (2) ... MA-1
Little Goodman Ridge—ridge ... OR-9
Little Goodwin Creek—stream ... AL-4
**Little Goose**—pop pl ... WA-9
Little Goose Bay—bay ... AK-9
Little Goose Bay—bay ... WA-9
Little Goose Bay Creek—stream ... MO-7
Little Gooseberry Creek—stream ... ID-8
Little Gooseberry Creek—stream ... WY-8
Little Gooseberry River—stream ... MN-6
Little Goose Campground—locale ... WA-9
Little Goose Campground—locale ... WY-8
Little Goose Ch—church ... KY-4
Little Goose Creek ... WY-8
Little Goose Creek—stream ... GA-3
Little Goose Creek—stream (2) ... ID-8
Little Goose Creek—stream (4) ... KY-4
Little Goose Creek—stream ... NV-8
Little Goose Creek—stream ... NC-3
Little Goose Creek—stream ... TN-4
Little Goose Creek—stream ... WA-9
Little Goose Creek—stream ... WY-8
Little Goose Dam—dam ... ND-7
Little Goose Dam—dam ... WA-9
Little Goose Dam Heliport—airport ... WA-9
Little Goose Dam Reservoir ... WA-9
Little Goose Island—island ... AK-9
Little Goose Lake ... WA-9
Little Goose Lake—lake (2) ... AR-4
Little Goose Lake—lake (3) ... MI-6
Little Goose Lake—lake (2) ... MN-6
Little Goose Lake—lake ... MT-8
Little Goose Lake—lake (2) ... WA-9
Little Goose Lake—reservoir ... CO-8
Little Goose Lake—reservoir ... ND-7
Little Goose Lock And Dam Airp—airport ... WA-9
Little Goose Natl Wildlife Ref—park ... ND-7
Little Goose Peak—summit ... WY-8
Little Goose Pond—lake ... MA-1
Little Goose Pond—lake ... NH-1
Little Goose Pond—lake ... NJ-2
Little Goose Pond—lake ... SC-3
Little goose Reservoir ... WA-9
Little Goose River—stream ... ND-7
Little Goose Spring—spring ... NV-8
Little Goosmus Creek—stream ... WA-9
Little Gordon Brook—stream ... ME-1
Little Gordon Hill—summit ... NH-1
Little Gordon Pond—lake ... ME-1
Little Goshen—summit ... TN-4
Little Goshen Reef—bar ... CT-1
Little Gott Island—island ... ME-1
Little Gough Spring—spring ... UT-8
Little Government Creek—stream ... CO-8
Little Governors Creek—stream ... NC-3
Little Grade Creek—stream ... WA-9
Little Graham Creek—stream ... IN-6
Little Grandad Run Trail—trail ... PA-2
Little Grandad Trail ... PA-2
Little Grand Bay—lake ... LA-4
Little Grand Bayou—stream ... LA-4
Little Grand Canyon—valley ... UT-8
Little Grand Canyon Rancho—locale ... AZ-5
Little Grande—summit ... NM-5
Little Grande Wash ... UT-8
Little Grandfather Mtn—summit ... NC-3
Little Grand Lake ... MI-6
Little Grand Lake—lake ... MN-6
Little Grandmother Mtn—summit ... NM-5
Little Grand Pierre Creek—stream ... IL-6
Little Grand River—stream ... SD-7
Little Grand Wash ... UT-8
Little Grand Wash—valley ... UT-8
Little Graneros Creek—stream ... CO-8
Little Granite Canyon—valley ... UT-8
Little Granite Creek ... WY-8
Little Granite Creek—stream (2) ... AK-9
Little Granite Creek—stream ... CA-9
Little Granite Creek—stream ... ID-8
Little Granite Creek—stream (2) ... OR-9
Little Granite Creek—stream ... WA-9
Little Granite Creek—stream ... WY-8
Little Granite Gulch—valley ... CO-8
Little Granite Lake—lake ... WI-6
Little Granite Mine (Inactive)—mine ... NM-5
Little Granite Mountain Trail Number Thiry Seven—trail ... AZ-5
Little Granite Mtn—summit (2) ... AZ-5
Little Granite Mtn—summit ... UT-8
Little Granite Mtn—summit ... WA-9
Little Granite Peak—summit ... CA-9
Little Granite Peak—summit ... MT-8
Little Granny Creek—stream ... AR-4
Little Grant Cem—cemetery ... WI-6
Little Grant Mine—mine ... WI-6
Little Grant River—stream ... WI-6
**Little Grant (Town of)**—pop pl ... WI-6
Little Granulated Mtn—summit ... MT-8
Little Grape Creek—stream (3) ... TX-5
Little Grapevine Canyon—valley ... AZ-5
Little Grapevine Creek—stream (2) ... CA-9
Little Grapevine Pond—lake ... ME-1
Little Grapevine Tank—reservoir ... AZ-5
Little Grass Creek—stream ... SD-7
Little Grass Creek—stream ... WY-8
Little Grass Field Tank—reservoir ... TX-5
Little Grasshopper Creek—stream ... KS-7
Little Grass Island—island ... FL-3

Little Grass Lake ... WI-6
Little Grass Lake—lake ... MI-6
Little Grass Lake—lake (2) ... TX-5
Little Grass Mtn—summit ... ID-8
Little Grass Mtn—summit ... MO-7
Little Grass Mtn—summit ... OR-9
Little Grass Pond ... RI-1
Little Grass Pond—lake ... ME-1
Little Grass Pond—lake ... RI-1
Little Grass Run—stream ... WV-2
Little Grass Valley—valley ... CA-9
Little Grass Valley—valley ... UT-8
Little Grass Valley Creek—stream ... CA-9
Little Grass Valley Rsvr—reservoir ... CA-9
Little Grass Valley Trail—trail ... CA-9
Little Grassy—flat ... UT-8
Little Grassy Bay—bay ... FL-3
Little Grassy Brake—swamp ... AR-4
Little Grassy Branch—stream ... KY-4
Little Grassy Butte—summit ... ID-8
Little Grassy Creek—stream ... IL-6
Little Grassy Creek—stream (2) ... MO-7
Little Grassy Creek—stream (2) ... NC-3
Little Grassy Creek—stream ... VA-3
Little Grassy Creek—stream ... WV-2
Little Grassy Island—island (2) ... FL-3
Little Grassy Key ... FL-3
Little Grassy Knob—summit ... GA-3
Little Grassy Lake—lake ... AR-4
Little Grassy Lake—lake ... FL-3
Little Grassy Lake—lake ... WI-6
Little Grassy Lake—reservoir ... IL-6
Little Grassy Lake—swamp ... LA-4
Little Grassy Mtn—summit ... OR-9
Little Grassy Pond—lake ... FL-3
Little Grassy Pond—lake ... IN-6
Little Grassy Pond—lake ... NY-2
Little Grassy Ridge—ridge ... ID-8
Little Grassy Rsvr—reservoir ... OR-9
Little Grassy Slough—gut ... OK-5
Little Grassy Valley—valley ... MO-7
Little Gratiot River—stream ... MI-6
Little Grave Creek—stream ... WV-2
Little Gravel Creek—stream ... AL-4
Little Gravelly ... AR-4
Little Gravelly Branch—stream ... MD-2
Little Gravel Mtn—summit ... CO-8
Little Gravel Slough—stream ... AR-4
Little Graves Creek—stream ... OR-9
Little Graveyard Hollow—valley ... KY-4
Little Gravois Creek—stream (2) ... MO-7
Little Grayback—summit ... CA-9
Little Grayback Creek—stream ... OR-9
Little Grayback Mtn—summit ... OR-9
Little Grayback Peak—summit ... OR-9
Little Gray Hill—summit ... AZ-5
Little Grayhorse Canyon—valley ... AZ-5
Little Gray Ridge—ridge ... ID-8
Little Grays Branch—stream ... KY-4
Little Grays Cove—cove ... AL-4
Little Grays River ... WY-8
Little Greasewood Creek—stream ... OR-9
Little Greasy Creek ... MS-4
Little Greasy Creek—stream ... MO-7
Little Greaves Creek—stream ... NJ-2
Little Greely Pond—lake ... ME-1
Little Green Brake—swamp ... TX-5
Little Greenbrier Creek—stream ... AR-4
Little Greenbrier Creek—stream ... GA-3
Little Greenbrier Creek—stream ... VA-3
Little Greenbrier Hill—summit ... AR-4
Little Greenbrier School-Church—hist pl ... TN-4
Little Greenbush Pond—lake ... ME-1
Little Green Creek—stream ... NC-3
Little Green Creek—stream ... PA-2
Little Green Creek—stream ... TX-5
Little Greenhorn Creek—stream ... CA-9
Little Green Island—island ... AK-9
Little Green Island—island (2) ... ME-1
Little Green Lake—lake ... MN-6
Little Green Lake—lake ... TX-5
Little Green Lake—lake ... WI-6
Little Greenland Lake—lake ... ME-1
Little Greenleaf Creek—stream ... OK-5
Little Greenlick Run—stream ... PA-2
Little Green Man Cave—cave ... AL-4
Little Green Mine—mine ... AZ-5
Little Green Mtn—summit ... CO-8
Little Green Mtn—summit (2) ... ID-8
Little Green Mtn—summit ... NC-3
Little Green Mtn—summit ... OR-9
Little Greenough Pond—lake ... NH-1
Little Greenough Pond—reservoir ... MA-1
Little Green Park—park ... MN-6
Little Green Pond—lake ... NY-2
Little Green River—stream ... WI-6
Little Green Sch—school ... AR-4
Little Greens Run—stream ... OH-6
Little Greenstone Beach—beach ... MI-6
**Little Green Store**—pop pl ... AR-4
Little Green Swamp—swamp ... NC-3
Little Green Tom Lake—lake (2) ... AR-4
Little Green Tom Slough—stream ... AR-4
Little Green Valley—valley ... AZ-5
Little Green Valley—valley ... CA-9
Little Greenwood Pond—lake ... ME-1
Little Greider Lake—lake ... WA-9
Little Grenadier Island—island ... NY-2
Little Gressy Creek ... MO-7
Little Greyback Mtn ... OR-9
Little Greys River—stream ... WY-8
Little Grider Creek—stream ... CA-9
Little Grief Creek ... OK-5
Little Griffin Bluff—cliff ... GA-3
Little Griffin Lake—reservoir ... AL-4
Little Grill Ridge—ridge ... NC-3
Little Grinders Creek—stream ... TN-4
Little Grindle Cave—cave ... AL-4
Little Grindstone Creek—stream ... NY-2
Little Grindstone Creek—stream ... TX-5
Little Grinnell Lake—lake ... CA-9
Little Grizzlie Spring—spring ... CA-9
Little Grizzly Basin—basin ... WY-8
Little Grizzly Canyon—valley ... CA-9
Little Grizzly Creek ... CA-9
Little Grizzly Creek—stream (7) ... CA-9
Little Grizzly Creek—stream ... CO-8
Little Grizzly Creek—stream ... ID-8
Little Grizzly Ditch—canal ... CO-8
Little Grizzly Flat—flat ... CA-9
Little Grizzly Lake—lake ... MT-8
Little Grizzly Mtn—summit ... CA-9
Little Grizzly Valley—basin ... CA-9
Little Grocery Creek—stream ... GA-3
Little Grooms Creek—stream ... FL-3
Little Gros Ventre River ... WY-8
Little Groundhog Mtn—summit ... OR-9
Little Groundhog Rsvr—reservoir ... OR-9
Little Grouse Creek—stream ... ID-8
Little Grouse Creek—stream ... OR-9
Little Grouse Rsvr—reservoir ... CO-8
Little Grove Cem—cemetery ... MO-7
Little Grove Cem—cemetery ... TN-4
Little Grove Ch—church (3) ... IL-6
Little Grove Ch—church ... NC-3
Little Grove Ch—church ... TN-4
Little Grove Creek—stream ... IL-6
Little Grove Creek—stream ... SC-3
Little Grover Branch—stream ... MO-7
Little Groves—locale ... IA-7
Little Grove Sch—school ... IL-6
Little Grove Sch—school ... WI-6
Little Grove Sch (historical)—school ... TN-4
Little Growler Rapids—rapids ... ID-8
Little Guagus Stream—stream ... ME-1
Little Guano Creek—stream ... WV-2
Little Guard Peak—summit ... ID-8
Little Guernsey Lakes—lake ... MI-6
Little Guess Creek ... TN-4
Little Guess Creek—stream ... TN-4
Little Guinea Creek—stream (2) ... VA-3
Little Gulch—valley ... AK-9
Little Gulch—valley (2) ... MT-8
Little Gulch—valley ... OR-9
Little Gulch Creek ... CO-8
Little Gulch Creek—stream ... ID-8
Little Gulch Lakes—lake ... MN-6
Little Gulf ... MS-4
Little Gulf Branch—stream ... AL-4
Little Gulf Stream—stream ... ME-1
Little Gull Island—island ... MI-6
Little Gull Island—island (2) ... NY-2
Little Gull Lake ... MN-6
Little Gull Reef—bar ... NY-2
Little Gully—valley ... IA-7
Little Gully Creek—stream ... FL-3
Little Gum Creek—stream ... FL-3
Little Gum Creek—stream ... GA-3
Little Gumhead Marsh—swamp ... FL-3
Little Gum Hollow—valley ... OH-6
Little Gum Hollow—valley ... TN-4
Little Gum Lake—lake ... FL-3
Little Gum Point—cape ... MD-2
Little Gum Pond—lake ... AR-4
Little Gum Swamp—swamp (2) ... FL-3
Little Gum Swamp Creek—stream ... GA-3
Little Gunflint Lake—lake ... MN-6
Little Gunnison Creek—stream ... CO-8
Little Gunnuk Creek—stream ... AK-9
Little Gunnysack Creek—stream ... WY-8
Little Gunpowder Creek—stream ... NC-3
Little Gunpowder Falls—stream ... MD-2
Little Gurr Lake—lake ... ND-7
Little Gurr Lake Natl Wildlife Ref—park ... ND-7
Little Gus Creek—stream ... KS-7
Little Gust James Wash—stream ... AZ-5
Little Gut—gut ... NC-3
Little Gut Creek—stream ... AR-4
Little Gutshall Spring—spring ... CO-8
Little Gyp Beds—bay ... NV-8
Little Gyp Creek—stream ... TX-5
Little Gypsum Creek—stream ... CO-8
Little Gypsum Valley—valley ... CO-8
Little Gypsy Lake—lake ... MI-6
Little Gypsy Lake—lake ... WI-6
Little Gyp Windmill—locale ... TX-5
Little Hackberry Canyon—valley ... TX-5
Little Hackberry Creek—stream (3) ... TX-5
Little Hackberry Draw—valley ... TX-5
Little Hackberry Tank—reservoir ... TX-5
Little Hackberry Wash—stream ... AZ-5
Little Hackberry Well—well ... AZ-5
Little Hackers Creek—stream ... WV-2
Little Hacking Run—stream ... WV-2
Little Hackney Creek—stream ... KY-4
Little Hack Point—cape ... MD-2
**Little Haddam**—pop pl ... CT-1
Little Hafey Brook—stream ... ME-1
Little Hagerman Lake—lake ... MI-6
Little Haha Bayou—gut ... LA-4
Little Hahnee Rsvr—reservoir ... OR-9
Little Halawaka Creek—stream ... AL-4
Little Halfmoon Bay—lake ... LA-4
Little Halfmoon Lake—lake ... FL-3
Little Halfmoon Lake—lake ... KS-7
Little Half Moon Lake—lake ... WY-8
Little Half Moon Pass—gap ... ID-8
Little Half Moon Spring—spring ... ID-8
Little Half Moon Trail—trail ... WY-8
Little Half Mountain Creek—stream ... KY-4
Little Half Mtn—summit ... KY-4
Little Halfway Pond—lake ... MA-1
Little Halfway Tank—reservoir ... TX-5
Little Halleck Creek—stream ... WY-8
Little Hall Lake—lake ... FL-3
Little Hall Lake—lake ... MN-6
Little Hall Park—locale ... GA-3
Little Halls Creek—stream ... AL-4
Little Ham Branch—stream ... TX-5
Little Ham Hole Spring—spring ... TX-5
Little Hamilton Island—island ... AK-9
Little Hamilton Windmill—locale ... NM-5
Little Ham Lake—lake ... MN-6
Little Hamlet Lake—lake ... MN-6
Little Hamlin Gulch—valley ... CO-8
Little Hammer Creek ... NC-3
Little Hammer Creek—stream ... ID-8
Little Hammock—island ... LA-4
Little Hammock Creek—stream ... NC-3
Little Hammond Point—cape ... NY-2
Little Hancock Lake—lake ... CA-9
Little Hanging Horn Lake—lake ... MN-6
Little Hangman Creek—stream ... ID-8
Little Hangman Creek—stream ... WA-9
Little Hannah Hill—summit ... KY-4
Little Hans Creek—stream ... NY-2
Little Hansen Lake—lake ... MN-6
Little Hans Lollik Island—island ... VI-3
Little Happy Creek ... OR-9
Little Harbor—bay ... CA-9
Little Harbor—bay ... CT-1
Little Harbor—bay ... ME-1
Little Harbor—bay ... MI-6
Little Harbor—bay ... NH-1
Little Harbor—bay ... WI-6
Little Harbor—cove (2) ... MA-1
Little Harbor—harbor ... MA-1
Little Harbor Beach—beach ... MA-1
**Little Harbor Beach**—pop pl ... MA-1
Little Harbor Brook—stream ... ME-1
Little Harbor Island—island ... NY-2
Little Harbor Marshes—swamp ... MA-1
**Little Harbor on the Hillsboro**—pop pl ... FL-3
Little Harbor Point—cape ... WI-6
Little Harbor Rsvr—reservoir ... MA-1
Little Harbor Run—stream ... PA-2
Little Harden Creek—stream ... FL-3
Little Hard Labor Creek—stream ... FL-3
Little Hardtime Lake—lake ... MS-4
Little Hardtrigger Creek—stream ... ID-8
Little Hardwick Creek—stream ... KY-4
Little Hardwood Hill—summit ... ME-1
Little Hardwood Hill—summit ... NY-2
Little Hardwood Island—island ... ME-1
Little Harkening Hill—summit ... VA-3
Little Harmon Cove—bay ... VA-3
Little Harper Lake—lake ... GA-3
Little Harpeth River—stream ... TN-4
Little Harpo Canyon—valley ... AZ-5
Little Harpo Tank—reservoir ... AZ-5
Little Harquahala Mountains—summit ... AZ-5
Little Harriett Lake—lake ... MN-6
Little Harris Branch—stream ... TN-4
Little Harris Creek—stream ... AL-4
Little Harris Creek—stream ... AK-9
Little Harris Creek—stream ... NC-3
Little Harrow Lake—lake ... ME-1
Little Harry Island—island ... SC-3
Little Hart Canyon—valley ... CA-9
Little Hart Creek ... WV-2
Little Hart Creek—stream ... ID-8
Little Harts Ch—church ... WV-2
Little Harts Creek—stream ... WV-2
Little Harvey Creek—stream ... WI-6
Little Harvey Mtn—summit ... CA-9
Little Harvey Valley—valley ... CA-9
Little Haskell Peak—summit ... CA-9
Little Hasparos Canyon ... NM-5
Little Hasperos Canyon—valley ... NM-5
Little Haste—rock ... MA-1
Little Hastings Tract—civil ... CA-9
Little Hatcase Pond—lake ... ME-1
Little Hatchapaloo Creek—stream ... MS-4
Little Hatch Canyon—valley ... UT-8
Little Hatchet Creek ... AL-4
Little Hatchet Creek—stream ... AL-4
Little Hatchet Creek—stream ... CA-9
Little Hatchet Creek—stream ... FL-3
Little Hatchet Mountains—other ... NM-5
Little Hatchie Cem—cemetery ... TN-4
Little Hatchie Ch—church (2) ... TN-4
Little Hatchie Creek—stream ... TN-4
Little Hatchie River—stream ... MS-4
Little Hat Creek ... ID-8
Little Hat Creek—stream ... ID-8
Little Hathorn Pond—lake ... ME-1
Little Hat Mtn—summit ... CA-9
Little Hat Mtn—summit ... NV-8
Little Hatton ... AL-4
Little Hauani Creek—stream ... OK-5
Little Hauken Run—stream ... NJ-2
Little Havana—post sta ... FL-3
Little Haven—locale ... VA-3
Little Haw Creek—stream ... FL-3
Little Haw Creek—stream ... IL-6
Little Haw Creek—stream ... IN-6
Little Haw Creek—stream ... MO-7
Little Haw Creek—swamp ... FL-3
Little Hawk Creek—stream ... MT-8
Little Hawk Lake—lake ... MT-8
Little Hawk Mtn—summit ... NC-3
Little Haw Knob—summit ... NC-3
Little Haw Knob—summit ... TN-4
Little Hawksbill Creek—stream ... VA-3
Little Hawk Spring—spring ... AZ-5
Little Haw Mtn—summit ... NC-3
Little Hay Brook—stream ... ME-1
Little Hay Creek—stream ... OR-9
Little Hay Creek—stream ... WI-6
Little Hayen—locale ... CA-9
Little Hayes Creek—stream ... AR-4
Little Haymeadow Creek ... WI-6
Little Hay Meadow Creek—stream ... WI-6
Little Haynes Creek—stream ... GA-3
Little Hays Creek—stream ... AL-4
Little Hay Spring—spring ... NM-5
Little Haystack—summit ... ID-8
Little Haystack—summit ... NM-5
Little Haystack—summit ... NY-2
Little Haystack Creek—stream ... ID-8
Little Haystack Mtn—summit ... AZ-5
Little Haystack Mtn—summit ... CO-8
Little Haystack Mtn—summit ... NH-1
Little Haystack Mtn—summit ... NM-5
Little Haystack Mtn—summit ... NY-2
Little Haystack Mtn—summit ... VT-1
Little Haystack Mtn—summit ... WA-9
Little Hazel Creek ... GA-3
Little Hazel Creek—stream ... GA-3
Little Hazel Creek—stream ... KY-4
Little Hazel Creek—stream (2) ... MO-7
Little Hazel Patch Creek—stream ... KY-4
Little Head—cliff ... CA-9
Little Head—summit ... ME-1
Little Heald Brook—stream ... ME-1
Little Hearst Branch—stream ... GA-3
Little Heart ... ND-7
**Little Heart**—pop pl ... ND-7
Little Heart Butte ... ND-7
Little Heart Flats—flat ... ND-7
Little Heart Lake—lake ... WA-9
Little Heart Rec Area—park ... ND-7
Little Heart River—stream ... ND-7
**Little Heaven**—pop pl ... DE-2
Little Hebe Crater—crater ... CA-9
Little Hebo—summit ... OR-9
Little He Creek—stream ... TN-4
Little Hedgehog—summit ... VT-1
Little Hefner Tank—reservoir ... NM-5
Little Hefren Run—stream ... PA-2
Little Heiser Tank—reservoir ... TX-5
Little Hell ... DE-2
Little Hell—swamp ... GA-3
Little Hell Canyon—valley ... CO-8
Little Hell Canyon Bridge—hist pl ... AZ-5
Little Hell Creek ... MS-4
Little Hell Creek—stream ... MS-4
Little Hell Creek—stream ... NC-3
Little Hell Gate—channel ... ME-1
Little Hellgate Creek ... VA-3
Little Hellgate Creek—stream ... VA-3
Little Hellgate Gulch—valley ... MT-8
Little Hellhole Bay—bay ... SC-3
Little Hellhole Bay—swamp ... SC-3
Little Hellhole Bayou—gut ... LA-4
Little Hellhole Dam—dam ... SC-3
Little Hellhole Reserve—reservoir ... SC-3
Little Hell Landing—locale ... SC-3
Little Hell Pond ... MA-1
Little Hell Pond—lake ... GA-3
Little Hellroaring Creek—stream ... ID-8
Little Hell Roaring Creek—stream ... MT-8
Little Hells Canyon—valley ... OR-9
Little Hells Creek—stream ... AL-4
Little Hells Gate—gap ... AZ-5
Little Hell Tank—reservoir ... TX-5
Little Hell Windmill—locale ... TX-5
Little Helton Ch—church ... NC-3
Little Helton Creek—stream ... NC-3
Little Helton Creek—stream ... VA-3
Little Hemlock—summit ... MA-1
Little Hemlock Creek—stream ... WI-6
Little Hemlock River—stream ... MI-6
Little Henderson Canyon—valley ... UT-8
Little Henderson Creek—stream ... CO-8
Little Henna Creek—stream ... MI-6
Little Henry Creek—stream ... CO-8
Little Henry Lake—lake ... FL-3
Little Hensley Branch—stream ... NC-3
Little Henson Creek—stream ... NC-3
Little Herman Creek—stream ... OR-9
Little Hermit Gulch—valley ... WY-8
Little Herring Pond—lake ... MA-1
Little Hester Lake—lake ... WA-9
Little Hewitt Creek—stream ... WV-2
Little Hichitee Creek—stream ... GA-3
Little Hickman—locale ... KY-4
Little Hickman Creek—stream ... KY-4
Little Hickman Sch—school ... KY-4
**Little Hickory**—pop pl ... PA-2
Little Hickory Bay—bay ... FL-3
Little Hickory Ch—church ... IL-6
Little Hickory Creek ... NC-3
Little Hickory Creek—stream (2) ... AR-4
Little Hickory Creek—stream (2) ... IL-6
Little Hickory Creek—stream ... KS-7
Little Hickory Creek—stream ... NC-3
Little Hickory Creek—stream (2) ... OK-5
Little Hickory Creek—stream ... TN-4
Little Hickory Creek—stream (2) ... TX-5
Little Hickory Island—island ... FL-3
Little Hickory Knob—summit ... NC-3
Little Hickory Lake—lake ... PA-2
Little Hickorynut Mtn—summit ... GA-3
Little Hickory Pass (historical)—channel ... FL-3
Little Hickory Pond ... PA-2
Little Hickory Ridge Cem—cemetery ... IN-6
Little Hickory Run—stream ... PA-2
Little Hickory Top—summit ... NC-3
Little Hidden Lake—lake ... WI-6
Little Higgenbotham Cove—cave ... TN-4
Little High Creek—stream ... CO-8
Little High Point Creek—stream ... TX-5
Little High Pond—lake ... NY-2
Little High Rock Canyon—valley ... NV-8
Little High Rock Creek—stream ... NV-8
Little High Rock Rsvr—reservoir ... NV-8
Little High Top—summit ... OK-5
Little Hightower Creek ... AR-4
Little Hightower Creek—stream ... GA-3
Little High Valley—valley ... CA-9
Little Highway Tank—reservoir ... NM-5
Little Hill ... MA-1
Little Hill—summit ... CO-8
Little Hill—summit ... ME-1
Little Hill—summit ... TN-4
Little Hill—summit (2) ... UT-8
Little Hillabe Creek ... AL-4
Little Hillabee Creek—stream (2) ... AL-4
Little Hillabee Watershed Dam Number 1 ... AL-4
Little Hillabee Watershed Dam Number 2 ... AL-4
Little Hillabee Watershed Dam Number 3—dam ... AL-4
Little Hillabee Watershed Dam Number 4—dam ... AL-4
Little Hillabee Watershed Dam Number 6—dam ... AL-4
Little Hillabi Creek ... AL-4
Little Hill Ch—church ... AL-4
Little Hill Ch—church ... DE-2
Little Hill Ch—church ... MS-4
Little Hill Ch—church ... PA-2
Little Hill Ch—church ... TX-5
Little Hilliby Creek—stream ... OK-5
Little Hill Mine—mine ... TN-4
Little Hill Mines Airp—airport ... AZ-5
Little Hill River ... MN-6
Little Hill River—stream ... MN-6
Little Hills—range ... NV-8
Little Hills—summit ... TX-5
Little Hill Sch (historical)—school ... AL-4
Little Hills Game Experiment Station—other ... CO-8
Little Hill Windmill—locale ... TX-5
Little Hils Game Experiment Station—other ... CO-8
Little Hindoo Creek—stream ... WA-9
Little Hitchen Creek—stream ... KS-7
Little H Lake—lake ... AR-4
Little Hobble Creek—stream ... UT-8
Little Hobbs Lake—lake ... FL-3
Little Hobo Spring—spring ... NM-5
**Little Hocking**—pop pl ... OH-6
Little Hocking River—stream ... OH-6
Little Hocter Tank—reservoir ... AZ-5
Little Hogan Creek ... IN-6
Little Hogan Creek—stream ... IN-6
Little Hogan Well—well ... AZ-5
Little Hogback—ridge ... MT-8
Little Hogback, The—ridge ... CO-8
Little Hogback, The—ridge ... NV-8
Little Hogback Creek ... NC-3
Little Hogback Creek—stream ... MT-8
Little Hogback Creek—stream ... NC-3
Little Hogback Lake—lake ... MI-6
Little Hogback Mtn—summit (2) ... NC-3
Little Hogback Mtn—summit ... VA-3
Little Hogback Ridge—ridge ... MT-8
Little Hog Bayou—gut ... TX-5
Little Hog Bayou—stream ... LA-4
Little Hog Butte—summit ... AK-9
Little Hog Creek—stream ... AL-4
Little Hog Creek—stream (2) ... GA-3
Little Hog Creek—stream ... MI-6
Little Hog Creek—stream ... MO-7
Little Hog Creek—stream ... OH-6
Little Hog Creek—stream ... TX-5
Little Hog Glade—swamp ... LA-4
Little Hog Hill Tank—reservoir ... AZ-5
Little Hog Island ... ME-1
Little Hog Island ... MA-1
Little Hog Island ... NC-3
Little Hog Island—island ... MI-6
Little Hogles Creek—stream ... MO-7
Little Hog Neck ... NY-2
Little Hog Neck—cape ... NY-2
Little Hogpen Run—stream ... VA-3
Little Hog Ranch Creek—stream ... NV-8
Little Hog Ranch Rsvr—reservoir ... NV-8
Little Hogsback—cape ... WA-9
Little Hogsback—ridge ... WY-8
Little Hogskin Creek—stream ... SC-3
Little Hog Slough—stream ... LA-4
Little Hog Swamp—swamp ... NC-3
Little Hog Tusk Creek—stream ... AR-4
Little Hogup Mountains ... UT-8
Little Hohnholz Lake—lake ... CO-8
Little Hoko River—stream ... WA-9
Little Holbrook Pond—lake ... ME-1
Little Hole—basin ... CO-8
Little Hole—basin ... UT-8
Little Hole—bay ... ID-8
Littlehole Creek—stream ... NH-1
Little Hole Draw—valley ... ID-8
Little Hole-In-The-Wall—area ... NM-5
Little Hole In The Wall—area ... NM-5
Little Hole In The Wall Creek—stream ... ID-8
Little Hole Rsvr—reservoir ... OR-9
Little Holes—lake ... UT-8
Little Hole Tank—reservoir ... AZ-5
Little Hole Trail—trail ... UT-8
Little Hole Wildlife Mngmt Area—park ... UT-8
Little Holiness Ch—church ... WV-2
Little Holland Bayou—stream ... LA-4
Little Holland Cem—cemetery ... MT-8
Little Holland Sch—school ... MT-8
Little Holland Tract—civil ... CA-9
Little Holley Creek ... SC-3
Little Hollow—locale ... NY-2
Little Hollow—valley ... PA-2
Little Hollow—valley ... TN-4
Little Hollow—valley ... UT-8
Little Hollow—valley ... VA-3
Little Hollow Creek ... SC-3
Little Hollow Creek—stream (2) ... SC-3
Little Hollow (historical)—valley ... AL-4
Little Hollow Place—basin ... AZ-5
Little Holly Branch—stream ... MS-4
Little Holly Cove ... ME-1
Little Holly Cove—bay ... ME-1
Little Holly Creek—stream ... AR-4
Little Hollywood Hist Dist—hist pl ... CT-1
**Little Hollywood Mobile Home Park**—pop pl ... PA-2
Little Holmes Bayou—stream ... LA-4
Little Holmes Lake—lake ... MS-4
Little Holmes Lake—lake ... NY-2
Little Home Hill—summit ... NH-1
Little Hominy Creek—stream ... OK-5
Little Homosasso River—gut ... FL-3
Little Honey Creek—stream ... IN-6
Little Honey Creek—stream ... OR-9
Little Honker Bay—bay ... CA-9
Little Honolulu Creek—stream ... AK-9
Little Hood Creek—stream ... KY-4
Little Hoodoo Creek—stream ... ID-8
Little Hoodoo Mtn—summit ... MT-8
Little Hoosic River—stream ... NY-2
Little Hoot Oil Field—oilfield ... CO-8
Little Hoover Island—island ... PA-2
Little Hope ... TN-4
Little Hope—locale ... TX-5
**Little Hope**—pop pl ... GA-3
**Little Hope**—pop pl ... PA-2
**Little Hope**—pop pl (2) ... TN-4
**Little Hope**—pop pl ... WI-6
Little Hope Baptist Church ... MS-4
Little Hope Baptist Church ... TN-4
Little Hope Cem ... MS-4
Little Hope Cem—cemetery ... AR-4
Little Hope Cem—cemetery ... MS-4
Little Hope Cem—cemetery ... TN-4
Little Hope Ch ... AL-4
Little Hope Ch—church (3) ... AL-4
Little Hope Ch—church ... AR-4
Little Hope Ch—church ... KY-4
Little Hope Ch—church ... LA-4
Little Hope Ch—church (2) ... MS-4
Little Hope Ch—church ... TN-4
Little Hope Ch—church (4) ... TX-5
Little Hope Ch—church ... VA-3
Little Hope Ch (historical)—church ... MS-4
Little Hope Creek—stream ... NC-3
Little Hope Mine—mine ... CA-9
Little Hope-Moore Community Center—locale ... TX-5
Little Hope Pond—lake ... NY-2
Little Hope Sch—school ... IL-6
Little Hope Sch—school ... TN-4
Little Hope Sch (historical)—school ... NC-3
Little Hopewell Baptist Church ... TN-4
Little Hopewell Church ... TN-4
Little Hop Island—island ... NC-3
Little Hopkins Mtn—summit ... NY-2
Little Hopp Canyon—valley ... UT-8
Little Hopper Camp Branch—stream ... TN-4
**Little Hoquiam**—pop pl ... WA-9
Little Hoquiam River—stream ... WA-9
Little HO Ranch—locale ... CO-8
Little Horn Bayou—stream ... LA-4
Little Horner Tank—reservoir ... AZ-5
Little Hornet Creek—stream ... WY-8
Little Hornet Ridge—ridge ... WA-9
Little Horn Lake—lake ... MN-6
Little Horn Lake—lake ... WI-6
Little Horn Mountains—summit ... AZ-5
Little Horn Peak—summit ... AZ-5
Little Horn Peak—summit ... CO-8
Little Horn River ... MT-8
Little Horn River ... WY-8
Little Horn Trail—trail ... WY-8
Little Horn Well—well ... AZ-5
Little Horse Basin—basin ... ID-8
Little Horse Basin Gap—gap ... ID-8
Little Horse Basin Rsvr—reservoir ... ID-8
Little Horse Bottom—bend ... UT-8
Little Horse Branch—stream ... NC-3
Little Horse Branch—stream ... SC-3
Little Horse Canyon—valley ... CA-9
Little Horse Canyon—valley ... NV-8
Little Horse Canyon—valley (2) ... UT-8
Little Horse Cave Run—stream ... WV-2
Little Horse Creek ... OR-9
**Little Horse Creek**—pop pl ... NC-3
Little Horse Creek—stream (2) ... AL-4
Little Horse Creek—stream (2) ... CO-8
Little Horse Creek—stream ... FL-3
Little Horse Creek—stream (3) ... GA-3
Little Horse Creek—stream (2) ... ID-8
Little Horse Creek—stream ... MS-4
Little Horse Creek—stream ... MT-8
Little Horse Creek—stream (3) ... NC-3
Little Horse Creek—stream ... OK-5
Little Horse Creek—stream (4) ... SC-3
Little Horse Creek—stream ... TN-4
Little Horse Creek—stream ... UT-8
Little Horse Creek—stream ... WV-2
Little Horse Creek—stream (4) ... WY-8
Little Horse Creek Cem—cemetery ... GA-3
Little Horse Creek Ch—church ... GA-3
Little Horse Creek Ch—church ... NC-3
Little Horse Creek Ch—church ... SC-3
Little Horse Creek No 4 Ditch—canal ... WY-8
Little Horse Draw—valley ... CO-8
Little Horse Gap—gap ... TN-4
Little Horse Gap—gap ... VA-3
Little Horsehead Lake ... WI-6
Little Horsehead Lake—lake ... WI-6
Little Horse Heaven—basin ... UT-8
Little Horse Heaven—summit ... VA-3
Little Horse Heaven Creek—stream ... OR-9
Little Horselog Branch—stream ... TN-4
Little Horse Meadows—flat ... CA-9
Little Horse Mesa—ridge ... NM-5
Little Horse Mtn—summit (2) ... CA-9
Little Horse Mtn—summit ... WY-8
Little Horse Opening—flat ... CA-9
Little Horse Park—flat (2) ... AZ-5
Little Horse Park—flat ... MT-8
Little Horse Peak—summit ... CA-9
Little Horse Peak—summit ... WY-8
Little Horsepen Bay—swamp ... SC-3
Little Horsepen Creek—stream ... LA-4
Little Horse Pen Creek—stream ... MS-4
Little Horsepen Creek—stream ... SC-3
Little Horsepen Creek—stream (2) ... VA-3
Little Horse Ridge—ridge ... UT-8
Little Horse Rsvr—reservoir ... CO-8
Little Horse Run—stream ... WV-2
Little Horseshoe—basin ... UT-8
Little Horseshoe—slope ... UT-8
Little Horseshoe Basin—basin ... MT-8
Little Horseshoe Bay—swamp ... NC-3
Little Horseshoe Bayou—gut ... WI-6
Little Horseshoe Bend—bend ... GA-3
Little Horseshoe Bend—bend ... TN-4
Little Horseshoe Brake—lake ... AR-4
Little Horseshoe Creek ... WY-8
Little Horseshoe Creek—stream ... MO-7
Little Horseshoe Creek—stream ... MT-8
Little Horseshoe Creek—stream ... WA-9
Little Horseshoe Lake ... WI-6
Little Horseshoe Lake—lake (2) ... AR-4
Little Horseshoe Lake—lake (2) ... MN-6
Little Horseshoe Lake—lake ... MS-4
Little Horseshoe Lake—lake ... ND-7
Little Horseshoe Lake—lake (3) ... WI-6
Little Horseshoe Mtn—summit ... OK-5
Little Horseshoe Park—flat ... CO-8
Little Horseshoe Park Trail—trail ... CO-8
Little Horseshoe Pond—lake ... ME-1
Little Horseshoe Spring—spring ... OR-9
Little Horseshoe Swamp—swamp ... NC-3
Little Horseshoe Trail—trail ... OK-5
Little Horse Spring—spring ... ID-8
Little Horse Spring—spring ... OR-9
Little Horse Tank—reservoir (2) ... AZ-5
Little Horsethief Canyon—valley ... CA-9
Little Horsethief Canyon—valley ... WY-8
Little Horsethief Creek—stream ... CO-8
Little Horsethief Creek—stream ... ID-8
Little Horsethief Ranch—locale ... CA-9
Little Horse Valley—valley (2) ... UT-8
Little Hosmer Pond—lake ... VT-1
Little Hot Creek—stream ... CA-9
Little Hotel Campground—park ... UT-8
Little Hoton Creek ... WI-6
Little Hot Spring—spring ... CA-9
Little Hot Springs ... CA-9
Little Hot Springs—spring ... NV-8
Little Hot Springs Valley ... CA-9
Little Hot Springs Valley—valley ... CA-9
Little Hot Spring Valley—valley ... CA-9
Little Houani Creek ... OK-5
Little Houghton Canal—canal ... CA-9
Little Houlka Creek—stream ... MS-4
Little Hound Creek ... VA-3
Little Hounds Creek—stream ... VA-3
Little House—hist pl ... TX-5
Little House Creek ... GA-3
Little House Creek (CCD)—cens area ... GA-3
Little House Mtn—summit ... VA-3
Little House Tank—reservoir ... NM-5
Little Houston Brook—stream ... ME-1
Little Houston Creek—stream ... CA-9
Little Houston Creek—stream ... WY-8
Little Houston Lake—lake ... OR-9
Little Houston Pond—lake ... ME-1
Little Howard Brook—stream ... ME-1
Little Howard Creek—stream ... CA-9

Little Howard Creek—*stream* .......... KY-4
Little Howard Pond—*lake* .......... NY-2
Little Howard Spring—*spring* .......... OR-9
Little Hoyle Creek—*stream* .......... NC-3
Little HQ Lake—*lake* .......... MI-6
Little HS—*school* .......... ME-1
Little Hubbard Ch—*church* .......... MS-4
*Little Hubbard Creek* .......... AL-4
Little Huckleberry Creek—*stream* .......... FL-3
Little Huckleberry Creek—*stream* .......... KY-4
Little Huckleberry Creek—*stream* .......... TN-4
Little Huckleberry Knob—*summit* .......... NC-3
Little Huckleberry Knob—*summit* .......... VA-3
Little Huckleberry Mtn—*summit* .......... NC-3
Little Huckleberry Mtn—*summit* .......... WA-9
Little Huckleberry Trail—*trail* .......... WA-9
Little Hudson Brook—*stream* .......... ME-1
Little Hudson Pond—*lake* .......... ME-1
Little Huff Creek—*stream* .......... WV-2
Little Huff Creek Ch—*church* (2) .......... WV-2
Little Huff Run—*stream* .......... KY-4
Little Huggins Branch—*stream* .......... NC-3
Little Huggins Creek—*stream* .......... NC-3
Little Hull Creek—*stream* .......... ID-8
Little Hull Tank—*reservoir* .......... AZ-5
Little Humboldt Ranch—*locale* .......... NV-8
Little Humboldt River—*stream* .......... NV-8
Little Humbug Creek—*stream* (2) .......... CA-9
Little Humbug Creek—*stream* .......... OR-9
Little Humbug Mtn—*summit* .......... NY-2
Little Hump—*summit* .......... WA-9
Little Humpback Lake—*lake* .......... AK-9
Little Humphrey Canyon—*valley* .......... NM-5
Little Humphrey Creek—*stream* .......... KY-4
Little Hump Mtn—*summit* (2) .......... NC-3
Little Hump Mtn—*summit* .......... TN-4
Little Humpy Peak—*summit* .......... OR-9
Little Hungry River—*stream* .......... NC-3
Little Hunter Creek—*stream* .......... PA-2
Little Hunting Creek—*stream* .......... MD-2
Little Hunting Creek—*stream* .......... NC-3
Little Hunting Creek—*stream* .......... VA-3
Little Hunting Run—*stream* .......... VA-3
Little Hunting Slough—*stream* .......... MO-7
Little Huntley Brook—*stream* .......... ME-1
Little Huntoon Valley—*basin* .......... NV-8
Little Hurd Hill—*summit* .......... NY-2
*Little Hurd Lake* .......... ME-1
Little Hurd Pond—*lake* (2) .......... ME-1
Little Huron Pond—*lake* .......... RI-1
Little Huron River—*stream* .......... MI-6
Little Hurrah Creek—*stream* .......... AK-9
*Little Hurricane Baptist Church* .......... AL-4
Little Hurricane Branch—*stream* .......... KY-4
Little Hurricane Branch—*stream* .......... NJ-2
Little Hurricane Branch—*stream* .......... VA-3
Little Hurricane Cem—*cemetery* .......... AL-4
Little Hurricane Cem—*cemetery* (2) .......... TN-4
Little Hurricane Ch—*church* .......... AL-4
Little Hurricane Ch—*church* (2) .......... TN-4
Little Hurricane Ch (historical)—*church* .......... TN-4
*Little Hurricane Creek* .......... IN-6
Little Hurricane Creek—*stream* .......... AL-4
Little Hurricane Creek—*stream* (3) .......... AR-4
Little Hurricane Creek—*stream* .......... GA-3
Little Hurricane Creek—*stream* .......... IL-6
Little Hurricane Creek—*stream* .......... IN-6
Little Hurricane Creek—*stream* (2) .......... KY-4
Little Hurricane Creek—*stream* .......... LA-4
Little Hurricane Creek—*stream* (4) .......... MO-7
Little Hurricane Creek—*stream* .......... NC-3
Little Hurricane Creek—*stream* .......... OR-9
Little Hurricane Creek—*stream* (6) .......... TN-4
Little Hurricane Creek—*stream* (2) .......... WV-2
Little Hurricane Fork—*stream* .......... KY-4
Little Hurricane Hill—*summit* .......... IN-6
Little Hurricane Island—*island* .......... KY-4
Little Hurricane Island—*island* .......... ME-1
Little Hurricane Lake—*lake* .......... AR-4
Little Hurricane Ridge—*ridge* .......... AZ-5
Little Hurricane Rim—*cliff* .......... AZ-5
Little Hurricane Sch (historical)—*school* .......... TN-4
Little Hurst Lake—*lake* .......... WI-6
Little Huston Creek—*stream* .......... AR-4
Little Hutch Spring—*spring* .......... AZ-5
Little Hyatt Rsvr—*reservoir* .......... OR-9
Little Ibex Peak—*summit* .......... MT-8
Little Ice Cave—*cave* .......... MT-8
Little Ice Cream Cone Hill—*summit* .......... AZ-5
Little Ice Creek—*stream* .......... OH-6
Little Ichawaynochaway Creek—*stream* .......... GA-3
Little Ichusa Creek—*stream* .......... MS-4
Little Idaho Canyon—*valley* .......... NV-8
Little Ike Spring—*spring* .......... NV-8
Little Ike Spring Wash—*stream* .......... NV-8
Little Iller Branch—*stream* .......... KY-4
*Little Illinois* .......... PA-2
Little Illinois River Falls—*falls* .......... OR-9
Little Independence Pond—*lake* .......... NY-2
Little Indian—*locale* .......... IL-6
Little Indian Bayou—*stream* (2) .......... LA-4
Little Indian Bog—*swamp* .......... ME-1
Little Indian Branch—*stream* .......... KY-4
Little Indian Branch—*stream* .......... MS-4
Little Indian Camp—*locale* .......... WY-8
Little Indian Canyon—*valley* .......... UT-8
*Little Indian Creek* .......... GA-3
*Little Indian Creek* .......... IN-6
*Little Indian Creek* .......... MD-2
*Little Indian Creek* .......... NV-8
*Little Indian Creek* .......... NC-3
*Little Indian Creek* .......... OR-9
Little Indian Creek—*stream* (4) .......... AL-4
Little Indian Creek—*stream* .......... AK-9
Little Indian Creek—*stream* .......... AR-4
Little Indian Creek—*stream* (4) .......... CA-9
Little Indian Creek—*stream* (3) .......... GA-3
Little Indian Creek—*stream* (2) .......... ID-8
Little Indian Creek—*stream* (5) .......... IL-6
Little Indian Creek—*stream* (10) .......... IN-6
Little Indian Creek—*stream* (4) .......... IA-7
Little Indian Creek—*stream* (3) .......... KS-7
Little Indian Creek—*stream* (4) .......... KY-4
Little Indian Creek—*stream* (2) .......... LA-4
Little Indian Creek—*stream* .......... MD-2
Little Indian Creek—*stream* (6) .......... MO-7
Little Indian Creek—*stream* .......... MT-8
Little Indian Creek*—*stream* .......... NE-7
Little Indian Creek—*stream* .......... NV-8
Little Indian Creek—*stream* .......... NY-2
Little Indian Creek—*stream* (3) .......... NC-3
Little Indian Creek—*stream* (5) .......... OH-6
Little Indian Creek—*stream* (4) .......... OR-9
Little Indian Creek—*stream* (5) .......... TN-4
Little Indian Creek—*stream* (7) .......... TX-5
Little Indian Creek—*stream* (2) .......... VA-3
Little Indian Creek—*stream* (2) .......... WV-2
Little Indian Creek—*stream* (3) .......... WY-8
Little Indian Creek Cem—*cemetery* .......... IL-6
Little Indian Creek Ch—*church* .......... AL-4
Little Indian Creek Ch—*church* .......... KY-4
*Little Indian Creek Primitive Baptist Ch* .......... AL-4
Little Indian Ditch—*canal* .......... ID-8
Little Indian Draw—*valley* .......... CO-8
Little Indian Draw—*valley* .......... WY-8
Little Indian Fork—*stream* .......... WV-2
Little Indian Guyan Creek—*stream* .......... OH-6
Little Indian Hill—*summit* .......... ME-1
Little Indian Hollow—*valley* .......... PA-2
*Little Indian Lake* .......... ME-1
Little Indian Lake—*lake* (2) .......... MI-6
Little Indian Pond—*lake* (5) .......... ME-1
*Little Indian Prairie* .......... MT-8
*Little Indian river* .......... MN-6
Little Indian River—*stream* .......... AK-9
Little Indian River—*stream* .......... MI-6
Little Indian Run—*stream* .......... OH-6
Little Indian Run—*stream* (2) .......... PA-2
Little Indian Run—*stream* .......... VA-3
Little Indian Run—*stream* (3) .......... WV-2
Little Indian Sioux River—*stream* .......... MN-6
Little Indian Spring—*spring* .......... NV-8
Little Indian Stream—*stream* .......... ME-1
Little Indian Swamp—*stream* .......... NC-3
Little Indian Tank—*reservoir* .......... AZ-5
Little Indian Valley—*basin* .......... CA-9
Little Indian Valley—*valley* .......... CA-9
Little Inky Lake—*lake* .......... MN-6
Little Inlet—*gut* .......... VA-3
Little Inlet—*stream* .......... ME-1
Little Inlet—*stream* .......... NY-2
Little Inskip Hill—*summit* .......... CA-9
Little Ioni Creek—*stream* .......... TX-5
Little Iowa River—*stream* .......... MN-6
*Little Ireland* .......... TN-4
Little Ireland Cem—*cemetery* .......... VT-1
Little Irish Bayou—*gut* .......... LA-4
Little Irish Creek—*stream* .......... VA-3
Little Irish Mtn—*summit* .......... VA-3
Little Irish Ridge—*ridge* .......... WI-6
Little Iron Island—*island* .......... ME-1
*Little Iron Lake* .......... MN-6
Little Iron Lake—*lake* .......... MN-6
Little Iron Ore Creek—*stream* .......... TX-5
*Little Iron River* .......... MI-6
Little Iron River—*stream* .......... MI-6
Little Ironsides Islands—*island* .......... NY-2
*Little Ironside Isles* .......... NY-2
Little Isaac Creek—*stream* (2) .......... WV-2
Little Isaacs Creek—*stream* .......... VA-3
Little Isabella River—*stream* .......... MN-6
*Little Island* .......... AL-4
*Little Island* .......... MD-2
*Little Island* .......... NY-2
*Little Island* .......... WA-9
Little Island—*area* .......... AR-4
Little Island—*bench* .......... NV-8
Little Island—*cape* (2) .......... MA-1
Little Island—*cape* .......... WA-9
Little Island—*flat* .......... MS-4
Little Island—*island* .......... AL-4
Little Island—*island* (2) .......... AK-9
Little Island—*island* .......... AR-4
Little Island—*island* .......... CA-9
Little Island—*island* .......... DC-2
Little Island—*island* (3) .......... GA-3
Little Island—*island* .......... ID-8
Little Island—*island* .......... IL-6
Little Island—*island* (3) .......... LA-4
Little Island—*island* (6) .......... ME-1
Little Island—*island* (3) .......... MD-2
Little Island—*island* (5) .......... MA-1
Little Island—*island* (2) .......... MI-6
Little Island—*island* .......... MS-4
Little Island—*island* (3) .......... NH-1
Little Island—*island* .......... NJ-2
Little Island—*island* (5) .......... NY-2
Little Island—*island* (2) .......... NC-3
Little Island—*island* .......... PA-2
Little Island—*island* .......... RI-1
Little Island—*island* .......... VA-3
Little Island—*island* .......... WA-9
Little Island—*island* (2) .......... WI-6
Little Island Bayou—*stream* .......... AR-4
Little Island Branch—*stream* .......... KY-4
Little Island Coast Guard Station—*locale* .......... VA-3
*Little Island Creek* .......... NC-3
*Little Island Creek* .......... VA-3
Little Island Creek—*stream* .......... GA-3
Little Island Creek—*stream* (2) .......... NC-3
Little Island Creek—*stream* .......... WV-2
Little Island (historical)—*island* .......... TN-4
Little Island Lake—*lake* .......... FL-3
Little Island Lake—*lake* (2) .......... MI-6
Little Island Lake—*lake* (3) .......... MN-6
Little Island Lake—*lake* (2) .......... WI-6
Little Island Mtn—*summit* .......... NV-8
Little Island Pass—*channel* .......... LA-4
*Little Island Pond* .......... MA-1
Little Island Pond—*lake* .......... ME-1
Little Island Pond—*lake* .......... NH-1
**Little Island Pond**—*pop pl* .......... NH-1
Little Island Run—*stream* .......... WV-2
Little Islands—*island* .......... LA-4
Little Israel Christian Ranch—*locale* .......... AL-4
Little Israel Pond—*lake* .......... MA-1
*Little Italy* .......... AR-4
Little Italy—*locale* .......... PA-2
Little Italy—*locale* .......... WV-2
**Little Italy**—*pop pl* .......... AR-4
**Little Italy**—*pop pl* .......... ME-1
**Little Italy**—*pop pl* .......... MS-4
**Little Italy**—*pop pl* .......... WV-2
Little Ivy Ch—*church* .......... NC-3
Little Ivy Creek—*stream* .......... GA-3
Little Ivy Creek—*stream* .......... NC-3
Little Ivy Creek—*stream* (2) .......... VA-3
Little Jabe Pond—*lake* .......... NY-2
Little Jackass Campground—*locale* .......... CA-9
Little Jackass Creek—*stream* (2) .......... CA-9
Little Jackass Mtn—*summit* .......... WA-9
Little Jackass Spring—*spring* .......... ID-8
Little Jack Bayou—*stream* .......... MS-4
**Little Jack Corners**—*pop pl* .......... PA-2
*Little Jack Creek* .......... WY-8
Little Jack Creek—*stream* .......... AK-9
Little Jack Creek—*stream* (2) .......... NV-8
Little Jack Creek—*stream* .......... TN-4
Little Jack Creek—*stream* .......... WY-8
Little Jack Creek Rsvr—*reservoir* .......... OR-9
Little Jacket Creek—*stream* .......... ID-8
Little Jack Falls—*stream* .......... OR-9
Little Jack Lake—*lake* .......... AR-4
Little Jacks Brook—*stream* .......... CT-1
Little Jacks Creek—*stream* .......... AL-4
Little Jacks Creek—*stream* .......... ID-8
Little Jacks Creek—*stream* .......... TX-5
Little Jacks Creek—*stream* .......... VA-3
Little Jacks Creek Basin—*basin* .......... ID-8
Little Jacks Lake—*lake* .......... CA-9
Little Jack Slough—*stream* .......... AK-9
Little Jackson Bayou—*stream* .......... MS-4
Little Jackson Canyon—*valley* .......... CA-9
Little Jackson Creek—*stream* .......... CA-9
Little Jackson Creek—*stream* .......... ID-8
Little Jackson Creek—*stream* .......... MT-8
Little Jackson Creek—*stream* .......... SC-3
Little Jackson Creek—*stream* .......... WA-9
Little Jackson Hollow—*valley* .......... PA-2
Little Jackson Lake—*lake* .......... CA-9
Little Jackson Mtn—*summit* .......... ME-1
Little Jackson Sch—*school* .......... MI-6
Little Jacob Creek—*stream* .......... TN-4
Little Jacobs Creek—*stream* .......... AL-4
Little Jacobs Creek—*stream* .......... NC-3
Little Jacob Swamp—*stream* .......... NC-3
Little Jake Hollow—*valley* .......... UT-8
*Little Jakes Creek* .......... IN-6
Little James Creek—*stream* .......... CO-8
Little Jameson Creek—*stream* .......... IN-6
Little Jamison Creek—*stream* .......... CA-9
Little Jammer Lake—*lake* .......... MN-6
Little Jara Windmill—*locale* .......... NM-5
Little Jardin Windmill—*locale* .......... TX-5
Little Jarrells Creek—*stream* .......... WV-2
*Little Jarrells Fork* .......... WV-2
Little Jarvis Glacier—*glacier* .......... AK-9
Little Jarvis Lake—*lake* .......... ID-8
Little Jawbone Canyon—*valley* .......... CA-9
Little Jay—*summit* .......... VT-1
Little Jay Gould Lake—*lake* .......... MN-6
Little Jeff Canyon—*valley* .......... CO-8
Little Jefferson Lake—*lake* .......... AR-4
Little Jeff Tank—*reservoir* .......... AZ-5
Little Jellison Hill Pond—*lake* .......... ME-1
Little Jelloway Creek—*stream* .......... OH-6
Little Jenkins Creek—*stream* .......... CO-8
Little Jenkins Mtn—*summit* .......... VA-3
LITTLE JENNIE (Chesapeake Bay bugeye)—*hist pl* .......... NY-2
*Little Jennings Creek* .......... TN-4
Little Jennings Creek Trail—*trail* .......... TN-4
Little Jennings Mtn—*summit* .......... NY-2
Little Jenny Branch—*stream* .......... WV-2
Little Jenny Creek—*stream* .......... NV-8
Little Jenny Lake—*lake* .......... WY-8
Little Jensay Creek—*stream* .......... MS-4
Little Jensen Pass—*gap* .......... UT-8
Little Jeptha Creek—*stream* .......... KY-4
Little Jernigan Lake—*lake* .......... TX-5
**Little Jersey**—*pop pl* .......... DE-2
*Little Jerusalem* .......... MS-4
Little Jerusalem AME Church—*hist pl* .......... PA-2
Little Jerusalem Ch—*church* .......... KY-4
Little Jerusalem Ch—*church* .......... MS-4
Little Jerusalem Ch of God—*church* .......... AL-4
Little Jerusalem Island—*island* .......... WA-9
Little Jesse James Canyon—*valley* .......... AZ-5
Little Jessie Island—*island* .......... FL-3
Little Jessie Lake—*lake* .......... MN-6
*Little Jet Creek* .......... NV-8
Little Jett Creek—*stream* .......... NV-8
Little Jewell Mine—*mine* .......... NV-8
Little Jicarita Peak—*summit* .......... NM-5
Little Jim Canyon—*valley* .......... UT-8
Little Jim Creek—*stream* (2) .......... WA-9
Little Jim Gulch—*valley* .......... OR-9
Little Jim Lake—*lake* .......... MN-6
Little Jimmerson Spring—*spring* .......... CA-9
Little Jim Mine—*mine* .......... OR-9
Little Jim Mission—*church* .......... OK-5
Little Jimmy Campground—*locale* .......... CA-9
*Little Jimmys Creek* .......... TX-5
Little Jimmys Creek—*stream* .......... TX-5
Little Jimmy Spring—*spring* .......... CA-9
Little Jim Pond—*lake* .......... ME-1
Little Jim Tank—*reservoir* (2) .......... AZ-5
Little Joaquin Valley—*valley* .......... CA-9
Little Jobs Creek—*stream* .......... IL-6
Little Jo Creek—*stream* .......... WY-8
Little Joe Bald—*summit* .......... MO-7
Little Joe Basin—*basin* .......... CO-8
Little Joe Butte—*summit* .......... ID-8
Little Joe Butte—*summit* .......... MT-8
Little Joe Campground—*locale* .......... MT-8
Little Joe Canyon—*valley* .......... CO-8
Little Joe Creek—*stream* .......... AK-9
Little Joe Creek—*stream* .......... AR-4
Little Joe Creek—*stream* (2) .......... IN-6
Little Joe Creek—*stream* .......... KY-4
Little Joe Creek—*stream* (3) .......... MT-8
Little Joe Creek—*stream* .......... OR-9
Little Joe Creek—*stream* .......... VA-3
Little Joe Creek—*stream* .......... WA-9
Little Joe Dam—*other* .......... WY-8
Little Joe Day Branch—*stream* .......... KY-4
Little Joe Draw—*valley* .......... AZ-5
Little Joe Draw—*valley* .......... CO-8
Little Joe Flat—*flat* .......... CA-9
Little Joe Gulch—*valley* .......... AK-9
Little Joe Gulch—*valley* .......... MT-8
*Little Joe Lake* .......... WI-6
Little Joe Lake—*lake* .......... GA-3
Little Joe Lake—*lake* .......... MI-6
Little Joe Lake—*lake* .......... MT-8
Little Joe Lake—*lake* .......... WA-9
Little Joe Lake—*reservoir* .......... AR-4
Little Joe Lookout Station—*locale* .......... MT-8
Little Joe May Canyon—*valley* .......... NV-8
Little Joe Meadows—*swamp* .......... MT-8
Little Joe Mine—*mine* .......... AZ-5
Little Joe Mine—*mine* .......... CO-8
Little Joe Mine—*mine* .......... NM-5
Little Joe Mtn—*summit* .......... ID-8
Little Joe Mtn—*summit* .......... MT-8
Little Joe Oil Field—*oilfield* .......... TX-5
Little Joe River—*stream* .......... MN-6
Little Joe Rsvr—*reservoir* .......... OR-9
Little Joe Run—*stream* .......... PA-2
Little Joes Ch—*church* .......... NC-3
Little Joes Fish Camp—*locale* .......... AL-4
Little Joe Spring—*spring* .......... AZ-5
Little Joe Spring—*spring* .......... CO-8
Little Joe Spring—*spring* .......... NV-8
Little Joe Spring—*spring* .......... SD-7
Little Joe Tank—*reservoir* (2) .......... AZ-5
Little Joe Tank—*reservoir* (2) .......... NM-5
Little Joe Windmill—*locale* .......... NM-5
Littlejohn, Joseph B., House—*hist pl* .......... NC-3
Littlejohn Branch—*stream* .......... TN-4
Littlejohn Cem—*cemetery* .......... AL-4
Littlejohn Cem—*cemetery* .......... AR-4
Little John Cem—*cemetery* .......... IN-6
Littlejohn Cem—*cemetery* .......... SC-3
Little John Cem—*cemetery* .......... TN-4
Littlejohn Cem—*cemetery* .......... TX-5
Littlejohn Ch—*church* .......... NC-3
Little John Creek—*stream* .......... GA-3
Little John Creek—*stream* .......... ID-8
Little John Creek—*stream* .......... KS-7
Little John Creek—*stream* .......... KY-4
Little John Creek—*stream* .......... NC-3
Little John Day Creek—*stream* .......... OR-9
*Little John Days River* .......... WY-8
Little John Dick Mtn—*summit* .......... GA-3
Littlejohn Hill—*summit* .......... TN-4
Little John Hollow—*valley* .......... MO-7
Littlejohn House—*building* .......... NC-3
Littlejohn Island—*island* .......... ME-1
**Littlejohn Island**—*pop pl* .......... ME-1
Little John Junior Lake—*lake* .......... WI-6
Littlejohn Lagoon—*bay* .......... AK-9
*Little John Lake* .......... MI-6
Littlejohn Lake—*lake* .......... MI-6
Little John Lake—*lake* (2) .......... MN-6
Little John Lake—*lake* .......... WI-6
Littlejohn Lateral—*canal* .......... ID-8
Little John Mann Creek—*stream* .......... TX-5
Littlejohn Mine Complex—*hist pl* .......... CO-8
Little John Mtn—*summit* .......... NY-2
Little Johnnie Mine—*mine* .......... WY-8
Little Johnnies Creek—*stream* .......... AR-4
Little Johnny Canyon—*valley* .......... UT-8
Little Johnny Mine—*mine* .......... AZ-5
Little Johnny Mine—*mine* .......... WA-9
Little Johnny Mtn—*summit* .......... MA-1
Little Johnny Windmill—*locale* .......... NM-5
Little John Ranch—*locale* .......... WY-8
Littlejohn Rock—*bar* .......... ME-1
Little John Rsvr—*reservoir* .......... OR-9
Little Johns Cabin—*locale* .......... CO-8
Littlejohn Sch—*school* .......... CA-9
Littlejohn Sch—*school* .......... IL-6
Little John Sch—*school* .......... NE-7
Littlejohns Creek—*stream* .......... AL-4
Littlejohns Creek—*stream* .......... CA-9
Little Johns Creek—*stream* .......... SC-3
Littlejohns Dam—*dam* .......... CA-9
Little Johnson Bayou—*bay* .......... FL-3
*Little Johnson Creek* .......... TN-4
Little Johnson Creek—*stream* .......... CO-8
Little Johnson Creek—*stream* .......... ID-8
Little Johnson Creek—*stream* .......... MS-4
Little Johnson Creek—*stream* .......... NC-3
Little Johnson Creek—*stream* .......... OR-9
Little Johnson Creek—*stream* .......... SC-3
Little Johnson Creek—*stream* .......... TN-4
Little Johnson Creek—*stream* .......... WA-9
Little Johnson Lake—*lake* .......... AR-4
Little Johnson Lake—*lake* .......... LA-4
Little Johnson Lake—*lake* .......... MN-6
Little Johnson Lake—*lake* .......... MT-8
Little Johnson Pond—*lake* .......... ME-1
Little Johnson Rsvr—*reservoir* .......... CO-8
Little Johnsontown—*locale* .......... VA-3
Littlejohn State Game Mngmt Area—*park* .......... NY-2
Little John Store (historical)—*locale* .......... MS-4
Little Johny Creek—*stream* .......... AK-9
Little Joiner Creek—*stream* .......... GA-3
Little Joker Island—*island* .......... AK-9
Little Joker Mine—*mine* .......... AZ-5
Little Joker Spring—*spring* .......... AZ-5
Little Jo Lake—*lake* .......... CA-9
Little Jollo Creek—*stream* .......... CA-9
Little Jonas Creek—*stream* .......... NC-3
Little Jonathan Creek—*stream* .......... KY-4
Little Jones Creek—*gut* .......... SC-3
Little Jones Creek—*stream* .......... CA-9
Little Jones Creek—*stream* .......... FL-3
Little Jones Creek—*stream* .......... GA-3
Little Jones Creek—*stream* .......... TN-4
Little Jones Gut—*stream* .......... MD-2
Little Jones Lake—*lake* .......... AR-4
Little Jones Pond—*lake* .......... AZ-5
Little Jordan Branch—*stream* .......... LA-4
Little Jordan Branch—*stream* .......... MO-7
Little Jordan Cem—*cemetery* .......... KY-4
Little Jordan Cem—*cemetery* .......... TX-5
Little Jordan Creek—*stream* .......... MS-4
Little Jordan Lake—*lake* .......... AR-4
Little Jordan Lake—*lake* .......... NY-2
*Little Jordan Creek* .......... MS-4
Little Jose Pond—*lake* .......... ME-1
Little Josh Canyon—*valley* .......... WY-8
Little Joshua Creek—*stream* .......... TX-5
Little Jo State Wildlife Mngmt Area—*park* .......... MN-6
Little Juan Creek—*stream* .......... CA-9
Little Juan Largo Canyon—*valley* .......... NM-5
Little Juan Tank—*reservoir* .......... AZ-5
Little Judith Islands—*island* .......... NC-3
Little Judy Creek—*stream* .......... AL-4
Little Jug Tank—*reservoir* .......... NM-5
Little Jug Tank—*reservoir* .......... TX-5
Little Julia Mine—*mine* .......... NM-5
Little Julia No 1 Mine—*mine* .......... NM-5
Little Jumbo Creek—*stream* .......... ID-8
Little Jump Bar (historical)—*bar* .......... AL-4
Little Jump Rapids—*rapids* .......... TN-4
*Little Jump River* .......... WI-6
Little Jump River—*stream* .......... WI-6
Little Juniata Creek—*stream* .......... PA-2
Little Juniata Natural Area—*area* .......... PA-2
Little Juniata River—*stream* .......... PA-2
Little Juniper Basin Rsvr—*reservoir* .......... ID-8
Little Juniper Bay—*swamp* .......... NC-3
Little Juniper Branch—*stream* .......... NC-3
Little Juniper Canyon—*valley* .......... OR-9
Little Juniper Creek—*stream* .......... AL-4
Little Juniper Creek—*stream* .......... CA-9
Little Juniper Creek—*stream* .......... FL-3
Little Juniper Creek—*stream* .......... GA-3
Little Juniper Creek—*stream* (2) .......... NC-3
Little Juniper Creek—*stream* .......... SC-3
Little Juniper Creek—*stream* .......... VA-3
Little Juniper Mtn—*summit* .......... CO-8
Little Juniper Mtn—*summit* (2) .......... OR-9
Little Juniper Peak—*summit* .......... NM-5
*Little Juniper Rsvr* .......... OR-9
Little Juniper Rsvr—*reservoir* .......... CA-9
Little Juniper Rsvr—*reservoir* .......... OR-9
Little Juniper Run—*stream* .......... NC-3
Little Juniper Spring—*spring* .......... OR-9
Little Junkyard Bay—*swamp* .......... SC-3
Little Jupiter Mine—*mine* .......... NV-8
Little Jureano Creek—*stream* .......... ID-8
Little Kabyai Creek—*stream* .......... CA-9
Little Kachess Lake—*lake* .......... WA-9
Little Kalama River—*stream* .......... WA-9
*Little Kalispell Creek* .......... WA-9
Little Kalusuk Creek—*stream* .......... AK-9
Little Kamishak River—*stream* .......... AK-9
*Little Kanahwa River* .......... WV-2
Little Kanaka Creek—*stream* .......... CA-9
Little Kanatak Creek—*stream* .......... AK-9
Little Kanawha River—*stream* .......... WV-2
Little Kandiyohi Lake—*lake* .......... MN-6
Little Kane Creek—*stream* .......... ID-8
Little Kane Spring—*spring* .......... ID-8
Little Kankakee River—*stream* .......... IN-6
Little Kansas—*locale* .......... PA-2
Little Kansas Cem—*cemetery* .......... CO-8
Little Kasigluk River—*stream* .......... AK-9
*Little Kate Lake* .......... MI-6
Little Kate Mine—*mine* .......... CO-8
Little Kates Lake—*lake* .......... MI-6
Little Kaukauna Lock and Dam—*dam* .......... WI-6
Little Kaw—*locale* .......... KS-7
*Little Kawahwa River* .......... WV-2
Little Kaw Creek—*stream* .......... KS-7
*Little Keaton Lake* .......... AL-4
Little Keaton Lake—*lake* .......... AL-4
Little Keechi Creek—*stream* (2) .......... TX-5
Little Keen Pond—*reservoir* .......... PA-2
Little Keen Pond Dam—*dam* .......... PA-2
Little Keg Creek—*stream* .......... GA-3
Little Keg Creek—*stream* .......... IA-7
Little Kekegama Lake—*lake* .......... WI-6
Little Kellen Hollow—*valley* .......... KY-4
Little Keller Lake—*lake* .......... IA-7
Little Kelley Creek—*stream* .......... MI-6
Little Kelley Tank—*reservoir* .......... AZ-5
**Little Kelly**—*pop pl* .......... NC-3
Little Kelly Pond—*lake* .......... ME-1
Little Kelsay Creek—*stream* .......... OR-9
Little Kennebago Lake—*lake* .......... ME-1
Little Kennebec Bay—*bay* .......... ME-1
Little Kennesaw Mtn—*summit* .......... GA-3
Little Kentawka Canal—*canal* .......... MS-4
Little Kentucky Oil Field—*oilfield* .......... TX-5
Little Kentucky River—*stream* .......... KY-4
Little Kerber Creek—*stream* .......... CO-8
Little Kernel Tree Branch—*stream* .......... NC-3
Little Kern Lake—*lake* .......... CA-9
Little Kern Lake Creek—*stream* .......... CA-9
Little Kern River—*stream* .......... CA-9
Little Kershaw Canyon—*valley* .......... NV-8
Little Ketchepedrakee Creek—*stream* .......... AL-4
Little Kettle—*basin* .......... PA-2
Little Kettle Creek—*stream* .......... GA-3
Little Kettle Creek—*stream* .......... MS-4
Little Kettle Creek—*stream* .......... OR-9
Little Kettle Creek—*stream* .......... PA-2
Little Kettle Lake—*lake* .......... MN-6
Little Kettle Mtn—*summit* .......... PA-2
Little Keyhole Lake—*lake* .......... WY-8
Little Kickapoo Creek—*stream* .......... IL-6
Little Kickapoo Creek—*stream* .......... WI-6
Little Kid Hollow—*valley* .......... TX-5
Little Kiesche Creek—*stream* .......... LA-4
Little Kiffer Point—*cape* .......... SC-3
Little Kiger Creek—*stream* .......... OR-9
*Little Kilbuck Creek* .......... IN-6
Little Kilbuck Creek—*stream* .......... OH-6
Little Kilby Lake—*lake* .......... MS-4
**Little Killarney Beach**—*pop pl* .......... MI-6
*Little Killbuck Creek* .......... IN-6
Little Killbuck Creek—*stream* .......... IN-6
Little Killbuck Creek—*stream* .......... OH-6
Little Killbuck Run—*stream* .......... PA-2
Little Killington—*summit* .......... VT-1
*Little Kiln Creek* .......... WV-2
Little Kilsock Bay—*swamp* .......... SC-3
Little Kimball Creek—*stream* .......... TX-5
Little Kimble Mine—*mine* .......... AZ-5
Little Kimbrough Creek—*stream* .......... OK-5
Little Kimshew Creek—*stream* .......... CA-9
Little Kincaid Windmill—*locale* .......... TX-5
Little Kinchlow Hollow—*valley* .......... MO-7
Little Kinchlow Hollow Cove—*bay* .......... MO-7
Little Kineo Mtn—*summit* .......... ME-1
Little-King Cem—*cemetery* .......... TN-4
Little Kingdom Ch—*church* .......... LA-4
Little Kingdom Come Ch (historical)—*church* .......... MS-4
Little King Lake—*lake* .......... ME-1
Little King Lake—*lake* .......... MI-6
Little King Mines—*mine* .......... WA-9
*Little King Reservoir* .......... WY-8
Little King Ridge—*ridge* .......... ME-1
Little Kings Creek—*stream* .......... NC-3
Little Kings Creek—*stream* .......... SC-3
Little Kingsley Creek—*stream* .......... MN-6
*Little Kingston* .......... AL-4
Little Kingston Creek—*bay* .......... MD-2
Little Kinkaid Creek—*stream* .......... IL-6
Little Kinnakeet—*locale* .......... NC-3
Little Kinterbish Creek—*stream* .......... AL-4
Little Kiokee Creek—*stream* .......... GA-3
Little Kiowa Creek—*stream* .......... OK-5
Little Kisatchie Bayou—*stream* .......... LA-4
Little Kishacoquillas Creek—*stream* .......... PA-2
Little Kiska Head—*cliff* .......... AK-9
Little Kiska Island—*island* .......... AK-9
Little Kitchens Ridge—*ridge* .......... NC-3
Little Kitoi Lake—*lake* .......... AK-9
Little Kitten Creek—*stream* .......... KS-7
Little Klacking Creek—*stream* .......... MI-6
*Little Klamath Lake* .......... CA-9
*Little Klamath Lake* .......... OR-9
Little Klickitat River—*stream* .......... WA-9
Little Kline Creek—*stream* .......... CO-8
*Little Klonaqua Lake* .......... WA-9
Little Klondike Mine—*mine* .......... ID-8
Little Knapp Lake—*reservoir* .......... IN-6
Little Knawl Creek—*stream* .......... WV-2
Little Knife River—*stream* (2) .......... MN-6
Little Knife River—*stream* (2) .......... ND-7
Little Knisely Canyon—*valley* .......... NM-5
*Little Knob* .......... TN-4
Little Knob—*summit* (2) .......... KY-4
Little Knob—*summit* .......... MD-2
Little Knob—*summit* .......... MO-7
Little Knob—*summit* (2) .......... NC-3
Little Knob—*summit* .......... OK-5
Little Knob—*summit* (2) .......... PA-2
Little Knob—*summit* .......... SC-3
Little Knob—*summit* .......... TN-4
Little Knob Creek—*stream* .......... NC-3
Little Knob Mtn—*summit* .......... NY-2
Little Knockemdown Key—*island* .......... FL-3
Little Knoll—*summit* .......... AZ-5
Little Knoll—*summit* .......... UT-8
Little Knox Island—*island* .......... MN-6
Little Knubble—*island* .......... ME-1
Little Kobuk Sand Dunes—*area* .......... AK-9
**Little Kohler**—*pop pl* .......... WI-6
Little Kolomoki Creek—*stream* .......... GA-3
Little Koniuji Island—*island* .......... AK-9
Little Kotlik River—*stream* .......... AK-9
Little Kowaliga Creek—*stream* .......... AL-4
Little K P Lake—*lake* .......... MI-6
Little Kyger Ch—*church* .......... OH-6
Little Kyger Creek—*stream* .......... OH-6
Little Kyger Grange—*locale* .......... OH-6
Little KY Tank—*reservoir* .......... AZ-5
Little Labette Creek—*stream* .......... KS-7
Little Labrador Pond—*lake* .......... ME-1
Little Lacassine Bayou—*gut* .......... LA-4
Little Lac Courte Oreilles—*lake* .......... WI-6
*Little Lacrosse Lake* .......... MI-6
Little LaCrosse River—*stream* .......... WI-6
Little Laddie Tank—*reservoir* .......... NM-5
Little Ladies Canyon—*valley* .......... CA-9
Little La Garita Creek—*stream* .......... CO-8
*Little Lagoon* .......... AL-4
Little Lagoon—*lake* (2) .......... AK-9
Little Lagoon—*lake* .......... CA-9
Little Lagoon—*lake* (2) .......... LA-4
Little La Grange—*hist pl* .......... VI-3
Little La Grange—*locale* .......... VI-3
Little LaGrue Bayou—*stream* .......... AR-4
*Little La Grue Creek* .......... AR-4
Little Laguna Lake—*lake* .......... CA-9
Little Lahey Creek—*stream* .......... TX-5
Little Laidlaw Park—*flat* .......... ID-8
*Little Laidlow Park* .......... ID-8
*Little Lake* .......... AL-4
*Little Lake* .......... CA-9
*Little Lake* .......... IL-6
*Little Lake* .......... IN-6
*Little Lake* .......... ME-1
*Little Lake* .......... MN-6
*Little Lake* .......... MS-4
*Little Lake* .......... NY-2
*Little Lake* .......... OH-6
*Little Lake* .......... OR-9
*Little Lake* .......... UT-8
Little Lake—*bay* .......... LA-4
Little Lake—*lake* (2) .......... AL-4
Little Lake—*lake* (4) .......... AK-9
Little Lake—*lake* (4) .......... AR-4
Little Lake—*lake* (4) .......... CA-9
Little Lake—*lake* (5) .......... FL-3
Little Lake—*lake* .......... GA-3
Little Lake—*lake* (3) .......... ID-8
Little Lake—*lake* (2) .......... IL-6
Little Lake—*lake* (2) .......... IN-6
Little Lake—*lake* (8) .......... LA-4
Little Lake—*lake* .......... ME-1
Little Lake—*lake* (18) .......... MI-6
Little Lake—*lake* (12) .......... MN-6
Little Lake—*lake* (4) .......... MS-4
Little Lake—*lake* (2) .......... MT-8
Little Lake—*lake* .......... NV-8
Little Lake—*lake* .......... NH-1
Little Lake—*lake* (2) .......... NM-5
Little Lake—*lake* (5) .......... NY-2
Little Lake—*lake* .......... NC-3
Little Lake—*lake* .......... OH-6
Little Lake—*lake* (4) .......... OR-9
Little Lake—*lake* .......... PA-2
Little Lake—*lake* (3) .......... SC-3
Little Lake—*lake* (6) .......... TX-5
Little Lake—*lake* (2) .......... UT-8
Little Lake—*lake* .......... VT-1
Little Lake—*lake* (6) .......... WA-9
Little Lake—*lake* (7) .......... WI-6
**Little Lake**—*pop pl* (2) .......... CA-9
**Little Lake**—*pop pl* .......... MI-6
Little Lake—*reservoir* .......... CA-9
Little Lake—*reservoir* .......... IN-6
Little Lake—*reservoir* .......... TN-4
Little Lake—*reservoir* .......... TX-5
Little Lake—*swamp* .......... MN-6
Little Lake Agnes—*lake* .......... FL-3
Little Lake Arrowhead—*reservoir* .......... VA-3
Little Lake Barton—*lake* .......... FL-3
Little Lake Batola—*lake* .......... LA-4
Little Lake Bayou—*gut* .......... AR-4
Little Lake Benoit—*lake* .......... LA-4
Little Lake Bryan—*lake* .......... FL-3
Little Lake Bryant—*lake* .......... FL-3
Little Lake Butte Des Morts—*lake* .......... WI-6
Little Lake Canyon—*valley* .......... CA-9
*Little Lake Cavanaugh* .......... WA-9
Little Lake Cem—*cemetery* (2) .......... CA-9
**Little Lake City**—*pop pl* .......... FL-3
Little Lake Clark—*lake* .......... AK-9

Little Mill Hollow—valley TN-4
Little Millican Creek—stream TN-4
**Little Milligan**—pop pl TN-4
Little Milligan Baptist Ch—church TN-4
Little Milligan Elem Sch—school TN-4
Little Millinocket Lake—lake ME-1
Little Mill Lake—lake MI-6
Little Mill Lake—lake MN-6
Little Mill Mtn—summit NY-2
Little Mill Point—cape AR-4
Little Mill Pond MD-2
Little Mill Pond—lake MA-1
Little Millpond—locale MD-2
Little Millrace—canal CA-9
Little Mill Run—stream MD-2
Little Mill Run—stream WV-2
Little Mills Creek—stream FL-3
Little Millseat Branch—stream KY-4
Little Mills Wells—well NM-5
Little Minam Creek OR-9
Little Minam Meadow—flat OR-9
Little Minam River—stream OR-9
Little Mincy Creek—stream MO-7
Little Mine Creek—stream SC-3
Little Mine Fork—stream KY-4
Little Mine Fork Sch—school KY-4
Little Mineral Arm—bay TX-5
Little Mineral Creek—stream NM-5
Little Mineral Creek—stream TX-5
Little Mineral Lake—lake GA-3
Little Mine Road Ch—church VA-3
Little Mine Run (historical)—stream PA-2
Little Minerva Branch—stream IA-7
Little Minerva Creek IA-7
Little Mingo Creek—stream AR-4
Little Mingo Creek—stream CA-9
Little Minister Pond—lake ME-1
Little Minister Run—stream PA-2
Little Mink Creek—stream MN-6
Little Mink Hole—lake MA-1
Little Mink Island NH-1
Little Mink Lake—lake AK-9
Little Mink Pond MA-1
Little Minnesota River—stream MN-6
Little Minnesota River—stream SD-7
Little Minnie Creek—stream NE-7
Little Minnow Creek AR-4
Little Minnow Creek—stream MS-4
Little Minook Creek—stream AK-9
Little Minook Junior Creek—stream AK-9
Little Minum River OR-9
Little Mioxes Pond—lake MA-1
Little Mirror Lake—lake MA-1
Little Mirror Lake—lake WI-6
Little Misale Bayou—gut LA-4
Little Misery Island—island MA-1
Little Misery River—stream MI-6
Little Mission—church GA-3
Little Mission Ch—church AL-4
Little Mission Ch—church KY-4
Little Mission Ch—church SC-3
Little Mission Chapel—church WI-6
Little Mission Church TN-4
Little Mission Creek—stream MT-8
Little Mission Creek—stream WA-9
Little Mission Temple—church NC-3
Little Mississinewa River—stream IN-6
Little Mississippi Cem—cemetery TX-5
Little Mississippi Creek—stream AL-4
Little Mississippi River—stream MN-6
Little Miss Muffet Sch—school FL-3
Little Missouri—cens area MT-8
**Little Missouri**—pop pl ND-7
Little Missouri Badlands—area ND-7
Little Missouri Bank Bldg—hist pl SD-7
Little Missouri Bend (historical)—bend ND-7
Little Missouri Creek—stream (2) IL-6
Little Missouri Creek—stream WI-6
Little Missouri Hollow—valley MO-7
Little Missouri Public Use Area—park ND-7
Little Missouri River SD-7
Little Missouri River WY-8
Little Missouri River—stream AR-4
Little Missouri River—stream MT-8
Little Missouri River—stream ND-7
Little Missouri River*—stream SD-7
Little Missouri River—stream WY-8
Little Missouri Sch—school IL-6
Little Mitchell Creek—stream WY-8
Little Mitchell Creek Breaks—range WY-8
Little Mitchell Slough—stream WY-8
Little Mitten Lake—reservoir NJ-2
Little Mitten Lake Dam NJ-2
Little Moccasin Branch—stream TN-4
Little Moccasin Canyon—valley CO-8
Little Moccasin Creek—stream FL-3
Little Moccasin Creek—stream IL-6
Little Moccasin Creek—stream KY-4
Little Moccasin Creek—stream (2) VA-3
Little Moccasin Gap—gap VA-3
Little Moccasin Lake—lake CA-9
Little Moccasin Lake—lake WI-6
Little Moccasin Lake—lake WY-8
Little Mod Run—stream WV-2
Little Moffat Gulch—valley MT-8
Little Mokelumne River—stream CA-9
Little Molas Lake—lake CO-8
Little Molasses River—stream MI-6
Little Molunkus Stream—stream ME-1
Little Monadnock Mtn—summit NH-1
Little Monday Creek—stream OH-6
Little Monday Creek—stream VA-3
Little Mondeaux Creek—stream WI-6
Little Monegaw Creek—stream MO-7
Little Money Key—island FL-3
Little Monica Canyon—valley NM-5
Little Monie Creek—stream MD-2
Little Moniteau Creek—stream MO-7
Little Monitor Creek—stream CO-8
Little Monitor Rsvr—reservoir CO-8
Little Monmt—pillar WY-8
Little Monocacy River—stream MD-2
Little Monocnoc Lake—lake MS-4
Little Monon Creek IN-6
Little Monroe Windmill—locale TX-5
Little Montana Creek—stream AK-9
Little Monte—summit UT-8
Little Monteocha Creek—stream FL-3
Little Montgomery—locale VA-3
Little Montgomery Street Hist Dist—hist pl MD-2
Little Montreal River MI-6
Little Monty Bay NY-2
Little Monument Canyon—valley UT-8
Little Moody Creek—stream VA-3
Little Mooney Creek—stream IL-6
Little Moon Lake MI-6
Little Moon Lake—lake AR-4
Little Moon Lake—lake FL-3
Little Moon Lake—lake MI-6
Little Moon Lake—lake WI-6
Little Moon Lake—lake WY-8
Little Moon Mtn—summit MA-1
Little Moonshine Creek—stream TX-5
Little Moorehead Ridge—ridge CA-9
Little Moores Run—stream PA-2
Little Moose Creek—stream AK-9
Little Moose Creek—stream (4) ID-8
Little Moose Creek—stream (2) MT-8
Little Moosehead Pond—lake NY-2
Little Moose Hill—summit ME-1
Little Moose Hill—summit MA-1
Little Moosehorn Creek—stream MT-8
Little Moose Island—island (2) ME-1
Little Moose Lake MN-6
Little Moose Lake—lake (4) MN-6
Little Moose Lake—lake (2) NY-2
Little Moose Lake—lake WI-6
Little Moose Lake—lake WY-8
Little Mooseleuk Stream—stream ME-1
Little Moose Mtn MA-1
Little Moose Mtn—summit (2) NY-2
Little Moose Outlet—stream NY-2
Little Moose Pond—lake ME-1
Little Moose Pond—lake (2) NY-2
Little Moose Ridge—ridge ID-8
Little Moose River—stream WI-6
Little Mopan Creek WA-9
Little Mopang Creek—stream WA-9
Little Mopang Stream—stream ME-1
Little Moqui Spring—spring AZ-5
Little Moreau Creek SD-7
Little Moreau Lake—reservoir SD-7
Little Moreau Lake Dam—dam SD-7
Little Moreau River—stream SD-7
Little Moreau State Rec Area—park SD-7
Little Morgan Branch—stream SC-3
Little Morgan Run—stream (2) MD-2
Little Mormon Lake—lake AZ-5
Little Mormon Meadow—flat CA-9
Little Mormon Tank—reservoir AZ-5
Little Morning Star Ch—church MS-4
Little Morongo Canyon—valley CA-9
Little Morongo Creek—stream CA-9
**Little Morongo Heights**—pop pl CA-9
Little Morongo Wash—stream CA-9
Little Morrell Lake—lake FL-3
Little Morris Island Creek—stream VA-3
Little Morrison Creek—stream CO-8
Little Morris Run—stream PA-2
Little Morris Trail—trail PA-2
Little Morro Creek—stream CA-9
Little Mosca Creek—stream CO-8
Little Moses Mtn—summit WA-9
Little Moshamnon PA-2
Little Moshannon PA-2
Little Moshannon Creek PA-2
Little Moshier Island—island ME-1
Little Mosquito Bayou—stream LA-4
Little Mosquito Canyon—valley OR-9
Little Mosquito Creek—stream AK-9
Little Mosquito Creek—stream CA-9
Little Mosquito Creek—stream IN-6
Little Mosquito Creek—stream (2) IA-7
Little Mosquito Creek—stream MD-2
Little Mosquito Creek—stream VA-3
Little Mosquito Lake MI-6
Little Mosquito Lake—lake MI-6
Little Mosquito Lake—lake WA-9
Little Mosquito Pass—channel LA-4
Little Moss Lake FL-3
Little Moss Lake—lake MI-6
Little Moss Lake—lake MN-6
Little Moss Lake—lake WY-8
Little Mossy Lake—lake AR-4
Little Mossy Lake—lake MS-4
Little Mott Lake—lake AR-4
Little Mouldy Pond—lake NY-2
Little Mound—summit IL-6
Little Mound—summit TX-5
Little Mound—summit WI-6
Little Mound Bayou—stream MS-4
Little Mound Cem—cemetery IA-7
Little Mound Cem—cemetery OH-6
Little Mound Creek—stream MS-4
Little Mound Creek—stream TX-5
Little Mound Lake—lake MN-6
Little Mound Missionary Ch—church TX-5
**Little Mount**—pop pl KY-4
Little Mount Adams—summit WA-9
Little Mountain—locale OH-6
Little Mountain—locale UT-8
**Little Mountain**—pop pl NC-3
**Little Mountain**—pop pl SC-3
Little Mountain—ridge AR-4
Little Mountain—ridge MT-8
Little Mountain—ridge TN-4
Little Mountain—ridge VA-3
Little Mountain—ridge (3) WV-2
Little Mountain, The—summit MD-2
Little Mountain Aircraft Dam—dam NC-3
Little Mountain Aircraft Lake—reservoir NC-3
Little Mountain Air Force Training Annex—military UT-8
Little Mountain Airp—airport NC-3
Little Mountain Branch—stream TN-4
**Little Mountain Canyon Condominium**—pop pl UT-8
Little Mountain Catcher Pond—lake ME-1
Little Mountain Cem—cemetery TN-4
Little Mountain Ch—church MS-4
Little Mountain Ch—church (2) NC-3
Little Mountain Ch—church (2) SC-3
Little Mountain Ch—church (2) TN-4
Little Mountain Ch—church VA-3
Little Mountain Creek—stream GA-3
Little Mountain Creek—stream (3) NC-3
Little Mountain Creek—stream OK-5
Little Mountain Creek—stream SC-3
Little Mountain Creek—stream (2) TX-5
Little Mountain Lookout—locale CA-9
Little Mountain Marina—locale AL-4
Little Mountain Meadow—flat CA-9
Little Mountain Mine—mine TN-4
Little Mountain Overlook—locale UT-8
Little Mountain Park MS-4
Little Mountain Ridge—ridge GA-3
Little Mountain Run—stream VA-3
Little Mountain Sch (historical)—school (2) TN-4
Little Mountain Spring—spring (2) UT-8
Little Mountain State Park AL-4
**Little Mountain Subdivision**—pop pl UT-8
Little Mountain Summit—locale UT-8
Little Mountaintown Creek GA-3
Little Mountain Trail—trail (2) PA-2
Little Mountain Trail—trail WV-2
Little Mountain USAF Heliports—airport UT-8
Little Mountain Village (Site)—locale AK-9
Little Mount Cem—cemetery IN-6
Little Mount Cem—cemetery KY-4
Little Mount Ch—church MS-4
Little Mount Ch—church (2) VA-3
Little Mount Creek MS-4
Little Mount Deception—summit NH-1
Little Mount Discovery—summit NY-2
Little Mount Grace—summit MA-1
Little Mount Haven Ch MS-4
Little Mount Hoffman—summit CA-9
Little Mount Olive Holiness Ch—church DE-2
Little Mount Ord—summit AZ-5
Little Mount Pleasant—summit VA-3
Little Mount Sch TN-4
Little Mount Sch (historical)—school MS-4
Little Mount Susitna—summit AK-9
Little Mount Tom—summit CT-1
Little Mount Zion Ch—church NC-3
Little Mount Zion Primitive Baptist Ch—church AL-4
Little Mount Zircon—summit ME-1
Little Mouse Creek—stream MS-4
Little Mowich Mtn—summit OR-9
Little Moxie Brook—stream ME-1
Little Moxie Pond—lake ME-1
Little Moyer Run—stream PA-2
Little Mtn NC-3
Little Mtn PA-2
Little Mtn SC-3
Little Mtn WV-2
Little Mtn—range (2) PA-2
Little Mtn—range (3) VA-3
Little Mtn—summit (10) AL-4
Little Mtn—summit (2) AK-9
Little Mtn—summit (2) AZ-5
Little Mtn—summit (3) AR-4
Little Mtn—summit (2) CA-9
Little Mtn—summit (2) CO-8
Little Mtn—summit (3) GA-3
Little Mtn—summit (2) ID-8
Little Mtn—summit KY-4
Little Mtn—summit (3) ME-1
Little Mtn—summit (2) MA-1
Little Mtn—summit (2) MS-4
Little Mtn—summit NV-8
Little Mtn—summit NH-1
Little Mtn—summit (5) NY-2
Little Mtn—summit (17) NC-3
Little Mtn—summit (2) OK-5
Little Mtn—summit (10) PA-2
Little Mtn—summit (4) SC-3
Little Mtn—summit (23) TN-4
Little Mtn—summit (14) UT-8
Little Mtn—summit (24) VA-3
Little Mtn—summit (6) WA-9
Little Mtn—summit (9) WV-2
Little Mtn—summit (5) WY-8
Little Mtn Baptist Church TN-4
Little Mtn Hill—summit VA-3
Little Mucalsea Pond—lake ME-1
Little Muchakinock Creek—stream IA-7
Little Muchinippi Creek—stream OH-6
Little Muckaloochee Creek—stream GA-3
Little Muckaway Creek—stream SC-3
Little Muckle Knob—summit NC-3
Little Mud Brook—stream ME-1
Little Mud Creek—gut FL-3
Little Mud Creek—stream (3) AL-4
Little Mud Creek—stream AR-4
Little Mud Creek—stream GA-3
Little Mud Creek—stream ID-8
Little Mud Creek—stream (2) IL-6
Little Mud Creek—stream IN-6
Little Mud Creek—stream (2) KY-4
Little Mud Creek—stream MI-6
Little Mud Creek—stream MS-4
Little Mud Creek—stream NC-3
Little Mud Creek—stream OR-9
Little Mud Creek—stream (2) TX-5
Little Mud Creek—stream WA-9
Little Mud Creek—stream WY-8
Little Muddy ND-7
Little Muddy Branch—stream NC-3
Little Muddy Ch—church KY-4
Little Muddy Creek IA-7
Little Muddy Creek MT-8
Little Muddy Creek ND-7
Little Muddy Creek OH-6
Little Muddy Creek PA-2
Little Muddy Creek—stream (3) CO-8
Little Muddy Creek—stream ID-8
Little Muddy Creek—stream IL-6
Little Muddy Creek—stream (2) IA-7
Little Muddy Creek—stream KS-7
Little Muddy Creek—stream (4) KY-4
Little Muddy Creek—stream (7) MO-7
Little Muddy Creek—stream (2) MT-8
Little Muddy Creek—stream (2) NE-7
Little Muddy Creek—stream NC-3
Little Muddy Creek—stream ND-7
Little Muddy Creek—stream (2) OH-6
Little Muddy Creek—stream (6) OR-9
Little Muddy Creek—stream PA-2
Little Muddy Creek—stream (2) TN-4
Little Muddy Creek—stream (2) WA-9
Little Muddy Creek—stream (4) WY-8
Little Muddy Cut-off (historical)—bend ND-7
Little Muddy Gulch—valley CO-8
Little Muddy Lake—lake MI-6
Little Muddy Lake—reservoir NC-3
**Little Muddy (Needmore)**—pop pl KY-4
Little Muddy Pond—lake MA-1
Little Muddy River—stream IL-6
Little Muddy River—stream ND-7
Little Muddy Run—stream PA-2
Little Mud Flat—flat CA-9
Little Mud Flat—flat OR-9
Little Mud Flat Rsvr—reservoir OR-9
Little Mud Grass Islands—island LA-4
Little Mud Hazel Creek GA-3
Little Mud Hen Lake—lake MN-6
Little Mudhole—lake NY-2
Little Mud Lake MI-6
Little Mud Lake MN-6
Little Mud Lake PA-2
Little Mud Lake WI-6
Little Mud Lake—lake CA-9
Little Mud Lake—lake GA-3
Little Mud Lake—lake (9) MI-6
Little Mud Lake—lake (5) MN-6
Little Mud Lake—lake OR-9
Little Mud Lake—lake TN-4
Little Mud Lake—lake WA-9
Little Mud Lake—lake (3) WI-6
Little Mud Lake—reservoir AR-4
Little Mud Lake Flooding—reservoir MI-6
Little Mud Lick PA-2
Little Mud Lick—stream KY-4
Little Mudlick Creek—stream PA-2
Little Mud Pond—lake CO-8
Little Mud Pond—lake (5) ME-1
Little Mud Pond—lake (2) NY-2
Little Mud Pond—lake (2) PA-2
Little Mud Pond—lake (4) VT-1
Little Mud Pond Dam—dam PA-2
Little Mud Pond Ridge—ridge PA-2
Little Mud Pond Swamp—swamp PA-2
Little Mud River—channel GA-3
Little Mud River—stream AK-9
Little Mud River—stream GA-3
Little Mud Rsvr—reservoir CO-8
Little Mud Spring—spring AZ-5
Little Mud Spring—spring (4) NV-8
Little Mud Spring—spring OR-9
Little Mud Spring—spring UT-8
Little Mud Spring—spring WA-9
Little Mud Springs—spring WA-9
Little Mud Thorofare—channel NJ-2
Little Mud Well—well AZ-5
Little Muela Creek—stream TX-5
Little Mugget Hill—summit MA-1
Little Muklung River—stream AK-9
Little Mulberry Branch—stream FL-3
Little Mulberry Ch—church TN-4
Little Mulberry Creek AL-4
Little Mulberry Creek GA-3
Little Mulberry Creek NC-3
Little Mulberry Creek—stream (2) AL-4
Little Mulberry Creek—stream (2) AR-4
Little Mulberry Creek—stream MS-4
Little Mulberry Creek—stream TN-4
Little Mulberry Creek—stream TX-5
Little Mulberry River AR-4
Little Mulberry River—stream (2) GA-3
Little Mulchatna River—stream AK-9
Little Mule Creek—stream CA-9
Little Mule Creek—stream KS-7
Little Mule Creek—stream OK-5
Little Mule Creek Windmill—locale TX-5
Little Mule Lake—lake MN-6
Little Mule Mountains—range CA-9
Little Mule Tank—reservoir TX-5
Little Muley—ridge OR-9
Little Muley Creek OR-9
Little Muley Creek—stream OR-9
Little Mulky Mtn—summit VA-3
Little Mullet Key—island FL-3
Little Mummy Island—island AK-9
Little Muncy Branch—stream WV-2
Little Muncy Creek—stream PA-2
Little Muniz Windmill—locale NM-5
Little Munsey Branch WV-2
Little Munson Creek—stream AK-9
Little Munsungan Lake—lake ME-1
Little Munsungan Stream—stream ME-1
Little Munuscong Lake MI-6
Little Munuscong River—stream MI-6
Little Munyon Island—island FL-3
Little Murphy Creek—stream MI-6
Little Murphy Lake—lake MI-6
Little Murray Mtn—summit TX-5
Little Muscamoot Bay—bay MI-6
Little Muscle Shoals (historical)—bar AL-4
Little Mushannon Creek PA-2
Little Music Creek—stream AR-4
Little Muskego Lake—reservoir WI-6
Little Muskegon Pond MI-6
Little Muskegon River—stream MI-6
Little Muskie Lake—lake (3) WI-6
Little Muskingum River—stream OH-6
Little Muskrat Lake—lake ID-8
Little Muskrat Lake—lake MI-6
Little Musquacook Stream—stream ME-1
Little Musquash Lake—lake ME-1
Little Musquash Stream—stream ME-1
Little Mussel Creek—stream MO-7
Little Mussy Lake—lake OH-6
Little Mustang Creek—stream CO-8
Little Mustang Creek—stream (3) TX-5
Little Mutau Creek—stream CA-9
Little Mutton Creek—stream IN-6
Little Myers Lake—lake MI-6
Little Myrtle Lake—lake WA-9
Little Mystery—summit WA-9
Little Mystic Channel—channel MA-1
Little Mystic River MA-1
Little Naches Campground—locale WA-9
Little Naches River WA-9
Little Naches River—stream WA-9
**Little Nahant**—pop pl MA-1
Little Nahant Beach MA-1
Little Nails Creek—stream GA-3
Little Naked Creek—stream NC-3
Little Namakan Lake MN-6
Little Namekan Lake MN-6
Little Namskaket Creek—stream MA-1
Little Namskaket River Marshes—swamp MA-1
Little Nancey Branch—stream AL-4
Little Nancy Canyon—valley UT-8
Little Nancy Ch—church KY-4
Little Nankoweap Canyon—valley AZ-5
Little Nankoweap Creek—stream AZ-5
Little Nanticoke Creek—stream NY-2
Little Narlap Island FM-9
Little Narragansett Bay—bay CT-1
Little Narragansett Bay—bay RI-1
Little Narraguagus River—stream ME-1
Little Narrows—channel AK-9
Little Narrows—channel NC-3
Little Narrows—channel WI-6
Little Narrows—gap AL-4
Little Narrows—gut VA-3
Little Narrows—other NM-5
Little Narrows—valley (2) CO-8
Little Narrows, The—channel NY-2
Little Nash Crater—crater OR-9
Little Nashville—locale AL-4
Little Nashville Point—cape AL-4
Little Nasty Creek—stream SD-7
Little Nasty Creek—stream TX-5
Little Natalbany Creek—stream LA-4
Little Natalbany River—stream LA-4
Little Nat Cave—cave AL-4
Little Natches Bayou—stream LA-4
Little Nation Hill—summit AK-9
Little Naukati Bay—bay AK-9
Little Naukeag Pond MA-1
Little Navajo River—stream CO-8
Little Neatman Creek—stream NC-3
Little Nebo Lake—reservoir IN-6
Little Neck MA-1
Little Neck RI-1
Little Neck—cape CT-1
Little Neck—cape (2) DE-2
Little Neck—cape (3) MA-1
Little Neck—cape (3) NY-2
Little Neck—cape (2) RI-1
Little Neck—cape VA-3
Little Neck—isthmus MA-1
**Little Neck**—pop pl (2) MA-1
**Little Neck**—pop pl NY-2
Little Neck Bay—bay NY-2
Little Neck Cemetery—hist pl RI-1
Little Neck Creek VA-3
Little Neck Creek—bay MD-2
Little Neck Creek—stream VA-3
Little Neck Island—island MD-2
Little Neck Lake—lake MN-6
Little Neck Point—cape MD-2
Little Neck Point—cape NY-2
Little Neck Pond—lake RI-1
Little Neck Run—stream NY-2
**Little Neck Village**—pop pl VA-3
Little Needle Lake—lake CA-9
Little Needles Eye—cliff NM-5
Little Needmore—locale KY-4
Little Negro Creek—stream IL-6
Little Negro Creek—stream KY-4
Little Negro Creek—stream NV-8
Little Negro Creek—stream SD-7
Little Negrohead—summit NC-3
Little Negro Lick—stream IL-6
Little Nelchina River—stream AK-9
Little Nellie Ditch—canal CO-8
Little Nellie Falls—falls CA-9
Little Nellie Mine—mine MT-8
Little Nelligan Lake—lake WI-6
Little Nell Knob—summit GA-3
Little Nelson Lake—lake AZ-5
Little Nelson Mtn—summit UT-8
Little Nelson Run—stream PA-2
Little Nelson Windmill—locale TX-5
Little Nemaha River—stream NE-7
Little Nenana River—stream AK-9
Little Neosho KS-7
Little Nesbit Lake—lake MI-6
Little Nescopeck Creek—stream (2) PA-2
Little Nescopeck Mtn—summit PA-2
Little Nesenkeag Brook NH-1
Little Neshaminy Creek—stream PA-2
Little Neshannock Creek—stream PA-2
Little Nesourdnahunk Lake ME-1
Little Nesowadnehunk Lake—lake ME-1
Little Nesowadnehunk Stream—stream ME-1
Little Nespelem River—stream WA-9
Little Nestucca Camp—locale OR-9
Little Nestucca County Park—park OR-9
Little Nestucca River—stream OR-9
Little Net Branch—stream GA-3
Little Net River—stream MN-6
Little Nettle Branch—stream NC-3
Little Newby Ditch—canal IN-6
Little Newfound Neck—cape DE-2
Little New River AL-4
Little New River—stream AL-4
Little New River Lake Number 1—reservoir AL-4
Little New River Lake Number 1 Dam—dam AL-4
Little New River Lake Number 2—reservoir AL-4
Little New River Lake Number 2 Dam—dam AL-4
Little New River Lake Number 3—reservoir AL-4
Little New River Lake Number 3 Dam—dam AL-4
Little Newton Lake—lake WI-6
Little New York MS-4
Little New York—locale AL-4
Little New York—locale TX-5
Little N Fk South Fk Coeur d'Alene River—stream ID-8
Little Niagara Creek—stream NC-3
Little Niagara Creek—stream WI-6
Little Niagara Falls—falls ME-1
Little Niagara Falls—falls OK-5
Little Niagara Falls—falls OR-9
Little Niagara Falls—falls WA-9
Little Niagra Falls—falls OR-9
Little Niangua Arm—bay MO-7
Little Niangua Ch—church MO-7
Little Niangua River—stream MO-7
Little Nickleson Branch—stream AR-4
Little Nigger Creek WA-9
Little Nigger Lick IL-6
Little Nine Mile Creek TN-4
Little Ninemile Creek—stream IL-6
Little Ninemile Creek—stream MT-8
Little Ninemile Creek—stream TN-4
Little Ninemile Creek—stream WA-9
Little Ninemile Fork—stream WV-2
Little Nineteen Mtn—summit NY-2
Little Nippletop—summit NY-2
Little Nishisakawick Creek—stream NJ-2
Little Nisqually River—stream WA-9
Little Nittany Valley—valley PA-2
Little Nixon Creek—stream TN-4
Little Njoo Mtn—summit AK-9
Little Noatak Slough—stream AK-9
Little No Business Creek—stream AL-4
Little No Creek—stream KY-4
Little No Creek—stream MO-7
Little Nogales Spring—spring AZ-5
Little Noix Creek—stream MO-7
Little Nokasippi River—stream MN-6
Little No Mans Mesa—summit UT-8
Little No Name Creek—stream IN-6
Little Noonday Creek—stream GA-3
Little Norkok Creek—stream WY-8
Little Norridgewock Stream—stream ME-1
Little Norris Creek—stream TN-4
Little Norris Spring—spring TX-5
Little North Basin—basin ME-1
Little North Creek KY-4
Little North Creek—stream MI-6
Little North Creek—stream (2) UT-8
Little Northeast Creek MD-2
Little Northeast Creek PA-2
Little North East Creek—stream MD-2
Little Northeast Creek—stream NC-3
Little North East Creek—stream PA-2
Little North Fork CA-9
Little North Fork OR-9
Little North Fork—stream CO-8
Little North Fork—stream MO-7
Little North Fork—stream MT-8
Little North Fork—stream WY-8
Little North Fork Albion River—stream CA-9
Little North Fork Big River—stream CA-9
Little North Fork Campground—locale CA-9
Little North Fork Campground—locale ID-8
Little North Fork Clearwater River—stream ID-8
Little North Fork Crazy Woman Creek—stream WY-8
Little North Fork East Creek—stream CA-9
Little North Fork Gualala River—stream CA-9
Little North Fork Navarro River—stream CA-9
Little North Fork Nehalem River—stream OR-9
Little North Fork North Branch North Fork El—stream CA-9
Little North Fork North Fork Dye Creek—stream CA-9
Little North Fork Noyo River—stream CA-9
Little North Fork of Middle Fork Feather Riv—stream CA-9
Little North Fork of Middle Fork of North Fork Yuba River CA-9
Little North Fork of Wilson River OR-9
Little North Fork Parker Creek—stream CA-9
Little North Fork River MO-7
Little North Fork Salmon River—stream CA-9
Little North Fork Silver Creek—stream OR-9
Little North Fork Tank—reservoir AZ-5
Little North Fork Ten Mile River—stream CA-9
Little North Fork White Oak Creek—stream OH-6
Little North Fork White River—stream AR-4
Little North Fork White River—stream MO-7
Little North Fork Wilson River—stream OR-9
Little North Indian Creek—stream MO-7
Little Northkill Creek—stream PA-2
Little North Lake—lake MN-6
Little North Mountains VA-3
Little North Mountain Trail—trail VA-3
Little North Mountain Wildlife Mngmt Ar—park VA-3
Little North Mouse Creek—stream TN-4
Little North Mtn VA-3
Little North Mtn—range (2) VA-3
Little North Mtn—summit (3) VA-3
Little North Pembina River—stream ND-7
Little North Prong—stream FL-3
Little North River—stream WA-9
Little North Santiam River—stream OR-9
Little North Star Lake—lake MN-6
Little North Valley Creek—stream CA-9
Little North Well—well TX-5
Little Northwest Creek—stream NY-2
Little Northwest Pond—lake ME-1
Little North Woahink Lake—lake OR-9
Little Norton Lake—lake MI-6
Little Norway—bay AK-9
**Little Norway**—pop pl CA-9
**Little Norway**—pop pl WI-6
Little Norway Ch—church MN-6
Little Norway Ch—church WI-6
Little Norway Creek—stream MI-6
Little Norway Lake—lake (2) MI-6
Little Nose—cliff NY-2
Little Notch—gap NM-5
Little Notch—gap UT-8
Little Notch Pond—lake ME-1
Little Notchy Creek—stream TN-4
Little Nottoway River—stream VA-3
Little Noxie Creek—stream KS-7
Little Noxubee Creek MS-4
Little Noxubee River—stream MS-4
Little Nugget Creek—stream AK-9
Little Nugget Gulch—valley NM-5
Little Nugget Lake—reservoir MA-1
Little Nugget Lake Dam—dam MA-1
Little Nutbush Creek—stream NC-3
Little Nut Spring—spring NV-8
Little Nutten Hook—cape NY-2
Little Oak—locale AL-4
Little Oak Bayou Sch (historical)—school MS-4
Little Oak Branch—stream TN-4
Little Oak Canyon—valley CA-9
Little Oak Canyon—valley NE-7
Little Oak Canyon—valley UT-8
Little Oak Cem—cemetery MN-6
Little Oak Ch—church AL-4
Little Oak Ch—church NC-3
Little Oak Creek—stream CO-8
Little Oak Creek—stream KS-7
Little Oak Creek—stream KY-4
Little Oak Creek—stream OR-9
Little Oak Creek—stream (2) SD-7

Little Pond—lake (5) VT-1
Little Pond—reservoir (2) AL-4
Little Pond—reservoir PA-2
Little Pond—reservoir UT-8
Little Pond Beach—beach ME-1
Little Pond Brook—stream NH-1
Little Pond Brook—stream NJ-2
Little Pond Brook—stream VT-1
Little Pond Cem—cemetery NH-1
Little Pond Cove—bay RI-1
Little Pond Creek—stream IL-6
Little Pond Creek—stream NJ-2
Little Pond Creek—stream TN-4
Little Pond Creek—stream TX-5
Little Pond Creek—stream WV-2
Little Pond Dam—dam SD-7
**Little Ponderosa**—pop pl OK-5
Little Pond Head—cape ME-1
Little Pond Island—island ME-1
Little Pond Mountain Trail—trail TN-4
Little Pond Mtn—summit TN-4
Little Pond Ridge—ridge WV-2
Little Pond Run—stream WV-2
*Little Pony* MN-6
Little Pony Meadows—flat ID-8
Little Pony River—stream MN-6
Little Poor Valley—basin VA-3
Little Poor Valley—valley (2) TN-4
Little Poor Valley—valley VA-3
Little Poor Valley Creek—stream TN-4
Little Poor Valley Ridge—ridge TN-4
Little Pootatuck Brook—stream CT-1
Little Pop Lake—lake OR-9
Little Poplar Creek—stream AL-4
Little Poplar Creek—stream KY-4
Little Poplar Creek—stream MS-4
Little Poplar Creek—stream NC-3
Little Poplar Creek—stream SC-3
Little Poplar Creek—stream VA-3
Little Poplar Creek Ch—church KY-4
Little Poplar Mtn—summit ME-1
Little Popo Agie Basin—basin WY-8
Little Popo Agie Canyon—valley WY-8
Little Popo Agie Cem—cemetery WY-8
Little Popo Agie River—stream WY-8
Little Popple Lake—lake WI-6
Little Popple River—stream (2) WI-6
*Little Porcupine Creek* MT-8
Little Porcupine Creek—stream (3) MT-8
Little Porcupine Creek—stream WY-8
Little Porcupine Gulch—valley CO-8
Little Porcupine Lake—lake WI-6
Little Porcupine Tank—reservoir CA-9
Little Porky Lake—lake MN-6
Little Porpoise Bay—bay NC-3
Little Porpoise Creek—stream FL-3
Little Porpoise Point—cape NC-3
**Littleport**—pop pl IA-7
**Little Port**—pop pl NC-3
Little Portage Bay—bay MN-6
Little Portage Creek—stream MI-6
Little Portage Creek—stream PA-2
*Little Portage Lake* MN-6
Little Portage Lake—lake (2) MI-6
Little Portage Lake—lake MN-6
Little Portage Lake—lake WI-6
Little Portage River—stream OH-6
Little Port Brook—stream NC-3
Little Porter Creek—stream NV-8
Little Porter Lake—lake FL-3
Little Porter Mtn—summit NY-2
*Little Porter Pond* FL-3
Little Portuguese Canyon—valley CA-9
Little Port Walter—cape AK-9
Little Porus Island—island ME-1
Little Posey Cave—cave AL-4
Little Posey Lake—lake MI-6
Little Poso Creek—stream CA-9
Little Poso Creek—stream NM-5
Little Poso Well—well NM-5
Little Possum Creek—stream TN-4
Little Post Bayou—stream AR-4
*Little Postoak Creek* TX-5
Little Post Oak Creek—stream OK-5
Little Post Oak Creek—stream TX-5
Little Post Office (historical)—building AL-4
Little Potamus Creek—stream OR-9
Little Potamus Well—locale OR-9
Little Potash Mtn—summit VT-1
Little Potato Butte—summit CA-9
*Little Potato Creek* GA-3
Little Potato Creek—stream (2) GA-3
Little Potato Creek—stream IN-6
Little Potato Creek—stream MI-6
Little Potatoe Hill—summit IL-6
Little Potato Slough—gut CA-9
Little Potato Valley—valley TN-4
Little Pot Creek—stream OR-9
Little Pothole Lake—lake CA-9
Little Potholes—spring NV-8
Little Potlatch Creek—stream ID-8
*Little Potlatch River* ID-8
Little Potomac Creek—stream IA-7
Little Potrero Creek—stream CA-9
Little Pott Creek—stream NC-3
Little Potter Mtn—summit NY-2
Little Pottsburg Creek—stream FL-3
Little Potts Run—stream PA-2
Little Poverty—summit NV-8
Little Poverty Canyon—valley NM-5
Little Poverty Pond—lake ME-1
Little Powderhorn Creek—stream CA-9
*Little Powder River* WY-8
Little Powder River—stream MT-8
Little Powder River—stream WY-8
Little Powder River Sch—school WY-8
Little Poxabogue Pond—lake NY-2
Little Pozega Lake—lake MT-8
Little Prairie—area CA-9
Little Prairie—area ND-7
Little Prairie—flat ID-8
Little Prairie—flat IL-6
Little Prairie—flat LA-4
Little Prairie—flat TX-5
Little Prairie—flat WA-9
**Little Prairie**—pop pl LA-4
**Little Prairie**—pop pl WI-6
Little Prairie Aa Flow—lava ID-8
Little Prairie Bend—bend TN-4
Little Prairie Cem—cemetery MO-7
Little Prairie Ch—church (3) IL-6
Little Prairie Ch—church MN-6
Little Prairie Ch—church ND-7
Little Prairie Community Lake—park MO-7
Little Prairie Creek—stream AL-4
Little Prairie Creek—stream LA-4
Little Prairie Dog Creek—stream SD-7
Little Prairie Lake—lake MN-6
Little Prairie Lake—reservoir MO-7
Little Prairie Ridge—ridge LA-4
Little Prairie Slough—gut MO-7
Little Prairie Township—civil MO-7
Little Prairie Waterhole—lake ID-8
Little Prater Creek—stream VA-3
Little Prather Meadow—flat CA-9
Little Prayer Cem—cemetery TX-5
Little Preacher Creek—stream AK-9
Little Presley Lake—lake ME-1
Little Presque Isle—island MI-6
Little Presque Isle Lake—lake MI-6
Little Presque Isle Lake—lake WI-6
Little Presque Isle River—stream MI-6
Little Prickly Pear Creek—stream MT-8
Little Priest—summit VA-3
Little Primrose Dam Rsvr—reservoir NV-8
Little Princess—locale VI-3
Little Proctor Creek—stream MO-7
Little Proctor Creek—stream TN-4
*Little Professor Mountain* CO-8
Little Profits Creek—stream MO-7
Little Prong—locale NC-3
Little Prong—stream NC-3
Little Prong—stream TX-5
Little Prong Creek—stream MS-4
Little Prospect Creek—stream WY-8
Little Prospect Mtn—summit WY-8
Little Providence Ch—church MS-4
*Little Provo Hole* UT-8
Little Pryor Creek—stream AL-4
Little Pryor Creek—stream OK-5
Little Ptarmigan Creek—stream AK-9
Little Pucketa Creek—stream PA-2
Little Pudding Brook—stream MA-1
Little Pudding River—stream OR-9
Little Puffin Bay—bay AK-9
Little Pug Tank—reservoir AZ-5
Little Pump Canyon—valley NM-5
Little Pumpkin Creek—gut FL-3
Little Pumpkin Creek—stream GA-3
Little Pumpkin Creek—stream MT-8
Little Pumpkinvine Creek—stream (2) GA-3
Little Puncheoncamp Branch—stream TN-4
Little Puncheon Creek—stream KY-4
Little Puncheon Creek—stream TN-4
Little Punderson Lake—lake OH-6
Little Pungers Creek—channel MD-2
Little Punky Pond—lake NY-2
Little Pup—stream AK-9
Little Pup Creek—stream MI-6
Little Puposky Lake—lake MN-6
Little Purcell Canyon—valley AZ-5
Little Purcell Tank—reservoir AZ-5
Little Purgatory—area UT-8
Little Purgatory Canyon—valley AZ-5
Little Purgatory Pond—lake ME-1
Little Pushaw Pond—lake ME-1
Little Puzzle Mtn—summit ME-1
Little Pybus Bay—bay AK-9
Little Pyramid—summit ID-8
Little Pyramids—pillar KS-7
Little Quabbin—summit MA-1
Little Quabbin Island—island MA-1
*Little Quabin Mountain* MA-1
Little Quadrant Mtn—summit WY-8
Little Quail Hill Mine—mine CA-9
Little Quail Spring—spring AZ-5
Little Quaking Asp Spring—spring CA-9
Little Quamino Rock—rock MA-1
Little Quankey Creek—stream NC-3
Little Queenie Creek—stream AK-9
Little Queens River—stream ID-8
Little Queenstown Creek—bay MD-2
Little Question Lake—lake AK-9
*Little Quicksand Creek* TX-5
Little Quicksand Creek—stream TX-5
Little Quien Sabe Valley—valley CA-9
Little Quilcene River—stream WA-9
Little Quilcene Trail—trail WA-9
Little Quinnesec Falls—falls WI-6
Little Quittacas Pond—lake MA-1
*Little Quittacus Pond* MA-1
Little Rabbit Bayou—stream AR-4
Little Rabbit Creek—stream AK-9
Little Rabbit Creek—stream NV-8
Little Rabbit Creek—stream TX-5
Little Rabbit Lake—lake MN-6
Little Rabbit River—stream MI-6
Little Rabbit Swamp—swamp DE-2
Little Rabbit Tank—reservoir AZ-5
*Little Rabbit Valley* CA-9
Little Rabbit Valley—valley CA-9
Little Rabideau Lake—lake MN-6
Little Raccoon Creek—stream AR-4
Little Raccoon Creek—stream GA-3
Little Raccoon Creek—stream (5) IN-6
Little Raccoon Creek—stream KY-4
Little Raccoon Creek—stream (2) OH-6
Little Raccoon Creek—stream VA-3
Little Raccoon Creek—stream WV-2
Little Raccoon Island—island LA-4
Little Raccoon Point—cape LA-4
Little Raccoon Run—stream PA-2
Little Raccoon Structure Number 11—dam IN-6
Little Raccoon Structure Number 15—dam IN-6
Little Raccoon Structure Number 16—dam IN-6
Little Raccoon Structure Number 2-C—dam IN-6
Little Raccoon Structure Number 3—dam IN-6
Little Raccoon Structure Number 8—dam IN-6
Little Racetrack Lake—lake MT-8
Little Racetrack Mtn—summit TX-5
*Little Radcliff Gulch* CO-8
Little Radford Cem—cemetery MO-7
Little Rafting Creek—stream SC-3
Little Raft Swamp—stream NC-3
Little Ragged Mtn—summit ME-1
Little Ragged Pond—lake ME-1
Little Rag Island—island IA-7
Little Ragland Tank—reservoir NM-5
Little Ragmuff Stream—stream ME-1
Little Rail Creek—stream OR-9
Little Rainbow Bridge—arch UT-8
Little Rainbow Lake—lake CO-8
Little Rainbow Lake—lake ID-8
Little Rainbow Park—flat UT-8
Little Rainbow Pond—lake NY-2
Little Rainbow Ridge—ridge CA-9
Little Rainbow Valley—valley AZ-5
Little Rain Tank—reservoir (2) AZ-5
Little Rainy Creek—stream AR-4
*Little Rainy Lake* MN-6
Little Rainy River—stream MI-6
*Little Raisin Drain* MI-6
Little Ram Creek—stream CA-9
Little Ramey Creek—stream ID-8
Little Ramhorn Branch—stream NC-3
Little Ram Island—island (3) ME-1
Little Ram Island—island MA-1
Little Ram Island—island NY-2
Little Ramme Creek—stream MT-8
Little Ram Pasture Point—cape MA-1
Little Ramsey Creek—stream MO-7
Little Ranch—locale AZ-5
Little Rancheria Creek—stream (2) CA-9
Little Ranch Spring—spring AZ-5
Little Randsburg Mine—mine CA-9
Little Range Sch—school IL-6
Little Ranier Lake—lake MN-6
Little Rankin Pond—lake NY-2
Little Rapid Creek—stream WY-8
Little Rapid River—stream MI-6
Little Rapids—channel MI-6
Little Rapids—locale NY-2
**Little Rapids**—pop pl WI-6
Little Rapids Channel—channel MI-6
Little Raspberry Island—island AK-9
Little Ratcliff Gulch—valley CO-8
Little Rat Creek—stream WY-8
Little Rat Lake—lake MN-6
*Little Rattlesnake Canyon* CA-9
Little Rattlesnake Canyon—valley NV-8
*Little Rattlesnake Creek* VA-3
Little Rattlesnake Creek—stream (2) CA-9
Little Rattlesnake Creek—stream ID-8
Little Rattlesnake Creek—stream NC-3
Little Rattlesnake Creek—stream (2) OR-9
Little Rattlesnake Creek—stream WA-9
Little Rattlesnake Gulch—valley CA-9
Little Rattlesnake Hill—summit NH-1
*Little Rattlesnake Island* NH-1
*Little Rattlesnake Lake* WA-9
Little Rattlesnake Mtn—summit CA-9
*Little Rattlesnake Pond* ME-1
Little Rattlesnake Spring—spring WA-9
Little Rattlesnake Tank—reservoir AZ-5
Little Ratz Creek—stream AK-9
Little Ratz Harbor—bay AK-9
Little Raven Hill—summit NY-2
Little Rawhide Butte—summit WY-8
Little Rawhide Creek—stream (2) WY-8
Little Rawhide Mtn—summit NV-8
Little Rayborn Canyon—valley OR-9
Little Ray Brook—stream NY-2
Littler Cem—cemetery OH-6
*Little Red* TX-5
Little Red—locale AR-4
Little Redbank Creek—stream LA-4
Little Red Bar—bar MS-4
Little Red Bill Hill—summit WY-8
Little Red Bluff Creek—stream (2) GA-3
Little Red Branch—stream TX-5
Little Red Butte—summit CO-8
Little Red Canyon—valley CO-8
Little Red Cap Gulch—valley CA-9
Little Red Cedar Wash—valley UT-8
Little Red Ch—church OK-5
*Little Red Creek* CO-8
Little Red Creek—stream (2) AL-4
Little Red Creek—stream AR-4
Little Red Creek—stream (2) CO-8
Little Red Creek—stream IN-6
Little Red Creek—stream (2) MS-4
Little Red Creek—stream UT-8
Little Red Creek—stream (4) WY-8
Little Reddon Lake—lake AR-4
Little Redfish—gut FL-3
Little Redfish Creek—stream FL-3
Little Redfish Lake—lake FL-3
Little Redfish Lake—lake (2) ID-8
Little Redfish Point—cape FL-3
Little Red Hill—summit NM-5
Little Red Hill—summit UT-8
Little Red Hills—spring MT-8
Little Red Hill Tank—reservoir AZ-5
Little Red Horse Creek—stream ID-8
Little Red Horse Lake—lake MN-6
Little Red Horse Wash—stream AZ-5
Little Red Kill—stream NY-2
Little Red Lake—lake NM-5
Little Red Lake—lake TX-5
Little Red Lake—reservoir TX-5
Little Red Lake (dry)—lake AZ-5
Little Redlands Tank—reservoir AZ-5
Little Red Mountain Creek—stream (2) CA-9
Little Red Mountain Creek—stream OR-9
Little Red Mtn—summit AL-4
Little Red Mtn—summit (2) CA-9
Little Red Mtn—summit GA-3
Little Red Mtn—summit OR-9
Little Red Mud Creek—stream TX-5
*Little Redoak Creek* GA-3
Little Red Park—flat CO-8
Little Red Pass—gut LA-4
Little Red Pine Canyon—valley UT-8
*Little Red River* AR-4
*Little Red River* CO-8
*Little Red River* OK-5
*Little Red River* TX-5
Little Red River—stream AR-4
Little Red River—stream TX-5
Little Red Rock Mtn—summit CA-9
Little Red Rsvr—reservoir CO-8
Little Red Sand Lake—lake MN-6
Little Red Sch—hist pl AZ-5
Little Red Sch—school (2) IL-6
Little Red Sch—school MD-2
Little Red Sch—school NY-2
Little Red Sch—school WI-6
Little Red Sch House 1835 District No. 7—hist pl NH-1
*Little Red School, The* SD-7
Little Red Schoolhouse—hist pl ME-1
Little Red Schoolhouse—hist pl NJ-2
Little Red Schoolhouse—hist pl WA-9
Little Red Schoolhouse—school NY-2
Little Red Schoolhouse, The—school CT-1
Little Red Schoolhouse Museum—building NH-1
Little Red S Fields—flat OR-9
Little Red Spring—spring UT-8
Little Redstone Ch—church PA-2
*Little Red Stone Creek* PA-2
Little Redstone Creek—stream PA-2
Little Redstone Presbyterian Ch—church PA-2
Little Redstone Sch (historical)—school PA-2
Little Red Tank—reservoir AZ-5
Little Red Tank—reservoir (2) NM-5
Little Red Tank—reservoir (2) TX-5
Little Redtop Windmill—locale TX-5
Little Red Wash—stream CO-8
Little Red Wash—stream NV-8
Little Red Water Lake—lake (2) FL-3
Little Red Windmill—locale NM-5
Little Redwood Campground—park OR-9
Little Redwood Creek—stream LA-4
Little Reedbrake Creek—stream AL-4
*Little Reed Creek* AR-4
Little Reed Creek—stream MS-4
Little Reed Creek—stream VA-3
Little Reed Heights—uninc pl CA-9
*Little Reed Island Creek* VA-3
Little Reed Island Creek—stream VA-3
Little Reed Pond—lake ME-1
Little Reed Pond—lake NY-2
Little Reedy Branch—stream (2) FL-3
Little Reedy Creek—stream (2) AL-4
Little Reedy Creek—stream FL-3
Little Reedy Creek—stream GA-3
Little Reedy Creek—stream KY-4
Little Reedy Creek—stream (2) SC-3
Little Reedy Creek—stream TN-4
Little Reedy Island—island DE-2
Little Reigan Gulch—valley CO-8
Little Reiley Lake—lake MN-6
Little Reilley Canyon—valley NV-8
Little Remington Creek—stream WY-8
Little Renderbrook Tank—reservoir TX-5
Little Renfro Creek—stream KY-4
Little Renfro Hollow—valley MO-7
Little Renfrow Top—summit TN-4
Little Renox Creek—stream KY-4
Little Renox Sch—school KY-4
Little Reservoir Basin—basin NV-8
Little Reservoir Campground—park UT-8
Little Reservoir Dam—dam AL-4
Little Reservoir Dam—dam UT-8
Littlerest—locale NY-2
**Little Rest**—pop pl MA-1
*Little Rest Hill* RI-1
Little Reynolds Creek—stream CA-9
Little Rhiney Creek—stream PA-2
Little Rhododendron Creek—stream TN-4
*Little Rhoton Spring* AZ-5
*Little Rhoton Wash* AZ-5
Little Rib Lake—lake WI-6
Little Rib River—stream WI-6
Little Rice Creek—stream FL-3
Little Rice Field—swamp GA-3
*Little Rice Lake* MN-6
Little Rice Lake—lake MI-6
Little Rice Lake—lake (10) MN-6
Little Rice Lake—lake (2) WI-6
Little Rice Lake—reservoir WI-6
Little Rice Pond—lake MN-6
Little Rice River—stream WI-6
**Little Rice (Town of)**—pop pl WI-6
Little Richard Creek—stream WI-6
Little Richard Mine—mine CO-8
Little Richardson Creek—stream NC-3
Little Rich Fork—stream WV-2
Little Richie Island—island MN-6
*Little Richies Island* MN-6
Little Richland Creek—stream IN-6
Little Richland Creek—stream (2) KY-4
Little Richland Creek—stream MO-7
Little Richland Creek—stream (3) TN-4
**Little Richmond**—pop pl NC-3
**Little Richmond**—pop pl OH-6
Little Richmond Tank—reservoir AZ-5
Little Rich Mtn—summit (2) NC-3
Little Rich Mtn—summit SC-3
**Little Richwood**—pop pl NC-3
Little Ricks Canyon—valley UT-8
Little Riddle Mountain—ridge OR-9
**Little Ridge**—pop pl TX-5
Little Ridge—ridge (2) AL-4
Little Ridge—ridge GA-3
Little Ridge—ridge NC-3
Little Ridge—ridge OK-5
Little Ridge—ridge (3) TN-4
Little Ridge—ridge VA-3
Little Ridge—ridge (2) WV-2
Little Ridge, The—ridge AZ-5
Little Ridge Ch—church IN-6
Little Ridge Creek—stream GA-3
Little Ridge Lake—flat OR-9
Little Ridge Park—park TX-5
Little Ridgepole Mtn—summit NC-3
Little Ridges—stream MD-2
Little Riffle Canyon—valley TX-5
*Little Right Fork* WV-2
Little Right Fork—stream WV-2
Little Righthand Canyon—valley AZ-5
Little Righthand Fork—stream WV-2
*Little Rigolets* LA-4
Little Riley Creek—stream (2) OH-6
Little Riley Lake—lake (2) WI-6
Little Rincon—basin UT-8
Little Rincon—valley CO-8
Little Rincon Mountains—summit AZ-5
Little Rincon Seco Windmill—locale TX-5
Little Riner Basin—basin OR-9
Little Ripley Lake—lake WI-6
Little Ripple Lake—lake MN-6
Little Ripstein Gulch—valley CA-9
Little Riser Creek—stream NV-8
*Little River* AL-4
*Little River* AR-4
*Little River* CT-1
*Little River* FL-3
*Little River* GA-3
*Little River* KS-7
*Little River* LA-4
*Little River* ME-1
*Little River* MA-1
*Little River* MN-6
*Little River* MS-4
*Little River* NC-3
*Little River* OH-6
*Little River* OK-5
*Little River* RI-1
*Little River* WI-6
Little River—bay ME-1
Little River—channel DC-2
Little River—channel MA-1
Little River—channel MN-6
Little River—channel (2) NY-2
Little River—gut GA-3
Little River—gut LA-4
Little River—locale AL-4
Little River—locale CT-1
Little River—locale GA-3
Little River—locale IA-7
Little River—locale NC-3
**Little River**—pop pl AL-4
**Little River**—pop pl AR-4
**Littleriver**—pop pl CA-9
**Little River**—pop pl FL-3
**Little River**—pop pl KS-7
**Little River**—pop pl MA-1
**Little River**—pop pl NC-3
**Little River**—pop pl OR-9
**Little River**—pop pl SC-3
**Little River**—pop pl TN-4
**Little River**—pop pl TX-5
Little River—stream (4) AL-4
Little River—stream (2) AK-9
Little River—stream (3) AR-4
Little River—stream (2) CA-9
Little River—stream (5) CT-1
Little River—stream DE-2
Little River—stream (7) FL-3
Little River—stream (7) GA-3
Little River—stream IN-6
Little River*—stream IA-7
Little River—stream KY-4
Little River—stream (8) LA-4
Little River—stream (16) ME-1
Little River—stream (9) MA-1
Little River—stream (2) MI-6
Little River—stream MN-6
Little River—stream (2) MS-4
Little River—stream (2) MO-7
Little River—stream (7) NH-1
Little River—stream (6) NY-2
Little River—stream (10) NC-3
Little River—stream (2) OK-5
Little River—stream (2) OR-9
Little River—stream (7) SC-3
Little River—stream TN-4
Little River—stream TX-5
Little River—stream VT-1
Little River—stream (8) VA-3
Little River—stream (2) WA-9
Little River—stream (2) WV-2
Little River—stream (2) WI-6
**Little River-Academy**—pop pl TX-5
Little River Access Point—locale GA-3
Little River Baptist Church—hist pl SC-3
Little River Bay—bay FL-3
Little River Bluff—cliff ME-1
Little River Bridge—bridge GA-3
Little River Camp Dam—dam NC-3
Little River Camp Lake—reservoir NC-3
Little River Canal—canal FL-3
Little River Canal Number C-7—canal FL-3
Little River Canyon—valley AL-4
Little River (CCD)—cens area GA-3
Little River (CCD)—cens area SC-3
Little River Cem—cemetery CA-9
Little River Cem—cemetery FL-3
Little River Cem—cemetery TX-5
Little River Cem—cemetery VA-3
Little River Ch—church (4) AL-4
Little River Ch—church AR-4
Little River Ch—church FL-3
Little River Ch—church GA-3
Little River Ch—church (4) KY-4
Little River Ch—church LA-4
Little River Ch—church MO-7
Little River Ch—church NH-1
Little River Ch—church (3) NC-3
Little River Ch—church (7) SC-3
Little River Ch—church TX-5
Little River Ch—church (3) VA-3
Little River Chapel—church AR-4
Little River Chapel—church NC-3
Little River Christian Camp—locale OR-9
Little River Community Park—park FL-3
Little River Country Club—other AR-4
Little River Country Club—other WI-6
**Little River (County)**—pop pl AR-4
Little River County Courthouse—hist pl AR-4
Little River Cove—bay ME-1
Little River Crossing—locale VA-3
Little River Cutoff—bend AR-4
Little River Dam—dam KS-7
Little River Dam—dam NC-3
Little River Elem Sch—school KS-7
Little River Falls—falls AL-4
Little River Golf Course—other CA-9
Little River Gorge—valley TN-4
*Little River Gulf* AL-4
*Little River Head* ME-1
Little River Hill—summit CA-9
Little River Hill—summit OK-5
**Little River Hills**—pop pl VA-3
Little River (historical)—locale MA-1
**Little River (historical)**—pop pl TN-4
Little River Inlet—bay SC-3
Little River Inlet—channel NC-3
*Little River Island* TN-4
Little River Island—island AR-4
Little River Island—island (2) ME-1
Little River Islands (historical)—island TN-4
*Little River Junior High School* FL-3
Little River Lake—lake AL-4
Little River Lake—lake AK-9
Little River Lake—lake FL-3
Little River Lake—lake LA-4
Little River Lake—lake ME-1
Little River Landing—locale GA-3
Little River Ledge—bar ME-1
Little River Ledges—bar ME-1
Little River Lighthouse—locale ME-1
Little River Light Station—hist pl ME-1
Little River Log Dam—dam OR-9
Little River Log Pond—reservoir OR-9
Little River Log Storage Rsvr—reservoir OR-9
Little River (Magisterial District)—fmr MCD VA-3
Little River Marina—locale AL-4
Little River Marshes—swamp (2) MA-1
*Little River Mission* TN-4
Little River Mtn—summit ME-1
Little River Mtn—summit OK-5
Little River Neck—cape SC-3
Little River Neck Sch—school SC-3
Little River Park—park FL-3
Little River Picnic Area—park NC-3
**Little River Pines (Ilda)**—pop pl VA-3
Little River Plaza—locale MA-1
*Little River Point* ME-1
Little River Point—cape ME-1
*Little River Pond* FL-3
Little River Post Office (historical)—building TN-4
*Little River Raisin* MI-6
Little River Raisin—stream MI-6
Little River Ranch—locale OK-5
Little River Rock—bar ME-1
Little River Rock—island CA-9
Little River Rsvr—reservoir (2) MA-1
Little River Sch—school AL-4
Little River Sch—school FL-3
Little River Sch—school NC-3
Little River Sch—school SC-3
Little River Sch (historical)—school MO-7
Little River Shoals—bar TN-4
Little River Springs—spring FL-3
Little River State Beach—beach CA-9
Little River State For—forest AL-4
*Little River State Park* AL-4
Little River State Park—park OK-5
Little River State Park Dam—dam AL-4
Little River Summit—summit WA-9
Little River Swamp—swamp NH-1
Little River Swamp—swamp SC-3
**Little River (Town of)**—pop pl WI-6
Little River Township—civil MO-7
**Little River Township**—pop pl KS-7
Little River (Township of)—fmr MCD (3) AR-4
Little River (Township of)—fmr MCD (6) NC-3
Little River Trail—trail WA-9
Little River Windmill—locale TX-5
Little River Winyah Bay Light One Hundred Fifty—locale SC-3
Little River Winyah Bay Light One Hundred Fifty-six—locale SC-3
Little River Winyah Bay Light One Hundred Fifty-two—locale SC-3
Little River Winyah Bay Light One Hundred Forty-eight—locale SC-3
Little Road Branch—stream WV-2
Little Road Run—stream WV-2
*Little Roanoke Creek* VA-3
Little Roaring Bayou—stream LA-4
Little Roaring Brook—stream (2) PA-2
*Little Roaring Creek* PA-2
Little Roaring Creek—stream CA-9
Little Roaring Creek—stream PA-2
Little Roaring Creek—stream TN-4
Little Roaring Creek—stream WV-2
Little Roaring River Lake—lake ID-8
Little Robbers Gulch—valley WY-8
Little Robbins Slough—stream TX-5
Little Robe Bayou—stream AR-4
Little Robe Creek—stream (2) OK-5
*Little Robertson Valley* CA-9
Little Roberts Pond—reservoir FL-3
Little Robin Branch—stream NJ-2
Little Robin Hood Lake Dam—dam MA-1
Little Robinson Canyon—valley AZ-5
Little Robinson Cow Camp—locale CO-8
Little Robinson Creek—stream CO-8
Little Robinson Creek—stream ID-8
Little Robinson Creek—stream (2) KY-4
Little Robinson Lake—lake MI-6
Little Robinsons Valley—valley CA-9
Little Roche a Cri Creek—stream WI-6
*Little Rock* CA-9
*Little Rock* WA-9
Little Rock—island AK-9
Little Rock—island CT-1
Little Rock—locale ID-8
**Little Rock**—pop pl AL-4
**Little Rock**—pop pl AR-4
**Littlerock**—pop pl CA-9
**Little Rock**—pop pl IL-6
**Little Rock**—pop pl IN-6
**Little Rock**—pop pl IA-7
**Little Rock**—pop pl KY-4
**Little Rock**—pop pl MN-6
**Little Rock**—pop pl (2) MS-4
**Little Rock**—pop pl SC-3
**Littlerock**—pop pl WA-9
Little Rock—summit KY-4
Little Rock—summit VA-3
Little Rock, The—hist pl AR-4
Little Rock Air Force Base—military AR-4
*Little Rock Assembly of God Church* MS-4
*Little Rock Baptist Church* TN-4
Little Rock Boys Club—hist pl AR-4
Little Rock Branch—stream NC-3
Little Rock Branch—stream TN-4
Little Rock Branch—stream VA-3
Little Rockcamp Ch—church WV-2
Little Rockcamp Run—stream (2) WV-2
Little Rock Canyon—valley NV-8
Little Rock Canyon—valley NM-5
Little Rock Canyon—valley (2) UT-8
Little Rockcastle Creek—stream KY-4
Little Rock Castle Creek—stream VA-3
Little Rockcastle River—stream KY-4
Little Rock (CCD)—cens area SC-3
Little Rock Cem—cemetery FL-3
Little Rock Cem—cemetery (4) MS-4

Little Rock Cem—*cemetery* OK-5
Little Rock Cem—*cemetery* TN-4
Little Rock Cem—*cemetery* VA-3
Little Rock Central Fire Station—*hist pl* AR-4
Little Rock Ch—*church* (10) AL-4
Little Rock Ch—*church* (2) FL-3
Little Rock Ch—*church* (4) GA-3
Little Rock Ch—*church* IL-6
Little Rock Ch—*church* (3) LA-4
Little Rock Ch—*church* (13) MS-4
Little Rock Ch—*church* (4) NC-3
Little Rock Ch—*church* OK-5
Little Rock Ch—*church* (3) SC-3
Little Rock Ch—*church* (2) TN-4
Little Rock Ch—*church* (4) TX-5
Little Rock Ch—*church* (3) VA-3
Little Rock Ch—*church* (2) WV-2
Little Rock Ch (historical)—*church* (2) AL-4
Little Rock Ch of Assembly of the Lord Jesus Christ—*church* AL-4
Little Rock Church—*locale* GA-3
Little Rock Church Cem—*cemetery* AL-4
Little Rock City—*locale* NY-2
Little Rock City Hall—*hist pl* AR-4
Little Rock City Park—*park* AL-4
Little Rock Coulee—*valley* MT-8
Little Rock Country Club—*other* AR-4
*Little Rock Creek* MN-6
*Little Rock Creek* MO-7
*Little Rock Creek* OK-5
*Little Rock Creek* OR-9
*Little Rock Creek* TN-4
*Little Rock Creek* WY-8
Little Rock Creek—*stream* (4) AL-4
Little Rock Creek—*stream* AZ-5
Little Rock Creek—*stream* (4) CA-9
Little Rock Creek—*stream* (2) CO-8
Little Rock Creek—*stream* (2) GA-3
Little Rock Creek—*stream* (2) ID-8
Little Rock Creek—*stream* (2) IL-6
Little Rock Creek—*stream* (2) IN-6
Little Rock Creek—*stream* KS-7
Little Rock Creek—*stream* (4) MN-6
Little Rock Creek—*stream* (2) MS-4
Little Rock Creek—*stream* (3) MO-7
Little Rock Creek—*stream* (5) MT-8
Little Rock Creek—*stream* NE-7
Little Rock Creek—*stream* NV-8
Little Rock Creek—*stream* NC-3
Little Rock Creek—*stream* OH-6
Little Rock Creek—*stream* (4) OK-5
Little Rock Creek—*stream* (7) OR-9
Little Rock Creek—*stream* (3) TN-4
Little Rock Creek—*stream* (2) TX-5
Little Rock Creek—*stream* (2) VA-3
Little Rock Creek—*stream* WI-6
Little Rock Creek—*stream* WY-8
Littlerock Creek—*stream* WY-8
Little Rock Creek Ch—*church* NC-3
Little Rock Creek Dam—*hist pl* CA-9
Little Rock Creek Lake—*lake* MT-8
Little Rock Creek (Township of)—*fmr MCD* NC-3
Little Rock Ditch—*canal* CA-9
Little Rock Falls—*falls* MN-6
*Little Rockfish Creek* NC-3
Little Rockfish Creek—*stream* NC-3
Little Rock Fish Creek—*stream* NC-3
Little Rock Flat—*flat* OR-9
Little Rock Gillett Levee—*levee* (2) AR-4
Little Rockhouse Branch—*stream* TN-4
Little Rockhouse Branch—*stream* VA-3
Little Rock House Canyon—*valley* UT-8
*Little Rockhouse Creek - in part* TN-4
Little Rock House Riffle—*rapids* UT-8
Little Rock HS—*hist pl* AR-4
*Little Rockies* MT-8
Little Rockies—*range* UT-8
Little Rockies Camp—*locale* MT-8
Little Rockies Natl Natural Landmark—*locale* UT-8
Little Rock Island—*island* AL-4
Little Rock Island—*island* IL-6
Little Rock Island—*island* TN-4
Little Rock Island Creek—*stream* VA-3
*Little Rock Island Run* VA-3
Little Rock Knob—*summit* NC-3
Little Rock Knob—*summit* TN-4
*Little Rock Lake* MN-6
Little Rock Lake—*lake* AZ-5
Little Rock Lake—*lake* CO-8
Little Rock Lake—*lake* (3) MN-6
Little Rock Lake—*lake* NY-2
Little Rock Lake—*lake* WA-9
Little Rock Lake—*lake* WI-6
Little Rock Landing—*locale* MO-7
Little Rock Lick Creek—*stream* (2) KY-4
*Littlerock Mills* TN-4
Little Rock Mills—*locale* TN-4
*Little Rock Mills Post Office* TN-4
Littlerock Mills Post Office (historical)—*building* TN-4
*Little Rock Missionary Baptist Church* MS-4
Little Rock Mtn—*summit* AK-9
Little Rock Mtn—*summit* SC-3
Little Rock-Palmdale Dam—*dam* CA-9
Little Rock Pond—*lake* (6) NY-2
Little Rock Pond—*lake* VT-1
Little Rock Post—*locale* AR-4
Little Rock Post Office (historical)—*building* AL-4
Little Rock River—*stream* MN-6
Little Rock (RR name for Littlerock)—*other* WA-9
**Littlerock (RR name Little Rock)**—*pop pl* WA-9
Little Rock Rsvr—*reservoir* CA-9
Little Rock Rsvr—*reservoir* UT-8
Little Rock Run—*stream* KY-4
*Little Rock Sch* AL-4
Little Rock Sch—*school* AL-4
Little Rock Sch—*school* FL-3
Little Rock Sch—*school* MS-4
Little Rock Sch—*school* OK-5
Little Rock Sch—*school* SC-3
Little Rock Sch (abandoned)—*school* PA-2
Little Rock Sch (historical)—*school* AL-4
Little Rock Sch (historical)—*school* MS-4
Little Rock Sch (historical)—*school* TN-4
*Little Rock School* TN-4
Little Rock Sink—*basin* GA-3
Little Rock Siphon—*canal* CA-9
Little Rocks Ponds—*lake* NY-2
Little Rock Spring—*spring* ID-8
Little Rock Spring—*spring* NV-8
Little Rock Spring—*spring* OR-9
Little Rock Spring—*spring* UT-8
Little Rock Spring—*spring* WY-8
*Little Rock Springs* ID-8
Little Rock Station—*locale* CA-9
Little Rock Swamp—*swamp* FL-3
*Little Rock Tank* AZ-5
Little Rock Tank—*reservoir* (2) AZ-5
**Little Rock (Township of)**—*pop pl* IL-6
**Little Rock (Township of)**—*pop pl* MN-6
Little Rock Wash—*stream* CA-9
Little Rocky—*summit* NY-2
Little Rocky—*summit* TN-4
Little Rocky Branch—*stream* KY-4
Little Rocky Branch—*stream* OH-6
Little Rocky Branch—*stream* (3) TN-4
Little Rocky Brook—*stream* ME-1
Little Rocky Canyon—*valley* MT-8
Little Rocky Canyon—*valley* NM-5
Little Rocky Canyon—*valley* UT-8
Little Rocky Cem—*cemetery* FL-3
Little Rocky Cem—*cemetery* TX-5
*Little Rocky Coulee* MT-8
*Little Rocky Creek* AR-4
*Little Rocky Creek* MT-8
*Little Rocky Creek* NC-3
*Little Rocky Creek* TX-5
Little Rocky Creek—*stream* (2) AL-4
Little Rocky Creek—*stream* AZ-5
Little Rocky Creek—*stream* AR-4
Little Rocky Creek—*stream* (4) FL-3
Little Rocky Creek—*stream* (4) GA-3
Little Rocky Creek—*stream* (2) MS-4
Little Rocky Creek—*stream* MO-7
Little Rocky Creek—*stream* MT-8
Little Rocky Creek—*stream* (3) NC-3
Little Rocky Creek—*stream* (2) SC-3
Little Rocky Creek—*stream* (6) TX-5
Little Rocky Creek—*stream* VA-3
Little Rocky Creek Ch—*church* FL-3
Little Rocky Creek Sch (abandoned)—*school* FL-3
*Little Rocky Fork* IN-6
*Little Rocky Fork* MT-8
Little Rocky Fork Creek—*stream* IN-6
**Little Rocky Hill**—*pop pl* NJ-2
Little Rocky Knob—*summit* NC-3
Little Rock Y.M.C.A.—*hist pl* AR-4
Little Rocky Mount Ch—*church* MS-4
Little Rocky Mtn—*summit* NY-2
Little Rocky Mtn—*summit* NC-3
Little Rocky Mtn—*summit* VA-3
Little Rocky Mtns—*range* MT-8
Little Rocky Point Branch—*stream* KY-4
Little Rocky Pond—*lake* (3) ME-1
Little Rocky Pond—*lake* MA-1
Little Rocky Pond—*lake* NH-1
Little Rocky Ridge—*ridge* PA-2
Little Rocky Row—*summit* VA-3
Little Rocky Run—*stream* NC-3
Little Rocky Run—*stream* VA-3
Little Rocky Run—*stream* WV-2
Little Rocky Tank—*reservoir* AZ-5
Little Rocky Tank—*reservoir* NM-5
Little Roden Spring—*spring* AZ-5
Little Roden Wash—*stream* AZ-5
Little Rodgers Tanks—*reservoir* AZ-5
Little Rod Tank—*reservoir* AZ-5
Little Rody Creek—*stream* CA-9
Little Roger Creek—*stream* WA-9
Little Rogers Ch—*church* GA-3
Little Rogg Island—*island* MI-6
Little Rollins Creek—*stream* IA-7
Little Rollins Creek—*stream* MO-7
Little Rolph Canyon—*valley* ID-8
Little Romney Creek—*stream* MD-2
Little Roney Pond—*lake* TN-4
Little Rooster Branch—*stream* KY-4
*Little Root Narrows* VA-3
Little Rosa Canyon—*valley* NM-5
Little Rosa Lake—*lake* WI-6
**Little Rose**—*pop pl* WI-6
Little Rosebud Spring—*spring* NV-8
Little Rose Ch—*church* KY-4
Little Rose Creek—*stream* AR-4
Little Rose Creek—*stream* GA-3
Little Rose Creek—*stream* NC-3
Little Rose Creek—*stream* WY-8
Little Rose Island—*island* AK-9
Little Rose Lake—*lake* (2) MN-6
Little Rose Lakes—*lake* WI-6
Little Rose Run—*stream* KY-4
Little Ross Branch—*stream* MS-4
Little Ross Cave—*cave* AL-4
Little Ross Lake—*lake* MI-6
Little Ross Rsvr—*reservoir* OR-9
Little Rotten Bayou Cem—*cemetery* MS-4
Little Rough Canyon—*valley* ID-8
Little Rough Canyon—*valley* NM-5
Little Rough Creek—*stream* MT-8
Little Rough Creek—*stream* (2) TX-5
Little Rough Gulch—*valley* CA-9
Little Rough Range—*range* UT-8
Little Rough Run—*stream* (2) WV-2
Little Round Bay—*bay* MD-2
*Little Round Bay Creek* MD-2
Little Round Butte—*summit* OR-9
Little Round Hill—*summit* KY-4
Little Round Hill Campground—*locale* MN-6
Little Round Island—*island* NY-2
*Little Round Lake* WI-6
Little Round Lake—*lake* MI-6
Little Round Lake—*lake* (4) MN-6
Little Round Lake—*lake* NY-2
Little Round Lake—*lake* (6) WI-6
Little Round Meadow—*swamp* OR-9
*Little Round Mountain* WA-9
Little Round Mountain Creek—*stream* CA-9
Little Round Mountain Spring—*spring* WY-8
Little Round Mountain Tank—*reservoir* NM-5
Little Round Mtn—*summit* AZ-5
Little Round Mtn—*summit* (3) AR-4
Little Round Mtn—*summit* (6) CA-9
Little Round Mtn—*summit* CO-8
Little Round Mtn—*summit* (3) KY-4
Little Round Mtn—*summit* MT-8
Little Round Mtn—*summit* NM-5
Little Round Mtn—*summit* (5) OK-5
Little Round Mtn—*summit* (2) TX-5
Little Round Mtn—*summit* WY-8
*Little Round Pond* ME-1
*Little Round Pond* MA-1
*Little Round Pond* NH-1
Little Round Pond—*lake* AR-4
Little Round Pond—*lake* DE-2
Little Round Pond—*lake* IL-6
Little Round Pond—*lake* (3) ME-1
Little Round Pond—*lake* NY-2
Little Round Prairie—*flat* OR-9
Little Round Prairie Spring—*spring* OR-9
Little Round Rock—*summit* AZ-5
Little Round Shoal—*bar* MA-1
*Little Round Top* CA-9
Little Roundtop—*locale* PA-2
Little Round Top—*summit* ID-8
Little Round Top—*summit* MA-1
Little Roundtop—*summit* (2) NY-2
Little Roundtop—*summit* OH-6
Little Round Top—*summit* (5) PA-2
Little Roundtop—*summit* TN-4
Little Round Top—*summit* TX-5
Little Roundtop—*summit* VT-1
Little Roundtop—*summit* (2) WA-9
*Little Round Top Mtn* WA-9
Little Round Top Mtn—*summit* AZ-5
Little Round Top Mtn—*summit* AR-4
Little Roundtop Mtn—*summit* NH-1
Little Roundtop Mtn—*summit* (2) NY-2
Little Roundtop Mtn—*summit* OR-9
Little Round Top Pond—*lake* RI-1
Little Round Top Tank—*reservoir* AZ-5
Little Round Valley—*basin* (3) CA-9
Little Round Valley—*basin* UT-8
Little Round Valley—*valley* AZ-5
Little Round Valley—*valley* CA-9
Little Rouse Pond—*reservoir* PA-2
*Little Rouze Lake* MI-6
*Little Rouzel Lake* MI-6
Little Rowell Creek—*stream* OR-9
Little Rowles Run—*stream* WV-2
Little Royal Oak Swamp—*stream* NC-3
Little Roycroft Gulch—*valley* CA-9
Littler River HS—*school* KS-7
Littlers Creek—*stream* IL-6
Little RS Spring—*spring* AZ-5
Little Rsvr—*reservoir* AL-4
Little Rsvr—*reservoir* (2) AZ-5
Little Rsvr—*reservoir* CA-9
Little Rsvr—*reservoir* NV-8
Little Rsvr—*reservoir* (2) OR-9
Little Rsvr—*reservoir* UT-8
Little Rsvr—*reservoir* WY-8
Little Rsvr Lake—*reservoir* MN-6
Little Rsvr Number Five—*reservoir* OR-9
Little Rsvr Number One—*reservoir* OR-9
Little Rsvr Number Six—*reservoir* OR-9
Little Rsvr Number Three—*reservoir* OR-9
Little Ruby Creek—*stream* WA-9
Little Ruby Gulch—*valley* CO-8
Little Ruby Lake—*lake* CO-8
Little Ruby Lake—*lake* MN-6
Little Ruddy Branch—*stream* SC-3
Little Ruin Canyon—*valley* UT-8
Little Ruin Creek—*stream* NC-3
*Little Rumstick Neck* RI-1
*Little Run* PA-2
Little Run—*stream* IN-6
Little Run—*stream* NC-3
Little Run—*stream* (2) OH-6
Little Run—*stream* (3) PA-2
Little Run—*stream* (5) WV-2
**Little Run Estates**—*pop pl* VA-3
Little Running Water Ditch—*canal* AR-4
Little Run Sch—*school* VA-3
*Little Rush Creek* OH-6
Little Rush Creek—*stream* AR-4
Little Rush Creek—*stream* IL-6
Little Rush Creek—*stream* OH-6
Little Rush Creek—*stream* OK-5
Little Rush Creek—*stream* TX-5
Little Rush Lake—*lake* MN-6
Little Rush Lake—*lake* SD-7
Little Rush Run—*stream* OH-6
Little Rush Wood Sch (historical)—*school* MO-7
Little Russell Creek—*stream* KY-4
Little Russell Creek—*stream* OR-9
Little Russell Creek—*stream* VA-3
Little Russell Mtn—*summit* (2) ME-1
Little Russell Stream—*stream* ME-1
Little Rusty Creek—*stream* AK-9
Little Rusty Gut—*stream* IN-6
Little Ruth Ch—*church* FL-3
Little Ruth Ch—*church* OH-6
Little R W Creek—*stream* WY-8
**Littles**—*pop pl* IN-6
Little Sabattus Mtn—*summit* ME-1
Little Sabattus Pond—*lake* ME-1
Little Sabine Bay—*bay* FL-3
Little Sable Creek—*stream* FL-3
*Little Sable Lake* MI-6
Little Sable Point—*cape* MI-6
Little Sable Point Light Station—*hist pl* MI-6
*Little Sable River* MI-6
Little Sac Branch—*stream* KS-7
Little Sachem Pond—*lake* RI-1
Little Sacony Creek—*stream* PA-2
Little Saco River—*stream* ME-1
Little Sacramento Gulch—*valley* CO-8
Little Sac River—*stream* MO-7
Little Saddle—*gap* AZ-5
Little Saddle—*gap* WA-9
Little Saddleback Pond—*lake* ME-1
Little Saddle Creek—*stream* TX-5
Little Saddle Mtn—*summit* WY-8
Little Safford Lake—*lake* NY-2
Little Sag, The—*basin* MT-8
Little Saganaga Lake—*lake* MN-6
Little Sage Creek—*stream* ID-8
Little Sage Creek—*stream* (3) MT-8
Little Sage Creek—*stream* (2) WY-8
Little Sage Hen Basin—*basin* ID-8
*Little Sage Hen Creek* OR-9
Little Sage Hen Creek—*stream* NV-8
Little Sage Hen Creek—*stream* OR-9
Little Sage Hen Flat—*flat* ID-8
Little Sage Hen Flat—*flat* OR-9
Little Sage Hen Spring—*spring* NV-8
Little Sage Hen Spring—*spring* OR-9
Little Sage Hill—*summit* CA-9
Little Sage Valley—*valley* (2) UT-8
*Little Sagus Lake* MN-6
Little Sahara Natl Rec Area—*park* UT-8
*Little Sahara Rec Area* UT-8
Little Sahara State Rec Area—*park* OK-5
Little Sailor Creek—*stream* CA-9
Little Saint Charles Creek—*stream* CO-8
Little Saint Francis River—*stream* MO-7
Little Saint George Island—*island* FL-3
Little Saint Germain Creek—*stream* WI-6
Little Saint Germain Lake—*lake* WI-6
Little Saint James Island—*island* VI-3
*Little Saint Joe Creek* MT-8
Little Saint John Ch—*church* FL-3
Little Saint John Lake—*lake* ME-1
*Little Saint Joseph River* IN-6
*Little Saint Louis* KS-7
**Little Saint Louis**—*pop pl* IN-6
Little Saint Marks River—*stream* FL-3
Little Saint Martin Island—*island* MI-6
*Little Saint Mary* MT-8
*Little Saint Mary Creek* MT-8
*Little Saint Mary Lake* MT-8
Little Saint Marys River—*stream* FL-3
Little Saint Michael Canal—*canal* AK-9
Little Saint Roch River—*stream* ME-1
Little Saint Simons Island—*island* GA-3
Little Saint Thomas—*cape* VI-3
Little Salado Creek—*stream* CA-9
Little Salamonie Ch—*church* IN-6
Little Salamonie River—*stream* IN-6
Little Salcha River—*stream* AK-9
Little Salem Ch—*church* NC-3
Little Salem Ch—*church* VA-3
Little Salem Creek—*stream* KY-4
*Little Salem River* NJ-2
*Little Salina Creek* OK-5
Little Saline Bayou—*stream* LA-4
Little Saline Branch—*stream* LA-4
Little Saline Ch—*church* IL-6
*Little Saline Creek* TX-5
Little Saline Creek—*stream* IL-6
Little Saline Creek—*stream* (2) MO-7
Little Saline Creek—*stream* OK-5
Little Saline Creek—*stream* (3) TX-5
Little Saline River—*stream* IL-6
Little Salisbury—*locale* VA-3
Little Salitre Tank—*reservoir* NM-5
Little Salkehatchie River—*stream* SC-3
Little Sallisaw Creek—*stream* OK-5
Little Sally Brook—*stream* NY-2
*Little Salmon Creek* CA-9
Little Salmon Creek—*stream* (2) CA-9
Little Salmon Creek—*stream* MT-8
Little Salmon Creek—*stream* NV-8
Little Salmon Creek—*stream* NY-2
Little Salmon Creek—*stream* OR-9
Little Salmon Creek—*stream* PA-2
Little Salmon Creek—*stream* WA-9
Little Salmon Lake—*lake* (2) NY-2
*Little Salmon Lasac Creek* WA-9
Little Salmon la Sac Creek—*stream* WA-9
Little Salmon Outlet—*stream* NY-2
Little Salmon Park—*flat* MT-8
*Little Salmon River* MT-8
Little Salmon River—*stream* AK-9
Little Salmon River—*stream* ID-8
Little Salmon River—*stream* (2) NY-2
Little Salmon River—*stream* OR-9
Little Salmon Stream—*stream* ME-1
Little Salmon Stream Lake—*lake* ME-1
Little Sal Mtn—*summit* GA-3
Little Salt—*fmr MCD* NE-7
Little Salt Branch—*stream* TX-5
Little Salt Branch Tank—*reservoir* TX-5
Little Salt Canyon—*valley* AZ-5
Little Salt Canyon—*valley* CA-9
*Little Salt Creek* KS-7
*Little Salt Creek* MI-6
Little Salt Creek—*stream* AK-9
Little Salt Creek—*stream* (4) CA-9
Little Salt Creek—*stream* IL-6
Little Salt Creek—*stream* (4) IN-6
Little Salt Creek—*stream* KS-7
Little Salt Creek—*stream* MI-6
Little Salt Creek—*stream* MT-8
Little Salt Creek—*stream* NE-7
Little Salt Creek—*stream* (2) OH-6
Little Salt Creek—*stream* (2) OK-5
Little Salt Creek—*stream* (2) TX-5
Little Salt Creek—*stream* UT-8
Little Salt Creek Cem—*cemetery* IN-6
Little Saltery Island—*island* AK-9
Little Salt House Canyon—*valley* NM-5
Little Salt House Well—*well* NM-5
Little Salt Lake—*lake* (2) NM-5
Little Salt Lake—*lake* UT-8
Little Salt Lick Creek—*stream* (2) TN-4
*Little Salt Lick Run* PA-2
Little Saltlick Run—*stream* PA-2
Little Salt Marsh—*swamp* KS-7
*Little Salt River* MI-6
Little Salt River Valley (inundated)—*valley* AZ-5
Little Salt Rock Creek—*stream* NC-3
Little Salt Rocks—*bar* MA-1
Little Salt Rsvr—*reservoir* OR-9
Little Salt Run—*stream* OH-6
Little Salt Spring—*lake* FL-3
Little Salt Spring—*spring* NV-8
Little Salt Springs—*hist pl* FL-3
Little Salt Wash—*stream* CO-8
Little Saluda Creek—*stream* IN-6
*Little Saluda River* SC-3
Little Saluda River—*stream* SC-3
*Little Salvages* MA-1
Little Salvages—*bar* MA-1
Little Sam Jack Creek—*stream* AL-4
Little Sam Knob—*summit* NC-3
Little Sam Moore Tank—*reservoir* AZ-5
Little Sam Mtn—*summit* NC-3
Little Sampson Creek—*stream* MO-7
Little Sampson Windmill—*locale* TX-5
Little Sam Sch (historical)—*school* AL-4
Little Sams Creek—*stream* ID-8
Little San Bernardino Mountains—*range* CA-9
Little San Bernard River—*stream* TX-5
Little Sancho Creek—*stream* WV-2
*Little Sand* GA-3
Little Sand Bay—*bay* MI-6
Little Sand Bay—*bay* NY-2
Little Sand Bay—*bay* WI-6
Little Sand Butte—*summit* CA-9
Little Sand Canyon—*valley* CA-9
*Little Sand Coulee* WY-8
Little Sand Coulee—*valley* WY-8
*Little Sand Creek* CA-9
*Little Sand Creek* IN-6
*Little Sand Creek* MN-6
*Little Sand Creek* UT-8
Little Sand Creek—*stream* CA-9
Little Sand Creek—*stream* (3) CO-8
Little Sand Creek—*stream* GA-3
Little Sand Creek—*stream* (3) ID-8
Little Sand Creek—*stream* IN-6
Little Sand Creek—*stream* MN-6
Little Sand Creek—*stream* (4) MS-4
Little Sand Creek—*stream* MT-8
Little Sand Creek—*stream* (4) OK-5
Little Sand Creek—*stream* OR-9
Little Sand Creek—*stream* TX-5
Little Sand Creek—*stream* UT-8
Little Sand Creek—*stream* WY-8
Little Sand Creek Cem—*cemetery* IN-6
Little Sand Creek Lakes—*lake* CO-8
Little Sand Draw—*valley* (4) WY-8
Little Sand Dunes—*summit* WY-8
Little Sand Flat—*flat* CA-9
Little Sand Flat—*flat* UT-8
Little Sand Island—*island* AL-4
*Little Sand Lake* WI-6
Little Sand Lake—*lake* FL-3
Little Sand Lake—*lake* (7) MN-6
Little Sand Lake—*lake* SD-7
Little Sand Lake—*lake* (6) WI-6
Little Sand Lake (Unorganized Territory of)—*unorg* MN-6
Little Sand Meadow—*flat* CA-9
Little Sand Mountain (CCD)—*cens area* GA-3
*Little Sand Mountain Plateau* GA-3
Little Sand Mtn—*summit* AL-4
Little Sand Mtn—*summit* CO-8
Little Sand Mtn—*summit* GA-3
Little Sand Mtn—*summit* ID-8
Little San Domingo Mine—*mine* AZ-5
Little San Domingo Wash—*stream* AZ-5
Little Sand Point State Campsite—*locale* NY-2
*Little Sand Pond* RI-1
Little Sand Pond—*lake* FL-3
Little Sandridge Canal—*canal* CA-9
Little Sandrock Gulch—*valley* OR-9
Little Sand Run—*stream* WV-2
*Little Sands Creek* OK-5
Little Sand Spring—*spring* CA-9
Little Sand Spring—*spring* WY-8
*Little Sand Spring Valley* NV-8
Little Sandstone Campground—*locale* WY-8
Little Sandstone Creek—*stream* WY-8
Little Sand Tank—*reservoir* AZ-5
Little Sand Tank—*reservoir* NM-5
Little Sand Truck Trail—*trail* CA-9
**Little Sandusky**—*pop pl* OH-6
Little Sandusky River—*stream* OH-6
Little Sand Valley—*valley* AL-4
Little Sand Valley Creek—*stream* (2) AL-4
Little Sand Wash—*stream* (2) AZ-5
Little Sand Windmill—*locale* TX-5
**Little Sandy**—*pop pl* AL-4
**Little Sandy**—*pop pl* KY-4
Little Sandy, Bayou—*stream* LA-4
*Little Sandy Baptist Church* AL-4
Little Sandy Bar Creek—*stream* CA-9
*Little Sandy Bay* MI-6
Little Sandy Bayou—*stream* LA-4
Little Sandy Bottom Pond—*lake* MA-1
Little Sandy Branch—*stream* LA-4
Little Sandy Branch—*stream* (2) TN-4
Little Sandy Campground—*locale* CA-9
Little Sandy Canal—*canal* WY-8
Little Sandy Canyon—*valley* WA-9
Little Sandy Cem—*cemetery* AL-4
Little Sandy Cem—*cemetery* KS-7
Little Sandy Ch—*church* AL-4
*Little Sandy Coulee* MT-8
*Little Sandy Creek* OK-5
*Little Sandy Creek* TX-5
*Little Sandy Creek* WI-6
Little Sandy Creek—*stream* (5) AL-4
Little Sandy Creek—*stream* AR-4
Little Sandy Creek—*stream* CA-9
Little Sandy Creek—*stream* FL-3
Little Sandy Creek—*stream* (7) GA-3
Little Sandy Creek—*stream* (3) IL-6
Little Sandy Creek—*stream* IN-6
Little Sandy Creek—*stream* (4) KS-7
Little Sandy Creek—*stream* KY-4
Little Sandy Creek—*stream* (5) LA-4
Little Sandy Creek—*stream* MI-6
Little Sandy Creek—*stream* (3) MO-7
Little Sandy Creek—*stream* MT-8
Little Sandy Creek—*stream* (4) NE-7
Little Sandy Creek—*stream* NY-2
Little Sandy Creek—*stream* NC-3
Little Sandy Creek—*stream* OH-6
Little Sandy Creek—*stream* (6) OK-5
Little Sandy Creek—*stream* (3) PA-2
Little Sandy Creek—*stream* SC-3
Little Sandy Creek—*stream* (14) TX-5
Little Sandy Creek—*stream* (2) VA-3
Little Sandy Creek—*stream* WA-9
Little Sandy Creek—*stream* (4) WV-2
Little Sandy Creek—*stream* WI-6
Little Sandy Creek—*stream* (2) WY-8
Little Sandy Diversion Dam—*dam* OR-9
Little Sandy Draw—*valley* (2) TX-5
Little Sandy Feeder Canal—*canal* WY-8
Little Sandy Gap—*gap* NC-3
Little Sandy Guard Station—*locale* OR-9
Little Sandy Hill Creek—*stream* GA-3
Little Sandy Hollow—*valley* FL-3
Little Sandy Hollow—*valley* PA-2
Little Sandy Keys—*island* FL-3
Little Sandy Lake—*lake* MN-6
Little Sandy Lake—*lake* WY-8
Little Sandy Mtn—*summit* TX-5
Little Sandymush Bald—*summit* NC-3
Little Sandymush Ch—*church* NC-3
Little Sandymush Creek—*stream* NC-3
Little Sandy Point—*cape* VA-3
*Little Sandy Pond* MA-1
Little Sandy Pond—*lake* (2) MA-1
Little Sandy Ridge Ch—*church* AL-4
*Little Sandy Ridge Presbyterian Ch* AL-4
Little Sandy River—*stream* KY-4
Little Sandy River—*stream* OR-9
Little Sandy River—*stream* SC-3
Little Sandy Rsvr—*reservoir* (2) OR-9
Little Sandy Rsvr No 2—*reservoir* WY-8
Little Sandy Rsvr No 3—*reservoir* WY-8
*Little Sandy Run* PA-2
*Little Sandy Run* WV-2
Little Sandy Run—*stream* OH-6
Little Sandy Run—*stream* (4) PA-2
Little Sandy Run—*stream* SC-3
Little Sandy Run Creek—*stream* GA-3
*Little Sandy School* AL-4
Little Sandy Spring—*spring* AZ-5
Little Sandy Stream—*stream* ME-1
Little Sandy Trail—*trail* OR-9
Little Sandy Trail—*trail* WY-8
*Little Sandy Wash* AZ-5
Little Sandy Well—*well* TX-5
Little Sanes Creek—*stream* IN-6
Little Sangamon River—*stream* IL-6
Little Sanger Peak—*summit* CA-9
Little Sang Kill—*stream* WV-2
Little San Gorgonio Creek—*stream* CA-9
Little San Gorgonio Peak—*summit* CA-9
Little San Miguel Creek—*stream* LA-4
Little San Nicholas Canyon—*valley* NM-5
Little San Pasqual Mtn—*summit* NM-5
Little Sans Bois Cem—*cemetery* OK-5
Little Sans Bois Creek—*stream* OK-5
Little Santa Anita Canyon—*valley* CA-9
Little Santa Anita Racetrack—*other* ID-8
Little Santa Cruz Spring—*spring* AZ-5
Little Santa Fe (historical)—*locale* KS-7
Little Santa Fe Lake—*lake* FL-3
Little Santa Maria Valley—*valley* CA-9
Little Santanoni Mtn—*summit* NY-2
Little Santeetlah Creek—*stream* NC-3
*Little Santiam River* OR-9
Little Sanusi Creek—*stream* AL-4
Little Sapelo Island—*island* GA-3
Little Sapony Creek—*stream* NC-3
Little Sarasota Bay—*bay* FL-3
*Little Sarasota Key* FL-3
Little Sarco Creek—*stream* TX-5
Little Sarco Windmill—*locale* TX-5
Little Sardine Creek—*stream* OR-9
Little Sardis Ch—*church* AL-4
Little Satan Ch (historical)—*church* AL-4
Little Satan Creek—*stream* TX-5
Little Satilla Creek—*stream* (2) GA-3
*Little Satilla River* GA-3
Little Satilla River—*stream* GA-3
Little Satilla River Swamp—*swamp* GA-3
*Little Sauble Lake* MI-6
*Little Sauble River* MI-6
Little Saucepan Creek—*stream* NC-3
Little Saucer Basin—*basin* UT-8
**Little Sauk**—*pop pl* MN-6
Little Sauk Ch—*church* MN-6
Little Sauk Lake—*lake* MN-6
**Little Sauk (Township of)**—*pop pl* MN-6
Little Saunders Run—*stream* PA-2
Little Sauty Creek—*stream* AL-4
*Little Sauvany* FL-3
Little Savage Creek—*stream* OR-9
Little Savage Mtn—*summit* MD-2
Little Savage Mtn—*summit* PA-2
Little Savage River—*stream* MD-2
Little Savannah Ch—*church* NC-3
Little Savannah Creek—*stream* NC-3
Little Savannah Pond—*swamp* SC-3
Little Savanna Lake—*lake* MN-6
Little Savanna Lake—*reservoir* MD-2
Little Savery Creek—*stream* WY-8
Little Savory Creek—*stream* NV-8
Little Sawgrass—*swamp* FL-3
Little Sawgrass Lake—*lake* FL-3
Little Sawmill Basin—*basin* (2) NV-8
Little Sawmill Canyon—*valley* ID-8
Little Sawmill Canyon—*valley* NV-8
Little Sawmill Canyon—*valley* UT-8
Little Sawmill Creek—*stream* (2) ID-8
Little Sawmill Creek—*stream* NV-8
Little Sawmill Lake—*lake* IA-7
Little Sawpit Gulch—*valley* MT-8
Little Sawtelle Pond—*lake* ME-1
Little Sawyer, Lake—*lake* FL-3
Little Saylers Creek—*stream* VA-3
Littles Bar—*bar* AL-4
*Littles Bayou* FL-3
Littles Bayou—*stream* FL-3
Littles Branch—*stream* KY-4
Littles Branch—*stream* MO-7
*Littles Bridge* MA-1
*Littles Brook* MA-1
**Littlesburg**—*pop pl* WV-2
Little Scaly—*summit* NC-3
Littles Campground and RV Park—*park* UT-8
Little Scandard Gulch—*valley* CO-8
*Littles Canyon* UT-8
Little Scarboro Creek—*stream* WI-6
Little Scarboro State Public Fishery Area—*park* WI-6
Little Scarboro State Public Hunting Grounds—*park* WI-6
Little Scarecorn Creek—*stream* GA-3
Little Scarham Creek—*stream* AL-4
*Little Scarran Creek* AL-4
*Little Scarum Creek* AL-4
Little Scary Creek—*stream* WV-2
Littles Cem—*cemetery* MA-1
Littles Cem—*cemetery* OH-6
Littles Cem—*cemetery* PA-2
Little Scenic Trail—*trail* MN-6
Little Sch—*school* AL-4
Little Sch—*school* KS-7
Little Sch—*school* MA-1
Little Sch—*school* MI-6
Little Sch—*school* NJ-2
Littles Chapel—*church* TX-5
Little Schenck Creek—*stream* OH-6
Little Schloss—*summit* VA-3

Little Schneider Creek—stream CA-9
Little Schoharie Creek—stream NY-2
Little Scholars Acad—school FL-3
Little Schoodic Stream—stream ME-1
Little School—locale MT-8
Little School, The—school DE-2
Little School Branch—stream TX-5
Little Schoolhouse—school FL-3
Little School Lot Lake—lake MI-6
Little Schooner Creek—stream OR-9
Little Schrader Creek—stream PA-2
Little Schultz Creek—stream AL-4
Little Schultz Pond—reservoir AZ-5
Little Schuylkill Dam—dam PA-2
Little Schuylkill River—stream PA-2
Little Schwar Creek—stream ID-8
*Little Scioto River* OH-6
Little Scioto River—stream (2) OH-6
Little Scirum Creek—stream AL-4
Little Scooba Creek—stream MS-4
*Littles Corner* PA-2
**Littles Corners**—pop pl PA-2
Little Scotch Bonnet—channel NJ-2
Little Scotia Campground—locale MO-7
*Little Scotia Canyon* WA-9
Little Scotia Pond—reservoir MO-7
Little Scott Brook—stream ME-1
Little Scott Deadwater—lake ME-1
Little Scottie Creek—stream AK-9
Little Scott Pond—lake ME-1
Little Scott Tank—reservoir AZ-5
Little Scotty Creek—stream OR-9
Little Scraggy Peak—summit CO-8
*Littles Creek* OH-6
Littles Creek—stream MA-1
Littles Creek—stream UT-8
Littles Creek—stream WV-2
Little Scrubgrass Creek—stream PA-2
Little Scrub Island—island GA-3
Little Scrub Ridge—ridge PA-2
*Little Scull Lick Creek* MO-7
Little Scull Shoal Creek—stream GA-3
Littles Dam—dam AL-4
Little Seal Creek—stream VA-3
Little Seatuck Creek—stream NY-2
Little Seavey Lake—lake ME-1
Little Sebago Lake—lake ME-1
Little Seboeis River—stream ME-1
Little Sebonac Creek—stream NY-2
Little Seco Creek—stream TX-5
Little Seco Tank—reservoir NM-5
Little Secret Canyon—valley CA-9
Little Sedge Island—island NJ-2
Little Seed Branch—stream SC-3
Little Seeley Spring—spring CA-9
*Little Seguana* FL-3
Little Selatna River—stream AK-9
*Little Self Creek* AL-4
Little Selle Gap—gap OR-9
Little Selle Gap Rsvr—reservoir OR-9
Little Selle Spring—spring OR-9
*Little Semoneaston Creek* VA-3
Little Senachwine Creek—stream IL-6
Little Seneca Creek—stream MD-2
Little Seneca Lake—lake WY-8
Little Sentinel Peak—summit ID-8
Little Sequatchie Cove—valley TN-4
Little Sequatchie River—stream TN-4
Little Service Creek—stream OR-9
Little Service Run—stream PA-2
Little Sespe Creek—stream CA-9
Little Sett Creek—stream SC-3
*Little Sevenmile Creek* MT-8
Little Sevenmile Creek—stream MT-8
Little Sevenmile Creek—stream OR-9
Little Sevenmile Creek—stream WV-2
Little Seventy-seven Tank—reservoir AZ-5
Little Sevy Draw Pond—reservoir AZ-5
Little Sewee Creek—stream TN-4
Little Sewell Ch—church WV-2
Little Sewell Creek—stream WV-2
Little Sewell Mtn—summit WV-2
Little Sewickley Creek—stream (2) PA-2
Little Sextons Creek—stream KY-4
Littles Ferry Bridge—bridge GA-3
Littles Flats—flat TX-5
Littles Fork—stream WY-8
Littles Fork Trail—trail UT-8
*Littles Grove* IA-7
Little Shabakunk Creek—stream NJ-2
Little Shaddox Creek—stream NC-3
Little Shade Run—stream MD-2
Little Shade Run—stream PA-2
Little Shades Creek—stream (2) AL-4
Little Shades Creek—stream PA-2
Little Shades Creek Bridge—bridge AL-4
Little Shades Mtn—summit AL-4
*Little Shadow Lake* WI-6
Little Shady Creek—stream CA-9
Little Shaggy Canyon—valley TX-5
Little Shag Lake—lake MI-6
Little Shakey Creek—stream MI-6
*Little Shaky Creek* MI-6
*Little Shallotte Creek* NC-3
*Little Shallotte River* NC-3
Little Shallow—lake NY-2
Little Shallow Lake—lake ME-1
Little Shamokin Creek—stream PA-2
Little Shamrock Cove—bay TX-5
Little Shanley Creek—stream MT-8
Little Shannon Run—stream PA-2
Little Shannon Windmill—locale TX-5
Little Shanty Mtn—summit ME-1
Little Sharkey Creek—stream MS-4
Little Shark River—stream FL-3
Little Sharp Point—cape TX-5
Little Shasta—locale CA-9
Little Shasta Cem—cemetery CA-9
Little Shasta Meadow—flat CA-9
Little Shasta River—stream CA-9
Little Shasta Spring—spring CA-9
*Little Shaver Creek* MO-7
Little Shaver Creek—stream MO-7
Little Shawangunk Kill—stream NY-2
Little Shaw Cem—cemetery MS-4
**Little Shawmut**—pop pl AL-4
Little Shawnee Creek—stream IN-6
Little Shawnee Creek—stream KS-7
Little Shawnee Creek—stream KY-4
Little Shawnee Creek—stream MO-7
Little Shawnette Creek—stream TN-4
Little Shay Mtn—summit CA-9
Little Sheen Rapids—rapids WI-6
Little Sheep Cliff—summit NC-3
Little Sheep Creek—stream AK-9
Little Sheep Creek—stream (2) ID-8
Little Sheep Creek—stream (3) MT-8
Little Sheep Creek—stream OR-9
Little Sheep Creek—stream WA-9
Little Sheepeater Creek—stream ID-8
Little Sheepeater Lake—lake ID-8
Little Sheepeater Point—summit ID-8
Little Sheep Hammock—island DE-2
*Little Sheephead Creek* NJ-2
Little Sheep Island—island (2) ME-1
Little Sheep Mtn—summit CO-8
Little Sheep Mtn—summit MT-8
Little Sheep Mtn—summit (2) WY-8
Little Sheep Ridge—ridge OR-9
Little Sheepscot River—channel ME-1
Little Sheepshead Creek—gut NJ-2
Little Shell—beach TX-5
Little Shell Ch—church ND-7
Little Shell Creek—stream ND-7
Little Shell Creek Public Use Area—park ND-7
Little Shell Island—island FL-3
Little Shell Lake—lake MN-6
Little Shell Lake—lake WY-8
Little Shellstone Creek—stream GA-3
Little Shelly—summit UT-8
*Little Shelly Baldy Peak* UT-8
Little Shelter Bay—bay MI-6
**Little Shenandoah**—pop pl AL-4
Little Shenango Dam—dam PA-2
Little Shenango Dam Rsvr—reservoir PA-2
Little Shenango River—stream PA-2
Little Shephard Creek—stream TX-5
Little Sheriff Lake—lake MN-6
Little Sherman Pond—lake NY-2
Little Sherwood Lake—lake MI-6
Little Shickshinny Creek—stream PA-2
Littles Hill—summit MA-1
Littles Hill—summit NH-1
Little Shiloh Ch—church VA-3
Little Shiloh Primitive Baptist Ch—church AL-4
Little Shiney Mtn—summit PA-2
Little Shingle Canyon—valley NM-5
Little Shingle Run—stream VA-3
Little Ship Island—island ME-1
Little Shipp Mtn—summit AZ-5
Little Shipp Wash—stream AZ-5
Little Shiprock Wash—stream NM-5
Little Shirttail Mesa—summit AZ-5
Little Shiver Creek—stream MN-6
**Little Shoal**—pop pl AL-4
Little Shoal Cem—cemetery MO-7
*Little Shoal Creek* AL-4
Little Shoal Creek—stream (3) AL-4
Little Shoal Creek—stream AR-4
Little Shoal Creek—stream (4) GA-3
Little Shoal Creek—stream IA-7
Little Shoal Creek—stream (4) MO-7
Little Shoal Creek—stream TN-4
Little Shoal Creek Public Use Area—park GA-3
Little Shoally Creek—stream SC-3
Little Shoals—bar FL-3
Little Shoal Sch—school MO-7
*Little Shoals Creek* AL-4
Little Shocco Creek—stream NC-3
Little Shoe Creek—stream WY-8
Little Shoe Heel Creek—stream NC-3
Little Shoeinhorse Mtn—summit CA-9
Little Shoepack Lake—lake MN-6
Little Shongelo Creek—stream MS-4
Little Shonot Spring—spring AZ-5
Little Short Creek—stream KY-4
Little Short Creek—stream OH-6
*Little Short Mountain* AR-4
Little Short Mtn—summit TN-4
Little Shotgun Creek—stream AK-9
Little Shotgun Creek—stream CA-9
Little Shot Mine—mine AZ-5
Little Shot Mine—mine CA-9
Little Shoulderbone Creek—stream GA-3
Little Shuckstack—summit NC-3
Little Shupac Lake—lake MI-6
Little Shuteye Pass—gap CA-9
Little Shuteye Peak—summit CA-9
Little Si—summit WA-9
Little Siberia Mine—mine OR-9
Little Sicily Run—stream PA-2
Little Siegel Creek—stream ID-8
*Little Signal* CA-9
Little Signal—summit CA-9
Little Signal Hills—other CA-9
Little Signal Peak—summit CA-9
Little Silly Tank—reservoir TX-5
**Little Silver**—pop pl NJ-2
Little Silver Basin—basin CO-8
Little Silver Cove—cove AL-4
*Little Silver Creek* MI-6
Little Silver Creek—stream AL-4
Little Silver Creek—stream (2) CA-9
Little Silver Creek—stream (2) ID-8
Little Silver Creek—stream (2) IL-6
Little Silver Creek—stream (2) IA-7
Little Silver Creek—stream LA-4
Little Silver Creek—stream MI-6
Little Silver Creek—stream NJ-2
Little Silver Creek—stream NC-3
Little Silver Creek—stream OK-5
Little Silver Creek—stream (2) OR-9
Little Silver Creek—stream (2) TX-5
Little Silver Creek—stream (2) WI-6
Little Silver Creek Lake—lake OR-9
Little Silver Dawn Lake—lake NY-2
*Little Silver Lake* WI-6
Little Silver Lake—lake (2) MI-6
Little Silver Lake—lake MN-6
Little Silver Lake—lake WI-6
Little Silver Lake—reservoir NJ-2
Little Silverleaf Creek—stream ID-8
**Little Silver Point**—pop pl NJ-2
Little Silver River—stream MI-6
Little Silver Sch—school NJ-2
*Little Silver Springs Creek* LA-4
Little Silver Station—hist pl NJ-2
Little Simi Valley—valley CA-9
*Little Simonds Creek* IN-6
Little Simoneaston Creek—stream VA-3
Little Simon Pond—lake (2) NY-2
*Little Simons Creek* IN-6
*Little Simons Pond* NY-2
Little Simpson Creek—stream CO-8
Little Simpson Creek—stream WY-8
Little Simpson River—stream FL-3
Little Simsquish Brook—stream ME-1
Little Singepole Mtn—summit ME-1
Little Singletary Lake—lake NC-3
Little Sink Branch—stream TN-4
Little Sink Cave—cave (2) AL-4
Little Sinker Creek—stream OR-9
Little Sinkhole—reservoir KS-7
Little Sinking Ch—church KY-4
*Little Sinking Creek* TN-4
Little Sinking Creek—stream (3) KY-4
Little Sinking Creek—stream MO-7
Little Sinking Creek—stream (4) TN-4
**Little Sioux**—pop pl IA-7
Little Sioux Bend—bend IA-7
Little Sioux Bend—bend NE-7
Little Sioux Cem—cemetery IA-7
Little Sioux Ch—church IA-7
Little Sioux Country Club—other IA-7
Little Sioux County Park—park IA-7
*Little Sioux River* IA-7
Little Sioux River—stream MN-6
Little Sioux River—stream WI-6
Little Sioux State Wildlife Mngmt Area—park MN-6
Little Sioux Township—fmr MCD (2) IA-7
Little Sioux Valley Cem—cemetery IA-7
Little Sippewissett Marsh—swamp MA-1
*Little Sippowisset Lake* MA-1
Little Sipsey Creek—stream MS-4
Little Sipson Island—island MA-1
*Little Sipsons Island* MA-1
Little Sis Creek—stream TX-5
Little Siseebakwet Lake—lake MN-6
Little Siskiwit Island—island MI-6
Little Siskiwit Lake—lake WI-6
Little Siskiwit River—stream MI-6
Littles Island—area MO-7
Littles Island (historical)—island AL-4
Little Sissabagama Lake—lake WI-6
Little Sister—island WA-9
Little Sister Bay—swamp SC-3
Little Sister Cem—cemetery WI-6
Little Sister Ch—church MS-4
Little Sister Creek—stream IL-6
Little Sister Creek—stream NY-2
Little Sister Lake—lake MT-8
Little Sister Mine—mine CA-9
Little Sister Peak—summit ID-8
Little Sister Sch—school IL-6
Little Sisters of the Poor—other CO-8
Little Sisters of the Poor Convent—church NY-2
Little Sisters of the Poor Home for the Aged—hist pl MN-6
Little Sisters of the Poor Home for the Aged—hist pl TN-4
Little Sitkin Island—island AK-9
Little Sitkin Pass—channel AK-9
Little Siuslaw Creek—stream OR-9
Little Sixmile Creek—stream AR-4
Little Sixmile Creek—stream FL-3
Little Sixmile Creek—stream KY-4
Little Sixmile Creek—stream LA-4
Little Sixmile Creek—stream NY-2
Little Sixmile Creek—stream OR-9
Little Sixmile Creek—stream TN-4
Little Sixmile Creek—stream TX-5
*Little Sixmile Island* NH-1
Little Sixmile Island—island NH-1
Little Sixteen, Lake—lake MI-6
Little Sixteenmile Creek—stream WV-2
Little Skedee Creek—stream OK-5
Little Skeenah Creek—stream GA-3
Little Skeleton Creek—stream ID-8
Little Skeleton Lake—lake MN-6
Little Skid Creek—stream TX-5
Little Skidder Hill—summit WA-9
Little Skidmore Fork—stream VA-3
Little Skidmore Trail—trail VA-3
Little Skillet Creek—stream TX-5
Little Skin Bayou—stream OK-5
Little Skin Creek—stream OK-5
Little Skin Creek—stream WV-2
Little Skinner Creek—stream LA-4
Little Skipper Creek—stream SC-3
Little Skippers Preschool/ Kindergarten—school (2) FL-3
*Little Skirum Creek* AL-4
Little Skookum Creek—stream WA-9
Little Skookum Inlet—bay WA-9
Little Skookum Lake—lake OR-9
Little Skull Canyon—valley NM-5
Little Skull Creek—stream OR-9
Little Skull Lake—lake NE-7
Little Skull Lick Creek—stream MO-7
Little Skull Mtn—summit NV-8
Little Skuna Creek—stream MS-4
Little Skunk Creek—stream MT-8
Little Skunk Lake—lake MN-6
*Little Skutahzis Pond* ME-1
*Little Skutarzy Pond* ME-1
Little Slab Creek—stream AL-4
Littles Lake—lake LA-4
Littles Lake—lake MI-6
Littles Lake—lake NY-2
Littles Lake—reservoir AL-4
Little Slash Mtn—summit NY-2
Little Slate Creek—stream CA-9
Little Slate Creek—stream ID-8
Little Slate Creek—stream KY-4
Little Slate Creek—stream WA-9
Little Slate Creek—stream WV-2
Little Slate Creek Saddle—gap ID-8
Little Slate Lake—lake WA-9
Little Slate Run—stream (2) PA-2
Little Slate Run Trail—trail PA-2
Little Slaughter Creek—stream GA-3
Little Slaunch Branch—stream WV-2
Little Sleeping Child Creek—stream MT-8
Little Sletten Lake—lake MN-6
Little Sleuter Hollow—valley MO-7
Little Slick Creek—stream WY-8
Little Slickrock Creek—stream TN-4
Little Slide Canyon—valley CA-9
Little Slide Canyon—valley UT-8
Little Slide Lake—lake OR-9
Little Sliding Run—stream WV-2
Little Sloop Channel—channel VA-3
Little Slough—gut ND-7
Little Slough—stream (2) IN-6
Little Slough—stream KS-7
Little Slough—stream (2) TX-5
*Little Slough Creek* IN-6
Little Slough Creek—stream KS-7
Little Slough Ditch—canal AR-4
Little Slough Gundy Rapids—rapids WI-6
Little Sluice Box—area CA-9
Little Sluice Mountain Trail—trail VA-3
Little Sluice Mtn—summit VA-3
Little Sluice Mtn—summit WV-2
Little Sly Brook—stream ME-1
Little Smackout Creek—stream WA-9
Little Smackover Creek—stream AR-4
Little Smalley Lake—reservoir IN-6
Little Smelt Pond—lake MA-1
Littles Mill—locale NC-3
Littles Mill Creek—stream AL-4
Littles Mill (historical)—locale AL-4
Little Smith Branch—stream KY-4
Little Smith Brook—stream (3) ME-1
Little Smith Creek—stream (2) ID-8
Little Smith Creek—stream MT-8
Little Smith Creek—stream WV-2
Little Smith Island—island AK-9
Little Smith Lake—lake MN-6
*Little Smith Mountain* CA-9
Little Smith Pond—lake ME-1
Little Smith Valley—valley NV-8
Little Smokehouse Key—island FL-3
Little Smokey—summit OR-9
*Little Smokey Valley* NV-8
Little Smoky Campground—locale ID-8
Little Smoky Creek—stream (2) CA-9
Little Smoky Creek—stream ID-8
Little Smoky Creek—stream NV-8
Little Smoky Creek—stream WI-6
Little Smoky Lake—lake MI-6
Little Smoky Valley—valley NV-8
Littles Mtn—summit ME-1
Little Snag—island FL-3
Little Snag Creek—stream KY-4
Little Snaggy Mtn—summit MD-2
Little Snake Creek—stream FL-3
Little Snake Creek—stream GA-3
Little Snake Creek—stream NY-2
Little Snake Creek—stream PA-2
Little Snake Creek—stream TN-4
Little Snake Creek—stream (2) VA-3
Little Snake Hill—summit NJ-2
Little Snake Pond—lake MA-1
*Little Snake River* CO-8
Little Snake River—stream CO-8
Little Snake River—stream (2) WY-8
Little Snapper Cut—channel FL-3
Little Snell Creek—stream KS-7
Little Sni-A-Bar Creek—stream MO-7
Little Snider Canyon—valley UT-8
Little Snipe Creek—stream IA-7
Little Snook Kill—stream NY-2
Little Snooks Lake—lake SC-3
Little Snowball Mtn—summit NC-3
Little Snowbird Creek—stream NC-3
Little Snow Creek—stream MS-4
Little Snow Creek—stream ID-8
Little Snow Lake—lake MN-6
Little Snow Lake—lake WA-9
Little Snow Lake—reservoir MS-4
*Little Snowmass Lake* CO-8
Little Snowshoe Creek—stream OR-9
Little Snowy Mtns—range MT-8
Little Snowy Top—summit ID-8
*Little Snowy Top Mountain* ID-8
Little Sny—gut IL-6
Little Soak Creek—stream TN-4
Little Soap Creek—stream IA-7
Little Soap Lake—lake (2) WA-9
Little Soap Park—flat CO-8
Little Soapstone Creek—stream LA-4
Little Socapatoy Creek—stream AL-4
Little Soda Canyon—valley CO-8
Little Soda Creek—stream (2) CA-9
Little Soda Lake—lake NV-8
Little Soda Lake—lake WY-8
Little Soda Springs Forest Camp—locale WA-9
Little Soddy Creek—stream TN-4
Little Sodus Bay—bay NY-2
Little Sodus Creek—stream NY-2
Little Soft Maple Creek—stream WI-6
Little Sohare Creek—stream WY-8
Little Soldier Creek—stream CA-9
Little Soldier Creek—stream ID-8
Little Soldier Creek—stream IA-7
Little Soldier Creek—stream KS-7
Little Soldier Creek—stream OK-5
Little Soldier Creek—stream SD-7
Little Soldier Mtn—summit ID-8
Little Soldier Pond—lake ME-1
Little Solier, Lake—lake LA-4
Little Solomon (historical)—locale AL-4
Little Solomon Lake—swamp SC-3
Little Sombrero Peak—summit AZ-5
Little Somo Creek—stream WI-6
Little Somo River—stream WI-6
Little Soos Creek—stream WA-9
Little Soto Tank—reservoir AZ-5
Little Sound—lake NJ-2
Little Sound Creek—stream MD-2
Little Sound Meadow—swamp NJ-2
Little Soup Lake Waterhole—reservoir OR-9
Little Sourdough Canyon—valley OR-9
Little Sourdough Creek—stream WY-8
Little Sous Creek—stream TX-5
Little South Branch Pere Marquette River—stream MI-6
Little South Branch Pike River—stream WI-6
*Little South Cache la Poudre River* CO-8
*Little Southeast Branch* ME-1
Little South Fork—stream AK-9
Little South Fork—stream (3) KY-4
Little South Fork—stream TN-4
Little South Fork Boise Creek—stream CA-9
Little South Fork Bottle Creek—stream NV-8
*Little South Fork Creek* KY-4
Little South Fork Dog Creek—stream CA-9
Little South Fork Elk River—stream CA-9
Little South Fork Hunter Creek—stream OR-9
Little South Fork Indian Creek—stream CA-9
Little South Fork Kilchis River—stream OR-9
Little South Fork Lake—lake CA-9
Little South Fork Lewis and Clark River—stream OR-9
Little South Fork Manti Canyon—valley UT-8
Little South Fork Provo River—stream UT-8
Little South Fork Salmon River—stream CA-9
Little South Fork Smith River—stream OR-9
Little South Mouse Creek—stream TN-4
Little South Pass—gut FL-3
Little South Pembina River—stream ND-7
*Little South Platte River* CO-8
Little South Pond—lake MA-1
Little South Tank—reservoir AZ-5
Little South Well—well TX-5
Little Southwest Branch Saint John River—stream ME-1
Little South West Rock—rock MA-1
Little South Windmill—locale TX-5
*Little Souwilpa Creek* AL-4
Little Souwilpa Creek—stream AL-4
Little Sowats Canyon—valley AZ-5
Little Sowats Spring—spring AZ-5
Little Spadra Creek—stream AR-4
Little Spangle Lake—lake ID-8
Little Spanish Creek—stream GA-3
Little Spanish Key—island FL-3
Little Spanish Key Mangrove—island FL-3
Little Spanish Lake—lake CA-9
Little Sparr Lake—lake MT-8
Littles Peak—summit WY-8
Little Spearfish Creek—stream SD-7
Little Spearfish Guard Station—locale SD-7
Little Spearfish Lake—lake WA-9
Little Spearfish Spring—spring SD-7
Little Specimen Gulch—valley AK-9
Little Spec Lake—lake MI-6
Little Spectacle Pond—lake MA-1
Little Spencer Creek—stream VA-3
Little Spencer Flat—flat UT-8
Little Spencer Mtn—summit ME-1
Little Spencer Pond—lake ME-1
Little Spencer Stream—stream ME-1
Little Spider Lake—lake (2) WI-6
Little Spirit Creek—stream GA-3
*Little Spirit Lake* MN-6
Little Spirit Lake—lake IA-7
Little Spirit Lake—lake MN-6
Little Spirit Lake State Game Mgt Area—park IA-7
Little Spivey Creek—stream NC-3
Little Spivey Creek—stream TN-4
Little Splice Creek—stream MO-7
Little Split Hand Lake—lake MN-6
Little Splunge Creek—stream MS-4
Littles Point—point MA-1
Little Spokane River—stream WA-9
Little Spoon Creek—stream VA-3
Little Spooner Lake—lake WI-6
Little Spoon Island—island ME-1
Little Spreader Tank—reservoir AZ-5
*Little Spring* AL-4
Little Spring—locale AZ-5
Little Spring—spring (11) AZ-5
Little Spring—spring (3) CA-9
Little Spring—spring FL-3
Little Spring—spring ID-8
Little Spring—spring NV-8
Little Spring—spring NC-3
Little Spring—spring (2) OR-9
Little Spring—spring (2) TN-4
Little Spring—spring WY-8
Little Spring Branch—stream TX-5
Little Spring Branch—stream WV-2
Little Spring Brook—stream (2) ME-1
Little Spring Brook—stream NY-2
Little Spring Brook Mtn—summit ME-1
Little Spring Canyon—valley AZ-5
Little Spring Canyon—valley CA-9
Little Spring Canyon—valley (2) UT-8
*Little Spring Creek* OK-5
Little Spring Creek—stream AL-4
Little Spring Creek—stream (3) CO-8
Little Spring Creek—stream FL-3
Little Spring Creek—stream (2) ID-8
Little Spring Creek—stream IL-6
Little Spring Creek—stream KY-4
Little Spring Creek—stream LA-4
Little Spring Creek—stream MS-4
Little Spring Creek—stream (2) MO-7
Little Spring Creek—stream (3) MT-8
Little Spring Creek—stream NE-7
Little Spring Creek—stream OK-5
Little Spring Creek—stream OR-9
Little Spring Creek—stream (3) TN-4
Little Spring Creek—stream WV-2
Little Spring Creek—stream WI-6
Little Spring Creek—stream WY-8
Little Spring Creek Rsvr—reservoir OR-9
Little Spring Creek Sch (historical)—school TN-4
Little Spring Fork—stream WV-2
Little Spring Gulch—valley CA-9
Little Spring Gulch—valley CO-8
Little Spring Gulch—valley MT-8
Little Spring Hill Baptist Ch—church MS-4
Little Spring Hollow—valley VA-3
Little Spring Lake—lake FL-3
Little Spring Lake—lake MI-6
Little Spring Lake—lake (3) MN-6
Little Spring Lake—lake (2) WI-6
Little Spring Landing—locale TN-4
Little Spring Pasture Windmill—locale NM-5
*Little Spring Pond* FL-3
*Little Spring River* MO-7
Little Springs—locale MS-4
Little Springs—spring NV-8
Little Springs Canyon—valley AZ-5
Little Springs Canyon—valley (2) CA-9
Little Springs Ch—church FL-3
Little Springs Ch—church IL-6
Little Springs Post Office (historical)—building MS-4
Little Springs Tank—reservoir AZ-5
Little Spring Tank—reservoir AZ-5
Little Spring Trick Tank—reservoir AZ-5
Little Sprite Creek—stream NY-2
Little Sproul Creek—stream CA-9
Little Sprouts Creek—stream VA-3
*Little Sprowl Creek* CA-9
Little Spruce Creek—stream AK-9
Little Spruce Creek—stream KY-4
*Little Sprucehead Island* ME-1
Little Spruce Head Island—island ME-1
Little Spruce Island—island ME-1
*Little Spruce Island Ledge* ME-1
Little Spruce Knob—summit WV-2
Little Spruce Lake—lake MI-6
Little Spruce Lake—lake MN-6
*Little Spruce Ledge* ME-1
Little Spruce Mtn—summit ME-1
Little Spruce Mtn—summit VT-1
*Little Spruce Mtn Brook* ME-1
Little Spruce Pine Branch—stream VA-3
Little Spruce Ridge—ridge NC-3
Little Spruce Ridge—ridge WV-2
Little Spruce Run—stream OH-6
Little Spruce Run—stream WV-2
Little Spur—ridge KY-4
Little Spur Mtn—summit NY-2
Little Spur Truck Trail—trail WA-9
Little Spy Mtn—summit VA-3
*Little Spy Pond* MA-1
Little Squam Lake—lake NH-1
Little Square Bay—bay NY-2
Little Square Pond—lake NY-2
Little Squaretop Butte—summit ND-7
Littles Quarters—locale NC-3
Little Squaw Back—ridge OR-9
Little Squaw Brook—stream ME-1
Little Squaw Brook—stream NY-2
*Little Squaw Creek* SD-7
Little Squaw Creek—stream AK-9
Little Squaw Creek—stream AZ-5
Little Squaw Creek—stream (2) CO-8
Little Squaw Creek—stream (4) ID-8
Little Squaw Creek—stream MI-6
Little Squaw Creek—stream MT-8
Little Squaw Creek—stream NV-8
Little Squaw Creek—stream OH-6
Little Squaw Creek—stream (2) OR-9
Little Squaw Creek—stream SD-7
Little Squaw Creek Spring—spring ID-8
Little Squaw Flat—swamp OR-9
Little Squaw Flat Rsvr—reservoir OR-9
Little Squaw-Humper Creek—stream SD-7
Little Squaw-Humper Table—summit SD-7
Little Squaw Lake—lake AK-9
Little Squaw Lake—lake MI-6
Little Squaw Lake—lake WI-6
Little Squaw Meadow—flat OR-9
Little Squaw Mtn—summit AZ-5
Little Squaw Mtn—summit ME-1
Little Squaw Peak—summit AK-9
Little Squaw Pond—lake ME-1
Little Squaw Spring—spring (2) OR-9
Little Squaw (Township of)—unorg ME-1
Little Squaw Valley—basin CA-9
Little Squaw Valley—flat NV-8
Littles Run—stream PA-2
Little-Stabler House—hist pl AL-4
Little Stacy Park—park TX-5
Little Stag Island—island MO-7
Little Stakey Mtn—summit SC-3
Little Stanchfield Lake—lake MN-6
Little Stanley Butte—summit AZ-5
Little Star Ch—church (2) LA-4
Little Star Ch—church (3) SC-3
Little Star Ch—church TN-4
Little Star Ch—church TX-5
Little Star Ch—church VA-3
Little Star Ch (historical)—church AL-4
Little Star Creek—stream MI-6
*Little Star Lake* MI-6
*Little Star Lake* WI-6
Little Star Lake—lake MI-6
Little Star Lake—lake MN-6
Little Star Lake—lake (4) WI-6
Little Star Mtn—summit AZ-5
Little Star Mtn—summit TX-5
Little Star Run—stream WV-2
Little Starvation Cove—bay FL-3
Little Starve Island—island TN-4
Little Star Well—well TX-5
Little Star Windmill—locale TX-5
*Little State Line Lake* MI-6
Little Station Canyon—valley ID-8
Little Station Creek—stream MS-4
Little Stave Hollow—valley KY-4
Little Steamboat Mtn—summit CA-9
Little Steamboat Point—cape OR-9
*Little Steel Bayou* MS-4
Little Steele Bayou—stream MS-4
Little Steele Lake—lake WI-6
Little Steeltrap Creek—stream NC-3
Little Steel Windmill—locale TX-5
Little Steen Marsh—swamp NE-7
Little Steer Creek—stream OR-9
*Little Steere Creek* OR-9
Little Steer Run—stream WV-2
Little Stemilt Creek—stream WA-9
Little Stevens—summit NY-2
*Little Stevens Creek* SC-3
Little Stevens Creek—stream SC-3
Little Stevens Creek Ch—church SC-3
Little Stevens Draw—valley NM-5
Little Stevens Lake—lake MI-6
*Little Steves Ranch* AZ-5
Little Stewart Canyon—valley OR-9
Little Stewart Creek—stream VA-3
*Little Stewart River* MN-6
Little Stewart River—stream MN-6
Little Stickney Creek—stream MT-8
Little Stillwater Creek—stream OH-6
Little Stillwater Creek—stream (2) OK-5
Little Stillwell Creek—stream WV-2
Little Stink Creek—stream TX-5
Little Stinkingwater Basin—basin OR-9
*Little Stinking Water Creek* OR-9
Little Stinkingwater Creek—stream OR-9
Little Stinnett Creek—stream KY-4
Little Stissing Mtn—summit NY-2
Little Stitchihatchie Branch—stream GA-3
Little Stock Creek—stream VA-3
Little Stocker Pond—lake NH-1
Little Stocking Head Creek—stream GA-3
Little Stoneberger Creek—stream NV-8

Little Stonecoal Run—stream WV-2
*Little Stone Creek* ND-7
Little Stone Gap—gap VA-3
Little Stone House Creek—stream NC-3
Little Stone Lake—lake MN-6
Little Stone Lake—lake (2) WI-6
Little Stone Mountain Ch—church NC-3
Little Stone Mountain Creek—stream GA-3
Little Stone Mtn—summit NC-3
Little Stone Mtn—summit TN-4
Little Stone Mtn—summit (2) VA-3
Little Stoner Creek—stream KY-4
*Little Stone Ridge* VA-3
Little Stonewall Creek—stream CA-9
Little Stonewall Pass—gap CA-9
Little Stonewall Peak—summit CA-9
Little Stoney Creek—stream IN-6
Little Stono Mtn—summit MO-7
Little Stony Brook—stream VT-1
*Little Stony Creek* MI-6
*Little Stony Creek* ND-7
Little Stony Creek—stream AK-9
Little Stony Creek—stream (2) CA-9
Little Stony Creek—stream MI-6
Little Stony Creek—stream MN-6
Little Stony Creek—stream MT-8
Little Stony Creek—stream NY-2
Little Stony Creek—stream (2) TN-4
Little Stony Creek—stream (5) VA-3
Little Stony Creek—stream (2) WV-2
Little Stony Creek Mine—mine TN-4
Little Stony Gap—gap TN-4
Little Stony Island—island PA-2
Little Stony Knob—summit MO-7
Little Stony Lake—lake MI-6
Little Stony Lake—lake MN-6
Little Stony Man—summit VA-3
Little Stony Point—cape NY-2
Little Stony Run—stream WV-2
Little Stony Run Branch—stream SC-3
Little Stony Sch (abandoned)—school CA-9
*Little Stoopingbush Island* CT-1
Little Stop Hollow—valley WV-2
Little Storm Lake—lake IA-7
Little Storm Lake—lake OR-9
Little Storm Lake Game Mngmt Area—park IA-7
Little Storms Creek—stream OH-6
**Littlestown**—pop pl PA-2
Littlestown Borough—civil PA-2
Little Straddle Branch—stream VA-3
Little Straightstone Creek—stream VA-3
*Little Stranger* KS-7
Little Stranger Ch—church KS-7
Little Stranger Creek—stream (2) KS-7
Little Stratton Creek—stream OR-9
Little Strawberry Creek—stream CA-9
Little Strawberry Creek—stream CO-8
Little Strawberry Island—island WI-6
Little Strawberry Lake—lake MI-6
Little Strawberry Lake—lake OR-9
Little Strawberry River—stream AR-4
Little Strawberry Valley—basin UT-8
Little Stray Horse Gulch—valley CO-8
**Little Sturgeon**—pop pl WI-6
Little Sturgeon Bay—bay WI-6
Little Sturgeon Creek—stream GA-3
Little Sturgeon Creek—stream KY-4
Little Sturgeon Lake—lake MN-6
Little Sturgeon River—stream MI-6
Little Stylus Lake—lake MI-6
**Little Suamico**—pop pl WI-6
Little Suamico River—stream WI-6
**Little Suamico (Town of)**—pop pl WI-6
*Little Succor Creek* ID-8
*Little Succor Creek* OR-9
Little Succor Creek—stream ID-8
Little Sucia Island—island WA-9
Little Sucker Brook—stream (2) NY-2
*Little Sucker Creek* MI-6
Little Sucker Creek—stream MI-6
Little Sucker Lake—lake MI-6
Little Sucker Lake—lake MN-6
Little Sucker River—stream MN-6
Little Sucker Run—stream CA-9
Little Suction Creek—stream MT-8
Little Sue Branch—stream KY-4
*Little Suee Creek* TN-4
Little Sugar Bush Lake—lake MN-6
Little Sugarbush Lake—lake WI-6
Little Sugar Camp Hollow—valley MO-7
*Little Sugar Creek* IL-6
*Little Sugar Creek* IN-6
Little Sugar Creek—gut LA-4
Little Sugar Creek—stream (2) AR-4
Little Sugar Creek—stream (4) GA-3
Little Sugar Creek—stream (5) IN-6
Little Sugar Creek—stream IA-7
Little Sugar Creek—stream KS-7
Little Sugar Creek—stream (2) KY-4
Little Sugar Creek—stream (4) MO-7
Little Sugar Creek—stream NC-3
Little Sugar Creek—stream (2) OH-6
Little Sugar Creek—stream (3) PA-2
Little Sugar Creek—stream SC-3
Little Sugar Creek—stream (2) TN-4
Little Sugar Creek—stream WV-2
Little Sugar Creek Cem—cemetery IN-6
Little Sugar Creek Ch—church IN-6
Little Sugar Creek Dam—dam PA-2
*Little Sugar Lake* MN-6
Little Sugar Loaf—bend NC-3
**Little Sugarloaf**—pop pl ID-8
Little Sugarloaf—summit ID-8
Little Sugarloaf—summit NH-1
Little Sugarloaf Creek—stream AR-4
Little Sugarloaf Creek—stream CA-9
Little Sugarloaf Gulch—valley CO-8
Little Sugarloaf Hill—summit RI-1
Little Sugarloaf Lake—lake MI-6
*Little Sugar Loaf Mtn* PA-2
Little Sugarloaf Mtn—summit CO-8
Little Sugarloaf Mtn—summit PA-2
Little Sugarloaf Peak—summit CA-9
Little Sugarloaf Peak—summit CO-8
Little Sugarloaf Peak—summit OR-9
Little Sugar Pine Mtn—summit CA-9
Little Sugar River—stream NH-1
Little Sugar River—stream WI-6
Little Sugar Run—stream PA-2
Little Sugar Run—stream VA-3
*Little Sugar Run Storage Dam* PA-2
Little Sugar Valley—valley PA-2
Little Sulfer Springs—spring AL-4
Little Sullivan Creek—stream CA-9
Little Sullivan Lake—lake WA-9
Little Sullivan Ridge—ridge CA-9
Little Sullivan Tank—reservoir AZ-5
Little Sulphur Branch—stream KY-4
Little Sulphur Canyon—valley CA-9
Little Sulphur Canyon—valley UT-8
Little Sulphur Creek—stream AR-4
Little Sulphur Creek—stream CA-9
Little Sulphur Creek—stream ID-8
Little Sulphur Creek—stream (2) IN-6
Little Sulphur Creek—stream KY-4
Little Sulphur Creek—stream OH-6
Little Sulphur Creek—stream TN-4
Little Sulphur Creek—stream TX-5
Little Sulphur Creek—stream WV-2
Little Sulphur Creek—stream WY-8
Little Sulphur Spring—spring (2) CA-9
Little Sulphur Windmill—locale TX-5
Little Summer Island—island MI-6
Little Summer Island Shoal—bar MI-6
Little Summit—gap NV-8
Little Summit—locale PA-2
**Little Summit**—pop pl (2) PA-2
Little Summit—summit NV-8
Little Summit—summit WA-9
Little Summit Campground—park OR-9
Little Summit Creek—stream OR-9
Little Summit (historical)—summit AZ-5
Little Summit Lake—lake CA-9
Little Summit Lake—lake ID-8
Little Summit Lake—lake MI-6
Little Summit Lake—lake OR-9
Little Summit Lake—lake WY-8
Little Summit Prairie—flat OR-9
Little Sumner Ditch—canal IN-6
Little Sunapee Lake—lake NH-1
Little Sunbeams Child Care Center—school FL-3
Little Suncook River—stream NH-1
*Little Sun Creek* TN-4
Little Sunday Creek—stream MT-8
Little Sunday Creek—stream (2) TX-5
Little Sundog Lake—lake MI-6
Little Sunfish Creek—stream OH-6
**Little Sunflower**—pop pl MS-4
*Little Sunflower Baptist Church* AL-4
*Little Sunflower Baptist Church Number Three* AL-4
Little Sunflower Ch—church AL-4
Little Sunflower Landing—locale MS-4
*Little Sunflower Missionary Baptist Ch* AL-4
Little Sunflower River—stream (2) MS-4
Little Sunlight Campground—locale WY-8
Little Sunlight Creek—stream WY-8
Little Sunrise Lake—lake MI-6
Little Sunshine Creek—stream OR-9
Little Superior Lake—lake UT-8
Little Supreme Bluff—cliff AK-9
Little Sur River—stream CA-9
Little Surveyor Run—stream PA-2
Little Survival Creek—stream AK-9
Little Susie Island—island MN-6
Little Susitna River—stream AK-9
Little Susitna Roadhouse—locale AK-9
Little Susybole Creek—stream SC-3
Little Sutton Mtn—summit MT-8
Little Suwanee Creek—stream GA-3
Little Suwannee Creek—stream (2) GA-3
*Little Swamp* NC-3
Little Swamp—stream (4) NC-3
Little Swamp—stream SC-3
Little Swamp—stream VA-3
Little Swamp—swamp NC-3
Little Swamp—swamp SC-3
*Little Swamp Branch* NC-3
Little Swamp Branch—stream NC-3
Little Swamp Ch—church SC-3
Little Swamp Creek—stream GA-3
Little Swamp Creek—stream MN-6
Little Swamp Creek—stream MT-8
Little Swamp Fork—stream WV-2
Little Swamp Run—stream PA-2
Little Swamp Sch—school SC-3
Little Swan—island ME-1
Little Swan—locale MN-6
Little Swan Cem—cemetery MN-6
Little Swan Ch—church TN-4
*Little Swan Creek* IN-6
Little Swan Creek—stream IL-6
Little Swan Creek—stream (3) MI-6
Little Swan Creek—stream MN-6
Little Swan Creek—stream OH-6
Little Swan Creek—stream (2) TN-4
Little Swan Island—island NC-3
*Little Swan Islands* NC-3
Little Swan Lake—lake IL-6
Little Swan Lake—lake (2) MN-6
Little Swan Lake—reservoir IL-6
Little Swan Lake State Wildlife Mngmt Area—park MN-6
Little Swannee Creek—stream FL-3
Little Swan Pond Slough—swamp KY-4
*Little Swan River* MN-6
Little Swartswood Lake—reservoir NJ-2
Little Swartswood Lake Dam—dam NJ-2
*Little Swash* NC-3
Little Swash Keys—island FL-3
Little Swash Opening—bay NC-3
*Little Swatara Creek* PA-2
Little Swatara Creek—stream PA-2
Little Swede Creek—stream AK-9
Little Swede Creek—stream CA-9
Little Swede Creek—stream KS-7
Little Swede Lake—lake AK-9
Little Sweden—flat WA-9
Little Swede Valley—basin NE-7
**Little Sweeden**—pop pl OR-9
Little Sweedlin Hill—summit WV-2
Little Sweetwater Cem—cemetery MS-4
Little Sweetwater Ch—church MS-4
Little Sweetwater Creek—stream FL-3
Little Sweetwater Creek—stream GA-3
Little Sweetwater Creek—stream MS-4
*Little Sweetwater Missionary Baptist Church* MS-4
Little Sweetwater River—stream WY-8
Little Sweetwater Trail—trail WY-8
Little Swens Canyon—valley UT-8
Little Swift Creek—channel NY-2
Little Swift Creek—stream AK-9
Little Swift Creek—stream (2) GA-3
Little Swift Creek—stream NC-3
Little Swift Creek—stream SC-3
Little Swift Lake—lake MN-6
Little Swift River Pond—lake ME-1
Little Switzerland—hist pl AR-4
**Little Switzerland**—pop pl (2) NC-3
**Little Switzerland**—pop pl OR-9
Little Switzerland Tunnel—tunnel NC-3
Little Sycamore Canyon—valley (4) CA-9
Little Sycamore Ch—church FL-3
Little Sycamore Ch—church TN-4
Little Sycamore Creek—stream AZ-5
Little Sycamore Creek—stream NM-5
Little Sycamore Creek—stream TN-4
Little Sycamore Creek—stream (3) VA-3
Little Sycamore Creek—stream WV-2
*Little Sycamore Missionary Baptist Church* TN-4
Little Sycamore Spring—spring AZ-5
Little Sycamore Wash—stream AZ-5
Little Syers Lake—lake MI-6
Little Sylco Branch—stream TN-4
Little Tabernacle—church VA-3
Little Tabernacle Ch—church IL-6
Little Tabernacle Ch—church WI-6
Little Table—summit NV-8
Little Table—summit UT-8
Little Tableland—flat CA-9
Little Table Mountain Spring—spring NV-8
Little Table Mtn—summit AZ-5
Little Table Mtn—summit CA-9
Little Table Mtn—summit ID-8
Little Table Mtn—summit MT-8
Little Table Mtn—summit NV-8
Little Table Mtn—summit OR-9
Little Table Mtn—summit (2) WY-8
Little Table Rock—summit CA-9
Little Table Rock Creek—stream SC-3
Little Table Rock Mtn—summit NC-3
Little Table Rock Mtn—summit SC-3
Little Table Top—summit AZ-5
*Little Table Top Mountains* AZ-5
Little Tabletop Mtn—summit NV-8
Little Tabo Creek—stream MO-7
Little Tackett Creek—stream TN-4
Little Tacoma Creek—stream WA-9
Little Tacony Creek (historical)—stream PA-2
Little Taft Creek—stream OR-9
Little Tahoma Peak—summit WA-9
Little Tahquitz Valley—valley CA-9
*Little Tahunga Canyon* CA-9
Little Tail Point—cape WI-6
Little Tail Swamp—swamp WI-6
Little Talbot Island—island FL-3
Little Talbot Island State Park—park FL-3
Little Tallahala Creek—stream MS-4
Little Tallahalla Creek—stream MS-4
*Little Tallahatchee Creek* AL-4
Little Tallahatchie Canal—canal MS-4
*Little Tallahatchie River* MS-4
Little Tallahatchie River—stream MS-4
Little Tallapoosa Lake—reservoir GA-3
Little Tallapoosa River—stream AL-4
Little Tallapoosa River—stream GA-3
*Little Tallasahatchee Creek* AL-4
Little Tallaseehatchee Creek—stream AL-4
Little Tallasseehatchee Creek—stream AL-4
Little Tallawampa Creek—stream AL-4
Little Talucah Cave—cave AL-4
Little Tamarack Creek—stream (3) WI-6
Little Tamarack Flowage—lake WI-6
Little Tamarack Lake—lake MI-6
Little Tamarack Lake—lake (2) MN-6
Little Tamarack Mtn—summit OR-9
Little Tamarack River—stream MN-6
Little Tamarac River—stream MN-6
Little Tanaga Island—island AK-9
Little Tanaga Strait—channel AK-9
Little Tanana Slough—stream AK-9
Little Tangipahoa River—stream MS-4
Little Tank—lake TX-5
Little Tank—reservoir (8) AZ-5
Little Tank—reservoir (7) NM-5
Little Tank—reservoir (4) TX-5
Little Tank Creek—stream OR-9
Little Tank Ridge—ridge AL-4
Little Tanks—reservoir AZ-5
Little Tank Wells—well TX-5
Little Tar Canyon—valley CA-9
Little Tarklin Branch—stream NC-3
*Little Tarkio Creek* IA-7
*Little Tarkio Creek* MO-7
Little Tarkio Creek—stream IA-7
Little Tarkio Creek—stream MO-7
*Little Tarkio Ditch* MO-7
Little Tar Springs—locale KY-4
*Little Tastine Swamp* VA-3
*Little Tater Valley* TN-4
Little Taum Sauk Creek—stream MO-7
Little Tavern Creek—stream (5) MO-7
Little Tavern Island—island CT-1
Little Tawcaw Creek—stream SC-3
Little Taylor Brook—stream ME-1
Little Taylor Creek—stream CO-8
Little Taylor Creek—stream GA-3
Little Taylor Lake—lake AR-4
Little Taylor Mountains—ridge AK-9
Little Tea Pond—lake ME-1
Little Teapot Creek—stream WY-8
Little Teasel Creek—stream OR-9
Little Tebo Creek—stream (2) MO-7
Little Tebo Creek State Wildlife Mngmt Area—park MO-7
Little Tecate Peak—summit CA-9
Little Teche, Bayou—stream LA-4
Little Techillas—reservoir NM-5
*Little Tedyuskung Lake* PA-2
Little Teedyuskung Lake—lake PA-2
Little Tehipite Valley—basin CA-9
Little Tehuacana Creek—stream (2) TX-5
Little Telephone Creek—stream NV-8
Little Telico Creek—stream AR-4
Little Telogia Creek—stream FL-3
Little Temecula—civil CA-9
Little Temple Oil and Gas Field—oilfield LA-4
Little Tenant Spring—spring CA-9
Little Tenasa Bayou—stream LA-4
*Little Tenmile Creek* KY-4
*Little Tenmile Creek* TX-5
Little Tenmile Creek—stream GA-3
Little Tenmile Creek—stream ID-8
Little Ten Mile Creek—stream KY-4
Little Tenmile Creek—stream OK-5
Little Tenmile Creek—stream PA-2
Little Tenmile Creek—stream WV-2
Little Tenmile Fork—stream WV-2
Little Tenmile Swamp—stream NC-3
Little Tennessee Presbyterian Ch (historical)—church TN-4
Little Tennessee River—stream GA-3
Little Tennessee River—stream NC-3
Little Tennessee River—stream TN-4
Little Tennessee Sch—school TN-4
Little Tensas Bayou—gut LA-4
Little Tensas Bayou—stream LA-4
Little Tensas River—stream LA-4
Little Teoc Creek—stream MS-4
Little Tepee Creek—stream ID-8
Little Tepee Creek—stream MT-8
Little Tepee Creek—stream SD-7
Little Tepee Creek—stream WY-8
Little Tepee Creek—valley MT-8
Little Tepee Creek Trail—trail MT-8
Little Tepee Pole Canyon—valley TX-5
Little Terrapin Branch—stream TN-4
Little Terrapin Creek—stream AL-4
Little Terrapin Creek—stream GA-3
Little Terrapin Mtn—summit NC-3
Little Terrapin Run—stream KY-4
Little Terre Rouge Creek—stream AR-4
Little Terrible Creek—stream MS-4
Little Terrible Creek—stream VA-3
*Little Terror Creek* CO-8
Little Terror Gulch—valley ID-8
*Little Tesnatee Creek* GA-3
Little Tesuque Camp—locale NM-5
Little Tesuque Creek—stream NM-5
Little Teton Creek—stream CA-9
Little Tetons—summit WY-8
*Little Texas* MS-4
*Little Texas* TN-4
Little Texas—locale AL-4
Little Texas—locale AR-4
Little Texas—locale TN-4
Little Texas—locale VA-3
**Little Texas**—pop pl KY-4
**Little Texas**—pop pl LA-4
**Little Texas**—pop pl MS-4
**Little Texas**—pop pl SC-3
Little Texas Bayou—stream LA-4
Little Texas Cem—cemetery AL-4
Little Texas Ch—church AL-4
Little Texas Ch—church AR-4
Little Texas Ch—church MS-4
Little Texas Hollow—valley OH-6
Little Texas Sch—school MS-4
Little Texas-Society Hill (CCD)—cens area AL-4
Little Texas-Society Hill Division—civil AL-4
Little Texas (Township of)—fmr MCD (2) AR-4
Little Texas Valley—valley GA-3
Little Thatcher Creek—stream CA-9
*Little Thatcher Island* MA-1
Little Thatch Island—island (2) MA-1
Little Theatre—hist pl NY-2
Little Therriault Lake—lake MT-8
Little Thicketty Creek—stream SC-3
Little Third Creek—stream MO-7
Little Third Fork—stream MO-7
*Little Third Fork Platte River* MO-7
Little Thirteenth Lake Mtn—summit NY-2
Little Thirtynine Creek—stream MN-6
Little Thomas Creek—stream ID-8
Little Thomas Mtn—summit CA-9
Little Thomas Wash—stream AZ-5
Little Thompson Branch—stream MS-4
Little Thompson Creek—stream ID-8
Little Thompson Creek—stream MS-4
Little Thompson Creek—stream MT-8
Little Thompson Ditch—canal CO-8
Little Thompson Draw—valley SD-7
Little Thompson Grange—locale CO-8
Little Thompson Gulch—valley ID-8
Little Thompson Peak—summit MT-8
Little Thompson River—stream CO-8
Little Thompson River—stream MT-8
*Little Thompsons Creek* MS-4
Little Thoms Creek—gut VA-3
*Little Thornapple Drain* MI-6
Little Thornapple River—stream (2) MI-6
Little Thornapple River—stream (2) WI-6
Little Thorn Creek—stream ID-8
Little Thorn Creek—stream WA-9
Little Thorne Mountains—summit CA-9
Little Thorne Spring—spring AZ-5
Little Thorn Hollow—valley OR-9
Little Thorny Creek—stream WV-2
Little Thorny Hollow—valley MO-7
Little Thorny Mtn—summit MO-7
Little Thorofare—channel ME-1
Little Thorofare—channel MD-2
Little Thorofare—channel NJ-2
Little Thorofare—channel VA-3
Little Thorofare—stream MD-2
Little Thorofare Run—stream WV-2
Little Thoroughfare—canal PA-2
Little Thoroughfare Bay (Carolina Bay)—swamp NC-3
Little Thorpe Creek—stream NV-8
Little Thrasher Gut—gut VA-3
Little Three Creek Lake—lake OR-9
Little Three Creek Lake Dam—dam OR-9
Little Threemile Canyon—valley ID-8
Little Threemile Creek—stream MT-8
Little Thumb Creek—stream WY-8
Little Thunder Creek—stream WY-8
Little Thunder Flowage—reservoir WI-6
*Little Thunderhole* TN-4
Little Thunder Lake—lake MN-6
*Little Thunder Ridge* WY-8
Little Thunder Rsvr—reservoir WY-8
*Little Tick Creek* AR-4
Little Tide Creek—stream FL-3
Little Tide Key—island FL-3
*Little Tidwell Reservoir* UT-8
*Little Tidwell Valley* UT-8
Little Tiffany Lake—lake WA-9
Little Tiger Bay—swamp FL-3
Little Tiger Bayou—stream LA-4
Little Tiger Creek—stream CA-9
Little Tiger Creek—stream (2) GA-3
Little Tiger Creek—stream MS-4
Little Tiger Creek—stream TX-5
Little Tiger Island—island FL-3
Little Tiger Spring—spring CA-9
Little Tigert Spring—spring ID-8
Little Timber Canyon—valley OR-9
*Little Timber Creek* TX-5
Little Timber Creek—stream ID-8
Little Timber Creek—stream (2) KS-7
Little Timber Creek—stream MT-8
Little Timber Creek—stream (2) NJ-2
Little Timber Creek—stream (2) TX-5
Little Timber Ridge—ridge (2) VA-3
Little Tim Island—island NC-3
Little Tinaja Spring—spring AZ-5
Little Tin Cup Creek—stream MT-8
Little Tinicum Island—island PA-2
Little Tinker Creek—stream ID-8
Little Tionesta Creek—stream PA-2
*Little Tippah Creek* MS-4
Little Tippah River LT-7-17 Dam—dam MS-4
*Little Tippecanoe Lake* IN-6
Little Tippo—gut MS-4
Little Tired Creek—stream GA-3
Little Titnuk Creek—stream AK-9
Little Tizer Creek—stream MT-8
Little Tizer Wildcat Mine—mine MT-8
Little Toad Lake—reservoir MN-6
Little Tobacco River—stream MI-6
Little Tobehanna Creek—stream NY-2
Little Tobesofkee Creek—stream GA-3
Little Tobin Creek—stream MT-8
Little Tobin Lake—lake MI-6
Little Tobin Spring—spring MT-8
Little Toby—locale PA-2
Little Toby Creek—stream (2) PA-2
Little Toby Creek—stream VA-3
*Little Tobyhanna Creek* NY-2
Little Toccoa Creek—stream GA-3
Little Todd Creek—stream OR-9
Little Todd Harbor—bay MI-6
Little Toe River—stream NC-3
Little Togiak Creek—stream AK-9
Little Togiak Lake—lake AK-9
*Little Togus Pond* ME-1
Little Togus Pond—lake ME-1
Little Tok River—stream AK-9
Little Tokyo Hist Dist—hist pl CA-9
Little Tomahawk Creek—stream NC-3
Little Tomahawk Creek—stream VA-3
Little Tomahawk Lake—lake MI-6
Little Tomahawk Lake—lake WI-6
Little Tomah Lake—lake ME-1
Little Tomah Stream—stream ME-1
*Little Tamaracack Mountain* OR-9
*Little Tombigby River - in part* AL-4
*Little Tombigby River - in part* MS-4
Little Tom Brown Branch—stream KY-4
*Little Tom Creek* CO-8
Little Tom Creek—stream AL-4
Little Tom Creek—stream GA-3
Little Tom Folley Creek—stream OR-9
*Little Tomhicken Creek* PA-2
Little Tomhicken Creek—stream PA-2
Little Tom Lake—lake MI-6
Little Tom Moore Tank—reservoir AZ-5
Little Tom Mtn—summit MT-8
Little Tommy Branch—stream NC-3
Little Tomoka River—stream FL-3
*Little Tom Sauk Mtn* MO-7
Little Toms Cove—bay VA-3
Little Toms Creek—stream VA-3
Little Toms Fish Camp—locale AL-4
Little Toms Fork—stream WV-2
Little Toms Run—stream WV-2
Little Tom Tunnel—tunnel VA-3
Little Tom Well—well NM-5
*Littleton* KS-7
*Littleton* TN-4
Littleton—locale NJ-2
Littleton—locale SC-3
Littleton—locale VA-3
**Littleton**—pop pl (2) AL-4
**Littleton**—pop pl CO-8
**Littleton**—pop pl IL-6
**Littleton**—pop pl IA-7
**Littleton**—pop pl KY-4
**Littleton**—pop pl ME-1
**Littleton**—pop pl MA-1
**Littleton**—pop pl NH-1
**Littleton**—pop pl NC-3
**Littleton**—pop pl UT-8
**Littleton**—pop pl WV-2
*Littleton and Bethlehem (Littleton)* NH-1
Little Tonawanda Creek—stream NY-2
Littleton Branch—stream KY-4
Littleton Canyon—valley NM-5
Littleton Cem—cemetery IL-6
Littleton Cem—cemetery KS-7
Littleton Cem—cemetery KY-4
Littleton Cem—cemetery MS-4
Littleton Cem—cemetery UT-8
Littleton (census name Littleton Common)—uninc pl MA-1
*Littleton Center* MA-1
**Littleton Common**—pop pl MA-1
Littleton Common (census name for Littleton)—CDP MA-1
**Littleton Compact (census name Littleton)**—pop pl NH-1
Littleton Creamery-Beatrice Foods Cold Storage Warehouse—hist pl CO-8
Littleton Creek—stream WA-9
Littleton Tongue River—stream WY-8
Littleton Hollow—valley KY-4
Littleton Hollow—valley TN-4
Littleton HS—school MA-1
Littleton Mine (underground)—mine AL-4
Little Tonoloway Creek—stream MD-2
Little Tonoloway Creek—stream PA-2
Littleton Ridge—ridge ME-1
Littleton Rsvr—reservoir NH-1
**Littletons**—pop pl AL-4
Littleton Sch—school AZ-5
Littleton-Sedalia Landing Area—airport CO-8
Little Tonshi Mtn—summit NY-2
Little Tonsina River—stream AK-9
Littletons Lake—reservoir TX-5
**Littleton Southeast**—pop pl CO-8
Littleton (sta.) (RR name for Harwood)—other MA-1
*Littleton Station* MA-1
Littleton Station—locale ME-1
Little Tonto Tank—reservoir AZ-5
Littleton Town Bldg—hist pl NH-1
Littleton Town Hall—hist pl CO-8
**Littleton (Town of)**—pop pl ME-1
**Littleton (Town of)**—pop pl MA-1
**Littleton (Town of)**—pop pl NH-1
Littleton (Township of)—fmr MCD NC-3
**Littleton (Township of)**—pop pl IL-6
*Littleton Village* MA-1
Little Tony Lake—lake MN-6
Little Tonzona River—stream AK-9
Little Too Much Lake—lake MN-6
Little Top—summit TN-4
Little Topashaw Creek—stream MS-4
Little Toper Ridge—ridge TN-4
Little Top Hat Butte—summit NM-5
Little Toponce Creek—stream ID-8
Little Topsail Inlet—bay NC-3
Little Topsail Inlet—channel NC-3
Little Topy Creek—stream LA-4
*Little Toqua Baptist Church* TN-4
Little Toqua Cem—cemetery TN-4
Little Toqua Creek—stream TN-4
Little Toqua Creek Ch—church TN-4
Little Tor—summit NY-2
Little Torch Key—island FL-3
**Little Torch Key**—pop pl FL-3
Little Torch Lake—lake MI-6
Little Tornado Mine (historical)—mine SD-7
Little Toroweap Rsvr—reservoir AZ-5
Little Torrey Canyon—valley TX-5
Little Torrey Windmill—locale TX-5
Little Tor Sch—school NY-2
Little Tory Camp Run—stream WV-2
Little Totem Bay—bay AK-9
Little Totten Key—island FL-3
Little Totuskey Creek—stream VA-3
Little Tough Creek—stream IN-6
Little Towaliga River—stream GA-3
*Little Town* KS-7
*Littletown* MA-1
*Littletown* NJ-2
Little Town—hist pl VA-3
Littletown—locale NJ-2
**Littletown**—pop pl AZ-5
**Littletown**—pop pl PA-2
**Little Town**—pop pl SC-3
**Little Town**—pop pl VA-3
Little Town Creek—stream NC-3
Little Town Creek—stream VA-3
Little Town Hill Creek—stream VA-3
Littletown Park—park AZ-5
Little Toxaway Creek—stream SC-3
Little Trace Branch—stream KY-4
Little Trace Creek—stream TN-4
Little Trace Run—stream WV-2
*Little Tracy Pond* CT-1
Little Tracys Pond—lake CT-1
Little Trade Lake—lake WI-6
*Little Trail Creek* UT-8
Little Trail Creek—stream MT-8
Little Trail Creek—stream OR-9
Little Trail Creek—stream UT-8
Little Trail Lake—lake MI-6
Little Trail Run—stream OH-6
Little Trammel Creek—stream KY-4
Little Trammel Creek—stream TN-4
*Little Trammel Fork* KY-4
*Little Trammel Fork* TN-4
Little Trap Falls—falls MI-6
Little Trapper Creek—stream MT-8
Little Trappe River—stream WI-6
Little Trapper Lake—lake WY-8
Little Trappers Lake—lake CO-8
Little Trap Ridge—ridge WV-2
Little Trap Spring—spring AZ-5
Little Trash Dam—dam AZ-5
Little Trash Dam Tank—reservoir AZ-5
Little Traverse Bay—bay (2) MI-6
Little Traverse Creek—stream PA-2
Little Traverse Lake—lake MI-6
*Little Traverse Run* PA-2
Little Traverse (Township of)—civ div MI-6
Little Tree Hill—summit UT-8
*Little Tree Point* RI-1
Little Tree Point—cape RI-1
Little Triangle—bench UT-8
Little Triangle Ledge—bar ME-1
Little Triangle Pass—channel TX-5
Little Tribble Creek—stream WV-2
Little Trickle Tube Dam—dam SD-7
**Little Trieste Subdivision**—pop pl UT-8
Little Trimbelle Creek—stream WI-6
Little Trimmer Creek—stream TX-5
*Little Trinity Lake* ID-8
Little Trinity Lake—lake ID-8
Little Trinity River—stream CA-9
Little Troublesome Creek—stream MO-7
Little Troublesome Creek—stream NC-3
Little Trough Canyon—valley CA-9
Little Trough Creek—stream AZ-5
Little Trough Creek—stream PA-2
Little Trough Spring—spring (2) AZ-5
Little Trout Brook—stream ME-1
Little Trout Brook—stream NY-2
*Little Trout Creek* MT-8
*Little Trout Creek* WA-9
Little Trout Creek—stream CA-9
Little Trout Creek—stream CO-8
Little Trout Creek—stream (2) FL-3
Little Trout Creek—stream ID-8
Little Trout Creek—stream (3) MT-8
Little Trout Creek—stream NC-3
Little Trout Creek—stream (2) OR-9
Little Trout Island—island MI-6
Little Trout Lake—lake (5) MI-6
Little Trout Lake—lake (4) MN-6
Little Trout Lake—lake NY-2
Little Trout Lake—lake WA-9
Little Trout Lake—lake WI-6
Little Trout Pond—lake NY-2
Little Trout River—stream FL-3

Little Trout River—*stream* ... MI-6
Little Trout River—*stream* ... NY-2
Little Trout Run—*stream* ... PA-2
Little Trout Valley—*valley* ... MN-6
Little Troxel Point—*cape* ... CA-9
Little Troy Cedar Lake—*lake* ... IN-6
Little Troy Meadow—*flat* ... CA-9
Little Truckee River—*stream* ... CA-9
Little Trudo Lake—*lake* ... LA-4
Little Trujillo Wash—*valley* ... CO-8
Little Trump Lake—*lake* ... MN-6
*Little Tucannon Creek* ... WA-9
Little Tucannon River—*stream* ... WA-9
Little Tuckahoe Creek—*stream* ... TN-4
Little Tuckahoe Creek—*stream* ... VA-3
Little Tucker Lake—*lake* ... TX-5
Little Tucker Lake—*reservoir* ... FL-3
*Little Tucson* ... AZ-5
*Little Tucson (Ali Chukson)* ... AZ-5
Little Tug—*summit* ... ID-8
Little Tujunga Canyon—*valley* ... CA-9
Little Tujunga Station—*locale* ... CA-9
Little Tuledad Canyon—*valley* ... CA-9
Little Tule Lake—*lake* ... CA-9
Little Tule Lake—*lake* ... NM-5
Little Tule Lake—*lake* ... TX-5
Little Tule Lake—*lake* ... WA-9
Little Tule River—*stream* ... CA-9
Little Tule Tank—*reservoir* ... AZ-5
Little Tule Well—*well* ... AZ-5
Little Tully Mtn—*summit* ... MA-1
Little Tulpehocken Ch—*church* ... PA-2
Little Tulsona Creek—*stream* ... AK-9
Little Tumbling Cove—*valley* ... VA-3
Little Tumbling Creek—*stream* (2) ... VA-3
Little Tungsten Mine—*mine* (2) ... NV-8
Little Tuni Creek—*stream* (2) ... NC-3
Little Tunk Pond—*lake* ... ME-1
Little Tunnel—*tunnel* ... TN-4
Little Tunnel Brook—*stream* ... NH-1
Little Tupper Lake—*lake* ... NY-2
Little Turkey—*locale* ... IA-7
*Little Turkey Creek* ... AL-4
*Little Turkey Creek* ... AZ-5
*Little Turkey Creek* ... KS-7
*Little Turkey Creek* ... MO-7
Little Turkey Creek—*stream* (3) ... AL-4
Little Turkey Creek—*stream* ... AZ-5
Little Turkey Creek—*stream* (2) ... CO-8
Little Turkey Creek—*stream* ... GA-3
Little Turkey Creek—*stream* ... IN-6
Little Turkey Creek—*stream* ... IA-7
Little Turkey Creek—*stream* (3) ... KS-7
Little Turkey Creek—*stream* ... LA-4
Little Turkey Creek—*stream* (4) ... MO-7
Little Turkey Creek—*stream* (3) ... NM-5
Little Turkey Creek—*stream* (4) ... OK-5
Little Turkey Creek—*stream* (5) ... SC-3
Little Turkey Creek—*stream* (3) ... TN-4
Little Turkey Creek—*stream* (2) ... TX-5
*Little Turkey Hill Brook* ... CT-1
Little Turkey Island—*island* ... FL-3
Little Turkey Knob—*summit* ... VA-3
Little Turkey Lake—*lake* (2) ... IN-6
Little Turkey Lake—*reservoir* ... MS-4
Little Turkey Mountain Brook—*stream* ... VT-1
Little Turkey Pack—*flat* ... NM-5
Little Turkey Pond—*reservoir* ... NH-1
Little Turkey River—*stream* (2) ... IA-7
Little Turkey Spring—*spring* (2) ... NM-5
Little Turkey Tail—*ridge* ... WA-9
Little Turkey Tank—*reservoir* ... AZ-5
Little Turkey Townhall—*building* ... IA-7
Little Turnbull Creek—*stream* ... NC-3
Little Turnbull Creek—*stream* ... TN-4
Little Turner Creek—*stream* ... WY-8
Little Turner Lake—*lake* ... KY-4
Little Turner Mtn—*summit* ... ME-1
Little Turner Pond—*lake* ... ME-1
Little Turners Hill—*summit* ... MA-1
Little Turney Draw—*valley* ... TX-5
Little Turniptown Creek—*stream* ... GA-3
Little Turnpike Creek—*stream* ... TX-5
Little Turtle Creek—*stream* ... IN-6
Little Turtle Creek—*stream* ... KY-4
Little Turtle Creek—*stream* ... MN-6
Little Turtle Creek—*stream* ... SD-7
Little Turtle Creek—*stream* ... WI-6
Little Turtle Flowage—*channel* ... WI-6
Little Turtle Gut—*gut* ... NJ-2
Little Turtle Island—*island* ... IA-7
*Little Turtle Lake* ... WI-6
Little Turtle Lake—*lake* (4) ... MN-6
Little Turtle River—*stream* ... WI-6
Little Turtle State Rec Area—*park* ... IN-6
Little Tusas Creek—*stream* ... NM-5
Little Tuscarora Creek—*stream* ... MD-2
*Little Tuscon* ... AZ-5
*Little Tusekiah Creek* ... VA-3
Little Tussekiah Creek—*stream* ... VA-3
Little Tutka Bay—*bay* ... AK-9
Little Tuttle Lake—*lake* ... MN-6
*Little Twelve Mile Creek* ... MT-8
Little Twelvemile Creek—*stream* ... NC-3
Little Twentyseven Pond—*bay* ... LA-4
Little Twin Branch—*stream* ... KY-4
Little Twin Branch—*stream* ... WV-2
Little Twin Butte Canyon—*valley* ... NM-5
Little Twin Creek—*stream* ... CA-9
Little Twin Creek—*stream* ... KY-4
Little Twin Creek—*stream* ... OH-6
Little Twin Creek—*stream* ... WY-8
Little Twin Dump Rsvr—*reservoir* ... CO-8
Little Twin Gulch—*valley* ... CA-9
*Little Twin Lake* ... MI-6
Little Twin Lake—*lake* (2) ... AR-4
Little Twin Lake—*lake* ... MI-6
Little Twin Lake—*lake* (2) ... MN-6
Little Twin Lake—*lake* ... WA-9
Little Twin Lake—*lake* (2) ... WI-6
Little Twin Lake—*swamp* ... AR-4
Little Twin Lake—*swamp* ... MN-6
Little Twin Lake—*swamp* ... WI-6
Little Twin Lakes—*lake* (2) ... WA-9
Little Twin Lakes—*lake* ... WI-6
Little Twins—*summit* ... CO-8
Little Twin Sister Peaks—*summit* ... TX-5
Little Twin State Wildlife Mngmt Area—*park* ... MN-6
Little Twist Creek—*stream* ... UT-8
Little Two Bayou—*stream* ... AR-4
Little Two Bush Island—*island* ... ME-1
Little Two Harbors—*bay* ... MN-6
Little Two Hearted Lakes—*lake* ... MI-6
Little Two Hearted River—*stream* ... MI-6
Little Twombly Ridge—*ridge* ... ME-1
*Little Twomile Creek* ... OR-9
Little Twomile Creek—*stream* ... WV-2
Little Two River—*stream* ... MN-6
Little Two Run—*stream* ... WV-2
Little Two Top Butte—*summit* ... SD-7
Little Tybee Creek—*channel* ... GA-3
*Little Tybee Island* ... GA-3
Little Tybee Island—*island* ... GA-3
Little Tygart Creek—*stream* ... WV-2
Little Tykle Cove—*bay* ... WA-9
*Little Tymochtee Creek* ... OH-6
Little Tymochtee Creek—*stream* (2) ... OH-6
Little Tyro Creek—*stream* ... AL-4
Little Uchee Bridge—*bridge* ... AL-4
*Little Uchee Church* ... AL-4
Little Uchee Creek—*stream* ... AL-4
Little Ugashik Creek—*stream* ... AK-9
Little Ugly Branch—*stream* (2) ... WV-2
Little Ugly Creek—*stream* ... AL-4
Little Ugly Creek—*stream* ... WV-2
Little Underhill Creek—*stream* ... AK-9
Little Union—*church* ... MS-4
Little Union Canal—*canal* ... ID-8
Little Union Ch—*church* ... AL-4
Little Union Ch—*church* ... GA-3
Little Union Ch—*church* ... IN-6
Little Union Ch—*church* (3) ... KY-4
Little Union Ch—*church* (2) ... LA-4
Little Union Ch—*church* (2) ... MO-7
Little Union Ch—*church* ... NC-3
Little Union Ch—*church* (3) ... VA-3
Little Union Ch—*church* ... WV-2
Little Union Community Center—*building* ... KY-4
*Little Union Creek* ... CO-8
Little Union Creek—*stream* ... CO-8
Little Union River—*stream* ... MI-6
Little Union Sch—*school* ... KY-4
Little Union School (Abandoned)—*locale* ... IL-6
Little Upton Creek—*stream* ... KS-7
*Little Uta Lake* ... UT-8
Little Ute Creek—*stream* ... CO-8
**Little Utica**—*pop pl* ... NY-2
Little Uvas Creek—*stream* ... CA-9
Little Uwharrie River—*stream* ... NC-3
*Little Vache Creek* ... AR-4
Little Vache Grasse Creek—*stream* ... AR-4
Little Valentine Lake—*lake* ... WY-8
*Little Valley* ... AZ-5
*Little Valley* ... CA-9
*Little Valley* ... NV-8
Little Valley—*area* ... NV-8
Little Valley—*basin* (3) ... CA-9
Little Valley—*basin* ... ID-8
Little Valley—*basin* (2) ... NV-8
Little Valley—*basin* (12) ... UT-8
Little Valley—*flat* ... CA-9
Little Valley—*locale* ... OR-9
**Little Valley**—*pop pl* ... CA-9
**Little Valley**—*pop pl* ... NY-2
Little Valley—*valley* ... AL-4
Little Valley—*valley* ... AZ-5
Little Valley—*valley* (5) ... CA-9
Little Valley—*valley* (3) ... ID-8
Little Valley—*valley* (2) ... NV-8
Little Valley—*valley* (4) ... OR-9
Little Valley—*valley* (2) ... PA-2
Little Valley—*valley* ... TN-4
Little Valley—*valley* ... TN-4
Little Valley—*valley* ... TN-4
Little Valley—*valley* (18) ... UT-8
Little Valley—*valley* (4) ... VA-3
Little Valley Bayou—*stream* ... LA-4
Little Valley Campground—*locale* ... UT-8
*Little Valley Canal* ... OR-9
*Little Valley Canyon* ... UT-8
Little Valley Canyon—*valley* (3) ... UT-8
Little Valley Cem—*cemetery* ... MN-6
Little Valley Cem—*cemetery* ... TN-4
Little Valley Ch—*church* ... GA-3
Little Valley Ch—*church* ... MS-4
Little Valley Ch—*church* ... MO-7
Little Valley Ch—*church* (2) ... TN-4
Little Valley Ch—*church* ... VA-3
Little Valley Ch—*church* ... WV-2
Little Valley Corral—*locale* ... UT-8
*Little Valley Creek* ... ID-8
Little Valley Creek—*stream* ... AL-4
Little Valley Creek—*stream* (2) ... CA-9
Little Valley Creek—*stream* ... NY-2
Little Valley Creek—*stream* (2) ... PA-2
Little Valley Creek—*stream* ... UT-8
Little Valley Creek—*stream* ... WA-9
Little Valley Ditch—*canal* ... UT-8
Little Valley Harbor—*harbor* ... UT-8
Little Valley Hills—*range* ... ID-8
Little Valley Hollow—*valley* ... MO-7
Little Valley Hollow—*valley* ... UT-8
Little Valley Lateral—*canal* ... OR-9
Little Valley Mtn—*summit* ... AL-4
Little Valley Park—*park* ... PA-2
**Little Valley Plantation**—*pop pl* ... LA-4
Little Valley Ridge—*ridge* ... VA-3
Little Valley Rod and Gun Club—*other* ... NY-2
Little Valley Rsvr—*reservoir* (2) ... ID-8
Little Valley Run—*stream* ... VA-3
Little Valleys—*basin* ... UT-8
Little Valley Sch—*school* (2) ... TN-4
Little Valley School—*locale* ... ID-8
Little Valley Spring—*spring* ... AZ-5
**Little Valley (Town of)**—*pop pl* ... NY-2
**Little Valley Township**—*pop pl* ... KS-7
Little Valley Wash—*valley* (3) ... UT-8
Little Valley Well—*well* ... UT-8
Little Van Buren Creek—*stream* ... ID-8
Little Vance Creek—*stream* ... WI-6
Little Vandamore Draw—*valley* ... CO-8
Little Vandemere Creek—*stream* ... NC-3
Little Vanderwhacker Brook—*stream* ... NY-2
Little Van Duzen River—*stream* ... CA-9
Little Van Lake—*lake* ... FL-3
Little Vanose Lake—*lake* ... MN-6
Little Van Zile Lake—*lake* ... WI-6
Little Varnell Creek—*stream* ... MS-4
Little Vasques Creek—*stream* ... CO-8
Little Vega Windmill—*locale* ... TX-5
Little Venice—*locale* ... MI-6
Little Venice Island—*island* ... CA-9
Little Venus Cutoff Trail—*trail* ... WY-8
*Little Verdigris River* ... KS-7
*Little Vermejo Creek* ... CO-8
Little Vermejo Creek—*stream* ... CO-8
Little Vermejo Creek—*stream* ... NM-5
Little Vermilion Ditch—*canal* ... IL-6
Little Vermilion Lake—*lake* ... MN-6
Little Vermilion Narrows—*channel* ... MN-6
Little Vermilion River—*stream* (2) ... IL-6
Little Vermilion River—*stream* ... IN-6
*Little Vermillion Lake* ... MN-6
Little Vermillion Lake—*lake* ... MN-6
*Little Vermillion River* ... IL-6
*Little Vermillion River* ... IN-6
Little Vermillion River—*stream* ... SD-7
Little V-H Draw—*valley* ... WY-8
Little Vian Creek—*stream* ... OK-5
**Little Vienna Estates**—*pop pl* ... VA-3
Little Viles Pond—*lake* ... ME-1
*Little Village* ... MO-7
Little Village Cem—*cemetery* ... LA-4
Little Village Creek Ditch—*canal* ... AR-4
*Little Village Ditch* ... AR-4
*Littleville* ... AL-4
Littleville—*locale* ... NY-2
**Littleville**—*pop pl* (2) ... AL-4
**Littleville**—*pop pl* ... KY-4
**Littleville**—*pop pl* ... MA-1
**Littleville**—*pop pl* ... NY-2
Littleville (CCD)—*cens area* ... AL-4
Littleville Dam—*dam* ... MA-1
Littleville Division—*civil* ... AL-4
Littleville Elem Sch—*school* ... AL-4
Littleville First Baptist Ch—*church* ... AL-4
Littleville Lake—*reservoir* ... MA-1
*Littleville Rsvr* ... MA-1
Little Vince Bayou—*stream* ... TX-5
**Littlevine**—*pop pl* ... VA-3
Little Vine Acad (historical)—*school* ... MS-4
Little Vine Cem—*cemetery* (2) ... AL-4
Little Vine Ch—*church* (4) ... AL-4
Little Vine Ch—*church* (3) ... GA-3
Little Vine Ch—*church* (2) ... KY-4
Little Vine Ch—*church* (6) ... MO-7
Little Vine Ch—*church* ... TX-5
Little Vine Ch—*church* ... VA-3
Little Vine Ch—*church* ... WV-2
Little Vine Creek—*stream* ... GA-3
*Little Vine Primitive Baptist Ch* ... AL-4
Little Vine Sch (abandoned)—*school* ... MO-7
Little Vineyard Run—*stream* ... PA-2
Little Virgin Peak—*summit* ... NV-8
**Little Vista Heights**—*pop pl* ... SC-3
Little Volcano—*summit* ... CA-9
Little Volga River—*stream* ... IA-7
Little Vulcan Lake—*lake* ... OR-9
Little Vulcan Mtn—*summit* ... WA-9
Little Wabana Lake—*lake* ... MN-6
Little Wabash Ch—*church* (2) ... IL-6
Little Wabash Creek—*stream* ... AK-9
*Little Wabash River* ... IN-6
Little Wabash River—*stream* ... IL-6
Little Wabasis Lake—*lake* ... MI-6
Little Wachusett—*summit* ... MA-1
*Little Wachusett Hill* ... MA-1
*Little Wachusett Mtn* ... MA-1
Little Wadleigh Pond—*lake* ... ME-1
Little Wadleigh Stream—*stream* ... ME-1
Little Wagner Tank—*reservoir* ... AZ-5
Little Wagon Bayou—*gut* ... AR-4
Little Wahoo Creek—*stream* ... GA-3
Little Waiska Creek—*stream* ... MI-6
Little Wakarusa Creek—*stream* ... KS-7
Little Wakatomika Creek—*stream* ... OH-6
Little Wakenda Creek—*stream* ... MO-7
*Little Walamontage Stream* ... ME-1
Little Waldren Fork—*stream* ... AK-9
Little Walesheba Creek—*stream* ... MS-4
**Little Walker**—*pop pl* ... AL-4
Little Walker Ch—*church* ... AL-4
*Little Walker CME Ch* ... AL-4
Little Walker Cowcamp—*locale* ... CA-9
Little Walker Creek—*stream* ... VA-3
Little Walker Lake—*lake* ... PA-2
Little Walker Mtn—*summit* ... OR-9
Little Walker Mtn—*summit* (2) ... VA-3
Little Walker River—*stream* ... CA-9
Little Wall, The—*ridge* ... CO-8
Little Wall, The—*ridge* ... NM-5
Little Wallace Bayou—*stream* ... LA-4
Little Wallace Canyon—*valley* ... CA-9
Little Wallace Lake—*lake* ... LA-4
Little Wallace Well—*well* ... NM-5
Little Wallace Windmill—*locale* ... AZ-5
Little Wallamatogue Stream—*stream* ... ME-1
*Little Walla Walla River* ... OR-9
*Little Walla Walla River* ... WA-9
Little Walla Walla River—*stream* ... OR-9
Little Wall Creek—*stream* ... MT-8
Little Wall Creek—*stream* ... OR-9
Little Wall Lake—*lake* ... IA-7
Little Wall Lake County Park—*park* ... IA-7
Little Wallooskee River—*stream* ... OR-9
Little Wall Pumping Station—*other* ... MT-8
Little Walls Lake—*lake* ... OR-9
*Little Walluski River* ... OR-9
*Little Walnut* ... KS-7
**Little Walnut**—*pop pl* ... OH-6
Little Walnut Branch—*stream* ... SC-3
Little Walnut Canyon—*valley* ... AZ-5
Little Walnut Cem—*cemetery* ... IN-6
Little Walnut Cem—*cemetery* ... KS-7
Little Walnut Ch—*church* ... KS-7
*Little Walnut Creek* ... KS-7
*Little Walnut Creek* ... OH-6
Little Walnut Creek—*stream* ... AR-4
Little Walnut Creek—*stream* (2) ... IN-6
Little Walnut Creek—*stream* (3) ... IA-7
Little Walnut Creek—*stream* (3) ... KS-7
Little Walnut Creek—*stream* (4) ... MO-7
Little Walnut Creek—*stream* (2) ... NM-5
Little Walnut Creek—*stream* ... OH-6
Little Walnut Creek—*stream* ... OK-5
Little Walnut Creek—*stream* (4) ... TX-5
Little Walnut Creek Structure Number 3—*dam* ... IN-6
Little Walnut Fork—*stream* ... IN-6
Little Walnut Isle—*island* ... OH-6
Little Walnut Picnic Area—*park* ... NM-5
Little Walnut Ridge—*ridge* ... TN-4
Little Walnut River—*stream* ... KS-7
Little Walnut Run—*stream* ... TX-5
Little Walnut Spring—*spring* (2) ... AZ-5
Little Walnut Tank—*reservoir* ... AZ-5
**Little Walnut Township**—*pop pl* ... KS-7
**Little Walnut Village**—*pop pl* ... NM-5
Little Walt Canyon—*valley* ... NM-5
Little Walters Lake—*lake* ... MI-6
Little Walt Spring—*spring* ... NM-5
*Little Wamatogue Stream* ... ME-1
Little Wambaw Swamp—*swamp* ... SC-3
Little Wampus Lake—*lake* ... MN-6
Little Wannagan Creek—*stream* ... ND-7
Little Wapato Lake—*lake* ... WI-6
Little Wapessening Creek—*stream* ... NY-2
Little Wapessening Creek—*stream* ... PA-2
Little Wapiti Creek—*stream* ... MT-8
Little Wapiti Creek Trail—*trail* ... MT-8
Little Wapoose Lake—*lake* ... WI-6
*Little Wappasening Creek* ... PA-2
Little Wappinger Creek—*stream* ... NY-2
Little Wapsipinicon River—*stream* (2) ... IA-7
Little Wapwallopen Creek—*stream* ... PA-2
Little War Creek—*stream* ... TN-4
Little Ward Canal—*canal* ... CA-9
Little Ward Island—*island* ... FL-3
Little Ward Lake—*lake* ... MI-6
Little Ward Lake—*lake* ... WI-6
Little Ware Point Creek—*gut* ... MD-2
Little Waresha Creek—*stream* ... OK-5
Little War Gap—*gap* ... TN-4
Little Warm Creek—*stream* (2) ... ID-8
Little Warm Creek—*stream* ... MT-8
Little Warm Rsvr—*reservoir* ... MT-8
Little Warm Spring—*spring* ... NV-8
Little Warm Spring Canyon—*valley* ... WY-8
*Little Warm Spring Creek* ... MT-8
Little Warm Spring Creek—*stream* ... WY-8
Little Warm Springs Creek—*stream* ... CA-9
Little Warrior—*locale* ... AL-4
*Little Warrior Creek* ... AL-4
Little Warrior Creek—*stream* ... NC-3
Little Warrior (historical)—*locale* ... AL-4
Little Warrior Mtn—*summit* ... NC-3
Little Warrior River—*stream* ... AL-4
Little Wash—*stream* ... AZ-5
Little Wash—*stream* ... CO-8
*Little Washboard Rsvr* ... OR-9
Little Washburn Creek—*stream* ... AR-4
Little Washburn Creek—*stream* ... NV-8
Little Washington—*locale* ... PA-2
**Little Washington**—*pop pl* ... OH-6
**Little Washington**—*pop pl* ... PA-2
Little Washington Creek—*stream* ... AK-9
Little Washington Creek—*stream* ... ID-8
Little Washita Indian Ch—*church* ... OK-5
Little Washita River—*stream* ... OK-5
Little Washoe Lake—*lake* ... NV-8
Little Washougal River—*stream* ... WA-9
Little Washout Creek—*stream* ... OR-9
Little Wash Pond—*lake* ... RI-1
Little Wasp Creek—*stream* ... GA-3
Little Wassataquoik Lake—*lake* ... ME-1
Little Wassaw Island—*island* ... GA-3
Little Wasson Lake—*lake* ... MN-6
Little Watab Lake—*lake* ... MN-6
*Little Watatick Mtn* ... MA-1
Little Watatic Mtn—*summit* ... MA-1
Little Watchic Pond—*lake* ... ME-1
Little Watch Island—*island* ... NY-2
Little Water—*area* ... AZ-5
Little Water—*lake* ... AZ-5
Little Water—*locale* ... NM-5
**Little Water**—*pop pl* ... UT-8
Little Water—*stream* ... CO-8
Little Water—*stream* ... UT-8
Little Water Branch—*stream* ... NC-3
Little Water Canyon—*valley* ... CA-9
Littlewater Canyon—*valley* ... CO-8
Little Water Canyon—*valley* ... MT-8
Little Water Canyon—*valley* (2) ... NV-8
Little Water Canyon—*valley* ... NM-5
Littlewater Creek—*stream* ... CO-8
Little Water Creek—*stream* ... MT-8
Little Water Creek—*stream* (2) ... NM-5
Little Water Creek—*stream* ... OR-9
Little Water Creek—*stream* ... TX-5
Little Water Creek—*stream* ... UT-8
Little Watered Hollow—*valley* ... TN-4
*Little Wateree Creek* ... SC-3
Little Wateree Creek—*stream* ... SC-3
Little Waterfall Bay—*bay* ... AK-9
Little Waterfall Well—*well* ... AZ-5
*Little Water Gap* ... PA-2
Little Water Gulch—*valley* ... ID-8
Little Water Gulch—*valley* ... UT-8
Little Water Hills—*summit* ... UT-8
Little Waterhole Creek—*stream* ... OK-5
Little Waterman Creek—*stream* ... IA-7
Little Water Mines—*mine* ... UT-8
Little Wateroak Round—*bend* ... GA-3
*Little Water Peak* ... UT-8
Little Water Peak—*summit* ... UT-8
Little Water Pond—*lake* ... GA-3
Littlewater Spring—*spring* ... CO-8
Little Water Spring—*spring* ... CO-8
Little Water Spring—*spring* ... NM-5
Little Water Spring—*spring* (2) ... UT-8
Little Water Tank—*reservoir* (2) ... AZ-5
Little Water Tank—*reservoir* ... NM-5
Little Water Tank—*reservoir* ... TX-5
Little Water Well—*well* (2) ... AZ-5
Little Wauksha Bayou—*stream* ... LA-4
Little Waumandee Creek—*stream* ... WI-6
Little Waupee Creek—*stream* ... WI-6
Little Waupon—*locale* ... WI-6
Little Wausaukee Creek—*stream* ... WI-6
Little Waverly Lake—*lake* ... MN-6
Little Wax Bayou—*stream* (2) ... LA-4
Little Wea Creek—*stream* ... IN-6
Little Weakfish Thorofare—*channel* ... NJ-2
Little Weasel Spring—*spring* ... OR-9
Little Weaubleau Creek—*stream* ... MO-7
Little Weaver Cave—*cave* ... AL-4
Little Weaver Run—*stream* ... PA-2
Little Webber Creek—*stream* ... AR-4
Little Webb Lake—*lake* ... MN-6
Little Webb Pond—*lake* ... ME-1
Little Weber Creek—*stream* ... UT-8
*Little Web Lake* ... MN-6
Little Weddle Creek—*stream* ... KY-4
Little Wedge Plateau—*plain* ... UT-8
Little Weesau Creek—*stream* ... IN-6
Little Wehadkee Branch—*stream* ... AL-4
Little Wehadkee Creek—*stream* ... AL-4
Little Wehadkee Creek—*stream* ... GA-3
Little Weidmann Lake—*lake* ... AR-4
*Little Weiker Run* ... PA-2
Little Weikert Run—*stream* ... PA-2
*Little Weirgor Creek* ... WI-6
Little Weirgor Creek—*stream* ... WI-6
Little Weiser River—*stream* ... ID-8
Little Weiser Trail—*trail* ... ID-8
*Little Weitas Butte* ... ID-8
Little Weitas Butte—*summit* ... ID-8
*Little Weitas Creek* ... ID-8
Little Weitas Creek—*stream* ... ID-8
Little Wekiva River—*stream* ... FL-3
Little Welch Point—*cape* ... MD-2
Little Welcome Baptist Ch—*church* ... AL-4
Little Well—*locale* ... NM-5
Little Well—*well* (3) ... AZ-5
Little Well—*well* (6) ... NM-5
Little Well—*well* (4) ... TX-5
Little Weller Pond—*lake* ... NY-2
Little Wellington Springs—*spring* ... NV-8
Little Wells—*well* (2) ... NM-5
*Little Wells Creek* ... KS-7
Little Wells Creek—*stream* ... KS-7
Little Wenatchee Ford Campground—*locale* ... WA-9
Little Wenatchee River—*stream* ... WA-9
Little Weoka Creek—*stream* ... AL-4
Little West Bayou—*bay* ... FL-3
*Little West Bay Pond* ... ME-1
Little West Blue Creek—*stream* ... OK-5
*Little West Branch* ... WI-6
Little West Branch Creek—*stream* ... WI-6
Little West Branch Escanaba River—*stream* ... MI-6
Little West Branch Huron River—*stream* ... MI-6
Little West Branch Little Hocking River—*stream* ... OH-6
*Little West Branch Wolf River* ... WI-6
Little West Branch Wolf River—*stream* ... WI-6
Little West Chavez Windmill—*locale* ... NM-5
Little West Creek—*stream* ... VA-3
Little Westfield Creek—*stream* ... SC-3
*Little West Fork* ... KY-4
*Little West Fork* ... TN-4
*Little West Fork* ... WY-8
Little West Fork—*stream* ... MT-8
Little West Fork—*stream* ... TN-4
Little West Fork—*stream* ... UT-8
*Little West Fork Baptist Church* ... TN-4
*Little West Fork Blacks Creek* ... WY-8
Little West Fork Blacks Fork—*stream* ... UT-8
Little West Fork Blacks Fork—*stream* ... WY-8
Little West Fork Campground—*locale* ... ID-8
Little West Fork Ch—*church* ... TN-4
*Little West Fork Creek* ... TN-4
Little West Fork Morgan Creek—*stream* ... ID-8
Little West Fork Ohio Brush Creek—*stream* ... OH-6
Little West Fork Plum Creek—*stream* ... TX-5
Little West Fork Trabing Dry Creek—*stream* ... WY-8
Little West Fork West Branch Feather River—*stream* ... CA-9
Little Westham Creek—*stream* ... VA-3
Little West Kill—*stream* ... NY-2
Little West Kill Cem—*cemetery* ... NY-2
Little West Kill Sch—*school* ... NY-2
Little West Locust Creek—*stream* ... MO-7
Little West Pass—*channel* ... TX-5
Little West Pond—*lake* ... CT-1
Little West Pond—*lake* ... MA-1
Little West Tank—*reservoir* ... NM-5
Little West Windmill—*locale* ... TX-5
Little Wet Hollow—*valley* ... MO-7
Little Wewoka Creek—*stream* ... OK-5
Little Whale—*pillar* ... RI-1
Little Whaleboat Island—*island* ... ME-1
Little Whaleboat Ledge—*bar* ... ME-1
Little Whaley Lake—*reservoir* ... NY-2
*Little Wheeler Branch* ... TX-5
Little Wheeler Lake—*lake* ... MI-6
Little Wheeler Pond—*lake* ... VT-1
Little Wheeling Creek—*stream* ... PA-2
Little Wheeling Creek—*stream* ... WV-2
Little Whetstone Branch—*stream* ... TN-4
Little Whetstone Creek—*stream* ... KY-4
Little Whetstone Creek—*stream* ... OR-9
Little Whetstone Run—*stream* ... WV-2
Little Whipping Creek—*stream* ... VA-3
Little Whippoorwill Creek—*stream* ... AL-4
Little Whippoorwill Creek—*stream* ... KY-4
Little Whisenant Cave—*cave* ... AL-4
*Little Whiskey Creek* ... OR-9
Little Whiskey Creek—*stream* ... CO-8
Little Whiskey Creek—*stream* ... NM-5
Little Whiskey Creek—*stream* ... OR-9
Little Whisky Creek—*stream* ... IA-7
Little Whisky Flat—*flat* ... NV-8
Little Whisky Mtn—*summit* ... WA-9
Little White Bird Creek—*stream* ... ID-8
Little White Breast Creek—*stream* ... IA-7
Little White Ch—*church* (2) ... FL-3
Little White Ch—*church* ... MI-6
Little White Ch—*church* ... MO-7
Little White Ch—*church* ... NY-2
Little White Ch—*church* ... NC-3
Little White Church Cem—*cemetery* ... TN-4
Little White Cone—*summit* ... NM-5
Little White Cone Lake—*reservoir* ... NM-5
Little White Country Church, The—*church* ... NC-3
*Little White Creek* ... AL-4
Little White Creek—*stream* ... AL-4
Little White Creek—*stream* ... NY-2
Little White Creek—*stream* ... VT-1
Little White Creek—*stream* ... WY-8
Little White Dam—*dam* ... AZ-5
Little White Deer Creek—*stream* ... CA-9
Little White Deer Valley—*valley* ... CA-9
Little Whiteface Mtn—*summit* ... NY-2
Little Whiteface River—*stream* (2) ... MN-6
*Little Whitefish Lake* ... MN-6
Little Whitefish Lake—*lake* ... MI-6
Little Whitefish Lake—*lake* ... MN-6
Little Whitefish Sch—*school* ... MI-6
Little White Gap—*gap* ... NM-5
Little White Goat Creek—*stream* ... ID-8
Little White Goat Lake—*lake* ... MI-6
Little White Head—*cape* ... MA-1
Little White Horse Canyon—*valley* ... NV-8
Little Whitehorse Creek—*stream* ... OR-9
Little White Horse Hills—*range* ... NV-8
Little White Horse Pass—*gap* ... NV-8
Little White Horse Spring—*spring* ... NV-8
Little White House—*hist pl* ... FL-3
Little White House, The—*building* ... GA-3
Little White House Canyon—*valley* ... AZ-5
Little White House Ruins—*locale* ... AZ-5
*Little White Lake* ... AR-4
Little White Lake—*bay* ... LA-4
Little White Lake—*lake* ... AR-4
Little Whiteley Creek—*stream* ... PA-2
Little Whiteman Creek—*stream* ... AK-9
Little White Mtn—*summit* ... WA-9
**Little White Oak**—*pop pl* ... TN-4
*Little Whiteoak Bayou* ... MS-4
Little White Oak Bayou—*stream* ... MS-4
Little Whiteoak Bayou—*stream* ... TX-5
Little White Oak Branch—*stream* ... WV-2
Little White Oak Ch—*church* ... WV-2
*Little White Oak Creek* ... AL-4
*Little Whiteoak Creek* ... MS-4
Little White Oak Creek—*stream* ... AL-4
Little White Oak Creek—*stream* (2) ... GA-3
Little White Oak Creek—*stream* (2) ... KY-4
Little White Oak Creek—*stream* ... MS-4
Little Whiteoak Creek—*stream* ... NC-3
Little White Oak Creek—*stream* ... NC-3
Little Whiteoak Creek—*stream* ... NC-3
Little White Oak Creek—*stream* ... NC-3
Little White Oak Creek—*stream* ... OH-6
Little White Oak Creek—*stream* ... OK-5
Little White Oak Creek—*stream* ... TN-4
Little White Oak Creek—*stream* (2) ... TX-5
Little White Oak Creek—*stream* (3) ... WV-2
Little White Oak Ditch—*canal* ... AR-4
Little White Oak Lake—*lake* ... MN-6
Little White Oak Mtn—*summit* ... NC-3
Little White Oak Mtn—*summit* ... OK-5
Little White Oak Ridge—*ridge* ... AR-4
Little White Oak Swamp—*stream* ... SC-3
Little White Pine Hollow—*valley* ... KY-4
Little White Pond—*reservoir* ... SC-3
*Little White River* ... UT-8
Little White River—*stream* ... FL-3
Little White River—*stream* ... IN-6
Little White River—*stream* ... SD-7
Little White River Dike Dam—*dam* ... SD-7
Little White River Pool Rsvr—*reservoir* ... SD-7
Little White River Project Dam—*dam* ... SD-7
*Little White Rock* ... NV-8
Little White Rock Canyon—*valley* ... UT-8
Little White Rock Cem—*cemetery* ... PA-2
Little White Rock Creek—*stream* ... TX-5
Little White Rock Mtn—*summit* ... NC-3
Little White Rock Spring—*spring* (2) ... NV-8
Little White Sage Canyon—*valley* ... NV-8
Little White Salmon Range Channel—*channel* ... OR-9
Little White Salmon River—*stream* ... WA-9
Little White Salmon Trail—*trail* ... WA-9
Little White Salom Range Channel—*channel* ... OR-9
*Little White Sand Creek* ... MS-4
Little White Schoolhouse—*hist pl* ... WI-6
Little White Schoolhouse—*school* ... FL-3
*Little Whites Creek* ... AL-4
Little Whites Creek—*stream* ... NC-3
Little White Snake Creek—*stream* ... CO-8
Little Whitestick Creek—*stream* ... WV-2
Little White Stone Ch—*church* ... MI-6
Little Whitetail Creek—*stream* ... MT-8
Little White Tanks—*reservoir* ... AZ-5
Little Whitewater Ch—*church* ... MO-7
Little Whitewater Creek—*stream* ... GA-3
Little Whitewater Creek—*stream* ... MO-7
Little Whitewater Creek—*stream* ... NM-5
Little Whitewater Creek—*stream* ... NC-3
*Little Whitewater River* ... MO-7
Little Whitewater Trail (Pack—*trail* ... NM-5
Little Whitford Lake—*lake* ... IN-6
Little Whiting Lake—*lake* ... MS-4
Little Whitley Gulch—*valley* ... ID-8
Little Whitney Creek—*stream* ... MT-8
*Little Whitney Gulch* ... ID-8
Little Whitney Meadow—*flat* ... CA-9
Little Whitney Prairie—*flat* ... FL-3
Little Whitten Brook—*stream* ... ME-1
Little Whittle Creek—*stream* ... VA-3
Little Whorl Lake—*lake* ... MI-6
Little Wichita River—*stream* ... OK-5
Little Wichita River—*stream* ... TX-5
Little Wickiup Creek—*stream* ... ID-8
Little Wickson Creek—*stream* ... TX-5
Little Wicomico River—*stream* ... VA-3
Little Wiconisco Creek—*stream* ... PA-2
Little Widgeon Creek—*stream* ... VA-3
Little Widgeon Pond—*lake* ... MA-1
Little Widger—*valley* ... PA-2
Little Widow Branch—*stream* ... KY-4
Little Wiemer Spring—*spring* ... NV-8
Little Wigwam Pond—*lake* ... MA-1
Little Wilcox Peak—*summit* ... VT-1
Little Wild Bill Tank—*reservoir* ... AZ-5
*Little Wildcat Canyon* ... AZ-5
Little Wildcat Canyon—*valley* ... AZ-5
Little Wildcat Canyon—*valley* ... WY-8
*Little Wildcat Creek* ... IN-6
Little Wildcat Creek—*stream* ... AR-4
Little Wildcat Creek—*stream* ... CA-9
Little Wildcat Creek—*stream* ... IN-6
Little Wild Cat Creek—*stream* ... KY-4
Little Wildcat Creek—*stream* ... NV-8
Little Wildcat Creek—*stream* ... WA-9
Little Wildcat Lake—*lake* ... MI-6
Little Wildcat Mtn—*summit* ... GA-3
Little Wildcat Mtn—*summit* ... NH-1
Little Wildcat Rapids—*rapids* ... OR-9
Little Wildcat Run—*stream* (2) ... WV-2
Little Wildcat Spring—*spring* ... TN-4
Little Wildcat Trail—*trail* ... WA-9
Little Wild Dog Creek—*stream* ... KY-4

Livingston Creek ... NY-2
Livingston Creek—stream ... AK-9
Livingston Creek—stream ... AR-4
Livingston Creek—stream ... FL-3
Livingston Creek—stream ... ID-8
Livingston Creek—stream (2) ... KY-4
Livingston Creek—stream ... MI-6
Livingston Creek—stream ... NC-3
Livingston Creek—stream ... ND-7
Livingston Creek—stream ... OR-9
Livingston Creek—stream ... VA-3
Livingston Creek Cem—cemetery ... AR-4
Livingston Creek Ch—church ... VA-3
Livingston-Delhi (CCD)—cens area ... CA-9
Livingston Ditch—canal ... MT-8
Livingston Division—civil ... AL-4
Livingston Division—civil ... TN-4
Livingston Drain—canal ... CA-9
Livingston Drain—canal ... MI-6
Livingston Draw—valley ... WY-8
Livingstone ... AL-4
Livingstone Channel—channel ... MI-6
Livingstone Coll—school ... NC-3
Livingstone College Hist Dist—hist pl ... NC-3
Livingstone Creek ... AR-4
Livingstone Creek ... ND-7
Livingstone Drain—canal ... MI-6
Livingstone Hollow ... TN-4
Livingstone Junior Acad—school ... OR-9
Livingstone Range ... MT-8
Livingston First Baptist Ch—church ... TN-4
**Livingston Grove**—pop pl ... MD-2
Livingston Hills—summit ... AZ-5
Livingston (historical)—locale ... KS-7
Livingston (historical P.O.)—locale ... IA-7
Livingston Hollow—valley ... AR-4
Livingston Hollow—valley ... TN-4
Livingston HS—school ... AL-4
Livingston Island ... NY-2
Livingston Island—island ... MT-8
Livingston JHS—school ... AL-4
Livingston JHS—school ... NJ-2
Livingston JHS—school ... NY-2
Livingston Knob ... TN-4
Livingston Lake—lake ... CO-8
Livingston Lake—lake ... NY-2
Livingston Lake—reservoir ... AL-4
Livingston Lake—reservoir ... ND-7
Livingston Lake Dam—dam ... AL-4
Livingston Lake Dam—dam ... MS-4
Livingston Landing ... NY-2
Livingston Lateral—canal ... AZ-5
Livingston Lookout—locale ... TX-5
Livingston (Magisterial District)—fmr MCD ... VA-3
**Livingston Manor**—pop pl ... NY-2
Livingston Memorial Baptist Church ... NC-3
Livingston Memorial Ch—church ... NC-3
Livingston Memorial Church and Burial Ground—hist pl ... NY-2
Livingston Memorial Gardens—cemetery ... AL-4
Livingston Mil—locale ... ID-8
Livingston Mill Sch—school ... SC-3
Livingston Mine—mine ... AZ-5
Livingston Mine—mine ... ID-8
Livingston MS—school ... TN-4
Livingston Mtn—summit ... WA-9
Livingston Municipal Airp—airport ... TN-4
Livingston-New Willard (CCD)—cens area ... TX-5
Livingston Oil Field—oilfield ... TX-5
**Livingston Parish**—pop pl ... LA-4
Livingston Park—flat ... CO-8
Livingston Park—park ... AL-4
Livingston Park—park ... CO-8
Livingston Park—park ... MS-4
Livingston Park—park ... NH-1
Livingston Park—park ... OH-6
**Livingston Park**—pop pl ... MD-2
**Livingston Park**—pop pl ... NJ-2
Livingston Park Sch—school ... NJ-2
Livingston Pass ... AZ-5
Livingston Peak—summit ... MT-8
Livingston Point—cape ... KY-4
Livingston Pond—lake ... NY-2
Livingston Pond—reservoir ... SC-3
Livingston Ponds—lake ... NJ-2
Livingston Pumping Station—other ... TX-5
**Livingston Quarters**—pop pl ... NC-3
Livingston Range—range ... MT-8
Livingston Rec Area—park ... AL-4
Livingston Reformed Cem—cemetery ... NY-2
Livingston Ridge—ridge ... NM-5
Livingston Sch—school ... FL-3
Livingston Sch—school ... GA-3
Livingston Sch—school ... IL-6
Livingston Sch—school ... IA-7
Livingston Sch—school ... KY-4
Livingston Sch—school ... NJ-2
Livingston Sch—school ... PA-2
Livingston Sch—school ... VA-3
Livingstons Creek ... NY-2
Livingston Shiawassee Drain—canal ... MI-6
Livingston South Oil Field—other ... IL-6
Livingstons Post Office—building ... TN-4
Livingston Spring—spring ... AL-4
Livingston Springs Pond—lake ... FL-3
**Livingstons Quarters**—pop pl ... NC-3
Livingstons Springs—spring ... FL-3
**Livingston Subdivision**—pop pl ... MS-4
**Livingston Subdivision (subdivision)**—pop pl ... AL-4
Livingston Substation—other ... CA-9
Livingston Tabernacle ... AL-4
**Livingston (Town of)**—pop pl ... NY-2
**Livingston (Township of)**—pop pl ... MI-6
**Livingston (Township of)**—pop pl ... NJ-2
Livingston Univ—school ... AL-4
**Livingstonville**—pop pl ... NY-2
Livingston Well—well ... AZ-5
Living Tabernacle Ch—church ... LA-4
Livington Creek ... NC-3
Living Water Assembly of God Ch—church ... MS-4
Living Water Ch—church ... AL-4
Living Waters Camp—locale ... PA-2
Living Waters Spring—spring ... AR-4
Living Word Christian Center—church ... UT-8
Living Word Fellowship Ch—church ... TN-4
Livity Ch—church ... TX-5
Livius Pond ... NH-1
Livona—locale ... ND-7
**Livonia**—pop pl ... IN-6
**Livonia**—pop pl ... LA-4
**Livonia**—pop pl ... MI-6
**Livonia**—pop pl ... MO-7
**Livonia**—pop pl ... NY-2
**Livonia**—pop pl ... PA-2
Livonia Baptist Church—hist pl ... NY-2
Livonia Cem—cemetery ... MI-6
Livonia Cem—cemetery ... MN-6
**Livonia Center**—pop pl ... NY-2
Livonia Oil Field—oilfield ... LA-4
Livonia Rsvr—reservoir ... NY-2
Livonia Station—locale ... NY-2
**Livonia (Town of)**—pop pl ... NY-2
**Livonia (Township of)**—pop pl ... MN-6
Livonia Yards—locale ... NY-2
Liwa Lake—lake ... AK-9
Lixard Pond ... NY-2
Lix Hollow—valley ... MO-7
**Lixville**—pop pl ... MO-7
Liyang ... MH-9
Liyang, I—slope ... MH-9
Liyang Falingum Hanun ... MH-9
Liyang Falingun Hanum ... MH-9
Liyeeg—summit ... FM-9
Liyeg ... FM-9
Liyeggow—bay ... FM-9
Liymowol—cape ... FM-9
Liyo—slope ... MH-9
Liyog—area ... GU-9
Liyog River—stream ... GU-9
Liza, Lake—lake ... OR-9
Liza Creek—stream ... CA-9
Liza Flats—flat ... TN-4
Liza Gap—gap ... VA-3
Liza Lake—lake ... SC-3
Liza Lumps—island ... NC-3
Liza Mtn—summit ... KY-4
**Lizana**—pop pl ... MS-4
Lizana Baptist Ch—church ... MS-4
Lizana Cem—cemetery ... MS-4
Lizana Elementary School ... MS-4
Lizana Sch—school ... MS-4
Lizang ... MH-9
Lizann Knob—summit ... WV-2
Lizard—locale ... AZ-5
Lizard—locale ... IA-7
Lizard—locale ... NM-5
**Lizard Acres**—pop pl ... AZ-5
**Lizard Acres (Circle One Ranch)**—pop pl ... AZ-5
Lizard Branch—stream ... KY-4
Lizard Butte—summit ... ID-8
Lizard Canyon—valley ... CA-9
Lizard Canyon—valley ... CO-8
Lizard Cem—cemetery ... IA-7
Lizard Creek ... ID-8
Lizard Creek ... IA-7
Lizard Creek ... WY-8
Lizard Creek—stream ... CA-9
Lizard Creek—stream ... ID-8
Lizard Creek—stream (3) ... IA-7
Lizard Creek—stream ... LA-4
Lizard Creek—stream ... MS-4
Lizard Creek—stream ... NC-3
Lizard Creek—stream ... OR-9
Lizard Creek—stream ... PA-2
Lizard Creek—stream ... VA-3
Lizard Creek—stream ... WV-2
Lizard Creek—stream ... WY-8
Lizard Creek Junction—locale ... PA-2
Lizard Creek Recreational Site—locale ... WY-8
Lizard Creek State Rec Area—park ... IA-7
Lizard Glade Cem—cemetery ... TN-4
Lizard Head—other ... CA-9
Lizard Head—summit ... CO-8
Lizard Head Creek—stream (2) ... CO-8
Lizard Head Meadows—flat ... CO-8
Lizard Head Meadows—flat ... WY-8
Lizard Head Pass—gap ... CO-8
Lizard Head Peak—summit ... WA-9
Lizard Head Peak—summit ... WY-8
Lizard Head Trail—trail ... CO-8
Lizard Head Trail—trail ... WY-8
Lizard Hills—summit ... NV-8
**Lizard (historical)**—pop pl ... IA-7
Lizard Lake ... ID-8
Lizard Lake ... MN-6
Lizard Lake—lake ... CO-8
Lizard Lake—lake ... IA-7
Lizard Lake—lake ... MN-6
Lizard Lake—lake ... MS-4
Lizard Lake—lake ... NE-7
Lizard Lake—lake (2) ... OR-9
Lizard Lake—lake (2) ... UT-8
Lizard Lake—lake (3) ... WA-9
Lizard Lake—reservoir ... ID-8
Lizard Lake Access—park ... IA-7
Lizard Lake Public Hunting Area—area ... IA-7
Lizard Lakes—lake ... ID-8
Lizard Lakes—lake ... MT-8
Lizard Lakes Creek ... ID-8
**Lizard Lick**—pop pl ... NC-3
Lizard Lope School ... AL-4
Lizard Mound State Park—hist pl ... WI-6
Lizard Mound State Park—park ... WI-6
Lizard Mtn—summit ... TX-5
Lizard Mtn—summit ... WA-9
Lizard Peak—summit ... ID-8
Lizard Point ... WY-8
Lizard Point—cape ... AZ-5
Lizard Point—lake ... NY-2
Lizard Point—summit ... KY-4
Lizard Point—summit ... OR-9
Lizard Ridge—ridge ... OR-9
Lizard Ridge Sch (historical)—school ... TN-4
Lizard Rock—summit ... AZ-5
Lizard Rock—summit ... UT-8
Lizard Rocks—island ... VI-3
Lizard Run—stream ... OH-6
Lizard Run—stream ... TX-5
Lizard Scrape Mtn—summit ... AL-4
Lizards Head ... CO-8
Lizard Spring—spring (2) ... AZ-5
Lizard Spring—spring ... CA-9
Lizard Spring—spring ... NV-8
Lizard Spring—spring ... OR-9
Lizard Spring Brook—stream ... NY-2
Lizard Spring (historical)—spring ... AZ-5
Lizard Township—fmr MCD ... IA-7
Lizard Township Hall—locale ... IA-7
Lizard Wash—stream ... AZ-5
Lizard Wash—valley ... AZ-5
Lizard Wash—valley ... UT-8
Lizard Wasteway—canal ... ID-8
Lizar Lateral—canal ... ID-8
Lizas (Barrio)—fmr MCD ... PR-3
Liz Branch—stream ... NC-3
Liz Butte—summit ... ID-8
Liz Creek—stream ... ID-8
Liz Creek Cabin—locale ... ID-8
Lize Branch—stream ... TN-4
Lize Creek—stream ... AL-4
Lizelia—locale ... MS-4
Lizelia Post Office (historical)—building ... MS-4
**Lizella**—pop pl ... GA-3
Lizella (CCD)—cens area ... GA-3
Lizemores—locale ... WV-2
Lizemores Ch—church ... WV-2
Lizenby Ditch—canal ... IN-6
Lizer Lake—lake ... MN-6
Liz Hill—summit ... GA-3
Lizonbee Administrative Site—locale ... UT-8
Lizonbee Springs—spring ... UT-8
Lizotte Brook—stream ... ME-1
Lizotte Lake—lake ... MN-6
**Lizton**—pop pl ... IN-6
Lizzamonde Pond—bay ... LA-4
Lizzard Creek ... AL-4
Lizzard Creek ... MS-4
Lizzard Creek ... OR-9
Lizzard Head Peak ... WY-8
Lizzard Lake ... MN-6
Lizzard Lake ... WA-9
Lizzard Lake—lake ... MN-6
Lizzard Lope Ch (historical)—church ... AL-4
Lizzard Mtn ... WA-9
Lizzard Mtn—summit ... OK-5
Lizzard Ridge—ridge ... AL-4
Lizzie—locale ... NC-3
Lizzie, Lake—lake ... FL-3
Lizzie, Lake—lake ... MN-6
Lizzie, Lake—lake ... WI-6
Lizzie, Mount—summit ... MA-1
Lizzie Branch—stream ... TN-4
Lizzie Ch—church ... MO-7
Lizzie Chapel—church ... GA-3
Lizzie Cotton Mills—uninc pl ... NC-3
Lizzie Creek—stream ... LA-4
Lizzie Creek—stream ... MN-6
Lizzie Creek—stream ... OR-9
Lizzie Creek—stream ... UT-8
Lizzie Ditch—canal ... CO-8
Lizzie Fork—stream ... KY-4
Lizzie Hart Sink—basin ... FL-3
Lizzie Hollow—valley ... KY-4
Lizzie Horn Elem Sch—school ... MS-4
Lizzie Judkins Sch (historical)—school ... AL-4
Lizzie Lake ... ND-7
Lizzie Lake—lake ... FL-3
Lizzie Lake—lake ... MN-6
Lizzie Lee Mine Spring—spring ... AZ-5
Lizzie Lozier Ditch—canal ... WY-8
Lizzie Lozier North Ditch—canal ... WY-8
Lizzie Mtn—summit ... MA-1
Lizzie Mtn—summit ... NC-3
Lizzies Basin—basin ... NV-8
Lizzies Bog—lake ... ME-1
Lizzies Branch—stream ... GA-3
Lizzies Branch—stream ... SC-3
Lizzies Pond ... MA-1
Lizzie Spring Creek—stream ... WY-8
Lizzies Roost Run—stream ... WV-2
**Lizzieville**—pop pl ... AL-4
Lizz Lake—lake ... MN-6
Lizzy Canyon—valley ... WA-9
Lizzy Harold Cem—cemetery ... GA-3
Lizzy Harold Ch—church ... GA-3
Lizzy Lake—lake ... MN-6
Lizzy Pauls Pond—reservoir ... WI-6
L. James Landing ... AL-4
L J Denny Lake Dam—dam ... MS-4
L J H Rsvr—reservoir ... OR-9
L Johnson Bayou ... FL-3
LJ Stanford Spring ... AL-4
L J Wilsons Landing (historical)—locale ... AL-4
**LKC Development**—pop pl ... UT-8
**LKC Jordan View Estates**—pop pl ... UT-8
L Kelly Ranch—locale ... NM-5
Lkes—island ... PW-9
L Kesling—locale ... TX-5
L Kirkbride Ranch—locale ... WY-8
LK Markel Ranch—locale ... NM-5
L Koch Dam—dam ... SD-7
Llader Ch—church ... CO-8
Llaga Creek ... CA-9
Llagas Creek—stream ... CA-9
Llagas Sch—school ... CA-9
Llagas-Uvas (CCD)—cens area ... CA-9
L Lake ... WA-9
L Lake—lake ... IN-6
L-Lake—lake ... MT-8
Llama Mtn—summit ... NV-8
Llambias House—hist pl ... FL-3
Llanada—locale ... CA-9
**Llanada**—pop pl ... PR-3
Llanadas (Barrio)—fmr MCD ... PR-3
**Llandaff**—pop pl ... MD-2
Llanda Landing—locale ... MS-4
L L Anderson Dam—dam ... CA-9
**Llandrilla**—pop pl ... PA-2
**Llanerch**—pop pl ... PA-2
Llanerch Country Club—other ... PA-2
**Llanerch Manor**—pop pl ... PA-2
Llanerch (RR name for Havertown)—other ... PA-2
Llanereh ... PA-2
**Llanfair**—pop pl ... PA-2
**Llangelan Hills**—pop pl ... PA-2
Llangollen (2) ... DE-2
**Llangollen Estates**—pop pl ... DE-2
**Llangollen Estates (Llangollen)**—pop pl ... DE-2
Llangollen Estates Park—park ... DE-2
Llanito Banco Number 14—levee ... TX-5
Llanito Creek—stream ... CA-9
Llanito de la Cruz—area ... NM-5
Llanito del Chapulin—other ... NM-5
Llanito Frio Tanks—reservoir ... NM-5
Llanitos—area ... NM-5
Llanito Well—well ... TX-5
Llanito Windmill—locale ... TX-5
**Llano**—pop pl (2) ... CA-9
**Llano**—pop pl ... NM-5
**Llano**—pop pl ... TX-5
Llano Ancho Tank—reservoir ... TX-5
Llano Ancho Windmill—locale ... TX-5
Llano (Barrio)—fmr MCD ... PR-3
Llano Blanco—area (2) ... NM-5
Llano Cem—cemetery ... TX-5
Llano City Lake—reservoir ... TX-5
Llano City Park—park ... TX-5
**Llano (County)**—pop pl ... TX-5
Llano County Courthouse and Jail—hist pl ... TX-5
Llano De Buena Vista—civil ... CA-9
Llano de la Yegua Cem—cemetery ... NM-5
**Llano Del Medio**—pop pl ... NM-5
Llano Del Tequisquita—civil ... CA-9
Llano Del Vado—area ... NM-5
Llano De Santa Rosa—civil ... CA-9
Llano Ditch—canal ... CO-8
Llano Ditch—canal (3) ... NM-5
Llano Grande Banco Number 112—levee ... TX-5
Llano Grande Canyon—valley ... CA-9
Llano Grande Country Club—other ... TX-5
Llano Grande Lake—lake ... TX-5
Llano Grande Tank—reservoir ... TX-5
Llano Grove Ch (historical)—church ... AL-4
**Llano (historical)**—pop pl ... OR-9
Llano Largo—gap ... NM-5
**Llano Largo**—pop pl ... NM-5
Llano Lobato—ridge ... NM-5
Llano North (CCD)—cens area ... TX-5
Llano Pens—locale ... NM-5
Llano Piedra Lumbre—area ... NM-5
**Llano Quemado**—pop pl ... NM-5
Llano Race Track—other ... CA-9
Llano River—stream ... TX-5
Llano Road Roadhouse—hist pl ... CA-9
**Llanos**—pop pl ... PR-3
Llano Santa Barbara Tract—civil ... NM-5
Llanos (Barrio)—fmr MCD (2) ... PR-3
Llano Sch—school ... NM-5
Llanos Costa (Barrio)—fmr MCD ... PR-3
Llano Seco—civil ... CA-9
Llano South (CCD)—cens area ... TX-5
Llano Spring—spring ... NM-5
**Llanos Township**—pop pl ... KS-7
**Llanos Tuna**—pop pl ... PR-3
Llanos Tuna (Barrio)—fmr MCD ... PR-3
Llano Tank—reservoir ... NM-5
Llano Tank—reservoir (2) ... TX-5
**Llano Viego (La Loma PO)**—pop pl ... NM-5
**Llano Viejo (La Loma Post Office)**—pop pl ... NM-5
Llano Well—well (2) ... TX-5
Llano Windmill—locale (8) ... TX-5
**Llanwellyn**—pop pl ... PA-2
Llao Bay—bay ... OR-9
Llao Rock—pillar ... OR-9
Llaos Hallway—area ... OR-9
Llaos Hallway—valley ... OR-9
L Lateral—canal ... CA-9
Llave (Barrio)—fmr MCD ... PR-3
Llaves—locale ... NM-5
**Llaves**—pop pl ... NM-5
Llave Tank—reservoir ... TX-5
Llave Windmill—locale ... TX-5
LL Bar Ranch—locale ... WY-8
L L Bennett Pond Dam—dam ... MS-4
L L Childress Lake Dam—dam ... MS-4
L L Draw—valley ... WY-8
Llebuchel—channel ... PW-9
Llegua, Canada De La —valley ... CA-9
Lleguas, Canoncito de las—valley ... NM-5
Llenroc—hist pl ... NY-2
Llerun Lake—lake ... AK-9
Llescosa Well (Flowing)—well ... TX-5
**Llewellyn**—pop pl ... PA-2
Llewellyn Canyon—valley ... UT-8
Llewellyn Cem—cemetery ... NC-3
Llewellyn Ch—church ... WV-2
**Llewellyn Corners**—pop pl ... PA-2
Llewellyn Creek—stream ... OR-9
Llewellyn Falls—falls ... CA-9
Llewellyn Gulch—valley ... UT-8
Llewellyn Island—island ... TN-4
Llewellyn Islands ... TN-4
Llewellyn Lake—reservoir ... IN-6
Llewellyn Millpond—lake ... SC-3
Llewellyn Mills ... PA-2
**Llewellyn Park**—pop pl ... NJ-2
Llewellyn Park Hist Dist—hist pl ... NJ-2
Llewellyn Run—stream ... WV-2
Llewellyn Sch—school ... OR-9
Llewellyns Corners ... PA-2
Llewellyns Schoals—bar ... TN-4
Llewellyn Station—locale ... NJ-2
**Llewelyn Corners**—pop pl ... PA-2
**Llewelyn (historical)**—pop pl ... OR-9
L L Gelder Fire Station—building ... TN-4
Llicho, Mount—summit ... GU-9
Lliff Cem—cemetery ... WI-6
Llis Oil and Gas Field—oilfield ... LA-4
Lllahee Camp—locale ... WA-9
L L Major Lake Dam—dam ... MS-4
Llorona Tank —reservoir ... TX-5
Lloron Windmill—locale ... TX-5
Lloyd ... MD-2
Lloyd—locale ... MT-8
**Lloyd**—pop pl ... FL-3
**Lloyd**—pop pl ... KY-4
**Lloyd**—pop pl ... NY-2
Lloyd, Harold, Estate—hist pl ... CA-9
Lloyd, Henry Demarest, House—hist pl ... IL-6
Lloyd, John Uri, House—hist pl ... OH-6
Lloyd, Joseph, House—hist pl ... NY-2
Lloyd, Lake—lake ... GA-3
Lloyd, Thomas F., Hist Dist—hist pl ... NC-3
Lloyd Bay—bay ... VA-3
Lloyd Bayou—stream ... MI-6
Lloyd Beach—beach ... NY-2
Lloyd Bend—bend ... TX-5
Lloyd-Bond House—hist pl ... FL-3
Lloyd Bottom—flat ... AR-4
Lloyd Branch ... GA-3
Lloyd Branch—stream ... GA-3
Lloyd Branch—stream ... MS-4
Lloyd Brook—stream ... MA-1
Lloyd Butte—summit ... MT-8
Lloyd Canyon—valley ... NM-5
Lloyd Canyon—valley ... TX-5
Lloyd Cave—cave ... TN-4
Lloyd Cem—cemetery ... AL-4
Lloyd Cem—cemetery (2) ... AR-4
Lloyd Cem—cemetery ... IN-6
Lloyd Cem—cemetery ... MO-7
Lloyd Cem—cemetery ... OH-6
Lloyd Cem—cemetery ... PA-2
Lloyd Cem—cemetery ... TN-4
Lloyd Cem—cemetery ... TX-5
Lloyd Chapel ... TN-4
Lloyd Church Lake—reservoir ... OK-5
**Lloyd Corners**—pop pl ... OH-6
Lloyd Cove—valley ... NC-3
Lloyd Creek—bay ... MD-2
Lloyd Creek—stream ... AR-4
Lloyd Creek—stream ... FL-3
Lloyd Creek—stream (2) ... GA-3
Lloyd Creek—stream (2) ... MD-2
Lloyd Creek—stream ... MT-8
Lloyd Creek—stream ... SC-3
Lloyd Creek—stream ... TX-5
Lloyd Creek—stream ... UT-8
Lloyd Creek—stream ... WI-6
Lloyd Creek—stream ... WY-8
**Lloyd Crossroads**—pop pl ... NC-3
Lloyd Ditch—canal ... ID-8
Lloyd Ditch—canal ... IN-6
Lloyd Drain—canal ... MI-6
Lloyd Drain—stream ... MD-2
**Lloydell**—pop pl ... PA-2
Lloydell Dam—dam ... PA-2
Lloyd Estates Elem Sch—school ... FL-3
**Lloydesville**—pop pl ... PA-2
Lloyd Ford—locale ... AR-4
Lloyd Fox Dam Number 3—dam ... SD-7
Lloyd Fox Number 2 Dam—dam ... SD-7
Lloyd Gift Dam—dam ... OR-9
Lloyd Hahn Lake—reservoir ... IN-6
Lloyd Hahn Lake Dam—dam ... IN-6
Lloyd Hall—locale ... IL-6
Lloyd Hall Sch (historical)—school ... MS-4
Lloyd Harbor—bay ... NY-2
**Lloyd Harbor**—pop pl ... NY-2
Lloyd Harbor Sch—school ... NY-2
Lloyd Hill—summit ... NE-7
Lloyd Hill—summit ... NY-2
Lloyd Hill Dam—dam ... OR-9
Lloyd Hollow—valley ... AR-4
Lloyd Hollow—valley ... KY-4
Lloyd Hollow—valley ... TN-4
Lloyd House—hist pl ... VA-3
Lloyd-Howe House—hist pl ... NC-3
Lloyd H Roland Memorial Park—park ... PA-2
Lloyd HS—school ... KY-4
Lloyd Island—island ... GA-3
Lloyd Lake ... MI-6
Lloyd Lake—lake ... CA-9
Lloyd Lake—lake ... ID-8
Lloyd Landing—locale ... MD-2
Lloyd Meadow Creek ... CA-9
Lloyd Meadows—flat ... CA-9
Lloyd Meadows Creek—stream ... CA-9
Lloyd Mine—mine (2) ... CA-9
Lloyd Mine—mine ... MI-6
Lloyd Mountain School (Abandoned)—locale ... TX-5
Lloyd Mtn—summit ... GA-3
Lloyd Mtn—summit ... TN-4
Lloyd Mtn—summit ... TX-5
Lloyd Neck—cape ... NY-2
Lloyd Neck Beach Club—other ... NY-2
Lloyd Nolan Hospital ... AL-4
Lloyd Park—park ... CA-9
Lloyd Park—park ... IL-6
Lloyd Park—park ... TX-5
Lloyd Place—uninc pl ... VA-3
Lloyd Point—cape (2) ... MD-2
Lloyd Point—cape ... NY-2
Lloyd Point—cape ... PA-2
Lloyd Pond—lake ... ME-1
Lloyd Post Office (historical)—building ... PA-2
Lloyd Ranch—locale ... WY-8
Lloyd Ridge—ridge ... KY-4
Lloyd Ridge—ridge ... NC-3
**Lloyd (Riggs)**—pop pl ... KY-4
Lloyd RR Depot—hist pl ... FL-3
Lloyd Run—stream ... PA-2
Lloyds ... MD-2
Lloyds—locale ... AL-4
Lloyds—locale ... MD-2
**Lloyds**—pop pl ... VA-3
Lloyds Bayou—swamp ... AR-4
Lloyds Brook ... MA-1
Lloyds Canyon—valley ... NM-5
Lloyds Ch ... AL-4
Lloyds Ch—church ... VA-3
Lloyd Sch—school (3) ... IL-6
Lloyd Sch—school ... MT-8
Lloyd Sch—school ... OH-6
Lloyds Chapel—church ... AL-4
Lloyds Chapel Baptist Ch ... AL-4
Lloyds Chapel Cem—cemetery ... AL-4
Lloyds Chapel Ch—church ... AL-4
Lloyds Corners—locale ... NY-2
Lloyds Coulee—valley ... ND-7
Lloyds Creek ... AR-4
Lloyds Drag Strip (historical)—other ... GA-3
**Lloyds Estates (subdivision)**—pop pl ... FL-3
Lloyd's Harbor ... NY-2
Lloyd Shoals ... GA-3
Lloyd Shoals Dam—dam ... GA-3
Lloyd Shoals Reservoir ... GA-3
Lloyds Lake—lake ... ID-8
Lloyds Lake—reservoir ... UT-8
Lloyd's Neck ... NY-2
Lloyd Spring—spring ... ID-8
Lloyd Spring—spring ... OR-9
Lloyd Square Park—park ... MT-8
Lloyds Run ... PA-2
Lloyds Run—stream ... VA-3
Lloyds Sch House (historical)—school ... AL-4
Lloyds School ... AL-4
Lloyds School ... TN-4
Lloyds Tank—reservoir ... AZ-5
Lloyd Star Consolidated Sch—school ... MS-4
Lloyd Street Sch—school ... WI-6
Lloyd Street Synagogue—hist pl ... MD-2
Lloydsville ... PA-2
Lloydsville—locale ... WV-2
**Lloydsville**—pop pl ... NY-2
**Lloydsville**—pop pl ... OH-6
**Lloydsville**—pop pl ... PA-2
Lloyd Tank—reservoir ... TX-5
**Lloyd (Town of)**—pop pl ... NY-2
Lloyd Township—fmr MCD ... IA-7
Lloyd Trail—trail ... PA-2
Lloyd Union Cem—cemetery ... NY-2
Lloydville—locale ... PA-2
Lloyd Vincent, Lake—reservoir ... OK-5
Lloyd-Watson Mine (underground)—mine ... AL-4
Lloyd Well—well ... NM-5
L L Ranch—locale ... AZ-5
L L Roberts Memorial Methodist Ch—church ... MS-4
Llseng Mtn—summit ... TX-5
Lluberas—post sta ... PR-3
L Luckie Ranch—locale ... TX-5
Lluveras—CDP ... PR-3
L Lyle Pond Dam—dam ... MS-4
Llynwood Sch—school ... TX-5
**Llyswen**—pop pl ... PA-2
**L Marlene Villa Subdivision**—pop pl ... UT-8
L Martin—locale ... TX-5
L M Bar Ranch—locale ... NM-5
LMB Spring—spring ... ID-8
L McKinney Ranch—locale ... NM-5
L McMurtry Lake Dam—dam ... MS-4
Lmetmellasch—stream ... PW-9
L M Hanson Dam—dam (2) ... SD-7
L M Lodge—locale ... MT-8
L'Moure ... ND-7
L M Smith Lake ... AL-4
L M Smith Reservoir ... AL-4
L & N Marine Terminal Bldg—hist pl ... FL-3
L Nobels Lake Dam—dam ... MS-4
L & N Passenger Depot—hist pl ... KY-4
L-N Ranch—locale ... NM-5
L & N RR Depot—hist pl ... KY-4
L N Spring—spring ... OR-9
L N Station—locale ... TN-4
L & N Steam Locomotive No. 152—hist pl ... KY-4
Loa ... HI-9
Loa—island ... MP-9
**Loa**—pop pl ... UT-8
Loa, Lae—cape ... HI-9
Loa, Mauna—summit (2) ... HI-9
Loa Cem—cemetery ... UT-8
**Loachapoka**—pop pl ... AL-4
Loachapoka Cem—cemetery ... AL-4
Loachapoka Hist Dist—hist pl ... AL-4
Loachapoka JHS—school ... AL-4
Loachapoka-Roxana (CCD)—cens area ... AL-4
Loachapoka-Roxana Division—civil ... AL-4
Loachapoka Sch—school ... AL-4
Loacke Ford—locale ... AL-4
Loa Cove—bay ... AS-9
**Load**—pop pl ... KY-4
Loading Chute Tank—reservoir ... AZ-5
Loading Creek—stream ... ID-8
Loading Pen Canyon—valley ... CO-8
Loa District Ranger Station—locale ... UT-8
Loa Division—civil ... UT-8
Load Post Office—locale ... KY-4
Loaf, The—summit ... WA-9
Loaf Creek—stream ... MT-8
Loafer—locale ... AR-4
Loafer Canyon—valley ... UT-8
Loafer Creek ... TX-5
Loafer Creek—stream ... CA-9
Loafer Creek—stream ... OR-9
Loafer Creek—stream ... TX-5
Loafer Creek Campground—locale ... CA-9
Loafer Dam—dam ... AZ-5
Loafer Draw—valley ... NM-5
Loafer Mountain Wildlife Mngmt Area—park ... UT-8
Loafer Mtn—summit ... UT-8
Loafer Ridge—ridge ... UT-8
Loafers Canyon—valley ... UT-8
**Loafers Corner**—pop pl ... TN-4
**Loafers Glory**—pop pl ... NC-3
**Loafers Station**—pop pl ... IN-6
Loafer Tank—reservoir ... AZ-5
Loafer Tank—reservoir ... NM-5
Loa Fish Hatchery—other ... UT-8
Loaf Island—island ... AK-9
Loafman Park—park ... WY-8
Loafman Springs—spring ... WY-8
Loaf Mtn—summit ... WY-8
Loaf of Bread Butte—summit ... MT-8
Loaf Ridge—summit ... AK-9
Loaf Rock—summit ... AZ-5
Loag—locale ... PA-2
Loags Corner ... PA-2
Loagy Bay—cove ... MA-1
Loagy Bay Marshes—swamp ... MA-1
Loa Hatchery ... UT-8
Loaine Lake—lake ... MN-6
Loa Island ... MP-9
Loa Island—island ... MP-9
**Loakfoma**—pop pl ... MS-4
Loakfoma Creek—stream ... MS-4
Loakfoma Lake—reservoir ... MS-4
Loakfoma Lake Dam—dam ... MS-4
Loal—locale ... FM-9
Loa Lake—lake ... ID-8
Loal Island—island ... FM-9
Loaloa—summit ... HI-9
Loaloa Heiau—hist pl ... HI-9
Loaloa Heiau—locale ... HI-9
Loam—locale ... KY-4
Loa Mae Mine—mine ... OR-9
**Loami**—pop pl ... IL-6
**Loami (Township of)**—pop pl ... IL-6
Loam Land Cem—cemetery ... LA-4
Loam Land Sch—school ... LA-4
**Loam Township**—pop pl ... ND-7
Loan Branch—stream ... TN-4
Loangais—unknown ... FM-9
Loangen Alemwet—locale ... FM-9
Loangen Enipein—civil ... FM-9
Loangen Nih Merepw—civil ... FM-9
Loangen Rehwei—locale ... FM-9
Loangen Rohi—locale ... FM-9
Loangen Semwei—locale ... FM-9

Lockland Branch—*stream* TX-5
Lock Landing—*locale* NC-3
**Lockland (subdivision)**—*pop pl* AL-4
Lockland (Township of)—*other* OH-6
Locklayer Cem—*cemetery* AL-4
Lockleaf Canyon—*valley* NM-5
Lockler Canyon—*valley* NM-5
Locklies—*locale* VA-3
Locklin Cem—*cemetery* GA-3
Locklin Cem—*cemetery* TX-5
*Locklin Lake* PA-2
Locklin Lake—*lake* FL-3
Locklin Pond—*lake* PA-2
Locklin Pond Dam—*dam* PA-2
Locklin Ranch—*locale* TX-5
Locklin Voc-Tech Center—*school* FL-3
Lockloma, Lake—*reservoir* MO-7
Lockloma Ch—*church* MS-4
Lock Lomond—*lake* CO-8
*Lock Lynn* MD-2
*Lock Lynn Heights* MD-2
Lockman—*locale* IA-7
Lockman Butte—*summit* ID-8
Lockman Gulch—*valley* ID-8
Lockman Park—*park* MI-6
Lockman Pass—*gap* WA-9
Lockman Sch—*school* MI-6
Lockmar Elem Sch—*school* FL-3
**Lockmiller Addition**—*pop pl* TN-4
Lockmiller Bridge (historical)—*bridge* TN-4
Lockmiller Springs—*spring* TN-4
**Lockmoor**—*pop pl* LA-4
Lock Mtn—*summit* NY-2
Lock Mtn—*summit* PA-2
*Lockner Creek* GA-3
Lockner Creek—*stream* GA-3
Lockner Ridge—*ridge* IN-6
**Lockney**—*pop pl* TX-5
**Lockney**—*pop pl* WV-2
Lockney (CCD)—*cens area* TX-5
Lockney (Site)—*locale* NM-5
Lock No 1—*dam* NC-3
Lock No. 1, North New River Canal—*hist pl* FL-3
Lock No 17—*other* WV-2
Lock No 19—*dam* IL-6
Lock No 19—*dam* IA-7
Lock No 2—*dam* NC-3
Lock No 2—*other* AR-4
Lock No 22—*dam* IL-6
Lock No 24—*dam* IL-6
Lock No 25—*dam* IL-6
Lock No 26—*dam* IL-6
Lock No. 26—*hist pl* OH-6
Lock No 27—*dam* IL-6
Lock No. 27—*hist pl* OH-6
Lock No 27—*other* IL-6
Lock No 28—*dam* IL-6
Lock No. 28—*hist pl* OH-6
Lock No. 28—*other* MD-2
Lock No 29—*dam* IL-6
Lock No. 29 and Aqueduct—*hist pl* OH-6
Lock No 3—*dam* NC-3
**Lock No. 3**—*pop pl* PA-2
Lock No 30—*dam* IL-6
Lock No. 30 and Feeder Dam—*hist pl* OH-6
Lock No 31—*dam* IL-6
Lock No. 31—*hist pl* OH-6
Lock No 32—*dam* IL-6
Lock No. 32—*hist pl* OH-6
Lock No. 33—*hist pl* OH-6
Lock No. 34—*hist pl* OH-6
Lock No. 35—*hist pl* OH-6
Lock No. 37 and Spillway—*hist pl* OH-6
Lock No. 38 and Spillway—*hist pl* OH-6
Lock No. 39 and Spillway—*hist pl* OH-6
Lock No. 4—*uninc pl* PA-2
Lock No 52—*other* IL-6
Lock Number Eight—*dam* PA-2
Lock Number Eight (historical)—*locale* AL-4
Lock Number Eleven (historical)—*locale* AL-4
Lock Number Fifteen (historical)—*locale* AL-4
Lock Number Five Left Bank Public Use Area—*park* AL-4
Lock Number Fourteen (historical)—*locale* AL-4
Lock Number Nine (historical)—*locale* AL-4
Lock Number Nine Left Bank Public Use Area—*park* AL-4
*Lock Number One* AL-4
Lock Number One—*dam* LA-4
Lock Number One Left Bank Public Use Area—*park* AL-4
Lock Number Seven—*dam* PA-2
Lock Number Seven (historical)—*locale* AL-4
Lock Number Seventeen (historical)—*locale* AL-4
Lock Number Six (historical)—*dam* AL-4
Lock Number Six Left Bank Public Use Area—*park* AL-4
Lock Number Sixteen (historical)—*locale* AL-4
Lock Number Sixty-Eight—*dam* PA-2
*Lock Number Thirteen* AL-4
Lock Number Thirteen (historical)—*locale* AL-4
Lock Number Three—*dam* LA-4
Lock Number Three (historical)—*locale* AL-4
Lock Number Twelve (historical)—*locale* AL-4
Lock Number Two—*dam* LA-4
Lock Number Two—*dam* (2) PA-2
Lock Number Two (historical)—*locale* AL-4
Lock Number Two Park—*park* AL-4
Lock Number 7—*dam* TX-5
*Lock Number 71 and 72* PA-2
*Lock One* AL-4
*Lock One Cut-off* AL-4
Lock One Hollow—*valley* AL-4
Lockourne Road Ch—*church* OH-6
Lockpit—*locale* NY-2
Lockpit Cem—*cemetery* NY-2
Lock Playground—*park* LA-4
*Lock Point* MI-6
Lock Point—*cape* LA-4
Lock Pond—*lake* IL-6
*Lockport* IN-6
*Lockport* PA-2
Lockport—*locale* MI-6
Lockport—*locale* PA-2
**Lockport**—*pop pl* IL-6
**Lockport**—*pop pl* IN-6
**Lockport**—*pop pl* KY-4
**Lockport**—*pop pl* LA-4
**Lockport**—*pop pl* NY-2
**Lock Port**—*pop pl* OH-6
**Lockport**—*pop pl* (4) PA-2
Lockport Air Force Station—*military* NY-2
Lockport Cem—*cemetery* IL-6
**Lockport Heights**—*pop pl* LA-4
Lockport Hist Dist—*hist pl* IL-6
Lockport (historical)—*locale* KS-7
Lockport Industrial District—*hist pl* NY-2
Lockport Junction—*locale* NY-2
**Lockport (Lockport Station)**—*pop pl* PA-2
Lockport Locks—*other* IL-6
Lockport Memorial Hosp—*hospital* NY-2
Lockport Oil and Gas Field—*oilfield* LA-4
Lockport Plaza—*locale* NY-2
Lockport Post Office (historical)—*building* TN-4
Lockport Road Cem—*cemetery* NY-2
**Lockport (sta.) (Rita)**—*pop pl* LA-4
Lockport Station—*building* PA-2
**Lockport (Town of)**—*pop pl* NY-2
**Lockport Township**—*pop pl* KS-7
**Lockport (Township of)**—*pop pl* IL-6
**Lockport (Township of)**—*pop pl* MI-6
Lockport West HS—*school* IL-6
*Lockprt* IN-6
*Lockridge* PA-2
Lockridge—*fmr MCD* NE-7
**Lockridge**—*pop pl* IA-7
**Lockridge**—*pop pl* PA-2
Lock Ridge—*ridge* PA-2
Lock Ridge—*ridge* TN-4
Lockridge Canyon—*valley* MT-8
Lockridge Cem—*cemetery* AL-4
Lockridge Cem—*cemetery* MO-7
Lockridge Cem—*cemetery* OK-5
Lockridge Creek Cutoff—*channel* MS-4
Lockridge Family Cem—*cemetery* AL-4
Lock Ridge Furnance Complex—*hist pl* PA-2
Lockridge Memorial Ch—*church* VA-3
Lockridge Mountain Trail—*trail* WV-2
Lockridge Mtn—*summit* WV-2
Lockridge Run—*stream* WV-2
Lockridge Spring—*spring* MT-8
Lockridge Township—*fmr MCD* IA-7
**Locks**—*pop pl* OH-6
Lock Sch—*school* IL-6
Lock Sch—*school* TN-4
Locks Corner—*locale* ME-1
**Locks Corner**—*pop pl* VA-3
*Locks Creek* MS-4
Locks Creek—*stream* CA-9
Locks Creek—*stream* NC-3
Locks Creek Ch—*church* NC-3
*Locks Crossing Church of Christ* AL-4
*Lock Seven East Park* AL-4
Lock Seven Public Use Area—*park* AL-4
Locks Hill—*summit* MA-1
Locks Hill—*summit* PA-2
Locks Hollow—*valley* PA-2
*Lock's Island* NH-1
Locks Island—*island* NH-1
**Lock Six**—*pop pl* AL-4
Lock Six Day Use Area—*park* AL-4
*Lock Six Public Use Area* AL-4
*Locks Lake* LA-4
Locksley—*locale* PA-2
**Locksley Park**—*pop pl* NY-2
Locks Mtn—*summit* TX-5
Locks-of-the-Mountain—*locale* WV-2
Locks Point—*cape* NC-3
*Locks Pond* MA-1
*Lockspring* MO-7
Lock Spring (historical P.O.)—*locale* IN-6
**Lock Springs**—*pop pl* MO-7
*Locks Sch* TN-4
*Locks Store* AL-4
Locks Swamp Creek—*stream* MD-2
**Locks Village**—*pop pl* MA-1
Locks Village (historical P.O.)—*locale* MA-1
Locks Watershed LT-9a-1 Dam—*dam* MS-4
Locks Watershed LT-9a-3 Dam—*dam* MS-4
Lock Tender's House and Inn—*hist pl* OH-6
**Lock Three**—*pop pl* AL-4
Lock Three Left Bank Public Use Area—*park* AL-4
Lock Three Right Bank Public Use Area—*park* AL-4
Lock Three Sch (historical)—*school* AL-4
**Locktown**—*pop pl* NJ-2
Locktown Baptist Church—*hist pl* NJ-2
Lock Twelve (historical)—*dam* AL-4
**Lock Two**—*pop pl* OH-6
Lock Two Park—*park* TN-4
*Lock Two Right Bank Rec Area* AL-4
**Lockview**—*pop pl* PA-2
*Lock Village* MA-1
Lock Village—*other* MA-1
**Lockville**—*pop pl* (2) OH-6
**Lockville**—*pop pl* PA-2
Lockville Canal Locks—*hist pl* OH-6
Lockville Dam, Canal and Powerhouse—*hist pl* NC-3
**Lockville Station**—*pop pl* OH-6
Lockwain Sch—*school* IL-6
Lockwood—*locale* KY-4
Lockwood—*locale* NE-7
Lockwood—*locale* NV-8
Lockwood—*locale* NJ-2
Lockwood—*locale* PA-2
**Lockwood**—*pop pl* CA-9
**Lockwood**—*pop pl* FL-3
**Lockwood**—*pop pl* MI-6
**Lockwood**—*pop pl* MO-7
**Lockwood**—*pop pl* MT-8
**Lockwood**—*pop pl* NY-2
**Lockwood**—*pop pl* OH-6
**Lockwood**—*pop pl* WV-2
Lockwood, J. C., House—*hist pl* OH-6
Lockwood, Point—*cape* AK-9
Lockwood Arroyo—*stream* CO-8
Lockwood Ave Sch—*school* CA-9
Lockwood Barn—*hist pl* WI-6
Lockwood Bay—*bay* NY-2
**Lockwood Beach**—*pop pl* MI-6
Lockwood-Boynton House—*hist pl* VT-1
Lockwood Branch—*stream* IN-6
Lockwood Brook—*stream* RI-1
Lockwood Brook—*stream* (2) VT-1
Lockwood Canyon—*valley* AZ-5
Lockwood Canyon—*valley* CO-8
Lockwood Canyon—*valley* OR-9
Lockwood Cave—*cave* TN-4
Lockwood Cem—*cemetery* CT-1
Lockwood Cem—*cemetery* KS-7
Lockwood Cem—*cemetery* KY-4
Lockwood Cem—*cemetery* OH-6
Lockwood Cem—*cemetery* TX-5
Lockwood Ch—*church* FL-3
Lockwood Ch—*church* MI-6
*Lockwood Corner* RI-1
Lockwood Corners—*locale* NY-2
**Lockwood Corners**—*pop pl* (2) OH-6
Lockwood Creek—*stream* (2) CA-9
Lockwood Creek—*stream* (2) ID-8
Lockwood Creek—*stream* KY-4
Lockwood Creek—*stream* MI-6
Lockwood Creek—*stream* WA-9
Lockwood Ditch—*canal* IN-6
Lockwood Ditch—*canal* MT-8
Lockwood Drain—*canal* MI-6
Lockwood Drain—*stream* MI-6
Lockwood Draw—*arroyo* AZ-5
Lockwood Flat—*flat* CA-9
*Lockwood Folly Inlet* NC-3
*Lockwood Folly River* NC-3
Lockwood Grove—*woods* CA-9
Lockwood Gulch—*valley* AZ-5
**Lockwood Heights (subdivision)**—*pop pl* TN-4
Lockwood Hill—*summit* OK-5
Lockwood Hills—*other* AK-9
Lockwood (historical)—*locale* SD-7
Lockwood Hollow—*valley* IL-6
Lockwood Hollow—*valley* PA-2
Lockwood Hosp—*hospital* TX-5
Lockwood JHS—*school* MT-8
Lockwood Lake—*lake* AK-9
Lockwood Lake—*lake* MI-6
Lockwood Lake—*lake* (2) MT-8
Lockwood Lake—*lake* TN-4
Lockwood Lake—*reservoir* MI-6
Lockwood-Mathews Mansion—*hist pl* CT-1
Lockwood Mesa—*summit* AZ-5
Lockwood Mesa Tank—*reservoir* AZ-5
*Lockwood Mills* IN-6
Lockwood Mine—*mine* WA-9
Lockwood Park—*flat* AZ-5
Lockwood Park—*park* IL-6
Lockwood Park—*park* TX-5
Lockwood Peak—*summit* AK-9
Lockwood Playground—*park* MN-6
Lockwood Point—*cliff* ID-8
Lockwood Point—*summit* MT-8
*Lockwood Pond* CT-1
Lockwood Pond—*lake* CT-1
Lockwood Pond—*lake* NY-2
Lockwood Ridge—*uninc pl* FL-3
Lockwood Rock, Point—*other* AK-9
Lockwood Run—*stream* NY-2
Lockwood Run—*stream* OH-6
Lockwood Saddle—*gap* ID-8
Lockwood Sch—*school* CA-9
Lockwood Sch—*school* DE-2
Lockwood Sch—*school* IL-6
Lockwood Sch—*school* MI-6
Lockwood Sch—*school* MO-7
Lockwood Sch—*school* ND-7
Lockwoods Creek—*stream* NC-3
*Lockwoods Crossing* OH-6
Lockwoods Folly Inlet—*channel* NC-3
Lockwoods Folly River—*stream* NC-3
Lockwoods Folly (Township of)—*fmr MCD* NC-3
Lockwood Spring—*spring* (3) AZ-5
**Lockwood (subdivision)**—*pop pl* (2) NC-3
Lockwood Swamp—*swamp* NY-2
Lockwood Tank—*reservoir* (2) AZ-5
**Lockwood Terrace**—*pop pl* GU-9
**Lockwood Township**—*pop pl* MO-7
**Lockwood Township**—*pop pl* ND-7
**Lockwood Township**—*pop pl* SD-7
Lockwood Valley—*valley* CA-9
Lockwood Well—*well* TX-5
Lockyear College—*hist pl* IN-6
Lock 1—*other* AR-4
Lock 18 of Enlarged Erie Canal—*hist pl* NY-2
Lock 21—*other* NY-2
Lock 22—*other* NY-2
Lock 23—*other* NY-2
Lock 32—*other* NY-2
Lock 5—*dam* WI-6
Lock 5 Sch (historical)—*school* AL-4
Lock 8—*other* AR-4
Lock 9—*dam* KY-4
Loco—*locale* LA-4
Loco—*locale* TX-5
**Loco**—*pop pl* GA-3
**Loco**—*pop pl* OK-5
Loco, Bayou—*gut* TX-5
Loco, Bayou—*stream* (2) TX-5
Locoallomi—*civil* CA-9
Loco Arroyo—*stream* NM-5
Loco Bill Canyon—*valley* CA-9
Loco Bottom Basin—*basin* WY-8
Loco Canyon—*valley* NM-5
Loco Canyon—*valley* OR-9
Loco Cem—*cemetery* OK-5
Loco Creek—*stream* AK-9
Loco Creek—*stream* AZ-5
Loco Creek—*stream* CA-9
Loco Creek—*stream* MT-8
Loco Creek—*stream* UT-8
Loco Creek—*stream* WY-8
**Locoda**—*pop pl* OR-9
Loco Draw—*stream* NM-5
Loco Draw—*valley* NM-5
Loco Draw—*valley* WY-8
Loco Hill—*summit* CO-8
Loco Hills—*other* NM-5
**Loco Hills**—*pop pl* NM-5
Loco Hills—*ridge* NM-5
Loco Hills (CCD)—*cens area* NM-5
Loco Hills Gasoline Plant—*other* NM-5
Loco Hills Landing Field—*other* NM-5
Loco Hills Oil Field—*other* NM-5
Loco (historical)—*locale* KS-7
Loco Holiness Ch—*church* GA-3
Loco Knoll—*summit* AZ-5
Loco Knoll Number Three Tank—*reservoir* AZ-5
Loco Knolls—*summit* AZ-5
Loco Knoll Tank—*reservoir* AZ-5
Loco Lake—*lake* MT-8
Loco Mesa—*summit* NM-5
*Locomotive Peak* UT-8
*Locomotive Peaks* AZ-5
Locomotive Point—*cape* UT-8
Locomotive Point—*cliff* CA-9
Locomotive Roadside Park—*park* AL-4
Locomotive Rock—*summit* AZ-5
Locomotive Springs—*spring* UT-8
*Locomotive Springs Bird Refuge* UT-8
Locomotive Springs Waterfowl Mngmt Area—*park* UT-8
Loco Mountain Tank—*reservoir* NM-5
Loco Mtn—*summit* CO-8
Loco Mtn—*summit* MT-8
Loco Mtn—*summit* (2) NM-5
Loco Park—*flat* CO-8
Loco Point—*cape* AZ-5
Locopolis Bayou—*gut* MS-4
Locopolis Ch—*church* MS-4
Locopolis Cut-Off—*bend* MS-4
**Locopolis (historical)**—*pop pl* MS-4
Locopolis Landing—*locale* MS-4
Loco Pool Spring—*spring* AZ-5
Loco Ridge—*ridge* CO-8
Loco Ridge—*ridge* MT-8
Loco Spring—*spring* OR-9
Loco Tank—*reservoir* AZ-5
Loco Tank—*reservoir* (3) NM-5
Locota Sch—*school* MI-6
Loco Twentynine Knoll Tank—*reservoir* AZ-5
L O Creek—*stream* (2) MT-8
Locum—*locale* MS-4
Locum Sch (historical)—*school* MS-4
*Locus Branch* AL-4
Locus Ditch—*canal* IN-6
*Locushatchee Creek* AL-4
*Locust* NC-3
*Locust* TN-4
Locust—*locale* IA-7
Locust—*locale* (2) KY-4
Locust—*locale* MO-7
Locust—*locale* PA-2
Locust—*locale* TX-5
Locust—*locale* WV-2
**Locust**—*pop pl* CA-9
**Locust**—*pop pl* NJ-2
**Locust**—*pop pl* NC-3
Locust, The—*hist pl* KY-4
Locust Ave—*hist pl* KY-4
Locust Ave Sch—*hist pl* CT-1
Locust Ave Sch—*school* CT-1
Locust Ave Sch—*school* NY-2
Locust Bay—*bay* LA-4
*Locust Bayou* AR-4
Locust Bayou—*gut* LA-4
**Locust Bayou**—*pop pl* AR-4
Locust Bayou—*stream* AR-4
Locust Bayou—*stream* MS-4
Locust Bayou Ch—*church* AR-4
Locust Bayou Oil Field—*oilfield* AR-4
Locust Bayou (Township of)—*fmr MCD* AR-4
Locust Bend—*bend* LA-4
Locust Bluff Ch—*church* AL-4
Locust Bluff Sch—*school* AL-4
Locust Bottom Ch—*church* (2) VA-3
Locust Branch—*locale* KY-4
Locust Branch—*stream* (2) AL-4
Locust Branch—*stream* (2) KY-4
Locust Branch—*stream* MO-7
Locust Branch—*stream* SC-3
Locust Branch—*stream* TN-4
Locust Branch—*stream* VA-3
Locust Branch Sch—*school* KY-4
Locust Butte Rsvr—*reservoir* OR-9
Locust Canyon—*valley* (2) AZ-5
Locust Cem—*cemetery* (3) NY-2
Locust Ch—*church* AR-4
Locust Ch—*church* MD-2
Locust Ch—*church* MO-7
Locust Chapel—*church* IN-6
Locust Corner—*locale* NJ-2
**Locust Corner**—*pop pl* OH-6
**Locust Corners**—*pop pl* MI-6
Locust Cove—*bay* MD-2
Locust Cove—*bay* VA-3
Locust Cove—*valley* (2) NC-3
Locust Cove—*valley* VA-3
Locust Cove Creek—*stream* VA-3
Locust Cove Gap—*gap* NC-3
*Locust Creek* AR-4
*Locust Creek* CO-8
*Locust Creek* OR-9
Locust Creek—*locale* VA-3
Locust Creek—*stream* AL-4
Locust Creek—*stream* (6) AR-4
Locust Creek—*stream* (2) IL-6
Locust Creek—*stream* (2) IN-6
Locust Creek—*stream* IA-7
Locust Creek—*stream* KS-7
Locust Creek—*stream* (4) KY-4
Locust Creek—*stream* (2) MO-7
Locust Creek—*stream* (3) NC-3
Locust Creek—*stream* OH-6
Locust Creek—*stream* OK-5
Locust Creek—*stream* (3) PA-2
Locust Creek—*stream* UT-8
Locust Creek—*stream* VT-1
Locust Creek—*stream* (2) VA-3
Locust Creek—*stream* WV-2
Locust Creek Cem—*cemetery* IL-6
Locust Creek Covered Bridge—*hist pl* MO-7
Locust Creek Covered Bridge—*hist pl* WV-2
Locust Creek Dam—*dam* PA-2
Locust Creek Ditch—*canal* (2) AR-4
Locust Creek House Complex—*hist pl* VT-1
Locust Creek Sch—*school* VT-1
Locust Creek Sch (abandoned)—*school* MO-7
Locust Creek Township—*civil* MO-7
*Locust Dale* PA-2
Locust Dale—*locale* VA-3
Locust Dale—*other* PA-2
**Locustdale**—*pop pl* PA-2
**Locustdale (Locust Dale)**—*pop pl* PA-2
Locustdale (Magisterial District)—*fmr MCD* VA-3
Locust Field Ch—*church* NC-3
Locust Ford—*locale* TN-4
*Locust Fork* TN-4
Locust Fork—*locale* OH-6
**Locust Fork**—*pop pl* AL-4
Locust Fork—*stream* IL-6
Locust Fork—*stream* KY-4
Locust Fork—*stream* TN-4
Locust Fork—*stream* VA-3
Locust Fork—*stream* WV-2
Locust Fork (CCD)—*cens area* AL-4
*Locust Fork Church* AL-4
Locust Fork Division—*civil* AL-4
Locust Fork HS—*school* AL-4
Locust Gap—*gap* AR-4
Locust Gap—*gap* (3) GA-3
Locust Gap—*gap* KY-4
Locust Gap—*gap* (8) NC-3
Locust Gap—*gap* PA-2
Locust Gap—*gap* (3) TN-4
**Locust Gap**—*pop pl* PA-2
Locust Gap Branch—*stream* NC-3
**Locust Gap Junction**—*pop pl* PA-2
*Locust Grove* NC-3
*Locust Grove* PA-2
*Locust Grove* VA-3
Locust Grove—*hist pl* KY-4
Locust Grove—*hist pl* MD-2
Locust Grove—*hist pl* NY-2
Locust Grove—*hist pl* NC-3
Locust Grove—*hist pl* PA-2
Locust Grove—*hist pl* TN-4
Locust Grove—*hist pl* TX-5
Locust Grove—*hist pl* (3) VA-3
Locust Grove—*locale* (2) KY-4
Locust Grove—*locale* MD-2
Locust Grove—*locale* OR-9
Locust Grove—*locale* PA-2
Locust Grove—*locale* TX-5
Locust Grove—*locale* (2) VA-3
Locustgrove—*other* VA-3
**Locust Grove**—*pop pl* AR-4
**Locust Grove**—*pop pl* GA-3
**Locust Grove**—*pop pl* IN-6
**Locust Grove**—*pop pl* (4) MD-2
**Locust Grove**—*pop pl* MS-4
**Locust Grove**—*pop pl* NJ-2
**Locust Grove**—*pop pl* (2) NY-2
**Locust Grove**—*pop pl* NC-3
**Locust Grove**—*pop pl* (3) OH-6
**Locust Grove**—*pop pl* OK-5
**Locust Grove**—*pop pl* (4) PA-2
**Locust Grove**—*pop pl* TN-4
Locust Grove Baptist Ch—*church* (2) MS-4
*Locust Grove Baptist Church* TN-4
**Locust Grove Beach**—*pop pl* MD-2
Locust Grove Brethren Ch—*church* PA-2
Locust Grove Canyon—*valley* OR-9
Locust Grove (CCD)—*cens area* GA-3
Locust Grove (CCD)—*cens area* OK-5
Locust Grove Cem—*cemetery* (2) AR-4
Locust Grove Cem—*cemetery* (4) IL-6
Locust Grove Cem—*cemetery* IN-6
Locust Grove Cem—*cemetery* IA-7
Locust Grove Cem—*cemetery* (4) KY-4
Locust Grove Cem—*cemetery* LA-4
Locust Grove Cem—*cemetery* (3) MA-1
Locust Grove Cem—*cemetery* (2) MS-4
Locust Grove Cem—*cemetery* MO-7
Locust Grove Cem—*cemetery* NJ-2
Locust Grove Cem—*cemetery* NM-5
Locust Grove Cem—*cemetery* (3) OH-6
Locust Grove Cem—*cemetery* PA-2
Locust Grove Cem—*cemetery* TN-4
Locust Grove Cem—*cemetery* TX-5
Locust Grove Ch—*church* AL-4
Locust Grove Ch—*church* (4) AR-4
Locust Grove Ch—*church* GA-3
Locust Grove Ch—*church* (3) IN-6
Locust Grove Ch—*church* (2) IA-7
Locust Grove Ch—*church* (16) KY-4
Locust Grove Ch—*church* LA-4
Locust Grove Ch—*church* MI-6
Locust Grove Ch—*church* (6) MS-4
Locust Grove Ch—*church* (2) MO-7
Locust Grove Ch—*church* (7) NC-3
Locust Grove Ch—*church* (3) OH-6
Locust Grove Ch—*church* (2) PA-2
Locust Grove Ch—*church* (4) TN-4
Locust Grove Ch—*church* (2) TX-5
Locust Grove Ch—*church* (7) VA-3
Locust Grove Ch—*church* (6) WV-2
Locust Grove Ch (historical)—*church* TN-4
*Locust Grove Ch of Christ* TN-4
*Locust Grove Cove* MD-2
Locust Grove Creek—*stream* TN-4
Locust Grove Ditch—*canal* CA-9
Locust Grove Elem Sch—*school* PA-2
Locust Grove (historical)—*locale* KS-7
**Locust Grove (historical)**—*pop pl* OR-9
Locust Grove Historical Home—*building* KY-4
Locust Grove Institute Academic Bldg—*hist pl* GA-3
Locust Grove Landing (historical)—*locale* MS-4
**Locust Grove (Locustgrove)**—*pop pl* VA-3
Locust Grove (Magisterial District)—*fmr MCD* VA-3
*Locust Grove Missionary Baptist Church* MS-4
Locust Grove Plantation (historical)—*locale* AL-4
Locust Grove Ridge—*ridge* WV-2
Locust Grove Sch—*school* CA-9
Locust Grove Sch—*school* ID-8
Locust Grove Sch—*school* (10) IL-6
Locust Grove Sch—*school* (2) IA-7
Locust Grove Sch—*school* (2) MS-4
Locust Grove Sch—*school* (6) MO-7
Locust Grove Sch—*school* NE-7
Locust Grove Sch—*school* NY-2
Locust Grove Sch—*school* (4) PA-2
Locust Grove Sch—*school* (2) TN-4
Locust Grove Sch—*school* WV-2
Locust Grove Sch—*school* WI-6
Locust Grove Sch (abandoned)—*school* (2) MO-7
Locust Grove Sch (abandoned)—*school* (3) PA-2
Locust Grove Sch (historical)—*school* MO-7
Locust Grove Sch (historical)—*school* (4) TN-4
Locust Grove School—*locale* IL-6
Locust Grove School (Abandoned)—*locale* MO-7
Locust Grove School (historical)—*locale* MO-7
Locust Grove Station—*locale* MD-2
Locust Grove Stock Farm—*hist pl* KY-4
**Locust Grove Subdivision**—*pop pl* UT-8
Locust Grove Township—*fmr MCD* (2) IA-7
Locust Grove (Township of)—*fmr MCD* AR-4
Locust Grove United Ch of Christ—*church* PA-2
Locust Hill—*hist pl* MO-7
Locust Hill—*hist pl* VA-3
Locust Hill—*locale* KY-4
Locust Hill—*locale* MO-7
Locust Hill—*locale* NC-3
**Locust Hill**—*pop pl* PA-2
**Locust Hill**—*pop pl* SC-3
**Locust Hill**—*pop pl* (2) VA-3
Locust Hill—*summit* (2) MA-1
Locust Hill—*summit* MT-8
Locust Hill—*summit* NY-2
Locust Hill—*summit* PA-2
Locust Hill—*summit* (2) TN-4
*Locust Hill Baptist Church* MS-4
Locust Hill Branch—*stream* MS-4
Locust Hill Cem—*cemetery* IN-6
Locust Hill Cem—*cemetery* KS-7
Locust Hill Cem—*cemetery* MA-1
Locust Hill Cem—*cemetery* MO-7
Locust Hill Cem—*cemetery* NJ-2
Locust Hill Cem—*cemetery* NY-2
Locust Hill Cem—*cemetery* WV-2
Locust Hill Cemetry—*cemetery* MA-1
Locust Hill Ch—*church* GA-3
Locust Hill Ch—*church* KY-4
Locust Hill Ch—*church* LA-4
Locust Hill Ch—*church* MS-4
Locust Hill Ch—*church* NC-3
Locust Hill Ch—*church* PA-2
Locust Hill Country Club—*other* NY-2
**Locust Hill Estates**—*pop pl* MD-2
Locust Hill Oil Field—*oilfield* MS-4
Locust Hill Plantation (historical)—*locale* TN-4
Locust Hill (Township of)—*fmr MCD* NC-3
Locust Hollow—*valley* TN-4
Locust Hollow—*valley* VA-3
Locust Island—*island* ME-1
Locust Junction—*locale* PA-2
Locust Knob—*summit* KY-4
Locust Knob—*summit* (6) NC-3
Locust Knob—*summit* PA-2
Locust Knob—*summit* (4) TN-4
Locust Knob—*summit* (2) VA-3
Locust Knob—*summit* (2) WV-2
Locust Knob Branch—*stream* TN-4
Locust Lake—*flat* AR-4
Locust Lake—*lake* MS-4
**Locust Lake**—*pop pl* OH-6
Locust Lake—*reservoir* NJ-2
Locust Lake—*reservoir* OH-6
Locust Lake—*reservoir* (2) PA-2
Locust Lake Dam—*dam* NJ-2
Locust Lake Dam—*dam* PA-2
Locust Lake State Park—*park* PA-2
**Locust Lakes Village**—*pop pl* PA-2
*Locust Lane* PA-2
**Locust Lane Acres (subdivision)**—*pop pl* PA-2
Locust Lane Ch—*church* IL-6
**Locust Lane Gardens (subdivision)**—*pop pl* PA-2
Locust Lane Sch—*school* WI-6
Locust Lawn—*hist pl* NC-3
Locust Lawn Estate—*hist pl* NY-2
*Locust Level* NC-3
Locust Level Sch—*school* PA-2
Locust Lick Branch—*stream* KY-4
Locust Lick Hollow—*valley* VA-3
Locust Licklog Gap—*gap* NC-3
Locust Log Branch—*stream* NC-3
Locust Log Gap—*gap* GA-3
*Locust Log Ridge* GA-3
Locust Log Ridge—*ridge* (3) GA-3
Locust Manor—*locale* NJ-2
**Locust Manor**—*pop pl* NY-2
**Locust Manor Mobile Home Park**—*pop pl* PA-2
Locust Meadow—*flat* NJ-2
**Locust Mound**—*pop pl* VA-3
**Locust Mount**—*pop pl* VA-3
Locust Mountain—*locale* TN-4
Locust Mount Post Office (historical)—*building* TN-4
Locust Mtn—*range* PA-2
Locust Mtn—*summit* AL-4
Locust Mtn—*summit* (3) AR-4
Locust Mtn—*summit* GA-3
Locust Mtn—*summit* NC-3
Locust Mtn—*summit* OK-5
Locust Mtn—*summit* PA-2
Locust Mtn—*summit* TN-4
Locust Mtn—*summit* VA-3
Locust Mtn—*summit* WV-2
Locust Pen Gap—*gap* NC-3
Locust Playground—*park* OK-5
*Locust Point* IN-6
*Locust Point* MD-2
Locust Point—*cape* FL-3
Locust Point—*cape* (6) MD-2
Locust Point—*cape* MI-6
Locust Point—*cape* NJ-2
Locust Point—*cape* NY-2
Locust Point—*cape* OH-6
Locust Point—*cliff* AZ-5
Locust Point—*cliff* OH-6
**Locust Point**—*pop pl* IN-6
**Locust Point**—*pop pl* NY-2
**Locust Point**—*pop pl* OH-6
**Locust Point**—*pop pl* PA-2
Locust Point—*uninc pl* MD-2
Locust Point Cem—*cemetery* OH-6
Locust Point Marine Terminal—*locale* MD-2
Locust Point Marsh—*swamp* MD-2
Locust Point Sch (abandoned)—*school* PA-2
Locust Pole Knob—*summit* TN-4
Locust Pond—*bay* LA-4
Locust Pond—*lake* MI-6
Locust Pond—*reservoir* MA-1
Locust Pond Dam—*dam* MA-1
Locust Prairie Community Center—*locale* MO-7
Locust Prairie Sch (abandoned)—*school* MO-7
*Locust Reach* ME-1
Locust Reef—*bar* OH-6
*Locust Ridge* NC-3
**Locust Ridge**—*pop pl* LA-4

**Locust Ridge**—pop pl OH-6
**Locust Ridge**—pop pl PA-2
Locust Ridge—ridge AL-4
Locust Ridge—ridge AR-4
Locust Ridge—ridge KY-4
Locust Ridge—ridge (6) NC-3
Locust Ridge—ridge (2) PA-2
Locust Ridge—ridge TN-4
Locust Ridge—ridge (3) VA-3
Locust Ridge—ridge (2) WV-2
Locust Ridge Branch—stream VA-3
Locust Ridge Cem—cemetery PA-2
Locust Ridge Cem—cemetery VT-1
Locust Ridge Ch—church TN-4
**Locust Ridge Manor (subdivision)**—pop pl PA-2
Locust Ridge Oil Field—oilfield LA-4
Locust Ridge Sch (abandoned)—school PA-2
Locust Ridge Sch (historical)—school MO-7
Locust Ridge Sch (historical)—school PA-2
Locust Rough Mtn—summit NC-3
Locust Rough Ridge—ridge NC-3
Locust Row Airp—airport PA-2
**Locust Run**—pop pl PA-2
Locust Run—stream (2) MD-2
Locust Run—stream PA-2
Locust Run—stream VA-3
Locust Run—stream WV-2
Locust Run Cem—cemetery PA-2
Locust Run (historical)—stream PA-2
Locust Sch—hist pl IA-7
Locust Sch—school IL-6
Locust Sch—school NE-7
Locust Sch—school NY-2
Locust Sch—school NC-3
Locust Sch—school TX-5
Locust Sch—school WI-6
Locust Sch (historical)—school MO-7
*Locust School* KY-4
Locust School Gap—gap GA-3
Locust School (Museum)—locale IA-7
Locust Shopes Cave—cave AL-4
Locust Site (33MU160)—hist pl OH-6
Locust Slough—stream AR-4
*Locust Spring* TN-4
**Locust Spring**—pop pl PA-2
Locust Spring—spring (4) AZ-5
Locust Spring Gap—gap NC-3
Locust Spring Post Office (historical)—building TN-4
Locust Spring Run—stream VA-3
Locust Spring Run Trail—trail VA-3
Locust Springs—locale TN-4
Locust Stake Gap—gap GA-3
Locust Street Baptist Ch—church MS-4
Locust Street Ch of Christ—church TN-4
Locust Street Park—park PA-2
**Locust Summit**—pop pl PA-2
Locust Summit Fines Plant Dam—dam PA-2
Locust Summit Retention Pond—reservoir PA-2
Locust Tank—reservoir AZ-5
Locust Thicket—stream KY-4
Locust Thicket—stream VA-3
Locust Thicket Lake—lake LA-4
Locust Thicket Mtn—summit VA-3
Locust Thorn Ridge—ridge TN-4
**Locust (Township of)**—pop pl IL-6
**Locust (Township of)**—pop pl PA-2
Locust Tree Branch—stream NC-3
Locust Tree Cem—cemetery MS-4
Locust Tree Gap—gap (2) NC-3
Locust Tree Landing—locale SC-3
Locust Tree Sch (historical)—school MS-4
Locust Valley—basin MD-2
Locust Valley—locale MD-2
Locust Valley—locale (2) PA-2
**Locust Valley**—pop pl NY-2
Locust Valley Ch—church MO-7
Locust Valley Country Club—locale MA-1
Locust Valley Country Club—other PA-2
*Locust Valley Golf Course* PA-2
Locust Valley HS—school NY-2
Locust Valley Sch (abandoned)—school PA-2
Locustville—locale DE-2
**Locustville**—pop pl RI-1
**Locustville**—pop pl VA-3
Locustville Pond—lake RI-1
Locustville Pond—reservoir RI-1
Locustville Pond Dam—dam RI-1
**Locustwood**—pop pl NJ-2
**Locustwood**—pop pl NY-2
Locustwood Cem—cemetery NJ-2
Locus 7 Site—hist pl PA-2
*Lod* FM-9
Loda—locale WV-2
**Loda**—pop pl IL-6
*Lodabar Church* MS-4
Lodabar Sch (historical)—school MS-4
Loda Center (historical)—locale KS-7
Loda Lake—lake MI-6
Lodal Creek—stream PA-2
Lodale—locale KY-4
**Loda Township**—pop pl KS-7
**Loda (Township of)**—pop pl IL-6
*Lodde's Mill* WI-6
Loddes Mill—locale WI-6
Loddes Mill Bluff—cliff WI-6
Lodebar—locale VA-3
Lodebar Cem—cemetery MS-4
Lodebar Ch—church MS-4
*Lodebar Methodist Ch* MS-4
Lode Creek—stream MI-6
**Lodema Township**—pop pl ND-7
Lodemia—locale IL-6
Lodemier Lake—lake MN-6
Loden Branch—stream TN-4
Loden Branch—stream TX-5
Loden Creek—stream MS-4
Loden Mtn—summit TN-4
Loden Ridge—ridge TN-4
Lo De Padilla Grant—civil NM-5
Lo De Padilla Grant (Peralta Tract)—civil NM-5
**Loder**—pop pl OK-5
Loder Creek—stream KY-4
*Loderick Creek* MD-2
Loder Sch—school NV-8
Loder Siding—locale OK-5
*Lodeson Church* TN-4
Lodestone Mine—mine CA-9
*Lodge* AR-4
Lodge—hist pl IN-6
Lodge—locale MO-7
Lodge—locale TN-4
**Lodge**—pop pl IL-6
**Lodge**—pop pl SC-3
**Lodge**—pop pl VA-3
Lodge, Henry Cabot, House—hist pl MA-1
Lodge, Lake—reservoir CO-8
Lodge, Mount—summit AK-9
Lodge, The—building TX-5
*Lodge Branch* VA-3
Lodge Campground—locale UT-8
Lodge Canyon—valley CA-9
Lodge Canyon—valley NM-5
Lodge (CCD)—cens area SC-3
Lodge Cem—cemetery MO-7
**Lodgecliffe**—pop pl MD-2
Lodgecliffe Canal—stream MD-2
**Lodge Corner**—pop pl AR-4
*Lodge Creek* GA-3
Lodge Creek—stream (3) ID-8
Lodge Creek—stream IN-6
Lodge Creek—stream MT-8
Lodge Creek—stream NC-3
Lodge Creek—stream OR-9
Lodge Creek—stream TX-5
Lodge Creek—stream VA-3
Lodge Creek—stream (2) WA-9
Lodge Elem Sch—school IN-6
**Lodge Forest**—pop pl MD-2
**Lodge Grass**—pop pl MT-8
Lodge Grass Canal Number One—canal MT-8
Lodge Grass Canal Number Two—canal MT-8
Lodge Grass Canyon—valley MT-8
Lodge Grass Cem—cemetery MT-8
Lodge Grass City Jail—hist pl MT-8
Lodge Grass Creek—stream MT-8
Lodge Grass Creek—stream WY-8
Lodge Grass Feeder Canal—canal MT-8
Lodge Grass Merchandise Company Store—hist pl MT-8
Lodge Grass Storage Rsvr—reservoir MT-8
**Lodge Hall**—pop pl SC-3
Lodge Hall Sch—school KY-4
Lodge Island—island AK-9
Lodge Lake—lake CO-8
Lodge Lake—lake LA-4
Lodge Lake—lake MI-6
Lodge Lake—lake WA-9
Lodge of the Pines—locale CO-8
Lodge Park (County Forest Preserve)—park IL-6
Lodge Playground—park MI-6
Lodge Point—cape NJ-2
Lodge Point—cape TN-4
Lodge Point—summit ID-8
*Lodgepole (2)* MT-8
Lodgepole—locale (2) CA-9
**Lodge Pole**—pop pl CA-9
**Lodge Pole**—pop pl MT-8
**Lodgepole**—pop pl NE-7
**Lodgepole**—pop pl SD-7
Lodge Pole Buttes—range SD-7
Lodgepole Campground—locale CO-8
Lodgepole Campground—locale ID-8
Lodgepole Campground—locale (2) MT-8
Lodge Pole Campground—locale UT-8
Lodgepole Campground—locale WA-9
Lodgepole Campground—park UT-8
Lodgepole Canal—canal UT-8
Lodgepole Canyon—valley UT-8
*Lodge Pole Creek* CO-8
*Lodgepole Creek* MT-8
*Lodge Pole Creek* SD-7
*Lodgepole Creek* WY-8
Lodgepole Creek—stream CO-8
Lodgepole Creek—stream (5) ID-8
Lodgepole Creek—stream (4) MT-8
Lodge Pole Creek—stream MT-8
Lodgepole Creek—stream (6) MT-8
Lodgepole Creek—stream NE-7
Lodge Pole Creek—stream OK-5
Lodgepole Creek—stream (2) OR-9
Lodgepole Creek—stream SD-7
Lodgepole Creek—stream (2) UT-8
Lodgepole Creek—stream (4) WA-9
Lodgepole Creek—stream (3) WY-8
Lodgepole Creek Oil Field—oilfield WY-8
Lodgepole Creek Trail—trail MT-8
Lodgepole Dam—dam SD-7
Lodgepole Guard Station—locale OR-9
Lodgepole Gulch—valley ID-8
Lodge Pole Hump—summit ID-8
Lodgepole Lake—lake (2) ID-8
Lodgepole Lake—lake OR-9
Lodgepole Lake—lake UT-8
Lodgepole Mtn—summit MT-8
Lodgepole Opera House—hist pl NE-7
Lodgepole Picnic Area—area CA-9
Lodgepole Point—summit ID-8
Lodgepole Rsvr—reservoir UT-8
Lodgepole Saddle—gap MT-8
Lodgepole Sch—school SD-7
Lodgepole Spring—spring CA-9
Lodgepole Spring—spring MT-8
Lodgepole Spring—spring (4) OR-9
Lodgepole Spring—spring WA-9
Lodgepole Springs—spring ID-8
**Lodgepole Township**—pop pl SD-7
Lodgepole Trail—trail (3) MT-8
Lodgepole Trail—trail WY-8
Lodgepole Trail (jeep)—trail OR-9
Lodgepole Wayside Park—park NE-7
Lodge Pool—lake NY-2
Lodge Post Office (historical)—building TN-4
Lodge Ranch—locale OR-9
Lodge Ridge—ridge OH-6
Lodge Ridge Cem—cemetery OH-6
Lodge Rsvr Number One—reservoir OR-9
Lodge Rsvr Number Two—reservoir OR-9
*Lodge Rsvr 1* OR-9
Lodge Sch—school IL-6
Lodge Sch—school IN-6
Lodge Sch—school MI-6
Lodge Sch—school SD-7
*Lodges Corners* AR-4
Lodge Trail—trail VA-3
Lodge Trail Ridge—ridge WY-8
**Lodgeville**—pop pl WV-2
**Lodgeville (Ocean Mines)**—pop pl WV-2
Lodge Zare Zapadu No. 44—hist pl MN-6
*Lodi* KS-7
*Lodi* TN-4
Lodi—locale AR-4
Lodi—locale CO-8
Lodi—locale MI-6
Lodi—locale MS-4
Lodi—locale NE-7
Lodi—locale OK-5
Lodi—locale PA-2
Lodi—locale SD-7
Lodi—locale TN-4
Lodi—locale TX-5
Lodi—locale VA-3
**Lodi**—pop pl CA-9
**Lodi**—pop pl IN-6
**Lodi**—pop pl MS-4
**Lodi**—pop pl MO-7
**Lodi**—pop pl NJ-2
**Lodi**—pop pl NY-2
**Lodi**—pop pl OH-6
**Lodi**—pop pl PA-2
**Lodi**—pop pl WI-6
Lodi Acad—school CA-9
Lodiana Cem—cemetery KS-7
Lodi Arch—hist pl CA-9
Lodi Branch—stream TX-5
Lodiburg—locale KY-4
Lodi Canyon—valley CA-9
Lodi (CCD)—cens area CA-9
Lodi Cem—cemetery CA-9
Lodi Cem—cemetery KS-7
Lodi Cem—cemetery MI-6
Lodi Cem—cemetery NE-7
Lodi Cem—cemetery NJ-2
Lodi Cem—cemetery SD-7
Lodi Cem—cemetery TX-5
Lodi Center—locale NY-2
Lodi Ch—church MI-6
Lodi Creek—stream MS-4
Lodi Creek—stream WA-9
*Lodi Gas Field* CA-9
Lodi Hills—range NV-8
Lodi (historical)—locale KS-7
Lodi Junction—locale CA-9
Lodi Junction—uninc pl NJ-2
Lodi Landing (historical)—locale MS-4
Lodi Marsh—swamp WI-6
Lodi Marsh State Wildlife Area—swamp WI-6
Lodi Methodist Church—hist pl NY-2
*Lodi Mill* WI-6
Lodi Municipal Lake Park—park CA-9
Lodi Point—cape NY-2
**Lodi Point**—pop pl NY-2
*Lodi Post Office* TN-4
Lodi Post Office (historical)—building MS-4
Lodi Post Office (historical)—building TN-4
Lodi Sch—school NE-7
Lodi Sch—school TX-5
Lodi Senior Sch—school CA-9
Lodi Station—locale NY-2
Lodi Tank—reservoir NV-8
**Lodi (Town of)**—pop pl NY-2
**Lodi (Town of)**—pop pl WI-6
**Lodi Township**—pop pl SD-7
**Lodi (Township of)**—pop pl MI-6
**Lodi (Township of)**—pop pl MN-6
**Lodi (Township of)**—pop pl OH-6
Lodi Valley—valley NV-8
*Lodj* MP-9
**Lodjic**—pop pl UT-8
Lodlow Revetment—levee AR-4
*Lodo* MP-9
**Lodoga**—pop pl CA-9
Lodoga Peak—summit CA-9
Lodomillo Township—fmr MCD IA-7
**Lodonberry Estates (subdivision)**—pop pl NC-3
Lodo Pond—lake NY-2
Lodore—locale VA-3
Lodore, Canyon—valley CO-8
Lodore, Lake—lake PA-2
*Lodore Creek* OR-9
Lodore Creek—stream OR-9
Lodore Mine—mine CO-8
Lodore Ranger Station—locale CO-8
Lodore Sch—school CO-8
Lodoso, Cerro—summit CA-9
LO Draw—valley AZ-5
**Lodwick**—pop pl TX-5
Lodwick Ch—church TX-5
Loe, Moku o—island HI-9
Loea Point—cape HI-9
**Loeb**—pop pl TX-5
Loeb, Alex, Bldg—hist pl MS-4
Loeb, Ernest, House—hist pl IL-6
Loeb, Nathan, House—hist pl OR-9
Loebau—locale TX-5
Loebau Siding—locale TX-5
Loeb Bay—bay MI-6
Loeb Cem—cemetery MO-7
Loeb Cem—cemetery TX-5
Loeb Creek—stream MI-6
Loeber Canyon—valley CA-9
Loeber Gulch—valley UT-8
*Loe Blue River* KS-7
Loeb Point—cape MI-6
Loeb Ranch—locale NE-7
Loebs Landing—locale NC-3
Loeck Sch—school IA-7
Loefler Ditch—canal IN-6
**Loehencove Ridge (subdivision)**—pop pl NC-3
Loehmann Cem—cemetery TX-5
Loehmanns (OPlaza (Shop Ctr)—locale MO-7
Loehmanns Plaza—locale MO-7
Loehmanns Plaza—locale NC-3
Loehmanns Plaza (Shop Ctr)—locale FL-3
Loehmann Village Shop Ctr—locale AL-4
Loehme—locale MI-6
Loehner Sch (abandoned)—school MO-7
**Loehr**—pop pl MO-7
*Loen* MP-9
Loerch—locale MN-6
Loerch State Wildlife Mngmt Area—park MN-6
Loers, Benjamin, House—hist pl WA-9
Loers Pond—lake WA-9
Loerzel Beer Hall—hist pl NY-2
Loesche Ridge—ridge MO-7
Loeser, Dr. Irwin D., Log Cabin—hist pl OK-5
Loes Lake—lake NE-7
Loes Rsvrs—reservoir OR-9
Loethers Plantation—locale AR-4
*Loet Island* NY-2
Loew, William Goadby, House—hist pl NY-2
Loew-Define Grocery Store and Home—hist pl OH-6
Loewen Creek—stream OR-9
Loewen Rsvr—reservoir OR-9
Loewenstein and Sons Hardware Bldg—hist pl WV-2
**Loewi (historical)**—pop pl OR-9
Loew Lake—reservoir IN-6
Loew Lake Dam South—dam IN-6
Loew's and United Artists State Theatre—hist pl KY-4
Loew's Midland Theater-Midland Bldg—hist pl MO-7
Loew's State Theater—hist pl NY-2
Loew's State Theatre—hist pl RI-1
Loew's Theatre—hist pl OH-6
Loews Theatre—hist pl VA-3
**Lofall**—pop pl WA-9
Lofdahl Springs—spring CO-8
Lofer Bench—bench AZ-5
Lofer Cienega—swamp AZ-5
Lofer Cienega Creek—stream AZ-5
Lofers Bend Park—park TX-5
Loff Bay—bay ID-8
Lofferts Airp (private)—airport PA-2
Lofferty Springs—spring AR-4
Lofgreen—locale UT-8
*Lofield Church* AL-4
Lofland, Peter, House—hist pl DE-2
Lofland Creek—stream AR-4
Lofland Ditch—canal IN-6
Lofland Gulch—valley CO-8
Lofland Lake—reservoir TX-5
LO Flat—flat AZ-5
Loflin—locale AL-4
Loflin Ch—church AL-4
Loflin Lake—reservoir NC-3
Loflin Lake Dam—dam MS-4
Loflin Lake Dam—dam NC-3
Loflin Sch—school NC-3
Loflins Pond—reservoir AL-4
Loflins Store—locale NC-3
Lofon—area GU-9
Loft, The—basin CO-8
Loften Bayou—stream LA-4
Loften Cem—cemetery AL-4
Loft Hist Dist North—hist pl MD-2
Loft Hist Dist South—hist pl MD-2
Loftin—other GA-3
**Loftin**—pop pl GA-3
Loftin Canyon—valley TX-5
Loftin Cem—cemetery MO-7
Loftin Cem—cemetery TN-4
Loftin Cem—cemetery TX-5
Loftin Ch (abandoned)—church MO-7
Loftin Creek—stream TX-5
Loftin Hill—summit TN-4
Loftin Sch (historical)—school MO-7
**Loftins Crossroad**—pop pl NC-3
**Loftins Crossroads**—pop pl NC-3
Loftis Cem—cemetery MO-7
Loftis Cem—cemetery TN-4
Loftis Creek—stream AR-4
Loftis Hollow—valley TN-4
Loftis Mtn—summit GA-3
Loft Lake—lake MN-6
Loft Mountain Campgrounds—locale VA-3
Loft Mountain Overlook—locale VA-3
Loft Mtn—summit VA-3
Lofton—locale AR-4
Lofton—locale LA-4
Lofton—locale VA-3
**Lofton**—pop pl TN-4
Lofton Cem—cemetery CA-9
Lofton Cem—cemetery FL-3
Lofton Cem—cemetery GA-3
Lofton Cem—cemetery LA-4
Lofton Ch—church GA-3
Lofton Creek—stream FL-3
Lofton Creek—stream OR-9
Lofton Dam—dam OR-9
Lofton Island—island FL-3
Lofton Lake—lake OR-9
Lofton Lake—reservoir IL-6
Lofton Lake—swamp AR-4
Lofton Point—cape FL-3
Lofton Pond—lake FL-3
Lofton Rsvr—reservoir OR-9
Loftons Branch—stream SC-3
Lofton Sch—school GA-3
*Lofts Creek* MS-4
Lofts Pond Park—park NY-2
*Loftus* CA-9
**Loftus**—pop pl CA-9
Loftus Canyon—valley CA-9
Loftus Creek—stream ID-8
Loftus Creek—stream OR-9
*Loftus Heights* MS-4
Loftus Mine—mine CA-9
**Lofty**—pop pl AL-4
**Lofty**—pop pl PA-2
Lofty Creek—stream PA-2
Lofty Gulch—valley AK-9
Lofty Lake—lake UT-8
Lofty Lake Trail—trail UT-8
Lofty Mtn—summit AK-9
Lofty Reservoir Dam—dam PA-2
Lofty Rsvr—reservoir PA-2
*Lofty Ruth Lake* UT-8
Lofty Tunnel—tunnel PA-2
*Log* MS-4
*Logaf* FM-9
Logah Meadow Campground—locale CA-9
*Logalap* FM-9
*Logan* AZ-5
*Logan* PA-2
Logan—fmr MCD (5) NE-7
Logan—locale AR-4
Logan—locale CA-9
Logan—locale CO-8
Logan—locale GA-3
Logan—locale NE-7
Logan—locale ND-7
Logan—locale OK-5
Logan—locale PA-2
Logan—locale TX-5
Logan—locale VA-3
**Logan**—pop pl (2) AL-4
**Logan**—pop pl IL-6
**Logan**—pop pl (2) IN-6
**Logan**—pop pl IA-7
**Logan**—pop pl KS-7
**Logan**—pop pl MO-7
**Logan**—pop pl MT-8
**Logan**—pop pl NM-5
**Logan**—pop pl NY-2
**Logan**—pop pl NC-3
**Logan**—pop pl OH-6
**Logan**—pop pl OR-9
**Logan**—pop pl PA-2
**Logan**—pop pl UT-8
**Logan**—pop pl WV-2
Logan, George W., House—hist pl NC-3
Logan, Henry, Memorial AME Church—hist pl WV-2
Logan, John, House—hist pl KY-4
Logan, Lake—lake FL-3
Logan, Lake—lake NC-3
Logan, Lake—reservoir NC-3
Logan, Lake—reservoir TN-4
Logan, Mount—summit AK-9
Logan, Mount—summit AZ-5
Logan, Mount—summit (2) CO-8
Logan, Mount—summit MT-8
Logan, Mount—summit OH-6
Logan, Mount—summit WA-9
Logan, Mount—summit WY-8
Logan, Thomas E., House—hist pl ID-8
Logan, W. W., House—hist pl KY-4
**Logana**—pop pl KY-4
Logan Aero Light—locale MA-1
Logan and Hyde Park Canal—canal UT-8
Logan Ave Elem Sch—school KS-7
Logan Basin—basin CA-9
Logan Bayou—stream LA-4
Logan Beach—beach AK-9
Logan Bluff—cliff AL-4
Logan Bluffs—cliff AK-9
Logan Bog—swamp ME-1
*Logan Branch* AL-4
*Logan Branch* TN-4
Logan Branch—stream AL-4
Logan Branch—stream GA-3
Logan Branch—stream (6) KY-4
Logan Branch—stream MN-6
Logan Branch—stream MS-4
Logan Branch—stream (3) MO-7
Logan Branch—stream NE-7
Logan Branch—stream NC-3
Logan Branch—stream PA-2
Logan Branch—stream TX-5
Logan Branch Marshall Univ—school WV-2
*Logan Branch Spring Creek* PA-2
*Logan Brook* PA-2
Logan Brook—stream (6) ME-1
*Logan Butte* OR-9
Logan Butte—summit OR-9
Logan Butte Dam—dam OR-9
Logan Butte Rsvr—reservoir OR-9
Logan-Cache Airp—airport UT-8
Logan Camp—locale OH-6
Logan Camp Branch—stream MO-7
Logan Canyon—valley (2) CA-9
Logan Canyon—valley NE-7
Logan Canyon—valley NV-8
Logan Canyon—valley NM-5
Logan Canyon—valley UT-8
Logan Cave—cave AR-4
Logan Cave—cave UT-8
Logan (CCD)—cens area AL-4
Logan Cem—cemetery (4) AL-4
Logan Cem—cemetery FL-3
Logan Cem—cemetery (2) IL-6
Logan Cem—cemetery (2) IN-6
Logan Cem—cemetery (2) IA-7
Logan Cem—cemetery KS-7
Logan Cem—cemetery KY-4
Logan Cem—cemetery (2) MI-6
Logan Cem—cemetery MS-4
Logan Cem—cemetery (3) MO-7
Logan Cem—cemetery MT-8
Logan Cem—cemetery (3) NE-7
Logan Cem—cemetery NM-5
Logan Cem—cemetery OH-6
Logan Cem—cemetery SD-7
Logan Cem—cemetery UT-8
**Logan Center**—pop pl ND-7
Logan Center Cem—cemetery ND-7
Logan Center Ch—church NE-7
Logan Center Dam—dam ND-7
Logan Center Sch—school NE-7
Logan Center Street Hist Dist—hist pl UT-8
**Logan Center Township**—pop pl ND-7
Logan Ch—church (2) AL-4
Logan Ch—church KS-7
Logan Ch—church MI-6
Logan Ch—church ND-7
Logan Ch—church OH-6
Logan Chapel—church NC-3
Logan Chapel—church (2) TN-4
Logan Chapel—church TX-5
Logan Chapel Sch (historical)—school TN-4
Logan Circle—locale DC-2
Logan Circle—locale PA-2
Logan Circle Hist Dist—hist pl DC-2
*Logan City* AZ-5
Logan City Dam—dam KS-7
Logan City Hall—hist pl OH-6
Logan City Lake—reservoir KS-7
Logan Coll (historical)—school AL-4
Logan Corners—locale MI-6
*Logan (corporate name Hanaford)* IL-6
Logan Country Club—other UT-8
Logan County—civil KS-7
Logan County—civil ND-7
**Logan (County)**—pop pl AR-4
**Logan (County)**—pop pl IL-6
**Logan (County)**—pop pl KY-4
**Logan (County)**—pop pl OH-6
**Logan (County)**—pop pl OK-5
**Logan (County)**—pop pl WV-2
Logan County Courthouse—hist pl CO-8
Logan County Courthouse—hist pl ND-7
Logan County Courthouse—hist pl OH-6
Logan County Courthouse—hist pl OK-5
Logan County Courthouse, Eastern District—hist pl AR-4
Logan County State Lake Dam—dam KS-7
Logan County State Park—park KS-7
Logan Cove—valley NC-3
*Logan Creek* ID-8
*Logan Creek* IN-6
*Logan Creek* MT-8
*Logan Creek* NE-7
*Logan Creek* PA-2
Logan Creek—stream AL-4
Logan Creek—stream AK-9
Logan Creek—stream (2) AR-4
Logan Creek—stream (4) CA-9
Logan Creek—stream FL-3
Logan Creek—stream GA-3
Logan Creek—stream ID-8
Logan Creek—stream IL-6
Logan Creek—stream (2) IN-6
Logan Creek—stream (2) KY-4
Logan Creek—stream (7) MO-7
Logan Creek—stream (5) MT-8
Logan Creek—stream NV-8
Logan Creek—stream (2) NC-3
Logan Creek—stream (3) OR-9
Logan Creek—stream TX-5
Logan Creek—stream VA-3
Logan Creek—stream WA-9
Logan Creek—stream (2) WI-6
Logan Creek—stream WY-8
Logan Creek Ch—church IN-6
*Logan Creek Ditch* NE-7
Logan Creek Dredge—canal NE-7
Logan Creek Patrol Cabin—hist pl MT-8
Logan Creek Sch (abandoned)—school MO-7
Logan Creek Site—hist pl NE-7
Logan Creek State For—forest MO-7
Logan Creek Trail—trail MT-8
*Logan Cross* IN-6
*Logan Crossroads* IN-6
Logan Cut—stream OR-9
Logandale—locale CA-9
**Logandale**—pop pl NV-8
Logandale Overton Interchange—crossing NV-8
Logan Dam—reservoir SD-7
Logan Demonstration Sch—hist pl PA-2
Logan Division—civil AL-4
Logan Division—civil UT-8
Logan Draw—valley NM-5
Logan Draw—valley (2) WY-8
Logan Draw Oil Field—other NM-5
Logan (Election Precinct)—fmr MCD IL-6
*Logan Elem Sch* PA-2
Logan Elem Sch—school KS-7
Logan Elem Sch—school PA-2
Logan Elm HS—school OH-6
Logan Elm State Memorial—park OH-6
Logan Family Cem—cemetery AL-4
Logan Field—park MA-1
Logan Field Municipal Airp—airport AL-4
Logan Fish Hatchery—other UT-8
Logan Fish Hatchery Caretaker's Residence—hist pl UT-8
Logan Fork—stream KY-4
Logan Fork—stream WV-2
Logan Furnace Mansion—hist pl PA-2
*Logan Gap* PA-2
Logan Gap—gap AR-4
Logan Gap—gap (3) KY-4
Logan Gap—gap NC-3
Logan Gap—gap PA-2
Logan Gap Mtn—summit AR-4
Logan Gas Field—other MI-6
Logan Glacier—glacier AK-9
Logan Glacier—glacier MT-8
Logan Grove Park—park KS-7
Logan Gulch—valley AK-9
Logan Gulch—valley (3) CA-9
Logan Gulch—valley MT-8
Logan Gulch—valley WY-8
Logan Gulch Oil Well No 1—locale WY-8
Logan Gulch Oil Well No 2—locale WY-8
Logan Hall Ch—church AR-4
**Logan Heights**—pop pl TX-5
**Logan Heights**—pop pl WV-2
Logan Heights—uninc pl CA-9
**Logan Heights (subdivision)**—pop pl TN-4
Logan Hill—summit (2) CO-8
Logan Hill—summit NY-2
Logan Hill—summit (2) TN-4
Logan Hill—summit WA-9
Logan Hill (CCD)—cens area WA-9
Logan Hill Ch—church WA-9
Logan Hill Sch (historical)—school PA-2
Logan Hollow—valley AR-4
Logan Hollow—valley IL-6
Logan Hollow—valley IN-6
Logan Hollow—valley (3) KY-4
Logan Hollow—valley OK-5
Logan Hollow—valley WY-8
Logan Hollow Ch—church IL-6
Logan House—hist pl DE-2
Logan House—hist pl KY-4
Logan House Creek—stream NV-8
Logan HS—school UT-8
Logan HS—school WI-6
Logan HS Gymnasium—hist pl UT-8
Logan Hyde Park and Smithfield Canal—canal UT-8
Logania Ch—church PA-2
Logan International Airport, General Edward Lawrence—airport MA-1
Loganita Lodge—locale WA-9
**Logan (Itom)**—pop pl NC-3
Logan Japanese Christian Ch—church UT-8
Logan JHS—school AL-4
Logan JHS—school IA-7
Logan Junction Rsvr—reservoir WY-8
*Logan Junior High School* KS-7
*Logan Lake* AL-4
*Logan Lake* OH-6
Logan Lake—lake CA-9
Logan Lake—lake ID-8
Logan Lake—lake MI-6
Logan Lake—lake MN-6
Logan Lake—lake MO-7
Logan Lake—reservoir GA-3
Logan Lakes—lake MI-6
Logan LDS Sixth Ward Church—hist pl UT-8
Logan (Magisterial District)—fmr MCD WV-2

Logan Martin Dam—*dam* AL-4
**Logan Martin Dam**—*pop pl* AL-4
Logan Martin Lake—*reservoir* AL-4
Logan Martin Lake Ch of Christ—*church* AL-4
**Logan Martin Lake Estates**—*pop pl* AL-4
**Logan Martin Pines**—*pop pl* AL-4
*Logan Martin Reservoir* AL-4
Logan Memorial Ch—*church* FM-9
**Logan Mills**—*pop pl* PA-2
Logan Mills Covered Bridge—*hist pl* PA-2
Logan Mills Gristmill—*hist pl* PA-2
Logan Mine—*mine* AZ-5
Logan Mine—*mine* CA-9
Logan Mine—*mine* CO-8
Logan Mine Spring—*spring* (2) AZ-5
Logan-Missouri Valley Country Club—*other* IA-7
*Logan Mountain* MT-8
Logan Mtn—*summit* AR-4
Logan Mtn—*summit* (2) CA-9
Logan Mtn—*summit* ID-8
Logan Mtn—*summit* (2) MO-7
Logan Mtn—*summit* NC-3
Logan Mtn—*summit* WY-8
Logan Municipal Slaughterhouse—*hist pl* UT-8
Logan-Nara Visa (CCD)—*cens area* NM-5
Logan Nine Hundred Forty-Five Ditch—*canal* IN-6
Logan Northern Canal—*canal* UT-8
Logan North Field Canal—*canal* UT-8
Logan Northwest Field Canal—*canal* UT-8
Logan Park—*park* AL-4
Logan Park—*park* KS-7
Logan Park—*park* MA-1
Logan Park—*park* MN-6
Logan Park—*park* NE-7
Logan Park—*uninc pl* VA-3
Logan Park Campground—*locale* MT-8
Logan Park Cem—*cemetery* IA-7
Logan Pass—*gap* MT-8
Logan Pass—*gap* NV-8
*Logan Peak* WA-9
Logan Peak—*summit* NV-8
Logan Peak—*summit* UT-8
Logan Place—*locale* WY-8
Logan Plant—*airport* NJ-2
Logan Point—*cape* AL-4
Logan Point—*cape* PA-2
Logan Point—*cliff* AR-4
Logan Point—*summit* AL-4
Logan Pond—*lake* FL-3
Logan Pond—*reservoir* LA-4
Logan Pond—*reservoir* SC-3
Logan Ponds—*lake* ME-1
*Loganport* IN-6
Logan Post Office—*building* AL-4
Logan Post Office—*building* UT-8
Logan Potrero—*flat* CA-9
Logan Pride Sch—*school* NE-7
Logan Ranch—*locale* CO-8
Logan Ranch—*locale* MT-8
Logan Ranch—*locale* NM-5
Logan Ranch—*locale* ND-7
Logan Ranch—*locale* TX-5
Logan Reef—*bar* AK-9
*Logan Reform Cemetery* SD-7
Logan Regional Hosp—*hospital* UT-8
Logan Regional Hospital Heliport—*airport* UT-8
Logan Ridge—*ridge* (2) CA-9
Logan Ridge—*ridge* KY-4
Logan Ridge—*ridge* MO-7
Logan River—*stream* ID-8
Logan River—*stream* UT-8
Logan-Rogersville HS—*school* MO-7
Logan Rsvr—*reservoir* WY-8
Logan Run—*stream* KY-4
Logan Run—*stream* (3) PA-2
Logan Run—*stream* (2) WV-2
*Logan Sch* PA-2
Logan Sch—*hist pl* SC-3
Logan Sch—*school* DC-2
Logan Sch—*school* (11) IL-6
Logan Sch—*school* IN-6
Logan Sch—*school* (2) IA-7
Logan Sch—*school* KY-4
Logan Sch—*school* MI-6
Logan Sch—*school* MS-4
Logan Sch—*school* (2) MO-7
Logan Sch—*school* NE-7
Logan Sch—*school* NC-3
Logan Sch—*school* ND-7
Logan Sch—*school* OR-9
Logan Sch—*school* (5) PA-2
Logan Sch—*school* SC-3
Logan Sch—*school* WA-9
Logan Sch (abandoned)—*school* (2) PA-2
Logans Chapel Cem—*cemetery* (2) TN-4
*Logans Chapel Methodist Church* TN-4
*Logans Chapel School* TN-4
*Logans Chapel United Methodist Church* TN-4
Logan Sch (historical)—*school* (2) MO-7
Logan Sch House K-834—*hist pl* DE-2
Logan Sch No 6—*school* IL-6
Logan School—*park* DE-2
Logan Senior HS—*school* KS-7
Logans Ferry—*locale* PA-2
**Logans Ferry Heights**—*pop pl* PA-2
Logan Shoals—*bar* NV-8
Logans Hollow—*valley* TN-4
**Logans Lake**—*pop pl* TN-4
Logans Lake—*reservoir* TN-4
Logans Lake Dam—*dam* TN-4
*Logans Landing* AL-4
Logan Slough—*stream* CA-9
Logan Slough—*stream* OR-9
Logansport—*locale* KY-4
**Logansport**—*pop pl* IN-6
**Logansport**—*pop pl* IA-7
**Logansport**—*pop pl* LA-4
**Logansport**—*pop pl* PA-2
**Logansport**—*pop pl* WV-2
Logansport Community HS—*school* IN-6
Logansport Gas Field—*oilfield* LA-4
Logansport Municipal Airp—*airport* IN-6
Logansport Oil and Gas Field—*oilfield* LA-4
Logansport Post Office (historical)—*building* PA-2
**Logansport Township**—*pop pl* KS-7
*Logan Spring* PA-2
Logan Spring—*spring* AR-4
Logan Spring—*spring* (5) CA-9
Logan Spring—*spring* (2) NV-8
Logan Spring—*spring* NM-5
Logan Spring Run—*stream* PA-2
*Logan Square* IL-6
Logan Square—*hist pl* PA-2
Logan Square—*park* IL-6
Logan Square Boulevards Hist Dist—*hist pl* IL-6
*Logans Run* PA-2
*Logans Shoals* AL-4
Logan State Fishing Lake and Wildlife Area—*park* KS-7
Logan Station—*locale* MA-1
Logan Store (Township of)—*fmr MCD* NC-3
Logan Street Sch—*school* CA-9
*Logansville* GA-3
*Logansville* PA-2
Logansville—*locale* NJ-2
**Logansville**—*pop pl* OH-6
Logan Tabernacle—*hist pl* UT-8
Logan Tank—*reservoir* NM-5
Logan Temple—*church* UT-8
Logan Temple—*hist pl* UT-8
Logan Temple African Methodist Episcopal Zion Ch—*church* TN-4
Logan Temple Barn—*hist pl* UT-8
Logan Thoene Number 1 Dam—*dam* SD-7
**Loganton**—*pop pl* PA-2
Loganton Borough—*civil* PA-2
**Loganton (historical)**—*pop pl* TN-4
Loganton Post Office (historical)—*building* TN-4
**Logantown**—*pop pl* KY-4
*Logan Township* KS-7
Logan Township—*civ div* KS-7
Logan Township—*civ div* NE-7
Logan Township—*civil* KS-7
Logan Township—*civil* (2) MO-7
Logan Township—*civil* (2) SD-7
Logan Township—*fmr MCD* (7) IA-7
Logan Township—*inact MCD* NV-8
**Logan Township**—*pop pl* (18) KS-7
**Logan Township**—*pop pl* (11) NE-7
**Logan Township**—*pop pl* ND-7
**Logan Township**—*pop pl* (7) SD-7
Logan Township Cem—*cemetery* (2) IA-7
Logan Township Hall—*building* SD-7
Logan (Township of)—*fmr MCD* (4) AR-4
**Logan (Township of)**—*pop pl* IL-6
**Logan (Township of)**—*pop pl* (3) IN-6
**Logan (Township of)**—*pop pl* (2) MI-6
**Logan (Township of)**—*pop pl* (2) MN-6
**Logan (Township of)**—*pop pl* NJ-2
**Logan (Township of)**—*pop pl* OH-6
**Logan (Township of)**—*pop pl* (3) PA-2
Logan Tunnel—*tunnel* ID-8
Logan Valley—*valley* OR-9
Logan Valley—*valley* PA-2
Logan Valley Cem—*cemetery* PA-2
Logan Valley Cem—*cemetery* TX-5
Logan Valley Ch—*church* TX-5
Logan Valley Mall—*locale* PA-2
Logan Valley Sch—*school* NE-7
*Loganville* PA-2
**Loganville**—*pop pl* CA-9
**Loganville**—*pop pl* GA-3
**Loganville**—*pop pl* OR-9
**Loganville**—*pop pl* PA-2
**Loganville**—*pop pl* WI-6
Loganville Borough—*civil* PA-2
Loganville (CCD)—*cens area* GA-3
Logan Wash—*stream* AZ-5
Logan Wash—*stream* CO-8
Logan Wash—*stream* NV-8
Logan Well—*well* NE-7
**Loganwood (subdivision)**—*pop pl* AL-4
Log Bay—*bay* MN-6
Log Bay Island—*island* NY-2
Log Bayou—*stream* (2) LA-4
*Log Branch* AL-4
*Log Branch* WV-2
Log Branch—*stream* LA-4
Log Branch—*stream* MS-4
Log Branch—*stream* (2) SC-3
Log Branch—*stream* TN-4
Log Branch—*stream* (2) WV-2
Log Bridge Campground—*locale* CA-9
Log Bridge Cem—*cemetery* SC-3
Log Bridge Creek—*stream* SC-3
Log Cabin—*island* NH-1
Log Cabin—*locale* CA-9
Log Cabin—*locale* CO-8
Log Cabin—*locale* GA-3
Log Cabin—*locale* NV-8
**Log Cabin**—*pop pl* LA-4
Log Cabin and Farm—*hist pl* NJ-2
Log Cabin Branch—*stream* MD-2
**Log Cabin Camp**—*pop pl* IL-6
Log Cabin Campground—*locale* CA-9
Log Cabin Canyon—*valley* CA-9
Log Cabin Canyon—*valley* NM-5
Log Cabin Ch—*church* KY-4
Log Cabin Ch—*church* OK-5
Log Cabin Chapel—*church* AL-4
Log Cabin Chapel—*church* TN-4
Log Cabin Country Club—*other* MO-7
*Log Cabin Creek* KS-7
Log Cabin Creek—*stream* AK-9
Log Cabin Creek—*stream* (2) CA-9
Log Cabin Creek—*stream* MT-8
Log Cabin Creek—*stream* NV-8
**Log Cabin Crossroads**—*pop pl* IN-6
Log Cabin Gulch—*valley* ID-8
**Log Cabin (historical)**—*pop pl* OR-9
Log Cabin Hollow—*valley* KY-4
Log Cabin Hollow—*valley* MO-7
Log Cabin Hollow—*valley* UT-8
Log Cabin Inn—*locale* AK-9
Log Cabin Island—*island* WA-9
Log Cabin Lake—*lake* (2) NE-7
Log Cabin Lake—*reservoir* TN-4
Log Cabin Lake Dam—*dam* TN-4
Log Cabin Lode—*mine* MT-8
Log Cabin Lodge—*hist pl* NJ-2
Log Cabin Meadow—*flat* CA-9
Log Cabin Mine—*mine* CA-9
Log Cabin Mine—*mine* NV-8
Log Cabin Peak—*summit* NM-5
Log Cabin Point—*cape* MI-6
Log Cabin Ranch—*locale* CA-9
Log Cabin Rapids—*rapids* UT-8
Log Cabin Ridge—*ridge* UT-8
Log Cabin Sch—*school* KY-4
Log Cabin Sch—*school* ME-1
Log Cabin Sch—*school* MI-6
Log Cabin Sch—*school* NC-3
Log Cabin Spring—*spring* (2) AZ-5
Log Cabin Spring—*spring* CA-9
Log Cabin Spring—*spring* NV-8
Log Cabin Spring—*spring* (2) OR-9
Log Cabin Spring—*spring* PA-2
Log Cabin Spring—*spring* UT-8
Log Cabin Station—*locale* MO-7
Log Cabin Tabernacle—*church* GA-3
Log Cabin Tabernacle—*church* TX-5
Log Cabin Tank—*reservoir* AZ-5
**Log Cabin (trailer park)**—*pop pl* DE-2
Log Camp—*locale* OR-9
Log Camp Hollow—*valley* TN-4
Log Camp Spring—*spring* CO-8
Log Camp Spring Rsvr—*reservoir* CO-8
Log Canyon—*valley* (2) CO-8
Log Canyon—*valley* ID-8
Log Canyon—*valley* (2) NV-8
Log Canyon—*valley* NM-5
Log Canyon—*valley* UT-8
Log Canyon Tank—*reservoir* AZ-5
Log Canyon Trail—*trail* NM-5
Log Cave—*cave* AL-4
Log Ch—*church* KY-4
Log Ch—*church* MO-7
Log Ch—*church* MT-8
Log Ch—*church* WV-2
Log Chain Creek—*stream* KS-7
Log Chapel—*church* MO-7
Log Chapel—*church* NY-2
Log Church Cem—*cemetery* IL-6
Log Church Cem—*cemetery* IN-6
Log Church Sch (abandoned)—*school* MO-7
Log Chute Gulch—*valley* ID-8
Log Chute Hollow—*valley* WV-2
Log Coll—*school* PA-2
Log Corral Canyon—*valley* AZ-5
Log Corral Creek—*stream* CO-8
Log Corral Meadow—*flat* CA-9
Log Corral Spring—*spring* AZ-5
Log Corral Spring—*spring* CA-9
Log Corral Wash—*stream* AZ-5
*Log Creek* AL-4
*Log Creek* CO-8
*Log Creek* IN-6
Log Creek—*gut* NJ-2
Log Creek—*stream* (2) AL-4
Log Creek—*stream* (4) ID-8
Log Creek—*stream* IN-6
Log Creek—*stream* KY-4
Log Creek—*stream* MO-7
Log Creek—*stream* MT-8
Log Creek—*stream* NV-8
Log Creek—*stream* NC-3
Log Creek—*stream* (7) OR-9
Log Creek—*stream* SC-3
Log Creek—*stream* WA-9
Log Creek—*stream* WI-6
Log Creek Basin—*basin* OR-9
Log Creek Basin Rsvr—*reservoir* OR-9
Log Creek Ch—*church* IN-6
Log Creek Ch—*church* MO-7
Log Creek Pond—*lake* FL-3
Log Creek Pond—*lake* NJ-2
Log Creek Sch—*school* MO-7
Log Creek Trail—*trail* WA-9
Log Dam Creek—*stream* GA-3
Logdell—*locale* OR-9
Log Draw—*valley* CO-8
Log Drive Creek—*stream* MN-6
Logee House—*hist pl* RI-1
Logemanns Creek—*stream* WI-6
Logfield Hollow—*valley* MO-7
Log Flat—*flat* UT-8
Loggains Branch—*stream* AL-4
Loggan Springs—*spring* OR-9
*Log Gaol* NJ-2
Logg Drain—*stream* MI-6
Logge Canyon—*valley* UT-8
Logged Canyon—*valley* ID-8
Logged Up Springs—*spring* ID-8
Logger Branch—*stream* VT-1
*Logger Brook* VT-1
Logger Brook—*stream* VT-1
Logger Butte—*summit* OR-9
Logger Canyon—*valley* WA-9
Logger Creek—*stream* MT-8
Loggerhead Canyon—*valley* OR-9
Loggerhead Creek—*stream* AL-4
Loggerhead Creek—*stream* MI-6
*Loggerhead Flat* MS-4
Loggerhead Fork—*stream* WV-2
Loggerhead Inlet—*gut* NC-3
Loggerhead Inlet (historical)—*channel* NC-3
*Loggerhead Key* FL-3
Loggerhead Key—*island* FL-3
Loggerhead Pond—*lake* NJ-2
Loggerhead Ridge—*ridge* WV-2
Loggerhead Shoal—*bar* MS-4
Loggerhead Spring—*spring* OR-9
Logger Lake—*lake* (2) MN-6
Logger Lake—*lake* (2) WI-6
Logger Mtn—*summit* AZ-5
Logger Point—*summit* CA-9
Loggers Cabin Park—*flat* UT-8
Loggers Delight Canyon—*valley* CA-9
Loggers Flat—*flat* TN-4
Loggers Fork—*stream* UT-8
Loggers Fork—*valley* UT-8
Loggers Fork Dam—*dam* UT-8
Loggers Fork Rsvr—*reservoir* UT-8
Loggers Lake—*reservoir* MO-7
Loggers Lake Campground—*locale* MO-7
Loggers Path—*trail* PA-2
Logger Spring—*spring* ID-8
Loggers Run Community MS—*school* FL-3
Loggers Tank—*reservoir* AZ-5
Logger Tank—*reservoir* AZ-5
Logger Tank—*reservoir* TX-5
Logger Waterhole—*reservoir* OR-9
Loggia Beach Park—*park* FL-3
Loggie Bayou—*stream* MS-4
Loggie Gulch—*valley* CO-8
Logging Bay—*swamp* FL-3
*Logging Branch* AR-4
Logging Cabin Creek—*stream* AK-9
Logging Camp—*locale* WY-8
Logging Camp Bay—*bay* AK-9
Logging Camp Cave—*cave* TN-4
Logging Camp Draw—*valley* CO-8
Logging Camp Draw Rsvr—*reservoir* CO-8
Logging Camp Ranch—*locale* ND-7
Logging Camp Seep Tank—*reservoir* AZ-5
Logging Camp Spring—*spring* CO-8
Logging Camp Spring—*spring* OR-9
Logging Canyon—*valley* CO-8
Logging Creek—*locale* MT-8
Logging Creek—*stream* (4) MT-8
Logging Creek—*stream* OR-9
Logging Creek—*stream* WI-6
Logging Creek Campground—*locale* MT-8
Logging Creek Ranger Station—*locale* MT-8
Logging Creek Ranger Station Hist Dist—*hist pl* MT-8
Logging Creek Rsvr—*reservoir* MT-8
Logging Creek Spring—*spring* MT-8
Logging Flat—*flat* CA-9
Logging Grove—*woods* UT-8
Logging Grove Draw—*valley* UT-8
Logging Gulch—*valley* CA-9
Logging Gulch—*valley* (2) ID-8
Logging Hollow—*valley* TN-4
Logging Lake—*lake* AK-9
Logging Lake—*lake* MT-8
Logging Mtn—*summit* MT-8
Logging Ridge—*ridge* MT-8
Logging Savanna—*swamp* SC-3
Logging Sleigh Lake—*lake* MN-6
Logging Slough—*gut* MO-7
Logging Spring—*spring* CO-8
Logging Swamp—*swamp* MA-1
Loggins Cem—*cemetery* (2) MS-4
Loggins Creek—*stream* TX-5
Loggins Spring—*spring* MT-8
Log Grade Trail—*trail* PA-2
*Log Gulch* MT-8
Log Gulch—*valley* CO-8
Log Gulch—*valley* ID-8
Log Gulch—*valley* (3) MT-8
Log Gulch—*valley* NV-8
Log Gully—*valley* TX-5
**Loggy Bayou**—*pop pl* LA-4
Loggy Bayou—*stream* (2) LA-4
Loggy Bayou—*swamp* AR-4
Loggy Bayou Ch—*church* AR-4
Loggy Bottom Branch—*stream* VA-3
Loggy Branch—*stream* (2) NC-3
Loggy Branch—*stream* WV-2
Loggy Creek—*stream* ID-8
Loggy Flats—*flat* GA-3
Loggy Gap—*gap* NC-3
Loggy Hollow—*valley* KY-4
Loggy Hollow—*valley* WV-2
Loggy Knob—*summit* NC-3
Loggy Lake—*lake* SC-3
Loggy Meadows—*flat* CA-9
Loggy Pond Swamp—*swamp* FL-3
Loggy Ridge—*ridge* (3) NC-3
Loghall Sch—*school* AR-4
**Log Haven Subdivision**—*pop pl* UT-8
Log Highway—*channel* MI-6
Log Hill Mesa—*summit* CO-8
Log Hole—*lake* MS-4
Log Hollow—*valley* ID-8
Log Hollow—*valley* (2) MO-7
Log Hollow—*valley* (2) PA-2
Log Hollow—*valley* TX-5
Log Hollow—*valley* (6) UT-8
Log Hollow Branch—*stream* NC-3
Log Hollow Divide—*ridge* UT-8
Log Hollow Run—*stream* WV-2
Log Hollow Spring—*spring* AL-4
Log Hollow Spring—*spring* UT-8
Log Hollow Trail—*trail* PA-2
Log House, Hiester House, and Market Annex—*hist pl* PA-2
Log House Brook—*stream* RI-1
*Log House Creek* CO-8
*Log House Draw* TX-5
Log House on Shun Pike—*hist pl* KY-4
Log House Rsvr—*reservoir* CO-8
Log House Spring—*spring* OR-9
Loghry State Park—*park* CA-9
Logia Adelphia—*hist pl* PR-3
Logia Masonica Hijos de la Luz—*hist pl* PR-3
Logia Union y Amparo No. 44—*hist pl* PR-3
*Logie Creek* WA-9
Logie Dam Dropped—*dam* MA-1
Logie Lake—*lake* CO-8
Logie Sch—*school* MT-8
*Log Jail* NJ-2
Logjam Creek—*stream* AK-9
Log Jam Landing—*locale* SC-3
*Log Lake* CA-9
Log Lake—*lake* AR-4
Log Lake—*lake* (2) CA-9
Log Lake—*lake* (3) GA-3
Log Lake—*lake* (2) MI-6
Log Lake—*lake* MS-4
Log Lake—*lake* OR-9
Log Landing—*locale* (3) AL-4
Log Landing—*locale* CA-9
Log Landing—*locale* FL-3
Log Landing—*locale* (2) GA-3
Log Landing—*locale* (2) NC-3
Log Landing—*locale* VA-3
Log Landing (historical)—*locale* AL-4
Log Landing Pond—*lake* ME-1
Log Landing Tank—*reservoir* AZ-5
**Log Lane Village**—*pop pl* CO-8
Log Lick—*locale* KY-4
**Loglick**—*pop pl* KY-4
Log Lick—*stream* KY-4
Log Lick Creek—*stream* IN-6
Log Lick Creek—*stream* KY-4
Loglick Run—*stream* (2) WV-2
Log Loader Chute—*gut* MS-4
Log Log Cave—*cave* AL-4
Log Meadow—*flat* CA-9
Log Mesa—*summit* CO-8
*Logmont* KY-4
**Logmont**—*pop pl* KY-4
**Log Mountain**—*pop pl* KY-4
Log Mountain—*ridge* TN-4
Log Mountains—*range* KY-4
Log Mountains—*ridge* TN-4
Log Mountain Trail—*trail* ID-8
Log Mtn—*summit* ID-8
Log Mtn—*summit* (2) TN-4
Logologo Point—*cape* AS-9
Logome Point—*cape* AS-9
*Logonda* KS-7
*Logoni Lake* MT-8
Logotala Hill—*summit* AS-9
Logoua Fall—*falls* AS-9
**Log Pile**—*pop pl* PA-2
Log Pile Ch—*church* OH-6
Logpile Flat—*flat* CO-8
Log Pile Ridge—*ridge* OH-6
Log Pile Sch—*school* PA-2
Log Pile Trail—*trail* OR-9
Log Pine Bay—*swamp* NC-3
Log Pipe Spring—*spring* OR-9
Log Point—*cape* AK-9
Log Point—*cape* (2) MD-2
Log Point—*cape* NC-3
Log Pond—*lake* DE-2
Log Pond—*lake* FL-3
Log Pond—*lake* GA-3
Log Pond—*lake* NY-2
Log Pond—*lake* WA-9
Log Pond—*reservoir* CA-9
Log Pond—*reservoir* OR-9
Log Pond Creek—*stream* NC-3
Log Pond Run—*stream* OH-6
Log Providence Ch—*church* MO-7
Log Ridge—*ridge* CA-9
Log Ridge—*ridge* ID-8
Log Ridge—*ridge* TN-4
Log Ridge Branch—*stream* TN-4
Log River—*stream* FL-3
Log Road Hollow—*valley* PA-2
Log Road Tank—*reservoir* AZ-5
*Log Run* WV-2
**Log Run**—*pop pl* DE-2
Log Run—*stream* IN-6
Log Run—*stream* PA-2
*Logsboro* NC-3
**Logsboro**—*pop pl* NC-3
Log Sch—*school* MT-8
Logsden—*locale* OR-9
Logsden Ridge—*ridge* OR-9
Logsdon Cem—*cemetery* KY-4
Logsdon Creek—*stream* WA-9
Logsdon Rsvr—*reservoir* TX-5
Logsdon Valley—*locale* KY-4
Logsdon Valley Cem—*cemetery* KY-4
Log Shoal—*bar* TN-4
Log Shoal Branch—*stream* KY-4
Logshoal Island—*island* TN-4
Logshoal Run—*stream* WV-2
Log Shoals—*bar* AL-4
Logslide Bluff—*cliff* MO-7
Log Slide Hollow—*valley* PA-2
Log Slide Trail—*trail* (2) PA-2
Log Slough—*lake* IL-6
Log Slough—*stream* AR-4
Logson Branch—*stream* IN-6
Log Spanned Shaft—*cave* TN-4
Log Spring—*spring* (2) AZ-5
Log Spring—*spring* CA-9
Log Spring—*spring* (2) ID-8
Log Spring—*spring* MT-8
Log Spring—*spring* (3) NV-8
Log Spring—*spring* NM-5
Log Spring—*spring* (5) OR-9
Log Spring—*spring* SD-7
Log Spring—*spring* WA-9
Log Spring Creek—*stream* CA-9
Log Spring Hollow—*valley* MO-7
Log Spring Ridge—*ridge* (2) CA-9
Log Springs—*spring* AZ-5
Log Springs—*spring* NM-5
Log Springs Mtn—*summit* NM-5
Log Spring Station—*locale* CA-9
Log Spur (historical)—*locale* MS-4
Logston Branch—*stream* TX-5
Logston Cem—*cemetery* WV-2
Logston Hollow—*valley* KY-4
Logston Run—*stream* WV-2
Log Swamp Branch—*stream* NJ-2
Log Table Camp—*locale* OR-9
Log Tank—*reservoir* (3) AZ-5
Log Tank—*reservoir* NM-5
Log Tavern Pond—*lake* PA-2
*Log Tavern Ponds* PA-2
Logton—*locale* AL-4
*Logtown* NJ-2
*Logtown* OH-6
*Logtown* PA-2
Logtown—*locale* CO-8
Logtown—*locale* NY-2
**Logtown**—*pop pl* GA-3
**Logtown**—*pop pl* LA-4
**Logtown**—*pop pl* MS-4
**Logtown**—*pop pl* OH-6
Logtown Branch—*stream* MO-7
Logtown Cem—*cemetery* MS-4
Log Town Cem—*cemetery* OR-9
Log Town Creek—*stream* OR-9
Logtown Hollow—*valley* KY-4
Log Town Hollow Picnic Area—*locale* WV-2
Logtown Plantation—*hist pl* LA-4
Log Town Pond—*lake* TX-5
Logtown Post Office (historical)—*building* MS-4
Logtown Ridge—*ridge* CA-9
Logtown Run—*stream* PA-2
Logtown Sch—*school* LA-4
Logtown (Site)—*locale* CA-9
Log Trough Canyon—*valley* AZ-5
Log Trough Spring—*spring* AZ-5
Log Trough Spring—*spring* CA-9
Log Trough Spring—*spring* ID-8
Log Trough Spring—*spring* NV-8
Logue—*locale* PA-2
Logue Airp—*airport* PA-2
Logue Cem—*cemetery* KS-7
Logue Lake—*reservoir* MO-7
Logue Pond Dam—*dam* AL-4
Logue Run—*stream* PA-2
Logues Cem—*cemetery* SC-3
Logue Sch—*school* (2) IL-6
Logues Pond—*reservoir* AL-4
*Logues Run* PA-2
Log Union Cem—*cemetery* KY-4
Log Union Cem—*cemetery* TN-4
*Logussock* RI-1
Log Verjeles Dam—*dam* CA-9
Logville—*locale* KY-4
Logville Sch—*school* KY-4
Logwater Branch—*stream* KS-7
Logway Run—*stream* PA-2
Log Well—*locale* AZ-5
Logwell Ch—*church* GA-3
Logwood Ch—*church* KY-4
Logwood Cove—*bay* RI-1
Logwood Creek—*stream* CA-9
Logwood Pond—*lake* DE-2
Logwood Ridge—*ridge* CA-9
*Logy* NC-3
Logyard Campsite—*park* MO-7
Logyard River Access—*locale* MO-7
Logyard Shoals—*bar* AL-4
Logy Creek—*stream* WA-9
Logy Creek Cow Camp—*locale* WA-9
Logy Creek Falls—*falls* WA-9
Lohali Basin—*basin* AZ-5
Lohali Mesa—*summit* AZ-5
Lohali Point—*cliff* AZ-5
Lohd, Dauen—*gut* FM-9
Lohd, Kepidau En—*bay* FM-9
Lohd, Pillap En—*stream* FM-9
Lohd Pah—*civil* FM-9
Lohd Powe—*civil* FM-9
Lohff Creek—*stream* KS-7
Lohff Creek—*stream* NE-7
Lohiaus House (Site)—*locale* HI-9
Lohi Creek—*stream* AK-9
**Lohman**—*pop pl* MO-7
**Lohman**—*pop pl* MT-8
**Lohman**—*pop pl* TN-4
Lohman Block—*hist pl* MT-8
*Lohman Canyon* NV-8
Lohman Coulee—*valley* (2) MT-8
Lohman Funeral Home and Livery Stable—*hist pl* WI-6
Lohman Ranch—*locale* CA-9
Lohman Ranch—*locale* ND-7
Lohman Ridge—*ridge* CA-9
Lohman Sch—*school* MI-6
Lohman's Landing Bldg—*hist pl* MO-7
**Lohmans Store (historical)**—*pop pl* TN-4
Lohmar, John, House—*hist pl* MN-6
Lohmer—*locale* MO-7
Lohn—*locale* TX-5
Lohn Cem—*cemetery* TX-5
Lohn Creek—*stream* WI-6
Lohner State Public Shooting Area—*park* SD-7
**Lohnes Township**—*pop pl* ND-7
Lohr, Charles and Mary, House—*hist pl* SD-7
Lohre (historical)—*locale* SD-7
Lohrey Sch—*school* OH-6
*Lohr Reservoir* CO-8
Lohr Sch—*school* OH-6
Lohrs Landing Strip—*airport* PA-2
*Lohrs Run* PA-2
**Lohrville**—*pop pl* IA-7
**Lohrville**—*pop pl* WI-6
Lohse PN Ferry—*locale* MT-8
Lohse Spring—*spring* MT-8
*Lohson* FM-9
Lohstroh Highline Ditch—*canal* CO-8
*Lohum River* OR-9
*Loi* MP-9
Loi—*island* MP-9
Loids Brook—*stream* ME-1
*Loi Island* MP-9
Loi Islands (not verified)—*island* MP-9
Loiloa Keopuka—*civil* HI-9
Loimbach Landing—*locale* MO-7
Loin, Bayou—*stream* LA-4
Loin Draw—*valley* NM-5
Loines Observatory—*building* MA-1
Loipunawai—*spring* HI-9
Loire—*locale* TX-5
Loire Creek—*stream* KS-7
Lois—*locale* CA-9
Lois—*locale* FL-3
Lois—*locale* MO-7
Lois—*locale* TX-5
Lois—*locale* VA-3
**Lois**—*pop pl* TN-4
**Lois**—*pop pl* TX-5
Lois, Key—*island* FL-3
Lois, Lake—*lake* CA-9
Lois Cem—*cemetery* TN-4
Lois Creek—*stream* AK-9
**Loisdale**—*pop pl* VA-3
**Loisdale Estates**—*pop pl* VA-3
Lois Dome—*summit* AK-9
Loisel—*locale* LA-4
*Loiselle Creek* SD-7
Loisels Post (historical)—*locale* SD-7
Lois Island—*island* OR-9
Lois Kilian Cave—*cave* AL-4
Lois Lake—*lake* CA-9
Lois Lake—*lake* CO-8
Lois Lake—*lake* MI-6
Lois Lake—*lake* MN-6
Lois Lake—*lake* OR-9
Lois Lake—*reservoir* MT-8
Lois Lake Bed—*flat* MN-6
Lois Sch (historical)—*school* TN-4
Lois Spring—*locale* AL-4
**Lois Subdivision**—*pop pl* UT-8
Loiten Lake—*lake* MN-6
Loiza—*CDP* PR-3
**Loiza**—*pop pl* (2) PR-3
**Loiza Aldea**—*pop pl* PR-3
Loiza (Municipio)—*civil* PR-3
Loiza (Pueblo)—*fmr MCD* PR-3
Loiza Street—*post sta* PR-3
**Loiza Valley**—*pop pl* (2) PR-3
*Loj* MP-9
Loj—*island* MP-9
*Lojan* MP-9
Lojan—*island* MP-9
*Lojiron Islet* MP-9
*Loj Island* MP-9
*Lojjaion* MP-9
*Lojjaiong* MP-9
Lojjairok—*island* MP-9

Lone Hill—*summit* .... CA-9
Lone Hill—*summit* (2) .... MO-7
Lone Hill—*summit* .... TX-5
Lone Hill—*summit* .... UT-8
*Lone Hill Baptist Church* .... TN-4
Lone Hill Cem—*cemetery* (2) .... AR-4
Lone Hill Cem—*cemetery* .... IL-6
Lone Hill Cem—*cemetery* .... WA-9
Lone Hill Ch—*church* .... GA-3
Lone Hill Ch—*church* (2) .... KY-4
Lone Hill Ch—*church* (2) .... LA-4
Lone Hill Ch—*church* .... TN-4
Lone Hill Lookout Tower—*tower* .... MO-7
Lone Hill Rsvr—*reservoir* .... WY-8
Lone Hill Sch—*school* .... CA-9
Lone Hill Sch—*school* .... NE-7
Lonehill Tank—*reservoir* .... AZ-5
Lone Hill (Township of)—*fmr MCD* .... AR-4
Lone Hill Windmill—*locale* .... NM-5
Lone Hollow—*valley* .... CO-8
Lone Holly—*locale* .... MD-2
Lone Indian, Lake of the—*lake* .... CA-9
Lone Indian Butte—*summit* .... MT-8
Lone Indian Mtn—*summit* .... AK-9
Lone Indian Peak—*summit* .... MT-8
*Lone Indian Point* .... MT-8
Lone Island—*island* (2) .... AK-9
Lone Island—*island* .... WI-6
**Lone Jack**—*pop pl* .... MO-7
**Lone Jack**—*pop pl* .... VA-3
Lone Jack Canyon—*valley* .... CO-8
Lone Jack Mine—*mine* .... AZ-5
Lone Jack Mine—*mine* .... CA-9
Lone Jack Mine—*mine* .... WA-9
Lone Jack Placer Mine—*mine* .... AZ-5
Lone Jack Pond—*lake* .... ME-1
Lone Jack Rsvr—*reservoir* .... CO-8
Lone Jack Sch—*school* .... KY-4
Lone Jack Station—*locale* .... VA-3
Lone Jack Waterhole—*reservoir* .... OR-9
Lone Jim Mtn—*summit* .... AK-9
Lone Joe Ranch—*locale* .... TX-5
Lone Juniper—*summit* .... OR-9
Lone Juniper Canyon—*valley* .... NV-8
Lone Juniper Canyon—*valley* .... OR-9
Lone Juniper Creek—*stream* .... ID-8
Lone Juniper Spring—*spring* .... AZ-5
Lone Juniper Spring—*spring* (2) .... NV-8
Lone Juniper Spring—*spring* .... OR-9
Lone Knob—*summit* .... ID-8
Lone Knob—*summit* .... NC-3
Lone Knob Creek—*stream* .... ID-8
*Lonelake* .... KS-7
*Lone Lake* .... MN-6
Lone Lake—*lake* .... CA-9
Lone Lake—*lake* .... ID-8
Lone Lake—*lake* .... MI-6
Lone Lake—*lake* (3) .... MN-6
Lone Lake—*lake* (3) .... MT-8
Lone Lake—*lake* .... WA-9
Lone Lake—*reservoir* .... MS-4
Lonelake (historical)—*locale* .... KS-7
*Lone Lane* .... KS-7
Lone Lick Creek—*stream* .... CO-8
Lone Lick Lakes—*lake* .... CO-8
**Lonelm**—*pop pl* .... AR-4
Lonely, Lake—*lake* .... NY-2
**Lonely Acres**—*pop pl* .... PA-2
Lonely Cedar Sch—*school* .... WI-6
Lonely Cem—*cemetery* .... KY-4
Lonely Creek—*stream* .... ID-8
*Lonely Dell* .... AZ-5
Lonely Dell Ranch Hist Dist—*hist pl* .... AZ-5
Lonely Gulch—*valley* .... CA-9
Lonely Hollow—*valley* .... AR-4
Lonely Lake—*lake* (2) .... AK-9
Lonely Lake—*lake* .... CA-9
Lonely Lake—*lake* .... MN-6
Lonely Lake—*lake* .... NH-1
Lonely Lakes—*lake* .... MT-8
Lonely Lee—*summit* .... TX-5
Lonely Mountain Tank—*reservoir* .... AZ-5
Lonely Mtn—*summit* .... AZ-5
Lonely Mtn—*summit* .... ID-8
Lonely Night Rsvr—*reservoir* .... MT-8
*Lonely Park Spring* .... UT-8
Lonely Post Office (historical)—*building* .... TN-4
Lonely Spring—*spring* .... UT-8
Lonely Trail—*trail* .... PA-2
Lonely Valley Ch—*church* .... MS-4
**Lonelyville**—*pop pl* .... NY-2
Lonelyville Lake—*lake* .... WA-9
Lonely Windmill—*locale* .... NM-5
Lone Man Butte—*summit* .... UT-8
Lone Man Coulee—*valley* .... MT-8
Loneman Creek—*stream* .... MT-8
Lone Man Creek—*stream* .... TX-5
Lone Man Draw—*valley* .... UT-8
Loneman Fire Lookout—*hist pl* .... MT-8
Loneman Mountain Trail—*trail* .... MT-8
Loneman Mtn—*summit* .... MT-8
Lone Man Mtn—*summit* .... TX-5
Loneman Mtn—*summit* .... TX-5
Lone Maple Sch—*school* .... IL-6
Lone Maple Sch (historical)—*school* .... TN-4
*Lone Meadow Creek* .... ID-8
Lone Meadow Spring—*spring* .... NV-8
Lone Mesa—*summit* (3) .... CO-8
Lone Mesa—*summit* .... NV-8
Lone Mesa—*summit* (2) .... NM-5
Lone Mesa Cem—*cemetery* .... NM-5
Lone Mesa Rsvr—*reservoir* .... CO-8
Lone Mesa Spring Number 1—*spring* .... CO-8
Lone Mesquite Hill—*summit* .... TX-5
*Lone Mill Creek* .... VA-3
Lone Mound Ch—*church* .... TX-5
*Lone Mountain* .... ID-8
Lone Mountain—*locale* .... TN-4
**Lone Mountain**—*pop pl* .... TN-4
**Lone Mountain**—*pop pl* .... TX-5
Lone Mountain—*ridge* .... NV-8
Lone Mountain—*ridge* (2) .... TN-4
Lone Mountain Baptist Ch—*church* .... TN-4
Lone Mountain Canyon—*valley* .... AZ-5
Lone Mountain Canyon—*valley* .... CO-8
Lone Mountain Canyon—*valley* .... NM-5
Lone Mountain Canyon—*valley* .... UT-8
Lone Mountain Cem—*cemetery* (2) .... NV-8
Lone Mountain Cem—*cemetery* .... TN-4
Lone Mountain Cem—*cemetery* .... TX-5
Lone Mountain Ch—*church* .... TN-4
Lone Mountain Creek—*stream* .... NV-8
Lone Mountain Creek—*stream* .... TN-4
Lone Mountain Creek—*stream* .... UT-8
Lone Mountain Dock—*locale* .... TN-4
Lone Mountain Methodis Ch—*church* .... TN-4
Lone Mountain Mine—*mine* .... NV-8
Lone Mountain Post Office—*building* .... TN-4
Lone Mountain Ranch—*locale* .... AZ-5
Lone Mountain Ridge—*ridge* .... TN-4
Lone Mountain Sch—*school* .... TN-4
Lone Mountain Sch (historical)—*school* .... TN-4
Lone Mountain Spring—*spring* (2) .... NV-8
Lone Mountain Tank—*reservoir* .... AZ-5
Lone Mountain Trail—*trail* .... MT-8
Lone Mountain Well—*well* .... AZ-5
*Lone Mtn* .... AZ-5
*Lone Mtn* .... TN-4
Lone Mtn—*range* .... TX-5
Lone Mtn—*summit* (3) .... AK-9
Lone Mtn—*summit* (6) .... AZ-5
Lone Mtn—*summit* .... CA-9
Lone Mtn—*summit* .... CO-8
Lone Mtn—*summit* (2) .... ME-1
Lone Mtn—*summit* (3) .... MT-8
Lone Mtn—*summit* (9) .... NV-8
Lone Mtn—*summit* (6) .... NM-5
Lone Mtn—*summit* .... NY-2
Lone Mtn—*summit* .... NC-3
Lone Mtn—*summit* .... OK-5
Lone Mtn—*summit* (2) .... OR-9
Lone Mtn—*summit* .... SD-7
Lone Mtn—*summit* (3) .... TN-4
Lone Mtn—*summit* (7) .... TX-5
Lone Mtn—*summit* (2) .... UT-8
Lone Mtn—*summit* .... VA-3
Lone Mtn—*summit* (3) .... WA-9
Lone Mtn—*summit* .... WY-8
*Lone Oak* .... TN-4
Lone Oak—*CDP* .... WA-9
Lone Oak—*locale* .... CO-8
Lone Oak—*locale* .... KS-7
Lone Oak—*locale* .... KY-4
Lone Oak—*locale* .... OK-5
Lone Oak—*locale* (4) .... TX-5
Lone Oak—*locale* .... VA-3
Lone Oak—*locale* .... WV-2
Lone Oak—*other* .... TN-4
**Lone Oak**—*pop pl* .... GA-3
**Lone Oak**—*pop pl* .... KY-4
**Lone Oak**—*pop pl* .... MD-2
**Lone Oak**—*pop pl* .... SC-3
**Lone Oak**—*pop pl* .... TN-4
**Lone Oak**—*pop pl* (2) .... TX-5
*Lone Oak Baptist Ch* .... MS-4
Lone Oak Bayou—*stream* .... LA-4
Lone Oak Bayou—*stream* .... TX-5
Lone Oak Branch—*stream* .... MO-7
Lone Oak Canal—*canal* .... CA-9
Lone Oak Canyon—*valley* .... CA-9
Lone Oak (CCD)—*cens area* .... TN-4
Lone Oak (CCD)—*cens area* .... TX-5
Lone Oak Cem—*cemetery* .... AR-4
Lone Oak Cem—*cemetery* .... CA-9
Lone Oak Cem—*cemetery* .... FL-3
Lone Oak Cem—*cemetery* .... IL-6
Lone Oak Cem—*cemetery* .... KY-4
Lone Oak Cem—*cemetery* .... MN-6
Lone Oak Cem—*cemetery* .... MS-4
Lone Oak Cem—*cemetery* .... OR-9
Lone Oak Cem—*cemetery* .... TN-4
Lone Oak Cem—*cemetery* (6) .... TX-5
Lone Oak Cem—*cemetery* .... WV-2
Lone Oak Ch—*church* (3) .... AR-4
Lone Oak Ch—*church* .... FL-3
Lone Oak Ch—*church* .... GA-3
Lone Oak Ch—*church* .... IL-6
Lone Oak Ch—*church* (4) .... MS-4
Lone Oak Ch—*church* .... MO-7
Lone Oak Ch—*church* .... NC-3
Lone Oak Ch—*church* (2) .... OK-5
Lone Oak Ch—*church* (3) .... TN-4
Lone Oak Ch—*church* (3) .... TX-5
Lone Oak Ch—*church* (2) .... VA-3
Lone Oak Ch—*church* (2) .... WV-2
Lone Oak Channel—*channel* .... NC-3
Lone Oak Ch (historical)—*church* .... TN-4
Lone Oak Ch of Christ—*church* .... TN-4
*Lone Oak Christian Church* .... TN-4
Lone Oak Community Center—*locale* .... TX-5
Lone Oak Community Hall—*locale* .... OK-5
Lone Oak Division—*civil* .... TN-4
Lone Oak Elem Sch—*school* .... TN-4
Lone Oak Landing (historical)—*locale* .... TN-4
Lone Oak Mill—*locale* .... VA-3
Lone Oak Mine—*mine* .... CA-9
Lone Oak Mtn—*summit* .... CA-9
Lone Oak Mtn—*summit* .... TX-5
Lone Oak Park—*park* .... KY-4
Lone Oak Point—*cape* .... FL-3
Lone Oak Point—*cape* .... MO-7
Lone Oak Ranch—*locale* .... TX-5
Lone Oaks—*hist pl* .... VA-3
Lone Oak Sch—*school* .... IL-6
Lone Oak Sch—*school* .... KY-4
Lone Oak Sch—*school* .... MD-2
Lone Oak Sch—*school* .... MO-7
Lone Oak Sch—*school* .... OK-5
Lone Oak Sch—*school* .... SC-3
Lone Oak Sch (historical)—*school* (2) .... TN-4
Lone Oak Slough—*gut* .... CA-9
Lone Oaks Ranch Airstrip—*airport* .... OR-9
**Lone Oak (subdivision)**—*pop pl* .... TN-4
**Lone Oak Township**—*pop pl* .... MO-7
Lone Palm Head—*island* .... FL-3
Lone Palm Island (historical)—*island* .... FL-3
Lone Park—*flat* .... MT-8
Lone Park Creek—*stream* .... ID-8
Lone Parson Hole—*flat* .... UT-8
Lone Passage—*channel* .... AK-9
*Lone Peak* .... NV-8
Lone Peak—*summit* .... AK-9
Lone Peak—*summit* .... CO-8
Lone Peak—*summit* .... OK-5
Lone Peak—*summit* .... UT-8
Lone Peak—*summit* .... WA-9
**Lone Peak Estates Subdivision**—*pop pl* .... UT-8
*Lone Peak Reservoir* .... UT-8
Lone Peak Sch—*school* .... UT-8
Lone Pilgrim Cem—*cemetery* .... MO-7
Lone Pilgrim Ch—*church* .... MS-4
Lone Pilgrim Ch—*church* .... MO-7
Lone Pilgrim School (historical)—*locale* .... MO-7
*Lonepine* .... LA-4
*Lone Pine* .... VA-3
Lone Pine—*hist pl* .... LA-4
Lone Pine—*hist pl* .... NC-3
Lone Pine—*locale* .... AR-4
Lone Pine—*locale* .... ID-8
Lone Pine—*locale* .... LA-4
Lone Pine—*locale* .... MS-4
Lone Pine—*locale* .... OK-5
Lone Pine—*locale* .... OR-9
Lone Pine—*locale* .... TX-5
Lone Pine—*locale* .... VA-3
Lone Pine—*locale* .... WA-9
**Lone Pine**—*pop pl* .... AR-4
**Lone Pine**—*pop pl* .... CA-9
**Lone Pine**—*pop pl* .... LA-4
**Lonepine**—*pop pl* .... LA-4
**Lonepine**—*pop pl* .... MT-8
**Lone Pine**—*pop pl* .... PA-2
**Lone Pine**—*pop pl* .... TX-5
**Lone Pine**—*pop pl* .... WA-9
Lone Pine Bar—*bar* .... CA-9
Lone Pine Basin—*basin* .... OR-9
Lone Pine Bridge—*bridge* .... OR-9
Lone Pine Butte—*summit* .... CA-9
Lone Pine Butte—*summit* (2) .... OR-9
Lone Pine Butte—*summit* .... WA-9
Lone Pine Camp—*locale* .... AL-4
Lone Pine Camp—*locale* .... CA-9
Lone Pine Campsite—*locale* .... ME-1
*Lone Pine Canyon* .... UT-8
*Lone Pine Canyon* .... WA-9
Lone Pine Canyon—*valley* (3) .... CA-9
Lone Pine Canyon—*valley* .... ID-8
Lone Pine Canyon—*valley* (2) .... NV-8
Lone Pine Canyon—*valley* .... NM-5
Lone Pine Canyon—*valley* .... OR-9
Lone Pine Canyon—*valley* (4) .... UT-8
Lone Pine Canyon—*valley* .... WA-9
Lone Pine (CCD)—*cens area* .... CA-9
Lone Pine Cem—*cemetery* .... AR-4
Lone Pine Cem—*cemetery* .... LA-4
Lone Pine Cem—*cemetery* .... MN-6
Lone Pine Cem—*cemetery* .... MS-4
Lone Pine Cem—*cemetery* (3) .... MO-7
Lone Pine Cem—*cemetery* .... MT-8
Lone Pine Cem—*cemetery* .... OR-9
Lone Pine Cem—*cemetery* .... TN-4
Lone Pine Cem—*cemetery* .... VA-3
Lone Pine Cem—*cemetery* (2) .... WA-9
Lone Pine Cem—*cemetery* (2) .... WI-6
Lone Pine Ch—*church* (2) .... AR-4
Lone Pine Ch—*church* (5) .... LA-4
Lone Pine Ch—*church* (2) .... MS-4
Lone Pine Ch—*church* (3) .... TX-5
Lone Pine Chapel—*church* .... VA-3
**Lone Pine Corner**—*pop pl* .... OR-9
Lone Pine Corrals—*locale* .... CA-9
*Lone Pine Creek* .... CO-8
*Lone Pine Creek* .... ID-8
Lone Pine Creek—*stream* .... AZ-5
Lone Pine Creek—*stream* (2) .... CA-9
Lone Pine Creek—*stream* (4) .... CO-8
Lone Pine Creek—*stream* (5) .... ID-8
Lone Pine Creek—*stream* .... MI-6
Lone Pine Creek—*stream* (3) .... MT-8
Lone Pine Creek—*stream* (2) .... OR-9
Lonepine Creek—*stream* .... OR-9
Lone Pine Creek—*stream* .... UT-8
Lone Pine Creek—*stream* .... WA-9
Lone Pine Dam—*dam* .... AZ-5
Lone Pine Ditch—*canal* (3) .... CO-8
Lone Pine Ditch—*canal* .... OR-9
Lone Pine Divide—*ridge* .... AZ-5
**Lone Pine Estates**—*pop pl* .... CO-8
Lone Pine Fire Tower—*locale* .... MS-4
Lone Pine Flat—*flat* .... OR-9
Lone Pine Flat—*flat* (2) .... UT-8
Lone Pine Gap—*gap* .... TN-4
Lone Pine Golf Course—*locale* .... PA-2
*Lone Pine Gulch* .... CO-8
Lone Pine Gulch—*valley* (2) .... CO-8
Lone Pine Gulch—*valley* (2) .... ID-8
Lone Pine Gulch—*valley* .... MT-8
Lone Pine Gulch—*valley* .... OR-9
Lone Pine Gulch—*valley* .... UT-8
Lone Pine Hill—*summit* .... NM-5
Lone Pine (historical)—*locale* .... MS-4
Lone Pine Island—*island* .... CA-9
Lone Pine Island—*island* .... NY-2
Lone Pine Island—*island* .... OR-9
Lone Pine Lake—*lake* (2) .... CA-9
Lone Pine Lake—*lake* .... CO-8
Lone Pine Lake—*lake* .... ID-8
Lone Pine Lake—*lake* (2) .... MN-6
Lone Pine Lake—*lake* (2) .... WA-9
Lone Pine Lake—*lake* (2) .... WI-6
Lone Pine Lake—*reservoir* .... CO-8
Lone Pine Lateral—*canal* .... CO-8
Lone Pine Lookout—*locale* .... CA-9
Lone Pine Meadow—*flat* .... CA-9
Lone Pine Mesa—*summit* .... NM-5
Lone Pine Mine—*mine* (2) .... ID-8
Lone Pine Mine—*mine* .... MT-8
Lone Pine Mine—*mine* .... UT-8
Lone Pine Mtn—*summit* .... AR-4
Lone Pine Mtn—*summit* (2) .... CA-9
Lone Pine Mtn—*summit* .... NC-3
Lone Pine Mtn—*summit* .... OK-5
Lone Pine Mtn—*summit* .... OR-9
Lone Pine Mtn—*summit* .... VA-3
Lone Pine Pass—*gap* .... ID-8
Lone Pine Peak—*summit* .... CA-9
Lone Pine Peak—*summit* .... ID-8
Lone Pine Peak—*summit* .... VA-3
Lone Pine Point—*cape* .... ME-1
Lone Pine Point—*cape* .... UT-8
Lone Pine Point—*cliff* .... ID-8
Lone Pine Prairie—*flat* .... MT-8
Lone Pine Quarry—*basin* .... OR-9
**Lone Pine Rancheria (Indian Reservation)**—*pop pl* .... CA-9
Lone Pine Ranch (historical)—*locale* .... ID-8
Lone Pine Rapids—*rapids* .... MT-8
Lone Pine Ridge—*ridge* (4) .... CA-9
Lone Pine Ridge—*ridge* .... ID-8
Lone Pine Ridge—*ridge* .... MN-6
Lone Pine Ridge—*ridge* .... MT-8
Lone Pine Ridge—*ridge* .... NC-3
Lone Pine Ridge—*ridge* .... OR-9
Lone Pine Ridge—*ridge* (2) .... UT-8
Lone Pine Ridge Lake—*lake* .... TX-5
Lone Pine Rsvr—*reservoir* .... CA-9
Lone Pine Rsvr—*reservoir* (2) .... CO-8
Lone Pine Rsvr—*reservoir* (2) .... OR-9
Lone Pine Saddle—*gap* (2) .... AZ-5
Lone Pine Saddle—*gap* .... OR-9
Lone Pine Sch—*school* .... CO-8
Lone Pine Sch—*school* .... MI-6
Lone Pine Sch—*school* (2) .... OR-9
Lone Pine Sch—*school* .... PA-2
Lone Pine Sch—*school* .... TX-5
Lone Pine Sch—*school* .... WI-6
Lone Pine Sch (historical)—*school* .... MO-7
Lone Pine Spring—*spring* (4) .... AZ-5
Lone Pine Spring—*spring* .... CA-9
Lone Pine Spring—*spring* (5) .... ID-8
Lone Pine Spring—*spring* .... MT-8
Lone Pine Spring—*spring* (2) .... NV-8
Lone Pine Spring—*spring* .... NM-5
Lone Pine Spring—*spring* (3) .... OR-9
Lone Pine Spring—*spring* (4) .... UT-8
Lone Pine Spring—*spring* .... WA-9
Lone Pine State Park—*park* .... MT-8
Lone Pine State Preserve—*park* .... MT-8
Lone Pine Station—*locale* .... CA-9
Lone Pine Stretch—*channel* .... TX-5
Lone Pine Swale—*valley* .... NV-8
Lone Pine Tank—*reservoir* (6) .... AZ-5
Lone Pine Tank Number One—*reservoir* .... AZ-5
Lone Pine Tank Number Two—*reservoir* .... AZ-5
Lone Pine Thicket—*woods* .... CA-9
Lone Pine (Township of)—*fmr MCD* .... AR-4
**Lone Pine (Township of)**—*pop pl* .... MN-6
Lone Pine Trail—*trail* .... AZ-5
Lone Pine Trail—*trail* .... CO-8
Lone Pine Trail—*trail* .... OR-9
Lone Pine Tree Hill—*summit* .... NM-5
Lone Pine Tree Ridge—*ridge* .... UT-8
Lone Pine Waterhole—*bay* .... OR-9
Lone Pine Water Trough—*canal* .... CA-9
Lone Pine Windmill—*locale* .... NM-5
*Lone Point* .... CA-9
*Lone Point* .... MT-8
Lone Point—*cape* .... AK-9
Lone Point—*cape* .... VA-3
Lone Point—*cliff* .... TX-5
Lone Point Light—*other* .... VA-3
Lone Pole Windmill—*locale* .... TX-5
Lone Pond—*lake* .... MD-2
Lone Pond—*lake* (2) .... NY-2
Lone Post Office (historical)—*building* .... AL-4
Lone Prairie Ch—*church* .... OK-5
Lone Prairie Ch (abandoned)—*church* .... MO-7
Lone Prairie Lookout Tower—*locale* .... OK-5
Lone Prairie Sch—*school* .... KS-7
Lone Rabbit Water Hole—*lake* .... OR-9
Lone Ranch Creek—*stream* .... OR-9
Lone Ranch Creek—*stream* .... WA-9
Lone Ranger Ranch—*locale* .... CO-8
Lone Range Sch—*school* .... NE-7
Lonergan—*fmr MCD* .... NE-7
Lonergan Creek—*stream* .... NE-7
Lonergan Lake—*lake* .... MN-6
*Lone Ridge* .... OR-9
*Lone Ridge* .... TN-4
Lone Ridge—*ridge* .... AK-9
Lone Ridge—*ridge* .... OR-9
Lone Ridge—*ridge* .... TN-4
Lone Ridge—*summit* .... TN-4
Lone Ridge Sch (abandoned)—*school* .... MO-7
*Lone Rock* .... OR-9
Lone Rock—*bar* .... CA-9
Lone Rock—*bar* .... MA-1
Lone Rock—*cliff* .... AR-4
Lone Rock—*gap* .... OK-5
Lone Rock—*island* (2) .... AK-9
Lone Rock—*island* .... AZ-5
Lone Rock—*island* .... OR-9
Lone Rock—*locale* .... AR-4
Lone Rock—*locale* .... ID-8
Lone Rock—*locale* .... WI-6
Lone Rock—*other* .... AK-9
Lone Rock—*pillar* .... CA-9
Lone Rock—*pillar* .... ID-8
Lone Rock—*pillar* .... KY-4
Lone Rock—*pillar* .... MI-6
Lone Rock—*pillar* .... OR-9
Lone Rock—*pillar* (4) .... UT-8
Lone Rock—*pillar* .... WA-9
Lone Rock—*pillar* .... WI-6
**Lone Rock**—*pop pl* .... IA-7
**Lonerock**—*pop pl* .... OR-9
**Lone Rock**—*pop pl* .... WI-6
Lone Rock—*rock* (4) .... MA-1
Lone Rock—*rock* .... UT-8
Lone Rock—*summit* (2) .... CO-8
Lone Rock—*summit* (2) .... MO-7
Lone Rock—*summit* .... NV-8
Lone Rock—*summit* .... OR-9
Lone Rock—*summit* .... UT-8
Lone Rock—*summit* .... WI-6
Lone Rock Basin—*basin* .... UT-8
Lone Rock Beach—*beach* .... UT-8
Lone Rock Bridge—*bridge* .... ID-8
Lone Rock Bridge—*bridge* .... OR-9
Lone Rock Camp—*locale* .... OR-9
Lone Rock Campground—*locale* .... CA-9
Lone Rock Campground—*locale* .... CO-8
Lone Rock Canyon—*valley* .... UT-8
Lonerock Cem—*cemetery* .... OR-9
Lone Rock Cem—*cemetery* .... SD-7
Lone Rock Cem—*cemetery* .... WI-6
Lone Rock Ch—*church* .... AR-4
Lone Rock Ch—*church* (2) .... MO-7
Lone Rock Ch—*church* .... SD-7
Lone Rock County Park—*park* .... OR-9
*Lone Rock Creek* .... MN-6
*Lone Rock Creek* .... OR-9
*Lone Rock Creek* .... SD-7
Lone Rock Creek—*stream* .... CA-9
Lone Rock Creek—*stream* .... CO-8
Lone Rock Creek—*stream* .... ID-8
Lone Rock Creek—*stream* .... MT-8
Lone Rock Creek—*stream* .... OR-9
Lone Rock Draw—*valley* .... CO-8
Lone Rock Hill—*summit* .... CO-8
Lone Rock Place—*locale* .... OR-9
Lone Rock Point—*cape* .... VT-1
Lone Rock Ravine—*valley* .... UT-8
Lone Rock Rsvr—*reservoir* .... ID-8
Lone Rock Sch—*school* (2) .... MO-7
Lone Rock Sch—*school* .... MT-8
Lone Rock Sch (historical)—*school* .... MO-7
**Lone Rock Township**—*pop pl* .... SD-7
Lone Rock (Township of)—*fmr MCD* .... AR-4
Lone Rock Valley—*valley* .... CA-9
Loner Siding—*locale* .... MD-2
Lone Rsvr—*reservoir* .... OR-9
Lone Rugged Tree Valley—*valley* .... AZ-5
*Lone Run* .... WV-2
Lone Sand Hill—*summit* .... WY-8
Lone Sassafras Cem—*cemetery* .... AR-4
Lone Sch—*school* .... WI-6
Lones Creek—*stream* .... OR-9
Lones Ditch—*canal* .... IN-6
Lone Sequoia Campground—*locale* .... CA-9
Lone Sharp Hill—*summit* .... AZ-5
Lonesome, Point—*cape* .... FL-3
Lonesome Bachelor, The—*summit* .... MT-8
Lonesome Bay—*bay* .... AK-9
Lonesome Bay—*bay* (3) .... NY-2
Lonesome Bayou—*gut* .... LA-4
Lonesome Beaver Campground—*park* .... UT-8
*Lonesome Beaver Rec Area* .... UT-8
*Lonesome Bend* .... AL-4
Lonesome Bottom—*bend* .... OR-9
Lonesome Branch—*stream* .... TN-4
Lonesome Butte—*summit* .... SD-7
Lonesome Cabin Draw—*valley* .... NM-5
Lonesome Cabin Tank—*reservoir* .... NM-5
Lonesome Camp Swamp—*swamp* .... FL-3
Lonesome Canyon—*valley* .... CA-9
*Lonesome Coulee* .... MT-8
Lonesome Coulee—*valley* .... MT-8
Lonesome Cove—*bay* .... WA-9
Lonesome Creek—*stream* (3) .... ID-8
Lonesome Creek—*stream* .... KY-4
Lonesome Creek—*stream* (2) .... MT-8
Lonesome Creek—*stream* .... ND-7
Lonesome Creek—*stream* (3) .... OR-9
Lonesome Creek—*stream* .... WA-9
Lonesome Dove Ch—*church* .... KY-4
Lonesome Dove Ch—*church* .... TX-5
Lonesome Dove Ch (historical)—*church* .... TN-4
Lonesome Dove Hollow—*valley* .... TN-4
Lonesome Duck Lake—*reservoir* .... AL-4
Lonesome Gulch—*valley* .... OR-9
Lonesome Gulch Pond—*reservoir* .... VA-3
Lonesome Hill Cem—*cemetery* .... MO-7
Lonesome Hills—*summit* .... AK-9
Lonesome Hill Sch (historical)—*school* .... MO-7
Lonesome Hollow—*valley* .... AR-4
Lonesome Hollow—*valley* .... IN-6
Lonesome Hollow—*valley* .... KY-4
Lonesome Island—*island* .... LA-4
Lonesome Knob Tank—*reservoir* .... AZ-5
*Lonesome Lake* .... MI-6
Lonesome Lake—*lake* .... AK-9
Lonesome Lake—*lake* .... AZ-5
Lonesome Lake—*lake* .... CA-9
Lonesome Lake—*lake* .... CO-8
Lonesome Lake—*lake* .... ID-8
Lonesome Lake—*lake* (2) .... MI-6
Lonesome Lake—*lake* (2) .... MT-8
Lonesome Lake—*lake* .... NH-1
Lonesome Lake—*lake* .... SD-7
Lonesome Lake—*lake* (2) .... WA-9
Lonesome Lake—*lake* (2) .... WY-8
Lonesome Lake—*reservoir* .... PA-2
Lonesome Lake Coulee—*valley* .... MT-8
Lonesome Lake Hut—*locale* .... NH-1
Lonesome Lake Trail—*trail* .... NH-1
Lonesome Lkae—*lake* .... CO-8
Lonesome Low Sch—*school* .... WV-2
Lonesome Meadow—*flat* .... OR-9
*Lonesome Meadows* .... OR-9
Lonesome Mine—*mine* .... AK-9
Lonesome Mine—*mine* .... NM-5
Lonesome Mtn—*summit* .... MT-8
Lonesome Mtn—*summit* .... NM-5
Lonesome Mtn—*summit* .... NC-3
Lonesome Mtn—*summit* .... VA-3
Lonesome Park—*flat* (2) .... UT-8
Lonesome Peak—*summit* .... AZ-5
Lonesome Peak—*summit* .... CO-8
Lonesome Peak—*summit* (2) .... MT-8
Lonesome Pine, Trail of the—*trail* .... NC-3
Lonesome Pine, Trail of the—*trail* .... TN-4
Lonesome Pine Cem—*cemetery* .... MS-4
Lonesome Pine Country Club—*other* .... VA-3
Lonesome Pine Flat—*flat* .... UT-8
Lonesome Pine Lake—*reservoir* .... VA-3
Lonesome Pine Sch—*school* .... TN-4
Lonesome Pine Trail, The—*trail* .... VA-3
Lonesome Pocket—*basin* .... AZ-5
Lonesome Pocket Tank—*reservoir* .... AZ-5
Lonesome Point—*cape* .... AK-9
Lonesome Point—*cape* .... MI-6
Lonesome Polecat Creek—*stream* .... MN-6
*Lonesome Pond* .... NY-2
Lonesome Pond—*lake* .... MT-8
Lonesome Pond—*lake* .... NY-2
Lonesome Pond—*lake* .... OR-9
Lonesome Prairie—*area* .... MT-8
Lonesome Ridge—*ridge* .... CA-9
Lonesome Ridge—*ridge* .... MT-8
Lonesome Ridge—*ridge* .... NH-1
Lonesome Ridge—*ridge* .... NM-5
Lonesome Ridge—*ridge* .... VA-3
Lonesome Ridge Sch—*school* .... NE-7
Lonesome Rock—*pillar* .... NM-5
Lonesome Sch (abandoned)—*school* .... MO-7
Lonesome Spring—*spring* .... OR-9
Lonesome Spring—*spring* .... WA-9
Lonesome Tank—*reservoir* .... AZ-5
Lonesome Valley—*valley* (3) .... AZ-5
Lonesome Valley—*valley* .... TN-4
*Lonesome Valley Church* .... TN-4
Lonesome Valley Creek—*stream* .... TN-4
*Lonesome Valley Elementary School* .... TN-4
Lonesome Valley Pond—*reservoir* .... AZ-5
Lonesome Valley Sch—*school* .... TN-4
Lonesome Wash—*stream* .... NV-8
Lonesome Well—*well* .... CO-8
Lones Pond—*swamp* .... TX-5
Lone Spring—*spring* .... CA-9
Lone Spring—*spring* .... CO-8
Lone Spring—*spring* .... NV-8
Lone Spring—*spring* .... OR-9
Lone Spring—*spring* .... UT-8
Lone Spring—*spring* .... WY-8
Lone Spring Butte—*summit* .... CO-8
Lone Spring Mtn—*summit* .... CA-9
Lone Spring Mtn—*summit* .... OR-9
Lone Spring Ridge—*ridge* .... CO-8
Lone Spring Ridge—*ridge* .... UT-8
Lone Spruce Draw—*valley* .... CO-8
Lone Spur—*ridge* .... KY-4
Lone Squaw Island—*island* .... MN-6
Lone Star—*locale* (2) .... AR-4
Lone Star—*locale* .... CA-9
Lone Star—*locale* .... CO-8
Lone Star—*locale* .... KY-4
Lone Star—*locale* .... MS-4
Lone Star—*locale* (2) .... MO-7
Lone Star—*locale* .... OR-9
Lone Star—*locale* (4) .... TX-5
Lone Star—*locale* .... VA-3
**Lone Star**—*pop pl* .... AZ-5
**Lone Star**—*pop pl* .... CA-9
**Lone Star**—*pop pl* .... ID-8
**Lone Star**—*pop pl* .... KS-7
**Lone Star**—*pop pl* (2) .... LA-4
**Lone Star**—*pop pl* .... SC-3
**Lone Star**—*pop pl* .... TN-4
**Lone Star**—*pop pl* (4) .... TX-5
Lone Star Army Ammun Plant—*military* .... TX-5
**Lone Star (Asander)**—*pop pl* .... TX-5
Lonestar Baptist Ch—*church* .... AL-4
Lone Star Baptist Ch—*church* .... MS-4
Lone Star Baptist Ch (historical)—*church* .... MS-4
Lone Star Baptist Ch (historical)—*church* .... TX-5
Lone Star Branch—*stream* .... TX-5
*Lone Star Brook* .... MA-1
Lone Star Camp—*locale* .... TX-5
Lone Star Canal—*canal* .... CA-9
Lone Star Canal—*canal* .... TX-5
Lone Star Cem—*cemetery* .... AL-4
Lone Star Cem—*cemetery* .... CA-9
Lone Star Cem—*cemetery* (5) .... KS-7
Lone Star Cem—*cemetery* (2) .... LA-4
Lone Star Cem—*cemetery* .... MN-6
Lone Star Cem—*cemetery* .... MS-4
Lone Star Cem—*cemetery* (2) .... MO-7
Lone Star Cem—*cemetery* (5) .... OK-5
Lone Star Cem—*cemetery* .... TN-4
Lone Star Cem—*cemetery* (4) .... TX-5
Lone Star Cemetery—*cemetery* .... AR-4
Lone Star Ch—*church* .... AL-4
Lone Star Ch—*church* (4) .... AR-4
Lone Star Ch—*church* .... IA-7
Lone Star Ch—*church* .... KS-7
Lone Star Ch—*church* (4) .... KY-4
Lone Star Ch—*church* (6) .... LA-4
Lone Star Ch—*church* (2) .... MS-4
Lone Star Ch—*church* (7) .... MO-7
Lone Star Ch—*church* (6) .... OK-5
Lone Star Ch—*church* (12) .... TX-5
Lone Star Ch—*church* (2) .... VA-3
Lone Star Ch—*church* (2) .... WV-2
Lone Star Ch (historical)—*church* .... TN-4
Lonestar Creek—*stream* .... AK-9
Lone Star Creek—*stream* .... CA-9
Lone Star Creek—*stream* .... WY-8
Lone Star Cumberland Presbyterian Ch (historical)—*church* .... AL-4
Lone Star Ditch—*canal* .... CO-8
Lone Star East Sch (historical)—*school* .... MO-7
Lone Star Elem Sch—*school* .... FL-3
Lone Star Geyser—*geyser* .... WY-8
Lone Star (historical)—*locale* .... SD-7
Lone Star Hollow—*valley* .... MO-7
Lone Star HS—*school* .... TX-5
*Lone Star Island* .... NY-2
Lone Star Junction—*locale* .... CA-9
Lone Star Lake—*lake* .... WI-6
Lone Star Lake—*reservoir* .... KS-7
Lone Star Lake—*reservoir* .... TX-5
Lone Star Lake Dam—*dam* .... KS-7
Lone Star Landing (historical)—*locale* .... MS-4
Lone Star Lookout Tower—*locale* .... KY-4
Lone Star Lookout Tower—*locale* .... WV-2
Lone Star Mine—*mine* (2) .... AZ-5
Lone Star Mine—*mine* (4) .... CA-9
Lone Star Mine—*mine* .... CO-8
Lone Star Mine—*mine* .... TX-5
Lone Star Mine (historical)—*mine* .... OR-9
Lone Star Mtn—*summit* .... AZ-5
Lone Star Private Sch—*school* .... TX-5
Lone Star Pumping Station—*other* .... TX-5
Lone Star Ranch—*locale* .... CA-9
Lone Star Ridge—*ridge* .... KY-4
Lone Star Ridge—*ridge* .... MO-7
Lone Star Road Shop Ctr—*locale* .... FL-3
Lone Star Sch—*school* .... CA-9
Lone Star Sch—*school* .... ID-8
Lone Star Sch—*school* (2) .... IL-6
Lone Star Sch—*school* .... IA-7
Lone Star Sch—*school* (2) .... KS-7
Lone Star Sch—*school* .... KY-4
Lone Star Sch—*school* .... MN-6
Lone Star Sch—*school* .... MS-4
Lone Star Sch—*school* (11) .... MO-7
Lone Star Sch—*school* (2) .... NE-7
Lone Star Sch—*school* (4) .... OK-5
Lone Star Sch—*school* .... SC-3
Lone Star Sch—*school* (4) .... SD-7
Lone Star Sch—*school* (5) .... TX-5
Lone Star Sch—*school* .... WV-2
Lone Star Sch (abandoned)—*school* (4) .... MO-7
Lone Star Sch (abandoned)—*school* .... PA-2
Lone Star Sch (historical)—*school* .... AL-4
Lone Star Sch (historical)—*school* .... MS-4
Lone Star Sch (historical)—*school* (9) .... MO-7
Lone Star Sch (historical)—*school* (2) .... TN-4
Lone Star School—*locale* .... MO-7
Lone Star School (Aban'd)—*locale* .... CA-9
Lone Star School (Abandoned)—*locale* .... MO-7
Lone Star School (abandoned)—*locale* .... MO-7
Lone Star School (Abandoned)—*locale* .... MO-7
Lone Star School (Abandoned)—*locale* .... NE-7
Lone Star School (historical)—*locale* (2) .... MO-7
Lone Star Spring—*spring* .... AR-4
Lone Star Spring—*spring* .... WA-9
Lone Star Steel Lake—*reservoir* .... OK-5

Lone Star Tank—reservoir ... TX-5
**Lone Star Township—pop pl** ... KS-7
**Lone Star Township—pop pl (2)** ... SD-7
**Lone Star (trailer park)—pop pl** ... DE-2
Lone Star United Methodist Ch—church ... MS-4
Lone Star Wash—stream ... AZ-5
Lone Star West Sch ... MO-7
Lone Star Windmill—locale ... TX-5
Lone Stone Creek—stream ... WI-6
Lone Stone Lake—lake ... WI-6
Lone Susan Island—island ... MI-6
Lone Sycamore Gulch—valley ... AZ-5
Lone Tank—reservoir ... AZ-5
Lonetot Corners—locale ... PA-2
Lonetree ... IN-6
Lone Tree ... KS-7
Lone Tree ... ND-7
Lonetree—hist pl ... MT-8
Lonetree—locale ... CO-8
Lone Tree—locale ... IL-6
Lone Tree—locale ... OR-9
Lone Tree—locale ... SD-7
Lone Tree—locale (2) ... UT-8
Lonetree—locale ... WV-2
Lone Tree—other ... CA-9
**Lone Tree—pop pl** ... IL-6
**Lone Tree—pop pl** ... IN-6
**Lonetree—pop pl** ... IN-6
**Lone Tree—pop pl** ... IA-7
**Lone Tree—pop pl** ... MO-7
**Lonetree—pop pl** ... ND-7
**Lonetree—pop pl** ... WY-8
Lone Tree—summit ... ID-8
Lone Tree Arroyo ... CO-8
Lone Tree Arroyo—stream ... CO-8
Lone Tree Bar—bar ... OR-9
Lone Tree Bayou—gut ... TX-5
Lone Tree Bench—bench ... MT-8
Lone Tree Bench Sch—school ... MT-8
Lone Tree Branch—stream (2) ... IA-7
Lone Tree Bridge—bridge ... OR-9
Lone Tree Campsite—locale ... UT-8
Lone Tree Canal—canal ... CA-9
Lone Tree Canyon ... CA-9
Lonetree Canyon—valley ... AZ-5
Lonetree Canyon—valley ... CA-9
Lonetree Canyon—valley ... CO-8
Lone Tree Canyon—valley ... KS-7
Lone Tree Canyon—valley ... UT-8
Lone Tree Canyon—valley ... WY-8
Lone Tree Cem—cemetery ... AR-4
Lone Tree Cem—cemetery ... CA-9
Lone Tree Cem—cemetery ... CO-8
Lone Tree Cem—cemetery ... IL-6
Lone Tree Cem—cemetery (3) ... IA-7
Lone Tree Cem—cemetery ... KS-7
Lone Tree Cem—cemetery (2) ... NE-7
Lone Tree Cem—cemetery ... OK-5
Lonetree Cem—cemetery ... WY-8
Lone Tree Ch—church ... KS-7
Lone Tree Ch—church ... OK-5
Lonetree Channel—canal (2) ... CA-9
Lone Tree Community Center—locale ... CA-9
Lone Tree Corners Cem—cemetery ... IL-6
Lone Tree Coulee—stream ... MT-8
Lone Tree Coulee—valley (3) ... MT-8
Lonetree Coulee—valley ... MT-8
Lone Tree Coulee—valley (3) ... MT-8
Lonetree Coulee—valley ... MT-8
Lone Tree Coulee—valley (2) ... MT-8
Lone Tree Coulee—valley ... ND-7
Lone Tree Creek ... MT-8
Lonetree Creek ... TX-5
Lone Tree Creek—bay ... NC-3
Lone Tree Creek—gut ... NJ-2
Lone Tree Creek—stream (5) ... CA-9
Lone Tree Creek—stream (2) ... CO-8
Lonetree Creek—stream ... CO-8
Lone Tree Creek—stream (5) ... CO-8
Lone Tree Creek—stream ... ID-8
Lone Tree Creek—stream ... IL-6
Lone Tree Creek—stream ... IA-7
Lone Tree Creek—stream (4) ... KS-7
Lone Tree Creek—stream ... MA-1
Lone Tree Creek—stream ... MN-6
Lone Tree Creek—stream (7) ... MT-8
Lonetree Creek—stream ... MT-8
Lone Tree Creek—stream (11) ... MT-8
Lone Tree Creek—stream (3) ... NE-7
Lone Tree Creek—stream ... NC-3
Lone Tree Creek—stream ... ND-7
Lone Tree Creek—stream ... OK-5
Lone Tree Creek—stream (3) ... OR-9
Lonetree Creek—stream ... SD-7
Lone Tree Creek—stream ... SD-7
Lonetree Creek—stream (2) ... SD-7
Lone Tree Creek—stream ... SD-7
Lonetree Creek—stream ... SD-7
Lone Tree Creek—stream (8) ... SD-7
Lone Tree Creek—stream (3) ... TX-5
Lone Tree Creek—stream ... WA-9
Lone Tree Creek—stream ... WY-8
Lonetree Creek—stream ... WY-8
Lone Tree Creek—stream (5) ... WY-8
Lonetree Creek—stream ... WY-8
Lone Tree Creek—stream (3) ... WY-8
Lonetree Creek—stream ... WY-8
Lone Tree Creek—stream (3) ... WY-8
Lonetree Creek—stream ... WY-8
Lone Tree Creek—stream (5) ... WY-8
Lone Tree Creek Oil Field—oilfield ... WY-8
Lone Tree Crossing—locale ... UT-8
Lone Tree Crossing—locale ... WY-8
Lone Tree Ditch—canal (3) ... CO-8
Lone Tree Ditch—canal ... SD-7
Lone Tree Ditch—canal ... WY-8
Lone Tree Draw—valley ... CO-8
Lone Tree Draw—valley ... NM-5
Lone Tree Draw—valley ... SD-7
Lone Tree Draw—valley (3) ... WY-8
Lone Tree Gulch—valley ... AK-9
Lone Tree Gulch—valley (4) ... CO-8
Lone Tree Gulch—valley (2) ... MT-8
Lone Tree Gulch—valley (3) ... WY-8
Lone Tree Gun Club—other ... CA-9
Lone Tree Hill—summit ... CA-9
Lone Tree Hill—summit (3) ... MA-1
Lone Tree Hill—summit ... MT-8
Lone Tree Hill—summit ... NV-8
Lone Tree Hill—summit ... NM-5
Lone Tree Hill—summit (2) ... TX-5
Lone Tree Hill—summit (2) ... VT-1
Lone Tree Hill—summit ... WA-9
Lone Tree Hill—summit (2) ... WY-8
Lone Tree (historical)—locale ... KS-7
Lone Tree Hollow—valley ... TX-5
Lone Tree Indian Mound—summit ... IL-6
Lone Tree Island—island ... AK-9
Lone Tree Island—island (2) ... MI-6
Lone Tree Island—island ... MN-6
Lone Tree Island—island ... NY-2
Lone Tree Island—island ... WA-9
Lone Tree Islet—island ... AK-9
Lonetree Knob—summit ... WV-2
Lone Tree Lake—flat ... OR-9
Lone Tree Lake—lake (3) ... MN-6
Lone Tree Lake—lake ... MT-8
Lone Tree Lake—lake ... NE-7
Lonetree Lake—lake ... NM-5
Lone Tree Lake—lake (2) ... ND-7
Lonetree Lake—lake ... ND-7
Lone Tree Lake—lake (2) ... ND-7
Lone Tree Lake—lake (2) ... SD-7
Lone Tree Lake—lake ... WA-9
Lone Tree Lake—lake ... WI-6
Lone Tree Lakebed—flat ... MN-6
Lone Tree Lake (historical)—lake ... IA-7
Lonetree Lake Post Office (historical)—building ... SD-7
Lone Tree Lake State Public Shooting Area—park ... SD-7
Lone Tree Mesa—summit ... AZ-5
Lone Tree Mesa—summit ... CO-8
Lone Tree Mineral Spring—spring ... CA-9
Lone Tree Mountain ... OR-9
Lone Tree Mtn—summit ... AR-4
Lonetree Mtn—summit ... CO-8
Lone Tree Mtn—summit ... MO-7
Lone Tree Mtn—summit ... NM-5
Lone Tree Mtn—summit ... UT-8
Lone Tree Mtn—summit ... WA-9
Lonetree Mtn—summit ... WV-2
Lone Tree Oil Field—oilfield ... WY-8
Lone Tree Park—flat ... CO-8
Lone Tree Park—flat (2) ... MT-8
Lone Tree Pass—gap (2) ... MT-8
Lone Tree Pass—gap ... OR-9
Lone Tree Pass—gap ... WA-9
Lone Tree Peak—summit ... ID-8
Lone Tree Peak—summit ... MT-8
Lone Tree Point ... RI-1
Lone Tree Point ... WI-6
Lonetree Point—cape ... AK-9
Lone Tree Point—cape ... AK-9
Lone Tree Point—cape ... CA-9
Lone Tree Point—cape ... IA-7
Lone Tree Point—cape ... MN-6
Lone Tree Point—cape ... OR-9
Lone Tree Point—cape ... TX-5
Lone Tree Point—cape ... WA-9
Lone Tree Point—cape ... WI-6
Lone Tree Pothole—lake ... AZ-5
Lone Tree Prong—stream ... WY-8
Lone Tree Ranch—locale ... ID-8
Lone Tree Ranch—locale ... NV-8
Lone Tree Ranch—locale ... OR-9
Lone Tree Ranch—locale ... WY-8
Lone Tree Ridge—ridge ... CA-9
Lone Tree Ridge—ridge ... MT-8
Lone Tree Ridge—ridge ... NY-2
Lone Tree Ridge—ridge ... OR-9
Lone Tree Road Overpass—crossing ... AZ-5
Lone Tree Rsvr—reservoir ... AZ-5
Lonetree Rsvr—reservoir ... CO-8
Lone Tree Rsvr—reservoir ... CO-8
Lone Tree Rsvr—reservoir ... MT-8
Lone Tree Rsvr—reservoir ... NV-8
Lone Tree Rsvr—reservoir ... OR-9
Lone Tree Rsvr—reservoir ... UT-8
Lone Tree Rsvr—reservoir ... WY-8
Lone Tree Rsvr No 1—reservoir ... WY-8
Lone Tree Rsvr No 2—reservoir ... WY-8
Lone Tree Rsvr Number One—reservoir ... MT-8
Lone Tree Rsvr Number Two—reservoir ... MT-8
Lone Tree Sag—basin ... MT-8
Lone Tree Sch—school (2) ... CA-9
Lone Tree Sch—school (2) ... CO-8
Lone Tree Sch—school ... ID-8
Lone Tree Sch—school ... IL-6
Lone Tree Sch—school (2) ... IA-7
Lone Tree Sch—school ... KS-7
Lone Tree Sch—school ... MI-6
Lone Tree Sch—school (2) ... MT-8
Lone Tree Sch—school (2) ... NE-7
Lone Tree Sch—school ... NV-8
Lone Tree Sch—school ... ND-7
Lone Tree Sch—school (4) ... SD-7
Lone Tree Sch—school ... TX-5
Lone Tree Sch (abandoned)—school ... MO-7
Lone Tree Sch Number 1—school ... ND-7
Lone Tree Sch Number 2—school ... ND-7
Lonetree School—locale ... MT-8
Lone Tree Section—other ... MT-8
Lone Tree Slough—swamp ... MN-6
Lone Tree Spring—spring (2) ... CO-8
Lone Tree Spring—spring ... ID-8
Lonetree Spring—spring ... ID-8
Lone Tree Spring—spring ... ID-8
Lone Tree Spring—spring ... NV-8
Lone Tree Spring—spring (2) ... SD-7
Lone Tree Spring—spring ... WY-8
Lone Tree Stage Station (site)—locale ... WY-8
Lone Tree Tank—reservoir ... AZ-5
Lone Tree Tank—reservoir (2) ... NM-5
Lone Tree Township—civil (2) ... SD-7
Lone Tree Township—fmr MCD ... IA-7
**Lone Tree Township—pop pl (2)** ... KS-7
**Lone Tree Township—pop pl** ... NE-7
**Lone Tree Township—pop pl** ... ND-7
**Lone Tree Township—pop pl (3)** ... SD-7
Lonetree Township (historical)—civil ... SD-7
**Lone Tree (Township of)—pop pl** ... MN-6
Lone Tree Valley—valley ... CA-9
Lone Tree Wedge—cape ... UT-8
Lone Tree Well—well ... CA-9
Lone Tree Well—well ... NV-8
Lone Tree Well—well (2) ... NM-5
Lone Tree Windmill—locale ... CO-8
Lone Tree Windmill—locale ... TX-5
Lone Trough Spring—spring ... NV-8
Lone Tule Wash—stream ... AZ-5
Lone Valley—basin ... CA-9
Lone Valley—basin ... NE-7
Lone Valley Branch—stream ... KY-4
Lone Valley Cem—cemetery (2) ... AR-4
Lone Valley Ch—church ... AR-4
Lone Valley Ch—church ... KY-4
Lone Valley Reservoir ... CA-9
Lone Valley Sch—school ... NE-7
Lone Valley Sch (historical)—school ... MO-7
Loneview—uninc pl ... OK-5
Lonewa Bayou—stream ... LA-4
Lone Walker Mtn—summit ... MT-8
Lone Walnut (historical)—locale ... KS-7
Lone Walnut Sch (historical)—school ... MO-7
Lone Wash—valley ... UT-8
Lone Well—well (2) ... NM-5
Lone Well Creek—stream ... SD-7
Lonewell Township (historical)—civil ... SD-7
Lone Willow—locale ... NV-8
Lone Willow—locale ... TX-5
Lone Willow Ch (historical)—church ... TN-4
Lone Willow Creek—stream ... IA-7
Lone Willow Creek—stream ... MT-8
Lone Willow Creek—stream ... OR-9
Lone Willow Island—island ... WI-6
Lone Willow Point—cape ... AR-4
Lone Willow Sch (historical)—school ... TN-4
Lone Willow Slough—gut ... CA-9
Lone Willow Spring—spring ... CA-9
Lone Willow Spring—spring ... ID-8
Lone Willow Spring—spring ... MT-8
Lone Willow Spring—spring (2) ... NV-8
Lone Willow Spring—spring ... OR-9
Lone Willow Springs ... OR-9
Lone Wolf—locale ... NM-5
**Lone Wolf—pop pl** ... OK-5
Lone Wolf—summit ... OR-9
Lone Wolf Bridge—bridge ... TX-5
Lone Wolf Camp—locale ... TX-5
Lone Wolf Camp—locale ... WA-9
Lone Wolf Canal—canal ... CO-8
Lone Wolf (CCD)—cens area ... OK-5
Lone Wolf Cem—cemetery ... TX-5
Lone Wolf Chapel—church ... OK-5
**Lone Wolf Colony—pop pl** ... CA-9
Lone Wolf Creek—stream ... TX-5
Lone Wolf Crossing Bridge—hist pl ... TX-5
Lone Wolf Lake—lake ... WI-6
Lone Wolf Mine—mine ... AZ-5
Lone Wolf Mine—mine ... MT-8
Lone Wolf Mine—mine ... NV-8
Lone Wolf Mtn—summit ... TX-5
Lone Wolf Windmills—locale ... NM-5
Lonewoman Creek—stream ... OR-9
Lone Woman Mtn—summit ... TX-5
Lonewood—locale ... TN-4
Lonewood Cem—cemetery ... TN-4
Lonewood Lake—lake ... WI-6
Lonewood Sch (historical)—school ... TN-4
Loney Creek—stream ... NC-3
Loney Lake—lake ... CA-9
Loney Meadow—flat ... CA-9
Lonez Well No 1—well ... NM-5
Lonfit—area ... GU-9
Lonfit River—stream ... GU-9
Long ... MI-6
Long ... MN-6
Long ... PA-2
Long—locale ... AR-4
Long—locale ... MS-4
Long—locale ... OK-5
Long—locale ... WA-9
Long—locale ... WV-2
Long—other ... VA-3
**Long—pop pl** ... AK-9
**Long—pop pl** ... MD-2
**Long—pop pl** ... OH-6
**Long—pop pl** ... OR-9
Long, Alexander, House—hist pl ... NC-3
Long, Bay—bay ... LA-4
Long, Bayou—gut (3) ... LA-4
Long, Bayou—stream (2) ... LA-4
Long, Chester I., House—hist pl ... KS-7
Long, Crawford W., Childhood Home—hist pl ... GA-3
Long, Crawford W., Memorial Hosp—hist pl ... GA-3
Long, D. T., House—hist pl ... KY-4
Long, George Parker, House—hist pl ... LA-4
Long, Huey P., Mansion—hist pl ... LA-4
Long, Lac—lake ... LA-4
Long, Lake—lake ... AK-9
Long, Lake—lake (2) ... LA-4
Long, R. A., House—hist pl ... MO-7
Long, Robert Alexander, HS—hist pl ... WA-9
Long, Samuel C., House—hist pl ... AZ-5
Long, William, Log House—hist pl ... MO-7
Long, William H., Memorial—hist pl ... NH-1
Long, William H., House—hist pl ... NC-3
Long A—stream ... TX-5
Longacoming ... NJ-2
**Longacre—pop pl** ... WV-2
Long Acre—ridge ... NC-3
Longacre Cem—cemetery ... AL-4
Long Acre Chapel—church ... NC-3
Longacre Draw—valley ... WA-9
Longacre Park—park ... IN-6
Long Acre Park—uninc pl ... PA-2
Long Acres—locale ... PA-2
**Long Acres—pop pl** ... DE-2
**Long Acres—pop pl** ... IN-6
Long Acres Branch—stream ... IN-6
Longacre Sch—school ... MI-6
Longacre Siding Station—locale ... PA-2
Longacres Park—park ... MI-6
**Longacres Park—pop pl** ... NV-8
Longacres Race Track—other ... WA-9
Longacres Sch—school ... NY-2
**Long Acres (subdivision)—pop pl** ... NC-3
Long Acre (Township of)—fmr MCD ... NC-3
Long Airp—airport ... IN-6
Long Alakline Lake—lake ... ND-7
Long Alec Creek—stream ... WA-9
Long Alex Creek ... WA-9
Long-Allen Bridge—bridge ... LA-4
Longamas—bar ... FM-9
Longan Branch—stream ... MO-7
Long and Derry Hill—summit ... CO-8
Long and Pierce Drain—canal ... MI-6
Long and Third Commercial Bldg—hist pl ... OH-6
Longan Sch—school ... MO-7
Longar ... MP-9
Long Arm ... TN-4
Long Arm—bay ... AK-9
Long Arm—cape ... FL-3
Long Arm—ridge ... TN-4
Long Arm—ridge ... VA-3
Longarm Branch—stream ... TN-4
Long Arm Branch—stream ... TX-5
Longarm Creek—stream ... AK-9
Long Arm Creek—stream ... PA-2
Long Arm Ditch—canal ... TN-4
Long Arm Hollow—valley ... VA-3
Longarm Mtn—summit ... NC-3
Long Arm Mtn—summit ... NC-3
Long Arm Mtn—summit ... VA-3
Long Arm Reservoir ... PA-2
Long Arm Ridge—ridge (2) ... NC-3
Longarm Ridge—ridge ... TN-4
Long Arroyo—stream ... NM-5
Long Arroyo Draw—valley ... NM-5
Long Arsenicker ... FL-3
Long Arsenicker Key—island ... FL-3
Long Ashepoo Creek—stream ... SC-3
Long A (Township of)—unorg ... ME-1
Long Ave Baptist Ch—church ... FL-3
Long Bald—summit ... MO-7
Long Bank Prospect—mine ... TN-4
Long Bar—bar ... CA-9
Long Bar—bar (2) ... FL-3
Long Bar—bar (2) ... MD-2
Long Bar—bar ... NY-2
Long Bar Harbor—harbor ... MD-2
**Long Bar Harbor—pop pl** ... MD-2
**Long Barn—pop pl** ... CA-9
Long Bar Point—cape ... DE-2
Long Bar Point—cape ... FL-3
Long Basin Light—locale ... MA-1
Long Bay ... AK-9
Long Bay ... NH-1
Long Bay—bay (2) ... AK-9
Long Bay—bay ... LA-4
Long Bay—bay ... NY-2
Long Bay—bay (2) ... NC-3
Long Bay—bay ... OK-5
Long Bay—bay ... SC-3
Long Bay—bay ... TX-5
Long Bay—bay ... WA-9
Long Bay—bay (2) ... VI-3
Long Bay—gut ... MO-7
Long Bay—lake ... GA-3
Long Bay—lake (2) ... LA-4
Long Bay—swamp (3) ... FL-3
Long Bay—swamp ... MS-4
Long Bay—swamp (4) ... NC-3
Long Bay—swamp (2) ... SC-3
Long Bay (Carolina Bay)—swamp ... NC-3
**Long Bay Estates—pop pl** ... SC-3
Long Bay Hollow—valley ... MO-7
Long Bayou ... FL-3
Long Bayou ... LA-4
Long Bayou—bay ... FL-3
Long Bayou—gut ... AL-4
Long Bayou—gut (2) ... LA-4
Long Bayou—gut ... MS-4
Long Bayou—gut ... TX-5
Long Bayou—stream ... FL-3
Long Bayou—stream (3) ... LA-4
Long Bayou—stream ... MS-4
Long Bayou-Greentree Rsvr—reservoir ... MS-4
Long Bay Point—cape ... NC-3
Long Bay Rec Area—park ... OK-5
Long Bays—swamp ... NC-3
Long Beach ... FL-3
Long Beach ... MA-1
Long Beach ... MI-6
Long Beach ... MH-9
Long Beach—beach (2) ... AK-9
Long Beach—beach (2) ... CT-1
Long Beach—beach ... FL-3
Long Beach—beach ... ME-1
Long Beach—beach (4) ... MA-1
Long Beach—beach ... NJ-2
Long Beach—beach (4) ... NY-2
Long Beach—beach ... NC-3
**Long Beach—pop pl** ... CA-9
**Longbeach—pop pl** ... FL-3
**Long Beach—pop pl** ... IN-6
**Long Beach—pop pl (2)** ... ME-1
**Long Beach—pop pl** ... MD-2
**Long Beach—pop pl** ... MA-1
**Long Beach—pop pl** ... MN-6
**Long Beach—pop pl** ... MS-4
**Long Beach—pop pl** ... MO-7
**Long Beach—pop pl** ... NJ-2
**Long Beach—pop pl** ... NY-2
**Long Beach—pop pl** ... NC-3
**Long Beach—pop pl** ... OH-6
**Long Beach—pop pl** ... WA-9
Long Beach Airp (Daugherty Field)—airport ... CA-9
Long Beach Bar Lighthouse—locale ... NY-2
Long Beach Bay—bay ... NY-2
**Long Beach (Beach Haven Park)—pop pl** ... NJ-2
Long Beach Breakwater—dam ... CA-9
Long Beach-Calvert Beach—CDP ... MD-2
Long Beach Ch—church ... FL-3
Long Beach Channel—channel ... CA-9
Long Beach City ... NJ-2
Long Beach City Coll—school ... CA-9
Long Beach City Hall—building ... MS-4
Long Beach Elem Sch—school ... IN-6
Long Beach First United Methodist Ch—church ... MS-4
Long Beach Harbor—harbor ... MS-4
Long Beach Hollow—valley ... NY-2
Long Beach Island ... NJ-2
Long Beach JHS—school ... MS-4
Long Beach JHS—school ... NY-2
Long Beach-Lakewood (CCD)—cens area ... CA-9
Long Beach Lido Beach HS—school ... NY-2
Long Beach Marina—locale ... MS-4
Long Beach Middle Harbor—bay ... CA-9
Long Beach Naval Regional Med Ctr—military ... CA-9
Long Beach Naval Shipyard—military ... CA-9
Long Beach Naval Station—military ... CA-9
**Long Beach Park—pop pl** ... NJ-2
Long Beach Plaza Shop Ctr—locale ... MS-4
Long Beach Point ... NY-2
Long Beach Point—cape ... MA-1
Long Beach Point—cape ... NY-2
Long Beach Public Library—building ... MS-4
**Long Beach Resort—pop pl** ... FL-3
Long Beach Rock—rock ... MA-1
Long Beach Senior HS—school ... MS-4
Long Beach Thorofare ... NY-2
**Long Beach (Township of)—pop pl** ... NJ-2
Long Beach Yacht Club—locale ... MS-4
Long Bed—basin ... IN-6
Long Bell Creek—stream ... OK-5
Long Bell State Game Ref—park ... CA-9
Long Bell Station—locale ... CA-9
Long Bench—bench (2) ... UT-8
Long Bench Creek ... OR-9
Long Bend ... TN-4
Long Bend—bend ... AL-4
Long Bend—bend ... AK-9
Long Bend—bend ... AZ-5
Long Bend—bend ... KY-4
Long Bend—bend ... TX-5
Long Bend Shoal—bar ... AL-4
Long Billy Spring—spring ... CA-9
Long Birch Creek—stream ... UT-8
Long Bluff—cliff ... FL-3
Long Bluff—summit ... WI-6
Long Bluff Cem—cemetery ... NC-3
Long Bluff Landing—locale ... NC-3
Longboat Creek—stream ... VA-3
Longboat Inlet ... FL-3
Longboat Key—island ... FL-3
**Longboat Key—pop pl** ... FL-3
Longboat Key (CCD)—cens area ... FL-3
Longboat Pass—channel ... FL-3
Long Bog—lake (3) ... ME-1
Long Bog—swamp (2) ... ME-1
Long Bog Brook—stream ... ME-1
Long Boggs Hollow—valley ... OK-5
Long Bog Run—stream ... NJ-2
Long Bottom—basin ... KY-4
Long Bottom—bend ... KY-4
Long Bottom—bend ... OH-6
Long Bottom—bend ... UT-8
Long Bottom—locale ... KY-4
**Long Bottom—pop pl** ... OH-6
**Longbottom—pop pl** ... VA-3
Long Bottom—valley ... WV-2
Long Bottom Branch—stream ... VA-3
Longbottom Canyon—valley ... NM-5
Long Bottom Cem—cemetery ... NC-3
Long Bottom Cem—cemetery ... TX-5
Long Bottom Creek—stream ... TX-5
Longbottom Creek—stream ... WV-2
Long Bottom Ford—locale ... GA-3
Long Bottom Ford—locale ... SC-3
Long Bottom Hollow—valley ... TN-4
Longbottom Polygonal Barn—hist pl ... IA-7
Long Bottoms—flat ... NC-3
Long Bottoms—valley ... AL-4
Long Bow Camp—locale ... OR-9
Long Bow Creek—stream ... MT-8
Long Bow Lake—lake ... MT-8
Long Bown Lake Dam—dam ... MA-1
Long Bow Reach—channel ... TX-5
Long Brake—swamp ... LA-4
Long Brake—swamp ... MS-4
Long Brake Creek—stream ... TX-5
Long Brake (historical)—swamp ... LA-4
Long Branch ... AL-4
Long Branch ... CT-1
Long Branch ... DE-2
Long Branch ... FL-3
Long Branch ... GA-3
Long Branch ... IN-6
Long Branch ... KS-7
Long Branch ... KY-4
Long Branch ... LA-4
Long Branch ... MD-2
Long Branch ... MO-7
Long Branch ... NC-3
Long Branch ... OH-6
Long Branch ... PA-2
Long Branch ... TN-4
Long Branch ... TX-5
Long Branch ... WV-2
Long Branch—bay ... MD-2
Long Branch—gut ... IL-6
Long Branch—hist pl ... VA-3
Long Branch—locale ... FL-3
Long Branch—locale ... IL-6
Long Branch—locale ... MS-4
Long Branch—locale ... NY-2
Long Branch—locale (2) ... TX-5
**Long Branch—pop pl** ... IL-6
**Long Branch—pop pl** ... KY-4
**Long Branch—pop pl** ... NJ-2
**Long Branch—pop pl** ... NC-3
**Long Branch—pop pl** ... PA-2
**Long Branch—pop pl (2)** ... SC-3
**Long Branch—pop pl (2)** ... TN-4
**Long Branch—pop pl** ... TX-5
**Long Branch—pop pl (3)** ... VA-3
**Longbranch—pop pl** ... WA-9
**Long Branch—pop pl (2)** ... WV-2
Long Branch—stream (27) ... AL-4
Long Branch—stream (15) ... AR-4
Long Branch—stream (3) ... CA-9
Long Branch—stream (2) ... CO-8
Long Branch—stream ... DE-2
Long Branch—stream (23) ... FL-3
Long Branch—stream (49) ... GA-3
Long Branch—stream (6) ... IL-6
Long Branch—stream (10) ... IN-6
Long Branch—stream (6) ... IA-7
Long Branch—stream (5) ... KS-7
Long Branch—stream (90) ... KY-4
Long Branch—stream (12) ... LA-4
Long Branch—stream (3) ... MD-2
Long Branch—stream (32) ... MS-4
Long Branch—stream (38) ... MO-7
Long Branch—stream (2) ... MT-8
Long Branch—stream ... NE-7
Long Branch—stream (2) ... NJ-2
Long Branch—stream (99) ... NC-3
Long Branch—stream (3) ... OH-6
Long Branch—stream (8) ... OK-5
Long Branch—stream (3) ... OR-9
Long Branch—stream (3) ... PA-2
Long Branch—stream (52) ... SC-3
Long Branch—stream (52) ... TN-4
Long Branch—stream (58) ... TX-5
Long Branch—stream (46) ... VA-3
Long Branch—stream (26) ... WV-2
Long Branch—swamp ... FL-3
Long Branch—swamp ... SC-3
Longbranch Annex—hist pl ... LA-4
Long Branch Baldy—summit ... CO-8
Long Branch Borough—civil ... PA-2
Long Branch Brook—stream ... CT-1
Long Branch Brook—stream ... MA-1
Long Branch Cem—cemetery (2) ... MS-4
Long Branch Cem—cemetery ... MO-7
Long Branch Cem—cemetery ... TX-5
Long Branch Ch—church (2) ... AL-4
Long Branch Ch—church ... FL-3
Long Branch Ch—church (2) ... GA-3
Long Branch Ch—church ... IN-6
Long Branch Ch—church ... KY-4
Long Branch Ch—church ... MS-4
Long Branch Ch—church (3) ... MO-7
Long Branch Ch—church (8) ... NC-3
Long Branch Ch—church (8) ... SC-3
Long Branch Ch—church (2) ... TN-4
Long Branch Ch—church ... TX-5
Long Branch Ch—church (2) ... VA-3
Long Branch Ch—church ... WV-2
Long Branch Chapel—church ... LA-4
Long Branch Ch (historical)—church ... TN-4
Long Branch Creek ... CO-8
Long Branch Creek ... KS-7
Long Branch Creek ... LA-4
Long Branch Creek ... OR-9
Long Branch Creek ... SC-3
Long Branch Creek ... WI-6
Longbranch Creek—stream ... AL-4
Long Branch Creek—stream ... CA-9
Long Branch Creek—stream ... FL-3
Long Branch Creek—stream ... MT-8
Long Branch Creek*—stream ... NE-7
Long Branch Creek—stream (2) ... OR-9
Long Branch Creek—stream ... SD-7
Long Branch Crossing—locale ... AL-4
Long Branch Dam—dam ... MO-7
Long Branch-Dotson (CCD)—cens area ... TX-5
Long Branch Draw ... KS-7
Long Branch Gap—gap ... TN-4
Long Branch Guard Station—locale ... CO-8
Long Branch Hill—summit ... PA-2
Long Branch Hollow—valley ... AR-4
Long Branch Hollow—valley ... OH-6
Longbranch Hotel Complex—hist pl ... LA-4
Long Branch HS—school ... NJ-2
Long Branch Lake—lake ... MT-8
Long Branch Lake—reservoir ... MO-7
**Long Branch Manor—pop pl** ... NY-2
Long Branch Methodist Church ... TN-4
Long Branch Mtn—summit ... VA-3
Long Branch Park—park ... MD-2
Long Branch Park—park ... NY-2
Long Branch Peninsula ... WA-9
Long Branch Picnic Area—park ... VA-3
Long Branch Reach—channel ... NJ-2
Long Branch Rec Area—park ... MS-4
Long Branch Rec Area—park ... TN-4
Long Branch Reservoir Dam—dam ... NC-3
Long Branch Rsvr—reservoir ... NC-3
Long Branch Rsvr—reservoir ... OR-9
Long Branch Run—stream ... NJ-2
Long Branch Sch—school (2) ... FL-3
Long Branch Sch—school ... IL-6
Long Branch Sch—school ... KY-4
Long Branch Sch—school ... MO-7
Long Branch Sch—school ... NY-2
Long Branch Sch—school (2) ... NC-3
Long Branch Sch—school ... TN-4
Long Branch Sch—school ... TX-5
Longbranch Sch—school ... WA-9
Long Branch Sch (abandoned)—school (2) ... MO-7
Longbranch Sch Gymnasium—hist pl ... WA-9
Long Branch Sch (historical)—school ... AL-4
Long Branch Sch (historical)—school ... MO-7
Long Branch Sch (historical)—school (3) ... TN-4
Long Branch Sch (reduced usage)—school ... TX-5
Long Branch Spring—spring ... OR-9
Long Branch Swamp—swamp ... SC-3
**Long Branch (Township of)—pop pl** ... IL-6
Long Branch Trail—trail ... TN-4
Longbridge ... LA-4
Long Bridge ... PA-2
Long Bridge—bridge ... AL-4
Long Bridge—bridge ... CA-9
Long Bridge—bridge ... DE-2
Long Bridge—bridge ... FL-3
Long Bridge—bridge (2) ... GA-3
Long Bridge—bridge ... TX-5
Long Bridge—bridge ... VA-3
Long Bridge—locale ... LA-4
Long Bridge—locale ... NJ-2
**Longbridge—pop pl** ... LA-4
**Long Bridge—pop pl** ... LA-4
**Long Bridge—pop pl** ... NY-2
**Longbridge—pop pl** ... PA-2
Long Bridge—uninc pl ... DC-2
Long Bridge Cem—cemetery ... NY-2
Long Bridge Community Ch—church ... FL-3
Long Bridge Creek—stream ... LA-4
Long Bridge Flat—flat ... NM-5
Long Bridge Gulch—valley ... CO-8
Long Bridge Hollow—valley ... OH-6
Longbridge Hollow—valley ... VA-3
Long Bridge Sch—school ... MI-6
Long-Briggs House—hist pl ... KY-4
Longbrook ... PA-2
Long Brook—locale ... PA-2
Long Brook—stream (2) ... CT-1
Long Brook—stream (2) ... ME-1
Long Brook—stream (2) ... NJ-2
Long Brook—stream ... OH-6
Long Brook—stream ... PA-2
Long Brook—stream ... RI-1
Long Brook Park—park ... CT-1
Long Brook Ridge—summit ... ME-1
Long Broughton Branch—stream ... MD-2
Long Brown Rock—island ... OR-9
Long Brush Hill ... MA-1
Long Bullet Branch—stream ... GA-3
Long Bullet Creek—stream ... GA-3

Long Bunk—ridge ... NC-3
Long Butte—summit ... AZ-5
Long Butte—summit ... ID-8
Long Butte—summit (2) ... MT-8
Long Butte—summit (2) ... ND-7
Long Butte—summit (2) ... OR-9
Long Butte—summit ... WY-8
Long Butte Cem—cemetery ... ND-7
Long Butte Sch—school ... SD-7
Long Cabbage Island—island ... FL-3
Long Cabin—locale ... CA-9
Long Cabin—locale ... ID-8
Long Cabin—locale ... OR-9
Long Camp ... NC-3
Long Camp—locale ... NC-3
Long Canal—canal ... SD-7
Long Canal—canal ... UT-8
Long Cane—locale ... GA-3
Long Cane Cem—cemetery ... AR-4
Long Cane Cem—cemetery ... SC-3
Long Cane Ch—church ... SC-3
Long Cane Creek—stream ... GA-3
Long Cane Creek—stream ... SC-3
Long Cane Hist Dist—hist pl ... GA-3
Long Cane Massacre Site—hist pl ... SC-3
Long Cane Sch—school (2) ... SC-3
Long Canes Creek ... SC-3
Long Canyon ... CA-9
Long Canyon ... CO-8
Long Canyon—valley (16) ... AZ-5
Long Canyon—valley (49) ... CA-9
Long Canyon—valley (9) ... CO-8
Long Canyon—valley (6) ... ID-8
Long Canyon—valley ... MT-8
Long Canyon—valley (24) ... NV-8
Long Canyon—valley (25) ... NM-5
Long Canyon—valley (6) ... OR-9
Long Canyon—valley (2) ... TX-5
Long Canyon—valley (22) ... UT-8
Long Canyon—valley ... WA-9
Long Canyon—valley (5) ... WY-8
Long Canyon Creek—stream (2) ... CA-9
Long Canyon Creek—stream ... ID-8
Long Canyon Creek—stream ... MT-8
Long Canyon Creek—stream ... TX-5
Long Canyon Draw ... WY-8
Long Canyon Fork Tank—reservoir ... AZ-5
Long Canyon Hill—summit ... CO-8
Long Canyon (historical)—valley ... KS-7
Long Canyon Overlook—locale ... UT-8
Long Canyon Pass—gap ... ID-8
Long Canyon Point—cape ... UT-8
Long Canyon Rsvr ... OR-9
Long Canyon Rsvr—reservoir ... NV-8
Long Canyon Spring—spring (2) ... AZ-5
Long Canyon Spring—spring ... NV-8
Long Canyon Tank—reservoir (3) ... AZ-5
Long Canyon Tank—reservoir (4) ... NM-5
Long Canyon Trail—trail ... AZ-5
Long Canyon Trail—trail ... CA-9
Long Canyon Trail—trail ... MT-8
Long Canyon Village Site—hist pl ... CA-9
Long Canyon Wash—valley ... AZ-5
Long Canyon Wash—valley ... UT-8
Long Carrying Place ... NY-2
Long Causeway—locale ... NJ-2
Long Causeway Branch—stream ... NJ-2
Long Causeway Brook—stream ... MA-1
Long Cem—cemetery (4) ... AL-4
Long Cem—cemetery ... AR-4
Long Cem—cemetery ... DE-2
Long Cem—cemetery ... FL-3
Long Cem—cemetery (3) ... GA-3
Long Cem—cemetery (3) ... IL-6
Long Cem—cemetery (2) ... IN-6
Long Cem—cemetery (6) ... KY-4
Long Cem—cemetery (2) ... MI-6
Long Cem—cemetery (3) ... MS-4
Long Cem—cemetery ... NY-2
Long Cem—cemetery ... NC-3
Long Cem—cemetery (5) ... OH-6
Long Cem—cemetery (2) ... PA-2
Long Cem—cemetery (19) ... TN-4
Long Cem—cemetery (5) ... TX-5
Long Cem—cemetery (4) ... VA-3
Long Cem—cemetery (3) ... WV-2
Long Cemeteries—cemetery ... MO-7
Long Ch—church ... AL-4
Long Ch—church ... NC-3
Long Ch—church ... OK-5
Long Ch—church ... TN-4
Long Chance Mine—mine ... CA-9
Long Channel—channel ... AK-9
Long Chapel—church ... GA-3
Long Chapel—church ... IN-6
Long Chapel—church (2) ... NC-3
Long Cherry Ch—church ... LA-4
Long Cienega—flat ... AZ-5
Long Cliff—cliff ... KY-4
Longcliff Hosp—hospital ... IN-6
**Long Cliff (State Mental Hospital)**—pop pl ... IN-6
Long Clove—gap ... NY-2
Longcommon Park—park ... IL-6
Longcore Sch—school ... MI-6
**Long Corner**—pop pl ... MD-2
Long Corners—locale ... NY-2
Long Coulee—stream ... MT-8
Long Coulee—valley (11) ... MT-8
Long Coulee—valley ... WI-6
Long Coulee Cem—cemetery ... WI-6
Long Coulee Park—park ... WI-6
**Long (County)**—pop pl ... GA-3
Long County Courthouse—hist pl ... GA-3
Long Cove ... ME-1
Long Cove ... MA-1
Long Cove—bay ... CT-1
Long Cove—bay ... GA-3
Long Cove—bay (17) ... ME-1
Long Cove—bay (6) ... MD-2
Long Cove—bay ... NY-2
Long Cove—bay ... NC-3
Long Cove—bay ... RI-1
Long Cove—bay ... VA-3
Long Cove—cove ... MA-1
Long Cove—locale ... TX-5
**Longcove**—pop pl ... ME-1
Long Cove—valley ... AL-4
Long Cove—valley ... GA-3
Long Cove—valley ... NC-3
Long Cove—valley (2) ... TN-4
Long Cove Branch—stream ... NC-3
Long Cove Brook—stream ... ME-1
Long Cove Creek—stream ... GA-3
Long Cove Creek—stream ... TN-4
Long Cove Ledge—bar ... ME-1
Long Cove Point—cape ... ME-1
Long Cove Ridge—ridge ... NC-3
Longcoy Sch—school ... OH-6
Long Creek ... AL-4
Long Creek ... AZ-5
Long Creek ... AR-4
Long Creek ... FL-3
Long Creek ... ID-8
Long Creek ... IL-6
Long Creek ... IN-6
Long Creek ... MD-2
Long Creek ... MI-6
Long Creek ... MS-4
Long Creek ... MT-8
Long Creek ... NV-8
Long Creek ... SC-3
Longcreek ... TN-4
Long Creek ... TX-5
Long Creek ... WV-2
Long Creek—bay (2) ... MD-2
Long Creek—bay ... NC-3
Long Creek—channel ... NY-2
Long Creek—gut ... VA-3
Long Creek—locale ... IA-7
Long Creek—locale (2) ... TN-4
**Long Creek**—pop pl ... IL-6
**Longcreek**—pop pl ... NC-3
**Long Creek**—pop pl ... NC-3
**Long Creek**—pop pl ... OR-9
**Longcreek**—pop pl ... SC-3
Long Creek—stream (4) ... AL-4
Long Creek—stream (3) ... AK-9
Long Creek—stream ... AZ-5
Long Creek—stream (8) ... AR-4
Long Creek—stream (2) ... CA-9
Long Creek—stream (3) ... CO-8
Long Creek—stream ... DE-2
Long Creek—stream (7) ... FL-3
Long Creek—stream (7) ... GA-3
Long Creek—stream (7) ... ID-8
Long Creek—stream (4) ... IL-6
Long Creek—stream ... IN-6
Long Creek—stream (3) ... IA-7
Long Creek—stream (4) ... KS-7
Long Creek—stream (7) ... KY-4
Long Creek—stream (2) ... ME-1
Long Creek—stream ... MD-2
Long Creek—stream ... MA-1
Long Creek—stream ... MN-6
Long Creek—stream (7) ... MS-4
Long Creek—stream (5) ... MO-7
Long Creek—stream (4) ... MT-8
Long Creek—stream ... NE-7
Long Creek—stream (2) ... NY-2
Long Creek—stream (18) ... NC-3
Long Creek—stream ... ND-7
Long Creek*—stream ... ND-7
Long Creek—stream (2) ... OH-6
Long Creek—stream (9) ... OK-5
Long Creek—stream (15) ... OR-9
Long Creek—stream (5) ... SC-3
Long Creek—stream (2) ... SD-7
Long Creek—stream (7) ... TN-4
Long Creek—stream (12) ... TX-5
Long Creek—stream ... UT-8
Long Creek—stream (9) ... VA-3
Long Creek—stream (4) ... WA-9
Long Creek—stream ... WI-6
Long Creek—stream (4) ... WY-8
Long Creek Acad—hist pl ... SC-3
Long Creek Acad—school ... SC-3
Long Creek Baptist Ch—church ... TN-4
Long Creek Baptist Church ... MS-4
Long Creek Bay—swamp ... FL-3
Long Creek (CCD)—cens area ... OR-9
Long Creek (CCD)—cens area ... SC-3
Long Creek Cem—cemetery (2) ... MS-4
Long Creek Cem—cemetery ... TX-5
Long Creek Ch—church ... AR-4
Long Creek Ch—church (2) ... GA-3
Long Creek Ch—church ... IA-7
Long Creek Ch—church (2) ... MS-4
Long Creek Ch—church (4) ... NC-3
Long Creek Ch—church ... ND-7
Long Creek Ch—church ... TN-4
Long Creek Ch—church ... TX-5
Long Creek Church ... AL-4
Long Creek Dam—dam ... NC-3
Long Creek Dam—dam ... ND-7
Long Creek Dam—dam ... OR-9
Long Creek Elementary School ... MS-4
Long Creek Grady Sch—school ... NC-3
Long Creek (historical)—locale ... SD-7
Long Creek - in part ... MO-7
Long Creek Lake—reservoir ... OK-5
Long Creek Landing—locale ... SC-3
Long Creek Lookout Tower—locale ... SC-3
Long Creek Memorial Ch—church ... NC-3
Long Creek Mill (historical)—locale ... TN-4
Long Creek Mtn—summit ... OR-9
Long Creek Mtn—summit ... WY-8
Long Creek Park—park ... MO-7
Long Creek Point—cape ... MD-2
Long Creek Point—cape ... NC-3
Long Creek Post Office ... TN-4
Longcreek Post Office (historical)—building ... TN-4
Long Creek Prospect—mine ... TN-4
Long Creek Public Use Area—locale ... MO-7
Long Creek Ranch—locale ... WY-8
Long Creek Recreation Center—locale ... MS-4
Long Creek Reservoir Dam—dam ... MS-4
Long Creek Ridge—ridge ... ID-8
Long Creek Rsvr—reservoir ... MS-4
Long Creek Rsvr—reservoir ... OR-9
Long Creek Sch ... NC-3
Long Creek Sch—school ... MS-4
Long Creek Sch—school ... NC-3
Long Creek Sch—school ... ND-7
Long Creek Sch (historical)—school ... AL-4
Long Creek Sch (historical)—school ... MS-4
Long Creek Sch (historical)—school ... NC-3
Long Creek Sch (historical)—school ... TN-4
Long Creek Sewage Disposal—locale ... NC-3
Long Creek Spring—spring ... ID-8
Long Creek Spring Number One—spring ... MT-8
Long Creek Structure Number 7 Dam—dam ... MS-4
Long Creek Structure 11 Dam—dam ... MS-4
Long Creek Temple—church ... AL-4
Long Creek Temple Ch ... AL-4
Long Creek Township—fmr MCD ... IA-7
**Long Creek Township**—pop pl ... ND-7
Long Creek (Township of)—fmr MCD (3) ... AR-4
Long Creek (Township of)—fmr MCD ... NC-3
**Long Creek (Township of)**—pop pl ... IL-6
Long Creek Trail—trail ... VA-3
Long Creek Watershed Structure 14 Dam—dam ... MS-4
Long Creek Watershed Structure 4 Dam—dam ... MS-4
Long Creek Watershed Y-11a-23 Dam—dam ... MS-4
Long Creek Watershed Y-11a-24 Dam—dam ... MS-4
Long Creek Watershed Y-11a-6 Dam—dam ... MS-4
Long Creek Watershed 3 Dam—dam ... MS-4
Longcrest Ch—church ... TN-4
Long Crossing—locale ... NY-2
Long Crossing—locale ... TX-5
Long Crossway Swamp—swamp ... MI-6
Long Cutoff—channel ... FL-3
Long Cutoff—channel ... LA-4
Long Cypress Slash—swamp (2) ... FL-3
Longdale—locale ... WV-2
**Longdale**—pop pl ... FL-3
**Longdale**—pop pl ... OK-5
**Long Dale**—pop pl ... VA-3
**Longdale**—pop pl (2) ... VA-3
Longdale Ch—church ... VA-3
Long Dale Furnace ... VA-3
**Longdale Furnace**—pop pl ... VA-3
Longdale Mountain ... VA-3
Longdale Rec Area—park ... OK-5
Longdale Rec Area—park ... VA-3
Long Dale Sch—school ... MS-4
Longdale Sch—school ... VA-3
Long Dam (historical)—dam ... ME-1
Long Dam Slough—gut ... MS-4
Long Dave Canyon—valley ... CA-9
Long Dave Valley—valley ... CA-9
Long Day Tank ... NM-5
Long Deep Marsh Island ... NC-3
Longden Sch—school ... CA-9
Long Devils Fork—stream ... AR-4
Long Dick Creek—stream ... IA-7
Long Dike—levee ... AZ-5
Long Ditch ... IN-6
Long Ditch—canal (5) ... IN-6
Long Ditch—canal ... OH-6
Long Divide—ridge ... UT-8
Long Doctor Spring—spring ... NV-8
Long Doe Ridge—ridge ... CA-9
Longdon Sch—school ... KY-4
Long Drain—canal ... MI-6
Long Drain—stream (3) ... WV-2
Long Drain Ch—church ... WV-2
Long Drain Ditch—stream ... DE-2
Long Drain Rsvr—reservoir ... OR-9
Long Draught Branch—stream ... MD-2
Long Draw ... TX-5
Long Draw—valley (4) ... AZ-5
Long Draw—valley (11) ... CO-8
Long Draw—valley (3) ... ID-8
Long Draw—valley (2) ... KS-7
Long Draw—valley ... MT-8
Long Draw—valley (2) ... NV-8
Long Draw—valley (4) ... NM-5
Long Draw—valley (2) ... OR-9
Long Draw—valley (5) ... SD-7
Long Draw—valley (4) ... TX-5
Long Draw—valley (3) ... UT-8
Long Draw—valley (2) ... WA-9
Long Draw—valley (12) ... WY-8
Long Draw, The—valley ... TX-5
Long Draw Campground—locale ... CO-8
Long Draw Canyon—valley ... UT-8
Long Draw Rsvr—reservoir (2) ... CO-8
Long Draw Tank—reservoir ... TX-5
Long Draw Trail—trail ... WA-9
Long Draw Water Catchment—basin ... AZ-5
Long Draw Well—well ... AZ-5
Long Drive Mtn—summit ... VA-3
Long Drive Ridge—ridge ... NC-3
Long Dry Canyon—valley ... NV-8
Long Dry Creek—stream ... TX-5
Long Duck Pond—lake ... MA-1
**Long Eddy**—pop pl ... NY-2
Longenbaugh, Mounta—summit ... AK-9
Longenecker Ch—church ... OH-6
Longenecker Ch—church ... PA-2
Longer Lake ... WI-6
Longer Park—park ... TX-5
Longevity ... TN-4
Longevity Post Office ... TN-4
Long Fall Creek—stream ... KY-4
Long Falls—falls ... ME-1
Long Falls Brook—stream ... NY-2
Long Falls Creek ... KY-4
Long Falls Creek—stream ... KY-4
Longfellow ... IA-7
Longfellow—locale ... TX-5
**Longfellow**—pop pl ... MD-2
**Longfellow**—pop pl ... PA-2
Longfellow, Henry, Sch—hist pl ... PA-2
Longfellow, Stephen, House—hist pl ... ME-1
Longfellow Brook—stream ... ME-1
Longfellow Camp—locale ... ME-1
Longfellow Cem—cemetery ... ME-1
Longfellow Creek—stream ... CA-9
Longfellow Creek—stream (2) ... MT-8
Longfellow Elem Sch—school ... AZ-5
Longfellow Elem Sch—school (2) ... IN-6
Longfellow Elem Sch—school (3) ... KS-7
Longfellow-Evangeline State Park—park ... LA-4
Longfellow Field—park ... MN-6
Longfellow Grade Sch—hist pl ... MT-8
Longfellow Gulch—valley ... CO-8
Longfellow Gulch—valley ... ID-8
Longfellow-Hastings House—hist pl ... CA-9
Longfellow Hill—summit ... WA-9
Longfellow Home—building ... MA-1
Longfellow House Natl Historical Site—park ... MS-4
Longfellow Intermediate Sch—school ... VA-3
Longfellow JHS—school ... NY-2
Longfellow JHS—school ... OK-5
Longfellow JHS—school ... TX-5
Longfellow JHS—school ... WI-6
Longfellow Lake ... ME-1
Longfellow Lake—lake ... ME-1
Longfellow Lake—lake ... NE-7
Longfellow Mine—mine ... CO-8
Longfellow Mine—mine ... MT-8
Longfellow Mine—mine ... NV-8
Longfellow Mtn—summit ... WA-9
Longfellow Natl Historic Site—hist pl ... MA-1
Longfellow Natl Historic Site—park ... MA-1
Longfellow Park—flat ... MT-8
Longfellow Park—park ... IL-6
Longfellow Park—park ... MA-1
Longfellow Park—park ... OH-6
Longfellow Peak—summit ... MT-8
Longfellow Pitch—cliff ... ME-1
Longfellow Pond—lake ... MA-1
Longfellow Ridge—ridge ... AZ-5
Longfellow Ridge Spring—spring ... AZ-5
Longfellow Sch—hist pl ... ID-8
Longfellow Sch—hist pl ... PA-2
Longfellow Sch—hist pl ... VT-1
Longfellow Sch—school (2) ... AZ-5
Longfellow Sch—school (10) ... CA-9
Longfellow Sch—school ... CO-8
Longfellow Sch—school ... CT-1
Longfellow Sch—school ... ID-8
Longfellow Sch—school (9) ... IL-6
Longfellow Sch—school (3) ... IN-6
Longfellow Sch—school (7) ... IA-7
Longfellow Sch—school (4) ... KY-4
Longfellow Sch—school (12) ... ME-1
Longfellow Sch—school (2) ... MA-1
Longfellow Sch—school (9) ... MI-6
Longfellow Sch—school (6) ... MN-6
Longfellow Sch—school (3) ... MO-7
Longfellow Sch—school (2) ... MT-8
Longfellow Sch—school (2) ... NE-7
Longfellow Sch—school ... NJ-2
Longfellow Sch—school (2) ... NM-5
Longfellow Sch—school (3) ... NY-2
Longfellow Sch—school ... ND-7
Longfellow Sch—school (9) ... OH-6
Longfellow Sch—school (3) ... OK-5
Longfellow Sch—school ... PA-2
Longfellow Sch—school (3) ... SD-7
Longfellow Sch—school (4) ... TX-5
Longfellow Sch—school ... UT-8
Longfellow Sch—school ... VT-1
Longfellow Sch—school (2) ... WA-9
Longfellow Sch—school (7) ... WI-6
Longfellow Sch (abandoned)—school ... PA-2
Longfellow Sch Number 28 ... IN-6
Longfellow Statue—park ... DC-2
**Longfellow Township**—pop pl ... ND-7
Longfellow Trail—trail ... PA-2
Long Ferry (historical)—crossing ... TN-4
Long Fibre County Park—park ... OR-9
Long Field—flat ... OR-9
Longfield—hist pl ... RI-1
Longfield—locale ... MD-2
Longfield Baptist Church ... TN-4
Long Field Branch—stream ... KY-4
Longfield Branch—stream ... KY-4
Longfield Branch—stream ... TN-4
Longfield Cem—cemetery ... TN-4
Longfield Ch—church ... TN-4
Longfield Hollow—valley ... TN-4
Long Field Pond—reservoir ... SC-3
Longfield Sandbar—bar ... MS-4
Long Flat—flat ... CA-9
Long Flat—flat (8) ... UT-8
Long Flat—flat ... WY-8
**Long Flat**—pop pl ... NY-2
Long Flat Canyon—valley ... UT-8
Long Flat Cem—cemetery ... NY-2
Long Flat Creek—stream ... FL-3
Long Flat Site—hist pl ... UT-8
Long Flat Wash—valley ... AZ-5
Long Ford—locale ... AL-4
Long Ford—locale (2) ... TN-4
**Longford**—pop pl ... KS-7
**Longford**—pop pl ... MD-2
**Longford**—pop pl ... VI-3
Longford Ch—church ... NC-3
Longford Elem Sch—school ... KS-7
Longford Lake—reservoir ... PA-2
Longford Lake Dam—dam ... PA-2
Long Fork ... TN-4
**Longfork**—pop pl ... VA-3
Long Fork—stream (21) ... KY-4
Long Fork—stream ... LA-4
Long Fork—stream ... OH-6
Long Fork—stream ... PA-2
Long Fork—stream (4) ... TN-4
Long Fork—stream ... VA-3
Long Fork—stream (5) ... WV-2
Long Fork Bear Creek—stream ... OH-6
Long Fork (CCD)—cens area ... KY-4
Long Fork Cem—cemetery ... TN-4
Long Fork Ch—church ... KY-4
Long Fork Ch—church ... TN-4
Long Fork Ch—church ... VA-3
Longfork Creek—stream ... MT-8
Long Fork Creek—stream ... TN-4
Long Fork Sch—school ... KY-4
Long Fork Silver Creek—stream ... ID-8
Long Fork Trail—trail ... PA-2
Long Fred Lake—lake ... AK-9
Long Gall Branch—stream ... SC-3
Long Gap—gap (2) ... GA-3
Long Gap—gap (2) ... NC-3
Long George Creek—stream ... OK-5
Long George Peak—summit ... MT-8
Long Glacier—glacier ... AK-9
Long Glade—flat ... CA-9
Long Glade—flat ... TX-5
Long Glade—valley ... CO-8
Long Glade—valley ... OR-9
Long Glade Branch—stream ... TX-5
Long Glade Canyon—valley ... NM-5
Long Glade Creek—stream ... VA-3
Long Glade Ditch—canal ... WV-2
Long Glade Lake—reservoir ... TX-5
Long Glade Run ... VA-3
Long Gone Lake—lake ... WA-9
Long Gore Creek—stream ... NY-2
Long Grade Canyon—valley ... CA-9
Long Grass Branch—stream ... NC-3
Long Grass Branch—stream ... VA-3
Long Grass Creek—stream ... MT-8
Long Grass Point—cape ... FL-3
Long Grassy Butte—ridge ... ND-7
Long Grassy Creek—stream ... FL-3
Long Gravel Branch—stream ... MO-7
**Long Green**—pop pl ... MD-2
Long Green Creek—stream ... MD-2
Long Green Station—locale ... MD-2
Long Green Valley Ch—church ... MD-2
Long Green Valley Hist Dist—hist pl ... MD-2
Long Grindle Cave—cave ... AL-4
Longgrove—other ... IL-6
**Long Grove**—pop pl ... IL-6
**Long Grove**—pop pl ... IA-7
Long Grove Branch—stream ... MO-7
Long Grove Cem—cemetery ... AR-4
Long Grove Cem—cemetery ... IL-6
Long Grove Ch—church ... IL-6
Long Grove Ch—church ... NC-3
Long Grove Creek—stream ... IL-6
Long Grove Sch—school ... IL-6
Long Grove Sch—school ... MO-7
Long Gulch ... CA-9
Long Gulch ... CO-8
Long Gulch—valley (2) ... AZ-5
Long Gulch—valley (30) ... CA-9
Long Gulch—valley (13) ... CO-8
Long Gulch—valley (17) ... ID-8
Long Gulch—valley (6) ... MT-8
Long Gulch—valley ... NE-7
Long Gulch—valley ... NV-8
Long Gulch—valley ... NM-5
Long Gulch—valley (10) ... OR-9
Long Gulch—valley ... WA-9
Long Gulch—valley ... WY-8
Long Gulch Creek ... ID-8
Long Gulch Guard Station—locale ... ID-8
Long Gulch Lake ... CA-9
Long Gulch Lake—lake ... CA-9
Long Gulch Ridge—ridge ... ID-8
Long Gulch Riffle—rapids ... OR-9
Long Gulch Rsvr—reservoir ... OR-9
Long Gulch Spring—spring (2) ... AZ-5
Long Gulch Spring—spring ... OR-9
Long Gulch Springs—spring ... OR-9
Long Gulch Tank—reservoir ... AZ-5
Long Gulch Trail—trail ... CO-8
Long Gully—stream (2) ... LA-4
Long Gut—stream ... MD-2
Longhair Smith Canyon—valley ... NV-8
Long Hammock—island (3) ... FL-3
Long Hammock—locale ... FL-3
Long Hammock Creek—stream ... FL-3
Longham Reservoir Outlet Dam—dam ... MA-1
Longham Rsvr—reservoir ... MA-1
Long Haul Creek—bay ... MD-2
Long Haul Creek—stream ... ID-8
Long Haul Hollow—valley ... TN-4
Long Haul Rsvr—reservoir ... OR-9
Longhaven West (trailer park)—locale ... AZ-5
**Longhaven West (trailer park)**—pop pl ... AZ-5
Long Hay Flat—flat ... CA-9
Long Heath—swamp ... ME-1
Long High Creek—stream ... CA-9
Long High Lake—lake ... CA-9
Long Hike Peak—summit ... ID-8
Long Hike Rock—summit ... ID-8
Long Hill (2) ... CT-1
Long Hill—hist pl ... MD-2
**Long Hill**—pop pl (4) ... CT-1
**Long Hill**—pop pl ... NJ-2
**Long Hill**—pop pl ... NC-3
Long Hill—summit ... CA-9
Long Hill—summit (6) ... CT-1
Long Hill—summit ... GA-3
Long Hill—summit (2) ... ME-1
Long Hill—summit (14) ... MA-1
Long Hill—summit (4) ... NH-1
Long Hill—summit (2) ... NJ-2
Long Hill—summit (3) ... PA-2
Long Hill—summit (2) ... SC-3
Long Hill—summit (2) ... UT-8
Long Hill—summit (3) ... VT-1
Long Hill—summit ... WA-9
**Long Hill Acres**—pop pl ... MA-1
Long Hill Brook—stream ... CT-1
Long Hill Cem—cemetery ... CT-1
Long Hill Cem—cemetery ... MA-1
Long Hill Cem—cemetery ... SD-7
Long Hill Ch—church ... NJ-2
Long Hill Ch—church ... NC-3
Long Hill Hosp—hospital ... CT-1
Long Hill Lookout Tower—locale ... MD-2
Long Hills—summit ... TX-5
Long Hill Sch—school ... CT-1
Long Hill Sch—school ... NC-3
Long Hill Swamp—stream ... VA-3
Long Hill Tank—reservoir ... TX-5
Long Hill (Township of)—fmr MCD ... NC-3
Long Hog Hollow Archeol District—hist pl ... TX-5
Long Hole—lake ... KY-4
Long Hole—lake ... MS-4
Long Hole—lake ... VT-1
Long Hole—reservoir ... TX-5
Long Hollow ... CO-8
Long Hollow ... TN-4
Long Hollow—basin ... OR-9
Long Hollow—locale ... TX-5
**Long Hollow**—pop pl ... TN-4
Long Hollow—valley (5) ... AL-4
Long Hollow—valley (2) ... AZ-5
Long Hollow—valley (7) ... AR-4
Long Hollow—valley (5) ... CA-9
Long Hollow—valley (2) ... CO-8
Long Hollow—valley ... FL-3
Long Hollow—valley (3) ... GA-3
Long Hollow—valley ... ID-8
Long Hollow—valley ... IL-6
Long Hollow—valley (9) ... KY-4
Long Hollow—valley ... MD-2
Long Hollow—valley (11) ... MO-7
Long Hollow—valley ... NV-8
Long Hollow—valley (2) ... NC-3
Long Hollow—valley (7) ... OH-6
Long Hollow—valley (13) ... OR-9
Long Hollow—valley (8) ... PA-2
Long Hollow—valley ... SD-7
Long Hollow—valley (33) ... TN-4
Long Hollow—valley (29) ... TX-5
Long Hollow—valley (12) ... UT-8
Long Hollow—valley (10) ... VA-3
Long Hollow—valley (2) ... WA-9
Long Hollow—valley (11) ... WV-2
Long Hollow—valley (3) ... WI-6
Long Hollow—valley (7) ... WY-8
Long Hollow Access Point—locale ... GA-3
Long Hollow Bay—bay ... WA-9
Long Hollow Branch—stream ... AL-4
Long Hollow Branch—stream ... KY-4
Long Hollow Branch—stream (3) ... TN-4
Long Hollow Canyon—valley ... TX-5
Long Hollow Cem—cemetery ... TX-5
Long Hollow Ch—church ... MO-7
Long Hollow Ch—church ... SD-7
Long Hollow Ch—church ... TN-4
Long Hollow Ch—church ... WV-2
Long Hollow Creek—stream ... AL-4
Long Hollow Creek—stream ... AR-4
Long Hollow Creek—stream (2) ... ID-8
Long Hollow Creek—stream (5) ... OR-9
Long Hollow Creek—stream ... SD-7
Long Hollow Creek—stream (2) ... TX-5
Long Hollow Dam—dam ... SD-7
Long Hollow Ditch—canal ... WY-8
Long Hollow Gap—gap ... NC-3
Long Hollow Golf Course—locale ... TN-4
Long Hollow Hill—summit ... IN-6
**Long Hollow (historical)**—pop pl ... TN-4
**Long Hollow Housing (subdivision)**—pop pl ... SD-7
Long Hollow Picnic Area—locale ... PA-2
Long Hollow Post Office (historical)—building ... TN-4
Long Hollow Ridge—ridge ... PA-2
Long Hollow Ridge—ridge ... VA-3
Long Hollow Rsvr—reservoir ... OR-9
Long Hollow Rsvr—reservoir ... UT-8
Long Hollow Run—stream ... PA-2
Long Hollow Run—stream (2) ... WV-2
Long Hollow Sch—school ... VA-3
Long Hollow Sch (historical)—school ... PA-2
Long Hollow Sch (historical)—school ... TN-4
Long Hollow Spring—spring (2) ... UT-8
Long Hollow Summit—gap ... OR-9
Long Hollow Tank—reservoir (2) ... AZ-5
Long Hollow Tank—reservoir ... TX-5
**Long Hollow Township**—pop pl ... SD-7
Long Hollow Trail—trail ... CO-8
Long Hollow Trail—trail (3) ... PA-2
Long Hollow Windmill—locale ... TX-5
Long Hook Creek—stream ... PA-2
Long Hope Creek—stream ... NC-3
Long Hope Falls—falls ... NC-3
Long Hope Mtn—summit ... NC-3
**Longhorn**—pop pl ... TX-5
Long Horn A Ranch—locale ... MT-8
Longhorn Army Ammun Plant—military ... TX-5
Longhorn Athletic Field—park ... TX-5
Long Horn Canyon—valley ... CA-9
Longhorn Cavern State Park—park ... TX-5
Longhorn Cem—cemetery ... TX-5
Longhorn Creek—stream ... OK-5
Longhorn Ditch—canal ... CO-8
Long Horn Lake Dam—dam ... MS-4
Longhorn Mine—mine ... WY-8
Longhorn Mtn—summit ... OK-5
Longhorn Oil Field—oilfield ... TX-5
Longhorn Ordnance Works—military ... TX-5
Longhorn Park—park ... TX-5
**Longhorn Park**—pop pl ... TX-5
Longhorn Ranch—locale ... NM-5
**Longhorn Ranch II (subdivision)**—pop pl (2) ... AZ-5
Longhorn Rsvr—reservoir ... NM-5
Longhorn Siding—locale ... TX-5
Longhorn Valley—valley ... TX-5
Long Hosp—hospital ... NC-3
Long House ... MS-4
Long House—hist pl ... FL-3
Long House—locale ... CO-8
Long House Cem—cemetery ... NY-2
Long House Creek—stream ... NJ-2
Long House Creek—stream ... NY-2
Long House Ruin—locale ... AZ-5
Long House Valley—valley ... AZ-5
Long H Ranch—locale ... AZ-5
Long Hungry Branch—stream ... NC-3
Long Hungry Creek—stream ... KY-4
Long Hungry Creek—stream (2) ... TN-4
Long Hungry Gulch—valley ... CO-8
Long Hungry Ridge—ridge ... NC-3
Long Hungry Ridge Trail—trail ... NC-3
**Longhurst**—pop pl ... NC-3
Longhurst (RR name for North Roxboro)—other ... NC-3
Longhurst Spring—spring ... UT-8
Long Indian Creek—stream ... GA-3
Longino—locale ... AR-4
**Longino**—pop pl ... MS-4
Longino, Dr. H. A., House—hist pl ... AR-4
Longino Baptist Church ... MS-4
Longino Ch—church ... MS-4
Longino Creek—stream ... GA-3
Longino House—hist pl ... MS-4
Longino Sch—school ... GA-3
Longino Sch (historical)—school ... MS-4
Long Interlaken ... WI-6
Long Interlaken Lake—lake ... WI-6
Long Island ... FL-3
Long Island ... GA-3
Long Island (2) ... ME-1
Long Island ... MI-6
Long-island ... NC-3
Long Island ... TX-5
Long Island—flat ... OR-9
Long Island—island (2) ... AL-4
Long Island—island (9) ... AK-9
Long Island—island ... CA-9
Long Island—island ... CT-1
Long Island—island (10) ... FL-3
Long Island—island (9) ... GA-3
Long Island—island ... ID-8
Long Island—island ... IL-6

Long Island—*island* (4) ... LA-4
Long Island—*island* (10) ... ME-1
Long Island—*island* (4) ... MA-1
Long Island—*island* (6) ... MI-6
Long Island—*island* (4) ... MN-6
Long Island—*island* (3) ... NE-7
Long Island—*island* (2) ... NH-1
Long Island—*island* (6) ... NY-2
Long Island—*island* (3) ... NC-3
Long Island—*island* ... OH-6
Long Island—*island* ... OR-9
Long Island—*island* ... PA-2
Long Island—*island* (5) ... SC-3
Long Island—*island* (4) ... TN-4
Long Island—*island* (3) ... TX-5
Long Island—*island* (3) ... VA-3
Long Island—*island* (2) ... WA-9
Long Island—*island* (6) ... WI-6
Long Island—*island* ... WY-8
Long Island—*locale* ... VA-3
Long Island—*other* ... ME-1
**Long Island**—*pop pl* ... AL-4
**Long Island**—*pop pl* ... AK-9
**Long Island**—*pop pl* ... KS-7
**Long Island**—*pop pl* ... ME-1
**Longisland**—*pop pl* ... NC-3
**Long Island**—*pop pl* ... NC-3
**Long Island**—*pop pl* ... TN-4
Long Island Access Area—*area* ... NC-3
Long Island Airp—*airport* ... NC-3
Long Island Bayou—*channel* ... TX-5
Long Island Bayou—*gut* ... LA-4
Long Island Beach—*beach* ... OH-6
Long Island Canal—*canal* ... ID-8
Long Island Cave—*cave* ... AL-4
Long Island (CCD)—*cens area* ... AL-4
Long Island Cem—*cemetery* ... KS-7
Long Island Cem—*cemetery* ... MN-6
Long Island Channel—*channel* ... AK-9
**Long Island City**—*pop pl* ... NY-2
Long Island City Courthouse
Complex—*hist pl* ... NY-2
Long Island Country Club—*other* ... NY-2
Long Island Cove—*basin* ... TX-5
Long Island Cove—*valley* ... AL-4
Long Island Creek—*stream* ... AL-4
Long Island Creek—*stream* ... GA-3
Long Island Creek—*stream* ... TX-5
Long Island Creek—*stream* ... VA-3
Long Island Ditch—*canal* ... CO-8
Long Island Ditch—*canal* ... LA-4
Long Island Division—*civil* ... AL-4
Long Island Dock—*locale* ... TN-4
Long Island Doctors Hosp—*hospital* ... NY-2
*Long Island Elementary School* ... TN-4
Long Island Elem Sch—*school* ... KS-7
Long Island Ferry (historical)—*locale* ... TN-4
*Long Island Head* ... ME-1
Long Island Head—*cliff* ... MA-1
*Long Island Headlight* ... MA-1
Long Island Head Light—*hist pl* ... MA-1
Long Island Head Light—*locale* ... MA-1
Long Island (historical)—*locale* ... MA-1
Long Island Hosp—*hospital* ... MA-1
Long Island HS—*school* ... NY-2
Long Island Hub—*cape* ... ME-1
Long Island Jewish Hosp—*hospital* ... NY-2
Long Island Lake—*lake* ... MN-6
Long Island Ledges—*bar* ... ME-1
Long Island MacArthur Airp—*airport* ... NY-2
*Long Island Marina* ... TN-4
Long Island Marina—*locale* ... NC-3
Long Island Marsh—*swamp* ... FL-3
Long Island Marsh Public Hunting
Area—*area* ... IA-7
Long Island Narrows—*channel* ... ME-1
Long Island Natl Cem—*cemetery* ... NY-2
Long Island of the Holston—*hist pl* ... TN-4
Long Island Passage—*channel* ... ME-1
Long Island Point—*cape* ... OR-9
Long Island Pond—*reservoir* ... MA-1
Long Island River—*stream* ... MN-6
Long Island Sch—*school* ... TN-4
Long Island Sch (historical)—*school* ... AL-4
Long Island Shoal—*bar* ... WA-9
Long Island Slough—*stream* ... WA-9
Long Island Sound—*bay* ... CT-1
Long Island Sound—*bay* ... NY-2
**Long Island Township**—*pop pl* ... KS-7
Long Island Univ—*school* ... NY-2
Long Island Univ C W Post Coll—*school* ... NY-2
Long Island Wildlife Mngmt Area—*park* ... TN-4
Long Island Woods—*woods* ... TX-5
Longist Forks—*locale* ... VA-3
Longjaw Coulee—*valley* ... MT-8
Long JHS—*school* ... SC-3
Long JHS—*school* (2) ... TX-5
Long Jim Canyon—*valley* ... AZ-5
Long John—*locale* ... AK-9
Long John Canyon—*valley* ... CA-9
*Long John Creek* ... MT-8
Long John Creek—*stream* (2) ... CA-9
Long John Creek—*stream* ... MT-8
Long John Creek—*stream* (2) ... OR-9
Long John Creek—*stream* ... TX-5
Long John Gulch—*valley* ... MT-8
Long John Hollow—*valley* ... TX-5
Long John Lagoon—*bay* ... AK-9
Long John Lake—*lake* ... WA-9
Long John Mine—*mine* ... CA-9
Long John Mtn—*summit* ... NC-3
Long John Mtn—*summit* ... WA-9
Longjohn Slough—*gut* ... IL-6
*Long Joseph's Point* ... MA-1
**Long Josephs Point**—*pop pl* ... MA-1
*Long Kent Creek* ... TX-5
Long Kent Creek—*stream* ... TX-5
*Long Key* ... FL-3
Long Key—*island* (4) ... FL-3
Long Key Bight—*bay* ... FL-3
*Long Key (corporate name Layton)* ... FL-3
Long Key Point—*cape* ... FL-3
Long Key State Park—*park* ... FL-3
Long Key Viaduct—*bridge* ... FL-3
Long Kill—*stream* ... NY-2
Long King Creek—*stream* ... TX-5
*Long Knife Creek* ... ND-7
Long Knife Creek—*stream* ... MT-8
Long Knob—*ridge* ... OH-6
Long Knob—*summit* ... MO-7
Long Knob—*summit* ... PA-2
Long Knob—*summit* (2) ... WV-2
Long Knoll—*summit* ... UT-8
Long Lagoon—*lake* ... LA-4
*Long Lake* ... CO-8
*Long Lake* ... CT-1
*Long Lake* ... ID-8
*Long Lake* ... IN-6
*Long Lake* ... LA-4
*Long Lake* ... MI-6
*Long Lake* ... MN-6
*Long Lake* ... MS-4
*Long Lake* ... NE-7
*Long Lake* ... NH-1
*Long Lake* ... NY-2
*Long Lake* ... OK-5
*Long Lake* ... PA-2
*Longlake* (2) ... SD-7
*Long Lake* ... WA-9
*Long Lake* ... WI-6
*Long Lake* ... WY-8
Long Lake—*bay* ... TX-5
Long Lake—*gut* (3) ... AR-4
Long Lake—*lake* (11) ... AK-9
Long Lake—*lake* (5) ... AZ-5
Long Lake—*lake* (20) ... AR-4
Long Lake—*lake* (16) ... CA-9
Long Lake—*lake* (7) ... CO-8
Long Lake—*lake* (13) ... FL-3
Long Lake—*lake* (7) ... GA-3
Long Lake—*lake* (4) ... ID-8
Long Lake—*lake* (13) ... IL-6
Long Lake—*lake* (7) ... IN-6
Long Lake—*lake* ... IA-7
Long Lake—*lake* (20) ... LA-4
Long Lake—*lake* (7) ... ME-1
Long Lake—*lake* (63) ... MI-6
Long Lake—*lake* (104) ... MN-6
Long Lake—*lake* (20) ... MS-4
Long Lake—*lake* (4) ... MO-7
Long Lake—*lake* (6) ... MT-8
Long Lake—*lake* (7) ... NE-7
Long Lake—*lake* ... NV-8
Long Lake—*lake* (3) ... NM-5
Long Lake—*lake* (7) ... NY-2
Long Lake—*lake* (2) ... NC-3
Long Lake—*lake* (13) ... ND-7
Long Lake—*lake* ... OH-6
Long Lake—*lake* (3) ... OK-5
Long Lake—*lake* (9) ... OR-9
Long Lake—*lake* ... SC-3
Long Lake—*lake* (8) ... SD-7
Long Lake—*lake* (2) ... TN-4
Long Lake—*lake* (15) ... TX-5
Long Lake—*lake* ... UT-8
Long Lake—*lake* (14) ... WA-9
Long Lake—*lake* (60) ... WI-6
Long Lake—*lake* (9) ... WY-8
Long Lake—*locale* ... WA-9
**Long Lake**—*pop pl* (2) ... IL-6
**Long Lake**—*pop pl* (2) ... IN-6
**Longlake**—*pop pl* ... LA-4
**Long Lake**—*pop pl* (4) ... MI-6
**Long Lake**—*pop pl* ... MN-6
**Long Lake**—*pop pl* (2) ... MS-4
**Long Lake**—*pop pl* ... NY-2
**Long Lake**—*pop pl* ... SD-7
**Long Lake**—*pop pl* ... TX-5
**Long Lake**—*pop pl* ... WA-9
**Long Lake**—*pop pl* ... WI-6
Long Lake—*reservoir* ... AZ-5
Long Lake—*reservoir* ... CA-9
Long Lake—*reservoir* ... CO-8
Long Lake—*reservoir* ... ID-8
Long Lake—*reservoir* ... IN-6
Long Lake—*reservoir* ... ME-1
Long Lake—*reservoir* (2) ... MN-6
Long Lake—*reservoir* (2) ... NC-3
Long Lake—*reservoir* ... ND-7
Long Lake—*reservoir* ... OR-9
Long Lake—*reservoir* (2) ... TX-5
Long Lake—*reservoir* ... UT-8
Long Lake—*reservoir* ... WA-9
Long Lake—*reservoir* (2) ... WI-6
Long Lake—*swamp* (3) ... AR-4
Long Lake—*swamp* ... FL-3
Long Lake—*swamp* (2) ... LA-4
Long Lake—*swamp* (2) ... MI-6
Long Lake—*swamp* ... MN-6
Long Lake—*swamp* ... MS-4
Long Lake—*swamp* ... MO-7
*Long Lake Bayou* ... LA-4
Long Lake Bayou—*stream* (2) ... LA-4
Long Lakebed—*flat* ... MN-6
*Long Lake Branch* ... FL-3
Long Lake Branch—*stream* ... WI-6
*Long Lake Branch Of White River* ... WI-6
Long Lake Camp—*locale* ... MN-6
Long Lake Camp—*locale* ... OR-9
Long Lake Campground—*locale* ... ME-1
Long Lake Cem—*cemetery* ... LA-4
Long Lake Cem—*cemetery* (2) ... MI-6
Long Lake Cem—*cemetery* ... NY-2
Long Lake Cem—*cemetery* (2) ... WI-6
Long Lake Ch—*church* ... AR-4
Long Lake Ch—*church* ... MI-6
Long Lake Ch—*church* (4) ... MN-6
Long Lake Ch—*church* ... WI-6
Long Lake Channel—*lake* ... OH-6
**Long Lake Colony**—*pop pl* ... SD-7
Long Lake Community Ch—*church* ... WA-9
Long Lake Cove—*bay* ... ME-1
*Long Lake Creek* ... MI-6
*Long Lake Creek* ... ND-7
*Long Lake Creek* ... WY-8
Long Lake Creek—*stream* (4) ... MI-6
Long Lake Creek—*stream* (3) ... MN-6
Long Lake Creek—*stream* ... ND-7
Long Lake Creek—*stream* ... WI-6
*Long Lake Dam* ... NC-3
*Long Lake Dam* ... WA-9
Long Lake Dam—*dam* ... ME-1
Long Lake Dam—*dam* (2) ... MS-4
Long Lake Dam—*dam* ... UT-8
Long Lake Dam—*dam* ... WA-9
Long Lake Ditch—*canal* ... CO-8
*Long Lake Drain* ... MI-6
Long Lake Drain—*canal* ... MI-6
**Long Lake Heights**—*pop pl* ... MI-6
Long Lake Hills—*other* ... AK-9
Long Lake Hydroelectric Power
Plant—*hist pl* ... WA-9
**Long Lake Island**—*pop pl* ... IN-6
Long Lake Lookout Lower—*locale* ... WI-6
Long Lake Narrows—*channel* ... MI-6
Long Lake Natl Wildlife Ref—*park* (3) ... ND-7
Long Lake Number Two—*lake* ... MN-6
Long Lake Oil Field—*oilfield* ... MS-4
Long Lake Oil Field—*oilfield* ... TX-5
Long Lake Outlet—*stream* (2) ... NY-2
Long Lake Outlet—*stream* ... WI-6
Long Lake Park—*park* ... MI-6
Long Lake Park—*park* ... MN-6
Long Lake Park—*park* ... WI-6
Long Lake Pictographs—*hist pl* ... WA-9
Long Lake Point—*summit* ... ID-8
Long Lake Public Access—*locale* ... WI-6
Long Lake Rec Area—*park* ... WI-6
Long Lake Recreation Grounds—*park* ... NE-7
Long Lake Recreation Hall—*hist pl* ... WA-9
*Long Lake Reservoir* ... WA-9
Long Lake Ridge—*ridge* ... ME-1
Long Lake Rsvr—*reservoir* ... NY-2
Long Lakes—*lake* ... AK-9
Long Lake Sch—*school* ... MI-6
Long Lake Sch—*school* ... MN-6
Long Lake Sch (historical)—*school* ... MS-4
Long Lake Sch Number 1—*school* ... ND-7
Long Lake Sch Number 2—*school* ... ND-7
**Long Lake Shores**—*pop pl* ... MI-6
Long Lake Slough—*gut* ... AR-4
Long Lake Slough—*gut* ... FL-3
Long Lake Slough—*gut* ... TX-5
Long Lake State Public Shooting Area—*park*
(2) ... SD-7
Long Lake State Wildlife Mngmt
Area—*park* ... MN-6
**Long Lake (Town of)**—*pop pl* ... NY-2
**Long Lake (Town of)**—*pop pl* (2) ... WI-6
Long Lake Township—*civil* ... SD-7
**Long Lake Township**—*pop pl* ... ND-7
**Long Lake (Township of)**—*pop pl* ... MI-6
**Long Lake (Township of)**—*pop pl* (2) ... MN-6
Long Lake Valley—*basin* ... OR-9
*Long Lake Village* ... MI-6
Long Lake Well—*well* ... NM-5
Long Lane—*locale* ... SC-3
**Long Lane**—*pop pl* ... MO-7
**Long Lane Acres (subdivision)**—*pop pl* ... PA-2
Long Lane Cem—*cemetery* ... PA-2
Long Lane Lookout Tower—*locale* ... SC-3
Long Lane Sch—*school* ... CT-1
**Longleaf**—*pop pl* ... LA-4
**Long Leaf Acres (subdivision)**—*pop pl* ... NC-3
Longleaf Ch—*church* ... NC-3
Longleaf Elem Sch—*school* ... FL-3
**Longleaf Estates**—*pop pl* ... AL-4
Longleaf Flat—*flat* ... UT-8
Long Leaf Lake—*reservoir* ... NC-3
Long Leaf Lake Dam—*dam* ... NC-3
Long Leaf Park—*uninc pl* ... NC-3
*Long Leaf Pine Hills* ... AL-4
*Long Leaf Pine Hills* ... MS-4
Long Leaf (RR name for Longleaf)—*other* ... LA-4
**Longleaf (RR name Long
Leaf)**—*pop pl* ... LA-4
Longleat—*hist pl* ... TN-4
Long Ledge—*bar* ... CT-1
Long Ledge—*bar* (11) ... ME-1
Long Ledge—*bar* ... MA-1
Long Ledge—*island* ... ME-1
Long Ledge Cove—*bay* ... ME-1
Longleg Lake—*lake* ... MN-6
Long Level—*flat* ... NY-2
Long Level—*locale* ... PA-2
**Longlevel**—*pop pl* ... PA-2
Long Level Ridge—*ridge* ... NC-3
Long Levels—*ridge* ... NC-3
Long Levels Branch—*stream* ... NC-3
**Longley**—*pop pl* ... OH-6
Longley, Howard, House—*hist pl* ... CA-9
Longley Brook—*stream* (2) ... ME-1
Longley Canyon—*valley* ... UT-8
Longley Cem—*cemetery* ... ME-1
Longley Covered Bridge—*hist pl* ... VT-1
Longley Hill—*summit* ... MA-1
Longley Lake—*lake* ... ME-1
Longley Lake—*reservoir* ... CA-9
Longley Meadow—*flat* ... CA-9
Longley Pass—*gap* ... CA-9
Longley Pond—*lake* ... ME-1
Longley Stream—*stream* ... ME-1
Longley Way Sch—*school* ... CA-9
*Long Lick* ... KY-4
Longlick—*locale* ... KY-4
Long Lick—*stream* ... KY-4
Longlick Branch—*stream* ... KY-4
Long Lick Branch—*stream* ... SC-3
Longlick Branch—*stream* ... WV-2
Long Lick Canyon—*valley* ... UT-8
Long Lick Creek—*stream* (3) ... KY-4
Long Lick Hill—*ridge* ... OH-6
Long Lick Mtn—*summit* ... UT-8
Long Lick Run—*stream* (2) ... WV-2
Long Liz Creek—*stream* ... ID-8
Long Liz Point—*summit* ... ID-8
Long Logan—*lake* ... ME-1
Long Logan—*swamp* ... ME-1
Long Log Lake—*lake* ... OK-5
Long Logs—*area* ... AZ-5
Longlois Sch—*school* ... IN-6
**Long (Longs Switch)**—*pop pl* ... MS-4
*Long Lookout Tower* ... GA-3
Long Lost Creek—*stream* ... ID-8
Long Lost Lake—*lake* ... MI-6
Long Lost Lake—*lake* ... MN-6
Long Lot Pond—*lake* ... RI-1
Long Lots JHS—*school* ... CT-1
Longly Sch of Music—*school* ... MA-1
Longman Sch (historical)—*school* ... SD-7
*Longmare Lake* ... AK-9
Long Marsh—*swamp* ... NY-2
Long Marsh—*swamp* ... NC-3
Long Marsh—*swamp* (2) ... TX-5
Long Marsh—*swamp* ... WA-9
Long Marsh Bay—*bay* ... VT-1
Longmarsh Brook—*stream* ... NH-1
Long Marsh Channel—*channel* ... VT-1
Long Marsh Creek—*stream* ... LA-4
Long Marsh Ditch—*canal* ... MD-2
Long Marshes—*swamp* ... MD-2
Long Marsh Island—*island* ... MD-2
Long Marsh (Magisterial
District)—*fmr MCD* ... VA-3
Longmarsh Point—*cape* ... MD-2
Long Marsh Run—*stream* ... VA-3
Long Marsh Run—*stream* ... WV-2
**Longmead Farms**—*pop pl* ... PA-2
*Long Meadow* (2) ... CA-9
*Long Meadow* ... IL-6
*Long Meadow* ... MA-1
*Long Meadow* ... OR-9
*Longmeadow* ... RI-1
Long Meadow—*flat* (12) ... CA-9
Long Meadow—*flat* ... ID-8
Long Meadow—*flat* (2) ... MT-8
Long Meadow—*flat* ... NY-2
Long Meadow—*flat* ... OR-9
Long Meadow—*flat* ... UT-8
Long Meadow—*hist pl* ... TN-4
**Long Meadow**—*pop pl* ... MD-2
**Longmeadow**—*pop pl* ... MA-1
**Longmeadow**—*pop pl* ... RI-1
Long Meadow—*stream* ... VA-3
Long Meadow—*swamp* ... MA-1
Long Meadow—*swamp* ... NJ-2
*Longmeadow, Town of* ... MA-1
*Long Meadow Brook* ... MA-1
Long Meadow Brook—*stream* ... ME-1
Longmeadow Brook—*stream* (2) ... MA-1
Long Meadow Brook—*stream* ... MA-1
Long Meadow Brook—*stream* ... PA-2
Long Meadow Brook—*stream* ... VT-1
Longmeadow Ccountry Club—*locale* ... MA-1
Long Meadow Cem—*cemetery* ... NH-1
Longmeadow Ch—*church* ... MD-2
Long Meadow Ch—*church* ... NH-1
Long Meadow Community Center—*locale* ... CO-8
Longmeadow Country Club Dam—*dam* ... MA-1
*Long Meadow Creek* ... ID-8
*Long Meadow Creek* ... VA-3
Long Meadow Creek—*stream* (3) ... CA-9
Long Meadow Creek—*stream* (3) ... ID-8
Long Meadow Creek—*stream* ... NV-8
Long Meadow Creek—*stream* (2) ... OR-9
**Long Meadow Estates**—*pop pl* ... MD-2
Long Meadow Farm—*hist pl* ... PA-2
Longmeadow Golf Club—*locale* ... MA-1
Long Meadow Grove—*woods* ... CA-9
Long Meadow Hill—*summit* ... VT-1
Long Meadow Hill JHS—*school* ... CT-1
Longmeadow Hist Dist—*hist pl* ... MA-1
Longmeadow Hollow—*valley* ... VA-3
Long Meadow Island—*island* ... NY-2
Long Meadow Lake—*lake* ... MN-6
Longmeadow Plaza—*locale* ... MA-1
Long Meadow Pond—*reservoir* (2) ... CT-1
Long Meadow Pond Brook—*stream* ... CT-1
Long Meadow Ranch—*locale* ... AZ-5
*Long Meadow River* ... VA-3
Long Meadow Run—*stream* ... WV-2
*Long Meadows* ... ID-8
Long Meadows—*flat* ... CO-8
Long Meadows—*flat* ... ID-8
Long Meadows—*flat* (2) ... OR-9
Long Meadows—*flat* ... WY-8
Long Meadows—*hist pl* ... MD-2
**Long Meadows**—*pop pl* ... TN-4
Long Meadows—*swamp* ... ME-1
Long Meadow Sch—*school* ... MI-6
Long Meadow Sch (abandoned)—*school* ... PA-2
Long Meadows Country Club—*other* ... TX-5
*Long Meadows Creek* ... ID-8
**Long Meadows Estates**—*pop pl* ... MD-2
Longmeadow Shops—*locale* ... MA-1
Long Meadow Swamp—*swamp* ... MA-1
Long Meadow Swamp—*swamp* ... NJ-2
**Longmeadow (Town of)**—*pop pl* ... MA-1
Longmead Sch—*school* ... OH-6
Long Memorial County Park—*park* ... IA-7
Long Memorial Methodist Episcopal Ch
(historical)—*church* ... AL-4
Longmere Lake—*lake* ... AK-9
Long Mesa—*summit* (2) ... AZ-5
Long Mesa—*summit* (3) ... CO-8
Long Mesa Ditch—*canal* ... CO-8
Long Mesa Tank—*reservoir* (3) ... AZ-5
*Longmeyer Church* ... TN-4
*Longmeyers Church* ... TN-4
Long Mile Lookout Tower—*locale* ... WI-6
Long Mill Cove—*bay* ... ME-1
Long Mine—*mine* ... NV-8
Long Mine (underground)—*mine* ... TN-4
*Longmire* ... TN-4
**Longmire**—*pop pl* ... WA-9
Longmire Bluff—*cliff* ... TN-4
Longmire Buildings—*hist pl* ... WA-9
Longmire Campground—*locale* ... WA-9
Longmire Cem—*cemetery* ... IA-7
Longmire Cem—*cemetery* ... MS-4
Longmire Cem—*cemetery* (3) ... TN-4
Longmire Ch—*church* ... TN-4
Longmire Meadow—*flat* (2) ... WA-9
*Longmire Post Office* ... TN-4
Longmire Sch—*school* ... IL-6
*Longmire Springs* ... WA-9
Longmire Wenas Canal—*canal* ... WA-9
**Longmont**—*pop pl* ... CO-8
Longmont College—*hist pl* ... CO-8
Longmont Filtration Plant—*other* ... CO-8
Longmont Fire Department—*hist pl* ... CO-8
Longmont Municipal Airp—*airport* ... CO-8
Longmont Power Plant—*hist pl* ... CO-8
Longmont Powerplant—*other* ... CO-8
Longmont Rsvr—*reservoir* ... CO-8
Longmont Supply Ditch—*canal* ... CO-8
Longmont Water Tank—*reservoir* ... CO-8
Long Moore Creek—*stream* ... UT-8
*Longmore Lake* ... AK-9
**Long Mott**—*pop pl* ... TX-5
Long Mott Oil Field—*oilfield* ... TX-5
Long Mound—*summit* ... KS-7
Long Mound—*summit* ... MO-7
Long Mound—*summit* ... OK-5
**Long Mountain**—*pop pl* ... OR-9
Long Mountain—*ridge* ... CA-9
Long Mountain—*ridge* ... MT-8
Long Mountain—*ridge* (2) ... NH-1
Long Mountain—*ridge* ... NC-3
Long Mountain Branch—*stream* ... NC-3
Long Mountain Brook—*stream* ... NH-1
Long Mountain Cem—*cemetery* ... CT-1
Long Mountain Cem—*cemetery* ... TX-5
Long Mountain Ch—*church* ... VA-3
Long Mountain Community
Center—*locale* ... TX-5
Long Mountain Creek—*stream* ... VA-3
Long Mountain Lake—*lake* ... ID-8
Long Mountain (Magisterial
District)—*fmr MCD* ... VA-3
Long Mountain Pond—*lake* ... NH-1
Long Mountain Ranch—*locale* ... AZ-5
Long Mountains—*summit* ... AK-9
Long Mountain Trail—*trail* ... PA-2
Long Mountain Wash—*stream* ... AZ-5
*Long Mtn* ... NC-3
Long Mtn—*range* ... GA-3
Long Mtn—*range* ... PA-2
Long Mtn—*summit* (2) ... AZ-5
Long Mtn—*summit* (6) ... AR-4
Long Mtn—*summit* ... CA-9
Long Mtn—*summit* (2) ... CO-8
Long Mtn—*summit* ... CT-1
Long Mtn—*summit* (2) ... GA-3
Long Mtn—*summit* (4) ... ID-8
Long Mtn—*summit* (4) ... ME-1
Long Mtn—*summit* ... MA-1
Long Mtn—*summit* ... MO-7
Long Mtn—*summit* (2) ... MT-8
Long Mtn—*summit* ... NY-2
Long Mtn—*summit* (6) ... NC-3
Long Mtn—*summit* (3) ... OK-5
Long Mtn—*summit* (3) ... OR-9
Long Mtn—*summit* (3) ... PA-2
Long Mtn—*summit* (3) ... SC-3
Long Mtn—*summit* (2) ... TN-4
Long Mtn—*summit* (7) ... TX-5
Long Mtn—*summit* (7) ... VA-3
Long Mtn—*summit* ... WA-9
Long Mtn—*summit* ... WV-2
Long-Mueller House—*hist pl* ... OH-6
*Long Neck* ... MA-1
*Long Neck* ... RI-1
Long Neck—*cape* ... CT-1
Long Neck—*cape* ... DE-2
Long Neck—*cape* ... MD-2
Long Neck—*cape* ... MA-1
Long Neck—*cape* ... UT-8
Long Neck Cabin—*locale* ... UT-8
Long Neck Cem—*cemetery* ... MA-1
Long Neck Ch—*church* ... DE-2
Long Neck Cove—*bay* ... RI-1
Long Neck Creek—*bay* ... MD-2
Long Neck Creek—*stream* ... NJ-2
**Longnecker**—*pop pl* ... IN-6
Longnecker Ditch—*canal* ... IN-6
Longneckers Ch—*church* ... PA-2
*Long Neck Islands* ... CT-1
*Long Neck Mesa* ... UT-8
Long Neck Point—*cape* ... CT-1
Long Neck Point—*cape* ... NC-3
**Long Neck Village (trailer
park)**—*pop pl* ... DE-2
Long Noble Lake—*lake* ... MI-6
Longnook Beach—*beach* ... MA-1
Long Nook Valley—*valley* ... MA-1
Longnose Creek—*stream* ... MN-6
Longnose Creek—*stream* ... SC-3
Longnose Mtn—*summit* ... SC-3
Long Oil Field—*oilfield* ... KS-7
Long Opening Creek—*stream* ... CA-9
Longora Windmill—*locale* ... TX-5
Longoreno Banco Number 3—*levee* ... TX-5
Longoria Banco Number 39—*levee* ... TX-5
Longoria Cem—*cemetery* (3) ... TX-5
Longoria Creek—*stream* ... TX-5
Longoria Windmill—*locale* ... TX-5
Longorlliano Well—*well* ... TX-5
Longort Spring—*spring* ... AZ-5
Longort Well—*well* ... AZ-5
Long Otter Creek—*stream* ... MT-8
*Long Park* ... MT-8
*Long Park* ... PA-2
Long Park—*flat* (3) ... AZ-5
Long Park—*flat* (9) ... CO-8
Long Park—*flat* (2) ... MT-8
Long Park—*flat* (2) ... UT-8
Long Park—*flat* (2) ... WY-8
Long Park—*locale* ... MT-8
Long Park—*park* ... NM-5
Long Park—*park* ... WA-9
Long Park—*park* ... WY-8
Long Park Creek—*stream* (2) ... CO-8
Long Park Creek—*stream* (2) ... WY-8
Long Park Dam—*dam* (2) ... UT-8
Long Park Ditch—*canal* ... CO-8
Long Park Lake—*lake* ... CO-8
Long Park No 6 Mine—*mine* ... CO-8
Long Park Rsvr—*reservoir* ... CO-8
Long Park Rsvr—*reservoir* (2) ... UT-8
Long Park Tank—*reservoir* ... AZ-5
Long Pass—*locale* ... OR-9
Long Pasture Run—*stream* ... WV-2
Long Pasture Windmill—*locale* ... TX-5
Longpatch Swamp—*swamp* ... PA-2
*Long Path Trail* ... PA-2
Long Path Trail—*trail* ... PA-2
Long Payne Cem—*cemetery* ... TN-4
Long Peak—*summit* ... MT-8
Long Peak—*summit* ... NV-8
Long Peak Trail—*trail* ... CO-8
Long Pine—*fmr MCD* ... NE-7
**Long Pine**—*pop pl* ... NE-7
**Long Pine**—*pop pl* ... NC-3
**Long Pine**—*pop pl* ... PA-2
Long Pine Ch—*church* ... NC-3
*Long Pine Creek* ... MS-4
Long Pine Creek—*stream* ... ID-8
Long Pine Creek—*stream* ... NE-7
Long Pine Key—*island* ... FL-3
Long Pine Key Lookout Tower—*tower* ... FL-3
Long Pine Mtn—*summit* ... NY-2
Long Pine Pond—*reservoir* ... NJ-2
*Long Pine Reservoir* ... PA-2
Long Pine Run—*stream* ... PA-2
Long Pine Run Dam—*dam* ... PA-2
Long Pine Run Rsvr—*reservoir* ... PA-2
Long Place Windmill—*locale* ... NM-5
**Long Plain**—*pop pl* ... MA-1
Long Plain Brook—*stream* ... MA-1
Long Plain Cem—*cemetery* ... MA-1
Long Plain Cemeteries—*cemetery* ... MA-1
Long Plain Friends
Meetinghouse—*hist pl* ... MA-1
Long Plantation—*locale* ... TX-5
Long Plantation Sch—*school* ... LA-4
Long Playground—*park* ... MA-1
*Long Pocket* ... TN-4
*Long Point* ... CA-9
*Long Point* ... ME-1
*Long Point* ... MD-2
*Long Point* ... MA-1
*Long Point* ... MN-6
*Long Point* ... NY-2
*Long Point* ... TX-5
*Long Point* ... VT-1
Long Point—*bar* ... MA-1
Long Point—*cape* (3) ... AK-9
Long Point—*cape* ... AR-4
Long Point—*cape* (10) ... CA-9
Long Point—*cape* (2) ... DE-2
Long Point—*cape* (13) ... FL-3
Long Point—*cape* ... GA-3
Long Point—*cape* ... ID-8
Long Point—*cape* (4) ... LA-4
Long Point—*cape* (15) ... ME-1
Long Point—*cape* (24) ... MD-2
Long Point—*cape* (10) ... MA-1
Long Point—*cape* (7) ... MI-6
Long Point—*cape* ... MN-6
Long Point—*cape* (2) ... MS-4
Long Point—*cape* (2) ... NH-1
Long Point—*cape* (4) ... NJ-2
Long Point—*cape* ... NM-5
Long Point—*cape* (12) ... NY-2
Long Point—*cape* (15) ... NC-3
Long Point—*cape* ... OR-9
Long Point—*cape* ... PA-2
Long Point—*cape* (3) ... RI-1
Long Point—*cape* (2) ... SC-3
Long Point—*cape* (3) ... TN-4
Long Point—*cape* (4) ... TX-5
Long Point—*cape* (3) ... UT-8
Long Point—*cape* (2) ... VT-1
Long Point—*cape* (7) ... VA-3
Long Point—*cape* ... WA-9
Long Point—*cape* (3) ... WV-2
Long Point—*cape* ... WI-6
Long Point—*cape* ... WY-8
Long Point—*cape* (3) ... VI-3
Long Point—*cliff* ... AL-4
Long Point—*cliff* ... AZ-5
Long Point—*cliff* ... CA-9
Long Point—*cliff* (2) ... CO-8
Long Point—*cliff* (2) ... TN-4
Long Point—*gut* ... FL-3
Long Point—*island* ... MA-1
Long Point—*island* ... WI-6
Long Point—*locale* ... IA-7
Long Point—*locale* ... SC-3
Long Point—*locale* ... TX-5
Longpoint—*locale* ... TX-5
**Long Point**—*pop pl* ... FL-3
**Long Point**—*pop pl* ... IL-6
**Long Point**—*pop pl* ... MI-6
**Long Point**—*pop pl* ... MN-6
**Long Point**—*pop pl* ... TX-5
**Long Point**—*pop pl* ... VT-1
Long Point—*ridge* ... AZ-5
Long Point—*ridge* (3) ... CA-9
Long Point—*ridge* ... CO-8
Long Point—*ridge* (2) ... OR-9
Long Point—*ridge* ... UT-8
Long Point—*summit* ... AR-4
Long Point—*summit* ... CO-8
Long Point—*summit* ... KY-4
Long Point—*summit* ... MT-8
Long Point—*summit* ... PA-2
Long Point—*summit* (2) ... TX-5
Long Point—*uninc pl* ... TX-5
Longpoint and Cotton Garden—*locale* ... VI-3
Long Point Bay—*bay* ... MI-6
Long Point Bay—*bay* ... VI-3
Long Point Bayou—*stream* ... LA-4
Long Point Branch—*stream* ... KY-4
Long Point Branch—*stream* ... VA-3
Long Point Bridge—*bridge* ... GA-3
Long Point Cem—*cemetery* ... WV-2
Longpoint Cem—*cemetery* ... WV-2
Long Point Ch—*church* (3) ... IL-6
Long Point Ch—*church* ... SC-3
Long Point Channel—*channel* ... NC-3
Long Point Channel—*channel* ... VA-3
Long Point Cove—*bay* ... ME-1
**Long Point Cove**—*pop pl* ... NY-2
*Long Point Creek* ... SC-3
*Longpoint Creek* ... WY-8
Long Point Creek—*gut* ... FL-3
Long Point Creek—*gut* ... NC-3
Long Point Creek—*stream* (4) ... IL-6
Long Point Creek—*stream* ... NJ-2
Long Point Creek—*stream* ... TX-5
Long Point Dam—*dam* ... AZ-5
Long Point Gully—*stream* ... LA-4
Long Point Gully—*valley* ... NY-2
Long Point (historical)—*cape* ... MA-1
*Long Point Island* ... CA-9
*Long Point Island* ... NJ-2
*Long Point Island* ... VA-3
Long Point Island—*island* ... ME-1
Long Point Island—*island* ... MD-2
Long Point Island—*island* ... VT-1
Long Point Key—*island* ... FL-3
Long Point Lake—*lake* ... LA-4
Long Point Landing—*locale* ... DE-2
Long Point Light—*locale* ... MD-2
Long Point Light—*locale* ... MA-1
Long Point Lighthouse—*locale* ... MA-1
Long Point Light Station—*hist pl* ... MA-1
Long Point Marsh—*swamp* ... FL-3
Long Point Marsh—*swamp* ... MD-2
Long Point Marshes—*swamp* ... MA-1
Long Point Mtn—*summit* ... CO-8
Long Point No 3 Rsvr—*reservoir* ... UT-8
*Long Point of Marsh* ... NC-3
Long Point of the Buckskins—*cape* ... UT-8
Long Point Plantation
(38CH321)—*hist pl* ... SC-3
Long Point Plaza Shop Ctr—*locale* ... TX-5
Long Point Pond—*lake* ... NC-3

Look West Hist Dist—hist pl ... WI-6
**Loom**—pop pl ... WV-2
Loombeam Creek—stream ... AL-4
Loombeam Gin (historical)—locale ... AL-4
Loom Brook—stream ... MA-1
**Loom Cemetery**—pop pl ... WV-2
Loom Creek—stream ... NC-3
Loomer Township—civil ... SD-7
Loom Hollow ... KY-4
Loom Hollow—valley ... KY-4
Loomhouse Branch—stream ... KY-4
Loomiller Park—park ... CO-8
**Loomis**—pop pl ... CA-9
**Loomis**—pop pl ... MI-6
**Loomis**—pop pl ... NE-7
**Loomis**—pop pl (2) ... NY-2
**Loomis**—pop pl ... OH-6
**Loomis**—pop pl ... SD-7
**Loomis**—pop pl ... WA-9
**Loomis**—pop pl ... WI-6
Loomis, Capt. James, House—hist pl ... CT-1
Loomis, Col. James, House—hist pl ... CT-1
Loomis, George G., House—hist pl ... CT-1
Loomis, Gordon, House—hist pl ... CT-1
Loomis, Horace, House—hist pl ... WI-6
Loomis, Ira, Jr., House—hist pl ... CT-1
Loomis Basin-Folsom Lake (CCD)—cens area ... CA-9
Loomis Brook—stream ... NY-2
Loomis Cem—cemetery ... NY-2
Loomis Cem—cemetery ... OH-6
Loomis Cem—cemetery (2) ... PA-2
Loomis Cem—cemetery ... VT-1
Loomis Corner—locale ... NY-2
Loomis Corners—locale (2) ... NY-2
**Loomis Corners**—pop pl ... CA-9
Loomis Coulee—valley (2) ... MT-8
Loomis Creek ... NY-2
Loomis Creek ... WV-2
Loomis Creek—stream ... NV-8
Loomis Creek—stream ... NY-2
Loomis Creek—stream ... WA-9
Loomis Drain—canal ... MI-6
Loomis Drain—stream ... MI-6
**Loomises**—pop pl ... NY-2
**Loomis Hill**—pop pl ... NY-2
Loomis Hill—summit ... ME-1
Loomis Hill—summit ... NY-2
Loomis Hill—summit ... VT-1
Loomis Hill Cem—cemetery ... VT-1
Loomis House—hist pl ... WA-9
Loomis Institute—school ... CT-1
Loomis Lake ... IN-6
Loomis Lake ... OH-6
Loomis Lake—lake ... CO-8
Loomis Lake—lake (2) ... MI-6
Loomis Lake—lake ... PA-2
Loomis Lake—lake ... WA-9
Loomis Lake—lake ... WY-8
Loomis Lake—reservoir (2) ... IN-6
Loomis Lake—reservoir ... PA-2
Loomis Lake Dam—dam ... IN-6
Loomis Lake Dam—dam ... PA-2
Loomis Memorial Park—park ... IA-7
Loomis Mine—mine ... CA-9
Loomis Mtn—summit ... NV-8
Loomis Mtn—summit ... NY-2
Loomis Mtn—summit ... WA-9
Loomis Park—flat ... WY-8
Loomis Park—park ... DC-2
Loomis Park—park ... MI-6
**Loomis Park**—pop pl ... PA-2
Loomis Park Ch—church ... MI-6
Loomis Pass—gut ... LA-4
Loomis Peak—summit ... CA-9
Loomis Pond—bay ... LA-4
Loomis Pond—lake ... NY-2
Loomis Ponds—lake ... NY-2
Loomis Ranch—locale ... CA-9
Loomis Ranch—locale ... WA-9
Loomis Rsvr—reservoir ... CA-9
Loomis Sch—school (3) ... MI-6
Loomis Sch—school ... OH-6
Loomis Sch—school (2) ... SD-7
Loomis School ... PA-2
Loomis School Number 85 ... IN-6
Loomis Spring—spring ... CO-8
Loomis Swamp—swamp ... NY-2
Loomis Swamp—swamp ... PA-2
Loomis Township—civil ... SD-7
Loomis Valley Brook—stream ... NH-1
Loomis Vistor Center, Bldg. 43—hist pl ... CA-9
Loom Lake ... MI-6
Loom Tree Hollow—valley (2) ... WV-2
Loon Bay ... NH-1
Loon Bay—bay ... ME-1
Loon Bay—bay ... MN-6
Loon Bay—bay (2) ... NY-2
Loon Beam Hollow ... AR-4
Loonbeam Hollow—valley ... AR-4
Loon Branch—stream ... FL-3
Loon Brook—stream ... CT-1
Loon Brook—stream ... NY-2
Loon Channel—channel ... VA-3
**Loon Cove**—pop pl ... NH-1
Loon Creek—stream ... AK-9
Loon Creek—stream (2) ... ID-8
Loon Creek—stream ... IN-6
Loon Creek—stream ... MI-6
Loon Creek—stream ... OR-9
Loon Creek—stream ... WI-6
Loon Creek Cem—cemetery ... IN-6
Loon Creek Guard Station—locale ... ID-8
Loon Creek Lookout—locale ... ID-8
Loon Creek Point—pillar ... ID-8
Loon Creek Summit—summit ... ID-8
**Loonewood**—pop pl ... TN-4
Looney—locale ... VA-3
Looney, Moses, Fort House—hist pl ... TN-4
Looney Branch—stream ... KY-4
Looney Branch—stream ... OK-5
Looney Branch—stream ... VA-3
Looney Butte—summit ... OR-9
Looney Cem—cemetery ... OR-9
Looney Cem—cemetery ... TX-5
Looney Cem—cemetery (4) ... VA-3
Looney Cem—cemetery (3) ... WV-2
Looney Chapel—church ... VA-3
Looney Creek ... TN-4
Looney Creek ... TX-5
Looney Creek—stream ... CA-9
Looney Creek—stream ... KY-4
Looney Creek—stream ... MN-6
Looney Creek—stream ... MO-7
Looney Creek—stream (2) ... OR-9
Looney Creek—stream (3) ... VA-3
Looney Creek—stream ... WA-9
Looney Creek Cem—cemetery ... VA-3
Looney Creek Ch—church ... VA-3
Looney Creek Sch—school ... VA-3
Looney Fork—stream ... VA-3
Looney Fork—stream ... WV-2
Looney Gap ... TN-4
Looney Gap—gap (3) ... AL-4
Looney Hollow—valley ... AL-4
Looney Hollow—valley ... AR-4
Looney Hollow—valley (3) ... TN-4
Looney House—hist pl ... AL-4
Looney Islands—island ... TN-4
Looney Lake—lake ... AR-4
Looney Lake—reservoir ... GA-3
Looney Mill Creek ... VA-3
Looney Mill Creek Site—hist pl ... VA-3
Looney Mine—mine ... NV-8
Looney Plantation (historical)—locale ... MS-4
Looney Point ... MI-6
Looney Ranch—locale ... TX-5
Looney Ridge—ridge ... KY-4
Looney Ridge—ridge ... TN-4
Looney Ridge—ridge ... VA-3
Looney Rsvr—reservoir ... OR-9
Looneys Cem—cemetery ... TN-4
Looney Sch—school ... IA-7
Looney Sch—school ... TX-5
Looneys Chapel—church ... TN-4
Looney School ... TN-4
**Looney's Creek**—pop pl ... VA-3
Looneys Creek—stream ... TN-4
Looneys Creek Methodist Church ... TN-4
Looneys Creek Post Office (historical)—building ... TN-4
Looneys Gap—gap ... TN-4
Looney Shoals—rapids ... TN-4
Looneys Island ... TN-4
Looneys Mill Creek ... VA-3
Looneys Mill (historical)—locale ... AL-4
Looney Spring—spring ... AZ-5
Looney Spring—spring ... ID-8
Looney Spring—spring ... OR-9
Looney Spring Campground—park ... OR-9
Looney Springs Cem—cemetery ... IL-6
Looneys Sch (historical)—school ... TN-4
Looney Valley—valley ... MN-6
Looney Valley Cem—cemetery ... MN-6
Looney Valley Ch—church ... MN-6
Looneyville—locale ... TX-5
Looneyville—locale ... WV-2
Loon Falls—falls ... MN-6
Loon Hill—summit ... MA-1
Loon Hole, The—swamp ... VT-1
Loon Hollows Pond—lake ... NY-2
Loon Island ... ID-8
Loon Island ... NH-1
Loon Island—island (5) ... ME-1
Loon Island—island ... MN-6
Loon Island—island (8) ... NH-1
Loon Island—island ... NY-2
Loon Island—island ... WI-6
Loon Islands—island ... NH-1
Loon Lake ... MA-1
Loon Lake (2) ... MI-6
Loon Lake ... MN-6
Loon Lake ... NY-2
Loon Lake ... WA-9
Loon Lake ... WI-6
Loon Lake—lake (5) ... AK-9
Loon Lake—lake ... ID-8
Loon Lake—lake (2) ... IL-6
Loon Lake—lake (3) ... IN-6
Loon Lake—lake (2) ... ME-1
Loon Lake—lake (28) ... MI-6
Loon Lake—lake (26) ... MN-6
Loon Lake—lake (6) ... MT-8
Loon Lake—lake (2) ... NH-1
Loon Lake—lake (5) ... NY-2
Loon Lake—lake ... ND-7
Loon Lake—lake (2) ... OR-9
Loon Lake—lake ... WA-9
Loon Lake—lake (17) ... WI-6
Loon Lake—lake ... WY-8
**Loon Lake**—pop pl ... IL-6
**Loon Lake**—pop pl ... IN-6
**Loon Lake**—pop pl ... NY-2
**Loon Lake**—pop pl ... WA-9
Loon Lake—reservoir ... CA-9
Loon Lake—reservoir ... ME-1
Loon Lake—reservoir ... WI-6
Loon Lake (CCD)—cens area ... WA-9
Loon Lake Chapel—church ... NY-2
Loon Lake Creek ... MI-6
Loon Lake Creek—stream ... MI-6
Loon Lake Dam—dam ... ME-1
**Loon Lake Junction**—pop pl ... NY-2
Loon Lake Lookout—locale ... OR-9
Loon Lake Mountains—ridge ... NY-2
Loon Lake Mtn—summit ... WA-9
Loon Lake Recreation Site—park ... OR-9
Loon Lake Rsvr ... CA-9
Loon Lakes—lake (2) ... AK-9
Loon Lake Sch—school ... MN-6
Loon Lake Sch Number 1—school ... ND-7
Loon Lake Sch Number 3—school ... ND-7
Loon Lake Sch Number 5—school ... ND-7
Loon Lake State Wildlife Area—park ... WI-6
**Loon Lake (Township of)**—pop pl ... MN-6
Loon Lake Trail—trail ... CA-9
Loon Ledge—bar ... ME-1
Loon Mountain ... ID-8
Loon Mountain—ridge ... NH-1
Loon Mtn—summit ... NY-2
Loon Peak—summit ... MT-8
Loon Point—cape ... AK-9
Loon Point—cape ... CA-9
Loon Point—cape ... ME-1
Loon Point—cape ... MI-6
Loon Point—cape ... NY-2
Loon Pond ... NH-1
Loon Pond—lake (6) ... ME-1
Loon Pond—lake (2) ... MA-1
Loon Pond—lake (2) ... NH-1
Loon Pond—lake ... NY-2
Loon Pond—reservoir (2) ... NH-1
Loon Pond Brook—stream (2) ... NH-1
Loon Pond Mtn—summit ... NY-2
Loon Rapids—rapids ... WI-6
Loon River—stream ... MN-6
Loon Rock—bar ... AK-9
Loon Shoal—bar ... AK-9
Loons Nest—island ... ME-1
Loonsong Lake—lake ... AK-9
Loon Stream—stream ... ME-1
Loon Stream Deadwater—lake ... ME-1
Loon Vly—swamp ... NY-2
Loony Creek—stream ... WA-9
Loop ... IL-6
Loop ... MN-6
Loop—locale ... AL-4
Loop—locale ... NC-3
Loop—locale ... PA-2
Loop—locale ... WV-2
**Loop**—pop pl ... CA-9
**Loop**—pop pl ... PA-2
**Loop**—pop pl ... TX-5
**Loop**—pop pl ... WV-2
Loop—uninc pl ... AL-4
Loop, Joseph M., House—hist pl ... MI-6
Loop, The—bend ... AK-9
Loop, The—bend ... KY-4
Loop, The—bend ... OR-9
Loop, The—bend ... TN-4
Loop, The—bend ... UT-8
Loop, The—bend ... WV-2
Loop, The—locale ... CA-9
Loop, The—locale ... MT-8
Loop, The—locale ... NV-8
Loop, The—locale ... NC-3
Loop, The—locale (2) ... TN-4
Loop, The—trail ... NY-2
Loop, The—valley ... PA-2
Loop Branch—stream ... WV-2
Loop Branch Ditch—canal ... IA-7
Loop Cabin Site—locale ... TN-4
Loop Camp—locale ... TX-5
Loop Campground—park ... UT-8
Loop Canyon—valley ... CA-9
Loop Ch—church ... VA-3
Loop Creek ... WV-2
Loop Creek—stream (2) ... ID-8
Loop Creek—stream ... IL-6
Loop Creek—stream ... VA-3
Loop Creek—stream ... WA-9
Loop Creek—stream ... WV-2
Loop Creek Ch—church ... WV-2
Loop Ditch—canal ... CA-9
Loop Ditch Number One—canal ... CA-9
Loop Ditch Number Two—canal ... CA-9
Loop Drain—stream ... IN-6
Loope—locale ... CA-9
Loope, The—bend ... VA-3
Loope, The—ridge ... VA-3
Loope, The—summit ... VA-3
Loope Canyon—valley ... CA-9
Loope Cem—cemetery ... NY-2
Loopemount—locale ... WV-2
Looper Branch—stream ... TN-4
Looper Cem—cemetery ... AR-4
Looper Cem—cemetery ... KY-4
Looper Cem—cemetery ... SC-3
Looper Cem—cemetery ... TN-4
Looper Hollow—valley ... AR-4
Looper Lake—reservoir ... GA-3
Loopers Bend—bend ... GA-3
Loopers Bridge—bridge ... GA-3
Loopers Mill Creek ... TN-4
Loopeville ... CA-9
Loop Firetower ... PA-2
Loop Hollow ... NY-2
Loop Hollow—valley (2) ... TN-4
**Loop Junction**—pop pl ... WV-2
Loop Lake—lake ... MN-6
Loop Lake—reservoir ... CO-8
Loop Lookout Tower—locale ... PA-2
Loop Loop Creek ... WA-9
Loop Mountain—ridge ... WV-2
Loop Mtn—summit ... PA-2
Loop Park—park ... OH-6
Loop Pond—lake ... MA-1
Loop Post Office (historical)—building ... AL-4
Loop Run—locale ... PA-2
Loop Run—stream ... PA-2
Loop Sch (abandoned)—school ... PA-2
Loops Road Ch—church ... WV-2
Loop Station—post sta ... IL-6
**Loop Station (Loop)**—pop pl ... PA-2
Loop Thru Cave—cave ... AL-4
Loop Trail—trail ... CA-9
Loop Trail—trail ... CO-8
Loop Trail—trail ... MD-2
Loop Trail—trail ... PA-2
Loop Wash—stream ... CA-9
Loosa ... MS-4
Loosa Hatchee River ... TN-4
Loosahatchie Bar—bar ... TN-4
Loosahatchie Bottom—basin ... TN-4
Loosa Hatchie River ... TN-4
Loosahatchie River—stream ... TN-4
Loosahatchie River Canal—canal ... TN-4
Loosahatchie River Drainage Canal ... TN-4
Loosahatchie River Drainage Canal—canal ... TN-4
Loosa Schoona ... MS-4
Loosa Shooner Creek ... MS-4
Looscan Sch—school ... TX-5
Loose, Jacob, House—hist pl ... MO-7
Loose Angel Cem—cemetery ... KY-4
**Loose Creek**—pop pl ... MO-7
Loose Creek—stream (2) ... MO-7
Loose Memorial Park—cemetery ... MO-7
Loose Mtn—summit ... NC-3
Loose Pulley Junction—locale ... IL-6
**Loosier**—pop pl ... AL-4
Loosier Ch—church ... AL-4
Loosier Hollow—valley ... AL-4
Loosier Sch (historical)—school ... AL-4
Loosing Swamp ... NC-3
Loosing Swamp—stream ... NC-3
Loosing Swamp—swamp ... SC-3
Loospililla Creek ... AL-4
Loos Pond—lake ... CT-1
Loos Sch—school ... IL-6
Loos Sch—school ... OH-6
Loosuckel ... AL-4
Loosuckelea Creek ... AL-4
Loosum Creek—stream ... ID-8
Looters Gulch—valley ... MT-8
Loothog—locale ... FM-9
Loowell Run ... SD-7
Loowit Creek—stream ... OR-9
Loowit Falls—falls ... OR-9
Loowit Glacier—glacier ... WA-9
**Looxahoma**—pop pl ... MS-4
Looxahoma Baptist Church ... MS-4
Looxahoma Cem—cemetery ... MS-4
Looxahoma Ch—church ... MS-4
Looxahoma Ch of Christ—church ... MS-4
Looxahoma Post Office (historical)—building ... MS-4
Looxapalia Post Office (historical)—building ... AL-4
looxapillila Creek ... AL-4
Lopa—locale ... HI-9
Lopa Gulch—valley ... HI-9
Lopas Canyon—valley ... AZ-5
**Lopatcong (Br. P.O.)**—pop pl ... NJ-2
Lopatcong Creek—stream ... NJ-2
**Lopatcong (Township of)**—pop pl ... NJ-2
Lopatcong Village ... NJ-2
Lopau Point ... ME-1
Lopaus Point—cape ... ME-1
Lop Ear Creek ... AZ-5
Lop Ear Creek—stream ... AZ-5
Lop Ear Spring—spring ... AZ-5
Lopena Artesian Well—well ... TX-5
Lopena Island ... TX-5
**Lopeno**—pop pl ... TX-5
Lopeno Gas Field —oilfield ... TX-5
Lopeno Island ... TX-5
**Loper**—pop pl ... AL-4
Loper Cem—cemetery ... IA-7
Loper Cem—cemetery ... KY-4
Loper Creek ... NY-2
Loper Creek—stream ... AK-9
Loper Creek—stream ... MS-4
Loper Creek—stream ... WA-9
Loper Creek—stream ... WI-6
Loper Ditch—canal ... CA-9
Loperfido Spring—spring ... OR-9
Loper Hollow—valley ... OH-6
Loper Island—island ... AK-9
Loper Peak—summit ... CA-9
Loper Pond—lake ... FL-3
Loper Pond—swamp ... TX-5
Loper Run—stream ... NJ-2
Lopers Cabin—locale ... UT-8
Loper Sch—school ... KY-4
Loper Sch (historical)—school ... AL-4
Loper School ... IN-6
Lopers Crossroads—locale ... SC-3
Lopers Gut—gut ... NJ-2
Lopers Sch—school ... WI-6
Lopers Spring—spring ... UT-8
Lope Spring—spring ... NV-8
Lopez—locale ... MO-7
Lopez—locale ... PA-2
Lopez—locale ... WA-9
Lopez, Hilario, House—hist pl ... NM-5
Lopez Adobe—hist pl ... CA-9
Lopez Arch—arch ... UT-8
Lopez Arroyo—stream ... NM-5
Lopez Artesian Well—well ... TX-5
Lopez Canyon ... AZ-5
Lopez Canyon—valley (3) ... CA-9
Lopez Canyon—valley ... CO-8
Lopez Canyon—valley (3) ... NM-5
Lopez Canyon Forest Station—locale ... CA-9
Lopez (CCD)—cens area ... WA-9
Lopez Creek—stream (2) ... CA-9
Lopez Creek—stream ... CO-8
Lopez Creek—stream ... PA-2
Lopez Creek—stream ... TX-5
Lopez Dam—dam (2) ... CA-9
Lopez Ditch—canal (2) ... CO-8
Lopez Draw—valley ... NM-5
Lopez Elementary School ... MS-4
Lopez Elem Sch—school ... FL-3
Lopez Flats—flat ... CA-9
Lopez Gulch—valley ... CO-8
Lopez Gulch—valley ... UT-8
Lopez Hill—summit ... WA-9
Lopez Island—island ... WA-9
Lopez Island Airp—airport ... WA-9
Lopez Lake—lake ... OR-9
Lopez Lake—reservoir ... CA-9
Lopez Lateral—canal ... NM-5
Lopez Mtn—summit ... CA-9
Lopez Oil Field—oilfield ... TX-5
Lopez Park—park ... KS-7
Lopez Pass—channel ... WA-9
Lopez Peak ... WA-9
Lopez Peaks—summit ... TX-5
Lopez Point—cape ... CA-9
Lopez Pond—lake ... PA-2
Lopez Pond Branch—stream ... PA-2
Lopez Ranch—locale ... AZ-5
Lopez Ranch—locale ... TX-5
Lopez Reservoir ... CA-9
Lopez River—gut ... FL-3
Lopez Rock—island ... CA-9
Lopez Sound—bay ... WA-9
Lopez Spring—spring (2) ... AZ-5
Lopez Spring—spring ... NM-5
Lopez Spring—spring ... TX-5
Lopez Tank—reservoir ... AZ-5
Lopez Tank—reservoir (2) ... NM-5
Lopez Tank—reservoir ... TX-5
**Lopezville**—pop pl ... TX-5
Lopezville Drain—canal ... NM-5
Lopez Wash—stream (2) ... AZ-5
Lopez Well—well (2) ... AZ-5
Lopez Well No 2—well ... NM-5
Lopez Wells—well ... AZ-5
Lopez Windmill—locale ... AZ-5
Lopez Windmill—locale ... NM-5
LO Pocket—basin ... AZ-5
LO Pocket Tank—reservoir ... AZ-5
Lopp Coulee—valley ... MT-8
Lopp Hollow—valley ... IN-6
Lopp Lagoon—lake ... AK-9
Lopps Chapel (historical)—church ... TN-4
Lopps Landing (historical)—locale ... IN-6
**Loquemont Township**—pop pl ... ND-7
Loque Sch (abandoned)—school ... PA-2
Lora—locale ... TX-5
Lora B Pearson Elem Sch—school ... IN-6
Loradale—locale ... KY-4
**Lorado**—pop pl ... AR-4
**Lorado**—pop pl ... WV-2
Lorah—locale ... IA-7
Lorah Cem—cemetery ... IA-7
Lorah Park Elem Sch—school ... FL-3
Lorain ... IN-6
Lorain (2) ... ND-7
**Lorain**—pop pl ... OH-6
**Lorain**—pop pl ... PA-2
Lorain, Lake—lake ... PA-2
Lorain Borough—civil ... PA-2
Lorain-Carnegie Bridge—hist pl ... OH-6
Lorain Ch—church ... WI-6
Lorain Country Club—other ... OH-6
**Lorain (County)**—pop pl ... OH-6
Lorain County Courthouse—hist pl ... OH-6
Lorain Detention Home—building ... OH-6
Loraine ... WI-6
**Loraine**—pop pl ... CA-9
**Loraine**—pop pl ... IL-6
**Loraine**—pop pl ... MS-4
**Loraine**—pop pl ... ND-7
**Loraine**—pop pl ... TX-5
**Loraine**—pop pl ... WI-6
Loraine, Lake—lake ... NY-2
Loraine, Lake—reservoir ... TX-5
Loraine Bldg—hist pl ... MI-6
Loraine (CCD)—cens area ... TX-5
Loraine Cem—cemetery ... IL-6
Loraine Creek—stream ... AK-9
Loraine Lake ... WI-6
Loraine Lake—reservoir ... NC-3
Loraine Lake Dam—dam ... NC-3
Loraine Sch—school ... IL-6
**Loraine (Township of)**—pop pl ... IL-6
**Loraine (Twin Oaks)**—pop pl ... CA-9
Lorain Fire Station No. 1—hist pl ... OH-6
Lorain Lighthouse—hist pl ... OH-6
Lorain Sch—school ... MO-7
**Lorain (Town of)**—pop pl ... WI-6
**Lorain (Township of)**—pop pl ... MN-6
Loraleno Windmill—locale ... TX-5
Loral Hills Memory Gardens ... MS-4
Loralin, Lake—lake ... FL-3
Lora Locke Hotel—hist pl ... KS-7
Loramie ... OH-6
Loramie—other ... OH-6
Loramie, Lake—reservoir ... OH-6
Loramie Creek—stream ... OH-6
Loramie Ditch ... OH-6
Loramie Reservoir ... OH-6
**Loramie (Township of)**—pop pl ... OH-6
**Loran**—pop pl ... IL-6
Lorance Cem—cemetery ... TN-4
Lorance Creek ... AR-4
Lorance Creek—stream ... AR-4
Lorance Township—civil ... MO-7
Loran Coast Guard Station—locale ... SC-3
Lorane—locale ... GA-3
**Lorane**—pop pl ... IN-6
**Lorane**—pop pl ... OR-9
**Lorane**—pop pl ... PA-2
Lorane Grange Cem—cemetery ... OR-9
Lorane Guard Station—locale ... OR-9
Lorane Sch—school ... OR-9
L'Orange Park—park ... HI-9
**Loranger**—pop pl ... LA-4
Loranger, Edward, House—hist pl ... MI-6
Loranger Cem—cemetery ... LA-4
Loranger Coulee—valley ... MT-8
Loranger Drain—stream ... MI-6
Loranger Lookout Tower—locale ... LA-4
Loranger Methodist Church—hist pl ... LA-4
Loran Radio Station (Abandoned)—locale ... AK-9
Loran Radio Tower (Abandoned)—locale ... AK-9
Loran Saint Ch—church ... OH-6
Loran Tower—locale ... HI-9
**Loran (Township of)**—pop pl ... IL-6
Lora Point—cape ... FL-3
Loras Coll—school ... IA-7
Loray—locale ... NV-8
**Loray**—pop pl ... NC-3
Loray Campground—locale ... NV-8
Loray Draw—valley ... NV-8
**Loray Mills**—pop pl ... NC-3
Lora Young Dam—dam ... NC-3
Lora Young Lake—reservoir ... NC-3
Loray Rsvr—reservoir ... NV-8
Lorays—locale ... AR-4
Loray Wash—stream ... NV-8
Lorbeer JHS—school ... CA-9
Lorberry—locale ... PA-2
Lorberry Creek—stream ... PA-2
Lorberry Junction—locale ... PA-2
**Lorcum Hills**—pop pl ... VA-3
**Lord**—pop pl ... TX-5
Lord, Capt. Nathaniel, Mansion—hist pl ... ME-1
Lord, C. J., Mansion—hist pl ... WA-9
Lord, Drew H., House—hist pl ... MN-6
Lord, James C., House—hist pl ... ME-1
Lord, Richard T. C., and William V. Wilcox House—hist pl ... IA-7
Lordamercy Cove—valley ... GA-3
Lord Baltimore Elem Sch—school ... DE-2
Lord Baltimore Hotel—hist pl ... MD-2
Lord Baltimore HS ... DE-2
Lord Bay ... CT-1
Lord-Baylies-Bennett House—hist pl ... MA-1
Lord Block—hist pl ... ME-1
Lord Botetourt HS—school ... VA-3
Lord Brook ... ME-1
Lord Brook—stream (2) ... ME-1
Lord Brook—stream ... MA-1
Lord Brook—stream (3) ... NH-1
Lord Brook—stream (2) ... VT-1
Lord Canyon—valley ... UT-8
Lord Cem—cemetery ... ME-1
Lord Cem—cemetery ... OK-5
Lord Cem—cemetery ... TX-5
Lord Cem—cemetery ... WI-6
Lord Coulee—valley ... MT-8
Lord Cove ... CT-1
Lord Cove—bay ... CT-1
Lord Cove—cove ... MA-1
Lord Cove Site—hist pl ... CT-1
Lord Creek—stream ... CT-1
Lord Creek—stream ... WI-6
Lord Delaware Bridge—bridge ... VA-3
Lord Ditch—canal ... WY-8
Lord Draw—valley ... MT-8
Lord-Ellis Summit—gap ... CA-9
Lorden Lake—lake ... MI-6
Lorden Sch—school ... MI-6
**Lord Fairfax Estates**—pop pl ... VA-3
Lord Farm—hist pl ... ME-1
Lord Flat—flat ... OR-9
Lord Flat Airp—airport ... OR-9
Lord Hill—summit ... CT-1
Lord Hill—summit (2) ... ME-1
Lord Hill—summit ... NH-1
Lord Hill—summit ... WA-9
Lord House—hist pl ... PA-2
Lordier Ditch—canal ... WY-8
Lordier Rsvr—reservoir ... WY-8
Lord Island ... ME-1
Lord Island—island ... CT-1
Lord Island—island (2) ... OR-9
Lord Islands—area ... AK-9
Lord JHS—school ... MA-1
**Lord (Klondike)**—pop pl ... MD-2
Lord Lake—lake ... FL-3
Lord Lake—lake ... GA-3
Lord Lake—lake ... MN-6
Lord Lake—lake ... SC-3
**Lordland (subdivision)**—pop pl ... FL-3
Lord Lutheran Sch—school ... FL-3
Lord M ... MP-9
Lord Mansion—hist pl ... ME-1
Lord Mine—mine ... TN-4
Lord Mtn—summit (2) ... ME-1
Lord Mulgave ... MP-9
Lord of Life Ch—church ... MN-6
Lord of Life Lutheran Ch—church ... FL-3
Lord of Life Lutheran Ch—church ... IN-6
Lord Pond—lake ... PA-2
Lord Pond—reservoir ... CT-1
Lord Ridge—ridge ... TN-4
Lord Rock—island ... AK-9
Lord Rsvr—reservoir ... CO-8
Lords, William L., House—hist pl ... IN-6
Lords Bay ... CT-1
Lords Branch—stream ... GA-3
Lords Brook—stream ... ME-1
Lords Brook—stream ... NH-1
**Lordsburg**—pop pl ... NM-5
Lordsburg Draw—valley ... NM-5
Lordsburg Golf Club—other ... NM-5
Lordsburg Mesa—area ... NM-5
Lordsburg Pumping State—locale ... NM-5
**Lordsburg Township**—pop pl ... ND-7
Lordsburg Valley—valley ... NM-5
Lords Cem—cemetery ... GA-3
Lords Corner—locale ... DE-2
**Lords Corners**—pop pl ... NY-2
Lords Cove ... CT-1
Lords Cove—bay ... ME-1
Lords Creek—channel ... MA-1
Lords Creek—stream ... NC-3
Lords Creek—stream ... PA-2
Lords Creek—stream ... VT-1
Lords Creek—stream ... WA-9
Lords Drain—stream ... MI-6
Lords Hill—summit ... ME-1
Lords Hill—summit ... MA-1
Lords Hill—summit ... NH-1
Lords Hill—summit ... NY-2
Lords Hill—summit ... VT-1
Lord's Hill Hist Dist—hist pl ... NH-1
**Lordship**—pop pl (2) ... CT-1
Lordship Beach—beach ... CT-1
Lords House Ch—church ... NC-3
Lords Island—island ... ME-1
Lords Lake—lake ... AK-9
Lords Lake—lake ... MN-6
Lords Lake—lake ... NV-8
Lords Lake—lake ... ND-7
Lords Lake—lake ... SD-7
Lords Lake—lake ... WA-9
Lords Lake—reservoir ... ND-7
Lords Lake Dam—dam ... ND-7
Lords Lake Natl Wildlife Ref—park ... ND-7
Lords Park—park ... IL-6
Lords' Park Manor ... IL-6
Lords Passage—channel ... NY-2
Lords Passage—channel ... RI-1
Lords Pocket—bay ... AK-9
Lords Point—cape ... CT-1
Lords Point—cape ... ME-1
**Lords Point**—pop pl ... CT-1
Lords Pond—lake ... ME-1
Lord Spring—spring ... CA-9
Lords Ranch—locale ... AZ-5
Lords Reservoir ... NY-2
Lords Sch—school ... AR-4
Lords Slough—gut ... MN-6
Lords Tabernacle, The—church ... AL-4
**Lordstown**—pop pl ... OH-6
Lordstown Milit Reservation—military ... OH-6
Lordstown (Township of)—other ... OH-6
Lords Trail—valley ... OR-9
**Lords Valley**—pop pl ... PA-2
Lords Valley—valley ... WA-9
Lords Valley Ch—church ... KY-4
**Lordville**—pop pl ... NY-2
**Lore**—pop pl ... IA-7
Lore, Charles B., Elem Sch—hist pl ... DE-2
Lore, J. C., Oyster House—hist pl ... MD-2
Lore, Seth and Irwinton Hist Dist (Boundary Increase)—hist pl ... AL-4
**Loreauville**—pop pl ... LA-4
Loreauville Canal—canal ... LA-4
**Lore City**—pop pl ... OH-6
**Loredell Subdivision**—pop pl ... UT-8
Loree—locale ... AL-4
**Loree**—pop pl ... IN-6
Loree Cem—cemetery ... MI-6
Loree Ch—church ... SC-3
**Loree Estates**—pop pl ... CA-9
Lore Hist Dist—hist pl ... AL-4
Lore Lake—lake ... MT-8
Lorelei, Lake—reservoir ... OH-6
**Lorelein**—pop pl ... LA-4
Lorelei Picnic Area—locale ... MT-8
**Loreley**—pop pl ... MD-2
**Lorella**—pop pl ... OR-9

Lorel Park—*park* IL-6
*Lore-n* MP-9
Lorena—*locale* KS-7
Lorena—*locale* MS-4
**Lorena**—*pop pl* TX-5
Lorena, Lake—*lake* UT-8
*Lorena Baptist Church* MS-4
Lorena Butte—*summit* WA-9
Lorena Cem—*cemetery* TX-5
Lorena Ch—*church* MS-4
Lorena Ditch—*canal* CO-8
Lorena Gulch—*valley* AZ-5
Lorena Saint Sch—*school* CA-9
Lorena Sch—*school* NY-2
Lorenaton Post Office (historical)—*building* TN-4
Lorence Creek—*stream* TX-5
Lorence Dam—*dam* OR-9
*Lorence Lake* OR-9
Lorence Rsvr—*lake* OR-9
Lorencito Canyo—*valley* CO-8
Lorencito Canyon—*valley* CO-8
Lorencito Canyon—*valley* NM-5
Lorene, Lake—*reservoir* AL-4
*Loren Johnson Hollow* MO-7
Lorenson Cem—*cemetery* MN-6
**Lorenton**—*pop pl* PA-2
**Lorentz**—*pop pl* WV-2
Lorenz Canyon—*valley* CA-9
Lorenz Cem—*cemetery* OK-5
**Lorenzen**—*pop pl* MS-4
Lorenzen Hill—*summit* ME-1
Lorenzen Post Office (historical)—*building* MS-4
Lorenz Hill—*summit* TX-5
Lorenzi Park—*park* NV-8
*Lorenzo* CA-9
Lorenzo—*hist pl* NY-2
Lorenzo—*locale* GA-3
**Lorenzo**—*pop pl* ID-8
**Lorenzo**—*pop pl* IL-6
**Lorenzo**—*pop pl* NE-7
**Lorenzo**—*pop pl* TX-5
Lorenzo Arroyo—*stream* (2) NM-5
Lorenzo Artesian Well—*well* TX-5
Lorenzo Beach—*beach* CA-9
Lorenzo Canyon—*valley* NM-5
Lorenzo (CCD)—*cens area* TX-5
Lorenzo Cem—*cemetery* TX-5
Lorenzo Creek—*stream* ID-8
Lorenzo Manor Sch—*school* CA-9
Lorenzo Pond—*reservoir* CT-1
Lorenzo Post Office (historical)—*building* TN-4
**Lorenzo Station**—*pop pl* CA-9
Lorenzo Vasquez Canyon—*valley* CA-9
Lorenzo Well—*well* NM-5
Lorenz Park—*CDP* NY-2
Lorenz Ranch—*locale* WY-8
Lorenz Schlichter Memorial Cem—*cemetery* KS-7
Lores Branch—*stream* NE-7
Lore Sch—*school* DE-2
Lores Island—*island* NJ-2
*Lores Landing* DE-2
Lores Mill—*locale* NJ-2
Loreta—*locale* WI-6
*Loreto* WI-6
Loreto Cem—*cemetery* WI-6
Loreto Sch—*school* NY-2
Loreto Shrine Chapel—*hist pl* WI-6
*Loret Resort Villa* TN-4
*Loretta* WI-6
**Loretta**—*pop pl* KS-7
**Loretta**—*pop pl* WI-6
Loretta, Lake—*lake* GA-3
Loretta Branch—*stream* MD-2
Loretta Cem—*cemetery* MN-6
Loretta Creek—*stream* WA-9
**Loretta Heights**—*pop pl* MD-2
Loretta Lake—*lake* NY-2
Loretta Lake—*reservoir* WI-6
Loretta Park Sch—*school* NY-2
Loretta Sch (historical)—*school* MS-4
Loretta Town Hall—*building* ND-7
**Loretta Township**—*pop pl* ND-7
*Loretto* KS-7
Loretto—*locale* IL-6
**Loretto**—*pop pl* AL-4
**Loretto**—*pop pl* FL-3
**Loretto**—*pop pl* KY-4
**Loretto**—*pop pl* MD-2
**Loretto**—*pop pl* MI-6
**Loretto**—*pop pl* MN-6
**Loretto**—*pop pl* NE-7
**Loretto**—*pop pl* PA-2
**Loretto**—*pop pl* TN-4
**Loretto**—*pop pl* VA-3
Loretto Acad—*hist pl* MO-7
Loretto Acad—*school* (2) MO-7
Loretto Borough—*civil* PA-2
Loretto Branch—*stream* TN-4
Loretto (CCD)—*cens area* KY-4
Loretto (CCD)—*cens area* TN-4
Loretto Cem—*cemetery* PA-2
Loretto Cem—*cemetery* TN-4
Loretto Ch of Christ—*church* TN-4
Loretto City Hall—*building* TN-4
Loretto Coll—*school* TX-5
Loretto Convent—*school* IL-6
Loretto Division—*civil* TN-4
Loretto Educational Center—*school* CO-8
Loretto Elem Sch—*school* TN-4
*Loretto Heights* CO-8
Loretto Heights Acad—*hist pl* CO-8
Loretto Heights Coll—*school* CO-8
Loretto Hosp—*hospital* MN-6
Loretto HS—*school* CA-9
Loretto HS—*school* KY-4
Loretto HS—*school* TN-4
*Loretto Methodist Episcopal Church South* TN-4
Loretto Mine—*mine* MI-6
Loretto Motherhouse—*hist pl* KY-4
Loretto Post Office—*building* TN-4
Loretto Post Office (historical)—*building* AL-4
Loretto Post Office (historical)—*building* PA-2
Loretto Rest—*building* NY-2
**Loretto Road**—*pop pl* PA-2
Loretto Sch—*school* FL-3
Loretto United Methodist Ch—*church* TN-4
Lorettta Post Office (historical)—*building* SD-7

Loret Villa—*locale* TN-4
Loretz House—*hist pl* NC-3
Lorewood Grove—*locale* DE-2
**Lorey**—*pop pl* CO-8
Loreys Cabins—*locale* MO-7
Lorez Canal—*canal* LA-4
**Lorfax Heights**—*pop pl* VA-3
Lorian Canyon—*valley* ID-8
*Lorian Lake* MI-6
**Lori Ann Estates Subdivision**—*pop pl* UT-8
Lorick, Preston C., House—*hist pl* SC-3
Lorick Branch—*stream* SC-3
Lorida—*locale* FL-3
Loridon Canyon—*valley* CA-9
**Lori Estates Subdivision**—*pop pl* UT-8
Lori Lake—*lake* WY-8
**Loriland (subdivision)**—*pop pl* TN-4
Lori Lane Shop Ctr—*locale* FL-3
Lorillard Beach—*uninc pl* NJ-2
Lorillard Snuff Mill—*hist pl* NY-2
Lorimer Park—*park* PA-2
Lorimer Sch—*school* IL-6
Lorimer Sch—*school* MO-7
Lorimier Cem—*cemetery* MO-7
**Lorimor**—*pop pl* IA-7
Lorimor Cem—*cemetery* IA-7
Lorimor City Park—*park* IA-7
Lorinda Brook—*stream* MA-1
Lorinda Cem—*cemetery* SD-7
Lorin Dam—*dam* MT-8
**Lorine**—*pop pl* AR-4
Lorin Farr Park—*park* UT-8
Lorin Farr Sch—*school* UT-8
Lorin Farr Tank—*reservoir* AZ-5
*Loring* MN-6
*Loring* SD-7
Loring—*locale* IA-7
Loring—*locale* LA-4
Loring—*locale* MS-4
Loring—*locale* MO-7
Loring—*locale* MT-8
Loring—*other* ME-1
**Loring**—*pop pl* AK-9
**Loring**—*pop pl* KS-7
Loring, Dr. David J., Residence and Clinic—*hist pl* IN-6
Loring, Harrison, House—*hist pl* MA-1
Loring AFB—*military* ME-1
Loring Arena—*locale* MA-1
*Loring Bogs* MA-1
Loring Branch—*stream* TX-5
Loring Cem—*cemetery* ND-7
Loring Cem—*cemetery* SC-3
Loring Cove—*bay* ME-1
Loring Creek—*stream* TX-5
**Loring Crossing**—*pop pl* NY-2
Loring Cut—*mine* NV-8
Loring Field—*park* MA-1
Loring-Greenough House—*hist pl* MA-1
*Loring Hill* MA-1
Loring Hill—*summit* ME-1
Loring Hill—*summit* (2) MA-1
Loring Lake—*reservoir* LA-4
Loring Millpond—*reservoir* SC-3
Loring Nickell Branch—*stream* KY-4
Loring Park—*park* MN-6
Loring Post Office (historical)—*building* MS-4
**Lorings**—*pop pl* NY-2
Lorings Bogs—*swamp* MA-1
Loring Sch—*school* KS-7
Loring Sch—*school* MN-6
Loring Sch—*school* MO-7
*Lorings Hill* MA-1
Loring Siding—*locale* SD-7
Loring Spring—*spring* NM-5
*Loring Station* KS-7
Lorinkono—*island* MP-9
Lorin Lake—*lake* OR-9
Lorio Lake Dam—*dam* MS-4
**Loris**—*pop pl* SC-3
Loris (CCD)—*cens area* SC-3
*Lorman* MS-4
**Lorman**—*pop pl* MS-4
Lorman, Lake—*reservoir* MS-4
Lormand Bluff—*cliff* LA-4
Lorman Mine—*mine* CA-9
Lorna Creek—*stream* AK-9
**Lornadale Subdivision**—*pop pl* UT-8
Lorna Doone, Lake—*lake* FL-3
Lorna Prieta Artesian Well—*well* TX-5
Lorne—*locale* MN-6
Lorne—*locale* VA-3
Lorne Street Sch—*school* CA-9
Lorona, Andronico, Second House—*hist pl* AZ-5
Lorona Lateral—*canal* AZ-5
Loron William Park—*park* GA-3
*Loror* FM-9
*Loror, Mount* FM-9
Lor-o Ranch—*locale* CA-9
*Lorrabb Creek* MI-6
*Lorrain* VA-3
Lorrain Cem—*cemetery* LA-4
Lorraine—*locale* FL-3
Lorraine—*locale* (2) LA-4
Lorraine—*locale* TN-4
Lorraine—*locale* VA-3
**Lorraine**—*pop pl* KS-7
**Lorraine**—*pop pl* MS-4
**Lorraine**—*pop pl* NY-2
**Lorraine**—*pop pl* PA-2
Lorraine—*uninc pl* NJ-2
Lorraine, Lake—*lake* AK-9
Lorraine, Lake—*lake* FL-3
Lorraine, Lake—*lake* GA-3
Lorraine, Lake—*lake* MA-1
Lorraine, Lake—*lake* NY-2
Lorraine, Lake—*lake* WA-9
Lorraine, Lake—*lake* WI-6
Lorraine, Lake—*reservoir* MI-6
Lorraine Ave Mennonite Ch—*church* KS-7
*Lorraine Baptist Church* TN-4
Lorraine Cem—*cemetery* KS-7
Lorraine Cem—*cemetery* TN-4
Lorraine Ch—*church* TN-4
Lorraine Creek—*stream* OR-9
Lorraine Field Airp—*airport* MO-7
Lorraine Gulf—*valley* NY-2
Lorraine Lake—*lake* FL-3
Lorraine Lake—*lake* MI-6

Lorraine Lake—*lake* MN-6
Lorraine Lake—*reservoir* TX-5
Lorraine Lodge—*hist pl* CO-8
Lorraine North Oil Field—*oilfield* KS-7
Lorraine Oil Field—*oilfield* KS-7
*Lorraine Park* IL-6
Lorraine Park—*park* MN-6
Lorraine Park Campground—*park* MA-1
Lorraine Park Cem—*cemetery* MD-2
Lorraine Park Cemetery Gate Lodge—*hist pl* MD-2
Lorraine Post Office (historical)—*building* TN-4
Lorraine Run—*stream* PA-2
Lorraine Station—*locale* NJ-2
**Lorraine (Town of)**—*pop pl* NY-2
**Lorraine Township**—*pop pl* ND-7
Lorraine Township (historical)—*civil* ND-7
Lorrain Gulch—*valley* CO-8
*Lorrain Lake* LA-4
Lorrain Sch (historical)—*school* MO-7
*Lorran Lake* LA-4
Lorran Lake—*lake* LA-4
Lorretta Acad (historical)—*school* AL-4
Lorrison Cem—*cemetery* KY-4
*Lorrisons Creek* TX-5
*Lorsbaugh Run* PA-2
Lort—*locale* CA-9
Lorta RR Station—*building* AZ-5
**Lorton**—*pop pl* AL-4
**Lorton**—*pop pl* VA-3
Lorton—*post sta* NE-7
Lorton Bridge—*other* IL-6
Lorton Ch—*church* IL-6
**Lorton Lick**—*pop pl* WV-2
Lorton Lick Creek—*stream* WV-2
**Lorton Valley**—*pop pl* VA-3
**Lorton Village**—*pop pl* NE-7
*Lort's Point* MD-2
Lorwood—*locale* MO-7
Lorwood—*uninc pl* GA-3
Lory—*locale* CO-8
**Lory**—*pop pl* WV-2
Lory, Lake—*lake* MI-6
Lory Ch—*church* WV-2
Lory Lake—*lake* MN-6
Lory Sch—*school* WV-2
Los Aceiteros Windmill—*locale* TX-5
Los Adaes—*hist pl* LA-4
Los Adaes State Commemorative Area—*park* LA-4
Los Adjuntas Banco Number 91—*levee* TX-5
Losa Island—*island* AK-9
Los Alamitos—*civil* CA-9
**Los Alamitos**—*pop pl* CA-9
Los Alamitos Canyon—*valley* NM-5
Los Alamitos Channel—*canal* CA-9
Los Alamitos Circle—*locale* CA-9
Los Alamitos Junction—*locale* CA-9
Los Alamitos Naval Air Station—*military* CA-9
Los Alamitos Racetrack—*other* CA-9
Los Alamitos Retarding Basin—*basin* CA-9
Los Alamitos Sch—*school* CA-9
Los Alamos—*CDP* NM-5
Los Alamos—*civil* CA-9
Los Alamos—*locale* NM-5
**Los Alamos**—*pop pl* CA-9
Los Alamos Canyon—*valley* CA-9
Los Alamos Canyon—*valley* NM-5
Los Alamos (CCD)—*cens area* NM-5
Los Alamos Cem—*cemetery* CA-9
**Los Alamos (County)**—*pop pl* NM-5
Los Alamos Creek—*stream* CA-9
Los Alamos Creek—*stream* NM-5
Los Alamos Ranch—*locale* CA-9
Los Alamos Ranch House—*hist pl* CA-9
Los Alamos Scientific Laboratory—*hist pl* NM-5
Los Alamos Spring—*spring* NM-5
Los Alamos Springs—*spring* NM-5
Los Alamos Truck Trail—*trail* CA-9
*Los Alamos Valley* CA-9
Los Alamos Valley—*valley* CA-9
Los Alamos Y Agua Caliente—*civil* CA-9
Los Alisos Canyon—*valley* CA-9
Los Alisos Sch—*school* CA-9
**Los Altos**—*pop pl* (2) CA-9
Los Altos Ch—*church* NM-5
Los Altos Country Club—*other* CA-9
**Los Altos Hills**—*pop pl* CA-9
Los Altos HS—*school* CA-9
Los Altos Park—*park* NM-5
Los Altos Sch—*school* (2) CA-9
Los Altos Sch—*school* NM-5
Los Altos Terrace—*uninc pl* CA-9
Los Amigos Gun Club—*other* CA-9
Los Amigos JHS—*school* CA-9
Los Amigos Park—*park* CA-9
**Los Amigos (Ranchos Los Amigos Hospital)**—*pop pl* CA-9
Los Amigos Sch—*school* CA-9
Los Amigos Windmill—*locale* TX-5
Los Amoles Creek—*stream* CA-9
Los Angeles—*locale* TX-5
**Los Angeles**—*pop pl* CA-9
**Los Angeles**—*pop pl* TX-5
**Los Angeles**—*pop pl* PR-3
Los Angeles Air Force Station—*military* CA-9
Los Angeles Amarillo Airway Beacon 17—*other* CA-9
Los Angeles Aqueduct—*canal* CA-9
Los Angeles Baptist HS—*school* CA-9
Los Angeles Canyon—*valley* UT-8
Los Angeles (CCD)—*cens area* CA-9
Los Angeles Central Library—*hist pl* CA-9
Los Angeles City Coll—*school* CA-9
Los Angeles Civic Center—*building* CA-9
Los Angeles Coliseum—*other* CA-9
Los Angeles Coll Aircraft Sch—*school* CA-9
Los Angeles Country Club—*other* CA-9
**Los Angeles (County)**—*pop pl* CA-9
Los Angeles County Fairgrounds—*locale* CA-9
Los Angeles County Hosp—*hospital* CA-9
Los Angeles Harbor Coll—*school* CA-9
Los Angeles Harbor General Hosp—*hospital* CA-9
Los Angeles Harbor Light Station—*hist pl* CA-9
**Los Angeles Heights**—*pop pl* TX-5
Los Angeles HS—*school* CA-9
Los Angeles International Airp—*airport* CA-9
Los Angeles Memorial Coliseum—*hist pl* CA-9

Los Angeles Mine—*mine* CA-9
Los Angeles Naval Support Activity—*other* CA-9
Los Angeles Outer Harbor—*harbor* CA-9
Los Angeles Pacific Coll—*school* CA-9
Los Angeles Pacific Company Ivy Park Substation—*hist pl* CA-9
Los Angeles Pet Cem—*cemetery* CA-9
Los Angeles Plaza Hist Dist—*hist pl* CA-9
Los Angeles Ranch—*locale* TX-5
Los Angeles River—*stream* CA-9
Los Angeles Tank—*reservoir* NM-5
Los Angeles Tank—*reservoir* TX-5
Los Angeles Union Passenger Terminal—*hist pl* CA-9
Los Angeles Valley Junior Coll—*school* CA-9
Los Angeles Wash—*stream* AZ-5
Los Angeles Windmill—*locale* NM-5
Los Angeles Windmill—*locale* (2) TX-5
Los Angeles Y M C A Camp—*locale* CA-9
Los Ansares Windmill—*locale* TX-5
*Losantiville* OH-6
Losantiville Country Club—*other* OH-6
**Losantville**—*pop pl* IN-6
Losantville Triangle—*locale* OH-6
Losap Island—*island* FM-9
Losap (Municipality)—*civ div* FM-9
Los Arboles Sch—*school* CA-9
Los Arcos Mall—*locale* AZ-5
Los Arrierous Cem—*cemetery* TX-5
Los Arroyos—*valley* TX-5
Los Avispas Ranch—*locale* AZ-5
Los Bancos de en Medio—*island* TX-5
**Los Banos**—*pop pl* CA-9
Los Banos (CCD)—*cens area* CA-9
Los Banos Cem—*cemetery* CA-9
Los Banos Creek—*stream* CA-9
Los Banos Detention Dam—*dam* CA-9
Los Banos Fire Control Station—*locale* CA-9
Los Banos Game Bird Farm—*other* CA-9
Los Banos Gun Club—*other* CA-9
Los Banos Odd Fellows Grove—*woods* CA-9
Los Banos Rsvr—*reservoir* CA-9
Los Banos State Waterfowl Area—*park* CA-9
Los Banos Valley—*valley* CA-9
Los Barrancos—*ridge* NM-5
Los Barreales Lake—*lake* NM-5
**Los Barreras**—*pop pl* TX-5
Los Barros—*summit* PR-3
Los Barrosos Creek—*stream* TX-5
Los Becerros—*flat* TX-5
**Los Berros (Berros)**—*pop pl* CA-9
Los Berros Canyon—*valley* CA-9
Los Berros Creek—*stream* CA-9
Los Borregos Banco Number 123—*levee* TX-5
Los Brazos Hist Dist—*hist pl* NM-5
Los Buellis Hills—*summit* CA-9
Los Bueyes Creek—*stream* CA-9
*Los Burrita Creek* TX-5
Los Burros—*locale* AZ-5
Los Burros Creek—*stream* CA-9
Los Burros Ranger Station—*hist pl* AZ-5
Los Burros Ranger Station—*locale* AZ-5
Los Caballos Campground—*locale* CA-9
Los Caballos Windmill—*locale* (2) TX-5
*Los Camotes* AZ-5
Los Candelarias—*uninc pl* NM-5
Los Candelarias Chapel-San Antonio Chapel—*hist pl* NM-5
**Los Canderlarias**—*pop pl* NM-5
Los Canoncitos—*other* NM-5
Los Canos—*valley* PR-3
**Los Caobos**—*pop pl* PR-3
Los Capitancillos—*civil* CA-9
*Los Capitancillos Creek* CA-9
Los Capitancillos Creek—*stream* CA-9
Los Caraneras Canyon—*valley* NM-5
Los Carneros (Little John)—*civil* CA-9
Los Carneros (McDougal)—*civil* CA-9
Los Cayos de la Mula—*lake* TX-5
Los Cedros Artesian Wells—*well* TX-5
Los Cedros Windmill—*locale* TX-5
*Los Cerrillos* NM-5
Los Cerrillos Grant—*civil* NM-5
Los Cerritos—*civil* CA-9
Los Cerritos—*locale* CO-8
Los Cerritos—*summit* (3) NM-5
Los Cerritos De La Cruz—*other* NM-5
Los Cerritos del Toro—*ridge* NM-5
Los Cerritos Park—*park* CA-9
Los Cerritos Ranch House—*hist pl* CA-9
Los Cerritos Sch—*school* (3) CA-9
Los Cerro Ranch—*locale* NM-5
Los Cerros—*summit* NM-5
Los Cerros Barril—*summit* NM-5
Los Cerros Casualidad—*other* PR-3
Los Cerros del Comandante—*summit* PR-3
Los Cerros Vinet—*other* PR-3
Los Charcos Tank—*reservoir* TX-5
**Los Chavez**—*pop pl* NM-5
Los Chavez Ditch—*canal* NM-5
Los Chavez Drain—*canal* NM-5
Los Chavez Lateral—*canal* NM-5
Los Chavez Well—*well* NM-5
Losch Hollow—*valley* PA-2
Los Chinos Spring—*spring* CA-9
*Loschi River* LA-4
**Loschs**—*pop pl* PA-2
Los Chupaderos—*area* NM-5
Los Cisneros—*locale* NM-5
Los Cobreros Mesa—*summit* NM-5
**Los Cocas**—*pop pl* NM-5
Los Coches—*civil* (2) CA-9
Los Coches Creek—*stream* CA-9
Los Coches Mtn—*summit* CA-9
Los Coches Rancho—*hist pl* CA-9
Los Coches Substation—*other* CA-9
**Los Colericas**—*pop pl* PR-3
**Los Colericos**—*pop pl* PR-3
Los Colorados Windmill—*locale* TX-5
*Los Comates* AZ-5
Los Compadres Well—*well* TX-5
**Los Cordovas**—*pop pl* NM-5
Los Corrales Windmill—*locale* TX-5
Los Corralitos—*civil* CA-9
Los Corrallos—*area* TX-5
*Los Corrientes Creek Spencer Creek* TX-5
Los Cortes Creek—*stream* TX-5
Los Cove—*valley* TN-4
Los Coyotes—*civil* CA-9

**Los Coyotes**—*pop pl* TX-5
Los Coyotes Country Club—*other* CA-9
Los Coyotes Gin—*locale* TX-5
**Los Coyotes Ind Res**—*pop pl* CA-9
Los Coyotes Ranch—*locale* TX-5
Los Coyotes Sch—*school* CA-9
Los Creek—*stream* CO-8
Los Cruces Cem—*cemetery* NM-5
**Los Cuates**—*pop pl* TX-5
Los Cuates Basin—*basin* NM-5
Los Cuates Canyon—*valley* NM-5
Los Cuates Windmill—*locale* (3) TX-5
Los Cuervos Windmill—*locale* TX-5
**Los Deltos**—*pop pl* CA-9
Los Deltos Ranch—*locale* CA-9
Los Deltos Sch—*school* CA-9
Los Diegos—*reservoir* NM-5
Los Dolores Cem—*cemetery* NM-5
Los Dos Pueblos—*civil* CA-9
**Los Duranes**—*pop pl* NM-5
Los Duranes Chapel—*hist pl* NM-5
**Los Ebanos**—*pop pl* TX-5
Losee—*locale* UT-8
Losee, Isaac, House—*hist pl* NY-2
Losee Canyon—*valley* (2) UT-8
Losee Lake—*lake* MI-6
*Losee Pond* NJ-2
Losees Hill—*summit* NY-2
Losekamp Lake—*lake* WY-8
Loseke Creek—*stream* NE-7
Los Encenitos—*civil* CA-9
Los Encinos Ranch—*locale* AZ-5
Los Encinos Sch—*school* TX-5
Los Encinos State Historical Monmt—*park* CA-9
Losen Slofe—*stream* NJ-2
*Losen Slofe Creek* NJ-2
Losenville Valley—*valley* KY-4
Lose Sch—*school* PA-2
Lose Sch (abandoned)—*school* PA-2
*Los Esteros Lake* NM-5
Losey Creek—*stream* PA-2
Losey Ditch—*canal* IA-7
Losey Lake—*lake* MI-6
Losey Ranch—*locale* WY-8
Losey Run—*stream* PA-2
Losey Trail—*trail* PA-2
Los Farallones—*island* PR-3
**Los Febres**—*pop pl* NM-5
Los Felis—*civil* CA-9
Los Feliz—*uninc pl* CA-9
Los Feliz Sch—*school* CA-9
Los Finados Lake—*lake* TX-5
*Los Flores Lake* CO-8
Los Flores Lake—*lake* CO-8
**Los Fresnos**—*pop pl* TX-5
Los Fresnos Banco Number 145—*levee* TX-5
Los Fresnos Canal (elevated)—*canal* TX-5
Los Fresnos Crossing—*locale* TX-5
Los Fresnos-Laureles (CCD)—*cens area* TX-5
Los Fresnos Pump Bend—*bend* TX-5
Los Fresnos Sch—*school* TX-5
**Los Fuertes**—*pop pl* CO-8
Los Fuertes (Ruins)—*locale* NM-5
**Los Garzas**—*pop pl* TX-5
Los Garzas Cem—*cemetery* TX-5
**Los Gatos**—*pop pl* AZ-5
**Los Gatos**—*pop pl* CA-9
Los Gatos Canyon—*valley* NM-5
Los Gatos Cem—*cemetery* CA-9
*Los Gatos Creek* CO-8
Los Gatos Creek—*stream* (2) CA-9
Los Gatos Creek County Park—*park* CA-9
Los Gatos Or Santa Rita—*civil* CA-9
Los Gatos Ravine—*valley* CA-9
Los Gavilanes Canyon—*valley* NM-5
Los Gemelos—*island* PR-3
Los Gerrio JHS—*school* CA-9
Los Gigantes—*cliff* NM-5
Los Girls Camp—*locale* AZ-5
**Los Griegos**—*pop pl* NM-5
Los Griegos—*summit* NM-5
Los Griegos Hist Dist—*hist pl* NM-5
Los Guicaches Windmill—*locale* TX-5
Los Guilicos—*civil* CA-9
Los Guilicos Sch For Girls—*school* CA-9
Los Guilicos Warm Springs—*spring* CA-9
Losher Ditch—*canal* IN-6
Los Hermanos—*post sta* PR-3
Los Hermanos Penitentes Cem—*cemetery* CO-8
Loshita Branch—*swamp* AR-4
Los Hornos—*summit* NM-5
Losh Ranch—*locale* NE-7
Losh Run—*locale* PA-2
Losh Run—*stream* PA-2
**Loshs Run**—*pop pl* PA-2
Los Huecos—*civil* CA-9
Los Huecos Ranch—*locale* CA-9
Los Huecos Rsvr—*reservoir* CA-9
**Los Hueros**—*pop pl* NM-5
Los Huerros—*locale* NM-5
Los Huerros Canyon—*valley* NM-5
Los Huerros Creek—*stream* NM-5
Los Huesos Tank—*reservoir* TX-5
Los Huesos Windmill—*locale* TX-5
Losiep Island—*island* FM-9
**Los Indios**—*pop pl* TX-5
**Los Indios**—*pop pl* PR-3
Los Indios Artesian Well—*well* TX-5
Los Indios Canyon—*valley* (2) NM-5
Los Indios Creek—*stream* TX-5
Los Indios Gas Field—*oilfield* TX-5
Los Indios Lake—*reservoir* TX-5
Los Indios Ranch—*locale* (2) TX-5
Los Indios Spring—*spring* NM-5
Los Indios Well (Windmill)—*locale* TX-5
Los Indios Windmill—*locale* (3) TX-5
*Los Isleto* TX-5
*Los Jaboncillos Creek* TX-5
Los Jaboncillos Ranch—*locale* TX-5
*Los Jardines* MH-9
Los Jardines—*uninc pl* TX-5
Los Jinetes—*locale* CA-9
Loski Ditch—*canal* WY-8
*Los Ladrones* MH-9
Los Lagos Reservoirs—*reservoir* CO-8
Los Lagos Reservoirs No 1—*reservoir* CO-8
Los Lagos Reservoirs No 2—*reservoir* CO-8
Los Lagos Reservoirs No 3—*reservoir* CO-8
Los Lasos Tank—*reservoir* TX-5

Los Laureles Canyon—*valley* CA-9
Los Laurelles (Beronda)—*civil* (2) CA-9
Los Laurelles (Ransom)—*civil* CA-9
*Los Laurells* CA-9
Los LeFebres—*locale* NM-5
**Los Lentes**—*pop pl* NM-5
Los Lentes Cem—*cemetery* NM-5
Los Lentes Drain—*canal* NM-5
*Los Lingos Creek* TX-5
Los Lingos Creek—*stream* TX-5
**Los Llanos**—*pop pl* PR-3
Los Llanos (Barrio)—*fmr MCD* PR-3
Los Lobos Creek—*stream* CA-9
*Los Lobos Oil Field* CA-9
Los Lobos Spring—*spring* CA-9
**Los Lomas**—*pop pl* TX-5
**Los Luceros**—*pop pl* NM-5
Los Luceros Ditch—*canal* NM-5
Los Luceros Hacienda—*hist pl* NM-5
**Los Lunas**—*pop pl* NM-5
Los Lunas (CCD)—*cens area* NM-5
Los Lunas Ditch—*canal* NM-5
Los Lunas Wasteway—*canal* NM-5
*Los M* MH-9
Los Machos Creek—*stream* CA-9
Los Machos Hills—*other* CA-9
Los Machos Pasture—*flat* TX-5
Los Machos Ranch—*locale* TX-5
Los Machos Well (Flowing)—*well* TX-5
**Los Maderas (subdivision)**—*pop pl* (2) AZ-5
**Los Maestros**—*pop pl* PR-3
**Los Magos**—*pop pl* (2) PR-3
Los Magueyes Windmill—*locale* TX-5
Los Marias—*locale* NM-5
Los Medanitos—*area* NM-5
Los Medanos—*area* NM-5
Los Medanos—*civil* CA-9
Los Medanos—*locale* CA-9
Los Medanos—*summit* CA-9
Los Medanos Coll—*school* CA-9
Los Medanos Sch—*school* CA-9
Los Medanos Windmill—*locale* TX-5
Los Medinas—*locale* NM-5
Los Meganos—*civil* CA-9
Los Mogotes—*area* NM-5
Los Mogotes—*summit* CO-8
**Los Molinos**—*pop pl* CA-9
**Los Molinos**—*pop pl* PR-3
Los Molinos Grange—*locale* CA-9
Los Molinos Sch—*school* CA-9
Los Monos Canyon—*valley* CA-9
Los Montecitos—*area* NM-5
Los Montes—*summit* TX-5
**Los Montoyas**—*pop pl* NM-5
*Los Moras Creek* TX-5
*Los Moras Mtn* TX-5
*Los Moras Spring* TX-5
Los Morones—*ridge* CA-9
**Los Muertos**—*pop pl* PR-3
Los Muertos Creek—*stream* CA-9
Los Muertos Pasture—*flat* TX-5
Los Muertos Valley—*valley* CA-9
Los Muertos Windmill—*locale* TX-5
**Los Naranjos**—*pop pl* PR-3
Los Naranjos Peak—*summit* NM-5
Los Negritos—*island* PR-3
Los Negritos Canyon—*valley* NM-5
Los Negros Creek—*stream* TX-5
Los Negros Windmill—*locale* TX-5
**Los Nietos**—*pop pl* CA-9
Los Nietos, Lake—*lake* CA-9
Los Nietos Junction—*locale* CA-9
Los Nietos Sch—*school* CA-9
Los Nietos Station—*locale* CA-9
Los Ninos Neighborhood Park —*park* AZ-5
Los Ninos Sch —*school* AZ-5
*Los Nogales* AZ-5
Los Nogales—*civil* CA-9
Los Nogales—*hist pl* TX-5
Los Norios Ranch—*locale* NM-5
Los Ocho Mine—*mine* CO-8
Los Ojitos—*civil* CA-9
Los Ojitos—*locale* NM-5
Los Ojitos—*spring* NM-5
Los Ojitos de Agua Salada Danosa—*spring* NM-5
**Los Ojos (Park View)**—*pop pl* NM-5
Los Ojos (Parkview) Fish Hatchery—*hist pl* NM-5
Los Ojos (Parkview) Hist Dist—*hist pl* NM-5
Los Ojuelos—*hist pl* TX-5
Los Ojuelos—*locale* TX-5
Los Ojuelos (The Springs)—*hist pl* NM-5
**Los Olivos**—*pop pl* CA-9
Los Olivos Park—*park* AZ-5
Los Olivos Senior Center—*building* AZ-5
*Los Olmas Creek* TX-5
Los Olmos Creek—*stream* (3) TX-5
*Loson* FM-9
Los Ositos Substation—*other* CA-9
**Los Osos**—*pop pl* CA-9
Los Osos Creek—*stream* CA-9
Los Osos Sch—*school* CA-9
Los Osos Valley—*valley* CA-9
Los Osos Valley Memorial Park (Cemetery)—*cemetery* CA-9
*Los Ovejo Creek* TX-5
**Losoya**—*pop pl* TX-5
Losoya Creek—*stream* TX-5
Los Pachecos—*locale* NM-5
**Los Padillas**—*pop pl* NM-5
Los Padillas Acequia—*canal* NM-5
Los Padillas Cem—*cemetery* NM-5
Los Padillas Drain—*canal* NM-5
Los Padres (CCD)—*cens area* CA-9
Los Padres Dam—*dam* CA-9
Los Padres (Mens Penal Colony)—*building* CA-9
Los Padres Mine—*mine* CA-9
Los Padres Sch—*school* CA-9
Los Padrinos Juvenile Hall—*other* CA-9
*Los Palos Verdes* CA-9
Los Palos Verdes—*civil* CA-9
**Los Pampanos**—*pop pl* (2) PR-3
Los Patos Gun Club—*other* CA-9
Los Patos Tank—*reservoir* TX-5
Lospe, Mount—*summit* CA-9
Los Pelados—*summit* CA-9
Los Penales Sch—*school* CA-9
**Los Penas**—*pop pl* (2) PR-3

Lost Lakes—lake AR-4
Lost Lakes—lake (3) CA-9
Lost Lakes—lake CO-8
Lost Lakes—lake ID-8
Lost Lakes—lake (3) MI-6
Lost Lakes—lake (2) MT-8
Lost Lakes—lake PA-2
Lost Lakes—reservoir CO-8
Lost Lakes—swamp MI-6
Lost Lake Saddle—gap OR-9
Lost Lake School (Abandoned)—locale WI-6
Lost Lake Slough—lake CO-8
Lost Lakes Peaks—summit CO-8
Lost Lake Spring—spring OR-9
**Lost Lake (subdivision)**—pop pl MS-4
Lost Lake Swamp—swamp MN-6
Lost Lake Tank—reservoir AZ-5
Lost Lake Tank—reservoir NM-5
Lost Lake Trail—trail AK-9
Lost Lake Trail—trail (3) CO-8
Lost Lake Trail—trail NM-5
Lost Lake Trail—trail OR-9
Lost Lake Trail—trail WA-9
Lost Lake Trail—trail WY-8
**Lost Lake (Trailer Park)**—pop pl CA-9
**Lost Lake Woods**—pop pl MI-6
*Lost Land* MD-2
Lost Land Lake—lake WI-6
Lostland Run—stream MD-2
Lost Lane Farm—hist pl OH-6
Lost Lick—stream (2) KY-4
Lostlick Branch—stream KY-4
Lostlick Run—stream WV-2
**Lost Lodge**—pop pl NM-5
Lost Logan—lake ME-1
Lost Long Lake—lake MN-6
Lost Lookout—cliff NY-2
Lost Man Campground—locale CO-8
Lost Man Canyon—valley NM-5
Lost Man Cave—cave MO-7
*Lost Man Creek* MT-8
Lost Man Creek—stream AZ-5
Lost Man Creek—stream (2) CA-9
Lost Man Creek—stream CO-8
Lost Man Creek—stream ID-8
Lost Man Creek—stream OK-5
Lost Man Lake—lake CO-8
Lost Man Lake—lake MN-6
Lost Man Rsvr—reservoir CO-8
*Lostmans Creek* CO-8
Lostmans Creek—stream FL-3
Lostmans Creek Number Three—stream FL-3
Lostmans Five—gut FL-3
Lostmans Five Bay—bay FL-3
Lostmans Key—island FL-3
Lost Mans Lake—lake WI-6
Lostmans Pines—woods FL-3
Lostman Spring—spring CA-9
Lostmans River—stream FL-3
Lostmans River Ranger Station—locale FL-3
Lostmans Slough—gut FL-3
Lostmans Trail—trail FL-3
Lost Man Tank—reservoir AZ-5
Lost Mare Creek—stream MT-8
Lost Marsh State Wildlife Mngmt Area—park MN-6
Lost McMenomey Rsvr—reservoir MT-8
Lost Meadow—flat (4) CA-9
Lost Meadow—flat OR-9
Lost Meadow—flat (2) WA-9
Lost Meadow Creek—stream ID-8
Lost Meadows—flat (2) CA-9
Lost Meadows—flat (2) ID-8
Lost Meadows—flat MT-8
Lost Meadows Creek—stream NV-8
Lost Meadows Lake—lake TX-5
Lost Meadows Ranch—locale TX-5
Lost Mesa—summit TX-5
Lost Mine Airp—airport MO-7
Lost Mine Canyon—valley ID-8
Lost Mine Canyon—valley MT-8
Lost Mine Creek—stream CO-8
Lost Mine Creek—stream ID-8
Lost Mine Peak—summit TX-5
Lost Mines Hill—summit NM-5
Lost Moose Lake—lake MN-6
Lost Mound—summit IL-6
Lost Mound Cem—cemetery IL-6
Lost Mound Sch—school IL-6
Lost Mountain—locale GA-3
**Lost Mountain**—pop pl TN-4
Lost Mountain Overlook—locale VA-3
Lost Mountain Post Office (historical)—building TN-4
Lost Mountain Sch—school TN-4
Lost Mtn—summit AZ-5
Lost Mtn—summit (5) AR-4
Lost Mtn—summit CO-8
Lost Mtn—summit GA-3
Lost Mtn—summit KY-4
Lost Mtn—summit MT-8
Lost Mtn—summit NY-2
Lost Mtn—summit (2) OK-5
Lost Mtn—summit PA-2
Lost Mtn—summit (2) TN-4
Lost Mtn—summit TX-5
Lost Mtn—summit VT-1
Lost Mtn—summit (4) VA-3
Lost Mtn—summit WA-9
*Lost Mtn Crossroads* GA-3
Lost Mule Canyon—valley TX-5
Lost Mule Cave—cave AL-4
Lost Mule Creek—stream AZ-5
Lost Mule Creek—stream ID-8
Lost Mule Creek—stream (2) TX-5
Lost Mule Spring—spring TX-5
Lost Mule Tank—reservoir AZ-5
Lost Mule Tank—reservoir NM-5
Lost Mule Windmill—locale TX-5
Lost Nation—locale NH-1
Lost Nation—locale VT-1
**Lost Nation**—pop pl IL-6
**Lost Nation**—pop pl IA-7
Lost Nation Country Club—other OH-6
Lost Nation Sch—school SD-7
Los Tomases Chapel—hist pl NM-5
Los Tomates Banco—levee TX-5
Loston Branch—stream AR-4
Loston Windmill—locale TX-5
Lost Orphan Mine—mine AZ-5
Los Torres Cem—cemetery NM-5
Los Torres Ditch—canal NM-5
Los Torres (Ruins)—locale NM-5
Los Torritos Gas Field—oilfield TX-5
Los Torritos North Gas Field—oilfield TX-5
Lost Owl Creek—stream ID-8
Lost Packer Lake—lake ID-8
Lost Packer Meadows—flat ID-8
Lost Packer Mine—mine ID-8
Lost Packer Peak—summit ID-8
*Lost Palms Canyon* CA-9
Lost Palms Canyon—valley CA-9
Lost Palms Oasis—spring CA-9
Lost Palms Trail—trail CA-9
Lost Park—flat (3) CO-8
Lost Park—flat (2) MT-8
Lost Park—flat (3) UT-8
Lost Park—locale WY-8
Lost Park—park IN-6
Lost Park Cow Camp—locale CO-8
*Lost Park Creek* CO-8
Lost Park Creek—stream MT-8
Lost Park Meadows—flat ID-8
Lost Park Rsvr—reservoir CO-8
Lost Park Spring—spring SD-7
Lost Pass—gap NH-1
Lost Pass—gap WA-9
*Lost Peak* NV-8
Lost Peak—summit CA-9
Lost Peak—summit ID-8
Lost Peak—summit (3) MT-8
Lost Peak—summit OR-9
Lost Peak—summit TX-5
Lost Peak—summit UT-8
Lost Peak—summit (2) WA-9
Lost Peak Spring—spring UT-8
Lost Peak Trail—trail OR-9
Lost Pete Creek—stream ID-8
Lost Pig Cave—cave TN-4
*Lost Pin Creek* OR-9
Lost Pin Creek—stream OR-9
Lost Pine Lake—reservoir TX-5
Lost Pipe Creek—stream CA-9
Lost Pit—cave AL-4
Lost Point—cape CA-9
Lost Point—cliff AZ-5
Lost Point—summit TX-5
Lost Point—summit WA-9
Lost Point Ridge—ridge WA-9
Lost Pond—lake CT-1
Lost Pond—lake KY-4
Lost Pond—lake (25) ME-1
Lost Pond—lake MA-1
Lost Pond—lake NM-5
Lost Pond—lake (19) NY-2
Lost Pond—lake (4) VT-1
Lost Pond—reservoir MA-1
Lost Pond—reservoir TX-5
Lost Pond—swamp TX-5
Lost Pond Brook—stream CT-1
Lost Pond Brook—stream ME-1
Lost Pond Hollow—valley MO-7
Lost Pond Mtn—summit NY-2
Lost Ponds—lake NH-1
Lost Ponds—lake NY-2
Lost Pond Sch (abandoned)—school MO-7
Lost Pond Trail—trail NY-2
Lost Pony Creek—stream MT-8
Lost Pony Mine—mine CA-9
Lost Poteau River—stream OK-5
Lost Prairie—flat IL-6
Lost Prairie—flat (2) MT-8
Lost Prairie—flat (2) OR-9
Lost Prairie—swamp OR-9
Lost Prairie Cem—cemetery OR-9
Lost Prairie Ch—church IL-6
Lost Prairie Ch—church (2) TX-5
Lost Prairie Creek—stream MT-8
Lost Prairie Forest Camp—locale OR-9
**Lost Prairie (historical)**—pop pl OR-9
Lost Prairie Lake—reservoir TX-5
Lost Prairie Rock—pillar OR-9
Lost Prairie Sch—school (2) IL-6
Lost Prairie Sch—school (2) TX-5
Lost Prong—stream TN-4
Los Trancos Canyon—valley CA-9
Los Trancos Creek—stream CA-9
Los Trancos Woods—locale FL-3
**Los Trancos Woods**—pop pl CA-9
*Los Traneos Creek* CA-9
Lost Ranger Peak—summit CO-8
Lost Ranger Top—summit WY-8
Lost Ranger Trail—trail CO-8
Lostra Ranch—locale NV-8
Lostra Spring—spring NV-8
*Lost Reed Creek* AL-4
Los Tres Picachos—summit PR-3
*Los Tres Picos* CA-9
Lost Ridge—ridge CA-9
Lost Ridge—ridge ID-8
Lost Ridge—ridge IN-6
Lost Ridge—ridge (2) MT-8
Lost Ridge—ridge (2) NC-3
Lost Ridge—ridge (2) TN-4
Lost Ridge—ridge VA-3
Lost Ridge—ridge WA-9
Los Trigos—civil NM-5
Los Trigos Dam—dam NM-5
Los Trigos Ditch—canal NM-5
*Lost River* IN-6
*Lost River* NM-5
*Lost River* VA-3
*Lost River* WV-2
Lost River—locale OR-9
Lost River—locale WV-2
**Lost River**—pop pl AK-9
**Lost River**—pop pl (2) ID-8
**Lost River**—pop pl IN-6
**Lost River**—pop pl KY-4
**Lost River**—pop pl NH-1
Lost River—stream (3) AK-9
Lost River—stream CA-9
Lost River—stream IN-6
Lost River—stream (5) MN-6
Lost River—stream MT-8
Lost River—stream NH-1
Lost River—stream (2) NM-5
Lost River—stream OR-9
Lost River—stream TX-5
Lost River—stream (2) WA-9
Lost River—stream WV-2
Lost River Archeol Cave—hist pl KY-4
Lost River Bayou—gut AR-4
Lost River Cave—cave WI-6
Lost River Caverns—cave PA-2
Lost River Cem—cemetery ID-8
Lost River Ch—church IN-6
Lost River Ch—church WV-2
Lost River Diversion Channel—channel OR-9
Lost River Diversion Dam—dam OR-9
Lost River Gorge—valley WA-9
Lost River Hosp—hospital ID-8
Lost River HS—school OR-9
Lost River (Magisterial District)—fmr MCD WV-2
Lost River Mine—mine TN-4
Lost River Mines—mine AK-9
Lost River Pool—reservoir OR-9
Lost River Range—range ID-8
Lost River Resort Airp—airport WA-9
Lost River Spring—spring OR-9
Lost River State Park—park WV-2
**Lost River (Township of)**—pop pl IN-6
*Lost River Valley* ID-8
Lost Rsvr—reservoir CA-9
Lost Rsvr—reservoir OR-9
Lost Rsvr—reservoir (2) WY-8
**Los Trujillos**—pop pl NM-5
*Lost Run* PA-2
Lost Run—stream IN-6
Lost Run—stream KY-4
Lost Run—stream (2) OH-6
Lost Run—stream (6) PA-2
Lost Run—stream VA-3
Lost Run—stream (10) WV-2
Lost Salt Canyon—valley AZ-5
Lost Salt Spring Number One—spring AZ-5
Lost Salt Spring Number Two—spring AZ-5
Lost Section—area TX-5
Lost Sheep Lake—lake MT-8
Lost Shirt Creek—stream KS-7
Lost Shirt Creek—stream MT-8
Lost Shirt Gulch—valley ID-8
Lost Sink Cave—cave AL-4
Lost Skull Cave—cave AL-4
Lost Slough—lake IA-7
Lost Slough—stream AK-9
Lost Solar Creek—stream CO-8
Lost Solar Park—flat CO-8
Lost Soldier Creek—stream MT-8
Lost Soldier Creek—stream WY-8
Lost Soldier Divide—ridge WY-8
Lost Soldier Lake—lake WY-8
Lost Soldier Oil Field—oilfield WY-8
Lost Soldier Rsvr—reservoir WY-8
Lost Soul Mtn—summit MT-8
Lost Spring—spring (6) AZ-5
Lost Spring—spring (4) CA-9
Lost Spring—spring (2) CO-8
Lost Spring—spring (3) ID-8
Lost Spring—spring KS-7
Lost Spring—spring MO-7
Lost Spring—spring (2) MT-8
Lost Spring—spring (4) NV-8
Lost Spring—spring (3) NM-5
Lost Spring—spring OK-5
Lost Spring—spring (8) OR-9
Lost Spring—spring SD-7
Lost Spring—spring (3) TX-5
Lost Spring—spring (13) UT-8
Lost Spring—spring WA-9
Lost Spring—spring WY-8
Lost Spring Campground—locale ID-8
Lost Spring Campsite—locale ME-1
Lost Spring Canyon—valley ID-8
Lost Spring Canyon—valley NM-5
Lost Spring Canyon—valley TX-5
Lost Spring Canyon—valley UT-8
Lost Spring Creek—stream ID-8
Lost Spring Draw—valley UT-8
Lost Spring Gap—gap AZ-5
Lost Spring Gap—gap UT-8
Lost Spring Hollow—valley TX-5
Lost Spring Hollow—valley UT-8
Lost Spring Mtn—summit AZ-5
Lost Spring Rsvr—reservoir (2) UT-8
Lost Springs—hist pl KS-7
Lost Springs—locale WY-8
**Lost Springs**—pop pl KS-7
Lost Springs—spring WA-9
Lost Springs Campground—locale WA-9
Lost Spring Sch (abandoned)—school MO-7
Lost Springs Creek—stream OK-5
Lost Springs Draw—valley WY-8
Lost Springs Oil Field—oilfield KS-7
Lost Springs Ranch—locale WA-9
**Lost Springs Township**—pop pl KS-7
Lost Spring Tank—reservoir AZ-5
Lost Spring Tank—reservoir NM-5
Lost Spring Wash—stream AZ-5
Lost Spring Wash—stream UT-8
Lost Spring Wash—valley (3) UT-8
Lost Spur Country Club—other MN-6
Lost Steers Mine—mine NV-8
Lost Stove Creek—stream MT-8
Lost Swamp—swamp GA-3
Lost Tank—reservoir (19) AZ-5
Lost Tank—reservoir (3) NM-5
Lost Tank—reservoir (7) TX-5
Lost Tank Canyon—valley (2) AZ-5
Lost Tank Ridge—ridge AZ-5
Lost Temper Creek—stream AK-9
Lost Tom Creek—stream OR-9
Lost Tom Mtn—summit OR-9
Lost Tooth Cabin—locale MT-8
Lost Town Creek—stream GA-3
Lost Trace Branch—stream KY-4
Lost Trail—trail PA-2
Lost Trail Camp—locale MT-8
Lost Trail Campground—locale CO-8
Lost Trail Creek—stream (2) CO-8
Lost Trail Pass—gap ID-8
Lost Trail Pass—gap MT-8
Lost Trail Ranch—locale CO-8
Lost Trail Spring—spring WA-9
Lost Trap Lake—lake AR-4
Lost Treasure Diggings—locale CO-8
Lost Treasure Ditch—canal CO-8
Lost Trough Canyon—valley CA-9
Lost Trout Creek—stream CA-9
*Lost Trout Meadow* CA-9
Lost Tubs Springs—spring TX-5
Lost Turtle Cave—cave AL-4
Lost Twin Lakes—lake WY-8
Los Tularcitos (Gomez)—civil CA-9
**Los Tules**—pop pl CA-9
Los Tullidos Well—well TX-5
Lost Umlaut Farm Airp—airport MO-7
*Lost Valley* CA-9
*Lost Valley* OR-9
Lost Valley—basin (2) CA-9
Lost Valley—flat CA-9
**Lost Valley**—pop pl NY-2
Lost Valley—stream CA-9
Lost Valley—valley (3) CA-9
Lost Valley—valley CO-8
Lost Valley—valley ID-8
Lost Valley—valley NH-1
Lost Valley—valley (3) OR-9
Lost Valley—valley UT-8
Lost Valley—valley VA-3
Lost Valley—valley (3) WA-9
Lost Valley Brook—stream NH-1
Lost Valley Cem—cemetery OR-9
Lost Valley Creek—stream CA-9
Lost Valley Creek—stream ID-8
Lost Valley Creek—stream (4) OR-9
Lost Valley Lakes—reservoir MO-7
Lost Valley Park—flat CO-8
Lost Valley Ranch—locale (2) CO-8
Lost Valley Rsvr—reservoir CA-9
Lost Valley Rsvr—reservoir ID-8
Lost Valley Springs—spring ID-8
Lost Valley State Park—park AR-4
Lost Valley Tank—reservoir TX-5
Lost Valley Trail—trail CA-9
Lost Village—locale NY-2
Lost Wallet Rim—cliff NV-8
Lost Watch Creek—stream OR-9
Lost Water Canyon—valley MT-8
Lost Water Creek—stream MT-8
Lost Waterhole Tank—reservoir TX-5
Lost Well—well (2) NM-5
Lost Wells Butte—summit WY-8
Lost Wells Lateral—canal WY-8
Lost Wheelbarrow Mine—mine ID-8
Lost Wilderness Lake—lake WY-8
Lost Wilderness Lake Northern Dam—dam MA-1
Lost Wilderness Lake Rsvr—reservoir MA-1
Lost Wilderness Lake Southern Dam—dam MA-1
Lost Wilson Mtn—summit AZ-5
Lost Windmill—locale TX-5
Lost Woman Canyon—valley CA-9
**Lostwood**—pop pl ND-7
Lostwood Natl Wildlife Ref—park ND-7
**Lostwood Township**—pop pl ND-7
Lost World Caverns—cave WV-2
Losty Canyon—valley UT-8
*Lostzand* MD-2
Los Ulpinos—civil CA-9
Los Vallecitos—valley CA-9
Los Vallecitos De San Marcos—civil CA-9
Los Valles—area NM-5
**Los Velas**—pop pl TX-5
Los Venados—summit NM-5
Los Verdes Golf Club—other CO-8
Los Verdes Golf Course—other CA-9
Los Verdes Park—park CA-9
Los Vergeles—civil CA-9
Los Viejos—summit CA-9
**Los Vigiles**—pop pl NM-5
Los Voces Windmill—locale TX-5
L Oswood Ranch—locale MT-8
**Los Ybanez**—pop pl TX-5
*Los Yeguas Creek* CA-9
*Lot* FM-9
Lot—locale KY-4
Lota—locale SC-3
Lotah Gulch—valley ID-8
Lotawana, Lake—reservoir MO-7
Lotawana Ch—church MO-7
Lotawata, Lake—reservoir KY-4
Lot Branch—stream SC-3
Lot Canal—canal NC-3
Lot Chapel—church TN-4
*Lot Cove* MA-1
Lotela, Lake—lake FL-3
Lotell Hollow Cove—bay MO-7
Loth, Joseph, Company Bldg—hist pl CT-1
*Lot Hafen* FM-9
*Lothair* MD-2
Lothair—locale KY-4
**Lothair**—pop pl GA-3
**Lothair**—pop pl MT-8
Lothair Spring—spring MT-8
*Lot Harbor* FM-9
*Lothian* MD-2
**Lothian**—pop pl MD-2
Lothian Sch—school MD-2
Lot (historical)—locale AL-4
*Lothog* FM-9
*Lot Hollow* TN-4
Lot Hollow—valley AL-4
Lot Hollow—valley KY-4
Lothrop—locale MT-8
Lothrop, Caleb, House—hist pl MA-1
Lothrop, H.B., Store—hist pl MA-1
Lothrop, Joseph, House—hist pl MA-1
Lothrop Hill Cem—cemetery MA-1
Lothrop Island—island ME-1
Lothrop Mansion—hist pl DC-2
Lothrop Memorial Building-G.A.R. Hall—hist pl MA-1
Lothrop Sch—school NE-7
*Lothrup* MT-8
Loties Canyon—valley NV-8
Lotj—island MP-9
*Lotj Island* MP-9
Lotj Island—island MP-9
Lot Lane—locale MD-2
Lotloh Creek—stream WA-9
Lotnon—other GU-9
*Loto* MP-9
Lotoaise Point—cape AS-9
*Lotoback* MP-9
Lotoen—locale MP-9
Lotofaaee Rock—pillar AS-9
*Lotoin* MP-9
Loto Point—cape AS-9
Lot Pond—lake (2) FL-3
Lot Pond—lake GA-3
Lot Run—swamp FL-3
Lots Branch—stream WV-2
*Lots Creek* KY-4
*Lots Creek* MS-4
**Lotsee**—pop pl OK-5
Lots Fork—stream SC-3
Lots Gap—gap VA-3
*Lots Landing* TN-4
Lots Mill Creek—stream FL-3
Lotspeachy Mill (historical)—locale TN-4
Lotspeich Prong Waddle Creek—stream WY-8
Lotspeich Valley—basin NE-7
Lotspelch Sch—school TX-5
Lotspiech Mine—mine ID-8
**Lott**—pop pl AL-4
**Lott**—pop pl TX-5
*Lotta* KS-7
Lotta—locale TX-5
Lotta, Lake—lake FL-3
Lotta Crabtree Fountain—hist pl CA-9
Lotta Creek—stream CA-9
*Lottaville* IN-6
**Lottaville**—pop pl IN-6
Lott Branch—stream AL-4
Lott Branch—stream (2) MS-4
Lott Canyon—valley UT-8
Lott-Carey Sch—school VA-3
Lott Cave—cave AL-4
Lott (CCD)—cens area TX-5
Lott Cem—cemetery AL-4
Lott Cem—cemetery FL-3
Lott Cem—cemetery (3) GA-3
Lott Cem—cemetery (9) MS-4
Lott Cem—cemetery SC-3
Lott Cem—cemetery (4) TX-5
Lott Cem—cemetery WV-2
Lott Ch—church MI-6
Lott Creek—stream GA-3
Lott Creek—stream MS-4
Lott Creek—stream SC-3
Lott Dead River—lake MS-4
Lot Ten Swamp—swamp NY-2
Lotterdale Cove Rec Area—park TN-4
Lotterdale Knob—summit TN-4
Lotter Drain—canal MI-6
*Lottery* RI-1
Lottery Bridge—bridge NH-1
*Lotteryville* RI-1
Lottes Lake—reservoir IN-6
Lottes Lake Dam—dam IN-6
*Lott Ferry Landing* AL-4
Lott Fork Ridge—ridge AL-4
Lott Hollow—valley (2) TN-4
**Lottick Corner**—pop pl IN-6
**Lottie**—pop pl (2) AL-4
**Lottie**—pop pl LA-4
Lottie Bay—bay WA-9
Lottie Ch—church AL-4
Lottie Creek—stream ID-8
Lottie Creek—stream NC-3
Lottie Creek—stream SD-7
Lottie Hollow—valley MO-7
Lottie Lake—lake ID-8
Lottie Lookout Tower—tower AL-4
Lottie Oil and Gas Field—oilfield LA-4
*Lotties Canyon* NV-8
Lotties Creek—stream AL-4
Lotties Draw—valley MT-8
Lotties Draw—valley WY-8
Lottieville—locale FL-3
Lottin, Port—harbor FM-9
Lottis Creek—stream CO-8
Lottis Creek Campground—locale CO-8
**Lottivue**—pop pl MI-6
Lott Lake—lake LA-4
Lott Lake—lake TX-5
Lott Landing—locale TN-4
Lott Lateral—canal AZ-5
Lott Memorial Cem—cemetery MS-4
Lott Mine—mine CA-9
Lott Oil Field—oilfield TX-5
Lotto Lake—lake MI-6
Lott Park—park AL-4
Lott Pettus Cem—cemetery TX-5
Lott Pond—lake PA-2
**Lottridge**—pop pl OH-6
Lottridge Cem—cemetery OH-6
Lott Road Assembly of God Ch—church AL-4
Lott Road Ch—church AL-4
Lott Road Revival Center Ch—church AL-4
Lott Rsvr—reservoir CO-8
Lotts—locale GA-3
*Lotts Bluff* MS-4
**Lottsburg**—pop pl VA-3
Lottsburg (Magisterial District)—fmr MCD VA-3
Lotts Cem—cemetery SC-3
Lott Sch—school AL-4
Lott Sch (historical)—school MS-4
Lott School (historical)—locale MO-7
*Lotts Creek* GA-3
*Lotts Creek* IN-6
**Lotts Creek**—pop pl IA-7
Lotts Creek—stream (3) GA-3
Lotts Creek*—stream IA-7
Lotts Creek—stream IA-7
Lotts Creek—stream KY-4
Lotts Creek—stream (2) MS-4
Lotts Creek—stream MO-7
Lotts Creek—stream SC-3
Lotts Creek Ch—church GA-3
*Lotts Creek Church* MS-4
Lotts Creek Community Ch—church KY-4
Lotts Creek Townhall—building IA-7
Lotts Creek Township—fmr MCD (2) IA-7
Lotts Crossroads—locale SC-3
Lotts Ferry (historical)—locale AL-4
Lottsford Branch—stream MD-2
Lotts Grove Ch—church MO-7
Lotts Grove Ch—church SC-3
Lotts (historical P.O.)—locale IA-7
Lotts Hosp—hospital MT-8
Lotts Island—island GA-3
Lotts Lake—lake CA-9
*Lotts Landing* TN-4
Lott Slough—stream AL-4
Lotts Mill Creek—stream AL-4
Lott Smith Cem (US-M962/Carnes/1958)—cemetery MS-4
Lotts Park—park IA-7
Lott Spring Cave—cave AL-4
Lotts Sch—school IL-6
Lott Store (historical)—locale TN-4
*Lottstown* MS-4
**Lottsville**—pop pl PA-2
Lottville Cem—cemetery MS-4
Lottville Ch—church MS-4
Lottville Creek—stream MS-4
Lott Windmill—locale TX-5
*Lotus* MS-4
Lotus—locale CA-9
Lotus—locale ID-8
Lotus—locale KY-4
Lotus—locale LA-4
**Lotus**—pop pl FL-3
**Lotus**—pop pl IL-6
**Lotus**—pop pl IN-6
Lotus, Lake—lake (2) FL-3
Lotus Bay—bay NY-2
Lotus Canal—canal CA-9
Lotus Drain—canal CA-9
*Lotus Island* NY-2
Lotus Island—island NY-2
*Lotus Lake* VT-1
Lotus Lake—lake (2) MI-6
Lotus Lake—lake MN-6
Lotus Lake—lake OR-9
Lotus Lake—lake (2) WI-6
Lotus Lake—reservoir NY-2
Lotus Lake County Park—park WI-6
Lotus Mine—mine CA-9
Lotus Mine—mine CO-8
LOTUS (motor vessel)—hist pl WA-9
Lotus Point—cape NY-2
Lotus Point—cliff ID-8
Lotus Post Office (historical)—building MS-4
**Lotus Woods**—pop pl IL-6
**Lotville**—pop pl NY-2
Lotz, Henry, Stone—hist pl OH-6
Lotz, J. H., House—hist pl WA-9
Lotz Creek—stream WI-6
Lotz House—hist pl TN-4
Lotz Lake—lake IN-6
Lotz Park—park WI-6
Lotz Pond—lake NJ-2
Lot 8 Creek—stream NY-2
Lou—locale AL-4
**Lou**—pop pl AR-4
**Lou**—pop pl FL-3
Lou, Lake—lake FL-3
Lou, Lake—reservoir AL-4
**Louann**—pop pl AR-4
Lou Anna S Paine Pond Dam—dam MS-4
Lou Ann Brook—stream ME-1
Lou Beverly Lake—lake CA-9
Lou Branch—stream KY-4
*Lou Chapel* TN-4
Louciles Elem Sch—school FL-3
Louck Ditch—canal IN-6
Louck Park—park KS-7
Loucks, Charles N., House—hist pl IL-6
Loucks Cem—cemetery OH-6
Louck Sch (abandoned)—school PA-2
Loucks Creek—stream CA-9
Loucks Ditch—canal IN-6
Loucks Grove Ch—church IA-7
Loucks Mills—locale PA-2
Loucks Park—park PA-2
Loucks Pond—lake NY-2
Loucks Sch—school IL-6
Loucks Sch—school MI-6
Lou Creek—stream AR-4
Lou Creek—stream CO-8
Lou Creek Pass—gap CO-8
Lou Creek Trail—trail CO-8
*Loud Basin* MI-6
Loud Brook—stream ME-1
Loud Cem—cemetery MI-6
Loud Creek—stream (3) MI-6
Loud Dam—dam MI-6
Loud Dam Pond—reservoir MI-6
**Lou Del**—pop pl IL-6
Louden—locale AK-9
Louden—locale KY-4
**Louden**—pop pl NJ-2
**Louden**—pop pl (2) OH-6
*Louden, Town of* MA-1
Loudenbeck Bridge—bridge IA-7
Louden Cem—cemetery NY-2
Louden Cem—cemetery OH-6
Louden Coulee—valley ND-7
Louden Cove—bay NY-2
**Loudendale**—pop pl WV-2
Louden Ditch—canal CO-8
**Louden Hill**—pop pl PA-2
Louden Hill—summit PA-2
Louden Lake—lake NE-7
Louden Lake—lake WA-9
Louden Ridge—ridge IN-6
Louden Sch (abandoned)—school PA-2
Loudens Chapel—church IN-6
Loudens Lager Sch—school NJ-2
Louden Slough—stream AK-9
**Loudenville**—pop pl WV-2
Louderback Cem—cemetery TN-4
Louderback Creek—stream TN-4
Louderback Gap—gap TN-4
Louderback Mtn—summit TN-4
Louderback Mtns—summit NV-8
*Louder Creek* UT-8
Louder Creek—stream KY-4
Loudermild Bend—bend NC-3
Loudermilk Creek—stream NC-3
Loudermilk Hollow—valley WV-2
*Loudermilk Prong* TN-4
Loudermilk Ridge—ridge NC-3
Loudermilk Wash—stream AZ-5
Louder Number 1 Dam—dam (2) SD-7
Louder Number 2 Dam—dam SD-7
Louder Number 3 Dam—dam SD-7
Louder Number 4 Dam—dam SD-7
Louder Ranger Station—locale UT-8
Louder Sch (historical)—school TN-4
Louder Sch Number 1 (historical)—school SD-7
Loudes Hosp—hospital NJ-2
Loud Island—island MI-6
*Loudon* CA-9

*Loudon* ... OH-6
*Loudon* ... PA-2
**Loudon**—*pop pl* ... NH-1
**Loudon**—*pop pl* (2) ... OH-6
**Loudon**—*pop pl* ... TN-4
Loudon Bridge—*bridge* ... NH-1
Loudon Bridge—*bridge* ... TN-4
Loudon (CCD)—*cens area* ... TN-4
**Loudon Center**—*pop pl* ... NH-1
Loudon Center Ch—*church* ... NH-1
Loudon Ch of the Nazarene—*church* ... TN-4
Loudon City Hall—*building* ... TN-4
**Loudon City Park**—*pop pl* ... TN-4
**Loudon County**—*pop pl* ... TN-4
Loudon County Courthouse—*building* ... TN-4
Loudon County Courthouse—*hist pl* ... TN-4
Loudon County Farm (historical)—*locale* ... TN-4
Loudon County Memorial Gardens—*cemetery* ... TN-4
Loudon County Prison Camp (historical)—*locale* ... TN-4
Loudon County Vocational Center—*school* ... TN-4
Loudon Creek—*stream* ... TN-4
Loudon Cumberland Presbyterian Ch—*church* ... TN-4
Loudon Division—*civil* ... TN-4
Loudon Elem Sch—*school* ... TN-4
*Loudon Gulch* ... CA-9
**Loudon Heights**—*pop pl* ... WV-2
Loudon HS—*school* ... TN-4
Loudon HS—*school* ... WV-2
Loudon JHS—*school* ... TN-4
Loudon Marine Park—*park* ... TN-4
Loudon Park—*uninc pl* ... MD-2
Loudon Park Cem—*cemetery* ... MD-2
Loudon Post Office—*building* ... TN-4
Loudon Ridge—*ridge* ... NH-1
Loudon Ridge Sch—*school* ... NH-1
Loudon Road Hist Dist—*hist pl* ... NY-2
Loudon Sch—*school* ... NH-1
Loudon Sch—*school* ... VA-3
Loudon Shoals—*bar* ... TN-4
**Loudon (Town of)**—*pop pl* ... NH-1
**Loudon (Township of)**—*pop pl* ... IL-6
**Loudon (Township of)**—*pop pl* (2) ... OH-6
Loudon United Methodist Ch—*church* ... TN-4
**Loudonville**—*pop pl* ... NY-2
**Loudonville**—*pop pl* ... OH-6
Loudoun Agricultural and Mechanical Institute—*hist pl* ... VA-3
Loudoun Country Club—*other* ... VA-3
**Loudoun (County)**—*pop pl* ... VA-3
Loudoun County HS—*school* ... VA-3
Loudoun Hall—*hist pl* ... KY-4
Loudoun Heights—*locale* ... VA-3
**Loudoun Heights**—*pop pl* ... VA-3
Loudoun Heights—*summit* ... WV-2
Loudoun Heights Trail—*trail* ... WV-2
Loudoun House—*hist pl* ... KY-4
Loudoun Valley—*valley* ... VA-3
Loudoun Valley Ch—*church* ... VA-3
Loudoun Valley HS—*school* ... VA-3
Loud Pond—*lake* ... NH-1
Loud Sch—*school* ... MI-6
*Louds Creek* ... NY-2
Louds Creek—*stream* ... NY-2
Louds Creek—*stream* ... PA-2
Louds Island—*island* ... ME-1
Loudsville Ch—*church* ... GA-3
Loud Thunder Forest Preserve—*park* ... IL-6
**Loud (Township of)**—*pop pl* ... MI-6
**Loudville**—*pop pl* ... ME-1
**Loudville**—*pop pl* ... MA-1
Loudville Cem—*cemetery* ... ME-1
*Louella* ... PA-2
Louella, Lake—*reservoir* ... GA-3
Louella Guard Station—*locale* ... WA-9
*Louelle* ... KS-7
Louellen—*locale* ... KY-4
Louellen, Lake—*reservoir* ... NC-3
Louemma Lake—*reservoir* ... AR-4
Louemma Lake—*reservoir* ... NJ-2
Loues Creek—*stream* ... SD-7
L'Ouest, Bayou De—*gut* ... LA-4
Louetta—*locale* ... TX-5
Lougee, George A., House—*hist pl* ... WI-6
Lougee Bog—*swamp* ... ME-1
Lougee Lake—*lake* ... MN-6
Lougee Pond—*lake* ... NH-1
Loughberry Lake—*lake* ... NY-2
**Loughboro**—*pop pl* ... MO-7
Loughborough Shop Ctr—*locale* ... MO-7
Lough Cem—*cemetery* ... IN-6
Lough Knob—*summit* ... WV-2
Loughlin Creek—*stream* ... MO-7
**Loughman**—*pop pl* ... FL-3
Loughman Lake—*lake* ... FL-3
*Lough Pond* ... AL-4
Loughrey Cem—*cemetery* ... MN-6
Loughridge Sch—*school* ... IL-6
Loughs Mine—*mine* ... OR-9
Lougis Ditch—*canal* ... IN-6
*Louhatten* ... MS-4
Lou Hollow—*valley* ... NC-3
Louie, Lake—*lake* ... MN-6
Louie and—*stream* ... MT-8
Louie Bluff—*cliff* ... WI-6
Louie Camp Branch—*stream* ... NC-3
Louie Creek—*stream* ... AK-9
Louie Creek—*stream* ... ID-8
Louie Creek—*stream* ... MT-8
Louie Creek—*stream* ... OR-9
Louie Creek—*stream* ... WA-9
Louie Englehardt Dam—*dam* (2) ... SD-7
Louie Entrican Lake Dam—*dam* ... MS-4
Louie Hughes Spring—*spring* ... OR-9
Louie Island—*island* ... LA-4
Louie Lake—*lake* ... AK-9
Louie Lake—*lake* ... ID-8
Louie Lake—*lake* ... OK-5
Louie Lake Trail—*trail* ... ID-8
Louie Lowe Basin—*basin* ... MT-8
Louie Pond—*lake* ... NY-2
Louie Pup—*stream* ... AK-9
Louies Bayou—*stream* ... LA-4
Louies Brake—*swamp* ... LA-4
Louies Cabin—*locale* ... CA-9
Louies Draw—*valley* ... OR-9
Louies Draw Rsvr—*reservoir* ... OR-9
Louie's Place—*hist pl* ... CA-9
Louie Way Gap—*gap* ... WA-9
Louie Well—*well* ... NM-5
**Louin**—*pop pl* ... MS-4
Louina—*locale* ... AL-4
Louin Baptist Ch—*church* ... MS-4
Louin Cem—*cemetery* ... MS-4
Louing Creek—*stream* ... GA-3
Louin Post Office—*building* ... MS-4
Louis—*locale* ... OK-5
Louis, Bayou—*gut* ... LA-4
Louis, Bayou—*stream* (2) ... LA-4
Louis, Lake—*lake* ... WA-9
*Louisa* ... LA-4
Louisa—*locale* ... IA-7
Louisa—*other* ... LA-4
**Louisa**—*pop pl* ... KY-4
**Louisa**—*pop pl* ... VA-3
Louisa, Lake—*lake* (2) ... FL-3
Louisa, Lake—*lake* (2) ... MN-6
Louisa, Lake—*reservoir* ... VA-3
Louisa Bend—*bend* ... FL-3
Louisa Canal—*canal* ... LA-4
Louisa (CCD)—*cens area* ... KY-4
Louisa Cem—*cemetery* ... IL-6
Louisa Chapel—*church* (2) ... NC-3
Louisa Chapel—*church* ... WV-2
Louisa Commercial Hist Dist—*hist pl* ... KY-4
**Louisa (County)**—*pop pl* ... VA-3
Louisa County Courthouse—*hist pl* ... IA-7
Louisa County Home—*building* ... IA-7
Louisa Creek—*stream* ... AK-9
Louisa Creek—*stream* ... ID-8
Louisa Creek—*stream* ... KS-7
Louisa Creek—*stream* ... MS-4
Louisa Creek—*stream* ... NE-7
*Louisa Fork* ... KY-4
*Louisa Fork* ... VA-3
*Louisa Furnace* ... TN-4
Louisa Furnace (40MT379)—*hist pl* ... TN-4
Louisa Jane Ch—*church* ... WV-2
Louisa Lake—*reservoir* ... MA-1
Louisa (Magisterial District)—*fmr MCD* ... VA-3
Louisa May Alcott Sch—*school* ... IL-6
Louisa-Muscatine HS—*school* ... IA-7
Louisa Pond—*lake* ... FL-3
Louisa Pond—*lake* ... NY-2
Louisa Residential Hist Dist—*hist pl* ... KY-4
*Louisa River* ... WV-2
Louisa Spring—*spring* ... FL-3
Louisa Spring Branch—*stream* ... VA-3
Louisa United Methodist Church—*hist pl* ... KY-4
Louis Ave Sch—*school* ... FL-3
Louis Barrett Sch—*school* ... CA-9
Louis Bay—*bay* ... AK-9
Louis Bayou—*gut* ... AL-4
Louis Beach Campground—*locale* ... WY-8
Louis B Hazelton Memorial Cem—*cemetery* ... AZ-5
Louis Bonhorst Number 1 Dam—*dam* ... SD-7
Louis Bonhorst Number 2 Dam—*dam* ... SD-7
Louis Bonhorst Number 3 Dam—*dam* ... SD-7
Louis Bonhorst Number 4 Dam—*dam* ... SD-7
Louis Bonhorst Number 5 Dam—*dam* ... SD-7
Louis Branch—*stream* ... AL-4
*Louis Brook* ... RI-1
**Louisburg**—*pop pl* ... KS-7
**Louisburg**—*pop pl* ... MN-6
**Louisburg**—*pop pl* ... MO-7
**Louisburg**—*pop pl* ... NC-3
**Louisburg**—*pop pl* ... WI-6
Louisburg City Dam—*dam* ... KS-7
Louisburg Coll—*school* ... NC-3
Louisburg Creek—*stream* ... WI-6
Louisburg Elem Sch—*school* ... KS-7
Louisburg Elem Sch—*school* ... NC-3
*Louisburgh* ... KS-7
*Louisburgh* ... NJ-2
*Louisburgh* ... TN-4
Louisburg Hist Dist—*hist pl* ... NC-3
Louisburg HS—*school* ... KS-7
Louisburg HS—*school* ... NC-3
Louisburg Lake—*reservoir* ... KS-7
Louisburg Sch—*hist pl* ... MN-6
Louisburg Square—*park* ... MA-1
**Louisburg Township**—*pop pl* ... KS-7
Louis Burtschi, Lake—*reservoir* ... OK-5
Louis Cabin Landing—*locale* ... MI-6
Louis Caldwell Dam*—*dam* ... SD-7
Louis Cem—*cemetery* ... OK-5
Louis Ch—*church* ... GA-3
Louis Chapel—*church* ... GA-3
Louis Clearing Bay—*bay* ... NY-2
*Louis Corner* ... WI-6
**Louis Corners**—*pop pl* ... WI-6
Louis Creek—*stream* (2) ... AK-9
Louis Creek—*stream* ... MT-8
Louis Creek—*stream* ... OR-9
Louis Creek—*stream* ... SD-7
Louis Creek—*stream* ... TX-5
Louis Creek—*stream* (2) ... WA-9
Louis Creek—*stream* ... WY-8
*Louis C Rimes Cemetery* ... MS-4
Louis C Ward Elem Sch—*school* ... IN-6
Louis D'Or Shaft—*mine* ... AZ-5
**Louise**—*pop pl* ... AR-4
**Louise**—*pop pl* ... FL-3
**Louise**—*pop pl* ... GA-3
**Louise**—*pop pl* ... IA-7
**Louise**—*pop pl* ... MS-4
**Louise**—*pop pl* ... TN-4
**Louise**—*pop pl* ... TX-5
**Louise**—*pop pl* ... WV-2
Louise, Lake—*lake* ... AL-4
Louise, Lake—*lake* (2) ... AK-9
Louise, Lake—*lake* ... CA-9
Louise, Lake—*lake* ... CO-8
Louise, Lake—*lake* ... CT-1
Louise, Lake—*lake* (9) ... FL-3
Louise, Lake—*lake* ... GA-3
Louise, Lake—*lake* ... IL-6
Louise, Lake—*lake* (5) ... MI-6
Louise, Lake—*lake* (2) ... MN-6
Louise, Lake—*lake* ... NJ-2
Louise, Lake—*lake* ... ND-7
Louise, Lake—*lake* ... OH-6
Louise, Lake—*lake* ... TN-4
Louise, Lake—*lake* ... UT-8
Louise, Lake—*lake* (3) ... WA-9
Louise, Lake—*lake* ... WI-6
Louise, Lake—*lake* (3) ... WY-8
Louise, Lake—*reservoir* (3) ... AL-4
Louise, Lake—*reservoir* ... GA-3
Louise, Lake—*reservoir* ... IN-6
Louise, Lake—*reservoir* ... KS-7
Louise, Lake—*reservoir* ... MD-2
Louise, Lake—*reservoir* (2) ... NJ-2
Louise, Lake—*reservoir* (2) ... NC-3
Louise, Lake—*reservoir* ... PA-2
Louise, Lake—*reservoir* ... SD-7
Louise, Lake—*reservoir* ... TX-5
Louise, Point—*cape* ... AK-9
Louise and Hunter Mine—*mine* ... SD-7
Louise Apartments—*hist pl* ... MO-7
Louise Attendance Center—*school* ... MS-4
Louise Cave—*cave* ... AL-4
Louise (CCD)—*cens area* ... TX-5
Louise Cem—*cemetery* ... AR-4
Louise Cem—*cemetery* ... GA-3
Louise Ch—*church* ... GA-3
Louise Chapel—*church* ... AR-4
Louise Cove—*bay* (2) ... AK-9
*Louise Creek* ... ID-8
*Louise Creek* ... ND-7
Louise Creek—*stream* ... AK-9
Louise Creek—*stream* (2) ... ID-8
Louise Creek—*stream* (2) ... OR-9
Louise Creek—*stream* ... TN-4
Louise Creek Trail—*trail* ... OR-9
Louise Dam—*dam* ... SD-7
Louis E Dieruff HS—*school* ... PA-2
Louise Furnace (historical)—*locale* ... TN-4
Louise Grove Ch—*church* ... NC-3
Louise Hays Park—*park* ... TX-5
**Louise Heights (subdivision)**—*pop pl* ... TN-4
Louise Home—*building* ... DC-2
Louise Home Hosp and Residence Hall—*hist pl* ... OR-9
**Louise Junction**—*pop pl* ... MD-2
*Louise Lake* ... ID-8
*Louise Lake* ... MN-6
*Louise Lake* ... WY-8
Louise Lake—*lake* ... AK-9
Louise Lake—*lake* ... FL-3
Louise Lake—*lake* (3) ... MI-6
Louise Lake—*lake* (3) ... MN-6
Louise Lake—*lake* ... MT-8
Louise Lake—*lake* ... WA-9
Louise Lake Dam—*dam* ... NJ-2
Louise Marie, Lake—*reservoir* ... NY-2
Louise Mine—*mine* ... MN-6
Louise Mine—*mine* ... MT-8
Louise Mine—*mine* ... UT-8
Louise Mtn—*summit* ... ME-1
Louise N Henking Sch—*school* ... IL-6
Louisenhoj—*locale* ... VI-3
Louise Obici Memorial Hosp—*hospital* ... VA-3
Louise Oil Field—*oilfield* ... TX-5
Louise Point—*summit* ... CA-9
Louise Post Office (historical)—*building* ... TN-4
Louise S McInnis Elem Sch—*school* ... FL-3
Louise Street—*uninc pl* ... LA-4
Louise United Methodist Ch—*church* ... TN-4
Louise Van Meter Sch—*school* ... CA-9
*Louiseville* ... AL-4
Louise Windmill—*locale* ... TX-5
Louise W. Moore Park—*park* ... PA-2
Louis Granger Place—*locale* ... TX-5
Louis Gulch—*valley* ... CO-8
Louis Hill—*cliff* ... MI-6
Louis Hill Lookout Tower—*tower* ... FL-3
Louis Hollow—*valley* ... OH-6
Louis Hollow—*valley* ... TN-4
Louis Hunt Tank—*reservoir* ... AZ-5
Louis Hunt Tank Draw—*valley* ... AZ-5
**Louisiana**—*pop pl* ... MO-7
Louisiana and Arkansas Junction—*uninc pl* ... LA-4
Louisiana Army Ammunition Plant—*military* ... LA-4
Louisiana Bar—*bar* ... CA-9
Louisiana Brook—*stream* ... MA-1
Louisiana Butte—*summit* ... CA-9
Louisiana Coll—*school* ... LA-4
Louisiana Correctional Institute—*locale* ... LA-4
*Louisiana Cypress Lumber Canal* ... LA-4
Louisiana Cypress Lumber Canal—*canal* ... LA-4
Louisiana Downs—*other* ... LA-4
Louisiana Gulch—*valley* ... AZ-5
Louisiana Gulch—*valley* ... MT-8
Louisiana (historical)—*locale* ... KS-7
Louisiana Irrigation Canal—*canal* ... LA-4
Louisiana Junction—*uninc pl* ... LA-4
Louisiana Lake—*lake* ... LA-4
Louisiana Lake—*lake* ... MS-4
Louisiana Lateral—*canal* ... NM-5
Louisiana Memorial Gardens—*cemetery* ... MO-7
Louisiana Mtn—*summit* ... MA-1
Louisiana Ordnance Plant—*military* ... LA-4
Louisiana Point—*cape* ... LA-4
Louisiana Poly Institute—*school* ... LA-4
Louisiana Prison Farm—*locale* ... LA-4
Louisiana Purchase Survey Marker—*hist pl* ... AR-4
Louisiana Saddle—*gap* ... WA-9
Louisiana State Bank Bldg—*hist pl* ... LA-4
Louisiana State Capitol Bldg and Gardens—*hist pl* ... LA-4
Louisiana State Penitentiary—*locale* ... LA-4
Louisiana State Univ And A&M Coll—*school* ... LA-4
Louisiana State Univ Dean Lee Agricultural Center—*school* ... LA-4
Louisiana State University—*other* ... LA-4
Louisiana State University, Baton Rouge—*hist pl* ... LA-4
Louisiana State University Camp—*locale* ... CO-8
Louisiana State University Experiment Station—*locale* ... LA-4
Louisiana State Univ (New Orleans Branch)—*school* ... LA-4
Louisiana Street/Seventh Ave Hist Dist—*hist pl* ... WI-6
Louisiana Training Istitute—*school* ... LA-4
Louisiana Windmill—*locale* ... TX-5
Louis Jeffers Hollow—*valley* ... TN-4
Louis Jordan Mine—*mine* ... CA-9
Louis Juvenile Hosp—*hospital* ... OR-9
*Louis Lake* ... MI-6
*Louis Lake* ... WY-8
Louis Lake—*lake* ... AK-9
Louis Lake—*lake* ... MN-6
Louis Lake—*lake* ... MT-8
Louis Lake—*lake* ... TX-5
Louis Lake—*lake* ... WA-9
Louis Lake—*lake* ... WY-8
Louis Lake—*reservoir* ... TN-4
Louis Lake Campground—*locale* ... WY-8
Louis Lake Dam—*dam* ... TN-4
Louis Lake Resort—*locale* ... WY-8
Louis Lake Trail—*trail* ... WY-8
Louis Lesmeister Dam—*dam* ... SD-7
Louis Lowe Gap—*gap* ... VA-3
Louis Main Hollow—*valley* ... PA-2
Louis Merwitzer Mesivta HS—*school* ... FL-3
Louis Murphy Dam—*dam* ... AL-4
Louis Nelson County Park—*park* ... WI-6
Louis Oil Field—*oilfield* ... OK-5
Louis Park—*park* ... CA-9
Louis P DeMartin Senior Memorial Bridge—*bridge* ... CA-9
Louis Point—*cape* ... MI-6
Louis (RR name for Louisville)—*other* ... IL-6
Louis Slough—*stream* ... OR-9
Louis Southwestern Railway Hosp—*hospital* ... AR-4
Louis Spring—*spring* ... WA-9
Louis S Sheffield Elem Sch—*school* ... FL-3
Louis Tank—*reservoir* ... AZ-5
Louisvilla, Lake—*reservoir* ... KY-4
*Louisville* ... DE-2
*Louisville* ... MS-4
Louisville—*locale* ... MT-8
Louisville—*locale* ... OH-6
**Louisville**—*pop pl* ... AL-4
**Louisville**—*pop pl* ... CO-8
**Louisville**—*pop pl* ... GA-3
**Louisville**—*pop pl* ... IL-6
**Louisville**—*pop pl* ... KS-7
**Louisville**—*pop pl* ... KY-4
**Louisville**—*pop pl* ... LA-4
**Louisville**—*pop pl* ... MD-2
**Louisville**—*pop pl* ... MS-4
**Louisville**—*pop pl* ... MO-7
**Louisville**—*pop pl* (2) ... NE-7
**Louisville**—*pop pl* ... NY-2
**Louisville**—*pop pl* ... OH-6
**Louisville**—*pop pl* ... TN-4
Louisville—*reservoir* ... IL-6
Louisville—*uninc pl* ... LA-4
Louisville Acad (historical)—*school* ... TN-4
Louisville AHP Airp—*airport* ... AL-4
Louisville and Nashville Depot—*hist pl* ... AL-4
Louisville and Nashville Depot—*hist pl* ... FL-3
Louisville and Nashville Depot—*hist pl* ... IL-6
Louisville And Nashville Depot—*locale* ... AL-4
Louisville and Nashville Freight Depot—*hist pl* ... TN-4
Louisville and Nashville Passenger Station—*hist pl* ... TN-4
Louisville and Nashville Passenger Station and Express Bldg—*hist pl* ... FL-3
Louisville and Nashville RR Depot—*hist pl* ... AL-4
Louisville and Nashville RR Depot—*hist pl* ... KY-4
Louisville and Nashville RR Depot—*hist pl* ... MS-4
Louisville and Nashville RR Depot at Ocean Springs—*hist pl* ... MS-4
Louisville and Nashville RR Office Bldg—*hist pl* ... KY-4
Louisville and Nashville RR Passenger Depot—*hist pl* ... KY-4
Louisville and Nashville RR Station—*hist pl* ... KY-4
Louisville and Nashville RR Station—*locale* ... AL-4
Louisville and Portland Canal—*canal* ... KY-4
Louisville Baptist Ch—*church* ... MS-4
Louisville Brook—*stream* ... NH-1
Louisville (CCD)—*cens area* ... AL-4
Louisville (CCD)—*cens area* ... GA-3
Louisville (CCD)—*cens area* ... KY-4
Louisville Cem—*cemetery* ... CO-8
Louisville Cem—*cemetery* ... KS-7
Louisville Cem—*cemetery* ... KY-4
Louisville Cem—*cemetery* ... MS-4
Louisville Cem—*cemetery* ... TN-4
Louisville Ch—*church* ... MO-7
Louisville Ch—*church* ... TN-4
Louisville Ch of Christ—*church* ... MS-4
Louisville City Hall—*building* ... MS-4
Louisville City Hall Complex—*hist pl* ... KY-4
Louisville Club Pond—*lake* ... AL-4
Louisville Club Pond Dam—*dam* ... AL-4
Louisville Collegiate Sch—*school* ... KY-4
Louisville Cotton Mills—*hist pl* ... KY-4
Louisville Country Club—*other* ... KY-4
Louisville Creek—*stream* ... AK-9
Louisville Creek—*stream* ... MO-7
Louisville Creek—*stream* ... TX-5
Louisville Division—*civil* ... AL-4
Louisville Dock—*locale* ... TN-4
Louisville Downs—*other* ... KY-4
*Louisville Ferry* ... TN-4
Louisville Free Public Library—*hist pl* ... KY-4
Louisville Free Public Library, Western Colored Branch—*hist pl* ... KY-4
Louisville Golf Club—*other* ... GA-3
Louisville Hist Dist—*hist pl* ... TN-4
Louisville HS—*school* ... AL-4
Louisville JHS (historical)—*school* ... TN-4
Louisville Junior Acad—*school* ... KY-4
Louisville Lagoon Dam—*dam* ... MS-4
Louisville Lakes State Rec Area—*park* ... NE-7
Louisville Landing Ch—*church* ... NY-2
Louisville Male HS—*hist pl* ... KY-4
Louisville Memorial Gardens—*cemetery* ... KY-4
Louisville Memorial Park—*cemetery* ... KY-4
Louisville MS—*school* ... MS-4
Louisville Municipal Bridge, Pylons and Administration Bldg—*hist pl* ... KY-4
Louisville Naval Ordnance Station—*military* ... KY-4
Louisville Point Park—*park* ... TN-4
Louisville Post Office—*building* ... MS-4
Louisville Post Office—*building* ... TN-4
Louisville Presbyterian Ch (historical)—*church* ... TN-4
Louisville Presbyterian Theological Seminary—*church* ... KY-4
Louisville Recreation Grounds—*park* ... NE-7
Louisville Rifle and Gun Club—*other* ... KY-4
Louisville Rsvr—*reservoir* ... CO-8
Louisville Sch—*school* ... IL-6
Louisville Sch—*school* (2) ... LA-4
Louisville Sch—*school* ... NY-2
Louisville Sch—*school* ... OH-6
Louisville Swamp—*swamp* ... MN-6
**Louisville (Town of)**—*pop pl* ... NY-2
**Louisville Township**—*pop pl* ... KS-7
**Louisville (Township of)**—*pop pl* ... IL-6
**Louisville (Township of)**—*pop pl* (2) ... MN-6
Louisville Trust Bldg—*hist pl* ... KY-4
Louisville War Memorial Auditorium—*hist pl* ... KY-4
Louisville Water Company Pumping Station—*hist pl* ... KY-4
Louisville Winston County Airp—*airport* ... MS-4
Louis Windmill—*locale* ... TX-5
Louis Windmills—*locale* ... NM-5
Louis Woods Hollow—*valley* ... MO-7
Louis Woodward Ranch—*locale* ... TX-5
Louj—*island* ... MP-9
Lou Jay Resort—*locale* ... CO-8
Louk Run—*stream* ... WV-2
Louler Creek—*stream* ... WI-6
*Lou-Lou Creek* ... MT-8
*Lou-Lou Pass* ... MT-8
**Loulynn**—*pop pl* ... KY-4
Louma Lake—*lake* ... MN-6
**Lou Mar Estates**—*pop pl* ... MD-2
Lou Mine, The—*mine* ... UT-8
Lounce Lookout—*park* ... AZ-5
Lou Nelson Ranch—*locale* ... CO-8
Lounge Lake—*lake* ... MN-6
**Lounsberry**—*pop pl* ... NY-2
Lounsberry Ch—*church* ... NY-2
*Lounsberry Creek* ... OR-9
Lounsberry (historical)—*locale* ... SD-7
Lounsbury, Phineas Chapman, House—*hist pl* ... CT-1
Lounsbury Corners—*locale* ... PA-2
Lounsbury Lake—*lake* ... WA-9
Lounsbury Pond—*lake* ... NY-2
Lou One Cave—*cave* ... AL-4
Loup—*fmr MCD* ... NE-7
Loup, Bayou—*stream* ... LA-4
*Loup Canal* ... NE-7
**Loup City**—*pop pl* ... NE-7
Loup City Rec Area—*park* ... NE-7
Loup City Township—*civ div* ... NE-7
*Loup Creek* ... WV-2
**Loup Ferry Township**—*pop pl* ... NE-7
Loup Fork—*fmr MCD* ... NE-7
Loup Loup Creek—*stream* ... WA-9
Loup Loup Rec Area—*locale* ... WA-9
Loup Loup Summit—*summit* ... WA-9
Lou Point—*cape* ... MN-6
Loup Park—*park* ... NE-7
*Loup Public Power District Canal* ... NE-7
Loup River—*stream* ... NE-7
Loup River Canal—*canal* ... NE-7
*Loup Run* ... PA-2
Loup Run—*stream* ... PA-2
Loup Sch—*school* ... SD-7
**Loup Township**—*pop pl* (4) ... NE-7
Loup Valley Cem—*cemetery* ... NE-7
**Lourdes**—*pop pl* ... IA-7
**Lourdes**—*pop pl* ... NM-5
Lourdes Acad—*school* ... OH-6
Lourdes Ch—*church* ... IL-6
Lourdes Ch—*church* ... LA-4
Lourdes Hosp—*hospital* ... NY-2
Lourdes HS—*school* ... IL-6
Lourdes HS—*school* ... MN-6
Lourdes HS—*school* ... NM-5
Lourdes HS—*school* ... WI-6
Lourdes Junior Coll—*school* ... OH-6
Lourdes Lake—*lake* ... TN-4
Lourdes Memorial Ch—*church* ... IA-7
Lourdes Memorial Sch—*school* ... IA-7
Lourdes Sch—*school* ... IL-6
Lourdes Sch—*school* ... NM-5
Loureys (historical)—*locale* ... AL-4
**Louriston (Township of)**—*pop pl* ... MN-6
*Lour Lake* ... MN-6
Lou RR Station—*locale* ... FL-3
Lourtown Sch—*school* ... PA-2
Loury Cem—*cemetery* ... VA-3
*Loury Fork* ... UT-8
Lous Chapel—*church* ... TN-4
Lous Crawl Cave—*cave* ... AL-4
Louse Camp—*locale* ... CA-9
Louse Camp Run—*stream* ... WV-2
Louse Canyon—*valley* ... CA-9
Louse Canyon—*valley* ... OR-9
*Louse Creek* ... IL-6
Louse Creek—*stream* (2) ... CA-9
Louse Creek—*stream* (7) ... ID-8
Louse Creek—*stream* ... MO-7
Louse Creek—*stream* ... MT-8
Louse Creek—*stream* ... NE-7
Louse Creek—*stream* (2) ... NV-8
Louse Creek—*stream* ... ND-7
Louse Creek—*stream* ... OR-9
Louse Creek—*stream* ... SD-7
Louse Creek—*stream* ... TN-4
Louse Creek—*stream* (3) ... VA-3
Louse Creek—*stream* ... WA-9
Louse Creek—*stream* (2) ... WY-8
Louse Flat—*flat* ... AZ-5
Louse Flat Tank—*reservoir* ... AZ-5
Louse Hollow—*valley* ... IA-7
Louse Hollow—*valley* ... TN-4
Louse Hollow Branch—*stream* ... TN-4
Louse Island—*island* ... ME-1
Louse Island—*island* ... NC-3
Louse Island—*island* ... OR-9
Louse Kill—*stream* ... NY-2
Louse Lake—*lake* ... AZ-5
Louse Lake—*lake* ... ID-8
Louse Lake—*lake* ... MN-6
Louse Lake—*lake* ... OR-9
Louse Point—*cape* ... NY-2
Louse Point—*cliff* ... ID-8
Louse River—*stream* ... MN-6
Louse Rock—*pillar* ... OR-9
Louse Run—*stream* ... IL-6
Louse Run—*stream* ... MO-7
Louse Run—*stream* ... TX-5
Louse Spring—*spring* ... CA-9
Louse Spring—*spring* ... NV-8
Louse Spring—*spring* ... OR-9
Louse Tank Number One—*reservoir* ... AZ-5
Lousetown Creek—*stream* ... NV-8
Lousetown (Site)—*locale* ... NV-8
Lousey Hollow—*valley* ... OR-9
Lousie—*locale* ... TN-4
Lousigmont Creek—*stream* ... OR-9
Lousignont Creek—*stream* (2) ... OR-9
*Lousignot Creek* ... OR-9
Lousley Hill—*summit* ... AZ-5
Lou Spring—*spring* ... NV-8
Lousy Branch—*stream* ... MO-7
Lousy Canyon—*valley* ... AZ-5
Lousy Creek—*stream* ... AK-9
Lousy Creek—*stream* ... CA-9
Lousy Creek—*stream* (2) ... MO-7
Lousy Creek—*stream* ... NC-3
Lousy Creek—*stream* ... WA-9
Lousy Creek—*stream* ... WI-6
Lousy George Spring—*spring* ... WY-8
Lousy Gulch—*valley* ... AZ-5
Lousy Jim Creek—*stream* ... UT-8
Lousy Level Landing (historical)—*locale* ... MS-4
Lousy Run—*stream* ... OH-6
Lousy Run—*stream* ... PA-2
Lousy Spring—*spring* ... CA-9
Lousy Springs—*spring* ... MT-8
Lousy Tank—*reservoir* (2) ... AZ-5
Louthan Tank—*reservoir* ... AZ-5
Louther—*locale* ... WV-2
Louther Ch—*church* ... WV-2
Louthers Run—*stream* ... WV-2
Lout Pond—*lake* ... MA-1
Loutre, Bayou de—*stream* ... AR-4
Loutre, Bayou de—*stream* ... LA-4
Loutre, Bayou la—*stream* ... LA-4
Loutre Island Cem—*cemetery* ... MO-7
Loutre Island Ch—*church* ... MO-7
Loutre Lick Access Area—*locale* ... MO-7
Loutre River—*stream* ... MO-7
Loutre Slough—*stream* ... MO-7
Loutre Township—*civil* (2) ... MO-7
Loutsenhizer Arroyo—*stream* ... CO-8
Loutsenhizer Canal—*canal* ... CO-8
Louts Lake—*lake* ... AL-4
Lou Two Cave—*cave* ... AL-4
**Louvale**—*pop pl* ... GA-3
Louvale Church Row Hist Dist—*hist pl* ... GA-3
Louvale Sch—*school* ... GA-3
**Louvale Station**—*pop pl* ... GA-3
Louvenia Cem—*cemetery* ... AR-4
L'Ouverture Sch—*school* ... KS-7
L'Ouverture Sch—*school* ... OK-5
Louviers—*hist pl* ... DE-2
**Louviers**—*pop pl* ... CO-8
Louviers Country Club—*locale* ... DE-2
Louviers Station—*locale* ... CO-8
**Lou-vre Estates Subdivision**—*pop pl* ... UT-8
Louwien, A. C., Bakery—*hist pl* ... TX-5
Loux Corner—*locale* ... PA-2
Loux Covered Bridge—*bridge* ... PA-2
Loux Covered Bridge—*hist pl* ... PA-2
Loux Sch—*school* ... IL-6
*Louxs Corner* ... PA-2
Louxs Corner—*locale* ... PA-2
Lou Yaeger, Lake—*reservoir* ... IL-6
*Louzers Lake* ... MN-6
Lovaas Ridge—*ridge* ... WI-6
Lovada—*locale* ... WV-2
Lovada Gap—*gap* ... NC-3
Lova Lake—*lake* ... MN-6
Lovall Valley—*valley* ... CA-9
Lovango Cay—*island* ... VI-3
Lovango Channel—*channel* ... VI-3
*Lova Pass* ... OR-9
**Lovato**—*pop pl* ... NM-5
Lovato Cem—*cemetery* ... NM-5
Lovato Dam—*dam* ... NM-5
Lovato Ditch—*canal* ... NM-5
Lovatt Butte—*summit* ... WY-8
Lovatt Creek—*stream* ... WY-8
Lovatt Ditch—*canal* ... WY-8
Lovatt Draw—*valley* ... WY-8
Lovatt Lake—*lake* ... WY-8
Lovawalla Spring—*spring* ... OR-9
Lova Windmill—*locale* ... TX-5
Lovdal—*locale* ... CA-9
Love—*locale* ... AZ-5
Love—*locale* ... IL-6
Love—*locale* ... KY-4
Love—*locale* (2) ... TX-5
Love—*locale* ... VA-3
**Love**—*pop pl* ... AZ-5
**Love**—*pop pl* ... AR-4
**Love**—*pop pl* ... MS-4
**Love**—*pop pl* ... VA-3
Love, Col. Thomas C., House—*hist pl* ... MO-7
Love, E. C., House—*hist pl* ... FL-3
Love, Emily Rockwell, House—*hist pl* ... MO-7
Love, Frank and Mellie, House—*hist pl* ... TX-5
Love, George Collins, House—*hist pl* ... TN-4
Love, Mount—*summit* ... TN-4
Love All Ch—*church* ... GA-3
Love and White Ditch—*canal* ... CO-8
Love Arroyo—*valley* ... TX-5
Loveberry Run—*stream* ... WV-2
**Loveberry Siding**—*pop pl* ... WV-2
Love Bluff—*cliff* ... TN-4
*Love Branch* ... MO-7
Love Branch—*canal* ... CA-9
Love Branch—*stream* (2) ... TN-4
Love Branch—*stream* ... TX-5
*Love Branch Dry Gulch* ... CA-9
Love Bridge—*bridge* ... TN-4
Love Cabin Spring—*spring* ... CA-9
Lovecamp Sch—*school* ... IL-6
Love Canal—*canal* ... FL-3
Love Canyon—*valley* ... WY-8
Love-Cass Ranch—*locale* ... TX-5
Love Cem—*cemetery* ... AL-4
Love Cem—*cemetery* (3) ... AR-4
Love Cem—*cemetery* ... GA-3
Love Cem—*cemetery* ... IN-6
Love Cem—*cemetery* (2) ... KY-4
Love Cem—*cemetery* (2) ... MS-4
Love Cem—*cemetery* (2) ... MO-7

Love Cem—cemetery (3) NC-3
Love Cem—cemetery (2) OK-5
Love Cem—cemetery OR-9
Love Cem—cemetery (8) TN-4
Love Ch—church GA-3
Love Ch—church MS-4
Love Ch—church NC-3
Love Ch—church OH-6
Love Ch—church OK-5
Love Chapel—church AL-4
Love Chapel—church LA-4
Love Chapel—church (2) NC-3
Love Chapel—church TN-4
Love Chapel—church TX-5
**Love Chapel**—pop pl TX-5
Love Chapel Cem—cemetery NC-3
Love Chapel Cem—cemetery TN-4
*Love Chapel Cemetery* AL-4
Love Chapel Elem Sch—school IN-4
Love-Charity Ch—church SC-3
Love Corners—locale PA-2
**Love (County)**—pop pl OK-5
Love County Courthouse—hist pl OK-5
Love Cove—bay ME-1
*Love Creek* MA-1
*Love Creek* UT-8
Love Creek—gut WI-6
Love Creek—locale AR-4
Love Creek—stream (3) AR-4
Love Creek—stream (2) CA-9
Love Creek—stream DE-2
Love Creek—stream MI-6
Love Creek—stream (2) MS-4
Love Creek—stream (3) OR-9
Love Creek—stream SC-3
Love Creek—stream TN-4
Love Creek—stream (2) TX-5
Love Creek Bridge—bridge DE-2
Love Crest Ch—church MS-4
Lovedale—locale FL-3
**Lovedale**—pop pl PA-2
Lovedale Ch—church KY-4
Lovedale Post Office (historical)—building TN-4
Love Dam—dam OR-9
Love Ditch—canal IN-6
Love Ditch—canal (2) OR-9
Love Ditch—stream AL-4
Love Draw—valley WY-8
**Love Field**—pop pl NC-3
Lovefield Branch—stream TN-4
*Love Gap* NC-3
Love Gap—gap TN-4
Lovegrass Windmill—locale NM-5
Love Grove Ch—church FL-3
Love Grove Ch—church (6) NC-3
Love Grove Sch—school FL-3
Love Grove Sch—school NC-3
**Love Grove (subdivision)**—pop pl NC-3
Love Gulch—valley CO-8
Love Hill—locale GA-3
**Love Hill**—pop pl AL-4
Love Hill—summit MT-8
Love Hill Ch—church AL-4
Love Hogback—ridge TX-5
Love Hollow—valley AR-4
Love Hollow—valley IN-6
Love Hollow—valley (3) TN-4
Love HS—school TX-5
Love Island—island MI-6
Loveitt Bridge—bridge ME-1
*Lovejoy* IL-6
*Lovejoy* KS-7
Lovejoy—locale NC-3
**Lovejoy**—pop pl GA-3
**Lovejoy**—pop pl PA-2
**Lovejoy**—pop pl TN-4
**Love Joy**—pop pl TN-4
Lovejoy, Carrie, House—hist pl OH-6
Lovejoy, Charles, House—hist pl MA-1
Lovejoy, Owen, Homestead—hist pl IL-6
Lovejoy and Merrill-Nowlan Houses—hist pl WI-6
Lovejoy Bridge—hist pl ME-1
Lovejoy Brook—stream ME-1
Lovejoy Brook—stream NH-1
Lovejoy Brook—stream VT-1
Lovejoy Buttes—summit CA-9
Lovejoy Camp—locale CA-9
Lovejoy Cem—cemetery (2) AL-4
Lovejoy Cem—cemetery GA-3
Lovejoy Cem—cemetery MI-6
Love Joy Cem—cemetery MS-4
Lovejoy Cem—cemetery NY-2
Lovejoy Cem—cemetery OH-6
Lovejoy Cem—cemetery TN-4
Lovejoy Cem—cemetery WV-2
Love Joy Ch—church (2) AL-4
Love Joy Ch—church GA-3
Love Joy Ch—church MS-4
Lovejoy Ch—church MS-4
*Lovejoy (corporate and RR name Brooklyn)* IL-6
Lovejoy Cove—bay ME-1
Lovejoy Creek—stream CA-9
Lovejoy Creek—stream GA-3
Lovejoy Creek—stream MO-7
Love Joy Ditch—canal IN-6
Lovejoy Drain—canal MI-6
Lovejoy Flats—flat NE-7
Lovejoy Hill—summit ME-1
Lovejoy Homestead—hist pl CA-9
Lovejoy Lake—lake MN-6
Lovejoy Lake—lake NE-7
Lovejoy Lake—lake WI-6
Lovejoy Lake—reservoir MS-4
Lovejoy Mtn—summit (2) ME-1
Lovejoy Narrows—channel ME-1
Lovejoy Point—cape WA-9
Lovejoy Pond—lake (2) ME-1
Lovejoy Pond—reservoir ME-1
Lovejoy Ranch—locale NE-7
Lovejoy Ranch—locale NM-5
Lovejoy Ridge—ridge ME-1
**Lovejoy Sands**—pop pl NH-1
Lovejoy Sch—school DC-2
Lovejoy Sch—school IL-6
Lovejoy Sch—school TX-5
Lovejoy Springs—spring CA-9
Lovejoy Stream—stream ME-1
**Lovejoy (Township of)**—pop pl IL-6
Lovekin Drain—canal CA-9
Love Knob—summit NC-3
*Lovelace* AL-4
Lovelace—locale GA-3
Lovelace—locale MS-4
Lovelace—locale NM-5
Lovelace—locale TN-4
**Lovelace**—pop pl GA-3
**Lovelace**—pop pl TX-5
Lovelace, Andrew, Jr., House—hist pl KY-4
*Lovelace Baptist Church* TN-4
Lovelace Bridge—bridge AL-4
Lovelace Canyon—valley CA-9
Lovelace Cem—cemetery AR-4
Lovelace Cem—cemetery GA-3
Lovelace Cem—cemetery KY-4
Lovelace Ch—church KY-4
Lovelace Ch—church TN-4
Lovelace Clinic—hospital NM-5
Lovelace Creek—stream AK-9
Lovelace Creek—stream (2) NC-3
Lovelace Creek—stream TX-5
**Lovelace Crossroads**—pop pl AL-4
Lovelace Fork—stream KY-4
Lovelace Gap—gap NC-3
**Lovelace (historical)**—pop pl NC-3
Lovelace Knob—summit NC-3
Lovelace Lake—lake LA-4
Lovelace Landing (historical)—locale AL-4
Lovelace Levee—levee CA-9
Lovelace Mine—mine KY-4
Lovelace Park—park FL-3
Lovelace Pond—lake PA-2
Lovelace Post Office (historical)—building TN-4
Lovelace Ranch—locale NM-5
Lovelace Ranch—locale TX-5
Lovelace Sch—school IL-6
Lovelace Sch (historical)—school AL-4
Lovelace Sch (historical)—school TN-4
Lovelace Spring—spring TN-4
Lovelace Tank—reservoir AZ-5
Lovelace (Township of)—fmr MCD NC-3
**Lovelaceville**—pop pl KY-4
*Love Ladies* NJ-2
**Loveladies**—pop pl NJ-2
Loveladies Harbor—harbor NJ-2
*Loveladies Island* NJ-2
**Loveladies (Long Beach Park)**—pop pl NJ-2
*Lovelady* NJ-2
*Lovelady* NC-3
**Love Lady**—pop pl TN-4
**Lovelady**—pop pl TX-5
Lovelady Branch—stream TN-4
Lovelady (CCD)—cens area TX-5
Lovelady Cem—cemetery (2) AL-4
Love Lady Cem—cemetery TN-4
Lovelady Cem—cemetery TN-4
Lovelady Ch—church (2) NC-3
Lovelady Ch—church OK-5
Lovelady Ch (historical)—church TN-4
Lovelady Creek—stream TX-5
Love Lady Creek—stream VA-3
Lovelady Creek—stream VA-3
Lovelady Draw—valley NM-5
Lovelady Gap—gap VA-3
Lovelady Gulch—valley CA-9
**Lovelady (historical)**—pop pl NC-3
*Love Lady Island* NJ-2
Lovelady Island—island NJ-2
Love Lady Mtn—summit VA-3
Lovelady Park—park TX-5
*Love Lady Ridge* CA-9
Lovelady Ridge—ridge (2) CA-9
Loveladys Mill (historical)—locale MS-4
Lovelady Spring—spring NM-5
Lovelady Spring—spring TN-4
Lovelady (Township of)—fmr MCD (2) NC-3
Lovelady Valley—valley VA-3
*Love Lake* MS-4
Love Lake—lake (2) CO-8
Love Lake—lake ME-1
Love Lake—lake (2) MN-6
Love Lake—lake OR-9
Love Lake—lake TX-5
Love Lake—lake WI-6
Love Lake—reservoir AZ-5
Love Lake—reservoir CO-8
Love Lake—reservoir MO-7
Love Lake Dam—dam MS-4
Loveland—locale NY-2
Loveland—locale WA-9
**Loveland**—pop pl CO-8
**Loveland**—pop pl IA-7
**Loveland**—pop pl OH-6
**Loveland**—pop pl OK-5
**Loveland**—pop pl TN-4
Loveland, Lake—reservoir CO-8
Loveland Airp—airport CO-8
Loveland and Greely Canal—canal CO-8
Loveland Baptist Ch—church TN-4
Loveland Brook—stream VT-1
Loveland Canyon—valley OR-9
Loveland Canyon—valley SD-7
Loveland Canyon Rsvr—reservoir OR-9
Loveland Cem—cemetery OK-5
Loveland Corners—locale WI-6
Loveland Creek—stream OR-9
Loveland Filtration Plant—other CO-8
Loveland Gulch—valley CA-9
**Loveland Heights**—pop pl CO-8
Loveland Hill—summit VT-1
Loveland Horse Camp—locale OR-9
Loveland Lateral—canal CO-8
Loveland Ledge—bench VT-1
Loveland-Miami Sch—school OH-6
Loveland Mountain Park—park CO-8
Loveland Mtn—summit CO-8
**Loveland Park**—pop pl OH-6
Loveland Pass—gap CO-8
Loveland Peak—summit MT-8
Loveland Peak Trail—trail MT-8
Loveland Powerplant—other CO-8
Loveland Rsvr—reservoir CA-9
Loveland Rsvr—reservoir CO-8
Loveland Sch—school FL-3
Loveland Sch—school NE-7
Loveland Ski Area—other CO-8
Loveland Thorofare—channel NJ-2
Loveland Water Tanks—other CO-8
*Love Lane Hill* RI-1
Love-Larson Opera House—hist pl NE-7
*Lovelass Spring* TN-4
Lovel Canyon—valley CA-9
Lovel Cem—cemetery OH-6
Lovel Cem—cemetery PA-2
*Lovel Creek* NC-3
*Lovel Creek* VA-3
**Loveless**—pop pl AL-4
**Loveless**—pop pl IL-6
Loveless Cem—cemetery GA-3
Loveless Cem—cemetery (2) IN-6
Loveless Cem—cemetery TX-5
Loveless Ch—church TN-4
Loveless Creek—stream AL-4
Loveless Creek—stream OR-9
Loveless Dredgings—locale CA-9
Loveless Hollow—valley TN-4
Loveless Homestead—locale OR-9
Loveless Lake—lake WI-6
**Loveless Park**—pop pl AL-4
Loveless Ranch—locale TX-5
Loveless Sch—school AL-4
Loveless Sch—school NY-2
Loveless Sch (historical)—school TN-4
Love Letter Spring—spring CA-9
Lovelkady Sch (historical)—school TN-4
Lovell—locale NV-8
Lovell—locale OH-6
Lovell—locale PA-2
**Lovell**—pop pl ME-1
**Lovell**—pop pl OK-5
**Lovell**—pop pl TN-4
**Lovell**—pop pl WY-8
Lovell, Capt. George, House—hist pl MA-1
Lovell, Ellen, M., House—hist pl MN-6
Lovell, Nehemiah, House—hist pl MA-1
Lovell Beach House—hist pl CA-9
Lovell Block—hist pl MA-1
Lovell Branch—stream GA-3
Lovell Branch—stream KY-4
Lovell Canal—canal WY-8
Lovell Canyon—valley CA-9
Lovell Canyon—valley NV-8
Lovell Cem—cemetery MO-7
Lovell Cem—cemetery TN-4
Lovell Cem—cemetery WY-8
Lovell Ch—church TN-4
Lovell Chapel (historical)—church AL-4
Lovell Corners—locale PA-2
**Lovell Corners**—pop pl MA-1
Lovell Creek—stream MI-6
Lovell Creek—stream TN-4
Lovell Ditch—canal CA-9
Lovell Draw—valley WY-8
Lovell Elem Sch—school FL-3
Lovell Field (Airport)—airport TN-4
Lovell Field (airport)—airport TN-4
Lovell Gulch—valley CO-8
Lovell Gulch—valley ID-8
**Lovell Heights**—pop pl TN-4
Lovell (historical)—locale SD-7
Lovell Hollow—valley AR-4
Lovell Hollow—valley TN-4
Lovell Hollow—valley UT-8
Lovell House—hist pl CA-9
Lovell Island—island LA-4
Lovell Island—island MA-1
Lovell Island—island MT-8
Lovell Lake—lake MN-6
Lovell Lake—lake NH-1
Lovell Lake—lake TX-5
**Lovell Lake**—pop pl TX-5
Lovell Lake—reservoir NC-3
Lovell Lake Dam—dam NC-3
Lovell Lake Oil Field—oilfield TX-5
Lovell Lakes—lake WY-8
Lovell Park—park PA-2
Lovell Peak—summit NV-8
*Lovell Pond* ME-1
*Lovell Pond* MA-1
Lovell Pond—lake MI-6
Lovell Reservoir Dam—dam MA-1
Lovell Reservoir Dike—dam MA-1
Lovell River—stream NH-1
Lovell Rsvr—reservoir MA-1
*Lovells* PA-2
**Lovells**—pop pl MI-6
Lovells Boat Dock—locale TN-4
Lovells Cem—cemetery MI-6
Lovell Sch—school CA-9
Lovell Sch—school CT-1
Lovell Sch (abandoned)—school PA-2
*Lovells Corner* MA-1
Lovells Grove Ch—church IL-6
Lovells Gulch—valley MT-8
*Lovells Island* MA-1
Lovells Island—island TN-4
Lovells Lake—lake MT-8
*Lovell's Pond* ME-1
Lovells Pond—lake MA-1
Lovell Square—park MN-6
Lovells Town Hall—locale MI-6
**Lovells (Township of)**—pop pl MI-6
Lovell Summit—summit NV-8
**Lovell (Town of)**—pop pl ME-1
Lovell Township—fmr MCD IA-7
**Lovell Township**—pop pl ND-7
Lovell Valley—valley ID-8
Lovell Village Church—hist pl ME-1
**Lovellville**—pop pl MA-1
*Lovell Wash* NV-8
Lovell Wash—stream (2) NV-8
Lovell-Webber House—hist pl MI-6
Lovelock—locale CA-9
**Lovelock**—pop pl NV-8
Lovelock Cave—hist pl NV-8
**Lovelock Colony**—pop pl NV-8
Lovelock Drain—canal NV-8
Lovelock Indian Caves—cave NV-8
*Lovelocks* NV-8
**Lovelock Subdivision**—pop pl UT-8
Love Loney Ditch—canal OR-9
Lovel Point—cape MD-2
*Lovels Creek* NC-3
*Lovels Creek* VA-3
*Lovels Island* MA-1
**Lovelton**—pop pl PA-2
Lovelund—locale VI-3
*Lovely* MH-9
**Lovely**—pop pl KY-4
**Lovely**—pop pl PA-2
Lovely, Lake—lake FL-3
Lovely Branch—stream KY-4
Lovely Branch—stream TN-4
Lovely Cem—cemetery KY-4
Lovely Cem—cemetery (2) TN-4
Lovely Ch—church AL-4
Lovely Cove—bay MD-2
Lovely Creek—stream NE-7
*Lovely Dale* IN-6
Lovely Grove Ch—church GA-3
Lovely Hill Cem—cemetery NC-3
Lovely Hill Ch—church NC-3
Lovely Hill Ch—church (2) SC-3
**Lovely (historical)**—pop pl OR-9
Lovely Hollow—valley TN-4
Lovely Lane Methodist Church—hist pl MD-2
Lovely Mill (historical)—locale TN-4
Lovely Pass—gap WY-8
Lovely Ranch—locale MT-8
Lovely Ridge Sch (historical)—school MO-7
Lovely Spring—spring (2) TN-4
Lovely Spring Branch—stream TN-4
Lovely Valley—valley NV-8
Lovely Valley Spring—spring NV-8
Loveman, Joseph, & Loeb Department Store—hist pl AL-4
Love Memorial Ch—church NC-3
Love Memorial Ch—church TN-4
*Love Memorial Elementary School* NC-3
Love Memorial Sch—school NC-3
Love Mesa—summit CO-8
**Love Mills**—pop pl VA-3
Love Mound Cem—cemetery MO-7
*Love Mountain* UT-8
*Love Mountain, The* TN-4
Love Mtn—summit NC-3
Love Mtn—summit TN-4
Lovenburg Sch—school TX-5
Love-N-Care Day Nurseries—school FL-3
Lovenia, Mount—summit UT-8
Lovenia Lake—lake UT-8
*Lovenia Lake Number Two Dam* UT-8
Loven Lake—lake MN-6
Lovenlund Bay—bay VI-3
Love of Christ Temple—church MS-4
Love of Peace Cem—cemetery MA-1
Love Oil Field—oilfield KS-7
Love Park—park TX-5
**Love Park (subdivision)**—pop pl NC-3
Love Place—locale AR-4
Love Point—cape MD-2
**Love Point**—pop pl MD-2
Love Point Lighthouse—locale MD-2
Lover—locale PA-2
*Lovera Lake* MN-6
Love Ranch—locale CO-8
Love Ranch—locale (4) TX-5
Love Ranch—locale WY-8
Love Ranch HQ—locale NM-5
Lover Cem—cemetery KY-4
Lover Ch—church PA-2
Lovercheck Canyon—valley WY-8
Lovercheck Ditch—canal WY-8
Loverens Mill—locale NH-1
Love Rest Cem—cemetery AR-4
Love Rest No 2 Ch—church AR-4
Loveridge—locale WV-2
Love Ridge—ridge KY-4
Love Ridge—ridge ME-1
Loveridge Bridge—bridge ID-8
Loveridge Flat—flat UT-8
Loveridge Gulch—valley ID-8
**Loveridge Heights**—pop pl FL-3
Loveridge Island—island ID-8
**Loveridge Mine**—pop pl WV-2
Loveridge Sch—school IL-6
Lovering, Joseph, House—hist pl MA-1
Lovering Brook—stream NH-1
Lovering Cem—cemetery (2) NH-1
Lovering Colony State Hosp—hospital MA-1
Lovering Hill—summit NH-1
Lovering Mtn—summit NH-1
Loverix Park—park MI-6
Lover Meadow—flat NH-1
Lovern—locale WV-2
**Lovernlund**—pop pl VI-3
Love Rock—summit MT-8
Lovers, The—pillar UT-8
Lovers Bluff—cliff WA-9
Lovers Brook—stream ME-1
Lovers Camp—locale CA-9
Lovers Cove—bay AK-9
Lovers Cove—bay NV-8
Lovers Cove—bay WA-9
Lovers Gap—gap VA-3
Lovers Glen Park—park IL-6
Lovers Gulch Creek—stream CA-9
Lovers Island—island CT-1
Lovers Island—island ME-1
Lovers Island—island MN-6
Lovers Key—island FL-3
Lovers Lake—lake MA-1
Lovers Lake—lake MN-6
Lovers Lane—trail WA-9
Lovers Lane Brook—stream CT-1
Lovers Lane Ch—church TX-5
Lover's Lane Hist Dist—hist pl MS-4
Lovers Leap—cliff (2) AL-4
Lovers Leap—cliff (3) CA-9
Lovers Leap—cliff (2) CO-8
Lovers Leap—cliff CT-1
Lovers Leap—cliff IN-6
Lovers Leap—cliff (3) KY-4
Lovers Leap—cliff MD-2
Lovers Leap—cliff MO-7
Lovers Leap—cliff NM-5
Lovers Leap—cliff NC-3
Lovers Leap—cliff TN-4
Lovers Leap—cliff (4) TX-5
Lovers Leap—cliff (4) VA-3
Lovers Leap—cliff WV-2
Lovers Leap—cliff WY-8
Lovers Leap—gap VA-3
Lovers Leap—locale AL-4
Lovers Leap—mine AZ-5
Lovers Leap—summit (2) CA-9
Lovers Leap—summit NE-7
Lovers Leap Bluff—cliff MO-7
Lover's Leap Bridge—hist pl CT-1
Lovers Leap Butte—summit NE-7
Lovers Leap Canyon—valley NM-5
Lovers Leap Ch—church TX-5
Loversleap Post Office (historical)—building TN-4
Lovers Leap Ridge—ridge NC-3
*Lovers Peak* NM-5
Lovers Point—cape CA-9
Lovers Point—cape MD-2
Lovers Resort—summit TX-5
Lovers Retreat Brook—stream MA-1
Lovers Rock—island NY-2
Lovers Rock—rock MA-1
Lovers Rock—summit PA-2
Lovers Rock—summit TX-5
Love Rsvr—reservoir MT-8
Love Rsvr—reservoir (2) OR-9
Love Run—stream MD-2
Love Run—stream OH-6
Love Run—stream (2) PA-2
Love Run Trail—trail PA-2
*Loves* MS-4
Loves—locale MD-2
Loves Branch—stream KY-4
Loves Branch—stream (2) TN-4
Loves Branch—stream TX-5
Loves Bridge—bridge GA-3
*Loves Brook* ME-1
Loves Camp—locale AZ-5
Loves Cem—cemetery KY-4
Loves Ch—church TN-4
Love Sch—school FL-3
Love Sch—school MS-4
Love Sch—school MO-7
Love Sch—school NY-2
Love Sch—school PA-2
Love Sch—school TN-4
Love Sch—school TX-5
Love Sch (abandoned)—school MO-7
Loves Chapel—church KY-4
Loves Chapel—church NC-3
Loves Chapel—church SC-3
Love Sch (historical)—school (2) MS-4
**Loves Corner**—pop pl IL-6
*Loves Creek* TN-4
Loves Creek—stream MS-4
Loves Creek—stream NC-3
Loves Creek—stream SC-3
Loves Creek Ch—church NC-3
Loves Falls—falls CA-9
*Loves Ferry* TN-4
Loves Ferry (historical)—crossing TN-4
Loves Ferry (historical)—locale TN-4
Loves Grove Ch—church (2) NC-3
Loves Hollow—valley PA-2
Loves Knob—summit KY-4
Loves Lake—lake MN-6
Loves Lake—reservoir NC-3
Loves Lookout Park—park TX-5
Loves Mill—locale (2) VA-3
Loves Mill (historical)—locale TN-4
Loves Mine—mine AZ-5
**Loves Park**—pop pl IL-6
Loves Park Schools—school IL-6
Loves Pond Dam—dam NC-3
Loves Pond Dam—reservoir NC-3
Love Spring—spring (2) TN-4
Love Spring—spring WY-8
Love Spring Ch—church SC-3
Loves Run—stream OH-6
Loves Run—stream VA-3
*Loves Shop* VA-3
Loves Shop—locale VA-3
*Loves Station* MS-4
*Loves Store* IL-6
**Love Station**—pop pl OR-9
**Love Station**—pop pl TN-4
Love Station Post Office (historical)—building MS-4
Love Street Sch—school FL-3
**Love Subdivision**—pop pl MS-4
Loves Valley—basin OK-5
Loves Valley—valley PA-2
Lovetown—locale TN-4
**Love (Township of)**—pop pl IL-6
Lovets Pond—lake IL-6
Lovets Shoal—bar TN-4
*Lovett* PA-2
Lovett—locale FL-3
Lovett—locale NM-5
**Lovett**—pop pl GA-3
**Lovett**—pop pl IN-6
Lovett Branch—stream GA-3
Lovett Bridge—bridge GA-3
Lovett Brook—stream MA-1
Lovett Cem—cemetery IL-6
Lovett Cem—cemetery LA-4
Lovett Cem—cemetery NC-3
Lovett Cem—cemetery (3) TN-4
Lovett Cem—cemetery TX-5
*Lovett Cemetery Number One* MS-4
Lovett Ch—church GA-3
Lovett Chapel—church WV-2
*Lovett Creek* AL-4
Lovette Branch—stream KY-4
Lovette Cem—cemetery MS-4
*Lovett Elementary School* MS-4
Lovett Hill Ch—church GA-3
Lovett Island—island MO-7
Lovett Island—island NC-3
Lovett Island—island TN-4
Lovett Lookout Tower—tower FL-3
Lovett Memorial Library—building PA-2
*Lovett Mine* AL-4
Lovett Point—cape VA-3
Lovett (RR name for Sidman)—other PA-2
Lovetts Branch—stream TN-4
Lovett's by Lafayette Brook—hist pl NH-1
Lovetts Cem—cemetery GA-3
Lovett Sch—school IL-6
Lovett Sch—school MS-4
Lovett Sch—school TX-5
Lovett Sch (historical)—school PA-2
*Lovetts Creek* MT-8
Lovetts Creek—stream AL-4
Lovett Site—hist pl NE-7
Lovetts Marsh—swamp VA-3
*Lovetts Point* VA-3
**Lovettsville**—pop pl VA-3
Lovettsville Union Cem—cemetery VA-3
Lovett Tank—reservoir NM-5
**Lovett (Township of)**—pop pl IN-6
**Lovettville**—pop pl AL-4
Love Valley—basin CA-9
**Love Valley**—pop pl NC-3
Love Valley—valley NC-3
Love Valley Ch—church NC-3
Love View Ch—church TX-5
*Loveville* TN-4
Loveville—locale DE-2
Loveville—locale MD-2
**Lovewell**—pop pl KS-7
Lovewell Ch—church MS-4
Lovewell Dam—dam KS-7
Lovewell Island—island ME-1
Lovewell Mtn—summit NH-1
Lovewell Pond—lake ME-1
Lovewell Pond—lake NH-1
Lovewell Pond—reservoir MA-1
Lovewell Pond Dam—dam MA-1
*Lovewell Reservoir* MA-1
Lovewell Rsvr—reservoir KS-7
*Lovewell's Pond* ME-1
Lovewell State Park—park KS-7
*Lovewell Station* KS-7
Lovewell Wildlife Area—park KS-7
Love-Wilburn Cem—cemetery AL-4
Love Windmill—locale NM-5
Love Windmill—locale TX-5
**Lovewood**—pop pl FL-3
Lovewood Ch—church FL-3
Lovewood Sch—school FL-3
*Loveyland Creek* NH-1
*Lovfall* WA-9
Lovi—locale PA-2
**Lovick**—pop pl AL-4
Lovick Sch—school LA-4
**Lovie (historical)**—pop pl TN-4
Lovie Mine—mine NV-8
Lovie Post Office (historical)—building TN-4
**Lovilia**—pop pl IA-7
**Lovill**—pop pl NC-3
Lovilla—locale IL-6
Lovills Creek—stream NC-3
Lovills Creek—stream VA-3
Lovills Creek Ch—church NC-3
Lovin and Withers Cottages—hist pl AZ-5
Lovin Branch—stream NC-3
Lovin Entry Branch—stream NC-3
Loving—locale GA-3
Loving—locale KY-4
Loving—locale OK-5
**Loving**—pop pl NM-5
**Loving**—pop pl NC-3
**Loving**—pop pl TX-5
Loving Branch—stream IL-6
Loving Branch—stream NC-3
Loving Branch—stream TX-5
Loving Care Cem—cemetery FL-3
Loving Care Nursery Sch And Kindergarten, Incorporated—school DE-2
Loving (CCD)—cens area NM-5
Loving Cem—cemetery OK-5
Loving Cem—cemetery TX-5
Loving Cem—cemetery VA-3
Loving Ch—church MO-7
Loving Chapel—church KY-4
**Loving (County)**—pop pl TX-5
*Loving Creek* NC-3
*Loving Creek* VA-3
Loving Creek—stream AR-4
Loving Creek—stream LA-4
Loving Creek—stream OK-5
Loving Creek—stream TX-5
Loving Fork—locale VA-3
Lovinggood Creek—stream GA-3
Loving Missionary Baptist Ch—church IN-6
Lovingood Cem—cemetery GA-3
*Lovingood Spring* TN-4
Loving Place (abandoned)—locale NM-5
Loving Ridge—ridge MO-7
Lovings Bogs—swamp MA-1
Loving Sch—school GA-3
Loving Spring Ch—church KY-4
**Lovingston**—pop pl VA-3
Lovingston (Magisterial District)—fmr MCD VA-3
Lovingston Sch—school VA-3
Loving Tank—reservoir NM-5
**Lovington**—pop pl IL-6
**Lovington**—pop pl IA-7
**Lovington**—pop pl NM-5
Lovington (CCD)—cens area NM-5
Lovington Cem—cemetery NM-5
Lovington Ch—church VA-3
Lovington Country Club—other NM-5
**Lovington (Township of)**—pop pl IL-6
Loving Union Ch—church VA-3
Lovingwood Spring—spring TN-4
Lovins Branch—stream KY-4
Lovin & Withers Investment House—hist pl AZ-5
Lovis Shore—island NC-3
Lovitt Hollow—valley KY-4
Lovlett Corral—locale OR-9
Lovlett Creek—stream OR-9
*Lovley Glen Reseort* CA-9
Lovon Windmill—locale TX-5
*Lovorn Town* MS-4
Lovvorn, Dr. James L., House—hist pl GA-3
Lovvorn Creek—stream GA-3
Lovvorn Sch—school KY-4
Low—bay FM-9
Low—locale UT-8
**Low**—pop pl KY-4
Low, Joseph W., House—hist pl ME-1
Low, Juliette Gordon, Birthplace—hist pl GA-3
Low, Loch—lake FL-3
Low, Morris, Bungalow—hist pl ID-8
Lowa Hill—summit OR-9
Lowa Hill School—locale OR-9
**Lowake**—pop pl TX-5
*Low And Burbank Grant* NH-1
Low And Burbanks Grant—civil NH-1
Lowary Lake—lake MT-8
Low Ash Hollow—valley KY-4
Lowa Slough—stream OR-9
Low Aziscohos Mtn—summit ME-1
Low Bay—bay FL-3
Low Beach—beach MA-1
**Lowber**—pop pl (2) PA-2

Lower Centennial Spring—spring CA-9
Lower Center Point Canal—canal ID-8
Lower Chadwick Creek—stream KY-4
Lower Chain Lake—lake ME-1
Lower Chain Lake—lake UT-8
Lower Chain Lake—reservoir UT-8
Lower Chain Lake Dam—dam UT-8
Lower Chamberino Lateral—canal NM-5
Lower Champaign Spring—spring AZ-5
**Lower Chanceford (Township of)**—pop pl PA-2
Lower Chandler Pond—lake MA-1
Lower Chandler Pond—reservoir MA-1
Lower Chandler Pond Dam—dam MA-1
Lower Chapman Dam—dam OR-9
Lower Chapman Rsvr—reservoir OR-9
Lower Charlebois Ditch—canal NV-8
Lower Charleston Canal—canal UT-8
Lower Charauqua Mine—mine CO-8
**Lower Chateaugay Lake**—pop pl NY-2
Lower Chateaugay Lake—reservoir NY-2
Lower Chatham Bridge—bridge NJ-2
Lower Checats Lake—lake AK-9
Lower Cherry Aqueduct—canal CA-9
Lower Cherum Spring—spring AZ-5
Lower Chestnut Flats—flat TN-4
Lower Chewaucan Marsh—swamp OR-9
Lower Chichester Township—CDP PA-2
**Lower Chichester (Township of)**—pop pl PA-2
Lower Chicken Cock Bar—bar AL-4
Lower Chicosa Rsvr—reservoir CO-8
Lower Chilhowee Cem—cemetery TN-4
Lower Chilhowee Ch—church TN-4
Lower Chilson Sch—school NY-2
Lower Chimney Ditch—canal UT-8
Lower Chimney Spring—spring NV-8
Lower China Windmills—locale TX-5
Lower Chipoak Creek VA-3
Lower Chippoak's creek VA-3
Lower Chippokes Creek—stream VA-3
Lower Chiquito Campground—locale CA-9
Lower Chloe Creek—other KY-4
Lower Chloe Creek—stream KY-4
Lower Christiana (CCD)—cens area DE-2
Lower Chub Lake—lake MI-6
Lower Chub Landing—locale MI-6
Lower Church—hist pl VA-3
Lower Church Hill—summit CT-1
Lower Church Lake—reservoir CO-8
Lower Cienega Creek AZ-5
**Lower Cincinnatus**—pop pl NY-2
Lower Circle Lake—lake LA-4
Lower City—locale CT-1
Lower City Cem—cemetery CT-1
Lower City Island—island TN-4
Lower Claar Ch—church PA-2
Lower Clam Lake—lake (2) WI-6
Lower Clapboard Island Ledge—bar ME-1
Lower Clark Rsvr—reservoir OR-9
Lower Clay Landing—locale FL-3
Lower Clay Spring—spring UT-8
Lower Clear Creek Canal—canal CO-8
Lower Clear Creek Ch—church KY-4
Lower Clear Creek Sch—school KY-4
Lower Clear Lake—lake LA-4
Lower Clear Lake—lake WI-6
Lower Cliff Lake—lake CA-9
Lower Clifty Creek—stream KY-4
Lower Clover Ranch—locale NV-8
Lower Club Lake—reservoir TX-5
Lower Coal Creek Rsvr—reservoir MT-8
Lower Coalfield Mine—mine AZ-5
Lower Coalport Ch—church KY-4
Lower Coalson Spring—spring AZ-5
Lower Coastal Plains Experimental Farm—other AL-4
Lower Cochran Rapids—rapids OR-9
Lower Coffee Pot Campground—locale ID-8
Lower Coffee Pot Lake WA-9
Lower Cogdill Lake—reservoir CO-8
Lower Cold Lake—lake MT-8
Lower Cold Spring—spring NM-5
Lower Cole Camp Spring—spring NV-8
**Lower Colonias**—pop pl NM-5
Lower Colorado River Authority Park—park TX-5
Lower Columbia Junior Coll—school WA-9
Lower Commerce Street Hist Dist—hist pl AL-4
Lower Commerce Street Hist Dist (Boundary Increase)—hist pl AL-4
Lower Comstock Lake—lake MN-6
Lower Concord Sch—school KY-4
Lower Coombs Island—island ME-1
Lower Coon Creek Sch—school WV-2
Lower Coon Mtn—summit CA-9
Lower Coon Valley Ch—church WI-6
Lower Copper Lake—lake AK-9
Lower Corner Cem—cemetery MA-1
Lower Corner Hist Dist—hist pl NH-1
Lower Corners NH-1
**Lower Corners**—pop pl NY-2
Lower Cornwall Well—well AZ-5
Lower Corral—locale AZ-5
Lower Corral—locale NV-8
Lower Corral—other NM-5
Lower Corral Canyon—valley AZ-5
Lower Corral Creek Spring—spring ID-8
Lower Corral Draw—valley AZ-5
Lower Corral Tank—reservoir AZ-5
Lower Corral Tank Number Two—reservoir AZ-5
Lower Corral Tanks—reservoir (2) AZ-5
Lower Cottonwood Rsvr—reservoir CO-8
Lower Cottonwood Spring—spring AZ-5
Lower Cottonwood Spring—spring (2) NV-8
Lower Cottonwood Tank—reservoir AZ-5
Lower Cottonwood Troughs—locale UT-8
Lower Cougar Camp—locale OR-9
Lower Courthouse Spring—spring UT-8
Lower Cove—basin NV-8
Lower Cove Run—stream WV-2
Lower Covington Flat—flat CA-9
Lower Cowcamp Spring—spring NV-8
Lower Cow Chip Spring—spring CA-9
Lower Cow Creek Lake OR-9
Lower Cow Lake—reservoir OR-9
Lower Cowlitz School—locale WA-9
Lower Cow Rsvr—reservoir OR-9
Lower Cox Brook Covered Bridge—hist pl VT-1
Lower Coyote Creek ND-7
Lower Coyote Rsvr—reservoir NV-8
Lower Coyote Spring—spring NV-8
Lower Coyote Spring—spring UT-8
Lower Coyote Well—well NM-5
Lower Coytee Shoals—bar TN-4
Lower CP Tank—reservoir AZ-5
Lower Crab Creek—stream AL-4
Lower Crab Creek—stream WA-9
Lower Cramer Lake—lake ID-8
Lower Cranberry Lake—lake ME-1
Lower Crandon Lake—reservoir NJ-2
Lower Crane Sch—school KY-4
Lower Crawford Creek—stream UT-8
Lower Cream Ridge—ridge ID-8
Lower Creek—stream (3) NC-3
Lower Creek—stream (2) WV-2
Lower Creek Airp—airport NC-3
Lower Creek Ch—church WV-2
Lower Creek Sch—school NC-3
Lower Creek (Township of)—fmr MCD (2) NC-3
Lower Crooked Lake—lake AR-4
Lower Crooked Shoal Branch—stream KY-4
Lower Crosno Ch (historical)—church MO-7
Lower Crosno Sch (historical)—school MO-7
Lower Crossing—reservoir AZ-5
Lower Crossing (Site)—locale CA-9
Lower Croton Windmill—locale TX-5
Lower Crow Rsvr—reservoir MT-8
Lower Crystal Lake—lake CO-8
Lower Crystal Lake—lake WA-9
Lower Crystal School (Abandoned)—locale ID-8
Lower Crystal Spring—spring ID-8
Lower Crystal Springs Rsvr—reservoir CA-9
Lower Cullen Lake—lake MN-6
Lower Cummings Cem—cemetery IN-6
Lower Cummings Rsvr—reservoir CA-9
Lower Cupsuptic (Township of)—unorg ME-1
Lower Curia Lake—lake AR-4
Lower Curry Cem—cemetery WV-2
Lower Curry Ch—church KY-4
Lower Curtis Glacier—glacier WA-9
Lower Cutoff—channel AL-4
Lower Cutoff—channel IL-6
Lower Cutoff Creek AR-4
Lower Cutoff Creek—stream AR-4
Lower Cynth Gap—gap GA-3
Lower Cypress Spring—spring AZ-5
Lower Cyrus Spring—spring OR-9
Lower Dallas Lateral—canal CA-9
Lower Dam PA-2
Lower Dam—dam AZ-5
Lower Dam—dam AR-4
Lower Dam—dam ME-1
Lower Dam—dam (3) PA-2
Lower Dam—dam WA-9
Lower Dam—reservoir PA-2
Lower Dam Sambo Creek—dam PA-2
Lower Dauphin HS—school PA-2
Lower Dauphin Senior HS PA-2
Lower Dauphin Street Hist Dist—hist pl AL-4
Lower Dauphin Street Hist Dist (Boundary Increase)—hist pl AL-4
Lower Davis Flat—swamp OR-9
Lower Deacon Flat Rsvr—reservoir OR-9
Lower Dead Cow Spring—spring AZ-5
Lower Deadman Spring—spring (2) NV-8
Lower Deadman Tank—reservoir AZ-5
Lower Dead Ox Flat—flat OR-9
Lower Dead River—stream MS-4
Lower Deadwater—lake (5) ME-1
Lower Deadwater—swamp ME-1
Lower Deadwater Creek—stream NC-3
Lower Deadwater Pond—lake (2) ME-1
Lower Deadwood Guard Station—locale ID-8
Lower Death Valley—basin UT-8
Lower Debris Basin—basin UT-8
Lower Decatur Bend—bend NE-7
Lower Decature Bend—bend IA-7
Lower Deep Bay—bay NY-2
Lower Deep Creek—gut NJ-2
Lower Deep Creek Rsvr—reservoir ID-8
Lower Deep Creek Spring—spring MT-8
Lower Deer Creek—stream MT-8
Lower Deer Creek—stream NM-5
Lower Deer Creek Canyon—valley WY-8
Lower Deer Creek Cem—cemetery IA-7
Lower Deer Creek Ch—church IN-6
Lower Deer Creek Ch—church IA-7
Lower Deer Creek - in part MS-4
Lower Deer Creek Spring—spring NV-8
Lower Deer Creek Well—well MT-8
Lower Deer Flat—flat ID-8
Lower Delaney Pond—reservoir MA-1
Lower Delaney Pond Dam—dam MA-1
Lower Delaney Tank—reservoir AZ-5
Lower Dells—valley WI-6
Lower Demlow Lake—lake WI-6
Lower Dempsey Branch—stream (2) WV-2
**Lower Dennysville**—pop pl ME-1
Lower Desdemona Shoal Channel—channel OR-9
Lower Desert—plain OR-9
Lower Desert Tank—reservoir CO-8
Lower Des Lacs Lake—reservoir ND-7
Lower Desolation Lake—lake CA-9
Lower Deus Lake—lake CO-8
Lower Devil Creek—stream KY-4
Lower Devils Lake—lake WI-6
Lower Devils Peak—summit CA-9
Lower Devils Swamp—swamp MS-4
Lower Dewey Lake—lake AK-9
Lower DeZarn Hollow—valley KY-4
Lower Diagonal Drain—canal NV-8
Lower Dianne Lake—lake FL-3
Lower Diehl Lake—lake OH-6
Lower Diggings—summit VT-1
Lower Dill Branch—stream KY-4
Lower Dillman Tank—reservoir AZ-5
Lower Disaster Falls—falls CO-8
Lower Ditch—canal CA-9
Lower Ditch—canal MT-8
Lower Ditch—canal OR-9
Lower Ditch—canal WY-8
Lower Division AZ-5
Lower Division NV-8
Lower Doame Lake—lake AK-9
Lower Doane Valley—valley CA-9
Lower Doe Lake—lake FL-3
Lower Doe Run Ch—church MO-7
Lower Dog Bluff—cliff SC-3
Lower Dog Tank—reservoir NM-5
Lower Domenichi Creek CA-9
Lower Dominici Creek—stream CA-9
Lower Donaldson PA-2
Lower Donkey Dam—dam UT-8
Lower Donkey Reservoir UT-8
Lower Donkey Rsvr—reservoir UT-8
Lower Donnally Branch—stream WV-2
Lower Double Branch—stream (3) KY-4
Lower Double Branch—stream NC-3
Lower Dougherty Spring—spring AZ-5
Lower Dowery Creek NC-3
Lower Dowery Point NC-3
Lower Dowry Creek—stream NC-3
Lower Dowry Point NC-3
Lower Dowry Point—cape NC-3
Lower Doyle Creek Campground—locale WY-8
Lower Doyle Windmill—locale CO-8
Lower Drain—canal TX-5
Lower Dry Bread Pond—lake UT-8
Lower Dry Hollow—valley PA-2
Lower Dry Lake—lake CA-9
Lower Dry Pasture Tank—reservoir AZ-5
Lower Dry Run—stream WV-2
Lower Dry Susie Spring—spring NV-8
Lower Duck Creek—stream NC-3
Lower Duck Hole—bay NY-2
Lower Duck Pond—lake AL-4
Lower Dugan Bluff—cliff MO-7
Lower Dug Bar Rapids—rapids ID-8
Lower Dug Bar Rapids—rapids OR-9
Lower Dugnut Creek NE-7
Lower Dugout Creek—stream NE-7
Lower Dugout Creek Rsvr—reservoir OR-9
Lower Dugout Spring—spring SD-7
Lower Dugout Spring—spring UT-8
Lower Dugway—gap WY-8
Lower Duhme Spring—spring CO-8
Lower Dunnville Bottoms—bend WI-6
Lower Dutch Creek—stream KS-7
Lower Dutch Creek Sch—school WI-6
Lower Dutch Tank—reservoir NM-5
**Lower Dutchtown**—pop pl PA-2
Lower Eagle Creek LA-4
Lower Eagle Creek—stream LA-4
Lower Eagle Nest Lake—gut AR-4
Lower Eagle Nest Lake—lake AR-4
Lower East Bend Bottom—bend KY-4
Lower East Fork Lateral Site Number Eleven—reservoir TX-5
Lower East Fork Lateral Site Number Five—reservoir TX-5
Lower East Fork Lateral Site Number One—reservoir TX-5
Lower East Fork Ranger Cabin No. 9—hist pl AK-9
Lower East Jewett Ch—church NY-2
Lower East Lateral—canal OR-9
Lower East Ragged Pond—lake ME-1
Lower East Tank—reservoir NM-5
Lower Eau Claire Lake—lake WI-6
Lower Ebbs Spring—spring UT-8
Lower Ebeemee Pond—lake ME-1
Lower Echo Lake—lake CA-9
Lower Eddeeleo Lake—lake OR-9
Lower Eddy—bay PA-2
Lower Egg Island MA-1
Lower Egg Lake—lake MN-6
Lower Egypt Landing (historical)—locale MS-4
Lower Eighteenmile Lake—lake MI-6
Lower Eighth Coulee—valley MT-8
Lower Eightmile Campground—park OR-9
Lower Eightmile Sch—school OR-9
Lower Elbow Pond—lake ME-1
Lower Elk Creek—locale VA-3
Lower Elk Creek—stream KY-4
Lower Elk Creek—stream VA-3
Lower Elk Hollow—valley WV-2
Lower Elk Lake—lake MN-6
Lower Elk Meadows—flat OR-9
Lower Elk River Sch (historical)—school TN-4
Lower Elk Sch—school KY-4
**Lower Elkton (historical)**—pop pl TN-4
Lower Elk Valley—basin NE-7
Lower Elk Well—locale NM-5
Lower Ella Lake—lake AK-9
Lower Elliot Lake—lake MT-8
Lower Ellis Place—locale MT-8
Lower Ellis Pond—lake ME-1
Lower Elm Creek—stream TX-5
Lower Elwah Ind Res—reserve WA-9
Lower Elwha—locale WA-9
**Lower Elwha Ind Res**—pop pl WA-9
Lower Embankment Drain—canal ID-8
Lower Emerald Lake—reservoir CA-9
Lower Empire Lake—lake OR-9
Lower Empire Lake—reservoir OR-9
Lower Empire Lake Dam—dam OR-9
Lower Enchanted Pond—lake ME-1
Lower Enchanted (Township of)—unorg ME-1
Lower End Camp—locale OR-9
Lower End Windmill—locale NM-5
Lower Engineers Camp—locale AK-9
Lower Enterprise Dam—dam UT-8
Lower Enterprise Rsvr—reservoir UT-8
Lower Erma Bell Lake—lake OR-9
Lower Evans Lake—lake MI-6
**Lower Exeter**—pop pl VA-3
Lower Factory (historical)—locale AL-4
Lower Fairforest Ch—church SC-3
Lower Fairmount—locale NJ-2
Lower Fairview Sch—school ID-8
Lower Fairview Spring—spring NV-8
Lower Fall Branch—stream TN-4
Lower Falling Branch—stream TN-4
Lower Falls ID-8
Lower Falls OR-9
Lower Falls UT-8
Lower Falls—falls AK-9
Lower Falls—falls CA-9
Lower Falls—falls ME-1
Lower Falls—falls (2) MI-6
Lower Falls—falls NH-1
Lower Falls—falls (2) NY-2
Lower Falls—falls NC-3
Lower Falls—falls SC-3
Lower Falls—falls TN-4
Lower Falls—falls WA-9
Lower Falls—falls WV-2
**Lower Falls**—pop pl WV-2
Lower Falls Creek Lake—lake MT-8
Lower Falls Little Minam River—falls OR-9
Lower Falls Mine (underground)—mine TN-4
Lower Falls of the Yellowstone River—falls WY-8
Lower Fandango—ridge NV-8
Lower Fandango Spring—spring NV-8
Lower Farmers Valley Sch—school WI-6
Lower Farm Hill Creek—stream MI-6
Lower Feltonville—uninc pl PA-2
Lower Fencepost Tank—reservoir TX-5
Lower Ferguson Spring—spring KY-4
Lower Fiddler Green Canal—canal CA-9
Lower Field Branch—stream (2) KY-4
Lowerfield Hollow—valley KY-4
Lower Firebox Tank—reservoir AZ-5
Lower Fire Lake—lake AK-9
Lower First Creek Spring—spring OR-9
Lower First Lake—lake WI-6
Lower First Saint John Pond—lake ME-1
Lower Fisher Lake—lake AL-4
Lower Fisher Lake—lake WA-9
Lower Fisher Long Ditch—canal OR-9
Lower Fishhole—swamp OR-9
Lower Fishhook Canyon—valley AZ-5
Lower Fishhook Tank Number One—reservoir AZ-5
Lower Fishhook Tank Number Two—reservoir AZ-5
Lower Fish Lake—lake AK-9
Lower Fish Lake—lake IN-6
Lower Fish Valley—valley CA-9
Lower Fivemile Creek—stream WV-2
Lower Fivemile Drain—canal ID-8
Lower Fivemile Sch—school OR-9
Lower Flag Pond—lake TX-5
Lower Flat—lake LA-4
Lower Flat Branch—stream MS-4
Lower Flat Creek Public Access—locale MO-7
Lower Flat Creek Sch—school KY-4
Lower Flat Lake—lake IL-6
Lower Flat Pond—lake IL-6
Lower Flat Seep—spring UT-8
Lower Flat Spring—spring ID-8
Lower Flat Spring—spring UT-8
Lower Flattop Hill—summit TX-5
Lower Flatwoods Run—stream WV-2
Lower Florence Lake—lake WA-9
Lower Flying E Ditch—canal WY-8
Lower Ford Lake—lake SC-3
**Lower Forge**—pop pl NJ-2
Lower Fork—stream TN-4
Lower Fork Cool Spring Branch KY-4
Lower Fork Cool Spring Branch—stream KY-4
Lower Forked Deer Landing—locale TN-4
Lower Forked Deer River—stream TN-4
Lower Forked Lake—lake AR-4
Lower Fork (Township of)—fmr MCD NC-3
Lower Fork Twelvemile Creek—stream AK-9
Lower Fork Whitaker Creek—stream AR-4
Lower Forni—locale CA-9
Lower Fort Creek Rsvr—reservoir OR-9
Lower Foster Island—island CA-9
Lower Four Lane Cave—cave AL-4
Lower Four Mile Creek WY-8
Lower Fourmile Draw—valley TX-5
Lower Fourmile Spring—reservoir WY-8
Lower Four Tank—reservoir AZ-5
Lower Fourth of July Spring—spring AZ-5
Lower Fowler—uninc pl WI-6
Lower Fowler Pond—lake ME-1
Lower Fox Creek Sch—hist pl KS-7
Lower Fox Lake—lake WA-9
Lower Foxtown Sch—school KY-4
Lower Foy Lake—lake MT-8
Lower Francis Pond—reservoir NY-2
**Lower Frankford (Township of)**—pop pl PA-2
**Lower Frederick (Township of)**—pop pl PA-2
Lower Fremont Glacier—glacier WY-8
Lower French Broad Baptist Church TN-4
Lower French Gulch Windmill—locale AZ-5
Lower Frenchman Hollow—valley MO-7
Lower Frenchman Spring—spring NV-8
Lower French Valley—valley CA-9
Lower Frijoles Falls—falls NM-5
Lower Frijole Tank—reservoir NM-5
Lower Frio Canyon Tank—reservoir AZ-5
Lower Frozen Lake—lake WY-8
Lower Fulton Park Pond—lake CT-1
Lower Galice Riffle—rapids OR-9
Lower Gangway Ledge—bar ME-1
Lower Gap—gap SC-3
Lower Gap—gap VA-3
Lower Gap—gap WV-2
Lower Gap Branch WV-2
Lower Gap Branch—stream (2) KY-4
Lower Gap Creek OR-9
Lower Gap Creek—stream OR-9
Lower Garden District—hist pl LA-4
Lower Gardner Meadow—flat CA-9
Lower Garfield Mountain Lake—lake WA-9
Lower Gar Lake—lake IA-7
Lower Gar Lake State Game Mngmt Area—park IA-7
Lower Gato Tank—reservoir TX-5
Lower Gause Bar—bar AL-4
Lower Genegantslet Cem—cemetery NY-2
**Lower Genegantslet Corner**—pop pl NY-2
Lower Genesee Lake—lake WI-6
Lower Genesee Street Hist Dist—hist pl NY-2
Lower George, Lake—lake AK-9
Lower George Lake—lake MN-6
Lower Georges Branch WV-2
Lower Geyser Basin—basin WY-8
Lower Gilead Sch—school IL-6
Lower Gillis Windmill—locale TX-5
Lower Gillmore—locale KY-4
Lower Gills Rock—summit NH-1
**Lower Gilmanton**—pop pl NH-1
Lower Girdner Sch (historical)—school MO-7
Lower Glacier Lake WA-9
Lower Glade Camp—locale CA-9
Lower Glade Cem—cemetery OH-6
Lower Glade Rsvr—reservoir CO-8
Lower Glaston Lake—lake MT-8
Lower Glendora Cut-Off—bend MS-4
Lower Glenn Mine—mine CA-9
Lower Glen Reservoir Dam—dam MA-1
Lower Glidden Lake—lake ID-8
Lower Goat Camp—locale AZ-5
Lower Goat Canyon Tank—reservoir NM-5
Lower Goat Tank—reservoir TX-5
Lower Goldwater Dam—dam AZ-5
Lower Goldwater Lake—reservoir AZ-5
Lower Golf Lateral—canal CA-9
Lower Gooch Valley—valley CA-9
Lower Gooseberry Reservoir Dam—dam UT-8
Lower Gooseberry Rsvr—reservoir UT-8
Lower Gooseberry Spring—spring MT-8
Lower Goose Creek Rsvr—reservoir ID-8
Lower Goose Island—island ME-1
Lower Goose Lake—lake WA-9
Lower Goose Lake—reservoir ID-8
Lower Goose Lake—reservoir TX-5
Lower Goose Pen Pool—reservoir MI-6
Lower Goose Pond MA-1
Lower Goose Pond—lake NY-2
Lower Gorge—valley OR-9
Lower Goshen Reservoir MA-1
Lower Gospel Lake—lake ID-8
Lower Granard Archeol District—hist pl VI-3
Lower Grand Bayou—gut LA-4
Lower Grand Coulee—valley WA-9
Lower Grand Gulf Landing—locale MS-4
Lower Grand Lagoon—CDP FL-3
Lower Grand River—stream LA-4
Lower Grand Trunk Rsvr—reservoir NV-8
Lower Grand Wash Cliffs AZ-5
Lower Grand Wash Ledge AZ-5
Lower Granite Dam Heliport—airport WA-9
Lower Granite Gorge AZ-5
Lower Granite Gorge—valley AZ-5
Lower Granite Lake—lake ID-8
Lower Granite Lake—lake WA-9
Lower Granite Lake—reservoir WA-9
Lower Granite Lake Dam—dam WA-9
Lower Granite Reservoir ID-8
Lower Granite Reservoir WA-9
Lower Granite State Airp—airport WA-9
**Lower Granville**—pop pl VT-1
Lower Grapes Spring—spring CA-9
Lower Grapevine Campground—locale CA-9
Lower Grapevine Spring—spring AZ-5
Lower Grass Flat Tank—reservoir AZ-5
Lower Grassy Branch—stream NC-3
Lower Grassy Cem—cemetery MO-7
Lower Grassy Sch—school KY-4
Lower Grassy Sch (historical)—school TN-4
Lower Graysville WV-2
Lower Green MA-1
Lower Green Bottom Ch—church WV-2
Lower Greenbrier Sch—school VA-3
Lower Green Creek Cem—cemetery TX-5
Lower Green Hill AL-4
Lower Green Point Dam—dam OR-9
Lower Green Ridge Lake WA-9
Lower Greens Cove—bay MD-2
Lower Gresham Lake—lake WI-6
Lower Grey Cloud Island—island MN-6
Lower Grindstone Spring—spring WI-6
Lower Group—area UT-8
Lower Group Mines—mine CO-8
Lower Grouse Rsvr—reservoir UT-8
Lower Grove Community Ch—church IA-7
Lower Grover Sch—school SC-3
Lower Guess Fork Sch—school VA-3
Lower Guide Levee—levee LA-4
Lower Gulch—valley CO-8
Lower Gulf Run—stream WV-2
Lower Gut Ache Tank—reservoir NM-5
Lower Gwynedd Sch—school PA-2
**Lower Gwynedd (Township of)**—pop pl PA-2
Lower Hackberry Spring—spring AZ-5
Lower Hackberry Windmill—locale TX-5
Lower Hackett Creek Rsvr—reservoir WY-8
Lower Hackleburg Cemetery AL-4
Lower Hadlock Pond—lake ME-1
Lower Halfway Lake—lake AK-9
Lower Hall Landing—locale AL-4
Lower Halls Branch—stream KY-4
Lower Hamakua Ditch—canal HI-9
Lower Hannah Branch—stream KY-4
Lower Hanover Canal—canal WY-8
Lower Hanson Lake—lake MN-6
Lower Hanson Spring—spring MT-8
Lower Harbor—harbor NY-2
Lower Harbor Keys—island FL-3
Lower Harden Creek—stream ID-8
Lower Hardscrabble Spring—spring NM-5
**Lower Harmony**—pop pl NJ-2
Lower Harper Spring—spring AL-4
Lower Harrison Lake—lake NE-7
Lower Hatchie Natl Wildlife Ref—park TN-4
Lower Hathan Bog—swamp ME-1
Lower Hather Bog ME-1
Lower Hauer Spring—spring WI-6
Lower Haw Knob—summit NC-3
Lower Hay Lake—lake MN-6
Lower Hazen Drain—canal NV-8
Lower Head—cape ME-1
Lower Head Dam MS-4
Lower Heaton Creek Ch—church TN-4
Lower Heglar Spring—spring ID-8
**Lower Heidelberg (Township of)**—pop pl PA-2
Lower Hell Gate—channel ME-1
Lower Hellhole—valley CA-9
Lower Helton Sch (historical)—school TN-4
Lower Hembrillo Spring—spring NM-5
Lower Hemlock Dam—dam PA-2
Lower Hemlock Lake—reservoir PA-2
Lower Hemlock Rapids—rapids MI-6
Lower Henderson Brook—stream ME-1
Lower Hendrix Sch—school KY-4
Lower Hensley Creek—stream WV-2
Lower Hepsida Sch—school MO-7
Lower Hereford Manor Dam—dam PA-2
Lower Herlihy Rsvr—reservoir OR-9
Lower Hermana Lateral—canal CO-8
Lower Hernandez Windmill—locale TX-5
Lower Herring Bay—bay AK-9
Lower Herring Brook Pond MA-1
Lower Herring Cove—bay ME-1
Lower Herring Lake—lake MI-6
Lower Hidden Spring—spring AZ-5
Lower Hidden Spring—spring TX-5
Lower High Creek Canal—canal UT-8
**Lower Highland**—pop pl OR-9
Lower Highland Rsvr—reservoir MA-1
Lower Highlands Hist Dist—hist pl MA-1
Lower Hightower GA-3
Lower Hightower Ch—church GA-3
Lower Hill Valley Sch (abandoned)—school PA-2
Lower Hillville—other PA-2
**Lower Hillville**—pop pl PA-2
Lower Hilton Windmill—well AZ-5
Lower Hist Dist—hist pl MA-1
Lower Hiwanka Lake—lake WI-6
Lower H N Trough—reservoir AZ-5
Lower Hoffman Lake—lake CO-8
Lower Hog Branch—stream KY-4
Lower Hog Camp Spring—spring CA-9
Lower Hog Canyon Tank—reservoir AZ-5
Lower Hog Canyon Windmill—locale AZ-5
Lower Hog Pen—bend GA-3
Lower Hogpen Spring—spring ID-8
Lower Hog Point—cape AR-4
Lower Hog Ponds MA-1
Lower Hoh Fire Camp—locale WA-9
Lower Holding Tank—reservoir AZ-5
Lower Holdout—basin AZ-5
Lower Hole Canyon Tank—reservoir AZ-5
Lower Holleman Island (historical)—island TN-4
Lower Holliman Island TN-4
Lower Hollimans Island TN-4
Lower Hollow—valley KY-4
**Lower Holly Creek**—pop pl TN-4
Lower Holly Lake—lake WI-6
Lower Holmes Canal—canal ID-8
Lower Holmes Lake—lake (2) MI-6
Lower Homewood MD-2
Lower Hominy (Township of)—fmr MCD NC-3
Lower Honey Branch—stream WV-2
Lower Honeymoon Lake—lake CA-9
Lower Hood Branch—stream KY-4
Lower Hooper Island—island MD-2
Lower Hoopers Island MD-2
Lower Hoot Owl Tank—reservoir AZ-5
Lower Hope Butte Rsvr—reservoir OR-9
Lower Hopewell—locale PA-2
Lower Hopkins Lake—lake CA-9
Lower Horse Creek Sch—school WI-6
Lower Horse Creek Spring—spring NM-5
Lower Horse Draw CO-8
Lower Horse Flats—flat UT-8
Lower Horse Lake OR-9
Lower Horse Lake—lake OR-9
Lower Horse Meadow—flat CA-9
Lower Horse Mesa Tank Number Two—reservoir AZ-5
Lower Horse Race Rapids—rapids ME-1
Lower Horseshoe Bend—bend NM-5
Lower Horseshoe Lake AR-4
Lower Horseshoe Lake—lake AK-9
Lower Horsethief Lake—lake CA-9
Lower Hosston Oil Pool—oilfield MS-4
Lower Hot Brook Lake—lake ME-1
Lower Howard Camp—locale OR-9
Lower Howard Creek—stream KY-4
Lower Hubbard Basin—basin NV-8
Lower Hudson Meadow—flat WY-8
Lower Hudson Pond—lake ME-1
Lower Hull Spring—spring AZ-5
Lower Hult Rsvr—reservoir OR-9
Lower Humbert Bridge—hist pl PA-2
Lower Humboldt Drain—canal NV-8
Lower Hungry Valley—valley CA-9
Lower Hunt Lake—lake MN-6
Lower Hunts Lake—lake UT-8
Lower Huron Metropolitan Park—park MI-6
Lower Hurricane Creek Sch (historical)—school TN-4
Lower Hurricane Rsvr—reservoir VT-1
Lower Hurricane Sch—school KY-4
Lower Hurricane Sch—school WV-2
Lower Hurricane Sch (historical)—school TN-4
Lower Hurricane Valley—valley AZ-5
Lower Hutcherson Spring—spring AZ-5
Lower Icefall—falls AK-9
Lower Ice Lake Basin—basin CO-8
Lower Imnaha Falls OR-9
Lower Indian Creek Rsvr—reservoir MT-8
Lower Indian Lake—lake CA-9
Lower Indian Spring—spring AZ-5
Lower Indian Spring—spring (3) NV-8
Lower Indian Spring—spring UT-8
Lower Indian Springs—spring NV-8
Lower Indian Tank—reservoir NM-5
Lower Indian Well—locale NM-5
Lower Ingram Sch—school TN-4
Lower Iron Bridge—bridge AL-4
Lower Island SD-7
Lower Island—island (2) LA-4
Lower Island—island TX-5
Lower Island Creek SD-7
Lower Island Creek—stream KY-4
Lower Island Lake—lake OR-9
Lower Island Lake—lake WI-6
Lower Island Point—cape (2) MD-2
Lowe River—stream AK-9
Lower Jacks Branch—stream KY-4
Lower Jacks Creek Sch—school KY-4
Lower Jack Springs Camp—locale CO-8
Lower Jack Tank—reservoir AZ-5
Lower Jade Lake—lake WY-8
Lower Janita Lake—reservoir NC-3
Lower Janita Lake Dam—dam NC-3
Lower Japan Tunnel—mine CO-8
Lower Jarvis Range Channel—channel OR-9
Lower Jean Lake—lake WY-8
Lower Jefferson Ditch—canal MT-8
Lower Jeptha Lake—lake MI-6
Lower Jeptha Lake Drain—stream MI-6
Lower Jerry Lake—lake MS-4
Lower Jerry Run—stream PA-2
Lower Jerry Run Natural Area—area PA-2
Lower J H D Sheds—locale WY-8
Lower Jobe Patch Branch—stream TN-4
Lower Jocko Canal—canal MT-8
Lower Jocko J Canal—canal MT-8
Lower Jocko Lake—lake MT-8
Lower Joe Fork—stream KY-4
Lower Joe Green Cabin—locale CA-9
Lower Joes Valley—valley UT-8

Lower Johnson Creek—stream ... OR-9
Lower Johnson Lake ... WA-9
Lower Johnson Mine—mine ... TN-4
Lower John Well—well ... NM-5
Lower Jo-Mary Lake—lake ... ME-1
Lower Jo-Mary Stream—stream ... ME-1
Lower Jones Canyon Rsvr—reservoir ... OR-9
Lower Jones Fork—stream ... KY-4
Lower Jones Lake—lake ... WI-6
Lower Jones Tract—civil ... CA-9
Lower Jones Valley—basin ... NE-7
Lower Jones Windmill—locale ... TX-5
Lower Jordan Lake—lake ... WA-9
Lower Josie ... AL-4
Lower Juan Miller Campground—park ... AZ-5
Lower Jug Creek Rsvr—reservoir ... ID-8
Lower Jug Lake—lake ... WA-9
Lower Jumbo Mine—mine ... AZ-5
Lower Jump—falls ... UT-8
Lower Jump Springs—spring ... AZ-5
Lower Jumpup Spring—spring ... AZ-5
Lower Junction Dam—dam ... AZ-5
Lower Junction Tank—reservoir ... AZ-5
Lower Junction Tank Dam—dam ... AZ-5
Lower Juniper Spring—spring ... TX-5
Lower Kaibito ... AZ-5
Lower Kakeout Dam—dam ... NJ-2
Lower Kalama River Falls—falls ... WA-9
**Lower Kalskag**—pop pl ... AK-9
Lower Kaubashine Lake—lake ... WI-6
Lower Kawita ... AL-4
Lower Keechi Creek—stream ... TX-5
Lower Keene Broad—channel ... MD-2
Lower Keener Lick—stream ... WV-2
Lower Kelly Lake—lake ... WI-6
Lower Kents Lake—lake ... UT-8
Lower Kern Creek Spring—spring ... OR-9
Lower Kern Spring—spring ... OR-9
Lower Ketchikan Lake—lake ... AK-9
Lower Key Memorial Hosp—hospital ... FL-3
Lower Keys (CCD)—cens area ... FL-3
Lower Keys Ch of Christ—church ... FL-3
Lower Keystone Tank—reservoir ... AZ-5
Lower Kiger Island—island ... OR-9
Lower Kimball Lake ... ME-1
Lower Kimball Lake ... NH-1
Lower Kimball Lake—lake ... WI-6
Lower Kimball Pond—lake ... ME-1
Lower Kimball Pond—lake ... NH-1
Lower Kimball Seep—spring ... UT-8
Lower Kimberly—locale ... UT-8
Lower Kimberly Mine—mine ... UT-8
Lower King and Queen Ch—church ... VA-3
**Lower Kings Addition**—pop pl ... KY-4
Lower Kings Bridge—bridge ... GA-3
Lower Kings Creek Meadow—flat ... CA-9
Lower Kings Creek Sch—school ... KY-4
Lower Kings River Ditch—canal ... CA-9
Lower Kings Run Sch—school ... PA-2
Lower Kinney Lake—lake ... CA-9
Lower Kintla Lake ... MT-8
Lower Kirby Rapids—rapids ... ID-8
Lower Kirby Rapids—rapids ... OR-9
Lower Kirkland Valley—valley ... AZ-5
Lower Kitsap Peninsula ... WA-9
Lower Kittanning Dam—dam ... PA-2
Lower Klamath Lake—lake ... CA-9
Lower Klamath Lake—lake ... OR-9
Lower Klamath Lake Sump—lake ... CA-9
Lower Klamath Natl Wildlife Ref—park ... CA-9
Lower Klamath Natl Wildlife Refuge—hist pl ... CA-9
Lower Klamath Natl Wildlife Refuge—hist pl ... OR-9
Lower Klamath Natl Wildlife Refuge—reserve ... OR-9
Lower Klondike Dam—dam ... PA-2
Lower Klondike Mine ... AL-4
Lower Klondike Pond—reservoir ... PA-2
Lower Klutuk Creek—stream ... AK-9
Lower Knob Lake—lake ... ID-8
Lower Knolls—ridge ... AZ-5
Lower Kobuk Canyon—area ... AK-9
Lower Kohanza Lake—reservoir ... CT-1
Lower Kolob Plateau—plateau ... UT-8
Lower Kuskokwim (Census Subarea)—cens area ... AK-9
Lower La Cinta Windmill—locale ... NM-5
Lower Ladysmith Spring—spring ... WY-8
Lower La Garde Ditch—canal ... CO-8
Lower Lagoon ... CT-1
Lower Lagoon—lake ... CT-1
Lower Lagoon, The—bay ... AK-9
Lower Lagrange Landing (historical)—locale ... TN-4
Lower Laguna Tank—reservoir ... AZ-5
Lower lake ... AZ-5
Lower Lake ... MA-1
Lower Lake ... MS-4
Lower lake ... NV-8
Lower Lake ... WA-9
Lower Lake ... WI-6
Lower Lake—lake (2) ... CA-9
Lower Lake—lake ... GA-3
Lower Lake—lake ... IN-6
Lower Lake—lake (3) ... MI-6
Lower Lake—lake ... MN-6
Lower Lake—lake ... MS-4
Lower Lake—lake ... MT-8
Lower Lake—lake ... NV-8
Lower Lake—lake (2) ... NY-2
Lower Lake—lake ... PA-2
Lower Lake—lake (2) ... WI-6
**Lower Lake**—pop pl ... CA-9
Lower Lake—reservoir ... AL-4
Lower Lake—reservoir ... AZ-5
Lower Lake—reservoir ... NJ-2
Lower Lake—reservoir ... NY-2
Lower Lake—reservoir ... NC-3
Lower Lake—reservoir ... OR-9
Lower Lake—reservoir (3) ... PA-2
Lower Lake—reservoir ... TX-5
Lower Lake—reservoir ... UT-8
Lower Lake Beach—beach ... MS-4
Lower Lake Beach Public Use Area—park ... MS-4
Lower Lake (ck other entry)—lake ... NV-8
Lower Lake Dam ... AL-4
Lower Lake Dam—dam (2) ... PA-2
Lower Lake Hominy—reservoir ... OK-5
Lower Lake Long Pass—channel ... LA-4
Lower Lake Louise—lake ... FL-3
Lower Lake Mary—reservoir ... AZ-5
Lower Lake Mary Dam—dam ... AZ-5
Lower Lake-Middletown (CCD)—cens area ... CA-9
Lower Lake Nemahbin ... WI-6
Lower Lake Swamp—swamp ... FL-3
Lower Lake Traverse ... MN-6
Lower Lake Traverse ... SD-7
Lower La Manga Windmill—locale ... NM-5
Lower Lamarck Lake—lake ... CA-9
Lower Lambert Bar—bar ... OR-9
Lower Lamphier Lake—lake ... CO-8
Lower Land Creek—stream ... OR-9
Lower Landing—locale ... ME-1
Lower Langston Landing—locale ... FL-3
Lower LaPomkeag Lake—lake ... ME-1
**Lower Laposada**—pop pl ... NM-5
**Lower La Posada**—pop pl ... NM-5
Lower Larga Flat—flat ... CA-9
Lower Lasalle Lake ... MN-6
Lower Last Chance Spring—spring ... AZ-5
Lower Latenache Church—cemetery ... LA-4
Lower Lateral—canal ... MT-8
Lower Lateral Number Four—canal ... CA-9
Lower Lateral Number Three—canal ... CA-9
Lower Lateral Number Two—canal ... CA-9
Lower Lateral Number Two And One Half—canal ... CA-9
Lower Latham Drain—canal ... CO-8
Lower Latham Outlet—canal ... CO-8
Lower Latham Rsvr—reservoir ... CO-8
Lower Laurel Branch—stream (2) ... KY-4
Lower Laurel Creek—stream ... KY-4
Lower Laurel Creek Sch—school ... KY-4
Lower Laurel Fork—stream ... WV-2
Lower Laurel Fork Ch—church ... KY-4
Lower Laurel Run—stream ... WV-2
Lower Laurel Sch—school (2) ... KY-4
Lower Laurel Sch—school ... WV-2
Lower Lawrence Lake—lake ... MN-6
Lower Lead King Lake—lake ... WA-9
Lower Lead Mountain Pond—lake ... ME-1
Lower Leavry Pond—lake ... NM-5
Lower Lebanon Branch ... NJ-2
Lower Ledbetter Hollow—valley ... TN-4
Lower Ledge Spring—spring ... AZ-5
Lower Legion Lake—reservoir ... SC-3
Lower Leitner Pond—reservoir ... GA-3
Lower Lester Cem—cemetery ... IL-6
Lower Letts Valley—basin ... CA-9
Lower Lettsworth ... LA-4
Lower Level Run—stream ... WV-2
Lower Lewis Run—stream ... VA-3
Lower Liberty Sch (historical)—school ... PA-2
Lower Lick—stream ... OH-6
Lower Lick Branch—stream ... KY-4
Lower Lick Branch—stream ... WV-2
Lower Lick Fork—stream (2) ... KY-4
Lower Lick Tank—reservoir ... NM-5
Lower Lihue Ditch—canal ... HI-9
Lower Lillies Spring—spring ... NM-5
Lower Lime Mountain Well—well ... NV-8
Lower Limestone Creek—stream ... IN-6
Lower Limestone Tank—reservoir (2) ... AZ-5
Lower Limestone Valley Creek—stream ... CA-9
Lower Line Sch (historical)—school ... MS-4
Lower Lion Spring—spring ... CA-9
Lower Lisbon Street Hist Dist—hist pl ... ME-1
Lower Lisbon Valley—valley ... UT-8
Lower Little Creek—stream ... MS-4
Lower Little Fish Lake ... NV-8
Lower Little Park—flat ... AZ-5
Lower Little River ... NC-3
Lower Little River—stream ... NC-3
Lower Little River Dam Number One—dam ... NC-3
Lower Little River Dam Number Two—dam ... NC-3
Lower Little Swatara Creek—stream ... PA-2
Lower Little York Lake—lake ... NY-2
Lower Lobo Well—well ... NM-5
Lower Locks Reservoir ... MA-1
Lower Lockwood Tank—reservoir ... AZ-5
Lower Lodgepole Meadow—flat ... ID-8
Lower Lodi Sch—school ... NE-7
Lower Log Canyon—valley ... CO-8
Lower Logging Lake Snowshoe Cabin—hist pl ... MT-8
Lower Log Road Campground—park ... AZ-5
Lower Lola Montez Lake—lake ... CA-9
Lower Loman Well—locale ... NM-5
Lower Lone Rock Valley—valley ... CA-9
Lower Lone Tree Rsvr—reservoir ... MT-8
Lower Long Branch—stream ... KY-4
Lower Long Creek Ch—church ... TN-4
Lower Long Creek Sch—school ... TN-4
Lower Long Draw Tank—reservoir ... AZ-5
Lower Long Fork Sch—school ... KY-4
Lower Long Lake—lake ... CA-9
Lower Long Lake—lake ... IN-6
Lower Long Lake—lake ... MI-6
Lower Long Lake—lake ... MN-6
Lower Long Lake—reservoir ... CO-8
Lower Long Pond—reservoir ... MA-1
Lower Long Pond Dam—dam ... MA-1
Lower Long Reach—gut ... NJ-2
**Lower Longswamp**—pop pl ... PA-2
Lower Longwood—locale ... NJ-2
Lower Loon Creek Bridge—bridge ... ID-8
Lower Loop Creek ... WV-2
Lower Lord Brook—stream ... ME-1
Lower Los Fresnos Crossing—locale ... TX-5
Lower Lost Camp Spring—spring ... NV-8
Lower Lost Parks—flat ... UT-8
Lower Lostwood Lake—lake ... ND-7
Lower Lotts Creek Ch—church ... GA-3
Lower Louviers and Chicken Alley—hist pl ... DE-2
**Lower Love**—pop pl ... VI-3
Lower Lovett Place—locale ... NM-5
Lower Lowe Bend—bend ... TN-4
Lower Lozier Spring—spring ... WA-9
Lower Lyman Ditch—canal ... AZ-5
Lower Lytle Creek Ridge—ridge ... CA-9
Lower Macedonia Ch—church ... SC-3
Lower Machodoc Creek—stream ... VA-3
Lower Machodoc River ... VA-3
Lower MacIntosh Sch—school ... KY-4
**Lower Macungie (Township of)**—pop pl ... PA-2
Lower Macungie Township Sch—school ... PA-2
Lower Macwahoc Lake—lake ... ME-1
Lower Madison Lodge—locale ... AL-4
Lower Magill Prospect—mine ... TN-4
**Lower Magothy Beach**—pop pl ... MD-2
**Lower Mahanoy (Township of)**—pop pl ... PA-2
Lower Maiden Spring—spring ... WA-9
Lower Main Canal—canal ... CA-9
Lower Main Street Commercial Hist Dist—hist pl ... ID-8
Lower Main Street Hist Dist—hist pl ... NY-2
Lower Makefield ... PA-2
**Lower Makefield (Township of)**—pop pl ... PA-2
Lower Malina Lake—lake ... AK-9
Lower Mammoth—mine ... UT-8
Lower Maple River Cem—cemetery ... ND-7
Lower Maple Spring—spring ... CA-9
Lower March Creek Cemetery ... PA-2
Lower Marilyn Lake—lake ... OR-9
Lower Market Street Hist Dist—hist pl ... DE-2
Lower Market Street Hist Dist (Boundary Increase)—hist pl ... DE-2
Lower Mark Island—island ... ME-1
**Lower Marlboro**—pop pl ... MD-2
Lower Marr Tank—reservoir ... NM-5
Lower Marsh—swamp ... TX-5
Lower Marsh Canal—canal ... OR-9
Lower Marsh Creek—stream ... PA-2
Lower Marsh Creek Cem—cemetery ... PA-2
Lower Marsh Creek Ch—church ... KY-4
Lower Marsh Creek Presbyterian Church—hist pl ... PA-2
Lower Marsh Creek Sch—school ... PA-2
Lower Martine Bar—bar ... OR-9
Lower Martinez Tank—reservoir ... AZ-5
Lower Massapoag Pond—reservoir ... MA-1
**Lower Matecumbe Beach**—pop pl ... FL-3
Lower Matecumbe Key—island ... FL-3
Lower McBride Springs—spring ... CA-9
Lower McCain Springs—spring ... OR-9
Lower McCall Lake—lake ... WI-6
Lower McCammon Island—island ... TN-4
Lower Mc Cauley Tank—reservoir ... AZ-5
Lower McDermit Spring—spring ... AZ-5
Lower McGregor Spring—spring ... AZ-5
Lower McKellars Pond—reservoir ... NC-3
Lower McKenzie Lake—lake ... WI-6
Lower McKinney Tank—reservoir ... AZ-5
Lower McNulty Rsvr—reservoir ... OR-9
Lower Meadow ... CA-9
Lower Meadow—flat ... CA-9
Lower Meadow—flat ... ID-8
Lower Meadow—flat ... UT-8
Lower Meadow Cem—cemetery ... MA-1
Lower Meadows—flat ... NH-1
Lower Meadows Campground ... UT-8
Lower Meadow Trail—trail ... CA-9
Lower Medicine Lodge Lake—lake ... WY-8
Lower Medio Windmill—locale ... NM-5
Lower Medley Well—well ... NM-5
Lower Melton Landing (historical)—locale ... TN-4
Lower Melville—locale ... NY-2
Lower Memorial Lake—reservoir ... FL-3
Lower Mendenhall Valley—uninc pl ... AK-9
Lower Menton Lake—lake ... MN-6
Lower Merced Pass Lake—lake ... CA-9
Lower Merchants Lake—reservoir ... NC-3
Lower Merchants Lake Dam—dam ... NC-3
Lower Merino Pond—reservoir ... MA-1
Lower Merino Pond Dam—dam ... MA-1
Lower Merion HS—school ... PA-2
Lower Merion Township—CDP ... PA-2
**Lower Merion (Township of)**—pop pl ... PA-2
Lower Merion Township Park—park ... PA-2
**Lower Merryall**—pop pl ... CT-1
Lower Mesa Falls—falls ... ID-8
Lower Meyersville ... TX-5
**Lower Miami**—pop pl ... AZ-5
Lower Miami Ch—church ... OH-6
Lower Midas Spring—spring ... NV-8
Lower Middle—bar ... MA-1
Lower Middle, The—bar ... DE-2
Lower Middle Branch Pond—lake ... ME-1
Lower Middle Ground—bar ... ME-1
Lower Middle Inlet—stream ... WI-6
Lower Middle Tank—reservoir ... AZ-5
**Lower Mifflin (Township of)**—pop pl ... PA-2
Lower Milford Elem Sch—school ... PA-2
Lower Milford Sch ... PA-2
**Lower Milford (Township of)**—pop pl ... PA-2
Lower Mill—hist pl ... NY-2
Lower Mill—locale ... NM-5
Lower Mill—locale ... TN-4
Lower Mill—other ... PA-2
**Lower Mill**—pop pl ... ME-1
**Lower Mill**—pop pl ... NJ-2
Lower Mill Branch—stream ... VA-3
Lower Mill Canyon—valley ... ID-8
Lower Mill Creek—stream (2) ... WV-2
Lower Mill Creek Sch—school (2) ... KY-4
Lower Mill Creek Sch—school ... WV-2
Lower Mill Creek Sch—school ... WY-8
Lower Mill Dam ... MA-1
Lower Millecoquin River ... MI-6
Lower Millecoquins River—stream ... MI-6
Lower Miller Creek—stream ... AK-9
Lower Miller Rsvr—reservoir ... OR-9
Lower Mill Lake—lake ... CA-9
Lower Mill Pond ... MA-1
Lower Mill Pond—lake ... MI-6
Lower Millpond—reservoir ... CT-1
Lower Millpond—reservoir (3) ... MA-1
Lower Millpond Dam—dam (2) ... MA-1
Lower Mill Pond Dam—dam ... MA-1
Lower Mill Run—stream ... WV-2
Lower Mills Creek Lake—lake ... CA-9
Lower Mills Pond ... MA-1
**Lower Mills (subdivision)**—pop pl ... MA-1
Lower Millstone Sch—school ... KY-4
Lower Milton Lake—lake ... MN-6
Lower Mint Spring—spring ... TN-4
Lower Miocene Canal—canal ... CA-9
Lower Mission Lake—lake ... MN-6
Lower Missouri Lake—lake ... WY-8
Lower Mockeson—locale ... TN-4
Lower Mohawk Lake—lake ... CO-8
Lower Monona Bend—bend ... IA-7
Lower Monona Bend—bend ... NE-7
Lower Monroe Lake—reservoir ... NC-3
Lower Monroe Lake Dam—dam ... NC-3
Lower Montana Ridge Cem—cemetery ... WI-6
Lower Montegut Sch—school ... LA-4
Lower Montgomery Creek Sch—school ... KY-4
Lower Montosa Well—well ... NM-5
Lower Montville—locale ... NJ-2
Lower Monumental Dam—dam ... WA-9
Lower Monumental Dam Heliport—airport ... WA-9
Lower Monumental Lake ... WA-9
Lower Monumental State Airp—airport ... WA-9
Lower Monument Creek—stream ... CO-8
Lower Moon Landing (historical)—locale ... TN-4
Lower Moore Lake—reservoir ... AR-4
Lower Moores Corner—locale ... DE-2
Lower Moose Creek ... PA-2
Lower Moose Pond—lake ... NY-2
Lower Moquitch Tank—reservoir ... AZ-5
Lower Moreland MS—school ... PA-2
Lower Moreland Park—park ... PA-2
Lower Moreland Sch—school ... NY-2
Lower Moreland Senior HS—school ... PA-2
Lower Moreland Township—CDP ... PA-2
**Lower Moreland (Township of)**—pop pl ... PA-2
Lower Morgan Lake—lake ... CA-9
Lower Morganton Shoals—bar ... TN-4
Lower Morgantown Shoals ... TN-4
Lower Mormon Spring—spring ... WY-8
Lower Morse Lake—reservoir ... NJ-2
Lower Morton Spring—spring ... OR-9
Lower Mosquito Creek Spring—spring ... OR-9
Lower Moss Branch—stream ... AR-4
Lower Moss Wash Well—well ... AZ-5
Lower Mound Cem—cemetery ... IN-6
Lower Mountain Lick—stream ... VA-3
Lower Mountain Pond—lake ... NH-1
**Lower Mount Bethel (Township of)**—pop pl ... PA-2
Lower Mount Glen Lake—reservoir ... NJ-2
Lower Mount Glen Lake Dam—dam ... NJ-2
Lower Mount Hope Spring—spring ... AZ-5
Lower Mount Pleasant Dam—dam ... PA-2
Lower Mount Pleasant Powerplant—other ... UT-8
Lower Mousetail Landing ... TN-4
Lower Mouth—locale ... NY-2
Lower Mouth Birch Creek—stream ... AK-9
Lower Mouth Porcupine River—stream ... AK-9
Lower Moyza Tank ... AZ-5
Lower Mtn—summit ... AK-9
Lower Mtn—summit ... UT-8
Lower Mtn—summit ... WV-2
Lower Mudabock ... NJ-2
Lower Mud Creek—stream ... AL-4
Lower Muddy Cem—cemetery ... IL-6
Lower Mud Lake ... WI-6
Lower Mud Lake—lake ... LA-4
Lower Mud Lake—lake ... ME-1
Lower Mud Lake—lake ... MN-6
Lower Mud Spring ... NV-8
Lower Mud Spring—spring ... AZ-5
Lower Mud Spring—spring (4) ... OR-9
Lower Mud Tank—reservoir ... AZ-5
Lower Muhlenburg Ch—church ... PA-2
Lower Mulberry Branch—stream ... KY-4
Lower Muldoon Tank—reservoir ... CA-9
Lower Mule Creek Spring—spring ... AZ-5
Lower Mule Tank ... NM-5
Lower Mule Windmill—locale ... NM-5
Lower Mungers Pond ... CT-1
Lower Myakka Lake—lake ... FL-3
Lower Mystic Lake—lake ... MA-1
Lower Naches Community Park—park ... WA-9
Lower Naches Grange—locale ... WA-9
Lower Naches Sch—school ... WA-9
Lower Naches Valley—valley ... WA-9
Lower Napier Cem—cemetery ... WV-2
Lower Narrows—channel (2) ... ME-1
Lower Narrows—channel (2) ... NH-1
Lower Narrows—channel ... VT-1
Lower Narrows—gap ... CA-9
Lower Narrows—gap ... UT-8
Lower Narrows—gap ... WI-6
**Lower Narrows**—pop pl ... VT-1
Lower Narrows—ridge ... MO-7
Lower Narrows—stream ... NV-8
Lower Narrows Campground—park ... UT-8
Lower Narrows Pond—lake ... ME-1
Lower Nashotah Lake—lake ... WI-6
Lower Nashota Lake ... WI-6
Lower Naukeag Lake—lake ... MA-1
Lower Naukeag Lake Dam—dam ... MA-1
Lower Naukeag Pond ... MA-1
Lower Naukeag Ponds ... MA-1
Lower Nazareth Elem Sch—school ... PA-2
**Lower Nazareth (Township of)**—pop pl ... PA-2
Lower Neches Valley Authority Canal—canal ... TX-5
Lower Neck—cape ... MA-1
Lower Neck, The ... MA-1
Lower Neck Cove—cove ... MA-1
Lower Neck Point ... MA-1
Lower Neely Branch—stream ... MO-7
Lower Neely Sch (historical)—school ... MO-7
Lower Negro Island—island ... ME-1
Lower Nehmabin Lake ... WI-6
Lower Nemahbin Lake—lake ... WI-6
**Lower Nemahbin Lake**—pop pl ... WI-6
Lower New Albion Cem—cemetery ... NY-2
Lower Newell Windmill—locale ... TX-5
Lower Newhouse Coulee—valley ... MT-8
Lower Newport—locale ... OH-6
Lower Newsome Spring—spring ... CA-9
Lower New York Bay ... NJ-2
Lower New York Bay ... NY-2
Lower Niagara River State Park—park ... NY-2
Lower Nichol Flat Rsvr—reservoir ... ID-8
Lower Nicut Run—stream ... WV-2
Lower Nidifer Branch—stream ... TN-4
Lower Nigh Lake ... MN-6
Lower Niklaremut Creek—stream ... AK-9
Lower Ninemile Creek—stream ... WV-2
Lower Ninemile Lake—lake ... WI-6
Lower Noland Cem—cemetery ... NC-3
Lower Northampton Ch—church ... VA-3
Lower North Eden Rsvr—reservoir ... UT-8
Lower North Falls—falls ... OR-9
Lower North Fork ... OR-9
Lower North Fork—stream ... OR-9
Lower North Star Tank—reservoir ... NM-5
Lower North Tank—reservoir ... AZ-5
Lower North (Township of)—fmr MCD ... AR-4
Lower Nunn Creek Trail—trail ... CO-8
**Lower Nutria**—pop pl ... NM-5
Lower Nutrias Sch—school ... NM-5
Lower Nyack Snowshoe Cabin—hist pl ... MT-8
Lower Nye Campground—locale ... CA-9
Lower Oak Creek Windmill—locale ... AZ-5
Lower O'Brien Campground—locale ... ID-8
Lower Odell Sch (abandoned)—school ... MO-7
Lower Ohmer Lake—lake ... AK-9
Lower Old Brake—lake ... AR-4
Lower Oldhouse Branch—stream ... KY-4
Lower Old River ... AR-4
Lower Old River—lake ... AR-4
Lower Old River—stream ... LA-4
Lower One Tank—reservoir ... AZ-5
Lower Open Brook Sch—school ... PA-2
Lower Ophelia Landing—locale ... AL-4
Lower Orange Rsvr—reservoir ... VT-1
**Lower Orchard**—pop pl ... PA-2
Lower Oso Campground—locale ... CA-9
Lower Oso Windmill—locale ... NM-5
**Lower Oswegatchie**—pop pl ... NY-2
Lower Otay Camping Area—locale ... CA-9
Lower Otay Filtration Plant—other ... CA-9
Lower Otay Lake—reservoir ... CA-9
Lower Otay Rsvr ... CA-9
Lower Otter Creek Overlook—locale ... VA-3
Lower Otter Sch—school ... KY-4
Lower Ottoson Lake—lake ... UT-8
Lower Ottoway Lake—lake ... CA-9
Lower Owl Creek Dam—dam ... PA-2
Lower Oxbrook Lake—lake ... ME-1
Lower Ox Creek—stream ... WI-6
**Lower Oxford (Township of)**—pop pl ... PA-2
Lower Oxhead Pond—lake ... ME-1
Lower Ox Lake—lake ... WI-6
Lower Pacifico Campground—locale ... CA-9
Lower Page Creek ... WA-9
Lower Pahranagat Lake—lake ... NV-8
**Lower Paia**—pop pl ... HI-9
Lower Painted Grotto—cave ... NM-5
Lower Paint Rock Lake—lake ... WY-8
Lower Palisade Lake ... ID-8
Lower Palisades Lake—lake ... ID-8
Lower Palisades Lake—lake ... WA-9
Lower Paloma Dam—dam ... AZ-5
Lower Panaca Lake—lake ... MN-6
Lower Panther Island—island ... AR-4
Lower Paradise Lake—lake ... AK-9
Lower Paradise Lake—reservoir ... IN-6
Lower Paradise Lake Dam—dam ... IN-6
Lower Pargoud—hist pl ... LA-4
Lower Parish Lake—lake ... AR-4
Lower Park—flat (2) ... CO-8
Lower Park Creek Patrol Cabin—hist pl ... MT-8
Lower Parker Sch—school ... MO-7
Lower Parson Well—well ... AZ-5
Lower Partridge Lake ... MN-6
Lower Partridge Pond—lake ... ME-1
Lower Pass—channel (2) ... LA-4
Lower Pass—gap ... WI-6
Lower Passage—channel ... AK-9
Lower Pass Creek—stream ... ID-8
Lower Pasture—flat ... UT-8
Lower Pasture Creek—stream ... NJ-2
Lower Pasture Tank—reservoir ... AZ-5
Lower Pasture Well—well ... TX-5
Lower Path Valley Cem—cemetery ... PA-2
Lower Patroon Island—island ... NY-2
Lower Patten Pond—lake ... ME-1
Lower Patten Pond—reservoir ... ME-1
Lower Pauls Lake—lake ... TX-5
Lower Pauness Lake ... MN-6
Lower Pauness Lake—lake ... MN-6
Lower Pawn Lake—lake ... WA-9
Lower Pawtucket Canal Dam—dam ... MA-1
Lower Pawtucket Canal Rsvr—reservoir ... MA-1
**Lower Paxton**—pop pl ... PA-2
Lower Paxton JHS—school ... PA-2
**Lower Paxton (Township of)**—pop pl ... PA-2
Lower Payette Ditch—canal ... ID-8
Lower Payette Valley—valley ... ID-8
Lower Peach Springs—spring ... AZ-5
Lower Peachtree ... AL-4
**Lower Peach Tree**—pop pl ... AL-4
Lower Peach Tree Cem—cemetery ... AL-4
Lower Peach Tree Ferry (historical)—locale ... AL-4
Lower Peachtree Landing—locale ... AL-4
Lower Peach Tree Sch—school ... AL-4
Lower Peach Valley Dam—dam ... CO-8
**Lower Peanut**—pop pl ... PA-2
Lower Peavine Creek—stream ... MO-7
Lower Peavine Flat—flat ... OR-9
Lower Peck Mine—mine ... TN-4
Lower Pecks Pond Dam—dam ... MA-1
Lower Pecos Canyon Archeol District—hist pl ... TX-5
Lower Peedee Mine—mine ... TN-4
Lower Peeler Lake—lake ... CO-8
Lower Peewink Mine—mine ... CO-8
Lower Peninsula (CCD)—cens area ... WA-9
Lower Pennridge HS—school ... PA-2
Lower Penns Neck (Township of) ... NJ-2
Lower Penstemon Campground—locale ... ID-8
Lower Pentsotau ... AL-4
Lower Peralta Riverside Drain—canal ... NM-5
Lower Perish Spring—spring ... NV-8
Lower Perkiomen Valley County Park—park ... PA-2
Lower Perry ... OR-9
Lower Pesquiera Well ... AZ-5
Lower Pesquira Well—well ... AZ-5
Lower Pete Branch—stream ... WV-2
Lower Peters Canyon Rsvr—reservoir ... CA-9
Lower Peterson Bay—swamp ... FL-3
Lower Peterson Rsvr—reservoir ... CO-8
Lower Pettibone Lake—lake ... MI-6
**Lower Pewabic**—pop pl ... MI-6
Lower Phantom Lake—reservoir ... WI-6
Lower Phillips Well—well ... NV-8
Lower Phoebe Lake—lake ... WA-9
Lower Phoenix Ditch—canal ... NM-5
Lower Pickensville Cemetery ... AL-4
Lower Pickerel ... MI-6
Lower Pickerel Lake—lake ... MI-6
Lower Piedra Campground—locale ... CO-8
Lower Pierce Ranch—locale ... CA-9
Lower Pierce Tank—reservoir ... AZ-5
Lower Pigeon Branch—stream ... KY-4
Lower Pigeon Lake—lake ... MN-6
Lower Pigeon Spring—spring ... AZ-5
Lower Piletas Canyon—valley ... CA-9
Lower Pilot Knob—summit ... MO-7
Lower Pinch Sch—school ... WV-2
Lower Pinebottom Run ... PA-2
Lower Pine Bottom Run—stream ... PA-2
Lower Pine Branch—stream ... TN-4
Lower Pine Branch Mines—mine ... TN-4
Lower Pine Creek ... TX-5
Lower Pine Creek—stream ... WI-6
Lower Pine Creek Sch—school ... OR-9
Lower Pine Grove—woods ... UT-8
Lower Pine Grove Cem—cemetery ... SC-3
Lower Pine Lake—lake ... WI-6
Lower Pine Lake—reservoir ... OR-9
Lower Pine Lake Dam—dam ... OR-9
Lower Pine Ridge—ridge (2) ... WY-8
Lower Pine Ridge Spring—spring ... OR-9
Lower Pine Run—stream ... PA-2
Lower Pine Run Sch (abandoned)—school ... PA-2
Lower Pines Campground—park ... UT-8
Lower Pine Spring—spring ... NM-5
Lower Pine Tunnel—tunnel ... NC-3
Lower Pine Windmill—locale ... NM-5
Lower Piney Falls—falls ... TN-4
Lower Piney Reach—channel ... FL-3
Lower Pistol Lake—lake ... ME-1
Lower Pitt Lake—lake ... OR-9
Lower Pittsburg Landing—locale ... ID-8
Lower Pittsburg Rapids—rapids ... ID-8
Lower Pittsburg Rapids—rapids ... OR-9
Lower Pitt-Taylor Rsvr—reservoir ... NV-8
Lower Plain ... MA-1
**Lower Plain**—pop pl ... VT-1
Lower Plain Piermont Station—locale ... VT-1
Lower Plains—flat ... NJ-2
Lower Platte and Beaver Ditch—canal ... CO-8
Lower Pleasant Site Cem—cemetery ... AL-4
Lower Pleasant Street District—hist pl ... MA-1
Lower Pleasant Valley—valley ... OR-9
Lower Pleasant Valley Canal—canal ... UT-8
Lower Pleasantview Rsvr—reservoir ... ID-8
Lower Plug—dam ... AL-4
Lower Plum Creek Sch (historical)—school ... PA-2
Lower Pocosin Mission—church ... VA-3
Lower Podunk Creek—stream ... UT-8
Lower Point ... MS-4
Lower Point—cape ... ID-8
Lower Point—cape ... OR-9
Lower Point—cape ... VA-3
Lower Point Clear ... MS-4
Lower Pointe au Chien Sch—school ... LA-4
Lower Point Mason Landing (historical)—locale ... TN-4
Lower Polecat—summit ... GA-3
Lower Pole Rsvr—reservoir ... CO-8
Lower Polls Creek Sch—school ... KY-4
Lower Pomeroy Lake ... CO-8
**Lower Pompey**—pop pl ... KY-4
Lower Pompey Branch—stream ... KY-4
Lower Pond ... MA-1
Lower Pond—lake (3) ... CT-1
Lower Pond—lake ... ME-1
Lower Pond—lake (2) ... MA-1
Lower Pond—lake (3) ... NY-2
Lower Pond—lake (2) ... UT-8
Lower Pond—reservoir (2) ... ME-1
Lower Pond—reservoir (2) ... MA-1
Lower Pond—reservoir ... NY-2
Lower Pond—reservoir ... VT-1
Lower Pond Lick—stream ... WV-2
Lower Pony Creek Dam—dam ... OR-9
Lower Pony Creek Rsvr ... OR-9
**Lower Poplar Ridge**—pop pl ... AR-4
Lower Poplar Sch—school ... NC-3
Lower Poquette Tank—reservoir ... AZ-5
Lower Portage Pond—lake ... ME-1
Lower Porter Pond—reservoir ... MA-1
Lower Porter Pond Dam—dam ... MA-1
Lower Portland Bar—bar ... AL-4
Lower Post Corral Spring—spring ... NV-8
Lower Post Lake—lake ... WI-6
Lower Potter ... PA-2
Lower Pottsgrove Elem Sch—school ... PA-2
**Lower Pottsgrove (Township of)**—pop pl ... PA-2
Lower Pound Swamp—swamp ... NY-2
Lower Pouness Lake ... MN-6
Lower Pouness LakeA VAR Dauness Lake ... MN-6
Lower Powder Spring—spring ... WY-8
Lower Powder Valley—basin ... OR-9
Lower Powell Canyon—valley ... NE-7
Lower Powerhouse—other ... HI-9
Lower Power Plant—other ... UT-8
Lower Prairie Creek Cem—cemetery ... MS-4
Lower Prairie Creek Ch—church ... MS-4
Lower Prairie Creek Missionary Baptist Ch ... MS-4
Lower Prairie Hollow Ch—church ... MO-7
Lower Prairie Lake—reservoir ... MN-6
Lower Preston Rsvr—reservoir ... NV-8
Lower Prey Meadows—flat ... NV-8
Lower Price Hill Hist Dist—hist pl ... OH-6
Lower Price Lake—lake ... NV-8
Lower Prichard Point ... FL-3
Lower Prior Lake—lake ... MN-6
Lower Pritchard Long Point—cape ... FL-3
Lower Prong—stream ... MS-4
Lower Providence Post Office (historical)—building ... PA-2
**Lower Providence (Township of)**—pop pl ... PA-2
Lower Providencia Tanks—reservoir ... AZ-5
Lower Provo Campground ... UT-8
Lower Provo River Campground—locale ... UT-8
**Lower Pueblo**—pop pl ... NM-5
Lower Pug Lake—lake ... ME-1
Lower Pug Stream—stream ... ME-1
Lower Pump Canal—canal ... OR-9
Lower Pungo Sch—school ... NC-3
Lower PV Trick Tank—reservoir ... AZ-5
Lower Quaker Hill Sch—school ... NY-2
Lower Quartz Lake—lake ... MT-8
Lower Quinn Lake—lake ... OR-9

Lower Quiver River—*stream* ... MS-4
Lower Racetrack Mesa—*summit* ... AZ-5
Lower Radical Mine—*mine* ... CO-8
Lower Rainbow Falls—*falls* ... CA-9
Lower Rainbow Lake—*lake* ... CO-8
Lower Rakes Branch—*stream* ... VA-3
Lower Ramey Meadows—*flat* ... ID-8
Lower Ramparts—*valley* ... AK-9
Lower Ramsey Lake—*lake* ... MS-4
Lower Ranch—*locale* ... NV-8
Lower Ranch—*slope* ... UT-8
Lower Ranch, The—*locale* ... AZ-5
Lower Rancheria Creek—*stream* ... CA-9
Lower Ranchito—*locale* ... NM-5
Lower Ranch (site)—*locale* ... NM-5
Lower Ranch Well—*well* ... AZ-5
Lower Range Lake—*lake* ... WI-6
Lower Range Pond—*lake* ... ME-1
Lower Ranger Station—*locale* ... ID-8
Lower Rattlesnake Tank—*reservoir* ... AZ-5
Lower Rattlesnake Tank—*reservoir* ... NM-5
Lower Rattlesnake Windmill—*locale* ... NM-5
Lower Rattling Springs Lake—*lake* ... MN-6
Lower Rausch Creek—*stream* ... PA-2
Lower Ray Cem—*cemetery* ... OK-5
**Lowerre**—*pop pl* ... NY-2
Lower Reach—*channel* ... VA-3
*Lower Reata Tank* ... AZ-5
*Lower Reata Water Tank* ... AZ-5
Lower Red Castle Lake—*lake* ... UT-8
Lower Red Cut Mine—*mine* ... TN-4
Lower Red Lake—*lake* ... AR-4
Lower Red Lake—*lake* ... MN-6
Lower Red Lake Canyon—*valley* ... UT-8
Lower Red Lake (Unorganized Territory of)—*unorg* ... MN-6
Lower Red Rock Lake—*lake* ... MT-8
Lower Reeder Spring—*spring* ... NV-8
Lower Reed Well—*well* ... NM-5
Lower Reedy Branch Lake—*lake* ... GA-3
Lower Relief Valley—*basin* ... CA-9
Lower Renderbrook Tank—*reservoir* ... TX-5
Lower Reserve—*reservoir* ... SC-3
*Lower Reservoir* ... CO-8
*Lower Reservoir* ... MT-8
*Lower Reservoir* ... UT-8
Lower Reservoir Dam—*dam* ... NJ-2
*Lower Rhoda Lake* ... NY-2
Lower Rhoda Pond—*lake* ... NY-2
Lower Rice Lake—*lake* ... MN-6
Lower Rice Lake Site—*hist pl* ... MN-6
Lower Rice Lake State Wildlife Mngmt Area—*park* ... MN-6
Lower Richardson Lake—*reservoir* ... ME-1
Lower Rich Branch—*stream* ... KY-4
Lower Richland Creek—*stream* ... NC-3
Lower Richland HS—*school* ... SC-3
Lower Richland Vocational Center—*school* . SC-3
Lower Richwoods Cem—*cemetery* ... IA-7
Lower Rickards Dam—*dam* ... PA-2
Lower Riddell Lake—*lake* ... MT-8
Lower Ridge—*ridge* ... ME-1
Lower Ridge Sch—*school* ... PA-2
Lower Riffles—*rapids* ... ME-1
Lower Rigdon Lake—*lake* ... OR-9
Lower Riggs Spring—*spring* ... NV-8
Lower Right Fork—*stream* ... WV-2
Lower Rines Lake—*lake* ... MS-4
Lower Ringtail Tank—*reservoir* ... AZ-5
Lower Ripshin Branch—*stream* ... NC-3
Lower River Ditch—*canal* ... MT-8
Lower River Rouge—*stream* ... MI-6
Lower River Trail—*trail* ... OR-9
Lower River Windmill—*locale* ... TX-5
*Lower Rivord Lake* ... WA-9
*Lower Roach Pond* ... ME-1
Lower Road Branch—*stream* ... WV-2
Lower Road Run—*stream* ... WV-2
*Lower Roads* ... NC-3
Lower Road Well—*well* ... TX-5
Lower Roberts Rsvr—*reservoir* ... CA-9
Lower Robinson Creek—*stream* ... UT-8
Lower Rochester—*locale* ... NV-8
**Lower Rociada**—*pop pl* ... NM-5
Lower Rock Bridge—*bridge* ... NC-3
Lower Rockcamp Run—*stream* ... WV-2
Lower Rock Canyon Spring—*spring* ... MT-8
Lower Rock Creek—*stream* ... CA-9
Lower Rock Creek—*stream* ... ID-8
Lower Rock Creek—*stream* ... MO-7
Lower Rock Fork Sch—*school* ... KY-4
Lower Rock Hollow Windmill—*locale* ... TX-5
Lower Rock House Windmill—*locale* ... TX-5
Lower Rock Lake—*lake* ... OR-9
Lower Rock Lake—*lake* ... UT-8
Lower Rock Lake—*reservoir* ... CA-9
Lower Rock Tank—*reservoir* ... NM-5
Lower Rocky Honcut Creek—*stream* ... CA-9
Lower Rocky Pass Spring—*spring* ... UT-8
Lower Rocky Point—*cape* ... NJ-2
Lower Rogers Dam—*dam* ... NC-3
Lower Rogers Lake—*reservoir* ... NC-3
Lower Romero Windmill—*locale* ... NM-5
Lower Rosary Lake—*lake* ... OR-9
Lower Rose Canyon Dam—*dam* ... AZ-5
Lower Rose Canyon Lake—*reservoir* ... AZ-5
Lower Rosedale Landing—*locale* ... MS-4
Lower Rose Hill Ch—*church* ... VA-3
Lower Rotten Draw—*valley* ... TX-5
**Lower Rotterdam**—*pop pl* ... NY-2
**Lower Rotterdam Junction**—*pop pl* ... NY-2
Lower Rouge Parkway—*park* ... MI-6
Lower Rough And Ready Ditch—*canal* ... CA-9
Lower Roundabout—*bend* ... GA-3
Lower Roxborough Rsvr—*reservoir* ... PA-2
Lower RR Spring—*spring* ... AZ-5
Lower RR Tank—*reservoir* ... AZ-5
*Lower Rsvr* ... MA-1
Lower Rsvr—*reservoir* ... AK-9
Lower Rsvr—*reservoir* ... AZ-5
Lower Rsvr—*reservoir* ... CO-8
Lower Rsvr—*reservoir* (3) ... MA-1
Lower Rsvr—*reservoir* ... MO-7
Lower Rsvr—*reservoir* (2) ... NY-2
Lower Rsvr—*reservoir* (2) ... OR-9
Lower Rsvr—*reservoir* ... UT-8
Lower Rsvr Bear Swamp—*reservoir* ... MA-1
Lower Ruby Creek—*stream* ... AK-9
Lower Rugg Spring—*spring* ... OR-9
*Lower Ruin* ... AZ-5
Lower Run—*stream* ... NC-3
Lower Run—*stream* (4) ... WV-2
Lower Run Ch—*church* ... WV-2
Lower Running Valley Cem—*cemetery* ... WI-6
Lower Rush Creek Campground—*locale* ... CA-9
Lower Russell Pond—*lake* ... ME-1
Lower Russian Lake—*lake* ... AK-9
Lower Russian Lake—*lake* ... CA-9
Lower Rustler Spring—*spring* ... AZ-5
Lower Rutherford Creek (CCD)—*cens area* . TN-4
Lower Rutherford Creek Division—*civil* ... TN-4
Lower Ruth Lake—*lake* ... CA-9
Lower Rutledge Bay—*basin* ... SC-3
*Lower Sabao* ... ME-1
Lower Sabao Lake—*lake* ... ME-1
Lower Sabinal Riverside Drain—*canal* ... NM-5
Lower Sackett Rsvr—*reservoir* ... MA-1
Lower Saddle Gap Pumping Station—*other* ... WA-9
Lower Saginaw Rsvr—*reservoir* ... AZ-5
**Lower Sagon**—*pop pl* ... PA-2
Lower Sahuarita Dam (historical)—*dam* ... AZ-5
Lower Saint Mary Lake—*lake* ... MT-8
Lower Saint Regis Lake—*reservoir* ... NY-2
Lowers Airp—*airport* ... NC-3
Lower Sakatah Lake—*lake* ... MN-6
Lower Salamatof Lake—*lake* ... AK-9
**Lower Salem**—*pop pl* ... OH-6
Lower Salem Ch—*church* ... IL-6
Lower Salford Elem Sch—*school* ... PA-2
**Lower Salford (Township of)**—*pop pl* ... PA-2
Lower Salmon Creek—*stream* ... WA-9
Lower Salmon Falls—*falls* ... ID-8
Lower Salmon Lake—*lake* ... CA-9
Lower Salmon Lake—*lake* ... OR-9
Lower Salmon River Archeol District—*hist pl* ... ID-8
Lower Salt Creek Resort—*locale* ... CA-9
Lower Salt House Tank—*reservoir* ... AZ-5
Lower Salty Spring—*spring* ... NM-5
Lower Sampson Pond—*reservoir* ... MA-1
Lower San Antonio Station—*locale* ... CA-9
Lower Sandbar Lake—*lake* ... CO-8
Lower Sand Brook—*stream* ... ME-1
Lower Sand Cove Dam—*dam* ... UT-8
Lower Sand Cove Rsvr—*reservoir* ... UT-8
Lower Sand Creek Lake—*reservoir* ... CO-8
*Lower Sand Lake* ... MN-6
Lower Sandlick Branch—*stream* ... WV-2
Lower Sandlick Creek—*stream* ... KY-4
Lower Sand Pond—*lake* ... FL-3
Lower Sand Ridge Sch—*school* ... IL-6
Lower Sand Slide—*slope* ... UT-8
Lower Sands Light—*locale* ... OR-9
Lower Sand Spring—*spring* ... CA-9
Lower Sand Spring—*spring* ... OR-9
Lower Sandstone Tank—*reservoir* ... AZ-5
*Lower Sandusky* ... OH-6
Lower Sand Valley—*valley* ... AL-4
Lower Sand Wash—*valley* ... UT-8
Lower Sandy Slough—*stream* ... IL-6
Lower Sanford Spring—*spring* ... NV-8
**Lower San Francisco Plaza**—*pop pl* ... NM-5
Lower San Jacinto Bay—*bay* ... TX-5
Lower San Juan Campground—*locale* ... CA-9
Lower San Juan Riverside Drain—*canal* ... NM-5
Lower San Luis Well—*well* ... AZ-5
Lower San Saba Watershed Rsvr—*reservoir* ... TX-5
Lower San Saba Watershed Rsvr No 10—*reservoir* ... TX-5
Lower San Saba Watershed Rsvr No 11—*reservoir* ... TX-5
Lower San Saba Watershed Rsvr No 12—*reservoir* ... TX-5
Lower San Saba Watershed Rsvr No 16—*reservoir* ... TX-5
Lower Sansavilla—*locale* ... GA-3
Lower Santa Clara Bench Canal—*canal* ... UT-8
Lower Santan Ch—*church* ... AZ-5
Lower Saranac Lake—*lake* ... NY-2
Lower Sardina Well—*well* ... AZ-5
Lower Sardine Lake—*lake* (2) ... CA-9
Lower Sassafras Gap—*gap* ... NC-3
**Lower Saucon**—*pop pl* ... PA-2
Lower Saucon Elem Sch—*school* ... PA-2
*Lower Saucon High S chool* ... PA-2
*Lower Saucon Sch* ... PA-2
Lower Saucon Sch (abandoned)—*school* ... PA-2
**Lower Saucon (Township of)**—*pop pl* ... PA-2
Lower Sauratown Plantation—*hist pl* ... NC-3
Lower Sawmill Tank—*reservoir* ... NM-5
Lowers Cem—*cemetery* ... WV-2
*Lower Scenic Lake* ... WA-9
Lower Schodack Island—*island* ... NY-2
*Lower School* ... TN-4
Lower Schoolhouse Hollow—*valley* ... MO-7
Lower Schooner Creek—*stream* ... IN-6
Lower Scioto Park—*park* ... OH-6
Lower Scotland Sch (historical)—*school* ... AL-4
Lower Scott Lake—*lake* ... MI-6
Lower Scott Springs—*spring* ... NV-8
*Lower Second Creek* ... NC-3
*Lower Section Ferry* ... AL-4
Lower Seibert Lake—*lake* ... AR-4
Lower Selle Spring—*spring* ... OR-9
*Lower Semoneaston Thorofare* ... VA-3
Lower Seven Lake—*lake* ... CA-9
Lower Sevenmile Creek—*stream* ... MT-8
Lower Sevenmile Sch—*school* ... MT-8
Lower Sevenmile Well—*well* ... AZ-5
Lower Seymour Lake—*lake* ... MT-8
Lower Shady Grove Ch—*church* ... MS-4
Lower Shake Campground—*locale* ... CA-9
Lower Shaker Lake—*lake* ... OH-6
*Lower Shaker Prairie Ditch* ... IN-6
Lower Shaker Prairie Ditch—*canal* ... IN-6
**Lower Shaker Village**—*pop pl* ... NH-1
Lower Shasta Costa Riffle—*rapids* ... OR-9
Lower Shawneetown—*hist pl* ... KY-4
Lower Shawneetown Archeol District—*hist pl* ... KY-4
Lower Shaw Pond—*lake* ... ME-1
Lower Sheep Basin Tank—*reservoir* ... NM-5
Lower Sheep Canyon Well—*well* ... NV-8
Lower Sheep Canyon Windmill—*locale* ... CO-8
Lower Sheep Cave—*cave* ... TN-4
Lower Sheep Spring—*spring* ... AZ-5
Lower Sheepy Rsvr—*reservoir* ... OR-9
Lower Sheets Run—*stream* ... WV-2
Lower Shellburg Falls—*falls* ... OR-9
Lower Shell Creek Crossing—*locale* ... WY-8
Lower Shell Sch House—*hist pl* ... WY-8
Lower Sheriff Run—*stream* ... PA-2
*Lower Sherriff Run* ... PA-2
Lower Shields Pond—*lake* ... NH-1
Lower Shields Valley Ditch—*canal* ... MT-8
Lower Shingle Creek Lake—*lake* ... UT-8
Lower Shin Pond—*lake* ... ME-1
Lower Shirley Corner—*locale* ... ME-1
Lower Shoals—*other* ... MO-7
Lower Shoe Lake—*lake* ... MI-6
Lower Shoepack Point—*summit* ... ID-8
Lower Short Creek—*stream* ... CO-8
Lower Shutup—*valley* ... TX-5
Lower Sibley Pond—*reservoir* ... MA-1
Lower Sibley Pond Dam—*dam* ... MA-1
Lower Sierrita Well—*well* ... AZ-5
Lower Signal Butte—*summit* ... CA-9
Lower Silas Lake—*lake* ... WY-8
Lower Silver Bluff—*cliff* ... SC-3
Lower Silvis Lake—*lake* ... AK-9
Lower Simmons Peak—*summit* ... AZ-5
Lower Simmons Well—*well* ... AZ-5
Lower Simon Bar—*bar* ... OR-9
Lower Simoneaston Thorofare—*channel* ... VA-3
Lower Sinepuxent Neck—*cape* ... MD-2
Lower Sinking Creek—*stream* ... KY-4
Lower Sinking Creek—*stream* ... TN-4
Lower Sioux Agency—*hist pl* ... MN-6
Lower Sioux Community (Indian Reservation)—*reserve* ... MN-6
Lower Sioux Indian Community—*reserve* . MN-6
Lower Sioux Ind Res—*reserve* ... MN-6
Lower Sister Bar—*bar* ... AL-4
Lower Sister Bluff Landing—*locale* ... GA-3
Lower Sister Creek—*stream* ... FL-3
Lower Sister Creek—*stream* ... OH-6
Lower Sister Island—*island* ... ME-1
Lower Sister Lake—*lake* ... NY-2
Lower Sizemore Spring—*spring* ... OR-9
Lower Skeleton Tank—*locale* ... AZ-5
Lower Skinner Tank—*reservoir* ... AZ-5
Lower Skippack Ch—*church* ... PA-2
Lower Sky High Lake—*lake* ... CA-9
Lower Slaughter Gulch Rsvr—*reservoir* ... OR-9
Lower Slavonia Mine—*mine* ... CO-8
Lower Sleith Fork—*stream* ... WV-2
Lower Sleith Sch—*school* ... WV-2
Lower Slickrock—*summit* ... UT-8
Lower Slick Rock Spring—*spring* ... AZ-5
Lower Slide Lake—*lake* ... WY-8
Lower Slim and Fatty Rsvr—*reservoir* ... OR-9
Lower Slough—*stream* ... CA-9
Lower Smith Ditch—*canal* ... CO-8
*Lower Smith Morehouse Campground* ... UT-8
Lower Smith River Cem—*cemetery* ... OR-9
Lower Smith Tank—*reservoir* ... AZ-5
Lower Smoke Creek—*locale* ... NV-8
Lower Smoke Creek Well—*well* ... NV-8
Lower Smyrna Ch—*church* ... AR-4
Lower Snake River Archaeol District—*hist pl* ... WA-9
Lower Snake Tank—*reservoir* ... NM-5
Lower Snively Spring—*spring* ... WA-9
Lower Snoqualmie Valley (CCD)—*cens area* ... WA-9
Lower Snowy Lake—*lake* ... WA-9
Lower Soap Holes—*bend* ... WY-8
Lower Soda Falls—*falls* ... OR-9
Lower Soda Lake Drain—*canal* ... NV-8
Lower Sound Point—*cape* ... FL-3
Lower Sourdough Spring—*spring* ... OR-9
Lower Southampton Township—*CDP* ... PA-2
**Lower Southampton (Township of)**—*pop pl* ... PA-2
Lower South Bay—*bay* ... NY-2
**Lower South Bay**—*pop pl* ... NY-2
**Lower South Bay (South Bay)**—*pop pl* ... NY-2
Lower South Branch Pond—*lake* ... ME-1
Lower South Branch Thunder Bay River—*stream* ... MI-6
Lower South Falls—*falls* ... OR-9
Lower South Fork Little River—*stream* ... CA-9
Lower South Park—*flat* ... CO-8
Lower South Pond—*lake* ... NY-2
*Lower Spaniards Point* ... MD-2
Lower Sparky Tank—*reservoir* ... AZ-5
Lower Spectacle Island—*island* ... MA-1
Lower Spectacle Pond—*reservoir* ... MA-1
Lower Spectacle Pond Dam—*dam* ... MA-1
Lower Spencer—*locale* ... KY-4
*Lower Spinney Unit* ... CO-8
Lower Spirit Lake—*lake* ... WI-6
Lower Spring—*spring* (2) ... AZ-5
Lower Spring—*spring* ... CO-8
Lower Spring—*spring* ... ID-8
Lower Spring—*spring* ... NV-8
Lower Spring—*spring* ... OR-9
Lower Spring—*spring* ... TN-4
Lower Spring—*spring* ... UT-8
Lower Spring—*spring* ... WA-9
Lower Spring Canyon—*valley* ... NM-5
*Lower Spring Creek* ... TX-5
Lower Spring Creek—*stream* ... NC-3
Lower Spring Creek Cem—*cemetery* ... AR-4
Lower Spring Creek Sch—*school* ... KY-4
Lower Springdale Estates Dam—*dam* ... NC-3
Lower Springdale Estates Lake—*reservoir* . NC-3
Lower Springhill Campground—*locale* ... CA-9
*Lower Spring Hollow Campground* ... UT-8
Lower Spring Lake—*lake* ... MN-6
Lower Spring Lake—*reservoir* ... IL-6
Lower Spring Lake—*reservoir* ... IN-6
Lower Spring Lake Dam—*dam* ... IN-6
Lower Spring Ponds—*lake* ... FL-3
Lower Springstead Lake—*lake* ... WI-6
Lower Spring Water Windmill—*well* ... AZ-5
Lower Springy Pond—*lake* ... ME-1
Lower Spruce Creek—*stream* ... KY-4
Lower Spruce Run—*stream* ... WV-2
Lower Spunk Lake—*lake* ... MN-6
**Lower Squankum**—*pop pl* ... NJ-2
Lower Squirrel Spring—*spring* ... NM-5
Lowers Ridge—*ridge* ... WI-6
Lower Stafford Marsh—*swamp* ... NY-2
Lower Stairs Brook—*stream* ... NH-1
Lower Standard Canal—*canal* ... CA-9
**Lower Stanley**—*pop pl* ... ID-8
Lower Star Sch (historical)—*school* ... PA-2
*Lower State Lake* ... AL-4
Lower State Lake Dam—*dam* ... AL-4
Lower State Spring—*spring* ... WY-8
Lower Station Spring—*spring* ... ID-8
Lower St. Croix Natl Scenic River (Also MN)—*park* ... WI-6
Lower St. Croix Natl Scenic River (Also WI)—*park* ... MN-6
Lower Stevens Lake—*lake* ... ID-8
Lower Stewart Creek Ch—*church* ... WV-2
Lower Stillwater—*lake* ... NH-1
Lower Stillwater Lake—*lake* ... MT-8
Lower Stinson Creek—*stream* ... KY-4
Lower St. Jones Neck Hist Dist—*hist pl* ... DE-2
*Lower Stockade Spring* ... NV-8
Lower Stockpile Rsvr—*reservoir* ... OR-9
Lower Stony Brook—*stream* ... ME-1
Lower Stony Brook—*stream* ... OR-9
Lower Store (historical)—*locale* ... MS-4
*Lower Story Lake* ... IN-6
Lower Story Lake—*lake* ... IN-6
Lower Straight Canyon—*valley* ... UT-8
Lower Straits Lake—*lake* ... MI-6
Lower Stringtown Branch—*stream* ... KY-4
Lower Sturgeon River Cem—*cemetery* ... MN-6
Lower Sucker Creek—*stream* ... AK-9
Lower Sugarbush Lake—*lake* ... WI-6
Lower Sugarloaf Channel—*channel* ... FL-3
Lower Sugarloaf Sound—*bay* ... FL-3
Lower Sullivan Tank—*reservoir* ... AZ-5
Lower Sully Landing (historical)—*locale* ... SD-7
Lower Sulpher Springs Cem—*cemetery* ... AL-4
Lower Sulphur Creek—*stream* ... TX-5
Lower Sulphur Spring—*spring* ... NM-5
Lower Sulphur Springs Ch—*church* ... AL-4
Lower Summerhouse Pond—*reservoir* ... SC-3
*Lower Summers Meadow* ... CA-9
Lower Summers Meadow—*flat* ... CA-9
Lower Summers Meadows—*flat* ... CA-9
Lower Summit Lake—*lake* ... AK-9
Lower Suncook Lake—*lake* ... NH-1
Lower Sunday River Sch—*hist pl* ... ME-1
Lower Sunk Lake—*lake* ... LA-4
Lower Sun River—*uninc pl* ... MT-8
Lower Sunset Lake—*lake* ... CA-9
**Lower Sunset Park**—*pop pl* ... IN-6
*Lower Sunshine Basin Ditch* ... WY-8
Lower Surrounded Hill (Township of)—*fmr MCD* ... AR-4
Lower Surry Cem—*cemetery* ... VA-3
Lower Suzy Q Creek—*stream* ... AK-9
Lowe Rsvr—*reservoir* ... OR-9
Lower Swale—*valley* ... ID-8
Lower Swale Cem—*cemetery* ... NY-2
Lower Swan Lake—*lake* ... AR-4
Lower Swan Lake—*lake* ... IL-6
**Lower Swatara (Township of)**—*pop pl* ... PA-2
Lower Swedish Cabin—*hist pl* ... PA-2
Lower Sweeney Lake—*lake* ... WY-8
Lower Sweetheart Lake—*lake* ... AK-9
Lower Swiss Spring—*spring* ... OR-9
Lower Switzer Campground—*locale* ... CA-9
Lower Sycamore Tank—*reservoir* ... AZ-5
Lower Sylvan Lake—*lake* ... WY-8
Lower Symes Pond—*reservoir* ... VT-1
Lower Table—*summit* ... WY-8
Lower Table Rock—*pillar* ... OR-9
Lower Tailholt Tank—*reservoir* ... AZ-5
Lower Talarik Creek—*stream* ... AK-9
Lower Tallahatchie River Y-10-35 Dam—*dam* ... MS-4
Lower Tallahatchie Y-10-37 Dam—*dam* ... MS-4
Lower Tamarack River—*stream* ... MN-6
Lower Tangle Lake—*lake* ... AK-9
Lower Tank—*reservoir* (11) ... AZ-5
Lower Tank—*reservoir* (4) ... NM-5
Lower Tank—*reservoir* ... TX-5
**Lower Tannersville**—*pop pl* ... PA-2
Lower Taos Canyon—*valley* ... NM-5
Lower Taylor—*summit* ... CA-9
Lower Taylor Brook—*stream* ... ME-1
Lower Taylor Ditch—*canal* ... NV-8
Lower Taylor Lake—*lake* ... AR-4
Lower Taylor Rsvr—*reservoir* ... MT-8
Lower Tazimina Lake—*lake* ... AK-9
Lower Tebay Lake—*lake* ... AK-9
Lower Teges Creek—*stream* ... KY-4
Lower Telida Lake—*lake* ... AK-9
Lower Temora Lake—*reservoir* ... NC-3
Lower Temora Lake Dam—*dam* ... NC-3
Lower Tenmile Ch—*church* ... WV-2
Lower Tenmile Ranch—*locale* ... NV-8
Lower Tenmile Sch (abandoned)—*school* .. MO-7
Lower Tent Meadow—*flat* ... CA-9
Lower Terrace—*flat* ... NV-8
**Lower Texas**—*pop pl* ... LA-4
Lower Thirteen Tank—*reservoir* ... AZ-5
Lower Thirty-six Bay—*bay* ... FL-3
*Lower Thomas Point* ... MD-2
Lower Thompson Lake—*lake* ... MT-8
Lower Thompson Mesa Tank—*reservoir* ... AZ-5
Lower Thompson Spring—*spring* ... AZ-5
Lower Thompson Well—*well* ... NM-5
*Lower Thom's Point* ... MD-2
*Lower Thorn point* ... MD-2
Lower Thorofare—*channel* ... MD-2
Lower Thorofare—*channel* ... NJ-2
Lower Threemile Fork—*stream* ... WV-2
Lower Threemile Rsvr—*reservoir* ... WY-8
Lower Threemile Sch—*school* ... MT-8
*Lower Three Run* ... PA-2
Lower Three Runs—*stream* ... PA-2
Lower Three Runs Ch—*church* ... SC-3
Lower Three Runs Creek—*stream* ... SC-3
Lower Thumb Rsvr—*reservoir* ... ID-8
Lower Tillicum Creek—*stream* ... WA-9
Lower Tillman—*locale* ... AZ-5
*Lower Timber Canyon* ... OR-9
Lower Timber Canyon—*valley* ... OR-9
Lower Tincup Spring—*spring* ... AZ-5
Lower Tippah River Lt-7-18—*dam* ... MS-4
Lower Tobias Meadow—*flat* ... CA-9
Lower Togue Pond—*lake* ... ME-1
Lower Togus Pond—*lake* ... ME-1
Lower Toklat River Ranger Cabin No. 18—*hist pl* ... AK-9
Lower Tomahawk Lake—*lake* ... MI-6
Lower Tom Brown Well—*well* ... AZ-5
Lower Tom Creek—*stream* ... WV-2
**Lower Tonsina**—*pop pl* ... AK-9
Lower Toogoodoo Creek—*stream* ... SC-3
Lower Topaz Rsvr—*reservoir* ... UT-8
Lower Topsaw Landing—*locale* ... SC-3
Lower Torrey Island—*island* ... ME-1
**Lower Towamensing (Township of)**—*pop pl* ... PA-2
Lower Tower Spring—*spring* ... NV-8
Lower Town—*locale* ... CA-9
Lower Town Creek Ch—*church* ... NC-3
*Lower Town Dock* ... NY-2
Lowertown Hist Dist—*hist pl* ... NY-2
Lowertown Historic Distruct—*hist pl* ... MN-6
Lower Town Landing—*locale* ... NY-2
Lower Town Neighborhood District—*hist pl* ... KY-4
**Lower (Township of)**—*pop pl* ... NJ-2
Lower Trace Branch—*stream* ... KY-4
Lower Trace Fork—*stream* ... WV-2
Lower Trace Fork Sch—*school* ... KY-4
Lower Trail—*trail* ... HI-9
Lower Trail Canyon—*valley* ... OR-9
Lower Trail Canyon—*valley* ... UT-8
Lower Trail Lake—*lake* ... AK-9
Lower Trail Ridge—*ridge* ... NC-3
Lower Trapper Flat—*flat* ... ID-8
Lower Trees Point—*cape* ... VA-3
Lower Trelipe Lake—*reservoir* ... MN-6
Lower Triangle Tank—*reservoir* ... AZ-5
Lower Trick Tank—*reservoir* ... AZ-5
Lower Trilby Lake—*lake* ... ID-8
Lower Trinity (CCD)—*cens area* ... CA-9
Lower Trinity Ranger Station—*locale* ... CA-9
Lower Troublesome Creek—*stream* ... KY-4
Lower Trough Spring—*spring* ... UT-8
Lower Trout Creek Meadows—*flat* ... ID-8
*Lower Trout Lake* ... MN-6
Lower Trout Lake—*reservoir* ... MI-6
Lower Tufts Spring—*spring* ... UT-8
Lower Tule Lake—*reservoir* ... CO-8
Lower Tumbling Run Dam—*dam* ... PA-2
Lower Tunnel—*mine* ... CA-9
Lower Turkey Creek Sch—*school* ... KY-4
Lower Turkey Creek Sch—*school* ... MO-7
Lower Turkey Creek Sch—*school* ... WV-2
Lower Turkey Creek Spring—*spring* ... AZ-5
**Lower Turkeyfoot (Township of)**—*pop pl* ... PA-2
Lower Turnage Landing—*locale* ... TN-4
Lower Turner Gulch—*valley* ... OR-9
Lower Turner Tank—*reservoir* ... NM-5
Lower Turquoise Lake—*lake* ... CO-8
Lower Turret Lake—*lake* ... CA-9
Lower Turtle Lake—*lake* ... WI-6
*Lower Tuscaloosa* ... AL-4
Lower Tuscarora Church and Cem—*cemetery* ... PA-2
Lower Tuscohatchie Lake—*lake* ... WA-9
Lower Tusquitee Bridge—*bridge* ... NC-3
Lower Twentieth Street Residential Hist Dist—*hist pl* ... AL-4
Lower Twenty-five Ditch—*canal* ... NV-8
Lower Twentymile Meadows—*flat* ... ID-8
Lower Twin Branch—*stream* (9) ... KY-4
Lower Twin Branch—*stream* ... TN-4
Lower Twin Branch—*stream* ... VA-3
Lower Twin Branch—*stream* (4) ... WV-2
Lower Twin Branch Sch—*school* ... KY-4
Lower Twin Bridge—*bridge* ... TN-4
Lower Twin Brook—*stream* ... NY-2
Lower Twin Campground—*park* ... OR-9
Lower Twin Canyon—*valley* ... UT-8
Lower Twin Creek—*stream* ... ID-8
Lower Twin Creek—*stream* ... KY-4
Lower Twin Creek—*stream* (2) ... MT-8
Lower Twin Creek—*stream* (2) ... OH-6
Lower Twin Creek—*stream* ... WA-9
Lower Twin Creek Cem—*cemetery* ... AR-4
Lower Twin Island—*island* ... MN-6
Lower Twin Island—*island* ... WV-2
*Lower Twin Lake* ... MN-6
*Lower Twin Lake* ... WI-6
Lower Twin Lake—*lake* (3) ... CA-9
Lower Twin Lake—*lake* ... CO-8
Lower Twin Lake—*lake* ... ID-8
Lower Twin Lake—*lake* ... MN-6
Lower Twin Lake—*lake* ... NY-2
Lower Twin Lake—*lake* ... WI-6
Lower Twin Lake—*reservoir* ... CO-8
Lower Twin Lake—*reservoir* ... PA-2
Lower Twin Lake Dam—*dam* ... PA-2
*Lower Twin Lakes* ... NE-7
Lower Twin Lakes—*lake* ... MN-6
Lower Two Calf Island—*island* ... MT-8
*Lower Two Lick* ... PA-2
Lower Two Medicine Lake—*lake* ... MT-8
Lower Twomile Creek—*stream* ... OR-9
Lower Twomile Run—*stream* ... PA-2
Lower Two Run—*stream* (4) ... WV-2
Lower Two Spring—*spring* ... AZ-5
Lower Two Spring Run—*stream* ... WV-2
Lower Two Tank—*reservoir* ... AZ-5
Lower Two Troughs Tank—*reservoir* ... AZ-5
Lower T X Ranch—*locale* ... NM-5
**Lower Tyrone (Township of)**—*pop pl* ... PA-2
Lower Ugashik Lake—*lake* ... AK-9
Lower Union Canal—*canal* ... UT-8
Lower Union Cem—*cemetery* ... IN-6
Lower Unknown Lake—*lake* ... ME-1
**Lower Vacherie**—*pop pl* ... LA-4
Lower Vag Hollow—*valley* ... PA-2
Lower Valley—*basin* ... OR-9
**Lower Valley**—*pop pl* ... NJ-2
Lower Valley—*valley* ... ID-8
Lower Valley—*valley* ... NV-8
Lower Valley Cem—*cemetery* ... TX-5
Lower Valley Ditch—*canal* ... OR-9
Lower Valley Golf Club—*other* ... WA-9
Lower Valley Memorial Gardens—*cemetery* ... WA-9
Lower Valley Sch—*school* ... TX-5
Lower Valley-Somers—*cens area* ... MT-8
Lower Velma Lake—*lake* ... CA-9
Lower Vermillion Lake—*lake* ... WI-6
Lower Vicinity Well—*well* ... NM-5
**Lower Village**—*pop pl* ... HI-9
**Lower Village**—*pop pl* ... ME-1
**Lower Village**—*pop pl* ... MA-1
**Lower Village**—*pop pl* (2) ... NH-1
**Lower Village**—*pop pl* ... VT-1
Lower Village District—*hist pl* ... NH-1
**Lower Village Three**—*pop pl* ... HI-9
Lower Violet Hollow—*valley* ... KY-4
Lower Wagner Tank—*reservoir* ... AZ-5
Lower Wagon Canyon—*valley* ... UT-8
Lower Wakefield Spring—*spring* ... AZ-5
Lower Walden Ditch—*canal* ... CO-8
Lower Waldorff Ranch—*locale* ... CA-9
Lower Wales Sch—*school* ... KY-4
Lower Walkerfield Spring—*spring* ... AZ-5
Lower Wall Canyon Rsvr—*reservoir* ... NV-8
Lower Wall Pack Cem—*cemetery* ... NJ-2
Lower Wanato Lake—*lake* ... WI-6
Lower Warm Springs—*spring* ... CA-9
Lower Warm Springs Campground—*locale* ... MT-8
Lower Wass Cove—*bay* ... ME-1
Lower Water—*spring* ... AZ-5
**Lower Waterford**—*pop pl* ... VT-1
Lower Waterford Cem—*cemetery* ... VT-1
Lower Water Hollow—*valley* ... UT-8
Lower Water Hollow Canyon—*valley* ... UT-8
Lower Waterman Lake—*lake* ... WI-6
Lower Water Spring—*spring* ... AZ-5
Lower Water Spring—*spring* (2) ... NM-5
Lower Water Spring—*spring* ... UT-8
Lower Water Stewart Creek Rsvr—*reservoir* ... WY-8
**Lower Websterville**—*pop pl* ... VT-1
Lower Wekiva River State Res—*reserve* ... FL-3
Lower Well—*well* (3) ... AZ-5
Lower Well—*well* ... CA-9
Lower Well—*well* (3) ... NM-5
Lower Wesley Sch—*school* ... ME-1
Lower West Bay Pond—*lake* ... ME-1
Lower Westboro Reservoir Dam—*dam* ... MA-1
Lower Westboro Rsvr—*reservoir* ... MA-1
Lower West Branch Priest River—*stream* ... ID-8
Lower West Branch Priest River—*stream* ... WA-9
Lower West Branch Sch—*school* ... NE-7
Lower West Ditch—*canal* ... ID-8
Lower West Ellis Cem—*cemetery* ... ME-1
Lower West Hollow Windmill—*locale* ... TX-5
Lower West Market Street District—*hist pl* ... KY-4
Lower Weston Cem—*cemetery* ... WI-6
Lower West Ragged Pond—*lake* ... ME-1
Lower West Side Santo Domingo Ditch—*canal* ... NM-5
Lower Wharton Ch—*church* ... AR-4
Lower Wheatfields—*locale* ... AZ-5
*Lower Wheeler Reservoir* ... WA-9
Lower Whetstone Sch—*school* ... KY-4
Lower Whipple Lake—*lake* ... MN-6
Lower Whit Branch—*stream* ... KY-4
Lower White Blotch Spring—*spring* ... NV-8
Lower Whitefish Lake—*lake* ... MN-6
Lower White Hills—*summit* ... CT-1
Lower White Hills Cem—*cemetery* ... CT-1
*Lower White Lake* ... AR-4
Lower White Lake—*lake* ... AR-4
Lower White Lake—*reservoir* ... TX-5
Lower White Oak Creek—*stream* ... KY-4
Lower White Oak Sch—*school* ... KY-4
*Lower White River Mill Pond* ... WI-6
Lower Whiterock Trail—*trail* ... TN-4
Lower Whitetail Park—*flat* ... MT-8
*Lower Whitewater Lake* ... WI-6
**Lower Whyel**—*pop pl* ... PA-2
Lower Wicker Tank—*reservoir* ... TX-5
Lower Wiedemann Dam—*dam* ... KS-7
Lower Wigwam Rapids—*rapids* ... ME-1
Lower Wilbur Rsvr—*reservoir* ... MT-8
Lower Wilcox Pond—*reservoir* ... PA-2
Lower Wildcat Lake—*lake* ... WA-9
Lower Wildcat Spring—*spring* ... NV-8
Lower Wildcat Tank—*reservoir* ... AZ-5
Lower Wildcat Windmill—*locale* ... TX-5
Lower Wild Rice and Red River Cem—*cemetery* ... ND-7
Lower Wildwood Lake Dam—*dam* ... IN-6
Lower Williams Ranch—*locale* ... NV-8
Lower Willow Cem—*cemetery* ... TX-5
Lower Willow Creek—*stream* ... AK-9
Lower Willow Creek—*stream* ... MT-8
Lower Willow Creek—*stream* ... WY-8
Lower Willow Creek Rsvr—*reservoir* ... MT-8
Lower Willow Creek Sch—*school* ... WY-8
Lower Willow Creek Spring—*spring* ... WY-8
Lower Willow Creek Trail Number Four—*trail* ... MT-8
Lower Willows—*flat* ... CA-9
Lower Wilson Marsh Flowage—*reservoir* ... WI-6
Lower Wilson Pond—*reservoir* ... ME-1
Lower Windmill—*locale* ... AZ-5
Lower Windmill—*locale* ... CO-8
Lower Windmill—*locale* ... NM-5
Lower Windmill—*locale* (5) ... TX-5
Lower Windrock Sch (historical)—*school* ... TN-4
Lower Windsor Ditch—*canal* ... MT-8
**Lower Windsor (Township of)**—*pop pl* ... PA-2
Lower Windy Creek Ranger Cabin No. 15—*hist pl* ... AK-9
Lower Windy Tank—*reservoir* ... AZ-5
Lower Winganhauppauge Lake—*lake* ... NY-2
**Lower Wire Village**—*pop pl* ... MA-1
Lower Wizard Run—*stream* ... WV-2
Lower Wolf Branch—*stream* ... KY-4
Lower Wolf Creek Campground—*park* ... AZ-5
Lower Wolf Creek Rsvr No. 1—*reservoir* ... CO-8
Lower Wolf Creek Rsvr No. 2—*reservoir* ... CO-8
Lower Wolf Creek Rsvr No. 3—*reservoir* ... CO-8
Lower Wolfjaw Mtn—*summit* ... NY-2
Lower Wolf Lake—*lake* ... AK-9
Lower Wolf Lake—*lake* ... WI-6
Lower Wolfpen Branch—*stream* ... KY-4
Lower Wood Camp Spring—*spring* ... AZ-5
Lower Woodcock Lake—*lake* ... MI-6
Lower Wood Pond Dam—*dam* ... PA-2
Lower Woods Pond—*reservoir* ... PA-2
*Lower Woolfolk Lake* ... AR-4
Lower Wooton Sch—*school* ... KY-4
Lower Wright Lake—*lake* ... CA-9
Lower Wroten Point—*cape* ... MD-2
*Lower Wugus* ... PA-2
*Lowery* ... MS-4
Lowery—*locale* ... AL-4
Lowery—*locale* ... GA-3
**Lowery**—*pop pl* ... AL-4
Lowery, Lake—*lake* ... FL-3

**Lowery Air Force Base**—pop pl CO-8
Lowery Branch—stream (2) AL-4
Lowery Branch—stream AR-4
Lowery Branch—stream TN-4
Lowery Cem—cemetery AL-4
Lowery Cem—cemetery GA-3
Lowery Cem—cemetery IN-6
Lowery Cem—cemetery KY-4
Lowery Cem—cemetery LA-4
Lowery Cem—cemetery (4) MS-4
Lowery Cem—cemetery (2) MO-7
Lowery Cem—cemetery (4) TN-4
Lowery Cem—cemetery TX-5
Lowery Ch—church MS-4
Lowery Ch—church OK-5
Lowery Chapel—church TN-4
Lowery Cove—valley NC-3
Lowery Creek—stream AL-4
Lowery Creek—stream CA-9
Lowery Creek—stream IN-6
Lowery Creek—stream LA-4
Lowery Creek—stream MS-4
Lowery Creek—stream (2) NC-3
Lowery Creek—stream WI-6
Lowery Creek Baptist Church MS-4
Lowery Creek Ch—church MS-4
Lowery Drain—stream MI-6
Lower Yellow Pine Lake—lake UT-8
Lowery Gulch—valley MT-8
**Lowery Hills**—pop pl VA-3
Lowery HS—school LA-4
Lowery Knob—summit NC-3
Lowery Knob—summit PA-2
Lower Y Lake—lake IA-7
Lowery Lake—reservoir NC-3
Lowery Mill Creek—stream NC-3
Lower Yoder Fire Tower—tower PA-2
**Lower Yoder (Township of)**—pop pl PA-2
Lower Yosemite Fall—falls CA-9
Lower Youngcane Creek—stream GA-3
Lowery Park—park AL-4
Lowery Point—cape VA-3
Lowery Ridge—ridge CA-9
Lowery Riffle—rapids OR-9
Lowery Rsvr—reservoir NE-7
Lowery Run—stream OH-6
Lowerys Chapel—church AL-4
Lowerys Mill AL-4
Lowery Spring AZ-5
Lowery Stand Cem—cemetery TN-4
Lowery Stand (historical)—locale TN-4
**Lowerytown**—pop pl AL-4
Lowery Town Ch—church AL-4
**Lowery Township**—pop pl ND-7
Lowery Well—well AZ-5
Lower Zachary Cem—cemetery NC-3
Lower 25th Street Hist Dist—hist pl UT-8
Lower 25th Street Hist Dist (Boundary Increase)—hist pl UT-8
Lowes DE-2
**Lowes**—pop pl (2) KY-4
Lowes Bend TN-4
**Lowes Boydsville**—pop pl AR-4
Lowes Branch—stream KY-4
Lowes Branch—stream MO-7
Lowes Bridge—bridge IN-6
Lowes Camp—locale NE-7
Lowes Canyon—valley CA-9
Lowes Canyon—valley NV-8
Lowes Cem—cemetery IN-6
Lowes Cem—cemetery OH-6
Lowes Ch—church NC-3
Lowes Ch—church TX-5
Lowe Sch—school IN-6
Lowe Sch—school MA-1
Lowe Sch—school MO-7
Lowes Chapel—church MS-4
Lowes Chapel—church TN-4
Lowes Chapel Sch—school MS-4
Lowes Corner—locale CA-9
Lowes Corners—locale NY-2
Lowe's Cove ME-1
Lowes Cove—bay ME-1
Lowes Creek—stream AR-4
Lowes Creek—stream MD-2
Lowes Creek—stream TN-4
Lowes Creek—stream WI-6
Lowes Creek Ch—church AR-4
Lowes Creek Sch—school WI-6
Lowes Crossing—locale GA-3
Lowes Crossroads—locale DE-2
Lowes Dam—dam AL-4
Lowes Ditch—canal NC-3
Lowes Ferry TN-4
Lowes Gap—gap KY-4
**Lowes Grove**—pop pl NC-3
Lowes Grove Elem Sch—school NC-3
Lowes Grove JHS—school NC-3
Lowes Island—island VA-3
Lowes Lake—lake NE-7
Lowes Lake—lake WI-6
Lowes Lake—reservoir AL-4
Lowes Lakeview Campground—locale DE-2
Lowes Landing Strip—airport TN-4
Lowes Path—trail NH-1
Lowes Point—cape MD-2
Lowes Pond MA-1
Lowes Pond—lake VA-3
Lowes Pond—reservoir MA-1
Lowes Pond Dam—dam MA-1
Lowe Spring—spring NM-5
Lowe Spring—spring OR-9
Lowe State Wildlife Mngmt Area—park MN-6
Lowe-Steen Site (22LW511)—hist pl MS-4
Lowes Temple Ch—church MS-4
Lowes Tinaja—lake TX-5
Lowes Valley—valley TX-5
Lowesville—locale VA-3
**Lowesville**—pop pl NC-3
**Lowesville**—pop pl VA-3
Loweth—locale MT-8
**Lowetown**—pop pl AL-4
**Lowe Township**—pop pl KS-7
**Lowe Township**—pop pl SD-7
**Lowe (Township of)**—pop pl IL-6
Lowe Valley—basin NE-7
Lowe Well—well UT-8
Lowe Windmill—locale TX-5
Lowey Gum Spring—spring KY-4
Low Family Cem—cemetery MS-4
Lowfield Ch AL-4
Low Field Ch—church AL-4
Low Gap AL-4
Low Gap CA-9
Low Gap NC-3
Low Gap TN-4
Low Gap—gap (7) AL-4
Low Gap—gap (7) AR-4
Low Gap—gap (13) CA-9
Low Gap—gap (7) GA-3
Low Gap—gap (3) IN-6
Low Gap—gap (3) KY-4
Low Gap—gap (10) MO-7
Low Gap—gap (16) NC-3
Low Gap—gap (2) OH-6
Low Gap—gap OK-5
Low Gap—gap (2) OR-9
Low Gap—gap (26) TN-4
Low Gap—gap (14) VA-3
Low Gap—gap (9) WV-2
Low Gap—locale (2) AL-4
Low Gap—locale (4) AR-4
Low Gap—locale KY-4
Low Gap—locale NC-3
Low Gap—locale (2) OH-6
Low Gap—locale WA-9
Low Gap—locale (2) WV-2
**Lowgap**—pop pl KY-4
**Low Gap**—pop pl MO-7
**Lowgap**—pop pl NC-3
**Low Gap**—pop pl VA-3
**Low Gap**—pop pl (2) WV-2
Low Gap—summit MO-7
Low Gap Baptist Church TN-4
Low Gap Branch—stream IN-6
Low Gap Branch—stream (9) KY-4
Low Gap Branch—stream NC-3
Low Gap Branch—stream (5) TN-4
Low Gap Branch—stream (4) VA-3
Low Gap Branch—stream (2) WV-2
Lowgap Branch—stream WV-2
Low Gap Branch—stream (3) WV-2
Low Gap Branch Prospect Number One—mine TN-4
Low Gap Branch Prospect Number Two—mine TN-4
Low Gap Cem—cemetery AR-4
Low Gap Ch—church AL-4
Low Gap Ch—church (3) AR-4
Low Gap Ch—church (2) KY-4
Low Gap Ch—church MO-7
Low Gap Ch—church (2) NC-3
Low Gap Ch—church OH-6
Low Gap Ch—church TN-4
Low Gap Ch—church (4) WV-2
Low Gap Creek—stream (6) CA-9
Low Gap Creek—stream GA-3
Low Gap Creek—stream OR-9
Low Gap Creek—stream WV-2
Low Gap Elem Sch—school NC-3
Low Gap Fork—stream (3) KY-4
Lowgap Fork—stream KY-4
Low Gap Fork—stream (2) KY-4
Lowgap Fork—stream WV-2
Low Gap Hollow—valley (2) KY-4
Low Gap Hollow—valley (5) MO-7
Low Gap Hollow—valley NC-3
Lowgap Hollow—valley TN-4
Low Gap Hollow—valley VA-3
Low Gap Hollow—valley WV-2
Lowgap Island—island KY-4
Low Gap Lake AL-4
Low Gap Mtn—summit AR-4
Low Gap Mtn—summit OK-5
Low Gap Pass—gap WA-9
Low Gap Point—cape TN-4
Low Gap Pumping Plant—other WA-9
Low Gap Ridge—ridge (2) MO-7
Low Gap Run—stream (3) WV-2
Low Gap Sch—school KY-4
Low Gap Sch—school VA-3
Low Gap Sch—school (2) WV-2
Low Gap School (historical)—locale MO-7
Low Gap Spring—spring AR-4
Low Gap Spring—spring TN-4
Low Gap Station—locale CA-9
Low Gap (Township of)—fmr MCD (2) AR-4
Low Gap Trail—trail CA-9
Low Gap Trail—trail OR-9
Low Gap Trail—trail TN-4
Low Gap Wildlife Club Dam—dam NC-3
Low Gap Wildlife Pond—reservoir NC-3
Low Gilchrist Spring—spring OR-9
Low Gravity Wickman Lateral—canal CA-9
Lowground—locale MO-7
Lowground Ch—church MO-7
Lowground Sch (historical)—school MO-7
Low Hampton—locale NY-2
Low Heywood Sch—school CT-1
Low Hill PA-2
**Lowhill**—pop pl PA-2
Lowhill—summit PA-2
Low Hill—uninc pl PA-2
Lowhill Ch—church PA-2
Low Hill Ridge—ridge TN-4
Low Hills—summit UT-8
Lowhill Sch (abandoned)—school PA-2
**Lowhill (Township of)**—pop pl PA-2
Low (historical)—locale AL-4
Low (historical)—locale MS-4
Low Hollow—valley AR-4
Low Hollow—valley MO-7
Low Hotel—hist pl UT-8
Low House—hist pl CT-1
Low House—hist pl NC-3
Lowica Ditch No 2 (Abandoned)—canal WY-8
Lowica Rsvr—reservoir WY-8
Lowing Bald—summit NC-3
Low Island OR-9
Low Island—island (2) AK-9
Low Island—island MN-6
Low Island—island NY-2
Low Island—island (2) WA-9
Low Island Anchorage—bay AK-9
Low John Creek—stream LA-4
Low Key—island FL-3
Low Knob—summit PA-2
Low Lake PA-2
Low Lake—lake (2) AK-9
Low Lake—lake MI-6
Low Lake—lake MN-6
Low Lake—lake WI-6
Low Lake—reservoir FL-3
Lowland PA-2
Lowland—locale TN-4
Lowland—locale VA-3
Lowland—locale WV-2
**Lowland**—pop pl CO-8
**Lowland**—pop pl NC-3
Lowland Campground—locale MT-8
Lowland Canal (historical)—canal AZ-5
Lowland Cem—cemetery MS-4
Lowland Cottage—hist pl VA-3
Lowland Creek—stream MT-8
Lowland Ditch—canal CO-8
Lowlander Tank—reservoir AZ-5
Lowland Lake—lake WI-6
Lowland Post Office—building TN-4
Lowland Post Office (historical)—building TN-4
**Lowlands**—pop pl LA-4
Lowlands—swamp MA-1
Lowland Sch—school ND-7
Lowland Sch—school WV-2
Lowland Sch (historical)—school MS-4
Lowland Sch (historical)—school TN-4
**Lowlands (subdivision), The**—pop pl TN-4
Lowlands Well No 1—well NM-5
Lowlands Well No 2—well NM-5
**Lowland Township**—pop pl ND-7
Lowlar Bend KY-4
Lowler Mines—mine AL-4
Lowler's Tavern—hist pl OH-6
Low Lift Lateral—canal CA-9
Low Lift Line—other ID-8
Lowline Canal—canal CO-8
Low Line Canal—canal ID-8
Lowline Canal—canal MT-8
Lowline Canal—canal NE-7
Low Line Canal—canal OR-9
Lowline Canal—canal UT-8
Low Line Canal—canal UT-8
Lowline Ditch—canal CO-8
Low Line Ditch—canal (2) OR-9
Lowline Trail—trail CO-8
Lowline Trail—trail UT-8
Lowline Trail—trail (2) WY-8
Low Lot Cem—cemetery GA-3
Lowman WV-2
**Lowman**—pop pl ID-8
**Lowman**—pop pl NY-2
**Lowman Beach Park**—pop pl WA-9
Lowman Cem—cemetery (2) IA-7
Lowman Ch—church WV-2
Lowman Chapel—church MO-7
**Lowman Corner**—pop pl IN-6
Lowman Creek—stream IN-6
Lowman Creek—stream MT-8
Lowmandale IN-6
**Lowmandale**—pop pl IN-6
Lowman Hall, South Carolina State College—hist pl SC-3
Lowman Hill Elem Sch—school KS-7
Lowman Pond—lake FL-3
Lowman Ridge—ridge WV-2
Lowman Sch—school CA-9
Lowman Sch (historical)—school PA-2
**Lowmansville**—pop pl KY-4
Lowman United Methodist Ch—church KS-7
Lowman Valley Ch—church VA-3
Lowman Well—well AZ-5
Lowmeister Bay ID-8
Lowmeister Bay—bay ID-8
Low Memorial Library, Columbia Univ—hist pl NY-2
Lowmiller Bench—bench WY-8
Low Moor—other VA-3
**Low Moor**—pop pl IA-7
**Low Moor**—pop pl NJ-2
**Lowmoor**—pop pl VA-3
Lowmoor Lake—lake MI-6
**Lowmoor (Low Moor)**—pop pl VA-3
**Low Mountain**—pop pl AZ-5
Low Mountain Airp—airport AZ-5
Low Mountain Gulch—valley CA-9
Low Mountain Rsvr—reservoir AZ-5
Low Mtn—summit (3) AZ-5
Low Mtn—summit CA-9
Low Mtn—summit WA-9
Lown, William Ernest, House—hist pl SD-7
Lowndes—locale MD-2
**Lowndes**—pop pl MO-7
Lowndes, Lake—reservoir MS-4
Lowndes Acad—school AL-4
Lowndes Airp—airport TN-4
Lowndesboro AL-4
Lowndesboro—hist pl AL-4
**Lowndesboro**—pop pl AL-4
Lowndesboro (CCD)—cens area AL-4
Lowndesboro Division—civil AL-4
Lowndesboro (sta.) (Saint Clair)—other AL-4
**Lowndes County**—pop pl AL-4
**Lowndes (County)**—pop pl GA-3
**Lowndes County**—pop pl MS-4
Lowndes County Area Vocational School AL-4
Lowndes County Courthouse—building MS-4
Lowndes County Courthouse—hist pl AL-4
Lowndes County Courthouse—hist pl GA-3
Lowndes County Elem Sch AL-4
Lowndes County Fairgrounds—locale MS-4
Lowndes County Farm (historical)—locale MS-4
Lowndes County HS—school AL-4
Lowndes County Park Lake Dam—dam MS-4
Lowndes County Riverside Industrial Park—locale MS-4
Lowndes County Sanitary Landfill—locale AL-4
Lowndes County Training School AL-4
Lowndes County Vocational Technical Sch—school MS-4
Lowndes Grove—hist pl SC-3
Lowndes Hill Ch—church SC-3
Lowndes Lake—lake SC-3
**Lowndes Landing**—pop pl SC-3
Lowndes Park—park WV-2
Lowndesport (historical)—locale AL-4
**Lowndesville**—pop pl SC-3
Lowndesville Lookout Tower—locale SC-3
Lowney—locale WV-2
Lowney Creek—stream MI-6
Low Notch—gap NC-3
Low Notch Gap—gap NC-3
Low Park—park CA-9
Low Pass—gap ID-8
Low Pass—gap (2) MT-8
Low Pass—gap OR-9
Low Pass—gap (2) UT-8
Low Pass—gap WA-9
**Low Pass**—pop pl OR-9
Low Pass Creek—stream CA-9
Low Pass Creek—stream UT-8
Low Pass Gulch—valley CO-8
Low Pass Lake—lake ID-8
Low Pass Spring—spring OR-9
Low Piney Spur—ridge NC-3
Low Place—gap WV-2
Low Place Branch—stream VA-3
Low Place Branch—stream WV-2
Low Place Run—stream VA-3
Low Plains KS-7
Low Point—cape (2) AK-9
Low Point—cape NY-2
Low Point—cape (2) VA-3
Low Point—cape (2) WA-9
**Low Point**—pop pl IL-6
Low Point Hollow—valley WV-2
**Lowpoint (RR name Low Point)**—pop pl IL-6
Low Pond NY-2
Low Pond—reservoir MA-1
Lowrance Hosp—hospital NC-3
Lowrance Lake—reservoir OK-5
Lowrance Mtn—summit TX-5
Lowrance Ranch—locale OK-5
Lowrance Ranch—locale TX-5
Lowrance Sch—school NC-3
Lowrance Springs—spring OK-5
Lowrance Springs Site—hist pl OK-5
Lowranch Hollow—valley TN-4
Lowrence Brook—stream NY-2
Lowrey AL-4
Lowrey—locale CA-9
Lowrey—locale MS-4
Lowrey—locale OK-5
Lowrey Cem—cemetery AL-4
Lowrey Cem—cemetery CA-9
Lowrey Cem—cemetery MS-4
Lowrey Cem—cemetery (2) OK-5
Lowrey Ch—church MS-4
Lowrey Creek—stream VA-3
Lowrey Draw—valley TX-5
Lowrey Lake—lake CA-9
Lowrey Memorial Baptist Ch—church MS-4
Lowrey Methodist Ch MS-4
Lowrey Mill MS-4
Lowrey Ranch—locale ID-8
Lowrey Ranch—locale NM-5
Lowrey Ridge CA-9
Lowrey Run—stream PA-2
Lowrey Sch—school CA-9
Lowrey Sch—school MI-6
Lowrey Sch—school OK-5
Lowreys Ferry TN-4
Lowrey Sheep Camp—locale NM-5
Lowrey Spring—spring AZ-5
Lowreytown NJ-2
Low Ridge—bar AK-9
Low Ridge—ridge NC-3
Low Ridge—ridge (2) OR-9
Lowrie—canal HI-9
Lowrie, Sen. Walter, House—hist pl PA-2
Lowrie Ditch—canal HI-9
Lowrie Island—island AK-9
Lowries Cem—cemetery OH-6
Lowrie Sch—school IL-6
Lowries Run—stream PA-2
Lowrimore Cem—cemetery MS-4
**Lowrimores Crossroads**—pop pl AL-4
Lowring Nickell Branch KY-4
Low Rock—island CA-9
Low Rock—island FL-3
Low Rock—other AK-9
Lowry—locale AR-4
Lowry—locale FL-3
Lowry—locale LA-4
Lowry—locale MT-8
Lowry—locale VA-3
**Lowry**—pop pl (2) GA-3
**Lowry**—pop pl MN-6
**Lowry**—pop pl MT-8
**Lowry**—pop pl SD-7
Lowry, James, House—hist pl TN-4
Lowry, William, House—hist pl IN-6
Lowry, William, House—hist pl TN-4
Lowry, William C., House—hist pl KY-4
Lowry AFB—military CO-8
Lowry AFB Bombing Range—military CO-8
Lowry Bayou—gut MS-4
Lowry Branch TN-4
Lowry Branch—stream GA-3
Lowry Branch—stream TN-4
Lowry Branch—stream WV-2
Lowry Brook—stream CT-1
Lowry Canyon—valley NV-8
Lowry Cem—cemetery AL-4
Lowry Cem—cemetery IN-6
Lowry Cem—cemetery NC-3
Lowry Cem—cemetery SD-7
Lowry Cem—cemetery (2) TN-4
**Lowry City**—pop pl MO-7
Lowry Cove—bay MD-2
Lowry Cove Trail—trail TN-4
Lowry Creek—stream TN-4
Lowry Creek—stream TX-5
Lowry Creek—stream WI-6
**Lowry Crossing**—pop pl TX-5
Lowry Ditch—canal IN-6
Lowry Ditch—canal WA-9
Lowry Draw—valley WY-8
Lowry Falls Trail—trail TN-4
Lowry Fork UT-8
Lowry Fork—valley UT-8
Lowry Gap—gap AL-4
Lowry Gap—gap TN-4
Lowry Gulch MT-8
Lowry Gulch—valley OR-9
Lowry Hill MN-6
Lowry Hill—summit IL-6
Lowry Hill Cem—cemetery IL-6
Lowry Island—island MS-4
Lowry Knob—summit OH-6
Lowry Lake FL-3
Lowry Lake—lake NM-5
Lowry Mill—locale AL-4
Lowry Park—park FL-3
Lowry Peak—summit VA-3
Lowry Public Sch—hist pl MN-6
Lowry Ruin—hist pl CO-8
Lowry Ruins Natl Historical Landmark—park CO-8
Lowry Run—stream OH-6
Lowry Run—stream VA-3
**Lowrys**—pop pl NC-3
**Lowrys**—pop pl SC-3
Lowrys Canyon—valley UT-8
Lowry Sch—school KS-7
Lowry Sch—school MN-6
Lowrys Ferry (historical)—locale TN-4
Lowrys Hill—locale VI-3
Lowrys Landing (historical)—locale TN-4
Lowry's Point VA-3
Lowry Spring—spring NV-8
Lowry State Wildlife Mngmt Area—park MN-6
Lowrysville SC-3
Lowry Top—summit TN-4
Lowry Top—summit UT-8
Lowryville SC-3
Lowryville—locale TN-4
Lowry Water—stream UT-8
Lowry Well—well NV-8
Lowry Wilson Sch—school SC-3
Low Saddle—gap ID-8
Lows Bay—bay FL-3
Lows Branch—stream IN-6
Lows Branch—stream TX-5
Lows Branch River IN-6
Lows Bridge—locale ME-1
Lows Brook RI-1
Lows Cem—cemetery IN-6
Lows Ch—church NC-3
Low Sch—school CA-9
Low Sch—school IL-6
Lows Creek TX-5
Lows Creek WI-6
Lows Creek—stream FL-3
Lows Creek—stream TX-5
**Lowsen (historical)**—pop pl OR-9
Lows Ferry TN-4
Lows Hollow—locale NJ-2
Lows Island TN-4
Lows Island—island PA-2
Lows Lake WI-6
Lows Lake—lake MN-6
Lows Lake—reservoir NY-2
Lows Point MD-2
Lows Pond MA-1
Low Spur—area UT-8
Low Spur Archeol Site (12J87)—hist pl IN-6
Lows Ranch—locale AZ-5
Lows Run—stream MD-2
Lows Store (historical)—locale MS-4
Lows Sulphur Springs Post Office (historical)—building TN-4
**Lowsville**—pop pl WV-2
Lows Water Lake FL-3
Low Tank—reservoir AZ-5
Lowther Cem—cemetery WV-2
Lowther Neuhaus Ditch—canal IN-6
Lowther-North MS—school KS-7
Lowther-South MS—school KS-7
**Lowther Station (historical)**—pop pl IA-7
Low Tide Rock—bar NY-2
Lowullo Butte—summit OR-9
Low Valley—basin AZ-5
**Lowville**—pop pl NY-2
**Lowville**—pop pl PA-2
**Lowville**—pop pl WI-6
Lowville Cem—cemetery WI-6
Lowville Center Sch—school WI-6
Lowville Rsvr—reservoir NY-2
Lowville State Wildlife Mngmt Areas—park MN-6
**Lowville (Town of)**—pop pl NY-2
**Lowville (Township of)**—pop pl MN-6
**Low Wassie**—pop pl MO-7
Low Water Bridge—bridge LA-4
Low Water Dam Public Use Area—park OK-5
Low Water Thorofare—channel NJ-2
Low Well—well NM-5
**Lox**—pop pl WY-8
**Loxa**—pop pl IL-6
**Loxahatchee**—pop pl FL-3
Loxahatchee Canal—canal FL-3
Loxahatchee Natl Wildlife Ref—park FL-3
Loxahatchee River—stream FL-3
Loxahatchee River Aquatic Preserve—park FL-3
Loxahatchee River Bend Park—park FL-3
Loxahatchee Slough—gut FL-3
**Loxco**—pop pl NC-3
**Loxley**—pop pl AL-4
Loxley Elem Sch—school AL-4
**Loxley Gardens**—pop pl VA-3
Loxley JHS—school AL-4
**Loxley Place**—pop pl VA-3
Loxley Sch—school AL-4
Lox Rsvr—reservoir WY-8
Loy—locale AR-4
Loya Branch—stream MS-4
**Loyal**—pop pl OK-5
**Loyal**—pop pl WI-6
Loyal, Lake—lake FL-3
**Loyalhanna**—pop pl PA-2
Loyalhanna Cave—cave PA-2
Loyal Hanna Creek PA-2
Loyalhanna Creek—stream PA-2
Loyalhanna Creek Cave—cave PA-2
Loyalhanna Dam—dam (2) PA-2
Loyalhanna Elem Sch—school PA-2
Loyalhanna Gorge—valley PA-2
Loyalhanna Lake—reservoir (2) PA-2
Loyalhanna Lake Natl Rec Area—park PA-2
Loyalhanna Reservoir PA-2
Loyalhanna School PA-2
**Loyalhanna (Township of)**—pop pl PA-2
**Loyalhanna Woodlands No. 1**—pop pl PA-2
**Loyalhanna Woodlands No. 2**—pop pl PA-2
Loyalhanna 6 Mile Stations—locale PA-2
**Loyal Heights**—pop pl WA-9
Loyal Heights Playground—park WA-9
Loyal Heights Sch—school WA-9
Loyal (historical)—locale KS-7
Loyalist Monmt—park NC-3
**Loyall**—pop pl KY-4
Loyal Lake—lake MI-6
Loyall (historical)—locale AL-4
Loyall Station AL-4
Loyal Mtn—summit TX-5
Loyal Oak OH-6
Loyal Oak Lake—lake OH-6
**Loyal (Pershing)**—pop pl IN-6
Loyalsack Creek PA-2
Loyal Sch—school MS-4
Loyal Sch—school NE-7
Loyalsock PA-2
Loyalsock Canyon Vista PA-2
Loyalsock Creek—stream PA-2
Loyalsock Creek Gorge—valley PA-2
**Loyalsock (historical)**—pop pl PA-2
Loyalsock State Game Farm—park PA-2
Loyalsock Township—civil PA-2
**Loyalsock (Township of)**—pop pl PA-2
Loyalsock Trail—trail PA-2
Loyalsock Valley Sch—school PA-2
**Loyalsockville**—pop pl PA-2
**Loyalton**—pop pl CA-9
**Loyalton**—pop pl PA-2
**Loyalton**—pop pl SD-7
Loyalton Cem—cemetery SD-7
**Loyal (Town of)**—pop pl WI-6
Loyalty Cem—cemetery CT-1
Loyalty Sch—school WI-6
Loyal Valley—locale TX-5
Loyalville—locale PA-2
Loy Branch—stream KY-4
Loy Butte—summit AZ-5
Loy Butte Five—trail AZ-5
Loy Butte Pueblo—hist pl AZ-5
Loy Canyon—valley AZ-5
Loyce—locale FL-3
Loyce Cem—cemetery FL-3
Loy Cem—cemetery AR-4
Loy Cem—cemetery TN-4
Loy Ch—church IL-6
Loy Creek—stream TX-5
Loyd NY-2
Loyd—locale CO-8
**Loyd**—pop pl MS-4
**Loyd**—pop pl WI-6
Loyd Branch—stream (2) TN-4
Loyd Cem—cemetery AL-4
Loyd Cem—cemetery IL-6
Loyd Cem—cemetery (2) MS-4
Loyd Cem—cemetery (4) TN-4
Loyd Ch—church GA-3
Loyd Chapel—church TN-4
Loyd Cove—valley TN-4
Loyd Creek GA-3
Loyd Creek SC-3
Loyd Creek—stream OR-9
Loyd-Dalton Oil Field—oilfield TX-5
Loyd Gap—gap TN-4
Loyd Hall Plantation—hist pl LA-4
Loyd Knob TN-4
Loyd Mill Branch—stream AL-4
Loyd Moncur Ranch—locale SD-7
Loyd Park—park TN-4
Loyd Post Office (historical)—building AL-4
Loyd Post Office (historical)—building MS-4
Loyd Ranch—locale NM-5
Loyd Ridge—ridge TN-4
Loyd Rodgers Rsvr—reservoir AR-4
**Loyds Bridge**—pop pl LA-4
Loyds Cem—cemetery AL-4
Loyd Sch—school TN-4
Loyds Corner—locale NJ-2
Loyds Dam—dam AL-4
Loyd Spring—spring (2) TN-4
Loyds School TN-4
**Loyd Star**—pop pl MS-4
Loydsville OH-6
Loyd Uhl Ranch—locale MT-8
Loyd Valley—basin NE-7
**Loyer**—pop pl MD-2
Loyfall WA-9
Loy Gulch—valley CO-8
Loyhead Lake—lake WI-6
Loy Island—island AK-9
Loy Lake—reservoir TX-5
Loy Memorial Ch—church TN-4
Loy Memorial United Methodist Ch TN-4
Loy Mine—mine OR-9
Loyning Sch—school MT-8
**Loyola**—pop pl PR-3
Loyola—uninc pl CA-9
Loyola Acad—school IL-6
**Loyola Beach**—pop pl TX-5
Loyola Coll—school FL-3
Loyola Coll—school MD-2
**Loyola Corners**—pop pl CA-9
Loyola Home AL-4
Loyola HS—school CA-9
Loyola HS—school MD-2
Loyola HS—school MN-6
Loyola (Loyola College)—uninc pl MD-2
Loyola Park—park IL-6
Loyola Sch—school CA-9
Loyola Sch—school CO-8
Loyola Seminary—school NY-2
Loyola Univ—school (2) CA-9
Loyola Univ—school IL-6
Loyola Univ—school LA-4
Loyola Villa—locale AL-4
Loyola Village Sch—school CA-9
Loy Park—park OH-6
Loy Park—park TX-5
Loy Place (Abandoned)—locale TX-5
**Loys**—pop pl MD-2
**Loysburg**—pop pl PA-2
**Loysburg Gap**—pop pl PA-2
Loy Sch—school IL-6
Loy Sch—school MT-8
**Loys Corners**—pop pl OH-6
Loys Cross Roads TN-4
Loys Cross Roads Post Office TN-4
Loyseth Millpond—reservoir SC-3
Loys Mill (historical)—locale TN-4
**Loy Spur**—pop pl MT-8
Loys Run—stream OH-6
Loyss Sch—school AL-4
Loys Station Covered Bridge—hist pl MD-2
Loyston Dike—dam TN-4

Lucky Ditch—*canal* IN-6
Lucky Ditch Creek—*stream* AK-9
Lucky Dog Creek—*stream* AK-9
Lucky Dog Creek—*stream* CA-9
Lucky Dog Creek—*stream* ID-8
Lucky Dog Mine—*mine* CO-8
Lucky Dollar Mine—*mine* MT-8
Lucky Draw—*valley* NM-5
Lucky Draw—*valley* WY-8
Lucky Find Mine—*mine* UT-8
Lucky Finn Lake—*lake* MN-6
Lucky Five Ranch—*locale* CA-9
Lucky Flats—*flat* UT-8
Lucky Flats Spring—*spring* UT-8
Lucky Flats Wash—*valley* UT-8
Lucky Fork—*locale* KY-4
Lucky Fork—*stream* KY-4
Lucky Fork Sch—*school* KY-4
Lucky Friday Mine—*mine* ID-8
Lucky Gap—*gap* AR-4
Lucky Gap Creek—*stream* OR-9
Lucky Gas Field—*oilfield* LA-4
*Lucky Gulch* ID-8
Lucky Gulch—*valley* (4) AK-9
Lucky Gulch—*valley* CO-8
Lucky Gulch—*valley* ID-8
Lucky Gulch—*valley* MT-8
Lucky Gulch—*valley* WY-8
Lucky Gulch Mine—*mine* ID-8
**Lucky Hill**—*pop pl* VA-3
Lucky Hill—*summit* AK-9
Lucky Hill—*summit* MT-8
Lucky Hill—*summit* NY-2
Lucky Hill—*summit* VA-3
Lucky Hill Mine—*mine* CA-9
Lucky Hill Mine—*mine* NV-8
Lucky Hill Ravine—*valley* CA-9
Lucky Hills Stock Ranch—*locale* AZ-5
Lucky (historical)—*locale* AL-4
Lucky Hit P. O. (historical)—*locale* AL-4
Lucky Hollow—*valley* AR-4
Lucky Hollow—*valley* KY-4
Lucky Hollow—*valley* OR-9
Lucky Jack—*ridge* AZ-5
Lucky Jack Mine—*mine* CA-9
Lucky Jack Mine—*mine* (2) CO-8
Lucky Jim Bluff—*cliff* WA-9
Lucky Jim Mine—*mine* (2) CA-9
Lucky Jim Wash—*stream* CA-9
Lucky Joe Mine—*mine* MT-8
Lucky Knob—*summit* TX-5
Lucky Knob Camp—*locale* TX-5
Lucky Knob Windmill—*locale* TX-5
Lucky Knock Mine—*mine* WA-9
Lucky Lad Mine—*mine* (2) ID-8
Lucky Lady Mine—*mine* WY-8
Lucky Lake—*lake* CA-9
Lucky Lake—*lake* FL-3
Lucky Lake—*lake* MI-6
Lucky Lake—*lake* MN-6
Lucky Lake—*lake* NM-5
Lucky Lake—*lake* OR-9
Lucky Lake—*lake* (2) WI-6
Lucky Lakes—*lake* NY-2
Lucky Lakes—*reservoir* AL-4
Lucky Lake Strand—*swamp* FL-3
Lucky Lake Trail—*trail* OR-9
**Lucky Landing**—*pop pl* ME-1
Lucky Lass Mine—*mine* OR-9
Lucky Ledge Mine—*mine* AZ-5
Lucky L Ranch—*locale* FL-3
Lucky Luke Mine—*mine* MT-8
Lucky Mac Camp—*locale* WY-8
**Lucky Mac Camp**—*pop pl* WY-8
Lucky Mac Uranium Mill—*locale* WY-8
Lucky Mine—*mine* (2) AZ-5
Lucky Mine—*mine* CO-8
Lucky Mine—*mine* (2) NM-5
Lucky Mound Ch—*church* ND-7
Lucky Mound Creek Bay—*bay* ND-7
Lucky Mtn—*summit* TX-5
Lucky Nell Mine—*mine* AK-9
Lucky Pardner Mine—*mine* CA-9
Lucky Pass—*gap* WA-9
Lucky Peak—*summit* ID-8
Lucky Peak Dam—*dam* ID-8
Lucky Peak Lake—*reservoir* ID-8
*Lucky Peak Reservoir* ID-8
Lucky Peak State Rec Area—*park* ID-8
Lucky Penny Ditch—*canal* CO-8
Lucky Point—*cape* (2) AK-9
Lucky Point—*cape* ME-1
Lucky Point—*cliff* IN-6
Lucky Point—*summit* CA-9
Lucky Point—*summit* MT-8
Lucky Pond—*lake* ME-1
Lucky Quartz Mine—*mine* CA-9
Lucky Queen Mine—*mine* OR-9
Lucky Queen (site)—*locale* OR-9
Lucky Ridge—*locale* TX-5
Lucky Ridge—*ridge* ID-8
Lucky Rsvr—*reservoir* (2) OR-9
Lucky Run—*stream* IN-6
Lucky Run—*stream* (2) PA-2
Lucky Run—*stream* (2) VA-3
Lucky Saddle Tank—*reservoir* NM-5
Lucky Sch (historical)—*school* MS-4
Lucky Seven Ranch—*locale* NV-8
Lucky Shoals Creek—*stream* GA-3
Lucky Shot Mine—*mine* AK-9
Lucky Six Creek—*stream* AK-9
Lucky Six Spring—*spring* OR-9
Lucky S Mine—*mine* CA-9
Lucky Spar Lode Mine—*mine* SD-7
Lucky Spring—*spring* (2) AZ-5
Lucky Spring—*spring* (2) CA-9
Lucky Spring—*spring* (3) OR-9
Lucky Spring—*spring* UT-8
Lucky Spring Canyon—*valley* AZ-5
Lucky Springs—*spring* NV-8
Lucky Star Lake—*reservoir* NY-2
Lucky Star Mine—*mine* NV-8
Lucky Star Mine—*mine* OR-9
Lucky Star Mine—*mine* UT-8
Lucky Star Prospect Mine—*mine* SD-7
Lucky Star Sch—*school* NE-7
Lucky Stone Mine—*mine* WA-9
**Lucky Stop**—*pop pl* (2) KY-4
Lucky Strike Bentonite Mine—*mine* WY-8
Lucky Strike Canyon—*valley* MT-8
Lucky Strike Canyon—*valley* NV-8
Lucky Strike Creek—*stream* AK-9
Lucky Strike Mine—*mine* AZ-5
Lucky Strike Mine—*mine* (5) CA-9
Lucky Strike Mine—*mine* CO-8
Lucky Strike Mine—*mine* ID-8
Lucky Strike Mine—*mine* (4) NV-8
Lucky Strike Mine—*mine* (2) OR-9
Lucky Strike Mine—*mine* (3) SD-7
Lucky Strike Mine—*mine* (2) UT-8
Lucky Strike Mine—*mine* WA-9
Lucky Strike Well—*locale* NM-5
Lucky Strike Well—*well* NM-5
Lucky Strike Well—*well* (2) TX-5
Lucky Strike Windmill—*locale* TX-5
Lucky Sunday Mine—*mine* CA-9
Lucky Swede Gulch—*valley* ID-8
Lucky Swede Mine (historical)—*mine* ID-8
Lucky Tank—*reservoir* (3) AZ-5
Lucky Tank—*reservoir* NM-5
Lucky Tank—*reservoir* (2) TX-5
Lucky Twenty Mine—*mine* CO-8
Lucky Valley—*locale* IA-7
Lucky Valley Cem—*cemetery* IA-7
Lucky Well—*well* AZ-5
Lucky Well—*well* NM-5
Lucky Windmill—*locale* (2) NM-5
Lucky Windmill—*locale* TX-5
**Luco**—*pop pl* WI-6
Luco Creek—*stream* WI-6
Luco Hill—*summit* CA-9
Lucol Hollow—*valley* CA-9
Lucon—*locale* PA-2
Lucore Hollow—*valley* PA-2
Luco Slough—*gut* CA-9
L U Cow Camp—*locale* WY-8
Lucre—*locale* MS-4
Lucre Post Office (historical)—*building* MS-4
**Lucretia**—*pop pl* WV-2
*Lucson* AZ-5
Luctor Cem—*cemetery* KS-7
Luctor Cem—*cemetery* MN-6
Luctor Ch—*church* KS-7
Luctor (historical)—*locale* KS-7
Lucullus—*locale* PA-2
Lucus Cem—*cemetery* TN-4
Lucus Run—*stream* PA-2
Lucus Store—*locale* KY-4
*Lucy* MP-9
Lucy—*locale* AL-4
Lucy—*locale* NM-5
**Lucy**—*pop pl* LA-4
**Lucy**—*pop pl* TN-4
Lucy, Lake—*lake* (2) FL-3
Lucy, Lake—*lake* MN-6
Lucy, Lake—*lake* PA-2
Lucy, Lake—*reservoir* AR-4
Lucy, Lake—*reservoir* GA-3
Lucy, the Margate Elephant—*hist pl* NJ-2
Lucy Albirdie Flat—*flat* OK-5
Lucy B Herring Elem Sch—*school* NC-3
Lucy Branch—*stream* AL-4
Lucy Branch—*stream* FL-3
Lucy Branch—*stream* (3) NC-3
*Lucy Branch County Park* AL-4
Lucy Brook—*stream* CT-1
Lucy Brook—*stream* MA-1
Lucy Brook—*stream* (2) NH-1
Lucy Brook Trail—*trail* NH-1
Lucy Cabin Hollow—*valley* VA-3
Lucy Canyon—*valley* AZ-5
Lucy Canyon—*valley* WA-9
Lucy Cem—*cemetery* AL-4
Lucy Cem—*cemetery* MO-7
Lucy Cem—*cemetery* TN-4
Lucy Chapel—*church* GA-3
Lucy Cobb Institute Campus—*hist pl* GA-3
Lucy Coulee—*valley* MT-8
Lucy Cove—*bay* MD-2
Lucy Cove—*valley* TN-4
Lucy Creek—*stream* KY-4
Lucy Creek—*stream* LA-4
Lucy Creek—*stream* MT-8
Lucy Creek—*stream* OK-5
Lucy Creek—*stream* TN-4
Lucy Creek—*stream* TX-5
**Lucy Crossing**—*pop pl* PA-2
Lucy Draft—*valley* WV-2
Lucy E Simms Sch—*school* VA-3
*Lucy Fork* UT-8
Lucy Fork—*stream* UT-8
**Lucy Furnace**—*pop pl* PA-2
Lucy Furnace Sch (abandoned)—*school* PA-2
Lucy Gap—*gap* NC-3
Lucy Gas Field—*oilfield* LA-4
Lucy Gastrell Bar—*bar* AL-4
Lucy Grey Mine—*mine* NV-8
Lucy Grey Mtns—*range* NV-8
Lucy Gulch—*valley* CA-9
Lucy Gulch—*valley* OR-9
Lucy Halls Park—*flat* CO-8
Lucy Hawkins Cave—*cave* TN-4
Lucy Hill Cem—*cemetery* AL-4
Lucy Jefferson Lewis Memorial
Bridge—*bridge* KY-4
Lucy Lake—*lake* AK-9
Lucy Lake—*lake* WI-6
Lucy Lay Hollow—*valley* KY-4
Lucy Lee Hospital Heliport—*airport* MO-7
Lucy Lee Lateral—*canal* ID-8
Lucy L Gulch—*valley* UT-8
*Lucy L Webb School* MS-4
Lucy Memorial Ch—*church* TN-4
Lucy Park—*flat* MT-8
Lucy Park—*park* TX-5
Lucy Payne Canyon—*valley* OR-9
Lucy Payne Spring—*spring* OR-9
Lucy Peak—*summit* AZ-5
Lucy Plantation—*locale* LA-4
Lucy Point—*cape* MD-2
Lucy Point—*cape* MA-1
Lucy Post Office (historical)—*building* AL-4
*Lucy Pounders Cemetery* AL-4
Lucy Ragsdale Senior HS—*school* NC-3
Lucy Ranch—*locale* WY-8
Lucy Run—*stream* OH-6
Lucy Run Cem—*cemetery* OH-6
Lucy Runyon Canyon—*valley* CA-9
Lucy Sch—*school* AL-4
Lucys Foot Pass—*gap* CA-9
Lucys Hill—*summit* AL-4
Lucys Pond—*reservoir* OH-6
Lucy Spring—*spring* MO-7
Lucy Springs Methodist Ch—*church* AL-4
**Lucy Township**—*pop pl* ND-7
Lucyville—*locale* PA-2
Lucyville Sch (historical)—*school* AL-4
Lucy W Detention Dam—*dam* NM-5
Ludaseska Creek—*stream* AK-9
Luda Siding—*locale* TN-4
Luda Tunnel—*tunnel* TN-4
**Ludden**—*pop pl* ND-7
Ludden Brook—*stream* ME-1
Ludden Cem—*cemetery* ND-7
*Ludden Dam* ND-7
Ludden HS—*school* NY-2
Ludden Mtn—*summit* AZ-5
Ludden Park—*park* AZ-5
Ludden Peak—*summit* WA-9
**Luddersville**—*pop pl* FL-3
*Luddington* IN-6
Luddington Rock Breakwater—*other* CT-1
*Luddington's Branch* IL-6
Luddock Cem—*cemetery* MS-4
Luddy Creek—*stream* MT-8
**Lude**—*pop pl* MN-6
*Lude Beach* MN-6
Ludecker Bald—*summit* MO-7
Ludecker Creek—*stream* MO-7
**Ludell**—*pop pl* KS-7
Ludell Cem—*cemetery* KS-7
**Ludell Township**—*pop pl* KS-7
*Ludel Wash* AZ-5
Luder Creek—*stream* OR-9
Luders Creek—*stream* CO-8
Luders Creek Campground—*locale* CO-8
**Ludevine**—*pop pl* LA-4
Ludger—*locale* LA-4
Ludicia Cem—*cemetery* TN-4
Luding Siding—*locale* AZ-5
Ludington—*locale* MT-8
**Ludington**—*pop pl* LA-4
**Ludington**—*pop pl* MI-6
**Ludington**—*pop pl* OH-6
**Ludington**—*pop pl* WI-6
**Ludington Beet Siding**—*pop pl* MT-8
Ludington Bldg—*hist pl* IL-6
Ludington Cem—*cemetery* IN-6
Ludington Cem—*cemetery* MI-6
Ludington Cem—*cemetery* WI-6
Ludington House—*hist pl* KS-7
Ludington Lake—*lake* WI-6
Ludington Park—*park* MI-6
Ludington Run—*stream* PA-2
Ludingtons Cove—*bay* MI-6
Ludington State Park—*park* MI-6
**Ludington (Town of)**—*pop pl* WI-6
**Ludingtonville**—*pop pl* NY-2
*Ludinton Ditch* IN-6
Ludlam—*uninc pl* FL-3
Ludlam Bay—*bay* NJ-2
Ludlam Beach—*beach* NJ-2
Ludlam Creek—*stream* NJ-2
Ludlam Elem Sch—*school* FL-3
Ludlam-Gratigny Plaza (Shop Ctr)—*locale* FL-3
*Ludlam Pond* NJ-2
*Ludlams Bay* NJ-2
*Ludlams Beach* NJ-2
Ludlams Pond—*reservoir* NJ-2
Ludlams Pond Dam—*dam* NJ-2
Ludlams Sch—*school* NJ-2
Ludlam Thorofare—*channel* NJ-2
*Ludleys Bay* NJ-2
*Ludleys Beach* NJ-2
*Ludlow* OH-6
Ludlow—*locale* CO-8
Ludlow—*locale* IA-7
Ludlow—*locale* OH-6
Ludlow—*locale* OK-5
**Ludlow**—*pop pl* CA-9
**Ludlow**—*pop pl* (2) IL-6
**Ludlow**—*pop pl* KY-4
**Ludlow**—*pop pl* ME-1
**Ludlow**—*pop pl* MA-1
**Ludlow**—*pop pl* MS-4
**Ludlow**—*pop pl* MO-7
**Ludlow**—*pop pl* NY-2
**Ludlow**—*pop pl* PA-2
**Ludlow**—*pop pl* SD-7
**Ludlow**—*pop pl* VT-1
Ludlow, Col. Jacob Lott, House—*hist pl* NC-3
Ludlow, James R., Sch—*hist pl* PA-2
Ludlow, Lake—*lake* NY-2
Ludlow, Port—*bay* WA-9
*Ludlow-Asbury (Asbury)* NJ-2
Ludlow Branch—*stream* SC-3
Ludlow Cave—*cave* SD-7
Ludlow Cem—*cemetery* IL-6
Ludlow Cem—*cemetery* OH-6
Ludlow Cem—*cemetery* OK-5
**Ludlow Center**—*pop pl* MA-1
Ludlow Center Cem—*cemetery* MA-1
Ludlow Center Hist Dist—*hist pl* MA-1
*Ludlow Centre* MA-1
Ludlow Ch—*church* IN-6
**Ludlow City**—*pop pl* MA-1
Ludlow Corners—*locale* (2) NY-2
Ludlow Country Club—*locale* MA-1
Ludlow Creek—*stream* NY-2
Ludlow Creek—*stream* (2) OH-6
Ludlow Creek—*stream* TX-5
Ludlow Dam—*dam* MA-1
Ludlow Dam—*dam* SD-7
Ludlowe HS—*school* CT-1
**Ludlow Falls**—*pop pl* OH-6
Ludlow Flats—*flat* VA-3
Ludlow Graded Sch—*hist pl* VT-1
Ludlow Hill—*summit* IN-6
Ludlow (historical)—*locale* SD-7
Ludlow (historical P.O.)—*locale* IN-6
Ludlow HS—*school* MA-1
Ludlow Lagoon Clubhouse—*hist pl* KY-4
Ludlow Lake—*lake* WA-9
Ludlow Lookout Tower—*locale* MN-6
Ludlow Memorial—*other* CO-8
*Ludlow Mfg Dam* MA-1
Ludlow Mtn—*summit* VT-1
Ludlow Park—*park* MN-6
*Ludlow Reservoir* MA-1
*Ludlows Beach* NJ-2
Ludlow Sch—*school* OH-6
Ludlow Sch—*school* PA-2
Ludlow Sch (historical)—*school* PA-2
Ludlows Creek—*stream* NY-2
Ludlow Shop Ctr—*locale* MA-1
Ludlow Shopping Plaza—*locale* MA-1
Ludlow Station—*locale* NJ-2
**Ludlow (subdivision)**—*pop pl* MA-1
Ludlow Swamp—*swamp* NY-2
Ludlow Tent Colony Site—*hist pl* CO-8
**Ludlow (Town of)**—*pop pl* ME-1
**Ludlow (Town of)**—*pop pl* MA-1
**Ludlow (Town of)**—*pop pl* VT-1
Ludlow Township—*fmr MCD* IA-7
**Ludlow (Township of)**—*pop pl* IL-6
**Ludlow (Township of)**—*pop pl* OH-6
Ludlow Trail—*trail* PA-2
**Ludlowville**—*pop pl* NY-2
Ludlowville (sta.) (RR name for
Myers)—*other* NY-2
Ludlum Ditch—*canal* IN-6
Ludlum Gut—*gut* NJ-2
Ludlum Pasture—*flat* NC-3
Ludlum Pond—*lake* NJ-2
Ludlum Sch—*school* NY-2
*Ludlums Pastures* NC-3
**Ludowici**—*pop pl* GA-3
Ludowici North (CCD)—*cens area* GA-3
Ludowici South (CCD)—*cens area* GA-3
Ludowici Well Pavilion—*hist pl* GA-3
*Ludowick Creek* MD-2
Ludowissi Lake—*lake* WI-6
Ludson Hollow—*valley* UT-8
Luds Point—*cape* ID-8
Ludtke Lake—*lake* WA-9
*Ludvich Lake* WA-9
Ludvick Lake—*lake* WA-9
Ludvik Lake—*lake* AK-9
**Ludville**—*pop pl* GA-3
Ludville (CCD)—*cens area* GA-3
**Ludvine**—*pop pl* LA-4
**Ludwick Acres (subdivision)**—*pop pl* NC-3
Ludwick Cabin—*locale* OR-9
Ludwick Cem—*cemetery* KS-7
Ludwick (historical)—*locale* KS-7
Ludwick Sch—*school* PA-2
Ludwig—*locale* AR-4
Ludwig—*locale* MO-7
Ludwig, Godfrey, House—*hist pl* ME-1
Ludwig, Isaac R., Historical Mill—*hist pl* OH-6
Ludwig Bar—*bar* ID-8
Ludwig Cem—*cemetery* (3) OH-6
*Ludwig Creek* MD-2
Ludwig Ditch—*canal* OH-6
Ludwig Gulch—*valley* ID-8
Ludwig Mine—*mine* ID-8
Ludwig Mine—*mine* NV-8
Ludwig Mtn—*summit* CO-8
**Ludwig Park**—*pop pl* IN-6
Ludwig Rapids—*rapids* ID-8
Ludwigs, George, House—*hist pl* WA-9
Ludwig Sch—*school* IL-6
Ludwig Sch—*school* (2) SD-7
**Ludwigs Corner**—*pop pl* PA-2
Ludwigs Hill—*summit* PA-2
Ludwig (Site)—*locale* NV-8
Ludwig Swamp—*swamp* MI-6
*Ludy* MH-9
Ludy Creek—*stream* KS-7
**Luebbering**—*pop pl* MO-7
Luebke Creek—*stream* OR-9
Luebke Lake—*lake* WI-6
Luebking Cem—*cemetery* IN-6
Luebner Lake—*lake* AK-9
Luebow Point—*cape* CA-9
*Luech* FM-9
Lueck Cem—*cemetery* WI-6
Lueck Lake—*lake* ND-7
Lueck Marsh Ditch—*canal* MT-8
Luecks Lake—*lake* WI-6
**Lueders**—*pop pl* TX-5
Lueders (CCD)—*cens area* TX-5
Lueders Cem—*cemetery* TX-5
Lueders Encampment—*locale* TX-5
Luedevitz Lake—*lake* WI-6
*Luedj* FM-9
Luedtke Slough—*lake* MN-6
Luedtke State Wildlife Mngmt
Area—*park* MN-6
*Luedvitz Lake* WI-6
Luehm Spring—*spring* WA-9
*Lueis* FM-9
Luelia, Lake—*lake* AK-9
*Luella* KS-7
Luella—*locale* LA-4
**Luella**—*pop pl* GA-3
**Luella**—*pop pl* TX-5
Luella Cem—*cemetery* TX-5
Luella Ch—*church* NC-3
Luella Lake—*lake* CA-9
Luella Mine—*mine* ID-8
Luella Park—*park* IL-6
Luella Sch—*school* IL-6
Luella Sch—*school* OK-5
Luelleman, William, House—*hist pl* OH-6
**Luellen**—*pop pl* PA-2
Luellen Station—*locale* PA-2
Luelling Ranch—*locale* CA-9
Luelling Spring—*spring* OR-9
*Luena Beach* WA-9
Luena Beach—*locale* WA-9
Luenbergen Cem—*cemetery* MO-7
Luenberger Drain—*canal* MI-6
Luera Mountains—*other* NM-5
Luera Peak—*summit* NM-5
Lueschen, John, House—*hist pl* IA-7
Luescher-Barnum State Wildlife Mngmt
Area—*park* MN-6
Luesse Lake—*lake* MO-7
Luesseville Lake—*reservoir* MO-7
Luethi Lake—*lake* MN-6
Luethstrom-Hurin House—*hist pl* OH-6
Luethye Mine—*mine* OR-9
*Luetj* FM-9
Luey Huey Camp—*locale* WY-8
*Luf* NC-3
Lufberg Canyon—*valley* TX-5
Lufbery Memorial Park—*cemetery* CT-1
Lufborrow Cem—*cemetery* IN-6
*Luffenfoltz Creek* CA-9
Luffenholtz Creek—*stream* CA-9
Luffman (historical)—*locale* SD-7
Luff Sch—*school* MO-7
Lufkin—*locale* WI-6
**Lufkin**—*pop pl* TX-5
Lufkin Bottom—*bend* ID-8
Lufkin (CCD)—*cens area* TX-5
Lufkin Creek—*stream* MA-1
Lufkin Junction—*uninc pl* TX-5
Lufkin Land-Long Bell-Buck
House—*hist pl* TX-5
Lufkin Pond—*lake* ME-1
Lufkin Spring—*spring* ID-8
Lufkin Water Plant—*other* TX-5
Lufman Brook—*stream* ME-1
Luft, Conrad, Sr., House—*hist pl* CO-8
Luftee Gap—*gap* NC-3
Luftee Knob—*summit* NC-3
Lugagi Island—*island* MP-9
*Lugalap* FM-9
*Lugan* FM-9
Lugana Lake—*reservoir* NC-3
*Lugan Flat* OR-9
Lugans Basin—*basin* CO-8
Lugar Creek—*stream* IN-6
Lugar Creek Ch—*church* IN-6
Lugaren Island—*island* MP-9
**Lugav**—*pop pl* FM-9
*Lugbill Addition* OH-6
Lugenbeal Creek—*stream* WA-9
Lugenbeel County (historical)—*civil* SD-7
*Lugenur* MP-9
**Luger**—*pop pl* WI-6
Luger Creek—*stream* ID-8
Luger Spring—*spring* OR-9
Lugert—*locale* OK-5
Lugert, Mount—*summit* OK-5
Lugert, Mtn—*summit* OK-5
*Lugert Lake* OK-5
**Lugerville**—*pop pl* WI-6
Lugerville Lookout Tower—*locale* WI-6
Lugg Sch—*school* MN-6
*Lugi* MH-9
Lugo—*locale* CA-9
**Lugo**—*pop pl* AL-4
Lugo—*uninc pl* CA-9
Lugo Canyon—*valley* CA-9
*Lugodj* MP-9
**Lugoff**—*pop pl* SC-3
Lugoff Sch—*school* SC-3
Lugoff Station—*locale* SC-3
Lugonia Sch—*school* CA-9
*Lugoon* MP-9
Lugo Park—*park* CA-9
Lugo Pond—*reservoir* AL-4
Lugo Sch—*school* CA-9
*Lugoun* MP-9
Lug Point—*cape* AK-9
Lugten Gully—*valley* MI-6
*Lugulus* FM-9
Luguna Channel—*stream* CA-9
Luhan, Mabel Dodge, House—*hist pl* NM-5
**Luhke**—*pop pl* FM-9
Luhke, Pilen—*stream* FM-9
Luhkeileng—*locale* FM-9
Luhr Beach—*locale* WA-9
Luhr Creek—*stream* WA-9
Luhr Creek Rsvr—*reservoir* WA-9
Luhr Hill—*summit* NV-8
Luhrig—*locale* OH-6
Luhr Sch—*school* KY-4
Luhrs Landing Strip—*airport* MO-7
Luhrwood Lakes—*lake* IL-6
Luhtasaari Ranch—*locale* SD-7
Luicks Creek—*stream* IA-7
Lui Hopper Ditch—*canal* CO-8
*Luijap* MP-9
**Luisa**—*pop pl* PR-3
Luisaga—*island* FM-9
*Luisa Island* RI-1
Luisap Island—*island* MP-9
Luis Canyon—*valley* CO-8
**Luis Cintron**—*pop pl* (2) PR-3
Luis Creek—*stream* SD-7
Luis Llorens Torres—*CDP* PR-3
**Luis Llorens Torres**—*pop pl* PR-3
**Luis Lopez**—*pop pl* NM-5
Luis Lopez And Drain B—*canal* NM-5
Luis Lopez Ditch—*canal* NM-5
Luis Lopez Drain—*canal* (2) NM-5
*Luis Lopez Ranch* NM-5
Luis Maria Baca Float Number Five—*civil* AZ-5
Luis Maria Baca Grant (float Number
Three)—*civil* AZ-5
Luis Maria Baca No 4—*civil* CO-8
Luis M. Cintron—*CDP* PR-3
*Luiss Creek* NC-3
Luis Well—*locale* NM-5
Luis Well—*well* NM-5
Lujan Canyon—*valley* (2) NM-5
Lujan Creek—*stream* CO-8
Lujane—*locale* CO-8
Lujan Windmill—*locale* NM-5
Lujenida Lake—*lake* MN-6
*Lujirok Island* MP-9
Lujor—*island* MP-9
*Lujor Island* MP-9
Lujuna Point—*cape* GU-9
**Lukachukai**—*pop pl* AZ-5
Lukachukai Airp—*airport* AZ-5
Lukachukai Boarding Sch—*school* AZ-5
Lukachukai Creek—*stream* AZ-5
Lukachukai Mountains—*range* AZ-5
Lukachukai Post Office—*building* AZ-5
Lukachukai Trading Post—*building* AZ-5
*Lukachukai Wash* AZ-5
Lukaigai Well—*well* AZ-5
Lu Kai le gei Well—*well* AZ-5
Lukai Spring—*spring* AZ-5
Lukai Wash—*stream* AZ-5
*Lukalap* FM-9
Lukan—*island* FM-9
Lukanin Bay—*bay* AK-9
Lukarilla—*locale* OR-9
*Lukasakad* AZ-5
*Lukasakad Spring* AZ-5
Lukas Canyon—*valley* NM-5
Lukas Creek—*stream* VA-3
Luka Spring—*spring* NM-5
*Luke* AZ-5
Luke—*locale* AL-4
Luke—*locale* GA-3
Luke—*other* PA-2
**Luke**—*pop pl* MD-2
**Luke**—*pop pl* VA-3
Luke AFB—*military* (2) AZ-5
Luke Air Force Auxiliary Field Number
One—*military* AZ-5
*Luke Branch* GA-3
Luke Canyon—*valley* NM-5
Luke Carroll Branch—*stream* KY-4
Luke Cem—*cemetery* AR-4
Luke Cem—*cemetery* GA-3
Luke Cem—*cemetery* LA-4
Luke Cem—*cemetery* OH-6
**Luke Chute**—*pop pl* OH-6
Luke Creek—*stream* AK-9
Luke Creek—*stream* LA-4
Luke Decker Claim—*reserve* IN-6
Lukefahr Sch (abandoned)—*school* MO-7
**Luke Fidler (Luke)**—*pop pl* PA-2
Luke Fluffer Creek—*stream* MS-4
Luke Ford Creek—*swamp* FL-3
Luke Hall Mill Branch—*stream* TN-4
Luke Hill—*summit* MS-4
**Luke (historical)**—*pop pl* TN-4
Luke Hollow—*valley* KY-4
Luke Knob—*summit* IN-6
Luke Lake—*lake* AK-9
Luke Lake—*lake* FL-3
Luke Landing—*locale* LA-4
*Luke Lea Cemetery* MS-4
Luke Mine—*mine* MT-8
Luke Mountain Tank—*reservoir* AZ-5
Luke Mtn—*summit* AZ-5
Luke Mtn—*summit* MT-8
Luke Mtn—*summit* TN-4
Luken Cem—*cemetery* IL-6
Luken Ditch—*canal* IN-6
Lukens—*locale* NC-3
**Lukens**—*pop pl* FL-3
Lukens, Mount—*summit* CA-9
Lukens, Theodore Parker, House—*hist pl* CA-9
Lukens Cem—*cemetery* OH-6
Lukens Creek—*stream* FL-3
Lukens Creek—*stream* OR-9
Lukens Hazel Mine—*mine* MT-8
Lukens Lake—*lake* CA-9
**Lukens Lake**—*pop pl* IN-6
Lukens Lake—*reservoir* IN-6
Lukens Main Office Bldg—*hist pl* PA-2
Lukens Sch (abandoned)—*school* PA-2
Luke Park—*park* KS-7
Lukepen Sapw—*unknown* FM-9
Luke Point—*cape* AK-9
Luke Prairie—*woods* CA-9
Luker Branch—*stream* TN-4
Luker Cem—*cemetery* AL-4
Luker Cem—*cemetery* TX-5
Luker Dam—*dam* AL-4
Luker Dam—*dam* TN-4
Luker Lake—*reservoir* AL-4
Luker Lake—*reservoir* TN-4
Lukes—*bar* PW-9
Lukes Branch—*stream* WV-2
Luke Sch—*school* AZ-5
Lukes Cove—*valley* NC-3
*Lukes Creek* NC-3
Lukes Hoist Mine—*mine* AZ-5
Lukes Island—*island* VA-3
Luke (site)—*locale* NV-8
Lukes Landing—*locale* AL-4
Lukes Mtn—*summit* VA-3
Lukes Pond—*lake* GA-3
Lukes Run—*stream* PA-2
Lukes Trail—*trail* PA-2
Luke Swamp—*stream* GA-3
*Luke Swamp Branch* GA-3
Luketown Cem—*cemetery* AL-4
**Lukeville**—*pop pl* AZ-5
**Lukeville**—*pop pl* LA-4
Luke Wash—*stream* AZ-5
Luke Watkins Hollow—*valley* KY-4
Luke Well—*well* AZ-5
Luke Wilson—*locale* TX-5
Lukewood Park—*park* FL-3
Lukey Fork—*stream* WV-2
*Lukfahata Creek* MS-4
Lukfapa Creek—*stream* MS-4
Lukfata Cem—*cemetery* OK-5
Lukfata Ch—*church* OK-5
Lukfata Creek—*stream* OK-5
Lukfata Sch—*school* OK-5
*Lukfodder Creek* MS-4
Lukingdom Ch—*church* TX-5
Lukins, F. L., House—*hist pl* NM-5
Lukins Cem—*cemetery* PA-2
Lukins Run—*stream* WV-2
**Lukin (Township of)**—*pop pl* IL-6
Lukken Sch—*school* WI-6
Lukluksukwik Lake—*lake* AK-9
*Lukonwor* MP-9
*Lukonwor Island* MP-9
*Lukop* FM-9
Lukopoas—*civil* FM-9
**Lukopoas**—*pop pl* FM-9
Luksokla Ch—*church* OK-5
Lukthlukrit Marsh—*swamp* AK-9
Lukuen Island—*island* MP-9
*Lukula* FM-9
*Lukuladjaw* FM-9
*Lukulefau* FM-9
Lukunlulem—*locale* FM-9
Lukunlulem, Infal—*stream* FM-9
Lukunor—*island* FM-9
Lukunor Atoll—*island* FM-9
Lukunor Island—*island* MP-9
Lukunor (Municipality)—*civ div* FM-9
Lukunor Passage—*channel* MP-9
*Lukunos* MP-9
Lukuth—*summit* FM-9
*Lukwoj* MP-9
*Lukwonwod* MP-9
Lula—*locale* LA-4
**Lula**—*pop pl* GA-3
**Lula**—*pop pl* LA-4
**Lula**—*pop pl* MS-4
**Lula**—*pop pl* OK-5
Lula Baptist Ch—*church* MS-4
Lula Bridge—*bridge* GA-3

Lula (CCD)—cens area GA-3
Lula Cem—cemetery MO-7
Lula Cem—cemetery OK-5
Lula Cemetery TN-4
Lula Ch—church MS-4
Lula Ch—church MO-7
Lula Falls—falls GA-3
Lulah SC-3
Lulahala Point—cape HI-9
Lulah Cem—cemetery TN-4
Lulah Ch (historical)—church TN-4
Lula Head Gap—gap GA-3
**Lula (historical)**—pop pl TN-4
Lula Lake—lake GA-3
Lula Lake—lake OR-9
Lula Methodist Episcopal Church TN-4
Lula Mine—mine CO-8
Lula Park—park GA-3
Lula Post Office (historical)—building TN-4
Lula Residential Hist Dist—hist pl GA-3
Lula -Rich Acad—school MS-4
Lula Rich Consolidated Sch MS-4
Lula Rich Sch MS-4
Lula Sch—school LA-4
Lula Sch—school MS-4
**Lulaton**—pop pl GA-3
Lulaula HI-9
Lula United Methodist Ch—church MS-4
Lulaville—locale TN-4
**Lulaville**—pop pl GA-3
Lulaville Post Office (historical)—building TN-4
Lulbegrud Creek—stream KY-4
**Luling**—pop pl LA-4
**Luling**—pop pl TX-5
Luling (CCD)—cens area TX-5
Luling Oil Field—oilfield (2) TX-5
Lull—locale TX-5
**Lull**—pop pl TX-5
Lullaby Creek—stream MN-6
Lullaby Lake—lake MN-6
Lulla Chapel—church GA-3
Lull Cem—cemetery NY-2
Lull Mine—mine TN-4
Lulls Brook—stream VT-1
Lullwater Beach—uninc pl FL-3
Lullwater Creek—stream GA-3
Lull-White Prospect—mine TN-4
Lulog—area GU-9
**Lulu**—pop pl FL-3
**Lulu**—pop pl MI-6
**Lulu**—pop pl MO-7
Lulu, Lake—lake (2) FL-3
Lulu, Lake—reservoir AL-4
Lulu Brook—stream MA-1
Lulu Butte SD-7
Lulu Canal—canal LA-4
Lulu Cascade—falls MA-1
Lulu Cem—cemetery MI-6
Lulu City—locale CO-8
Lulu City Site—hist pl CO-8
Lulu Creek—stream (2) AK-9
Lulu Creek—stream CO-8
Lulu Fairbanks, Mount—summit AK-9
Lulu Falls Cem—cemetery OH-6
Lulu Gulch—valley MT-8
Lulu Island—island AK-9
Luluku Stream—stream HI-9
Luluku Tunnel—cave HI-9
Lulu Lake OR-9
Lulu Lake—lake MN-6
Lulu Lake—lake (2) WI-6
Lulumahu Stream—stream HI-9
Lulu Mine—mine UT-8
Lulu Mountain CO-8
Lulu M. Ross Elem Sch—school DE-2
Lulu Mtn—summit CO-8
Lulu Pass CO-8
Lulu Pass—gap MT-8
Lulu Rsvr—reservoir ID-8
Lu Lu Temple Country Club—other PA-2
**Lulu Township**—pop pl KS-7
Lulu Valley KS-7
Lum—locale AL-4
**Lum**—pop pl MI-6
**Luma**—pop pl AS-9
**Lumaghi Heights**—pop pl IL-6
Lumahai—civil HI-9
Lumahai Beach—beach HI-9
Lumahai River—stream HI-9
Luman Butte—summit WY-8
Luman Creek—stream (2) WY-8
Luman Ditch—canal WY-8
Luman Draw—valley WY-8
Luman Ranch—locale WY-8
Luman Rim—cliff WY-8
Luman Rsvr—reservoir WY-8
Luman Rsvr No 1—reservoir WY-8
Luman Rsvr No 2—reservoir WY-8
Luman Well—well (2) WY-8
Lumar Park—locale PA-2
Lumbards Cove MA-1
Lum Barn Hollow—valley MO-7
Lum Bayou—stream MS-4
Lumbee Recreation Center—park NC-3
Lumbee River NC-3
Lumber PA-2
Lumber—locale AR-4
Lumber—other PA-2
Lumber Bay—bay (2) AK-9
Lumber Branch—stream LA-4
**Lumber Bridge**—pop pl NC-3
Lumber Bridge Sch (abandoned)—school PA-2
Lumber Bridge (Township of)—fmr MCD NC-3
Lumber Camp Springs—spring FL-3
Lumber Canyon—valley CA-9
Lumber Canyon—valley NM-5
**Lumber City**—pop pl GA-3
**Lumber City**—pop pl (2) PA-2
Lumber City Borough—civil PA-2
Lumber City (CCD)—cens area GA-3
Lumber City Landing—locale GA-3
**Lumber City (Lumber)**—pop pl PA-2
Lumber Company Rsvr—reservoir CO-8
Lumber Cove—bay AK-9
Lumber Creek OR-9
Lumber Creek—stream AK-9
Lumber Creek—stream FL-3
Lumber Exchange Bldg—hist pl MN-6
Lumber Exchange Bldg—hist pl WA-9
Lumberg Sch—school CO-8
Lumber Hollow—valley TN-4
Lumber House Spring No 1—spring NM-5
Lumber House Spring No 2—spring NM-5
Lumberjack Creek—stream ID-8
Lumber Jack Lake MI-6
Lumberjack Lake—lake MI-6
Lumberjacks Park—park MI-6
Lumber Key—island FL-3
**Lumberland (Town of)**—pop pl NY-2
Lumberman Bay—bay MI-6
Lumber Marsh—swamp MD-2
Lumbermens Memorial Monument MI-6
Lumbermens Monument Visitor
Center—locale MI-6
Lumbermens Museum—building MI-6
Lumber Mill—locale NC-3
**Lumberport**—pop pl WV-2
Lumber Ridge—ridge TN-4
Lumber River—stream NC-3
Lumber River—stream SC-3
Lumber Rock—rock MA-1
Lumber Rocks MA-1
Lumber Run—stream VA-3
Lumbert Hill—summit NY-2
Lumberton—locale VA-3
**Lumberton**—pop pl FL-3
**Lumberton**—pop pl MS-4
**Lumberton**—pop pl NJ-2
**Lumberton**—pop pl NM-5
**Lumberton**—pop pl NC-3
**Lumberton**—pop pl OH-6
**Lumberton**—pop pl TX-5
Lumberton Citizens Hosp—hospital MS-4
Lumberton City Cem—cemetery MS-4
Lumberton Creek NJ-2
Lumberton Elem Sch—school MS-4
Lumberton Golf Club—locale NC-3
Lumberton (historical)—locale AL-4
Lumberton HS—school MS-4
Lumberton JHS—school NC-3
Lumberton MS—school NC-3
Lumberton Municipal Airp—airport NC-3
Lumberton P.O. AL-4
Lumberton Senior HS—school NC-3
Lumberton (Township of)—fmr MCD NC-3
**Lumberton (Township of)**—pop pl NJ-2
Lumberton United Methodist Ch—church MS-4
**Lumber (Township of)**—pop pl PA-2
Lumbert Pond—lake MA-1
Lumberts Cove MA-1
Lumberts Pond MA-1
**Lumberville**—pop pl PA-2
Lumberville Dam—dam NJ-2
Lumberville Hist Dist—hist pl PA-2
Lumber Yard PA-2
Lumberyard Landing (historical)—locale TN-4
Lumberyard Ranger Station—locale CA-9
Lumbix Cem—cemetery TN-4
Lumbo Ledge—bar ME-1
Lumbre Canyon—valley NM-5
Lumbrook—locale DE-2
Lumbull—locale AL-4
Lumbus Bar—bar AL-4
Lumbustown Cem—cemetery KY-4
Lumbustown Sch—school KY-4
Lum Drain—canal MI-6
Lumen Chapel—church OH-6
Lumen Lake—lake WI-6
Lumer—locale CA-9
Lumgrey Creek—stream CA-9
Lum Hollow Creek—stream IA-7
Lumiaiwai Waterhole—lake HI-9
Lumico—area GU-9
Luminao Reef—bar GU-9
Luminary—locale TN-4
Luminary Cem—cemetery TN-4
Luminary Ch—church TN-4
Luminary Sch (historical)—school TN-4
Luminary United Methodist Church TN-4
Lumis Ch—church MS-4
Lumis Chapel Ch MS-4
**Lumite**—pop pl GA-3
Lumkins—locale TX-5
Lum Lake—lake (2) MN-6
Lumley Branch—stream MO-7
Lumley Cem—cemetery TX-5
Lumley Lake—lake NM-5
Lumley School—locale IL-6
Lumleys Stand (historical)—locale TN-4
Lumley Stand Ch—church TN-4
Lumlick Ridge—ridge GA-3
**Lumm**—pop pl TX-5
Lummi Bay—bay WA-9
Lummi Cem—cemetery WA-9
Lummi Flats—flat WA-9
**Lummi Ind Res**—pop pl WA-9
Lummi Island—island WA-9
**Lummi Island**—pop pl WA-9
Lummi Island (CCD)—cens area WA-9
Lummi Marine Park—park WA-9
Lummi Peak—pillar WA-9
Lummi Point—cape WA-9
Lummi Reservation (CCD)—cens area WA-9
Lummi River—stream WA-9
Lummi Rocks—island WA-9
Lummis—locale VA-3
Lummis Canyon—valley NM-5
Lummi Sch—school WA-9
Lummis Home—building CA-9
Lummis House—hist pl CA-9
Lummis Lake Lower Dam—dam NJ-2
Lummis Lakes—reservoir NJ-2
Lummis Marsh Branch—stream NJ-2
Lummis Mill NJ-2
Lummis Ranch—locale WY-8
Lummistown—locale NJ-2
**Lummisville**—pop pl NY-2
Lummus Pond DE-2
Lummus Cem—cemetery TX-5
Lummus Island—island FL-3
Lummus Park—park FL-3
Lump, The—summit NC-3
Lum Park—park MN-6
Lump Gulch—valley CO-8
Lump Gulch—valley MT-8
Lump Island—island AK-9
Lumpkin—locale CA-9
Lumpkin—locale GA-3
**Lumpkin**—pop pl GA-3
Lumpkin, Gov. Wilson, House—hist pl GA-3
Lumpkin, Joseph Henry, House—hist pl GA-3
Lumpkin Branch—stream TN-4
Lumpkin (CCD)—cens area GA-3
Lumpkin Cem—cemetery (3) MS-4
Lumpkin Cem—cemetery TX-5
Lumpkin Commercial Hist Dist—hist pl GA-3
Lumpkin Company Park—park GA-3
**Lumpkin (County)**—pop pl GA-3
Lumpkin County Jail—hist pl GA-3
Lumpkin Creek—stream AR-4
Lumpkin Creek—stream GA-3
Lumpkin Mill Creek—stream AL-4
Lumpkin Ridge—ridge CA-9
Lumpkin Ridge—ridge GA-3
Lumpkin Sch (historical)—school MS-4
Lumpkins Fork—stream MO-7
Lumpkin Spring—spring GA-3
**Lumpkin Subdivision**—pop pl MS-4
Lumpkin Tank—reservoir AZ-5
Lumpmouth Creek—stream OK-5
Lump Mtn—summit AK-9
Lump Mtn—summit NC-3
Lump Overlook, The—locale NC-3
Lumpson Creek—stream MI-6
Lumps Spring, The—spring NV-8
Lumptown—locale NC-3
Lumpy Ridge—ridge CO-8
Lumreau Creek—stream CA-9
Lumreau Mtn—summit CA-9
Lum River IL-6
Lumrum Butte—summit OR-9
Lums—locale LA-4
Lums Canyon—valley UT-8
Lums Cem—cemetery TX-5
Lum Sch—school CA-9
Lums Chapel—locale TX-5
Lum Sch (historical)—school AL-4
Lumsden, W. H., House—hist pl CA-9
Lumsden Bend—bend TN-4
Lumsden-Boone Bldg—hist pl NC-3
Lumsden Canyon—valley CO-8
Lumsden Cem—cemetery TN-4
Lumsdens Rsvr—reservoir AR-4
Lumsley Fork—stream TN-4
Lum's Mill House—hist pl DE-2
Lums Millpond DE-2
Lums Pond—lake DE-2
**Lums Pond Estates II**
**(subdivision)**—pop pl DE-2
Lums Pond State Park—park DE-2
Lumstead—locale PA-2
**Lumtie**—pop pl MO-7
Lumuna—summit GU-9
Lum Wash—stream AZ-5
Luna—locale AR-4
Luna—locale LA-4
Luna—locale MN-6
Luna—locale MO-7
Luna—locale NM-5
Luna—locale TX-5
**Luna**—pop pl NM-5
**Luna**—pop pl TN-4
Luna, Lake—reservoir GA-3
Luna, Lake—reservoir MO-7
Luna, Tranquilino, House—hist pl NM-5
Luna Bar—bar MS-4
Luna Branch—stream OK-5
Luna Butte—summit OR-9
Luna Butte—summit WA-9
Luna Canyon—valley CA-9
Luna Cem—cemetery MS-4
Luna Cem—cemetery (2) TN-4
Luna Cem—cemetery TX-5
Luna Ch—church LA-4
Luna Ch—church MO-7
**Luna (County)**—pop pl NM-5
Luna County Courthouse and
Park—hist pl NM-5
Luna Creek—stream NM-5
Luna Creek—stream WA-9
Lunada Bay—bay CA-9
Lunada Bay—uninc pl CA-9
Lunada Bay Sch—school CA-9
Luna Dam—dam AZ-5
Luna Drain—canal NM-5
Lunaford Branch TN-4
Luna Gulch—valley WA-9
Lunah—locale KY-4
Luna (historical)—locale AL-4
Luna Hollow—valley TN-4
Luna Jacal—hist pl TX-5
Luna Lake—lake CO-8
Luna Lake—lake MN-6
Luna Lake—lake OH-6
Luna Lake—lake WA-9
Luna Lake—lake WI-6
Luna Lake—reservoir AZ-5
Luna Lake Campground—park AZ-5
Luna Landing—locale AR-4
Lunalilo Home—building HI-9
Lunalilo Sch—school HI-9
Luna Lookout Tower—locale LA-4
Luna Mtn—summit CA-9
Lunanca Tank—reservoir TX-5
Lunan Mine—mine AZ-5
Luna Park—flat NM-5
Luna Park—uninc pl NY-2
Luna Park Campground—locale NM-5
Luna Peak—summit WA-9
**Luna Pier**—pop pl MI-6
Luna Ranger Station—locale NM-5
Lunar Crater—crater NV-8
Lunar Creek—stream KY-4
Lunar Creek—stream WA-9
Lunar Cuesta—ridge NV-8
Lunar Lake—flat NV-8
Lunar Lake—lake MN-6
Lunar Landing Research Facility—hist pl VA-3
Lunas—locale TX-5
Lunas Lake—reservoir NM-5
Luna Spring—spring CA-9
Luna Tank—reservoir NM-5
LUNA (tugboat)—hist pl MA-1
Luna Valley—valley NM-5
**Lunaville**—pop pl HI-9
Luna-White Deer Campground—locale WI-6
Lunay Creek WV-2
Lunbeck Cem—cemetery OH-6
Lunby Cem—cemetery MN-6
Lunby Lake—lake ND-7
Lunce Branch—stream KY-4
Lunceford Branch—stream GA-3
Lunceford Canyon—valley OR-9
Lunceford Cem—cemetery AR-4
Lunceford Cem—cemetery NC-3
Lunch Box Spring—spring MT-8
Lunch Creek WA-9
Lunch Creek—stream AK-9
Lunch Creek—stream (3) CA-9
Lunch Creek—stream (2) CO-8
Lunch Creek—stream (8) ID-8
Lunch Creek—stream (2) MT-8
Lunch Creek—stream (3) OR-9
Lunch Creek—stream (3) WA-9
Lunch Creek—stream WI-6
Lunch Creek—stream WY-8
Lunchford Point AR-4
Lunch Gulch—valley AK-9
Lunch Gulch—valley CA-9
Lunch (historical)—locale MS-4
Lunch Island—island ME-1
Lunch Island—island SC-3
Lunch Lake—lake AK-9
Lunch Lake—lake MN-6
Lunch Lake—lake OR-9
Lunch Lake—lake WA-9
Lunch Lake—lake WY-8
Lunch Meadow—flat (2) CA-9
Lunch Peak—summit ID-8
Lunch Ridge—ridge OR-9
Lunch Spring—spring ID-8
Lunch Spring—spring OR-9
Lunch Tree Hill—summit WY-8
Lunch Valley—valley NV-8
Lund—locale ID-8
**Lund**—pop pl NV-8
**Lund**—pop pl TX-5
**Lund**—pop pl UT-8
**Lund**—pop pl WI-6
Lund, John G., House—hist pl MN-6
Lund, Jon, Site—hist pl ME-1
Lunda—locale OH-6
Lunda Head—cape AK-9
**Lundale**—pop pl WV-2
Lundale Spring—spring UT-8
Lunday—locale NC-3
Lunday Cem—cemetery MO-7
Lundberg—locale GA-3
Lundberg Lake—lake MN-6
Lundberg Ranch—locale WY-8
Lundberg Slough—gut MN-6
Lund Bldg—hist pl WA-9
Lund Brook—stream VT-1
Lundburg, George H., House—hist pl OR-9
Lund Canyon Well—well NV-8
Lund Cem—cemetery MN-6
Lund Ch—church KS-7
Lund Ch—church MN-6
Lund Ch—church ND-7
Lund Coulee—valley MT-8
Lund Creek—stream ID-8
Lund Creek—stream IA-7
Lund Creek—stream OR-9
Lund Creek—stream (2) WI-6
Lund Draw—valley NM-5
Lundeberg, Lake—lake MN-6
Lundeby Cem—cemetery MN-6
Lunde Ch—church ND-7
Lunde Creek—stream ID-8
Lundeen Creek—stream UT-8
Lundeen Lake—lake (2) MN-6
Lundeen Rsvr—reservoir OR-9
**Lundell**—pop pl AR-4
Lundell Canyon—valley OR-9
Lundell Oil Field—oilfield TX-5
Lundell Spring—spring UT-8
Lundell Tank—reservoir AZ-5
Lunden Dam—dam MA-1
Lunde Peak—summit ID-8
Lunder Ch—church MN-6
Lunde Ridge—ridge ID-8
Lunde State Wildlife Mngmt Area—park MN-6
Lunde Valley MO-7
Lund Flats—flat UT-8
Lundgren—locale IA-7
**Lundgren**—pop pl KY-4
Lundgren Canyon—valley ID-8
Lundgren Creek OR-9
Lundgren Creek (historical)—stream OR-9
Lundgren Elem Sch—school KS-7
Lundgren Hereford Ranch Airp—airport KS-7
Lundgren Lake—lake WI-6
Lundgren Oil Field—oilfield KS-7
Lundgren Pond—lake AZ-5
Lundgren 2 Dam—dam SD-7
Lund (historical)—locale KS-7
Lund (historical)—locale SD-7
Lund House—hist pl TX-5
Lundies Crossroads AL-4
Lundimo Meadows—flat WA-9
Lundin Airstrip—airport SD-7
Lundin Peak—summit WA-9
Lund Lake—lake (2) MN-6
Lund Lake—lake (3) WI-6
Lund Motte—other TX-5
**London Street Condo**—pop pl UT-8
Lund Park—locale OR-9
Lund Park—park MN-6
Lund Pasture Tank—reservoir AZ-5
Lundquist, Lake—reservoir SD-7
Lundquist Lake—lake MN-6
Lund Ranch—locale WY-8
Lundring Service Station—hist pl MN-6
**Lunds**—pop pl WI-6
Lunds Cabin (historical)—locale UT-8
Lunds Campground—park UT-8
Lund Sch—school KS-7
Lund Sch—school SD-7
Lunds Corner—uninc pl MA-1
Lundsford Cem—cemetery WV-2
Lundsford Corner—locale AR-4
Lunds Gulch—valley WA-9
Lund Sheep Camp—locale WY-8
Lunds Landing—locale ND-7
Lunds Point—cape WI-6
Lund Spring—spring NV-8
Lundsted Cem—cemetery MN-6
**Lundstrom Heights**—pop pl IA-7
Lundstrum Ford Bridge—other MO-7
**Lunds Valley**—pop pl ND-7
Lund Township—civil SD-7
Lund Township—inact MCD NV-8
**Lund Township**—pop pl ND-7
**Lund (Township of)**—pop pl MN-6
Lundvall Brothers Landing Field—airport CO-8
Lund Valley Ch—church TX-5
Lundvall Ranch—locale WY-8
**Lundy**—pop pl CA-9
**Lundy**—pop pl FL-3
Lundy, Benjamin, House—hist pl OH-6
Lundy Ann Branch—stream AL-4
Lundy Canyon—valley CA-9
Lundy Cem—cemetery TN-4
Lundy Chapel—church GA-3
Lundy Chapel—church TN-4
Lundy Creek—stream GA-3
Lundy Crossroads—locale SC-3
Lundy Divide—gap OK-5
Lundy Draw—valley MT-8
Lundy Hollow—valley TN-4
Lundy Knob—summit VA-3
Lundy Lake—lake CA-9
Lundy Lake—lake IL-6
Lundy Mtn—summit KY-4
Lundy Pass—gap CA-9
Lundy Pond—lake WI-6
Lundy Post Office (historical)—building MS-4
Lundy Post Office (historical)—building TX-5
Lundy Ridge—ridge TN-4
Lundys Airp—airport MS-4
Lundy Sch—school MO-7
Lundy Sch (historical)—school TX-5
Lundys Creek—stream IA-7
**Lundys Lane**—pop pl PA-2
Lundys Lane P. O. (historical)—building PA-2
**Lundys Lane (Wellsburg)**—pop pl PA-2
Lundy Slough—stream LA-4
Lundy Spring—spring OR-9
Lune, Lac du—lake WI-6
LuNeack House—hist pl OH-6
Lunebuoshah (historical)—locale MS-4
Lune Creek ID-8
Luneluah Creek—stream MS-4
Lunenburg—locale VA-3
**Lunenburg**—pop pl AR-4
**Lunenburg**—pop pl MA-1
**Lunenburg**—pop pl VT-1
Lunenburg Country Club—other VA-3
**Lunenburg (County)**—pop pl VA-3
Lunenburg Courthouse Hist Dist—hist pl VA-3
Lunenburg Hist Dist—hist pl MA-1
Lunenburg HS—school VA-3
Lunenburg Junior-Senior HS—school MA-1
Lunenburg (sta.) (RR name for South
Lunenburg)—other VT-1
**Lunenburg Station**—pop pl MA-1
**Lunenburg (Town of)**—pop pl MA-1
**Lunenburg (Town of)**—pop pl VT-1
Lunenburg (Township of)—fmr MCD AR-4
Luner—locale KY-4
Lunestone Creek AL-4
Lunet—locale AR-4
Lunetta Lake—lake MN-6
Luneville NC-3
Luney Creek WV-2
Luney Point—cape MI-6
Lunga Rsvr—reservoir VA-3
**Lungerville**—pop pl PA-2
Lunging Island—island NH-1
Lung Island—island AK-9
Lungren Island—island FL-3
Lungrun Cove—bay FL-3
Lungs, The—lake FL-3
Lungur Island FM-9
**Lun (historical)**—pop pl OR-9
Lunice Creek WV-2
Lunice Creek—stream WV-2
**Luning**—pop pl NV-8
Luning Arroyo—stream CO-8
Lunis Creek—stream TX-5
**Lunita**—pop pl LA-4
Lunkenheimer, Frederick, House—hist pl OH-6
Lunker Lake—lake MN-6
Lunker Lake—lake WA-9
Lunker Lake—reservoir AL-4
Lunksoos Camp—locale ME-1
Lunksoos Lake—lake ME-1
Lunksoos Mtn—summit ME-1
Lunksoos Stream—stream ME-1
Lunn—locale SC-3
Lunn Cem—cemetery MS-4
Lunn Creek TX-5
Lunney Rsvr—reservoir CO-8
Lunn Hollow—valley TN-4
Lunni (historical P.O.)—locale IA-7
Lunn-Musser Octagon Barn—hist pl NY-2
Lunn Point Post Office
(historical)—building TN-4
Lunns Branch—stream TN-4
Lunns Store—locale TN-4
Lunns Store Post Office
(historical)—building TN-4
Lunn's Tavern—hist pl PA-2
Lunn Store TN-4
Lunn Tank—reservoir AZ-5
**Lunnville**—pop pl OR-9
Lunsard Cem—cemetery WV-2
Lunsbury Creek—stream OR-9
Lunsford AL-4
Lunsford KY-4
Lunsford—locale IA-7
**Lunsford**—pop pl AR-4
Lunsford Branch TN-4
Lunsford Branch—stream TN-4
Lunsford Canyon OR-9
Lunsford Cem—cemetery TN-4
Lunsford Ditch—canal IN-6
Lunsford Gap—gap GA-3
Lunsford Hill—summit VA-3
Lunsford Hollow—valley TN-4
Lunsford Point—cape AR-4
Lunsford Pond Dam—dam AL-4
Lunsford-Pulcher Archeol Site—hist pl IL-6
Lunsford Spring—spring CA-9
Lunsford (Township of)—fmr MCD AR-4
Lunt—locale VA-3
Lunt Branch—stream TN-4
Lunte Creek—stream IL-6
Lunt Harbor—bay ME-1
Lunt Hollow—valley UT-8
Lunt-Lattimer Spring—spring UT-8
Lunt Ledge—bench NH-1
Lunt Memorial Cem—cemetery ME-1
Lunt Mountain VA-3
Lunt Point—cape ME-1
Lunt Rock—rock MA-1
Lunt Rocks MA-1
**Lunts Corner**—pop pl ME-1
Luntsfords Mtn—summit VA-3
Lunts Hill—summit ME-1
Lunts Horse Pasture—flat UT-8
Luntz, Lake—lake FL-3
Luntz Cem—cemetery PA-2
Lunx Creek—stream AK-9
Luoma Ranch—locale MT-8
Lupatcong Creek NJ-2
Lupea Kipuka—summit HI-9
Lupea Trail—trail HI-9
Lupehu—civil HI-9
Luper Cem—cemetery TX-5
**Luper (historical)**—pop pl OR-9
Luper Mtn—summit TN-4
Lupe Spring—spring CA-9
Lupe Springs—spring ID-8
Lupe Tank—reservoir NM-5
Lupe Well—well AZ-5
Lupfer—locale MT-8
Lupfer Glacier—glacier MT-8
Lupher Chapel—church PA-2
Luphers Run—stream PA-2
Lupien Spring—spring MT-8
Lupine Campground—locale CA-9
Lupine Creek—stream ID-8
Lupine Creek—stream (2) MT-8
Lupine Creek—stream OR-9
Lupine Creek—stream WY-8
Lupine Gulch—valley (2) ID-8
Lupine Lake MT-8
Lupine Lake—lake MT-8
Lupine Meadows—flat WY-8
Lupine Mtn—summit ID-8
Lupine Point—cliff CA-9
Lupine River—stream AK-9
Lupine Spring MT-8
**Lupine Village Subdivision**—pop pl UT-8
Lupog MH-9
**Lupog**—pop pl GU-9
Lupok—slope MH-9
Lupold Cem—cemetery IN-6
Luppatatong Creek—stream NJ-2
Luppatcong Creek NJ-2
Lupper Cem—cemetery TN-4
Lupperts Flume Bridge
(historical)—bridge TN-4
Luptn City Church TN-4
Lupton CO-8
Lupton TN-4
**Lupton**—pop pl AL-4
**Lupton**—pop pl AZ-5
**Lupton**—pop pl KY-4
**Lupton**—pop pl MI-6
**Lupton**—pop pl NC-3
Lupton Bottom Ditch—canal CO-8
Lupton Bottoms Ditch—canal CO-8
Lupton Cem—cemetery NC-3
Lupton Chapter House—building AZ-5
Lupton Church AL-4
**Lupton City**—pop pl TN-4
Lupton City Post Office—building TN-4
Lupton City Sch (historical)—school TN-4
Lupton Creek—stream CA-9
Lupton Cross Roads—locale TN-4
Lupton Ditch—canal IN-6
Lupton Drive Baptist Ch—church TN-4
Lupton Interchange—crossing AZ-5
Lupton Junior High School AL-4
Lupton Lake—reservoir NC-3
Lupton Lake Dam—dam NC-3
Lupton Point—cape NC-3
Lupton Post Office (historical)—building TN-4
Lupton Sch—school AL-4
Lupton Shore—beach NC-3
**Lupus**—pop pl MO-7
Lupus Lake—lake MN-6
Lu Queen Cem—cemetery TX-5
**Luquillo**—pop pl PR-3
Luquillo (Municipio)—civil PR-3
Luquillo (Pueblo)—fmr MCD PR-3
Lura KS-7
Lura, Lake—lake MN-6
Lura Bldg—hist pl ND-7
Lura Cem—cemetery MN-6
Lura Lake—lake MN-6
Lurance Canyon—valley NM-5
**Lurand**—pop pl MS-4
**Lura Township**—pop pl SD-7
**Lura (Township of)**—pop pl MN-6
Luraville—locale FL-3
Luray—locale IA-7
Luray—locale (2) OH-6
**Luray**—pop pl IN-6
**Luray**—pop pl KS-7
**Luray**—pop pl MO-7
**Luray**—pop pl SC-3
**Luray**—pop pl TN-4
**Luray**—pop pl VA-3
Luray Caverns—cave VA-3
Luray (CCD)—cens area TN-4
Luray Division—civil TN-4
Luray-Lucas Elem Sch—school KS-7
Luray (Magisterial District)—fmr MCD VA-3
Luray Post Office—building TN-4
Luray Rsvr—reservoir VA-3
Luray Sch (historical)—school TN-4
**Luray Township**—pop pl KS-7
Lure, Lake—lake FL-3
Lure, Lake—lake MI-6
Lure, Lake—reservoir GA-3
Lure, Lake—reservoir NC-3
Lure Lake—lake AK-9
Luretha KY-4
Luretta Ch—church TN-4
**Lurgan**—pop pl PA-2
**Lurgan (sta.)**—pop pl PA-2
**Lurgan (Township of)**—pop pl PA-2
Luria Plaza (Shop Ctr)—locale FL-3
Lurias Plaza (Shop Ctr)—locale FL-3
Lurich—locale VA-3
Lurker Hollow—valley MO-7
Lurleen, Lake—reservoir AL-4

Lyeffion (CCD)—cens area AL-4
Lyeffion Ch—church AL-4
Lyeffion Division—civil AL-4
Lyeffion Elem Sch—school AL-4
Lyeffion HS—school AL-4
**Lyeffiou**—pop pl AL-4
Lyehopper Hollow—valley WV-2
Lye Lake MN-6
Lye Lake—lake ID-8
Lyell—uninc pl NY-2
Lyell, Mount—summit CA-9
Lyell Airp—airport MO-7
Lyell Branch—stream VA-3
Lyell Butte—summit AZ-5
Lyell Canyon—valley CA-9
Lyell Fork—stream CA-9
Lyell Fork Merced River—stream CA-9
Lyell Glacier—glacier CA-9
Lyells—locale VA-3
Lyells Chapel—church VA-3
Lyendecker Lake—lake MN-6
Lye Pond—lake TN-4
Lyerle Chapel—church IL-6
**Lyerly**—pop pl GA-3
Lyerly (CCD)—cens area GA-3
Lyerly Cem—cemetery GA-3
Lyerly Cem—cemetery IL-6
Lyerly Ch—church NC-3
Lyerol Peak CA-9
Lye Run—stream PA-2
**Lyford**—pop pl IN-6
**Lyford**—pop pl TX-5
Lyford (CCD)—cens area TX-5
Lyford Corner—locale ME-1
Lyford Cove—bay ME-1
**Lyford Crossing**—pop pl NH-1
Lyford Dike and Levee Association Ditch—canal IN-6
Lyford Landing—locale MD-2
Lyford Pond—lake NH-1
Lyford Pond—lake VT-1
Lyfords Siding—locale NH-1
Lyford's Stone Tower—hist pl CA-9
Lyford Swamp—swamp ME-1
Lyga Valley—valley WI-6
Lygay Oil Field—oilfield TX-5
Lyges Fork—stream UT-8
Lygia TN-4
Lykens—locale WI-6
**Lykens**—pop pl OH-6
**Lykens**—pop pl PA-2
Lykens Cem—cemetery IN-6
Lykens Creek WV-2
Lykens Lake—lake WI-6
**Lykens (Township of)**—pop pl OH-6
**Lykens (Township of)**—pop pl PA-2
**Lykers**—pop pl NY-2
Lykers Cem—cemetery NY-2
Lykes—locale SC-3
Lykes Brothers Pond—lake FL-3
Lykes Cave—cave AL-4
Lykes Cove—valley AL-4
**Lykesland (Lykes)**—pop pl SC-3
Lykes Lookout Tower (fire tower)—tower FL-3
**Lykes (Lykesland)**—pop pl SC-3
Lykes Memorial Hosp—hospital FL-3
Lykins OH-6
Lykins—locale KY-4
Lykins Branch—stream KY-4
Lykins County KS-7
Lykins Creek—stream WV-2
Lykins Gulch—valley CO-8
Lykins Square—park MO-7
Lykow Flat—flat ID-8
**Lyla**—pop pl CA-9
Lyla Marsh—reservoir IA-7
Lyla Marsh Dam—dam IA-7
Lyle IN-6
Lyle KS-7
Lyle TN-4
Lyle—locale AL-4
Lyle—locale KS-7
**Lyle**—pop pl IN-6
**Lyle**—pop pl MN-6
**Lyle**—pop pl PA-2
**Lyle**—pop pl VA-3
**Lyle**—pop pl WA-9
Lyle Acad (historical)—school AL-4
Lyle Branch—stream AL 4
Lyle Branch—stream KY-4
Lyle Branch—stream MO-7
Lyle Branch—stream TN-4
Lyle Canyon AZ-5
Lyle Canyon—valley AZ-5
Lyle Canyon Trail One Hundred Twenty—trail AZ-5
Lyle Cem AL-4
Lyle Cem—cemetery (3) AL-4
Lyle Cem—cemetery GA-3
Lyle Cem—cemetery (4) TN-4
Lyle Cem—cemetery WA-9
Lyle Center Sch—school MN-6
Lyle Ch—church VA-3
Lyle Corner—locale FL-3
Lyle Covered Bridge—hist pl PA-2
Lyle Creek—stream AR-4
Lyle Creek—stream CO-8
Lyle Creek—stream ID-8
Lyle Creek—stream NC-3
Lyle Creek—stream OR-9
Lyle Creek—stream VA-3
Lyle Creek—stream WA-9
Lyle Dam—dam OR-9
Lyle Dam—dam TN-4
Lyle Drain—canal MI-6
Lyle Gap—gap OR-9
Lyle Gulch—valley ID-8
Lyle JHS—school MA-1
Lyle Knob—summit NC-3
Lyle Knob Mine—mine NC-3
Lyle Lake—lake CO-8
Lyle Lake—lake LA-4
Lyle Lake—lake MI-6
Lyle Lake—lake WA-9
Lyle Lake—lake WI-6
Lyle Lake—reservoir TN-4
Lyle Lake Dam—dam MS-4
Lyle Lane Ch—church TN-4
Lyle Lewton Dam—dam SD-7
Lyle Memorial Ch—church SC-3
Lyle Mtn—summit VA-3
Lyle Park—park AR-4
Lyle Peak—summit AZ-5
Lyle Point—cape WA-9
Lyle Retz Memorial County Park—park IA-7
Lyle Ridge—ridge CA-9
Lylerle Sch—school IL-6
Lyle (RR name for Lyles)—other TN-4
Lyle Rsvr—reservoir OR-9
Lyle Rsvr—reservoir WY-8
Lyles PA-2
**Lyles**—pop pl IN-6
**Lyles**—pop pl TN-4
Lyles Bay—cove MA-1
Lyles Bend TN-4
Lyles Branch TN-4
Lyles Branch—stream AL-4
Lyles Branch—stream SC-3
Lyles Cem—cemetery (2) LA-4
Lyles Cem—cemetery (3) TN-4
Lyles Cem—cemetery TX-5
Lyle Sch—school GA-3
Lyle Sch—school MI-6
Lyle Sch—school MN-6
Lyle Sch—school OR-9
Lyle Sch—school SD-7
Lyle Sch (historical)—school MO-7
Lyles Creek NC-3
Lyles Creek—stream LA-4
Lyles Creek—stream TN-4
Lyles Dam—dam AL-4
Lyles Farm—locale NM-5
Lyles-Gudmundson House—hist pl SC-3
Lyles Hole Spring—spring UT-8
Lyles Lake—lake NC-3
Lyles Lake—lake TN-4
Lyles Lake—reservoir AL-4
Lyles Memorial Library—building AL-4
Lyles Mine—mine TN-4
Lyles Old Field—flat GA-3
Lyles Post Office—building TN-4
Lyle Spring—spring ID-8
Lyle Spring—spring UT-8
Lyles Prospect—mine TN-4
Lyles Ranch—locale (3) TX-5
Lyles Ridge—ridge GA-3
**Lyles (RR name Lyle)**—pop pl TN-4
Lyles-Sanders Cem—cemetery TX-5
Lyles Sch (historical)—school TN-4
Lyles Spring—spring NV-8
Lyle Station IN-6
Lyles Wrigley TN-4
Lyles-Wrigley (CCD)—cens area TN-4
Lyles-Wrigley Division—civil TN-4
**Lyle (Township of)**—pop pl MN-6
**Lyleville**—pop pl PA-2
Lyman NE-7
Lyman NH-1
Lyman—locale MN-6
Lyman—locale NC-3
Lyman—locale OK-5
Lyman—locale SD-7
**Lyman**—pop pl ID-8
**Lyman**—pop pl IA-7
**Lyman**—pop pl MS-4
**Lyman**—pop pl NE-7
**Lyman**—pop pl NH-1
**Lyman**—pop pl SC-3
**Lyman**—pop pl UT-8
**Lyman**—pop pl VT-1
**Lyman**—pop pl WA-9
**Lyman**—pop pl WY-8
Lyman—unorg reg ND-7
Lyman, David, II, House—hist pl CT-1
Lyman, Rev. D. B., House—hist pl HI-9
Lyman, Thomas, House—hist pl CT-1
Lyman, William, House—hist pl OH-6
Lyman Anchorage—bay AK-9
Lyman Bayou—gut AL-4
Lyman Block—hist pl MA-1
Lyman Brook NH-1
Lyman Brook—stream CT-1
Lyman Brook—stream ME-1
Lyman Brook—stream MA-1
Lyman Brook—stream (2) NH-1
Lyman Brook—stream NY-2
Lyman Brook—stream (2) VT-1
Lyman Camp—locale WA-9
Lyman Canyon—valley (2) UT-8
Lyman Cem—cemetery MN-6
Lyman Cem—cemetery NH-1
Lyman Cem—cemetery NY-2
Lyman Cem—cemetery PA-2
Lyman Cem—cemetery UT-8
Lyman Circle—locale OH-6
Lyman County—civil SD-7
Lyman Cow Camp—locale WY-8
Lyman Creek WY-8
Lyman Creek—stream MI-6
Lyman Creek—stream MO-7
Lyman Creek—stream (2) MT-8
Lyman Creek—stream (2) OR-9
Lyman Creek—stream PA-2
Lyman Creek—stream WA-9
Lyman Creek Rsvr—reservoir MT-8
Lyman Crossing—locale NV-8
Lyman Dam—dam AZ-5
Lyman Ditch—canal AZ-5
Lyman Ditch—canal UT-8
Lyman Draw—valley SD-7
Lyman Draw—valley WY-8
Lyman Elem Sch—school KS-7
Lyman Elem Sch—school MS-4
Lyman Estate—building MA-1
Lyman Ferry (Site)—locale WA-9
Lyman Fork—stream AK-9
Lyman Gap—gap PA-2
Lyman Gap Trail—trail PA-2
Lyman Glacier—glacier (2) WA-9
Lyman Hall HS—school CT-1
Lyman Hall Sch—school GA-3
Lyman-Hamilton (CCD)—cens area WA-9
Lyman Hill—summit TN-4
Lyman Hill—summit VT-1
Lyman Hill—summit WA-9
Lyman (historical)—locale SD-7
**Lyman (historical)**—pop pl OR-9
Lyman House—hist pl CT-1
Lyman HS—school FL-3
Lyman Island CT-1
Lyman Island—island MN-6
Lyman Lake—lake MI-6
Lyman Lake—lake (2) WA-9
Lyman Lake—lake (2) WI-6
Lyman Lake—reservoir AZ-5
Lyman Lake—reservoir SC-3
Lyman Lake—reservoir UT-8
Lyman Lake Marina—locale AZ-5
Lyman Lakes—lake MN-6
Lyman Lake State Park—park AZ-5
Lyman Land Trail—trail PA-2
Lyman Log Trail—trail PA-2
Lyman Marsh—swamp WI-6
Lyman Meadow—flat OR-9
Lyman Meadow Brook—stream CT-1
Lyman Meadow Spring—spring OR-9
Lyman Mill Pond Dam—dam MA-1
Lyman Mountain—ridge NH-1
Lyman Mtn—summit OR-9
Lyman Number 1 Dam—dam SD-7
Lyman Number 2 Dam—dam SD-7
Lyman Number 3 Dam—dam SD-7
Lyman Number 4 Dam—dam SD-7
Lyman Number 5 Dam—dam SD-7
Lyman Number 6 Dam—dam SD-7
Lyman Park—park VA-3
Lyman Park (Military Housing)—uninc pl VA-3
Lyman Pass—gap ID-8
Lyman Pass—gap WA-9
Lyman Point—cape AK-9
Lyman Pond PA-2
Lyman Pond—reservoir (2) MA-1
Lyman Post Office (historical)—building SD-7
Lyman Prairie Cem—cemetery MN-6
Lyman Ranch (historical)—locale SD-7
Lyman Rapids—rapids WA-9
Lyman Reservoir AZ-5
Lyman Rock—other AK-9
Lyman Rsvr No 1—reservoir WY-8
Lyman Run—locale PA-2
Lyman Run—stream (2) PA-2
Lyman Run Camp—locale PA-2
Lyman Run Dam—dam PA-2
Lyman Run Rsvr—reservoir PA-2
Lyman Run State Park—park PA-2
Lyman Sch—school CA-9
Lyman Sch—school IL-6
Lyman Sch—school WI-6
Lyman Sch (historical)—school SD-7
Lymans Creek—stream ID-8
Lymans Lake—lake MI-6
Lymans Mill RI-1
Lymans Pond MA-1
Lymans Pond—lake CT-1
Lymans Pond—lake MA-1
Lyman Spring—spring HI-9
Lyman Spring—spring UT-8
Lyman Springs—spring CA-9
Lymans Run Station—locale PA-2
Lyman State Sch—school MA-1
**Lymansville**—pop pl PA-2
**Lymansville**—pop pl RI-1
Lymansville Dam—dam RI-1
Lyman Terrace—hist pl NE-7
**Lymantown**—pop pl WI-6
**Lyman (Town of)**—pop pl ME-1
**Lyman (Town of)**—pop pl NH-1
**Lyman (Township of)**—pop pl IL-6
Lyman Viaduct—hist pl CT-1
Lymanville RI-1
**Lymanville**—pop pl PA-2
Lyman Ward Military Acad—school AL-4
Lyman Well—well UT-8
Lymanwood Hollow—valley PA-2
Lyme CT-1
**Lyme**—pop pl NH-1
**Lyme (Black Hall)**—pop pl CT-1
Lyme Cem—cemetery OH-6
**Lyme Center**—pop pl NH-1
Lyme Common Hist Dist—hist pl NH-1
Lyme Emery Hill—summit VT-1
Lyme Hill—summit NH-1
**Lymehurst**—pop pl (2) PA-2
Lyme Sch—school OH-6
**Lyme Station**—pop pl CT-1
**Lyme (Town of)**—pop pl CT-1
**Lyme (Town of)**—pop pl NH-1
**Lyme (Town of)**—pop pl NY-2
**Lyme (Township of)**—pop pl OH-6
Lym Lake—lake UT-8
Lymnology Lab—school FL-3
Lymp Creek—stream OR-9
**Lympus**—pop pl VT-1
Lynam Creek—stream KY-4
Lynam Creek Sch—school KY-4
**Lynbrook**—pop pl MD-2
**Lynbrook**—pop pl NY-2
**Lynbrook (historical)**—pop pl OR-9
Lynbrook HS—school CA-9
Lynbrook Sch—school MD-2
Lynbrook Sch—school VA-3
Lynbye Slough State Public Shooting Area—park SD-7
Lynces Junction—locale PA-2
Lynch WA-9
Lynch—locale LA-4
Lynch—locale PA-2
**Lynch**—pop pl KY-4
**Lynch**—pop pl MD-2
**Lynch**—pop pl NE-7
**Lynch**—pop pl VA-3
**Lynch**—pop pl WY-8
Lynch—post sta OR-9
Lynch—uninc pl AR-4
Lynch, Matthew, House—hist pl RI-1
**Lynch and Glassmans Subdivision**—pop pl UT-8
Lynch Archeol Site—hist pl NE-7
Lynch Bar—bar OR-9
Lynch Bayou—stream AR-4
Lynch Beach—locale NC-3
Lynch Branch—stream NC-3
Lynch Branch—stream SC-3
Lynch Branch—stream (2) TN-4
Lynch Branch—stream WI-6
Lynchburg—locale FL-3
Lynchburg—locale (2) MS-4
Lynchburg—locale ND-7
**Lynchburg**—pop pl MO-7
**Lynchburg**—pop pl (2) OH-6
**Lynchburg**—pop pl SC-3
**Lynchburg**—pop pl TN-4
**Lynchburg**—pop pl TX-5
Lynchburg Canal TX-5
Lynchburg Canal—canal TX-5
Lynchburg (CCD)—cens area SC-3
Lynchburg (CCD)—cens area TN-4
Lynchburg Cem—cemetery NE-7
Lynchburg City Cem—cemetery TN-4
Lynchburg Coll—school VA-3
Lynchburg Courthouse—hist pl VA-3
Lynchburg Covered Bridge—hist pl OH-6
Lynchburg Division—civil TN-4
Lynchburg Elem Sch—school TN-4
**Lynchburg (Four Corners)**—pop pl TX-5
Lynchburgh TN-4
Lynchburg Hill—summit CA-9
**Lynchburg (ind. city)**—pop pl VA-3
Lynchburg Interchange crossing ND-7
Lynchburg Landing—locale TX-5
Lynchburg Municipal-Preston Glenn Field (Airport)—airport VA-3
Lynchburg Post Office (historical)—building MS-4
Lynchburg Rsvr—reservoir VA-3
**Lynchburg (Township of)**—pop pl IL-6
Lynchburg Training School And Hosp—hospital VA-3
Lynch Canyon—valley (3) CA-9
Lynch Cem—cemetery AL-4
Lynch Cem—cemetery AR-4
Lynch Cem—cemetery CO-8
Lynch Cem—cemetery IL-6
Lynch Cem—cemetery KY-4
Lynch Cem—cemetery MS-4
Lynch Cem—cemetery MO-7
Lynch Cem—cemetery NY-2
Lynch Cem—cemetery NC-3
Lynch Cem—cemetery (6) TN-4
Lynch Cem—cemetery (3) TX-5
Lynch Cem—cemetery (2) VA-3
Lynch Cem—cemetery (2) WV-2
Lynch Ch—church ND-7
Lynch Ch—church OH-6
Lynch Chapel—church MS-4
Lynch Chapel—church WV-2
Lynch Chapel Methodist Ch—church MS-4
Lynch Coulee—valley (3) MT-8
Lynch Coulee—valley WA-9
Lynch Coulee Squaw Creek MT-8
Lynch Cove—bay MD-2
Lynch Cove—bay WA-9
Lynch Cove—valley NC-3
Lynch Creek MT-8
Lynch Creek NC-3
Lynch Creek—stream AL-4
Lynch Creek—stream (4) CA-9
Lynch Creek—stream (2) CO-8
Lynch Creek—stream ID-8
Lynch Creek—stream MI-6
Lynch Creek—stream MN-6
Lynch Creek—stream MS-4
Lynch Creek—stream MT-8
Lynch Creek—stream NV-8
Lynch Creek—stream (3) NC-3
Lynch Creek—stream OK-5
Lynch Creek—stream (2) OR-9
Lynch Creek—stream (5) TX-5
Lynch Creek—stream VA-3
Lynch Creek—stream WA-9
Lynch Creek—stream WI-6
Lynch Creek Forest Camp—locale OR-9
Lynch Dam—dam CA-9
Lynch Ditch—canal CO-8
Lynch Drain—canal MI-6
Lynch Draw OR-9
Lynch Drive Sch—school AR-4
Lynch Elem Sch—school FL-3
Lynches Creek NC-3
Lynches Creek SC-3
Lynches Key FL-3
Lynches Mill—locale SC-3
Lynches River—stream NC-3
Lynches River—stream SC-3
Lynch Field—other PA-2
Lynchfield Landing (historical)—locale MS-4
Lynch Flat—flat OR-9
Lynch Fork—stream WV-2
Lynch-Frizzell Cem TN-4
Lynch Gap—gap CA-9
Lynch Glacier—glacier WA-9
Lynch Gulch—valley ID-8
Lynch Gulch—valley (2) OR-9
Lynch Gulch Waterhole—reservoir OR-9
**Lynch Heights**—pop pl DE-2
Lynch Hill—summit CT-1
Lynch Hill—summit PA-2
Lynch Hill—summit TN-4
Lynch Hill—summit TX-5
Lynch Hill—summit WA-9
Lynch Hollow—valley AR-4
Lynch Hollow—valley MO-7
Lynch Hollow—valley PA-2
Lynch Hollow—valley TN-4
Lynch Hollow—valley WV-2
Lynch HS—school KY-4
Lynch Island MD-2
Lynch JHS—school MA-1
Lynch Lake AL-4
Lynch Lake MN-6
Lynch Lake—lake MI-6
Lynch Lake—lake (5) MN-6
Lynch Lake—lake MT-8
Lynch Lake—lake ND-7
Lynch Lake—lake WA-9
Lynch Lake—lake WI-6
Lynch Meadows—flat CA-9
Lynch Mtn—summit GA-3
Lynch Mtn—summit (2) NY-2
Lynch-O'Gorman House—hist pl MA-1
Lynch Park—park MA-1
Lynch Park Sch—school OR-9
Lynch Pinnacle—pillar TN-4
Lynch Plaza Sch—school OR-9
Lynch Point—cape MD-2
Lynch Point—cape VA-3
**Lynch Point**—pop pl MD-2
Lynch Point Cem—cemetery WV-2
Lynch Pond—lake CT-1
Lynch Ponds—lake PA-2
Lynch-Probst House—hist pl TX-5
Lynch Ranch—locale (4) NM-5
Lynch Ranch—locale SD-7
Lynch Ranch—locale TX-5
Lynch Ranch—locale WY-8
Lynch Ridge—ridge UT-8
Lynch Ridge—ridge WV-2
Lynch River NC-3
Lynch River SC-3
Lynch River—stream VA-3
Lynch Road Sch—school GA-3
Lynch Run—stream PA-2
Lynch Run—stream (2) WV-2
Lynch Sch—school CA-9
Lynch Sch—school IL-6
Lynch Sch—school IN-6
Lynch Sch—school MA-1
Lynch Sch—school (2) MI-6
Lynch Sch—school MO-7
Lynch Sch—school OR-9
Lynchs Chapel—church TX-5
Lynchs Corner—locale NC-3
**Lynchs Corner**—pop pl MD-2
Lynch's Island MD-2
Lynchs Landing Strip—airport PA-2
Lynchs Pond—lake NY-2
Lynch Spring—spring MT-8
Lynch Spring—spring (3) OR-9
Lynch Spring—spring WA-9
Lynchs Rim—ridge OR-9
Lynchs River NC-3
Lynchs River SC-3
**Lynch Station**—pop pl VA-3
**Lynch Station (RR name Clarion)**—pop pl VA-3
Lynch Street CME Ch—church MS-4
Lynchs Woods Park—park SC-3
Lynch Thicket—woods DE-2
Lynch Town Sch—school KY-4
**Lynch Township**—pop pl MO-7
**Lynch Township**—pop pl NE-7
Lynchtown (Township of)—unorg ME-1
**Lynch Tract**—pop pl NY-2
Lynch Valley—valley MO-7
Lynchview Sch—school OR-9
Lynchville—locale ME-1
**Lynchville**—pop pl PA-2
Lynch Whatley Lake AL-4
Lynchwood Dam—dam PA-2
Lynchwood Lake—reservoir PA-2
Lynchwood Sch—school OR-9
Lynco—locale WV-2
Lyncourt—CDP NY-2
Lyncourt Sch—school NY-2
**Lyncrest**—pop pl TX-5
Lyncrest Park—park NJ-2
Lyncrest Sch—school NJ-2
**Lynd**—pop pl MN-6
Lynda, Lake—reservoir MS-4
Lyndale MN-6
Lyndale—locale IA-7
**Lyndale**—pop pl KY-4
**Lyndale**—pop pl MN-6
**Lyndale Acres (subdivision)**—pop pl NC-3
Lyndale Farmstead—park MN-6
Lyndale Field—park MN-6
Lyndale Junction MN-6
Lyndale Park—park MN-6
Lyndale Sch—school (2) MN-6
**Lyndalia**—pop pl DE-2
Lynd Cem—cemetery MN-6
Lynde Basins—lake MA-1
Lyndeboro Mtn NH-1
**Lyndeborough**—pop pl NH-1
Lyndeborough Center Hist Dist—hist pl NH-1
Lyndeborough Mtn—summit NH-1
**Lyndeborough (Town of)**—pop pl NH-1
Lynde Brook—stream (2) MA-1
Lynde Brook Reservoir Dam—dam MA-1
Lynde Brook Reservoir Dike—dam MA-1
Lynde Brook Rsvr—reservoir MA-1
Lynde Draw—valley WY-8
Lynde Hill MA-1
Lyndell—locale PA-2
**Lynden**—pop pl WA-9
Lynden Airp—airport WA-9
Lynden (CCD)—cens area WA-9
Lynden Cem—cemetery NF-7
Lynden Cem—cemetery WA-9
Lynden Creek—stream AK-9
Lynden Gun Club—other WA-9
**Lynden (Township of)**—pop pl MN-6
Lynde Point—cape CT-1
Lynde Rsvr—reservoir OR-9
Lyndes Brook MA-1
Lynde Sch—school VT-1
Lyndhurst MA-1
Lyndhurst SC-3
Lyndhurst—hist pl NY-2
**Lyndhurst**—pop pl NJ-2
**Lyndhurst**—pop pl OH-6
**Lyndhurst**—pop pl SC-3
**Lyndhurst**—pop pl VA-3
**Lyndhurst**—pop pl WI-6
Lyndhurst Mayfield—post sta OH-6
Lyndhurst-Mayfield Heights OH-6
Lyndhurst Plantation—hist pl FL-3
Lyndhurst Station—locale NJ-2
**Lyndhurst (Township of)**—pop pl NJ-2
Lyndon WI-6
**Lyndon**—pop pl IL-6
**Lyndon**—pop pl KS-7
**Lyndon**—pop pl KY-4
**Lyndon**—pop pl NY-2
**Lyndon**—pop pl OH-6
**Lyndon**—pop pl PA-2
**Lyndon**—pop pl VT-1
Lyndon, Loch—lake NH-1
Lyndon Baines Johnson Memorial Grove On The Potomac—park DC-2
Lyndon B Johnson, Lake—reservoir TX-5
Lyndon B Johnson Causeway—bridge TX-5
Lyndon B Johnson JHS—school FL-3
Lyndon B Johnson Lake—lake TX-5
Lyndon B Johnson Natl Grassland—park TX-5
Lyndon B. Johnson Natl Historical Park—hist pl TX-5
Lyndon B Johnson Natl Historic Site—park TX-5
Lyndon B Johnson Sch—school TX-5
Lyndon B. Johnson Space Center (NASA)—building TX-5
Lyndon Canyon—valley CA-9
Lyndon Carnegie Library—hist pl KS-7
Lyndon Cem—cemetery KS-7
Lyndon Cem—cemetery OH-6
Lyndon Cem—cemetery WI-6
Lyndon Center—locale MI-6
**Lyndon Center**—pop pl VT-1
Lyndon City Dam—dam KS-7
**Lyndon Corners**—pop pl VT-1
Lyndon Creek—stream OR-9
Lyndon Creek—stream WI-6
**Lyndon Dale**—pop pl WI-6
Lyndon Elem Sch—school KS-7
Lyndoner NC-3
Lyndon Gulch—valley NV-8
Lyndon Hill Sch—school MD-2
Lyndon HS—school KS-7
Lyndon (RR name for Lyndon Station)—other WI-6
Lyndon Sch—school MA-1
Lyndon Station—locale KS-7
**Lyndon Station**—pop pl WI-6
Lyndon Teachers Coll—school VT-1
**Lyndon (Town of)**—pop pl NY-2
**Lyndon (Town of)**—pop pl VT-1
**Lyndon (Town of)**—pop pl (2) WI-6
**Lyndon (Township of)**—pop pl IL-6
**Lyndon (Township of)**—pop pl MI-6
Lyndon Valley Sch—school KS-7
**Lyndonville**—pop pl NY-2
**Lyndonville**—pop pl VT-1
**Lyndora**—pop pl PA-2
Lyndora Elem Sch—school PA-2
Lyndover—locale NC-3
**Lynd (Township of)**—pop pl MN-6
Lyne, Thomas, House—hist pl KY-4
Lyne, Walter C., House—hist pl UT-8
Lyne Cem—cemetery KY-4
Lynelle Meadows—uninc pl NY-2
Lyne Ranch—locale TX-5
Lynes Cem—cemetery NY-2
Lynes Ranch—locale ID-8
Lynes Saddle—gap ID-8
Lynette, Lake—lake MD-2
Lyneville—locale GA-3
Lynfeld—hist pl NY-2
Lynford Gulch—valley CA-9
**Lynford (subdivision)**—pop pl DE-2
Lynhams—locale VA-3
Lynhaven—locale GA-3
**Lynhaven**—pop pl VA-3
Lynhaven Inlet VA-3
Lynhaven Lodge—locale TX-5
Lynhaven Sch—school CA-9
**Lyn Hills**—pop pl GA-3
Lynholm Gulch—valley OR-9
Lynhurst—locale GA-3
**Lynhurst**—pop pl IN-6
Lynhurst Baptist Ch—church IN-6
Lyn Knoll Sch—school CO-8
Lynmore Ch—church GA-3
Lynmore Estates—uninc pl GA-3
Lynn TN-4
Lynn WV-2
Lynn—locale CO-8
Lynn—locale (2) GA-3
Lynn—locale NE-7
Lynn—locale NH-1
Lynn—locale OH-6
Lynn—locale UT-8
**Lynn**—pop pl AL-4
**Lynn**—pop pl AR-4
**Lynn**—pop pl FL-3
**Lynn**—pop pl IN-6
**Lynn**—pop pl KY-4
**Lynn**—pop pl MA-1
**Lynn**—pop pl NM-5
**Lynn**—pop pl NC-3
**Lynn**—pop pl (2) PA-2
**Lynn**—pop pl TN-4
**Lynn**—pop pl UT-8
**Lynn**—pop pl WV-2
**Lynn**—pop pl WI-6
Lynn, Armory—hist pl MA-1
Lynn, City of—civil MA-1
Lynn, Lake—lake NC 3
Lynn, Lake—reservoir (3) NC-3
Lynn, Town of MA-1
**Lynn Acres**—pop pl AL-4
**Lynn Addition**—pop pl OK-5
Lynn Ave Sch—school TN-4
Lynn Bank Block—hist pl MA-1
Lynn Bark Fork—stream KY-4
Lynn Bark Sch—school KY-4
Lynn Bayou—stream TX-5
Lynn Beach MA-1
Lynn Beach—beach MA-1
Lynn Beals Dam—dam SD-7
Lynn Branch—stream (3) KY-4
Lynn Branch—stream MO-7
Lynn Branch—stream (2) NC-3
Lynn Branch—stream TN-4
Lynn Branch—stream VA-3
Lynn Branch—stream WV-2
Lynn Branch Ch—church IL-6
Lynn Brothers—island AK-9
**Lynncamp**—pop pl KY-4
**Lynn Camp**—pop pl WV-2
Lynn Camp Branch—stream (2) KY-4
Lynn Camp Branch—stream NC-3
Lynn Camp Ch—church KY-4
Lynn Camp Creek—stream (2) KY-4
Lynn Camp Creek—stream (2) VA-3
Lynn Camp Mtn—summit VA-3
Lynn Camp Prong—stream TN-4
Lynncamp Run WV-2
Lynn Camp Run—stream WV-2
Lynncamp Run—stream (4) WV-2
Lynn Camp Run—stream WV-2
Lynncamp Run—stream WV-2
Lynn Camp Run—stream WV-2
Lynncamp Run—stream (3) WV-2
Lynn Camp Sch—school KY-4
Lynn Canal—canal UT-8
Lynn Canal—channel AK-9
Lynn Canyon—valley TX-5
Lynn Canyon Windmill—locale TX-5
Lynn Carden Mtn—summit TN-4

Lynn Cartlage Lake Dam—dam MS-4
Lynn (CCD)—cens area AL-4
Lynn Cem TN-4
Lynn Cem—cemetery (3) GA-3
Lynn Cem—cemetery (3) KY-4
Lynn Cem—cemetery MT-8
Lynn Cem—cemetery PA-2
Lynn Cem—cemetery (4) TN-4
Lynn Cem—cemetery UT-8
Lynn Cem—cemetery WV-2
Lynn Cem—cemetery WI-6
**Lynn Center**—pop pl IL-6
Lynn Ch—church IN-6
Lynn Chapel TN-4
Lynn Chapel—church (2) WV-2
**Lynn Christie**—pop pl TN-4
**Lynn City**—pop pl KY-4
Lynn City Hall—building MA-1
Lynn Common—park MA-1
Lynn Common Station (historical)—locale MA-1
Lynn Corner Sch—school MI-6
**Lynn (County)**—pop pl TX-5
Lynn County Courthouse—hist pl TX-5
Lynn Cove—valley NC-3
Lynn Cove—valley TX-5
Lynncreek MS-4
Lynn Creek NC-3
Lynn Creek TX-5
Lynn Creek WV-2
Lynn Creek—locale MS-4
Lynn Creek—stream (2) AL-4
Lynn Creek—stream AK-9
Lynn Creek—stream (2) AR-4
Lynn Creek—stream GA-3
Lynn Creek—stream (2) IL-6
Lynn Creek—stream IN-6
Lynn Creek—stream KS-7
Lynn Creek—stream LA-4
Lynn Creek—stream (2) MS-4
Lynn Creek—stream NV-8
Lynn Creek—stream TN-4
Lynn Creek—stream (6) TX-5
Lynn Creek—stream UT-8
Lynn Creek—stream (2) WV-2
Lynn Creek—stream WI-6
Lynn Creek Cem—cemetery KS-7
Lynn Creek Cem—cemetery MS-4
Lynn Creek Ch—church MS-4
Lynn Creek Chapel—church TX-5
Lynn Creek Cumberland Presbyterian Ch MS-4
Lynn Creek Methodist Ch MS-4
Lynn Creek Post Office (historical)—building MS-4
Lynn Creek Shelter—hist pl AR-4
Lynn Crossing AL-4
**Lynn Crossing**—pop pl AL-4
**Lynn Crossroads**—pop pl NC-3
**Lynndale**—pop pl AL-4
**Lynndale**—pop pl TN-4
**Lynndale Estates**—pop pl VA-3
**Lynndale Estates (subdivision)**—pop pl NC-3
Lynndale Sch—school MD-2
Lynndale Sch—school MN-6
Lynndale Sch—school WA-9
Lynn Dale Sch—school WV-2
Lynndale Sch (historical)—school PA-2
Lynn Dam—dam AL-4
Lynn Deming Park—park CT-1
Lynn Divide—ridge WV-2
Lynn Division—civil AL-4
Lynn Drain—canal MI-6
Lynn Draw—valley WY-8
**Lynndyl**—pop pl UT-8
Lynndyl Cem—cemetery UT-8
Lynne UT-8
Lynne—locale FL-3
Lynne, Lake—lake FL-3
**Lynne Acres**—pop pl MD-2
Lynne Cem—cemetery LA-4
Lynne Lake—lake AK-9
Lynne Lake—lake WA-9
Lynn Elton Cem—cemetery ND-7
Lynn End MA-1
Lynn End, Town of MA-1
Lynne Oak Cem—cemetery MO-7
Lynne Oak Ch—church MO-7
Lynne Sch—school ND-7
**Lynn Estates (subdivision)**—pop pl MS-4
**Lynne (Town of)**—pop pl WI-6
Lynnewood—post sta PA-2
Lynnewood Elem Sch—school PA-2
**Lynnewood Gardens**—pop pl PA-2
Lynnewood Sch PA-2
Lynnewood Sch—school PA-2
Lynnfield MA-1
Lynn Field—airport GA-3
**Lynnfield**—pop pl DE-2
**Lynnfield**—pop pl MA-1
Lynnfield Center MA-1
Lynnfield Center Golf Club—locale MA-1
Lynnfield Center (RR name for Lynnfield)—other MA-1
Lynnfield Center Sch—school MA-1
Lynnfield Centre MA-1
Lynnfield (historical P.O.)—locale MA-1
Lynnfield HS—school MA-1
Lynnfield JHS—school MA-1
Lynnfield (RR name Lynnfield Center)—CDP MA-1
Lynnfield South Sch—school MA-1
Lynnfield Station (historical)—locale MA-1
**Lynnfield (Town of)**—pop pl MA-1
Lynn Flat TX-5
Lynnford-Lyndon Hall—hist pl KY-4
Lynn Fork—stream (3) KY-4
Lynn Fork—stream (3) WV-2
Lynn Gap—gap NC-3
Lynn Gap—gap TN-4
Lynn Gap Branch—stream TN-4
**Lynn Garden**—pop pl TN-4
Lynn Garden Elem Sch—school TN-4
Lynn Garden Post Office—building TN-4
Lynn Gardens TN-4
**Lynn Gardens**—pop pl IL-6
Lynngate Plaza (Shop Ctr)—locale MA-1
Lynn Grove—locale TX-5
**Lynn Grove**—pop pl KY-4
**Lynn Grove**—pop pl VA-3
Lynn Grove Branch—stream IL-6
Lynn Grove Cem—cemetery IL-6
Lynn Grove Cem—cemetery IA-7
Lynn Grove Sch—school IL-6
Lynn Grove Township—fmr MCD IA-7
Lynn Gulch—valley WA-9
Lynn Harbor—harbor MA-1
Lynn Haslem Dam—dam UT-8
Lynn Haslem Rsvr—reservoir UT-8
**Lynn Haven**—pop pl FL-3
**Lynnhaven**—pop pl (2) VA-3
Lynnhaven Acres—locale VA-3
Lynnhaven Bay VA-3
Lynnhaven Bay—bay VA-3
Lynn Haven Bayou—bay FL-3
Lynn Haven (CCD)—cens area FL-3
Lynn Haven Cem—cemetery FL-3
Lynn Haven Ch—church VA-3
Lynnhaven Ch—church VA-3
**Lynnhaven Colony**—pop pl VA-3
Lynn Haven Elem Sch—school FL-3
Lynn Haven Golf Course—locale FL-3
**Lynn Haven Hills**—pop pl VA-3
Lynn Haven Inlet VA-3
Lynnhaven Inlet—bay VA-3
Lynnhaven Lake—reservoir VA-3
Lynn Haven River VA-3
Lynnhaven Roads—bay VA-3
Lynnhaven Sch—school VA-3
**Lynnhaven Shores**—pop pl VA-3
**Lynn Haven (subdivision)**—pop pl AL-4
**Lynnhaven Subdivision**—pop pl UT-8
Lynn Hill—summit NC-3
Lynn (historical)—locale SD-7
Lynn (historical P.O.)—locale IA-7
Lynn Hollow—valley AR-4
Lynn Hollow—valley KY-4
Lynn Hollow—valley (3) TN-4
Lynn Hollow—valley TX-5
Lynn Hollow—valley (3) VA-3
Lynn Hollow—valley WV-2
Lynn Hosp—hospital MA-1
Lynn HS—school AL-4
**Lynnhurst**—pop pl MA-1
Lynnhurst, Lake—reservoir IL-6
Lynnhurst Cem—cemetery TN-4
Lynnhurst Ch—church KY-4
Lynnhurst Field—park MN-6
Lynnhurst Lake—reservoir TN-4
Lynn Island—island PA-2
Lynn JHS—school NM-5
Lynn Kirk Sch—school OH-6
Lynn Knob—summit GA-3
Lynn Knob—summit WV-2
Lynn Knob Trail—trail WV-2
Lynn Lake—lake MI-6
Lynn Lake—lake SD-7
Lynn Lake—lake (2) WA-9
Lynn Lake—lake WI-6
Lynn Lake State Public Shooting Area—park SD-7
**Lynn Lane**—pop pl OK-5
**Lynn Lee (subdivision)**—pop pl NC-3
**Lynn Lee Village (trailer park)**—pop pl DE-2
Lynn Lick—stream TN-4
Lynn Lick Fork—stream KY-4
Lynn Lick Hollow—valley WV-2
Lynn Lick Run—stream WV-2
Lynn Log Branch—stream KY-4
Lynn Low Place—gap WV-2
Lynn Masonic Hall—hist pl MA-1
Lynn Mill Creek—stream AL-4
Lynn Mill Pond—reservoir AL-4
Lynn Mine—mine CA-9
Lynn Mine (underground)—mine AL-4
Lynn Mtn—summit NC-3
Lynn Mtn—summit OK-5
Lynn Mtn—summit TN-4
Lynn Mussey Drain—canal MI-6
**Lynn Oaks**—pop pl NJ-2
Lynn Park AL-4
Lynn Park—park AL-4
Lynn Park—park OH-6
Lynn Park Dam AL-4
Lynn Point TN-4
Lynn Point—cape WA-9
Lynn Pond MA-1
**Lynnport**—pop pl PA-2
Lynn Post Office (historical)—building AL-4
Lynn Public Library—hist pl MA-1
Lynn Realty Company Bldg No. 2—hist pl MA-1
Lynn Reservoir Dam—dam MA-1
Lynn River—stream IN-6
Lynn Road Elem Sch—school NC-3
Lynn Rock Ch—church VA-3
Lynn (RR name for Lynn Center)—other IL-6
Lynn Rsvr—reservoir MA-1
Lynn Rsvr—reservoir MT-8
Lynn Rsvr—reservoir UT-8
Lynn Run—stream IN-6
Lynn Run—stream (2) WV-2
Lynn Run Hollow—valley PA-2
Lynns AL-4
Lynn Sch—school AZ-5
Lynn Sch—school (3) IL-6
Lynn Sch—school MI-6
Lynn Sch—school OK-5
Lynn Sch—school UT-8
Lynn Sch—school VA-3
Lynn Sch (abandoned)—school MO-7
Lynns Chapel Sch—school TN-4
Lynn Sch (historical)—school AL-4
Lynn Sch (historical)—school (2) TN-4
Lynn School MS-4
**Lynns Corners**—pop pl OH-6
Lynns Crossing AL-4
Lynns Ditch—canal (2) OR-9
**Lynn Shores**—pop pl VA-3
Lynn Sisters—island AK-9
Lynns Knob—summit PA-2
**Lynns Park**—pop pl AL-4
Lynns Pond—lake UT-8
Lynn Spring—locale VA-3
Lynn Spring—spring AL-4
Lynn Spring—spring TX-5
Lynn Spring—spring UT-8
Lynn Spring Gap—gap VA-3
Lynn Springs—spring TN-4
Lynn Springs Sch—school TN-4
Lynn Stand Hollow—valley VA-3
Lynn State Fishing Lake and Wildlife Area—park KS-7
Lynn Station—locale MA-1
Lynn Station—locale PA-2
Lynn Tank—reservoir AZ-5
Lynn Tank—reservoir TX-5
**Lynntown**—pop pl AL-4
**Lynn (Town of)**—pop pl WI-6
Lynn Township—fmr MCD IA-7
**Lynn Township**—pop pl NE-7
**Lynn Township**—pop pl ND-7
**Lynn Township**—pop pl (3) SD-7
Lynn Township (historical)—civil SD-7
**Lynn (Township of)**—pop pl (2) IL-6
**Lynn (Township of)**—pop pl IN-6
**Lynn (Township of)**—pop pl MI-6
**Lynn (Township of)**—pop pl MN-6
**Lynn (Township of)**—pop pl OH-6
**Lynn (Township of)**—pop pl PA-2
Lynntrough Branch—stream KY-4
Lynnvale Sch—school KY-4
Lynn Valley—valley TN-4
Lynn Valley Baptist Church TN-4
Lynn Valley Ch—church TN-4
**Lynnview**—pop pl KY-4
**Lynnview**—pop pl OH-6
Lynn View HS—school TN-4
Lynn View MS TN-4
Lynn Village MA-1
Lynnville IN-6
**Lynnville**—pop pl IL-6
**Lynnville**—pop pl IN-6
**Lynnville**—pop pl IA-7
**Lynnville**—pop pl KY-4
**Lynnville**—pop pl PA-2
**Lynnville**—pop pl TN-4
Lynnville (CCD)—cens area TN-4
Lynnville Cem—cemetery IN-6
Lynnville Ch—church PA-2
Lynnville Division—civil TN-4
Lynnville (Election Precinct)—fmr MCD IL-6
Lynnville Elem Sch—school IN-6
Lynnville Hist Dist—hist pl TN-4
Lynnville Mill and Dam—hist pl IA-7
Lynnville Mine—mine IN-6
Lynnville Post Office (historical)—building AL-4
Lynnville Sch—school IL-6
Lynnville Station TN-4
**Lynnville (Township of)**—pop pl IL-6
Lynn Waterways Dam—dam MA-1
Lynnwood IL-6
Lynnwood—locale NY-2
Lynnwood—locale VA-3
**Lynnwood**—pop pl GA-3
**Lynnwood**—pop pl IL-6
**Lynnwood**—pop pl (2) PA-2
**Lynnwood**—pop pl VA-3
**Lynnwood**—pop pl WA-9
Lynnwood Branch—stream TN-4
Lynnwood Cem—cemetery IA-7
Lynnwood Cem—cemetery TN-4
Lynnwood Ch—church AR-4
Lynnwood Ch—church TN-4
Lynnwood Ch of Christ TN-4
Lynnwood Farm—hist pl OH-6
**Lynnwood Gardens**—pop pl PA-2
Lynnwood Golf Club—other VA-3
Lynnwood Hollow—valley TN-4
Lynnwood Hollow Gap—gap TN-4
Lynnwood Lake—reservoir NC-3
**Lynn Woodoaks**—pop pl NJ-2
**Lynnwood Park**—pop pl PA-2
Lynnwood Place Shop Ctr—locale TN-4
Lynnwood-Pricedale—CDP PA-2
Lynnwood Shop Ctr—locale ID-8
Lynn Woods Sch—school MA-1
**Lynoak**—pop pl PA-2
**Lynobrook**—pop pl VA-3
Lyn River MA-1
Lyns Cem—cemetery AR-4
Lynside Ch—church VA-3
Lynus Vly—lake NY-2
Lynus Vly Outlet—stream NY-2
**Lynville**—pop pl MS-4
Lynville Attendance Center (historical)—school MS-4
Lynville Creek—stream VA-3
Lynville Mtn—summit VA-3
Lynville Ridge Ch—church VA-3
**Lynwinn**—pop pl WV-2
**Lynwood**—pop pl CA-9
**Lynwood**—pop pl IL-6
**Lynwood**—pop pl MN-6
**Lynwood**—pop pl ND-7
**Lynwood**—pop pl PA-2
**Lynwood**—pop pl SC-3
**Lynwood**—pop pl VA-3
Lynwood Acad—school CA-9
**Lynwood Acres (subdivision)**—pop pl TN-4
**Lynwood Acres Subdivision**—pop pl UT-8
Lynwood Ave Sch—school NY-2
Lynwood Cem—cemetery TX-5
**Lynwood Center**—pop pl WA-9
Lynwood Ch—church FL-3
Lynwood East Park—park TX-5
**Lynwood Estates**—pop pl NY-2
**Lynwood Estates (subdivision)**—pop pl NC-3
Lynwood Farm Purdue Univ—school IN-6
**Lynwood Gardens**—pop pl CA-9
**Lynwood Gardens (subdivision)**—pop pl AL-4
**Lynwood Hills**—pop pl CA-9
**Lynwood (historical)**—pop pl MS-4
Lynwood HS—school CA-9
Lynwood Lake—reservoir NC-3
Lynwood Lake Dam—dam NC-3
Lynwood Lakes Ch—church NC-3
Lynwood Main Post Office—building CA-9
Lynwood Pacific Electric Railway Depot—hist pl CA-9
Lynwood Park Sch—school GA-3
**Lynwood Park (subdivision)**—pop pl AL-4
Lynwood Post Office (historical)—building MS-4
Lynwood Sch—school CA-9
Lynwood Sch—school IN-6
Lynwood State Public Access Area—park SD-7
Lynwood Station—locale CA-9
**Lynwood Terrace (subdivision)**—pop pl AL-4
**Lynx**—pop pl OH-6
Lynx Brook—stream ME-1
Lynx Campground—park AZ-5
Lynx Cat Mtn—summit CA-9
Lynx Creck District—hist pl AZ-5
Lynx Creek WY-8
Lynx Creek—stream (4) AK-9
Lynx Creek—stream AZ-5
Lynx Creek—stream CO-8
Lynx Creek—stream (3) ID-8
Lynx Creek—stream (4) MT-8
Lynx Creek—stream OR-9
Lynx Creek—stream (2) WA-9
Lynx Creek—stream (2) WY-8
Lynx Creek Bridge—hist pl AZ-5
Lynx Creek Campground—locale WY-8
Lynx Creek Dam—dam AZ-5
Lynx Creek Flats—flat MT-8
Lynx Creek Lookout—locale WA-9
Lynx Dome—summit AK-9
**Lynx Estates**—pop pl AZ-5
Lynxfield Pond—lake NH-1
Lynx Gulch—valley CA-9
Lynx Hollow—valley OR-9
Lynx Hollow Sch—school OR-9
Lynx Lake MN-6
Lynx Lake—lake (3) AK-9
Lynx Lake—lake MI-6
Lynx Lake—lake MN-6
Lynx Lake—lake (2) WI-6
Lynx Lake—reservoir AZ-5
Lynx Lake Dam—dam AZ-5
Lynx Meadows—flat ID-8
Lynx Mtn—summit WA-9
Lynx Park—flat WY-8
Lynx Pass—gap CO-8
Lynx Peak—summit AK-9
**Lynxville**—pop pl WI-6
Lynxville Cem—cemetery WI-6
Lyod Ranch—locale NM-5
**Lyon**—pop pl MS-4
**Lyon**—pop pl MO-7
**Lyon**—pop pl NC-3
Lyon, Chittenden P., Jr., House—hist pl KY-4
Lyon, Thomas, House—hist pl CT-1
Lyon, T.U., House—hist pl MA-1
Lyona—locale KS-7
Lyona—locale PA-2
Lyon And Dean Drain—canal MI-6
Lyon and Hoag Ranch—locale CA-9
Lyon Baptist Ch—church MS-4
Lyon Bayou—stream LA-4
Lyon Branch—stream NC-3
Lyon Brook—stream CT-1
Lyon Brook—stream (2) NY-2
Lyon Canyon CA-9
Lyon Canyon—valley CA-9
Lyon Canyon—valley MT-8
Lyon Cem—cemetery AL-4
Lyon Cem—cemetery KY-4
Lyon Cem—cemetery NY-2
Lyon Cem—cemetery TN-4
Lyon Cem—cemetery WV-2
Lyon Ch (historical)—church AL-4
Lyon Corner—locale NY-2
Lyon County—civil KS-7
Lyon County—civil NV-8
**Lyon (County)**—pop pl KY-4
**Lyon (County)**—pop pl MN-6
Lyon County Courthouse—hist pl IA-7
Lyon County Courthouse—hist pl NV-8
Lyon County State Lake—reservoir KS-7
Lyon County State Lake Dam—dam KS-7
Lyon Creek NC-3
Lyon Creek—stream AK-9
Lyon Creek—stream (2) ID-8
Lyon Creek—stream KS-7
Lyon Creek—stream (2) MS-4
Lyon Creek—stream (2) MT-8
Lyon Creek—stream NY-2
Lyon Creek—stream NC-3
Lyon Creek—stream OK-5
Lyon Creek—stream PA-2
Lyon Creek—stream TN-4
Lyon Creek—stream WA-9
Lyon Creek Ch—church TN-4
Lyon Creek Divide Rsvr—reservoir MT-8
Lyon Creek Spring—spring MT-8
Lyon Creek Well—well MT-8
Lyon Ditch—canal IN-6
Lyon Garden TN-4
Lyon Gulch MT-8
Lyon Gulch—valley (2) MT-8
Lyon Health Center—building NV-8
Lyon Hill—summit CT-1
Lyon Hill—summit PA-2
Lyon Hollow—valley NY-2
Lyon Hollow Cem—cemetery NY-2
Lyon HS—school OH-6
Lyonia—other KY-4
Lyon Lake MI-6
Lyon Lake—lake (2) MI-6
Lyon Lake—lake (2) NY-2
**Lyon Lake**—pop pl MI-6
Lyon Lake Ch—church MI-6
Lyon Lakes—lake IL-6
Lyon-Lamar House—hist pl AL-4
Lyon Landing—locale NC-3
Lyon Lateral—canal AZ-5
Lyon (Magisterial District)—fmr MCD WV-2
**Lyon Manor**—pop pl MI-6
Lyon Marker—locale MO-7
Lyon Meadow Pond CT-1
**Lyon Mountain**—pop pl NY-2
Lyon Mtn—summit (3) NY-2
Lyon Park—park MO-7
Lyon Park—park NY-2
Lyon Park—park SD-7
**Lyon Park**—pop pl VA-3
Lyon Park Sch—school NC-3
Lyon Peak—summit CA-9
Lyon Peak—summit NV-8
Lyon Plain CT-1
Lyon Plains CT-1
Lyon Plat Sch—school OH-6
Lyon Point—cape ME-1
Lyon Pond MA-1
Lyon Pond—lake MA-1
Lyon Prospect—mine TN-4
Lyon Ridge—ridge OH-6
Lyon Run—stream OH-6
Lyons TN-4
Lyons—locale (2) LA-4
Lyons—locale NC-3
Lyons—locale ND-7
Lyons—locale OK-5
Lyons—locale VA-3
Lyons—locale WA-9
**Lyons**—pop pl CO-8
**Lyons**—pop pl GA-3
**Lyons**—pop pl (2) IL-6
**Lyons**—pop pl IN-6
**Lyons**—pop pl (2) IA-7
**Lyons**—pop pl KS-7
**Lyons**—pop pl KY-4
**Lyons**—pop pl MI-6
**Lyons**—pop pl MO-7
**Lyons**—pop pl NE-7
**Lyons**—pop pl NJ-2
**Lyons**—pop pl NY-2
**Lyons**—pop pl OH-6
**Lyons**—pop pl (2) OR-9
**Lyons**—pop pl PA-2
**Lyons**—pop pl SD-7
**Lyons**—pop pl TX-5
**Lyons**—pop pl WI-6
Lyons, Horace G., House—hist pl KS-7
Lyons, Oscar F., House—hist pl UT-8
Lyons Ave Sch—school MI-6
Lyons Bar—bar ID-8
Lyons Bay—bay FL-3
Lyons Bayou—stream MS-4
Lyons Bend—bend TN-4
Lyons Bluff—cliff MS-4
Lyons Bluff—cliff MO-7
Lyon's Bluff Site—hist pl MS-4
Lyons Borough—civil PA-2
Lyons Branch—stream AR-4
Lyons Branch—stream (3) KY-4
Lyons Branch—stream (2) TN-4
Lyons Branch—stream WV-2
Lyons Bridge—bridge MA-1
Lyons Bridge—bridge MT-8
Lyons Brook—stream MA-1
Lyonsburg Cem—cemetery NY-2
Lyons Butte—summit MT-8
Lyons Camp—locale NY-2
Lyons Canal—canal NE-7
Lyons Canyon—valley AZ-5
Lyons Canyon—valley (3) OR-9
Lyons Cem—cemetery AR-4
Lyons Cem—cemetery IL-6
Lyons Cem—cemetery IN-6
Lyons Cem—cemetery IA-7
Lyons Cem—cemetery KY-4
Lyons Cem—cemetery (2) MN-6
Lyons Cem—cemetery NE-7
Lyons Cem—cemetery NY-2
Lyons Cem—cemetery OH-6
Lyons Cem—cemetery PA-2
Lyons Cem—cemetery SD-7
Lyons Cem—cemetery (3) TN-4
Lyons Cem—cemetery (3) TX-5
Lyons Cem—cemetery (2) WV-2
Lyons Cem—cemetery WI-6
Lyons Ch—church AR-4
Lyon Sch—school (4) IL-6
Lyon Sch—school (2) KY-4
Lyon Sch—school MA-1
Lyon Sch—school MI-6
Lyon Sch—school (2) MS-4
Lyon Sch—school (2) MO-7
Lyon Sch—school TN-4
Lyons Chapel—church KY-4
Lyons Chapel—church TN-4
Lyon Sch Community MS-4
Lyon Sch (historical)—school MO-7
Lyons Chute—stream IA-7
**Lyons Corner**—pop pl MD-2
**Lyons Corners**—pop pl NY-2
**Lyons (corporate and RR name for Lyon Station)**—pop pl PA-2
Lyons Coulee—valley MT-8
Lyons Creek KS-7
Lyons Creek TN-4
**Lyons Creek**—pop pl (2) MD-2
Lyons Creek—stream AR-4
Lyons Creek—stream (3) CA-9
Lyons Creek—stream ID-8
Lyons Creek—stream IA-7
Lyons Creek—stream MD-2
Lyons Creek—stream MI-6
Lyons Creek—stream MS-4
Lyons Creek—stream MT-8
Lyons Creek—stream NC-3
Lyons Creek—stream OR-9
Lyons Creek—stream SC-3
Lyons Creek—stream (2) TN-4
Lyons Creek—stream VA-3
Lyons Creek—stream WI-6
Lyons Creek Baptist Church TN-4
Lyons Creek Cem—cemetery AR-4
Lyons Creek Fischers—locale MD-2
Lyons Creek Wharf—locale MD-2
Lyons Crossing—locale CA-9
**Lyonsdale**—pop pl NY-2
**Lyonsdale (Town of)**—pop pl NY-2
Lyons Ditch—canal WY-8
Lyons Drain—canal (2) MI-6
Lyons Draw—valley SD-7
**Lyons Falls**—pop pl NY-2
Lyons Farms NJ-2
Lyons Ferry—locale WA-9
Lyons Ferry State Park—park WA-9
Lyons Field—airport KS-7
Lyons Ford—locale AR-4
Lyons Ford—locale TN-4
Lyons Fork—stream AZ-5
Lyons Fork—stream VA-3
Lyons Fork Spring—spring AZ-5
Lyons Fulton Bridge—bridge IA-7
Lyons Fulton Bridge—other IL-6
Lyons Gap—gap VA-3
Lyons Garage—hist pl ND-7
Lyons Gulch—valley CA-9
Lyons Gulch—valley CO-8
Lyons Gulch—valley (2) MT-8
Lyons Gulch—valley OR-9
Lyons Head CT-1
Lyons Hill—summit GA-3
Lyons Hill—summit WA-9
Lyons Hill Sch—school ME-1
Lyons (historical)—locale KS-7
Lyons (historical)—locale SD-7
**Lyons Homes**—pop pl MD-2
Lyons Homestead—locale NM-5
Lyons House—hist pl LA-4
Lyons HQ (Site)—locale CA-9
Lyons HS—school KS-7
Lyons Island—island TN-4
Lyons JHS—school KS-7
Lyons Knob—summit TN-4
Lyons Lake OH-6
Lyons Lake—lake CA-9
Lyons Lake—lake IL-6
Lyons Lake—lake (5) MI-6
Lyons Lake—lake MS-4
Lyons Lake Dam—dam (2) MS-4
Lyons Marsh—swamp NY-2
Lyons Meadow—flat OR-9
Lyon's Meadow Pond CT-1
Lyons Meadow Pond—lake CT-1
Lyons Mtn—summit AR-4
Lyons Mtn—summit OK-5
Lyons Park—park AL-4
Lyons Park—park IL-6
Lyons Park—park IA-7
Lyons Park—park MI-6
Lyons Park—park MN-6
Lyons Park—park NY-2
Lyons Park—park WI-6
**Lyons Park Estates**—pop pl CO-8
**Lyons Park (subdivision)**—pop pl FL-3
Lyons Peak—summit (3) CA-9
Lyons Place—locale NE-7
**Lyons Plain**—pop pl CT-1
Lyons Plains CT-1
**Lyons Plains**—pop pl CT-1
Lyons Point—cape NC-3
Lyons Point—cliff AZ-5
**Lyons Point**—pop pl LA-4
Lyons Point Gully—stream LA-4
Lyons Pond—lake MA-1
Lyons Pond—lake NY-2
Lyons Pond—reservoir NY-2
Lyons (P.O.) (Veterans Administration Hospital)—hospital NJ-2
Lyon Spring—spring AZ-5
Lyon Spring—spring CA-9
Lyon Spring—spring MT-8
Lyon Spring—spring WA-9
Lyon Spring Number One—spring AZ-5
Lyons-Quinn Oil And Gas Field—oilfield OK-5
Lyons Red Tank—reservoir NM-5
Lyons-Rice County Municipal Airp—airport KS-7
Lyons Ridge—ridge OR-9
Lyons RR Depot—hist pl CO-8
Lyons Rsvr—reservoir CA-9
Lyons Rsvr—reservoir CO-8
Lyons Rsvr—reservoir (2) OR-9
Lyons Run—stream (3) PA-2
**Lyons Run Mine**—pop pl PA-2
Lyons Rural Cem—cemetery NY-2
Lyons Sandstone Buildings—hist pl CO-8
Lyons Sch—school AZ-5
Lyons Sch—school GA-3
Lyons Sch—school KS-7
Lyons Sch—school KY-4
Lyons Sch—school LA-4
Lyons Sch—school MA-1
Lyons Sch—school NY-2
Lyons Sch—school OR-9
Lyons Sch (historical)—school MS-4
Lyons Shoals—bar TN-4
Lyons Shop Ctr—locale FL-3
Lyonss Island TN-4
Lyons (Site)—locale CA-9
Lyons-Slater Ranch—locale NM-5
Lyons Spring—spring AL-4
Lyons Spring—spring NV-8
Lyons Spring—spring SD-7
Lyons Spring Campground—locale MT-8
Lyonss Shoals TN-4
Lyons State For—forest MN-6
Lyons Station IN-6
Lyons Station—hist pl NJ-2
**Lyons Station**—pop pl NJ-2
**Lyons Store (historical)**—pop pl TN-4
Lyons Store Post Office (historical)—building TN-4
Lyons Street Cem—cemetery PA-2
Lyons Street Ch—church PA-2
Lyons Swamp—swamp CT-1
Lyons Tank—reservoir (2) NM-5
Lyon Station (corporate and RR name Lyons) PA-2
Lyon Station (historical)—locale PA-2
**Lyonstown**—pop pl PA-2
**Lyons (Town of)**—pop pl NY-2
**Lyons (Town of)**—pop pl WI-6
Lyons Township—fmr MCD IA-7
**Lyons Township**—pop pl SD-7
Lyons Township Hall—hist pl IL-6
**Lyons (Township of)**—pop pl IL-6
**Lyons (Township of)**—pop pl MI-6
**Lyons (Township of)**—pop pl (2) MN-6
Lyon's Turning Mill—hist pl MA-1
Lyons Valley—stream CA-9
Lyons Valley—valley CA-9
Lyons Valley—valley WY-8
Lyons Valley Creek—stream CA-9
**Lyons View**—pop pl TN-4
Lyons View Sch (historical)—school TN-4
Lyonsville—locale NJ-2
**Lyonsville**—pop pl CA-9
**Lyonsville**—pop pl IN-6
**Lyonsville**—pop pl MA-1
**Lyonsville**—pop pl NY-2
**Lyonsville**—pop pl WV-2
Lyonsville Ch—church IL-6
Lyonsville Pond—reservoir NY-2
Lyon Swamp—swamp NC-3
Lyon Swamp Canal—canal NC-3
Lyons West Oil and Gas Field—oilfield KS-7
Lyons Woman's Club House—hist pl GA-3
Lyon Thorofare—channel NC-3

**Lyonton**—*pop pl* TN-4
Lyonton Post Office (historical)—*building* TN-4
*Lyontown* IN-6
Lyon Township—*civil* (3) MO-7
Lyon Township—*fmr MCD* (2) IA-7
**Lyon Township**—*pop pl* (5) KS-7
**Lyon Township**—*pop pl* ND-7
**Lyon Township**—*pop pl* SD-7
**Lyon (Township of)**—*pop pl* (2) MI-6
Lyon United Methodist Ch—*church* MS-4
Lyon Valley—*locale* PA-2
Lyon Valley—*valley* WI-6
Lyon Valley Sch—*school* OK-5
Lyon Valley Sch (abandoned)—*school* PA-2
**Lyon Village**—*pop pl* VA-3
*Lyonville* PA-2
Lyonville—*locale* SD-7
Lyonville (historical)—*locale* SD-7
**Lyoth**—*pop pl* CA-9
**Lyoth (Sharpe Army Depot Tracy Annex)**—*pop pl* CA-9
Lype Cem—*cemetery* TN-4
Lyra—*locale* TX-5
**Lyra**—*pop pl* OH-6
Lyra Cem—*cemetery* MN-6
**Lyra (Township of)**—*pop pl* MN-6
Lyratta Dock—*locale* FL-3
Lyre River—*stream* WA-9
Lyric Falls—*falls* CO-8
Lyric Theater—*hist pl* MO-7
Lyric Theatre—*hist pl* AL-4
Lyric Theatre—*hist pl* MD-2
**Lysander**—*pop pl* NY-2
**Lysander New Community**—*pop pl* NY-2
**Lysander (Town of)**—*pop pl* NY-2
*Lyseng Lake* MN-6
Lysing Lake—*lake* MN-6
**Lysite**—*pop pl* WY-8
Lysite Creek—*stream* WY-8
Lysite Mtn—*summit* WY-8
Lysliornes Brook—*stream* ME-1
Lysne Cem—*cemetery* MN-6
Lysne Ch—*church* MN-6
Lysock-View County Home—*building* PA-2
Lystair Lake—*lake* WA-9
Lyster Cem—*cemetery* ND-7
Lyster Ch—*church* WI-6
Lyster Field—*airport* ND-7
Lyster Ranch—*locale* CA-9
Lyster Sch—*school* MI-6
*Lystra* AL-4
Lystra Ch—*church* (2) AL-4
Lystra Ch—*church* KY-4
Lystra Ch—*church* NC-3
**Lystra Farms**—*pop pl* MD-2
Lystria Ch—*church* GA-3
Lytch Cem—*cemetery* NC-3
Lytchs Pond—*reservoir* NC-3
Lyter Sch—*school* PA-2
Lytle—*locale* AL-4
Lytle—*locale* GA-3
Lytle—*locale* TX-5
**Lytle**—*pop pl* OH-6
**Lytle**—*pop pl* TX-5
**Lytle**—*pop pl* WI-6
Lytle, Lake—*lake* OR-9
Lytle, Robert F., House—*hist pl* OR-9
Lytle Bay—*swamp* AL-4
Lytle Branch—*stream* NC-3
Lytle Camp—*locale* ID-8
Lytle Cem—*cemetery* (2) IA-7
Lytle City (historical)—*locale* IA-7
Lytle Clemons Ditch—*canal* MT-8
Lytle Cove—*basin* TX-5
*Lytle Creek* TX-5
**Lytle Creek**—*pop pl* CA-9
Lytle Creek—*stream* (2) CA-9
Lytle Creek—*stream* IA-7
Lytle Creek—*stream* OH-6
Lytle Creek—*stream* OK-5
Lytle Creek—*stream* (4) OR-9
Lytle Creek—*stream* (3) TN-4
Lytle Creek—*stream* TX-5
Lytle Creek—*stream* WA-9
Lytle Creek—*stream* WY-8
Lytle Creek Channel—*canal* CA-9
Lytle Creek Park—*park* CA-9
Lytle Creek Ranger Station—*locale* CA-9
Lytle Creek Sch—*school* CA-9
Lytle Creek Sch—*school* WY-8
Lytle Creek Wash—*stream* CA-9
Lytle Ditch—*canal* OH-6
Lytle Gap—*gap* TX-5
Lytle Hill—*summit* MT-8
Lytle Hill—*summit* WY-8
Lytle Lake—*reservoir* TX-5
Lytle Mtn—*summit* CA-9
Lytle Park—*park* OH-6
Lytle Park Hist Dist—*hist pl* OH-6
Lytle Prairie—*flat* OR-9
Lytle Pumping—*other* OR-9
Lytle Run—*stream* PA-2
**Lytles**—*pop pl* WI-6
Lytles Bend—*bend* TN-4
Lytle Sch—*school* CO-8
Lytle Sch—*school* FL-3
Lytle Sch—*school* SD-7
Lytle Sch (abandoned)—*school* PA-2
*Lytles Creek* TN-4
Lytles Creek—*stream* IA-7
*Lytles Creek Cumberland Presbyterian Church* TN-4
Lytles Fork—*stream* KY-4
Lytle Spring—*spring* AZ-5
Lyton Ranch—*locale* TX-5
Lytten—*locale* KY-4
Lytten Canyon—*valley* NM-5
Lytten Cem—*cemetery* KY-4
Lytten Well—*well* NM-5
*Lytters Creek* TX-5
*Lyttle Creek* OH-6
**Lytton**—*pop pl* CA-9
**Lytton**—*pop pl* IA-7
**Lytton**—*pop pl* OH-6
Lytton Creek—*stream* CA-9
Lytton Creek—*stream* TX-5
Lytton Industrial Home—*building* CA-9
*Lytton Lake* CA-9
Lytton Lake—*lake* CA-9
Lytton Rancheria—*locale* CA-9
**Lytton (Salvation Army Home)**—*pop pl* CA-9
Lytton Sch—*school* CA-9
**Lytton Springs**—*pop pl* TX-5
Lytton Springs Cem—*cemetery* TX-5
Lytton Springs Creek—*stream* TX-5
Lytton Springs Oil Field—*oilfield* TX-5
Lzaak Walton Lake—*lake* IA-7
L-Z Bravo Airp—*airport* MO-7
L-1 Canal—*canal* FL-3
L-2 Canal—*canal* FL-3
L 2 Canal—*canal* MT-8
L-40 Canal—*canal* FL-3
L-65 Canal—*canal* FL-3
L-7 Canal—*canal* FL-3
L 7 Ranch—*locale* NM-5
L-8 Canal—*canal* FL-3
L 9 Canal—*canal* MT-8

# M

M — TX-5
Ma — FM-9
Maa — FM-9
Maabuug—cape — FM-9
Maabuuq—locale — FM-9
Maacama Creek—stream — CA-9
**Maach Addition (subdivision)**—pop pl — UT-8
Maackworths Island — ME-1
Maackworths Point — ME-1
Maafee Island—island — AS-9
Maagas River—stream — GU-9
Maageruappu To — FM-9
Maahs Ranch—locale — NE-7
Maaje — MP-9
Maaje—island — MP-9
Maaji-To — MP-9
Maajiya — MH-9
Maak'eef—summit — FM-9
Maak'eefnigaaq—bay — FM-9
Maak'eefniqachiig—bay — FM-9
**Maakiy**—pop pl — FM-9
Maakole—cape — HI-9
Maakua Gulch—valley — HI-9
Maal'—summit — FM-9
**Maalaea**—pop pl — HI-9
Maalaea Bay—bay — HI-9
Maalaea Small Boat Harbor—bay — HI-9
Maalatetele Rocks (Black Rock)—island — AS-9
**Maalehu**—pop pl — HI-9
Maalo—civil — HI-9
Maalo Gulch—valley — HI-9
Maaloon—locale — FM-9
Maamaa Cove—bay — AS-9
Maangrar—island — MP-9
Maanimit—summit — FM-9
Maan Pa' — FM-9
Maap' — FM-9
Maap—civil — FM-9
Maap—island — FM-9
Maap' Elem Sch—school — FM-9
Maaq—locale — FM-9
**Maaq**—pop pl — FM-9
Maarsharu Shoto — MP-9
Maaryaar—summit — FM-9
Maas Cem—cemetery (2) — IA-7
Maasen Creek—stream — MO-7
Maas Mine—mine — MI-6
Maat — MP-9
Maatsuraido To — FM-9
Maatulaumea Point—cape — AS-9
Maatulua Ridge—ridge — AS-9
Maau — HI-9
Maawech — FM-9
MAB Airp—airport — PA-2
Maba Lake—lake — UT-8
Mabana—locale — WA-9
Maban Coulee—valley — MT-8
**Mabank**—pop pl — TX-5
Mabank Cem—cemetery — TX-5
Mabank City Lake—reservoir — TX-5
**Mabbettsville**—pop pl — NY-2
Mabbit Spring—spring — TN-4
Mabbott Pond—reservoir — MD-2
Mab Branch—stream — LA-4
Mabe—locale — VA-3
Mabee — OH-6
**Mabee**—pop pl — OH-6
Mabee Cem—cemetery — OH-6
Mabee Corner—locale — OH-6
Mabee House—hist pl — NY-2
Mabee-Mayberry House—hist pl — OR-9
Mabee Oil Field—oilfield — TX-5
Mabee Ranch—locale — TX-5
Mabees Corner — OH-6
Mabe Hollow—valley — TN-4
Mabel—locale — FL-3
Mabel—locale — IL-6
Mabel—locale — PA-2
**Mabel**—pop pl — MN-6
**Mabel**—pop pl — MO-7
**Mabel**—pop pl — NC-3
**Mabel**—pop pl — OR-9
Mabel, Lake—lake (2) — FL-3
Mabel, Lake—lake — MN-6
Mabel Bay—bay — AK-9
Mabel Bedsole Ward Trust Lake—reservoir — AL-4
Mabel Bedsole Ward Trust Lake Dam—dam — AL-4
Mabel Cem—cemetery — MN-6
Mabel Cem—cemetery — ND-7
Mabel Cem—cemetery — OR-9
Mabel Creek—stream (3) — AK-9
Mabel Creek—stream — OR-9
Mabel Creek—stream — WY-8
Mabel Elem Sch—school — NC-3
Mabel (historical)—locale — KS-7
Mabel Island—island (2) — AK-9
Mabel Lake—lake — MI-6
Mabel Lake—lake — MN-6
Mabel Lake—lake — WI-6
Mabel Lake—lake — WY-8
Mabel Lake Campground—locale — MN-6
Mabelle—locale — TX-5
Mabelle Hill—summit — ID-8
Mabel L Mine—mine — OR-9
Mabel Melear Sch—school — TX-5
Mabel Memorial Ch—church — VA-3
Mabel Mine—mine — AK-9
Mabel Mine—mine — CO-8
Mabel Park—park — OR-9
Mabel Porter Pond—lake — FL-3
Mabel Rsvr—reservoir — ID-8
Mabel Rush Sch—school — OR-9
Mabel Spring—spring — OR-9
Mabelton—locale — VA-3
**Mabel Township**—pop pl — ND-7
**Mabelvale**—pop pl — AR-4
Maben — AL-4
Maben—locale — WV-2
**Maben**—pop pl — AL-4
**Maben**—pop pl — MS-4
Maben Cem—cemetery — AL-4
Maben Cem—cemetery — MS-4
Maben Ch of Christ—church — MS-4
Maben Elem Sch—school — MS-4
Maben Elem Sch (historical)—school — AL-4
Maben First Baptist Ch—church — MS-4
Maben Hill—summit — NY-2
Maben HS—school — MS-4
Maben JHS—school — MS-4
Maben Line Consolidated HS — MS-4
Maben Lookout Tower—locale — MS-4
Maben United Methodist Ch—church — MS-4
Maberg Lake — MN-6
**Maberry**—pop pl — AR-4
Maberry Cem—cemetery — MO-7
Maberry Run—stream — WV-2
Maberry Sch—school — TN-4
Mabert Hollow—valley — OH-6
**Mabery (historical)**—pop pl — OR-9
Mabe Sch (historical)—school — AL-4
Mabey Canyon — ID-8
Mabey Canyon—valley — CA-9
Mabey Canyon—valley — ID-8
Mabey Creek—stream — ID-8
Mabey Spring—spring — ID-8
Mabey Spring No 2—spring — ID-8
**Mabi**—pop pl (3) — PR-3
Mabie—locale — CA-9
**Mabie**—pop pl — WV-2
Mabie Canyon — ID-8
Mabie Creek — ID-8
Mabie Sch—school — MA-1
Mabin Island—island — MS-4
Mabin Lodge—locale — MS-4
Mab Island—island — AK-9
**Mable**—pop pl — MI-6
**Mable**—pop pl — PA-2
Mable, Lake—lake — WI-6
Mable, Robert, House and Cemetery—hist pl — GA-3
Mable Canyon — ID-8
Mable Creek — OR-9
Mable Dean — TX-5
**Mable Hill**—pop pl — PA-2
Mable Hill Ch—church — AL-4
Mable Lake — IN-6
Mable Lake — WY-8
Mable Lake—lake — WI-6
Mable Lakes—lake — ID-8
Mable Mine—mine — NV-8
Mable Mine (underground)—mine — AL-4
Mable Mtn—summit — AK-9
Mable Mtn—summit — NV-8
Mable Pond—lake — AZ-5
Mable Ranch—locale — WY-8
**Mableton**—pop pl — GA-3
Mableton (CCD)—cens area — GA-3
Mabone Cem—cemetery — TN-4
Mabrey Bridge—bridge — NC-3
Mabrey Cem—cemetery — AR-4
**Mabrico**—pop pl — NC 3
Mabry—locale — TX-5
Mabry—uninc pl — TX-5
Mabry, H. S., Barn—hist pl — AR-4
Mabry Branch—stream — TN-4
Mabry Cem—cemetery — KY-4
Mabry Cem—cemetery — MO-7
Mabry Cem—cemetery (2) — TN-4
Mabry Creek—stream — GA-3
Mabry Gap—gap — AR-4
Mabry Lake—reservoir — OK-5
Mabry Manor—uninc pl — FL-3
Mabry Mill—locale — VA-3
Mabry Sch—school — FL-3
Mabry School — TN-4
Mabry-Van Pelt House—hist pl — UT-8
**Mabscott**—pop pl — WV-2
**Mabson**—pop pl — AL-4
Mabson Ch—church — AL-4
**Mabton**—pop pl — WA-9
Mabton (CCD)—cens area — WA-9
Mabton Cem—cemetery — WA-9
Mabton East Lateral—canal — WA-9
Mabton Feeder Lateral—canal — WA-9
Mabton HS—hist pl — WA-9
Mabton Siphon—canal — WA-9
Mabton West Lateral—canal — WA-9
Mabu' — FM-9
Mabu (Barrio)—fmr MCD — PR-3
Mabuu — FM-9
Mabyabu — PW-9
Mac—locale — KY-4
Mac—locale — PA-2
Mac, Lake—lake — FL-3
Macabee — KY-4
Macabee Cem—cemetery — WA-9
MacAbee Mine—mine — OR-9
Macabo Lake—reservoir — IN-6
Macachack Creek — OH-6
Macacheak Creek — OH-6
Macachee, Lake—lake — OH-6
Macacheek Castle—locale — OH-6
Macacheek Creek — OH-6
**Macada (subdivision)**—pop pl — PA-2
Macaddey Creek — IN-6
Macadonia Ch—church — GA-3
Macadoo Creek — IN-6
MacAdoo Dam—dam — KS-7
Macadues Mill (historical)—locale — TN-4
MacAfee Flat—flat — CA-9
Macafee Hill—summit — WA-9
Macaffee Brook—stream — MN-6
Macajahs Pond — MA-1
Macajna, Mount—summit — GU-9
Macalester Coll—school — MN-6
MacAlister — OK-5
Mac Alister Draw—valley — MT-8
MacAllister — OK-5
MacAllister Cove—bay — ME-1
MacAlpin Park—park — AL-4
MacAlpin (RR name for McAlpin)—other — WV-2
Macam Springs — CA-9
**Macana**—pop pl (2) — PR-3
Macana (Barrio)—fmr MCD (2) — PR-3
Macana Windmill—locale — TX-5
Mac and Nellie Branch—stream — KY-4
MacAndrews Lake—lake — MI-6
Macanie—locale — VA-3
Macanippuck Run—stream — NJ-2
Macarisqui — FL-3
Macaroni Creek—stream — AK-9
Macaroni Creek—stream — ID-8
Macaroni Lake—lake — MT-8
Macaroni Pit—reservoir — WY-8
Macaroni Spring—spring — NV-8
Macarte Creek—stream — ID-8
**MacArthur**—pop pl — WV-2
MacArthur—uninc pl — PA-2
MacArthur, Lake—reservoir — NC-3
MacArthur Branch—stream — KS-7
MacArthur Bridge—other — MI-6
MacArthur Bridge—other — MO-7
Mac Arthur Bridge (Toll)—other — IL-6
MacArthur Elem Sch—school — KS-7
MacArthur HS—school — IL-6
MacArthur HS—school — MI-6
MacArthur Junior High—school — TX-5
Macarthur Lake—lake — ID-8
**MacArthur Manor**—pop pl — NJ-2
MacArthur Park—park — AR-4
MacArthur Park—park (3) — CA-9
MacArthur Park—park — MI-6
MacArthur Park—park — NY-2
**MacArthur Park**—pop pl — TX-5
MacArthur Park Hist Dist—hist pl — AR-4
MacArthur Sch—school — CA-9
MacArthur Sch—school — IL-6
MacArthur Sch—school — KS-7
MacArthur Sch—school — MA-1
MacArthur Sch—school — MI-6
MacArthur Sch—school — NM-5
MacArthur Sch—school — NY-2
MacArthur Sch—school — TX-5
MacArthur Sch—school — VA-3
MacArthur Sch—school — WI-6
MacArthur School — IN-6
**MacArthurs Junction**—pop pl — SC-3
MacArthur Stadium—other — NY-2
MacArthur Tank—reservoir — NM-5
Macarty Sch—school — LA-4
**Macatawa**—pop pl — MI-6
Macatawa, Lake—lake — MI-6
Macatawa Bay—bay — MI-6
Macatawa River—stream — MI-6
Macatee Bldg—hist pl — TX-5
Macaulay Cem—cemetery — NY-2
Macaulay Creek—stream — WA-9
Macauley Creek—stream — IN-6
Macauley Creek—stream — WI-6
Macayaqui — FL-3
Mac Bain—locale — TX-5
Mac Bayou—gut — TX-5
MacBeth — WV-2
**Macbeth**—pop pl — SC-3
Macbeth Creek—stream — SC-3
MacBeth Ranch—locale — NE-7
Maccabee Cem—cemetery — MN-6
Maccabees Bldg—hist pl — MI-6
Maccabees Home—building — PA-2
MacCall—locale — WA-9
Mac Canyon—valley — NV-8
MacCartees Lake—reservoir — AL-4
MacCartees Lake Dam—dam — AL-4
Mac Carter Creek—stream — AL-4
Mac Cash Branch—stream — TN-4
MacCeffery Bridge—bridge — ND-7
Mac Cem—cemetery — NC-3
**Macclenny**—pop pl — FL-3
Macclenny (CCD)—cens area — FL-3
Macclenny Elem Sch—school — FL-3
**Macclesfield**—pop pl — NC-3
MacCochague Sch—school — KS-7
Macco Creek—stream — WI-6
MacColl Ridge—ridge — AK-9
MacColman Creek — MI-6
Maccongy — PA-2
MacConnell Lake—lake — NC-3
Mac Coon County Park—park — IA-7
**MacCorkle (McCorkle)**—pop pl — WV-2
Mac Coulee—valley — MT-8
Mac Cowan Cemetery — TN-4
MaCcrady — VA-3
MacCrady Gap — VA-3
Mac Creek—stream — ID 8
Mac Creek—stream — OR-9
Mac Creek—stream — WA-9
MacCreel Creek—stream — AK-9
MacCulloch Sch—school — MI-6
**Macdale**—pop pl — WV-2
MacDavid Lake — AL-4
MacDavid Millpond Branch—stream — MS-4
MacDill AFB—military — FL-3
MacDill AFB (MacDill Field)—military — FL-3
MacDill Field—other — FL-3
MacDill RR Station—locale — FL-3
**Macdoel**—pop pl — CA-9
**Macdona**—pop pl — TX-5
MacDonald—locale — WV-2
**Macdonald**—pop pl — WV-2
MacDonald, Flora, College—hist pl — NC-3
MacDonald Brook—stream — ME-1
MacDonald Camp—locale — MN-6
MacDonald Camp—locale — NM-5
Macdonald Canyon — AZ-5
MacDonald Canyon—valley — OR-9
Mac Donald Cem—cemetery — AR-4
MacDonald Creek—stream — FL-3
MacDonald Creek—stream — ID-8
MacDonald Creek—stream — MT-8
MacDonald Farm—hist pl — NY-2
MacDonald Hollow—valley — AL-4
MacDonald Knob—summit — KY-4
MacDonald Knolls Sch—school — MD-2
MacDonald Lake — WI-6
MacDonald Lake—lake — WI-6
**Macdonald (MacDonald)**—pop pl — WV-2
MacDonald Memorial Park—park — CT-1
MacDonald Merchandise Bldg—hist pl — NM-5
MacDonald Pass—gap — MT-8
MacDonald Pass Campground—locale — MT-8
MacDonald Pond—lake — MT-8
MacDonald Reservoir — MT-8
MacDonald-Robinson Prospect—mine — TN-4
MacDonald Sch—school — MA-1
MacDonald Sch—school — MI-6
MacDonalds No 1—locale — ID-8
MacDonald Spit—bar — AK-9
MacDonald Swamp—swamp — NC-3
MacDonald-Todd House—hist pl — MN-6
**Macdonaldton**—pop pl — PA-2
**MacDonald Woods (subdivision)**—pop pl — NC-3
Macdonell House—hist pl — OH-6
**MacDonnell Heights**—pop pl — NY-2
MacDonough — DE-2
MacDonough, Comdr. Thomas, House—hist pl — DE-2
Macdonough Point—cape — VT-1
Macdonough Sch — DE-2
**MacDougal**—pop pl — WV-2
MacDougal Bay—bay — MN-6
MacDougal Branch—stream — MO-7
**MacDougall**—pop pl — NY-2
Mac Dougall Canyon—valley — NM-5
MacDougall Creek—stream — AK-9
MacDougall Ditch—canal — IN-6
Macdougall Pond—lake — ME-1
MacDougall Youth Correction Center—building — SC-3
Macdougall Youth Correction Center—building — SC-3
MacDougal Spring — AZ-5
MacDougal-Sullivan Gardens Hist Dist—hist pl — NY-2
MacDowell Chapel—church — KY-4
MacDowell Colony—hist pl — NH-1
**MacDowell Colony**—pop pl — NH-1
MacDowell Rsvr—reservoir — NH-1
MacDowell Sch—school — CA-9
MacDowell Sch—school — MI-6
Macduff Peak—summit — OR-9
MacDunn — WV-2
**MacDunn**—pop pl — WV-2
Mace — IN-6
Mace—locale — ID-8
Mace—locale — NM-5
Mace—locale — WV-2
**Mace**—pop pl — IN-6
Mace, Garwin, Lime Kilns—hist pl — WI-6
Mace, Garwin A., House—hist pl — WI-6
Mace, Ulysses S., House—hist pl — NC-3
Maceasin Pond—lake — MD-2
Mace Branch—stream — MO-7
Mace Branch—stream — NC-3
Mace Brook—stream — ME-1
Mace Cem—cemetery — OH-6
Mace Cem—cemetery — SC-3
Mace Creek—stream — ID-8
Mace Creek—stream — MO-7
Mace Creek—stream — OR-9
Maceday Lake—lake — MI-6
Macedoina Ch—church — OH-6
Macedomia Ch—church — GA-3
Macedon—locale — SC-3
**Macedon**—pop pl — NY-2
**Macedon**—pop pl — OH-6
Macedona Ch—church — GA-3
Macedona Ch—church — VA-3
Macedon Canyon—valley — CA-9
**Macedon Center**—pop pl — NY-2
Macedon Center Cem—cemetery — NY-2
Macedonia — AL-4
Macedonia — MS-4
Macedonia—fmr MCD — NE-7
Macedonia—locale (2) — AL-4
Macedonia—locale (2) — AR-4
Macedonia—locale — FL-3
Macedonia—locale (2) — GA-3
Macedonia—locale — MS-4
Macedonia—locale (2) — NC-3
Macedonia—locale — OH-6
Macedonia—locale — PA-2
Macedonia—locale — SC-3
Macedonia—locale (3) — TN-4
Macedonia—locale (4) — TX-5
**Macedonia**—pop pl (4) — AL-4
**Macedonia**—pop pl — AR-4
**Macedonia**—pop pl — CT-1
**Macedonia**—pop pl — GA-3
**Macedonia**—pop pl — IL-6
**Macedonia**—pop pl — IN-6
**Macedonia**—pop pl — IA-7
**Macedonia**—pop pl (3) — KY-4
**Macedonia**—pop pl (4) — MS-4
**Macedonia**—pop pl — MO-7
**Macedonia**—pop pl — NJ-2
**Macedonia**—pop pl (2) — NC-3
**Macedonia**—pop pl — OH-6
**Macedonia**—pop pl — PA-2
**Macedonia**—pop pl — SC-3
**Macedonia**—pop pl (4) — TN-4
**Macedonia**—pop pl — TX-5
**Macedonia**—pop pl — VA-3
Macedonia African Methodist Episcopal Church — AL-4
Macedonia African Methodist Episcopalian Ch—church — DE-2
Macedonia Baptist Ch — AL-4
Macedonia Baptist Ch — MS-4
Macedonia Baptist Ch — TN-4
Macedonia Baptist Ch—church (7) — AL-4
Macedonia Baptist Ch—church (6) — FL-3
Macedonia Baptist Ch—church (3) — MS-4
Macedonia Baptist Ch—church (5) — TN-4
Macedonia Baptist Ch (historical)—church (2) — AL-4
Macedonia Baptist Ch (historical)—church — MS-4
Macedonia Baptist Church—hist pl — LA-4
Macedonia Baptist Church—hist pl — NY-2
Macedonia Baptist Church—hist pl — TX-5
Macedonia Bottom—basin — TN-4
Macedonia Branch—stream — AL-4
Macedonia Branch—stream — TN-4
Macedonia Branch—stream — TX-5
Macedonia Brook—stream — CT-1
Macedonia Brook State Park—park — CT-1
Macedonia Canyon—valley — CA-9
Macedonia (CCD)—cens area — GA-3
Macedonia (CCD)—cens area — SC-3
Macedonia (CCD)—cens area — TN-4
Macedonia Cem — AL-4
Macedonia Cem—cemetery (21) — AL-4
Macedonia Cem—cemetery (22) — AR-4
Macedonia Cem—cemetery (7) — GA-3
Macedonia Cem—cemetery — IL-6
Macedonia Cem—cemetery (2) — IN-6
Macedonia Cem—cemetery (4) — LA-4
Macedonia Cem—cemetery (21) — MS-4
Macedonia Cem—cemetery (6) — MO-7
Macedonia Cem—cemetery — NC-3
Macedonia Cem—cemetery (2) — OH-6
Macedonia Cem—cemetery — OK-5
Macedonia Cem—cemetery (3) — SC-3
Macedonia Cem—cemetery (12) — TN-4
Macedonia Cem—cemetery (12) — TX-5
Macedonia Cem—cemetery — VA-3
Macedonia Ch — AL-4
Macedonia Ch — MS-4
Macedonia Ch — TN-4
Macedonia Ch—church (76) — AL-4
Macedonia Ch—church (31) — AR-4
Macedonia Ch—church (13) — FL-3
Macedonia Ch—church (69) — GA-3
Macedonia Ch—church (7) — IL-6
Macedonia Ch—church (3) — IN-6
Macedonia Ch—church (19) — KY-4
Macedonia Ch—church (11) — LA-4
Macedonia Ch—church — MD-2
Macedonia Ch—church (56) — MS-4
Macedonia Ch—church (10) — MO-7
Macedonia Ch—church — NJ-2
Macedonia Ch—church (46) — NC-3
Macedonia Ch—church (4) — OH-6
Macedonia Ch—church (4) — OK-5
Macedonia Ch—church (2) — PA-2
Macedonia Ch—church (25) — SC-3
Macedonia Ch—church (24) — TN-4
Macedonia Ch—church (17) — TX-5
Macedonia Ch—church (20) — VA-3
Macedonia Ch—church (6) — WV-2
Macedonia Chapel—church — AR-4
Macedonia Chapel—church — MS-4
Macedonia Ch (historical)—church (4) — AL-4
Macedonia Ch (historical)—church — MS-4
Macedonia Ch (historical)—church (2) — TN-4
Macedonia Ch of Christ — AL-4
Macedonia Church—hist pl — OH-6
Macedonia Church (abandoned)—locale — MO-7
Macedonia Creek — IL-6
Macedonia Creek — SC-3
Macedonia Creek—stream — AR-4
Macedonia Creek—stream — IN-6
Macedonia Creek—stream — MS-4
Macedonia Cumberland Presbyterian Ch—church — AL-4
Macedonia Division—civil — TN-4
Macedonia Free Public School — MS-4
Macedonia Freewill Ch—church — AL-4
Macedonia Gap—gap — AL-4
Macedonia Gap—gap — PA-2
Macedonia (historical)—locale — MS-4
**Macedonia (historical)**—pop pl — MS-4
Macedonia (historical P.O.)—locale — IA-7
Macedonia Hollow—valley — AR-4
Macedonia Lookout—locale — MO-7
Macedonia Mercer Cem—cemetery — TN-4
Macedonia Methodist Church — AL-4
Macedonia Methodist Church — MS-4
Macedonia Missionary Baptist Ch — MS-4
Macedonia Missionary Baptist Ch—church (2) — FL-3
Macedonia Missionary Baptist Ch—church — MS-4
Macedonia Missionary Baptist Church — AL-4
Macedonia Missionary Baptist Church*—church — KS-7
Macedonia Missionary Ch—church — AL-4
Macedonia Missionary Ch—church — SC-3
Macedonia MS—school — SC-3
Macedonia Mtn—summit — AL-4
Macedonian Cem—cemetery — AR-4
Macedonia Neighborhood Center—building — AL-4
Macedonian Sch—school — OK-5
Macedonia Number 5 Mine (surface)—mine — AL-4
Macedonia Post Office (historical)—building — MS-4
Macedonia Post Office (historical)—building — TN-4
Macedonia Primitive Baptist Ch — AL-4
Macedonia Primitive Baptist Ch—church — AL-4
Macedonia Primitive Baptist Ch—church (2) — FL-3
Macedonia Primitive Baptist Church — TN-4
Macedonia Revival Center — MS-4
Macedonia Ridge—ridge — WV-2
Macedonia Run—stream — PA-2
Macedonia Sch — MS-4
Macedonia Sch—school (4) — AL-4
Macedonia Sch—school (4) — AR-4
Macedonia Sch—school (3) — GA-3
Macedonia Sch—school (2) — IL-6
Macedonia Sch—school — KY-4
Macedonia Sch—school — LA-4
Macedonia Sch—school (5) — MS-4
Macedonia Sch—school (2) — MO-7
Macedonia Sch—school — NC-3
Macedonia Sch—school — OK-5
Macedonia Sch—school (2) — SC-3
Macedonia Sch—school (6) — TN-4
Macedonia Sch—school — TX-5
Macedonia Sch—school — WV-2
Macedonia Sch (abandoned)—school — MO-7
Macedonia Sch (historical)—school (7) — AL-4
Macedonia Sch (historical)—school (7) — MS-4
Macedonia Sch (historical)—school (3) — TN-4
Macedonia School (historical)—locale — MO-7
Macedonia Slough—stream — GA-3
Macedonia Spring—spring — CA-9
Macedonia Spring—spring — MO-7
Macedonia Township—fmr MCD — IA-7
Macedonia (Township of)—other — OH-6
Macedonia Union Ch—church — MS-4
Macedonia United Freewill Baptist Ch—church — FL-3
Macedonia United Methodist Ch—church — MS-4
Macedonia United Methodist Church — TN-4
Macedonie CME Ch—church — AL-4
Macedonina Post Office (historical)—building — TN-4
Macedon Mine—mine — CA-9
Macedon Ridge—ridge — CA-9
**Macedon (Town of)**—pop pl — NY-2
Macedon Tunnel—mine — CA-9
Mace Fork—stream — KY-4
Mace Hill—summit — NY-2
Mace Hill—summit — VT-1
Mace Hollow—valley — OH-6
Mace Institute (historical)—school — TN-4
Mace Knob—summit — WV-2
**Macel**—pop pl — MS-4
Mace Lake—lake — CA-9
Mace Lake—lake — WA-9
Mac Elroy Gap — AR-4
MacElroy Heath—swamp — ME-1
Macelva Creek—stream — LA-4
Mace Meadow—flat — CA-9
Mace Meadows—flat — ID-8
Mace Mine—mine — MN-6
Mace Mtn—summit — OR-9
Mace Number One Mine—mine — MN-6
**Maceo**—pop pl — KY-4
Maceo Park—park — FL-3
Mace Ranch—locale — CO-8
Mace Sch (abandoned)—school — MO-7
Maces Creek—stream — KY-4
**Mace's Hill**—pop pl — TN-4
Maces Hill—summit — TN-4
Maces Hill Ch—church — TN-4
Maces Hill Missionary Baptist Ch — TN-4
Maces Hill Sch (historical)—school — TN-4
Maces Pond—lake — ME-1

Mad Inlet Creek NC-3
Madira Bickel Mounds—hist pl FL-3
Mad Island—island MI-6
Mad Island Bayou—channel TX-5
Mad Island Lake—lake TX-5
Mad Island Reef—bar TX-5
Mad Island Slough—stream TX-5
Madison IA-7
Madison PA-2
Madison TN-4
Madison TX-5
Madison—locale IA-7
**Madison**—pop pl (3) AL-4
**Madison**—pop pl AR-4
**Madison**—pop pl CA-9
**Madison**—pop pl CT-1
**Madison**—pop pl FL-3
**Madison**—pop pl GA-3
**Madison**—pop pl IL-6
**Madison**—pop pl IN-6
**Madison**—pop pl KS-7
**Madison**—pop pl ME-1
**Madison**—pop pl MD-2
**Madison**—pop pl MN-6
**Madison**—pop pl MS-4
**Madison**—pop pl MO-7
**Madison**—pop pl NE-7
**Madison**—pop pl NH-1
**Madison**—pop pl NJ-2
**Madison**—pop pl NY-2
**Madison**—pop pl NC-3
**Madison**—pop pl OH-6
**Madison**—pop pl PA-2
**Madison**—pop pl (2) SC-3
**Madison**—pop pl SD-7
**Madison**—pop pl TN-4
**Madison**—pop pl VA-3
**Madison**—pop pl WV-2
**Madison**—pop pl WI-6
Madison, Lake—lake SD-7
Madison, Mount—summit NH-1
Madison, Port—bay WA-9
Madison Acad—school AL-4
Madison Acad—school TN-4
Madison and Woodburn Hist Dist—hist pl OH-6
Madison Arm—bay MT-8
Madison Arm Resort—locale MT-8
Madison Ave Baptist Ch—church IN-6
Madison Ave Baptist Ch—church TN-4
Madison Ave Ch—church NJ-2
Madison Ave Ch—church NC-3
Madison Ave Facade of the Squadron A Armory—hist pl NY-2
Madison Avenue OH-6
Madison Ave Sch—school CA-9
Madison Ave Sch—school OH-6
Madison Ave Temple—church PA-2
Madison Aviation Airp—airport AZ-5
Madison Baptist Ch—church AL-4
Madison Baptist Ch—church TN-4
Madison Barracks—hist pl NY-2
Madison Bay—bay MD-2
Madison Bay—lake LA-4
Madison-Bean Cem—cemetery MS-4
Madison Borough—civil PA-2
Madison Boulder—pillar NH-1
Madison Branch TN-4
Madison Branch—stream TX-5
Madison Branch—stream WV-2
Madison Bridge—bridge IN-6
Madison Bridge—bridge NE-7
Madison Brook NH-1
Madison Brook—stream VT-1
Madison Buffalo Jump State Monmt—hist pl MT-8
**Madisonburg**—pop pl OH-6
**Madisonburg**—pop pl PA-2
Madisonburgh PA-2
Madison Butte—summit OR-9
Madison Butte Trail (pack)—trail OR-9
Madison Campground—locale MT-8
Madison Canal—canal LA-4
Madison Canyon—valley CA-9
Madison Canyon—valley UT-8
Madison Canyon—valley WY-8
Madison Carnegie Library—hist pl MN-6
Madison (CCD)—cens area AL-4
Madison (CCD)—cens area FL-3
Madison (CCD)—cens area GA-3
Madison Cem—cemetery (2) AL-4
Madison Cem—cemetery (5) IA-7
Madison Cem—cemetery MO-7
Madison Cem—cemetery NH-1
Madison Cem—cemetery NY-2
Madison Cem—cemetery OH-6
Madison Cem—cemetery OK-5
Madison Cem—cemetery (3) TN-4
Madison Cem—cemetery VA-3
**Madison Center**—pop pl MI-6
**Madison Center**—pop pl NY-2
Madison Center Cem—cemetery IA-7
Madison Center (census name Madison)—other ME-1
**Madison Center (census name Madison)**—pop pl CT-1
Madison Ch—church AL-4
Madison Ch—church GA-3
Madison Ch—church IN-6
Madison Ch—church (2) IA-7
Madison Ch—church (3) OH-6
Madison Ch—church PA-2
Madison Ch—church SC-3
Madison Ch—church WA-9
Madison Chapel—church GA-3
Madison Chapel—church IA-7
Madison Ch of Christ—church AL-4
Madison Ch of God—church AL-4
Madison Ch of the Nazarene—church AL-4
Madison Church MS-4
Madison City Hall—building MS-4
Madison City Hall—hist pl MN-6
Madison City Lake Dam—dam MS-4
Madison Coll—school VA-3
Madison College—uninc pl TN-4
Madison Coll (historical)—school TN-4
Madison Country Club—locale FL-3
Madison Country Club—other IN-6
Madison Country Club—other KY-4
Madison County—civil MO-7
**Madison County**—pop pl AL-4
**Madison (County)**—pop pl AR-4
**Madison County**—pop pl FL-3
**Madison (County)**—pop pl GA-3
**Madison (County)**—pop pl IL-6
**Madison County**—pop pl IN-6
**Madison (County)**—pop pl KY-4
**Madison County**—pop pl MS-4
**Madison (County)**—pop pl MO-7
**Madison (County)**—pop pl NY-2
**Madison County**—pop pl NC-3
**Madison (County)**—pop pl OH-6
**Madison County**—pop pl TN-4
**Madison (County)**—pop pl TX-5
**Madison (County)**—pop pl VA-3
Madison County Courthouse—building AL-4
Madison County Courthouse—building TN-4
Madison County Courthouse—hist pl GA-3
Madison County Courthouse—hist pl ID-8
Madison County Courthouse—hist pl IA-7
Madison County Courthouse—hist pl KY-4
Madison County Courthouse—hist pl NC-3
Madison County Courthouse—hist pl OH-6
Madison County Courthouse—hist pl VA-3
Madison County Courthouse Hist Dist—hist pl VA-3
Madison County Dragway—locale AL-4
Madison County Fairgrounds—hist pl MT-8
Madison County Home (historical)—building TN-4
Madison County HS—school AL-4
Madison County HS—school FL-3
Madison County Industrial Park—locale AL-4
Madison County Industrial Park—locale TN-4
Madison County Jail—hist pl MS-4
Madison County Lake—reservoir AL-4
Madison County Lake Dam—dam MS-4
Madison County Memorial Gardens—cemetery KY-4
Madison County Memorial Hosp—hospital FL-3
Madison County Memorial Hosp—hospital IA-7
Madison County MS—school FL-3
Madison County Nature Study Center—park AL-4
Madison County Nature Trail Dam—dam AL-4
Madison County Nature Trail Lake—reservoir AL-4
Madison County Nursing Home—hospital MT-8
Madison County Park and Boat Harbor—harbor AL-4
Madison County Public Lake AL-4
Madison County Public Lake Dam—dam AL-4
Madison County Sheriff's House and Jail—hist pl IL-6
Madison County Sky Park—airport AL-4
Madison County Technical Center AL-4
Madison County Technical Sch—school AL-4
Madison County Vocational Sch—school TN-4
Madison County Wayside—locale OR-9
Madison Creek KS-7
Madison Creek WI-6
Madison Creek—stream AK-9
Madison Creek—stream ID-8
Madison Creek—stream IL-6
Madison Creek—stream IN-6
Madison Creek—stream KS-7
Madison Creek—stream MT-8
Madison Creek—stream (2) NY-2
Madison Creek—stream OR-9
Madison Creek—stream TN-4
Madison Creek—stream VA-3
Madison Creek—stream WA-9
Madison Creek—stream WV-2
Madison Creek—stream WY-8
Madison Creek Baptist Church TN-4
Madison Creek Ch—church TN-4
Madison Creek Sch—school WY-8
Madison Creek Sch (historical)—school TN-4
Madison Cross Roads AL-4
**Madison Crossroads**—pop pl AL-4
Madison Crossroads (CCD)—cens area AL-4
Madison Crossroads Ch—church AL-4
Madison Crossroads Division—civil AL-4
Madison Cross Roads Post Office (historical)—building AL-4
Madison Crossroads Sch—school AL-4
Madison Dike—levee MT-8
Madison Ditch—canal OH-6
Madison Division—civil AL-4
Madison Drain MI-6
Madison Drain—canal MI-6
Madison Draw—valley SD-7
Madison East—post sta MN-6
Madison East (CCD)—cens area KY-4
Madison Elem Sch—hist pl PA-2
Madison Elem Sch—hist pl UT-8
Madison Elem Sch—school IN-6
Madison Elem Sch—school KS-7
Madison Elem Sch—school NC-3
Madison Elem Sch—school PA-2
Madison Fort—hist pl OH-6
Madison Gap—swamp MI-6
Madison Golf Course—other KS-7
Madison Golf Course—other NJ-2
**Madison Golf Lakelands**—pop pl OH-6
Madison Grade—summit MT-8
Madison Grade Sch—hist pl MT-8
Madison Green Hist Dist—hist pl CT-1
Madison Grove Ch—church NC-3
Madison Gulch—valley CA-9
Madison Gulch—valley CO-8
Madison Gulch—valley (2) MT-8
Madison Gulch—valley OR-9
Madison Gulf—trail NH-1
Madison Gulf—valley NH-1
**Madison Hall**—pop pl TN-4
Madison Heights AL-4
**Madison Heights**—pop pl MI-6
**Madison Heights**—pop pl NJ-2
**Madison Heights**—pop pl VA-3
Madison Heights—uninc pl AL-4
Madison Heights HS—school IN-6
Madison Heights Sch—school AZ-5
**Madison Heights (subdivision)**—pop pl MS-4
**Madison Highlands (subdivision)**—pop pl AL-4
Madison Hill CO-8
**Madison Hill**—pop pl NJ-2
**Madison Hill**—pop pl OH-6
Madison Hist Dist—hist pl GA-3
Madison Hist Dist—hist pl IN-6
Madison Hist Dist—hist pl SD-7
Madison (historical)—locale IA-7
Madison Hollow—stream PA-2
Madison Hollow—valley AR-4
Madison Hollow—valley (2) PA-2
Madison Hollow—valley VA-3
Madison Hotel—hist pl NJ-2
Madison Hotel and Cafe—hist pl MT-8
Madison House—hist pl CA-9
Madison HS—school CA-9
Madison HS—school IL-6
Madison HS—school KS-7
Madison HS—school KY-4
Madison HS—school MI-6
Madison HS—school NJ-2
Madison HS—school (2) NY-2
Madison HS—school NC-3
Madison HS—school (3) OH-6
Madison HS—school OR-9
Madison HS—school PA-2
Madison HS—school (3) TX-5
Madison HS—school VA-3
Madison Industrial Park—locale AL-4
Madison Island WV-2
Madison JHS—school (2) CA-9
Madison JHS—school (2) FL-3
Madison JHS—school IA-7
Madison JHS—school MI-6
Madison JHS—school NE-7
Madison JHS—school NJ-2
Madison JHS—school NM-5
Madison JHS—school (2) OK-5
Madison JHS—school UT-8
Madison Junction—locale WY-8
Madison Lake—lake MI-6
Madison Lake—lake NY-2
Madison Lake—lake WY-8
**Madison Lake**—pop pl MN-6
**Madison Lake**—pop pl OH-6
Madison Lake—reservoir IL-6
Madison Lake—reservoir MN-6
Madison Lake—reservoir OH-6
**Madison Lake Area**—pop pl OH-6
Madison Lakes—lake CT-1
Madison Lake State Park—park OH-6
Madison Lake State Res—park OH-6
Madison Livestock Investment Lake Dam—dam MS-4
**Madison (Madison Park)**—pop pl AL-4
Madison (Magisterial District)—fmr MCD (7) VA-3
Madison Mall Shop Ctr—locale AL-4
**Madison Manor**—pop pl VA-3
Madison Manor Park—park VA-3
Madison-Marianna Diversion—channel AR-4
Madison-Mayodan HS—school NC-3
Madison-Mayodan JHS—school NC-3
Madison Meadow—swamp MT-8
Madison Meadows Sch—school AZ-5
Madison Memorial Cem—cemetery OH-6
Madison Memorial Heliport—airport MO-7
Madison Memorial HS—school OH-6
Madison Memorial Park—park WV-2
Madison Memorial Sch—school WI-6
Madison Mill Branch—stream VA-3
Madison Mills—locale VA-3
**Madison Mills**—pop pl OH-6
Madison Mills Cem—cemetery OH-6
Madison Mine—mine AR-4
Madison Missionary Ch—church OH-6
Madison-Monroe Hist Dist—hist pl TN-4
Madison MS—school AL-4
Madison Mtn—summit AK-9
Madison Municipal Airp—airport IN-6
Madison Municipal Airp—airport SD-7
Madison Museum—hist pl WY-8
**Madison North**—pop pl OH-6
Madison North (CCD)—cens area KY-4
Madison on the Lake OH-6
Madison-On-The-Lake—lake OH-6
**Madison-on-the-Lake**—pop pl OH-6
**Madison Parish**—pop pl LA-4
Madison Park AL-4
Madison Park—park AZ-5
Madison Park—park CA-9
Madison Park—park (2) IL-6
Madison Park—park IN-6
Madison Park—park IA-7
Madison Park—park LA-4
Madison Park—park MN-6
Madison Park—park (2) MT-8
Madison Park—park (2) OH-6
Madison Park—park TN-4
Madison Park—park UT-8
Madison Park—park WI-6
**Madison Park**—pop pl NJ-2
**Madison Park**—pop pl NY-2
**Madison Park**—pop pl WA-9
Madison Park—post sta IL-6
Madison Park—uninc pl LA-4
Madison Park Apartments—hist pl CA-9
Madison Park Sch—school AL-4
Madison Park Sch—school AZ-5
Madison Park Sch—school IL-6
Madison Park Sch—school MI-6
Madison Park Sch—school OH-6
Madison Park Sch—school OK-5
Madison Park Shoal—bar IL-6
Madison Park Shop Ctr—locale AZ-5
Madison Park Shop Ctr—locale TN-4
**Madison Park (subdivision)**—pop pl NC-3
Madison Pike Sch—school AL-4
Madison Plateau—area WY-8
Madison Plateau—plain MT-8
Madison Plaza Shop Ctr—locale AL-4
**Madison Point (subdivision)**—pop pl AL-4
Madison Pond ME-1
Madison Pond—lake NY-2
Madison Pond—lake RI-1
Madison Pond—reservoir VA-3
Madison Post Office—building AL-4
Madison Post Office—building MS-4
Madison Powerhouse—other MT-8
Madison Primary Sch—school FL-3
Madison Public Library—building MS-4
Madison Public Library and the James Bldg—hist pl NJ-2
Madison-Putnam-60th Place Hist Dist—hist pl NY-2
Madison Ranch—locale SD-7
Madison Range—range MT-8
Madison Range Overlook—locale WY-8
Madison-Ridgeland Acad—school MS-4
Madison-Ridgeland HS—school MS-4
Madison-Ridgeland Public Sch—hist pl MS-4
Madison River—stream MT-8
Madison River—stream WY-8
Madison River Lodge—locale MT-8
Madison River Lookout—locale WY-8
Madison Run VA-3
Madison Run—locale VA-3
**Madison Run**—pop pl WV-2
Madison Run—stream OH-6
Madison Run—stream (2) VA-3
Madison Run—stream WV-2
Madison Saint Sch—school WI-6
Madison Sch—school (15) CA-9
Madison Sch—school CO-8
Madison Sch—school CT-1
Madison Sch—school DC-2
Madison Sch—school FL-3
Madison Sch—school GA-3
Madison Sch—school ID-8
Madison Sch—school (7) IL-6
Madison Sch—school (5) IA-7
Madison Sch—school KS-7
Madison Sch—school KY-4
Madison Sch—school (6) MI-6
Madison Sch—school (5) MN-6
Madison Sch—school MO-7
Madison Sch—school NE-7
Madison Sch—school NV-8
Madison Sch—school (3) NJ-2
Madison Sch—school (2) NY-2
Madison Sch—school ND-7
Madison Sch—school (9) OH-6
Madison Sch—school (2) OK-5
Madison Sch—school (2) OR-9
Madison Sch—school (3) PA-2
Madison Sch—school SD-7
Madison Sch—school UT-8
Madison Sch—school (5) VA-3
Madison Sch—school (6) WA-9
Madison Sch—school (2) WV-2
Madison Sch—school (7) WI-6
Madison Sch (abandoned)—school MO-7
Madison Sch (abandoned)—school PA-2
Madison Sch (historical)—school AL-4
Madison Sch Number One—school AZ-5
Madison Sch Number Two—school AZ-5
Madison School IN-6
Madison School, District No. 1—hist pl NH-1
Madison Seminary—school NC-3
Madison Seminary And Home—hist pl OH-6
Madison Settlement Cem—cemetery IA-7
Madison Slide—valley MT-8
Madison South Shopping Plaza—locale TN-4
Madison Springs—spring MS-4
Madison Square MI-6
Madison Square—fmr MCD NE-7
Madison Square—uninc pl NY-2
**Madison Square Addition (subdivision)**—pop pl UT-8
Madison Square Cem—cemetery NE-7
Madison Square Garden—building NY-2
Madison Square Garden Tank—reservoir NM-5
Madison Square Mall Shop Ctr—locale AL-4
Madison Square Park—park NY-2
Madison Square Park—park TX-5
Madison Square Sch—school NE-7
Madison Square (Shop Ctr)—locale FL-3
Madison Square Shop Ctr—locale IN-6
Madison Square Shop Ctr—locale NC-3
Madison Square-West Main Street Hist Dist—hist pl NY-2
Madison (sta.) (RR name for Darragh)—other PA-2
Madison State Hosp—hospital IN-6
Madison Station MS-4
Madison Station—hist pl NJ-2
Madison Station—locale NJ-2
Madison Station Post Office AL-4
Madison-Stewart Hist Dist—hist pl OH-6
Madison Street Baptist Ch—church AL-4
Madison Street Baptist Ch—church TN-4
Madison Street Cem—cemetery NY-2
Madison Street Ch of Christ—church TN-4
Madison Street Methodist Church—hist pl TN-4
Madison Street Sch—school KY-4
Madison Street United Methodist Ch—church TN-4
Madisons Woodyard Landing—locale MS-4
Madison Theatre—hist pl IL-6
**Madison (Town of)**—pop pl CT-1
**Madison (Town of)**—pop pl ME-1
**Madison (Town of)**—pop pl NH-1
**Madison (Town of)**—pop pl NY-2
**Madison (Town of)**—pop pl WI-6
Madison Township—civil (4) MO-7
Madison Township—fmr MCD (13) IA-7
**Madison Township**—pop pl (3) KS-7
**Madison Township**—pop pl (3) MO-7
**Madison Township**—pop pl NE-7
**Madison Township**—pop pl ND-7
**Madison Township**—pop pl (2) SD-7
Madison (Township of) NJ-2
Madison (Township of)—fmr MCD (3) AR-4
Madison (Township of)—fmr MCD (2) NC-3
**Madison (Township of)**—pop pl IL-6
**Madison (Township of)**—pop pl (14) IN-6
**Madison (Township of)**—pop pl MI-6
**Madison (Township of)**—pop pl MN-6
**Madison (Township of)**—pop pl (21) OH-6
**Madison (Township of)**—pop pl (4) PA-2
Madison Union Cem—cemetery PA-2
Madison Union Ch—church IN-6
Madison Union Clay Washington (Magisterial District)—fmr MCD WV-2
Madison United Methodist Ch—church AL-4
Madison Valley—cens area MT-8
Madison Valley—valley MT-8
Madison Valley—valley WY-8
Madison Valley Hosp—hospital MT-8
Madison Valley HS—school MT-8
Madison Valley Presbyterian Ch—church MT-8
Madisonville OH-6
Madisonville—locale MS-4
Madisonville—locale MO-7
Madisonville—locale VA-3
**Madisonville**—pop pl KY-4
**Madisonville**—pop pl LA-4
**Madisonville**—pop pl NJ-2
**Madisonville**—pop pl OH-6
**Madisonville**—pop pl PA-2
**Madisonville**—pop pl TN-4
**Madisonville**—pop pl TX-5
Madisonville Bank—hist pl LA-4
Madisonville (CCD)—cens area KY-4
Madisonville (CCD)—cens area TN-4
Madisonville (CCD)—cens area TX-5
Madisonville Cem—cemetery KY-4
Madisonville Cem—cemetery MO-7
Madisonville Cem—cemetery TN-4
Madisonville Ch—church VA-3
Madisonville Commercial Hist Dist—hist pl KY-4
Madisonville Division—civil TN-4
Madisonville Elem Sch—school TN-4
Madisonville HS—school TN-4
Madisonville Industrial Park—locale TN-4
Madisonville JHS—school TN-4
Madisonville Lake—reservoir TN-4
Madisonville Lake Dam TN-4
Madisonville Lookout Tower—locale TN-4
Madisonville Methodist Episcopal Church South TN-4
Madisonville Post Office—building TN-4
Madisonville Presbyterian Ch—church TN-4
Madisonville Public Library—hist pl KY-4
Madisonville School (historical)—locale MO-7
Madisonville Shop Ctr—locale TN-4
Madison Waterworks—hist pl WI-6
Madison Wayside—locale VA-3
Madison West (CCD)—cens area KY-4
Madison West Industrial Park—locale TN-4
**Madison Woods (subdivision)**—pop pl NC-3
Madjado MP-9
Madjuro MP-9
Madkin Bayou—gut LA-4
Madkin Branch TX-5
Madkin Creek—stream TX-5
Madkin Mtn—summit AL-4
Mad Lake MN-6
Mad Lake—lake WA-9
Madlay FM-9
Madlener, Albert F., House—hist pl IL-6
**Madley**—pop pl PA-2
Madley Creek ID-8
Mad Lick Ridge—ridge VA-3
Madman Coulee—valley MT-8
Mad Mares Neck—swamp MA-1
Mad Meadow—flat WA-9
Madmosuk Island PW-9
Mad Mule Gulch—valley CA-9
Mad Mule Mtn—summit CA-9
Madnan's Neck NY-2
Madoc—locale MT-8
Madofan River—stream GU-9
Madog MH-9
Madog—other GU-9
Madog Cliffs MH-9
Madog Point MH-9
Madog River—stream GU-9
Madoira HS—school OH-6
Madola—locale GA-3
Madola Mill Creek—stream GA-3
Madolenihmw FM-9
Madolenihmw—civil FM-9
Madolenihmw Harbor FM-9
Madolenihmw (Municipality)—civ div FM-9
Madol Peidak—locale FM-9
Madol Peidi—locale FM-9
Madon FM-9
Madon Branch—stream KY-4
Madon Hollow—valley TN-4
Madonna—locale MD-2
Madonna, Mount—summit CA-9
Madonna Acad—school FL-3
Madonna Cem—cemetery PA-2
Madonna Chapel—church LA-4
Madonna Coll—school MI-6
Madonna Creek—stream CA-9
Madonna Del Sasso Sch—school CA-9
Madonna Hall for Girls—school MA-1
Madonna Heights Sch—school NY-2
Madonna Home—locale NE-7
Madonna HS—school (2) IL-6
Madonna HS—school NY-2
Madonna HS—school WV-2
Madonna Lake—reservoir NC-3
Madonna Peak—summit VT-1
Madonna Sch—school MI-6
**Madonna (Smuggles Notch) (Ski Resort)**—pop pl VT-1
**Madonnaville**—pop pl IL-6
Madonnaville Cem—cemetery IL-6
Madora Lake—lake CA-9
Madoren—locale MP-9
Mad Ox Gulch—valley CA-9
Mad Ox Mine—mine CA-9
Mad Pahra—bar FM-9
Madra—locale SD-7
Madragil FM-9
Madranio Canyon—valley CA-9
Madras—locale TX-5
**Madras**—pop pl GA-3
**Madras**—pop pl OR-9
Madras (CCD)—cens area OR-9
Madras Elem Sch—school OR-9
Madras HS—school OR-9
Madras JHS—school OR-9
Madras Sch—school TX-5
**Madras Station**—pop pl OR-9
Madraw Branch—stream SC-3
**Madray Springs**—pop pl GA-3
Madre, Laguna—lake (2) TX-5
Madre, Laguna—reservoir TX-5
Madre de Dios Island—island AK-9
Madre de Oro Mine—mine CA-9
Madre Dolorosa Cem—cemetery TX-5
Madre Mtn—summit NM-5
Madren Draw—valley WY-8
Madre Pond—reservoir GA-3
Madrich FM-9
Madrid CO-8
Madrid—locale CO-8
Madrid—locale KY-4
**Madrid**—pop pl AL-4
**Madrid**—pop pl IA-7
**Madrid**—pop pl ME-1
**Madrid**—pop pl NE-7
**Madrid**—pop pl NM-5
**Madrid**—pop pl NY-2
**Madrid**—pop pl VA-3
Madrid Bar—island KY-4
Madrid Bend Ch—church KY-4
Madrid Bldg—hist pl KY-4
Madrid Canyon—valley (2) CO-8
Madrid (CCD)—cens area AL-4
Madrid Cem—cemetery NM-5
Madrid Division—civil AL-4
Madrid Falls—falls TX-5
Madrid Hist Dist—hist pl NM-5
Madrid JHS—school AL-4
Madrid Junction—locale ME-1
Madrid Peak—summit NM-5
Madrid Post Office (historical)—building AL-4
Madrid Ranch—locale TX-5
Madrid Sch—school AZ-5
Madrid Spring—spring TX-5
**Madrid Springs**—pop pl NY-2
Madrid Tank—reservoir NM-5
**Madrid (Town of)**—pop pl ME-1
**Madrid (Town of)**—pop pl NY-2
Madrid-Waddington HS—school NY-2
Madrid Well—well (2) NM-5
Madriguera, Loma de la—summit TX-5
Madrigueras Windmill—locale TX-5
Madrillon—other VA-3
**Madrillon Farms**—pop pl VA-3
**Madrillon Farms (Madrillon)**—pop pl VA-3
Madril Peak—summit AZ-5
Madril Ranch—locale AZ-5
Madril Wash—stream AZ-5
Mad River—locale CA-9
Mad River—stream (3) CA-9
Mad River—stream (2) CT-1
Mad River—stream IL-6
Mad River—stream ME-1
Mad River—stream MA-1
Mad River—stream (3) NH-1
Mad River—stream (2) NY-2
Mad River—stream OH-6
Mad River—stream VT-1
Mad River—stream WA-9
Mad River—stream WI-6
Mad River Block—hist pl OH-6
Mad River Butte CA-9
Mad River Buttes—summit CA-9
Mad River Campground—locale CA-9
Mad River (CCD)—cens area CA-9
Mad River Dam—dam CT-1
Mad River Falls—falls ME-1
Mad River Falls—falls NY-2
Mad River Fish Hatchery—locale CA-9
**Mad River Glen**—pop pl VT-1
Mad River Glen Ski Area—other VT-1
Mad River JHS—school OH-6
Mad River Notch—gap NH-1
**Mad River (Ohio Edison Power Plant)**—pop pl OH-6
Mad River Ranger Station—locale CA-9
Mad River Ridge—ridge CA-9
Mad River Rock—pillar CA-9
Mad River Sch—school NH-1
Mad River Sch—school OH-6
Mad River Slough—stream CA-9
**Mad River (Township of)**—pop pl (3) OH-6
**Madrona**—pop pl WA-9
Madrona Beach—locale WA-9
Madrona Canyon—valley AZ-5
Madrona Canyon—valley CA-9
Madrona Creek—stream TX-5
Madrona JHS—school WA-9
Madrona Knoll Rancho District—hist pl CA-9
Madrona Park—park OR-9
Madrona Park—park WA-9
Madrona Point—cape (2) WA-9
Madrona Ranger Station—locale AZ-5
Madrona Sch—school CA-9
Madrone—locale NM-5
**Madrone**—pop pl CA-9
Madrone Campground—locale CA-9
Madrone Canyon—valley AZ-5
Madrone Creek—stream CA-9
Madrone Guard Station—locale CA-9
Madrone Lake—reservoir CA-9
Madrone Mine—mine CA-9
Madrone Ranch—locale CA-9
Madrone Sch—school (2) CA-9
Madrone Soda Springs—spring CA-9
Madrone Spring—spring (2) CA-9
Madronia Cem—cemetery CA-9
Madron Lake—lake MI-6
Madron (not verified)—island MP-9
Madrono Spring—spring AZ-5
Madron Sch—school NE-7
Mad Run—stream IN-6
Mad Run—stream PA-2
Mad Run—stream VA-3
Mad Rushing Water TN-4
Madry—locale MO-7
Madry Cem—cemetery NC-3
Madschero MP-9
Madschidscho FM-9
Madsen—locale UT-8
Madsen—locale WI-6
**Madsen Beach**—pop pl SD-7
Madsen Ditch—canal UT-8
Madsen Lake—lake UT-8
Madsen Park UT-8
Madsen Pool—reservoir MN-6
Madsen Rsvr—reservoir UT-8
Madsen Rsvr—reservoir WY-8
Madsen State Wildlife Mngmt Area—park MN-6
**Madsen Subdivision**—pop pl UT-8
Mad Sheep—summit VA-3
Mad Sheep Ridge—ridge WV-2
Madson—locale WA-9
Madson Mtn—summit AK-9
Mad Spring Branch AL-4
Madstone Cabin—locale OR-9
Madstone Creek—stream OR-9
Mad Tom—summit VA-3
Mad Tom—summit WV-2
Mad Tom Brook—stream (2) NY-2

Mad Tom Brook—stream ... VT-1
Mad Tom Lake—lake ... NY-2
Mad Tom Notch—gap ... VT-1
Mad Tom Trail—trail ... VT-1
Madulce Guard Station—locale ... CA-9
Madulce Guard Station and Site—hist pl .. CA-9
Madulce Peak—summit ... CA-9
Madulce Trail—trail ... CA-9
Madura Cem—cemetery ... KS-7
Maduskeag Stream—stream ... ME-1
Madvernize Ch—church ... MS-4
Madwin Creek—stream ... AL-4
Mad Wolf Mtn—summit ... MT-8
Mad Woman Spring—spring ... CA-9
Madwor ... FM-9
Madzo Ranch—locale ... ND-7
Mae ... MP-9
Mae—locale ... MN-6
Mae—locale ... WA-9
Mae Creek—stream ... ID-8
Maedonia Ch—church (3) ... GA-3
Maedriich—cape ... FM-9
Maeduwor—bay ... FM-9
Mae Eanes Junior High School ... AL-4
Maefu Cove—bay ... AS-9
Maegly, A. H., House—hist pl ... OR-9
Mae Hall Pond Dam—dam ... MS-4
Mae Island ... MP-9
Mae Island—island ... MP-9
Maele Rsvr—reservoir ... HI-9
Maelieli Hill ... HI-9
Maemae Sch—school ... HI-9
Maemong River—stream ... GU-9
Mae Nesbit Sch—school ... CA-9
Maen Island ... MP-9
Maen-to ... MP-9
Maeo—bar ... FM-9
Maercker Sch—school ... IL-6
Maeriiw—cape ... FM-9
Maertens Wyngart ... MA-1
Maerur ... FM-9
Maeruru ... FM-9
Maes—locale ... NM-5
**Maes**—pop pl ... MO-7
Maesar-Fairview Cemetery ... UT-8
Maes Arroyo—stream ... NM-5
Maesburg Ranch—locale ... NE-7
Maes Cem—cemetery ... NM-5
Maes Creek—stream ... CO-8
Maes Creek Cem—cemetery ... CO-8
**Maeser**—pop pl ... UT-8
Maeser, Reinhard, House—hist pl ... UT-8
Maeser Sch—hist pl ... UT-8
Maeser Sch—school (2) ... UT-8
Mae Shima ... FM-9
Mae Shoal—bar ... FM-9
Mae Simmons Park—park ... TX-5
Maes Mesa ... CO-8
Maes Oil Field—oilfield ... KS-7
Maes Spring—spring ... CO-8
Maes Spring—spring ... NM-5
Maestas ... NM-5
Maestas Canyon—valley ... NM-5
Maestas Creek—stream ... NM-5
Maestas East Well—well ... NM-5
Maestas Lake—lake ... NM-5
Maestas Park—flat ... NM-5
Maestas Ridge—ridge ... NM-5
Maestas Sch—school ... NM-5
Maestas West Well—well ... NM-5
Maestro Tank—reservoir ... TX-5
Mae-to ... MP-9
Mae Valley—basin ... WA-9
Mae Well—well ... NM-5
Mae West Lake—lake ... AK-9
Mae West Peaks—summit ... AZ-5
Maeys (Maeystown Station)—locale ... IL-6
**Maeystown**—pop pl ... IL-6
Maeystown Creek—stream ... IL-6
Maeystown Hist Dist—hist pl ... IL-6
**Maeystown (sta.) (Maeys)**—pop pl ... IL-6
Maez Place—locale ... NM-5
Mafafa—locale ... AS-9
Maffet Cem—cemetery ... KY-4
Maffett Street Sch—school ... PA-2
Maffitt Ledge—rock ... MA-1
Mafler Creek—stream ... OR-9
Mafnagan ... MH-9
Mafnas Nete—area ... GU-9
Mafolie—locale ... VI-3
Mafolie Great House—hist pl ... VI-3
Maftin C Tant Lake—reservoir ... MS-4
Maga—summit ... MH-9
Magaaf—locale ... FM-9
Magachagiiru ... FM-9
Magachagil ... FM-9
Magachaguill ... FM-9
Magachaquill ... FM-9
Magachgil—locale ... FM-9
Magachin ... PW-9
Magadanz School ... SD-7
Magado Creek—stream ... NM-5
Magagnet ... GA-3
Magahee Ponds—reservoir ... GA-3
Maga Hill ... MH-9
Magaktlek Creek—stream ... AK-9
**Magalia**—pop pl ... CA-9
Magalia Camp—locale ... CA-9
Magalia Community Church—hist pl ... CA-9
Magalia Mine—mine ... CA-9
Magalia Rsvr—reservoir ... CA-9
Magallon—locale ... WA-9
Magallon Mtn—summit ... KY-4
Magalloway Mtn—summit ... NH-1
Magalloway (Plantation of)—civ div ... ME-1
Magalloway River—stream ... ME-1
Magalloway River—stream ... NH-1
Magalloway Sch—school ... ME-1
Magan—locale ... KY-4
Maga Point—cape ... AS-9
Magaretta Furnace Sch—school ... PA-2
Magargee Run—stream ... PA-2
Magary Camp—locale ... ID-8
**Magas Abajo**—pop pl ... PR-3
**Magas Arriba**—pop pl ... PR-3
Magas (Barrio)—fmr MCD ... PR-3
**Magasco**—pop pl ... TX-5
Mag Ashe Branch—stream ... NC-3
Magason Branch—stream ... LA-4
Magassi Cem—cemetery ... IL-6

Maga Stream—stream ... AS-9
Magatjagil ... FM-9
Magatjugil ... FM-9
Magazille, Bayou—stream ... LA-4
**Magazine**—pop pl ... AL-4
**Magazine**—pop pl ... AR-4
Magazine Branch—stream (3) ... NC-3
Magazine Branch—stream ... WV-2
Magazine Brook—stream ... ME-1
Magazine Canyon—valley ... AZ-5
Magazine Canyon—valley ... CA-9
Magazine Canyon—valley ... KS-7
Magazine Canyon—valley ... UT-8
Magazine Dam ... PA-2
Magazine Ditch—canal ... DE-2
Magazine Hollow—valley (2) ... TN-4
Magazine (Magazine Point)—uninc pl ... AL-4
Magazine Mesa—summit ... AZ-5
Magazine Mountain Lodge—locale ... AR-4
Magazine Mtn—summit ... AR-4
Magazine Point—cape ... AL-4
Magazine Point—cape ... FL-3
Magazine Point (Magazine) ... AL-4
Magazine Pond ... CT-1
Magazine Road Park—park ... TN-4
Magazine Spring—spring ... AZ-5
Magazine Tank—reservoir ... AZ-5
Magazine Tank Number One—reservoir ... AZ-5
Magazine Tank Number Two—reservoir ... AZ-5
Magazine (Township of)—fmr MCD ... AR-4
Magbee Bend—bend ... AL-4
Magbee Branch—stream ... TN-4
Magbee Creek ... TX-5
Magbee Island—island ... MN-6
Magby Creek—stream ... AL-4
Magby Creek—stream ... MS-4
Magby Creek—stream ... TX-5
Magby Gap—gap ... GA-3
**Magby Gap**—pop pl ... GA-3
Magbys Creek ... MS-4
Mag Creek—stream ... GA-3
Mag Creek—stream ... MO-7
Mag Creek—stream ... OR-9
Mag Creek Pond—reservoir ... GA-3
**Magda**—pop pl ... LA-4
Magda, Lake—lake ... MN-6
Magdalen—school ... IL-6
Magdalena ... AZ-5
**Magdalena**—pop pl ... NM-5
**Magdalena**—pop pl ... PR-3
Magdalena Butte—summit ... NM-5
Magdalena (CCD)—cens area ... NM-5
Magdalena Mountains—range ... NM-5
Magdalena Peak—summit (2) ... NM-5
Magdalene, Lake—lake ... FL-3
Magdalene Cem—cemetery ... SC-3
Magdalene Ch—church ... SC-3
Magdalene Ch (historical)—church ... AL-4
Magdalene Gulch—valley ... CO-8
Magdalene Lake—lake ... WY-8
Magdalene Mine—mine ... CO-8
Magdalene Sch—school ... OK-5
Magdalen Island ... NY-2
Magdalen Island—island ... NY-2
Magdalen Sch—school ... KS-7
Magdaline House—hist pl ... NM-5
Magdanz Creek—stream ... WI-6
Magden Sch—school ... MI-6
Magee—locale ... CO-8
Magee—locale ... PA-2
**Magee**—pop pl ... IN-6
**Magee**—pop pl ... MS-4
**Magee**—pop pl ... NY-2
Magee, Jacob, House—hist pl ... AL-4
MaGee, Merrill, House—hist pl ... NY-2
Magee, Nehemiah, House—hist pl ... LA-4
Magee, Robert D., House—hist pl ... LA-4
Magee Branch—stream ... FL-3
Magee Branch—stream ... TX-5
Magee Canal—canal ... LA-4
Magee Cem ... MS-4
Magee Cem—cemetery (6) ... LA-4
Magee Cem—cemetery (6) ... MS-4
Magee Cem—cemetery (2) ... MO-7
Magee Cemetery—locale ... MT-8
Magee Chapel—church ... MD-2
Magee Chapel—church ... TX-5
Magee Ch of God—church ... MS-4
Magee City Hall—building ... MS-4
Magee Creek—stream ... AL-4
Magee Creek—stream ... CA-9
Magee Creek—stream ... ID-8
Magee Creek—stream ... MS-4
Magee Creek—stream ... MT-8
Magee Creek—stream ... WA-9
Magee Creek—stream ... WI-6
Magee Ditch—canal ... IN-6
Magee Ditch—canal ... MT-8
Magee Eddy—bay ... PA-2
Magee Elem Sch—school ... MS-4
Magee General Hosp—hospital ... MS-4
Mageehee Lake Dam—dam ... MS-4
Magee Hill Ch—church ... MS-4
Magee Historic Site—park ... ID-8
Magee Hollow—valley ... MO-7
Magee Hosp—hospital ... PA-2
Magee HS—school ... MS-4
Magee JHS—school ... AZ-5
Magee JHS—school ... MS-4
Magee Lake—lake ... CA-9
Magee Lake—lake ... IA-7
Magee Lake Dam—dam ... MS-4
Magee Marsh Wildlife Area—park ... OH-6
Magee Municipal Airp—airport ... MS-4
Magee Oil Field—oilfield ... MS-4
Magee Peak ... CA-9
Magee Peak ... ID-8
Magee Peak—summit ... CA-9
Magee Peak—summit ... ID-8
Magee Playground—park ... PA-2
Magee Presbyterian Ch—church ... MS-4
Magee Ranch—locale ... MT-8
Magee Ranger Station—hist pl ... ID-8
Magee Ridge—ridge ... CA-9
Mageeruikku To ... FM-9
Magee Run ... PA-2
Magee Sch—school ... CA-9
Magee Sch—school ... WI-6
Magees Creek ... MS-4
Magees Creek—stream ... MS-4

Magees Creek Baptist Church ... MS-4
Magees Creek Cem—cemetery ... MS-4
Magees Creek Ch—church (2) ... MS-4
Magees Creek Water Park—park ... MS-4
Magees Hill—summit ... NY-2
Magees Mill (historical)—locale ... MS-4
Magee Spring—spring ... CA-9
Magee Spring—spring ... MT-8
Magee Springs—locale ... KY-4
Mageetown Corners—locale ... PA-2
Magee Trail—trail ... CA-9
Magee Trail—trail ... PA-2
Magee Trail (Pack)—trail ... CA-9
Magee-Womens Hospital Airp—airport ... PA-2
Mageik, Mount—summit ... AK-9
Mageik Creek—stream ... AK-9
Mageik Landslide—area ... AK-9
Magelby Rsvr—reservoir ... UT-8
Magella (historical)—locale ... AL-4
Magella Mine (undeground)—mine ... AL-4
Magellan Canal—canal ... LA-4
Magellan Monument—other ... GU-9
Magellan Post Office
(historical)—building ... TN-4
Magelssen Bluff Park—park ... MN-6
Magendanz Falls—falls ... TN-4
Magens Bay—bay ... VI-3
Magens Bay Archeol District—hist pl ... VI-3
Magenta—locale ... LA-4
Magenta—locale ... MS-4
**Magenta**—pop pl ... LA-4
Magenta—uninc pl ... WI-6
Magenta, Bayou—stream ... LA-4
Magenta Canal—canal ... LA-4
Magenta Landing (historical)—locale ... MS-4
Magenta Station ... MS-4
Mager Cem—cemetery ... TN-4
Mager Cem—cemetery ... TX-5
Magererik Island—island ... FM-9
Mager Hollow—valley ... TN-4
Magerle Gulch ... OR-9
Magerle Rsvr—reservoir ... OR-9
Magerly Gulch—valley ... OR-9
Magers Crossing—locale ... TX-5
Magers Pond—reservoir ... TX-5
Magers Rsvr—reservoir ... CO-8
Mageruruppu To ... FM-9
Magetti Flats—flat ... CA-9
Magevney House—hist pl ... TN-4
Maggard—locale ... KY-4
Maggard Branch—stream (5) ... KY-4
Maggard Branch Sch—school ... KY-4
Maggard Cabin—locale ... MO-7
Maggard Cem—cemetery ... KY-4
Maggard Cem—cemetery ... MO-7
**Maggard (historical)**—pop pl ... OR-9
Maggard Ridge—ridge ... TN-4
Maggard Sch—school ... KY-4
Maggart ... TN-4
**Maggart**—pop pl ... TN-4
Maggarte Branch—stream ... TN-4
**Maggarte (historical)**—pop pl ... TN-4
Maggart Post Office (historical)—building . TN-4
Maggart Sch (historical)—school ... TN-4
Maggarts Ridge ... TN-4
Maggart United Methodist Ch—church ... TN-4
Maggett Spring—spring ... AZ-5
Maggie—locale ... VA-3
Maggie—locale ... WV-2
**Maggie**—pop pl ... KY-4
**Maggie**—pop pl ... NC-3
Maggie, Lake—lake ... FL-3
Maggie, Lake—lake ... WA-9
Maggie Bend—bend ... ID-8
Maggie Branch—stream ... TX-5
Maggie Butte—summit ... ID-8
Maggie Canyon—valley ... AZ-5
Maggie Chapel—church ... NC-3
Maggie Creek ... OR-9
Maggie Creek—stream ... AK-9
Maggie Creek—stream ... CO-8
Maggie Creek—stream ... ID-8
Maggie Creek—stream ... MI-6
Maggie Creek—stream ... MN-6
Maggie Creek—stream (4) ... MT-8
Maggie Creek—stream (2) ... NV-8
Maggie Creek—stream ... TX-5
Maggie Creek—stream (2) ... WA-9
Maggie Creek—stream ... WI-6
Maggie Creek—stream ... WY-8
Maggie Creek Canyon—valley ... NV-8
Maggie Creek Spring—spring ... NV-8
Maggie Creek Trail—trail ... WA-9
Maggie Dam—reservoir ... AZ-5
Maggie Ditch—canal ... CO-8
Maggie Gulch—valley (2) ... CO-8
Maggie Gulch—valley ... NV-8
Maggie Hummocks—island ... GA-3
Maggie Jones Tank—reservoir ... AZ-5
Maggie Lake—lake ... MI-6
Maggie Lake—lake ... MN-6
Maggie Lakes—lake ... CA-9
Maggie Lakes—lake ... MI-6
MAGGIE LEE—hist pl ... MD-2
Maggie L Walker Natl Historic Site—park . VA-3
Maggie May Spring—spring ... AZ-5
Maggie Memorial Ch—church ... KY-4
Maggie Mine—mine (3) ... AZ-5
Maggie Mtn—summit ... CA-9
Maggie Post Office (historical)—building ... TN-4
Maggie Rock—pillar ... CO-8
Maggies Canyon—valley ... AZ-5
Maggies Cove—bay ... TX-5
Maggie Shaft—mine ... NM-5
Maggies Island—island ... WI-6
Maggie's Islands ... GA-3
Maggies Knob—summit ... CO-8
Maggies Mill—locale ... TN-4
MAGGIE S. MYERS (schooner)—hist pl ... DE-2
Maggies Nipple—summit (2) ... CO-8
Maggies Peaks—summit ... CA-9
Maggies Point—cape ... TX-5
Maggie Spring—spring ... OR-9
Maggie Springs—spring ... WY-8
Maggies Riffle—rapids ... OR-9
Maggie Summit—summit ... NV-8
Maggies Well—well ... AZ-5
Maggie Tank—reservoir (2) ... AZ-5
Maggie Valley—valley ... NC-3
**Maggie Valley (Maggie)**—pop pl ... NC-3

Maggie Wash—stream ... AZ-5
Maggie Well—well ... AZ-5
Maggini Ranch—locale ... NV-8
Maggio Estate Dam Number Two—dam ... PA-2
Maggiore, Lake—lake (2) ... FL-3
Maggis 84—locale ... PA-2
Maggity Branch—stream ... IN-6
Maggodee Creek ... VA-3
Maggodee Creek—stream ... VA-3
Maggot Creek—stream ... IL-6
Maggot Ridge—ridge ... NC-3
Maggot Spring—spring ... MT-8
Maggot Spring—spring ... OR-9
Maggot Spring Branch—stream ... NC-3
Maggot Spring Gap—gap ... NC-3
Maggotty Creek ... VA-3
Maggotty Creek—stream ... VA-3
Maggoty Run—stream ... WV-2
Maggs Bluff—cliff ... AL-4
Maghera Glass-Ormsby Hall—hist pl ... KY-4
Mag Hollow—valley ... TN-4
Magic—locale ... ID-8
Magic—post sta ... TX-5
**Magic City**—pop pl ... ID-8
**Magic City**—pop pl ... TX-5
Magic Creek—stream ... MS-4
Magic Dam—dam ... ID-8
Magic (historical)—locale ... KS-7
Magic Hole—bay ... TN-4
Magic Hot Springs—spring ... ID-8
Magician Lake—lake ... MI-6
Magiciene Bay ... MH-9
Magicienne Bay ... MH-9
Magicienne Bucht ... MH-9
Magic Island—island ... WV-2
Magic Lake—lake ... KY-4
Magic Lake—lake ... MN-6
Magiclantern Creek ... OR-9
Magic Lantern Creek—stream ... OR-9
MAGIC (log canoe)—hist pl ... MD-2
Magic Mountain Site—hist pl ... CO-8
Magic Mountain Ski Area—locale ... ID-8
Magic Mtn—summit ... CA-9
Magic Mtn—summit ... WA-9
Magic Place Shop Ctr, The—locale ... AL-4
**Magic Resort**—pop pl ... ID-8
Magic Rsvr—reservoir ... ID-8
Magic Sch—school ... KS-7
Magic Springs—locale ... AR-4
**Magic Valley**—pop pl ... KY-4
Magic Valley Hosp—hospital ... TX-5
Magic Valley Industrial Park—locale ... TN-4
Magie Creek—stream ... AR-4
Magie Mountain ... AL-4
Magill—locale ... MO-7
**Magill**—pop pl ... IA-7
Magill, Bayou—stream ... LA-4
Magill, Henry, House—hist pl ... CT-1
Magill Cem—cemetery ... MO-7
Magill Cem—cemetery ... TN-4
Magill Cem—cemetery ... TX-5
Magill Creek ... TX-5
Magill Creek—stream ... OR-9
Magill Creek—stream ... TX-5
**Magill Heights**—pop pl ... PA-2
Magill Hollow—valley ... MO-7
Magill Island ... NY-2
Magill Lagoon—lake ... LA-4
Magill Memorial Cem—cemetery ... TX-5
Magill Memorial Ch—church ... TN-4
Magill Mtn—summit ... TX-5
Magills Island ... NY-2
Maginnis Creek—stream ... MT-8
Maginnis Mine—mine ... MT-8
Maginnis Mtn—summit ... MT-8
Magistrate Canyon—valley ... UT-8
Magitchlie Creek—stream ... AK-9
Magitchlie Range—range ... AK-9
Magkpie Creek—stream ... ID-8
Maglab—uninc pl ... TX-5
Magladry Sch—school ... OR-9
Magleby Dam—dam ... UT-8
Magleby Pass—gap ... UT-8
**Magley**—pop pl ... IN-6
Magloire Delande Creek ... CO-8
Maglreng ... PW-9
Maglrong ... PW-9
Magma—locale ... AZ-5
Magma Copper Mines—mine ... AZ-5
Magma Dam—dam ... AZ-5
Magma Hosp—hospital ... AZ-5
Magma Mine—mine ... WA-9
Magma Retarding Dam—dam ... AZ-5
Magma RR Station—building ... AZ-5
Magma Tailings Dam Number Five—dam . AZ-5
Magma Tailings Dam Number Six—dam ... AZ-5
Magma Tailings Dam Numbers One and
Two—dam ... AZ-5
Magma Tailings Dam Numbers Three and
Four—dam ... AZ-5
Magma Wash—arroyo ... AZ-5
Magma Well—well ... AZ-5
Magmont Mine—mine ... MO-7
Magmont Mine and Mill ... MO-7
**Magna**—pop pl ... UT-8
**Magna Addition Subdivision**—pop pl ... UT-8
Magna Community Baptist
Church—hist pl ... UT-8
Magna Community Ch—church ... UT-8
Magna Creek ... MT-8
Magna Division—civil ... UT-8
**Magna Manors Subdivision**—pop pl ... UT-8
Magna Mill—locale ... UT-8
Magna Mine—mine ... AZ-5
Magna Mine—mine ... MT-8
Magnani Canyon—valley ... KS-7
Magna Sch—school ... UT-8
Magna View Baptist Ch ... TN-4
Magna View Ch—church ... TN-4
Magna Vista—locale ... MS-4
**Magner**—pop pl ... IL-6
Magner Park—flat ... NM-5
Magner Spring ... NM-5
Magnesia Creek—stream ... MT-8
Magnesia Pass—channel ... FL-3
Magnesia Spring—spring ... CA-9
Magnesia Spring Canyon—valley ... CA-9
Magnesia Springs—locale ... AR-4
Magnesia Springs—spring ... AR-4
Magnesia Springs—spring ... FL-3

Magnesite Wash—stream ... NV-8
Magnesium Queen Mines—mine ... AZ-5
Magnesium Spring—spring ... PA-2
Magnesium Springs—spring ... AZ-5
**Magness**—pop pl ... AR-4
Magness Cem—cemetery (2) ... AR-4
Magness Cem—cemetery ... MS-4
Magness Ch—church ... AR-4
Magness Chapel ... TN-4
Magness Chapel—church ... AR-4
Magness Cove—bay ... GA-3
Magness Creek ... AR-4
Magness Creek—stream (2) ... AR-4
Magness Creek—stream ... NC-3
Magness Draw—valley ... TX-5
Magness Lake—reservoir ... AR-4
Magness Mills (historical)—locale ... TN-4
Magness Mills Post Office
(historical)—building ... IN-4
Magness (Township of)—fmr MCD (2) ... AR-4
Magnet ... AR-4
Magnet—locale ... GA-3
Magnet—locale ... IL-6
Magnet—locale ... TX-5
Magnet—locale ... VA-3
**Magnet**—pop pl ... AR-4
**Magnet**—pop pl ... IN-6
**Magnet**—pop pl ... NE-7
Magnet Cem—cemetery ... NE-7
**Magnet Cove**—pop pl ... AR-4
**Magnet Cove**—pop pl ... FL-3
**Magnet Cove**—pop pl ... WY-8
Magnet Cove Ch—church ... AR-4
**Magnet Cove (Magnet)**—pop pl ... AR-4
Magnet Cove RR Station—locale ... FL-3
Magnet Cove Sch—school ... AR-4
Magnet Creek ... MT-8
Magnet Creek—stream (3) ... AK-9
Magnet Creek—stream ... WA-9
Magnet Creek Trail—trail ... WA-9
Magnet Ditch—canal ... IN-6
Magnetic Gulch—valley ... CO-8
Magnetic Hill—summit ... HI-9
Magnetic Island—island ... AK-9
Magnetic Laboratories Airp—airport ... PA-2
Magnetic Lake—lake ... MN-6
Magnetic Mesa—summit ... AZ-5
Magnetic Mine—mine ... WA-9
Magnetic Peak—summit ... HI-9
Magnetic Point—cape ... AK-9
Magnetic Post Office
(historical)—building ... TN-4
Magnetic Spring—spring ... AR-4
**Magnetic Springs**—pop pl ... IN-6
**Magnetic Springs**—pop pl ... OH-6
Magnet Island—island ... MN-6
Magnet Lake ... MS-4
Magnet Lake—lake ... MN-6
Magnet Mine—mine ... CO-8
Magnet Mountain ... MO-7
Magnet Park—flat ... CO-8
Magnet Rock—island ... AK-9
Magnet Tank—reservoir ... AZ-5
Magnet (Township of)—fmr MCD ... AR-4
Magney Park—park ... MN-6
Magnic Gap ... GA-3
Magnificent, Mount—summit ... AK-9
Magnison Butte—summit ... WA-9
Magnola Mine—mine ... CA-9
Magnolia ... AL-4
Magnolia ... KS-7
Magnolia ... MS-4
Magnolia ... WI-6
Magnolia—church ... SC-3
Magnolia—hist pl ... LA-4
Magnolia—hist pl ... NC-3
Magnolia—hist pl (2) ... SC-3
Magnolia—locale ... CA-9
Magnolia—locale ... CO-8
Magnolia—locale ... GA-3
Magnolia—locale (3) ... LA-4
Magnolia—locale ... ND-7
Magnolia—locale ... TN-4
Magnolia—locale ... TX-5
**Magnolia**—pop pl ... AL-4
**Magnolia**—pop pl ... AR-4
**Magnolia**—pop pl ... CA-9
**Magnolia**—pop pl ... DE 2
**Magnolia**—pop pl ... GA-3
**Magnolia**—pop pl ... IL-6
**Magnolia**—pop pl ... IN-6
**Magnolia**—pop pl ... IA-7
**Magnolia**—pop pl ... KY-4
**Magnolia**—pop pl (4) ... LA-4
**Magnolia**—pop pl ... MD-2
**Magnolia**—pop pl ... MA-1
**Magnolia**—pop pl ... MN-6
**Magnolia**—pop pl ... MS-4
**Magnolia**—pop pl ... MO-7
**Magnolia**—pop pl (3) ... NJ-2
**Magnolia**—pop pl ... NY-2
**Magnolia**—pop pl (2) ... NC-3
**Magnolia**—pop pl ... OH-6
**Magnolia**—pop pl ... TX-5
**Magnolia**—pop pl ... VA-3
**Magnolia**—pop pl (2) ... WV-2
**Magnolia**—pop pl ... WI-6
Magnolia—post sta ... CA-9
Magnolia—uninc pl ... WA-9
Magnolia, Bayou—gut ... LA-4
Magnolia, Bayou—stream ... LA-4
Magnolia Acad—school ... MS-4
Magnolia Airp—airport ... MS-4
**Magnolia Ave**—pop pl ... CA-9
Magnolia Ave Ch of Christ—church ... MS-4
Magnolia Ave Sch—school ... CA-9
Magnolia Ave United Methodist
Ch—church ... TN-4
Magnolia Baptist Ch—church ... FL-3
Magnolia Baptist Ch—church ... MS-4
Magnolia Baptist Church ... AL-4
Magnolia Bay ... FL-3
Magnolia Beach—beach ... SC-3
Magnolia Beach—locale ... FL-3
Magnolia Beach—locale ... WA-9
**Magnolia Beach**—pop pl ... AL-4
**Magnolia Beach**—pop pl ... TN-4
**Magnolia Beach**—pop pl ... TX-5
Magnolia Bend—bay ... MS-4
Magnolia Bldg—hist pl ... TX-5

Magnolia Bluff—cliff ... FL-3
Magnolia Bluff—cliff ... GA-3
Magnolia Bluff—cliff ... WA-9
**Magnolia Bluff**—pop pl ... WA-9
Magnolia Bluff Landing ... AL-4
Magnolia Bluffs—locale ... FL-3
Magnolia Branch—stream ... SC-3
Magnolia Branch—stream ... TX-5
Magnolia Camp—locale ... CO-8
Magnolia Canal—canal ... CA-9
Magnolia Canal—canal (2) ... LA-4
Magnolia (CCD)—cens area ... TX-5
Magnolia Cem ... MS-4
Magnolia Cem—cemetery (9) ... AL-4
Magnolia Cem—cemetery (3) ... FL-3
Magnolia Cem—cemetery (4) ... GA-3
Magnolia Cem—cemetery ... IA-7
Magnolia Cem—cemetery (4) ... LA-4
Magnolia Cem—cemetery ... MA-1
Magnolia Cem—cemetery (7) ... MS-4
Magnolia Cem—cemetery ... MO-7
Magnolia Cem—cemetery ... NC-3
Magnolia Cem—cemetery ... OK-5
Magnolia Cem—cemetery ... PA-2
Magnolia Cem—cemetery (7) ... SC-3
Magnolia Cem—cemetery (3) ... TN-4
Magnolia Cem—cemetery (6) ... TX-5
Magnolia Cem—cemetery ... VA-3
Magnolia Cemetery—hist pl ... LA-4
Magnolia Cemetery—hist pl ... SC-3
Magnolia Cemetery including Mobile Natl
Cemetery—hist pl ... AL-4
Magnolia Center—uninc pl ... CA-9
Magnolia Ch—church (11) ... AL-4
Magnolia Ch—church ... AR-4
Magnolia Ch—church (5) ... FL-3
Magnolia Ch—church (9) ... GA-3
Magnolia Ch—church (12) ... LA-4
Magnolia Ch—church (10) ... MS-4
Magnolia Ch—church (3) ... NC-3
Magnolia Ch—church ... SC-3
Magnolia Ch—church ... TN-4
Magnolia Ch—church (5) ... TX-5
Magnolia Ch (historical)—church (5) ... AL-4
Magnolia Ch (historical)—church ... MO-7
Magnolia City Oil Field—oilfield ... TX-5
Magnolia College ... MS-4
Magnolia Community Center—building ... MS-4
Magnolia Company Filling
Station—hist pl ... AR-4
Magnolia Country Club—other ... AR-4
**Magnolia Courts**—pop pl ... AL-4
Magnolia Creek ... TX-5
Magnolia Creek—stream ... AK-9
Magnolia Creek—stream ... CA-9
Magnolia Creek—stream ... FL-3
Magnolia Creek—stream ... LA-4
Magnolia Creek—stream ... OK-5
Magnolia Creek—stream (4) ... TX-5
Magnolia Ditch—canal ... CA-9
Magnolia Drain—canal ... CA-9
Magnolia Elem Sch—school ... MS-4
Magnolia Ferry (historical)—locale ... AL-4
Magnolia Freewill Baptist Church ... AL-4
Magnolia Garden Cem—cemetery ... MS-4
Magnolia Gardens—park ... SC-3
**Magnolia Gardens**—pop pl ... FL-3
**Magnolia Gardens**—pop pl ... PA-2
**Magnolia Gardens**—pop pl ... TX-5
**Magnolia Gardens**—pop pl ... PR-3
Magnolia Gardens—uninc pl ... VA-3
Magnolia Gas Storage Field—oilfield ... KY-4
Magnolia Grange—hist pl ... VA-3
Magnolia Grove—building ... MS-4
Magnolia Grove—hist pl ... AL-4
Magnolia Grove—hist pl ... NC-3
Magnolia Grove Ch—church ... TX-5
Magnolia Harbor—harbor ... MA-1
Magnolia Heights—locale ... WA-9
Magnolia Heights Acad—school ... MS-4
Magnolia Heights Baptist Church ... MS-4
Magnolia Heights Ch—church ... MS-4
Magnolia Heights Hist Dist—hist pl ... FL-3
**Magnolia Heights (subdivision)**—pop pl
(2) ... MS-4
Magnolia High School ... MS-4
Magnolia Hill—building ... MS-4
Magnolia Hill hist pl ... MS 4
**Magnolia Hill**—pop pl ... PA-2
Magnolia Hill—summit ... CT-1
Magnolia Hill Ch—church ... TX-5
Magnolia Hills—locale ... TX-5
Magnolia (historical)—locale ... MS-4
Magnolia Holiness Church ... AL-4
Magnolia Hollow—valley ... MO-7
Magnolia Hollow—valley ... TN-4
Magnolia Hosp—hospital ... CA-9
Magnolia Hosp—hospital ... MS-4
Magnolia Hotel—hist pl ... MS-4
Magnolia HS—school ... CA-9
Magnolia HS—school ... LA-4
Magnolia HS—school ... NC-3
Magnolia Island—island ... FL-3
Magnolia Island—island ... GA-3
Magnolia JHS—school ... GA-3
Magnolia JHS—school (2) ... MS-4
Magnolia Lagoon—lake ... LA-4
Magnolia Lake—lake (2) ... FL-3
Magnolia Lake—lake ... LA-4
Magnolia Lake—lake ... TX-5
Magnolia Lake—lake ... WY-8
Magnolia Lake—reservoir ... KS-7
Magnolia Lake—reservoir ... MS-4
Magnolia Lake—reservoir ... NJ-2
Magnolia Lake—reservoir ... TX-5
Magnolia Lake Dam—dam ... MS-4
Magnolia Lake Dam—dam ... NJ-2
Magnolia Lake State Park—park ... FL-3
Magnolia Landing—locale ... FL-3
Magnolia Landing—locale ... NC-3
**Magnolia Landing**—pop pl ... LA-4
Magnolia Landing (historical)—locale ... AL-4
Magnolia Landing (historical)—locale ... NC-3
Magnolia Lane Plantation House—hist pl ... LA-4
Magnolia Lateral—canal ... CA-9
Magnolia Lawns Cem—cemetery ... AL-4
Magnolia (Magisterial District)—fmr MCD
(2) ... WV-2
Magnolia Mall Shop Ctr—locale ... MS-4
Magnolia Manor—hist pl ... AR-4

Magnolia Manor—*hist pl* IL-6
Magnolia Manor—*hist pl* MS-4
Magnolia Memorial Gardens—*cemetery* MS-4
Magnolia Memorial Park—*cemetery* GA-3
Magnolia Memorial Roadside Park—*park* MS-4
*Magnolia Middle School* MS-4
Magnolia Mill—*locale* CO-8
Magnolia Mill (historical)—*locale* TN-4
Magnolia Mine—*locale* CO-8
Magnolia Mine—*mine* CA-9
Magnolia Mine—*mine* NV-8
Magnolia Mine—*mine* OR-9
Magnolia Mine—*mine* UT-8
Magnolia Mine (Site)—*locale* CA-9
**Magnolia Mobile Home Park**—*pop pl* DE-2
Magnolia Mound—*hist pl* LA-4
Magnolia Mound—*summit* LA-4
Magnolia Mound Plantation Dependency—*hist pl* LA-4
Magnolia Mound Plantation House—*hist pl* LA-4
Magnolia Museum—*building* MS-4
Magnolia Oil And Gas Field—*oilfield* AR-4
Magnolia Oil Field—*oilfield* MS-4
Magnolia Park—*park* AL-4
Magnolia Park—*park* CA-9
Magnolia Park—*park* GA-3
Magnolia Park—*park* PA-2
Magnolia Park—*park* TX-5
Magnolia Park—*park* WA-9
**Magnolia Park**—*pop pl* CA-9
**Magnolia Park**—*pop pl* GA-3
**Magnolia Park**—*pop pl* SC-3
**Magnolia Park**—*pop pl* TX-5
Magnolia Park Cem—*cemetery* GA-3
Magnolia Park (county park)—*park* FL-3
Magnolia Park Elem Sch—*school* MS-4
Magnolia Park (Shop Ctr)—*locale* FL-3
Magnolia Petroleum Bldg—*hist pl* OK-5
Magnolia Place—*hist pl* NC-3
**Magnolia Place (subdivision)**—*pop pl* TN-4
*Magnolia Plantation* AL-4
Magnolia Plantation—*hist pl* LA-4
Magnolia Plantation—*hist pl* MD-2
**Magnolia Plantation**—*pop pl* LA-4
Magnolia Plantation and Gardens—*hist pl* SC-3
Magnolia Plantation (historical)—*locale* MS-4
Magnolia Playground—*park* WA-9
Magnolia Plaza—*locale* NC-3
Magnolia Plaza (Shop Ctr)—*locale* FL-3
Magnolia Plaza Shop Ctr—*locale* MS-4
Magnolia Point—*cape* (3) FL-3
Magnolia Point—*cape* MA-1
Magnolia Post Office (historical)—*building* TN-4
Magnolia Presbyterian Ch—*church* MS-4
Magnolia Pumping Station—*other* TX-5
Magnolia Ranch—*hist pl* KS-7
Magnolia Ranch—*locale* FL-3
Magnolia Recreation Park—*park* LA-4
Magnolia Ridge—*ridge* MS-4
Magnolia Ridge—*ridge* SC-3
Magnolia Ridge Country Club—*other* TX-5
Magnolia River—*stream* AL-4
Magnolia-Rose Hill Sch—*school* NC-3
Magnolias, The—*hist pl* LA-4
Magnolias, The—*hist pl* MS-4
Magnolias, The—*hist pl* TX-5
*Magnolia Sch* FL-3
*Magnolia Sch* MS-4
Magnolia Sch—*school* (7) CA-9
Magnolia Sch—*school* FL-3
Magnolia Sch—*school* (3) GA-3
Magnolia Sch—*school* KS-7
Magnolia Sch—*school* (5) LA-4
Magnolia Sch—*school* MI-6
Magnolia Sch—*school* (3) MS-4
Magnolia Sch—*school* NJ-2
Magnolia Sch—*school* TN-4
Magnolia Sch—*school* (3) TX-5
Magnolia Sch—*school* WA-9
Magnolia Sch (historical)—*school* (2) AL-4
Magnolia Sch (historical)—*school* (2) MS-4
Magnolia Sch (historical)—*school* TN-4
Magnolia Sealy Oil Field—*oilfield* TX-5
**Magnolia Shores**—*pop pl* AL-4
Magnolia Shores Lake Dam—*dam* AL-4
**Magnolia Shores (subdivision)**—*pop pl* DE-2
Magnolia Slough—*channel* FL-3
Magnolia Spring—*spring* GA-3
Magnolia Spring—*spring* MD-2
Magnolia Spring—*spring* MO-7
**Magnolia Springs**—*pop pl* AL-4
**Magnolia Springs**—*pop pl* FL-3
**Magnolia Springs**—*pop pl* TX-5
Magnolia Springs Cem—*cemetery* GA-3
Magnolia Springs Ch—*church* AL-4
Magnolia Springs Ch—*church* TX-5
Magnolia Springs Country Club—*other* GA-3
Magnolia Springs Elem Sch (historical)—*school* AL-4
Magnolia Springs State Nursery—*other* TX-5
Magnolia Springs State Park—*park* GA-3
**Magnolia (sta.)**—*pop pl* WI-6
Magnolia State Game Mngmt Area—*park* ND-7
*Magnolia Station* AL-4
*Magnolia Station* WI-6
Magnolia Swamp—*swamp* GA-3
Magnolia Tank—*reservoir* TX-5
Magnolia Terminal—*locale* AL-4
**Magnolia Terrace (subdivision)**—*pop pl* MS-4
Magnolia Tower (fire tower)—*tower* FL-3
**Magnolia (Town of)**—*pop pl* WI-6
Magnolia Township—*fmr MCD* IA-7
Magnolia (Township of)—*fmr MCD* AR-4
Magnolia (Township of)—*fmr MCD* NC-3
**Magnolia (Township of)**—*pop pl* IL-6
**Magnolia (Township of)**—*pop pl* MN-6
Magnolia Trail—*trail* MD-2
Magnolia Union Sch—*school* CA-9
Magnolia United Methodist Ch—*church* DE-2
Magnolia United Methodist Ch—*church* MS-4
Magnolia-Upton (CCD)—*cens area* KY-4
Magnolia Vacuum Canal—*canal* LA-4
Magnolia Vale—*hist pl* MS-4
**Magnolia West Subdivision**—*pop pl* UT-8
Magnolia White Place (historical)—*locale* MS-4
Magnolia Windmill—*locale* (3) TX-5
**Magnolia Woods**—*pop pl* LA-4
Magnolia Woods Sch—*school* LA-4
Magnona Memorial Park—*cemetery* AR-4
Magnor Lake—*lake* WI-6
**Magnum (historical)**—*pop pl* TN-4
Magnum Spring—*spring* NM-5
Magnum Springs Ranger Station—*locale* AZ-5
Magnus Branch—*stream* TX-5
Magnus Farm—*locale* IL-6
Magnuson Ditch—*canal* MN-6
Magnuson Field—*airport* ND-7
Magnuson Number 1 Dam—*dam* SD-7
Magnuson Number 2 Dam—*dam* SD-7
Magnuson Ranch—*locale* NV-8
*Magnusons* NV-8
Magnuson Sch—*school* SD-7
*Magnusons Island* MN-6
Magnusons Island—*island* MN-6
*Magnussen Island* MN-6
Magnusson Branch—*stream* AL-4
Magnusson Hollow—*valley* AL-4
Magnusson Hollow—*valley* TN-4
Magnusson State Wildlife Mngmt Area—*park* MN-6
Magnus Windmill—*locale* NM-5
**Magoffin (County)**—*pop pl* KY-4
Magoffin Homestead—*hist pl* TX-5
Magoffin Institute—*school* KY-4
*Magoffins Store* AL-4
*Magoffinsville* TX-5
Magoffin West (CCD)—*cens area* KY-4
Magog, Mount—*summit* UT-8
Magog Lake—*lake* ND-7
*Magog Pond* MA-1
Magog Rock—*pillar* CO-8
*Magolel* FM-9
Magomiscock Hill—*summit* MA-1
Magone Lake—*lake* OR-9
Magone Lake Forest Camp—*locale* OR-9
Magonigal Camp—*locale* CA-9
Magonigal Summit—*summit* CA-9
Magonk Point—*cape* CT-1
Magoon Brook—*stream* ME-1
Magoon Creek—*stream* CA-9
Magoon Creek—*stream* MI-6
Magoon Hill—*summit* CA-9
Magoon Hill—*summit* MA-1
Mago Point—*cape* CT-1
Magor Township—*fmr MCD* IA-7
Magos (Barrio)—*fmr MCD* PR-3
Magote Peak—*summit* NM-5
Magote Ridge—*ridge* NM-5
Magote Spring—*spring* NM-5
Magote Tank—*reservoir* NM-5
Magotha—*locale* VA-3
Magothy Bay—*bay* VA-3
**Magothy Beach**—*pop pl* MD-2
Magothy Narrows—*channel* MD-2
Magothy Park Beach—*locale* MD-2
Magothy River—*stream* MD-2
Magothy River Light—*locale* MD-2
Magothy Sch—*school* MD-2
Magotito—*summit* NM-5
Magot Point—*cape* AK-9
*Magotsa Creek* UT-8
Magot Slough—*stream* AR-4
Magotsu Creek—*stream* UT-8
Magotty Hill—*summit* MA-1
Magotty Meadow Brook—*stream* ME-1
Magoun—*locale* TX-5
Magoun Cem—*cemetery* MA-1
Magoun Islands—*area* AK-9
Magoun Park—*park* MA-1
Magoun Pond—*reservoir* MA-1
Magoun Pond Dam—*dam* MA-1
Magoun Square—*locale* MA-1
**Mago Vista Beach**—*pop pl* MD-2
**Mago Vista (Mago Vista Beach)**—*pop pl* MD-2
Magowah Creek—*stream* MS-4
**Magowan**—*pop pl* VT-1
Magowan, Abraham, House—*hist pl* KY-4
Magowan Cem—*cemetery* KY-4
*Magoy Creek* TX-5
Magoy Creek—*stream* TX-5
Magpetco—*uninc pl* TX-5
*Magpi* MH-9
*Magpi Beach* MH-9
*Magpi Cliff* MH-9
*Magpi Cliffs* MH-9
Magpie Basin—*basin* ID-8
Magpie Butte—*summit* OR-9
*Magpie Campground* UT-8
Magpie Canyon—*valley* CO-8
Magpie Canyon—*valley* ID-8
Magpie Canyon—*valley* MT-8
Magpie Canyon—*valley* (5) UT-8
Magpie Canyon Spring—*spring* UT-8
Magpie Coulee—*valley* (2) MT-8
*Magpie Creek* ID-8
*Magpie Creek* UT-8
Magpie Creek—*stream* AK-9
Magpie Creek—*stream* CA-9
Magpie Creek—*stream* (4) ID-8
Magpie Creek—*stream* (6) MT-8
Magpie Creek—*stream* ND-7
Magpie Creek—*stream* (4) OR-9
Magpie Creek—*stream* (2) SD-7
Magpie Creek—*stream* UT-8
Magpie Creek—*stream* (4) WY-8
Magpie Creek Campsite—*locale* ID-8
Magpie Flats Heliport—*airport* WA-9
Magpie Gulch—*valley* (2) CO-8
Magpie Gulch—*valley* ID-8
Magpie Gulch—*valley* MT-8
Magpie Gulch—*valley* OR-9
Magpie Gulch—*valley* SD-7
Magpie Gulch—*valley* WY-8
Magpie Hill—*summit* NV-8
Magpie Hollow—*valley* UT-8
Magpie Hopkins Cottonwood Creek—*stream* UT-8
Magpie No 2 Mine—*mine* CO-8
Magpie Peak—*summit* OR-9
Magpie Picnic Ground—*locale* UT-8
Magpie Rec Area—*locale* MT-8
Magpie Rsvr—*reservoir* ID-8
Magpie Spring—*spring* (3) ID-8
Magpie Spring—*spring* (2) MT-8
Magpie Spring—*spring* NV-8
Magpie Spring—*spring* OR-9
Magpie Spring Creek—*stream* MT-8
Magpie Spring No 2—*spring* ID-8
Magpie Springs—*spring* ID-8
Magpie Table—*basin* OR-9
*Magpi Point* MH-9
*Magpi Ravine* MH-9
*Magpi Valley* MH-9
*Magpo* MH-9
Magpo—*area* GU-9
*Magpog Brook* MA-1
Magpogugae—*ridge* GU-9
*Magpo Wells* MH-9
Magra—*locale* CA-9
Magrath Sch—*school* CT-1
Mag Rsvr—*reservoir* NV-8
Magruda Creek—*stream* GA-3
Magruda Mines—*mine* GA-3
*Magruder* MD-2
*Magruder* OK-5
Magruder—*locale* GA-3
**Magruder**—*pop pl* OK-5
**Magruder**—*pop pl* VA-3
Magruder Bldg—*hist pl* OH-6
Magruder Branch—*stream* MD-2
Magruder Campground—*locale* ID-8
Magruder Cem—*cemetery* MS-4
Magruder Cem—*cemetery* VA-3
Magruder Ch—*church* VA-3
*Magruder Creek* ID-8
Magruder Creek—*stream* ID-8
Magruder Hosp—*hospital* OH-6
Magruder Landing—*locale* MD-2
Magruder Massacre Site—*locale* ID-8
Magruder-Morrissey House—*hist pl* MS-4
Magruder Mtn—*summit* ID-8
Magruder Mtn—*summit* NV-8
Magruder-Newsom House—*hist pl* MS-4
Magruder Park—*park* MD-2
Magruder Plots—*hist pl* OK-5
Magruder Ranch—*locale* MT-8
Magruder Ranch—*locale* (2) TX-5
Magruder Ranger Station—*locale* ID-8
Magruder Ridge—*ridge* ID-8
Magruder Rsvr—*reservoir* MT-8
Magruder Run—*stream* WV-2
Magruder Saddle—*gap* ID-8
Magruder Sch—*school* CA-9
Magruder Sch—*school* (2) VA-3
**Magruder (sta.)**—*pop pl* VA-3
Mags Hole—*bay* FL-3
Magsig JHS—*school* OH-6
Mags Ledge—*bar* ME-1
Mags Path—*trail* PA-2
Magtail Branch—*stream* GA-3
Maguagua—*area* GU-9
*Maguan Pond* MA-1
**Maguayo**—*pop pl* PR-3
Maguayo (Barrio)—*fmr MCD* PR-3
Maguelles Pasture—*flat* TX-5
Maguelles Windmill—*locale* TX-5
*Maguerrewoc Mountain* ME-1
*Maguerrowock* ME-1
Magueyal Artesian Well—*well* TX-5
*Magueyas Creek* TX-5
Maguey Creek—*stream* TX-5
**Magueyes**—*pop pl* (2) PR-3
Magueyes, Arroyo De—*valley* TX-5
Magueyes (Barrio)—*fmr MCD* (2) PR-3
Magueyes Urbano (Barrio)—*fmr MCD* PR-3
Maguey Tank—*reservoir* TX-5
Magugun—*area* GU-9
Maguire—*locale* OK-5
Maguire, Don, Duplex—*hist pl* UT-8
Maguire, Patrick, House—*hist pl* TN-4
Maguire Branch—*stream* LA-4
Maguire Canyon—*valley* UT-8
Maguire Cem—*cemetery* TN-4
Maguire Creek—*stream* AK-9
Maguire Gulch—*valley* WA-9
Maguire Islands—*area* AK-9
MaGuire Park—*park* OK-5
Maguire Peaks—*summit* CA-9
**Maguires Subdivision**—*pop pl* UT-8
Magulpin Channel—*channel* MI-6
*Magulwuk* ME-1
Magunco Hill—*summit* MA-1
*Maguncook* MA-1
**Magunden**—*pop pl* CA-9
*Magunkaquog* MA-1
*Maguntchi* PA-2
Maguriak Creek—*stream* AK-9
Magur Island—*island* FM-9
Magur Islands—*island* FM-9
Magur (Municipality)—*civ div* FM-9
Magurrewock Lakes—*lake* ME-1
Magurrewock Mtn—*summit* ME-1
Magurrewock Stream—*stream* ME-1
*Magurrewoc Stream* ME-1
*Magus Hill* MA-1
Magutex Oil Field—*oilfield* TX-5
Magwalt—*locale* TX-5
Magwire Lake—*lake* KS-7
Maha—*locale* TX-5
Maha Creek—*stream* TX-5
**Mahaffey**—*pop pl* PA-2
Mahaffey Borough—*civil* PA-2
Mahaffey Cem—*cemetery* PA-2
Mahaffey Cem—*cemetery* TX-5
Mahaffey Creek—*stream* WA-9
Mahaffey Hollow—*valley* KY-4
**Mahaffey Junction**—*pop pl* PA-2
Mahaffey Junction Station—*locale* (2) PA-2
Mahaffey Knob—*summit* AR-4
Mahaffey Lake—*lake* CO-8
Mahaffey Lake—*reservoir* SC-3
Mahaffey Racetrack—*other* PA-2
Mahaffie, J. B., House—*hist pl* KS-7
Mahaffy Drain—*stream* MI-6
*Mahagony Mountain* CA-9
*Mahagony Springs* CA-9
Mahaikona Valley—*valley* HI-9
Mahailey Crossroads—*locale* GA-3
Mahaiula—*civil* HI-9
Mahaiula—*locale* HI-9
Mahaiula Bay—*bay* HI-9
Mahala, Jacob and Herman, Homestead—*hist pl* ID-8
Mahala Chapel—*church* GA-3
Mahala Creek—*stream* NV-8
Mahala Creek—*stream* OK-5
Mahala Ditch—*canal* ID-8
Mahalang—*slope* MH-9
Mahalang, Laderan—*cliff* MH-9
Mahalani Cem—*cemetery* HI-9
Mahala Run—*stream* PA-2
Mahala Sloughs—*swamp* NV-8
**Mahalasville**—*pop pl* IN-6
Mahala Tank—*reservoir* AZ-5
Mahaley Park—*park* NC-3
Mahamenui—*civil* HI-9
Maham Lake—*lake* SC-3
Maham Sch (abandoned)—*school* PA-2
Maham Swamp—*swamp* SC-3
*Mahan* KS-7
Mahan—*locale* DE-2
Mahan—*locale* LA-4
**Mahan**—*pop pl* OR-9
**Mahan**—*pop pl* WV-2
Mahana—*civil* HI-9
Mahana—*locale* HI-9
Mahana—*summit* HI-9
Mahana Archeol District (50HA10230)—*hist pl* HI-9
Mahana Bay—*bay* HI-9
Mahanaloa Valley—*valley* HI-9
Mahan and Hoyt Rsvr—*reservoir* MT-8
Mahana Peak—*summit* CO-8
Mahan Branch—*stream* (2) AL-4
Mahan Branch—*stream* GA-3
Mahan Camp—*locale* ME-1
Mahan Canyon—*valley* NM-5
Mahan Cem—*cemetery* AL-4
Mahan Cem—*cemetery* MO-7
Mahan Cem—*cemetery* (3) TN-4
Mahan Corners—*locale* PA-2
Mahan Creek—*stream* AL-4
**Mahan Crossing**—*pop pl* IN-6
**Mahan Crossroads**—*pop pl* AL-4
Mahan Draw—*valley* CO-8
Mahan-Ellison Mine (underground)—*mine* TN-4
*Mahaney* PA-2
Mahaney Cave—*cave* TN-4
Mahaney Lake—*lake* MI-6
Mahaney Mtn—*summit* OK-5
Mahaney Pit—*cave* TN-4
Mahaney Public Use Area—*locale* PA-2
Mahan Gap—*gap* TN-4
Mahan Hill—*summit* IN-6
Mahan (historical)—*locale* AL-4
Mahan Lake—*lake* CA-9
Mahan Lake—*lake* CO-8
Mahan Mtn—*summit* AZ-5
Mahanna Cobble—*summit* MA-1
Mahannah Cabin—*locale* ID-8
Mahannah Oil Field—*oilfield* KS-7
Mahannon Creek—*stream* PA-2
Mahanon Brook—*stream* ME-1
*Mahanoy* PA-2
**Mahanoy City**—*pop pl* PA-2
Mahanoy City Borough—*civil* PA-2
Mahanoy Creek—*stream* PA-2
Mahanoy Dam Number Two—*dam* PA-2
Mahanoy Hill—*summit* PA-2
Mahanoy (historical)—*locale* PA-2
Mahanoy Mtn—*summit* PA-2
**Mahanoy Plane**—*pop pl* PA-2
Mahanoy Ridge—*ridge* PA-2
Mahanoy Rsvr Number Two—*reservoir* PA-2
Mahanoy Sch—*school* PA-2
Mahanoy Township Dam Number Two—*dam* PA-2
**Mahanoy (Township of)**—*pop pl* PA-2
Mahanoy Township Reservoirs—*reservoir* PA-2
Mahanoy Tunnel Station—*locale* PA-2
Mahanoy Union Ch—*church* PA-2
Mahan Park—*flat* AZ-5
Mahan Park Tank—*reservoir* AZ-5
Mahan Plaque—*other* CA-9
Mahan Pond—*lake* NY-2
Mahan Ranch—*locale* AZ-5
Mahan Roadside Park—*park* MO-7
Mahan Run—*stream* (2) WV-2
Mahan Sch—*school* MI-6
Mahan Sch—*school* WV-2
Mahan Sch (abandoned)—*school* PA-2
Mahans Creek—*stream* MO-7
*Mahans Gap* TN-4
Mahan Spring—*spring* AZ-5
Mahan Spring—*spring* CO-8
Mahan Swamp—*swamp* MI-6
Mahantango—*locale* PA-2
Mahantango—*other* PA-2
*Mahantango Creek* PA-2
Mahantango Creek—*stream* PA-2
Mahantango Mtn—*summit* PA-2
Mahantango Valley Sch—*school* PA-2
Mahan Tank—*reservoir* (2) AZ-5
**Mahan Village**—*pop pl* TN-4
Mahar, Lake—*lake* FL-3
Mahar Creek—*stream* WA-9
*Mahard Creek* TX-5
Mahar HS—*school* MA-1
Mahar Point—*cape* ME-1
Mahar Pond—*lake* ME-1
Maharris Post Office (historical)—*building* MS-4
Mahar Sch—*school* MI-6
*Mahars Point* ME-1
**Mahaska**—*pop pl* KS-7
Mahaska Cem—*cemetery* KS-7
Mahaska County Courthouse—*hist pl* IA-7
Mahaska County Farm—*building* IA-7
Mahaska County Farm Cem—*cemetery* IA-7
Mahaska Sch (abandoned)—*school* MO-7
Mahata Creek—*stream* CA-9
Mahathy Hill Sch—*school* TN-4
Ma-ha Tuak Park—*park* AZ-5
Ma Ha Tuak Range—*range* AZ-5
Mahaulepu—*civil* HI-9
*Mahaulepuu* HI-9
Mahaw Branch—*stream* MS-4
Maha Well—*well* AZ-5
*Mahead Cem* TX-5
Ma-He-Go, Lake—*lake* NJ-2
*Mahenauli* HI-9
*Maheo* HI-9
Maheo—*summit* HI-9
Maher—*locale* CO-8
**Maher**—*pop pl* WV-2
Maher, George W., House—*hist pl* IL-6
Maheras Memorial Playground—*park* MI-6
Maher Canyon—*valley* CA-9
Maher Creek—*stream* OK-5
Maher Dam—*dam* OR-9
Maher Field—*park* VA-3
*Maherg Branch* AL-4
Maher Hill—*summit* IL-6
Maher Rsvr—*reservoir* OR-9
Maher Sch—*school* IL-6
Maher Sch—*school* SD-7
**Mahers Quarry**—*pop pl* GA-3
Maherville (historical)—*locale* KS-7
*Mahetog Deep Ravine* MH-9
*Mahetog Place* MH-9
Mahettok, As—*slope* MH-9
Maheu Lake—*lake* MN-6
Mahewalu Point—*cape* HI-9
Mahgiae—*area* GU-9
Mahgre State Wildlife Mngmt Area—*park* MN-6
Mahican Brook—*stream* MA-1
Mahiehie—*area* HI-9
Mahie Point—*cape* HI-9
Mahikea Island—*island* HI-9
Mahiki Point—*cape* HI-9
Mahila Chapel—*church* WV-2
Mahinaakaka Heiau—*locale* HI-9
*Mahinahina* HI-9
**Mahinahina Camp**—*pop pl* HI-9
Mahinahina Four—*civil* HI-9
Mahinahina One-Two-Three—*civil* HI-9
Mahinahina Point—*cape* HI-9
Mahinakaka Gulch—*valley* HI-9
Mahina Kehau—*summit* HI-9
Mahinakehau Ridge—*ridge* HI-9
Mahinanui—*island* HI-9
Mahinauli Gulch—*valley* HI-9
*Mahinauli Valley* HI-9
**Mahinui**—*pop pl* HI-9
Mahi Waterway—*gut* FL-3
**Mahkeenac Heights**—*pop pl* MA-1
Mah-kin Rapids—*rapids* WA-9
**Mahkonce**—*pop pl* MN-6
**Mahl**—*pop pl* TX-5
Mahlac River—*stream* GU-9
Mahla Lake—*swamp* MN-6
Mahla Lakes—*lake* MN-6
Mahle Ditch—*canal* CA-9
Mahlep—*locale* AL-4
Mahler Creek—*stream* IN-6
Mahler Pond—*reservoir* NC-3
Mahlers Cem—*cemetery* MO-7
Mahlers Creek—*stream* NC-3
Mahlers Pond Dam—*dam* NC-3
Mahles Run—*stream* PA-2
*Mahlin Bayou* LA-4
Mahlin Bayou—*stream* LA-4
Mahlo, Mount—*summit* AK-9
Mahlon Sweet Field—*airport* OR-9
Mahlon Sweet Field (Airport)—*airport* OR-9
Mahlo River—*stream* AK-9
Mahls Pond—*lake* NY-2
*Mahn-ah-wauk Seepe* WI-6
*Mahn-a-waukee Seepe* WI-6
*Mahn-a-waukie* WI-6
Mahncke Park—*park* TX-5
*Mahncke Point* WA-9
Mahnckes Point—*cape* WA-9
**Mahnd**—*pop pl* FM-9
Mahnd, Dauen—*gut* FM-9
Mahnd, Pilap En—*stream* FM-9
**Mahned**—*pop pl* MS-4
Mahned Ch—*church* MS-4
Mahnes Ch—*church* WV-2
Mahnke House—*hist pl* IA-7
**Mahnomen**—*pop pl* MN-6
Mahnomen City Hall—*hist pl* MN-6
**Mahnomen (County)**—*pop pl* MN-6
Mahnomen County Country Club—*other* MN-6
Mahnomen County Courthouse—*hist pl* MN-6
Mahnomen Number One Mine—*mine* MN-6
Mahnomen Number Three Mine—*mine* MN-6
Mahnomen Number Two Mine—*mine* MN-6
Maho, Lake—*lake* AZ-5
Maho Bay—*bay* VI-3
Maho Bay—*locale* VI-3
Mahockanock Island—*island* ME-1
*Maho Creek* NC-3
*Maho Creek* VA-3
Mahoelua—*summit* HI-9
*Mahoe Mtn* HI-9
Mahoe Pali—*cliff* HI-9
Mahoe Spring—*spring* HI-9
Mahoganies, The—*range* NV-8
Mahogany Basin—*basin* ID-8
Mahogany Basin—*basin* NV-8
Mahogany Basin Spring—*spring* ID-8
*Mahogany Butte* ID-8
*Mahogany Butte* NV-8
Mahogany Butte—*summit* (2) ID-8
Mahogany Butte—*summit* (5) OR-9
Mahogany Butte—*summit* WY-8
Mahogany Canyon—*valley* ID-8
Mahogany Canyon—*valley* (3) UT-8
Mahogany Cove Campground—*park* UT-8
*Mahogany Creek* NV-8
*Mahogany Creek* UT-8
Mahogany Creek—*stream* CA-9
Mahogany Creek—*stream* (4) ID-8
Mahogany Creek—*stream* (4) NV-8
Mahogany Creek—*stream* (3) OR-9
Mahogany Creek—*stream* (2) UT-8
Mahogany Creek—*stream* WY-8
Mahogany Draw—*valley* UT-8
Mahogany Elephant Butte—*summit* NV-8
Mahogany Flat—*flat* (3) CA-9
Mahogany Flat—*flat* NV-8
Mahogany Flat—*flat* (2) OR-9
Mahogany Gap—*gap* OR-9
Mahogany Gap—*gap* VA-3
Mahogany Grove Picnic Area—*locale* NV-8
Mahogany Gulch—*valley* (3) ID-8
Mahogany Gulch—*valley* NV-8
Mahogany Hammock—*island* FL-3
Mahogany Hill—*summit* ID-8
Mahogany Hill—*summit* NV-8
Mahogany Hill—*summit* (3) UT-8
Mahogany Hills—*ridge* UT-8
Mahogany Hills—*summit* NV-8
Mahogany Hollow—*valley* (2) UT-8
Mahogany Hotel Spring—*spring* NV-8
Mahogany Knoll—*summit* (2) UT-8
Mahogany Knoll Rsvr—*reservoir* NV-8
Mahogany Lake—*lake* CA-9
Mahogany Lake—*lake* NV-8
Mahogany Long Draw Rsvr—*reservoir* OR-9
*Mahogany Mountains* OR-9
Mahogany Mountain Spring—*spring* NV-8
*Mahogany Mtn* CA-9
Mahogany Mtn—*summit* (2) CA-9
Mahogany Mtn—*summit* (5) NV-8
Mahogany Mtn—*summit* (5) OR-9
Mahogany Mtn—*summit* UT-8
Mahogany Pass—*gap* NV-8
Mahogany Peak—*summit* CA-9
Mahogany Peak—*summit* (2) NV-8
Mahogany Peaks—*summit* UT-8
Mahogany Point—*cape* UT-8
Mahogany Point—*cliff* OR-9
Mahogany Point—*summit* UT-8
Mahogany Range—*summit* UT-8
*Mahogany Ridge* OR-9
*Mahogany Ridge* UT-8
Mahogany Ridge—*ridge* (3) CA-9
Mahogany Ridge—*ridge* (2) ID-8
Mahogany Ridge—*ridge* (2) NV-8
Mahogany Ridge—*ridge* (2) OR-9
Mahogany Ridge—*ridge* (3) UT-8
Mahogany Ridge—*ridge* WY-8
Mahogany Ridge Rsvr—*reservoir* OR-9
Mahogany Rim—*cliff* OR-9
Mahogany Rock Mtn—*summit* NC-3
Mahogany Rock Overlook—*locale* NC-3
Mahogany Rsvr—*reservoir* (2) OR-9
Mahogany Run—*stream* WV-2
Mahogany Seep—*spring* UT-8
Mahogany Spring—*spring* ID-8
Mahogany Spring—*spring* (6) NV-8
Mahogany Spring—*spring* (6) OR-9
Mahogany Spring—*spring* (3) UT-8
Mahogany Spring Branch—*stream* VA-3
Mahogany Springs—*spring* CA-9
Mahogany Tank—*reservoir* NM-5
Mahogany Troughs—*spring* NV-8
Maholm Sch—*school* OH-6
Mahomet—*locale* TX-5
**Mahomet**—*pop pl* IL-6
Mahomet Cem—*cemetery* TX-5
Mahomet Gas Storage Area—*other* IL-6
Mahomet Graded Sch—*hist pl* IL-6
**Mahomet (Township of)**—*pop pl* IL-6
Mahon—*locale* KS-7
Mahon—*locale* MS-4
**Mahon**—*pop pl* IN-6
*Mahonay Spur* ND-7
Mahon Branch—*stream* TN-4
Mahon Canyon—*valley* UT-8
Mahon Cem—*cemetery* IL-6
Mahon Cem—*cemetery* WV-2
Mahon Company—*facility* MI-6
Mahon Creek—*stream* (2) OR-9
Mahon Creek Rsvr—*reservoir* OR-9
Mahone—*locale* WV-2
Mahone Branch—*stream* GA-3
Mahone Branch—*stream* WV-2
Mahone Chapel—*church* WV-2
*Mahone Creek* AL-4
Mahone Creek—*stream* AL-4
Mahone Creek—*stream* WV-2
**Mahone (historical)**—*pop pl* TN-4
*Mahone Peak* AZ-5
Mahone Post Office (historical)—*building* TN-4
Mahone Sch—*school* GA-3
Mahoney—*locale* TX-5
Mahoney—*uninc pl* KS-7
Mahoney, W. P., House—*hist pl* AZ-5
*Mahoney Administrative Site* NV-8
Mahoney Bldg—*hist pl* NM-5
Mahoney Brook—*stream* MA-1
Mahoney Brook—*stream* MN-6
Mahoney Butte—*summit* ID-8
Mahoney Canyon—*valley* CA-9
Mahoney Canyon—*valley* NV-8
Mahoney Cem—*cemetery* KY-4
Mahoney Cem—*cemetery* LA-4
Mahoney Cem—*cemetery* TN-4
Mahoney-Clark House—*hist pl* OK-5
Mahoney Creek—*stream* (4) ID-8
Mahoney Creek—*stream* MI-6
Mahoney Creek—*stream* SD-7
Mahoney Creek Lookout—*locale* ID-8
Mahoney Dome Oil Field—*oilfield* WY-8
Mahoney Draw—*valley* (3) WY-8
Mahoney Flat—*flat* ID-8
Mahoney Gulch—*valley* CA-9
Mahoney Hill—*summit* ME-1
Mahoney Hill—*summit* MT-8
Mahoney Hollow—*valley* TN-4
Mahoney House and Garage—*hist pl* OK-5
Mahoney Island—*island* ME-1
Mahoney Lake—*lake* AK-9
Mahoney Lake—*lake* MI-6
Mahoney Lake—*lake* (2) WY-8
Mahoney Lakes—*lake* WY-8
Mahoney Ledge—*bar* ME-1
Mahoney Meadows—*flat* OR-9
**Mahoney Mill**—*pop pl* TN-4
Mahoney Mine—*mine* AK-9
Mahoney Mine—*mine* NV-8
Mahoney Mines—*other* (2) NM-5
Mahoney Mtn—*summit* AK-9
Mahoney Park—*flat* NM-5
Mahoney Park—*park* IL-6
Mahoney Pond—*lake* CT-1
Mahoney Ranch—*locale* (2) MT-8
Mahoney Ranch—*locale* WY-8
Mahoney Ranch HQ—*locale* WY-8
Mahoney Ranger Station—*locale* NV-8
Mahoney Ridge—*ridge* AZ-5
Mahoney Rsvr—*reservoir* OR-9
Mahoney Rsvr—*reservoir* WY-8
Mahoneys Bend—*bend* IA-7
Mahoney Sch—*school* FL-3
Mahoney Sch—*school* IL-6
Mahoneys Hill—*summit* CT-1
Mahoney Site (20SA193)—*hist pl* MI-6
*Mahoneys Mill* TN-4

Mahoney Spring—*spring* NV-8
Mahoney Spring—*spring* WY-8
**Mahoneyville**—*pop pl* NJ-2
Mahoney Wash—*stream* AZ-5
Mahon Hill—*summit* WA-9
*Mahoning* IN-6
*Mahoning* PA-2
Mahoning—*locale* MN-6
**Mahoning**—*pop pl* OH-6
**Mahoning**—*pop pl* (2) PA-2
Mahoning Ave Hist Dist—*hist pl* OH-6
Mahoning Ave Hist Dist (Boundary Increase)—*hist pl* OH-6
Mahoning Ch—*church* (3) PA-2
Mahoning Cooper Elem Sch—*school* PA-2
**Mahoning (County)**—*pop pl* OH-6
Mahoning County Courthouse—*hist pl* OH-6
*Mahoning Creek* PA-2
Mahoning Creek—*stream* OH-6
Mahoning Creek—*stream* (3) PA-2
Mahoning Creek Dam—*dam* PA-2
Mahoning Creek Lake—*lake* PA-2
Mahoning Creek Lake—*reservoir* PA-2
Mahoning Creek Lake Rec Area—*park* PA-2
Mahoning Creek Mines Dam One and Two—*dam* PA-2
*Mahoning Creek Reservoir* PA-2
*Mahoning Dam* PA-2
**Mahoning Furnace**—*pop pl* PA-2
Mahoning Hills—*summit* PA-2
Mahoning-Hull-Rust Mine—*mine* MN-6
Mahoning Lakes—*lake* MN-6
Mahoning Mine—*mine* IL-6
Mahoning Mine—*mine* MN-6
Mahoning Mines—*mine* IL-6
Mahoning Mtn—*summit* PA-2
Mahoning Natl Bank Bldg—*hist pl* OH-6
Mahoning River—*stream* OH-6
Mahoning River—*stream* PA-2
Mahoning Road Plaza—*locale* OH-6
Mahoning Sch—*school* PA-2
Mahoning Sch (historical)—*school* PA-2
Mahoning Station—*locale* PA-2
**Mahoningtown**—*pop pl* PA-2
**Mahoning (Township of)**—*pop pl* (4) PA-2
Mahoning Valley—*valley* PA-2
Mahoning Valley Camp—*park* IN-6
*Mahoning Valley Interchange* PA-2
*Mahon Lake* MI-6
Mahonney Creek—*stream* PA-2
*Mahonoy Ridge* PA-2
Mahon River—*stream* DE-2
Mahon Rsvr—*reservoir* OR-9
Mahon Run—*stream* PA-2
*Mahons* DE-2
Mahon Sch—*school* IL-6
*Mahons Creek* OR-9
*Mahons Creek Rsvr* OR-9
Mahons Dam—*dam* OR-9
*Mahons Gap* TN-4
*Mahons River* DE-2
Mahons Rsvr—*reservoir* OR-9
Mahood Rsvr—*reservoir* CO-8
Mahood Run—*stream* PA-2
Mahoosuc Arm—*summit* ME-1
Mahoosuc Mtn—*summit* ME-1
Mahoosuc Notch—*gap* ME-1
Mahoosuc Range—*range* ME-1
Mahoosuc Range—*range* NH-1
Mahoosuc Trail—*trail* ME-1
Mahoosuc Trail—*trail* NH-1
**Mahopac**—*pop pl* NY-2
Mahopac, Lake—*lake* NY-2
**Mahopac Falls**—*pop pl* NY-2
Mahopac Golf Club—*other* NY-2
**Mahopac Hills**—*pop pl* NY-2
**Mahopac Mines**—*pop pl* NY-2
Mahopac Point—*cape* NY-2
**Mahopac Point**—*pop pl* NY-2
**Mahopac Ridge**—*pop pl* NY-2
*Mahopac Station* NY-2
Maho Point—*cape* VI-3
Mahoras Brook—*stream* NJ-2
**Mahou Riviera**—*pop pl* CA-9
Mahpiyata Island—*island* MN-6
Mahrt—*locale* AL-4
Mahrud (historical)—*locale* MS-4
Mahrud Landing (historical)—*locale* MS-4
Mahsetka Indian Ch—*church* OK-5
Mahskeekee Lake—*lake* MI-6
Mahtkwingak Slough—*gut* AK-9
Mahto—*locale* SD-7
**Mahtomedi**—*pop pl* MN-6
Mahtotopa Mtn—*summit* MT-8
**Mahto Township**—*pop pl* SD-7
**Mahtowa**—*pop pl* MN-6
**Mahtowa (Township of)**—*pop pl* MN-6
Mahtson-pi—*locale* AZ-5
Mahue Cem—*cemetery* MS-4
Mahuka Bay—*bay* HI-9
Mahukona—*civil* HI-9
**Mahukona**—*pop pl* HI-9
Mahukona Harbor—*bay* HI-9
Mahukona Park—*park* HI-9
Mahukuolo—*civil* HI-9
Mahurin Cem—*cemetery* KY-4
Mahurin Creek—*stream* TX-5
*Mahustan Peak* UT-8
**Mahwah**—*pop pl* NJ-2
Mahwah River—*stream* NJ-2
Mahwah River—*stream* NY-2
**Mahwah (Township of)**—*pop pl* NJ-2
**Maia**—*pop pl* AS-9
Maiakii Ditch—*canal* HI-9
Maiakii Stream—*stream* HI-9
Maiben Creek—*stream* AL-4
Maiben Landing (historical)—*locale* AL-4
Maibucker Ditch—*canal* IN-6
**Maida**—*pop pl* ND-7
Mai Dagi—*valley* AZ-5
Maidco—*locale* LA-4
*Maiden* MT-8
**Maiden**—*pop pl* MT-8
**Maiden**—*pop pl* NC-3
Maiden Bend—*bend* KY-4
Maiden Bridge—*bridge* MA-1
Maiden Butte—*summit* NV-8
Maiden Canyon—*valley* MT-8
Maiden Cem—*cemetery* TN-4
Maiden Chapel—*church* NC-3
Maiden Choice Sch—*school* MD-2
Maiden Cliff—*cliff* ME-1
Maiden Cove—*bay* ME-1
*Maiden Creek* AK-9
*Maiden Creek* NE-7
*Maiden Creek* NC-3
*Maiden Creek* OR-9
*Maidencreek* PA-2
*Maiden Creek* UT-8
Maiden Creek—*locale* PA-2
Maiden Creek—*stream* AK-9
Maiden Creek—*stream* CO-8
Maiden Creek—*stream* (2) GA-3
Maiden Creek—*stream* (2) ID-8
Maiden Creek—*stream* MT-8
Maiden Creek—*stream* NC-3
Maiden Creek—*stream* PA-2
Maiden Creek—*stream* VA-3
Maiden Creek—*stream* WA-9
Maiden Creek—*stream* WI-6
Maiden Creek Ch—*church* PA-2
Maiden Creek Sch—*school* PA-2
Maiden Creek Station (historical)—*locale* PA-2
**Maidencreek (Township of)**—*pop pl* PA-2
Maiden Doe Bayou—*stream* LA-4
Maidendown Bay—*swamp* SC-3
Maidendown Swamp—*stream* SC-3
Maiden Elem Sch—*school* NC-3
Maiden Fair Trail—*trail* MD-2
Maiden Flat—*flat* CA-9
Maidenform Peak—*summit* WY-8
Maiden Fur Farm—*locale* MT-8
Maiden Gulch—*valley* OR-9
Maidenhair Falls—*falls* CA-9
Maidenhair Falls—*falls* (2) NC-3
Maidenhair Spring—*spring* CA-9
*Maidenhead* NJ-2
Maidenhead Branch—*stream* VA-3
Maidenhead Canyon—*valley* AZ-5
Maiden Hill—*summit* MA-1
Maiden Hollow—*valley* UT-8
Maiden HS—*school* NC-3
Maiden Lady Cove—*bay* NH-1
*Maiden Lake* FL-3
Maiden Lake—*lake* AK-9
Maiden Lake—*lake* MN-6
Maiden Lake—*lake* OR-9
Maiden Lake—*lake* (2) WA-9
Maiden Lake—*lake* WI-6
Maiden Lane Sch—*school* WI-6
Maiden Lane Shops—*locale* MO-7
*Maiden Mine* SD-7
Maiden Paps (historical)—*island* NC-3
Maiden Park—*park* TN-4
Maiden Peak—*summit* (2) MT-8
Maiden Peak—*summit* OR-9
Maiden Peak—*summit* WA-9
Maiden Peak Saddle—*gap* OR-9
Maiden Peak Trail—*trail* OR-9
Maiden Point—*cape* NC-3
Maiden Pup—*stream* AK-9
Maiden Ridge—*ridge* KY-4
Maiden Rock—*cape* ID-8
Maiden Rock—*pillar* WI-6
**Maiden Rock**—*pop pl* MT-8
**Maiden Rock**—*pop pl* WI-6
Maiden Rock—*summit* (2) WI-6
Maiden Rock Cem—*cemetery* WI-6
Maiden Rock Mine—*mine* MT-8
*Maidenrock Siding* MT-8
**Maiden Rock (Town of)**—*pop pl* WI-6
Maiden Run—*stream* IN-6
Maidens—*locale* VA-3
Maiden Sch—*school* MT-8
Maidens Chapel—*church* NC-3
Maiden Sch (historical)—*school* MS-4
Maidens Choice Run—*stream* MD-2
Maidens Dream Mine—*mine* OR-9
Maidens Grave Cem—*cemetery* NV-8
Maidens Leap—*summit* NE-7
*Maiden Spring* NV-8
Maiden Spring—*locale* VA-3
Maiden Spring—*spring* CO-8
Maiden Spring—*spring* OR-9
Maiden Spring—*spring* WA-9
Maiden Spring Creek—*stream* VA-3
Maiden Spring (Magisterial District)—*fmr MCD* VA-3
Maiden Springs—*spring* NV-8
Maiden Springs—*spring* WA-9
Maiden Valley—*valley* CA-9
Maiden Valley Sch—*school* NE-7
Maidenwater—*stream* UT-8
*Maidenwater Creek* UT-8
Maiden Water Plant Lake—*reservoir* NC-3
Maiden Water Plant Lake Dam—*dam* NC-3
Maidenwater Rsvr—*reservoir* UT-8
Maidenwater Sands—*bar* UT-8
*Maiden Water Spring* UT-8
Maidenwater Spring—*spring* (2) UT-8
Maide Tank—*reservoir* TX-5
Maidford River—*stream* RI-1
*Maidi* MP-9
Maid Island—*island* AK-9
Maid Lake—*lake* AK-9
Maidlow Cem—*cemetery* OH-6
Maidlow Ditch—*canal* IN-6
Maid of Orleans Mine—*mine* CA-9
Maid of Orleans Mine—*mine* CO-8
Maid of the Mist Creek—*stream* MT-8
Maid of the Mist Mine—*mine* OR-9
Maid of the Mist Mtn—*summit* MT-8
Maid-Rite Sandwich Shop—*hist pl* IL-6
Maids Park—*park* NC-3
Maids Run—*stream* IL-6
*Maidstone* IN-6
Maidstone—*hist pl* MD-2
Maidstone—*locale* VT-1
Maidstone Branch—*stream* DE-2
Maidstone Brook—*stream* VT-1
Maidstone Hill—*summit* VT-1
Maidstone Lake—*lake* VT-1
**Maidstone Lake**—*pop pl* VT-1
Maidstone Manor Farm—*hist pl* WV-2
**Maidstone Park**—*pop pl* NY-2
Maidstone Park Beach—*beach* NY-2
*Maidstone State Forest* VT-1
Maidstone State Park—*forest* VT-1
**Maidstone (Town of)**—*pop pl* VT-1
**Maidsville**—*pop pl* WV-2
Maid Tank—*reservoir* AZ-5
Maidu Lake—*lake* OR-9
Maidu Lake Way—*trail* OR-9
Maier, Peter Augustus, House—*hist pl* IN-6
Maier Gulch—*valley* MT-8
Maier HS—*school* CA-9
Maier Lake—*lake* ND-7
Maier Lake—*reservoir* AL-4
Maier Lake Dam—*dam* AL-4
Maiers Butte—*ridge* OR-9
Maier Sch—*school* NE-7
Maigatter Knob—*summit* CO-8
Maigo Fahang, Isleta—*island* MH-9
*Maigo Fahang Island* MH-9
Maigo' Lu'ao, Isleta—*island* MH-9
*Maigo Luau Island* MH-9
Maihi Bay—*bay* HI-9
Maihi One-Two—*civil* HI-9
Maiitoh—*spring* AZ-5
Mail Bay—*bay* WA-9
Mail Bay—*bay* VI-3
Mailboat Channel—*channel* TX-5
Mailboat Cove—*bay* AK-9
Mailboat Harbor—*bay* VA-3
Mailboat Slough—*stream* WA-9
Mailbox, The—*locale* UT-8
Mailbox Branch Blue Creek—*stream* CO-8
Mailbox Canyon—*valley* AZ-5
Mailbox Canyon—*valley* OR-9
Mailbox Canyon Rsvr—*reservoir* OR-9
Mailbox Creek—*stream* AK-9
Mail Box Draw—*valley* CO-8
Mailbox Draw—*valley* TX-5
Mailbox Gulch—*valley* MT-8
Mail Box Hill—*summit* MT-8
Mailbox Hill—*summit* TN-4
Mailbox Mesa—*summit* AZ-5
Mailbox Park—*flat* CO-8
Mailbox Tank—*reservoir* TX-5
Mailbox Trail—*trail* CO-8
Mailbox Well—*well* AZ-5
Mailbox Well—*well* TX-5
Mail Building, The—*hist pl* SD-7
Mail Cabin Creek—*stream* WY-8
Mail Camp Ranger Station—*locale* WY-8
Mail Canyon—*valley* OR-9
Mail Canyon—*valley* UT-8
Mail Carrier Lake—*lake* NM-5
Mail Carrier Spring—*spring* AZ-5
Mail Creek—*stream* AZ-5
Mail Creek—*stream* CO-8
Mail Creek—*stream* OR-9
Mail Creek—*stream* WY-8
Mail Creek Ditch—*canal* CO-8
Mail Draw—*valley* UT-8
Mailehahei—*summit* HI-9
Mailelii—*summit* HI-9
Mailepai—*civil* HI-9
Mailepai Stream—*stream* HI-9
Mailey Ditch—*canal* MT-8
*Mailey Hollow* TN-4
Mail Ford—*locale* AR-4
Mail Hollow—*valley* (2) MO-7
Mail Hollow—*valley* NM-5
Mail Hollow—*valley* OK-5
Mail Hollow—*valley* TN-4
**Maili**—*pop pl* HI-9
Maili—*summit* HI-9
Mailiilii Beach Park—*park* HI-9
Mailiilii Stream—*stream* HI-9
Maili Point—*cape* HI-9
Maili Stream—*stream* HI-9
Maillet Cem—*cemetery* MT-8
Mailliard Ranch—*locale* CA-9
Mailliard Redwoods State Park—*park* CA-9
Mailly Pond—*lake* NH-1
*Mailog Point* MH-9
Mail Point Hill—*summit* WV-2
Mail Point Run—*stream* WV-2
Mailrider Branch—*stream* AL-4
*Mailrider Creek* OK-5
Mail Rider Creek—*stream* OK-5
Mail Ridge—*ridge* (2) CA-9
Mailroute Hollow—*valley* MO-7
Mail Route Hollow—*valley* (2) MO-7
Mail Route Mtn—*summit* AL-4
Mail Route Trail—*trail* WV-2
Mail Shack Creek—*stream* SD-7
Mail Slough—*stream* AK-9
Mail Spring—*spring* CA-9
Mail Station Draw—*valley* AZ-5
Mail Station Wash—*valley* UT-8
Mail Summit—*gap* NV-8
Mail Trail—*trail* AR-4
Mail Trail—*trail* CA-9
Mailtrail Creek—*stream* TX-5
Mail Trail Draw—*valley* TX-5
Mail Trail Mesa—*summit* CO-8
Mail Trail Mesa—*summit* UT-8
Mail Trail Pond—*lake* CA-9
Mail Trail Tank Number Two—*reservoir* AZ-5
Mail Xpress—*post sta* FL-3
Maimai—*area* GU-9
Maimai—*bar* FM-9
*Maime Creek* UT-8
Maimes Creek—*stream* WY-8
Maimonides-Elmont Cem—*cemetery* NY-2
Maimonides Hosp—*hospital* (2) NY-2
Maimonides Sch—*school* MA-1
Main, Point Of—*cape* ME-1
Maina—*CDP* GU-9
**Maina**—*pop pl* GU-9
Main and Military Plazas Hist Dist—*hist pl* TX-5
Main and Third Street Cluster—*hist pl* OH-6
Mainard Branch—*stream* FL-3
Main Ashe Lateral—*canal* CA-9
Main Ash Rsvr—*reservoir* MT-8
Main Ash Spring—*spring* MT-8
*Main Asphalt Canyon* UT-8
*Main Asphalt Wash* UT-8
Maina Spring—*spring* GU-9
Main Ave—*uninc pl* (2) NJ-2
Main Ave Grammar Sch—*school* AL-4
Main Ave Hist Dist—*hist pl* CO-8
Main Ave Sch—*school* CA-9
Main Bay—*bay* AK-9
*Main Bay Ch* VA-3
Main Beaver Dam Ditch—*canal* IN-6
Main Beaver Ditch—*canal* IN-6
Main Bldg—*hist pl* CA-9
Main Bldg—*hist pl* OH-6
Main Bldg—*hist pl* WV-2
Main Bldg of Dixie College—*hist pl* UT-8
Main Bottom Canyon—*valley* UT-8
Main Boulder Ranger Station—*locale* MT-8
Main Box Elder Picnic Ground—*locale* UT-8
*Main Branch* NJ-2
Main Branch—*stream* KY-4
*Main Branch Kettle Creek* NJ-2
Main Branch Northeast Canal—*canal* TX-5
*Main Branch of Westport River* MA-1
*Main Branch Toms River* NJ-2
*Main Branch White River* WI-6
Main-Broad-Grove Streets Hist Dist—*hist pl* NY-2
*Main Broad River* NC-3
Main Brook—*stream* CT-1
*Main Bryce Amphitheater* UT-8
Main Building, Arkansas Baptist College—*hist pl* AR-4
Main Building, Blinn College—*hist pl* TX-5
Main Building, Concordia College—*hist pl* MN-6
Main Building, Louisburg College—*hist pl* NC-3
Main Building, Mitchell College—*hist pl* NC-3
Main Building, Southwest Texas Normal Sch—*hist pl* TX-5
Main Building, Tempe Normal Sch—*hist pl* AZ-5
Main Building, U.S. Bureau of Mines—*hist pl* PA-2
Main Building, Vassar College—*hist pl* NY-2
Main Camp Spring—*spring* NV-8
Main Campus Complex, Roanoke College—*hist pl* VA-3
Main Camp Well—*well* AZ-5
*Main Canal* KS-7
Main Canal—*canal* AZ-5
Main Canal—*canal* (3) AR-4
Main Canal—*canal* (15) CA-9
Main Canal—*canal* FL-3
Main Canal—*canal* (2) ID-8
Main Canal—*canal* (2) LA-4
Main Canal—*canal* MS-4
Main Canal—*canal* (5) MT-8
Main Canal—*canal* NV-8
Main Canal—*canal* (2) NM-5
Main Canal—*canal* NC-3
Main Canal—*canal* ND-7
Main Canal—*canal* OR-9
Main Canal—*canal* TX-5
Main Canal—*canal* (3) WA-9
Main Canal A—*canal* MT-8
Main Canal B—*canal* MT-8
Main Canal Extension—*canal* WA-9
Main Canal No. 1—*canal* CO-8
Main Canal No. 2—*canal* CO-8
*Main Canyon* UT-8
Main Canyon—*valley* AZ-5
Main Canyon—*valley* CO-8
Main Canyon—*valley* ID-8
Main Canyon—*valley* NM-5
Main Canyon—*valley* (6) UT-8
Main Canyon Creek—*stream* UT-8
Main Canyon Spring—*spring* ID-8
Main Canyon Tank—*reservoir* AZ-5
Main Cem—*cemetery* IN-6
Main Cem—*cemetery* NE-7
Main Cem—*cemetery* OH-6
Main Cem—*cemetery* WV-2
Main Chandon Lateral—*canal* CA-9
*Main Channel* MS-4
*Main Channel* NJ-2
Main Channel—*channel* AL-4
Main Channel—*channel* AK-9
Main Channel—*channel* CA-9
Main Channel—*channel* (2) FL-3
Main Channel—*channel* MA-1
Main Channel—*channel* NJ-2
Main Channel—*channel* NC-3
Main Channel—*channel* OR-9
Main Channel Cut B Range Front Light—*locale* FL-3
Main Channel Way—*channel* ME-1
Main Chapel—*church* OH-6
Main City—*locale* MO-7
Main City Sch—*school* MO-7
Main Cokedale Mine—*mine* CO-8
Main Consolidated Oil And Gas Field—*other* IL-6
Main Cove—*valley* TN-4
*Main Creek* UT-8
Main Creek—*gut* SC-3
Main Creek—*stream* (2) AK-9
Main Creek—*stream* MD-2
Main Creek—*stream* NY-2
Main Creek—*stream* OK-5
Main Creek—*stream* UT-8
Main Creek—*stream* VA-3
Main Creek—*stream* WI-6
Main Creek Sch (abandoned)—*school* PA-2
Main Creek Trail—*trail* OR-9
Main Dam Campground—*locale* CA-9
Main District Canal—*canal* CA-9
*Main Ditch* MO-7
Main Ditch—*canal* (5) AR-4
Main Ditch—*canal* (6) IL-6
Main Ditch—*canal* MN-6
Main Ditch—*canal* (8) MO-7
Main Ditch—*canal* NJ-2
Main Ditch—*canal* NM-5
Main Ditch—*canal* (2) WI-6
Main Ditch A—*canal* CA-9
Main Ditch A—*canal* MS-4
Main Ditch B—*canal* CA-9
Main Ditch B—*canal* MS-4
Main Ditch District No 10—*canal* MO-7
Main Ditch District No 17—*canal* MO-7
Main Ditch District No 2—*canal* MO-7
*Main Ditch Lateral* AR-4
Main Ditch North—*canal* IL-6
Main Ditch No 1—*canal* AR-4
Main Ditch No 1—*canal* MO-7
Main Ditch No 10—*canal* MO-7
Main Ditch No 2—*canal* AR-4
Main Ditch No 2—*canal* MO-7
Main Ditch No 36—*canal* MO-7
Main Ditch No 6—*canal* IA-7
Main Ditch No 6—*canal* MO-7
Main Ditch No 8—*canal* MO-7
Main Ditch Number Six—*canal* MO-7
Main Ditch Number Two—*canal* TX-5
Main Divide Truck Trail—*trail* CA-9
*Main Doubling* TN-4
Main Drain—*canal* AZ-5
Main Drain—*canal* (2) CA-9
Main Drain—*canal* ID-8
Main Drain—*stream* ID-8
Main Drainage Canal—*canal* CA-9
Main Drainage Ditch—*canal* IL-6
Main Drain Extension—*canal* AZ-5
*Maine* AZ-5
Maine—*locale* AZ-5
Maine—*locale* IA-7
Maine—*locale* ME-1
**Maine**—*pop pl* MN-6
**Maine**—*pop pl* NY-2
**Maine**—*pop pl* NC-3
Maine, Desert Of—*area* ME-1
Maine, Gulf Of—*bay* ME-1
Maine, Gulf of—*bay* MA-1
Main Eagle Bridge Campground—*locale* OR-9
Maine Archeol Site No. 9-16—*hist pl* ME-1
Maine Archeol Survey Site—*hist pl* ME-1
Main East Canal—*canal* ID-8
Maine Bar—*bar* CA-9
Maine Bar Canyon—*valley* CA-9
Maine Branch—*stream* NC-3
*Maine Canal* FL-3
Maine Cem—*cemetery* IL-6
Maine Cem—*cemetery* NY-2
Maine Cem—*cemetery* NC-3
Maine Cem—*cemetery* WI-6
Maine Central RR General Office Bldg—*hist pl* ME-1
Maine Ch—*church* MN-6
Main Edlin Ditch—*canal* IN-6
Maine-Endwell HS—*school* NY-2
Maine Eye and Ear Infirmary—*hist pl* ME-1
Maine Forestry Service—*building* ME-1
Maine Historical Society—*hist pl* ME-1
Maine Insane Hosp—*hist pl* ME-1
Main Elk Creek—*stream* CO-8
Maine Med Ctr—*hospital* ME-1
Maine Mine—*mine* AZ-5
Maine New Hampshire Bridge—*bridge* ME-1
Maine-New Hampshire Bridge—*bridge* NH-1
Maine Park—*park* IL-6
**Maine (Parks)e for Parks)**—*pop pl* AZ-5
*Maine Praire Gas Field* CA-9
Maine Prairie—*locale* CA-9
Maine Prairie Cem—*cemetery* MN-6
Maine Prairie Sch—*school* CA-9
Maine Prairie Slough—*stream* CA-9
Maine Prairie (Township of)—*civ div* MN-6
Mainer Branch—*stream* TX-5
Maine River—*stream* ME-1
*Maines* ME-1
**Maines**—*pop pl* MO-7
**Mainesburg**—*pop pl* PA-2
Mainesburg Cem—*cemetery* PA-2
Maine Sch—*school* WI-6
Maine Sch For the Deaf—*school* ME-1
Maines Field—*park* MA-1
Maine Site (47MR22)—*hist pl* WI-6
*Maines Pass* MT-8
Maine State Bldg—*hist pl* ME-1
Maine State House—*hist pl* ME-1
Maine State Wildlife Area—*park* WI-6
Maine Supply Company Bldg—*hist pl* ME-1
**Maine (Town of)**—*pop pl* NY-2
**Maine (Town of)**—*pop pl* (2) WI-6
Maine Township—*fmr MCD* IA-7
**Maine Township**—*pop pl* ND-7
**Maine (Township of)**—*pop pl* (2) IL-6
**Maine (Township of)**—*pop pl* MN-6
Maine Trolley Cars—*hist pl* ME-1
*Maineville* PA-2
**Maineville**—*pop pl* OH-6
Maine Vocational Technical Institute—*school* ME-1
Maine Woods Office—*hist pl* ME-1
Mainey Branch—*stream* NC-3
Main Flat—*flat* UT-8
Main Floodway—*basin* TX-5
*Main Fork* TX-5
Main Fork—*stream* ID-8
Main Fork—*stream* UT-8
Main Fork Happy Canyon—*valley* UT-8
Main Fork Little Creek—*stream* MT-8
*Main Fork Little Lost River* ID-8
*Main Fork Sawmill Creek* ID-8
Main Fork Silver Creek—*stream* NV-8
Main Fork Trail—*trail* CO-8
Main Fork Trail—*trail* WY-8
Main Fox Ditch—*canal* NV-8
*Ma-In-Gan Lake* MI-6
Maingan Lake—*lake* MN-6
Main Gate, Washington Navy Yard—*hist pl* DC-2
Maingate Outlet Mall—*locale* FL-3
Main Gate Shop Ctr—*locale* MA-1
Main Gulch—*valley* CO-8
Main Gulch—*valley* MT-8
Main Hall—*hist pl* MS-4
Main Hall—*hist pl* SD-7
Main Hall—*hist pl* WI-6
Main Hall, Lawrence Univ—*hist pl* WI-6
Main Hall, Randolph-Macon Women's College—*hist pl* VA-3
Main Hall/La Crosse State Normal Sch—*hist pl* WI-6
*Main Hanging Woman Creek* MT-8
*Main Hanging Woman Creek* WY-8
Main Harbor—*locale* MS-4
Main Hartel Drain—*canal* MI-6
Main Hay Creek—*stream* MT-8
Main Hubbard Creek—*stream* CO-8
Main Impoundment—*reservoir* PA-2
Main Island Canal—*canal* CA-9
Main Jackson Ditch—*canal* MT-8
Main JHS—*school* AK-9
Main Key—*island* FL-3
*Main Lagoon* MP-9
*Main Lake* PA-2
Main Lake—*lake* MN-6
Main Lake—*reservoir* PA-2
*Main Lake Dam* PA-2
Mainland—*locale* PA-2
Mainland—*uninc pl* FL-3
Mainland Cove—*bay* ME-1
Mainland HS—*school* FL-3
Mainland Memorial Cem—*cemetery* TX-5
Mainland Point—*cape* NY-2
Mainlands Center—*post sta* FL-3
Mainlands Village (Shop Ctr)—*locale* FL-3
*Main Lateral* AR-4
Main Lateral—*canal* AZ-5
Main Lateral—*canal* NM-5
Main Library—*hist pl* PA-2
Main Lift—*canal* CA-9
Main Line Airp—*airport* PA-2
Main Line Canal—*canal* TX-5
Mainline Creek—*stream* WI-6
Mainline Dam No. 1—*dam* OR-9
Mainline Dam No. 2—*dam* OR-9
Mainline Dam No. 3—*dam* OR-9
Main Line Ditch—*canal* SC-3
Main Line Grand Valley Canal—*canal* CO-8
Mainline Lake—*lake* WI-6
Mainline Rsvr Number One—*reservoir* OR-9
Mainline Rsvr Number Three—*reservoir* OR-9
Mainline Rsvr Number Two—*reservoir* OR-9
Main Line Trail—*trail* MT-8
Mainline Well—*well* NV-8
Main Lot Hollow—*valley* PA-2
Main Mall Row—*hist pl* NY-2
Main Marsh Creek—*stream* NJ-2
Main Marsh Thorofare—*channel* NJ-2
Main Martinton Ditch No 3—*canal* IL-6
**Main-Mill**—*pop pl* NY-2
Main Mountain Mine (underground)—*mine* TN-4
Main Mtn—*summit* AR-4
*Main North Branch of Cedar Creek* NJ-2
Main North Side Canal—*canal* ID-8
Main Number One—*canal* CA-9
Main Number Two—*canal* CA-9
Main Office of the New Castle Leather Company—*hist pl* DE-2
Main Outfall Canal—*canal* LA-4
Main Outlet Drain—*canal* (2) AZ-5
Main Overcup Ditch—*canal* AR-4
Main Paint Rock Trail—*trail* WY-8
Main-Partition Streets Hist Dist—*hist pl* NY-2
*Main Pass* TX-5
Main Pass—*channel* (2) LA-4
*Main Passage* MP-9
Main Passage—*channel* FM-9
Main Place—*uninc pl* TX-5
Main Plaza—*park* TX-5
*Main Poamoho Stream* HI-9
Main Point—*cape* NJ-2
**Main Point Condominium**—*pop pl* UT-8
**Main Point South Subdivision**—*pop pl* UT-8
Main Pond—*reservoir* NY-2
Main Post Area, Fort Riley—*hist pl* KS-7
Main Post Office—*building* IL-6
Main Post Office—*hist pl* NJ-2
Main Post Office and Federal Bldg—*hist pl* CA-9
Main Prong—*stream* NC-3
Main Prong Big Buffalo Creek—*stream* AR-4
Main Prong Dry Fork Piceance Creek—*stream* CO-8
*Main Quihi Creek* TX-5
Main Quihi Creek—*stream* TX-5
Main Range Trail—*trail* CO-8
Main Ridge—*ridge* CA-9
Main Ridge—*ridge* VA-3
Main Road—*hist pl* GA-3
Main Rsvr—*reservoir* (2) CO-8
*Main Run* AZ-5
Main Saint Sch—*school* NC-3
Main Salt Lake City Post Office—*building* UT-8
Main Sawmill—*hist pl* CT-1
Mains Branch—*stream* TN-4
*Mainsburg* PA-2
Main Sch—*school* (2) IN-6
Main Sch—*school* NE-7
Main Sch (abandoned)—*school* PA-2
Mains Creek—*stream* VA-3
*Mainsdale* VA-3
Mainses Pond—*lake* PA-2
**Main Settlement**—*pop pl* NY-2
Mains Gap—*gap* AL-4
Mains Gulch—*valley* CO-8
*Main Ship Channel* AL-4
*Main Ship Channel* FL-3
*Main Ship Channel* NJ-2
Main Ship Channel—*channel* (2) FL-3
Main Ship Shoal Channel—*channel* VA-3
Main Shore (Township of)—*fmr MCD* AR-4
Main Siphon Canal—*canal* MT-8
*Main South Branch Oconto River* WI-6
Main South Side Canal—*canal* ID-8
Main Spring—*spring* (2) AZ-5
Main Spring—*spring* OR-9
Main Spring—*spring* TX-5
Main Spruce Canal—*canal* CA-9
Mains Ridge—*ridge* ID-8
Mains Run—*stream* PA-2
**Mainstream**—*pop pl* ME-1
Main Stream—*stream* (2) ME-1
Mainstream Mall Shop Ctr—*locale* MS-4
Mainstream Mtn—*summit* ME-1
Mainstream Pond—*lake* ME-1
Main Stream Sebasticook River—*stream* ME-1
Mainstream Station—*locale* ME-1
Main Street—*post sta* MA-1
Main Street—*uninc pl* AR-4
Main Street—*uninc pl* KY-4
Main Street—*uninc pl* MD-2
Main Street—*uninc pl* NC-3
Main Street Baptist Ch—*church* AL-4
Main Street Baptist Ch—*church* (3) MS-4
Main Street Bridge—*bridge* FL-3
Main Street Bridge—*hist pl* CT-1
Main Street Bridge—*hist pl* NY-2
Main Street Bridge—*hist pl* RI-1
Main Street Building, United Church of Ovid—*hist pl* MI-6
Main Street Buildings—*hist pl* OH-6
Main Street Canyon—*valley* CA-9
Main Street Cem—*cemetery* (2) MA-1
Main Street Cemetery—*summit* MA-1
Main Street Ch—*church* NC-3
Main Street Ch—*church* VA-3

Main Street-College Street Hist Dist—hist pl ... VT-1
Main Street Comerical District—hist pl ... AL-4
Main Street Commercial Bldg—hist pl ... NM-5
Main Street Commercial Buildings—hist pl ... MN-6
Main Street Commercial District—hist pl ... KY-4
Main Street Commercial Hist Dist—hist pl ... WI-6
Main Street District, Expanded—hist pl ... KY-4
Main Street Elementary School ... PA-2
Main Street Elem Sch ... MS-4
Main Street Elem Sch—school ... MS-4
Main Street Elem Sch—school ... TN-4
Main Street Freewill Baptist Ch—church ... MS-4
Main Street Hist Dist—hist pl ... AL-4
Main Street Hist Dist—hist pl (3) ... CT-1
Main Street Hist Dist—hist pl ... IL-6
Main Street Hist Dist—hist pl ... KY-4
Main Street Hist Dist—hist pl (2) ... LA-4
Main Street Hist Dist—hist pl (2) ... ME-1
Main Street Hist Dist—hist pl (3) ... MA-1
Main Street Hist Dist—hist pl ... MI-6
Main Street Hist Dist—hist pl (2) ... MS-4
Main Street Hist Dist—hist pl ... MT-8
Main Street Hist Dist—hist pl ... NE-7
Main Street Hist Dist—hist pl (9) ... NY-2
Main Street Hist Dist—hist pl ... OH-6
Main Street Hist Dist—hist pl ... RI-1
Main Street Hist Dist—hist pl ... SC-3
Main Street Hist Dist—hist pl ... TX-5
Main Street Hist Dist—hist pl (4) ... WI-6
Main Street Hist Dist—hist pl ... WY-8
Main Street Hist Dist (Boundary Increase)—hist pl ... NY-2
Main Street Hist Dist No. 2—hist pl ... CT-1
Main Street Historic Commercial District (Boundary Increase)—hist pl ... KY-4
**Main Street Island View Subdivision**—pop pl ... UT-8
Main Street-Locke—hist pl ... MA-1
Main Street/Market Square Hist Dist—hist pl ... TX-5
Main Street/Market Square Hist Dist (Boundary Increase)—hist pl ... TX-5
Main Street Plaza (Shop Ctr)—locale ... FL-3
Main Street Post Office—hist pl ... MI-6
Main Street Professional Plaza—locale ... UT-8
Main Street Sch—hist pl ... NY-2
Main Street Sch—school ... CA-9
Main Street Sch—school ... GA-3
Main Street Sch—school ... IL-6
Main Street Sch—school ... IA-7
Main Street Sch—school ... MA-1
Main Street Sch—school ... MI-6
Main Street Sch—school ... MS-4
Main Street Sch—school ... NH-1
Main Street Sch—school (4) ... NY-2
Main Street Sch—school (2) ... OH-6
Main Street Sch—school (2) ... PA-2
Main Street Sch—school ... TN-4
Main Street (Shop Ctr)—locale ... FL-3
Main Street Shop Ctr—locale (2) ... MA-1
Main Street Station—locale ... PA-2
Main Street Station—locale ... VA-3
Main Street Station and Trainshed—hist pl ... VA-3
Main Street United Methodist Ch—church (2) ... MS-4
Main Street Valley—valley ... AZ-5
Main Street Wash—stream ... CA-9
Main Supply Canal—canal ... TX-5
Main Supply Canal (elevated)—canal ... TX-5
**Mainsville**—pop pl ... OH-6
**Mainsville**—pop pl ... PA-2
Mainsville Elem Sch—school ... PA-2
Main Tank—reservoir ... AZ-5
Maintop Mtn—summit ... VA-3
Maintop (Site)—locale ... CA-9
**Main (Township of)**—pop pl ... PA-2
Main Trail—trail ... VA-3
Main Tule Creek ... CA-9
Main Tuolumne Ditch—canal ... CA-9
Main Turning Basin—harbor ... TX-5
Main Union Special Ditch—canal ... IL-6
Main Uno Ch—church ... VA-3
Mainview Sch—school ... LA-4
Main Village—post sta ... NY-2
Mainville ... OH-6
**Mainville**—pop pl ... PA-2
Mainville Ch—church ... NC-3
Main Wash ... UT-8
Main Weaver ... CA-9
Main West Canal—canal ... ID-8
Main-Yankee Street Hist Dist—hist pl ... AL-4
Maipalaoa Beach Park—park ... HI-9
Maipoina Oe Iau Beach Park—park ... HI-9
Maire Sch—school ... MI-6
Maire Sch—school ... NE-7
Mairey Branch—stream ... NC-3
Mair Point Neck ... ME-1
Mairs Branch—stream ... MO-7
Mairs Mill—locale ... MD-2
Mair Spring—spring ... UT-8
Mais Canyon—valley (2) ... CA-9
Maise Creek—stream ... TN-4
Maiser, Charles, House—hist pl ... MN-6
Maish ... AZ-5
Maish House—hist pl ... IA-7
Mai Shima ... FM-9
Maishpvaxia ... AZ-5
Maish-vaxia ... AZ-5
**Maish Vaya**—pop pl ... AZ-5
**Maison**—pop pl ... TN-4
Maison De Marie Therese—hist pl ... LA-4
Maison Institute (historical)—school ... TN-4
Maisou Island ... MI-6
Maisou Island—island ... MI-6
Maispvaxia ... AZ-5
**Maite**—pop pl ... GU-9
Maitio Spring ... AZ-5
Maitland—locale ... SD-7
**Maitland**—pop pl ... CO-8
**Maitland**—pop pl ... FL-3
**Maitland**—pop pl ... MO-7
**Maitland**—pop pl ... OH-6
**Maitland**—pop pl ... PA-2
**Maitland**—pop pl ... WV-2
Maitland, Lake—lake ... FL-3
Maitland Arroyo—stream ... CO-8
Maitland Art Center—hist pl ... FL-3
Maitland Cave—cave ... PA-2
Maitland Ch—church ... LA-4
Maitland Ch—church ... PA-2
Maitland Draw—valley ... SD-7
Maitland Gin (historical)—locale ... AL-4
Maitland (historical)—locale (2) ... SD-7
Maitland JHS—school ... FL-3
Maitland Landing—locale ... LA-4
Maitland Mine—mine ... CO-8
Maitland Plaza (Shop Ctr)—locale ... FL-3
Maitland Public Library—building ... FL-3
Maitland Sch—school ... LA-4
Maitland Sch—school ... SD-7
Maitland Sch (historical)—school ... PA-2
Maitland Spring—spring ... OR-9
Maitland Spring—spring ... SD-7
Maitlen Creek—stream ... WA-9
Maito—spring ... AZ-5
Mai to Spring ... AZ-5
Maivayi—locale ... AZ-5
Maiyumerak Creek—stream ... AK-9
Maiyumerak Mountains—other ... AK-9
**Maizales**—pop pl ... PR-3
Maizales (Barrio)—fmr MCD ... PR-3
**Maize**—pop pl ... KS-7
Maize Cem—cemetery ... KS-7
Maizefield—hist pl ... NY-2
Maize Hollow—valley ... VA-3
Maize HS—school ... KS-7
Maize Landing Field—airport ... KS-7
Maizeland Sch—school ... CA-9
Maize Road Sch—school ... OH-6
Maize Run—stream ... IN-6
Maize Sch (abandoned)—school ... MO-7
Maizetown—locale ... IL-6
Maizeville—locale ... PA-2
Maizie Ridge—ridge ... TN-4
Maj—island ... MP-9
Majada Windmill—locale ... TX-5
Majaga—basin ... GU-9
Majagmag—other ... GU-9
Majalcas Ranch—locale ... AZ-5
Majarera Creek ... TX-5
Majaroya Creek ... TX-5
Majeaj ... MP-9
Majej—other ... MP-9
Majenbwu—island ... MP-9
**Majenica**—pop pl ... IN-6
Majenica Creek—stream ... IN-6
**Majeriks Corners**—pop pl ... PA-2
Majerus, Michael, House—hist pl ... MN-6
Majeski Airp—airport ... KS-7
**Majestic**—pop pl ... AL-4
**Majestic**—pop pl ... KY-4
Majestic, Mount—summit ... UT-8
**Majestic Acres Subdivision**—pop pl ... UT-8
Majestic Bldg—hist pl ... IN-6
**Majestic Canyon Estates**—pop pl ... UT-8
**Majestic Cove Subdivision**—pop pl ... UT-8
**Majestic Grove Subdivision**—pop pl ... UT-8
Majestic Heights Sch—school ... CO-8
**Majestic Heights Subdivision**—pop pl (2) ... UT-8
**Majestic Heights Subdivisions**—pop pl ... UT-8
**Majestic Heights Subdivision 10**—pop pl ... UT-8
Majestic High School ... AL-4
Majestic Hotel—hist pl ... MO-7
Majestic Lake—lake ... MN-6
Majestic Mine—mine ... CO-8
Majestic Mine—mine ... WA-9
Majestic Mine Group—mine ... CA-9
Majestic Mine (undergound)—mine ... AL-4
Majestic Mountain ... UT-8
Majestic Mtn—summit ... WA-9
Majestic Sch—school ... AL-4
Majestic Sch—school ... UT-8
Majestic Theatre—hist pl ... IL-6
Majestic Theatre—hist pl (2) ... TX-5
**Majestic View Homes Subdivision**—pop pl ... UT-8
**Majestic View Subdivision**—pop pl ... UT-8
**Majestic Village Subdivision**—pop pl ... UT-8
Majet Cem—cemetery ... MS-4
Majet Lake ... MS-4
**Majette**—pop pl (2) ... FL-3
Majette Lookout Tower—tower ... FL-3
Majetto Island ... MP-9
Majieeshi ... MP-9
Majieeshi-To ... MP-9
Majieshi Island ... MP-9
Majieshi Island—island ... MP-9
Majijo ... FM-9
Majijo Peak ... FM-9
Majijo-San ... FM-9
Majikin ... MP-9
Majikin-To ... MP-9
Majil ... MP-9
Majill ... MP-9
Majinkin-to ... MP-9
Majiris Windmill—locale ... TX-5
Majishou ... FM-9
Maj Island ... MP-9
Majjen ... MP-9
Majkein ... MP-9
Majokoryaan Island—island ... MP-9
Majokoryaan-To ... MP-9
**Majolica**—pop pl ... NC-3
Major ... LA-4
Major—locale ... GA-3
Major—locale ... VA-3
**Major**—pop pl ... KY-4
**Major**—pop pl ... LA-4
**Major**—pop pl ... TN-4
**Major**—pop pl ... VA-3
Major, Mount—summit ... NH-1
Majo Ranch—locale ... WY-8
Major Basin—basin ... WY-8
Major Basin Draw—valley ... WY-8
Major Branch—stream ... KY-4
Major Branch—stream ... NC-3
Major Branch—stream ... TN-4
Majorca Mine—mine ... MN-6
Major Canyon—valley ... CA-9
Majorca Oil Field—oilfield ... MS-4
Major Cem—cemetery ... KY-4
Major Cem—cemetery ... NC-3
Major Cem—cemetery (3) ... TN-4
**Major (County)**—pop pl ... OK-5
Major County Courthouse—hist pl ... OK-5
Major Cove ... MA-1
Major Creek ... AL-4
Major Creek—stream ... AK-9
Major Creek—stream ... CA-9
Major Creek—stream (2) ... CO-8
Major Creek—stream ... OR-9
Major Creek—stream ... TX-5
Major Creek—stream ... WA-9
Major Ditch—canal ... IN-6
Major Ditch—canal ... NE-7
Major Draw—valley ... KS-7
Majores Plantation (historical)—locale ... MS-4
Major Evans Gulch—valley ... UT-8
Major Fenn Picnic Area—locale ... ID-8
Major General, The—pillar ... CA-9
Major George S. Welch Elem Sch—school ... DE-2
Major Gulch—valley ... NV-8
Major Harris Mtn—summit ... AR-4
Major Hartwick Museum—building ... MI-6
Major Hill Hollow—valley ... TN-4
Major Hole Bay—bay ... VA-3
Major Hole Creek—stream ... VA-3
Major Hollow—valley ... MO-7
Major Hosp—hospital ... IN-6
Major HS (historical)—school ... TN-4
Majorie Wash—arroyo ... AZ-5
Major Island—island ... CT-1
Major Island—island ... ME-1
Major Johnson Springs—spring ... NM-5
Major Lake—lake (2) ... FL-3
Major Lake—reservoir ... SD-7
Major Lewis Landing (historical)—locale ... TN-4
Major Mine—mine ... CO-8
Major Mtn—summit ... NH-1
Major Mtn—summit ... NC-3
Major Outside Pond—bay ... LA-4
Major Pit—cave ... AL-4
Major Pond ... FL-3
Major Post Office (historical)—building ... TN-4
Major Prairie—flat ... OR-9
Major Ranch—locale ... CO-8
Major Run—stream ... NJ-2
Majors ... NV-8
Majors—locale ... AR-4
Majors—locale ... CA-9
Majors—locale ... LA-4
Majors—locale ... TX-5
**Majors**—pop pl ... LA-4
Majors, Alexander, House—hist pl ... MO-7
Majors, Thomas J., Farmstead—hist pl ... NE-7
Majors Branch—stream ... LA-4
Majors Branch—stream ... TX-5
Majors Cem—cemetery ... CO-8
Majors Cem—cemetery ... NE-7
Majors Cem—cemetery (2) ... TN-4
Major Sch—school ... TN-4
Majors Chapel—church ... TX-5
Major School ... IN-6
Majors Cove—bay ... MA-1
Majors Creek—stream ... AL-4
Majors Creek—stream ... CA-9
Majors Creek Sch—school ... AL-4
Majors Gulch—valley ... SD-7
Majors Harbor—bay ... NY-2
Major Shear Pond—lake ... FL-3
Majors Hollow—valley ... MO-7
Major's Inn and Gilbert Block—hist pl ... NY-2
Majors Lake—reservoir ... AL-4
Major Slough—gut ... FL-3
Major Slough Lake—lake ... FL-3
Majors Place—locale ... NV-8
Majors Point—cape ... NY-2
Majors Pond—reservoir ... NJ-2
Major Spring—spring ... CO-8
Major Spring—spring ... NM-5
Majors Rock—island ... NH-1
Majors Run ... NJ-2
Majors Run—stream ... KY-4
Majors Shoal—bar ... MI-6
Major Steele Backbone—ridge ... MT-8
**Major Subdivision**—pop pl ... UT-8
Majorsville—locale ... WV-2
Majors Wharf—locale ... NJ-2
Majorville—locale ... MO-7
Majorville Ch—church ... IL-6
Major Walsh Sch—school ... MA-1
Major Windmill—locale ... NM-5
Majoshou Shan ... FM-9
Majotto (not verified)—island ... MP-9
Majro ... MP-9
Majruon—island ... MP-9
Majruondik—island ... MP-9
Majruonrik ... MP-9
Maju ... MP-9
Majuba Canyon—valley ... NV-8
Majuba Hill Mine—mine ... NV-8
Majuba Mtn—summit ... NV-8
Majuba Mtns—summit ... NV-8
Majuba Placers—mine ... NV-8
Majulosna—area ... GU-9
Majure Ch—church ... MS-4
Majuro ... MP-9
Majuro Atoll—island (2) ... MP-9
**Majuro (County-equivalent)**—pop pl ... MP-9
Majuro Inseln ... MP-9
Majuro Island—island ... MP-9
Majuro Lagoon—lake ... MP-9
Majuruk ... MP-9
Mak ... MP-9
Makaaikuloa Point—cape ... HI-9
Makaakini ... HI-9
Makaakini Point—cape ... HI-9
Makaalae—cape ... HI-9
Makaalae Point ... HI-9
Makaalae Point—cape ... HI-9
Makaalia—summit ... HI-9
Makaa Stream—stream ... HI-9
Makachak Creek ... OH-6
Maka Creek—stream ... AK-9
Makada Lake—lake ... MN-6
Makaeha—civil ... HI-9
Makaeleele Gulch—valley ... HI-9
Makaha—civil ... HI-9
**Makaha**—pop pl ... HI-9
Makaha Beach Park—park ... HI-9
Makah Air Force Station—locale ... WA-9
Makahalau ... HI-9
Makahalau—locale ... HI-9
Makahalau Pump Station—other ... HI-9
Makahanaloa—civil ... HI-9
Makahanu Pali—cliff ... HI-9
Makaha Playground—park ... HI-9
Makaha Point—cape ... HI-9
Makaha Ridge—ridge ... HI-9
Makaha Stream—stream ... HI-9
Makahauena—cape ... HI-9
Makaha Valley—valley (2) ... HI-9
Makah Bay—bay ... WA-9
Makahiki Point—cape ... HI-9
Makahiloa Stream—stream ... HI-9
**Makah Ind Res**—pop pl ... WA-9
Makahoa Point—cape (2) ... HI-9
Makahoa Ridge—ridge ... HI-9
Makah Peaks—summit ... WA-9
Makah Tepee ... SD-7
Makahuena ... HI-9
Makahuena Point—cape ... HI-9
Makahuene Point ... HI-9
Makahuna Gulch—valley (2) ... HI-9
Makaihuaa ... HI-9
Makaihuwaa—cliff ... HI-9
Makailola ... HI-9
Makaiwa—cape ... HI-9
Makaiwa Bay—bay (2) ... HI-9
Makaiwa Gulch—valley ... HI-9
Makaka Creek—stream ... AK-9
Makaka Kopu Moaula—civil ... HI-9
Makaka Lakes—lake ... AK-9
Makaka Point—cape ... AK-9
Makaka Ravine—valley ... HI-9
Makakilo ... HI-9
**Makakilo (alternate name Makakilo City)**—pop pl ... HI-9
**Makakilo City**—pop pl ... HI-9
Makakilo City (alternate name for Makakilo)—CDP ... HI-9
Makakilo Crater ... HI-9
Makakilo Gulch—valley ... HI-9
Makakiloia—summit ... HI-9
Makaktuk Lake—lake ... AK-9
Makakupaia—civil ... HI-9
Makakupaia (Government)—civil ... HI-9
Makakupu—civil ... HI-9
Makakupu Gulch—valley ... HI-9
Makal—locale ... FM-9
Makalapa Crater—crater ... HI-9
Makalapa Gulch—valley ... HI-9
Makala Stream ... HI-9
Makalawena—civil ... HI-9
Makalawena—locale ... HI-9
Makalawena Bank—bar ... HI-9
Makaleha—summit ... HI-9
Makaleha Ditch—canal ... HI-9
Makaleha Mountains—summit ... HI-9
Makaleha Stream—stream (2) ... HI-9
Makalihua—summit ... HI-9
Makalii—cape ... HI-9
Makalii—summit ... HI-9
Makaliihanau—summit ... HI-9
Makalii Point—cape ... HI-9
Makalina Ravine—valley ... HI-9
Makaluapuna Point—cape ... HI-9
Makamah Beach—beach ... NY-2
Makamakaole Stream—stream ... HI-9
Makamsom Cem—cemetery ... TX-5
Makana—summit ... HI-9
Makanaka ... HI-9
Makanali Gulch—valley ... HI-9
Makanaloa ... HI-9
Makanalua—civil ... HI-9
Makanao ... HI-9
Makanao Butte ... HI-9
Makanau—summit ... HI-9
Makanau Butte ... HI-9
**Makanda**—pop pl ... IL-6
**Makanda (Township of)**—pop pl ... IL-6
Makanikahio One—civil ... HI-9
Makanikahio Two—civil ... HI-9
Makano ... HI-9
Makao—civil ... HI-9
Makaohule Point—cape ... HI-9
Makaokahai Point—cape ... HI-9
Makaophi ... HI-9
Makaopihi—summit ... HI-9
Makaopuhi Crater—crater ... HI-9
Makapala—civil ... HI-9
**Makapala**—pop pl ... HI-9
Makapehu—civil ... HI-9
Makapili ... HI-9
Makapili Rock—cape ... HI-9
Makapipi Gulch ... HI-9
Makapipi Stream—stream ... HI-9
Makapua Point ... HI-9
Makapuu—civil ... HI-9
Makapuu Head ... HI-9
Makapuu Head—summit ... HI-9
Makapuu Point—cape ... HI-9
Makar ... PW-9
Makar—island ... MP-9
Makarius Bay—bay ... AK-9
Makaroyu ... MH-9
Makaru Island ... MP-9
Makaru Island—island ... MP-9
Makaru-to ... MP-9
Makasan Ch—church ... SD-7
Makatoka—locale ... NC-3
Makaua—civil ... HI-9
Makaukiu ... HI-9
Makaukiu Point—cape ... HI-9
Makaula—civil ... HI-9
Makaula-Ooma Mauka Tract—civil ... HI-9
Maka Ulaula—area ... HI-9
Makawana Point ... HI-9
Makawao—civil ... HI-9
**Makawao**—pop pl ... HI-9
Makawao For Res—forest ... HI-9
Makawao-Paia (CCD)—cens area ... HI-9
Makawao Stream—stream ... HI-9
Makawao Union Church—hist pl ... HI-9
Makawea Stream—stream ... HI-9
Makawehi—beach ... HI-9
Makaweli ... HI-9
Makaweli—civil ... HI-9
Makaweli Landing—locale ... HI-9
**Makaweli (Pakala)**—pop pl ... HI-9
Makaweli River—stream ... HI-9
Makay Lake—lake ... MS-4
Makeahua Gulch—valley ... HI-9
Makeanehu—civil ... HI-9
Makea Stream—stream ... HI-9
Maked Creek ... GA-3
Makeeff Landing Strip—airport ... ND-7
Makee Township—fmr MCD ... IA-7
Makee Township Cem—cemetery ... IA-7
Makeever Huff Ditch—canal ... IN-6
Makef ... FM-9
Makefield Elem Sch—school ... PA-2
Makefield Meeting—hist pl ... PA-2
Makefield Park—park ... PA-2
**Makefield Village**—pop pl ... PA-2
Makef Ni Ga ... FM-9
Mak'ef Ni Ichig ... FM-9
Makel Lake—lake ... MI-6
Makelulu Mountain ... PW-9
Makelyville ... NC-3
Makemanaku ... MH-9
Makemie Park—locale ... VA-3
Makemson, W. K. and Kate, House—hist pl ... TX-5
Maken—locale ... WV-2
Makena—civil ... HI-9
**Makena**—pop pl ... HI-9
Makeopihi ... HI-9
Make Peace—hist pl ... MD-2
Makepeace, D. E., Company—hist pl ... MA-1
Makepeace, George, House—hist pl ... IN-6
Makepeace Lake—reservoir ... NJ-2
Makepeace Lake Dam—dam ... NJ-2
Makepeace Number 1 Dam—dam (2) ... MA-1
Makepeace Number 2 Dam—dam (2) ... MA-1
Makepeace Number 4 Dam—dam ... MA-1
Makepeace Rsvr Number Two—reservoir ... MA-1
Makepeace Stream—stream ... NJ-2
Makeruru Mountain ... PW-9
Maketewah Country Club—other ... OH-6
Makey Creek—stream ... MT-8
Mak'f Niichig ... FM-9
Makgum Havoka—locale ... AZ-5
Makhnati Island—area ... AK-9
Makhnati Islands—area ... AK-9
Makhnati Rock—other ... AK-9
Makholm Lake—lake ... WI-6
Maki ... FM-9
Maki, Jacob, Homestead—hist pl ... ID-8
Maki Cabin—locale ... MT-8
Maki Creek—stream ... MI-6
Maki Creek—stream (2) ... MN-6
Maki Creek—stream ... WY-8
Makiki ... HI-9
Makiki—civil ... HI-9
Makiki Fire Station—hist pl ... HI-9
**Makiki Heights**—pop pl ... HI-9
Makiki Japanese Language Sch—school ... HI-9
Makikiki—summit ... HI-9
Makiki Springs—spring ... HI-9
Makiki Stream—stream ... HI-9
Makila—civil ... HI-9
Maki Lake—lake ... ID-8
Maki Lake—lake (2) ... MI-6
Maki Lake—lake ... MN-6
Maki Lake—lake ... WI-6
Makila Reservoir Ditch—canal ... HI-9
Makila Rsvr—reservoir ... HI-9
Makila (site)—locale ... HI-9
Makiloa—civil ... HI-9
Maki Mine—mine ... WA-9
Makin ... MP-9
**Makin**—pop pl ... IN-6
Makin Creek—stream ... OR-9
Makinen—locale ... MN-6
Makinen, John J., Bottle House—hist pl ... MI-6
Makins Creek—stream ... MI-6
Makinson Island—island ... FL-3
Maki Ranch—locale ... MT-8
Makisin Lake ... MI-6
Mak Island ... MP-9
Makiwa Gulch—valley ... HI-9
Makiy ... FM-9
Makku—island ... MP-9
Makkui ... MP-9
Makku (not verified)—island ... MP-9
Maklaks Crater—summit ... OR-9
Maklaks Creek—stream ... OR-9
Maklaks Mtn—summit ... OR-9
Maklaks Pass—gap ... OR-9
Maklaks Spring—spring ... OR-9
Makleys Corner—locale ... VA-3
**Makleyville**—pop pl ... NC-3
Maknek River—stream ... AK-9
Maknik Lagoon—lake ... AK-9
Maknockanut Lake—lake ... LA-4
Makole—cape ... HI-9
Makole—locale ... HI-9
Makolea Point—cape ... HI-9
Makolelau—civil ... HI-9
Makoloaka ... HI-9
Makoloaka Island—island ... HI-9
Makoloaka Point ... HI-9
Makomis Mtn—summit ... NY-2
Makomis Pond—lake ... NY-2
Makonikey Head—cliff ... MA-1
Makoniky Head ... MA-1
Mako Ridge—ridge ... AS-9
**Makoti**—pop pl ... ND-7
Makoti Municipal Airp—airport ... ND-7
Makoy Oil Field—oilfield ... TX-5
Makpe'—slope ... MH-9
Makpe', Kannat—stream ... MH-9
Makpe', Laderan—cliff ... MH-9
Makpe', Puntan—cape ... MH-9
Makpe', Unai—beach ... MH-9
Makpik, Lake—lake ... AK-9
Makpik Creek—stream ... AK-9
Makpo', Kanadan—basin ... MH-9
Makpo', Sisonyan—swamp ... MH-9
Makpo' Wells—well ... MH-9
Maktak Mtn—summit ... AK-9
Makua—civil ... HI-9
Makuaeae ... HI-9
Makua Keaau For Res—forest ... HI-9
Makua Milit Reservation—military ... HI-9
Makua (Site)—locale ... HI-9
Makua Stream—stream ... HI-9
Makua Valley—valley ... HI-9
Maku Gulch—valley ... HI-9
Makuku—summit ... HI-9
Makuku Stream—stream ... HI-9
Makuleia Bay—bay ... HI-9
Makumivooka ... AZ-5
Makuone Valley ... HI-9
Makushin—locale ... AK-9
Makushin Bay—bay ... AK-9
Makushin Point—cape ... AK-9
Makushin Valley—valley ... AK-9
Makushin Volcano—summit ... AK-9
Makuu—civil ... HI-9
Makuu (Site)—locale ... HI-9
Makuyu To ... FM-9
Makwa Lake—lake ... MN-6
Mal' ... FM-9
**Mala**—pop pl ... HI-9
Malaa—area ... GU-9
Malaaf—locale ... FM-9
**Mal'aay**—pop pl ... FM-9
Malabang Trail—trail ... TX-5
**Malabar**—pop pl ... FL-3
Malabar, Cape—cape ... FL-3
Malabar Branch—hist pl ... CA-9
Malabar (CCD)—cens area ... FL-3
Malabar Farm—hist pl ... OH-6
Malabar Saint Sch—school ... CA-9
Malabon Sch—school ... OR-9
Malacal ... PW-9
Malacan ... PW-9
Malacca Lake—lake ... MI-6
Malaccan ... PW-9
Malacheck Cave—cave ... AL-4
Malachi Branch—stream ... KY-4
Malachi Chapel—church ... NC-3
Malachite—locale ... CO-8
Malachite, Lake—lake ... WA-9
Malachite Mine—mine ... NV-8
Malachite Peak—summit ... WA-9
Malachy Lake—lake ... MN-6
Malachys Ch—church ... WI-6
Malachy School ... IN-6
Malackan ... PW-9
Malad (2) ... ID-8
**Malad City**—pop pl ... ID-8
Malad City Cem—cemetery ... ID-8
Malade ... ID-8
Malade City ... ID-8
Malade River ... ID-8
Malade River ... UT-8
Malad Pass—gap ... ID-8
Malad Range—range ... ID-8
Malad River ... ID-8
Malad River—stream (3) ... ID-8
Malad River—stream ... UT-8
Malad Second Ward Tabernacle—hist pl ... ID-8
Malad Substation—other ... ID-8
Malad Summit—summit ... ID-8
Malad Valley—valley ... ID-8
Malad Valley—valley ... UT-8
Malady Bush Island—island ... SC-3
**Malae**—pop pl ... HI-9
Malaea Point ... HI-9
Malae Gulch—valley ... HI-9
Malae Heiau—locale (2) ... HI-9
**Malaeimi**—pop pl ... AS-9
Malaeimi Valley—basin ... AS-9
Malaekahan ... HI-9
Malaekahana—civil ... HI-9
Malaekahana Stream—stream ... HI-9
Malaekahaua ... HI-9
Malaeloa—cape ... HI-9
**Malaeloa**—pop pl ... AS-9
Malae Point—cape ... HI-9
Malaetia Stream—stream ... AS-9
Malaf ... FM-9
Malaga—locale ... KY-4
Malaga—locale ... WA-9
**Malaga**—pop pl ... CA-9
**Malaga**—pop pl ... NJ-2
**Malaga**—pop pl ... NM-5
**Malaga**—pop pl ... OH-6
Malaga Bend—bend ... NM-5
Malaga Branch—stream ... NJ-2
Malaga Camp—locale ... NJ-2
Malaga Canal—canal ... CA-9
Malaga Canyon—valley ... CA-9
Malaga (CCD)—cens area ... KY-4
Malaga (CCD)—cens area ... WA-9
Malaga Cove—bay ... CA-9
Malaga Cove Sch—school ... CA-9
Malaga Creek ... CA-9
Malaga Dam—dam ... NJ-2
Malaga Island—island (2) ... ME-1
Malagal ... PW-9
Malaga Lake—reservoir ... NJ-2
Malagal Hafen ... PW-9
Malaga Point ... CA-9
Malaga Sch—school ... KY-4
Malagasco Brook—stream ... MA-1
Malagateine Stream—stream ... AS-9
Malagatiga Ridge—ridge ... AS-9
**Malaga (Township of)**—pop pl ... OH-6
Malage ... OH-6
Malagro Springs—spring ... NM-5
Malaguerra Winery—hist pl ... CA-9
Malahini Cave—cave ... HI-9
Malaikahana ... HI-9
Malaio ... FM-9
Malaj ... FM-9
Malaja River—stream ... GU-9
Malakal—harbor ... PW-9
Malakal—island ... PW-9
Malakal Durchfahrt ... PW-9
Malakal Hafen ... PW-9
Malakal Harbor ... PW-9
Malakal Island ... PW-9
Malakal Pass ... PW-9
Malakal Passage ... PW-9
Malaka Township—fmr MCD ... IA-7
**Malakoff**—pop pl ... TX-5
Malakoff Cem—cemetery ... TX-5
Malakoff Diggings—mine ... CA-9
Malakoff Diggins-North Bloomfield Hist Dist—hist pl ... CA-9
Malakoff Landing—locale ... AL-4
Malalii Point ... HI-9
**Malaloa**—pop pl ... AS-9
Malaloto Ridge—ridge ... AS-9
Malalowaiaole Gulch—valley ... HI-9
**Malam**—pop pl ... FM-9
Malama Homesteads—civil ... HI-9
Malama-Ki—civil ... HI-9
Malama-Ki For Res—forest ... HI-9
Malamalamaiki—summit ... HI-9

Malamamalamaiki One—civil HI-9
Malamamalamaiki 2—civil HI-9
Malama Point—cape AS-9
Malama Spring—spring AS-9
Malam Branch Canal—canal LA-4
Mala Mill Stack—other HI-9
Malamute Creek—stream ID-8
Malamute Fork—stream AK-9
Malamute Point—summit ID-8
Malanahae—civil HI-9
Malanahae Gulch—valley HI-9
Malanaj FM-9
Malan Canal—canal CA-9
Malaney Creek—stream WA-9
Malaney Flat—flat CA-9
Malang—area GU-9
Malangith—summit FM-9
Malanglang PW-9
Malang Ni P'ul—island FM-9
Malans Basin—basin UT-8
Malans Peak—summit UT-8
Malapai Cliffs AZ-5
Malapai Hill—summit CA-9
Malapai Mesa NV-8
Malapais Hills AZ-5
Malapais Mtn—summit AZ-5
Malapais Tank—well AZ-5
Malapai Tank—reservoir (3) AZ-5
**Malapardis**—pop pl NJ-2
Malapardis Brook—stream NJ-2
Malapartis Creek—stream NJ-2
Malapi Spring—spring CA-9
Malapi Tank—reservoir NM-5
Malaquite Beach—beach TX-5
Malaquite Beach Development—locale TX-5
Malarcher Plantation—locale LA-4
Malardi Lake—lake MN-6
Malarky Lake—lake OR-9
Malaruni Creek—stream MO-7
Malasia Park—park OH-6
Malaspina Glacier—glacier AK-9
**Mala Subdivision**—pop pl UT-8
Mala Suerte Windmill—locale (4) TX-5
Malat Draw—valley ID-8
Malaudos Creek—stream LA-4
Malavary Swamp—swamp RI-1
Mala Vista Ranch—locale NV-8
Malawaay—locale FM-9
Mala Wharf—locale HI-9
Malay FM-9
Malay Canyon—valley AZ-5
Malay Creek—stream AZ-5
Malay Gap—gap AZ-5
Malay Lake—lake MI-6
Malay Spring—spring AZ-5
Malay Tank—reservoir (2) AZ-5
**Malba**—pop pl NY-2
Malberg Lake—lake MN-6
Malbis—locale AL-4
Malbis Cem—cemetery AL-4
Malbis Ch—church AL-4
Malbis Fire Tower—tower AL-4
Malboeuf, Bayou—stream LA-4
Malbone—hist pl RI-1
Malbone, Francis, House—hist pl RI-1
Malbone Cem—cemetery NY-2
**Malbons Mills**—pop pl ME-1
Malbon Swamp—stream VA-3
**Malbrook**—pop pl VA-3
Malburg Drain—canal MI-6
Malburn Creek—stream AK-9
Malby Corners—locale NY-2
Malby Creek Church AL-4
Malby Crossing—locale CA-9
Malby Lake—lake WI-6
Malby Post Office (historical)—building AL-4
Malbys Crossroads Ch—church NC-3
Malchi Lake MI-6
Malchom Ammons Dam—dam AL-4
Malchom Ammons Lake AL-4
Malchow Ditch—canal IN-6
Malco FL-3
Malco WV-2
Malco Airp—airport PA-2
Malcolm—locale MI-6
Malcolm—locale MN-6
**Malcolm**—pop pl AL-4
**Malcolm**—pop pl MD-2
**Malcolm**—pop pl NE-7
**Malcolm**—pop pl VA-3
Malcolm Baptist Church AL-4
Malcolm Bay—bay WI-6
Malcolm Branch—stream GA-3
Malcolm Branch—stream ME-1
Malcolm Cem—cemetery NE-7
Malcolm Ch—church (2) AL-4
Malcolm Ch—church ND-7
Malcolm Chapel—church AR-4
Malcolm Creek—stream KY-4
Malcolm Creek—stream WA-9
Malcolm Creek Camp—locale KY-4
Malcolm Fork—stream WV-2
**Malcolm (historical)**—pop pl MS-4
Malcolm Ledge—bar ME-1
Malcolm Mtn—summit WA-9
Malcolm P.O. (historical)—building MS-4
Malcolm Ridge—ridge OR-9
Malcolm River—stream AK-9
Malcolm Sch—school MD-2
Malcolm Spring—spring WY-8
**Malcolm Township**—pop pl ND-7
Malcolm X House Site—hist pl NE-7
Malcoln Cem—cemetery MO-7
**Malcom**—pop pl IA-7
Malcom Cem—cemetery (2) OH-6
Malcom Creek—stream ID-8
Malcom Creek Cabin Area KY-4
Malcome Springs—other WV-2
Malco Mine—mine AZ-5
Malcom Martin Park—park TN-4
**Malcom Spring Heights**—pop pl WV-2
Malcom Tank—reservoir NM-5
Malcom Township—fmr MCD IA-7
Malcon—locale NY-2
Malco Pass FL-3
Malcum Post Office (historical)—building MS-4
**Malden**—pop pl IL-6
**Malden**—pop pl IN-6
**Malden**—pop pl MA-1
**Malden**—pop pl MO-7
**Malden**—pop pl WA-9
**Malden**—pop pl WV-2
Malden, City of—civil MA-1
Malden AFB (abandoned)—military MO-7
Malden Air Force Base MO-7
Malden Branch—stream GA-3
Malden Branch—stream TN-4
**Malden Bridge**—pop pl NY-2
Malden Brook—stream MA-1
**Malden Centre**—pop pl MA-1
Malden City Hall—building MA-1
Malden City Hall—building MO-7
Malden City Infirmary—hospital MA-1
Malden Creek—stream AR-4
Malden Creek—stream MO-7
Malden Creek—stream VA-3
**Malden Highlands**—pop pl MA-1
Malden Hill—summit MA-1
Malden Hist Dist—hist pl WV-2
Malden Hollow—valley MO-7
Malden Hosp—hospital MA-1
Malden HS—school MA-1
Malden HS—school MO-7
Malden Inn—hist pl PA-2
Malden Island—island ME-1
Malden Mtn—summit WV-2
Malden Municipal Airp—airport MO-7
Malden-on-Hudson NY-2
**Malden on Hudson**—pop pl NY-2
Malden-on-Hudson (RR name Malden On Hudson)—other NY-2
Malden Place—locale PA-2
Malden River—stream MA-1
Malden Spring—spring MO-7
Malden Square—park MA-1
Malden Station (historical)—locale MA-1
Malden Towers—hist pl IL-6
Maldonado Canyon—valley NM-5
Maldonado Cem—cemetery NM-5
Maldon Run—stream WV-2
Male Acad—hist pl KY-4
**Malecon**—pop pl (2) PR-3
Maledy Cem—cemetery MO-7
Maledy Ford—locale MO-7
Ma Leg Island—island MD-2
Male HS—school KY-4
Malekule—crater HI-9
Malekun FM-9
Maleky Branch—stream VA-3
Malel MP-9
**Malem**—pop pl FM-9
Malem, Infal—stream FM-9
Malem (Municipality)—civ div FM-9
Malen Dapengen Penlew—plain FM-9
Malen Dauen—plain FM-9
Malen Dolen Pahniep—plain FM-9
Malen Hollow—valley KY-4
Malen Karpwiolap—plain FM-9
Malen Karpwietik—plain FM-9
Malen Kullop—plain FM-9
Malen Likin Peisokele—plain FM-9
Malen Loange Peidak—plain FM-9
Malen Pahnpe—plain FM-9
Malen Pitalap—plain FM-9
Malen Pitetik—plain FM-9
Malen Pohras—plain FM-9
Malen Uhmwe—plain FM-9
Malen Wapar—plain FM-9
Maleo MP-9
Male Point—cape AK-9
Males Sch—school AL-4
Male Store—locale MI-6
**Malesus**—pop pl TN-4
Malesus Baptist Ch—church TN-4
Malesus Elem Sch—school TN-4
Malesus Post Office (historical)—building TN-4
Malesus United Methodist Ch—church TN-4
Maleta Windmill—locale TX-5
Maletin FM-9
Maletiu FM-9
Malett Cem—cemetery MS-4
Malette Canyon—valley NM-5
Maletti Hill—summit WA-9
Malett Sch (historical)—school MS-4
Malewe—locale FM-9
Malewehlap—locale FM-9
Maley Creek—stream OR-9
Maley Hill—summit PA-2
Maley Hollow—valley PA-2
Maley Hollow—valley TN-4
Maley Oil Field—oilfield TX-5
Maley School—locale IL-6
**Maleza**—pop pl PR-3
Maleza Alta (Barrio)—fmr MCD PR-3
Maleza Baja (Barrio)—fmr MCD PR-3
Malezas (Barrio)—fmr MCD PR-3
Malfordar Brook—stream MA-1
Malferd Sch (historical)—school AL-4
Malga Bay—bay AK-9
Malgosa Canyon—valley AZ-5
Malgosa Creek—stream AZ-5
Malgosa Crest—summit AZ-5
Malheur OR-9
Malheur Butte—summit OR-9
Malheur Butte Ch—church OR-9
Malheur Canyon—valley OR-9
Malheur Cave—cave OR-9
Malheur City—locale OR-9
**Malheur County**—pop pl OR-9
Malheur Dam—dam OR-9
Malheureux Point—cape LA-4
Malheur Ford—locale OR-9
Malheur Ford Camp (historical)—locale OR-9
Malheur Gap—gap OR-9
Malheur Job Corps Conservation Center—locale OR-9
Malheur Junction—locale OR-9
Malheur Junction (CCD)—cens area OR-9
Malheur Lake—lake OR-9
Malheur Lake Basin OR-9
Malheur Natl For—forest OR-9
Malheur Natl Wildlife Ref HQ—park OR-9
Malheur River OR-9
Malheur River—stream OR-9
Malheur River Basin OR-9
Malheur Rsvr—reservoir OR-9
Malheur Siphon—canal OR-9
Malheur Slough—stream (2) OR-9
Malheur Spring—spring OR-9
Malhiglum Creek TX-5
Malholms Creek—stream GA-3
Malhuldy Creek OK-5
Mali HI-9
Maliba Sequit Creek Topanga Malibu Sequit Creek CA-9
Maliba Sequit Point CA-9
Malibo Creek CA-9
Malibo Point CA-9
Malibou Lake Mountain Club—other CA-9
**Malibu**—pop pl CA-9
**Malibu**—pop pl VA-3
Malibu Beach—beach MA-1
**Malibu Beach**—pop pl CA-9
**Malibu Bowl**—pop pl CA-9
Malibu Campground—locale UT-8
**Malibu Canyon Homes**—pop pl CA-9
Malibu Club—other TX-5
Malibu Creek—stream CA-9
Malibu Drain—stream AZ-5
Malibu Fire Station—locale CA-9
Malibu Hills—locale CA-9
Malibu Junction—locale CA-9
Malibu Lake—reservoir CA-9
Malibu Park—park TX-5
Malibu Point—cape CA-9
Malibu Rsvr—reservoir CA-9
Malibu Sch—school CA-9
**Malibu Valley (subdivision)**—pop pl NC-3
**Malibu Vista**—pop pl CA-9
Malice, Lake—lake OR-9
Malice Ditch—canal CO-8
Malicious Gap—gap AZ-5
Malickson Airp—airport PA-2
Malicky Oil Field—oilfield TX-5
Maliefetaliai Ridge—ridge AS-9
Malikfik Bay—bay AK-9
Malik Island MP-9
Maliko Bay—bay HI-9
Malikoff Hill—summit TX-5
Maliko Gulch—valley HI-9
Maliko Stream HI-9
Malilog Point—cape GU-9
Malilok, Puntan—cape MH-9
Malin OK-5
**Malin**—pop pl OR-9
Malin, A., House—hist pl MI-6
Malin, Millard F., House—hist pl UT-8
Malina Bay—bay AK-9
Malina Creek—stream AK-9
Malin Airstrip—airport OR-9
Malina Point—cape AK-9
Malina Sch—school SC-3
Malin (CCD)—cens area OR-9
Malin Cem—cemetery OR-9
Malin Cem—cemetery TN-4
Malinchak Airp (private)—airport PA-2
Malin Creek—stream ID-8
Malinda Bridge—bridge TN-4
Malinda Gulch—valley CA-9
Maline Creek—stream MO-7
Maline Sch—school MO-7
Malino, Heiau o—locale HI-9
Malin Point—summit ID-8
**Malins**—pop pl PA-2
Malin Sch—school IL-6
Malins Store (historical)—locale TN-4
**Malinta**—pop pl OH-6
Malio House—hist pl OH-6
Malipai Windmill—locale AZ-5
Malish Playground—park MI-6
Mal Island FM-9
Maliuga Point—cape AS-9
Maliu Point—cape HI-9
**Maljamar**—pop pl NM-5
Maljamar Oil Field—other NM-5
Malk, Rois—summit PW-9
Malka Bay—bay AK-9
Malkal Harbor PW-9
Malkerson Island—island MN-6
Malkim Sch—school MI-6
Malkintooh Creek—channel GA-3
Malkowski Ranch—locale ND-7
Malks Cem—cemetery NY-2
Mall—island FM-9
**Mall**—pop pl NJ-2
Mall—post sta MN-6
Mall—post sta NY-2
Mall—post sta PA-2
Mall—post sta TN-4
Mall, The—locale (2) KS-7
Mall, The—park DC-2
Mall, The—park NY-2
Mall, The—post sta MS-4
Mallacomes Or Moristul—civil CA-9
Mallacomes or Moristul Y Plan De Agua Caliente—civil CA-9
Mallady Hollow—valley MO-7
Mallagh Landing—locale CA-9
Mallahau Ch—church TX-5
Mallakaset Bay MA-1
Mal Lake—lake WA-9
Mallalap—plain FM-9
Mallalieu, Lake—reservoir WI-6
Mallalieu Ch—church MS-4
Mallalieu Oil Field—oilfield MS-4
Mallalieu Pumping Station—building MS-4
Mallalieu Seminary (historical)—school MS-4
Mallalieu United Methodist Ch—church MS-4
Mall Allap—plain FM-9
Mallard—locale CA-9
Mallard—locale IL-6
Mallard—locale LA-4
Mallard—locale TX-5
Mallard—locale WI-6
**Mallard**—pop pl IA-7
Mallard Airp—airport AL-4
Mallard Arm—bay OR-9
Mallard Bay—bay (3) AK-9
Mallard Bay—bay LA-4
Mallard Bay—bay MN-6
Mallard Bay—bay UT-8
**Mallard Bay**—pop pl OK-5
Mallard Bay Island—island LA-4
Mallard Bay Oil and Gas Field—oilfield LA-4
Mallard Bayou—stream LA-4
Mallard Bay Rec Area—park OK-5
Mallard Branch GA-3
Mallard Branch—stream LA-4
Mallard Cem—cemetery GA-3
Mallard Cem—cemetery MO-7
Mallard Cem—cemetery TX-5
Mallard Chapel—church AL-4
Mallard Chapel Cem—cemetery AL-4
Mallard Cove—bay AK-9
Mallard Cove Landing—locale NC-3
Mallard Creek AL-4
Mallard Creek NC-3
Mallard Creek—locale NC-3
Mallard Creek—stream AL-4
Mallard Creek—stream IL-6
Mallard Creek—stream MI-6
Mallard Creek—stream MS-4
Mallard Creek—stream MT-8
Mallard Creek—stream (3) NC-3
Mallard Creek—stream OR-9
Mallard Creek—stream TX-5
Mallard Creek—stream WY-8
Mallard Creek Ch—church NC-3
Mallard Creek Community House—locale NC-3
Mallard Creek Elem Sch—school NC-3
Mallard Creek Falls—falls ID-8
Mallard Creek Ranch—locale ID-8
Mallard Dam SD-7
Mallard Duck Bay—bay AK-9
Mallard Flowage—reservoir (2) WI-6
Mallard Fork—gut AL-4
Mallard-Fox Creek Wildlife Mngmt Area—park AL-4
Mallard Gulch—valley CA-9
Mallard Gulch—valley OR-9
Mallard Haven Natl Wildlife Mgt Area—park NE-7
Mallard Head—cape AK-9
Mallard Hill—summit MA-1
Mallard Hole Lake—lake WI-6
Mallard Hole State Wildlife Mngmt Area—park MN-6
Mallard Island—island CA-9
Mallard Island—island MD-2
Mallard Island—island ND-7
**Mallard Junction**—pop pl LA-4
Mallard Lagoon—bay CA-9
Mallard Lake AL-4
Mallard Lake MT-8
Mallard Lake TX-5
Mallard Lake—lake (2) AK-9
Mallard Lake—lake (2) CA-9
Mallard Lake—lake FL-3
Mallard Lake—lake (2) ID-8
Mallard Lake—lake LA-4
Mallard Lake—lake (6) MI-6
Mallard Lake—lake (9) MN-6
Mallard Lake—lake MS-4
Mallard Lake—lake NE-7
Mallard Lake—lake (2) ND-7
Mallard Lake—lake TX-5
Mallard Lake—lake WA-9
Mallard Lake—lake (3) WI-6
Mallard Lake—lake WY-8
Mallard Lake—reservoir NY-2
Mallard Lake—reservoir NC-3
Mallard Lake—reservoir SD-7
Mallard Lake—reservoir TN-4
Mallard Lake Dam—dam AL-4
Mallard Lake Dam—dam TN-4
Mallard Lake For Preserve—forest IL-6
Mallard Lake Lookout Tower—locale MI-6
Mallard Lake Lower—reservoir NC-3
Mallard Lake Lower Dam—dam NC-3
**Mallard Lakes (subdivision)**—pop pl NC-3
Mallard Lake Trail—trail WY-8
Mallard Lake Upper—reservoir NC-3
Mallard Lake Upper Dam—dam NC-3
Mallard Marsh—lake MO-7
Mallard Marsh—swamp WA-9
Mallard Marsh Campground—park OR-9
Mallard Marsh Dam Number One—dam IA-7
Mallard Marsh Dam Number Three—dam IA-7
Mallard Marsh Swamp—swamp IA-7
Mallard Oil Field—oilfield TX-5
Mallard Peak—summit ID-8
Mallard Peak Lookout—hist pl ID-8
Mallard Point—cape AR-4
Mallard Point—cape MI-6
Mallard Point—cape MN-6
Mallard Point—cape NJ-2
Mallard Pond—bay NC-3
Mallard Pond—lake AR-4
Mallard Pond—lake FL-3
Mallard Pond—lake KS-7
Mallard Pond—lake MD-2
Mallard Pond—lake MI-6
Mallard Pond—lake MO-7
Mallard Pond—lake MT-8
Mallard Pond—lake UT-8
Mallard Pool—reservoir UT-8
Mallard Rsvr—reservoir CA-9
Mallard Sch—school PA-2
Mallards Creek—stream AL-4
Mallards Dozen Archeol Site (40HA147)—hist pl TN-4
Mallard Slough WI-6
Mallard Slough—gut CA-9
Mallard Slough—gut ID-8
Mallard Slough—lake SD-7
Mallard Slough—stream AK-9
Mallard Slough—stream WA-9
Mallard Slough—swamp FL-3
Mallard Slough—swamp SD-7
Mallards Mill—locale GA-3
Mallards Pond—lake GA-3
Mallards Rest Rec Area—locale MT-8
**Mallard Subdivision**—pop pl UT-8
Mallard West IL-6
Mallard Windmill—locale TX-5
Mallardy Creek—stream WA-9
Mallardy Ridge—ridge WA-9
Mallascham Branch SC-3
Mall at Chestnut Hill, The—locale MA-1
Mall at 163rd Street—locale FL-3
Mall Bldg—hist pl TN-4
Mall Creek—stream KS-7
Mall Creek—stream NC-3
Malle—island MP-9
Mallego Brook—stream NH-1
Mallego Plains—flat NH-1
Mallels Mill (historical)—locale AL-4
Mallen Mine—mine MN-6
Mallepwou—plain FM-9
Maller Ditch—canal WY-8
Mallery Cem—cemetery MI-6
Mallery Granger Ditch—canal IN-6
Mallery Lake—reservoir TX-5
Mallet, Bayou—stream (2) LA-4
Mallet, Joseph, House—hist pl IA-7
Mallet Bayou—bay FL-3
Mallet Branch—stream KY-4
Mallet Branch—stream MS-4
**Mallet Creek**—pop pl OH-6
Mallet Creek—stream OH-6
Mallethead Rock—pillar CA-9
Mallet Pond—reservoir NM-5
**Mallets Bay**—pop pl VT-1
Mallets Cem—cemetery GA-3
Mallets Creek—stream GA-3
Mallets Landing—locale GA-3
Mallett—locale OR-9
Mallett—locale TX-5
Mallett, David, Jr., House—hist pl CT-1
Mallett, E. B., Office Bldg—hist pl ME-1
Mallett, George W., House—hist pl AR-4
Mallett Cem—cemetery TN-4
Mallett Creek AL-4
Mallett Drain—canal OR-9
Mallette, Orin, Cabin—hist pl NM-5
Mallette, Sylvester M., Cabin—hist pl NM-5
Mallette Campground—locale NM-5
Mallette Cem—cemetery GA-3
Mallette Creek—stream NM-5
Mallettown AR-4
Mallet Town—locale AR-4
Mallet Town Cem—cemetery AR-4
Mallett Playground—park MI-6
Malletts Bay—bay VT-1
**Malletts Bay**—pop pl VT-1
Malletts Creek AL-4
Malletts Creek—stream VT-1
Malletts Head—summit VT-1
Mallet Vega Camp—locale CO-8
Mallewe—unknown FM-9
Malley Drive Sch—school CO-8
Malley Gulch—valley MT-8
Malleys Pond—lake CT-1
Mall Fork WV-2
Mall Hill—summit IN-6
Mall Hollow—valley KY-4
Mallicoat Cave—cave TN-4
Mallicoat Cem—cemetery TN-4
Mallie—locale KY-4
Malligoyoke PW-9
Mallin—locale LA-4
Mallinckrodt Convent—church NJ-2
Mallini Bayou—stream (2) MS-4
Mallini Point—cape MS-4
Mallis Chapel Ch—church AL-4
Mall Island FM-9
**Mallison Falls**—pop pl ME-1
Mallman Creek MI-6
Malloby Hollow—valley TN-4
Mallo Camp—locale WY-8
Malloch Sch—school CA-9
Mallok MP-9
Mallon Brook—stream ME-1
Mallon Ditch—canal CO-8
Mallon Ditch No. 2—canal CO-8
Mallonee JHS—school VA-3
Mallon Extension CO-8
Mallon Ranch—locale CO-8
Malloons Creek—stream OH-6
Mallo Pass Creek—stream CA-9
Mallory KS-7
Mallory MS-4
Mallory—locale TN-4
**Mallory**—pop pl AR-4
**Mallory**—pop pl MN-6
**Mallory**—pop pl NY-2
**Mallory**—pop pl SC-3
**Mallory**—pop pl WV-2
Mallory—uninc pl TN-4
Mallory, Mount—summit CA-9
Mallory, Ogden, House—hist pl OH-6
Mallory Branch—stream GA-3
Mallory Branch—stream IN-6
Mallory Brook—stream (2) CT-1
Mallory Brook—stream MA-1
Mallory Brook—stream (3) NY-2
Mallory Brook—stream VT-1
Mallory Canyon—valley NV-8
Mallory Cove AL-4
Mallory Cem—cemetery AL-4
Mallory Cem—cemetery (2) IL-6
Mallory Cem—cemetery IA-7
Mallory Cem—cemetery KY-4
Mallory Cem—cemetery TN-4
Mallory Ch—church NC-3
Mallory Ch—church TN-4
Mallory Corner—locale NY-2
Mallory Creek—stream ID-8
Mallory Creek—stream NY-2
Mallory Creek—stream NC-3
Mallory Creek—stream OR-9
Mallory Creek—stream PA-2
Mallory Creek—stream TX-5
Mallory Creek—stream (2) VA-3
Mallory Detention Dam—dam AZ-5
Mallory Dock—locale FL-3
Mallory Drain—canal MI-6
Mallory Draw—valley AZ-5
Mallory Family Cem—cemetery MS-4
Mallory Ford—locale VA-3
Mallory Gulch—valley SD-7
Mallory Gulch—valley WY-8
Mallory Heights Sch—school TN-4
**Mallory Heights (subdivision)**—pop pl FL-3
Mallory Hill—summit CT-1
Mallory Hill—summit NY-2
Mallory (historical)—locale AL-4
Mallory (historical)—locale KS-7
Mallory Island—island NY-2
Mallory Key—island FL-3
Mallory Lake—lake GA-3
Mallory Lake—lake MI-6
Mallory Lake—reservoir AL-4
Mallory Lake Dam—dam AL-4
Mallory Lake Drain—stream MI-6
Mallory Mill (historical)—locale AL-4
Mallory Mtn—summit AL-4
Mallory Point VA-3
Mallory Pond—lake NY-2
Mallory Ridge—ridge WA-9
Mallory Rsvr—reservoir OR-9
Mallorys TN-4
**Mallorys**—pop pl TN-4
Mallory Sch—school PA-2
Mallory Sch—school TN-4
Mallory Sch—school (2) VA-3
Mallorys Corners—locale (2) NY-2
Mallorys Creek—stream VA-3
Mallory Shaft—mine AZ-5
Mallorys Point—cape VA-3
Mallory Spring—spring AZ-5
Mallory Spring—spring CA-9
Mallory Spring—spring (2) OR-9
**Mallory Spur**—pop pl AR-4
Mallory Station TN-4
Mallory Station—locale NY-2
Mallorysville—locale GA-3
Mallory Swamp—swamp FL-3
Mallory Technical Institute—school IN-6
Mallory Township—fmr MCD IA-7
Malloryville—locale NY-2
**Mallot Park (historical)**—pop pl IN-6
Mallott Ditch—canal IN-6
**Mallow**—pop pl VA-3
Mallow Bay MD-2
Mallow Cem—cemetery IN-6
Mallow Cem—cemetery OH-6
Mallow Knob—summit WV-2
Mallow Lake—lake MI-6
Mallow Perrill Cem—cemetery OH-6
Mallow Run—stream IN-6
Mallows Bay—bay MD-2
Mallow School (historical)—locale MO-7
Malloxville Sch (historical)—school MS-4
**Malloy**—pop pl AR-4
Malloy Branch—stream FL-3
Malloy Bridge—bridge TX-5
Malloy Brook—stream NY-2
Malloy Cabin—locale OR-9
Malloy Cave Number Four—cave TN-4
Malloy Cave Number Three—cave TN-4
Malloy Cave Number Two—cave TN-4
Malloy Cem—cemetery FL-3
Malloy Cem—cemetery MS-4
Malloy Cem—cemetery NC-3
Malloy Chapel—church GA-3
Malloy Creek—stream WA-9
Malloy Hollow—valley OK-5
Malloy Lake—lake WI-6
Malloy Lateral—canal AZ-5
Malloy Mine—mine CA-9
Malloy Prairie—flat WA-9
Malloy Ranch—locale OR-9
Malloy Sch—school FL-3
Malloy Spring—spring OR-9
Mall Playground—park SC-3
Mall Shop Ctr, The—locale AL-4
Mallson Ditch—canal MI-6
Malls Shop Ctr, The—locale KS-7
Mallula State Game Production Area—park SD-7
**Mallwood**—pop pl WI-6
Mally Lake—lake NE-7
Mallys Weh-Weh Neh-Kee Park—park IA-7
Malmaison—locale MS-4
**Malmaison**—pop pl VA-3
Malmaison Ch—church MS-4
Malmaison Ch—church VA-3
Malmaison Site—hist pl MS-4
Malmaison State Wildlife Mngmt Area—park MS-4
Malman Marsh—swamp MI-6
Malmborg Sch—hist pl MT-8
Malmborg Sch—school MT-8
Malm Cem—cemetery MN-6
Malmedal Lake—lake MN-6
Malmgren Lake—lake MN-6
Malm Gulch—valley ID-8
Malmo—locale NC-3
**Malmo**—pop pl MN-6
**Malmo**—pop pl NE-7
Malmo Airp—airport PA-2
Malmo Bay—bay MN-6
Malmo Cem—cemetery MN-6
Malmo Mounds and Village Site—hist pl MN-6
Malmon Creek MI-6
**Malmo (Township of)**—pop pl MN-6
Malm Spring—spring ID-8
Malmsten Peak—summit UT-8
Malmstrom AFB—military MT-8
Malmstrom Air Force Base Rec Area—park MT-8
Malngith FM-9
Malnouri Creek ND-7
Malnourie Creek—stream ND-7
Malo—locale WA-9
Maloata—locale AS-9
Maloata Bay—bay AS-9
Maloata Stream—stream AS-9
Malo Beach—locale VA-3
Malochomy Lake—lake TX-5
Malo Creek—stream CA-9
Maloe FM-9
Maloelab Araktcheeff MP-9
Maloelab Island MP-9
Maloelap Atoll—island MP-9
Maloelap (County-equivalent)—civil MP-9
Maloelapj MP-9
Maloelap Lagoon (not verified)—lake MP-9
Maloin Ranch—locale WY-8
Maloit Park—flat CO-8
Malojloj—area GU-9
Malojloj Falls—falls GU-9
Malojloj Spring—spring GU-9
Malok MP-9
Malok Island MP-9
Malo Lake—lake WA-9
Malolos Site—hist pl GU-9
Malon FM-9
Malone AL-4
Malone PA-2
Malone—airport NJ-2
Malone—locale AL-4
Malone—locale IA-7
Malone—locale KY-4
Malone—locale MT-8
Malone—locale OR-9
Malone—locale TN-4
Malone—locale UT-8
**Malone**—pop pl AL-4
**Malone**—pop pl FL-3

**Malone**—*pop pl* ... IA-7
**Malone**—*pop pl* ... MS-4
**Malone**—*pop pl* ... NY-2
**Malone**—*pop pl* ... SC-3
**Malone**—*pop pl* ... TX-5
**Malone**—*pop pl* ... WA-9
**Malone**—*pop pl* ... WI-6
Malone, Lake—*reservoir* ... KY-4
Malone Archeol Site—*hist pl* ... KS-7
Malone Baptist Ch—*church* ... AL-4
Malone Bay—*bay* ... MD-2
Malone Bay—*bay* ... MI-6
Malone Bay Campground—*locale* ... MI-6
Malone Branch—*stream* ... AR-4
Malone Branch—*stream* ... TX-5
Malone (CCD)—*cens area* ... FL-3
Malone Cem—*cemetery* (6) ... AL-4
Malone Cem—*cemetery* (2) ... AR-4
Malone Cem—*cemetery* ... GA-3
Malone Cem—*cemetery* ... KY-4
Malone Cem—*cemetery* (3) ... MS-4
Malone Cem—*cemetery* ... OH-6
Malone Cem—*cemetery* (6) ... TN-4
Malone Cem—*cemetery* ... VA-3
Malone Ch—*church* ... AL-4
Malone Ch—*church* ... IL-6
Malone Chapel—*church* ... SC-3
Malone Chapel—*church* ... TN-4
Malone Coll—*school* ... OH-6
Malone Coulee—*valley* ... MT-8
*Malone Creek* ... AL-4
Malone Creek—*gut* ... AL-4
Malone Creek—*stream* ... AL-4
Malone Creek—*stream* ... CA-9
Malone Creek—*stream* ... FL-3
Malone Creek—*stream* ... IA-7
Malone Creek—*stream* ... KS-7
Malone Creek—*stream* ... MN-6
Malone Creek—*stream* ... MO-7
Malone Creek—*stream* ... MT-8
Malone Creek—*stream* ... WA-9
Malone Dam—*dam* ... OR-9
Malone Diversion Dam—*dam* ... OR-9
Malone Draw—*valley* ... NM-5
Malonee Mill—*locale* ... NC-3
Malone Ferry (historical)—*locale* ... AL-4
Malone Freight Depot—*hist pl* ... NY-2
Malone Gap—*gap* (2) ... TN-4
Malone Hammock Branch—*stream* ... FL-3
Malone Hollow—*valley* ... AL-4
Malone Hollow—*valley* ... KS-7
Malone Hollow—*valley* ... OH-6
Malone Hollow—*valley* (3) ... TN-4
Malone HS—*school* ... FL-3
Malone Island—*island* ... FL-3
Malone Island—*island* ... MI-6
Malone Island—*island* ... MN-6
**Malone Junction**—*pop pl* ... NY-2
Malone Lake—*lake* ... MS-4
Malone Lake—*lake* ... WI-6
Malone Lake—*reservoir* ... TN-4
Malone Lake Dam—*dam* ... TN-4
*Malone Landing* ... MS-4
Malone Mill Creek—*stream* ... AL-4
Malone Mines—*mine* ... NM-5
Malone Mountain Cem—*cemetery* ... MS-4
Malone Mountains—*summit* ... TX-5
Malone Park—*park* ... AL-4
Malone Park—*park* ... MA-1
Malone Park—*park* ... MO-7
Malone Park—*park* ... TN-4
Malone Peak—*summit* ... OR-9
Malone-Penelope (CCD)—*cens area* ... TX-5
Malone Point—*cape* ... FL-3
Malone Pond—*lake* ... IN-6
Malone Pool—*reservoir* ... OR-9
Malone-Porter (CCD)—*cens area* ... WA-9
Malone Ridge—*ridge* ... KY-4
*Malones Bayou* ... FL-3
Malones Bridge (historical)—*bridge* ... AL-4
Malones Cave—*cave* ... AL-4
Malone Sch—*school* ... MN-6
Malone Sch—*school* ... SD-7
*Malones Chapel Missionary Baptist Church* ... TN-4
Malones Creek—*stream* ... NC-3
Malones Pond—*lake* ... CT-1
Malone Spring—*spring* ... OR-9
Malone Spring—*spring* (3) ... TN-4
**Malone Spur**—*pop pl* ... MT-8
Malones Store (historical)—*locale* ... TN-4
*Malone Station* ... MS-4
*Malones Woodyard Landing* ... AL-4
Malone Tank—*reservoir* ... NM-5
Maloneton—*locale* ... KY-4
**Malone (Town of)**—*pop pl* ... NY-2
**Malone (Township of)**—*pop pl* ... IL-6
Malone Well—*well* ... TX-5
Maloney—*locale* ... KY-4
Maloney, Lake—*reservoir* ... NE-7
Maloney Basin—*valley* ... MT-8
Maloney Brook—*stream* ... CT-1
Maloney Brook—*stream* ... NY-2
Maloney Canyon—*valley* ... CA-9
Maloney Cem—*cemetery* ... TX-5
Maloney Ch—*church* ... SC-3
Maloney Coulee—*valley* ... MT-8
Maloney Creek—*stream* ... ID-8
Maloney Creek—*stream* ... MI-6
Maloney Creek—*stream* ... SD-7
Maloney Creek—*stream* ... TX-5
Maloney Creek—*stream* ... WA-9
Maloney Ditch—*canal* ... IN-6
Maloney Farm Preserve—*park* ... IL-6
**Maloney Heights**—*pop pl* ... TN-4
Maloney Hill—*summit* ... MT-8
Maloney Hollow—*valley* ... MO-7
Maloney HS—*school* ... CT-1
Maloney Island—*island* ... NY-2
Maloney Lakes—*lake* ... WA-9
Maloney Mtn—*summit* ... WA-9
Maloney Park—*flat* ... MT-8
Maloney Park—*park* ... PA-2
Maloney Point—*summit* ... TN-4
Maloney Post Office (historical)—*building* ... TN-4
Maloney Ranch—*locale* ... MT-8
Maloney Ranch—*locale* ... NM-5
*Maloney Reservoir* ... NE-7
Maloney Ridge—*ridge* ... WA-9
Maloney Rsvr—*reservoir* ... CA-9
Maloney Sch—*school* ... CA-9
Maloney Sch—*school* ... NY-2
Maloney Sch—*school* ... SD-7
Maloney Sch (historical)—*school* ... TN-4
Maloney Siding—*locale* ... VA-3
Maloneys Landing—*locale* ... DE-2
Maloney Spring—*spring* ... MT-8
Maloney Trail Number 5—*trail* ... MT-8
**Maloneyville**—*pop pl* ... TN-4
*Maloneyville Station* ... TN-4
Malon Swamp—*swamp* ... PA-2
Malony Branch—*stream* ... IA-7
Malony (historical)—*locale* ... AZ-5
Malony Lake—*lake* ... ID-8
Malony Lake—*lake* ... MI-6
Malo Point—*cape* ... AS-9
**Malore Gardens (subdivision)**—*pop pl* ... FL-3
Malory Hollow—*valley* ... VA-3
Malosky Creek—*stream* ... CA-9
Malo Suerte Tank—*reservoir* ... TX-5
Malotel—*island* ... FM-9
**Malott**—*pop pl* ... WA-9
Malott—*uninc pl* ... CA-9
*Malott Park* ... IN-6
Malo Vega Creek—*stream* ... CO-8
*Malowai* ... FM-9
Maloy—*locale* ... CO-8
**Maloy**—*pop pl* ... IA-7
Maloy, Lake—*lake* ... MI-6
Maloya, Lake—*reservoir* ... CO-8
Maloya, Lake—*reservoir* ... NM-5
Maloy Bayou—*gut* ... AR-4
Maloy Bayou—*stream* ... AR-4
Maloy Brook—*stream* ... MA-1
Maloy Lake—*lake* ... AR-4
Maloy Mine—*mine* ... NV-8
Maloy Mtn—*summit* ... ME-1
Maloy Park—*area* ... UT-8
Malpais—*locale* ... NM-5
Malpais—*summit* ... NV-8
Malpais, The—*area* (3) ... NM-5
Malpais Arroyo—*stream* ... NM-5
Malpais Camp—*locale* ... NM-5
Malpais Canyon—*valley* ... AZ-5
Malpais Cliffs—*cliff* ... AZ-5
Malpais Creek—*stream* ... CA-9
Malpais Flattop Mesa—*summit* ... AZ-5
Malpais Hill—*summit* (4) ... AZ-5
Malpais Hill—*summit* ... NM-5
*Malpais Hills* ... AZ-5
Malpais Hills—*other* ... NM-5
Malpais Hills—*summit* ... AZ-5
Malpais Mesa—*summit* (2) ... AZ-5
Malpais Mesa—*summit* ... CA-9
Malpais Mesa—*summit* ... NV-8
*Malpais Mtn* ... AZ-5
Malpais Mtn—*summit* ... AZ-5
Malpais Spring—*spring* (4) ... AZ-5
Malpais Spring—*spring* (3) ... NM-5
Malpais Springs—*spring* ... CA-9
Malpais Tank—*reservoir* (6) ... AZ-5
Malpais Tank—*reservoir* (2) ... NM-5
Malpais Well—*well* ... NM-5
Malpais Windmill—*locale* (2) ... NM-5
Mal Paso (Barrio)—*fmr MCD* ... PR-3
Malpaso Creek—*stream* ... CA-9
Mal Pass—*gap* ... CA-9
Malpass Cem—*cemetery* (2) ... NC-3
Malpass Corner—*locale* ... NC-3
**Malpica**—*pop pl* ... PR-3
Malpie Lake—*lake* ... NM-5
Malpie Mtn—*summit* ... NM-5
*Malpus Brook* ... MA-1
Malsonic Cem—*cemetery* ... CA-9
M Alspach Dam—*dam* ... SD-7
Malstead Breaker (historical)—*building* ... PA-2
Malstrom Ranch—*locale* ... NM-5
**Malsu**—*pop pl* ... FM-9
Malsu, Foko—*reef* ... FM-9
Malta—*locale* ... CO-8
Malta—*locale* ... SC-3
**Malta**—*pop pl* ... AL-4
**Malta**—*pop pl* ... ID-8
**Malta**—*pop pl* ... IL-6
**Malta**—*pop pl* ... IA-7
**Malta**—*pop pl* ... MI-6
**Malta**—*pop pl* ... MT-8
**Malta**—*pop pl* ... NY-2
**Malta**—*pop pl* ... OH-6
**Malta**—*pop pl* ... PA-2
**Malta**—*pop pl* ... TX-5
**Malta Bend**—*pop pl* ... MO-7
Malta Bend Cem—*cemetery* ... MO-7
Malta Cem—*cemetery* ... ID-8
Malta Cem—*cemetery* ... IL-6
Malta Cem—*cemetery* ... OH-6
Malta HS—*school* ... IL-6
Maltanner Creek—*stream* ... NY-2
*Malta Range* ... ID-8
**Malta Ridge**—*pop pl* ... NY-2
Malta Ridge—*ridge* ... NY-2
Malta Station (historical P.O.)—*locale* ... IN-6
Malta Substation—*locale* ... CO-8
**Malta (Town of)**—*pop pl* ... NY-2
**Malta (Township of)**—*pop pl* ... IL-6
**Malta (Township of)**—*pop pl* ... MN-6
**Malta (Township of)**—*pop pl* ... OH-6
**Maltaville**—*pop pl* ... NY-2
Maltazan Tank—*reservoir* ... AZ-5
Maltbie, Lake—*lake* ... FL-3
**Maltbie Heights**—*pop pl* ... NY-2
Maltby—*locale* ... CA-9
Maltby—*locale* ... KS-7
Maltby—*locale* ... NC-3
**Maltby**—*pop pl* ... WA-9
Maltby—*uninc pl* ... PA-2
Maltby, Henry, House—*hist pl* ... OH-6
Maltby (CCD)—*cens area* ... WA-9
Maltby Cem—*cemetery* ... NY-2
Maltby Colliery Station—*locale* ... PA-2
Maltby Creek—*stream* ... OR-9
Maltby Hollow Brook—*stream* ... NY-2
Maltby Lake—*lake* ... CA-9
Maltby Lake—*lake* ... CT-1
Maltby Lake—*lake* ... MI-6
Maltby Mine—*mine* ... CA-9
Maltbys Mound—*summit* ... MT-8
Maltbys Swamp—*swamp* ... MI-6
Maltby Station—*locale* ... PA-2
**Maltby Township**—*pop pl* ... SD-7
Malterna Creek—*stream* ... NY-2
**Maltersville**—*pop pl* ... IN-6
Maltese Cross Ranch—*locale* ... ND-7
Maltha—*locale* ... CA-9
*Malthey* ... NC-3
*Malt House Brook* ... CT-1
Malt House Brook—*stream* ... CT-1
Malton Field—*other* ... CA-9
Maltrud Lake—*lake* ... MN-6
**Maltsberger (historical)**—*pop pl* ... TN-4
Maltsberger Post Office
(historical)—*building* ... TN-4
Malt Well—*well* ... NM-5
Malty Branch—*stream* ... TN-4
Maluaka—*cape* ... HI-9
Maluaka—*civil* ... HI-9
*Maluaka Point* ... HI-9
*Malualae* ... HI-9
*Malualai* ... HI-9
Maluapopoki Stream—*stream* ... HI-9
Maluatia Hill—*summit* ... AS-9
Malugin Cem—*cemetery* (2) ... TN-4
Malugin Hollow—*valley* (3) ... TN-4
Maluhia Camp—*locale* ... HI-9
**Maluhia Camp**—*pop pl* ... HI-9
Maluhianaiwi Gulch—*valley* ... HI-9
Maluikeao—*area* ... HI-9
Malum Ridge—*ridge* ... CA-9
Malung—*locale* ... MN-6
Malung Cem—*cemetery* ... MN-6
Malung Hall—*building* ... MN-6
**Malung (Township of)**—*pop pl* ... MN-6
Malvado—*locale* ... TX-5
Malva Drain—*canal* ... CA-9
Malva Drain One—*canal* ... CA-9
Malva Drain Two—*canal* ... CA-9
Malva Lateral—*canal* ... CA-9
Malva Lateral One—*canal* ... CA-9
Malva Lateral Two—*canal* ... CA-9
Malva Real Anchorage—*bay* ... CA-9
Malvern—*locale* ... TX-5
Malvern—*locale* ... WI-6
**Malvern**—*pop pl* ... AL-4
**Malvern**—*pop pl* ... AR-4
**Malvern**—*pop pl* ... GA-3
**Malvern**—*pop pl* ... IL-6
**Malvern**—*pop pl* ... IA-7
**Malvern**—*pop pl* ... MD-2
**Malvern**—*pop pl* ... OH-6
**Malvern**—*pop pl* ... PA-2
**Malvern**—*pop pl* ... TX-5
Malvern, Lake—*reservoir* ... TN-4
Malvern Borough—*civil* ... PA-2
Malvern Cem—*cemetery* ... IA-7
Malvern Country Club—*other* ... AR-4
Malvern Dam—*dam* ... TN-4
**Malverne**—*pop pl* ... NY-2
**Malvern & Freeo Valley
Junction**—*pop pl* ... AR-4
Malvern Hall—*hist pl* ... PA-2
Malvern Hill—*hist pl* ... VA-3
Malvern Hill—*summit* ... VA-3
Malvern Hill Battlefield—*locale* ... VA-3
Malvern Hill Sch—*school* ... SC-3
Malvern Hills Park—*park* ... NC-3
**Malvern Hills (subdivision)**—*pop pl* ... NC-3
Malvern Institute—*building* ... PA-2
Malvern Preparatory Sch—*school* ... PA-2
Malvern Road Sch—*hist pl* ... MA-1
Malvern Sch—*school* ... AL-4
Malvern Sch—*school* ... OH-6
**Malvic Manor**—*pop pl* ... NY-2
Malvik Ch—*church* ... MN-6
Malville Cem—*cemetery* ... OK-5
*Malvin* ... AL-4
Malvina—*locale* ... MS-4
Malviney Creek—*stream* ... WI-6
Malvin Hill—*summit* ... KY-4
Malvin Hill Ch—*church* ... KY-4
*Malway* ... FM-9
M A Lynch Dam—*dam* ... SD-7
M. A. Lynch Sch—*school* ... OR-9
Malzon Bay—*bay* ... WI-6
*Mama* ... AL-4
Mamaalawe Point—*cape* ... HI-9
Mama Bear Lake—*lake* ... AK-9
*Mamacock Creek* ... CT-1
Mamacoke Cove—*bay* ... CT-1
Mamacoke Hill—*summit* ... CT-1
*Mamacuck Creek* ... CT-1
Mamaewa Gulch—*valley* ... HI-9
Mam-A-Gah Picnic Area—*locale* ... AZ-5
*Mama Gaylord Creek* ... MT-8
Mamagnak Mountains—*other* ... AK-9
*Mamaiahoa* ... HI-9
Mamajuda Island Shoal—*bar* ... MI-6
*Mamakating Hollow* ... NY-2
**Mamakating Park**—*pop pl* ... NY-2
**Mamakating (Town of)**—*pop pl* ... NY-2
Mamaki—*area* ... HI-9
Mamala Bay—*bay* ... HI-9
Mamalahoa—*summit* ... HI-9
Mamalahoa Trail—*trail* ... HI-9
*Mamaloa* ... HI-9
*Mamaloa Point* ... HI-9
*Mamaloose Island* ... ID-8
*Mamaloos Island* ... ID-8
*Mamalose Island* ... ID-8
*Mamalos Island* ... ID-8
*Mamalos Island* ... OR-9
*Mamalos Lake* ... OR-9
Mamalu, Pali o—*cliff* ... HI-9
Mamalu Bay—*bay* ... HI-9
*Mamalu Pali* ... HI-9
Mamanasco Lake—*lake* ... CT-1
Mamaon Channel—*channel* ... GU-9
**Mamaroneck**—*pop pl* ... NY-2
Mamaroneck Ave Sch—*school* ... NY-2
Mamaroneck Harbor—*bay* ... NY-2
Mamaroneck River—*stream* ... NY-2
Mamaroneck Rsvr—*reservoir* ... NY-2
**Mamaroneck (Town of)**—*pop pl* ... NY-2
Mamatgun Point—*summit* ... GU-9
*Mamatotk Mountains* ... AZ-5
*Mamatotk Peak* ... AZ-5
Mama Windmill—*locale* ... TX-5
Mambiche (Barrio)—*fmr MCD* ... PR-3
Mambrino—*locale* ... TX-5
Mamby Sch—*school* ... MI-6
*Mamcoc River* ... CT-1
*Mam Creek* ... CO-8
Mamelak Creek—*stream* ... AK-9
Mamelak Mtn—*summit* ... AK-9
Mamelles, Les—*range* ... MO-7
*Mameloose Island* ... ID-8
Mameluke Hill—*summit* ... CA-9
**Mamers**—*pop pl* ... NC-3
Mames, Bo'bo'—*spring* ... MH-9
Mames, Saddock—*stream* ... MH-9
*Mameweta Pons* ... NY-2
**Mameyal**—*pop pl* ... PR-3
Mameyal (Barrio)—*fmr MCD* ... PR-3
Mamey (Barrio)—*fmr MCD* (5) ... PR-3
Mameyes Abajo (Barrio)—*fmr MCD* ... PR-3
Mameyes Arriba (Barrio)—*fmr MCD* ... PR-3
Mameyes I (Barrio)—*fmr MCD* ... PR-3
Mameyes II (Barrio)—*fmr MCD* ... PR-3
**Mameyes (Palmer PO)**—*pop pl* ... PR-3
Mamey Peak—*summit* ... VI-3
**Mamie**—*pop pl* ... AL-4
**Mamie**—*pop pl* ... NC-3
Mamie, Lake—*lake* ... CA-9
Mamie, Lake—*lake* ... FL-3
Mamie Agnes Jones Elem Sch—*school* ... FL-3
Mamie Bayou—*stream* ... TX-5
Mamie Canyon—*valley* ... NM-5
*Mamie Creek* ... AZ-5
*Mamie Creek* ... UT-8
Mamie Creek—*stream* ... AZ-5
Mamie Creek—*stream* ... IA-7
Mamie Creek—*stream* (2) ... MT-8
Mamie Creek—*stream* ... UT-8
Mamie D Eisenhower Park—*park* ... CO-8
Mamie Lake—*lake* ... WI-6
*Mamie L Martin Elementary School* ... MS-4
Mamie Mine—*mine* ... AK-9
Mamie Pass—*gap* ... WA-9
MAMIE S. BARRETT (towboat)—*hist pl* ... KY-4
Mamies Chapel—*church* ... AL-4
Mamies Garden—*woods* ... UT-8
Mamirelund Cem—*cemetery* ... IA-7
Mamma, Mount—*summit* ... CO-8
Mammal Cem—*cemetery* ... OH-6
*Mammal Lake* ... MN-6
*Mammas Creek* ... TN-4
Mam-Maw Lake—*lake* ... WV-2
*Mamm Creek* ... CO-8
Mamm Creek—*stream* ... CO-8
**Mammen**—*pop pl* ... IA-7
Mammenga State Wildlife Mngmt
Area—*park* ... MN-6
Mammen Gulch—*valley* ... ID-8
Mammings Sch (historical)—*school* ... NC-3
Mammon Mine—*mine* ... AZ-5
Mammoth—*locale* ... CA-9
**Mammoth**—*pop pl* ... AZ-5
**Mammoth**—*pop pl* ... FL-3
**Mammoth**—*pop pl* ... MO-7
**Mammoth**—*pop pl* ... MT-8
**Mammoth**—*pop pl* ... PA-2
**Mammoth**—*pop pl* ... UT-8
**Mammoth**—*pop pl* ... WV-2
**Mammoth**—*pop pl* ... WY-8
Mammoth Bar—*bar* ... CA-9
Mammoth Bayou—*stream* ... MS-4
Mammoth Bridge—*other* ... MO-7
Mammoth Butte—*summit* ... CA-9
*Mammoth Camp* ... AZ-5
Mammoth Canal—*canal* (2) ... UT-8
Mammoth Canyon—*valley* (2) ... ID-8
Mammoth Canyon—*valley* ... UT-8
Mammoth Cave—*cave* ... CA-9
Mammoth Cave—*cave* ... IL-6
Mammoth Cave—*cave* ... KY-4
Mammoth Cave—*cave* ... MO-7
Mammoth Cave—*cave* ... UT-8
Mammoth Cave—*locale* ... KY-4
Mammoth Cave Ch—*church* ... KY-4
Mammoth Cave Natl Park—*park* ... KY-4
Mammoth Cave Ridge—*ridge* ... KY-4
Mammoth Cave Sch—*school* ... KS-7
Mammoth Cem—*cemetery* ... MO-7
Mammoth Ch—*church* ... OK-5
Mammoth Ch—*church* ... WV-2
Mammoth Consolidated Mine—*mine* ... CA-9
Mammoth Copper Corporation
Hosp—*hospital* ... AZ-5
Mammoth County Park—*park* ... PA-2
Mammoth Crater—*crater* ... CA-9
Mammoth Creek—*stream* (2) ... AK-9
Mammoth Creek—*stream* ... CA-9
Mammoth Creek—*stream* ... ID-8
Mammoth Creek—*stream* (2) ... MO-7
Mammoth Creek—*stream* ... MT-8
Mammoth Creek—*stream* ... OK-5
Mammoth Creek—*stream* ... TX-5
Mammoth Creek—*stream* ... UT-8
Mammoth Creek Ridge—*ridge* ... MT-8
Mammoth Creek Rsvr—*reservoir* ... CO-8
Mammoth Crest—*ridge* ... CA-9
Mammoth Ditch—*canal* ... MT-8
Mammoth Ditch—*canal* ... WY-8
Mammoth Dome Sink—*basin* ... KY-4
Mammoth Elem Sch—*school* ... AZ-5
Mammoth Eureka Mines—*mine* ... CA-9
Mammoth Fork Ditch—*canal* ... MT-8
Mammoth Furnace Bay—*bay* ... KY-4
*Mammoth Furnace Creek* ... KY-4
Mammoth Furnace Creek—*stream* ... KY-4
Mammoth Glacier—*glacier* ... WY-8
Mammoth Gulch—*valley* ... CO-8
Mammoth Gulch—*valley* ... ID-8
Mammoth Gulch—*valley* ... MT-8
Mammoth Gulch—*valley* ... UT-8
Mammoth Hill—*summit* ... CO-8
Mammoth Hist Dist—*hist pl* ... UT-8
Mammoth Hollow—*flat* ... WY-8
Mammoth Hot Springs—*obs name* ... WY-8
Mammoth Hot Springs—*spring* ... WY-8
Mammoth Incline—*bend* ... AZ-5
Mammoth Junction—*locale* ... UT-8
Mammoth Lake—*lake* ... CA-9
Mammoth Lake—*reservoir* ... PA-2
Mammoth Lake Dam—*dam* ... PA-2
Mammoth Lakes—*lake* ... CA-9
**Mammoth Lakes**—*pop pl* ... CA-9
Mammoth Lode Mine—*mine* ... OR-9
Mammoth Lode Mine—*mine* ... UT-8
Mammoth Mart Shop Ctr—*locale* ... MA-1
Mammoth Mart (Shop Ctr)—*locale* ... NC-3
Mammoth Mill (Ruins)—*locale* ... CA-9
Mammoth Mine—*mine* (3) ... AZ-5
Mammoth Mine—*mine* (5) ... CA-9
Mammoth Mine—*mine* (2) ... CO-8
Mammoth Mine—*mine* (2) ... ID-8
Mammoth Mine—*mine* ... MT-8
Mammoth Mine—*mine* (2) ... NV-8
Mammoth Mine—*mine* ... OR-9
Mammoth Mine—*mine* ... UT-8
Mammoth Mine (underground)—*mine* ... AL-4
Mammoth Mountain Ski Lodge—*locale* ... CA-9
Mammoth Mtn—*summit* ... CA-9
Mammoth Mtn—*summit* (2) ... CO-8
Mammoth Mtn—*summit* ... ID-8
**Mammoth Oak**—*pop pl* ... VA-3
Mammoth Onyx Cave—*cave* ... KY-4
Mammoth Pass—*gap* ... CA-9
Mammoth Peak—*summit* ... CA-9
Mammoth Peak—*summit* ... UT-8
Mammoth Pool Dam—*dam* ... CA-9
Mammoth Pool Rsvr—*reservoir* ... CA-9
Mammoth Ranger Station—*locale* ... CA-9
Mammoth Ranger Station—*locale* ... UT-8
Mammoth Revenue Mine—*mine* ... CO-8
Mammoth Ridge—*ridge* ... UT-8
Mammoth Rock—*pillar* ... CA-9
Mammoth Rock Sch—*school* ... CA-9
Mammoth RR Station (historical)—*locale* ... FL-3
Mammoth Sch—*school* ... CA-9
Mammoth Sch—*school* ... MO-7
Mammoth Shaft—*mine* ... UT-8
Mammoth (Site)—*locale* ... ID-8
Mammoth Softball Field Park—*park* ... AZ-5
Mammoth Spar Mine—*mine* ... AZ-5
**Mammoth Spring**—*pop pl* ... AR-4
Mammoth Spring—*spring* ... AR-4
Mammoth Spring—*spring* ... CA-9
Mammoth Spring—*spring* (2) ... OR-9
Mammoth Spring—*spring* (2) ... PA-2
Mammoth Spring—*spring* ... UT-8
Mammoth Spring—*spring* ... WI-6
Mammoth Spring Mine—*mine* ... CA-9
Mammoth Springs—*spring* ... CA-9
Mammoth Springs—*spring* ... MS-4
Mammoth Springs—*spring* ... NV-8
Mammoth Springs Campground—*park* ... UT-8
Mammoth Spring (Township
of)—*fmr MCD* ... AR-4
Mammoth Summit—*summit* ... UT-8
Mammoth Swimming Pool—*other* ... AZ-5
Mammoth Tunnel—*tunnel* ... CA-9
Mammoth Tusk Spring—*spring* ... WA-9
Mammoth Valley View Cem—*cemetery* ... AZ-5
Mammoth Wash—*stream* (3) ... AZ-5
Mammoth Wash—*stream* ... CA-9
*Mammouth Bayou* ... MS-4
Mammouth Ch—*church* ... AL-4
Mammouth Ditch—*canal* ... CO-8
Mammouth Gulch—*valley* ... CO-8
*Mammouth Mountain* ... ID-8
Mammouth Spring—*spring* ... OR-9
Mammouth Springs Campground—*locale* ... ID-8
*Mammouth Wash* ... CA-9
Mammua Caves—*cave* ... PA-2
*Mammy* ... TN-4
Mammy Cem—*cemetery* ... TN-4
*Mammy Creek* ... TN-4
Mammy Hi Run—*stream* ... PA-2
Mammy Judy Bayou—*stream* ... MS-4
*Mammy Morgans Hill* ... PA-2
Mammy Pond—*lake* ... TN-4
*Mammy Post Office* ... TN-4
Mammys Creek—*stream* ... TN-4
Mamnie Windmill—*locale* ... CO-8
*Mamo* ... HI-9
Mamo, Lae—*cape* ... HI-9
Mamochonap—*bar* ... FM-9
Mamoits Spring—*spring* ... UT-8
*Mamolokama* ... HI-9
*Mamolokama Peak* ... HI-9
**Mamont**—*pop pl* ... PA-2
Mamont Sch—*school* ... PA-2
*Mamotamu Island* ... MP-9
*Mamotamu-To* ... MP-9
**Mamou**—*pop pl* ... LA-4
Mamou Canal—*canal* (2) ... LA-4
Mamou Oil Field—*oilfield* ... LA-4
Mamouth Mine—*mine* ... NV-8
Mamre Baptist Ch—*church* ... AL-4
Mamre Cem—*cemetery* ... IA-7
Mamre Cem—*cemetery* ... MN-6
Mamre Cem—*cemetery* ... WI-6
Mamre Ch—*church* ... NE-7
Mamre Ch—*church* ... ND-7
Mamre Ch—*church* ... OH-6
Mamre Ch—*church* ... WI-6
Mamre Lake—*lake* ... MN-6
Mamre Lund Ch—*church* ... MN-6
Mamrelund Ch—*church* ... MN-6
**Mamre (Township of)**—*pop pl* ... MN-6
Mamsella Bayou—*stream* ... LA-4
Mams Slough—*stream* ... MO-7
*Mamtotk Peak* ... AZ-5
Mamtotk Peak—*summit* ... AZ-5
*Mamwhauge Swamp* ... MA-1
**Man**—*pop pl* ... WV-2
*Mana* ... HI-9
*Mana* ... PA-2
Mana—*locale* ... HI-9
**Mana**—*pop pl* ... HI-9
Mana, Moku—*island* ... HI-9
*Manaa Point* ... HI-9
Mana (Barrio)—*fmr MCD* ... PR-3
Mana Bay—*bay* ... GU-9
Manabezho Falls—*falls* ... MI-6
**Manaca**—*pop pl* ... GU-9
*Manacassee Creek* ... PA-2
*Manachagu* ... MH-9
*Manachles Creek* ... IN-6
**Manack**—*pop pl* ... AL-4
Manack Bar—*bar* ... AL-4
Manacke Creek—*stream* ... WI-6
*Manacks* ... AL-4
*Manacks Creek* ... AL-4
Manacks Island (historical)—*island* ... AL-4
Manacle Creek—*stream* ... MO-7
*Manacock Creek* ... CT-1
Manada Creek—*stream* ... PA-2
Manada Flat—*flat* ... ID-8
Manada Furnace Ch—*church* ... PA-2
Manada Gap—*gap* ... PA-2
Manada Gap—*locale* ... PA-2
Manada Golf Course—*locale* ... PA-2
Manadahill—*locale* ... PA-2
Manadalay Sch—*school* ... NY-2
Manadier—*locale* ... MD-2
**Mana Estates (subdivision)**—*pop pl* ... TN-4
*Manaffey Lake* ... CO-8
*Managachsink Creek* ... PA-2
Managaha, Isleta—*island* ... MH-9
Managaha Island Historic
District—*hist pl* ... MH-9
*Managaja* ... MH-9
Managam—*area* ... GU-9
*Managasa Island* ... MH-9
*Managassa* ... MH-9
*Managassi Creek* ... PA-2
*Manahan Creek* ... WA-9
Manahan Creek—*stream* ... TX-5
Manahath Cem—*cemetery* ... NJ-2
*Manahawken Lake* ... NJ-2
Manahawkin—*airport* ... NJ-2
**Manahawkin**—*pop pl* ... NJ-2
Manahawkin Baptist Church—*hist pl* ... NJ-2
Manahawkin Bay—*bay* ... NJ-2
Manahawkin Creek—*stream* ... NJ-2
Manahawkin Fish and Wildlife Mngmt
Area—*park* ... NJ-2
Manahawkin Lake—*reservoir* ... NJ-2
Manahawkin Lake Dam—*dam* ... NJ-2
**Manahawkin Terrace**—*pop pl* ... NJ-2
Mana Heiau—*locale* ... HI-9
Manahoa Rock—*pillar* ... HI-9
*Manahocking* ... NJ-2
*Manaho Creek* ... MD-2
Manahowic Creek—*stream* ... MD-2
Manahuilla Creek—*stream* ... TX-5
Manaige Spring—*spring* ... MT-8
Manaiki Stream—*stream* ... HI-9
*Manainam Ditch* ... HI-9
**Manaio**—*pop pl* ... FM-9
Manakaa Point—*cape* ... HI-9
Manakacha Point—*cliff* ... AZ-5
*Manakasie Creek* ... PA-2
*Manakasy Creek* ... PA-2
Manake Lake—*lake* ... MI-6
Manakiki, Lake—*reservoir* ... WI-6
Manakiki Country Club—*locale* ... OH-6
Manakiki Falls—*falls* ... MI-6
**Manakin**—*pop pl* (2) ... VA-3
Manakin Ch—*church* ... VA-3
**Manakin Farms**—*pop pl* ... VA-3
*Manakin Sabot* ... VA-3
**Manakin-Sabot**—*pop pl* ... VA-3
*Manakintown* ... VA-3
*Manakisy Hill* ... PA-2
**Manalapan**—*pop pl* ... FL-3
**Manalapan**—*pop pl* ... NJ-2
Manalapan, Lake—*reservoir* ... NJ-2
Manalapan Brook—*stream* ... NJ-2
*Manalapan Creek* ... NJ-2
Manalapan Lake Dam—*dam* ... NJ-2
**Manalapan (Township of)**—*pop pl* ... NJ-2
*Manalapan Village* ... NJ-2
Manalo Gulch—*valley* ... HI-9
*Manamanack Pond* ... NH-1
*Manamet Point* ... MA-1
*Manamoit* ... MA-1
*Manamoyik* ... MA-1
Manana—*civil* ... HI-9
Manana Grande—*uninc pl* ... AZ-5
*Manana Gulch* ... HI-9
Manana Island—*island* ... ME-1
Manana Island (State Bird
Refuge)—*island* ... HI-9
Mananana—*slope* ... MH-9
Manana Stream—*stream* ... HI-9
Man And Boy Buttes—*summit* ... WY-8
Man and Boy Channel—*channel* ... VA-3
Man and Boy Marsh—*swamp* ... VA-3
*Mananiet* ... MA-1
**Manannah**—*pop pl* ... MN-6
Manannah Cem—*cemetery* ... MN-6
**Manannah (Township of)**—*pop pl* ... MN-6
Mananole Stream—*stream* ... HI-9
*Manans Creek* ... MO-7
*Manantico* ... NJ-2
*Manantico Lake* ... NJ-2
*Manao* ... MH-9
*Manapailon* ... FM-9
Manapaqua Branch—*stream* ... NJ-2
*Mana Point* ... HI-9
Mana Point—*cape* ... HI-9
Man Apu Hill—*summit* ... GU-9
Manara—*locale* ... OH-6
**Manard**—*pop pl* ... OK-5
Manard, Bayou—*stream* ... OK-5
*Manard Bay* ... LA-4
Manard Cem—*cemetery* ... ID-8
Manard Sch—*school* ... ID-8
*Manard Slough* ... SD-7
*Mana Ridge* ... HI-9
Mana Ridge—*ridge* ... HI-9
Mana Rsvr—*reservoir* ... HI-9
Manary Creek—*stream* ... MI-6
Manasco Branch—*stream* ... MS-4
Manasco Cem—*cemetery* ... AL-4
Manasco Post Office (historical)—*building* ... AL-4
Mana Shaft—*reservoir* ... HI-9
*Manashoak* ... ME-1
**Manasota**—*pop pl* ... FL-3
**Manasota Beach**—*pop pl* ... FL-3
Manasota Bridge—*bridge* ... FL-3
*Manasota Fire Control HQ* ... FL-3
Manasota Key—*CDP* ... FL-3
Manasota Key—*island* ... FL-3
*Manasota Peninsula* ... FL-3
**Manasquan**—*pop pl* ... NJ-2
Manasquan Fish and Wildlife Mngmt
Area—*park* ... NJ-2
Manasquan Inlet—*channel* ... NJ-2
**Manasquan Park**—*pop pl* ... NJ-2
Manasquan River—*stream* ... NJ-2
Manasquan River Golf Club—*other* ... NJ-2
Manasquan Sch—*school* ... NY-2
**Manasquan Shores**—*pop pl* ... NJ-2
**Manassa**—*pop pl* ... CO-8
Manassa Ch—*church* ... PA-2
Manassa Ditch—*canal* ... CO-8
Manassa Eastfield Ditch—*canal* ... CO-8
**Manassas**—*pop pl* ... GA-3

**Manassas**—*pop pl* VA-3
Manassas, Lake—*reservoir* VA-3
Manassas Ch—*church* NC-3
Manassa Sch (abandoned)—*school* PA-2
Manassas Gap—*gap* PA-2
Manassas Gap—*gap* VA-3
Manassas Gap Shelter—*locale* VA-3
Manassas Guth Covered Bridge—*bridge* PA-2
Manassas Hills Country Club—*other* VA-3
Manassas Hist Dist—*hist pl* VA-3
Manassas HS—*school* TN-4
**Manassas (ind. city)**—*pop pl* VA-3
Manassas Natl Battlefield Park—*park* (2) VA-3
**Manassas Park (ind. city)**—*pop pl* VA-3
Manassas Run—*stream* VA-3
Manassas Sch (historical)—*school* PA-2
Manasseh Cutler Hall, Ohio Univ—*hist pl* OH-6
Manasse Mansion—*hist pl* LA-9
Manasses Guth Covered Bridge—*hist pl* PA-2
Manastash (CCD)—*cens area* WA-9
Manastash Cow Camp—*locale* WA-9
Manastash Creek—*stream* WA-9
Manastash Lake—*lake* WA-9
Manastash Ridge—*ridge* WA-9
Manastash Ridge Trail—*trail* WA-9
Manataba Park—*park* AZ-5
*Manatacat River* MA-1
Manataka Lake—*lake* PA-2
*Manatauk Point* NY-2
**Manatawna**—*pop pl* PA-2
**Manatawny**—*pop pl* PA-2
Manatawny Creek—*stream* PA-2
Manatawny Park—*park* PA-2
**Manatawny (Pleasantville)**—*pop pl* PA-2
Manatawny Station (historical)—*locale* PA-2
**Manatee**—*pop pl* FL-3
Manatee, Lake—*reservoir* FL-3
Manatee Agricultural Center (Fairgrounds)—*locale* FL-3
Manatee Area Vocational and Technical Center—*school* FL-3
Manatee Baptist Ch—*church* FL-3
Manatee Bay—*bay* (2) FL-3
**Manatee County**—*pop pl* FL-3
Manatee County Beach—*beach* FL-3
Manatee County Beach—*locale* FL-3
Manatee County Courthouse—*hist pl* FL-3
Manatee County Shop Ctr—*locale* FL-3
Manatee Creek—*gut* FL-3
Manatee Creek—*stream* FL-3
Manatee (historical)—*locale* FL-3
Manatee HS—*school* FL-3
Manatee Junior Coll—*school* FL-3
Manatee Keys—*island* FL-3
Manatee Memorial Cem—*cemetery* FL-3
Manatee Memorial Cemetary—*cemetary* FL-3
Manatee Memorial Hosp—*hospital* FL-3
Manatee Pass—*channel* FL-3
Manatee Plaza (Shop Ctr)—*locale* FL-3
Manatee Pocket—*lake* FL-3
Manatee Point—*cape* FL-3
Manatee River—*stream* FL-3
Manatee Southern Baptist Ch—*church* FL-3
Manatee Springs—*spring* FL-3
Manatee Springs State Park—*park* FL-3
**Manatheka (historical)**—*pop pl* IA-7
Manati—*CDP* PR-3
**Manati**—*pop pl* PR-3
*Manatick Mountain* CT-1
*Manatico Creek* NJ-2
*Manaticut River* MA-1
Manati (Municipio)—*civil* PR-3
Manati (Pueblo)—*fmr MCD* PR-3
*Manatiquot River* MA-1
*Manatook Lake* CT-1
*Manatoquot River* MA-1
Manatua Cem—*cemetery* AL-4
*Manatuck Mountain* CT-1
*Manatuck Springs* CT-1
Manaugh Sch—*school* CO-8
Manaugh Spring—*spring* CO-8
Manautou House—*hist pl* TX-5
**Manavista (subdivision)**—*pop pl* FL-3
*Manawa* IA-7
*Mana'wa* WI-6
**Manawa**—*pop pl* WI-6
Manawa, Lake—*lake* IA-7
Manawa Bend—*bend* IA-7
Manawa Bend—*bend* NE-7
*Manawahua* HI-9
*Manawahua Peak* HI-9
Manawai—*cape* HI-9
Manawai—*civil* HI-9
Manawai Gulch—*valley* (2) HI-9
*Manawaiiao* HI-9
Manawaiiao Gulch—*valley* HI-9
Manawaikeae Gulch—*valley* HI-9
Manawainui—*cape* HI-9
Manawainui—*civil* (2) HI-9
Manawainui Gulch—*valley* (3) HI-9
Manawainui Stream—*stream* HI-9
Manawainui Valley—*basin* HI-9
Manawaiopuna Falls—*falls* HI-9
Manawaipueo Gulch—*valley* HI-9
*Manawaki* WI-6
*Manawau* WI-6
Manayagavik Slough—*stream* AK-9
**Manayunk**—*pop pl* PA-2
Manayunk Main Street Hist Dist—*hist pl* PA-2
Manaza Hill Ch—*church* VA-3
*Manazana* AZ-5
Manbeck Cem—*cemetery* PA-2
Manbeck Ch—*church* PA-2
*Manbee Creek* OK-5
*Manbee Creek* TX-5
Manbess Ch—*church* SC-3
Manbone Branch—*stream* GA-3
Manbone Branch—*stream* KY-4
Manbone Cave—*cave* AL-4
Manbone Creek—*stream* AL-4
Manbone Creek—*stream* TN-4
Manbone Island—*island* MD-2
Manbone Ridge—*ridge* AL-4
Manbone Ridge—*ridge* TN-4
Manbur—*locale* VA-3
Manbury Mtn—*summit* NY-2
Manby Hot Springs—*spring* NM-5
Manby Lake—*lake* CO-8
Manby Stream—*stream* AK-9
Mance—*locale* PA-2

**Mancelona**—*pop pl* MI-6
**Mancelona (Township of)**—*pop pl* MI-6
**Manchac**—*pop pl* LA-4
Manchac, Bayou—*stream* LA-4
Manchaca—*locale* TX-5
Manchac Point—*cape* LA-4
Mancha Creek—*stream* AK-9
Manchac (RR name for Akers)—*other* LA-4
*Manchage* MA-1
**Manchaug**—*pop pl* MA-1
*Manchaugas* MA-1
*Manchauge* MA-1
*Manchaug Factory Village* MA-1
Manchaug Pond—*reservoir* MA-1
Manchaug Pond Dam—*dam* MA-1
*Manchaug Village* MA-1
Manchenil Bay—*bay* VI-3
Mancher Creek—*stream* AL-4
*Manchester* AL-4
*Manchester* IN-6
*Manchester* KS-7
*Manchester* MS-4
*Manchester* NJ-2
*Manchester* TN-4
*Manchester* VT-1
Manchester—*CDP* CT-1
Manchester—*fmr MCD* NE-7
Manchester—*locale* AL-4
Manchester—*locale* IA-7
Manchester—*locale* MT-8
**Manchester**—*pop pl* AL-4
**Manchester**—*pop pl* CA-9
**Manchester**—*pop pl* CT-1
**Manchester**—*pop pl* GA-3
**Manchester**—*pop pl* IL-6
**Manchester**—*pop pl* (2) IN-6
**Manchester**—*pop pl* IA-7
**Manchester**—*pop pl* KS-7
**Manchester**—*pop pl* KY-4
**Manchester**—*pop pl* LA-4
**Manchester**—*pop pl* ME-1
**Manchester**—*pop pl* MD-2
**Manchester**—*pop pl* MA-1
**Manchester**—*pop pl* MI-6
**Manchester**—*pop pl* MN-6
**Manchester**—*pop pl* MO-7
**Manchester**—*pop pl* NH-1
**Manchester**—*pop pl* NY-2
**Manchester**—*pop pl* NC-3
**Manchester**—*pop pl* (2) OH-6
**Manchester**—*pop pl* OK-5
**Manchester**—*pop pl* (2) PA-2
**Manchester**—*pop pl* SD-7
**Manchester**—*pop pl* TN-4
**Manchester**—*pop pl* (2) TX-5
**Manchester**—*pop pl* VT-1
**Manchester**—*pop pl* VA-3
**Manchester**—*pop pl* WA-9
**Manchester**—*pop pl* WI-6
Manchester, Isaac, House—*hist pl* PA-2
Manchester, Mount—*summit* CA-9
Manchester Airp (Grenier Industrial Airport)—*airport* NH-1
Manchester Apartments—*hist pl* MI-6
Manchester Ave Sch—*school* CA-9
Manchester Bay—*bay* MA-1
**Manchester Beach**—*pop pl* PA-2
Manchester Beach State Park—*park* CA-9
Manchester Borough—*civil* PA-2
Manchester Branch—*stream* KY-4
**Manchester Bridge**—*pop pl* NY-2
Manchester Brook—*stream* VT-1
Manchester (CCD)—*cens area* AL-4
Manchester (CCD)—*cens area* GA-3
Manchester (CCD)—*cens area* KY-4
Manchester (CCD)—*cens area* TN-4
Manchester (CCD)—*cens area* TX-5
Manchester Cem—*cemetery* AR-4
Manchester Cem—*cemetery* IN-6
Manchester Cem—*cemetery* (2) OH-6
Manchester Cem—*cemetery* TN-4
Manchester Center—*locale* NY-2
**Manchester Center**—*pop pl* VT-1
*Manchester Center Depot* VT-1
Manchester Ch—*church* AL-4
Manchester Ch—*church* AR-4
Manchester Ch—*church* IL-6
Manchester Ch—*church* OH-6
Manchester Ch—*church* PA-2
Manchester Channel—*channel* MA-1
Manchester City Hall—*building* IA-7
Manchester City Hall—*building* TN-4
Manchester City Hall—*hist pl* NH-1
Manchester Coll—*school* IN-6
Manchester Coll (historical)—*school* TN-4
Manchester Corners—*locale* NY-2
Manchester Cotton and Wool Manufacturing Co.—*hist pl* VA-3
Manchester Country Club—*other* CT-1
Manchester Country Club—*other* NH-1
Manchester Creek—*stream* CO-8
Manchester Creek—*stream* SC-3
Manchester Cumberland Presbyterian Ch—*church* TN-4
**Manchester Depot**—*pop pl* VT-1
Manchester Division—*civil* AL-4
Manchester Division—*civil* TN-4
Manchester (Election Precinct)—*fmr MCD* IL-6
Manchester Elem Sch—*school* PA-2
**Manchester Estates**—*pop pl* MD-2
Manchester First Freewill Baptist Ch—*church* TN-4
Manchester First Presbyterian Ch—*church* TN-4
Manchester First United Methodist Ch—*church* TN-4
Manchester Fish and Wildlife Mngmt Area—*park* NJ-2
*Manchester Furnace* NJ-2
Manchester Golf and Country Club—*locale* TN-4
**Manchester Green**—*pop pl* CT-1
Manchester Harbor—*cove* MA-1
Manchester Hill—*summit* TN-4
Manchester Hist Dist—*hist pl* PA-2
Manchester HS—*school* IN-6
Manchester HS—*school* MA-1
Manchester HS—*school* VA-3
Manchester Island No 1—*island* KY-4
Manchester Island No 2—*island* KY-4
Manchester JHS—*school* IN-6

Manchester JHS—*school* OH-6
*Manchester Lake* TN-4
Manchester Lake—*reservoir* CO-8
Manchester Landing (historical)—*locale* MS-4
Manchester Male and Female Coll (historical)—*school* TN-4
Manchester Methodist Episcopal Church—*hist pl* MO-7
Manchester Mine—*mine* CO-8
Manchester Mine (surface)—*mine* AL-4
Manchester Natl Fish Hatchery—*other* IA-7
Manchester Normal Sch (historical)—*school* TN-4
Manchester Park—*park* CA-9
**Manchester Park**—*pop pl* TN-4
*Manchester Point* ME-1
Manchester Point—*cape* ME-1
**Manchester (Point Arena) Rancheria**—*pop pl* CA-9
*Manchester Pond* MA-1
Manchester Pond—*reservoir* MA-1
Manchester Pond Dam—*dam* MA-1
Manchester Pond East Dike—*dam* MA-1
Manchester Pond Rsvr—*reservoir* MA-1
Manchester Post Office—*building* TN-4
Manchester Post Office (historical)—*building* AL-4
Manchester Post Office (historical)—*building* SD-7
Manchester Rancheria (Indian Reservation)—*reserve* CA-9
Manchester Run—*stream* VA-3
Manchester Sch—*school* (2) CA-9
Manchester Sch—*school* IL-6
Manchester Sch—*school* MI-6
Manchester Sch—*school* MO-7
Manchester Sch—*school* NJ-2
Manchester Sch—*school* VT-1
Manchester Sch—*school* VA-3
Manchester Sch (historical)—*school* TN-4
**Manchester School**—*pop pl* MO-7
Manchester Schoolhouse—*hist pl* CA-9
Manchester Schoolhouse (historical)—*school* PA-2
Manchester Shop Ctr—*locale* CA-9
Manchester Shop Ctr—*locale* TN-4
Manchester Speedway—*other* NH-1
Manchester Square—*park* MN-6
**Manchester (sta.) (Manchester Depot)**—*pop pl* VT-1
Manchester State For—*forest* SC-3
Manchester State Forest HQ—*locale* SC-3
*Manchester Station* KS-7
*Manchester Station* PA-2
Manchester Street Bridge—*hist pl* WI-6
**Manchester (subdivision)**—*pop pl* NC-3
**Manchester (Town of)**—*pop pl* ME-1
**Manchester (Town of)**—*pop pl* MA-1
**Manchester (Town of)**—*pop pl* NY-2
**Manchester (Town of)**—*pop pl* VT-1
**Manchester (Town of)**—*pop pl* (2) WI-6
**Manchester Township**—*pop pl* SD-7
Manchester (Township of)—*fmr MCD* AR-4
Manchester (Township of)—*fmr MCD* NC-3
**Manchester (Township of)**—*pop pl* IL-6
**Manchester (Township of)**—*pop pl* IN-6
**Manchester (Township of)**—*pop pl* MI-6
**Manchester (Township of)**—*pop pl* MN-6
**Manchester (Township of)**—*pop pl* NJ-2
**Manchester (Township of)**—*pop pl* (2) OH-6
**Manchester (Township of)**—*pop pl* (2) PA-2
Manchester United Pentacostal Ch—*church* TN-4
*Manchester Village* MA-1
Manchester Village Hist Dist—*hist pl* VT-1
*Manchinikan Island* MP-9
Manchinikon Island—*island* MP-9
Manch Sch—*school* NV-8
Mancil Cem—*cemetery* MS-4
Mancil Creek—*stream* AL-4
Mancill Cem—*cemetery* AL-4
Mancil Mill Creek—*stream* AL-4
Mancini Park—*park* CA-9
**Manco (Allegheny)**—*pop pl* KY-4
Manco Burro Pass—*gap* NM-5
Mancon Park—*flat* CO-8
**Mancos**—*pop pl* CO-8
Mancos Canyon—*valley* CO-8
Mancos Canyon—*valley* UT-8
**Mancos Creek**—*pop pl* CO-8
Mancos Jim Butte—*summit* UT-8
Mancos Mesa—*summit* UT-8
Mancos Opera House—*hist pl* CO-8
Mancos River—*stream* CO-8
Mancos River—*stream* NM-5
Mancos River Trading Post—*locale* CO-8
Mancos Rsvr No. 1—*reservoir* CO-8
Mancos Rsvr No. 2—*reservoir* CO-8
Mancos Rsvr No. 3—*reservoir* CO-8
Mancos Rsvr No. 4—*reservoir* CO-8
Mancos Spring—*spring* CO-8
Mancos Valley—*valley* CO-8
Mancos Valley Overlook—*locale* CO-8
**Mancourt**—*pop pl* IN-6
*Man Creek* GA-3
Man Creek—*stream* WY-8
Mand—*locale* WV-2
**Manda**—*pop pl* KY-4
**Manda**—*pop pl* TX-5
*Manda Furnace* PA-2
Mandal—*locale* VI-3
**Mandal**—*pop pl* VI-3
**Mandalay**—*pop pl* AR-4
**Mandalay**—*pop pl* FL-3
**Mandalay**—*pop pl* LA-4
**Mandalay**—*pop pl* NJ-2
Mandalay Beach—*beach* CA-9
Mandalay Channel—*channel* FL-3
**Mandalay Gardens**—*pop pl* CO-8
Mandalay Spring—*spring* NV-8
**Mandalay Terrace Subdivision**—*pop pl* UT-8
Mandal Bay—*bay* VI-3
Mandale—*locale* NC-3
**Mandale**—*pop pl* OH-6
Mandal Hill—*summit* VI-3
Mandall Creek—*stream* CO-8
Mandall Pass—*gap* CO-8
Mandal Point—*cape* VI-3
Mandal Ranch—*locale* ND-7

Mandamus Oil Field—*oilfield* MS-4
**Mandan**—*pop pl* MI-6
**Mandan**—*pop pl* ND-7
**Mandana**—*pop pl* NY-2
Mandan Bay—*bay* ND-7
Mandan Commercial Hist Dist—*hist pl* ND-7
Mandan County (historical)—*civil* SD-7
Mandan Lake—*lake* ND-7
Mandan Municipal Airp—*airport* ND-7
**Mandan Township**—*pop pl* ND-7
**Mandaree**—*pop pl* ND-7
*Mandares Creek* MD-2
**Mandarin**—*pop pl* FL-3
Mandarin Baptist Ch—*church* FL-3
Mandarin Cem—*cemetery* FL-3
Mandarin First Assembly of God Ch—*church* FL-3
Mandarin Landing (Shop Ctr)—*locale* FL-3
*Mandarin Orange Island* FM-9
Mandarin Point—*cape* FL-3
Mandarin South Shop Ctr—*locale* FL-3
Manda Sch (abandoned)—*school* MO-7
**Mandata**—*pop pl* PA-2
Mand Canyon—*valley* CA-9
**Mande**—*pop pl* IL-6
Mandell Hill—*summit* MA-1
Mandell Sch—*school* IL-6
**Mandels (historical)**—*pop pl* TN-4
*Manden Creek* WA-9
*Manderes Creek* MD-2
**Manderfield**—*pop pl* UT-8
Manderfield Dam—*dam* UT-8
Manderfield Ditch—*canal* UT-8
Manderfield Rsvr—*reservoir* UT-8
Manderfield Sch—*school* NM-5
Manderly, Lake—*reservoir* GA-3
Mandernach and Carlson Number Two Dam—*dam* SD-7
Mandernach and Carlson Number 1 Dam—*dam* SD-7
Mandernach and Carlson Number 3 Dam—*dam* SD-7
Mandernach and Carlson Number 4 Dam—*dam* SD-7
Mandernach and Carlson Number 5 Dam—*dam* SD-7
Mandernach and Carlson Number 6 Dam—*dam* SD-7
Mandernach and Carlson Number 7 Dam—*dam* SD-7
Mandernach and Carlson Number 8 Dam—*dam* SD-7
Mandernach and Carlson Number 9 Dam—*dam* SD-7
**Manderson**—*pop pl* SD-7
**Manderson**—*pop pl* WY-8
Manderson Cem—*cemetery* WY-8
Manderson Oil Field—*oilfield* WY-8
Manderson Sch—*school* NE-7
Mandeville—*locale* GA-3
Mandeville—*locale* WV-2
**Mandeville**—*pop pl* AR-4
**Mandeville**—*pop pl* FL-3
**Mandeville**—*pop pl* LA-4
**Mandeville**—*pop pl* MO-7
Mandeville, Bayou—*gut* LA-4
Mandeville Canyon—*valley* CA-9
Mandeville Cut—*canal* CA-9
Mandeville House—*hist pl* NY-2
Mandeville Island—*island* CA-9
Mandeville JHS—*school* MI-6
Mandeville Lake—*reservoir* MO-7
Mandeville Park—*park* IL-6
Mandeville Point—*cape* CA-9
Mandeville Reach—*channel* CA-9
Mandeville Sch—*school* LA-4
Mandeville Tip County Park—*park* CA-9
Mand (historical)—*locale* KS-7
M and H Junction Station—*locale* PA-2
M And K Junction—*uninc pl* WV-2
Mandl, Joseph, House—*hist pl* ID-8
M and M Country Club—*other* IA-7
M and M Creek—*stream* OR-9
M and M Fish Farm Lake Dam—*dam* MS-4
M and M Minnow Farm—*other* TX-5
M and M Pond—*lake* AZ-5
M and M Ranch—*locale* NM-5
**Mandolin Condominium**—*pop pl* UT-8
Mandolin Creek—*stream* ID-8
Mandolin Island—*island* NY-2
Mandolin Spring—*spring* ID-8
*Mandon Lake* MI-6
Mandon Lake—*lake* MI-6
M and O Ranch Airp—*airport* NV-8
Mandrake Hill—*summit* NY-2
*Mandrill Lake* OK-5
M and R Quarry—*mine* SC-3
M And S Montoya—*civil* NM-5
**Mandt**—*pop pl* ND-7
Mandt Ch—*church* MN-6
**Mandt (Township of)**—*pop pl* MN-6
Mandy Bay—*swamp* FL-3
Mandy Branch—*stream* GA-3
Mandy Branch—*stream* TN-4
Mandy Cotton Spring—*spring* AR-4
**Mandy Farms (subdivision)**—*pop pl* NC-3
Mandy Fork—*stream* KY-4
Mandy Gulch—*valley* MT-8
Mandy Holland Fork—*stream* KY-4
Mandy Hollow—*valley* IN-6
Mandy Hollow—*valley* TN-4
Mandy Lake—*lake* MN-6
Mandy Lake—*lake* TX-5
Mandys Pit—*cave* AL-4
Mandy Warren Lake—*lake* AL-4
Manealaang—*summit* FM-9
Man Eaten Lake—*lake* CA-9
Maneater Creek—*stream* WY-8
Manees, E. O., House—*hist pl* AR-4
Manekara—*island* FM-9
*Manekun* FM-9
*Manelang* FM-9
Manell Channel—*channel* GU-9
Manell Point—*cape* GU-9
Manell River—*stream* GU-9
Manengon—*area* GU-9
Manengon River—*stream* GU-9
*Maneopapa* HI-9
Maneopapa Gulch—*valley* HI-9
*Maner* PA-2

Manera Wash—*valley* UT-8
Maner Ch—*church* OK-5
Manere Mtn—*summit* TX-5
Maner Park—*park* OH-6
**Manes**—*pop pl* MO-7
Manes, Calloway, Homestead—*hist pl* MO-7
Manes Cem—*cemetery* MO-7
Mane Sch—*school* WI-6
Manes Hollow—*valley* MO-7
Manes Hollow—*valley* OK-5
Manes Nord Creek—*stream* MN-6
**Maness**—*pop pl* VA-3
Maness Branch—*stream* MS-4
Maness Branch—*stream* NC-3
Maness Cem—*cemetery* (2) MO-7
Maness Creek—*stream* AL-4
Maness Hollow—*valley* VA-3
Maness Mtn—*summit* AZ-5
Maness Mtn—*summit* NM-5
Maness Peak—*summit* AZ-5
Maness Sch—*school* MO-7
Maness Sch (historical)—*school* TN-4
Manes Town Sch—*school* AR-4
Manet Beach—*beach* MA-1
*Manetock Hill* CT-1
Manetta, Lake—*reservoir* NJ-2
Manette—*uninc pl* WA-9
Manette Bridge—*bridge* WA-9
**Manette Heights**—*pop pl* DE-2
Manette Pond—*lake* AL-4
Manette Sch—*school* WA-9
*Manetto* MP-9
*Manettos* PA-2
*Manetto-to* MP-9
*Manetuck Hill* CT-1
Manetuck Sch—*school* NY-2
Maney—*locale* MN-6
Maney Branch—*stream* GA-3
Maney Branch—*stream* NC-3
Maney Cem—*cemetery* AR-4
Maney Cem—*cemetery* (3) NC-3
Maney Cem—*cemetery* VA-3
Maney Ch—*church* AR-4
Maney Cove—*basin* GA-3
Maney Cove—*valley* NC-3
Maney Gap—*gap* NC-3
Maney Hist Dist—*hist pl* OK-5
Maney Sch—*school* NE-7
Maney-Sidway House—*hist pl* TN-4
Maneys Neck (Township of)—*fmr MCD* NC-3
Maney Well—*well* NM-5
Manfeltree Brook—*stream* NH-1
Manford Gas Field—*oilfield* TX-5
Manfred—*locale* AR-4
**Manfred**—*pop pl* ND-7
**Manfred Township**—*pop pl* ND-7
**Manfred (Township of)**—*pop pl* MN-6
Manfull Ch—*church* OH-6
Man Full of Troubles Tavern—*building* PA-2
*Mang* MH-9
Manga Canyon—*valley* NM-5
*Mangal* FM-9
*Mangalang* PW-9
Mangalar Spring—*spring* CA-9
*Mangal'lakl* PW-9
*Mangal'lang* PW-9
*Mangalyap* FM-9
Mangan Branch—*stream* TN-4
Mangan Cove—*locale* PA-2
Manganese—*locale* MN-6
Manganese, Lake—*lake* MI-6
*Manganese Creek* CO-8
Manganese Creek—*stream* OR-9
Manganese Draw—*valley* SD-7
Manganese Gulch—*valley* (2) CO-8
*Manganese Mesa* AZ-5
Manganese Mine—*mine* AZ-5
Manganese Peak—*summit* CO-8
Manganese Spring—*spring* MT-8
Manganese Spring—*spring* NV-8
Manganese Spring—*spring* UT-8
Manganese Wash—*stream* NV-8
Manganese Wash—*valley* UT-8
Manganika Lake—*lake* MN-6
Mangan Park—*park* CA-9
*Mangapeilong* FM-9
Mangas—*locale* NM-5
Mangas Creek—*stream* (2) NM-5
Mangas Flowing Well—*well* TX-5
Mangas Lake—*lake* NM-5
*Mangas Mountain* AZ-5
Mangas Mountain Lookout Complex—*hist pl* NM-5
Mangas Mountains—*other* NM-5
Mangas Mtn—*summit* NM-5
Mangas Mtn (historical)—*summit* AZ-5
Mangas Springs—*locale* NM-5
Mangas Valley—*valley* NM-5
Mangas Waterlot Tank—*reservoir* TX-5
Mang Dam—*dam* PA-2
*Mange* MP-9
Mange Cem—*cemetery* MO-7
Mangejang—*island* FM-9
Mangels, William F., Four-Row Carousel—*hist pl* OR-9
Mangel Sch—*school* PA-2
Mangels Gulch—*valley* CA-9
Mangel Windmill—*locale* TX-5
Manger Cem—*cemetery* ND-7
Manger Ch—*church* ND-7
Manger Ch—*church* OK-5
Manger Hill—*summit* NV-8
Manger of Bethlehem Ch—*church* MO-7
Manger Park—*flat* MT-8
Mang Field—*park* MO-7
**Mangham**—*pop pl* LA-4
Mangham Lakes—*reservoir* GA-3
Mangham State Bank Bldg—*hist pl* LA-4
Mangilao—*CDP* GU-9
Mangilao (Election District)—*fmr MCD* GU-9
*Mangiyor* FM-9
*Mangle* FM-9
*Mangles Creek* CA-9
Mangliil—*summit* FM-9
*Manglil* FM-9
Mangliyep—*cape* FM-9
**Mango**—*pop pl* FL-3
Mangoak River—*stream* AK-9
*Mango Creek* MI-6
Mango Creek—*stream* NC-3

Mango Elem Sch—*school* FL-3
Mangohick—*locale* VA-3
Mangohick Church—*hist pl* VA-3
Mangohick (Magisterial District)—*fmr MCD* VA-3
**Mango Hills**—*pop pl* FL-3
Mango Lake—*lake* FL-3
Mangold Hollow—*valley* IA-7
Mangold School (Abandoned)—*locale* IA-7
Mangonia, Lake—*lake* FL-3
**Mangonia Park**—*pop pl* FL-3
Mango Ridge—*ridge* LA-4
Mangoright Point—*cape* VA-3
Mango Sch—*school* CA-9
Mango-Seffner—*CDP* FL-3
Mangpang, Laderan—*cliff* MH-9
Mangpang, Sabanetan—*slope* MH-9
Manq Pond—*reservoir* PA-2
*Mang-rar* MP-9
Mangriff Lake—*lake* OR-9
*Mangrove Banks* FL-3
Mangrove Bay—*lake* LA-4
*Mangrove Bayou* LA-4
Mangrove Bayou—*stream* LA-4
Mangrove Island—*island* FL-3
Mangrove Key—*island* FL-3
Mangrove Lagoon—*bay* VI-3
*Mangrove Point* FL-3
Mangrove Point—*cape* (6) FL-3
Mangrove Point—*cape* LA-4
Mangrove Preserve—*park* FL-3
Mangrove Square—*post sta* FL-3
**Mangrum**—*pop pl* AR-4
Mangrum Cem—*cemetery* AR-4
Mangrum Cem—*cemetery* (2) TN-4
Mangrum Ch—*church* AR-4
Mangrum Hollow—*valley* TN-4
Mangrum Spring—*spring* AZ-5
*Mangs* MH-9
Mangue, Bayou de—*gut* LA-4
*Man Gulch* CA-9
*Mangum* MS-4
*Mangum* TN-4
Mangum—*locale* KY-4
Mangum—*locale* TX-5
**Mangum**—*pop pl* ID-8
**Mangum**—*pop pl* MI-6
**Mangum**—*pop pl* (2) NC-3
**Mangum**—*pop pl* OK-5
Mangum, James, House—*hist pl* NC-3
Mangum Branch—*stream* (2) SC-3
Mangum Camp—*spring* AZ-5
Mangum Canyon—*valley* AZ-5
Mangum (CCD)—*cens area* OK-5
Mangum Cem—*cemetery* AL-4
Mangum Cem—*cemetery* KY-4
Mangum Cem—*cemetery* TN-4
Mangum Chapel—*church* LA-4
Mangum Cove—*bay* GA-3
Mangum Manor Park—*park* TX-5
Mangum Post Office (historical)—*building* TN-4
**Mangums**—*pop pl* SC-3
Mangum Sch—*school* NC-3
*Mangum Spring* AZ-5
*Mangum Springs* AZ-5
Mangum Springs—*locale* AZ-5
*Mangum Station* MI-6
**Mangum Store**—*pop pl* NC-3
Mangum (Township of)—*fmr MCD* NC-3
Mangun Arm—*canal* IN-6
Mangus Cem—*cemetery* WV-2
Man Gut—*gut* MD-2
Mangy Branch—*stream* GA-3
Mangyoer—*bay* FM-9
*Mangyor* FM-9
*Manham River* MA-1
*Manhan Branch* MA-1
*Manhan Brook* MA-1
Manhan Meadows—*flat* MA-1
Manhanock Pond—*lake* ME-1
Manhan Peak—*summit* CA-9
Manhan River—*stream* MA-1
Manhan River Dam—*dam* MA-1
Manhan River Rsvr—*reservoir* MA-1
*Manhan Supply Dam* MA-1
Manhard Creek—*stream* UT-8
**Manhasset**—*pop pl* NY-2
Manhasset Bay—*bay* NY-2
**Manhasset Hills**—*pop pl* NY-2
Manhasset Mart Shop Ctr—*locale* AZ-5
Manhasset Neck—*cape* NY-2
Manhassett Creek—*stream* NJ-2
Manhasset Valley Sch—*school* NY-2
*Manhattan* KY-4
*Manhattan* OH-6
Manhattan—*locale* CO-8
Manhattan—*locale* FL-3
Manhattan—*locale* PA-2
**Manhattan**—*pop pl* IL-6
**Manhattan**—*pop pl* IN-6
**Manhattan**—*pop pl* KS-7
**Manhattan**—*pop pl* MS-4
**Manhattan**—*pop pl* MT-8
**Manhattan**—*pop pl* NV-8
Manhattan Acad—*school* MS-4
*Manhattan Airport* KS-7
Manhattan Arm—*bay* AK-9
Manhattan Baptist Ch—*church* FL-3
Manhattan Beach—*locale* FL-3
**Manhattan Beach**—*pop pl* CA-9
**Manhattan Beach**—*pop pl* MD-2
**Manhattan Beach**—*pop pl* MN-6
**Manhattan Beach**—*pop pl* NY-2
**Manhattan Beach**—*pop pl* OR-9
Manhattan Beach Park—*park* NY-2
Manhattan Beach State Park—*park* CA-9
Manhattan Bldg—*hist pl* IL-6
Manhattan Bldg—*hist pl* MN-6
Manhattan Bldg—*hist pl* OK-5
**Manhattan (Borough of New York City)**—*pop pl* NY-2
Manhattan Bridge—*bridge* NY-2
Manhattan Bridge—*hist pl* NY-2
Manhattan Carnegie Library Bldg—*hist pl* KS-7
Manhattan Cem—*cemetery* CO-8
Manhattan Cem—*cemetery* NE-7
Manhattan Christian Coll—*school* KS-7
Manhattan Coll—*school* NY-2
Manhattan Consolidated Mine—*mine* NV-8
Manhattan Creek—*stream* CA-9

Manhattan Creek—*stream* ... CO-8
Manhattan Creek—*stream* (2) ... ID-8
Manhattan Farms—*locale* ... FL-3
Manhattan Gap—*gap* ... NV-8
Manhattan Group—*island* ... NY-2
Manhattan Gulch—*valley* ... NV-8
Manhattan Gulch—*valley* ... WY-8
Manhattan Heights Hist Dist—*hist pl* ... TX-5
Manhattan Heights Sch—*school* ... CA-9
Manhattan Hotel—*hist pl* ... CO-8
Manhattan Island—*island* ... IN-6
Manhattan Island—*island* ... NY-2
Manhattan Island—*island* ... SD-7
Manhattan JHS—*school* ... KS-7
*Manhattan Junction* ... OH-6
Manhattan Lake—*lake* ... AK-9
Manhattan Mine—*mine* (2) ... CA-9
Manhattan Mountain—*ridge* ... NV-8
Manhattan Mtn—*summit* ... WA-9
Manhattan Municipal Airp—*airport* ... KS-7
Manhattan Park—*uninc pl* ... NY-2
Manhattan Place Sch—*school* ... CA-9
Manhattan Point—*cape* ... IA-7
Manhattan Robbins Lake Park—*park* ... IA-7
Manhattan Sch—*school* ... FL-3
Manhattan Sch—*school* ... MI-6
Manhattan Spring—*spring* ... OR-9
Manhattan State Hosp—*hospital* ... NY-2
**Manhattan (subdivision)**—*pop pl* ... NY-2
**Manhattan Subdivision**—*pop pl* ... UT-8
**Manhattan Township**—*pop pl* ... KS-7
**Manhattan (Township of)**—*pop pl* ... IL-6
Manhattan Tunnel—*mine* ... NV-8
Manhattanville—*uninc pl* ... NY-2
Manhattanville Coll—*school* ... NY-2
Manhatten Covered Bridge—*bridge* ... IN-6
Manhatten (historical P.O.)—*locale* ... IA-7
Manhaven Ch—*church* ... SC-3
*Man Head* ... AZ-5
Man Head—*summit* ... AZ-5
Manhead Mesa—*summit* ... NM-5
Manhead Mtn—*summit* ... CO-8
Manhead Mtn—*summit* ... MT-8
*Manhead Peak* ... MT-8
Manhead Sound—*bay* ... GA-3
Manheim—*locale* ... TX-5
**Manheim**—*pop pl* ... PA-2
**Manheim**—*pop pl* ... WV-2
Manheim Borough—*civil* ... PA-2
**Manheim Center**—*pop pl* ... NY-2
Manheim Central JHS—*school* ... PA-2
Manheim Central Senior HS—*school* ... PA-2
Manheim HS—*school* ... PA-2
Manheim JHS—*school* ... PA-2
Manheim Post Office
(historical)—*building* ... PA-2
Manheim Sch—*school* ... PA-2
**Manheim (Town of)**—*pop pl* ... NY-2
Manheim Township Community
Park—*park* ... PA-2
*Manheim Township High School* ... PA-2
*Manheim Township Middle School* ... PA-2
**Manheim (Township of)**—*pop pl* (2) ... PA-2
Manhole Cave—*cave* ... AL-4
Manhollow Ch—*church* ... NC-3
Man HS—*school* ... WV-2
**Mani**—*pop pl* (2) ... PR-3
*Maniagaha* ... MH-9
*Maniagaha Islet* ... MH-9
Maniania Ditch—*canal* ... HI-9
Maniania Pali—*cliff* ... HI-9
*Manianiaula* ... HI-9
Manido Falls—*falls* ... MI-6
Manidokan Camp—*locale* ... MD-2
Maniece Bayou—*stream* ... AR-4
Maniece Creek—*stream* ... ID-8
Manienie—*civil* ... HI-9
Manienie Gulch—*valley* (2) ... HI-9
Manienieula—*area* ... HI-9
Manierre Sch—*school* ... IL-6
**Manifest**—*pop pl* ... LA-4
Manifest Ch—*church* ... LA-4
**Manifold**—*pop pl* ... PA-2
Manifold Branch—*stream* ... TN-4
Manifold Ditch—*canal* ... IN-6
**Manifold Manor**—*pop pl* ... PA-2
Manifold Sch (abandoned)—*school* ... PA-2
Manigault, Joseph, House—*hist pl* ... SC-3
*Manigault Branch* ... SC-3
Manigault Neck—*cape* ... SC-3
Manila—*locale* ... AL-4
Manila—*locale* ... AZ-5
Manila—*locale* ... CO-8
Manila—*locale* ... MO-7
Manila—*locale* ... TN-4
**Manila**—*pop pl* ... AL-4
**Manila**—*pop pl* ... AR-4
**Manila**—*pop pl* ... CA-9
**Manila**—*pop pl* ... KY-4
**Manila**—*pop pl* ... UT-8
**Manila**—*pop pl* ... WV-2
Manila Airp—*airport* ... UT-8
Manila Bay—*bay* ... OH-6
Manila Bayou—*gut* ... LA-4
Manila Canyon—*valley* ... AZ-5
Manila Canyon—*valley* ... CA-9
Manila Cem—*cemetery* ... OK-5
Manila Cem—*cemetery* ... UT-8
Manila Ch—*church* ... UT-8
Manila Creek—*stream* (2) ... AK-9
Manila Creek—*stream* ... MI-6
Manila Creek—*stream* ... WA-9
Manila Creek—*stream* ... WV-2
Manila HS—*school* ... UT-8
Manila Mine—*mine* ... AZ-5
**Manila (North Samoa)**—*pop pl* ... CA-9
Manila Park—*flat* ... UT-8
Manila Petroglyphs—*hist pl* ... UT-8
Manila Post Office—*locale* ... KY-4
Manila Post Office (historical)—*building* ... TN-4
Manila Ranger Station—*locale* ... UT-8
Manila Ridge—*ridge* ... WV-2
Manila Sch—*school* ... CA-9
Manila Sch—*school* ... UT-8
Manila Sch—*school* ... WV-2
Manila Sch (historical)—*school* ... TN-4
Manila Spring—*spring* ... NV-8
Manila Village Oil Field—*oilfield* ... LA-4
Manila Wash—*stream* ... AZ-5
**Manilla**—*pop pl* ... IN-6
**Manilla**—*pop pl* ... IA-7
Manilla Branch—*stream* ... IN-6
Manilla Chapel Baptist Ch—*church* ... TN-4
Manilla Elem Sch—*school* ... IN-6
Manilla Mine—*mine* ... WY-8
Manilla Spring—*spring* ... WA-9
**Manilla Township**—*pop pl* ... ND-7
*Manimin* ... MN-6
Maninglik River—*stream* ... AK-9
Manini Gulch—*valley* ... HI-9
*Maniniowala* ... HI-9
Maniniowali—*civil* ... HI-9
Manini Pali—*cliff* ... HI-9
Maniobra Valley—*valley* ... CA-9
**Manion**—*pop pl* ... OK-5
Manion Cem—*cemetery* ... IL-6
Manion Cem—*cemetery* ... MO-7
Manion Oil Field—*oilfield* ... OK-5
Manion Run—*stream* ... WV-2
Manion Sch—*school* ... IL-6
Maniscalcos Cactus Farm—*locale* ... CA-9
Manis Cem—*cemetery* ... TN-4
Manis Creek—*stream* ... OR-9
Manis Hollow—*valley* ... TN-4
*Man Island* ... FM-9
Man Island—*island* ... ME-1
Man Island—*island* ... VA-3
Manis Mastodon Site—*hist pl* ... WA-9
*Manisses Island* ... RI-1
Manistee—*locale* ... AL-4
**Manistee**—*pop pl* ... MI-6
Manistee Central Business
District—*hist pl* ... MI-6
**Manistee (County)**—*pop pl* ... MI-6
Manistee County-Blacker Airp—*airport* ... MI-6
Manistee County Courthouse
Fountain—*hist pl* ... MI-6
Manistee Creek—*stream* ... MI-6
Manistee Lake—*lake* (2) ... MI-6
Manistee Natl For—*forest* ... MI-6
Manistee River—*stream* ... MI-6
Manistee River State Game Area—*park* ... MI-6
**Manistee (Township of)**—*pop pl* ... MI-6
*Manistique* ... MI-6
**Manistique**—*pop pl* ... MI-6
*Manistique Creek* ... MI-6
Manistique Lake—*lake* ... MI-6
Manistique Pumping Station—*hist pl* ... MI-6
Manistique River—*stream* ... MI-6
Manistique River State For—*forest* ... MI-6
**Manistique (Township of)**—*pop pl* ... MI-6
*Manitau Lake* ... IN-6
*Manitick Lake* ... CT-1
*Manitick Mountain* ... CT-1
*Manitiu* ... FM-9
Manito—*locale* ... WA-9
**Manito**—*pop pl* ... IL-6
**Manito**—*pop pl* ... PA-2
Manitoba Gulch—*valley* ... MT-8
Manitoba Junction—*locale* ... MN-6
Manitoba Sch—*school* ... WI-6
Manito Ch—*church* ... KY-4
Manitock Hill—*summit* ... CT-1
**Manitock Spring**—*pop pl* ... CT-1
**Manito Club Estates**—*pop pl* ... WA-9
Manito Ditch—*canal* ... IL-6
Manito Golf Country Club—*other* ... WA-9
Manito Lake—*lake* ... MI-6
Manitook Lake—*lake* ... CT-1
Manitook Mtn—*summit* ... CT-1
Manito Park—*flat* ... WA-9
Manito Playground—*park* ... WA-9
**Manito (sta.)**—*pop pl* ... WA-9
**Manito (Township of)**—*pop pl* ... IL-6
*Manitou* ... CO-8
*Manitou* ... MN-6
Manitou—*locale* ... MN-6
**Manitou**—*pop pl* ... KY-4
**Manitou**—*pop pl* ... NY-2
**Manitou**—*pop pl* ... ND-7
**Manitou**—*pop pl* ... OK-5
**Manitou**—*pop pl* ... WA-9
Manitou, Lake—*lake* ... IN-6
Manitou, Lake—*lake* ... MI-6
Manitou, Mount—*summit* (2) ... CO-8
Manitou Bathhouse—*hist pl* ... CO-8
*Manitou Bay* ... NY-2
*Manitou Beach* ... MI-6
**Manitou Beach**—*pop pl* (2) ... MI-6
**Manitou Beach**—*pop pl* ... NY-2
**Manitou Beach**—*pop pl* ... WA-9
Manitou Camp—*hist pl* ... WI-6
Manitou Cave—*cave* ... AL-4
Manitou Chapel—*church* ... NY-2
*Manitou Creek* ... MN-6
Manitou Experimental For—*forest* ... CO-8
Manitou Experimental Forest HQ—*locale* ... CO-8
*Manitou Falls* ... WI-6
Manitou Falls Ch—*church* ... WI-6
Manitou Hill—*summit* ... AZ-5
Manitou Island—*island* ... MI-6
Manitou Island—*island* ... MN-6
Manitou Island—*island* ... WI-6
Manitou Island Lighthouse—*locale* ... MI-6
Manitou Island Light Station—*hist pl* ... MI-6
Manitou Junction—*locale* ... MN-6
**Manitou Junction**—*pop pl* ... CO-8
*Manitou Lake* ... WI-6
Manitou Lake—*lake* ... MI-6
Manitou Lake—*lake* ... WI-6
Manitou Lake Sch—*school* ... WI-6
Manitou Mtn—*summit* ... NY-2
*Manitou Park* ... WA-9
Manitou Park—*park* ... AL-4
**Manitou Park**—*pop pl* ... NJ-2
Manitou Park Grange—*locale* ... CO-8
Manitou Park Lake—*reservoir* ... CO-8
Manitou Park Rec Area—*park* ... CO-8
Manitou Passage—*channel* ... MI-6
Manitou Payment Highbanks—*cliff* ... MI-6
Manitou Payment Point—*cape* ... MI-6
*Manitou Point* ... NY-2
*Manitou Rapid* ... MN-6
Manitou Rapids—*rapids* ... MN-6
*Manitou River* ... WI-6
Manitou River—*stream* ... MN-6
Manitou Rsvr—*reservoir* ... CO-8
Manitou Sch—*school* ... NY-2
**Manitou Springs**—*pop pl* ... CO-8
Manitou Springs Bridges (2)—*hist pl* ... CO-8
Manitou Springs Hist Dist—*hist pl* ... CO-8
Manitou Sunlight Mine—*mine* ... CO-8
**Manitou Township**—*pop pl* ... ND-7
**Manitowish**—*pop pl* ... WI-6
Manitowish River—*stream* ... WI-6
**Manitowish Waters**—*pop pl* ... WI-6
Manitowish Waters Sch—*school* ... WI-6
**Manitowish Waters (Town of)**—*pop pl* ... WI-6
**Manitowoc**—*pop pl* ... WI-6
**Manitowoc (County)**—*pop pl* ... WI-6
Manitowoc County Airp—*airport* ... WI-6
Manitowoc County Courthouse—*hist pl* ... WI-6
Manitowoc Harbor—*harbor* ... WI-6
Manitowoc Mine—*mine* ... AZ-5
**Manitowoc Rapids**—*pop pl* ... WI-6
Manitowoc Rapids (Rapids)—*uninc pl* ... WI-6
**Manitowoc Rapids (Town of)**—*pop pl* ... WI-6
Manitowoc River—*stream* ... WI-6
Manitowoc Shoal—*bar* ... WI-6
**Manitowoc (Town of)**—*pop pl* ... WI-6
Manitt Lake—*lake* ... MI-6
**Manitto Haven**—*pop pl* ... PA-2
*Manituck Mtn* ... CT-1
Maniwaki Creek—*stream* ... MN-6
Maniwaki Lake—*lake* ... MN-6
Manix—*locale* ... CA-9
**Manix**—*pop pl* ... IL-6
Manix Wash—*stream* ... CA-9
*Maniy* ... FM-9
Manjarres House—*hist pl* ... AZ-5
Manjo, Lake—*reservoir* ... PA-2
Mankakvik Creek—*stream* ... AK-9
Mankameyer Spring—*spring* ... MT-8
Manka RR Station—*locale* ... FL-3
**Mankas Corner**—*pop pl* ... CA-9
**Mankas Corners**—*pop pl* ... CA-9
**Mankato**—*pop pl* ... KS-7
**Mankato**—*pop pl* ... MN-6
Mankato Airp—*airport* ... KS-7
Mankato Creek—*stream* ... WA-9
Mankato East HS—*school* ... MN-6
Mankato Elem Sch—*school* ... KS-7
Mankato Golf Club—*other* ... MN-6
Mankato Holstein Farm Barn—*hist pl* ... MN-6
Mankato Junior-Senior HS—*school* ... KS-7
Mankato Mtn—*summit* ... WA-9
Mankato Municipal Airp—*airport* ... MN-6
Mankato Public Library and Reading
Room—*hist pl* ... MN-6
Mankato Spring—*spring* ... MN-6
Mankato State Coll—*school* ... MN-6
**Mankato (Township of)**—*pop pl* ... MN-6
Mankato Union Depot—*hist pl* ... MN-6
Manker Canyon—*valley* ... CA-9
Manker Creek—*stream* ... AK-9
Manker Flat—*flat* ... CA-9
Manker Patten Tennis Center
(UTC)—*locale* ... TN-4
*Man Key* ... FL-3
Man Key—*island* ... FL-3
Mankey Slough—*lake* ... SD-7
Mankie Island—*island* ... MN-6
Mankiller Bay—*bay* ... NJ-2
Man Killer Branch—*stream* ... NJ-2
Mankiller Island—*island* ... NJ-2
**Mankin**—*pop pl* ... TX-5
Mankin Ch—*church* ... TX-5
*Mankin Creek* ... CA-9
Mankin Draw—*valley* ... WY-8
*Mankin Flat* ... CA-9
Mankin Rsvr—*reservoir* ... WY-8
**Mankins**—*pop pl* ... TX-5
Mankins Creek—*stream* ... CA-9
Mankins Flat—*flat* (2) ... CA-9
Mankins Mill—*locale* ... TX-5
*Mankin Springs* ... CA-9
Mankins Spring—*spring* ... CA-9
**Mankinville**—*pop pl* ... TN-4
Manklin Creek—*stream* ... MD-2
*Manklins Creek* ... MD-2
Mankomen Lake—*lake* ... AK-9
Manks Corner—*locale* ... ME-1
Mankus Lake—*lake* ... MN-6
Man Lake—*lake* ... MI-6
Man Lake—*lake* ... MN-6
Manley—*locale* ... IL-6
Manley—*locale* ... MN-6
**Manley**—*pop pl* ... DE-2
**Manley**—*pop pl* ... NE-7
**Manley**—*pop pl* ... WI-6
Manley, William M., House—*hist pl* ... MA-1
Manley Branch—*stream* (2) ... KY-4
Manley Branch—*stream* ... NC-3
Manley Camp—*locale* ... MT-8
Manley Cem—*cemetery* ... GA-3
Manley Cem—*cemetery* (2) ... MO-7
Manley Cem—*cemetery* (3) ... TN-4
Manley Ch—*church* ... WV-2
*Manley Chapel* ... TN-4
*Manley Chapel Cem* ... TN-4
Manley Chapel Cem—*cemetery* ... TN-4
Manley Chapel (historical)—*church* ... TN-4
*Manley Chapel Methodist Ch* ... TN-4
Manley Chapel Sch—*school* ... TN-4
*Manley Creek* ... KS-7
Manley Creek—*stream* ... ID-8
Manley Creek—*stream* ... KS-7
Manley Creek—*stream* ... WA-9
Manley Creek—*stream* ... WI-6
*Manley Crossroad* ... AL-4
Manley Crossroads—*locale* ... AL-4
Manley Ditch—*canal* ... MT-8
*Manley Elem Sch* ... TN-4
Manley Gap—*gap* ... GA-3
Manley Grove Ch—*church* ... NC-3
Manley (historical)—*locale* ... KS-7
Manley Hollow—*valley* ... AR-4
Manley Hollow—*valley* ... KY-4
**Manley Hot Springs**—*pop pl* ... AK-9
Manley Hot Springs ANV850—*reserve* ... AK-9
Manley Hot Springs Dome—*summit* ... AK-9
Manley HS—*school* ... IL-6
Manley Infirmary—*hospital* ... TN-4
Manley Island—*island* ... ME-1
Manley Park—*flat* ... MT-8
Manley Point—*cape* ... NC-3
Manley Ranch—*locale* ... MT-8
Manley Sch—*school* (2) ... MI-6
Manley Sch—*school* ... TN-4
Manleys Chapel—*church* ... TN-4
Manleys Chapel Cem—*cemetery* ... TN-4
*Manleys Chapel School* ... TN-4
Manley Sch Number 3—*school* ... ND-7
**Manleys Church**—*pop pl* ... WV-2
**Manleys Corner**—*pop pl* ... MA-1
Manley Siding—*locale* ... MI-6
Manleys Landing—*locale* ... AL-4
*Manley Spring* ... MO-7
Manley Village Shop Ctr—*locale* ... TN-4
Manleyville—*locale* ... AK-9
**Manleyville**—*pop pl* ... TN-4
Manleyville Cem—*cemetery* ... TN-4
*Manley Vines Camp* ... AL-4
Manley Windmill—*locale* ... TX-5
Manlin Hammock—*island* ... FL-3
**Manlius**—*pop pl* ... IL-6
**Manlius**—*pop pl* ... NY-2
Manlius Cem—*cemetery* ... IL-6
Manlius Center—*locale* ... NY-2
Manlius Sch—*school* ... NY-2
**Manlius (Town of)**—*pop pl* ... NY-2
**Manlius (Township of)**—*pop pl* (2) ... IL-6
**Manlius (Township of)**—*pop pl* ... MI-6
Manlius Village Hist Dist—*hist pl* ... NY-2
Manlove—*locale* ... CA-9
Manlove, Bartholomew, House—*hist pl* ... TX-5
Manlove Branch—*stream* ... VA-3
Manlove Butte—*summit* ... MT-8
Manlove Cem—*cemetery* ... TN-4
Manlove Lake—*reservoir* ... IN-6
Manlove Park—*park* ... IN-6
Manlove Park Dam—*dam* ... IN-6
**Manly**—*pop pl* ... IA-7
**Manly**—*pop pl* ... NC-3
Manly Cem—*cemetery* ... TX-5
Manly Coal Bed Mine
(underground)—*mine* ... AL-4
Manly Draw—*valley* ... CO-8
Manly Fall—*locale* ... CA-9
Manly Gulch—*valley* ... CA-9
Manly Hill—*summit* ... WY-8
Manly JHS—*school* ... KY-4
Manly-McCann House—*hist pl* ... IL-6
Manly Pass—*gap* ... CA-9
Manly Peak—*summit* ... CA-9
*Manlys Creek* ... KS-7
*Manly Station* ... NC-3
Manly Taylor Elem Sch—*school* ... GA-3
*Manlyville* ... AZ-5
*Manlyville* ... TN-4
**Manlyville (Manleyville)**—*pop pl* ... TN-4
Manlyville Post Office
(historical)—*building* ... TN-4
Manmont Post Office
(historical)—*building* ... AL-4
Man Mound—*hist pl* ... WI-6
Man Mound Park—*park* ... WI-6
Man Mtn—*summit* ... TX-5
Mann—*island* ... MP-9
Mann—*locale* ... MT-8
Mann—*locale* ... TX-5
**Mann**—*pop pl* ... AL-4
**Mann**—*pop pl* ... OH-6
**Mann**—*pop pl* ... PA-2
**Mann**—*pop pl* ... WI-6
Mann, Andrew, Inn—*hist pl* ... NY-2
Mann, George R., Bldg—*hist pl* ... AR-4
Mann, Henry, House—*hist pl* ... NM-5
Mann, John, House—*hist pl* ... WI-6
Mann, John T., House—*hist pl* ... GA-3
Mann, John Wesley, House—*hist pl* ... TX-5
Mann, Lake—*lake* ... FL-3
Mann, Lake—*lake* ... ND-7
Mann, R. N., House—*hist pl* ... TN-4
Mann, William, Sch—*hist pl* ... PA-2
Mann, William G., House—*hist pl* ... WI-6
**Manna Acres Subdivision**—*pop pl* ... UT-8
Manna Creek—*stream* ... AK-9
*Mannahardts Pond* ... CT-1
Mann Airp—*airport* ... IN-6
Mannais—*civil* ... FM-9
Mannan Cem—*cemetery* ... IN-6
Mannassa—*locale* ... MS-4
Mannassa Cem—*cemetery* ... MS-4
Mannassa Methodist Ch—*church* ... MS-4
Mannassa Post Office
(historical)—*building* ... MS-4
Mannassa Sch (historical)—*school* ... MS-4
*Mannatuck Mtn* ... CT-1
*Man-na-wah-kie* ... WI-6
Mannayunk Kill—*stream* ... NY-2
Mann Bog—*swamp* ... ME-1
Mannboro—*locale* ... VA-3
*Mann Branch* ... KY-4
*Mann Branch* ... SC-3
Mann Branch—*stream* ... AL-4
Mann Branch—*stream* ... KY-4
Mann Branch—*stream* ... MS-4
Mann Branch—*stream* (2) ... VA-3
Mann Brook—*stream* ... CT-1
Mann Brook—*stream* ... ME-1
Mann Brook—*stream* ... NY-2
Mann Butte—*summit* ... WA-9
Mann Canyon—*valley* ... CA-9
Mann Cem—*cemetery* ... AL-4
Mann Cem—*cemetery* ... AR-4
Mann Cem—*cemetery* (2) ... GA-3
Mann Cem—*cemetery* (2) ... IL-6
Mann Cem—*cemetery* ... IN-6
Mann Cem—*cemetery* (3) ... KY-4
Mann Cem—*cemetery* ... MS-4
Mann Cem—*cemetery* (3) ... MO-7
Mann Cem—*cemetery* (3) ... OH-6
Mann Cem—*cemetery* ... SC-3
Mann Cem—*cemetery* (2) ... TN-4
Mann Cem—*cemetery* ... TX-5
Mann Cem—*cemetery* ... VA-3
*Mann Chapel* ... IL-6
Mann Chapel—*church* ... AL-4
Mann Chapel—*church* ... TX-5
Mann Chapel Ch—*church* ... AL-4
*Mann Creek* ... OR-9
Mann Creek—*stream* ... CA-9
Mann Creek—*stream* ... CO-8
Mann Creek—*stream* ... GA-3
Mann Creek—*stream* (5) ... ID-8
Mann Creek—*stream* ... IN-6
Mann Creek—*stream* (3) ... MI-6
Mann Creek—*stream* (3) ... OR-9
Mann Creek—*stream* ... TN-4
Mann Creek—*stream* ... VA-3
Mann Creek—*stream* ... WI-6
Mann Creek—*stream* ... WY-8
Mann Creek Cem—*cemetery* ... ID-8
Mann Creek Guard Station—*locale* ... ID-8
Mann Creek Ridge—*ridge* ... ID-8
Mann Crossing—*locale* ... TX-5
Mann Ditch—*canal* (2) ... IN-6
Mann Draw—*valley* ... CO-8
Mann Draw—*valley* ... TX-5
Manne Bldg—*hist pl* ... SC-3
Mannel Branch—*stream* ... IL-6
Mannen Cem—*cemetery* ... KS-7
Mannens Branch—*stream* ... WV-2
*Manner* ... PA-2
Mannerheim Tank—*reservoir* ... AZ-5
Mannering Creek—*stream* ... ID-8
*Manner Run* ... PA-2
Manners Cem—*cemetery* ... TN-4
Manners Dam Run—*stream* ... PA-2
*Manners Run* ... PA-2
Manners Sch—*school* ... IL-6
Mannetto Hills—*summit* ... NY-2
Mannetto Hills Sch—*school* ... NY-2
*Manney Lake* ... MI-6
*Manneys Ferry* ... NC-3
**Mannford**—*pop pl* ... OK-5
**Mann Ford**—*pop pl* ... VA-3
Mannford Ramp Rec Area—*park* ... OK-5
Mannford Rsvr—*reservoir* ... OK-5
Mann Gulch—*valley* ... MT-8
Mann Hall Playground—*locale* ... MI-6
Mannhan Canyon—*valley* ... SD-7
*Mannhardt Pond* ... CT-1
*Mannhardts Pond* ... CT-1
*Mannhassett Village* ... OH-6
*Mannheim* ... IL-6
Mannheim—*hist pl* ... MD-2
Mannheim Sch—*school* ... IL-6
Mannheim Sch—*school* ... SC-3
Mann Hill—*summit* ... IN-6
Mann Hill—*summit* (3) ... ME-1
Mann Hill—*summit* ... MA-1
Mann Hill—*summit* ... NH-1
Mann Hill—*summit* ... VT-1
**Mann Hill Beach**—*pop pl* ... MA-1
Mann (historical P.O.)—*locale* ... MS-4
Mann Home—*building* ... OR-9
Mann House—*hist pl* ... AR-4
Mann House—*hist pl* ... MI-6
Mannie Baird Mine—*mine* ... NM-5
Mannie Cem—*cemetery* ... TN-4
Mannie Lake—*lake* ... ND-7
*Mannie Mines Cem* ... TN-4
*Mannikaja Point* ... AZ-5
*Mannikin* ... VA-3
Mannila Camp—*locale* ... MN-6
Manning—*locale* ... FL-3
Manning—*locale* ... MI-6
Manning—*locale* ... TX-5
Manning—*locale* ... VA-3
Manning—*locale* ... WA-9
**Manning**—*pop pl* ... AR-4
**Manning**—*pop pl* ... IA-7
**Manning**—*pop pl* ... KS-7
**Manning**—*pop pl* ... NY-2
**Manning**—*pop pl* ... ND-7
**Manning**—*pop pl* ... OK-5
**Manning**—*pop pl* ... OR-9
**Manning**—*pop pl* ... SC-3
**Manning**—*pop pl* ... WI-6
Manning, Charles, House—*hist pl* ... MA-1
Manning, Jacob, House—*hist pl* ... MA-1
Manning, Lake—*lake* ... FL-3
Manning, Lee and Moore Law
Office—*hist pl* ... AR-4
Manning, Levi H., House—*hist pl* ... AZ-5
Manning, Mount—*summit* ... ID-8
Manning, S. A., Bldg—*hist pl* ... OR-9
Manning Archeol Site—*hist pl* ... SC-3
Manning Basin—*lake* ... FL-3
Manning Bay—*swamp* ... SC-3
Manning Bay Racetrack—*other* ... VI-3
Manning Bottoms—*bend* ... MT-8
Manning Branch—*stream* ... SC-3
Manning Branch—*stream* (2) ... TX-5
Manning Branch—*stream* (2) ... WV-2
Manning Branch (historical)—*stream* ... TN-4
Manning Bridge—*bridge* ... ID-8
Manning Brook—*stream* (2) ... MA-1
Manning Cabin—*hist pl* ... AZ-5
Manning Cabin—*locale* ... NM-5
Manning Camp—*locale* ... AZ-5
Manning Canyon—*valley* ... NM-5
Manning Canyon—*valley* ... UT-8
Manning (CCD)—*cens area* ... SC-3
Manning Cem—*cemetery* (3) ... AL-4
Manning Cem—*cemetery* (3) ... AR-4
Manning Cem—*cemetery* ... GA-3
Manning Cem—*cemetery* ... MS-4
Manning Cem—*cemetery* ... MO-7
Manning Cem—*cemetery* ... NY-2
Manning Cem—*cemetery* (3) ... NC-3
Manning Cem—*cemetery* ... OK-5
Manning Cem—*cemetery* ... PA-2
Manning Cem—*cemetery* ... TN-4
Manning Ch—*church* ... TX-5
Manning Chapel Sch—*school* ... TN-4
Manning Coal Mines—*mine* ... CO-8
Manning Corral Rsvr—*reservoir* ... MT-8
Manning Correctional Institute—*other* ... SC-3
Manning Creek—*stream* ... CA-9
Manning Creek—*stream* ... FL-3
Manning Creek—*stream* ... GA-3
Manning Creek—*stream* ... ID-8
Manning Creek—*stream* ... OR-9
Manning Creek—*stream* ... TX-5
Manning Creek—*stream* ... UT-8
Manning Crossing—*locale* ... KY-4
*Manning Crossroads* ... NY-2
**Manning Crossroads**—*pop pl* ... SC-3
Manning-Denton Cem—*cemetery* ... TN-4
*Manning Ditch* ... IN-6
Manning East (CCD)—*cens area* ... SC-3
Manning Farmlife Sch—*school* ... NC-3
Manning Ferry—*locale* ... TN-4
Manning Ferry (historical)—*locale* ... NC-3
Manning Flat—*flat* ... CA-9
Manning Flat—*flat* ... WY-8
Manning Gulch—*valley* ... OR-9
Manningham—*locale* ... AL-4
Manningham Cem—*cemetery* ... AL-4
Manning Hill—*summit* ... MI-6
Manning Hollow—*valley* ... PA-2
Manning Hollow—*valley* ... UT-8
Manning House—*hist pl* ... MA-1
*Manning Island* ... NY-2
Manning JHS—*school* ... CO-8
Manning Junction—*locale* ... PA-2
Manning Knob—*summit* ... WV-2
Manning Lake—*lake* ... AK-9
Manning Lake—*lake* ... LA-4
Manning Lake—*lake* ... MI-6
Manning Lake—*lake* ... MT-8
Manning Lake—*lake* ... NH-1
Manning Lake—*reservoir* ... GA-3
*Manning Landing* ... TN-4
Manning Library—*hist pl* ... SC-3
Manning Manse—*hist pl* ... MA-1
*Manning Meadow* ... UT-8
*Manning Meadow Dam* ... UT-8
*Manning Meadow Reservoir* ... UT-8
Manning Meadows—*flat* ... UT-8
Manning Meadows Dam—*dam* ... UT-8
Manning Meadows Rsvr—*reservoir* ... UT-8
Manning Mountains—*summit* ... TX-5
Manning Park—*park* ... CA-9
Manning Park—*park* ... MI-6
**Manning Park (subdivision)**—*pop pl* ... NC-3
Manning Point—*cape* (2) ... AK-9
Manning Pond—*lake* ... FL-3
Manning Ranch—*locale* ... TX-5
Manning Ranch—*locale* (3) ... WY-8
Manning Range—*flat* ... MD-2
Manning Ridge—*ridge* ... OR-9
Manning Ridge—*ridge* ... WY-8
Manning Rocks—*bar* ... AK-9
Manning Rsvr—*reservoir* ... NV-8
Manning Run—*stream* ... OH-6
Manning-Rye Covered Bridge—*hist pl* ... WA-9
**Mannings**—*pop pl* ... WV-2
Manning Sch—*school* ... MA-1
Manning Sch—*school* ... MN-6
Manning Sch—*school* ... MS-4
Manning Sch—*school* ... NC-3
Manning Sch (abandoned)—*school* ... MO-7
Mannings Chapel—*church* ... AL-4
Mannings Chapel Baptist Ch—*church* ... TN-4
Mannings Chapel Cem—*cemetery* ... MO-7
*Mannings Chapel School* ... TN-4
Manning Sch (historical)—*school* ... TN-4
Manning Sch Number 1—*school* ... ND-7
Manning School (Abandoned)—*locale* ... OK-5
**Mannings Cove**—*pop pl* ... NY-2
Mannings Creek—*stream* ... AL-4
Mannings Farm—*island* ... ME-1
Mannings Flats—*flat* ... CA-9
Mannings Hollow—*valley* ... TN-4
Manning (Site)—*locale* ... UT-8
Mannings Landing—*locale* ... TN-4
Manning Spring—*spring* ... AL-4
Manning Spring—*spring* ... MT-8
Manning Spring—*spring* ... TN-4
Mannings Store (historical)—*locale* ... AL-4
Mannings (Township of)—*fmr MCD* ... NC-3
Manning Tank—*reservoir* ... AZ-5
Manning Tank—*reservoir* ... NM-5
Mannington—*locale* ... KY-4
**Mannington**—*pop pl* ... KY-4
**Mannington**—*pop pl* ... WV-2
Mannington Creek—*stream* ... NJ-2
Mannington (Magisterial
District)—*fmr MCD* ... WV-2
Mannington Meadow—*lake* ... NJ-2
Mannington Memorial Cem—*cemetery* ... WV-2
**Mannington Mills**—*pop pl* ... NJ-2
**Mannington (Township of)**—*pop pl* ... NJ-2
**Manningtown**—*pop pl* ... GA-3
**Manning Township**—*pop pl* ... ND-7
Manning Trail—*trail* ... NH-1
**Manningville**—*pop pl* ... NY-2
Manning Well—*well* ... MT-8
Mann Inside Pond—*bay* ... LA-4
Mannis Branch—*stream* ... TN-4
Mannis Creek—*stream* ... MI-6
Mannis Duck Pond—*lake* ... NJ-2
**Mannitto Haven**—*pop pl* ... PA-2
Mannitto Lake—*reservoir* ... PA-2
Mannix Park—*flat* ... MT-8
*Mannix Point* ... ME-1
Mann JHS—*school* ... AR-4
Mann JHS—*school* (2) ... CA-9
Mann JHS—*school* ... FL-3
Mann JHS—*school* ... OH-6
Mann JHS—*school* ... WI-6
*Mann Junior High School* ... UT-8
Mann Knob—*summit* (2) ... WV-2
Mann Knob Cem—*cemetery* ... WV-2
Mann Knob Sch—*school* ... WV-2
*Mann Lake* ... MN-6
Mann Lake—*lake* ... ID-8
Mann Lake—*lake* ... IL-6
Mann Lake—*lake* ... MI-6
Mann Lake—*lake* ... MN-6
Mann Lake—*lake* ... OR-9
Mann Lake—*lake* ... WI-6
Mann Lake—*reservoir* ... GA-3
Mann Lake—*reservoir* ... IN-6
Mann Lake—*reservoir* ... TX-5
Mann Lateral—*canal* ... AZ-5
**Mann (Mann Station)**—*pop pl* ... AL-4
Mann Meadow—*swamp* ... ME-1
Mann-Monroe Sch—*school* ... PA-2
Mann Mound—*hist pl* ... OH-6
*Mann Mtn* ... WV-2
Mann Mtn—*summit* ... ME-1
Mann Mtn—*summit* ... WV-2
Mann Music Center—*building* ... PA-2
Mann Narrows—*gap* ... PA-2
Mannon—*locale* ... IL-6
Mannon Cem—*cemetery* ... IL-6
**Mannoni**—*pop pl* ... VA-3
Mannon Run—*stream* ... OH-6
Mannon Run—*stream* ... WV-2
Mannon Valley—*basin* ... NE-7
*Mannot Creek* ... CA-9
Man (not verified)—*island* ... MP-9
Mann Outside Pond—*bay* ... LA-4
Mann Park—*park* ... IL-6
Mann Passage—*channel* ... MP-9

Mann Point—*cape* NC-3
Mann Pond—*lake* FL-3
Mann Pond—*lake* ME-1
Mann Pond—*lake* MA-1
Mann Ranch—*locale* (2) CA-9
Mann Ranch—*locale* TX-5
Mann Recreation Center—*park* PA-2
Mann Ridge—*ridge* OR-9
Mann-Roshe Cem—*cemetery* KY-4
*Manns* MS-4
Manns Acad (historical)—*school* MS-4
Manns Branch—*stream* NE-7
Manns Branch—*stream* SC-3
Manns Camp Branch—*stream* WV-2
Manns Cem—*cemetery* NC-3
*Mann Sch* IN-6
*Mann Sch* PA-2
Manns Ch—*church* AR-4
Mann Sch—*school* (3) CA-9
Mann Sch—*school* (3) IL-6
Mann Sch—*school* IN-6
Mann Sch—*school* (3) IA-7
Mann Sch—*school* (2) MA-1
Mann Sch—*school* (3) MI-6
Mann Sch—*school* (3) MN-6
Mann Sch—*school* (3) MO-7
Mann Sch—*school* NJ-2
Mann Sch—*school* NY-2
Mann Sch—*school* OH-6
Mann Sch—*school* (3) OK-5
Mann Sch—*school* (4) PA-2
Mann Sch—*school* (3) SD-7
Mann Sch—*school* TX-5
Mann Sch—*school* (2) WA-9
Mann Sch—*school* (2) WI-6
Mann Sch (abandoned)—*school* MO-7
Manns Chapel—*church* IL-6
Manns Chapel—*church* (2) NC-3
Manns Chapel Cem—*cemetery* NC-3
Mann Sch Number 13—*school* IN-6
**Manns Choice**—*pop pl* PA-2
Manns Choice Borough—*civil* PA-2
Manns Corner—*locale* NY-2
Manns Creek—*stream* PA-2
Manns Creek—*stream* TN-4
Manns Creek—*stream* WV-2
**Mannsdale**—*pop pl* MS-4
*Mannsdale Plantation* MS-4
Manns Draw—*valley* WY-8
Mannser Creek—*stream* WA-9
*Manns Ferry* AL-4
Manns Ferry (historical)—*locale* AL-4
Manns Flat—*flat* WY-8
Manns Ford (historical)—*crossing* TN-4
Manns Fork Salt Creek—*stream* OH-6
Manns Harbor—*bay* NC-3
**Manns Harbor**—*pop pl* NC-3
Manns Hill—*summit* NY-2
Manns (historical)—*locale* MS-4
Mann-Simons Cottage—*hist pl* SC-3
Mann Site—*hist pl* IN-6
*Manns Lake* OR-9
Manns Old Landing (historical)—*locale* AL-4
Manns Peak—*summit* UT-8
Manns Pond—*lake* OR-9
Manns Pond—*reservoir* MA-1
Manns Pond Dam—*dam* MA-1
Mann Spring—*spring* MO-7
Mann Spring—*spring* OR-9
Manns Run—*stream* OH-6
Manns Spring—*spring* UT-8
Manns Spur—*locale* FL-3
**Manns Township**—*pop pl* ND-7
Manns Tunnel—*tunnel* WV-2
**Mannsville**—*pop pl* KY-4
**Mannsville**—*pop pl* NY-2
**Mannsville**—*pop pl* OK-5
**Mannsville**—*pop pl* PA-2
Mannsville (CCD)—*cens area* KY-4
Mannsville Sch—*school* PA-2
Manntown—*locale* KY-4
Manntown Ch—*church* FL-3
**Mann (Township of)**—*pop pl* PA-2
Mannuis Cem—*cemetery* AR-4
Mann Valley—*valley* WI-6
Mann Valley Cem—*cemetery* WI-6
*Mannville* SC-3
Mannville—*locale* FL-3
**Mannville**—*pop pl* NY-2
Mannville (historical)—*locale* MA-1
*Mannville Reservoir* MA-1
Manny Cem—*cemetery* IL-6
**Manny Corners**—*pop pl* NY-2
Manny Furnace (historical)—*locale* TN-4
Manny Gonzales Park—*park* AZ-5
Manny Ranch—*locale* TX-5
Manny Run—*stream* PA-2
Mannys Prairie—*flat* WA-9
Mann-Zwonecek House—*hist pl* NE-7
Mano—*island* FM-9
Mano—*locale* MO-7
**Manoa**—*pop pl* PA-2
Manoa Elem Sch—*school* PA-2
Manoa Falls—*falls* HI-9
**Manoa Heights**—*pop pl* PA-2
Manoa Japanese Language Sch—*school* HI-9
Manoa-Palolo Drainage Canal—*canal* HI-9
Manoa Sch—*school* HI-9
*Manoa School* PA-2
*Manoa Spring* CO-8
Manoa Springs—*spring* CO-8
Manoa Stream—*stream* (2) HI-9
Manoa Triangle—*park* HI-9
Manoa Tunnel—*cave* HI-9
Manoa Valley—*valley* HI-9
Manoa Valley Park—*park* HI-9
Manocknut Plantation (historical)—*locale* MS-4
Manofa—*island* AS-9
Man of War Brook—*stream* ME-1
Man of War Channel—*channel* FL-3
Man of War Harbor—*bay* FL-3
Man of War Harbor—*bay* MS-4
Man of War Key—*island* FL-3
Man-of-War Peak—*summit* AK-9
Manogue HS—*school* NV-8
Manoka Lake—*lake* MI-6
Manokin—*locale* MD-2
**Manokin**—*pop pl* MD-2
Manokinak River—*stream* AK-9
Manokin Branch—*stream* MD-2
Manokin Hist Dist—*hist pl* MD-2
**Manokin (Jamestown)**—*pop pl* MD-2
Manokin Presbyterian Church—*hist pl* MD-2
Manokin River—*stream* MD-2
*Manokisy Hill* PA-2
*Manok-nok-en'* MP-9
**Manokotak**—*pop pl* AK-9
Manoku Fishpond—*lake* HI-9
**Manolith**—*pop pl* CA-9
Manoloa—*cape* HI-9
Manoloa—*civil* HI-9
*Manoloa Point* HI-9
Manoloa Stream—*stream* HI-9
*Manoment Bay* MA-1
**Manomet**—*pop pl* MA-1
**Manomet Beach**—*pop pl* MA-1
**Manomet Bluffs**—*pop pl* MA-1
**Manomet Heights**—*pop pl* MA-1
Manomet Hill—*summit* MA-1
Manomet (historical P.O.)—*locale* MA-1
Manomet Life Saving Station—*locale* MA-1
Manomet Point—*cape* MA-1
*Manomet River* MA-1
Manomet Shop Ctr—*locale* MA-1
Manomin Creek—*stream* MN-6
*Manomin Lake* MN-6
Manomin Lake—*lake* MN-6
*Manomonack Pond* MA-1
Manon Canyon—*valley* UT-8
*Manononack Pond* MA-1
Manono Ridge—*ridge* HI-9
Mano Point—*cape* HI-9
Mano Prieto Mtn—*summit* TX-5
*Manor* MD-2
Manor—*locale* MD-2
Manor—*locale* WA-9
**Manor**—*pop pl* CA-9
**Manor**—*pop pl* DE-2
**Manor**—*pop pl* GA-3
**Manor**—*pop pl* (2) PA-2
**Manor**—*pop pl* TX-5
Manor, The—*hist pl* SC-3
Manor, The—*hist pl* WV-2
**Manor Acres (subdivision)**—*pop pl* PA-2
**Manora Estates (subdivision)**—*pop pl* AL-4
Manor and Cottages—*hist pl* NC-3
Manor Ave Sch—*school* OH-6
Manor Baptist Ch—*church* AL-4
Manor Borough—*civil* PA-2
*Manor Branch* AL-4
**Manor by the Lake**—*pop pl* MD-2
Manor (CCD)—*cens area* GA-3
Manor Cem—*cemetery* MD-2
Manor Ch—*church* MD-2
Manor Ch—*church* (2) PA-2
Manor Country Club—*other* MD-2
**Manor Creek**—*pop pl* KY-4
Manor Creek—*stream* MD-2
Manor Creek—*stream* PA-2
Manor Creek—*stream* SC-3
Manor Creek—*stream* WA-9
*Manor Creek Assembly of God Church* MS-4
*Manordale* PA-2
Manordale—*locale* PA-2
*Manor Elem Sch* PA-2
Manor Elem Sch—*school* PA-2
**Manor Estates Subdivision**—*pop pl* UT-8
Manor Fork—*stream* PA-2
Manor Foundation Sch—*school* MI-6
Manor Golf Course—*locale* PA-2
**Manorhaven**—*pop pl* NY-2
**Manor Haven (subdivision)**—*pop pl* AL-4
**Manor Heights**—*pop pl* PA-2
Manor Heights—*uninc pl* WI-6
**Manor Hill**—*pop pl* PA-2
Manor Hill—*summit* MD-2
Manor Hills—*range* PA-2
Manor Hills—*uninc pl* PA-2
Manor Hill Sch—*school* MO-7
Manor Hill Sch—*school* PA-2
**Manor Hill (subdivision)**—*pop pl* NC-3
Manor House—*hist pl* IL-6
Manor House—*hist pl* ME-1
Manor House—*hist pl* WI-6
Manor House, The—*building* NC-3
Manor HS—*school* TX-5
Manor Joint HS—*school* PA-2
Manor Junior Coll—*school* PA-2
*Manor Kill* NY-2
**Manor Kill**—*pop pl* NY-2
**Manorkill**—*pop pl* NY-2
Manor Kill—*stream* NY-2
Manorkill Falls—*falls* NY-2
Manor Knoll Airp (private)—*airport* PA-2
Manor Lake—*lake* NY-2
Manor Lake—*lake* TX-5
Manor Lake—*reservoir* IN-6
Manor Lake—*reservoir* PA-2
Manor Lake Dam—*dam* AL-4
Manor Lake Dam—*dam* PA-2
*Manor Lakes, The* PA-2
Manor Meeting House—*building* PA-2
*Manor Number One* MD-2
Manor Oaks Hosp—*hospital* FL-3
Manor Oaks Sch—*school* NY-2
*Manor Of Bentley* NY-2
*Manor Park* FL-3
Manor Park—*park* (2) IL-6
Manor Park—*park* MI-6
Manor Park—*park* MN-6
**Manor Park**—*pop pl* DE-2
**Manor Park**—*pop pl* DC-2
**Manor Park**—*pop pl* MD-2
**Manor Park**—*pop pl* NJ-2
**Manor Park Apartments**—*pop pl* DE-2
Manor Park Sch—*school* PA-2
**Manor Park Terrace**—*pop pl* PA-2
Manor Plains Sch—*school* NY-2
**Manor Ridge**—*pop pl* PA-2
Manor Rock—*rock* NY-2
**Manors, The**—*pop pl* VA-3
*Manor Sch* PA-2
Manor Sch—*school* CA-9
Manor Sch—*school* MI-6
Manor Sch—*school* (2) PA-2
Manor Shop Ctr—*locale* FL-3
Manor Slough—*stream* CA-9
Manor Street Elem Sch—*hist pl* PA-2
Manorton—*locale* NY-2
Manor Township Community Park—*park* PA-2
**Manor (Township of)**—*pop pl* (2) PA-2
Manor Valley Golf Course—*locale* PA-2
**Manor View**—*pop pl* MD-2
*Manorville* PA-2
**Manorville**—*pop pl* (2) NY-2
**Manorville**—*pop pl* PA-2
Manorville Borough—*civil* PA-2
**Manor Woods**—*pop pl* IN-6
**Manor Woods**—*pop pl* MD-2
Manos Creek—*stream* TX-5
Manos Spring—*spring* TX-5
Manowaialee—*civil* HI-9
Manowaialee For Res—*forest* HI-9
Manowaikohau—*civil* HI-9
Manowainui—*civil* HI-9
Manowaiopae—*civil* HI-9
Manowaiopae Homesteads—*civil* HI-9
Manowaiopae Stream—*stream* HI-9
Man-O-War Monmt—*pillar* KY-4
Mano Windmill—*locale* NM-5
**Manown**—*pop pl* PA-2
**Manown**—*pop pl* WV-2
Manoy Creek—*stream* AL-4
Man Peak—*summit* WY-8
Manqanpaaq—*bay* FM-9
**Manquin**—*pop pl* VA-3
*Manquin Creek* VA-3
*Manquin Pond* VA-3
Manresa—*locale* MD-2
Manresa Grotto—*cave* WA-9
Manresa Hall—*hist pl* WA-9
Manresa House of Retreats/Jefferson
College—*hist pl* LA-4
Manresa Island—*island* CT-1
Manresa Retreat—*locale* CA-9
Manresa Retreat—*locale* LA-4
Manresa State Beach—*park* CA-9
Man Ridge—*ridge* CA-9
Manring—*locale* TN-4
Manring Post Office (historical)—*building* TN-4
*Manrissa Island* CT-1
Man Run—*stream* IN-6
Manry—*locale* VA-3
Mansada Ranch—*locale* CA-9
Mansakenning—*hist pl* NY-2
Mansard Island Resort—*locale* TN-4
Mansard Roof House—*hist pl* NC-3
Mansberger Sch—*school* PA-2
*Mans Branch* FL-3
Mansbridge (historical)—*locale* SD-7
Mansco Hollow—*valley* MO-7
Manse—*locale* KY-4
Manse, The—*hist pl* MA-1
Manse, The—*hist pl* MS-4
Manse Branch—*stream* NC-3
Manse Creek—*stream* WY-8
Mansell Brook—*stream* (2) ME-1
Mansell Cem—*cemetery* TX-5
Mansell Creek—*stream* MS-4
Mansell Creek—*stream* TX-5
Mansell Lake Dam—*dam* MS-4
Mansell Mtn—*summit* ME-1
Mansell Pond—*lake* ME-1
Mansel Wolf Dam—*dam* AL-4
Mansel Wolf Lake—*reservoir* AL-4
Manse Meadow—*flat* (2) CA-9
Mansen Lake—*lake* WI-6
Manse Ranch—*locale* NV-8
**Manset**—*pop pl* ME-1
*Mansfield* CT-1
Mansfield—*hist pl* KY-4
Mansfield—*hist pl* PA-2
Mansfield—*hist pl* VA-3
Mansfield—*locale* AK-9
Mansfield—*locale* KS-7
Mansfield—*locale* MI-6
**Mansfield**—*pop pl* AL-4
**Mansfield**—*pop pl* AR-4
**Mansfield**—*pop pl* GA-3
**Mansfield**—*pop pl* IL-6
**Mansfield**—*pop pl* IN-6
**Mansfield**—*pop pl* LA-4
**Mansfield**—*pop pl* MA-1
**Mansfield**—*pop pl* MN-6
**Mansfield**—*pop pl* MO-7
**Mansfield**—*pop pl* NJ-2
**Mansfield**—*pop pl* NC-3
**Mansfield**—*pop pl* OH-6
**Mansfield**—*pop pl* PA-2
**Mansfield**—*pop pl* (2) SD-7
**Mansfield**—*pop pl* TN-4
**Mansfield**—*pop pl* TX-5
**Mansfield**—*pop pl* WA-9
**Mansfield**—*pop pl* WV-2
Mansfield, Judge, House—*hist pl* OH-6
Mansfield, Lake—*lake* AK-9
Mansfield, Lake—*reservoir* VT-1
Mansfield, Mount—*summit* VT-1
Mansfield, Murdock and Co.
Store—*hist pl* UT-8
Mansfield, Richard, House—*hist pl* CT-1
*Mansfield Academy* TN-4
Mansfield Airp—*airport* WA-9
Mansfield and Enlargement Ditch—*canal* CO-8
Mansfield Baptist Ch—*church* TN-4
Mansfield Battle Memorial Park—*park* LA-4
Mansfield Battle Park—*hist pl* LA-4
Mansfield Bend—*bend* KY-4
Mansfield Bluff—*cliff* AR-4
Mansfield Borough—*civil* PA-2
*Mansfield Branch* VA-3
Mansfield Branch—*stream* (2) TN-4
Mansfield Bridge—*hist pl* IN-6
Mansfield Cabin—*locale* CO-8
Mansfield Canal—*canal* CA-9
Mansfield Canyon—*valley* AZ-5
Mansfield Canyon—*valley* CA-9
Mansfield Canyon—*valley* ID-8
Mansfield (CCD)—*cens area* GA-3
Mansfield Cem—*cemetery* (2) IL-6
Mansfield Cem—*cemetery* NJ-2
Mansfield Cem—*cemetery* (2) OH-6
Mansfield Cem—*cemetery* TN-4
Mansfield Cem—*cemetery* TX-5
**Mansfield Center**—*pop pl* CT-1
Mansfield Center Hist Dist—*hist pl* CT-1
Mansfield Central Sch—*school* MA-1
Mansfield Ch—*church* PA-2
Mansfield Cheatham House—*hist pl* TN-4
Mansfield City—*locale* CT-1
Mansfield Cow Camp—*locale* MT-8
Mansfield Creek—*stream* AK-9
Mansfield Creek—*stream* CO-8
Mansfield Creek—*stream* ME-1
Mansfield Creek—*stream* (3) MI-6
Mansfield Creek—*stream* MT-8
Mansfield Creek—*stream* NY-2
Mansfield Creek—*stream* OR-9
Mansfield Cut Underwater Archeol
District—*hist pl* TX-5
Mansfield Dam—*dam* TX-5
Mansfield Dam—*other* TX-5
**Mansfield Depot**—*pop pl* CT-1
Mansfield Ditch—*canal* CO-8
Mansfield Ditch—*canal* OH-6
Mansfield Ditch—*canal* OR-9
Mansfield Ditch—*canal* WY-8
Mansfield Ditch Trail—*trail* CO-8
Mansfield Draw—*valley* CO-8
Mansfield Forest State Wildlife Mngmt
Area—*park* MO-7
**Mansfield Four Corners**—*pop pl* CT-1
Mansfield Gap—*gap* TN-4
**Mansfield Gap**—*pop pl* TN-4
*Mansfield Gap Baptist Church* TN-4
Mansfield Gap Ch—*church* TN-4
Mansfield Group—*mine* AZ-5
Mansfield Gulf—*valley* TN-4
Mansfield Hill—*summit* CO-8
Mansfield Hill—*summit* PA-2
Mansfield Hill—*summit* TN-4
Mansfield Hist Dist—*hist pl* LA-4
Mansfield (historical)—*locale* KS-7
**Mansfield Hollow**—*pop pl* CT-1
Mansfield Hollow—*valley* CT-1
Mansfield Hollow—*valley* MO-7
Mansfield Hollow—*valley* OH-6
Mansfield Hollow Hist Dist—*hist pl* CT-1
Mansfield Hollow Lake—*lake* CT-1
*Mansfield Hollow Reservoir* CT-1
Mansfield House—*hist pl* TX-5
Mansfield HS—*school* MA-1
Mansfield I (41OL50)—*hist pl* TX-5
Mansfield JHS—*school* AZ-5
*Mansfield Lake* IN-6
*Mansfield Lake* MA-1
Mansfield Lake—*lake* AR-4
Mansfield Lake—*lake* MN-6
Mansfield Lake—*reservoir* AR-4
Mansfield Ledge—*bench* ME-1
Mansfield Location—*locale* MI-6
Mansfield Lookout—*locale* OR-9
Mansfield Meadows—*flat* UT-8
Mansfield Memorial Park—*cemetery* OH-6
Mansfield Memorial Park—*park* MA-1
Mansfield Mine Location Hist
Dist—*hist pl* MI-6
Mansfield Monmt—*park* MD-2
*Mansfield Mtn* VT-1
Mansfield Mtn—*summit* OR-9
Mansfield Municipal Airp—*airport* MO-7
Mansfield Park—*park* AZ-5
Mansfield Park—*park* IL-6
Mansfield Park—*park* MI-6
Mansfield Park—*park* NC-3
Mansfield Peninsula—*cape* AK-9
Mansfield Plantation—*hist pl* SC-3
Mansfield Plantation—*locale* SC-3
Mansfield Point—*cape* CT-1
Mansfield Pond—*lake* FL-3
Mansfield Pond—*lake* ME-1
Mansfield Pond—*lake* (2) MA-1
Mansfield Pond—*lake* OR-9
Mansfield Post Office—*building* TN-4
Mansfield Post Office
(historical)—*building* AL-4
Mansfield-Prohosky Ditch—*canal* MT-8
Mansfield Ramp—*locale* IN-6
Mansfield Ranch—*locale* (2) TX-5
*Mansfield Reservoir* IN-6
Mansfield Savings Bank—*hist pl* OH-6
Mansfield Sch—*school* TX-5
Mansfield Sch (historical)—*school* TN-4
Mansfield Seep—*spring* NM-5
*Mansfield Southeast* OH-6
Mansfield Spring—*spring* TX-5
**Mansfield Square**—*pop pl* NJ-2
*Mansfield (sta.) (Mansfield Depot)* CT-1
*Mansfield State College* PA-2
Mansfield Street Archeol Site—*hist pl* TX-5
*Mansfield (Town name for Mansfield
Center)* CT-1
**Mansfield (Town of)**—*pop pl* CT-1
**Mansfield (Town of)**—*pop pl* MA-1
**Mansfield (Town of)**—*pop pl* NY-2
**Mansfield Township**—*pop pl* ND-7
Mansfield (Township of)—*other* OH-6
**Mansfield (Township of)**—*pop pl* MI-6
**Mansfield (Township of)**—*pop pl* MN-6
**Mansfield (Township of)**—*pop pl* (2) NJ-2
Mansfield Trail—*trail* OR-9
Mansfield Training Sch and Hosp—*hist pl* CT-1
Mansfield Univ of Pennsylvania—*school* PA-2
Mansfield Wash—*stream* NM-5
Mansfield Waterworks—*other* OH-6
Mansfield Woman's Club—*hist pl* OH-6
*Mansfield Woodhouse* NJ-2
Mansford—*locale* LA-4
Mansford—*locale* WA-9
*Mansford Bridge* TN-4
**Mansford (historical)**—*pop pl* TN-4
Mans Fork—*stream* OH-6
Man Shanty Brook—*stream* NY-2
Mans Head—*summit* MT-8
Manship Ch—*church* DE-2
Manship House—*hist pl* LA-4
Manship House—*hist pl* MS-4
Manship House (Boundary
Increase)—*hist pl* MS-4
Mans Hollow—*valley* TN-4
Mansion—*locale* VA-3
Mansion Beach—*beach* RI-1
Mansion Cem—*cemetery* MO-7
**Mansion Heights Addition
Subdivision**—*pop pl* UT-8
Mansion Hill Hist Dist—*hist pl* KY-4
Mansion Hill Hist Dist (Boundary
Increase)—*hist pl* KY-4
Mansion Hist Dist—*hist pl* NY-2
Mansion House—*building* NY-2
Mansion House—*hist pl* NJ-2
Mansion House, The—*hist pl* ME-1
Mansion House Hotel—*hist pl* CA-9
Mansion Mall—*locale* MO-7
Mansion Memorial Park—*cemetary* FL-3
Mansion Memorial Park—*cemetery* FL-3
*Mansion Of Health* NJ-2
Mansion Park—*park* PA-2
Mansion Row Hist Dist—*hist pl* IN-6
Mansion Square Park—*park* NY-2
Mansion Trail—*trail* VA-3
Mansion Truss Bridge—*hist pl* VA-3
**Mansion View**—*pop pl* AL-4
Mansker Cem—*cemetery* MO-7
Mansker Creek—*stream* AR-4
Mansker Creek—*stream* TN-4
Mansker Island—*island* TN-4
Mansker Lake—*reservoir* TX-5
*Manskers Creek* TN-4
*Manskers Island* TN-4
Manskers Island—*uninc pl* TN-4
Manslaughter Slough—*stream* AK-9
Manslick Road Cem—*cemetery* KY-4
Manso Lake—*lake* TX-5
Manson—*locale* ID-8
Manson—*locale* TX-5
**Manson**—*pop pl* AR-4
**Manson**—*pop pl* IN-6
**Manson**—*pop pl* IA-7
**Manson**—*pop pl* MT-8
**Manson**—*pop pl* NC-3
**Manson**—*pop pl* TN-4
**Manson**—*pop pl* WA-9
Manson Branch—*stream* GA-3
Manson Branch—*stream* IA-7
Manson Branch—*stream* TX-5
Manson (CCD)—*cens area* WA-9
Manson Cem—*cemetery* IN-6
Manson Corner—*locale* ME-1
**Manson Corner**—*pop pl* MA-1
Manson Creek—*stream* CA-9
Manson Creek—*stream* TX-5
Manson Elem Sch—*school* IA-7
Manson Ford—*locale* IL-6
*Manson Gulch* CO-8
Manson Hill—*summit* NH-1
Manson HS—*school* IA-7
Manson Kingery Ditch—*canal* IN-6
Manson Lake—*lake* NJ-2
Manson Lake—*lake* WI-6
Manson Mesa—*summit* AZ-5
Manson Post Office (historical)—*building* TN-4
Manson Saltpeter Cave—*cave* TN-4
Mansons Ch—*church* VA-3
Manson Sch—*school* (2) MO-7
Manson Sch—*school* TN-4
*Mansons Creek* TX-5
Manson Spring—*spring* GA-3
Manson-Wolf River (CCD)—*cens area* TN-4
Manson-Wolf River Division—*civil* TN-4
*Mans Peak* UT-8
Manston Cem—*cemetery* MN-6
Manston State Wildlife Mngmt
Area—*park* MN-6
**Manston (Township of)**—*pop pl* MN-6
Mansunita—*locale* AZ-5
*Mansun Lake* MN-6
**Mansura**—*pop pl* LA-4
Mansura Junction—*uninc pl* LA-4
Mansur Bay—*bay* WI-6
Mansur Boy Scout Camp—*locale* IL-6
Mansur Brook—*stream* ME-1
Mansure Pond—*lake* CT-1
Mansur Reef—*bar* WI-6
*Mansville* OK-5
*Mansville* PA-2
**Mansville**—*pop pl* PA-2
Mant—*island* FM-9
Manta—*locale* GA-3
**Mantachie**—*pop pl* MS-4
Mantachie Airp—*airport* MS-4
Mantachie Cem—*cemetery* MS-4
Mantachie Creek—*stream* MS-4
Mantachie First Baptist Ch—*church* MS-4
Mantachie Sch—*school* MS-4
**Mantador**—*pop pl* ND-7
Mantan Cem—*cemetery* TX-5
Mantansas—*locale* KS-7
*Mantanzas* KS-7
Mantanza Well—*well* TX-5
*Mantapeitak* FM-9
*Mantapeitak Island* FM-9
*Mantapeiti* FM-9
*Mantapeiti Island* FM-9
Mantapike—*locale* VA-3
Mantapike Creek—*stream* VA-3
*Mant Channel* FM-9
**Manteca**—*pop pl* CA-9
Manteca (CCD)—*cens area* CA-9
Manteca Gun Club—*other* CA-9
Manteca Junction—*locale* CA-9
**Mantee**—*pop pl* MS-4
Mantee Baptist Ch—*church* MS-4
Mantee Lake—*reservoir* MS-4
Mantee Lake Dam—*dam* MS-4
Mantee Post Office—*building* MS-4
*Mant Einfahrt* FM-9
Mantel Lake—*lake* OR-9
Manteno—*locale* IA-7
**Manteno**—*pop pl* IL-6
Manteno, Lake—*lake* IL-6
Manteno Community Hall—*locale* KS-7
Manteno County Park—*park* IA-7
Manteno (historical)—*locale* KS-7
Manteno State Hosp—*hospital* IL-6
**Manteno (Township of)**—*pop pl* IL-6
Manteo—*locale* VA-3
**Manteo**—*pop pl* NC-3
Manteo Airp—*airport* NC-3
*Manteo-Oregon Inlet Channel* NC-3
**Manteo (subdivision)**—*pop pl* NC-3
Manteo Well Field Site—*locale* NC-3
Mantequilla Lake—*lake* NM-5
**Manter**—*pop pl* KS-7
Manter Cem—*cemetery* KS-7
Manter Creek—*stream* CA-9
Manter Elem Sch—*school* KS-7
Manter Hill—*summit* ME-1
Manter Meadow—*flat* CA-9
Manternach Coulee—*valley* MT-8
Manterola Tank—*reservoir* AZ-5
Manter Sch—*school* ME-1
Manters Hole—*lake* MA-1
Manters Point—*cape* MA-1
Manter Township—*civil* KS-7
Mantes Canyon—*valley* CA-9
Mantey—*locale* KS-7
Manteys Chapel—*church* TN-4
Manteys Chapel Cem—*cemetery* TN-4
*Mant-Hafen* FM-9
*Mant Harbor* FM-9
Manthey Brook—*stream* CT-1
Manthos Ranch—*locale* WY-8
*Manti* AL-4
Manti—*locale* IA-7
**Manti**—*pop pl* UT-8
Manti Campground—*park* UT-8
Manti Canyon—*valley* UT-8
**Manti Canyon Summer
Homes**—*pop pl* UT-8
Manti Carnegie Library—*hist pl* UT-8
Manti Cem—*cemetery* IA-7
Manti Cem—*cemetery* UT-8
*Manti City Cemetery* UT-8
Manti City Hall—*hist pl* UT-8
*Mantick Mountain* CT-1
Manti Communtiy Campground—*locale* UT-8
Manti Dump Wildlife Mngmt Area—*park* UT-8
Mantie Hollow—*valley* AR-4
Manti-Ephraim Airp—*airport* UT-8
Manti Face Wildlife Mngmt Area—*park* UT-8
Manti HS—*school* UT-8
Mantila Camp—*locale* MI-6
Manti-La Sal Natl For—*forest* CO-8
Manti-La Sal Natl Forest-La Sal
Division—*forest* UT-8
Manti-LaSal Natl Forest-Manti
Division—*forest* UT-8
**Mantilla**—*pop pl* PR-3
Mantilo Branch—*stream* VA-3
Manti Meadows Waterfowl Mngmt
Area—*park* UT-8
Manti Mtn—*summit* UT-8
Manti Natl Guard Armory—*hist pl* UT-8
*Mant Inseln* FM-9
*Mantiock* PA-2
Manti Post Office—*building* UT-8
Manti Presbyterian Church—*hist pl* UT-8
Manti Ridge—*ridge* UT-8
Manti Sch—*school* UT-8
*Mant Islands* FM-9
Manti Temple—*church* UT-8
Manti Temple—*hist pl* UT-8
Mantkin Spring—*spring* AZ-5
Mantle Branch—*stream* AL-4
Mantle Branch—*stream* MO-7
Mantle Cave—*cave* CO-8
Mantle Ditch—*canal* IN-6
Mantle Ditch—*canal* MT-8
Mantle Gulch—*valley* UT-8
Mantle Lake—*lake* MN-6
Mantle Mine—*mine* CO-8
Mantle Mine—*mine* MT-8
Mantle Ranch—*locale* CO-8
Mantle Ranch—*locale* MT-8
Mantle Rock—*cliff* KY-4
Mantle Sch—*school* CO-8
Mantle Spring—*spring* CO-8
Mantle Summer Camp—*locale* CO-8
*Manto* FM-9
*Manto Creek* NJ-2
**Mantoloking**—*pop pl* (2) NJ-2
**Mantoloking Estates**—*pop pl* NJ-2
**Mantoloking Shores**—*pop pl* NJ-2
*Mantols Creek* NJ-2
*Manton* RI-1
Manton—*island* FM-9
Manton—*locale* KY-4
**Manton**—*pop pl* CA-9
**Manton**—*pop pl* MI-6
**Manton**—*pop pl* RI-1
Manton Coulee—*valley* MT-8
Manton Creek—*stream* MI-6
Manton Creek—*stream* TX-5
Manton Fire Control Station—*locale* CA-9
Manton-Hunt-Farnum Farm—*hist pl* RI-1
Manton (Mars Station)—*locale* KY-4
Manton Pond—*lake* ME-1
**Manton (RR name Mars)**—*pop pl* KY-4
*Manton Village* RI-1
Mantooth Cem—*cemetery* TN-4
**Mantorville**—*pop pl* MN-6
Mantorville Hist Dist—*hist pl* MN-6
**Mantorville (Township of)**—*pop pl* MN-6
*Mantos Creek* NJ-2
*Manto Suido* FM-9
*Manto To* FM-9
Mantown Cem—*cemetery* FL-3
Mant Passage—*channel* FM-9
Mantrap Fork—*stream* MT-8
Mantrap Gut—*gut* VA-3
Mantrap Lake—*lake* MN-6
**Mantrap (Township of)**—*pop pl* MN-6
Mantu—*locale* TX-5
Mantua—*CDP* VA-3
Mantua—*locale* AL-4
Mantua—*locale* MD-2
Mantua—*locale* WY-8
**Mantua**—*pop pl* NJ-2
**Mantua**—*pop pl* OH-6
**Mantua**—*pop pl* UT-8
**Mantua**—*pop pl* VA-3
Mantua—*uninc pl* PA-2
Mantua Cem—*cemetery* UT-8
**Mantua Center**—*pop pl* OH-6
Mantua Center District—*hist pl* OH-6
*Mantua Church* AL-4
**Mantua Corners**—*pop pl* OH-6
Mantua Creek—*stream* NJ-2
Mantua Draw—*valley* WY-8
Mantua Ferry—*locale* VA-3
Mantua Grove—*locale* NJ-2
Mantua Guard Station—*locale* UT-8
Mantua Gulch—*valley* CA-9
**Mantua Heights**—*pop pl* NJ-2
**Mantua Hills**—*pop pl* VA-3
Mantua (Magisterial District)—*fmr MCD* VA-3
Mantua Mounds—*summit* MS-4
Mantua Oil Field—*oilfield* MS-4
Mantua Rsvr—*reservoir* UT-8

Mantua Sch—school VA-3
Mantua Station Brick Commercial District—hist pl OH-6
**Mantua Terrace**—pop pl NJ-2
Mantua Terrace Sch—school NJ-2
Mantua Township—fmr MCD IA-7
**Mantua (Township of)**—pop pl NJ-2
**Mantua (Township of)**—pop pl OH-6
Mantua-West Greene (CCD)—cens area AL-4
Mantua-West Greene Division—civil AL-4
Mantyla Cem—cemetery MN-6
**Mantyla Subdivision**—pop pl UT-8
Manty Mtn—summit AK-9
**Mantyranta**—pop pl MA-1
**Mantz**—pop pl PA-2
Mantz Creek WY-8
Mantz Dam PA-2
Mantz Sch (abandoned)—school PA-2
Mantzville—locale PA-2
Manu, Moku (State Bird Refuge)—island HI-9
Manu'a (District)—civil AS-9
Manuahi Ridge—ridge HI-9
Manuahi Valley—valley HI-9
Manual Arts HS—school CA-9
Manual Arts Sch—school IA-7
Manual Church AL-4
Manual HS—school CO-8
Manual HS—school MO-7
Manual Training HS for Negroes—hist pl OK-5
Manual Training Sch—school IL-6
Manuel—locale KY-4
Manuel—uninc pl CA-9
Manuel, Bayou—gut (2) LA-4
Manuel, Bayou—stream LA-4
**Manuela**—pop pl PR-3
Manuel Arroyo—stream NM-5
**Manuela Subdivision**—pop pl UT-8
Manuel Bayou—stream AL-4
Manuel Bonafay Grant—civil FL-3
Manuel Branch—stream FL-3
Manuel Branch—stream NC-3
Manuel Canal—canal LA-4
Manuel Canyon—valley (2) CA-9
Manuel Canyon—valley NM-5
Manuel Canyon—valley TX-5
Manuel Cem—cemetery LA-4
Manuel Cem—cemetery OH-6
Manuel Ch—church SC-3
Manuel Creek WA-9
Manueles Canyon—valley NM-5
Manueles Creek—stream NM-5
Manuel Fuentes Well—well NM-5
Manuel Gap—gap WY-8
Manuel Gonzales Grant—civil FL-3
Manuel Hollow—valley WA-9
Manuelitas—locale NM-5
Manuelitas Creek—stream NM-5
Manuelito—locale NM-5
Manuelito Canyon—valley NM-5
Manuelito Complex—hist pl NM-5
Manuelito Place—locale NM-5
Manuelito Plateau (reduced usage)—area NM-5
Manuel Lake—lake WI-6
Manuella Lake—lake MN-6
Manuel Luis Ditch—canal HI-9
Manuel Mill—locale CA-9
Manuel Mine—mine MN-6
Manuelo Rock—island AS-9
Manuel Peak—summit CA-9
Manuel Peak Trail—trail CA-9
Manuel Point—cape AL-4
Manuel Seep—spring AZ-5
Manuel Seep Draw—valley AZ-5
Manuel Spring—spring (2) NM-5
Manuels Well AZ-5
Manuels Well—locale AZ-5
Manuel Tank—reservoir (2) NM-5
Manuel Tank—reservoir (2) TX-5
Manuel Ulibarri Ranch—locale NM-5
Manuel Wash—arroyo AZ-5
Manuel Well—well (2) NM-5
Manuel Windmill—locale (2) TX-5
Manufacturers Bldg—hist pl NC-3
Manufacturers Country Club—other PA-2
Manufacturer's Natl Bank—hist pl ME-1
Manuhonohono HI-9
Manuhonuhonu—summit HI-9
Manuhonuhonu Rsvr—reservoir HI-9
Manuka—civil HI-9
Manuka, Lake—lake MI-6
Manuka Bay—bay HI-9
Manuka Bay Petroglyphs—hist pl HI-9
Manuka Mauka House—locale HI-9
Manukani—summit HI-9
Manuka State Park—park HI-9
Manukun—locale FM-9
**Manukun**—pop pl FM-9
Manukun, Oror En—locale FM-9
Manukun, Unun En—bar FM-9
Manumpco Creek MD-2
Manumsco Creek—stream MD-2
Manumsico Creek MD-2
Manumuskin—locale NJ-2
Manumuskin Manor NJ-2
Manumuskin River—stream NJ-2
Manunka Chunk—locale NJ-2
Manunka Chunk Island NJ-2
Manunka Chunk Junction NJ-2
Manunu—other GU-9
Manunu Ridge—ridge AS-9
Manuohule—cape HI-9
Manup—summit FM-9
Manure Canyon—valley NV-8
Manure River KS-7
Manursing Island—island NY-2
Manursing Island Park—park NY-2
**Manus**—pop pl WV-2
Manus Cem—cemetery OK-5
Manus Creek—stream TN-4
Manus Run—stream PA-2
**Manus Town (historical)**—pop pl TN-4
Manu Temple—summit AZ-5
Manuwaiahu Gulch—valley HI-9
Manuwaikaalio Gulch—valley HI-9
Manuwish River WI-6
**Manvel**—pop pl ND-7
**Manvel**—pop pl TX-5
Manvel Canal—canal CO-8
Manvel Cem—cemetery TX-5
Manvel Oil Field—oilfield TX-5
Manvel Sch—school TX-5
Manver—locale PA-2
Manver Station—locale PA-2
Manville AL-4
**Manville**—pop pl IL-6
**Manville**—pop pl IN-6
**Manville**—pop pl NJ-2
**Manville**—pop pl RI-1
**Manville**—pop pl SC-3
**Manville**—pop pl VA-3
**Manville**—pop pl WY-8
Manville Bridge—other IL-6
Manville Dam—dam RI-1
Manville Ditch—canal CO-8
Manville Ditch No. 2—canal CO-8
Manville Draw—valley CO-8
Manville-Finderne NJ-2
**Manville-Finderne**—pop pl NJ-2
Manville Ranch—locale CO-8
Manville Sch—school IL-6
Manville Sch—school VA-3
Manville Shaft—mine PA-2
Manwaring Cem—cemetery IL-6
Manwarring Cem—cemetery OK-5
Manwell Gully—stream LA-4
Manwhague Plain—plain MA-1
Manwhague Swamp—swamp MA-1
Manwhauge Plain MA-1
Manxanedo Lake—reservoir PA-2
**Many**—pop pl LA-4
Many Arm Lake—lake MN-6
Many Arrow Wash—stream NM-5
Manyaska Lakebed—flat MN-6
**Manyaska (Township of)**—pop pl MN-6
Many Bobcats Hill—summit AZ-5
Many Branch—stream LA-4
Many Cherry Canyon—valley AZ-5
Many Coyote Mesa—summit AZ-5
Many Devils Wash—stream NM-5
Manydraw Rsvr—reservoir OR-9
Many Falls Trail—trail MT-8
**Many Farms**—pop pl AZ-5
Many Farms Boarding Sch—school AZ-5
Many Farms Child Development Center—school AZ-5
Many Farms Dam—dam AZ-5
Many Farms Elem Sch—school AZ-5
Many Farms HS—school AZ-5
Many Farms Lake—reservoir AZ-5
Many Farms Lake Campground—park AZ-5
Many Farms Public Sch—school AZ-5
Many Farms Spring—spring AZ-5
Many Farms Trading Post—locale AZ-5
Many Fork Branch—stream MD-2
Many Forks Ch—church GA-3
Many Ghosts Hill—summit AZ-5
Many Glacier—locale MT-8
Many Glacier Entrance Station—locale MT-8
**Many Glacier Hotel**—pop pl MT-8
Many Glacier Hotel Hist Dist—hist pl MT-8
Many Greasewood Valley—valley AZ-5
Many Island Lake—lake CA-9
**Many Islands**—pop pl AR-4
Many Ladders Trail—trail AZ-5
Many Mexican Spring—spring NM-5
Many Mind Creek—stream NJ-2
Many Minds Brook NJ-2
Many Minds Creek NJ-2
Manymoon Lake—lake MN-6
Many Owl Canyon—valley AZ-5
Many Parks Curve—locale CO-8
Many Point Lake—reservoir MN-6
Many Post Camp—locale TX-5
Many Sheep Valley—valley AZ-5
Many Sinks Cave—cave (2) AL-4
Many Skull Spring—spring AZ-5
Many Skulls Trail—trail AZ-5
Many Springs—locale MO-7
Many Springs Branch—stream MO-7
Many Springs Ch—church OK-5
Many Thunders Mtn—summit CO-8
Many Trails Peak—summit WA-9
Many Trails Ranch—locale SD-7
Many Winds, Lake—lake CO-8
**Manzana**—pop pl CA-9
Manzana Camp—locale CA-9
Manzana Campground—locale CA-9
Manzana Creek—stream CA-9
Manzana Mountain AZ-5
Manzana Narrows Camp—locale CA-9
Manzanar—locale CA-9
Manzanares, Tony, House—hist pl NM-5
Manzanares Cabin—locale NM-5
Manzanares Campground—locale NM-5
Manzanares Canyon—valley NM-5
Manzanares Creek—stream CO-8
Manzanares Lake—lake CO-8
Manzanares Mesa—summit NM-5
Manzanarez Canyon—valley NM-5
Manzanar War Relocation Center—hist pl CA-9
Manzana Trail—trail CA-9
Manzanedo Dam—dam PA-2
**Manzanillo**—pop pl PR-3
Manzanillo Sch—school CA-9
Manzanita—locale CA-9
Manzanita—locale (2) WA-9
**Manzanita**—pop pl (2) CA-9
**Manzanita**—pop pl OR-9
Manzanita Bay—bay AK-9
Manzanita Bay—bay WA-9
Manzanita Camp Cabin—locale AK-9
Manzanita Campground—park AZ-5
Manzanita Canyon—valley AZ-5
Manzanita Canyon—valley (2) CA-9
Manzanita Canyon—valley (2) NM-5
Manzanita Cem—cemetery CA-9
Manzanita Chute—stream CA-9
Manzanita Creek—stream AK-9
Manzanita Creek—stream (2) AZ-5
Manzanita Creek—stream (3) CA-9
Manzanita Creek—stream NM-5
Manzanita Creek—stream OR-9
Manzanita Fire Station—locale CA-9
Manzanita Flat—flat (4) CA-9
Manzanita Hill—summit (3) CA-9
**Manzanita Ind Res**—pop pl CA-9
Manzanita Island—island AK-9
Manzanita Island—island NY-2
Manzanita Knob—summit CA-9
Manzanita Lake—lake AK-9
Manzanita Lake—lake CA-9
**Manzanita Lake**—pop pl CA-9
Manzanita Lake—reservoir CA-9
Manzanita Lake—reservoir NV-8
Manzanita Mine—mine AZ-5
Manzanita Mine—mine (2) CA-9
Manzanita Mountains—other NM-5
Manzanita Mtn CA-9
Manzanita Mtn—summit AZ-5
Manzanita Mtn—summit (2) CA-9
Manzanita Park AZ-5
Manzanita Park—park AZ-5
Manzanita Park—park CA-9
Manzanita Peak—summit AK-9
Manzanita Point—cape CA-9
Manzanita Point—cliff AZ-5
Manzanita Ranch—locale CA-9
Manzanita Ridge—ridge (5) CA-9
Manzanita Ridge—ridge NM-5
Manzanitas Canyon—valley NM-5
Manzanita Sch—school (2) AZ-5
Manzanita Sch—school (8) CA-9
Manzanita Spring—spring (3) AZ-5
Manzanita Spring—spring (2) CA-9
Manzanita Spring—spring TX-5
Manzanita Springs—spring CA-9
Manzanita Tank—reservoir (2) AZ-5
Manzanita Wash—stream CA-9
Manzanita Winston Reynolds Park—park AZ-5
**Manzano**—pop pl NM-5
Manzano—post sta NM-5
Manzano Base—other NM-5
**Manzanola**—pop pl CO-8
Manzanola Bridge—hist pl CO-8
Manzano Lookout Tower—locale NM-5
Manzano Mountain—other NM-5
Manzano Mountains—range NM-5
Manzano Peak—summit NM-5
Manzar Cem—cemetery PA-2
Manzenita Island NY-2
Manziel Oil Field—oilfield TX-5
Manzone Well—well NV-8
Manzoro—locale AZ-5
Manzo Sch—school AZ-5
Mao MH-9
Maonakomalie—civil HI-9
Ma'oputasi (County of)—civ div AS-9
Mao Spring—spring GU-9
Maos Trail—trail AZ-5
Map FM-9
Mapao—area GU-9
Mapas—area GU-9
**Mapaville**—pop pl MO-7
Mapel Fork Branch—stream NC-3
Mapel Park Cem—cemetery MO-7
Mapes—locale NY-2
**Mapes**—pop pl ND-7
Mapes Canyon—valley CA-9
Mapes Cem—cemetery MO-7
Mapes Cow Camp—locale CA-9
Mapes Creek—stream (2) OR-9
Mapes Creek—stream PA-2
Mapes Drain—canal MI-6
Mapes (historical)—locale PA-2
Mapes Hotel and Casino—hist pl NV-8
Mapes Island—island IL-6
Mapes Lake TX-5
Mapes Ranch—locale CA-9
Mapes Rsvr—reservoir CA-9
Mapes Spring—spring CA-9
Mapes Tank—reservoir AZ-5
Mapes Township (historical)—civil ND-7
Mapies Branch—stream MO-7
Mapinger Canyon UT-8
Map' Island FM-9
Map Islands FM-9
Mapking Island MA-1
Maple MI-6
Maple TN-4
Maple—locale AR-4
Maple—locale IL-6
Maple—locale IA-7
Maple—locale KY-4
Maple—locale (2) MN-6
Maple—locale WV-2
**Maple**—pop pl NC-3
**Maple**—pop pl OH-6
**Maple**—pop pl OK-5
**Maple**—pop pl PA-2
**Maple**—pop pl SC-3
**Maple**—pop pl (2) TX-5
**Maple**—pop pl WI-6
**Maple Acre**—pop pl WV-2
**Maple Acres**—pop pl WV-2
**Maple Acres Subdivision**—pop pl UT-8
Maple Ave Baptist Ch—church AL-4
Maple Ave Cem—cemetery NH-1
Maple Ave Ch—church OH-6
Maple Ave Dam NJ-2
Maple Ave District—hist pl KY-4
Maple Ave Hist Dist—hist pl MA-1
Maple Ave Lake—reservoir IN-6
Maple Ave Lake Dam—dam IN-6
Maple Ave Maple Lane Hist Dist—hist pl IL-6
Maple Ave Park—park NY-2
Maple Ave Playground—park IL-6
Maple Ave Sch—school CA-9
Maple Ave Sch—school IN-6
Maple Ave Sch—school NH-1
Maple Ave Sch—school NJ-2
Maple Ave Sch—school NY-2
Maple Ave Sch—school NC-3
Maple Ave Station—locale NJ-2
Maple Bald Creek—stream NC-3
Maple Bay—bay MI-6
Maple Bay—bay (2) NY-2
**Maple Bay**—pop pl MN-6
**Maple Bay**—pop pl NY-2
Maple Bay—swamp NC-3
Maple Bay—swamp SC-3
Maple Bayou—gut AL-4
Maple Bayou—stream (2) LA-4
Maple Beach—beach WA-9
Maple Beach—locale MI-6
**Maple Beach**—pop pl NY-2
**Maple Beach**—pop pl PA-2
**Maple Beach**—pop pl (2) WA-9
Maple Beach Campground—park UT-8
Maple Beach Park—park OH-6
Maple Bench—bench UT-8
Maple Bench Campground—locale UT-8
Maple Bend—bend (2) TN-4
Maple Bend—bend VT-1
Maple Bend Island—island NY-2
Maple Birch Golf Course—other WI-6
Maple Bluff—cliff WI-6
**Maple Bluff**—pop pl WI-6
Maple Branch TN-4
Maple Branch—stream (4) AL-4
Maple Branch—stream CA-9
Maple Branch—stream DE-2
Maple Branch—stream (5) GA-3
Maple Branch—stream IL-6
Maple Branch—stream LA-4
Maple Branch—stream MS-4
Maple Branch—stream (7) NC-3
Maple Branch—stream SC-3
Maple Branch—stream (9) TN-4
Maple Branch—stream (2) TX-5
Maple Branch—stream (5) VA-3
Maple Branch—stream WV-2
Maple Branch Gas Field—oilfield MS-4
Maple Branch Sch—school TN-4
Maple Bridge RI-1
Maple Bridge (historical)—bridge AL-4
Maplebrook IL-6
Maple Brook MI-6
Maple Brook NJ-2
Maple Brook—stream NJ-2
Maple Brook—stream PA-2
Maple Brook—stream VT-1
**Maple Brook Lane**—pop pl OH-6
Maplebrook Sch—school NY-2
Maple Brook Trail—trail PA-2
Maple Camp—locale AZ-5
Maple Camp Bald—summit NC-3
Maple Camp Creek—stream NC-3
Maple Camp Lead—ridge TN-4
Maple Camp Ridge—ridge NC-3
Maple Canal—canal CA-9
Maple Cane Ch—church SC-3
Maple Cane Sch—school SC-3
Maple Cane Swamp—swamp SC-3
Maple Canyon ID-8
Maple Canyon—valley (2) AZ-5
Maple Canyon—valley (6) CA-9
Maple Canyon—valley (3) ID-8
Maple Canyon—valley NM-5
Maple Canyon—valley TX-5
Maple Canyon—valley (11) UT-8
Maple Canyon—valley WA-9
Maple Canyon Campground—park UT-8
Maple Canyon Creek—stream UT-8
Maple Canyon Lake—lake UT-8
Maple Canyon Slide—valley UT-8
Maple Canyon Spring—spring ID-8
Maple Cave Park Airp—airport PA-2
Maple Cem—cemetery AL-4
Maple Cem—cemetery IL-6
Maple Cem—cemetery IN-6
Maple Cem—cemetery IA-7
Maple Cem—cemetery MI-6
Maple Cem—cemetery (2) MO-7
Maple Cem—cemetery NE-7
Maple Cem—cemetery NY-2
Maple Cem—cemetery NC-3
Maple Cem—cemetery OH-6
Maple Cem—cemetery VT-1
Maple Center—locale MA-1
Maple Center Sch—school NE-7
Maple Ch—church WI-6
Maple Chapel—church AR-4
Maple Chapel—church OK-5
Maple City—locale KS-7
**Maple City**—pop pl MI-6
Maple City Cem—cemetery KS-7
**Maple City Subdivision**—pop pl UT-8
Maple Cliff—cliff ID-8
Maple Corner—locale OH-6
Maple Corner—other VT-1
**Maple Corner**—pop pl AR-4
Maple Corners PA-2
Maple Corners—locale NY-2
**Maple Corners (Calais Post Office)**—pop pl VT-1
Maple Corner Sch—school WI-6
Maple Court Apartments—hist pl IL-6
Maple Cove Campground—locale UT-8
Maple Cove Picnic Ground—locale UT-8
Maple Cove Recreation Site UT-8
**Maple Cove Subdivision**—pop pl UT-8
Maple Creek AL-4
Maple Creek CA-9
Maple Creek MI-6
Maple Creek SD-7
Maple Creek WA-9
Maple Creek WI-6
Maple Creek—fmr MCD (2) NE-7
**Maple Creek**—pop pl CA-9
Maple Creek—stream (2) AR-4
Maple Creek—stream (9) CA-9
Maple Creek—stream FL-3
Maple Creek—stream (2) GA-3
Maple Creek—stream (4) ID-8
Maple Creek—stream IL-6
Maple Creek—stream IN-6
Maple Creek—stream IA-7
Maple Creek—stream (2) KS-7
Maple Creek—stream KY-4
Maple Creek—stream (3) MI-6
Maple Creek—stream (2) MN-6
Maple Creek—stream MT-8
Maple Creek—stream (2) NE-7
Maple Creek—stream (2) NJ-2
Maple Creek—stream (4) NC-3
Maple Creek—stream ND-7
Maple Creek—stream (2) OH-6
Maple Creek—stream (13) OR-9
Maple Creek—stream (3) PA-2
Maple Creek—stream SC-3
Maple Creek—stream TN-4
Maple Creek—stream TX-5
Maple Creek—stream (5) UT-8
Maple Creek—stream VA-3
Maple Creek—stream (9) WA-9
Maple Creek—stream (2) WI-6
Maple Creek—stream WY-8
Maple Creek Campground UT-8
Maple Creek Cem—cemetery NE-7
Maple Creek Cem—cemetery PA-2
Maple Creek Cemetery Number 2—hospital WI-6
Maple Creek Cem No 2—cemetery WI-6
Maple Creek Cem Number 1—cemetery WI-6
Maple Creek Ch—church NC-3
Maple Creek Dam—dam TN-4
Maple Creek Lake—reservoir TN-4
Maple Creek (locale)—locale PA-2
Maple Creek Lookout Tower—locale TN-4
Maple Creek Post Office (historical)—building TN-4
Maple Creek Sch—school KY-4
**Maple Creek (Town of)**—pop pl WI-6
**Maplecrest**—pop pl DE-2
**Maplecrest**—pop pl MD-2
**Maplecrest**—pop pl NJ-2
**Maplecrest**—pop pl NY-2
**Maple Crest**—pop pl PA-2
**Maple Crest Acres**—pop pl TX-5
Maple Crest Ch—church IN-6
Maple Crest Elementary and MS—school IN-6
**Maple Crest (Glenmar Manor)**—pop pl MD-2
Maple Crest Golf Club—other IL-6
Maplecrest Lake Golf Club—other IL-6
Maplecrest Park—park MO-7
Maplecrest Park—park NJ-2
Maple Crest Sch IN-6
Maplecrest Sch—school MO-7
**Maple Crest Subdivision**—pop pl UT-8
Maplecroft - Charles M. Allen House—building MA-1
**Maple Crossroads**—pop pl SC-3
Maplecypress—locale NC-3
**Maple Cypress**—pop pl NC-3
Mapledale—locale (3) NY-2
Mapledale—locale WV-2
**Mapledale**—pop pl PA-2
**Mapledale**—pop pl WI-6
Maple Dale—valley WI-6
Maple Dale Cem—cemetery IL-6
Maple Dale Country Club—other DE-2
Mapledale Park—park MI-6
Mapledale Sch—school MO-7
Mapledale Sch—school OH-6
Maple Dale Sch—school OH-6
Maple Dale Sch—school (2) WI-6
Mapledale Sch—school WI-6
**Maple Dell**—pop pl VT-1
Maple Dell Camp—locale UT-8
Maple Dell Cem—cemetery OH-6
Maple Dell Creek OR-9
Maple Dell Gap—gap OR-9
Maple Ditch—canal AR-4
Maple Drain—canal CA-9
Maple Draw—valley AZ-5
Maple Elem Sch—school IN-6
Maple Falls—falls CA-9
Maple Falls—falls NJ-2
Maple Falls—falls WA-9
Maple Falls—locale WA-9
Maple Falls Brook—stream NH-1
Maple Flat—flat (2) CA-9
Maple Flat—flat (2) UT-8
Maple Flat Ponds—reservoir VA-3
Maple Flats—flat IN-6
Maple Flats—flat UT-8
Maple Flats—locale NY-2
Maple Flats Branch—stream VA-3
Maple Ford—locale AL-4
Maple Forest Cem—cemetery MI-6
Maple Forest Township Hall—locale MI-6
Maple Forest (Township of)—civ div MI-6
**Maple Fork**—pop pl WV-2
Maple Fork—stream LA-4
Maple Fork—stream UT-8
Maple Fork—stream (2) WV-2
Maple Forks—locale AL-4
Maple Gap—gap NC-3
Maple Gap—gap TX-5
Maple Gap—gap VA-3
Maple Glen—locale NY-2
**Maple Glen**—pop pl (2) PA-2
Maple Glen Ch—church (2) PA-2
**Maple Glen (Mapleglen)**—pop pl PA-2
Maple Glenn Sch—school IA-7
Maple Glen Sch—school MD-2
Maple Glen Sch—school WI-6
Maple Glen (Shoring)—uninc pl PA-2
**Maple Glen Subdivision**—pop pl UT-8
Maple Grange—locale NJ-2
Maplegrove ME-1
Maple Grove (2) MI-6
Maple Grove—fmr MCD NE-7
Maple Grove—hist pl MO-7
Maple Grove—locale CA-9
Maple Grove—locale GA-3
Maple Grove—locale IL-6
Maple Grove—locale IA-7
Maple Grove—locale KY-4
Maple Grove—locale MD-2
Maple Grove—locale MI-6
Maple Grove—locale NJ-2
Maple Grove—locale NY-2
Maple Grove—locale NC-3
Maple Grove—locale (2) OH-6
Maple Grove—locale OR-9
Maple Grove—locale (2) PA-2
Maple Grove—locale (2) TN-4
Maple Grove—locale UT-8
Maple Grove—locale (2) VA-3
**Maple Grove**—pop pl AL-4
**Maple Grove**—pop pl AR-4
**Maple Grove**—pop pl ME-1
**Maple Grove**—pop pl MA-1
**Maple Grove**—pop pl MI-6
**Maple Grove**—pop pl MN-6
**Maplegrove**—pop pl MO-7
**Maple Grove**—pop pl MO-7
**Maple Grove**—pop pl (3) NY-2
**Maple Grove**—pop pl OH-6
**Maple Grove**—pop pl (6) PA-2
**Maple Grove**—pop pl (2) TN-4
**Maple Grove**—pop pl (2) VA-3
**Maple Grove**—pop pl WA-9
**Maple Grove**—pop pl (2) WI-6
Maple Grove—valley UT-8
**Maple Grove Acres (subdivision)**—pop pl NC-3
Maple Grove Arena—other PA-2
Maple Grove Baptist Ch TN-4
Maple Grove Baptist Ch—church TN-4
Maple Grove Beach—beach WA-9
Maple Grove Branch Church MO-7
Maple Grove Cabins—locale MI-6
Maple Grove Camp—park IN-6
Maple Grove Camp Ground—locale CA-9
Maple Grove Campground—locale ME-1
Maple Grove Campground—park UT-8
Maple Grove Cem—cemetery AR-4
Maple Grove Cem—cemetery CT-1
Maple Grove Cem—cemetery (4) IL-6
Maple Grove Cem—cemetery (8) IN-6
Maple Grove Cem—cemetery (5) IA-7
Maple Grove Cem—cemetery (12) KS-7
Maple Grove Cem—cemetery (2) KY-4
Maple Grove Cem—cemetery (10) ME-1
Maple Grove Cem—cemetery (3) MA-1
Maple Grove Cem—cemetery (10) MI-6
Maplegrove Cem—cemetery MI-6
Maple Grove Cem—cemetery (11) MI-6
Maple Grove Cem—cemetery (5) MN-6
Maple Grove Cem—cemetery MO-7
Maple Grove Cem—cemetery (4) NE-7
Maple Grove Cem—cemetery NH-1
Maple Grove Cem—cemetery NJ-2
Maple Grove Cem—cemetery (27) NY-2
Maple Grove Cem—cemetery (19) OH-6
Maple Grove Cem—cemetery (2) OK-5
Maple Grove Cem—cemetery (5) PA-2
Maple Grove Cem—cemetery TN-4
Maple Grove Cem—cemetery (4) VT-1
Maple Grove Cem—cemetery WV-2
Maple Grove Cem—cemetery (6) WI-6
Maple Grove Cemetery—hist pl MI-6
Maple Grove Ch—church AL-4
Maple Grove Ch—church GA-3
Maple Grove Ch—church (8) IN-6
Maple Grove Ch—church (3) IA-7
Maple Grove Ch—church (3) KS-7
Maple Grove Ch—church (4) KY-4
Maple Grove Ch—church ME-1
Maple Grove Ch—church (2) MD-2
Maple Grove Ch—church (5) MI-6
Maple Grove Ch—church (7) MO-7
Maple Grove Ch—church (9) NC-3
Maple Grove Ch—church (7) OH-6
Maple Grove Ch—church OK-5
Maple Grove Ch—church (6) PA-2
Maple Grove Ch—church (6) TN-4
Maple Grove Ch—church TX-5
Maple Grove Ch—church (9) VA-3
Maple Grove Ch—church WV-2
Maple Grove Ch—church WI-6
Maple Grove Ch (historical)—church MO-7
Maple Grove Ch (historical)—church PA-2
Maple Grove Ch (historical)—church TN-4
Maple Grove Country Club—other WI-6
Maple Grove Creek—stream CA-9
Maple Grove Creek—stream OH-6
Maple Grove Downs MI-6
Maple Grove Elementary School TN-4
**Maple Grove Estates**—pop pl VA-3
Maple Grove Farm—hist pl DE-2
Maple Grove For Preserve—forest IL-6
Maple Grove Freewill Baptist Ch AL-4
Maple Grove (historical)—locale SD-7
Maple Grove (historical P.O.)—locale IA-7
Maple Grove Hollow—valley UT-8
Maple Grove Hot Springs—spring ID-8
Maple Grove Oil Field—other IL-6
Maple Grove Park—park PA-2
Maple Grove Post Office TN-4
Maple Grove Post Office (historical)—building AL-4
Maplegrove Post Office (historical)—building TN-4
Maple Grove Recreation Site UT-8
Maple Grove Rsvr—reservoir CO-8
Maple Grove Sch—school (2) CO-8
Maple Grove Sch—school (2) ID-8
Maple Grove Sch—school (29) IL-6
Maple Grove Sch—school IN-6
Maple Grove Sch—school (4) IA-7
Maple Grove Sch—school (2) KS-7
Maple Grove Sch—school (2) KY-4
Maple Grove Sch—school (3) MI-6
Maplegrove Sch—school MI-6
Maple Grove Sch—school (9) MI-6
Maple Grove Sch—school (2) MN-6
Maple Grove Sch—school (2) MO-7
Maple Grove Sch—school (10) NE-7
Maple Grove Sch—school (2) NC-3
Maple Grove Sch—school (2) OH-6
Maple Grove Sch—school OR-9
Maple Grove Sch—school (7) PA-2
Maple Grove Sch—school (2) TN-4
Maple Grove Sch—school VT-1
Maple Grove Sch—school VA-3
Maple Grove Sch—school (5) WI-6
Maple Grove Sch (abandoned)—school (7) MO-7
Maple Grove Sch (abandoned)—school (3) PA-2
Maple Grove Sch (historical)—school (2) AL-4
Maple Grove Sch (historical)—school (6) MO-7
Maple Grove Sch (historical)—school (3) PA-2
Maple Grove Sch (historical)—school (2) TN-4
Maple Grove School (Abandoned)—locale IL-6
Maple Grove School (abandoned)—locale MO-7
Maple Grove Spring—spring CA-9
**Maple Grove (Town of)**—pop pl (3) WI-6
**Maple Grove (Township of)**—pop pl (3) MI-6
**Maple Grove (Township of)**—pop pl (2) MN-6
Maple Gulch CA-9
Maple Gulch—valley (2) CA-9
Maple Gulch—valley (4) OR-9
Maple Gulch—valley UT-8
Maple Hall—hist pl VA-3
Maple Hall—locale VA-3
Maple Head Creek—stream FL-3
Maple Head Pond—lake FL-3
**Maple Heights**—pop pl IA-7
**Maple Heights**—pop pl (2) OH-6
**Maple Heights**—pop pl WI-6
Maple Heights Park—park OH-6

*Maplehill* ... KS-7
*Maple Hill* ... ME-1
Maple Hill—*hist pl* ... KY-4
Maple Hill—*locale* ... IA-7
Maple Hill—*locale* ... MO-7
Maple Hill—*locale* ... NY-2
Maple Hill—*locale* (2) ... PA-2
Maple Hill—*locale* ... WI-6
**Maple Hill**—*pop pl* ... AL-4
**Maple Hill**—*pop pl* ... CT-1
**Maple Hill**—*pop pl* ... KS-7
**Maple Hill**—*pop pl* ... MI-6
**Maple Hill**—*pop pl* ... MN-6
**Maple Hill**—*pop pl* ... NE-7
**Maple Hill**—*pop pl* ... NY-2
**Maple Hill**—*pop pl* ... NC-3
**Maple Hill**—*pop pl* ... PA-2
**Maple Hill**—*pop pl* (2) ... TN-4
Maple Hill—*summit* ... IN-6
Maple Hill—*summit* ... ME-1
Maple Hill—*summit* (2) ... MA-1
Maple Hill—*summit* (2) ... MI-6
Maple Hill—*summit* (2) ... MN-6
Maple Hill—*summit* ... NJ-2
Maple Hill—*summit* (5) ... NY-2
Maple Hill—*summit* ... OR-9
Maple Hill—*summit* (2) ... PA-2
Maple Hill—*summit* ... TN-4
Maple Hill—*summit* (3) ... VT-1
Maple Hill—*summit* (2) ... WI-6
Maple Hill Baptist Ch—*church* ... TN-4
Maple Hill Cem—*cemetery* ... AL-4
Maple Hill Cem—*cemetery* (2) ... IL-6
Maple Hill Cem—*cemetery* (2) ... IN-6
Maple Hill Cem—*cemetery* (3) ... IA-7
Maple Hill Cem—*cemetery* ... KS-7
Maple Hill Cem—*cemetery* ... KY-4
Maple Hill Cem—*cemetery* ... MA-1
Maple Hill Cem—*cemetery* (6) ... MI-6
Maple Hill Cem—*cemetery* (2) ... MN-6
Maple Hill Cem—*cemetery* ... MO-7
Maple Hill Cem—*cemetery* (5) ... NY-2
Maple Hill Cem—*cemetery* (4) ... OH-6
Maple Hill Cem—*cemetery* ... PA-2
Maple Hill Cem—*cemetery* ... TN-4
Maple Hill Cem—*cemetery* (2) ... VT-1
Maple Hill Cem—*cemetery* ... VA-3
Maple Hill Cem—*cemetery* (2) ... WI-6
Maple Hill Ch—*church* ... IN-6
Maple Hill Ch—*church* ... KS-7
Maple Hill Ch—*church* (2) ... KY-4
Maple Hill Ch—*church* ... MI-6
Maple Hill Ch—*church* (2) ... MN-6
Maple Hill Ch—*church* ... NC-3
Maple Hill Ch—*church* ... OH-6
Maple Hill Ch—*church* ... TN-4
Maple Hill Ch—*church* ... TX-5
Maple Hill Ch—*church* ... WV-2
Maple Hill Ch (historical)—*church* ... TN-4
*Maple Hill Ch of Christ* ... TN-4
Maple Hill Fire Tower—*locale* ... PA-2
Maple Hill Golf Course—*other* ... MI-6
Maple Hill Park—*park* ... MN-6
Maple Hill Ridge—*ridge* ... TN-4
*Maple Hills* ... TN-4
**Maple Hills**—*pop pl* ... VA-3
Maple Hill Sch—*school* (2) ... IL-6
Maple Hill Sch—*school* (3) ... MI-6
Maple Hill Sch—*school* (2) ... MN-6
Maple Hill Sch—*school* ... NE-7
Maple Hill Sch—*school* ... TN-4
Maple Hill Sch—*school* ... WI-6
Maple Hill Sch (abandoned)—*school* ... PA-2
Maple Hill Seminary (historical)—*school* ... TN-4
**Maple Hills Estates Subdivision**—*pop pl* ... UT-8
Maple Hills Golf Course—*other* ... MI-6
Maple Hill Shop Ctr—*locale* ... KS-7
Maple Hills Shop Ctr—*locale* ... MO-7
**Maple Hills Subdivision**—*pop pl* ... UT-8
**Maple Hills Subdivision (Plat 1)**—*pop pl* ... UT-8
**Maple Hills Subdivision (Plat 2A-4A)**—*pop pl* ... UT-8
**Maple Hill Township**—*pop pl* ... KS-7
*Maple Hollow* ... CT-1
Maple Hollow—*locale* ... CT-1
Maple Hollow—*valley* (2) ... ID-8
Maple Hollow—*valley* (2) ... KY-4
Maple Hollow—*valley* ... MO-7
Maple Hollow—*valley* (4) ... PA-2
Maple Hollow—*valley* ... TN-4
Maple Hollow—*valley* (6) ... UT-8
Maple Hollow—*valley* ... VA-3
Maple Hollow Branch—*stream* ... NJ-2
*Maple Hollow Creek* ... UT-8
Maple Hollow Picnic Area—*park* ... UT-8
Maple Hollow Sch (historical)—*school* ... PA-2
Maple Hollow Spring—*spring* ... ID-8
Maple Hollow Trail—*trail* ... PA-2
Maple HQ Dam—*dam* ... OR-9
Maple HQ Rsvr—*reservoir* ... OR-9
*Maplehurst* ... MI-6
Maplehurst—*hist pl* ... KY-4
**Maplehurst**—*pop pl* ... MI-6
**Maplehurst**—*pop pl* ... NY-2
**Maplehurst**—*pop pl* ... TN-4
Maplehurst, Lake—*lake* ... MI-6
Maplehurst Cem—*cemetery* ... NY-2
Maplehurst Cem—*cemetery* ... WI-6
Maplehurst Golf Course—*other* ... NY-2
Maplehurst Sch—*school* ... OH-6
**Maplehurst (Town of)**—*pop pl* ... WI-6
*Maple Island* ... NY-2
Maple Island—*island* ... IL-6
Maple Island—*island* ... LA-4
Maple Island—*island* (4) ... MI-6
Maple Island—*island* (2) ... MN-6
Maple Island—*island* ... MO-7
Maple Island—*island* ... NJ-2
Maple Island—*island* (4) ... NY-2
Maple Island—*island* ... PA-2
Maple Island—*locale* ... MN-6
**Maple Island**—*pop pl* ... MI-6
**Maple Island**—*pop pl* ... MN-6
Maple Island Conservation Area—*park* ... MO-7
Maple Island Sch—*school* ... MI-6
Maple Juice Cove—*bay* ... ME-1
Maple Knob—*summit* ... VA-3
Maple Knoll—*summit* ... OR-9
Maple Knoll Cem—*cemetery* ... MN-6
*Maple Lake* (2) ... MI-6
*Maple Lake* ... MN-6
Maple Lake—*lake* ... ID-8
Maple Lake—*lake* ... IL-6
Maple Lake—*lake* ... KY-4
Maple Lake—*lake* (3) ... MI-6
Maple Lake—*lake* (11) ... MN-6
Maple Lake—*lake* ... MO-7
Maple Lake—*lake* (2) ... NY-2
Maple Lake—*lake* ... PA-2
Maple Lake—*lake* (2) ... WI-6
**Maple Lake**—*pop pl* ... MN-6
**Maple Lake**—*pop pl* ... OH-6
**Maplelake**—*pop pl* ... PA-2
**Maple Lake**—*pop pl* ... PA-2
**Maple Lake**—*pop pl* ... WV-2
Maple Lake—*reservoir* (3) ... NJ-2
Maple Lake—*reservoir* (3) ... PA-2
Maple Lake—*reservoir* ... TN-4
Maple Lake—*reservoir* ... UT-8
Maple Lake—*swamp* ... MN-6
Maple Lake Ch—*church* ... MN-6
*Maple Lake Dam* ... NJ-2
Maple Lake Dam—*dam* (2) ... NJ-2
Maple Lake Dam—*dam* (3) ... PA-2
Maple Lake Dam—*dam* ... UT-8
Maple Lake Ridge—*ridge* ... ID-8
Maple Lake Sch—*school* ... MN-6
**Maple Lake (Township of)**—*pop pl* ... MN-6
**Maple Landing (historical)**—*pop pl* ... IA-7
**Maple Lane**—*pop pl* ... IL-6
**Maple Lane**—*pop pl* ... IN-6
**Maple Lane**—*pop pl* ... OR-9
Maple Lane Cem—*cemetery* ... OR-9
Maple Lane Ch—*church* ... WV-2
Maple Lane Elem Sch—*school* ... DE-2
Maple Lane Golf Club—*other* ... MI-6
*Maple Lane Sch* ... DE-2
Maple Lane Sch—*school* ... OR-9
Maple Lateral—*canal* ... CA-9
Maple Law Cem—*cemetery* ... IN-6
Maple Lawn—*hist pl* ... NY-2
Maple Lawn Cem—*cemetery* (4) ... IN-6
Maplelawn Cem—*cemetery* ... KY-4
Maple Lawn Cem—*cemetery* ... MI-6
Maple Lawn Cem—*cemetery* ... MN-6
Maple Lawn Cem—*cemetery* ... NY-2
Maplelawn Cem—*cemetery* ... NY-2
Maple Lawn Cem—*cemetery* (3) ... NY-2
Maple Lawn Cem—*cemetery* (2) ... OH-6
Maple Lawn Cem—*cemetery* ... TN-4
Maple Lawn Ch—*church* ... IN-6
Maple Lawn Ch—*church* ... NC-3
Maple Lawn Golf Course—*other* ... NY-2
Maple Lawn Hosp—*hospital* (2) ... MI-6
Maple Lawn Sch—*school* ... TX-5
Maple Lawn Sch—*school* ... WI-6
Maple Lawn Sch (abandoned)—*school* ... MO-7
Maple Lawn School (Abandoned)—*locale* ... WI-6
Maple Leaf—*locale* ... SD-7
**Maple Leaf**—*pop pl* ... IA-7
**Maple Leaf**—*pop pl* ... MI-6
**Mapleleaf**—*pop pl* ... WA-9
Maple Leaf Campground—*locale* ... WA-9
Maple Leaf Cem—*cemetery* ... OH-6
Maple Leaf Cem—*cemetery* ... WA-9
Maple Leaf Golf Course—*other* ... NH-1
Maple Leaf Lake—*lake* ... MN-6
Maple Leaf Lake—*reservoir* ... KY-4
Maple Leaf Mine—*mine* ... CO-8
Maple Leaf Sch—*school* (2) ... MN-6
Mapleleaf Sch—*school* ... WA-9
Maple Lick Run—*stream* ... MD-2
Maple Lode Mine (inactive)—*mine* ... CA-9
**Maple Manor**—*pop pl* ... PA-2
Maple Marsh—*swamp* ... LA-4
Maple Marsh and Beaver Dam Branch—*stream* ... DE-2
Maple-McLeod Cem—*cemetery* ... MS-4
**Maple Meade**—*pop pl* ... NJ-2
Maple Meade Sch—*school* ... NJ-2
Maple Meadow—*locale* ... WV-2
Maple Meadow—*swamp* ... ME-1
*Maplemeadow Brook* ... MA-1
Maple Meadow Brook—*stream* ... MA-1
Maple Meadow Creek—*stream* ... WV-2
**Maple Meadows Subdivision**—*pop pl* ... UT-8
Maplemere Sch—*school* ... NY-2
Maple Mine—*mine* ... CA-9
Maple Mine (underground)—*mine* ... AL-4
Maplemoor Golf Club—*other* ... NY-2
Maple Mound—*summit* ... FL-3
Maple Mound Cem—*cemetery* ... OH-6
Maple Mound Rsvr—*reservoir* ... OR-9
**Maple Mount (Mount St. Joseph)**—*pop pl* ... KY-4
Maple Mtn—*summit* ... ME-1
Maple Mtn—*summit* ... NH-1
Maple Mtn—*summit* (2) ... NY-2
Maple Mtn—*summit* ... WA-9
Maple No 2—*locale* ... IA-7
Maple Park—*park* ... CA-9
Maple Park—*park* ... MN-6
Maple Park—*park* ... MO-7
Maple Park—*park* ... OK-5
Maple Park—*park* ... OR-9
**Maple Park**—*pop pl* ... IL-6
**Maple Park**—*pop pl* ... MA-1
**Maple Park**—*pop pl* ... MO-7
**Maple Park**—*pop pl* ... OH-6
Maple Park Bogs—*swamp* ... MA-1
Maple Park Cem—*cemetery* ... MO-7
Maple Park Cem—*cemetery* ... WV-2
Maple Park Elem Sch—*school* (2) ... IN-6
Maple Park JHS—*school* ... MO-7
Maple Park Sch—*school* ... MI-6
Maple Park Sch—*school* ... OH-6
Maple Park Sch—*school* ... PA-2
Maple Park Sch—*school* ... WA-9
Maple Peak—*summit* ... AZ-5
Maple Peak—*summit* ... ID-8
Maple Peak—*summit* ... UT-8
Maple Pit—*mine* ... WA-9
**Maple Plain**—*pop pl* ... MN-6
**Maple Plains**—*pop pl* ... MD-2
Maple Plains Fish Hatchery—*other* ... WI-6
**Maple Plain (Town of)**—*pop pl* ... WI-6
Maple Point—*cape* ... MI-6
Maple Point—*cape* ... WA-9
Maple Point—*cape* ... WI-6
Maple Point—*locale* ... IL-6
**Maple Point**—*pop pl* ... NY-2
**Maple Point**—*pop pl* ... PA-2
**Maple Point**—*pop pl* ... WV-2
Maple Point HS—*school* ... PA-2
Maplepole Run—*stream* ... PA-2
Maple Pond—*lake* ... SC-3
Maple Pond (historical)—*lake* ... TN-4
Maple Ranch—*locale* ... WY-8
**Maple Rapids**—*pop pl* (2) ... MI-6
Maple Rest Cem—*cemetery* ... NY-2
*Maple Ridge* ... PA-2
**Maple Ridge**—*pop pl* ... IN-6
**Maple Ridge**—*pop pl* ... MA-1
**Maple Ridge**—*pop pl* ... MI-6
**Maple Ridge**—*pop pl* ... OH-6
**Maple Ridge**—*pop pl* ... PA-2
Maple Ridge—*ridge* ... KY-4
Maple Ridge—*ridge* (3) ... ME-1
Maple Ridge—*ridge* ... NH-1
Maple Ridge—*ridge* (3) ... NY-2
Maple Ridge—*ridge* (2) ... PA-2
Maple Ridge—*ridge* (2) ... UT-8
Maple Ridge—*ridge* (6) ... WI-6
Maple Ridge Cem—*cemetery* (2) ... IL-6
Maple Ridge Cem—*cemetery* ... IN-6
Maple Ridge Cem—*cemetery* (2) ... ME-1
Maple Ridge Cem—*cemetery* (2) ... MI-6
Maple Ridge Cem—*cemetery* ... OH-6
Maple Ridge Cem—*cemetery* (2) ... PA-2
Maple Ridge Ch—*church* ... MN-6
Maple Ridge Ch—*church* ... NY-2
Maple Ridge Ch—*church* ... SC-3
Maple Ridge Club—*other* ... MI-6
Maple Ridge County Park—*park* ... MI-6
Maple Ridge Elem Sch—*school* ... PA-2
Maple Ridge Historic Residential District—*hist pl* ... OK-5
Maple Ridge Island—*island* ... ME-1
*Maple Ridge Sch* ... PA-2
Maple Ridge Sch—*school* ... ME-1
Maple Ridge Sch—*school* (3) ... MI-6
Maple Ridge Sch (abandoned)—*school* ... PA-2
**Maple Ridge (Township of)**—*pop pl* (2) ... MI-6
**Maple Ridge (Township of)**—*pop pl* (2) ... MN-6
*Maple River* ... MI-6
*Maple River* ... ND-7
**Maple River**—*pop pl* ... IA-7
Maple River—*stream* ... FL-3
Maple River—*stream* ... IA-7
Maple River—*stream* (2) ... MI-6
Maple River—*stream* ... MN-6
Maple River—*stream* (2) ... ND-7
Maple River—*stream* ... SD-7
Maple River Cem—*cemetery* (2) ... MI-6
Maple River Dam—*dam* ... ND-7
**Maple River Junction**—*pop pl* ... IA-7
Maple River Lake—*reservoir* ... ND-7
Maple River Natl Wildlife Ref—*park* ... ND-7
Maple River State Game Area—*park* ... MI-6
*Maple River Township* ... ND-7
Maple River Township—*fmr MCD* ... IA-7
**Maple River Township**—*pop pl* ... ND-7
**Maple River (Township of)**—*pop pl* ... MI-6
Maple Root Branch—*stream* ... NJ-2
Maple Root Pond—*reservoir* ... RI-1
*Maple Root Swamp* ... NJ-2
**Maple Root Village (Trailer Park)**—*pop pl* ... RI-1
**Maple Row Estates (subdivision)**—*pop pl* ... TN-4
Maple Row Shop Ctr—*locale* ... TN-4
Maple Rsvr—*reservoir* ... AZ-5
Maple Run—*stream* (2) ... IN-6
Maple Run—*stream* ... MD-2
Maple Run—*stream* (2) ... NJ-2
Maple Run—*stream* ... OH-6
Maple Run—*stream* (5) ... PA-2
Maple Run—*stream* ... VA-3
Maple Run—*stream* (7) ... WV-2
Maple Run Ch—*church* ... IN-6
Maple Run Ch—*church* ... WV-2
Maples—*hist pl* ... DE-2
Maples—*locale* ... TN-4
**Maples**—*pop pl* ... IN-6
**Maples**—*pop pl* ... MO-7
**Maples**—*pop pl* ... NY-2
Maples, The—*hist pl* ... MD-2
Maples, The—*hist pl* (2) ... NY-2
Maples, The—*locale* ... OR-9
Maples, The—*park* ... DC-2
**Maples, The**—*pop pl* ... NJ-2
**Maples, The (subdivision)**—*pop pl* ... TN-4
Maple Saint Sch—*school* ... GA-3
*Maples Camp Ground* ... OR-9
*Maples Campground* ... UT-8
*Maples Campground, The* ... UT-8
Maples Cem—*cemetery* (3) ... AL-4
Maples Cem—*cemetery* ... LA-4
Maples Cem—*cemetery* ... MS-4
Maples Cem—*cemetery* ... TN-4
Maples Cemetery, The—*cemetery* ... NY-2
Maple Sch—*school* (5) ... CA-9
Maple Sch—*school* (4) ... IL-6
Maple Sch—*school* ... IN-6
Maple Sch—*school* ... ME-1
Maple Sch—*school* ... MA-1
Maple Sch—*school* ... MI-6
Maple Sch—*school* ... NY-2
Maple Sch—*school* (3) ... OH-6
Maple Sch—*school* (2) ... OK-5
Maple Sch—*school* (2) ... OR-9
Maple Sch—*school* ... SC-3
Maple Sch (abandoned)—*school* ... MO-7
Maple Sch (historical)—*school* ... AL-4
Maple School (Abandoned)—*locale* ... WI-6
Maples Corner—*locale* ... KY-4
Maples Corners Sch—*school* ... WI-6
Maples Cottage—*hist pl* ... MA-1
Maples Creek—*stream* ... MS-4
Maple Seep—*spring* ... UT-8
Maples Forest Camp—*locale* ... OR-9
*Mapleshade* ... OH-6
**Maple Shade**—*pop pl* (2) ... NJ-2
**Maple Shade**—*pop pl* ... NY-2
**Mapleshade**—*pop pl* ... OH-6
**Maple Shade**—*pop pl* (2) ... PA-2
Maple Shade Cem—*cemetery* ... MI-6
Maple Shade Cem—*cemetery* ... OH-6
Maple Shade Ch—*church* ... AR-4
Maple Shade Ch—*church* ... VA-3
*Maple Shade Farm* ... NY-2
Mapleshade Sch—*school* ... MA-1
Maple Shade Sch—*school* ... MO-7
Maple Shade Sch—*school* ... WI-6
Maple Shade Sch (abandoned)—*school* ... PA-2
**Maple Shade (Township of)**—*pop pl* ... NJ-2
Maple Shady Grove Ch—*church* ... MS-4
Maple Shaft—*mine* ... UT-8
Maple-Sheyenne Ch—*church* ... ND-7
**Maples (historical)**—*pop pl* ... OR-9
**Maples (historical)**—*pop pl* ... TN-4
Maples Hollow—*valley* ... TN-4
Mapleside—*locale* ... IA-7
Mapleside—*uninc pl* ... MD-2
*Maples Lake* ... AL-4
Maples Lake Dam—*dam* ... AL-4
Maple Slash—*lake* ... MO-7
Maple Slash Slough—*stream* ... TN-4
Maples Library—*building* ... TN-4
*Maple Slide Canyon* ... UT-8
*Maple Slough* ... AR-4
*Maple Slough* ... MO-7
Maple Slough—*gut* (2) ... AR-4
Maple Slough—*gut* ... IL-6
Maple Slough—*gut* ... LA-4
Maple Slough—*gut* (2) ... TX-5
Maple Slough—*stream* (2) ... AR-4
Maple Slough—*stream* ... TX-5
Maple Slough—*swamp* ... TX-5
*Maple Slough Ditch* ... AR-4
Maple Slough Ditch—*canal* ... AR-4
Maple Slough Ditch—*canal* ... MO-7
*Maple Slough Lateral* ... MO-7
Mapleslush Branch—*stream* ... TN-4
Maples Memorial United Methodist Ch—*church* ... MS-4
**Maples Mill**—*pop pl* ... IL-6
Maples Picnic Area—*locale* ... UT-8
Maples Post Office (historical)—*building* ... AL-4
Maples Post Office (historical)—*building* ... TN-4
Maple Spring—*locale* (2) ... TN-4
**Maple Spring**—*pop pl* ... TN-4
Maple Spring—*spring* (8) ... AZ-5
Maple Spring—*spring* ... AR-4
Maple Spring—*spring* (10) ... CA-9
Maple Spring—*spring* (2) ... ID-8
Maple Spring—*spring* (3) ... OR-9
Maple Spring—*spring* (3) ... TN-4
Maple Spring—*spring* (13) ... UT-8
Maple Spring—*spring* ... VA-3
Maple Spring—*spring* ... WI-6
Maple Spring Branch—*stream* ... GA-3
Maple Spring Branch—*stream* ... KY-4
Maple Spring Branch—*stream* (2) ... NC-3
Maple Spring Branch—*stream* (2) ... VA-3
*Maple Spring Brok* ... MA-1
Maple Spring Brook—*stream* ... PA-2
Maple Spring Canyon—*valley* ... UT-8
Maple Spring Cem—*cemetery* ... WV-2
Maple Spring Ch—*church* (2) ... GA-3
Maple Spring Ch—*church* ... KY-4
Maple Spring Ch—*church* ... WV-2
*Maple Spring Church* ... TN-4
Maple Spring Fire Trail—*trail* ... TN-4
Maple Spring Gap—*gap* ... GA-3
Maple Spring Gap—*gap* ... NC-3
Maple Spring Gap—*gap* (2) ... TN-4
Maple Spring Hollow—*valley* ... TN-4
Maple Spring Hollow—*valley* (4) ... UT-8
Maple Spring Pond—*reservoir* ... MA-1
Maple Spring Pond Dam—*dam* ... MA-1
Maple Spring Run—*stream* ... VA-3
*Maple Springs* ... UT-8
Maple Springs—*locale* ... MN-6
Maple Springs—*locale* ... NC-3
Maple Springs—*locale* ... TX-5
**Maple Springs**—*pop pl* ... AR-4
**Maple Springs**—*pop pl* ... NY-2
**Maple Springs**—*pop pl* ... NC-3
Maple Springs Acad (historical)—*school* ... MS-4
*Maple Springs Baptist Church* ... TN-4
Maple Springs Bog—*swamp* ... MA-1
Maple Springs Branch—*stream* ... NC-3
Maple Springs Branch—*stream* ... TN-4
Maple Springs Brook—*stream* ... MA-1
Maple Springs Brook Number 1 Dam—*dam* ... MA-1
Maple Springs Brook Rsvr—*reservoir* ... MA-1
Maple Springs Cem—*cemetery* ... GA-3
Maple Springs Cem—*cemetery* ... MS-4
*Maple Springs Ch* ... AL-4
Maple Springs Ch—*church* ... AL-4
Maple Springs Ch—*church* (2) ... AR-4
Maple Springs Ch—*church* ... LA-4
Maple Springs Ch—*church* (6) ... NC-3
Maple Springs Ch—*church* (2) ... PA-2
Maple Springs Ch—*church* (4) ... TN-4
Maple Springs Ch—*church* (2) ... TX-5
Maple Springs Ch (historical)—*church* ... TN-4
Maple Spring Sch (historical)—*school* (2) ... TN-4
Maple Springs Gap—*gap* ... TN-4
Maple Springs Hollow—*valley* ... VA-3
Maple Springs Post Office (historical)—*building* ... TN-4
Maple Springs Ranger Station—*locale* ... KY-4
Maple Springs Sch—*school* ... OK-5
Maple Springs Sch (historical)—*school* ... MS-4
Maple Springs Sch (historical)—*school* ... TN-4
*Maple Springs School* ... TN-4
**Maple Springs Subdivision**—*pop pl* ... UT-8
Maple Spring Tank—*reservoir* ... AZ-5
Maple Spring Truck Trail—*trail* ... CA-9
Maple Station (historical)—*locale* ... PA-2
Maple Store—*locale* ... AL-4
Maple Street Cem—*cemetery* ... MA-1
Maple Street Ch—*church* ... NC-3
Maple Street Hist Dist—*hist pl* ... WV-2
Maple Street Pond—*reservoir* ... MA-1
Maple Street Pond Dam—*dam* ... MA-1
Maple Street Sch—*school* ... IL-6
Maple Street Sch—*school* ... MA-1
Maple Street Sch—*school* ... MI-6
Maple Street Sch—*school* ... NH-1
Maple Street Sch—*school* ... NY-2
Maple Street Sch—*school* ... OH-6
**Maple (subdivision)**—*pop pl* ... PA-2
Maple Sugar Gap—*gap* ... NC-3
Maple Sugar Gap—*gap* ... TN-4
Maple Summit—*locale* ... PA-2
Maple Summit Ch—*church* (2) ... PA-2
Maple Summit Sch—*school* ... PA-2
Maplesville—*locale* ... KY-4
**Maplesville**—*pop pl* ... AL-4
Maplesville (CCD)—*cens area* ... AL-4
Maplesville Community Ch—*church* ... AL-4
Maplesville Division—*civil* ... AL-4
Maplesville HS—*school* ... AL-4
*Maple Swamp* ... NC-3
Maple Swamp—*reservoir* ... VA-3
Maple Swamp—*stream* ... NJ-2
Maple Swamp—*stream* ... NC-3
Maple Swamp—*stream* (2) ... SC-3
Maple Swamp—*swamp* ... AL-4
Maple Swamp—*swamp* ... CT-1
Maple Swamp—*swamp* ... KY-4
Maple Swamp—*swamp* ... ME-1
Maple Swamp—*swamp* (4) ... MA-1
Maple Swamp—*swamp* ... NJ-2
Maple Swamp—*swamp* ... NY-2
Maple Swamp—*swamp* ... NC-3
Maple Swamp—*swamp* ... PA-2
Maple Swamp—*swamp* ... SC-3
Maple Swamp Branch—*stream* ... AL-4
Maple Swamp Branch—*stream* ... VA-3
Maple Swamp Brook—*stream* ... ME-1
Maple Swamp Creek—*stream* ... VA-3
Maple Swamp Ditch—*canal* ... OH-6
Maple Swamp Drain—*canal* ... MI-6
Maple Syrup Well—*well* ... NV-8
Maple Tank—*reservoir* ... AZ-5
**Maple Terrace**—*pop pl* (2) ... VA-3
*Mapleton* ... IN-6
*Mapleton* ... MO-7
Mapleton—*hist pl* ... NY-2
Mapleton—*locale* ... MI-6
Mapleton—*locale* ... TX-5
**Mapleton**—*pop pl* ... ID-8
**Mapleton**—*pop pl* ... IL-6
**Mapleton**—*pop pl* ... IN-6
**Mapleton**—*pop pl* ... IA-7
**Mapleton**—*pop pl* ... KS-7
**Mapleton**—*pop pl* ... ME-1
**Mapleton**—*pop pl* (2) ... MI-6
**Mapleton**—*pop pl* ... MN-6
**Mapleton**—*pop pl* ... NH-1
**Mapleton**—*pop pl* (2) ... NY-2
**Mapleton**—*pop pl* ... NC-3
**Mapleton**—*pop pl* ... ND-7
**Mapleton**—*pop pl* ... OH-6
**Mapleton**—*pop pl* ... OR-9
**Mapleton**—*pop pl* ... PA-2
**Mapleton**—*pop pl* ... UT-8
**Mapleton**—*pop pl* ... VA-3
**Mapleton**—*pop pl* ... WI-6
Mapleton Borough—*civil* ... PA-2
Mapleton Cem—*cemetery* ... IN-6
Mapleton Cem—*cemetery* ... ND-7
Mapleton Ch—*church* ... PA-2
**Mapleton Corner**—*pop pl* ... IN-6
**Mapleton (corporate and RR name for Mapleton Depot)**—*pop pl* ... PA-2
*Mapleton Depot* ... PA-2
*Mapleton Depot (corporate and RR name Mapleton)* ... PA-2
Mapleton First Baptist Ch—*church* ... IN-6
**Mapleton Hills**—*pop pl* ... TN-4
Mapleton HS—*school* ... CO-8
Mapleton Junction—*locale* ... PA-2
Mapleton Junction Station—*locale* ... PA-2
Mapleton Lateral—*canal* ... UT-8
Mapleton Mine—*mine* ... MT-8
Mapleton Ranger Station—*locale* ... OR-9
Mapleton Sch—*school* ... CO-8
Mapleton Sch—*school* ... KY-4
Mapleton Sch—*school* ... PA-2
Mapleton Sch—*school* ... UT-8
Mapleton Sch—*school* ... WI-6
Mapleton Siding—*locale* ... UT-8
**Mapleton (Town of)**—*pop pl* ... ME-1
**Mapleton Township**—*pop pl* ... ND-7
**Mapleton Township**—*pop pl* ... SD-7
**Mapleton (Township of)**—*pop pl* ... MN-6
Mapleton-Union Elem Sch—*school* ... PA-2
**Mapletown**—*pop pl* ... PA-2
**Mapletown (Blaine)**—*pop pl* ... NY-2
**Maple (Town of)**—*pop pl* ... WI-6
Maple Township—*fmr MCD* (2) ... IA-7
**Maple Township**—*pop pl* ... KS-7
**Maple Township**—*pop pl* ... NE-7
**Maple Township**—*pop pl* ... ND-7
**Maple (Township of)**—*pop pl* ... MN-6
Maple Trail—*trail* ... PA-2
Maple Transit—*post sta* ... NY-2
*Maple Tree Island* ... FM-9
Maple Tree Sch—*school* ... WI-6
Maple Tree Shop Ctr—*locale* ... MO-7
Maple-Union Corners—*hist pl* ... MA-1
Maplevale Ch—*church* ... AR-4
*Maple Valley* ... OH-6
Maple Valley—*locale* ... OH-6
Maplevalley—*other* ... WA-9
**Maple Valley**—*pop pl* ... IN-6
**Maple Valley**—*pop pl* ... MI-6
**Maple Valley**—*pop pl* ... NY-2
**Maple Valley**—*pop pl* ... WA-9
Maple Valley Cem—*cemetery* (3) ... MI-6
Maple Valley Cem—*cemetery* ... WI-6
Maple Valley Ch—*church* ... WV-2
Maple Valley Country Club—*other* ... MN-6
**Maple Valley (Maplevalley)**—*pop pl* ... WA-9
Maple Valley Park—*park* ... PA-2
Maple Valley Sch—*school* ... WA-9
Maple Valley Sch—*school* ... WI-6
Maple Valley Sch (historical)—*school* ... TN-4
Maple Valley School—*other* ... OH-6
**Maple Valley (Town of)**—*pop pl* ... WI-6
Maple Valley Township—*fmr MCD* ... IA-7
Maple Valley (Township of)—*civ div* (2) ... MI-6
**Maple View**—*pop pl* ... MD-2
**Mapleview**—*pop pl* ... MN-6
**Maple View**—*pop pl* ... NY-2
**Mapleview**—*pop pl* ... TN-4
**Maple View**—*pop pl* ... WV-2
**Mapleview Acres**—*pop pl* ... TN-4
Mapleview Campsite—*locale* ... TN-4
Mapleview Cem—*cemetery* ... KY-4
Maple View Cem—*cemetery* (3) ... NY-2
Mapleview Cem—*cemetery* ... TN-4
Mapleview Ch—*church* ... MI-6
Mapleview Ch—*church* ... MO-7
Mapleview Park—*park* ... MN-6
Maple View Public Use Area—*park* ... TN-4
Mapleview Sch—*school* ... MI-6
Mapleview Sch—*school* ... OH-6
Mapleview Sch—*school* ... PA-2
Maple View Sch—*school* ... WI-6
**Mapleville**—*pop pl* (2) ... MD-2
**Mapleville**—*pop pl* ... NC-3
**Mapleville**—*pop pl* ... RI-1
Maple Well—*well* ... IL-6
*Maplewood* ... IL-6
*Maplewood* ... MI-6
*Maplewood* ... NH-1
Maplewood—*hist pl* ... KY-4
Maplewood—*hist pl* ... MO-7
Maplewood—*hist pl* ... OH-6
Maplewood—*locale* ... MI-6
Maplewood—*locale* ... NY-2
Maplewood—*locale* ... VA-3
Maplewood—*locale* ... WA-9
**Maplewood**—*pop pl* (2) ... AL-4
**Maplewood**—*pop pl* (2) ... IN-6
**Maplewood**—*pop pl* ... LA-4
**Maplewood**—*pop pl* ... ME-1
**Maplewood**—*pop pl* (3) ... MD-2
**Maplewood**—*pop pl* ... MA-1
**Maplewood**—*pop pl* ... MN-6
**Maplewood**—*pop pl* ... MO-7
**Maplewood**—*pop pl* (2) ... NH-1
**Maplewood**—*pop pl* ... NJ-2
**Maplewood**—*pop pl* (3) ... NY-2
**Maplewood**—*pop pl* ... NC-3
**Maplewood**—*pop pl* ... OH-6
**Maplewood**—*pop pl* ... OR-9
**Maplewood**—*pop pl* ... PA-2
**Maplewood**—*pop pl* ... TN-4
**Maplewood**—*pop pl* ... WA-9
**Maplewood**—*pop pl* ... WV-2
**Maplewood**—*pop pl* ... WI-6
Maplewood—*uninc pl* ... DE-2
Maplewood—*uninc pl* ... PA-2
Maplewood Acad—*school* ... MN-6
**Maplewood Addition (subdivision)**—*pop pl* ... UT-8
*Maplewood Baptist Church* ... TN-4
Maplewood Branch—*stream* ... VA-3
Maplewood Cem—*cemetery* ... AR-4
Maplewood Cem—*cemetery* ... CT-1
Maplewood Cem—*cemetery* (3) ... IL-6
Maplewood Cem—*cemetery* (3) ... IN-6
Maplewood Cem—*cemetery* ... IA-7
Maplewood Cem—*cemetery* (2) ... KS-7
Maplewood Cem—*cemetery* ... KY-4
Maplewood Cem—*cemetery* (3) ... ME-1
Maplewood Cem—*cemetery* (6) ... MA-1
Maplewood Cem—*cemetery* (4) ... MI-6
Maplewood Cem—*cemetery* ... MN-6
Maplewood Cem—*cemetery* (3) ... MO-7
Maplewood Cem—*cemetery* ... MT-8
Maplewood Cem—*cemetery* (3) ... NH-1
Maplewood Cem—*cemetery* ... NJ-2
Maplewood Cem—*cemetery* (2) ... NY-2
Maple Wood Cem—*cemetery* ... NY-2
Maplewood Cem—*cemetery* (13) ... NY-2
Maplewood Cem—*cemetery* (5) ... NC-3
Maplewood Cem—*cemetery* (4) ... OH-6
Maplewood Cem—*cemetery* (2) ... OR-9
Maplewood Cem—*cemetery* ... PA-2
Maplewood Cem—*cemetery* (3) ... TN-4
Maplewood Cem—*cemetery* (2) ... VT-1
Maplewood Cem—*cemetery* (3) ... VA-3
Maplewood Cem—*cemetery* ... WV-2
Maplewood Ch—*church* ... MN-6
Maplewood Ch—*church* ... TN-4
Maplewood Ch—*church* ... WV-2
Maplewood Chapel—*hist pl* ... MN-6
Maplewood Christian Sch—*school* ... MI-6
Maplewood Elem Sch—*school* ... FL-3
Maplewood Elem Sch—*school* (2) ... IN-6
**Maplewood Estates (subdivision)**—*pop pl* ... TN-4
**Maplewood Estates (subdivision)**—*pop pl* ... UT-8
**Maplewood Forest (subdivision)**—*pop pl* ... NC-3
Maplewood Golf Course—*other* ... NJ-2
Maplewood Golf Course—*other* ... WA-9
**Maplewood Heights**—*pop pl* ... PA-2
**Maplewood Heights**—*pop pl* ... TN-4
Maplewood Hotel—*hist pl* (2) ... MA-1
Maplewood HS—*school* ... NJ-2
Maplewood HS—*school* ... TN-4
Maplewood JHS—*school* ... CT-1
Maplewood Lake—*reservoir* ... PA-2
*Maplewood (Maplewood Park)* ... IL-6
Maplewood Park—*park* ... AL-4
Maplewood Park—*park* ... IL-6
Maplewood Park—*park* ... MA-1
Maplewood Park—*park* ... MI-6
Maplewood Park—*park* ... NY-2
**Maplewood Park**—*pop pl* ... IL-6
**Maplewood Park**—*pop pl* ... IN-6
**Maplewood Park**—*pop pl* ... PA-2
Maplewood Plaza—*locale* ... IN-6
Maplewood Point—*cape* ... NY-2
Maplewood Rec Area—*park* ... MI-6
Maplewood Sanitorium—*hist pl* ... OH-6
Maplewood Sch—*school* ... CO-8
Maplewood Sch—*school* ... CT-1
Maplewood Sch—*school* (2) ... IL-6
Maplewood Sch—*school* ... MA-1
Maplewood Sch—*school* (6) ... MI-6
Maplewood Sch—*school* ... MO-7
Maplewood Sch—*school* (2) ... NY-2
Maplewood Sch—*school* ... OH-6
Maplewood Sch—*school* ... OR-9
Maplewood Sch—*school* ... TX-5
Maplewood Sch—*school* ... WA-9
Maplewood Sch—*school* ... WV-2
Maplewood Sch (historical)—*school* ... AL-4
Maplewood Shop Ctr—*locale* ... TX-5
Maplewood Site—*hist pl* ... MN-6
Maplewood Spring—*spring* ... WA-9
Maplewood State Park—*park* ... MN-6
Maplewood Station—*locale* ... NJ-2
**Maplewood (subdivision)**—*pop pl* ... DE-2

**Maplewood (subdivision)**—*pop pl* MA-1
**Maplewood (subdivision)**—*pop pl* NC-3
**Maplewood (subdivision)**—*pop pl* TN-4
Maplewood Swamp—*swamp* WI-6
**Maplewood Terrace**—*pop pl* PA-2
**Maplewood (Township of)**—*pop pl* MN-6
**Maplewood (Township of)**—*pop pl* NJ-2
Map (Municipality)—*civ div* FM-9
Mapoleon Pass—*gap* CO-8
Mappa Hall—*hist pl* NY-2
*Mappi* MH-9
*Mappii* MH-9
*Mappi Mountain* MH-9
*Mappi-san* MH-9
Mapple Hollow—*valley* KY-4
Mapps—*locale* NE-7
**Mappsburg**—*pop pl* VA-3
Mapps Creek—*stream* FL-3
Mapps Point—*cape* VA-3
**Mappsville**—*pop pl* VA-3
*Mappu To* FM-9
Map Rock—*rock* ID-8
Map Rock Petroglyphs Hist Dist—*hist pl* ID-8
Mapsa, Lake—*lake* AK-9
*Maps Creek* VA-3
Mapsico Cem—*cemetery* VA-3
Mapsico Creek—*stream* VA-3
Mapsorak Creek—*stream* AK-9
Mapsorak Hill—*summit* AK-9
Mapsorak Lagoon—*bay* AK-9
Maptigak Mtn—*summit* AK-9
Mapulehu—*civil* HI-9
Mapulehu Stream—*stream* HI-9
**Mapusaga**—*pop pl* AS-9
**Mapusagafou**—*pop pl* AS-9
Mapusagatuai Stream—*stream* AS-9
**Maqanpaaq**—*pop pl* FM-9
**Maquam**—*pop pl* VT-1
Maquam Bay—*bay* VT-1
Maquam Creek—*stream* VT-1
Maquan Pond—*lake* MA-1
Maquan Sch—*school* MA-1
Maquelles Tank—*reservoir* TX-5
Maques Place—*locale* AZ-5
Maquette Park—*park* IL-6
Maquinita Canyon—*valley* NM-5
Maquinna Cove—*bay* AK-9
Maquire Hill—*summit* ME-1
Maquoit Bay—*bay* ME-1
Maquoit Cem—*cemetery* ME-1
Maquoit Ch—*church* ME-1
**Maquoketa**—*pop pl* IA-7
Maquoketa Caves State Park—*park* IA-7
Maquoketa City Hall—*building* IA-7
*Maquoketa River* IA-7
Maquoketa River—*stream* IA-7
Maquoketa Township—*fmr MCD* IA-7
**Maquon**—*pop pl* IL-6
Maquon Cem—*cemetery* IL-6
**Maquon (Township of)**—*pop pl* IL-6
**Maqweach**—*pop pl* FM-9
*Mar* MP-9
Mara—*uninc pl* TX-5
Maraalaay'—*summit* FM-9
Maraba—*other* FM-9
Marabilla Island—*island* AK-9
Marable, George, House—*hist pl* AZ-5
Marable Creek—*stream* GA-3
Marable Hollow—*valley* TN-4
Maraboeuf Lake—*lake* MN-6
Maraboeuf Lake Portage—*trail* MN-6
**Marabou Meadows**—*pop pl* DE-2
**Maracayo**—*pop pl* PR-3
Maracha—*summit* FM-9
Marack Lake—*lake* AK-9
Maracossic Creek—*stream* VA-3
Marada Golf Course—*locale* PA-2
Marae, Lake—*lake* FL-3
Maraen—*island* MP-9
*Maraen Island* MP-9
Marafio Spring—*spring* ID-8
*Maragai* MP-9
*Maragai-to* MP-9
**Maraguez**—*pop pl* (2) PR-3
Maraguez (Barrio)—*fmr MCD* PR-3
Marahu—*civil* FM-9
*Maraie D'Ogee* IL-6
**Marais Croche**—*pop pl* MO-7
Marais Croche—*swamp* MO-7
Marais de Saint Feriole—*gut* WI-6
*Marais De Saint Friol* WI-6
*Marais Des Cygens Waterfowl Area* KS-7
*Marais Des Cygnes* KS-7
*Marais des Cygnes Creek* KS-7
Marais des Cygnes Elem Sch—*school* (2) KS-7
Marais des Cygnes HS—*school* KS-7
*Marais des Cygnes Massacre Park* KS-7
Marais des Cygnes Massacre Site—*hist pl* KS-7
Marais des Cygnes MS—*school* KS-7
Marais des Cygnes River—*stream* KS-7
Marais des Cygnes River—*stream* MO-7
Marais des Cygnes Waterfowl Area—*park* KS-7
Marais Lake—*lake* WI-6
Marais Long—*lake* LA-4
Marais Saline—*lake* AR-4
*Marais Saline Lake* AR-4
Marais Temps Clair—*swamp* MO-7
Marak—*locale* TX-5
*Marakaru* PW-9
*Marakaru-Su* PW-9
*Marakaru To* PW-9
*Marakau Harbor* PW-9
Mara Kill—*stream* NY-2
Mar-A-Lago Natl Historic Landmark—*hist pl* FL-3
Mar-A-Lago Natl Historic Site—*park* FL-3
*Maralai* PW-9
*Mara Lake* MN-6
*Maralay* FM-9
Maraldo Lake—*reservoir* IL-6
Marall Chrome Mine—*mine* CA-9
Maraman Cem—*cemetery* KY-4
**Maramec**—*pop pl* OK-5
Maramec Cem—*cemetery* MO-7
Maramech Hill—*summit* IL-6
Maramec Iron Works District—*hist pl* MO-7
Maramec Lake—*reservoir* OK-5
Maramec Spring—*spring* MO-7
**Maramosok**—*pop pl* FM-9
**Marana**—*pop pl* AZ-5
Marana Airpark—*airport* AZ-5
Marana Air Park Interchange—*crossing* AZ-5
*Marana Airport* AZ-5
Marana Artesian Well—*well* (2) TX-5
Marana Auxillary Landing Field—*airport* AZ-5
Marana Camp—*locale* TX-5
Marana (CCD)—*cens area* AZ-5
Maranacook—*locale* ME-1
Maranacook Camp—*locale* ME-1
Maranacook Lake—*lake* ME-1
Marana Elem Sch—*school* AZ-5
Marana HS—*school* AZ-5
Marana Interchange—*crossing* AZ-5
Marana JHS—*school* AZ-5
Marana Park—*park* AZ-5
Marana Post Office—*building* AZ-5
Marana RR Station—*building* AZ-5
Marana Sheriffs Office—*building* AZ-5
Marana (siding)—*locale* AZ-5
Maranatha Baptist Ch—*church* DE-2
Maranatha Baptist Ch—*church* (2) FL-3
Maranatha Baptist Ch—*church* IN-6
Maranatha Baptist Ch—*church* UT-8
*Maranatha Baptist Church* TN-4
Maranatha Bible Camp—*locale* NE-7
Maranatha Ch—*church* AL-4
Maranatha Ch—*church* FL-3
Maranatha Ch—*church* GA-3
Maranatha Ch—*church* MI-6
Maranatha Ch—*church* MO-7
Maranatha Ch—*church* NC-3
Maranatha Ch—*church* PA-2
Maranatha Ch—*church* (3) TN-4
Maranatha Chapel—*church* (2) FL-3
Maranatha Chapel—*church* MI-6
Maranatha Christian Acad—*school* FL-3
Maranatha Christian Ch—*church* FL-3
Maranatha Faith Center—*church* MS-4
Marana Trap—*summit* TX-5
*Maranda Run* PA-2
Maranda Run—*stream* PA-2
Marandus Brook—*stream* CT-1
Marangi—*bar* FM-9
Marano Windmill—*locale* TX-5
Marantette House—*hist pl* MI-6
Marantha Ch—*church* GA-3
Marantha Ch—*church* IN-6
Marantha FWB Ch—*church* NC-3
Maranville Canal—*canal* NE-7
Marap—*locale* FM-9
*Marapa River* SD-7
*Maraposa Canyon* NV-8
Mararski Lake—*lake* CO-8
Mararski Mine—*mine* CO-8
Maras—*unknown* FM-9
Marasaras—*unknown* FM-9
Maraspin Creek—*stream* MA-1
Maraspin Creek Entrance Light—*locale* MA-1
Marasu—*locale* MH-9
Maratanza, Lake—*lake* NY-2
**Marathon**—*pop pl* FL-3
**Marathon**—*pop pl* IA-7
**Marathon**—*pop pl* LA-4
**Marathon**—*pop pl* MS-4
**Marathon**—*pop pl* NY-2
**Marathon**—*pop pl* OH-6
**Marathon**—*pop pl* TX-5
**Marathon**—*pop pl* WI-6
Marathon (CCD)—*cens area* TX-5
*Marathon City* WI-6
Marathon City (RR name for Marathon)—*other* WI-6
**Marathon (County)**—*pop pl* WI-6
Marathon County Fairgrounds—*hist pl* WI-6
Marathon Creek—*stream* MI-6
Marathon Gap—*gap* TX-5
Marathon HS—*school* FL-3
*Marathon Lake* MI-6
Marathon Lake—*lake* MN-6
Marathon Lake—*reservoir* MS-4
Marathon Lake Dam—*dam* MS-4
Marathon Lake Rec Area—*locale* MS-4
Marathon Lookout Tower—*locale* WI-6
**Marathon (Marathon City)**—*pop pl* WI-6
Marathon Mtn—*summit* AK-9
Marathon Poland Park—*park* IA-7
Marathon Sch—*school* NY-2
**Marathon Shores**—*pop pl* FL-3
Marathon Shores Christian Acad—*school* FL-3
**Marathon (Town of)**—*pop pl* NY-2
**Marathon (Town of)**—*pop pl* WI-6
**Marathon (Township of)**—*pop pl* MI-6
*Maratooker Pond* NY-2
Maratta Creek—*stream* WA-9
Maravialla Sur (Barrio)—*fmr MCD* PR-3
Maravilla—*uninc pl* FL-3
Maravilla Este (Barrio)—*fmr MCD* PR-3
Maravilla Norte (Barrio)—*fmr MCD* PR-3
**Maravilla Park**—*pop pl* CA-9
Maravillas Canyon—*valley* TX-5
Maravillas Creek—*stream* TX-5
Maravillas Gap—*gap* TX-5
Maravillas Well—*well* TX-5
*Maravista* MA-1
**Mara Vista**—*pop pl* MA-1
Mara Wash—*stream* NV-8
Mar Bar L Farms—*airport* NJ-2
Marbel Mountain Trail—*trail* WY-8
Marberry Branch—*stream* TN-4
Marberry Cem—*cemetery* TN-4
*Marberry Point* DC-2
Marble—*locale* NV-8
Marble—*locale* WA-9
**Marble**—*pop pl* AR-4
**Marble**—*pop pl* CO-8
**Marble**—*pop pl* MN-6
**Marble**—*pop pl* NC-3
**Marble**—*pop pl* PA-2
Marble, Jerome, House—*hist pl* MA-1
Marble Bath—*spring* CA-9
Marble Beach—*beach* IA-7
Marble Bluff—*cliff* NV-8
Marble Bluff—*cliff* TN-4
Marble Bluffs—*cliff* AK-9
Marble Branch—*stream* AR-4
Marble Branch—*stream* IN-6
Marble Bridge—*other* MO-7
Marble Brook—*stream* ME-1
Marble Brook—*stream* MA-1
Marble Butte—*summit* ID-8
Marble Cabin—*building* IA-7
*Marble Canon* AZ-5
**Marble Canyon**—*pop pl* AZ-5
Marble Canyon—*valley* (2) AZ-5
Marble Canyon—*valley* (5) CA-9
Marble Canyon—*valley* NM-5
Marble Canyon—*valley* TX-5
Marble Canyon—*valley* (2) UT-8
Marble Canyon Airp—*airport* AZ-5
Marble Canyon Lodge—*building* AZ-5
Marble Canyon Natl Monmt—*park* AZ-5
Marble Canyon Peak—*summit* UT-8
Marble Canyon Pit—*mine* CA-9
Marble Cave—*cave* MO-7
Marble Cave—*cave* PA-2
Marble Cave—*cave* TN-4
Marble Caves—*cave* CA-9
Marble Caves Trail—*trail* CA-9
Marble Cem—*cemetery* CO-8
Marble Cem—*cemetery* MI-6
Marble Cem—*cemetery* MS-4
Marble Cem—*cemetery* WI-6
Marble Ch—*church* MN-6
*Marble City* AL-4
**Marble City**—*pop pl* OK-5
**Marble City**—*pop pl* PA-2
**Marble City**—*pop pl* TN-4
*Marble City Baptist Ch* AL-4
Marble City Baptist Ch—*church* TN-4
Marble City Cem—*cemetery* OK-5
Marble City Ch—*church* (2) AL-4
Marble City Christian Sch—*school* AL-4
Marble City Heights—*uninc pl* AL-4
Marble City Lake—*lake* AL-4
Marble City Plaza Shop Ctr—*locale* AL-4
Marble City Quarry—*mine* AL-4
Marble City (Township of)—*fmr MCD* AR-4
**Marble Cliff**—*pop pl* OH-6
Marble Cliffs—*cliff* AK-9
Marble Collegiate Reformed Church—*hist pl* NY-2
Marble Cone—*cliff* CA-9
Marble Corner Cem—*cemetery* IN-6
Marble Cove—*bay* AK-9
*Marble Creek* OK-5
*Marble Creek* OR-9
*Marble Creek* WA-9
*Marble Creek* WY-8
Marble Creek—*locale* ID-8
Marble Creek—*stream* (4) AK-9
Marble Creek—*stream* (7) CA-9
Marble Creek—*stream* (3) ID-8
Marble Creek—*stream* IN-6
Marble Creek—*stream* KY-4
Marble Creek—*stream* (2) MO-7
Marble Creek—*stream* MT-8
Marble Creek—*stream* (2) NV-8
Marble Creek—*stream* NC-3
Marble Creek—*stream* OK-5
Marble Creek—*stream* (5) OR-9
Marble Creek—*stream* SD-7
Marble Creek—*stream* TX-5
Marble Creek—*stream* (5) WA-9
Marble Creek Camp—*locale* WA-9
Marble Creek Campground—*locale* MO-7
Marble Creek Campground—*locale* WA-9
Marble Creek Cem—*cemetery* MO-7
Marble Creek Sch (historical)—*school* MO-7
Marble Creek Spring—*spring* OR-9
**Marble Dale**—*pop pl* CT-1
**Marbledale**—*pop pl* TN-4
Marbledale Ch—*church* TN-4
Marble Ditch—*canal* IN-6
Marble Dow Ditch—*canal* CO-8
Marble Drain—*stream* MI-6
Marble Elem Sch—*school* NC-3
*Marble Falls* (2) AR-4
Marble Falls—*falls* AR-4
Marble Falls—*falls* CA-9
**Marble Falls**—*pop pl* TX-5
Marble Falls, Lake—*reservoir* TX-5
Marble Falls Canyon—*valley* NV-8
Marble Falls (CCD)—*cens area* TX-5
Marble Falls Spring—*spring* AR-4
Marble Flats—*flat* AZ-5
Marble Fork—*stream* AR-4
*Marble Fork Creek* CA-9
Marble Fork Kaweah River—*stream* CA-9
*Marble Fork of Kaweah River* CA-9
Marble Front Sch—*school* ID-8
**Marble Furnace**—*pop pl* OH-6
*Marble Gorge* AZ-5
Marble Grove Cem—*cemetery* KS-7
Marble Gulch—*stream* WA-9
Marble Gulch—*valley* (3) CA-9
Marble Gulch—*valley* SD-7
Marble Gulch—*valley* UT-8
Marble Hall—*locale* TN-4
**Marble Hall**—*pop pl* PA-2
Marble Hall Post Office (historical)—*building* TN-4
Marble Hall Sch (historical)—*school* TN-4
*Marble Harbor* MA-1
*Marble Harbor, Town of* MA-1
**Marblehead**—*pop pl* IL-6
**Marblehead**—*pop pl* MA-1
**Marblehead**—*pop pl* OH-6
**Marblehead**—*pop pl* UT-8
**Marblehead**—*pop pl* WI-6
Marble Head—*summit* MI-6
*Marblehead Beach* MA-1
*Marblehead Channel* MA-1
Marblehead Channel—*channel* MA-1
Marblehead Creek—*stream* MI-6
Marblehead Harbor—*harbor* MA-1
Marblehead Hist Dist—*hist pl* MA-1
Marblehead Island—*island* ME-1
Marblehead Lake—*lake* MI-6
Marblehead Light—*hist pl* MA-1
Marblehead Light—*locale* MA-1
Marblehead Lighthouse—*hist pl* OH-6
Marblehead Lighthouse—*locale* OH-6
**Marblehead Lighthouse**—*pop pl* MA-1
**Marblehead Neck**—*pop pl* MA-1
Marblehead Plant—*locale* UT-8
Marblehead Quarry—*mine* OH-6
Marblehead Quarry—*mine* UT-8
Marblehead Rock—*island* MA-1
**Marblehead (Town of)**—*pop pl* MA-1
*Marble Hill* AZ-5
Marble Hill—*locale* NJ-2
Marble Hill—*locale* TN-4
**Marblehill**—*pop pl* GA-3
**Marble Hill**—*pop pl* (2) IN-6
**Marble Hill**—*pop pl* MD-2
**Marble Hill**—*pop pl* MO-7
**Marble Hill**—*pop pl* TN-4
Marble Hill—*summit* AL-4
Marble Hill—*summit* AR-4
Marble Hill—*summit* MA-1
Marble Hill—*summit* NY-2
Marble Hill—*summit* TN-4
Marble Hill—*summit* UT-8
Marble Hill—*uninc pl* (2) NY-2
Marble Hill Cem—*cemetery* MO-7
Marble Hill Ch—*church* MS-4
Marble Hill Ch—*church* VA-3
Marble Hill Nuclear Power Station—*locale* IN-6
*Marble Hills* AZ-5
*Marble Hills* TN-4
Marble Hill Sch (historical)—*school* MO-7
Marble Hill Sch (historical)—*school* TN-4
Marble Hill United Methodist Ch—*church* TN-4
Marble Hot Springs—*spring* CA-9
Marble House—*hist pl* RI-1
Marble Island—*island* AK-9
Marble Island—*island* VT-1
Marble Islet—*island* AK-9
*Marble Lake* ID-8
*Marble Lake* WI-6
Marble Lake—*lake* IA-7
Marble Lake—*lake* MI-6
Marble Lake—*lake* (3) MN-6
Marble Lake—*lake* MT-8
**Marble Lake**—*pop pl* MI-6
Marble Lake State Game Mngmt Area—*park* IA-7
Marble Landmark Ch—*church* AR-4
Marble Lateral—*canal* AZ-5
Marble Ledge—*cliff* VT-1
Marble Lookout Tower—*locale* MN-6
Marble Meadow—*flat* WA-9
Marble Mill Site—*hist pl* CO-8
Marble Mine—*mine* AZ-5
Marble Mine Ridge—*ridge* CA-9
**Marblemount**—*pop pl* WA-9
*Marble Mountain* AZ-5
Marble Mountains—*range* (2) CA-9
Marble Mountain Trail—*trail* CO-8
Marble Mtn—*summit* AK-9
Marble Mtn—*summit* (2) CA-9
Marble Mtn—*summit* (3) CO-8
Marble Mtn—*summit* (2) ID-8
Marble Mtn—*summit* ME-1
Marble Mtn—*summit* NJ-2
Marble Mtn—*summit* (2) NY-2
Marble Mtn—*summit* (2) OR-9
Marble Mtn—*summit* (2) WA-9
*Marble Mtn Range* CA-9
Marble Park—*flat* MT-8
Marble Park Cem—*cemetery* MI-6
Marble Pass—*flat* WA-9
Marble Passage—*channel* AK-9
Marble Peak—*summit* AZ-5
Marble Peak—*summit* CA-9
Marble Peak—*summit* WA-9
Marble Peak Trail—*trail* CA-9
Marble Place—*locale* CA-9
Marble Plains—*locale* TN-4
Marble Plains Cem—*cemetery* TN-4
Marble Plains Ch—*church* TN-4
Marble Point—*cape* (3) AK-9
Marble Point—*cape* CA-9
Marble Point—*cape* ND-7
Marble Point—*cape* WI-6
Marble Point—*cliff* ID-8
Marble Point—*cliff* OR-9
Marble Point—*summit* CA-9
Marble Point—*summit* OR-9
Marble Point Ch—*church* VA-3
Marble Pond—*lake* (2) ME-1
Marble Pond—*reservoir* (2) MA-1
Marble Pond Dam—*dam* (2) MA-1
Marble Pond Dam—*dam* MS-4
Marble Quarries—*mine* CA-9
Marble Quarry—*mine* AZ-5
Marble Quarry—*mine* (2) CA-9
Marble Quarry—*mine* (2) WA-9
Marble Quarry Creek—*stream* WY-8
Marble Quarry Gulch—*valley* CO-8
*Marble Quarry Hot Springs* CA-9
Marble Rapids—*rapids* WA-9
Marble Ridge—*ridge* WI-6
Marble Ridge Station—*locale* MA-1
**Marble Ridge Station**—*pop pl* MA-1
*Marble River* VA-3
Marble River—*stream* NY-2
**Marble Rock**—*pop pl* IA-7
Marble Rock Bank—*hist pl* IA-7
Marble Rock Ch—*church* MS-4
Marble Rock Sch (historical)—*school* MS-4
Marble Rsvr—*reservoir* NV-8
Marble Rsvr—*reservoir* OR-9
Marbles Brook—*stream* MA-1
Marble Sch—*school* (2) MI-6
Marble Sch—*school* MN-6
Marble Sch (historical)—*school* MO-7
Marble Shaft Monmt—*park* IA-7
Marble Sinkhole—*basin* AZ-5
Marble (site)—*locale* NV-8
*Marble Spring* AL-4
Marble Spring—*spring* AZ-5
Marble Spring—*spring* GA-3
Marble Spring—*spring* NV-8
Marble Spring—*spring* UT-8
Marble Spring—*spring* VA-3
Marble Spring Canyon—*valley* CA-9
Marble Spring Mine—*mine* (2) CA-9
Marble Springs—*hist pl* TN-4
Marble Springs—*spring* AL-4
Marble Springs—*spring* (2) CA-9
Marble Springs Acad (historical)—*school* AL-4
Marble Spring Shelter—*locale* VA-3
Marble Springs Hist Dist—*hist pl* MS-4
Marble Springs (historical)—*locale* AL-4
Marble Springs (John Sevier Home)—*locale* TN-4
Marble Stone Ch—*church* MS-4
Marble Stone Ch (historical)—*church* AL-4
Marble Stone Sch—*school* AL-4
Marble Swamp—*swamp* WI-6
Marble Switch—*locale* TN-4
Marble Switch Post Office (historical)—*building* TN-4
Marbleton—*locale* TN-4
**Marbleton**—*pop pl* WY-8
Marbleton Sch—*school* TN-4
**Marbleton (Shadtown)**—*pop pl* TN-4
*Marble Top* UT-8
Marbletop—*summit* UT-8
Marble Top Sch—*school* GA-3
**Marbletown**—*pop pl* (2) NY-2
Marbletown Ch—*church* NY-2
Marbletown Sch—*school* IL-6
Marbletown Sch—*school* NY-2
**Marble Township**—*pop pl* NE-7
Marble (Township of)—*fmr MCD* (2) AR-4
**Marble (Township of)**—*pop pl* MN-6
**Marbletown (Town of)**—*pop pl* NY-2
Marble Valley—*basin* CA-9
Marble Valley—*locale* AL-4
Marble Valley—*locale* VA-3
Marble Valley—*valley* CA-9
Marble Valley—*valley* WA-9
Marble Valley Cem—*cemetery* AL-4
Marble Valley Cem—*cemetery* IA-7
Marble Valley Guard Station—*locale* CA-9
Marble Viewpoint—*locale* AZ-5
Marble Wash—*stream* CO-8
Marble Wash—*valley* (2) UT-8
Marble Well—*well* NV-8
**Marblewood Subdivision**—*pop pl* UT-8
Marbleyard Ridge—*ridge* NC-3
Marbo Annex—*CDP* GU-9
Marbo Cave—*cave* GU-9
**Marboe Township**—*pop pl* ND-7
Marbolite Mine—*mine* CA-9
Marbo Pumping Station—*other* GU-9
**Marborough West**—*pop pl* PA-2
Marbridge School, The—*school* TX-5
Marburg—*locale* PA-2
Marburg, Lake—*reservoir* PA-2
*Marburg Creek* GA-3
Marburg Ditch—*canal* CO-8
Marburg Lake—*reservoir* PA-2
**Marbury**—*pop pl* AL-4
**Marbury**—*pop pl* MD-2
Marbury (CCD)—*cens area* AL-4
Marbury Cem—*cemetery* TN-4
Marbury Creek—*stream* GA-3
Marbury Division—*civil* AL-4
Marbury Point—*cape* DC-2
Marbury Run—*stream* MD-2
Marbury Sch—*school* AL-4
Marbut Cave—*cave* AL-4
Marbuts—*locale* TN-4
Marbuts Post Office (historical)—*building* TN-4
Marby Chapel (historical)—*church* MS-4
Marca Canyon—*valley* CA-9
Marcado Creek—*stream* TX-5
Marcalus Manufacturing Company Dam—*dam* MA-1
Marcan Pond—*lake* MA-1
Marcarco—*locale* LA-4
M A R Cave—*cave* PA-2
Marce—*locale* LA-4
Marceaux Cem—*cemetery* (2) LA-4
Marceaux Island—*island* LA-4
Marcel—*locale* CA-9
Marcelais Mine—*mine* CA-9
Marceleno Tank—*reservoir* NM-5
Marcelina—*uninc pl* CA-9
Marcelina Artesian Well—*well* TX-5
Marcelina Ch—*church* TX-5
Marcelinas Creek—*stream* TX-5
Marcelinas Hills—*summit* TX-5
**Marceline**—*pop pl* MO-7
Marceline Municipal Airp—*airport* MO-7
Marceline Rsvr—*reservoir* MO-7
**Marceline Township**—*pop pl* MO-7
Marcelin Spring—*spring* CA-9
**Marcell**—*pop pl* MN-6
Marcella—*locale* NJ-2
**Marcella**—*pop pl* AR-4
**Marcella**—*pop pl* MS-4
Marcella Cem—*cemetery* MS-4
Marcella Cem—*cemetery* NJ-2
Marcella Cem—*cemetery* TN-4
Marcella Ch—*church* MS-4
Marcella Church & Sch—*hist pl* AR-4
Marcella Creek—*stream* MT-8
*Marcella Falls* TN-4
Marcella Falls—*falls* TN-4
Marcella Falls Ch—*church* TN-4
Marcella Falls Post Office (historical)—*building* TN-4
Marcella Falls Spring—*spring* TN-4
**Marcella (historical)**—*pop pl* TN-4
Marcel Lake—*reservoir* PA-2
Marcel Lake Dam—*dam* PA-2
Marcel Lake Estate—*locale* PA-2
Marcella Lake—*lake* CA-9
Marcella Landing (historical)—*locale* MS-4
Marcella Quarters Landing (historical)—*locale* MS-4
Marcelle Canyon—*valley* AZ-5
Marcelle Spring—*spring* AZ-5
Marcellina Mtn—*summit* CO-8
**Marcelline**—*pop pl* IL-6
Marcellini Draw—*valley* NV-8
**Marcellon**—*pop pl* WI-6
Marcellon Sch—*school* WI-6
**Marcellon (Town of)**—*pop pl* WI-6
Marcello Windmill—*locale* TX-5
Marcell Sch—*school* TX-5
**Marcell (Township of)**—*pop pl* MN-6
*Marcellus* IN-6
Marcellus—*locale* KY-4
Marcellus—*locale* WA-9
**Marcellus**—*pop pl* MI-6
**Marcellus**—*pop pl* NY-2
Marcellus Cave—*cave* MO-7
**Marcellus Falls**—*pop pl* NY-2
**Marcellus (Town of)**—*pop pl* NY-2
**Marcellus (Township of)**—*pop pl* MI-6
Marcem—*locale* VA-3
Marcer County Fair Ground—*locale* IL-6
Marcer County Hosp—*hospital* IL-6
*March* CA-9
*March* WI-6
March—*locale* MN-6
**March**—*pop pl* MO-7
March, Bayou—*stream* LA-4
March, George, House—*hist pl* (2) OH-6
March AFB—*military* CA-9
Marchainville, Mount—*summit* AK-9
*Marchand* PA-2
**Marchand**—*pop pl* OH-6
**Marchand**—*pop pl* PA-2
Marchand Bayou—*stream* TX-5
March and Trees Ditch—*canal* IN-6
*Marchandville* LA-4
**Marchandville**—*pop pl* PA-2
Marchant—*locale* CA-9
Marchant, Henry, Farm—*hist pl* RI-1
Marchant Branch—*stream* AL-4
Marchant Cem—*cemetery* VA-3
Marchant Creek—*stream* VA-3
*Marchant Hill* HI-9
Marchant Park—*park* CA-9
Marchant Tank—*reservoir* AZ-5
Marchbank Park—*park* CA-9
Marchbanks Cem—*cemetery* MS-4
**Marchbanks (historical)**—*pop pl* TN-4
March Branch—*stream* AL-4
March Branch—*stream* AR-4
*March Creek* ID-8
March Creek—*stream* GA-3
March Creek—*stream* IN-6
March Creek—*stream* WA-9
*March Creek Ch* PA-2
March Creek Ch—*church* PA-2
March Ditch—*canal* IN-6
Marche—*locale* AR-4
March Elem Sch—*school* PA-2
Marchell Spring—*spring* NV-8
Marches Bridge—*bridge* SC-3
*Marches Pond* NH-1
Marches Zion Ch—*church* TN-4
Marcheta Hill—*summit* AL-4
Marcheta Lake—*lake* MT-8
Marchetti Park—*park* CA-9
**March Field**—*pop pl* CA-9
**March Field (March Air Air Force Base)**—*pop pl* CA-9
March Hill—*summit* NH-1
Marching Men—*area* UT-8
Marchison Creek—*stream* TX-5
*March Lake* ID-8
March Lake—*lake* MN-6
*Marchlandville* LA-4
Marchman Cem—*cemetery* GA-3
Marchman Ch (historical)—*church* AL-4
Marchmans Dam—*dam* NC-3
Marchmans Lake—*reservoir* NC-3
March Point—*cape* WA-9
March Point Light—*locale* WA-9
March Pond—*lake* NH-1
**March Rapids**—*pop pl* WI-6
March Ridge—*ridge* KY-4
March Ridge—*ridge* OK-5
March Rock—*island* CA-9
March Run—*stream* OH-6
*March Sch* PA-2
March Sch (abandoned)—*school* PA-2
Marchs Pond—*lake* NH-1
Marchs Pond—*lake* TX-5
March Swamp—*stream* VA-3
**March Trailer Court**—*pop pl* TX-5
Marchwood Shop Ctr—*locale* PA-2
**Marcia**—*pop pl* NM-5
Marcia, Lake—*lake* NJ-2
Marcial Canyon—*valley* NM-5
Marcial Creek—*stream* TX-5
Marcial Lake—*lake* ME-1
Marcial Tank—*reservoir* TX-5
Marciano Stadium—*building* MA-1
Marcia (pullman car)—*hist pl* CO-8
Marclare—*hist pl* MS-4
Marclay Sch—*school* PA-2
*Marcles Run* WV-2
Marco—*locale* MO-7
Marco—*locale* TX-5
**Marco**—*pop pl* FL-3
**Marco**—*pop pl* IN-6
**Marco**—*pop pl* LA-4
Marco Bay—*cove* FL-3
Marco Beach—*beach* FL-3
Marco Cem—*cemetery* IN-6
Marco Cem—*cemetery* LA-4
Marco Christian Fellowship Ch—*church* FL-3
Marco Creek—*stream* ID-8
Marco Creek—*stream* OR-9
Marcoe—*locale* IL-6
Marcoe Ch—*church* IL-6
Marco Flat Bridge—*bridge* MT-8
Marco Flat Picnic Area—*park* MT-8
Marco Island—*island* FL-3
Marco Island—*other* FL-3
Marco Island Christian Sch—*school* FL-3
**Marcola**—*pop pl* OR-9
Marcola (CCD)—*cens area* OR-9
Marcola Cem—*cemetery* OR-9
Marco Lake—*lake* FL-3
Marco Lutheran Ch—*church* FL-3
Marco (Marco Island)—*CDP* FL-3
Marco Millpond—*reservoir* SC-3
*Marco Muddies* FL-3
Marcone Sch (historical)—*school* TN-4
**Marconi**—*pop pl* CA-9
**Marconi Area**—*pop pl* HI-9
Marconi Memorial Field—*other* NY-2
Marconi Park—*park* AL-4
Marconi Plaza—*locale* PA-2
Marconi Sch—*school* IL-6
Marconi Slough—*stream* AK-9
Marconi Station Site—*building* MA-1
Marconi Wireless Station Site—*hist pl* MA-1
*Marcon River* PW-9
*Marcoosee* FL-3
Marcoot—*locale* AL-4
Marcoot—*locale* MO-7
Marcoot Lookout—*locale* MO-7
*Marco Pass* FL-3
Marco School (historical)—*locale* MO-7
Marcos de Niza HS—*school* AZ-5
*Marcos Monument* AZ-5
Marco Spring—*spring* ID-8
Marcos Terrace—*bench* AZ-5

Marcot Park Rsvr—reservoir CO-8
Marcott—locale CO-8
Marcott Creek—stream CO-8
Marcott Creek—stream MT-8
Marcott Ditch—canal CO-8
Marcotte Nursing Home—hist pl ME-1
Marcott Lakes—lake MN-6
Marcou Crater AZ-5
Marcou Mesa—summit AZ-5
Marcou Tank—reservoir TX-5
Marcou Windmill—locale TX-5
Marcoux Corners—locale MN-6
Mar Creek OR-9
Marcroft Canyon—valley ID-8
Marcum—locale KY-4
Marcum Bluff—cliff KY-4
Marcum Branch—stream GA-3
Marcum Branch—stream IL-6
Marcum Branch—stream KY-4
Marcum Branch—stream TN-4
Marcum Branch—stream WV-2
Marcum Branch North Public Use Area—locale IL-6
Marcum Branch South Public Use Area—locale IL-6
Marcum Cem—cemetery (5) KY-4
Marcum Cem—cemetery OH-6
Marcum Cem—cemetery TN-4
Marcum Cem—cemetery (2) VA-3
Marcum Cem—cemetery (6) WV-2
Marcum Creek AZ-5
Marcum Creek—stream MS-4
Marcum Creek—stream OK-5
Marcum Creek—stream TN-4
Marcum Creek—stream WY-8
Marcum Gap—gap TN-4
Marcum Hollow—valley VA-3
Marcum Island—island KY-4
Marcum Lake—lake KY-4
Marcum Mtn—summit MT-8
Marcum Pond—lake ME-1
Marcumville (historical)—locale AL-4
Marcus (2) AR-4
Marcus—locale IL-6
Marcus—locale KY-4
**Marcus**—pop pl IA-7
**Marcus**—pop pl NC-3
**Marcus**—pop pl SD-7
**Marcus**—pop pl WA-9
Marcus, Bayou—stream FL-3
Marcus, Dr. Carl, House—hist pl MT-8
Marcus-Amherst Cem—cemetery IA-7
Marcus Baker, Mount—summit AK-9
Marcus Baker Glacier—glacier AK-9
Marcus Cem—cemetery NE-7
Marcus Community Golf Club—other IA-7
Marcus Cooke Memorial Park—cemetery CT-1
Marcus Cook Peak—summit ID-8
Marcus Draw—valley WY-8
Marcus Duncan Cemetery MS-4
Marcus Foster—post sta CA-9
Marcus Grove Ch—church NC-3
Marcus Hill Ch—church AR-4
Marcus (historical)—locale AL-4
**Marcus Hook**—pop pl PA-2
Marcus Hook Bar—bar DE-2
Marcus Hook Borough—civil PA-2
Marcus Hook Creek—stream PA-2
Marcus Hook Elem Sch at Trainer—school PA-2
Marcus Hook Range—channel PA-2
Marcus Island—island WA-9
Marcus J Lawrence Memorial Hosp—hospital AZ-5
Marcus J Lawrence Memorial Hospital Heliport—airport AZ-5
Marcus Lake—lake MN-6
Marcus Memorial Cem—cemetery MO-7
Marcus Mine—mine NM-5
Marcuson Creek—stream WA-9
Marcus Peak—summit WA-9
Marcus Ranch—locale NM-5
**Marcus (RR name Halo)**—pop pl WV-2
Marcus Run—stream OH-6
Marcus Tank—reservoir NM-5
Marcus Township—fmr MCD IA-7
Marcus Wash—stream CA-9
Marcus Whitman Cowiche Sch—school WA-9
Marcus Whitman JHS—school WA-9
Marcus Whitman Sch—school WA-9
Marcy OH-6
Marcy—locale FL-3
Marcy—locale PA-2
**Marcy**—pop pl NY-2
**Marcy**—pop pl (2) OH-6
**Marcy**—pop pl WI-6
Marcy—uninc pl NY-2
Marcy, Mount—summit CO-8
Marcy, Mount—summit MA-1
Marcy, Mount—summit NY-2
Marcy Brook CT-1
Marcy Brook MA-1
Marcy Brook—stream NY-2
Marcy Ch—church PA-2
**Marcy Colony**—pop pl SD-7
Marcy Dam—dam NY-2
Marcy Gulch—valley CO-8
Marcy Hill—summit NH-1
Marcy Hill—summit NY-2
Marcy (historical)—locale IA-7
Marcy Landing—locale NY-2
**Marcy (Marcy State Hospital)**—pop pl NY-2
Marcy Point—summit PA-2
Marcys KY-4
Marcy Sch—school CA-9
Marcy Sch—school MI-6
Marcy Sch—school MN-6
Marcy Sch—school TX-5
Marcy Swamp—swamp NY-2
**Marcy (Town of)**—pop pl NY-2
Marcy Township—fmr MCD IA-7
Mardee Lake—lake WA-9
**Mardela Springs**—pop pl MD-2
Mardella Branch—stream MD-2
Mardella Springs MD-2
**Mardell (historical)**—pop pl ND-7
**Mardell Manor**—pop pl IL-6
Mardem Canyon—valley NM-5
Marden, Lake—lake FL-3
Mardenboro Point—cape VI-3
Marden Brook—stream NH-1
Marden Hill—summit ME-1
**Mardenis**—pop pl IN-6
Marden Lake Bayou—gut LA-4
Marden Pond—lake ME-1
Mardens Hill—summit NH-1
Marders, Jefferson, House—hist pl KY-4
**Mardin**—pop pl PA-2
Mardis Branch—stream AL-4
Mardis Branch—stream AR-4
Mardis Cem—cemetery AL-4
Mardis Ferry AL-4
Mardis Ranch—locale MT-8
Mardis Run—stream PA-2
**Mardisville**—pop pl AL-4
Mardisville Cem—cemetery AL-4
Mardisville P.O. AL-4
Mardisville Sch—school AL-4
Mardillis Canyon—valley UT-8
Mardle Quarry Creek WY-8
Mardock Mission—hist pl OK-5
Mardorf Ch—church PA-2
Mardot Antique Shop—hist pl OH-6
Mardow Creek—stream AK-9
Mardow Lake—lake AK-9
**Maready**—pop pl NC-3
Mare Basin—basin CA-9
Mare Branch—stream (2) FL-3
Mare Branch—stream GA-3
Mare Branch—stream (2) KY-4
Mare Branch—stream (3) NC-3
Mare Branch—stream SC-3
Mare Branch—stream TX-5
Mare Branch—stream (3) WV-2
Mare Brook—stream ME-1
Mare Canyon—valley CO-8
Mare Canyon Crossing—locale TX-5
Mare Creek KY-4
Mare Creek—other KY-4
Mare Creek—stream FL-3
Mare Creek—stream KY-4
Mare Creek—stream TX-5
Mare Creek (CCD)—cens area KY-4
Mare Creek Sch—school KY-4
Maredith Mill—locale CA-9
Maree, Lake—reservoir NC-3
Maree Michel Canal—canal LA-4
Mareep Creek—stream CA-9
Mareere Island MP-9
Mareere Island—island MP-9
Mareet Creek—stream ID-8
Mare Fork—stream KY-4
Mare Island—island CA-9
Mare Island—island MI-6
Mare Island—post sta CA-9
Mare Island Naval Shipyard—hist pl CA-9
Mare Island Naval Shipyard—military CA-9
Mare Island Strait—channel CA-9
Marek Canyon—valley CA-9
Mareks Lake—lake MN-6
Marekville—other TX-5
Mare Lake—lake (2) NM-5
Marella Cem—cemetery OK-5
Marella Ch—church OK-5
Marell Lake—lake MI-6
Maremar MP-9
Mare Marsh—swamp DE-2
Mare Meadow Reservoir Dam—dam MA-1
Mare Meadow Rsvr—reservoir MA-1
**Maremont**—pop pl AL-4
Marena KS-7
Marena—locale IA-7
Marena—locale OK-5
Marena Cem—cemetery OK-5
Marena (historical P.O.)—locale IA-7
**Marena Township**—pop pl KS-7
Marenci AZ-5
**Marene Village (subdivision)**—pop pl PA-2
Marenge Lake WI-6
Marengo AL-4
Marengo KS-7
Marengo—locale NE-7
Marengo—locale VA-3
Marengo—locale (2) WA-9
**Marengo**—pop pl AL-4
**Marengo**—pop pl IL-6
**Marengo**—pop pl (2) IN-6
**Marengo**—pop pl IA-7
**Marengo**—pop pl MI-6
**Marengo**—pop pl NY-2
**Marengo**—pop pl OH-6
**Marengo**—pop pl PA-2
**Marengo**—pop pl WI-6
Marengo Bend—bend MS-4
Marengo Cem—cemetery OH-6
Marengo Chute—channel AL-4
Marengo City PA-2
**Marengo County**—pop pl AL-4
Marengo County Hosp—hospital AL-4
Marengo County Lake Dam—dam AL-4
Marengo County Sch—school AL-4
Marengo County Training Sch—school AL-4
Marengo County Vocational Center AL-4
Marengo Gardens—hist pl CA-9
Marengo HS—school AL-4
Marengo Island—island OH-6
**Marengo Junction**—pop pl WI-6
Marengo Lake—lake MS-4
Marengo Lake—lake WI-6
Marengo Lake—reservoir AL-4
Marengo Lake Dam AL-4
Marengo Lookout Tower—locale WI-6
Marengo Memorial Cem—cemetery MI-6
Marengo Military Acad (historical)—school AL-4
Marengo Plantation House—hist pl LA-4
Marengo Post Office (historical)—building TN-4
Marengo River—stream (2) WI-6
Marengo Sch—school CA-9
**Marengo (Town of)**—pop pl WI-6
Marengo Township—fmr MCD IA-7
**Marengo (Township of)**—pop pl IL-6
**Marengo (Township of)**—pop pl MI-6
Marengo Valley Sch—school WI-6
Marengo Village Cem—cemetery MI-6
**Marenisco**—pop pl MI-6
Marenisco Creek—stream MI-6
Marenisco Lookout Tower—locale MI-6
**Marenisco (Township of)**—pop pl MI-6
Marent Gulch—valley MT-8
Marentis House—hist pl CA-9
Marent Trestle—other MT-8
Mare Pasture—flat NV-8
Mare Pasture Gulch—valley MT-8
Mare Pasture Ridge—ridge CA-9
Mare Pasture Spring—spring NV-8
Mare Pasture Tank—reservoir AZ-5
Mare Pasture Tank—reservoir TX-5
Mare Pasture Well—well NM-5
Mare Pasture Well No 1—well CO-8
Mare Pasture Well No 2—well CO-8
Mare Pasture Windmill—locale WY-8
Mare Point ME-1
Mare Point—cape NC-3
Marepoint Bay ME-1
Mare Point Neck ME-1
Mare Pond MA-1
Mare Pond—lake MA-1
Mare Prairie—gut FL-3
Marere—island MP-9
Mareredik—island MP-9
Mareri MP-9
Mareri—island MP-9
Mareri Island MP-9
Mareri-To MP-9
Mare Run—stream NJ-2
Mare Run—stream OH-6
Mare Run—stream VA-3
Mare Run—stream WV-2
Mare Run Trail—trail VA-3
Mares Branch—stream MD-2
Mares Canyon—valley NM-5
Mares Cem—cemetery NM-5
Mares Egg Spring—spring OR-9
Mares Hill—summit CT-1
Maresh Sch—school SD-7
Mares Lake—lake SC-3
Mares Pond—lake MA-1
Mare Spring—spring (2) CA-9
Mare Springs—spring AZ-5
Mares Tail Canyon—valley UT-8
Maresua (Barrio)—fmr MCD PR-3
Mares Windmill—locale NM-5
Mare Tank—reservoir AZ-5
Mare Tank—reservoir (2) TX-5
Maretburg—locale KY-4
Maretburg Sch—school KY-4
Maret Cem—cemetery GA-3
Mare Trap Windmill—locale (2) TX-5
Maret Sch—school DC-2
Maretta Church AL-4
Marettico DE-2
Maretts—locale GA-3
Mare Windmill—locale (2) TX-5
Mareyon FM-9
Marez Spring—spring NM-5
**Marfa**—pop pl TX-5
Marfa (CCD)—cens area TX-5
Marfa Municipal Golf Course—other TX-5
Marfell Lakes—reservoir CO-8
Marfield Creek ND-7
**Marford**—pop pl VA-3
Marfork—locale WV-2
**Marfrance**—pop pl WV-2
Margalloway River ME-1
Margalloway River NH-1
Marganza LA-4
Marganza Crevasse LA-4
Marganza Landing LA-4
Margaret NC-3
Margaret MP-9
Margaret—locale KS-7
Margaret—locale PA-2
Margaret—locale WV-2
**Margaret**—pop pl AL-4
**Margaret**—pop pl NC-3
**Margaret**—pop pl TX-5
Margaret, Lake—lake CA-9
Margaret, Lake—lake CO-8
Margaret, Lake—lake (2) FL-3
Margaret, Lake—lake MI-6
Margaret, Lake—lake (2) MN-6
Margaret, Lake—lake NY-2
Margaret, Lake—lake (2) WA-9
Margaret, Lake—reservoir ND-7
Margaret, Lake—reservoir OH-6
Margaret, Lake—reservoir VA-3
Margaret, Lake—reservoir WA-9
Margaret, Mount—summit AK-9
Margaret, Mount—summit CO-8
Margaret, Mount—summit ID-8
Margaret, Mount—summit TX-5
Margaret, Mount—summit (2) WA-9
Margaret Ann Spring—spring CA-9
Margaret Arch—arch AZ-5
Margaret Basin—valley TX-5
Margaret Block—hist pl MT-8
Margaret Branch—stream NC-3
Margaret Cem—cemetery TX-5
Margaret Cliff—cliff NY-2
Margaret Creek—stream (3) AK-9
Margaret Creek—stream MT-8
Margaret Creek—stream OH-6
Margaret Creek—stream WA-9
Margarete, Lake—reservoir GA-3
MARGARET EMILIE (schooner)—hist pl MS-4
Margaret Falls—falls WA-9
Margaret Greene Ranch NV-8
Margaret Green JHS—school MS-4
Margaret Hall—hist pl KY-4
Margaret Hall—school KY-4
**Margarethe Subdivision**—pop pl UT-8
Margaret Hill—summit VI-3
**Margaret (historical)**—pop pl OR-9
Margaret Hollow—valley KY-4
Margaret Hollow—valley TN-4
Margaret Hollow—valley VA-3
Margaret Key—island FL-3
Margaret K Lewis Exceptional Education Center—school FL-3
Margaret Lake MN-6
Margaret Lake—lake AK-9
Margaret Lake—lake CA-9
Margaret Lake—lake CO-8
Margaret Lake—lake FL-3
Margaret Lake—lake MN-6
Margaret Lake—lake (3) MT-8
Margaret Lake—lake PA-2
Margaret Lake—lake (2) WA-9
Margaret Lake—lake (3) WI-6
Margaret Lake—reservoir AL-4
Margaret Lakes—lake CA-9
Margaret Lee Swamp—swamp VA-3
Margaret Martin JHS MS-4
Margaret McFarland Elem Sch—school IN-6
Margaret Mine—mine MN-6
Margaret Mine (underground)—mine AL-4
Margaret Mitchell Sch—school GA-3
Margaret Newton Elem Sch—school TN-4
Margaret Number 11 Mine (underground0—mine AL-4
Margaret Number 12 Mine AL-4
Margaret Peak TX-5
Margaret Post Office (historical)—building TN-4
Margaret Road Ch—church TN-4
Margaret (RR name for Margaretsville)—other NC-3
Margaret Run—stream PA-2
Margaret Sarah Rsvr—reservoir WY-8
Margaret Sch—school KS-7
Margaret Sch (historical)—school AL-4
Margaret Scott Sch—school OR-9
Margarets Draw—valley WY-8
Margarets Grove Ch—church GA-3
Margaret Slough—stream AK-9
Margarets Rock—summit MA-1
Margaret S. Sterck Sch—school DE-2
Margaretsville NC-3
**Margaretsville (RR name Margaret)**—pop pl NC-3
Margaretta—locale FL-3
Margaretta, Lake—lake FL-3
**Margaretta Furnace**—pop pl PA-2
Margaretta Islands MP-9
**Margaretta (Township of)**—pop pl OH-6
Margarette Falls Trail—trail TN-4
**Margaret Township**—pop pl ND-7
Margaret Trainor Cem—cemetery MO-7
Margaretts NC-3
**Margaretville**—pop pl NY-2
Margaret Wash—stream AZ-5
Margaret Willis Elementary School NC-3
Margaret Wines Park—park UT-8
Margarita—locale PR-3
**Margarita**—pop pl (3) PR-3
Margarita Canyon—valley NM-5
Margarita Lookout Tower—locale CA-9
Margarita Peak—summit CA-9
Margarita Sch—school CA-9
Margarita Tank—reservoir AZ-5
Margarita Tank—reservoir NM-5
Margarita Tank—reservoir (2) TX-5
Margarite, Lake—lake NY-2
Margarito Peak—summit NM-5
Margarito Ulibarri Ranch—locale NM-5
Margarot M Seylar Elementary School PA-2
Margarretta MP-9
Margate FL-3
**Margate**—pop pl FL-3
**Margate**—pop pl MD-2
Margate, Lake—lake FL-3
Margate (CCD)—cens area FL-3
Margate Ch of the Nazarene—church FL-3
**Margate City**—pop pl NJ-2
**Margate City (Margate)**—pop pl NJ-2
Margate Elem Sch—school FL-3
**Margate Estates**—pop pl FL-3
Margate MS—school FL-3
Margate Pier—locale NJ-2
Margate Plaza (Shop Ctr)—locale FL-3
Margate Plaza (Shop Ctr)—locale IN-6
Margate Sch—school CA-9
Margate Shop Ctr—locale FL-3
Margate Swamp—swamp SC-3
Margate Village Square (Shop Ctr)—locale FL-3
Marge, Lake—lake AK-9
Marge, Lake—reservoir PA-2
Marge Lake—lake MN-6
Margerie Glacier—glacier AK-9
Margerie Lake Rsvr—reservoir CT-1
Margerie Manor CT-1
**Margerie Manor**—pop pl CT-1
Margerita Craig Dam—dam TN-4
Margerita Craig Lake—reservoir TN-4
**Margerum**—pop pl AL-4
Margerum Creek—stream WA-9
Margerum Sch—school AL-4
Margerum Switch AL-4
Margerum United Methodist Ch—church AL-4
Margery, Lake—lake CA-9
Margery Run—stream WV-2
Marges Delight Creek—stream WY-8
Margeson Creek—stream MI-6
Margesson Ranch—locale NE-7
Marget Lake—lake MN-6
Marget Lake State Wildlife Mngmt Area—park MN-6
Margheim Oil Field—oilfield KS-7
Marghton AL-4
Margie—locale TX-5
**Margie**—pop pl MN-6
Margiebell Lake—reservoir GA-3
Margie Cem—cemetery MN-6
Margie Lake—lake UT-8
Margie Lou Branch—stream TX-5
Margie Mine—mine CO-8
Margie Rock—island ME-1
Margies Cove—valley AZ-5
Margies Peak—summit AZ-5
Margil Sch—school TX-5
Marginal Brook—stream MA-1
Margin St. Hist Dist—hist pl MS-4
Margisen—locale ME-1
**Margison**—pop pl ME-1
Marg Lake OR-9
Margloba Dam—dam AL-4
Marg Mtn—summit NC-3
Margo—locale VA-3
Margo Canyon UT-8
Margo Frankel Woods State Park—park IA-7
**Margo Gardens**—pop pl PA-2
Margo Lake—lake MT-8
Margo Lake—lake UT-8
Margona Village MO-7
Margot Creek—stream AK-9
Margot Fish Shoal—bar FL-3
Margots—hist pl VA-3
Marg Pond—lake MO-7
**Margrace**—pop pl NC-3
Margrave Goddard Cem—cemetery TN-4
Margrave Meadow—flat NE-7
Margrave Valley—valley TN-4
Margret—locale GA-3
Margrethe, Lake—lake MI-6
Margret Lake—lake MI-6
**Margretta Subdivision**—pop pl UT-8
Margrette Park—park CO-8
Margs Draw AZ-5
Margs Draw—valley AZ-5
Margson Creek MI-6
Marguerita Sch—school CA-9
Marguerita Sch (historical)—school TN-4
Marguerite—locale LA-4
Marguerite—locale TN-4
**Marguerite**—pop pl PA-2
Marguerite, Lake—lake MA-1
Marguerite, Lake—reservoir NJ-2
Marguerite, Point—cape NY-2
Marguerite Creek—stream AK-9
Marguerite Creek—stream CO-8
Marguerite Dam—dam PA-2
Marguerite Draw—valley WY-8
Marguerite Falls—falls CO-8
Marguerite H. Burnett JHS—school DE-2
**Marguerite (historical)**—pop pl MS-4
**Marguerite (Klondike)**—pop pl PA-2
Marguerite Lake MA-1
Marguerite Lake MN-6
Marguerite Lake—lake AZ-5
Marguerite Mine—mine MT-8
Marguerite Number Two Mine—mine NV-8
Marguerite Rsvr—reservoir PA-2
Marguerite S Howell Lake—reservoir AL-4
Marguerite S Howell Lake Dam—dam AL-4
Marguette Spring—spring WA-9
Marguretta Drake Station FL-3
Margurette Lake—lake OR-9
Marheime Creek—stream WI-6
**Maria**—pop pl PA-2
**Maria**—pop pl PR-3
Maria, Bayou—gut LA-4
Maria, Bayou—stream LA-4
Maria, Lake—lake FL-3
Maria, Lake—lake MI-6
Maria, Lake—lake (2) MN-6
Maria, Lake—lake WI-6
Maria, Mount—summit AK-9
Maria, Mount—summit ID-8
Maria, Mount—summit MI-6
Maria, Mount—summit NE-7
Maria Antonia—CDP PR-3
**Maria Antonia**—pop pl PR-3
Maria Assumpta Acad—school MA-1
Maria Bluff—cliff VI-3
Maria Bottoms—bend CO-8
Maria Branch AL-4
Maria Branch—stream FL-3
Maria Branch—stream KY-4
Maria Cem—cemetery LA-4
Maria Cem—cemetery ND-7
Maria Chapel—church MN-6
Maria Chapel—church NC-3
Maria Chavez Windmill—locale TX-5
Maria C Jackson Park—park OR-9
Maria Creek—stream AK-9
Maria Creek—stream IN-6
Maria Creek—stream OR-9
Maria Creek Ch—church IN-6
Mariadahl Cem—cemetery KS-7
Mariadahl (historical)—locale KS-7
Maria de Molaree Grant—civil FL-3
Maria Estella Artesian Well—well TX-5
Maria Forge (historical)—locale AL-4
Maria Forge P.O. AL-4
**Maria Furnace**—pop pl PA-2
Mariah Branch—stream AL-4
Mariah Cem—cemetery TN-4
Mariah Fork—stream KY-4
**Mariah Hill**—pop pl IN-6
Maria Hill—summit VI-3
Maria (historical)—locale KS-7
Mariah Pond IN-6
Maria HS—school IL-6
Maria HS—school WI-6
Mariahs Ch—church WV-2
Maria Immaculata Convent—church IL-6
Maria Inez Banco Number 46—levee TX-5
Mariais Des Cygnes Drainage Ditch—canal MO-7
**Maria Jimenez**—pop pl (2) PR-3
Marial—locale OR-9
Maria Lake—lake (5) MN-6
**Mariam**—pop pl TX-5
Mariam, Lake—lake FL-3
Mariama Yama MH-9
Mariam Cem—cemetery NE-7
Maria Mine—mine CA-9
Maria Mountains CA-9
Mariam Smith Sch—school GA-3
Mariams Sch—school NY-2
Marian CA-9
Marian, Lake—lake FL-3
Marian, Lake—lake NY-2
Marian, Lake—reservoir (2) MO-7
**Mariana**—pop pl (2) PR-3
Mariana (Barrio)—fmr MCD (2) PR-3
Mariana Butte—summit CO-8
Mariana Creek—stream CA-9
Mariana Creek—stream TX-5
Mariana Islands—island MH-9
Marian Apartments—hist pl IN-6
Mariana Sch—school CA-9
Marianas HS—school MH-9
Marian Center—locale NE-7
Marian Center Sch—school FL-3
Marian Coll—school IN-6
Marian Coll—school NY-2
Marian Coll—school WI-6
Marian Creek OR-9
Marian Creek—stream CA-9
Marian Creek—stream FL-3
**Mariandale**—pop pl NY-2
Mariane Gulch—valley CA-9
Mariane Lake—lake MT-8
Marian Fathers Monastery—church IL-6
Marian Fathers Monastery, The—church MA-1
Marian Hill Ch—church MO-7
Marianhill HS—school MA-1
Marian HS—school CA-9
Marian HS—school (2) IL-6
Marian HS—school IN-6
Marian HS—school (2) MA-1
Marian HS—school MI-6
Marian HS—school MN-6
**Mariani**—pop pl PR-3
Marian Island—island MN-6
Marianist Sch—school NY-2
**Marian Manor**—pop pl IN-6
**Marian Meadows Subdivision**—pop pl UT-8
Marianna AL-4
Marianna—locale MS-4
**Marianna**—pop pl AR-4
**Marianna**—pop pl FL-3
**Marianna**—pop pl PA-2
**Marianna**—pop pl WV-2
Marianna Ave Sch—school CA-9
Marianna Borough—civil PA-2
Marianna (CCD)—cens area FL-3
Marianna Ch—church AL-4
Marianna Creek—stream GA-3
Marianna Fire Control HQ (fire tower)—tower FL-3
Marianna Hist Dist—hist pl PA-2
Marianna HS—school FL-3
Marianna Memorial Park Cem—cemetery AR-4
Marianna MS—school FL-3
Marianna Spring Wash CO-8
Marianna Square Shop Ctr—locale FL-3
**Marianne**—pop pl PA-2
Marianne Channel—channel MS-4
**Marianne Condominium (subdivision)**—pop pl UT-8
Marianne Sch (abandoned)—school ME-1
Mariannes Corner—locale NJ-2
Mariano—locale CO-8
Mariano Colon—CDP PR-3
Mariano Creek TX-5
Mariano Draw—valley NM-5
Mariano Hill—summit NM-5
Mariano Lake—lake NM-5
Mariano Lake—locale NM-5
**Mariano Lake (Trading Post)**—pop pl NM-5
Mariano Mesa—summit NM-5
Marianopolis Coll—school CT-1
Mariano Springs—spring NM-5
Mariano Wash—stream CO-8
Marian Place—locale CA-9
Marian Sch—school CA-9
Marian Sch—school PA-2
Marian Sch for Exceptional Children—school FL-3
Marioon—island FM-9
Maria Petra Artesian Well—well TX-5
Maria Pond—lake IN-6
Mariar Cem—cemetery KY-4
Maria Regina HS—school NY-2
Maria Regina Sch—school CA-9
Maria Regina Sch—school NY-2
Maria Rsvr—reservoir CO-8
Maria Sanchez Lake—lake FL-3
Maria Santisima del Carmen—civil AZ-5
Marias (Barrio)—fmr MCD (3) PR-3
Marias Branch—stream LA-4
Marias Canyon—valley NM-5
Marias Creek—stream WA-9
Marias Creek Trail—trail WA-9
Marias Fairground—locale MT-8
Marias Mtn—summit MT-8
Marias Pass MT-8
Marias Pass—gap MT-8
Maria's River MT-8
Marias River—stream MT-8
Marias Sch—school MT-8
**Maria Stein**—pop pl OH-6
Maria Stein Catholic Church and Rectory—hist pl OH-6
Maria Stein Convent—hist pl OH-6
Maria Stein Shrine—other OH-6
Maria Stella Windmill—locale TX-5
Marias Valley Golf and Country Club—building MT-8
**Mariasville**—pop pl PA-2
Mariaville—locale ME-1
**Mariaville**—pop pl NE-7
**Mariaville**—pop pl NY-2
Mariaville Hist Dist—hist pl NY-2
Mariaville Lake—lake NY-2
Mariaville Sch—school NE-7
**Mariaville (Town of)**—pop pl ME-1
Maria Vista Retreat—church MO-7
Maria Windmill—locale TX-5
Maria Ygnacio Creek—stream CA-9
Marib MP-9
**Mariba**—pop pl KY-4
Mariba Ch—church KY-4
Mariba Fork—stream KY-4
**Maribel**—pop pl NC-3
**Maribel**—pop pl WI-6
Maribel Caves County Park—park WI-6
Maribel Sch—school NC-3
Maribel Sch—school TX-5
Marib Island MP-9
Maribw—island MP-9
Maricamp—locale FL-3
Maricamp (County Correctional Institution)—building FL-3
**Maricao**—pop pl PR-3
Maricao—post sta PR-3
Maricao Afuera (Barrio)—fmr MCD PR-3
Maricao (Barrio)—fmr MCD PR-3
Maricao (Municipio)—civil PR-3
Maricao (Pueblo)—fmr MCD PR-3
M A Richard Dam—dam AL-4
Mariconeag Sound ME-1
Maricopa AZ-5
Maricopa—civil AZ-5
**Maricopa**—pop pl AZ-5
**Maricopa**—pop pl CA-9
Maricopa Cem—cemetery AZ-5
Maricopa County AZ-5
**Maricopa County**—pop pl AZ-5
Maricopa County Accomodation Sch—school AZ-5
Maricopa County Cem—cemetery (2) AZ-5
Maricopa County Community Services—building AZ-5
Maricopa County General Hosp—hospital AZ-5
Maricopa County Highway Department—building AZ-5

Maricopa County Jail Annex—*building* AZ-5
Maricopa County Juvenile Detention Home—*building* AZ-5
Maricopa County Municipal Water Conservation District Number One—*building* AZ-5
Maricopa County Veterninary Center—*building* AZ-5
Maricopa Flat—*flat* CA-9
Maricopa General Hospital Heliport—*airport* AZ-5
Maricopa HS—*school* AZ-5
*Maricopa Ind Res* AZ-5
Maricopa Ind Res (Ak Chin)—*reserve* AZ-5
*Maricopa Junction* AZ-5
Maricopa Lake—*lake* AZ-5
Maricopa Mine—*mine* AZ-5
Maricopa Mission—*church* AZ-5
*Maricopa Mountains* AZ-5
Maricopa Mountains—*summit* AZ-5
Maricopa Peak—*summit* (2) AZ-5
Maricopa Point—*cliff* AZ-5
Maricopa RR Station—*building* AZ-5
Maricopa-Stanfield (CCD)—*cens area* AZ-5
*Maricopa Station* AZ-5
Maricopa Tank—*reservoir* AZ-5
Maricopa Unified Sch—*school* AZ-5
**Maricopa Village**—*pop pl* AZ-5
*Maricopaville* AZ-5
Maricopa Wells—*locale* AZ-5
*Mari Creek* MI-6
Marics Canyon—*valley* AZ-5
**Marie**—*pop pl* AR-4
**Marie**—*pop pl* MS-4
**Marie**—*pop pl* WV-2
Marie, Frank, House—*hist pl* TX-5
Marie, Lake—*lake* (3) FL-3
Marie, Lake—*lake* ID-8
Marie, Lake—*lake* IL-6
Marie, Lake—*lake* (2) MN-6
Marie, Lake—*lake* NY-2
Marie, Lake—*lake* (3) OR-9
Marie, Lake—*lake* WA-9
Marie, Lake—*lake* WI-6
Marie, Lake—*lake* WY-8
Marie, Lake—*reservoir* CA-9
Marie, Lake—*reservoir* (2) CO-8
Marie, Lake—*reservoir* CT-1
Marie, Lake—*reservoir* MN-6
Marie, Lake—*reservoir* MO-7
Marie, Lake—*reservoir* NY-2
Marie, Mount—*summit* ME-1
Marie Branch—*stream* WV-2
Marie Cem—*cemetery* OK-5
Marie Ch—*church* GA-3
*Marie Creek* IN-6
Marie Creek—*bay* NC-3
Marie Creek—*stream* (2) AK-9
Marie Creek—*stream* CA-9
Marie Creek—*stream* ID-8
Marie Creek—*stream* MT-8
Marie Curie Sch—*school* CA-9
Marie-Eileen Lake—*lake* PA-2
Marie Falls—*falls* WA-9
Marie Gulch—*valley* NV-8
Marie Gully—*stream* TX-5
**Marie Heights**—*pop pl* WV-2
Marie Hollow—*valley* MO-7
Marie Island—*island* WY-8
Marie Joseph Acad—*school* ME-1
*Marie Lake* WI-6
Marie Lake—*lake* AK-9
Marie Lake—*lake* CA-9
Marie Lake—*lake* (2) MN-6
Marie Lake—*lake* TN-4
Marie Lake—*lake* WA-9
Marie Lake—*reservoir* AL-4
Marie Lake—*reservoir* GA-3
Marie Lake—*reservoir* TN-4
Marie Lake Dam—*dam* TN-4
Marie Lakes—*lake* CA-9
Mariel Creek—*stream* OR-9
Marie Louise, Mount—*summit* CA-9
Marie Louise Chapel—*church* WI-6
Marie Louise Pond—*lake* NY-2
Marie Miller Ranch—*locale* NV-8
Marie Mine—*mine* MT-8
**Mariemont**—*pop pl* OH-6
Mariemont Embankment And Village Site—*hist pl* OH-6
Mariemont Hist Dist—*hist pl* OH-6
Mariemont Sch—*school* CA-9
Mariemont (Township of)—*other* OH-6
Marie Mtn—*summit* AK-9
*Marien* PA-2
Mariendal—*locale* VI-3
Marienette—*locale* MS-4
Marienfeld Camp—*locale* NH-1
**Marienthal**—*pop pl* KS-7
Marienthal HS—*school* KS-7
**Marienville**—*pop pl* PA-2
Marie Saline (Township of)—*fmr MCD* AR-4
Maries Canyon—*valley* (2) AZ-5
Maries Canyon—*valley* UT-8
Marie Sch (historical)—*school* MS-4
Marie Scott Camp—*locale* CO-8
Maries County—*civil* MO-7
**Maries (County)**—*pop pl* MO-7
Maries County Memorial Park—*park* MO-7
Maries Creek—*stream* MO-7
Maries Island—*island* MN-6
Marie (Site)—*locale* TX-5
Maries Neck—*cape* NY-2
Marie Spring—*spring* UT-8
Maries River—*stream* MO-7
Maries Rsvr—*reservoir* AZ-5
Mariesville (historical)—*locale* AL-4
*Marietta* IN-6
*Marietta* NE-7
*Marietta* PA-2
Marietta—*CDP* WA-9
Marietta—*locale* NV-8
Marietta—*locale* SD-7
**Marietta**—*pop pl* AL-4
**Marietta**—*pop pl* FL-3
**Marietta**—*pop pl* GA-3
**Marietta**—*pop pl* IL-6
**Marietta**—*pop pl* IN-6
**Marietta**—*pop pl* IA-7
**Marietta**—*pop pl* KS-7
**Marietta**—*pop pl* MN-6
**Marietta**—*pop pl* MS-4
**Marietta**—*pop pl* NY-2
**Marietta**—*pop pl* NC-3
**Marietta**—*pop pl* OH-6
**Marietta**—*pop pl* OK-5
**Marietta**—*pop pl* PA-2
**Marietta**—*pop pl* SC-3
**Marietta**—*pop pl* TX-5
**Marietta**—*pop pl* WA-9
Marietta, Lake—*lake* FL-3
*Marietta Air Force Base* PA-2
Marietta Air Force Station—*military* PA-2
Marietta Baptist Ch—*church* FL-3
Marietta Borough—*civil* PA-2
Marietta Campground—*locale* GA-3
Marietta (CCD)—*cens area* GA-3
Marietta Cem—*cemetery* AL-4
Marietta Cem—*cemetery* AR-4
Marietta Cem—*cemetery* IA-7
Marietta Cem—*cemetery* MS-4
Marietta Cem—*cemetery* NC-3
Marietta Ch—*church* (2) AL-4
Marietta Ch—*church* AR-4
Marietta Ch—*church* GA-3
Marietta Ch—*church* NE-7
Marietta Ch—*church* TN-4
Marietta Coll—*school* OH-6
Marietta Creek—*stream* CO-8
Marietta Creek—*stream* WA-9
Marietta-Douglassville (CCD)—*cens area* TX-5
Marietta Falls—*falls* WA-9
*Marietta High School* MS-4
Marietta Hist Dist—*hist pl* OH-6
Marietta Hist Dist—*hist pl* PA-2
Marietta Hist Dist (Boundary Increase)—*hist pl* PA-2
Marietta (historical)—*locale* KS-7
Marietta Lookout Tower—*locale* MS-4
*Marietta Mine* NV-8
Marietta Mine—*mine* MT-8
Marietta Mines—*mine* NV-8
Marietta Mine (underground)—*mine* AL-4
Marietta New (Township of)—*civ div* OH-6
Marietta Number 2 Sch (historical)—*school* AL-4
Marietta Post Office (historical)—*building* AL-4
*Marietta Run* WV-2
Marietta Run—*stream* OH-6
Marietta Run—*stream* WV-2
Marietta Sch—*school* AL-4
Marietta Sch—*school* KY-4
Marietta Sch—*school* MS-4
Marietta Sch—*school* NC-3
Marietta Sch—*school* SD-7
Marietta Sch (historical)—*school* AL-4
Marietta State For Nursery—*forest* OH-6
**Marietta (Town of)**—*pop pl* WI-6
Marietta Township—*fmr MCD* IA-7
**Marietta Township**—*pop pl* NE-7
Marietta Township (historical)—*civil* SD-7
Marietta (Township of)—*fmr MCD* NC-3
Marietta Valley—*valley* WI-6
Mariette Creek—*stream* CA-9
**Marieville**—*pop pl* RI-1
**Marie White Subdivision**—*pop pl* TN-4
Marigold—*locale* AL-4
Marigold—*locale* CA-9
Marigold—*locale* CO-8
Marigold—*locale* IL-6
**Marigold**—*pop pl* KS-7
Marigold Bar (inundated)—*bar* UT-8
Marigold Bldg—*hist pl* HI-9
Marigold Drain—*canal* CA-9
Marigold Lake—*lake* CO-8
Marigold Lateral—*canal* CA-9
Marigold Mine—*mine* (2) NV-8
Marigold Mines (surface)—*mine* AL-4
Marigold Pond—*lake* CO-8
Marigold Sch—*school* CA-9
Marihen Creek—*stream* IN-6
Marihers Museum Park—*park* VA-3
Mariich—*summit* FM-9
*Mariiru* MH-9
*Mariiru Point* MH-9
*Mariiru-saki* MH-9
*Mariiyu* MH-9
*Mariiyu Point* MH-9
Marijilda Canyon—*valley* AZ-5
Marijilda Canyon Prehistoric Archeol District—*hist pl* AZ-5
*Marijilda Creek* AZ-5
Marijilda Creek—*stream* AZ-5
Marijilda Picnic Grounds—*park* AZ-5
Marijilda Wash—*stream* AZ-5
Marijuana Tank—*reservoir* NM-5
Marijuna Tank—*reservoir* AZ-5
*Marikku-to* MP-9
Marila Gun Club—*other* CA-9
Marilee—*locale* TX-5
Mari-linn Sch—*school* OR-9
Marilla—*locale* MI-6
Marilla—*locale* TX-5
**Marilla**—*pop pl* NY-2
Marilla Brook—*stream* PA-2
Marilla Brook Sch—*school* PA-2
Marilla Cem—*cemetery* MI-6
Marilla Cem—*cemetery* NY-2
Marilla Ch—*church* MI-6
*Marilla Creek* PA-2
Marillac Sch—*school* MO-7
Marillac Seminary—*school* MO-7
Marilla Park—*locale* IL-6
Marilla Recreation Center—*park* WV-2
**Marilla (Town of)**—*pop pl* NY-2
**Marilla (Township of)**—*pop pl* MI-6
**Marilyn**—*pop pl* CA-9
**Marilyn Acres Subdivision**—*pop pl* UT-8
*Marilyn Lake* CA-9
Marilyn Napier Cem—*cemetery* WV-2
Marimac Lakes—*reservoir* GA-3
*Marimado To* FM-9
**Marimont**—*pop pl* TN-4
*Marina* MP-9
Marina—*CDP* GU-9
**Marina**—*pop pl* CA-9
Marina—*uninc pl* CA-9
Marina, Lake—*lake* MI-6
Marina Basin—*harbor* NY-2
Marina Boat Launch—*locale* PA-2
Marina Cove—*bay* OK-5
Marina Creek—*stream* NC-3
Marina del Ray—*CDP* CA-9
Marina del Rey JHS—*school* CA-9
**Marina District**—*pop pl* CA-9
*Marina Dunes* IN-6
Marina Gate—*locale* CA-9
Marina Golf Course—*other* CA-9
Marina Green—*park* CA-9
**Marina Hills**—*pop pl* TN-4
Marina HS—*school* (2) CA-9
Marina JHS—*school* CA-9
Marina Lakes Shop Ctr—*locale* KS-7
Marina Park Hist Dist—*hist pl* CT-1
*Marina Passage* CA-9
Marina Shoal—*bar* WI-6
Marina Site—*hist pl* WI-6
**Marina Terrace**—*pop pl* IL-6
**Marina Village**—*pop pl* IL-6
Marin (Barrio)—*fmr MCD* PR-3
**Marin City**—*pop pl* CA-9
Marin Country Club Estates—*uninc pl* CA-9
**Marin (County)**—*pop pl* CA-9
Marin County Civic Center—*building* CA-9
Marin County Day Sch—*school* CA-9
Marin County Hosp—*hospital* CA-9
Marindahl Dam—*dam* SD-7
Marindahl (historical)—*locale* SD-7
Marindahl Lake—*reservoir* SD-7
Marindahl Post Office—*hist pl* SD-7
**Marindahl Township**—*pop pl* SD-7
Marindahl Township Hall—*hist pl* SD-7
*Marine* MN-6
Marine—*locale* WV-2
**Marine**—*pop pl* IL-6
Marine Air Terminal—*hist pl* NY-2
Marine Barracks—*hist pl* PA-2
Marine Base Slough—*bay* TX-5
Marine Basin—*basin* CT-1
Marine Basin—*basin* NJ-2
Marine Bayou—*stream* LA-4
*Marine Beach* MH-9
Marine Cem—*cemetery* (2) IL-6
Marine Cem—*cemetery* ME-1
Marine Chapter House—*hist pl* IL-6
**Marine City**—*pop pl* MI-6
Marine City City Hall—*hist pl* MI-6
Marine City Drain—*stream* MI-6
Marine City Oil Field—*other* MI-6
Marine City South Oil And Gas Field—*other* MI-6
Marine Corp Barracks—*military* DC-2
*Marine Corps Air Station* AZ-5
*Marine Corps Air Station* CA-9
*Marine Corps Air Station* SC-3
*Marine Corps Air Station H* NC-3
*Marine Corps Air Station H New River* NC-3
Marine Corps Base—*other* VA-3
*Marine Corps Base (Twentynine Palms)* CA-9
Marine Corps Logistics Base, LANT—*military* GA-3
Marine Corps Memorial Museum—*building* PA-2
*Marine Corps Recruit Depot* CA-9
Marine Corps Reserve Center—*military* CA-9
Marine Corps Supply Activity—*hist pl* PA-2
Marine Corps Supply Annex—*military* CA-9
Marine Corps Supply Center (Nebo Area)—*military* CA-9
*Marine Corps Supply Center (Nebo Center)* CA-9
Marine Corps Supply Center (Yermo Area)—*military* CA-9
Marine Creek—*stream* AK-9
Marine Creek—*stream* OR-9
Marine Creek—*stream* TX-5
**Marine Drive**—*pop pl* WA-9
Marine Education Center and Museum—*building* MS-4
**Marine Hills**—*pop pl* WA-9
Marine Hosp—*hist pl* ME-1
Marine Hosp—*hospital* OH-6
Marine Hosp (historical)—*hospital* AL-4
Marine Hosp (historical)—*hospital* MS-4
Marine Hospital—*uninc pl* NY-2
**Marine Junction**—*pop pl* NC-3
Marine Lake—*lake* NJ-2
Marineland—*park* CA-9
**Marineland**—*pop pl* FL-3
**Marineland Gardens**—*pop pl* IN-6
Marine Memorial Airplane Crash Monmt—*park* WA-9
*Marine Mills* MN-6
Marine Mill Site—*hist pl* MN-6
Marine Mine—*mine* AZ-5
Marine Museum—*building* ME-1
Marine Museum—*building* OH-6
Marine Oil Field—*other* IL-6
*Marine-on-Saint Croix* MN-6
**Marine on Saint Croix**—*pop pl* MN-6
**Marine-on-St. Croix**—*pop pl* MN-6
Marine on St. Croix Hist Dist—*hist pl* MN-6
*Marine On St. Croix (RR name Marine)* MN-6
Marine Park—*airport* NJ-2
Marine Park—*park* CA-9
Marine Park—*park* MA-1
Marine Park—*park* TX-5
Marine Parkway Bridge—*bridge* NY-2
Marine Playland Dock—*locale* TN-4
**Mariner**—*pop pl* ME-1
Mariner—*uninc pl* CA-9
Mariner Creek—*stream* AK-9
Marine Ridge—*ridge* OR-9
Mariner Island—*island* AL-4
Mariner Lake—*lake* FL-3
Mariner Ledge—*bar* ME-1
Mariner Mall—*locale* FL-3
Mariner Outlet Mall—*locale* FL-3
Mariner Plaza (Shop Ctr)—*locale* FL-3
Marine (RR name for Marine On St. Croix)—*other* MN-6
**Mariners**—*pop pl* MD-2
Mariners Basin—*bay* CA-9
**Mariners (Bedsworth)**—*pop pl* MD-2
Mariners Bethel United Methodist Ch—*church* DE-2
Mariner Sch—*school* MT-8
Mariner's Church—*hist pl* ME-1
Mariners' Church—*hist pl* MI-6
**Mariners Harbor**—*pop pl* NY-2
Mariners Hosp—*hospital* FL-3
*Mariners Lake* FL-3
Mariners Point—*cape* CA-9
Mariners Point Campground—*locale* CA-9
Mariners Sch—*school* CA-9
Mariner's Temple—*hist pl* NY-2
Mariners Village Shop Ctr—*locale* AZ-5
Marines—*locale* NC-3
Marines Cem—*cemetery* TX-5
Marine Science Education Center—*school* FL-3
Marine Science Station—*school* FL-3
Marine Spring—*spring* WY-8
Marine Spring Branch—*stream* VA-3
Marine Stadium—*harbor* CA-9
Marine Stadium—*locale* FL-3
Marine Studios—*hist pl* FL-3
Marine Supply and Hardware Complex—*hist pl* WA-9
Marine Theater—*building* NY-2
**Marine (Township of)**—*pop pl* IL-6
*Marinette* AZ-5
**Marinette**—*pop pl* WI-6
**Marinette (County)**—*pop pl* WI-6
Marinette Heading Canal—*canal* AZ-5
Marinette RR Station—*building* AZ-5
Marinette Substation—*locale* AZ-5
**Marine View Estates**—*pop pl* WA-9
Marine World—*park* CA-9
Marinez Creek—*stream* NM-5
Marinez Springs—*spring* NM-5
Marin Garden Club Grove—*woods* CA-9
*Maring Creek* AL-4
Marin General Hosp—*hospital* CA-9
Maringer Canyon—*valley* UT-8
Maringo Creek—*stream* AL-4
**Maringouin**—*pop pl* LA-4
Maringouin, Bayou—*gut* LA-4
Maringouin, Bayou—*stream* LA-4
Maringouin Sch—*school* LA-4
Marin Headlands State Park—*park* CA-9
Marin HS—*school* CA-9
Marin Junior Coll—*school* CA-9
Marino Canyon—*valley* CA-9
Marino Mine—*mine* CA-9
Marino Pond—*reservoir* CT-1
Marino Windmill—*locale* TX-5
Marin Peninsula—*cape* CA-9
Marin Range—*other* AK-9
Marin Sch—*school* (2) CA-9
Marin Sierra Boy Scout Camp—*locale* CA-9
Marinuka Lake—*reservoir* WI-6
Marinus Canyon—*valley* (2) UT-8
Marinville Ranch—*locale* WY-8
Marinwood—*uninc pl* CA-9
Mario Creek—*stream* IN-6
Mario Johnson Dam—*dam* SD-7
*Marion* CA-9
*Marion* KS-7
*Marion* MS-4
*Marion* PA-2
Marion—*locale* FL-3
Marion—*locale* (2) GA-3
Marion—*locale* ID-8
Marion—*locale* NC-3
Marion—*locale* WV-2
**Marion**—*pop pl* AL-4
**Marion**—*pop pl* AR-4
**Marion**—*pop pl* CT-1
**Marion**—*pop pl* IL-6
**Marion**—*pop pl* (2) IN-6
**Marion**—*pop pl* IA-7
**Marion**—*pop pl* KS-7
**Marion**—*pop pl* KY-4
**Marion**—*pop pl* LA-4
**Marion**—*pop pl* ME-1
**Marion**—*pop pl* MD-2
**Marion**—*pop pl* MA-1
**Marion**—*pop pl* MI-6
**Marion**—*pop pl* MN-6
**Marion**—*pop pl* MS-4
**Marion**—*pop pl* (2) MO-7
**Marion**—*pop pl* MT-8
**Marion**—*pop pl* NE-7
**Marion**—*pop pl* NJ-2
**Marion**—*pop pl* NY-2
**Marion**—*pop pl* NC-3
**Marion**—*pop pl* ND-7
**Marion**—*pop pl* OH-6
**Marion**—*pop pl* OR-9
**Marion**—*pop pl* PA-2
**Marion**—*pop pl* SC-3
**Marion**—*pop pl* SD-7
**Marion**—*pop pl* (2) TN-4
**Marion**—*pop pl* TX-5
**Marion**—*pop pl* UT-8
**Marion**—*pop pl* VA-3
**Marion**—*pop pl* WV-2
**Marion**—*pop pl* (2) WI-6
Marion, Lake—*lake* AK-9
Marion, Lake—*lake* (4) FL-3
Marion, Lake—*lake* IN-6
Marion, Lake—*lake* (2) MI-6
Marion, Lake—*lake* (2) MN-6
Marion, Lake—*lake* WY-8
Marion, Lake—*reservoir* CA-9
Marion, Lake—*reservoir* GA-3
Marion, Lake—*reservoir* SC-3
Marion, Mount—*summit* NY-2
Mariona—*hist pl* CA-9
Marion Acad—*school* AL-4
*Marion Academy* TN-4
Marion-Adams HS—*school* IN-6
Marion And Genoa Drain—*stream* MI-6
Marion Archeol District—*hist pl* KS-7
Mariona Tower—*locale* GA-3
Marion Ave Sch—*school* CA-9
Marion Ave Sch—*school* WA-9
Marion Baptist Acad—*school* AL-4
Marion Baptist Ch (historical)—*church* TN-4
Marion Bay—*bay* MN-6
Marion Branch—*stream* (3) KY-4
Marion Branch—*stream* NC-3
Marion Branch—*stream* SC-3
Marion Branch—*stream* TN-4
Marion Bridge—*hist pl* PA-2
Marion Brooks Natural Area—*area* PA-2
Marion Butte—*summit* NM-5
Marion Butte—*summit* OR-9
Marion Canyon—*valley* CA-9
Marion Castle, Terre Bonne—*hist pl* CT-1
Marion (CCD)—*cens area* AL-4
Marion (CCD)—*cens area* KY-4
Marion (CCD)—*cens area* SC-3
Marion (CCD)—*cens area* TX-5
Marion Cem—*cemetery* AL-4
Marion Cem—*cemetery* CO-8
Marion Cem—*cemetery* ID-8
Marion Cem—*cemetery* (2) IN-6
Marion Cem—*cemetery* KS-7
Marion Cem—*cemetery* KY-4
Marion Cem—*cemetery* MO-7
Marion Cem—*cemetery* OH-6
Marion Cem—*cemetery* OR-9
Marion Cem—*cemetery* TX-5
Marion Cem—*cemetery* UT-8
Marion Cem—*cemetery* WI-6
Marion (census name for Marion Center)—*CDP* MA-1
*Marion Center* KS-7
**Marion Center**—*pop pl* PA-2
Marion Center Area Elem Sch—*school* PA-2
Marion Center Area HS—*school* PA-2
Marion Center Borough—*civil* PA-2
Marion Center Cem—*cemetery* IA-7
Marion Center (census name Marion)—*other* MA-1
Marion Center Sch (historical)—*school* MO-7
Marion Center Speedway—*other* PA-2
Marion Center Speedway Airp—*airport* PA-2
*Marion Central School* MS-4
*Marion Centre* KS-7
Marion Ch—*church* (2) IN-6
Marion Ch—*church* LA-4
Marion Ch—*church* OH-6
Marion Ch—*church* VA-3
Marion Ch—*church* WI-6
*Marion Church* AL-4
**Marion Circle**—*pop pl* IL-6
Marion City Hall—*building* AL-4
Marion City Hall—*building* IA-7
Marion Clayton Mtn—*summit* GA-3
Marion Coll—*school* IN-6
Marion Coll—*school* VA-3
Marion Correctional Institution—*building* OH-6
Marion Coulee—*valley* MT-8
Marion Country Club—*locale* NC-3
Marion Country Club—*other* AL-4
Marion Country Club—*other* OH-6
Marion County—*civil* KS-7
Marion County—*civil* MO-7
**Marion County**—*pop pl* AL-4
**Marion (County)**—*pop pl* AR-4
**Marion County**—*pop pl* FL-3
**Marion (County)**—*pop pl* GA-3
**Marion (County)**—*pop pl* IL-6
**Marion County**—*pop pl* IN-6
**Marion (County)**—*pop pl* KY-4
**Marion County**—*pop pl* MS-4
**Marion (County)**—*pop pl* MO-7
**Marion (County)**—*pop pl* OH-6
**Marion County**—*pop pl* OR-9
**Marion (County)**—*pop pl* SC-3
**Marion County**—*pop pl* TN-4
**Marion (County)**—*pop pl* TX-5
**Marion (County)**—*pop pl* WV-2
Marion County Airp—*airport* AL-4
Marion County-Brown Field (airport)—*airport* TN-4
Marion County Courthouse—*building* AL-4
Marion County Courthouse—*building* MS-4
Marion County Courthouse—*building* TN-4
Marion County Courthouse—*hist pl* GA-3
Marion County Courthouse—*hist pl* IA-7
Marion County Courthouse—*hist pl* KS-7
Marion County Courthouse—*hist pl* OH-6
Marion County Courthouse and Sheriff's House—*hist pl* WV-2
Marion County Dam—*dam* KS-7
Marion County Fairground—*locale* IA-7
*Marion County Game Mngmt Area* MS-4
Marion County General Hosp—*hospital* AL-4
Marion County General Hosp—*hospital* MS-4
Marion County Home (historical)—*building* TN-4
Marion County Housing Committee Demonstration House—*hist pl* OR-9
Marion County HS—*school* AL-4
Marion County HS—*school* MS-4
Marion County HS—*school* TN-4
Marion County Infirmary—*other* MO-7
*Marion County Lake* AL-4
**Marion County Lake**—*pop pl* KS-7
Marion County Lake—*reservoir* KS-7
*Marion County Memorial Cemetery* AL-4
Marion County Memorial Gardens—*cemetery* AL-4
*Marion County Memory Garden* AL-4
Marion County Park—*park* IA-7
Marion County Park—*park* KS-7
Marion County Park—*park* TN-4
Marion County Public Lake Dam—*dam* AL-4
Marion County State Wildlife Mngmt Area—*park* MS-4
*Marion County Vocational Complex* MS-4
Marion County Vocational Sch—*school* MS-4
Marion Cove Public Use Area—*park* KS-7
*Marion Creek* MN-6
Marion Creek—*stream* (2) AK-9
Marion Creek—*stream* (2) CA-9
Marion Creek—*stream* ID-8
Marion Creek—*stream* (2) MI-6
Marion Creek—*stream* MN-6
Marion Creek—*stream* (2) MT-8
Marion Creek—*stream* (5) OR-9
Marion Creek—*stream* SC-3
Marion Dam—*dam* KS-7
Marion Davis Park—*park* SC-3
Marion Ditch—*canal* OR-9
Marion Ditch—*canal* WY-8
Marion Division—*civil* AL-4
Marion Drain—*canal* WA-9
**Marion East**—*pop pl* OH-6
Marion East (CCD)—*cens area* TX-5
**Marion East (census name East Marion)**—*pop pl* NC-3
Marion Elem Sch—*school* AL-4
Marion Elem Sch—*school* IN-6
Marion Elem Sch*—*school* KS-7
Marion Elem Sch—*school* NC-3
Marion Engineer Depot—*locale* OH-6
Marion Falls—*falls* OR-9
Marion Female Seminary (historical)—*school* AL-4
Marion Fish Hatchery Dam Number One—*dam* AL-4
Marion Fish Hatchery Number One—*reservoir* AL-4
Marion Fish Hatchery Number Two—*reservoir* AL-4
Marion Fish Hatchery Number Two Dam—*dam* AL-4
Marion Flat—*flat* CO-8
Marion Flats—*flat* SD-7
Marion Fork—*stream* KY-4
**Marion Forks**—*pop pl* OR-9
*Marion Fork Santiam River* OR-9
Marion-Franklin HS—*school* OH-6
Marion Furnace (historical)—*locale* TN-4
Marion Furnace (40WY61)—*hist pl* TN-4
Mariong Island—*island* FM-9
Marion Grange—*locale* WA-9
Marion Gulch—*valley* CO-8
Marion Haws Draw—*valley* AZ-5
**Marion Heights**—*pop pl* IN-6
**Marion Heights**—*pop pl* PA-2
Marion Heights Borough—*civil* PA-2
**Marion Heights (Keiser)**—*pop pl* PA-2
Marion Heights (OPlaza (Shop Ctr)—*locale* MO-7
Marion Heights Plaza—*locale* MO-7
Marion Herthel Hill—*summit* IN-6
**Marion Hill**—*pop pl* PA-2
**Marion Hill**—*pop pl* VA-3
Marion Hill Ch—*church* KS-7
*Marion Hills* IL-6
Marion Hill Spring—*spring* WA-9
Marion Hills Sch—*school* IL-6
Marion Hills Seminary—*school* IL-6
**Marion Hill (Township name Pulaski)**—*pop pl* PA-2
Marion Hist Dist—*hist pl* CT-1
Marion Hist Dist—*hist pl* SC-3
Marion Hist Dist (Boundary Increase)—*hist pl* SC-3
**Marion (historical)**—*pop pl* OR-9
Marion (historical P.O.)—*locale* MA-1
Marion Homes—*uninc pl* GA-3
Marion Hotel—*hist pl* FL-3
Marion HS—*school* IN-6
Marion HS—*school* KS-7
Marion HS—*school* LA-4
Marion HS—*school* OH-6
Marion HS—*school* PA-2
Marion HS—*school* TX-5
*Marion Hyder Branch* TN-4
Marion Institute—*school* AL-4
Marion Institute (historical)—*school* TN-4
**Marion Interchange (Croxton Yards)**—*pop pl* NJ-2
Marion Iosco Drain—*canal* MI-6
Marion Island—*island* FL-3
Marion Island—*island* ME-1
Marion Island—*island* MI-6
Marion Island (historical)—*island* SD-7
Marion Jordan Trail (pack)—*trail* OR-9
*Marion Junction* (2) SD-7
**Marion Junction**—*pop pl* AL-4
Marion Lake—*lake* AR-4
Marion Lake—*lake* CA-9
Marion Lake—*lake* ID-8
Marion Lake—*lake* MI-6
Marion Lake—*lake* (5) MN-6
Marion Lake—*lake* MT-8
Marion Lake—*lake* NY-2
Marion Lake—*lake* OR-9
Marion Lake—*lake* WA-9
Marion Lake—*lake* (3) WI-6
Marion Lake—*lake* (2) WY-8
Marion Lake—*reservoir* CO-8
Marion Lake—*reservoir* KS-7
Marion Lake—*reservoir* NJ-2
Marion Lake Guard Station—*locale* OR-9
Marion Lakes—*lake* ND-7
Marion Lake Trail—*trail* OR-9
*Marion Landing* MS-4
*Marion Landing Field* KS-7
Marion Lea Sch—*school* FL-3
Marion Lookout Tower—*locale* AL-4
Marion Mackey Knob—*summit* MO-7
**Marion Manor**—*pop pl* IN-6
**Marion (Marion Station)**—*pop pl* MD-2
Marion Meadows—*flat* ID-8
Marion Memorial Bridge—*bridge* TN-4
Marion Methodist Ch—*church* AL-4
*Marion Military Institute* AL-4
**Marion Mills**—*pop pl* IN-6
Marion Mine—*mine* CO-8
Marion Mine (underground)—*mine* AL-4
Marion Mountain Camp—*locale* CA-9
Marion Mtn—*summit* CA-9
Marion Mtn—*summit* OR-9
Marion Municipal Airp—*airport* IN-6
Marion Municipal Airp—*airport* KS-7
Marion Natl Fish Hatchery—*other* AL-4
**Marion Oaks (subdivision)**—*pop pl* FL-3
Marion Park—*park* MI-6
Marion Park—*park* WI-6
*Marion Park Elem Sch* MS-4
Marion Park Pavilion—*hist pl* WI-6
Marion Park Sch—*school* MS-4
Marion Peak—*summit* CA-9
Marion Peak—*summit* OR-9
Marion Perry Lake Dam—*dam* MS-4
Marion Plaza (Shop Ctr)—*locale* IN-6
Marion Point—*cape* AZ-5
Marion Point—*cliff* OR-9
Marion Point—*summit* OR-9
Marion Pond—*lake* NY-2
Marion Pond—*reservoir* WI-6
Marion Post Office—*building* AL-4
Marion Public Sch (historical)—*school* AL-4
Marion Ravine—*valley* CA-9
Marion Reach—*channel* NJ-2
*Marion Reservoir* KS-7
Marion Ridge—*ridge* CA-9
Marion Ridge Ch—*church* OH-6
Marion River—*stream* NY-2
Marion Robinette Memorial Ch—*church* TN-4
Marion Rsvr—*reservoir* IL-6
Marion Sanders Lake Dam—*dam* AL-4
**Marions Camp**—*pop pl* MA-1

Marion Sch—*school* ... IL-6
Marion Sch—*school* ... IA-7
Marion Sch—*school* (2) ... MO-7
Marion Sch—*school* ... NC-3
Marion Sch—*school* ... OH-6
Marion Sch—*school* ... OR-9
Marion Sch—*school* ... SC-3
Marion Sch (historical)—*school* ... MS-4
Marion Sch (historical)—*school* ... TN-4
Marion School (historical)—*locale* ... MO-7
Marion Scott Cove—*bay* ... VA-3
Marion (Siding)—*locale* ... ID-8
Marion (site)—*locale* ... TX-5
Marion Slough—*gut* ... TX-5
Marion Spring—*spring* ... AZ-5
Marion Spring Number One—*spring* ... AZ-5
Marion Springs—*locale* ... MI-6
Marion Spur—*uninc pl* ... OR-9
Marion Square—*park* ... SC-3
Marion Square Park—*park* ... OR-9
*Marion Station* ... MD-2
*Marion Station* ... MS-4
Marion Station (historical)—*locale* ... MA-1
*Marion Station (Marion)* ... MD-2
Marion Street Ch—*church* ... SC-3
Marion Street Sch—*school* ... ME-1
Marion Street Sch—*school* ... NY-2
Marion Street Sch—*school* ... OH-6
Marions View Ch—*church* ... VA-3
Marion Top—*summit* ... NC-3
Marion Townhall—*building* ... IA-7
**Marion (Town of)**—*pop pl* ... MA-1
**Marion (Town of)**—*pop pl* ... NY-2
**Marion (Town of)**—*pop pl* (3) ... WI-6
Marion Township—*civil* (6) ... MO-7
Marion Township—*fmr MCD* (10) ... IA-7
**Marion Township**—*pop pl* (5) ... KS-7
**Marion Township**—*pop pl* (5) ... MO-7
**Marion Township**—*pop pl* ... NE-7
**Marion Township**—*pop pl* ... ND-7
**Marion Township**—*pop pl* ... SD-7
Marion Township (historical)—*civil* ... SD-7
Marion (Township of)—*fmr MCD* (7) ... AR-4
Marion (Township of)—*fmr MCD* ... NC-3
**Marion (Township of)**—*pop pl* (2) ... IL-6
**Marion (Township of)**—*pop pl* (12) ... IN-6
**Marion (Township of)**—*pop pl* (5) ... MI-6
**Marion (Township of)**—*pop pl* ... MN-6
**Marion (Township of)**—*pop pl* (12) ... OH-6
**Marion (Township of)**—*pop pl* (4) ... PA-2
Marion (Township of)—*unorg* ... ME-1
Marion Twin Mine—*mine* ... AK-9
Marion United Methodist Ch—*church* ... MS-4
Marion United Methodist Ch—*church* ... TN-4
**Marion Village Subdivision**—*pop pl* ... UT-8
**Marionville**—*pop pl* ... MO-7
**Marionville**—*pop pl* ... VA-3
Marion-Walthall HS (historical)—*school* ... MS-4
Marion Weissinger Lake Dam Number 1—*dam* ... AL-4
Marion Weissinger Lake Dam Number 2—*dam* ... AL-4
Marion Weissinger Lake No. 2—*reservoir* ... AL-4
Marion Weissinger Lake Number One—*reservoir* ... AL-4
Marion Wells—*well* ... TX-5
Marion West (CCD)—*cens area* ... TX-5
Marion Wildlife Area—*park* ... KS-7
Mari-Osa State Wildlife Area—*park* ... MO-7
*Mariot Creek* ... AL-4
Mariposa—*locale* ... NY-2
**Mariposa**—*pop pl* ... CA-9
**Mariposa**—*pop pl* ... NC-3
Mariposa Ave Sch—*school* ... CA-9
Mariposa Bypass—*canal* ... CA-9
Mariposa Canyon—*valley* ... AZ-5
Mariposa Canyon—*valley* ... NV-8
Mariposa (CCD)—*cens area* ... CA-9
**Mariposa (County)**—*pop pl* ... CA-9
Mariposa County Courthouse—*hist pl* ... CA-9
*Mariposa Creek* ... CO-8
Mariposa Creek—*stream* ... AK-9
Mariposa Creek—*stream* (2) ... CA-9
Mariposa Grove—*woods* ... CA-9
Mariposa Grove Museum—*hist pl* ... CA-9
Mariposa Guard Station—*locale* ... CA-9
Mariposa Key—*island* ... FL-3
Mariposa Lake—*lake* ... WY-8
Mariposa Mine—*mine* (3) ... CA-9
Mariposa Mine—*mine* ... TX-5
Mariposa Oil Field—*oilfield* ... TX-5
Mariposa Park—*park* ... AZ-5
Mariposa Peak—*summit* ... CA-9
Mariposa Ranch—*locale* ... TX-5
Mariposa Ranger Station—*locale* ... CA-9
Mariposa Reef—*bar* ... AK-9
Mariposa Rock—*other* ... AK-9
Mariposa Rsvr—*reservoir* ... CA-9
Mariposa Sch—*school* (2) ... CA-9
Mariposa Slough—*gut* ... CA-9
Mariposa Spring—*spring* ... CA-9
Mariposa Tank—*reservoir* ... NM-5
Mariposa Township—*fmr MCD* ... IA-7
**Mariposa Township**—*pop pl* ... NE-7
Maris Acad—*school* ... CA-9
Mariscal Canyon—*valley* ... TX-5
Mariscal Mine—*hist pl* ... TX-5
Mariscal Mine—*mine* ... TX-5
Mariscal Mtn—*summit* ... TX-5
Maris Coll—*school* ... GA-3
*Marisdale* ... VA-3
Maris HS—*school* ... NY-2
**Marissa**—*pop pl* ... IL-6
Marissa Cem—*cemetery* ... IL-6
**Marissa (Township of)**—*pop pl* ... IL-6
Marissa Waterworks—*other* ... IL-6
Maris Sch—*school* ... PA-2
Marist Brothers Seminary—*school* ... NY-2
Marist Coll—*school* ... MA-1
Marist HS—*school* ... NJ-2
**Maris Town**—*pop pl* ... MS-4
Marist Preparatory Sch—*school* ... NY-2
Marist Seminary—*school* ... MA-1
*Marisville* ... PA-2
Marita Shoal—*bar* ... MP-9
Marit Cem—*cemetery* ... SC-3
Maritime Acad—*school* ... ME-1
Maritime Bay—*bay* ... WI-6
Maritime Museum—*building* ... MA-1
Maritime Museum—*building* ... PA-2
Maritime Reservation—*military* ... CA-9
Maritje Kill—*stream* ... NY-2
Maritz, Incorporated (Warehouse)—*facility* ... MO-7
Marivue Park—*park* ... AZ-5
*Mariw* ... FM-9
*Mariyar* ... FM-9
*Mariych* ... FM-9
Marja Sch (historical)—*school* ... AL-4
Mar-Jeanne Farm Lake—*reservoir* ... TN-4
Mar-Jeanne Lake Dam—*dam* ... TN-4
Mar-Jean Shop Ctr—*locale* ... IN-6
Marjoe Key—*island* ... FL-3
Mar-Jon Golf Course—*locale* ... PA-2
Marjon Mine—*mine* ... CA-9
Marjorie—*locale* ... TX-5
Marjorie, Lake—*lake* ... CA-9
Marjorie Ann Mine—*mine* ... CO-8
Marjorie K Rawlings Elem Sch—*school* ... FL-3
Marjorie Lake—*lake* ... WA-9
Marjorie Lake—*reservoir* ... UT-8
Marjorie Lake Dam—*dam* ... UT-8
Marjorie Webster Junior Coll—*school* ... DC-2
Marjory, Lake—*lake* ... MI-6
Marjum Canyon—*valley* ... UT-8
Marjum Pass—*gap* ... UT-8
*Mark* ... KS-7
Mark—*locale* ... ID-8
Mark—*locale* ... KY-4
Mark—*locale* ... LA-4
Mark—*locale* ... MO-7
**Mark**—*pop pl* ... IL-6
**Mark**—*pop pl* ... IA-7
**Mark**—*pop pl* ... MI-6
Mark, Caroline, House—*hist pl* ... IL-6
Mark, Lake—*reservoir* ... CT-1
Marka Bay—*bay* ... AK-9
**Mark Acres**—*pop pl* ... PA-2
*Markagunk Plateau* ... UT-8
Markagunt Plateau—*plateau* ... UT-8
*Markam Creek* ... OR-9
Mark Anton Airp—*airport* ... TN-4
Mark Antony Motor Hotel—*hist pl* ... OR-9
Mark Bay—*bay* ... SC-3
Mark Beach Bayou—*stream* ... AR-4
Mark Beach Bayou—*stream* ... LA-4
Mark Branch—*stream* ... GA-3
Mark Branch—*stream* ... MO-7
Mark Cem—*cemetery* ... OH-6
**Mark Center**—*pop pl* ... OH-6
Mark Centre (RR name for Mark Center)—*other* ... OH-6
Mark Ch—*church* ... IA-7
Mark Clark Golf Course—*other* ... OR-9
Mark Conley Pit Number One—*cave* ... TN-4
Mark Conley Pit Number Two—*cave* ... TN-4
Mark Creek—*stream* ... AK-9
Mark Creek—*stream* ... MN-6
Mark Ditch—*canal* ... OH-6
*Mark Edson Reservoir* ... CA-9
**Marked Tree**—*pop pl* ... AR-4
Marked Tree Cem—*cemetery* ... AR-4
Marked Tree Lock and Siphons—*hist pl* ... AR-4
Markee—*locale* ... LA-4
Markee Creek—*stream* ... PA-2
Markee Creek—*stream* ... WI-6
Markee Lake—*lake* ... MN-6
Markeen Mtn—*summit* ... AZ-5
Markee Rsvr—*reservoir* ... OR-9
Markee Sch (abandoned)—*school* ... PA-2
Markee Site—*hist pl* ... WI-6
Markee Spring—*spring* ... WI-6
**Markeeta**—*pop pl* ... AL-4
*Markeeta Church* ... AL-4
Markeeta Mine (underground)—*mine* ... AL-4
*Markeham Lake* ... MN-6
Markel Canal—*canal* ... NC-3
Mark Elem Sch—*school* ... IN-6
Markel Lake—*lake* ... MI-6
Markel Run—*stream* ... PA-2
Markel Sch (abandoned)—*school* ... PA-2
**Markelsville**—*pop pl* ... PA-2
*Markelville* ... PA-2
Markem Branch—*stream* ... TN-4
Marker Branch—*stream* ... TN-4
Marker Ch—*church* ... ND-7
Marker Ditch—*canal* ... IN-6
Marker Drain—*canal* ... MI-6
**Marker Estates**—*pop pl* ... DE-2
Marker Hill—*summit* ... CO-8
Marker Lake—*lake* ... MI-6
Marker Lake—*reservoir* ... CO-8
Marker Mtn—*summit* ... AK-9
Marker Sch—*school* ... PA-2
Marker Sch (abandoned)—*school* ... PA-2
*Markers Hill* ... MD-2
Marker Spring—*spring* ... NV-8
**Markes**—*pop pl* ... PA-2
**Markesan**—*pop pl* ... WI-6
Market—*locale* ... NY-2
Market—*locale* ... WV-2
**Market**—*pop pl* ... HI-9
**Market**—*pop pl* ... NY-2
**Market**—*pop pl* ... OR-9
Market—*uninc pl* ... CA-9
Market Bldg—*hist pl* ... GA-3
**Marketboro Condostor Condominium**—*pop pl* ... UT-8
**Marketboro Subdivision**—*pop pl* ... UT-8
Market Branch—*stream* ... GA-3
Market Bridge—*bridge* ... MS-4
**Market Center**—*pop pl* ... SC-3
Market Center Shop Ctr—*locale* ... TX-5
Market Corners—*locale* ... NY-2
Market-Fire House—*building* ... NC-3
Market Gulch—*valley* ... MT-8
Market Hall and Sheds—*hist pl* ... SC-3
Market House—*hist pl* ... KY-4
Market House—*hist pl* ... NY-2
Market House—*hist pl* ... NC-3
Market House—*hist pl* ... RI-1
Market House Square District—*hist pl* ... NC-3
Market Lake—*reservoir* ... ID-8
Market Lake Slough—*gut* ... ID-8
Market Lake State Wildlife Mngmt Area—*park* ... ID-8
Market on Harbor Island, The—*locale* ... FL-3
Marketown—*locale* ... WA-9
Marketplace, The—*locale* ... FL-3
Market Place, The—*locale* ... FL-3
Marketplace, The—*locale* ... MA-1
Market Place, The (Shop Ctr)—*locale* (2) ... FL-3
Market Place at Hobe Sound, The—*locale* ... FL-3
Market Place North II (Shop Ctr)—*locale* ... FL-3
Marketplace of Delray (Shop Ctr)—*locale* ... FL-3
Market Place (Shop Ctr)—*locale* (2) ... FL-3
Market Place Shop Ctr—*locale* ... IL-6
Market Place Shop Ctr—*locale* ... KS-7
Market Place Shop Ctr—*locale* ... NC-3
Market Place West (Shop Ctr)—*locale* ... FL-3
Market Point—*cape* ... MO-7
Market Sch—*school* ... OH-6
Market Sch (historical)—*school* ... MS-4
Market Square—*hist pl* ... OH-6
Market Square—*locale* ... ND-7
Market Square—*locale* ... PA-2
Market Square—*park* ... TN-4
Market Square—*uninc pl* ... PA-2
Market Square Commercial Hist Dist—*hist pl* ... TN-4
Market Square Hist Dist—*hist pl* ... ME-1
Market Square Hist Dist—*hist pl* ... MA-1
Market Square-Patten Parkway—*hist pl* ... TN-4
Market Square Shop Ctr—*locale* ... AL-4
Market Square (Shop Ctr)—*locale* (2) ... FL-3
Market Square Shop Ctr—*locale* ... IN-6
Market Street—*uninc pl* ... PA-2
Market Street Bridge—*bridge* ... PA-2
Market Street Bridge—*hist pl* (2) ... PA-2
Market Street Ch—*church* ... MI-6
Market Street Ch of Christ—*church* ... AL-4
Market Street Ch of Christ—*church* ... TN-4
Market Street Hist Dist—*hist pl* ... NJ-2
Market Street Hist Dist—*hist pl* (3) ... NY-2
Market Street Mansion District—*hist pl* ... NC-3
Market Street Row—*hist pl* ... NY-2
Market Street Sch—*school* ... NJ-2
Market Street Sch—*school* ... OH-6
Market Street Sch—*school* ... PA-2
Market Street Sch—*school* ... TN-4
Market Street Shop Ctr—*locale* ... TN-4
Market Street-Suburb Ste. Mary Hist Dist—*hist pl* ... MS-4
Market Street Theatre and Loft District—*hist pl* ... CA-9
Market Street Warehouse Hist Dist—*hist pl* ... TN-4
Market Swamp—*stream* ... VA-3
*Marketta* ... AL-4
Marketta Baptist Ch—*church* ... AL-4
**Markette**—*pop pl* ... MS-4
Markey Beach—*beach* ... ME-1
Markey Cem—*cemetery* ... MI-6
Markey Ch—*church* ... MI-6
Markey House—*hist pl* ... AR-4
Markey Lake—*lake* ... MI-6
Markey Park—*park* ... MI-6
**Markey (Township of)**—*pop pl* ... MI-6
Mark Fischer Dam—*dam* ... SD-7
Mark Flight Memorial Sch—*school* ... FL-3
Markgrafs Lake—*lake* ... MN-6
Markgras Springs—*spring* ... WI-6
Mark Hall—*hist pl* ... GA-3
*Markham* ... TN-4
Markham—*locale* ... CO-8
Markham—*locale* ... IL-6
Markham—*locale* ... MN-6
Markham—*locale* ... OK-5
Markham—*locale* ... PA-2
Markham—*locale* ... VA-3
Markham—*locale* ... WA-9
**Markham**—*pop pl* ... FL-3
**Markham**—*pop pl* ... IL-6
**Markham**—*pop pl* ... MS-4
**Markham**—*pop pl* ... TN-4
**Markham**—*pop pl* ... TX-5
**Markham**—*pop pl* ... VA-3
Markham, Lake—*lake* ... FL-3
Markham, Mount—*summit* ... CA-9
Markham, Mount—*summit* ... NY-2
Markham Arroyo—*stream* ... CO-8
*Markham Branch* ... WV-2
Markham Canyon—*valley* ... AZ-5
Markham Cave—*cave* ... TN-4
Markham Cem—*cemetery* ... AR-4
Markham Cem—*cemetery* ... MI-6
Markham Cem—*cemetery* ... TN-4
Markham Ch—*church* ... MS-4
Markham Ch—*church* ... VA-3
*Markham City* ... IL-6
Markham City Oil Field—*other* ... IL-6
Markham Creek—*stream* ... AZ-5
Markham Creek—*stream* ... ID-8
Markham Creek—*stream* ... MS-4
Markham Creek—*stream* ... OR-9
Markham Creek—*stream* ... WI-6
Markham Dam—*dam* ... AZ-5
Markham Drain—*canal* ... MI-6
Markham Draw—*valley* ... WY-8
Markham (Election Precinct)—*fmr MCD* ... IL-6
Markham Elem Sch—*school* ... PA-2
Markham Ferry Ch—*church* ... OK-5
*Markham Ferry Reservoir* ... OK-5
Markham Fork—*stream* ... KY-4
Markham Gulch—*valley* ... UT-8
Markham Hollow—*valley* ... KY-4
Markham Hollow—*valley* ... MO-7
Markham Hollow—*valley* ... NY-2
Markham House—*hist pl* ... NH-1
Markham JHS—*school* (2) ... CA-9
Markham Lake—*lake* ... MN-6
Markham Ledge—*rock* ... MA-1
Markham Mound—*hist pl* ... OH-6
Markham Mtn—*summit* ... AR-4
Markham Mtn—*summit* ... VT-1
Markham Park—*park* ... FL-3
Markham Park Sch—*school* ... IL-6
*Markham Peak* ... UT-8
Markham Peak—*summit* ... UT-8
*Markham Plantation* ... MS-4
Markham Point—*cape* ... NY-2
Markham Pond—*lake* ... ME-1
Markham Ravine—*valley* ... CA-9
Markham Ridge—*ridge* ... CA-9
Markham Run—*stream* ... PA-2
**Markhams**—*pop pl* ... NY-2
Markham Sch—*school* (2) ... CA-9
Markham Sch—*school* ... OR-9
Markham Sch—*school* ... VA-3
Markham Sch—*school* ... WA-9
Markham Sch and Teacherage—*hist pl* ... OK-5
Markham Sch Annex—*school* ... OR-9
Markham Sch (historical)—*school* ... TN-4
*Markham School* ... PA-2
Markhams Ferry (historical)—*locale* ... MS-4
Markhams Pond—*lake* ... IA-7
Markham Spring—*spring* ... MO-7
Markham Spring—*spring* ... NM-5
Markham Spring Rec Area—*park* ... MO-7
Markham Street Interchange—*other* ... AR-4
*Markham Wash* ... AZ-5
Markham Wash—*arroyo* ... AZ-5
Markham Wash—*stream* ... AZ-5
Markham Well—*well* ... AZ-5
Markham Windmill—*locale* ... NM-5
Markham Woods Seventh Day Adventist Ch—*church* ... FL-3
Mark Hanna, Lake—*lake* ... AL-4
Mark Haven Beach—*locale* ... VA-3
Mark Hoard Memorial Airfield—*airport* ... KS-7
Mark Hollow—*valley* ... KY-4
Mark Howell Sch—*school* ... NM-5
Markillie Cem—*cemetery* ... OH-6
Markin Fork—*stream* ... OH-6
Marking Corral Springs—*spring* ... OR-9
Marking Corral Summit—*summit* ... NV-8
Marking Pen Creek—*stream* ... WY-8
*Mark Island* ... ME-1
Mark Island—*island* (5) ... ME-1
Mark Island—*island* ... NH-1
Mark Island Ledge—*bar* (2) ... ME-1
Mark James Park—*park* ... TN-4
Mark Lake—*lake* ... AK-9
Mark Lake—*lake* (2) ... MN-6
Markla Lake—*lake* ... MI-6
*Markland* ... IN-6
Markland—*hist pl* ... FL-3
**Markland**—*pop pl* ... IN-6
Markland Canyon—*valley* ... CA-9
Markland Cem—*cemetery* ... TN-4
Markland Dam—*dam* ... IN-6
Markland Locks and Dam—*dam* ... KY-4
Marklay Mine—*mine* ... CA-9
Markle—*airport* ... NJ-2
**Markle**—*pop pl* ... IN-6
**Markle**—*pop pl* ... PA-2
Markle, George and Eugene, House—*hist pl* ... MI-6
Markle Cem—*cemetery* ... IL-6
Markle Cem—*cemetery* ... MT-8
Markle Cem—*cemetery* (2) ... PA-2
Markle Ditch—*canal* ... WY-8
Marklee Island—*island* ... LA-4
**Marklee Village**—*pop pl* ... CA-9
**Markleeville**—*pop pl* ... CA-9
Markleeville (CCD)—*cens area* ... CA-9
*Markleeville Creek* ... CA-9
Markleeville Creek—*stream* ... CA-9
Markleeville Peak—*summit* ... CA-9
Markle Gap—*gap* ... PA-2
Markle Hill—*summit* ... MT-8
Markle Hollow—*valley* ... AR-4
Markle House and Mill Site—*hist pl* ... IN-6
*Markle Lake* ... MI-6
Marklelys Pond—*lake* ... PA-2
Markle Mine—*mine* ... AR-4
Markle Pass—*gap* ... MT-8
Markle-Pittock House—*hist pl* ... OR-9
**Markles**—*pop pl* ... IN-6
**Marklesburg**—*pop pl* ... PA-2
Marklesburg Borough—*civil* ... PA-2
**Marklesburg (corporate name for James Creek)**—*pop pl* ... PA-2
Markles Cem—*cemetery* ... IN-6
Markles Point—*cape* ... MT-8
Markle Spring—*spring* ... AR-4
*Markles Station* ... IN-6
Markle State Rec Area—*park* ... IN-6
**Markleton**—*pop pl* ... PA-2
**Markleville**—*pop pl* ... IN-6
Markley—*locale* ... TX-5
Markley Canyon—*valley* (2) ... CA-9
Markley Cem—*cemetery* ... AR-4
Markley Cem—*cemetery* ... IL-6
Markley Corners—*locale* ... PA-2
Markley Ditch—*canal* (3) ... IN-6
Markley Hill—*summit* ... WY-8
Markley Lake—*lake* ... MI-6
Markley Lake—*lake* ... MN-6
Markley Ranch—*locale* ... WY-8
Markley Rocks—*summit* ... VA-3
**Markleysburg**—*pop pl* ... PA-2
Markleysburg Borough—*civil* ... PA-2
Marklin Cem—*cemetery* ... TN-4
Mark Loves Landing (historical)—*locale* ... MS-4
Mark Means Park—*park* ... ID-8
*Mark Mountain* ... MA-1
Mark Mtn—*summit* ... TN-4
Marko—*uninc pl* ... NC-3
Markoma Bible Acad—*school* ... OK-5
Mark One Tank—*reservoir* ... AZ-5
Markout—*locale* ... TX-5
Mark Pine—*locale* ... NC-3
Mark Pine Bay—*swamp* ... NC-3
Mark Pine Canal—*stream* ... NC-3
Mark Point—*cape* ... UT-8
Mark Reed Hospital Heliport—*airport* ... WA-9
Markrider Cem—*cemetery* ... TX-5
Mark Rsvr—*reservoir* ... OR-9
Mark Run—*stream* ... IN-6
Mark Run—*stream* ... WV-2
Marks—*locale* ... MI-6
**Marks**—*pop pl* ... MS-4
Marks, M. J., House—*hist pl* ... ID-8
Marks, Morris, House—*hist pl* ... OR-9
Marks Bend—*bend* ... TX-5
**Marksboro**—*pop pl* ... NJ-2
Marks Branch—*stream* ... AL-4
Marks Branch—*stream* ... IA-7
Marks Branch—*stream* ... MO-7
Marks Branch—*stream* ... TN-4
Marks Branch—*stream* ... WV-2
Marks Brook—*stream* ... CT-1
Marksburg Hollow—*valley* ... AR-4
Marksbury—*locale* ... KY-4
Marksbury Gulch—*valley* ... CO-8
Marksbury Spring—*spring* ... OR-9
Marks Butte—*summit* ... CO-8
Marks Butte—*summit* ... ID-8
Marks Cabin—*locale* ... OR-9
Marks Camp—*locale* ... NY-2
Marks Canal—*canal* ... NY-2
Marks Cem—*cemetery* ... AR-4
Marks Cem—*cemetery* ... IN-6
Marks Cem—*cemetery* (2) ... TN-4
Marks Ch—*church* ... GA-3
Marks Ch—*church* ... KY-4
Marks Ch of Christ—*church* ... MS-4
*Mark School* ... AL-4
Marks Corner—*locale* ... ME-1
Marks Corners—*locale* ... NY-2
Marks Corners Cem—*cemetery* ... NY-2
Marks Cove—*cove* ... MA-1
Marks Cove Marshes—*swamp* ... MA-1
Marks Creek—*stream* ... AK-9
Marks Creek—*stream* ... IL-6
Marks Creek—*stream* ... MI-6
Marks Creek—*stream* (3) ... NC-3
Marks Creek—*stream* (5) ... OR-9
Marks Creek—*stream* ... SC-3
Marks Creek—*stream* (2) ... TN-4
Marks Creek Ch—*church* ... NC-3
Marks Creek (Township of)—*fmr MCD* (2) ... NC-3
Marks Cut-Off—*bend* ... MS-4
Marks Ditch—*canal* ... IN-6
*Marks Elementary School* ... MS-4
Marks-Family House—*hist pl* ... OH-6
**Marks Garrison**—*pop pl* ... MA-1
*Marks High School* ... MS-4
Marks Hollow—*valley* ... CT-1
Marks Hollow—*valley* ... TN-4
Marks Hollow Point—*cape* ... CT-1
Marks House—*hist pl* ... AZ-5
Mark Simmons Lake Dam—*dam* ... MS-4
Marks Island—*island* ... ME-1
Marks Island—*island* ... OR-9
Marks Island—*island* ... VA-3
Marks Knob—*summit* ... NC-3
Marks Knob—*summit* ... WV-2
Marks Lake—*lake* ... ME-1
Marks Lake—*reservoir* ... OR-9
Marks Lake Dam—*dam* ... OR-9
Marks Memorial Cem—*cemetery* ... MO-7
Marks Memorial Park—*cemetery* ... OR-9
*Marks Mill* ... PA-2
Marks Mill Pond—*reservoir* ... GA-3
Marks' Mills Battlefield Park—*hist pl* ... AR-4
*Marks Mtn* ... MA-1
Marks Mtn—*summit* ... MA-1
Marks Mtn—*summit* (2) ... NC-3
Marks Oil Field—*oilfield* ... TX-5
Marks Park—*park* ... MI-6
Marks Place—*locale* ... CA-9
Marks Pond—*lake* ... UT-8
Marks Prairie—*flat* ... OR-9
Marks Presbyterian Ch—*church* ... MS-4
Marks Ranch—*locale* ... MT-8
Marks Ranch—*locale* ... SD-7
Marks Ridge—*ridge* ... KY-4
Marks Ridge—*ridge* ... OR-9
Marks Run—*stream* ... PA-2
Marks Run—*stream* ... WV-2
Marks Sch—*school* ... FL-3
Marks Sch—*school* ... NY-2
Marks Sch—*school* ... SC-3
Marks Sch (historical)—*school* ... AL-4
Marks Slough—*gut* ... OR-9
Marks Slough—*stream* ... OR-9
*Marks Store Landing* ... MS-4
Markstein (historical)—*locale* ... AL-4
*Marks Thompson Mine* ... OR-9
Marks-Thompson Mine—*mine* ... OR-9
Mark Street Sch—*school* ... OH-6
Marks United Methodist Ch—*church* ... MS-4
**Marks Village**—*pop pl* ... AL-4
Marksville—*locale* ... MS-4
Marksville—*locale* ... VA-3
**Marksville**—*pop pl* ... LA-4
**Marksville**—*pop pl* ... SD-7
Marksville B Cut-Off—*bend* ... MS-4
Marksville Commercial Hist Dist—*hist pl* ... LA-4
Marksville Landing (historical)—*locale* ... MS-4
Marksville (Magisterial District)—*fmr MCD* ... VA-3
Marksville Post Office (historical)—*building* ... MS-4
Marksville Prehistoric Indian Site—*hist pl* ... LA-4
Mark Tank—*reservoir* (2) ... AZ-5
*Mark Thomas Church* ... MS-4
**Markton**—*pop pl* ... AL-4
**Markton**—*pop pl* ... PA-2
**Markton**—*pop pl* ... WI-6
Marktown Hist Dist—*hist pl* ... IN-6
Mark Town Park—*park* ... IN-6
*Mark Town School* ... IN-6
**Mark (Township of)**—*pop pl* ... OH-6
Mark Twain Air Park—*airport* ... MO-7
Mark Twain Air Strip—*airport* ... MO-7
Mark Twain Birthplace State Historic Site—*park* ... MO-7
Mark Twain Cabin—*locale* ... CA-9
Mark Twain Camp (site)—*locale* ... NV-8
Mark Twain Cave—*cave* ... MO-7
Mark Twain Elem Sch—*school* ... KS-7
Mark Twain Hist Dist—*hist pl* ... MO-7
Mark Twain Hosp—*hospital* ... CA-9
Mark Twain Hotel—*hist pl* ... MO-7
Mark Twain Intermediate Sch—*school* ... VA-3
Mark Twain JHS—*school* (2) ... CA-9
Mark Twain JHS—*school* ... NY-2
Mark Twain JHS—*school* ... TX-5
Mark Twain Lake Mngmt Office—*building* ... MO-7
Mark Twain Landing Field (abandoned)—*airport* ... MO-7
Mark Twain Mall—*locale* ... MO-7
Mark Twain Memorial Bridge—*other* ... IL-6
Mark Twain Memorial Bridge—*other* ... MO-7
Mark Twain Mine—*mine* ... AZ-5
Mark Twain Natl For—*forest* ... MO-7
Mark Twain Natl Wildlife Ref—*park* ... IL-6
Mark Twain Natl Wildlife Ref—*park* ... IA-7
Mark Twain Park—*park* ... CA-9
Mark Twain Park—*park* ... MI-6
Mark Twain Sch—*school* (9) ... CA-9
Mark Twain Sch—*school* ... CO-8
Mark Twain Sch—*school* (2) ... CT-1
Mark Twain Sch—*school* (5) ... IL-6
Mark Twain Sch—*school* (2) ... IA-7
Mark Twain Sch—*school* (4) ... MI-6
Mark Twain Sch—*school* (13) ... MO-7
Mark Twain Sch—*school* ... NJ-2
Mark Twain Sch—*school* ... NM-5
Mark Twain Sch—*school* (2) ... OH-6
Mark Twain Sch—*school* (2) ... OK-5
Mark Twain Sch—*school* ... SD-7
Mark Twain Sch—*school* (2) ... TX-5
Mark Twain State Park—*park* ... MO-7
Mark Twain State Park Picnic Shelter at Buzzard's Roost—*hist pl* ... MO-7
Mark Twain Wildlife Ref—*park* ... IL-6
Mark Twan Sch—*school* ... MO-7
Mark Two Tank—*reservoir* ... AZ-5
Markum Brook—*stream* ... NY-2
Markum Hollow—*valley* ... AR-4
Markums Cave—*cave* ... TN-4
*Markum Wash* ... AZ-5
Markunas Dam—*dam* ... PA-2
Markus Ranch—*locale* ... CO-8
Markus Sch—*school* ... SD-7
Markus Wold Dam—*dam* ... ND-7
**Mark View (subdivision)**—*pop pl* ... NC-3
*Markville* ... LA-4
**Markville**—*pop pl* ... MN-6
**Markvue Manor**—*pop pl* ... PA-2
Markwald—*locale* ... MS-4
Markwed Sch—*school* ... SD-7
*Markwell* ... MS-4
Markwell Cem—*cemetery* ... KY-4
Markwell Sch—*school* ... MN-6
Mark West—*locale* ... CA-9
Mark West Creek—*stream* ... CA-9
Mark West Creek Rancheria—*locale* ... CA-9
Mark West Sch—*school* ... CA-9
**Mark West Springs**—*pop pl* ... CA-9
Mark Windmill—*locale* ... TX-5
**Markwood**—*pop pl* ... WV-2
Markwood Ch—*church* ... WV-2
Markwood Chapel Sch (historical)—*school* ... TN-4
Markwood Creek—*stream* ... CA-9
Markwood Meadow—*flat* ... CA-9
**Markwood (subdivision)**—*pop pl* ... NC-3
Marl—*locale* ... AL-4
**Marl**—*pop pl* ... MD-2
Marla Bay—*bay* ... NV-8
*Marla Cove* ... NV-8
**Marlain Acres**—*pop pl* ... OH-6
**Marlaing Addition**—*pop pl* ... WV-2
Mar Lake—*lake* ... NE-7
Marlake—*lake* ... WA-9
**Marlan Acres**—*pop pl* ... OH-6
Marlan Creek—*stream* ... AK-9
Marland—*locale* ... FL-3
**Marland**—*pop pl* ... OK-5
Marland, E. W., Mansion—*hist pl* ... OK-5
Marland Cem—*cemetery* ... KS-7
Marl and Clay Bed (historical)—*locale* ... MA-1
**Marland Heights**—*pop pl* ... WV-2
Marland Hill—*summit* ... MO-7
Marland-Paris House—*hist pl* ... OK-5
Marland Peat Pits—*mine* ... OH-6
**Marlands**—*pop pl* ... WI-6
**Marlan Forest**—*pop pl* ... VA-3
Marlar Branch—*stream* ... MS-4
Marlar Creek—*stream* ... MS-4
**Marlar Township**—*pop pl* ... SD-7
Marlay Cem—*cemetery* ... MO-7
**Marlbank**—*pop pl* ... VA-3
Marl Bay—*bay* ... WI-6
Marl Bed Flats—*flat* ... FL-3
Marl Bed Lake—*lake* ... MI-6
Marlbed Lake—*lake* ... MI-6
Marl Bed Point—*cape* ... FL-3
Marl Bed Slough—*gut* ... FL-3
*Marlboro* ... MA-1
*Marlboro* ... NH-1
*Marlboro* ... NJ-2
Marlboro—*airport* ... NJ-2
Marlboro—*locale* ... CA-9
Marlboro—*locale* ... NJ-2
Marlboro—*locale* ... PA-2
Marlboro—*locale* ... VA-3
**Marlboro**—*pop pl* ... ME-1
**Marlboro**—*pop pl* ... MA-1
**Marlboro**—*pop pl* (2) ... NJ-2
**Marlboro**—*pop pl* ... NY-2
**Marlboro**—*pop pl* (2) ... NC-3
**Marlboro**—*pop pl* ... OH-6
**Marlboro**—*pop pl* ... SC-3
**Marlboro**—*pop pl* ... VT-1
**Marlboro**—*pop pl* ... VA-3
Marlboro—*uninc pl* ... NY-2
Marlboro Acad—*school* ... SC-3
Marlboro Academy—*cape* ... MA-1
Marlboro Beach—*beach* ... ME-1
Marlboro Branch—*stream* ... VT-1
Marlboro Canyon—*valley* ... TX-5
Marlboro Cem—*cemetery* ... OH-6
Marlboro Ch—*church* ... NJ-2
Marlboro Ch—*church* (2) ... NC-3
Marlboro Ch—*church* ... OH-6
Marlboro Coll—*school* ... VT-1
**Marlboro (County)**—*pop pl* ... SC-3
**Marlboro Forest (subdivision)**—*pop pl* ... NC-3
Marlboro HS—*school* ... OH-6
Marlboro Hunt Club—*other* ... MD-2
*Marlboro Junction* ... MA-1
Marlboro Marina—*harbor* ... NJ-2
Marlboro Mtn—*summit* ... NY-2
Marlboro Park Hist Dist—*hist pl* ... NJ-2
Marlboro Point—*cape* ... VA-3
Marlboro (RR name for Marlborough)—*other* ... MA-1
Marlboro (RR name Marlborough)—*CDP* ... NY-2
Marlboro Sch—*school* ... SC-3
Marlboro Sch—*school* ... TX-5
Marlboro Speedway—*other* ... MD-2
Marlboro State Hosp—*hospital* ... NJ-2
Marlboro Station—*locale* ... MD-2
**Marlboro (Town of)**—*pop pl* ... VT-1
**Marlboro (Township of)**—*pop pl* ... NJ-2
**Marlboro (Township of)**—*pop pl* (2) ... OH-6
Marlboro Trail—*trail* ... NH-1
*Marlborough* ... MA-1
*Marlborough* ... NJ-2
**Marlborough**—*pop pl* ... CT-1
**Marlborough**—*pop pl* ... MA-1
**Marlborough**—*pop pl* ... MI-6
**Marlborough**—*pop pl* (2) ... MO-7
**Marlborough**—*pop pl* ... NH-1

Marlborough, City of—civil MA-1
Marlborough, The—hist pl MI-6
Marlborough, Town of MA-1
Marlborough Cem—cemetery TN-4
**Marlborough Center**—pop pl CT-1
Marlborough City Hall—building MA-1
**Marlborough Compact (census name Marlborough)**—pop pl NH-1
Marlborough Hist Dist—hist pl MI-6
Marlborough HS—school MA-1
Marlborough JHS—school MA-1
**Marlborough Junction**—pop pl MA-1
**Marlborough Meadows (subdivision)**—pop pl (2) AZ-5
**Marlborough Mesa (subdivision)**—pop pl (2) AZ-5
**Marlborough Park (subdivision)**—pop pl (2) AZ-5
Marlborough Point VA-3
Marlborough Post Office—building MA-1
Marlborough Post Office (historical)—building TN-4
**Marlborough (RR name Marlboro)**—pop pl MA-1
Marlborough Sch—school CA-9
Marlborough Sch—school MO-7
Marlborough Sch (historical)—school TN-4
Marlborough Sewage Disposal—locale MA-1
Marlborough Tavern—hist pl CT-1
**Marlborough (Town of)**—pop pl CT-1
**Marlborough (Town of)**—pop pl NH-1
**Marlborough (Town of)**—pop pl NY-2
**Marlborough (Township of)**—pop pl PA-2
Marlboroughville PA-2
Marlboro (Upper Marlboro) MD-2
**Marlboro Village**—pop pl NJ-2
**Marlboroville**—pop pl PA-2
Marl Branch—stream AL-4
Marl Branch—stream LA-4
Marlbrook—locale VA-3
Marlbrook Ch—church AR-4
Marlbrook Ch—church VA-3
Marlbrook Creek—stream AR-4
Marlbrook Creek—stream VA-3
Marl Cave—cave PA-2
Marl City—locale OH-6
Marl Creek—stream MI-6
Marl Creek—stream MT-8
Marl Creek—stream (2) VA-3
Marle Canyon—valley CA-9
Marlee Lake—lake FL-3
Mar Lee Manor Shop Ctr—other CO-8
MarLee Sch—school MI-6
Marlen Branch—stream TN-4
Marlene Lake—lake WA-9
Marlene Sch Number 2 (historical)—school SD-7
**Marlene Village**—pop pl OR-9
**Marler**—pop pl NC-3
Marler Bayou—bay FL-3
Marler Branch—stream MO-7
Marler Cem—cemetery LA-4
Marler Chapel—church MO-7
Marler Creek—stream TX-5
Marler Knob—summit KY-4
Marler Spring—spring TN-4
**Marlette**—pop pl MI-6
Marlette Cem—cemetery MI-6
Marlette Creek—stream NV-8
Marlette Lake—reservoir NV-8
Marlette Peak—summit NV-8
Marlette Rsvr—reservoir NV-8
Marlette Sch (abandoned)—school SD-7
**Marlette (Township of)**—pop pl MI-6
Marley—locale IL-6
Marley—locale ND-7
**Marley**—pop pl IL-6
**Marley**—pop pl MD-2
Marley Brook—stream ME-1
Marley Cem—cemetery MS-4
Marley Cem—cemetery NC-3
Marley Creek—stream IL-6
Marley Creek—stream MD-2
Marley Creek—stream OR-9
Marley Creek—stream TX-5
Marley Draw—valley NM-5
Marley Farm—locale NM-5
Marley Gulch—valley CA-9
Marley JHS—school MD-2
Marley Knob—summit NC-3
**Marley Mill**—pop pl AL-4
Marley Millpond—reservoir AL-4
Marley Neck—cape MD-2
Marley Peaks—summit TX-5
Marley Ranch—locale NM-5
Marley Ranch—locale TX-5
Marleys Branch—stream NC-3
Marleysburg PA-2
Marley Sch—school MD-2
Marley Sch (historical)—school MS-4
Marley Station—locale ID-8
Marley Well—well (2) NM-5
Marl Hill Ch—church VA-3
**Marlin**—pop pl PA-2
**Mar Lin**—pop pl PA-2
**Marlin**—pop pl TX-5
Marlin Branch—stream IN-6
Marlin Branch—stream LA-4
Marlin Branch—stream MO-7
Marlin Branch—stream TX-5
Marlin Canyon—valley OR-9
Marlin (CCD)—cens area TX-5
Marlin Cem MO-7
Marlin Cem—cemetery IN-6
Marlin Cem—cemetery MO-7
Marlin Cem—cemetery (2) TN-4
Marlin City Lake TX-5
Marlin City Lake—reservoir TX-5
Marlin (corporate name Krupp) WA-9
Marlin Country Club—other TX-5
Marlin Creek GA-3
Marlin Creek—stream ID-8
Marlin Creek—stream MO-7
Marlin Creek—stream TN-4
**Marlinda West Subdivision**—pop pl UT-8
Marlin Elem Sch—school IN-6
**Marlin Forest**—pop pl VA-3
Marling—locale MO-7
Marling, Lake—lake NY-2
**Marling Farms**—pop pl MD-2
Marlington WV-2
Marlington HS—school OH-6
**Marlin Hills**—pop pl IN-6
**Marlin Hills**—pop pl PA-2
Marlin Hollow—valley WA-9
Marlin Knob—summit NC-3
**Marlin (Krupp)**—pop pl WA-9
Marlin Lake—lake PA-2
Marlin Lake Dam—dam MS-4
Marlin Lick Run—stream WV-2
Marlin Mine—mine CO-8
Marlin Mountain Trail—trail WV-2
Marlin Mtn—summit WV-2
Mar-Linn Log Pond—reservoir OR-9
Mar-Linn Timber Corporation Log Pond—reservoir OR-9
Mar-Linn Timber Corporation Log Pond Dike—dam OR-9
Marlin Park—park MN-6
Marlin Run—stream WV-2
Marlinsburg PA-2
Marlin Sch (historical)—school MO-7
Marlin Spring—spring ID-8
Marlin Spring—spring (3) OR-9
**Marlinton**—pop pl WV-2
Marlinton Chesapeake and Ohio RR Station—hist pl WV-2
Marlin Windmill—locale NM-5
Marl Lake MI-6
Marl Lake WI-6
Marl Lake—lake IN-6
Marl Lake—lake (7) MI-6
Marl Lake—lake MT-8
Marl Lake—lake (4) WI-6
Marl Lake Creek—stream MT-8
Marl Lakes—lake MI-6
Marl Lakes—lake NJ-2
Marlman—locale CO-8
Marl Mountains—other CA-9
**Marlo**—pop pl MO-7
**Marlo Heights**—pop pl VA-3
Marlo Johnson Dam—dam (2) SD-7
Marloma—uninc pl CA-9
Marlon, Lake—lake FL-3
**Mar Lon Hills Number One (subdivision)**—pop pl UT-8
Mar-lon Hills Sch—school UT-8
Marlors Station RI-1
Marlow—locale KY-4
Marlow—locale SD-7
**Marlow**—pop pl AL-4
**Marlow**—pop pl GA-3
**Marlow**—pop pl IL-6
**Marlow**—pop pl NH-1
**Marlow**—pop pl OK-5
**Marlow**—pop pl TN-4
Marlow Bay MD-2
Marlow Branch—stream AL-4
Marlow Branch—stream AR-4
Marlow Branch—stream LA-4
Marlow Branch—stream NC-3
Marlow Branch—stream (2) TN-4
Marlow Camp—locale CA-9
Marlow Canyon—valley UT-8
Marlow (CCD)—cens area OK-5
Marlow Cem—cemetery LA-4
Marlow Cem—cemetery MS-4
Marlow Cem—cemetery (3) TN-4
Marlow Cemetry—cemetery TN-4
Marlow Ch—church AL-4
Marlow Ch—church AR-4
Marlow Ch—church LA-4
Marlow Ch—church MS-4
Marlow Chapel (historical)—church MO-7
Marlow Ch of Christ MS-4
Marlow Creek—stream AR-4
Marlow Creek—stream ID-8
Marlow Creek—stream OR-9
Marlow Creek Drainage Ditch—canal MS-4
Marlowe SD-7
**Marlowe**—pop pl KY-4
**Marlowe**—pop pl WV-2
Marlowe Branch—stream GA-3
Marlowe Cem—cemetery MS-4
Marlowe Cem—cemetery SC-3
Marlowe Creek—stream MO-7
Marlowe Creek—stream NC-3
Marlowe Creek—stream SC-3
Marlow Elem Sch—school TN-4
Marlowe Sch—school KY-4
Marlow Field Cem—cemetery TN-4
**Marlow Heights**—pop pl MD-2
Marlow Hill—summit NH-1
Marlow Hollow—valley KY-4
Marlow Hollow—valley TN-4
**Marlow Junction**—pop pl NH-1
Marlow Lake—lake WI-6
Marlow Lateral—canal ID-8
Marlow Mesa—summit (2) AZ-5
Marlow Mesa Tank—reservoir AZ-5
Marlow Mtn—summit MO-7
Marlow Park—park CA-9
Marlow Place Bungalows District—hist pl KY-4
Marlow Post Office (historical)—building TN-4
Marlow Ranch—locale WY-8
Marlow Run—stream WV-2
Marlow Sch—school GA-3
Marlow Sch—school TN-4
Marlow Sch—school TX-5
Marlow Sch (historical)—school MS-4
Marlow Shoemake Dam—dam MS-4
**Marlow Subdivision**—pop pl UT-8
**Marlow (Town of)**—pop pl NH-1
Marl Pit—basin (2) MI-6
Marl Pit—mine NJ-2
Marlpit Brook—stream NJ-2
Marl Pond—lake VT-1
Marls Bluff Ch—church TN-4
Marl Spring—spring CA-9
**Marlton**—pop pl MD-2
**Marlton**—pop pl NJ-2
Marlton Cem—cemetery NJ-2
**Marlton Heights**—pop pl NJ-2
**Marlton Hills**—pop pl NJ-2
**Marlton Lakes**—pop pl NJ-2
Marlton Lakes—reservoir NJ-2
Marlton Lakes Upper Dam—dam NJ-2
Marlton Recreation Center—park MD-2
Marlu Lake—reservoir MN-6
Marlu Lake—reservoir NJ-2
Marlu Lake Dam—dam NJ-2
Marlum Hollow—valley AR-4
Mar-Lu-Ridge Conference and Educational Center—school MD-2
**Marlwood Acre**—pop pl NC-3
Marlwood Dam—dam NC-3
Marlwood Lake—reservoir NC-3
**Marly**—pop pl TX-5
**Marlyn Hills**—pop pl TN-4
**Marlyn Manor**—pop pl NJ-2
**Marlywood**—pop pl MD-2
Mar-Mac—CDP NC-3
Marmac—locale WA-9
Mar-Mac Lake—lake IN-6
**Mar-Mac Village (subdivision)**—pop pl NC-3
Marmad MP-9
Marmaduke—locale NC-3
**Marmaduke**—pop pl AR-4
Marmaduke Spring—spring ID-8
**Marmalade Condominium**—pop pl UT-8
Marma Lake—lake CO-8
Marmande Canal—canal LA-4
Marmande Ridge—ridge LA-4
**Marman Terrace (subdivision)**—pop pl NC-3
**Marmarth**—pop pl ND-7
**Marmaton**—pop pl KS-7
Marmaton Bridge—hist pl KS-7
Marmaton Cem—cemetery KS-7
Marmaton River—stream KS-7
Marmaton River—stream MO-7
**Marmaton Township**—pop pl (2) KS-7
Marmaton Valley HS—school KS-7
Marme—island MP-9
Marme Ch AL-4
Marmee Mine—mine AZ-5
Marmes Rockshelter—hist pl WA-9
**Marmet**—pop pl WV-2
Marmet Locks—other WV-2
Marmion—hist pl VA-3
Marmion (historical)—locale AL-4
Marmion Island—island AK-9
Marmion Military Acad—school IL-6
Marmitaw Creek KS-7
Marmiton KS-7
Marmiton Creek KS-7
Marmiton River KS-7
Marm Johns Pond MA-1
Marm Lake—lake WI-6
Marmolejo Creek—stream CA-9
Marmo-lejo Flats—flat CA-9
Marmon—locale NM-5
Marmon—locale ND-7
Marmon, Martin, House—hist pl OH-6
Marmon Creek TX-5
Marmonier Ditch—canal AZ-5
Marmon Ranch—locale NM-5
Marmon Valley—valley OH-6
Marmon Valley Cem—cemetery OH-6
Marmor—locale TN-4
**Marmora**—pop pl NJ-2
**Marmora**—pop pl VA-3
Marmora Ch—church VA-3
Marmosa, Lake—reservoir GA-3
Marmot—locale OR-9
Marmot Basin WA-9
Marmot Bay—bay AK-9
Marmot Butte—summit OR-9
Marmot Cape—cape AK-9
Marmot Creek—stream WA-9
Marmot Diversion Dam—dam OR-9
Marmot Island—island AK-9
Marmot Lake MT-8
Marmot Lake—lake CA-9
Marmot Lake—lake WA-9
Marmot Lakes—lake MT-8
Marmot Lakes—lake WA-9
Marmot Mtn—summit (3) MT-8
Marmot Pass—gap OR-9
Marmot Pass—gap WA-9
Marmot Peak—summit CO-8
Marmot Peak—summit MT-8
Marmot Point—summit CO-8
Marmot Ridge—ridge WA-9
Marmot Strait—channel AK-9
Marmount IN-6
Marna—locale MN-6
Marna, Lac—lake LA-4
Marnach, Nicholas, House—hist pl MN-6
Marna Station MN-6
Marncy KS-7
Marne AR-4
Marne—locale CA-9
Marne—locale WV-2
**Marne**—pop pl IA-7
**Marne**—pop pl MI-6
**Marne**—pop pl OH-6
Marne Creek—stream SD-7
Marne For—woods WA-9
Marnel—locale CO-8
Marnel Well—well CO-8
**Marne No.02**—pop pl KY-4
Marnett—locale CO-8
Marney Bluff—cliff TN-4
Marney Branch—stream MO-7
Marney Cem—cemetery TN-4
Marney Creek—stream TN-4
Marney (historical)—locale KS-7
Marnie—locale WV-2
Marny Bluff TN-4
**Maroa**—pop pl IL-6
Maroai FM-9
Maroa Sch—school ID-8
**Maroa (Township of)**—pop pl IL-6
Maroco Lookout Tower—tower FL-3
Maroco Mine—mine MN-6
Maroerappu-to MP-9
Maroga Canyon—valley AZ-5
Marok MP-9
Marok Channel—channel MP-9
Maroken—island MP-9
Marokku MP-9
Marokku Island MP-9
Marokku Island—island MP-9
Marokku Pass MP-9
Marokku-suido MP-9
Marokku-To MP-9
Marolf And Walker Ditch No 1—canal WY-8
Marolt Diich—canal CO-8
Marolt Rsvr—reservoir CO-8
Maromas CT-1
Maromas—locale CT-1
Maromas Cem—cemetery CT-1
Maromiyocknowhosunkatankshunk CT-1
Maron—island MP-9
Marone, Bayou—stream MS-4
Marone Landing Field—airport SD-7
Maronen Creek—stream MI-6
Marone Point—cape LA-4
Maroney Creek—stream OR-9
Maroney Gulch—valley AZ-5
Maroney Hollow—valley TN-4
Maroney Ranch—locale MT-8
Maroney Sch—school NE-7
Maroney Top—summit TN-4
Maroney Well—well AZ-5
**Marongo**—pop pl IN-6
Maron Island MP-9
Maronlik—island MP-9
Maronlik Island MP-9
Maron-to MP-9
Maroon Bells—ridge CO-8
Maroon Branch—stream TN-4
Maroon Cliffs—cliff NM-5
Maroon Crater—crater AZ-5
Maroon Creek CO-8
Maroon Creek—stream CO-8
Maroon Creek Bridge—hist pl CO-8
Maroon Creek Campground 1—locale CO-8
Maroon Creek Campground 2—locale CO-8
Maroon Creek Campground 3—locale CO-8
Maroon Creek Campground 4—locale CO-8
Maroon Gap—gap TN-4
Maroon Hole—bay VI-3
Maroon Lake—lake CO-8
Maroon Lake Campground—locale CO-8
Maroon Mtn—summit AZ-5
Maroon Peak—summit CO-8
Maroon Ridge—ridge VI-3
Maroon Sch (historical)—school TN-4
Maroon Stadium—other TX-5
Maroon Valley—valley TN-4
Maro Reef—bar HI-9
Maros AL-4
Marott Hotel—hist pl IN-6
Marott Park—park IN-6
Marott's Shoes Bldg—hist pl IN-6
Marpi MH-9
Marpi Beach MH-9
Marpi Hill MH-9
Marpi Peak MH-9
Marpi Point MH-9
Marple—locale PA-2
**Marple**—pop pl PA-2
Marple Canyon—valley CA-9
Marple Cem—cemetery OH-6
Marple Cem—cemetery WV-2
Marple Ch—church PA-2
Marple Creek—stream WA-9
Marple Dam—dam SD-7
**Marple Gardens**—pop pl PA-2
**Marple Heights**—pop pl PA-2
Marple-Newton Senior HS—school PA-2
Marple-Newtown HS PA-2
Marple-Newtown JHS (abandoned)—school PA-2
Marple Slough—lake ND-7
Marple State Wildlife Mngmt Area—park MN-6
**Marple Summit Estates**—pop pl PA-2
Marpleton—locale WV-2
Marple Township—CDP PA-2
**Marple (Township of)**—pop pl PA-2
**Marple Woods**—pop pl PA-2
Marpo Number Two MH-9
Marpo Point MH-9
Marpo Valley MH-9
Marpo Wells MH-9
**Marquam**—pop pl OR-9
Marquam Creek—stream OR-9
Marquam Dry Lake Canal—canal OR-9
Marquam Gulch—valley OR-9
**Marquam Hill**—pop pl OR-9
Marquam Lake—lake OR-9
Marquam Rsvr—reservoir OR-9
Marquams Lake OR-9
Marquand OH-6
**Marquand**—pop pl MO-7
Marquand Mill OH-6
Marquand Mills—locale OH-6
Marquand Township—civil MO-7
Marquardt Cem—cemetery MI-6
Marquardt Cem—cemetery WI-6
Marquardt Ch—church IN-6
Marquardt Ditch—canal IN-6
Marquardt Farm—hist pl NY-2
Marquardt Sch—school IL-6
Marquardt Sch—school MI-6
Marquart-Mercer Farm—hist pl OH-6
Marquat Ditch IN-6
**Marques**—pop pl PR-3
Marquesas Keys—island FL-3
Marquesas Rock—bay FL-3
Marques Hollow—valley MO-7
Marquess—locale WV-2
Marquess Branch—stream IN-6
Marquetta Pass AZ-5
Marquette—locale IL-6
**Marquette**—pop pl IA-7
**Marquette**—pop pl KS-7
**Marquette**—pop pl MI-6
**Marquette**—pop pl MO-7
**Marquette**—pop pl NE-7
**Marquette**—pop pl NY-2
**Marquette**—pop pl WI-6
Marquette, Lake—lake MN-6
Marquette Bay—bay (2) MI-6
Marquette Beach IN-6
Marquette Bldg—hist pl IL-6
Marquette Cem—cemetery KS-7
Marquette City Hall—hist pl MI-6
**Marquette (County)**—pop pl MI-6
**Marquette (County)**—pop pl WI-6
Marquette County Airp—airport MI-6
Marquette County Courthouse—hist pl MI-6
Marquette County Courthouse, Sheriff's Office, and Jail—hist pl WI-6
Marquette Creek—stream ID-8
Marquette Creek—stream WY-8
Marquette Elem Sch—school IN-6
**Marquette Farm**—pop pl IN-6
Marquette Glacier—glacier AK-9
Marquette Harbor Light Station—hist pl MI-6
**Marquette Heights**—pop pl IL-6
Marquette Hotel—hist pl MO-7
Marquette HS—school IL-6
Marquette HS—school IN-6
Marquette HS—school KS-7
Marquette HS—school WA-9
Marquette Island—island MI-6
Marquette Island—island MO-7
Marquette Lake—reservoir PA-2
Marquette Lakes—reservoir MO-7
Marquette Mall—post sta IN-6
Marquette Mine—mine AZ-5
Marquette Park—park IL-6
Marquette Park—park IN-6
Marquette Park—park MI-6
Marquette Park—park MO-7
Marquette Park—park (2) WI-6
Marquette Park Beach—beach IN-6
Marquette Park Municipal Beach IN-6
Marquette Sch—school (3) IL-6
Marquette Sch—school (3) MI-6
Marquette Sch—school MO-7
Marquette Sch—school (2) WI-6
Marquette School IN-6
Marquette State Prison—other MI-6
Marquette Street Archaeol District—hist pl MI-6
**Marquette (Town of)**—pop pl WI-6
**Marquette Township**—pop pl KS-7
**Marquette (Township of)**—pop pl (2) MI-6
Marquette Unit Stadium—other WI-6
Marquette Univ—school WI-6
Marquette Univ HS—school WI-6
**Marquez**—pop pl TX-5
Marquez Canyon—valley NM-5
Marquez Ranch—locale (2) NM-5
Marquez Tank—reservoir NM-5
Marquez Wash—stream NM-5
Marquis—locale OH-6
Marquis Basin—bay FL-3
Marquis Creek—gut NJ-2
**Marquis Hills (subdivision)**—pop pl NC-3
Marquis (historical)—locale AL-4
Marquis Opera House—hist pl NE-7
Marquiss Cem—cemetery IL-6
Marquiss Ranch—locale WY-8
Marquiss Rsvr—reservoir WY-8
Marquiss Sch—school NE-7
**Marquisville**—pop pl IA-7
Marquitta Mine—mine AZ-5
Marquitta Pass—gap AZ-5
Marr PA-2
Marr—locale OH-6
Marr, James, House and Farm—hist pl IN-6
Marr, Lake—lake OR-9
Marr, Mount—summit (2) AK-9
Marracossic Creek VA-3
Marrana Pasture—flat TX-5
Marranos Tank—reservoir TX-5
Marranos Windmill—locale TX-5
Marrano Windmill—locale (2) TX-5
Marratooka Point—cape NY-2
Marratooka Pond—lake NY-2
Marr Branch—stream NC-3
Marr Branch—stream (2) TN-4
Marr Branch—stream WV-2
Marr Bridge—bridge KS-7
Marr Cem—cemetery (3) KY-4
Marr Ch—church MI-6
Marr Creek—stream AR-4
Marr Creek—stream OR-9
Marr Ditch No 1—canal CO-8
Marr Ditch No 2—canal CO-8
Marre, Angelo, House—hist pl AR-4
Marre Canyon—valley CA-9
Marrell Creek TN-4
Marrell Spring TN-4
Marre Ranch—locale CA-9
**Marrero**—pop pl LA-4
Marrett, Daniel, House—hist pl ME-1
Marr Field (airport)—airport OR-9
Marr Field Bar—bar MO-7
Marr Flat—flat OR-9
Marr Flat—flat VT-1
Marr Gap—gap NC-3
Marr Hill—summit ME-1
Marr Hollow TN-4
Marriage, Sylvanus, Octagonal Barn—hist pl ND-7
Marriage Ground Ridge—ridge TN-4
Marricossick Creek VA-3
Marrina Windmill—locale TX-5
Marriner Run—stream VA-3
Marriners Brook—stream ME-1
**Marriott**—pop pl UT-8
Marriott Canal—canal UT-8
Marriott Creek—stream AL-4
Marriott Hill—locale MD-2
Marriott Post Office (historical)—building AL-4
Marriott Sch—school IL-6
Marriott Sch—school VA-3
Marriotts Landing (historical)—locale AL-4
Marriottsville—locale MD-2
Marr Island—island ME-1
Marr Island—island MN-6
Marrith Sch (historical)—school AL-4
Marritt Pond—reservoir SC-3
Marr Mine—mine CO-8
Marron—locale PA-2
Marron, Bayou—gut LA-4
Marron, Bayou—stream LA-4
Marron, Mount—summit CA-9
Marron Canyon—valley CA-9
Marron Creek—stream MT-8
Marrone, Isle—island LA-4
Marron Sch—school MI-6
Marron Valley—valley CA-9
Marrowback Hill—summit NY-2
Marrowbone—locale TN-4
**Marrowbone**—pop pl (2) KY-4
Marrowbone Branch VA-3
Marrowbone Ch—church KY-4
Marrowbone Creek—stream IL-6
Marrowbone Creek—stream IA-7
Marrowbone Creek—stream (3) KY-4
Marrowbone Creek—stream MO-7
Marrow Bone Creek—stream SC-3
Marrowbone Creek—stream TN-4
Marrowbone Creek—stream (3) VA-3
Marrowbone Creek—stream WV-2
Marrowbone Dam—dam TN-4
**Marrowbone Heights**—pop pl VA-3
Marrowbone Hist Dist—hist pl KY-4
Marrowbone Lake—lake TN-4
Marrowbone Lake—reservoir TN-4
Marrowbone Post Office (historical)—building TN-4
Marrowbone Round—bend GA-3
Marrowbone (RR name for Regina)—other KY-4
Marrowbone Rsvr—reservoir VA-3
Marrowbone Run—stream PA-2
Marrowbone Sch—school KY-4
Marrowbone Sch—school WV-2
Marrowbone Sch (historical)—school TN-4
Marrow Bone Slough—stream AR-4
Marrow Bone Spring Archeol Site—hist pl TX-5
Marrow Bone Swamp Creek—stream SC-3
**Marrowbone (Township of)**—pop pl IL-6
Marrow Cove—valley NC-3
Marrow Creek CA-9
Marrow Creek NC-3
Marrow Gap—gap TN-4
Marrow HS—school PA-2
Marrow Marsh—swamp TX-5
Marrow Run—stream WV-2
Marrows Cem—cemetery TN-4
Marrows Chapel—church NC-3
Marrowstone Island—island WA-9
Marrowstone Point—cape WA-9
Marr Park—park IA-7
Marr Point—cape ME-1
Marr Pond—lake ME-1
Marr Ranch—locale CA-9
Marr Ranch—locale NE-7
Marr Ridge GA-3
Marrs Branch—stream TN-4
**Marrs Center**—pop pl IN-6
Marr Sch—school IL-6
Marr Sch—school MO-7
Marrs Field—airport KS-7
Marrs Field Bar MO-7
Marrs Hill AL-4
Marrs Hill—summit ME-1
Marrs Hill Cem—cemetery TN-4
Marrs Hill Church AL-4
Marrs Hill (Township of)—fmr MCD AR-4
Marrs Hollow TN-4
Marrs Hollow—valley TN-4
Marrs Lake—lake MI-6
Marrs Landing Post Office (historical)—building TN-4
Marrs Mclean Gas Field—oilfield TX-5
Marrs Memorial Ch—church KY-4
Marrs Mine—mine CA-9
Marrs Spring—spring NM-5
**Marrs (Township of)**—pop pl IN-6
Marr Tanks—reservoir TX-5
Marr Towhead—bar TN-4
Marrtown—locale ME-1
**Marrtown**—pop pl WV-2
**Marruecos**—pop pl PR-3
Marr Well—well NM-5
Marr Windmill—locale TX-5
Marryat Inlet—bay AK-9
Marry Branch Bay—swamp NC-3
Mars IL-6
**Mars**—pop pl FL-3
**Mars**—pop pl PA-2
Mars, Mount—summit CA-9
Marsac Creek—stream MI-6
Marsac Elem Sch—hist pl UT-8
Marsac Point—cape MI-6
Marsac Sch—school UT-8
Marsa Drain—canal MI-6
**Marsalis**—pop pl LA-4
Marsalis Cem—cemetery MS-4
Marsalis Park—park TX-5
Marsalis Ponds—lake LA-4
Marsalis Sch—school TX-5
Mars Area Senior HS—school PA-2
Marsa Tank—lake NM-5
**Mars Bluff**—pop pl SC-3
Mars Bluff Bridge—bridge SC-3
Mars Bluff Firetower—locale SC-3
Mars Bluff Sch—school SC-3
Mars Borough—civil PA-2
Mars Branch—stream AR-4
Mars Branch—stream LA-4
Mars Branch—stream (2) TX-5
Mars Branch—swamp SC-3
Mars Cem—cemetery PA-2
Mars Cem—cemetery WV-2
Marschall Creek—stream (2) TX-5
Marschall Islands MP-9
Marschall Meusebach—cemetery TX-5
Marschall Spring—spring TX-5
Marschner Bldg—hist pl TX-5
Marsden—locale AR-4
Marsden—locale OK-5
Marsden Lake—swamp MN-6
Marsden Park—park WI-6
Marsden Slough—gut IL-6
Marsden Spring—spring UT-8
Marsden Station—locale NC-3
**Marsden Subdivision**—pop pl UT-8
Mars Ditch—canal IN-6
Marse—locale WY-8
Marsee Branch—stream KY-4
Marsee Cem—cemetery TN-4
Marseillaise Bayou—stream LA-4
Marseille, Lake—lake LA-4
**Marseilles**—pop pl IL-6
**Marseilles**—pop pl OH-6
Marseilles Canal—canal IL-6
Marseilles Dam—dam IL-6
Marseilles Lock—other IL-6
**Marseilles (Township of)**—pop pl OH-6
Marsell, Mount—summit UT-8
Marsell Canyon—valley UT-8
Marsellino Windmill—locale NM-5
Marsellis House—hist pl NJ-2
Marsell Lake—lake UT-8
Marsena—locale AR-4
Marsen Branch—stream MS-4
Marsen Knob—summit GA-3

**Mars Estates**—*pop pl* MD-2
Mars Estates Sch—*school* MD-2
*Marsh* MI-6
Marsh—*locale* AZ-5
Marsh—*locale* MI-6
Marsh—*locale* MT-8
Marsh—*locale* PA-2
Marsh—*locale* TX-5
**Marsh**—*pop pl* (2) IA-7
**Marsh**—*pop pl* PA-2
**Marsh**—*pop pl* WI-6
Marsh, Alexander, House—*hist pl* MA-1
Marsh, Bayou—*stream* LA-4
Marsh, George B., Bldg—*hist pl* AZ-5
Marsh, George H., Homestead and the Marsh Foundation Sch—*hist pl* OH-6
Marsh, George Perkins, Boyhood Home—*hist pl* VT-1
Marsh, John, House—*hist pl* CA-9
Marsh, Joseph, House—*hist pl* OH-6
Marsh, Lake—*lake* SD-7
Marsh, Martin Luther, House—*hist pl* CA-9
Marsh, Othniel C., House—*hist pl* CT-1
Marsh, Peter, House—*hist pl* DE-2
Marsh, Point of—*cape* VA-3
Marsh, The—*swamp* ME-1
Marsh, The—*swamp* (2) MA-1
Marsh, The—*swamp* NY-2
Marsh, The—*swamp* TX-5
Marsh, The—*swamp* VT-1
Marsh, William W., House—*hist pl* IL-6
Marsha Bay—*bay* AK-9
Marsha Bottom—*bend* KY-4
Marsh Airstrip—*airport* AZ-5
Marshal And Magruder Pond—*reservoir* GA-3
Marshal Bonanza Mine—*mine* NM-5
Marshal Chapel Cem—*cemetery* PA-2
*Marshal Creek* OR-9
Marshal Creek—*stream* GA-3
Marshal Gulch—*valley* AK-9
*Marshall* AL-4
*Marshall* IA-7
*Marshall* KS-7
*Marshall* ND-7
Marshall—*locale* (2) AL-4
Marshall—*locale* GA-3
Marshall—*locale* (2) NY-2
Marshall—*locale* TN-4
Marshall—*locale* UT-8
Marshall—*locale* WY-8
**Marshall**—*pop pl* AK-9
**Marshall**—*pop pl* AR-4
**Marshall**—*pop pl* CA-9
**Marshall**—*pop pl* CO-8
**Marshall**—*pop pl* IL-6
**Marshall**—*pop pl* IN-6
**Marshall**—*pop pl* (2) KY-4
**Marshall**—*pop pl* MI-6
**Marshall**—*pop pl* MN-6
**Marshall**—*pop pl* MO-7
**Marshall**—*pop pl* NC-3
**Marshall**—*pop pl* ND-7
**Marshall**—*pop pl* OH-6
**Marshall**—*pop pl* OK-5
**Marshall**—*pop pl* PA-2
**Marshall**—*pop pl* TX-5
**Marshall**—*pop pl* VA-3
**Marshall**—*pop pl* WA-9
**Marshall**—*pop pl* (2) WV-2
**Marshall**—*pop pl* WI-6
Marshall, Benjamin, House—*hist pl* NH-1
Marshall, David, House—*hist pl* OH-6
Marshall, Humphry, House—*hist pl* PA-2
Marshall, James, House—*hist pl* WV-2
Marshall, James E., House—*hist pl* OH-6
Marshall, James W., House—*hist pl* NJ-2
Marshall, John, House—*hist pl* VA-3
Marshall, John, House Site—*hist pl* IL-6
Marshall, John, Sch—*hist pl* PA-2
Marshall, John, Sr., House—*hist pl* KY-4
Marshall, Lake—*lake* MN-6
Marshall, Lake—*lake* MT-8
Marshall, Mount—*summit* NY-2
Marshall, Mount—*summit* VA-3
Marshall, Mount Reese—*summit* AK-9
Marshall, Paul, House—*hist pl* NY-2
Marshall, Thomas, House—*hist pl* PA-2
Marshall, Thomas R., House—*hist pl* IN-6
Marshall Airfield—*airport* (2) KS-7
*Marshall Air Force Base* KS-7
Marshall and Hayes Drain—*canal* MI-6
Marshall And Son Ranch—*locale* NE-7
Marshall And Wilcox Drain—*canal* MI-6
*Marshall Archipelago* MP-9
Marshall Arsenal, CSA—*hist pl* TX-5
Marshall Ash Pond—*reservoir* NC-3
Marshall Ash Pond Dam—*dam* NC-3
Marshall Baptist Camp—*locale* AL-4
Marshall Basin—*basin* CO-8
Marshall Bay—*bay* FL-3
Marshall Bay—*swamp* NC-3
Marshall Bend—*bend* TN-4
**Marshallberg**—*pop pl* NC-3
Marshallberg (Township of)—*fmr MCD* NC-3
*Marshall Bluff* AL-4
Marshall Branch—*stream* (3) AL-4
Marshall Branch—*stream* (3) AR-4
Marshall Branch—*stream* IL-6
Marshall Branch—*stream* (4) KY-4
Marshall Branch—*stream* MS-4
Marshall Branch—*stream* MO-7
Marshall Branch—*stream* SC-3
Marshall Branch—*stream* TN-4
Marshall Branch—*stream* TX-5
Marshall Branch—*stream* VA-3
Marshall Branch Ch—*church* KY-4
Marshall Branch Sch—*school* KY-4
Marshall Bridge—*bridge* TN-4
Marshall Bridge—*hist pl* IN-6
Marshall Brook—*stream* ME-1
Marshall Brook—*stream* NH-1
Marshall Brook—*stream* NY-2
Marshall-Bryan House—*hist pl* KY-4
**Marshall (Buffalo)**—*pop pl* WV-2
*Marshallburg* NC-3
Marshall Butte—*summit* AZ-5
Marshall Butte—*summit* OR-9
*Marshall Cabin Area* KY-4
Marshall Cabin Area—*locale* KY-4
Marshall Canyon—*valley* (2) CA-9
Marshall Canyon—*valley* ID-8
Marshall Canyon—*valley* MT-8
Marshall Canyon—*valley* NV-8
Marshall Canyon—*valley* UT-8
Marshall Canyon Regional Park—*park* CA-9
Marshall (CCD)—*cens area* TX-5
Marshall (CCD)—*cens area* WA-9
Marshall Cem—*cemetery* (2) AL-4
Marshall Cem—*cemetery* (2) AR-4
Marshall Cem—*cemetery* GA-3
Marshall Cem—*cemetery* IL-6
Marshall Cem—*cemetery* IA-7
Marshall Cem—*cemetery* KS-7
Marshall Cem—*cemetery* (4) KY-4
Marshall Cem—*cemetery* LA-4
Marshall Cem—*cemetery* ME-1
Marshall Cem—*cemetery* MN-6
Marshall Cem—*cemetery* (2) MS-4
Marshall Cem—*cemetery* (3) MO-7
Marshall Cem—*cemetery* NH-1
Marshall Cem—*cemetery* (2) NY-2
Marshall Cem—*cemetery* (3) NC-3
Marshall Cem—*cemetery* OH-6
Marshall Cem—*cemetery* (3) OK-5
Marshall Cem—*cemetery* TN-4
Marshall Cem—*cemetery* (2) TX-5
Marshall Cem—*cemetery* WA-9
Marshall Cem—*cemetery* WV-2
Marshall Center Cem—*cemetery* KS-7
Marshall Ch—*church* FL-3
Marshall Ch—*church* GA-3
Marshall Ch—*church* NC-3
*Marshall Chapel* TN-4
Marshall Chapel—*church* LA-4
Marshall Chapel—*church* NC-3
Marshall Chapel—*church* SC-3
Marshall Chapel—*church* TN-4
Marshall Chapel Sch—*school* NC-3
Marshall Church Cem—*cemetery* MN-6
**Marshall Corner**—*pop pl* MA-1
**Marshall Corner**—*pop pl* NH-1
Marshall Corners—*locale* PA-2
Marshall Country Club—*other* MI-6
Marshall County—*civil* KS-7
Marshall County—*civil* SD-7
**Marshall County**—*pop pl* AL-4
**Marshall (County)**—*pop pl* IL-6
**Marshall County**—*pop pl* IN-6
**Marshall (County)**—*pop pl* KY-4
**Marshall (County)**—*pop pl* MN-6
**Marshall County**—*pop pl* MS-4
**Marshall (County)**—*pop pl* OK-5
**Marshall County**—*pop pl* TN-4
**Marshall (County)**—*pop pl* WV-2
Marshall County Courthouse—*building* AL-4
Marshall County Courthouse—*building* MS-4
Marshall County Courthouse—*building* TN-4
Marshall County Court House—*hist pl* IN-6
Marshall County Courthouse—*hist pl* IA-7
Marshall County Courthouse—*hist pl* KS-7
Marshall County Courthouse—*hist pl* OK-5
Marshall County Farm (historical)—*locale* TN-4
Marshall County Home—*building* IA-7
Marshall County Hosp—*hospital* MS-4
Marshall County HS—*school* TN-4
Marshall County HS (historical)—*school* AL-4
Marshall County Memory Garden—*cemetery* KY-4
Marshall County Nursing Home—*hospital* AL-4
Marshall County Park—*park* AL-4
Marshall County Plaza Shop Ctr—*locale* TN-4
Marshall County Recreation Center and Golf Club—*building* TN-4
Marshall County Sch—*school* MS-4
Marshall County State Conservation Areas—*park* IL-6
Marshall County Technical Sch—*school* AL-4
Marshall County Vocational Center—*school* TN-4
*Marshall County Vocational Sch* AL-4
**Marshall Courts**—*pop pl* VA-3
*Marshall Creek* AL-4
*Marshall Creek* PA-2
*Marshall Creek* TX-5
**Marshall Creek**—*pop pl* TX-5
Marshall Creek—*stream* AL-4
Marshall Creek—*stream* AK-9
Marshall Creek—*stream* AR-4
Marshall Creek—*stream* (4) CA-9
Marshall Creek—*stream* (2) CO-8
Marshall Creek—*stream* (2) FL-3
Marshall Creek—*stream* GA-3
Marshall Creek—*stream* ID-8
Marshall Creek—*stream* (2) KS-7
Marshall Creek—*stream* LA-4
Marshall Creek—*stream* MD-2
Marshall Creek—*stream* MS-4
Marshall Creek—*stream* (2) MO-7
Marshall Creek—*stream* (4) MT-8
Marshall Creek—*stream* NM-5
Marshall Creek—*stream* NC-3
Marshall Creek—*stream* OH-6
Marshall Creek—*stream* (3) OR-9
Marshall Creek—*stream* SD-7
Marshall Creek—*stream* (6) TN-4
Marshall Creek—*stream* (2) TX-5
Marshall Creek—*stream* (2) VA-3
Marshall Creek—*stream* (2) WA-9
Marshall Creek—*stream* WI-6
Marshall Creek—*stream* WY-8
Marshall Creek Campground—*locale* ID-8
Marshall Creek Canal—*canal* MT-8
Marshall Creek Ch—*church* IL-6
Marshall Creek Dam—*dam* KS-7
Marshall Crossing Creek—*stream* CA-9
Marshall Cummins Pond—*lake* MO-7
Marshalldale—*hist pl* TN-4
Marshall Dam—*dam* NC-3
*Marshall District* MP-9
Marshall Ditch—*canal* IN-6
Marshall Ditch—*canal* MD-2
Marshall Ditch—*canal* (2) UT-8
Marshall Ditch Number Three—*canal* MT-8
Marshall Draft—*valley* VA-3
Marshall Draft Trail—*trail* VA-3
Marshall Draw—*valley* CO-8
Marshall Draw—*valley* UT-8
Marshall Draw Wildlife Mngmt Area—*park* UT-8
*Marshall Elementary School* MS-4
Marshall Elem Sch—*school* NC-3
**Marshall Estates**—*pop pl* TN-4
*Marshall Falls* PA-2
Marshall Falls—*falls* PA-2
**Marshall Farms**—*pop pl* NH-1
**Marshall Farms**—*pop pl* VA-3
Marshall Ferry Cem—*cemetery* IL-6
Marshall Ferry Landing—*locale* AL-4
Marshall Field—*park* KY-4
Marshall Field and Company Store—*hist pl* IL-6
Marshall Field Company Store—*hist pl* IL-6
Marshall Flat—*flat* MT-8
Marshall Flat—*flat* NM-5
Marshall Flat Tank—*reservoir* AZ-5
**Marshall Ford**—*pop pl* TX-5
**Marshall Ford (Mansfield Dam)**—*pop pl* TX-5
Marshall Fork Branch—*stream* IN-4
Marshall Gap—*gap* NM-5
Marshall Gap—*gap* VA-3
Marshall Gas Field—*oilfield* TX-5
Marshall Gin (historical)—*locale* MS-4
Marshall Gin Landing—*locale* AL-4
Marshall Glacier—*glacier* AK-9
Marshall Grove Ch—*church* GA-3
*Marshall-Gruppe* MP-9
Marshall Gulch—*valley* AK-9
Marshall Gulch—*valley* AZ-5
Marshall Gulch—*valley* CA-9
Marshall Gulch—*valley* CO-8
Marshall Gulch—*valley* SD-7
Marshall Gulch Picnic Area—*park* AZ-5
Marshall Hall—*hist pl* MD-2
Marshall Hall—*locale* MD-2
Marshall-Harris-Richardson House—*hist pl* NC-3
**Marshall Heights**—*pop pl* DC-2
**Marshall Heights**—*pop pl* PA-2
**Marshall Heights**—*pop pl* TN-4
**Marshall Heights**—*pop pl* VA-3
**Marshall Heights Subdivision**—*pop pl* UT-8
Marshall Hill—*locale* TN-4
Marshall Hill—*summit* CA-9
Marshall Hill—*summit* NH-1
Marshall Hill—*summit* TN-4
*Marshall Hill Baptist Church* TN-4
Marshall Hill Ch—*church* TN-4
Marshall Hills—*other* TX-5
Marshall Hill Sch—*school* OK-5
Marshall (historical)—*locale* AL-4
Marshall (historical)—*locale* KS-7
**Marshall (historical)**—*pop pl* IA-7
Marshall Hollow—*locale* PA-2
Marshall Hollow—*valley* AR-4
Marshall Hollow—*valley* (3) PA-2
Marshall Hollow—*valley* (4) TN-4
Marshall Hollow—*valley* WV-2
Marshall Hosp—*hospital* NY-2
Marshall Hotel—*hist pl* MO-7
Marshall House—*hist pl* AR-4
Marshall House—*hist pl* KY-4
Marshall House—*hist pl* NY-2
Marshall HS—*school* AL-4
Marshall HS—*school* FL-3
Marshall HS—*school* IL-6
Marshall HS—*school* (2) MN-6
Marshall HS—*school* NY-2
Marshall HS—*school* OH-6
Marshall HS—*school* OK-5
Marshall HS—*school* TX-5
Marshall HS—*school* VA-3
Marshallia Ranch—*locale* CA-9
Marshall I Diggs State Wildlife Mngmt A—*park* MO-7
*Marshall Inselnshallinseln* MP-9
Marshall Institute Ch (historical)—*church* MS-4
Marshall Island—*island* AK-9
Marshall Island—*island* DE-2
Marshall Island—*island* ME-1
Marshall Island—*island* OR-9
Marshall Island—*island* (2) PA-2
Marshall Islands—*island* MP-9
**Marshall Islands District**—*pop pl* MP-9
Marshall Islands War Memorial Park—*hist pl* MP-9
Marshall JHS—*school* (3) CA-9
Marshall JHS—*school* KS-7
Marshall JHS—*school* (2) MI-6
Marshall JHS—*school* MN-6
Marshall JHS—*school* TX-5
Marshall JHS—*school* WA-9
Marshall Junction—*locale* CA-9
**Marshall Junction**—*pop pl* MO-7
**Marshall Junction (sta.)**—*pop pl* MO-7
Marshall Junction State Wildlife Area—*park* MO-7
Marshall King Lake—*reservoir* IN-6
Marshall King Lake Dam—*dam* IN-6
Marshall Knob—*summit* TN-4
Marshall Knobs—*summit* TN-4
Marshall Lake—*flat* OR-9
Marshall Lake—*lake* AK-9
Marshall Lake—*lake* AZ-5
Marshall Lake—*lake* CA-9
Marshall Lake—*lake* FL-3
Marshall Lake—*lake* (2) ID-8
Marshall Lake—*lake* (2) MI-6
Marshall Lake—*lake* (3) MN-6
Marshall Lake—*lake* UT-8
Marshall Lake—*lake* WA-9
Marshall Lake—*lake* WI-6
Marshall Lake—*reservoir* CO-8
Marshall Lake—*reservoir* NC-3
Marshall Lake—*reservoir* OK-5
Marshall Lake—*reservoir* (2) PA-2
Marshall Lake Brook—*stream* CT-1
Marshall Lake Dam—*dam* MS-4
Marshall Lake Dam—*dam* PA-2
Marshall Lakes—*lake* FL-3
Marshall Landing—*locale* IL-6
Marshall Lane Sch—*school* CA-9
Marshall Ledge—*bar* ME-1
Marshall (Magisterial District)—*fmr MCD* (3) VA-3
Marshall McCay Lake Dam—*dam* AL-4
Marshall Meadow—*flat* CA-9
Marshall Meadow—*flat* ID-8
Marshall Meadow—*flat* UT-8
Marshall Memorial Cem—*cemetery* AL-4
Marshall Memorial Ch—*church* SC-3
Marshall Memorial Municipal Airp—*airport* MO-7
Marshall Mesa Tank—*reservoir* AZ-5
Marshall Mid Sch—*school* IL-6
Marshall Mill (historical)—*locale* AL-4
Marshall Millpond—*reservoir* DE-2
Marshall Millpond Dam—*dam* DE-2
Marshall Mill Run—*stream* MD-2
Marshall Mine—*mine* CA-9
Marshall Mine—*mine* NV-8
Marshall Mtn—*summit* AK-9
Marshall Mtn—*summit* AZ-5
Marshall Mtn—*summit* ID-8
Marshall Mtn—*summit* MT-8
Marshall Mtn—*summit* NY-2
**Marshall(native name for Fortuna Ledge)ANV852**—*pop pl* AK-9
Marshall-Nemaha Sch—*school* KS-7
Marshall Opening—*flat* CA-9
Marshall Park—*park* CA-9
Marshall Park—*park* FL-3
Marshall Park—*park* MA-1
Marshall Park—*park* MI-6
Marshall Park—*park* MS-4
Marshall Park—*park* SC-3
Marshall Park Campground—*locale* CO-8
Marshall Pass—*gap* AK-9
Marshall Pass—*gap* CO-8
Marshall Patterson Dam—*dam* AL-4
Marshall Peak—*pillar* ID-8
Marshall Peak—*summit* AZ-5
Marshall Peak—*summit* CA-9
Marshall Place—*locale* OR-9
Marshall Place Hist Dist—*hist pl* MO-7
**Marshall Plantation (historical)**—*pop pl* FL-3
Marshall Point—*cape* (4) ME-1
Marshall Point—*cape* MD-2
Marshall Point Light Station—*hist pl* ME-1
Marshall Pond—*lake* FL-3
Marshall Pond—*lake* ME-1
Marshall Pond—*lake* MI-6
Marshall Pond—*lake* NH-1
Marshall Pond—*lake* NJ-2
Marshall Pond—*lake* UT-8
Marshall Pond—*reservoir* GA-3
Marshall Pond—*reservoir* MA-1
Marshall Post Office (historical)—*building* TN-4
Marshall Primary Sch—*school* NC-3
Marshall Ranch—*locale* AZ-5
Marshall Ranch—*locale* CA-9
Marshall Ranch—*locale* CO-8
Marshall Ranch—*locale* TX-5
Marshall Ridge—*ridge* AZ-5
Marshall Ridge—*ridge* KY-4
Marshall Ridge—*ridge* NC-3
Marshall Road Sch—*school* PA-2
Marshall Road Sch—*school* VA-3
Marshall Roberts Ditch—*canal* CO-8
Marshall Rock—*pillar* CA-9
Marshall Rsvr—*reservoir* MA-1
Marshall Run—*stream* (2) PA-2
Marshall Run—*stream* VA-3
*Marshalls* MP-9
Marshalls—*locale* NY-2
Marshall Saddle—*gap* AZ-5
*Marshall's Archipel Marshalls* MP-9
**Marshalls Beach**—*pop pl* VA-3
Marshalls Bluff—*cliff* AL-4
Marshall's Bridge—*hist pl* PA-2
Marshalls Ch—*church* SC-3
Marshall Sch—*school* (2) AZ-5
Marshall Sch—*school* (13) CA-9
Marshall Sch—*school* (2) IL-6
Marshall Sch—*school* IA-7
Marshall Sch—*school* KY-4
Marshall Sch—*school* (5) MI-6
Marshall Sch—*school* MN-6
Marshall Sch—*school* (2) MS-4
Marshall Sch—*school* MO-7
Marshall Sch—*school* (2) NJ-2
Marshall Sch—*school* (2) OH-6
Marshall Sch—*school* (2) OR-9
Marshall Sch—*school* (2) PA-2
Marshall Sch—*school* SD-7
Marshall Sch—*school* TX-5
Marshall Sch—*school* VT-1
Marshall Sch—*school* (2) VA-3
Marshall Sch—*school* WI-6
Marshall Sch (historical)—*school* MS-4
Marshall Sch (historical)—*school* TN-4
*Marshall School* IN-6
*Marshalls Corner* MA-1
**Marshalls Corner**—*pop pl* MD-2
**Marshalls Corner**—*pop pl* NJ-2
*Marshalls Corners* NJ-2
*Marshalls Creek* MO-7
**Marshalls Creek**—*pop pl* PA-2
Marshalls Creek—*stream* AL-4
Marshalls Creek—*stream* NJ-2
Marshalls Creek—*stream* PA-2
*Marshalls Cross Roads* AL-4
*Marshalls District* MP-9
*Marshalls Falls* PA-2
Marshalls Falls—*falls* PA-2
Marshalls Ferry (historical)—*crossing* TN-4
Marshalls Ferry Post Office (historical)—*building* TN-4
Marshalls Ford (historical)—*crossing* TN-4
Marshall's Grove—*hist pl* AL-4
Marshalls (historical)—*locale* AZ-5
Marshalls Home Depot (Shop Ctr)—*locale* FL-3
Marshall Site (15CE27)—*hist pl* KY-4
Marshall Ski Area—*other* MT-8
*Marshalls Knob* TN-4
Marshall Slough—*stream* IL-6
Marshall Slough—*stream* OR-9
*Marshalls Millpond* DE-2
Marshall Smith Lake Dam—*dam* (2) MS-4
Marshall Space Flight Center (NASA)—*military* AL-4
*Marshall's Point* ME-1
*Marshalls Pond* DE-2
Marshalls Pond Dam Number One—*dam* NC-3
Marshalls Pond Number One—*reservoir* NC-3
Marshall Spring—*spring* CA-9
Marshall Spring—*spring* MT-8
Marshall Spring—*spring* NM-5
Marshall Spring—*spring* OR-9
Marshall Springs—*locale* TX-5
Marshall Springs—*spring* UT-8
Marshall Springs Cem—*cemetery* TX-5
Marshall Square—*park* PA-2
Marshall Square Hist Dist—*hist pl* AR-4
Marshalls Shoals—*bar* TN-4
Marshall State Forest—*park* NH-1
Marshall State Hosp—*hospital* MO-7
Marshall State Sch—*school* MO-7
**Marshall Station (Grabners)**—*pop pl* CA-9
Marshall Steam Station—*building* NC-3
Marshall Street Hist Dist—*hist pl* MI-6
Marshall Street Park—*park* CA-9
*Marshallsville* NJ-2
Marshall Swamp—*swamp* (2) FL-3
Marshall Tank—*reservoir* (5) AZ-5
Marshall Tank—*reservoir* NM-5
*Marshall Tavern* NC-3
**Marshall Terrace**—*pop pl* PA-2
**Marshall Terrace**—*pop pl* WV-2
**Marshall Terrace (Carnegie)**—*pop pl* WV-2
**Marshallton**—*pop pl* DE-2
**Marshallton**—*pop pl* (2) PA-2
**Marshallton Green**—*pop pl* DE-2
**Marshallton Heights II**—*pop pl* DE-2
Marshallton Hist Dist—*hist pl* PA-2
Marshallton Inn—*hist pl* PA-2
Marshallton United Methodist Church—*hist pl* DE-2
Marshalltown—*locale* NJ-2
Marshalltown—*locale* VA-3
**Marshalltown**—*pop pl* IA-7
**Marshalltown (historical)**—*pop pl* SD-7
**Marshall (Town of)**—*pop pl* NY-2
**Marshall (Town of)**—*pop pl* (2) WI-6
Marshalltown Sch (historical)—*school* SD-7
Marshall Township—*civil* (2) MO-7
Marshall Township—*fmr MCD* (4) IA-7
**Marshall Township**—*pop pl* NE-7
**Marshall Township**—*pop pl* ND-7
Marshall (Township of)—*fmr MCD* AR-4
**Marshall (Township of)**—*pop pl* IL-6
**Marshall (Township of)**—*pop pl* IN-6
**Marshall (Township of)**—*pop pl* MI-6
**Marshall (Township of)**—*pop pl* MN-6
**Marshall (Township of)**—*pop pl* OH-6
**Marshall (Township of)**—*pop pl* PA-2
Marshall Tunnel—*mine* CO-8
Marshall Tunnel—*tunnel* WV-2
Marshall Univ—*school* WV-2
Marshall Upper Landing—*locale* AL-4
*Marshallville* NJ-2
Marshallville—*locale* KY-4
**Marshallville**—*pop pl* GA-3
**Marshallville**—*pop pl* NJ-2
**Marshallville**—*pop pl* OH-6
Marshallville (CCD)—*cens area* GA-3
Marshallville Commercial District—*hist pl* GA-3
Marshallville Ditch—*canal* CO-8
Marshall Watershed Lake—*reservoir* NC-3
Marshall Well—*well* AZ-5
Marshall Well—*well* UT-8
Marshall Williams Park—*park* FL-3
Marshal Meeks Number 3 Mine (underground)—*mine* TN-4
Marshal Sch—*school* CA-9
*Marshalton* PA-2
Marshalton (historical)—*locale* MS-4
Marshan Lake—*lake* MN-6
**Marshan (Township of)**—*pop pl* MN-6
*Marshapauge Pond* CT-1
Marsha Peak—*summit* AK-9
*Marshapogge River* CT-1
Marshatt Creek—*stream* MI-6
Marsh Ave Park—*park* OH-6
Marshbank Metropolitan Park—*park* MI-6
Marshbanks Cem—*cemetery* NC-3
Marsh Bay—*bay* AK-9
Marsh Bay—*bay* FL-3
Marsh Bay—*bay* ME-1
Marsh Bay—*swamp* NC-3
Marsh Bay Creek—*bay* FL-3
Marsh Bay Creek—*stream* MI-6
Marsh Bayou—*gut* MS-4
Marsh Bayou—*stream* LA-4
Marsh Bayou Cutoff—*bend* LA-4
Marsh Bay Point—*cape* FL-3
Marsh Baywood—*swamp* NJ-2
Marsh Berea Ch—*church* MS-4
Marsh Bog Brook—*stream* NJ-2
*Marsh Branch* NC-3
*Marsh Branch* TN-4
Marsh Branch—*stream* (2) AL-4
Marsh Branch—*stream* FL-3
Marsh Branch—*stream* KY-4
Marsh Branch—*stream* (2) NC-3
Marsh Branch—*stream* TX-5
Marsh Bridges—*bridge* ME-1
*Marsh Brook* MA-1
*Marsh Brook* PA-2
Marshbrook—*locale* PA-2
Marsh Brook—*stream* (2) CT-1
Marsh Brook—*stream* (2) ME-1
Marsh Brook—*stream* MA-1
Marsh Brook—*stream* (2) NH-1
Marsh Brook—*stream* VT-1
**Marshburg**—*pop pl* PA-2
Marshburg Oil Field—*oilfield* PA-2
Marshburn Cem—*cemetery* NC-3
Marshburn Cemeteries—*cemetery* NC-3
Marsh Butte—*summit* AZ-5
Marsh Canal—*canal* LA-4
Marsh Canal—*canal* NC-3
Marsh Canyon—*valley* ID-8
Marsh Cem—*cemetery* (2) AL-4
Marsh Cem—*cemetery* AR-4
Marsh Cem—*cemetery* ID-8
Marsh Cem—*cemetery* IL-6
Marsh Cem—*cemetery* IN-6
Marsh Cem—*cemetery* MO-7
Marsh Cem—*cemetery* (2) OH-6
Marsh Cem—*cemetery* SC-3
Marsh Cem—*cemetery* (3) TN-4
Marsh Cem—*cemetery* (2) TX-5
Marsh Cem—*cemetery* WV-2
Marsh Center—*locale* ID-8
Marsh Center Cem—*cemetery* ID-8
*Marsh Channel* VA-3
Marsh Chapel—*church* TN-4
Marsh Concrete Rainbow Arch Bridge—*hist pl* MN-6
*Marsh Corner* PA-2
Marsh Corner—*locale* ME-1
Marsh Corner—*locale* MI-6
Marsh Corner—*locale* NY-2
**Marsh Corner**—*pop pl* MA-1
Marsh Corners—*locale* NY-2
Marsh Corners—*locale* PA-2
Marsh Coulee—*valley* (2) MT-8
Marsh Cove—*bay* (2) ME-1
Marsh Cove Head—*cape* ME-1
*Marsh Cove Island* ME-1
Marsh Cove Ledges—*bar* ME-1
Marsh Cove Point—*cape* ME-1
*Marsh Creek* MI-6
*Marsh Creek* MT-8
*Marsh Creek* NJ-2
*Marsh Creek* NY-2
*Marsh Creek* OR-9
*Marsh Creek* PA-2
*Marsh Creek* SC-3
*Marsh Creek* SD-7
*Marsh Creek* WI-6
*Marsh Creek* WY-8
Marsh Creek—*locale* MO-7
**Marsh Creek**—*pop pl* PA-2
Marsh Creek—*stream* (3) AK-9
Marsh Creek—*stream* AZ-5
Marsh Creek—*stream* (2) CA-9
Marsh Creek—*stream* GA-3
Marsh Creek—*stream* (6) ID-8
Marsh Creek—*stream* IN-6
Marsh Creek—*stream* IA-7
Marsh Creek—*stream* (2) KS-7
Marsh Creek—*stream* KY-4
Marsh Creek—*stream* (2) ME-1
Marsh Creek—*stream* (2) MD-2
Marsh Creek—*stream* (5) MI-6
Marsh Creek—*stream* MN-6
Marsh Creek—*stream* MO-7
Marsh Creek—*stream* (2) MT-8
Marsh Creek—*stream* (2) NV-8
Marsh Creek—*stream* (5) NY-2
Marsh Creek—*stream* NC-3
Marsh Creek—*stream* (3) OR-9
Marsh Creek—*stream* (7) PA-2
Marsh Creek—*stream* SC-3
Marsh Creek—*stream* SD-7
Marsh Creek—*stream* (2) TN-4
Marsh Creek—*stream* WA-9
Marsh Creek—*stream* (5) WI-6
Marsh Creek—*stream* WY-8
Marsh Creek Airp—*airport* PA-2
Marsh Creek Ch—*church* PA-2
Marsh Creek Ch—*church* TN-4
Marsh Creek Ch (historical)—*church* PA-2
*Marsh Creek Dam* PA-2
Marsh Creek Hollow—*valley* PA-2
Marsh Creek Mine—*mine* ID-8
Marsh Creek Pond—*reservoir* OR-9
Marsh Creek Pool—*reservoir* MI-6
Marsh Creek Ranch—*locale* AZ-5
Marsh Creek Rsvr—*reservoir* CA-9
Marsh Creek Sch—*school* PA-2
**Marsh Creek Springs**—*pop pl* CA-9
Marsh Creek State Park—*park* PA-2
Marsh Creek Tank—*reservoir* AZ-5
**Marsh Creek (Township of)**—*pop pl* MN-6
Marsh Creek Trail—*trail* PA-2
Marsh Crossing—*locale* GA-3
**Marshdale**—*pop pl* CO-8
*Marshdale Park* CO-8
**Marshdale Park**—*pop pl* CO-8
Marsh Ditch—*canal* (4) IN-6
Marsh Ditch—*canal* MT-8
Marsh Ditch—*canal* NY-2
Marsh Ditch—*canal* WY-8
*Marsh Drain* MI-6
Marsh Drain—*canal* MI-6
Marsh Draw—*valley* WY-8
*Marshe Creek* MI-6
Marshel Chapel—*church* NC-3
Marshelder Channel—*channel* NJ-2
Marshelder Island—*island* NJ-2
Marsh Elder Island—*island* NJ-2
Marshelder Islands—*island* NJ-2
Marshelder Point—*cape* NJ-2
Marshelder Pond—*lake* NJ-2
Marsh Elem Sch—*school* IN-6
*Marshell Lake* UT-8
Marshell (Township of)—*fmr MCD* AR-4
*Marshepaug River* CT-1
Marshepaug River—*stream* CT-1
Marsher, The—*swamp* NY-2
*Marshes* WV-2
Marshes, The—*swamp* ME-1
Marshes, The—*swamp* MD-2
Marshes, The—*swamp* MI-6
Marshes Ch—*church* OH-6
Marshes Creek—*stream* NJ-2
*Marshes Lake* MI-6
Marshes of Glynn Overlook Park—*park* GA-3
Marshes of Glynn Park—*park* GA-3
Marshes Ponds—*reservoir* AL-4
**Marshes Siding**—*pop pl* KY-4
*Marshfield* OR-9
*Marshfield* PA-2
Marshfield—*locale* ME-1
Marsh Field—*park* MI-6
**Marshfield**—*pop pl* (2) IN-6
**Marshfield**—*pop pl* MA-1
**Marshfield**—*pop pl* MO-7
**Marshfield**—*pop pl* NY-2
**Marshfield**—*pop pl* VT-1
**Marshfield**—*pop pl* WI-6
Marshfield Brook—*stream* VT-1
Marshfield Canal—*canal* LA-4
Marshfield (census name for Marshfield Compact)—*CDP* MA-1
**Marshfield Center**—*pop pl* MA-1
*Marshfield Centre* MA-1
Marshfield Centre (historical P.O.)—*locale* MA-1
Marshfield Centre Station (historical)—*locale* MA-1
Marshfield Channel—*channel* OR-9
Marshfield Compact (census name Marshfield)—*other* MA-1
Marshfield Elks Temple—*hist pl* OR-9

Martin Sch (historical)—*school* MO-7
Martin Sch Number 1 (historical)—*school* SD-7
Martin School (abandoned)—*locale* MO-7
*Martin School Cem* TN-4
Martin School (historical)—*locale* MO-7
Martins Corner—*locale* ME-1
Martins Corner—*locale* MD-2
Martins Corner—*locale* (2) VA-3
**Martins Corner**—*pop pl* NH-1
**Martins Corner**—*pop pl* PA-2
Martins Coulee—*valley* MT-8
Martins Cove—*basin* WY-8
Martins Cove—*bay* MD-2
Martin's Cove—*hist pl* WY-8
Martins Cow Camp—*locale* CA-9
*Martins Creek* MI-6
*Martins Creek* MS-4
*Martins Creek* PA-2
*Martins Creek* TN-4
*Martins Creek* TX-5
Martins Creek—*gut* NJ-2
**Martins Creek**—*pop pl* NJ-2
**Martins Creek**—*pop pl* NC-3
**Martins Creek**—*pop pl* PA-2
Martins Creek—*stream* (2) AL-4
Martins Creek—*stream* AR-4
Martins Creek—*stream* (2) KY-4
Martins Creek—*stream* OH-6
Martins Creek—*stream* (3) PA-2
Martins Creek—*stream* TX-5
Martins Creek—*stream* (4) VA-3
Martins Creek Cem—*cemetery* TX-5
Martins Creek Ch—*church* OH-6
Martins Creek Elem Sch—*school* NC-3
Martins Creek Ferry (historical)—*locale* PA-2
Martins Creek Junction—*locale* PA-2
Martins Creek Sch—*school* KY-4
*Martins Creek School* TN-4
Martins Creek Station—*locale* NJ-2
Martins Creek Station (historical)—*building* PA-2
*Martins Crossroads* NC-3
Martins Crossroads—*locale* AL-4
Martins Crossroads—*locale* (2) GA-3
Martins Crossroads—*locale* MD-2
Martins Crossroads—*locale* SC-3
**Martins Crossroads**—*pop pl* PA-2
*Martins Crossroads P.O.* AL-4
**Martinsdale**—*pop pl* MT-8
**Martinsdale Colony**—*pop pl* MT-8
*Martinsdale Lake* MT-8
Martinsdale-Ringling—*cens area* MT-8
Martinsdale Rsvr—*reservoir* MT-8
Martins Dam—*dam* AL-4
Martins Dam—*dam* PA-2
Martins Ditch—*canal* ID-8
*Martins Draft* VA-3
Martinsen Lake—*lake* ND-7
Martin's Evangelical Church—*hist pl* SD-7
*Martins Ferry* AL-4
Martins Ferry—*locale* AR-4
**Martins Ferry**—*pop pl* OH-6
**Martins Ferry**—*pop pl* PA-2
Martins Ferry Bridge—*bridge* CA-9
Martins Ferry Sch—*school* CA-9
Martins Flat—*flat* UT-8
*Martins Ford* TN-4
Martins Ford—*crossing* TN-4
Martins Ford (historical)—*locale* TN-4
*Martins Ford Shoals* TN-4
Martins Fork—*locale* KY-4
Martins Fork—*stream* KY-4
Martins Fork Cumberland River—*stream* KY-4
Martins Gap—*gap* NC-3
Martins Hill—*summit* KY-4
Martins Hill—*summit* WV-2
Martin-Shiloh Ch—*church* TX-5
Martins Hollow—*valley* KY-4
**Martin Siding**—*pop pl* VA-3
Martins Island—*island* FL-3
Martins Island—*island* LA-4
Martin Site—*hist pl* KY-4
Martin Site—*hist pl* VA-3
Martins Knob Lookout Tower—*locale* GA-3
*Martins Lake* MI-6
Martins Lake—*lake* NY-2
Martins Lake—*lake* OR-9
Martins Lake—*lake* SC-3
Martins Lake—*reservoir* (2) AL-4
Martins Lake—*reservoir* NC-3
Martins Lake Dam—*dam* NC-3
Martins Lakes—*lake* WA-9
*Martins Landing* TN-4
Martins Landing—*locale* LA-4
Martins Landing—*locale* MI-6
Martins Landing—*locale* MS-4
Martins Landing—*locale* NJ-2
Martins Landing—*locale* (2) SC-3
Martins Landing (historical)—*locale* MS-4
Martins Location—*civil* NH-1
Martin Slough—*gut* AL-4
Martin Slough—*gut* LA-4
Martin Slough—*stream* CA-9
Martin Slough—*stream* NV-8
Martin Slough—*stream* WA-9
Martins Low Gap—*gap* NC-3
Martins Mill—*locale* AL-4
Martins Mill—*locale* OR-9
Martins Mill—*locale* PA-2
**Martins Mill**—*pop pl* TX-5
Martins Mill Covered Bridge—*bridge* PA-2
Martin's Mill Covered Bridge—*hist pl* (2) PA-2
Martin's Mill Covered Bridge—*hist pl* VT-1
Martins Mill (historical)—*locale* AL-4
Martins Mill (historical)—*locale* MS-4
Martins Mill (historical)—*locale* (3) TN-4
Martins Mill Pond—*lake* FL-3
*Martins Mills* TX-5
**Martins Mills**—*pop pl* TN-4
**Martins Mills**—*pop pl* TX-5
Martins Mills Post Office (historical)—*building* TN-4
Martins Mills Sch—*school* TX-5
Martins Mills Sch (historical)—*school* TN-4
Martins Mtn—*summit* (2) VA-3
Martinson Cem—*cemetery* SD-7
Martinson Christian Ch—*church* KS-7
Martinson Gap—*gap* WA-9
Martinson HS—*school* MA-1
Martinson Island—*island* MN-6
Martinson Sch—*school* KS-7
Martins Park—*flat* WA-9
*Martins Point* SC-3
Martins Point—*cape* RI-1
Martins Point—*cape* SC-3
Martins Point—*cape* TN-4
Martins Point Landing—*locale* SC-3
*Martins Pond* SC-3
Martins Pond—*lake* MA-1
Martins Pond—*lake* NY-2
Martins Pond—*lake* VT-1
Martins Pond—*reservoir* GA-3
Martins Pond—*reservoir* MA-1
Martins Pond Brook—*stream* MA-1
Martins Pond Dam—*dam* MA-1
Martins Pond Site—*hist pl* MD-2
Martin Spring—*locale* AR-4
Martin Spring—*spring* AL-4
Martin Spring—*spring* (3) AZ-5
Martin Spring—*spring* CA-9
Martin Spring—*spring* (2) ID-8
Martin Spring—*spring* KY-4
Martin Spring—*spring* (2) MO-7
Martin Spring—*spring* (2) MT-8
Martin Spring—*spring* (3) NV-8
Martin Spring—*spring* (3) OR-9
Martin Spring—*spring* (5) TN-4
Martin Spring—*spring* (2) WA-9
Martin Spring—*spring* (2) WY-8
Martin Spring Branch—*stream* AL-4
Martin Spring Branch—*stream* TX-5
Martin Spring Ch—*church* TX-5
Martin Spring Draw—*valley* WY-8
Martin Spring Hollow—*valley* AR-4
Martin Springs—*locale* TX-5
**Martin Springs**—*pop pl* TN-4
Martin Springs—*spring* CA-9
Martin Springs—*spring* TN-4
Martin Springs Baptist Ch—*church* TN-4
Martin Springs Cave—*cave* TN-4
Martin Springs Cem—*cemetery* LA-4
*Martin Springs Cemetery* TN-4
Martin Springs High Hole—*cave* TN-4
Martin Springs Sch (historical)—*school* TN-4
**Martin Spur**—*pop pl* CO-8
Martin's Ranch—*locale* MT-8
Martins Ranch—*locale* WY-8
*Martin's Reef* MI-6
*Martins Run* KY-4
Martins Run—*stream* (2) OH-6
Martins Run—*stream* PA-2
Martins Run—*stream* (2) WV-2
Martins Sch (abandoned)—*school* PA-2
Martins Sch (historical)—*school* MS-4
Martins Sch (historical)—*school* TN-4
Martins Schoolhouse Methodist Ch (historical)—*church* TN-4
Martins Shoal—*bar* TN-4
Martins Shoals—*bar* TN-4
Martins Siding—*locale* ME-1
**Martins Siding**—*pop pl* VA-3
*Martins Spring* OR-9
*Martins Stand* AL-4
*Martins Station* AL-4
*Martins Store* AL-4
Martins Store—*locale* AR-4
Martins Store—*locale* NC-3
**Martins Store**—*pop pl* (3) VA-3
Martins Store (historical)—*locale* AL-4
Martins Store (historical)—*locale* TN-4
*Martins Stores* NC-3
**Martins Subdivision**—*pop pl* UT-8
Martins Swamp—*stream* AL-4
Martin Stadium—*other* AL-4
Martin State For—*forest* IN-6
*Martin Station* AL-4
*Martin Station* WA-9
Martin Station Sch—*school* AL-4
Martin Stewart Sch (historical)—*school* AL-4
Martin Store (historical)—*locale* AL-4
Martin Store (historical)—*locale* MS-4
Martinstown—*locale* IA-7
**Martinstown**—*pop pl* MO-7
*Martins Trail* PA-2
Martin Strand—*swamp* GA-3
Martin Stream—*stream* (4) ME-1
*Martinsville* GA-3
*Martinsville* PA-2
Martinsville—*locale* KY-4
Martinsville—*locale* MS-4
Martinsville—*locale* OH-6
**Martinsville**—*pop pl* IL-6
**Martinsville**—*pop pl* IN-6
**Martinsville**—*pop pl* ME-1
**Martinsville**—*pop pl* MI-6
**Martinsville**—*pop pl* MO-7
**Martinsville**—*pop pl* NJ-2
**Martinsville**—*pop pl* (2) NY-2
**Martinsville**—*pop pl* OH-6
**Martinsville**—*pop pl* PA-2
**Martinsville**—*pop pl* TX-5
**Martinsville**—*pop pl* WI-6
Martinsville Cem—*cemetery* MI-6
Martinsville Cem—*cemetery* MS-4
Martinsville Country Club—*other* IN-6
Martinsville Fish Dam—*hist pl* VA-3
Martinsville Ford—*locale* KY-4
Martinsville HS—*school* IN-6
Martinsville HS Gymnasium—*hist pl* IN-6
**Martinsville (ind. city)**—*pop pl* VA-3
Martinsville Industries Park—*facility* VA-3
Martinsville (Magisterial District)—*fmr MCD* VA-3
Martinsville Post Office (historical)—*building* PA-2
Martinsville Ridge—*ridge* WV-2
Martinsville Road Covered Bridge—*hist pl* OH-6
Martinsville Rsvr—*reservoir* VA-3
Martinsville Sch—*school* TX-5
Martinsville Sch (historical)—*school* MS-4
Martinsville Speedway—*other* VA-3
Martinsville (Township of)—*civ div* IL-6
Martin Swamp—*stream* NC-3
Martins Well—*cove* MA-1
Martins Well—*well* CA-9
**Martins Woods**—*pop pl* MD-2
Martin Tabernacle Ch—*church* GA-3
Martin Tank—*reservoir* (2) AZ-5
Martin Tank—*reservoir* (9) NM-5
Martin Tank—*reservoir* (3) TX-5
Martin Technical Coll—*school* FL-3
Martin Temple Ch of God in Christ—*church* KS-7
Martin Tidwell Sch (historical)—*school* TN-4
Martin T Krueger JHS—*school* IN-6
**Martinton**—*pop pl* IL-6
Martinton Ditch No 3—*canal* IL-6
**Martinton (Township of)**—*pop pl* IL-6
Martin Towhead—*island* IL-6
Martintown—*locale* PA-2
**Martintown**—*pop pl* (2) AL-4
**Martintown**—*pop pl* MS-4
**Martintown**—*pop pl* WI-6
Martin Town Hall—*building* ND-7
Martintown Recreational Lake Dam—*dam* MS-4
Martin Township—*civil* KS-7
**Martin Township**—*pop pl* KS-7
**Martin Township**—*pop pl* NE-7
**Martin Township**—*pop pl* (2) ND-7
**Martin Township**—*pop pl* SD-7
Martin (Township of)—*fmr MCD* (2) AR-4
**Martin (Township of)**—*pop pl* (2) IL-6
**Martin (Township of)**—*pop pl* MI-6
**Martin (Township of)**—*pop pl* MN-6
Martin Trail—*trail* (2) PA-2
Martin Tunnel—*tunnel* VA-3
Martin Tunnel—*tunnel* WV-2
Martinus Cem—*cemetery* SD-7
Martinus Ch—*church* SD-7
Martinus Corner—*locale* CA-9
Martin Valley—*valley* SD-7
Martin Valley (historical)—*locale* SD-7
Martin Valley Sch (abandoned)—*school* SD-7
Martin Van Buren Homestead—*locale* NY-2
Martin Van Buren HS—*school* NY-2
Martin Van Buren Natl Historic Site—*park* NY-2
Martin View Ch—*church* NC-3
**Martin Village Subdivision**—*pop pl* UT-8
Martinville—*locale* AL-4
Martinville—*locale* MS-4
**Martinville**—*pop pl* AR-4
Martinville Cem—*cemetery* AR-4
Martinville Ch—*church* AL-4
Martinville Ch—*church* AR-4
Martinville Ch—*church* GA-3
Martinville Oil Field—*oilfield* MS-4
Martinville Sch—*school* WI-6
Martinville Sch (historical)—*school* AL-4
Martin Wash—*stream* AZ-5
Martin Way—*trail* OR-9
Martin Weiss Park—*park* TX-5
Martin Well—*well* (2) AZ-5
Martin Well—*well* (3) NM-5
Martin Well—*well* TX-5
Martin Well—*well* UT-8
Martin Well (flowing)—*well* AZ-5
Martin West (CCD)—*cens area* KY-4
Martin West Sch—*school* KS-7
Martin Windmill—*locale* NM-5
Martin Windmill—*locale* (2) TX-5
**Martinwood Estates (subdivision)**—*pop pl* AL-4
*Martin Wyngaard* MA-1
Martiny Cem—*cemetery* MI-6
Martiny Lake—*reservoir* MI-6
Martin-Youngman Ditch—*canal* IN-6
**Martiny (Township of)**—*pop pl* MI-6
Martin Zion Ch—*church* AL-4
Martirena Ranch—*locale* WY-8
Martis Branch—*stream* KY-4
**Martisco**—*pop pl* NY-2
Martis Creek—*stream* CA-9
Martis Peak—*summit* CA-9
Martis Valley—*valley* CA-9
*Martlaers Island* NY-2
Martland—*locale* NE-7
Martland Gulch—*valley* CO-8
Martland Med Ctr—*hospital* NJ-2
**Mart Law Seminole Village**—*pop pl* FL-3
**Martling**—*pop pl* AL-4
Martling Branch—*stream* AL-4
Martling Cem—*cemetery* AL-4
Martling Ch—*church* AL-4
Martling Lake—*lake* NY-2
Martling Sch (historical)—*school* AL-4
Martlnad Peak—*summit* CO-8
Mart Meade Branch—*stream* KY-4
Mart Miller Draw—*valley* WY-8
*Marton Brook* ME-1
Marton Homestead—*locale* PA-2
Marton Ranch—*locale* TX-5
**Martorell**—*pop pl* PR-3
Martos Tank—*reservoir* NM-5
Marts Branch—*stream* KY-4
Marts Hollow—*valley* WV-2
Mart Shop Ctr—*locale* MO-7
Marts Pasture—*flat* UT-8
Martt Cem—*cemetery* OH-6
**Martville**—*pop pl* NY-2
Martville Cem—*cemetery* NY-2
Mart Whitt Fork—*stream* KY-4
Martwick—*locale* KY-4
Marty—*locale* OK-5
**Marty**—*pop pl* MN-6
**Marty**—*pop pl* SD-7
*Marty Lake* MI-6
Marty Lake—*lake* NE-7
Marty Lake—*lake* WI-6
Marty Lake—*swamp* MN-6
Martyn HS—*school* LA-4
Marty Ranch—*locale* SD-7
Martyrs Cem—*cemetery* WI-6
Martyrs Ch—*church* PA-2
Martyrs Cross—*other* NM-5
Marty Sch—*school* SD-7
Martys Island—*island* PA-2
*Marty's Lake* WI-6
*Martz* IN-6
Martzahn, August F., House—*hist pl* IA-7
Martz Creek—*stream* IN-6
Martz Ditch—*canal* IN-6
**Martz (Middlebury)**—*pop pl* IN-6
Martz Sch (abandoned)—*school* PA-2
Martzville—*locale* PA-2
Maruca Canyon—*valley* NM-5
Maruca Spring—*spring* NM-5
Maruche Canyon—*valley* NM-5
Marueno—*CDP* PR-3
**Marueno**—*pop pl* PR-3
Marueno (Barrio)—*fmr MCD* PR-3
Marufa Vega Trail—*trail* TX-5
Marugg Company—*hist pl* TN-4
Marugg Creek—*stream* CO-8
*Maru Island* FM-9
*Marukiyoku* PW-9
*Marukurabeshiku Mtn* PW-9
*Marukurabeshiku-San* PW-9
*Marumaru-to* MP-9
Marumsco—*locale* MD-2
**Marumsco Acres**—*pop pl* VA-3
Marumsco Acres Creek—*stream* VA-3
Marumsco Acres Lake—*lake* VA-3
Marumsco Creek—*stream* MD-2
Marumsco Creek—*stream* VA-3
**Marumsco Hills**—*pop pl* VA-3
Marumsco Hills Sch—*school* VA-3
Marumsco Marsh—*swamp* MD-2
*Marumsco Point* MD-2
Marumsco Sch—*school* VA-3
**Marumsco Village**—*pop pl* VA-3
**Marumsco Woods**—*pop pl* VA-3
Maru Mtn—*summit* MH-9
Marun Sch—*school* MO-7
*Marupo Saki* MH-9
*Maruppu Island* MP-9
Maruppu Island—*island* MP-9
*Maruppu-to* MP-9
Maruqruq—*slope* FM-9
Maruro Lake—*lake* AK-9
*Maru'ru'* FM-9
*Maru-to* FM-9
*Maruuru* FM-9
Marval—*locale* OR-9
Marva Lakes—*lake* OH-6
*Marvel* OH-6
*Marvel* OR-9
Marvel—*locale* WV-2
**Marvel**—*pop pl* AL-4
**Marvel**—*pop pl* CO-8
Marvel, Theodore L., House—*hist pl* MA-1
Marvel Canyon—*valley* CA-9
Marvel Cave—*cave* (2) MO-7
Marvel Cave—*locale* MO-7
Marvel Cave Hollow—*valley* MO-7
Marvel Cave Park—*post sta* MO-7
Marvel Cem—*cemetery* CO-8
Marvel Cem—*cemetery* MS-4
Marvel Ch—*church* AL-4
**Marvel Creek**—*pop pl* AK-9
Marvel Creek—*stream* AK-9
Marvel Creek—*stream* IA-7
Marvel Dome—*summit* AK-9
**Marvel Gardens**—*pop pl* PA-2
**Marvell**—*pop pl* AR-4
Marvell Acad—*school* AR-4
**Marvella Heights Subdivision**—*pop pl* UT-8
Marvell Creek—*stream* MT-8
Marvel Number 2 Slope Mine (underground)—*mine* AL-4
Marvel Park—*park* KS-7
Marvel Ranch—*locale* (2) NV-8
*Marvel Rock Baptist Church* MS-4
Marvel Rsvr—*reservoir* OR-9
**Marvels**—*pop pl* TX-5
*Marvels Cross Roads* DE-2
Marvels Crossroads—*locale* DE-2
Marve Well—*well* NM-5
Marvey Ch—*church* GA-3
**Mar Vian Subdivision**—*pop pl* UT-8
*Marvin* AL-4
*Marvin* KS-7
Marvin—*locale* MO-7
Marvin—*locale* TN-4
Marvin—*locale* (2) TX-5
Marvin—*locale* VA-3
**Marvin**—*pop pl* NY-2
**Marvin**—*pop pl* NC-3
**Marvin**—*pop pl* SD-7
Marvin, Dr. J. B., House—*hist pl* KY-4
Marvin, Lake—*reservoir* GA-3
Marvin, Lake—*reservoir* TX-5
**Marvina**—*pop pl* FL-3
Marvin Allen Ch—*church* TX-5
Marvin Ave Sch—*school* CA-9
Marvin Branch—*stream* NC-3
Marvin Butte—*summit* SD-7
Marvin Cem—*cemetery* (2) AL-4
Marvin Cem—*cemetery* AR-4
Marvin Cem—*cemetery* KS-7
Marvin Cem—*cemetery* (3) MS-4
Marvin Cem—*cemetery* PA-2
Marvin Ch—*church* AL-4
Marvin Ch—*church* (2) GA-3
Marvin Ch—*church* MS-4
Marvin Ch—*church* (3) NC-3
Marvin Ch—*church* TX-5
Marvin Ch—*church* VA-3
Marvin Chapel—*church* (3) AL-4
Marvin Chapel—*church* MS-4
Marvin Chapel—*church* (3) MO-7
Marvin Chapel—*church* (3) TN-4
Marvin Chapel—*church* VA-3
Marvin Chapel—*church* (7) WV-2
Marvin Chapel—*locale* TN-4
Marvin Chapel (abandoned)—*church* MO-7
*Marvin Chapel Assembly of God Ch* AL-4
Marvin Chapel Cem—*cemetery* (2) AL-4
Marvin Chapel Cem—*cemetery* CA-9
Marvin Chapel Cem—*cemetery* TX-5
*Marvin Chapel Church* AL-4
Marvin Chapel Sch (historical)—*school* TN-4
Marvin Ch (historical)—*church* MS-4
Marvin College Boys Dormitory—*hist pl* KY-4
Marvin Creek—*stream* (2) PA-2
*Marvin Creek Dam* PA-2
Marvin Creek Oil Field—*oilfield* PA-2
Marvin D Adams Waterway—*canal* FL-3
**Marvindale**—*pop pl* PA-2
Marvin Draw—*valley* MT-8
Marvine, Mount—*summit* UT-8
*Marvine Creek* UT-8
Marvine Creek—*stream* CO-8
Marvine Creek Campground—*locale* CO-8
Marvine Elem Sch—*school* PA-2
Marvine Glacier—*glacier* AK-9
Marvine Lakes—*lake* CO-8
*Marvine Mountain* CO-8
*Marvine Peak* CO-8
*Marvine Sch* PA-2
Marvine Shaft—*mine* PA-2
Marvin Fast Dam—*dam* OR-9
Marvin Fast Rsvr—*reservoir* OR-9
Marvin Hill—*summit* NH-1
Marvin Hill Cem—*cemetery* AL-4
Marvin Hill Cem—*cemetery* MS-4
Marvin Hill Ch—*church* AL-4
Marvin Hill Ch—*church* MS-4
*Marvin Hill Congregational Methodist Ch* MS-4
Marvin Hollow—*valley* NY-2
Marvin Hollow—*valley* TN-4
Marvin Huff Cem—*cemetery* MS-4
*Marvin Island* NH-1
Marvin Key—*island* FL-3
Marvin Lake—*lake* KS-7
Marvin Lake—*lake* MN-6
Marvin Lake—*reservoir* MN-6
Marvin Memorial Library—*hist pl* OH-6
*Marvin Methodist Church* MS-4
Marvin Park—*park* NY-2
*Marvin Parker Lake* AL-4
Marvin Parker Lake Dam Number Two—*dam* AL-4
Marvin Parker Lake Dam Number 1—*dam* AL-4
Marvin Parker Lake Number One—*reservoir* AL-4
Marvin Parker Lake Number Two—*reservoir* AL-4
Marvin Pass—*gap* CA-9
Marvin Place—*locale* WY-8
Marvin Playground—*park* OH-6
Marvin Pond—*lake* FL-3
Marvin Pond—*lake* NY-2
Marvin Ranch—*locale* CA-9
Marvin Reinhold Dam Number 1—*dam* SD-7
Marvin Ridge—*ridge* CT-1
Marvin Run—*stream* PA-2
*Marvins Bluff* TN-4
Marvins Bluff Landing—*locale* TN-4
Marvin Sch—*school* AR-4
Marvin Sch—*school* CA-9
Marvin Sch—*school* CT-1
Marvin Sch—*school* MA-1
Marvin Sch—*school* (2) MO-7
Marvin Sch—*school* TX-5
*Marvins Chapel* AL-4
Marvins Chapel—*church* KY-4
**Marvins Chapel**—*pop pl* MS-4
Marvins Chapel Cem—*cemetery* TN-4
*Marvins Chapel Methodist Church* MS-4
*Marvins Chapel United Methodist Church* TN-4
Marvin Sch (historical)—*school* MS-4
*Marvin Schnose Number 1 Dam* SD-7
*Marvin Schnose Number 2 Dam* SD-7
Marvins Creek—*stream* MN-6
Marvin Spring—*spring* UT-8
Marvins Store—*locale* GA-3
**Marvins Subdivision**—*pop pl* UT-8
Marvin Tank—*reservoir* AZ-5
Marvin Tavern—*hist pl* CT-1
*Marvin Terrace* MO-7
Marvin United Methodist Ch—*church* MS-4
Marvin United Methodist Ch—*church* TN-4
Marvinville—*locale* AR-4
**Mar Vista**—*pop pl* CA-9
Mar Vista HS—*school* CA-9
Mar Vista JHS—*school* CA-9
Mar Vista Recreation Center—*park* CA-9
Mar Vista Sch—*school* (2) CA-9
**Mar Vista Subdivision**—*pop pl* UT-8
Marvon Creek—*stream* MI-6
*Marvricio Canyon* CO-8
*Marvricio Creek* CO-8
**Marvyn**—*pop pl* AL-4
Marvyn Lake (historical)—*lake* AL-4
Marwin, Lake—*lake* OH-6
Marwitz Windmill—*locale* CO-8
**Marwood**—*pop pl* PA-2
Marwood Cem—*cemetery* MS-4
*Marwood Church* IN-6
Marwood Southern Baptist Ch—*church* IN-6
*Marx* MS-4
Marx Coulee—*valley* MN-6
Marx Dam—*dam* OR-9
Marxhausen Sch—*school* MI-6
**Marx (historical)**—*pop pl* OR-9
Marx House—*hist pl* MI-6
Marx Playground—*park* MI-6
Marx Pond—*reservoir* NY-2
Marx Rsvr—*reservoir* OR-9
**Marxville**—*pop pl* WI-6
*Mary* KS-7
*Mary* MP-9
Mary—*locale* AL-4
Mary—*locale* KY-4
**Mary**—*pop pl* SC-3
Mary, Lake—*lake* AL-4
Mary, Lake—*lake* AK-9
Mary, Lake—*lake* CA-9
Mary, Lake—*lake* (5) FL-3
Mary, Lake—*lake* (3) MI-6
Mary, Lake—*lake* (9) MN-6
Mary, Lake—*lake* MT-8
Mary, Lake—*lake* (2) ND-7
Mary, Lake—*lake* OR-9
Mary, Lake—*lake* SD-7
Mary, Lake—*lake* (2) WA-9
Mary, Lake—*lake* (4) WI-6
Mary, Lake—*reservoir* AL-4
Mary, Lake—*reservoir* (2) AZ-5
Mary, Lake—*reservoir* CA-9
Mary, Lake—*reservoir* CO-8
Mary, Lake—*reservoir* (2) GA-3
Mary, Lake—*reservoir* MS-4
Mary, Lake—*reservoir* TX-5
Mary, Lake—*reservoir* UT-8
Mary, Lake (Old River Lake)—*lake* MS-4
Mary, Point—*cape* FL-3
*Mary A Alley Hospital* MA-1
Mary Abbott Sch—*school* CT-1
Mary A Canyon—*valley* AZ-5
**Mary Alice**—*pop pl* KY-4
Mary Alice, Lake—*lake* CO-8
Mary Alice Creek—*stream* CO-8
Mary Alice Park—*park* GA-3
Mary Alice Rsvr—*reservoir* WY-8
Mary Allen Coll—*school* TX-5
*Mary Allen Junior Coll* TX-5
*Mary Allen Seminary* TX-5
Mary Allen Seminary for Colored Girls, Administration Bldg—*hist pl* TX-5
Mary Anderson Bay—*bay* AK-9
Mary and Joseph Ch—*church* MN-6
Mary and Martha Ch—*church* NC-3
**Maryan Estates Subdivision**—*pop pl* UT-8
Mary Anna Mine—*mine* CA-9
Mary Ann Canyon—*valley* NV-8
Mary Ann Ch—*church* SC-3
Mary Ann Creek—*stream* MN-6
Maryann Creek—*stream* MT-8
Mary Ann Creek—*stream* NJ-2
Mary Ann Creek—*stream* WA-9
Mary Ann Davis Grant—*civil* (2) FL-3
Mary Ann Drake Dam—*dam* AL-4
Mary Ann Draw—*valley* OR-9
Mary Anne Branch—*stream* GA-3
Mary Anne Branch—*stream* SC-3
Maryanne Mine—*mine* NV-8
Maryanne Spring—*spring* OR-9
*Mary Ann Furnace* PA-2
Mary Ann Furnace—*locale* NJ-2
Mary Ann Garber Elem Sch—*school* TN-4
Mary Ann Gulch—*valley* MT-8
Mary Ann Hollow—*valley* AL-4
Mary Ann Lake—*lake* WA-9
Mary Ann Mine—*mine* CO-8
Mary Ann Mine—*mine* MT-8
Maryann Mine—*mine* NV-8
Mary Ann Pond—*swamp* FL-3
Mary Ann Ridge—*ridge* CA-9
*Mary Ann Rock* MA-1
Mary Ann Rocks—*bar* MA-1
Mary Ann Run—*stream* WV-2
Mary Ann Sch—*school* OH-6
Mary Anns Pond—*bay* NC-3
**Mary Ann (Township of)**—*pop pl* OH-6
Mary A Oil Field—*oilfield* KS-7
*Maryar* FM-9
Maryatta Ch—*church* WV-2
Mary Austin, Mount—*summit* CA-9
Mary Baker Lake—*lake* MT-8
Mary Baldwin Coll—*school* VA-3
Mary Baldwin College, Main Bldg—*hist pl* VA-3
Mary B Austin Elem Sch—*school* AL-4
Mary Bay—*bay* WY-8
*Mary Beck School* IN-6
Marybelle Ch—*church* FL-3
Mary Belle Falls—*falls* WA-9
Mary Belle Mines—*mine* KY-4
Mary Bethel Ch—*church* (2) MS-4
**Mary Beth Park (subdivision)**—*pop pl* NC-3
*Mary Bethune Elementary School* MS-4
Marybill—*locale* WV-2
Mary Bird Branch—*stream* VA-3
Mary B Island—*island* MT-8
Mary Blaine Meadow—*flat* CA-9
Mary Blaine Mtn—*summit* CA-9
Mary Blue Mine—*mine* ID-8
Mary Bowers Pond—*bay* LA-4
Mary Branan Ch—*church* GA-3
Mary Branch—*stream* AL-4
Mary Branch—*stream* FL-3
Mary Branch—*stream* (2) KY-4
Mary Branch—*stream* (2) LA-4
Mary Branch—*stream* (2) NC-3
Mary Branch—*stream* SC-3
Mary Branch—*stream* TN-4
Mary Branch—*stream* WV-2
Mary Branch Ch—*church* WV-2
Mary Bray Ditch—*canal* CO-8
Mary Brown Bridge—*bridge* MN-6
Mary Brown Brook—*stream* CT-1
Mary Brown Brook—*stream* RI-1
Mary Brown Pond—*reservoir* CT-1
Mary B Sharpe Elem Sch—*school* PA-2
Mary Bull Hollow—*valley* TN-4
Mary Calder Golf Course—*other* GA-3
Mary Cane Lake—*lake* LA-4
Mary Carol Lake—*reservoir* KY-4
Mary Cashem Canyon—*valley* UT-8
Mary Ch—*church* NY-2
*Mary Chapel* AL-4
Mary Chapel—*church* NC-3
Mary Chapel—*church* OH-6
Mary Chapel—*church* (2) TN-4
Mary Chapel—*church* VA-3
Mary Chapel—*church* WV-2
**Mary Chapel**—*pop pl* TN-4
Mary Chapel Cem—*cemetery* NC-3
Mary Chapel Sch—*school* TN-4
Mary Church, The—*church* KY-4
Mary Clara Ch—*church* TN-4
Marycliff Acad—*school* MA-1
Marycliff-Cliff Park Hist Dist—*hist pl* WA-9
Marycliff HS—*school* WA-9
**Mary College**—*pop pl* ND-7
Mary Cooper Creek—*stream* WY-8
Mary Cove—*bay* GA-3
Mary Cox Bridge—*bridge* LA-4
Mary Crabtree Sch (historical)—*school* TN-4
Mary Crawford, Lake—*reservoir* MS-4
Mary Crawford Lake Dam—*dam* MS-4
Mary Creek—*bay* VI-3
Mary Creek—*stream* (2) AK-9
Mary Creek—*stream* GA-3
Mary Creek—*stream* WI-6
*Mary Crest* IL-6
Marycrest—*locale* NY-2
Marycrest Coll—*school* IA-7
Marycrest HS—*school* OR-9
Marycrest Sch—*school* CO-8
Marycrest Sch—*school* IL-6
Marycrest Sch—*school* OH-6
Mary C Williams Elem Sch—*school* NC-3
Mary C Womack HS—*school* TX-5
*Mary d* KS-7
*Mary-D* PA-2
**Maryd**—*pop pl* PA-2
Marydale—*locale* IL-6
Marydale—*locale* KY-4
Marydale Lake—*lake* LA-4
*Marydale Manor* IL-6
Marydale Plantation—*locale* LA-4
Marydale Scout Camp—*locale* LA-4
**Marydale (subdivision)**—*pop pl* DE-2
Mary Davis Branch—*stream* WV-2

Mason Valley—*basin* ... NV-8
Mason Valley—*locale* ... AR-4
Mason Valley—*valley* ... CA-9
Mason Valley Mine—*mine* ... NV-8
Mason Valley Township—*inact MCD* ... NV-8
Mason Valley (Township of)—*fmr MCD* ... AR-4
Mason Valley Truck Trail—*trail* ... CA-9
Mason Valley Wildlife Mngmt Area—*park* ... NV-8
*Masonville* ... RI-1
Masonville—*locale* ... KY-4
Masonville—*locale* ... WV-2
**Masonville**—*pop pl* ... AR-4
**Masonville**—*pop pl* ... CO-8
**Masonville**—*pop pl* ... IA-7
**Masonville**—*pop pl* ... KY-4
**Masonville**—*pop pl* ... MI-6
**Masonville**—*pop pl* ... NJ-2
**Masonville**—*pop pl* ... NY-2
**Masonville**—*pop pl* ... VA-3
Masonville—*uninc pl* ... MD-2
Masonville Ch—*church* ... PA-2
*Masonville Creek* ... NY-2
Masonville Creek—*stream* ... NY-2
Masonville (historical)—*locale* ... AL-4
*Masonville Methodist Church* ... AL-4
Masonville Post Office—*locale* ... CO-8
Masonville Sch—*school* ... KY-4
Masonville Sch—*school* ... VA-3
**Masonville (Town of)**—*pop pl* ... NY-2
**Masonville (Township of)**—*pop pl* ... MI-6
Mason-Watkins House—*hist pl* ... NH-1
Mason Well—*well* ... AZ-5
*Mason Wells Baptist Church* ... TN-4
Mason Wells Ch—*church* ... TN-4
Mason West (CCD)—*cens area* ... TX-5
Mason Windmill—*locale* ... NM-5
Mason Woods Village—*locale* ... MO-7
Mason Woods Village (Shop Ctr)—*locale* ... MO-7
Masopia Post Office (historical)—*building* ... SD-7
*Masorogu* ... MH-9
*Maspenock River* ... MA-1
**Maspeth**—*pop pl* ... NY-2
Maspeth Creek—*bay* ... NY-2
Maspeth Yards—*locale* ... NY-2
*Masphilion Creek* ... DE-2
*Maspillon Creek* ... DE-2
*Masquachug River* ... RI-1
*Masquetuc* ... NC-3
*Masquetuck* ... MA-1
*Mass* ... MI-6
**Mass**—*pop pl* ... MI-6
Massa—*locale* ... TX-5
*Massabeset River* ... CT-1
**Massabesic**—*pop pl* ... NH-1
Massabesic Lake—*lake* ... NH-1
Massac—*locale* ... KY-4
Massac Cem—*cemetery* ... KY-4
**Massac (County)**—*pop pl* ... IL-6
Massac Creek—*stream* ... IL-6
Massac Creek—*stream* ... KY-4
Massac Hosp—*hospital* ... IL-6
Massachuetts Hornfels-Braintree Slate Quarry—*hist pl* ... MA-1
*Massachusets Bay* ... MA-1
*Massachusett* ... MA-1
Massachusetts—*hist pl* ... IN-6
*Massachusetts Audubon Sanctuary* ... MA-1
Massachusetts Ave Baptist Ch—*church* ... FL-3
Massachusetts Ave Commercial District—*hist pl* ... IN-6
Massachusetts Ave Hist Dist—*hist pl* ... DC-2
Massachusetts Ave Hist Dist—*hist pl* ... MA-1
Massachusetts Bay—*bay* ... MA-1
Massachusetts Bay Community Coll—*school* ... MA-1
Massachusetts Block—*hist pl* ... WI-6
Massachusetts Bog—*reservoir* ... ME-1
Massachusetts Bog Stream—*stream* ... ME-1
Massachusetts Correctional Institute—*building* (2) ... MA-1
Massachusetts Correctional Institute Walpole—*locale* ... MA-1
Massachusetts Correctional Institution—*locale* ... MA-1
Massachusetts Correctional Institution Forestry Camp—*locale* ... MA-1
*Massachusotts Fort* ... MA-1
Massachusetts General Hosp—*hist pl* ... MA-1
Massachusetts Gore—*unorg* ... ME-1
Massachusetts Grove—*woods* ... CA-9
Massachusetts Hall, Bowdoin College—*hist pl* ... ME-1
Massachusetts Hall, Harvard Univ—*hist pl* ... MA-1
*Massachusetts Hill* ... MA-1
Massachusetts Historical Society Bldg—*hist pl* ... MA-1
Massachusetts Institute Of Technology—*school* ... MA-1
Massachusetts Maritime Acad—*school* ... MA-1
Massachusetts Mill—*locale* ... MA-1
Massachusetts Mtn—*summit* ... NV-8
Massachusetts Natl Gaurd Supply Depot—*locale* ... MA-1
Massachusetts Soldiers Home—*building* ... MA-1
Massachusetts State Archives—*building* ... MA-1
Massachusetts State Coll—*school* (2) ... MA-1
Massachusetts State Fish Hatchery—*locale* (3) ... MA-1
Massachusetts State Game Farm—*park* ... MA-1
Massachusetts State Hosp—*hospital* (3) ... MA-1
Massachusetts State Hospital Sch—*school* ... MA-1
Massachusetts Statehouse—*hist pl* ... MA-1
Massachusetts State Industrial Sch for Boys—*school* ... MA-1
Massachusetts State Industrial Sch For Girls—*school* ... MA-1
Massachusetts State Muster Ground (historical)—*locale* ... MA-1
Massachusetts State Pier—*locale* ... MA-1
Massachusetts State Service Center—*building* ... MA-1
Massachusetts Wasteway—*canal* ... MA-1
Massachusetts Youth Institution—*school* ... MA-1
*Massack* ... KY-4
**Massack**—*pop pl* ... CA-9
*Massack Creek* ... KY-4
Massack Creek—*stream* ... CA-9
*Massacocia Creek* ... VA-3
Massacoe Forest Pavilion—*hist pl* ... CT-1
Massacoe Spring—*spring* ... CT-1
Massacoe State For—*forest* ... CT-1
**Massacre**—*pop pl* ... IN-6
Massacre Bay—*bay* ... AK-9
Massacre Bay—*bay* ... WA-9
Massacre Bay—*bay* ... AS-9
Massacre Beach—*beach* ... AK-9
*Massacre Canyon* ... OR-9
Massacre Canyon—*valley* ... CA-9
Massacre Canyon—*valley* ... NE-7
Massacre Canyon—*valley* ... NM-5
Massacre Canyon Battlefield—*hist pl* ... NE-7
Massacre Canyon Historical Monument*—*park* ... NE-7
Massacre Cave—*cave* ... AZ-5
Massacre Cave Overlook—*locale* ... AZ-5
*Massacre Cave Ruins* ... AZ-5
*Massacre Creek* ... TX-5
Massacre Creek—*stream* ... ID-8
Massacre Creek—*stream* ... NV-8
Massacre Gap—*gap* ... NM-5
Massacre Grounds—*area* ... AZ-5
Massacre Hill—*summit* (2) ... WY-8
*Massacre Island* ... AL-4
*Massacre Island* ... MS-4
Massacre Lake—*lake* ... NV-8
Massacre Memorial State Park—*park* ... KS-7
*Massacre Mountain* ... OR-9
Massacre Mtn—*summit* ... ID-8
Massacre Peak—*summit* (2) ... NM-5
Massacre Point—*cliff* ... AZ-5
Massacre Pond—*lake* ... ME-1
Massacre Ranch—*locale* ... NV-8
Massacre Rocks—*summit* ... ID-8
Massacre Rocks State Park—*park* ... ID-8
Massacre Spring—*spring* ... NV-8
**Massac (sta.)**—*pop pl* ... KY-4
*Massad Dam* ... PA-2
**Massadona**—*pop pl* ... CO-8
*Massadonia Baptist Church* ... AL-4
Massadonia Ch—*church* ... NC-3
Massaemett Mtn—*summit* ... MA-1
Massai Point—*summit* ... AZ-5
Massalene Sch—*school* ... FL-3
Massalina Bayou—*bay* ... FL-3
*Massanamisco Plantation* ... MA-1
Massanetta Springs—*locale* ... VA-3
Massanova Ch—*church* ... VA-3
Massanutten Caverns—*cave* ... VA-3
Massanutten Military Acad—*school* ... VA-3
*Massanutten Mountains* ... VA-3
Massanutten Mountain Trail—*trail* ... VA-3
Massanutten Mtn—*range* ... VA-3
Massanutten Peak—*summit* ... VA-3
*Massanuttin Mtn* ... VA-3
Massanutton Heights—*hist pl* ... VA-3
*Massanutton Mountain* ... VA-3
Massapeag—*locale* ... CT-1
**Massapequa**—*pop pl* ... NY-2
Massapequa Creek—*stream* ... NY-2
Massapequa HS—*school* ... NY-2
Massapequa Lake—*reservoir* ... NY-2
**Massapequa Park**—*pop pl* ... NY-2
Massapequa Preserve—*park* ... NY-2
**Massapoag**—*pop pl* ... NC-3
Massapoag Brook—*stream* ... MA-1
Massapoag Lake—*lake* ... MA-1
*Massapoag Pond* ... MA-1
Massapoag Pond—*lake* ... MA-1
Massapoag Pond—*reservoir* ... MA-1
Massapoag Pond Dam—*dam* ... MA-1
Massapoag Ponds—*reservoir* ... MA-1
*Massapog Pond* ... MA-1
*Massapomock Creek* ... VA-3
Massaponax—*locale* ... VA-3
**Massaponax**—*pop pl* ... VA-3
Massaponax Creek—*stream* ... VA-3
*Massaponax River* ... VA-3
**Massaponax (sta.)**—*pop pl* ... VA-3
Massar and Koenig Cem—*cemetery* ... OH-6
**Massard**—*pop pl* ... AR-4
Massard Creek—*stream* ... AR-4
Massaro Park—*park* ... NY-2
*Massasal Mountains* ... AZ-5
Massasecum, Lake—*lake* ... NH-1
*Massasinaway River* ... IN-6
*Massasoit* ... KS-7
Massasoit Coll—*school* ... MA-1
Massasoit Creek—*stream* ... KS-7
Massasoit Fire House No. 5—*hist pl* ... MA-1
*Massasoit Lake* ... MA-1
**Massasoit (subdivision)**—*pop pl* ... MA-1
**Massa Subdivision**—*pop pl* ... UT-8
*Massatayun Creek* ... NY-2
Massa Tunnel—*tunnel* ... CA-9
**Massawepie**—*pop pl* ... NY-2
Massawepie Creek—*stream* ... NY-2
Massawepie Lake—*lake* ... NY-2
Massawepie Pond—*lake* ... NY-2
Massawippa, Lake—*lake* ... NY-2
**Massbach**—*pop pl* ... IL-6
Massbach Cem—*cemetery* ... IL-6
Mass Canyon—*valley* ... ID-8
Mass Canyon—*valley* ... MT-8
**Mass City**—*pop pl* ... MI-6
*Mass Creek* ... OK-5
Mass Creek—*stream* ... MT-8
Mass Creek—*stream* ... TX-5
*Masscuppic Lake* ... MA-1
Masse Branch—*stream* ... GA-3
*Masse Creek* ... TX-5
Masse Creek—*stream* ... MN-6
**Massee**—*pop pl* ... GA-3
Massee Lane—*hist pl* ... GA-3
**Massena**—*pop pl* ... IA-7
**Massena**—*pop pl* ... NY-2
Massena, Lake—*reservoir* ... OK-5
Massena Beach—*beach* ... NY-2
*Massena Canal* ... NY-2
Massena Cem—*cemetery* ... IA-7
**Massena Center**—*pop pl* ... NY-2
Massena-Cornwall International Bridge—*bridge* ... NY-2
Massena Country Club—*other* ... NY-2
Massena Intake Dam—*dam* ... NY-2
Massena Power Canal—*canal* ... NY-2
**Massena Springs**—*pop pl* ... NY-2
**Massena (Town of)**—*pop pl* ... NY-2
Massena Township—*fmr MCD* ... IA-7
Massenburg-Henderson Cem—*cemetery* ... AL-4
Massenburg Plantation—*hist pl* ... NC-3
*Massengale Mill* ... TN-4
Massengale Mtn—*summit* ... TN-4
Massengale Point—*cape* ... TN-4
Massengill Airp—*airport* ... NC-3
Massengill Bend—*bend* ... TN-4
Massengill Branch—*stream* ... TN-4
Massengill Bridge—*bridge* ... TN-4
Massengill Cave—*cave* ... TN-4
Massengill Cem—*cemetery* (2) ... TN-4
Massengill Hollow—*valley* (2) ... TN-4
Massengill Island (historical)—*island* ... TN-4
Massengill Lake Dam—*dam* ... MS-4
Massengill Memorial—*other* ... TN-4
Massengill Mill—*locale* ... TN-4
Massengill Mill Pond—*reservoir* ... NC-3
Massengill Mill Pond Dam—*dam* ... NC-3
Massengill Spring—*spring* ... TN-4
Massengill Spring Branch—*stream* ... TN-4
*Massenteean Brook* ... NH-1
Masses Chapel—*church* ... NC-3
**Massey**—*pop pl* ... AL-4
**Massey**—*pop pl* ... IA-7
**Massey**—*pop pl* ... MD-2
Massey, Louise, House—*hist pl* ... NM-5
Massey, Thomas, House—*hist pl* ... PA-2
Massey Bar—*bar* ... AR-4
Massey Bench—*bench* ... CO-8
*Massey Branch* ... CO-8
Massey Branch—*stream* (2) ... AL-4
Massey Branch—*stream* ... CO-8
Massey Branch—*stream* ... DE-2
Massey Branch—*stream* ... MD-2
Massey Branch—*stream* ... MS-4
Massey Branch—*stream* ... MO-7
Massey Branch—*stream* ... NC-3
Massey Branch—*stream* (2) ... TN-4
Massey Branch—*stream* (3) ... TX-5
**Masseyburg**—*pop pl* ... PA-2
Massey Cabin—*locale* ... CO-8
Massey Cave—*cave* ... TN-4
Massey Cem—*cemetery* (2) ... AL-4
Massey Cem—*cemetery* (3) ... AR-4
Massey Cem—*cemetery* ... GA-3
Massey Cem—*cemetery* (2) ... IN-6
Massey Cem—*cemetery* ... KY-4
Massey Cem—*cemetery* ... MS-4
Massey Cem—*cemetery* (3) ... NC-3
Massey Cem—*cemetery* ... OK-5
Massey Cem—*cemetery* (5) ... TN-4
Massey Cem—*cemetery* (3) ... WV-2
Massey Chapel—*church* ... DE-2
Massey Chapel—*church* ... NC-3
Massey Chapel (historical)—*church* ... TN-4
*Massey Cove* ... AL-4
Massey Creek—*stream* ... AL-4
Massey Creek—*stream* ... AR-4
Massey Creek—*stream* (2) ... IN-6
Massey Creek—*stream* ... MD-2
Massey Creek—*stream* ... MS-4
Massey Creek—*stream* ... MO-7
Massey Creek—*stream* ... MT-8
Massey Creek—*stream* ... OK-5
Massey Creek—*stream* ... OR-9
Massey Creek—*stream* (2) ... VA-3
Massey Ditch—*canal* ... DE-2
Massey Draughton Business Coll—*school* ... AL-4
Massey Draw—*valley* ... CO-8
Massey Draw—*valley* ... WY-8
Massey-Ferguson Plant—*facility* ... OH-6
Massey-Ferguson Pond—*reservoir* ... GA-3
Massey-Good Branch—*stream* ... TX-5
Massey Gulch—*valley* ... CO-8
*Massey Hill* ... NH-1
Massey Hill—*locale* ... GA-3
Massey Hill—*uninc pl* ... NC-3
Massey Hill Athletic Field—*locale* ... NC-3
Massey Hill Sch—*school* ... NC-3
*Massey Hollow* ... TN-4
Massey Hollow—*valley* ... AR-4
Massey Hollow—*valley* ... OH-6
Massey Hollow—*valley* ... TN-4
Massey Hollow—*valley* (2) ... TX-5
Massey Hollow—*valley* ... WV-2
Massey Hotel—*hist pl* ... AR-4
Massey Lake—*lake* ... MI-6
Massey Lake—*lake* (2) ... TX-5
Massey Lake—*locale* ... TX-5
Massey Lake—*reservoir* ... AL-4
Massey Lake—*reservoir* ... TN-4
Massey Lake Dam—*dam* ... MS-4
Massey Lake Slough—*gut* ... TX-5
Massey Landing—*locale* ... DE-2
**Masseyline**—*pop pl* ... AL-4
Massey Marsh—*swamp* ... DE-2
*Massey Mill* ... GA-3
Massey Mine (underground)—*mine* ... AL-4
Massey Mtn—*summit* ... AR-4
Massey Mtn—*summit* ... TX-5
**Massey Point**—*pop pl* ... OK-5
Massey Pond Dam—*dam* ... MS-4
Massey Ponds—*reservoir* ... TX-5
Massey Post Office (historical)—*building* ... AL-4
Massey Ranch—*locale* ... FL-3
Massey Sch—*school* ... IA-7
Massey Sch (historical)—*school* ... AL-4
Massey Sch (historical)—*school* ... MS-4
Massey Sewage Lagoon Dam—*dam* ... MS-4
Masseys Lake—*reservoir* ... GA-3
*Masseys Landing* ... DE-2
Masseys Mill (historical)—*locale* ... TN-4
Masseys Millpond—*reservoir* ... DE-2
Masseys Pond—*reservoir* ... AL-4
Massey Spring—*spring* ... KY-4
Massey Tank—*reservoir* (2) ... NM-5
Masseyville—*locale* ... GA-3
**Masseyville**—*pop pl* ... TN-4
**Masseyville**—*pop pl* ... WV-2
Masseyville Cem—*cemetery* ... TN-4
Masseyville Post Office (historical)—*building* ... TN-4
Masseyville Sch (historical)—*school* ... TN-4
Massey Well—*well* ... AZ-5
Massey Wharf—*locale* ... VA-3
Massey Windmill—*locale* ... WY-8
Massey Yard—*locale* ... NY-2
Mass Grave of the Mexican Miners—*hist pl* ... OK-5
*Massick's Creek* ... OH-6
**Massie**—*pop pl* ... NV-8
**Massie**—*pop pl* ... VA-3
Massie Branch—*stream* ... VA-3
Massie Common Sch House—*hist pl* ... GA-3
*Massie Creek* ... OH-6
Massie Creek—*stream* ... MO-7
Massie Field—*park* ... MI-6
Massie Gap—*gap* ... NC-3
Massie Gap—*gap* ... VA-3
Massie House—*hist pl* ... VA-3
Massie Island—*island* ... MO-7
Massie Knob—*summit* ... OH-6
Massie Lagoon—*swamp* ... NE-7
Massie Lake—*lake* ... WA-9
Massie (Magisterial District)—*fmr MCD* ... VA-3
Massie Memorial Ch—*church* ... VA-3
Massie Pond—*reservoir* ... VA-3
Massie Ranch—*locale* ... SD-7
Massie Ridge—*ridge* ... WV-2
Massie Run—*stream* ... OH-6
Massies Chapel—*church* ... KY-4
Massies Corner—*locale* ... VA-3
*Massie's Creek* ... OH-6
Massies Creek—*stream* ... OH-6
Massies Creek Cem—*cemetery* (2) ... OH-6
Massies Heaven—*summit* ... OH-6
Massie Slough—*swamp* ... NV-8
**Massies Mill**—*pop pl* ... VA-3
Massies Mill (Magisterial District)—*fmr MCD* ... VA-3
Massies Mill Sch—*school* ... VA-3
Massies Mtn—*summit* (2) ... VA-3
**Massie (Township of)**—*pop pl* ... OH-6
**Massieville**—*pop pl* ... OH-6
Massieville Cem—*cemetery* ... OH-6
Massie West Ranch—*locale* ... TX-5
*Massif, The* ... UT-8
*Massillion* ... OH-6
Massillon—*locale* ... AL-4
Massillon—*locale* ... IA-7
**Massillon**—*pop pl* ... IA-7
**Massillon**—*pop pl* ... OH-6
Massillon Cemetery Bldg—*hist pl* ... OH-6
Massillon Township—*fmr MCD* ... IA-7
Massilon Bridge—*other* ... IL-6
Massilon Cem—*cemetery* ... IN-6
Massilon (Township of)—*other* ... OH-6
**Massilon (Township of)**—*pop pl* ... IL-6
Massingale Branch—*stream* ... TN-4
Massingale Creek—*stream* ... TN-4
Massinger Corner—*locale* ... OR-9
Massingill Cem—*cemetery* ... TX-5
*Massive* ... UT-8
Massive, Mount—*summit* ... CO-8
Mass Lake—*lake* ... MN-6
Massman Sch (abandoned)—*school* ... MO-7
Mass Mtn—*summit* ... WY-8
Masso—*area* ... GU-9
Masson, Paul, Mountain Winery—*hist pl* ... CA-9
*Massongills Mill* ... TN-4
Masson Sch—*school* ... OH-6
Massopoag Ch—*church* ... NC-3
Masso River—*stream* ... GU-9
*Mass Pond* ... MD-2
Mass Spring—*spring* ... MT-8
**Mass (sta.)**—*pop pl* ... MI-6
Mass Station—*locale* ... MI-6
Massy Creek—*stream* ... NC-3
Massy Gulch—*valley* ... CO-8
Mast—*locale* ... NC-3
Masta Bay—*bay* ... MI-6
Mastadon Creek—*stream* ... AK-9
Mastadon Mine—*mine* ... AZ-5
Mastbaum Sch—*school* ... PA-2
Mast Bridge—*bridge* ... VA-3
*Mast Brook* ... ME-1
Mast Cem—*cemetery* (2) ... IN-6
Mast Cem—*cemetery* ... NC-3
Mast Cem—*cemetery* ... PA-2
Mast Cove—*bay* (2) ... ME-1
Mast Creek—*stream* ... AR-4
Mast Creek—*stream* ... OR-9
Mast Ditch—*canal* ... MT-8
Mastellar Ditch—*canal* ... IN-6
*Masten* ... DE-2
Masten—*locale* ... PA-2
Masten Butte—*summit* ... OR-9
Masten Cem—*cemetery* ... OR-9
Masten Creek—*stream* ... MN-6
*Masten Lake* ... NY-2
**Masten Lake**—*pop pl* ... NY-2
*Masten Pond* ... NY-2
Masten Ranch—*locale* ... TX-5
Mastens Corner—*locale* ... DE-2
**Masten's Corner**—*pop pl* ... DE-2
*Mastens Corners* ... DE-2
**Mastens Heights (trailer park)**—*pop pl* ... DE-2
Mastens Lake—*lake* ... NY-2
Masterbone Pond—*reservoir* ... CT-1
Master Feeders Eleven Incoporated Airp—*airport* ... KS-7
Master Key Mine—*mine* ... CO-8
Master Key of Countryside (Shop Ctr)—*locale* ... FL-3
Master Knob—*summit* ... TN-4
Masterman, Lake—*lake* ... MN-6
Masterman Hill—*summit* ... ME-1
Masterman Island—*island* ... ME-1
Master Mechanic's House—*hist pl* ... AZ-5
Master Mine—*mine* ... MT-8
Master Mining Camp—*locale* ... MT-8
Mastern Cut—*gap* ... GA-3
Masters—*locale* ... CO-8
**Masters**—*pop pl* ... LA-4
**Masters**—*pop pl* ... MO-7
Masters Bayou—*bay* ... FL-3
Masters Brook—*stream* ... ME-1
Masters Cem—*cemetery* ... AL-4
Masters Cem—*cemetery* (3) ... KY-4
Masters Cem—*cemetery* ... NC-3
Masters Cem—*cemetery* ... OH-6
Masters Cem—*cemetery* ... TX-5
Masters Ch—*church* ... GA-3
Master Sch (abandoned)—*school* ... PA-2
Masters Church, The—*church* ... OH-6
*Masters Corners* ... DE-2
Masters Creek—*stream* ... AK-9
Masters Creek—*stream* ... KY-4
Masters Creek—*stream* ... LA-4
Masters Field—*airport* ... KS-7
Masters Fork—*stream* ... IL-6
Masters Hill—*summit* ... CA-9
Masters Hill—*summit* ... MO-7
Masters Island—*island* ... FL-3
Masters Island—*island* ... ME-1
Masters Island—*island* ... MO-7
Masters Landing—*locale* ... FL-3
**Masters Landing (historical)**—*pop pl* ... OR-9
Masters Mill (historical)—*locale* ... TN-4
Masters Mtn—*summit* ... VT-1
*Masterson* ... AL-4
Masterson—*locale* ... TX-5
**Masterson**—*pop pl* ... TX-5
Masterson, Dr. J. R., House—*hist pl* ... NV-8
Masterson, Richard, House—*hist pl* ... KY-4
Masterson, Robert, House—*hist pl* ... MO-7
Masterson Campground—*locale* ... CA-9
Masterson Cem—*cemetery* ... AL-4
Masterson Cem—*cemetery* ... AR-4
Masterson Cem—*cemetery* ... TN-4
Masterson Ch—*church* ... AL-4
Masterson Creek—*stream* ... AL-4
Masterson Hollow—*valley* ... CA-9
Masterson Hollow—*valley* ... TN-4
Masterson Lake—*reservoir* ... TX-5
Masterson Meadow—*flat* ... CA-9
Masterson Meadow Creek—*stream* ... CA-9
Masterson Meadow Lake—*lake* ... CA-9
**Masterson Mill**—*pop pl* ... AL-4
Masterson Mill Lake Dam—*dam* ... AL-4
Masterson Oil Field—*oilfield* ... TX-5
Masterson Point—*cape* ... TX-5
Masterson Post Office (historical)—*building* ... AL-4
Masterson Sch—*school* ... TX-5
Masterson Sch (historical)—*school* ... AL-4
*Mastersons Creek* ... AL-4
Masterson Spring—*spring* ... NM-5
Masterson Spring—*spring* ... OR-9
**Mastersonville**—*pop pl* ... PA-2
Mastersonville Post Office (historical)—*building* ... PA-2
Masters Post Office—*locale* ... CO-8
Masters Run—*stream* ... WV-2
Masters Sch—*school* ... ND-7
Masters Sch (historical)—*school* ... AL-4
Masters School, The—*school* ... NY-2
Masterton Cem—*cemetery* ... OH-6
Masterton-Dusenberry House—*hist pl* ... NY-2
Mast Farm—*hist pl* ... NC-3
Mast Farm Inn—*park* ... NC-3
Mast Gap—*gap* ... NC-3
Mast General Store—*hist pl* ... NC-3
Mast General Store—*park* ... NC-3
*Mast Heath* ... ME-1
*Mast Hope* ... PA-2
**Masthope**—*pop pl* ... PA-2
Masthope Creek—*stream* ... PA-2
**Masthope Rapids**—*pop pl* ... PA-2
Masthope Ski Area—*locale* ... PA-2
**Mastic**—*pop pl* ... NY-2
**Mastic Beach**—*pop pl* ... NY-2
Mastick Sch—*school* ... CA-9
*Mastic River* ... NY-2
Mastic Rock—*other* ... AK-9
**Mastic-Shirley (sta.)**—*pop pl* ... NY-2
Mastiff, Mount—*summit* ... WA-9
Mastiff Mine—*mine* ... SD-7
*Mastin* ... KS-7
Mastin Brook—*stream* ... NH-1
Mastin Corners—*locale* ... NY-2
Mastin Lake Ch of Christ—*church* ... AL-4
Mastin Lake Ch of the Nazarene—*church* ... AL-4
Mastin Lake Park—*park* ... AL-4
Mastin Lake Sch—*school* ... AL-4
Mastins Corner—*locale* ... VA-3
*Mastinyale Creek* ... MT-8
Mast Knob—*summit* ... NC-3
Mast Lake—*lake* ... MI-6
**Mast Landing**—*pop pl* ... ME-1
Mast Mtn—*summit* ... AR-4
Mastodon—*locale* ... MI-6
Mastodon—*locale* ... NM-5
Mastodon Creek—*stream* (2) ... AK-9
Mastodon Creek—*stream* ... MI-6
Mastodon Dome—*summit* ... AK-9
Mastodon Fork—*stream* ... AK-9
Mastodon (historical)—*locale* ... MS-4
Mastodon Lake—*lake* ... IL-6
Mastodon Lake—*lake* ... MI-6
Mastodon Lake—*lake* ... NJ-2
Mastodon Mine—*mine* ... CA-9
Mastodon Mine—*mine* ... ID-8
Mastodon Mtn—*summit* ... ID-8
Mastodon Peak—*summit* ... CA-9
Mastodon Post Office (historical)—*building* ... MS-4
Mastodon State Park—*park* ... MO-7
**Mastodon (Township of)**—*pop pl* ... MI-6
Maston Creek—*stream* ... AK-9
Maston House—*hist pl* ... DE-2
Maston I (410L256)—*hist pl* ... TX-5
Maston Lake—*lake* ... MI-6
Maston No. 13 Stone Wall (410L249)—*hist pl* ... TX-5
Maston No. 52 (410L235)—*hist pl* ... TX-5
Maston Run—*stream* ... WV-2
Mastons Mill (historical)—*locale* ... AL-4
Mast Point—*cape* ... MI-6
Mastricola Sch—*school* ... NH-1
Mast Run—*stream* ... PA-2
Mastuxet Brook—*stream* ... RI-1
Mastuxet Cove—*bay* ... RI-1
Mast Yard—*locale* ... NH-1
Mast Yard State For—*forest* ... NH-1
Masu Creek—*stream* ... AK-9
Masukatalik Creek—*stream* ... AK-9
Masuk HS—*school* ... CT-1
*Ma-su-la Creek* ... MT-8
Masur House—*hist pl* ... LA-4
**Masury**—*pop pl* ... OH-6
Masury Estate Ballroom—*hist pl* ... NY-2
Masury Point—*cape* ... NY-2
*Masu-Shima* ... FM-9
*Masushima To* ... FM-9
*Masu Sima* ... FM-9
*Masu To* ... FM-9
*Mat* ... MP-9
Mata—*area* ... GU-9
**Mata**—*pop pl* ... PR-3
Mataae Point—*cape* ... AS-9
Mataalaosagamai Ridge—*ridge* ... AS-9
Mataala Ridge—*ridge* ... AS-9
Mataalii Stream—*stream* ... AS-9
Mat'aan—*summit* ... FM-9
Mataavaloa Point—*cape* ... AS-9
*Matabezeke River* ... CT-1
*Mataches* ... MS-4
*Mataches Creek* ... MS-4
*Matacomba Key* ... FL-3
*Matacumba Key* ... FL-3
*Matacumbe Key* ... FL-3
*Matacut Harbor* ... MA-1
*Matade, Mount* ... FM-9
Mata de Canas (Barrio)—*fmr MCD* ... PR-3
*Matade Hill* ... FM-9
Mata de Platano (Barrio)—*fmr MCD* ... PR-3
*Matade Queen* ... VA-3
Matadequin Creek—*stream* ... VA-3
Matadero Canal—*canal* ... CA-9
Matadero Creek—*stream* ... CA-9
*Matade-san* ... FM-9
**Matador**—*pop pl* ... TX-5
Matador Camp—*locale* ... TX-5
Matador Coulee—*valley* ... MT-8
Matador North (CCD)—*cens area* ... TX-5
Matador Ranch—*locale* ... MT-8
Matador South (CCD)—*cens area* ... TX-5
Matador Tank—*reservoir* ... TX-5
Matador Wildlife Mngmt Area—*park* ... TX-5
Matador Windmill—*locale* ... TX-5
Matafanua JHS—*school* ... AS-9
Matafaofafine Peak—*summit* ... AS-9
Matafao Peak—*summit* ... AS-9
Matagamon Tote Road—*trail* ... ME-1
Matagimalie Stream—*stream* ... AS-9
Matagorda—*locale* ... MS-4
**Matagorda**—*pop pl* ... TX-5
*Matagorda Bay* ... TX-5
Matagorda Cem—*cemetery* ... TX-5
Matagorda Club—*other* ... TX-5
**Matagorda (County)**—*pop pl* ... TX-5
Matagorda Island—*island* ... TX-5
Matagorda Island AFB—*military* ... TX-5
Matagorda Island Bombing And Gunnery Range—*military* ... TX-5
Matagorda Island Lighthouse—*hist pl* ... TX-5
Matagorda Peninsula—*cape* ... TX-5
Matagorda-Sargent (CCD)—*cens area* ... TX-5
Mataguac—*area* ... GU-9
Mataguac Hill—*summit* ... GU-9
Mataguac Hill Command Post—*hist pl* ... GU-9
*Matagua Creek* ... CA-9
Mataguac Spring—*spring* ... GU-9
Matagual Creek—*stream* ... CA-9
Matagual Valley—*valley* ... CA-9
*Matagua Valley* ... CA-9
*Mataguay Creek* ... CA-9
*Mataguay Valley* ... CA-9
Matague—*area* ... GU-9
Matahpi Peak—*summit* ... MT-8
Matahunk Neck—*cape* ... VA-3
Matai Mtn—*summit* ... AS-9
Mataitaotao—*area* ... GU-9
Mataitutua Rock—*island* ... AS-9
*Matajuai Creek* ... CA-9
*Matajuai Valley* ... CA-9
*Matakees* ... MA-1
*Matakeeset Bay* ... MA-1
*Matakessett Bay* ... MA-1
Matala—*area* ... GU-9
*Matalai* ... PW-9
*Matalanim* ... FM-9
Matalanim Harbor—*harbor* ... FM-9
*Matalanin* ... FM-9
Matala Point—*cape* ... GU-9
*Matal Eigad* ... PW-9
Matalesolo Point—*cape* ... AS-9
Matalia Point—*island* ... AS-9
Matamaoaki—*bar* ... FM-9
Matamat Island—*island* ... MP-9
*Matamoras* ... OH-6
**Matamoras**—*pop pl* ... IN-6
**Matamoras**—*pop pl* (2) ... PA-2
Matamoras Borough—*civil* ... PA-2
**Matamoras (corporate name for New Matamoras)**—*pop pl* ... OH-6
Matamoras Post Office (historical)—*building* ... TN-4
Matamoras School and Ch—*church* ... PA-2
Matamoros Banco Number 121—*levee* ... TX-5
Matamoros Windmill—*locale* (2) ... NM-5
*Mat'an* ... FM-9
Matansa—*slope* ... MH-9
Matanuska—*locale* ... AK-9
Matanuska Glacier—*glacier* ... AK-9
Matanuska Lake—*lake* ... AK-9
Matanuska Peak—*summit* ... AK-9
Matanuska River—*stream* ... AK-9
**Matanuska-Susitna (Borough)**—*pop pl* ... AK-9
Matanuska-Susitna (Census Subarea)—*cens area* ... AK-9
Matanuska Valley—*valley* ... AK-9
*Matanza River* ... FL-3
*Matanzas* ... FL-3
Matanzas—*locale* ... IL-6
**Matanzas**—*pop pl* ... KY-4
**Matanzas Beach**—*pop pl* ... IL-6
Matanzas (CCD)—*cens area* ... FL-3
Matanzas Ch—*church* ... IL-6
Matanzas Creek—*stream* ... CA-9
Matanzas Inlet—*channel* ... FL-3
Matanzas Island—*island* ... IL-6
Matanzas Lake—*lake* ... IL-6
Matanzas Pass—*channel* ... FL-3
Matanzas River—*stream* ... FL-3
Matanzas Sch—*school* ... CA-9
Matanza Windmill—*locale* (2) ... TX-5
*Matapan* ... MA-1
Matapeake—*locale* ... MD-2
Matape Hill—*summit* ... AS-9
Mataponi Creek—*stream* ... MD-2
Matarana Gulch—*valley* ... CA-9
*Mataranimu* ... FM-9
*Mataranimu-Ko* ... FM-9
*Mataranium* ... FM-9
Mata Redonda—*island* ... PR-3
Mata Siete Spring—*spring* ... AZ-5
Matasina Stream—*stream* ... AS-9

*Mata Site Spring* AZ-5
Mata Spring—*spring* NM-5
*Matate Creek* TX-5
Matatula, Cape—*cape* AS-9
Matautuele Point—*cape* AS-9
Matautuloa Point—*cape* AS-9
Matautuloa Ridge—*ridge* AS-9
Matautuotafuna Point—*cape* AS-9
Matautu Point—*cape* AS-9
Matautu Ridge—*ridge* AS-9
Mataututele Point—*cape* AS-9
Matavai Point—*cape* AS-9
Matavai Stream—*stream* AS-9
Matavalu Ridge—*ridge* AS-9
Matawa Lake—*reservoir* NY-2
*Matawan* PA-2
**Matawan**—*pop pl* MN-6
**Matawan**—*pop pl* NJ-2
Matawan, Lake—*reservoir* NJ-2
Matawan Creek—*stream* NJ-2
*Matawan Lake* NJ-2
Matawan Point—*cape* NJ-2
Matawan Station—*hist pl* NJ-2
Matawan Station—*locale* NJ-2
*Matawan (Township of)* NJ-2
*Matayan* NJ-2
*Matayan Creek* NJ-2
*Matayan Point* NJ-2
Matay Canyon—*valley* CA-9
**Mata y Orsini**—*pop pl* PR-3
*Matazal Peak* AZ-5
*Matazals Mountains* AZ-5
*Mat-a-zell Mountains* AZ-5
**Match**—*pop pl* GA-3
**Match**—*pop pl* TN-4
*Matchamacormack Creek* NC-3
Matchaponix—*locale* NJ-2
Matchaponix Brook—*stream* NJ-2
Matcharak, Lake—*lake* AK-9
Match Creek—*stream* MI-6
Matche, Bayou—*gut* AL-4
Matchett Cem—*cemetery* FL-3
Matchett Lake—*lake* FL-3
Matchett Lake—*lake* MI-6
Matchett Point—*cape* FL-3
Matchett Sch—*school* MI-6
Matchetts Landing—*locale* AR-4
*Matchi Lake* MI-6
Matchin—*locale* CA-9
Matchless Gulch—*valley* ID-8
Matchless Mine—*mine* CO-8
Matchless Mtn—*summit* CO-8
Matchless Trail—*trail* CO-8
Matchotank Creek—*stream* VA-3
Match Pine Hollow—*valley* PA-2
Matchwood—*locale* MI-6
Matchwood Lookout Tower—*locale* MI-6
**Matchwood (Township of)**—*pop pl* MI-6
Matdan—*other* GU-9
Mate Cabin—*locale* OR-9
Matecjek Dam—*dam* ND-7
*Mate Creek* CA-9
Mate Creek—*stream* WV-2
Matecumbe Bight—*bay* FL-3
Matecumbe Harbor—*bay* FL-3
Matecumbe Keys—*island* FL-3
Matecumbe United Methodist Ch—*church* FL-3
*Mateen* SD-7
Mateer—*locale* PA-2
Mate Island—*island* NC-3
Matelot Gulch—*valley* CA-9
Matelot Rsvr—*reservoir* CA-9
Mateo Coast State Beaches—*beach* CA-9
Mateo Well (Windmill)—*locale* TX-5
Mater—*locale* NM-5
Mater—*other* KY-4
Mater Chrish HS—*school* NY-2
Mater Christi Sch—*school* IL-6
Mater Christi Seminary—*school* NY-2
Mater Cleri Seminary—*church* WA-9
Mater Dei Coll—*school* NY-2
Mater Dei HS—*school* CA-9
Mater Dei HS—*school* IL-6
Mater Dei HS—*school* IN-6
Mater Dei Provincial Lake—*reservoir* IN-6
Mater Dei Provincial Lake Dam—*dam* IN-6
*Mater Dei Sch* IN-6
Mater Dei Sch—*school* IN-6
Mater Delorosa Sch—*school* CA-9
Mater Dolorosa Cem—*cemetery* OR-9
Mater Dolorosa Sch—*school* PA-2
Mater Dolorosa Seminary—*school* IL-6
Materion Park—*park* MN-6
Mater Misericordia Acad—*school* PA-2
Maternity Cem—*cemetery* IL-6
Maternity Hill—*summit* ID-8
Maternity Hosp—*hist pl* MN-6
Maternity Well—*well* AZ-5
*Mates Branch* GA-3
*Mates Knob* GA-3
**Matewan**—*pop pl* WV-2
**Matfield**—*pop pl* MA-1
**Matfield Corner**—*pop pl* MA-1
**Matfield Green**—*pop pl* KS-7
Matfield Green Cem—*cemetery* KS-7
Matfield Green Service Facility—*locale* KS-7
Matfield (historical P.O.)—*locale* MA-1
**Matfield Junction**—*pop pl* MA-1
Matfield River—*stream* MA-1
Matfield Station (historical)—*locale* MA-1
**Matfield Township**—*pop pl* KS-7
Matgue—*area* GU-9
Matgue River—*stream* GU-9
Matgue River Valley Battle Area—*hist pl* GU-9
Mat Gulch—*valley* CO-8
Mat Gut—*gut* NJ-2
*Matha'* FM-9
Mathaag—*summit* FM-9
*Mathaaq* FM-9
Mathaire Park—*park* MN-6
*Mathakesett Bay* MA-1
Mathas Creek—*stream* OR-9
Mathay Dam (Pa-459)—*dam* PA-2
Mathay Run—*stream* PA-2
Mathay Run Pond—*reservoir* PA-2
*Math Branch* TN-4
Math Branch—*stream* MO-7
Math Branch—*stream* TN-4
**Mathena**—*pop pl* MS-4
Mathena Brake—*swamp* MS-4
Mathena Cem—*cemetery* MS-4
Mathena Cem—*cemetery* VA-3
Mathena Ch—*church* MS-4
*Matheny* WV-2
**Matheny**—*pop pl* (2) WV-2
Matheny Branch—*stream* TN-4
Matheny Camp—*locale* TN-4
Matheny Cem—*cemetery* KY-4
Matheny Cem—*cemetery* WV-2
Matheny Creek—*stream* OR-9
Matheny Creek—*stream* WA-9
Matheny Field—*airport* ND-7
**Matheny Grove**—*pop pl* TN-4
Matheny Grove Cem—*cemetery* TN-4
Matheny Grove Ch—*church* TN-4
Matheny Gulch—*valley* WA-9
Matheny Hollow—*valley* VA-3
Matheny Ridge—*ridge* WA-9
Matheny Sch—*school* IL-6
*Mather* CA-9
**Mather**—*pop pl* CA-9
**Mather**—*pop pl* PA-2
**Mather**—*pop pl* WI-6
Mather, Flora Stone, College District—*hist pl* OH-6
Mather, Mount—*summit* AK-9
Mather, Stephen Tyng, House—*hist pl* CT-1
Mather AFB—*military* CA-9
Mather Brothers Ranch—*locale* MT-8
Mather Building/Franklin & DeHaven Jewelers—*hist pl* WV-2
Mather Camp—*locale* OH-6
Mather (CCD)—*cens area* CA-9
Mather Cem—*cemetery* VT-1
Mather Creek—*stream* CA-9
Mather Ditch—*canal* (2) IN-6
**Mather Field**—*pop pl* CA-9
**Mather Field (Mather Air Force Base)**—*pop pl* CA-9
Mather Gorge—*valley* MD-2
Mather Grove—*woods* CA-9
**Mather Heights**—*pop pl* CA-9
Mather Heights Sch—*school* CA-9
Mather Homestead—*hist pl* CT-1
Mather HS—*school* IL-6
Mather Inn—*hist pl* MI-6
Mather JHS—*school* CT-1
Mather-Kirkland House—*hist pl* TX-5
Mather Lake—*reservoir* CA-9
Mather Lateral—*canal* IN-6
Matherly Cem—*cemetery* TN-4
Mather Memorial Hosp—*hospital* NY-2
Mather Mine A—*mine* MI-6
Mather Mine B—*mine* MI-6
Matherne, Bayou—*stream* LA-4
Matherne Cem—*cemetery* LA-4
Mather Park—*park* IL-6
Mather Park—*park* PA-2
Mather Pass—*gap* CA-9
*Mather Peak* WY-8
Mather Peaks—*summit* WY-8
Mather Point—*cliff* AZ-5
Mather Ranger Station—*locale* CA-9
Mathers Bridge—*bridge* FL-3
Mathers Cem—*cemetery* OH-6
Mather Sch—*school* SC-3
Mathers Chapel—*church* IN-6
Mathers Cove—*bay* FL-3
Mathers Mill—*locale* KY-4
Matherson Branch—*stream* NC-3
Matherson Brook—*stream* ME-1
Matherson Creek—*stream* NC-3
Matherson Pond—*lake* ME-1
Mathers Pond—*lake* CT-1
Mathers Run Trail—*trail* PA-2
**Matherton**—*pop pl* (2) MI-6
Matherville—*locale* MS-4
**Matherville**—*pop pl* IL-6
**Matherville**—*pop pl* MS-4
Matherville, Lake—*reservoir* IL-6
Matherville Cem—*cemetery* MS-4
Mathes Acad (historical)—*school* AL-4
*Mathes Canyon* UT-8
Mathes Cem—*cemetery* NH-1
Mathes Cem—*cemetery* TN-4
Mathes Hill—*summit* IN-6
Mathes Hill—*summit* MS-4
Matheson—*locale* CA-9
**Matheson**—*pop pl* CO-8
Matheson Cove—*valley* NC-3
*Matheson Creek* WY-8
Matheson Creek—*stream* MI-6
Matheson Creek—*stream* WY-8
Matheson Ditch—*canal* MT-8
Matheson Hammock County Park—*park* FL-3
Matheson Hill—*summit* CO-8
Matheson House—*hist pl* FL-3
Matheson Ranch—*locale* CA-9
Matheson Rsvr—*reservoir* CO-8
Matheson Sch—*school* UT-8
*Mathesons Mill* AL-4
Mathesons Millpond—*lake* SC-3
*Mathew* TN-4
Mathew Brown Branch—*stream* MO-7
Mathew Cem—*cemetery* MI-6
Mathew Cem—*cemetery* TN-4
Mathew Creek—*stream* NY-2
Mathew Creek—*stream* WA-9
Mathew Drop Structure—*dam* NV-8
Mathew Henson Park—*park* AZ-5
Mathew Kilgore Cem—*cemetery* CA-9
Mathew Meadow—*flat* WA-9
Mathew Mound—*hist pl* OH-6
Mathew Post Office (historical)—*building* TN-4
**Mathews**—*pop pl* GA-3
**Mathews**—*pop pl* LA-4
**Mathews**—*pop pl* ND-7
**Mathews**—*pop pl* PA-2
**Mathews**—*pop pl* VA-3
Mathews—*uninc pl* SC-3
Mathews, David, House—*hist pl* NY-2
Mathews, David, House—*hist pl* VT-1
Mathews, G. A., House—*hist pl* SD-7
Mathews, John Frank, Plantation—*hist pl* GA-3
Mathews, Lake—*reservoir* CA-9
Mathews, Nelson and Margret, House—*hist pl* OR-9
Mathews Arm—*ridge* VA-3
Mathews Brake—*lake* LA-4
Mathews Brake Natl Wildlife Ref—*park* MS-4
*Mathews Branch* KS-7
Mathews Branch—*stream* AL-4
Mathews Branch—*stream* NC-3
Mathews Branch—*stream* (2) TN-4
Mathews Bridge—*bridge* FL-3
Mathews Bridge—*bridge* TN-4
Mathews Brothers Number 1 Dam—*dam* SD-7
Mathews Brothers Number 2 Dam—*dam* SD-7
Mathews Canyon—*valley* NV-8
Mathews Canyon—*valley* NM-5
Mathews Canyon Dam—*dam* NV-8
Mathews Canyon Rsvr—*reservoir* NV-8
*Mathews Cem* MS-4
Mathews Cem—*cemetery* (3) AL-4
Mathews Cem—*cemetery* (2) GA-3
Mathews Cem—*cemetery* IL-6
Mathews Cem—*cemetery* KS-7
Mathews Cem—*cemetery* KY-4
Mathews Cem—*cemetery* MS-4
Mathews Cem—*cemetery* MO-7
Mathews Cem—*cemetery* NM-5
Mathews Cem—*cemetery* SC-3
Mathews Cem—*cemetery* WV-2
Mathews Ch—*church* AL-4
Mathews Ch—*church* NC-3
Mathews Ch—*church* VA-3
Mathews Chapel—*church* GA-3
Mathews Chapel—*church* MS-4
Mathews Chapel—*church* NC-3
Mathews Chapel—*church* VA-3
Mathews Corner—*locale* WA-9
Mathews Corners—*locale* DE-2
**Mathews (County)**—*pop pl* VA-3
Mathews County Courthouse Square—*hist pl* VA-3
**Mathews Courthouse**—*pop pl* VA-3
Mathews Cove—*bay* ME-1
Mathews Creamery (historical)—*locale* SD-7
*Mathews Creek* CA-9
*Mathews Creek* GA-3
*Mathews Creek* LA-4
Mathews Creek—*gut* SC-3
Mathews Creek—*stream* AL-4
Mathews Creek—*stream* AR-4
Mathews Creek—*stream* GA-3
Mathews Creek—*stream* NC-3
Mathews Creek—*stream* VA-3
*Mathews Creek - in part* TN-4
Mathews Crossing—*locale* MS-4
**Mathews Crossroads**—*pop pl* NC-3
Mathews Cut—*channel* SC-3
Mathews Dam—*dam* CA-9
Mathews Dam—*dam* VA-3
Mathews Dike—*levee* CA-9
Mathews Ditch—*canal* CA-9
Mathews Ditch—*canal* CO-8
Mathews Ditch—*canal* (2) IN-6
Mathews Dome—*summit* AK-9
Mathews Drain—*canal* MI-6
Mathews Eastern Ditch—*canal* CO-8
*Mathews Guard Station* OR-9
**Mathews Heights**—*pop pl* SC-3
*Mathews High School for Negroes* AL-4
Mathews Hill—*summit* ME-1
Mathews Hill Ch—*church* SC-3
Mathews (historical)—*locale* AL-4
Mathews House—*hist pl* OH-6
Mathews Island—*island* FL-3
Mathews Island—*island* ME-1
*Mathews Lake* NJ-2
Mathews Lake—*lake* WA-9
Mathews Lake—*reservoir* GA-3
Mathews Lake—*reservoir* TN-4
Mathews Lake—*reservoir* VA-3
Mathews Lake Dam—*dam* TN-4
**Mathews (Matthews)**—*pop pl* AL-4
Mathews Memorial Ch—*church* TN-4
Mathews Mill—*locale* CA-9
Mathews Mill (historical)—*locale* TN-4
Mathews Millpond—*lake* ME-1
Mathew-Smith Cem—*cemetery* OH-6
*Mathewson* KS-7
Mathewson Brook—*stream* VT-1
Mathewson Cem—*cemetery* OK-5
*Mathewson Cemetery* TN-4
Mathewson Hill—*summit* NY-2
Mathewson Hill—*summit* VT-1
Mathewson JHS—*school* KS-7
*Mathewson Pond* RI-1
*Mathewson Wash* AZ-5
Mathews Park—*park* KS-7
**Mathews Park**—*pop pl* KS-7
*Mathews Peak* CA-9
Mathews Point—*cape* WA-9
*Mathews Pond* ME-1
*Mathews Pond* MA-1
Mathews Pond—*reservoir* CT-1
Mathews Pond—*reservoir* NC-3
Mathews Post Office (historical)—*building* SD-7
Mathews-Powell House—*hist pl* TX-5
Mathew Spring—*spring* OR-9
Mathew Spring—*spring* UT-8
Mathews Raceway—*other* VA-3
Mathews Ranch—*locale* TX-5
Mathews River—*stream* AK-9
*Mathews Run* PA-2
Mathews Run—*stream* NJ-2
Mathews Run—*stream* OH-6
Mathews Sch—*school* TN-4
Mathews Sch—*school* TX-5
Mathews Sch (historical)—*school* PA-2
*Mathews School* IN-6
Mathews Slough—*stream* AL-4
Mathews Slough—*stream* AK-9
Mathews Spring—*spring* NV-8
Mathews Spring—*spring* TN-4
**Mathews Subdivision**—*pop pl* UT-8
Mathews Tank No 1—*reservoir* NM-5
Mathews Tank No 2—*reservoir* NM-5
**Mathews Township**—*pop pl* SD-7
**Mathews Village**—*pop pl* SC-3
*Mathewsville Wash* AZ-5
*Mathews Wash* AZ-5
Mathews Windmill—*locale* TX-5
*Mathey* NC-3
Matheys Branch—*stream* NC-3
**Mathias**—*pop pl* WV-2
Mathias, John, House—*hist pl* WV-2
Mathias, Mount—*summit* WA-9
Mathias Branch—*stream* KY-4
Mathias Branch—*stream* TN-4
Mathias Canyon—*valley* UT-8
Mathias Cem—*cemetery* GA-3
Mathias Cem—*cemetery* NC-3
Mathias Cove—*bay* MD-2
Mathias Creek—*stream* MT-8
Mathias Ditch—*canal* (2) IN-6
Mathias Lake—*lake* KS-7
Mathias Mitchell Public Square-Main Street Hist Dist—*hist pl* WI-6
Mathias Point—*cape* VA-3
Mathias Point Neck—*cape* VA-3
Mathias Run—*stream* WV-2
**Mathias (Township of)**—*pop pl* MI-6
Mathias Young Ditch—*canal* IN-6
*Mathie* AZ-5
Mathie, Karl, House—*hist pl* WI-6
Mathie Branch—*stream* AL-4
Mathiers Point—*cape* MD-2
Mathiesen House—*hist pl* SD-7
**Mathies Manor (subdivision)**—*pop pl* MA-1
Mathieson Spring—*spring* OR-9
Mathiessen Park—*park* NY-2
Mathieu Creek—*stream* OR-9
**Mathieu Place Condominium**—*pop pl* UT-8
Mathiews Cem—*cemetery* TX-5
*Mathis* GA-3
*Mathis* NC-3
Mathis—*other* NC-3
**Mathis**—*pop pl* TX-5
Mathis, T. H., House—*hist pl* TX-5
Mathis Bayou—*gut* MS-4
Mathis Brake—*swamp* MS-4
Mathis Branch—*stream* AL-4
Mathis Branch—*stream* TN-4
Mathis Branch—*stream* TX-5
Mathis Canyon—*valley* UT-8
Mathis (CCD)—*cens area* TX-5
*Mathis Cem* TN-4
Mathis Cem—*cemetery* (3) AL-4
Mathis Cem—*cemetery* (2) GA-3
Mathis Cem—*cemetery* LA-4
Mathis Cem—*cemetery* (2) MS-4
Mathis Cem—*cemetery* NC-3
Mathis Cem—*cemetery* (3) TN-4
Mathis Cem—*cemetery* (2) TX-5
Mathis Ch—*church* MO-7
Mathis Chapel—*church* AL-4
Mathis Chapel—*church* GA-3
Mathis Chapel—*reservoir* NC-3
Mathis Chapel Sch (historical)—*school* GA-3
**Mathis Corner**—*pop pl* SC-3
Mathis Creek—*stream* AL-4
Mathis Creek—*stream* MS-4
Mathis Creek—*stream* SC-3
Mathis Creek—*stream* TN-4
Mathis Creek—*stream* TX-5
Mathis Dam—*dam* NC-3
Mathisen Ranch—*locale* WY-8
Mathis Field (Airport)—*airport* TX-5
Mathis Hill—*summit* NC-3
Mathis Hill—*summit* TN-4
Mathis Hollow—*valley* AR-4
Mathis Hollow—*valley* (2) MO-7
Mathis Hollow—*valley* (3) TN-4
Mathis Hollow Mine—*mine* TN-4
Mathis House—*hist pl* GA-3
Mathis Lake—*lake* (3) GA-3
Mathis Lake—*lake* SC-3
Mathis Lake—*lake* WI-6
Mathis Lake—*reservoir* GA-3
Mathis Lake—*reservoir* NC-3
Mathis Mill—*building* TN-4
Mathis Mill Branch—*stream* NC-3
Mathis Mill Branch—*stream* TX-5
Mathis Mtn—*summit* AL-4
Mathis Mtn—*summit* NC-3
Mathis Mtn—*summit* TX-5
*Mathison Attendance Center* MS-4
Mathison Baptist Ch—*church* MS-4
Mathison Colored Sch (historical)—*school* MS-4
Mathison Creek—*stream* FL-3
*Mathison HS* MS-4
Mathison Lake—*reservoir* AL-4
*Mathison Line Special Consolidated Sch* MS-4
*Mathison Mill Bridge* AL-4
Mathison Peak—*summit* CA-9
Mathison Ranch—*locale* MT-8
Mathison Rsvr—*reservoir* WA-9
Mathison Sch—*school* WI-6
Mathison State Wildlife Mngmt Area—*park* MN-6
Mathison United Methodist Ch—*church* MS-4
Mathis Pond—*lake* SC-3
Mathis Pond—*swamp* NC-3
Mathis Ranch—*locale* NM-5
Mathis Ridge—*ridge* WV-2
Mathis Sch—*school* MS-4
Mathis Sch—*school* MO-7
Mathis Slough—*lake* AR-4
Mathis Spring—*spring* AZ-5
Mathis Spring—*spring* OR-9
Mathis Store (historical)—*building* MS-4
Mathis Thorofare—*channel* NJ-2
**Mathiston**—*pop pl* MS-4
*Mathis Town* MS-4
Mathis Wash—*valley* UT-8
Mathlamar Ch—*church* GA-3
Mathles Creek—*stream* CA-9
*Mathonguchen* FM-9
Mathson Sch—*school* CA-9
Mathuldy Creek—*stream* OK-5
*Math'unguchan* FM-9
Math'uunguchaan—*cape* FM-9
Mathy Lake—*lake* WI-6
Matia Island—*island* WA-9
*Matia Islands* WA-9
Matia Island State Park—*park* WA-9
**Matias**—*pop pl* PR-3
Matias Peak—*summit* SD-7
*Matiee Creek* NV-8
Matignon HS—*school* MA-1
Matilda—*locale* TX-5
**Matilda**—*pop pl* LA-4
Matilda Bay—*bay* NY-2
Matilda Canyon—*valley* UT-8
Matilda Creek—*stream* WY-8
Matilda (historical)—*locale* AL-4
Matilda Island—*island* NY-2
Matilda Jackson State Park—*park* WA-9
Matilda Perkins Oil Field—*oilfield* TX-5
Matilda Roy Draw—*valley* NM-5
Matilda Tunnel—*mine* NV-8
*Matildaville* AL-4
**Matilde**—*pop pl* (2) PR-3
Matilija Creek—*stream* CA-9
Matilija Dam—*dam* CA-9
Matilija Springs—*locale* CA-9
Matilla Gulch—*valley* CA-9
*Matin* MP-9
Matinburg—*locale* TX-5
**Matinburg**—*pop pl* TX-5
Matin Cem—*cemetery* IN-6
**Matinecock**—*pop pl* NY-2
Matinecock Friends Meetinghouse—*hist pl* NY-2
Matinecock Point—*cape* NY-2
*Matinicock Point* NY-2
**Matinicus**—*pop pl* ME-1
Matinicus Harbor—*bay* ME-1
Matinicus Island—*island* ME-1
Matinicus Isle (Plantation of)—*civ div* ME-1
Matinicus Roads—*channel* ME-1
Matinicus Rock—*island* ME-1
Matinicus Rock Light Station—*hist pl* ME-1
Matin Peak—*summit* (2) AK-9
Mati Point—*cape* GU-9
Mati Ranch—*locale* AZ-5
Matire Park—*park* AL-4
Matis Lake—*lake* NM-5
*Mat Island* MP-9
Matis Well—*well* NM-5
*Matkatameeba Canyon* AZ-5
Matkatamiba Canyon—*valley* AZ-5
Matkatamiba Mesa—*summit* AZ-5
Matkatamiba Rapids—*rapids* AZ-5
Matkin Cem—*cemetery* IN-6
Matkin Cem—*cemetery* MO-7
**Matkins**—*pop pl* MO-7
**Matkins**—*pop pl* NC-3
Matkins Cem—*cemetery* AL-4
Matkins Ch—*church* MO-7
Matkins Chapel—*church* AL-4
*Matkins Chapel Cumberland Presbyterian Ch* AL-4
**Matlacha**—*pop pl* FL-3
Matlacha Pass—*channel* FL-3
Matlacha Pass Aquatic Preserve—*park* FL-3
Matlacha Pass Natl Wildlife Ref—*park* FL-3
Matlack, Enoch, House—*hist pl* PA-2
Matley Hollow—*valley* PA-2
Matley Run—*stream* PA-2
Matley Spring—*spring* NV-8
Matlin—*locale* UT-8
Matlin Basin—*basin* UT-8
Matlin Mtns—*summit* UT-8
*Matlin Siding* UT-8
Matlock—*locale* KY-4
Matlock—*locale* WA-9
**Matlock**—*pop pl* IA-7
Matlock Acad—*school* FL-3
Matlock Bald—*summit* NC-3
Matlock Bend—*bend* TN-4
Matlock Bend Industrial Park—*locale* TN-4
Matlock Branch—*stream* (2) TN-4
Matlock Bridge—*bridge* OR-9
Matlock Bridge—*bridge* WA-9
Matlock-Brownfield Bldg—*hist pl* OR-9
Matlock Canyon—*valley* OR-9
Matlock Cem—*cemetery* AL-4
Matlock Cem—*cemetery* GA-3
Matlock Cem—*cemetery* (2) IN-6
Matlock Cem—*cemetery* (3) MO-7
Matlock Cem—*cemetery* (3) TN-4
Matlock Ch—*church* SC-3
Matlock Creek—*stream* (2) NC-3
Matlock Creek—*stream* OR-9
Matlock Flat—*flat* OR-9
Matlock Ford—*locale* TN-4
*Matlock Heights* IN-6
Matlock Hill—*summit* OR-9
Matlock Hills—*summit* TX-5
Matlock Island—*island* TN-4
Matlock Lake—*lake* CA-9
Matlock Plaza—*locale* KS-7
Matlock Post Office (historical)—*building* TN-4
Matlock Prairie—*flat* OR-9
Matlock Ridge—*ridge* TN-4
Matlock Sch—*school* MO-7
Matlock Sch (historical)—*school* TN-4
Matlock Valley—*valley* TN-4
Matlock Waterhole—*lake* OR-9
Matlock Water Hole Camp—*locale* OR-9
Matlock Well—*well* TX-5
Mat Martin Point—*cape* UT-8
Matmon RR Station (historical)—*locale* FL-3
Matmos, As—*slope* MH-9
*Matmos Point* MH-9
Matne Hollow—*valley* MO-7
Matney—*locale* NC-3
Matney—*locale* VA-3
**Matney**—*pop pl* OR-9
Matney Branch—*stream* AL-4
Matney Branch—*stream* IL-6
Matney Branch—*stream* KY-4
Matney Branch—*stream* VA-3
Matney Cem—*cemetery* WV-2
Matney Creek—*stream* WA-9
Matney Flat—*flat* OR-9
Matney Flat—*flat* VA-3
Matney Knob—*summit* AR-4
Matney Post Office (historical)—*building* TN-4
Matney Ranch—*locale* AK-9
Matneys Branch—*stream* VA-3
Matney Spring—*spring* WA-9
**Matneys Spur**—*pop pl* WA-9
Matneys Spurs—*locale* WA-9
Matney (Township of)—*fmr MCD* AR-4
*Mato* SD-7
Mato—*island* MP-9
**Matoaca**—*pop pl* VA-3
Matoaca HS—*school* VA-3
Matoaca (Magisterial District)—*fmr MCD* VA-3
Matoaka—*locale* FL-3
Matoaka—*locale* OK-5
**Matoaka**—*pop pl* WV-2
Matoaka Lake—*reservoir* VA-3
*Matochshoning* NJ-2
Matodd Branch—*stream* IL-6
Matogak River—*stream* AK-9
*Matoisa* MH-9
*Mato Island* MP-9
*Matoisu* MH-9
**Matojillo**—*pop pl* PR-3
*Matol* PW-9
*Matolen* MP-9
*Matolenim* FM-9
*Matomkin* VA-3
*Matomkin Point* VA-3
*Matomy Hill* RI-1
Maton Abajo (Barrio)—*fmr MCD* PR-3
Maton Arriba (Barrio)—*fmr MCD* PR-3
Maton de la Jara—*area* NM-5
Matonoso Creek—*stream* TX-5
Matoon Creek—*stream* NY-2
*Matoonoc* RI-1
Mato Oso Tank—*reservoir* TX-5
*Matoroen* MP-9
Matoroen—*island* MP-9
*Matoroen-To* MP-9
*Matosiu* MH-9
*Matouchin* NJ-2
Matovich Cem—*cemetery* WV-2
Matovich Ranch—*locale* (3) MT-8
*Matowepesack River* CT-1
Matoy—*locale* OK-5
Matoy Cem—*cemetery* OK-5
*Matpit* MH-9
Matpo—*slope* MH-9
Matquaw Flat—*flat* CA-9
Mat Rice Branch—*stream* WV-2
**Matrimony**—*pop pl* NC-3
Matrimony Ch—*church* NC-3
Matrimony Creek—*stream* NC-3
Matrimony Creek—*stream* VA-3
Matrimony Point—*cape* ME-1
Matrimony Spring—*spring* UT-8
Matriotti Creek—*stream* WA-9
Mat River—*stream* VA-3
Matron Cem—*cemetery* TN-4
*Mat Ruk I Salat* FM-9
Mat Run—*stream* IN-6
Mats Basin—*basin* UT-8
Matsell Bridge Public Access—*park* IA-7
Matsen Cem—*cemetery* WI-6
Matsen Creek—*stream* WA-9
Matsen Ranch—*locale* CA-9
Matsingale Creek—*stream* MT-8
Matsler Cem—*cemetery* IL-6
Matsler Cem—*cemetery* TX-5
Mats Mats Bay—*bay* WA-9
**Mats Mats (Port Ludlow PO)**—*pop pl* (2) WA-9
Mats Mats Quarry—*mine* WA-9
*Matson* ND-7
**Matson**—*pop pl* MO-7
Matson Cem—*cemetery* IN-6
Matson Cem—*cemetery* MO-7
Matson Chapel—*church* VA-3
Matson Creek—*stream* AK-9
Matson Creek—*stream* (3) OR-9
Matson Dam—*dam* SD-7
Matson Ditch—*canal* IN-6
Matson Field—*park* MN-6
Matson Hill—*summit* NY-2
Matson Island—*island* MN-6
Matson Lake—*lake* (2) MN-6
Matson Lake—*lake* WI-6
Matson Park—*park* OR-9
Matson Pond—*lake* IA-7
Matson Ranch—*locale* WY-8
Matson Rsvr—*reservoir* SD-7
Matson Run—*stream* DE-2
Matson Sch—*school* SD-7
Matson Slough—*lake* ND-7
Matson Spring—*spring* PA-2
Matson Spring—*spring* WA-9
Matson Tank—*reservoir* AZ-5
Matson Trail—*trail* PA-2
Matsonville (historical)—*locale* AL-4
*Matsum Point* MH-9
*Matsunk* PA-2
Matsunk Creek—*stream* PA-2
*Matsu Shima* FM-9
Matsutnak River—*stream* AK-9
*Matt* CT-1
Matt—*locale* GA-3
*Mattabasset River* CT-1
*Mattabeset River* CT-1
*Mattabesicke River* CT-1
*Mattabesic River* CT-1
Mattabesset River—*stream* CT-1
Mattabesset Trail—*trail* (2) CT-1
*Mattabessett River* CT-1
Mattacheese MS—*school* MA-1
*Mattacheeset* MA-1
*Mattacheeset, Town of* MA-1
*Mattacocy Creek* VA-3
*Mattacomack Creek* NC-3
Mattagodus Stream—*stream* ME-1
*Mattak* MA-1
*Mattakeeset Herring Creek* MA-1
Mattakeset Bay—*cove* MA-1
*Mattakeset Herring Brook* MA-1
Mattakeset Herring Creek—*canal* MA-1
*Mattakeset Herring Run* MA-1
*Mattakesett* MA-1
*Mattaket* MA-1
*Mattakeunk Pond* ME-1
Mattakeunk Stream—*stream* ME-1
*Mattallak Pond* ME-1
*Mattametto-to* MP-9
Mattamiscontis Club Camp—*locale* ME-1
Mattamiscontis Lake—*lake* ME-1
Mattamiscontis Mtn—*summit* ME-1
Mattamiscontis Stream—*stream* ME-1
Mattamiscontis (Township of)—*unorg* ME-1
*Mattamuij* MP-9
Mattamuskeeet High—*school* NC-3
Mattamuskeet, Lake—*lake* NC-3
Mattamuskeet Natl Wildlife Ref—*park* NC-3
Mattamuskeet Natl Wildlife Refuge HQ—*building* NC-3
*Mattamuskett* NC-3
Mattanawcook Acad—*school* ME-1
Mattanawcook Island—*island* ME-1
Mattanawcook Pond—*lake* ME-1
Mattanawcook Stream—*stream* ME-1
Mat Tank—*reservoir* NV-8
Mattano Park—*park* NJ-2

*Mattapan* MA-1
Mattapan Station—*locale* MA-1
**Mattapan (subdivision)**—*pop pl* MA-1
Mattapany (historical)—*area* DE-2
Mattapany-Sewall Archeol Site—*hist pl* MD-2
Mattapex—*locale* MD-2
*Mattapoiset Neck* MA-1
*Mattapoiset River* MA-1
Mattapoiset Rock—*bar* MA-1
**Mattapoisett**—*pop pl* MA-1
Mattapoisett (census name for Mattapoisett Center)—*CDP* MA-1
Mattapoisett Center (census name Mattapoisett)—*other* MA-1
Mattapoisett Harbor—*bay* MA-1
Mattapoisett (historical P.O.)—*locale* MA-1
Mattapoisett Historical Society Bldg—*building* MA-1
Mattapoisett Ledge—*rock* MA-1
Mattapoisett Neck—*cape* MA-1
Mattapoisett Neck Marshes—*swamp* MA-1
Mattapoisett River—*stream* MA-1
Mattapoisett River Marshes—*swamp* MA-1
Mattapoisett Shipyard Park—*park* MA-1
**Mattapoisett (Town of)**—*pop pl* MA-1
*Mattapoissett* MA-1
**Mattaponi**—*pop pl* VA-3
Mattaponi Ch—*church* VA-3
Mattaponi Church—*hist pl* VA-3
Mattaponi Creek—*stream* MD-2
**Mattaponi Ind Res**—*pop pl* VA-3
Mattaponi Landing—*locale* MD-2
Mattaponi River—*stream* VA-3
Mattapony—*uninc pl* MD-2
*Mattapony River* VA-3
*Mattapuyst* MA-1
Matta River—*stream* VA-3
Mattaseunk Dam—*dam* ME-1
Mattaseunk Lake—*lake* ME-1
Mattaseunk Stream—*stream* ME-1
Mattassee Branch—*stream* SC-3
Mattassee Lake—*lake* SC-3
Mattatuck State For—*forest* CT-1
Mattatuck Trail—*trail* (2) CT-1
Mattatuxet River—*stream* RI-1
**Mattawa**—*pop pl* WA-9
Mattawa, Lake—*reservoir* MA-1
Mattawa Air Strip Airp—*airport* WA-9
**Mattawamkeag**—*pop pl* ME-1
Mattawamkeag Hill—*summit* ME-1
Mattawamkeag Lake—*lake* ME-1
Mattawamkeag River—*stream* ME-1
**Mattawamkeag (Town of)**—*pop pl* ME-1
*Mattawan* NJ-2
**Mattawan**—*pop pl* MI-6
Mattawana—*locale* AL-4
**Mattawana**—*pop pl* PA-2
Mattawana Cem—*cemetery* PA-2
**Mattawana (RR name McVeytown (sta.))**—*pop pl* PA-2
*Mattawan Creek* NJ-2
*Mattawan Point* NJ-2
**Mattawoman**—*pop pl* MD-2
Mattawoman Creek—*stream* MD-2
Mattawoman Creek—*stream* VA-3
Matt Ayers Lake—*lake* MN-6
Matt-Bahls House—*hist pl* IA-7
Matt Bluff—*cliff* MO-7
Matt Branch—*stream* GA-3
Matt Branch—*stream* NC-3
Matt Brooks Dam—*dam* NC-3
Matt Brooks Lake—*reservoir* NC-3
*Matt Creek* AR-4
*Matt Creek* MO-7
Matt Creek—*stream* CO-8
Matt Creek—*stream* (2) MT-8
Matt Davis Cove—*valley* NC-3
*Matte* FM-9
Matteawan—*uninc pl* NY-2
Matteawan State Hosp—*hospital* NY-2
Mattei—*locale* CA-9
Matten Island—*island* MP-9
*Matten-to* MP-9
Matter Creek—*stream* SD-7
Matter Dam—*dam* SD-7
Matterds Prospects—*mine* KY-4
Matterhorn—*other* CA-9
Matterhorn—*summit* AZ-5
Matterhorn—*summit* NV-8
Matterhorn—*summit* OR-9
Matterhorn Canyon—*valley* CA-9
Matterhorn Creek—*stream* CO-8
Matterhorn Drifts—*mine* CO-8
Matterhorn Peak—*summit* CA-9
Matterhorn Peak—*summit* CO-8
Matterhorn Point—*cape* MT-8
Matter Lake—*lake* SD-7
Mattern Cem—*cemetery* OH-6
Mattern Junction (historical)—*locale* PA-2
**Matternville**—*pop pl* PA-2
Matternville Sch—*school* PA-2
Matter Oil Field—*oilfield* KS-7
Matter Park—*park* IN-6
Matter Run—*stream* PA-2
**Matterstown**—*pop pl* PA-2
Matter Trail—*trail* PA-2
**Mattese**—*pop pl* MO-7
Mattese Creek—*stream* MO-7
**Matteson**—*pop pl* IL-6
**Matteson**—*pop pl* MI-6
Matteson Cem—*cemetery* KS-7
Matteson Cem—*cemetery* MI-6
Matteson Ch—*church* MI-6
Matteson Creek—*stream* ID-8
Matteson Creek—*stream* WI-6
Matteson Gin—*locale* AR-4
Matteson Lake—*lake* MI-6
**Matteson Lake**—*pop pl* MI-6
Matteson Mine—*mine* ID-8
Matteson Pond—*lake* RI-1
Matteson Ranch—*locale* WY-8
Matteson Ridge—*ridge* ID-8
Matteson Sch—*school* IL-6
**Matteson (Town of)**—*pop pl* WI-6
**Matteson (Township of)**—*pop pl* MI-6
Mattey, Joseph, House—*hist pl* OR-9
Matt Gulch—*valley* MT-8
Matthes Crest—*ridge* CA-9
Matthes Glacier—*glacier* AK-9
Matthes Glaciers—*glacier* CA-9
Matthes Lake—*lake* CA-9
Matthew—*locale* KY-4
Matthew—*locale* WA-9
**Matthew**—*pop pl* TN-4
Matthew Anaker Ditch—*canal* IN-6
Matthew Bluff—*cliff* NC-3
Matthew Branch—*stream* TN-4
Matthew Cem—*cemetery* AL-4
Matthew Cem—*cemetery* WV-2
Matthew Ch—*church* MD-2
Matthew Chapel—*church* NC-3
Matthew Creek—*stream* TN-4
Matthew Dolan Ch—*church* SC-3
Matthew Gulch—*valley* OR-9
**Matthew (historical)**—*pop pl* NC-3
Matthew Howell Ditch—*canal* IN-6
Matthew Mtn—*summit* TN-4
Matthew Place (abandoned)—*locale* NM-5
Matthew Point—*cape* NY-2
Matthew Pond Dam—*dam* NC-3
Matthew Run—*stream* MD-2
*Matthews* VA-3
Matthews—*airport* NJ-2
Matthews—*locale* AL-4
Matthews—*locale* CO-8
Matthews—*locale* IL-6
Matthews—*locale* MT-8
Matthews—*locale* TX-5
**Matthews**—*pop pl* GA-3
**Matthews**—*pop pl* IN-6
**Matthews**—*pop pl* MD-2
**Matthews**—*pop pl* (2) MS-4
**Matthews**—*pop pl* MO-7
**Matthews**—*pop pl* NJ-2
**Matthews**—*pop pl* NC-3
**Matthews**—*pop pl* PA-2
**Matthews**—*pop pl* WA-9
Matthews, Dr. James O., Office—*hist pl* NC-3
Matthews, Lake—*reservoir* GA-3
Matthews, Pleasant L., House—*hist pl* TN-4
Matthews and Willard Factory—*hist pl* CT-1
*Matthews Arm* VA-3
Matthews-Atwood House—*hist pl* TX-5
Matthews Bar—*bar* AL-4
Matthews Bayou—*stream* MS-4
Matthews Beach—*beach* WA-9
Matthews Bend—*bend* MS-4
Matthews Bluff—*cliff* SC-3
Matthews Branch—*stream* KY-4
Matthews Branch—*stream* MO-7
Matthews Branch—*stream* NJ-2
Matthews Branch—*stream* TN-4
Matthews Branch—*stream* WV-2
*Matthews Brook* NJ-2
Matthews Brook—*stream* NJ-2
Matthews Cabins—*locale* MO-7
Matthews Canal—*canal* SC-3
Matthews Cave—*cave* AL-4
*Matthews Cem* MS-4
*Matthews Cem* TN-4
Matthews Cem—*cemetery* (2) AL-4
Matthews Cem—*cemetery* (2) GA-3
Matthews Cem—*cemetery* (2) MS-4
Matthews Cem—*cemetery* (2) MO-7
Matthews Cem—*cemetery* (7) TN-4
Matthews Cem—*cemetery* TX-5
Matthews Cem—*cemetery* WV-2
*Matthews Ch* AL-4
Matthews Ch—*church* AL-4
Matthews Ch—*church* (2) SC-3
Matthew Sch—*school* SD-7
Matthews Chapel—*church* AL-4
Matthews Chapel—*church* LA-4
Matthews Chapel—*church* NC-3
Matthews Chapel—*church* VA-3
Matthews Chapel (historical)—*church* AL-4
*Matthew School* KS-7
*Matthew School* TN-4
*Matthews Church* TN-4
*Matthews Corner* DE-2
Matthews Cove—*bay* MD-2
Matthews Cove—*bay* VA-3
Matthews Cove—*valley* AL-4
*Matthews Creek* MS-4
*Matthews Creek* MO-7
*Matthews Creek* OR-9
*Matthews Creek* TN-4
Matthews Creek—*stream* AL-4
Matthews Creek—*stream* (2) CA-9
Matthews Creek—*stream* MS-4
Matthews Creek—*stream* (2) NC-3
Matthews Creek—*stream* SC-3
Matthews Creek—*stream* WA-9
Matthews Creek Campground—*locale* CA-9
Matthews Crossing (historical)—*locale* MS-4
**Matthews Crossroads**—*pop pl* NC-3
Matthews Dam—*dam* AL-4
Matthews Ditch—*canal* IN-6
Matthews Draw—*valley* WY-8
*Matthews Elementary School* AL-4
Matthews Elem Sch—*school* IN-6
Matthews Elem Sch—*school* NC-3
Matthews Ferry (historical)—*locale* MS-4
Matthews Fulling Mill Site—*hist pl* MA-1
Matthews Gap—*gap* TN-4
Matthews Guard Station—*locale* OR-9
Matthews Hall—*hist pl* AZ-5
Matthews Hill—*summit* TX-5
Matthews Hill—*summit* VA-3
Matthews Hill—*summit* WY-8
Matthews (historical)—*locale* MS-4
*Matthews Hollow* TN-4
Matthews Hollow—*valley* TN-4
Matthews House—*hist pl* AR-4
Matthews House—*hist pl* GA-3
Matthews JHS—*school* TX-5
Matthews Junction—*locale* IL-6
Matthews Lake—*lake* TN-4
Matthews Lake—*lake* WA-9
Matthews Lake—*lake* WI-6
Matthews Lake—*reservoir* AL-4
Matthews Lake—*reservoir* KY-4
Matthews Lake—*reservoir* NJ-2
Matthews Lake—*reservoir* (2) NC-3
Matthews Lake Dam—*dam* (2) NC-3
Matthews Landing—*locale* AL-4
Matthew Slough—*gut* NC-3
Matthews (Mathews)—*other* AL-4
Matthews Memorial Ch—*church* VA-3
Matthews Millpond—*reservoir* SC-3
*Matthews Mine Tailings Dam* TN-4
*Matthews Mine Water Supply Dam* TN-4
Matthews Mtn—*summit* AK-9
Matthews Mtn—*summit* MO-7
*Matthewson Landing* AL-4
Matthewson Sawmill (historical)—*locale* AL-4
Matthewsons Bar—*bar* AL-4
Matthews Park—*park* AL-4
**Matthews Park (subdivision)**—*pop pl* NC-3
Matthews Peak—*summit* AZ-5
Matthews Place—*hist pl* NC-3
Matthews Place—*locale* TX-5
Matthews Plaza—*locale* NC-3
Matthews Point—*cape* NY-2
Matthews Point—*cape* VA-3
*Matthews Pond* ME-1
Matthews Pond—*lake* ME-1
Matthews Pond—*lake* MA-1
Matthews Pond—*lake* NH-1
Matthews Post Office (historical)—*building* MS-4
Matthew Springs—*spring* NV-8
Matthews Prospect—*mine* TN-4
Matthews Ranch—*locale* TX-5
Matthews Ranch—*locale* WY-8
**Matthews Run**—*pop pl* PA-2
Matthews Run—*stream* PA-2
Matthews Sch—*school* AL-4
Matthews Sch—*school* GA-3
Matthews Sch—*school* MO-7
Matthews Sch—*school* PA-2
Matthews Sch (historical)—*school* AL-4
Matthews Sch (historical)—*school* MO-7
Matthews Sch (historical)—*school* (2) TN-4
*Matthews School* TN-4
Matthews Scippio Sch—*school* FL-3
Matthews-South Elem Sch—*school* IN-6
Matthews Tabernacle—*church* SC-3
Matthews-Templeton House—*hist pl* TX-5
**Matthewstown**—*pop pl* MD-2
**Matthewstown**—*pop pl* NC-3
Matthews Township Festival Center—*locale* NC-3
Matthews (Township of)—*fmr MCD* AR-4
Matthews (Township of)—*fmr MCD* NC-3
*Matthewsville* AZ-5
Matthews Wash—*stream* AZ-5
Matthew Welsh Bridge—*bridge* IN-6
Matthew Welsh Bridge—*bridge* KY-4
Matthie—*locale* AZ-5
Matthies Cem—*cemetery* TX-5
Matthiesen Sch—*school* WA-9
Matthiessen Sch—*school* IL-6
Matthiessen State Park—*park* IL-6
Matthie Tank—*reservoir* AZ-5
*Matthieu Lakes* OR-9
Matthieu Lakes—*lake* OR-9
Matthis, Fleet, Farm—*hist pl* NC-3
Matthis Branch—*stream* IL-6
Matthis Lake—*lake* FL-3
Matt Hollow—*valley* TN-4
Matt Hollow Creek—*stream* AL-4
Mattic Creek—*stream* MS-4
Mattice Cem—*cemetery* NY-2
Mattice Homestead—*locale* MT-8
Mattice Tank—*reservoir* NM-5
Mattice Tunnel—*tunnel* WY-8
Mattick Spring—*spring* MT-8
**Mattie**—*pop pl* PA-2
Mattie, Lake—*lake* (2) FL-3
*Mattie Akin Elementary School* MS-4
Mattie Canyon—*valley* AZ-5
Mattie Ch—*church* KY-4
Mattie Clark Bayou—*stream* MS-4
*Mattie Creek* MS-4
Mattie Gap—*gap* WV-2
Mattie Js Pond—*reservoir* SC-3
Mattie Lake—*lake* CA-9
Mattie Lake—*lake* MI-6
Mattie Randolph Hollow—*valley* TN-4
Mattier Creek—*stream* NV-8
Mattie Real Park—*park* OK-5
Mattie Roberts Memorial Cem—*cemetery* MO-7
Mattier Ranch—*locale* NV-8
Matties Ark—*flat* OR-9
Mattiese Shop Ctr—*locale* MO-7
Mattie Spring—*spring* OR-9
Mattie T Blount HS—*school* AL-4
*Mattie Thompson Elementary School* MS-4
Mattie Thompson Sch—*school* MS-4
Mattie V Creek—*stream* MT-8
Mattie Wells Sch—*school* GA-3
Mattigan Point—*cape* ME-1
Mattimo Place—*locale* ME-1
Mattingly—*locale* KY-4
Mattingly Branch—*stream* KY-4
Mattingly Creek—*stream* ID-8
Mattingly Ditch—*canal* IN-6
Mattingly House—*hist pl* KY-4
Mattingly Park—*park* FL-3
Mattingly Peak—*summit* ID-8
Mattingly Spring—*spring* OR-9
*Mattison* AL-4
Mattison Cem—*cemetery* NY-2
Mattison Drain—*stream* MI-6
Mattison (historical)—*locale* KS-7
Mattison Hollow—*valley* NY-2
Mattison Mine—*mine* CA-9
*Mattison Quarry* AL-4
Mattison Township—*civil* SD-7
Mattis Park—*park* IL-6
**Mattituck**—*pop pl* NY-2
Mattituck Creek—*stream* NY-2
Mattituck Hills—*summit* NY-2
Mattituck Inlet—*gut* NY-2
Mattituck Light—*locale* NY-2
Mattituck Park District Beach—*park* NY-2
*Mattituck Pond* NY-2
Mattix Branch—*stream* IA-7
**Mattix Corner**—*pop pl* IN-6
Mattix Creek—*stream* MI-6
Mattix Run—*stream* NJ-2
*Mattler Creek* NV-8
Mattley Creek—*stream* CA-9
Mattley Meadow—*flat* CA-9
Mattlia Lake—*lake* MN-6
Mattlin JHS—*school* NY-2
Matt Mtn—*summit* MT-8
Matt Mtn—*summit* NC-3
Mattney Point—*cape* MD-2
*Mattnicunk Island* NJ-2
Mattoax—*locale* VA-3
Mattoax Ch—*church* VA-3
*Matt Och Lake* WI-6
Matt Ochs Lake—*lake* WI-6
*Mattock Bay* AR-4
Mattock Ditch—*canal* OH-6
Mattock Gulch—*valley* OR-9
Mattock Hollow—*valley* MO-7
Mattocks (RR name for East Baldwin)—*other* ME-1
Mattocks Sch—*school* MN-6
Mattocks Site—*hist pl* NM-5
Mattock Well—*well* NM-5
Mattole Beach—*beach* CA-9
Mattole Canyon—*valley* CA-9
Mattole Point—*cape* CA-9
Mattole River—*stream* CA-9
Matton, Lake—*reservoir* IL-6
Matton Creek—*stream* KY-4
Matton Creek—*stream* VA-3
Mattons Grove Ch—*church* NC-3
Mattoon—*locale* MS-4
**Mattoon**—*pop pl* IL-6
**Mattoon**—*pop pl* KY-4
**Mattoon**—*pop pl* WI-6
Mattoon Cabin—*hist pl* WA-9
Mattoon Creek—*stream* KS-7
Mattoon Creek—*stream* KY-4
Mattoon Swamp—*swamp* WI-6
**Mattoon (Township of)**—*pop pl* IL-6
Mattos Drain—*canal* CA-9
Mattos Gulch—*valley* CA-9
Mattos Sch—*school* CA-9
Mattox—*locale* FL-3
Mattox—*locale* GA-3
Mattox—*locale* TX-5
Mattox Branch—*stream* AL-4
Mattox Canyon—*valley* CA-9
Mattox Cem—*cemetery* (2) TN-4
Mattox Cem—*cemetery* (2) TX-5
Mattox Ch—*church* NC-3
Mattox Creek—*stream* AL-4
Mattox Creek—*stream* GA-3
Mattox Creek—*stream* OR-9
Mattox Creek—*stream* (2) VA-3
Mattox Creek—*stream* WY-8
*Mattox Ditch* IN-6
Mattox Draw—*valley* KS-7
Mattox Ford—*locale* GA-3
Mattox Hollow—*valley* TN-4
*Mattox Island* MD-2
Mattox Sch (historical)—*school* MS-4
Mattox Store (historical)—*locale* AL-4
**Mattoxtown**—*pop pl* KY-4
Mattox Well—*well* NM-5
Matt Phillips Cem—*cemetery* TN-4
*Mattpoiset* MA-1
Mattress Cienega—*flat* AZ-5
Mattress Drain—*stream* FL-3
Mattress Head Branch—*stream* FL-3
Mattrich Lake—*lake* WI-6
*Matts* WV-2
Matts Branch—*stream* MO-7
Matts Branch—*stream* NC-3
Matts Chapel Ch—*church* MS-4
Matts Creek—*stream* VA-3
Matts Creek—*stream* WV-2
Matts Creek Shelter—*locale* VA-3
*Matts Hollow* TN-4
Matts Landing—*locale* NJ-2
Matts Mtn—*summit* NY-2
Mattson—*locale* MN-6
Mattson—*locale* TX-5
**Mattson**—*pop pl* MS-4
Mattson, Lake—*lake* MN-6
Mattson Bay—*bay* MN-6
Mattson Creek—*stream* MI-6
Mattson Lake—*lake* MN-6
*Mattsons Run* DE-2
Matts Pond—*reservoir* NY-2
Matt Spring—*spring* CO-8
Matts Sch—*school* MS-4
Matts Summit—*summit* UT-8
Matts Well—*well* OR-9
Matt Trail—*trail* CO-8
Mattubby Creek—*stream* MS-4
*Mattuby Creek* MS-4
Matt Warner Dam—*dam* UT-8
Matt Warner Rsvr—*reservoir* UT-8
Matt Well—*well* TX-5
Matt Windmill—*locale* TX-5
Matty Cem—*cemetery* KY-4
Matty Cem—*cemetery* MO-7
**Mattydale**—*pop pl* NY-2
Matty Ditch—*gut* DE-2
Matty Ferguson Branch—*stream* WV-2
Matty Ferguson Cem—*cemetery* WV-2
Matty Hersee Hosp—*hospital* MS-4
Matty Price Hill—*summit* NJ-2
Mattys Fork—*stream* AZ-5
*Matubba Creek* MS-4
*Matubbie Creek* MS-4
*Matubby Creek* MS-4
*Matucjek Dam* ND-7
*Mat'uft'uf* FM-9
Mat'uft'uuf—*summit* FM-9
**Matugan**—*pop pl* GU-9
Matuis, As—*summit* MH-9
*Matuis Place* MH-9
Matulich Meadow—*flat* CA-9
Matuli Point—*cape* AS-9
Matumbla, Mount—*summit* NY-2
*Matunuc* RI-1
**Matunuck**—*pop pl* RI-1
Matunuck Point—*cape* RI-1
Maturango Peak—*summit* CA-9
Matushka Island—*island* AK-9
*Matusky Brook* IL-6
Matusky Hollow—*valley* IL-6
**Matuta (historical)**—*pop pl* TN-4
Matuta Post Office (historical)—*building* TN-4
**Matu'u**—*pop pl* AS-9
**Matuu**—*pop pl* AS-9
Matuyas Alto (Barrio)—*fmr MCD* PR-3
Matuyas Bajo (Barrio)—*fmr MCD* PR-3
**Matville**—*pop pl* OH-6
Matville Ch—*church* WV-2
Matwell Windmill—*locale* TX-5
Matz Draw—*stream* OR-9
Matze Oil Field—*oilfield* TX-5
Matzie Airp—*airport* MO-7
Matzke Lake Dam—*dam* SD-7
Matzke Sch—*school* TX-5
Matz-Tagatz Cem—*cemetery* WI-6
*Maubila Boy Scout Camp* AL-4
Maubila Boy Scout Lake—*reservoir* AL-4
Maubila Boy Scout Lake Dam—*dam* AL-4
Maubila Camp—*locale* AL-4
Maubry Cave—*cave* AL-4
Mauch Cem—*cemetery* MI-6
*Mauch Chunk* PA-2
Mauch Chunk—*other* PA-2
Mauch Chunk and Summit Hill Switchback RR—*hist pl* PA-2
Mauch Chunk Creek—*stream* PA-2
Mauch Chunk Dam—*dam* PA-2
Mauch Chunk Lake—*reservoir* PA-2
Mauch Chunk Ridge—*ridge* PA-2
Mauch Chunk Tower—*tower* PA-2
Mauch Chunk (Township of)—*civ div* PA-2
Maucher Sch—*school* SD-7
Mauchlinville Branch—*stream* WV-2
**Mauch Township**—*pop pl* ND-7
**Mauck**—*pop pl* VA-3
Mauck, Rudolph, House—*hist pl* KY-4
Mauck Cem—*cemetery* IN-6
Maucki Coulee—*valley* MT-8
**Mauckport**—*pop pl* IN-6
Mauck Run—*stream* IN-6
Mauck Sch—*school* MI-6
**Maucks (historical)**—*pop pl* TN-4
Mauck's Meetinghouse—*hist pl* VA-3
Maucks Pond—*lake* IN-6
*Mauckspor*t IN-6
Mau Creek—*stream* NV-8
*Maud* AL-4
*Maud* KS-7
Maud—*locale* (2) AL-4
Maud—*locale* IA-7
Maud—*locale* KY-4
Maud—*locale* WA-9
**Maud**—*pop pl* IL-6
**Maud**—*pop pl* MS-4
**Maud**—*pop pl* MO-7
**Maud**—*pop pl* OH-6
**Maud**—*pop pl* OK-5
**Maud**—*pop pl* TX-5
**Maud**—*pop pl* WV-2
Maud, Lake—*lake* MN-6
Maud, Mount—*summit* MN-6
Maud Bay—*bay* MI-6
Maud (CCD)—*cens area* OK-5
Maud Ch—*church* AL-4
Maud Creek—*stream* AK-9
Maud Creek—*stream* ID-8
Maude—*locale* LA-4
Maude, Lake—*lake* AK-9
Maude, Lake—*lake* FL-3
Maude, Lake—*reservoir* GA-3
Maude, Mount—*summit* WA-9
Maude Canyon—*valley* NV-8
Maude Chapel—*church* WV-2
*Maude Creek* ID-8
Maude Creek—*stream* MN-6
Maude Creek—*stream* OR-9
Maude Lake—*lake* ID-8
Maude Lake—*lake* MN-6
Maude Lake—*lake* OR-9
Maud-Elliot Creek (CCD)—*cens area* TX-5
Maude Mtn—*summit* OR-9
*Mauden Creek* WA-9
*Maudener's Creek* NY-2
Maude Oakerman Spring—*spring* OR-9
Maude Ridge—*ridge* ID-8
Maude Sanders Elem Sch—*school* FL-3
Maudes Canyon—*valley* NM-5
Maude- S Mine—*mine* OR-9
Maud Hill—*summit* AZ-5
Maud (historical)—*locale* KS-7
Maud Hollow—*valley* MO-7
Mau Ditch—*canal* WY-8
Maud Lake—*lake* CA-9
Maud Lake—*lake* ID-8
Maud Lake—*lake* MI-6
Maud Lake—*lake* WA-9
Maud Lake—*lake* WI-6
Maudlin Cem—*cemetery* AL-4
*Maudlin Chapel* AL-4
*Maudlin Gulch* CO-8
Maudlin Gulch—*valley* CO-8
Maudlin Gulch Oil Field—*oilfield* CO-8
Maudlin (historical)—*locale* AL-4
Maudlin Park—*park* MI-6
*Maudlin P.O.* AL-4
*Maudlow* TX-5
**Maudlow**—*pop pl* MT-8
Maudlowe—*locale* TX-5
Maudlow Sch—*hist pl* MT-8
Maud Mine—*mine* CO-8
Maud Mtn—*summit* ID-8
Maud Point—*cape* AK-9
Maud Post Office (historical)—*building* MS-4
Maud Post Office (historical)—*building* PA-2
**Maudru**—*pop pl* MT-8
Maudru House—*hist pl* OH-6
Maud Run—*stream* WV-2
Maudru Spur—*locale* MT-8
Maud S Mine—*mine* NM-5
Maud-S Mine—*mine* UT-8
Mauds (RR name for Maud)—*other* OH-6
Mauds Well—*well* NV-8
Maud Williamson State Park—*park* OR-9
Maudwin—*hist pl* MS-4
Maud Wise Rsvr—*reservoir* CO-8
Mauele Bay—*bay* HI-9
*Mauer Creek* WI-6
*Maues Cemetery* TX-5
Maue Sch—*school* IL-6
*Mauga* MH-9
Maugaele Ridge—*ridge* AS-9
Maugaleoo Ridge—*ridge* AS-9
Maugaloa Ridge—*ridge* AS-9
Maugansville—*CDP* MD-2
**Maugansville**—*pop pl* MD-2
Maugaoalii Ridge—*ridge* AS-9
Maugaopea Point—*cape* AS-9
Maugaotula Peak—*summit* AS-9
Maugasaa Ridge—*ridge* AS-9
Maugatele Rock—*cape* AS-9
Maugham Sch—*school* NJ-2
Maughan Hollow—*valley* UT-8
*Maug Inseln* MH-9
*Maug Island* MH-9
Maug Islands—*island* MH-9
Maugs Cave—*cave* TN-4
Maugus Hill—*summit* MA-1
Mauh Nah Tee-See Country Club—*other* IL-6
*Maui* MH-9
Maui—*island* HI-9
Maui Childrens Home—*locale* HI-9
Maui Country Club—*other* HI-9
**Maui (County)**—*pop pl* HI-9
Maui County Farm—*locale* HI-9
Maui HS—*school* HI-9
Maui Jinsha Mission—*hist pl* HI-9
Mauiloa—*summit* HI-9
Maui Mall—*post sta* HI-9
Maui Radio Range Station—*locale* HI-9
Maui Veterans Cem—*cemetery* HI-9
Maui Vocational Sch—*school* HI-9
**Mauk**—*pop pl* GA-3
Mauka Ditch Tunnel—*tunnel* HI-9
Maukaloa Camp—*locale* HI-9
**Mauka Loa (Maukaloa)**—*pop pl* HI-9
*Maukanu* HI-9
Mauka Powerhouse—*other* HI-9
Mauka Rsvr—*reservoir* HI-9
Mauk Branch—*stream* TX-5
Mauk Cem—*cemetery* TN-4
Maukey Gulch—*valley* MT-8
Mauk & Hammer/Houghton Elevator—*hist pl* MI-6
**Mauk (Mauk Mines)**—*pop pl* PA-2
Mauk Sch—*school* IA-7
Mauk Sch—*school* KY-4
Mauland Bottoms—*bend* MT-8
Mauland Ranch—*locale* MT-8
Mauland Rapstad Ditch—*canal* MT-8
Mauland-Westervelt Ditch—*canal* MT-8
*Maula Nui* HI-9
Maulap River—*stream* GU-9
Maulbridge Apartments—*hist pl* CA-9
Maulden—*locale* KY-4
Maulden Branch—*stream* KY-4
Maulden Branch—*stream* SC-3
*Maulden Mill Creek* GA-3
Maulden P O—*locale* KY-4
Maulden Sch—*school* KY-4
Mauldentown Cem—*cemetery* IN-6
*Maulder Mill Creek* GA-3
**Mauldin**—*pop pl* SC-3
Mauldin Airstrip—*airport* AZ-5
Mauldin Branch—*stream* MS-4
Mauldin Cem—*cemetery* AL-4
Mauldin Creek—*stream* AL-4
Mauldin Creek—*stream* GA-3
Mauldin Gap—*gap* GA-3
Maulding Millpond—*reservoir* SC-3
Mauldin-Hall House—*hist pl* NM-5
Mauldin Hills—*summit* TX-5
Mauldin House—*hist pl* GA-3
Mauldin Mill Creek—*stream* GA-3
Mauldin Mine—*mine* MT-8
Mauldin Mountain—*ridge* AR-4
Mauldin Mtn—*summit* MD-2
Mauldin Mtn—*summit* SC-3
**Mauldins Mill**—*pop pl* SC-3
Mauldin Spring—*spring* NM-5
Mauldin Springs—*spring* ID-8
Mauldon Branch—*stream* KY-4
**Maule Addition Subdivision**—*pop pl* UT-8
Maulecamp Run—*stream* WV-2
Maule Coulee—*valley* WI-6
Mauled Cedar Tank—*reservoir* NM-5
Maule Lake—*lake* FL-3
Maule Mines—*mine* CA-9
Maules Point—*cape* NC-3
Maul Fork—*stream* WV-2
Maul Fork Sch—*school* WV-2
Maul Hammock Lake—*lake* GA-3
Maul Hammock Prairie—*swamp* GA-3
Maul Hill—*summit* TX-5
*Maulii* HI-9
Maulili—*civil* (3) HI-9
Maulili Bay—*bay* HI-9
*Mauliola* HI-9
Maull, Thomas, House (Boundary Increase)—*hist pl* DE-2
Maul Lake—*lake* CA-9
Maul Lake Dam—*dam* MS-4
Maull House—*hist pl* DE-2
Maulls Wharf (historical)—*locale* DE-2
*Maul Reservoir* CA-9
Maul Run—*stream* NC-3
Maulsby—*locale* MO-7
**Maulsby**—*pop pl* IA-7
*Mauls Point* NC-3
Mauls Swamp—*stream* NC-3
Maultbys Point—*cape* NC-3
Mault Cem—*cemetery* OH-6
Maulua Bay—*bay* HI-9
*Maulua Gulch* HI-9
Maulua Iki—*civil* HI-9
Maulua Nui—*civil* HI-9
Maulua Stream—*stream* HI-9
Maulua Trail—*trail* HI-9
**Maulua (Weloka)**—*pop pl* HI-9
Maululu Stream—*stream* AS-9
Maumau—*civil* HI-9
Maumau Point—*cape* HI-9
*Maume Beach* HI-9
**Maumee**—*pop pl* AR-4
**Maumee**—*pop pl* IN-6
**Maumee**—*pop pl* (2) OH-6
Maumee Bay—*bay* OH-6
Maumee Cem—*cemetery* OH-6
Maumee Ch—*church* IN-6
*Maumee Creek* IN-6
Maumee Crossing—*locale* AR-4
Maumee Ditch—*canal* IN-6
Maumee Hill—*summit* IN-6
Maumee Hollow—*valley* AR-4
Maumee Mine—*mine* (2) CA-9
Maumee River—*stream* IN-6
Maumee River—*stream* OH-6
Maumee Sidecut—*hist pl* OH-6
Maumee State For—*forest* OH-6
Maumee Swamp—*swamp* NY-2

Maumee (Township of)—*fmr MCD* AR-4
**Maumee (Township of)**—*pop pl* IN-6
Maumee Uptown Hist Dist—*hist pl* OH-6
Maumee Valley Sch—*school* OH-6
**Maumelle**—*pop pl* AR-4
Maumelle, Lake—*reservoir* AR-4
Maumelle Harbor—*bay* AR-4
**Maumelle New Town**—*pop pl* AR-4
Maumelle Ordnance Plant (U.S. Army)—*other* AR-4
Maumelle Pinnacles—*ridge* AR-4
Maumelle Prairie—*flat* AR-4
Maumelle Public Use Area—*park* AR-4
Maumelle River—*stream* AR-4
Maumelle (Township of)—*fmr MCD* (2) AR-4
Maunaanu Waterhole—*lake* HI-9
**Maunabo**—*pop pl* PR-3
Maunabo (Municipio)—*civil* PR-3
Maunabo (Pueblo)—*fmr MCD* PR-3
*Mauna Eeka* HI-9
*Mauna Halakala* HI-9
*Mauna Haleakala* HI-9
Maunahina Stream—*stream* HI-9
*Mauna Hualalai* HI-9
Maunahui—*summit* HI-9
Mauna Iki Trail—*trail* HI-9
*Mauna Kaala* HI-9
*Mauna Kala* HI-9
Mauna Kea Adz Quarry—*hist pl* HI-9
Mauna Kea For Res—*forest* HI-9
Mauna Kea-Humuula Trail—*trail* HI-9
Mauna Kea Memorial Park—*cemetery* HI-9
Mauna Kea Umikoa Trail—*trail* HI-9
*Mauna Kea Volcano* HI-9
Maunakini—*summit* HI-9
Maunalaha Stream—*stream* HI-9
**Maunalani Heights**—*pop pl* HI-9
Maunalani Hosp—*hospital* HI-9
Maunalan Playground—*park* HI-9
Maunalei—*area* HI-9
Maunalei—*civil* HI-9
Maunalei Gulch—*valley* HI-9
*Maunaloa* HI-9
**Mauna Loa**—*pop pl* HI-9
Mauna Loa, Lake—*lake* MI-6
Mauna Loa Cem—*cemetery* HI-9
Maunaloa (census name for Mauna Loa)—*CDP* HI-9
**Mauna Loa (census name Maunaloa)**—*pop pl* HI-9
Mauna Loa For And Game Res—*forest* HI-9
Mauna Loa Trail—*trail* HI-9
*Mauna Loa Volcano* HI-9
Mauna Lua—*civil* HI-9
**Maunalua**—*pop pl* HI-9
Maunalua Bay—*bay* HI-9
Maunanu—*summit* HI-9
Mauna o Ahi Ridge—*ridge* HI-9
*Mauna o Ecka* HI-9
*Mauna o Eeka* HI-9
*Mauna o Eka* HI-9
Maunaolu Coll—*school* HI-9
Maunaoluolu—*summit* HI-9
Maunaoluolu Gulch—*valley* HI-9
*Maunaolu Seminary* HI-9
Maunaoni—*civil* HI-9
Maunapuluo—*summit* HI-9
*Mauna Roa* HI-9
Maunatome Mtn—*summit* PA-2
Maunauna—*summit* HI-9
*Maunauna Mtn* HI-9
Maunawai—*other* HI-9
**Maunawili**—*pop pl* HI-9
Maunawili Ditch—*canal* HI-9
Maunawili Sch—*school* HI-9
Maunawili Stream—*stream* HI-9
Maunawili Valley—*valley* HI-9
Maunders Corners—*locale* NY-2
Mauneluk River—*stream* AK-9
Maunesha River—*stream* WI-6
Mauney Branch—*stream* NC-3
Mauney Cem—*cemetery* NC-3
Mauney Chapel—*church* KY-4
Mauney Cove—*valley* NC-3
Mauney Cove Branch—*stream* NC-3
Mauney Creek—*stream* NC-3
Mauney Gap—*gap* NC-3
**Maunie**—*pop pl* IL-6
Maunie North Oil Field—*other* IL-6
Maunie South Oil Field—*other* IL-6
Maunu Sch—*school* SD-7
*Mauo* MH-9
Maupas Pond—*lake* CT-1
*Maupers Island* AL-4
**Maupin**—*pop pl* MO-7
**Maupin**—*pop pl* OR-9
Maupin Ave Ch—*church* NC-3
Maupin Bend—*bend* KY-4
Maupin Branch—*stream* MO-7
Maupin Butte—*summit* (2) OR-9
Maupin Cem—*cemetery* MO-7
Maupin Cem—*cemetery* OR-9
Maupin Cem—*cemetery* (2) TN-4
Maupin Cem—*cemetery* WV-2
Maupin Ch—*church* KY-4
Maupin Cow Camp—*locale* CO-8
Maupin Creek—*stream* MO-7
Maupin Creek—*stream* MT-8
Maupin Field Shelter—*locale* VA-3
Maupin Flat—*flat* AR-4
Maupin Flat—*flat* CA-9
Maupin Flat—*flat* SD-7
Maupin Gap—*gap* KY-4
Maupin Gulch—*valley* CA-9
Maupin Hollow—*valley* TN-4
Maupin-Maury House—*hist pl* VA-3
Maupin Ranch—*locale* TX-5
Maupin Ranch—*locale* WY-8
**Maupin Row**—*pop pl* TN-4
Maupin Row Ch—*church* TN-4
Maupin Sch—*school* OR-9
Maupin Sch—*school* SD-7
*Maupins Station* TN-4
Maupin Trail Canyon—*valley* OR-9
Maupua—*locale* AS-9
Maupua Stream—*stream* AS-9
Maureen Lake—*reservoir* AZ-5
Maure Hollow—*valley* CO-8
Maurelle Islands—*area* AK-9
*Maurells Inlet* SC-3
**Maurepas**—*pop pl* LA-4
Maurepas, Lake—*lake* LA-4
Maurepas Ch—*church* LA-4
Maurer—*locale* NJ-2
Maurer, Lake—*lake* MO-7
*Maurer Creek* WI-6
Maurer Creek—*stream* MT-8
Maurer Creek—*stream* WI-6
Maurer Ranch—*locale* (2) CO-8
Maurer Ranch—*locale* WY-8
Maurer Sch—*school* MI-6
Maurer Sch—*school* SD-7
Maurer Sch (abandoned)—*school* PA-2
**Maurertown**—*pop pl* VA-3
Maurey Ditch—*canal* IN-6
Maurglen P. O. (historical)—*building* PA-2
Maur Hill Prep Sch—*school* KS-7
Maurice—*locale* KY-4
Maurice—*locale* SD-7
**Maurice**—*pop pl* IA-7
**Maurice**—*pop pl* LA-4
Maurice, Bayou—*gut* LA-4
Maurice, Bayou—*stream* LA-4
*Maurice Bayou* LA-4
Maurice Brengle Dam—*dam* SD-7
Maurice Canyon—*valley* TX-5
Maurice C Cash Sch—*school* AZ-5
Maurice Cem—*cemetery* MT-8
*Maurice Creek* NJ-2
Maurice Creek—*stream* ID-8
Maurice Creek—*stream* MT-8
Maurice Gulch—*valley* SD-7
Maurice K Goddard State Park—*park* PA-2
*Maurice Lake* NE-7
Maurice Mount—*summit* MT-8
Maurice Mtn—*summit* MT-8
Maurice Park—*park* NY-2
Maurice Pond—*lake* MT-8
Maurice River—*locale* NJ-2
Maurice River—*stream* NJ-2
Maurice River Cove—*bay* NJ-2
Maurice River Neck—*cape* NJ-2
**Maurice River (Township of)**—*pop pl* NJ-2
**Mauricetown**—*pop pl* NJ-2
Mauricetown Station—*locale* NJ-2
**Mauriceville**—*pop pl* TX-5
Mauriceville (CCD)—*cens area* TX-5
Mauricio Canyon—*valley* CO-8
*Maurie Creek* MT-8
**Maurin**—*pop pl* TX-5
*Maurine* MS-4
Maurine—*locale* MO-7
**Maurine**—*pop pl* SD-7
Maurine Lake—*reservoir* SD-7
Mauris-Earnest Fort House—*hist pl* TN-4
Maurita Spring—*spring* TX-5
Mauritz Lake—*lake* MN-6
Mau Rsvr—*reservoir* HI-9
*Maury* WA-9
Maury—*locale* WA-9
**Maury**—*pop pl* NC-3
Maury Cem—*cemetery* TN-4
Maury Cem—*cemetery* VA-3
Maury Chapel—*church* TN-4
**Maury City**—*pop pl* TN-4
Maury City (CCD)—*cens area* TN-4
Maury City Division—*civil* TN-4
Maury City Elem Sch—*school* TN-4
Maury City First Baptist Ch—*church* TN-4
Maury City Post Office—*building* TN-4
Maury City Primary Sch—*school* TN-4
**Maury County**—*pop pl* TN-4
Maury County Airp—*airport* TN-4
Maury County Hosp—*hospital* TN-4
Maury County Park—*park* TN-4
Maury Creek—*stream* OR-9
Maury Elem Sch—*hist pl* TN-4
Maury Guard Station—*locale* OR-9
*Maury HS* TN-4
Maury HS—*school* VA-3
Maury Island—*island* WA-9
Maury Junction—*locale* TN-4
*Maury Middle School* TN-4
Maury Monument—*other* VA-3
*Maury Mountain* OR-9
Maury Mountain Mines—*mine* OR-9
Maury Mountains—*range* OR-9
Maury Peak—*summit* AK-9
Maury Place—*uninc pl* VA-3
Maury Pond—*lake* MO-7
Maury River—*stream* VA-3
Maury Sch—*school* DC-2
Maury Sch—*school* (2) TN-4
Maury Sch—*school* (3) VA-3
*Maury's Island* WA-9
Maus Cem—*cemetery* MO-7
**Mausdale**—*pop pl* PA-2
Mauser Glade—*flat* CA-9
Mauser Island Campsite—*locale* ME-1
Mauser Lake—*lake* MN-6
Mauser Mill—*locale* MO-7
Mausert Block—*hist pl* MA-1
Mauserts Pond—*reservoir* MA-1
Mauserts Pond North Dam—*dam* MA-1
Mauserts Pond South Dam—*dam* MA-1
Mauses Creek—*stream* PA-2
Maushie Creek—*stream* MI-6
Maus Hog Windmill—*locale* TX-5
**Maushop Village**—*pop pl* MA-1
Maus Lake—*lake* MO-7
Maus Lake—*reservoir* MO-7
Mausolus, Mount—*summit* AK-9
Maust Hill—*summit* PA-2
**Mauston**—*pop pl* WI-6
Maustown—*locale* OH-6
Mauthe Lake—*lake* WI-6
Mauthe Lake Rec Area—*park* WI-6
Mauuloa—*summit* HI-9
Mauumae Beach—*beach* HI-9
Mauumae Ridge—*ridge* HI-9
*Mauvais Accueil* FM-9
Mauvais Bois, Bayou—*stream* LA-4
*Mauvais Coulee* ND-7
Mauvais Coulee—*arroyo* ND-7
*Mauvaises Terres* SD-7
Mauvaise Terre Creek—*stream* IL-6
Mauvaise Terre Lake—*reservoir* IL-6
Mauvaise Terre Sch—*school* IL-6
Mauvais Lac—*lake* LA-4
*Mauvais Lake* LA-4
*Mauv Canyon* AZ-5
Mauvella—*other* MS-4
*Mauvila Boy Scout Camp* AL-4
**Mauvilla**—*pop pl* AL-4
Mauvilla Cem—*cemetery* AL-4
Mauvilla Community Ch of God—*church* AL-4
**Mauvilla Forest Estates (subdivision)**—*pop pl* AL-4
Mauwee Brook—*stream* CT-1
Mauweehoo, Lake—*reservoir* CT-1
*Mauweehoo Lake* CT-1
Mauwee Peak—*summit* CT-1
*Mauwi* HI-9
Maux Branch—*stream* KY-4
Mauze Gulch—*valley* AK-9
Mauzey Creek—*stream* MT-8
Mauzy—*locale* VA-3
**Mauzy**—*pop pl* IN-6
Mauzy Trading Post—*locale* NM-5
*Mavarick Spring* NM-5
*MA VAR Kilpatrick Lake* MN-6
**Mavaton**—*pop pl* NC-3
Mav Company—*canal* TX-5
*Maver Creek* WI-6
Maverick—*locale* AZ-5
**Maverick**—*pop pl* TX-5
Maverick-Altgelt Ranch and Fenstermaker-Fromme Farm—*hist pl* TX-5
Maverick Basin—*basin* (3) AZ-5
Maverick Basin—*basin* MT-8
Maverick Basin—*valley* AZ-5
Maverick Basin Tank—*reservoir* AZ-5
Maverick Bayou—*gut* TX-5
Maverick Bottom—*bend* UT-8
Maverick Bridge—*other* UT-8
Maverick Butte—*summit* (3) AZ-5
Maverick Butte—*summit* WY-8
Maverick Camp—*locale* AZ-5
Maverick Canyon—*valley* (3) AZ-5
Maverick Canyon—*valley* CO-8
Maverick Canyon—*valley* NV-8
Maverick Canyon—*valley* (8) NM-5
Maverick Canyon—*valley* TX-5
Maverick Canyon—*valley* (2) UT-8
Maverick Canyon Corral—*locale* AZ-5
Maverick Cem—*cemetery* TX-5
Maverick Cienega—*swamp* AZ-5
**Maverick (County)**—*pop pl* TX-5
*Maverick County Canal* TX-5
Maverick County Courthouse—*hist pl* TX-5
Maverick County Lake—*reservoir* TX-5
Maverick Creek—*stream* CO-8
Maverick Creek—*stream* ID-8
Maverick Creek—*stream* NM-5
Maverick Creek—*stream* OR-9
Maverick Creek—*stream* (4) TX-5
Maverick Creek—*stream* WY-8
Maverick Creek Windmill—*locale* TX-5
Maverick Dam—*dam* TX-5
Maverick Ditch—*canal* WY-8
Maverick Draw—*valley* CO-8
Maverick Draw—*valley* TX-5
Maverick Draw—*valley* UT-8
Maverick Flat—*flat* AZ-5
Maverick Flat—*flat* NM-5
Maverick Flat—*flat* TX-5
Maverick Flats—*flat* CO-8
Maverick Flat Tank—*reservoir* AZ-5
Maverick Gap Spring—*spring* AZ-5
Maverick Gulch—*valley* (2) CO-8
Maverick Hill—*summit* AZ-5
Maverick Hill Tank—*reservoir* AZ-5
Maverick Irrigation District Canal—*canal* TX-5
Maverick Lake—*lake* AZ-5
Maverick Lake—*lake* NE-7
Maverick Mesa—*bench* NM-5
Maverick Mines—*mine* CO-8
Maverick Mountain Ski Area—*area* MT-8
Maverick Mountain Wash—*stream* AZ-5
Maverick Mtn—*summit* (6) AZ-5
Maverick Mtn—*summit* MT-8
Maverick Mtn—*summit* NM-5
Maverick Mtn—*summit* TX-5
*Maverick Natural Bridge* UT-8
Maverick Park—*park* TX-5
Maverick Peak—*summit* AZ-5
Maverick Peak—*summit* NM-5
Maverick Peak—*summit* WA-9
Maverick Point—*cape* (2) UT-8
Maverick Prong—*stream* MT-8
Maverick Ranger Station—*locale* TX-5
Maverick Rsvr—*reservoir* MT-8
Maverick Saddle—*gap* WA-9
Maverick Sch—*school* (2) TX-5
*Maverick Spring* TX-5
Maverick Spring—*spring* (8) AZ-5
Maverick Spring—*spring* CO-8
Maverick Spring—*spring* (5) NM-5
Maverick Spring—*spring* TX-5
Maverick Spring—*spring* (2) UT-8
Maverick Spring—*spring* WY-8
Maverick Spring Branch—*stream* TX-5
Maverick Spring Canyon—*valley* AZ-5
Maverick Spring Dome—*summit* WY-8
Maverick Spring Dome Oil Field—*oilfield* WY-8
*Maverick Spring Draw* WY-8
Maverick Spring Draw—*valley* WY-8
Maverick Springs—*spring* NV-8
*Maverick Springs Canyon* AZ-5
Maverick Springs Range—*range* NV-8
Maverick Tank—*reservoir* (7) AZ-5
Maverick Tank—*reservoir* NM-5
Maverick Tank—*reservoir* (3) TX-5
Maverick Well—*well* (2) AZ-5
Maverick Windmill—*locale* TX-5
Maveric Tank—*reservoir* AZ-5
**Mavie**—*pop pl* MN-6
Mavilla (Barrio)—*fmr MCD* PR-3
Mavin Hill—*summit* OR-9
**Mavis**—*pop pl* WV-2
**Mavisdale**—*pop pl* VA-3
Mavis Island—*island* AK-9
Mavis Lake—*lake* CA-9
Mavis Lake—*lake* MN-6
**Mavis Subdivision**—*pop pl* UT-8
Mavis Wash—*stream* AZ-5
Mavity—*locale* KY-4
Mavity Landing—*locale* TN-4
Mavo—*locale* KY-4
Mavreeso Campground—*locale* CO-8
Mavreeso Canyon—*valley* CO-8
Mavreeso Creek—*stream* CO-8
Mavriat Rsvr—*reservoir* CO-8
*Mawae* HI-9
Mawae—*area* HI-9
Mawae Gate—*gap* HI-9
Mawah Creek—*stream* CA-9
*Mawai* HI-9
Mawavi Camp No 2—*locale* VA-3
Maw Bay—*bay* NC-3
Mawdesley Lake—*lake* MI-6
Mawdsley, Capt. John, House—*hist pl* RI-1
Mawell Chapel—*church* TN-4
Mawer Lateral—*canal* SD-7
*Mawhee* HI-9
Mawl Springs—*locale* SD-7
Mawney Brook—*stream* RI-1
Maw Point—*cape* NC-3
Maw Point Creek—*bay* NC-3
Maw Point Shoal—*bar* NC-3
Mawres Landing (historical)—*locale* MS-4
*Mawrglen* PA-2
Maws Gulch—*valley* ID-8
Mawson Bridge—*bridge* CA-9
Maws Spring—*spring* MT-8
Max—*locale* MN-6
Max—*locale* MO-7
Max—*locale* VA-3
**Max**—*pop pl* ID-8
**Max**—*pop pl* IN-6
**Max**—*pop pl* IA-7
**Max**—*pop pl* NE-7
**Max**—*pop pl* ND-7
Maxada Sch—*school* PA-2
Maxam Drain—*canal* MI-6
*Maxams* IN-6
Maxam Sch—*school* (2) MI-6
**Maxatawny**—*pop pl* PA-2
Maxatawny Township Elem Sch—*school* PA-2
**Maxatawny (Township of)**—*pop pl* PA-2
*Maxay Pond* MA-1
**Maxbass**—*pop pl* ND-7
Maxbass Cem—*cemetery* ND-7
Max Branch—*stream* FL-3
Max Bruner, Junior JHS—*school* FL-3
Max Canyon—*valley* CO-8
Max Cem—*cemetery* NE-7
*Maxcey* MS-4
Max Cove—*bay* AK-9
**Max Creek**—*pop pl* VA-3
Max Creek—*stream* AK-9
Max Creek—*stream* IL-6
Max Creek—*stream* IA-7
Max Creek—*stream* MO-7
Max Creek—*stream* MT-8
Max Creek—*stream* OR-9
Maxcy Pond—*lake* MA-1
**Maxcy Quarters**—*pop pl* FL-3
Maxdale—*locale* TX-5
Maxdale Community Center—*locale* TX-5
Max Dalton Artesian Well—*well* UT-8
Max Ditch—*canal* WY-8
Maxedon Branch—*stream* TN-4
Maxewell Branch—*stream* KY-4
*Maxey* AZ-5
Maxey—*locale* MO-7
**Maxey**—*pop pl* TN-4
**Maxey**—*pop pl* TX-5
Maxey, Samuel Bell, House—*hist pl* TX-5
Maxey Bayou—*gut* MS-4
Maxey Branch—*stream* MS-4
Maxey Cem—*cemetery* CO-8
Maxey Cem—*cemetery* IL-6
Maxey Cem—*cemetery* (2) MS-4
Maxey Cem—*cemetery* OK-5
Maxey Cem—*cemetery* TN-4
Maxey Ch—*church* CO-8
Maxey Community Center—*building* TN-4
Maxey Creek—*stream* AR-4
Maxey Creek—*stream* KY-4
Maxey Creek—*stream* TX-5
Maxey Ditch—*canal* MT-8
Maxey Dock—*locale* TN-4
Maxey Elem Sch—*school* FL-3
Maxey Flats—*flat* KY-4
Maxey (historical)—*locale* MS-4
Maxey Knob—*summit* (2) KY-4
Maxey Lateral—*canal* AZ-5
Maxey Mill Creek—*stream* VA-3
Maxey Mine—*mine* MT-8
Maxey Mines—*mine* MT-8
*Maxey Mtn* AR-4
Maxey Mtn—*summit* AR-4
*Maxey Pond* MA-1
Maxey Pond—*lake* NY-2
Maxey Ranch—*locale* CA-9
Maxey Ranch—*locale* NM-5
Maxey Ridge—*ridge* MT-8
**Maxeys**—*pop pl* GA-3
Maxeys (CCD)—*cens area* GA-3
Maxey Sch (historical)—*school* TN-4
Maxeys Creek—*stream* VA-3
*Maxeys Mill* MS-4
*Maxeys Pond* MA-1
Maxey Town—*locale* TX-5
Maxey (Township of)—*fmr MCD* AR-4
Maxey Valley Sch—*school* KY-4
**Maxeyville**—*pop pl* CO-8
Maxfield Basin—*basin* UT-8
Maxfield Brook—*stream* (2) ME-1
Maxfield Creek—*stream* ID-8
Maxfield Creek—*stream* OR-9
Maxfield Creek—*stream* (2) WA-9
Maxfield (historical P.O.)—*locale* IA-7
*Maxfield Lake* MI-6
Maxfield Lake—*lake* MI-6
Maxfield Lodge—*locale* UT-8
Maxfield Mine—*mine* NV-8
Maxfield Mine—*mine* UT-8
Maxfield Point—*cape* VT-1
Maxfield Prairie—*flat* WA-9
Maxfield Sch—*school* (2) IL-6
Maxfield Sch—*school* ME-1
Maxfield Sch—*school* NH-1
*Maxfield's Point* VT-1
**Maxfield Subdivision**—*pop pl* UT-8
**Maxfield (Town of)**—*pop pl* ME-1
Maxfield Township—*fmr MCD* IA-7
Max Gulch—*valley* OR-9
Maxham Sch—*school* MA-1
Max Hoeck Back Creek—*gut* FL-3
Max Hoeck Creek—*gut* FL-3
Max Hollow—*valley* VA-3
**Maxie**—*pop pl* (2) KY-4
**Maxie**—*pop pl* LA-4
**Maxie**—*pop pl* MS-4
**Maxie**—*pop pl* VA-3
Maxie Branch—*stream* MO-7
Maxie Cem—*cemetery* IL-6
Maxie Cem—*cemetery* MS-4
Maxie Ch—*church* LA-4
Maxie Creek—*stream* MS-4
Maxie Fire Tower—*locale* MS-4
Maxie Lake Dam—*dam* MS-4
*Maxie Lookout Tower* MS-4
Maxie Oil and Gas Field—*oilfield* LA-4
Maxie Oil And Gas Field—*oilfield* MS-4
Maxie Pond—*lake* ME-1
Maxie Ridge—*summit* TN-4
Maxies Hill Ch—*church* GA-3
Maxie Tank—*reservoir* AZ-5
Maxim—*locale* GA-3
Maxim—*locale* NJ-2
**Maxim Corner**—*pop pl* MA-1
Maxim Corner Pond—*reservoir* MA-1
Maximilian Gulch—*valley* CO-8
Maximilian Township (historical)—*civil* SD-7
Maxim Lake—*lake* MN-6
**Maximo**—*pop pl* OH-6
Maximo Bridge—*bridge* FL-3
Maximo Channel—*channel* FL-3
Maximo Elem Sch—*school* FL-3
Maximo Heights Baptist Ch—*church* FL-3
Maximo Moorings—*locale* FL-3
Maximo Point—*cape* FL-3
Maxine—*locale* KY-4
**Maxine**—*pop pl* AL-4
**Maxine**—*pop pl* KS-7
**Maxine**—*pop pl* WV-2
Maxine, Lake—*reservoir* IN-6
Maxine Bridge—*bridge* AL-4
Maxine Creek—*stream* MT-8
Maxine East Oil Field—*oilfield* TX-5
*Maxine Elementary School* AL-4
Maxine Lake—*lake* MN-6
Maxine Lake Dam—*dam* IN-6
Maxine Mines (surface)—*mine* AL-4
Maxine Mine (underground)—*mine* AL-4
Maxine Oil Field—*oilfield* TX-5
Maxine Point—*summit* MT-8
Maxine Sch—*school* MI-6
Maxine Sch (historical)—*school* AL-4
*Maxine Tailings Pond* AL-4
Maxine Tailings Pond Dam—*dam* AL-4
**Maxinkuckee**—*pop pl* IN-6
Maxinkuckee, Lake—*reservoir* IN-6
Max Lake—*lake* AK-9
Max Lake—*lake* MI-6
Maxler, Lake—*reservoir* IN-6
Max Lopez Spring—*spring* NM-5
**Max Meadows**—*pop pl* VA-3
Maxmillian Hollow—*valley* IL-6
Maxmore Creek—*bay* MD-2
Maxon—*locale* KY-4
**Maxon**—*pop pl* IA-7
Maxon Basin—*basin* WY-8
Maxon Cem—*cemetery* MI-6
Maxon Cem—*cemetery* WI-6
Maxon Ch—*church* KY-4
Maxon Corners—*locale* NY-2
Maxon Creek—*stream* NY-2
Maxon Creek—*stream* TX-5
Maxon Crossing—*locale* KY-4
Maxon Hill—*summit* RI-1
Maxon Ranch—*locale* WY-8
Maxon Ridge—*ridge* NY-2
Maxon (RR name for West Paducah)—*other* KY-4
Maxon Rsvr—*reservoir* IA-7
Maxon Sch—*school* IA-7
Maxon Sch—*school* NJ-2
Maxon Station—*locale* KY-4
Max Patch Mtn—*summit* NC-3
*Maxs Arch* OR-9
Max Seep—*spring* AZ-5
*Max Slough* WA-9
Maxson Crater—*other* NM-5
Maxson Dome—*summit* CA-9
Maxson Lake—*lake* AK-9
Maxson Lake—*lake* CA-9
Maxson Meadows—*flat* CA-9
Maxson Sch—*school* CA-9
Max Spring—*spring* OR-9
Max Spring Branch—*stream* FL-3
Max Starcke Dam—*dam* TX-5
Max Starcke Park—*park* TX-5
Max Tank—*reservoir* AZ-5
Maxted Draw—*valley* WY-8
**Maxton**—*pop pl* NC-3
Maxton Cem—*cemetery* IL-6
Maxton Hollow—*valley* MO-7
Maxton Lookout Tower—*locale* MI-6
Maxton Plains—*flat* MI-6
Maxton P.O. (historical)—*building* AL-4
Maxton Pond—*reservoir* NC-3
Maxton Pond Dam—*dam* NC-3
Maxton (Township of)—*fmr MCD* NC-3
**Maxtown**—*pop pl* OH-6
Max Township—*civ div* NE-7
**Max (Township of)**—*pop pl* MN-6
*Maxville* KY-4
*Maxville* MS-4
*Maxville* MO-7
Maxville—*locale* OR-9
**Maxville**—*pop pl* AR-4
**Maxville**—*pop pl* FL-3
**Maxville**—*pop pl* (2) IN-6
**Maxville**—*pop pl* KY-4
**Maxville**—*pop pl* (2) MO-7
**Maxville**—*pop pl* MT-8
**Maxville**—*pop pl* OH-6
**Maxville**—*pop pl* WI-6
Maxville Assembly of God Ch—*church* FL-3
Maxville Cem—*cemetery* WI-6
Maxville Ch—*church* AR-4
Maxville Ch—*church* IN-6
Maxville Sch—*school* AR-4
**Maxville (Town of)**—*pop pl* WI-6
*Maxwall* OR-9
*Maxwell* OR-9
Maxwell—*locale* (2) GA-3
Maxwell—*locale* (2) IL-6
Maxwell—*locale* KY-4
Maxwell—*locale* NJ-2
Max Well—*locale* NM-5
Maxwell—*locale* NY-2
Maxwell—*locale* NC-3
Maxwell—*locale* VA-3
**Maxwell**—*pop pl* AL-4
**Maxwell**—*pop pl* CA-9
**Maxwell**—*pop pl* (2) IN-6
**Maxwell**—*pop pl* IA-7
**Maxwell**—*pop pl* NE-7
**Maxwell**—*pop pl* NM-5
**Maxwell**—*pop pl* OK-5
**Maxwell**—*pop pl* PA-2
**Maxwell**—*pop pl* (2) TN-4
**Maxwell**—*pop pl* TX-5
**Maxwell**—*pop pl* WV-2
Maxwell, Art and Frieda, Barn—*hist pl* ID-8
Maxwell, Ebenezer, House—*hist pl* PA-2
Maxwell, James O., Farmstead—*hist pl* OR-9
Maxwell, R. G., House—*hist pl* CO-8
Maxwell Acad—*school* TN-4
**Maxwell Acres**—*pop pl* WV-2
Maxwell Air Force Base—*airport* AL-4
Maxwell Air Force Base Senior Officer's Quarters Hist Dist—*hist pl* AL-4
Maxwell Baptist Ch—*church* TN-4
Maxwell Basin—*basin* OR-9
Maxwell Bay—*bay* MN-6
Maxwell Bay—*bay* NY-2
Maxwellborn—*locale* AL-4
Max Wellborn Cave—*cave* AL-4
Maxwellborn Spring—*spring* AL-4
Maxwell Branch—*stream* AL-4
Maxwell Branch—*stream* AR-4
Maxwell Branch—*stream* GA-3
Maxwell Branch—*stream* IN-6
Maxwell Branch—*stream* KY-4
Maxwell Branch—*stream* MS-4
Maxwell Branch—*stream* (2) TN-4
Maxwell Branch—*stream* TX-5
Maxwell Bridge—*bridge* CA-9
Maxwell Bridge—*bridge* SC-3
Maxwell Brook—*stream* ME-1
Maxwell Brook—*stream* (2) MA-1
Maxwell Brook—*stream* NY-2
Maxwell Butte—*summit* MT-8
Maxwell Butte—*summit* OR-9
Maxwell Canal—*canal* OR-9
Maxwell Canyon—*valley* UT-8
Maxwell Cave—*cave* TN-4
Maxwell Cem—*cemetery* (3) AL-4
Maxwell Cem—*cemetery* (2) AR-4
Maxwell Cem—*cemetery* CA-9
Maxwell Cem—*cemetery* (2) GA-3
Maxwell Cem—*cemetery* IL-6
Maxwell Cem—*cemetery* IN-6
Maxwell Cem—*cemetery* (2) ME-1
Maxwell Cem—*cemetery* MS-4
Maxwell Cem—*cemetery* MO-7
Maxwell Cem—*cemetery* (2) NC-3
Maxwell Cem—*cemetery* OK-5
Maxwell Cem—*cemetery* (6) TN-4
Maxwell Cem—*cemetery* TX-5
Maxwell Cem—*cemetery* WV-2
Maxwell Ch—*church* OK-5
Maxwell Chapel—*church* AL-4
Maxwell Chapel—*church* NC-3
Maxwell Chapel—*church* TN-4
Maxwell Chapel Cem—*cemetery* TN-4
*Maxwell Chapel United Methodist Church* TN-4
Maxwell Ch (historical)—*church* AL-4
Maxwell Childrens Home—*building* SC-3
**Maxwell Colony**—*pop pl* SD-7
Maxwell Community Cem—*cemetery* TN-4
Maxwell Coulee—*valley* MT-8
Maxwell Cove—*bay* (2) ME-1
Maxwell Cove—*valley* AL-4
Maxwell Cove—*valley* NC-3
*Maxwell Creek* AR-4
Maxwell Creek—*stream* AL-4
Maxwell Creek—*stream* AK-9
Maxwell Creek—*stream* AR-4
Maxwell Creek—*stream* (6) CA-9
Maxwell Creek—*stream* (2) CO-8
Maxwell Creek—*stream* GA-3
Maxwell Creek—*stream* ID-8
Maxwell Creek—*stream* IL-6
Maxwell Creek—*stream* MT-8
Maxwell Creek—*stream* NY-2
Maxwell Creek—*stream* NC-3
Maxwell Creek—*stream* (2) OK-5
Maxwell Creek—*stream* OR-9
Maxwell Creek—*stream* (2) TX-5
Maxwell Creek—*stream* WY-8
Maxwell Crossing—*locale* TX-5
Maxwell Ditch—*canal* (2) OR-9
Maxwell Ditch—*stream* IN-6
Maxwell Ditch No 19 and 20—*canal* CO-8
Maxwell Drain—*canal* MI-6
Maxwell Draw—*valley* WY-8
Maxwell Drift (historical)—*mine* PA-2
Maxwell Falls Picnic Grounds—*locale* CO-8
*Maxwell Field (Maxwell Air Force Base)* AL-4
*Maxwell Game Preserve* KS-7
Maxwell Gap—*gap* (2) AL-4
Maxwell Gap—*gap* WV-2
**Maxwell Garden**—*pop pl* VA-3
*Maxwell Grant* CO-8
Maxwell Gulch—*valley* ID-8
*Maxwell-Gunter Air Force Base Rec Area* AL-4
Maxwell-Gunter Rec Area—*park* AL-4
Maxwell Hall—*hist pl* MD-2
Maxwell Hamilton Cem—*cemetery* MS-4
*Maxwell Heights* MO-7
**Maxwell Heights (subdivision)**—*pop pl* AL-4
Maxwell Hill—*summit* IN-6
Maxwell Hill—*summit* MT-8
Maxwell Hill—*summit* TN-4
Maxwell Hill—*summit* WA-9
Maxwell Hill Sch—*school* WV-2
Maxwell-Hinman House—*hist pl* AR-4
Maxwell (historical)—*locale* MS-4
Maxwell (historical)—*locale* UT-8
**Maxwell (historical)**—*pop pl* OR-9
Maxwell Hollow—*valley* AL-4
Maxwell Hollow—*valley* (2) AR-4

Maxwell Hollow—*valley* TN-4
Maxwell House—*hist pl* KY-4
Maxwell House—*hist pl* NC-3
Maxwell Island—*island* ME-1
Maxwell JHS—*school* AZ-5
Maxwell Lake—*lake* CA-9
Maxwell Lake—*lake* CO-8
Maxwell Lake—*lake* (3) OR-9
Maxwell Lake—*reservoir* GA-3
Maxwell Lake—*reservoir* TN-4
Maxwell Lake (historical)—*lake* AZ-5
Maxwell Lock—*dam* PA-2
Maxwell Lock and Dam—*dam* PA-2
*Maxwell Locks and Dam* PA-2
**Maxwell Mill**—*pop pl* NC-3
Maxwell Millpond—*reservoir* (2) NC-3
Maxwell Mine—*mine* CA-9
Maxwell Mine—*mine* OR-9
Maxwell Mine—*mine* TN-4
Maxwell MS—*school* IN-6
Maxwell Mtn—*summit* (2) AL-4
Maxwell Mtn—*summit* OK-5
Maxwell Mtn—*summit* TN-4
Maxwell Mtn—*summit* TX-5
Maxwell Natl Wildlife Ref—*park* NM-5
Maxwell Park—*flat* AZ-5
Maxwell Park—*park* MI-6
Maxwell Park—*park* OK-5
Maxwell Park Sch—*school* CA-9
*Maxwell Peak* OR-9
Maxwell Place—*hist pl* KY-4
Maxwell Point—*cape* ME-1
Maxwell Point—*cape* MD-2
Maxwell Point—*cape* OR-9
Maxwell Point—*summit* ID-8
Maxwell Pond—*lake* OR-9
Maxwell Pond—*reservoir* OR-9
Maxwell Pool—*reservoir* PA-2
Maxwell Post Office (historical)—*building* TN-4
Maxwell Ranch—*locale* CA-9
Maxwell Ranch—*locale* CO-8
Maxwell Ranch—*locale* MT-8
Maxwell Ranch—*locale* OR-9
Maxwell Ridge—*ridge* WV-2
Maxwell Rsvr—*reservoir* CO-8
Maxwell Rsvr—*reservoir* OR-9
Maxwell Run—*stream* (2) PA-2
Maxwell Run—*stream* (2) WV-2
Maxwell Run Cem—*cemetery* PA-2
Maxwell Saint Sch—*school* KY-4
Maxwell Sawmill (Inactive)—*locale* CA-9
Maxwells Branch—*stream* MS-4
Maxwell Sch—*school* AL-4
Maxwell Sch—*school* (3) CA-9
Maxwell Sch—*school* IL-6
Maxwell Sch—*school* NV-8
Maxwell Sch—*school* NC-3
Maxwell Sch—*school* (2) PA-2
Maxwell Sch (abandoned)—*school* PA-2
Maxwell Sch (historical)—*school* TN-4
Maxwell School—*locale* CO-8
Maxwells Creek—*stream* UT-8
*Maxwells Landing* AL-4
Maxwells Landing (historical)—*locale* MS-4
*Maxwells Mill Pond* NC-3
Maxwell Spring—*spring* (2) AZ-5
Maxwell Spring—*spring* KS-7
Maxwell Spring—*spring* MT-8
Maxwell Spring—*spring* (2) OR-9
Maxwell Spring—*spring* TN-4
Maxwell Spring—*spring* WI-6
Maxwells Slough—*bay* TX-5
Maxwell's Slough Bridge—*hist pl* KS-7
Maxwells Store (historical)—*locale* AL-4
Maxwell State Game Ref—*park* KS-7
Maxwell Storage Annex—*military* AL-4
Maxwell Swamp—*swamp* ME-1
Maxwell-Sweet House—*hist pl* AR-4
Maxwell Tank—*reservoir* (4) AZ-5
*Maxwellton* WA-9
**Maxwell (Township of)**—*pop pl* IL-6
**Maxwell (Township of)**—*pop pl* MN-6
Maxwell Trail—*trail* OR-9
Maxwell Vocational HS—*school* NY-2
Maxwell Vocational HS Annex—*school* NY-2
Maxwell Well—*well* MT-8
Maxwelton—*hist pl* TN-4
**Maxwelton**—*pop pl* WA-9
**Maxwelton**—*pop pl* WV-2
Maxwelton Golf Club—*other* IN-6
Maxx Plaza, The (Shop Ctr)—*locale* FL-3
Maxy Brook—*stream* ME-1
Maxy Canyon—*valley* CA-9
*May* AL-4
*May* NC-3
*May* ND-7
*May* FM-9
*May* MH-9
May—*locale* KY-4
May—*locale* MO-7
May—*locale* TX-5
May—*locale* WV-2
**May**—*pop pl* CA-9
**May**—*pop pl* ID-8
**May**—*pop pl* MI-6
**May**—*pop pl* OK-5
**May**—*pop pl* SC-3
**May**—*pop pl* TX-5
May, Asa, House—*hist pl* FL-3
May, Bayou—*stream* (2) LA-4
May, Cape—*cape* NJ-2
May, David L., House—*hist pl* KY-4
May, Eli, House—*hist pl* WI-6
May, George, House—*hist pl* MT-8
May, Lake—*lake* FL-3
May, Lake—*lake* MI-6
May, Lake—*lake* MN-6
May, Lake—*lake* WA-9
May, Lake—*swamp* FL-3
May, Mount—*summit* MT-8
May, Point—*bar* MA-1
May, Robert, House—*hist pl* KY-4
May, Samuel, House—*hist pl* KY-4
May, Sophie, House—*hist pl* ME-1
*Maya* MH-9
Ma'ya—*slope* MH-9
Maya, Mesa de—*summit* CO-8
*Mayacamas Mountains* CA-9
**Mayacas (historical)**—*pop pl* FL-3
Mayacmas Mountains—*range* CA-9
**May Acres**—*pop pl* TN-4
Mayaguez—*CDP* PR-3
**Mayaguez**—*pop pl* PR-3
Mayaguez, Bahia de—*bay* PR-3
Mayaguez Airp—*airport* PR-3
Mayaguez Arriba (Barrio)—*fmr MCD* PR-3
Mayaguez (Ciudad)—*fmr MCD* PR-3
Mayaguez (Municipio)—*civil* PR-3
**Mayaguez Terrace**—*pop pl* (2) PR-3
**Mayaimi (historical)**—*pop pl* FL-3
May Airp—*airport* MO-7
May Airp—*airport* NC-3
Mayall St Sch—*school* CA-9
Mayall Telescope (158 Inch)—*building* AZ-5
May and Akers Cem—*cemetery* AL-4
May and Cooney Dry Goods Company—*hist pl* AL-4
May and White Drain—*canal* MI-6
Mayan Lake—*lake* FL-3
Mayan Peak—*summit* CA-9
Mayapple Branch—*stream* KY-4
Mayapple Brook—*stream* CT-1
May Apple Ch—*church* KY-4
Mayapple Gap—*gap* NC-3
Mayapple Hill—*summit* NJ-2
May Apple (historical)—*locale* AL-4
May Apple (historical P.O.)—*locale* AL-4
Mayapple Knob—*summit* GA-3
**Mayaro**—*pop pl* CA-9
Mayason Ch—*church* SD-7
*Mayate Canyon* CA-9
Mayatte Creek—*stream* MS-4
**Mayaya**—*pop pl* GU-9
Maybank—*locale* MS-4
May Basin—*basin* OR-9
Maybea Cave—*cave* AL-4
*Maybe Canyon* ID-8
*Maybe Creek* ID-8
Maybe Creek—*stream* (2) AK-9
*Maybee* OH-6
**Maybee**—*pop pl* MI-6
**Maybee**—*pop pl* OH-6
Maybee Branch—*stream* MO-7
Maybee Meadows—*flat* MT-8
Maybee Sch—*school* MI-6
*Maybell* MS-4
**Maybell**—*pop pl* CO-8
**Maybell**—*pop pl* MS-4
Maybell Canyon—*valley* TX-5
Maybell Ditch—*canal* CO-8
Maybelle B. Avery Elem Sch—*school* CT-1
Maybelle Ch—*church* OK-5
*Maybelle Lake* WY-8
Maybelle Lake—*lake* WY-8
Maybell Mine—*mine* CA-9
Maybell-Powder Wash—*cens area* CO-8
Maybe Nasty Cave—*cave* PA-2
Mayberry—*locale* IL-6
Mayberry—*locale* NE-7
**Mayberry**—*pop pl* MD-2
**Mayberry**—*pop pl* VA-3
Mayberry, Henry H., House—*hist pl* TN-4
Mayberry, H. G. W., House—*hist pl* TN-4
Mayberry Brake—*woods* AR-4
Mayberry Branch—*stream* IL-6
Mayberry Branch—*stream* MO-7
Mayberry Branch—*stream* (3) TN-4
Mayberry Branch Access Park—*park* TN-4
Mayberry Canyon—*valley* NM-5
Mayberry Cem—*cemetery* AR-4
Mayberry Cem—*cemetery* KS-7
Mayberry Cem—*cemetery* ME-1
Mayberry Cem—*cemetery* (3) MO-7
Mayberry Cem—*cemetery* (3) TN-4
Mayberry Cem—*cemetery* TX-5
Mayberry Ch—*church* AL-4
Mayberry Ch—*church* VA-3
Mayberry Ch—*church* WV-2
Mayberry Creek—*stream* AL-4
Mayberry Creek—*stream* VA-3
Mayberry Cut—*canal* CA-9
Mayberry Elem Sch (historical)—*school* AL-4
Mayberry Gully—*valley* AL-4
*Mayberry Hill* MA-1
**Mayberry Hill**—*pop pl* ME-1
Mayberry Hill—*summit* ME-1
Mayberry (historical)—*locale* SD-7
**Mayberry (historical)**—*pop pl* TN-4
Mayberry Hollow—*valley* MO-7
Mayberry Hollow—*valley* (4) TN-4
Mayberry JHS—*school* KS-7
Mayberry Lake—*reservoir* KS-7
Mayberry Mound and Village Site—*hist pl* IL-6
Mayberry Mtn—*summit* TX-5
Mayberry Park—*park* CA-9
Mayberry Park Dam—*dam* SD-7
Mayberry Pond—*lake* NH-1
Mayberry Ridge—*ridge* AR-4
Mayberry Run—*stream* WV-2
Mayberry Sch—*school* CT-1
Mayberry Sch (historical)—*school* TN-4
Mayberry Slough—*gut* AR-4
Mayberry Slough—*gut* CA-9
Mayberry Spring—*spring* AZ-5
Mayberry Spring—*spring* CO-8
Mayberry Spring—*spring* TN-4
Mayberry Street Sch—*school* CA-9
**Mayberry (Township of)**—*pop pl* IL-6
**Mayberry (Township of)**—*pop pl* PA-2
**Mayberry Village**—*pop pl* CT-1
**Mayberry Wells**—*pop pl* MD-2
Maybeso Creek—*stream* AK-9
Maybe Tank—*reservoir* AZ-5
Maybet Pond—*lake* FL-3
**Maybeury**—*pop pl* WV-2
Maybeury Sch—*school* VA-3
Maybin Mtn—*summit* NC-3
**Maybinton**—*pop pl* SC-3
Maybird Gulch—*valley* UT-8
May B. Leasure Elem Sch—*school* DE-2
May Bohm Ditch—*canal* CO-8
*May Branch* AR-4
*May Branch* TN-4
May Branch—*stream* (2) AL-4
May Branch—*stream* AR-4
May Branch—*stream* (2) GA-3
May Branch—*stream* IL-6
May Branch—*stream* (5) KY-4
May Branch—*stream* LA-4
May Branch—*stream* (3) MO-7
May Branch—*stream* (2) NC-3
May Branch—*stream* (3) TN-4
May Branch—*stream* TX-5
May Branch—*stream* WV-2
May Branch Ch—*church* GA-3
May Branch Lateral—*canal* AR-4
Maybrick P.O. (historical)—*building* AL-4
**Maybrook**—*pop pl* NY-2
**Maybrook**—*pop pl* VA-3
May Brook—*stream* (2) CT-1
May Brook—*stream* (2) ME-1
May Brook—*stream* (2) MA-1
May Brook—*stream* MO-7
May Brook—*stream* NH-1
Maybrook Sch—*school* CA-9
**Maybrook Subdivision**—*pop pl* UT-8
Maybrook Yards—*locale* NY-2
**Mayburg**—*pop pl* PA-2
Mayburn Corners—*locale* OH-6
May Burner Trail—*trail* WV-2
Mayburn Lodge—*locale* LA-4
Maybury—*uninc pl* CA-9
Maybury Brook—*stream* NY-2
Maybury Highway—*channel* MI-6
Maybury Hill—*hist pl* NJ-2
Maybury Mills—*locale* NY-2
Maybury Sanitarium—*hospital* MI-6
Maybury Sch—*school* MI-6
Maybury Sch—*school* OH-6
*Mayby Creek* AL-4
*Mayby Creek* MS-4
May Canyon—*valley* CA-9
May Canyon—*valley* CO-8
May Canyon—*valley* OR-9
May Canyon Saddle—*gap* CA-9
May (CCD)—*cens area* TX-5
*May Cem* AL-4
*May Cem* MS-4
*May Cem* TN-4
May Cem—*cemetery* (2) AL-4
May Cem—*cemetery* (2) AR-4
May Cem—*cemetery* (4) KY-4
May Cem—*cemetery* (4) MS-4
May Cem—*cemetery* NE-7
May Cem—*cemetery* NC-3
May Cem—*cemetery* OK-5
May Cem—*cemetery* (4) TN-4
May Cem—*cemetery* TX-5
May Cem—*cemetery* VA-3
May Cem—*cemetery* (2) WV-2
May Cemetery—*cemetery* AR-4
May Chapel—*church* IL-6
May Chapel—*church* WV-2
*May Church* PA-2
**May City**—*pop pl* IA-7
Maycock Draw—*valley* WY-8
Maycock Mtn—*summit* PA-2
Maycocks Point—*cape* VA-3
Maycock Spring—*spring* WY-8
May Company—*hist pl* OH-6
May Company Department Store Bldg—*hist pl* MO-7
**May Corner**—*pop pl* WI-6
May Coulee—*valley* WI-6
*May Creek* AL-4
*May Creek* CO-8
May Creek—*locale* AK-9
May Creek—*locale* WA-9
May Creek—*stream* (4) AK-9
May Creek—*stream* AR-4
May Creek—*stream* CA-9
May Creek—*stream* (2) CO-8
May Creek—*stream* FL-3
May Creek—*stream* ID-8
May Creek—*stream* IN-6
May Creek—*stream* (2) MS-4
May Creek—*stream* (2) MT-8
May Creek—*stream* (4) OR-9
May Creek—*stream* TN-4
May Creek—*stream* (4) WA-9
May Creek Compground—*locale* MT-8
May Creek Ch—*church* AL-4
May Creek Church Cem—*cemetery* AL-4
*May Creek Methodist Church* AL-4
*Maycrest* NY-2
**Mayd**—*pop pl* TX-5
Maydale Cem—*cemetery* KS-7
*May Day* CO-8
*Mayday* KS-7
May Day—*locale* KS-7
Mayday—*locale* MS-4
Mayday—*locale* TN-4
**Mayday**—*pop pl* CO-8
**Mayday**—*pop pl* GA-3
May Day Cem—*cemetery* KS-7
Mayday Cem—*cemetery* MS-4
Mayday Landing (historical)—*locale* MS-4
Mayday Mine—*mine* CO-8
May Day Mine—*mine* (2) MT-8
Mayday Mine—*mine* NV-8
Mayday Mine—*mine* UT-8
Mayday No 2—*mine* NM-5
Mayday No 3—*mine* NM-5
May Day Peak—*summit* AZ-5
Mayday Post Office (historical)—*building* TN-4
Mayday Shaft—*mine* UT-8
May Day Spring—*spring* KS-7
*Mayday Township* KS-7
**May Day Township**—*pop pl* KS-7
Maydee Post Office (historical)—*building* TN-4
**Maydelle**—*pop pl* TX-5
**Maydell Township**—*pop pl* SD-7
May Ditch—*canal* IN-6
May Ditch—*canal* OH-6
Maydole Logan (Oxbow)—*bend* MN-6
May Draw—*valley* WY-8
Maye Cem—*cemetery* AL-4
Maye Creek—*stream* AL-4
Maye Creek—*stream* MI-6
*Maye Jima* FM-9
*Mayencopi* AZ-5
Mayer—*locale* TX-5
**Mayer**—*pop pl* AZ-5
**Mayer**—*pop pl* MN-6
Mayer, Lake—*lake* GA-3
Mayer, S. C., House—*hist pl* OH-6
Mayer Boot and Shoe Company Bldg—*hist pl* WI-6
Mayer Branch—*stream* DE-2
Mayer Branch—*stream* MD-2
Mayer Bryden Ranch—*locale* TX-5
Mayer Canal—*canal* LA-4
Mayer Cem—*cemetery* TX-5
Mayer Creek—*stream* TX-5
Mayer Dam—*dam* SD-7
Mayer Ditch—*canal* OH-6
Mayer Ditch—*canal* WY-8
Mayer Elem Sch—*school* AZ-5
Mayer Farms—*locale* CA-9
Mayer Gulch—*valley* CO-8
Mayer HS—*school* AZ-5
Mayer Number Nine Ranch—*locale* TX-5
Mayer Peak—*summit* AK-9
Mayer Post Office—*building* AZ-5
Mayer Ranch—*locale* (2) TX-5
Mayer Rsvr—*reservoir* CO-8
**Mayers**—*pop pl* LA-4
Mayers Cem—*cemetery* AL-4
Mayers Cem—*cemetery* ME-1
Mayers Cem—*cemetery* MO-7
Mayer Sch—*school* IL-6
Mayers Dome—*summit* VT-1
Mayer State Park—*park* OR-9
**Mayersville**—*pop pl* MS-4
Mayersville Archeol Site—*hist pl* MS-4
*Mayes* AL-4
Mayes—*locale* PA-2
Mayes Branch—*stream* MO-7
Mayes Branch—*stream* TX-5
Mayes Bridge—*bridge* OK-5
Mayes Bridge—*bridge* PA-2
Mayesburg—*locale* MO-7
Mayes Cabin—*locale* OR-9
*Mayes Cave* PA-2
*Mayes Cem* TN-4
Mayes Cem—*cemetery* AL-4
Mayes Cem—*cemetery* GA-3
Mayes Cem—*cemetery* (4) MO-7
Mayes Cem—*cemetery* OH-6
Mayes Cem—*cemetery* TN-4
Mayes Cem—*cemetery* TX-5
Mayes Cem—*cemetery* VA-3
Mayes Chapel—*church* (2) TN-4
Mayes Chapel Cem—*cemetery* TX-5
*Mayes Chapel United Methodist Ch* TN-4
**Mayes (County)**—*pop pl* OK-5
Mayes Creek—*stream* MO-7
Mayes Creek—*stream* TN-4
*Mayes Creek Baptist Church* MS-4
**Mayes Crossroad**—*pop pl* AL-4
*Mayes Elementary School* TN-4
Mayes Hill—*summit* MO-7
Mayes Homestead Airp—*airport* MO-7
Mayes-Hutton House—*hist pl* TN-4
Mayes Islands (historical)—*island* TN-4
*Mayes Lake* TX-5
Mayes Lake—*lake* MS-4
Mayes Lake—*lake* TX-5
Mayes Lake—*reservoir* TN-4
Mayes Mill (historical)—*locale* TN-4
Mayes Ranch (Abandoned)—*locale* NM-5
Mayes Rsvr—*reservoir* OR-9
Mayes Spring—*spring* NM-5
Mayes Tank—*reservoir* AZ-5
**Mayesville**—*pop pl* SC-3
Mayesville Hist Dist—*hist pl* SC-3
Mayes Wash—*stream* NM-5
*Mayesworth* NC-3
*Mayeta* AZ-5
*Maye To* MP-9
**Mayetta**—*pop pl* KS-7
**Mayetta**—*pop pl* NJ-2
Mayetta Cem—*cemetery* KS-7
Mayetta Elem Sch—*school* KS-7
May Evergreen Ch—*church* OK-5
*Mayfair* IL-6
Mayfair—*hist pl* SC-3
Mayfair—*locale* PA-2
**Mayfair**—*pop pl* (2) AL-4
**Mayfair**—*pop pl* CA-9
**Mayfair**—*pop pl* DE-2
**Mayfair**—*pop pl* GA-3
**Mayfair**—*pop pl* IL-6
**Mayfair**—*pop pl* LA-4
**Mayfair**—*pop pl* PA-2
**Mayfair**—*pop pl* SC-3
**Mayfair**—*pop pl* TX-5
Mayfair—*post sta* NY-2
Mayfair—*uninc pl* CA-9
Mayfair Apartments—*hist pl* IL-6
**Mayfair At Marlton**—*pop pl* NJ-2
Mayfair Baptist Ch—*church* FL-3
Mayfair Ch—*church* AL-4
*Mayfair Ch of Christ* AL-4
Mayfair Country Club—*other* OH-6
**Mayfair Gardens**—*pop pl* AL-4
Mayfair Hotel—*hist pl* MO-7
Mayfair House—*hist pl* PA-2
Mayfair HS—*school* CA-9
Mayfair in the Grove (Shop Ctr)—*locale* FL-3
*Mayfair Mill* SC-3
*Mayfair Park* OH-6
Mayfair Park—*park* AL-4
Mayfair Park—*park* CA-9
Mayfair Park—*park* IL-6
**Mayfair Place**—*pop pl* VA-3
Mayfair Plaza Shop Ctr—*locale* AZ-5
Mayfair Plaza (Shop Ctr)—*locale* FL-3
Mayfair Sch—*school* (2) CA-9
Mayfair Sch—*school* LA-4
Mayfair Sch—*school* MI-6
Mayfair Sch—*school* NV-8
Mayfair Sch—*school* (2) OH-6
Mayfair Sch—*school* OK-5
Mayfair Sch—*school* PA-2
Mayfair Shop Ctr—*locale* AZ-5
**Mayfair (subdivision)**—*pop pl* AL-4
**Mayfair (subdivision)**—*pop pl* MS-4
**Mayfair (subdivision)**—*pop pl* (2) NC-3
**Mayfair Subdivision**—*pop pl* UT-8
Mayfalfa Farm (historical)—*locale* MS-4
May Farm Branch—*stream* KY-4
*Mayfield* OH-6
Mayfield—*locale* AR-4
Mayfield—*locale* ID-8
Mayfield—*locale* OK-5
Mayfield—*locale* SD-7
Mayfield—*locale* TX-5
**Mayfield**—*pop pl* DE-2
**Mayfield**—*pop pl* GA-3
**Mayfield**—*pop pl* IN-6
**Mayfield**—*pop pl* KS-7
**Mayfield**—*pop pl* KY-4
**Mayfield**—*pop pl* (2) MD-2
**Mayfield**—*pop pl* MI-6
**Mayfield**—*pop pl* MO-7
**Mayfield**—*pop pl* NY-2
**Mayfield**—*pop pl* NC-3
**Mayfield**—*pop pl* (2) OH-6
**Mayfield**—*pop pl* (2) PA-2
**Mayfield**—*pop pl* TX-5
**Mayfield**—*pop pl* UT-8
**Mayfield**—*pop pl* (2) VA-3
**Mayfield**—*pop pl* WA-9
**Mayfield**—*pop pl* WI-6
Mayfield, John, House—*hist pl* KY-4
Mayfield and Oregon Drain—*canal* MI-6
Mayfield Borough—*civil* PA-2
Mayfield Branch—*stream* AL-4
Mayfield Branch—*stream* KY-4
Mayfield Branch—*stream* TX-5
Mayfield Bridge—*bridge* SC-3
Mayfield Canyon—*valley* AZ-5
Mayfield Canyon—*valley* (2) TX-5
Mayfield Cave—*cave* TX-5
Mayfield (CCD)—*cens area* GA-3
Mayfield (CCD)—*cens area* KY-4
Mayfield Cem—*cemetery* AR-4
Mayfield Cem—*cemetery* KS-7
Mayfield Cem—*cemetery* KY-4
Mayfield Cem—*cemetery* MS-4
Mayfield Cem—*cemetery* (2) MO-7
Mayfield Cem—*cemetery* (2) OH-6
Mayfield Cem—*cemetery* OK-5
Mayfield Cem—*cemetery* SC-3
Mayfield Cem—*cemetery* TX-5
Mayfield Cem—*cemetery* UT-8
Mayfield Cem—*cemetery* (2) WI-6
Mayfield Center HS—*school* OH-6
Mayfield Ch—*church* AL-4
Mayfield Ch—*church* GA-3
Mayfield Ch—*church* IL-6
Mayfield Ch—*church* MS-4
Mayfield Ch—*church* TN-4
Mayfield Ch—*church* TX-5
Mayfield Chapel—*church* SC-3
*Mayfield Ch of Christ* MS-4
Mayfield Corner—*locale* ME-1
Mayfield Corners—*locale* OH-6
Mayfield Cottage—*hist pl* VA-3
Mayfield Country Club—*other* OH-6
*Mayfield Creek* ID-8
Mayfield Creek—*stream* ID-8
Mayfield Creek—*stream* KY-4
Mayfield Creek—*stream* LA-4
Mayfield Creek—*stream* MO-7
Mayfield Creek—*stream* NY-2
Mayfield Creek—*stream* OR-9
Mayfield Creek—*stream* (2) TX-5
Mayfield Creek—*stream* WY-8
Mayfield Creek Ch—*church* KY-4
*Mayfield Cumberland Presbyterian Ch* TN-4
Mayfield Ditch—*canal* OR-9
Mayfield Downtown Commercial District—*hist pl* KY-4
Mayfield Draw—*valley* TX-5
Mayfield Dugout—*hist pl* TX-5
**Mayfield East**—*pop pl* PA-2
*Mayfield Elementary School* TN-4
Mayfield Face Wildlife Mngmt Area—*park* UT-8
**Mayfield Farms**—*pop pl* VA-3
Mayfield Golf Course—*locale* PA-2
*Mayfield Grammar School* TN-4
Mayfield Gulch—*valley* MT-8
**Mayfield Heights**—*pop pl* OH-6
Mayfield Hills—*range* TX-5
Mayfield (historical)—*locale* SD-7
**Mayfield (historical)**—*pop pl* TN-4
Mayfield Hollow—*valley* KY-4
Mayfield HS—*school* NM-5
Mayfield Ice Cave—*cave* CA-9
Mayfield Junior Sch—*school* CA-9
Mayfield Knob—*summit* KY-4
Mayfield Lake—*reservoir* WA-9
Mayfield Lake Dam—*dam* MS-4
Mayfield Memorial Park Cem—*cemetery* IL-6
Mayfield Memory Garden—*cemetery* KY-4
Mayfield Mine (underground)—*mine* AL-4
Mayfield Mtn—*summit* OK-5
Mayfield Park—*park* CA-9
Mayfield Peak—*summit* ID-8
Mayfield Pond—*lake* ME-1
Mayfield Pond—*lake* OR-9
Mayfield Pond—*reservoir* MI-6
Mayfield Post Office (historical)—*building* TN-4
Mayfield Ranch—*locale* OR-9
Mayfield Ranch—*locale* (7) TX-5
Mayfield Road Sch—*school* OH-6
Mayfield Sch—*school* (2) CA-9
Mayfield Sch—*school* (2) KY-4
Mayfield Sch—*school* (2) MI-6
Mayfield Sch—*school* MN-6
Mayfield Sch—*school* TN-4
Mayfield Sch (historical)—*school* AL-4
Mayfield Sch (historical)—*school* IA-7
Mayfield Sch (historical)—*school* MO-7
Mayfield Slough—*gut* CA-9
Mayfields Mill (historical)—*locale* TN-4
Mayfield Spring—*spring* AZ-5
Mayfield Spring—*spring* CA-9
Mayfield Spring—*spring* MO-7
Mayfield Spring—*spring* TN-4
Mayfields Ranch—*locale* WY-8
Mayfields Station (historical)—*locale* TN-4
Mayfields Store (historical)—*locale* AL-4
Mayfield Store (historical)—*locale* MS-4
**Mayfield Subdivision**—*pop pl* UT-8
**Mayfield (Town of)**—*pop pl* NY-2
Mayfield Township—*civil* MO-7
**Mayfield Township**—*pop pl* NE-7
**Mayfield Township**—*pop pl* SD-7
**Mayfield (Township of)**—*pop pl* IL-6
**Mayfield (Township of)**—*pop pl* (2) MI-6
**Mayfield (Township of)**—*pop pl* MN-6
Mayfield (Township of)—*unorg* ME-1
May Flat—*flat* UT-8
*Mayflower* LA-4
*Mayflower* ND-7
Mayflower—*locale* LA-4
Mayflower—*locale* (2) TX-5
Mayflower—*locale* VA-3
**Mayflower**—*pop pl* AR-4
**Mayflower**—*pop pl* KY-4
**Mayflower**—*pop pl* MI-6
Mayflower—*uninc pl* CA-9
Mayflower (CCD)—*cens area* KY-4
Mayflower Cem—*cemetery* AR-4
Mayflower Cem—*cemetery* IA-7
Mayflower Cem—*cemetery* KS-7
Mayflower Cem—*cemetery* (2) LA-4
Mayflower Cem—*cemetery* MA-1
Mayflower Ch—*church* FL-3
Mayflower Ch—*church* KS-7
Mayflower Ch—*church* LA-4
Mayflower Ch—*church* TN-4
Mayflower Ch—*church* VA-3
**Mayflower Condominium**—*pop pl* UT-8
Mayflower Creek—*stream* AK-9
Mayflower Creek—*stream* CO-8
Mayflower Creek—*stream* ID-8
Mayflower Creek—*stream* OR-9
Mayflower Drain—*canal* CA-9
Mayflower Gospel Chapel—*church* IA-7
**Mayflower Grove**—*pop pl* MA-1
Mayflower Gulch—*valley* (2) CO-8
Mayflower Gulch—*valley* ID-8
Mayflower Gulch—*valley* MT-8
Mayflower Gulch—*valley* NV-8
**Mayflower Heights**—*pop pl* MA-1
Mayflower Hill—*summit* CO-8
Mayflower Hill—*summit* ME-1
Mayflower Hill Cem—*cemetery* MA-1
Mayflower Hills Ch—*church* VA-3
**Mayflower (historical)**—*pop pl* TN-4
Mayflower Hotel—*hist pl* DC-2
Mayflower II (museum)—*park* MA-1
Mayflower Lake—*lake* AK-9
Mayflower Lake—*lake* MI-6
Mayflower Lake—*lake* (3) WI-6
Mayflower Lakes—*lake* CO-8
Mayflower Lateral—*canal* CA-9
Mayflower Ledge—*rock* MA-1
Mayflower Lookout—*locale* TX-5
Mayflower Meadow—*swamp* OR-9
**Mayflower Meadows**—*pop pl* IN-6
Mayflower Mill—*locale* CO-8
Mayflower Mine—*mine* (2) CA-9
Mayflower Mine—*mine* (2) CO-8
Mayflower Mine—*mine* (2) ID-8
Mayflower Mine—*mine* MT-8
Mayflower Mine—*mine* NV-8
Mayflower Mine—*mine* OR-9
Mayflower Mine—*mine* UT-8
*Mayflower Park* MA-1
Mayflower Park—*park* CA-9
Mayflower Park—*park* PA-2
Mayflower Park Station (historical)—*locale* MA-1
Mayflower Ranch—*locale* (2) CA-9
Mayflower Road Dam—*dam* MA-1
**Mayflower (Sardis)**—*pop pl* VA-3
Mayflower Sch—*hist pl* AK-9
Mayflower Sch—*school* CA-9
Mayflower Sch—*school* IL-6
Mayflower Sch—*school* IA-7
Mayflower Sch—*school* KY-4
Mayflower Sch—*school* LA-4
Mayflower Sch—*school* MA-1
Mayflower Sch—*school* MI-6
Mayflower Sch—*school* MN-6
Mayflower Sch—*school* NE-7
Mayflower Sch—*school* NY-2
Mayflower Sch—*school* OH-6
Mayflower Sch (historical)—*school* MO-7
Mayflower Sch (historical)—*school* NC-3
Mayflower School (Abandoned)—*locale* IA-7
Mayflower Spring—*spring* AZ-5
**Mayflower (subdivision)**—*pop pl* AL-4
Mayflower Tank—*reservoir* AZ-5
**Mayflower Terrace (subdivision)**—*pop pl* (2) AZ-5
Mayflower Trail—*trail* OR-9
*Mayflower Village* OH-6
Mayflower Village—*CDP* CA-9
**Mayflower Village**—*pop pl* OH-6
Mayfly Lake—*lake* MN-6
May Fork—*stream* KY-4
May Fork—*stream* WV-2
**Mayger**—*pop pl* OR-9
Mayger Downing Cem—*cemetery* OR-9
Mayginnis Sch—*school* KS-7
*May Gog Mountain* CO-8
May Gulch—*valley* AK-9
Mayhall Cem—*cemetery* MS-4
*Mayhall Creek* GA-3
May Hall Creek—*gut* GA-3
May Hall Island—*island* GA-3
*Mayhall Marsh* TX-5
Mayhall Pond—*lake* FL-3
Mayhall Pond—*lake* GA-3
Mayham Hollow—*valley* MO-7
Mayham Lake—*lake* CO-8
Mayham Pond—*reservoir* NY-2
Mayhan Branch—*stream* (2) MO-7
Mayhan Hollow—*valley* TN-4
*Mayhard Creek* TX-5
Mayhaw—*locale* GA-3
Mayhaw Bayou—*stream* TX-5
Mayhaw Brake—*swamp* LA-4
Mayhaw Branch—*stream* (4) LA-4
Mayhaw Branch—*stream* MS-4
Mayhaw (CCD)—*cens area* GA-3
Mayhaw Creek—*stream* TX-5
Mayhaw Glade—*stream* LA-4
Mayhaw Lakes—*lake* GA-3
Mayhaw Marsh—*swamp* TX-5
Mayhaw Pond—*lake* FL-3
Mayhaw Pond—*lake* TX-5
May Haw Pond Slough—*stream* TX-5
Mayhaw Prairie—*flat* TX-5
Mayhaw Slough—*stream* LA-4
Mayhaw Slough—*stream* TX-5
*Mayheue Creek* TX-5
Mayhew—*locale* CA-9
Mayhew—*locale* OK-5
**Mayhew**—*pop pl* KY-4
**Mayhew**—*pop pl* MN-6
**Mayhew**—*pop pl* MS-4
**Mayhew**—*pop pl* NC-3

Mayhew, Carmelita, House—hist pl AZ-5
Mayhew Canyon—valley CA-9
Mayhew Cem—cemetery KY-4
Mayhew Cem—cemetery MS-4
Mayhew Chapel MS-4
Mayhew Chapel—church MA-1
Mayhew Creek—stream MN-6
Mayhew Creek—stream MS-4
Mayhew Creek—stream NV-8
Mayhew Creek—stream OK-5
Mayhew Flats—flat KY-4
Mayhew Hollow—valley LA-4
Mayhew Island—island NH-1
Mayhew Lake—lake MN-6
Mayhew Lake—lake NE-7
Mayhew Lake—reservoir MN-6
**Mayhew Lake (Township of)**—pop pl MN-6
Mayhew Landing—locale LA-4
Mayhew Mission Cem—cemetery MS-4
Mayhew Mission (historical)—church MS-4
Mayhew Run—stream WV-2
Mayhews Station MS-4
May-Hickey House—hist pl TX-5
**Mayhill**—pop pl NM-5
**May Hill**—pop pl OH-6
**Mayhill**—pop pl TX-5
May Hill—summit VT-1
May Hill—summit WA-9
Mayhill Cem—cemetery NM-5
May Hill Ch—church OH-6
Mayhill Ranger Station—other NM-5
May Hill Sch—school TN-4
May Hill Sch—school TX-5
May Hilltop—locale SC-3
May (historical)—locale SD-7
Mayhoffer Ranch—locale CO-8
**Mayhoff Springs (historical)**—pop pl MS-4
May Hollow VA-3
May Hollow—valley AR-4
May Hollow—valley KY-4
May Hollow—valley MA-1
May Hollow—valley TN-4
May Hollow—valley UT-8
May Hollow—valley VA-3
May Hollow Run—stream PA-2
May Hollow YCC Camp—locale MO-7
May Homestead—locale WY-8
Mayhorn Bayou—stream AR-4
Mayhorn Hollow—valley TN-4
Mayhue Creek—stream MI-6
Mayhurst—hist pl VA-3
Mayhurst Sch—school KY-4
Mayich—summit FM-9
May Junction—locale WA-9
**Mayking**—pop pl KY-4
Mayking Creek—stream WI-6
May Knob—summit (2) KY-4
May Lake—lake AK-9
May Lake—lake CA-9
May Lake—lake ID-8
May Lake—lake LA-4
May Lake—lake (2) MI-6
May Lake—lake MN-6
May Lake—lake MT-8
May Lake—lake (2) OR-9
May Lake—lake WA-9
May Lake—lake (2) WI-6
May Lake Dam—dam MS-4
May Lake High Sierra Camp—locale CA-9
**Mayland**—pop pl TN-4
**Mayland**—pop pl VA-3
Mayland Baptist Ch—church TN-4
Mayland Cave—hist pl WI-6
Mayland Cem—cemetery TN-4
Mayland Lake—reservoir TN-4
Mayland Lake Dam—dam TN-4
Mayland-Pleasant Hill (CCD)—cens area TN-4
Mayland-Pleasant Hill Division—civil TN-4
Mayland Post Office (historical)—building TN-4
Mayland Sch—school TN-4
Mayland Town Hall—building TN-4
**Mayland Township**—pop pl ND-7
May Lateral—canal CO-8
Mayle MS-4
Mayle Cem—cemetery MD-2
May Lee Ch (historical)—church AL-4
Mayleeno—hist pl IN-6
Maylender Creek—stream NY-2
Maylender Pond—reservoir NY-2
**Maylene**—pop pl AL-4
Maylene Cem—cemetery AL-4
Maylene Elem Sch (historical)—school AL-4
Maylene Mine (underground)—mine AL-4
May-Lewis, Benjamin, House—hist pl NC-3
May-Lillie Mine—mine MT-8
Mayline—locale KS-7
Maylor Point—cape WA-9
Mayluck Brook CT-1
May Lundy Mine—mine (2) CA-9
Maymay Lake—lake MN-6
Maymead—locale TN-4
May Memorial Cem—cemetery NY-2
Maymens Flat—flat CA-9
May Mill Creek—stream FL-3
May Mines—mine KY-4
Maymont—hist pl VA-3
Maymont Park—park VA-3
Maymont Sch—school VA-3
May Mtn—summit ID-8
**Mayna**—pop pl LA-4
Maynadier Creek MT-8
Maynadier Creek—bay MD-2
Maynadler Creek MT-8
Maynard IN-6
Maynard KS-7
Maynard—locale KY-4
Maynard—locale NY-2
**Maynard**—pop pl AR-4
**Maynard**—pop pl IN-6
**Maynard**—pop pl IA-7
**Maynard**—pop pl ME-1
**Maynard**—pop pl MA-1
**Maynard**—pop pl MN-6
**Maynard**—pop pl NY-2
**Maynard**—pop pl OH-6
**Maynard**—pop pl TX-5
**Maynard**—pop pl WA-9
Maynard, Lake—lake FL-3
Maynard, Powell C., House—hist pl TX-5
Maynard, Thomas, House—hist pl MD-2
Maynard, W. E., House—hist pl TX-5
Maynard Border Ditch—canal MT-8
Maynard Branch—stream (3) KY-4
Maynard Branch—stream TN-4
Maynard Branch—stream WV-2
Maynard Brook—stream MA-1
Maynard Burn Way—trail WA-9
Maynard Canyon—valley UT-8
Maynard Cave—cave TN-4
Maynard Cem—cemetery AR-4
Maynard Cem—cemetery (3) KY-4
Maynard Cem—cemetery MS-4
Maynard Cem—cemetery MO-7
Maynard Cem—cemetery PA-2
Maynard Cem—cemetery (5) WV-2
Maynard Ch—church GA-3
Maynard Chapel (historical)—church AL-4
Maynard Corners—locale NY-2
Maynard Coulee—valley MT-8
Maynard Cove—locale AL-4
Maynard Cove—valley AL-4
Maynard Cove Cem—cemetery AL-4
Maynard Creek—stream CA-9
Maynard Creek—stream (2) MT-8
Maynard Creek—stream OR-9
Maynard Creek—stream (2) TN-4
Maynard Creek—stream TX-5
Maynard Ditch—canal IN-6
Maynard Elementary School TN-4
Maynard Elem Sch—school KS-7
Maynard E Traviss Vocational Technical Center—school FL-3
Maynard Flat—flat OR-9
Maynard Fork—stream (2) KY-4
Maynard Glacier—glacier AK-9
Maynard Glen Park—park TN-4
Maynard Gulch—valley CO-8
Maynard Gulch—valley ID-8
Maynard Hill—locale PA-2
Maynard Hill—summit (2) CT-1
Maynard Hill—summit PA-2
Maynard Hollow—valley (2) KY-4
Maynard Hollow—valley NY-2
Maynard Hollow—valley PA-2
Maynard Hollow—valley TN-4
Maynard Homestead—locale WY-8
Maynard HS—school MA-1
Maynardier Ridge—ridge MD-2
Maynardier Ridge Ch—church MD-2
Maynardier Ridge Sch—school MD-2
Maynard-Jacksonville Pass WI-6
Maynard Lake—lake IL-6
Maynard Lake—lake (2) MI-6
Maynard Lake—lake MN-6
Maynard Lake—lake NV-8
**Maynard Lake**—pop pl IL-6
Maynard Lake—reservoir NC-3
Maynard Lake Sch—school MN-6
Maynard Mill Bridge—bridge GA-3
Maynard Mine—mine MT-8
Maynard Mtn—summit AK-9
Maynard Park—park IA-7
Maynard Pass WI-6
Maynard Peak—summit WA-9
Maynard Pond—reservoir MA-1
Maynard Ranch—locale TX-5
Maynard Ridge—ridge VA-3
Maynards Brook MA-1
Maynard Sch—school IL-6
Maynard Sch—school MA-1
Maynard Sch—school MI-6
Maynard Sch—school NH-1
Maynard Sch—school PA-2
Maynard Sch—school SC-3
Maynard Sch—school TN-4
**Maynards Cove**—pop pl AL-4
Maynards Crossroads—locale VA-3
Maynards Hill MA-1
Maynard Spring—spring NV-8
Maynard Spring—spring TN-4
Maynards Ranch—locale CA-9
Maynards Run PA-2
Maynardsville TN-4
Maynard Tank—reservoir AZ-5
**Maynard (Town of)**—pop pl MA-1
Maynard Trace Branch—stream KY-4
**Maynardville**—pop pl TN-4
Maynardville Baptist Ch—church TN-4
Maynardville (CCD)—cens area TN-4
Maynardville Ch (historical)—church TN-4
Maynardville Division—civil TN-4
Maynardville Elem Sch—school TN-4
Mayn Cem—cemetery MT-8
Mayne—locale CO-8
Mayne Arroyo—stream CO-8
Mayne Cem—cemetery GA-3
Mayne Creek—stream NC-3
Maynedier Creek MD-2
Mayne Ranch—locale MT-8
Mayner Branch—stream AR-4
Mayner Creek MS-4
Mayne Sch—school CA-9
Maynes Chapel—church KY-4
Maynes Creek—stream IA-7
Maynes Grove Cem—cemetery IA-7
Maynes Spring—spring CO-8
Maynew Windmill—locale TX-5
Mayngaite IL-6
**Maynor**—pop pl WV-2
Maynor Branch—stream WV-2
Maynor Cem—cemetery NC-3
Maynor Cem—cemetery WV-2
Maynor Creek—stream MS-4
Maynor Creek Ch—church MS-4
Maynor Creek Water Park—park MS-4
Maynor Creek Water Park Dam—dam MS-4
Maynor Gap—gap AL-4
Maynor Hollow—valley TN-4
Maynor Spring—spring AL-4
Mayns Creek—stream MT-8
Mayo LA-4
Mayo—locale LA-4
Mayo—locale OR-9
Mayo—locale VA-3
Mayo—locale PR-3
Mayo—other VT-1
**Mayo**—pop pl CA-9
**Mayo**—pop pl FL-3
**Mayo**—pop pl KY-4
**Mayo**—pop pl MD-2
**Mayo**—pop pl SC-3
**Mayo**—pop pl TX-5
**Mayo**—pop pl VA-3
Mayo, Dr. William J., House—hist pl MN-6
Mayo, Dr. William W., House—hist pl MN-6
Mayo, John C. C., Mansion and Office—hist pl KY-4
Mayo, Mount—summit VT-1
Mayo Airp—airport NC-3
Mayo Bar Dam—dam GA-3
Mayo Beach—beach MD-2
Mayo Beach—beach MA-1
**Mayo Beach**—pop pl MA-1
Mayo Bldg—hist pl VT-1
Mayo Brake—swamp LA-4
Mayo Branch—stream AL-4
Mayo Branch—stream (4) MS-4
Mayo Branch—stream (2) TN-4
Mayo (CCD)—cens area FL-3
Mayo (CCD)—cens area SC-3
Mayo Cem—cemetery AL-4
Mayo Cem—cemetery IN-6
Mayo Cem—cemetery KY-4
Mayo Cem—cemetery LA-4
Mayo Cem—cemetery MS-4
Mayo Cem—cemetery WV-2
Mayo Ch—church (3) VA-3
Mayo Chapel—church KY-4
Mayo Chapel—church VA-3
Mayo Clinic—hospital MN-6
Mayo Clinic Buildings—hist pl MN-6
**Mayo Corners**—pop pl MA-1
Mayo Correctional Institute—building FL-3
Mayo Cove—bay WA-9
Mayo Creek—stream LA-4
Mayo Creek—stream MN-6
Mayo Creek—stream MT-8
Mayo Creek—stream NC-3
Mayo Creek—stream SC-3
Mayo Creek—stream (2) VA-3
Mayo Creek—stream WA-9
Mayo Creek Cem—cemetery MN-6
**Mayodan**—pop pl NC-3
Mayodan Camp—locale NC-3
Mayo Ditch—canal AR-4
Mayoeak River—stream AK-9
Mayo Family Cem—cemetery AL-4
Mayo Grove Ch—church VA-3
Mayo Gulch—valley MT-8
Mayo Hill—summit MA-1
Mayo (historical)—locale SD-7
**Mayo (historical)**—pop pl OR-9
**Mayo (historical)**—pop pl TN-4
Mayo Hotel—hist pl OK-5
Mayo Island—island IL-6
Mayo JHS—school MS-4
Mayo Junction—locale FL-3
Mayo Key—island FL-3
Mayo Lake—lake MI-6
Mayo Lake—lake MN-6
Mayo Lookout Tower—tower FL-3
Mayo Mill Branch—stream FL-3
Mayo Mill Creek—stream AL-4
Mayo Mill Number 1 Pond Dam—dam MA-1
**Mayo Mills**—pop pl SC-3
Mayo Mountain Ch—church VA-3
Mayo Mtn—summit AL-4
Mayo Mtn—summit VA-3
Mayo Park—park FL-3
Mayo Park—park MN-6
Mayo Point—cape ME-1
Mayo Point—cape MD-2
Mayo Pond—reservoir MA-1
Mayo Post Office (historical)—building TN-4
Mayoriak River—stream AK-9
Mayo River NC-3
Mayo River VA-3
Mayo River—stream NC-3
Mayo River (Magisterial District)—fmr MCD VA-3
Mayo River Sluice—hist pl NC-3
Mayor Memorial Park—park IL-6
Mayor Ranch—locale WY-8
Mayo Rsvr—reservoir NC-3
Mayo Rsvr—reservoir WY-8
Mayos Beach MA-1
Mayos Beach Light—locale MA-1
Mayos Bridge—bridge VA-3
Mayos Cabin—locale UT-8
Mayos Cem—cemetery TN-4
Mayo Sch—school CA-9
Mayo Sch—school (2) IL-6
Mayo Sch—school MD-2
Mayo Sch—school MI-6
Mayo Sch—school SC-3
Mayo Sch—school SD-7
Mayo Sch—school VA-3
**Mayos Crossroads**—pop pl NC-3
Mayo'S Hill MA-1
Mayos Island—island VA-3
Mayo Slough—stream MS-4
Mayos Mill (historical)—locale AL-4
Mayo's Point ME-1
Mayo Spring—spring AR-4
Mayo Spur—locale CA-9
Mayos Toll Bridge (historical)—bridge AL-4
Mayo Tank—reservoir NM-5
Mayo Town MS-4
Mayo (Township of)—fmr MCD NC-3
Mayous Bayou—stream LA-4
**Mayo Village**—pop pl KY-4
Mayoville (historical)—locale MS-4
Mayowood Hist Dist—hist pl MN-6
Mayowood Lake—lake MN-6
Mayoworth—locale WY-8
Mayoworth Junction WY-8
May Park—park GA-3
**May Park**—pop pl OR-9
May Park Ditch—canal OR-9
Mayparty Spring—spring UT-8
**Maypearl**—pop pl TX-5
Maypearl (CCD)—cens area TX-5
Maypens—locale NM-5
May-Peoples Cem—cemetery TN-4
May Place—locale ID-8
May Plantation (historical)—locale AL-4
May Point—cape VI-3
Maypole, The—cape ME-1
Maypole Hill—summit AK-9
May Pond—lake ME-1
May Pond—lake NH-1
May Pond—lake VT-1
May Pond—reservoir MO-7
May Pond Brook—stream VT-1
May Pond Mtn—summit VT-1
May Ponds—lake CT-1
Maypop MP-9
Maypop Cem—cemetery FL-3
**Mayport**—pop pl FL-3
**Mayport**—pop pl PA-2
Mayport Airp—airport PA-2
Mayport Basin—basin FL-3
Mayport Basin Range Front Light—locale FL-3
Mayport Carrier Basin FL-3
Mayport Cem—cemetery FL-3
Mayport Elem Sch—school FL-3
Mayport JHS—school FL-3
Mayport Naval Station—military FL-3
May Prairie—lake FL-3
May Queen Mine—mine NV-8
May Queen Mine—mine OR-9
May Ranch—locale CO-8
May Ranch—locale NE-7
May Ranch—locale WY-8
Mayrant Cem—cemetery TX-5
Mayrant Lead—stream SC-3
Mayrants Reserve—reservoir SC-3
May Realty Bldg—hist pl OH-6
May Ridge TN-4
**May Ridge**—pop pl IN-6
May Ridge—post sta OK-5
May River—stream SC-3
May River Ch—church SC-3
May Roberts Sch—school OR-9
May Rock—pillar CA-9
Mayronne Canal—canal LA-4
May Rsvr—reservoir OR-9
May Run—stream PA-2
Mays TN-4
Mays—locale IL-6
**Mays**—pop pl AL-4
**Mays**—pop pl IN-6
Mays, Blaney Covered Bridge—hist pl PA-2
Mays, Terry, House—hist pl MO-7
May Sands Sch—school FL-3
Mays Bar—bar AL-4
Mays Bay—swamp GA-3
Mays Bayou—stream LA-4
Mays Bend—bend MO-7
**Mays Bend**—pop pl AL-4
Mays Bluff GA-3
Mays Bluff—cliff AR-4
Mays Bluff—cliff MO-7
Mays Bluff—locale GA-3
Mays Bluff Branch (historical)—swamp GA-3
Mays-Boddie House—hist pl GA-3
Mays Branch TX-5
Mays Branch—stream (2) AR-4
Mays Branch—stream IN-6
Mays Branch—stream KY-4
Mays Branch—stream TN-4
Mays Branch—stream (2) VA-3
Mays Branch—stream WV-2
Mays Bridge—bridge TN-4
Mays Brook—stream ME-1
Mays Canyon—valley CA-9
Mays Canyon—valley OR-9
Mays Canyon Creek—stream OR-9
Mays Cem—cemetery (4) AL-4
Mays Cem—cemetery (2) AR-4
Mays Cem—cemetery FL-3
Mays Cem—cemetery (4) KY-4
Mays Cem—cemetery (2) MS-4
Mays Cem—cemetery OH-6
Mays Cem—cemetery (4) TN-4
Mays Cem—cemetery TX-5
Mays Cem—cemetery (5) VA-3
Mays Cem—cemetery WV-2
Mays Ch—church PA-2
Mays Ch—church WV-2
May Sch—school (3) IL-6
May Sch—school IA-7
May Sch—school MA-1
May Sch—school MO-7
May Sch—school OR-9
Mays Chapel TN-4
Mays Chapel—CDP MD-2
Mays Chapel—church AL-4
Mays Chapel—church KY-4
Mays Chapel—church MD-2
Mays Chapel—church MS-4
Mays Chapel—church (3) NC-3
Mays Chapel—church PA-2
Mays Chapel—church (2) TN-4
Mays Chapel—church WV-2
Mays Chapel African Methodist Episcopal Ch. TN-4
Mays Chapel Cem—cemetery TN-4
May Sch (historical)—school MS-4
Mays Creek—stream (2) ID-8
Mays Creek—stream KY-4
Mays Creek—stream (2) MS-4
Mays Creek—stream TX-5
Mays Creek Ch—church MS-4
Mays Creek Ch (historical)—church MS-4
Mays Crossing—locale TX-5
Mays Crossroads AL-4
Mays Crossroads—locale AL-4
Mays Crossroads—locale NC-3
Mays Dam—dam SD-7
Mays Draft—stream WV-2
Mayse Cem—cemetery KY-4
Mayse Cem—cemetery MO-7
**Maysel**—pop pl WV-2
Mays Elem Sch—school IN-6
Mayse Sch—school KY-4
Mays Field—park CA-9
**Maysfield**—pop pl TX-5
Maysfield Creek—stream TX-5
Maysfield Sch—school TX-5
Mays Flat—flat CA-9
Mays Ford TN-4
Mays Ford Islands TN-4
Mays Ford Shoals—bar TN-4
Mays Fork—stream OH-6
Mays Gap WV-2
Mays Gap—gap AZ-5
Mays Gap—gap WV-2
Mays Gap Tunnel Spring AZ-5
Mays Gap Well—well AZ-5
Mays General Store—hist pl AR-4
Mays Grade Canyon—valley OR-9
Mays Grove Cem—cemetery KY-4
Mays Grove Ch—church GA-3
Mays Gulf AL-4
Mays Gulf (historical)—locale AL-4
Mays Hill PA-2
Mays Hill Ch (historical)—church TN-4
Mays Hills—summit AZ-5
Mays Hill School TN-4
Mays Hollow—valley KY-4
Mays Hollow—valley (2) VA-3
Mays Island—island FL-3
May's Island Hist Dist—hist pl IA-7
Mays JHS—school FL-3
Mays Knob—summit WV-2
Mays Lake MN-6
Mays Lake—lake (2) AR-4
Mays Lake—lake MN-6
Mays Lake—lake WY-8
Mays Lake—reservoir NC-3
Mays Lake Dam—dam NC-3
Mays Lakes—lake IL-6
Maysland—locale FL-3
Mays Landing MS-4
Mays Landing—locale TN-4
**Mays Landing**—pop pl NJ-2
Mays Landing (historical)—locale (3) AL-4
Mays Landing Presbyterian Church—hist pl NJ-2
**Mays Lick**—pop pl KY-4
Mays Lick (CCD)—cens area KY-4
Mays Lick Consolidated Sch—hist pl KY-4
Mays-McCracken Cemetery TN-4
Mays Memorial Ch—church VA-3
Mays Memorial Church AL-4
Mays Mill (historical)—locale AL-4
Mays Millpond—reservoir GA-3
Mays Mills PA-2
Mays Mills—locale NY-2
Mays Mtn—summit VT-1
Mays Mtn—summit (3) VA-3
Mays Oil Field—oilfield TX-5
**Mayson**—pop pl SC-3
Mayson—uninc pl GA-3
Mayson Crossroads—locale SC-3
Maysonia MS-4
Mayson Sch—school GA-3
Mays Patch Hollow—valley TN-4
Mays Peak—summit CO-8
Mays Point NC-3
Mays Point—cape AL-4
Mays Point—locale NY-2
Mays Pond—lake (2) FL-3
Mays Pond—lake GA-3
Mays Pond—lake NY-2
Mays Pond—reservoir AL-4
Mays Prairie Ch—church TX-5
May Spring TN-4
**May Spring**—pop pl MS-4
May Spring—spring CA-9
May Spring—spring OR-9
May Spring—spring TN-4
May Spring Branch—stream TN-4
May Spring Post Office (historical)—building TN-4
May Spring Run—stream VA-3
May Springs—spring MT-8
May Springs Branch TN-4
May Springs Campground—locale TN-4
**May Springs (historical)**—pop pl TN-4
Mays Ranch—locale NM-5
Mays Ridge—ridge TN-4
Mays Rock—pillar OR-9
Mays Rsvr—reservoir OR-9
Mays Run—stream KY-4
Mays Run—stream VA-3
Mays Run—stream WV-2
Mays Sch—school (2) TN-4
Mays Sch (historical)—school AL-4
Mays Sch (historical)—school (2) TN-4
Mays Spring—spring CO-8
Mays Store—locale KY-4
Mays Store—locale NC-3
**Mays Subdivision**—pop pl TN-4
Mays Tank—reservoir AZ-5
Mayston Hill—summit VT-1
May Street Hist Dist—hist pl MA-1
May Street Park—park IL-6
May Street Park—park TN-4
May Street School OR-9
May String Branch—stream KY-4
Mays Valley TN-4
Maysville AZ-5
Maysville IN-6
Maysville MS-4
Maysville PA-2
Maysville SC-3
Maysville UT-8
Maysville—locale IL-6
Maysville—locale ME-1
Maysville—locale (2) OH-6
Maysville—locale SC-3
**Maysville**—pop pl AL-4
**Maysville**—pop pl AR-4
**Maysville**—pop pl CO-8
**Maysville**—pop pl GA-3
**Maysville**—pop pl IN-6
**Maysville**—pop pl IA-7
**Maysville**—pop pl KY-4
**Maysville**—pop pl MO-7
**Maysville**—pop pl NC-3
**Maysville**—pop pl (3) OH-6
**Maysville**—pop pl OK-5
**Maysville**—pop pl (3) PA-2
**Maysville**—pop pl WV-2
Maysville-Aberdeen Bridge—hist pl KY-4
Maysville Canyon—valley NV-8
Maysville (CCD)—cens area (2) GA-3
Maysville (CCD)—cens area KY-4
Maysville (CCD)—cens area OK-5
Maysville Cem—cemetery IN-6
Maysville Cem—cemetery IA-7
Maysville Cem—cemetery OK-5
Maysville Center—other ME-1
Maysville Ch—church KY-4
Maysville Ch—church OH-6
Maysville Country Club—other KY-4
**Maysville Crossing**—pop pl IN-6
Maysville Downtown Hist Dist—hist pl KY-4
Maysville Hist Dist—hist pl GA-3
Maysville (Magisterial District)—fmr MCD VA-3
Maysville (Maysville Center) ME-1
Maysville Oil Field—oilfield OK-5
Maysville Post Office—building AL-4
Maysville Schoolhouse—hist pl IA-7
Maysville Station—locale IL-6
Maysville Summit—summit NV-8
Mays Wash—stream AZ-5
Mayswell Canyon—valley AZ-5
Mayswell Peak—summit AZ-5
Mays Woodyard Landing (historical)—locale AL-4
Maytag Lake Number Two—reservoir AL-4
Maytag Lake Number 1—reservoir AL-4
Maytag Lake Number 1 Dam—dam AL-4
Maytag Number 2 Dam—dam AL-4
Maytag Park—park IA-7
Maytags Lake—reservoir AL-4
Maytag Spring, The—spring WY-8
May Tank—reservoir (2) AZ-5
May Tank—reservoir NM-5
May Tank Canyon—valley AZ-5
May Tank Pocket—basin AZ-5
Mayten CA-9
Mayter Lake—lake NM-5
May-Thomas Cem—cemetery TN-4
Mayton—locale AR-4
Mayton—locale MS-4
Mayton Cemetery MS-4
Mayton (historical)—locale AL-4
Maytown KY-4
Maytown—locale IL-6
Maytown—locale KY-4
Maytown—locale PA-2
**Maytown**—pop pl AL-4
**Maytown**—pop pl FL-3
**Maytown**—pop pl PA-2
**Maytown**—pop pl VA-3
**Maytown**—pop pl WA-9
Maytown Elem Sch—school PA-2
Maytown Post Office (historical)—building PA-2
Maytown (RR name for Langley)—other KY-4
May Township—civil MO-7
**May Township**—pop pl NE-7
**May (Township of)**—pop pl (2) IL-6
**May (Township of)**—pop pl (2) MN-6
Maytown Station KY-4
Maytown-Sylvan Springs (CCD)—cens area AL-4
Maytown-Sylvan Springs Division—civil AL-4
May Trail—trail PA-2
Maytubby Cem—cemetery OK-5
Maytubby Springs—spring OK-5
Maytum Cem—cemetery NM-5
Mayu FM-9
Mayuasanik Creek—stream AK-9
Mayukuit Mtn—summit AK-9
May Valley—locale CO-8
May Valley—valley CO-8
May Valley—valley TN-4
May Valley Sch—school CO-8
May Van Canyon—valley CA-9
Mayvaxi AZ-5
Mayview—locale AR-4
Mayview—locale WA-9
**Mayview**—pop pl IL-6
**Mayview**—pop pl MO-7
**Mayview**—pop pl PA-2
**Mayview Acres (subdivision)**—pop pl NC-3
Mayview Cem—cemetery MO-7
Mayview Cem—cemetery WA-9
Mayview Ch—church KS-7
**Mayview Heights**—pop pl TN-4
Mayview (historical)—locale KS-7
**Mayview Manor (subdivision)**—pop pl DE-2
**Mayview Park**—pop pl NC-3
Mayview Sch—school KS-7
Mayview Sch—school MO-7
Mayview State Hosp—hospital PA-2
Mayville AL-4
Mayville PA-2
Mayville—locale MN-6
**Mayville**—pop pl ME-1
**Mayville**—pop pl MI-6
**Mayville**—pop pl NJ-2
**Mayville**—pop pl NY-2
**Mayville**—pop pl ND-7
**Mayville**—pop pl OR-9
**Mayville**—pop pl PA-2
**Mayville**—pop pl WI-6
Mayville Blanchard Drain—canal ND-7
Mayville Cem—cemetery OR-9
**Mayville Crossing**—pop pl NC-3
Mayville Dam—dam ND-7
Mayville Drain Number 19—canal ND-7
Mayville Golf Course—locale ND-7
Mayville Hist Dist—hist pl ND-7
Mayville Lake—lake MI-6
Mayville Municipal Airp—airport ND-7
Mayville Public Library—hist pl ND-7
Mayville Sch (historical)—school OR-9
Mayville Spring—spring OR-9
Mayville State Coll—school ND-7
Mayville Town Hall—building ND-7
**Mayville (Town of)**—pop pl WI-6
**Mayville Township**—pop pl ND-7
Mayville Township (historical)—civil ND-7
**Mayville (Township of)**—pop pl MN-6
May Water—lake CO-8
Mayweed Corner—locale NY-2
May Well—well NM-5
May Windmill—locale TX-5
Maywood IN-6
Maywood MI-6
Maywood—locale KS-7
Maywood—locale MI-6
Maywood—locale NY-2
Maywood—locale WA-9
Maywood—locale WV-2
**Maywood**—pop pl CA-9
**Maywood**—pop pl IL-6
**Maywood**—pop pl IN-6
**Maywood**—pop pl KS-7
**Maywood**—pop pl KY-4
**Maywood**—pop pl MS-4
**Maywood**—pop pl (2) MO-7
**Maywood**—pop pl NE-7
**Maywood**—pop pl NJ-2
**Maywood**—pop pl NY-2

**Maywood**—pop pl .... OR-9
Maywood Camp—locale .... AL-4
Maywood Cem—cemetery .... MN-6
Maywood Cem—cemetery .... MO-7
Maywood Ch—church .... MN-6
Maywood Elem Sch—school .... IN-6
Maywood Grove—woods .... IL-6
Maywood Hill Sch—school .... WA-9
**Maywood Hills Subdivision**—pop pl .... UT-8
**Maywood (historical)**—pop pl .... SD-7
Maywood Lake—reservoir .... MS-4
Maywood Park—park .... IL-6
Maywood Park—park .... IN-6
Maywood Park—park .... IA-7
**Maywood Park**—pop pl .... OR-9
Maywood Park Racetrack—other .... IL-6
Maywood Ridge—ridge .... MT-8
Maywood Rod and Gun Club—other .... CA-9
Maywood Sch—school .... IA-7
Maywood Sch—school .... VA-3
Maywood Sch—school .... WI-6
Maywood Shop Ctr—locale .... MS-4
Maywood Sportsmans Club—other .... IL-6
**Maywood (Township of)**—pop pl .... MN-6
Mayworth .... NC-3
**Maza**—pop pl .... ND-7
Mazama—locale .... OR-9
Mazama—locale .... WA-9
Mazama, Mount—summit .... OR-9
Mazama Camp—locale .... WA-9
Mazama Campground—park .... OR-9
Mazama Creek—stream .... OR-9
Mazama Creek Campground—park .... OR-9
Mazama Dome—summit .... WA-9
Mazama Falls—falls .... WA-9
Mazama Glacier .... WA-9
Mazama Glacier—glacier (2) .... WA-9
Mazama Junction—locale .... OR-9
Mazama Lake—lake (2) .... WA-9
Mazama Park—flat .... WA-9
Mazama Ridge—ridge .... WA-9
Mazama Rock—summit .... OR-9
Mazama Timber Pad (heliport)—airport .... OR-9
Mazarick Park—park .... NC-3
Mazarn—locale .... AR-4
**Mazarn**—pop pl .... AR-4
Mazarn Chapel Cem—cemetery .... AR-4
Mazarn Creek—stream .... AR-4
Mazarn Mtn—summit .... AR-4
Mazarn (Township of)—fmr MCD (2) .... AR-4
Mazaska Lake—lake .... MN-6
**Maza Township**—pop pl .... ND-7
Mazatzal Divide—trail .... AZ-5
Mazatzal Divide Trail—trail .... AZ-5
Mazatzal Divide 23—trail .... AZ-5
Mazatzal Mountains—range .... AZ-5
Mazatzal Peak—summit .... AZ-5
Mazatzal Range .... AZ-5
Mazatzal Wash—stream .... AZ-5
Maz-at-zark Mountains .... AZ-5
Mazda—locale .... ND-7
Mazda Brook Golf Course—other .... NJ-2
Maze .... UT-8
**Maze**—pop pl .... PA-2
Maze, The—area .... UT-8
Maze Cem—cemetery .... IN-6
Maze Cem—cemetery .... TX-5
Maze Cem—cemetery .... WV-2
Maze Creek—stream .... IN-6
Maze Creek—stream .... MO-7
Maze Hill—summit .... PA-2
Maze Lake—lake .... MN-6
Mazelin Cem—cemetery .... IN-6
Maze Overlook—locale .... UT-8
**Mazeppa**—pop pl .... MN-6
**Mazeppa**—pop pl .... NC-3
**Mazeppa**—pop pl .... PA-2
Mazeppa Cem—cemetery .... SD-7
Mazeppa Hill .... SD-7
Mazeppa State Public Shooting Area—park .... SD-7
Mazeppa State Wildlife Mngmt Area—park .... MN-6
**Mazeppa Township**—pop pl .... SD-7
**Mazeppa (Township of)**—pop pl .... MN-6
Mazeroski Park—park .... OH-6
Maze Stone Historical Marker—park .... CA-9
Mazey Lake .... ND-7
Mazie—locale .... KY-4
**Mazie**—pop pl .... OK-5
Mazie Branch—stream .... KY-4
Mazie Canyon—valley .... NV-8
Mazie C Gable Elem Sch—school .... PA-2
Mazie Ch—church .... KY-4
Mazie Creek—stream .... ID-8
Mazie Creek—stream .... MT-8
Mazie Landing Public Use Area—park .... OK-5
Mazies Chapel Missionary Baptist Church .... TN-4
Mazie Spring—spring .... NV-8
Maziki .... MP-9
Mazo Manie .... WI-6
**Mazomanie**—pop pl .... WI-6
Mazomanie State Wildlife Area—park .... WI-6
Mazomanie Town Hall—hist pl .... WI-6
**Mazomanie (Town of)**—pop pl .... WI-6
**Mazon**—pop pl .... IL-6
Mazon Camp—locale .... NM-5
Mazonia—locale .... IL-6
Mazon River—stream .... IL-6
**Mazon (Township of)**—pop pl .... IL-6
Mazourka Canyon—valley .... CA-9
Mazuki point—cape .... UT-8
Mazuma Creek—stream .... AK-9
Mazuma (historical)—locale .... NV-8
Mazuma Mine—mine .... NV-8
Mazure Drain—canal .... MI-6
Mazy Lake—lake .... WI-6
M Bar C Landing Field .... SD-7
M-Bar-J Ranch—locale .... CA-9
M Bar Ranch—locale (2) .... WY-8
M B Ditch—canal .... NM-5
M B Lamar Sch—school .... TX-5
Mb Ranch Airp—airport .... MO-7
MB Smith Tank—reservoir .... AZ-5
Mbul .... FM-9
M Butler Ranch—locale .... SD-7
Mbuul—summit .... FM-9
McAbee .... PA-2
McAbee Falls—falls .... ID-8
McAdam—locale .... WA-9
**McAdam**—pop pl .... VA-3
McAdam Branch—stream .... WI-6
McAdam Cem—cemetery .... TN-4
McAdam Creek—stream (2) .... AK-9
McAdam Creek—stream .... CA-9
McAdam Ranch—locale .... SD-7
**McAdams**—pop pl .... MS-4
**McAdams**—pop pl .... PA-2
McAdams and Morford Bldg—hist pl .... KY-4
McAdams Baptist Ch—church .... MS-4
McAdams Cem .... TN-4
McAdams Cem—cemetery .... AR-4
McAdams Cem—cemetery .... SC-3
McAdams Cem—cemetery .... TN-4
McAdams Cem—cemetery (3) .... TX-5
McAdams HS—school .... MS-4
McAdams Lake—lake .... MI-6
McAdams Methodist Ch—church .... MS-4
McAdams Park—park .... KS-7
McAdams Peak—summit .... IL-6
McAdams Peak—summit .... TX-5
McAdams Pond—reservoir .... OK-5
McAdam Spring Branch—stream .... TX-5
McAdams Station .... PA-2
**McAddry**—pop pl .... AL-4
McAdensville .... NC-3
**McAdenville**—pop pl .... NC-3
McAdenville Elem Sch—school .... NC-3
McAdenville Junction—locale .... NC-3
McAdenville Lake—reservoir .... NC-3
McAdenville Lake Dam—dam .... NC-3
McAdie, Mount—summit .... CA-9
McAding—locale .... AL-4
**McAdoo**—pop pl .... PA-2
**McAdoo**—pop pl .... TX-5
McAdoo, William Gibbs, House—hist pl .... GA-3
McAdoo Borough—civil .... PA-2
McAdoo Branch—stream .... TN-4
McAdoo Cem—cemetery (2) .... TN-4
McAdoo Cem—cemetery .... TX-5
McAdoo Ch—church .... TN-4
McAdoo Creek—stream .... IN-6
McAdoo Creek—stream .... KY-4
McAdoo Creek—stream (2) .... MO-7
McAdoo Cumberland Presbyterian Ch .... TN-4
**Mc Adoo Heights**—pop pl .... NC-3
**McAdoo Heights**—pop pl .... PA-2
McAdoo Heights—uninc pl .... NC-3
McAdoo Mine—mine .... NV-8
McAdoo Ranch—locale .... TX-5
McAdoo Ridge—ridge .... WV-2
McAdoo Sch (historical)—school .... TN-4
McAdoo Tank—reservoir (2) .... TX-5
**McAdoo Township**—pop pl .... KS-7
McAdory—locale .... AL-4
McAdory, Thomas, House—hist pl .... AL-4
McAdory Bldg—hist pl .... AL-4
McAdory Elem Sch—school .... AL-4
McAdory HS—school .... AL-4
McAdow, Perry, House—hist pl .... MI-6
McAdows Canyon—valley .... MT-8
McAfee—locale .... NJ-2
**McAfee**—pop pl .... GA-3
**McAfee**—pop pl .... KY-4
**McAfee**—pop pl .... MS-4
McAfee, George, House—hist pl .... KY-4
McAfee, James, House—hist pl .... KY-4
McAfee Basin—basin .... UT-8
McAfee Bluff—cliff .... TN-4
McAfee Branch—stream .... TN-4
McAfee Canyon—valley .... NV-8
McAfee Canyon—valley .... NM-5
McAfee Cem—cemetery .... MS-4
McAfee Ch—church .... GA-3
McAfee Creek—stream .... AL-4
McAfee Creek—stream .... AR-4
McAfee Creek—stream .... CA-9
McAfee Creek—stream .... MI-6
McAfee Creek—stream (2) .... NV-8
McAfee Creek—stream .... TN-4
McAfee Gap—gap .... VA-3
McAfee Godwin Vega—flat .... CO-8
McAfee Gulch—valley .... CA-9
McAfee Hill—summit .... TN-4
McAfee Knob—summit .... VA-3
McAfee Meadow—flat .... CA-9
McAfee Peak—summit .... NV-8
McAfee Place Unit Two Mini Park—park .... AZ-5
McAfee Place Unit Two Water Retention Basin—reservoir .... AZ-5
McAfee Ranch—locale .... NV-8
McAfee Ridge—ridge .... UT-8
McAfee Run—stream .... VA-3
McAfee Sch—school .... KY-4
McAfees Landing (historical)—locale .... MS-4
McAfee Spring Branch—stream .... AL-4
McAfee Stol Patch Airp—airport .... TN-4
McAfee Valley .... NJ-2
McAfee Windmill—locale .... CO-8
McAffees Ferry (historical)—locale .... MS-4
McAhren Gap .... PA-2
McAlear-Sawden Sch—school .... MI-6
McAleer Creek—stream .... WA-9
**McAlester**—pop pl .... OK-5
McAlester, Lake—reservoir .... OK-5
McAlester Armory—hist pl .... OK-5
McAlester Army Ammun Plant—military .... OK-5
McAlester (CCD)—cens area .... OK-5
McAlester Cem—cemetery .... OK-5
McAlester Ch—church .... OK-5
McAlester Creek—stream .... WA-9
McAlester DX—hist pl .... OK-5
McAlester House—hist pl .... OK-5
McAlester Lake—lake .... WA-9
McAlester Mtn—summit .... WA-9
McAlester Municipal Airp—airport .... OK-5
McAlester Pass—gap .... WA-9
McAlester Scottish Rite Temple—hist pl .... OK-5
**McAlevys Fort**—pop pl .... PA-2
McAlexander Cem—cemetery .... MS-4
McAlexander Lake Number One—reservoir .... TN-4
McAlexander Lake Number One Dam—dam .... TN-4
McAlexander-Stephenson Cem .... MS-4
McAley Creek .... TN-4
McAlhaney Sch—school .... SC-3
McAlhany Pond—swamp .... TX-5
McAlister—locale .... NM-5
McAlister, Bo, Site—hist pl .... OK-5
McAlister Cem—cemetery .... GA-3
McAlister Cem—cemetery .... NM-5
McAlister Creek—stream .... CA-9
McAlister Creek—stream .... OR-9
McAlister Ditch—canal .... OR-9
McAlister Gap—gap .... PA-2
McAlister Lake—lake .... NE-7
McAlister Point—cape .... ME-1
McAlister Ridge—ridge .... OR-9
McAlisters Crossroads—locale .... PA-2
McAlister Slough—stream (2) .... OR-9
McAlister Spring—spring .... OR-9
**McAlisterville**—pop pl .... PA-2
McAlister Well—locale .... NM-5
McAllaster—locale .... KS-7
McAllaster Landing—locale .... FL-3
**McAllaster Township**—pop pl .... KS-7
**McAllen**—pop pl .... TX-5
McAllen Gas Field—oilfield .... TX-5
McAllen-Hidalgo-Reynosa Toll Bridge—bridge .... TX-5
McAllen Main Canal—canal .... TX-5
McAllen-Pharr (CCD)—cens area .... TX-5
McAllen Pumping Station—other .... TX-5
McAllen Ranch—locale .... TX-5
McAllester Lake .... WA-9
McAllis Point—cape .... TX-5
McAllister .... PA-2
**McAllister**—pop pl .... FL-3
**Mc Allister**—pop pl .... MT-8
**McAllister**—pop pl .... WI-6
McAllister, Archibald, House—hist pl .... PA-2
McAllister,James G., House—hist pl .... UT-8
McAllister, Lake—lake .... NE-7
McAllister-Beaver House—hist pl .... PA-2
McAllister Branch—stream (2) .... TN-4
McAllister Branch Workings—mine .... TN-4
McAllister Bridge—bridge .... VA-3
McAllister Bridge—hist pl .... IN-6
Mc Allister Butte—summit .... MT-8
Mc Allister Cem—cemetery .... AR-4
McAllister Cem—cemetery (2) .... MS-4
McAllister Cem—cemetery (2) .... TN-4
McAllister Cem—cemetery .... VA-3
McAllister Chapel—church .... SC-3
McAllister Cove .... AL-4
McAllister Creek .... OR-9
McAllister Creek—stream .... AK-9
McAllister Creek—stream .... IA-7
McAllister Creek—stream .... KS-7
McAllister Creek—stream .... MI-6
McAllister Creek—stream (2) .... MS-4
McAllister Creek—stream .... NC-3
McAllister Creek—stream (2) .... OR-9
McAllister Creek—stream (3) .... WA-9
McAllister Creek—stream .... WI-6
McAllister Creek Glacier .... WA-9
McAllister Ditch .... OR-9
McAllister Ditch—canal (2) .... IN-6
McAllister Drain—canal .... NM-5
McAllister Draw—valley .... NM-5
McAllister Glacier—glacier .... WA-9
McAllister Gulch—valley .... AK-9
Mc Allister Gulch—valley .... CO-8
**McAllister Hill**—pop pl .... TN-4
McAllister Hollow—valley .... PA-2
McAllister Hollow—valley .... TN-4
McAllister House—hist pl .... CO-8
McAllister Lake .... WA-9
McAllister Lake—lake .... NM-5
McAllister Lake—lake .... WI-6
McAllister Landing .... FL-3
McAllister Mtn—summit .... AL-4
McAllister Park—park .... TX-5
McAllister Pond—reservoir .... VT-1
McAllister Pond—reservoir .... WI-6
McAllister Ranch—locale .... MT-8
McAllister Range—range .... AZ-5
McAllister Rapids—rapids .... WA-9
McAllister Ridge .... OR-9
McAllister Ridge—ridge .... CA-9
McAllister Rod Gun Club—other .... WA-9
McAllister Sch—school (2) .... IL-6
McAllister Sch—school .... KS-7
Mc-Allister Sch—school .... NC-3
McAllister Sch—school (2) .... WI-6
McAllister School and Ch—church .... PA-2
McAllisters Covered Bridge—bridge .... IN-6
McAllisters Crossroads—locale .... TN-4
McAllisters Crossroads Post Office (historical)—building .... TN-4
McAllisters Folly .... PA-2
McAllister Sink Cave—cave .... AL-4
McAllister Sinks—basin .... AL-4
McAllister Slough .... OR-9
McAllister Slough—gut .... OR-9
McAllister Slough—stream .... TX-5
McAllister Spring .... OR-9
McAllister Spring—spring .... AZ-5
McAllister Spring—spring (3) .... OR-9
McAllister Springs—spring .... MO-7
McAllister Springs—spring .... WA-9
McAllister Springs Access Point—locale .... MO-7
McAllister Trail—trail .... WA-9
McAllister Wash—stream .... AZ-5
McAllistor Cem—cemetery .... GA-3
McAllistor Mill Creek—stream .... GA-3
McAlloyd Branch—stream .... TN-4
McAlly Cem—cemetery .... AR-4
McAllys Ferry (historical)—crossing .... TN-4
McAlmond Canyon—valley .... CA-9
McAlmond House—hist pl .... WA-9
**Mcalmond Township**—pop pl .... ND-7
**McAlmont**—pop pl .... AR-4
McAlpin .... WV-2
McAlpin—locale .... WV-2
**McAlpin**—pop pl .... FL-3
**McAlpin**—pop pl .... WV-2
McAlpin Bend—bend .... AL-4
McAlpin Cem—cemetery .... IL-6
McAlpin Cem—cemetery .... TN-4
McAlpin Ch—church .... FL-3
**McAlpine**—pop pl .... MD-2
McAlpine Bluff—cliff .... AL-4
McAlpine Brook—stream .... CT-1
McAlpine Creek—stream .... MI-6
McAlpine Creek—stream .... NC-3
McAlpine Creek—stream .... SC-3
McAlpine Creek Greenway Park—park .... NC-3
McAlpine Dam—dam .... KY-4
McAlpine Lake—lake .... MN-6
McAlpine Lake—lake .... MS-4
McAlpine Locks—other .... KY-4
McAlpine Mine—mine .... CA-9
Mcalpine Mountain .... CO-8
McAlpine Mtn—summit .... NC-3
McAlpine Pond—lake .... MI-6
McAlpines Bluff .... AL-4
McAlpines Bluff—cliff .... AL-4
Mc Alpine Sch—school .... NC-3
McAlpines Ferry .... AL-4
McAlpines Ferry (historical)—locale (2) .... AL-4
McAlpines Landing (historical)—locale .... AL-4
McAlpin Hill—summit .... AL-4
McAlpin Landing—locale .... FL-3
Mc Alpin Mtn—summit .... CO-8
McAlpin Pond .... NH-1
**McAlpin (RR name MacAlpin)**—pop pl .... WV-2
McAlpin Sch—school .... OR-9
McAlpins Creek .... MS-4
McAlpins Creek .... NC-3
McAlpins Landing .... AL-4
McAlpin-Wellborn (CCD)—cens area .... FL-3
McAltas Mills .... PA-2
McAlvey Ridge—ridge .... CA-9
McAlvin Pond—lake .... NH-1
M Canal—canal .... FL-3
M Canal—canal .... ID-8
M Canal—canal .... OR-9
McAnally, William, House—hist pl .... OK-5
McAnally Break—swamp .... TX-5
Mc Andrew Gulch—valley .... CO-8
**McAndrews**—pop pl .... KY-4
McAndrews-Gallaher House—hist pl .... WV-2
Mc Andrews Lake—lake .... CO-8
McAndrews Playground—park .... MN-6
McAndrew Spring—spring .... TN-4
**McAndrews (RR name Pinson)**—pop pl .... KY-4
McAnear Cem—cemetery .... AL-4
McAnear Creek—stream .... AL-4
McAnear Creek—stream .... TX-5
McAnear Spring Creek .... AL-4
McAnelly Bend—bend .... TX-5
McAnelly Branch—stream .... KY-4
McAnelly Cem—cemetery .... AL-4
McAnelly Creek—stream .... TX-5
McAnerney (historical)—locale .... MS-4
McAninch Sch (abandoned)—school (2) .... PA-2
**McAnna**—pop pl .... TN-4
McAnnally Cove—valley .... AL-4
McAnnally Mtn—summit .... AL-4
McAnnally Ridge—ridge .... TN-4
McAnn Cove .... NC-3
McAnnelly Bend .... TX-5
McAnnely Bend .... TX-5
McAnnuley Sch .... PA-2
McAnnulty Elem Sch—school .... PA-2
McAntee Creek—stream .... AK-9
McAnulty—locale .... AL-4
McAnulty Creek .... WY-8
McAnulty Creek—stream .... WY-8
McAra, John, House—hist pl .... MI-6
Mcardle—fmr MCD .... NE-7
McArdle Bay—bay .... WA-9
McArdle House—hist pl .... GA-3
McArdle Mine (underground)—mine .... AL-4
McArdle Sch—school .... NE-7
McArron Ranch—locale .... NM-5
McArtan Cem—cemetery .... NC-3
McArther Sch—school .... OH-6
**McArthers Crossroads**—pop pl .... NC-3
McArthur—locale .... CA-9
McArthur—locale .... ND-7
**McArthur**—pop pl .... AR-4
**McArthur**—pop pl .... CA-9
**Mcarthur**—pop pl .... ID-8
**McArthur**—pop pl .... OH-6
McArthur, Lake—reservoir .... NC-3
McArthur, Mount—summit .... AK-9
McArthur Bank—bar .... WA-9
McArthur Brook—stream .... VT-1
McArthur-Burney Falls State Park—park .... CA-9
McArthur Canyon—valley .... WA-9
McArthur Cem—cemetery (2) .... GA-3
McArthur Cem—cemetery (2) .... NY-2
McArthur Cem—cemetery .... OH-6
McArthur Chapel—church .... OH-6
McArthur-Council House—hist pl .... NC-3
McArthur Cove—bay .... AK-9
McArthur Cow Camp—locale .... CA-9
McArthur Creek .... ID-8
McArthur Creek—stream .... AK-9
McArthur Creek—stream .... CA-9
McArthur Creek—stream .... OR-9
**McArthur Crossroads**—pop pl .... NC-3
McArthur Ditch—canal .... UT-8
McArthur Diversion Canal—canal .... CA-9
McArthur Drain—canal .... MI-6
McArthur Elevator—locale .... ND-7
**McArthur Estates (subdivision)**—pop pl .... NC-3
McArthur Flats—flat .... AK-9
McArthur Frandsen Canal—canal .... UT-8
McArthur Glacier—glacier .... AK-9
Mc Arthur Gulch—valley .... CO-8
McArthur Heights Ch—church .... AL-4
McArthur HS—school .... FL-3
McArthur Interchange—crossing .... ND-7
McArthur Lake—lake .... NC-3
McArthur Lake—lake .... WI-6
McArthur Lake—reservoir .... ID-8
Mc Arthur Lake—reservoir .... IL-6
McArthur Lake Dam—dam .... MS-4
**McArthur Manor (subdivision)**—pop pl .... NC-3
McArthur-Martin Hexadecagon Barn—hist pl .... NY-2
McArthur Memorial State Park .... CA-9
McArthur Mtn—summit .... AR-4
Mc Arthur Mtn—summit .... CO-8
McArthur Pass—channel (2) .... AK-9
McArthur Pond—lake .... FL-3
Mc Arthur Ranch—locale .... CO-8
McArthur Ranch—locale .... MT-8
McArthur Reef—bar (2) .... AK-9
McArthur River—stream .... AK-9
McArthur Run—stream .... PA-2
McArthur Sch—school .... AL-4
McArthur Sch—school .... OH-6
McArthur Sch—school .... OK-5
McArthurs Friends Ch—church .... AR-4
McArthur Spring—spring (3) .... OR-9
McArthurs River .... ID-8
McArthur Stadium—other .... NY-2
McArthur Swamp—swamp .... CA-9
**McArthur (Township of)**—pop pl .... OH-6
McArthur Well—locale .... NM-5
McArtor Cem—cemetery .... IA-7
McArtur Spring .... OR-9
McAshan Mtn—summit .... AL-4
McAshan Ranch—locale (2) .... NM-5
McAsh Spring—spring .... NM-5
McAskill Cem—cemetery .... WI-6
McAskill Spring—spring .... TN-4
McAtee Bar—bar .... CA-9
McAtee Basin—basin .... MT-8
McAtee Bridge—bridge .... MT-8
McAtee Bridge Sportsmans Access—locale .... MT-8
McAtee Creek—stream .... MT-8
McAteer Branch—stream .... AL-4
McAteer Branch—stream .... SC-3
McAteer Cem—cemetery .... TN-4
McAtee Run—stream .... OH-6
McAttee Spring—spring .... OR-9
**McAuley**—pop pl .... PA-2
McAuley Brook—stream .... NY-2
McAuley Cem—cemetery .... MI-6
McAuley HS—school .... MO-7
McAuley HS—school (2) .... OH-6
McAuley Mountain .... PA-2
**McAuley Park**—pop pl .... MD-2
McAuley Sch—school .... IL-6
McAuley Sch District No. 27—hist pl .... IL-6
McAuleys Lake—lake .... NY-2
McAuly HS—school .... NY-2
McAvan—locale .... OH-6
McAvity Bay—bay .... MN-6
McAvity Lake—lake .... MN-6
McAvoy—locale .... CA-9
McAvoy Boat Harbor—locale .... CA-9
McAvoy Dam—dam .... MA-1
McAvoy Lake—lake .... MI-6
McAvoy Mtn—summit .... TX-5
McAvoy Pond .... MA-1
McAvoy Pond—lake .... ME-1
McAvoy Ranch—locale .... CA-9
McAvoy Run—stream .... WV-2
McAvoy Sch (abandoned)—school .... PA-2
McAvoys Pond .... MA-1
**McBain**—pop pl .... MI-6
McBain, Newman, House—hist pl .... GA-3
**McBaine**—pop pl .... MO-7
McBaine Sch—school .... MO-7
McBain Flat—flat .... OR-9
McBain Flat Spring—spring .... OR-9
McBain Spring—spring .... WA-9
**McBean**—pop pl .... GA-3
McBean Cem—cemetery .... GA-3
McBean Creek—stream .... GA-3
McBee—locale .... OR-9
**McBee**—pop pl .... SC-3
McBee Branch—stream .... TX-5
McBee Bridge—bridge .... TN-4
McBee (CCD)—cens area .... SC-3
McBee Cem—cemetery .... AR-4
McBee Cem—cemetery (4) .... TN-4
McBee Cem—cemetery .... TX-5
McBee Cem—cemetery .... WV-2
McBee Chapel—church .... MO-7
McBee Creek—stream .... OR-9
McBee Creek—stream .... TX-5
McBee Ferry (historical)—crossing .... TN-4
McBee Ford—crossing .... TN-4
McBee Hill—summit .... TN-4
McBee Hollow—valley .... TN-4
McBee Island—island .... OR-9
McBee Island—island .... TN-4
McBee Lake—lake (2) .... OR-9
McBee Landing—locale .... AR-4
McBee Methodist Church—hist pl .... SC-3
McBee Rsvr—reservoir .... OR-9
McBees Creek .... TX-5
McBees Ferry .... TN-4
McBees Ferry (historical)—locale .... MS-4
McBee Slu—gut .... OR-9
McBees Shoals—bar .... TN-4
McBee Trail—trail .... OR-9
McBee Union Ch—church .... MS-4
McBee Windmill—locale .... NM-5
McBeth .... SC-3
**McBeth**—pop pl .... TX-5
McBeth, Sue, Cabin—hist pl .... ID-8
McBeth Cem—cemetery .... NY-2
McBeth Spring—spring .... AZ-5
McBinley Bridge—locale .... OH-6
McBirney, James H., House—hist pl .... OK-5
McBirney Lateral—canal .... ID-8
McBlair Shoal—bar .... MA-1
McBlairs Shoal .... MA-1
**McBrayer**—pop pl .... KY-4
McBrayer, Dr. Victor, House—hist pl .... NC-3
Mc Brayer and Fenner Ditch—canal .... CO-8
McBrayer Branch—stream (2) .... AL-4
McBrayer Cem—cemetery .... KY-4
McBrayer Cem—cemetery .... NC-3
McBrayer-Clark House—hist pl .... KY-4
Mc Brayer Ditch—canal .... CO-8
McBrayer Lake—reservoir .... AL-4
McBrayer Lake Dam .... AL-4
McBreers Slope Mine (underground)—mine .... AL-4
McBriar Branch—stream .... GA-3
McBriar Ditch—canal .... CA-9
McBribe Canyon—valley .... CA-9
McBride—locale .... GA-3
McBride—locale .... MS-4
McBride—locale .... PA-2
McBride—locale .... TX-5
**McBride**—pop pl .... IA-7
**McBride**—pop pl .... LA-4
**McBride**—pop pl .... MO-7
**McBride**—pop pl .... OK-5
McBride, Lake—lake .... FL-3
McBride, Lake—reservoir .... IA-7
McBride Bay—bay .... VT-1
McBride Branch—stream .... AL-4
McBride Branch—stream .... FL-3
McBride Branch—stream .... IN-6
McBride Branch—stream .... NC-3
McBride Branch—stream .... TN-4
McBride Butte—summit .... CO-8
McBride Canyon—valley .... NM-5
McBride Canyon—valley .... TX-5
McBride Canyon Ruin—hist pl .... TX-5
McBride Cave—cave .... AL-4
McBride Cem—cemetery .... AL-4
McBride Cem—cemetery (2) .... AR-4
McBride Cem—cemetery .... GA-3
McBride Cem—cemetery (2) .... IL-6
McBride Cem—cemetery .... KS-7
McBride Cem—cemetery (2) .... LA-4
McBride Cem—cemetery .... MI-6
McBride Cem—cemetery .... OR-9
McBride Cem—cemetery (5) .... TN-4
McBride Cem—cemetery .... TX-5
McBride Ch—church .... MO-7
McBride Ch—church .... NC-3
McBride Corners—locale .... SC-3
McBride Creek—stream .... CA-9
McBride Creek—stream .... CO-8
Mc Bride Creek—stream .... CO-8
McBride Creek—stream .... ID-8
McBride Creek—stream .... MT-8
McBride Creek—stream (3) .... OR-9
McBride Crossing—bridge .... SC-3
Mcbride Dam—dam .... AL-4
McBride Dam—dam .... AL-4
McBride Ditch—canal .... OH-6
McBride Ditch—canal .... OR-9
McBride Drain—stream (2) .... MI-6
McBride Elementary School .... MS-4
McBride Flat—flat .... NV-8
McBride Gap—gap .... PA-2
McBride Glacier—glacier .... AK-9
McBride Guard Station—locale .... OR-9
**McBride Heights**—pop pl .... IN-6
McBride-Hickey House—hist pl .... IA-7
McBride Hollow—valley .... WV-2
McBride House—hist pl .... KY-4
McBride Lake—lake .... WA-9
McBride Lake—lake .... WY-8
McBride Lake—reservoir .... AL-4
McBride Lake—reservoir .... OH-6
McBride Mines—mine .... AR-4
McBride Monmt—pillar .... KS-7
McBride Park—park (2) .... OH-6
McBride Point—cape .... TX-5
McBride Pond—lake .... NY-2
McBride Post Office (historical)—building .... TN-4
McBride Ranch (Historical Site)—locale .... TX-5
McBride Ranch House—hist pl .... TX-5
McBride Recreational Camp .... AL-4
McBride Rsvr—reservoir .... OR-9
McBride Run—stream (2) .... OH-6
McBrides Bluff—cliff .... IN-6
McBrides Branch .... TN-4
McBrides Bridge—bridge .... GA-3
McBrides Cem—cemetery .... IN-6
McBrides Cem—cemetery .... MI-6
McBride Sch—school .... LA-4
McBride Sch—school .... ME-1
McBride Sch—school .... MI-6
McBride Sch—school .... MS-4
McBride Sch—school .... OR-9
McBride Sch—school .... SD-7
McBride Sch (historical)—school .... TN-4
McBrides Gulch—valley .... CA-9
McBrides Long Valley Well—well .... NV-8
McBride Slough—stream .... FL-3
**McBrides (McBride)**—pop pl .... MI-6
McBrides Mill (historical)—locale .... NC-3
McBride Spring—spring .... AZ-5
McBride Spring—spring .... MT-8
McBride Spring—spring .... UT-8
McBride Spring—spring .... WA-9
McBride Springs—spring .... CA-9
McBride Springs—spring .... NV-8
McBrides Run—stream .... KY-4
McBrides Sheep Well—well .... NV-8
McBrides Spring—spring .... NV-8
McBride Station—locale .... PA-2
McBride Tank—reservoir .... AZ-5
McBride Tank—reservoir (2) .... NM-5
McBride Well—well .... NM-5
McBride Windmill—locale .... NM-5
McBridge Canyon—valley .... AZ-5
McBridge Ch—church .... GA-3
McBridge Hollow—valley .... AR-4
McBridy Spring—spring .... MT-8
McBrien-Burdett Cem—cemetery .... TN-4
McBrien Elementary School .... TN-4
McBrien Sch—school .... TN-4
McBrite Sch—school .... MI-6
McBroom Administrative Study Plot—other .... OR-9
McBroom Branch—stream .... TN-4
McBroom Cem—cemetery .... AR-4
McBroom Cem—cemetery .... IA-7
McBroom Cem—cemetery .... LA-4
McBroom Cem—cemetery .... OH-6
McBroom Cem—cemetery .... TN-4
McBroom Chapel—church .... TN-4
McBroom Chapel Ch of Christ .... TN-4
McBroom Cove—valley .... AL-4
McBroom Ranch—locale .... OR-9
McBrooms Mill (historical)—locale .... TN-4
McBroom Spring—spring .... OR-9
McBrown Mtn—summit .... TX-5
McBryant Corner—locale .... VA-3
McBryde Cem—cemetery .... NC-3
**McBryde Farm (subdivision)**—pop pl .... NC-3
McBryde Rsvr—reservoir .... AZ-5
McBrydes—locale .... AL-4
McBryde-Screws-Tyson House—hist pl .... AL-4
**McBurg**—pop pl .... TN-4
McBurg Ch of Christ—church .... TN-4
McBurg Community Center—building .... TN-4
McBurg Post Office (historical)—building .... TN-4
McBurg United Methodist Ch—church .... TN-4
McBurnett Ford (historical)—locale .... AL-4
McBurnett Ranch—locale .... TX-5
McBurney Well—well .... OR-9
McBurrel Hollow—valley .... AR-4
McCaa Cem—cemetery .... AL-4
McCaa Cem—cemetery .... MS-4
**McCabe**—pop pl .... MT-8
McCabe Bldg—hist pl .... TX-5
McCabe Bldg—hist pl .... WA-9
McCabe Cabin Waterhole .... OR-9
McCabe Canyon—valley .... CA-9

McCabe Cem—*cemetery* IN-6
McCabe Cem—*cemetery* KS-7
McCabe Cem—*cemetery* TN-4
McCabe Ch—*church* WV-2
McCabe Chapel—*church* IL-6
McCabe Chapel—*church* PA-2
McCabe Creek—*stream* (2) CA-9
Mc Cabe Creek—*stream* CO-8
McCabe Creek—*stream* MO-7
McCabe Creek—*stream* (2) MT-8
McCabe Creek—*stream* OH-6
McCabe Creek—*stream* WA-9
McCabe Dam—*dam* NM-5
Mccabe Ditch—*canal* DE-2
McCabe Flat—*flat* CA-9
McCabe Hollow—*valley* AL-4
McCabe Hollow—*valley* MO-7
McCabe Hollow—*valley* NY-2
*McCabe Lake* CA-9
McCabe Lake—*lake* (2) WI-6
McCabe Lake Creek Trail—*trail* MT-8
McCabe Lakes—*lake* CA-9
McCabe Meadow—*flat* MT-8
McCabe Mtn—*summit* ME-1
McCabe Mtn—*summit* MT-8
McCabe Oil Field—*oilfield* TX-5
McCabe Park—*park* OH-6
McCabe Park—*park* TN-4
McCabe Point—*summit* CA-9
McCabe Point—*summit* MT-8
McCabe Pond—*lake* NY-2
McCabe Pond—*reservoir* NC-3
Mc Cabe Ranch—*locale* CO-8
McCabe Ranch—*locale* NM-5
McCabe Ridge—*ridge* CA-9
Mc Cabe Rsvr—*reservoir* (2) CO-8
McCabe Run—*stream* (2) PA-2
McCabe Sch—*school* CA-9
McCabe Sch—*school* MD-2
McCabe Sch (abandoned)—*school* PA-2
McCabe Spring—*spring* TN-4
*McCabes Run* PA-2
McCabe Union Sch—*school* CA-9
McCadden Hollow—*valley* UT-8
McCaddin Sch—*school* NY-2
McCadley Cem—*cemetery* TX-5
McCaferdy Run—*stream* PA-2
McCaffary, John, House—*hist pl* WI-6
McCafferty, William, Farmhouse—*hist pl* OH-6
McCafferty Canyon—*valley* AZ-5
McCafferty Cem—*cemetery* MI-6
McCafferty Hollow—*valley* AR-4
McCafferty Hollow—*valley* MO-7
McCafferty Village—*uninc pl* PA-2
McCaffery Lookout Tower—*locale* MT-8
McCaffery Pond—*reservoir* OR-9
McCaffery Slough—*stream* OR-9
*McCafferys Slough* OR-9
McCaffree Park—*park* NE-7
McCaffrey House—*hist pl* IA-7
McCagar Draw—*valley* WY-8
McCager Point—*cape* TN-4
McCahan Gap—*gap* PA-2
**McCahill Estates**—*pop pl* MD-2
McCaig Branch—*stream* AL-4
McCaig Cem—*cemetery* AL-4
McCaig Hollow—*valley* AL-4
*McCain* PA-2
McCain, Henry Hicks, House—*hist pl* TX-5
*McCain Branch* AL-4
McCain Cem—*cemetery* AL-4
McCain Cem—*cemetery* KY-4
McCain Cem—*cemetery* MS-4
McCain Cem—*cemetery* MO-7
McCain Cem—*cemetery* NE-7
*McCain Creek* TX-5
McCain Creek—*stream* AL-4
McCain Creek—*stream* LA-4
McCain Creek—*stream* OR-9
McCain Creek—*stream* TX-5
McCain Creek—*stream* WA-9
McCain Creek—*stream* WY-8
McCain Creek Park—*park* TX-5
McCain Creek Rsvr—*reservoir* OR-9
McCain Dam—*dam* AL-4
McCain Drain—*canal* MI-6
McCaine Creek—*stream* MS-4
McCain Guard Station—*locale* WY-8
McCain Hill—*summit* KY-4
McCain (historical)—*locale* MS-4
McCain Hollow—*valley* TX-5
McCain Lake—*lake* FL-3
McCain Library—*building* MS-4
McCain Lookout Tower—*tower* FL-3
**McCain(North Carolina Sanatorium,RR name Sanatorium)**—*pop pl* NC-3
McCain Ranch—*locale* CA-9
McCain Rsvr Number One—*reservoir* OR-9
McCain Rsvr Number Two—*reservoir* OR-9
**McCains**—*pop pl* TN-4
McCain Sch—*school* ME-1
McCains Chapel Methodist Ch (historical)—*church* AL-4
McCain Sch (historical)—*school* PA-2
McCains Lake—*reservoir* AL-4
McCain Slough—*gut* AR-4
McCain Spring—*spring* NM-5
McCain Spring—*spring* WY-8
*McCains School* TN-4
*McCainsville* NJ-2
McCain Valley—*valley* CA-9
*McCainville* NJ-2
McCainville—*locale* AL-4
McCainville Cem—*cemetery* AL-4
McCainville Creek—*stream* AL-4
McCaleb, John, House—*hist pl* AR-4
McCaleb, Mount—*summit* ID-8
McCaleb Cem—*cemetery* TN-4
McCaleb Hollow—*valley* TN-4
McCaleb Mill—*locale* AL-4
McCaleb Ranch—*locale* OR-9
McCalebs Landing—*locale* MS-4
McCaleb Spring—*spring* TN-4
*McCaleb Station* MS-4
McCalip Sch—*school* TN-4
McCalips Chapel—*church* TN-4
McCalips Chapel Cem—*cemetery* TN-4
*McCall* FL-3
*McCall* KY-4
McCall—*locale* IL-6
McCall—*locale* WA-9
McCall—*other* MS-4
**McCall**—*pop pl* ID-8
**McCall**—*pop pl* LA-4
**McCall**—*pop pl* WA-9
McCall, Clarence, House—*hist pl* SC-3
McCall, John, House—*hist pl* OR-9
McCall, Mount—*summit* AK-9
**McCalla**—*pop pl* AL-4
McCalla Ave Baptist Ch—*church* TN-4
McCalla Baptist Ch—*church* AL-4
McCalla Chapel—*church* AL-4
McCalla Creek—*stream* ID-8
McCalla Creek—*stream* MT-8
McCalla Creek—*stream* WA-9
McCalla Island—*island* GA-3
McCalla Lake Dam—*dam* AL-4
McCalla Ridge—*ridge* ID-8
McCalla Sch—*school* IN-6
McCalla Station (historical)—*locale* AL-4
McCallay—*church* GA-3
McCall Bar—*bar* OR-9
McCall Basin—*basin* (2) WA-9
McCall Bayou—*stream* LA-4
*McCall Branch* TN-4
McCall Branch—*stream* AL-4
McCall Branch—*stream* FL-3
McCall Branch—*stream* (2) NC-3
McCall Branch—*stream* (2) SC-3
McCall Branch—*stream* (2) TN-4
McCall Branch—*stream* TX-5
McCall Bridge—*bridge* GA-3
McCall Bridge—*other* MO-7
McCall Canyon—*valley* OR-9
McCall Cem—*cemetery* FL-3
McCall Cem—*cemetery* GA-3
McCall Cem—*cemetery* (2) MS-4
McCall Cem—*cemetery* (4) NC-3
McCall Cem—*cemetery* SC-3
McCall Cem—*cemetery* (6) TN-4
McCall Cem—*cemetery* TX-5
McCall Ch—*church* MS-4
*McCall Ch of God* MS-4
**McCall Creek**—*pop pl* MS-4
McCall Creek—*stream* AK-9
McCall Creek—*stream* (2) MS-4
McCall Creek—*stream* NV-8
McCall Creek—*stream* OH-6
McCall Creek—*stream* (2) OR-9
McCall Creek—*stream* TX-5
McCall Creek—*stream* (2) WI-6
**McCall Creek (McCall)**—*pop pl* MS-4
McCall Dam State Park—*park* PA-2
McCall Dipping Vat Spring—*spring* OR-9
McCall Ditch—*canal* CA-9
McCall Drain—*canal* CA-9
McCall Drain Five—*canal* CA-9
McCall Drain Five A—*canal* CA-9
McCall Drain Five B—*canal* CA-9
McCall Drain Four—*canal* CA-9
McCall Drain One—*canal* CA-9
McCall Drain One B—*canal* CA-9
McCalley Lake Dam—*dam* MS-4
McCalleys Creek—*stream* SC-3
McCall Field—*park* PA-2
*McCall Fork* VA-3
McCall Gap—*gap* NC-3
McCall Gap—*gap* (2) VA-3
**McCall Gap**—*pop pl* VA-3
McCall Glacier—*glacier* AK-9
McCall Glacier—*glacier* WA-9
McCall Gulch—*valley* CA-9
McCall Gulch—*valley* WA-9
**McCall Heights (subdivision)**—*pop pl* NC-3
McCall Hill—*summit* MI-6
McCall Hill—*summit* WA-9
McCall Hollow—*valley* KY-4
McCall Hosp—*hospital* GA-3
McCall House—*hist pl* NC-3
**McCallie**—*pop pl* GA-3
McCallie Cem—*cemetery* (2) TN-4
McCallie Creek—*stream* AK-9
McCallie Gap—*gap* GA-3
McCallie Hollow—*valley* AL-4
McCallie Lake—*lake* GA-3
McCallie Lake—*lake* TN-4
McCallie Landing—*locale* TN-4
*McCallie Tunnel* TN-4
McCallie Tunnel Prospect—*mine* TN-4
McCallister, John E., House—*hist pl* KY-4
McCallister Cem—*cemetery* IL-6
McCallister Cem—*cemetery* MO-7
McCallister Cem—*cemetery* WV-2
McCallister-Gash Farmhouse—*hist pl* OR-9
McCallister Hill—*summit* IN-6
McCallister Soda Spring Forest Camp—*locale* OR-9
McCall JHS—*school* MA-1
*McCall Junior High School* AL-4
McCall Knob—*summit* KY-4
*Mccall Lake* WI-6
McCall Lake—*lake* NC-3
McCall Lake—*lake* TX-5
McCall Lake—*lake* (3) WI-6
Mc Call Lake—*reservoir* CO-8
McCall Lake—*reservoir* TN-4
McCall Lake Dam—*dam* TN-4
McCall Landing—*locale* MS-4
McCall Mtn—*summit* NC-3
McCall Mtn—*summit* PA-2
McCall Mtn—*summit* WA-9
*McCallocks Creek* AL-4
McCallop Creek—*stream* GA-3
McCall Point—*summit* OR-9
McCall Pond—*lake* NY-2
McCall Pond—*swamp* GA-3
Mc Call Ranch—*locale* CO-8
McCall River—*gut* MS-4
McCall Rsvr—*reservoir* NM-5
McCall Run—*stream* WV-2
McCall Sand Flats—*flat* FL-3
*McCalls Bayou* LA-4
McCalls Branch—*stream* AR-4
McCalls Branch—*stream* IL-6
McCalls Branch—*stream* MO-7
McCalls Branch—*stream* SC-3
**Mccallsburg**—*pop pl* IA-7
McCalls Cem—*cemetery* GA-3
McCalls Cem—*cemetery* OH-6
McCall Sch—*school* AL-4
McCall Sch—*school* IL-6
McCall Sch—*school* LA-4
McCall Sch—*school* MI-6
McCall Sch—*school* NV-8
McCall Sch—*school* OK-5
McCall Sch—*school* PA-2
McCall Sch—*school* TN-4
McCalls Chapel—*church* FL-3
*McCalls Creek* MS-4
McCalls Creek—*stream* AL-4
McCalls Creek Precinct (historical)—*locale* MS-4
*McCalls Ferry* PA-2
*McCalls Lake* AL-4
McCalls Lake—*reservoir* SC-3
Mc Calls Lake Dam—*dam* AL-4
McCalls Mill (historical)—*locale* AL-4
McCalls Millpond—*lake* SC-3
McCalls Pond—*reservoir* AL-4
McCall Spring—*spring* (2) OR-9
McCalls Sch—*school* TN-4
McCalls Sch (historical)—*school* TN-4
*McCalls School* AL-4
McCall Street Hist Dist—*hist pl* WI-6
McCall Substation—*locale* CA-9
McCall Swamp—*swamp* NC-3
**McCallum**—*pop pl* MS-4
McCallum Bay—*swamp* FL-3
McCallum Branch—*stream* FL-3
McCallum Ch—*church* MI-6
McCallum Creek—*stream* AK-9
McCallum Creek—*stream* MI-6
McCallum Drain—*canal* MI-6
McCallum Glacier—*glacier* AK-9
McCallum Grove—*woods* CA-9
McCallum HS—*school* TX-5
McCallum Manor—*hist pl* PA-2
McCallum Playground—*locale* MI-6
McCallum Pond—*lake* GA-3
McCallum Post Office (historical)—*building* MS-4
McCallum Sch—*school* MI-6
McCall Woods—*woods* WA-9
McCally Creek—*stream* AK-9
McCalmont—*locale* PA-2
McCalmont Sch—*school* PA-2
**McCalmont (Township of)**—*pop pl* PA-2
**McCaln**—*pop pl* FL-3
McCalvy Hill—*summit* PA-2
McCamant Creek—*stream* AK-9
McCamant Hill—*summit* VA-3
McCamant Hills—*ridge* AZ-5
McCambridge Park—*park* CA-9
*Mccameron Creek* MT-8
*McCameron Township* IN-6
**McCamey**—*pop pl* TX-5
McCamey (CCD)—*cens area* TX-5
McCamey Oil Field—*oilfield* TX-5
McCamey Windmill—*locale* TX-5
McCamish Cem—*cemetery* KY-4
**McCamish Township**—*pop pl* KS-7
McCamley Post Office (historical)—*building* SD-7
**McCammon**—*pop pl* ID-8
McCammon, Samuel, House—*hist pl* TN-4
McCammon Branch—*stream* KY-4
McCammon Cem—*cemetery* IN-6
McCammon Cem—*cemetery* TN-4
McCammon State Bank Bldg—*hist pl* ID-8
**McCampbell**—*pop pl* CA-9
McCampbell Ch—*church* TN-4
McCampbell Gap—*gap* (2) NC-3
McCampbell Gap—*gap* TN-4
McCampbell Knob—*summit* NC-3
McCampbell Knob—*summit* TN-4
McCampbell Oil Field—*oilfield* TX-5
McCampbell Sch—*school* TN-4
McCampbells Chapel Cem—*cemetery* TN-4
*McCampbells Chapel Methodist Church* TN-4
McCampbell Slough—*gut* TX-5
McCampbell Spring—*spring* TN-4
McCamy Branch—*stream* TN-4
McCamy Cem—*cemetery* AL-4
McCamy Dam—*dam* TN-4
McCamy Dam—*reservoir* TN-4
McCamy Ridge—*ridge* TN-4
*McCamys Ford* TN-4
McCamy Spring—*spring* TN-4
McCan Branch—*stream* KY-4
**McCance**—*pop pl* OH-6
**McCance**—*pop pl* PA-2
**McCance (Long Bridge)**—*pop pl* PA-2
McCandless Airp—*airport* PA-2
McCandless Archeol Site—*hist pl* MD-2
McCandless Bridge (historical)—*bridge* TN-4
McCandless Cem—*cemetery* KY-4
McCandless Cem—*cemetery* PA-2
McCandless Cem—*cemetery* TN-4
McCandless Cleghorn Ditch—*canal* IA-7
McCandless Cleghorn Outlet—*canal* IA-7
McCandless Ditch—*canal* HI-9
McCandless Elem Sch—*school* KS-7
McCandless Gulch—*valley* CA-9
McCandless Sch—*school* CA-9
McCandless Township—*CDP* PA-2
**McCandless (Township of)**—*pop pl* PA-2
*McCandy* MS-4
*McCanee Creek* WA-9
*McCanes Creek* WA-9
McCaneys Mill (historical)—*locale* TN-4
McCan Gulch—*valley* ID-8
*McCanico* AL-4
McCanless Cem—*cemetery* KY-4
McCanless Cem—*cemetery* TN-4
McCanless Creek—*stream* GA-3
McCanless Golf Course—*locale* NC-3
McCanless Hollow—*valley* TN-4
McCanless Memorial Ch—*church* VA-3
McCanless-Williams House—*hist pl* TX-5
*McCann* AL-4
McCann—*locale* CA-9
McCann, Benjamin, House—*hist pl* KY-4
McCann, Neal, House—*hist pl* KY-4
McCann, Thomas, House—*hist pl* OR-9
**McCanna**—*pop pl* ND-7
McCanna-Hubbell Bldg—*hist pl* NM-5
*McCanna Run* PA-2
McCanna Run—*stream* PA-2
*McCanna Run - in part* PA-2
McCan-Nave House—*hist pl* TX-5
McCann Bayou—*gut* MS-4
McCann Bluff—*cliff* TN-4
McCann Branch—*stream* KY-4
McCann Branch—*stream* TN-4
McCann Branch—*stream* (2) TX-5
McCann Bridge—*other* MO-7
McCann Butte—*summit* MT-8
McCann Canyon—*valley* KS-7
McCann Canyon—*valley* (2) NE-7
McCann Canyon—*valley* (2) NV-8
McCann Cave—*cave* MO-7
McCann Cem—*cemetery* MS-4
McCann Cem—*cemetery* MO-7
McCann Cem—*cemetery* TN-4
McCann Cem—*cemetery* (2) TX-5
*McCann Creek* MS-4
McCann Creek—*stream* AK-9
McCann Creek—*stream* CA-9
McCann Creek—*stream* IN-6
McCann Creek—*stream* NV-8
McCann Creek—*stream* OK-5
McCann Creek—*stream* TX-5
McCann Creek—*stream* WI-6
McCann Creek Mtn—*summit* NV-8
Mc Cann Ditch—*canal* CO-8
McCann Draw—*valley* WY-8
McCann Field—*park* AL-4
McCann Ford—*locale* IL-6
McCann Gulch—*valley* NM-5
McCann Hill—*summit* AK-9
McCann Hollow—*valley* AR-4
Mc Cann Hollow—*valley* NY-2
McCann Lake—*lake* MS-4
McCann Lake—*lake* WI-6
McCann Lake—*lake* WY-8
McCann Lake—*reservoir* AL-4
McCann Lake—*swamp* MN-6
McCann Landing—*locale* MO-7
McCann Mill—*locale* ID-8
McCann Mtn—*summit* OK-5
McCann Pass—*gap* WY-8
McCann Ranch—*locale* WY-8
McCann Run—*stream* WV-2
McCann Run Ch—*church* WV-2
McCann Sch—*school* MI-6
McCann Sch—*school* MS-4
McCann Sch—*school* TN-4
McCann Sch (historical)—*school* MO-7
McCanns Corner—*locale* MD-2
McCann Spring—*spring* OR-9
McCann Spring—*spring* TX-5
McCann Spring Tank—*reservoir* AZ-5
McCann Station (site)—*locale* NV-8
**McCannsville (subdivision)**—*pop pl* AL-4
McCann Technical Sch—*school* MA-1
*McCannville* AL-4
*McCant Creek* MS-4
McCants Creek—*stream* MS-4
McCants Millpond—*reservoir* GA-3
McCants Ranch—*locale* NM-5
McCants Sch—*school* SC-3
McCants Sch (historical)—*school* AL-4
M C Canyon—*valley* AZ-5
McCanyon—*valley* WA-9
McCard Brook—*stream* MA-1
McCardell Lake—*swamp* TX-5
McCardle Gulch—*valley* CA-9
McCardle Island—*island* FL-3
McCardney Ferry (historical)—*locale* AL-4
McCards Lake—*lake* GA-3
McCardy Canyon—*valley* UT-8
*McCardy Hollow* TN-4
McCardy Spring—*spring* UT-8
*McCarens Lake* WI-6
McCargar Place—*locale* WY-8
McCargo Branch—*stream* AR-4
*McCargo Cove* MI-6
McCargo Creek—*stream* AR-4
*McCargo-Crutcher Cemetery* AL-4
McCargoe Cove—*bay* MI-6
McCargoe Cove Campground—*locale* MI-6
McCargo Lake—*lake* NY-2
**McCarley**—*pop pl* MS-4
McCarley Cem—*cemetery* AL-4
McCarley Community Center—*building* MS-4
McCarley Sch (historical)—*school* MS-4
McCarmack Windmill—*locale* TX-5
McCarmel Branch—*stream* TN-4
McCarn, Noah, House—*hist pl* AR-4
McCarne Mtn—*summit* AL-4
McCarn Hollow—*valley* MO-7
*McCaroy Hill* MT-8
McCarr—*locale* KY-4
**McCarr**—*pop pl* WV-2
McCarrahan Lake—*lake* MN-6
McCarran International Airport—*airport* NV-8
McCarr (CCD)—*cens area* KY-4
McCarrell Cem—*cemetery* TN-4
McCarrell Memorial Cem—*cemetery* AZ-5
McCarrell Spring—*spring* TN-4
McCarren Campsite—*locale* ME-1
McCarren Park—*park* NY-2
McCarroll Corner—*locale* PA-2
McCarroll Hill Ch—*church* KY-4
McCarroll Interchange—*crossing* AZ-5
McCarroll Sch—*school* MI-6
McCarrol Mtn—*summit* NC-3
McCarrol Mtn—*summit* SC-3
McCarrols Mill (historical)—*locale* AL-4
McCarron—*locale* MI-6
McCarron Ch—*church* MI-6
*McCarron Lake* MN-6
McCarrons Lake—*lake* MN-6
McCarrons Lake Filtration Plant—*other* MN-6
McCarrty Canyon—*valley* OR-9
McCarry Lake—*lake* WI-6
McCarrys Knob—*summit* PA-2
McCarson Cem—*cemetery* NC-3
McCarteney Creek—*stream* WA-9
McCarter, Tyson, Place—*hist pl* TN-4
McCarter Branch—*stream* KY-4
McCarter Cem—*cemetery* MO-7
McCarter Cem—*cemetery* TN-4
McCarter Cem—*cemetery* VA-3
McCarter Creek—*stream* ID-8
McCarter Ditch—*canal* IN-6
McCarter Elem Sch—*school* KS-7
McCarter Hollow—*valley* MO-7
McCarter Lake—*lake* AR-4
McCarter Sch—*school* KS-7
Mc Carters Lake—*lake* MT-8
*McCartersville* PA-2
McCarter Well—*locale* NM-5
*McCart Gap* TN-4
McCartha Branch—*stream* SC-3
*McCarth Creek* MT-8
**McCarthey**—*pop pl* PA-2
McCarthey Lake—*lake* MN-6
McCarthy—*locale* ID-8
**McCarthy**—*pop pl* AK-9
McCarthy, Judge Charles P., House—*hist pl* ID-8
McCarthy, Margaret, Homestead—*hist pl* MT-8
McCarthy, Patrick F., House—*hist pl* IA-7
McCarthy, T. G., House—*hist pl* CO-8
**McCarthy Addition**—*pop pl* IN-6
McCarthy Bar—*bend* CA-9
McCarthy Beach State Park—*park* MN-6
McCarthy Bldg—*hist pl* IL-6
McCarthy Bldg—*hist pl* NY-2
McCarthy-Blosser-Dillon Bldg—*hist pl* OH-6
McCarthy Branch—*stream* TX-5
McCarthy Bridge—*bridge* GA-3
McCarthy Butte—*summit* OR-9
McCarthy Camp—*locale* VA-3
McCarthy Cem—*cemetery* KY-4
McCarthy Cem—*cemetery* TN-4
*McCarthy Chapel* TN-4
McCarthy Chapel Cem—*cemetery* TX-5
*McCarthy Creek* CA-9
*McCarthy Creek* MT-8
McCarthy Creek—*stream* AK-9
McCarthy Creek—*stream* (2) CA-9
McCarthy Creek—*stream* (2) MI-6
McCarthy Creek—*stream* MN-6
McCarthy Creek—*stream* MT-8
McCarthy Creek—*stream* OR-9
McCarthy Creek—*stream* WI-6
McCarthy Creek Glacier—*glacier* AK-9
McCarthy Ditch—*canal* ID-8
McCarthy Drain—*stream* MI-6
McCarthy General Store—*hist pl* AK-9
Mc Carthy Gulch—*valley* CO-8
McCarthy Gulch—*valley* MT-8
McCarthy Hill—*summit* MA-1
McCarthy Homestead Cabin—*hist pl* MT-8
*McCarthy Lake* MN-6
McCarthy Lake—*lake* FL-3
McCarthy Lake—*lake* (2) MI-6
McCarthy Lake—*lake* (2) MN-6
McCarthy Lake—*lake* NE-7
McCarthy Lake—*lake* (3) WI-6
McCarthy Lake—*reservoir* IL-6
McCarthy Lake—*swamp* MN-6
McCarthy Lake State Wildlife Mngmt Area—*park* MN-6
McCarthy Marsh—*swamp* AK-9
*McCarthy Mountain* MT-8
McCarthy Mtn—*summit* NY-2
McCarthy-Platt House—*hist pl* NV-8
McCarthy Point—*cape* CA-9
McCarthy Point—*cape* ME-1
McCarthy Pond—*lake* MA-1
McCarthy Power Plant—*hist pl* AK-9
Mc Carthy Ranch—*locale* CO-8
McCarthy Ranch—*locale* WY-8
Mc Carthy Reservoir—*locale* CO-8
McCarthy Ridge—*ridge* OR-9
McCarthy Run—*stream* PA-2
McCarthys Brook—*stream* CT-1
McCarthy Sch—*school* CA-9
McCarthy Sch—*school* NE-7
McCarthy Sch—*school* NY-2
*McCarthys Corner* PA-2
**McCarthys Corner**—*pop pl* VA-3
McCarthys Lake—*lake* NY-2
McCarthys Lakes—*reservoir* NJ-2
McCarthys Landing (historical)—*locale* MS-4
McCarthy Slough—*stream* OR-9
McCarthy Spring—*spring* (2) OR-9
Mc Carthy Trail—*trail* CO-8
McCarthy Well—*well* WY-8
McCartie Hill—*summit* CA-9
McCartie Ranch—*locale* (2) OR-9
McCartie Rsvr—*reservoir* OR-9
McCartie Spring—*spring* OR-9
McCartney—*locale* WI-6
**McCartney**—*pop pl* PA-2
McCartney, R. W., Music Hall—*hist pl* IL-6
McCartney-Bone House—*hist pl* AL-4
McCartney Branch—*stream* WI-6
McCartney Bridge—*bridge* TX-5
McCartney Cem—*cemetery* (2) AL-4
McCartney Cem—*cemetery* LA-4
McCartney County Park—*park* OR-9
McCartney Creek—*stream* (2) MT-8
McCartney Creek—*stream* WA-9
McCartney House—*hist pl* TX-5
McCartney Island—*island* TX-5
McCartney Lake—*lake* LA-4
McCartney Lake—*lake* WI-6
Mc Cartney Mesa—*summit* CO-8
*McCartney Mountain* MT-8
McCartney Mtn—*summit* MT-8
McCartney Peak—*summit* WA-9
McCartney Sch—*school* IL-6
McCartney Sch—*school* OH-6
McCartney Sch (historical)—*school* MO-7
McCartney Springs—*spring* MT-8
McCart Slough—*lake* SD-7
McCartt Cem—*cemetery* TN-4
McCartt Gap—*gap* TN-4
*McCarty* TN-4
McCarty—*locale* ME-1
**McCarty**—*pop pl* IN-6
**McCarty**—*pop pl* MO-7
**McCarty**—*pop pl* TN-4
McCarty, John, Round Barn—*hist pl* IL-6
McCarty, Mount—*summit* AK-9
*McCarty Arm* AK-9
Mc Carty Basin—*basin* CO-8
McCarty Bayou—*stream* MS-4
Mc Carty Bench—*bench* CO-8
McCarty Branch—*stream* (2) KY-4
McCarty Branch—*stream* (2) TN-4
McCarty Bridge—*other* MI-6
McCarty Butte—*summit* OR-9
McCarty Cabin Waterhole—*reservoir* OR-9
McCarty Canyon—*valley* UT-8
McCarty Canyon—*valley* WY-8
*McCarty Cem* TN-4
McCarty Cem—*cemetery* AL-4
McCarty Cem—*cemetery* IN-6
McCarty Cem—*cemetery* KY-4
McCarty Cem—*cemetery* (2) LA-4
McCarty Cem—*cemetery* MS-4
McCarty Cem—*cemetery* OH-6
McCarty Cem—*cemetery* OK-5
McCarty Cem—*cemetery* (3) TN-4
McCarty Cem—*cemetery* (3) TX-5
McCarty Ch—*church* MO-7
McCarty Ch—*church* TN-4
McCarty Chapel—*church* TN-4
McCarty Chapel—*church* TX-5
McCarty Coulee—*valley* MT-8
McCarty Cove—*bay* ME-1
Mc Carty Cow Camp—*locale* CO-8
*McCarty Creek* CA-9
*McCarty Creek* MT-8
McCarty Creek—*stream* (3) CA-9
McCarty Creek—*stream* IA-7
McCarty Creek—*stream* KY-4
McCarty Creek—*stream* MO-7
McCarty Creek—*stream* (3) MT-8
McCarty Creek—*stream* OK-5
McCarty Creek—*stream* (3) OR-9
McCarty Creek—*stream* TX-5
McCarty Creek—*stream* (2) WA-9
McCarty Creek—*stream* WY-8
McCarty Ditch—*canal* IN-6
*McCarty Draw* AZ-5
McCarty Draw—*valley* AZ-5
McCarty Draw—*valley* TX-5
McCarty Ferry (historical)—*locale* AL-4
McCarty Field—*flat* OR-9
McCarty Fiord—*bay* AK-9
McCarty Flat—*flat* CA-9
McCarty Flat—*flat* NM-5
McCarty Flat—*flat* OR-9
McCarty Ford—*locale* AL-4
McCarty Glacier—*glacier* (2) AK-9
*McCarty Gulch* OR-9
McCarty Gulch—*valley* ID-8
McCarty Gulch—*valley* (2) OR-9
McCarty Hill—*summit* MT-8
McCarty Hill—*summit* NY-2
McCarty Hollow—*valley* TN-4
McCarty Hollow—*valley* VA-3
McCarty Island—*island* MS-4
McCarty Lagoon—*bay* AK-9
McCarty Lake—*lake* MN-6
McCarty Lake—*lake* (2) NE-7
McCarty Lake—*reservoir* TX-5
McCarty-Lilley House—*hist pl* NE-7
McCarty Meadow—*swamp* OR-9
M C Carty Mesa—*summit* NM-5
McCarty Mine—*mine* AK-9
McCarty Mine—*mine* (3) CA-9
*McCarty Mountain* MT-8
McCarty Mtn—*summit* ME-1
Mc Carty Park—*flat* CO-8
McCarty Park—*park* IL-6
McCarty Park—*park* WI-6
McCarty Pond—*lake* WA-9
McCarty Ranch—*locale* CA-9
McCarty Ranch—*locale* (2) NM-5
McCarty Ranch—*locale* WY-8
McCarty Ridge—*ridge* AZ-5
McCarty Ridge—*ridge* AR-4
McCarty Ridge—*ridge* TN-4
McCarty River—*stream* MN-6
McCarty Road Ch—*church* MI-6
McCarty Rsvr—*reservoir* OR-9
**McCartys**—*pop pl* (2) NM-5
McCartys Bluff—*cliff* AL-4
McCarty Sch—*school* NE-7
McCarty Sch—*school* WI-6
McCarty Sch Number 1—*school* LA-4
McCarty Sch Number 48—*school* IN-6
**McCartys Corner**—*pop pl* PA-2
McCartys Ferry (historical)—*crossing* TN-4
McCartys Ferry (historical)—*locale* AL-4
*McCartys Ferry Landing* AL-4
McCarty Site—*hist pl* TX-5
McCartys Landing—*locale* AL-4
McCartys Landing—*locale* (2) TN-4
McCarty Spring—*spring* (2) NV-8
McCarty Spring—*spring* (2) OR-9
McCarty Spring—*spring* TN-4
McCartys Run—*stream* IN-6
McCartys Siding—*locale* NM-5
McCarty Station—*locale* TN-4
McCartysville Flats—*flat* MT-8
McCarty Tank—*reservoir* AZ-5
McCarty Tank—*reservoir* NM-5
*McCarty United Methodist Church* TN-4
**McCartyville**—*pop pl* OH-6
McCarty Well—*locale* NM-5
McCarty Well—*well* NM-5
McCarty West Camp—*locale* NM-5
McCarty Wharf—*locale* MD-2
McCarty Windmill—*locale* NM-5
McCarver, Morton Matthew, House—*hist pl* OR-9
McCarvers Bar—*bar* TN-4
McCarver Sch—*school* WA-9
McCarvey—*locale* PA-2
McCarvey Creek—*stream* CA-9
McCary Cem—*cemetery* MO-7
McCash Fork—*stream* CA-9
McCash Lake—*lake* CA-9
McCaskey Cem—*cemetery* OH-6
McCaskey Drain—*stream* WY-8
McCaskey Graves—*cemetery* PA-2
McCaskey HS—*school* PA-2
McCaskey Lateral—*canal* NM-5
McCaskey Ridge—*ridge* TX-5
McCaskill—*locale* SC-3
**McCaskill**—*pop pl* AR-4
McCaskill Cem—*cemetery* AL-4
McCaskill Cem—*cemetery* SC-3
McCaskill Ch—*church* LA-4
McCaskill Creek—*stream* SC-3
McCaskill Pond—*reservoir* NC-3
McCaskills Crossing—*locale* TX-5
McCaskin Run—*stream* PA-2
McCasland and Schiller Number 1 Dam—*dam* SD-7
McCasland and Schiller Number 2 Dam—*dam* SD-7

McCasland and Schiller Number 3 Dam—dam ... SD-7
McCasland and Schiller Number 4 Dam—dam ... SD-7
McCasland Branch—stream ... TN-4
McCasland Cem—cemetery ... TN-4
McCasland Creek—stream ... LA-4
**McCaslin**—pop pl ... PA-2
McCaslin, William Henry and Lucinda, Farm House—hist pl ... MI-6
McCaslin Branch—stream ... AR-4
McCaslin Brook—stream ... WI-6
McCaslin Lake—lake ... MI-6
McCaslin Lake—lake ... WI-6
Mc Caslin Lake—reservoir ... CO-8
McCaslin Lookout Tower—locale ... WI-6
McCaslin Marsh—swamp ... WA-9
McCaslin Mtn—summit ... WI-6
McCaslin Spring—spring ... WI-6
McCaslin Stream—stream ... ME-1
McCasslin Valley—basin ... PA-2
McCathern Spring—spring ... TN-4
McCathey Hollow—valley ... AL-4
McCathrine Mtn—summit ... TX-5
McCaughan, John, House—hist pl ... KY-4
McCaughan Park—park ... TX-5
McCauley—locale ... PA-2
McCauley—locale ... WV-2
**McCauley**—pop pl ... PA-2
McCauley, Henry, Farm—hist pl ... MD-2
McCauley, H. M., House—hist pl ... WA-9
McCauley, John, House—hist pl ... KY-4
McCauley and Meyer Barns—hist pl ... CA-9
McCauley Bay—bay ... MI-6
McCauley Bridge—hist pl ... KS-7
McCauley Butte—summit ... MT-8
McCauley Cabin—hist pl ... CA-9
McCauley Cem—cemetery ... KS-7
McCauley Cem—cemetery ... KY-4
McCauley Cem—cemetery ... MO-7
McCauley Cem—cemetery ... NC-3
McCauley Cem—cemetery ... OH-6
McCauley Ch—church ... AR-4
McCauley Chapel—church ... AL-4
McCauley Chapel Methodist Ch ... AL-4
McCauley Creek ... OK-5
McCauley Creek ... WA-9
McCauley Creek—stream (2) ... ID-8
McCauley Creek—stream ... OR-9
Mc Cauley Ditch—canal ... CO-8
McCauley Ditch—canal ... MT-8
McCauley Falls—falls ... WA-9
McCauley Hill—summit ... CA-9
McCauley Lake—reservoir ... NC-3
McCauley Lake Dam—dam ... NC-3
McCauley Mount—summit ... NC-3
McCauley Mtn—summit ... AL-4
McCauley Mtn—summit (2) ... NY-2
McCauley Mtn—summit ... PA-2
McCauley-Murphy Ditch ... MT-8
McCauley Park—flat ... MT-8
McCauley Park—park ... ID-8
McCauley Peak—summit ... CO-8
McCauley Point—cape ... MI-6
McCauley Pond—lake ... NY-2
McCauley Pond—reservoir ... DE-2
McCauley Pond—reservoir ... NC-3
McCauley Pond Dam—dam ... NC-3
McCauley Ranch—locale ... MT-8
McCauley Ranch—locale (3) ... NM-5
McCauley Ranch (Old Stage Station)—locale ... CA-9
McCauley Run—stream (2) ... PA-2
McCauley Run—stream (2) ... WV-2
McCauleys Bluff—cliff ... TN-4
McCauleys Bluff Landing—locale ... TN-4
McCauley Sch—school ... IL-6
McCauley Sinks—basin ... AZ-5
**McCauleyville**—pop pl ... MN-6
McCauleyville (Township of)—civ div ... MN-6
McCauley Well—well ... TX-5
McCauliff Ditch—canal ... IN-6
**McCaulley**—pop pl ... TX-5
McCaulley Branch—stream ... TN-4
McCaulley (CCD)—cens area ... TX-5
McCausey Branch—stream ... MI-6
McCausey Ridge—ridge ... KY-4
McCausey Ridge Cem—cemetery ... KY-4
McCausey Ridge Lookout Tower—locale ... KY-4
McCausey Ridge Sch—school ... KY-4
**McCausland**—pop pl ... IA-7
McCausland, Gen. John, House—hist pl ... WV-2
McCausland, Mount—summit ... WA-9
McCausland Cem—cemetery ... LA-4
McCausland Run—stream ... WV-2
McCautry Run—stream ... PA-2
McCavanaugh Pond—lake ... NY-2
McCave Sch—school ... PA-2
McCavick Mine—mine ... CA-9
McCavley Tank—reservoir ... NM-5
McCawleys Mill (historical)—locale ... TN-4
McCaw Sch—school ... NV-8
McCay, Mount—summit ... WA-9
McCaybe Cem—cemetery ... OK-5
McCay Branch—stream ... AL-4
McCay Cem—cemetery ... MS-4
McCay Creek—stream ... WA-9
McCayhan Cem—cemetery ... SC-3
McCay Lake—reservoir ... AL-4
McCays ... TN-4
McCays Post Office ... TN-4
**McCaysville**—pop pl ... GA-3
McCaysville (CCD)—cens area ... GA-3
McCay Trail—trail ... WA-9
Mccearys Creek ... MS-4
McCellan Canyon—valley ... CA-9
McCellan Cem—cemetery ... AL-4
McCelland Lake ... UT-8
McCellan Sch—school ... IL-6
McCellan Sch—school ... PA-2
McChapel Ch—church ... FL-3
McChapel Sch—school ... FL-3
McCharen Field (airport)—airport ... MS-4
**McChesney Heights**—pop pl ... VA-3
McChesney Hill—summit (2) ... KY-4
McChesney JHS—school ... CA-9
McChesney Mountain ... CA-9
McChesney Ridge—ridge ... OH-6
McChesney Rsvr—reservoir ... MT-8
McChesney Spring—spring ... WA-9
McChesneytown—uninc pl ... PA-2
McChesneytown-Loyalhanna—CDP ... PA-2
Mcchesny Ridge ... OH-6
McChester Shaft Mine (underground)—mine ... AL-4
Mc Chivvis Rsvr—reservoir ... CO-8
McChord—other ... WA-9
McChord, William C., House—hist pl ... KY-4
Mcchord Afb Airp—airport ... WA-9
McChord Air Force Base—military ... WA-9
McChord Butte—summit ... ID-8
McChord Field—other ... WA-9
McChord Run—stream ... WV-2
McChristian Creek—stream ... CA-9
McChune Branch—stream ... SC-3
**McClaimsville**—pop pl ... OH-6
McClain—locale ... MT-8
McClain—locale ... WV-2
McClain Bay—swamp ... GA-3
McClain Branch—stream ... AL-4
McClain Branch—stream ... AR-4
McClain Branch—stream ... GA-3
McClain Branch—stream ... KY-4
McClain Branch—stream ... TN-4
McClain Canyon—valley ... TX-5
McClain Cem—cemetery ... AR-4
McClain Cem—cemetery ... MS-4
McClain Cem—cemetery (2) ... MO-7
McClain Cem—cemetery (5) ... TN-4
McClain Ch—church ... IL-6
McClain Ch—church ... WV-2
McClain Chapel—church ... MS-4
McClain Coulee—stream ... MT-8
**McClain (County)**—pop pl ... OK-5
McClain County Courthouse—hist pl ... OK-5
McClain Creek—stream ... MT-8
McClain Ditch—canal ... IN-6
McClaine House—hist pl ... IA-7
McClaine Lake—lake (2) ... WI-6
McClain-Ellison House—hist pl ... TN-4
McClain Grocery Company (Warehouse)—facility ... OH-6
McClain Hill—summit ... NE-7
McClain HS—school ... OH-6
McClain Lake—lake ... MN-6
McClain Lake—lake ... MT-8
McClain Lake—lake ... WA-9
McClain Mtn—summit ... VA-3
McClain Peaks ... WA-9
McClain Ranch—locale ... CA-9
McClain Ranch (reduced usage)—locale ... TX-5
McClain Rsvr—reservoir ... CO-8
McClain Run ... PA-2
McClain Sch ... TN-4
McClains Chapel ... TN-4
McClains Chapel Cem—cemetery ... TN-4
McClains Chapel Sch (historical)—school ... TN-4
McClain Shop Ctr—locale ... TN-4
McClains Sch—school ... AL-4
McClainsville Sch—school ... IN-6
**McClainville**—pop pl ... OH-6
McClain Windmill—locale ... TX-5
McClair Slough—gut ... KY-4
McClam Crossroads ... NC-3
**McClam Crossroads**—pop pl ... NC-3
**McClamerys Stand**—pop pl ... TN-4
McClamory Key—island ... FL-3
McClamrock Ditch—canal ... IN-6
McClam Sch—school ... SC-3
McClam X-Roads ... NC-3
McClanahan ... WV-2
McClanahan—locale ... TX-5
McClanahan Branch—stream ... TN-4
McClanahan Cem—cemetery ... AR-4
McClanahan Cem—cemetery ... IL-6
McClanahan Cem—cemetery (3) ... TN-4
McClanahan Cem—cemetery ... VA-3
McClanahan Cem—cemetery ... WV-2
McClanahan Creek—stream ... MO-7
McClanahan Ditch—canal ... CA-9
McClanahan Draw—valley ... WY-8
McClanahan Ferry (historical)—locale ... TN-4
McClanahan Hill—summit ... TN-4
McClanahan Hollow—valley (2) ... TN-4
McClanahan Lake—lake ... WY-8
McClanahan Meadow—flat ... OR-9
McClanahan Post Office (historical)—building ... AL-4
McClanahan Sch (abandoned)—school ... MO-7
McClanahan Spring—spring ... NV-8
**McClane City**—pop pl ... LA-4
McClane Creek—stream ... GA-3
McClane Creek—stream ... KY-4
McClane Lake—reservoir ... KS-7
McClappin Spring—spring ... CA-9
McClarem Lake—lake ... SD-7
McClaren Cem—cemetery ... AR-4
McClaren Hollow—valley ... TN-4
McClaren Lake ... WI-6
McClarens Run—stream ... PA-2
McClarin Hollow—valley ... TN-4
McClarity Branch—stream ... WV-2
McClarity Branch Ch—church ... WV-2
Mcclark Bayou ... MS-4
McClarney Cem—cemetery ... KS-7
McClaron Mine—mine ... CA-9
**McClarran**—pop pl ... PA-2
McClary Cem—cemetery ... NH-1
McClary Hill—summit ... NH-1
McClary House—hist pl ... DE-2
McClary Island—island ... WI-6
McClary Islands—island ... TN-4
McClary Ranger Station—locale ... MT-8
McClarys Islands ... TN-4
McClary Spring—spring ... TN-4
McClarys Spring ... TN-4
McClaster Pit—cave ... AL-4
McClatchey-Gettys Farm—hist pl ... TN-4
McClatchy Cemetery ... MS-4
McClatchy HS—school ... CA-9
McClatchy Park—park ... CA-9
McClathy Cem—cemetery ... MS-4
McClaughrey Drain—stream ... MI-6
McClaughry Sch—school ... IL-6
McClaughry Springs Woods—woods ... IL-6
Mc Clave—locale ... MT-8
**McClave**—pop pl ... CO-8
Mc Clave Drainage Ditch—canal ... CO-8
**McClaveville**—pop pl ... CT-1
McClay Coulee—valley ... MT-8
McClay Orchard—locale ... IL-6
McClay Sch—school ... PA-2
McClays Peak—summit ... PA-2
McClay's Twin Bridge (East)—hist pl ... PA-2
McClay's Twin Bridge (West)—hist pl ... PA-2
Mcclayville ... CT-1
**McClean**—pop pl ... MI-6
McClean Creek ... MT-8
Mcclean Lake—reservoir ... AL-4
Mcclean Lake Dam—dam ... AL-4
McClean Sch—school ... TN-4
McCleans Corner—locale ... MD-2
McClean Site—hist pl ... NE-7
McClearen Hollow—valley ... TN-4
McClear Ranch—locale ... WY-8
McCleary—locale ... PA-2
McCleary—other ... OH-6
**McCleary**—pop pl ... WA-9
McCleary, Henry, House—hist pl ... WA-9
McCleary Bluff—cliff ... IL-6
McCleary Brook—stream ... VT-1
McCleary Canyon—valley ... AZ-5
McCleary (CCD)—cens area ... WA-9
McCleary Cem—cemetery ... IA-7
McCleary Cem—cemetery ... OH-6
McCleary Elem Sch—hist pl ... PA-2
McCleary Junction—locale ... WA-9
McCleary Peak—summit ... AZ-5
McCleary Rsvr—reservoir ... WY-8
McCleary Sch—school ... NY-2
McCleary Sch—school ... PA-2
McCleary Sch (abandoned)—school ... MO-7
McCleary Sch (historical)—school ... PA-2
McCleary School (historical)—locale ... MO-7
McCleary Well Number One—well ... NV-8
McCleary Well Number Two—well ... NV-8
McCleary Sch—school ... WA-9
McClede Mtn—summit ... NM-5
McClede Spring—spring ... NM-5
McClerey Creek—stream ... IA-7
McCleery Gulch—valley ... MT-8
McCleery Sch—school ... IL-6
McClees Creek—stream ... NJ-2
McClehan Lake ... UT-8
McClellan ... AZ-5
**McClellan**—pop pl ... PA-2
**McClellan**—pop pl ... WV-2
McClellan, E. W., House—hist pl ... AR-4
McClellan, Lake—reservoir ... TX-5
McClellan AFB—military ... CA-9
McClellan-Andere Cem—cemetery ... IL-6
McClellan Brook—stream ... MA-1
McClellan Brothers Dam—dam ... SD-7
McClellan Butte—summit ... WA-9
McClellan Canyon ... CA-9
McClellan Canyon—valley ... NM-5
McClellan Cem—cemetery ... AL-4
McClellan Cem—cemetery ... AR-4
McClellan Cem—cemetery (2) ... FL-3
McClellan Cem—cemetery ... MS-4
McClellan Cem—cemetery (3) ... TN-4
McClellan Cem—cemetery ... VA-3
McClellan Chapel—church ... VA-3
McClellan Circle—locale ... NY-2
McClellan Creek ... MT-8
McClellan Creek ... NV-8
McClellan Creek—stream ... MS-4
McClellan Creek—stream ... MT-8
McClellan Creek—stream ... NV-8
Mc Clellan Creek—stream ... NC-3
McClellan Creek—stream ... OK-5
McClellan Creek—stream (3) ... OR-9
McClellan Creek—stream ... TX-5
McClellan Creek—stream ... WA-9
McClellan Creek Quarry—mine ... MT-8
McClelland ... VA-3
McClelland—locale ... TX-5
**McClelland**—pop pl ... AR-4
**McClelland**—pop pl ... IA-7
McClelland, Gov. Robert, House—hist pl ... MI-6
McClelland, Harry S., House—hist pl ... OH-6
McClelland, J. T. and Minnie, House—hist pl ... TX-5
McClelland Beach—beach ... IA-7
McClelland Cem—cemetery ... GA-3
McClelland Cem—cemetery ... MS-4
McClelland Cem—cemetery ... NY-2
McClelland Cem—cemetery (2) ... OH-6
McClelland Cem—cemetery ... PA-2
McClelland Creek ... NV-8
McClelland-Davis House—hist pl ... NC-3
McClelland Drain—canal ... MI-6
McClelland Elem Sch—school ... IN-6
McClelland Lake—lake ... MS-4
McClelland-Layne House—hist pl ... IN-6
Mc Clelland Mtn—summit ... CO-8
McClelland Park—park ... MO-7
McClelland Peak—summit ... NV-8
McClelland Ridge—ridge ... KY-4
McClelland Rsvr—reservoir ... CA-9
Mc Clellands—locale ... CO-8
McClelland Sch—school ... MO-7
McClelland Sch—school ... SD-7
McClelland Sch—school ... TX-5
McClelland Sch Number 10 ... IN-6
McClelland School (Abandoned)—locale ... MN-6
McClelland Slough—gut ... IA-7
McClellandsville ... DE-2
**McClellandtown**—pop pl ... PA-2
**McClellandville**—pop pl ... DE-2
McClellan Elem Sch—school ... PA-2
McClellan Fickle Ditch—canal ... IN-6
Mc Clellan Field Airp—airport ... WA-9
McClellan Flats—bar ... AK-9
McClellan Group—area ... AK-9
McClellan Gulch—valley ... MT-8
McClellan Gulch—valley ... OR-9
McClellan Gulch—valley ... WY-8
**McClellan Heights**—pop pl ... PA-2
McClellan Heights Historic District—hist pl ... IA-7
McClellan Heights United Ch—church ... IA-7
McClellan Hollow—valley ... TN-4
McClellan House—hist pl ... CO-8
McClellan HS—school ... AR-4
McClellan Lake—lake ... FL-3
McClellan Lake—lake ... MN-6
McClellan Lake—lake ... MS-4
McClellan Lake—reservoir ... TX-5
McClellan Lake—reservoir ... UT-8
McClellan Lake Dam—dam ... UT-8
McClellan (Magisterial District)—fmr MCD ... WV-2
McClellan Mart Shop Ctr—locale ... AL-4
McClellan Meadow—flat ... OR-9
McClellan Meadows—flat ... WA-9
McClellan Mine—mine ... AZ-5
McClellan Mountain—ridge ... CO-8
McClellan Mtn—summit ... CA-9
McClellan Mtn—summit (2) ... OR-9
McClellan Mtn—summit ... WA-9
McClellan Peak—summit ... WA-9
McClellan Place—locale ... CA-9
McClellan Ranch—locale ... CA-9
McClellan Ranch—locale ... WY-8
McClellan Ranger Station—locale ... MT-8
McClellan Rock—island ... AK-9
McClellan Rock—summit ... CA-9
Mc Clellan Rsvr—reservoir ... CO-8
McClellan Run—stream ... MI-6
McClellan Run—stream ... PA-2
McClellan Run Creek ... MI-6
McClellans Butte ... WA-9
McClellans Cave ... AL-4
McClellan Sch—school ... CA-9
McClellan Sch—school ... IL-6
McClellan Sch—school ... ME-1
McClellan Sch—school ... MI-6
McClellan Sch—school ... MN-6
McClellan School Number 91 ... IN-6
McClellans Creek ... NV-8
**McClellans Creek**—pop pl ... MT-8
McClellans Number 1 Cave ... AL-4
McClellan Spring—spring ... OR-9
McClellan Spring—spring ... UT-8
McClellan Statue—park ... DC-2
McClellans Wash ... AZ-5
McClellan Tanks—reservoir ... AZ-5
**McClellan Township**—pop pl ... ND-7
**McClellan (Township of)**—pop pl ... IL-6
**McClellan (Township of)**—pop pl ... IN-6
**McClellanville**—pop pl ... SC-3
McClellanville (CCD)—cens area ... SC-3
McClellanville Hist Dist—hist pl ... SC-3
McClellan Wash—stream (3) ... AZ-5
McClellan Wash—valley ... UT-8
McClellen Branch—stream ... LA-4
McClellen House—hist pl ... KY-4
McClellens Chapel ... AL-4
McClellen Tower—pillar ... LA-4
McClellon Gulch—valley ... CA-9
McClenagan Lateral—canal ... ID-8
McClenahan Cem—cemetery ... IL-6
McClenahan House—hist pl ... NC-3
McClenden Spring—spring ... ID-8
McClendon ... AL-4
**McClendon**—pop pl ... LA-4
McClendon-Abney Hardware Company—hist pl ... TX-5
McClendon Branch—stream ... AR-4
McClendon Cave—cave ... AL-4
McClendon Cem—cemetery (2) ... AL-4
McClendon Cem—cemetery (3) ... AR-4
McClendon Cem—cemetery ... LA-4
McClendon Cem—cemetery ... MS-4
McClendon Cem—cemetery ... TN-4
McClendon Christian Methodist Episcopal Tabernacle—church ... IN-6
McClendon Creek—stream ... GA-3
McClendon Gap—gap ... AL-4
McClendon Gulch—valley ... CA-9
McClendon (historical)—locale ... AL-4
McClendon Lake—lake ... FL-3
McClendon Pond Dam—dam ... MS-4
McClendon Ridge—ridge ... KY-4
**McClendons Corner**—pop pl ... AR-4
McClendon Spring—spring ... OR-9
McClendon Swamp—swamp ... GA-3
McClendon Tank—reservoir ... AZ-5
McClennan ... GA-3
McClennan County Courthouse—hist pl ... TX-5
McClennen Branch—stream ... NC-3
McClennen Grove Ch—church ... MS-4
McClennens Church ... AL-4
McClenney Lake—reservoir ... GA-3
McClennon Draw ... NM-5
McClennon Ranch ... NM-5
McClenny ... FL-3
McClenny Sch—school ... AL-4
McCleod Flat—flat ... CA-9
McCleod House—hist pl ... AR-4
McClernand Sch—school ... IL-6
McCleskey Cem—cemetery ... MS-4
McCleskey Hill—summit ... AL-4
McCless Hollow—valley (2) ... KY-4
McCleve Canyon—valley ... AZ-5
McCleve Tank—reservoir ... AZ-5
McClew, Alexander, Farm House—hist pl ... MI-6
McClimans Cem—cemetery ... IL-6
**McClimansville**—pop pl ... OH-6
McClinery Ridge—ridge ... ID-8
Mcclinic Point ... ME-1
McClintic Bridge—bridge ... VA-3
McClintic Cem—cemetery ... IN-6
McClintic Sch—school ... MI-6
Mc Clintock—locale ... CO-8
**Mcclintock**—pop pl ... CO-8
**McClintock**—pop pl ... PA-2
McClintock Arroyo—valley ... TX-5
McClintock Branch—stream ... TN-4
McClintock Cem—cemetery ... ME-1
McClintock Cem—cemetery ... MO-7
McClintock Ch—church ... NC-3
Mc Clintock County Park—park ... WI-6
McClintock Creek—stream ... OR-9
McClintock Creek—stream ... WI-6
McClintock Draw—valley ... AZ-5
McClintock Hall—hist pl ... PA-2
McClintock House—hist pl ... AR-4
McClintock HS—school ... AZ-5
McClintock JHS—school ... NC-3
McClintock Lake—reservoir ... OH-6
**McClintock Manor (subdivision)**—pop pl (2) ... AZ-5
**McClintock (McClintockville)**—pop pl ... PA-2
McClintock Peak—summit ... MT-8
McClintock Ranch—locale ... NE-7
McClintock Ridge—ridge ... AZ-5
McClintock Run—stream ... PA-2
McClintock Run—stream (2) ... WV-2
**McClintocksburg**—pop pl ... OH-6
McClintock Spring—spring ... AZ-5
McClintock Storage Warehouse—hist pl ... CA-9
Mcclintousville ... PA-2
McClish Lake—lake ... IN-6
McClister Airp—airport ... PA-2
McCloe Pond—lake ... PA-2
McCloons Creek ... MS-4
Mcclory Creek ... TN-4
McClorys Branch ... TN-4
McCloskey Creek—stream ... WA-9
McCloskey Ditch—canal ... IN-6
McCloskey Hollow—valley ... PA-2
McCloskey Island—island ... PA-2
McCloskey Run—stream (2) ... PA-2
Mc Closkey Sch—school ... PA-2
McCloskey Trail—trail ... PA-2
McCloskie Bar—bar ... OR-9
McClosky Run ... PA-2
McCloud—locale ... MT-8
**McCloud**—pop pl ... CA-9
**McCloud**—pop pl ... TN-4
**McCloud**—pop pl ... WV-2
McCloud Baptist Ch—church ... TN-4
McCloud Bay—swamp (2) ... FL-3
McCloud Branch—stream ... AL-4
McCloud Branch—stream ... NC-3
McCloud Branch—stream ... WV-2
McCloud Bridge—bridge ... MS-4
McCloud Bridge Guard Station—locale ... CA-9
McCloud Camp—locale ... CA-9
McCloud Cave—cave ... TN-4
McCloud Cem—cemetery ... GA-3
McCloud Cem—cemetery (2) ... TN-4
McCloud Cem—cemetery ... WV-2
McCloud Cemetery ... MS-4
McCloud Ch—church ... GA-3
McCloud Ch—church ... WV-2
McCloud Creek—stream ... AK-9
McCloud Creek—stream ... CA-9
McCloud Creek—stream ... MI-6
McCloud Creek—stream ... MN-6
McCloud Creek—stream ... WA-9
McCloud Creek—stream ... WI-6
McCloud-Field Rsvr—reservoir ... OR-9
McCloud Flat—flat ... CA-9
McCloud Glacier ... CA-9
McCloud Gulch—valley ... ID-8
McCloud Head—cliff ... AK-9
McCloud Hollow—valley ... TN-4
McCloud Hood Rsvr—reservoir ... TX-5
McCloud Lake ... CA-9
McCloud Lake—lake ... AR-4
McCloud Lake—lake ... CA-9
McCloud Lake—lake ... MN-6
McCloud Lake—lake ... WI-6
McCloud Lake—reservoir ... TX-5
McCloud Landing—locale ... MS-4
McCloud-Medicine Lake (CCD)—cens area ... CA-9
McCloud Mine—mine ... CA-9
McCloud Mountains—summit ... AZ-5
McCloud Mtn—summit ... ME-1
McCloud Peak ... MT-8
McCloud Post Office (historical)—building ... TN-4
McCloud Ranch—locale ... NE-7
McCloud Ranch Creek—stream ... AK-9
McCloud River—stream ... CA-9
McCloud River Arm—bay ... CA-9
McCloud River Club—other ... CA-9
McCloud Rsvr ... OR-9
McCloud Run—stream ... WV-2
McCloud Sch—school ... IL-6
McCloud Sch (historical)—school ... MS-4
McClouds Landing—locale ... AL-4
McCloud Spring—spring ... AZ-5
McCloud Spring—spring ... NV-8
McCloud Spring—spring ... OR-9
McClough Chapel ... TN-4
McClough Grove Ch—church ... GA-3
McClough Hollow—valley ... TN-4
McClown Mtn—summit ... KY-4
McCloy Creek—stream ... GA-3
**McCloy (historical)**—pop pl ... IA-7
McCloy Park—park ... AR-4
McCloy Ranch—locale ... NM-5
McClue Cem—cemetery ... TN-4
McCluer Council Sch ... MS-4
McCluer HS—school ... VA-3
McCluer Sch—school ... MS-4
McClugage Bridge—other ... IL-6
McCluney Branch—stream ... SC-3
McCluney Cave—cave ... AL-4
**McCluney (historical)**—pop pl ... MS-4
McClung—locale ... VA-3
McClung Branch—stream ... WV-2
McClung Canyon—valley ... OR-9
McClung Cem—cemetery ... WV-2
McClung Creek ... AL-4
McClung Creek—stream ... TX-5
McClung Gap—gap ... AL-4
McClung House—hist pl ... OK-5
McClung Mill—locale ... VA-3
McClung Mtn—summit ... VA-3
McClung Museum—building ... TN-4
McClung Park—park ... MO-7
McClung Post Office (historical)—building ... AL-4
McClung Ranch—locale ... MT-8
McClung Ridge—ridge ... VA-3
McClung Sch—school ... AR-4
McClung Sch—school ... IL-6
McClung Sch (abandoned)—school ... MO-7
McClung Sch (historical)—school ... AL-4
McClungs Creek—stream ... AL-4
McClungs Hole—cave ... AL-4
Mcclungs Mill ... VA-3
McClure ... MS-4
Mcclure ... PA-2
McClure—locale ... AL-4
McClure—locale ... KY-4
McClure—locale ... MI-6
McClure—locale ... OK-5
**McClure**—pop pl ... IL-6
**McClure**—pop pl ... KY-4
**McClure**—pop pl ... NY-2
**McClure**—pop pl ... OH-6
**McClure**—pop pl (2) ... PA-2
**McClure**—pop pl ... VA-3
Mcclure—unorg reg ... SD-7
McClure, Alexander K., Sch—hist pl ... PA-2
McClure, Lake—lake ... PA-2
McClure, Lake (Exchequer Reservoir)—reservoir ... CA-9
McClure Airp—airport ... PA-2
McClure-Barbee House—hist pl ... KY-4
McClure Bay—bay ... AK-9
McClure Bend—bend ... TN-4
McClure Bend Sch (historical)—school ... TN-4
McClure Borough—civil ... PA-2
McClure Branch—stream ... GA-3
McClure Branch—stream ... KY-4
McClure Branch—stream ... NC-3
McClure Branch—stream ... TN-4
McClure Branch—stream ... VA-3
McClure Branch—stream ... WV-2
McClure Bridge—bridge ... GA-3
McClure Bridge—bridge ... NC-3
McClure Bridge—hist pl ... WA-9
McClure Burn—area ... CA-9
McClure Butte—summit ... MI-8
McClure Camp—locale ... CO-8
McClure Canyon—valley ... AZ-5
McClure Canyon—valley (2) ... CA-9
McClure Canyon—valley ... CO-8
McClure Canyon—valley ... NV-8
McClure Cave—cave ... MO-7
McClure Cave—cave ... PA-2
McClure Cem—cemetery ... AL-4
McClure Cem—cemetery (3) ... IL-6
McClure Cem—cemetery (2) ... IN-6
McClure Cem—cemetery ... IA-7
McClure Cem—cemetery (3) ... KY-4
McClure Cem—cemetery ... MI-6
McClure Cem—cemetery (3) ... NC-3
McClure Cem—cemetery (3) ... OH-6
McClure Cem—cemetery ... OK-5
McClure Cem—cemetery (3) ... PA-2
McClure Cem—cemetery ... TN-4
McClure Cem—cemetery ... TX-5
McClure Cem—cemetery (3) ... VA-3
McClure Cem—cemetery (2) ... WV-2
McClure Cemetery ... GA-3
McClure Ch—church ... MI-6
McClure Ch—church ... NY-2
McClure Chapel—church ... KY-4
McClure Cove—bay ... NC-3
McClure Cove—valley ... NC-3
McClure Creek ... VA-3
McClure Creek—stream (3) ... CA-9
Mc Clure Creek—stream ... CO-8
McClure Creek—stream (2) ... GA-3
McClure Creek—stream ... IA-7
McClure Creek—stream (2) ... MT-8
McClure Creek—stream ... NC-3
McClure Creek—stream ... OK-5
McClure Creek—stream ... OR-9
McClure Creek—stream ... SC-3
McClure Creek—stream ... TX-5
McClure Creek—stream ... VA-3
McClure Dam—dam ... MI-6
McClure Dam—dam ... SD-7
McClure Ditch—canal (2) ... IN-6
McClure Drain—stream ... MI-6
McClure (Election Precinct)—fmr MCD ... IL-6
McClure Flat—flat ... CA-9
McClure Fork—stream ... KY-4
McClure Gap—gap ... GA-3
McClure Gulch—valley ... CA-9
Mc Clure Gulch—valley ... CO-8
McClure Gulch—valley ... MT-8
McClure Hill—summit ... FL-3
McClure Hollow ... TN-4
McClure Hollow—valley ... NY-2
McClure Hollow—valley ... TN-4
McClure Hollow—valley ... WV-2
McClure House—hist pl ... CO-8
McClure House—hist pl ... KY-4
McClure Islands—area ... AK-9
McClure Knob—summit ... KY-4
McClure Lake—lake ... AZ-5
McClure Lake—lake ... CA-9
McClure Lake—lake ... OR-9
McClure Lake—lake ... WA-9
McClure Lake—reservoir ... GA-3
McClure Landing (historical)—locale ... TN-4
McClure Meadow—flat ... CA-9
McClure Mill—locale ... NC-3
Mc Clure Mtn—summit ... CO-8
McClure Mtn—summit ... NM-5
McClure Mtn—summit ... WA-9
Mc Clure Murray Ditch—canal ... CO-8
McClure Park—park ... OK-5
Mc Clure Pass—gap ... CO-8
McClure Peak—summit ... VA-3
McClure Place—locale (2) ... CA-9
McClure Pond—lake ... ME-1
McClure Quarry—mine ... TN-4
McClure Ranch—locale ... CA-9
McClure Ranch—locale ... SD-7
McClure Ranch—locale ... TX-5
McClure Ranch—locale (2) ... WY-8
McClure Ridge—ridge ... NC-3
McClure Ridge Trail—trail ... PA-2
McClure River—stream ... VA-3
McClure Rock—summit ... WA-9
Mc Clure Rsvr—reservoir ... CO-8
McClure Rsvr—reservoir ... MT-8
McClure Run—stream ... PA-2
McClure Run Trail—trail ... PA-2
McClures ... MI-6
McClures Airp—airport ... IN-6
McClures Beach—beach ... CA-9
McClures Bend ... TN-4
**McClures Bend**—pop pl ... TN-4
McClures Branch—stream ... SC-3
McClure Sch—school (2) ... IL-6
McClure Sch—school ... KS-7
McClure Sch—school ... KY-4
McClure Sch—school ... OK-5
McClure Sch—school ... PA-2
McClure Sch—school ... TX-5
McClure Sch—school ... WA-9
McClures Chapel—church ... VA-3
McClure Sch (historical)—school ... MO-7
McClures Creek—stream ... SC-3
McClure's Fork ... VA-3
McClures Gap—gap ... PA-2
McClures Gap Cem—cemetery ... PA-2
McClures Gap Ch—church ... PA-2
McClures Gap Sch (abandoned)—school ... PA-2
McClure-Shelby House—hist pl ... KY-4

McClure Site (39HU7)—hist pl ... SD-7
McClures Lake—lake ... IN-6
Mcclures Pass ... CO-8
Mcclure's Point ... ME-1
Mcclures Pond ... ME-1
McClure Spring—spring ... AZ-5
McClure Spring—spring (2) ... CA-9
McClure Spring—spring ... NV-8
McClures Ranch (historical)—locale ... SD-7
McClures Switch ... MS-4
McClure Station ... PA-2
McClure Storage Basin—reservoir ... MI-6
McClure Tank—reservoir ... AZ-5
McCluret Ditch—canal ... IN-6
**McClure Town**—pop pl ... AL-4
McClure Township—civil ... SD-7
**Mcclure Township**—pop pl ... NE-7
McClure Trail—trail ... ID-8
McClure Trail—trail ... PA-2
McClure Tunnel—tunnel ... VA-3
Mcclure Well—well ... NM-5
McClure Windmill—locale ... NM-5
**McClurg**—pop pl (2) ... MO-7
McClurg Airp—airport ... MO-7
McClurg Bldg—hist pl ... IL-6
McClurg Bldg—hist pl ... WI-6
McClurg Branch—stream ... KY-4
Mcclurkin Lake—reservoir ... AL-4
McClurkin Lake Number Three—reservoir ... AL-4
McClurkin Lake Number Two—reservoir ... AL-4
McClurkin Number 2 Dam—dam ... AL-4
McClurkin Number 3 Dam—dam ... AL-4
McClurkin Sch—school ... AL-4
McCluskey Brook—stream (2) ... ME-1
McCluskey Cave—cave ... AL-4
McCluskey Cem—cemetery ... MO-7
McCluskey Hollow—valley ... AL-4
McCluskey Hollow—valley ... PA-2
McCluskey Mtn—summit ... TX-5
**McClusky**—pop pl ... IL-6
**McClusky**—pop pl ... ND-7
McClusky Brook—stream (2) ... ME-1
McClusky Canal—canal ... ND-7
McClusky Creek—stream ... NV-8
McClusky Hill—summit ... GA-3
McClusky Lake—lake ... ME-1
McClusky Mtn—summit ... MT-8
McClusky Municipal Airp—airport ... ND-7
McClusky Pass—gap ... NV-8
McClusky Peak—summit ... NV-8
McClusky Slough—gut ... CA-9
McCluskys Mill (historical)—locale ... AL-4
**Mcclusky Township**—pop pl ... ND-7
McClymonds HS—school ... CA-9
Mccnnis Bayou ... MS-4
McCobb Hill—summit ... ME-1
McCobb-Hill-Minott House—hist pl ... ME-1
McCoe Lake—lake ... IL-6
McCoffey Sch—school ... OH-6
McCoin Creek—stream ... OR-9
McCoin School ... TN-4
**McCoinsville**—pop pl ... TN-4
McCoinsville Post Office (historical)—building ... TN-4
McCoinsville Sch (historical)—school ... TN-4
McCold Draw—valley ... WY-8
McCole Cem—cemetery ... OH-6
McColeman Creek ... MI-6
McColgan Cem—cemetery ... TN-4
McColgan Low Gap—gap ... WV-2
McColgin Cem—cemetery ... IN-6
McColgin Creek—stream ... IN-6
McColl—locale ... CA-9
**McColl**—pop pl ... SC-3
**McColl**—pop pl ... TX-5
McColl, Anthony M., House—hist pl ... IA-7
McColl, James, House—hist pl ... MI-6
McCollam Sch—school ... CA-9
McColl Branch—stream ... NC-3
McColl (CCD)—cens area ... SC-3
McColley, James, House—hist pl ... DE-2
McColley Branch ... DE-2
McColley Canyon—valley ... NV-8
McColley Ch—church ... DE-2
McColley Lake—lake ... IN-6
McColleys Branch ... DE-2
McColleys Branch—stream ... DE-2
McColleys Millpond ... DE-2
McColleys Pond ... DE-2
McColl-Fletcher Memorial HS—school ... SC-3
McCollin Ranch—locale ... NE-7
McCollins Run—stream ... WV-2
McCollister, James, Farmstead—hist pl ... IA-7
McCollister Hill—summit ... ME-1
Mccoll Lake ... WI-6
McCollom Drain—canal ... MI-6
McCollom Elem Sch—school ... KS-7
McCollom Hill—summit ... NH-1
**McColloms**—pop pl ... NY-2
Mccolloms Pond—lake ... NY-2
McCollough ... GA-3
McCollough Branch—stream ... AL-4
McCollough Branch—stream ... FL-3
McCollough Cem—cemetery ... AL-4
McCollough Cem—cemetery ... AR-4
McCollough Ch—church ... SC-3
McCollough Hollow—valley ... AR-4
McCollough Island ... NE-7
McCollough Lake ... WI-6
McCollough Sch (historical)—school ... AL-4
McColl Sch—school ... MI-6
McColls Mill Pond ... SC-3
McCollum—locale ... GA-3
**McCollum**—pop pl ... AL-4
McCollum, Elmer V., House—hist pl ... MD-2
McCollum, Robert, House—hist pl ... ID-8
McCollum Branch—stream ... GA-3
McCollum Cem—cemetery ... AL-4
McCollum Cem—cemetery ... MO-7
McCollum Cem—cemetery ... PA-2
McCollum Cem—cemetery (4) ... TN-4
McCollum Ch—church ... AL-4
McCollum-Chidester House—hist pl ... AR-4
McCollum County Park—park ... TX-5
McCollum Creek—stream ... MT-8
McCollum Creek—stream ... OR-9
McCollum Dairy—locale ... TX-5
McCollum Farm—hist pl ... TN-4
McCollum Fish Weir—hist pl ... SC-3
McCollum Gap—gap ... TN-4
McCollum Hill—summit ... NY-2
McCollum Hill—summit ... TN-4
**McCollum (historical)**—pop pl ... OR-9
McCollum Hollow—valley (2) ... TN-4
McCollum HS—school ... TX-5
McCollum Lake—lake ... MI-6
McCollum Lake—lake ... MN-6
McCollum Lookout Tower—locale ... GA-3
McCollum Mine (surface)—mine ... AL-4
McCollum Mine (underground)—mine ... AL-4
McCollum Mound—hist pl ... SC-3
McCollum Ranch—locale ... NM-5
McCollum Rsvr—reservoir ... OR-9
McCollum Sch—school ... IL-6
McCollum Sch (historical)—school ... AL-4
McCollum Sch (historical)—school ... MO-7
McCollums Pond—reservoir ... GA-3
McColly Covered Bridge—hist pl ... OH-6
McColly Ditch ... IN-6
McColman Creek—stream ... MI-6
McColm Ch—church ... OH-6
McColough Cem—cemetery ... AL-4
Mc Col Place ... IN-6
**McCol Place**—pop pl ... IN-6
McColskey Bay—swamp ... NC-3
**McColsky**—pop pl ... FL-3
McColvey Cemetery ... TX-5
**McComas**—pop pl ... MD-2
**McComas**—pop pl ... WV-2
**McComas Beach**—pop pl ... MD-2
McComas Branch—stream (3) ... WV-2
McComas Cem—cemetery ... MO-7
McComas Cem—cemetery ... WV-2
McComas Chapel—church ... PA-2
McComas Creek—stream ... OR-9
McComas Institute—hist pl ... MD-2
McComas Institute—school ... MD-2
McComas-Lees Summit Municipal Airp—airport ... MO-7
McComas (Magisterial District)—fmr MCD ... WV-2
McComas Meadows—flat ... ID-8
McComas Mtn—summit ... WV-2
McComas Ridge—ridge ... WV-2
McComas Sch—school (2) ... WV-2
McComb ... AL-4
McComb ... OK-5
**McComb**—pop pl ... MS-4
**McComb**—pop pl ... OH-6
McComb Branch—stream ... MS-4
Mc Comb Branch—stream ... NC-3
McComb Butte—summit ... OR-9
Mc Comb Campbell Ditch—canal ... MT-8
McComb Canyon—valley ... TX-5
McComb Cave—cave ... TN-4
McComb Ch of God—church ... MS-4
McComb City Hall—building ... MS-4
McComb Corner—locale ... MI-6
McComb Creek—stream ... TX-5
McComb Drain—canal ... MI-6
McComb Draw—valley ... MT-8
McCombe Branch—stream ... TX-5
McComber—locale ... MN-6
McComber Gulch—valley ... ID-8
McComber Sch—school ... CA-9
McComb Ford—locale ... AL-4
McComb High School ... MS-4
McComb Lake—lake ... LA-4
McComb Lake—lake ... MI-6
McComb Lake—lake ... WI-6
McComb Middle School ... MS-4
McComb Oil Field—oilfield ... MS-4
McComb-Pike County-John E Lewis Field (airport)—airport ... MS-4
McCombs—locale ... AL-4
McCombs—locale ... KY-4
McCombs Branch—stream ... AL-4
McCombs Branch—stream ... KY-4
McCombs Camp—locale ... CA-9
McCombs Cem—cemetery ... AL-4
McCombs Cem—cemetery ... WI-6
McCombs Chapel—church ... AL-4
McComb Sch (historical)—school ... MS-4
McCombs Creek—stream ... TX-5
McCombs Cut ... GA-3
McComb Sewage Lagoon Dam—dam ... MS-4
McCombs Lake ... MI-6
McComb South (census name Bear Town)—other ... MS-4
McComb Spring—spring ... TX-5
McCombs Ranch—locale ... NM-5
McCombs Sch—school ... IL-6
McComic Cem—cemetery ... LA-4
McComico Bar—bar ... AL-4
McCompsey Canyon—valley ... WY-8
McCompsey Pass—gap ... WY-8
McCompsey Spring—spring ... WY-8
McConachie Lake—lake ... MI-6
McConahay Bldg—hist pl ... MO-7
McConaughy, Lake—reservoir ... NE-7
McConaughy Gulch—valley ... CA-9
McConaughy Lake—reservoir ... NE-7
**McConchie**—pop pl ... MD-2
**McCondy**—pop pl ... MS-4
McCondy Baptist Church ... MS-4
McCondy Church ... MS-4
McCondy Sch (historical)—school ... MS-4
McCone Creek—stream ... MT-8
McConegal Creek—stream ... AL-4
McCone Heights—plain ... MT-8
McCone Residence—hist pl ... MT-8
McCongle Canyon—valley ... ID-8
McConico Cem—cemetery ... AL-4
McConico Cemetery ... TN-4
McConico (historical)—locale ... AL-4
McConkey Cem—cemetery ... IL-6
McConkey Cem—cemetery ... OH-6
McConkey Cem—cemetery ... WV-2
McConkey Ch—church ... WV-2
McConkey Sch—school ... TN-4
McConkeys Ferry ... NJ-2
McConkie Ranch—locale ... UT-8
McConkie Ranch Petroglyphs—hist pl ... UT-8
McConnahas Creek ... CA-9
McConnahas Mill Creek—stream ... CA-9
McConnahue Gulch ... CA-9
McConnaughhay Cem—cemetery ... IL-6
McConn Creek—stream ... ID-8
Mc Connel, Mount—summit ... CO-8
McConnel Branch—stream ... KY-4
McConnel Canal ... NV-8
McConnel Canyon—valley ... NV-8
Mc Connel Cem—cemetery ... AR-4
McConnel Cem—cemetery ... TX-5
McConnel Creek—stream ... OH-6
McConnel Ditch—canal ... IN-6
McConnell ... GA-3
McConnell—locale ... VA-3
**McConnell**—pop pl ... CA-9
**McConnell**—pop pl ... IL-6
**McConnell**—pop pl (2) ... NC-3
**McConnell**—pop pl ... TN-4
**McConnell**—pop pl ... WV-2
McConnell, James, House—hist pl ... KY-4
McConnell, Lake—lake ... TX-5
McConnell, William, House—hist pl ... KY-4
McConnell, W. J., House—hist pl ... ID-8
McConnell AFB—military ... KS-7
McConnell Baptist Ch—church ... TN-4
McConnell Bar—bar ... CA-9
McConnell Branch—stream ... AL-4
McConnell Branch—stream ... AR-4
McConnell Branch—stream ... TN-4
McConnell Branch—stream ... VA-3
McConnell Brook—stream ... ME-1
McConnell Canyon—valley ... CA-9
McConnell Canyon—valley (2) ... NV-8
McConnell Cem ... TN-4
McConnell Cem—cemetery ... IL-6
McConnell Cem—cemetery ... KY-4
McConnell Cem—cemetery ... MO-7
McConnell Cem—cemetery ... NY-2
Mc Connell Cem—cemetery ... NC-3
McConnell Cem—cemetery ... TN-4
McConnell Cem—cemetery (3) ... VA-3
McConnell Ch—church ... GA-3
McConnell Ch—church ... VA-3
McConnell Chapel—church ... VA-3
McConnell Corners—locale ... NY-2
McConnell Creek—stream ... NV-8
McConnell Creek—stream ... NY-2
McConnell Creek—stream ... PA-2
McConnell Dam—dam ... MI-6
McConnell (historical)—locale ... AL-4
McConnell (historical)—locale ... ND-7
McConnell Hollow—valley ... PA-2
McConnell Hollow—valley ... VA-3
McConnell Homestead (abandoned)—locale ... MT-8
McConnell House—hist pl ... PA-2
McConnell House, Law Office, and Slave Quarters—hist pl ... KY-4
McConnell Island—island ... WA-9
McConnell Lake—lake ... CA-9
Mcconnell Lake Dam—dam ... PA-2
McConnell Lateral—canal ... WI-6
McConnell Livingston Lateral—canal ... CA-9
McConnell-McGuire Bldg—hist pl ... ID-8
McConnell Memorial Ch—church ... OK-5
McConnell Mill—locale ... VA-3
McConnell Mine—mine ... NV-8
McConnell Mine (underground)—mine ... AL-4
McConnell Mtn—summit ... ID-8
McConnell Mtn—summit ... MT-8
McConnell-Neve House—hist pl ... VA-3
McConnell Peak—summit ... CA-9
McConnell Peak—summit ... NV-8
McConnell Pond—lake ... VT-1
McConnell Pond—reservoir ... PA-2
McConnell Ridge—ridge ... AK-9
McConnell Ridge—ridge ... VA-3
McConnell Road Ch—church ... NC-3
McConnell Rsvr—reservoir ... OR-9
McConnell Run—stream ... KY-4
McConnell Run—stream ... PA-2
**McConnells**—pop pl ... SC-3
**McConnellsburg**—pop pl ... PA-2
McConnellsburg Borough—civil ... PA-2
McConnells (CCD)—cens area ... SC-3
McConnell Sch—school (2) ... MI-6
McConnell Sch—school ... WI-6
McConnell Sch (abandoned)—school ... PA-2
McConnells Mill—locale ... PA-2
**McConnells Mill**—pop pl ... PA-2
McConnell's Mill Covered Bridge—hist pl ... PA-2
**McConnells Mills**—pop pl ... PA-2
McConnells Mill State Park—park ... PA-2
McConnell Spring—spring ... ID-8
McConnell Spring—spring ... NV-8
McConnell Springs—hist pl ... KY-4
McConnell Springs—spring ... OR-9
McConnell State Park—park ... CA-9
**McConnellstown**—pop pl ... PA-2
McConnellstown Quarry Cave Number One—cave ... PA-2
McConnellsville ... PA-2
McConnellsville ... SC-3
**McConnellsville**—pop pl ... NY-2
McConnell-Woodson-Philips House—hist pl ... KY-4
McConnel Meadow—flat ... CA-9
McConnel Place—locale ... CA-9
McConnel Ridge—ridge ... AR-4
McConnel Run—stream ... OH-6
McConnel Spring—spring ... NV-8
**McConnelsville**—pop pl ... OH-6
McConnelsville Hist Dist—hist pl ... OH-6
McConnico ... AL-4
McConnico—locale ... AZ-5
McConnico Cem—cemetery ... AL-4
McConnico Cem—cemetery ... TN-4
McConnico Creek—stream ... AL-4
McConnico P.O. ... AL-4
McConnico-Steele Cem—cemetery ... AL-4
McConville Gulch—valley ... OR-9
McConville Lake—lake ... WI-6
McConville Nudist Camp (private)—locale ... CA-9
McConville Peak—summit ... OR-9
McCoo HS—school ... AL-4
Mccook ... SD-7
**McCook**—pop pl ... IL-6
**McCook**—pop pl ... NE-7
**McCook**—pop pl ... TX-5
McCook, Daniel, House—hist pl ... OH-6
Mc Cook Cem—cemetery ... GA-3
McCook Coll—school ... NE-7
McCook County—civil ... SD-7
McCook Lake—lake ... SD-7
McCook Lake—locale ... SD-7
**McCook Lake (subdivision)**—pop pl ... SD-7
Mccook Municipal Airp—airport ... NE-7
McCook Point—cape ... CT-1
McCook Public-Carnegie Library—hist pl ... NE-7
McCook Ridge—ridge ... UT-8
McCook Sch—school ... SD-7
McCookville—locale ... TN-4
McCook Windmill—locale ... NM-5
McCool ... IN-6
McCool ... MD-2
McCool ... NE-7
**McCool**—pop pl ... IN-6
**McCool**—pop pl ... MS-4
McCool Butte—summit ... OR-9
McCool Cem—cemetery ... AR-4
McCool Cem—cemetery ... GA-3
McCool Cem—cemetery ... MS-4
McCool Ditch—canal ... IN-6
**McCoole**—pop pl ... MD-2
**McCool Junction**—pop pl ... NE-7
McCool Junction Cem—cemetery ... NE-7
McCool Lookout Tower—locale ... MS-4
McCool Sch—school ... SD-7
McCools Creek—stream ... KY-4
McCoon Creek—stream ... OR-9
McCoon Crossing—locale ... NY-2
McCoppin Hill—summit ... OH-6
**McCoppin Mill**—pop pl ... OH-6
McCord ... MI-6
McCord—locale ... AK-9
McCord—locale ... WI-6
**McCord**—pop pl ... OK-5
McCord, William Harrison, House—hist pl ... TN-4
McCord Bay—bay ... AK-9
McCord Bluff—cliff ... TN-4
McCord-Braden (CCD)—cens area ... OK-5
McCord Branch—stream (2) ... MO-7
McCord Cabin Spring—spring ... OR-9
McCord Canyon—valley ... NE-7
McCord Cem—cemetery ... AL-4
McCord Cem—cemetery (2) ... IL-6
McCord Cem—cemetery ... IN-6
McCord Cem—cemetery ... KY-4
McCord Cem—cemetery (2) ... MS-4
McCord Cem—cemetery ... OH-6
McCord Cem—cemetery (5) ... TN-4
McCord Cem—cemetery ... TX-5
McCord Ch—church ... AR-4
McCord Ch—church ... NC-3
McCord Creek—stream (2) ... AK-9
McCord Creek—stream ... IN-6
McCord Creek—stream ... OR-9
McCord Creek—stream ... SC-3
**McCord Crossroads**—pop pl ... AL-4
McCord Ditch—canal ... OR-9
McCord Hollow—valley ... TN-4
McCord House—hist pl ... SC-3
McCordick Brook—stream ... NH-1
McCord Knob—summit ... TN-4
McCord-Laible State Wildlife Mngmt—park ... MN-6
McCord Mill Hollow—valley ... MO-7
McCord Park—park ... FL-3
Mc Cord Pass—gap ... CO-8
McCord Place—locale (2) ... NM-5
McCord Pond—reservoir ... IA-7
McCord Pond State Wildlife Mngmt Area—park ... IA-7
McCord Prairie—flat ... CA-9
**McCords**—pop pl ... MI-6
McCord Sch—school ... CA-9
McCord Sch—school ... MI-6
McCord Sch—school ... OK-5
McCord Sch—school ... TN-4
McCord School ... PA-2
McCords Creek ... IN-6
McCords Creek—stream ... MI-6
McCord Spring ... OR-9
**McCordsville**—pop pl ... IN-6
McCorkel Cem—cemetery ... TN-4
**McCorkle**—pop pl ... VA-3
**McCorkle**—pop pl ... WV-2
McCorkle, Almon G., House—hist pl ... OH-6
McCorkle Branch—stream ... AL-4
McCorkle Canyon—valley ... CA-9
McCorkle Cave—cave ... AL-4
McCorkle Cem—cemetery ... IL-6
McCorkle Cem—cemetery ... OK-5
McCorkle Cem—cemetery (2) ... TN-4
McCorkle-Cockrill Cem ... TN-4
McCorkle Creek—stream ... IL-6
McCorkle Dam—dam ... NC-3
McCorkle-Fewell-Long House—hist pl ... SC-3
Mc Corkle Gulch—valley ... CO-8
McCorkle Lake—reservoir ... NC-3
McCorkle Mtn—summit ... AL-4
McCorkle Sch—school ... WV-2
McCorkles Gap—gap ... AL-4
McCorkles Landing ... TN-4
McCorkles Mill (historical)—locale ... TN-4
McCorkle Spring—spring ... OR-9
McCorkle Spring—spring ... TN-4
McCormac—locale ... OR-9
McCormach Slough—gut ... OR-9
McCormack, J., Farm—hist pl ... DE-2
McCormack Cem—cemetery ... AL-4
McCormack Cem—cemetery ... LA-4
McCormack Cem—cemetery (2) ... MO-7
McCormack Ch—church ... KY-4
McCormack Chapel—church ... NC-3
McCormack Church—hist pl ... KY-4
**McCormack Corners**—pop pl ... NY-2
McCormack Creek ... WA-9
McCormack Crossing—locale ... TN-4
McCormack Hill—summit ... PA-2
McCormack Hollow—valley (2) ... MO-7
McCormack Lake—lake ... MN-6
McCormack Lake—reservoir ... MO-7
McCormack Lake (Unorganized Territory of)—unorg ... MN-6
McCormack Park—park ... IL-6
McCormack Pass—gap ... MT-8
McCormack Ranch—locale ... CA-9
McCormack Ridge—ridge ... ID-8
McCormack Rsvr—reservoir ... TX-5
McCormacks Cem—cemetery ... OH-6
McCormack Spring—spring (2) ... MO-7
McCormack Spring—spring ... NV-8
McCormacks Well—well ... AZ-5
McCormic-Bishop House—hist pl ... TX-5
McCormick ... PA-2
McCormick ... UT-8
McCormick—locale ... WA-9
**McCormick**—pop pl ... AR-4
**McCormick**—pop pl (2) ... IL-6
**McCormick**—pop pl ... OH-6
**McCormick**—pop pl ... PA-2
**McCormick**—pop pl ... SC-3
McCormick, Colin, House—hist pl ... MI-6
McCormick, Cyrus, Farm and Workshop—hist pl ... VA-3
McCormick, John B., House—hist pl ... PA-2
McCormick Apartments—hist pl ... DC-2
McCormick Bridge—bridge ... FL-3
McCormick Brook—stream ... IN-6
McCormick Cabin—locale ... CO-8
McCormick Cabin Site—hist pl ... IN-6
McCormick Canyon—valley ... AZ-5
McCormick Cave—cave ... MO-7
McCormick (CCD)—cens area ... SC-3
McCormick Cem—cemetery ... AR-4
McCormick Cem—cemetery ... FL-3
McCormick Cem—cemetery (3) ... IL-6
McCormick Cem—cemetery ... IA-7
McCormick Cem—cemetery (2) ... KY-4
McCormick Cem—cemetery ... LA-4
McCormick Cem—cemetery ... MS-4
McCormick Cem—cemetery ... TN-4
**McCormick (County)**—pop pl ... SC-3
McCormick County Courthouse—hist pl ... SC-3
McCormick Creek—gut ... FL-3
McCormick Creek—stream (4) ... CA-9
McCormick Creek—stream ... FL-3
McCormick Creek—stream ... ID-8
McCormick Creek—stream ... KY-4
McCormick Creek—stream (2) ... MT-8
McCormick Creek—stream ... OK-5
McCormick Creek—stream (2) ... TX-5
McCormick Creek—stream (4) ... WA-9
McCormick Creek—stream ... WY-8
McCormick Creek Trail—trail ... MT-8
**McCormick Crossroads**—pop pl ... SC-3
McCormick Cutoff—gut ... MS-4
McCormick Dam ... SD-7
McCormick Distillery—hist pl ... MO-7
McCormick Drain—canal ... MI-6
McCormick Gap—gap ... VA-3
McCormick Gap Overlook—locale ... VA-3
McCormick Gulch—valley ... OR-9
McCormick Hall—hist pl ... NE-7
McCormick Hill—summit ... MT-8
McCormick Hollow—valley ... TN-4
McCormick Island ... PA-2
McCormick Island—island ... FL-3
McCormick JHS—school ... WY-8
McCormick Lake—lake ... FL-3
McCormick Lake—lake ... ID-8
McCormick Lake—lake (3) ... MI-6
McCormick Lake—lake ... MN-6
McCormick Lake—lake ... MO-7
McCormick Lake—lake ... WI-6
McCormick Lake Dam—dam (2) ... MS-4
McCormick Lookout—locale ... CA-9
McCormick Lookout Tower—locale ... IL-6
McCormick Lookout Tower—locale ... SC-3
McCormick Meadow—flat ... WA-9
McCormick Meadows—flat ... CA-9
McCormick Meadows—flat ... ID-8
McCormick Mine—mine ... CA-9
McCormick Observatory—other ... VA-3
McCormick Park—flat ... MT-8
McCormick Park—park ... AZ-5
McCormick Park—park ... IL-6
McCormick Park—park ... MT-8
McCormick Peak—summit ... MT-8
McCormick Place—locale ... IL-6
McCormick Pocket—basin ... CA-9
McCormick Pond—lake ... NJ-2
McCormick Pond—reservoir ... NC-3
McCormick Ranch—locale ... NM-5
**McCormick Ranch**—pop pl ... AZ-5
McCormick Ranch Golf Course—other ... AZ-5
McCormick Reef—bar ... MI-6
McCormick Ridge—ridge ... ID-8
McCormick Ridge—ridge (2) ... TN-4
McCormick Rocks—bar ... MI-6
McCormick RR Park—park ... AZ-5
McCormick Rsvr—reservoir ... OR-9
McCormick Run—stream ... OH-6
McCormick Run—stream ... PA-2
McCormick Sch—hist pl ... KS-7
McCormick Sch—school ... IL-6
McCormick Sch—school ... KS-7
McCormick Sch—school ... MD-2
McCormick Sch—school ... MI-6
McCormick Sch—school ... NM-5
McCormick Sch (abandoned)—school ... MO-7
McCormick Sch Number 30—school ... IN-6
McCormicks Creek—stream ... IN-6
McCormicks Creek Ch—church ... IN-6
McCormicks Creek State Park—park ... IN-6
McCormick Seminary—school ... IL-6
McCormicks Island—island ... PA-2
McCormick's Livery and Feed Stable Sign—hist pl ... MT-8
McCormick Slough—gut ... KY-4
McCormicks Mill (historical)—locale ... TN-4
McCormick Spring—spring ... AZ-5
**McCormick Subdivision**—pop pl ... UT-8
McCormick Swamp—swamp ... MD-2
McCormick Train Station—hist pl ... SC-3
McCormick Wash—stream ... AZ-5
Mc Cormick Windmill—locale ... CO-8
McCormic Lake—lake ... MN-6
McCormic Mine—mine ... UT-8
McCormmach—locale ... OR-9
McCormmach Creek—stream ... OR-9
McCornack Point—cape ... OR-9
McCornack Sch—school ... OR-9
McCorn Creek—stream ... NY-2
McCorney Hollow ... MO-7
McCornick—locale ... UT-8
McCornick Bldg—hist pl ... UT-8
McCorrie Point—cape ... RI-1
McCorskey Cem—cemetery ... AL-4
Mc Corskie Ch—church ... MO-7
McCort Canyon—valley ... WY-8
McCort Hill—summit ... MI-6
McCort HS—school ... PA-2
McCortle Cem—cemetery ... GA-3
McCortney Run—stream ... OH-6
McCory Creek—stream ... GA-3
McCosh Grist Mill—hist pl ... AL-4
McCosh Mill—locale ... AL-4
McCosh Sch—school ... IL-6
McCostill Mill Creek—stream ... FL-3
McCosumne ... CA-9
McCotter Point—cape ... NC-3
McCouen Cem—cemetery ... MS-4
McCouley Run—stream ... PA-2
McCoullock Spring—spring ... ID-8
McCoullough Marsh—swamp ... WI-6
McCourt, Peter, House—hist pl ... CO-8
McCourteneys Fork ... PA-2
McCourtney Creek—stream ... OR-9
McCourtney Hollow—valley ... MO-7
McCourtney Run—stream ... PA-2
McCoury Rock Ch—church ... NC-3
McCovey Gulch—valley ... CA-9
McCovey Ranch—locale ... CA-9
McCowan Bend—bend ... LA-4
McCowan Branch—stream ... WV-2
McCowan Cem—cemetery ... AR-4
McCowan Cem—cemetery ... MS-4
McCowan Cem—cemetery ... TX-5
McCowan Creek—stream ... AL-4
McCowan Creek—stream ... TN-4
McCowan Creek Ch—church ... TN-4
McCowan Spring—locale ... VA-3
McCowan Valley—bend ... TX-5
McCowan Valley Park—locale ... TX-5
McCowen Cem—cemetery ... GA-3
McCowens Creek ... MS-4
McCowers Creek ... MS-4
McCowleys Ch (historical)—church ... TN-4
McCown—locale ... IL-6
McCown Cem—cemetery ... IL-6
McCown Cem—cemetery ... VA-3
McCown Ch—church ... VA-3
McCown Mill Pond ... SC-3
McCowns Millpond—reservoir ... SC-3
Mccoy ... IA-7
McCoy ... LA-4
McCoy—locale ... KY-4
McCoy—locale ... NV-8
McCoy—locale (2) ... TX-5
McCoy—locale ... WA-9
**Mc Coy**—pop pl ... CO-8
**McCoy**—pop pl ... CO-8
**McCoy**—pop pl ... IN-6
**McCoy**—pop pl ... OR-9
**McCoy**—pop pl (3) ... TX-5
**McCoy**—pop pl ... VA-3
McCoy, Andrew, House—hist pl ... KY-4
McCoy, Benjamin, House—hist pl ... SC-3
McCoy, Harvey, House—hist pl ... NM-5
McCoy, Lake—lake (2) ... FL-3
McCoy, Lake—reservoir ... IN-6
McCoy AFB—military ... FL-3
McCoy Airp—airport ... PA-2
McCoy Ave Sch—school ... NM-5
McCoy Bay—swamp ... SC-3
McCoy Big Mary Mine (surface)—mine ... TN-4
McCoy Branch—stream ... AR-4
McCoy Branch—stream ... FL-3
McCoy Branch—stream ... IL-6
McCoy Branch—stream (3) ... KY-4
McCoy Branch—stream (2) ... NC-3
McCoy Branch—stream (6) ... TN-4
McCoy Branch—stream ... TX-5
McCoy Branch—stream ... VA-3
McCoy Branch Cove—bay ... MO-7
McCoy Bridge—bridge ... AZ-5
McCoy Bridge—bridge ... NC-3
McCoy Cabin—locale ... ID-8
McCoy Canyon—valley (3) ... CA-9
Mc Coy Canyon—valley ... CO-8
McCoy Canyon—valley ... ID-8
McCoy Canyon—valley ... WA-9
McCoy Cave—cave ... AL-4
McCoy Cave—cave (2) ... TN-4
McCoy Cem—cemetery (3) ... AL-4
Mc Coy Cem—cemetery ... AR-4
McCoy Cem—cemetery ... AR-4
Mc Coy Cem—cemetery ... CO-8
McCoy Cem—cemetery ... IL-6
McCoy Cem—cemetery (2) ... IN-6
McCoy Cem—cemetery (6) ... KY-4
McCoy Cem—cemetery (2) ... LA-4
McCoy Cem—cemetery (2) ... MS-4
McCoy Cem—cemetery ... NH-1
McCoy Cem—cemetery ... OH-6
McCoy Cem—cemetery ... OK-5
McCoy Cem—cemetery ... PA-2
McCoy Cem—cemetery (4) ... TN-4
McCoy Cem—cemetery (4) ... VA-3
McCoy Cem—cemetery ... WA-9
McCoy Cem—cemetery (5) ... WV-2
McCoy Ch—church ... TX-5
McCoy Ch—church ... WV-2
McCoy Chapel—church ... NC-3
McCoy Chapel—church ... VA-3
McCoy Corners ... PA-2
McCoy Cove—valley ... NC-3
Mccoy Creek ... ME-1
McCoy Creek ... TX-5
McCoy Creek—stream ... AK-9
McCoy Creek—stream ... AR-4
McCoy Creek—stream (3) ... CA-9
Mc Coy Creek—stream (2) ... CO-8
McCoy Creek—stream ... FL-3
McCoy Creek—stream ... ID-8
McCoy Creek—stream ... IN-6
McCoy Creek—stream ... MI-6
McCoy Creek—stream ... MO-7
McCoy Creek—stream (2) ... MT-8
McCoy Creek—stream ... NV-8
McCoy Creek—stream ... NC-3
McCoy Creek—stream (5) ... OR-9
McCoy Creek—stream (2) ... TX-5
McCoy Creek—stream (3) ... WA-9
McCoy Creek Campground—locale ... ID-8
McCoy Crossing—locale ... ME-1
McCoy Dam—dam ... OR-9
McCoy Ditch—canal ... AR-4
McCoy Ditch—canal ... IN-6
McCoy Drain—canal ... IN-6
McCoy Drain—canal ... MI-6
McCoy Drain—stream ... MI-6
McCoy Elem Sch—school ... FL-3
McCoy Farmhouse—hist pl ... WI-6

McCoy Ferry (historical)—*locale* ... AL-4
McCoy Flat—*flat* (2) ... CA-9
McCoy Flat—*flat* ... UT-8
McCoy Flat—*flat* ... WA-9
McCoy Flat Corral—*other* ... UT-8
McCoy Flat Rsvr—*reservoir* ... CA-9
McCoy Flats—*flat* ... OR-9
McCoy Ford Bridge—*bridge* ... KY-4
McCoy Gas and Oil Field—*oilfield* ... TX-5
McCoy Grove Ch—*church* ... AL-4
Mc Coy Grove Ch—*church* ... NC-3
Mc Coy Gulch—*valley* (2) ... CO-8
McCoy Gulch—*valley* ... ID-8
McCoy Hill—*summit* ... IL-6
McCoy Hill—*summit* ... IN-6
McCoy Hill—*summit* ... TN-4
*Mccoy Hills* ... CO-8
McCoy Hollow—*valley* (2) ... KY-4
McCoy Hollow—*valley* ... OH-6
McCoy Hollow—*valley* (3) ... TX-5
McCoy Hollow—*valley* ... WV-2
McCoy House—*hist pl* ... DE-2
McCoy House—*hist pl* ... PA-2
McCoy House—*hist pl* ... WV-2
McCoy Island—*island* ... IL-6
McCoy Knolls—*summit* ... UT-8
McCoy Lake—*lake* (2) ... MI-6
McCoy Lake—*lake* (2) ... MN-6
McCoy Lake—*lake* ... MS-4
McCoy Lake—*lake* ... SD-7
McCoy Lake—*lake* ... WA-9
McCoy Lake—*reservoir* ... KS-7
McCoy Lake—*reservoir* ... WV-2
McCoy Lakes—*reservoir* ... MO-7
McCoy Lake State Public Shooting
Area—*park* ... SD-7
McCoy Lateral—*canal* ... CA-9
*Mccoy Ledges* ... ME-1
McCoy-Maddox House—*hist pl* ... NM-5
McCoy Memorial Ch—*church* ... IN-6
McCoy Memorial United Methodist
Ch—*church* ... AL-4
McCoy Methodist Ch—*church* ... AL-4
McCoy Mill—*hist pl* ... WV-2
*McCoy Mine* ... TN-4
McCoy Mine—*mine* ... ID-8
McCoy Mine—*mine* (2) ... NV-8
McCoy Mining Camp—*locale* ... NV-8
McCoy Mountains—*range* ... CA-9
McCoy Mtn—*summit* ... AL-4
McCoy Mtn—*summit* ... NH-1
Mc Coy Park—*flat* ... CO-8
McCoy Park—*flat* ... UT-8
McCoy Park—*park* ... GA-3
McCoy Park—*park* ... WI-6
McCoy Peak—*summit* ... CA-9
McCoy Peak—*summit* ... WA-9
McCoy Pit—*cave* ... AL-4
McCoy Plaza (Shop Ctr)—*locale* ... FL-3
McCoy Polygonal Barn—*hist pl* ... IA-7
McCoy Pond—*reservoir* ... CT-1
McCoy Ranch—*locale* ... CO-8
McCoy Ranch—*locale* ... KS-7
McCoy Ranch—*locale* ... NV-8
McCoy Ranch—*locale* ... SD-7
McCoy Ridge—*ridge* ... CA-9
McCoy Ridge—*ridge* ... NV-8
McCoy Ridge—*ridge* ... OH-6
McCoy Ridge—*ridge* ... OR-9
McCoy Ridge—*ridge* ... TN-4
McCoy Rocks—*cliff* ... TN-4
McCoy Rsvr—*reservoir* ... OR-9
McCoy Rsvr No 1—*reservoir* ... UT-8
McCoy Rsvr No 2—*reservoir* ... UT-8
McCoy Run—*stream* ... OH-6
McCoy Run—*stream* ... PA-2
McCoy Run—*stream* (2) ... WV-2
McCoys Branch—*stream* ... GA-3
McCoys Branch—*stream* ... SC-3
**McCoysburg**—*pop pl* ... IN-6
McCoys Cabin—*locale* ... CA-9
McCoy Sch—*school* ... CA-9
McCoy Sch—*school* ... IL-6
McCoy Sch—*school* ... KY-4
McCoy Sch—*school* ... MI-6
McCoy Sch—*school* (2) ... MO-7
McCoy Sch—*school* ... TX-5
McCoy Sch (abandoned)—*school* (2) ... PA-2
McCoy Sch (historical)—*school* ... AL-4
McCoy Sch Number 24—*school* ... IN-6
McCoys Corner—*locale* ... NJ-2
**McCoys Corners**—*pop pl* ... PA-2
McCoys Cove—*bay* ... OR-9
*McCoys Creek* ... NC-3
McCoys Creek—*stream* ... GA-3
McCoys Cut—*channel* ... GA-3
McCoys Cut—*channel* ... SC-3
McCoys Ferry—*locale* ... MD-2
McCoys Fishing Lake—*lake* ... NC-3
McCoys Ford—*locale* ... VA-3
McCoys Ford (historical)—*locale* ... PA-2
McCoys Fork—*stream* ... KY-4
McCoy-Shoemaker Farm—*hist pl* ... PA-2
McCoys Island (historical)—*island* ... AL-4
McCoys Knob—*summit* ... NY-2
*McCoy Slough* ... CA-9
McCoy Spring—*spring* (2) ... CA-9
Mc Coy Spring—*spring* ... CO-8
McCoy Spring—*spring* ... ID-8
McCoy Spring—*spring* ... NV-8
McCoy Spring—*spring* ... OR-9
McCoy Spring Archeol Site—*hist pl* ... CA-9
*McCoy Springs* ... ID-8
McCoy Springs—*spring* ... NV-8
*McCoys Station* ... IN-6
**Mccoy Subdivision**—*pop pl* ... CO-8
**McCoysville**—*pop pl* ... PA-2
McCoysville Cem—*cemetery* ... PA-2
**McCoytown**—*pop pl* ... PA-2
McCoy Wash—*stream* ... CA-9
McCoy Water Pit—*well* ... CA-9
McCoy Well—*well* ... NV-8
McCrabb Cem—*cemetery* ... FL-3
McCrabb Cem—*cemetery* ... TX-5
McCrabb Ch—*church* ... FL-3
McCrabb Landing—*locale* ... FL-3
**McCracken**—*pop pl* ... KS-7
**McCracken**—*pop pl* ... MO-7
**McCracken**—*pop pl* (2) ... PA-2
McCracken Branch—*stream* ... KS-7
McCracken Branch—*stream* ... NC-3
McCracken Branch—*stream* ... TN-4
McCracken Canyon—*valley* ... NM-5
McCracken Canyon—*valley* ... UT-8
McCracken Cem—*cemetery* ... AR-4
McCracken Cem—*cemetery* ... KS-7
McCracken Cem—*cemetery* ... MO-7
McCracken Corners—*locale* ... OH-6
**McCracken (County)**—*pop pl* ... KY-4
McCracken Creek—*stream* ... AL-4
McCracken Creek—*stream* ... IN-6
McCracken Creek—*stream* ... KY-4
McCracken Creek—*stream* ... VA-3
McCracken Ditch—*canal* ... AR-4
McCracken Draw—*valley* ... CO-8
*McCracken Gap* ... PA-2
**McCracken Heights**
**(subdivision)**—*pop pl* ... NC-3
McCracken Hills—*summit* ... AR-4
McCracken Hollow—*valley* ... KY-4
McCracken Knoll Number One—*summit* ... AZ-5
McCracken Knoll Number Three—*summit* ... AZ-5
McCracken Knoll Number Two—*summit* ... AZ-5
McCracken Knoll Number Two
(historical)—*summit* ... AZ-5
McCracken Knolls—*summit* ... AZ-5
McCracken Lake—*lake* ... TX-5
McCracken-McFarland House—*hist pl* ... OH-6
*McCracken Mesa* ... UT-8
McCracken Mesa—*summit* ... UT-8
McCracken Mine—*mine* ... AZ-5
McCracken Mound—*summit* ... TX-5
McCracken Mountains—*range* ... AZ-5
McCracken Mtn—*summit* ... AL-4
McCracken Northwest (CCD)—*cens area* ... KY-4
McCracken Peak—*summit* ... AZ-5
McCracken Point—*cape* ... WA-9
McCracken Point—*summit* ... UT-8
McCracken Ranch—*locale* (2) ... NM-5
McCracken Rsvr—*reservoir* ... CA-9
McCracken Run—*stream* ... OH-6
McCracken Run—*stream* (3) ... PA-2
McCracken Sch—*school* ... IL-6
McCracken Sch (abandoned)—*school* ... PA-2
McCracken Sch (historical)—*school* ... PA-2
McCracken Sch (historical)—*school* ... TN-4
McCracken-Scott House—*hist pl* ... OH-6
McCracken-Sells House—*hist pl* ... OH-6
McCracken Southwest (CCD)—*cens area* ... KY-4
McCracken Spring—*spring* ... UT-8
*McCracken Station* ... KS-7
**McCracken (Sugar Grove)**—*pop pl* ... PA-2
McCracken Tank—*reservoir* ... AZ-5
McCracken Township—*civil* ... MO-7
*McCracken Wash* ... UT-8
McCracken-Wilgus House—*hist pl* ... KY-4
McCracker Hollow—*valley* ... PA-2
McCrackin, Cyrus, House and
Quarters—*hist pl* ... KY-4
McCrackin Distillery and Mill—*hist pl* ... KY-4
McCraddy Fork—*stream* ... WV-2
*McCrady* ... VA-3
**McCrady**—*pop pl* ... VA-3
McCrady, Lake—*reservoir* ... NC-3
McCrady Draw—*valley* ... WY-8
McCrady Hill—*summit* ... TN-4
*McCrady Hollow* ... MO-7
McCrady's Tavern and Long
Room—*hist pl* ... SC-3
McCrae Cem—*cemetery* ... WV-2
McCrae Mine—*mine* ... ID-8
McCrae Park—*park* ... MI-6
McCrae Rsvr—*reservoir* ... OR-9
McCrain Cem—*cemetery* ... MS-4
McCraken Cem—*cemetery* ... MS-4
McCraken Cem—*cemetery* ... OH-6
McCraken Knob—*summit* ... WV-2
McCraken Spring—*spring* ... KY-4
McCrakin Lake—*lake* ... TX-5
McCraney Creek—*stream* ... IL-6
McCraney Diversion Ditch—*canal* ... IL-6
McCraney Lake—*lake* ... MN-6
McCraney Run—*stream* (2) ... PA-2
McCranie's Turpentine Still—*hist pl* ... GA-3
McCrary—*locale* ... AL-4
**McCrary**—*pop pl* ... MS-4
McCrary, DeWitt, House—*hist pl* ... GA-3
McCrary, Lake—*reservoir* ... AL-4
McCrary Access Area—*park* ... NC-3
**McCrary Acres (subdivision)**—*pop pl* ... NC-3
McCrary Branch—*stream* ... NC-3
McCrary Cave—*cave* ... AL-4
*McCrary Cem* ... AL-4
McCrary Cem—*cemetery* (2) ... AL-4
McCrary Cem—*cemetery* (2) ... TN-4
McCrary Ch—*church* ... AL-4
McCrary Cove—*bay* ... FL-3
McCrary Creek—*stream* ... AL-4
McCrary Creek—*stream* ... MS-4
McCrary Creek—*stream* ... NC-3
McCrary Dam—*dam* ... AL-4
McCrary House—*hist pl* ... AL-4
McCrary Lake—*lake* ... TX-5
McCrary Minnow Farm—*other* ... GA-3
McCrary Oil Field—*oilfield* ... TX-5
McCrary Point—*cape* ... AL-4
McCrary Ranch—*locale* ... TX-5
McCrarys Branch—*stream* ... AL-4
McCrary Sch—*school* ... GA-3
McCrary Sch—*school* ... NC-3
McCrary Settlement—*locale* ... GA-3
McCrary Side Ditch—*canal* ... CA-9
McCrary Spring—*spring* ... AL-4
**McCrary Subdivision**—*pop pl* ... TN-4
McCratic Hollow—*valley* ... MO-7
McCraven Cem—*cemetery* ... MS-4
McCravy Cem—*cemetery* ... AL-4
McCraw Cem—*cemetery* ... AR-4
McCraw Cem—*cemetery* ... MO-7
McCraw Cem—*cemetery* ... TN-4
McCraw Chapel—*church* ... TX-5
McCraw Chapel Sch—*school* ... TX-5
*McCraw Creek* ... TN-4
McCraw Mtn—*summit* ... NC-3
*McCray* ... PA-2
McCray—*locale* ... NC-3
McCray Bluff—*cliff* ... MS-4
McCray Cem—*cemetery* ... IN-6
McCray Ch—*church* ... PA-2
McCray Chapel—*church* ... VA-3
McCray Creek—*stream* ... WV-2
McCray Creek Trail—*trail* ... WV-2
McCray Draw—*valley* ... WY-8
McCray Hollow—*valley* ... AR-4
McCray Lake—*reservoir* ... SC-3
McCray Mtn—*summit* ... CA-9
McCray Mtn—*summit* ... NY-2
McCray Park—*park* ... CA-9
Mc Cray Ridge—*ridge* ... AR-4
McCray Ridge—*ridge* ... WV-2
McCray Run—*stream* ... IN-6
McCray Run—*stream* ... PA-2
McCrays—*locale* ... PA-2
McCrays Branch—*stream* ... DE-2
McCray Sch—*hist pl* ... NC-3
McCray Sch (abandoned)—*school* ... PA-2
*McCrays Chapel Church* ... AL-4
McCrays Draft—*valley* ... VA-3
McCray Well—*well* (2) ... AZ-5
*McCrea* ... ND-7
**McCrea**—*pop pl* ... LA-4
**McCrea**—*pop pl* ... PA-2
McCrea, Matthew, House—*hist pl* ... OH-6
McCrea Branch—*stream* ... TX-5
McCrea Bridge Campground—*locale* ... ID-8
McCrea Cem—*cemetery* ... PA-2
McCrea Creek—*stream* ... ID-8
McCrea Creek—*stream* ... WA-9
McCrea Dead River—*gut* ... MS-4
McCrea Drain—*canal* ... MI-6
**McCready**—*pop pl* ... VA-3
McCready Cem—*cemetery* ... VA-3
McCready Gap—*gap* ... VA-3
McCready Gulch—*valley* ... CA-9
McCready Memorial Hosp—*hospital* ... MD-2
McCready Ranch—*locale* ... OR-9
McCreadys Cove—*bay* ... MD-2
McCreadys Creek—*stream* ... MD-2
McCreadys Point—*cape* ... MD-2
McCrea Furnace—*locale* ... PA-2
McCrea Hill—*summit* ... IN-6
McCrea Hill—*summit* ... MI-6
McCrea House—*hist pl* ... CA-9
McCrea Lake—*lake* ... LA-4
McCrea Mills—*locale* ... NJ-2
McCreanor—*locale* ... AR-4
McCrea Place—*locale* ... ID-8
McCrea Playground—*park* ... MI-6
McCrea Ranch—*locale* ... ID-8
McCrea Ranch—*locale* ... MT-8
McCrea Row—*locale* ... PA-2
McCrea Run—*stream* (2) ... PA-2
McCreary—*locale* ... KY-4
McCreary-Burnworth House—*hist pl* ... OH-6
McCreary Cem—*cemetery* ... AL-4
McCreary Cem—*cemetery* ... MS-4
McCreary Cem—*cemetery* ... MO-7
**McCreary (County)**—*pop pl* ... KY-4
*McCreary Creek* ... MS-4
McCreary Drain—*canal* ... NE-7
McCreary Glade—*flat* ... CA-9
McCreary Lake—*reservoir* ... CA-9
McCreary Lake—*reservoir* ... TX-5
McCreary Meadow—*flat* ... CA-9
McCreary Ridge—*ridge* ... IN-6
McCreary Run—*stream* ... PA-2
McCreary Sch—*school* ... WI-6
McCreary Sch (historical)—*school* ... AL-4
*Mccrearys Creek* ... MS-4
McCrea Sch—*school* ... PA-2
*McCreas Furnace* ... PA-2
McCrea Tank—*reservoir* ... TX-5
McCreath Creek—*stream* ... IA-7
McCreath Ranch—*locale* ... NE-7
**McCrea (Township of)**—*pop pl* ... MN-6
McCreaville Ch—*church* ... TX-5
McCrea Windmill—*locale* ... AZ-5
*McCredie* ... MO-7
McCredie—*locale* (2) ... WA-9
McCredie, William, House—*hist pl* ... OR-9
McCredie Creek—*stream* ... OR-9
McCredie Hot Springs—*spring* ... OR-9
McCredie Springs—*locale* ... OR-9
**McCredie (subdivision)**—*pop pl* ... MO-7
McCredie Township—*civil* ... MO-7
*McCree Branch* ... WA-9
McCree Cem—*cemetery* ... TX-5
*Mccree Creek* ... WA-9
McCreedie Lake—*lake* ... MI-6
McCreedy Creek—*stream* ... WA-9
McCreery—*locale* ... WV-2
McCreery Hollow—*valley* ... WV-2
McCreery Ranch—*locale* ... CA-9
**McCreight**—*pop pl* ... KY-4
McCreight Run—*stream* ... PA-2
McCreight Sch (historical)—*school* ... PA-2
McCreless Shop Ctr—*locale* ... TX-5
McCrie Shoal—*bar* ... NJ-2
McCright Branch—*stream* ... AR-4
McCrillian Brook—*stream* ... ME-1
McCrills Trail—*trail* ... NH-1
McCrimon Cem—*cemetery* ... GA-3
McCristy-Knox Mansion—*hist pl* ... OK-5
McCrite Cem—*cemetery* (2) ... IL-6
McCroans Bridge—*bridge* ... GA-3
*Mccrone Branch* ... AL-4
*McCrone Branch* ... FL-3
McCrorey Liston Sch—*school* ... SC-3
**McCrory**—*pop pl* ... AR-4
McCrory Bldg—*hist pl* ... OH-6
McCrory Cem—*cemetery* ... TX-5
McCrory Creek—*stream* (3) ... TN-4
McCrory-Deas-Buckley House—*hist pl* ... MS-4
McCrory Gap—*gap* ... AL-4
McCrory Lake Dam—*dam* ... MS-4
McCrory-Mayfield House—*hist pl* ... TN-4
McCrory Ranch—*locale* ... TX-5
McCrory Sch (historical)—*school* ... TN-4
McCrory Stores Airp—*airport* ... PA-2
McCrory Village—*uninc pl* ... AL-4
*McCrosby Creek* ... MO-7
McCroskey—*locale* ... TX-5
McCroskey, John, Cabin—*hist pl* ... TX-5
McCroskey, R. C., House—*hist pl* ... WA-9
**McCroskey Addition**
**(subdivision)**—*pop pl* ... SD-7
McCroskey Cem—*cemetery* ... AL-4
McCroskey Cem—*cemetery* ... VA-3
McCroskey Cem—*cemetery* ... WV-2
McCroskey Spring—*spring* ... AL-4
McCroskie Ch—*church* ... MO-7
McCroskie Creek—*stream* ... MO-7
Mc Crosky Gulch—*valley* ... CO-8
McCrosky Island—*island* ... TN-4
McCrosky Run—*stream* ... WV-2
McCrossen Lake—*lake* ... WI-6
McCrowey Hollow—*valley* ... TN-4
McCroy 4-H Camp—*locale* ... TN-4
McCrutchen Hollow—*valley* ... TN-4
McCrystal Creek—*stream* ... NM-5
McCrystal Place—*locale* ... NM-5
McCuan Branch—*stream* ... TX-5
McCubbin Basin—*basin* ... OR-9
McCubbin Cem—*cemetery* (2) ... KY-4
McCubbin Creek—*stream* ... OK-5
McCubbin Creek—*stream* (2) ... OR-9
*McCubbin Gulch* ... OR-9
McCubbin Hollow—*valley* ... MO-7
McCubbins Cem—*cemetery* ... IN-4
McCubbins Gulch—*valley* ... OR-9
McCubbins Point—*cape* ... MO-7
*McCue* ... KS-7
McCue Cem—*cemetery* ... WV-2
McCue Hollow—*valley* ... MO-7
McCue Medsker Ditch—*canal* ... IN-6
McCuen Canyon—*valley* ... NM-5
McCuen Creek—*stream* ... MN-6
McCuen Pond—*lake* ... NY-2
McCuen Pond Outlet—*stream* ... NY-2
McCue Ranch—*locale* ... WY-8
Mccue Ridge—*ridge* ... WA-9
McCue Spring—*spring* ... OR-9
McCue Spring—*spring* ... WA-9
McCuetown—*locale* ... WV-2
McCuistion Camp—*locale* ... NM-5
McCuistion Cem—*cemetery* (2) ... TN-4
McCuistion Springs—*spring* ... NV-8
McCuiston Cem—*cemetery* ... KY-4
McCulgan Cem—*cemetery* ... OH-6
McCuligan Butte—*summit* ... NE-7
McCuligan Canyon—*valley* ... NE-7
McCulla Cem—*cemetery* ... MO-7
*Mccullach Creek* ... CO-8
*McCullach Creek* ... FL-3
McCullagh-Jones House—*hist pl* ... CA-9
*Mccullah* ... AL-4
McCullah Hill—*summit* ... AR-4
McCullah Hollow—*valley* ... MO-7
McCulla House—*hist pl* ... LA-4
*McCullah Reservoir* ... AZ-5
McCullah Spring—*spring* ... CA-9
McCullan Rsvr—*reservoir* ... AZ-5
McCullar Cem—*cemetery* ... TN-4
McCullar Ch (historical)—*church* ... TN-4
McCullars (historical)—*locale* ... AL-4
McCullars Lake Number Two—*reservoir* ... AL-4
McCullars Lake Number 1—*reservoir* ... AL-4
McCullars Number 1 Dam—*dam* ... AL-4
McCullars Number 2 Dam—*dam* ... AL-4
McCullars Spring—*spring* ... AL-4
**McCullen**—*pop pl* ... NC-3
McCullen Bluff—*cliff* ... WY-8
McCullen Cem—*cemetery* ... MO-7
McCullen Gulch—*valley* ... WY-8
McCullen Run—*stream* ... PA-2
McCullens Branch—*stream* ... NC-3
McCullen Spring—*spring* ... MT-8
McCullen Temple—*church* ... GA-3
McCuller Island—*island* ... ME-1
**McCullers**—*pop pl* ... NC-3
McCullers Cem—*cemetery* ... NC-3
McCullers Cove—*bay* ... FL-3
**McCullers Crossroads**—*pop pl* ... NC-3
**McCulley**—*pop pl* ... AL-4
McCulley Cem—*cemetery* ... AL-4
McCulley Cem—*cemetery* ... MO-7
McCulley Cem—*cemetery* (3) ... TN-4
McCulley Creek—*stream* ... AL-4
McCulley Creek—*stream* ... ID-8
McCulley Creek—*stream* ... SC-3
*McCulley Hill* ... AL-4
**McCulley Hill**—*pop pl* ... AL-4
McCulley Hill Ch—*church* ... AL-4
McCulley Mtn—*summit* ... TN-4
McCulley Ridge—*ridge* ... TN-4
Mc Culley Sch (historical)—*school* ... MO-7
*McCulleys Pond* ... AL-4
McCulley Spring—*spring* ... TN-4
*McCulleys Spring* ... AL-4
**Mcculley Township**—*pop pl* ... ND-7
McCulloch, Hugh, House—*hist pl* ... IN-6
McCulloch, Lake—*reservoir* ... IN-6
McCulloch Branch—*stream* ... TN-4
McCulloch Cem—*cemetery* ... IA-7
McCulloch Cem—*cemetery* (2) ... OR-9
McCulloch Cem—*cemetery* ... WV-2
**McCulloch (County)**—*pop pl* ... TX-5
McCulloch County Courthouse—*hist pl* ... TX-5
Mc Culloch Creek—*stream* ... CO-8
Mc Culloch Creek Ditch—*canal* ... CO-8
McCulloch Elem Sch—*school* ... IN-6
McCulloch House—*hist pl* ... TX-5
McCulloch Park—*park* (2) ... IN-6
*McCulloch Post Office* ... TN-4
McCullochs Bar—*bar* ... TN-4
*McCulloch Sch* ... IN-6
McCulloch Sch—*school* ... IN-6
McCulloch Sch—*school* ... MA-1
McCulloch Sch—*school* ... MI-6
McCulloch Sch Number 5—*school* ... IN-6
*McCullochs Creek* ... TN-4
McCulloch's Gold Mill—*hist pl* ... NC-3
**McCullochs Mills**—*pop pl* ... PA-2
*McCullock Creek* ... FL-3
McCullock Ranch—*locale* ... NE-7
McCullocks Fort (historical)—*locale* ... TN-4
**McCullocks Mills**—*pop pl* ... PA-2
McCullock Stadium—*other* ... OR-9
Mc Cullogh Canyon—*valley* ... CO-8
Mc Cullogh Rsvr—*reservoir* ... CO-8
Mc Cullogh Spring—*spring* ... CO-8
McCulloh—*locale* ... AL-4
McCulloh—*locale* ... CA-9
McCulloh Spring—*spring* ... CA-9
McCullom Lake—*lake* ... IL-6
**McCullom Lake**—*pop pl* ... IL-6
McCullom Mtn—*summit* ... AR-4
*McCullon Creek* ... TX-5
McCullouch Park—*park* ... IN-6
*McCullough* ... OH-6
McCullough—*locale* ... GA-3
McCullough—*locale* ... VA-3
**McCullough**—*pop pl* ... AL-4
**McCullough**—*pop pl* ... PA-2
**McCullough**—*pop pl* ... TN-4
McCullough, Charles S., House—*hist pl* ... SC-3
McCullough, John, House—*hist pl* ... PA-2
McCullough Bend—*bend* ... TN-4
*McCullough Branch* ... TN-4
McCullough Branch—*stream* ... AR-4
McCullough Branch—*stream* ... NC-3
McCullough Bridge—*bridge* ... OR-9
McCullough Cem—*cemetery* ... AL-4
McCullough Cem—*cemetery* ... AR-4
McCullough Cem—*cemetery* ... IA-7
McCullough Cem—*cemetery* (2) ... MS-4
McCullough Cem—*cemetery* (2) ... MO-7
McCullough Cem—*cemetery* ... NE-7
McCullough Cem—*cemetery* ... IN-4
*McCullough Ch* ... TN-4
McCullough Ch—*church* ... MO-7
McCullough Chapel—*church* ... TN-4
McCullough Creek—*stream* (2) ... FL-3
McCullough Creek—*stream* ... GA-3
McCullough Creek—*stream* ... OH-6
McCullough Creek—*stream* ... OR-9
McCullough Creek—*stream* ... TX-5
McCullough Ditch—*canal* (2) ... IN-6
McCullough Ditch—*canal* ... MT-8
McCullough Drain—*canal* ... MI-6
McCullough Ford—*locale* ... MO-7
McCullough Fork—*stream* ... KY-4
McCullough Fork—*stream* ... TN-4
McCullough Gap—*gap* ... AL-4
McCullough Grove Ch—*church* ... IN-6
Mc Cullough Gulch—*valley* ... CO-8
McCullough Gulch—*valley* ... ID-8
McCullough Hill—*summit* ... NV-8
McCullough Hollow—*valley* ... AR-4
McCullough-Huxford (CCD)—*cens area* ... AL-4
McCullough-Huxford Division—*civil* ... AL-4
McCullough Island—*island* ... NE-7
McCullough JHS—*school* ... MS-4
McCullough Lake—*lake* ... MI-6
McCullough Lake—*lake* ... TX-5
McCullough Lake—*lake* ... WI-6
McCullough Millpond—*reservoir* ... GA-3
McCullough Mtn—*summit* ... NV-8
McCullough Mtn—*summit* ... TN-4
McCullough Number 2 Sch—*school* ... ND-7
McCullough Number 3 Sch—*school* ... ND-7
McCullough Pass—*gap* ... NV-8
*Mccullough Peak* ... WY-8
McCullough Peaks—*summit* ... WY-8
McCullough Ranch—*locale* ... MT-8
McCullough Ranch—*locale* ... SD-7
McCullough Range—*range* ... NV-8
Mc Cullough Rsvr—*reservoir* ... CO-8
McCullough Run—*stream* ... KY-4
McCullough Run—*stream* (2) ... OH-6
McCullough Run—*stream* ... PA-2
McCulloughs Butte—*summit* ... NV-8
McCullough Sch—*school* ... ND-7
McCullough Sch—*school* (2) ... PA-2
*McCulloughs Chapel Baptist Church* ... TN-4
McCullough Sch (historical)—*school* (2) ... TN-4
McCullough Slough—*gut* ... TX-5
McCulloughs Mine (underground)—*mine* ... TN-4
McCullough Spring—*spring* ... NV-8
McCullough Spring—*spring* ... OR-9
McCulloughs Spring—*spring* ... NV-8
Mc Cullough Tunnel—*tunnel* ... CO-8
*McCullough-Walker Cemetery* ... MS-4
*McCullum* ... AL-4
*McCullum* ... MS-4
**McCullum**—*pop pl* ... AL-4
McCullum Cem—*cemetery* ... KY-4
McCullum Creek—*stream* ... TX-5
McCullum Post Office
(historical)—*building* ... AL-4
McCullums Pond—*reservoir* ... NC-3
McCully, David, House—*hist pl* ... OR-9
McCully Basin—*basin* ... OR-9
McCully Branch—*stream* ... TN-4
McCully Cabin—*locale* ... NV-8
McCully Cem—*cemetery* ... AL-4
McCully Cem—*cemetery* ... MA-1
McCully Community Center—*building* ... HI-9
*McCully Creek* ... SC-3
McCully Creek—*stream* ... OR-9
McCully Fork—*stream* ... OR-9
McCully Forks Campground—*park* ... OR-9
McCully Lake—*lake* ... MI-6
McCully Log House—*hist pl* ... OH-6
McCully Mill (historical)—*locale* ... AL-4
McCully Mtn—*summit* ... OR-9
McCully Ridge—*ridge* ... MT-8
McCully Spring—*spring* ... NV-8
McCumber Branch—*stream* ... TX-5
McCumber Cem—*cemetery* ... MI-6
McCumber Creek—*stream* ... AK-9
McCumber Flat—*flat* ... CA-9
McCumber Hollow—*valley* ... WI-6
McCumber Rsvr—*reservoir* ... CA-9
*McCumber Run* ... WV-2
McCumber Run—*stream* ... WV-2
McCumber Sch—*school* ... MT-8
McCumber Sch—*school* ... SD-7
McCumber Spring—*spring* ... WA-9
McCume Run—*stream* ... WV-2
McCumsey Spring—*spring* ... SD-7
*McCune* ... KS-7
McCune—*locale* ... MO-7
McCune—*locale* ... NM-5
McCune—*locale* ... PA-2
**Mc Cune**—*pop pl* ... KS-7
**Mccune**—*pop pl* ... KS-7
**McCune**—*pop pl* ... TX-5
McCune, Alfred W., Mansion—*hist pl* ... UT-8
McCune Canyon—*valley* ... UT-8
Mc Cune Cem—*cemetery* ... KS-7
McCune Cem—*cemetery* (2) ... MO-7
McCune Cem—*cemetery* ... OH-6
McCune Cem—*cemetery* ... TX-5
McCune Creek—*stream* ... CA-9
McCune Creek—*stream* ... MT-8
McCune Glacier—*glacier* ... AK-9
McCune Hollow—*valley* ... UT-8
McCune Home for Boys—*other* ... MO-7
McCune JHS—*school* ... OR-9
McCune Lake—*lake* ... WI-6
McCune Mound and Village Site—*hist pl* ... IL-6
McCune Pass—*gap* ... UT-8
McCune Ridge—*ridge* ... OH-6
McCune Run—*stream* (2) ... PA-2
McCunes Cem—*cemetery* ... MO-7
McCune Site—*hist pl* ... MA-1
McCune Springs—*spring* ... WY-8
*McCunes Station* ... MO-7
*McCune Station* ... MO-7
McCune's Villa—*hist pl* ... OH-6
McCune Tunnel—*mine* ... UT-8
**McCuneville**—*pop pl* ... OH-6
McCuran Creek—*stream* ... MI-6
*McCurdy* ... WV-2
McCurdy Bldg (Sears, Roebuck and Company
Building)—*hist pl* ... IN-6
*McCurdy Branch* ... TN-4
McCurdy Bridge—*bridge* ... AL-4
McCurdy Campground—*park* ... OR-9
McCurdy Cem—*cemetery* ... IA-7
McCurdy Cem—*cemetery* ... TN-4
McCurdy Ch—*church* ... NM-5
McCurdy Creek—*stream* ... AK-9
Mc Curdy Creek—*stream* ... CO-8
McCurdy Creek—*stream* ... IN-6
Mccurdy Creek—*stream* ... NV-8
McCurdy Creek—*stream* (2) ... OR-9
McCurdy Draw—*valley* ... MT-8
McCurdy Gap—*gap* ... AL-4
McCurdy Garden—*area* ... NV-8
McCurdy Gulch—*valley* ... SD-7
**McCurdy (historical)**—*pop pl* ... OR-9
McCurdy Hotel—*hist pl* ... IN-6
McCurdy Log House—*hist pl* ... NC-3
Mc Curdy Mtn—*summit* ... CO-8
Mc Curdy Park—*flat* ... CO-8
McCurdy Point—*cape* ... ME-1
McCurdy Point—*cape* ... WA-9
McCurdy Pond—*lake* ... ME-1
McCurdy Sch—*school* ... IL-6
McCurdy Sch—*school* ... NM-5
McCurdy Sch—*school* ... PA-2
McCurdy Sch—*school* ... SD-7
McCurdy Sch (historical)—*school* ... PA-2
McCurdy Trail—*trail* ... CA-9
**McCurdyville**—*pop pl* ... WV-2
McCure Cem—*cemetery* ... LA-4
McCurg Cem—*cemetery* ... KY-4
McCurley Cem—*cemetery* ... AL-4
McCurran Ranch—*locale* ... SD-7
McCurry—*locale* ... MO-7
McCurry Branch—*stream* ... IN-6
McCurry Cem—*cemetery* ... GA-3
McCurry Cem—*cemetery* ... TN-4
McCurry Creek—*stream* ... GA-3
McCurry Creek—*stream* ... OR-9
McCurry-Kidd House—*hist pl* ... GA-3
*McCurry Point* ... RI-1
Mc Curry Rsvr—*reservoir* ... CO-8
**McCurtain**—*pop pl* ... OK-5
McCurtain, Edmund, House—*hist pl* ... OK-5
McCurtain, Green, House—*hist pl* ... OK-5
McCurtain (CCD)—*cens area* ... OK-5
**McCurtain (County)**—*pop pl* ... OK-5
McCurtain County Game Res—*park* ... OK-5
McCurtain Creek—*stream* ... MS-4
McCurtain Creek Ch—*church* ... MS-4
*McCurtains Creek* ... MS-4
McCurtie Branch—*stream* ... TN-4
*Mc Curtin Creek* ... AL-4
McCurtin Creek—*stream* ... AL-4
McCurtin Creek Cem—*cemetery* ... MS-4
*McCurtins Creek* ... MS-4
*McCurtney Creek* ... MT-8
McCurtney Creek—*stream* ... MT-8
McCurvey Hollow—*valley* ... PA-2
McCusker Bridge—*bridge* ... ND-7
McCusker Pond—*lake* ... MA-1
McCuster Brook—*stream* ... RI-1
*McCutchan* ... IN-6
*McCutchan Station* ... IN-6
**McCutchanville**—*pop pl* ... IN-6
*McCutchanville Station* ... IN-6
**McCutchen**—*pop pl* ... GA-3
McCutchen, Bayou—*gut* ... LA-4
McCutchen Branch—*stream* ... AL-4
Mccutchen Branch Clear Creek—*stream* ... TX-5
McCutchen Ch—*church* ... VA-3
McCutchen Ch (historical)—*church* ... AL-4
**Mccutchen Crossroads**—*pop pl* ... SC-3
McCutchen Gap—*gap* ... AR-4
**McCutchen Heights**—*pop pl* ... TN-4
McCutchen Hill—*summit* ... AR-4
McCutchen Meadows—*hist pl* ... KY-4
McCutchen Ranch—*locale* ... ND-7
McCutchens Crossroads—*locale* ... SC-3
McCutchen Spring—*spring* ... NV-8
**McCutchenville**—*pop pl* ... OH-6
**McCutcheon**—*pop pl* ... MS-4
McCutcheon Canyon—*valley* ... TX-5
McCutcheon Cem—*cemetery* ... WV-2
McCutcheon Ch—*church* ... WV-2
McCutcheon Corners—*locale* ... NH-1
McCutcheon Cove—*bay* ... GA-3
McCutcheon Creek—*stream* ... MI-6
McCutcheon Creek—*stream* ... NV-8
McCutcheon Creek—*stream* ... TN-4
McCutcheon Field—*post sta* ... NC-3
McCutcheon Flat—*flat* ... OR-9
McCutcheon Lake—*reservoir* ... MI-6
McCutcheon Mtn—*summit* ... AL-4
McCutcheon Pond—*lake* ... NH-1
McCutcheon Run—*stream* ... PA-2
McCutcheon Run—*stream* ... WV-2
McCutcheon Sch—*school* ... SC-3
McCutchin Canyon—*valley* ... CA-9
McCutchin Cem—*cemetery* ... WV-2
McCutchum Windmill—*locale* ... TX-5
McCuteheon Bayou—*stream* ... MS-4
McCuthen Cem—*cemetery* ... TN-4
McCuthen Oil Field—*oilfield* ... TX-5
McCuthen Ranch—*locale* ... TX-5
McDade—*locale* ... AL-4
McDade—*locale* ... LA-4
**McDade**—*pop pl* ... NC-3
**McDade**—*pop pl* ... TX-5
McDade, Lake—*lake* ... FL-3
McDade Branch—*stream* ... MO-7
McDade Cache—*basin* ... OR-9

McDade Cem—cemetery ... IN-6
McDade Cem—cemetery ... WV-2
McDade Ch—church ... AL-4
McDade Creek—stream ... FL-3
McDade Pond—reservoir ... GA-3
McDade Rsvr—reservoir ... OR-9
McDade Sch—school ... AL-4
McDade Sch—school ... IL-6
McDade Sch—school ... TX-5
McDade Spring ... OR-9
McDade Spring—spring ... MO-7
McDade Springs—spring ... OR-9
McDaid Springs (site)—locale ... OR-9
McDainels—locale ... GA-3
McDaires Cove—valley ... NC-3
McDaires Ridge—ridge ... NC-3
McDale Branch—stream ... KY-4
McDale Hollow ... TN-4
McDale Sch (historical)—school ... TN-4
McDame Creek—stream ... AK-9
McDanial Cem—cemetery ... MS-4
McDaniel ... NC-3
Mcdaniel ... OH-6
McDaniel—locale ... GA-3
McDaniel—locale ... TN-4
**McDaniel**—pop pl ... IN-6
**McDaniel**—pop pl ... MD-2
**McDaniel**—pop pl ... NC-3
McDaniel, Delaplaine, Sch—hist pl ... PA-2
McDaniel, Delaplane, House—hist pl ... DE-2
McDaniel, J., Farm—hist pl ... DE-2
McDaniel Annex Ch—church ... TN-4
McDaniel Bald—summit ... NC-3
McDaniel Branch ... AL-4
McDaniel Branch—stream ... AL-4
McDaniel Branch—stream ... MS-4
McDaniel Branch—stream (2) ... SC-3
McDaniel Branch—stream ... TN-4
McDaniel Branch—stream ... TX-5
McDaniel Bridge—bridge ... AL-4
McDaniel Canyon—valley ... WA-9
McDaniel Caves—cave ... TN-4
McDaniel Cem—cemetery (2) ... AL-4
McDaniel Cem—cemetery (4) ... AR-4
McDaniel Cem—cemetery (2) ... GA-3
McDaniel Cem—cemetery ... IN-6
McDaniel Cem—cemetery ... IA-7
McDaniel Cem—cemetery (5) ... KY-4
McDaniel Cem—cemetery (3) ... LA-4
McDaniel Cem—cemetery (2) ... MS-4
McDaniel Cem—cemetery (2) ... MO-7
McDaniel Cem—cemetery ... OH-6
McDaniel Cem—cemetery (3) ... TN-4
McDaniel Cem—cemetery (2) ... TX-5
McDaniel Ch—church ... AR-4
McDaniel Ch—church ... PA-2
McDaniel Chapel—church ... KY-4
McDaniel Chapel (historical)—church ... TN-4
McDaniel Cimarron Place—locale ... NM-5
McDaniel Cove—bay ... WA-9
McDaniel Creek—stream ... AL-4
McDaniel Creek—stream ... GA-3
McDaniel Creek—stream ... OR-9
McDaniel Creek—stream ... TX-5
McDaniel Crest ... DE-2
McDaniel Crossroad—locale ... OH-6
McDaniel Field—airport ... AZ-5
McDaniel Gas Field—oilfield ... TX-5
**McDaniel Heights**—pop pl ... DE-2
McDaniel Hill—summit ... NH-1
McDaniel Hollow—valley (2) ... TN-4
McDaniel Hollow—valley ... VA-3
McDaniel Knob—summit ... TN-4
McDaniel Lake—lake ... FL-3
McDaniel Lake—lake ... WA-9
McDaniel Lake—reservoir ... MO-7
McDaniel Lake Dam—dam ... MS-4
McDaniel-McElveen Cem—cemetery ... MS-4
McDaniel-Moore Cem—cemetery ... TN-4
McDaniel Mound—hist pl ... OH-6
McDaniel Mtn—summit ... TX-5
McDaniel Mtn—summit ... WA-9
McDaniel Pond—lake ... FL-3
McDaniel Ranch—locale ... NE-7
McDaniel Ranch—locale (3) ... NM-5
McDaniel Ranch—locale ... TX-5
McDaniel Ridge—ridge ... TN-4
Mcdaniels ... OH-6
**McDaniels**—pop pl ... GA-3
**McDaniels**—pop pl ... KY-4
**McDaniels**—pop pl ... MS-4
**McDaniels**—pop pl ... NC-3
McDaniels Bluff—cliff ... GA-3
McDaniels Bridge—bridge ... GA-3
McDaniels Cem—cemetery ... IN-6
McDaniels Ch—church ... NC-3
McDaniel Sch—school ... IL-6
McDaniel Sch—school ... KY-4
McDaniel Sch—school ... MO-7
McDaniel Sch—school ... PA-2
McDaniel Sch—school ... SD-7
McDaniel Sch (abandoned)—school ... MO-7
McDaniels Chapel (historical)—church ... MS-4
McDaniel School ... MS-4
McDaniels Creek—stream ... VA-3
McDaniels Elem Sch ... PA-2
McDaniels Farm—locale ... AR-4
McDaniels Ferry ... AL-4
McDaniels Field Airp—airport ... IN-6
McDaniels Hill—summit ... ME-1
McDaniel Slough—stream ... CA-9
McDaniel Slough—stream ... TN-4
McDaniels Mill ... AL-4
McDaniels Pond Dam—dam ... MS-4
McDaniel Spring—spring ... MO-7
McDaniels Ranch—locale ... NM-5
McDaniels Sch—school ... PA-2
**McDaniels (subdivision)**—pop pl ... NC-3
McDaniels (Township of)—fmr MCD ... NC-3
McDaniel Street Hist Dist—hist pl ... GA-3
McDaniel Tank—reservoir ... AZ-5
McDaniel Tank—reservoir ... NM-5
McDaniel-Tichenor House—hist pl ... GA-3
McDaniel-Travis Cem—cemetery ... MS-4
McDaniel Well—well ... AZ-5
McDaniel Windmill—locale ... TX-5
McDanile Bald ... NC-3
McDannald Homestead—hist pl ... OH-6
McDannel Sch—school ... OH-6
McDauw's Well—locale ... NM-5
**McDavid**—pop pl ... FL-3
**McDavid**—pop pl ... KY-4
McDavid Branch—stream ... IL-6
McDavid Branch—stream ... TN-4
McDavid Cem—cemetery ... KY-4
McDavid Cem—cemetery ... MS-4
McDavid Cem—cemetery ... VA-3
McDavid Ch—church ... FL-3
McDavid Creek—stream (2) ... FL-3
McDavid Grove Baptist Church ... TN-4
McDavid Grove Cem—cemetery ... TN-4
McDavid Grove Ch—church ... TN-4
McDavid Hollow—valley ... MO-7
McDavid Lake—reservoir ... AL-4
McDavid Lake Dam—dam ... AL-4
McDavid Point Cem—cemetery ... IL-6
McDavids Branch ... TN-4
McDavids Cemetery ... TN-4
McDavid Sch—school ... FL-3
McDavid Sch (historical)—school ... TN-4
McDavids Grove Sch ... TN-4
McDavids Sch ... TN-4
**McDavitt (Township of)**—pop pl ... MN-6
McDay Cem—cemetery ... PA-2
McDearman Post Office (historical)—building ... TN-4
McDearmon Sch—school ... MI-6
McDeed Creek ... NC-3
McDeed Creek—stream ... MT-8
McDeeds Creek—stream ... NC-3
McDees (historical)—locale ... MS-4
McDermaid Tank—reservoir ... AZ-5
McDermand, Lake—lake ... CA-9
McDerment Cem—cemetery ... WV-2
McDerments Cave ... AL-4
McDermid Cone ... OR-9
McDermid Creek—stream ... NV-8
McDermid Drive—area ... FL-3
McDermid Ranch—locale ... NV-8
McDermit ... NV-8
McDermit ... OR-9
McDermit Canyon—valley ... AZ-5
McDermit Creek ... NV-8
McDermit Creek ... OR-9
McDermit Lake—lake ... AZ-5
McDermit Spring—spring ... AZ-5
Mc Dermitt ... NV-8
**McDermitt**—pop pl ... NV-8
**McDermitt**—pop pl ... OR-9
McDermitt Cem—cemetery ... NV-8
McDermitt Cem—cemetery ... OH-6
McDermitt Creek ... NV-8
McDermitt Creek ... OR-9
McDermitt Creek—stream ... NV-8
McDermitt Creek—stream ... OR-9
McDermitt Mine—mine ... NV-8
McDermitt Ranch ... NV-8
McDermitt Spring—spring ... NV-8
McDermitt State Airp—airport ... OR-9
Mcdermitt Township—inact MCD ... NV-8
McDermon Hollow—valley ... AR-4
McDermont Ranch—locale ... CA-9
McDermont Spring—spring ... CA-9
McDermoth Sch—school ... WA-9
McDermott—locale ... PA-2
**McDermott**—pop pl ... OH-6
Mc Dermott Arroyo—stream ... CO-8
McDermott Arroyo—stream ... NM-5
McDermott Branch—stream ... TX-5
McDermott Brook—stream ... WI-6
McDermott Camp—locale ... CA-9
McDermott Cem—cemetery ... WV-2
McDermott Creek—stream ... AK-9
McDermott Creek—stream ... CA-9
McDermott Creek—stream ... MN-6
McDermott Creek—stream ... MT-8
McDermott Creek—stream ... WI-6
McDermott Ditch—canal (2) ... NM-5
McDermott Elem Sch—school ... KS-7
McDermott Gulch—valley ... MT-8
McDermott House—hist pl ... MS-4
McDermott Lake—lake ... MI-6
McDermott Lake—lake (2) ... WI-6
McDermott Mine—mine ... MT-8
McDermott Mtn—summit ... AL-4
McDermott Park—park ... WI-6
McDermott Point Lighthouse (abandoned)—locale ... WA-9
McDermott Ravine—valley ... CA-9
McDermotts Butte—summit ... WY-8
McDermott Sch—school ... IL-6
McDermott Sch (abandoned)—school ... PA-2
McDermotts Gulch ... WY-8
McDermotts Gulch—valley ... WY-8
McDermott Trail—trail ... MT-8
McDermott Wells—locale ... NM-5
McDevitt Branch—stream ... NC-3
McDevitt Cem—cemetery ... NC-3
McDevitt Creek—stream ... ID-8
McDevitt Sch—school ... MI-6
McDevitt Springs—spring ... OR-9
McDiarmid, William, House—hist pl ... NC-3
McDiermid Guard Station—locale ... CA-9
McDill—locale ... IA-7
McDill, Mount—summit ... CA-9
McDill Cem—cemetery ... OH-6
McDill Cem—cemetery ... WI-6
McDilley Ridge—ridge ... WI-6
McDill Hollow—valley ... TN-4
McDill Point—summit ... AL-4
McDill Pond—reservoir ... WI-6
McDill Sch—school ... WI-6
McDoel Peak—summit ... AK-9
McDonald ... AL-4
McDonald ... MS-4
McDonald ... WV-2
McDonald—locale ... MD-2
McDonald—locale ... MT-8
McDonald—locale ... OH-6
McDonald—locale ... OR-9
McDonald—locale ... TX-5
McDonald—locale ... WA-9
**McDonald**—pop pl ... AR-4
**McDonald**—pop pl ... FL-3
**McDonald**—pop pl ... KS-7
**McDonald**—pop pl ... MI-6
**McDonald**—pop pl (2) ... MS-4
**McDonald**—pop pl ... NJ-2
**McDonald**—pop pl ... NM-5
**McDonald**—pop pl ... NC-3
**McDonald**—pop pl ... OH-6
**McDonald**—pop pl ... PA-2
**McDonald**—pop pl ... TN-4
**McDonald**—pop pl ... WA-9
McDonald, David, House—hist pl ... UT-8
McDonald, D. C., Bldg—hist pl ... CA-9
McDonald, Irving, House—hist pl ... NV-8
McDonald, J. D., House—hist pl ... NE-7
McDonald, J. G., Chocolate Company Bldg—hist pl ... UT-8
McDonald, Lake—lake ... AK-9
McDonald, Lake—lake ... MT-8
McDonald, Lake—lake ... ND-7
McDonald, Lake—lake ... WA-9
McDonald, Mount—summit ... AK-9
McDonald Acres—locale ... GA-3
McDonald Anticline Oil Field—oilfield ... CA-9
McDonald Anti-Cline Oil Field—oilfield ... CA-9
McDonald Arm—bay ... AK-9
McDonald Baptist Church ... MS-4
McDonald Bar—bar ... AK-9
McDonald Basin—basin (3) ... MT-8
McDonald Basin—basin ... UT-8
McDonald Bayou—stream ... LA-4
McDonald Bayou—stream ... TX-5
McDonald Bend—bend ... TN-4
McDonald-Bolner House—hist pl ... TN-4
McDonald Borough—civil (2) ... PA-2
McDonald Branch ... NJ-2
McDonald Branch—stream (2) ... AL-4
McDonald Branch—stream (2) ... FL-3
McDonald Branch—stream ... GA-3
McDonald Branch—stream (2) ... MS-4
McDonald Branch—stream ... MO-7
McDonald Branch—stream ... OK-5
McDonald Branch—stream ... TN-4
McDonald Branch—stream ... TX-5
McDonald Branch—stream ... VA-3
McDonald Brook—stream (2) ... ME-1
McDonald Brook—stream ... MA-1
McDonald Brother Tank—reservoir ... NM-5
McDonald Butte—summit (2) ... MT-8
McDonald Cabin—locale ... CA-9
McDonald Cabin—locale ... WY-8
McDonald Cabins—locale ... WY-8
McDonald Camp—locale ... TX-5
McDonald Camp (site)—locale ... OR-9
McDonald Canal—canal ... FL-3
McDonald Canyon—valley ... AZ-5
McDonald Canyon—valley (2) ... CA-9
McDonald Canyon—valley ... OR-9
McDonald Canyon—valley ... UT-8
McDonald Cem—cemetery (3) ... AL-4
McDonald Cem—cemetery (5) ... AR-4
McDonald Cem—cemetery (4) ... GA-3
McDonald Cem—cemetery ... KY-4
McDonald Cem—cemetery (2) ... LA-4
McDonald Cem—cemetery (6) ... MS-4
McDonald Cem—cemetery (2) ... MO-7
McDonald Cem—cemetery ... NM-5
McDonald Cem—cemetery ... NY-2
McDonald Cem—cemetery ... OH-6
McDonald Cem—cemetery (9) ... TN-4
McDonald Cem—cemetery (5) ... TX-5
McDonald Cem—cemetery (2) ... WV-2
McDonald Cem—cemetery ... WI-6
McDonald Ch—church (2) ... AR-4
McDonald Ch—church ... GA-3
McDonald Ch—church ... IN-6
McDonald Ch—church ... KY-4
McDonald Ch—church ... LA-4
McDonald Ch—church ... MS-4
McDonald Ch—church ... NC-3
McDonald Chapel ... AL-4
McDonald Chapel ... MS-4
McDonald Chapel—church ... TN-4
**McDonald Chapel**—pop pl ... AL-4
McDonald Chapel Cem ... MS-4
McDonald Chapel Elem Sch—school ... AL-4
McDonald Chase Cem—cemetery ... IA-7
McDonald Chute—stream ... IL-6
**McDonald Condo**—pop pl ... UT-8
**McDonald (corporate name for McDonalds)**—pop pl ... NC-3
McDonald County—civil ... MO-7
**McDonald (County)**—pop pl ... MO-7
McDonald Cove—bay ... AK-9
Mc Donald Cove—bay ... CO-8
McDonald Creek ... MT-8
McDonald Creek—stream ... AL-4
McDonald Creek—stream (3) ... AK-9
McDonald Creek—stream ... AZ-5
McDonald Creek—stream (5) ... CA-9
Mc Donald Creek—stream ... CO-8
McDonald Creek—stream ... CO-8
McDonald Creek—stream (2) ... ID-8
McDonald Creek—stream ... IL-6
McDonald Creek—stream ... IA-7
McDonald Creek—stream ... LA-4
McDonald Creek—stream (2) ... MI-6
McDonald Creek—stream ... MN-6
McDonald Creek—stream ... MS-4
McDonald Creek—stream (11) ... MT-8
McDonald Creek—stream (3) ... NV-8
McDonald Creek—stream ... NY-2
McDonald Creek—stream (2) ... OR-9
McDonald Creek—stream (4) ... TX-5
McDonald Creek—stream (3) ... WA-9
McDonald Creek—stream (2) ... WI-6
McDonald Creek—stream ... WY-8
McDonald Creek Trail—trail ... MT-8
McDonald Cunningham Ditch—canal ... IN-6
McDonald Dam—dam ... ND-7
Mc Donald Ditch—canal ... CO-8
McDonald Ditch—canal ... IN-6
McDonald Ditch—canal ... MT-8
McDonald Ditch—canal ... OR-9
McDonald Drain—canal (5) ... MI-6
McDonald Draw—valley ... NM-5
McDonald Draw—valley ... UT-8
McDonald Draw—valley ... WA-9
McDonald Draw—valley ... WY-8
McDonald Drive Ch of Christ—church ... TN-4
McDonald East View Cem—cemetery ... TN-4
McDonald Elem Sch ... TN-4
McDonald Elem Sch—school ... TN-4
McDonald Falls—falls ... MT-8
McDonald Flat—flat ... AZ-5
McDonald Flat—flat ... NM-5
Mcdonald Flat Recreation Site—locale ... ID-8
McDonald Fork—stream ... WV-2
McDonald Glacier—glacier ... MT-8
McDonald Golf Club—locale ... TN-4
McDonald Green Sch—school ... SC-3
McDonald Grove Ch—church ... MS-4
McDonald Gulch—valley (2) ... CA-9
McDonald Gulch—valley (2) ... ID-8
McDonald Hay Draw Tank—reservoir ... NM-5
**McDonald Heights**—pop pl ... PA-2
**McDonald Hill**—pop pl ... TN-4
McDonald Hill—ridge ... OH-6
McDonald Hill—summit ... ME-1
McDonald Hollow—valley ... AL-4
McDonald Hollow—valley (2) ... PA-2
McDonald Hollow—valley (4) ... TN-4
McDonald Hollow—valley ... VA-3
McDonald Hollow Landfill—locale ... AL-4
McDonald Hollow Trail—trail ... PA-2
McDonald House—hist pl ... LA-4
McDonald House—hist pl (2) ... TX-5
McDonald Inlet—stream ... NY-2
McDonald Island—island ... GA-3
McDonald Island—island ... IL-6
McDonald Island—island ... MI-6
McDonald Island Ferry—locale ... CA-9
McDonald Islands—area ... AK-9
McDonald Lagoon—bay ... AK-9
McDonald Lake ... MI-6
McDonald Lake ... MN-6
McDonald Lake ... WA-9
McDonald Lake ... WI-6
McDonald Lake—lake ... AR-4
McDonald Lake—lake ... CA-9
McDonald Lake—lake ... ID-8
McDonald Lake—lake ... IN-6
McDonald Lake—lake (5) ... MI-6
McDonald Lake—lake (5) ... MN-6
McDonald Lake—lake ... MT-8
McDonald Lake—lake ... NM-5
McDonald Lake—lake ... ND-7
McDonald Lake—lake ... TX-5
McDonald Lake—lake ... WA-9
McDonald Lake—lake (3) ... WI-6
McDonald Lake—reservoir (2) ... UT-8
McDonald Lake Dam—dam ... UT-8
McDonald Landing—locale ... AL-4
McDonald Lateral—canal ... ID-8
McDonald Lower Landing—locale ... AL-4
McDonald Mansion—hist pl ... CA-9
McDonald Meadow—flat ... MT-8
McDonald Meadow—flat ... OR-9
McDonald Mesa—summit ... CO-8
McDonald Mill—locale ... NC-3
McDonald Mill Creek—stream ... WV-2
McDonald Mine—mine ... MT-8
McDonald Mountain Tank—reservoir ... AZ-5
McDonald Mountian—summit (3) ... WA-9
McDonald Mtn—summit ... AZ-5
McDonald Mtn—summit ... ME-1
McDonald Mtn—summit ... MT-8
McDonald Mtn—summit ... TX-5
McDonald Mtn—summit (3) ... WA-9
McDonald Natl Wildlife Mngmt Area—park ... ND-7
McDonald Number 2 Cem—cemetery ... MS-4
McDonald Observatory—building ... TX-5
McDonald Oil Field—oilfield ... TX-5
McDonald Outlet—stream ... NY-2
McDonald Park—flat ... MT-8
McDonald Park—park ... AZ-5
McDonald Park—park ... CA-9
McDonald Park—park (2) ... FL-3
McDonald Park—park ... KS-7
McDonald Park Congregation Jehovahs Witnesses—church ... KS-7
McDonald Pass ... MT-8
McDonald Peak—summit (2) ... CA-9
McDonald Peak—summit (2) ... ID-8
McDonald Peak—summit ... MT-8
McDonald Peak—summit ... OR-9
McDonald Pocket—basin ... AZ-5
McDonald Point—cape ... AK-9
McDonald Point—cape ... ID-8
McDonald Pond—lake ... NY-2
McDonald Pond—lake ... OR-9
McDonald Pond—reservoir ... GA-3
McDonald Pond Dam—dam ... MS-4
McDonald Ponds Dam—dam ... MS-4
McDonald Post Office—building ... TN-4
McDonald Presbyterian Church ... MS-4
McDonald Ranch—hist pl ... WY-8
McDonald Ranch—locale ... AZ-5
McDonald Ranch—locale ... MT-8
McDonald Ranch—locale ... NE-7
McDonald Ranch—locale ... NM-5
McDonald Ranch—locale ... OR-9
McDonald Ranch—locale ... TX-5
McDonald Ranch—locale (2) ... WY-8
McDonald Ranch HQ—locale ... NM-5
Mc Donald Ridge—ridge ... NC-3
McDonald Ridge—ridge ... OR-9
McDonald Ridge—ridge ... WA-9
McDonald Rock—other ... AK-9
Mc Donald Rsvr—reservoir (3) ... CO-8
McDonald Rsvr—reservoir ... OR-9
McDonald Rsvr—reservoir ... WY-8
McDonald Run ... PA-2
McDonald Run—stream (5) ... PA-2
McDonalds ... NC-3
McDonalds ... TN-4
McDonalds Airp—airport ... PA-2
McDonalds Branch—stream ... NJ-2
McDonalds Cem—cemetery ... MS-4
McDonalds Cem—cemetery ... PA-2
McDonald Sch ... TN-4
McDonalds Ch—church ... MS-4
McDonald Sch—school ... FL-3
McDonald Sch—school ... IL-6
Mc Donald Sch—school ... IL-6
McDonald Sch—school (2) ... MI-6
McDonald Sch—school ... NE-7
McDonald Sch—school ... NH-1
McDonald Sch—school ... OR-9
McDonald Sch—school (2) ... SD-7
McDonald Sch—school ... TN-4
McDonald Sch—school ... WA-9
McDonald Sch—school ... WY-8
McDonalds Chapel ... AL-4
McDonalds Chapel—church ... NC-3
McDonald Sch (historical)—school ... TN-4
McDonalds (corporate name McDonald) ... NC-3
McDonalds Crossroad ... DE-2
McDonalds Crossroads—locale ... DE-2
McDonalds Farm Airport ... PA-2
McDonalds Fishing Camp ... AL-4
McDonald Siding ... WA-9
McDonald's-Kline's Mill—hist pl ... NJ-2
McDonalds Little Valley—valley ... UT-8
McDonald Slough—channel ... IA-7
McDonalds Mill—locale ... VA-3
McDonalds Mill Ch (historical)—church ... MS-4
McDonalds Mill (historical)—locale ... AL-4
McDonalds Mill (historical)—locale ... MS-4
McDonalds Mill (historical)—locale ... TN-4
McDonalds North Well—well ... NM-5
McDonald South Well—well ... NM-5
McDonalds Pond—reservoir ... NC-3
McDonalds Ponds—reservoir ... NJ-2
McDonald Spring—spring (2) ... AL-4
McDonald Spring—spring ... AZ-5
Mc Donald Spring—spring ... CO-8
McDonald Spring—spring ... ID-8
McDonald Spring—spring ... NV-8
McDonald Spring—spring (2) ... OR-9
McDonald Spring—spring ... TN-4
McDonald Spring—spring (2) ... WA-9
McDonald Spring Branch—stream ... AL-4
McDonald Spur ... WA-9
**McDonald's Small Farms**—pop pl ... VA-3
McDonalds Station ... AL-4
McDonalds Store (historical)—locale ... MS-4
McDonald State For—forest ... OR-9
**McDonald Subdivision**—pop pl ... UT-8
**McDonaldsville**—pop pl ... OH-6
McDonaldsville (Township of)—civ div ... MN-6
McDonald Swamp—swamp ... CT-1
McDonald Tank—reservoir ... AZ-5
McDonald Tank—reservoir (2) ... NM-5
McDonald Theater Bldg—hist pl ... OR-9
McDonaldtown ... PA-2
McDonald Township—civil (2) ... MO-7
**McDonald (Township of)**—pop pl ... OH-6
McDonald Trail—trail ... VA-3
McDonald Tunnel—tunnel ... NM-5
McDonald United Methodist Ch—church ... MS-4
McDonaldville—locale ... ID-8
McDonald-Wait-Newton House—hist pl ... AR-4
McDonald Wash ... UT-8
McDonald Wash—valley ... UT-8
McDonald Waterhole—lake ... OR-9
McDonald Waterworks—locale ... PA-2
McDonald Well—well ... CA-9
McDonald Well—well (2) ... NM-5
McDonald Windmill—locale ... NM-5
McDonell, Mount—summit ... AK-9
McDonell Central HS—school ... WI-6
McDonell HS—hist pl ... WI-6
McDonell Peak ... OR-9
McDonld Basin—basin ... UT-8
McDonnal Mill (historical)—locale ... MS-4
McDonnel Field—park ... MS-4
McDonnell Airp—airport ... MO-7
McDonnell Ave Sch—school ... CA-9
McDonnell Cem—cemetery ... AL-4
McDonnell Chapel—church ... AL-4
McDonnell Creek—stream ... CA-9
McDonnell Elementary School ... AL-4
McDonnell Hollow—valley ... TN-4
McDonnell Ranch—locale ... MT-8
McDonnell Sch—school ... AL-4
McDonnel Mtn—summit ... NY-2
McDonogh—locale ... MD-2
McDonogh HS—school ... LA-4
**McDonogh (McDonogh School)**—pop pl ... MD-2
McDonogh Number 1 Sch—school ... LA-4
McDonogh Number 10 Sch—school ... LA-4
McDonogh Number 11 Sch—school ... LA-4
McDonogh Number 14 Sch—school ... LA-4
McDonogh Number 15 Sch—school ... LA-4
McDonogh Number 16 Sch—school ... LA-4
McDonogh Number 19 Sch—school ... LA-4
McDonogh Number 26 Sch—school ... LA-4
McDonogh Number 27 Sch—school ... LA-4
McDonogh Number 28 Sch—school ... LA-4
McDonogh Number 31 Sch—school ... LA-4
McDonogh Number 32 Sch—school ... LA-4
McDonogh Number 37 Sch—school ... LA-4
McDonogh Number 42 Sch—school ... LA-4
McDonogh Number 45 Sch—school ... LA-4
McDonogh Sch—school (2) ... LA-4
McDonogh Sch For Boys—school ... MD-2
McDonogh Sch No. 6—hist pl ... LA-4
**McDonoghville**—pop pl ... LA-4
McDonoghville Cem—cemetery ... LA-4
McDonold Peak ... OR-9
McDonough—locale ... DE-2
**McDonough**—pop pl ... GA-3
**McDonough**—pop pl ... MI-6
**McDonough**—pop pl ... NY-2
**McDonough**—pop pl ... TX-5
Mcdonough, Lake—reservoir ... CT-1
McDonough Brook—stream ... NH-1
McDonough (CCD)—cens area ... GA-3
McDonough Corners—locale ... MI-6
**McDonough (County)**—pop pl ... IL-6
McDonough County Courthouse—hist pl ... IL-6
McDonough Lake—lake ... IL-6
McDonough Lake—lake ... MN-6
McDonough Park—flat ... CO-8
Mc Donough Park—park ... CO-8
McDonough Peak—summit ... AK-9
McDonough Playground—park ... WI-6
McDonough Ranch—locale ... CO-8
McDonough Rsvr—reservoir ... CO-8
McDonough Rsvr No 2—reservoir ... CO-8
McDonoughs—airport ... NJ-2
McDonoughs—uninc pl ... NJ-2
McDonough Sch—school ... MA-1
McDonough's Island ... WA-9
**McDonough (Town of)**—pop pl ... NY-2
McDorman Well—well ... NM-5
**McDougal**—pop pl ... AR-4
McDougal, Mount—summit ... WY-8
McDougal, Stiles, House—hist pl ... KY-4
McDougal (Abandoned)—locale ... AK-9
McDougal Basin—basin ... MT-8
McDougal Branch—stream ... MS-4
McDougal Cem—cemetery ... OK-5
McDougal Cem—cemetery ... TN-4
McDougal Creek ... TX-5
Mc Dougal Creek—stream ... AK-9
McDougal Creek—stream ... ID-8
McDougal Creek—stream ... KY-4
McDougal Creek—stream ... MS-4
McDougal Creek—stream ... NY-2
McDougal Creek—stream ... OR-9
McDougal Creek—stream ... WY-8
McDougald, John A., House—hist pl ... GA-3
McDougald Branch—stream (2) ... NC-3
McDougal Draw—valley ... TX-5
McDougal Flat—flat ... AZ-5
McDougal Flat Tank—reservoir ... AZ-5
McDougal Gulch—valley ... MT-8
McDougal Gulch—valley ... WY-8
McDougal-Jones House—hist pl ... TX-5
McDougal Lake—lake ... AR-4
McDougal Lake—lake ... FL-3
McDougal Lake—lake ... MN-6
McDougall Branch—stream ... OH-6
McDougall Camp—locale ... OR-9
McDougall Ch—church ... OH-6
Mc Dougall Creek—stream ... AK-9
McDougall Island—island ... MN-6
McDougall Lake—lake ... NY-2
McDougall Lake—lake ... WI-6
McDougall Peak ... WY-8
McDougal Mountain ... MA-1
McDougal Pass—gap ... WY-8
McDougal Pond—lake ... ME-1
McDougal Spring—spring ... AZ-5
McDougal Spring—spring ... TX-5
McDougal Springs—spring ... WI-6
McDougal Tank—reservoir ... NM-5
McDougal Wash—stream ... AZ-5
McDougle Cem—cemetery (2) ... TX-5
McDougle Cem—cemetery ... WV-2
McDougle Lake—lake ... TX-5
McDow Branch ... TX-5
Mc Dow Creek—stream ... OR-9
McDow Creek—stream ... SC-3
McDowel Bridge—bridge ... WI-6
McDowell ... AZ-5
McDowell ... KS-7
McDowell—locale ... AL-4
**McDowell**—pop pl ... IL-6
**McDowell**—pop pl ... KY-4
**McDowell**—pop pl ... MO-7
**McDowell**—pop pl ... VA-3
**McDowell**—pop pl ... WV-2
McDowell—uninc pl ... AZ-5
McDowell—uninc pl ... TN-4
McDowell, Austin, House—hist pl ... OH-6
McDowell, Dr. Ephraim, House—hist pl ... KY-4
McDowell, Mount—summit ... AZ-5
McDowell and Black Grant—civil ... FL-3
McDowell Bat Cave ... AL-4
McDowell Branch—stream ... KY-4
McDowell Branch—stream ... LA-4
McDowell Branch—stream ... MO-7
McDowell Branch—stream ... NC-3
McDowell Branch—stream ... VA-3
McDowell Branch—stream ... WV-2
McDowell Bridge—bridge ... NC-3
McDowell Bridge—other ... MO-7
McDowell Butte—summit ... OR-9
McDowell Butte Rsvr—reservoir ... OR-9
McDowell Camp—locale ... CA-9
McDowell Canyon—valley ... CA-9
McDowell Canyon—valley ... NE-7
McDowell Canyon—valley ... WA-9
McDowell (CCD)—cens area ... KY-4
McDowell Cem—cemetery ... AL-4
McDowell Cem—cemetery ... AR-4
McDowell Cem—cemetery ... IL-6
Mc Dowell Cem—cemetery ... IA-7
McDowell Cem—cemetery ... KY-4
McDowell Cem—cemetery ... ME-1
McDowell Cem—cemetery (5) ... MS-4
McDowell Cem—cemetery ... MO-7
McDowell Cem—cemetery (2) ... PA-2
McDowell Cem—cemetery ... SC-3
McDowell Cem—cemetery ... TN-4
McDowell Cem—cemetery (2) ... VA-3
Mc Dowell Ch—church ... NC-3
McDowell Chapel—church ... TN-4
McDowell Corners—locale ... PA-2
**McDowell County**—pop pl ... NC-3
**McDowell (County)**—pop pl ... WV-2
McDowell County Courthouse—hist pl ... NC-3
McDowell County Courthouse—hist pl ... WV-2
McDowell County Plaza (Shop Ctr)—locale ... NC-3
McDowell Creek ... KS-7
McDowell Creek—stream ... AL-4
McDowell Creek—stream ... CA-9
McDowell Creek—stream ... KS-7
McDowell Creek—stream ... KY-4
McDowell Creek—stream (2) ... NC-3
McDowell Creek—stream ... OH-6
McDowell Creek—stream (2) ... OR-9
McDowell Creek—stream ... SC-3
McDowell Creek—stream (3) ... TX-5
McDowell Creek—stream ... VA-3
McDowell Creek Camp—locale ... OR-9
McDowell Creek Sch—school ... KS-7
McDowell Creek Sch—school ... OR-9
McDowell Dam—dam ... ND-7
McDowell Ditch—canal ... IN-6
McDowell Draw—valley ... TX-5
McDowell Exhibit Plaza—park ... AZ-5
McDowell Falls County Park—park ... OR-9
McDowell Ferry—locale ... AL-4
McDowell Flat—flat ... WY-8
McDowell Grove—park ... IL-6
Mc Dowell Gulch—valley ... CO-8
McDowell Hill—summit ... WA-9
Mcdowell HS—school ... NC-3
McDowell HS—school ... PA-2
McDowell Island—island ... SC-3
McDowell Island—island ... WI-6
McDowell Lake—lake ... MI-6
McDowell Lake—lake (2) ... WA-9
Mcdowell Lake—reservoir ... AL-4
McDowell Lake—reservoir ... IA-7
McDowell Lake Dam One—dam ... IA-7
McDowell Landing—locale ... AL-4
McDowell Lateral—canal ... ID-8
McDowell Lateral—canal ... WI-6
McDowell Memorial Chapel—church ... AL-4

McDowell Memorial Park—cemetery NC-3
McDowell Mountain AZ-5
McDowell Mountain Regional Park—park AZ-5
McDowell Mountains UT-8
McDowell Mountains—range AZ-5
McDowell Mountains—summit AZ-5
McDowell Mtn—summit NC-3
Mc Dowell Park—flat CO-8
McDowell Park—park NC-3
McDowell Pass—gap AZ-5
McDowell Peak—summit AZ-5
McDowell Peak—summit OR-9
McDowell Plaza Shop Ctr—locale AZ-5
McDowell Pocket—lake MS-4
McDowell Point—cape (2) TX-5
Mc Dowell Ranch—locale CO-8
McDowell Ranch—locale NM-5
McDowell Ranch—locale TX-5
McDowell Road Baptist Ch—church MS-4
McDowell Run—stream (2) PA-2
McDowell Run—stream WV-2
McDowell Sch—school IL-6
McDowell Sch—school IN-6
McDowell Sch—school KY-4
McDowell Sch—school MI-6
McDowell Sch—school TN-4
McDowell Sch (historical)—school PA-2
McDowell-Schmid Airp—airport MO-7
McDowell Senior HS PA-2
McDowell Shoal—bar TN-4
McDowell Site—hist pl SC-3
McDowells Landing—locale AL-4
McDowells Mill Post Office
(historical)—building TN-4
McDowell Spring—spring CA-9
McDowell Spring—spring MT-8
McDowell Spring—spring OR-9
McDowell Spring Branch—stream AL-4
McDowell Square Shop Ctr—locale AZ-5
McDowell Square Shop Ctr—locale MS-4
McDowells Run—stream KY-4
McDowells Run—stream PA-2
McDowells Spring Cave—cave AL-4
McDowell Station AL-4
McDowell Station Post Office—building AZ-5
McDowell Tank—reservoir AZ-5
McDowell Tank—reservoir (2) NM-5
McDowell Township—civil MO-7
McDowell Trail—trail PA-2
McDowell Trailer Village—locale AZ-5
McDowell Valley—stream CA-9
McDuff—locale VA-3
McDuff Branch—stream AL-4
McDuffee Brook—stream CT-1
McDuffee Creek—stream MI-6
McDuffees Gin AL-4
McDuffey Ferry AL-4
McDuffie, Mount—summit CA-9
McDuffie Cem—cemetery (2) AL-4
McDuffie Cem—cemetery GA-3
McDuffie Church AL-4
**McDuffie (County)**—pop pl GA-3
McDuffie Creek—stream NC-3
McDuffie Ferry AL-4
McDuffie Island—island AL-4
McDuffie Memorial Ch—church NC-3
McDuffie Park—park NM-5
**McDuffie Town**—pop pl NY-2
McDuff Rapids—rapids ID-8
McDuff Rapids—rapids WA-9
McDuff Spring Branch—stream AL-4
McDuff Windmill—locale TX-5
McDuffy Branch—stream TX-5
McDuffy Creek—stream NY-2
McDuffy Gulch—valley NV-8
McDuffy Opening—flat CA-9
McDuffy Sch—school PA-2
**McDunn**—pop pl WV-2
McEachera Spring—lake MI-6
McEacher Branch—stream NC-3
McEachern Cem—cemetery MS-4
McEachern Creek—stream MI-6
McEachin Hollow—valley OK-5
McEachins Landing—locale GA-3
McEamee Cem—cemetery OH-6
McEbright Sch—school OH-6
McEchron, William, House—hist pl NY-2
McElderry—locale AL-4
McElderrys Station AL-4
McElder Sch (historical)—school AL-4
McEldowney Cem—cemetery KY-4
McEleny Mtn—summit ID-8
McElfee Creek AL-4
McElfish Creek—stream AK-9
McElhaney Bluff—cliff AR-4
McElhaney Branch—stream MO-7
Mc Elhaney Canyon—valley CO-8
McElhaney Creek—stream IA-7
McElhaney Drain—canal WY-8
McElhaneys Island—island PA-2
McElhaney Tank—reservoir AZ-5
Mc Elhaney Windmill—locale CO-8
**McElhany**—pop pl MO-7
McElhany Spring—spring NV-8
**McElhattan**—pop pl PA-2
McElhattan Creek—stream PA-2
Mcelhattan Dam PA-2
Mcelhattan Rsvr PA-2
McElhattan Rsvr—reservoir PA-2
McElheneys Crossroads—locale GA-3
McElhenney Ch—church WV-2
McElheny Tank—reservoir AZ-5
McElhiney Cem—cemetery TN-4
McElhinney Drain—canal MI-6
McElhinny House—hist pl IA-7
McElla Church MS-4
McEllen Canyon—valley NV-8
McElligott Canyon—valley OR-9
McElmerry Cem—cemetery MO-7
**Mcelmo**—pop pl CO-8
McElmo Canyon—valley CO-8
Mc Elmo Creek—stream CO-8
McElmo Creek—stream UT-8
Mc Elmo Falls—falls CO-8
McElmoyle Sch—school SC-3
McElmurray Grove Ch—church GA-3
McElmurray Pond—lake SC-3
McElmurrays Pond SC-3
McElmurroy Pond SC-3
McElmurry Creek—stream KY-4
McElory Mtn—summit GA-3
McElprang Canyon—valley UT-8
McElprang Wash—valley UT-8
McElrath Cem—cemetery IN-6
Mc Elrath Chapel—church NC-3
McElrath Creek—stream AR-4
McElrath Lake—reservoir NC-3
**McElrath Subdivision**
**(subdivision)**—pop pl AL-4
McElrow Tank—reservoir TX-5
McElroy—locale LA-4
McElroy—locale TN-4
McElroy—locale TX-5
**McElroy**—pop pl AR-4
**McElroy**—pop pl MT-8
McElroy, H. E., House—hist pl ID-8
McElroy, Mount—summit TX-5
Mc Elroy Airp—airport CO-8
McElroy Branch—stream NC-3
McElroy Branch—stream SC-3
McElroy Branch—stream TN-4
McElroy Butte—summit ID-8
McElroy Canyon WA-9
McElroy Cave—cave TN-4
McElroy Cem—cemetery AL-4
McElroy Cem—cemetery AR-4
Mc Elroy Cem—cemetery NC-3
McElroy Cem—cemetery OH-6
McElroy Cem—cemetery (2) TN-4
McElroy Cem—cemetery (2) TX-5
McElroy Ch—church GA-3
McElroy Ch—church TN-4
McElroy Coulee—valley WA-9
McElroy Cove—valley NC-3
McElroy Creek—stream CA-9
McElroy Creek*—stream IA-7
McElroy Creek—stream KY-4
McElroy Creek—stream MS-4
McElroy Creek—stream MO-7
McElroy Creek—stream WA-9
McElroy Creek—stream WV-2
McElroy Drain—canal WY-8
McElroy Draw—valley ID-8
McElroy Ferry (historical)—crossing TN-4
McElroy Flat—flat CA-9
McElroy Ford—locale KY-4
McElroy Ford (historical)—crossing TN-4
McElroy Gap—gap AR-4
McElroy Hill—summit IN-6
McElroy Hollow TN-4
McElroy Lake—lake WA-9
McElroy Lake—lake WI-6
McElroy Lake Dam—dam MS-4
McElroy (Magisterial District)—fmr MCD WV-2
McElroy Octagon House—hist pl CA-9
McElroy Oil Field—oilfield TX-5
McElroy Park—park ND-7
McElroy Post Office (historical)—building TN-4
McElroy Ranch—locale TX-5
McElroy Ridge—ridge LA-4
McElroy Run—stream PA-2
McElroys Lake—lake MS-4
McElroys Mill—locale GA-3
McElroy Spring AL-4
McElroys Run—stream WV-2
McElroy Trap Windmill—locale TX-5
McElroy Well—well (2) TX-5
McElroy Windmill—locale TX-5
McElvain Camp—locale FL-3
McElvain Cem—cemetery IL-6
McElvain Sch—school IL-6
McElveen—locale MS-4
McElveen Cem—cemetery LA-4
McElvey Branch—stream GA-3
McElvoy Canyon—valley CA-9
McElwain Baptist Ch—church AL-4
McElwain Cem—cemetery (2) MO-7
McElwain Creek—stream MT-8
McElwain Creek—stream SC-3
McElwain Elementary School AL-4
McElwain House—hist pl ME-1
McElwain Sch—school AL-4
Mc Elwain Sch—school CO-8
McElwain Sch—school MA-1
McElwain Spring—spring MO-7
McElwee Cem—cemetery MS-4
McElwee Cem—cemetery MO-7
McElwee Chapel—church VA-3
McElwee Ferry TN-4
McElwee Houses—hist pl NC-3
McElwee Landing (historical)—locale TN-4
McElwee Mill (historical)—locale TN-4
McElwin Lake—lake MI-6
McElyea Place—locale MO-7
McElyea Sch—school MO-7
McEnary Tunnel—tunnel AZ-5
Mc Endree Ranch—locale CO-8
McEnery Lake—lake LA-4
McEniry Earth and Life Sciences
Bldg—building NC-3
McEnniery Lake—lake WA-9
McEntee Spring—spring WA-9
McEntire Air Natl Guard Base—military SC-3
McEntire Lake—reservoir OK-5
McEntire Ranch—locale TX-5
McEnturff Creek—stream TX-5
McEntyre—locale AL-4
McEntyre Ch AL-4
McEntyre Chapel—church AL-4
McEtheren Spring TN-4
McEuen Cem—cemetery AZ-5
McEvan, Mathew, House—hist pl UT-8
McEvans Sch—school MS-4
McEver Field—locale NC-3
McEver Lake—reservoir GA-3
McEvers Branch—stream GA-3
McEver Sch—school GA-3
McEvory Park—park OH-6
Mc Evoy Lakes—lake CO-8
McEwan, Peter, Warehouse—hist pl WI-6
McEwan Canyon—valley NM-5
McEwan Flat—flat UT-8
McEwan Spring—spring NM-5
McEwan Tank—reservoir NM-5
McEwen—locale OR-9
**McEwen**—pop pl TN-4
McEwen, Christopher, House—hist pl TN-4
McEwen, David, House—hist pl TN-4
McEwen Branch—stream TN-4
McEwen Butte—summit OR-9
McEwen (CCD)—cens area TN-4
McEwen Cem—cemetery AR-4
McEwen Cem—cemetery MS-4
McEwen Cem—cemetery NC-3
McEwen Cem—cemetery (3) TN-4
McEwen Creek—stream NV-8
McEwen Creek—stream OR-9
McEwen Ditch—canal UT-8
McEwen Division—civil TN-4
McEwen Draw—valley TX-5
McEwen Estate Dam—dam NC-3
McEwen First Baptist Ch—church TN-4
McEwen HS—school OR-9
McEwen Industrial Park—locale TN-4
McEwen Lake—lake MI-6
McEwen Lake—reservoir NC-3
McEwen Post Office—building TN-4
McEwen Prairie—flat WA-9
McEwen Ranch—locale OR-9
McEwen Rsvr—reservoir OR-9
McEwen Run—stream PA-2
McEwens TN-4
McEwens, John F., House—hist pl WI-6
McEwen-Samuels-Marr House—hist pl IN-6
McEwen Sch—school TN-4
McEwens Corner—locale NY-2
**McEwens Corners**—pop pl NY-2
McEwen Spring—spring AL-4
McEwen Spring—spring (2) OR-9
McEwen Spring—spring UT-8
**McEwensville**—pop pl PA-2
McEwensville Borough—civil PA-2
McEwen Trap Spring—spring AZ-5
McEwen Valley Ditch—canal OR-9
McEwin Cem—cemetery TX-5
Mcfadden—fmr MCD NE-7
McFadden—locale AR-4
**McFadden**—pop pl TX-5
**McFadden**—pop pl WY-8
McFadden, O. B., House—hist pl WA-9
McFadden Bayou—stream TX-5
McFadden Bend Cutoff TX-5
McFadden Bend Cutoff—channel TX-5
McFadden Branch—stream KS-7
McFadden Branch—stream SC-3
McFadden Branch—stream TN-4
McFadden Cem—cemetery (2) AR-4
McFadden Cem—cemetery IL-6
McFadden Cem—cemetery IN-6
McFadden Cem—cemetery KY-4
McFadden Cem—cemetery MI-6
McFadden Creek—stream AZ-5
Mc Fadden Creek—stream CO-8
McFadden Creek—stream IN-6
McFadden Ditch—canal IL-6
McFadden Ditch—canal IN-6
McFadden Ditch—canal MT-8
McFadden Falls—falls OK-5
McFadden Ford—locale VA-3
McFadden Horse Mtn—summit AZ-5
McFadden Junoir HS—school CA-9
McFadden Landing—locale MO-7
McFadden Marsh—swamp OR-9
McFadden Memorial Gardens—cemetery AL-4
McFadden Peak—summit AZ-5
McFadden Peak Lookout—tower AZ-5
McFadden Point—cape MI-6
McFadden Point—cliff ID-8
McFadden Ranch—locale TX-5
McFadden Rsvr No 3—reservoir WY-8
McFadden Run—stream OH-6
McFadden Sch—school CA-9
McFaddens Ferry (historical)—locale MS-4
McFadden Spring—spring NV-8
McFadden Trail—trail PA-2
**McFaddin**—pop pl TX-5
McFaddin, James, House—hist pl TX-5
McFaddin Cem—cemetery OH-6
McFaddin Creek—stream TX-5
McFaddin House Complex—hist pl TX-5
McFaddin Oil Field—oilfield TX-5
McFaddin Ranch—locale TX-5
McFade Waterhole Draw—valley WY-8
McFadin Cem—cemetery TX-5
McFadin House—hist pl TX-5
McFadyen Lake—reservoir NC-3
McFait Canyon—valley UT-8
Mcfall AL-4
**McFall**—pop pl MO-7
McFall Branch—stream TX-5
McFall Cem TN-4
McFall Cem—cemetery FL-3
McFall Cem—cemetery MO-7
McFall Cem—cemetery OH-6
McFall Cem—cemetery PA-2
McFall Cem—cemetery SC-3
McFall Cem—cemetery TN-4
McFall Chapel Sch (historical)—school TN-4
McFall Crags—cliff AZ-5
McFall Creek—stream MO-7
McFall Creek—stream OR-9
McFall Draw—valley TX-5
McFall Fork—stream VA-3
McFall Hollow—valley TN-4
McFall House—hist pl SC-3
McFall Lake—lake MI-6
McFall Lake—lake (2) NE-7
McFall (railroad station)—locale FL-3
McFall Ranch—locale NE-7
McFall Rsvr—reservoir OR-9
McFalls Branch—stream TN-4
McFalls Cem—cemetery TN-4
McFalls Ch—church TN-4
McFalls Chapel (historical)—church TN-4
McFalls Creek—stream VA-3
McFalls Hollow—valley TN-4
McFalls Mtn VA-3
McFalls Mtn—summit VA-3
McFalls Ridge—ridge TN-4
McFalls Ridge—ridge VA-3
McFalls Sch (historical)—school TN-4
McFall Station AL-4
McFall Tank—reservoir TX-5
McFall (Township of)—fmr MCD AR-4
McFann—locale PA-2
McFaran Branch—stream AR-4
McFarlain Cem—cemetery LA-4
**McFarlan**—pop pl NC-3
McFarlan, George, House—hist pl CA-9
McFarlan Cem—cemetery GA-3
McFarlan Cem—cemetery IA-7
McFarland—locale TN-4
**McFarland**—pop pl CA-9
**McFarland**—pop pl KS-7
**McFarland**—pop pl MI-6
**McFarland**—pop pl NC-3
**McFarland**—pop pl WI-6
McFarland—post sta AL-4
McFarland, William, House—hist pl MA-1
McFarland Airp (private)—airport PA-2
Mc Farland Bench—bench MT-8
McFarland Bottoms—flat AL-4
McFarland Bottoms Park AL-4
McFarland Brake—swamp AR-4
McFarland Branch—stream KY-4
McFarland Branch—stream TN-4
McFarland Brook—stream MA-1
McFarland Butte—summit OR-9
McFarland Canyon—valley AZ-5
McFarland Canyon—valley NE-7
McFarland Canyon—valley NV-8
McFarland Cave—cave AL-4
McFarland Cem—cemetery AL-4
McFarland Cem—cemetery AR-4
McFarland Cem—cemetery IL-6
McFarland Cem—cemetery (2) KS-7
McFarland Cem—cemetery (3) KY-4
McFarland Cem—cemetery MI-6
McFarland Cem—cemetery MS-4
McFarland Cem—cemetery NC-3
McFarland Cem—cemetery OH-6
McFarland Cem—cemetery OR-9
McFarland Cem—cemetery (3) TN-4
McFarland Cem—cemetery (2) TX-5
McFarland Ch—church MS-4
Mcfarland Cove ME-1
McFarland Creek—stream CA-9
McFarland Creek—stream ID-8
McFarland Creek—stream IN-6
McFarland Creek—stream (3) KY-4
McFarland Creek—stream (2) MI-6
McFarland Creek—stream MT-8
McFarland Creek—stream OH-6
McFarland Creek—stream TN-4
McFarland Creek—stream (2) TX-5
McFarland Creek—stream WA-9
McFarland-Delano (CCD)—cens area CA-9
McFarland Detention Dam—dam KS-7
McFarland Ditch—canal (3) IN-6
McFarland Ditch—canal WY-8
McFarland Divide—ridge WY-8
McFarland East Oil Field—oilfield TX-5
McFarland Gap—gap GA-3
McFarland Gulch—valley CA-9
McFarland Gulch—valley MT-8
McFarland Hill—summit TX-5
McFarland Hill Cem—cemetery ME-1
McFarland Hill Ch—church GA-3
McFarland Hollow—valley AL-4
McFarland Hollow—valley MO-7
McFarland Hollow—valley (2) TN-4
McFarland Hosp—hospital TN-4
McFarland House—hist pl KY-4
McFarland House—hist pl WI-6
McFarland Island—island KY-4
McFarland Island—island ME-1
McFarland Island—island (2) TX-5
McFarland Islands—area AK-9
McFarland Lake—lake MN-6
McFarland Lake—lake OR-9
McFarland Lake—reservoir IA-7
McFarland Lake—reservoir (2) NC-3
McFarland Lake Dam—dam IA-7
McFarland Lake Dam—dam NC-3
McFarland Lake Park—park IA-7
McFarland Mtn—summit ME-1
McFarland Oil Field—oilfield TX-5
McFarland Park—park AL-4
McFarland Park—park TN-4
McFarland Peak—summit NV-8
McFarland Place—locale TX-5
Mcfarland Point ME-1
McFarland Point—cape OR-9
McFarland Pond—lake MO-7
McFarland Pond—reservoir CO-8
McFarland Post Office
(historical)—building TN-4
McFarland Presbyterian Ch MS-4
McFarland Ranch—locale CA-9
McFarland Ranch—locale WY-8
McFarland Ravine—valley CA-9
McFarland-Render House—hist pl GA-3
McFarland Rsvr—reservoir MT-8
Mc Farland Rsvr No 1—reservoir CO-8
McFarland Rsvr No 2—reservoir CO-8
McFarland Run—stream WV-2
McFarlands MI-6
McFarlands—locale NM-5
McFarland Sch—school IL-6
McFarland Sch—school KY-4
McFarland Sch—school ME-1
McFarland Sch—school NC-3
McFarland Sch—school OR-9
McFarland Sch—school SD-7
McFarland Sch—school TN-4
McFarland Sch—school TX-5
McFarland Sch (abandoned)—school PA-2
McFarland Sch (historical)—school MS-4
McFarlands Corner—locale ME-1
**McFarlands Corners**—pop pl OH-6
McFarlands Cove—bay ME-1
McFarlands Ledges—bar ME-1
McFarlands Point—cape ME-1
McFarland Spring—spring AZ-5
McFarland Spring—spring NV-8
McFarland Spring—spring TX-5
McFarland Spring Cave—cave AL-4
McFarland Springs—spring AL-4
McFarlands Run—stream PA-2
McFarland Tank—reservoir TX-5
McFarland Trail—trail OK-5
McFarland Well—locale NM-5
McFarland-White Ranch—locale MT-8
McFarlane Branch TN-4
McFarlane Branch—stream VA-3
McFarlane-Bredt House—hist pl NY-2
McFarlane Cem—cemetery AL-4
McFarlane Cem—cemetery VA-3
McFarlane Chapel—church WV-2
Mc Farlane Creek—stream CO-8
McFarlane Creek—stream WY-8
McFarlane Ditch—canal CA-9
McFarlan (Election Precinct)—fmr MCD IL-6
McFarlane Mountain UT-8
McFarlane Mtn—summit UT-8
McFarlane Ravine—valley CA-9
McFarlane Sch—school MI-6
McFarlane Sch—school OH-6
McFarlanes Creek TN-4
McFarlane State Park—park IA-7
McFarlan Park—park MI-6
McFarlen IN-6
McFarlen Cem—cemetery LA-4
McFarlin—locale OK-5
McFarlin, John Lee, House—hist pl FL-3
McFarlin, Robert M., House—hist pl OK-5
McFarlin Bldg—hist pl OK-5
McFarlin Bridge—bridge GA-3
McFarlin Cem—cemetery TN-4
McFarline Mountain UT-8
Mcfarling's Cove ME-1
Mcfarling's Point ME-1
**McFarlin (historical)**—pop pl OR-9
McFarlin Memorial Auditorium—hist pl TX-5
McFarlin Pond—reservoir GA-3
McFarney Spring—spring ID-8
McFarren Cem—cemetery IN-6
McFarren Ditch—canal IN-6
McFarren Gulch—valley ID-8
McFarren Hill—summit IN-6
McFates Canyon—valley ID-8
McFaul Creek—stream NV-8
McFayden Lake NC-3
McFayden Lake Dam NC-3
McFayden Pond—reservoir NC-3
McFee Cem—cemetery NY-2
McFee Creek—stream MT-8
McFee Creek—stream OR-9
McFee Lake—lake MI-6
McFeeters Knob—summit PA-2
McFeeters Knob—summit WV-2
McFerran, J. B., Sch—hist pl KY-4
McFerran Sch—school KY-4
McFerren, Lake—reservoir NM-5
McFerren Park—park IL-6
**McFerrin**—pop pl AR-4
McFerrin Cem—cemetery AR-4
McFerrin Cem—cemetery (3) TN-4
McFerrin Ch—church (2) TN-4
McFerrin Coll (historical)—school TN-4
McFerrin Park—park TN-4
McFerrin Plantation—locale AR-4
McFerron Sch (abandoned)—school PA-2
McFetridge Island—island WI-6
McFrey Crossroads—locale AL-4
McFry Ford—locale MO-7
**McGaffey**—pop pl NM-5
McGaffey Canyon—valley NM-5
McGaffey Cem—cemetery NM-5
McGaffey Cem—cemetery TX-5
McGaffey Ditch—canal IN-6
McGaffey Lake—reservoir NM-5
McGaffey Lookout Tower—locale NM-5
McGaffey Mtn—summit ME-1
McGaffey Rec Area—park NM-5
McGaffey Ridge—ridge NM-5
**McGaha**—pop pl KY-4
McGaha Cem—cemetery NC-3
McGaha Chapel—church TN-4
McGaha Hollow—valley TN-4
**Mcgahan Township**—pop pl ND-7
McGaha Sch—school TX-5
McGahee Creek—stream WA-9
**McGaheysville**—pop pl VA-3
McGalasson Cem—cemetery TX-5
**McGalin**—pop pl TX-5
McGalliard Creek—stream NC-3
McGann Bog—swamp ME-1
McGann Gulch—valley CA-9
McGann Lake—lake MI-6
McGann Mtn—summit NY-2
McGann Springs—spring CA-9
**McGarey**—pop pl PA-2
**McGareys**—pop pl PA-2
McGargels Ford—locale IA-7
McGargle Rocks—summit ME-1
McGarity Lake—lake FL-3
McGarr Hollow—valley MO-7
McGarrity Bay—swamp GA-3
McGarr Meadows—flat OR-9
McGarr Ridge—ridge MO-7
McGarr Spring—spring MO-7
McGarry Canyon—valley ID-8
McGarry House—hist pl MO-7
McGarrys Wash—stream AZ-5
McGars Pond—lake GA-3
McGarva Rsvr—reservoir CA-9
McGarva Rsvr Two—reservoir CA-9
McGarvey, Dr. John, House—hist pl KY-4
Mc Garvey Cem—cemetery PA-2
McGarvey Creek—stream CA-9
McGarvey Gulch—valley CA-9
McGarvey Park—park CA-9
**McGary**—pop pl IN-6
McGary Butte—summit ID-8
McGary Creek—stream ID-8
McGary Creek—stream TX-5
McGary Ditch—canal IN-6
McGary Elementary and JHS—school IN-6
McGary Sch IN-6
Mcgathery Island ME-1
McGath Lake—lake UT-8
McGath Point—summit UT-8
McGath Point Bench—bench UT-8
McGaugh Cem—cemetery MO-7
McGaughey Cem—cemetery GA-3
McGaughey Ch—church GA-3
McGaughey Ditch—canal IN-6
McGaughey Lookout Tower—locale GA-3
McGaughey Swamp—swamp KY-4
McGaugh Sch—school CA-9
McGaugh Slough—stream CA-9
McGaughty Sch—school IL-6
McGaughy Lake—reservoir MS-4
McGaughys Windmill—locale NM-5
McGauhee Creek WA-9
McGauley Drain—canal MI-6
McGaurik Cem—cemetery MS-4
McGaver Creek—stream WI-6
McGavin Peak—summit CA-9
McGavock Cem—cemetery TN-4
McGavock Creek—stream (2) VA-3
McGavock Family Cemetery—hist pl VA-3
McGavock-Gaines House—hist pl TN-4
McGavock-Grider Memorial Park—park AR-4
McGavock Run—stream VA-3
McGavock Sch—school TN-4
McGavock (Township of)—fmr MCD AR-4
**McGaw**—pop pl OH-6
**McGaw Park**—pop pl IL-6
McGaw Sch—school IL-6
McGeach Creek—stream MI-6
McGeachy Cem—cemetery FL-3
McGeahy Bldg—hist pl NC-3
McGeary Creek—stream AK-9
McGeath Ditch—canal IN-6
McGee—locale MO-7
McGee—locale OK-5
McGee—locale SD-7
**McGee**—pop pl WV-2
McGee, John, House—hist pl KY-4
McGee, Mount—summit CA-9
McGee Bayou—stream LA-4
McGee Bend—bend GA-3
McGee Bend—bend TX-5
McGee Bend Dam—dam TX-5
McGee Bend Reservoir TX-5
McGee Branch—stream KY-4
McGee Branch—stream LA-4
McGee Branch—stream MO-7
McGee Branch—stream SC-3
McGee Burnett Cem—cemetery MS-4
McGee Canyon—valley (3) CA-9
McGee Canyon—valley (2) NM-5
McGee Canyon—valley OR-9
McGee Cave—cave TN-4
McGee Cem—cemetery (4) AL-4
McGee Cem—cemetery AR-4
McGee Cem—cemetery GA-3
McGee Cem—cemetery IL-6
McGee Cem—cemetery IA-7
McGee Cem—cemetery (2) KY-4
McGee Cem—cemetery (3) LA-4
McGee Cem—cemetery (4) MS-4
McGee Cem—cemetery MO-7
McGee Cem—cemetery NC-3
McGee Cem—cemetery (3) OH-6
McGee Cem—cemetery SC-3
McGee Cem—cemetery (3) TN-4
McGee Cem—cemetery (2) TX-5
McGee Ch—church MO-7
McGee Ch—church NC-3
McGee Ch—church OK-5
McGee Chapel—church MS-4
McGee Chapel—church MO-7
McGee Chapel—church OK-5
McGee Chapel—church TN-4
McGee Coulee—valley MT-8
McGee County KS-7
McGee Cove—valley TN-4
McGee Creek IL-6
McGee Creek WA-9
McGee Creek—stream AR-4
McGee Creek—stream (3) CA-9
McGee Creek—stream MS-4
McGee Creek—stream MO-7
McGee Creek—stream (2) MT-8
McGee Creek—stream NC-3
McGee Creek—stream (2) OK-5
McGee Creek—stream (2) OR-9
McGee Creek—stream TX-5
McGee Creek—stream WA-9
McGee Creek—stream WI-6
**McGee Crossroads**—pop pl NC-3
McGee Dam SD-7
McGee Dam—dam AL-4
McGee Dam—dam NC-3
McGee Dam—reservoir NC-3
McGee Ditch—canal CA-9
McGee Ditch—stream DE-2
McGee Flat—flat CA-9
McGee Grade—trail NV-8
Mc Gee Gulch—valley CO-8
McGee Gulch—valley WY-8
McGee Gully—valley TX-5
McGeehee MS-4
McGee Hill—cliff MT-8
McGee Hill—summit IL-6
McGee Hill—summit NY-2
McGee Hill—summit TX-5
McGee (historical)—locale AL-4
McGee Hole—cave TN-4
McGee Hollow—valley AR-4
McGee Hollow—valley OK-5
McGee Hollow—valley (3) TN-4
McGee House—hist pl NM-5
McGee-Hudson House—hist pl MS-4
McGee Island—island ME-1
McGee Lake CA-9
McGee Lake—lake (3) CA-9
McGee Lake—lake TX-5
McGee Lake—lake WI-6
McGee Lake—reservoir (2) AL-4
McGee Lake—reservoir WI-6
McGee Meadow—flat (2) CA-9
McGee Meadow—flat MT-8
McGee Meadow Overlook—locale MT-8
McGee Mill—locale NC-3
McGee Mill Hollow TN-4
McGee Mission—church LA-4
McGee Mountain Spring—spring NV-8
McGee Mtn—summit AZ-5
McGee Mtn—summit CA-9
McGee Mtn—summit NV-8
McGee Mtn—summit TN-4
McGee Pass—gap CA-9
McGee-Payne Cem—cemetery MO-7
McGee Peak—summit MT-8
McGee Point—cliff AR-4
McGee Pond—reservoir NC-3
McGee Ranch—locale AZ-5
McGee Ranch—locale NM-5
McGee Ranch—locale OR-9
McGee Ranger Station—locale ID-8
McGee Rsvr—reservoir WY-8
McGee Run PA-2
McGee Run—stream PA-2
McGee Run—stream VA-3
McGee Run—stream (3) WV-2
McGee Run Trail—trail WV-2

McGees Branch—*stream* AL-4
McGee Sch—*school* AL-4
McGee Sch—*school* AZ-5
McGee Sch—*school* MO-7
McGees Chapel—*church* WV-2
McGee Sch (historical)—*school* TN-4
*McGees Creek* MS-4
*McGees Creek* WA-9
McGees Ferry (historical)—*locale* AL-4
McGees (historical)—*locale* MS-4
McGees Landing (historical)—*locale* TN-4
McGee Slough—*stream* OR-9
*McGees Meadow* MT-8
McGees Mill Pond Dam—*dam* NC-3
**McGees Mills**—*pop pl* PA-2
McGees Mills Covered Bridge—*hist pl* PA-2
**McGees Mills (RR name McGees)**—*pop pl* PA-2
McGee Spring—*spring* NM-5
Mc Gee Spring—*spring* NC-3
McGee Spring—*spring* (2) TN-4
McGee Spring Cave—*cave* (2) TN-4
McGee Springs Cem—*cemetery* OK-5
McGees (RR name for McGees Mills)—*other* PA-2
*McGees Run* PA-2
*McGees Sliding* SD-7
McGees Station—*locale* PA-2
McGeetown—*locale* TN-4
**McGee Town**—*pop pl* AL-4
McGee Valley—*valley* OK-5
McGee Wash—*valley* AZ-5
McGee Well—*well* AZ-5
McGee Windmill—*locale* AZ-5
Mc Gee Windmill—*locale* CO-8
McGee Windmill—*locale* NM-5
McGegers Branch—*stream* NC-3
**McGehee**—*pop pl* AR-4
**McGehee**—*pop pl* MS-4
McGehee Bayou—*gut* AR-4
McGehee Branch—*stream* TN-4
*McGehee Cem* MS-4
McGehee Cem—*cemetery* AR-4
McGehee Cem—*cemetery* KS-7
McGehee Cem—*cemetery* (2) LA-4
McGehee Cem—*cemetery* (6) MS-4
McGehee Cem—*cemetery* OH-6
McGehee Coll for Girls (historical)—*school* MS-4
McGehee Creek—*stream* (3) MS-4
**McGehee Estates (subdivision)**—*pop pl* AL-4
McGehee Hall, Southeastern Louisiana State Univ—*hist pl* LA-4
McGehee Hollow—*valley* TX-5
McGehee House—*hist pl* LA-4
McGehee House—*hist pl* MS-4
McGehee Mtn—*summit* AL-4
**McGehees**—*pop pl* AL-4
McGehee Sch—*school* LA-4
McGehees Chapel Cem—*cemetery* MS-4
*McGehees Chapel Methodist Church* MS-4
McGehees (Hope Hull)—*other* AL-4
*McGehees Landing* MS-4
McGehees Mill—*locale* NC-3
McGehee Spring—*spring* AL-4
*McGehees Station* AL-4
*McGehees Switch* AL-4
McGehee-Stringfellow House—*hist pl* AL-4
McGehee Well—*well* NM-5
McGehee-Woodall House—*hist pl* GA-3
McGellairds Brook—*stream* NJ-2
McGenis Mine (underground)—*mine* AL-4
McGeorge Cem—*cemetery* KY-4
McGeorge Pond—*reservoir* VA-3
**Mcgeorges**—*pop pl* ME-1
McGeorge Sch of Law—*school* CA-9
**McGerrow Village**—*pop pl* HI-9
McGery Canyon—*valley* NV-8
McGhee—*locale* MS-4
**McGhee**—*pop pl* AL-4
**McGhee**—*pop pl* TN-4
*McGhee Branch* TN-4
McGhee Branch—*stream* AR-4
McGhee-Carson House Ruins—*locale* TN-4
McGhee Cem—*cemetery* (2) AL-4
McGhee Cem—*cemetery* AR-4
McGhee Cem—*cemetery* IL-6
Mc Ghee Cem—*cemetery* NC-3
McGhee Cem—*cemetery* (3) TN-4
McGhee Cem—*cemetery* VA-3
McGhee Chapel—*church* GA-3
*McGhee Creek* DE-2
McGhee Creek—*stream* VA-3
McGhee Gap—*gap* TN-4
McGhee Gulch—*valley* MT-8
McGhee Hollow—*valley* TN-4
McGhee Island—*island* TN-4
McGhee Lake—*lake* AR-4
McGhee Lake Number Two—*reservoir* AL-4
McGhee Peak—*summit* NM-5
Mcghee Pond—*dam* AL-4
McGhee Post Office (historical)—*building* AL-4
McGhee Post Office (historical)—*building* TN-4
**McGhees Bend**—*pop pl* AL-4
McGhee Sch—*school* PA-2
*McGhees Ferry* TN-4
*McGhees Island* TN-4
McGhees Station Post Office (historical)—*building* TN-4
McGhee Tyson Airp—*airport* TN-4
McGhee Wells—*locale* NM-5
McGibney Sch—*school* PA-2
McGibneys Lake—*lake* MN-6
McGiffert Cem—*cemetery* AL-4
McGiffin Hollow—*valley* TN-4
McGifford Branch—*stream* LA-4
McGifford (historical)—*locale* AL-4
McGilberry Branch—*stream* TX-5
McGilberry Cem—*cemetery* TX-5
McGilberry Lake—*lake* TX-5
McGilbert House—*hist pl* TX-5
*McGill* CA-9
*McGill* PA-2
*McGill* SD-7
McGill—*locale* CA-9
**McGill**—*pop pl* NV-8
**McGill**—*pop pl* OH-6
**McGill**—*pop pl* WV-2
McGill, Andrew R., House—*hist pl* MN-6
McGill, John H., House—*hist pl* MA-1
McGill Airstrip—*airport* OR-9
*McGill Bay* FL-3
McGill Branch—*stream* MO-7
McGill Branch—*stream* NC-3
McGill Branch—*stream* SC-3
McGill Branch—*stream* TN-4
McGill Bridge—*bridge* WY-8
McGill Canyon—*valley* (2) NV-8
McGill Cem—*cemetery* AL-4
McGill Cem—*cemetery* (2) AR-4
McGill Cem—*cemetery* IN-6
McGill Cem—*cemetery* KS-7
McGill Cem—*cemetery* MS-4
McGill Cem—*cemetery* NE-7
McGill Cem—*cemetery* NC-3
McGill Cem—*cemetery* TN-4
*McGill Creek* CA-9
McGill Creek—*stream* (2) CA-9
McGill Creek—*stream* MD-2
McGill Creek—*stream* MS-4
McGill Creek—*stream* MO-7
McGill Creek—*stream* NE-7
McGill Creek—*stream* NC-3
McGill Creek—*stream* TN-4
*McGill Cutoff* FL-3
McGill Ditch—*canal* ID-8
McGillem Cem—*cemetery* IN-6
McGill Gulf—*valley* TN-4
McGill Hole—*lake* TX-5
McGill Hollow—*valley* AR-4
Mc Gill Hollow—*valley* MO-7
McGill Hollow—*valley* TN-4
McGillian Hollow—*valley* IL-6
McGillicuddys Duck Pond—*lake* WA-9
McGilligan Creek—*stream* KY-4
McGill Institute—*school* AL-4
*McGillis Creek* ND-7
McGillis Creek—*stream* MI-6
*McGill Island* FL-3
McGillivray Cem—*cemetery* IL-6
McGillivray Draw—*valley* NM-5
McGill Junction—*locale* NV-8
McGill Lake—*reservoir* OK-5
McGill Lakes—*lake* WY-8
*McGill Meadow* CA-9
*McGill Memorial Church* TN-4
McGill Mtn—*summit* AR-4
McGill Pond—*reservoir* GA-3
McGill Ranch—*locale* TX-5
McGill Ranch—*locale* (2) WY-8
McGill Ridge—*ridge* CA-9
McGill Run—*stream* MD-2
McGill Run—*stream* OH-6
**McGills Addition (subdivision)**—*pop pl* UT-8
McGills Bridge (historical)—*bridge* MS-4
McGill Sch—*school* MI-6
McGill Sch—*school* MS-4
McGill Sch—*school* MO-7
McGill Sch—*school* PA-2
McGill Sch—*school* TX-5
*McGills Creek* TN-4
McGills Creek—*stream* KY-4
*McGills Hill* AL-4
*McGills Island* FL-3
McGills Lake—*reservoir* GA-3
McGills Pond—*reservoir* GA-3
McGill Spring—*spring* NV-8
McGill Spring—*spring* TN-4
McGill Spring (Swimming Pool)—*spring* NV-8
McGillstown—*locale* PA-2
McGillvery Sch—*school* SD-7
McGilton Branch—*stream* KY-4
McGilvary Cem—*cemetery* MS-4
McGilvery, Capt. John, House—*hist pl* ME-1
McGilvery, Capt. William, House—*hist pl* ME-1
McGilvery Canyon—*valley* OR-9
McGilvery Creek—*stream* AK-9
McGilvery Creek—*stream* WA-9
McGilvery Island—*island* TX-5
McGilvery Lake—*lake* MI-6
McGilvrary Lake—*lake* MT-8
McGilvra Sch—*school* WA-9
McGilvra Spring—*spring* WA-9
McGilvray Lateral—*canal* CA-9
McGilvrey Creek—*stream* MT-8
*Mcgilvrey Pond* ME-1
McGilvry Pond—*lake* ME-1
McGinley Cem—*cemetery* TN-4
Mc Ginley Creek—*stream* CO-8
Mc Ginley Gulch—*valley* CO-8
McGinley Gulch—*valley* MT-8
Mc Ginley Hill—*summit* PA-2
Mc Ginley Mine—*mine* CO-8
McGinley Ranch—*locale* (2) NE-7
Mc Ginley Spring—*spring* CO-8
McGinley Spring—*spring* TN-4
McGinn Brook—*stream* NY-2
McGinn Brook—*stream* VT-1
McGinn Creek—*stream* CA-9
McGinn Creek—*stream* MI-6
Mc Ginn Ditch—*canal* CO-8
McGinnel Spring—*spring* AZ-5
**Mcginnes**—*pop pl* MD-2
*Mcginness* MD-2
McGinness, Lake—*lake* MO-7
McGinness, Lake—*reservoir* MO-7
McGinness Airp—*airport* PA-2
McGinness Mine—*mine* NV-8
McGinness Ranch—*locale* ID-8
McGinnet Corners—*locale* PA-2
*Mcginneys Ford* TN-4
McGinn Hill—*summit* CA-9
McGinn Hill—*summit* NY-2
McGinnis—*airport* NJ-2
**McGinnis**—*pop pl* MD-2
McGinnis, J. S., Bldg—*hist pl* ID-8
McGinnis Branch—*stream* KY-4
McGinnis Branch—*stream* TN-4
McGinnis Branch—*stream* WV-2
McGinnis Butte—*summit* MT-8
McGinnis Canyon—*valley* WA-9
McGinnis Cem—*cemetery* GA-3
McGinnis Cem—*cemetery* IL-6
McGinnis Cem—*cemetery* (3) KY-4
McGinnis Cem—*cemetery* MO-7
McGinnis Cem—*cemetery* ND-7
McGinnis Cem—*cemetery* (3) TN-4
McGinnis Cem—*cemetery* TX-5
McGinnis Cem—*cemetery* (2) WV-2
McGinnis Chapel—*church* MS-4
McGinnis Creek—*stream* AK-9
McGinnis Creek—*stream* (2) CA-9
McGinnis Creek—*stream* ID-8
McGinnis Creek—*stream* (5) MT-8
McGinnis Creek—*stream* (3) OR-9
McGinnis Creek—*stream* WA-9
McGinnis Creek—*stream* (3) WI-6
**McGinnis Crossroads**—*pop pl* NC-3
McGinnis Ditch—*canal* IN-6
McGinnis Ditch—*canal* MT-8
McGinnis Ford—*locale* TN-4
McGinnis Glacier—*glacier* AK-9
McGinnis Harrell Cem—*cemetery* TN-4
McGinnis Hollow—*valley* PA-2
*Mc Ginnis Lake* CO-8
Mc Ginnis Lake—*lake* CO-8
McGinnis Lake—*lake* (2) MI-6
McGinnis Lake—*lake* WA-9
McGinnis Lake—*lake* (2) WI-6
McGinnis Lake—*reservoir* WI-6
McGinnis Levee—*levee* IN-6
McGinnis Meadows—*flat* MT-8
McGinnis Mtn—*summit* AK-9
McGinnis Pass—*gap* WY-8
McGinnis Peak—*summit* AK-9
McGinnis Point—*cape* TX-5
McGinnis Pond—*reservoir* DE-2
Mcginnis Pond Dam—*dam* DE-2
McGinnis Ranch—*locale* NV-8
McGinnis Ravine—*valley* CA-9
*Mcginnis Run* PA-2
McGinnis Sch—*school* MO-7
McGinnis Sch—*school* NJ-2
McGinnis Spring—*spring* TX-5
McGinnis Springs—*spring* CA-9
**Mcginnis Township**—*pop pl* ND-7
McGinnity Pond—*lake* NY-2
McGinn Lake—*lake* MI-6
McGinn Meadows—*swamp* NY-2
*Mcginn's Gulch* CO-8
*McGinny Chapel* MS-4
McGinty—*locale* LA-4
**McGinty**—*pop pl* AL-4
**McGinty**—*pop pl* LA-4
McGinty Bayou—*stream* MS-4
McGinty Canyon—*valley* UT-8
McGinty Cove—*bay* MI-6
McGinty Creek—*stream* (2) ID-8
McGinty Creek—*stream* MI-6
Mc Ginty Creek—*stream* NC-3
McGinty Gulch—*valley* MT-8
McGinty Hollow—*valley* MO-7
McGinty Mtn—*summit* CA-9
McGinty Point—*cape* AK-9
McGinty Point—*cape* CA-9
McGinty Ridge—*ridge* ID-8
McGinty Ridge—*ridge* UT-8
McGinty Rsvr—*reservoir* CA-9
McGinty Sch—*school* LA-4
McGintytown—*locale* AR-4
**McGirk**—*pop pl* MO-7
McGirk Cem—*cemetery* TX-5
McGirk Island—*area* MO-7
McGirk School—*locale* TX-5
**McGirr**—*pop pl* IL-6
McGirr Sch—*school* IL-6
McGirts Creek—*stream* FL-3
McGirts Creek—*stream* SC-3
McGirts Millpond—*reservoir* SC-3
*Mcgirts River* FL-3
*Mcgiven Run* PA-2
*McGiven Run* WV-2
McGivern Park—*park* MN-6
McGlamery Cem—*cemetery* TN-4
**McGlamerys Stand**—*pop pl* TN-4
McGlannan Sch and Language Arts Center—*school* FL-3
McGlannon Sch—*school* FL-3
McGlashan Point—*summit* CA-9
McGlasson Cem—*cemetery* KY-4
McGlasson Cem—*cemetery* TX-5
McGlathery Island—*island* ME-1
McGlathery Sch—*school* MS-4
McGlauflin House—*hist pl* MT-8
McGlaughlin Peak—*summit* MT-8
McGlawin Creek—*stream* MS-4
McGlen Buttes—*spring* MT-8
*Mcglendon Gap* AL-4
**McGlendon Mill**—*pop pl* AR-4
*McGlennen Church* MS-4
McGlinchey Spring—*spring* CA-9
McGlinn Island—*island* WA-9
McGloin, James, Homestead—*hist pl* TX-5
McGloin, James, Homestead (Boundary Increase)—*hist pl* TX-5
McGloins Bluff—*cliff* TX-5
McGlone—*locale* WV-2
**McGlone**—*pop pl* KY-4
McGlone Fork—*stream* (2) KY-4
**Mcglone Heights**—*pop pl* MT-8
McGlothin Cem—*cemetery* VA-3
McGlothlin Cem—*cemetery* (2) VA-3
McGloughlin Cem—*cemetery* LA-4
McGlynn Creek—*stream* OR-9
McGlynn Creek—*stream* WI-6
McGlynn Dam—*dam* MT-8
*McGlynn Island* WA-9
McGolrick, Monsignor, Park and Shelter Pavilion—*hist pl* NY-2
McGolrick Park—*park* NY-2
McGonagall Gulch—*valley* AK-9
McGonagall Mtn—*summit* AK-9
McGonagall Pass—*gap* AK-9
McGonagle Site, RI-1227—*hist pl* RI-1
McGonigal Cem—*cemetery* MS-4
**McGonigle**—*pop pl* OH-6
McGonigle Canyon—*valley* CA-9
McGonigle Cem—*cemetery* KS-7
McGooden Ranch—*locale* NE-7
McGoon Pond—*lake* ME-1
McGooseley Pond—*lake* ME-1
McGoragill Ranch—*locale* NM-5
McGormley Cem—*cemetery* OH-6
McGothy Channel—*channel* VA-3
McGougan Cem—*cemetery* NC-3
McGough New Slope Mine (underground)—*mine* AL-4
McGough Pond—*reservoir* AL-4
McGough Sch (historical)—*school* AL-4
McGough Springs—*spring* TX-5
McGouirk Dam—*dam* AL-4
McGouirk Lake—*reservoir* AL-4
McGourvey Run—*stream* PA-2
**McGovern**—*pop pl* PA-2
McGovern Brook—*stream* MA-1
McGovern Creek—*stream* (2) MT-8
McGovern Gap—*gap* CA-9
McGovern Park—*park* WI-6
Mc Govern Ridge—*ridge* CA-9
McGovern Sch—*school* PA-2
McGoverns Creek—*stream* MI-6
**McGovernsville**—*pop pl* PA-2
McGowan—*locale* KY-4
McGowan—*locale* WA-9
**McGowan**—*pop pl* AL-4
McGowan Basin—*basin* ID-8
McGowan Branch—*stream* AL-4
McGowan Branch—*stream* GA-3
McGowan Branch—*stream* TN-4
McGowan Bridge—*bridge* AL-4
McGowan Brook—*stream* RI-1
McGowan Brook—*stream* VT-1
McGowan Butte—*summit* ID-8
McGowan Butte—*summit* WA-9
McGowan Canyon—*valley* CA-9
McGowan Chapel—*church* MS-4
McGowan Chapel Cem—*cemetery* MS-4
**McGowan Corners**—*pop pl* RI-1
*McGowan Creek* SC-3
McGowan Creek—*stream* ID-8
McGowan Creek—*stream* NC-3
McGowan Creek—*stream* OR-9
McGowan Ditch—*canal* ID-8
Mc Gowan Homestead—*locale* CO-8
McGowan Hunting Club—*locale* AL-4
McGowan Lake—*lake* CA-9
McGowan Lake—*lake* MN-6
*McGowan Mountain* SC-3
McGowan Mountain Trail—*trail* WV-2
McGowan Mountain Way—*trail* OR-9
McGowan Mtn—*summit* OR-9
McGowan Mtn—*summit* WV-2
McGowan Park—*park* IA-7
McGowan Pond—*lake* ME-1
Mc Gowan Rsvr—*reservoir* CO-8
*McGowans* WA-9
McGowan Sch—*school* MI-6
McGowans Channel—*channel* OR-9
**McGowans Crossing**—*pop pl* IL-6
McGowans Ferry (historical)—*locale* AL-4
McGowans Lake—*lake* PA-2
McGowansville Post Office (historical)—*building* TN-4
McGowen Brake—*swamp* LA-4
McGowen Cave—*cave* AR-4
McGowen Cem—*cemetery* LA-4
McGowen Cem—*cemetery* MS-4
McGowen Pond—*lake* FL-3
McGowen Sch (historical)—*school* AL-4
*McGowers Creek* MS-4
McGowin Branch—*stream* AL-4
McGowin Bridge—*locale* AL-4
McGowin Cem—*cemetery* AL-4
McGowin Ch—*church* AL-4
McGowin Dam—*dam* AL-4
McGowin Ferry Cem—*cemetery* AL-4
Mcgowin Field (airport)—*airport* AL-4
McGowin Lake—*reservoir* AL-4
Mcgowin Pond Dam—*dam* AL-4
McGown, Floyd, House—*hist pl* TX-5
McGown Cem—*cemetery* TX-5
McGown Creek—*stream* ID-8
McGown Lakes—*lake* ID-8
McGown Peak—*summit* ID-8
Mc Grade Sch—*school* MT-8
**McGrady**—*pop pl* NC-3
McGrady Bend—*bend* GA-3
McGrady Cem—*cemetery* AL-4
McGrady Cem—*cemetery* MO-7
McGrady Cem—*cemetery* TX-5
*McGrady Creek* KY-4
McGrady Creek—*stream* KY-4
McGrady Creek Ch—*church* KY-4
*McGrady Ditch* IN-6
McGrady Lake—*lake* MN-6
McGrae Swamp—*swamp* NY-2
McGraff Canyon—*valley* NV-8
McGraft Park—*park* MI-6
McGrain JHS—*school* MI-6
**McGrann**—*pop pl* PA-2
McGrann Playground—*park* MA-1
McGrary Cem—*cemetery* OH-6
McGrass Creek—*stream* WI-6
**McGrath**—*pop pl* AK-9
**McGrath**—*pop pl* MN-6
**McGrath**—*pop pl* MS-4
McGrath Airp—*airport* AK-9
McGrath Ditch—*canal* WY-8
McGrath-Holy Cross (Census Subarea)—*cens area* AK-9
*McGrath Lake* UT-8
McGrath Lake—*lake* CA-9
McGrath Lake—*lake* WI-6
McGrath Point—*cape* NY-2
McGrath Pond—*lake* ME-1
McGrath School (Abandoned)—*locale* MN-6
McGraugh Ranch—*locale* WY-8
McGravey Lakes—*lake* WA-9
*Mcgraw* ME-1
*McGraw* WV-2
McGraw—*locale* KS-7
**McGraw**—*pop pl* NY-2
McGraw Bottom—*bend* UT-8
McGraw Butte—*summit* MT-8
*McGraw Cem* MS-4
McGraw Cem—*cemetery* MS-4
McGraw Cem—*cemetery* OH-6
McGraw Cem—*cemetery* WV-2
McGraw Ch—*church* KS-7
McGraw Copper Mine—*mine* WY-8
McGraw Corners—*locale* NY-2
McGraw Corners—*locale* PA-2
McGraw Coulee—*valley* (2) MT-8
*McGraw Creek* TN-4
McGraw Creek—*stream* MI-6
McGraw Creek—*stream* OR-9
McGraw Creek—*stream* (2) TX-5
McGraw Drain—*canal* MI-6
McGraw Flats—*flat* WY-8
McGraw Gap—*gap* VA-3
McGraw Hill—*summit* KY-4
McGraw-Hill Bldg—*hist pl* NY-2
McGraw Hollow—*valley* VA-3
Mcgraw House—*hist pl* OH-6
McGraw Lake—*lake* MI-6
McGraw Lake—*lake* TX-5
McGraw Lake—*lake* WI-6
McGraw Lake Dam—*dam* (2) MS-4
McGraw Memorial Hall—*locale* IL-6
McGraw Mountain—*ridge* AR-4
McGraw Mtn—*summit* GA-3
**McGraw Park (Industrial Area)**—*pop pl* IL-6
Mc Graw Ranch—*locale* CO-8
McGraw Ranch—*locale* NE-7
McGraw Run—*stream* (2) WV-2
McGraws—*locale* NY-2
**McGraws**—*pop pl* WV-2
McGraw Sch—*school* AZ-5
McGraw Sch—*school* MI-6
McGraw Sch—*school* NJ-2
McGraw Sch—*school* WV-2
McGraw Sch (abandoned)—*school* PA-2
*McGraws Creek* TX-5
McGraws Mill (historical)—*locale* AL-4
**McGrawsville**—*pop pl* IN-6
McGraw Swamp—*swamp* NY-2
*McGrawville* NY-2
McGrawville—*locale* NY-2
McGrawville Rural Cem—*cemetery* NY-2
McGray—*locale* ME-1
McGray Ditch—*canal* IN-6
McGray Park—*park* AL-4
*McGready* VA-3
McGready, Rev. James, House—*hist pl* KY-4
McGreevy School—*locale* IL-6
McGreggor Place—*locale* NM-5
McGregor—*hist pl* MS-4
Mc Gregor—*locale* CO-8
McGregor—*locale* GA-3
**McGregor**—*pop pl* AR-4
**McGregor**—*pop pl* IA-7
**McGregor**—*pop pl* MI-6
**McGregor**—*pop pl* MN-6
**McGregor**—*pop pl* ND-7
**McGregor**—*pop pl* PA-2
**McGregor**—*pop pl* TX-5
McGregor, George, Cabin—*hist pl* AK-9
McGregor, Walker, Farmstead—*hist pl* SD-7
McGregor Apartments—*hist pl* UT-8
McGregor Baptist Ch—*church* FL-3
McGregor Bluff—*cliff* AL-4
McGregor Brake—*swamp* AR-4
McGregor Branch—*stream* NC-3
McGregor Cabin—*locale* AK-9
McGregor Canyon—*valley* CA-9
McGregor (CCD)—*cens area* TX-5
McGregor Cem—*cemetery* GA-3
McGregor Cem—*cemetery* KY-4
McGregor Cem—*cemetery* TN-4
McGregor Chapel—*church* MS-4
McGregor Country Club—*other* NY-2
McGregor Creek—*stream* MI-6
McGregor Creek—*stream* MT-8
McGregor Creek—*stream* TN-4
McGregor Creek—*stream* WA-9
Mcgregor Dam—*dam* AL-4
McGregor Dam—*dam* ND-7
McGregor Dam*—*dam* SD-7
McGregor Downs Lake—*reservoir* NC-3
McGregor Downs Lake Dam—*dam* NC-3
McGregor Flat—*flat* CA-9
**McGregor Gardens**—*pop pl* FL-3
McGregor Groves—*locale* FL-3
Mc Gregor Gulch—*valley* MT-8
McGregor Heights—*locale* IA-7
McGregor Island—*island* OR-9
McGregor Lake—*lake* MT-8
McGregor Lake—*lake* WI-6
Mcgregor Lake—*reservoir* AL-4
McGregor Meadows—*flat* WA-9
McGregor Mill—*locale* ME-1
McGregor Mines—*mine* PA-2
*McGregor Mountain* CO-8
McGregor Mtn—*summit* NY-2
McGregor Mtn—*summit* WA-9
McGregor Oil and Gas Field—*oilfield* ND-7
McGregor Park—*flat* WY-8
McGregor Park—*park* OR-9
McGregor Park—*park* TN-4
McGregor Park—*park* TX-5
McGregor Peak—*summit* MT-8
McGregor Point—*cape* HI-9
McGregor Point—*cape* VT-1
McGregor Point—*cape* WI-6
McGregor Point Shop Ctr—*locale* FL-3
McGregor Ranch—*hist pl* WA-9
McGregor Ranch—*locale* NM-5
McGregor Ranch—*locale* TX-5
McGregor Ranch—*locale* WA-9
McGregor Ridge—*ridge* CA-9
McGregor Run—*stream* WV-2
McGregor Sch—*school* (2) MI-6
McGregor Sch—*SCHOOL* MN-6
McGregor Sch—*school* MO-7
McGregor Sch—*school* (2) OH-6
*McGregors Chapel Free Will Baptist Ch* MS-4
**McGregors Hill**—*pop pl* IN-6
McGregors Pond—*lake* NH-1
McGregor Spring—*spring* NV-8
**McGregor (Township of)**—*pop pl* MN-6
McGregory Brook—*stream* NY-2
McGregory Buttes—*range* ND-7
McGregory Creek—*stream* MS-4
*McGrew* MI-6
McGrew—*locale* NE-7
**McGrew**—*pop pl* NE-7
McGrew Branch—*stream* TX-5
McGrew Cem—*cemetery* IN-6
McGrew Cem—*cemetery* MO-7
McGrew Ch—*church* KY-4
McGrew Creek—*stream* TN-4
McGrew Hollow—*valley* TN-4
McGrew Junction—*locale* MI-6
McGrew Point—*cape* HI-9
**Mcgrew Point (Capehart Housing)**—*pop pl* HI-9
Mc Grew Rsvr—*reservoir* CO-8
McGrews Ferry (historical)—*locale* AL-4
McGrews Fort (historical)—*military* AL-4
McGrew Spring—*spring* AZ-5
McGrew Spring—*spring* CA-9
McGrews Shoals—*bar* AL-4
McGrew Tank—*reservoir* NM-5
McGrew Well—*well* TX-5
McGribble Campground—*park* OR-9
McGribble Guard Station—*locale* OR-9
*McGriffin Fork* MT-8
McGriff Lakes—*lake* CA-9
McGrillis Hill—*summit* NH-1
*McGrits Creek* SC-3
McGroarty Park—*park* CA-9
McGrogan Creek—*stream* WI-6
*McGrory Gap* AL-4
McGruder Creek—*stream* IA-7
McGruder Hill—*summit* NM-5
McGruder Hollow—*valley* TN-4
McGruder Mine—*mine* CO-8
McGruder Ranch—*locale* TX-5
McGruders Landing—*locale* MS-4
McGruder Spring—*spring* NM-5
McGrue Creek—*stream* TX-5
*McGuaine Hollow* NY-2
McGuane Field—*park* CT-1
McGuane Park—*park* IL-6
McGuan Hollow—*valley* NY-2
McGuff Creek—*stream* VA-3
**McGuffey**—*pop pl* OH-6
McGuffey, William H., Boyhood Home Site—*hist pl* OH-6
McGuffey, William H., House—*hist pl* OH-6
McGuffey Branch—*stream* TN-4
*McGuffey Heights* OH-6
**McGuffey Heights**—*pop pl* OH-6
McGuffey Sch—*school* (3) OH-6
McGuffey Sch—*school* VA-3
McGuffie Mine—*mine* AZ-5
McGuffin Branch—*stream* KY-4
McGuffin Ranch—*locale* NM-5
McGuffintown Bridge—*bridge* PA-2
McGuffin Trail—*trail* VA-3
McGuffy Creek—*stream* CA-9
McGuffy Plaza—*locale* OH-6
*McGugin Field* KS-7
McGugin Tunnel—*tunnel* PA-2
McGuill Cem—*cemetery* TX-5
McGuill Lake—*lake* TX-5
McGuilons Bar—*bar* AL-4
McGuiness Pond—*lake* MO-7
McGuinness Sch—*school* NY-2
McGuinnis Cem—*cemetery* KY-4
McGuinns Ferry (historical)—*locale* AL-4
McGuir Cabin—*locale* AK-9
*McGuire* NJ-2
**McGuire**—*pop pl* ID-8
**McGuire**—*pop pl* MO-7
McGuire, Mount—*summit* ID-8
McGuire AFB—*military* NJ-2
Mc Guire AFB—*military* NJ-2
McGuire Branch—*stream* (2) KY-4
McGuire Branch—*stream* (2) MO-7
McGuire Brook—*stream* NY-2
*McGuire Canyon* OR-9
*McGuire Canyon* UT-8
McGuire Canyon—*valley* TX-5
McGuire Cem—*cemetery* KY-4
McGuire Cem—*cemetery* (4) MO-7
McGuire Cem—*cemetery* NE-7
McGuire Cem—*cemetery* NC-3
Mc Guire Cem—*cemetery* NC-3
McGuire Cem—*cemetery* OK-5
McGuire Cem—*cemetery* TN-4
McGuire Cem—*cemetery* VA-3
McGuire Ch—*church* IA-7
McGuire Circle—*locale* VA-3
Mc Guire Creek—*stream* CO-8
McGuire Creek—*stream* (3) ID-8
McGuire Creek—*stream* MI-6
McGuire Creek—*stream* (2) MT-8
McGuire Creek—*stream* OH-6
McGuire Creek—*stream* TN-4
McGuire Creek—*stream* VA-3
McGuire Creek—*stream* WA-9
McGuire Creek Bay—*bay* MT-8
McGuire Crossing—*locale* AZ-5
McGuire Dam—*dam* OR-9
McGuire Ditch—*canal* OH-6
McGuire Ford—*locale* AL-4
McGuire Fork—*stream* KY-4
McGuire Gilliland Ditch—*canal* OH-6
McGuire Gulch—*valley* CA-9
McGuire Gulch—*valley* MT-8
McGuire Gulch—*valley* OR-9
McGuire Hammock—*island* FL-3
McGuire Hill—*summit* CA-9
McGuire Hill—*summit* MT-8
McGuire Hollow—*valley* UT-8
McGuire Hollow—*valley* VA-3
McGuire Island—*island* OR-9
McGuire Island—*island* PA-2
*McGuire Lake* CA-9
*McGuire Lake* WI-6
McGuire Lake—*lake* AR-4
McGuire Lake—*lake* MN-6
McGuire Lake—*reservoir* NC-3
McGuire Lake—*reservoir* TX-5
McGuire Lake Dam—*dam* NC-3
McGuire Lake Number One—*lake* LA-4
McGuire Lake Number Two—*lake* LA-4
McGuire Lakes—*lake* CA-9
McGuire Mine—*mine* TN-4
McGuire Mountain—*locale* WV-2
McGuire Mtn—*summit* CA-9
McGuire Mtn—*summit* MT-8
McGuire Mtn—*summit* NY-2
McGuire Nuclear Station—*building* NC-3
McGuire Park—*park* MN-6
**McGuire Park**—*pop pl* WV-2
McGuire Peak—*summit* CA-9
McGuire Point—*cape* ME-1
McGuire Ranch—*locale* NM-5
McGuire Ridge—*ridge* CA-9
McGuire Ridge—*ridge* IN-6
McGuire Rsvr—*reservoir* OR-9
McGuire Run—*stream* PA-2
*McGuires* MO-7
McGuires—*locale* NC-3
McGuire Sch—*school* ID-8
McGuire Sch—*school* IL-6
McGuire Sch—*school* MI-6

McGuire Sch—*school* ... MO-7
McGuire Sch (abandoned)—*school* ... PA-2
McGuires Chapel—*church* ... AL-4
McGuire Sch (historical)—*school* ... AL-4
McGuire Sch (historical)—*school* ... MO-7
McGuire Spring—*spring* ... AL-4
McGuire Spring—*spring* ... ID-8
McGuire Spring—*spring* ... OR-9
McGuire Spring—*spring* ... TX-5
McGuires Sch—*hist pl* ... ID-8
McGuires ( Siding)—*locale* ... ID-8
McGuires Slough—*stream* ... NE-7
McGuires Wharf—*locale* ... VA-3
McGuire Tank—*reservoir* ... TX-5
McGuire Valley—*valley* ... VA-3
McGuire Veterans Hosptial—*hospital* ... VA-3
**McGuireville**—*pop pl* ... AZ-5
McGuireville Interchange—*crossing* ... AZ-5
McGuire Well—*well* ... TX-5
McGuirks Tanks—*reservoir* ... TX-5
*McGuirs Hollow* ... UT-8
McGulley Branch—*stream* ... KY-4
McGullion Mtn—*summit* ... SC-3
McGulpin Point—*cape* ... MI-6
*McGulpin's* ... MI-6
McGunnegle Tank—*reservoir* ... TX-5
McGurdy Stream—*stream* ... ME-1
McGurk Cabin—*hist pl* ... CA-9
McGurk Meadow—*flat* ... CA-9
McGuyer Branch—*stream* ... TX-5
McGuyer Cave—*cave* ... AL-4
**McHaddon**—*pop pl* ... PA-2
McHaffey Windmill—*locale* ... NM-5
McHaffie, Melville F., Farm—*hist pl* ... IN-6
McHaffie Cem—*cemetery* ... MO-7
*McHaffie Cemetery* ... TN-4
McHaffie Ch—*church* ... MO-7
McHaffie Gap—*gap* ... TN-4
McHaffie Sch (abandoned)—*school* ... MO-7
**McHale**—*pop pl* ... MI-6
McHale (historical)—*locale* ... KS-7
McHaley Creek—*stream* ... KY-4
McHaley Creek—*stream* ... OR-9
McHan Cem—*cemetery* ... NC-3
McHan Cove—*valley* ... NC-3
*McHan Creek* ... ID-8
McHaney Branch—*stream* ... TN-4
**McHaney (historical)**—*pop pl* ... TN-4
McHaney Post Office (historical)—*building* ... TN-4
McHan Gulch—*valley* ... ID-8
McHan Knob—*summit* ... NC-3
McHann Lake Dam—*dam* (2) ... MS-4
McHan Rsvr—*reservoir* ... ID-8
McHarg—*locale* ... MI-6
McHarg—*locale* ... TN-4
McHarg, Joseph S., House—*hist pl* ... IA-7
McHarg Creek—*stream* ... ID-8
McHarg Sch—*school* ... VA-3
McHargue—*locale* ... KY-4
McHargue Ditch—*canal* ... IN-6
McHargue Mtn—*summit* ... NC-3
McHarry Hill—*summit* ... IN-6
McHarry Pond—*reservoir* ... IL-6
McHat Tank—*reservoir* ... AZ-5
Mc Hatten Creek—*stream* ... CO-8
Mc Hatten Rsvr—*reservoir* ... CO-8
McHattie—*locale* ... TX-5
Mc Hatton Rsvr—*reservoir* ... CO-8
McHayneys Mill Creek—*stream* ... TN-4
McHayneys Mill (historical)—*locale* ... TN-4
McHeard Brook—*stream* ... ME-1
McHeffy Butte—*summit* ... AZ-5
McHendree Cem—*cemetery* ... MO-7
McHenry—*locale* ... CA-9
McHenry—*locale* ... ID-8
McHenry—*locale* ... VA-3
**McHenry**—*pop pl* ... IL-6
**McHenry**—*pop pl* ... KY-4
**McHenry**—*pop pl* ... MD-2
**McHenry**—*pop pl* ... MS-4
**McHenry**—*pop pl* ... ND-7
McHenry, George Austin, House—*hist pl* ... MS-4
McHenry, William A., House—*hist pl* ... IA-7
McHenry Anchorage—*bay* ... AK-9
Mchenry Branch—*stream* ... AR-4
McHenry Branch stroam ... AR-4
McHenry Branch—*stream* ... MS-4
McHenry Canyon—*valley* ... UT-8
McHenry Cem—*cemetery* ... IL-6
McHenry Cem—*cemetery* (2) ... MO-7
McHenry Cem—*cemetery* ... PA-2
McHenry Cem—*cemetery* ... TX-5
McHenry Cem—*cemetery* ... WV-2
McHenry Ch—*church* ... IL-6
*McHenry Church* ... PA-2
McHenry County—*civil* ... ND-7
**McHenry (County)**—*pop pl* ... IL-6
McHenry County Courthouse—*hist pl* ... ND-7
*McHenry Creek* ... AR-4
McHenry Creek—*stream* ... AR-4
McHenry Creek—*stream* (2) ... VA-3
McHenry Dam—*dam* ... SD-7
McHenry Dam Number 1—*dam* ... ND-7
McHenry Dam State Park—*park* ... IL-6
McHenry Ditch—*canal* ... IL-6
McHenry Ditch—*canal* ... IN-6
McHenry Flat—*flat* ... OR-9
McHenry Fork—*stream* ... VA-3
McHenry Hollow—*valley* ... MO-7
McHenry Inlet—*bay* ... AK-9
McHenry Island—*island* ... WI-6
McHenry JHS—*school* ... GA-3
McHenry Lake—*lake* ... AK-9
McHenry Lake—*lake* ... IN-6
McHenry Lateral—*canal* ... ID-8
McHenry Ledge—*bar* ... AK-9
McHenry Lookout Tower—*locale* ... MS-4
McHenry Mansion—*hist pl* ... CA-9
*McHenry Mountain* ... TN-4
McHenry Park—*park* ... IA-7
McHenry-Rockport (CCD)—*cens area* ... KY-4
McHenry RR Loop—*hist pl* ... ND-7
McHenry Sch—*school* ... MD-2
*McHenry Shores* ... IL-6
**McHenry Shores**—*pop pl* ... IL-6
McHenry Slough—*gut* ... IL-6
McHenry Slough—*stream* ... IL-6
Mc Henrys Notch—*gap* ... CO-8
Mc Henrys Peak—*summit* ... CO-8
McHenry Spring—*spring* ... OR-9
**Mchenry Township**—*pop pl* ... ND-7
**McHenry (Township of)**—*pop pl* ... IL-6
**McHenry (Township of)**—*pop pl* ... PA-2
McHenry Valley Creek—*stream* ... NY-2
McHessor Creek—*stream* ... MT-8
McHill Gap—*gap* ... NC-3
Mchochaeo—*island* ... PW-9
McHone Cem—*cemetery* ... NC-3
McHone Creek—*stream* ... AR-4
McHood Park—*park* ... AZ-5
McHose Park—*park* ... IA-7
**McHue**—*pop pl* ... AR-4
McHue (Township of)—*fmr MCD* ... AR-4
*McHugh* ... ND-7
**McHugh**—*pop pl* ... LA-4
McHugh-Andrews House—*hist pl* ... CO-8
McHugh Bayou—*gut* ... TX-5
McHugh Cem—*cemetery* ... LA-4
McHugh Creek—*stream* (2) ... AK-9
McHugh Hill Ch—*church* ... GA-3
McHugh Lake—*reservoir* ... AL-4
McHugh Lake Dam—*dam* ... AL-4
McHugh Peak—*summit* ... AK-9
McHugh Sch—*school* ... MO-7
McHugh Slough—*lake* ... ND-7
McHugh Windmill—*locale* ... TX-5
*M'chwewormink* ... PA-2
McIdoo Cem—*cemetery* ... IN-6
McIgee Creek—*stream* ... MI-6
McIihenny Sch—*school* ... SC-3
McIiwee Ridge—*ridge* ... VA-3
**McIlhaney**—*pop pl* ... PA-2
McIlhaney Hill—*summit* ... VA-3
**McIlhenny**—*pop pl* ... LA-4
*McIlhenny Canal* ... LA-4
McIlhenny Canal—*canal* ... LA-4
McIlhennys Pond (historical)—*reservoir* ... NC-3
McIlheran Cem—*cemetery* ... TN-4
*McIllhearn Cem* ... TN-4
**McIllwain**—*pop pl* ... TN-4
McIllwain Methodist Ch—*church* ... TN-4
McIllwain Post Office (historical)—*building* ... TN-4
McIllwain Sch (historical)—*school* ... TN-4
McIlquham Lake—*lake* ... WI-6
McIlraby Ranch—*locale* ... SD-7
McIlroy Canyon—*valley* ... WA-9
McIlroy Cem—*cemetery* ... AR-4
McIlroy Ch—*church* ... AR-4
McIlroy Creek—*stream* ... AR-4
McIlroy State Game Mngmt Area—*park* ... AR-4
McIlroy (Township of)—*fmr MCD* ... AR-4
McIlvain, Francis, House—*hist pl* ... PA-2
*McIlvaine Bay* ... FL-3
McIlvain Tank—*reservoir* ... TX-5
McIlvane Bay—*bay* ... FL-3
*McIlwaine Creek* ... MT-8
McIlwaine House—*hist pl* ... VA-3
McIlwain Lake—*lake* ... MT-8
**McIndoe Falls (McIndoes Station)**—*pop pl* ... VT-1
McIndoe Hill—*summit* ... TX-5
McIndoes Acad—*hist pl* ... VT-1
McIndoes (RR name for McIndoe Falls)—*other* ... VT-1
McInerney Drain—*stream* ... MI-6
McInernie Creek—*stream* ... MT-8
McInerny Ranch—*locale* ... SD-7
McInerny Spring—*spring* ... SD-7
McInguale Lake Dam—*dam* ... MS-4
McIngvale Clock Museum—*building* ... MS-4
McInnes Lake—*lake* ... MI-6
McInnes Norton Ridge—*ridge* ... OR-9
*McInness Creek* ... MS-4
McInnes Spring—*spring* ... OR-9
McInnis Bayou—*gut* ... MS-4
McInnis Bridge—*bridge* ... SC-3
McInnis Cem—*cemetery* ... AL-4
McInnis Cem—*cemetery* (2) ... MS-4
Mcinnis Cem—*cemetery* ... MS-4
McInnis Cem—*cemetery* ... MS-4
*McInnis Creek* ... MS-4
McInnis Creek—*stream* ... MS-4
McInnis Ferry (historical)—*locale* ... MS-4
McInnis Lake—*lake* (2) ... MS-4
McInnis Mill (historical)—*locale* ... MS-4
McInnis Sch—*school* ... AL-4
McInnis Spring—*spring* ... CA-9
McInnis Springs—*spring* ... MS-4
McInnus Sch (historical)—*school* ... AL-4
McInteer Villa—*hist pl* ... KS-7
McIntier Branch—*stream* ... KY-4
**McIntire**—*pop pl* ... IA-7
**McIntire**—*pop pl* ... WV-2
McIntire, Levi, House—*hist pl* ... MO-7
McIntire Basin—*basin* ... OR-9
McIntire Branch—*stream* ... GA-3
McIntire Brook—*stream* ... ME-1
McIntire Cem—*cemetery* ... IN-6
McIntire Cem—*cemetery* ... IA-7
McIntire Cem—*cemetery* (3) ... KY-4
McIntire Cem—*cemetery* ... MO-7
McIntire Cem—*cemetery* ... OH-6
McIntire Cem—*cemetery* ... PA-2
McIntire Cem—*cemetery* ... TN-4
McIntire Creek—*stream* ... CA-9
McIntire Creek—*stream* ... KS-7
McIntire Fork—*stream* ... WV-2
McIntire Fork Cem—*cemetery* ... WV-2
McIntire Fork Ch—*church* ... WV-2
McIntire Garrison House—*hist pl* ... ME-1
McIntire Hollow—*valley* ... KY-4
McIntire Lake—*lake* ... MI-6
*McIntire Mountains* ... NY-2
McIntire Municipal Park—*park* ... VA-3
McIntire Pond—*lake* ... ME-1
McIntire Run—*stream* ... PA-2
McIntire Sch—*school* ... MO-7
McIntire Sch—*school* ... VA-3
Mc Intire Spring—*spring* ... CO-8
McIntire Terrace Hist Dist—*hist pl* ... OH-6
McIntosh—*locale* ... AK-9
McIntosh—*locale* ... MO-7
McIntosh—*locale* ... NM-5
**McIntosh**—*pop pl* ... AL-4
**McIntosh**—*pop pl* ... FL-3
**McIntosh**—*pop pl* ... GA-3
**McIntosh**—*pop pl* ... IL-6
**McIntosh**—*pop pl* ... MN-6
**McIntosh**—*pop pl* ... SD-7
McIntosh, Roger D., House—*hist pl* ... TX-5
McIntosh Acad—*school* ... AL-4
McIntosh Bayou—*gut* ... LA-4
McIntosh Bayou—*stream* ... LA-4
McIntosh Beaton Ditch—*canal* ... WY-8
McIntosh Bldg—*hist pl* ... MA-1
McIntosh Bluff—*cliff* ... AL-4
McIntosh Branch—*stream* ... FL-3
McIntosh Branch—*stream* ... KY-4
McIntosh Branch—*stream* ... MO-7
McIntosh Branch—*stream* ... NC-3
McIntosh Branch Big Creek—*stream* ... AR-4
McIntosh Bridge—*bridge* ... NY-2
McIntosh Brook—*stream* ... ME-1
McIntosh Camp—*locale* ... NM-5
McIntosh (CCD)—*cens area* ... AL-4
McIntosh Cem cemetery ... AL-4
McIntosh Cem—*cemetery* ... GA-3
McIntosh Cem—*cemetery* (2) ... IA-7
McIntosh Cem—*cemetery* (2) ... KY-4
McIntosh Cem—*cemetery* ... MS-4
McIntosh Cem—*cemetery* ... MO-7
McIntosh Cem—*cemetery* ... NY-2
McIntosh Cem—*cemetery* (2) ... OK-5
McIntosh Cem—*cemetery* ... SD-7
McIntosh Cem—*cemetery* (3) ... TN-4
McIntosh Cemeteries—*cemetery* ... KY-4
McIntosh Ch—*church* ... GA-3
McIntosh Chapel—*church* ... KY-4
McIntosh Chapel—*church* ... OK-5
McIntosh Coulee—*valley* ... ND-7
McIntosh County—*civil* ... ND-7
**McIntosh (County)**—*pop pl* ... GA-3
**McIntosh (County)**—*pop pl* ... OK-5
McIntosh County Courthouse—*hist pl* ... ND-7
McIntosh County Courthouse—*hist pl* ... OK-5
McIntosh Cove—*bay* ... NC-3
McIntosh Creek—*stream* (2) ... GA-3
McIntosh Creek—*stream* ... MI-6
McIntosh Creek—*stream* ... NY-2
McIntosh Creek—*stream* ... NC-3
McIntosh Division—*civil* ... AL-4
McIntosh Draw—*valley* ... WY-8
McIntosh Fork—*stream* ... KY-4
McIntosh Grange—*locale* ... WA-9
*Mcintosh Hill* ... ME-1
McIntosh Hill—*summit* ... CA-9
McIntosh Hill—*summit* ... FL-3
McIntosh Hill—*summit* ... IN-6
McIntosh Hist Dist—*hist pl* ... FL-3
McIntosh (historical)—*locale* ... KS-7
McIntosh Hollow—*valley* ... PA-2
McIntosh Hollow—*valley* ... TN-4
McIntosh Lake—*lake* ... MI-6
McIntosh Lake—*lake* ... WA-9
Mc Intosh Lake—*reservoir* ... CO-8
McIntosh Lake—*reservoir* ... SD-7
McIntosh Lake Dam—*dam* ... SD-7
McIntosh Landing—*locale* ... AL-4
McIntosh Landing (Site)—*locale* ... CA-9
McIntosh Lateral—*canal* ... NM-5
McIntosh Ledge—*bar* ... ME-1
McIntosh Log Church—*hist pl* ... AL-4
McIntosh Meadows—*flat* ... WY-8
McIntosh Millpond—*reservoir* ... SC-3
**McIntosh Mill Village**—*pop pl* ... GA-3
Mc Intosh Mtn—*summit* ... CO-8
McIntosh Municipal Airp—*airport* ... SD-7
McIntosh Park—*park* ... MI-6
McIntosh Peak—*summit* ... AK-9
McIntosh Peak—*summit* ... WY-8
McIntosh Place—*locale* ... NV-8
Mc Intosh Ranch—*locale* ... CO-8
McIntosh Ranch—*locale* ... TX-5
McIntosh Ranch—*locale* (2) ... WY-8
McIntosh Run—*stream* ... MD-2
McIntosh Run—*stream* ... WV-2
*McIntoshs* ... MS-4
*McIntosh Sch* ... AL-4
McIntosh Sch—*school* ... CA-9
McIntosh Sch—*school* ... GA-3
McIntosh Sch—*school* ... IL-6
McIntosh Sch—*school* ... NE-7
McIntosh Sch (abandoned)—*school* ... PA-2
McIntosh Sch (historical)—*school* ... MS-4
McIntosh Slough—*bay* ... OR-9
McIntosh Spring—*spring* ... NM-5
McIntosh Spring—*spring* ... OR-9
McIntosh Spring—*spring* ... TN-4
*McIntosh Station* ... KS-7
McIntosh Station—*locale* ... AL-4
McIntosh Student Center—*school* ... FL-3
McIntosh Trail (Camp)—*locale* ... NY-2
*McIntosh Union School* ... AL-4
*McIntoshville* ... MS-4
McIntosh Well—*well* ... CA-9
McIntosh Windmill—*locale* ... NM-5
McIntosh Woods State Park—*park* ... IA-7
McIntrye Creek—*stream* ... OR-9
McIntrye Hill—*summit* ... ME-1
McIntrye Lookout—*locale* ... OR-9
McIntrye Sch—*school* ... MS-4
*McInturf* ... VA-3
McInturff Cem—*cemetery* ... IL-6
McInturff Cem—*cemetery* (2) ... TN-4
*McInturff Creek* ... TX-5
Mc Inturf Mesa—*summit* ... CO-8
McInturf Spring—*spring* ... AZ-5
McInturf Trick Tank—*reservoir* ... AZ-5
McIntyers Bluff—*cliff* ... AL-4
McIntyers Shoals—*bar* ... AL-4
*McIntyre* ... AL-4
McIntyre—*locale* ... FL-3
McIntyre—*locale* ... UT-8
**McIntyre**—*pop pl* ... GA-3
**McIntyre**—*pop pl* ... LA-4
**McIntyre**—*pop pl* ... NY-2
**McIntyre**—*pop pl* ... OH-6
**McIntyre**—*pop pl* ... PA-2
McIntyre, J., Farm—*hist pl* ... DE-2
McIntyre and Willing Drain—*canal* ... MI-6
McIntyre Bldg—*hist pl* ... UT-8
**McIntyre Building Condominium**—*pop pl* ... UT-8
McIntyre Canal—*canal* ... ID-8
McIntyre Canal—*canal* ... UT-8
McIntyre Canyon—*valley* ... AZ-5
McIntyre Canyon—*valley* (2) ... CO-8
McIntyre Canyon—*valley* ... UT-8
McIntyre Cem—*cemetery* (2) ... GA-3
McIntyre Cem—*cemetery* ... MI-6
McIntyre Cem—*cemetery* ... MS-4
McIntyre Cem—*cemetery* ... MO-7
McIntyre Ch—*church* ... MS-4
*McIntyre Creek* ... OH-6
McIntyre Creek—*stream* ... CA-9
Mc Intyre Creek—*stream* ... CO-8
McIntyre Creek—*stream* ... FL-3
McIntyre Creek—*stream* ... ID-8
McIntyre Creek—*stream* ... IN-6
McIntyre Creek—*stream* ... NC-3
McIntyre Creek—*stream* ... OH-6
McIntyre Creek—*stream* ... TX-5
Mc Intyre Ditch—*canal* ... CO-8
McIntyre Ditch—*stream* ... AL-4
McIntyre Drain—*stream* (2) ... MI-6
McIntyre Draw—*valley* ... ID-8
McIntyre Draw—*valley* ... WY-8
McIntyre Fork—*stream* ... WV-2
McIntyre Grove—*woods* ... CA-9
McIntyre Gulch—*valley* (2) ... CA-9
Mc Intyre Gulch—*valley* ... CO-8
McIntyre Gulch—*valley* ... CO-8
Mc Intyre Gulch—*valley* (2) ... CO-8
McIntyre Gulch—*valley* (2) ... CO-8
McIntyre Gulch—*valley* (2) ... ID-8
McIntyre Gulch—*valley* ... MT-8
McIntyre Gymnasium—*building* ... NC-3
McIntyre Hill—*summit* ... ID-8
Mc Intyre Hills—*summit* ... CO-8
**McIntyre (historical)**—*pop pl* ... MS-4
McIntyre House—*hist pl* ... AR-4
McIntyre House—*hist pl* ... UT-8
McIntyre Island—*island* ... MI-6
*McIntyre Junior High School* ... AL-4
Mc Intyre Lake—*lake* ... CO-8
McIntyre Lake—*lake* ... LA-4
McIntyre Lake—*lake* (2) ... MI-6
McIntyre Lake—*lake* ... MS-4
Mc Intyre Lake Trail—*trail* ... CO-8
**McIntyre Landing**—*pop pl* ... MI-6
McIntyre Lateral—*canal* ... ID-8
McIntyre Lead—*ridge* ... TN-4
McIntyre Mine—*mine* ... NV-8
*McIntyre Mountain* ... NY-2
*McIntyre Mountains* ... NY-2
Mc Intyre Mtn—*summit* ... CO-8
McIntyre Park—*park* ... GA-3
McIntyre Peak—*summit* ... CO-8
McIntyre Pond—*lake* ... MA-1
McIntyre Ranch—*locale* ... WY-8
Mc Intyre Ridge—*ridge* ... CO-8
McIntyre Ridge—*ridge* (2) ... OR-9
McIntyre Rsvr—*reservoir* (2) ... MT-8
McIntyre Rsvr—*reservoir* ... OR-9
Mcintyre Rsvr Number Two—*reservoir* ... OR-9
McIntyres Bluff—*cliff* ... NY-2
*Mcintyre's Brook* ... CT-1
McIntyres Brook—*stream* ... CT-1
McIntyre Scatters—*swamp* ... MS-4
McIntyre Sch—*school* ... MI-6
McIntyre Sch—*school* (2) ... PA-2
McIntyre Sch (abandoned)—*school* ... PA-2
McIntyre Sch (historical)—*school* ... AL-4
McIntyre Sch (historical)—*school* ... MS-4
*McIntyre Slough* ... OR-9
McIntyre Slough—*stream* ... NV-8
Mc Intyre Spring—*spring* ... CO-8
McIntyre Spring—*spring* ... NM-5
McIntyre Spring—*spring* ... OR-9
McIntyre Spring—*spring* ... UT-8
*McIntyres Switch* ... TN-4
McIntyre Summit—*gap* ... NV-8
McIntyre Tank—*reservoir* ... AZ-5
**McIntyre (Township of)**—*pop pl* ... PA-2
McIntyre Well—*well* ... AZ-5
McIntyre Wild Area—*area* ... PA-2
McIroy Cem—*cemetery* ... AR-4
Mc Isaac Ditch No 2—*canal* ... CO-8
*McIthelinny Canal* ... LA-4
McIver Bight—*bay* ... AK-9
McIver Branch—*stream* ... FL-3
McIver Brook—*stream* ... MA-1
McIver Camp—*locale* ... WI-6
McIver Canal—*canal* ... CA-9
McIver Cem—*cemetery* ... MS-4
McIver Ch—*church* ... MS-4
McIver Creek—*stream* ... KY-4
McIver Lake—*lake* ... MN-6
McIver North Tank—*reservoir* ... NM-5
McIver Pond—*reservoir* ... SC-3
McIver Ranch—*locale* ... NM-5
*McIvers Bluff* ... TN-4
McIvers Cabin—*locale* ... CA-9
Mc Iver Sch—*school* ... NC-3
McIver Sch—*school* (2) ... NC-3
Mciver Sch—*school* ... NC-3
McIver Sch (historical)—*school* ... NC-3
McIvers Grant Public Library—*building* ... TN-4
McIvers Pring—*spring* ... CA-9
McIvers Road (jeep)—*trail* ... CA-9
McIvers Sch (historical)—*school* ... AL-4
McIver Tank—*reservoir* ... NM-5
**McIvor**—*pop pl* ... MI-6
**McIvor**—*pop pl* ... MS-4
*McIvor Baptist Church* ... MS-4
*Mcivor Canal* ... MS-4
McIvor Cem—*cemetery* ... MS-4
McIvor Cem—*cemetery* ... VA-3
McIvor Ch—*church* ... MS-4
McIvor Drainage Canal—*canal* ... MS-4
*Mcivor Lake* ... MN-6
McIvor Post Office (historical)—*building* ... MS-4
McIvor Tank—*reservoir* ... TX-5
McJester—*locale* ... AR-4
McJester (Township of)—*fmr MCD* ... AR-4
McJohnston Chapel and Cemetery—*hist pl* ... IN-6
McJonkin Branch—*stream* ... KY-4
McJunkin Cem—*cemetery* ... TN-4
Mc Junkin Creek—*stream* ... CO-8
McJunkins Branch—*stream* ... AR-4
McJunkins Cem—*cemetery* ... AL-4
McKabe Flat—*flat* ... CA-9
*McKacken Mesa* ... UT-8
McKaig—*locale* ... MD-2
McKaig Cem—*cemetery* ... GA-3
McKaig Gulf—*valley* ... GA-3
McKain Brook—*stream* ... ME-1
McKain Corners—*locale* ... MI-6
McKain Creek—*stream* ... TX-5
McKale Canyon—*valley* ... WA-9
McKalester Cem—*cemetery* ... VA-3
McKamey Cem—*cemetery* (2) ... TN-4
McKamey Forge (historical)—*locale* ... TN-4
**McKamie**—*pop pl* ... AR-4
McKamie Patton Oil Field—*oilfield* ... AR-4
*McKane Lake* ... MI-6
McKane Lake—*lake* ... MI-6
McKanna Spring—*spring* ... MT-8
McKanna Spring Creek—*stream* ... MT-8
McKans Bay—*bay* ... VA-3
McKaskel Lake—*lake* ... WI-6
McKaskey Creek—*stream* ... GA-3
*McKathan Lake* ... FL-3
McKathnie Sch—*school* ... NE-7
McKaughan, Isaac Harrison, House—*hist pl* ... NC-3
*McKay* ... TN-4
McKay—*hist pl* ... IN-6
McKay—*locale* ... CA-9
McKay—*locale* ... OR-9
McKay—*locale* ... WA-9
McKay—*other* ... WA-9
**McKay**—*pop pl* ... CA-9
**McKay**—*pop pl* ... OH-6
McKay, Claude, Residence—*hist pl* ... NY-2
McKay, Donald, House—*hist pl* ... MA-1
McKay, John A., House and Manufacturing Company—*hist pl* ... NC-3
McKay, Lake—*reservoir* ... NC-3
McKay, Moses, House—*hist pl* ... OH-6
McKay Bay—*bay* ... FL-3
McKay Bay—*bay* ... MI-6
**McKay Beach**—*pop pl* ... MD-2
McKay Branch—*stream* ... AL-4
McKay Branch—*stream* ... GA-3
McKay Branch—*stream* ... LA-4
McKay Branch—*stream* ... MS-4
McKay Branch—*stream* ... TN-4
McKay Bridge—*bridge* ... TX-5
*McKay Brook* ... MI-6
McKay Butte—*summit* ... CA-9
McKay Butte—*summit* ... OR-9
McKay Camp—*locale* ... CA-9
Mc Kay Canyon—*valley* ... CO-8
McKay Cem—*cemetery* ... AR-4
McKay Cem—*cemetery* ... GA-3
McKay Cem—*cemetery* ... IL-6
McKay Cem—*cemetery* (3) ... IN-6
McKay Cem—*cemetery* (2) ... LA-4
McKay Cem—*cemetery* ... MI-6
McKay Cem—*cemetery* ... MS-4
McKay Cem—*cemetery* ... MT-8
McKay Cem—*cemetery* ... OH-6
Mc Kay Coulee—*valley* ... MT-8
McKay Cove—*bay* ... MD-2
*McKay Creek* ... IN-6
*McKay Creek* ... WA-9
McKay Creek—*stream* ... AK-9
McKay Creek—*stream* (2) ... CA-9
McKay Creek—*stream* ... FL-3
McKay Creek—*stream* ... ID-8
Mckay Creek—*stream* ... ID-8
McKay Creek—*stream* ... ID-8
McKay Creek—*stream* ... MI-6
McKay Creek—*stream* (3) ... MT-8
McKay Creek—*stream* (5) ... OR-9
McKay Creek—*stream* (2) ... TX-5
McKay Creek—*stream* (2) ... WA-9
McKay Creek—*stream* ... WY-8
McKay Creek Cem—*cemetery* ... OR-9
McKay Creek Forest Camp—*locale* ... OR-9
McKay Creek Natl Wildlife Ref—*reserve* ... OR-9
*McKay Creek Reservoir* ... FL-3
McKay Creek Sch—*school* ... OR-9
McKay Dam—*dam* ... OR-9
McKay-Dee Hosp—*hospital* ... UT-8
McKay-Dee Hospital Center Airp—*airport* ... UT-8
Mc Kay Ditch—*canal* ... CO-8
McKay Ditch—*canal* ... MI-6
McKay Drain—*canal* ... MI-6
McKay Dredge Ditch—*canal* ... IN-6
McKay Ferry (historical)—*locale* ... MS-4
McKay Flat—*flat* ... CA-9
McKay Flat—*flat* ... UT-8
Mc Kay Fork—*stream* ... CO-8
McKay Gulch—*valley* ... CA-9
Mc Kay Gulch—*valley* ... CO-8
McKay Gulch—*valley* ... ID-8
McKay Gulch—*valley* ... MT-8
McKay Hill—*summit* ... WA-9
McKay Hollow—*valley* ... AL-4
McKay Hollow—*valley* ... UT-8
McKay Hollow—*valley* ... WA-9
McKay House—*hist pl* ... KY-4
McKay Inlet—*bay* ... AK-9
McKay Island—*island* ... NC-3
*McKay Lake* ... OR-9
McKay Lake—*lake* (2) ... FL-3
McKay Lake—*lake* ... MI-6
McKay Lake—*lake* (2) ... MN-6
McKay Lake—*lake* ... NY-2
McKay Lake—*lake* ... WY-8
McKay Lake—*reservoir* ... AL-4
McKay Lake—*reservoir* ... CO-8
McKay Lake—*reservoir* ... GA-3
McKay Lake Dam—*dam* ... AL-4
McKay Lake Dam—*dam* ... MS-4
McKay Marine Ways—*hist pl* ... AK-9
McKay Mtn—*summit* ... MT-8
McKay-Nealis Park—*park* ... IL-6
McKay Oil Field—*oilfield* ... KS-7
*McKay Peak* ... AZ-5
McKay Point—*cape* ... FL-3
McKay Ranch—*locale* ... MT-8
McKay Ranch—*locale* ... SD-7
McKay Reservoirs—*reservoir* ... WY-8
McKay Ridge—*ridge* ... AR-4
McKay Ridge—*ridge* ... CA-9
McKay Ridge—*ridge* ... UT-8
McKay Ridge—*ridge* ... WA-9
McKay Rsvr—*reservoir* ... AZ-5
McKay Rsvr—*reservoir* (3) ... OR-9
McKay Saddle—*gap* ... OR-9
*McKays Bay Creek* ... MI-6
McKays Bridge—*bridge* ... SC-3
McKays Butte—*summit* ... WA-9
McKay Sch—*school* ... IL-6
McKay Sch—*school* ... MO-7
McKay Sch—*school* ... OR-9
McKays Corners—*locale* ... DE-2
**McKays Corners**—*pop pl* ... OH-6
*McKays Creek* ... MI-6
McKays (historical)—*locale* ... MS-4
McKays Mill Creek—*stream* ... AL-4
McKays Peak—*summit* ... AZ-5
*McKays Point* ... SC-3
McKays Point—*cape* ... CA-9
McKays Point—*cliff* ... CA-9
McKay Spring—*spring* ... AZ-5
McKay Spring—*spring* ... CA-9
McKay Spring—*spring* ... MT-8
McKay Spring—*spring* ... TN-4
McKay Springs—*spring* ... CA-9
*McKays Run* ... PA-2
McKays Spur—*locale* ... WI-6
**McKays Trailer Court (subdivision)**—*pop pl* ... SD-7
McKay Tank—*reservoir* ... AZ-5
McKay-Thornberry House—*hist pl* ... KY-4
McKay Wash—*stream* ... NV-8
McKay Well—*well* ... OR-9
McKay Windmill—*locale* ... NM-5
McKeachnie Ranch—*locale* ... UT-8
McKeadney Mine—*mine* ... CA-9
McKeag—*locale* ... NE-7
Mckeage Dam—*dam* ... PA-2
McKeages Crossing—*locale* ... PA-2
**McKeages Subdivision**—*pop pl* ... UT-8
McKeags Meadow—*swamp* ... NY-2
McKeal Meadows—*flat* ... WY-8
*McKean* ... PA-2
McKean—*locale* (2) ... PA-2
McKean Borough—*civil* ... PA-2
McKean Corners—*locale* ... PA-2
**McKean County**—*pop pl* ... PA-2
*McKean Elementary School* ... PA-2
**McKean Estates Subdivision**—*pop pl* ... UT-8
McKean Memorial Park Cem—*cemetery* ... PA-2
**McKean (Middleboro)**—*pop pl* ... PA-2
McKean P O and Station—*locale* ... PA-2
*McKean Post Office and Station* ... PA-2
**McKeansburg**—*pop pl* ... PA-2
McKean Sch—*school* ... OH-6
McKean Sch—*school* ... PA-2
McKean Sch (abandoned)—*school* ... PA-2
McKean Sch (historical)—*school* ... MO-7
McKean Sch (historical)—*school* ... PA-2
Mc Kean Spring—*spring* ... CO-8
McKean Swamp—*swamp* ... PA-2
**McKean (Township of)**—*pop pl* ... OH-6
**McKean (Township of)**—*pop pl* ... PA-2
*McKeaver* ... MI-6
McKechnie Field—*park* ... FL-3
McKechnie Meadow—*flat* ... WY-8
McKechnie Ranch—*locale* ... WY-8
McKechnie River Ranch—*locale* ... WY-8
McKecknie Creek—*stream* ... KY-4
*McKee* ... MN-6
*McKee* ... NC-3
McKee—*locale* ... GA-3
McKee—*locale* ... PA-2
**McKee**—*pop pl* ... KY-4
**McKee**—*pop pl* ... OR-9
**McKee**—*pop pl* ... PA-2
**McKee**—*pop pl* ... TX-5
McKee, John, House—*hist pl* ... KY-4
McKee Basin—*basin* ... OR-9
McKee Bench—*bench* ... UT-8
McKee Bend—*bend* ... KY-4
McKee Branch—*stream* ... IL-6
McKee Branch—*stream* ... KY-4
McKee Branch—*stream* (2) ... NC-3
McKee Branch—*stream* ... OH-6
McKee Bridge—*hist pl* ... OR-9
**McKee Bridge**—*pop pl* ... OR-9
McKee Bridge Camp—*locale* ... OR-9
McKee Brook—*stream* ... MA-1
McKeeby, Dr. Gilbert, House—*hist pl* ... NE-7
McKee Cabin—*locale* ... OR-9
McKee Canyon—*valley* ... CA-9
McKee (CCD)—*cens area* ... KY-4
McKee Cem—*cemetery* ... AL-4
McKee Cem—*cemetery* ... GA-3
McKee Cem—*cemetery* ... IL-6
McKee Cem—*cemetery* ... IN-6
McKee Cem—*cemetery* ... KS-7
McKee Cem—*cemetery* ... MS-4
McKee Cem—*cemetery* ... OH-6
McKee Cem—*cemetery* (3) ... TN-4
McKee Cem—*cemetery* ... VA-3
McKee Chapel—*church* ... MO-7
McKee Chapel—*church* ... PA-2
**McKee City**—*pop pl* ... NJ-2
McKee City Sch—*school* ... NJ-2
McKee City Station—*locale* ... NJ-2
*Mckee Creek* ... MS-4
*McKee Creek* ... TX-5
McKee Creek—*stream* (2) ... CA-9
McKee Creek—*stream* ... ID-8
McKee Creek—*stream* ... IL-6
McKee Creek—*stream* ... MS-4
McKee Creek—*stream* ... NC-3
McKee Creek—*stream* ... OH-6
McKee Creek—*stream* ... WV-2
Mc Kee Ditch—*canal* ... IN-6
McKee Ditch—*cemetery* ... IN-6
*McKee Draw* ... UT-8
McKee Draw—*valley* ... CO-8
McKee Draw—*valley* ... TX-5
McKee Draw—*valley* ... UT-8
McKee Elem Sch—*school* ... PA-2
McKeefer Canyon—*valley* ... NM-5
**McKeefrey**—*pop pl* ... WV-2
*McKee Gap* ... PA-2
McKee Gap—*gap* ... PA-2
McKee Grave Creek—*stream* ... WY-8
Mc Kee Gulch—*valley* ... CO-8
*McKee Half Falls* ... PA-2
**McKee Half Falls**—*pop pl* ... PA-2
McKeehan Cem—*cemetery* ... IA-7
McKeehan Cem—*cemetery* (2) ... TN-4
McKee Hill—*summit* ... CA-9
McKee Hill—*summit* ... NY-2
Mc Kee Hill—*summit* ... PA-2
McKee Hollow—*valley* ... KY-4
McKee Hollow—*valley* ... MO-7
McKee Hollow—*valley* ... OH-6

McKinney Branch—stream (2) TN-4
McKinney Branch Ch—church GA-3
Mc Kinney Bridge—bridge GA-3
McKinney Bridge—bridge NC-3
McKinney Butte—summit ID-8
McKinney Butte—summit OR-9
McKinney Canyon—valley AZ-5
McKinney Canyon—valley CA-9
McKinney Cove—cave AL-4
McKinney (CCD)—cens area TX-5
McKinney Cem—cemetery (4) AL-4
McKinney Cem—cemetery AZ-5
McKinney Cem—cemetery (3) AR-4
McKinney Cem—cemetery (2) IL-6
McKinney Cem—cemetery (2) IN-6
McKinney Cem—cemetery (7) KY-4
McKinney Cem—cemetery LA-4
McKinney Cem—cemetery MS-4
McKinney Cem—cemetery (2) MO-7
McKinney Cem—cemetery NC-3
Mc Kinney Cem—cemetery NC-3
McKinney Cem—cemetery NC-3
McKinney Cem—cemetery OH-6
McKinney Cem—cemetery OK-5
McKinney Cem—cemetery (12) TN-4
McKinney Cem—cemetery TX-5
McKinney Cem—cemetery VA-3
McKinney Cemetery—hist pl ND-7
McKinney Cem Number 2 AL-4
McKinney Chapel—church IL-6
McKinney Chapel—church MS-4
McKinney Chapel—church SC-3
McKinney Cliff—cliff KY-4
McKinney Club Lake—reservoir TX-5
McKinney Commercial Hist Dist—hist pl TX-5
McKinney Cotton Compress Plant—hist pl TX-5
McKinney Cotton Mill Hist Dist—hist pl TX-5
**McKinney Cove**—pop pl NC-3
McKinney Cove—valley NC-3
McKinney Creek—stream (3) AR-4
McKinney Creek—stream (4) CA-9
McKinney Creek—stream ID-8
McKinney Creek—stream KY-4
McKinney Creek—stream (2) MO-7
McKinney Creek—stream MT-8
McKinney Creek—stream (2) NC-3
McKinney Creek—stream OH-6
McKinney Creek—stream OK-5
McKinney Creek—stream (6) OR-9
McKinney Creek—stream SC-3
McKinney Creek—stream TX-5
McKinney Creek—stream WY-8
McKinney Dam—dam (2) AZ-5
McKinney Ditch—canal IN-6
McKinney Ditch—canal MT-8
Mc Kinney Draw—valley CO-8
McKinney Eddy—other MO-7
McKinney Fork—stream TN-4
McKinney Gap—gap (2) NC-3
McKinney Gap—gap (3) TN-4
McKinney Gulch—valley CA-9
Mc Kinney Gulch—valley CO-8
McKinney Gulch—valley MT-8
McKinney-Helm House—hist pl KY-4
McKinney Hill—summit AR-4
McKinney Hill—summit IL-6
McKinney Hill—summit NY-2
McKinney Hills—summit TX-5
McKinney Hollow—valley AR-4
McKinney Hollow—valley TN-4
McKinney Hollow—valley WI-6
McKinney Homestead—hist pl TX-5
McKinney Hospital, Old—hist pl TX-5
McKinney House—hist pl IA-7
McKinney Island TN-4
McKinney Islands—island TN-4
McKinney Knob—summit KY-4
McKinney Lake—lake AK-9
McKinney Lake—lake CA-9
McKinney Lake—lake MN-6
McKinney Lake—lake MN-6
McKinney Lake—lake WI-6
McKinney Lake—reservoir NC-3
McKinney Lake—reservoir TN-4
McKinney Lake—reservoir TX-5
McKinney Lake Dam—dam NC-3
McKinney Lake Dam—dam TN-4
McKinney Lake Fish Hatchery—locale NC-3
McKinney-McDonald House—hist pl TX-5
McKinney Military Reservation—area WY-8
McKinney Mill Bridge—bridge NC-3
McKinney Mine—mine TN-4
McKinney Mountains TX-5
McKinney Mtn—summit AL-4
McKinney Mtn—summit AZ-5
McKinney Mtn—summit KY-4
McKinney Mtn—summit (2) SC-3
McKinney Mtn—summit TX-5
McKinney Mtn—summit WA-9
McKinney Mtns—range NV-8
McKinney Park—park TX-5
McKinney Pass—gap NV-8
McKinney Pit Cave—cave AL-4
McKinney Playground—locale MA-1
McKinney Point—cape ME-1
McKinney Pond—lake GA-3
McKinney Pond—lake PA-2
McKinney Pond—reservoir NY-2
Mc Kinney Ranch—locale MT-8
McKinney Ranch—locale WY-8
McKinney Ranch (historical)—locale SD-7
McKinney Residential Hist Dist—hist pl TX-5
McKinney Ridge TN-4
McKinney Ridge—ridge TN-4
Mc Kinney Rsvr—reservoir CO-8
McKinney Run—stream PA-2
McKinney Run—stream WV-2
**McKinneys**—pop pl NY-2
McKinneysburg—locale KY-4
McKinney Sch—school CA-9
McKinney Sch—school (2) IL-6
McKinney Sch—school KY-4
McKinney Sch—school ME-1
McKinney Sch (historical)—school TN-4
McKinneys Creek—stream SC-3
McKinneys Islands—island TN-4
McKinney Slough—gut OR-9
McKinneys Mtn—summit SC-3
McKinneys Point—cape NY-2
**McKinneys Point**—pop pl NY-2
McKinney Spring TX-5
McKinney Spring—spring AZ-5
McKinney Spring—spring PA-2
McKinney Springs—spring TX-5
McKinney Springs—locale TX-5
McKinneys Shoals—bar TN-4
McKinney Stand (historical)—locale TN-4
McKinney Tank—reservoir (2) AZ-5
McKinney Tanks—reservoir NV-8
McKinney Tanks Summit—gap NV-8
**Mckinney Township**—pop pl ND-7
McKinney Trail—trail PA-2
McKinneyville MS-4
McKinney Windmill—locale TX-5
McKinnie Cem—cemetery IL-6
McKinnie Creek—stream TN-4
McKinnie Creek—stream WY-8
McKinnie Rsvr—reservoir WY-8
McKinnis Cem—cemetery MS-4
Mc Kinnis Creek—stream CO-8
McKinnis Creek—stream (2) MS-4
McKinnish Branch—stream NC-3
McKinnneysburg Sch—school KY-4
McKinnon—locale FL-3
**McKinnon**—pop pl GA-3
**McKinnon**—pop pl TN-4
**McKinnon**—pop pl WY-8
McKinnon, Mount—summit UT-8
McKinnon and Millers Claim Mine—mine SD-7
McKinnon Branch—stream FL-3
McKinnon Branch—stream GA-3
McKinnon Branch—stream PA-2
McKinnon Branch—stream TX-5
McKinnon Brook—stream ME-1
McKinnon Cem—cemetery GA-3
McKinnon Cem—cemetery MS-4
McKinnon Cem—cemetery NC-3
McKinnon Cem—cemetery WY-8
McKinnon Ch—church WV-2
McKinnon Coulee—valley MT-8
Mc Kinnon Creek—stream CO-8
McKinnon Creek—stream ID-8
McKinnon Creek—stream OR-9
McKinnon Creek—stream (2) WA-9
McKinnon Creek—stream WY-8
McKinnon Dam—dam TN-4
McKinnon Enterprises Airfield—airport OR-9
McKinnon Family Cem—cemetery AL-4
McKinnon Hill—summit FL-3
McKinnon Junction—locale WY-8
McKinnon Lake—reservoir TN-4
McKinnon Lake Dam—dam MS-4
**McKinnon (McKinnonville)**—pop pl FL-3
McKinnon Mill (historical)—locale MS-4
McKinnon Park—park NY-2
McKinnon Point AZ-5
McKinnon Post Office—building TN-4
McKinnon Sch—school CA-9
McKinnon Sch—school TN-4
McKinnon Spring—spring UT-8
**Mckinnon Township**—pop pl ND-7
McKinnsey Rsvr—reservoir MT-8
McKinny-Leigh Cemetery TN-4
McKinsey Branch—stream KY-4
McKinsey Cem—cemetery NC-3
McKinsey Ditch—canal IN-6
McKinsey Draw—valley MT-8
McKinsey Homestead—locale MT-8
McKinsey Ridge—ridge CA-9
McKinsey Slough—stream OK-5
McKinsey Valley—valley AK-9
McKinsman Creek CA-9
McKinstrey House—hist pl MA-1
McKinstry Brook—stream MA-1
McKinstry Canyon—valley WA-9
McKinstry Cem—cemetery IN-6
McKinstry Cem—cemetery NY-2
McKinstry Creek—stream NY-2
McKinstry Drain—stream MI-6
McKinstry Hill—summit VT-1
**McKinstry Hollow**—pop pl NY-2
McKinstry Lake—lake CA-9
McKinstry Meadow—flat CA-9
McKinstry Mounds and Village Site—hist pl MN-6
McKinstry Peak—summit CA-9
McKinstry Pond—reservoir MA-1
McKinstry Ranch—locale NM-5
McKinstry Sch—school IA-7
McKinstry Sch—school MI-6
**McKinstrys Mill**—pop pl MD-2
**McKinstrys Mills**—pop pl MD-2
McKinstry Trail—trail CA-9
McKintosh Ranch—locale CA-9
McKinzey Gulch—valley CA-9
McKinzie Bridge OR-9
McKinzie Cem—cemetery MS-4
McKinzie Ch—church TX-5
McKinzie Creek MI-6
McKinzie Creek—stream (2) ID-8
McKinzie Creek—stream MI-6
McKinzie Creek—stream NC-3
McKinzie Ditch—canal IN-6
McKinzie Mine—mine AZ-5
Mc Kinzie Pond—lake NC-3
McKinzie Sch—school SD-7
McKinzter Homestead—locale MT-8
McKirahan Lake—lake NE-7
McKisic Creek—stream AR-4
McKissack Cut FL-3
McKissack Ponds—lake FL-3
McKissack Sch—school TN-4
McKissacks Ferry (historical)—locale AL-4
McKissacks Grove—locale IA-7
McKissick Cem—cemetery TN-4
McKissick Island—island NE-7
McKissick Lake—reservoir TN-4
McKissick Ponds FL-3
McKissick Spring—spring CA-9
McKissick Spring—spring NV-8
McKissock Island NE-7
McKisson, Robert, House—hist pl OH-6
McKittrick MO-7
McKittrick, Dr., House—hist pl OH-6
McKittrick, Dr., Office—hist pl OH-6
McKittrick Creek AZ-5
McKitterick Cem—cemetery OH-6
**McKittrick**—pop pl CA-9
**McKittrick**—pop pl MO-7
McKittrick Branch VA-3
McKittrick Canyon TX-5
Mckittrick Canyon—valley TX-5
McKittrick Canyon Draw—valley NM-5
McKittrick Canyon Draw—valley TX-5
McKittrick Cave—cave NM-5
McKittrick Creek—stream AZ-5
McKittrick Hill—summit NM-5
McKittrick Ranch—locale CA-9
McKittricks Branch—stream VA-3
McKittrick Spring—spring NM-5
McKittricks Ridge—ridge VA-3
McKittrick Summit—summit CA-9
McKittrick Valley—valley CA-9
McKleroy-Wilson-Kirby House—hist pl AL-4
McKnally Ford—locale AL-4
McKnally Ford Bridge—bridge AL-4
McKnatt Corners—locale DE-2
McKnay Cem—cemetery IL-6
**McKneeley**—pop pl LA-4
McKneeley Spur LA-4
McKneely Spur—locale LA-4
McKnight—locale OK-5
McKnight—locale TN-4
McKnight—locale (2) TX-5
**McKnight**—pop pl AR-4
**McKnight**—pop pl PA-2
McKnight, Lake—lake MT-8
**McKnight Acres**—pop pl CA-9
**McKnight and Bay (subdivision)**—pop pl MA-1
McKnight and Cooper Ranch—locale NM-5
McKnight and Richards Ferry AL-4
McKnight Branch—stream AL-4
McKnight Branch—stream IL-6
McKnight Branch—stream (3) TN-4
McKnight Branch—stream TX-5
McKnight Cabin—locale NV-8
McKnight Canyon—valley MT-8
McKnight Canyon—valley NM-5
McKnight Cem—cemetery AR-4
McKnight Cem—cemetery IL-6
McKnight Cem—cemetery IN-6
McKnight Cem—cemetery (3) KY-4
McKnight Cem—cemetery LA-4
McKnight Cem—cemetery MS-4
McKnight Cem—cemetery MO-7
McKnight Cem—cemetery OK-5
McKnight Cem—cemetery (4) TN-4
McKnight Ch—church TX-5
McKnight Corners—locale NY-2
McKnight Creek—stream KY-4
McKnight Creek—stream (2) OR-9
McKnight Creek—stream WY-8
McKnight Crossing—locale LA-4
McKnight District MA-1
McKnight District—hist pl MA-1
McKnight District (Boundary Increase)—hist pl MA-1
McKnight Ditch—canal NY-2
McKnight Drain—canal MI-6
McKnight-Ebb House—hist pl TX-5
McKnight Elem Sch—school PA-2
McKnight Fire Cabin—locale NM-5
McKnight Gap—gap PA-2
McKnight Gulch—valley MT-8
McKnight Hollow—valley AR-4
McKnight Hollow—valley IN-6
McKnight Hollow—valley (2) TN-4
McKnight Homestead—locale MT-8
McKnight Lake—reservoir AL-4
McKnight Lake Dam—dam AL-4
McKnight Mtn—summit NM-5
McKnight Ranch—locale (2) NM-5
McKnight Run—stream PA-2
McKnights Branch TN-4
McKnight Sch—school MO-7
McKnight Sch—school NC-3
McKnight Sch—school SC-3
McKnight Sch (abandoned)—school PA-2
McKnight School PA-2
McKnights Ditch—canal NC-3
McKnights Mill—locale VA-3
McKnights Placer Mine—mine NV-8
McKnights Point—locale IA-7
McKnight Spring—spring WY-8
Mcknight Springs CO-8
McKnight Springs—spring NV-8
McKnight State Sanatorium—hospital TX-5
McKnight State Tuberculosis Hospital—hospital TX-5
**McKnightstown**—pop pl PA-2
**McKnightstown Station**—pop pl PA-2
McKnight Swamp—stream SC-3
McKnights Well—well UT-8
**McKnight Village**—pop pl PA-2
McKnight Village Ch—church PA-2
McKnobe Creek—stream OR-9
McKnob Tank—reservoir TX-5
McKnown Well—well MT-8
McKomey Dam—dam TN-4
McKomey Lake—reservoir TN-4
McKone Creek AR-4
McKonkey Creek—stream MT-8
McKoozie Canyon MT-8
McKosato Cem—cemetery OK-5
McKosta Cem—cemetery OK-5
McKowen Ch—church LA-4
McKowen Creek—stream LA-4
McKown, Gilbert and Samuel, House—hist pl WV-2
McKown Cem—cemetery NY-2
McKown Cem—cemetery WV-2
McKown Creek—stream WV-2
McKown Creek Chapel—church WV-2
McKown Creek Oil Field—other WV-2
**McKown Park**—pop pl NY-2
McKown Point—cape ME-1
McKowns Creek—stream SC-3
McKown Slough—stream AR-4
McKowns Mountain Ch—church SC-3
McKowns Mtn—summit SC-3
**McKownville**—pop pl NY-2
**McKownville Estates**—pop pl NY-2
McKoy—locale NC-3
McKoy Cem—cemetery NC-3
McKoy Creek ID-8
McKume PA-2
McKune Lake—lake UT-8
McKune Spring—spring UT-8
McKusic Hill—summit WV-2
McKusick, Ivory, House—hist pl MN-6
McKusick, Lake—lake MN-6
McLachlan, William, Farmhouse—hist pl UT-8
McLachlan Hills—range MI-6
McLachlan Pond—lake NY-2
McLachlen Bldg—hist pl DC-2
McLaden Creek—stream OR-9
McLafferty Creek—stream OR-9
McLagan Airstrip—airport OR-9
McLain—locale LA-4
McLain—locale OK-5
**McLain**—pop pl MS-4
McLain, Carrie, House—hist pl AK-9
McLain, Dr. Andrew D., Office and Drug Store—hist pl AL-4
McLain, Lake—lake WY-8
McLain and Wade Cem—cemetery MS-4
McLain Attendance Center—school MS-4
McLain Branch TN-4
McLain Branch—stream NC-3
McLain Branch—stream TX-5
McLain Bridge—bridge AL-4
McLain Bridge—bridge NE-7
McLain Brook VT-1
McLain Cem—cemetery (2) GA-3
McLain Cem—cemetery MI-6
McLain Cem—cemetery MS-4
McLain Cem—cemetery (2) OK-5
McLain Cem—cemetery (2) TX-5
McLain Ch—church WV-2
McLain Chapel—church MS-4
McLain Chapel—church TN-4
McLain Creek—stream WY-8
McLaine Canyon—valley WA-9
**McLaines Mountain Subdivision**—pop pl UT-8
McLain-Gillmer House—hist pl OH-6
McLain Gulch—valley OR-9
McLain HS—school OK-5
McLain Lake—lake AK-9
McLain Lake—lake WI-6
McLain Mtn—summit ME-1
McLain Park—flat WY-8
Mclain Park—locale CA-9
McLain Peaks WA-9
McLain Reservoir MT-8
McLain Ridge—stream WV-2
McLain Run—stream OH-6
McLain Run—stream PA-2
Mclains—locale KS-7
McLains Chapel—church MO-7
McLains Sewage Lagoon Dam—dam MS-4
McLain Spring—spring (3) CA-9
Mclains Sch—school KS-7
McLain State Park—park MI-6
**McLallen Corners**—pop pl PA-2
Mclamar Canyon—valley NM-5
McLamb Airp—airport NC-3
McLamb Crossroads—locale NC-3
McLam Brook—stream VT-1
McLambs Pond—reservoir (2) NC-3
McLambs Pond Dam—dam (2) NC-3
McLam Pond—lake VT-1
**McLane**—pop pl PA-2
McLane, Louis, House—hist pl DE-2
McLane Bridge—bridge PA-2
McLane Cove—bay WA-9
McLane Creek—stream AK-9
McLane Creek—stream WA-9
McLane Draw—valley NM-5
McLane HS—school CA-9
McLane JHS—school FL-3
McLane Sch—school WA-9
McLane Sch—school WI-6
McLanes Creek—stream AK-9
McLane Spring—spring PA-2
McLane Tank—reservoir NM-5
McLaneton NC-3
McLaney Cem—cemetery TN-4
McLaran, Charles, House—hist pl MS-4
McLard Hill—summit MO-7
McLaren—uninc pl CA-9
McLaren Coulee—valley MT-8
McLaren Drain—canal MI-6
McLaren Gulch—valley ID-8
McLaren Hosp—hospital MI-6
McLaren Lake—lake MI-6
McLaren Lake—lake WI-6
McLarens Landing—locale AL-4
Mc Larens Mines—mine MT-8
McLaren (Township of)—fmr MCD AR-4
McLarer Sch—school IL-6
M Clarkson Ranch—locale SD-7
McLarry Cem—cemetery TX-5
**McLarty**—pop pl AL-4
McLary Creek—stream MI-6
McLatchy Creek—stream MT-8
McLatchy Draw Well—well MT-8
McLatchy Rsvr—reservoir MT-8
McLatchy Well—well MT-8
McLauchlin Creek MT-8
McLauchlin (Township of)—fmr MCD NC-3
McLaughan Lake—lake MI-6
McLaughin Cem—cemetery GA-3
**McLaughlin**—pop pl SD-7
McLaughlin, Charles D., House—hist pl NE-7
McLaughlin, Key—island (2) FL-3
McLaughlin Acres—locale PA-2
McLaughlin Bridge—other NM-5
McLaughlin Canyon WA-9
McLaughlin Canyon—valley CA-9
McLaughlin Cem—cemetery AR-4
McLaughlin Cem—cemetery IN-6
McLaughlin Cem—cemetery MO-7
McLaughlin Cem—cemetery NC-3
McLaughlin Cem—cemetery OK-5
McLaughlin Cem—cemetery WV-2
McLaughlin Chapel—church NC-3
**McLaughlin Corners**—pop pl PA-2
McLaughlin Creek—stream CA-9
McLaughlin Creek—stream (2) MT-8
McLaughlin Creek—stream OK-5
McLaughlin Creek—stream PA-2
McLaughlin Creek—stream (2) TX-5
McLaughlin Crossroads—locale SC-3
Mclaughlin Ditch IN-6
McLaughlin Ditch—canal IN-6
Mc laughlin Ditch—canal WY-8
McLaughlin Ditch No 5—canal WY-8
McLaughlin Ditch No 6—canal WY-8
McLaughlin Draw—valley WY-8
McLaughlin Hill—summit GA-3
McLaughlin Hollow—valley PA-2
McLaughlin Hollow—valley WV-2
McLaughlin Lake—lake MI-6
McLaughlin Lake—lake ND-7
McLaughlin Lake—lake TN-4
McLaughlin Lake—lake WY-8
Mc Laughlin Mine—mine CO-8
McLaughlin Mound—hist pl OH-6
McLaughlin Mtn—summit TX-5
McLaughlin Municipal Airp—airport SD-7
McLaughlin Pond—reservoir CT-1
McLaughlin Pond—reservoir OR-9
McLaughlin Ranch—locale CA-9
McLaughlin Rsvr No 2—reservoir WY-8
McLaughlin Run—stream (2) PA-2
McLaughlin Sch—school IL-6
McLaughlin Sch—school (2) MI-6
McLaughlin Sch—school NC-3
McLaughlin Sch—school OR-9
McLaughlins Creek TX-5
McLaughlin Site—hist pl OK-5
McLaughlin Spring—spring UT-8
McLaughlin Springs—spring CA-9
McLaughlinstown PA-2
McLaughlinsville PA-2
Mc Laughlin Township—civ div SD-7
McLaughlin Township—civil SD-7
McLaughlin-Waugh-Dovey House—hist pl NE-7
McLauren Creek—stream MS-4
**McLaurin**—pop pl MS-4
**McLaurin Acres (subdivision)**—pop pl NC-3
McLaurin Cem—cemetery (2) MS-4
McLaurin Cem—cemetery SC-3
**McLaurin Heights**—pop pl MS-4
McLaurin Heights Baptist Ch—church MS-4
McLaurin Heights United Methodist Ch—church MS-4
McLaurin House—hist pl SC-3
McLaurin HS—school MS-4
McLaurin JHS—school SC-3
McLaurin Mill Creek MS-4
McLaurin Shop Ctr—locale MS-4
McLaurins Millpond—lake SC-3
McLaurins Millpond—reservoir SC-3
McLaurin United Methodist Ch—church MS-4
McLaurlin Heights—uninc pl MS-4
McLavey Lake—lake MI-6
McLead Bay MI-6
McLead Hill—summit ID-8
McLead Lake—lake CA-9
McLean CA-9
**McLean**—pop pl IL-6
**McLean**—pop pl NE-7
**McLean**—pop pl NY-2
**McLean**—pop pl TX-5
**McLean**—pop pl VA-3
**McLean**—pop pl WV-2
McLean, Henry, House—hist pl NC-3
McLean, Isaac, House—hist pl MA-1
McLean, John S., House—hist pl NC-3
McLean, Robert and Lucy, House—hist pl OR-9
McLean Arm—bay AK-9
Mc Lean Basin—basin CO-8
McLean Bend—bend TN-4
McLean Bible Ch—church VA-3
McLean Bottom—bend AR-4
McLean Bottom Cutoff—channel AR-4
McLean Branch—stream NC-3
McLean Bridge—bridge NC-3
McLean Brook—stream (2) ME-1
McLean Brothers Airp—airport NC-3
McLean Canyon CA-9
McLean (CCD)—cens area TX-5
McLean Cem—cemetery GA-3
McLean Cem—cemetery MO-7
McLean Cem—cemetery (3) NC-3
McLean Cem—cemetery SC-3
McLean Cem—cemetery (3) TN-4
McLean Ch—church MS-4
McLean Ch—church NC-3
McLean Coulee—valley MT-8
McLean County—civil ND-7
**McLean (County)**—pop pl IL-6
**McLean (County)**—pop pl KY-4
McLean County Courthouse—hist pl ND-7
McLean County Courthouse and Square—hist pl IL-6
McLean Creek—stream (2) AK-9
McLean Creek—stream GA-3
McLean Creek—stream MO-7
McLean Creek—stream MT-8
McLean Creek—stream NC-3
McLean Creek—stream WI-6
McLean Dam NC-3
Mc Lean Drain—canal CO-8
McLean Drain—canal MI-6
McLean Draw OR-9
McLeane Coulee MT-8
Mclean Elem Sch—school KS-7
**McLean Estates**—pop pl VA-3
McLean Field—park KS-7
Mc Lean Game Ref—park CT-1
**McLean Gardens**—pop pl DC-2
McLean Gulch Rsvr—reservoir WY-8
McLean Gut—gut VA-3
**McLean Hamlet**—pop pl VA-3
McLean Heights—uninc pl NY-2
McLean Hill—summit VT-1
**McLean (historical)**—pop pl TN-4
McLean Hollow—valley MO-7
McLean Hosp—hospital MA-1
McLean House—building VA-3
McLean House—hist pl AR-4
McLean HS—school VA-3
McLean JHS—school IN-6
McLean JHS—school TX-5
McLean Lake—flat CA-9
McLean Lake—lake AL-4
McLean Lake—lake ME-1
McLean Lake—lake WI-6
McLean Lake Number 1—reservoir AL-4
**McLean Manor**—pop pl VA-3
McLean Meadows—flat WY-8
McLean Mine—mine ID-8
McLean Mine (underground)—mine AL-4
McLean Mountain VA-3
McLean Mtn—summit ME-1
McLean Mtn—summit OR-9
McLean Park—park TX-5
McLean Place—locale OR-9
McLean Point—cape AK-9
McLean Point—cape OR-9
McLean Pond—reservoir SC-3
McLean Reservoir Dam—dam MA-1
McLean Ridge—ridge ME-1
McLean Rock—pillar TN-4
McLean Rsvr—reservoir MA-1
McLean Rsvr—reservoir MT-8
McLeans—locale NV-8
McLeans Bay—bay ID-8
**McLeansboro**—pop pl IL-6
McLeansboro, Lake—reservoir IL-6
McLeansboro Golf Club—other IL-6
**McLeansboro (Township of)**—pop pl IL-6
McLeans Branch—stream NC-3
McLeans Ch—church NC-3
McLean Sch—school AL-4
McLean Sch—school (2) MI-6
McLeans Creek—stream ID-8
McLeans Creek—stream NC-3
McLean Site (22LF513)—hist pl MS-4
McLean Slough—stream OR-9
McLean Spring—spring CA-9
McLean Spur—locale MS-4
McLeans Station—locale PA-2
**McLeansville**—pop pl NC-3
McLeansville Ch—church NC-3
McLeansville MS—school NC-3
McLeansville Post Office TN-4
**McLean (Township of)**—pop pl OH-6
McLean Well—well OR-9
McLearn Hollow TN-4
McLearns Coulee MT-8
McLear Resort—locale CA-9
McLeary Brook—stream ME-1
McLeary Cem—cemetery (2) TN-4
McLedd Lake—reservoir ND-7
McLees Lake—lake AK-9
McLees Ranch—locale WY-8
**McLeish**—pop pl OH-6
McLeish Canyon—valley WA-9
McLeish Cem—cemetery MI-6
McLeish Cem—cemetery MT-8
McLeish Landing Strip—airport ND-7
McLellan NJ-2
McLellan Bay—swamp FL-3
McLellan Cem—cemetery FL-3
McLellan Cem—cemetery SC-3
McLellan Ch—church FL-3
McLellan Cove—bay ME-1
McLellan Creek—stream AK-9
McLellan Creek—stream GA-3
McLellan Dam—dam AZ-5
McLellan House—hist pl ME-1
McLellan Lake—lake MI-6
McLellan Pass—gap AK-9
McLellan Peak—summit AK-9
McLellan Pond—lake ME-1
McLellan Rsvr—reservoir AZ-5
McLellan Siding Tank—reservoir AZ-5
McLellan-Sweat Mansion—hist pl ME-1
McLellen FL-3
**McLellen**—pop pl FL-3
McLemmonsville TN-4
McLemmonsville Post Office TN-4
McLemore MS-4
McLemore—uninc pl OK-5
McLemore Branch—stream (2) AL-4
McLemore Branch—stream MS-4
McLemore Branch—stream TX-5
McLemore Cem—cemetery AL-4
McLemore Cem—cemetery AR-4
McLemore Cem—cemetery MS-4
McLemore Cem—cemetery TN-4
McLemore Cem—cemetery TX-5
McLemore Cemetery—hist pl MS-4
McLemore Cove—valley GA-3
McLemore Hills—summit TX-5
**McLemore Point Subdivision (subdivision)**—pop pl AL-4
McLemore Sch—school AL-4
McLemore Sch (historical)—school MS-4
McLemore-Sharpe Farmstead—hist pl GA-3
McLemore Site—hist pl OK-5
McLemores Landing MS-4
McLemore Station MS-4
**McLemoresville**—pop pl TN-4
McLemoresville Baptist Ch—church TN-4
McLemoresville Post Office—building TN-4
McLemoresville Sch (historical)—school TN-4
McLenathan Bay—bay NY-2
McLenden Draw—valley NM-5
McLendon—locale TX-5
**McLendon**—pop pl AL-4
McLendon Branch—stream AR-4
McLendon Branch—stream TX-5
McLendon Butte—summit ID-8
McLendon Cem—cemetery AL-4
McLendon Cem—cemetery TN-4
**McLendon-Chisholm**—pop pl TX-5
McLendon Crossroads—locale GA-3
McLendon Park—park AL-4
McLendon Peak—summit AZ-5
McLendon Ranch—locale NM-5
McLendons Creek—stream NC-3
McLennan Canyon—valley OR-9
McLennan Cem—cemetery TX-5
**McLennan (County)**—pop pl TX-5
McLennen Mtn—summit OR-9
McLennon Pit—cave AL-4
McLennon Spring Number One—spring MT-8
McLennon Spring Number Two—spring MT-8
**McLeod**—pop pl LA-4
**McLeod**—pop pl MS-4
**McLeod**—pop pl MT-8
**McLeod**—pop pl ND-7
**McLeod**—pop pl OR-9
**McLeod**—pop pl TX-5
McLeod, Angus, House—hist pl AR-4
McLeod, Lake—lake FL-3
McLeod, Point—cape AK-9
McLeod Arroyo—stream NM-5
McLeod Basin—basin (2) MT-8
McLeod Bay—bay AK-9
McLeod Branch—stream (2) MS-4
McLeod Bridge MS-4
McLeod Cem—cemetery AR-4
McLeod Cem—cemetery (6) MS-4

McLeod Ch—*church* ... SC-3
*McLeod Chapel* ... MS-4
McLeod Chapel—*church* ... SC-3
**McLeod (County)**—*pop pl* ... MN-6
McLeod County Courthouse—*hist pl* ... MN-6
*McLeod Creek* ... NC-3
*McLeod Creek* ... SC-3
McLeod Creek—*stream* ... AL-4
McLeod Creek—*stream* ... AK-9
McLeod Creek—*stream* ... CA-9
McLeod Creek—*stream* ... ID-8
McLeod Creek—*stream* (2) ... MS-4
McLeod Creek—*stream* ... NV-8
McLeod Creek—*stream* ... NC-3
McLeod Creek—*stream* (2) ... OR-9
McLeod Creek—*stream* ... UT-8
McLeod Ditch—*canal* ... MI-6
McLeod Ditch—*canal* ... MT-8
McLeod Ditch—*canal* ... NV-8
McLeod Draw—*valley* ... NM-5
*McLeod Elementary School* ... MS-4
McLeod Family Rural Complex—*hist pl* ... NC-3
McLeod Grave—*cemetery* ... GA-3
McLeod Guard Station—*locale* ... OR-9
McLeod Gulch—*valley* (2) ... MT-8
McLeod Hill—*summit* ... NV-8
McLeod Hills—*ridge* ... NM-5
McLeod Honor Farm—*area* ... OK-5
McLeod Honor Farm—*other* ... OK-5
*McLeod Lake* ... WI-6
McLeod Lake—*lake* (3) ... AK-9
McLeod Lake—*lake* ... CA-9
McLeod Lake—*lake* ... ND-7
McLeod Lake—*lake* ... WA-9
McLeod Lake—*lake* ... WI-6
McLeod Memorial Cem—*cemetery* ... NC-3
*McLeod Mill Branch* ... NC-3
McLeod Mill Branch—*stream* ... NC-3
McLeod Mountian—*summit* ... WA-9
McLeod Park—*park* ... MT-8
*Mcleod Peak* ... WA-9
McLeod Peak—*summit* ... MT-8
McLeod Plantation—*hist pl* ... SC-3
McLeod Point—*cape* ... AK-9
McLeod Pond—*reservoir* ... MA-1
McLeod Pond—*reservoir* ... MS-4
McLeod Pond Dam—*dam* ... MA-1
McLeod Post Office (historical)—*building* ... MS-4
Mc Leod Ranch—*locale* ... CO-8
McLeod Ranch—*locale* ... NV-8
McLeod Ranch—*locale* ... SD-7
McLeod Ridge—*ridge* ... CA-9
McLeod Ridge—*ridge* ... OR-9
McLeod Sch—*school* ... MS-4
McLeod Sch—*school* ... MT-8
McLeod Sch—*school* ... SD-7
McLeods Chapel—*church* ... MS-4
**McLeods Corner**—*pop pl* ... MI-6
*McLeods Creek* ... NC-3
*McLeods Creek* ... SC-3
McLeods Lake—*reservoir* ... NC-3
McLeod Slough—*stream* ... WA-9
McLeods Mill—*locale* ... GA-3
McLeods Pond—*lake* ... SC-3
McLeods Pond—*reservoir* ... SC-3
McLeod Spring House—*hist pl* ... KY-4
*McLeods River* ... OR-9
McLeods Slough—*gut* ... MN-6
McLeod State Park—*park* ... OR-9
McLeod Tank—*reservoir* ... NM-5
*McLeon Coulee* ... MT-8
*McLeoud Peak* ... MT-8
McLeroys Store (historical)—*locale* ... AL-4
McLery Cem—*cemetery* ... WI-6
McLester Cem—*cemetery* ... TN-4
McLester Cem—*cemetery* ... TX-5
McLewean Square (Shop Ctr)—*locale* ... NC-3
McLewis Sch—*school* ... TX-5
McLiesh Cem—*cemetery* ... OH-6
McLin Cem—*cemetery* ... LA-4
McLin Cem—*cemetery* ... VA-3
McLin Creek—*stream* ... NC-3
M Cline Ranch—*locale* ... NE-7
McLin Notch—*gap* ... KY-4
McLin Notch—*gap* ... VA-3
*McLins Corner* ... TN-4
**McLin's Corner (Hodson)**—*pop pl* ... TN-4
M'Clintock House—*hist pl* ... NY-2
McLish and Carpenter Drain—*canal* ... MI-6
McLish Sch—*school* ... OK-5
McLishs Stand (historical)—*locale* ... TN-4
McLlhenny Elem Sch—*school* ... GA-3
McLlheran Cem—*cemetery* ... TN-4
McLlroy Canyon—*valley* ... WA-9
Mcllroy Knob—*summit* ... MO-7
Mc Llvoy Park—*park* ... CO-8
McLntosh Cem—*cemetery* ... IL-6
McLoad Cem—*cemetery* ... KY-4
M C Log S B Pac—*post sta* ... CA-9
McLorn Well—*locale* ... NM-5
**McLoud**—*pop pl* ... OK-5
McLoud Cem—*cemetery* ... OK-5
McLoud Gas Field—*oilfield* ... OK-5
*McLoud Hill* ... ID-8
**McLoughlin**—*pop pl* ... WA-9
McLoughlin, Mount—*summit* ... OR-9
McLoughlin Airfield—*airport* ... OR-9
McLoughlin Canyon—*valley* ... WA-9
McLoughlin Falls—*falls* ... WA-9
**McLoughlin Heights**—*pop pl* ... WA-9
*McLoughlin Home Natl Historic Site* ... OR-9
McLoughlin House Natl Historic
Site—*park* ... OR-9
McLoughlin HS—*school* ... OR-9
McLoughlin JHS—*school* (2) ... WA-9
McLoughlin Spring—*spring* ... WA-9
McLoughlin Substation—*locale* ... OR-9
*McLouglin Spring* ... WA-9
**McLouth**—*pop pl* ... KS-7
McLouth Elem Sch—*school* ... KS-7
McLouth HS—*school* ... KS-7
McLouth Park—*park* ... MI-6
McLucas Cem—*cemetery* ... ME-1
McLuin Seymour Dam—*dam* ... SD-7
**McLuney**—*pop pl* ... OH-6
McLuney Cem—*cemetery* ... OH-6
McLuney Creek—*stream* ... OH-6
McLung Lateral—*canal* ... SD-7
*McLure* ... AL-4
McMaban Cem—*cemetery* ... TN-4
McMackin Mine—*mine* ... SD-7
McMackins Cem—*cemetery* ... TN-4
McMahan—*locale* ... TN-4
**McMahan**—*pop pl* ... TN-4
**McMahan**—*pop pl* ... TX-5
McMahan, Daniel, House—*hist pl* ... TN-4
*McMahan Branch* ... OR-9
McMahan Branch—*stream* ... OR-9
McMahan Branch—*stream* ... TN-4
*McMahan Calvary Baptist Church* ... TN-4
McMahan Cem—*cemetery* ... AL-4
McMahan Cem—*cemetery* ... MO-7
McMahan Cem—*cemetery* ... OK-5
McMahan Cem—*cemetery* ... TN-4
McMahan Cem—*cemetery* ... TX-5
McMahan Ch—*church* (2) ... TN-4
McMahan Chapel—*church* ... TX-5
*McMahan Ch of Christ* ... TN-4
McMahan Cove—*valley* ... AL-4
McMahan Creek—*stream* ... ID-8
McMahan Creek—*stream* ... TN-4
McMahan Ditch—*canal* ... IN-6
McMahan Drain—*canal* (2) ... MI-6
McMahan Homestead—*hist pl* ... NY-2
McMahan House—*hist pl* ... KY-4
McMahan Knob—*summit* ... TN-4
McMahan Ranch—*locale* ... NV-8
*McMahans* ... OH-6
McMahan Sch—*school* ... MO-7
McMahan Sch (historical)—*school* ... TN-4
McMahans Ferry (historical)—*locale* ... AL-4
McMahan Spring—*spring* ... MO-7
McMahen Creek—*stream* ... MI-6
McMahill Cem—*cemetery* ... IL-6
McMahon, John, House—*hist pl* ... AL-4
McMahon Arroyo—*stream* ... CO-8
McMahon Canal—*canal* ... LA-4
McMahon Corners—*locale* ... NY-2
*McMahon Cove* ... AL-4
McMahon Creek—*stream* ... CA-9
McMahon Creek—*stream* ... ID-8
McMahon Creek—*stream* ... OH-6
McMahon Drain—*canal* ... MI-6
McMahone Park—*flat* ... WY-8
Mc Mahon Field Airp—*airport* ... WA-9
McMahon Hollow—*valley* ... TN-4
McMahon House—*hist pl* ... IA-7
McMahon HS—*school* ... CT-1
McMahon HS—*school* ... NY-2
McMahon Lake—*lake* ... MI-6
McMahon Lake—*lake* ... MN-6
McMahon Memorial Bldg—*building* ... OK-5
McMahon Mine—*mine* ... CA-9
McMahon Ridge—*ridge* ... NV-8
Mc Mahon Rsvr—*reservoir* ... CO-8
*McMahon's* ... OH-6
McMahon Sch—*school* ... ME-1
McMahon Sch—*school* ... MA-1
McMahon Sch—*school* ... MI-6
McMahons Pond—*lake* ... NH-1
McMahon Swamp—*stream* ... VA-3
McMahon Woods—*flat* ... OK-5
McMahon Woods—*woods* ... IL-6
McMain JHS—*school* ... LA-4
McMains Cem—*cemetery* ... OK-5
McMakin, William, House—*hist pl* ... KY-4
McMakin Creek—*stream* ... MO-7
McMakin's Tavern—*hist pl* ... SC-3
McMammon Ditch—*canal* ... IN-6
McManas Hollow—*valley* ... PA-2
**McMan (Dundee)**—*pop pl* ... OK-5
McManigal Canyon—*valley* ... NE-7
McMannaman Lake—*lake* ... WA-9
*McMannamay Run* ... VA-3
McMannamy Draw—*valley* ... MT-8
McMannaway Run—*stream* ... VA-3
McMann Creek—*stream* ... WA-9
McMannen Ch—*church* ... NC-3
McMann Hollow—*valley* ... PA-2
McMannis Creek—*stream* ... MT-8
McMann Island (historical)—*island* ... TN-4
McMann Lake—*lake* ... ND-7
McMann Sch—*school* ... SD-7
McManns Sch—*school* ... NJ-2
McManus—*locale* ... CA-9
**McManus**—*pop pl* ... AR-4
**McManus**—*pop pl* ... GA-3
**McManus**—*pop pl* ... LA-4
McManus, George, House—*hist pl* ... MI-6
McManus, Patrick F., House—*hist pl* ... OR-9
McManus Brook—*stream* ... ME-1
McManus Camp—*locale* ... ME-1
McManus Corner—*locale* ... MI-6
*McManus Creek* ... TX-5
McManus Creek—*stream* ... AK-9
McManus Creek—*stream* ... MT-8
McManus Creek—*stream* ... TX-5
McManus Dam—*dam* ... AL-4
*McManus-Darlington Drain* ... MI-6
McManus Ditch—*canal* ... IN-6
McManus Drain—*canal* ... MI-6
McManus Gulch—*valley* ... MT-8
McManus House—*hist pl* ... IA-7
*Mcmanus Island* ... MN-6
McManus Island—*island* ... MN-6
McManus Lake—*lake* ... CT-1
McManus Mine—*mine* ... TN-4
McManus Park—*park* ... CA-9
McManus P.O. (historical)—*building* ... MS-4
McManus Pond—*reservoir* ... AL-4
McManus Ridge—*ridge* ... WI-6
McManus Sch—*school* ... CA-9
McManus Spring—*spring* ... NV-8
McManus Spur—*locale* ... AR-4
McMara Ranch—*locale* ... NE-7
McMaster Corners—*locale* ... NY-2
McMaster Creek—*stream* ... IA-7
McMaster Creek—*stream* ... MI-6
McMaster Hill—*summit* ... VT-1
McMaster House—*hist pl* ... NY-2
McMaster Park—*park* ... CA-9
McMaster Rsvr—*reservoir* ... WY-8
McMasters Bridge—*other* ... MI-6
McMaster Sch—*school* ... SC-3
McMasters Creek—*stream* ... MI-6
McMasters Crossing—*locale* ... NY-2
McMasters Run—*stream* ... PA-2
McMath-Hulbert Observatory—*building* ... MI-6
McMath Millpond—*lake* ... GA-3
McMath Pond—*reservoir* ... GA-3
*McMaths* ... AL-4
McMath Solar Telescope—*building* ... AZ-5
McMaughn Canyon—*valley* ... NV-8
M C M Ch—*church* ... TN-4
McMeans Ranch—*locale* ... NM-5
**McMechen**—*pop pl* ... WV-2
McMechen Cem—*cemetery* ... WV-2
McMechen Hill—*summit* ... OH-6
McMeckens Run—*stream* ... WV-2
McMeekin—*locale* ... FL-3
McMeekin Drain—*canal* ... MI-6
McMeekin Lake—*lake* ... FL-3
McMeekin Ranch—*locale* ... ID-8
McMeekin Rock Shelter—*hist pl* ... SC-3
McMeekin Rsvr—*reservoir* ... NE-7
McMeen Branch—*stream* ... TN-4
McMeen Creek—*stream* ... OR-9
Mc Meen Sch—*school* ... CO-8
McMeen Spring—*spring* ... OR-9
*McMeikles Creek* ... PA-2
McMenomey Ranch—*locale* ... MT-8
**McMichael**—*pop pl* ... PA-2
McMichael Cem—*cemetery* ... GA-3
McMichael Cem—*cemetery* ... LA-4
McMichael Cem—*cemetery* ... PA-2
McMichael Cem—*cemetery* ... TN-4
McMichael Ch—*church* ... LA-4
McMichael Creek—*stream* ... OH-6
McMichael Creek—*stream* ... PA-2
McMichael Draw—*valley* ... WY-8
McMichael Run—*stream* ... PA-2
*McMichaels* ... PA-2
**McMichaels**—*pop pl* ... PA-2
McMichael Sch—*school* ... PA-2
*Mcmichaels Creek* ... PA-2
*McMicheals Creek* ... PA-2
McMicken—*locale* ... AZ-5
McMicken Dam—*dam* ... AZ-5
McMicken Dam Outlet Channel—*canal* ... AZ-5
Mcmicken Ditch—*canal* ... WY-8
**McMicken Heights**—*pop pl* ... WA-9
McMicken House—*hist pl* ... KY-4
McMicken Island—*island* ... WA-9
McMickin Lake—*lake* ... TX-5
*McMickle Dam* ... NJ-2
*McMickles Pond* ... NJ-2
**McMilan Corner**—*pop pl* ... AR-4
McMillan—*locale* ... ID-8
McMillan—*locale* ... MS-4
McMillan—*locale* ... NC-3
McMillan—*locale* ... OK-5
McMillan—*locale* ... TN-4
**McMillan**—*pop pl* ... MI-6
**McMillan**—*pop pl* ... MS-4
**McMillan**—*pop pl* ... PA-2
**McMillan**—*pop pl* ... WV-2
McMillan, David, House—*hist pl* ... WI-6
McMillan, Lake—*reservoir* ... AL-4
McMillan, Lake—*reservoir* ... NM-5
McMillan, Reuben, Free Library—*hist pl* ... OH-6
McMillan, Robert, House—*hist pl* ... GA-3
McMillan, Samuel, House—*hist pl* ... KY-4
McMillan Bluff—*cliff* ... FL-3
McMillan Branch—*stream* ... TX-5
McMillan Cabin—*locale* ... CA-9
McMillan Camp—*locale* ... MI-6
*McMillan Canyon* ... CA-9
McMillan Canyon—*valley* ... CA-9
McMillan Canyon—*valley* ... NM-5
McMillan Canyon—*valley* ... OR-9
McMillan Cem—*cemetery* ... AL-4
McMillan Cem—*cemetery* (2) ... GA-3
McMillan Cem—*cemetery* ... KY-4
McMillan Cem—*cemetery* ... MS-4
McMillan Cem—*cemetery* (2) ... NC-3
McMillan Cem—*cemetery* ... OK-5
McMillan Cem—*cemetery* (2) ... TN-4
McMillan Cem—*cemetery* ... TX-5
McMillan Ch—*church* ... NC-3
McMillan Ch—*church* ... TN-4
McMillan Chapel—*church* ... ID-8
McMillan Corner—*locale* ... MI-6
*McMillan Creek* ... CA-9
McMillan Creek—*stream* ... MI-6
McMillan Creek—*stream* ... MS-4
McMillan Creek—*stream* ... MT-8
McMillan Creek—*stream* ... NY-2
McMillan Creek—*stream* ... OR-9
McMillan Creek—*stream* ... WA-9
McMillan Dam—*dam* (2) ... AL-4
McMillan Ditch—*canal* ... IN-6
McMillan Draw—*valley* ... WY-8
McMillan Forest Camp—*locale* ... NM-5
McMillan Fork—*stream* ... MD-2
McMillan-Garrison House—*hist pl* ... GA-3
McMillan Hill—*summit* ... WA-9
McMillan Hollow—*valley* ... AR-4
McMillan Hollow—*valley* ... MO-7
McMillan House—*hist pl* ... AL-4
McMillan House—*hist pl* ... SC-3
*McMillan Island* ... TN-4
McMillan Island—*island* ... GA-3
McMillan Island—*island* ... IA-7
McMillan Lake—*lake* ... CA-9
Mc Millan Lake—*lake* ... CO-8
McMillan Lake—*lake* ... FL-3
McMillan Lake—*lake* ... GA-3
McMillan Manor—*uninc pl* ... CA-9
McMillan Marsh—*swamp* ... WI-6
McMillan Marsh State Public Hunting
Grounds—*park* ... WI-6
**McMillan Meadows
Subdivision**—*pop pl* ... UT-8
McMillan Memorial Hosp—*hospital* ... AL-4
**McMillan Mesa**—*pop pl* ... AZ-5
McMillan Mine—*mine* ... AZ-5
McMillan Mines—*mine* ... AK-9
McMillan Mountains—*summit* ... TX-5
McMillan Mtn—*summit* ... MT-8
McMillan Mtn—*summit* ... WA-9
McMillan Park—*flat* ... WA-9
McMillan Park—*park* ... AL-4
McMillan Park—*park* ... SC-3
Mc Millan Peak—*summit* ... CO-8
McMillan Pond—*lake* ... AL-4
McMillan Pond—*reservoir* ... AL-4
McMillan Post Office (historical)—*building* ... TN-4
McMillan Rsvr—*reservoir* ... DC-2
McMillan Rsvr—*reservoir* ... WY-8
*McMillans* ... NC-3
McMillans Acad—*school* ... PA-2
*McMillan Sch* ... PA-2
McMillan Sch—*school* ... CA-9
McMillan Sch—*school* (2) ... IL-6
McMillan Sch—*school* (2) ... MI-6
McMillan Sch—*school* ... MO-7
McMillan Sch—*school* ... UT-8
McMillan Sch (historical)—*school* ... AL-4
McMillan Sch (historical)—*school* ... TN-4
McMillans Corners—*locale* ... NY-2
McMillans Ferry—*locale* ... KY-4
McMillans Landing (historical)—*locale* ... AL-4
McMillan Spire—*pillar* ... WA-9
McMillan Spring—*spring* (2) ... CA-9
McMillan Spring—*spring* ... TN-4
McMillan Springs Campground—*park* ... UT-8
*McMillans Switch* ... MS-4
*McMillan Swamp* ... WI-6
**McMillan (Town of)**—*pop pl* ... WI-6
**McMillan (Township of)**—*pop pl* (2) ... MI-6
McMillanville Town Well—*well* ... AZ-5
McMillan Woods—*woods* ... PA-2
McMillen, George, House—*hist pl* ... SD-7
McMillen Cem—*cemetery* ... KY-4
McMillen Coy Township—*civil* ... MO-7
McMillen Ditch—*canal* ... NM-5
McMillen Hollow—*valley* ... MO-7
McMillen Hollow—*valley* ... PA-2
McMillen Lake—*lake* ... OH-6
McMillen Park—*park* (2) ... IN-6
McMillen Ranch—*locale* (2) ... NE-7
McMillen Ranch—*locale* ... NM-5
McMillen Spring—*spring* ... OR-9
McMillen Tiff Township—*civil* ... MO-7
McMillen Wash—*stream* ... AZ-5
McMiller Corners—*locale* ... NY-2
McMillian Bayou—*stream* ... LA-4
McMillian Branch—*stream* ... SC-3
McMillian Cem—*cemetery* ... AR-4
McMillian Cem—*cemetery* ... LA-4
McMillian Cem—*cemetery* ... MS-4
McMillian Cem—*cemetery* ... NC-3
McMillian Cem—*cemetery* (2) ... TN-4
McMillian JHS—*school* ... FL-3
McMillian Park—*park* ... FL-3
McMillian Park—*park* ... MS-4
McMillianville—*locale* ... AZ-5
**McMillin**—*pop pl* ... TX-5
**McMillin**—*pop pl* ... WA-9
McMillin Bridge—*hist pl* ... WA-9
McMillin Cem—*cemetery* ... TN-4
McMillin Cem—*cemetery* (2) ... TX-5
McMillin Creek—*stream* ... OR-9
McMillin Rsvr—*reservoir* ... WA-9
McMillin Sch—*hist pl* ... WA-9
*McMillin Spring Rec Area* ... UT-8
McMillion Cabin—*locale* ... CA-9
McMillion Cem—*cemetery* ... AR-4
McMillion Cem—*cemetery* ... LA-4
McMillion Ch—*church* ... WV-2
McMillion Creek—*stream* (2) ... WV-2
*McMillon Creek* ... FL-3
McMilly Swamp—*stream* ... NC-3
*McMinn* ... PA-2
McMinn Airp—*airport* ... AL-4
McMinn Bench—*bench* ... MT-8
McMinn Branch—*stream* ... MS-4
McMinn Canal—*canal* ... UT-8
McMinn Cem—*cemetery* ... MS-4
McMinn Cem—*cemetery* ... NY-2
McMinn Cem—*cemetery* ... TX-5
McMinn Central HS—*school* ... TN-4
**McMinn County**—*pop pl* ... TN-4
McMinn County Airp—*airport* ... TN-4
McMinn County Cem—*cemetery* ... TN-4
McMinn County Courthouse—*building* ... TN-4
McMinn County HS—*school* ... TN-4
McMinn Field—*park* ... TN-4
McMinn Gap—*gap* ... AR-4
*McMinn High School* ... TN-4
McMinn Hollow—*valley* ... AR-4
McMinn Knob—*summit* ... AR-4
McMinn Lake Dam—*dam* ... MS-4
McMinn Memory Gardens—*cemetery* ... TN-4
McMinn Ridge—*ridge* ... TN-4
McMinn Sch—*school* ... MO-7
McMinn Shop Ctr—*locale* ... TN-4
McMinn Spring—*spring* ... MO-7
McMinns Summit—*locale* ... PA-2
**McMinnville**—*pop pl* ... OR-9
**McMinnville**—*pop pl* (2) ... TN-4
McMinnville (CCD)—*cens area* ... OR-9
McMinnville (CCD)—*cens area* ... TN-4
McMinnville City Hall—*building* ... TN-4
McMinnville Division—*civil* ... TN-4
McMinnville Downtown Hist Dist—*hist pl* ... OR-9
McMinnville First Baptist Ch—*church* ... TN-4
McMinnville First Presbyterian Ch—*church* ... TN-4
McMinnville Grange Hall—*locale* ... OR-9
McMinnville Municipal Airp—*airport* ... OR-9
McMinnville Plaza Shop Ctr—*locale* ... TN-4
McMinnville Post Office—*building* ... TN-4
*McMinnville Rsvr* ... OR-9
McMinnville Water Supply Dam—*dam* ... TN-4
McMinnville Water Supply
Lake—*reservoir* ... TN-4
*M C M Missionary Baptist Church* ... TN-4
*Mcmocin Hill* ... OH-6
McMonies Run—*stream* ... OH-6
McMoran Flat—*flat* ... CA-9
McMordie Pens—*locale* ... TX-5
**McMorran**—*pop pl* ... OH-6
M C M Sch—*school* ... TN-4
McMullan Branch—*stream* ... MS-4
McMullan Cem—*cemetery* ... GA-3
*McMullan Creek* ... CA-9
McMullan Lake Dam—*dam* ... MS-4
McMullan Lakes—*lake* ... MI-6
McMullan Peak—*summit* ... MT-8
McMullan-Skinner House—*hist pl* ... AL-4
*McMullans Lake* ... MI-6
*Mc Mullans Landing* ... OR-9
McMullans Landing—*locale* ... OR-9
McMullan-Vickery Farm—*hist pl* ... GA-3
McMullen—*locale* ... VA-3
**McMullen**—*pop pl* ... AL-4
McMullen, John, House—*hist pl* ... CA-9
McMullen Airp—*airport* ... KS-7
McMullen Basin—*basin* ... ID-8
McMullen Bay—*lake* ... GA-3
McMullen Branch—*gut* ... FL-3
McMullen Branch—*stream* ... MO-7
McMullen Brook—*stream* ... NY-2
McMullen Cem—*cemetery* ... FL-3
McMullen Cem—*cemetery* ... MO-7
McMullen Cem—*cemetery* (2) ... VA-3
*McMullen Cemetery* ... MS-4
**McMullen (County)**—*pop pl* ... TX-5
McMullen Cove—*bay* ... AK-9
McMullen Cow Camp—*locale* ... ID-8
McMullen Creek—*stream* ... CA-9
McMullen Creek—*stream* ... FL-3
McMullen Creek—*stream* ... ID-8
McMullen Creek—*stream* ... NC-3
McMullen Creek—*stream* (3) ... OR-9
McMullen Creek Market—*locale* ... NC-3
McMullen Ditch—*canal* ... OR-9
McMullen Drain—*canal* ... MI-6
McMullen Drain—*stream* ... MI-6
McMullen Flat—*flat* ... CA-9
McMullen Hill—*summit* ... WI-6
*McMullen Hollow* ... MO-7
*McMullen Lake* ... TX-5
McMullen Lake—*lake* ... MI-6
McMullen Lake—*lake* ... MN-6
McMullen Lake—*lake* ... TX-5
McMullen Lake Dam—*dam* (2) ... MS-4
*McMullen Lakes* ... MI-6
McMullen Mtn—*summit* ... CA-9
McMullen Peak—*summit* ... NM-5
McMullen Pond—*lake* ... NY-2
McMullen Quarry—*mine* (2) ... TN-4
McMullen Ridge—*ridge* ... MO-7
*McMullen Run* ... PA-2
McMullens—*locale* ... TN-4
McMullen School (abandoned)—*locale* ... MO-7
*McMullens Creek* ... FL-3
McMullen Spring—*spring* (2) ... OR-9
*McMullen Station* ... TN-4
*McMullen Valley* ... AZ-5
McMullen Valley—*valley* ... AZ-5
McMullin—*locale* ... VA-3
**McMullin**—*pop pl* ... MO-7
McMullin, Maj. James W., House—*hist pl* ... IA-7
McMullin Cem—*cemetery* ... KY-4
Mc Mullin Cem—*cemetery* ... KY-4
McMullin Creek—*stream* ... OR-9
*McMullin Ranch Gas Field* ... CA-9
McMullin Sch (abandoned)—*school* ... MO-7
McMullins Landing—*stream* ... OR-9
Mc Mullin Spring—*spring* ... CO-8
McMullin-Warren House—*hist pl* ... KY-4
McMunns Point—*cape* ... MA-1
McMurdie Hollow—*valley* ... UT-8
McMurdo Cabin—*locale* ... OR-9
Mc Murdo Gulch—*valley* ... CO-8
McMurdo Ranch—*locale* ... MT-8
McMurdy Brook—*stream* ... NY-2
McMurdy Hill—*summit* ... NY-2
McMurphy Cem—*cemetery* ... MO-7
McMurphy Creek—*stream* ... WA-9
**McMurray**—*pop pl* ... PA-2
**McMurray**—*pop pl* ... WA-9
McMurray, Lake—*lake* ... WA-9
McMurray Camp—*locale* ... AL-4
McMurray Cem—*cemetery* ... OH-6
McMurray Cem—*cemetery* (2) ... TN-4
McMurray Cem—*cemetery* (2) ... VA-3
McMurray Chapel—*church* ... KY-4
McMurray Creek—*stream* ... NY-2
McMurray Creek—*stream* ... WY-8
McMurray Dam—*dam* (2) ... AL-4
McMurray Hollow—*valley* ... TN-4
McMurray House—*hist pl* ... GA-3
McMurray House—*hist pl* ... TX-5
McMurray JHS—*school* ... TN-4
McMurray Lake—*lake* ... CA-9
McMurray Lake—*reservoir* (2) ... AL-4
McMurray (McMurry College)—*uninc pl* ... TX-5
McMurray Run—*stream* ... PA-2
McMurray Sch—*school* ... TX-5
McMurray Shoals—*bar* ... TN-4
McMurrays Lake—*lake* ... PA-2
*McMurrays Mill* ... NJ-2
*McMurrays Mill* ... TN-4
McMurray Spring—*spring* ... TN-4
McMurrin Branch—*stream* ... GA-3
McMurrin Gap—*gap* ... PA-2
McMurrin Pond—*lake* ... GA-3
McMurrin Run—*stream* ... PA-2
*Mcmurry* ... PA-2
McMurry Cem—*cemetery* ... KY-4
McMurry Cem—*cemetery* ... MS-4
McMurry Cem—*cemetery* (3) ... TN-4
McMurry Coll—*school* ... TX-5
McMurry Lake—*reservoir* ... GA-3
McMurry Meadows—*flat* ... CA-9
Mc Murry Ranch—*locale* ... CO-8
McMurry Spring—*spring* ... CA-9
McMurry Spring—*spring* ... MO-7
McMurtery Branch—*stream* ... OK-5
McMurtrey Creek—*stream* ... MO-7
McMurtrey Creek—*stream* ... OK-5
McMurtrey Marsh—*swamp* ... NE-7
McMurtrey Township—*civil* ... MO-7
McMurtrie Cem—*cemetery* ... TN-4
McMurtrie Lake—*reservoir* ... IN-6
McMurtry, Lake—*reservoir* ... OK-5
McMurtry Bayou—*stream* ... TX-5
McMurtry Canyon—*valley* ... TX-5
McMurtry Cem—*cemetery* (2) ... TN-4
McMurtry Creek—*stream* ... MT-8
McMurtry Farm—*locale* ... TX-5
McMurtry Hollow—*valley* ... TN-4
McMurtry Ranch—*locale* (3) ... TX-5
McMurtry Windmill—*locale* ... TX-5
*McMurty Creek* ... MO-7
McNab—*locale* ... OR-9
**McNab**—*pop pl* ... AR-4
**McNabb**—*pop pl* ... IL-6
**Mcnabb**—*pop pl* ... IL-6
McNab Bank Bldg—*hist pl* ... AL-4
McNabb Bluff—*cliff* ... TN-4
McNabb Branch—*stream* ... TN-4
McNabb Cem—*cemetery* ... MS-4
McNabb Cem—*cemetery* (2) ... TN-4
McNabb Cem—*cemetery* ... TX-5
McNabb Creek—*stream* ... ID-8
McNabb Creek—*stream* ... KY-4
McNabb Creek—*stream* ... OR-9
McNabb Creek—*stream* ... TN-4
McNabb Creek Trail—*trail* ... TN-4
McNabb Hollow—*valley* ... IL-6
McNabb Island—*island* ... TX-5
*McNabb Mine* ... TN-4
McNabb Mines—*mine* ... TN-4
McNabb Sch (historical)—*school* (2) ... TN-4
*McNabbs Mill* ... TN-4
McNabbs Point—*cliff* ... ID-8
McNabb Spring—*spring* ... TN-4
McNab Creek—*stream* ... CA-9
McNab Creek—*stream* ... MS-4
McNab Hollow—*valley* ... MO-7
McNab Lake—*lake* ... TX-5
McNab Park—*park* ... FL-3
McNab Post Office (historical)—*building* ... AL-4
McNab Ranch—*locale* ... CA-9
McNab Ranch—*locale* ... NM-5
McNab Sch—*school* ... FL-3
McNab Sch—*school* ... NY-2
McNair—*locale* ... AR-4
McNair—*locale* ... MN-6
**McNair**—*pop pl* (2) ... MS-4
**McNair**—*pop pl* ... NC-3
**McNair**—*pop pl* ... TX-5
McNair Branch—*stream* ... AL-4
McNair Branch—*stream* ... FL-3
McNair Branch—*stream* ... MS-4
McNair Cem—*cemetery* ... FL-3
McNair Cem—*cemetery* ... MS-4
McNair Cem—*cemetery* ... NC-3
McNair Cem—*cemetery* ... TN-4
McNair Creek—*stream* ... AL-4
McNair Creek—*stream* ... OR-9
McNair Crossing—*locale* ... NC-3
McNair Cut—*gap* ... TN-4
McNaire Spring—*spring* ... NM-5
*McNair Falls* ... TN-4
McNair Fishpond—*reservoir* ... NC-3
McNair Lake—*reservoir* ... NC-3
McNair Lake Dam—*dam* ... NC-3
McNair Meadow—*flat* ... CA-9
*McNair Meadows* ... CA-9
McNair Mill (historical)—*locale* ... MS-4
*McNair Mill Pond* ... MS-4
McNair Millpond—*reservoir* ... MS-4
McNair Plantation—*hist pl* ... MS-4
McNair Pond—*reservoir* ... NC-3
McNair Post Office (historical)—*building* ... MS-4
McNair Saddle—*gap* ... CA-9
McNair Sch—*school* ... IL-6
McNair Sch—*school* (2) ... MI-6
*McNairs Mill Pond* ... SC-3
Mc Nairs Millpond—*reservoir* ... SC-3
*McNairs Pond* ... NC-3
McNair Tower—*locale* ... LA-4
**McNair Village**—*pop pl* ... TX-5
McNair Woods—*woods* ... AK-9
**McNairy**—*pop pl* ... TN-4
*McNairy Cemetery* ... AL-4
McNairy Central HS—*school* ... TN-4
**McNairy County**—*pop pl* ... TN-4
McNairy County Farm—*locale* ... TN-4
McNairy County General Hosp—*hospital* ... TN-4
McNairy Cypress Watershed Dam Number
Seventeen—*dam* ... TN-4
McNairy Point—*cape* ... AK-9
McNairy Post Office—*building* ... TN-4
McNairy Sch (historical)—*school* ... AL-4
*McNairy Station* ... TN-4
*McNairy Station Post Office* ... TN-4
McNalley Brook—*stream* ... NY-2
McNalley Tank—*reservoir* ... AZ-5
McNalley Tank—*reservoir* ... TX-5
McNalley Windmill—*locale* ... TX-5
**McNalls**—*pop pl* ... NY-2
McNally—*locale* ... ME-1
**McNally**—*pop pl* ... IA-7
McNally Brook—*stream* ... ME-1
McNally Cem—*cemetery* ... IL-6
*McNally Creek* ... AR-4
McNally Creek—*stream* ... AK-9
McNally Creek—*stream* ... AR-4
Mc Nally Creek—*stream* ... CO-8
McNally Creek—*stream* ... MT-8
McNally Deadwater—*swamp* ... ME-1
McNally Drain—*canal* ... MI-6
McNally Lake—*lake* ... MI-6
McNally Memorial Park—*park* ... CA-9
Mc Nally Mine—*mine* ... CO-8
McNally Park—*park* ... AL-4
McNally Park—*park* ... IL-6
McNally Playground—*park* ... MA-1
McNally Ranch—*locale* ... NM-5
McNally Ridge—*ridge* ... ME-1
McNally Sch—*school* (2) ... CA-9
McNally's Windemere Ranch HQ—*hist pl* ... CA-9
McNamara—*locale* ... MT-8
McNamara Bridge—*bridge* ... MT-8
McNamara Butte—*summit* ... MT-8
McNamara Cem—*cemetery* ... OH-6
McNamara Hollow—*valley* ... PA-2
McNamara HS—*school* ... MD-2
McNamara Lake—*lake* ... NV-8
McNamara Mine—*mine* ... NV-8
McNamara Monmt—*pillar* ... MI-6
McNamara-O'Conner House—*hist pl* ... TX-5
McNamara Park—*park* ... CA-9
McNamara Pond—*lake* ... MI-6
McNamara Ranch—*locale* ... CA-9
McNamara Ranch—*locale* ... NE-7
McNamara Sch—*school* ... NY-2
McNamaras Corners—*locale* ... PA-2
McNamaras Ferry (historical)—*locale* ... MS-4
McNamara Spring—*spring* ... NV-8
McNamar Bldg—*hist pl* ... OR-9
McNamar Lake—*lake* ... WI-6
McNamar-McLure-Miller
Residence—*hist pl* ... OH-6
McNamee Cem—*cemetery* ... IN-6
McNamee Gulch—*valley* ... OR-9
McNamee Hill—*summit* ... MD-2
Mc Namee Peak—*summit* ... CO-8
McNamers Chapel Methodist Ch
(historical)—*church* ... TN-4
McNary—*locale* ... KY-4
**McNary**—*pop pl* ... AZ-5
**McNary**—*pop pl* ... LA-4
**McNary**—*pop pl* ... OR-9
**McNary**—*pop pl* ... PA-2

**McNary**—*pop pl* ... TX-5
McNary Air Natl Guard Field—*military* ... OR-9
McNary Annex Sch—*school* ... AZ-5
McNary Beach—*beach* ... OR-9
McNary Branch—*stream* ... IL-6
McNary Branch—*stream* ... OR-9
McNary Creek—*stream* (2) ... OR-9
McNary Dam—*dam* ... OR-9
McNary Dam—*dam* ... WA-9
**McNary Dam**—*pop pl* ... OR-9
McNary Ditch—*canal* ... AZ-5
McNary Drain—*canal* ... MI-6
McNary Elem Sch—*school* ... AZ-5
McNary Field—*airport* ... OR-9
McNary Field (Airport)—*airport* ... OR-9
McNary Golf Course—*other* ... OR-9
McNary Heights Sch—*school* ... OR-9
McNary HS—*school* ... AZ-5
McNary Lake—*lake* ... OR-9
McNary Lateral—*canal* ... TX-5
McNary Lock and Dam—*dam* ... OR-9
McNary Natl Wildlife Ref—*park* ... WA-9
McNary Place—*locale* ... AZ-5
McNary Range Channel—*channel* ... OR-9
McNary Reservation—*park* ... AL-4
McNary RR Station—*building* ... AZ-5
McNary Sch—*school* ... OH-6
McNary Siphon—*canal* ... AZ-5
McNary Tank—*reservoir* ... AZ-5
McNaspy Stadium—*locale* ... LA-4
Mc Nasser Gulch—*valley* ... CO-8
McNaths—*locale* ... AL-4
**McNatt**—*pop pl* ... MO-7
McNatt Cem—*cemetery* ... AL-4
McNatt Cem—*cemetery* ... KY-4
McNatt Cem—*cemetery* ... TN-4
McNatt Falls—*locale* ... GA-3
McNatt Hollow—*valley* ... TN-4
McNatt Ranch—*locale* ... NM-5
**McNatts**—*pop pl* ... IN-6
McNatts Ch—*church* ... IN-6
McNatt Spring—*spring* ... NM-5
McNatts Station—*locale* ... NC-3
*McNaugher Middle School* ... PA-2
McNaugher Special Education
Center—*school* ... PA-2
McNaughton—*locale* ... WI-6
McNaughton Draw—*valley* ... WY-8
McNaughton Lake—*lake* ... WI-6
McNaughton Park—*park* ... IN-6
McNaughton Point—*cape* ... AK-9
McNaughton Spring—*spring* ... OR-9
McNaughton Spring Campground—*locale* ... OR-9
McNaulty Cem—*cemetery* ... OK-5
*McNay Creek* ... WY-8
McNay Creek—*stream* ... WY-8
McNeal—*locale* ... MS-4
**McNeal**—*pop pl* ... AZ-5
**McNeal**—*pop pl* ... FL-3
McNeal Bayou—*gut* ... TX-5
McNeal Branch—*stream* ... MO-7
McNeal Cem—*cemetery* ... NY-2
McNeal Cem—*cemetery* (3) ... OH-6
Mc Neal Chapel—*church* ... SC-3
McNeal Creek—*stream* ... CA-9
McNeal Ditch—*canal* ... OH-6
*McNeal Elementary School* ... MS-4
McNeal Generating Plant—*locale* ... AZ-5
McNeal Gulch—*valley* ... MT-8
McNeal Lake—*lake* ... TX-5
McNeally Cem—*cemetery* ... FL-3
McNeal Mine—*mine* ... CA-9
McNeal Post Office—*building* ... AZ-5
McNeal Run—*stream* ... PA-2
McNeals Branch—*stream* ... NJ-2
McNeal Sch—*school* ... MS-4
McNeals Corner—*locale* ... VA-3
McNeals Landing (historical)—*locale* ... AL-4
McNealy Cem—*cemetery* ... KY-4
McNealy Cem—*cemetery* ... WV-2
McNealy Pond—*swamp* ... FL-3
*McNealy Spring* ... AZ-5
*McNear* ... CA-9
McNear—*locale* ... CA-9
McNear, Erskine, B., House—*hist pl* ... CA-9
*McNear Landing* ... CA-9
McNearney Lake—*lake* ... MI-6
McNearney Lake Tower—*locale* ... MI-6
**McNears Beach**—*pop pl* ... CA-9
McNear Sch—*school* ... CA-9
McNear Sch (historical)—*school* ... AL-4
McNeary Creek—*stream* ... ID-8
McNeece Cem—*cemetery* ... LA-4
*McNeece Flat* ... OR-9
McNeece Hollow—*valley* ... TN-4
McNeel Cem—*cemetery* ... NE-7
McNeel Creek—*stream* ... ID-8
McNeel Creek—*stream* ... WY-8
*McNeeley* ... LA-4
*McNeeley Cemetery* ... TN-4
McNeeley Creek—*stream* ... AR-4
McNeeley Creek—*stream* ... MT-8
McNeeley Ford—*locale* ... AR-4
McNeeley Peak—*summit* ... MT-8
McNeeley Peak—*summit* ... WA-9
*McNeeley Spur* ... LA-4
McNeel Mill—*hist pl* ... WV-2
McNeely—*locale* ... LA-4
McNeely Brake—*swamp* ... AR-4
McNeely Branch—*stream* ... NC-3
McNeely Cem—*cemetery* ... KY-4
McNeely Cem—*cemetery* ... OH-6
McNeely Cem—*cemetery* ... TN-4
McNeely Cem—*cemetery* (2) ... TX-5
McNeely Cem—*cemetery* ... WV-2
McNeely Ch—*church* ... SC-3
McNeely Chapel—*church* ... IN-6
*McNeely Creek* ... AR-4
McNeely House—*hist pl* ... LA-4
McNeely Lake—*lake* ... TX-5
Mc Neely Lake—*reservoir* ... KY-4
McNeely Lake Park—*park* ... KY-4
McNeely Playground—*park* ... LA-4
McNeely Sch (historical)—*school* ... MO-7
McNeely Spring—*spring* ... TN-4
McNeely-Strachan House—*hist pl* ... NC-3
**McNeely Township**—*pop pl* ... SD-7
**McNees**—*pop pl* ... PA-2
McNees Draw—*valley* ... WY-8
McNeese Cem—*cemetery* ... TN-4
McNeese Draw—*valley* ... WY-8
McNeese Flat—*flat* ... OR-9
McNeese State Coll—*school* ... LA-4
McNeese University—*post sta* ... LA-4
McNees Park—*park* ... CA-9
McNees Ranch—*locale* (2) ... WY-8
McNeil—*locale* ... TX-5
McNeil—*other* ... FL-3
McNeil—*other* ... MS-4
**McNeil**—*pop pl* ... AR-4
**McNeil**—*pop pl* ... TX-5
McNeil, Harriet and Charlie,
House—*hist pl* ... TX-5
McNeil, Marcellus, House—*hist pl* ... TX-5
McNeil Baptist Ch—*church* ... AL-4
*McNeil Bay* ... VT-1
McNeil Bay—*bay* ... NC-3
McNeil Bayou—*stream* ... MS-4
McNeil Canyon—*valley* ... AK-9
McNeil Canyon—*valley* ... WA-9
McNeil Cem—*cemetery* (2) ... KY-4
McNeil Cem—*cemetery* ... MS-4
McNeil Cem—*cemetery* (2) ... TN-4
McNeil Cem—*cemetery* (2) ... TX-5
*McNeil Cemetery* ... AL-4
*McNeil Ch* ... MS-4
McNeil Ch—*church* ... IL-6
McNeil Ch—*church* ... MS-4
McNeil Chapel—*church* ... MS-4
McNeil Chapel—*church* ... MO-7
McNeil Cove—*bay* ... AK-9
McNeil Cove—*bay* ... VT-1
*McNeil Creek* ... CA-9
McNeil Creek—*stream* ... AK-9
McNeil Creek—*stream* ... AR-4
McNeil Creek—*stream* (2) ... CA-9
McNeil Creek—*stream* ... MI-6
McNeil Creek—*stream* ... NY-2
McNeil Creek—*stream* ... OR-9
McNeil Creek—*stream* (2) ... TX-5
McNeil Creek—*stream* ... WA-9
McNeil Ditch—*canal* ... IA-7
McNeil Drain—*canal* (2) ... MI-6
McNeil Head—*cape* ... AK-9
McNeil Hollow—*valley* ... KY-4
McNeil Homestead—*hist pl* ... VT-1
*McNeil Island* ... WA-9
**McNeil Island**—*pop pl* ... WA-9
McNeil Island (Federal
Penitentiary)—*island* ... WA-9
McNeil Islet—*cape* ... AK-9
McNeill—*locale* ... WV-2
**McNeill**—*pop pl* ... MS-4
McNeill, Lake—*reservoir* ... NC-3
McNeil Lake—*lake* ... AK-9
McNeil Lake—*lake* ... MI-6
McNeil Lake—*lake* ... MS-4
*McNeil Landing* ... AL-4
McNeill Branch—*stream* ... NC-3
McNeill Cem—*cemetery* ... IL-6
McNeill Cem—*cemetery* ... MS-4
McNeill Cem—*cemetery* ... MO-7
McNeill Cem—*cemetery* (3) ... NC-3
McNeill Cem—*cemetery* ... TX-5
McNeill Creek—*stream* ... AK-9
McNeill Island—*island* ... WA-9
McNeill Lake—*reservoir* ... NC-3
McNeill Lake Dam—*dam* ... NC-3
McNeill-McGee House—*hist pl* ... MS-4
**McNeill (McNeil)**—*pop pl* ... MS-4
*McNeill Peak* ... WA-9
McNeill Pond—*reservoir* (2) ... NC-3
McNeill Sch—*school* ... KY-4
McNeill Sch—*school* ... MA-1
*McNeills Lake* ... NC-3
McNeills Mill Creek—*stream* ... NC-3
McNeilly Rsvr—*reservoir* ... NV-8
McNeil Oil Field—*oilfield* ... TX-5
McNeil Peak—*summit* ... WA-9
*McNeil Point* ... NY-2
McNeil Point—*cape* ... FL-3
McNeil Point—*summit* ... OR-9
McNeil Pond—*lake* ... AL-4
McNeil Pond—*reservoir* ... NC-3
McNeil Pond Dam—*dam* ... NC-3
McNeil Ranch—*locale* ... CA-9
McNeil River—*stream* ... AK-9
McNeil River State Game
Sanctuary—*park* ... AK-9
McNeil Rsvr—*reservoir* ... MT-8
*McNeils* ... FL-3
McNeils Bar—*bar* ... AL-4
McNeils Bridge—*bridge* ... NC-3
McNeil Sch—*school* ... AL-4
McNeil Sch—*school* ... AR-4
McNeil Sch—*school* ... SD-7
McNeil Sch (abandoned)—*school* ... PA-2
McNeil Sch (historical)—*school* (2) ... TN-4
*McNeils Landing* ... AL-4
McNeils Landing (historical)—*locale* ... AL-4
McNeil Slough—*lake* ... MT-8
McNeil Slough—*stream* ... MS-4
McNeil South Oil Field—*oilfield* ... TX-5
McNeils Point Campsite—*locale* ... NY-2
McNeil Spring—*spring* ... CA-9
McNeil Spring—*spring* (2) ... WA-9
McNeils Spring—*spring* ... OR-9
McNeils Store (historical)—*locale* ... MS-4
McNeil Tank—*reservoir* ... AZ-5
McNeil (Township of)—*fmr MCD* ... AR-4
McNeil Windmill—*locale* ... NM-5
*McNella Creek* ... AR-4
McNellis Bayou—*stream* ... IL-6
McNell Point—*cape* ... ME-1
McNelly Cem—*cemetery* ... AR-4
McNelly Sch—*school* ... KS-7
McNelty Spring—*spring* ... AZ-5
*McNene Memorial Church* ... AL-4
McNenny Fish Hatchery (USDA)—*locale* ... SD-7
McNenny Sch—*school* ... SD-7
McNerney Dam—*dam* ... PA-2
McNerney Run—*stream* ... PA-2
McNerny Branch—*stream* ... PA-2
McNess Crossing—*locale* ... NM-5
*McNett Corners* ... DE-2
McNett Creek—*stream* ... TX-5
McNett Ditch—*canal* ... OH-6
McNett Fork—*stream* ... AK-9
McNett School—*locale* ... MI-6
*McNetts Corner* ... DE-2
**McNett (Township of)**—*pop pl* ... PA-2
McNew, Thornton, House—*hist pl* ... MO-7
McNew Branch—*stream* ... TN-4
McNew Cem—*cemetery* ... AR-4
McNew Cem—*cemetery* (2) ... TN-4
McNew Cem—*cemetery* (2) ... VA-3
McNew Feeder Tank—*reservoir* ... NM-5
McNew Gap—*gap* ... TN-4
McNew Hill—*summit* ... AK-9
McNew Hollow—*valley* (2) ... TN-4
McNew South Tank—*reservoir* ... NM-5
Mc New West Camp—*locale* ... NM-5
McNicholas Cem—*cemetery* ... PA-2
McNicholas Sch—*school* ... OH-6
**McNichol Place (subdivision)**—*pop pl* ... DE-2
McNichols Hollow—*valley* ... TN-4
Mc Nichols Park—*park* ... CO-8
McNickle Cem—*cemetery* ... MO-7
McNicol MS—*school* ... FL-3
McNider Park—*park* ... IA-7
McNie Creek—*stream* ... AR-4
*McNiel Canyon* ... WA-9
McNiel Cem—*cemetery* ... TX-5
McNierney—*locale* ... NM-5
McNik Cem—*cemetery* ... OK-5
McNinch Creek—*stream* ... MT-8
McNinch Ditch—*canal* ... WY-8
McNinch No 1 Rsvr—*reservoir* ... WY-8
McNinch No 2 Rsvr—*reservoir* ... WY-8
McNinch Supply Ditch—*canal* ... WY-8
McNinch Wash—*valley* ... WY-8
McNinch Well—*well* ... NV-8
McNir Chapel—*church* ... NC-3
McNish Branch—*stream* ... AL-4
McNish House—*hist pl* ... OR-9
McNitt Cave—*cave* ... PA-2
McNitt Cem—*cemetery* ... MI-6
McNitt Ditch—*canal* ... IN-6
McNitt Gap—*gap* ... PA-2
McNitt Sch—*school* ... MI-6
McNitt Sch (historical)—*school* ... PA-2
McNitt Trail—*trail* ... PA-2
McNiven Creek—*stream* ... MN-6
McNiven Farm Complex—*hist pl* ... NY-2
McNiven Lake—*lake* ... MN-6
McNiven Lateral—*canal* ... WY-8
*McNoel* ... IL-6
McNoel—*other* ... IL-6
**McNorton**—*pop pl* ... TX-5
McNorton Branch—*stream* ... TX-5
*McNorton Creek* ... TX-5
McNott Island—*island* ... WI-6
McNuff Branch—*stream* ... PA-2
McNuff Trail—*trail* ... PA-2
McNulta—*locale* ... IL-6
**McNulty**—*pop pl* ... OR-9
McNulty Basin—*basin* ... OR-9
McNulty Bottoms—*bend* ... MT-8
McNulty Cem—*cemetery* ... TX-5
Mc Nulty Creek—*stream* ... CO-8
McNulty Creek—*stream* ... OR-9
McNulty Creek—*stream* ... WY-8
McNulty Lake—*lake* ... AR-4
McNulty Mine—*mine* ... CA-9
McNulty Park—*park* ... MA-1
McNulty Ridge—*ridge* ... CA-9
McNulty Rsvr—*reservoir* ... OR-9
McNulty Slough—*gut* ... CA-9
McNulty Spring—*spring* ... CA-9
McNush Park—*park* ... NE-7
*McNut* ... LA-4
McNutt—*locale* ... WV-2
**McNutt**—*pop pl* ... LA-4
**McNutt**—*pop pl* ... MS-4
McNutt Branch—*stream* (2) ... MS-4
McNutt Cem—*cemetery* (2) ... AR-4
McNutt Cem—*cemetery* ... IN-6
McNutt Cem—*cemetery* ... KY-4
McNutt Cem—*cemetery* ... LA-4
McNutt Cem—*cemetery* ... MS-4
McNutt Cem—*cemetery* ... TN-4
McNutt Creek—*stream* ... GA-3
McNutt Creek—*stream* (2) ... ID-8
McNutt Creek—*stream* ... TX-5
McNutt Ditch—*canal* ... ID-8
McNutt Ditch—*canal* ... IN-6
McNutt Flat—*flat* ... OR-9
McNutt Gulch—*valley* ... CA-9
McNutt Hill—*summit* ... LA-4
McNutt House—*hist pl* ... MS-4
McNutt Lake—*lake* (2) ... MS-4
McNutt Memorial Ch—*church* ... AL-4
McNutt Ranch—*locale* ... CA-9
McNutt Ranch—*locale* ... NE-7
McNutt Ranch—*locale* ... WY-8
McNutt Run—*stream* ... NY-2
McNutt Rural Hist Dist—*hist pl* ... LA-4
McNutt Sch—*school* ... MO-7
McNutt Sch (abandoned)—*school* ... MO-7
McNutt Shoals—*rapids* ... TN-4
McNutt Windmill—*locale* ... TX-5
McNutty Reservation—*reserve* ... AL-4
McOlothen Cem—*cemetery* ... TN-4
McOmber Sch—*school* ... MI-6
*McParland Butte* ... OR-9
McPartland Mtn—*summit* ... MT-8
**McPaul**—*pop pl* ... IA-7
McPeace Valley—*valley* ... WI-6
McPeak Branch—*stream* ... KY-4
McPeak Creek—*stream* ... ND-7
McPeak Sch—*school* ... KY-4
McPeak Spring—*spring* ... ND-7
McPeek State Public Shooting
Area—*park* ... SD-7
McPete Branch—*stream* ... AR-4
McPete Point—*cape* ... MN-6
McPeters Branch—*stream* ... AL-4
McPeters Hollow—*valley* ... TN-4
McPete Sch—*school* ... MS-4
McPhail, Jonas, House and McPhail, Annie,
Store—*hist pl* ... NC-3
McPhail Branch—*stream* ... MS-4
McPhail Branch—*stream* ... NC-3
McPhail Butte Historic Monmt—*park* ... ND-7
McPhail Cem—*cemetery* (3) ... MS-4
McPhail Draw—*valley* ... WY-8
McPhail Sch—*school* ... CA-9
McPhail Slough—*lake* ... ND-7
McPhails Peak—*summit* ... CA-9
*McPhails Slough* ... ND-7
McPhatter Cem—*cemetery* ... NC-3
McPhaul, Lake—*reservoir* ... NC-3
McPhaul Bridge—*bridge* ... AZ-5
McPhaul Ranch—*locale* (2) ... NM-5
McPhaul Suspension Bridge—*hist pl* ... AZ-5
**McPhearson**—*pop pl* ... AR-4
McPhearson Cem—*cemetery* ... KY-4
*McPhearson Creek* ... ID-8
McPhearson Creek—*stream* ... ID-8
McPhee and McGinnity Bldg—*hist pl* ... CO-8
Mc Phee Creek—*stream* ... CO-8
McPhee Creek—*stream* ... ID-8
McPhee Creek—*stream* ... MI-6
McPhee Drain—*stream* ... MI-6
Mc Phee Gulch—*valley* ... CO-8
McPhee Gulch—*valley* ... ID-8
Mc Phee Park—*flat* ... CO-8
McPhee Rsvr—*reservoir* ... CO-8
McPhee Sch—*school* ... MI-6
McPhee Sch—*school* ... NE-7
McPhees Landing—*locale* ... MI-6
McPheeter Bend—*bend* ... TN-4
McPheeter Bend—*locale* ... TN-4
*McPheeter Bend School* ... TN-4
McPheeter Ch—*church* ... TN-4
McPheeters, Charles, House—*hist pl* ... KY-4
*McPheeters Bend Baptist Ch* ... TN-4
McPheeters Bend Elem Sch—*school* ... TN-4
*McPheeter Sch* ... TN-4
Mc Pheeter Sch—*school* ... TN-4
McPheron Branch—*stream* ... TN-4
McPherren Cem—*cemetery* ... IL-6
McPherren Ditch—*canal* ... IN-6
McPherrin Camp—*locale* ... CA-9
**McPherron**—*pop pl* ... PA-2
McPherron Creek—*stream* ... IA-7
*McPherson* ... MS-4
McPherson—*locale* ... AR-4
McPherson—*locale* ... CA-9
McPherson—*locale* ... FL-3
McPherson—*locale* ... GA-3
McPherson—*locale* ... IA-7
McPherson—*locale* ... NJ-2
**McPherson**—*pop pl* ... IA-7
**McPherson**—*pop pl* ... KS-7
**McPherson**—*pop pl* ... MD-2
Mcpherson, Maj. Gen. James B.,
House—*hist pl* ... OH-6
McPherson, Mount—*summit* ... AK-9
McPherson Airp—*airport* ... KS-7
McPherson Bay—*bay* ... AK-9
McPherson Bayou—*bay* ... FL-3
McPherson Bayou—*gut* ... LA-4
McPherson Branch—*stream* ... KY-4
McPherson Branch—*stream* ... WI-6
McPherson Brook—*stream* ... ME-1
McPherson Canal—*canal* ... AZ-5
McPherson Canyon—*valley* ... ID-8
McPherson Canyon—*valley* ... OR-9
McPherson Canyon—*valley* ... UT-8
McPherson Canyon—*valley* ... WA-9
McPherson Cem—*cemetery* ... AL-4
McPherson Cem—*cemetery* ... AR-4
McPherson Cem—*cemetery* ... IL-6
McPherson Cem—*cemetery* ... KS-7
McPherson Cem—*cemetery* ... KY-4
McPherson Cem—*cemetery* ... MN-6
McPherson Cem—*cemetery* ... MS-4
McPherson Cem—*cemetery* ... NC-3
McPherson Cem—*cemetery* ... OH-6
McPherson Cem—*cemetery* ... SC-3
McPherson Cem—*cemetery* (3) ... TN-4
McPherson Cem—*cemetery* ... VA-3
McPherson Cem—*cemetery* ... WV-2
McPherson Cem—*cemetery* ... WI-6
McPherson Ch—*church* ... NC-3
McPherson Coll—*school* ... KS-7
McPherson Country Club—*other* ... KS-7
McPherson County—*civil* ... KS-7
McPherson County—*civil* ... SD-7
McPherson County Courthouse—*hist pl* ... KS-7
McPherson County Courthouse—*hist pl* ... SD-7
McPherson County State Lake—*reservoir* ... KS-7
McPherson County State Lake
Dam—*dam* ... KS-7
**McPherson Cove**—*pop pl* ... NY-2
*McPherson Creek* ... ID-8
McPherson Creek—*stream* ... NC-3
McPherson Creek—*stream* ... OR-9
McPherson Creek—*stream* ... PA-2
McPherson Creek—*stream* ... SC-3
McPherson Creek—*stream* ... SD-7
McPherson Dam—*dam* ... AL-4
McPherson Ditch—*canal* ... OR-9
McPherson Drain—*canal* ... MI-6
McPherson Draw—*valley* ... WY-8
**McPherson Estates**
**(subdivision)**—*pop pl* ... NC-3
McPherson Glacier—*glacier* ... AK-9
McPherson Gulch—*valley* ... OR-9
McPherson Hill—*summit* ... NY-2
McPherson-Holland House—*hist pl* ... MO-7
McPherson Hollow—*valley* ... PA-2
McPherson Hollow—*valley* ... TN-4
McPherson Hosp—*hospital* ... MI-6
McPherson HS—*school* ... KS-7
McPherson JHS—*school* ... CA-9
McPherson JHS*—*school* ... KS-7
McPherson Lake—*lake* ... IN-6
McPherson Lake—*lake* ... ME-1
McPherson Lake—*lake* ... MI-6
McPherson Lake—*reservoir* ... AL-4
McPherson Landing—*locale* ... AL-4
McPherson Landing—*locale* ... TN-4
Mc Pherson Mine—*mine* ... CO-8
McPherson Mine—*mine* ... TN-4
McPherson Mine—*mine* ... WA-9
McPherson Mtn—*summit* ... AL-4
McPherson Number 1 Dam—*dam* ... AL-4
McPherson Oil Field—*oilfield* ... KS-7
McPherson Opera House—*hist pl* ... KS-7
McPherson Park—*park* ... SC-3
McPherson Pass—*gap* ... AZ-5
McPherson Passage—*channel* ... AK-9
McPherson Peak—*summit* ... CA-9
McPherson Playground—*park* ... MA-1
**McPherson Point**—*pop pl* ... NY-2
McPherson Pond—*lake* ... ME-1
McPherson Post Office
(historical)—*building* ... TN-4
McPherson Ranch—*locale* ... UT-8
McPherson Range—*range* ... UT-8
McPherson Run—*stream* ... OH-6
McPherson Run—*stream* ... PA-2
McPherson Sch—*school* ... CA-9
McPherson Sch—*school* ... IL-6
McPherson Sch—*school* ... MI-6
McPherson Sch—*school* ... NE-7
McPherson Sch—*school* ... WI-6
McPhersons Corner—*locale* ... PA-2
McPhersons Island—*island* ... OR-9
McPherson Spring—*spring* ... SD-7
McPherson Spring—*spring* ... WA-9
McPherson Springs—*spring* ... WY-8
McPherson's Purchase—*hist pl* ... MD-2
McPherson Square—*park* ... DC-2
McPherson Square—*park* ... PA-2
McPherson Square Metro Station—*locale* ... DC-2
McPherson Tank—*reservoir* ... AZ-5
McPherson Town Hist Dist—*hist pl* ... OH-6
**McPherson Township**—*pop pl* (2) ... KS-7
**McPherson (Township of)**—*pop pl* ... MN-6
**McPhersonville**—*pop pl* ... SC-3
McPherson Wash—*stream* ... AZ-5
McPheters Ford (historical)—*locale* ... MO-7
McPheters Lake—*lake* ... UT-8
*McPhillips School* ... SD-7
McPike Branch—*stream* ... IN-6
McPike Cem—*cemetery* ... MO-7
McQuaddy Branch—*stream* ... GA-3
*McQuade Bayou* ... FL-3
McQuade Brook—*stream* ... NH-1
McQuade Creek—*stream* ... OR-9
McQuade Gulch—*valley* ... ID-8
McQuade Lake—*lake* ... MN-6
**McQuady**—*pop pl* ... KY-4
McQuage Bayou—*stream* ... FL-3
McQuage Branch—*stream* ... FL-3
McQuage Cem—*cemetery* ... SC-3
McQuagge Mill Creek—*stream* ... AL-4
*McQuagg Mill Branch* ... AL-4
McQuaid HS—*school* ... NY-2
*McQuaig Bayou* ... FL-3
McQuaig Drain—*canal* ... MI-6
McQuaig (historical)—*locale* ... SD-7
McQuaig Lake—*lake* ... FL-3
McQuarrie Spur—*locale* ... MT-8
McQuarry Ridge—*ridge* ... KY-4
McQuay Ditch—*canal* ... OH-6
McQuay Ranch—*locale* ... WY-8
McQue—*flat* ... NM-5
Mc Queary Creek—*stream* ... CO-8
McQueary Lake—*lake* ... CO-8
McQue Draw—*valley* ... WY-8
McQueen—*locale* ... AZ-5
McQueen—*locale* ... IL-6
McQueen—*locale* ... OK-5
**McQueen**—*pop pl* ... AL-4
**McQueen**—*pop pl* ... IL-6
**McQueen**—*pop pl* ... MT-8
McQueen Bend—*bend* ... MO-7
McQueen Branch—*stream* ... TN-4
McQueen Branch—*stream* ... VA-3
McQueen Branch Prospect—*mine* ... TN-4
McQueen Bridge—*bridge* ... SC-3
McQueen Cem—*cemetery* ... AL-4
McQueen Cem—*cemetery* ... LA-4
McQueen Cem—*cemetery* ... NC-3
McQueen Cem—*cemetery* ... TN-4
McQueen Chapel—*church* ... NC-3
McQueen Creek—*stream* ... FL-3
McQueen Creek—*stream* ... NY-2
McQueen Crossroads—*locale* ... SC-3
McQueen Drain—*canal* ... MI-6
**McQueeney**—*pop pl* ... TX-5
McQueeney, Lake—*reservoir* ... TX-5
McQueen Gap—*gap* ... TN-4
McQueen Gap—*gap* ... VA-3
McQueen Hammock—*island* ... GA-3
McQueen Hollow—*valley* ... TN-4
McQueen Inlet—*bay* ... GA-3
McQueen Knob—*summit* ... TN-4
McQueen Knob—*summit* ... VA-3
McQueen Lateral—*canal* ... CA-9
McQueen Run—*stream* ... OH-6
**McQueens**—*pop pl* ... NY-2
Mcqueens Dam—*dam* ... AL-4
McQueens Island—*island* ... GA-3
McQueens Pond—*reservoir* (2) ... AL-4
McQueen Spring—*spring* ... WY-8
**McQueens Village (historical)**—*pop pl* ... FL-3
McQueen Swamp—*swamp* ... FL-3
McQuen Hollow—*valley* ... PA-2
McQuery Canyon—*valley* ... NM-5
**McQueston Corners**—*pop pl* ... PA-2
McQuiddy Cem—*cemetery* ... MO-7
McQuiddy Cem—*cemetery* (2) ... TN-4
McQuiddy Curves—*locale* ... TX-5
McQuiddy Sch—*school* ... CA-9
McQuidys Mill (historical)—*locale* ... TN-4
McQuie, Peter and Isabelle McCulloch,
Milkhouse—*hist pl* ... IA-7
McQuiggin Corners—*locale* ... NY-2
McQuilkin, James Greer, Round
Barn—*hist pl* ... IA-7
McQuinn Cem—*cemetery* ... KY-4
McQuinn Cem—*cemetery* ... OR-9
**McQuinn Estates**—*pop pl* ... IN-6
McQuinney Branch—*stream* ... LA-4
McQuire Cem—*cemetery* ... WV-2
McQuire Lake—*lake* ... AR-4
McQuirk Gulch—*valley* ... MT-8
McQuirter Bayou—*stream* ... MS-4
McQuirter Creek—*stream* ... MS-4
McQuirt Mtn—*summit* ... TX-5
McQuistan Sch—*school* ... NE-7
McQuisten Creek—*stream* ... AK-9
McQuistion Elem Sch—*school* ... PA-2
*McQuistion Sch* ... PA-2
McQuiston Corners—*locale* ... PA-2
McQuithy Gulch—*valley* ... MT-8
McQuoid Cem—*cemetery* ... MO-7
McQuoid Coulee—*valley* ... MT-8
McQuown, Lafayette, House—*hist pl* ... MI-6
McRae—*locale* ... AL-4
McRae—*locale* ... VA-3
**McRae**—*pop pl* ... AR-4
**McRae**—*pop pl* ... FL-3
**McRae**—*pop pl* ... GA-3
McRae, D. L., House—*hist pl* ... AR-4
McRae, K. G., House—*hist pl* ... AR-4
McRae, T. C., House—*hist pl* ... AR-4
McRae Arroyo—*stream* ... CO-8
McRae Bay—*bay* ... MI-6
McRae Branch—*stream* ... MS-4
McRae Branch—*stream* ... NC-3
McRae Canyon—*valley* ... NM-5
McRae Canyon—*valley* ... TX-5
McRae Cem—*cemetery* ... GA-3
McRae Cem—*cemetery* ... MI-6
McRae Cem—*cemetery* (3) ... MS-4
McRae Cem—*cemetery* ... NC-3
McRae Cemeteries—*cemetery* ... GA-3
McRae Ch—*church* ... GA-3
McRae Ch—*church* ... TX-5
McRae Chapel—*church* ... TN-4
*McRae Creek* ... WA-9
McRae Creek—*stream* ... ID-8
McRae Creek—*stream* ... MI-6
McRae Creek—*stream* ... OR-9
McRae Creek—*stream* ... TX-5
McRae Dam—*dam* ... AL-4
McRae Gap—*gap* ... WY-8
McRae-Helena (CCD)—*cens area* ... GA-3
McRae Homestead—*locale* ... OR-9
*McRae Hosital* ... MS-4
McRae House—*hist pl* ... AR-4
**McRae Junction**—*pop pl* ... GA-3
McRae Lake—*reservoir* ... AL-4
McRae Lake—*reservoir* ... MS-4
*McRae Lake Dam* ... AL-4
McRae Lake Dam—*dam* ... MS-4
McRae-McQueen House—*hist pl* ... NC-3
McRae Meadow—*flat* ... CA-9
McRae Mill Creek—*stream* ... AL-4
McRae Park—*park* ... AR-4
McRae Park—*park* ... MI-6
McRae Park—*park* ... MN-6
*McRae Peak* ... NC-3
*McRae Pond* ... NC-3
McRae Pond Dam—*dam* ... MS-4
McRae Post Office (historical)—*building* ... AL-4
McRae Ridge—*ridge* ... CA-9
McRae Sch—*school* ... AR-4
McRae Sch—*school* ... NC-3
McRae Sch—*school* ... TX-5
McRaes Chapel—*church* ... NC-3
*McRaes Chapel Cemetery* ... TN-4
*McRaes Chapel Methodist Ch* ... TN-4
McRae Slough—*stream* ... OR-9
Mc Rae Springs—*spring* ... MT-8
McRae Street Methodist Ch—*church* ... AL-4
McRae Tank—*reservoir* (2) ... AZ-5
McRae (Township of)—*fmr MCD* ... AR-4
McRainey Lake Dam—*dam* ... MS-4
M C Ranch—*locale* ... OR-9
McRaney—*locale* ... MS-4
McRany Branch—*stream* ... NC-3
McRary Creek—*stream* ... NC-3
**McRaven**—*pop pl* ... MS-4
McRaven Post Office
(historical)—*building* ... MS-4
*Mcraven Station* ... MS-4
McRay Point—*cape* ... NY-2
McRay Site (15CH139)—*hist pl* ... KY-4
McRea Cem—*cemetery* ... ID-8
McRea Cem—*cemetery* ... MS-4
McRea Island—*island* ... ID-8
McRee, James Price, House—*hist pl* ... GA-3
McRee Cem—*cemetery* ... TN-4
M Creek—*stream* ... WY-8
McRee Ranch—*locale* ... NM-5
McRenolds Rsvr—*reservoir* ... ID-8
McReynolds Branch—*stream* ... TN-4
McReynolds Cem—*cemetery* ... AR-4
McReynolds Cem—*cemetery* (2) ... TN-4
McReynolds Cem—*cemetery* (2) ... VA-3
McReynolds Cem—*cemetery* ... WI-6
McReynolds Crossroads—*locale* ... AL-4
McReynolds House—*hist pl* ... KY-4
McReynolds Island—*island* ... FL-3
McReynolds Island (historical)—*island* ... TN-4
McReynolds JHS—*school* ... TX-5
McReynolds Point—*cape* ... MD-2
McReynolds Ranch—*locale* ... MT-8
McReynolds Sch—*school* ... FL-3
McReynolds Spring—*spring* ... TX-5
McReynolds Valley—*valley* ... CA-9
*McRight Cemetery* ... AL-4
M Crighton Ranch—*locale* ... ND-7
McRitchie Mill—*locale* ... AL-4
**McRitchie Mill**—*pop pl* ... AL-4
**McRoberts**—*pop pl* ... KY-4
McRoberts Sch—*school* ... TX-5
McRoe Branch—*stream* ... MS-4
McRoe Hollow—*valley* ... KY-4
McRoey Well—*well* ... NM-5
McRorie Lake—*lake* ... NY-2
**McRoss**—*pop pl* ... WV-2
M Cross Ranch—*locale* ... ND-7
McRoy—*locale* ... TX-5
M C Rsvr—*reservoir* ... OR-9
McSauba, Mount—*summit* ... MI-6
**McShan**—*pop pl* ... AL-4
McShan Cem—*cemetery* ... TX-5
Mc Shane Home—*locale* ... CO-8
McShane State Public Shooting
Area—*park* ... SD-7
McShan Lake—*reservoir* ... AL-4
*McShan Lake Number One* ... AL-4
McShan Lake Number Three—*reservoir* ... AL-4
McShan Lake Number Two—*reservoir* ... AL-4
McShann Sch (historical)—*school* ... MS-4
McShea—*locale* ... ME-1
*McSherlay Branch* ... TN-4
McSherley Branch—*stream* ... TN-4
**McSherry**—*pop pl* ... PA-2
McSherry Creek—*stream* ... OR-9
McSherry Mtn—*summit* ... VT-1
**McSherrystown**—*pop pl* ... PA-2
McSherrystown Borough—*civil* ... PA-2
McSorley, Patrick J., House—*hist pl* ... GA-3
McSorley Ranch—*locale* ... CA-9
McSorley Sch—*school* ... ID-8
McSpadden Branch—*stream* ... TN-4
McSpadden Cem—*cemetery* ... TX-5
McSpadden Hollow—*valley* ... MO-7
McSpadden Lake—*lake* ... TX-5
McSpadden Pumping Station—*other* ... TX-5
McSpadden Spring—*spring* ... TN-4

Meadow Swamp—swamp GA-3
**Meadowsweet**—pop pl CA-9
Meadows Yard—locale NJ-2
Meadow Tank—reservoir (2) AZ-5
Meadow Tanks—reservoir NM-5
**Meadowthorpe**—pop pl KY-4
Meadowthorpe Sch—school KY-4
Meadow Tithing Granary—hist pl UT-8
Meadow Township—fmr MCD (2) IA-7
**Meadow Township**—pop pl ND-7
**Meadow Township**—pop pl SD-7
Meadow (Township of)—fmr MCD NC-3
**Meadow (Township of)**—pop pl MN-6
**Meadow Trace (subdivision)**—pop pl AL-4
Meadow Trail—trail CA-9
Meadow Tunnel—mine UT-8
Meadow Upper Feeder—stream CA-9
**Meadow Vale**—pop pl KY-4
**Meadowvale Manor**—pop pl MD-2
Meadow Vale Sch—school NE-7
Meadowvale Sch—school OH-6
**Meadowvale (subdivision)**—pop pl (2) AZ-5
**Meadowvale (subdivision)**—pop pl TN-4
Meadow Valley UT-8
Meadow Valley—locale WI-6
**Meadow Valley**—pop pl CA-9
Meadow Valley—valley AZ-5
Meadow Valley—valley NV-8
Meadow Valley Cem—cemetery WI-6
Meadow Valley Ch—church PA-2
Meadow Valley Ch—church WV-2
**Meadow Valley Condominium**—pop pl UT-8
Meadow Valley Creek—stream CA-9
Meadow Valley Creek—stream UT-8
Meadow Valley Drainage Ditch SD-7
Meadow Valley Flat—flat AZ-5
Meadow Valley Flowage—reservoir WI-6
Meadow Valley Mine—mine AZ-5
Meadow Valley Mountains NV-8
Meadow Valley Mtns—range NV-8
Meadow Valley Range NV-8
Meadow Valley Rec Area—park NV-8
Meadow Valley Sch—school (2) OH-6
Meadow Valley State Wildlife Area—park WI-6
Meadow Valley State Wildlife Mngmt Area—park WI-6
**Meadow Valley Subdivision**—pop pl UT-8
Meadow Valley Tank—reservoir AZ-5
Meadow Valley Wash—stream NV-8
Meadowview IL-6
Meadowview—locale ME-1
Meadow View—locale OR-9
**Meadowview**—pop pl IN-6
**Meadowview**—pop pl KS-7
**Meadowview**—pop pl KY-4
**Meadowview**—pop pl MD-2
**Meadowview**—pop pl NJ-2
**Meadowview**—pop pl NC-3
**Meadowview**—pop pl PA-2
**Meadowview**—pop pl TN-4
**Meadow View**—pop pl TN-4
**Meadowview**—pop pl (2) TN-4
**Meadow View**—pop pl VA-3
**Meadowview**—pop pl (2) VA-3
Meadowview—uninc pl KS-7
**Meadow View Addition (subdivision)**—pop pl SD-7
Meadowview Baptist Ch TN-4
Meadowview Baptist Ch—church MS-4
Meadowview Baptist Ch—church TN-4
Meadowview Campground—locale CA-9
Meadowview Cem—cemetery MT-8
Meadow View Cem—cemetery NH-1
Meadow View Cem—cemetery UT-8
Meadow View Cem—cemetery WV-2
Meadowview Ch TN-4
Meadowview Ch—church KY-4
Meadow View Ch—church NC-3
Meadow View Ch—church (4) TN-4
Meadow View Ch—church (2) VA-3
Meadowview Community Center—locale TX-5
Meadowview Country Club—other IA-7
Meadowview Elementary School TN-4
Meadow View Elem Sch—school KS-7
**Meadowview Estates**—pop pl KY-4
**Meadowview Estates**—pop pl PA-2
Meadowview Gardens—uninc pl TN-4
Meadow View Golf Course—locale TN-4
Meadow View Guard Station—locale CA-9
**Meadowview Heights Subdivision - Number 4**—pop pl UT-8
Meadowview Hosp—hospital MS-4
Meadow View Lake—lake FL-3
Meadowview Memorial Park—cemetery NC-3
Meadow View Midddle Sch—school TN-4
Meadowview Mission—church TN-4
**Meadowview Park**—pop pl MD-2
**Meadowview Park**—pop pl TX-5
Meadowview Park—uninc pl LA-4
Meadow View Peak—summit CA-9
Meadow View (RR Name For Meadowview)—uninc pl VA-3
Meadowview (RR name Meadow View)—other VA-3
Meadowview Sch TN-4
Meadow View Sch—school CA-9
Meadowview Sch—school LA-4
Meadowview Sch—school MI-6
Meadow View Sch—school NE-7
Meadow View Sch—school NC-3
Meadowview Sch—school TN-4
Meadowview Sch—school (2) WI-6
Meadow View Sch (historical)—school TN-4
**Meadowview (subdivision)**—pop pl MS-4
**Meadowview (subdivision)**—pop pl (2) TN-4
**Meadow View Subdivision**—pop pl UT-8
Meadowview United Methodist Church TN-4
**Meadow Village**—pop pl NJ-2
Meadowville TN-4
Meadowville—locale UT-8
Meadowville—locale (2) VA-3
**Meadowville**—pop pl ME-1
**Meadowville**—pop pl WV-2
Meadowville Cem—cemetery MN-6
Meadowville Cem—cemetery UT-8
Meadowville Channel VA-3
Meadowville Creek—stream UT-8
Meadowville Post Office TN-4
Meadowville Sch—school NE-7
Meadowville Valley UT-8
Meadowville Valley—valley UT-8
**Meadow Vista**—pop pl CA-9
Meadow Vista—uninc pl NM-5
**Meadow Vista (subdivision)**—pop pl DE-2
Meadow Wash—stream AZ-5
Meadow Waterhole—lake OR-9
Meadow Well—well (2) NM-5
Meadow Windmill—locale AZ-5
Meadow Windmill—locale NM-5
Meadow Windmill—locale TX-5
Meadow Wood—locale NY-2
**Meadow Wood**—pop pl PA-2
Meadow Wood Acad—school FL-3
**Meadowwood Acres (subdivision)**—pop pl TN-4
**Meadow Wood Estates (subdivision)**—pop pl UT-8
Meadowwood Memorial Park—cemetery FL-3
Meadow Wood Sch—school TX-5
Meadow Woods Plantation (historical)—locale MS-4
Meadowwoods Point—cape WI-6
**Meadow Wood (subdivision)**—pop pl AL-4
Mead Park—park OH-6
Mead Park—park PA-2
Mead Park—park TN-4
Mead Park—park WI-6
Mead Point—cape FL-3
Mead Pond MA-1
Mead Pond NH-1
Mead Pond—lake NY-2
Mead Ridge—ridge IN-6
Mead River AK-9
Mead Rsvr—reservoir CO-8
Mead Rsvr—reservoir NY-2
Mead Run—stream (4) PA-2
Meads MI-6
Meads—locale KY-4
Meads—locale WY-8
Meads Cem—cemetery OH-6
Meads Ch—church OH-6
Mead Sch—school CA-9
Mead Sch—school CT-1
Mead Sch—school MI-6
Mead Sch—school NE-7
Mead Sch—school WI-6
Mead Sch (abandoned)—school PA-2
Meads Chapel—church TN-4
Meads Corner—locale NC-3
**Meads Corner**—pop pl MA-1
**Meads Corners**—pop pl NY-2
**Meads Creek**—pop pl NY-2
Meads Creek—stream NY-2
Meads Flat—flat OR-9
Meads Hollow—valley KY-4
Meads Lake MN-6
Meads Lake—lake WI-6
**Meads Landing**—pop pl MI-6
Mead's Peak ID-8
Mead Spring—spring WA-9
Meads Run PA-2
Meads Store—locale VA-3
Meadstown Airstrip—airport NC-3
Mead Substation Heliport—airport NV-8
Meadsville (Magisterial District)—fmr MCD VA-3
Meads Wash—valley UT-8
**Mead (Town of)**—pop pl WI-6
**Mead Township**—pop pl NE-7
**Mead (Township of)**—pop pl OH-6
**Mead (Township of)**—pop pl PA-2
Mead Trail—trail NH-1
**Mead Valley**—pop pl CA-9
Mead Valley—valley CA-9
**Meadview**—pop pl AZ-5
Meadvilla—hist pl MS-4
Mead Village IN-6
Meadville—locale AL-4
Meadville—locale VA-3
**Meadville**—pop pl MS-4
**Meadville**—pop pl MO-7
**Meadville**—pop pl NE-7
**Meadville**—pop pl (2) PA-2
**Meadville**—pop pl WV-2
Meadville Area HS—school PA-2
Meadville Area JHS—school PA-2
Meadville Branch—stream MS-4
Meadville Cem—cemetery MS-4
Meadville City—civil PA-2
Meadville Dam—dam PA-2
Meadville Downtown Hist Dist—hist pl PA-2
Meadville Junction—locale PA-2
Meadville Mall—locale PA-2
Meadville Sch—school PA-2
Meadville Sch—school VA-3
Meadwood, Lake—reservoir AL-4
**Meadwood Heights**—pop pl AL-4
Mead-Zimmerman House—hist pl OH-6
Meager Spring Branch—stream TN-4
Meagher Bridge—bridge ND-7
Meagher Gulch—valley MT-8
Meaghersville WA-9
**Meagsville**—pop pl TN-4
Meagsville Post Office (historical)—building TN-4
Meahagh, Lake—lake NY-2
Meahers Landing—locale AL-4
Meaher-Zoghby House—hist pl AL-4
Meahl Cem—cemetery KY-4
Meairs Sch—school CA-9
Meak Cem—cemetery IA-7
Meaker Pond PA-2
Meaker Ranch—locale CO-8
Meakerville (Eyak)—other AK-9
Meal Camp Hollow—valley TN-4
Meal Creek—stream GA-3
Mealer Lake (historical)—lake MS-4
Mealey, Tobias G., House—hist pl MN-6
Mealey Hollow—valley PA-2
Mealing Cem—cemetery GA-3
Mealing Grove Ch—church SC-3
Mealing Park—park SC-3
Meally—locale KY-4
**Meally**—pop pl KY-4
Meal Run—stream IN-6
Meals Cem—cemetery MO-7
Meals Creek—stream TN-4
Mealy Mounds Archeol Site—hist pl MO-7
Meamber Creek—stream CA-9
Meamber Gulch—valley CA-9
Meamber Sch—school CA-9
Mean—island MP-9
Mean Bayou—gut LA-4
**Mean Crossroads**—pop pl SC-3
Meander MS-4
Meander Along Creek—stream OR-9
Meander Canyon—valley UT-8
Meander Creek CA-9
Meander Creek—stream MI-6
Meander Creek—stream MN-6
Meander Creek—stream WA-9
Meander Creek Rsvr—reservoir OH-6
Meander Lake OH-6
Meander Lake—lake MI-6
Meander Lake—lake (2) MN-6
Meander Lake—lake ND-7
Meander Lake Picnic Area—locale MN-6
Meander Meadow—flat WA-9
Meander Post Office MS-4
Meander Rsvr OH-6
Meane Spring—spring MO-7
Mean Island MP-9
Mean Lake—lake LA-4
Mean Lake Oil Field—oilfield LA-4
Mean Ranch—locale NM-5
Mean Rock—island AK-9
Means—locale KY-4
Means—other OH-6
Means, Emily, House—hist pl ME-1
Means Branch—stream MO-7
Means Branch—stream SC-3
Means Bridge—bridge AL-4
Means Brook—stream CT-1
Means Brook Rsvr—reservoir CT-1
Means Canal—canal WY-8
Means Cem—cemetery AR-4
Means Cem—cemetery IN-6
Means Cem—cemetery MO-7
Means Cem—cemetery TX-5
Means Chapel—church NC-3
Means Chapel—church SC-3
Means Court Elem Sch—school FL-3
Means Creek PA-2
Means Creek—stream CO-8
Means Creek—stream GA-3
Means Creek—stream NC-3
Means (historical)—locale AL-4
Means Hollow—valley TN-4
Means House—hist pl SC-3
Means-Justiss House—hist pl TX-5
Means Lake—flat CA-9
Means Lake—reservoir AL-4
Means Lane Cem—cemetery GA-3
Means North Oil Field—oilfield TX-5
Means Oil Field—oilfield TX-5
Means Pond MA-1
Means Ranch—locale TX-5
Means Ridge—ridge WV-2
Means Run PA-2
Means Sch—school IL-6
Means Sch (historical)—school AL-4
Means Tank—reservoir NM-5
Means Tunnel—tunnel KY-4
**Meansville**—pop pl GA-3
Meansville (CCD)—cens area GA-3
Meansville Cem—cemetery GA-3
Means Well—well CA-9
Means Windmill—locale NM-5
Meant Community Center—building MS-4
Mean-to MP-9
Meany , Mount—summit WA-9
Meany Crest—summit WA-9
Meares—locale CA-9
Meares, Cape—cape OR-9
Meares Bay—swamp (2) NC-3
Meares Cem—cemetery (2) NC-3
Meares Cem—cemetery SC-3
Meares Glacier—glacier AK-9
Meares Island—island AK-9
Meares Millpond—reservoir NC-3
Meares Passage—channel AK-9
Meares Point—cape AK-9
Mearney Creek—stream ID-8
Mearoor—cape FM-9
**Mears**—pop pl MI-6
**Mears**—pop pl VA-3
**Mears**—pop pl WI-6
Mears, Charles, Silver Lake Boardinghouse—hist pl MI-6
Mears Brook—stream ME-1
Mears Cem—cemetery IN-6
Mears Cem—cemetery NC-3
Mears Cem—cemetery OH-6
Mears Cem—cemetery TN-4
Mears Corner—locale VA-3
Mears Cove—bay ME-1
Mears Cove—bay MD-2
Mears Creek—stream CA-9
Mears Creek—stream MD-2
Mears Ditch—canal SD-7
Mears Fork—stream NC-3
Mears Hall—hist pl IA-7
Mears Hollow—valley AR-4
Mears Hollow—valley VT-1
Mears House—hist pl KY-4
Mears Junction—locale CO-8
Mears Meadow—flat CA-9
Mearson Spring—spring FL-3
Mears Park—park KS-7
Mears Peak—summit CO-8
Mears Ridge—ridge CA-9
Mears Sch—school WI-6
**Mears Station**—pop pl VA-3
**Mearsville**—pop pl VA-3
Mease Gap—gap NC-3
Mease Hosp and Clinic—hospital FL-3
Mease Hosp Countryside—hospital FL-3
Measel Spring Rsvr—reservoir WY-8
Measels Spring—spring CA-9
Measer UT-8
Measle Fork—stream WV-2
Measles Gulf Cave—cave TN-4
Measles Memorial Cem—cemetery AR-4
Measley Creek—stream CA-9
Meason, Isaac, House—hist pl PA-2
Meason Flat—flat NM-5
Meason Spring—spring NM-5
Meason Tank—reservoir NM-5
Measure Island FM-9
Meat Bayou—stream LA-4
Meatblock Canyon—valley NM-5
Meatbox Run—stream WV-2
**Meat Camp**—pop pl NC-3
Meat Camp Ch—church NC-3
Meat Camp Creek—stream NC-3
Meat Camp (Township of)—fmr MCD NC-3
Meath Dam—dam AZ-5
**Meath (historical)**—pop pl AZ-5
Meat Hollow—valley MS-4
Meat Hollow—valley OK-5
Meathook Fork WV-2
Meat Hook Number 1 Dam—dam SD-7
Meat Hook Ranch—locale SD-7
Meathook Spring—spring SD-7
Meathouse Branch—stream WV-2
Meathouse Creek—stream KY-4
Meathouse Fork—stream KY-4
Meathouse Fork—stream (3) WV-2
Meathouse Fork Ch—church KY-4
Meath RR Station—building AZ-5
Meath Spring—spring AZ-5
Meath Tank—reservoir AZ-5
Meath Wash—stream AZ-5
Meat Island—island GA-3
Meat Lake—lake MN-6
Meat Mtn—summit AK-9
Meat Point—cliff AZ-5
Meatrack Creek—stream MT-8
Meatscaffold Branch—stream KY-4
Meatscaffold Ch—church KY-4
Meatskin Branch—stream KY-4
Meatte Cem—cemetery MO-7
Meatte Park—park MO-7
**Meauwataka**—pop pl MI-6
Meauwataka Lake—lake MI-6
**Meaux**—pop pl LA-4
Meaux Canal—canal LA-4
**Meay**—pop pl FM-9
Meazels Creek—stream LA-4
**Mebane**—pop pl NC-3
Mebane Cem—cemetery (2) TN-4
Mebane HS—school FL-3
Mebane-Nuckolls House—hist pl TN-4
Mebane Ridge—ridge AR-4
Mebee Pass—gap WA-9
Mebens Lake—reservoir NC-3
Mebens Lake Dam—dam NC-3
Me Campbell Ranch—locale TX-5
Mecan—locale WI-6
Mecan River—stream WI-6
Mecan Springs—spring WI-6
**Mecan (Town of)**—pop pl WI-6
Mecate Meadow—area NM-5
Mecate Mountain CA-9
Mecawee Pond—lake VT-1
Mecca—locale OR-9
Mecca—locale TN-4
Mecca—locale TX-5
**Mecca**—pop pl CA-9
**Mecca**—pop pl (2) FL-3
**Mecca**—pop pl GA-3
**Mecca**—pop pl IN-6
**Mecca**—pop pl MO-7
**Mecca**—pop pl OH-6
**Mecca Acres**—pop pl KS-7
Mecca Bridge—hist pl IN-6
Mecca Elem Sch—school IN-6
Mecca Gulch—valley MT-8
Mecca Hammock—island FL-3
Mecca Hills—range CA-9
Mecca (historical)—locale AL-4
Mecca Junction (railroad station)—locale FL-3
Mecca Lake—lake NJ-2
Mecca Mills IN-6
Mecca Pass Tunnels—tunnel CA-9
Mecca Post Office (historical)—building TN-4
Mecca Springs Baptist Church AL-4
Mecca Temple—hist pl NY-2
**Mecca (Township of)**—pop pl OH-6
Mecentell Gully LA-4
Mech—bar FM-9
Mechacebe River MS-4
Mechakamiut (Summer Camp)—locale AK-9
Mecham Canyon NE-7
Mecham Creek—stream NV-8
Mecham Creek—stream UT-8
Mecham Hill—summit ME-1
Mechancisburg PA-2
**Mechang**—pop pl PW-9
**Mechanic**—pop pl NC-3
Mechanical Engineering Hall, Vanderbilt Univ—hist pl TN-4
Mechanic Branch—stream AL-4
Mechanic Chapel AL-4
Mechanic Creek—stream AK-9
Mechanic Creek—stream SC-3
Mechanic Falls—CDP ME-1
**Mechanic Falls Center**—pop pl ME-1
**Mechanic Falls (Town of)**—pop pl ME-1
**Mechanic Grove**—pop pl PA-2
Mechanic Grove Ch—church PA-2
**Mechanic Hill**—pop pl GA-3
Mechanic Institute—hist pl ME-1
Mechanic Ridge Cem—cemetery WI-6
Mechanics And Miners Cem—cemetery WV-2
Mechanics' Bank and Trust Company Bldg—hist pl TN-4
Mechanics Bldg and Loan Company—hist pl OH-6
Mechanics Block—building MA-1
Mechanics Block Hist Dist—hist pl MA-1
Mechanics Block Hist Dist (Boundary Increase)—hist pl MA-1
Mechanics Brook CT-1
Mechanics Building/Masonic Bldg—hist pl CO-8
Mechanicsburg IN-6
Mechanicsburg PA-2
Mechanicsburg—locale MS-4
Mechanicsburg—locale OH-6
Mechanicsburg—locale PA-2
Mechanicsburg—locale WV-2
**Mechanicsburg**—pop pl IL-6
**Mechanicsburg**—pop pl (5) IN-6
**Mechanicsburg**—pop pl (3) OH-6
**Mechc icsburg**—pop pl (2) PA-2
**Mechanicsburg**—pop pl VA-3
Mechanicsburg Area HS—school PA-2
Mechanicsburg Area Intermediate Sch—school PA-2
Mechanicsburg Baptist Church—hist pl OH-6
Mechanicsburg Borough—civil PA-2
Mechanicsburg Cave—cave PA-2
Mechanicsburg Cem—cemetery IN-6
Mechanicsburg Chapel—church IL-6
Mechanicsburg Commercial Hist Dist—hist pl OH-6
Mechanicsburg Commercial Hist Dist—hist pl PA-2
Mechanicsburg Drain—stream IN-6
Mechanicsburgh IN-6
Mechanicsburgh MS-4
Mechanicsburg (Magisterial District)—fmr MCD VA-3
Mechanicsburg Post Office (historical)—building MS-4
Mechanicsburg Sch—school MI-6
Mechanicsburg (Township of)—civ div IL-6
Mechanics Cem—cemetery VA-3
Mechanics Creek SC-3
Mechanics Grove PA-2
**Mechanics Grove**—pop pl PA-2
Mechanics Grove Post Office (historical)—building PA-2
Mechanics' Hall—hist pl ME-1
Mechanics Hall—hist pl MA-1
Mechanics' Hall District—hist pl MA-1
Mechanics Hill NC-3
Mechanics Mill—hist pl MA-1
Mechanics Pond—reservoir MA-1
Mechanics Pond Dam—dam MA-1
**Mechanicstown**—pop pl NY-2
**Mechanicstown**—pop pl OH-6
**Mechanicstown**—pop pl WV-2
**Mechanicstown (census name East Middletown)**—pop pl NY-2
Mechanic Street Hist Dist—hist pl CT-1
Mechanic Street (historical)—locale PA-2
Mechanics Valley MD-2
**Mechanics Valley**—pop pl PA-2
Mechanicsville NJ-2
Mechanicsville NY-2
Mechanicsville NC-3
Mechanicsville PA-2
Mechanicsville TN-4
Mechanicsville VT-1
Mechanicsville VA-3
Mechanicsville WV-2
Mechanicsville—locale AL-4
Mechanicsville—locale PA-2
Mechanicsville—locale (2) VA-3
**Mechanicsville**—pop pl (2) CT-1
**Mechanicsville**—pop pl DE-2
**Mechanicsville**—pop pl GA-3
**Mechanicsville**—pop pl IN-6
**Mechanicsville**—pop pl IA-7
**Mechanicsville**—pop pl (2) MD-2
**Mechanicsville**—pop pl MA-1
**Mechanicsville**—pop pl (3) NJ-2
**Mechanicsville**—pop pl OH-6
**Mechanicsville**—pop pl (9) PA-2
**Mechanicsville**—pop pl (2) SC-3
**Mechanicsville**—pop pl TN-4
**Mechanicsville**—pop pl VT-1
**Mechanicsville**—pop pl (2) VA-3
Mechanicsville—uninc pl LA-4
Mechanicsville Borough—civil PA-2
Mechanicsville Cem—cemetery AL-4
Mechanicsville (census name for Danville East)—CDP PA-2
Mechanicsville Ch—church SC-3
Mechanicsville Elem Sch—school AL-4
**Mechanicsville (Frampton)**—pop pl PA-2
Mechanicsville Hist Dist—hist pl TN-4
Mechanicsville (Magisterial District)—fmr MCD VA-3
Mechanicsville Post Office (historical)—building TN-4
Mechanicsville Sch—hist pl GA-3
Mechanicsville Sch—hist pl PA-2
Mechanicsville Sch—school MD-2
Mechanicsville Sch—school PA-2
Mechanicsville Sch (historical)—school TN-4
**Mechanicsville (subdivision)**—pop pl AL-4
Mechanicsville Swamp—swamp SC-3
**Mechanic (Township of)**—pop pl OH-6
**Mechanic Valley**—pop pl MD-2
**Mechanicville**—pop pl NY-2
Mechanicville Rsvr—reservoir NY-2
Mechanicville Sch—school LA-4
Mechanisville Ch—church LA-4
Mechan River WI-6
Mechant, Lake—lake LA-4
Mechasipi River MS-4
Mechaw Creek—stream SC-3
Mechebechubl PW-9
Mechedchudelbad—harbor PW-9
Mechengin—bar FM-9
Me chen-to MP-9
Mecherchar—island PW-9
Mechescatauxin Branch NJ-2
**Mechesneytown**—pop pl PA-2
Mechetsemoi Creek—stream OK-5
Mech Fork—stream WV-2
Mechikku FM-9
Mechitiu FM-9
Mechitiv FM-9
**Mechitiw**—pop pl FM-9
**Mechlenberg Heights**—pop pl WV-2
**Mechlin**—pop pl AL-4
Mechlin Cem—cemetery OH-6
**Mechling and Fleming Subdivision**—pop pl UT-8
Mechling Hill—summit WV-2
Mechling Run—stream WV-2
Mechlings Corner—locale NJ-2
Mechlins Corner Tavern—hist pl NJ-2
Mechoech, Bkul A—bar PW-9
Mechoglan Lake—lake NE-7
Mechol FM-9
Mechool FM-9
Mechoru FM-9
Mechum Creek VA-3
Mechumps Creek—stream VA-3
Mechum River VA-3
Mechums creek VA-3
Mechums River—locale VA-3
Mechums River—stream VA-3
Mechunk Creek—stream VA-3
M. E. Church, South—hist pl KY-4
Mecier Cem—cemetery GA-3
Mecikalski General Store, Saloon, and Boardinghouse—hist pl WI-6
Meck—island MP-9
Meckauer Park—park CT-1
Meck Creek—stream PA-2
Meckel Coulee—valley MT-8
Meckel Draw—valley TX-5
Meckel Gas Field—oilfield TX-5
Meckell Sch—school IL-6
Meckel Ranch—locale TX-5
Meckelroy Branch—stream TX-5
Meckel Sch—school MT-8
Mecker Run—stream PA-2
**Meckesville**—pop pl PA-2
Meckesville Sch (abandoned)—school PA-2
Meckinock ND-7
Meck-Insel MP-9
Meck Island MP-9
Mecklenberg TN-4
Mecklenberg County NC-3
Mecklenberg Wildlife Club Lake—reservoir NC-3
Mecklenburg TN-4
**Mecklenburg**—pop pl NY-2
Mecklenburg Cem—cemetery MN-6
Mecklenburg Complex Department of Correction—locale NC-3
Mecklenburg Country Club—other VA-3
**Mecklenburg County**—pop pl NC-3
**Mecklenburg (County)**—pop pl VA-3
Mecklenburg County Courthouse—hist pl NC-3
Mecklenburg County Courthouse—hist pl VA-3
Mecklenburg County Park—park NC-3
Mecklenburg Investment Company Bldg—hist pl NC-3
Mecklenburg Ridge MN-6
Mecklenburg Sanatorium—hospital NC-3
Mecklenburg's Garden—hist pl OH-6
Mecklenburg Wayside—locale VA-3
Mecklenburg Wildlife Club Lake Dam—dam NC-3
Meckler Drain—stream MI-6
Meckley Lake ID-8
Meckleyville NC-3
Mecklin Cem—cemetery MO-7
**Meckling**—pop pl SD-7
Meckling Cem—cemetery SD-7
Meckling Hill WV-2
Meckling Run WV-2
**Meckling Township**—pop pl SD-7
**Mecks Corner**—pop pl PA-2
Meckville—locale PA-2
Meckville Ch—church PA-2
**Meco**—pop pl NY-2
Meco Lake—lake NY-2
Mecom Cut—channel LA-4
**Mecosta**—pop pl (2) MI-6
Mecosta, Lake—lake MI-6
**Mecosta (County)**—pop pl MI-6
Mecosta Lookout Tower—locale MI-6
Mecosta-Remus HS—school MI-6
**Mecosta (Township of)**—pop pl MI-6
**Mecox**—pop pl NY-2
Mecox Bay—bay NY-2
Mecum Branch—stream AR-4
Mecum Cem—cemetery NC-3
Mecumps Creek VA-3
Meda—locale GA-3
Meda—locale OR-9
Meda Bridge—bridge OR-9
Medac MO-7
**Medalaii**—pop pl PW-9
Medal (historical)—locale MO-7
Medalist Park IL-6
Medallaiechad—falls PW-9
Medalline IN-6
**Medallion Acres (subdivision)**—pop pl TN-4
**Medallion Cove Subdivision**—pop pl UT-8
Medallion Field Airp—airport IN-6
**Medanales**—pop pl NM-5
Medanito Artesian Well—well TX-5
Medanito Well—well TX-5
Medanito Windmill—locale (4) TX-5
Medano Creek CO-8
Medano Creek—stream CO-8
Medano Ditch—canal CO-8
Medano Lake—lake CO-8
Medano Pass CO-8
Medano Pass—gap CO-8
Medano Peak CO-8
Medano Ranch—locale CO-8
Medanoso Windmill—locale NM-5
Medano Windmill—locale NM-5
Medano Windmill—locale TX-5
Meda Pass—gap NV-8
Medaris Cem—cemetery OH-6
Medart—locale FL-3
Medart Assembly of God Ch—church FL-3
Medary—locale SD-7
**Medary**—pop pl WI-6
Medary Creek—stream MN-6
Medary Creek—stream SD-7
Medary Monmt—park SD-7
**Medary (Town of)**—pop pl WI-6
**Medary Township**—pop pl SD-7
**Medaryville**—pop pl IN-6
Medas (historical)—locale SD-7
Medas Lake—lake MN-6
**Medberry**—pop pl CO-8
**Medberry**—pop pl ND-7
Medberrys Lake—reservoir NC-3
Medberrys Lake Dam—dam NC-3
Medbery Park—park MI-6
Medbury Brook—stream VT-1
Medbury Hill—summit ID-8
Medbury Pond—lake CT-1
Medbu.y's-Grove Lawn Subdivisions Hist Dist—hist pl MI-6
**Medburyville**—pop pl VT-1
Medcalf Lake—stream FL-3
Medcalf Ranch—locale CA-9
Medca Pond—lake OR-9
Medco No. 3 Dam—dam OR-9
Medco Number 3 Pond—reservoir OR-9
Meddas Cem—cemetery GA-3
Medden Hollow—valley VA-3
Medders Cem—cemetery IL-6

Medders Tanks—*reservoir* NM-5
Meddleberger Branch—*stream* MO-7
Meddler Point—*cape* AZ-5
Meddler Wash—*stream* AZ-5
Meddler Wash Well—*well* AZ-5
Meddlin Creek—*stream* TX-5
**Meddo**—*pop pl* ME-1
Meddough Drain—*stream* MI-6
**Meddybemps**—*pop pl* ME-1
Meddybemps Heath—*flat* ME-1
Meddybemps Lake—*reservoir* ME-1
**Meddybemps (Town of)**—*pop pl* ME-1
Medea Creek—*stream* CA-9
*Medeinizya* MH-9
Medelmans Lake—*lake* NE-7
Medenhause Creek—*stream* LA-4
Medenuhra—*bar* FM-9
Meder, Lew M., House—*hist pl* NV-8
*Meder Creek* CA-9
Meder Lake—*lake* WI-6
Medermel—*cape* PW-9
**Mederville**—*pop pl* IA-7
**Medfield**—*pop pl* MA-1
**Medfield**—*pop pl* NC-3
Medfield Center—*hospital* FL-3
*Medfield Centre* MA-1
**Medfield Estates (subdivision)**—*pop pl* NC-3
Medfield JHS—*school* MA-1
**Medfield Junction**—*pop pl* MA-1
Medfield Rhododendron Reservation—*park* MA-1
Medfield Shops—*locale* MA-1
Medfield State Hosp—*hospital* MA-1
Medfield State Hospital Cem—*cemetery* MA-1
**Medfield (Town of)**—*pop pl* MA-1
*Medford* IN-6
*Medford* ND-7
Medford—*locale* ME-1
**Medford**—*pop pl* IN-6
**Medford**—*pop pl* MD-2
**Medford**—*pop pl* MA-1
**Medford**—*pop pl* MN-6
**Medford**—*pop pl* MO-7
**Medford**—*pop pl* NJ-2
**Medford**—*pop pl* NY-2
**Medford**—*pop pl* OK-5
**Medford**—*pop pl* OR-9
**Medford**—*pop pl* TN-4
**Medford**—*pop pl* WI-6
Medford, City of—*civil* MA-1
Medford Aqueduct—*canal* OR-9
Medford Ave Sch—*school* NY-2
Medford Bathhouse and Swimming Pool—*hist pl* OK-5
Medford Branch—*stream* AL-4
Medford Branch—*stream* (2) NC-3
Medford Branch—*stream* TX-5
Medford Carnegie Library—*hist pl* OR-9
Medford (CCD)—*cens area* OK-5
Medford (CCD)—*cens area* OR-9
Medford Cem—*cemetery* MS-4
Medford Cem—*cemetery* MO-7
Medford Cem—*cemetery* NC-3
Medford Cem—*cemetery* (2) TX-5
Medford (census name Medford Center)—*other* NJ-2
**Medford Center**—*pop pl* ME-1
**Medford Center (census name for Medford)**—*pop pl* NJ-2
Medford Ch—*church* IA-7
Medford Ch—*church* OK-5
Medford Chapel—*church* TN-4
Medford Cove—*valley* NC-3
Medford Creek—*stream* MN-6
Medford Drain—*stream* IN-6
Medford Elem Sch—*school* TN-4
**Medford Farms**—*pop pl* NJ-2
Medford Fish and Wildlife Mngmt Area—*park* NJ-2
Medford Flowage—*reservoir* WI-6
Medford Forest Nursery Dam (historical)—*dam* OR-9
Medford Forest Nursery Rsvr (historical)—*reservoir* OR-9
Medford Golf Course—*other* OK-5
**Medford Hillside (subdivision)**—*pop pl* MA-1
Medford (historical)—*locale* ND-7
Medford HS—*school* MA-1
Medford HS (North)—*school* MA-1
Medford HS (South)—*school* MA-1
Medford Irrigation District Canal—*canal* OR-9
Medford Island—*island* CA-9
Medford-Jackson County Airp—*airport* OR-9
Medford Junction—*uninc pl* MA-1
*Medford Lake* MO-7
**Medford Lakes**—*pop pl* NJ-2
Medford Lakes Sch Number 2—*school* NJ-2
Medford Lookout Tower—*locale* ME-1
Medford Mtn—*summit* NC-3
Medford Park—*park* NJ-2
Medford Sch—*school* WI-6
Medford Shop Ctr—*locale* MA-1
Medford Spring—*spring* CO-8
Medford Square—*park* MA-1
*Medford Station* NY-2
Medford Station—*locale* TN-4
Medford Station (historical)—*locale* MA-1
**Medford (Town of)**—*pop pl* ME-1
**Medford (Town of)**—*pop pl* WI-6
**Medford Township**—*pop pl* KS-7
**Medford Township**—*pop pl* ND-7
**Medford (Township of)**—*pop pl* MN-6
**Medford (Township of)**—*pop pl* NJ-2
Medford Valley—*valley* CA-9
**Medford West**—*pop pl* OR-9
**Medfra**—*pop pl* AK-9
Med Hollow—*valley* KY-4
**Media**—*pop pl* AL-4
**Media**—*pop pl* IL-6
**Media**—*pop pl* PA-2
Media Agua Creek—*stream* CA-9
Media Borough—*civil* PA-2
Media Cem—*cemetery* PA-2
Media Chapel—*church* PA-2
Media Creek—*stream* ID-8
Media Elem Sch—*school* PA-2
*Media Heights Country Club* PA-2
Media Heights Golf Club—*other* PA-2
Media (historical)—*locale* KS-7
Mediak Lake—*lake* MN-6
Medial Creek—*stream* AK-9
Media Luna (Barrio)—*fmr MCD* PR-3
Media Luna Well—*well* TX-5
Media Mine—*mine* CO-8
**Mediania Alta**—*pop pl* (2) PR-3
Mediania Alta (Barrio)—*fmr MCD* PR-3
Mediania Baja (Barrio)—*fmr MCD* PR-3
Media Park—*park* CA-9
**Media Park**—*pop pl* VA-3
**Mediapolis**—*pop pl* IA-7
**Mediapolis***—*pop pl* IA-7
Media Providence Friends Sch—*school* PA-2
**Media Quijada**—*pop pl* PR-3
*Mediar Lake* MN-6
*Media Sch* PA-2
Media Sch—*school* PA-2
**Media Township**—*pop pl* SD-7
**Media (Township of)**—*pop pl* IL-6
Media Well—*well* AZ-5
Medical Art Center—*locale* NM-5
Medical Arts Bldg—*hist pl* AZ-5
Medical Arts Bldg—*hist pl* AR-4
Medical Arts Bldg—*hist pl* OR-9
Medical Arts Bldg—*hist pl* (2) TN-4
Medical Arts Bldg and Garage—*hist pl* TN-4
Medical Arts Hosp—*hospital* TX-5
Medical Center—*post sta* PR-3
Medical Center—*uninc pl* TX-5
*Medical Center Helistop* UT-8
Medical Center Hosp—*hospital* AL-4
Medical Center Hosp—*hospital* FL-3
Medical Center of Manchester—*hospital* TN-4
Medical Center Shop Ctr—*locale* TN-4
Medical Centre Bldg—*hist pl* OH-6
Medical Coll—*school* KY-4
*Medical College of Alabama* AL-4
Medical Coll Of South Carolina—*school* SC-3
Medical Coll Of Virginia—*school* VA-3
**Medical Drive Condominium**—*pop pl* UT-8
Medical Hall Hist Dist—*hist pl* MD-2
Medical Hosp—*hospital* TX-5
Medical Hot Spring—*spring* OR-9
*Medical Lake* WA-9
Medical Lake—*lake* WA-9
**Medical Lake**—*pop pl* WA-9
Medical Lake (CCD)—*cens area* WA-9
Medical Lake Cem—*cemetery* WA-9
Medical Lake Cheney Interchange—*locale* WA-9
Medical Lake Interchange—*locale* WA-9
Medical Lake Waterfront Park—*park* WA-9
Medical Museum Bldg—*building* DC-2
*Medical Park Hospital* TN-4
Medical Spring—*spring* CA-9
Medical Spring—*spring* KY-4
Medical Springs—*locale* OR-9
Medical Square—*park* AZ-5
Medicine—*fmr MCD* NE-7
Medicine Bluffs—*cliff* OK-5
Medicine Bluffs—*hist pl* OK-5
**Medicine Bow**—*pop pl* WY-8
Medicine Bow Breaks—*range* WY-8
*Medicine Bow Creek* MT-8
Medicine Bow Curve—*locale* CO-8
Medicine Bow Ditch—*canal* CO-8
Medicine Bow Lodge—*locale* WY-8
*Medicine Bow Mountains* CO-8
Medicine Bow Mtns—*range* CO-8
Medicine Bow Natl For—*forest* WY-8
Medicine Bow Peak—*summit* WY-8
*Medicine Bow Range* CO-8
Medicine Bow River—*stream* WY-8
Medicine Bow Ski Area—*locale* WY-8
Medicine Bow Trail—*trail* CO-8
Medicine Bow Union Pacific Depot—*hist pl* WY-8
Medicine Branch—*stream* OK-5
Medicine Brook—*stream* WI-6
Medicine Bulls Camp (historical)—*locale* SD-7
*Medicine Butte* SD-7
Medicine Butte—*summit* AZ-5
Medicine Butte—*summit* ND-7
Medicine Butte—*summit* SD-7
Medicine Butte—*summit* WY-8
Medicine Butte (historical)—*summit* (2) SD-7
Medicine Butte Tank—*reservoir* AZ-5
Medicine Butte Tank Number Two—*reservoir* AZ-5
Medicine Butte Wells—*well* AZ-5
Medicine Cabin Park—*park* WY-8
*Medicine Creek* MT-8
*Medicine Creek* SD-7
*Medicine Creek* WA-9
Medicine Creek—*stream* (3) AK-9
Medicine Creek—*stream* AZ-5
Medicine Creek—*stream* CA-9
Medicine Creek—*stream* CO-8
Medicine Creek—*stream* ID-8
Medicine Creek—*stream* (3) KS-7
Medicine Creek—*stream* MO-7
Medicine Creek—*stream* (3) NE-7
Medicine Creek—*stream* NV-8
Medicine Creek—*stream* (3) OK-5
Medicine Creek—*stream* (3) OR-9
Medicine Creek—*stream* (4) SD-7
Medicine Creek—*stream* (4) WA-9
Medicine Creek—*stream* WY-8
Medicine Creek Archeol District—*hist pl* SD-7
Medicine Creek Cem—*cemetery* SD-7
Medicine Creek Dam—*dam* NE-7
*Medicine Creek Reservoir* NE-7
Medicine Creek Roadside Park—*park* SD-7
Medicine Elk Creek—*stream* MT-8
Medicine Flat—*flat* WY-8
Medicine Flat Creek—*stream* WY-8
Medicine Grizzly Lake—*lake* MT-8
Medicine Grizzly Peak—*summit* MT-8
Medicine Grizzly Trail—*trail* MT-8
Medicine Hill—*summit* CA-9
Medicine Hill Cem—*cemetery* ND-7
Medicine Hill Cem—*cemetery* SD-7
Medicine Hill Sch Number 3—*school* ND-7
**Medicine Hill Township**—*pop pl* ND-7
Medicine Hole—*locale* ND-7
**Medicine Hot Springs**—*pop pl* MT-8
Medicine Island (historical)—*island* SD-7
Medicine Knoll—*summit* SD-7
*Medicine Knoll Creek* SD-7
Medicine Knoll Creek—*stream* SD-7
*Medicine Knoll River* SD-7
*Medicine Lake* MT-8
*Medicine Lake* UT-8
*Medicine Lake* WI-6
Medicine Lake—*lake* AK-9
Medicine Lake—*lake* CA-9
Medicine Lake—*lake* FL-3
Medicine Lake—*lake* ID-8
Medicine Lake—*lake* (2) MN-6
Medicine Lake—*lake* MT-8
Medicine Lake—*lake* NE-7
Medicine Lake—*lake* (2) ND-7
Medicine Lake—*lake* SD-7
Medicine Lake—*lake* WA-9
Medicine Lake—*lake* WI-6
Medicine Lake—*lake* WY-8
**Medicine Lake**—*pop pl* MN-6
**Medicine Lake**—*pop pl* MT-8
Medicine Lake—*reservoir* MT-8
Medicine Lake Cem—*cemetery* MT-8
Medicine Lake Ch—*church* MN-6
Medicine Lake Glass Flow—*reserve* CA-9
**Medicine Lake Lodge**—*pop pl* CA-9
Medicine Lake Natl Wildlife Ref—*park* MT-8
Medicine Lakes—*lake* UT-8
Medicine Lake Sch—*school* NE-7
**Medicine Lodge**—*pop pl* KS-7
Medicine Lodge Airp—*airport* KS-7
Medicine Lodge Canyon—*valley* WY-8
*Medicine Lodge Creek* MT-8
*Medicine Lodge Creek* OK-5
Medicine Lodge Creek—*stream* ID-8
Medicine Lodge Creek—*stream* MT-8
Medicine Lodge Creek—*stream* WY-8
Medicine Lodge Creek Site—*hist pl* WY-8
Medicine Lodge HS—*school* KS-7
Medicine Lodge Intermediate Sch—*school* KS-7
*Medicine Lodge Pass* ID-8
Medicine Lodge Peace Treaty Site—*hist pl* KS-7
Medicine Lodge Peak—*summit* MT-8
Medicine Lodge Primary Sch—*school* KS-7
Medicine Lodge River—*stream* KS-7
Medicine Lodge River—*stream* OK-5
Medicine Lodge Sch Number 1—*school* ND-7
Medicine Lodge Sch Number 3—*school* ND-7
Medicine Lodge Sch Number 4—*school* ND-7
**Medicine Lodge Township**—*pop pl* KS-7
Medicineman Creek—*stream* AK-9
Medicine Man Creek—*stream* AK-9
Medicine Man Reach—*channel* TX-5
Medicine Mine—*mine* CO-8
**Medicine Mound**—*pop pl* TX-5
Medicine Mounds—*summit* TX-5
Medicine Mountain Ranch—*locale* SD-7
*Medicine Mtn* CA-9
Medicine Mtn—*summit* (2) CA-9
Medicine Mtn—*summit* MT-8
Medicine Mtn—*summit* OR-9
Medicine Mtn—*summit* SD-7
Medicine Mtn—*summit* WY-8
Medicine Owl Creek—*stream* MT-8
Medicine Owl Lake—*lake* MT-8
Medicine Owl Peak—*summit* MT-8
**Medicine Park**—*pop pl* OK-5
Medicine Park Hotel and Annex—*hist pl* OK-5
*Medicine Peak* MT-8
Medicine Pipe State Wildlife Mngmt Area—*park* MN-6
Medicine Point—*cliff* MT-8
Medicine Pole Hills—*range* ND-7
Medicine Range—*range* NV-8
Medicine Ridge—*ridge* WA-9
Medicine Rite Cem—*cemetery* MN-6
*Medicine River* KS-7
*Medicine River* OK-5
Medicine Rock—*pillar* OR-9
Medicine Rock—*summit* ND-7
Medicine Rock Creek—*stream* MT-8
Medicine Rock State Historic Site—*hist pl* ND-7
Medicine Root Creek—*stream* SD-7
Medicine Sink—*basin* GA-3
Medicine Spring—*spring* NV-8
Medicine Spring—*spring* WA-9
*Medicine Springs* MT-8
*Medicine Springs* NV-8
**Medicine Springs**—*pop pl* MT-8
Medicine Springs—*spring* MT-8
Medicine Springs—*spring* OK-5
Medicine Springs Rsvr—*reservoir* WY-8
Medicine Stone Bay—*bay* ND-7
Medicine Stone Cem—*cemetery* ND-7
Medicine Stone Public Use Area—*park* ND-7
Medicine Tail Coulee Ford—*locale* MT-8
Medicine Tail Creek—*valley* MT-8
Medicine Tank—*reservoir* OK-5
*Medicine Township* KS-7
**Medicine Township**—*pop pl* (3) MO-7
Medicine Tree Creek—*stream* MT-8
Medicine Tree Hill—*summit* MT-8
Medicine Valley—*valley* AZ-5
Medicine Valley—*valley* WA-9
Medicineville Cem—*cemetery* IA-7
Medicine Wheel—*hist pl* WY-8
Medicine Wheel ( Archeol Site)—*locale* WY-8
Medicine Wheel Ranger Station—*locale* WY-8
Medicis Island—*island* FL-3
Medico-Dental Bldg—*hist pl* CA-9
Medieros Windmill—*locale* TX-5
Medill—*locale* MO-7
Medill—*locale* TX-5
Medill, William, House—*hist pl* OH-6
Medill Bair HS—*school* PA-2
Medill Cem—*cemetery* MO-7
Medill Sch—*school* DE-2
Medill Sch—*school* IL-6
Medill Sch—*school* OH-6
**Medimont**—*pop pl* ID-8
*Medina* MN-6
Medina—*locale* AR-4
Medina—*locale* KS-7
Medina—*locale* WV-2
**Medina**—*pop pl* MI-6
**Medina**—*pop pl* NY-2
**Medina**—*pop pl* ND-7
**Medina**—*pop pl* OH-6
**Medina**—*pop pl* TN-4
**Medina**—*pop pl* TX-5
**Medina**—*pop pl* WA-9
**Medina**—*pop pl* WI-6
**Medina**—*pop pl* PR-3
Medina, Mount—*summit* TX-5
Medina Base—*military* TX-5
Medina Base (Military Reservation)—*uninc pl* TX-5
Medina Canyon—*valley* CO-8
Medina Canyon—*valley* (2) NM-5
Medina (CCD)—*cens area* TN-4
Medina (CCD)—*cens area* TX-5
Medina Cem—*cemetery* (2) WI-6
Medina Ch—*church* ND-7
Medina Childrens Home—*building* TX-5
Medina Ch of Christ—*church* TN-4
**Medina (corporate name for Hamel)**—*pop pl* MN-6
**Medina (County)**—*pop pl* OH-6
**Medina (County)**—*pop pl* TX-5
Medina County Courthouse—*hist pl* OH-6
Medina Dam—*dam* TX-5
Medina Dam—*hist pl* TX-5
Medina Division—*civil* TN-4
Medina Drain—*stream* MI-6
Medina Elem Sch—*school* TN-4
Medina First Baptist Ch—*church* TN-4
**Medinah**—*pop pl* IL-6
Medinah Country Club—*other* IL-6
**Medina Heights**—*pop pl* WA-9
*Medinah on the Lake* IL-6
Medina Irrigation Canal—*canal* TX-5
Medina JHS—*school* OH-6
Medina Junction—*locale* WI-6
Medina Lake—*lake* CO-8
Medina Lake—*lake* WY-8
Medina Lake—*other* TX-5
Medina Lake—*reservoir* TX-5
Medina Lake State Fish Hatchery—*other* TX-5
Medina Meadows—*area* NM-5
Medina Mesa—*summit* NM-5
Medina Methodist Ch—*church* TN-4
Medina Mtn—*summit* WY-8
**Medina Plaza**—*pop pl* CO-8
Medina Post Office—*building* TN-4
Medina Public Square Hist Dist—*hist pl* OH-6
*Medina River* TX-5
Medina River—*stream* TX-5
Medina River Ch—*church* TX-5
Medina Rsvr—*reservoir* NY-2
Medina Sch—*school* WA-9
*Medina Station* KS-7
Medina Tank—*reservoir* TX-5
**Medina (Town of)**—*pop pl* WI-6
**Medina (Township of)**—*pop pl* IL-6
**Medina (Township of)**—*pop pl* IN-6
**Medina (Township of)**—*pop pl* MI-6
**Medina (Township of)**—*pop pl* OH-6
Medina Valley Sch—*school* TX-5
Medina Windmill—*locale* NM-5
*Mediniija-to* MH-9
*Medinilla Insel* MH-9
*Medinilla Isl* MH-9
*Medino Plaza* CO-8
Medio—*locale* NM-5
Medio—*uninc pl* OK-5
Medio, Arroyo—*valley* TX-5
Medio Canyon—*valley* (3) NM-5
Medio Canyon Windmill—*locale* NM-5
Medio Creek—*stream* NM-5
Medio Creek—*stream* (3) TX-5
Medio Creek Bridge—*hist pl* TX-5
Medio de Llano Tank—*reservoir* TX-5
Medio dia Canyon—*valley* NM-5
Medio Dia Trail—*trail* NM-5
Medio Flowing Well—*well* TX-5
Medio Island—*island* TX-5
Medio Lake—*reservoir* TX-5
Medio Millon Well—*well* TX-5
*Mediopolis* IA-7
Medio Shipping Pasture Windmill—*locale* NM-5
Medio Well—*well* TX-5
Medio Windmill—*locale* TX-5
Meditation Lake—*lake* MN-6
Meditation Mtn—*summit* NC-3
Meditation Point Campground—*park* OR-9
Mediterranean Style House—*hist pl* AZ-5
Medium Cem—*cemetery* TN-4
*Medium Lake* IA-7
Medium Post Office (historical)—*building* TN-4
Medium Sch—*school* TN-4
Medium Sch (historical)—*school* TN-4
Medium Security Prison—*building* WV-2
Medium United Methodist Ch—*church* TN-4
*Mediuro* MP-9
**Medix Run**—*pop pl* PA-2
Medix Run—*stream* PA-2
*Medjado* MP-9
*Medjae* MP-9
*Medjato* MP-9
*Medjeol* FM-9
*Medjeronn* MP-9
*Medjill* MP-9
*Medjit* MP-9
*Medjruen* MP-9
*Medjuron* MP-9
Medke—*island* MP-9
*Medkin Creek* TX-5
Medla Cem—*cemetery* TX-5
Medlan Branch—*stream* TX-5
Medlan Cem—*cemetery* TX-5
Medlan Chapel—*church* TX-5
Medlar Spring—*spring* AZ-5
Medlen Creek—*stream* (2) MO-7
**Medler**—*pop pl* NM-5
Medler Cem—*cemetery* IL-6
Medlers Seep—*spring* AZ-5
**Medley**—*pop pl* FL-3
**Medley**—*pop pl* VA-3
**Medley**—*pop pl* WV-2
Medley Bar—*bar* MO-7
Medley Branch—*stream* VA-3
Medley Camp—*locale* VA-3
Medley Canyon—*valley* TX-5
Medley Canyon—*valley* WA-9
Medley Cave—*cave* TN-4
Medley Cem—*cemetery* NM-5
*Medley Creek* MD-2
Medley Creek—*stream* ID-8
Medley Double Wells—*well* TX-5
Medley Draw—*valley* TX-5
Medley Fork—*stream* KY-4
Medley Fork—*stream* WV-2
Medley Hill—*summit* AL-4
Medley Hills Park—*park* MN-6
**Medley (historical)**—*pop pl* OR-9
Medley Hollow—*valley* (2) MO-7
Medley Hollow—*valley* TN-4
Medley House—*hist pl* KY-4
Medley Lake—*lake* CA-9
Medley Lake—*lake* MN-6
*Medley Lakes Reservoir* CA-9
Medley Landing—*locale* MO-7
*Medley Neck* MD-2
*Medley Point* MD-2
Medley Ridge—*ridge* TN-4
Medley Sch—*school* IL-6
Medleys Creek—*stream* MD-2
Medleys Neck—*cape* MD-2
Medleys Pond—*reservoir* GA-3
Medley Trap Well—*well* TX-5
Medley Valley—*basin* VA-3
Medley Well—*well* (2) NM-5
Medlicott Dome—*summit* CA-9
*Medlin Branch* TX-5
Medlin Branch—*stream* NC-3
Medlin Cem—*cemetery* TX-5
*Medlin Creek* MO-7
*Medline Baptist Church* AL-4
Medline Cem—*cemetery* AL-4
Medline Ch—*church* AL-4
Medline (historical)—*locale* AL-4
Medlin Mtn—*summit* SC-3
Medlin Place—*locale* NM-5
Medlin Ranch—*locale* (2) NM-5
Medlin Sch—*school* NC-3
Medlock—*locale* AR-4
Medlock Branch—*stream* KY-4
Medlock Branch—*stream* MS-4
Medlock Branch—*stream* TN-4
Medlock Bridge—*bridge* GA-3
Medlock Cave—*cave* MO-7
Medlock Cem—*cemetery* AR-4
Medlock Cem—*cemetery* KY-4
Medlock Cem—*cemetery* MS-4
Medlock Ch—*church* MS-4
Medlock Creek—*stream* KY-4
Medlock Hollow—*valley* (2) MO-7
Medlock Hollow—*valley* TN-4
*Medlock Methodist Ch* MS-4
Medlock Spring—*spring* AL-4
*Medlocks Store* TN-4
Medo—*locale* WV-2
**Medoc**—*pop pl* MO-7
Medo Center Cem—*cemetery* MN-6
Medo Ch—*church* MN-6
Medoc Lookout Tower—*locale* NC-3
**Medoe**—*pop pl* MO-7
**Medomak**—*pop pl* ME-1
*Medomak Pond* ME-1
Medomak Pond—*lake* ME-1
Medomak River—*stream* ME-1
Medo-McPherson Cem—*cemetery* MN-6
**Medon**—*pop pl* TN-4
Medon Acad (historical)—*school* TN-4
Medon (CCD)—*cens area* TN-4
Medon Ch—*church* TN-4
Medon Division—*civil* TN-4
Medon Post Office—*building* TN-4
Medon Sch (historical)—*school* TN-4
*Medora* NC-3
**Medora**—*pop pl* IL-6
**Medora**—*pop pl* IN-6
**Medora**—*pop pl* IA-7
**Medora**—*pop pl* KS-7
**Medora**—*pop pl* KY-4
**Medora**—*pop pl* NC-3
Medora, Lake—*lake* FL-3
Medora, Lake—*lake* MI-6
Medora Cem—*cemetery* ND-7
Medora Elementary and HS—*school* IN-6
**Medora (historic Medora)**—*pop pl* ND-7
Medora Lake—*lake* CA-9
Medora River—*stream* MI-6
Medora Sch—*school* KY-4
**Medora Township**—*pop pl* KS-7
**Medorm**—*pop pl* PW-9
Medorm, Bkul A—*cape* PW-9
Medorm, Troch Ra—*gut* PW-9
*Medorom* PW-9
**Medo (Township of)**—*pop pl* MN-6
*Medow Creek* TX-5
Medow Island Ditch No. 1—*canal* CO-8
Medra Creek—*stream* WA-9
Medren—*island* (2) MP-9
Medrick Beach—*beach* ME-1
Medric Rock—*bar* ME-1
Medrith Branch—*stream* NC-3
Medron Windmill—*locale* TX-5
Medsger Pass—*gap* NV-8
Med Short Branch—*stream* KY-4
*Medskar Canyon* WA-9
Medsker Canyon—*valley* WA-9
Medsker Cem—*cemetery* IL-6
Medsker Spring—*spring* WA-9
Meduele Ranch—*locale* AZ-5
**Medulla**—*pop pl* FL-3
Medulla Assembly of God Ch—*church* FL-3
Medulla Cem—*cemetery* FL-3
Medulla Ch—*church* (2) FL-3
Medulla Elem Sch—*school* FL-3
Meduncook River—*stream* ME-1
Medunkeunk Lake—*lake* ME-1
Medunkeunk Stream—*stream* ME-1
*Meduro Island* MP-9
**Medusa**—*pop pl* NY-2
Medusa Cem—*cemetery* NY-2
Meduu—*island* PW-9
*Meduxmikeag River* ME-1
Meduxnekeag Lake—*lake* ME-1
Meduxnekeag Mtn—*summit* ME-1
*Meduxnekeag River* ME-1
Meduxnekeag River—*stream* ME-1
Meduxnekeag Stream—*stream* ME-1
Medvejie Lake—*lake* AK-9
Medvilles Mudhole—*cave* PA-2
*Medvilloe Attendance Center* MS-4
*Medway* VT-1
Medway—*hist pl* SC-3
Medway—*locale* KS-7
**Medway**—*pop pl* ME-1
**Medway**—*pop pl* MA-1
**Medway**—*pop pl* NY-2
**Medway**—*pop pl* OH-6
**Medway (census name Medway Center)**—*pop pl* MA-1
Medway Center (census name Medway)—*other* MA-1
Medway Ch—*church* OH-6
Medway (historical P.O.)—*locale* MA-1
Medway Lake—*lake* OH-6
Medway River—*stream* GA-3
Medway Sch—*school* MA-1
Medway Shop Ctr—*locale* MA-1
Medway Spit—*bar* GA-3
Medway Station (historical)—*locale* MA-1
**Medway (Town of)**—*pop pl* ME-1
**Medway (Town of)**—*pop pl* MA-1
Medway Township—*fmr MCD* KS-7
*Medway Village* MA-1
Medyado Island—*island* MP-9
Medyai Island—*island* MP-9
Medyeron Channel—*channel* MP-9
Medyeron Island—*island* MP-9
*Medyeron Pass* MP-9
Medyil Island—*island* MP-9
Mee, Joe, House—*hist pl* AZ-5
Meeboer Lake—*lake* WY-8
Meeboer Ranch—*locale* WA-9
Mee Canyon—*valley* CO-8
Meece—*locale* KY-4
Meece Sch—*school* KY-4
Meechan-Nunally Cem—*cemetery* MS-4
Meech Cem—*cemetery* NY-2
*Meechien To* MP-9
Meechoqol—*locale* FM-9
**Mee Corners**—*pop pl* ME-1
Mee Cove—*valley* OR-9
Meed Lake—*lake* WI-6
Meeds Lake—*lake* MN-6
**Meege Crossroads**—*pop pl* NC-3
**Meeham**—*pop pl* WI-6
Meehan—*locale* AK-9
**Meehan**—*pop pl* MS-4
**Meehan**—*pop pl* WI-6
Meehan, Thomas, Sch—*hist pl* PA-2
*Meehan Airfield* PA-2
Meehan Airp—*airport* PA-2
Meehan/Gaar House—*hist pl* AZ-5
Meehan Hill—*summit* VT-1
*Meehan Junction* MS-4
Meehan Junction—*other* MS-4
**Meehan (Meehan Junction)**—*pop pl* MS-4
Meehl Draw—*valley* WY-8
Meehl Sch—*school* MN-6
*Meek* AL-4
**Meek**—*pop pl* NE-7
Meek, J.F., Buildings—*hist pl* OH-6
Meek, Mount—*summit* AK-9
Meek, Mount—*summit* WY-8
Meek Branch—*stream* VA-3
*Meek Cem* TN-4
Meek Cem—*cemetery* GA-3
Meek Cem—*cemetery* IN-6
Meek Cem—*cemetery* KY-4
Meek Cem—*cemetery* OH-6
Meek Cem—*cemetery* (3) TN-4
Meek Cem—*cemetery* VA-3
Meek Ch—*church* AL-4
*Meek Ditch* IN-6
Meeker—*locale* PA-2
Meeker—*locale* TX-5
Meeker—*locale* WA-9
Meeker—*locale* WV-2
**Meeker**—*pop pl* CO-8
**Meeker**—*pop pl* LA-4
**Meeker**—*pop pl* (2) OH-6
**Meeker**—*pop pl* OK-5
**Meeker**—*pop pl* WI-6
Meeker—*uninc pl* WI-6
Meeker, Ezra, Mansion—*hist pl* WA-9
Meeker, Mount—*summit* CO-8
Meeker Airp—*airport* CO-8
Meeker Canal—*canal* NE-7
Meeker (CCD)—*cens area* OK-5
Meeker Cem—*cemetery* LA-4
Meeker Cem—*cemetery* MN-6
Meeker Cem—*cemetery* NY-2
**Meeker (County)**—*pop pl* MN-6
Meeker Creek—*stream* CA-9
Meeker Creek—*stream* ID-8
Meeker Ditch—*canal* CO-8
Meeker Ditch—*canal* IL-6
Meeker Dome—*summit* CO-8
Meeker Extension Canal—*canal* NE-7
Meeker Hill—*summit* (2) NY-2
Meeker Hollow—*valley* NY-2
Meeker Hollow—*valley* PA-2
Meeker JHS—*school* CO-8
Meeker JHS—*school* WA-9
Meeker Lake—*lake* MI-6
Meeker Lake—*lake* PA-2
*Meeker Lakes* WA-9
Meeker Massacre—*locale* CO-8
Meeker Memorial Museum—*hist pl* CO-8
Meeker Memorial Museum—*other* CO-8
Meeker Mountain Rsvr—*reservoir* OR-9
Meeker Mountian—*summit* WA-9
Meeker Mtn—*summit* OR-9
Meeker Park—*park* OK-5
**Meeker Park**—*pop pl* CO-8
Meeker Peak—*summit* NV-8
Meeker Point—*cliff* ID-8
Meeker Ridge—*ridge* CO-8
Meeker Ridge—*ridge* ID-8
Meeker Run—*stream* PA-2
Meeker Run Lake—*lake* WI-6
**Meekers**—*pop pl* OH-6
Meekers Cem—*cemetery* MO-7
Meeker Sch—*school* IA-7
Meeker Sch—*school* WA-9
Meekers Creek—*stream* AL-4
Meekers Creek—*stream* MN-6
Meekers Grove—*locale* WI-6
Meeker's Hardware—*hist pl* CT-1
Meekers Hill—*summit* CT-1
Meekers Hill—*summit* NY-2
*Meeker's Island* MN-6
*Meekers Pond* PA-2
Meekers Sch—*school* KS-7

Meeker Sugar Refinery—*hist pl* LA-4
Meeker Swamp—*swamp* CT-1
*Meekertown Brook* CT-1
Meeker Tree—*locale* CO-8
Meeker Valley—*basin* NE-7
Meek Field—*flat* GA-3
Meek Hollow—*valley* KY-4
Meek HS—*school* AL-4
Meekin Brook—*stream* MA-1
*Meekin Neck* MD-2
Meekins, Thedore S., House—*hist pl* NC-3
Meekins Barn—*hist pl* SC-3
*Meekins Brook* MA-1
*Meekins Cove* MD-2
Meekins Creek—*bay* MD-2
Meekins Creek Marsh—*swamp* MD-2
*Meekin's Neck* MD-2
Meekins Neck—*cape* MD-2
Meekins Roadhouse—*locale* AK-9
Meek Lake—*lake* MI-6
Meek Lake—*lake* OR-9
Meek Lookout Tower—*locale* AL-4
Meek Mansion and Carriage House—*hist pl* CA-9
Meek-Miller House—*hist pl* KY-4
Meek Rsvr—*reservoir* CO-8
*Meeks* AR-4
Meeks—*locale* IL-6
Meeks—*locale* SC-3
Meeks—*locale* TX-5
**Meeks**—*pop pl* GA-3
**Meeks**—*pop pl* MS-4
Meeks Bay—*bay* CA-9
**Meeks Bay**—*pop pl* CA-9
Meeks Bend—*bend* TX-5
Meeks Branch—*stream* (2) AR-4
Meeks Branch—*stream* KY-4
Meeks Branch—*stream* TN-4
Meeks Branch—*stream* TX-5
Meeks Branch—*stream* WV-2
Meeks Cabin Dam—*dam* WY-8
Meeks Cabin ( Historical)—*locale* WY-8
Meeks Cabin Rsvr—*reservoir* UT-8
Meeks Cabin Rsvr—*reservoir* WY-8
Meeks Camp—*locale* TX-5
Meeks Canyon—*valley* NM-5
Meeks Cem—*cemetery* (2) GA-3
Meeks Cem—*cemetery* (2) IN-6
Meeks Cem—*cemetery* NY-2
Meeks Cem—*cemetery* NC-3
Meeks Cem—*cemetery* TN-4
Meeks Cem—*cemetery* WV-2
Meek Sch—*school* IL-6
Meek Sch—*school* OR-9
Meeks Chapel—*church* OK-5
*Meeks Cliff* UT-8
Meeks Cliffs—*cliff* UT-8
*Meeks Creek* PA-2
Meeks Creek—*stream* AR-4
Meeks Creek—*stream* CA-9
Meeks Creek—*stream* WY-8
*Meeks Ditch* IN-6
Meeks Draw—*valley* UT-8
Meeks Ferry (historical)—*locale* MS-4
Meek's Flour Mill—*hist pl* IA-7
Meeks Grove Cem—*cemetery* TN-4
Meeks Grove Ch—*church* TN-4
Meeks Hill—*summit* NY-2
*Meeks Lake* CA-9
Meeks Lake—*lake* FL-3
Meeks Lake—*lake* (2) UT-8
Meeks Lake—*lake* WY-8
Meeks Meadow Creek—*stream* CA-9
Meeks Meadow Lake—*lake* CA-9
Meeks Mesa—*summit* UT-8
Meeks Mtn—*summit* AL-4
Meeks Mtn—*summit* AR-4
Meeks Point—*cape* MD-2
Meeks Pond—*lake* AK-9
Meeks Post Office (historical)—*building* AL-4
Meeks Ranch—*locale* AZ-5
Meeks Ranch—*locale* NM-5
Meeks Ranch—*locale* WY-8
Meeks Rsvr—*reservoir* AZ-5
Meeks Rsvr No 1—*reservoir* CO-8
Meeks Rsvr No 2—*reservoir* CO-8
Meeks Run—*stream* PA-2
**Meeks Settlement**—*pop pl* AR-4
Meeks Spring—*spring* AZ-5
Meeks Table—*summit* WA-9
**Meeksville**—*pop pl* AL-4
Meeman-Shelby Forest State Park—*park* TN-4
Meeme—*locale* WI-6
Meeme Center Cem—*cemetery* WI-6
*Meeme Creek* WI-6
Meeme Creek—*stream* WI-6
Meeme River—*stream* WI-6
**Meeme (Town of)**—*pop pl* WI-6
Meems—*locale* VA-3
Meems Bottom—*bend* VA-3
Meems Bottom Covered Bridge—*hist pl* VA-3
Meenach Hollow—*valley* KY-4
Meenahga, Mount—*summit* NY-2
Meenahga Mtn—*summit* NY-2
Meengs Canyon—*valley* OR-9
Meengs Spring—*spring* OR-9
**Meenon (Town of)**—*pop pl* WI-6
Meentzen Gulch—*valley* CA-9
Meer—*locale* FM-9
Meer Ranch—*locale* WY-8
Meers—*locale* OK-5
Meers Cem—*cemetery* OK-5
Meerschaum Canyon—*valley* NM-5
Meerschaum Mine—*mine* NM-5
Meerschaum Tank—*reservoir* NM-5
Meerscheidt, Otto, House—*hist pl* TX-5
**Meersman**—*pop pl* IL-6
Meers Mining Camp—*hist pl* OK-5
Meers Township—*civil* SD-7
*Meerur* FM-9
Meese Ch—*church* IN-6
*Meeshawn* MA-1
Meesing Nature Center—*locale* PA-2
Meesville Post Office (historical)—*building* TN-4
**Meeteetse**—*pop pl* WY-8
Meeteetse Creek—*stream* WY-8
Meeteetse Draw—*valley* WY-8
Meeteetse Rim—*cliff* WY-8
*Meethouse Fork* WV-2

Meeting Bend—*bend* TN-4
Meeting Branch—*stream* TX-5
**Meeting Creek**—*pop pl* KY-4
Meeting Creek—*stream* KY-4
Meeting Creek Ch—*church* KY-4
Meeting Grove Cem—*cemetery* SC-3
Meeting Hall—*hist pl* UT-8
*Meeting House* MA-1
Meetinghouse, The—*hist pl* NH-1
Meetinghouse Bay—*swamp* FL-3
Meeting House Bay—*swamp* GA-3
Meeting House Bluff—*cliff* MS-4
*Meeting House Branch* TN-4
Meetinghouse Branch—*stream* AL-4
Meeting House Branch—*stream* (2) AL-4
Meetinghouse Branch—*stream* (2) GA-3
Meetinghouse Branch—*stream* (10) KY-4
Meetinghouse Branch—*stream* MD-2
Meetinghouse Branch—*stream* MS-4
Meetinghouse Branch—*stream* (2) NC-3
Meeting House Branch—*stream* (2) SC-3
Meetinghouse Branch—*stream* (2) SC-3
Meetinghouse Branch—*stream* (3) TN-4
Meetinghouse Branch—*stream* TX-5
Meetinghouse Branch—*stream* VA-3
Meetinghouse Branch—*stream* (2) WV-2
Meetinghouse Brook—*stream* CT-1
Meetinghouse Brook—*stream* (2) NH-1
Meetinghouse Canyon—*valley* (2) UT-8
Meeting House Cave—*cave* MO-7
Meetinghouse Ch—*church* NC-3
Meetinghouse Common District—*hist pl* MA-1
Meetinghouse Cove—*bay* (2) ME-1
Meeting House Creek—*stream* AL-4
Meetinghouse Creek—*stream* NY-2
Meetinghouse Creek—*stream* NC-3
Meetinghouse Creek—*stream* PA-2
Meetinghouse Gap—*gap* VA-3
Meeting House Green—*locale* NY-2
Meetinghouse Green Hist Dist—*hist pl* MA-1
Meeting House Hall—*summit* MA-1
*Meeting House Hill* DE-2
*Meeting House Hill* MA-1
**Meeting House Hill**—*pop pl* DE-2
Meeting House Hill—*summit* CT-1
Meetinghouse Hill—*summit* (2) ME-1
Meetinghouse Hill—*summit* MA-1
Meeting House Hill—*summit* MA-1
Meetinghouse Hill—*summit* MA-1
Meeting House Hill—*summit* MA-1
Meetinghouse Hill—*summit* (4) NH-1
Meeting House Hill—*summit* NH-1
Meetinghouse Hill—*summit* (2) NH-1
Meetinghouse Hill—*summit* RI-1
Meetinghouse Hill—*summit* TN-4
Meetinghouse Hill—*summit* (3) VT-1
Meeting House Hill Hist Dist—*hist pl* CT-1
**Meeting House Hill (subdivision)**—*pop pl* MA-1
Meetinghouse Hollow—*valley* (4) TN-4
Meetinghouse Hollow—*valley* WV-2
Meetinghouse Hollow Mine—*mine* TN-4
Meetinghouse Knob—*summit* KY-4
Meeting House Lane Cem—*cemetery* MA-1
**Meeting House Meadows**—*pop pl* DE-2
Meetinghouse Mtn—*summit* NC-3
Meetinghouse Mtn—*summit* VA-3
Meetinghouse of the Central Congregational Church—*hist pl* IL-6
Meetinghouse Point—*cape* ME-1
*Meetinghouse Pond* MA-1
Meetinghouse Pond—*lake* ME-1
Meeting House Pond—*lake* MA-1
Meetinghouse Pond—*lake* (2) NH-1
Meetinghouse Pond—*reservoir* MA-1
Meetinghouse Pond Dam—*dam* MA-1
Meetinghouse Ridge—*ridge* GA-3
Meetinghouse Ridge—*ridge* IN-6
Meetinghouse Rips—*rapids* ME-1
Meetinghouse Run—*stream* NY-2
Meetinghouse Run—*stream* PA-2
Meetinghouse Run—*stream* WV-2
*Meeting House Swamp* MA-1
Meetinghouse Swamp—*swamp* MA-1
Meeting of the Pines Natural Area—*area* PA-2
Meeting-of-the-Waters—*hist pl* TN-4
Meeting of the Waters—*stream* NC-3
Meeting of the Waters Plantation (historical)—*locale* TN-4
Meeting Pond—*reservoir* FL-3
Meeting Reach—*channel* SC-3
Meeting Sch—*school* NH-1
**Meeting Street**—*pop pl* SC-3
Meetze—*locale* VA-3
Meetze, Maj. Henry A., House—*hist pl* SC-3
*Meeyero Creek* WY-8
Meffert Creek—*stream* PA-2
Mefford Branch—*stream* KY-4
Mefford Hollow—*valley* KY-4
Mefford Hollow—*valley* MO-7
Mefford Hollow—*valley* OH-6
Meffords Branch—*stream* KY-4
Meffords Run—*stream* OH-6
Mefford Wash—*stream* CO-8
Mefford Wash—*stream* NM-5
**Meg**—*pop pl* AR-4
*Megalloway Reservoir* ME-1
**Megansett**—*pop pl* MA-1
Megansett Harbor—*bay* MA-1
**Megargee**—*pop pl* PA-2
**Megargel**—*pop pl* AL-4
**Megargel**—*pop pl* TX-5
*Megargle* TX-5
*Megarly Gulch* OR-9
Megaron—*post sta* TX-5
Megeath—*locale* NE-7
Megee Cem—*cemetery* MS-4
*Megee Switch* MS-4
Me George Spring—*spring* SD-7
Meggers—*locale* WI-6
**Meggers**—*pop pl* WI-6
**Meggett**—*pop pl* SC-3
Meggett Sch—*school* SC-3
Megginnis Arm—*bay* FL-3
Megginson Cem—*cemetery* VA-3
Megginson Gulch—*valley* WA-9
Megginson Park—*park* AL-4
Meggs Bay—*swamp* VA-3
Meggs Cem—*cemetery* (2) MS-4
Megler—*locale* WA-9

Megli Cem—*cemetery* NE-7
Meglin Creek—*stream* NE-7
*Megonko* MA-1
Megotsol Island—*island* AK-9
Megquier Hill—*summit* ME-1
Megquier Island—*island* ME-1
Megram Cabin—*locale* CA-9
Megram Ridge—*ridge* CA-9
Megrew Cem—*cemetery* MO-7
Megs Mud Spring—*spring* CA-9
Megunticook, Mount—*summit* ME-1
Megunticook Lake—*lake* ME-1
Megunticook River—*stream* ME-1
Meguzee Point—*cape* MI-6
Megwil Point—*cape* CA-9
**Mehaffey**—*pop pl* AL-4
Mehaffey House—*hist pl* AR-4
*Mehama* AL-4
**Mehama**—*pop pl* AL-4
**Mehama**—*pop pl* OR-9
**Mehan**—*pop pl* OK-5
*Mehaphy* AL-4
Meharg—*locale* PA-2
Meharg Drain—*stream* MI-6
Meharry AG Service Airp—*airport* IN-6
Meharry Cem—*cemetery* IL-6
Meharry Cem—*cemetery* IN-6
Meharry Medical Coll—*school* TN-4
*Mehebehubl* PW-9
Meherg Branch—*stream* AL-4
Meherg Sch (historical)—*school* AL-4
**Meherrin**—*pop pl* VA-3
Meherrin Ch—*church* NC-3
Meherrin Ch—*church* VA-3
Meherrin (Magisterial District)—*fmr MCD* VA-3
Meherrin-Powellton Sch—*school* VA-3
*Meherrin River* VA-3
Meherrin River—*stream* NC-3
Meherrin River—*stream* VA-3
Meherrin Sch—*school* NC-3
Mehert Creek—*stream* MI-6
Mehixen Creek—*stream* VA-3
Mehl Creek—*stream* OR-9
Mehles Springs—*spring* WI-6
Mehl Hill—*summit* TX-5
Mehlhorn Butte—*summit* OR-9
Mehlhorn Mill—*building* OR-9
Mehlhorn Rsvr—*reservoir* OR-9
Mehl Lake—*lake* MI-6
Mehlow Ditch—*canal* OH-6
Mehlschau Creek—*stream* CA-9
**Mehlville**—*pop pl* (2) MO-7
Mehlville HS—*school* MO-7
M E Home for the Aged—*building* PA-2
**Mehoopany**—*pop pl* PA-2
Mehoopany Creek—*stream* PA-2
Mehoopany Fire Tower—*locale* PA-2
Mehoopany Mtn—*summit* PA-2
Mehoopany Station—*locale* PA-2
**Mehoopany (Township of)**—*pop pl* PA-2
Mehr—*locale* MS-4
Mehrer Creek—*stream* ND-7
Mehrley Cem—*cemetery* OH-6
Mehrten Creek—*stream* (2) CA-9
Mehrten Meadow—*flat* CA-9
Mehrten Spring—*spring* CA-9
**Mehurin (Township of)**—*pop pl* MN-6
*Mei* FM-9
*Meiamon, Mount* FM-9
Meichen—*island* MP-9
Meichen Channel—*channel* MP-9
*Meichen Island* MP-9
*Meichen Pass* MP-9
*Meichikku* FM-9
Meidinger Square—*locale* ND-7
Meidj—*island* MP-9
*Meidj Island* MP-9
Meieneo—*tunnel* FM-9
**Meier**—*pop pl* WY-8
Meier, Fred W., Round Barn—*hist pl* IA-7
Meier, George Philip, House—*hist pl* IN-6
Meier, Isaac, Homestead—*hist pl* PA-2
Meier, William G., Warehouse—*hist pl* KY-4
Meier and Frank Bldg—*hist pl* OR-9
Meier Branch—*stream* TX-5
Meier Canyon—*valley* CA-9
*Meier Creek* OR-9
Meier Creek—*stream* TX-5
Meier Ditch—*canal* IN-6
Meier Hills—*summit* TX-5
Meier Lodge—*locale* AK-9
Meier Memorial Park—*park* IA-7
Meier Oil Field—*oilfield* KS-7
Meier Sch—*school* WI-6
*Meier School* SD-7
Meier Settlement Ch—*church* TX-5
Meiers Lake—*lake* AK-9
Meiers Lake—*lake* SD-7
Meifo, Unun En—*cape* FM-9
Meighan Bridge—*bridge* AL-4
**Meighen**—*pop pl* WV-2
Meigh Ranch—*locale* WY-8
**Meigs**—*pop pl* GA-3
**Meigs**—*pop pl* (2) OH-6
*Meigs Bay* CA-9
Meigs-Bishop House—*hist pl* CT-1
**Meigs Cabin Area**—*pop pl* TN-4
Meigs (CCD)—*cens area* GA-3
Meigs Ch—*church* OH-6
*Meigs Consolidated School* TN-4
**Meigs (County)**—*pop pl* OH-6
**Meigs County**—*pop pl* TN-4
Meigs County Bank—*hist pl* TN-4
Meigs County Courthouse—*building* TN-4
Meigs County Courthouse—*hist pl* TN-4
Meigs County Fairgrounds, Grandstand and Racetrack—*hist pl* OH-6
Meigs County HS Gymnasium—*hist pl* TN-4
Meigs County Park—*park* TN-4
Meigs County Sch—*school* TN-4
*Meigs Creek* CA-9
Meigs Creek—*stream* (2) OH-6
Meigs Creek—*stream* TN-4
Meigs Field—*park* IL-6
Meigs JHS—*school* FL-3
Meigs Key—*island* FL-3
Meigs Mountain Trail—*trail* TN-4
Meigs Mtn—*summit* TN-4
Meigs Peak—*summit* AK-9
Meigs Pond—*lake* PA-2

Meigs Post Prong—*stream* TN-4
Meigs Ranch—*locale* MT-8
Meigs Sch—*school* TN-4
*Meigs Subdivision* TN-4
**Meigs (Township of)**—*pop pl* (2) OH-6
*Meigsville Post Office* TN-4
**Meigsville (Township of)**—*pop pl* OH-6
*Meik Island* MP-9
Meiklejohn Pass—*gap* AK-9
Meiklejohn Peak—*summit* NV-8
Meikle Windmill—*locale* NM-5
**Meiks**—*pop pl* IN-6
*Meiku* MP-9
*Meiku-to* MP-9
Meilap—*cape* FM-9
Meile Dietrich Point—*cape* TX-5
Meili Coulee—*valley* MT-8
Meilke Lake—*lake* WI-6
Meill Ditch—*canal* MT-8
*Meilop* FM-9
Meilvaig JHS—*school* WA-9
Meinaw—*bar* FM-9
Meinecke Cem—*cemetery* TX-5
Meine Cow Camp—*locale* MT-8
**Meiners Oak**—*pop pl* CA-9
Meiners Oaks—*uninc pl* CA-9
Meiners Oaks-Mira Monte—*CDP* CA-9
Meiners Oaks-Ojai (CCD)—*cens area* CA-9
**Meinert**—*pop pl* CA-9
**Meinert**—*pop pl* IL-6
**Meinert**—*pop pl* MO-7
*Meinert Branch* MO-7
Meinert Branch—*stream* MO-7
Meinert Park—*park* MI-6
Meinert Ranch Cabin—*hist pl* ID-8
**Meinhard**—*pop pl* GA-3
Meinhardt Cem—*cemetery* AL-4
Mein Hope Ch—*church* TX-5
Meinig Glove Factory-Meinig, E. Richard, Co.—*hist pl* PA-2
Meinopar, Ochen—*bar* FM-9
Meinrad Hollow—*valley* IN-6
Meins Landing—*locale* CA-9
Meints Cem—*cemetery* IL-6
Meints Sch—*school* IA-7
*Meinwa Island* MP-9
Meinzine Branch—*stream* AL-4
Meipat, Dolen—*unknown* FM-9
Meipun—*bar* FM-9
Meir Cem—*cemetery* TX-5
**Meire Grove**—*pop pl* MN-6
Meirop, Unun En—*bar* FM-9
Meisakot—*unknown* FM-9
Meisch House—*hist pl* NE-7
Meisenheimer Cem—*cemetery* IL-6
*Meiser* PA-2
Meiser Creek—*stream* WY-8
Meiser Drug Store—*hist pl* IA-7
**Meiser (Globe Mills)**—*pop pl* PA-2
Meiser Lake—*lake* WY-8
**Meiser Station**—*pop pl* PA-2
**Meisertown**—*pop pl* PA-2
**Meiserville**—*pop pl* PA-2
Meismer Ranch—*locale* NE-7
Meisner, George, House—*hist pl* NE-7
Meiss—*locale* CA-9
Meiss Lake—*lake* (2) CA-9
Meissner Island—*island* IL-6
Meissner Lookout—*locale* OR-9
Meissner-Pleasants House—*hist pl* TX-5
Meiss Ranch—*locale* CA-9
Meister Branch—*stream* MO-7
Meister Mine—*mine* NV-8
Meister Pond—*lake* NY-2
Meister Sch—*school* MN-6
*Meister School* IN-6
Meitik—*civil* FM-9
Meitik, Pilen—*stream* FM-9
Meitzen House—*hist pl* TX-5
**Meiuhpw**—*pop pl* FM-9
*Meiungs* PW-9
Meixell Trail—*trail* PA-2
*Meixsell Creek* PA-2
*Mej* MP-9
*Mejaddo* MP-9
*Mejado-to* MP-9
*Mejae* MP-9
*Mejai-to* MP-9
Mejan Mesa—*summit* NM-5
*Mejatto* MP-9
Mejatto—*island* MP-9
Mejatto Island—*island* MP-9
*Mejatto-To* MP-9
*Mejdit Island* MP-9
*Mejejok* MP-9
*Mejetto Island* MP-9
**Mejias**—*pop pl* PR-3
*Mejichi-to* MP-9
*Mejieruen-suido* MP-9
*Mejieruen-to* MP-9
*Mejiiru-to* MP-9
*Mejiruiku* MP-9
*Mejiruon* MP-9
*Mejiruon Island* MP-9
Mejiruon Island—*island* MP-9
*Mejiruon-To* MP-9
*Mejiruriku* MP-9
*Mejiruriku-To* MP-9
*Mejisebu* MP-9
*Mejisenbu* MP-9
*Mejisenbu-To* MP-9
Mejit—*island* MP-9
*Mejit Atoll* MP-9
Mejit (County-equivalent)—*civil* MP-9
*Mejit Island* MP-9
*Mejiyai To* MP-9
*Mejiyatto-to* MP-9
*Mejjen* MP-9
Mejor Tank—*reservoir* AZ-5
*Mejrwirok* MP-9
*Mejurirok* MP-9
*Mejuro-to* MP-9
*Mejurwon* MP-9
*Mejurwon Channel* MP-9
*Mejurwon Island* MP-9
*Mejyai To* MP-9
Mekaeb—*channel* PW-9
Mekanac Point—*cape* WI-6
Mekasukey Acad—*hist pl* OK-5
*Mekasuki* FL-3

Mekaud, Omoachel Ra—*stream* PW-9
Mekeald—*bar* PW-9
Mekee—*locale* IA-7
*Meker* PW-9
Meketchum Creek—*stream* AK-9
**Meketii**—*pop pl* PW-9
**Mekinock**—*pop pl* ND-7
Mekinock Sch—*school* ND-7
**Mekinock Township**—*pop pl* ND-7
Mekirong—*summit* PW-9
Mekko—*locale* OK-5
Mekko Ch—*church* OK-5
**Mekoryuk**—*pop pl* AK-9
Mekoryuk River—*stream* AK-9
Mekusukey Ch—*church* OK-5
*Me-kwah-mooks Point* WA-9
Melado, Arroyo—*valley* TX-5
Melager Cove—*gut* TX-5
Melaken, Lake—*reservoir* AL-4
Melakwa Creek—*stream* ID-8
Melakwa Lake—*lake* OR-9
Melakwa Lake—*lake* WA-9
Melakwa Pass—*gap* WA-9
Melaleuca Elem Sch—*school* FL-3
Melaleuca Head—*summit* FL-3
**Melaleuca Isle**—*pop pl* FL-3
Melaleuca Trail—*trail* FL-3
**Melalevca Isles (subdivision)**—*pop pl* FL-3
Melan Bridge—*hist pl* IA-7
Melancholy Bayou—*stream* MS-4
*Melanchthon* NC-3
Melanchthon Chapel—*church* VA-3
**Melanchton**—*pop pl* NC-3
Melancthon Creek—*stream* WI-6
*Melancton* NC-3
Melandco—*locale* NV-8
*Melang* MP-9
Melanie, Lake—*reservoir* AL-4
**Melanie Acres Subdivision**—*pop pl* UT-8
*Melanie Dam* AL-4
**Melanie (subdivision)**—*pop pl* DE-2
Melankton Cem—*cemetery* ND-7
Melanson Lake—*lake* AK-9
Melargo Windmill—*locale* TX-5
*Melasa Point* MH-9
Melat Cem—*cemetery* PA-2
Melatolik Creek—*stream* AK-9
Melatone Tank—*reservoir* AZ-5
*Melattach Brook* ME-1
*Melba* AR-4
Melba—*locale* MS-4
**Melba**—*pop pl* ID-8
**Melba**—*pop pl* (2) MS-4
Melba Creek—*stream* AK-9
Melba Drain—*canal* ID-8
Melba Island—*island* FL-3
Melba Sch (historical)—*school* MS-4
**Melber**—*pop pl* KY-4
**Melbern**—*pop pl* OH-6
Melbern Lake—*lake* NY-2
Melbert Ranch—*well* TX-5
**Melbeta**—*pop pl* NE-7
Melbeth Tank—*reservoir* TX-5
**Melborne**—*pop pl* AL-4
**Melborne Heights**—*pop pl* NC-3
Melborne Post Office (historical)—*building* AL-4
*Melbourne* AL-4
Melbourne—*locale* CA-9
**Melbourne**—*pop pl* AR-4
**Melbourne**—*pop pl* FL-3
**Melbourne**—*pop pl* IA-7
**Melbourne**—*pop pl* KY-4
**Melbourne**—*pop pl* MO-7
**Melbourne**—*pop pl* TN-4
**Melbourne**—*pop pl* WA-9
**Melbourne Beach**—*pop pl* FL-3
Melbourne Beach Pier—*hist pl* FL-3
Melbourne Cave—*cave* AR-4
Melbourne (CCD)—*cens area* FL-3
Melbourne Cem—*cemetery* IA-7
Melbourne Ch—*church* IA-7
Melbourne Ch—*church* LA-4
Melbourne Dam—*dam* AZ-5
Melbourne Flats—*hist pl* OH-6
**Melbourne Gardens (subdivision)**—*pop pl* FL-3
Melbourne Golf and Country Club—*locale* FL-3
Melbourne Heights Ch—*church* KY-4
Melbourne Heights Sch—*school* KY-4
Melbourne (historical)—*locale* SD-7
Melbourne HS—*school* FL-3
Melbourne Lake—*lake* WA-9
Melbourne Memorial Garden Cem—*cemetery* IA-7
Melbourne Plaza (Shop Ctr)—*locale* FL-3
Melbourne Regional Airp—*airport* FL-3
Melbourne Sch—*school* CA-9
Melbourne Seventh-Day Adventist Sch—*school* FL-3
Melbourne Shop Ctr—*locale* FL-3
Melbourne Shores-Floridana Beach (CCD)—*cens area* FL-3
**Melbourne Shores (subdivision)**—*pop pl* FL-3
Melbourne Square (Shop Ctr)—*locale* FL-3
Melbourne Tillman Canal—*canal* FL-3
**Melbourne Village**—*pop pl* FL-3
*Melbs Cut* TX-5
Melburn Tank—*reservoir* AZ-5
*Melby* ND-7
**Melby**—*pop pl* MN-6
Melbye Lake—*lake* MN-6
Melbye State Wildlife Mngmt Area—*park* MN-6
Melby Hills—*range* ND-7
Melby JHS—*school* MI-6
Melby Lake—*lake* MN-6
Melby Private Airstrip—*airport* ND-7
Melbys Slough—*gut* ND-7
*Melchar Branch* AR-4
*Melcher* IA-7
**Melcher**—*pop pl* IA-7
Melcher Bridge—*hist pl* IN-6
Melcher Cem—*cemetery* TX-5
*Melcher Dallas* IA-7
**Melcher-Dallas**—*pop pl* IA-7
Melcher Hills—*summit* IL-6
**Melcher (historical)**—*pop pl* IN-6
Melcher Mine—*locale* ID-8

Melcher Mine (underground)—*mine* AL-4
Melcher Number 11 Mine (underground)—*mine* AL-4
Melcher Ranch—*locale* SD-7
Melcher Sch—*school* MO-7
Melchers Point—*cape* MI-6
Melchers Sch—*school* VA-3
Melches Branch—*stream* LA-4
Melchoir Hotel and Brewery Ruins—*hist pl* WI-6
Melchoir Park—*park* NY-2
*Melchor Branch* AR-4
Melchor Branch—*stream* NC-3
Melchor Creek—*stream* AR-4
**Melchris Wood**—*pop pl* PA-2
Melco Lake—*lake* OH-6
Melco Landing—*locale* OR-9
**Melcore Acres Subdivision (subdivision)**—*pop pl* SD-7
**Melco Subdivision**—*pop pl* MS-4
Melcott Rsvr—*reservoir* MT-8
Melcourt—*uninc pl* NY-2
**Melcroft**—*pop pl* PA-2
Meldah—*locale* WV-2
Meldahl Dam—*building* OH-6
**Meldahls**—*pop pl* WV-2
Meldal Cem—*cemetery* SD-7
**Melder**—*pop pl* LA-4
Melder Cem—*cemetery* LA-4
Melder Draw—*valley* ID-8
Meldo Park—*park* TX-5
**Meldrim**—*pop pl* GA-3
Meldrim Cem—*cemetery* GA-3
Meldrim Cem—*cemetery* OH-6
*Meldrim Millpond* GA-3
**Meldrim Park**—*pop pl* FL-3
Meldrim Point—*cape* WA-9
*Meldrin Mill Pond* GA-3
Meldrin Millpond—*reservoir* GA-3
Meldrum—*locale* TX-5
**Meldrum**—*pop pl* KY-4
Meldrum Canyon—*valley* OR-9
Meldrum Drain—*stream* (2) MI-6
Meldrum Mtn—*summit* MT-8
Meldrum Park—*park* SD-7
Meldrum Tunnel—*mine* CO-8
Melear—*post sta* TX-5
Melechalb, Bkul A—*cape* PW-9
*Meledeconk River* NJ-2
*Melekeiok* PW-9
Melekeiok (County-equivalent)—*civil* PW-9
*Melekeiok Point* PW-9
*Melekejok* PW-9
**Melekeok**—*pop pl* PW-9
Melekeok Elem Sch—*school* PW-9
*Melekiok Municipality* PW-9
*Melekoi* MP-9
*Melekyok* PW-9
*Melemmar Island* MP-9
Melena—*locale* NM-5
*Melendreth Pass* AZ-5
Melendrez Pass—*gap* AZ-5
Melendrez Well—*well* AZ-5
Melendy—*locale* TX-5
*Melendy Ferry* TN-4
Melendy Pond—*lake* NH-1
Melendy Ranch—*locale* CA-9
Melendy Ridge—*ridge* OR-9
Melendys Pond—*lake* NH-1
Meleskie Camp—*locale* WY-8
*Meletecunk River* NJ-2
M E Levy Grant—*civil* FL-3
**Melfa**—*pop pl* VA-3
Mel Fieldings Ditch—*canal* ID-8
Melford—*hist pl* MD-2
*Melga* CA-9
Melgaard Park—*park* SD-7
Melga Canal—*canal* CA-9
Melges Bakery—*hist pl* MN-6
**Melham**—*pop pl* SD-7
Melham (historical)—*locale* SD-7
Melhany Creek—*stream* NC-3
Melhase Ditch—*canal* OR-9
Mel Hodge Park—*park* IL-6
Melhomes Creek—*stream* TX-5
*Melhomes Mill Creek* TX-5
*Melhoms Creek* TX-5
Melhorn-Bassett Dam—*dam* OR-9
Melhorn Ford—*locale* TN-4
Melhorn Gulch—*valley* MT-8
Melhorn Mill (historical)—*locale* TN-4
*Melhorn Rsvr* OR-9
*Melhouns Creek* TX-5
Melhus Cem—*cemetery* SD-7
*Meli* MP-9
Melia—*locale* NE-7
Melia-Forest City—*fmr MCD* NE-7
Melick Mound—*hist pl* OH-6
*Meligeok* PW-9
**Melillas**—*pop pl* PR-3
Melina—*locale* CO-8
Melin Branch—*stream* MO-7
Melinda Bar—*bar* AR-4
*Melinda Ferry* TN-4
Melindas Prairie Cem—*cemetery* WI-6
Melior (historical)—*locale* KS-7
*Melis* MS-4
Melis—*locale* MS-4
Melis Lake—*lake* NE-7
Melis Lake—*lake* OR-9
**Melissa**—*pop pl* TX-5
**Melissa**—*pop pl* WV-2
Melissa, Lake—*lake* IL-6
Melissa, Lake—*lake* MN-6
Melissa Cem—*cemetery* TX-5
Melissa Ditch—*canal* IN-6
Melissa Ditch—*canal* OH-6
*Melissa Manning Elementary School* MS-4
**Melissaville (historical)**—*pop pl* IN-6
Melita—*locale* MI-6
**Melita**—*pop pl* CA-9
Melita Ch—*church* MI-6
Melita Island—*island* MT-8
**Melitota**—*pop pl* MD-2
Melius-Bentley House—*hist pl* NY-2
Melius Creek—*stream* WI-6
Melius Sch—*school* SD-7
Meliville Dam—*dam* ND-7
Melix Spring—*spring* OR-9
Melke Brothers Ranch—*locale* WY-8

Mennenga Lake—lake MN-6
Menne Ranch—locale CA-9
Mennetaga Lake—lake MN-6
*Mennets Run* IN-6
Mennets Run—stream IN-6
Menninger Clinic Bldg—hist pl KS-7
Menning Golf Course—other CA-9
**Menno**—pop pl PA-2
**Menno**—pop pl SD-7
Menno, Lake—lake SD-7
Menno Cem—cemetery KS-7
Menno Colony (historical)—locale SD-7
Menno Dam—dam SD-7
Menno (historical)—locale KS-7
Menno Municipal Airp—airport SD-7
Mennonite Brethern Ch—church CO-8
Mennonite Cem—cemetery (3) IL-6
Mennonite Cem—cemetery (3) IA-7
Mennonite Cem—cemetery (7) KS-7
Mennonite Cem—cemetery MI-6
Mennonite Cem—cemetery (2) MN-6
Mennonite Cem—cemetery (2) NE-7
Mennonite Cem—cemetery OH-6
Mennonite Cem—cemetery (2) OK-5
Mennonite Cem—cemetery OR-9
Mennonite Cem—cemetery (2) PA-2
Mennonite Cem—cemetery WI-6
Mennonite Ch—church (2) IL-6
Mennonite Ch—church IA-7
Mennonite Ch—church (2) KS-7
Mennonite Ch—church LA-4
Mennonite Ch—church (3) MI-6
Mennonite Ch—church (2) MN-6
Mennonite Ch—church MS-4
Mennonite Ch—church (2) NE-7
Mennonite Ch—church (2) ND-7
Mennonite Ch—church OH-6
Mennonite Ch—church (3) OK-5
Mennonite Ch—church PA-2
Mennonite Ch—church SD-7
Mennonite Ch—church WI-6
Mennonite Ch (abandoned)—church PA-2
Mennonite Ch of God in Christ—church MS-4
Mennonite Home—building PA-2
Mennonite Meetinghouse—hist pl PA-2
**Mennonite Mission**—pop pl AZ-5
Mennonite Mission—school AZ-5
Mennonite Sch—school AR-4
Mennonite Sch—school IA-7
Mennonite Sch—school MI-6
Mennonite Sch—school MS-4
Mennonite Sch—school SD-7
*Mennonite Village* SD-7
**Menno Township**—pop pl KS-7
Menno Township (historical)—civil SD-7
**Menno (Township of)**—pop pl PA-2
Mennoville Mennonite Church—hist pl OK-5
Menn-Treude Cem—cemetery TX-5
Meno—locale NY-2
**Meno**—pop pl OK-5
**Meno**—pop pl OR-9
Meno Adams Ranch (reduced usage)—locale NM-5
Menoah Cem—cemetery VA-3
Menoher Hill—summit OK-5
Menoken—locale KS-7
Menoken—locale WA-9
**Menoken**—pop pl ND-7
Menoken Indian Village Site—hist pl ND-7
Menoken Sch—school CO-8
Menoken Sch—school KS-7
**Menoken Township**—pop pl KS-7
**Menoken Township**—pop pl ND-7
Menokin—hist pl VA-3
Menokin Bay—bay VA-3
Menokin Ch—church VA-3
Menokin Landing—locale VA-3
*Menoknoken* MP-9
Menokwnokwen—island MP-9
**Menola**—pop pl NC-3
Menola Ch—church NC-3
Men-O-Lan Camp—locale PA-2
Menomin, Lake—reservoir WI-6
*Menominee* WI-6
**Menominee**—pop pl IL-6
**Menominee**—pop pl MI-6
**Menominee**—pop pl NE-7
**Menominee (County)**—pop pl MI-6
**Menominee (County)**—pop pl WI-6
Menominee County Courthouse—hist pl MI-6
Menominee Creek—stream WI-6
Menominee Ind Res—reserve WI-6
Menominee-Marinette Twin County Airp—airport MI-6
*Menominee Park* MI-6
Menominee Park—park WI-6
Menominee Public Fishing Area—park IN-6
*Menominee River* WI-6
Menominee River—stream IL-6
Menominee River—stream MI-6
Menominee River—stream (2) WI-6
Menominee Slough—stream IL-6
*Menominee State Fishing Area* IN-6
*Menominee State Forest* MI-6
Menominee State Wetlands—park IN-6
Menominee (Station)—locale IL-6
**Menominee (Town of)**—pop pl WI-6
**Menominee (Township of)**—pop pl IL-6
**Menominee (Township of)**—pop pl MI-6
Menomin Lake—lake MN-6
*Menomonee* MI-6
*Menomonee* WI-6
**Menomonee Falls**—pop pl WI-6
Menomonee Falls City Hall—hist pl WI-6
Menomonee Golf Club—hist pl WI-6
Menomonee River—stream WI-6
Menomonee River Parkway—park WI-6
**Menomonie**—pop pl WI-6
Menomonie Campground—locale WI-6
Menomonie Country Club—other WI-6
Menomonie Downtown Hist Dist—hist pl WI-6
**Menomonie Junction**—pop pl WI-6
Menomonie Junction—uninc pl WI-6
*Menomonie River* WI-6
**Menomonie (Town of)**—pop pl WI-6
**Menonaqua Beach**—pop pl MI-6
Menonite Cem—cemetery ND-7
Menonite Ch—church ND-7
Menorah Cem—cemetery NJ-2
Menorah Gardens—cemetery IL-6
Menorah Hosp—hospital MO-7
Menorah Hosp—hospital NY-2
Menorkenut Slough No 16—stream MO-7
Menorkenut Slough No 19—stream MO-7
Menor's Ferry—hist pl WY-8
Menors Ferry—locale WY-8
Menoti (historical P.O.)—locale IA-7
Menotl Creek—stream AK-9
*Menotomy* MA-1
*Menotomy, Town of* MA-1
Menotomy Rocks Park—park MA-1
*Menotonomy, Town of* MA-1
Mens Burial Point—cape MD-2
Mensch Dam—dam SD-7
Mensell Bayou—gut TX-5
*Mensendick MS* AZ-5
Menser Cem—cemetery KY-4
Mensis Point—cape AK-9
Mensler Creek—stream FL-3
Mensor Windmill—locale NM-5
Mentanontli River—stream AK-9
Mentasta Creek—stream (2) AK-9
Mentasta Lake—lake AK-9
Mentasta Lake ANV856—reserve AK-9
Mentasta (Mentasta Lake)—other AK-9
Mentasta Mountains—other AK-9
Mentasta Pass—gap AK-9
Mentch—locale PA-2
**Mentcle**—pop pl PA-2
Mentelle Park—hist pl KY-4
Menter Canyon—valley NV-8
Menter Draw—valley WY-8
Menter Hill—summit WY-8
Menter Knob—summit WY-8
Menteth Gully—valley NY-2
Menteth Point—cape NY-2
**Menteth Point**—pop pl NY-2
*Menth* PA-2
**Mentha**—pop pl MI-6
**Mentmore**—pop pl NM-5
**Mentone**—pop pl AL-4
**Mentone**—pop pl CA-9
**Mentone**—pop pl IN-6
**Mentone**—pop pl TX-5
**Mentone**—pop pl WI-6
Mentone Airp—airport IN-6
Mentone (CCD)—cens area TX-5
Mentone Ch—church AL-4
Mentone Elem Sch—school IN-6
*Mentone Revival Center* AL-4
Mentone Sch—school CA-9
Mentone Springs Hotel—hist pl AL-4
Menton Hollow—valley AL-4
**Mentor**—pop pl IN-6
**Mentor**—pop pl KS-7
**Mentor**—pop pl KY-4
**Mentor**—pop pl MN-6
**Mentor**—pop pl MO-7
**Mentor**—pop pl OH-6
**Mentor**—pop pl TN-4
Mentor Ave Cem—cemetery OH-6
Mentor Ave District—hist pl OH-6
Mentor Cem—cemetery IA-7
Mentor Cem—cemetery WI-6
Mentor Ch—church OH-6
Mentor Community Park—park TN-4
*Mentor Headlands* OH-6
**Mentor Headlands**—pop pl OH-6
Mentor (historical P.O.)—locale IA-7
Mentor Marsh—swamp OH-6
**Mentor-on-the-Lake**—pop pl OH-6
Mentor-on-the-Lake (Township of)—other OH-6
Mentor Plains Ch—church OH-6
Mentor Post Office—building TN-4
Mentor Recreation Park—park OH-6
Mentor Sch—school PA-2
Mentor Sch—school SD-7
Mentor Sch—school TN-4
Mentor Shore Sch—school OH-6
**Mentor (Town of)**—pop pl WI-6
Mentor Township—civil SD-7
**Mentor Township**—pop pl ND-7
Mentor (Township of)—other OH-6
**Mentor (Township of)**—pop pl (2) MI-6
Mentow—locale VA-3
Mentz—locale TX-5
Mentz Corners—locale NY-2
Mentzel Canyon—valley NM-5
Mentzel Ditch—canal NM-5
Mentzer—locale OH-6
**Mentzer**—pop pl PA-2
Mentzer, Joseph P., House—hist pl IA-7
Mentzer Bldg—hist pl PA-2
Mentzer Cem—cemetery IA-7
Mentzer Ch—church OH-6
Mentzer Sch—school IL-6
**Mentz (Town of)**—pop pl NY-2
Menual Sch—school NM-5
Menuckatuck Rsvr—reservoir CT-1
Menudo, Arroyo—stream CA-9
Menunketesuck Island—island CT-1
Menunketesuck River—stream CT-1
Menzel Gulch—valley CA-9
Menzel Lake—lake WA-9
Menzer Run—stream SC-3
Menzie—locale KY-4
**Menzie**—pop pl IN-6
Menzie, Lake—lake FL-3
Menzie Creek—stream TX-5
Menzie Crossing—locale NY-2
Menzie (historical P.O.)—locale IA-7
Menzie Lake—lake IN-6
Menzie Mtn—summit NY-2
Menzies Girl Scout Camp—locale CA-9
*Menzies Island* OR-9
*Menzies Trail* HI-9
Menz Sch—school ND-7
**Menz Township**—pop pl ND-7
Meore Cem—cemetery OK-5
M E Orphanage—building PA-2
Me Own Hill—summit NM-5
Me Own Tank—reservoir NM-5
**Mepkin**—pop pl SC-3
Mepkin Creek—stream SC-3
**Meppen**—pop pl IL-6
Meppen Canal—canal ID-8
**Meqruur**—pop pl FM-9
Mequithy Lake—lake WI-6
**Mequon**—pop pl WI-6
Mequon Cem—cemetery WI-6
Mequon Sch—school WI-6
*Mer* FM-9
M E Ragsdale Pond Dam—dam MS-4
*Meramac Spring* MO-7
Meramec Caverns—cave MO-7
Meramec Community Coll—school MO-7
Meramec Park Lake—reservoir MO-7
Meramec River—stream MO-7
Meramec Sch—school (2) MO-7
*Meramec Spring* MO-7
Meramec State Park—park MO-7
Meramec State Park Lookout House/ Observation Tower—hist pl MO-7
Meramec State Park Pump House—hist pl MO-7
Meramec State Park Shelter House—hist pl MO-7
Meramec Township—civil (6) MO-7
**Meraux**—pop pl LA-4
Merazo—locale CA-9
*Merbert Creek* MI-6
Mer Branch Mississippi State Univ—school MS-4
**Mercado**—pop pl PR-3
Mercado de las Carnes—hist pl PR-3
Mercado Shop Ctr—locale FL-3
Mercantile Bayou—gut LA-4
Mercantile Trust and Deposit Company—hist pl MD-2
**Merced**—pop pl CA-9
Merced, Lake—lake CA-9
Merced (CCD)—cens area CA-9
**Merced (County)**—pop pl CA-9
Merced County Courthouse—hist pl CA-9
Merced County HS—hist pl CA-9
**Mercedes**—pop pl TX-5
Mercedes District Settling Basin—reservoir TX-5
Mercedes Executive Park and Arcade Shoppes—locale FL-3
Mercedes Floodway Bridge—bridge TX-5
Mercedes Gulch—valley SD-7
Mercedes Lake—lake (2) MI-6
Mercedes Pump—other TX-5
Mercedes Windmill—locale TX-5
Merced Falls—locale CA-9
Merced Falls Diversion Dam—dam CA-9
Merced Golf Club—other CA-9
Merced Gorge—valley CA-9
Merced Grove—woods CA-9
Merced Grove Ranger Station—hist pl CA-9
Merced Hosp—hospital CA-9
**Mercedita**—pop pl PR-3
Mercedita Airp—airport PR-3
Merced Lake—lake CA-9
Merced Lake Ranger Station—locale CA-9
Merced Lateral—canal CA-9
Merced Natl Wildlife Ref—park CA-9
Merced Pass—gap CA-9
Merced Peak—summit CA-9
*Merced Peak Creek* CA-9
Merced Peak Fork—stream CA-9
*Merced River* CA-9
Merced River—stream CA-9
Merced Sch—school CA-9
Merced Sewage Disposal—other CA-9
Merced Substation—other CA-9
Mercer—locale FL-3
Mercer—locale IA-7
Mercer—locale KY-4
**Mercer**—pop pl ME-1
**Mercer**—pop pl MO-7
**Mercer**—pop pl NE-7
**Mercer**—pop pl NC-3
**Mercer**—pop pl ND-7
**Mercer**—pop pl OH-6
**Mercer**—pop pl PA-2
**Mercer**—pop pl TN-4
**Mercer**—pop pl WI-6
Mercer, Dr. Samuel D., House—hist pl NE-7
Mercer Area Elem Sch—school PA-2
Mercer Area JHS—school PA-2
Mercer Ave Ch—church GA-3
Mercer Bay—swamp FL-3
Mercer Bayou—gut AR-4
Mercer Borough—civil PA-2
*Mercer Bottom* WV-2
Mercer Brake—swamp LA-4
Mercer Branch—stream FL-3
Mercer Branch—stream NC-3
Mercer Brook—stream NY-2
Mercer Canyon—valley NM-5
Mercer Canyon—valley UT-8
Mercer Cave—cave CA-9
Mercer Cem—cemetery (2) GA-3
Mercer Cem—cemetery IA-7
Mercer Cem—cemetery (3) KY-4
Mercer Cem—cemetery MO-7
Mercer Cem—cemetery NJ-2
Mercer Cem—cemetery TN-4
Mercer Cem—cemetery WI-6
Mercer Ch—church IA-7
Mercer County—airport NJ-2
Mercer County—civil ND-7
**Mercer (County)**—pop pl IL-6
**Mercer (County)**—pop pl KY-4
**Mercer County**—pop pl MO-7
**Mercer County**—pop pl NJ-2
**Mercer (County)**—pop pl OH-6
**Mercer County**—pop pl PA-2
**Mercer (County)**—pop pl WV-2
Mercer County Airp—airport WV-2
Mercer County Community Coll—school NJ-2
Mercer County Courthouse—hist pl IL-6
Mercer County Courthouse—hist pl WV-2
Mercer County Home (historical)—building MO-7
Mercer County Park—park NJ-2
*Mercer County Reservoir* OH-6
*Mercer Creek* AL-4
Mercer Creek—stream GA-3
Mercer Creek—stream (2) KS-7
Mercer Creek—stream (3) OR-9
Mercer Creek—stream (2) TX-5
Mercer Creek—stream WA-9
Mercer Cut—bend NC-3
Mercer Dam—dam OR-9
Mercer Ditch—canal IN-6
Mercer Draw—valley WY-8
Mercer Field—park CT-1
Mercer Fire Tower—tower FL-3
Mercer Grove Ch—church (2) GA-3
Mercer Hall—hist pl TN-4
Mercer Healing Springs—locale WV-2
**Mercer (historical)**—pop pl MS-4
**Mercer (historical)**—pop pl OR-9
Mercer Hollow—valley TN-4
Mercer Hollow—valley UT-8
Mercer Hosp—hospital NJ-2
Mercer House—hist pl MS-4
Mercer Island—island MS-4
Mercer Island—island WA-9
**Mercer Island**—pop pl WA-9
Mercer Island HS—school WA-9
**Mercer Island Town**—pop pl WA-9
Mercer Island (town)—uninc pl WA-9
Mercer Lake—lake AR-4
Mercer Lake—lake OR-9
Mercer Lake—lake (2) WI-6
Mercer Lake—reservoir MO-7
Mercer Lake Park—park OR-9
Mercer Lakes—lake MI-6
Mercer Landing—locale NC-3
Mercer Log House—hist pl OH-6
Mercer (Magisterial District)—fmr MCD VA-3
Mercer Med Ctr—airport NJ-2
Mercer Millpond—lake GA-3
Mercer Minnow Ponds—reservoir OK-5
Mercer Mtn—summit AL-4
Mercer Mtn—summit CA-9
Mercer Mtn—summit NY-2
Mercer Museum—hist pl PA-2
Mercer Number 1 Dam—dam SD-7
Mercer Oil Field—oilfield MS-4
Mercer Park—park NE-7
Mercer Pond—lake FL-3
Mercer Post Office (historical)—building TN-4
Mercer Public Golf Course—locale PA-2
Mercer Ranch—locale AZ-5
*Mercer Road* PA-2
*Mercer Rsvr* OR-9
Mercer Rsvr—reservoir OR-9
Mercer Run—stream WV-2
**Mercers Bottom**—pop pl WV-2
Mercers Bridge (historical)—bridge AL-4
**Mercersburg**—pop pl PA-2
Mercersburg Acad—hist pl PA-2
Mercersburg Acad—school PA-2
Mercersburg Borough—civil PA-2
Mercersburg Elem Sch—school PA-2
Mercersburg Hist Dist—hist pl PA-2
Mercersburg Junction—locale PA-2
Mercersburg Rsvr—reservoir (2) PA-2
Mercer Sch—school MA-1
Mercer Sch—school NE-7
Mercer Sch—school OH-6
Mercer Sch—school TN-4
Mercer Sch—school (2) WV-2
**Mercer's Gap**—pop pl TX-5
Mercer Slough—gut WA-9
Mercer's Mill Covered Bridge—hist pl PA-2
Mercers Pond—lake CT-1
Mercer Spring—spring AZ-5
**Mercer Square**—pop pl MA-1
Mercers Store (historical)—locale AL-4
Mercer Street Friends Center—hist pl NJ-2
**Mercersville**—pop pl MD-2
**Mercer (Town of)**—pop pl ME-1
**Mercer (Town of)**—pop pl WI-6
Mercer Township—fmr MCD IA-7
**Mercer Township**—pop pl ND-7
Mercer Township (historical)—civil SD-7
**Mercer (Township of)**—pop pl IL-6
**Mercer (Township of)**—pop pl PA-2
Mercer Tunnel Spring—spring AZ-5
Mercer Univ—school GA-3
Mercer Univ Administration Bldg—hist pl GA-3
Mercer View Sch—school WA-9
**Mercerville**—pop pl NJ-2
**Mercerville**—pop pl OH-6
Mercerville-Hamilton Square—CDP NJ-2
Mercey Creek—stream CA-9
**Mercey Hot Springs**—pop pl CA-9
Mercey Mine—mine CA-9
Mercham Hollow—valley ID-8
*Merchandise Mart* IL-6
Merchandise Mart—locale IL-6
Merchandise Mart—post sta TX-5
Merchant—locale VA-3
**Merchant**—pop pl SC-3
Merchant Branch—stream LA-4
Merchant Brook—stream ME-1
Merchant Canal—canal NV-8
Merchant Cem—cemetery MS-4
Merchant Corners—locale PA-2
*Merchant Creek* VA-3
Merchant Creek—stream MS-4
Merchant Creek—stream UT-8
Merchant Hollow—valley UT-8
Merchant Hope Ch—church VA-3
*Merchant Island* MA-1
Merchant Island—island ME-1
*Merchant Mountain* WA-9
*Merchant Oil Field* TX-5
Merchant Peak—summit WA-9
Merchant Ranch—locale NM-5
Merchant Row—channel ME-1
Merchant Run—stream WV-2
Merchants—uninc pl MD-2
Merchants' and Drovers' Tavern—hist pl NJ-2
Merchants and Farmers Bank Bldg—hist pl MS-4
Merchants and Farmers Natl Bank Bldg—hist pl NC-3
Merchants and Manufacturers Bldg—hist pl TX-5
Merchants and Planters Bank—hist pl AR-4
Merchants and Planters Bank Bldg—hist pl AR-4
Merchants Ave Hist Dist—hist pl WI-6
Merchants Bank Bldg—hist pl FL-3
Merchants Bank Bldg—hist pl RI-1
Merchants Basin—basin WA-9
Merchants Beach—beach OR-9
Merchants Bldg—hist pl MI-6
Merchants Bridge—other IL-6
Merchants Bridge—other MO-7
Merchant Sch—school IL-6
Merchant Sch (abandoned)—school MO-7
Merchants Corners—locale NY-2
Merchants Exchange—building PA-2
Merchants & Farmers Bank—hist pl AR-4
Merchants Hill—summit NY-2
Merchant's Hope Church—hist pl VA-3
Merchant's Hotel—hist pl KY-4
*Merchants Island* ME-1
*Merchants Island* MA-1
Merchant Slough—stream TX-5
Merchants Mill Creek—stream SC-3
Merchants Mill (historical)—locale NC-3
Merchants Millpond—reservoir NC-3
Merchants' Natl Bank—hist pl IA-7
Merchants Natl Bank—hist pl (2) MN-6
Merchants Natl Bank and Annex—hist pl IN-6
Merchants Park Shop Ctr—other CO-8
Merchants Pointe Shop Ctr—locale FL-3
Merchants Refrigerating Company Warehouse—hist pl NY-2
Merchant Street Hist Dist—hist pl HI-9
Merchants Village Shop Ctr—locale TN-4
Merchants Walk—post sta GA-3
Merchant Tank—reservoir AZ-5
**Merchantville**—pop pl NJ-2
**Merchiston**—pop pl NE-7
Merchiston Sch—school NE-7
Mer Ch of Christ—church MS-4
Mer Ch of God—church MS-4
Mercia Ditch—canal OH-6
**Mercier**—pop pl KS-7
Mercier, Bayou—gut LA-4
**Mercier Township**—pop pl SD-7
Mer City Hall—building MS-4
Merck Athletic Field—park NJ-2
Merck Cem—cemetery OK-5
Merck Ch—church AR-4
*Merckley Sch* IN-6
Mer Coll (historical)—school MS-4
Mercur—locale PA-2
Mercur—locale UT-8
Mercur Canyon—valley UT-8
Mercur Cem—cemetery PA-2
Mercur Creek—stream UT-8
Mercuria Mine—mine AZ-5
Mercur Peak—summit CA-9
**Mercury**—pop pl AL-4
**Mercury**—pop pl NV-8
**Mercury**—pop pl TX-5
Mercury Belle Mine—mine CA-9
*Mercury Creek* OR-9
Mercury Creek—stream CO-8
Mercury Creek—stream (2) ID-8
Mercury Creek—stream OR-9
Mercury Fishing Club—other MI-6
Mercury Lake—lake MI-6
Mercury Mine—mine CO-8
Mercury Mine Sch—school AZ-5
Mercury Mtn—summit CA-9
Mercury Post Office (historical)—building AL-4
Mercury Ridge—ridge NV-8
Mercury Valley—basin NV-8
Mercuryville—locale CA-9
Mercuson Creek—stream MS-4
Mercy Acad—school OH-6
Mercy Baptist Temple—church IN-6
Mercy Branch—stream VA-3
Mercy Ch—church GA-3
Mercy Ch—church LA-4
Mercy Chapel at Mill Run—hist pl MD-2
Mercy Coll—school MI-6
Mercy Coll—school NY-2
*Mercy Creek* CA-9
Mercycrest Hosp—hospital OH-6
Mercy Cross HS—school MS-4
Mercy General Hosp—hospital NY-2
Mercy Hosp—hospital (5) CA-9
Mercy Hosp—hospital (2) CO-8
Mercy Hosp—hospital (2) FL-3
Mercy Hosp—hospital (2) IL-6
Mercy Hosp—hospital IN-6
Mercy Hosp—hospital (6) IA-7
Mercy Hosp—hospital (2) KS-7
Mercy Hosp—hospital LA-4
Mercy Hosp—hospital ME-1
Mercy Hosp—hospital MD-2
Mercy Hosp—hospital MA-1
Mercy Hosp—hospital (6) MI-6
Mercy Hosp—hospital MN-6
Mercy Hosp—hospital MS-4
Mercy Hosp—hospital (3) NY-2
Mercy Hosp—hospital NC-3
Mercy Hosp—hospital (2) OH-6
Mercy Hosp—hospital OK-5
Mercy Hosp—hospital (5) PA-2
Mercy Hosp—hospital (5) TX-5
Mercy Hosp—hospital WI-6
Mercy Hosp and Elizabeth McDowell Bialy Memorial House—hist pl MI-6
Mercy Hosp Medical Park—hospital NC-3
*Mercy Hot Springs* CA-9
Mercy HS—school (2) CA-9
Mercy HS—school CT-1
Mercy HS—school IL-6
Mercy HS—school MO-7
Mercy HS—school NE-7
Mercy HS—school NY-2
Mercy HS—school WI-6
Mercyhurst Coll—school PA-2
Mercy Med Ctr—hospital PA-2
Mercy Medical Mission—church FL-3
*Mercy Mine* CA-9
Mercy Mission—church TX-5
Mercy Oil Field—oilfield TX-5
Mercy Park—park MN-6
*Mercy Regional Med Ctr* MS-4
Mercy San Juan Hosp—hospital CA-9
*Mercy Seat Baptist Ch* MS-4
Mercy Seat Baptist Ch—church MS-4
Mercy Seat Cem—cemetery AR-4
Mercy Seat Cem—cemetery MS-4
Mercy Seat Ch—church GA-3
Mercy Seat Ch—church (7) MS-4
Mercy Seat Ch—church TX-5
Mercy Seat Ch—church (3) VA-3
*Mercy Seat Missionary Baptist Ch* MS-4
Mercy Seat Missionary Baptist Ch—church MS-4
Mercy Seat Sch (historical)—school MS-4
Mercy See Ch—church VA-3
Mercy Tank—reservoir AZ-5
Mercy Temple—church MS-4
Mercyville—locale MO-7
Mercyville Sanitarium—hospital IL-6
Mercywood Hosp—hospital MI-6
Merden Lake—lake MN-6
Merdian Lake—lake IL-6
Mereda Branch—stream KY-4
Meredith—locale CO-8
Meredith—locale IL-6
Meredith—locale KY-4
Meredith—locale PA-2
Meredith—locale WA-9
**Meredith**—pop pl MI-6
**Meredith**—pop pl NH-1
**Meredith**—pop pl NY-2
**Meredith**—pop pl OH-6
**Meredith**—pop pl PA-2
**Meredith**—pop pl VA-3
**Meredith**—pop pl WV-2
Meredith, Daniel, House—hist pl PA-2
Meredith, Dr. Owen, House—hist pl GA-3
Meredith, Lake—lake CO-8
Meredith, Lake—reservoir TX-5
Meredith, Mount—summit NY-2
Meredith, Simon, House—hist pl PA-2
Meredith, William M., Sch—hist pl PA-2
Meredith Ammer Canal—canal NE-7
Meredith Bay—bay NH-1
Meredith Bend—bay NC-3
Meredith Branch—stream DE-2
Meredith Branch—stream KY-4
Meredith Branch—stream (2) VA-3
Meredith Branch—stream WV-2
Meredith Brook—stream PA-2
Meredith Canal—canal NE-7
Meredith Cave—cave TN-4
**Meredith Cave**—pop pl TN-4
Meredith Cem—cemetery IN-6
Meredith Cem—cemetery (3) TN-4
Meredith Cem—cemetery TX-5
Meredith Cem—cemetery (2) VA-3
*Meredith Cemetery* AL-4
**Meredith Center**—pop pl NH-1
Meredith Ch—church KS-7
Meredith Coll—school NC-3
**Meredith Compact (census name Meredith)**—pop pl NH-1
Meredith Creek—stream KY-4
Meredith Creek—stream MD-2
*Meredith Ditch* IN-6
Meredith Ditch—canal IN-6
Meredith Drive Ch—church IA-7
Meredith Ford—locale TN-4
Meredith Fork—stream WV-2
Meredith Heights Ch—church LA-4
Meredith Hill—summit CO-8
Meredith Hill—summit NH-1
Meredith (historical)—locale KS-7
**Meredith (historical)**—pop pl OR-9
Meredith Hollow—valley (3) TN-4
*Meredith Island* OR-9
Meredith JHS—school IA-7
**Meredith Manor**—pop pl FL-3
Meredith-McDowal House—hist pl TX-5
Meredith Natl Recreation Area, Lake—park TX-5
Meredith Neck—cape NH-1
Meredith Nicholson Elem Sch—school IN-6
Meredith Plantation (historical)—locale MS-4
Meredith Pond—swamp FL-3
Meredith Public Library—hist pl NH-1
Meredith Run—stream PA-2
Merediths—locale FL-3
Meredith Sch—school PA-2
*Merediths Corners* DE-2
*Merediths Cove* MD-2
Merediths Mill (historical)—locale TN-4
**Meredith Springs**—pop pl WV-2
**Meredith Square (subdivision)**—pop pl NC-3
*Merediths Shop* DE-2
**Meredith Townes (subdivision)**—pop pl NC-3
**Meredith (Town of)**—pop pl NH-1
**Meredith (Town of)**—pop pl NY-2
**Meredith Township**—pop pl KS-7
Meredith (Township of)—fmr MCD NC-3
Meredith Trail—trail PA-2
Meredithville—locale VA-3
**Meredith Woods (subdivision)**—pop pl NC-3
*Meredosha* IL-6
**Meredosia**—pop pl IL-6
Meredosia Ditch—canal IL-6
Meredosia Island—island IL-6
Meredosia Lake—lake IL-6
Meredosia Slough—stream IL-6
Meredosia (Township of)—civ div IL-6
*Meren* MP-9
*Merengo Lake* MS-4
*Me'reniw* FM-9
Mere Point—cape ME-1
**Merepoint**—pop pl ME-1
*Mere Point Bay* ME-1
Merepoint Bay—bay ME-1
*Mere Point Neck* ME-1
Merepoint Neck—cape ME-1
Merestead—hist pl NY-2
**Mereta**—pop pl TX-5
Mereta Oil Field—oilfield TX-5
Merewi—unknown FM-9
Merewi, Dolen—summit FM-9
Merford Ridge—ridge OK-5
Mergagan Point—summit GU-9
**Merganser (historical)**—pop pl OR-9
Merganser Lake—lake MN-6
Mergelmann Cow Camp—locale CO-8
Merger Mine—mine NV-8
Mer HS—school MS-4
Merial Lake—lake FL-3
Meriam, Lake—reservoir CO-8
**Meriams Corner**—pop pl MA-1
*Meriams Hill* MA-1
Merical Hollow—valley WV-2
Merical Run—stream WV-2
Mericoma Quicksilver Mine—mine CA-9
*Mericoneag Sound* ME-1
*Mericourt Park* TN-4
Meri Court Park—park TN-4
Merida—locale ND-7
Merida Lake—lake IL-6

**Meridale**—*pop pl* NY-2
Meridale Baptist Ch—*church* MS-4
Meridale Camp—*locale* MS-4
**Meridan**—*pop pl* FL-3
*Meridan Creek* NE-7
Meridan Docks—*facility* GA-3
**Meridan Heights**—*pop pl* WA-9
Meridan Island—*island* AK-9
Meridan Mansions—*hist pl* DC-2
**Meridan Park**—*pop pl* VA-3
Meridan Peak—*summit* MT-8
Meridan PO—*locale* WY-8
**Meridean**—*pop pl* WI-6
Meridean Slu—*stream* WI-6
Meriden—*locale* NJ-2
Meriden—*locale* WV-2
**Meriden**—*pop pl* CT-1
**Meriden**—*pop pl* IL-6
**Meriden**—*pop pl* IA-7
**Meriden**—*pop pl* KS-7
**Meriden**—*pop pl* MN-6
**Meriden**—*pop pl* NH-1
**Meriden**—*pop pl* WY-8
Meriden Avenue-Oakland Road Hist Dist—*hist pl* CT-1
Meriden Bridge—*hist pl* NH-1
Meriden Cem—*cemetery* IA-7
Meriden Curtain Fixture Company Factory—*hist pl* CT-1
Meriden Hebrew Cem—*cemetery* CT-1
*Meriden Hill* CO-8
**Meriden Hill**—*pop pl* NH-1
Meriden (Town of)—*civ div* CT-1
*Meriden Township* KS-7
**Meriden (Township of)**—*pop pl* IL-6
**Meriden (Township of)**—*pop pl* MN-6
*Merideth Bay* NC-3
Merideth Branch—*stream* MO-7
Merideth Cem—*cemetery* TN-4
Merideth Ch—*church* MO-7
Merideth Creek—*stream* TX-5
Merideth Ditch—*canal* UT-8
Merideth Ranch—*locale* MT-8
Meridian—*civil* KS-7
Meridian—*fmr MCD* NE-7
Meridian—*locale* AR-4
Meridian—*locale* KY-4
Meridian—*locale* LA-4
Meridian—*locale* MI-6
Meridian—*locale* TN-4
**Meridian**—*pop pl* (4) CA-9
**Meridian**—*pop pl* FL-3
**Meridian**—*pop pl* GA-3
**Meridian**—*pop pl* ID-8
**Meridian**—*pop pl* MS-4
**Meridian**—*pop pl* NY-2
**Meridian**—*pop pl* (2) OK-5
**Meridian**—*pop pl* PA-2
**Meridian**—*pop pl* TX-5
**Meridian**—*pop pl* WA-9
Meridian, Lake—*lake* WA-9
Meridian Ave Baptist Ch—*church* KS-7
*Meridian Baptist Church* TN-4
Meridian Baptist Seminary—*hist pl* MS-4
Meridian Butte—*summit* AZ-5
Meridian Campground—*locale* CO-8
Meridian Cave—*cave* AL-4
Meridian (CCD)—*cens area* TX-5
Meridian Cem—*cemetery* ID-8
Meridian Cem—*cemetery* KS-7
Meridian Cem—*cemetery* NE-7
Meridian Cem—*cemetery* OK-5
Meridian Cem—*cemetery* OR-9
Meridian Cem—*cemetery* (2) TN-4
Meridian Ch—*church* KS-7
Meridian Ch—*church* LA-4
Meridian Ch—*church* (2) TN-4
Meridiancheri Mobile Home Park—*locale* AZ-5
Meridian Ch of God—*church* IN-6
Meridian Creek—*stream* AK-9
Meridian Creek—*stream* ID-8
Meridian Creek—*stream* IN-6
Meridian Creek—*stream* KS-7
Meridian Creek—*stream* LA-4
Meridian Creek—*stream* MS-4
Meridian Creek—*stream* MT-8
Meridian Creek—*stream* NE-7
Meridian Creek—*stream* OK-5
Meridian Creek—*stream* (2) TN-4
Meridian Creek—*stream* (2) TX-5
Meridian Creek Dam One—*dam* TN-4
Meridian Creek Dam Two—*dam* TN-4
Meridian Creek Lake One—*reservoir* TN-4
Meridian Creek Lake Two—*reservoir* TN-4
Meridian Depot District—*hist pl* MS-4
Meridian Drain—*canal* MI-6
Meridian Elem Sch—*school* PA-2
Meridian Exchange Bank—*hist pl* ID-8
Meridian For Preserve—*forest* IL-6
Meridian Gulch—*valley* ID-8
*Meridian Heights* IL-6
**Meridian Heights**—*pop pl* WA-9
Meridian Hill—*summit* CO-8
Meridian Hill—*summit* WA-9
Meridian Hill Park—*hist pl* DC-2
**Meridian Hills**—*pop pl* IN-6
Meridian Hills Country Club—*other* IN-6
Meridian House—*hist pl* DC-2
Meridian HS—*school* IL-6
Meridian HS—*school* WA-9
Meridian Junior Coll—*school* MS-4
Meridian Knob—*summit* AL-4
Meridian Lake—*lake* AK-9
Meridian Lake—*lake* CO-8
Meridian Lake—*lake* FL-3
Meridian Lake—*lake* OR-9
Meridian Lake—*reservoir* OH-6
Meridian Lookout—*locale* WA-9
Meridian Lookout Tower—*locale* LA-4
Meridian Male Coll (historical)—*school* MS-4
Meridian Monmt—*park* UT-8
Meridian Mtn—*summit* AL-4
Meridian Mtn—*summit* (2) TX-5
Meridian Museum of Art—*hist pl* MS-4
Meridian Naval Air Station (McCain Field)—*airport* MS-4
Meridian Oil Field—*oilfield* TX-5
Meridian Park Hosp—*hospital* OR-9
Meridian Peak—*summit* ID-8
Meridian Peak—*summit* UT-8
Meridian Ridge—*ridge* CA-9
Meridian-Robbins (CCD)—*cens area* CA-9
Meridian Sch—*school* (2) CA-9
Meridian Sch—*school* IL-6
Meridian Sch—*school* KS-7
Meridian Sch—*school* MI-6
Meridian Sch—*school* NE-7
Meridian Sch—*school* WA-9
Meridian Sch (historical)—*school* MO-7
Meridian Sch (historical)—*school* (2) TN-4
*Meridian School* IN-6
*Meridian School* KS-7
Meridian State Park—*locale* TX-5
Meridian Street Elem Sch—*school* IN-6
Meridian Street United Methodist Ch—*church* IN-6
Meridian Tower—*summit* UT-8
**Meridian Township**—*pop pl* KS-7
**Meridian (Township of)**—*pop pl* IL-6
**Meridian (Township of)**—*pop pl* MI-6
Meridian Urban Center Hist Dist—*hist pl* MS-4
**Meridianville**—*pop pl* AL-4
Meridianville Baptist Ch—*church* AL-4
Meridianville Bottom Ch—*church* AL-4
Meridianville Bottom Sch (historical)—*school* AL-4
Meridianville Cem—*cemetery* AL-4
Meridianville Ch of Christ—*church* AL-4
Meridianville (historical)—*locale* MS-4
Meridianville JHS—*school* AL-4
Meridianville Post Office—*building* AL-4
Meridianville Primitive Baptist Ch—*church* AL-4
Meridian Woods Baptist Ch—*church* IN-6
Meridith Cem—*cemetery* TX-5
Meridith Ch—*church* TX-5
Meridith Lake—*reservoir* AL-4
Meridith Lake Dam—*dam* AL-4
Meridith Nicholson Elem Sch—*school* IN-6
*Merie Mounte* MA-1
Merieult House—*hist pl* LA-4
Merigale-Paul Oil Field—*oilfield* TX-5
*Merige* MP-9
Merige—*island* MP-9
*Merige-To* MP-9
**Merigold**—*pop pl* MS-4
Merigold Brake—*swamp* MS-4
Merigold Post Office (historical)—*building* AL-4
Merigold Sch—*school* MS-4
Merigold Sewage Lagoon Dam—*dam* MS-4
Merihew Cem—*cemetery* MI-6
Merihew Sch—*school* MI-6
Merikay Mine—*mine* WA-9
Merill Branch—*stream* KY-4
Merillon Ave—*uninc pl* NY-2
Merill Road Shop Ctr—*locale* FL-3
*Merimack* MA-1
Meriman Sch—*school* NY-2
Merimax Bldg—*hist pl* TX-5
Merimere Rsvr—*reservoir* CT-1
*Merino* MA-1
Merino—*locale* MT-8
Merino—*locale* WY-8
**Merino**—*pop pl* CO-8
**Merino**—*pop pl* RI-1
Merino, Mount—*summit* NY-2
Merino Bench—*bench* MT-8
Merino Cem—*cemetery* CO-8
Merino Creek—*stream* ID-8
Merino Hill House and Farm—*hist pl* NJ-2
Merino Oil Field—*oilfield* CO-8
Merino Pond—*reservoir* MA-1
Merino Pond Dam—*dam* MA-1
Merino Village (census name Dudley)—*other* MA-1
**Merino Village (historical)**—*pop pl* MA-1
**Merino Village (subdivision)**—*pop pl* MA-1
Merion Cricket Club—*hist pl* PA-2
Merion Cricket Club—*other* PA-2
*Merion Elementary School* PA-2
**Merion Golf Manor**—*pop pl* PA-2
**Merion Hills**—*pop pl* PA-2
Merion Memorial Park—*park* PA-2
*Merion Mercy Academy* PA-2
**Merion Park**—*pop pl* PA-2
Merion (RR name for Merion Station)—*other* PA-2
Merion Sch—*school* PA-2
*Merion Square* PA-2
**Merion Square**—*pop pl* PA-2
Merion Square Sch—*school* PA-2
Merion Station—*locale* PA-2
**Merion Station (RR name Merion)**—*pop pl* PA-2
**Merion View**—*pop pl* PA-2
*Merionville* PA-2
*Meriperip* FM-9
*Meripirip* FM-9
Meripirip—*bar* FM-9
Merir—*island* PW-9
*Meriren-to* MP-9
Merit—*locale* MS-4
**Merit**—*pop pl* TX-5
Merit Cave—*cave* AL-4
Merit Cem—*cemetery* MS-4
Merit Cem—*cemetery* TX-5
Merithew Cem—*cemetery* NY-2
Merit Meadows—*flat* OR-9
Merit Meadows Spring—*spring* OR-9
Merito—*locale* TX-5
Merit Oil And Gas Field—*oilfield* MS-4
Merit Sch—*school* IL-6
Merit Spring—*spring* AZ-5
Merit-Tandy Farmstead—*hist pl* IN-6
*Meritt Butte* AZ-5
Meritt Cem—*cemetery* TN-4
Meritt Island—*island* FL-3
Meritt Landing—*locale* FL-3
Meriweather Branch—*stream* TN-4
*Meriwether* AL-4
Meriwether—*locale* GA-3
Meriwether—*locale* MT-8
**Meriwether**—*pop pl* SC-3
Meriwether, Dr. Willis, House—*hist pl* AL-4
Meriwether, Point—*cape* OR-9
*Meriwether Bend* TN-4
Meriwether Branch—*stream* TX-5
*Meriwether Canyon* MT-8
Meriwether Canyon—*valley* MT-8
Meriwether Cem—*cemetery* AL-4
Meriwether Cem—*cemetery* TX-5
**Meriwether (County)**—*pop pl* GA-3
Meriwether County Courthouse—*hist pl* GA-3
Meriwether County Jail—*hist pl* GA-3
Meriwether Creek—*stream* VA-3
**Meriwether Farms**—*pop pl* PA-2
Meriwether Golf Course—*other* OR-9
Meriwether Lewis Natl Monmt—*park* TN-4
Meriwether Lewis Sch—*school* VA-3
Meriwether Lookout Tower—*locale* GA-3
Meriwether Picnic Area—*locale* MT-8
Meriwether Pond—*reservoir* AR-4
*Meriwether Reef* AL-4
Meriwether Sch—*school* MO-7
Meriwether Spring—*spring* GA-3
Meriwether White Sulphur—*locale* GA-3
**Meriwether White Sulphur Springs**—*pop pl* GA-3
Meriwhitica Canyon—*valley* AZ-5
Meriwhitica Springs—*spring* AZ-5
Meriwhitica Tank—*reservoir* AZ-5
**Merizo**—*pop pl* GU-9
Merizo Bell Tower—*hist pl* GU-9
Merizo Catholic Cem—*cemetery* GU-9
Merizo Cockpit—*other* GU-9
Merizo Conbento—*hist pl* GU-9
Merizo (Election District)—*fmr MCD* GU-9
Merizo Martyrs Memorial Sch—*school* GU-9
Merizo Martyrs Monument—*other* GU-9
Merizo Sch—*school* GU-9
Merk, Nels, Farmstead—*hist pl* SD-7
Merk Canyon—*valley* CA-9
*Merkel* AL-4
**Merkel**—*pop pl* TX-5
Merkel,lake—*reservoir* SC-3
Merkel Branch—*stream* SC-3
Merkel Canyon—*valley* WA-9
Merkel (CCD)—*cens area* TX-5
Merkel Creek—*stream* TX-5
Merkel Dam—*dam* SD-7
Merkel Ditch No 1—*canal* WY-8
Merkel Pumping Station—*locale* TX-5
**Merkel Township**—*pop pl* ND-7
Merker Hills—*summit* CO-8
Merker Sch—*school* KY-4
Merkey Cem—*cemetery* KS-7
Merkey Ch—*church* PA-2
Merkle Bay—*bay* NC-3
Merkle Bay Point—*cape* NC-3
Merkle Cem—*cemetery* ND-7
Merkle Creek—*stream* OK-5
Merkle Hammock—*bar* NC-3
Merkle Hammock Creek—*bay* NC-3
*Merkle Lake* MI-6
Merkle Sch—*school* (3) IL-6
Merkle Station (abandoned)—*building* PA-2
Merkle Swamp—*stream* NC-3
Merkley Drop—*falls* UT-8
Merkley Lake—*lake* ID-8
*Merkley Mountain* ID-8
Merkley Mtn—*summit* ID-8
Merkley Park—*park* UT-8
Merkley Ranch—*locale* NV-8
Merkley Rsvr—*reservoir* UT-8
Merkley Spring—*spring* UT-8
Merkl Island—*island* AL-4
Merkl Mtn—*summit* AL-4
Merk Ranch—*locale* TX-5
Merkt Creek—*stream* CO-8
Merkwan, John, Jr., Rubblestone House—*hist pl* SD-7
Merkwan, John and Kate, Log and Rubblestone House—*hist pl* SD-7
Merkwan, John and Kate, Rubblestone House-Barn—*hist pl* SD-7
Merkwan, Mathias, Rubblestone Barn—*hist pl* SD-7
Mer-Lauderdale County Industrial Park—*locale* MS-4
Merlau Ditch—*canal* IN-6
Merl Cem—*cemetery* AR-4
Merle—*locale* OR-9
Merle—*locale* TX-5
**Merle**—*pop pl* IA-7
**Merle**—*pop pl* PR-3
Merle Beach—*locale* MI-6
Merle Branch—*stream* OK-5
Merle Burn—*area* OR-9
Merle Creek—*stream* WY-8
Merle Davies Sch—*school* OR-9
Merledes Executive Park and Arcade Shoppes—*locale* FL-3
Merle Findlay Tank—*reservoir* AZ-5
Merle Gulch—*valley* OR-9
Merle J Abbett Elem Sch—*school* IN-6
Merle Junction—*locale* IA-7
Merle Lake—*lake* OR-9
Merle Palmer Lake Dam—*dam* MS-4
Merle Ranch—*locale* CA-9
Merles Chapel—*church* MO-7
Merle Sidener JHS—*school* IN-6
Merles Pond—*lake* ID-8
Merle West Med Ctr Helipad—*airport* OR-9
Merlie Butte—*summit* OR-9
Merlie Table—*summit* OR-9
Merlin—*locale* CA-9
Merlin—*locale* PA-2
**Merlin**—*pop pl* LA-4
**Merlin**—*pop pl* OR-9
Merlin Abyss—*valley* AZ-5
Merlinda Sch—*school* CA-9
Merlin Gut—*gut* MD-2
**Merlin Heights Addition (subdivision)**—*pop pl* UT-8
Merlin Lake—*lake* WA-9
Merlin Sanitarium—*hospital* OR-9
Merlo Mine—*mine* AZ-5
Merlyn Lake—*lake* AZ-5
Mermaid—*locale* DE-2
**Mermaid**—*pop pl* PA-2
Mermaid House Hotel—*hist pl* IL-6
Mermaid Island—*island* AK-9
Mermaid Lake—*lake* PA-2
Mermaid Lake—*lake* WI-6
Mermaid Point—*cape* FL-3
Mermaid Riffle—*rapids* OR-9
**Mermaid Run**—*pop pl* DE-2
Mermaids Chair—*other* VI-3
Mermaid Swim and Golf Club—*locale* PA-2
Mermaid Swimming Pool—*other* TX-5
Mermaid Tavern—*hist pl* DE-2
**Mermentau**—*pop pl* LA-4
Mermentau River—*stream* LA-4
*Mermenteau* LA-4
*Mermenteau River* LA-4
*Mermenton* LA-4
*Mermenton River* LA-4
**Mermet**—*pop pl* IL-6
Mermet Lake—*reservoir* IL-6
Mermet Lake State Conservation Area—*park* IL-6
**Mermill**—*pop pl* OH-6
Mermont Plaza—*locale* PA-2
Mermoud Cem—*cemetery* IN-6
Merna—*locale* MO-7
Merna—*locale* WY-8
**Merna**—*pop pl* IL-6
**Merna**—*pop pl* NE-7
Merna Butte—*summit* WY-8
Merna Cem—*cemetery* NE-7
Merna Post Office (historical)—*building* SD-7
Merna (RR name for Coalgood)—*other* KY-4
Merna Sch—*school* IL-6
Mernill Pond State Reservation—*park* MA-1
**Meroa**—*pop pl* IA-7
**Merom**—*pop pl* IN-6
Merom Bluff—*range* IN-6
Merom Island—*island* IN-6
Meromr, Bkul A—*cape* PW-9
Merom Site and Fort Azatlan—*hist pl* IN-6
**Merom (sta)**—*pop pl* IN-6
**Merom Station**—*pop pl* IN-6
*Meron* FM-9
Meroney—*locale* AR-4
Merong—*slope* PW-9
Meronies Ch—*church* NC-3
Meron Island—*island* MP-9
*Meror* FM-9
Merora (historical P.O.)—*locale* MS-4
Merow Spring—*spring* SD-7
Meroyuk River—*stream* AK-9
Mer Parish United Methodist Ch—*church* MS-4
Mer. Park Hospital Heliport—*airport* OR-9
Mer Post Office—*building* MS-4
Merquin Sch—*school* CA-9
Merrbach Cem—*cemetery* MD-2
Mer Regional Hosp—*hospital* MS-4
Merrehope—*hist pl* MS-4
Merrehope Hist Dist—*hist pl* MS-4
Merrell, Capt. Nelson, House—*hist pl* TX-5
**Merrell Beach**—*pop pl* AL-4
Merrell Cem—*cemetery* TN-4
Merrell Cem—*cemetery* TX-5
Merrell Ch—*church* WV-2
Merrell Creek—*stream* TX-5
Merrell Lake—*lake* MT-8
Merrell Ridge—*ridge* OH-6
Merrell Ridge Ch—*church* OH-6
Merrell Rsvr—*reservoir* OR-9
Merrell Tavern—*hist pl* MA-1
Merrellton—*locale* AL-4
Merrellton Sch (historical)—*school* AL-4
Merrelltown—*locale* TX-5
*Merrelton* AL-4
Merren Creek—*stream* AR-4
Merrett Canyon—*valley* NM-5
Merrett Cem—*cemetery* TN-4
Merrett Creek—*stream* GA-3
Merrett Park—*park* FL-3
Merrett Pond—*reservoir* (2) GA-3
Merrials Pond—*lake* UT-8
Merriam—*locale* MN-6
Merriam—*locale* OH-6
**Merriam**—*pop pl* IL-6
**Merriam**—*pop pl* IN-6
**Merriam**—*pop pl* KS-7
Merriam, C. Hart, Base Camp Site—*hist pl* AZ-5
Merriam, Galen, House—*hist pl* MA-1
Merriam, Henry W., House—*hist pl* NJ-2
Merriam, Mount—*summit* AK-9
Merriam Beach—*beach* MA-1
Merriam Boy Scout Camp—*locale* WI-6
Merriam Brook—*stream* MA-1
Merriam Brook—*stream* NH-1
Merriam Cem—*cemetery* IN-6
Merriam Chapel—*church* IN-6
*Merriam Crater* AZ-5
*Merriam Creek* IN-6
Merriam Creek—*stream* CO-8
Merriam Drain—*canal* CA-9
Merriam Elem Sch—*school* KS-7
Merriam Hill—*summit* (2) MA-1
Merriam Hill—*summit* NH-1
Merriam Lake—*lake* CA-9
Merriam Lake—*lake* NY-2
Merriam Lake—*reservoir* ID-8
Merriam Meadows—*flat* WY-8
Merriam Mountains—*range* CA-9
Merriam Mtn—*summit* AZ-5
*Merriam Park* MN-6
Merriam Peak—*summit* CA-9
Merriam Peak—*summit* ID-8
Merriam Point—*cape* OR-9
Merriam Ranch—*locale* WY-8
*Merriams Corner* MA-1
*Merriams Creek* IN-6
*Merriams Hill* MA-1
Merriam Swamp—*swamp* NY-2
Merriam Swamp—*swamp* WI-6
Merriam Terrace Park—*park* MN-6
**Merriam Woods**—*pop pl* MO-7
Merrian—*locale* PA-2
Merrian Sch—*school* IL-6
*Merrians Pond* MA-1
Merri Belle Lake—*lake* AK-9
*Merrical Run* WV-2
Merrick—*locale* KS-7
Merrick—*locale* OK-5
Merrick—*locale* TX-5
**Merrick**—*pop pl* IN-6
**Merrick**—*pop pl* MA-1
**Merrick**—*pop pl* NY-2
Merrick Art Gallery—*hist pl* PA-2
Merrick Ave JHS—*school* NY-2
Merrick Ave Sch—*school* NY-2
Merrick Bay—*bay* NY-2
Merrick Boys Camp—*locale* MD-2
Merrick Branch—*stream* WV-2
Merrick Brook—*stream* CT-1
Merrick Butte—*summit* AZ-5
Merrick Cem—*cemetery* KY-4
Merrick Cem—*cemetery* MD-2
Merrick Cem—*cemetery* MO-7
Merrick Corner—*locale* NY-2
*Merrick Creek* WV-2
Merrick Creek—*stream* NY-2
Merrick Creek—*stream* WV-2
Merrick Island—*summit* MA-1
Merrick JHS—*school* OH-6
*Merrick Lake* NE-7
Merrick Lake—*lake* MI-6
Merrick Lake—*lake* NM-5
Merrick-Moore Sch—*school* NC-3
Merrick Park—*park* FL-3
Merrick Park—*park* IL-6
Merrick Point—*cape* NY-2
Merrick Pond—*lake* NY-2
Merrick Road Park—*park* NY-2
*Merricks* AL-4
Merrick Sch—*school* FL-3
Merrick Sch—*school* NY-2
Merricks Creek—*stream* NC-3
Merrick-Simmons House—*hist pl* FL-3
*Merricks Lake* NE-7
Merrick Special Education Center—*school* FL-3
Merrick Spring—*spring* WY-8
Merrick Spring Trail—*trail* PA-2
Merrick State Park—*park* WI-6
*Merrickton* MD-2
**Merrickville**—*pop pl* NY-2
Merrick Well—*well* OR-9
Merriconeag Sound—*bay* ME-1
Merriconegan Farm—*hist pl* ME-1
**Merricourt**—*pop pl* ND-7
Merricourt Cem—*cemetery* ND-7
Merridun—*hist pl* SC-3
Merrie Christmas Park—*park* FL-3
*Merriewold* NY-2
**Merriewold**—*pop pl* NY-2
Merriewold Lake—*CDP* NY-2
Merriewold Lake—*lake* NY-2
Merriewold Lake—*reservoir* NY-2
**Merriewold Park**—*pop pl* NY-2
*Merrie Wood Camp* NC-3
Merrie Woode Camp—*locale* NC-3
Merriewood Sch—*school* CA-9
Merrifield—*locale* KY-4
Merrifield—*locale* NY-2
**Merrifield**—*pop pl* MN-6
**Merrifield**—*pop pl* ND-7
**Merrifield**—*pop pl* (2) VA-3
Merrifield, Samuel B., House—*hist pl* KY-4
Merrifield Bay—*bay* AK-9
Merrifield Brook—*stream* ME-1
Merrifield-Cass House—*hist pl* IN-6
Merrifield Cem—*cemetery* ME-1
Merrifield Cove—*bay* WA-9
Merrifield Creek—*stream* ND-7
Merrifield House—*hist pl* MA-1
Merrifield Run—*stream* WV-2
Merrigan Creek—*stream* PA-2
Merrihew, Harry B., Drugstore—*hist pl* UT-8
Merrihew Ranch—*locale* NE-7
Merril, Lake—*lake* FL-3
Merriland Ridge—*ridge* ME-1
*Merriland River* ME-1
Merriland River—*stream* ME-1
Merril Cove—*basin* NC-3
Merril Creek—*stream* OR-9
Merril Draw—*valley* WY-8
Merril Flat—*flat* UT-8
Merrilis Hill—*summit* CA-9
Merrill—*locale* MD-2
Merrill—*locale* PA-2
**Merrill**—*pop pl* CA-9
**Merrill**—*pop pl* IA-7
**Merrill**—*pop pl* MI-6
**Merrill**—*pop pl* MS-4
**Merrill**—*pop pl* NY-2
**Merrill**—*pop pl* OR-9
**Merrill**—*pop pl* WI-6
Merrill, Cape—*cape* MA-1
Merrill, Capt. Reuben, House—*hist pl* ME-1
Merrill, Levi, House—*hist pl* WI-6
Merrill, R. D., House—*hist pl* WA-9
*Merril Lake* TX-5
**Merrillan**—*pop pl* WI-6
Merrill And Ring Creek—*stream* WA-9
Merrillat, J. C. M., House—*hist pl* VA-3
Merrill Ave Hist Dist—*hist pl* MT-8
Merrill Branch—*stream* AL-4
Merrill Branch—*stream* FL-3
Merrill Branch—*stream* MS-4
Merrill Branch—*stream* (2) TN-4
Merrill Brook—*stream* (8) ME-1
Merrill Brook—*stream* (5) NH-1
Merrill Burn—*area* CA-9
Merrill Cabin—*locale* CA-9
*Merrill Canyon* TX-5
Merrill Canyon—*valley* (2) OR-9
Merrill Canyon—*valley* TX-5
Merrill (CCD)—*cens area* OR-9
Merrill Cem—*cemetery* FL-3
Merrill Cem—*cemetery* (4) ME-1
Merrill Cem—*cemetery* (2) MS-4
Merrill Cem—*cemetery* MO-7
Merrill Cem—*cemetery* NH-1
Merrill Cem—*cemetery* (2) NY-2
Merrill Cem—*cemetery* NC-3
Merrill Cem—*cemetery* TX-5
Merrill Cem—*cemetery* VT-1
Merrill Ch—*church* MI-6
Merrill City Hall—*hist pl* WI-6
Merrill Columbus Ditch—*canal* MT-8
Merrill Coquille—*bar* MS-4
Merrill Corner—*locale* ME-1
Merrill Corner—*locale* VT-1
**Merrill Corner**—*pop pl* VT-1
*Merrill Corners* NY-2
**Merrill Corners**—*pop pl* NH-1
Merrill Cove—*bay* ME-1
Merrill Cove—*valley* NC-3
Merrill Cove Creek—*stream* NC-3
Merrill Crater—*summit* AZ-5
*Merrill Creek* AZ-5
*Merrill Creek* NC-3
Merrill Creek—*stream* AL-4
Merrill Creek—*stream* (3) CA-9
Merrill Creek—*stream* MT-8
Merrill Creek—*stream* NJ-2
Merrill Creek—*stream* (2) NY-2
Merrill Creek—*stream* NC-3
Merrill Creek—*stream* (2) OR-9
Merrill Creek—*stream* TX-5
Merrill Double House—*hist pl* MA-1
Merrill Estate—*hist pl* MA-1
Merrill Field—*park* NY-2
Merrill Fork—*stream* TX-5
Merrill Hall—*hist pl* ME-1
*Merrill Hill* CT-1
*Merrill Hill* VT-1
Merrill Hill—*summit* (5) ME-1
Merrill Hill—*summit* (2) NH-1
Merrill Hill Cem—*cemetery* ME-1
Merrill Hollow—*valley* MO-7
Merrill Hollow—*valley* UT-8
Merrill House—*hist pl* AR-4
Merrill HS—*school* AR-4
*Merrill IOOF Cemetery* OR-9
Merrill Island—*island* ME-1
Merrill Island—*island* NH-1
Merrill JHS—*school* CO-8
Merrill JHS—*school* IA-7
Merrill Karlen Number 1 Dam—*dam* SD-7
*Merrill Lake* TX-5
Merrill Lake—*lake* CA-9
Merrill Lake—*lake* (3) MI-6
Merrill Lake—*lake* MN-6
Merrill Lake—*lake* NE-7
Merrill Lake—*lake* OR-9
Merrill Lake—*lake* WA-9
Merrill Lake—*lake* WI-6
*Merrill Lakes* MI-6
Merrill Ledge—*bar* ME-1
Merrill Lock No. 6—*hist pl* PA-2
Merrill-Maley House—*hist pl* MS-4
Merrill Mill—*locale* AL-4
Merrill Mtn—*summit* AL-4
Merrill Mtn—*summit* (2) CA-9
Merrill Mtn—*summit* ME-1
Merrill Mtn—*summit* NC-3
Merrill Park—*park* IL-6
Merrill Park—*park* NJ-2
Merrill Park—*park* WI-6
Merrill Pass—*gap* AK-9
Merrill Peak—*summit* AZ-5
Merrill Pickering Lake Dam—*dam* MS-4
Merrill Place—*locale* NM-5
Merrill Point—*cape* ME-1
*Merrill Pond* ME-1
*Merrill Pond* NY-2
Merrill Pond—*lake* ME-1
Merrill Pools—*flat* CA-9
Merrill-Poor House—*hist pl* ME-1
Merrill Post Office (historical)—*building* MS-4
Merrill Prospect—*mine* CA-9
Merrill Ranch—*locale* CA-9
Merrill Ranch—*locale* NM-5
Merrill Ranch—*locale* UT-8
Merrill Reservation—*reserve* AL-4
Merrill River—*stream* AK-9
Merrill Road Day Sch—*school* FL-3
Merrills Branch—*stream* MO-7
*Merrills Brook* ME-1
Merrill Sch—*school* CA-9
Merrill Sch—*school* FL-3
Merrill Sch—*school* IL-6
Merrill Sch—*school* MA-1
Merrill Sch—*school* (2) MI-6
Merrill Sch—*school* MO-7
Merrill Sch—*school* TN-4
Merrill Sch—*school* (2) WI-6
Merrill Sch (historical)—*school* PA-2
Merrill Sch Number 25—*school* IN-6
*Merrills Coquille* MS-4
Merrills Grove Cem—*cemetery* IA-7
Merrills Hill—*summit* NY-2
Merrill Siding—*locale* OR-9
Merrills Lake—*lake* TX-5
Merrills Landing—*locale* CA-9
*Merrill Spring* MT-8
*Merrill Spring* TN-4
Merrill Spring—*spring* CA-9
Merrill Spring—*spring* OR-9
Merrill Spring—*spring* WY-8
Merrill Springs—*spring* OR-9
Merrill Springs Rim—*cliff* OR-9
Merrills Shell Bank Lighthouse—*locale* MS-4
Merrills Slough—*lake* ND-7
Merrills Springs Creek—*stream* MT-8
Merrill's Store—*hist pl* MS-4
Merrill Station—*locale* PA-2
Merrill Strip—*unorg* ME-1
Merrillsville—*locale* NY-2
**Merrillsville**—*pop pl* NY-2
Merrillsville Cem—*cemetery* NY-2
Merrill's Wharf Hist Dist—*hist pl* MA-1
**Merrill (Town of)**—*pop pl* ME-1
**Merrill (Town of)**—*pop pl* WI-6
**Merrill Township**—*pop pl* ND-7
**Merrill (Township of)**—*pop pl* MI-6
Merrill Valley—*basin* CA-9
*Merrillville* NY-2
**Merrillville**—*pop pl* GA-3
**Merrillville**—*pop pl* IN-6
Merrill Wash—*stream* AZ-5
Merril P Barber Bridge—*bridge* FL-3
Merril Point—*cape* MI-6
Merrils Camp Spring—*spring* UT-8
*Merrilville* NY-2
**Merrilville**—*pop pl* NY-2
*Merril Wash* AZ-5
Merrilyn Dam—*dam* AZ-5
*Merrimac* MA-1
Merrimac—*locale* CA-9
Merrimac—*locale* IA-7
Merrimac—*locale* VA-3
**Merrimac**—*pop pl* FL-3
**Merrimac**—*pop pl* IL-6
**Merrimac**—*pop pl* KY-4
**Merrimac**—*pop pl* MA-1
**Merrimac**—*pop pl* VA-3
**Merrimac**—*pop pl* WV-2
**Merrimac**—*pop pl* WI-6
Merrimac Branch—*stream* AL-4
Merrimac Butte—*summit* UT-8
Merrimac Cem—*cemetery* KY-4
Merrimac Ferry—*hist pl* WI-6
Merrimac Gulch—*valley* ID-8

Mesa Sarca—*summit* NM-5
Mesa Sarcio—*summit* NM-5
Mesa Sch—*school* (3) CA-9
Mesa Sch—*school* CO-8
Mesa Sch—*school* NE-7
Mesas Cuatas—*summit* NM-5
*Mesas de Mal Pais* AZ-5
Mesa Seco—*summit* CO-8
Mesa Segura—*summit* NM-5
Mesa Shadows East Mobile Home Park—*locale* AZ-5
Mesa Shadows Mobile Home Park—*locale* AZ-5
Mesa Side Tank—*reservoir* AZ-5
Mesa Siding—*locale* ID-8
Mesa Six Drain—*canal* CA-9
Mesas Mojinas—*summit* NM-5
Mesa Sola—*summit* NM-5
Mesa Spring—*spring* AZ-5
Mesa Spring—*spring* CA-9
Mesa Spring—*spring* NM-5
Mesa Spring—*spring* (2) WY-8
Mesa Spring Hunter Campground—*locale* CO-8
Mesa Spring No 1—*spring* CO-8
Mesa Spring No 2—*spring* CO-8
Mesa Springs—*spring* OR-9
Mesa Spur Drain—*canal* TX-5
Mesa Substation—*locale* AZ-5
Mesa Tank—*lake* NM-5
Mesa Tank—*reservoir* (24) AZ-5
Mesa Tank—*reservoir* (12) NM-5
Mesa Tank—*reservoir* (2) TX-5
Mesa Tank, La—*reservoir* AZ-5
Mesa Tank Farm—*other* TX-5
Mesa Tank Number Two—*reservoir* AZ-5
Mesa Tanks—*reservoir* AZ-5
Mesatchee Creek—*stream* (2) WA-9
Mesa Three Drain—*canal* CA-9
Mesa Tierra Number Three Subdivision Mini Park—*park* AZ-5
Mesa Tierra Number Three Subdivision Water Retetion Basin—*reservoir* AZ-5
Mesa Tinaja—*summit* NM-5
Mesa Top Mine—*mine* NM-5
Mesa Trail—*trail* CO-8
Mesa Trail Valley—*valley* AZ-5
Mesa Trail Wash—*valley* AZ-5
Mesa Travelodge Mobile Home Park—*locale* AZ-5
Mesa Valley Farm—*locale* CA-9
Mesa Venado—*bench* NM-5
**Mesa Verde**—*pop pl* CA-9
Mesa Verde—*uninc pl* TX-5
Mesa Verde Administrative District—*hist pl* CO-8
Mesa Verde Country Club—*other* CA-9
**Mesa Verde Estates (subdivision)**—*pop pl* (2) AZ-5
Mesa Verde Landing Strip—*airport* KS-7
Mesa Verde Mine—*mine* CO-8
Mesa Verde Natl Park—*hist pl* CO-8
Mesa Verde Natl Park—*park* CO-8
Mesa Verde Sch—*school* CA-9
Mesa Verde Sch—*school* NM-5
Mesa Verde West Rim—*cliff* CO-8
Mesa Vibora—*summit* NM-5
Mesa View Ch—*church* CO-8
Mesa View Ranch—*locale* CO-8
*Mesa Village* FM-9
**Mesa Village**—*pop pl* NM-5
Mesa Village Park—*park* AZ-5
Mesa Villas Number Two Mini Park—*park* AZ-5
Mesa Villas Number Two Water Retention Basin—*reservoir* AZ-5
Mesaville—*locale* CA-9
Mesa Vista—*uninc pl* TX-5
Mesa Wash—*stream* (2) AZ-5
Mesa Well—*well* (4) AZ-5
Mesa Well—*well* (4) NM-5
Mesa Well Canyon—*valley* NM-5
Mesa Well No 1—*well* WY-8
Mesa Wells—*well* NM-5
Mesa Windmill—*locale* AZ-5
Mesa Windmill—*locale* CO-8
Mesa Windmill—*locale* (2) NM-5
Mesa Windmill—*locale* TX-5
Mesa 36—*hist pl* WA-9
Mesbelau—*cape* PW-9
Mescal—*locale* AZ-5
Mescal Arroyo—*valley* AZ-5
Mescal Artesian Well—*well* TX-5
Mescal Bajada—*pass* CA-9
Mescal Campground—*locale* CA-9
Mescal Canyon—*valley* AZ-5
Mescal Canyon—*valley* NM-5
Mescal Creek—*stream* (3) AZ-5
Mescal Creek—*stream* CA-9
Mescal Creek—*stream* TX-5
Mescal Dam—*dam* AZ-5
**Mescalero**—*pop pl* NM-5
**Mescalero Apache Ind Res**—*pop pl* NM-5
Mescalero (CCD)—*cens area* NM-5
Mescalero Indian Cem—*cemetery* NM-5
Mescalero Oil Field—*other* NM-5
Mescalero Point—*cliff* AZ-5
Mescalero Point—*summit* NM-5
Mescalero Ridge (The Caprock)—*ridge* NM-5
Mescalero Ridge The Caprock pp—*ridge* NM-5
Mescalero Sands—*area* NM-5
Mescalero Spring—*spring* NM-5
Mescalero Windmills—*locale* TX-5
Mescal Gulch—*valley* AZ-5
Mescal Interchange—*crossing* AZ-5
Mescalitan Island—*island* CA-9
Mescalito Windmill—*locale* TX-5
Mescal Mountains—*ridge* AZ-5
Mescal Mtn—*summit* (2) AZ-5
Mescal Peak—*summit* AZ-5
Mescal Pit—*locale* AZ-5
Mescal Pit Catchment Basin—*reservoir* AZ-5
Mescal Pit Spring—*spring* AZ-5
Mescal Pit Tank—*reservoir* AZ-5
*Mescal Range* AZ-5
Mescal Range—*range* CA-9
Mescal Ridge—*ridge* AZ-5
Mescal Ridge—*ridge* CA-9
Mescal Ridge Tank—*reservoir* AZ-5
Mescal Ridge Tank Number One—*reservoir* AZ-5
Mescal Spring—*spring* (5) AZ-5
Mescal Spring—*spring* NM-5
Mescal Tank—*reservoir* (7) AZ-5
Mescal Warm Spring—*spring* AZ-5
*Mescan Bar* UT-8
Mesco Windmill—*locale* TX-5
Mese, Pilen—*stream* FM-9
Meseal Cem—*cemetery* NE-7
*Mesearaan* FM-9
*Meseeyog* FM-9
*Mesegon Island* FM-9
*Mesegou* FM-9
*Meseichok* FM-9
Meseichuk—*summit* FM-9
Meseiku—*locale* FM-9
Meseinom—*bar* FM-9
Meseinom Renong—*bar* FM-9
Meseinom Rewu—*bar* FM-9
*Meseinon* FM-9
*Meseiren* FM-9
Meseirong—*swamp* FM-9
Meseirong—*well* FM-9
*Mesejo* FM-9
*Mese la Oso* AZ-5
Mesemai—*bar* FM-9
Mesena—*locale* GA-3
**Mesenieng**—*pop pl* FM-9
Mesenikau—*spring* FM-9
**Meseniko**—*pop pl* FM-9
Meseno—*spring* FM-9
Mesenon—*well* FM-9
Mesenpal—*locale* FM-9
*Mesenpali* FM-9
Meseong—*island* FM-9
**Mesepa**—*pop pl* AS-9
*Meseram* FM-9
Meseran—*island* FM-9
**Meseran**—*pop pl* FM-9
Meserole Sch—*school* MI-6
*Meserve Brook* ME-1
Meserve Brook—*stream* NH-1
Meserve Drain—*canal* CA-9
Meserve Head—*summit* ME-1
Meserve Lake—*lake* IN-6
**Meservey**—*pop pl* (2) IA-7
Meservey Hill—*summit* NY-2
Meservey Sch—*school* MO-7
Meseta Blanca—*summit* NM-5
Meshach Lake—*reservoir* IL-6
Meshack—*locale* KY-4
Meshack Creek—*stream* KY-4
*Meshaddock Brook* CT-1
*Meshamasick Mountain* CT-1
*Meshamasic Mountain* CT-1
*Meshanticut* RI-1
**Meshanticut**—*pop pl* RI-1
Meshanticut Brook—*stream* RI-1
*Meshanticut RR Station* RI-1
*Meshapock Brook* CT-1
*Mesh Barrel Spring* AZ-5
**Meshik**—*pop pl* AK-9
Meshik Lake—*lake* AK-9
Meshik (Port Heiden)—*other* AK-9
Meshik River—*stream* AK-9
*Meshikun Channel* PW-9
Meshingomesia Cem—*cemetery* IN-6
Meshingomesta Country Club—*other* IN-6
*Meshobe* VT-1
*Meshomac Point* NY-2
*Meshomasick Mountain* CT-1
Meshomasic Mtn—*summit* CT-1
Meshomasic State For—*forest* CT-1
*Meshomuck Point* NY-2
**Meshoppen**—*pop pl* PA-2
Meshoppen Borough—*civil* PA-2
Meshoppen Creek—*stream* PA-2
**Meshoppen (Township of)**—*pop pl* PA-2
**Mesic**—*pop pl* NC-3
Mesic Creek—*stream* NC-3
**Mesick**—*pop pl* MI-6
Mesick House—*hist pl* CA-9
*Mesid* MP-9
*Mesieiren* FM-9
*Mesieng* FM-9
Mesier Park—*park* NY-2
*Mesihou* FM-9
*Mesihsou* FM-9
Mesihsou—*civil* FM-9
Mesikm—*channel* PW-9
**Mesilla**—*pop pl* NM-5
Mesilla Civil Colony—*civil* NM-5
Mesilla Civil Colony Tract No 1—*civil* NM-5
Mesilla Civil Colony Tract No 2—*civil* NM-5
**Mesilla (corporate name for La Mesilla)**—*pop pl* NM-5
Mesilla Diversion Dam—*dam* NM-5
Mesilla Drain—*canal* NM-5
Mesilla Lateral—*canal* NM-5
**Mesilla Park**—*pop pl* NM-5
**Mesilla Park**—*pop pl* TX-5
Mesilla Plaza—*hist pl* NM-5
Mesilla Valley—*valley* NM-5
Mesilla Valley—*valley* TX-5
**Mesita**—*pop pl* CO-8
**Mesita**—*pop pl* NM-5
Mesita Americana—*summit* NM-5
Mesita Blanca—*summit* (3) NM-5
Mesita Camp—*locale* NM-5
Mesita Cocida—*summit* NM-5
Mesita Colorado—*summit* NM-5
Mesita Contadero—*summit* NM-5
Mesita Cortada—*summit* (2) NM-5
Mesita Creek—*stream* NM-5
Mesita de Guadalupe—*summit* NM-5
Mesita De Juana Lopez—*civil* NM-5
Mesita de la Madera—*summit* NM-5
Mesita del Anil—*summit* NM-5
Mesita de la Ventana—*summit* NM-5
Mesita del Buey—*summit* NM-5
Mesita del Gato—*summit* NM-5
Mesita del Gavilan—*summit* NM-5
Mesita del Medio—*summit* NM-5
Mesita de Los Alamos—*summit* NM-5
Mesita de los Ladrones—*summit* NM-5
Mesita del Potrillo—*summit* NM-5
Mesita De Yeso—*summit* NM-5
Mesita Gato—*summit* NM-5
Mesita Hill—*summit* CO-8
Mesita Leon—*summit* NM-5
*Mesita Mesa* NM-5
Mesita Negra—*bench* NM-5
Mesita Negra—*summit* CO-8
Mesita Sch—*school* NM-5
Mesita Sch—*school* TX-5
Mesita Tank—*reservoir* NM-5
Mesita Tierra Blanca—*summit* NM-5
Mesita Trementina—*summit* NM-5
Mesito Rsvr—*reservoir* CO-8
Meskelat—*stream* PW-9
Mesken Bar (inundated)—*bar* UT-8
*Meskenthine Creek* NE-7
Mesker Park—*park* IN-6
Mesker Park Cem—*cemetery* IN-6
Meskill—*locale* WA-9
Meskill—*post sta* TX-5
Meskill Pit—*locale* WA-9
*Meskin Bar* UT-8
Meskin Bar (historical)—*bay* UT-8
*Mesler* MO-7
Mesler Creek—*stream* MT-8
**Mesler (Messler)**—*pop pl* MO-7
Mesling Dam—*dam* ND-7
Mesman Creek—*stream* OR-9
**Mesmer**—*pop pl* CA-9
Mesnard, Mount—*summit* MI-6
Mesner Branch—*stream* MO-7
Meso Island—*island* MI-6
*Mesomersic Mountain* CT-1
**Mesopotamia**—*pop pl* OH-6
Mesopotamia Cem—*cemetery* AL-4
Mesopotamia Cem—*cemetery* MN-6
Mesopotamia Ch—*church* SC-3
*Mesopotamia Church* AL-4
*Mesopotamia Female Academy* AL-4
*Mesopotamia Female Seminary* AL-4
Mesopotamia (historical)—*locale* AL-4
*Mesopotamia P.O.* AL-4
**Mesopotamia (Township of)**—*pop pl* OH-6
Mesopotamia Village District—*hist pl* OH-6
Mesor—*locale* FM-9
Mesoydez Homestead—*locale* MT-8
Mespiah Cem—*cemetery* SC-3
Mesquakie Indian Burial Grounds—*cemetery* IA-7
Mesquakie Indian Settlement—*locale* IA-7
*Mesqual* AZ-5
Me-Squa-L-Cum-E Park—*flat* MI-6
*Mesquit* AZ-5
Mesquital Tank—*reservoir* NM-5
Mesquite—*locale* CA-9
Mesquite—*locale* TX-5
**Mesquite**—*pop pl* NV-8
**Mesquite**—*pop pl* NM-5
**Mesquite**—*pop pl* TX-5
Mesquite, Loma del—*summit* TX-5
Mesquite Bay—*bay* TX-5
Mesquite Branch—*stream* (4) TX-5
Mesquite Canyon—*valley* AZ-5
Mesquite Canyon—*valley* CA-9
Mesquite Canyon—*valley* TX-5
Mesquite Canyon Spring—*spring* AZ-5
Mesquite Cem—*cemetery* (2) TX-5
*Mesquite Creek* TX-5
Mesquite Creek—*stream* AZ-5
Mesquite Creek—*stream* (14) TX-5
Mesquite Creek—*stream* WY-8
Mesquite Ditch—*canal* NV-8
Mesquite Drain—*canal* CA-9
Mesquite Drain—*canal* NM-5
Mesquite Drain Five—*canal* CA-9
Mesquite Drain Four—*canal* CA-9
Mesquite Drain One—*canal* CA-9
Mesquite Drain Seven—*canal* CA-9
Mesquite Drain Three—*spring* CA-9
Mesquite Drain Two—*canal* CA-9
Mesquite Drain 3—*canal* CA-9
Mesquite Flat—*flat* (2) AZ-5
Mesquite Flat—*flat* (2) CA-9
Mesquite Flat Spring—*spring* AZ-5
*Mesquite Gray Well* AZ-5
Mesquite Gray Well—*well* AZ-5
Mesquite Hill—*summit* TX-5
Mesquite Hills—*range* CA-9
Mesquite Hunting Club—*other* CA-9
Mesquite Island—*island* TX-5
Mesquite Jim Well—*well* AZ-5
Mesquite Knoll—*summit* TX-5
*Mesquite Lake* TX-5
Mesquite Lake—*flat* (2) CA-9
Mesquite Lake—*lake* TX-5
Mesquite Lake—*reservoir* NM-5
Mesquite Lateral—*canal* CA-9
Mesquite Mountains—*other* CA-9
Mesquite Mountains—*ridge* AZ-5
Mesquite Mtn—*summit* AZ-5
Mesquite Oasis—*locale* CA-9
Mesquite Park—*park* TX-5
Mesquite Pass—*gap* CA-9
Mesquite Point—*cliff* TX-5
Mesquite Pond—*lake* TX-5
Mesquite Ranch—*locale* TX-5
Mesquite Rincon—*island* TX-5
Mesquite Seep—*spring* AZ-5
Mesquite Sewage Disposal—*other* TX-5
Mesquite Spring—*spring* (3) AZ-5
Mesquite Spring—*spring* (2) CA-9
Mesquite Spring—*spring* NM-5
Mesquite Spring—*spring* TX-5
Mesquite Spring Campground—*locale* CA-9
Mesquite Springs—*spring* CA-9
Mesquite Springs Campground—*park* AZ-5
Mesquite Spring Tank—*reservoir* AZ-5
Mesquite Street Original Townsite Hist Dist—*hist pl* NM-5
Mesquites Windmill—*locale* TX-5
Mesquite Tank—*reservoir* (7) AZ-5
Mesquite Tank—*reservoir* (3) NM-5
Mesquite Tank—*reservoir* (4) TX-5
Mesquite Tanks—*reservoir* AZ-5
Mesquite Thicket Spring—*spring* AZ-5
Mesquite Township—*inact MCD* NV-8
*Mesquite Valley* CA-9
Mesquite Valley—*basin* NV-8
Mesquite Valley—*valley* CA-9
Mesquite Wash—*stream* AZ-5
Mesquite Wash—*valley* UT-8
Mesquite Well—*well* (4) AZ-5
Mesquite Well—*well* TX-5
Mesquite Well (Windmill)—*locale* TX-5
Mesquite Windmill—*locale* AZ-5
Mesquite Windmill—*locale* NM-5
Mesquite Windmill—*locale* (7) TX-5
Mesquitin Well (Flowing)—*well* TX-5
Mesquitoso Creek—*stream* TX-5
Mesquito Spring—*spring* CA-9
**Messa**—*pop pl* FM-9
Messa, Oror En—*locale* FM-9
*Messagosquelgamook* ME-1
Messalonskee Lake—*lake* ME-1
Messalonskee Stream—*stream* ME-1
Messamer Ridge—*ridge* PA-2
*Messanamisco, Town of* MA-1
Messanger Mtn—*summit* TX-5
Messbox Creek—*stream* TX-5
Mess Box Mesa—*summit* NM-5
Mess Ditch—*canal* OH-6
Messenger, William C., House—*hist pl* MI-6
Messenger Bay—*bay* NY-2
**Messenger Bay**—*pop pl* NY-2
Messenger Branch—*stream* WV-2
Messenger Bridge—*bridge* ME-1
*Messenger Canyon* CA-9
Messenger Canyon—*valley* CA-9
Messenger Cem—*cemetery* IL-6
Messenger Cem—*cemetery* (2) WV-2
Messenger Ch—*church* WV-2
Messenger Creek—*stream* MS-4
Messenger Creek—*stream* (2) NE-7
Messenger Creek—*stream* WI-6
Messenger Flats—*flat* CA-9
Messenger Gulch—*valley* CA-9
Messenger Gulch—*valley* CO-8
Messenger Lake—*lake* MI-6
Messenger Post Office (historical)—*building* TN-4
Messenger Run—*stream* PA-2
*Messengers Brook* MA-1
Messenger Shoal—*bar* NY-2
Messengerville—*locale* NY-2
Messenger Woods—*woods* IL-6
Messer—*locale* OK-5
Messer Barn—*hist pl* TN-4
*Messer Branch* NC-3
*Messer Branch* WV-2
Messer Branch—*stream* (2) KY-4
Messer Branch—*stream* (5) NC-3
Messer Branch—*stream* TN-4
Messer Brook—*stream* MI-6
Messer Brook—*stream* NH-1
Messer Cem—*cemetery* IA-7
Messer Cem—*cemetery* KS-7
Messer Cem—*cemetery* KY-4
Messer Cem—*cemetery* MI-6
Messer Cem—*cemetery* OK-5
Messer Cem—*cemetery* WV-2
Messer Creek—*stream* AR-4
Messer Creek—*stream* GA-3
Messer Creek—*stream* LA-4
Messer Creek—*stream* MO-7
Messer Creek—*stream* NC-3
Messer Flat—*flat* CO-8
Messer Fork—*stream* KY-4
Messer Fork—*stream* NC-3
Messer Gap—*gap* NC-3
*Messerger Creek* NE-7
Messer Hammock—*island* FL-3
Messer (historical)—*locale* KS-7
Messerly Cem—*cemetery* MT-8
Messer Mtn—*summit* NC-3
Messer Mtn—*summit* TN-4
Messer Pond—*lake* ME-1
Messer Pond—*lake* NH-1
Messer Prairie—*flat* FL-3
Messer Ranch—*locale* CA-9
Messer Ridge—*ridge* GA-3
Messer Ridge—*ridge* NC-3
*Messer Run* OH-6
*Messer Run* PA-2
Messer Run—*stream* WV-2
Messer Sawgrass—*swamp* FL-3
Messers Bridge—*bridge* GA-3
Messer Sch—*school* KS-7
Messer Sch—*school* KY-4
Messer Sch—*school* MI-6
Messer Sch—*school* NY-2
Messerschmidt Coulee—*valley* MT-8
Messerschmidt Pond—*reservoir* CT-1
Messerschmidt Sch—*school* PA-2
*Messers Creek* AR-4
Messersmith Cem—*cemetery* IN-6
Messersmith Creek—*stream* IN-6
Messers Pond—*reservoir* SC-3
Messers Run—*stream* PA-2
Messer Swamp—*swamp* MI-6
Messer Trail—*trail* TN-4
**Messex**—*pop pl* CO-8
Messhoss Creek—*stream* KS-7
Messhouse Creek—*stream* OR-9
Messiah African Methodist Episcopal Zion Temple—*church* IN-6
Messiah Baptist Ch—*church* KS-7
Messiah Cem—*cemetery* SD-7
*Messiah Ch* IN-6
Messiah Ch—*church* AL-4
Messiah Ch—*church* GA-3
Messiah Ch—*church* IN-6
Messiah Ch—*church* MD-2
Messiah Ch—*church* (2) MI-6
Messiah Ch—*church* NE-7
Messiah Ch—*church* NC-3
Messiah Ch—*church* (5) PA-2
Messiah Ch—*church* SC-3
Messiah Ch—*church* (2) SD-7
Messiah Ch—*church* TN-4
Messiah Ch—*church* VA-3
Messiah Coll—*post sta* PA-2
Messiah Evangelical Lutheran Ch—*church* KS-7
Messiah Lutheran Ch—*church* (2) FL-3
Messiah Lutheran Ch—*church* IN-6
Messiah Lutheran Ch—*church* SD-7
Messiah Park—*park* IL-6
Messiah Sch—*school* IL-6
Messiah Sch—*school* MI-6
Messiah Sch—*school* TX-5
Messiah Sch—*school* WI-6
Messiah United Methodist Ch—*church* PA-2
Messiah Village—*locale* PA-2
*Messick* DE-2
*Messick* LA-4
**Messick**—*pop pl* IN-6
**Messick**—*pop pl* LA-4
Messick, Dr. John W., House and Office—*hist pl* DE-2
Messick Branch—*stream* AL-4
Messick Cem—*cemetery* MO-7
**Messick Development (subdivision)**—*pop pl* DE-2
Messick Ditch—*canal* MD-2
Messick HS—*school* TN-4
Messick Lake—*lake* CA-9
Messick Lake—*lake* IN-6
Messick Point—*cape* VA-3
Messick Pond—*reservoir* AL-4
Messicks Ditch—*canal* MD-2
Messic Mtn—*summit* CA-9
Messiers Creek—*stream* GA-3
Messilla Valley—*valley* CA-9
Messilla Valley Sch—*school* CA-9
*Messina* NY-2
*Messina Mine* AL-4
Messing Creek—*stream* OR-9
Messinger Creek—*stream* (2) OR-9
Messinger Dam—*dam* NC-3
Messinger Lake—*reservoir* NC-3
Messinger Lower Range Channel—*channel* OR-9
Messinger Middle Range Channel—*channel* OR-9
Messinger Upper Range Channel—*channel* OR-9
Messinger Windmill—*locale* NM-5
Messing Sch—*school* OK-5
Messing Sch (historical)—*school* SD-7
Messir Cem—*cemetery* WV-2
Messix Canyon—*valley* UT-8
Messix Peak—*summit* UT-8
**Messler**—*pop pl* MO-7
Messler Lateral—*canal* ID-8
Messmer HS—*school* WI-6
**Messmore**—*pop pl* PA-2
Messmore Cem—*cemetery* OH-6
Messmore Cronk Drain—*canal* MI-6
Messmore Sch—*school* MI-6
Messner—*locale* OR-9
*Messner Branch* MO-7
Messner Cabin—*locale* CA-9
Messner Gulch—*valley* CA-9
Messner Hill—*summit* NY-2
Messner Marsh—*swamp* OR-9
**Messongo**—*pop pl* VA-3
Messongo Bridge—*locale* VA-3
Messongo Creek—*stream* VA-3
Mess Ridge Cem—*cemetery* MS-4
Mess Township—*civil* SD-7
Messy Slough—*gut* AK-9
Mestad Spring—*spring* IA-7
Mesta Park—*hist pl* OK-5
Mestas, Mount—*summit* CO-8
Mestas Canyon—*valley* NM-5
Mestas Cem—*cemetery* CO-8
Mestas Ditch—*canal* CO-8
Mestas Ditch—*canal* NM-5
Mestayer—*locale* LA-4
Mestayer Point—*cape* LA-4
Mestena Artesian Well—*well* TX-5
Mestenas Canyon—*valley* NM-5
Mestenas Mesa—*summit* NM-5
Mestenas Peak—*summit* NM-5
Mestenito Cem—*cemetery* NM-5
Mestenito Valley—*valley* NM-5
Mesteno Camp—*locale* NM-5
Mesteno Draw—*valley* NM-5
Mesteno Lake —*lake* TX-5
Mesteno Windmill —*locale* TX-5
Mestice Ranch—*locale* NM-5
**Mesto**—*pop pl* CA-9
Mesubedumail—*bay* PW-9
Meszaros Slough—*gut* ND-7
Meszler Hill—*summit* NY-2
**Meta**—*pop pl* KY-4
**Meta**—*pop pl* MO-7
*Metacombe Key* FL-3
Metacomet Lake—*lake* MA-1
Metacomet Sch—*school* CT-1
Metacomet Trail—*trail* CT-1
*Metacumbe Key* FL-3
**Metairie**—*pop pl* LA-4
Metairie Cem—*cemetery* LA-4
Metairie Outfall Canal—*canal* LA-4
Metairie Park Sch—*school* LA-4
Metairie Sch—*school* LA-4
**Metairie Terrace**—*pop pl* LA-4
**Metal**—*pop pl* PA-2
Metalak, Lake—*lake* NH-1
Meta Lake—*lake* WA-9
Meta Lake—*lake* WI-6
*Metalanim* FM-9
*Metalanim Hafen* FM-9
*Metalanim Harbor* FM-9
Metal Ch—*church* PA-2
Metal Creek—*stream* AK-9
Metal Creek—*stream* OR-9
Metal Creek Glacier—*glacier* AK-9
Metal Ford—*locale* (2) TN-4
**Metaline**—*pop pl* WA-9
**Metaline Falls**—*pop pl* WA-9
Metaline Falls Sch—*hist pl* WA-9
Metallak Brook—*stream* ME-1
Metallak Island—*island* ME-1
Metallak Island—*island* NH-1
Metallak Mtn—*summit* ME-1
Metallak Pond—*lake* ME-1
*Metallak's island* NH-1
Metallak Stream—*stream* ME-1
Metal Landing—*locale* TN-4
Metallic Accident Mine—*mine* AZ-5
*Metallic Brook* ME-1
Metallic City (Site)—*locale* NV-8
*Metallic Island* NH-1
*Metallic Pond* ME-1
Metallic Streak Mine—*mine* SD-7
*Metalluc Island* NH-1
*Metalluck Brook* ME-1
Metal Queen Mine—*mine* UT-8
Metal Shop—*hist pl* IL-6
**Metals Park (American Society of Metals)**—*pop pl* OH-6
Metal Tank Well—*locale* NM-5
Metalton—*locale* AR-4
**Metalton**—*pop pl* WV-2
**Metalton (Semoco)**—*pop pl* WV-2
**Metal Township**—*pop pl* PA-2
Metam, Lake—*lake* WA-9
*Metamora* PA-2
**Metamora**—*pop pl* IL-6
**Metamora**—*pop pl* IN-6
**Metamora**—*pop pl* MI-6
**Metamora**—*pop pl* OH-6
Metamora, Lake—*reservoir* MI-6
Metamora Cem—*cemetery* MI-6
Metamora Courthouse—*hist pl* IL-6
Metamora Crossroads Hist Dist—*hist pl* MI-6
Metamora-Hadley State Rec Area—*park* MI-6
Metamora Rsvr—*reservoir* OH-6
*Metamora Siding* PA-2
**Metamora Station**—*pop pl* PA-2
**Metamora (Township of)**—*pop pl* IL-6
**Metamora (Township of)**—*pop pl* IN-6
**Metamora (Township of)**—*pop pl* MI-6
Meta Mtn—*summit* TX-5
*Metan Lake* WA-9
Metaregato Channel—*channel* FM-9
**Meta (sta.)**—*pop pl* KY-4
Metasville—*locale* GA-3
Metasville Ch—*church* GA-3
Metasville HS—*school* GA-3
Metate Arch—*arch* UT-8
*Metate Creek* TX-5
Metate Creek—*stream* TX-5
Metate Dam—*dam* AZ-5
Metate Flat—*flat* CA-9
Metate Hill—*summit* CA-9
Metate Mine—*mine* AZ-5
Metate Peak—*summit* AZ-5
Metate Rsvr—*reservoir* NM-5
Metate Spring—*spring* AZ-5
Metate Tank—*reservoir* (4) AZ-5
Meta Tower Site—*locale* MO-7
*Metatuxet River* RI-1
*Metau* FM-9
Metauque, Lake—*lake* NY-2
Metberry Gulch—*valley* CO-8
Metcalf—*locale* KS-7
**Metcalf**—*pop pl* GA-3
**Metcalf**—*pop pl* IL-6
**Metcalf**—*pop pl* MA-1
**Metcalf**—*pop pl* NC-3
**Metcalf**—*pop pl* (2) PA-2
Metcalf, Isaac, House—*hist pl* KY-4
Metcalf, Rev. Harlan, House—*hist pl* OH-6
Metcalf, Thomas, House—*hist pl* KY-4
Metcalf Bay—*bay* CA-9
Metcalf Bend—*bend* TX-5
Metcalf Bottoms—*bend* TN-4
Metcalf Branch—*stream* LA-4
Metcalf Branch—*stream* MO-7
Metcalf Branch—*stream* VA-3
Metcalf Brook—*stream* CT-1
Metcalf Brook—*stream* NY-2
Metcalf Canyon—*valley* NM-5
Metcalf Cem—*cemetery* AZ-5
Metcalf Cem—*cemetery* ME-1
Metcalf Cem—*cemetery* (2) MO-7
Metcalf Cem—*cemetery* NC-3
Metcalf Cem—*cemetery* OK-5
Metcalf Chain of Lakes—*lake* NY-2
Metcalf Creek—*stream* AL-4
Metcalf Creek—*stream* CA-9
Metcalf Creek—*stream* CO-8
Metcalf Creek—*stream* GA-3
Metcalf Creek—*stream* MA-1
Metcalf Dam—*dam* ND-7
Metcalf Ditch—*canal* CO-8
Metcalf Ditch—*canal* (2) IN-6
Metcalf Ditch—*canal* UT-8
Metcalf Dock—*locale* TN-4
*Metcalfe* GA-3
**Metcalfe**—*pop pl* KY-4
**Metcalfe**—*pop pl* MS-4
Metcalfe Canyon—*valley* CA-9
Metcalfe Cem—*cemetery* MS-4
**Metcalfe (County)**—*pop pl* KY-4
Metcalfe County Sch—*school* KY-4
Metcalfe Dam—*dam* TX-5
Metcalfe Hist Dist—*hist pl* GA-3
Metcalfe House—*hist pl* AR-4
Metcalfe Island—*island* VT-1
Metcalfe Moraine—*ridge* WA-9
Metcalfe Sch—*school* FL-3
Metcalf Ferry (historical)—*locale* AL-4
Metcalf Gap—*gap* CA-9
Metcalf Gap—*gap* TX-5
Metcalf Gap—*locale* TX-5
Metcalf Gap Oil Field—*oilfield* TX-5
Metcalf Grove—*locale* CA-9
Metcalf Gulch—*valley* WY-8
Metcalf Hill—*summit* AR-4
Metcalf Hill—*summit* NY-2
Metcalf Hill—*summit* VT-1
Metcalf Hosp—*hospital* NJ-2
Metcalf Island—*island* WI-6
Metcalf JHS—*school* MN-6
Metcalf Lake—*lake* FL-3
Metcalf Lake—*lake* MI-6
Metcalf Lake—*lake* MT-8
Metcalf Lake—*lake* NY-2
Metcalf Lake—*lake* (2) WA-9
Metcalf Lake—*lake* (2) WI-6
Metcalf Marsh—*swamp* WA-9
Metcalf Mill Bridge—*bridge* AL-4
Metcalf Mtn—*summit* NY-2
*Metcalf Point* ME-1
Metcalf Point—*cape* FL-3
Metcalf Pond—*lake* VT-1
Metcalf Post Office (historical)—*building* TN-4
Metcalf Ranch—*locale* CA-9
Metcalf Range—*range* NY-2
*Metcalfs* MA-1
**Metcalfs**—*pop pl* MA-1
*Metcalfs Brook* CT-1
Metcalf Sch—*school* CA-9
Metcalf Sch—*school* MA-1
Metcalf Sch (abandoned)—*school* MO-7
Metcalf Sch (historical)—*school* MS-4
Metcalf Sch (historical)—*school* MO-7
Metcalf Siding—*locale* NY-2
Metcalf (site)—*locale* AZ-5
Metcalf Slough—*stream* WA-9
*Metcalfs Mill* AL-4
Metcalf South Shop Ctr—*locale* KS-7

Metcalf Spring—spring ID-8
Metcalf Spring—spring UT-8
Metcalf State Wildlife Mngmt Area—park NE-7
Metcalf Wildlife Marsh—reservoir RI-1
Metcalf Wildlife Marsh Dam—dam RI-1
Metcalf 75 Shop Ctr—locale KS-7
Metcall Cem—cemetery MO-7
**Metea**—pop pl IN-6
Metea Ch—church IN-6
**Metedeconk**—pop pl NJ-2
Metedeconk Lake NJ-2
Metedeconk Neck—cape NJ-2
**Metedeconk Park**—pop pl NJ-2
**Metedeconk Pines**—pop pl NJ-2
Metedeconk River NJ-2
Metedeconk River—stream NJ-2
Metediu FM-9
Meteer Lake—lake IN-6
Meteer Spring—spring OR-9
Meteer Store House—hist pl DE-2
Meteochol PW-9
**Meteolchol**—pop pl PW-9
Meteor—locale ID-8
Meteor—locale WA-9
**Meteor**—pop pl ID-8
**Meteor**—pop pl WI-6
Meteor City—locale AZ-5
Meteor Crater—crater AZ-5
Meteor Crater Interchange—crossing AZ-5
Meteor Crater Ranch—locale AZ-5
Meteor Crater Rest Area—park AZ-5
Meteor Hill—summit WI-6
Meteor Hills Radio Tower—locale WI-6
Meteorite Crater—crater NV-8
Meteorite Mountain AZ-5
Meteorite Mtn—summit AK-9
Meteorite Tank—reservoir CA-9
Meteor Lake—lake CA-9
Meteor Mountain AZ-5
Meteorokoru PW-9
Meteor Peak—summit AK-9
Meteor Tank—reservoir AZ-5
Meteor Tank—reservoir TX-5
Meteorukoru PW-9
METEOR (Whaleback carrier)—hist pl WI-6
Meter—locale VA-3
Meter Bight—bay AK-9
Meter Meadow—flat CA-9
Meter Station—other OR-9
Metervik Bay—bay AK-9
Metetcunk River NJ-2
Metetecunk River NJ-2
Meteu 'L Klechem—hist pl PW-9
Meteulogol PW-9
Metew PW-9
Metewemesick MA-1
Metford, Town of MA-1
Methacton HS—school PA-2
Methacton Senior HS PA-2
Metham—locale OH-6
Metham Sch (historical)—school MO-7
Metheglin Creek—stream TX-5
Metheny Park—flat CO-8
Methnen Central Sch—school MA-1
**Method**—pop pl NC-3
Methodist Airp—airport TN-4
Methodist Branch—stream WV-2
Methodist Camp—locale AZ-5
**Methodist Camp**—pop pl IA-7
Methodist Camp Ground ME-1
Methodist Camp Ground Cem—cemetery TN-4
Methodist Camp Lake—reservoir NC-3
Methodist Camp Lake Dam—dam NC-3
Methodist Cem—cemetery (3) MS-4
Methodist Cem—cemetery (5) MO-7
Methodist Cem—cemetery (2) WI-6
Methodist Ch—church KS-7
Methodist Ch—church MS-4
Methodist Ch—church NC-3
Methodist Ch—church WI-6
Methodist Chapel—church MS-4
Methodist Childrens Home—building AL-4
Methodist Childrens Home—locale NC-3
Methodist Ch of Micanopy—church FL-3
Methodist Ch Parkwny United—church FL-3
Methodist Church—hist pl AR-4
Methodist Church—hist pl MA-1
Methodist Church—hist pl NY-2
Methodist Church, Old—hist pl OH-6
Methodist Church, The—church LA-4
Methodist Church-Big Pine United—church FL-3
Methodist Church Concord—hist pl TX-5
Methodist Church of Marshall—hist pl OK-5
Methodist Coll—school NC-3
Methodist Conference Grounds—other MO-7
Methodist Cove—bay NE-7
Methodist Creek—stream AZ-5
Methodist Creek—stream CA-9
Methodist Creek—stream ID-8
Methodist Creek—stream NE-7
Methodist Creek—stream WY-8
Methodist Early Childhood Education—school FL-3
Methodist Episcopal Ch (historical)—church (2) SD-7
Methodist Episcopal Church—hist pl AZ-5
Methodist Episcopal Church—hist pl CT-1
Methodist Episcopal Church—hist pl ID-8
Methodist Episcopal Church—hist pl KY-4
Methodist Episcopal Church—hist pl MN-6
Methodist Episcopal Church—hist pl MT-8
Methodist Episcopal Church—hist pl NY-2
Methodist Episcopal Church—hist pl OH-6
Methodist Episcopal Church—hist pl SD-7
Methodist-Episcopal Church—hist pl VT-1
Methodist Episcopal Church—hist pl WY-8
Methodist Episcopal Church, South—hist pl AL-4
Methodist Episcopal Church, South—hist pl (2) OK-5
Methodist Episcopal Church and Parsonage—hist pl MT-8
Methodist Episcopal Church at Half Moon Bay—hist pl CA-9
Methodist-Episcopal Church of Marysville—hist pl MT-8
Methodist Episcopal Church of Payette—hist pl ID-8
Methodist Episcopal Church of Pescadero—hist pl CA-9
Methodist Episcopal Church of West Martinsburg—hist pl NY-2
Methodist Episcopal Church Parsonage—hist pl MI-6
Methodist Episcopal Church South—hist pl KY-4
Methodist Episcopal Church South—hist pl (2) OR-9
Methodist Episcopal Parsonage—hist pl OR-9
Methodist Epscopal Church of Port Hadlock—hist pl WA-9
Methodist Farm—locale NY-2
Methodist Grove Cem—cemetery IA-7
Methodist Gulch—valley ID-8
Methodist Hill—summit NH-1
Methodist Hill—summit NY-2
Methodist Hill—summit PA-2
Methodist Hill Sch—school NH-1
**Methodist (historical)**—pop pl TN-4
Methodist Hollow—valley NY-2
Methodist Home for Children—building PA-2
Methodist Home Park—park NC-3
Methodist Hosp—hospital CA-9
Methodist Hosp—hospital FL-3
Methodist Hosp—hospital IN-6
Methodist Hosp—hospital KY-4
Methodist Hosp—hospital MN-6
Methodist Hosp—hospital (2) MS-4
Methodist Hospital Helistop—airport IN-6
Methodist Hosp of Dyersburg—hospital TN-4
Methodist Hosp of McKenzie—hospital TN-4
Methodist Hosp of Middle Mississippi—hospital MS-4
Methodist Hosp of Middle Tennessee TN-4
Methodist Hosp of Stone County—hospital MS-4
Methodist Manse—hist pl AR-4
Methodist Med Ctr of Oak Ridge—hospital TN-4
Methodist Memorial Ch—church AL-4
**Methodist Memorial Home**—pop pl IN-6
Methodist Mesa—summit AZ-5
Methodist Mesa Tank—reservoir AZ-5
Methodist Mission Home—other TX-5
Methodist Mission Parsonage—hist pl OR-9
Methodist Mission Res—park MI-6
Methodist Mission Sch—school AL-4
Methodist Mtn AZ-5
Methodist Mtn—summit AZ-5
Methodist Mtn—summit CO-8
Methodist Parsonage—hist pl AZ-5
Methodist Parsonage, Old—hist pl OH-6
Methodist Parsonage House—hist pl MS-4
Methodist-Protestant Campgrounds—locale MS-4
Methodist Ridge—ridge OH-6
Methodist Sch—school CA-9
Methodist Sch—school TX-5
Methodist Tabernacle—hist pl GA-3
Methodist Tabernacle—hist pl VA-3
Methodist Training Camp—locale PA-2
Methodist Univ AL-4
Methodonia Ch—church LA-4
Methol—locale NY-2
**Methow**—pop pl WA-9
Methow Cem—cemetery WA-9
Methow Pass—gap WA-9
Methow Rapids—rapids WA-9
Methow River ID-8
Methow River—stream WA-9
Methow Street Park—park WA-9
Methow Valley—valley WA-9
Methow Valley (CCD)—cens area WA-9
Methow Valley State Airp—airport WA-9
**Methuen**—pop pl MA-1
Methuen Falls MA-1
Methuen Mall—locale MA-1
Methuen Memorial Music Hall—hist pl MA-1
**Methuen (Town of)**—pop pl MA-1
Methuen Water Works—hist pl MA-1
Methven Drain—canal MI-6
Methvin—locale LA-4
Methvin Cem—cemetery GA-3
Methvin Memorial Mission—church OK-5
Methvins—locale GA-3
Metias Tank—reservoir AZ-5
Metier Cem—cemetery IA-7
Metigoshe Lake—lake ND-7
Metiki, Cape FM-9
Metina Cem—cemetery TX-5
Metinic Green Island—island ME-1
Metinic Island—island ME-1
Metinic Island Ledge—bar ME-1
Metipw, Dolen—summit FM-9
Metipw En Awak—locale FM-9
Metipw En Uh—locale FM-9
Metiticonk River NJ-2
Metitiu FM-9
Metiul Einfahrt PW-9
Metjodo MP-9
Metjeol FM-9
Metlakahtla (Metlakatla)—other AK-9
**Metlakatla**—pop pl AK-9
Metlako Falls—falls OR-9
Metlar House—hist pl NJ-2
Metleol FM-9
Metler Ridge—ridge PA-2
Metlock Hills TX-5
Meto—locale AR-4
Meto, Bayou—stream AR-4
Metocinah Creek IN-6
Metocinah Creek—stream IN-6
Meto Creek—stream MI-6
Metocunk River NJ-2
Metogga Lake—lake MN-6
Metolenim Hafen FM-9
**Metolius**—pop pl OR-9
Metolius Bench—bench OR-9
Metolius Canyon—valley OR-9
Metolius River—stream OR-9
Metolius Spring—spring OR-9
**Metomen (Town of)**—pop pl WI-6
Metomkin VA-3
**Metomkin**—pop pl VA-3
Metomkin Bay VA-3
Metomkin Inlet VA-3
Metomkin Island VA-3
Metomkin Point—cape VA-3
**Metompkin**—pop pl VA-3
Metompkin Bay—bay VA-3
Metompkin Ch—church VA-3
Metompkin Inlet—bay VA-3
Metompkin Islands—island VA-3
Metompkin (Magisterial District)—fmr MCD VA-3
Metonga, Lake—lake IL-6
Metonga Lake—reservoir WI-6
Metonia MS-4
Metorikku MP-9
Metorikku Island MP-9
Metorikku Island—island MP-9
Metorikku-To MP-9
Metory—locale OK-5
Metory Spring—spring OK-5
Metote Pit Tank—reservoir AZ-5
Motour Gulch MT-8
Metralla Canyon—valley CA-9
**Metreco**—pop pl WA-9
Metro—post sta CA-9
Metro-Aire Industrial Park—locale TN-4
Metro Airport Industrial Park—locale MS-4
Metro Airport South Terminal—post sta MI-6
Metro Center—post sta AZ-5
Metrocenter Mall Shop Ctr—locale MS-4
Metro Center Metro Station—locale DC-2
Metrocenter Shop Ctr—locale AZ-5
Metrofania Creek—stream AK-9
Metro Industrial Park—locale MS-4
Metrolina Fairgrounds—locale NC-3
**Metro Main**—pop pl CA-9
Metro-Meridian HS—school KS-7
Metro North Mall—locale MO-7
**Metropark**—pop pl NJ-2
**Metro Park (subdivision)**—pop pl TN-4
Metropilitan Park—park OK-5
**Metropolis**—pop pl IL-6
**Metropolis**—pop pl LA-4
Metropolis Cem—cemetery NV-8
Metropolis Country Club—other IL-6
Metropolis Country Club—other NY-2
Metropolis Junction IL-6
Metropolis Lake—lake KY-4
Metropolis No. 1 (Election Precinct)—fmr MCD IL-6
Metropolis No. 2 (Election Precinct)—fmr MCD IL-6
Metropolis No. 3 (Election Precinct)—fmr MCD IL-6
Metropolis No. 4 (Election Precinct)—fmr MCD IL-6
Metropolis Post Office (historical)—building AL-4
Metropolis Reservoir NV-8
Metropolis (Site)—locale NV-8
Metropolitan—locale CA-9
Metropolitan—locale MI-6
Metropolitan—uninc pl CA-9
Metropolitan—uninc pl NY-2
Metropolitan African Methodist Episcopal Church—hist pl DC-2
Metropolitan Airport—other MI-6
Metropolitan AME Ch—church AL-4
Metropolitan Apartments—hist pl NE-7
Metropolitan Atlanta Industrial Park—facility GA-3
Metropolitan Baptist Ch—church FL-3
Metropolitan Baptist Ch—church KS-7
Metropolitan Baptist Ch—church MS-4
Metropolitan Bar—bar MT-8
Metropolitan Beach—park MI-6
Metropolitan Block—hist pl OH-6
Metropolitan Camps—locale NY-2
Metropolitan Ch—church (2) FL-3
Metropolitan Ch—church MD-2
Metropolitan Ch—church NC-3
Metropolitan Ch—church SC-3
Metropolitan Ch—church VA-3
Metropolitan Community Ch—church FL-3
Metropolitan Community Ch—church KS-7
Metropolitan Community Ch of Indianapolis—church IN-6
Metropolitan Community Church-Joy—church FL-3
Metropolitan Correctional Center (Federal Bureau of Prisons)—locale FL-3
Metropolitan Dade Agriculture Center—building FL-3
Metropolitan Dade Police Training Center—locale FL-3
Metropolitan District Commission Pumping House—hist pl MA-1
Metropolitan District Commission Stable—hist pl MA-1
Metropolitan Edison Airp—airport PA-2
Metropolitan Edison Bldg—hist pl PA-2
Metropolitan Edison Three Mile Island Airp—airport PA-2
Metropolitan General Hosp—hospital FL-3
**Metropolitan Government (CCD)**—pop pl TN-4
Metropolitan Government Division—civil TN-4
Metropolitan Grove—locale MD-2
Metropolitan Hosp—hospital NY-2
Metropolitan Hosp—hospital TN-4
Metropolitan Hosp Springfield Division—hospital PA-2
Metropolitan HS—school AR-4
Metropolitan HS—school CA-9
Metropolitan Junior Coll—school CA-9
Metropolitan Junior Coll—school KS-7
Metropolitan Junior Coll—school MO-7
Metropolitan Life Insurance Company—hist pl NY-2
Metropolitan Memorial Park—cemetery MI-6
Metropolitan Museum of Art—building NY-2
Metropolitan Museum of Art—hist pl NY-2
Metropolitan Oakland International Airp—airport CA-9
Metropolitan Opera House—hist pl IA-7
Metropolitan Opera House—hist pl PA-2
Metropolitan Park—park (2) OH-6
Metropolitan Savings Bank—hist pl NY-2
Metropolitan Stadium—other MN-6
Metropolitan State Hosp—hospital CA-9
Metropolitan State Hosp—hospital MA-1
Metropolitan State Junior Coll—school MN-6
Metropolitan Tabernacle—church TX-5
Metropolitan Theatre—hist pl MA-1
Metropolitan Theatre—hist pl WV-2
Metropolitan United Methodist Ch—church DE-2
Metropolitan United Methodist Church—hist pl MI-6
Metropolitan Youth Education Center—school CO-8
Metropolitan Zoo—park FL-3
Metro Sch of Gymnastics—school MS-4
Metro South Hist Dist—hist pl CT-1
Metroz Lake—reservoir CO-8
Metroz Mtn—summit CO-8
Metser Creek—stream MI-6
Metsker Spring—spring OR-9
**Mettacahonts**—pop pl NY-2
Mettacahonts Creek—stream NY-2
Mettah Creek—stream CA-9
Metta Lake WA-9
Mettallack Island NH-1
Mettalock Brook ME-1
Mettam Memorial Baptist Church—hist pl MD-2
Mettapaset MA-1
Mettasaset MA-1
**Mettawa**—pop pl IL-6
Mettawee, The—summit VT-1
Mettawee River—stream NY-2
Mettawee River—stream VT-1
Mettawee Valley Cem—cemetery NY-2
Mettawee Valley Cem—cemetery VT-1
Mett Bay—swamp GA-3
Mettconk River NJ-2
Metteer Canyon—valley OR-9
Mettel Field—airport IN-6
Mettenpherg Creek—stream AK-9
**Metter**—pop pl GA-3
Metter (CCD)—cens area GA-3
Mettetal Sch—school MI-6
Mettick Creek—stream CA-9
Mett Lake MN-6
**Mettler**—pop pl CA-9
**Mettler**—pop pl NJ-2
Mettler Coulee—valley MT-8
Mettman Creek—stream OR-9
Metton Pond—lake MD-2
Metton Pond Creek—stream MD-2
Mettowee River NY-2
Mettowee River VT-1
Metts Bluff—cliff FL-3
Metts Creek—stream FL-3
Metts Pond—lake FL-3
**Metuchen**—pop pl NJ-2
Metuchen HS—school NJ-2
Metuchen Station—locale NJ-2
Metuchen Yard—locale NJ-2
Metuck Springs—spring AZ-5
Metuck Tank—reservoir AZ-5
Metuker Bay PW-9
Metuker Petikl Bay PW-9
Metuker Risong PW-9
Metukeruikull—summit PW-9
Metum—locale WA-9
Metz OK-5
Metz—locale CA-9
Metz—locale IA-7
Metz—locale TX-5
Metz—locale WI-6
**Metz**—pop pl IN-6
**Metz**—pop pl MI-6
**Metz**—pop pl MO-7
**Metz**—pop pl WV-2
Metz Airp—airport PA-2
Metz Branch—stream SC-3
Metz Canyon—valley CO-8
Metz Cem—cemetery IN-6
Metz Cem—cemetery TN-4
Metz Cem—cemetery WV-2
Metz Creek—stream CO-8
Metz Creek—stream IL-6
Metz Creek—stream IA-7
Metz Creek—stream MS-4
Metz Ditch—canal ID-8
Metzelaar Bay—bay MI-6
Metzel Creek—stream MT-8
Metzel Ranch—locale MT-8
Metzel West Side Ditch—canal MT-8
Metz Gap—gap KY-4
Metzgar OR-9
Metzgar Cem—cemetery OH-6
Metzgar Elem Sch—school PA-2
**Metzger**—pop pl OH-6
**Metzger**—pop pl OR-9
Metzger, Charles, Mound—hist pl OH-6
Metzger Cem—cemetery IN-6
Metzger Creek—stream TX-5
Metzger House—hist pl AL-4
Metzger Lake—lake WI-6
Metzger Lake—reservoir TX-5
Metzger Marsh Wildlife Area—park OH-6
Metzger Pond—lake IN-6
Metzger Ranch—locale NE-7
Metzger Sch—school (2) MI-6
Metzger Sch—school OR-9
Metzgers Indian Cave—cave PA-2
Metzger Tank—reservoir AZ-5
Metzger Trail—trail PA-2
Metzgerville—locale SD-7
Metzger Windmill—locale TX-5
Metz Hill Cem—cemetery OR-9
Metz (historical)—locale KS-7
Metz Hollow—valley UT-8
Metzig Garden Site (47WN283)—hist pl WI-6
Metz Lake—lake IL-6
Metz Lake—reservoir IN-6
**Metzler**—pop pl PA-2
Metzler Airp—airport PA-2
Metzler Brook—stream NJ-2
Metzler Creek—stream OR-9
Metzlers Brook NJ-2
Metzler Sch—school CA-9
Metzler Sch—school PA-2
Metzner Ditch—canal IN-6
Metz Oil Field—oilfield TX-5
Metz Park—park TX-5
Metz Pond—lake NY-2
Metz Ranch—locale NE-7
Metz Run Overlook—locale VA-3
Metz Sch—school CO-8
Metz Sch—school IL-6
Metz Sch—school NE-7
Metz Sch—school TX-5
Metz Spring—spring SD-7
Metz Springs—spring CO-8
Metz Tank—reservoir AZ-5
**Metz Township**—pop pl MO-7
**Metz (Township of)**—pop pl MI-6
Met 75 Shops—locale KS-7
Meungs PW-9
Meungs, Bkul A—cape PW-9
Meuret Airstrip—airport OR-9
Meusebach Cem—cemetery TX-5
Meusebach Creek—stream (2) TX-5
Meusebach Mtn—summit TX-5
Meusebach Sch—school TX-5
Meuser Park—park PA-2
Meuset Creek MA-1
Meuwissen Lake—lake MN-6
Meux Corner—locale TN-4
Meux Hill—summit TN-4
Meux House—hist pl CA-9
Meva Cove—valley VA-3
**Meva (historical)**—pop pl OR-9
**Mevers**—pop pl CA-9
Mew—bar FM-9
Mew—locale VA-3
M E Wash—valley AZ-5
Mewborn Crossroads NC-3
Mewborns Crossroads—locale NC-3
Mew Cem—cemetery SC-3
Mew Cove—bay AK-9
Mewhinney Cem—cemetery (2) IN-6
Mewhinney Creek—stream CA-9
Mew Sch—school VA-3
Mewshaw—locale TX-5
**Mexboro**—pop pl AL-4
Mex Creek—stream ID-8
Mexhoma—locale OK-5
Mexhoma Ch—church OK-5
**Mexia**—pop pl AL-4
**Mexia**—pop pl TX-5
Mexia, Lake—reservoir TX-5
Mexia (CCD)—cens area TX-5
Mexia Country Club—other TX-5
Mexia Creek—stream (2) TX-5
**Mexia Crossing**—pop pl AL-4
Mexia Oil Field—oilfield TX-5
Mexia State Sch—school TX-5
Mexican American Baptist Ch—church KS-7
Mexican Baptist Ch—church KS-7
Mexican Bend—bend TX-5
Mexican Bend—bend UT-8
Mexican Butte—summit NV-8
Mexican Cabin Spring—spring CO-8
Mexican Calvary Ch—church MI-6
Mexican Camp—locale CA-9
Mexican Camp (Site)—locale NV-8
Mexican Canyon—valley (3) AZ-5
Mexican Canyon—valley CA-9
Mexican Canyon—valley (2) CO-8
Mexican Canyon—valley (4) NM-5
Mexican Canyon—valley UT-8
Mexican Canyon Trestle—hist pl NM-5
Mexican Cem—cemetery MS-4
Mexican Cem—cemetery (3) TX-5
**Mexican Colony**—pop pl CA-9
Mexican Consulate—building AZ-5
Mexican Consulate—hist pl AZ-5
Mexican Cooking Canyon—valley NM-5
Mexican Creek—stream CO-8
Mexican Creek—stream SD-7
Mexican Creek—stream (4) TX-5
Mexican Creek—stream (2) WY-8
Mexican Cry Mesa—summit AZ-5
Mexican Cry Mine—mine AZ-5
Mexican Dam—dam AZ-5
Mexican Dam—dam NV-8
Mexican Ditch—canal CO-8
Mexican Ditch—canal NV-8
Mexican Ditch—canal (2) NM-5
Mexican Draw—valley (3) WY-8
Mexican Embassy Bldg—building DC-2
Mexican Field—flat NV-8
Mexican Flat—flat WY-8
Mexican Flats—flat WY-8
Mexican Flats Rsvr No 1—reservoir WY-8
Mexican Gap—gap TX-5
Mexican Gulch—valley AZ-5
Mexican Gulch—valley (2) CA-9
Mexican Gulch—valley (2) CO-8
Mexican Gulch—valley MT-8
Mexican Gulf Canal LA-4
Mexican Gully—valley TX-5
**Mexican Hat**—pop pl UT-8
Mexican Hat—summit NM-5
Mexican Hat Hill—summit TX-5
Mexican Hat Mtn—summit AZ-5
Mexican Hat Rock—pillar UT-8
Mexican Hat Sch—school UT-8
Mexican Hay Lake—reservoir AZ-5
Mexican Hay Lake Dam—dam AZ-5
Mexican Hill—summit NM-5
Mexican Hill—summit TX-5
Mexican Hill—summit WY-8
Mexican Hollow—valley AZ-5
Mexican Hollow—valley (2) TX-5
Mexican Hollow—valley UT-8
Mexican Hollow Wash—stream AZ-5
Mexican Jack Tank—reservoir AZ-5
Mexican Joe Creek—stream MT-8
Mexican Joe Gulch—valley CO-8
Mexican Joe Hill—summit WY-8
Mexican Joe Tank—reservoir AZ-5
Mexican John Creek—stream MT-8
Mexican Lake—lake AZ-5
Mexican Lake—lake CO-8
Mexican Lake—lake NM-5
Mexican Lakes—lake WY-8
Mexican Lake Wells—well NM-5
Mexican Mine—mine (3) CA-9
Mexican Mine Canyon—valley AZ-5
Mexican Mtn—summit UT-8
Mexican-Nest Tank—reservoir AZ-5
Mexican Park—flat CO-8
Mexican Pass—gap WY-8
Mexican Place—locale ID-8
Mexican Place—locale WY-8
Mexican Pocket—basin AZ-5
Mexican Prisoners Grave—cemetery TX-5
Mexican Rest Peak—summit AZ-5
Mexican Rest Spring—spring AZ-5
Mexican Ridge—ridge (2) CO-8
Mexican Rsvr—reservoir CO-8
Mexican Saddle (historical)—summit AZ-5
Mexican Seep—spring AZ-5
Mexican Seep—spring UT-8
Mexican Sink—flat AZ-5
Mexican Spring—spring (2) AZ-5
Mexican Spring—spring (2) CA-9
Mexican Spring—spring (2) CO-8
Mexican Spring—spring (2) NV-8
Mexican Spring—spring (2) TX-5
Mexican Spring—spring WY-8
**Mexican Springs**—pop pl NM-5
Mexican Springs—spring NM-5
Mexican Springs—stream WY-8
Mexican Springs Branch Greasewood Arroyo—stream CO-8
**Mexican Springs (Nakaibito)**—pop pl NM-5
Mexican Spring Wash—stream NM-5
Mexican Tank AZ-5
Mexican Tank—locale AZ-5
Mexican Tank—reservoir (8) AZ-5
Mexican Tank—reservoir (2) NM-5
Mexican Tank—reservoir TX-5
**Mexican Town**—pop pl AZ-5
Mexican War Streets—locale PA-2
Mexican War Streets Historic District, —hist pl PA-2
Mexican Water—locale AZ-5
Mexican Water Rec Area—park AZ-5
Mexican Water Spring—spring CA-9
Mexican Water Trading Post—locale AZ-5
Mexican Well—well CA-9
Mexican Well—well (2) NM-5
Mexican Well—well TX-5
Mexico—locale PA-2
**Mexico**—pop pl IN-6
**Mexico**—pop pl KY-4
**Mexico**—pop pl ME-1
**Mexico**—pop pl MD-2
**Mexico**—pop pl MO-7
**Mexico**—pop pl NY-2
**Mexico**—pop pl OH-6
**Mexico**—pop pl PA-2
**Mexico**—pop pl SC-3
**Mexico**—pop pl TX-5
Mexico, Gulf of—bay AL-4
Mexico, Gulf of—bay FL-3
Mexico, Gulf Of—bay MS-4
Mexico, Gulf of—bay TX-5
Mexico, Mount—summit NH-1
Mexico Bay—bay NY-2
**Mexico Beach**—pop pl FL-3
Mexico Beach (CCD)—cens area FL-3
Mexico Bottom—bend IN-6
Mexico Cem—cemetery SC-3
Mexico Center (census name Mexico)—other ME-1
Mexico Country Club—other MO-7
Mexico Creek WI-6
Mexico Creek—stream OK-5
Mexico Creek—stream WI-6
Mexico Crossing—locale GA-3
Mexico (historical)—civil DC-2
Mexico Hollow—valley WV-2
Mexico HS—school ME-1
Mexico Memorial Airp—airport MO-7
Mexico Mines—mine CO-8
Mexico Point—cape AK-9
Mexico Point—cape NY-2
Mexico Point—cape UT-8
Mexico Primitive Cem—cemetery NY-2
Mexico Ridge—ridge CA-9
Mexico Ridge—ridge IN-6
Mexico Ridge Trail—trail NH-1
Mexico Sch—school KY-4
Mexico Sch (historical)—school PA-2
**Mexico (Town of)**—pop pl ME-1
**Mexico (Town of)**—pop pl NY-2
Mex-i-min-e Falls—falls MI-6
Mex Mtn—summit ID-8
Mey FM-9
Meyano Creek KS-7
Meydenbauer Bay—bay WA-9
Meyer—locale IL-6
**Meyer**—pop pl (3) IL-6
**Meyer**—pop pl IA-7
**Meyer**—pop pl OK-5
Meyer—uninc pl GA-3
Meyer, August, House—hist pl MO-7
Meyer, Frederick A. E., House—hist pl UT-8
Meyer, Henry A., House—hist pl WI-6
Meyer, Incorporated (Warehouse)—facility MI-6
Meyer, Joseph Ernest, House—hist pl IN-6
Meyer, Lake—lake IA-7
Meyer, Lake—lake MN-6
Meyer, Maurice, Barracks—hist pl OK-5
Meyer, R. W., Sugar Mill—hist pl HI-9
Meyer, Starke, House—hist pl WI-6
Meyer Airp—airport PA-2
Meyer Basin—basin WY-8
Meyer Bayou—gut TX-5
Meyer Branch TN-4
Meyer Branch—stream AR-4
**Meyer Camp**—pop pl HI-9
Meyer Canyon TX-5
Meyer Canyon—valley CA-9
Meyer Cem—cemetery AL-4
Meyer Cem—cemetery IN-6
Meyer Cem—cemetery IA-7
Meyer Cem—cemetery MI-6
Meyer Cem—cemetery (2) MO-7
Meyer Cem—cemetery (2) PA-2
Meyer Cem—cemetery (3) TX-5
Meyer Ch—church PA-2
Meyer Clinic—hospital IL-6
**Meyercord**—pop pl WV-2
Meyer County (historical)—civil SD-7
Meyer Creek ID-8
Meyer Creek MT-8
Meyer Creek OR-9
Meyer Creek—stream AK-9
Meyer Creek—stream OR-9
Meyer Ditch—canal (2) IN-6
Meyer Ditch—canal OH-6
Meyer Grove Ch—church TN-4
Meyer Gulch—valley (2) CA-9
Meyer Gulch—valley (2) ID-8
Meyer Hill—summit MT-8

Meyerhofer Cobblestone House—*hist pl* WI-6
Meyerhoff, John, House—*hist pl* NJ-2
Meyerholz Lake—*lake* IA-7
Meyerholz Sch—*school* CA-9
Meyer House—*hist pl* MO-7
Meyer House—*hist pl* OH-6
Meyer House—*hist pl* WA-9
Meyering Park—*park* IL-6
Meyer Lake—*lake* HI-9
Meyer Lake—*lake* MI-6
Meyer Lake—*lake* (2) MN-6
Meyer Lake—*lake* MT-8
Meyer Lake—*lake* SC-3
Meyer Lake—*lake* (3) WI-6
Meyer Lake—*reservoir* IN-6
Meyer Lake Dam—*dam* (2) IN-6
Meyer Lakes—*lake* NE-7
**Meyerland**—*pop pl* TX-5
Meyerland Shop Ctr—*locale* TX-5
Meyer Lookout—*summit* WY-8
*Meyerly Spring Cave* PA-2
**Meyer Manor**—*pop pl* MD-2
*Meyer Mill* TN-4
Meyer Mtn—*summit* MT-8
Meyer No 2 Sch—*school* IL-6
Meyer Park—*park* AZ-5
Meyer Park—*park* TX-5
Meyer Park—*park* (2) WI-6
Meyer Pond—*lake* IN-6
Meyer Ranch—*locale* TX-5
Meyer Ranch—*locale* WA-9
Meyer Ravine—*valley* CA-9
Meyer Ridge—*ridge* WA-9
Meyer Riverside Airpark—*airport* OR-9
Meyers—*locale* AR-4
Meyers—*locale* CA-9
Meyers—*other* CA-9
**Meyers**—*pop pl* MS-4
Meyers, Albertus L., Bridge—*hist pl* PA-2
Meyers, Elias, House—*hist pl* MI-6
*Meyers and Tolles Addition* UT-8
*Meyers Bay* MS-4
Meyers Bay—*bay* MN-6
**Meyers Bay**—*pop pl* IL-6
*Meyers Bay Creek* MS-4
Meyers Bayou—*gut* LA-4
Meyers Bayou—*stream* MS-4
**Meyers Beach**—*pop pl* MI-6
Meyers Bend Ch—*church* LA-4
*Meyers Bluff* AL-4
Meyers Branch—*stream* MO-7
Meyers Branch—*stream* SC-3
Meyers Branch—*stream* TN-4
Meyers Branch—*stream* TX-5
Meyersburg Sch—*school* MT-8
Meyers Butte—*summit* OR-9
Meyers Cabin—*locale* CA-9
Meyers Canal—*canal* LA-4
*Meyers Canyon* TX-5
Meyers Canyon—*valley* CA-9
Meyers Canyon—*valley* OR-9
Meyers Canyon—*valley* TX-5
Meyers Cem—*cemetery* CO-8
Meyers Cem—*cemetery* IL-6
Meyers Cem—*cemetery* KS-7
Meyers Cem—*cemetery* MI-6
Meyers Cem—*cemetery* MO-7
Meyers Cem—*cemetery* OR-9
Meyers Cem—*cemetery* TN-4
Meyers Cem—*cemetery* (2) WV-2
Meyers Ch—*church* WV-2
Meyer Sch—*school* AZ-5
Meyer Sch—*school* CA-9
Meyer Sch—*school* DC-2
Meyer Sch—*school* LA-4
Meyer Sch—*school* (2) SD-7
Meyer Sch—*school* TX-5
Meyers Chuck—*bay* AK-9
**Meyers Chuck**—*pop pl* AK-9
Meyers Corner—*locale* CO-8
Meyers Corners—*locale* (2) NY-2
Meyers Cove—*basin* ID-8
Meyers Cove—*bay* FL-3
Meyers Cove Point—*cliff* ID-8
*Meyers Creek* ID-8
*Meyers Creek* MS-4
*Meyers Creek* NV-8
Meyers Creek—*locale* MT-8
Meyers Creek—*stream* AR-4
Meyers Creek—*stream* CA-9
Meyers Creek—*stream* (3) MT-8
Meyers Creek—*stream* (2) WI-6
Meyers Creek Ch—*church* AR-4
**Meyersdale**—*pop pl* PA-2
Meyersdale Airp—*airport* PA-2
Meyersdale Borough—*civil* PA-2
Meyersdale HS—*school* PA-2
Meyers Dam—*dam* MT-8
Meyers Ditch—*canal* IN-6
Meyers Drain—*canal* MI-6
Meyers Draw—*valley* KS-7
Meyers Draw—*valley* TX-5
Meyers Falls—*falls* WA-9
Meyers Falls Cem—*cemetery* WA-9
Meyers Falls Rsvr—*reservoir* WA-9
*Meyers Flat* CA-9
Meyers Fork—*stream* KY-4
Meyers Fork Sch—*school* KY-4
*Meyers Gulch* CO-8
Meyers Gulch—*valley* CO-8
Meyers Gulch—*valley* (3) MT-8
Meyers Gulch—*valley* WY-8
*Meyers Hill* PA-2
Meyers Hill—*summit* MT-8
Meyers Hill—*summit* NY-2
Meyers Hill—*summit* OR-9
Meyers Hollow—*valley* (2) MO-7
Meyers Hollow—*valley* OH-6
Meyers HS—*school* PA-2
Meyers Island—*island* AK-9
Meyer Site—*hist pl* MD-2
*Meyers Lake* AL-4
*Meyers Lake* IL-6
Meyers Lake—*lake* IL-6
Meyers Lake—*lake* IA-7
Meyers Lake—*lake* MI-6
Meyers Lake—*lake* MN-6
Meyers Lake—*lake* WI-6
**Meyers Lake**—*pop pl* OH-6
Meyers Lake Dam—*dam* SD-7
Meyers Lakes—*reservoir* NJ-2
*Meyers Landing* CA-9
*Meyers Landing* TN-4
Meyer Slough—*gut* IL-6
Meyer Slough—*lake* SD-7
**Meyers Mill**—*pop pl* SC-3
Meyers Mill (historical)—*locale* TN-4
Meyers Mtn—*summit* PA-2
Meyers Park—*park* CA-9
Meyers Park—*park* TX-5
Meyers Peak—*summit* CA-9
Meyers Place—*locale* (2) CA-9
Meyers Pond—*lake* IL-6
Meyers Pond—*lake* NJ-2
Meyers Pond—*lake* NY-2
Meyers Pond—*lake* OR-9
Meyers Pond—*reservoir* CT-1
*Meyer Spring* CA-9
Meyer Spring—*spring* NM-5
Meyers Ranch—*locale* CA-9
Meyers Ranch—*locale* WY-8
Meyers-Rapstad-Rudd Ditch—*canal* MT-8
Meyers Ravine—*valley* CA-9
*Meyers Ridge* TN-4
Meyers Ridge—*ridge* WY-8
Meyers Rsvr—*reservoir* NV-8
Meyers Run—*stream* PA-2
Meyers Sch—*school* AZ-5
Meyers Sch—*school* CA-9
Meyers Sch—*school* (2) IL-6
Meyers Sch—*school* MI-6
Meyers Sch—*school* (2) PA-2
Meyers Sch—*school* WI-6
Meyers Sch (abandoned)—*school* SD-7
Meyers Speedway—*other* TX-5
Meyers Spring—*spring* CA-9
Meyers Spring—*spring* MO-7
Meyers Spring—*spring* NV-8
Meyers Spring—*spring* TX-5
Meyers Springs Pictograph Site—*hist pl* TX-5
Meyers Stream—*stream* AK-9
Meyerstown—*locale* MO-7
Meyerstown—*locale* WV-2
Meyers Valley—*valley* OH-6
Meyers Valley—*valley* WI-6
*Meyersville* TX-5
Meyersville—*locale* PA-2
**Meyersville**—*pop pl* NJ-2
**Meyersville**—*pop pl* TX-5
Meyersville Cem—*cemetery* NJ-2
Meyersville Gas Field—*oilfield* TX-5
Meyers Windmill—*locale* TX-5
**Meyer Township**—*pop pl* ND-7
Meyer Township Natl Wildlife Ref—*park* ND-7
**Meyer (Township of)**—*pop pl* MI-6
Meyer Wash—*stream* AZ-5
Meyer Windmill—*locale* NM-5
**Meyhew Lake**—*pop pl* MN-6
**Meyle Estates (subdivision)**—*pop pl* DE-2
Meyler Run—*stream* PA-2
Meyler Street Sch—*school* CA-9
Meylert Creek—*stream* PA-2
Meylor Sch—*school* WI-6
Meysan Lake—*lake* CA-9
Meysan Trail—*trail* CA-9
*Meyson Lake* CA-9
Meystre Canyon—*valley* WA-9
**Meyungs**—*pop pl* PW-9
*Mezeppa* PA-2
Mezes Plaza—*park* CA-9
*Mezetchoku* MP-9
Mezetchoku Passage—*channel* MP-9
*Mezetchoku-Suido* MP-9
*Mezick Cove* MD-2
Mezick Ponds—*lake* MD-2
*Mezicks Pond* MD-2
Mezicks Pond—*reservoir* AL-4
*Mezicks Ponds* MD-2
*Mezieruen* MP-9
Mezik Creek—*stream* MI-6
Mezik Lake—*lake* MI-6
*Meziti To* MP-9
*Mezitiu* FM-9
*Meziyatto To* MP-9
*Mezquit Bay* TX-5
*Mezquite Flat* AZ-5
*Mezyuro To* MP-9
M Feist Ranch—*locale* SD-7
M F Harris Pond Dam—*dam* MS-4
M. F. H. Textiles—*facility* GA-3
M Fisher Dam—*dam* SD-7
M Flynn Ranch—*locale* ND-7
M F Mtn—*summit* CO-8
M-Four Ranch—*locale* TX-5
M F Ranch—*locale* AZ-5
M Frank Farm—*locale* TX-5
M F S Homestead Wells—*well* WY-8
M F Tucker Sch (historical)—*school* AL-4
*Mgadernal* PW-9
*M'Gees Creek* MS-4
M G L Mines—*mine* NV-8
MGM Studios—*other* CA-9
M Graham Clark Airp—*airport* (2) MO-7
M Griffin Ranch—*locale* ND-7
M Hague Dam—*dam* SD-7
*M Hall Ditch* IN-6
M Hamilton Ranch—*locale* SD-7
*M Harvey Taylor Bridge* PA-2
*Mhoon* MS-4
Mhoon Bend—*bend* AR-4
Mhoon Bend—*bend* MS-4
Mhoon Bend Revetment—*levee* MS-4
Mhoon Landing—*locale* MS-4
*Mhoons* MS-4
Mhoon Sch—*school* MS-4
Mhoons Farm Sch—*school* MS-4
**Mhoons Valley**—*pop pl* MS-4
**Mhoontown**—*pop pl* AL-4
*Mhoontown Church* AL-4
*Mhoon Valley* MS-4
M H Tank—*reservoir* AZ-5
Miacomet Pond—*lake* MA-1
Miacomet Rip—*bar* MA-1
**Miad**—*pop pl* FL-3
*Miadi Island* MP-9
Miah Maull Range—*channel* NJ-2
Miah Maull Shoal—*bar* NJ-2
*Miakka* FL-3
**Miakka**—*pop pl* FL-3
Miakka Ch—*church* FL-3
*Miakka City* FL-3
*Miakka River* FL-3
Miakka Sch House—*hist pl* FL-3
*Mialoquo Island* TN-4
Mialoquo Site—*hist pl* TN-4
Miam, Lake—*lake* AK-9
Miamarina North Pier Light—*locale* FL-3
Miamarina South Pier Light—*locale* FL-3
*Miama River* FL-3
Miam Hollow—*valley* PA-2
*Miami* OH-6
Miami—*locale* IA-7
**Miami**—*pop pl* AZ-5
**Miami**—*pop pl* FL-3
**Miami**—*pop pl* IN-6
**Miami**—*pop pl* MO-7
**Miami**—*pop pl* NM-5
**Miami**—*pop pl* OH-6
**Miami**—*pop pl* OK-5
**Miami**—*pop pl* TX-5
**Miami**—*pop pl* WV-2
Miami Aerospace Acad—*school* (2) FL-3
Miami Agricultural Sch—*school* FL-3
Miami And Erie Canal—*canal* OH-6
Miami And Erie Canal, Deep Cut—*hist pl* OH-6
Miami Arena—*locale* FL-3
Miami Bar—*bar* OR-9
Miami Beach—*beach* NJ-2
Miami Beach—*beach* WA-9
**Miami Beach**—*pop pl* FL-3
**Miami Beach**—*pop pl* MD-2
**Miami Beach**—*pop pl* MI-6
**Miami Beach**—*pop pl* NJ-2
**Miami Beach**—*pop pl* WA-9
Miami Beach Architectural District—*hist pl* FL-3
Miami Beach (CCD)—*cens area* FL-3
Miami Beach Coast Guard Base—*military* FL-3
Miami Beach First Baptist Ch—*church* FL-3
Miami Beach Recreational Youth Center—*park* FL-3
Miami Beach Senior HS—*school* FL-3
Miami Beach Theater of the Performing Arts—*building* FL-3
**Miami Bend**—*pop pl* IN-6
Miami-Biltmore Hotel—*hist pl* FL-3
Miami Bldg—*hist pl* PR-3
Miami Branch—*stream* TN-4
Miami Canal—*canal* FL-3
Miami Canal Number C-6—*canal* (2) FL-3
Miami Carol City Senior HS—*school* FL-3
Miami (CCD)—*cens area* AZ-5
Miami (CCD)—*cens area* FL-3
Miami (CCD)—*cens area* OK-5
Miami (CCD)—*cens area* TX-5
Miami Cem—*cemetery* GA-3
Miami Cem—*cemetery* IN-6
Miami Cem—*cemetery* NM-5
Miami Cem—*cemetery* (2) OH-6
Miami Central HS—*school* FL-3
Miami Ch—*church* IN-6
Miami Ch—*church* KS-7
Miami Ch—*church* NC-3
Miami Chapel Sch—*school* OH-6
Miami Childrens Hosp—*hospital* FL-3
Miami Ch of Religious Science—*church* FL-3
Miami Christian Coll—*school* FL-3
Miami Christian Sch—*school* FL-3
*Miami City* OH-6
Miami City Hospital, Bldg No. 1—*hist pl* FL-3
*Miami City Stockade* FL-3
Miami Concentrator—*locale* AZ-5
Miami Coral City HS—*school* FL-3
Miami Coral Park Senior HS—*school* FL-3
Miami Country Club—*locale* FL-3
Miami Country Day Sch—*school* FL-3
Miami County—*civil* KS-7
**Miami County**—*pop pl* IN-6
**Miami (County)**—*pop pl* OH-6
Miami County Courthouse—*hist pl* KS-7
Miami County Courthouse and Power Station—*hist pl* OH-6
Miami County State Lake—*reservoir* KS-7
Miami County State Lake Dam—*dam* KS-7
Miami County State Park—*park* KS-7
Miami Cove—*bay* OR-9
Miami Creek—*stream* CA-9
Miami Creek—*stream* MO-7
Miami Creek—*stream* NY-2
*Miami Crossing* OH-6
Miami-Dade C C Preschool Laboratory—*school* FL-3
Miami-Dade Community Coll—*school* FL-3
Miami-Dade Community College (North Campus)—*building* FL-3
Miami-Dade Community College (South Campus)—*building* FL-3
Miami-Dade Community Coll (Medical Center Campus)—*school* FL-3
Miami Dade Community Coll (North Campus)—*school* FL-3
Miami-Dade Community Coll (North Campus)—*school* FL-3
Miami-Dade Community Coll (South Campus)—*school* FL-3
Miami-Dade Community Coll (Wolfson New World Center Campus)—*school* FL-3
Miami-Dade Public Library—*building* FL-3
Miami Ditch—*canal* WY-8
Miami Dorsey Skill Center—*school* FL-3
Miami Douglas MacArthur Senior, North—*school* FL-3
Miami Douglas MacArthur Senior HS, South—*school* FL-3
Miami Drainage Ditch—*canal* MO-7
Miami East HS—*school* OH-6
Miami East JHS—*school* OH-6
Miami-Edison HS—*school* FL-3
Miami Edison MS—*school* FL-3
Miami Edison Senior HS—*hist pl* FL-3
Miami Edison Senior HS—*school* FL-3
Miami Elem Sch—*school* IN-6
Miami Erie Canal—*canal* OH-6
Miami-Erie Canal Lock No. 70—*hist pl* OH-6
Miami-Erie Canal Site Hist Dist—*hist pl* OH-6
Miami Erie Feeder Canal—*canal* OH-6
Miami Fire and Rescue Training Center—*building* FL-3
Miami Flat—*flat* AZ-5
**Miami Fort**—*pop pl* OH-6
Miami Free Zone—*building* FL-3
**Miami Gardens**—*pop pl* AZ-5
**Miami Gardens**—*pop pl* FL-3
Miami Gardens Ch of Christ—*church* FL-3
Miami Gardens Elem Sch—*school* FL-3
Miami Gardens Shopping Plaza—*locale* FL-3
Miami Gardens-Utopia-Carver—*CDP* FL-3
Miami General Hosp—*hospital* (2) FL-3
Miami Gliderport Landing Strip—*airport* FL-3
Miami Grand Prix Track—*locale* FL-3
Miami Grove—*locale* OH-6
Miami Halfway House—*building* FL-3
Miami Heart Institute—*hospital* FL-3
Miami Heights—*locale* OH-6
Miami Heights Elem Sch—*school* FL-3
Miami Hills Sch—*school* OH-6
Miami (historical)—*locale* KS-7
Miami HS—*school* AZ-5
Miami HS—*school* MO-7
Miami-Inspiration Hosp—*hospital* AZ-5
Miami Interchange—*other* OK-5
Miami International Airp—*airport* FL-3
Miami International Mall—*locale* FL-3
Miami Jackson Senior HS—*school* FL-3
Miami Jewish Home and Hosp for the Aged—*hospital* FL-3
Miami Job Corp Center—*school* FL-3
Miami Killian Senior HS—*school* FL-3
Miami Lake—*reservoir* NM-5
*Miami Lake Public Hunting Area* IA-7
**Miami Lakes**—*pop pl* FL-3
Miami Lakes Congregational Church Preschool—*school* FL-3
Miami Lakes Country Club—*locale* FL-3
Miami Lakes Elem Sch—*school* FL-3
Miami Lakes JHS—*school* FL-3
Miami Lakes Picnic Park—*park* FL-3
**Miami Lakes (subdivision)**—*pop pl* FL-3
Miami Lake State Game Mngmt Area—*area* IA-7
Miami Lakes Technical Education Center—*school* FL-3
Miami Lakes United Methodist Preschool—*school* FL-3
Miami Memorial—*cemetery* FL-3
Miami Memorial Cem—*cemetery* OH-6
Miami Memorial Park Cem—*cemetery* FL-3
Miami Military Acad (historical)—*school* FL-3
Miami Mtn—*summit* CA-9
Miami Mtn—*summit* NC-3
Miami-Norland HS—*school* FL-3
Miami Northwestern Senior HS—*school* FL-3
Miami Number One Day Care/Church of God of Prophecy—*school* FL-3
Miami Palmetto Senior HS—*school* FL-3
**Miami Park**—*pop pl* MI-6
Miami Park—*uninc pl* FL-3
*Miami Park Beach* MI-6
**Miami Park Beach**—*pop pl* MI-6
Miami Park RR Station—*locale* FL-3
Miami Park Sch—*school* FL-3
**Miami Plantation**—*pop pl* FL-3
Miami Plantation Station RR Station—*locale* FL-3
Miami Police Benevolent Association Park—*park* FL-3
Miami Post Office—*building* AZ-5
Miami Preparatory Sch—*school* FL-3
Miami Private Sch—*school* (2) FL-3
Miami Ranch Sch (historical)—*school* FL-3
Miami Res Christian Camp—*park* IN-6
*Miami River* IN-6
*Miami River* OH-6
Miami River—*stream* FL-3
Miami River—*stream* NY-2
Miami River—*stream* OR-9
Miami River Leanto—*locale* NY-2
Miami River Rapids Mini Park—*park* FL-3
Miami RR Station—*building* AZ-5
**Miamisburg**—*pop pl* OH-6
Miamisburg Mound—*hist pl* OH-6
Miamisburg Mound State Memorial—*park* OH-6
Miami Senior HS—*school* FL-3
**Miami Shores**—*pop pl* FL-3
**Miami Shores (Arch Creek)**—*pop pl* FL-3
Miami Shores Baptist Ch—*church* FL-3
Miami Shores Ch of Christ—*church* FL-3
Miami Shores Community Church Day Care—*school* FL-3
Miami Shores Country Club—*locale* FL-3
Miami Shores Elem Sch—*school* FL-3
Miami Shores Preparation Sch—*school* FL-3
Miami Skill Center—*school* FL-3
Miami South Cannel—*channel* FL-3
Miami Southridge HS—*school* FL-3
Miami Southridge Senior HS—*school* FL-3
Miami Speedway Park—*locale* FL-3
*Miamisport* IN-6
**Miami Springs**—*pop pl* FL-3
Miami Springs Baptist Ch—*church* FL-3
Miami Springs Baptist Church Kindergarten—*school* FL-3
Miami Springs Country Club—*locale* FL-3
**Miami Springs (Country Club Estates)**—*pop pl* FL-3
Miami Springs Elem Sch—*school* FL-3
Miami Springs JHS—*school* FL-3
Miami Springs Recreation Center—*park* FL-3
Miami Springs Senior HS—*school* FL-3
Miami Stadium—*locale* FL-3
Miami State Fishing Lake and Wildlife Area—*park* KS-7
Miami State Rec Area—*park* IN-6
Miami Station—*locale* MO-7
Miami Street Grade Sch—*hist pl* OH-6
Miami Sunset Senior HS—*school* FL-3
Miami Tailings Dam Number Two—*dam* AZ-5
Miami Tailings Pond—*reservoir* AZ-5
Miami Technical Coll—*school* (2) FL-3
*Miami Town* IN-6
**Miamitown**—*pop pl* OH-6
Miami Township—*civil* (2) MO-7
**Miami Township**—*pop pl* (2) KS-7
**Miami (Township of)**—*pop pl* IN-6
**Miami (Township of)**—*pop pl* (5) OH-6
Miami Trace HS—*school* OH-6
*Miami Trails* IN-6
**Miami Trails Addition**—*pop pl* IN-6
Miami Univ—*school* OH-6
*Miami University* OH-6
Miami Univ Middletown Branch—*school* OH-6
Miami Valley—*locale* GA-3
Miami Valley Camp—*locale* OH-6
Miami Valley Golf Club—*locale* OH-6
Miami Valley Memorial Garden—*cemetery* OH-6
Miami Valley Memory Garden—*cemetery* OH-6
Miami Valley Sch—*school* OH-6
**Miami Villa**—*pop pl* OH-6
**Miamiville**—*pop pl* OH-6
Miami Wash—*stream* AZ-5
Miami Whitewater For—*forest* OH-6
Miami Women's Club—*hist pl* FL-3
Miami Woods—*woods* IL-6
Miamogue Lagoon—*lake* NY-2
Miamogue Point—*cape* NY-2
Miam Run—*stream* PA-2
Mian—*island* MP-9
Miana Point—*cape* HI-9
*Mian To* MP-9
Miantonomi Hill—*summit* RI-1
Miantonomi Memorial Park—*hist pl* RI-1
*Miantonomy Hill* RI-1
**Mianus**—*pop pl* CT-1
Mianus Gorge—*valley* NY-2
Mianus Pond—*lake* CT-1
Mianus River—*stream* CT-1
Mianus River—*stream* NY-2
Mianus River RR Bridge—*hist pl* CT-1
Mianus Rsvr—*reservoir* CT-1
Mianus Rsvr—*reservoir* NY-2
Miari—*locale* FM-9
*Miatt Creek* AR-4
*Miatt Creek* MO-7
*Miaturn* CO-8
Mica—*locale* GA-3
Mica—*locale* ID-8
Mica—*locale* VA-3
**Mica**—*pop pl* WA-9
Mica, Mount—*summit* ME-1
Mica Basin—*basin* CO-8
Mica Basin Trail—*trail* CO-8
Mica Bay—*bay* ID-8
Mica Bay—*bay* MN-6
Mica Butte—*summit* CA-9
Mica Butte—*summit* CO-8
Mica Canyon—*valley* NV-8
Mica Canyon—*valley* NM-5
Mica Cem—*cemetery* WA-9
Mica Ch—*church* GA-3
Mica City Creek—*stream* NC-3
Mica Creek—*stream* CO-8
Mica Creek—*stream* (4) ID-8
Mica Creek—*stream* MT-8
Mica Creek—*stream* WA-9
Mica Creek Cem—*cemetery* WA-9
Micadale Ch—*church* NC-3
Mica Flats—*flat* ID-8
Mica Gem Mine—*mine* CA-9
Mica Giant Mine—*mine* AZ-5
Mica Gulch—*valley* CA-9
Mica Hill—*summit* ID-8
Micah Pond—*lake* MA-1
*Micahs Pond* MA-1
Mica Island—*island* MN-6
Micajah—*locale* WV-2
Micajah Pond—*lake* MA-1
Micajah Ridge—*ridge* (2) WV-2
*Micajahs Pond* MA-1
Mica King Mine—*mine* SD-7
Mica King Number 3 Claim Mine—*mine* SD-7
Mica Knob—*summit* NC-3
Mica Lake—*lake* AR-4
Mica Lake—*lake* CO-8
Mica Lake—*lake* WA-9
Mica Lake—*lake* WY-8
Mica Lakes—*lake* NY-2
Micale Bayou—*gut* LA-4
Mica Meadow—*flat* AZ-5
Mica Meadows—*flat* ID-8
*Mica Mine* SD-7
Mica Mine—*mine* (2) AZ-5
Mica Mine—*mine* ID-8
Mica Mine—*mine* MT-8
Mica Mine—*mine* SD-7
Mica Mine Gulch—*valley* CO-8
Mica Mine Hill—*summit* NH-1
Mica Mine Ridge—*ridge* CO-8
Mica Mine Windmill—*locale* TX-5
Mica Mtn—*summit* AZ-5
Mica Mtn—*summit* ID-8
Mica Mtn—*summit* WA-9
**Micanopy**—*pop pl* FL-3
Micanopy (CCD)—*cens area* FL-3
Micanopy Hist Dist—*hist pl* FL-3
Micanopy Junction—*locale* FL-3
Micanopy Tower—*tower* FL-3
Mican Pond—*reservoir* PA-2
Mica Peak—*locale* WA-9
Mica Peak—*summit* ID-8
Mica Peak—*summit* NV-8
Mica Peak Air Force Station—*military* WA-9
Mica Peak Cem—*cemetery* WA-9
Mica Pit—*basin* NC-3
Mica Queen Number 1 Prospect Mine—*mine* SD-7
Mica Ridge—*ridge* ID-8
Mica Saddle—*gap* ID-8
Mica Tank—*reservoir* AZ-5
**Micaville**—*pop pl* AL-4
**Micaville**—*pop pl* NC-3
Micaville Ch (historical)—*church* AL-4
Micaville Elem Sch—*school* NC-3
Micawber—*locale* OK-5
Micawber Cem—*cemetery* OK-5
*Micayune Creek* MT-8
Micayune Gulch—*valley* MT-8
Micca House—*hist pl* NV-8
**Micco**—*pop pl* FL-3
**Micco**—*pop pl* WV-2
**Miccosukee**—*pop pl* FL-3
Miccosukee, Lake—*reservoir* FL-3
Miccosukee Cem—*cemetery* FL-3
**Miccosukee Ind Res**—*pop pl* FL-3
Miccosukee Sch—*school* FL-3
Miccosukee Tribe HQ—*locale* FL-3
Miccosukee Tribe Island—*island* FL-3
*Micco Town* FL-3
Mice Creek—*stream* AK-9
Micek Playground—*park* IL-6
*Micenuckchuwat* MA-1
*Mice Run* VA-3
*Michael* NC-3
**Michael**—*pop pl* IL-6
**Michael**—*pop pl* NC-3
Michael, Bayou—*gut* LA-4
Michael, Enos, House—*hist pl* IN-6
Michael, John, Farm—*hist pl* PA-2
Michael, Lake—*lake* LA-4
Michael, Lake—*lake* NC-3
Michael, Lake—*reservoir* NC-3
Michael-Ann Russell Jewish Community Center—*building* FL-3
Michael Ann Russell Jewish Community Center—*building* FL-3
*Michaelbach Tank* AZ-5
*Michael Branch* LA-4
Michael Branch—*stream* (2) LA-4
Michael Branch—*stream* NC-3
Michael Branch—*stream* WV-2
Michael Breen Mine—*mine* CO-8
Michael Brook—*stream* NY-2
Michael Cem—*cemetery* GA-3
Michael Cem—*cemetery* IL-6
Michael Cem—*cemetery* IN-6
Michael Cem—*cemetery* KY-4
Michael Cem—*cemetery* NC-3
Michael Cem—*cemetery* WV-2
Michael Cem—*cemetery* WI-6
Michael Creek—*gut* FL-3
Michael Creek—*stream* AK-9
Michael Creek—*stream* CA-9
Michael Creek—*stream* ID-8
Michael Creek—*stream* IL-6
Michael Creek—*stream* NC-3
Michael Creek—*stream* OR-9
Michael Creek—*stream* PA-2
Michael Creek Ch—*church* NC-3
Michael Ditch—*canal* IN-6
Michael Ditch—*canal* MT-8
Michael Farm Airp—*airport* MO-7
Michael Gap—*gap* NC-3
Michael Gulch—*valley* MT-8
Michael Hallihan Ditch—*canal* IN-6
Michael Hole Bay—*swamp* SC-3
Michael Hollow—*valley* AL-4
Michael Hollow—*valley* TX-5
Michaelis Cem—*cemetery* KS-7
Michael Island—*island* FL-3
Michaelis Park—*park* WI-6
Michaelis Ranch—*locale* TX-5
Michael J. Kirwan Rsvr—*reservoir* OH-6
Michael Lake—*lake* WA-9
Michael Lake—*lake* WI-6
Michael Landing Public Access—*locale* IL-6
Michael Marsh—*swamp* VA-3
*Michael Memorial Baptist Church* MS-4
Michael Memorial Ch—*church* MS-4
Michael Mtn—*summit* WV-2
Michael Ranch—*locale* CA-9
Michael Ranch—*locale* NM-5
Michael Rsvr—*reservoir* OR-9
Michael Run—*stream* PA-2
*Michaels* IN-6
**Michaels**—*pop pl* IN-6
*Michaels Branch* NJ-2
Michaels Cem—*cemetery* IN-6
Michaels Cem—*cemetery* PA-2
Michaels Cem—*cemetery* WV-2
Michael Sch—*school* NY-2
Michaels Chapel—*church* WV-2
Michaels Creek—*stream* AK-9
Michaels Creek—*stream* CA-9
Michaels Creek—*stream* IA-7
Michaels Ditch—*canal* IN-6
Michaels Draw—*valley* CO-8
Michaels Draw—*valley* MT-8
Michaelsen Creek—*stream* CO-8
Michaelsen Rsvr—*reservoir* CO-8
Michaels Farm—*hist pl* OH-6
Michaels Hill—*summit* CA-9
Michaels Kindergarten—*school* FL-3
Michaels Lake—*lake* MN-6
Michaels Lake—*lake* NE-7
Michaels Mill—*locale* MD-2
*Michaelson Reservoir* CO-8
Michaelson Springs—*spring* UT-8
Michael Spring—*spring* MT-8
Michaels Ranch—*locale* WA-9
*Michaels Ridge* PA-2
Michaels Run—*stream* MD-2
Michaels Run—*stream* NJ-2
Michaels-Stern Bldg—*hist pl* NY-2
Michaels Sword—*summit* AK-9
Michael Stream—*stream* (2) ME-1
Michaelsville—*locale* MD-2
**Michaelsville**—*pop pl* IN-6
Michael Tank—*reservoir* NM-5
Michael Valley Sch (abandoned)—*school* PA-2
**Michaelwood**—*pop pl* VA-3
Michale, Lake—*reservoir* IL-6
Michales Hill—*summit* MS-4
Michallas Canyon—*valley* NM-5
Michalski Drain—*stream* MI-6
*Michanicsville* MA-1
*Michaud* ME-1
Michaud—*locale* ID-8
**Michaud**—*pop pl* ME-1
Michaud Camp—*locale* ME-1
Michaud Creek—*stream* ID-8
Michaud Farm—*locale* ME-1
Michaud Flats—*flat* ID-8
Michaud Hill—*summit* ME-1
Michaud Island—*island* ME-1
Michaud Lake—*lake* MI-6
Michaud Lake—*lake* MN-6
Michaud Siding—*locale* ME-1
Michauds Mill—*locale* ME-1
Michauk Creek—*stream* VA-3
Michaux—*locale* VA-3
Michaux Bridge—*bridge* VA-3
Michaux State For—*forest* PA-2
Micheal Cem—*cemetery* NY-2
*Micheaud* LA-4
Micheew—*locale* FM-9
Mich-E-Ke-Wis Park—*park* MI-6
Michelbach Ranch—*locale* AZ-5
Michelbach Tank—*reservoir* (2) AZ-5
**Michele Estates (subdivision)**—*pop pl* AL-4

Middle Branch Queens Run—*stream* PA-2
Middle Branch Red Cedar River—*stream* MI-6
Middle Branch Ridge—*ridge* ME-1
Middle Branch Riley Creek—*stream* TX-5
Middle Branch River—*stream* MI-6
Middle Branch Rockhouse Creek—*stream* KY-4
Middle Branch Rock Run—*stream* PA-2
Middle Branch Rocky Creek—*stream* VA-3
*Middle Branch Root River* MN-6
Middle Branch Root River—*stream* MN-6
Middle Branch (RR name for Middlebranch)—*other* OH-6
Middle Branch Rsvr—*reservoir* NY-2
Middle Branch Rush River—*stream* MN-6
Middle Branch Russian Gulch—*valley* CA-9
Middle Branch Saint Martin River—*stream* MD-2
Middle Branch Salt Slough—*gut* CA-9
Middle Branch Sandy Creek—*stream* OH-6
Middle Branch Sees Creek—*stream* MO-7
Middle Branch Shamokin Creek—*stream* PA-2
Middle Branch South Branch Kishwaukee River—*stream* IL-6
Middle Branch South Branch Tule River—*stream* CA-9
*Middle Branch South Fork North River* MO-7
Middle Branch South Fork South Eden Canyon—*valley* UT-8
Middle Branch Squaw Creek—*stream* MO-7
Middle Branch Stony Run—*stream* IN-6
Middle Branch Stutts Creek—*stream* MI-6
*Middle Branch Sugar Creek* PA-2
Middle Branch Swift Brook—*stream* ME-1
Middle Branch Swift River—*stream* MA-1
Middle Branch Thompson Creek—*stream* NE-7
Middle Branch Thoroughfare Brook—*stream* ME-1
*Middle Branch Thoroughfare Stream* ME-1
Middle Branch Tioughnioga Creek—*stream* NY-2
Middle Branch Tittabawassee River—*stream* MI-6
Middle Branch Tobacco River—*stream* MI-6
*Middle Branch Toppenish Creek* WA-9
Middle Branch (Township of)—*civ div* MI-6
Middle Branch Trout River—*stream* NY-2
Middle Branch Twomile Run—*stream* PA-2
*Middle Branch Two River* MN-6
Middle Branch Two Rivers—*stream* MN-6
Middle Branch Union River—*stream* ME-1
Middle Branch Verdigre Creek—*stream* NE-7
Middle Branch Verdigree Creek*—*stream* NE-7
Middle Branch Wakarusa River—*stream* KS-7
Middle Branch Wapsinonoc Creek—*stream* IA-7
Middle Branch Ward Creek—*stream* CA-9
Middle Branch Wards Fork Creek—*stream* VA-3
Middle Branch West Branch Caldwell Creek—*stream* PA-2
Middle Branch West Branch Copperas Creek—*stream* IL-6
Middle Branch Westfield River—*stream* MA-1
*Middle Branch White Clay Creek* DE-2
Middle Branch White Clay Creek—*stream* PA-2
Middle Branch Wilhite Creek—*stream* MS-4
Middle Branch Wilkinson Creek—*stream* NC-3
Middle Branch Williams River—*stream* VT-1
Middle Branch Willow Run—*stream* MI-6
Middle Branch Wilson Run—*stream* PA-2
Middle Branch Wyalusing Creek—*stream* PA-2
*Middle Branch Zumbro River* MN-6
Middle Branigan Lake—*lake* CA-9
Middle Breaker—*bar* AK-9
Middle Breakers—*bar* MA-1
Middle Breakwater—*dam* CA-9
Middle Brewster Island—*island* MA-1
Middle Bridge—*bridge* KY-4
Middle Bridge—*bridge* TN-4
Middle Bridge—*locale* OR-9
**Middle Bridge**—*pop pl* NY-2
Middlebrook—*hist pl* TN-4
**Middlebrook**—*pop pl* AR-4
**Middlebrook**—*pop pl* MD-2
**Middlebrook**—*pop pl* MO-7
**Middlebrook**—*pop pl* VA-3
Middle Brook—*stream* IN-6
Middle Brook—*stream* (7) ME-1
Middle Brook—*stream* MA-1
Middle Brook—*stream* NH-1
Middle Brook—*stream* (3) NJ-2
Middle Brook—*stream* (2) NY-2
Middle Brook—*stream* TN-4
Middle Brook—*stream* (2) VT-1
**Middlebrook Acres**—*pop pl* TN-4
Middle Brook Bog—*swamp* ME-1
Middlebrook Cem—*cemetery* GA-3
*Middlebrook Church* TN-4
Middlebrook Creek—*stream* MO-7
Middlebrook Dam—*dam* TN-4
**Middle Brooke**—*pop pl* MD-2
Middlebrook Encampment Site—*hist pl* NJ-2
**Middlebrook Heights**—*pop pl* TN-4
Middlebrook Heights—*ridge* NJ-2
Middlebrook Hill—*summit* MO-7
Middle Brook Hill—*summit* NY-2
Middle Brook Hill—*summit* TX-5
Middlebrook Hist Dist—*hist pl* VA-3
Middlebrook HS—*hist pl* VA-3
Middlebrook Industrial Park—*locale* TN-4
Middlebrook Lake—*reservoir* TN-4
Middle Brook Mtn—*summit* ME-1
*Middlebrook Pike Baptist Church* TN-4
Middlebrook Pike Ch—*church* TN-4
*Middlebrook Pike United Methodist Ch* TN-4
**Middle Brook Place**—*pop pl* TN-4
Middlebrook Point—*cape* AL-4
Middle Brook Pond—*lake* ME-1
**Middle Brook (RR name Middlebrook)**—*pop pl* MO-7
Middlebrooks Cem—*cemetery* GA-3
Middlebrooks Cem—*cemetery* TX-5
Middlebrook Sch—*hist pl* VA-3
Middlebrook Sch—*school* CT-1
*Middle Brooks Cross Road* AL-4
Middle Brooks Crossroads—*locale* AL-4
**Middle Brooks Cross Roads**—*pop pl* AL-4
**Middlebrook (subdivision)**—*pop pl* NC-3
Middle Brother—*flat* CA-9
Middle Brothers Creek—*stream* NJ-2
Middle Brownlee Creek—*stream* ID-8
*Middle Bruff Creek* CO-8
Middle Bruff Creek—*stream* CO-8
Middle Brush Creek—*stream* (2) CO-8
Middle Brushy Creek—*stream* MO-7
Middle Buck Creek—*stream* IA-7
Middle Buck Trap Windmill—*locale* NM-5
Middle Buffalo Creek—*stream* KS-7
Middle Buffalo Creek—*stream* OK-5
Middle Buffalo Windmill—*locale* TX-5
*Middlebum* TN-4
*Middleburg* NY-2
*Middleburg* OK-5
*Middleburg* PA-2
*Middleburg* TN-4
Middleburg—*locale* TX-5
Middleburg—*other* PA-2
**Middleburg**—*pop pl* FL-3
**Middleburg**—*pop pl* IA-7
**Middleburg**—*pop pl* KY-4
**Middleburg**—*pop pl* MD-2
**Middleburg**—*pop pl* NC-3
**Middleburg**—*pop pl* (4) OH-6
**Middleburg**—*pop pl* (2) PA-2
**Middleburg**—*pop pl* (2) TN-4
**Middleburg**—*pop pl* VA-3
Middleburg Baptist Ch—*church* TN-4
Middleburg Borough—*civil* PA-2
Middleburg (CCD)—*cens area* KY-4
Middleburg Cem—*cemetery* (2) IA-7
Middleburg Cem—*cemetery* OH-6
Middleburg-Clay Hill (CCD)—*cens area* FL-3
*Middleburg (corporate and Town name Middleburgh)* NY-2
Middleburg Elem Sch—*school* FL-3
*Middleburgh* TN-4
**Middleburgh (corporate name for Middleburg)**—*pop pl* NY-2
**Middleburg Heights**—*pop pl* OH-6
*Middleburgh Heights* OH-6
Middleburg Hist Dist—*hist pl* VA-3
Middleburg (historical P.O.)—*locale* IA-7
*Middleburgh Post Office* TN-4
Middleburg HS—*school* FL-3
**Middleburgh (Town of)**—*pop pl* NY-2
Middleburg-Nutbush (Township of)—*fmr MCD* NC-3
Middleburg Plantation—*hist pl* SC-3
Middleburg Plantation—*locale* SC-3
Middleburg Post Office (historical)—*building* TN-4
Middleburg Sch—*school* IA-7
Middleburg Sch—*school* NE-7
Middleburg Sch (historical)—*school* TN-4
Middleburg Training Track—*other* VA-3
Middle Burning Creek—*stream* WV-2
Middle Burnt Corral Tank—*reservoir* AZ-5
Middle Burro Canyon Sch—*school* CO-8
*Middlebury* IL-6
**Middlebury**—*pop pl* CT-1
**Middlebury**—*pop pl* IL-6
**Middlebury**—*pop pl* (2) IN-6
**Middlebury**—*pop pl* OH-6
**Middlebury**—*pop pl* VT-1
Middlebury Acad—*hist pl* NY-2
Middlebury Brook—*stream* NY-2
Middlebury Cem—*cemetery* CT-1
Middlebury Cem—*cemetery* MI-6
**Middlebury Center**—*pop pl* PA-2
Middlebury Center Hist Dist—*hist pl* CT-1
**Middlebury Center (Township and RR name Middlebury)**—*5pop pl* PA-2
*Middlebury Centre* PA-2
Middlebury Ch—*church* MI-6
Middlebury Ch—*church* WI-6
Middlebury Coll—*school* VT-1
Middlebury College Snow Bowl—*area* VT-1
Middlebury Country Club—*other* VT-1
Middlebury Elem Sch—*school* (2) IN-6
Middlebury Gap—*gap* VT-1
*Middlebury River* VT-1
Middlebury River—*stream* VT-1
Middlebury (RR name for Middlebury Center)—*other* PA-2
Middlebury Swamp—*swamp* VT-1
**Middlebury (Town of)**—*pop pl* CT-1
**Middlebury (Town of)**—*pop pl* NY-2
**Middlebury (Town of)**—*pop pl* VT-1
**Middlebury (Township of)**—*pop pl* IN-6
**Middlebury (Township of)**—*pop pl* MI-6
**Middlebury (Township of)**—*pop pl* OH-6
**Middlebury (Township of)**—*pop pl* PA-2
Middlebury Union Cem—*cemetery* PA-2
Middlebury Village Hist Dist—*hist pl* VT-1
Middlebury Village Hist Dist (Boundary Increase)—*hist pl* VT-1
Middlebury Water Supply—*reservoir* VT-1
Middlebury Waterworks—*other* VT-1
**Middlebush**—*pop pl* NJ-2
Middlebush Brook—*stream* NJ-2
Middlebush Cem—*cemetery* NY-2
Middle Butler Creek—*stream* TN-4
Middle Butte—*summit* CA-9
Middle Butte—*summit* (2) ID-8
Middle Butte—*summit* (2) MT-8
Middle Butte—*summit* OR-9
Middle Butte—*summit* UT-8
Middle Butte—*summit* WA-9
Middle Butte—*summit* (2) WY-8
Middle Butte Cave—*cave* ID-8
Middle Butte Creek—*stream* CA-9
Middle Butte Mine—*mine* CA-9
Middle Bywy Creek—*stream* MS-4
Middle Caddo Creek—*stream* TX-5
Middle Camp—*locale* OR-9
Middle Camp—*locale* WY-8
Middle Camp Baisley-Elkhorn Mine—*mine* OR-9
Middle Camp Branch—*stream* VA-3
Middle Camp Mtn—*summit* AZ-5
Middle Campsite—*locale* CA-9
Middle Canal—*canal* NY-2
Middle Canal—*canal* NC-3
Middle Cane Creek—*stream* TN-4
*Middle Caney Creek* KS-7
*Middle Caney Creek* OK-5
Middle Caney Creek—*stream* AR-4
Middle Caney Creek—*stream* KS-7
Middle Caney Creek—*stream* OK-5
*Middle Caney River* KS-7
Middle Canyon—*valley* (5) AZ-5
Middle Canyon—*valley* (5) CA-9
Middle Canyon—*valley* CO-8
Middle Canyon—*valley* (3) ID-8
Middle Canyon—*valley* NV-8
Middle Canyon—*valley* (9) NM-5
Middle Canyon—*valley* (2) OR-9
Middle Canyon—*valley* SD-7
Middle Canyon—*valley* (3) TX-5
Middle Canyon—*valley* (11) UT-8
Middle Canyon—*valley* WA-9
Middle Canyon—*valley* (2) WY-8
*Middle Canyon Creek* ID-8
*Middle Canyon Creek* WY-8
Middle Canyon Spring—*spring* NV-8
Middle Canyon Tank—*reservoir* AZ-5
Middle Canyon Tank No 1—*reservoir* NM-5
Middle Canyon Tank No 2—*reservoir* NM-5
Middle Canyon Wash—*stream* AZ-5
Middle Canyon Well—*well* TX-5
Middle Cape—*cape* AK-9
Middle Cape—*cape* FL-3
Middle Cape Canal—*canal* FL-3
Middle Carry Pond—*lake* ME-1
*Middle Carter Creek* OK-5
Middle Carter Creek—*stream* OK-5
Middle Carter Mtn—*summit* CO-8
Middle Carter Mtn—*summit* NH-1
Middle Cascade Glacier—*glacier* WA-9
Middle Catherine Creek—*stream* OR-9
Middle Cat Pond—*lake* NY-2
Middle Cave—*cave* UT-8
Middle Cave Ridge—*ridge* VA-3
Middle CCC Pool—*reservoir* MN-6
Middle Cedar Creek—*stream* AZ-5
Middle Cedar Creek—*stream* KS-7
Middle Cedar Creek—*stream* WY-8
Middle Cem—*cemetery* MA-1
Middle Center Lake—*lake* IN-6
Middle Ch—*church* AL-4
Middle Ch—*church* PA-2
Middle Chain Lake—*lake* UT-8
Middle Chain Lake—*reservoir* ME-1
Middle Channel—*channel* AL-4
Middle Channel—*channel* (2) AK-9
Middle Channel—*channel* FL-3
Middle Channel—*channel* NJ-2
Middle Channel—*channel* TX-5
Middle Channel—*channel* VA-3
Middle Channel—*channel* (2) WA-9
Middle Channel Dike—*levee* OR-9
Middle Channel Kiwalk River—*stream* AK-9
Middle Channel Muskegon River—*stream* MI-6
Middle Channel Platte River—*stream* NE-7
Middle Channel Porcupine River—*stream* AK-9
Middle Channel Willamette River—*channel* OR-9
*Middle Charley Creek* MT-8
Middle Charlie Creek—*stream* MT-8
Middle Chester Cem—*cemetery* ME-1
Middle Cheyenne Creek—*stream* TX-5
Middle China Windmill—*locale* TX-5
Middle Chin Creek Rsvr—*reservoir* NV-8
Middle Chugwater Creek—*stream* WY-8
**Middle Churches**—*pop pl* PA-2
**Middle City**—*pop pl* TN-4
Middle City—*uninc pl* PA-2
Middle Clear Creek—*stream* WY-8
Middle Cliff—*cliff* KY-4
Middle Cloud Peak Lake—*lake* WY-8
Middle Clump—*bar* NY-2
Middle Clyde Ditch—*canal* NM-5
Middle Coffee Creek—*stream* TX-5
Middle Colly Sch—*school* KY-4
Middle Colony Creek—*stream* CO-8
Middle Colyell Creek—*stream* LA-4
Middle Concho River—*stream* TX-5
*Middle Cone* ID-8
Middle Cone Lake—*lake* MN-6
Middle Coon Bayou—*gut* AR-4
Middle Coon Valley Ch—*church* WI-6
Middle Copperas Creek—*stream* TX-5
Middle Copper Canyon—*valley* NM-5
Middle Cormorant Lake—*lake* MN-6
*Middle Corners* OH-6
Middle Cottonwood Creek—*stream* CO-8
Middle Cottonwood Creek—*stream* MT-8
Middle Cottonwood Draw—*valley* CO-8
Middle Cottonwood Rsvr—*reservoir* CO-8
Middle Cottonwood Tank—*reservoir* AZ-5
*Middle Cotuit Pond* MA-1
Middle Coulee—*valley* (4) MT-8
Middle Cove—*bay* CA-9
Middle Cove—*bay* CT-1
Middle Cove—*bay* FL-3
Middle Cove—*bay* OR-9
Middle Cove Ch—*church* PA-2
Middle Cowan Creek Sch—*school* KY-4
*Middle Cow Creek* CO-8
*Middle Cow Creek* KS-7
Middle Cow Creek—*stream* AR-4
*Middle Crab Creek* WA-9
Middle Craig Point—*cape* AK-9
Middle Cramer Lake—*lake* ID-8
*Middle Crane Creek* NC-3
*Middle Crazy Woman Creek* WY-8
*Middle Creek* CA-9
*Middle Creek* CO-8
*Middle Creek* KS-7
*Middle Creek* MN-6
*Middle Creek* MO-7
*Middle Creek* MT-8
*Middle Creek* NE-7
*Middle Creek* NV-8
*Middle Creek* NC-3
*Middle Creek* OR-9
*Middlecreek* PA-2
*Middle Creek* UT-8
*Middle Creek* WA-9
*Middle Creek* WV-2
Middle Creek—*bay* (2) NC-3
Middle Creek—*fmr MCD* NE-7
Middle Creek—*gut* FL-3
Middle Creek—*gut* MS-4
Middle Creek—*gut* NC-3
Middlecreek—*other* KY-4
**Middle Creek**—*pop pl* CA-9
**Middle Creek**—*pop pl* IL-6
**Middle Creek**—*pop pl* KY-4
**Middle Creek**—*pop pl* PA-2
**Middle Creek**—*pop pl* TN-4
Middle Creek—*stream* (5) AL-4
Middle Creek—*stream* (4) AK-9
Middle Creek—*stream* (4) AR-4
Middle Creek—*stream* (17) CA-9
Middle Creek—*stream* (9) CO-8
Middle Creek—*stream* (6) FL-3
Middle Creek—*stream* (4) GA-3
Middle Creek—*stream* (6) ID-8
Middle Creek—*stream* (8) IL-6
Middle Creek—*stream* (2) IN-6
Middle Creek—*stream* (2) IA-7
Middle Creek—*stream* (5) KS-7
Middle Creek—*stream* (4) KY-4
Middle Creek—*stream* (2) LA-4
Middle Creek—*stream* (4) MD-2
Middle Creek—*stream* MI-6
Middle Creek—*stream* (3) MN-6
Middle Creek—*stream* (2) MS-4
Middle Creek—*stream* (2) MO-7
Middle Creek—*stream* (10) MT-8
Middle Creek—*stream* (6) NE-7
Middle Creek—*stream* (4) NV-8
Middle Creek—*stream* (6) NC-3
Middle Creek—*stream* ND-7
Middle Creek—*stream* (2) OH-6
Middle Creek—*stream* OK-5
Middle Creek—*stream* (7) OR-9
Middle Creek—*stream* (9) PA-2
Middle Creek—*stream* (5) SD-7
Middle Creek—*stream* (10) TN-4
Middle Creek—*stream* (12) TX-5
Middle Creek—*stream* (2) UT-8
Middle Creek—*stream* (7) VA-3
Middle Creek—*stream* (6) WA-9
Middle Creek—*stream* (3) WV-2
Middle Creek—*stream* WI-6
Middle Creek—*stream* (12) WY-8
Middle Creek Association Ditch—*canal* MT-8
*Middle Creek Baptist Church* TN-4
Middle Creek Basin Creek—*stream* FL-3
Middle Creek Butte—*summit* ID-8
Middle Creek Butte—*summit* SD-7
Middle Creek Camp—*locale* CA-9
Middle Creek Camp—*locale* MT-8
Middle Creek Campground—*locale* (2) CA-9
Middle Creek Cave—*cave* PA-2
Middle Creek Cem—*cemetery* KS-7
Middle Creek Cem—*cemetery* PA-2
Middle Creek Ch—*church* (4) IL-6
Middle Creek Ch—*church* KY-4
Middle Creek Ch—*church* LA-4
Middle Creek Ch—*church* MN-6
Middle Creek Ch—*church* NC-3
Middle Creek Ch—*church* OH-6
Middle Creek Ch—*church* OK-5
Middle Creek Ch—*church* (3) PA-2
Middle Creek Ch—*church* TN-4
Middle Creek Ch—*church* WV-2
Middle Creek County Park—*park* OR-9
Middle Creek Cow Camp—*locale* MT-8
Middle Creek Dam—*dam* MT-8
Middle Creek Dam—*dam* (2) PA-2
Middle Creek Ditch—*canal* AR-4
Middle Creek Ditch—*canal* MT-8
Middle Creek Falls—*falls* OR-9
Middle Creek Flat—*flat* CA-9
Middle Creek Flat Trail—*trail* CA-9
Middlecreek Golf Course—*locale* PA-2
**Middle Creek (historical)**—*pop pl* PA-2
Middle Creek (historical)—*stream* PA-2
*Middle Creek - in part* PA-2
Middle Creek Lake—*reservoir* MT-8
Middle Creek Lake—*reservoir* PA-2
Middle Creek Levisa Fork—*stream* KY-4
Middle Creek Meadows—*flat* CA-9
Middle Creek Mill—*locale* NC-3
Middle Creek Mtn—*summit* PA-2
Middle Creek Recreation Site—*park* OR-9
Middle Creek Ridge—*ridge* CA-9
Middle Creek Ridge—*ridge* VA-3
Middle Creek Rsvr—*reservoir* PA-2
Middle Creek Rsvr—*reservoir* WY-8
Middle Creek Sch—*school* MT-8
Middle Creek Sch—*school* SD-7
Middle Creek Sch—*school* (2) WV-2
*Middle Creek Southern Mountains* ID-8
Middle Creek Spring—*spring* MT-8
Middle Creek Spring—*spring* WY-8
Middle Creek Stock Driveway—*trail* CO-8
**Middle Creek Township**—*pop pl* KS-7
Middle Creek (Township of)—*fmr MCD* NC-3
**Middlecreek (Township of)**—*pop pl* (2) PA-2
Middle Creek Tributary Bridge—*hist pl* KS-7
Middle Creek Valley—*valley* CA-9
Middle Creek Warden Station—*locale* OR-9
Middle Creek Well—*well* TX-5
Middle Creek Windmill—*locale* TX-5
Middle Crescent Canyon—*valley* UT-8
Middle Crooked Lake—*lake* AR-4
Middle Cross Ch—*church* NC-3
Middle Crossing—*locale* TX-5
Middle Crossing Tank—*reservoir* AZ-5
Middle Croton Windmill—*locale* TX-5
Middle Crow Camp—*locale* WY-8
*Middle Crow Creek* MT-8
Middle Crow Creek—*stream* MT-8
Middle Crow Creek—*stream* WY-8
Middle Crow Island—*island* NY-2
Middle Cullen Lake—*lake* MN-6
Middle Cunningham Creek—*stream* CO-8
*Middle Cypress Congregation* AL-4
Middle Cypress Creek—*stream* AL-4
Middle Cypress Creek—*stream* TN-4
Middle Cypress Pond—*lake* GA-3
Middle Dairy—*locale* ID-8
Middle Dallas Lateral—*canal* CA-9
Middle Dam—*dam* PA-2
**Middledam**—*pop pl* ME-1
**Middle Dam**—*pop pl* ME-1
Middle Dam Creek—*stream* NC-3
Middle Dam Pond—*reservoir* RI-1
Middle Darrs Creek—*stream* TX-5
Middle Davenport Rsvr—*reservoir* UT-8
Middle Deadwater—*lake* ME-1
Middle Decatur Bend—*bend* NE-7
Middle Decature Bend—*bend* IA-7
*Middle Deep Creek* TX-5
Middle Deep Creek—*stream* TX-5
Middle Deep Creek—*stream* UT-8
Middle Deer Creek—*stream* IN-6
Middle Deer Creek—*stream* UT-8
Middle Deer Island—*island* TX-5
Middle Deer Pond—*lake* IN-6
Middle Delaware Natl Scenic and Recreational River—*park* PA-2
Middle Desert—*plain* UT-8
*Middle Desert Wash* UT-8
Middle Desert Wash—*valley* UT-8
Middle Des Lacs Lake—*reservoir* ND-7
Middle Devils Peak—*summit* CA-9
Middle Diamond Creek—*stream* NM-5
Middle Diamond Spring—*spring* WY-8
Middle Diamond Springs Draw—*valley* WY-8
Middle Dipping Vat Well—*well* NM-5
Middle District Ch—*church* NC-3
Middle District Ch—*church* OH-6
Middle Ditch—*canal* AK-9
Middle Ditch—*canal* CA-9
Middle Ditch—*canal* ID-8
Middle Ditch—*canal* NV-8
Middle Ditch—*canal* (2) NM-5
Middle Ditch—*canal* OR-9
Middle Ditch—*canal* UT-8
Middle Ditch—*canal* VA-3
Middle Ditch—*stream* WY-8
*Middle Division* AZ-5
Middle Dixon Creek—*stream* TX-5
Middle Dog Canyon—*valley* NM-5
Middle Dolan Creek—*stream* TX-5
Middle Dome—*ridge* CA-9
Middle Dome—*summit* AK-9
Middle Donkey Dam—*dam* UT-8
*Middle Donkey Reservoir* UT-8
Middle Drain—*canal* (2) TX-5
Middle Drain—*gut* DE-2
Middle Drain Ditch—*canal* NM-5
Middle Draw—*valley* NM-5
Middle Draw—*valley* (2) TX-5
Middle Draw Rsvr—*reservoir* NV-8
*Middle Dry Creek* KS-7
Middle Dry Creek—*stream* CA-9
Middle Dry Creek—*stream* ID-8
Middle Dry Creek—*stream* KS-7
Middle Dry Fork—*stream* CO-8
Middle Dry Fork Sch—*school* KY-4
Middle Duck Creek—*stream* KS-7
Middle Duck Creek—*stream* OK-5
Middle Dutch Creek—*stream* CO-8
Middle East Windmill—*locale* WY-8
Middle Eau Claire Lake—*lake* WI-6
Middle Eighteenmile Lake—*lake* MI-6
Middle Eighth Coulee—*valley* MT-8
Middle Eighth Ridge—*ridge* MT-8
Middle Elbow Pond—*lake* ME-1
Middle Elk Creek—*stream* KY-4
Middle Elk Creek—*stream* VA-3
Middle Elk Mtn—*summit* NC-3
Middle Ellerson Lake—*lake* WI-6
Middle Ellis Creek—*stream* WV-2
Middle Emigrant Lake—*lake* CA-9
Middle Emma Creek—*stream* KS-7
Middle Empire Lake—*reservoir* OR-9
Middle Empire Lake Dam—*dam* OR-9
Middle English River—*stream* IA-7
Middle Entrance—*channel* MI-6
Middle Entrance Point—*cape* MI-6
Middle Erma Bell Lake—*lake* OR-9
*Middle Fabius River* MO-7
Middle Fabius River—*stream* MO-7
Middle Fabius Sch—*school* MO-7
*Middle Falls* OR-9
Middle Falls—*falls* CA-9
Middle Falls—*falls* MN-6
Middle Falls—*falls* NY-2
Middle Falls—*falls* NC-3
Middle Falls—*falls* WA-9
**Middle Falls**—*pop pl* NY-2
Middle False Bottom Sch—*school* SD-7
Middle Farallon—*island* CA-9
Middle Farmhouse—*hist pl* NY-2
Middle Farms Pond—*lake* NY-2
Middle Ferrell Cem—*cemetery* WV-2
*Middlefield* MA-1
**Middlefield**—*pop pl* CT-1
**Middlefield**—*pop pl* MA-1
**Middlefield**—*pop pl* NY-2
**Middlefield**—*pop pl* OH-6
Middlefield-Becket Stone Arch RR Bridge District—*hist pl* MA-1
Middle Field Canyon—*valley* NV-8
*Middlefield Center* CT-1
**Middlefield Center**—*pop pl* NY-2
Middlefield Center Cem—*cemetery* MA-1
Middlefield District No. 1 Sch—*hist pl* NY-2
Middlefield Fork—*stream* KY-4
Middlefield Hamlet Hist Dist—*hist pl* NY-2
Middlefield (historical)—*locale* IA-7
*Middle Field Land* MA-1
**Middlefield Road**—*pop pl* CA-9
Middlefield Rsvr—*reservoir* CA-9
Middlefield Sch—*school* MA-1
**Middlefield (sta.)**—*pop pl* MA-1
Middlefield State For—*forest* MA-1
*Middlefield Station* MA-1
**Middlefield (Town of)**—*pop pl* CT-1
**Middlefield (Town of)**—*pop pl* MA-1
**Middlefield (Town of)**—*pop pl* NY-2
Middlefield Township—*fmr MCD* IA-7
**Middlefield (Township of)**—*pop pl* OH-6
Middle Field Windmill—*locale* TX-5
Middle Firehole Canyon—*valley* WY-8
Middle Fish Creek—*stream* CO-8
Middle Fishhole—*swamp* OR-9
Middle Fishhook Canyon—*valley* AZ-5
Middle Fish Lake—*lake* MI-6
Middle Flat—*lake* LA-4
Middle Flat Creek Sch—*school* KY-4
Middle Flats—*flat* MA-1
Middle Flow—*lake* NY-2
Middle Flume Spring—*spring* HI-9
Middleford—*locale* DE-2
**Middleford Acres (subdivision)**—*pop pl* DE-2
Middle Forest River Cem—*cemetery* ND-7
*Middle Fork* AZ-5
*Middle Fork* CA-9
*Middle Fork* CO-8
*Middle Fork* IN-6
*Middle Fork* KY-4
*Middle Fork* MN-6
*Middle Fork* MS-4
*Middle Fork* MT-8
*Middle Fork* NC-3
*Middle Fork* OH-6
*Middle Fork* OK-5
*Middle Fork* OR-9
*Middle Fork* PA-2
*Middlefork* TN-4
*Middle Fork* UT-8
*Middle Fork* WA-9
*Middle Fork* WY-8
Middle Fork—*locale* (2) WV-2
**Middlefork**—*pop pl* (2) IN-6
**Middlefork**—*pop pl* KY-4
**Middle Fork**—*pop pl* NC-3
**Middle Fork**—*pop pl* TN-4
Middle Fork—*stream* CA-9
Middle Fork—*stream* IN-6
Middle Fork—*stream* (2) KY-4
Middle Fork—*stream* MO-7
Middle Fork—*stream* NM-5
Middle Fork—*stream* WA-9
Middle Fork—*stream* (3) WV-2
*Middle Fork Adams Creek* WA-9
Middle Fork Ahtanum Creek—*stream* WA-9
*Middle Fork Alder Creek* CO-8
Middle Fork Alder Creek—*stream* (2) CA-9
Middle Fork Allen Creek—*stream* MT-8
Middle Fork Allison Creek—*stream* NV-8
Middle Fork Alpine Gulch—*valley* CO-8
Middle Fork American Fork—*stream* MT-8
Middle Fork American River—*stream* CA-9
Middle Fork Amos Canyon—*valley* UT-8
*Middle Fork Anderson Creek* IN-6
Middle Fork Anderson Creek—*stream* AL-4
Middle Fork Anderson River—*stream* IN-6
Middle Fork Annie Creek—*stream* OR-9
*Middle Fork Antanam Creek* WA-9
*Middle Fork Antelope Creek* ID-8
Middle Fork Antelope Creek—*stream* CA-9
Middle Fork Apple Creek—*stream* TX-5
Middle Fork Applegate River—*stream* CA-9
Middle Fork Arapaho Creek—*stream* CO-8
Middle Fork Arkansas Creek—*stream* WY-8
Middle Fork Arthurs Creek—*stream* UT-8
Middle Fork Ash Creek—*stream* OR-9
Middle Fork Badger Creek—*stream* WY-8
Middle Fork Bad Route Creek—*stream* MT-8
*Middle Fork Bald Mountain Creek* OR-9
*Middle Fork Balleus Creek* NC-3
Middle Fork Barkers Creek—*stream* NC-3
Middle Fork Battle Butte Creek—*stream* MT-8
*Middle Fork Battle Creek* WY-8
Middle Fork Bayou D'Arbonne—*stream* LA-4
Middle Fork Bayou Loco—*stream* TX-5
Middle Fork Bayou Long—*stream* LA-4
*Middle Fork Bayou Pierre* MS-4
Middle Fork Bear Canyon—*valley* CO-8
Middle Fork Bear Creek—*stream* ID-8
Middle Fork Bear Creek—*stream* (2) MT-8
Middle Fork Beargrass Creek—*stream* KY-4
Middle Fork Bear Gulch—*valley* MT-8
*Middle Fork Beaver Creek* CO-8
*Middle Fork Beaver Creek* IA-7
*Middle Fork Beaver Creek* KS-7
*Middle Fork Beaver Creek* WA-9
Middle Fork Beaver Creek—*stream* (2) MT-8
Middle Fork Beaver Creek—*stream* OR-9
Middle Fork Beaver Creek—*stream* UT-8
Middle Fork Beaver Creek—*stream* (2) WY-8
Middle Fork Beaverdam Creek—*stream* TN-4
Middle Fork Beaverdam Creek—*stream* VA-3
Middle Fork Beefhide Creek—*stream* KY-4
Middle Fork Beegum Creek—*stream* CA-9
Middle Fork Bergher Creek—*stream* TX-5
Middle Fork Berry Creek—*stream* OR-9
Middle Fork Big Bear Creek—*stream* ID-8
*Middle Fork Big Boulder Creek* WA-9
Middle Fork Big Cabin Creek—*stream* OK-5
Middle Fork Big Camas Creek—*stream* MT-8
Middle Fork Big Canyon—*valley* NM-5
Middle Fork Big Canyon—*valley* TX-5
*Middle Fork Big Creek* IN-6
*Middle Fork Big Creek* MT-8
Middle Fork Big Creek—*stream* ID-8
Middle Fork Big Creek—*stream* MO-7
Middle Fork Big Creek—*stream* MT-8
Middle Fork Big Creek—*stream* WA-9
Middle Fork Big Creek—*stream* WV-2
Middle Fork Big Creek—*stream* WY-8
Middle Fork Big Elk Creek—*stream* MT-8
*Middle Fork Big Flatrock River* IN-6
*Middle Fork Big Hat Creek* ID-8
*Middle Fork Big Muddy Creek* MT-8
Middle Fork Big Muddy River—*stream* IL-6
Middle Fork Big Pine Creek—*stream* ID-8
Middle Fork Big Sandy Creek—*stream* WV-2
Middle Fork Big Sheep Creek—*stream* OR-9
Middle Fork Big Spring Creek—*stream* CO-8
Middle Fork Big Spring Creek—*stream* MT-8
Middle Fork Big Timber Creek—*stream* MT-8
*Middle Fork Big Vermillion River* IL-6
Middle Fork Big Walnut Creek—*stream* IN-6
*Middle Fork Birch Creek* OR-9
Middle Fork Birch Creek—*stream* MT-8
Middle Fork Birch Creek—*stream* UT-8
Middle Fork Bird Creek—*stream* CA-9
Middle Fork Bishop Creek—*stream* CA-9
*Middle Fork Bitch Creek* WY-8
Middle Fork Bitter Creek—*stream* UT-8
*Middle Fork Black River* MI-6
Middle Fork Black River—*stream* MO-7
Middle Fork Blacks Fork—*stream* UT-8
Middle Fork Blacktail Deer Creek—*stream* MT-8
Middle Fork Blackwood Creek—*stream* CA-9
Middle Fork Blood River—*stream* TN-4
Middle Fork Bloomington Creek—*stream* ID-8
Middle Fork Blubber Creek—*stream* UT-8
Middle Fork Blue Creek—*stream* WV-2
Middle Fork Blue River—*stream* IN-6
*Middle Fork Boise River* ID-8
Middle Fork Boise River—*stream* ID-8
Middle Fork Borrego Palm Canyon—*valley* CA-9
*Middle Fork Boulder Creek* WA-9
Middle Fork Boulder Creek—*stream* ID-8
Middle Fork Boulder Creek—*stream* WA-9
Middle Fork Boulder Creek—*stream* WY-8
Middle Fork Boundary Gulch—*valley* WY-8
Middle Fork Box Creek—*stream* UT-8

Middle Fork Sanders Creek—*stream* ... KY-4
Middle Fork Sandy Creek—*stream* ... UT-8
Middle Fork San Francisco Creek—*stream* ... CO-8
Middle Fork San Gabriel River—*stream* ... TX-5
*Middle Fork San Joaquin River* ... CA-9
Middle Fork San Joaquin River—*stream* ... CA-9
Middle Fork San Pedro Creek—*stream* ... CA-9
Middle Fork San Pedro Creek—*stream* ... TX-5
Middle Fork Sanpoil River—*stream* ... WA-9
Middle Fork Santa Clara River—*stream* ... UT-8
Middle Fork Sappa Creek—*stream* ... KS-7
Middle Fork Sardine Creek—*stream* ... OR-9
Middle Fork Satsop River—*stream* ... WA-9
Middle Fork Savanac Creek—*stream* ... MT-8
Middle Fork Sawmill Gulch—*valley* ... CO-8
*Middle Fork Sch* ... TN-4
Middle Fork Sch—*school* ... ID-8
Middlefork Sch—*school* ... IL-6
Middle Fork Sch—*school* ... TN-4
Middlefork Sch (historical)—*school* ... TN-4
Middle Fork Schwartz Creek—*stream* ... MT-8
*Middle Fork Scott Creek* ... MI-6
Middle Fork Scriver Creek—*stream* ... ID-8
Middle Fork Seedtick Branch—*stream* ... KY-4
Middle Fork Shafer Canyon—*valley* ... UT-8
Middle Fork Shannon Canyon—*valley* ... CA-9
Middle Fork Shawnee Creek—*stream* ... WY-8
Middle Fork Sheeds Creek—*stream* ... TN-4
Middle Fork Sheep Creek—*stream* ... UT-8
Middle Fork Sheep Creek—*stream* (2) ... WY-8
Middle Fork Sheridan Creek—*stream* ... ID-8
*Middle Fork Shoal Creek* ... TN-4
Middle Fork Shoal Creek—*stream* ... IL-6
Middle Fork Shoal Creek—*stream* ... MO-7
Middle Fork Shoshone Creek—*stream* ... ID-8
Middle Fork Silesia Creek—*stream* ... WA-9
*Middle Fork Silver Creek* ... CA-9
Middle Fork Siwash Creek—*stream* ... WA-9
Middle Fork Sixes River—*stream* ... OR-9
Middle Fork Sixteenmile Creek—*stream* ... MT-8
Middle Fork Slate Creek—*stream* ... WY-8
Middle Fork Sleepy Creek—*stream* ... VA-3
Middle Fork Sleepy Creek—*stream* ... WV-2
Middle Fork Smith Creek—*stream* (2) ... ID-8
Middle Fork Smith Creek—*stream* ... NV-8
Middle Fork Smith River—*stream* ... CA-9
Middle Fork Snoqualmie River—*stream* ... WA-9
Middle Fork Soldier Creek—*stream* ... CO-8
Middle Fork Soldier Creek—*stream* ... ID-8
Middle Fork Soldier Creek—*stream* ... NE-7
Middle Fork South Arkansas River—*stream* ... CO-8
Middle Fork South Beaver Creek—*stream* ... IA-7
Middle Fork South Canyon—*valley* ... ID-8
Middle Fork South Creek—*stream* ... UT-8
*Middle Fork South Fork Beaver Creek* ... WA-9
Middle Fork South Fork Chambers Creek—*stream* ... TX-5
Middle Fork South Fork New River—*stream* ... NC-3
*Middle Fork South Fork Owl Creek* ... WY-8
Middle Fork South Fork Provo River—*stream* ... UT-8
Middle Fork South Fork Rock Creek—*stream* ... MT-8
Middle Fork South Fork Sultan River—*stream* ... WA-9
*Middle Fork South Fork Wildcat Creek* ... IN-6
Middle Fork South Piney Creek—*stream* ... WY-8
Middle Fork South Platte River—*stream* ... CO-8
Middle Fork Spirit Creek—*stream* ... GA-3
Middle Fork Split Creek—*stream* ... ID-8
Middle Fork Spotted Dog Creek—*stream* ... MT-8
Middle Fork Spring—*spring* ... AZ-5
Middle Fork Spring—*spring* (2) ... CA-9
Middle Fork Spring—*spring* ... NV-8
Middle Fork Spring Creek—*stream* ... CO-8
Middle Fork Spring Creek—*stream* ... MT-8
Middle Fork Spring Creek—*stream* ... TN-4
Middle Fork Spring Creek—*stream* ... TX-5
Middle Fork Spruce Branch—*stream* ... KY-4
Middle Fork Spruce Fork—*stream* ... WV-2
Middle Fork Spruce Pine Creek—*stream* ... VA-3
*Middle Fork Squaw Creek* ... MT-8
Middle Fork Squaw Creek—*stream* ... AZ-5
Middle Fork Squaw Creek—*stream* ... MT-8
Middle Fork Squaw Creek—*stream* ... WY-8
*Middle Fork Stanislaus River* ... CA-9
Middle Fork Stanislaus River—*stream* ... CA-9
*Middle Fork Station Camp Creek* ... TN-4
Middle Fork Station Camp Creek—*stream* ... KY-4
Middle Fork Stell Creek—*stream* ... OR-9
*Middle Fork Stewart Gulch* ... CO-8
Middle Fork Stewart Gulch—*valley* ... CO-8
*Middle Fork Stillwater River* ... MT-8
Middle Fork Stinking Creek—*stream* ... KY-4
Middle Fork Stone Creek—*stream* ... MT-8
*Middle Fork Stone River* ... TN-4
Middle Fork Stones River—*stream* ... TN-4
Middle Fork Stony Creek—*stream* ... CA-9
Middle Fork Story Gulch—*valley* ... CO-8
*Middle Fork Stotts Creek* ... IN-6
Middle Fork Stovall Creek—*stream* ... VA-3
Middle Fork Street Creek—*stream* ... OR-9
*Middle Fork Stuart Gulch* ... CO-8
Middle Fork Sturgill Creek—*stream* ... ID-8
Middle Fork Sugar Creek—*stream* ... IL-6
Middle Fork Sugar Creek—*stream* ... KY-4
Middle Fork Sugar Creek—*stream* ... OH-6
Middle Fork Sugar Creek—*stream* ... TN-4
Middle Fork Sullivan Canyon—*valley* ... UT-8
Middle Fork Sulphur Creek—*stream* ... WY-8
Middle Fork Summerville Wash—*valley* ... UT-8
Middle Fork Sunshine Creek—*stream* ... OR-9
Middle Fork Suwannee River—*stream* ... GA-3
Middle Fork Swan River—*stream* ... CO-8
Middle Fork Swayze Creek—*stream* ... OR-9
Middle Fork Sweet Grass Creek—*stream* (2) ... MT-8
*Middle Fork Sybille Creek* ... WY-8
Middle Fork Sycamore Creek—*stream* ... TN-4
Middle Fork Tank—*reservoir* (3) ... AZ-5
Middle Fork Tank—*reservoir* (2) ... NM-5
*Middle Fork Tarkie River* ... IA-7
Middle Fork Tauy Creek—*stream* ... KS-7
Middle Fork Taylor Creek—*stream* ... UT-8
Middle Fork Taylor Creek—*stream* ... WA-9
Middle Fork Teanaway River—*stream* ... WA-9
Middle Fork Tebo Creek—*stream* ... MO-7
Middle Fork Tenmile Creek—*stream* ... MT-8
Middle Fork Tenmile Creek—*stream* ... WY-8
Middle Fork Ten Mile River—*stream* ... CA-9
Middle Fork Terry Branch—*stream* ... KY-4
Middle Fork Third Fork Rock Creek—*stream* ... ID-8
Middle Fork Thistle Creek—*stream* ... UT-8
*Middle Fork Thompson Creek* ... LA-4
Middle Fork Thompson Creek—*stream* ... LA-4
Middle Fork Thompson Creek—*stream* ... MS-4
Middle Fork Thorn Creek—*stream* ... ID-8
Middle Fork Threemile Creek—*stream* ... TX-5
Middle Fork Threemile Creek—*stream* ... UT-8
*Middle Fork Thumb Run* ... VA-3
Middle Fork Ticaboo Creek—*stream* ... UT-8
Middle Fork Timber Swamp Brook—*stream* ... NJ-2
Middle Fork Titus Creek—*stream* ... CA-9
Middle Fork Toats Coulee Creek—*stream* ... WA-9
*Middle Fork Tom Beal Creek* ... ID-8
Middle Fork Tom Beall Creek—*stream* ... ID-8
*Middle fork Tom Bell Creek* ... ID-8
Middle Fork Tommys Draw—*valley* ... CO-8
Middle Fork Toponce Creek—*stream* ... ID-8
*Middle Fork Toppenish Creek* ... WA-9
Middle Fork Township—*civil* ... MO-7
Middlefork Township—*civil* ... MO-7
Middle Fork Township—*fmr MCD* ... IA-7
Middle Fork (Township of)—*fmr MCD* ... NC-3
**Middlefork (Township of)**—*pop pl* ... IL-6
Middle Fork Trabing Dry Creek—*stream* ... WY-8
Middle Fork Trail—*trail* ... ID-8
Middle Fork Trail—*trail* ... NM-5
Middle Fork Trail—*trail* (2) ... WA-9
Middle Fork Trail—*trail* ... WY-8
Middle Fork Trail Creek—*stream* ... MT-8
Middle Fork Trout Creek—*stream* ... OR-9
Middle Fork Trujillo Creek—*stream* ... CO-8
Middle Fork Tufts Creek—*stream* ... UT-8
Middle Fork Tule River—*stream* ... CA-9
Middle Fork Tumalo Creek—*stream* ... OR-9
*Middle Fork Tuolumne River* ... CA-9
Middle Fork Turkey Creek—*stream* ... TX-5
*Middle Fork Twelvemile Creek* ... OR-9
Middle Fork Twelvemile Creek—*stream* ... SC-3
Middle Fork Twentymile Creek—*stream* ... WA-9
Middle Fork Two Leggins Creek—*stream* ... MT-8
Middle Fork Upper Creek—*stream* ... NC-3
Middle Fork Upper Deer Creek—*stream* ... MT-8
Middle Fork Upper Twin Branch—*stream* ... VA-3
Middle Fork Ute Canyon—*valley* ... CO-8
*Middle Fork Vermilion River* ... IL-6
*Middle Fork Vermilion River* ... IN-6
Middle Fork Vermilion River—*stream* ... IL-6
*Middle Fork Vermillion River* ... IL-6
*Middle Fork Vermillion River* ... IN-6
Middle Fork Walnut Creek—*stream* ... KS-7
*Middle Fork Waptus River* ... WA-9
Middle Fork Warm Springs Creek—*stream* (2) ... ID-8
Middle Fork Warm Springs Creek—*stream* (3) ... MT-8
Middle Fork Warm Springs Creek—*stream* ... WY-8
Middle Fork Water Canyon—*valley* ... UT-8
Middle Fork Waterhole—*reservoir* ... NM-5
Middle Fork Watts Creek—*stream* ... KY-4
Middle Fork Webb Creek—*stream* ... MO-7
Middle Fork Weber River—*stream* (2) ... UT-8
Middle Fork Weiser River—*stream* ... ID-8
Middle Fork West Creek—*stream* ... AR-4
Middle Fork West Fork Gallatin River—*stream* ... MT-8
Middle Fork West Virginia Fork Dunkard Creek—*stream* ... WV-2
Middle Fork Wheeler Creek—*stream* ... UT-8
Middle Fork Whisky Creek—*stream* ... OR-9
*Middle Fork White River* ... UT-8
Middle Fork White River—*stream* ... AK-9
Middle Fork White River—*stream* ... AR-4
Middle Fork White River—*stream* ... UT-8
Middle Fork Whitetail Creek—*stream* ... MT-8
*Middle Fork Whitewater River* ... CA-9
*Middle Fork Whitewater River* ... IN-6
Middle Fork Whitewater River—*stream* ... CA-9
Middle Fork Whitewater River—*stream* ... MN-6
Middle Fork Wichita River—*stream* ... TX-5
Middle Fork Widow Woman Canyon—*valley* ... CO-8
Middle Fork Wildcat Creek—*stream* (2) ... IN-6
Middle Fork Wild Cow Creek—*stream* ... WY-8
Middle Fork Wilkins Creek—*stream* ... OR-9
Middle Fork Willamette River—*stream* ... OR-9
Middle Fork Williams Creek—*stream* ... TX-5
Middle Fork Williams Fork—*stream* ... CO-8
*Middle Fork Williams Fork River* ... CO-8
*Middle Fork Williamson Creek* ... TX-5
*Middle Fork Williams River* ... CO-8
Middle Fork Williams River—*stream* ... WV-2
Middle Fork Willis Canyon—*valley* ... AZ-5
*Middle Fork Willow Creek* ... OR-9
Middle Fork Willow Creek—*stream* ... AK-9
Middle Fork Willow Creek—*stream* (2) ... MT-8
Middle Fork Willow Creek—*stream* ... NV-8
Middle Fork Willow Creek—*stream* ... SD-7
Middle Fork Wilson Creek—*stream* ... WV-2
Middle Fork Wind Creek—*stream* ... WY-8
Middle Fork Winters Creek—*stream* ... NV-8
Middle Fork Wolf Creek—*stream* ... CO-8
Middle Fork Wolf Creek—*stream* ... MT-8
Middle Fork Wolf Creek—*stream* ... OR-9
Middle Fork Wolf Creek—*stream* ... TN-4
Middle Fork Wolf River—*stream* ... KS-7
Middle Fork Wood River—*stream* ... WY-8
Middle Fork Wounded Man Creek—*stream* ... MT-8
Middle Fork Yager Creek—*stream* ... CA-9
Middle Fork Yancy Creek—*stream* ... TX-5
Middle Fork Yanubbee Creek—*stream* ... OK-5
*Middle Fork Yellow River* ... AL-4
*Middle Fork Yellow River* ... IN-6
Middle Fork Yellow River—*stream* ... IN-6
*Middle Fork Yuba River* ... CA-9
Middle Fork Zumbro River—*stream* ... MN-6
Middle Foster Creek—*stream* ... WA-9
Middle Fowler Pond—*lake* ... ME-1
Middle Fowler Tank—*reservoir* ... TX-5
Middle Fox Creek—*stream* ... VA-3
Middle Fox Lake—*lake* ... FL-3
Middle Foy Lake—*lake* ... MT-8
Middle French Creek—*stream* ... WY-8
Middle Gambill Dam—*dam* ... NC-3
Middle Gambill Lake—*reservoir* ... NC-3
Middle Gap—*gap* ... NM-5
Middle Gap—*gap* ... NC-3
Middle Gap—*gut* ... FL-3
Middle Gap Channel—*channel* ... VA-3
Middle Garber Creek—*stream* ... CO-8
Middlegate—*gap* ... NV-8
Middle Gate—*gut* ... MA-1
Middle Gate—*locale* ... AL-4
Middlegate—*locale* ... NV-8
Middle Gate Sch—*school* ... CT-1
Middle Gato Tank—*reservoir* ... TX-5
Middle Genesee Lake—*lake* ... WI-6
Middle Georgia Coll—*school* ... GA-3
Middle Georgia Memorial Gardens—*cemetery* ... GA-3
Middle Georgia Raceway—*other* ... GA-3
Middle Glacier Creek—*stream* ... AK-9
*Middle Goodwin Creek* ... AZ-5
*Middle Goodwin Wash* ... AZ-5
Middle Gooseberry Creek—*stream* ... WY-8
Middle Gooseberry Gulch—*valley* ... CO-8
*Middle Goose Creek* ... TN-4
Middle Granite Gorge—*valley* ... AZ-5
**Middle Granville**—*pop pl* ... NY-2
**Middle Grave Creek**—*pop pl* ... WV-2
Middle Grave Creek—*stream* ... WV-2
Middle Grenier Pond—*lake* ... ME-1
Middle Gresham Lake—*lake* ... WI-6
Middle Griever Creek—*stream* ... OK-5
*Middle Ground* ... NC-3
Middle Ground—*bar* ... AL-4
Middle Ground—*bar* (3) ... FL-3
Middle Ground—*bar* ... GA-3
Middle Ground—*bar* (5) ... ME-1
Middle Ground—*bar* (3) ... MA-1
Middle Ground—*bar* (2) ... MS-4
Middle Ground—*bar* (2) ... NY-2
Middle Ground—*bar* (2) ... NC-3
Middle Ground—*bar* ... TX-5
Middle Ground—*bar* ... VA-3
Middle Ground—*bay* ... LA-4
Middle Ground—*harbor* ... GU-9
Middle Ground—*island* ... FL-3
Middle Ground—*island* ... MA-1
Middle Ground—*island* ... MI-6
Middle Ground—*island* ... MS-4
Middle Ground—*ridge* ... ME-1
Middle Ground—*rock* ... MA-1
Middle Ground—*swamp* ... ME-1
Middle Ground—*swamp* ... MI-6
Middle Ground, The—*island* ... WA-9
Middleground Cem—*cemetery* ... CT-1
Middle Ground Ch—*church* ... GA-3
Middleground Ch—*church* ... GA-3
Middle Ground Ch—*church* ... GA-3
Middle Ground Flats—*island* ... NY-2
Middle Ground Island—*island* ... CA-9
Middle Ground Island—*island* ... MS-4
Middle Ground Reef—*bar* ... MI-6
Middle Ground Rock—*bar* ... ME-1
Middle Grounds—*bay* ... VA-3
Middle Grounds—*swamp* ... MI-6
Middle Grounds, The—*flat* ... ME-1
Middle Grounds Ch—*church* ... GA-3
Middle Ground Shoal—*bar* (2) ... AK-9
Middle Grounds Island—*island* ... MI-6
Middle Group Mines—*mine* ... CO-8
**Middlegrove**—*pop pl* ... IL-6
**Middle Grove**—*pop pl* ... MO-7
**Middle Grove**—*pop pl* ... NY-2
**Middle Grove**—*pop pl* ... OR-9
Middle Grove Ch—*church* ... ND-7
Middle Grove (RR name for Middlegrove)—*other* ... IL-6
Middle Grove Sch—*school* ... IL-6
Middle Grove Sch—*school* ... OR-9
Middle Gulch—*valley* (2) ... CA-9
Middle Gulch—*valley* (3) ... CO-8
Middle Gut—*gut* ... AL-4
**Middle Haddam**—*pop pl* ... CT-1
Middle Haddam Hist Dist—*hist pl* ... CT-1
Middleham Chapel—*church* ... MD-2
Middleham Chapel—*hist pl* ... MD-2
Middle Hanagita Lake—*lake* ... AK-9
Middle Hanks Lake—*lake* ... OR-9
Middle Hanson Lake—*lake* ... MN-6
Middle Harbor—*bay* ... OH-6
Middle Hardscrabble Creek—*stream* ... CO-8
Middle Hardwood Island—*island* ... ME-1
Middle Harris Trail—*trail* ... OK-5
Middle Haw Creek—*stream* ... FL-3
Middle Haw Creek—*swamp* ... FL-3
Middle Hay Ranch—*locale* ... WY-8
Middle Hector Sch—*school* ... KY-4
*Middlehell Creek* ... CA-9
Middle Henderson Creek—*stream* ... IL-6
Middle Henderson Well—*well* ... TX-5
Middle Herlihy Rsvr—*reservoir* ... OR-9
*Middle Hero* ... VT-1
Middle Hickory Creek—*stream* ... PA-2
Middle Hidden Lake—*lake* ... WA-9
*Middle Hill* ... CT-1
*Middle Hill* ... HI-9
Middle Hill—*summit* ... AZ-5
Middle Hill—*summit* ... NV-8
Middle Hill—*summit* ... NH-1
Middle Hill—*summit* ... NM-5
Middle Hill—*summit* (2) ... NY-2
Middle Hill—*summit* (2) ... PA-2
Middle Hill Ch—*church* ... GA-3
Middle Hills—*range* ... CA-9
Middle Hill Trail—*trail* (2) ... PA-2
Middle Hollow—*valley* ... CA-9
Middle Hollow—*valley* ... KY-4
Middle Hollow—*valley* (2) ... MO-7
Middle Hollow—*valley* ... WV-2
Middle Hollow Cove—*bay* ... MO-7
Middle Hollow Trail—*trail* ... VA-3
Middle Hollybush Sch—*school* ... KY-4
Middle Hooper Island—*island* ... MD-2
**Middle Hope**—*pop pl* ... NY-2
Middle Hope (census name for Middlehope)—*CDP* ... NY-2
Middlehope (census name Middle Hope)—*uninc pl* ... NY-2
Middle Hope Sch—*school* ... NY-2
Middle Horse Camp Tank—*reservoir* ... TX-5
Middle Horse Canyon—*valley* ... UT-8
*Middle Horse Lake* ... OR-9
Middle Horse Lake—*lake* ... OR-9
Middle Hosston Oil Pool—*oilfield* ... MS-4
Middle Hubbard Creek—*stream* ... CO-8
Middle Huisache Tank—*reservoir* ... TX-5
*Middle Hunt Creek* ... CO-8
Middle Hunt Creek—*stream* ... CO-8
Middle Hurricane Sch—*school* ... KY-4
Middle Hurricane Sch—*school* ... WV-2
*Middle Indian Creek* ... IN-6
Middle Indian Creek—*stream* (2) ... MO-7
Middle Indian Creek—*stream* ... TX-5
Middle Indian Field—*island* ... FL-3
Middle Indian Sch—*school* ... KY-4
Middle Indian Spring—*spring* ... NV-8
**Middle Inlet**—*pop pl* ... WI-6
Middle Inlet—*stream* ... WI-6
Middle Inlet Lookout Tower—*locale* ... WI-6
**Middle Inlet (Town of)**—*pop pl* ... WI-6
Middle Intervale—*locale* ... ME-1
Middle Island—*flat* ... AR-4
Middle Island—*island* (4) ... AK-9
Middle Island—*island* ... DE-2
Middle Island—*island* (2) ... FL-3
Middle Island—*island* ... GA-3
Middle Island—*island* (3) ... LA-4
Middle Island—*island* (2) ... ME-1
Middle Island—*island* (4) ... MI-6
Middle Island—*island* ... NJ-2
Middle Island—*island* (2) ... NY-2
Middle Island—*island* ... NC-3
Middle Island—*island* ... WV-2
**Middle Island**—*pop pl* ... NY-2
Middle Island Ch—*church* ... NY-2
Middle Island Ch—*church* ... WV-2
*Middle Island Channel* ... MI-6
Middle Island Country Club—*other* ... NY-2
Middle Island Creek—*stream* ... WV-2
Middle Island Lake—*lake* ... MN-6
Middle Island Point—*cape* ... MI-6
**Middle Island Point**—*pop pl* ... MI-6
Middle Islands—*area* ... AK-9
Middle Islands—*island* ... MI-6
Middle Island Sch—*school* ... WV-2
Middle Islands Passage—*channel* ... MI-6
Middle Island State Game Farm—*park* ... NY-2
Middle Jack Creek—*stream* ... SD-7
Middle Jerry Run—*stream* ... PA-2
Middle JHS—*school* ... IA-7
Middle Jo-Mary Lake—*lake* ... ME-1
Middle Jones Canyon—*valley* ... NM-5
Middle Kehl Canyon—*valley* ... AZ-5
*Middle Kenilworth Corners* ... OH-6
*Middle Key* ... FL-3
Middle Key—*island* (3) ... FL-3
Middle Keys—*island* ... FL-3
Middle Keys (CCD)—*cens area* ... FL-3
Middle Kickapoo Creek—*stream* (2) ... TX-5
Middle Kiffer Point—*cape* ... GA-3
Middle Kiln Brook—*stream* ... NY-2
Middle Kilns—*locale* (2) ... NY-2
Middle Kilns Brook—*stream* ... NY-2
Middle Kimball Lake—*lake* ... WI-6
Middle Kings Creek—*stream* ... TX-5
Middle Kiowa Creek—*stream* ... KS-7
Middle Kirby Rapids—*rapids* ... ID-8
Middle Kirby Rapids—*rapids* ... OR-9
Middle Knappie Canyon—*valley* ... SD-7
Middle Kneebone Draw—*arroyo* ... SD-7
Middle Knob—*summit* ... CA-9
Middle Knob—*summit* ... CO-8
Middle Knob—*summit* ... KY-4
Middle Knob—*summit* (2) ... VA-3
Middle Knob—*summit* ... WV-2
Middle Knob Lake—*lake* ... ID-8
Middle Knoll—*summit* ... AZ-5
Middle La Cinta Windmill—*locale* ... NM-5
Middle Ladder Creek—*stream* ... KS-7
Middle Lagoon—*bay* ... AK-9
*Middle Lake* ... AZ-5
*Middle Lake* ... CA-9
*Middle Lake* ... GA-3
*Middle Lake* ... MI-6
*Middle Lake* ... OR-9
Middle Lake—*lake* (2) ... AL-4
Middle Lake—*lake* (3) ... AK-9
Middle Lake—*lake* (3) ... CA-9
Middle Lake—*lake* ... CO-8
Middle Lake—*lake* (3) ... FL-3
Middle Lake—*lake* ... ID-8
Middle Lake—*lake* ... KY-4
Middle Lake—*lake* (3) ... LA-4
Middle Lake—*lake* (12) ... MI-6
Middle Lake—*lake* (3) ... MN-6
Middle Lake—*lake* ... MS-4
Middle Lake—*lake* ... MT-8
Middle Lake—*lake* ... NE-7
Middle Lake—*lake* (2) ... NV-8
Middle Lake—*lake* (4) ... NM-5
Middle Lake—*lake* (2) ... NY-2
Middle Lake—*lake* (3) ... OR-9
Middle Lake—*lake* (2) ... TX-5
Middle Lake—*lake* (4) ... WI-6
Middle Lake—*lake* ... WY-8
Middle Lake—*reservoir* ... CA-9
Middle Lake—*reservoir* ... NC-3
Middle Lake—*reservoir* ... OK-5
Middle Lake—*reservoir* ... PA-2
Middle Lake Creek—*stream* ... CO-8
Middle Lake Dam—*dam* ... OR-9
Middle Lake Dam—*dam* ... PA-2
Middle Lake Hamilton—*lake* ... FL-3
Middle Lake (historical)—*lake* ... MO-7
Middle Lake (historical)—*lake* ... TX-5
Middle Lakes—*lake* ... WA-9
Middle Lake Waterhole—*lake* ... OR-9
**Middle Lancaster**—*pop pl* ... PA-2
Middleland (historical)—*locale* ... KS-7
Middle Landing—*locale* ... TN-4
Middle Lands—*locale* ... WA-9
*Middle LaSalle Lake* ... MN-6
Middle LaSalle Lake—*lake* ... MN-6
Middle Lateral—*canal* ... CA-9
Middle Lateral—*canal* ... ID-8
Middle Lateral—*canal* ... NM-5
Middle Laurel Ch—*church* ... NC-3
Middle Lead Mountain Pond—*lake* ... ME-1
Middle Leatherwood Creek—*stream* ... OH-6
Middle Ledge—*bar* ... ME-1
Middle Ledge—*bar* ... MA-1
Middle Ledge—*rock* (2) ... MA-1
Middle Ledge (historical)—*bar* ... MA-1
*Middle Ledges* ... ME-1
Middle Ledges—*bar* ... ME-1
Middle Leigh Creek—*stream* ... ID-8
Middle Leonard Canyon—*valley* ... AZ-5
Middle Leon Creek—*stream* ... CO-8
Middle Lick Branch—*stream* ... KY-4
Middlelick Branch—*stream* ... WV-2
Middle Lick Creek—*stream* ... MO-7
Middle Lick Gulch—*valley* ... CA-9
Middle Lilly Creek—*stream* ... TX-5
Middle Limestone Creek—*stream* ... KS-7
*Middle Line Canal* ... OR-9
Middle Line Canal—*canal* ... ID-8
Middle Line Island—*island* ... NY-2
Middle Little River—*stream* ... NC-3
Middle Loch—*bay* ... HI-9
*Middle Lodge Pole Creek* ... WY-8
Middle Lodgepole Creek—*stream* ... WY-8
Middle Logan Creek—*stream* ... NE-7
Middle Long Hollow—*valley* ... OR-9
Middle Lost Creek—*stream* ... UT-8
*Middle Lots* ... PA-2
*Middle Loup River* ... NE-7
Middle Loup River*—*stream* ... NE-7
Middle Lyman Ditch—*canal* ... AZ-5
Middle Lynch Oil Field—*other* ... NM-5
*Middle Mam Creek* ... CO-8
Middle Mamm Creek—*stream* ... CO-8
Middle Mancos River—*stream* ... CO-8
Middleman Falls—*falls* ... CA-9
Middleman Mine—*mine* ... ID-8
Middleman Mtn—*summit* ... MT-8
Middlemarch Canyon—*valley* ... AZ-5
Middlemarch Pass—*gap* ... AZ-5
Middle Mark Island—*island* ... ME-1
*Middle Marsh* ... FL-3
*Middle Marsh* ... MD-2
Middle Marsh—*reservoir* ... WI-6
Middle Marsh Brook—*stream* ... VA-3
Middle Marsh Creek—*stream* ... NJ-2
Middle Marsh Creek—*stream* ... WY-8
Middle Marshes—*swamp* ... NC-3
Middle Marsh Island—*island* ... GA-3
Middle Marsh Island—*island* ... SC-3
Middle Marsh Islands—*island* ... GA-3
Middle Marsh Lake—*lake* ... NE-7
Middle Martis Creek—*stream* ... CA-9
Middle McKenzie Lake—*lake* ... WI-6
Middle Meadow—*flat* ... ID-8
Middle Meadows—*flat* ... ID-8
Middle Meherrin River—*stream* ... VA-3
*Middle Mesa* ... AZ-5
Middle Mesa—*summit* (3) ... AZ-5
Middle Mesa—*summit* ... CA-9
Middle Mesa—*summit* (3) ... CO-8
Middle Mesa—*summit* (5) ... NM-5
Middle Mesa—*summit* ... UT-8
Middle Mesa Canyon—*valley* ... NM-5
Middle Mesa Tank—*reservoir* (2) ... AZ-5
Middle Mesa Tank—*reservoir* ... NM-5
*Middle Mill Creek* ... IA-7
Middle Mill Creek—*stream* ... IA-7
Middle Mill Creek Sch—*school* ... KY-4
Middle Miller Creek—*stream* ... CO-8
Middle Mill Hist Dist—*hist pl* ... NY-2
*Middle Mill Pond* ... MA-1
Middle Millstone Sch—*school* ... KY-4
*Middle Mill Trail* ... PA-2
Middle Mineral Creek—*stream* ... CO-8
Middle Minerva Creek—*stream* ... IA-7
Middlemist Creek—*stream* ... CO-8
Middlemist Oil Field—*oilfield* ... CO-8
Middle Moat Mtn—*summit* ... NH-1
**Middle Moaula Camp**—*pop pl* ... HI-9
Middle Modoc Creek—*stream* ... ID-8
Middle Mohave Wash—*stream* ... AZ-5
Middle Mongaup River—*stream* ... NY-2
Middle Moody Canyon—*valley* ... UT-8
Middlemoor—*swamp* ... MD-2
Middlemoor Ditch—*canal* ... MD-2
*Middlemoor Island* ... MD-2
Middlemoor Thorofare—*channel* ... MD-2
Middle Moriah Mtn—*summit* ... NH-1
Middle Moss Wash Well—*well* ... AZ-5
Middle Mound—*summit* ... WI-6
*Middle Mountain* ... CO-8
Middle Mountain—*ridge* ... AR-4
Middle Mountain—*ridge* (2) ... CA-9
Middle Mountain—*ridge* ... OR-9
Middle Mountain—*ridge* (5) ... WV-2
Middle Mountain Campground—*locale* ... CO-8
Middle Mountain Creek—*stream* ... OR-9
Middle Mountain Firebreak—*trail* ... CA-9
Middle Mountains—*ridge* ... AZ-5
Middle Mountain Seep—*spring* ... UT-8
Middle Mountain Spring—*spring* ... CO-8
Middle Mountain Tank—*reservoir* (2) ... AZ-5
Middle Mountain Trail—*trail* ... CO-8
Middle Mountain Trail—*trail* (2) ... VA-3
Middle Mountain Trail—*trail* (3) ... WV-2
Middle Mouth—*gut* ... VA-3
*Middle Mtn* ... OR-9
*Middle Mtn* ... VA-3
Middle Mtn—*range* ... ID-8
Middle Mtn—*range* ... UT-8
Middle Mtn—*summit* ... AL-4
Middle Mtn—*summit* (3) ... AK-9
Middle Mtn—*summit* (4) ... AZ-5
Middle Mtn—*summit* ... AR-4
Middle Mtn—*summit* (2) ... CA-9
Middle Mtn—*summit* (9) ... CO-8
Middle Mtn—*summit* ... GA-3
Middle Mtn—*summit* (3) ... ID-8
Middle Mtn—*summit* (3) ... ME-1
Middle Mtn—*summit* ... MS-4
Middle Mtn—*summit* ... MO-7
Middle Mtn—*summit* (4) ... MT-8
Middle Mtn—*summit* (3) ... NH-1
Middle Mtn—*summit* ... NM-5
Middle Mtn—*summit* (3) ... NY-2
Middle Mtn—*summit* (6) ... NC-3
Middle Mtn—*summit* (4) ... OK-5
Middle Mtn—*summit* (2) ... OR-9
Middle Mtn—*summit* (2) ... PA-2
Middle Mtn—*summit* (10) ... UT-8
Middle Mtn—*summit* (2) ... VT-1
Middle Mtn—*summit* (12) ... VA-3
Middle Mtn—*summit* (3) ... WA-9
Middle Mtn—*summit* (3) ... WV-2
Middle Mtn—*summit* ... WY-8
Middle Mud Creek—*stream* ... ID-8
Middle Mud Creek—*stream* ... OR-9
*Middle Muddy Creek* ... CO-8
Middle Muddy Creek—*stream* ... CO-8
Middle Mud Spring—*spring* ... UT-8
*Middle Mulberry Creek* ... AL-4
Middle Mule Tank—*reservoir* ... TX-5
Middle Mustang Creek—*stream* (2) ... TX-5
Middle Narrows—*channel* ... IN-6
Middle Naturita Creek—*stream* ... CO-8
Middle Neck—*cape* (2) ... MD-2
Middle Neck Branch—*stream* ... MD-2
Middle Neebish Channel—*channel* ... MI-6
Middle Needham Windmill—*locale* ... TX-5
Middle Nemah—*locale* ... WA-9
Middle Nemah River—*stream* ... WA-9
Middle Newark Reach—*channel* ... NJ-2
Middle Ninemile Creek—*stream* ... WV-2
Middle Nodaway River—*stream* ... IA-7
*Middle Noland Creek* ... TX-5
Middle North Falls—*falls* ... OR-9
Middle North Star Tank—*reservoir* ... NM-5
Middle Nugget Gulch—*valley* ... SD-7
Middle Oak Ch—*church* ... VA-3
Middle Oak Creek—*stream* ... KS-7
Middle Oak Creek—*stream* (2) ... NE-7
Middle Oak Point—*cliff* ... AZ-5
*Middle Oconee River* ... GA-3
Middle Oconee River—*stream* ... GA-3
Middle Octorara Ch—*church* ... PA-2
*Middle Octoraro Ch* ... PA-2
*Middle-of-the-Shore* ... NJ-2
Middle Old River—*lake* ... AR-4
Middle Old River—*stream* ... AR-4
Middle One Creek—*stream* ... OK-5
*Middle One Hundred And Two river* ... IA-7
Middle Osborne Lake—*lake* ... NE-7
Middle Otter Creek—*stream* ... IA-7
Middle Otter Creek Overlook—*locale* ... VA-3
Middle Oval Lake—*lake* ... WA-9
Middle Oxhead Pond—*lake* ... ME-1
Middle Paddy Creek—*stream* ... CA-9
Middle Paddy Creek—*stream* ... OH-6
*Middle Painter Creek* ... KS-7
*Middle Painterhood Creek* ... KS-7
Middle Paint Rock Creek—*stream* ... WY-8
Middle Palisade—*summit* ... CA-9
Middle Palisade Glacier—*glacier* ... CA-9
Middle Palmyra Island—*area* ... MS-4
Middle Park—*basin* ... CA-9
Middle Park—*flat* ... CO-8
Middle Park—*flat* ... UT-8
Middle Park Canyon—*valley* ... CA-9
Middle Parker Spring—*spring* ... NV-8
Middle Parks Creek—*stream* ... ID-8
*Middle Pass* ... AZ-5
*Middle Pass* ... ID-8
*Middle Pass* ... MT-8
*Middle Pass* ... TX-5
Middle Pass—*bay* ... TX-5
Middle Pass—*channel* (2) ... LA-4
Middle Pass—*channel* ... TX-5
Middle Pass—*gap* ... NV-8
Middle Pass—*gap* (2) ... TX-5
Middle Pass—*gap* ... UT-8
Middle Passage—*channel* ... VI-3
Middle Pass Rsvr—*reservoir* ... NV-8
Middle Pass Spring—*spring* ... NV-8
Middle Pasture (historical)—*civil* ... MA-1
Middle Pasture Lake—*reservoir* ... TX-5
Middle Pasture Tank—*reservoir* ... AZ-5
Middle Pasture Tank—*reservoir* (2) ... NM-5
Middle Pasture Well—*well* ... MT-8
Middle Pasture Well—*well* ... TX-5
Middle Pasture Windmill—*locale* (2) ... NM-5
Middle Pasture Windmill—*locale* ... TX-5
Middle Patent Ch—*church* ... NY-2
Middle Patent Golf Course—*other* ... NY-2
Middle Patent Rural Cem—*cemetery* ... NY-2
Middle Patent Sch—*school* ... NY-2
Middle Patuxent River—*stream* ... MD-2
**Middle Paxton (Township of)**—*pop pl* ... PA-2
Middle Peachtree Creek—*stream* ... NC-3
Middle Peach Valley Dam—*dam* ... CO-8
*Middle Peak* ... CA-9
*Middle Peak* ... CO-8
Middle Peak—*summit* (2) ... AK-9
Middle Peak—*summit* (3) ... CA-9
Middle Peak—*summit* ... CO-8
Middle Peak—*summit* ... MT-8
Middle Peak—*summit* ... NH-1
Middle Peak—*summit* ... NM-5
Middle Peak—*summit* ... UT-8
Middle Peak—*summit* (2) ... WA-9
Middle Peak Loop Trail—*trail* ... CA-9
Middle Pea Porridge Pond—*lake* ... NH-1
Middle Pearl Creek—*stream* ... SD-7
Middle Pease River—*stream* ... TX-5
Middle Pen Swamp—*stream* ... SC-3
Middle Pens Windmill—*locale* ... TX-5
Middle Pen Windmill—*locale* ... TX-5
Middle Peralta Ditch—*canal* ... NM-5
Middle Percha Creek—*stream* ... NM-5
Middle Phillips Creek—*stream* ... MT-8
*Middle Pickerel* ... MI-6
Middle Pickerel Lake—*lake* ... MI-6
Middle Piece Mtn—*summit* ... VA-3
Middle Pigeon Lake—*lake* ... MN-6
Middle Pine Creek—*stream* ... MT-8
Middle Pine Creek—*stream* ... UT-8
*Middle Pine Lake* ... WI-6
Middle Pine Lake—*lake* ... MI-6
Middle Piney Creek—*stream* ... WY-8
Middle Piney Lake—*lake* ... WY-8
Middle Piney Lake Campground—*locale* ... WY-8
Middle Pipe Creek—*stream* ... KS-7
*Middle Pipe Lake* ... MN-6
Middle Pistol Lake—*lake* ... ME-1
Middle Pitman Creek—*stream* ... KY-4
Middle Pittsburg Rapids—*rapids* ... OR-9
Middle Place—*locale* ... GA-3
Middle Place Windmills—*locale* ... NM-5
Middle Platte River—*stream* ... IA-7
Middle Plum Creek—*stream* ... CO-8
*Middle Point* ... DE-2
*Middle Point* ... FL-3
*Middle Point* ... MD-2
*Middle Point* ... WA-9

Middle Point—*cape* (2) ... AL-4
Middle Point—*cape* (5) ... AK-9
Middle Point—*cape* ... CA-9
Middle Point—*cape* (3) ... FL-3
Middle Point—*cape* ... ME-1
Middle Point—*cape* ... MI-6
Middle Point—*cape* ... NV-8
Middle Point—*cape* ... NY-2
Middle Point—*cape* ... NC-3
Middle Point—*cape* (2) ... OR-9
Middle Point—*cape* (2) ... TN-4
Middle Point—*cape* (2) ... UT-8
Middle Point—*cape* ... WA-9
Middle Point—*cape* ... WV-2
Middle Point—*cliff* ... VA-3
Middlepoint—*locale* ... IL-6
Middle Point—*locale* ... WV-2
**Middlepoint**—*pop pl* ... MD-2
**Middle Point**—*pop pl* ... OH-6
Middle Point—*ridge* ... CO-8
Middle Point Bay—*bay* ... NY-2
Middle Point Cem—*cemetery* ... MO-7
*Middlepoint (corporate and RR name Middle Point)* ... OH-6
Middle Point Cove—*cove* ... MA-1
Middle Point Divide—*ridge* ... OR-9
Middle Point Island—*island* ... FL-3
Middle Point Islands—*island* ... NV-8
**Middlepoint (Middle Point)**—*pop pl* ... MD-2
Middle Point of the Buckskins—*cape* ... UT-8
Middle Point Ridge—*ridge* (2) ... WA-9
Middle Point Tank—*reservoir* ... AZ-5
Middle Point Trail—*trail* ... CO-8
Middle Polecat Canyon—*valley* ... AZ-5
Middle Polles Tank—*reservoir* ... AZ-5
*Middle Pond* ... CT-1
*Middle Pond* ... MA-1
Middle Pond—*lake* ... CO-8
Middle Pond—*lake* ... DE-2
Middle Pond—*lake* ... FL-3
Middle Pond—*lake* ... IA-7
Middle Pond—*lake* ... ME-1
Middle Pond—*lake* (4) ... MA-1
Middle Pond—*lake* (3) ... NH-1
Middle Pond—*lake* (3) ... NY-2
Middle Pond—*lake* ... RI-1
Middle Pond—*reservoir* ... AZ-5
Middle Pond—*reservoir* ... AR-4
Middle Pond—*reservoir* ... CT-1
Middle Pond—*reservoir* ... ME-1
Middle Pond—*reservoir* ... SC-3
Middle Pond—*reservoir* ... TX-5
Middle Pond—*stream* ... GA-3
Middle Pond Rsvr—*reservoir* ... NV-8
Middle Ponil Creek—*stream* ... NM-5
Middle Poplar Branch—*stream* ... IN-6
Middle Popo Agie River—*stream* ... WY-8
*Middleport* ... WV-2
**Middleport**—*pop pl* (2) ... NY-2
**Middleport**—*pop pl* ... OH-6
**Middleport**—*pop pl* ... PA-2
Middleport Borough—*civil* ... PA-2
*Middle Port Cove* ... RI-1
Middleport Ditch No 1—*canal* ... IL-6
Middleport Hill Cem—*cemetery* ... OH-6
Middleport Mine—*mine* ... WA-9
Middleport Public Library—*hist pl* ... OH-6
Middleport Rsvr—*reservoir* ... NY-2
**Middleport (Township of)**—*pop pl* ... IL-6
Middle Poso Well—*well* ... NM-5
*Middle Potlatch* ... ID-8
Middle Potlatch Creek—*stream* ... ID-8
Middle Prairie—*lake* ... LA-4
Middle Price Lake—*lake* ... WI-6
*Middle Prong* ... KY-4
*Middle Prong* ... TN-4
*Middle Prong* ... WY-8
Middle Prong—*bay* ... FL-3
Middle Prong—*gut* ... AR-4
Middle Prong—*stream* ... NC-3
Middle Prong Alamocitos Creek—*stream* ... TX-5
Middle Prong Big Brushy Creek—*stream* ... KY-4
Middle Prong Big Creek—*stream* ... KY-4
Middle Prong Bogue Falaya—*stream* ... LA-4
Middle Prong Brushy Creek—*stream* ... MO-7
Middle Prong Catfish Creek—*stream* ... TX-5
Middle Prong Clear Creek—*stream* ... NC-3
Middle Prong Collins River—*stream* ... TN-4
Middle Prong Creek—*stream* ... AZ-5
Middle Prong Crooked Creek—*stream* ... MO-7
Middle Prong Cypress Creek—*stream* ... NC-3
Middle Prong Dead Horse Creek—*stream* ... WY-8
Middle Prong Doe Creek—*stream* ... TN-4
Middle Prong Glade Creek—*stream* ... NC-3
Middle Prong Green Creek—*stream* ... IN-6
Middle Prong Gulf Creek—*stream* ... TN-4
Middle Prong Hamer Creek—*stream* ... NC-3
Middle Prong Hanging Woman Creek—*stream* ... WY-8
Middle Prong Hayden Creek—*stream* ... CO-8
Middle Prong Horse Creek—*stream* ... GA-3
Middle Prong Horse Creek—*stream* ... TX-5
Middle Prong Indian Creek—*stream* ... GA-3
Middle Prong Jerigan Creek—*stream* ... TX-5
Middle Prong Left Fork Soque River—*stream* ... GA-3
Middle Prong Little Bridge Branch—*stream* ... NC-3
Middle Prong Little Creek—*stream* ... MO-7
Middle Prong Little Pigeon River—*stream* ... TN-4
Middle Prong Little River—*stream* ... TN-4
Middle Prong Pamlico River—*stream* ... NC-3
Middle Prong Parch Corn Creek—*stream* ... TN-4
Middle Prong Pegamore Creek—*stream* ... GA-3
Middle Prong Pumpkin Creek—*stream* ... WY-8
Middle Prong Red Creek—*stream* ... WY-8
Middle Prong Roaring River—*stream* ... NC-3
Middle Prong Rsvr—*reservoir* ... WY-8
Middle Prong Saint Marys River—*stream* ... FL-3
Middle Prong Silver Creek—*stream* ... MS-4
Middle Prong Sneeds Creek—*stream* ... AR-4
Middle Prong Spring—*spring* (2) ... AZ-5
Middle Prong Sturgeon Creek—*stream* ... GA-3
Middle Prong Tank—*reservoir* ... AZ-5
Middle Prong Tauler Creek—*stream* ... AL-4
Middle Prong West Fork Pigeon River—*stream* ... NC-3
Middle Prong Wild Horse Creek—*stream* (2) ... WY-8
Middle Prong Wolf Creek—*stream* ... TX-5
Middle Quarter Cove—*bay* ... MD-2
Middle Quartz Creek—*stream* ... CO-8
Middle Quartz Lake—*lake* ... MT-8
Middle Raccoon River—*stream* ... IA-7
Middle Rainbow Lake—*lake* ... CO-8
Middle Rainbow Lake—*lake* ... ID-8
Middle Ranch—*locale* (2) ... CA-9
Middle Ranch Canyon—*valley* ... CO-8
Middle Ranch Windmill—*locale* ... NM-5
Middle Range—*range* (2) ... UT-8
Middle Range Pond—*lake* ... ME-1
Middle Ravine—*valley* ... CA-9
Middle Rawhide Butte—*summit* ... WY-8
Middle Reach—*channel* ... VA-3
Middle Red Creek—*stream* ... AZ-5
Middle Red Creek—*stream* ... CO-8
Middle Red Wash—*stream* ... CO-8
Middle Red Well—*well* ... TX-5
*Middle Reef* ... NY-2
Middle Reef—*bar* ... AK-9
Middle Reef—*bar* ... NY-2
Middle Reef—*bar* ... VT-1
Middle Reefs—*bar* ... NY-2
Middle Reservoir Dike—*dam* ... MA-1
Middle Richland Creek—*stream* ... MO-7
*Middle Richland Creek - in part* ... MO-7
*Middle Ridge* ... ID-8
*Middle Ridge* ... UT-8
**Middleridge**—*pop pl* ... VA-3
**Middle Ridge**—*pop pl* ... WI-6
Middle Ridge—*ridge* (2) ... AL-4
Middle Ridge—*ridge* ... AR-4
Middle Ridge—*ridge* (13) ... CA-9
Middle Ridge—*ridge* (2) ... GA-3
Middle Ridge—*ridge* (2) ... ID-8
Middle Ridge—*ridge* (2) ... KY-4
Middle Ridge—*ridge* ... MD-2
Middle Ridge—*ridge* (2) ... MO-7
Middle Ridge—*ridge* (2) ... MT-8
Middle Ridge—*ridge* (10) ... NC-3
Middle Ridge—*ridge* (2) ... OH-6
Middle Ridge—*ridge* ... OK-5
Middle Ridge—*ridge* (5) ... OR-9
Middle Ridge—*ridge* (8) ... PA-2
Middle Ridge—*ridge* (8) ... TN-4
Middle Ridge—*ridge* ... TX-5
Middle Ridge—*ridge* (7) ... UT-8
Middle Ridge—*ridge* (7) ... VA-3
Middle Ridge—*ridge* (4) ... WA-9
Middle Ridge—*ridge* (14) ... WV-2
Middle Ridge—*ridge* ... WI-6
Middle Ridge—*ridge* ... WY-8
Middle Ridge Bald—*ridge* ... NC-3
Middle Ridge Branch—*stream* ... NC-3
Middle Ridge Cem—*cemetery* (2) ... OH-6
Middle Ridge Cem—*cemetery* ... PA-2
Middle Ridge Ch—*church* ... PA-2
Middle Ridge Ch—*church* ... WV-2
Middle Ridge Exclosure—*locale* ... UT-8
Middle Ridge Hollow—*valley* ... WV-2
Middle Ridge Mine—*mine* ... TN-4
Middle Ridges, The—*ridge* ... AL-4
Middle Ridge Sch—*school* ... WV-2
Middle Ridge Swamp—*swamp* ... PA-2
Middle Ridge Trail—*trail* (5) ... PA-2
Middle Rifle Creek—*stream* ... CO-8
Middle Rim Rsvr—*reservoir* ... OR-9
Middle Rincon Tank—*reservoir* ... NM-5
*Middle River* ... IA-7
*Middle River* ... MI-6
*Middle River* ... VA-3
Middle River—*gut* ... AL-4
Middle River—*locale* ... CA-9
Middle River—*locale* ... NC-3
**Middle River**—*pop pl* ... FL-3
**Middle River**—*pop pl* ... MD-2
**Middle River**—*pop pl* ... MN-6
Middle River—*stream* ... AL-4
Middle River—*stream* ... AK-9
Middle River—*stream* ... CA-9
Middle River—*stream* ... CT-1
Middle River—*stream* ... FL-3
Middle River—*stream* ... GA-3
Middle River—*stream* ... IA-7
Middle River—*stream* (2) ... LA-4
Middle River—*stream* ... ME-1
Middle River—*stream* ... MD-2
Middle River—*stream* ... MA-1
Middle River—*stream* ... MN-6
Middle River—*stream* ... MS-4
Middle River—*stream* ... MO-7
Middle River—*stream* ... NJ-2
Middle River—*stream* (2) ... NC-3
Middle River—*stream* ... VA-3
Middle River—*stream* ... WI-6
Middle River Canal—*canal* ... FL-3
Middle River Cem—*cemetery* ... MO-7
Middle River Ch—*church* ... GA-3
Middle River Ch—*church* ... IA-7
Middle River Ch—*church* ... MD-2
Middle River Ch—*church* ... SC-3
Middle River Ch—*church* (2) ... VA-3
Middle River Ch (abandoned)—*church* ... MO-7
Middle River Chapel—*church* ... VA-3
Middle River Ditch—*canal* ... NV-8
Middle River (historical P.O.)—*locale* ... IA-7
Middle River Island—*island* ... LA-4
Middle River JHS—*school* ... MD-2
Middle River (Magisterial District)—*fmr MCD* ... VA-3
**Middle River Manor**—*pop pl* ... FL-3
Middle River Neck—*cape* ... MD-2
Middle River Park—*park* ... MA-1
Middle River Rouge—*stream* ... MI-6
Middle River Sanitorium—*hospital* ... WI-6
Middle River Sch—*school* ... MO-7
Middle River School (Abandoned)—*locale* ... IA-7
Middle River (Township of)—*civ div* ... MN-6
**Middle River Vista**—*pop pl* ... FL-3
*Middle Roach Pond* ... ME-1
Middle Road Ch—*church* ... NY-2
Middle Road Sch—*school* ... IN-6
Middle Roaring Creek—*stream* ... OK-5
Middle Roberts Canyon—*valley* ... CO-8
Middle Rock—*bar* (2) ... ME-1
Middle Rock—*bar* ... NY-2
Middle Rock—*bar* ... WA-9
Middle Rock—*island* ... AK-9
Middle Rock—*island* (2) ... CA-9
Middle Rock—*island* (3) ... CT-1
Middle Rock—*other* ... AK-9
Middle Rock Creek—*stream* ... MT-8
Middle Rock Creek—*stream* ... OK-5
Middle Rock Creek—*stream* ... UT-8
Middle Rock Creek—*stream* ... WY-8
Middle Rock House Tank—*reservoir* ... TX-5
Middle Rock Lake—*lake* ... OR-9
Middle Rock Lake—*lake* ... UT-8
Middle Rock Light—*other* ... AK-9
Middle Rocky Arroyo—*stream* ... NM-5
Middle Rocky Creek—*stream* ... FL-3
Middle Rosary Lake—*lake* ... OR-9
Middle Rouge Parkway—*park* ... MI-6
*Middlers Gut* ... NC-3
Middle Rsvr—*reservoir* (2) ... AZ-5
Middle Rsvr—*reservoir* (2) ... CO-8
Middle Rsvr—*reservoir* (2) ... CT-1
Middle Rsvr—*reservoir* ... MA-1
Middle Rsvr—*reservoir* ... NV-8
Middle Rsvr—*reservoir* ... OR-9
Middle Rsvr—*reservoir* ... UT-8
Middle Rsvr—*reservoir* (2) ... WY-8
Middle Ruckels Branch—*stream* ... NJ-2
Middle Rugg Spring—*spring* ... OR-9
*Middle Run* ... PA-2
Middle Run—*locale* ... WV-2
Middle Run—*stream* ... DE-2
Middle Run—*stream* ... IN-6
Middle Run—*stream* ... KY-4
Middle Run—*stream* (3) ... MD-2
Middle Run—*stream* ... NC-3
Middle Run—*stream* (5) ... OH-6
Middle Run—*stream* (4) ... PA-2
Middle Run—*stream* (2) ... VA-3
Middle Run—*stream* (12) ... WV-2
Middle Run Cem—*cemetery* ... WV-2
Middle Run Ch—*church* ... OH-6
Middle Run Valley Park—*park* ... DE-2
*Middle Rush Creek* ... CO-8
Middle Rush Creek—*stream* ... CO-8
Middle Rushing Creek—*stream* ... TN-4
Middle Russell Pond—*lake* ... ME-1
*Middle Saint Charles River* ... CO-8
Middle Saint Vrain Campground—*locale* ... CO-8
Middle Saint Vrain Creek—*stream* ... CO-8
*Middle Salmon Creek* ... WA-9
Middle Salt Creek—*stream* ... CA-9
Middle Salt Lagoon—*lake* ... AK-9
Middle Saluda River—*stream* ... SC-3
Middle Sanborn Park Rsvr—*reservoir* ... CO-8
Middle Sand Canyon—*valley* ... CO-8
*Middle Sandies Creek* ... TX-5
Middle Sand Lake—*lake* ... MI-6
*Middle Sandy Creek* ... TX-5
Middle Sandy Creek—*stream* ... TX-5
Middle Sanford Spring—*spring* ... NV-8
Middle Santa Ynez Campground—*locale* ... CA-9
Middle Santiam River—*stream* ... OR-9
Middle Saranac Lake—*lake* ... NY-2
Middle Sardina Dam—*dam* ... AZ-5
Middle Sawmill Creek—*stream* ... WY-8
Middle Sawtooth Mtn—*summit* ... WY-8
**Middlesboro**—*pop pl* ... KY-4
*Middlesboro (corporate name Middlesborough)* ... KY-4
Middlesboro Downtown Commercial District—*hist pl* ... KY-4
*Middlesborough* ... KY-4
Middlesborough (CCD)—*cens area* ... KY-4
**Middlesborough (corporate name for Middlesboro)**—*pop pl* ... KY-4
*Middle Sch* ... TN-4
Middle Sch—*school* ... AL-4
Middle Sch—*school* ... AZ-5
Middle Sch—*school* (2) ... AR-4
Middle Sch—*school* ... CA-9
Middle Sch—*school* ... FL-3
Middle Sch—*school* ... IA-7
Middle Sch—*school* ... KY-4
Middle Sch—*school* ... ME-1
Middle Sch—*school* (3) ... MI-6
Middle Sch—*school* ... MN-6
Middle Sch—*school* (2) ... MO-7
Middle Sch—*school* (3) ... NY-2
Middle Sch—*school* (3) ... NC-3
Middle Sch—*school* ... OH-6
Middle Sch—*school* (2) ... SC-3
Middle Sch—*school* (2) ... TN-4
Middle Sch—*school* (2) ... TX-5
Middle Sch—*school* ... WA-9
Middle Sch—*school* (3) ... WI-6
Middle Sch North—*school* ... NC-3
Middle Schroeder Butte—*summit* ... AZ-5
Middle Sch South—*school* ... NC-3
Middle Sch West—*school* ... PA-2
Middle Seamen Tank—*reservoir* ... TX-5
Middle Seco Canyon—*valley* ... NM-5
Middle Seco Creek—*stream* ... NM-5
Middle Seco Spring—*spring* ... NM-5
Middle Sedge—*island* (2) ... NJ-2
Middleset Hollow—*valley* ... TN-4
**Middle Settlement**—*pop pl* ... TN-4
*Middle Settlement Church* ... TN-4
Middle Settlement Community Center—*building* ... TN-4
Middle Settlement Creek—*stream* ... NY-2
Middle Settlement Elem Sch—*school* ... TN-4
Middle Settlement Lake—*lake* ... NY-2
*Middlesettlements* ... TN-4
Middlesettlements Cem—*cemetery* ... TN-4
Middle Settlement Sch (historical)—*school* ... TN-4
Middlesettlements Methodist Ch—*church* ... TN-4
Middle Sevenmile Tank—*reservoir* ... AZ-5
Middle Seven Rivers—*stream* ... NM-5
*Middlesex* ... MA-1
*Middlesex* ... NJ-2
*Middlesex* ... PA-2
Middlesex—*locale* ... VA-3
**Middlesex**—*pop pl* ... MD-2
**Middlesex**—*pop pl* ... NJ-2
**Middlesex**—*pop pl* ... NY-2
**Middlesex**—*pop pl* ... NC-3
**Middlesex**—*pop pl* ... PA-2
**Middlesex**—*pop pl* ... VT-1
**Middlesex Beach**—*pop pl* ... DE-2
Middlesex Canal—*canal* ... MA-1
Middlesex Canal—*hist pl* ... MA-1
Middlesex Cem—*cemetery* ... NC-3
Middlesex Cem—*cemetery* ... PA-2
Middlesex Center—*locale* ... VT-1
Middlesex Center Cem—*cemetery* ... VT-1
Middlesex Ch—*church* ... NC-3
Middlesex Ch—*church* ... PA-2
**Middlesex County**—*pop pl* ... NJ-2
**Middlesex (County)**—*pop pl* ... VA-3
Middlesex County Courthouse—*hist pl* ... VA-3
Middlesex County Hosp—*hospital* ... MA-1
**Middlesex County (in (P)MSA 1120,2600, 4560)**—*pop pl* ... MA-1
**Middlesex County (in (P)MSA 3280,5020, 5480)**—*pop pl* ... CT-1
Middlesex County Training Sch—*school* ... MA-1
Middlesex Dam—*dam* ... MA-1
**Middlesex Downs**—*pop pl* ... NJ-2
Middlesex Elem Sch—*school* ... NC-3
Middlesex Elem Sch—*school* (2) ... PA-2
Middlesex Fells—*range* ... MA-1
Middlesex Fells Reservation—*park* ... MA-1
Middlesex HS—*school* ... VA-3
Middlesex Intermediate Sch—*school* ... PA-2
Middlesex JHS—*school* ... CT-1
Middlesex Junction (historical)—*locale* ... MA-1
Middlesex Mall—*locale* ... MA-1
Middlesex Memorial Cem—*cemetery* ... VA-3
Middlesex Memorial Gardens—*cemetery* ... NC-3
Middlesex (Middlesex Village)—*uninc pl* ... MA-1
Middlesex Milling Dam—*dam* ... NJ-2
Middlesex Mine—*mine* ... NV-8
Middlesex Notch—*summit* ... VT-1
Middlesex Reservoir Dam—*dam* ... NJ-2
Middlesex Rsvr—*reservoir* ... NJ-2
Middlesex Rumney Sch—*school* ... VT-1
*Middlesex Sch* ... PA-2
Middlesex Sch—*school* ... MD-2
Middlesex Sch—*school* ... MA-1
**Middlesex (Town of)**—*pop pl* ... NY-2
**Middlesex (Town of)**—*pop pl* ... VT-1
**Middlesex (Township of)**—*pop pl* (2) ... PA-2
Middlesex Valley Central Sch—*school* ... NY-2
**Middlesex Village (subdivision)**—*pop pl* ... MA-1
Middle Shaser Creek—*stream* ... WA-9
Middle Shaser Trail—*trail* ... WA-9
Middle Shingle Canyon—*valley* ... NM-5
Middle Shoal—*bar* ... NJ-2
Middle Shoal—*bar* ... NY-2
Middle Shoal—*bar* ... NC-3
Middle Shoal—*bar* ... WI-6
Middle Shoal Creek—*bay* ... NC-3
Middle Shoal Rock—*bar* ... NY-2
Middle Shoals—*other* ... MO-7
Middle Shoo Fly Creek—*stream* ... KS-7
Middle Silver Creek—*stream* ... IA-7
Middle Sink—*basin* ... UT-8
*Middle Sister* ... OR-9
Middle Sister—*summit* ... CA-9
Middle Sister—*summit* ... NV-8
Middle Sister—*summit* ... OR-9
Middle Sister Bar—*bar* ... AL-4
Middle Sister Creek—*stream* ... OR-9
Middle Sister Peak—*summit* ... ID-8
*Middle Sisters* ... OR-9
Middle Sister Trail—*trail* ... NH-1
Middle Siuslaw-Triangle Lake (CCD)—*cens area* ... OR-9
Middle Slaughter Canyon—*valley* ... NM-5
Middle Slide Canyon—*valley* ... UT-8
Middle Slough—*channel* ... CA-9
Middle Slough—*channel* ... IA-7
Middle Slough—*gut* (2) ... AK-9
Middle Slough—*gut* ... CA-9
Middle Slough—*gut* ... FL-3
Middle Slough—*gut* ... IL-6
Middle Slough—*stream* ... AR-4
Middle Smithfield Ch—*church* ... PA-2
*Middle Smithfield Elementary School* ... PA-2
Middle Smithfield Sch—*school* ... PA-2
**Middle Smithfield (Township of)**—*pop pl* ... PA-2
Middle Smith Tank—*reservoir* ... AZ-5
Middle Soldier River—*stream* ... IA-7
Middle Sound—*bay* ... NC-3
Middle Sound Ch—*church* ... NC-3
Middle South Branch Forest River Number 1 Dam—*dam* ... ND-7
Middle South Branch Forest River Number 4 Dam—*dam* ... ND-7
Middle South Pond—*lake* ... NY-2
Middle Spit—*bar* ... MS-4
*Middle Spring* ... MH-9
**Middle Spring**—*pop pl* ... PA-2
Middle Spring—*spring* (5) ... AZ-5
Middle Spring—*spring* (3) ... CA-9
Middle Spring—*spring* ... CO-8
Middle Spring—*spring* ... ID-8
Middle Spring—*spring* (5) ... NV-8
Middle Spring—*spring* (2) ... NM-5
Middle Spring—*spring* ... OR-9
Middle Spring—*spring* ... TX-5
Middle Spring—*spring* (4) ... UT-8
Middle Spring—*spring* ... WY-8
*Middle Spring Beach* ... MH-9
Middle Spring Creek—*stream* ... CA-9
Middle Spring Creek—*stream* ... PA-2
*Middle Spring Grasslands* ... MH-9
Middle Spring Lake—*lake* ... UT-8
*Middle Spring Ridge* ... MH-9
Middle Spring Ridge—*ridge* ... TN-4
*Middle Spring Stream* ... MH-9
Middle Spring Wash—*valley* ... UT-8
Middle Springy Pond—*lake* ... ME-1
Middle Sprite—*locale* ... NY-2
Middle Sprite Creek—*stream* ... NY-2
Middle Spunk Lake—*lake* ... MN-6
Middle Spy Windmill—*locale* ... NM-5
Middle Squabble Sch—*school* ... KY-4
Middle Squaw Brook—*stream* ... ME-1
Middle Stack Mtn—*summit* ... NV-8
*Middle Stoddard Lake* ... CA-9
Middlestown—*locale* ... KY-4
Middle Straits Lake—*lake* ... MI-6
Middle Strange Island—*island* ... GA-3
Middle Sugarbush Lake—*lake* ... WI-6
Middle Sugarloaf—*summit* ... NH-1
Middle Sulphur Canyon—*valley* ... ID-8
Middle Sulphur Creek—*stream* ... MO-7
Middle Sulphur River—*stream* ... TX-5
Middle Summit Mount Jefferson—*summit* ... NV-8
Middle Supply Creek—*stream* ... CO-8
Middle Supply Ditch—*canal* ... MT-8
Middle Susie Creek—*stream* ... NV-8
*Middle Swamp* ... NC-3
Middle Swamp—*stream* (3) ... NC-3
Middle Swamp—*stream* ... SC-3
Middle Swamp—*swamp* (3) ... NC-3
Middleswart Cem—*cemetery* ... OH-6
Middleswarth—*locale* ... PA-2
Middleswart Spring—*spring* ... OR-9
Middle Sweeney Lake—*lake* ... WY-8
**Middlesworth**—*pop pl* ... IL-6
Middlesworth, Isaac R., Farm House—*hist pl* ... MI-6
Middle Sybille Creek—*stream* ... WY-8
Middle Sycamore Creek—*stream* ... TX-5
Middle Tallahassee Creek—*stream* ... CO-8
Middle Tallawampa Creek—*stream* ... AL-4
*Middle Tank* ... AZ-5
Middle Tank—*lake* ... NM-5
Middle Tank—*lake* ... TX-5
Middle Tank—*reservoir* (26) ... AZ-5
Middle Tank—*reservoir* (20) ... NM-5
Middle Tank—*reservoir* (14) ... TX-5
Middle Tanks—*reservoir* ... AZ-5
Middle Tanks—*reservoir* ... NM-5
Middle Tarkio Creek—*stream* ... IA-7
Middle Tarkio Creek—*stream* ... MO-7
*Middle Tarkio River* ... IA-7
*Middle Tarkio River* ... MO-7
Middle Taylor Creek—*stream* ... CO-8
**Middle Taylor (Township of)**—*pop pl* ... PA-2
Middle Tebay Lake—*lake* ... AK-9
Middle Tennessee Agricultural Experiment Station—*locale* ... TN-4
Middle Tennessee Agricultural Station—*stream* ... TN-4
Middle Tennessee Hosp—*hospital* ... TN-4
Middle Tennessee State Coll—*school* ... TN-4
*Middle Tennessee State Normal Sch* ... TN-4
*Middle Tennessee State Teachers Coll* ... TN-4
*Middle Tennessee State Univ* ... TN-4
Middle Tensleep Creek—*stream* ... WY-8
Middle Terrapin Creek—*stream* ... OK-5
Middle Teton—*summit* ... WY-8
Middle Teton Glacier—*glacier* ... WY-8
Middle Thompson Creek—*stream* ... CO-8
Middle Thompson Lake—*lake* ... MT-8
Middle Thompson Park—*flat* ... CO-8
Middle Thorofare—*channel* (4) ... NJ-2
Middle Thorofare Island—*island* ... NJ-2
Middle Three Forks Creek—*stream* ... WY-8
Middle Three Meadow—*flat* ... CA-9
Middle Threemile Creek—*stream* ... ID-8
Middle Thurmon Creek—*stream* ... ID-8
Middle Tiffany Mtn—*summit* ... WA-9
*Middle Tillatoba Creek - in part* ... MS-4
Middle Timber Creek—*stream* ... IA-7
*Middle Timberlake Creek* ... CO-8
Middle Tios Tank—*reservoir* ... TX-5
*Middleton* ... DE-2
*Middleton* ... IN-6
*Middleton* ... NH-1
*Middleton* ... NJ-2
*Middleton* ... OH-6
*Middleton* ... TN-4
*Middleton* ... VA-3
Middleton—*locale* ... AL-4
Middleton—*locale* ... AR-4
Middleton—*locale* ... CA-9
Middleton—*locale* ... CO-8
Middleton—*locale* ... GA-3
Middleton—*locale* ... IL-6
Middleton—*locale* ... MS-4
Middleton—*locale* ... OK-5
Middleton—*locale* ... TX-5
Middleton—*locale* ... UT-8
**Middleton**—*pop pl* ... ID-8
**Middleton**—*pop pl* ... KY-4
**Middleton**—*pop pl* ... MA-1
**Middleton**—*pop pl* (2) ... MI-6
**Middleton**—*pop pl* ... MO-7
**Middleton**—*pop pl* ... NH-1
**Middleton**—*pop pl* (3) ... OH-6
**Middleton**—*pop pl* ... OR-9
**Middleton**—*pop pl* ... PA-2
**Middleton**—*pop pl* ... TN-4
**Middleton**—*pop pl* (2) ... VA-3
**Middleton**—*pop pl* ... WI-6
Middleton, Dr. George McLelland, House and Garage—*hist pl* ... IA-7
Middleton, Henri, House—*hist pl* ... KY-4
Middleton, Jesse, House—*hist pl* ... KY-4
Middleton, Mount—*summit* ... AK-9
Middleton Black Ridge—*ridge* ... UT-8
Middleton Branch—*stream* ... IL-6
Middleton Branch—*stream* (2) ... KY-4
Middleton Canal—*canal* ... ID-8
Middleton (CCD)—*cens area* ... TN-4
Middleton Cem—*cemetery* (3) ... AL-4
Middleton Cem—*cemetery* ... AR-4
Middleton Cem—*cemetery* ... CA-9
Middleton Cem—*cemetery* ... GA-3
Middleton Cem—*cemetery* (3) ... KY-4
Middleton Cem—*cemetery* (2) ... MS-4
Middleton Cem—*cemetery* ... OK-5
Middleton Cem—*cemetery* ... OR-9
Middleton Cem—*cemetery* ... SC-3
Middleton Cem—*cemetery* ... TN-4
Middleton Cem—*cemetery* ... VA-3
Middleton Ch—*church* ... GA-3
Middleton Ch—*church* ... MS-4
Middleton Ch—*church* ... MO-7
Middleton City Hall—*building* ... TN-4
**Middleton Colony**—*pop pl* ... MA-1
Middleton Corner—*locale* ... OH-6
**Middleton Corners**—*pop pl* ... NH-1
Middleton Creek—*stream* ... AZ-5
Middleton Creek—*stream* ... CA-9
Middleton Creek—*stream* ... ID-8
Middleton Creek—*stream* ... MS-4
Middleton Creek—*stream* ... NC-3
Middleton Creek—*stream* ... TN-4
Middleton Creek Cem—*cemetery* ... MS-4
Middleton Creek Ch—*church* ... MS-4
*Middleton Creek Primitive Baptist Ch* ... MS-4
Middleton Cut—*channel* ... SC-3
Middleton Division—*civil* ... TN-4
Middleton Drain—*canal* ... MI-6
Middleton Elem Sch—*school* ... TN-4
**Middleton Farm**—*pop pl* ... MD-2
Middleton Field (airport)—*airport* ... AL-4
Middleton Field Cem—*cemetery* ... MS-4
Middleton Fork—*stream* ... WV-2
Middleton Gap—*gap* ... KY-4
Middleton Gap—*gap* ... VA-3
Middleton Gardens—*uninc pl* ... VA-3
Middleton Grove Ch—*church* ... MS-4
Middleton Gulch—*valley* ... CA-9
**Middleton Heights**—*pop pl* ... KY-4
**Middleton Heights**—*pop pl* ... NC-3
Middleton Hill—*summit* ... TX-5
Middleton (historical)—*locale* (2) ... MS-4
Middleton (historical P.O.)—*locale* ... MA-1
Middleton Hollow—*valley* ... MO-7
Middleton HS—*school* ... FL-3
Middleton HS—*school* ... TN-4
Middleton Hunt Club—*other* ... SC-3
Middleton Island—*island* ... AK-9
Middleton Island—*island* ... IL-6
**Middleton Junction**—*pop pl* ... WI-6
Middleton Lake—*lake* ... GA-3
Middleton Lake—*lake* ... NM-5
Middleton Lake—*reservoir* ... AL-4
Middleton Lake Dam—*dam* (2) ... MS-4
Middleton Memorial Ch—*church* ... TX-5
Middleton Mesa—*summit* ... AZ-5
Middleton Mesa Spring—*spring* ... AZ-5
Middleton Mesa Tank—*reservoir* ... AZ-5
*Middleton Methodist Church* ... MS-4
Middleton Mill Canal—*canal* ... ID-8
Middleton Mill Ditch—*canal* ... ID-8
Middleton Place—*cemetery* ... SC-3
Middleton Place—*hist pl* ... SC-3
Middleton P.O. (historical)—*locale* ... AL-4
Middleton P. O. (historical)—*locale* ... AL-4
Middleton Pond—*lake* ... MA-1
Middleton Pond—*reservoir* ... TX-5
Middleton Pond Outlet Dam—*dam* ... MA-1
Middleton Post Office (historical)—*building* ... AL-4
Middleton Post Office (historical)—*building* ... MS-4
Middleton Ranch—*locale* ... WY-8
Middleton Sch—*school* ... IL-6
Middleton Sch—*school* ... KS-7
Middleton Sch—*school* ... MS-4
Middleton Sch—*school* ... MT-8
Middleton Sch—*school* ... WI-6
Middleton Sch (abandoned)—*school* ... PA-2
Middletons Corner—*locale* ... VA-3
Middleton Seeps—*spring* ... NV-8
Middleton Shop Ctr—*locale* ... FL-3
Middleton's Plantation—*hist pl* ... SC-3
*Middletons Station* ... IN-6
*Middleton Station* ... TN-4
*Middleton Station Post Office* ... TN-4
Middleton Street Sch—*school* ... CA-9
Middleton Substation—*hist pl* ... ID-8
*Middletons (West Middleton)* ... IN-6
**Middleton (Town of)**—*pop pl* ... MA-1
**Middleton (Town of)**—*pop pl* ... NH-1
**Middleton (Town of)**—*pop pl* ... WI-6
Middleton Township—*civil* ... MO-7
**Middleton Township**—*pop pl* ... SD-7
Middleton Township (historical)—*civil* ... SD-7
**Middleton (Township of)**—*pop pl* (2) ... OH-6
Middleton Valley Sch—*school* ... MD-2
Middleton Wash—*valley* ... UT-8
Middleton Well—*well* ... NM-5
Middle Top—*summit* ... NC-3
Middle Torch Key—*island* ... FL-3
*Middletown* ... AL-4
*Middle Town* ... DE-2
*Middletown* (2) ... IN-6
*Middletown* ... MA-1
*Middletown* ... NJ-2
*Middletown* ... PA-2
*Middletown* ... VT-1
Middletown—*locale* ... KS-7
Middletown—*locale* ... MD-2
Middletown—*locale* ... NJ-2
Middletown—*locale* ... PA-2
Middletown—*locale* ... WV-2
**Middletown**—*pop pl* ... CA-9
**Middletown**—*pop pl* ... CT-1
**Middletown**—*pop pl* ... DE-2
**Middletown**—*pop pl* ... IL-6
**Middletown**—*pop pl* (3) ... IN-6
**Middletown**—*pop pl* ... IA-7
**Middletown**—*pop pl* (3) ... KY-4
**Middletown**—*pop pl* (2) ... MD-2
**Middletown**—*pop pl* ... MO-7
**Middletown**—*pop pl* (2) ... NJ-2
**Middletown**—*pop pl* ... NY-2
**Middletown**—*pop pl* ... NC-3
**Middletown**—*pop pl* (3) ... OH-6
**Middletown**—*pop pl* (6) ... PA-2
**Middletown**—*pop pl* ... RI-1
**Middletown**—*pop pl* ... VT-1
**Middletown**—*pop pl* (2) ... VA-3
Middletown—*uninc pl* ... WV-2
*Middletown, Town of* ... MA-1
**Middletown, (Township of)**—*pop pl* ... NJ-2
Middletown Acad—*hist pl* ... DE-2
Middletown Alms House—*hist pl* ... CT-1
Middletown Anchorage—*bay* ... NC-3
Middletown Area HS—*school* ... PA-2
Middletown Borough—*civil* ... PA-2
Middletown Branch—*stream* (2) ... MD-2
Middletown Brook—*stream* ... NY-2
Middle Town Cem—*cemetery* ... TX-5
Middletown Cem—*cemetery* (3) ... VT-1
Middletown Center—*locale* ... PA-2
Middletown Ch—*church* ... KY-4
Middletown Ch—*church* ... MD-2
Middletown Ch—*church* ... VA-3
*Middletown Creek* ... NJ-2
Middletown Creek—*stream* ... NC-3
Middletown Drain—*stream* ... IN-6
**Middletowne Farms**—*pop pl* ... VA-3
Middletown Elem Sch—*school* ... IN-6
**Middletown Farm**—*pop pl* ... VA-3
Middletown Heights—*locale* ... KY-4
Middletown Heights—*locale* ... PA-2
**Middletown Heights**—*pop pl* ... MD-2
Middletown Hist Dist—*hist pl* ... DE-2
Middletown Hist Dist—*hist pl* ... IL-6
Middletown Hist Dist (Boundary Increase)—*hist pl* ... IL-6
Middletown (historical)—*locale* ... KS-7

Middletown HS—school ... DE-2
Middletown HS—school ... NJ-2
Middletown Hydraulic Canal—canal ... OH-6
Middletown Inn—hist pl ... KY-4
**Middletown Junction**—pop pl ... OH-6
Middletown Lake—reservoir ... MO-7
Middletown Meetinghouse—church ... PA-2
Middletown-Odessa (CCD)—cens area ... DE-2
**Middletown Park**—pop pl ... IN-6
Middletown Point ... NJ-2
Middletown Point—cape ... NY-2
**Middletown Rancheria (Indian Reservation)**—pop pl ... CA-9
Middletown Rsvr—reservoir ... MD-2
Middletown Sch (historical)—school ... MO-7
Middle (Township of)—fmr MCD ... AR-4
**Middle (Township of)**—pop pl ... IN-6
**Middle (Township of)**—pop pl ... NJ-2
Middletown South Green Hist Dist—hist pl ... CT-1
**Middletown Springs**—pop pl ... VT-1
Middletown Springs Hist Dist—hist pl ... VT-1
**Middletown Springs (Town of)**—pop pl ... VT-1
Middletown State Hospital—uninc pl ... NY-2
Middletown (Town of)—civ div ... CT-1
**Middletown (Town of)**—pop pl ... NY-2
**Middletown (Town of)**—pop pl ... RI-1
Middletown Township—CDP ... PA-2
**Middletown (Township of)**—pop pl ... MN-6
**Middletown (Township of)**—pop pl (3) ... PA-2
**Middletown & Unionville Junction**—pop pl ... NY-2
Middletown United Methodist Church—hist pl ... KY-4
Middletown Upper Houses Hist Dist—hist pl ... CT-1
Middletown Valley—valley ... MD-2
Middle Trabajo Creek—stream ... NM-5
Middle Trace Fork—stream ... WV-2
Middle Trail—trail ... UT-8
Middle Trail—trail ... WY-8
Middle Trail Canyon—valley ... AZ-5
Middle Trail Creek—stream ... OR-9
Middle Trail Ridge—ridge ... NC-3
Middle Trail Tank—reservoir ... AZ-5
Middle Trap Spring—spring ... AZ-5
Middle Trap Windmill—locale ... TX-5
Middle Trilby Lake—lake ... ID-8
Middle Trough Tank—reservoir ... AZ-5
Middle Trout Creek—stream ... CO-8
Middle Truchas Peak—summit ... NM-5
Middle Tschuddi Gulch—valley ... CO-8
Middle Tsid-weza—area ... NM-5
Middle Tule Draw—valley ... TX-5
Middle Tulip Creek—stream ... MS-4
Middle Tunnel (abandoned)—tunnel ... SC-3
Middle Tuolumne River—stream ... CA-9
Middle Turkey Creek—stream ... TX-5
Middle Turret Lakes—lake ... CA-9
Middle Twin Creek—stream ... ID-8
Middle Two Tank—reservoir ... AZ-5
Middle Tyger River—stream ... SC-3
Middle Underwood Windmill—locale ... TX-5
Middle Unknown Lake—lake ... ME-1
Middle Ute Creek—stream ... CO-8
Middle Ute Lake—lake ... CO-8
Middle Valley—basin ... NE-7
Middle Valley—basin ... OR-9
**Middle Valley**—pop pl ... NJ-2
**Middle Valley**—pop pl ... TN-4
Middle Valley—valley ... ID-8
Middle Valley—valley ... MN-6
Middle Valley—valley ... NJ-2
Middle Valley—valley ... TX-5
Middle Valley Baptist Ch—church ... TN-4
Middle Valley (CCD)—cens area ... TN-4
Middle Valley Cem—cemetery ... NJ-2
Middle Valley Ch—church ... TN-4
Middle Valley Ch of Christ—church ... TN-4
Middle Valley Division—civil ... TN-4
**Middle Valley Estates**—pop pl ... TN-4
Middle Valley Prong—stream ... TX-5
Middle Valley Rec Area—park ... TN-4
Middle Valley Sch—school ... NJ-2
Middle Valley Sch—school ... OR-9
Middle Valley School ... TN-4
Middle Velma Lake—lake ... CA-9
**Middle Verde**—pop pl ... AZ-5
Middle Verde Cem—cemetery ... AZ-5
Middle Verde Creek ... TX-5
Middle Verde Creek—stream ... TX-5
Middle Verde Substation—locale ... AZ-5
Middle Village—locale ... MI-6
**Middle Village**—pop pl (2) ... NY-2
**Middle Village Three**—pop pl ... HI-9
Middleville ... NJ-2
Middleville—locale ... NJ-2
**Middleville**—pop pl ... MI-6
**Middleville**—pop pl (2) ... NY-2
Middleville Ch—church ... MN-6
Middleville Ch—church ... WV-2
Middleville JHS—school ... NY-2
Middleville State Game Area—park ... MI-6
Middleville Township Hall—hist pl ... MN-6
**Middleville (Township of)**—pop pl ... MN-6
Middle Wakefield Spring—spring ... AZ-5
Middle Wallace Tank—reservoir ... AZ-5
Middle Walnut Creek—stream ... IA-7
Middle Warm Creek Point—ridge ... UT-8
Middle Warrior Creek—stream ... FL-3
Middle Wash—stream ... AZ-5
Middle Water—locale ... TX-5
Middle Water—spring ... AZ-5
Middle Water—stream ... CO-8
Middle Water Canyon—valley ... AZ-5
Middlewater Creek—stream ... AZ-5
Middle Water Creek—stream ... CO-8
Middle Water Hole—spring ... ID-8
Middle Watering—area ... TX-5
Middlewater Pumping Station—other ... CA-9
Middlewaters Campground—locale ... CA-9
Middle Water Spring—spring (3) ... AZ-5
Middle Water Springs—spring ... NM-5
Middle Water Tank—reservoir ... AZ-5
Middle Waterway—bay ... WA-9
Middlewater Windmill—locale ... AZ-5
**Middleway**—pop pl ... WV-2
Middleway Hist Dist—hist pl ... WV-2
Middleway (Magisterial District)—fmr MCD ... WV-2
Middle Well—locale (5) ... NM-5
Middlewell—locale ... TX-5
Middle Well—well (5) ... AZ-5
Middle Well—well ... NV-8
Middle Well—well (20) ... NM-5
Middle Well—well (11) ... TX-5
Middle Well ( Artesian)—well ... WY-8
Middle Wells—locale ... NM-5
Middle Wells—well ... TX-5
Middle West Hotel—hist pl ... MO-7
Middle West Windmill—locale ... TX-5
Middle Wheeling Creek ... WV-2
Middle Wheeling Creek—stream ... PA-2
Middle Wheeling Creek—stream ... WV-2
Middle White Oak Fork—stream ... KY-4
Middle White Peak—summit ... CO-8
Middle Wide Mesa—summit ... AZ-5
Middle Wild Horse Mesa—summit ... UT-8
Middle Willow Creek—stream (3) ... CO-8
Middle Willow Creek—stream ... IA-7
Middle Willow Creek—stream ... MT-8
Middle Willow Creek—stream ... OR-9
Middle Willows—flat ... CA-9
Middle Windmill—locale (2) ... AZ-5
Middle Windmill—locale ... CO-8
Middle Windmill—locale ... ID-8
Middle Windmill—locale (9) ... NM-5
Middle Windmill—locale (26) ... TX-5
Middle Windsor Ditch—canal ... MT-8
Middle Witch Canyon—valley ... AZ-5
Middle Wolf Creek—stream ... IL-6
Middlewood Creek—stream ... WY-8
Middlewood Hill—summit ... WY-8
Middlewood Ranch—locale ... WY-8
Middley Bridge—bridge ... OR-9
Middle Yegua Creek—stream ... TX-5
Middle Yoke Creek—stream ... AK-9
Middle Yuba River—stream ... CA-9
Middle Zapata Creek ... CO-8
Middle Zapata Creek—stream ... CO-8
Middle Zapata Creek Lake—lake ... CO-8
Middllton Creek—stream ... CO-8
Middlton Post Office—building ... TN-4
Middough Creek—stream ... OR-9
Middy Point—cape ... AK-9
Mideity—locale ... TX-5
Mideke Supply Bldg—hist pl ... OK-5
Midel A Tank—reservoir ... AZ-5
**Midfield**—pop pl ... AL-4
**Midfield**—pop pl ... TX-5
Midfield City Hall—building ... AL-4
Midfield Elem Sch—school ... AL-4
Midfield Lake—reservoir ... AL-4
Midfield Oil Field—oilfield ... TX-5
Midfield Park Shop Ctr—locale ... AL-4
Midfield Plantation—hist pl ... SC-3
Midfield Plaza Shop Ctr—locale ... AL-4
**Midfields**—pop pl ... TN-4
Midfield Senior HS—school ... AL-4
Mid-Florida Assembly Grounds—church ... FL-3
Mid-Florida Golf Course—locale ... FL-3
Mid-Florida Technical Institute—school ... FL-3
Midford Township—civil ... ND-7
Mid Fork Panther Creek—stream ... OR-9
Mid-Fork Pine Creek ... OR-9
Mid Fork Rattlesnake Creek—stream ... OR-9
Mid Fork Trout Creek—stream ... OR-9
Midge Creek—stream ... CA-9
Midge Creek—stream ... MT-8
Midge Lake—lake ... CA-9
Midge Lake—lake ... MN-6
Midgely Bridge Picnic Area—park ... AZ-5
Midges Court (trailer park)—locale ... AZ-5
**Midges Court (trailer park)**—pop pl ... AZ-5
Midget, Lake—lake (2) ... FL-3
Midget Creek—stream ... ID-8
Midget Creek—stream ... MT-8
Midget Creek—stream ... OR-9
Midget Creek—stream ... TX-5
Midget Creek—stream ... WA-9
Midget Draw—valley ... AZ-5
Midget Lake—lake (2) ... MI-6
Midget Lake—lake ... MN-6
Midget Lake—lake ... OR-9
Midget Lake—lake (3) ... WI-6
Midget Mesa—summit ... NM-5
Midget Mine—mine ... AZ-5
Midget Peak—summit ... ID-8
Midget Pond—lake ... NY-2
Midgett Cove—bay ... NC-3
Midgette Creek—stream ... NC-3
Midgette Point—cape ... NC-3
Midgett Island—island ... NC-3
Midgley Bridge—bridge ... AZ-5
Mid Griffith Lake—lake ... CO-8
**Midhampton**—pop pl ... NY-2
Mid Hills—other ... CA-9
Mid (historical)—locale ... AL-4
Mid-Hudson Bridge—bridge ... NY-2
Midian—locale ... KS-7
Midimber Lake—lake ... AK-9
Mid Island Hosp—hospital ... NY-2
Midjigei, Cape ... FM-9
**Midkiff**—pop pl ... TX-5
**Midkiff**—pop pl ... WV-2
Midkiff Camp—locale ... TX-5
Midkiff Cem—cemetery ... KY-4
Midkiff Cem—cemetery ... NC-3
Midkiff Cem—cemetery (2) ... WV-2
Midkiff Creek—stream ... LA-4
Midkiff Gas Plant—oilfield ... TX-5
**Midkiff (Hadacol Corners)**—pop pl ... TX-5
Midkiff Sch—school ... WV-2
Midkiff Sch—school ... AS-9
Mid Lake—lake (2) ... MI-6
Mid Lake—lake ... UT-8
Mid Lake—lake ... WI-6
Midlake—locale ... UT-8
**Midlake**—pop pl ... CA-9
Midlakes—locale ... WA-9
Midlake Substation—other ... CA-9
Midland ... MN-6
Midland ... MO-7
Midland—fmr MCD (2) ... NE-7
Midland—locale ... CO-8
Midland—locale ... KS-7
Midland—locale ... KY-4
Midland—locale ... NE-7
Midland—locale ... OR-9
**Midland**—pop pl ... AR-4
**Midland**—pop pl ... CA-9
**Midland**—pop pl ... GA-3
**Midland**—pop pl ... IN-6
**Midland**—pop pl ... IA-7
**Midland**—pop pl ... KS-7
**Midland**—pop pl ... KY-4
**Midland**—pop pl ... LA-4
**Midland**—pop pl ... MD-2
**Midland**—pop pl ... MA-1
**Midland**—pop pl ... MI-6
**Midland**—pop pl ... NC-3
**Midland**—pop pl ... OH-6
**Midland**—pop pl (2) ... PA-2
**Midland**—pop pl ... SD-7
**Midland**—pop pl ... TN-4
**Midland**—pop pl ... TX-5
**Midland**—pop pl ... VA-3
**Midland**—pop pl ... WA-9
**Midland**—pop pl ... WV-2
Midland—uninc pl ... KS-7
Midland Acres—uninc pl ... WA-9
Midland Annex Sch—school ... NY-2
Midland Beach—beach ... NY-2
**Midland Beach**—pop pl ... NY-2
Midland Borough ... PA-2
Midland Borough—civil ... PA-2
Midland Branch RR Depot—hist pl ... LA-4
Midland Campground—locale ... CO-8
Midland Canal—canal ... CO-8
Midland Canal—canal ... LA-4
Midland (CCD)—cens area ... TX-5
Midland Cem—cemetery ... IA-7
Midland Cem—cemetery ... OK-5
Midland Cem—cemetery ... PA-2
Midland Cem—cemetery ... SD-7
Midland Cem—cemetery ... VA-3
Midland Center—hospital ... SC-3
Midland Ch—church ... KS-7
Midland Ch—church (2) ... MI-6
Midland Ch—church ... MO-7
Midland Ch—church ... OH-6
Midland Ch—church ... OK-5
**Midland City**—pop pl ... AL-4
**Midland City**—pop pl ... AZ-5
**Midland City**—pop pl ... IL-6
Midland City (RR name for Midland)—other ... OH-6
Midland Coll—school ... NE-7
Midland Corner ... NE-7
Midland Country Club—other ... TX-5
**Midland (County)**—pop pl ... MI-6
**Midland (County)**—pop pl ... TX-5
Midland County Courthouse—hist pl ... MI-6
Midland County Park—park ... TX-5
**Midland Court Condominium**—pop pl ... UT-8
Midland Dam—dam ... SD-7
Midland Depot—hist pl ... AR-4
Midland Ditch—canal ... CO-8
Midland Draw—valley ... TX-5
Midland Fairview Mission—church ... PA-2
Midland Farms North Oil Field—oilfield ... TX-5
Midland Farms Oil Field—oilfield ... TX-5
**Midland Farms Subdivision**—pop pl ... UT-8
**Midland Five Acre Plat (subdivision)**—pop pl ... UT-8
Midland Flats—flat ... ME-1
Midland Gas Field—oilfield ... LA-4
Midland-Gilmore Rsvr—reservoir ... MD-2
Midland Hill—summit ... CO-8
Midland Hill—summit ... NY-2
**Midland Hills**—pop pl ... IL-6
Midland Hills Country Club—other ... IL-6
Midland Hills Country Club—other ... MN-6
Midland (historical)—locale ... SD-7
Midland Junction ... MD-2
Midland Junction—locale ... MN-6
**Midland Junction**—pop pl ... IN-6
**Midland Junction**—pop pl ... MD-2
**Midland Junction**—pop pl ... WI-6
Midland Lake ... WA-9
Midland Mine—mine ... CO-8
Midland Mine—mine ... MO-7
**Midland Mine**—pop pl ... WV-2
Midland Missionary Ch—church ... MI-6
Midland Overland Canal—canal (2) ... NE-7
Midland Packing Company—hist pl ... IA-7
Midland Park—park ... NE-7
**Midland Park**—pop pl ... KS-7
**Midland Park**—pop pl ... MI-6
**Midland Park**—pop pl ... NJ-2
**Midland Park**—pop pl (2) ... SC-3
Midland Peak—summit (2) ... AR-4
Midland Pumping Station—other ... TX-5
Midland Regional Airp—airport ... TX-5
Midland Rural (CCD)—cens area ... TX-5
Midlands—hist pl ... KY-4
Midland Sch—hist pl ... NJ-2
Midland Sch—school ... AZ-5
Midland Sch—school (3) ... CA-9
Midland Sch—school ... CO-8
Midland Sch—school ... MA-1
Midland Sch—school ... MI-6
Midland Sch—school ... NE-7
Midland Sch—school ... NJ-2
Midland Sch—school ... NY-2
Midland Sch—school ... OH-6
Midland Sch—school ... TN-4
Midland Sch—school ... UT-8
Midland Sch—school ... WA-9
Midland Sch (abandoned)—school ... MO-7
Midland Sch Number 1—school ... NJ-2
Midland Sewage Disposal Ponds—other ... TX-5
Midland Shop Ctr—locale ... NC-3
Midland Shop Ctr—locale ... TN-4
Midland Speedway (historical)—building ... NC-3
**Midland Square Subdivision**—pop pl ... UT-8
Midland Store ... NE-7
Midland Street Commercial District—hist pl ... MI-6
Midland Supply Ditch—canal ... CO-8
Midland Technical Education Center—school ... SC-3
Midland Terminal RR Depot—hist pl ... CO-8
Midland Terminal RR Roundhouse—hist pl ... CO-8
**Midland Tower**—pop pl ... KS-7
Midland Townhall—building ... IA-7
Midland Town Hall—building ... ND-7
Midland Township—civil ... MO-7
Midland Township—fmr MCD ... IA-7
**Midland Township**—pop pl (2) ... NE-7
**Midland Township**—pop pl ... ND-7
**Midland Township**—pop pl ... SD-7
**Midland (Township of)**—pop pl ... MI-6
Midland Trail—trail ... ID-8
Midland Trail—trail ... NV-8
Midland Trail—trail ... WV-2
**Midland Valley**—pop pl ... SC-3
Midlawn Memorial Gardens—cemetery ... MO-7
Midletown ... PA-2
Midlien Baptist Ch—church ... AL-4
Midline—locale ... TX-5
Mid Lothian ... KS-7
**Midlothian**—pop pl ... IL-6
**Midlothian**—pop pl ... MD-2
**Midlothian**—pop pl ... OK-5
**Midlothian**—pop pl ... TX-5
**Midlothian**—pop pl ... VA-3
Midlothian (CCD)—cens area ... TX-5
Midlothian Ch—church ... VA-3
Midlothian Country Club—other ... IL-6
Midlothian Creek—stream ... IL-6
Midlothian (Magisterial District)—fmr MCD ... VA-3
Midlothian Meadows—woods ... IL-6
Midmermac Ditch—canal (2) ... WY-8
Mid Minerva Creek ... IA-7
Midmont—locale ... PA-2
Mid Mountain Ranch—locale ... CA-9
Mid Mtn—summit ... MT-8
Midnight—locale ... ID-8
**Midnight**—pop pl ... MS-4
Midnight Brook—stream ... ME-1
Midnight Cabin—locale ... NM-5
Midnight Canyon—valley (2) ... AZ-5
Midnight Canyon—valley ... MT-8
Midnight Canyon—valley ... NM-5
Midnight Cave—cave ... TX-5
Midnight Cove—bay ... AK-9
Midnight Creek—stream (2) ... AK-9
Midnight Creek—stream ... AZ-5
Midnight Creek—stream (2) ... ID-8
Midnight Creek—stream ... MT-8
Midnight Creek—stream ... NM-5
Midnight Creek—stream ... WA-9
Midnight Dam—dam ... AZ-5
Midnight Dome—summit ... AK-9
Midnight Gulch—valley ... OR-9
Midnight Hill—summit ... AK-9
Midnight Hill—summit ... MT-8
Midnight Hollow—valley ... MO-7
Midnight Hollow—valley ... TN-4
Midnight Lake—lake ... CA-9
Midnight Lake—lake ... ID-8
Midnight Lake—lake ... OR-9
Midnight Mesa—summit ... AZ-5
Midnight Mine—mine (2) ... AZ-5
Midnight Mine—mine ... CO-8
Midnight Mine—mine ... MT-8
Midnight Mine—mine (2) ... NM-5
Midnight Mound Site (22HU509)—hist pl ... MS-4
Midnight Mtn—summit (2) ... AK-9
Midnight Mtn—summit ... ID-8
Midnight Mtn—summit (2) ... WA-9
Midnight Owl Mine—mine ... AZ-5
Midnight Pass—channel (2) ... FL-3
Midnight Pond—lake ... ME-1
Midnight Sch (historical)—school ... MS-4
Midnight Shoal—bar ... NC-3
Midnight Spring—spring ... ID-8
Midnight Spring—spring ... NM-5
Midnight Spring—spring ... OR-9
Midnight Tank—reservoir ... AZ-5
Midnight Thicket—locale ... DE-2
Midnight Wash—stream ... NV-8
Midnight Well—well ... NM-5
Midnite Mine—mine ... AZ-5
Midnite Shaft—mine ... CO-8
Midnite Spring—spring ... AZ-5
Midnite Test Mine—mine ... AZ-5
Mid-Ohio Industrial Park—facility ... OH-6
Mid-Ohio Race Course—other ... OH-6
Midoil—locale ... CA-9
Mid Pacific Country Club—other ... HI-9
Mid Pacific Institute—school ... HI-9
Mid Painterhood Creek—stream ... KS-7
Midpark ... OH-6
Midpark HS—school ... OH-6
Mid Penn Mine Station—locale ... PA-2
**Midpine**—pop pl ... NC-3
Midpines—locale ... CA-9
Mid Pines Lake—reservoir ... NC-3
Mid Pines Lake Dam—dam ... NC-3
Midpipe Lake ... MN-6
Mid Plains Technical Coll—school ... NE-7
Mid Point—cape ... AK-9
Midred Lake—lake ... WI-6
Mid Reef—bar ... AK-9
**Midridge**—pop pl ... MO-7
Mid Ridge—ridge ... CA-9
Midriver—locale ... GA-3
**Mid River**—pop pl ... IA-7
Midriver (Mid River Farms)—uninc pl ... FL-3
Mid River Public Use Area—park ... IA-7
Midrivers Mall—locale ... MO-7
Midrivers Mall (Shop Ctr)—locale ... MO-7
Mids Branch—stream ... TN-4
Mid Settlements Elementary School ... TN-4
Mids Gap—gap ... TN-4
Midshipman Point—cape ... CA-9
Midship Rock—pillar ... RI-1
Mid Slough—stream ... OR-9
Mid-South Bible Center ... TN-4
Mid-South Bible Coll—school ... TN-4
Mid-South Coll—school ... MS-4
Mid-South Factory Outlet Shop Ctr—locale ... MS-4
Mid Springs Creek—stream ... TX-5
Midsprings Sch—school ... KY-4
Mid-State Airp—airport ... PA-2
Mid-State Mall—locale ... KS-7
Midstate Mill—other ... NC-3
**Midstreams**—pop pl ... NJ-2
**Midstreams Park**—pop pl ... NJ-2
Midtown ... OH-6
Midtown ... TN-4
**Midtown**—pop pl ... NC-3
**Midtown**—pop pl ... TN-4
Midtown—post sta ... GA-3
Midtown—uninc pl ... CA-9
Midtown—uninc pl ... NJ-2
Midtown—uninc pl ... NY-2
Midtown—uninc pl ... VA-3
Midtown Ch—church ... TN-4
Midtown Dock—locale ... TN-4
Midtown Elem Sch—school ... TN-4
Midtown Harrisburg Hist Dist—hist pl ... PA-2
Midtown Heights—locale ... TN-4
Mid-Town Hist Dist—hist pl ... MS-4
Midtown Hist Dist—hist pl ... MO-7
Mid Town Mall (Shop Ctr)—locale ... MA-1
**Midtown (Pine Grove)**—pop pl ... TN-4
Mid Town Plaza—post sta ... FL-3
Midtown Plaza—post sta ... NY-2
Midtown Sch—school ... CA-9
Midtown Shop Ctr—locale ... AL-4
Midtown Shop Ctr—locale ... AZ-5
Mid Town Shop Ctr—locale ... MS-4
Midtown Shop Ctr—locale ... TN-4
Midtown Shopping Plaza—locale ... NC-3
Midtown Station—building ... PA-2
Midtown Tunnel—tunnel ... VA-3
Midun Island—island ... AK-9
Mid Vail—locale ... CO-8
**Midval**—pop pl ... WY-8
Midvale—fmr MCD ... NE-7
Midvale—locale ... PA-2
Midvale—locale ... WA-9
Midvale—locale ... WV-2
Midvale—locale ... WY-8
**Midvale**—pop pl ... DE-2
**Midvale**—pop pl ... ID-8
**Midvale**—pop pl ... IA-7
**Midvale**—pop pl ... MN-6
**Midvale**—pop pl ... MO-7
**Midvale**—pop pl ... OH-6
**Midvale**—pop pl ... PA-2
**Midvale**—pop pl ... TN-4
**Midvale**—pop pl ... UT-8
**Midvale**—pop pl ... VA-3
Midvale—uninc pl ... NJ-2
Midvale Airfield—airport ... UT-8
Midvale Cem—cemetery ... ID-8
Midvale City Cem—cemetery ... UT-8
Midvale Corner—locale ... WA-9
Midvale Creek—stream ... MT-8
Midvale Dam—dam ... NJ-2
Midvale MS—school ... UT-8
Midvale (Nicetown)—uninc pl ... PA-2
Midvale Plaza (Shop Ctr)—locale ... UT-8
Midvale Post Office—building ... UT-8
Midvale Sch—school ... MI-6
Midvale Sch—school ... NE-7
Midvale Sch—school ... UT-8
Midvale Sch—school ... WI-6
Midvale Station—locale ... OH-6
**Midvale Terrace Subdivision**—pop pl ... UT-8
**Midvalf (subdivision)**—pop pl ... DE-2
Mid Vallee Golf Course—other ... WI-6
**Midvalley**—pop pl ... CA-9
**Midvalley**—pop pl ... PA-2
Mid Valley—valley ... NV-8
Midvalley Bible Ch—church ... UT-8
Midvalley Ch—church ... PA-2
**Midvalley Estates Subdivision**—pop pl ... UT-8
Mid Valley Industrial Park—locale ... PA-2
Mid Valley Intermediate Elem Sch—school ... PA-2
**Midvalley Manors Subdivision**—pop pl ... UT-8
Midvalley Sch—school ... UT-8
**Midvalley Subdivision**—pop pl ... UT-8
**Midvalley Terrace Subdivision**—pop pl ... UT-8
Midvals Golf Club—other ... NY-2
Mid Venice—post sta ... FL-3
Midview Ch—church ... NC-3
Midview Dam—dam ... UT-8
Midview Ditch—canal ... UT-8
Midview HS—school ... OH-6
Midview Lateral—canal ... UT-8
Midview Reservoir ... UT-8
**Midville**—pop pl ... GA-3
Midville (CCD)—cens area ... GA-3
Midville Site—locale ... UT-8
Midway ... AL-4
Midway ... GA-3
Midway ... IN-6
Midway (2) ... MN-6
Midway ... NC-3
Midway ... ND-7
Midway ... OR-9
Midway ... SD-7
Midway ... TN-4
Midway ... TX-5
Midway ... WV-2
Midway—hist pl ... VA-3
Midway—locale (6) ... AL-4
Midway—locale (2) ... AZ-5
Midway—locale (4) ... AR-4
Midway—locale (2) ... CA-9
Midway—locale (5) ... CO-8
Midway—locale ... CT-1
Midway—locale (2) ... FL-3
Midway—locale (6) ... GA-3
Midway—locale ... ID-8
Midway—locale ... IL-6
Midway—locale (4) ... KS-7
Midway—locale (3) ... KY-4
Midway—locale (2) ... LA-4
Midway—locale (2) ... MS-4
Midway—locale (2) ... MO-7
Midway—locale ... MT-8
Midway—locale ... NE-7
Midway—locale ... NV-8
Midway—locale ... NM-5
Midway—locale ... NY-2
Midway—locale ... NC-3
Midway—locale ... ND-7
Midway—locale (3) ... OH-6
Midway—locale (4) ... OK-5
Midway—locale ... OR-9
Midway—locale ... PA-2
Midway—locale ... SC-3
Midway—locale (3) ... SD-7
Midway—locale (8) ... TN-4
Midway—locale (18) ... TX-5
Midway—locale (7) ... VA-3
Midway—locale (2) ... WA-9
Midway—locale ... WI-6
Midway—locale ... WY-8
Midway—mine ... NV-8
Midway—other ... VA-3
Midway—other ... WV-2
**Midway**—pop pl (7) ... AL-4
**Midway**—pop pl (10) ... AR-4
**Midway**—pop pl (2) ... CA-9
**Midway**—pop pl ... CO-8
**Midway**—pop pl ... DE-2
**Midway**—pop pl (2) ... FL-3
**Midway**—pop pl (2) ... GA-3
**Midway**—pop pl ... ID-8
**Midway**—pop pl (4) ... IL-6
**Midway**—pop pl (6) ... IN-6
**Midway**—pop pl (3) ... IA-7
**Midway**—pop pl (2) ... KS-7
**Midway**—pop pl (2) ... KY-4
**Midway**—pop pl (3) ... LA-4
**Midway**—pop pl ... ME-1
**Midway**—pop pl (2) ... MN-6
**Midway**—pop pl (4) ... MS-4
**Midway**—pop pl (2) ... MO-7
**Midway**—pop pl ... NE-7
**Midway**—pop pl ... NM-5
**Midway**—pop pl ... NY-2
**Midway**—pop pl (9) ... NC-3
**Midway**—pop pl (3) ... OH-6
**Midway**—pop pl (2) ... OK-5
**Midway**—pop pl (4) ... OR-9
**Midway**—pop pl (4) ... PA-2
**Midway**—pop pl (4) ... SC-3
**Midway**—pop pl (15) ... TN-4
**Midway**—pop pl (7) ... TX-5
**Midway**—pop pl ... UT-8
**Midway**—pop pl ... WA-9
**Midway**—pop pl (4) ... WV-2
**Midway**—pop pl (2) ... WI-6
**Midway**—pop pl ... WY-8
Midway—uninc pl ... GA-3
Midway Airp—airport ... IN-6
Midway Airp—airport ... NC-3
Midway Air Park—airport ... KS-7
Midway Asembly of God Ch—church ... DE-2
Midway Baptist Ch ... MS-4
Midway Baptist Ch ... TN-4
Midway Baptist Ch—church (2) ... AL-4
Midway Baptist Ch—church ... KS-7
Midway Baptist Ch—church (3) ... MS-4
Midway Baptist Ch—church (2) ... TN-4
Midway Bay—bay ... AK-9
**Midway Beach**—pop pl ... IA-7
Midway Bluff—cliff ... WY-8
Midway Borough—civil ... PA-2
Midway Branch ... NC-3
Midway Branch—stream ... AL-4
Midway Branch—stream ... FL-3
Midway Branch—stream ... MD-2
Midway Branch—stream ... MO-7
Midway Branch—stream (2) ... TX-5
Midway Branch—stream ... VA-3
Midway Butte—summit ... NM-5
**Midway (Calhoun)**—pop pl ... WV-2
Midway Camp—locale ... TX-5
Midway Camp—locale ... WA-9
Midway Canal—canal (2) ... CA-9
Midway Canal—canal ... LA-4
Midway Canyon—valley ... AZ-5
Midway Canyon—valley ... CA-9
Midway Canyon—valley ... NE-7
**Midway (Carroll)**—pop pl ... AR-4
Midway (CCD)—cens area ... AL-4
Midway (CCD)—cens area ... GA-3
Midway (CCD)—cens area ... KY-4
Midway (CCD)—cens area ... TN-4
Midway (CCD)—cens area ... TX-5
Midway Cem—cemetery (4) ... AL-4
Midway Cem—cemetery ... AR-4
Midway Cem—cemetery (3) ... GA-3
Midway Cem—cemetery (2) ... KY-4
Midway Cem—cemetery (3) ... LA-4
Midway Cem—cemetery ... MN-6
Midway Cem—cemetery (10) ... MS-4
Midway Cem—cemetery ... MO-7
Midway Cem—cemetery ... NC-3
Midway Cem—cemetery ... OH-6
Midway Cem—cemetery ... OK-5
Midway Cem—cemetery (3) ... TX-5
Mid Way Cem—cemetery ... TX-5
Midway Cem—cemetery (2) ... TX-5
Midway Cem—cemetery ... UT-8
Midway Cem Number One—cemetery ... MS-4
Midway Cem Number Three—cemetery ... MS-4
Midway Cem Number Two—cemetery ... MS-4
Midway Center ... SD-7
Midway Ch ... TN-4
Midway Ch—church (20) ... AL-4
Midway Ch—church (13) ... AR-4
Midway Ch—church ... DE-2
Midway Ch—church (11) ... FL-3
Midway Ch—church (37) ... GA-3
Midway Ch—church (2) ... IN-6
Midway Ch—church ... IA-7
Midway Ch—church (6) ... KY-4
Midway Ch—church (10) ... LA-4
Midway Ch—church (2) ... MI-6
Midway Ch—church (21) ... MS-4
Midway Ch—church (4) ... MO-7
Midway Ch—church (18) ... NC-3
Midway Ch—church (8) ... OK-5
Midway Ch—church (9) ... SC-3
Midway Ch—church ... SD-7
Midway Ch—church (18) ... TN-4
Midway Ch—church (12) ... TX-5
Midway Ch—church (11) ... VA-3
Midway Ch—church ... WV-2
Midway Chapel—church ... KS-7
Midway Ch of Christ ... AL-4
Midway Ch of Christ ... TN-4
Midway Ch of Christ—church ... MS-4
Midway Ch of Christ—church ... TN-4
Midway Church Cem—cemetery ... TN-4
**Midway City**—pop pl ... CA-9
Midway City Cemetery ... UT-8
Midway City Sch—school ... CA-9
Midway Community Center—locale ... MT-8
Midway Community Center—locale ... OK-5

Military Cem—*cemetery* ... WA-9
Military Ch—*church* ... OK-5
Military Chapel—*church* ... MS-4
Military Chapel Cem—*cemetery* ... MS-4
Military Circle Shop Ctr—*locale* ... VA-3
Military Creek—*lake* ... WI-6
Military Creek—*stream* ... AK-9
Military Creek—*stream* ... OR-9
Military Creek—*stream* ... WI-6
Military Creek—*stream* ... WY-8
Military Crossing—*locale* ... OR-9
Military Crossing—*locale* ... TX-5
Military Crossing Cem—*cemetery* ... MO-7
Military Ditch—*canal* ... WY-8
Military Donations—*reserve* ... IN-6
Military Drill Hall and Men's
  Gymnasium—*hist pl* ... IL-6
Military Grove Ch—*church* ... AL-4
Military Gulch—*valley* ... ID-8
Military Heights Sch—*school* ... NM-5
Military Hill—*summit* ... AZ-5
Military Hill—*summit* ... WI-6
**Military Junction**—*pop pl* ... CO-8
*Military Lake* ... NE-7
Military Lake—*lake* ... NY-2
Military Mtn—*summit* ... TX-5
*Military Ocean Terminal* ... NJ-2
Military Ocean Terminal Sunny
  Point—*military* ... NC-3
Military Park—*hist pl* ... IN-6
Military Park—*park* ... NJ-2
**Military Park**—*pop pl* ... FL-3
Military Park Brannons Redoubt—*locale* ... TN-4
Military Park General Bragg HQ—*locale* ... TN-4
Military Park Rsvr—*reservoir* ... CO-8
Military Pass—*gap* ... CA-9
Military Plaza Park—*park* ... AZ-5
*Military Point* ... FL-3
Military Point—*cape* ... FL-3
Military Pond—*lake* (2) ... NY-2
Military Ridge—*ridge* ... WI-6
Military Road, The—*trail* ... NM-5
Military Road Sch—*school* ... DC-2
Military Road Sch—*school* ... WI-6
Military Rsvr—*reservoir* ... OR-9
Military Run—*stream* ... NY-2
Military Run—*stream* ... OH-6
Military Sch—*school* ... IL-6
Military Sinkhole—*basin* ... AZ-5
Military Slough—*stream* ... OR-9
Military Spring—*spring* ... OR-9
Military Springs Post Office
  (historical)—*building* ... AL-4
Military Springs Reservation—*reserve* ... UT-8
Military Street Sch—*school* ... MA-1
Military Tank—*reservoir* ... AZ-5
Military Township—*fmr MCD* ... IA-7
Military Trail Sch—*school* ... FL-3
*Militia Bluff* ... AL-4
**Militia Hill**—*pop pl* ... PA-2
Militia Hill—*summit* ... TN-4
Militia Hollow—*valley* ... IA-7
Militia HQ Bldg—*hist pl* ... GA-3
Militia Springs—*spring* ... TN-4
Militia Springs Post Office
  (historical)—*building* ... TN-4
Milk, Lemuel, Carriage House—*hist pl* ... IL-6
Milk And Mush Creek—*stream* ... KY-4
Milk And Water Creek—*stream* ... PA-2
Milk And Water Ridge—*ridge* ... PA-2
Milk Branch—*stream* ... WV-2
Milk Brook—*stream* ... IN-6
Milk Cabin Gulch—*valley* ... CO-8
Milk Camp—*locale* ... CA-9
Milkcan Spring—*spring* ... CA-9
Milk Canyon—*valley* ... CA-9
Milk Canyon—*valley* ... OR-9
Milk Canyon—*valley* ... WA-9
Milk Coulee Bay—*bay* ... MT-8
Milk Cow Pass—*gap* ... CO-8
*Milk Creek* ... MT-8
*Milk Creek* ... WY-8
Milk Creek—*stream* (2) ... AK-9
Milk Creek—*stream* (4) ... AZ-5
Milk Creek—*stream* (3) ... CA-9
Milk Creek—*stream* (6) ... CO-8
Milk Creek—*stream* (6) ... ID-8
Milk Creek—*stream* ... MI-6
Milk Creek—*stream* (3) ... MT-8
Milk Creek—*stream* (8) ... OR-9
Milk Creek—*stream* (3) ... UT-8
Milk Creek—*stream* (6) ... WA-9
Milk Creek—*stream* ... WY-8
Milk Creek Rsvr—*reservoir* ... CO-8
Milk Creek Rsvr—*reservoir* ... UT-8
Milk Creek Trail—*trail* ... ID-8
Milken Canyon—*valley* ... NE-7
*Milkers Landing* ... FL-3
*Milkey Creek* ... AR-4
Milk Glacier—*glacier* ... AK-9
Milkhouse Bar—*bar* ... AL-4
Milkhouse Creek—*stream* ... AL-4
Milkhouse Creek—*stream* ... NV-8
Milkhouse Draw—*valley* ... NM-5
Milkhouse Flat—*flat* ... CA-9
Milkhouse Ford—*locale* ... DC-2
Milkhouse Hollow—*valley* ... MD-2
Milkhouse Hollow—*valley* ... WV-2
Milkhouse Mesa—*summit* ... NM-5
*Milkhouse Spring* ... NV-8
Milk House Spring—*spring* ... NV-8
Milk Island—*island* ... MA-1
Milk Island Bar—*bar* ... MA-1
*Milk Isle* ... MA-1
Milk Lake—*lake* ... CA-9
Milk Lake—*lake* (2) ... ID-8
Milk Lake—*lake* ... MI-6
Milk Lake—*lake* ... NM-5
Milk Lake—*lake* (2) ... UT-8
Milk Lake—*lake* (3) ... WA-9
Milk Lake—*reservoir* ... UT-8
Milk Lake Dam—*dam* ... UT-8
Milk Lake Glacier—*glacier* ... WA-9
Milk Lakes—*lake* ... WA-9
Milk Landing—*locale* ... VA-3
Milk Lateral—*canal* ... ID-8
Milkmaid Mine—*mine* ... CA-9
Milkmaid Riffle—*rapids* ... OR-9
Milk Pond—*lake* ... MA-1
Milk Pond—*lake* ... WA-9
Milk Pond Picnic Grounds—*locale* ... WA-9
Milk Ranch—*locale* (2) ... AZ-5
Milk Ranch—*locale* (2) ... CA-9
Milk Ranch Boulder Creek—*stream* ... OR-9
Milk Ranch Canyon—*valley* (2) ... CA-9
Milk Ranch Canyon—*valley* ... NV-8
Milk Ranch Canyon—*valley* ... NM-5
Milk Ranch Creek—*stream* ... AZ-5
Milk Ranch Creek—*stream* (3) ... CA-9
Milk Ranch Creek—*stream* ... NV-8
Milkranch Gulch—*valley* ... CO-8
Milk Ranch Gulch—*valley* ... ID-8
*Milk Ranch Meadow* ... CA-9
Milk Ranch Meadow—*flat* ... CA-9
Milk Ranch Meadows—*flat* ... CA-9
Milk Ranch Peak—*summit* ... CA-9
Milk Ranch Point—*cape* ... UT-8
Milk Ranch Point—*cliff* ... AZ-5
Milk Ranch (Site)—*locale* ... CA-9
Milk Ranch Spring—*spring* ... AZ-5
Milk Ranch Spring—*spring* ... CA-9
Milk Ranch Spring—*spring* (2) ... NV-8
Milk Ranch Spring—*spring* ... WA-9
Milk Ranch Springs—*spring* ... NV-8
Milk Ranch Tank—*reservoir* ... AZ-5
Milk Ranch Wash—*valley* ... WY-8
Milk Ranch Well—*well* ... NV-8
Milk River—*stream* ... MI-6
Milk River—*stream* ... MT-8
Milk River Badlands—*area* ... MT-8
Milk River Canal A—*canal* ... MT-8
Milk River Coulee—*valley* (2) ... MT-8
Milk River Hills—*spring* ... MT-8
Milk River Mine—*mine* ... MT-8
Milk River Ridge—*ridge* ... MT-8
Milk River Valley Ch—*church* ... MT-8
Milks Camp—*locale* ... SD-7
Milks Camp Park—*park* ... SD-7
Milks Grove Ch—*church* ... IL-6
**Milks Grove (Township of)**—*pop pl* ... IL-6
Milk Shakes—*summit* ... OR-9
Milksick Cove—*cave* ... TN-4
Milksick Cove—*basin* ... GA-3
Milksick Cove—*valley* (2) ... GA-3
Milksick Cove—*valley* (5) ... NC-3
Milksick Cove Knob—*summit* ... GA-3
Milksick Hollow—*valley* (2) ... TN-4
Milksick Knob—*summit* (2) ... NC-3
Milksick Mtn—*summit* ... TN-4
Milksick Ridge—*ridge* ... NC-3
Milk Spring—*spring* ... AL-4
Milk Spring—*spring* ... CA-9
Milk Spring—*spring* ... ID-8
Milk Spring—*spring* ... NV-8
Milk Spring—*spring* (3) ... OR-9
Milk Spring Hollow—*valley* ... AL-4
*Milk Springs* ... AL-4
**Milk Springs**—*pop pl* ... AL-4
*Milk Stream* ... MT-8
Milkwater—*locale* ... AZ-5
Milkweed Canyon—*valley* ... AZ-5
Milkweed Lake—*lake* ... TX-5
Milkweed Spring—*spring* ... AZ-5
*Milk White Lake* ... MI-6
*Milky Creek* ... AR-4
Milky Creek—*stream* ... ID-8
Milky Creek—*stream* ... MS-4
Milky Creek—*stream* ... WA-9
Milky Creek—*stream* ... WY-8
Milky Falls—*falls* ... UT-8
Milky Fork—*stream* ... OR-9
Milky House—*locale* ... AZ-5
*Milky Lake* ... MT-8
Milky Lake—*lake* ... MN-6
Milky Lakes—*lake* ... WY-8
Milky Ridge—*ridge* ... WY-8
Milky River—*stream* ... AK-9
Milky Spring—*spring* ... CA-9
Milky Stream—*stream* ... MT-8
Milky Tank—*reservoir* (2) ... AZ-5
Milky Wash—*stream* ... AZ-5
Milky Wash Bridge—*bridge* ... AZ-5
Milky Way—*locale* ... TN-4
Milky Way Farm—*hist pl* ... TN-4
Milky Way Farm—*locale* ... TN-4
Milky Way Tank—*reservoir* ... AZ-5
*Mill* ... AL-4
*Mill* ... LA-4
*Mill* ... UT-8
Mill—*fmr MCD* ... NE-7
Mill—*locale* ... TX-5
**Mill**—*pop pl* ... LA-4
Milla—*locale* ... IL-6
**Mill A**—*pop pl* ... WA-9
Mill A Basin—*basin* ... UT-8
*Mill A Basin Peak* ... UT-8
**Milladore**—*pop pl* ... WI-6
**Milladore (Town of)**—*pop pl* ... WI-6
*Mill A Flat* ... WA-9
Mill A Flat—*flat* ... WA-9
Mill Agent's House—*hist pl* ... ME-1
*Millageville Church* ... AL-4
Mill A Hollow—*valley* ... UT-8
*Millakietekwu River* ... WA-9
Millam Creek—*stream* ... MO-7
Millan Hollow—*valley* ... MO-7
Millan Sch—*school* ... FL-3
Millanville-Skinners Falls Bridge—*hist pl* ... NY-2
Millanville-Skinners Falls Bridge—*hist pl* ... PA-2
Millaquaka Lake—*lake* ... MI-6
Millar Bay—*bay* ... FL-3
*Millard* ... KS-7
*Millard* ... NE-7
Millard—*locale* ... KS-7
Millard—*locale* ... MS-4
Millard—*locale* ... SD-7
**Millard**—*pop pl* ... KY-4
**Millard**—*pop pl* ... MO-7
**Millard**—*pop pl* ... NE-7
**Millard**—*pop pl* ... WV-2
**Millard**—*pop pl* ... WI-6
Millard, George Madison, House—*hist pl* ... IL-6
Millard, Sylvester, House—*hist pl* ... IL-6
Millard Acad—*hist pl* ... UT-8
Millard Airp—*airport* ... PA-2
Millard Area Vocational Sch—*school* ... KY-4
Millard Branch—*stream* ... OR-9
Millard Brook—*stream* ... CT-1
Millard Brook—*stream* ... VT-1
*Millard Canyon* ... NV-8
Millard Canyon—*valley* (2) ... CA-9
Millard Canyon—*valley* ... UT-8
*Millard Canyon Bench* ... UT-8
Millard Canyon Benches—*bench* ... UT-8
Millard Canyon Guard Station—*locale* ... CA-9
Millard Canyon Overlook—*locale* ... UT-8
Millard (CCD)—*cens area* ... KY-4
Millard Cem—*cemetery* ... SD-7
Millard Cem—*cemetery* ... WI-6
Millard Corral—*locale* ... CA-9
Millard County—*civil* ... UT-8
*Millard Creek* ... NV-8
Millard Creek—*stream* ... AK-9
Millard Creek—*stream* ... NJ-2
Millard Creek—*stream* ... PA-2
Millard Ditch—*canal* ... WY-8
Millard Fillmore Hosp—*hospital* ... NY-2
Millard Hill Sch—*school* ... LA-4
Millard House—*hist pl* ... CA-9
Millard HS—*school* ... KY-4
Millard HS—*school* ... UT-8
Millard HS Gymnasium—*hist pl* ... UT-8
Millard Island—*island* ... FL-3
Millard Lake—*lake* ... AK-9
Millard-McCarty House—*hist pl* ... FL-3
Millard Oil Field—*oilfield* ... TX-5
Millard Peuther Chapel—*church* ... VA-3
Millard Picnic Area—*locale* ... CA-9
Millard Pond—*lake* ... CT-1
Millard Ridge—*ridge* ... SD-7
Millard Sch—*school* ... CA-9
Millard Sch—*school* (2) ... OR-9
Millard Sch—*school* ... SD-7
Millard Sch—*school* ... TX-5
Millard Sch (historical)—*school* ... TN-4
Millards Mill—*locale* ... MD-2
Millard-Souther-Green House—*hist pl* ... MA-1
Millards Prairie—*flat* ... WI-6
Millards Prairie Ch—*church* ... WI-6
Millard Spring—*spring* ... NV-8
Millards Quarry Pond—*lake* ... PA-2
**Millard Subdivision**—*pop pl* ... UT-8
**Millardsville**—*pop pl* ... PA-2
*Millardsville Lake* ... PA-2
*Millard Wash* ... UT-8
Millard Windmill—*locale* ... NM-5
*Millar Gas Field* ... CA-9
*Millar Hill* ... UT-8
Millarich, Martin, Hall—*hist pl* ... UT-8
Millark Millpond—*reservoir* ... IN-6
Millark Millpond Dam—*dam* ... IN-6
*Millar Marsh* ... MI-6
*Millar Point* ... CA-9
Millar Rocks—*area* ... AK-9
*Millar's Mountain* ... CO-8
Millars School—*locale* ... PA-2
*Millarsville* ... IN-6
**Millarton**—*pop pl* ... ND-7
Mill A Sch—*school* ... WA-9
Millaudon Canal—*canal* ... LA-4
Millay Hill—*summit* ... ME-1
Millay Sch—*school* ... ME-1
Millbach—*locale* ... PA-2
Millbach Ch—*church* ... PA-2
Millbach Sch—*school* ... PA-2
Millbach Springs—*locale* ... PA-2
Millball Gulch—*valley* ... CO-8
**Millbank**—*pop pl* (2) ... PA-2
Millbank Cem—*cemetery* ... PA-2
Millbank Creek—*stream* ... VA-3
*Millbank Mills* ... PA-2
Millbank Mills—*locale* ... PA-2
Mill Basin—*basin* ... CO-8
Mill Basin—*bay* ... NY-2
Mill Basin Bridge—*bridge* ... NY-2
Mill Bay—*bay* ... AK-9
Mill Bay—*bay* ... FL-3
Mill Bay—*bay* ... NY-2
Mill Bay—*swamp* (3) ... NC-3
Mill Bay—*swamp* (4) ... SC-3
*Mill Bay Creek* ... SC-3
Mill Bay (historical)—*swamp* ... FL-3
*Mill Bayou* ... AR-4
*Mill Bayou* ... LA-4
*Mill Bayou* ... TX-5
Mill Bayou—*bay* ... FL-3
Mill Bayou—*gut* (3) ... LA-4
**Mill Bayou**—*pop pl* ... FL-3
Mill Bayou—*stream* (4) ... AR-4
Mill Bayou—*stream* ... FL-3
Mill Bayou—*stream* (6) ... LA-4
Mill Bayou—*stream* ... MS-4
Mill Bayou—*stream* ... TX-5
Mill Bayou (Township of)—*fmr MCD* ... AR-4
Mill B Canyon—*valley* ... UT-8
**Millbell**—*pop pl* ... PA-2
Mill Bend—*bend* ... IL-6
Mill Bend Post Office
  (historical)—*building* ... TN-4
Millberry Brook—*stream* ... ME-1
Millberry Canyon—*valley* ... CA-9
Millberry Creek—*stream* ... CA-9
Mill Bethel Ch—*church* ... GA-3
Mill B Flat—*flat* ... UT-8
Mill B Flat—*flat* ... WA-9
Mill Bight—*bay* ... WA-9
Millbite, Lake—*lake* ... FL-3
Mill Bluff—*cliff* ... AL-4
Mill Bluff—*cliff* (3) ... MO-7
Mill Bluff—*cliff* ... TN-4
Mill Bluff Cave—*cave* ... AL-4
Mill Bluff Hollow—*valley* ... TN-4
Mill Bluff State Park—*park* ... WI-6
Mill B North Fork—*stream* ... UT-8
**Millboro**—*pop pl* ... NC-3
**Millboro**—*pop pl* ... SD-7
**Millboro**—*pop pl* (2) ... VA-3
Millboro (Magisterial District)—*fmr MCD* ... VA-3
*Millboro Spring* ... VA-3
Millboro Spring—*other* ... VA-3
Millboro Springs—*locale* ... VA-3
**Millboro Springs (Millboro
  Spring)**—*pop pl* ... VA-3
**Millboro Township**—*pop pl* ... SD-7
Millboro Tunnel—*tunnel* ... VA-3
Mill Boulder Creek—*stream* ... OR-9
**Millbourne**—*pop pl* ... PA-2
Millbourne Borough—*civil* ... PA-2
**Millbrae**—*pop pl* ... CA-9
**Millbrae Meadows**—*pop pl* ... CA-9
Millbrae Sch—*school* ... CA-9
*Mill Branch* ... AL-4
*Mill Branch* ... DE-2
*Mill Branch* ... GA-3
*Mill Branch* ... IA-7
*Mill Branch* ... SC-3
*Mill Branch* ... TN-4
*Mill Branch* ... TX-5
*Mill Branch* ... VA-3
Mill Branch—*locale* ... NC-3
Mill Branch—*locale* ... SC-3
Mill Branch—*stream* (19) ... AL-4
Mill Branch—*stream* (18) ... AR-4
Mill Branch—*stream* ... DE-2
Mill Branch—*stream* (11) ... FL-3
Mill Branch—*stream* (26) ... GA-3
Mill Branch—*stream* ... IN-6
Mill Branch—*stream* ... IA-7
Mill Branch—*stream* (46) ... KY-4
Mill Branch—*stream* (5) ... LA-4
Mill Branch—*stream* (3) ... MD-2
Mill Branch—*stream* (11) ... MS-4
Mill Branch—*stream* (6) ... MO-7
Mill Branch—*stream* (2) ... NJ-2
Mill Branch—*stream* ... NY-2
Mill Branch—*stream* (47) ... NC-3
Mill Branch—*stream* (2) ... OH-6
Mill Branch—*stream* (2) ... PA-2
Mill Branch—*stream* (29) ... SC-3
Mill Branch—*stream* (31) ... TN-4
Mill Branch—*stream* (25) ... TX-5
Mill Branch—*stream* (16) ... VA-3
Mill Branch—*stream* (21) ... WV-2
Mill Branch—*stream* ... WI-6
Mill Branch—*swamp* ... TX-5
*Mill Branch Baptist Church* ... TN-4
Mill Branch Cave—*cave* ... TN-4
Mill Branch Ch—*church* ... KY-4
Mill Branch Ch—*church* (5) ... NC-3
Mill Branch Ch—*church* ... TN-4
Mill Branch Ch—*church* ... VA-3
Mill Branch Hollow—*valley* ... KY-4
Mill Branch Ridge—*ridge* ... VA-3
Mill Branch Sch—*school* ... KY-4
Mill Branch Sch—*school* (2) ... SC-3
Mill Branch Sch (historical)—*school* ... AL-4
Mill Branch Swamp—*stream* ... NC-3
Mill Branch Trail—*trail* ... TN-4
Mill Branch Water Wheel
  (historical)—*building* ... TX-5
Mill Branch Workings—*mine* ... TN-4
Mill Break Creek—*stream* ... TX-5
*Mill Bridge* ... ME-1
*Millbridge* ... NC-3
Mill Bridge—*bridge* ... TN-4
**Millbridge**—*pop pl* ... NJ-2
**Mill Bridge**—*pop pl* ... NC-3
**Millbridge**—*pop pl* ... NC-3
Millbridge Ch—*church* ... NJ-2
Mill Bridge Dam—*dam* ... NE-7
Millbrig Hollow—*valley* ... IL-6
*Mill Brook* ... CT-1
*Mill Brook* ... MA-1
*Mill Brook* ... NH-1
*Millbrook* ... NJ-2
*Mill Brook* ... NY-2
*Mill Brook* ... NC-3
*Mill Brook* ... PA-2
*Mill Brook* ... RI-1
*Mill Brook* ... VT-1
Mill Brook—*locale* ... CT-1
Mill Brook—*locale* ... ME-1
Mill Brook—*locale* ... NJ-2
Millbrook—*locale* ... NJ-2
Millbrook—*locale* ... PA-2
Mill Brook—*locale* ... TN-4
Millbrook—*locale* ... VT-1
Millbrook—*locale* ... WV-2
Millbrook—*locale* ... WY-8
**Millbrook**—*pop pl* ... AL-4
**Millbrook**—*pop pl* ... CT-1
**Millbrook**—*pop pl* ... IL-6
**Millbrook**—*pop pl* ... KS-7
**Millbrook**—*pop pl* ... MA-1
**Millbrook**—*pop pl* ... MI-6
**Millbrook**—*pop pl* ... MO-7
**Millbrook**—*pop pl* ... NJ-2
**Millbrook**—*pop pl* ... NY-2
**Millbrook**—*pop pl* ... NC-3
**Millbrook**—*pop pl* ... OH-6
**Millbrook**—*pop pl* ... PA-2
Mill Brook—*stream* (9) ... CT-1
Mill Brook—*stream* (29) ... ME-1
Mill Brook—*stream* ... MD-2
Mill Brook—*stream* (23) ... MA-1
Mill Brook—*stream* (15) ... NH-1
Mill Brook—*stream* (6) ... NJ-2
Mill Brook—*stream* (15) ... NY-2
Mill Brook—*stream* ... PA-2
Mill Brook—*stream* (17) ... VT-1
Mill Brook—*stream* ... WI-6
Millbrook—*uninc pl* ... MD-2
Mill Brook—*uninc pl* ... NY-2
Millbrook Baptist Ch—*church* ... AL-4
Millbrook Branch—*stream* ... MO-7
Mill Brook Cascade—*falls* ... NH-1
Millbrook Ch—*church* ... SC-3
Mill Brook Ch—*church* ... WV-2
Millbrook Ch of Christ—*church* ... AL-4
Millbrook Community Center—*building* ... AL-4
Millbrook Country Club—*locale* ... MS-4
Millbrook Creek—*stream* ... MA-1
Millbrook Creek—*stream* ... MS-4
Millbrooke Ch—*church* ... KY-4
Millbrook Elem Sch—*school* ... NC-3
Millbrooke Sch—*school* ... KY-4
**Millbrook Estates (subdivision)**—*pop pl*
  (2) ... NC-3
**Millbrook Heights**—*pop pl* ... NY-2
Millbrook (historical)—*locale* ... KS-7
Millbrook (historical P.O.)—*locale* ... MA-1
Millbrook Hollow—*valley* ... NY-2
Millbrook HS—*school* ... NC-3
Millbrook JHS—*school* ... AL-4
Millbrook Methodist Ch—*church* ... AL-4
*Millbrook Mountains* ... NY-2
Millbrook MS—*school* ... AL-4
**Millbrook Park**—*pop pl* ... NJ-2
Millbrook Park Sch—*school* ... NJ-2
Millbrook Plantation (historical)—*locale* ... MS-4
Mill Brook Pond—*lake* ... ME-1
Millbrook Pond—*lake* ... RI-1
Mill Brook Pond—*reservoir* ... PA-2
Millbrook Pond—*reservoir* ... RI-1
Millbrook Pond Dam—*dam* ... RI-1
Mill Brook Post Office
  (historical)—*building* ... TN-4
Millbrook Presbyterian Ch—*church* ... AL-4
Mill Brook Ridge—*ridge* ... NY-2
Mill Brook Rsvr—*reservoir* (2) ... MA-1
Millbrook Rsvr No 1—*reservoir* ... WY-8
Millbrook Rsvr No 2—*reservoir* ... WY-8
Millbrook Sch—*school* ... MI-6
Millbrook Sch—*school* ... NY-2
Millbrook Sch—*school* ... SC-3
Millbrook Sch—*school* ... WY-8
Millbrook Sch (historical)—*school* ... MS-4
Millbrook Station (historical)—*locale* ... MA-1
Mill Brook Stream—*stream* ... MA-1
**Millbrook (subdivision)**—*pop pl* ... NC-3
**Mill Brook (subdivision)**—*pop pl* ... NC-3
**Millbrook (subdivision)**—*pop pl* (2) ... NC-3
Millbrook Swamp—*swamp* ... MA-1
**Millbrook Township**—*pop pl* ... KS-7
**Millbrook (Township of)**—*pop pl* ... IL-6
**Millbrook (Township of)**—*pop pl* ... MI-6
Mill Brook Trail—*trail* ... NH-1
**Millbrool**—*pop pl* ... MI-6
Mill B South Fork—*stream* ... UT-8
Mill B South Fork Picnic Ground—*locale* ... UT-8
*Millbum Creek* ... NY-2
**Millburg**—*pop pl* ... MI-6
Millburg Cem—*cemetery* ... MI-6
*Millburn* ... UT-8
Millburn—*locale* ... WA-9
**Millburn**—*pop pl* ... IL-6
**Millburn**—*pop pl* ... NJ-2
**Millburn**—*pop pl* ... PA-2
*Millburn Brook* ... MA-1
Millburn Cem—*cemetery* ... IL-6
Millburn Chapel—*church* ... KY-4
*Millburn Creek* ... NY-2
Millburne—*locale* ... WY-8
Millburne Cem—*cemetery* ... WY-8
Millburn Hist Dist—*hist pl* ... IL-6
Millburn Sch—*school* ... IL-6
Millburn Sch (abandoned)—*school* ... PA-2
Millburn Station—*locale* ... NJ-2
**Millburn (Township of)**—*pop pl* ... NJ-2
**Millbury**—*pop pl* ... MA-1
**Millbury**—*pop pl* ... OH-6
Millbury Center Sch—*school* ... MA-1
*Millbury Centre* ... MA-1
Millbury HS—*school* ... MA-1
**Millbury Junction**—*pop pl* ... MA-1
Millbury Ledge—*bar* ... ME-1
**Millbury (Town of)**—*pop pl* ... MA-1
Mill Butte—*summit* ... WA-9
Mill Camp—*locale* ... WA-9
**Mill Camps**—*pop pl* ... HI-9
Mill Camp Valley—*basin* ... NE-7
*Mill Canyon* ... ID-8
*Mill Canyon* ... NV-8
*Mill Canyon* ... OR-9
*Mill Canyon* ... UT-8
Mill Canyon—*valley* (2) ... AZ-5
Mill Canyon—*valley* (5) ... CA-9
Mill Canyon—*valley* ... CO-8
Mill Canyon—*valley* (11) ... ID-8
Mill Canyon—*valley* ... MT-8
Mill Canyon—*valley* (7) ... NV-8
Mill Canyon—*valley* (2) ... NM-5
Mill Canyon—*valley* (16) ... UT-8
Mill Canyon—*valley* (3) ... WA-9
*Mill Canyon Creek* ... MT-8
*Mill Canyon Creek* ... UT-8
Mill Canyon Mine—*mine* ... NV-8
Mill Canyon Peak—*summit* ... UT-8
Mill Canyon Sch—*school* ... NV-8
Mill Canyon Spring—*spring* ... OR-9
Mill Canyon Spring—*spring* (2) ... UT-8
Mill Canyon Spring—*spring* ... WA-9
Mill-Castle Trail—*trail* ... CO-8
Mill Cave—*cave* (3) ... TN-4
Mill Cem—*cemetery* ... IN-6
Mill Cem—*cemetery* ... ME-1
Mill Cem—*cemetery* ... NH-1
Mill Cem—*cemetery* ... SC-3
Mill Cem—*cemetery* ... WV-2
**Mill Center**—*pop pl* ... WI-6
Mill Center Cem—*cemetery* ... WI-6
*Mill City* ... AZ-5
*Mill City* ... PA-2
**Mill City**—*pop pl* ... CA-9
**Mill City**—*pop pl* ... NV-8
**Mill City**—*pop pl* ... OR-9
**Mill City**—*pop pl* (2) ... PA-2
Mill City (CCD)—*cens area* (2) ... OR-9
Mill City Creek—*stream* ... UT-8
Mill City Ghost Town—*locale* ... UT-8
Mill Cliff Branch—*stream* ... KY-4
Mill Club Dam—*dam* ... PA-2
Mill Corner—*locale* ... NC-3
*Mill Coulee* ... MT-8
Mill Coulee—*stream* ... MT-8
Mill Coulee—*valley* ... WI-6
Mill Coulee Canal—*canal* ... MT-8
Mill Coulee Creek—*stream* ... MT-8
Mill Cove—*bay* ... CT-1
Mill Cove—*bay* (2) ... FL-3
Mill Cove—*bay* (12) ... ME-1
Mill Cove—*bay* ... MD-2
Mill Cove—*bay* ... RI-1
Mill Cove—*cove* ... MA-1
Mill Cove—*valley* (3) ... NC-3
*Mill Cove Creek* ... RI-1
Mill Covered Bridge—*hist pl* (2) ... VT-1
*Mill Creek* ... AR-4
*Mill Creek* ... CA-9
*Mill Creek* ... CO-8
*Mill Creek* ... CT-1
*Mill Creek* ... DE-2
*Mill Creek* ... FL-3
*Mill Creek* ... GA-3
*Mill Creek* ... ID-8
*Mill Creek* (2) ... IL-6
*Mill Creek* ... IN-6
*Mill Creek* ... IA-7
*Mill Creek* ... KS-7
*Mill Creek* ... KY-4
*Mill Creek* ... LA-4
*Mill Creek* ... MD-2
*Mill Creek* ... MA-1
*Mill Creek* ... MI-6
*Mill Creek* ... MS-4
*Mill Creek* ... MO-7
*Mill Creek* ... MT-8
*Mill Creek* ... NV-8
*Mill Creek* ... NJ-2
*Mill Creek* ... NY-2
*Mill Creek* ... NC-3
*Mill Creek* ... OH-6
*Mill Creek* ... OK-5
*Mill Creek* ... OR-9
*Mill Creek* ... PA-2
*Mill Creek* ... SC-3
*Mill Creek* ... TN-4
*Mill Creek* ... TX-5
*Mill Creek* ... UT-8
*Mill Creek* ... VA-3
*Mill Creek* ... WA-9
*Mill Creek* ... WV-2
*Mill Creek* ... WI-6
*Mill Creek* ... WY-8
Mill Creek—*bay* ... AL-4
Mill Creek—*bay* (2) ... MD-2
Mill Creek—*bay* ... NY-2
Mill Creek—*bay* ... NC-3
Mill Creek—*gut* ... CT-1
Mill Creek—*gut* (2) ... FL-3
Mill Creek—*gut* ... NY-2
Mill Creek—*gut* ... SC-3
Mill Creek—*lake* ... WA-9
Mill Creek—*locale* ... DE-2
Mill Creek—*locale* ... GA-3
Millcreek—*locale* ... MS-4
Mill Creek—*locale* ... NC-3
Mill Creek—*locale* (3) ... PA-2
Mill Creek—*locale* (3) ... TN-4
Mill Creek—*locale* ... TX-5
Mill Creek—*locale* (2) ... VA-3
Mill Creek—*other* ... IL-6
**Mill Creek**—*pop pl* (2) ... AR-4
**Mill Creek**—*pop pl* ... CA-9
**Millcreek**—*pop pl* ... FL-3
**Mill Creek**—*pop pl* ... IL-6
**Mill Creek**—*pop pl* (2) ... IN-6
**Mill Creek**—*pop pl* ... KY-4
**Mill Creek**—*pop pl* ... LA-4
**Mill Creek**—*pop pl* (2) ... MS-4
**Millcreek**—*pop pl* ... MO-7
**Mill Creek**—*pop pl* ... MT-8
**Mill Creek**—*pop pl* (2) ... NC-3
**Mill Creek**—*pop pl* ... OK-5
**Mill Creek**—*pop pl* (2) ... PA-2
**Mill Creek**—*pop pl* (4) ... TN-4
**Mill Creek**—*pop pl* ... WA-9
**Mill Creek**—*pop pl* ... WV-2
Mill Creek—*stream* (75) ... AL-4
Mill Creek—*stream* (2) ... AK-9
Mill Creek—*stream* ... AZ-5
Mill Creek—*stream* (71) ... AR-4
Mill Creek—*stream* (88) ... CA-9
Mill Creek—*stream* (19) ... CO-8
Mill Creek—*stream* ... CT-1
Mill Creek—*stream* (3) ... DE-2
Mill Creek—*stream* (26) ... FL-3
Mill Creek—*stream* (67) ... GA-3
Mill Creek—*stream* (34) ... ID-8
Mill Creek—*stream* (18) ... IL-6
Mill Creek—*stream* (21) ... IN-6
Mill Creek—*stream* (10) ... IA-7
Mill Creek—*stream* (10) ... KS-7
Mill Creek—*stream* (47) ... KY-4
Mill Creek—*stream* (41) ... LA-4
Mill Creek—*stream* (4) ... ME-1
Mill Creek—*stream* (17) ... MD-2
Mill Creek—*stream* (5) ... MA-1
Mill Creek—*stream* (16) ... MI-6
Mill Creek—*stream* (3) ... MN-6
Mill Creek—*stream* (69) ... MS-4
Mill Creek—*stream* (44) ... MO-7
Mill Creek—*stream* (24) ... MT-8
Mill Creek—*stream* (4) ... NE-7
Mill Creek—*stream* (11) ... NV-8
Mill Creek—*stream* ... NH-1
Mill Creek—*stream* (14) ... NJ-2
Mill Creek—*stream* (2) ... NM-5
Mill Creek—*stream* (35) ... NY-2
Mill Creek—*stream* (82) ... NC-3
Mill Creek—*stream* (16) ... OH-6
Mill Creek—*stream* (14) ... OK-5
Mill Creek—*stream* (63) ... OR-9
Mill Creek—*stream* (54) ... PA-2
Mill Creek—*stream* (2) ... RI-1
Mill Creek—*stream* (39) ... SC-3
Mill Creek—*stream* ... SD-7
Mill Creek—*stream* (45) ... TN-4
Mill Creek—*stream* (64) ... TX-5
Mill Creek—*stream* (16) ... UT-8
Mill Creek—*stream* (80) ... VA-3
Mill Creek—*stream* (28) ... WA-9
Mill Creek—*stream* (28) ... WV-2
Mill Creek—*stream* (13) ... WI-6
Mill Creek—*stream* (24) ... WY-8
Mill Creek—*swamp* ... FL-3
Millcreek—*uninc pl* ... UT-8
**Mill Creek Addition
  (subdivision)**—*pop pl* ... UT-8
Millcreek Baptist Ch—*church* ... UT-8
Mill Creek Baptist Ch (historical)—*church* ... AL-4
*Mill Creek Baptist Church* ... MS-4
*Mill Creek BaptistChurch* ... TN-4
Mill Creek Basin—*basin* (2) ... CO-8
Mill Creek Bay—*swamp* ... GA-3
Mill Creek Bend—*bend* ... AR-4
Mill Creek Borough—*civil* ... PA-2
Mill Creek Branch—*stream* ... KY-4
Mill Creek Branch—*stream* ... TN-4
Millcreek Branch Post Office—*building* ... UT-8
Mill Creek Bridge—*bridge* ... UT-8
Mill Creek Bridge—*hist pl* ... IN-6
*Mill Creek Butte* ... OR-9
Mill Creek Buttes—*ridge* ... OR-9
Mill Creek Cabin Area—*locale* ... MS-4
Mill Creek Camp and Picnic
  Grounds—*locale* ... MT-8
Mill Creek Campground—*locale* (2) ... ID-8
Mill Creek Campground—*locale* ... MT-8
Mill Creek Campgrounds—*locale* ... CA-9

Mill Creek Campsite—*locale* MO-7
Mill Creek Canal—*canal* OR-9
Mill Creek Canyon—*valley* CA-9
Mill Creek Canyon—*valley* MT-8
Mill Creek Canyon—*valley* (2) UT-8
Mill Creek Cem—*cemetery* AL-4
Mill Creek Cem—*cemetery* (2) AR-4
Mill Creek Cem—*cemetery* GA-3
Mill Creek Cem—*cemetery* IL-6
Mill Creek Cem—*cemetery* IN-6
Mill Creek Cem—*cemetery* KS-7
Mill Creek Cem—*cemetery* KY-4
Mill Creek Cem—*cemetery* LA-4
Mill Creek Cem—*cemetery* MS-4
Mill Creek Cem—*cemetery* (2) MO-7
Mill Creek Cem—*cemetery* OH-6
Mill Creek Cem—*cemetery* OK-5
Mill Creek Cem—*cemetery* OR-9
Millcreek Cem—*cemetery* PA-2
Mill Creek Cem—*cemetery* PA-2
Mill Creek Cem—*cemetery* SC-3
Mill Creek Cem—*cemetery* (2) WI-6
Mill Creek Ch—*church* (2) AL-4
Mill Creek Ch—*church* (2) AR-4
Mill Creek Ch—*church* FL-3
Mill Creek Ch—*church* (6) GA-3
Mill Creek Ch—*church* (2) IN-6
Mill Creek Ch—*church* (5) KY-4
Mill Creek Ch—*church* (2) LA-4
Mill Creek Ch—*church* (2) MS-4
Mill Creek Ch—*church* (4) MO-7
Mill Creek Ch—*church* (7) NC-3
Mill Creek Ch—*church* OK-5
Mill Creek Ch—*church* (2) PA-2
Mill Creek Ch—*church* (4) SC-3
Mill Creek Ch—*church* (4) TN-4
Mill Creek Ch—*church* (5) TX-5
Mill Creek Ch—*church* (9) VA-3
Mill Creek Ch—*church* (3) WV-2
Mill Creek Chapel (historical)—*church* TN-4
Mill Creek Ch of God—*church* MS-4
**Mill Creek Community**—*pop pl* WI-6
Mill Creek Corner—*locale* PA-2
**Mill Creek Corners (subdivision)**—*pop pl* MS-4
*Millcreek (corporate name Mill Creek)* IL-6
Mill Creek Cove—*bay* DE-2
Mill Creek Cove—*bay* NJ-2
Mill Creek Cutoff—*stream* KY-4
*Mill Creek Dam* NC-3
*Mill Creek Dam* UT-8
Mill Creek Dam—*dam* OR-9
Mill Creek Dam—*dam* (2) PA-2
Mill Creek Ditch—*canal* CA-9
Mill Creek Ditch—*canal* (2) IN-6
Mill Creek Divide—*ridge* OR-9
Mill Creek Dock—*locale* MS-4
Mill Creek Drain—*canal* WY-8
Mill Creek East Elem Sch—*school* IN-6
Mill Creek (Election Precinct)—*fmr MCD* IL-6
Mill Creek Elem Sch—*school* IN-6
**Millcreek Estates Subdivision**—*pop pl* UT-8
Mill Creek Falls—*falls* (2) CA-9
Mill Creek Falls—*falls* (2) OR-9
**Mill Creek Falls**—*pop pl* PA-2
Mill Creek Falls Campground—*locale* CA-9
Mill Creek Field—*airport* OR-9
Mill Creek Flat—*flat* OR-9
Mill Creek Flat Ditch—*canal* MT-8
Mill Creek Flat Sch—*school* MT-8
*Mill Creek Forest Service Station* UT-8
Millcreek Forest Service Station—*locale* UT-8
Mill Creek Friends Meetinghouse—*hist pl* DE-2
Mill Creek Gap—*gap* CA-9
Mill Creek Gap—*gap* GA-3
Mill Creek Gap—*gap* TN-4
Mill Creek Guard Station—*locale* MT-8
Mill Creek Guard Station—*locale* UT-8
Mill Creek Guard Station—*locale* (3) WA-9
*Millcreek Heights Subdivision* UT-8
**Mill Creek Heights Subdivision**—*pop pl* UT-8
Mill Creek Hill Cem—*cemetery* PA-2
Mill Creek Hills—*summit* TX-5
Mill Creek Hist Dist—*hist pl* PA-2
Mill Creek Hist Dist—*hist pl* WV-2
**Mill Creek (historical)**—*pop pl* TN-4
Millcreek HS—*school* UT-8
Mill Creek Hundred—*civil* DE-2
*Mill Creek - in part* MO-7
*Mill Creek - in part* NV-8
Mill Creek Intake Dam—*dam* PA-2
Mill Creek Island—*island* WV-2
Millcreek JHS—*school* UT-8
Mill Creek Jumpoff—*gap* CA-9
**Mill Creek Junction**—*pop pl* WV-2
Mill Creek Lake—*lake* CA-9
Mill Creek Lake—*lake* NY-2
Mill Creek Lake—*reservoir* GA-3
Mill Creek Lake—*reservoir* ID-8
Mill Creek Lake—*reservoir* IA-7
Mill Creek Lake—*reservoir* KY-4
Mill Creek Lake Dam—*dam* IA-7
Mill Creek Lakes—*lake* CA-9
Mill Creek Landing—*locale* VA-3
Mill Creek Lateral—*canal* OR-9
Mill Creek Lodge—*locale* CO-8
Mill Creek (Magisterial District)—*fmr MCD* (2) WV-2
Mill Creek Mall—*locale* FL-3
Millcreek Mall—*locale* PA-2
**Millcreek Manor Condominium**—*pop pl* UT-8
**Mill Creek Manor (subdivision)**—*pop pl* DE-2
Mill Creek Meadows—*flat* CA-9
Mill Creek Meetinghouse—*church* DE-2
Mill Creek Methodist Ch—*church* MS-4
Mill Creek Mine (Quarry)—*mine* CA-9
Mill Creek Mine (surface)—*mine* AL-4
Mill Creek Mine (underground)—*mine* AL-4
Mill Creek Missionary Baptist Ch—*church* FL-3
*Mill Creek Missionary Baptist Church* AL-4
Mill Creek Mountain—*ridge* AR-4
Mill Creek Mountain—*ridge* WV-2
Mill Creek Mtn—*summit* (2) AR-4
Mill Creek Mtn—*summit* GA-3
Mill Creek Mtn—*summit* PA-2
Mill Creek Mtn—*summit* WV-2
*Mill Creek Neck* VA-3
Mill Creek No 3—*stream* NC-3
Mill Creek Number Two Dam—*dam* PA-2
Mill Creek Oil And Gas Field—*oilfield* PA-2
Mill Creek Park—*park* (2) MO-7
Mill Creek Park—*park* OH-6
Mill Creek Park—*park* OR-9
**Mill Creek Park**—*pop pl* VA-3
**Mill Creek Park (Mountain Home Village)**—*pop pl* CA-9
Mill Creek Park Suspension Bridge—*hist pl* OH-6
Mill Creek Pass—*gap* MT-8
Mill Creek Picnic Grounds—*locale* CA-9
**Mill Creek Place (subdivision)**—*pop pl* MS-4
Mill Creek Plateau—*plain* CA-9
Mill Creek Point—*cliff* WA-9
*Mill Creek Pond* NY-2
Mill Creek Ponds—*lake* CA-9
*Mill Creek Post Office* TN-4
Millcreek Post Office (historical)—*building* TN-4
Mill Creek Public Use Area—*locale* MO-7
Mill Creek Ranch—*locale* MT-8
Mill Creek Ranger Station—*locale* CA-9
Mill Creek Rec Area—*park* AR-4
Mill Creek Rec Area—*park* OH-6
Mill Creek Recreation Site—*park* OR-9
*Mill Creek Reservoir* UT-8
Mill Creek Ridge—*ridge* (3) CA-9
Mill Creek Ridge—*ridge* NC-3
Mill Creek Ridge—*ridge* (2) OR-9
Mill Creek Rim—*cliff* CA-9
**Mill Creek Road**—*pop pl* WV-2
Mill Creek Roughs—*area* GA-3
Mill Creek Rsvr—*reservoir* NV-8
Mill Creek Rsvr—*reservoir* OR-9
Mill Creek Rsvr—*reservoir* (3) PA-2
Mill Creek Rsvr—*reservoir* WV-2
Mill Creek Sch—*school* CA-9
Mill Creek Sch—*school* FL-3
Mill Creek Sch—*school* GA-3
Mill Creek Sch—*school* (3) KY-4
Mill Creek Sch—*school* MS-4
Mill Creek Sch—*school* MO-7
Mill Creek Sch—*school* (3) OR-9
Mill Creek Sch—*school* (2) PA-2
Mill Creek Sch—*school* SC-3
Mill Creek Sch—*school* TX-5
Millcreek Sch—*school* UT-8
Mill Creek Sch—*school* VA-3
Mill Creek Sch—*school* WA-9
Mill Creek Sch—*school* (2) WV-2
Mill Creek Sch (abandoned)—*school* MO-7
Mill Creek Sch (abandoned)—*school* PA-2
Mill Creek Sch (historical)—*school* MS-4
Mill Creek Sch (historical)—*school* (2) MO-7
Mill Creek Sch (historical)—*school* PA-2
Mill Creek Sch (historical)—*school* (3) TN-4
*Mill Creek School* UT-8
Mill Creek School (historical)—*locale* MO-7
Mill Creek Shop Ctr—*locale* DE-2
Mill Creek Site—*hist pl* MS-4
**Mill Creek South**—*pop pl* MD-2
Mill Creek Spring—*spring* AZ-5
Mill Creek Spring—*spring* CO-8
Mill Creek Spring—*spring* MO-7
Mill Creek Spring—*spring* (2) NV-8
Mill Creek Spring—*spring* OR-9
Mill Creek State Park—*park* IA-7
Mill Creek Stock Drive—*trail* CO-8
**Mill Creek (subdivision)**—*pop pl* MS-4
Mill Creek Summit—*gap* CA-9
Mill Creek Summit—*summit* (2) ID-8
Mill Creek Summit—*summit* NV-8
Mill Creek Thorofare—*channel* NJ-2
Millcreek Tower—*tower* FL-3
**Mill Creek Towne**—*pop pl* MD-2
Mill Creek Township—*civil* MO-7
Mill Creek Township—*civil* PA-2
**Mill Creek Township**—*pop pl* (4) KS-7
Mill Creek (Township of)—*fmr MCD* (8) AR-4
**Millcreek (Township of)**—*pop pl* IN-6
**Millcreek (Township of)**—*pop pl* OH-6
**Mill Creek (Township of)**—*pop pl* (2) OH-6
**Mill Creek (Township of)**—*pop pl* PA-2
**Millcreek (Township of)**—*pop pl* (2) PA-2
**Mill Creek (Township of)**—*pop pl* PA-2
**Millcreek (Township of)**—*pop pl* PA-2
Millcreek Township Police Airp—*airport* PA-2
Mill Creek Trail—*trail* CA-9
Mill Creek Trail—*trail* ID-8
Mill Creek Trail—*trail* MT-8
Mill Creek Trail—*trail* OR-9
Mill Creek Trail—*trail* (2) WA-9
Mill Creek Trout Rearing Station—*other* GA-3
Mill Creek Truck Trail—*trail* WA-9
Mill Creek Tube—*other* PA-2
Mill Creek Valley—*valley* GA-3
Mill Creek Valley Park—*park* PA-2
Mill Creek Well—*well* AZ-5
Mill Creek Zanja—*hist pl* CA-9
Millcrest Park—*park* OH-6
Mill Crossroads—*locale* NC-3
Mill Cut—*gut* WI-6
*Milldale* NJ-2
Milldale—*locale* VA-3
**Milldale**—*pop pl* CT-1
**Milldale**—*pop pl* LA-4
**Milldale**—*pop pl* TN-4
Milldale Cem—*cemetery* MS-4
Milldale Ch—*church* OH-6
Milldale Drift Mine (underground)—*mine* AL-4
Milldale Hollow—*valley* OH-6
Milldale Post Office (historical)—*building* TN-4
Milldale Ranch—*locale* NE-7
*Mill Dam* PA-2
Mill Dam—*dam* NJ-2
Mill Dam—*dam* (4) PA-2
Mill Dam Branch—*stream* FL-3
Milldam Branch—*stream* NC-3
Mill Dam Branch—*stream* TN-4
*Milldam Creek* VA-3
Mill Dam Creek—*stream* (2) FL-3
Mill Dam Creek—*stream* GA-3
Mill Dam Creek—*stream* (2) NC-3
Milldam Creek—*stream* (2) VA-3
Mill Dam Creek—*stream* (3) VA-3
Mill Dam Hill—*ridge* OH-6
Milldam Hollow—*valley* MO-7
Mill Dam Hollow—*valley* TN-4
Mill Dam Lake—*lake* FL-3
Milldam Marsh (historical)—*swamp* MA-1
Mill Dam Park—*park* NJ-2
Mill Dam Park—*park* NY-2
Milldam Rice Mill and Rice Barn—*hist pl* SC-3
Mill Dam Ridge—*ridge* TN-4
Mill Dam Run—*stream* MD-2
*Millde Fork Bull Creek* ID-8
Mill Den Creek—*gut* SC-3
Mill Diich—*canal* CO-8
*Mill Ditch* OR-9
Mill Ditch—*canal* AR-4
Mill Ditch—*canal* (2) CA-9
Mill Ditch—*canal* IL-6
Mill Ditch—*canal* (2) MT-8
Mill Ditch—*canal* (2) OR-9
Mill Ditch—*canal* UT-8
Mill Ditch, The—*canal* OR-9
Mill D North Fork—*stream* UT-8
Mill Draw—*valley* MT-8
Mill D South Fork—*stream* UT-8
*Mille* MP-9
Mille, Lake—*reservoir* MS-4
*Mille Atoll* MP-9
**Millecoquins**—*pop pl* MI-6
*Millecoquins Lake* MI-6
Millecoquins Lake—*lake* MI-6
**Millecoquins Lake**—*pop pl* MI-6
Millecoquins Point—*cape* MI-6
Millecoquins Pond—*lake* MI-6
Millecoquins Reefs—*bar* MI-6
Millecoquins River—*stream* MI-6
Mille Crag Bend—*bend* UT-8
*Mille Craig Bend* UT-8
Milledge Ave Hist Dist—*hist pl* GA-3
Milledge Circle Hist Dist—*hist pl* GA-3
Milledge Sch—*school* GA-3
*Milledgeville* TN-4
Milledgeville—*locale* IA-7
Milledgeville—*locale* KY-4
**Milledgeville**—*pop pl* GA-3
**Milledgeville**—*pop pl* IL-6
**Milledgeville**—*pop pl* IN-6
**Milledgeville**—*pop pl* OH-6
**Milledgeville**—*pop pl* PA-2
**Milledgeville**—*pop pl* TN-4
Milledgeville Baptist Ch—*church* TN-4
Milledgeville Cem—*cemetery* PA-2
Milledgeville Cem—*cemetery* TN-4
Milledgeville Country Club—*other* GA-3
Milledgeville Hist Dist—*hist pl* GA-3
Milledgeville-Midway-Hardwick (CCD)—*cens area* GA-3
Milledgeville Plymouth Cem—*cemetery* OH-6
Milledgeville Post Office—*building* TN-4
Millegan—*locale* MT-8
Millegan Hill—*summit* MT-8
*Mille Inseln* MP-9
*Mille Island* MP-9
**Mille Lacs (County)**—*pop pl* MN-6
Mille Lacs County Courthouse—*hist pl* MN-6
Mille Lacs Ind Res—*reserve* MN-6
Mille Lacs Kathio State Park—*park* MN-6
Mille Lacs Lake—*lake* MN-6
Mille Lacs Lookout Tower—*locale* MN-6
Mille Lacs Meadows—*swamp* MN-6
Mille Lacs Natl Wildlife Ref—*park* MN-6
Mille Lacs Sch—*school* MN-6
Mille Lacs State Wildlife Mngmt Area—*park* MN-6
**Millen**—*pop pl* GA-3
**Millen**—*pop pl* WV-2
Millen Bay—*bay* NY-2
**Millen Bay**—*pop pl* NY-2
**Millenbeck**—*pop pl* VA-3
Millenbeck Prong—*stream* VA-3
Millen Hill—*summit* NH-1
Millen Lake—*lake* NH-1
Millen Natl Fish Hatchery—*other* GA-3
**Millennium**—*pop pl* NC-3
Millennium Ch—*church* NC-3
**Millennium Church**—*pop pl* NC-3
*Millens Bay* NY-2
Millen Sch (abandoned)—*school* PA-2
*Millens Channel* NV-8
Millens Channel—*channel* NV-8
Millen-Schmidt House—*hist pl* OH-6
Millens Landing—*locale* NV-8
**Millen (Township of)**—*pop pl* MI-6
*Miller* IN-6
*Miller* PA-2
*Miller* WV-2
Miller—*fmr MCD* NE-7
Miller—*locale* (3) AL-4
Miller—*locale* CA-9
Miller—*locale* FL-3
Miller—*locale* IL-6
Miller—*locale* KY-4
Miller—*locale* MD-2
Miller—*locale* MT-8
Miller—*locale* OK-5
Miller—*locale* (3) OR-9
Miller—*locale* PA-2
Miller—*locale* TN-4
Miller—*locale* WY-8
**Miller**—*pop pl* (2) AR-4
**Miller**—*pop pl* (2) IN-6
**Miller**—*pop pl* IA-7
**Miller**—*pop pl* KS-7
**Miller**—*pop pl* MI-6
**Miller**—*pop pl* MS-4
**Miller**—*pop pl* MO-7
**Miller**—*pop pl* NE-7
**Miller**—*pop pl* OH-6
**Miller**—*pop pl* SD-7
**Miller**—*pop pl* TN-4
Miller—*spring* OR-9
Miller—*uninc pl* TX-5
Miller, A. J., House—*hist pl* VA-3
Miller, Alexander McVeight, House—*hist pl* WV-2
Miller, Alvin, House—*hist pl* IA-7
Miller, Charles A., House—*hist pl* OH-6
Miller, C. W., House—*hist pl* VA-3
Miller, Daniel, House—*hist pl* OH-6
Miller, Daniels, House—*hist pl* OH-6
Miller, Dr. Thomas B., House—*hist pl* GA-3
Miller, Ezekial and Mary Jane, House—*hist pl* TX-5
Miller, F. H., House—*hist pl* IA-7
Miller, Frederick, House—*hist pl* KY-4
Miller, Frederick A., House-Broad Gables—*hist pl* OH-6
Miller, George A., House—*hist pl* NJ-2
Miller, George H., House—*hist pl* IL-6
Miller, George McA., House—*hist pl* FL-3
Miller, Hannah, House—*hist pl* VA-3
Miller, Harrison, Farmhouse—*hist pl* MN-6
Miller, Harvey, Residence—*hist pl* OH-6
Miller, Henry, House—*hist pl* ID-8
Miller, Henry, House—*hist pl* VA-3
Miller, Henry, House—*hist pl* WI-6
Miller, Hugo, House—*hist pl* AZ-5
Miller, Issac, House—*hist pl* MO-7
Miller, Jacob, House—*hist pl* MI-6
Miller, James, House—*hist pl* PA-2
Miller, J.F., House—*hist pl* OH-6
Miller, J. K., Homestead—*hist pl* MT-8
Miller, Johannes, House—*hist pl* NY-2
Miller, John, Farmhouse—*hist pl* MN-6
Miller, John Andrew, House—*hist pl* KY-4
Miller, John Hickman, House—*hist pl* TX-5
Miller, John J., House—*hist pl* WA-9
Miller, Joseph, House—*hist pl* IL-6
Miller, Justice Samuel Freeman, House—*hist pl* IA-7
Miller, Lake—*lake* CA-9
Miller, Lake—*lake* MI-6
Miller, Lake—*lake* ND-7
Miller, Lake—*lake* TX-5
Miller, L. D., Funeral Home—*hist pl* SD-7
Miller, Lewis, Cottage, Chautauqua Institution—*hist pl* NY-2
Miller, Lewis, House—*hist pl* OH-6
Miller, Longdon L., Covered Bridge—*hist pl* PA-2
Miller, Mount—*summit* AK-9
Miller, Norris, House—*hist pl* IA-7
Miller, Paschal, House—*hist pl* NY-2
Miller, Peter, House—*hist pl* OH-6
Miller, Robert H., House—*hist pl* KS-7
Miller, Severin, House—*hist pl* IA-7
Miller, William, Chapel and Ascension Rock—*hist pl* NY-2
Miller, William, Place—*hist pl* KY-4
Miller, William Davis, House—*hist pl* RI-1
Miller, William M., House—*hist pl* KY-4
Miller Academy Ch—*church* GA-3
Miller Airp—*airport* (2) IN-6
Miller Airp—*airport* MO-7
Miller Airp—*airport* NC-3
Miller Airp—*airport* (3) PA-2
Miller Airstrip—*airport* OR-9
**Millerama View Subdivision**—*pop pl* UT-8
Miller and Herriott House—*hist pl* CA-9
Miller and Lux Ranch—*locale* CA-9
Miller and Lux Spring—*spring* (2) NV-8
Miller and Lux Well—*well* NV-8
Miller And Malosh Drain—*stream* MI-6
Miller and McGirl Ditch—*canal* MT-8
Miller and Sons Farm Supply Airp—*airport* IN-6
Miller Arm—*bay* OR-9
Miller Arm—*canal* IN-6
Miller Army Air Field Hist Dist—*hist pl* NY-2
Miller Ave Ch—*church* TX-5
Miller Ave Sch—*school* (2) NY-2
Miller Ave Sch—*school* PA-2
Miller Bar—*bar* OR-9
*Miller Basin* NV-8
Miller Basin—*basin* (3) NV-8
Miller Basin Wash—*stream* NV-8
Miller Bay—*bay* (2) MN-6
Miller Bay—*bay* (2) WA-9
Miller Bay—*swamp* FL-3
Miller Bayou—*bay* WI-6
Miller Bayou—*gut* LA-4
Miller Bayou—*stream* AR-4
Miller Bayou—*stream* FL-3
*Miller Beach* IN-6
Miller Bench—*bench* NV-8
Miller Bend—*bend* KY-4
Miller Bend—*bend* TX-5
Miller Bend—*locale* FL-3
**Millerberg Subdivision**—*pop pl* UT-8
Miller Bldg—*hist pl* IA-7
Miller Block—*hist pl* AZ-5
Miller Block—*hist pl* OH-6
Miller Bluff—*cliff* FL-3
Miller Bluff—*cliff* LA-4
Miller Bluff—*cliff* TN-4
Miller Bluff—*cliff* WI-6
Miller Bog—*swamp* ME-1
Millerboro Cem—*cemetery* NE-7
Miller Bottom—*bend* AL-4
Miller Bottoms—*bend* MT-8
*Miller Branch* MS-4
*Miller Branch* TX-5
Miller Branch—*stream* (9) AL-4
Miller Branch—*stream* (4) AR-4
Miller Branch—*stream* (2) GA-3
Miller Branch—*stream* IL-6
Miller Branch—*stream* (4) IN-6
Miller Branch—*stream* (14) KY-4
Miller Branch—*stream* (4) LA-4
Miller Branch—*stream* MD-2
Miller Branch—*stream* MS-4
Miller Branch—*stream* (5) MO-7
Miller Branch—*stream* NE-7
Miller Branch—*stream* (6) NC-3
Miller Branch—*stream* (2) SC-3
Miller Branch—*stream* (16) TN-4
Miller Branch—*stream* (6) TX-5
Miller Branch—*stream* (4) VA-3
Miller Branch—*stream* WV-2
Miller Branch—*stream* WI-6
Miller Branch Sch—*school* KY-4
Miller-Brewer House—*hist pl* WA-9
Miller Bridge—*bridge* MS-4
Miller Bridge—*bridge* NC-3
Miller Bridge—*bridge* SC-3
*Miller Brook* TN-4
Miller Brook—*stream* CT-1
Miller Brook—*stream* ME-1
Miller Brook—*stream* (5) MA-1
Miller Brook—*stream* NH-1
Miller Brook—*stream* (3) NY-2
Miller Brook—*stream* PA-2
Miller Brook—*stream* VT-1
Miller Brothers Bldg—*hist pl* KY-4
Miller Brothers Dam—*dam* SD-7
Miller Brothers Dam Number One—*dam* AL-4
Miller Brothers Dam Number Three—*dam* AL-4
Miller Brothers Dam Number Two—*dam* AL-4
Miller Brothers Department Store—*hist pl* TN-4
Miller Brothers Farm—*hist pl* GA-3
Miller Brothers Lake Number One—*reservoir* AL-4
Miller Brothers Lake Number Three—*reservoir* AL-4
Miller Brothers Lake Number Two—*reservoir* AL-4
Miller Brothers Mine—*mine* ID-8
Millerburg Sch—*school* MI-6
Miller Butte—*summit* MT-8
Miller Butte—*summit* (2) OR-9
Miller Butte—*summit* SD-7
Miller Buttes—*summit* CA-9
Miller Cabin—*hist pl* WY-8
Miller Cabin—*locale* DC-2
Miller Cabin—*locale* OR-9
Miller Cabin—*locale* SD-7
Miller Cabin—*locale* WY-8
**Miller Calioon Addition**—*pop pl* UT-8
Miller Camp—*locale* AK-9
Miller Camp—*locale* SD-7
Miller Camp (historical)—*locale* SD-7
Miller Camp Lake—*lake* WI-6
Miller Canal—*canal* (2) ID-8
Miller Canal—*canal* KS-7
*Miller Canon* NV-8
*Miller Canyon* NV-8
*Miller Canyon* OR-9
*Miller Canyon* WY-8
Miller Canyon—*valley* (3) AZ-5
Miller Canyon—*valley* (7) CA-9
Miller Canyon—*valley* (2) CO-8
Miller Canyon—*valley* ID-8
Miller Canyon—*valley* (2) NV-8
Miller Canyon—*valley* (7) NM-5
Miller Canyon—*valley* (2) OR-9
Miller Canyon—*valley* TX-5
Miller Canyon—*valley* (6) UT-8
Miller Canyon Camp—*locale* CA-9
*Miller Canyon - in part* UT-8
Miller Canyon Rec Area—*park* AZ-5
Miller Canyon Rsvr—*reservoir* UT-8
Miller Canyon Trail—*trail* (2) CA-9
Miller Cave—*cave* AL-4
Miller Cave—*cave* KY-4
*Miller Cem* AL-4
*Miller Cem* TN-4
Miller Cem—*cemetery* (13) AL-4
Miller Cem—*cemetery* (5) AR-4
Miller Cem—*cemetery* CO-8
Miller Cem—*cemetery* (2) FL-3
Miller Cem—*cemetery* (4) GA-3
Miller Cem—*cemetery* ID-8
Miller Cem—*cemetery* (15) IL-6
Miller Cem—*cemetery* (17) IN-6
Miller Cem—*cemetery* (5) IA-7
Miller Cem—*cemetery* (3) KS-7
Miller Cem—*cemetery* (13) KY-4
Miller Cem—*cemetery* (9) LA-4
Miller Cem—*cemetery* ME-1
Miller Cem—*cemetery* MI-6
Miller Cem—*cemetery* (5) MS-4
Miller Cem—*cemetery* (8) MO-7
Miller Cem—*cemetery* NJ-2
Miller Cem—*cemetery* (5) NY-2
Miller Cem—*cemetery* (4) NC-3
Miller Cem—*cemetery* (15) OH-6
Miller Cem—*cemetery* (6) OK-5
Miller Cem—*cemetery* (4) OR-9
Miller Cem—*cemetery* (7) PA-2
Miller Cem—*cemetery* (4) SC-3
Miller Cem—*cemetery* SD-7
Miller Cem—*cemetery* (30) TN-4
Miller Cem—*cemetery* (12) TX-5
Miller Cem—*cemetery* VT-1
Miller Cem—*cemetery* (5) VA-3
Miller Cem—*cemetery* (15) WV-2
Miller Cem—*cemetery* (3) WI-6
Miller Cemetery Church—*hist pl* OR-9
Miller Cemeterys—*cemetery* GA-3
*Miller Ch* AL-4
Miller Ch—*church* AR-4
Miller Ch—*church* KY-4
Miller Ch—*church* LA-4
Miller Ch—*church* MS-4
Miller Ch—*church* NE-7
Miller Ch—*church* (2) NC-3
Miller Ch—*church* OH-6
Miller Ch—*church* SC-3
Miller Ch—*church* TN-4
Miller Ch—*church* VA-3
Miller Ch—*church* WV-2
*Miller Chapel* MO-7
Miller Chapel—*church* (2) AL-4
Miller Chapel—*church* AR-4
Miller Chapel—*church* GA-3
Miller Chapel—*church* IL-6
Miller Chapel—*church* IA-7
Miller Chapel—*church* (2) KY-4
Miller Chapel—*church* LA-4
Miller Chapel—*church* (4) NC-3
Miller Chapel—*church* (5) TN-4
Miller Chapel—*church* VA-3
Miller Chapel—*church* WV-2
Miller Chapel (abandoned)—*church* MO-7
Miller Chapel Cem—*cemetery* TN-4
Miller Chapel Cem—*cemetery* VA-3
Miller Chapel Ch—*church* GA-3
Miller Chapel (historical)—*church* (3) TN-4
Miller-Chapman Ditch—*canal* CO-8
Miller Ch (historical)—*church* AL-4
*Miller City* TN-4
**Miller City**—*pop pl* IL-6
**Miller City**—*pop pl* OH-6
Miller City Cutoff—*canal* OH-6
Miller-Claytor House—*hist pl* VA-3
**Miller Colony**—*pop pl* MT-8
Miller Community Lake State Wildlife Area—*park* MO-7
Miller-Coon Cem—*cemetery* OR-9
Miller Corner—*locale* ME-1
**Miller Corner**—*pop pl* ME-1
*Miller Corners* KY-4
**Miller Corners**—*pop pl* NY-2
Miller Corral—*locale* NV-8
Miller-Cory House—*hist pl* NJ-2
Miller Coulee—*stream* MT-8
Miller Coulee—*valley* (8) MT-8
Miller Coulee—*valley* ND-7
Miller Coulee—*valley* WI-6
**Miller (County)**—*pop pl* AR-4
**Miller (County)**—*pop pl* GA-3
**Miller County**—*pop pl* MO-7
Miller Cove—*bay* VA-3
Miller Cove—*cove* MA-1
Miller Cove—*locale* TN-4
Miller Cove—*valley* GA-3
Miller Cove—*valley* (2) NC-3
Miller Cove—*valley* (3) TN-4
Miller Cove—*valley* UT-8
Miller Cove—*valley* VA-3
Miller Cove Branch—*stream* GA-3
Miller Cove Ch—*church* TN-4
*Miller Cove Methodist Ch* TN-4
Miller Cove Mtn—*summit* TN-4
Miller Cow Camp—*locale* MT-8
*Miller Creek* AL-4
*Miller Creek* AZ-5
*Miller Creek* AR-4
*Miller Creek* CO-8
*Miller Creek* DE-2
*Miller Creek* ID-8
*Miller Creek* MN-6
*Miller Creek* NC-3
*Miller Creek* OR-9
*Miller Creek* TN-4
*Miller Creek* TX-5
*Miller Creek* WI-6
Miller Creek—*bay* DE-2
Miller Creek—*gut* FL-3
Miller Creek—*stream* (5) AL-4
Miller Creek—*stream* (7) AK-9
Miller Creek—*stream* (2) AZ-5
Miller Creek—*stream* (5) AR-4
Miller Creek—*stream* (14) CA-9
Miller Creek—*stream* (10) CO-8
Miller Creek—*stream* DE-2
Miller Creek—*stream* (2) FL-3
Miller Creek—*stream* (3) GA-3
Miller Creek—*stream* (11) ID-8
Miller Creek—*stream* (7) IL-6
Miller Creek—*stream* (3) IN-6
Miller Creek—*stream* (6) IA-7
Miller Creek—*stream* KS-7
Miller Creek—*stream* (2) KY-4
Miller Creek—*stream* (3) LA-4
Miller Creek—*stream* ME-1
Miller Creek—*stream* MD-2
Miller Creek—*stream* (8) MI-6
Miller Creek—*stream* (4) MN-6
Miller Creek—*stream* (3) MS-4
Miller Creek—*stream* (2) MO-7
Miller Creek—*stream* (16) MT-8
Miller Creek—*stream* (3) NV-8
Miller Creek—*stream* NJ-2
Miller Creek—*stream* NM-5
Miller Creek—*stream* (3) NY-2
Miller Creek—*stream* (3) NC-3
Miller Creek—*stream* ND-7
Miller Creek—*stream* (3) OH-6
Miller Creek—*stream* (2) OK-5
Miller Creek—*stream* (25) OR-9
Miller Creek—*stream* SC-3
Miller Creek—*stream* SD-7
Miller Creek—*stream* (4) TN-4
Miller Creek—*stream* (11) TX-5
Miller Creek—*stream* (3) UT-8
Miller Creek—*stream* (3) VA-3
Miller Creek—*stream* (9) WA-9
Miller Creek—*stream* (5) WV-2
Miller Creek—*stream* (3) WI-6
Miller Creek—*stream* (11) WY-8
Miller Creek Cem—*cemetery* ID-8
Miller Creek Cem—*cemetery* MO-7
Miller Creek Cem—*cemetery* (2) TX-5
Miller Creek Cem—*cemetery* WY-8
Miller Creek Cove—*slope* UT-8
Miller Creek Cow Camp—*locale* CO-8
Miller Creek Ditch—*canal* CO-8
Miller Creek Lake—*reservoir* GA-3
Miller Creek Oil Field—*oilfield* WY-8
**Miller Creek Park (trailer park)**—*pop pl* DE-2
Miller Creek Rec Area—*park* NE-7
Miller Creek Sch—*school* KY-4
Miller Creek Sch—*school* WY-8
Miller Creek Sch (historical)—*school* MO-7
Miller Creek Sch Indian Mound—*hist pl* CA-9
Miller Creek Settlement—*locale* ID-8
Miller Creek Spring—*spring* OR-9
Miller Creek Trail—*trail* MT-8
Miller Creek Trail—*trail* WY-8
**Millercrest (subdivision)**—*pop pl* TN-4
Miller Crossing—*locale* CA-9
**Miller Crossing**—*pop pl* SC-3
Miller Crossing Well—*well* NV-8
Miller Crossroads—*locale* FL-3
Miller Crossroads—*locale* SC-3
Miller-Curtis House—*hist pl* TX-5
Miller Cutoff—*bend* OH-6
*Millerdale* IA-7
**Miller Dale Colony**—*pop pl* SD-7
Miller Dam—*dam* AL-4
Miller Dam—*dam* KS-7
Miller Dam—*dam* NC-3
Miller Dam—*dam* (2) OR-9
Miller Dam—*dam* PA-2
Miller Dam—*dam* SD-7
Miller Dam—*dam* WI-6
Miller Dam Branch—*stream* SC-3
Miller Dam Tank—*reservoir* AZ-5
Miller-Davidson House—*hist pl* WI-6
Miller-Davis Law Buildings—*hist pl* IL-6
*Miller Ditch* IN-6
Miller Ditch—*canal* CA-9
Miller Ditch—*canal* (4) CO-8
Miller Ditch—*canal* ID-8
Miller Ditch—*canal* (22) IN-6
Miller Ditch—*canal* (4) MT-8
Miller Ditch—*canal* NM-5
Miller Ditch—*canal* OH-6
Miller Ditch—*canal* (2) OR-9
Miller Ditch—*canal* SD-7
Miller Ditch—*canal* (4) WY-8
Miller Diversion Dam—*dam* OR-9

Miller Drain—*canal* (4) MI-6
Miller Drain—*stream* (4) MI-6
Miller Drain Number 29—*canal* ND-7
Miller Draw—*valley* (2) TX-5
Miller Draw—*valley* (5) WY-8
Miller Draw Rsvr—*reservoir* MT-8
Miller Drive Park—*park* FL-3
Miller (Election Precinct)—*fmr MCD* IL-6
Miller Elem Sch—*school* KS-7
Miller Elem Sch—*school* PA-2
Miller-Ellyson House—*hist pl* TX-5
Miller Farm—*hist pl* OH-6
Miller Farm—*locale* PA-2
Miller Farm Airp—*airport* KS-7
**Miller Farms**—*pop pl* CA-9
Miller Ferry Bar (historical)—*bar* AL-4
Miller Field—*airport* ND-7
Miller Field—*locale* MA-1
Miller Field—*park* NY-2
Miller Field—*park* OH-6
Miller Field Airp—*airport* IN-6
Miller Field Branch—*stream* SC-3
Millerfield Ch—*church* KY-4
Millerfield Ridge—*ridge* KY-4
Miller Flat—*flat* AZ-5
Miller Flat—*flat* (4) CA-9
Miller Flat—*flat* NV-8
Miller Flat—*flat* (4) OR-9
Miller Flat Creek—*stream* OR-9
Miller Flat Creek—*stream* UT-8
Miller Flat Dam—*dam* UT-8
Miller Flat Rsvr—*reservoir* UT-8
Miller Flats—*area* CA-9
Miller Flats—*flat* NM-5
Miller Flats—*flat* TN-4
Miller Flats—*locale* TN-4
Miller Flat Spring—*spring* OR-9
Miller Ford (historical)—*locale* MO-7
Miller Fork—*stream* AK-9
Miller Fork—*stream* CA-9
Miller Fork—*stream* CO-8
Miller Fork—*stream* IN-6
Miller Fork—*stream* (4) KY-4
Miller Fork—*stream* WV-2
Miller Fork Carmel River—*stream* CA-9
Miller Fourmile Ditch—*canal* CO-8
Miller Gap—*gap* (3) GA-3
Miller Gap—*gap* NM-5
Miller Gap—*gap* (4) NC-3
Miller Gap—*gap* PA-2
Miller Gap—*gap* TN-4
Miller Gap Sch—*school* NC-3
Miller-Gibson Dam No 3—*dam* NM-5
Miller-Gibson Dam No 4—*dam* NM-5
Miller-Gibson Detention Dam No 1—*dam* NM-5
Miller-Gibson Detention Dam No 2—*dam* NM-5
Miller Glacier—*glacier* AK-9
Miller Glade—*flat* CA-9
Miller Grove—*locale* OH-6
**Miller Grove**—*pop pl* (2) TX-5
Miller Grove Ch—*church* (2) GA-3
Miller Grove Ch—*church* TN-4
Miller Grove Sch (abandoned)—*school* MO-7
Miller Gulch—*valley* (2) AK-9
Miller Gulch—*valley* (4) CA-9
Miller Gulch—*valley* (3) CO-8
Miller Gulch—*valley* (2) ID-8
Miller Gulch—*valley* (7) MT-8
Miller Gulch—*valley* NV-8
Miller Gulch—*valley* NM-5
Miller Gulch—*valley* (5) OR-9
Miller Gulch—*valley* UT-8
Miller Gulch—*valley* WA-9
Miller Gulch Creek—*stream* CO-8
Miller Gulch Spring—*spring* CO-8
Miller Gully—*valley* LA-4
Miller Hall—*hist pl* NE-7
Miller Hall—*hist pl* PA-2
Miller Heights Elem Sch—*school* PA-2
**Miller Heights (Heights)**—*pop pl* PA-2
Miller Heights Sch—*school* TX-5
*Miller Heights School* PA-2
Miller Hereford Ranch—*locale* CO-8
**Miller Hill**—*pop pl* SC-3
Miller Hill—*post sta* MN-6
Miller Hill—*ridge* AZ-5
Miller Hill—*summit* AL-4
Miller Hill—*summit* AR-4
Miller Hill—*summit* CA-9
Miller Hill—*summit* (2) CO-8
Miller Hill—*summit* CT-1
Miller Hill—*summit* (2) KY-4
Miller Hill—*summit* MD-2
Miller Hill—*summit* (4) MA-1
Miller Hill—*summit* MO-7
Miller Hill—*summit* (6) NY-2
Miller Hill—*summit* OH-6
Miller Hill—*summit* OR-9
Miller Hill—*summit* PA-2
Miller Hill—*summit* SD-7
Miller Hill—*summit* UT-8
Miller Hill—*summit* (2) VT-1
Miller Hill—*summit* VA-3
Miller Hill—*summit* (2) WA-9
Miller Hill—*summit* WY-8
Miller Hill Cem—*cemetery* CO-8
Miller Hill Ch—*church* AL-4
Miller Hill Ch—*church* NC-3
Miller Hill Draw—*valley* CO-8
Miller Hill Lake—*lake* WY-8
Miller Hills—*range* WY-8
Miller Hill Tunnel—*mine* UT-8
**Miller (historical)**—*pop pl* MO-7
**Miller (historical)**—*pop pl* OR-9
*Miller Hollow* TN-4
Miller Hollow—*valley* (4) AR-4
Miller Hollow—*valley* IN-6
Miller Hollow—*valley* (5) KY-4
Miller Hollow—*valley* (3) MO-7
Miller Hollow—*valley* (2) NY-2
Miller Hollow—*valley* NC-3
Miller Hollow—*valley* (3) PA-2
Miller Hollow—*valley* (5) TN-4
Miller Hollow—*valley* UT-8
Miller Hollow—*valley* VA-3
Miller Hollow—*valley* (5) WV-2
Miller Hollow—*valley* WI-6
Miller Hollow Cove—*bay* MO-7
Miller Homestead—*hist pl* AR-4
Miller Homestead—*locale* CO-8
Miller Hosp—*hospital* (2) MN-6
Miller House—*hist pl* CO-8
Miller House—*hist pl* NY-2
Miller House—*hist pl* TN-4
Miller House—*hist pl* TX-5
Miller House—*hist pl* (2) WI-6
Miller House (Post Office)—*locale* AK-9
Miller HS—*school* GA-3
Miller HS—*school* MI-6
Miller HS—*school* TX-5
Miller Huggins Field—*park* FL-3
Miller International Airp—*airport* TX-5
*Miller Island* ME-1
*Miller Island* MD-2
*Miller Island* UT-8
Miller Island—*island* AK-9
Miller Island—*island* ME-1
Miller Island—*island* MN-6
Miller Island—*island* (3) MO-7
Miller Island—*island* OR-9
Miller Island—*island* (3) TN-4
Miller Island—*island* WA-9
Miller Island Canal—*canal* LA-4
Miller Islands—*island* ME-1
Millerite Ledges—*cliff* ME-1
Miller-Jackson Bldg—*hist pl* OK-5
Miller & Jackson Spring—*spring* OR-9
Miller JHS—*school* CO-8
Miller JHS—*school* TX-5
Miller JHS—*school* WA-9
Miller-Kingsland House—*hist pl* NJ-2
Miller-Kite House—*hist pl* VA-3
Miller Knob—*summit* KY-4
Miller Knob—*summit* TN-4
Miller Knob—*summit* (2) VA-3
Miller Knob—*summit* WV-2
Miller Knobs—*summit* TN-4
Miller Knoll—*summit* UT-8
*Miller Lake* AR-4
*Miller Lake* IN-6
*Miller Lake* MI-6
*Miller Lake* WI-6
*Miller Lake* WY-8
Miller Lake—*lake* AL-4
Miller Lake—*lake* AK-9
Miller Lake—*lake* AR-4
Miller Lake—*lake* (2) CA-9
Miller Lake—*lake* (2) FL-3
Miller Lake—*lake* (2) GA-3
Miller Lake—*lake* IN-6
Miller Lake—*lake* KY-4
Miller Lake—*lake* (2) LA-4
Miller Lake—*lake* (11) MI-6
Miller Lake—*lake* (12) MN-6
Miller Lake—*lake* MS-4
Miller Lake—*lake* (4) MT-8
Miller Lake—*lake* (2) NE-7
Miller Lake—*lake* NY-2
Miller Lake—*lake* ND-7
Miller Lake—*lake* OH-6
Miller Lake—*lake* (4) OR-9
Miller Lake—*lake* TN-4
Miller Lake—*lake* TX-5
Miller Lake—*lake* UT-8
Miller Lake—*lake* (2) WA-9
Miller Lake—*lake* (6) WI-6
Miller Lake—*lake* (3) WY-8
**Miller Lake**—*pop pl* IL-6
Miller Lake—*reservoir* AL-4
Miller Lake—*reservoir* CA-9
Miller Lake—*reservoir* (2) IL-6
Miller Lake—*reservoir* (3) IN-6
Miller Lake—*reservoir* LA-4
Miller Lake—*reservoir* (2) MO-7
Miller Lake—*reservoir* (2) TN-4
Miller Lake—*reservoir* (2) TX-5
Miller Lake—*reservoir* VA-3
Miller Lake—*swamp* MI-6
Miller Lake Creek—*stream* OR-9
Miller Lake Cut Off—*channel* GA-3
Miller Lake Dam—*dam* (2) IN-6
Miller Lake Dam—*dam* OR-9
Miller Lake Dam—*dam* (2) TN-4
Miller Lakes—*lake* TX-5
*Miller Landing* MS-4
Miller Landing—*locale* FL-3
Miller Landing—*locale* KY-4
Miller Landing—*locale* MS-4
Miller Landing—*locale* NC-3
Miller Landing—*locale* VA-3
Miller Lateral—*canal* AZ-5
Miller Lateral—*canal* ID-8
Miller-Leuser Log House—*hist pl* OH-6
Miller Line Sch (historical)—*school* MS-4
Miller-Lowery Cem—*cemetery* SC-3
Miller Mall—*locale* IN-6
**Miller Manor**—*pop pl* PA-2
Miller Marsh—*swamp* MI-6
Miller Marsh—*swamp* NY-2
Miller Marsh Drain—*stream* MI-6
Miller-Martin Town House—*hist pl* AL-4
Miller-Mast Cem—*cemetery* OH-6
Miller Mausoleum—*other* MO-7
Miller Meadow—*flat* CA-9
Miller Meadow—*flat* OR-9
Miller Meadow—*flat* WA-9
Miller Meadow Campground—*locale* CA-9
Miller Meadows—*flat* CA-9
Miller Meadows—*flat* IL-6
Miller Meadows—*flat* UT-8
Miller Memorial Airpark—*airport* OR-9
Miller Memorial Cem—*cemetery* AL-4
Miller Memorial Cem—*cemetery* MD-2
Miller Memorial Cem—*cemetery* TX-5
Miller Memorial Ch—*church* VA-3
Miller Mesa—*summit* (2) CO-8
Miller Mesa—*summit* NM-5
Miller Mesa Tank—*reservoir* NM-5
Miller Mill Run—*stream* WV-2
Miller Mine—*mine* AK-9
Miller Mine—*mine* (2) MT-8
Miller Mine—*mine* NV-8
Miller Mine—*mine* OR-9
Miller Mine Branch—*stream* TN-4
Miller Mine (historical)—*mine* ID-8
Miller Mines—*mine* AZ-5
Miller Mines—*mine* KY-4
Miller Mine (underground)—*mine* (2) AL-4
Miller Mound—*summit* AR-4
Miller Mountain Mine—*mine* OR-9
Miller Mtn—*summit* AL-4
Miller Mtn—*summit* (2) AZ-5
Miller Mtn—*summit* (3) AR-4
Miller Mtn—*summit* (4) CA-9
Miller Mtn—*summit* CO-8
Miller Mtn—*summit* ID-8
Miller Mtn—*summit* ME-1
Miller Mtn—*summit* (2) MT-8
Miller Mtn—*summit* (2) NV-8
Miller Mtn—*summit* NY-2
Miller Mtn—*summit* (5) NC-3
Miller Mtn—*summit* (3) OR-9
Miller Mtn—*summit* (2) PA-2
Miller Mtn—*summit* (4) TN-4
Miller Mtn—*summit* (3) TX-5
Miller Mtn—*summit* UT-8
Miller Mtn—*summit* VA-3
Miller Mtn—*summit* WA-9
Miller Mtn—*summit* (3) WY-8
Miller Municipal Airp—*airport* SD-7
Miller Narrows—*gap* CA-9
Miller Neck—*cape* DE-2
*Miller Neck Brook* MA-1
Miller-Nelson Cem—*cemetery* TN-4
Miller-O'Donnell House—*hist pl* AL-4
Miller Park—*flat* WY-8
Miller Park—*park* (2) CA-9
Miller Park—*park* GA-3
Miller Park—*park* IL-6
Miller Park—*park* IN-6
Miller Park—*park* IA-7
Miller Park—*park* MI-6
Miller Park—*park* (2) MN-6
Miller Park—*park* MT-8
Miller Park—*park* (3) NE-7
Miller Park—*park* NJ-2
Miller Park—*park* (2) NC-3
Miller Park—*park* (2) OH-6
Miller Park—*park* OR-9
Miller Park—*park* TN-4
Miller Park—*park* UT-8
Miller Park—*park* VA-3
Miller Park—*park* (2) WA-9
Miller Park Sch—*school* GA-3
Miller Park Sch—*school* MO-7
Miller Park Sch—*school* NE-7
Miller-Patterson Cem—*cemetery* AL-4
*Miller Peak* UT-8
Miller Peak—*summit* AK-9
Miller Peak—*summit* AZ-5
Miller Peak—*summit* CA-9
Miller Peak—*summit* (2) ID-8
Miller Peak—*summit* MT-8
Miller Peak—*summit* NM-5
Miller Peak—*summit* WA-9
*Miller Peak Trail* AZ-5
Miller Peak Trail—*trail* AZ-5
Miller Peak Trail—*trail* WA-9
Miller Peninsula—*cape* WA-9
Miller Perry Annex Sch—*school* TN-4
*Miller Perry Elem Sch* TN-4
Miller Perry Sch—*school* TN-4
Miller Place—*locale* CA-9
Miller Place—*locale* OR-9
**Miller Place**—*pop pl* NY-2
Miller Place Beach—*beach* NY-2
Millerplace Branch—*stream* VA-3
Miller Place Cem—*cemetery* AL-4
Miller Place Hist Dist—*hist pl* NY-2
Miller Plantation House—*hist pl* MS-4
Miller Plaza Shop Ctr—*locale* AZ-5
Miller Plaza (Shop Ctr)—*locale* FL-3
Miller Pocket—*basin* WY-8
*Miller Point* WA-9
Miller Point—*cape* AK-9
Miller Point—*cape* FL-3
Miller Point—*cape* LA-4
Miller Point—*cape* (2) ME-1
Miller Point—*cape* MI-6
Miller Point—*cape* (2) MN-6
Miller Point—*cape* MS-4
Miller Point—*cape* MT-8
Miller Point—*cape* NC-3
Miller Point—*cape* TX-5
Miller Point—*cape* UT-8
Miller Point—*cape* (2) WA-9
Miller Point—*cliff* WA-9
Miller Point—*flat* LA-4
*Miller Pond* CT-1
*Miller Pond* IL-6
*Miller Pond* NY-2
Miller Pond—*lake* AL-4
Miller Pond—*lake* CT-1
Miller Pond—*lake* FL-3
Miller Pond—*lake* GA-3
Miller Pond—*lake* IL-6
Miller Pond—*lake* LA-4
Miller Pond—*lake* MA-1
Miller Pond—*lake* MI-6
Miller Pond—*lake* NH-1
Miller Pond—*lake* NJ-2
Miller Pond—*lake* (3) NY-2
Miller Pond—*lake* PA-2
Miller Pond—*lake* VT-1
Miller Pond—*lake* (2) WA-9
Miller Pond—*reservoir* CT-1
Miller Pond—*reservoir* NY-2
Miller Pond—*reservoir* OR-9
Miller Pond—*reservoir* (2) PA-2
Miller Pond—*reservoir* SC-3
Miller Pond Dam—*dam* MS-4
Miller Pond Dam—*dam* PA-2
Miller Pond (historical)—*lake* TN-4
Miller Ponds—*reservoir* SC-3
Miller Pond Sch—*school* IL-6
Miller-Porter-Lacy House—*hist pl* MO-7
Miller Post Office (historical)—*building* MS-4
Miller Prairie—*area* CA-9
Miller Prairie—*flat* OR-9
Miller Prong—*stream* AR-4
Miller Pugh Ditch—*canal* IN-6
Miller Purdue Agricultural Center—*school* IN-6
Miller Quarry—*mine* TN-4
Miller Ranch—*locale* (2) AZ-5
Miller Ranch—*locale* (5) CA-9
Miller Ranch—*locale* (3) CO-8
Miller Ranch—*locale* ID-8
Miller Ranch—*locale* (4) MT-8
Miller Ranch—*locale* (4) NE-7
Miller Ranch—*locale* NV-8
Miller Ranch—*locale* (5) NM-5
Miller Ranch—*locale* (2) ND-7
Miller Ranch—*locale* OR-9
Miller Ranch—*locale* (3) SD-7
Miller Ranch—*locale* (5) TX-5
Miller Ranch—*locale* (2) WY-8
Miller Ranch Creek—*stream* AR-4
Miller Ranch HQ—*locale* NM-5
Miller Ranch (reduced usage)—*locale* TX-5
Miller Ranch (Site)—*locale* CA-9
Miller Ravine—*valley* CA-9
Miller Red Creek Canal—*canal* WY-8
Miller Ree Creek Bridge—*hist pl* SD-7
Miller Retarding Basin—*basin* CA-9
Miller Rhinehart Washer—*locale* AR-4
Miller-Richter State Wildlife Mngmt Area—*park* MN-6
Miller Ridge—*ridge* AL-4
Miller Ridge—*ridge* AZ-5
Miller Ridge—*ridge* (2) CA-9
Miller Ridge—*ridge* IN-6
Miller Ridge—*ridge* ME-1
Miller Ridge—*ridge* MN-6
Miller Ridge—*ridge* MO-7
Miller Ridge—*ridge* NC-3
Miller Ridge—*ridge* OK-5
Miller Ridge—*ridge* (5) TN-4
Miller Ridge—*ridge* UT-8
Miller Ridge—*ridge* (5) WV-2
*Miller River* MA-1
*Miller River* RI-1
*Miller River* WA-9
**Miller River**—*pop pl* WA-9
Miller River—*stream* WA-9
Miller River Campground—*locale* WA-9
Miller Road Shopping Plaza—*locale* FL-3
Miller Rock—*cape* WV-2
Miller Rock—*summit* CO-8
Miller Round Barn—*hist pl* IA-7
Miller Rsvr—*reservoir* AZ-5
Miller Rsvr—*reservoir* (3) CO-8
Miller Rsvr—*reservoir* MT-8
Miller Rsvr—*reservoir* (3) OR-9
Miller Rsvr—*reservoir* WA-9
*Miller Run* PA-2
**Miller Run**—*pop pl* PA-2
Miller Run—*stream* KY-4
Miller Run—*stream* (2) MD-2
Miller Run—*stream* (2) OH-6
Miller Run—*stream* (14) PA-2
Miller Run—*stream* VT-1
Miller Run—*stream* (2) VA-3
Miller Run—*stream* (5) WV-2
Miller Run Ch—*church* OH-6
Miller Run Natural Area—*area* PA-2
Miller Run Station—*locale* PA-2
Miller Run Trail—*trail* PA-2
Miller Run Trail—*trail* WV-2
*Millers* IN-6
*Millers* PA-2
*Millers* TN-4
Millers—*locale* AL-4
Millers—*locale* AR-4
Millers—*locale* MO-7
Millers—*locale* NV-8
Millers—*locale* PA-2
Millers—*locale* TX-5
**Millers**—*pop pl* MD-2
**Millers**—*pop pl* (2) MI-6
**Millers**—*pop pl* NY-2
**Millers**—*pop pl* NC-3
**Millers**—*pop pl* (2) PA-2
Miller Saddle—*gap* MT-8
*Millers Airport* NC-3
Millers Anchor Marina—*locale* AL-4
Miller Sands—*island* OR-9
Miller Sands Channel—*channel* OR-9
Millers Bar—*bar* AL-4
Millers Bay—*bay* IA-7
Millers Bay—*bay* WI-6
Millers Bay—*swamp* FL-3
*Millers Bayou* LA-4
Millers Bayou—*lake* FL-3
Millers Beach—*beach* NY-2
*Millers Bend* AL-4
Millers Bend—*bend* MD-2
Millers Bend—*bend* WV-2
Millers Bend—*ridge* TN-4
Millers Bluff—*cliff* LA-4
Millers Bluff—*cliff* TX-5
Millers Bluff—*locale* AR-4
Millers Boat Dock—*locale* TN-4
Millers Branch—*stream* GA-3
Millers Branch—*stream* IN-6
Millers Branch—*stream* KY-4
Millers Branch—*stream* SC-3
Millers Branch—*stream* TX-5
Millers Bridge—*bridge* AL-4
Millers Bridge—*bridge* MD-2
Millers Bridge—*bridge* NC-3
Millers Brook—*stream* MA-1
*Millersburg* IN-6
*Millersburg* PA-2
Millersburg—*locale* MN-6
**Millersburg**—*pop pl* IL-6
**Millersburg**—*pop pl* (4) IN-6
**Millersburg**—*pop pl* IA-7
**Millersburg**—*pop pl* KY-4
**Millersburg**—*pop pl* MI-6
**Millersburg**—*pop pl* MO-7
**Millersburg**—*pop pl* OH-6
**Millersburg**—*pop pl* OR-9
**Millersburg**—*pop pl* PA-2
*Millersburg Baptist Church* TN-4
Millersburg Borough—*civil* PA-2
Millersburg Branch—*stream* KY-4
Millersburg (CCD)—*cens area* KY-4
Millersburg Cem—*cemetery* TN-4
Millersburg Ch—*church* TN-4
Millersburg Elem Sch—*school* IN-6
*Millersburgh* IN-6
*Millersburgh* TN-4
Millersburg Hist Dist—*hist pl* KY-4
Millersburg Hist Dist—*hist pl* OH-6
Millersburg Military Institute—*school* KY-4
Millersburg Sch—*school* OR-9
**Millersburg (Township of)**—*pop pl* IL-6
Millers Butte—*summit* WY-8
Millers Camp—*locale* ME-1
Millers Camp—*locale* NY-2
Millers Canal—*canal* CA-9
Millers Canal—*canal* LA-4
Millers Cave—*cave* AL-4
Millers Cave—*cave* AZ-5
Millers Cave—*cave* NM-5
Millers Cem—*cemetery* AL-4
Millers Cem—*cemetery* MO-7
Millers Cem—*cemetery* PA-2
*Miller Sch* IN-6
Millers Ch—*church* MD-2
Millers Ch—*church* PA-2
Millers Ch—*church* TX-5
Miller Sch—*school* AZ-5
Miller Sch—*school* (2) AR-4
Miller Sch—*school* (4) CA-9
Miller Sch—*school* CO-8
Miller Sch—*school* (2) FL-3
Miller Sch—*school* GA-3
Miller Sch—*school* ID-8
Miller Sch—*school* (14) IL-6
Miller Sch—*school* (5) IN-6
Miller Sch—*school* IA-7
Miller Sch—*school* (3) KY-4
Miller Sch—*school* ME-1
Miller Sch—*school* MA-1
Miller Sch—*school* (6) MI-6
Miller Sch—*school* (8) MO-7
Miller Sch—*school* (2) NE-7
Miller Sch—*school* NV-8
Miller Sch—*school* NJ-2
Miller Sch—*school* OH-6
Miller Sch—*school* OK-5
Miller Sch—*school* (7) PA-2
Miller Sch—*school* (4) SD-7
Miller Sch—*school* TN-4
Miller Sch—*school* (4) TX-5
Miller Sch—*school* (2) VA-3
Miller Sch—*school* (5) WV-2
Miller Sch (abandoned)—*school* (4) MO-7
Miller Sch (abandoned)—*school* (8) PA-2
*Millers Chapel* TN-4
Millers Chapel—*church* AL-4
Millers Chapel—*church* (2) AR-4
Millers Chapel—*church* (2) GA-3
Millers Chapel—*church* MS-4
Millers Chapel—*church* MO-7
Millers Chapel—*church* (3) NC-3
Millers Chapel—*church* SC-3
Millers Chapel—*church* TN-4
Millers Chapel—*church* VA-3
*Millers Chapel Baptist Ch* TN-4
Millers Chapel Cem—*cemetery* OH-6
*Millers Chapel Ch* AL-4
Millers Chapel Ch—*church* TN-4
Millers Chapel (historical)—*church* TN-4
Millers Chapel Post Office (historical)—*building* TN-4
Millers Chapel Sch—*school* (2) TN-4
Miller Sch (historical)—*school* (2) AL-4
Miller Sch (historical)—*school* (5) MS-4
Miller Sch (historical)—*school* (3) MO-7
Miller Sch (historical)—*school* (5) PA-2
Miller Sch of Albemarle—*hist pl* VA-3
Miller School—*locale* CO-8
Miller School—*locale* MI-6
Miller School (Abandoned)—*locale* (2) IL-6
**Miller School (Boarding School)**—*pop pl* VA-3
Millers City (RR name for Miller City)—*other* OH-6
Millers Corner—*locale* NY-2
Millers Corner—*locale* PA-2
*Millers Corners* NY-2
Millers Corners—*locale* (2) NY-2
Millers Corners—*locale* PA-2
**Millers Corners**—*pop pl* CA-9
**Millers Corners**—*pop pl* NY-2
**Millers Corners**—*pop pl* (2) OH-6
Millers Corners Cem—*cemetery* NY-2
Miller Scott Spring—*spring* NM-5
Millers Coulee—*valley* MT-8
*Millers Cove* MA-1
*Millers Cove* TN-4
**Miller's Cove**—*pop pl* TN-4
**Miller's Cove**—*pop pl* TX-5
Millers Cove—*valley* VA-3
*Millers Cove Baptist Church* TN-4
Millers Cove Cem—*cemetery* TN-4
*Millers Cove Ch* TN-4
Millers Cove Ch—*church* TN-4
Millers Cove Post Office (historical)—*building* TN-4
Millers Cove Presbyterian Ch (historical)—*church* TN-4
*Millers Creek* AL-4
*Millers Creek* KS-7
*Millers Creek* LA-4
*Millers Creek* TN-4
*Millers Creek* TX-5
Millers Creek—*locale* KY-4
**Millers Creek**—*pop pl* NC-3
Millers Creek—*stream* AL-4
Millers Creek—*stream* (3) KY-4
Millers Creek—*stream* MO-7
Millers Creek—*stream* (4) NC-3
Millers Creek—*stream* OH-6
Millers Creek—*stream* TN-4
Millers Creek—*stream* (2) TX-5
Millers Creek—*stream* UT-8
Millers Creek—*stream* VA-3
Millers Creek Ch—*church* MO-7
Millers Creek (historical)—*locale* IA-7
Millers Creek (historical P.O.)—*locale* IA-7
Millers Crossing—*locale* AR-4
Millers Crossing—*locale* ME-1
Millers Crossing—*locale* NY-2
Millers Crossroads—*locale* SC-3
**Millers Crossroads**—*pop pl* PA-2
**Millers Crossroads (Prescott)**—*pop pl* SC-3
**Millersdale**—*pop pl* PA-2
Millers Defeat—*mine* CA-9
**Millers Eddy**—*pop pl* PA-2
Miller Seep—*spring* UT-8
Miller Seep Tank—*reservoir* AZ-5
*Millers Falls* MA-1
Millers Falls—*falls* NY-2
**Millers Falls**—*pop pl* MA-1
Millers Ferry—*locale* AL-4
Millers Ferry—*locale* FL-3
Millers Ferry (historical)—*locale* (4) AL-4
Millers Ferry Lock and Dam—*dam* AL-4
Millers Ferry (P O)—*locale* FL-3
Millers Field Airp—*airport* WA-9
*Millers Flat Reservoir* UT-8
Millers Ford—*locale* AL-4
Millers Ford—*locale* SC-3
Millers Ford (historical)—*locale* MO-7
*Millers Fork* IN-6
*Millers Fork* SC-3
Millers Fork—*stream* OH-6
Millers Fork—*stream* SC-3
Millers Fork—*stream* (2) WV-2
Millers Furnace (historical)—*locale* TN-4
Millers Gap—*gap* (2) PA-2
Millers Gin (historical)—*locale* AL-4
*Millers Grove* KS-7
*Millers Grove* PA-2
Millers Gulch—*valley* CO-8
Millers Gulch—*valley* OR-9
Miller Shaft—*locale* PA-2
Millers Head—*summit* VA-3
*Millers Hill* HI-9
*Millers Hill* MA-1
Millers Hill—*summit* (3) MA-1
Millers Hill—*summit* MS-4
*Millers Hill Church* AL-4
**Millers (historical)**—*pop pl* OR-9
Miller Shoals—*bar* TN-4
Miller's House at Mortonsville Mill—*hist pl* KY-4
Miller's House at Red Mills—*hist pl* NY-2
Miller's House at Ruddels Mills—*hist pl* KY-4
Miller-Sibley Field—*park* PA-2
Miller Siding—*locale* NC-3
Miller Siding (historical)—*locale* TN-4
*Millers Island* MD-2
*Millers Island* OR-9
*Millers Island* TN-4
Millers Island—*island* MD-2
Millers Island—*island* MO-7
Millers Island—*island* OH-6
**Millers Island (Swan Point)**—*pop pl* MD-2
Millers Knob—*summit* KY-4
Millers Knob—*summit* VA-3
*Millers Lake* PA-2
*Millers Lake* WI-6
Millers Lake—*lake* IN-6
Millers Lake—*lake* (2) MI-6
Millers Lake—*lake* MO-7
Millers Lake—*lake* TX-5
Millers Lake—*reservoir* GA-3
Millers Lake—*reservoir* IN-6
Millers Lake—*reservoir* LA-4
Millers Lake—*reservoir* TN-4
Millers Lake Dam—*dam* IN-6
Millers Lake Dam—*dam* TN-4
Millers Landing—*locale* AK-9
Millers Landing—*locale* CA-9
Millers Landing—*locale* MS-4
Millers Landing (historical)—*locale* (2) AL-4
Miller Slate Pond—*reservoir* PA-2
Miller Slough—*gut* IL-6
Miller Slough—*stream* AL-4
Miller Slough—*stream* CA-9
Miller Slough—*stream* TN-4
Millers Marsh—*lake* MI-6
Millers Mill—*locale* GA-3
Millers Mill—*locale* SC-3
Millers Mill (historical)—*locale* PA-2
**Millers Mills**—*pop pl* NY-2
Millers Mills Crossing—*locale* NY-2
Millers Mine—*mine* MT-8
Miller's Mountain House—*hist pl* OR-9
*Millers Mtn* VA-3
Millers Neck Brook—*stream* MA-1
*Millers Park* MI-6
Millers Park—*park* AL-4
*Millers Peak* CA-9
Millers Pocket—*basin* AZ-5
Millers Point—*cape* AR-4
Millers Point—*cape* CA-9
Millers Point—*cape* TX-5
Millers Point—*summit* NV-8
*Millers Pond* MA-1
*Millers Pond* PA-2
Millers Pond—*lake* (2) CT-1
Millers Pond—*lake* NV-8
Millers Pond—*lake* NY-2
Millers Pond—*lake* SC-3
Millers Pond—*reservoir* (2) GA-3
Millers Pond—*reservoir* MS-4
Millers Pond—*reservoir* NY-2
Millers Pond—*reservoir* SC-3
Millers Pond—*reservoir* VA-3
Millers Pond Dam—*dam* PA-2
Millers Pond Park—*park* FL-3
Millers Pond Park—*park* TX-5
Millers Pond State Park—*park* CT-1
*Millersport* OH-6
Millersport—*locale* WV-2
**Millersport**—*pop pl* IN-6
**Millersport**—*pop pl* NY-2
**Millersport**—*pop pl* OH-6
*Miller Spring* OR-9
Miller Spring—*reservoir* AZ-5
Miller Spring—*spring* AL-4
Miller Spring—*spring* (7) AZ-5
Miller Spring—*spring* (4) CA-9
Miller Spring—*spring* CO-8
Miller Spring—*spring* KY-4
Miller Spring—*spring* MO-7
Miller Spring—*spring* (2) MT-8
Miller Spring—*spring* (2) NV-8
Miller Spring—*spring* (3) NM-5
Miller Spring—*spring* (7) OR-9
Miller Spring—*spring* SD-7
Miller Spring—*spring* (2) TN-4
Miller Spring—*spring* (2) UT-8
Miller Spring—*spring* (3) WY-8
*Miller Spring Branch* AL-4
Miller Spring Branch—*stream* AL-4
Miller Spring Branch—*stream* TN-4
Miller Spring Cabin—*locale* NM-5
Miller Spring Canyon—*valley* NM-5
Miller Spring Lake—*reservoir* IL-6
Miller Spring Park—*park* TX-5
Miller Spring Run—*stream* VA-3
Miller Springs—*spring* CA-9

Miller Springs—spring GA-3
Miller Springs—spring TX-5
Miller Springs—stream TX-5
Miller Springs Cem—cemetery MS-4
Miller Springs Ch—church MS-4
Miller Springs Missionary Baptist Ch MS-4
Miller Springs Trail (Pack)—trail NM-5
Miller Springs Windmill—locale TX-5
Miller Spring Wash—stream NV-8
Millers Public Landing—locale FL-3
Miller Spur—canal TX-5
Miller Square (Shop Ctr)—post sta FL-3
Millers Ranch—locale MT-8
Millers Ranch—pop pl CA-9
Millers Rest Area—locale NV-8
Millers River MD-2
Millers River MA-1
Millers River—stream (3) MA-1
Millers River—stream RI-1
Millers River Rsvr—reservoir (3) MA-1
Millers Roadhouse (Abandoned)—locale AK-9
Millers Rock—bar NY-2
Millers Rock—summit KY-4
Millers Run PA-2
Millers Run—stream KY-4
Millers Run—stream MD-2
Millers Run—stream (4) OH-6
Millers Run—stream (7) PA-2
Millers Run Ch—church PA-2
Miller's Run Hist Dist—hist pl KY-4
Millers Sawmill—locale MD-2
Millers Sch—school (3) PA-2
Millers Sch (historical)—school AL-4
Millers Shop Ctr—locale UT-8
Millers Spring—spring CA-9
Millers Spring—spring NV-8
Millers Spring—spring OH-6
Millers Springs—spring WY-8
Millers Spur—locale ND-7
Millers Spur—pop pl MT-8
Millers Station TN-4
Millers Station—locale MI-6
Millers Station—pop pl IN-6
Millers Station—pop pl PA-2
Millers Store GA-3
Millers Store—locale NC-3
Millers Store (historical)—locale MS-4
Millers Store (historical)—locale TN-4
Miller Stand (historical)—locale TN-4
Miller State Forest Nursery—locale AL-4
Miller State Park—park NH-1
Miller State Wildlife Mngmt Area—park AL-4
Miller Station TN-4
Miller Station—locale OH-6
Miller's Tavern—hist pl WV-2
Millers Tavern—pop pl VA-3
Miller Steam Plant—building AL-4
Miller Steam Plant Ash Pond—reservoir AL-4
Miller Steam Plant Ash Pond Dam—dam AL-4
Miller Steam Plant Water
Storagep—reservoir AL-4
Millers Tomb—cemetery PA-2
Miller Store (historical)—locale TN-4
Millerstown PA-2
Millerstown—locale PA-2
Millerstown—pop pl KY-4
Millerstown—pop pl OH-6
Millerstown—pop pl (4) PA-2
Millerstown Borough—civil PA-2
Millerstown (CCD)—cens area KY-4
Millers (Township of)—fmr MCD NC-3
Miller Street Hist Dist—hist pl NJ-2
Miller Street Sch—school CA-9
Miller Sireet Sch—school NJ-2
Miller Subdivision
(subdivision)—pop pl AL-4
Millers Union Ch—church MS-4
Millers Union Sch—school MS-4
Millersview—pop pl TX-5
Millersview Cem—cemetery TX-5
Millersville AL-4
Millersville IN-6
Millersville—locale IL-6
Millersville—locale MI-6
Millersville—locale WY-8
Millersville—pop pl CA-9
Millersville—pop pl IN-6
Millersville—pop pl MD-2
Millersville—pop pl MO-7
Millersville—pop pl NC-3
Millersville—pop pl OH-6
Millersville—pop pl PA-2
Millersville—pop pl TN-4
Millersville—pop pl WV-2
Millersville—uninc pl WI-6
Millersville Borough—civil PA-2
Millersville Borough Park—park PA-2
Millersville Cem—cemetery IL-6
Millersville Ch—church MO-7
Millersville Elem Sch—school TN-4
Millersville (historical)—locale AL-4
Millersville Post Office
(historical)—building PA-2
Millersville Sch—school MO-7
Millersville Univ of Pennsylvania—school PA-2
Miller Swamp—stream SC-3
Miller Swamp—swamp MA-1
Miller Swamp—swamp NY-2
Miller Swamp—swamp WA-9
Miller Swamp Ch—church SC-3
Millers Well Number One—well NV-8
Millers Windmill—locale AZ-5
Millers Windmill—locale NM-5
Millers Woodyard Landing
(historical)—locale AL-4
Millersylvania State Park—park WA-9
Miller Tank—reservoir (8) AZ-5
Miller Tank—reservoir (3) NM-5
Miller Tank—reservoir (2) TX-5
Millerton—locale CA-9
Millerton—locale KS-7
Millerton—locale MI-6
Millerton—pop pl IA-7
Millerton—pop pl LA-4
Millerton—pop pl NY-2
Millerton—pop pl OK-5
Millerton—pop pl PA-2
Millerton Dam—dam UT-8
Millerton Gulch—valley CA-9
Millerton (historical)—pop pl NC-3
Millerton Lake—reservoir CA-9
Millerton Lake Fire Control
Station—other CA-9
Millerton Lake State Rec Area—park CA-9
Millerton Point—cape CA-9
Millerton Ridge—ridge CA-9
Millerton Rsvr—reservoir UT-8
Miller Top—summit GA-3
Millertown PA-2
Millertown—locale OH-6
Millertown—pop pl AL-4
Millertown—pop pl NY-2
Millertown—pop pl (2) PA-2
Millertown—pop pl TN-4
Millertown—pop pl WV-2
Miller Town Ch—church AL-4
Millertown Ch—church KY-4
Miller Town Hall—hist pl IN-6
Millertown Sch (historical)—school PA-2
Miller Township—civil (6) MO-7
Miller Township—fmr MCD IA-7
Miller Township—pop pl MO-7
Miller Township—pop pl NE-7
Miller Township—pop pl (2) SD-7
Miller Township (historical)—civil SD-7
Miller (Township of)—fmr MCD (2) AR-4
Miller (Township of)—pop pl IL-6
Miller (Township of)—pop pl IN-6
Miller (Township of)—pop pl OH-6
Miller (Township of)—pop pl (2) PA-2
Millertown (Site)—locale CA-9
Millertown (Site)—locale TX-5
Miller Trail—trail CA-9
Miller Trail—trail MT-8
Miller Trail—trail (2) PA-2
Miller Trough—spring NV-8
Miller Valley—pop pl AZ-5
Miller Valley—valley (2) CA-9
Miller Valley—valley MN-6
Miller Valley—valley WI-6
Miller Valley Post Office—building AZ-5
Miller Valley Sch—school AZ-5
Miller View Ch—church VA-3
Millerville NV-8
Millerville—locale AR-4
Millerville—pop pl AL-4
Millerville—pop pl (2) LA-4
Millerville—pop pl MA-1
Millerville—pop pl MN-6
Millerville Cem—cemetery TX-5
Millerville Cem—cemetery WV-2
Millerville Elem Sch—school AL-4
Millerville-Hollins (CCD)—cens area AL-4
Millerville-Hollins Division—civil AL-4
Millerville Sch—school WV-2
Millerville (Township of)—pop pl MN-6
Miller-Walker House—hist pl MI-6
Miller Wall Sch—school LA-4
Miller Wash—stream (3) AZ-5
Miller Wash—stream NV-8
Miller Wash—valley UT-8
Miller-Washington Sch—hist pl OK-5
Miller Wash Reservoir AZ-5
Miller Wash Tank—reservoir (2) AZ-5
Miller Water—stream ID-8
Miller Water Table—summit ID-8
Miller Water Tank—reservoir AZ-5
Miller W Boyd Sch—school TN-4
Miller Well—well AZ-5
Miller Well—well (2) NM-5
Miller Well No 1—well NM-5
Miller Wells—well NM-5
Miller Wells—well TX-5
Miller Windmill—locale AZ-5
Miller Windmill—locale (2) NM-5
Miller Windmill—locale (2) TX-5
Miller Woods—pop pl IL-6
Miller Woods—woods WA-9
Miller Yard—locale VA-3
Milleson—pop pl WV-2
Milleson Draw—valley WY-8
Millesons Mill—pop pl WV-2
Millesville—locale NC-3
Millesville—pop pl PA-2
Millet Canyon—valley UT-8
Millet Canyon—valley WY-8
Millet Cem—cemetery MN-6
Millet Island—island ID-8
Millet Island—island ME-1
Millet Point—cliff UT-8
Millet Pond—lake MI-6
Millets Point—cape AK-9
Millets Swamp—swamp MA-1
Millet Swale—stream AZ-5
Millet Swale Dam—dam AZ-5
Millet Swale Rsvr—reservoir AZ-5
Millett NV-8
Millett—pop pl MI-6
Millett—pop pl SC-3
Millett—pop pl TX-5
Millett, Bayou—gut LA-4
Millett (CCD)—cens area SC-3
Millett Creek—stream AK-9
Millett Opera House—hist pl TX-5
Millett Ranch—locale NV-8
Millettville SC-3
Millet Windmill—locale NM-5
Milleville Beach—pop pl MI-6
Mill Fall Branch—stream WV-2
Mill Fall Run—stream WV-2
Mill Farm Run—stream VA-3
Mill Farms—pop pl VA-3
Mill F East Fork—valley UT-8
Mill F Flat—flat UT-8
Mill Field—area UT-8
Millfield—pop pl OH-6
Millfield Ch—church VA-3
Millfield-Hilltop Cem—cemetery OH-6
Mill Field Hollow—valley MO-7
Millfield Mtn—summit AL-4
Mill Flat—flat CA-9
Mill Flat—flat (2) OR-9
Mill Flat—flat (4) UT-8
Mill Flat Campground—locale UT-8
Mill Flat Creek—stream CA-9
Mill Flat Creek—stream OR-9
Millford PA-2
Mill Ford—locale AR-4
Millford—pop pl SC-3
Millford (historical)—pop pl OR-9
Mill Ford Post Office (historical)—building AL-4
Millford Township—civil SD-7
Millfork UT-8
Mill Fork—locale UT-8
Mill Fork—stream (2) KY-4
Mill Fork—stream MT-8
Mill Fork—stream (2) OH-6
Mill Fork—stream (4) UT-8
Mill Fork—stream (5) WV-2
Mill Fork—valley ID-8
Mill Fork—valley UT-8
Mill Fork Cem—cemetery UT-8
Mill Fork Ch—church OH-6
Mill Fork Creek—stream (2) MT-8
Mill Fork Creek—stream UT-8
Mill Fork Eightmile Creek—stream ID-8
Mill Fork Ridge—ridge UT-8
Mill F South Fork—valley UT-8
Mill Gann Branch—stream AL-4
Mill Gap VA-3
Mill Gap—gap KY-4
Mill Gap—gap NC-3
Mill Gap—gap PA-2
Mill Gap—gap VA-3
Mill Gap—gap WV-2
Mill Gap—pop pl VA-3
Mill Gap Run—stream WV-2
Mill Green—locale MD-2
Mill Grove IN-6
Mill Grove MI-6
Mill Grove NY-2
Mill Grove NC-3
Millgrove PA-2
Mill Grove—hist pl PA-2
Mill Grove—locale OH-6
Mill Grove—locale PA-2
Millgrove—pop pl IN-6
Mill Grove—pop pl IN-6
Millgrove—pop pl MI-6
Mill Grove—pop pl MI-6
Mill Grove—pop pl MO-7
Mill Grove—pop pl NY-2
Millgrove—pop pl NY-2
Mill Grove—pop pl NC-3
Mill Grove—pop pl (2) PA-2
Mill Grove Cem—cemetery IA-7
Mill Grove Ch—church IN-6
Mill Grove Ch—church (2) NC-3
Mill Grove Creek—stream SC-3
Mill Grove (historical)—locale AL-4
Mill Grove (historical P.O.)—locale IA-7
Mill Grove Post Office
(historical)—building AL-4
Mill Grove Sch—school IL-6
Mill Grove Sch (abandoned)—school PA-2
Millgrove (Township of)—pop pl IN-6
Mill Gulch MT-8
Mill Gulch—valley (7) CA-9
Mill Gulch—valley (10) CO-8
Mill Gulch—valley ID-8
Mill Gulch—valley (4) MT-8
Mill Gulch—valley NV-8
Mill Gulch—valley (2) OR-9
Mill Gulch—valley UT-8
Mill Gulch Station—locale MT-8
Mill Gut—gut MD-2
Mill Gut—gut NC-3
Mill Gut—gut RI-1
Mill Hall—pop pl PA-2
Mill Hall Borough PA-2
Mill Hall Borough—civil PA-2
Millham Brook—stream MA-1
Millham Rsvr—reservoir MA-1
Mill Hardy Branch—stream TN-4
Millhausens—pop pl MD-2
Mill Haven LA-4
Millhaven—pop pl GA-3
Millhaven—pop pl LA-4
Millhaven (CCD)—cens area GA-3
Millhayes Meadow—flat OR-9
Millheim—locale TX-5
Millheim—pop pl MO-7
Millheim—pop pl PA-2
Millheim Borough—civil PA-2
Millheim Cem—cemetery TX-5
Millheim Ch—church OH-6
Millheim Creek TX-5
Millheim Gas Field—oilfield TX-5
Millheim Hist Dist—hist pl PA-2
Mill Hill CT-1
Mill Hill NJ-2
Mill Hill—hist pl NC-3
Mill Hill—pop pl CT-1
Mill Hill—summit CO-8
Mill Hill—summit (2) CT-1
Mill Hill—summit (4) MA-1
Mill Hill—summit MO-7
Mill Hill—summit OR-9
Mill Hill—summit (2) PA-2
Mill Hill—summit SC-3
Mill Hill—summit TN-4
Mill Hill—summit UT-8
Mill Hill—summit VA-3
Mill Hill Branch VA-3
Mill Hill Cem—cemetery NH-1
Mill Hill Ch—church NC-3
Mill Hill Hist Dist—hist pl NJ-2
Mill Hill (historical)—pop pl (2) NC-3
Mill Hill Run PA-2
Mill Hill Sch—school CT-1
Millhiser-Baker Farm—hist pl NM-5
Mill (historical)—locale AL-4
Mill (historical P.O.)—locale IA-7
Mill Hole—basin TN-4
Mill Hole—cave AL-4
Mill Hole Cave—cave TN-4
Mill Hole Farm—hist pl KY-4
Mill Hollow—locale NH-1
Mill Hollow—pop pl NH-1
Mill Hollow—valley (4) AL-4
Mill Hollow—valley (11) AR-4
Mill Hollow—valley (2) ID-8
Mill Hollow—valley IN-6
Mill Hollow—valley (10) KY-4
Mill Hollow—valley (13) MO-7
Mill Hollow—valley MT-8
Mill Hollow—valley NY-2
Mill Hollow—valley (2) OH-6
Mill Hollow—valley OR-9
Mill Hollow—valley (3) PA-2
Mill Hollow—valley (22) TN-4
Mill Hollow—valley TX-5
Mill Hollow—valley (13) UT-8
Mill Hollow—valley (3) VA-3
Mill Hollow—valley (4) WV-2
Mill Hollow—valley WY-8
Mill Hollow Branch—stream IN-6
Mill Hollow Branch—stream TN-4
Mill Hollow Brook—stream NY-2
Mill Hollow Campground—park UT-8
Mill Hollow Cave—cave AL-4
Mill Hollow Creek UT-8
Mill Hollow Dam—dam UT-8
Mill Hollow Forest Service Station UT-8
Mill Hollow Granite Sch Center—school UT-8
Mill Hollow Guard Station—locale UT-8
Mill Hollow House, The—hist pl OH-6
Mill Hollow Rsvr—reservoir UT-8
Mill Hollow Run—stream PA-2
Mill Hollow Trail—trail PA-2
Mill Home WI-6
Millhome—pop pl WI-6
Mill Hook—pop pl NY-2
Millhopper Center—post sta FL-3
Mill Hopper Creek—stream PA-2
Millhopper Montessori Sch—school FL-3
Millhopper Shop Ctr—locale FL-3
Millhopper Square (Shop Ctr)—locale FL-3
Mill House—hist pl DE-2
Mill House—hist pl ME-1
Mill House—hist pl NY-2
Mill House—hist pl VA-3
Mill House—hist pl WA-9
Millhouse Bayou—bay MI-6
Millhouse Blacksmith Shop—hist pl IL-6
Millhouse Ditch—canal MS-4
Millhouse Hollow—valley WV-2
Millhousen—pop pl IN-6
Millhurst—locale IL-6
Millhurst—pop pl IL-6
Millhurst—pop pl NJ-2
Millhurst Dam—dam NJ-2
Millhurst Pond—reservoir NJ-2
Millians Creek—stream AL-4
Milliard NE-7
Millican TN-4
Millican—locale OR-9
Millican—pop pl TN-4
Millican—pop pl TX-5
Millican Airstrip—airport OR-9
Millican Cem—cemetery IL-6
Millican Cem—cemetery TX-5
Millican Crater—crater OR-9
Millican Crater Trail—trail OR-9
Millican Creek—stream OR-9
Millican Creek—stream TN-4
Millican Creek—stream TX-5
Millican Grove—pop pl TN-4
Millican Hills—summit TX-5
Millican Mountains—summit TX-5
Millican Oil Field—oilfield TX-5
Millican Park—park GA-3
Millican Valley—basin OR-9
Millican Well—well NM-5
Millicent, Lake—lake WI-6
Millicent, Mount—summit UT-8
Millicent Library—building MA-1
Millicent Library—hist pl MA-1
Millich Ditch—canal CA-9
Millichetah Creek—stream AK-9
Millick Canyon—valley NV-8
Millick Gulch—valley ID-8
Millicoma Fork OR-9
Millicoma JHS—school OR-9
Millicoma Myrtle Grove State Park—park OR-9
Millicoma River—stream OR-9
Millicoma River Rearing Pond—reservoir OR-9
Millicoma River Rearing Pond Dam—dam OR-9
Millie Bluff—cliff AR-4
Millie Branch—stream (2) AL-4
Millie Branch—stream VA-3
Millie Hill—summit MI-6
Millie (historical)—locale AL-4
Millie Lake—lake CA-9
Millier Creek—stream GA-3
Millies Hill—summit WY-8
Millie Spring—spring UT-8
Millieville Ch—church AL-4
Milligan TN-4
Milligan—locale CA-9
Milligan—locale TX-5
Milligan—pop pl FL-3
Milligan—pop pl IN-6
Milligan—pop pl NE-7
Milligan—pop pl OH-6
Milligan—pop pl TN-4
Milligan, Bayou—stream LA-4
Milligan, Cuthbert, House—hist pl OH-6
Milligan, Lake—lake IL-6
Milligan Alexander Cem—cemetery TN-4
Milligan Arroyo—stream CO-8
Milligan Barranca—valley CA-9
Milligan Bend—bend OK-5
Milligan Block—hist pl AL-4
Milligan Branch—stream AL-4
Milligan Branch—stream MO-7
Milligan Branch—stream (2) TN-4
Milligan Canyon CO-8
Milligan Canyon—valley MT-8
Milligan Cave—cave TN-4
Milligan Cem—cemetery IL-6
Milligan Cem—cemetery (2) NC-3
Milligan Cem—cemetery TN-4
Milligan Cem—cemetery (2) TX-5
Milligan Ch (historical)—church TN-4
Milligan Coll—school TN-4
Milligan College Post Office—building TN-4
Milligan College Spring—spring TN-4
Milligan Cove—bay TX-5
Milligan Cove—valley AL-4
Milligan Cove—valley PA-2
Milligan Cove Ch—church PA-2
Milligan Creek—stream AZ-5
Milligan Creek—stream (3) FL-3
Milligan Creek—stream (2) GA-3
Milligan Creek—stream ID-8
Milligan Creek—stream MI-6
Milligan Creek—stream MO-7
Milligan Creek—stream (2) MT-8
Milligan Creek—stream (2) NV-8
Milligan Creek—stream TN-4
Milligan Creek—stream WV-2
Milligan Creek - in part NV-8
Milligan Ditch—canal CO-8
Milligan Draw—valley (2) TX-5
Milligan Gulch—valley ID-8
Milligan Gulch—valley NM-5
Milligan Hill—summit IL-6
Milligan House—hist pl AZ-5
Milligan Knoll—summit AZ-5
Milligan Lake—lake AZ-5
Milligan Lakes—lake CO-8
Milligan Mesa—bench NM-5
Milligan Mountain AR-4
Milligan Mtn—summit NM-5
Milligan Park—park IN-6
Milligan Peak—summit AZ-5
Milligan Peak—summit NM-5
Milligan Point LA-4
Milligan Pond—lake FL-3
Milligan Post Office (historical)—building TN-4
Milligan Ridge—pop pl AR-4
Milligan Ridge—ridge AR-4
Milligan Ridge—ridge PA-2
Milligan Ridge Ch—church AR-4
Milligan Ridge Sch—school AR-4
Milligan Run PA-2
Milligan Run—stream (2) PA-2
Milligan Sch—school CA-9
Milligan Sch—school PA-2
Milligan Sch (historical)—school (2) TN-4
Milligan School (historical)—locale MO-7
Milligans Creek GA-3
Milligans Creek NV-8
Milligans Knob—summit PA-2
Milligan Slough—gut AR-4
Milligans Pond—reservoir AL-4
Milligan Springs Cem—cemetery MS-4
Milligan Springs Ch—church MS-4
Milligan Springs Lake—reservoir MS-4
Milligantown—pop pl PA-2
Milligan Valley—valley AZ-5
Milligan Windmill—locale WY-8
Milligen Gulch ID-8
Milligen Point—cape LA-4
Milligon Well—well CO-8
Millikan, Robert A., House—hist pl IL-6
Millikan HS—school CA-9
Millikan JHS—school CA-9
Milliken—pop pl CO-8
Milliken—pop pl WV-2
Milliken Bend MS-4
Milliken Bluff—cliff TX-5
Milliken Branch TN-4
Milliken Bridge—bridge CA-9
Milliken Bridge—bridge KY-4
Milliken Brook—stream ME-1
Milliken Brook—stream NH-1
Milliken Canyon—valley CA-9
Milliken Chapel—church KY-4
Milliken Cove—bay SC-3
Milliken Creek MI-6
Milliken Creek—stream CA-9
Milliken Creek—stream IL-6
Milliken Creek—stream MN-6
Milliken Farm—locale ME-1
Milliken Hill—summit ME-1
Milliken Hill—summit NH-1
Milliken Lake—lake AR-4
Milliken Mills—pop pl ME-1
Milliken Peak—summit CA-9
Milliken Pond RI-1
Milliken Pond—lake ME-1
Milliken Rsvr—reservoir CA-9
Millikens—pop pl PA-2
Millikens Bend—bend MS-4
Millikens Chapel—church KY-4
Millikens Knob PA-2
Milliken Sloughs—swamp MT-8
Millikens Station—locale PA-2
Milliken Swamp—stream NC-3
Milliken Swamp—swamp KY-4
Millikin—pop pl LA-4
Millikin, James, House—hist pl IL-6
Millikin Bay—swamp GA-3
Millikin Lake—lake MI-6
Millikin Sch—school CA-9
Millikin Sch—school KS-7
Millikin Univ—school IL-6
Millikin Woods—park OH-6
Millilli Inseln MP-9
Millimagassett Lake—lake ME-1
Millimagassett Ridge—ridge ME-1
Millimagassett Stream—stream ME-1
Millimocket Lake ME-1
Millin Draw Well—well NM-5
Millinery Hill MA-1
Mill Ingalls Creek Trail—trail WA-9
Millingar Sch (historical)—school PA-2
Milling Crossroad Cem—cemetery SC-3
Millingport—pop pl NC-3
Millingport Sch—school NC-3
Millington—locale CT-1
Millington—locale MS-4
Millington—locale VA-3
Millington—pop pl IL-6
Millington—pop pl MD-2
Millington—pop pl MI-6
Millington—pop pl NJ-2
Millington—pop pl OR-9
Millington—pop pl TN-4
Millington Brook—stream NY-2
Millington (CCD)—cens area TN-4
Millington Cem—cemetery CT-1
Millington Ch—church TN-4
Millington Creek—stream MI-6
Millington Creek—stream VA-3
Millington Division—civil TN-4
Millington (historical)—pop pl MA-1
Millington Newark Cem—cemetery IL-6
Millington Post Office
(historical)—building MS-4
Millington Station—hist pl NJ-2
Millington (Township of)—pop pl MI-6
Millington Wildlife Demonstration
Area—park MD-2
Millinocket—pop pl ME-1
Millinocket Airp—airport ME-1
Millinocket Falls—falls ME-1
Millinocket Lake—lake ME-1
Millinocket Lake—reservoir ME-1
Millinocket Lake Tote Road—trail ME-1
Millinocket Ridge—ridge (2) ME-1
Millinocket Stream—stream (2) ME-1
Millinockett ME-1
Millinockett Lake ME-1
Millinocket (Town of)—pop pl ME-1
Millinockett Stream ME-1
Millinoket ME-1
millinoket Lake ME-1
Millinoket Stream ME-1
Millinokett ME-1
Millinokett Lake ME-1
Millinokett Stream ME-1
Millin Rsvr—reservoir ID-8
Millins Mill (historical)—locale MS-4
Mill in the Flat Pond—lake TX-5
Million—locale KY-4
Million Acre Swamp—swamp WI-6
Millionaire Camp—locale CA-9
Millionaire Gulch—valley CO-8
Millionaire Mine—mine OR-9
Millionaire's Row Hist Dist—hist pl PA-2
Million Branch—stream TX-5
Million Brook—stream IN-6
Million Cem—cemetery KY-4
Million Creek MO-7
Million Creek—stream MO-7
Million Creek—stream WY-8
Million Dollar Bridge—other AK-9
Million Dollar Canyon—valley CA-9
Million Dollar Canyon—valley TX-5
Million Dollar Creek—stream CA-9
Million Dollar Lake—reservoir AL-4
Million Dollar Lake Estates—pop pl AL-4
Million Dollar Lakes Church of God AL-4
Million Dollar Pier—locale NJ-2
Million Dollar Spring—spring CA-9
Million Dollar Theater—hist pl CA-9
Million Dollar Water Hole—spring CO-8
Million Gulch—valley MT-8
Million Hill—summit TN-4
Million Hills—range NV-8
Million Hills—summit AZ-5
Million Hills Wash—stream NV-8
Million Hills Wash—valley AZ-5
Million Lake—lake MN-6
Million McCleland Ditch IN-6
Million Rsvr—reservoir CO-8
Millions Cem—cemetery IL-6
Milliorn Cem—cemetery OR-9
Milliorn Hill—summit OR-9
Milliorn (historical)—pop pl OR-9
Millipede Cave—cave AL-4
Mill Iron—locale MI-6
Mill Iron—pop pl MT-8
Milliron Cem—cemetery OH-6
Milliron Cem—cemetery PA-2
Mill Iron Ch—church VA-3
Mill Iron Creek—stream AR-4
Mill Iron Creek—stream SD-7
Milliron Draw—valley CO-8
Milliron Park—pop pl MI-6
Millis—pop pl MA-1
Millis—pop pl WY-8
Millis Beach—pop pl NE-7
Millis-Clicquot—CDP MA-1
Mill Island—hist pl WV-2
Mill Island—island ME-1
Mill Island—island MN-6
Mill Island—island NC-3
Mill Island—island SC-3
Mill Island—island VA-3
Millis Peak—summit CA-9
Millis Road Elem Sch—school NC-3
Millis Sch—school MI-6
Millis Shop Ctr—locale MA-1
Millis Swamp—stream NC-3
Millis (Town of)—pop pl MA-1
Mill Knob—summit KY-4
Mill Knob—summit (3) NC-3
Mill Knob—summit SC-3
Mill Knob—summit VA-3
Mill Knob—summit WV-2
Mill Lake MI-6
Mill Lake WI-6
Mill Lake—lake (4) AR-4
Mill Lake—lake CO-8
Mill Lake—lake (2) FL-3
Mill Lake—lake (2) ID-8
Mill Lake—lake LA-4
Mill Lake—lake (7) MI-6
Mill Lake—lake (4) MN-6
Mill Lake—lake MT-8
Mill Lake—lake ND-7
Mill Lake—lake TX 5
Mill Lake—lake (3) WI-6
Mill Lake—pop pl MI-6
Mill Lake—reservoir IN-6
Mill Lake—reservoir MS-4
Mill Lake—reservoir TN-4
Mill Lake Cem—cemetery ND-7
Mill Lake Dam—dam MS-4
Mill Landing—locale NC-3
Mill Landing Creek—stream NC-3
Mill Lane—locale PA-2
Mill Lane Brook CT-1
Mill Lane JHS—school NY-2
Mill Ledge—rock MA-1
Mill Log Creek—stream FL-3
Millman—pop pl IA-7
Millman Hollow—valley MO-7
Millman Island—island MI-6
Millman Lake MI-6
Millman Lake—lake IL-6
Millman Pond—lake NY-2
Millman Ranch—locale NM-5
Millmans Corners—locale NY-2
Millman South Well—well NM-5
Mill-Mar Ranch—locale OR-9
Mill Meadow—swamp MA-1
Mill Meadow Dam—dam UT-8
Mill Meadow Rsvr—reservoir (2) UT-8
Mill Meadows—swamp CT-1
Mill Meadows Reservoir UT-8
Mill Mine—mine NM-5
Mill Mine Junction—locale MI-6
Millmont—pop pl (2) PA-2
Millmont Farm—hist pl PA-2
Millmont Red Bridge—hist pl PA-2

Millmont Sch—*school* PA-2
Mill Mountain—*ridge* VA-3
Mill Mountain Park—*park* VA-3
Mill Mountain Trail—*trail* VA-3
Mill Mountain Trail—*trail* WV-2
Mill Mtn VA-3
Mill Mtn—*summit* AL-4
Mill Mtn—*summit* (2) AR-4
Mill Mtn—*summit* GA-3
Mill Mtn—*summit* ID-8
Mill Mtn—*summit* MO-7
Mill Mtn—*summit* (2) NH-1
Mill Mtn—*summit* (3) NY-2
Mill Mtn—*summit* (2) NC-3
Mill Mtn—*summit* SC-3
Mill Mtn—*summit* (6) VA-3
Mill Mtn—*summit* (2) WV-2
Mill Neck—*cape* NY-2
**Mill Neck**—*pop pl* NY-2
**Mill Neck**—*pop pl* NC-3
Mill Neck Ch—*church* VA-3
Mill Neck Creek—*stream* NY-2
Mill Neck Manor Sch—*school* NY-2
Millner Creek—*stream* CA-9
Millner Lake MT-8
Millnerville—*locale* IA-7
Mill No 2 Mine—*mine* CO-8
Mill No 4 Mine—*mine* CO-8
Mill Office and Post Office—*hist pl* OH-6
**Millonocket Center**—*pop pl* ME-1
Mill on the Fence—*locale* NM-5
Millot Sch—*school* IL-6
Millouri Flat Cem—*cemetery* OR-9
Millowakee MO-7
Mill Park—*flat* AZ-5
Mill Park—*flat* CO-8
Mill Park—*flat* (2) UT-8
Mill Park—*park* CA-9
Mill Park—*park* IN-6
**Mill Park**—*pop pl* PA-2
Mill Park Sch—*school* OR-9
Mill Park Tank—*reservoir* AZ-5
Mill Peak—*summit* CA-9
Mill-Pine Neighborhood Hist Dist—*hist pl* OR-9
Mill Place—*locale* NM-5
Mill Plain CT-1
Mill Plain—*flat* WA-9
**Mill Plain**—*pop pl* (3) CT-1
Mill Plain Cem—*cemetery* (2) CT-1
Mill Plain Sch—*school* WA-9
Mill Plain Swamp—*swamp* CT-1
Mill Pocket—*basin* MT-8
Mill Pocket Creek—*stream* MT-8
Mill P. O. (historical)—*locale* AL-4
Mill Point ID-8
Mill Point ME-1
Mill Point MD-2
Mill Point RI-1
Millpoint TN-4
Millpoint WV-2
Mill Point—*cape* AL-4
Mill Point—*cape* FL-3
Mill Point—*cape* (2) ME-1
Mill Point—*cape* MI-6
Mill Point—*cape* (5) NC-3
Mill Point—*cape* RI-1
Mill Point—*cape* (3) VA-3
Mill Point—*cape* WA-9
Mill Point—*cliff* KY-4
Mill Point—*cliff* MT-8
Millpoint—*locale* MD-2
Mill Point—*locale* NY-2
**Mill Point**—*pop pl* TN-4
**Mill Point**—*pop pl* WV-2
Mill Point—*summit* MT-8
Mill Point Island—*island* NC-3
Millpoint Post Office (historical)—*building* TN-4
Millpoint Ridge—*ridge* TN-4
Mill Point Sch—*school* MT-8
Mill Point Tank—*reservoir* AZ-5
Millpon Creek—*stream* NC-3
Mill Pond AL-4
Mill Pond CT-1
Mill Pond IN-6
Mill Pond MA-1
Mill Pond MI-6
Mill Pond NJ-2
Mill Pond NY 2
Mill Pond VA-3
Mill Pond WI-6
Mill Pond—*bay* (2) ME-1
Mill Pond—*bay* MA-1
Mill Pond—*hist pl* MO-7
Mill Pond—*lake* CA-9
Mill Pond—*lake* (4) CT-1
Mill Pond—*lake* (8) FL-3
Mill Pond—*lake* GA-3
Mill Pond—*lake* KY-4
Mill Pond—*lake* LA-4
Mill Pond—*lake* (11) ME-1
Mill Pond—*lake* (2) MD-2
Mill Pond—*lake* (14) MA-1
Mill Pond—*lake* (16) MI-6
Mill Pond—*lake* (4) MN-6
Mill Pond—*lake* MS-4
Mill Pond—*lake* NE-7
Mill Pond—*lake* NH-1
Mill Pond—*lake* NJ-2
Mill Pond—*lake* (10) NY-2
Millpond—*lake* OH-6
Mill Pond—*lake* OR-9
Mill Pond—*lake* (3) RI-1
Mill Pond—*lake* TN-4
Mill Pond—*lake* (2) TX-5
Mill Pond—*lake* (2) UT-8
Mill Pond—*lake* (3) VT-1
Mill Pond—*lake* (4) WA-9
Mill Pond—*lake* (5) WI-6
Millpond—*locale* CT-1
Mill Pond—*locale* KY-4
**Mill Pond**—*pop pl* TX-5
Mill Pond—*reservoir* (2) CT-1
Mill Pond—*reservoir* MD-2
Mill Pond—*reservoir* (14) MA-1
Millpond—*reservoir* MA-1
Mill Pond—*reservoir* (8) MA-1
Mill Pond—*reservoir* (3) MI-6
Mill Pond—*reservoir* MN-6
Mill Pond—*reservoir* MS-4
Mill Pond—*reservoir* NE-7
Mill Pond—*reservoir* NH-1
Mill Pond—*reservoir* (2) NJ-2
Millpond—*reservoir* NY-2
Mill Pond—*reservoir* (8) NY-2
Mill Pond—*reservoir* (3) NC-3
Mill Pond—*reservoir* RI-1
Mill Pond—*reservoir* (2) TX-5
Millpond—*reservoir* TX-5
Mill Pond—*reservoir* UT-8
Mill Pond—*reservoir* (6) WI-6
Mill Pond—*stream* NC-3
Mill Pond—*swamp* FL-3
Millpond—*swamp* ME-1
Mill Pond—*swamp* NC-3
Millpond, The—*stream* NC-3
**Millpond Acres**—*pop pl* DE-2
**Mill Pond Acres (subdivision)**—*pop pl* DE-2
Millpond Bay—*swamp* NC-3
Mill Pond Branch—*stream* AR-4
Mill Pond Branch—*stream* FL-3
Mill Pond Branch—*stream* MS-4
Millpond Branch—*stream* NC-3
Millpond Branch—*stream* (4) SC-3
Millpond Branch—*stream* TN-4
Millpond Branch—*stream* (2) VA-3
Millpond Branch—*swamp* GA-3
Mill Pond Bridge—*bridge* AL-4
Millpond Brook NJ-2
Mill Pond Brook—*stream* (2) VT-1
Millpond Campground—*park* OR-9
Mill Pond Cem—*cemetery* NC-3
Millpond Cem—*cemetery* SC-3
Millpond Creek NC-3
Mill Pond Creek—*stream* AL-4
Mill Pond Creek—*stream* FL-3
Mill Pond Creek—*stream* MI-6
Mill Pond Creek—*stream* (2) NC-3
Millpond Creek—*stream* (3) VA-3
Mill Pond Dam AL-4
Mill Pond Dam—*dam* (2) MA-1
Millpond Dam—*dam* MA-1
Mill Pond Dam—*dam* (13) MA-1
Mill Pond Dam—*dam* RI-1
Mill Pond Dam Number 1—*dam* MA-1
Millpond Drain—*stream* MI-6
Mill Pond Farm—*locale* UT-8
Millpond Field—*flat* NC-3
Mill Pond (historical)—*lake* MA-1
Mill Pond Hollow—*valley* (2) KY-4
Millpond Hot Spring—*spring* OR-9
Mill Pond lake IN-6
Mill Pond Lake WI-6
Millpond Lake—*lake* MN-6
Mill Pond Lake—*lake* WI-6
Mill Pond Lake—*lake* WY-8
Millpond Lake—*reservoir* CA-9
Mill Pond Lower Dam—*dam* MA-1
Mill Pond Main Dam—*dam* MA-1
Mill Pond Marshes—*swamp* (2) MA-1
**Mill Pond Meadows (subdivision)**—*pop pl* NC-3
Mill Pond North Dike—*dam* MA-1
Millpond Number One—*reservoir* PA-2
Millpond Park—*park* NY-2
Millpond Plantation—*hist pl* GA-3
Millpond Ridge—*ridge* GA-3
Mill Ponds MA-1
Mill Pond South Dike—*dam* MA-1
Mill Pond Spring—*spring* FL-3
Mill Pond Stevens Pond—*reservoir* MA-1
Millpond Swamp—*stream* VA-3
Mill Pond Upper MA-1
**Mill Pond Village (subdivision)**—*pop pl* NC-3
Mill Port NY-2
Millport PA-2
Millport—*locale* KY-4
Millport—*locale* MO-7
Millport—*locale* PA-2
**Millport**—*pop pl* AL-4
**Millport**—*pop pl* IN-6
**Millport**—*pop pl* NY-2
**Millport**—*pop pl* (2) OH-6
**Millport**—*pop pl* PA-2
Millport (CCD)—*cens area* AL-4
Millport Division—*civil* AL-4
Millport HS—*school* AL-4
Millport Landing (historical)—*locale* MS-4
Millport Sch—*school* PA-2
Millport Slough—*stream* OR-9
Mill Potrero—*swamp* CA-9
Mill Priveledge Brook—*stream* ME-1
Mill Privilege Lake—*lake* ME-1
Mill Prong—*hist pl* NC-3
Mill Prong—*stream* AR-4
Mill Prong—*stream* VA-3
Mill Prong Trail—*trail* VA-3
Mill Race—*canal* AR-4
Mill Race—*canal* IA-7
Mill Race—*canal* KS-7
Mill Race—*stream* GA-3
Mill Race—*stream* IA-7
Mill Race—*stream* NE-7
Mill Race—*stream* NC-3
Mill Race—*stream* OR-9
Millrace—*stream* OR-9
Mill Race—*stream* PA-2
Mill Race—*stream* TX-5
Mill Race—*stream* UT-8
Mill Race—*stream* VA-3
Mill Race—*stream* WI-6
Mill Race Canal—*canal* UT-8
Mill Race Creek TX-5
Millrace Creek—*stream* CA-9
Millrace Creek—*stream* GA-3
Mill Race Ditch—*canal* (2) UT-8
Millrace Drain—*stream* SC-3
Mill Race Golf Course—*locale* PA-2
Millrace Islands—*island* SC-3
Millrace Site, RI-1039—*hist pl* RI-1
Millrace Slough—*stream* IL-6
Millrace Stream—*gut* SC-3
**Millrace Subdivision**—*pop pl* UT-8
Mill Ranch Creek CA-9
Mill Rice Trail—*trail* PA-2
Mill Ridge AL-4
Mill Ridge—*ridge* AL-4
Mill Ridge—*ridge* (2) AR-4
Mill Ridge—*ridge* GA-3
Mill Ridge—*ridge* IN-6
Mill Ridge—*ridge* KY-4
Mill Ridge—*ridge* (5) NC-3
Mill Ridge—*ridge* OR-9
Mill Ridge—*ridge* (3) TN-4
Mill Ridge—*ridge* (2) VA-3
Mill Ridge—*ridge* (2) WV-2
Mill Ridge Ch—*church* NC-3
Millridge Creek—*stream* WA-9
Mill Ridge Sch—*school* CT-1
Millridge Sch—*school* OH-6
**Mill Ridge (subdivision)**—*pop pl* NC-3
Mill Ridge Trail—*trail* WV-2
**Millrift**—*pop pl* PA-2
Mill river CT-1
Mill River MA-1
Mill River—*gut* ME-1
**Mill River**—*pop pl* (2) MA-1
Mill River—*stream* (3) CT-1
Mill River—*stream* (2) ME-1
Mill River—*stream* (10) MA-1
Mill River—*stream* (3) NY-2
Mill River—*stream* (2) VT-1
Mill River Cemetery—*island* MA-1
Mill River Ch—*church* ME-1
Mill River Country Club—*other* CT-1
Mill River Country Club—*other* NY-2
Mill River Culvert And Tide Gate Dam—*dam* MA-1
Mill River Dam—*dam* (2) MA-1
Mill River Diversion—*canal* MA-1
Mill River Diversion Rsvr—*reservoir* MA-1
Mill River Rsvr—*reservoir* (2) MA-1
Mill River West Branch MA-1
**Mill Road**—*pop pl* PA-2
Mill Road Bowstring Bridge—*hist pl* OH-6
Mill Road Branch—*stream* KY-4
Mill Road Elementary School PA-2
Mill Road Gap—*gap* AL-4
Mill Road Sch—*school* CT-1
Mill Road Sch—*school* PA-2
Mill Rock—*island* NY-2
Mill Rock—*pillar* RI-1
**Millrock**—*pop pl* IA-7
**Mill Rock**—*pop pl* OH-6
Mill Rock—*rock* MA-1
Mill Rock—*summit* CT-1
Millrock Ch—*church* GA-3
Mill Rock Ch—*church* SC-3
Mill Rock Creek—*stream* MO-7
Millrock Ford—*locale* MO-7
Mill Rock Hollow—*valley* TN-4
Millrock Sch (historical)—*school* TN-4
Millrose Creek NE-7
Mill Rsvr—*reservoir* HI-9
Mill Rsvr—*reservoir* OR-9
Mill Run IN-6
Mill Run MD-2
Mill Run NC-3
Mill Run OH-6
Mill Run PA-2
Mill Run VA-3
Mill Run WV-2
Mill Run—*channel* OH-6
**Mill Run**—*pop pl* MD-2
**Mill Run**—*pop pl* (4) PA-2
**Mill Run**—*pop pl* TN-4
**Mill Run**—*pop pl* WV-2
Mill Run—*stream* IN-6
Mill Run—*stream* (6) MD-2
Mill Run—*stream* NJ-2
Mill Run—*stream* (8) NC-3
Mill Run—*stream* (6) OH-6
Mill Run—*stream* (20) PA-2
Mill Run—*stream* SC-3
Mill Run—*stream* UT-8
Mill Run—*stream* (16) VA-3
Mill Run—*stream* (27) WV-2
**Mill Run Acres**—*pop pl* VA-3
**Mill Run Acres (subdivision)**—*pop pl* DE-2
Millrun Branch—*stream* VA-3
Mill Run Brook—*stream* NY-2
Mill Run Ch—*church* MD-2
Mill Run Ch—*church* PA-2
Mill Run Ch—*church* WV-2
Mill Run Dam—*dam* PA-2
Mill Run Hollow Trail—*trail* PA-2
**Mill Run Junction**—*pop pl* PA-2
Mill Run Lake—*lake* PA-2
Mill Run (Magisterial District)—*fmr MCD* WV-2
Mill Run Pond—*reservoir* VA-3
Mill Run Rsvr—*reservoir* (2) PA-2
Mill Run Sch (abandoned)—*school* (2) PA-2
**Millrun (subdivision)**—*pop pl* MS-4
Mill Run Trail PA-2
**Millry**—*pop pl* AL-4
Millry (CCD)—*cens area* AL-4
Millry Division—*civil* AL-4
Millry HS—*school* AL-4
Mills KY-4
Mills—*fmr MCD* NE-7
Mills—*locale* CA-9
Mills—*locale* KY-4
Mills—*locale* NM-5
Mills—*locale* OH-6
Mills—*locale* OK-5
**Mills**—*pop pl* CA-9
**Mills**—*pop pl* IA-7
**Mills**—*pop pl* (2) MI-6
**Mills**—*pop pl* NE-7
**Mills**—*pop pl* PA-2
**Mills**—*pop pl* TX-5
**Mills**—*pop pl* UT-8
**Mills**—*pop pl* VA-3
**Mills**—*pop pl* WY-8
Mills, Clark, Studio—*hist pl* SC-3
Mills, Davis, House—*hist pl* MA-1
Mills, Elijah, House—*hist pl* CT-1
Mills, Enos, Homestead Cabin—*hist pl* CO-8
Mills, Florence, House—*hist pl* NY-2
Mills, Gen. William A., House—*hist pl* NY-2
Mills, Henry Clay, House—*hist pl* AR-4
Mills, James, Stonehouse—*hist pl* VA-3
Mills, Lake—*reservoir* WA-9
Mills, Lewis H., House—*hist pl* OR-9
Mills, Mount—*summit* AK-9
Mills, Mount—*summit* CA-9
Mills, Mount—*summit* ID-8
Mills, Oliver W., House—*hist pl* CT-1
Mills, Simeon, House—*hist pl* WI-6
Mills, Timothy, House—*hist pl* NJ-2
Mills, Timothy Dwight, House—*hist pl* CT-1
Mills, William, House—*hist pl* KS-7
Mills, W. P., House—*hist pl* AK-9
Mills and Prichard Drain—*canal* MI-6
**Millsap**—*pop pl* TX-5
Millsap Branch—*stream* TN-4
Millsap Bridge—*other* MO-7
Millsap Cem—*cemetery* CA-9
Millsap Ch—*church* GA-3
Mill Sap Creek AL-4
Millsap Creek—*stream* MO-7
Millsap Hill—*summit* KY-4
Millsap Hollow—*valley* TN-4
Millsap Mtn—*summit* GA-3
**Millsaps**—*pop pl* CA-9
Millsaps Branch—*stream* TN-4
Millsaps-Buie House—*hist pl* MS-4
Millsaps Cem—*cemetery* GA-3
Millsaps Cem—*cemetery* MS-4
Millsaps Cem—*cemetery* TN-4
Millsaps Ch (historical)—*church* TN-4
Millsaps Coll—*school* MS-4
Millsaps Creek AL-4
Millsaps (historical)—*locale* MS-4
Millsaps Hollow—*valley* TN-4
Mill Saps Knob AR-4
Millsaps Knob—*summit* AR-4
Millsaps Spring TN-4
Mills Arroyo—*stream* CO-8
Mills Bay—*bay* AK-9
Mills Bay—*swamp* FL-3
Mills Bayou—*gut* AR-4
Mills Bayou—*gut* MS-4
Mills Bayou—*stream* (2) MS-4
Mills Bayou Ditch—*canal* AR-4
Mills Bayou Junction MS-4
Mills Bennett—*locale* TX-5
Mills Bldg—*hist pl* WA-9
Mills Bldg and Tower—*hist pl* CA-9
Millsboro—*locale* WV-2
**Millsboro**—*pop pl* DE-2
**Millsboro**—*pop pl* OH-6
**Millsboro**—*pop pl* (2) PA-2
Millsboro (CCD)—*cens area* DE-2
Millsboro Cem—*cemetery* DE-2
Millsboro Ch—*church* DE-2
Millsboro Pond—*reservoir* DE-2
Millsborough DE-2
Mills Branch—*stream* AR-4
Mills Branch—*stream* FL-3
Mills Branch—*stream* (2) KY-4
Mills Branch—*stream* LA-4
Mills Branch—*stream* MD-2
Mills Branch—*stream* MS-4
Mills Branch—*stream* MO-7
Mills Branch—*stream* (2) NC-3
Mills Branch—*stream* OH-6
Mills Branch—*stream* (2) TN-4
Mills Branch—*stream* (2) TX-5
Mills Branch—*stream* VA-3
Mills Bridge—*bridge* NE-7
Mills Bridge—*bridge* NC-3
Mills Brook NJ-2
Mills Brook—*stream* (2) ME-1
Mills Brook—*stream* NH-1
Mills Brook—*stream* VT-1
Mills Brothers Catfish Ponds Dam—*dam* MS-4
Millsburg KS-7
**Millsburg**—*pop pl* NY-2
Millsburg (historical)—*locale* ND-7
Millsburgh Township (historical)—*civil* ND-7
Millsbury Landing (historical)—*locale* AL-4
Mills Canyon NV-8
Mills Canyon—*valley* AZ-5
Mills Canyon—*valley* NM-5
Mills Canyon—*valley* WA-9
Mills Canyon Campground—*locale* (2) NM-5
Mills Cem—*cemetery* AR-4
Mills Cem—*cemetery* (2) GA-3
Mills Cem—*cemetery* IN-6
Mills Cem—*cemetery* KS-7
Mills Cem—*cemetery* (3) KY-4
Mills Cem—*cemetery* ME-1
Mills Cem—*cemetery* (2) MI-6
Mills Cem—*cemetery* (2) MS-4
Mills Cem—*cemetery* (3) MO-7
Mills Cem—*cemetery* NM-5
Mills Cem—*cemetery* (3) NY-2
Mills Cem—*cemetery* NC-3
Mills Cem—*cemetery* OH-6
Mills Cem—*cemetery* OK-5
Mills Cem—*cemetery* (2) TN-4
Mills Cem—*cemetery* (4) WV-2
**Mills Center**—*pop pl* WI-6
Mills Ch FL-3
Mill Sch IN-6
Mills Ch—*church* IN-6
Mills Ch—*church* FL-3
Mill Sch—*school* (2) CA-9
Mill Sch—*school* IL-6
Mill Sch—*school* IN-6
Mill Sch—*school* NE-7
Mill Sch—*school* OH-6
Mill Sch—*school* SC-3
Mills Chapel—*church* AL-4
Mills Chapel—*church* NC-3
Mills Chapel—*church* WV-2
Mills Chapel (historical)—*church* MS-4
Mill Sch (historical)—*school* AL-4
Mill Sch (historical)—*school* TN-4
Mill Sch (historical)—*school* TX-5
Mills Coll—*school* CA-9
Mills Community Ch—*church* MS-4
Mills Community House—*hist pl* MI-6
**Mills Corners**—*pop pl* NY-2
Mills Coulee—*valley* MT-8
**Mills (County)**—*pop pl* TX-5
Mills County Jailhouse—*hist pl* TX-5
Mills Cove—*valley* NC-3
Mills Cove Area—*bay* AZ-5
Mills Creek AL-4
Mills Creek FL-3
Mills Creek MA-1
Mills Creek MS-4
Mills Creek TN-4
Mills Creek—*stream* AL-4
Mills Creek—*stream* (2) AK-9
Mills Creek—*stream* AR-4
Mills Creek—*stream* (6) CA-9
Mills Creek—*stream* (3) FL-3
Mills Creek—*stream* (2) GA-3
Mills Creek—*stream* IN-6
Mills Creek—*stream* KY-4
Mills Creek—*stream* (2) MI-6
Mills Creek—*stream* (2) MS-4
Mills Creek—*stream* MO-7
Mills Creek—*stream* (2) MT-8
Mills Creek—*stream* (2) NC-3
Mills Creek—*stream* OH-6
Mills Creek—*stream* OK-5
Mills Creek—*stream* (4) OR-9
Mills Creek—*stream* PA-2
Mills Creek—*stream* (2) SC-3
Mills Creek—*stream* TN-4
Mills Creek—*stream* (3) TX-5
Mills Creek—*stream* VA-3
Mills Creek—*stream* WA-9
Mills Creek—*stream* (2) WY-8
Mills Creek Ch—*church* SC-3
Mills Creek Sch—*school* KY-4
Mills Creek Sch (historical)—*school* MO-7
Mills Creek Trail—*trail* VA-3
Millsdale—*locale* IL-6
**Millsdale**—*pop pl* CA-9
Mills Dam Number 1—*dam* OR-9
Mills Dam Number 2—*dam* OR-9
Mills Dam Number 3—*dam* OR-9
Mills-Darden Cem—*cemetery* TN-4
Mills Ditch IN-6
Mills Ditch—*canal* IN-6
Mills Ditch—*canal* MI-6
Mills Ditch—*canal* MS-4
Mills Divide—*gap* NM-5
Mills Drain—*canal* MI-6
Mills Draw—*valley* TX-5
Millsea Branch—*stream* TN-4
Mill Seat—*locale* TN-4
**Millseat**—*pop pl* KY-4
Millseat Branch—*stream* AR-4
Millseat Branch—*stream* KY-4
Mill Seat Branch—*stream* KY-4
Millseat Branch—*stream* KY-4
Mill Seat Branch—*stream* KY-4
Millseat Branch—*stream* NC-3
Millseat Branch—*stream* (3) TX-5
Millseat Branch—*stream* (2) WV-2
Millseat Creek—*stream* CA-9
Mill Seat Creek—*stream* FL-3
Mill Seat Creek—*stream* KY-4
Mill Seat Creek—*stream* TN-4
Millseat Lake AR-4
Mill Seat Landing—*locale* NC-3
Millseat Run—*stream* WV-2
Mill Seat Run—*stream* WV-2
Millseat Run—*stream* WV-2
Millseat Sch—*school* KY-4
Mill Seat Spring—*spring* AL-4
Mill Seat Spring Cave—*cave* AL-4
Millseed Hollow—*valley* IL-6
Millseed Lake—*lake* AR-4
Millseep Branch—*stream* KY-4
Mill Set Branch—*stream* KY-4
Mill Set Gully—*valley* TX-5
Millset Rsvr—*reservoir* CO-8
Millset Spring—*spring* NM-5
Mills Falls Reservoir MA-1
Mills Family Cem—*cemetery* AL-4
Mills Family Cem—*cemetery* MS-4
Mills Field—*park* MA-1
**Millsfield**—*pop pl* TN-4
Millsfield Pond—*lake* NH-1
Millsfield Pond Brook—*stream* NH-1
Millsfield Sch (historical)—*school* TN-4
Millsfield (Township of)—*fmr MCD* NH-1
Mills Flat—*flat* CA-9
Mills Flat—*flat* UT-8
Mills Flat—*flat* WA-9
Mills Fork—*stream* KY-4
Mills Fremont Ditch—*canal* IA-7
Mills Gap—*gap* NC-3
Mills Gap—*gap* WV-2
Mills Gap Overlook—*locale* VA-3
Mills Glacier—*glacier* CO-8
Mills Goat Ranch—*locale* NM-5
Mills Grove Ch—*church* GA-3
Mills-Hale-Owen Blocks—*hist pl* MA-1
Mills Hall—*hist pl* CA-9
**Mills Heights Subdivision**—*pop pl* UT-8
Mills Hill—*summit* CA-9
Mills Hill—*summit* MA-1
Mills Hill—*summit* NY-2
Mills (historical)—*locale* AL-4
Mill Shoal Ch—*church* GA-3
Mill Shoal Creek—*stream* AL-4
Mill Shoal Creek—*stream* GA-3
Millshoal Creek—*stream* GA-3
Mill Shoal Creek—*stream* GA-3
**Mill Shoals**—*pop pl* IL-6
Mill Shoals—*rapids* TN-4
Mill Shoals Creek—*stream* SC-3
Mill Shoals Oil Field—*other* IL-6
**Mill Shoals (Township of)**—*pop pl* IL-6
Millshoal (Township of)—*fmr MCD* NC-3
Mills Hollow—*valley* (2) AL-4
Mills Hollow—*valley* AR-4
Mills Hollow—*valley* MA-1
Mills Hollow—*valley* MO-7
Mills Hollow—*valley* NY-2
Mills Home Cem—*cemetery* NC-3
Mills House—*hist pl* AK-9
Mills House—*hist pl* GA-3
Mills House—*hist pl* NM-5
Mills House and Smokehouse—*hist pl* GA-3
Mills HS—*school* AR-4
Mills HS—*school* CA-9
Mills HS—*school* FL-3
**Millside**—*pop pl* DE-2
Millside—*uninc pl* NC-3
Millside Ch—*church* NC-3
**Millside Heights**—*pop pl* NJ-2
**Millside Manor**—*pop pl* NJ-2
Mill Siding—*locale* MT-8
Mills Island—*island* AK-9
Mills Island—*island* MD-2
Mills Island—*island* TN-4
Mills Island Bar—*bar* TN-4
Mills Island Creek—*gut* MD-2
Mill (site)—*locale* ID-8
Mill Site Bluff—*cliff* MO-7
Mill Site Campground—*park* UT-8
Millsite Canyon—*valley* (2) AZ-5
Millsite Canyon—*valley* NM-5
Millsite Creek—*stream* NM-5
Millsite Creek—*stream* OR-9
Millsite Dam—*dam* UT-8
Millsite Lake—*lake* FL-3
Millsite Lake—*lake* NY-2
Millsite Rsvr—*reservoir* UT-8
Millsite Run—*stream* WV-2
Millsite Spring—*spring* (2) NV-8
Millsite State Park—*park* UT-8
Mills JHS—*school* CA-9
Mills Junction—*locale* UT-8
Mills Knob—*summit* KY-4
Mills Knob—*summit* (2) NC-3
Mills Lake—*lake* CA-9
Mills Lake—*lake* CO-8
Mills Lake—*lake* FL-3
Mills Lake—*lake* MI-6
Mills Lake—*lake* MN-6
Mills Lake—*lake* MT-8
Mills Lake—*lake* WI-6
Mills Lake—*swamp* MI-6
Mills Lake Dam Lower—*dam* AL-4
Mills Lake Lower—*reservoir* AL-4
Mills Landing—*locale* CA-9
Mills Landing Field—*airport* KS-7
Mills Landing Strip—*airport* KS-7
Mills Lick Creek AL-4
Mill Slough—*gut* (2) IL-6
Mill Slough—*stream* AR-4
Mill Slough—*stream* FL-3
Mill Slough—*stream* ID-8
Mill Slough—*stream* IA-7
Mill Slough—*stream* MO-7
Mill Slough—*stream* OR-9
Mill Slough Swamp IL-6
Mills McKillip Cem—*cemetery* OH-6
Mills Meadows Waterfowl Mngmt Area—*park* UT-8
Mills Memorial Cem—*cemetery* VT-1
Mills Memorial Ch—*church* NC-3
Mills Memorial Hosp—*hospital* CA-9
Mills Memorial State Park—*park* NY-2
Mills Mill—*hist pl* SC-3
Mills Mill Ch—*church* SC-3
**Mills Mills**—*pop pl* NY-2
Mills Moraine—*ridge* CO-8
Mills Mountain AL-4
Mills Mountain—*ridge* WV-2
Mills Mountain Ch—*church* WV-2
Mills Mtn—*summit* VA-3
Millsone Mountain MA-1
Millsop Sch—*school* WV-2
**Mills Orchard**—*pop pl* CA-9
Mills Orchards—*locale* CA-9
Mills Park—*park* IL-6
Mills Park—*park* TX-5
Mills Pasture—*flat* KS-7
Millspaugh—*locale* CA-9
Mills Peak—*summit* NM-5
Mills Place—*locale* WY-8
Mills Point—*cape* ME-1
Mills Point—*cape* (2) MD-2
Mills Point—*cape* NH-1
Mills Point—*cape* NY-2
Mills Point—*cape* VT-1
Mills Point, Bay—*cape* MI-6
Mills Pond NC-3
Mills Pond—*lake* NY-2
Mills Pond—*lake* TN-4
Mills Pond—*reservoir* CO-8
Mills Pond—*reservoir* LA-4
Mills Pond—*reservoir* SC-3
Mills Pond District—*hist pl* NY-2
Mills Pond Sch—*school* NY-2
Mills Prairie—*flat* IN-6
Mills Prairie Sch—*school* IL-6
Mill Spring AL-4
Millspring TN-4
Mill Spring—*locale* TN-4
**Millspring**—*pop pl* FL-3
**Mill Spring**—*pop pl* IL-6
**Mill Spring**—*pop pl* MO-7
**Mill Spring**—*pop pl* NC-3
Mill Spring—*spring* AZ-5
Mill Spring—*spring* (2) CA-9
Mill Spring—*spring* KY-4
Mill Spring—*spring* (2) MO-7
Mill Spring—*spring* MT-8
Mill Spring—*spring* (2) NV-8
Mill Spring—*spring* OR-9
Mill Spring—*spring* (4) TN-4
Mill Spring—*spring* (2) UT-8
Mill Spring—*stream* IL-6
Mill Spring Branch (historical)—*stream* TN-4
Mill Spring Creek—*stream* MO-7
Mill Spring Creek—*stream* TN-4
Mill Spring Elementary—*school* NC-3
Mill Spring Hill—*summit* FL-3
Mill Spring Mill—*locale* TN-4
Mill Spring Post Office (historical)—*building* TN-4
Mill Springs TN-4
**Mill Springs**—*pop pl* KY-4
Mill Springs Baptist Ch—*church* TN-4
Mill Springs Battlefield—*park* KY-4
Mill Springs (CCD)—*cens area* KY-4
Mill Springs Cem—*cemetery* MS-4
Mill Springs Ch—*church* FL-3
Millsprings Ch—*church* MS-4
Mill Spring Sch (historical)—*school* TN-4
Mill Springs Mill—*hist pl* KY-4
Mill Springs Natl Cem—*cemetery* KY-4
Mill Springs State Park—*park* KY-4
Mill Spring Township—*civil* MO-7
Mill Spur—*locale* CA-9
Mill Spur—*ridge* KY-4
Mills Quarry—*mine* AZ-5
Mills Ranch—*locale* AZ-5
Mills Ranch—*locale* CA-9
Mills Ranch—*locale* KS-7
Mills Ranch—*locale* MT-8
Mills' Ranch—*locale* MT-8
Mills Ranch—*locale* (2) TX-5
Mills Ranch Airp—*airport* KS-7
Mills (Rancho Cordova) CA-9
Mills Ridge—*locale* NC-3
Mills Ridge—*ridge* ME-1
Mills Ridge Tank—*reservoir* AZ-5

**Mills River**—*pop pl* NC-3
Mills River—*stream* NC-3
Mills River Bridge—*bridge* NC-3
Mills River Cem—*cemetery* NC-3
Mills River Ch—*church* NC-3
Mills River Chapel—*church* NC-3
Mills River Chapel—*hist pl* NC-3
Mills River Sch—*school* NC-3
Mills River (Township of)—*fmr MCD* NC-3
Mills' Row—*hist pl* OH-6
Mills (RR name for Harford Mills)—*other* NY-2
*Mills Rsvr* OR-9
Mills Sch—*school* CA-9
Mills Sch—*school* IL-6
Mills Sch—*school* ME-1
Mills Sch—*school* (2) MI-6
Mills Sch—*school* NE-7
Mills Sch—*school* NC-3
Mills Sch—*school* (2) OH-6
Mills Sch—*school* OR-9
Mills Sch—*school* TN-4
Mills Sch (abandoned)—*school* MO-7
*Mills School* IN-6
Mills-Screven Plantation—*hist pl* NC-3
Mills Slough—*gut* (2) AR-4
Mills Smokehouse Pond—*lake* FL-3
Mills Spring—*spring* (2) CA-9
Mills Spring—*spring* MO-7
Mills Spring—*spring* MT-8
Mills Spring—*spring* OR-9
Mills Spring Branch—*stream* AL-4
Mills Spring Branch—*stream* TN-4
Mills Spring (historical)—*locale* AL-4
**Mills Spur**—*pop pl* AL-4
Mills Stadium—*other* GA-3
Mills-Stebbins Villa—*hist pl* MA-1
Mills Store—*locale* PA-2
**Mills Subdivision**—*pop pl* TN-4
**Mills Subdivision, The**—*pop pl* UT-8
*Mills Swamp* FL-3
*Mills Swamp* MD-2
Mills Swamp—*stream* SC-3
**Millstadt**—*pop pl* IL-6
Millstadt Junction—*locale* IL-6
**Millstadt (Township of)**—*pop pl* IL-6
Mills Tank—*reservoir* AZ-5
Mill Station Creek—*stream* NC-3
Millstead Branch—*stream* TX-5
*Millsteed Branch* TX-5
**Millston**—*pop pl* WI-6
*Millstone* PA-2
Millstone—*locale* PA-2
Millstone—*locale* TN-4
Millstone—*locale* VA-3
**Millstone**—*pop pl* CT-1
**Millstone**—*pop pl* KY-4
**Millstone**—*pop pl* (2) NJ-2
**Millstone**—*pop pl* (2) WV-2
Millstone Bayou—*stream* MS-4
Millstone Bluff—*hist pl* IL-6
Millstone Bluff—*summit* IL-6
*Millstone Branch* TN-4
Millstone Branch—*stream* GA-3
Millstone Branch—*stream* (6) KY-4
Millstone Branch—*stream* SC-3
Millstone Branch—*stream* (2) TN-4
Millstone Branch—*stream* (4) VA-3
Millstone Branch—*stream* (2) WV-2
Millstone Cem—*cemetery* TN-4
Millstone Ch—*church* GA-3
Millstone Ch—*church* IN-6
Millstone Ch—*church* MO-7
Millstone Ch—*church* VA-3
Millstone Ch—*church* (2) WV-2
Millstone Ch of Christ—*church* TN-4
*Millstone Creek* MS-4
*Millstone Creek* PA-2
Millstone Creek—*stream* GA-3
Millstone Creek—*stream* (2) IN-6
Millstone Creek—*stream* KY-4
Millstone Creek—*stream* (4) NC-3
Millstone Creek—*stream* (2) PA-2
Millstone Creek—*stream* (3) TN-4
Millstone Creek—*stream* VA-3
Millstone Creek—*stream* (3) WV-2
Millstone Flats—*flat* TN-4
Millstone Gap—*gap* (2) TN-4
Millstone Gap Lookout Tower—*locale* TN-4
Millstone Gap Ridge—*ridge* WV-2
*Mill Stone Hill* MA-1
Millstone Hill—*summit* CT-1
Millstone Hill—*summit* (3) MA-1
Millstone Hill—*summit* NH-1
Millstone Hill—*summit* NJ-2
Millstone Hill—*summit* VT-1
Millstone Hist Dist—*hist pl* NJ-2
Millstone Hollow—*valley* (2) MO-7
Millstone Hollow—*valley* (2) TN-4
Millstone Hollow—*valley* (2) VA-3
Millstone Hollow—*valley* WV-2
Millstone HS (abandoned)—*school* PA-2
Millstone Island—*island* ME-1
Millstone Island—*island* PA-2
Millstone Knob—*summit* TN-4
Millstone Lake—*lake* MN-6
Millstone Lake—*reservoir* NC-3
Mill Stone Landing—*locale* SC-3
Millstone Landing Public Access—*locale* MN-6
Millstone (Moffet Station)—*locale* MD-2
Millstone Mountain Ch—*church* AL-4
Millstone Mtn—*summit* AL-4
Millstone Mtn—*summit* NC-3
Millstone Mtn—*summit* PA-2
Millstone Mtn—*summit* TN-4
Millstone Point—*cape* CT-1
Millstone Point—*cape* MD-2
Millstone Point—*cape* NH-1
Millstone Post Office (historical)—*building* TN-4
Millstone Ridge—*ridge* KY-4
Millstone Ridge—*ridge* TN-4
Millstone Ridge—*ridge* VA-3
Millstone River—*stream* NJ-2
*Mill Stone Run* PA-2
Millstone Run—*stream* (2) OH-6
Millstone Run—*stream* PA-2
Millstone Run—*stream* VA-3
Millstone Run—*stream* (7) WV-2
Millstone Sch—*school* WV-2
Millstone Sch (historical)—*school* TN-4
**Millstone (Township of)**—*pop pl* NJ-2
**Millstone (Township of)**—*pop pl* PA-2
Millstone Valley Agricultural District—*hist pl* NJ-2
**Millston (Town of)**—*pop pl* WI-6
**Mills (Township of)**—*pop pl* IL-6
**Mills (Township of)**—*pop pl* (2) MI-6
*Mill Stream* ME-1
*Mill Stream* MA-1
Mill Stream—*stream* CA-9
Mill Stream—*stream* (13) ME-1
Mill Stream—*stream* (3) NY-2
Mill Stream—*stream* UT-8
Mill Stream—*stream* VA-3
Mill Stream Branch—*stream* MD-2
**Millstream Condominium Phase 1-4**—*pop pl* UT-8
*Millstream Creek* IN-6
Mill Stream Drain—*stream* MI-6
Mill Stream Spring—*spring* KY-4
Mill Stream Swamp—*swamp* FL-3
*Mill Street Dam* MA-1
Mill Street-North Clover Street Hist Dist—*hist pl* NY-2
Mill Street-North Clover Street Hist Dist (Boundary Increase)—*hist pl* NY-2
Mill Street Sch—*school* NJ-2
Mill Street Station—*locale* PA-2
**Mill Street (subdivision)**—*pop pl* MA-1
Mills Tributary Number Two—*canal* IN-6
*Mills Valley* AL-4
Mills Valley—*basin* UT-8
Mills Valley—*valley* NE-7
Mills Valley—*valley* WV-2
*Mills Variety* AL-4
**Millsville**—*pop pl* TX-5
*Mill Swamp* FL-3
*Mill Swamp* NC-3
**Mill Swamp**—*pop pl* MD-2
Mill Swamp—*stream* MD-2
Mill Swamp—*stream* (5) NC-3
Mill Swamp—*stream* (6) VA-3
Mill Swamp—*swamp* (4) NC-3
Mill Swamp—*swamp* SC-3
Mill Swamp Branch—*stream* MD-2
Mill Swamp Branch—*stream* NC-3
Mill Swamp Ch—*church* VA-3
*Mill Swamp Creek* NC-3
Mill Swamp Creek—*stream* NC-3
Mill Swamp Sch—*school* SC-3
Mill Swan Sch—*school* MA-1
Mills Well—*well* CO-8
Mills Well—*well* WY-8
Millswitch Creek—*stream* CO-8
**Millswood Estates (subdivision)**—*pop pl* TN-4
Milltail Creek—*stream* NC-3
Milltail Creek—*stream* VA-3
*Mill Tail Pond* RI-1
Mill Tail Swamp—*swamp* RI-1
Mill Tail Swamp And Pond—*reservoir* RI-1
Mill Tanks—*reservoir* TX-5
Mill Thorofare—*channel* NJ-2
Mill Timber Branch—*stream* KY-4
Mill Timber Creek—*stream* NC-3
*Millton* UT-8
*Milltown* CA-9
*Milltown* ME-1
*Mill Town* MD-2
*Mill Town* MS-4
*Milltown* NJ-2
*Mill Town* NC-3
Milltown—*locale* DE-2
Milltown—*locale* (2) KY-4
Milltown—*locale* MO-7
Milltown—*locale* (3) NJ-2
Milltown—*locale* NY-2
Milltown—*locale* PA-2
Milltown—*locale* (2) TN-4
Milltown—*locale* VA-3
Milltown—*locale* WA-9
**Milltown**—*pop pl* AL-4
**Milltown**—*pop pl* AR-4
**Milltown**—*pop pl* FL-3
**Milltown**—*pop pl* IN-6
**Milltown**—*pop pl* ME-1
**Milltown**—*pop pl* MS-4
**Milltown**—*pop pl* MT-8
**Milltown**—*pop pl* (3) NJ-2
**Milltown**—*pop pl* NC-3
**Milltown**—*pop pl* (4) PA-2
**Milltown**—*pop pl* SD-7
**Mill Town**—*pop pl* TN-4
**Milltown**—*pop pl* TN-4
**Mill Town**—*pop pl* TX-5
**Milltown**—*pop pl* WV-2
**Milltown**—*pop pl* WI-6
Mill Town—*uninc pl* MS-4
Milltown Bay—*swamp* GA-3
Milltown (CCD)—*cens area* AL-4
Milltown Cem—*cemetery* AL-4
Milltown Cem—*cemetery* NY-2
Mill Town Cem—*cemetery* SC-3
Milltown Cem—*cemetery* SD-7
Milltown Ch—*church* AL-4
Mill Town Ch—*church* AR-4
Milltown Ch—*church* AR-4
Milltown Ch—*church* GA-3
Milltown Ch—*church* KY-4
Milltown Ch (historical)—*church* TN-4
Milltown Collegiate Institute (historical)—*school* AL-4
Milltown Colony (historical)—*locale* SD-7
Milltown Creek—*stream* VA-3
Milltown Dam—*dam* MT-8
Milltown Dam—*dam* PA-2
Milltown Division—*civil* AL-4
**Milltown (Dycus)**—*pop pl* TN-4
*Milltown High School* AL-4
Milltown Hill—*summit* OR-9
Milltown Hill Bridge—*bridge* OR-9
Milltown (historical)—*locale* UT-8
Milltown Hutterite Colony—*hist pl* SD-7
Milltown India Rubber Company—*hist pl* NJ-2
Milltown Island—*island* WA-9
Milltown Landing—*locale* MD-2
Milltown Rsvr—*reservoir* PA-2
Milltown Sch—*school* IN-6
Milltown Sch—*school* WV-2
Milltown Sch—*school* WI-6
Mill (Township of)—*fmr MCD* (2) AR-4
**Mill (Township of)**—*pop pl* IN-6
**Mill (Township of)**—*pop pl* OH-6
Milltown (site)—*locale* AZ-5
**Milltown (Town of)**—*pop pl* WI-6
**Milltown Township**—*pop pl* SD-7
Milltown Township (historical)—*civil* (2) SD-7
*Mill Track* DC-2
Mill Tract Farm—*hist pl* PA-2
Mill Trail Ridge—*ridge* MO-7
Mill Tunnel—*mine* CO-8
Millux—*locale* CA-9
**Millvale**—*pop pl* ME-1
**Millvale**—*pop pl* PA-2
Millvale Borough—*civil* PA-2
Millvale Reservoir Dam—*dam* MA-1
Millvale Rsvr—*reservoir* MA-1
Millvale Sch—*school* OH-6
Millvale Station—*building* PA-2
**Mill Valley**—*pop pl* CA-9
**Mill Valley**—*pop pl* MA-1
Mill Valley—*valley* (2) CA-9
Mill Valley—*valley* NY-2
Mill Valley—*valley* TN-4
Mill Valley Air Force Station—*military* CA-9
Mill Valley Campground—*locale* CA-9
Mill Valley Creek—*stream* OR-9
Mill Valley Sch—*school* WI-6
Millview—*locale* PA-2
**Millview**—*pop pl* FL-3
**Millview**—*pop pl* TN-4
Millview Cem—*cemetery* PA-2
Millview Ch—*church* FL-3
Millview Community Center—*building* TN-4
Millview Community Club—*building* WI-6
Millview (historical)—*locale* MS-4
Millview Post Office (historical)—*building* MS-4
Millview Sch—*school* CA-9
*Mill Village* MA-1
*Mill Village* NH-1
Mill Village—*locale* NH-1
**Mill Village**—*pop pl* AL-4
**Mill Village**—*pop pl* MA-1
**Mill Village**—*pop pl* NH-1
**Mill Village**—*pop pl* PA-2
**Mill Village**—*pop pl* (4) VT-1
Mill Village—*uninc pl* SC-3
Mill Village Borough—*civil* PA-2
Mill Village Chapel—*church* VT-1
Mill Village Hist Dist—*hist pl* MA-1
Mill Village Hist Dist—*hist pl* VT-1
Mill Village Shop Ctr—*locale* MA-1
*Millville* AL-4
*Millville* CT-1
*Millville* NJ-2
*Millville* OH-6
*Millville* PA-2
*Millville* WV-2
Millville—*locale* AR-4
Millville—*locale* IL-6
Millville—*locale* MI-6
Millville—*locale* TN-4
Millville—*locale* VA-3
Millville—*locale* WI-6
**Millville**—*pop pl* AL-4
**Millville**—*pop pl* CA-9
**Millville**—*pop pl* CT-1
**Millville**—*pop pl* DE-2
**Millville**—*pop pl* FL-3
**Millville**—*pop pl* IL-6
**Millville**—*pop pl* (2) IN-6
**Millville**—*pop pl* IA-7
**Millville**—*pop pl* KY-4
**Millville**—*pop pl* MA-1
**Millville**—*pop pl* MI-6
**Millville**—*pop pl* MN-6
**Millville**—*pop pl* MS-4
**Millville**—*pop pl* MO-7
**Millville**—*pop pl* NH-1
**Millville**—*pop pl* (2) NJ-2
**Millville**—*pop pl* NY-2
**Millville**—*pop pl* (2) OH-6
**Millville**—*pop pl* (2) PA-2
**Millville**—*pop pl* RI-1
**Millville**—*pop pl* UT-8
**Millville**—*pop pl* WV-2
Millville Borough—*civil* PA-2
Millville Canyon—*valley* UT-8
Millville Cem—*cemetery* FL-3
Millville Cem—*cemetery* IL-6
Millville Cem—*cemetery* NH-1
Millville Cem—*cemetery* NY-2
Millville Cem—*cemetery* OH-6
**Millville Center**—*pop pl* MA-1
Millville Ch—*church* AL-4
Millville Ch—*church* GA-3
Millville Ch—*church* MI-6
Millville Ch—*church* MS-4
Millville Ch—*church* TX-5
Millville City Cem—*cemetery* UT-8
Millville Creek—*stream* MD-2
Millville Creek—*stream* NE-7
Millville Creek—*stream* WI-6
Millville Drain—*stream* IN-6
Millville Face Wildlife Mngmt Area—*park* UT-8
Millville (historical)—*locale* AL-4
Millville Historic and Archaeol District—*hist pl* NJ-2
**Millville Lake**—*pop pl* NH-1
Millville Lake—*reservoir* NH-1
Millville Municipal—*airport* NJ-2
Millville Peak—*summit* UT-8
Millville Plains—*plain* CA-9
*Millville P. O.* MS-4
Millville Post Office (historical)—*building* TN-4
Millville Providence Canal—*canal* UT-8
Millville Sch—*hist pl* NH-1
Millville Sch—*school* CA-9
Millville Sch—*school* FL-3
Millville Sch—*school* KY-4
Millville Sch—*school* NH-1
Millville Sch—*school* SC-3
Millville Sch—*school* UT-8
Millville's First Bank Bldg—*hist pl* NJ-2
**Millville Siding**—*pop pl* IA-7
**Millville (Town of)**—*pop pl* MA-1
**Millville (Town of)**—*pop pl* WI-6
Millville Township—*fmr MCD* IA-7
Millward Sch—*school* PA-2
Millward Slough—*gut* ID-8
Mill Wash—*stream* AZ-5
Mill Water Dam—*dam* PA-2
Mill Watershed LT-14b-1 Dam—*dam* MS-4
Mill Watershed LT-14b-2 Dam—*dam* MS-4
Mill Watershed LT-14b-5 Dam—*dam* MS-4
**Millway**—*pop pl* PA-2
Millway Ch—*church* SC-3
Mill Way Hist Dist—*hist pl* MA-1
Millway Post Office (historical)—*building* PA-2
Millwee Cem—*cemetery* AR-4
Millwee Creek—*stream* AR-4
Millwee Creek—*stream* SC-3
Mill-Willow Bypass—*canal* MT-8
*Millwood* TN-4
Millwood—*hist pl* KY-4
Millwood—*hist pl* SC-3
Millwood—*locale* AR-4
Millwood—*locale* (2) CO-8
Millwood—*locale* KS-7
Millwood—*locale* OR-9
Millwood—*locale* TX-5
**Millwood**—*pop pl* AL-4
**Millwood**—*pop pl* FL-3
**Millwood**—*pop pl* GA-3
**Millwood**—*pop pl* KY-4
**Millwood**—*pop pl* MD-2
**Millwood**—*pop pl* MO-7
**Millwood**—*pop pl* NY-2
**Millwood**—*pop pl* OH-6
**Millwood**—*pop pl* PA-2
**Millwood**—*pop pl* SC-3
**Millwood**—*pop pl* VA-3
**Millwood**—*pop pl* WA-9
**Millwood**—*pop pl* WV-2
Millwood Cem—*cemetery* AL-4
Millwood Cem—*cemetery* FL-3
Millwood Cem—*cemetery* KY-4
Millwood Cem—*cemetery* OH-6
Millwood Ch—*church* DE-2
Millwood Ch—*church* KY-4
Millwood Ch—*church* PA-2
Millwood Chapel—*church* IN-6
Millwood Country Club—*other* VA-3
Millwood Creek—*stream* KY-4
Millwood Ditch—*canal* CO-8
**Millwood Gardens**—*pop pl* SC-3
Millwood Lake—*reservoir* AR-4
Millwood Lake—*swamp* MN-6
Millwood Landing—*locale* AL-4
Millwood Park—*park* MN-6
Millwood Park—*park* WA-9
Millwood Pond—*lake* AL-4
Millwood Pond—*reservoir* SC-3
Millwood Post Office (historical)—*building* TN-4
Millwood Primitive Baptist Ch—*church* AL-4
Millwood Recreation Center—*park* MD-2
*Millwood Rsvr* AR-4
Mill Woods—*woods* MA-1
Millwoods Cem—*cemetery* NH-1
Millwood Sch—*school* OK-5
Millwood Sch—*school* PA-2
Millwood Sch—*school* SC-3
Millwood Sch—*school* WA-9
Millwoods Island—*island* IL-6
Millwood (Site)—*locale* CA-9
Mill Woods Park—*park* CT-1
Millwood Township—*civil* MO-7
**Millwood (Township of)**—*pop pl* MN-6
**Millwood (Township of)**—*pop pl* OH-6
Milly Cem—*cemetery* OK-5
Milly Creek—*stream* MT-8
Milly Lake—*lake* FL-3
**Milly Plantation**—*pop pl* LA-4
*Millys Creek* AL-4
Millys Foot Pass—*gap* CA-9
Milma Branch—*stream* GA-3
**Milmay**—*pop pl* NJ-2
**Milmine**—*pop pl* IL-6
**Milmont**—*pop pl* PA-2
*Milmont (Milmont Park)* PA-2
Milmont Park—*locale* PA-2
**Milmont Park (Milmont)**—*pop pl* PA-2
Milmont Station—*locale* PA-2
Milne—*locale* IL-6
Milne, James, House—*hist pl* OR-9
Milne, John, House—*hist pl* NM-5
Milne, Robert, House—*hist pl* IL-6
Milneburg—*uninc pl* LA-4
Milne-Bush Ranch—*hist pl* NM-5
Milne Lake—*lake* CA-9
Milne Municipal Boys Home—*building* LA-4
Milne Point—*cape* AK-9
*Milner* AL-4
*Milner* TN-4
Milner—*locale* AL-4
Milner—*locale* ID-8
**Milner**—*pop pl* CO-8
**Milner**—*pop pl* GA-3
**Milner**—*pop pl* KY-4
Milne Ranch—*locale* (3) WY-8
Milner Arm—*canal* IN-6
Milner Brook—*stream* GA-3
Milner Butte—*summit* ID-8
Milner (CCD)—*cens area* GA-3
Milner Cem—*cemetery* GA-3
Milner Cem—*cemetery* MO-7
Milner Cem—*cemetery* TX-5
*Milner Cemetery* AL-4
*Milner Chapel* AL-4
*Milner Creek* CA-9
Milner Crest Sch—*school* OR-9
**Milner Crossroads**—*pop pl* GA-3
**Milner Cross Roads**—*pop pl* GA-3
Milner Dam—*dam* ID-8
Milner Dam and the Twin Falls Main Canal—*hist pl* ID-8
Milner Draw—*valley* NM-5
Milner Glade—*valley* CO-8
Milner Gooding Canal—*canal* ID-8
Milner (historical)—*locale* (2) AL-4
Milner House—*hist pl* MS-4
*Milner Lake* MT-8
Milner Lake—*lake* NM-5
Milner Lake—*lake* TX-5
Milner Lake—*reservoir* (2) GA-3
Milner Lake—*reservoir* ID-8
Milner Low Lift Main Canal—*canal* ID-8
Milner Mine (underground)—*mine* (2) AL-4
Milner Mtn—*summit* CO-8
Milner Pass—*gap* CO-8
Milner Pass Road Camp—*locale* CO-8
Milner Pass Road Camp Mess Hall and House—*hist pl* CO-8
Milner Pond—*lake* AL-4
Milner Rosenwald Acad—*school* FL-3
Milners Chapel—*church* AL-4
**Milners Corner**—*pop pl* IN-6
Milners Neck—*cape* VA-3
Milner Spring Creek—*stream* CO-8
Milners Switch—*locale* TN-4
Milnersville—*other* OH-6
*Milner Tank* TX-5
**Milnes**—*pop pl* MI-6
Milnesand—*locale* NM-5
Milnesand Oil Field—*other* NM-5
Milnes Sch—*school* CA-9
Milnes Sch—*school* MI-6
Milnes Sch—*school* NJ-2
*Milnesville* VA-3
**Milnesville**—*pop pl* PA-2
**Milnor**—*pop pl* ND-7
**Milnor**—*pop pl* PA-2
Milnor Cem—*cemetery* OH-6
Milnor Lake—*lake* MT-8
Milnor Municipal Airp—*airport* ND-7
**Milnor Township**—*pop pl* ND-7
Milny Lake—*lake* WI-6
*Milo* AL-4
*Milo* NY-2
Milo—*locale* AR-4
Milo—*locale* CA-9
Milo—*locale* KS-7
Milo—*locale* KY-4
Milo—*locale* OR-9
Milo—*locale* WV-2
Milo—*locale* WY-8
**Milo**—*pop pl* ID-8
**Milo**—*pop pl* IL-6
**Milo**—*pop pl* IN-6
**Milo**—*pop pl* IA-7
**Milo**—*pop pl* ME-1
**Milo**—*pop pl* MO-7
**Milo**—*pop pl* OK-5
**Milo**—*pop pl* TN-4
Milo Acad Bridge—*hist pl* OR-9
Milo Bible Ch—*church* MI-6
Milo Canyon—*valley* ID-8
Milo Canyon—*valley* NM-5
Milo Cem—*cemetery* ID-8
Milo Cem—*cemetery* KS-7
Milo Cem—*cemetery* MN-6
Milo Cem—*cemetery* OK-5
Milo Center—*locale* TX-5
**Milo Center**—*pop pl* NY-2
Milo Center (census name Milo)—*other* ME-1
**Milo Center (Milo)**—*pop pl* NY-2
Milo Cove—*bay* HI-9
Milo Creek—*stream* ID-8
Milo Dry Farm—*locale* ID-8
Milo Gard Cem—*cemetery* OR-9
Mil Ojos Camp—*locale* TX-5
Milokrawlok Creek—*stream* AK-9
Milokrawlok Mtn—*summit* AK-9
Milo Lake—*lake* MT-8
Milo Landing (historical)—*locale* MS-4
*Milo Lemert Memorial Bridge* TN-4
Milolii—*civil* HI-9
**Milolii**—*pop pl* HI-9
Milolii Bay—*bay* HI-9
*Milolii Gulch* HI-9
Milolii Ridge—*ridge* HI-9
Milolii State Park—*park* HI-9
Milolii Valley—*valley* HI-9
Miloma—*locale* MN-6
Milo McIver State Park—*park* OR-9
Milo Mills—*locale* NY-2
Milomilo Mtn—*summit* AS-9
Milo P.O. (historical)—*locale* AL-4
Milo Point—*cape* HI-9
Milo Post Office (historical)—*building* TN-4
Milo Ray State Wildlife Area—*park* IA-7
Milord Point—*cape* VI-3
Milos Butte—*summit* AZ-5
Milo Sch—*school* MO-7
Milo Sch—*school* OH-6
Milo Sch—*school* WV-2
Milos Kitchen—*basin* UT-8
Milo Station—*locale* NY-2
**Milo Subdivision**—*pop pl* UT-8
*Milotk* PW-9
**Milo (Town of)**—*pop pl* ME-1
**Milo (Town of)**—*pop pl* NY-2
Milo Township—*fmr MCD* IA-7
**Milo (Township of)**—*pop pl* IL-6
**Milo (Township of)**—*pop pl* MN-6
**Milo Village**—*pop pl* HI-9
Milo Wood Pond—*lake* WA-9
Milpas—*uninc pl* CA-9
Milpa Tank—*reservoir* AZ-5
Mil Pesos Well—*well* TX-5
*Milpitas* AZ-5
Milpitas—*civil* CA-9
**Milpitas**—*pop pl* CA-9
Milpitas (Alviso)—*civil* CA-9
Milpitas Draw—*valley* NM-5
Milpitas Ranchhouse—*hist pl* CA-9
Milpitas Sewage Disposal—*other* CA-9
Milpitas Wash—*stream* CA-9
Milpitas Well—*well* NM-5
*Milqer* FM-9
*Milridge Creek* WA-9
**Milro (historical)**—*pop pl* MS-4
Milrose—*locale* AR-4
Milrose Creek—*stream* NE-7
Milrose Trail—*trail* ME-1
Milroy—*locale* IL-6
Milroy—*locale* ND-7
Milroy—*locale* WV-2
**Milroy**—*pop pl* IN-6
**Milroy**—*pop pl* MN-6
**Milroy**—*pop pl* MS-4
**Milroy**—*pop pl* PA-2
Milroy, John, House—*hist pl* TX-5
Milroy Access Area—*park* IA-7
Milroy Block—*hist pl* MN-6
Milroy Cem—*cemetery* IN-6
Milroy Creek—*stream* AK-9
Milroy Elementary and JHS—*school* IN-6
Milroy Hosp—*hospital* TX-5
Milroy House—*hist pl* TX-5
Milroy (Magisterial District)—*fmr MCD* WV-2
Milroy-Muller House—*hist pl* TX-5
Milroy Number One Cave—*cave* PA-2
Milroy Number Two Cave—*cave* PA-2
Milroy Park—*park* TX-5
Milroy Park—*park* WA-9
Milroy Sch—*school* OH-6
Milroy State Bank Bldg—*hist pl* MN-6
**Milroy (Township of)**—*pop pl* IN-6
Milsap Bar—*bar* CA-9
Milsap Creek—*stream* CO-8
Milsap Gap—*gap* GA-3
*Milsap Hollow* TN-4
Milsaps Cem—*cemetery* MS-4
Milstead—*locale* AL-4
**Milstead**—*pop pl* GA-3
Milstead Branch—*stream* MS-4
*Milstead Cemetery* AL-4
Milstead Creek—*gut* VA-3
Milstead Lookout Tower—*locale* AL-4
Milstead Park—*park* OK-5
Milstead Post Office (historical)—*building* AL-4
*Milt Adkins Branch* WV-2
Milt Adkins Fork—*stream* WV-2
Milt-ann, Lake—*reservoir* GA-3
Milt Creek—*stream* WA-9
**Milteer Acres (subdivision)**—*pop pl* VA-3
Miltimore House—*hist pl* CA-9
Miltmore Lake—*lake* IL-6
*Milton* AR-4
*Milton* KS-7
*Milton* MD-2
*Milton* NJ-2
*Milton* OH-6
*Milton* PA-2
*Milton* UT-8
Milton—*CDP* MA-1
Milton—*hist pl* MD-2
Milton—*locale* AL-4
Milton—*locale* CT-1
Milton—*locale* MO-7
Milton—*locale* NJ-2
Milton—*locale* OK-5
Milton—*locale* (2) VA-3
Milton—*other* OH-6
**Milton**—*pop pl* CA-9
**Milton**—*pop pl* DE-2
**Milton**—*pop pl* FL-3
**Milton**—*pop pl* IL-6
**Milton**—*pop pl* (2) IN-6
**Milton**—*pop pl* IA-7
**Milton**—*pop pl* KS-7
**Milton**—*pop pl* KY-4
**Milton**—*pop pl* LA-4
**Milton**—*pop pl* ME-1
**Milton**—*pop pl* MD-2
**Milton**—*pop pl* MA-1
**Milton**—*pop pl* MI-6
**Milton**—*pop pl* MS-4
**Milton**—*pop pl* MO-7
**Milton**—*pop pl* NE-7
**Milton**—*pop pl* NH-1
**Milton**—*pop pl* (2) NY-2
**Milton**—*pop pl* NC-3
**Milton**—*pop pl* ND-7
**Milton**—*pop pl* (2) PA-2
**Milton**—*pop pl* SC-3
**Milton**—*pop pl* TN-4
**Milton**—*pop pl* TX-5
**Milton**—*pop pl* UT-8
**Milton**—*pop pl* VT-1
**Milton**—*pop pl* WA-9
**Milton**—*pop pl* WV-2
**Milton**—*pop pl* WI-6
Milton—*uninc pl* OR-9
Milton, Lake—*reservoir* OH-6
**Miltona**—*pop pl* MN-6
Miltona, Lake—*lake* MN-6
**Miltona (Township of)**—*pop pl* MN-6
Milton Ave Sch—*school* GA-3
Milton Ave Sch—*school* NJ-2
Milton Ave Sch—*school* NY-2
*Milton Bluff* AL-4
Milton Bluff—*cliff* AL-4
**Miltonboro**—*pop pl* VT-1
Milton Borough—*civil* PA-2
Milton-Bowman Tunnel—*tunnel* CA-9
Milton-Bradley Company—*hist pl* MA-1
Milton Branch—*stream* AL-4
Milton Branch—*stream* IL-6
Milton Branch—*stream* TN-4
Milton Branch—*stream* WV-2
Milton Camp (historical)—*locale* PA-2
Milton Canyon—*valley* NV-8
Milton Carter Dam—*dam* AL-4
Milton Cave—*cave* TN-4
Milton (CCD)—*cens area* DE-2
Milton (CCD)—*cens area* FL-3
Milton (CCD)—*cens area* KY-4
Milton Cem—*cemetery* CT-1
Milton Cem—*cemetery* (2) FL-3
Milton Cem—*cemetery* IN-6
Milton Cem—*cemetery* LA-4
Milton Cem—*cemetery* MN-6
Milton Cem—*cemetery* PA-2
Milton Cem—*cemetery* (2) TN-4
Milton Cem—*cemetery* UT-8
**Milton Center**—*pop pl* NY-2
Milton Center Hist Dist—*hist pl* CT-1
**Milton Center (RR name Milton)**—*pop pl* OH-6
**Milton Center (subdivision)**—*pop pl* MA-1
Milton Centre Hist Dist—*hist pl* MA-1
Milton Ch—*church* AL-4
Milton Ch—*church* KY-4
Milton Chapel—*church* SC-3
Milton College Hist Dist—*hist pl* WI-6
*Milton Creek* OR-9
Milton Creek—*stream* CA-9
Milton Creek—*stream* CO-8
Milton Creek—*stream* LA-4
Milton Creek—*stream* MT-8
Milton Creek—*stream* OR-9
Milton Creek—*stream* SC-3
Milton Creek—*stream* TX-5
**Miltondale**—*pop pl* MO-7
Milton Dam—*dam* OH-6
Milton Ditch—*canal* OR-9
Milton Drain—*stream* IN-6
Milton Elem Sch—*school* IN-6

Milton Fairgrounds—*locale* ... PA-2
Milton Federal Street Elem Sch—*school* ... DE-2
Milton Female Acad (historical)—*school* ... MS-4
Milton Ford—*locale* ... AR-4
Milton Frank Farms—*locale* ... TX-5
Milton Frank Stadium—*park* ... AL-4
**Milton-Freewater**—*pop pl* ... OR-9
Milton Freight Station—*hist pl* ... PA-2
**Milton Grove**—*pop pl* ... PA-2
Milton Grove Cem—*cemetery* ... PA-2
Milton Grove Ch—*church* ... TN-4
Milton Harbor—*bay* ... NY-2
Milton Hershey HS—*school* ... PA-2
*Milton Hershey Intermediate Sch* ... PA-2
*Milton Hill* ... TN-4
**Milton Hill**—*pop pl* ... MA-1
Milton Hill—*summit* ... MA-1
Milton Hill—*summit* ... OR-9
*Milton Hill Dam* ... TN-4
Milton Hist Dist—*hist pl* ... DE-2
Milton Hist Dist—*hist pl* ... FL-3
Milton Hist Dist—*hist pl* ... NC-3
Milton Hist Dist—*hist pl* ... PA-2
Milton (historical)—*locale* ... AL-4
Milton (historical)—*locale* ... KS-7
*Milton Hollow* ... AL-4
Milton Hollow—*valley* ... TN-4
Milton HS—*school* ... FL-3
*Milton J Brecht Elem Sch* ... PA-2
Milton JHS—*school* ... DE-2
Milton JHS—*school* ... MI-6
**Milton Junction**—*pop pl* ... WI-6
Milton Junction—*uninc pl* ... WI-6
Milton Lake—*lake* ... AK-9
Milton Lake—*reservoir* ... NJ-2
Milton Lake Dam—*dam* ... NJ-2
Milton Lake Park—*park* ... NJ-2
Milton Lawn Memorial Park—*cemetery* ... WI-6
Milton Littman Memorial Bridge—*bridge* ... FL-3
*Milton Lower Mills* ... MA-1
Milton Masonic Lodge and County General Store—*hist pl* ... KY-4
Milton Memorial Cem—*cemetery* ... ND-7
**Milton Mills**—*pop pl* ... NH-1
Milton Mills Cem—*cemetery* ... NH-1
*Milton Mills Village* ... MA-1
Milton Mine—*hist pl* ... AZ-5
Milton Mtn—*summit* ... ME-1
Milton Mtn—*summit* ... WA-9
Milton Olive Sch—*school* ... NY-2
Milton-Otto Field (airport)—*airport* ... AL-4
Milton Park—*park* ... OR-9
**Milton (Phoenix)**—*pop pl* ... PA-2
*Milton Poadpis* ... MA-1
Milton Point—*cape* (2) ... NY-2
*Milton Pond* ... DE-2
Milton Pond—*lake* ... CT-1
Milton Pond—*lake* ... ME-1
Milton Pond—*lake* ... NH-1
Milton Pond—*lake* ... VT-1
Milton Ranch—*locale* ... NV-8
Milton Ranch—*locale* ... WY-8
Milton Ray Tank—*reservoir* ... AZ-5
*Milton Reservoir* ... OH-6
Milton Ridge—*ridge* ... NH-1
*Milton River* ... CT-1
*Milton River* ... MA-1
Milton (RR name for Milton Center)—*other* ... OH-6
Milton Rsvr—*reservoir* ... CA-9
Milton Rsvr—*reservoir* ... CO-8
Milton R Young Powerplant—*locale* ... ND-7
**Miltonsburg**—*pop pl* ... OH-6
Miltonsburg Cem—*cemetery* ... OH-6
Milton Sch—*school* ... MO-7
Milton Sch—*school* ... NJ-2
Milton Sch—*school* ... OH-6
Milton Sch—*school* ... TX-5
Milton Schaeffers Lake—*reservoir* ... TN-4
Milton Schaeffers Lake Dam—*dam* ... TN-4
Miltons Island—*island* ... LA-4
Milton Spring—*spring* ... AL-4
Milton Spring—*spring* ... NV-8
Milton Square (Shop Ctr)—*locale* ... FL-3
Milton State Bank—*hist pl* ... NC-3
Milton Stateline Sch—*school* ... OR-9
Milton State Park—*park* ... PA-2
**Milton Station**—*pop pl* ... IN-6
Milton Store—*locale* ... NE-7
*Milton Stream* ... CT-1
Milton Substation—*locale* ... OR-9
Milton Town House—*hist pl* ... NH-1
**Milton (Town of)**—*pop pl* ... MA-1
**Milton (Town of)**—*pop pl* ... NH-1
**Milton (Town of)**—*pop pl* ... NY-2
**Milton (Town of)**—*pop pl* ... VT-1
**Milton (Town of)**—*pop pl* (2) ... WI-6
**Milton Township**—*pop pl* (2) ... KS-7
Milton (Township of)—*fmr MCD* ... NC-3
**Milton (Township of)**—*pop pl* ... IL-6
**Milton (Township of)**—*pop pl* ... IN-6
**Milton (Township of)**—*pop pl* (2) ... MI-6
**Milton (Township of)**—*pop pl* ... MN-6
**Milton (Township of)**—*pop pl* (5) ... OH-6
Milton (Township of)—*unorg* ... ME-1
Milton Trask Dam—*dam* ... SD-7
Milton (Unorganized Territory of)—*unorg* ... ME-1
**Milton Upper Mills (subdivision)**—*pop pl* ... MA-1
**Miltonvale**—*pop pl* ... KS-7
Miltonvale Cem—*cemetery* ... KS-7
Miltonvale Elem Sch—*school* ... KS-7
Miltonvale HS—*school* ... KS-7
Milton Valley Cem—*cemetery* ... VA-3
**Milton Village (subdivision)**—*pop pl* ... MA-1
*Miltonville* ... KS-7
*Miltonville* ... MS-4
**Miltonville**—*pop pl* ... OH-6
Miltonville Cem—*cemetery* (2) ... OH-6
Milton Wright Cave—*cave* ... PA-2
Milu—*island* ... MP-9
Miluet Creek—*stream* ... AK-9
*Milu Island* ... MP-9
Milum Cem—*cemetery* ... AR-4
Milum Creek—*stream* ... WI-6
*Milu Pass* ... MP-9
Milu Pass—*channel* ... MP-9
Milur—*bay* ... FM-9
Miluveach River—*stream* ... AK-9
Milvid—*locale* ... TX-5
*Milward* ... MA-1
*Milwaukee* ... MO-7
*Milwaukee* ... OR-9
**Milwaukee**—*pop pl* ... NC-3
**Milwaukee**—*pop pl* ... PA-2
**Milwaukee**—*pop pl* ... WI-6
Milwaukee Ave Hist Dist—*hist pl* ... MN-6
Milwaukee Bay—*bay* (2) ... WI-6
Milwaukee Childrens Hosp—*hospital* ... WI-6
Milwaukee City Hall—*hist pl* ... WI-6
Milwaukee Coast Guard Base—*military* ... WI-6
Milwaukee Coulee—*valley* ... MT-8
Milwaukee Country Club—*other* ... WI-6
**Milwaukee (County)**—*pop pl* ... WI-6
Milwaukee County Courthouse—*hist pl* ... WI-6
Milwaukee County Dispensary and Emergency Hosp—*hist pl* ... WI-6
Milwaukee County Historical Center—*hist pl* ... WI-6
Milwaukee County Institutes—*other* ... WI-6
Milwaukee Creek—*stream* ... MI-6
Milwaukee Creek—*stream* ... NY-2
Milwaukee Depot—*hist pl* ... MT-8
Milwaukee Downer Coll—*school* ... WI-6
Milwaukee-Downer "Quad"—*hist pl* ... WI-6
Milwaukee Fire Department High Pressure Pumping Station—*hist pl* ... WI-6
Milwaukee Hill—*summit* ... CO-8
Milwaukee (historical)—*locale* ... KS-7
Milwaukee Hosp—*hospital* ... WI-6
*Milwaukee Junction* ... MI-6
**Milwaukee Junction**—*pop pl* ... WA-9
Milwaukee Junction (historical)—*locale* ... SD-7
Milwaukee Junior Acad—*school* ... WI-6
Milwaukee Lake—*lake* ... MI-6
Milwaukee Lake—*lake* ... SD-7
Milwaukee Lutheran HS—*school* ... WI-6
Milwaukee News Bldg and Milwaukee Abstract Association Bldg—*hist pl* ... WI-6
Milwaukee Normal School-Milwaukee Girls' Trade and Technical High School—*hist pl* ... WI-6
Milwaukee Pass—*gap* ... MT-8
Milwaukee Peak—*summit* ... CO-8
Milwaukee River—*stream* ... WI-6
Milwaukee Road Hist Dist—*hist pl* ... MT-8
Milwaukee Sch (historical)—*school* ... SD-7
Milwaukee (Town of)—*other* ... WI-6
Milwaukee Waterway—*bay* ... WA-9
**Milwaukie**—*pop pl* ... OR-9
Milwaukie Cem—*cemetery* ... OR-9
**Milwaukie Heights**—*pop pl* ... OR-9
Milwaukie Plywood Corp. Log Pond—*reservoir* ... OR-9
Milwaukie Plywood Corp. Dam—*dam* ... OR-9
Milwaukie Sch—*school* ... OR-9
*Milwee Creek* ... AL-4
Milwee MS—*school* ... FL-3
*Milwood* ... MI-6
**Milwood**—*pop pl* ... MI-6
Milwood Sch—*school* ... MI-6
Milyard Slough—*gut* ... IL-6
Mima—*locale* ... KY-4
Mima—*locale* ... WA-9
Mima Branch—*stream* ... GA-3
Mima Creek—*stream* ... WA-9
*Mimaloose Island* ... OR-9
*Mimaloose Lake* ... OR-9
Mima Prairie—*flat* ... WA-9
Mimbreno Point—*cliff* ... AZ-5
Mimbres—*locale* (2) ... NM-5
Mimbres Canyon—*valley* ... NM-5
Mimbres (CCD)—*cens area* ... NM-5
Mimbres Hot Springs—*other* ... NM-5
Mimbres Lake—*lake* ... NM-5
Mimbres Memorial Hosp—*hospital* ... NM-5
Mimbres Mountains—*range* ... NM-5
Mimbres Peak—*summit* ... NM-5
Mimbres River—*stream* ... NM-5
Mimbres Sch—*hist pl* ... NM-5
Mimbres Tank—*reservoir* ... NM-5
Mimbroso, Arroyo—*valley* ... TX-5
Mimbs Ch—*church* ... GA-3
*Mim Cross Roads* ... AL-4
Mimes Branch—*stream* ... MS-4
Mimes Tank—*reservoir* ... NM-5
Mimi, Lake—*lake* ... NY-2
Mimi Lake—*lake* ... WI-6
*Mimina Reservoir* ... HI-9
*Mimina Stream* ... HI-9
Mimino Ditch—*canal* ... HI-9
Mimino Gulch—*valley* ... HI-9
Mimino Rsvr—*reservoir* ... HI-9
Mimino Stream—*stream* ... HI-9
Mimmossa Lake Dam—*dam* ... MS-4
*Mimms* ... MS-4
**Mimms**—*pop pl* ... MS-4
Mimms—*uninc pl* ... TN-4
Mimms Lake—*lake* ... AL-4
Mimms Well—*well* ... NM-5
Mimosa—*locale* ... TN-4
Mimosa, Lake—*reservoir* ... GA-3
Mimosa Cem—*cemetery* ... TN-4
Mimosa Cove—*locale* ... MD-2
Mimosa Creek—*stream* ... NM-5
**Mimosa Estates**—*pop pl* ... TN-4
Mimosa Hall—*hist pl* ... TX-5
Mimosa Hall Cem—*cemetery* ... TX-5
**Mimosa Heights**—*pop pl* ... TN-4
**Mimosa Lake**—*pop pl* ... NJ-2
Mimosa Lake—*reservoir* ... AL-4
Mimosa Lakes—*reservoir* ... NJ-2
**Mimosa Park**—*pop pl* ... LA-4
Mimosa Park Country Club—*other* ... AL-4
Mimosa Park Dam—*dam* ... AL-4
*Mimosa Park Lake* ... AL-4
**Mimosa Park (subdivision)**—*pop pl* ... NC-3
Mimosa-Pines Cem—*cemetery* ... LA-4
Mimosa Place Ch—*church* ... TX-5
Mimosa Ridge—*ridge* ... NM-5
Mimosa Sch—*hist pl* ... TN-4
Mimosa Sch (historical)—*school* ... TN-4
**Mimosa Shores**—*pop pl* ... NC-3
**Mims**—*pop pl* ... FL-3
**Mims**—*pop pl* ... MS-4
**Mims**—*pop pl* ... TX-5
Mims—*uninc pl* ... AL-4
Mims Acad—*school* ... SC-3
Mims Branch—*stream* (2) ... GA-3
Mims Branch—*stream* ... KY-4
Mims Branch—*stream* ... SC-3
Mims Cem—*cemetery* ... FL-3
Mims Cem—*cemetery* ... GA-3
Mims Chapel—*church* ... GA-3
Mims Chapel—*church* (2) ... TX-5
Mims Chapel Lookout Tower—*locale* ... TX-5
Mims Creek—*stream* ... AL-4
Mims Creek—*stream* ... GA-3
Mims Creek—*stream* (2) ... LA-4
Mims Creek—*stream* ... TX-5
Mims Crossroads (historical)—*locale* ... AL-4
Mims Elem Sch—*school* ... FL-3
Mims Ferry—*locale* ... AL-4
Mims Grove Ch—*church* ... SC-3
**Mims (historical)**—*pop pl* ... TN-4
Mims HS—*school* ... SC-3
Mimsh Wahia—*spring* ... AZ-5
Mims Island—*island* ... GA-3
*Mims Lake* ... TX-5
Mims Lake—*lake* ... NM-5
Mims Lake—*lake* ... SC-3
Mims Lake—*reservoir* ... OH-6
Mims Lake Dam—*dam* ... MS-4
Mims Memorial Ch—*church* ... TX-5
Mims Millpond—*lake* ... GA-3
*Mims Mine* ... TN-4
Mims Post Office (historical)—*building* ... TN-4
Mim Springs Ch—*church* ... LA-4
Mims Sch—*school* ... TX-5
Mims Sch (historical)—*school* ... AL-4
Mims Sch Number 2—*school* ... SC-3
Mims Sch Number 3—*school* ... SC-3
*Mims School* ... AL-4
Mimsville—*locale* ... GA-3
Mimulus Spring—*spring* ... CA-9
Mina—*locale* ... CA-9
Mina—*locale* ... KY-4
Mina—*locale* ... OH-6
Mina—*locale* ... PA-2
**Mina**—*pop pl* ... NV-8
**Mina**—*pop pl* ... NY-2
**Mina**—*pop pl* ... SD-7
Mina—*uninc pl* ... GA-3
Mina, Lake—*lake* ... MN-6
Mina Airp—*airport* ... NV-8
*Mina Bay* ... TX-5
Mina Cem—*cemetery* ... NV-8
Mina Cem—*cemetery* ... NY-2
Minachage—*gap* ... MH-9
Mina Chapel—*church* ... OH-6
*Mina Colorado* ... AZ-5
Mina Creek—*stream* ... AK-9
Mina Creek—*stream* ... OR-9
Mina Dam—*dam* ... SD-7
Mina de Terra Mine—*mine* ... NM-5
Min'aeg—*cape* ... FM-9
*Min'ag* ... FM-9
Minahan Stadium—*other* ... WI-6
Mina Hill—*summit* ... PA-2
Minaker Island—*island* (2) ... OR-9
Minakokosa, Lake—*lake* ... AK-9
Minakwa Country Club—*other* ... MN-6
Mina Lake—*lake* (2) ... MN-6
Minaloosa Valley—*valley* ... ID-8
**Minam**—*pop pl* ... OR-9
Minam Falls—*falls* ... OR-9
Minam Hill—*summit* ... OR-9
*Minami* ... FM-9
*Minami* ... MH-9
*Minami* ... MP-9
*Minami-Kaku* ... MP-9
*Minami Misaki* ... FM-9
Mina Mine—*mine* ... MT-8
Mina Mine—*mine* ... NV-8
*Minami-Shima* ... FM-9
*Minami Suido* ... FM-9
*Minami-suido* ... MP-9
Minam Lake—*lake* ... OR-9
Minam Lake Dam—*dam* ... OR-9
Minam Lodge—*locale* ... OR-9
Minam Lodge Airstrip—*airport* ... OR-9
*Minamoto Jima* ... FM-9
Minam Peak—*summit* ... OR-9
Minam River—*stream* ... OR-9
*Minamshu Cove* ... MA-1
Minam State Rec Area—*park* ... OR-9
Minam Summit—*summit* ... OR-9
*Minandeo School* ... PA-2
*Minani Jima* ... FM-9
*Minani Suido* ... FM-9
Minaogut Lake—*lake* ... AK-9
*Minard* ... MI-6
**Minard**—*pop pl* ... MI-6
Minard Drain—*canal* ... MI-6
Minard Lake—*lake* ... MI-6
Minard Lake—*lake* ... MN-6
*Minard Mills* ... MI-6
Minard Run—*stream* ... PA-2
Minard Run Sch—*school* ... PA-2
Minard Sch—*school* ... MI-6
Minard Sch—*school* ... NY-2
Minards Mill—*locale* ... MI-6
Minards Pond—*lake* ... VT-1
Mina Rec Area—*park* ... SD-7
*Minaret Bridge* ... UT-8
Minaret Creek—*stream* ... CA-9
Minaret Falls—*falls* ... CA-9
Minaret Falls Campground—*locale* ... CA-9
*Minaret Lake* ... CA-9
Minaret Lake—*lake* ... CA-9
*Minaret Meadow* ... CA-9
Minaret Mine—*mine* ... CA-9
Minaret Peak—*summit* ... MT-8
Minaret Ranger Station—*locale* ... CA-9
Minarets—*summit* ... CA-9
Minaret Summit—*summit* ... CA-9
Mina Sauk Falls—*falls* ... MO-7
*minas Bay* ... TX-5
Minas del Chupadero—*summit* ... NM-5
Mina Tank—*reservoir* ... NM-5
**Minatare**—*pop pl* ... NE-7
Minatare, Lake—*reservoir* ... NE-7
Minatare Canal—*canal* ... NE-7
Minatare Drain—*stream* ... NE-7
*Minatare Reservoir* ... NE-7
Minato Bashi—*bridge* ... PW-9
**Mina (Town of)**—*pop pl* ... NY-2
Mina Township—*inact MCD* ... NV-8
Minatra Cem—*cemetery* ... TN-4
Minausin, Lake—*reservoir* ... PA-2
*Minaville* ... MO-7
**Minaville**—*pop pl* ... MO-7
**Minaville**—*pop pl* ... NY-2
**Minawa Beach**—*pop pl* ... WI-6
**Minburn**—*pop pl* ... IA-7
Mince Branch—*stream* ... NC-3
Mince Cove—*valley* ... NC-3
Mincey Canyon—*valley* ... CA-9
Mincey Cem—*cemetery* ... TN-4
Minch Ditch—*canal* ... IN-6
*Minchel* ... IN-6
Minchey Cem—*cemetery* ... TN-4
Minchin—*locale* ... TX-5
*Minch Lake* ... MI-6
Minch Sch—*school* ... IL-6
Minchumina, Lake—*lake* ... AK-9
Mincke Hollow—*valley* ... MO-7
Minckler Cem—*cemetery* ... WI-6
Minckler Mine—*mine* ... MI-6
Mincks-Adams Hotel—*hist pl* ... OK-5
Mincle Mtn—*summit* ... GA-3
**Minco**—*pop pl* ... OK-5
Minco (CCD)—*cens area* ... OK-5
Mincoff Ranch—*locale* ... MT-8
**Mincoka**—*pop pl* ... AL-4
**Mincoll**—*pop pl* ... FL-3
**Minco Township**—*pop pl* ... ND-7
Mincy—*locale* ... MO-7
Mincy Branch—*stream* ... FL-3
Mincy Cem—*cemetery* ... MO-7
Mincy Creek—*stream* ... MO-7
Mincy Full Gospel Ch—*church* ... MO-7
Mincy Public Hunting Area—*locale* ... MO-7
Mincy Wildlife Area—*park* ... MO-7
Mindack Creek—*stream* ... MI-6
Mindack Lake—*lake* ... MI-6
Mindale—*locale* ... IL-6
Mindalina Island—*island* ... AK-9
Mindego Creek—*stream* ... CA-9
Mindego Hill—*summit* ... CA-9
Mindego Lake—*lake* ... CA-9
Mindeman—*locale* ... CO-8
**Mindeman (Helmick)**—*pop pl* ... OK-5
*Minden* ... MO-7
*Minden* ... SD-7
*Minden* ... VT-1
**Minden**—*pop pl* ... IA-7
**Minden**—*pop pl* ... LA-4
**Minden**—*pop pl* ... NE-7
**Minden**—*pop pl* ... NV-8
**Minden**—*pop pl* ... TX-5
**Minden**—*pop pl* ... WV-2
Minden Butter Manufacturing Company—*hist pl* ... NV-8
**Minden City**—*pop pl* ... MI-6
Minden City Cem—*cemetery* ... MI-6
Minden City State Game Area—*park* ... MI-6
*Minden Creek* ... TX-5
Minden Creek—*stream* ... TX-5
Minden Elementary and HS—*school* ... TX-5
Minden Flour Milling Company—*hist pl* ... NV-8
Minden (historical)—*locale* ... AL-4
Minden Inn—*hist pl* ... NV-8
**Mindenmines**—*pop pl* ... MO-7
Mindenmines Cem—*cemetery* ... MO-7
*Minden P.O.* ... AL-4
Minden Prairie Cem—*cemetery* ... NE-7
**Minden (Town of)**—*pop pl* ... NY-2
Minden Township—*fmr MCD* ... IA-7
**Minden (Township of)**—*pop pl* ... MI-6
**Minden (Township of)**—*pop pl* ... MN-6
**Mindenville**—*pop pl* ... NY-2
Minden Wool Warehouse—*hist pl* ... NV-8
**Mindoro**—*pop pl* ... WI-6
Mindowaskin Park—*park* ... NJ-2
Mine a Breton Creek—*stream* ... MO-7
Minear Cem—*cemetery* (2) ... OH-6
Minear Creek—*stream* ... ID-8
Minear Lake—*lake* ... IL-6
Minear Run—*stream* ... WV-2
Mineau, Francis, House—*hist pl* ... WA-9
Mine Bank Creek—*stream* ... VA-3
Minebank Ford—*locale* ... VA-3
Mine Bank Mtn—*summit* ... VA-3
Mine Bank Ridge—*ridge* ... PA-2
Minebank Run—*stream* ... MD-2
Minebank Schoolhouse (historical)—*school* ... PA-2
Mine Branch—*stream* ... AL-4
Mine Branch—*stream* ... GA-3
Mine Branch—*stream* (2) ... KY-4
Mine Branch—*stream* ... MO-7
Mine Branch—*stream* (6) ... NC-3
Mine Branch—*stream* (3) ... TN-4
Mine Branch—*stream* (2) ... VA-3
*Mine Brook* ... MA-1
Mine Brook—*locale* ... NJ-2
Mine Brook—*stream* ... CT-1
Mine Brook—*stream* (4) ... MA-1
Mine Brook—*stream* (3) ... NJ-2
Mine Brook—*stream* (3) ... NY-2
Mineca Hollow—*valley* ... MO-7
Mine Camp—*locale* ... WY-8
Mine Camp Peak—*summit* ... UT-8
*Mine Canyon* ... WA-9
Mine Canyon—*valley* (3) ... AZ-5
Mine Canyon—*valley* (7) ... CA-9
Mine Canyon—*valley* ... CO-8
Mine Canyon—*valley* (4) ... ID-8
Mine Canyon—*valley* ... NV-8
Mine Canyon—*valley* (4) ... NM-5
Mine Canyon—*valley* ... TX-5
Mine Canyon—*valley* ... UT-8
Mine Canyon Spring—*spring* ... CA-9
Minechoag Brook—*stream* ... MA-1
Minechoag Mtn—*summit* ... MA-1
Minechoag Pond—*lake* ... MA-1
Minecke Draw—*valley* ... WY-8
**Mineco**—*pop pl* ... FL-3
Mineco RR Station—*locale* ... FL-3
Mine Coulee—*valley* ... MT-8
Mine Cove—*bay* ... MD-2
Mine Cove—*valley* ... TN-4
*Mine Creek* ... TN-4
Mine Creek—*bay* ... MD-2
Mine Creek—*stream* (2) ... AR-4
Mine Creek—*stream* (3) ... CA-9
Mine Creek—*stream* ... CO-8
Mine Creek—*stream* (2) ... ID-8
Mine Creek—*stream* ... KS-7
Mine Creek—*stream* ... LA-4
Mine Creek—*stream* ... MO-7
Mine Creek—*stream* ... MT-8
Mine Creek—*stream* (2) ... NC-3
Mine Creek—*stream* ... OK-5
Mine Creek—*stream* (3) ... OR-9
Mine Creek—*stream* ... SC-3
Mine Creek—*stream* ... TN-4
Mine Creek—*stream* (3) ... TX-5
Mine Creek—*stream* (2) ... WA-9
*Mine Creek Battlefield* ... KS-7
Mine Creek Battlefield Park—*park* ... KS-7
Mine Creek Bridge—*hist pl* ... KS-7
Mine Creek Ch—*church* ... NC-3
Mine Creek Ch—*church* ... SC-3
*Mine Creek Grove Spring* ... OR-9
Mine Creek (Township of)—*fmr MCD* ... AR-4
Mine del Candelario—*mine* ... NM-5
Mine Disaster Memorial—*park* ... WY-8
Mine Ditch—*canal* ... ID-8
Mined Land Wildlife Area—*park* ... KS-7
Mine Draw—*valley* ... UT-8
Mine Draw Spring—*spring* ... OR-9
Mine Dump Spring—*spring* ... ID-8
Mineef—*locale* ... FM-9
*Minef* ... FM-9
Minefield—*locale* ... MD-2
Mine Flat—*flat* ... TN-4
Minefork—*locale* ... KY-4
Mine Fork—*stream* ... NC-3
Mine Fork Branch—*stream* ... NC-3
Mine Fork Sch—*school* ... NC-3
Minefree Sch—*school* ... MO-7
Minegan Cem—*cemetery* ... OK-5
Mine Gap—*gap* ... NC-3
Mine Gap—*gap* ... PA-2
Mine Gap—*gap* ... VA-3
Mine Gap Run—*stream* ... PA-2
Minega Sch—*school* ... MI-6
Mine Gulch—*valley* ... CA-9
Mine Gulch—*valley* (2) ... CO-8
Mine Gulch—*valley* ... ID-8
Mine Gulch—*valley* ... MT-8
Mine Gulch Camp—*locale* ... CA-9
Minehaha, Lake—*lake* ... NC-3
Minehan Slough—*lake* ... ND-7
Mine Harbor—*bay* ... AK-9
Minehart Dam—*dam* ... PA-2
Minehart Rsvr—*reservoir* ... PA-2
Minehart Run—*stream* ... PA-2
*Minehead* ... VT-1
Minehead (railroad station)—*locale* ... FL-3
**Mine Hill**—*pop pl* ... NJ-2
Mine Hill—*ridge* ... CA-9
Mine Hill—*summit* ... AR-4
Mine Hill—*summit* (2) ... CA-9
Mine Hill—*summit* ... CT-1
Mine Hill—*summit* (2) ... MA-1
Mine Hill—*summit* (2) ... NH-1
Mine Hill—*summit* (2) ... NY-2
Mine Hill—*summit* ... NC-3
Mine Hill—*summit* (2) ... PA-2
Mine Hill—*summit* ... WY-8
Mine Hill Reservoir Dam—*dam* ... NJ-2
Mine Hill Rsvr—*reservoir* ... NJ-2
Mine Hills—*range* ... MO-7
Mine Hills—*range* ... WY-8
**Mine Hill (Township of)**—*pop pl* ... NJ-2
Minehole Gap—*gap* ... NC-3
Mine Hole Ridge—*ridge* ... TN-4
Mine Hole Run—*stream* ... PA-2
Mine Hollow—*valley* (3) ... AR-4
Mine Hollow—*valley* (2) ... ID-8
Mine Hollow—*valley* (4) ... MO-7
Mine Hollow—*valley* (3) ... NY-2
Mine Hollow—*valley* ... NC-3
Mine Hollow—*valley* ... OH-6
Mine Hollow—*valley* ... TN-4
Mine Hollow—*valley* ... TX-5
Mine Hollow—*valley* (6) ... UT-8
Mine Hollow—*valley* ... VA-3
Mine Hollow—*valley* ... WV-2
Mine House Spring—*spring* ... NM-5
*Minei'* ... FM-9
Mine Island—*island* ... MD-2
**Mine Junction**—*pop pl* ... CO-8
Mine Kill—*stream* ... NY-2
Mine Kill Falls—*falls* ... NY-2
Mine Knob—*summit* ... NC-3
Mine Lake—*lake* ... MN-6
Mine Lake—*lake* ... MT-8
Mine Lake—*lake* ... NY-2
Mine Lake—*lake* ... TX-5
Mine LaMotte—*mine* ... MO-7
**Mine La Motte**—*pop pl* ... MO-7
Mine La Motte Cem—*cemetery* ... MO-7
Mine La Motte Ch—*church* ... MO-7
Mine La Motte Lake—*reservoir* ... MO-7
Mine La Motte Township—*civil* ... MO-7
Mine Ledge—*bench* (2) ... NH-1
Mine Lick Baptist Ch (historical)—*church* ... TN-4
Mine Lick Creek—*stream* ... TN-4
Mine Lot Falls—*falls* ... NY-2
**Mine Mountain Estates (subdivision)**—*pop pl* ... NC-3
Mine Mountain Junction—*locale* ... NV-8
Mine Mountain Spring—*spring* ... AZ-5
Mine Mtn—*summit* ... AK-9
Mine Mtn—*summit* ... AZ-5
Mine Mtn—*summit* ... CA-9
Mine Mtn—*summit* (3) ... CT-1
Mine Mtn—*summit* ... GA-3
Mine Mtn—*summit* (2) ... NV-8
Mine Mtn—*summit* ... NJ-2
Mine Mtn—*summit* ... NY-2
Mine Mtn—*summit* (4) ... NC-3
Mine Mtn—*summit* ... TX-5
Mine Mtn—*summit* ... VA-3
Mine Notch—*gap* ... ME-1
*Mine No. 1* ... IL-6
Mine No 10—*mine* ... MO-7
Mine No 17—*mine* ... NM-5
Mine No 21—*mine* ... OK-5
Mine No 24—*mine* ... NM-5
Mine No 25—*mine* ... MO-7
*Minens Gulch* ... UT-8
Mine Number Six-Pond Six Dam—*dam* ... PA-2
Mine Number Sixty-Pond Five Dam—*dam* ... PA-2
Mine Number Sixty Rsvr—*reservoir* ... PA-2
**Mine Number 36**—*pop pl* ... PA-2
**Mine Number 42**—*pop pl* ... PA-2
Mine Number 8—*mine* ... PA-2
*Mineola* ... KS-7
*Mineola* ... NC-3
Mineola—*locale* ... AL-4
Mineola—*locale* ... AR-4
Mineola—*locale* ... GA-3
**Mineola**—*pop pl* ... IA-7
**Mineola**—*pop pl* ... MO-7
**Mineola**—*pop pl* ... NY-2
**Mineola**—*pop pl* ... NC-3
**Mineola**—*pop pl* ... TX-5
Mineola, Lake—*lake* ... PA-2
Mineola Bay—*bay* ... IL-6
Mineola (CCD)—*cens area* ... TX-5
Mineola Cem—*cemetery* ... AL-4
Mineola Ch—*church* ... AL-4
Mineola Club Lake—*reservoir* ... TX-5
Mineola Hotel—*hist pl* ... IL-6
Mineola Hunting Camp—*locale* ... ME-1
*Mineola Mountain* ... NH-1
Mineola Rec Area—*park* ... TX-5
Mineola State Wildlife Area—*park* ... MO-7
*Mineold* ... GA-3
Mineota Ditch—*canal* ... CO-8
Mine Peak—*summit* ... MT-8
*Mine Pit Hill* ... MA-1
Mine Point—*cape* ... MI-6
Mine Point Mesa—*summit* ... TX-5
*Mine Pond* ... MA-1
Mine Pond—*lake* ... IN-6
Mine Pond—*lake* ... ME-1
Miner—*locale* ... MT-8
**Miner**—*pop pl* ... IA-7
**Miner**—*pop pl* ... MO-7
**Miner**—*pop pl* ... WI-6
Miner, Mount—*summit* ... NH-1
Miner, Samuel, House—*hist pl* ... CT-1
Miner, Selden, House—*hist pl* ... MI-6
Minera—*locale* ... TX-5
*Mineral* ... KS-7
Mineral—*locale* ... AR-4
Mineral—*locale* ... NV-8
Mineral—*locale* ... OH-6
Mineral—*locale* ... OR-9
**Mineral**—*pop pl* ... CA-9
**Mineral**—*pop pl* ... ID-8
**Mineral**—*pop pl* ... IL-6
**Mineral**—*pop pl* ... IN-6
**Mineral**—*pop pl* ... TX-5
**Mineral**—*pop pl* ... VA-3
**Mineral**—*pop pl* ... WA-9
Mineral, Mount—*summit* ... MA-1
Mineral Area Hosp—*hospital* ... MO-7
Mineral Basin—*basin* (2) ... CO-8
Mineral Basin—*basin* ... UT-8
Mineral Bayou—*stream* ... OK-5
**Mineral Bluff**—*pop pl* ... GA-3
Mineral Bluff (CCD)—*cens area* ... GA-3
Mineral Bluff House of Prayer—*church* ... GA-3
*Mineral Bottom* ... UT-8
Mineral Bottom—*bend* ... UT-8
Mineral Branch—*gut* ... FL-3
Mineral Branch—*stream* ... AL-4
Mineral Branch—*stream* ... GA-3
Mineral Branch—*stream* ... IA-7
Mineral Branch—*stream* ... LA-4
Mineral Branch—*stream* ... MS-4
Mineral Branch—*stream* ... MO-7
Mineral Branch—*stream* ... TX-5
Mineral Brook—*stream* ... VT-1
Mineral Butte—*summit* ... AZ-5
Mineral Butte—*summit* ... WA-9
Mineral Buttes—*summit* ... NV-8
Mineral Canyon—*valley* ... AZ-5
Mineral Canyon—*valley* ... NV-8
Mineral Canyon—*valley* ... OR-9
Mineral Canyon—*valley* (2) ... UT-8
Mineral (CCD)—*cens area* ... WA-9
Mineral Cem—*cemetery* ... TX-5
Mineral Center—*locale* ... MN-6
Mineral Ch—*church* ... WV-2
*Mineral City* ... AZ-5
*Mineral City* ... FL-3
**Mineral City**—*pop pl* ... IN-6
**Mineral City**—*pop pl* ... MO-7
**Mineral City**—*pop pl* ... OH-6
**Mineral City**—*pop pl* ... WV-2
Mineral City ( Site)—*locale* ... WA-9
Mineral County—*civil* ... NV-8
**Mineral (County)**—*pop pl* ... WV-2
Mineral County Courthouse—*hist pl* ... NV-8
Mineral County HS—*school* ... NV-8
*Mineral Creek* ... AZ-5
*Mineral Creek* ... TX-5
*Mineral Creek* ... WA-9
**Mineral Creek**—*pop pl* ... AZ-5
Mineral Creek—*stream* (3) ... AK-9
Mineral Creek—*stream* (5) ... AZ-5
Mineral Creek—*stream* ... CA-9
Mineral Creek—*stream* (5) ... CO-8
Mineral Creek—*stream* (5) ... ID-8
Mineral Creek—*stream* ... IL-6
Mineral Creek—*stream* (2) ... IA-7
Mineral Creek—*stream* ... MS-4
Mineral Creek—*stream* ... MO-7
Mineral Creek—*stream* (2) ... MT-8
Mineral Creek—*stream* (3) ... NM-5
Mineral Creek—*stream* ... NC-3
Mineral Creek—*stream* ... ND-7
Mineral Creek—*stream* (4) ... OR-9
Mineral Creek—*stream* ... SC-3
Mineral Creek—*stream* (2) ... TX-5
Mineral Creek—*stream* ... UT-8
Mineral Creek—*stream* (7) ... WA-9
Mineral Creek—*stream* ... WI-6
Mineral Creek Arch Dam—*dam* ... AZ-5
Mineral Creek Bridge—*hist pl* ... AZ-5
Mineral Creek Cem—*cemetery* ... MO-7
Mineral Creek Dam Tank—*reservoir* ... AZ-5
Mineral Creek Diversion Dam—*dam* ... AZ-5
Mineral Creek Glacier—*glacier* ... AK-9
Mineral Creek Islands—*island* ... AK-9
Mineral Creek Trail—*trail* ... MT-8
Mineral Creek Trail—*trail* ... NM-5
Mineral Creek Well—*well* ... NM-5
Mineral Ditch—*canal* ... AZ-5
*Mineral Draw* ... AZ-5
Mineral Farm—*locale* ... CO-8

Mineral Farms Canyon—*valley* NM-5
Mineral Feeder Pond—*reservoir* FL-3
Mineral Flat—*flat* UT-8
Mineral Flat Tunnels—*mine* UT-8
Mineral Fork—*stream* MO-7
Mineral Fork—*stream* UT-8
*Mineral Gap* NC-3
*Mineral Gap* TN-4
Mineral Gap—*gap* NC-3
Mineral Gap—*gap* TN-4
Mineral Gap Branch—*stream* NC-3
Mineral Gas Field—*oilfield* TX-5
Mineral Gulch—*valley* ID-8
Mineral Gulch—*valley* UT-8
Mineral Hall—*hist pl* MO-7
**Mineral Heights**—*pop pl* TX-5
Mineral Heights—*uninc pl* OK-5
*Mineral Hill* MA-1
Mineral Hill—*island* KY-4
Mineral Hill—*locale* NM-5
Mineral Hill—*summit* AK-9
Mineral Hill—*summit* (2) AZ-5
Mineral Hill—*summit* AR-4
Mineral Hill—*summit* (2) CA-9
Mineral Hill—*summit* (2) CO-8
Mineral Hill—*summit* (2) ID-8
Mineral Hill—*summit* (2) MO-7
Mineral Hill—*summit* (3) MT-8
Mineral Hill—*summit* NV-8
Mineral Hill—*summit* NM-5
Mineral Hill—*summit* OR-9
Mineral Hill—*summit* UT-8
Mineral Hill—*summit* WA-9
Mineral Hill—*summit* WY-8
Mineral Hill Ch—*church* VA-3
Mineral Hill Fork—*stream* OR-9
Mineral Hill Mine—*mine* AZ-5
Mineral Hill Mine—*mine* CO-8
Mineral Hill Mine—*mine* ID-8
Mineral Hill Mines—*mine* AZ-5
**Mineral Hills**—*pop pl* MI-6
Mineral Hills—*summit* MA-1
Mineral Hill Tank—*reservoir* AZ-5
**Mineral (historical)**—*pop pl* OR-9
Mineral Hollow—*valley* AR-4
Mineral Hollow—*valley* MO-7
Mineral Hollow—*valley* TN-4
**Mineral Hot Springs**—*pop pl* CO-8
**Mineralking**—*pop pl* CA-9
Mineral King Game Ref—*park* CA-9
Mineral King Guard Station—*locale* CA-9
Mineral Lake—*lake* AK-9
Mineral Lake—*lake* AZ-5
Mineral Lake—*lake* KS-7
Mineral Lake—*lake* MN-6
Mineral Lake—*lake* WA-9
Mineral Lake—*lake* WI-6
Mineral Lake—*reservoir* MO-7
Mineral Lake Lookout Tower—*locale* WI-6
Mineral Lakes—*lake* CA-9
Mineral Log Lodge—*hist pl* WA-9
Mineral (Magisterial District)—*fmr MCD* VA-3
Mineral Marsh Ditch—*canal* IL-6
Mineral Mountain Creek—*stream* MT-8
Mineral Mountain Mine—*mine* ID-8
Mineral Mountain Mine—*mine* NM-5
Mineral Mountain Mine (Inactive)—*mine* NM-5
*Mineral Mtn* WA-9
Mineral Mtn—*summit* AK-9
Mineral Mtn—*summit* AZ-5
Mineral Mtn—*summit* (2) CA-9
Mineral Mtn—*summit* (2) CO-8
Mineral Mtn—*summit* (2) ID-8
Mineral Mtn—*summit* (3) MT-8
Mineral Mtn—*summit* (2) UT-8
Mineral Mtn—*summit* (3) WA-9
Mineral Mtn—*summit* WY-8
Mineral Mtns—*range* UT-8
Mineral Number 14 Sch—*school* PA-2
Mineral Palace Park—*park* CO-8
Mineral Park—*flat* (2) CO-8
Mineral Park—*locale* (2) AZ-5
**Mineral Park**—*pop pl* TN-4
Mineral Park Campground—*locale* WA-9
Mineral Park Cem—*cemetery* AZ-5
Mineral Park Chapel—*church* TN-4
Mineral Park Mine—*mine* CO-8
Mineral Park Municipal Golf Course—*other* AL-4
Mineral Park Post Office (historical)—*building* TN-4
Mineral Pasture—*flat* TX-5
*Mineral Peak* NV-8
Mineral Peak—*summit* AZ-5
Mineral Peak—*summit* CA-9
Mineral Peak—*summit* MT-8
Mineral Peak—*summit* NV-8
Mineral Point—*cape* AK-9
Mineral Point—*cape* ID-8
Mineral Point—*cape* UT-8
Mineral Point—*cliff* CO-8
Mineral Point—*locale* CO-8
Mineral Point—*locale* WI-6
**Mineral Point**—*pop pl* MO-7
**Mineral Point**—*pop pl* PA-2
**Mineral Point**—*pop pl* WI-6
Mineral Point—*ridge* CA-9
Mineral Point—*ridge* UT-8
Mineral Point—*summit* (2) CO-8
Mineral Point—*summit* NV-8
Mineral Point Branch—*stream* WI-6
Mineral Point Ch—*church* MO-7
Mineral Point Hill—*hist pl* WI-6
Mineral Point Hist Dist—*hist pl* WI-6
Mineral Point (historical)—*locale* KS-7
*Mineral Point School* MO-7
Mineral Point School (historical)—*locale* MO-7
**Mineral Point (Town of)**—*pop pl* WI-6
Mineral Range—*range* CA-9
*Mineral Ridge* IA-7
Mineral Ridge—*locale* IA-7
**Mineral Ridge**—*pop pl* OH-6
Mineral Ridge—*ridge* (2) MT-8
Mineral Ridge—*ridge* NV-8
Mineral Ridge—*ridge* (2) VA-3
Mineral Ridge—*ridge* WA-9
Mineral Ridge Cem—*cemetery* IA-7
*Mineral River* MI-6
Mineral River—*stream* MI-6
Mineral Run—*stream* PA-2
Mineral Sch—*school* CA-9
Mineral Siding—*locale* OH-6
Mineral Slide—*locale* CA-9
*Mineral Spring* PA-2
Mineral Spring—*locale* MD-2
Mineral Spring—*locale* PA-2
**Mineral Spring**—*pop pl* MO-7
**Mineral Spring**—*pop pl* PA-2
Mineral Spring—*spring* AK-9
Mineral Spring—*spring* AZ-5
Mineral Spring—*spring* (2) CA-9
Mineral Spring—*spring* GA-3
Mineral Spring—*spring* MS-4
Mineral Spring—*spring* MO-7
Mineral Spring—*spring* ND-7
Mineral Spring—*spring* (2) OR-9
Mineral Spring—*spring* TN-4
Mineral Spring—*spring* (2) UT-8
Mineral Spring—*spring* (2) WA-9
*Mineral Spring Branch* GA-3
*Mineral Spring Branch* MS-4
Mineral Spring Branch—*stream* (2) GA-3
Mineral Spring Branch—*stream* LA-4
Mineral Spring Branch—*stream* (2) SC-3
Mineral Spring Brook—*stream* CT-1
Mineral Spring Brook—*stream* (2) NY-2
Mineral Spring Brook—*stream* VT-1
Mineral Spring Campground—*locale* UT-8
Mineral Spring Canyon—*valley* NV-8
Mineral Spring Canyon—*valley* NM-5
Mineral Spring Ch—*church* AL-4
Mineral Spring Ch—*church* KY-4
Mineral Spring Ch—*church* MO-7
Mineral Spring Ch—*church* NC-3
Mineral Spring Ch—*church* TN-4
Mineral Spring Creek—*stream* IL-6
**Mineral Spring (historical)**—*pop pl* NC-3
Mineral Spring Hollow—*valley* GA-3
Mineral Spring Park—*park* PA-2
Mineral Spring Pond—*reservoir* AL-4
Mineral Spring Ravine—*valley* CA-9
*Mineral Springs* AL-4
*Mineral Springs* OR-9
Mineral Springs—*locale* AR-4
Mineral Springs—*locale* KS-7
Mineral Springs—*locale* LA-4
Mineral Springs—*locale* OH-6
Mineral Springs—*locale* TN-4
**Mineral Springs**—*pop pl* (2) AL-4
**Mineral Springs**—*pop pl* AR-4
**Mineral Springs**—*pop pl* FL-3
**Mineral Springs**—*pop pl* IL-6
**Mineral Springs**—*pop pl* IN-6
**Mineral Springs**—*pop pl* MS-4
**Mineral Springs**—*pop pl* NY-2
**Mineral Springs**—*pop pl* (2) NC-3
**Mineral Springs**—*pop pl* (2) PA-2
**Mineral Springs**—*pop pl* TN-4
**Mineral Springs**—*pop pl* WV-2
Mineral Springs—*spring* AL-4
Mineral Springs—*spring* AK-9
Mineral Springs—*spring* AZ-5
Mineral Springs—*spring* (2) CA-9
Mineral Springs—*spring* GA-3
Mineral Springs—*spring* ID-8
Mineral Springs—*spring* IL-6
Mineral Springs—*spring* ND-7
Mineral Springs—*spring* OR-9
Mineral Springs—*spring* UT-8
Mineral Springs—*spring* WY-8
Mineral Springs Baptist Ch—*church* TN-4
*Mineral Springs Baptist Church* MS-4
Mineral Springs Branch—*stream* AL-4
Mineral Springs Branch—*stream* GA-3
Mineral Springs Branch—*stream* IA-7
Mineral Springs Branch—*stream* MS-4
Mineral Springs Branch—*stream* MO-7
Mineral Springs Branch—*stream* (2) TN-4
Mineral Springs Branch—*stream* VA-3
Mineral Springs Campground—*locale* WA-9
Mineral Springs (CCD)—*cens area* AL-4
Mineral Springs Cem—*cemetery* AR-4
Mineral Springs Cem—*cemetery* MS-4
Mineral Springs Ch—*church* (4) AL-4
Mineral Springs Ch—*church* (2) GA-3
Mineral Springs Ch—*church* LA-4
Mineral Springs Ch—*church* (2) MS-4
Mineral Springs Ch—*church* (3) NC-3
Mineral Springs Ch—*church* OK-5
Mineral Springs Ch—*church* TX-5
Mineral Springs Ch—*church* VA-3
Mineral Spring Sch—*school* AR-4
Mineral Spring Sch—*school* KY-4
Mineral Spring Sch (historical)—*school* PA-2
Mineral Springs Creek—*stream* GA-3
Mineral Springs Division—*civil* AL-4
*Mineral Springs Elem Sch* NC-3
Mineral Springs Elem Sch—*school* NC-3
Mineral Springs Elem Sch (historical)—*school* AL-4
Mineral Springs First Baptist Ch—*church* TN-4
Mineral Springs Ford—*locale* MO-7
Mineral Springs Gulch—*valley* CO-8
Mineral Springs Hollow—*valley* MO-7
Mineral Springs Mtn—*summit* NC-3
Mineral Springs Oil Field—*other* MI-6
Mineral Springs Park—*park* IL-6
Mineral Springs Park—*park* MN-6
Mineral Springs Park—*park* MS-4
Mineral Springs Park—*park* NC-3
**Mineral Springs Park**—*pop pl* SC-3
Mineral Springs Resort—*spring* WA-9
Mineral Springs Sanatorium—*hospital* MN-6
Mineral Springs Sch—*school* (2) NC-3
Mineral Springs Sch—*school* ND-7
Mineral Springs Sch—*school* WI-6
Mineral Springs Sch (historical)—*school* AL-4
Mineral Springs Sch (historical)—*school* (2) MS-4
**Mineral Springs Township**—*pop pl* ND-7
Mineral Springs (Township of)—*fmr MCD* AR-4
Mineral Springs (Township of)—*fmr MCD* NC-3
Mineral Springs (Watson)—*other* AL-4
Mineral Summit—*summit* CA-9
Mineral Tank—*reservoir* AZ-5
Mineral Township—*civil* (2) MO-7
**Mineral Township**—*pop pl* KS-7
Mineral (Township of)—*fmr MCD* AR-4
**Mineral (Township of)**—*pop pl* IL-6
**Mineral (Township of)**—*pop pl* PA-2
Mineral Valley—*stream* NV-8
Mineral Wash—*stream* AZ-5
Mineral Well Park—*hist pl* MI-6
*Mineral Wells* WV-2
**Mineral Wells**—*pop pl* MS-4
**Mineral Wells**—*pop pl* TX-5
**Mineralwells**—*pop pl* WV-2
Mineral Wells, Lake—*reservoir* TX-5
Mineral Wells Baptist Ch—*church* MS-4
Mineral Wells (CCD)—*cens area* TX-5
Mineralwells Ch—*church* WV-2
Mineral Wells Methodist Ch—*church* MS-4
Mineral Wonder Gulch—*valley* CO-8
Mineral Wonder Mine—*mine* OR-9
Mineral Yager Spring—*spring* MT-8
Miner Basin—*basin* CO-8
Miner Basin—*basin* OR-9
Miner Basin Creek—*stream* OR-9
Miner Branch—*stream* AL-4
Miner Brook—*stream* CT-1
Miner Brook—*stream* (2) ME-1
Miner Brook—*stream* MA-1
Miner Brook Bog—*swamp* ME-1
Miner Brothers Store—*hist pl* NE-7
Miner Canyon—*valley* ID-8
Miner Cem—*cemetery* AR-4
Miner Cem—*cemetery* (2) CT-1
Miner Cem—*cemetery* IN-6
Miner Cem—*cemetery* MI-6
Miner Cem—*cemetery* MO-7
**Miner City**—*pop pl* IN-6
Miner County—*civil* SD-7
Miner Cove—*bay* AK-9
*Miner Creek* WA-9
*Miner Creek* WY-8
Miner Creek—*stream* (2) AK-9
Miner Creek—*stream* (3) CA-9
Miner Creek—*stream* ID-8
Miner Creek—*stream* MI-6
Miner Creek—*stream* (4) MT-8
Miner Creek—*stream* (4) OR-9
Miner Creek—*stream* WA-9
Miner Creek—*stream* (2) WY-8
Miner Creek Trail—*trail* MT-8
*Minerd Lake* MN-6
Mine Rescue Station Bldg—*hist pl* OK-5
Miner Flat—*flat* AZ-5
Miner Gulch—*valley* CO-8
Miner Gulch—*valley* OR-9
*Miner Hill* VA-3
Miner Hill—*summit* AK-9
Miner Hill—*summit* NY-2
Miner Hill—*summit* UT-8
Miner (historical)—*locale* SD-7
Miner Hollow—*valley* AL-4
Miner Hollow—*valley* (2) KY-4
Miner House—*hist pl* NE-7
*Mine Ridge* WA-9
Mine Ridge—*ridge* NY-2
Mine Ridge—*ridge* (3) NC-3
Mine Ridge—*ridge* OR-9
Mine Ridge—*ridge* PA-2
Mine Ridge—*ridge* (2) TN-4
Mine Ridge—*ridge* WA-9
Mine Ridge Spring—*spring* OR-9
Miner Island—*island* AK-9
Miner JHS—*school* IL-6
Miner Lake—*lake* ID-8
Miner Lake—*lake* (2) MI-6
Miner Lake—*lake* MT-8
Miner Lake—*lake* WI-6
Miner Lake—*lake* WY-8
**Miner Lake**—*pop pl* MI-6
Miner Lake—*reservoir* NY-2
Miner Lake Sch—*school* MI-6
Miner Lake State Park—*park* NY-2
*Miner Mills* PA-2
Miner Mill Vly—*swamp* NY-2
Minero—*locale* NM-5
Mine Road Canyon—*valley* NM-5
Mine Road Ch—*church* VA-3
Mine Road Spring—*spring* AZ-5
Minero Canyon—*valley* CA-9
Miner Park—*flat* CO-8
Miner Park—*park* PA-2
*Miner Pass* CO-8
Miner Point Tank—*reservoir* NM-5
Miner Pond—*lake* CT-1
Miner Pond—*lake* OR-9
Miner Ranch—*locale* NE-7
Miner Ridge—*ridge* (2) CA-9
Miners Basin—*basin* OR-9
Miners Basin—*basin* UT-8
Miners Basin—*basin* WA-9
Miners Basin—*valley* UT-8
Miners Bay—*bay* AK-9
Miners Bay—*bay* CA-9
Miners Bend (historical)—*bend* SD-7
Miners Bowl—*basin* CA-9
Miners Branch—*stream* KY-4
Miners Butte—*summit* OR-9
Miners Cabin—*locale* OR-9
Miners Cabin Spring—*spring* CA-9
Miners Cabin Spring—*spring* OR-9
Miners Cabin Wash—*valley* UT-8
*Miners Canon* NV-8
Miners Canyon—*valley* AZ-5
Miners Canyon—*valley* CO-8
Miners Canyon—*valley* NV-8
Miners Canyon—*valley* (4) UT-8
Miners Canyon—*valley* WY-8
*Miners Castle* MI-6
Miners Castle Point—*cape* MI-6
Miners Cem—*cemetery* IL-6
Miner Sch—*school* CA-9
Miner Sch—*school* DC-2
Miner Sch—*school* IL-6
Miner Sch—*school* IN-6
Miner Sch—*school* MT-8
Miners Chapel Cem—*cemetery* IL-6
Miners Circle Cem—*cemetery* TN-4
Miners Corral—*locale* WA-9
Miners Coulee—*valley* (2) MT-8
Miners Cove—*bay* NV-8
Miners Cow Creek Ranch—*locale* NV-8
*Miners Creek* MT-8
*Miners Creek* WA-9
*Miners Creek* WY-8
Miners Creek—*stream* (3) CA-9
Miners Creek—*stream* (4) CO-8
Miners Creek—*stream* (2) ID-8
Miners Creek—*stream* IA-7
Miners Creek—*stream* (3) MT-8
Miners Creek—*stream* (3) OR-9
Miners Creek—*stream* (5) WA-9
Miners Creek Spring—*spring* ID-8
Miners Creek Trail—*trail* CO-8
Miners Creek Trail—*trail* WA-9
Miners Delight—*locale* WY-8
Miners Delight Creek—*stream* ID-8
Miners Delight Mine—*mine* WY-8
Miners Draw—*valley* CO-8
Miners Draw—*valley* OR-9
Miners Draw—*valley* UT-8
Miners Draw Waterhole—*reservoir* OR-9
Miners Falls—*falls* MI-6
*Miners Fork* OH-6
Miners Fork—*stream* MT-8
Miners Fork—*stream* OH-6
Miners Gold Mine—*mine* NV-8
*Miners Gulch* MT-8
*Miners Gulch* UT-8
Miners Gulch—*valley* AZ-5
Miners Gulch—*valley* (2) CA-9
Miners Gulch—*valley* CO-8
Miners Gulch—*valley* (5) MT-8
Miners Gulch—*valley* UT-8
Miners Gulch—*valley* WY-8
Miners Gulch Campground—*locale* UT-8
Miners Hill—*summit* NY-2
Miners Hill Rsvr—*reservoir* UT-8
Miners Hollow—*valley* UT-8
Miners Hosp—*hospital* IL-6
Miners Hosp—*hospital* NM-5
Miners Hosp—*hospital* PA-2
Miners Institute Bldg—*hist pl* IL-6
Miners Lake—*lake* AK-9
Miners Lake—*lake* MI-6
Miners Lake—*reservoir* CO-8
Miners Lakes—*lake* WA-9
Miner Slough—*stream* CA-9
Miners Memorial Cem—*cemetery* IL-6
**Miners Mills**—*pop pl* PA-2
Miners Mtn—*summit* UT-8
Miners Mtn—*summit* VA-3
Miners Needle—*summit* AZ-5
Miners Nose—*summit* CA-9
Miners Park—*flat* NM-5
*Miners Peak* CA-9
Miners Peak—*summit* CO-8
Miners Peak—*summit* ID-8
Miners Peak—*summit* UT-8
Miners Peak Trail—*trail* ID-8
Miners Point—*cape* AK-9
Miners Point—*cape* CA-9
Miner Spring—*spring* OR-9
Miners Ranch Canal—*canal* CA-9
Miners Ranch Rsvr—*reservoir* CA-9
Miners Ranch Tunnel—*tunnel* CA-9
*Miners Range* WA-9
Miners Ravine—*valley* CA-9
Miners Ridge—*ridge* CA-9
Miners Ridge—*ridge* (2) UT-8
Miners Ridge—*ridge* (3) WA-9
Miners Ridge Lookout—*hist pl* WA-9
Miners Ridge Trail—*trail* CA-9
Miners River—*stream* AK-9
Miners River—*stream* MI-6
Miners Run—*stream* PA-2
*Miners Run Creek* WA-9
Miners Run Creek—*stream* WA-9
Miners Shop Ctr—*locale* FL-3
*Miners Spring* AZ-5
Miners Spring—*spring* AZ-5
Miners Spring—*spring* NV-8
**Miners Spur**—*pop pl* MI-6
Miners Square—*park* CA-9
Miners Stairs—*other* UT-8
**Miners Store**—*pop pl* VA-3
Miners Summit—*summit* AZ-5
Miner's Supply Store—*hist pl* OH-6
Miners Tank—*reservoir* AZ-5
Miners Trail—*trail* AZ-5
Miner Street Bridge—*hist pl* CO-8
Miners Union Cem—*cemetery* ID-8
Miners Union Hall—*hist pl* MT-8
*Miners Village* PA-2
**Miners Village**—*pop pl* PA-2
*Minersville* WV-2
Minersville—*locale* NE-7
Minersville—*locale* PA-2
Minersville—*locale* TN-4
Minersville—*other* WV-2
**Minersville**—*pop pl* OH-6
**Minersville**—*pop pl* (2) PA-2
**Minersville**—*pop pl* UT-8
**Minersville**—*pop pl* WI-6
Minersville Borough—*civil* PA-2
Minersville Campground—*park* UT-8
Minersville Canal—*canal* UT-8
Minersville Cem—*cemetery* UT-8
Minersville Ch (historical)—*church* TN-4
Minersville City Hall—*hist pl* UT-8
*Minersville Dam* PA-2
Minersville Dam Number Four—*dam* PA-2
Minersville Hill Cem—*cemetery* OH-6
Minersville (historical)—*locale* KS-7
**Minersville (historical)**—*pop pl* OR-9
*Minersville Lake State Rec Area* UT-8
Minersville Reservation Recreation Site—*park* UT-8
*Minersville Reservoir* UT-8
Minersville Rsvr—*reservoir* PA-2
Minersville Rsvr—*reservoir* UT-8
Minersville Sch—*school* UT-8
Minersville State Park—*park* UT-8
*Minersville Water Companys Dam* PA-2
Miner Tank—*reservoir* (2) NM-5
Minerton—*locale* OH-6
Minerton Ch—*church* OH-6
**Miner Township**—*pop pl* SD-7
Miner Township (historical)—*civil* SD-7
Mine Run—*locale* VA-3
Mine Run—*stream* OH-6
Mine Run—*stream* (2) PA-2
Mine Run—*stream* (5) VA-3
Mine Run Branch—*stream* VA-3
Minerva—*locale* IA-7
Minerva—*locale* MN-6
Minerva—*locale* NV-8
Minerva—*locale* OR-9
Minerva—*locale* WV-2
**Minerva**—*pop pl* KY-4
**Minerva**—*pop pl* LA-4
**Minerva**—*pop pl* MS-4
**Minerva**—*pop pl* NY-2
**Minerva**—*pop pl* OH-6
**Minerva**—*pop pl* TX-5
Minerva Bar—*bar* CA-9
Minerva Bond Long-Lake Helen Elem Sch—*school* FL-3
Minerva Canyon—*valley* NV-8
Minerva Ch—*church* IA-7
Minerva Club of Santa Maria—*hist pl* CA-9
*Minerva Creek* IA-7
Minerva Creek—*stream* IA-7
Minerva Creek—*stream* MT-8
Minerva (historical)—*locale* KS-7
Minerva (historical P.O.)—*locale* IA-7
**Minerva Jct.**—*pop pl* IA-7
*Minerva Junction* OH-6
Minerva Junction—*locale* OH-6
Minerva Lake—*lake* MI-6
Minerva Lake—*lake* (2) MN-6
Minerva Lake—*lake* NY-2
Minerva Lake—*reservoir* WI-6
Minerva Lake Golf Club—*other* OH-6
Minerva Lusk Cem—*cemetery* TN-4
Minerva Memorial Ch—*church* AL-4
*Minerva Memorial Methodist Ch* AL-4
*Minerva Mill* NV-8
Minerva Mine—*mine* (2) ID-8
Minerva Mine—*mine* SD-7
Minerva Mine No 1—*mine* IL-6
Minerva Mtn—*summit* AK-9
**Minerva Park**—*pop pl* OH-6
Minerva Peak—*summit* ID-8
Minerva Peak—*summit* NV-8
**Minerva Plantation**—*pop pl* LA-4
Minerva Post Office (historical)—*building* MS-4
Minerva Ridge—*ridge* ID-8
Minerva-Rockdale Oil Field—*oilfield* TX-5
Minerva Stream—*stream* NY-2
Minerva Substation—*other* TX-5
**Minerva (Town of)**—*pop pl* NY-2
Minerva Township—*fmr MCD* IA-7
**Minerva (Township of)**—*pop pl* MN-6
Minerville—*locale* PA-2
Miner Well—*well* (3) NM-5
Mines—*mine* NM-5
Mine Safety Car 5—*hist pl* AK-9
Mines Branch—*stream* VA-3
Mines Canyon—*valley* ID-8
Mines Creek—*stream* NC-3
Mines Creek—*stream* VA-3
Mines Creek—*stream* WI-6
Minese Gap—*gap* NM-5
Minese Mesa—*summit* NM-5
Mine Shaft Mill—*locale* NM-5
Mine Shaft Saddle—*gap* CA-9
Mine Shaft Spring—*spring* AZ-5
Mineshaft Spring—*spring* (2) AZ-5
Mineshaft Well—*well* AZ-5
Mine Shaft Windmill—*locale* AZ-5
*Minesha Point Spring* AZ-5
Minesinger Cem—*cemetery* IL-6
Minesinger Creek—*stream* MT-8
Minesinger Ridge—*ridge* MT-8
**Minesite**—*pop pl* PA-2
Mines of Spain—*park* IA-7
Mines of Spain Area Rural Community Archeol District—*hist pl* IA-7
Mines of Spain Lead Mining Community Archeol District—*hist pl* IA-7
Mines of Spain Prehistoric District—*hist pl* IA-7
Mines of Spain State Park—*park* IA-7
Mine Spring—*spring* (2) AZ-5
Mine Spring—*spring* (2) NV-8
Mine Spring—*spring* (2) OR-9
Mine Spring—*spring* VA-3
Mine Spring—*spring* WY-8
Mine Spring Run—*stream* VA-3
Mines Run—*stream* VA-3
Mines Run Trail—*trail* VA-3
Mines Sch (historical)—*school* TN-4
Mine Swamp—*swamp* CT-1
Mines Windmill—*locale* (2) NM-5
Mine Tank—*reservoir* (7) AZ-5
Mine Tank—*reservoir* (3) NM-5
Mine Tank Number Two—*reservoir* AZ-5
Mineta Ridge—*ridge* AZ-5
*Minet Bay* AL-4
*Minet Creek* AL-4
Mine Ten Ridge—*ridge* KY-4
Minetop Trail—*trail* OR-9
*Minetta Bay* AL-4
Minetta Branch—*gut* FL-3
Minette, Bay—*bay* AL-4
*Minette Bay* AL-4
*Minette Bayou* AL-4
*Minette Creek* AL-4
Minette Creek—*stream* OR-9
Minette Lake—*lake* WI-6
Minett Island—*island* AK-9
**Minetto**—*pop pl* NY-2
Minetto Cem—*cemetery* NY-2
**Minetto (Town of)**—*pop pl* NY-2
Mine Valley—*valley* UT-8
Mine Valley Rsvr—*reservoir* UT-8
**Mineville**—*pop pl* NY-2
Mineville-Witherbee—*CDP* NY-2
*Mine Wash* UT-8
Mine Wash—*stream* CA-9
Mine Well—*well* AZ-5
Mine Well—*well* NV-8
Mine Windmill—*well* AZ-5
Miney Branch—*stream* PA-2
Mine 51 Pond Three Dam—*dam* PA-2
**Minford**—*pop pl* OH-6
Ming, A.B., House—*hist pl* AZ-5
Minga Branch—*stream* MS-4
Mingamahone Brook—*stream* NJ-2
Mingay Sch—*school* CA-9
Ming Bar—*bar* MT-8
Ming Bend—*bend* TX-5
Ming Bend Cem—*cemetery* TX-5
Ming Coulee—*valley* (2) MT-8
Ming Coulee Ridge—*ridge* MT-8
Minge Branch—*stream* FL-3
Minge Brook—*stream* NH-1
Minge Cove—*bay* NH-1
*Minge Pond* FL-3
Minges Brook—*stream* MI-6
Minges Brook Sch—*school* MI-6
*Mingey Pond* FL-3
Mingkoket, Lake—*lake* AK-9
Mingkoket Lake—*lake* AK-9
Ming Lake Dam—*dam* MS-4
Mingle Branch—*stream* TN-4
Mingle Ditch—*canal* IN-6
Mingle Hill—*summit* TN-4
Mingle HIll Ch—*church* NC-3
Minglewood Farm—*hist pl* TN-4
*Mingo* PA-2
Mingo—*locale* MS-4
Mingo—*locale* MO-7
Mingo—*locale* PA-2
Mingo—*locale* TX-5
**Mingo**—*pop pl* IA-7
**Mingo**—*pop pl* KS-7
**Mingo**—*pop pl* (2) NC-3
**Mingo**—*pop pl* OH-6
**Mingo**—*pop pl* OK-5
**Mingo**—*pop pl* WV-2
Mingo Beach—*beach* MA-1
Mingo Bible Ch—*church* KS-7
Mingo Branch—*stream* AL-4
Mingo Branch—*stream* MD-2
Mingo Branch—*stream* MS-4
Mingo Branch—*stream* SC-3
Mingo Branch—*stream* TN-4
Mingo Cay—*island* VI-3
Mingo Cem—*cemetery* FL-3
Mingo Cem—*cemetery* KS-7
Mingo Ch—*church* (2) PA-2
Mingo City (historical)—*locale* MS-4
**Mingo (County)**—*pop pl* WV-2
*Mingo Creek* CA-9
Mingo Creek—*stream* CA-9
Mingo Creek—*stream* MS-4
Mingo Creek—*stream* (2) MO-7
Mingo Creek—*stream* (2) NC-3
Mingo Creek—*stream* OK-5
Mingo Creek—*stream* (3) PA-2
Mingo Creek—*stream* VA-3
Mingo Creek—*stream* WA-9
Mingo Creek County Park—*park* PA-2
Mingo Ditch—*canal* MO-7
Mingo Falls—*falls* NC-3
Mingo Flats—*flat* WV-2
Mingo Gulch—*valley* CO-8
Mingo Hill Ch—*church* NC-3
Mingo Hollow—*valley* KY-4
Mingo Hollow—*valley* NY-2
Mingo Hollow—*valley* TN-4
**Mingo Junction**—*pop pl* OH-6
Mingo Knob—*summit* WV-2
Mingo Lake—*lake* WI-6
Mingo Lake—*reservoir* PA-2
Mingo Lake Dam—*dam* PA-2
Mingo Lookout Tower—*locale* WV-2
Mingo (Magisterial District)—*fmr MCD* WV-2
*Mingo Mountain* TN-4
Mingo Mountains—*ridge* TN-4
Mingo Mtn—*summit* WA-9
Mingona—*locale* KS-7
Mingo Natl Wildlife Ref—*park* MO-7
Mingo Natl Wildlife Refuge Archeology District—*hist pl* MO-7
**Mingona Township**—*pop pl* KS-7
Mingo Park—*park* OH-6
**Mingo Park Subdivision**—*pop pl* UT-8
Mingo Pond—*lake* TN-4
Mingo Primitive Ch—*church* NC-3
*Mingo River* MO-7
Mingo Rock—*island* ME-1
Mingo Run—*stream* (2) WV-2
Mingo Sch—*school* OH-6
Mingo Sch—*school* PA-2
Mingo Sch (historical)—*school* TN-4
**Mingo Springs**—*pop pl* ME-1
Mingo Swamp—*stream* NC-3
Mingo Swamp—*swamp* MO-7
Mingo Swamp—*swamp* SC-3
Mingo Swamp—*swamp* TN-4
**Mingo Township**—*pop pl* MO-7
Mingo (Township of)—*fmr MCD* NC-3
**Mingoville**—*pop pl* PA-2
Mingoville Post Office (historical)—*building* PA-2
Ming Run—*stream* WV-2
*Mings Canyon* OR-9
Mings Cem—*cemetery* TX-5
Mings Chapel—*church* TX-5
**Mings Chapel**—*pop pl* TX-5
Mings Chenoweth and Wolverton Ditch—*canal* CO-8
Ming School (abandoned)—*locale* MO-7
*Ming Spur* AZ-5
Mings Ranch—*locale* AZ-5
Mingsville—*locale* MO-7
**Mingus**—*pop pl* TX-5
Mingus, Joseph H., Farm—*hist pl* NC-3
Mingus, Lake—*reservoir* TX-5
Mingus, Mount—*summit* TN-4
Mingus Branch—*stream* NC-3
Mingus Creek—*stream* NC-3
Mingus Lake—*lake* AZ-5
Mingus Lead—*ridge* TN-4
Mingus Lookout Complex—*hist pl* AZ-5
Mingus Mountain Campground—*park* AZ-5
Mingus Mountain (CCD)—*cens area* AZ-5
*Mingus Mountains* AZ-5
Mingus Mtn—*summit* AZ-5
Mingus Park—*park* OR-9
Mingus Park Creek—*stream* OR-9
Mingus Park Lake—*reservoir* OR-9
Mingus Ridge—*ridge* NC-3
Mingus Spring—*spring* TX-5
Mingus Springs Ranch—*locale* AZ-5
Mingus Substation—*locale* AZ-5
Mingus Union HS—*school* AZ-5
Mingvk Lake—*lake* AK-9
*Mingy Pond* FL-3
*Minhan River* MA-1
*Mini* FM-9
**Miniard**—*pop pl* KY-4
Miniatulik Creek—*stream* AK-9
Miniatulik River—*stream* AK-9
*Miniature Grand Canyon* HI-9

Minnow Run—stream (3) PA-2
Minnow Slough—gut AL-4
Minnow Slough—stream IL-6
Minnow Spring—spring TX-5
Minnow Springs WV-2
Minny Lake—lake MN-6
Minoa—pop pl NY-2
Minoch Ch—church TX-5
Minocqua—pop pl WI-6
Minocqua Lake—lake WI-6
Minocqua (Town of)—pop pl WI-6
Mino Creek—stream AK-9
Min'og FM-9
Minoi-Sandiage Cem—cemetery MO-7
Minola Administrative Site—locale NV-8
Minoletti Creek—stream NV-8
Minoletti Shaft—mine NV-8
Minoletti Spring—spring NV-8
Minom Sog—swamp FL-3
Minon Creek—stream CA-9
Minong—pop pl WI-6
Minong Flowage—channel WI-6
Minong Island—island MI-6
Minong Mine—mine MI-6
Minong Mine Hist Dist—hist pl MI-6
Minong Ridge—ridge MI-6
Minong Ridge Fire Manway—trail (2) MI-6
Minong (Town of)—pop pl WI-6
Minonk—pop pl IL-6
Minonk Junction—pop pl IL-6
Minonk Lake—lake WI-6
Minonk (Township of)—pop pl IL-6
Minon Run—stream PA-2
Minooka—pop pl AL-4
Minooka—pop pl IL-6
Minooka—pop pl PA-2
Minooka County Park—park WI-6
Minooka Park Rec Area—park KS-7
Minook Creek—stream AK-9
Minook Island—island AK-9
Minor—locale KY-4
Minor—locale VA-3
Minor—pop pl AL-4
Minor, Canal (historical)—canal AZ-5
Minor, Charles, House—hist pl MO-7
Minor, J. R., House—hist pl KY-4
Minor Beach—pop pl MI-6
Minor Bridge—other WV-2
Minor Brook—locale CT-1
Minorca—locale LA-4
Minorca—pop pl AR-4
Minorca—pop pl MN-6
Minorca Cem—cemetery LA-4
Minorca Nut Lake—lake MS-4
Minorcas Creek Par 3 Golf Course—park NC-3
Minor Cem—cemetery AL-4
Minor Cem—cemetery (2) KY-4
Minor Cem—cemetery LA-4
Minor Cem—cemetery MO-7
Minor Cem—cemetery WV-2
Minor Ch—church AL-4
Minor Ch—church IL-6
Minor Creek—stream CA-9
Minor Creek—stream ID-8
Minor Creek—stream IA-7
Minor Creek—stream KY-4
Minor Creek—stream MO-7
Minor Ditch—canal CO-8
Minore, Lake—lake FL-3
Minorea—locale AR-4
Minor Farm—locale CA-9
Minor First Baptist Ch—church AL-4
Minorga Mine—mine MN-6
Minor Gulch—valley OR-9
Minorhill TN-4
Minor Hill—pop pl TN-4
Minor Hill—summit TN-4
Minor Hill—summit VA-3
Minor Hill (CCD)—cens area TN-4
Minor Hill Cem—cemetery AL-4
Minor Hill Cem—cemetery TN-4
Minor Hill Ch—church AL-4
Minor Hill Division—civil TN-4
Minor Hill First Baptist Ch—church TN-4
Minorhill Post Office TN-4
Minor Hill Post Office—building TN-4
Minor Hill Sch—school TN-4
Minor Hill Sch (historical)—school AL-4
Minor House—hist pl IN-6
Minor HS—school AL-4
Minor Island—island WA-9
Minor Knob—summit KY-4
Minor Lake—lake AK-9
Minor Lake—lake KY-4
Minor Lake—lake MT-8
Minor Lake Dam—dam MS-4
Minor Lane Heights—pop pl KY-4
Minor Memorial Ch—church MS-4
Minor Notch Ranch—locale CO-8
Minor Park—park MO-7
Minor Pond—reservoir CT-1
Minor Ranch—locale NV-8
Minors Canal—canal LA-4
Minor Sch—school AL-4
Minor Sch—school IL-6
Minor Sch (abandoned)—school MO-7
Minor School (historical)—locale MO-7
Minors Creek—stream KY-4
Minors Hill VA-3
Minors Lane Sch—school KY-4
Minor Slough—gut KY-4
Minors Millpond—reservoir GA-3
Minor Spring—spring OR-9
Minorsville—pop pl KY-4
Minorsville Cem—cemetery KY-4
Minor Terrace—pop pl AL-4
Minor Thornton Ditch—canal CA-9
Minortown—locale CT-1
Minorville (historical)—locale AL-4
Minorville (historical)—pop pl FL-3
Minor Well—well NV-8
Minoso Farm—locale AR-4
Minot—pop pl ME-1
Minot—pop pl MA-1
Minot—pop pl MS-4
Minot—pop pl ND-7
Minot, George R., House—hist pl MA-1
Minot AFB—military ND-7
Minotaur Lake—lake WA-9
Minot Base ND-7
Minot Beach—beach MA-1
Minot Brook—stream MA-1
Minot Carnegie Library—hist pl ND-7
Minot Chapel Missionary Baptist Church AL-4
Minot Commercial Hist Dist—hist pl ND-7
Minot Country Club—locale ND-7
Minot Creek—stream ME-1
Minot Forest Beach—beach MA-1
Minot Forest Sch—school MA-1
Minot Industrial Hist Dist—hist pl ND-7
Minot International Airp—airport ND-7
Minot Island—island ME-1
Minotocloga Lake—lake AK-9
Minotola—pop pl NJ-2
Minoto Ranch—locale AZ-5
Minot Peak—summit WA-9
Minot Plaza—locale ND-7
Minot Post Office (historical)—building MS-4
Minot's Ledge MA-1
Minots Ledge—bar MA-1
Minot's Ledge Light—hist pl MA-1
Minots Ledge Light—locale MA-1
Minot's Light—tower MA-1
Minot State Coll—school ND-7
Minott, William, House—hist pl ME-1
Minott Corners—locale NY-2
Minotti Creek—stream OR-9
Minot (Town of)—pop pl ME-1
Minott Pond—reservoir MA-1
Minott Pond Dam—dam MA-1
Minott Spring—spring OR-9
Minot Water Supply Dam—dam ND-7
Minpro—pop pl NC-3
Minquadale—pop pl DE-2
Minquadale Assembly of God—church DE-2
Minquadle Trailer Village—pop pl DE-2
Minque Hollow—valley OH-6
Minschew Branch—stream GA-3
Minsell Creek FL-3
Minshall—pop pl IN-6
Minsi PA-2
Minsi, Mount—summit PA-2
Minsi Lake—reservoir PA-2
Minsi Lake Dam—dam PA-2
Minsi Trail Bridge—bridge PA-2
Minski Place—locale OR-9
Minson Cem—cemetery IL-6
Minsteed—pop pl NY-2
Minster—pop pl OH-6
Minster, The—pillar CA-9
Minster Elem Sch—hist pl OH-6
Minster Hill VT-1
Minstral Hole—cave AL-4
Mint—locale AZ-5
Mint—pop pl TN-4
Minta PA-2
Minta Cem—cemetery IL-6
Mint Branch—stream NC-3
Mint Brook—stream CT-1
Mint Canyon—pop pl CA-9
Mint Canyon—valley CA-9
Mint Canyon Campground—locale CA-9
Mint Canyon Spring—locale CA-9
Mint Cem—cemetery MI-6
Mint Creek—stream IL-6
Mint Creek—stream KY-4
Mint Creek—stream OR-9
Mintdale Community Club—other MI-6
Minter—locale TX-5
Minter—locale WA-9
Minter—pop pl AL-4
Minter—pop pl GA-3
Minter—pop pl SC-3
Minter, George W., House—hist pl CA-9
Minter Branch—stream TX-5
Minterburn Mill—hist pl CT-1
Minter Cem—cemetery (2) GA-3
Minter Cem—cemetery MS-4
Minter Cem—cemetery TX-5
Minter City—pop pl MS-4
Minter City Junction—locale MS-4
Minter City Landing (historical)—locale MS-4
Minter Community Center—building WA-9
Minter Creek—stream AL-4
Minter Creek—stream VA-3
Minter Creek—stream (2) WA-9
Minter Hill—summit CO-8
Minter Hill—summit GA-3
Minter Hill—summit MS-4
Minter Hill—summit MO-7
Minter Lake—lake MS-4
Minter (Minters)—pop pl AL-4
Minter Point—cape VA-3
Minter (RR name for Lollie)—other GA-3
Minters Chapel—locale TX-5
Minters Church TX-5
Minters Corral—locale NM-5
Minters Creek AL-4
Minters (Minter) AL-4
Minter Spring—spring TX-5
Minter Village—pop pl CA-9
Mint Glacier—glacier AK-9
Mint Hill—locale MO-7
Mint Hill—pop pl NC-3
Mint Hill Ch—church MO-7
Mint Hill Festival Center—locale NC-3
Mint Hill-Matthews Airport NC-3
Mint Hill Municipal Park—park NC-3
Mint Hollow—valley TN-4
Mint Hollow (subdivision)—pop pl NC-3
Minthorn—locale OR-9
Minthorn, Dr. Henry J., House (Herbert Hoover House)—hist pl OR-9
Mint Lake—reservoir NC-3
Mint Lake Dam—dam NC-3
Mintle—locale NE-7
Mintmere—hist pl LA-4
Mint Mine—mine AZ-5
Mint Mine—mine NV-8
Mint Museum—building NC-3
Minto—locale (2) OR-9
Minto—pop pl NV-8
Minto—pop pl ND-7
Minto, John and Douglas, Houses—hist pl OR-9
Minto ANV857—reserve AK-9
Minto-Brown Island Park—park OR-9
Minto Canyon—valley NV-8
Minto Cem—cemetery ND-7
Minto Creek—stream (2) OR-9
Minto Dam—dam ND-7
Minto Dam—dam OR-9
Minto (historical)—locale MS-4
Minto Island—island OR-9
Minto Lakes—lake AK-9
Min-Tom Childrens Home—building TN-4
Minto Mtn—summit OR-9
Minto Municipal Airp—airport ND-7
Minton—locale GA-3
Minton Bayou—gut MS-4
Minton Branch—stream KY-4
Minton Branch—stream (2) TN-4
Minton Canyon—valley NM-5
Minton Cem—cemetery KY-4
Minton Cem—cemetery MO-7
Minton Cem—cemetery OH-6
Minton Cem—cemetery TN-4
Minton Cem—cemetery (2) VA-3
Minton Chapel—church GA-3
Minton Cove—basin OR-9
Minton Creek—stream AK-9
Minton Creek—stream CA-9
Minton Creek—stream MT-8
Minton Creek—stream SC-3
Minton Creek Pass—gap MT-8
Minto (New)—locale AK-9
Minton Hollow—valley KY-4
Minton Hollow—valley (2) TN-4
Minton Hollow—valley VA-3
Minton Mill—locale SC-3
Minton Mill—locale TN-4
Minton Peak—summit MT-8
Minton Prospect—mine TN-4
Minton Rsvr—reservoir NY-2
Mintons—pop pl KY-4
Mintons Branch AL-4
Minton Sch—school GA-3
Mintons Corner—pop pl FL-3
Mintons Corner Shop Ctr—locale FL-3
Minton's Playhouse—hist pl NY-2
Minton Springs Ch—church GA-3
Mintons Store—locale NC-3
Minton-Strawn Oil Field—oilfield TX-5
Mintonsville—pop pl NC-3
Mintonsville (Township of)—fmr MCD NC-3
Minton Township—civil MO-7
Mintonville—locale KY-4
Mintonville Point—cliff VA-3
Mintonye Cem—cemetery IN-6
Minto Park—park OR-9
Minto Pass—gap OR-9
Minto Pass Trail—trail OR-9
Minto Township—pop pl ND-7
Minto Valley Sch—school CO-8
Mint Post Office (historical)—building (2) TN-4
Mint River—stream AK-9
Mint Shaft—mine AZ-5
Mint Shaft—mine NV-8
Mint Spring—locale AL-4
Mint Spring—pop pl VA-3
Mint Spring—spring AL-4
Mint Spring—spring (3) AZ-5
Mint Spring—spring (4) MO-7
Mint Spring—spring OR-9
Mint Spring—spring (3) TN-4
Mint Spring Branch—stream AR-4
Mint Spring Branch—stream KY-4
Mint Spring Branch—stream MS-4
Mint Spring Branch—stream TN-4
Mint Spring Cem—cemetery TN-4
Mint Spring (historical)—pop pl TN-4
Mint Spring Hollow—valley MO-7
Mintspring Hollow—valley TN-4
Mint Spring Hollow—valley TN-4
Mint Spring Post Office (historical)—building TN-4
Mint Springs—locale AL-4
Mint Springs—locale KY-4
Mint Springs—spring AL-4
Mint Springs—spring KY-4
Mint Spring Sch (historical)—school AL-4
Mint Springs Missionary Ch—church KY-4
Mint Springs Rec Area—locale VA-3
Mint Tank—reservoir AZ-5
Mintubbe Lake—lake OK-5
Minturn—locale SC-3
Minturn—locale WY-8
Minturn—pop pl AR-4
Minturn—pop pl CA-9
Minturn—pop pl CO-8
Minturn—pop pl ME-1
Minturn-Red Cliff—cens area CO-8
Mint Wash—stream AZ-5
Mint Well—well NV-8
Mintz—locale NC-3
Mintz Cem—cemetery NC-3
Mintzers PA-2
Mintzers—pop pl PA-2
Mintzers Siding—locale PA-2
Mintz (Mints)—pop pl NC-3
Mintz Pond—reservoir NC-3
Mintz Pond Dam—dam NC-3
Minue Sch—school NJ-2
Minum River OR-9
Minunn—pop pl ME-1
Minute Creek—stream OR-9
Minute Man Monmt—park MA-1
Minute Man Natl Historical Park—park MA-1
Minute Tank—reservoir NM-5
Minvale—pop pl AL-4
Minwah Stream ME-1
Minx Creek WY-8
Minx Island ME-1
Minx Islands—area AK-9
Minx Spring Branch—stream TX-5
Minya Peak—summit AK-9
Minyard Branch—stream KY-4
Minzies Creek—stream NC-3
Mio—pop pl MI-6
Mio AuSable Sch—school MI-6
Mio Cem—cemetery MI-6
Miocene Ditch—canal AK-9
Mio Dam Pond—reservoir MI-6
Miola—locale (2) PA-2
Miola Cem—cemetery PA-2
Miola Lake—reservoir KS-7
Miola Lake Dam—dam KS-7
Miomi Park Beach MI-6
Mio Mtn—summit MI-6
Miona—locale VA-3
Miona, Lake—lake FL-3
Miona Ferry—other GA-3
Miona Springs—spring GA-3
Mio Pond MI-6
Mioxes Pond—lake MA-1
Miqernael—summit FM-9
Miqiw FM-9
Miqiy—bay FM-9
Miques LA-4
Miquon—pop pl PA-2
Miquon Hills—pop pl PA-2
Miquon Sch—school PA-2
Mira—locale IL-6
Mira—pop pl LA-4
Mira, Lake—lake FL-3
Mirabales (Barrio)—fmr MCD PR-3
Miraballes, Point—cape AK-9
Mirabal Mine—mine NM-5
Mirabal Windmill—locale NM-5
Mirabeau Sch—school LA-4
Mirabel Heights—pop pl CA-9
Mirabel Mine—mine CA-9
Mirabel Park—pop pl CA-9
Mirabel Spring—spring NM-5
Mirabile—pop pl MO-7
Mirabile Center Sch—school MO-7
Mirabile Township—pop pl MO-7
Mira Catalina Sch—school CA-9
Miracerros Park—park NM-5
Miracle—locale (2) KY-4
Miracle Camp—locale LA-4
Miracle Cem—cemetery KY-4
Miracle Ch—church IN-6
Miracle Ch—church NC-3
Miracle Ch—church TN-4
Miracle Ch—church TX-5
Miracle City Mall—locale FL-3
Miracle Deliverance Tabernacle Ch—church AL-4
Miracle Haven Ch (ACLF)—church FL-3
Miracle Hill—summit CA-9
Miracle Hill Ch—church AL-4
Miracle Hills Ranch (Youth Camp)—locale MO-7
Miracle Hills Ranch (youth camp)—park MO-7
Miracle Hot Springs—pop pl CA-9
Miracle Hot Springs (Hobo Hot Springs)—pop pl CA-9
Miracle Lighthouse Ch of God—church TN-4
Miracle Lodge Number 84 Cem—cemetery MT-8
Miracle Mall—locale SD-7
Miracle Mall Shop Ctr—locale TN-4
Miracle Manor—pop pl CA-9
Miracle Mart (Shop Ctr)—locale FL-3
Miracle Mile—post sta CA-9
Miracle Mile—post sta FL-3
Miracle Mile Exchange—locale AZ-5
Miracle Mile Shop Ctr—locale FL-3
Miracle Mile Shop Ctr—locale PA-2
Miracle Mission—church MI-6
Miracle Missionary Baptist Ch—church TN-4
Miracle Plaza (Shop Ctr)—locale (2) FL-3
Miracle Pond—lake TN-4
Miracle Prayer House Ch—church AL-4
Miracle Revival Center—church KS-7
Miracle Ridge—ridge VA-3
Miracle Rock—pillar CO-8
Miracle Rock Ch—church UT-8
Miracle Rock Picnic Ground—locale CO-8
Miracle Run WV-2
Miracle Run—locale WV-2
Miracle Run—stream WV-2
Miracle Run Cem—cemetery WV-2
Miracle Run Ch—church WV-2
Miracle Shop Ctr—locale PA-2
Miracle Temple—church NC-3
Miracle Temple Apostolic Holiness Ch—church FL-3
Miracle Temple Cem—cemetery MS-4
Miracle Temple Ch—church AL-4
Miracle Temple Ch of Deliverance—church MS-4
Miracle Temple Ch of God in Christ—church FL-3
Miracle Temple Christian Sch—school FL-3
Miracle Temple Deliverance Ch—church MS-4
Miracle Valley—pop pl AZ-5
Miracle Valley Airstrip—airport AZ-5
Miracosta Coll—school CA-9
Mira Costa HS—school CA-9
Mira Creek—stream NE-7
Mirada Hills CA-9
Miradero (Barrio)—fmr MCD (2) PR-3
Mirador—hist pl VA-3
Mirador—locale CA-9
Miradores Ranch—locale TX-5
Mirador (subdivision)—pop pl (2) AZ-5
Miraflores—locale PR-3
Miraflores—pop pl PR-3
Miraflores (Barrio)—fmr MCD (2) PR-3
Miraflores Park—park FL-3
Mira Fork—stream VA-3
Mira Fork Chapel—church VA-3
Mirage NV-8
Mirage—fmr MCD NE-7
Mirage—locale CO-8
Mirage—locale NM-5
Mirage, Lake—lake WY-8
Mirage Cem—cemetery CO-8
Mirage Creek—stream ID-8
Mirage Dam—dam SD-7
Mirage Flats Canal—canal NE-7
Mirage (historical)—locale KS-7
Mirage Lake CA-9
Mirage Lake MN-6
Mirage Lake—lake MN-6
Mirage Lake—reservoir SD-7
Mirage Sch—school KS-7
Mirage Township—pop pl KS-7
Mirage Township—pop pl NE-7
Mirage Valley CA-9
Miralejos Artesian Well—well TX-5
Miralejos Windmill—locale TX-5
Miralesta Subdivision UT-8
Miraleste—pop pl CA-9
Miraleste Canyon—valley CA-9
Miraleste Subdivision—pop pl UT-8
Miralia—pop pl GA-3
Mira Linda Sch—school CA-9
Mira Loma—pop pl CA-9
Mira Loma Detention Facility (LA County)—other CA-9
Mira Loma HS—school CA-9
Miraloma Sch—school CA-9
Mira Loma (sta.)—pop pl CA-9
Mira Lookout Tower—locale LA-4
Miramar MS-4
Miramar—locale (2) CA-9
Miramar—pop pl CA-9
Miramar—pop pl FL-3
Miramar—pop pl MA-1
Miramar—pop pl NJ-2
Miramar—pop pl (3) PR-3
Miramar, Lake—reservoir CA-9
Miramar, Mount—summit AK-9
Miramar Beach—beach CA-9
Miramar Beach—pop pl FL-3
Miramar Country Club—locale FL-3
Miramar Elem Sch—school FL-3
Miramar HS—school FL-3
Miramar Naval Air Station—military CA-9
Miramar Park—park MS-4
Miramar Park Associates (Shop Ctr)—locale FL-3
Miramar-Pembroke Pines (CCD)—cens area FL-3
Miramar Reservoir CA-9
Miramar Sch—school FL-3
Miramar Shop Ctr—locale FL-3
Miramar Terrace—pop pl FL-3
Mira Mesa—pop pl CA-9
Miramichi—locale CT-1
Miramichi Lake—lake MI-6
Miramichi Pond MA-1
Miramont—hist pl CO-8
Miramontas Point CA-9
Mira Monte—pop pl CA-9
Miramonte—pop pl CA-9
Miramonte—pop pl CO-8
Miramonte Acres—uninc pl AZ-5
Mira Monte Club—other CA-9
Miramonte Conservation Camp—locale CA-9
Miramonte HS—school CA-9
Miramonte Mtn—summit CO-8
Miramonte Rsvr—reservoir CO-8
Miramontes—civil CA-9
Miramonte Sch—school (3) CA-9
Miramontes Point—cape CA-9
Mira Mountain—ridge NV-8
Miranda—pop pl CA-9
Miranda—pop pl SD-7
Miranda—pop pl (2) PR-3
Miranda, Jesus, Homestead—hist pl AZ-5
Miranda Cabin—locale CA-9
Miranda Canyon—valley CA-9
Miranda Cem—cemetery SD-7
Miranda Creek CA-9
Miranda Creek—stream OR-9
Miranda Hill PA-2
Miranda Hill—summit PA-2
Miranda (historical)—pop pl NC-3
Miranda (historical)—pop pl TN-4
Miranda Lake—lake FL-3
Miranda Pine Campground—locale CA-9
Miranda Pine Creek CA-9
Miranda Pine Mtn—summit CA-9
Miranda Pine Spring—spring CA-9
Miranda Post Office (historical)—building TN-4
Miranda Run—stream (2) OH-6
Miranda Spring—spring OR-9
Mirando City—pop pl TX-5
Mirando City Oil Field—oilfield TX-5
Mirandy, Lake—reservoir AR-4
Mira Pond—reservoir LA-4
Mira Slough—stream CA-9
Mirasol (Barrio)—fmr MCD PR-3
Mirasol Creek—stream TX-5
Mirasol Ditch—canal CA-9
Mirasol Drain—canal CA-9
Mirasoles Windmill—locale TX-5
Mirasol Park—park AZ-5
Mirasol Ranch—locale CA-9
Mirasol Windmill—locale TX-5
Miraso Ranch—locale TX-5
Mirassou Sch—school CA-9
Mira Vista—uninc pl CA-9
Mira Vista Park—park CA-9
Mira Vista Sch—school CA-9
Mirawood Day Sch—school FL-3
Mire—pop pl LA-4
Mire Bayou—stream LA-4
Mire Branch—stream IN-6
Mire Branch—stream (3) NC-3
Mire Branch—stream (3) TN-4
Mire Branch—stream (2) VA-3
Mire Canal—canal LA-4
Mire Cem—cemetery LA-4
Mire Creek—stream ID-8
Mired FM-9
Mireed—cape FM-9
Mireeniiw—locale FM-9
Mire Hollow—valley MO-7
Mirehouse Ranch—locale MT-8
Mireles Windmill—locale NM-5
Mire Lick Creek—stream MO-7
Mireniw FM-9
Mires Creek—stream WA-9
Mire-to MP-9
Mirey Branch—stream AR-4
Mirey Branch—stream DE-2
Mirey Branch—stream (3) NC-3
Mirey Brook—stream MA-1
Mirey Brook—stream NH-1
Mirey Creek—stream KY-4
Mirey Fork—stream MO-7
Mirey Run—stream NJ-2
Mirey's Brook CT-1
Miriam IN-6
Miriam—locale NV-8
Miriam, Lake—reservoir (2) AL-4
Miriam Creek—stream WA-9
Miriam Heights (subdivision)—pop pl AL-4
Miriam Lake—lake WA-9
Miriam Lake—lake WI-6
Miriam Orr Pond Dam—dam MS-4
Miriam Peak—summit WY-8
Miriamr HS—school FL-3
Miriamville AL-4
Mirienda Windmill—locale TX-5
Mirikattan MH-9
Mirimar Center (Shop Ctr)—locale FL-3
Mirimar Elem Sch—school FL-3
Mirimichi, Lake—reservoir MA-1
Mirimich Pond MA-1
Miri To MP-9
Mirl, Lake—reservoir NC-3
Miron Sch (historical)—school AL-4
Mirrell Creek TN-4
Mirrell Spring TN-4
Mirre Point—cape MI-6
Mirre's MI-6
Mirror, Lake—lake (2) FL-3
Mirror Bay—bay AK-9
Mirror Creek OR-9
Mirror Creek—stream AK-9
Mirror Creek—stream CO-8
Mirror Creek—stream (3) ID-8
Mirror Fork—stream WY-8
Mirror Harbor—harbor AK-9
Mirror Lake MA-1
Mirror Lake NC-3
Mirror Lake—flat CA-9
Mirror Lake—lake (4) AK-9
Mirror Lake—lake (5) CA-9
Mirror Lake—lake (7) CO-8
Mirror Lake—lake (3) CT-1
Mirror Lake—lake (9) FL-3
Mirror Lake—lake (4) ID-8
Mirror Lake—lake (2) IL-6
Mirror Lake—lake (5) IN-6
Mirror Lake—lake LA-4
Mirror Lake—lake (2) ME-1
Mirror Lake—lake (3) MA-1
Mirror Lake—lake (9) MI-6
Mirror Lake—lake (4) MN-6
Mirror Lake—lake MS-4
Mirror Lake—lake (2) MT-8
Mirror Lake—lake (5) NH-1
Mirror Lake—lake NM-5
Mirror Lake—lake (6) NY-2
Mirror Lake—lake ND-7
Mirror Lake—lake OH-6
Mirror Lake—lake (2) OR-9
Mirror Lake—lake TX-5
Mirror Lake—lake (2) UT-8
Mirror Lake—lake VT-1
Mirror Lake—lake (7) WA-9
Mirror Lake—lake (12) WI-6
Mirror Lake—lake (5) WY-8
Mirror Lake—locale WA-9
Mirror Lake—pop pl NH-1
Mirror Lake—pop pl WA-9
Mirror Lake—reservoir CA-9
Mirror Lake—reservoir CO-8
Mirror Lake—reservoir GA-3
Mirror Lake—reservoir MA-1
Mirror Lake—reservoir (3) NJ-2
Mirror Lake—reservoir NY-2
Mirror Lake—reservoir NC-3
Mirror Lake—reservoir (2) PA-2
Mirror Lake—reservoir SC-3
Mirror Lake—reservoir TX-5
Mirror Lake—reservoir (3) WI-6
Mirror Lake Campground—locale UT-8
Mirror Lake Dam—dam MA-1
Mirror Lake Dam—dam NJ-2
Mirror Lake Dam—dam NC-3
Mirror Lake Dam—dam ND-7
Mirror Lake Drain—canal MI-6
Mirror Lake Elem Sch—school FL-3
Mirror Lake Forest Service Station UT-8
Mirror Lake Guard Station—locale UT-8
Mirror Lake Lookout Tower—locale MN-6
Mirror Lake Recreation Site—park UT-8
Mirror Lakes—lake NC-3
Mirror Lakes—lake WA-9
Mirror Lakes—reservoir AL-4
Mirror Lakes—reservoir KY-4
Mirror Lake Sch—school WA-9
Mirror Lake State Park—park WI-6
Mirror Lake/Tomlinson Adult Education Center—school FL-3
Mirror Lake Trail—trail CO-8
Mirror Lake Trail—trail (2) OR-9
Mirror Mountain AZ-5
Mirror Park (subdivision)—pop pl NC-3
Mirror Peak—summit ID-8
Mirror Plateau—area WY-8
Mirror Pond NH-1
Mirror Pond—lake ME-1
Mirror Pond—lake MT-8
Mirror Pond—lake OR-9
Mirror Pond—reservoir NJ-2
Mirror Pond—reservoir OR-9
Mirror Slough—gut AK-9
Mirror Spring—spring UT-8
Mirrow Lake—lake ID-8
Mirrow Lake Dam—dam MS-4
Mirrow Lake (subdivision)—locale FL-3
Mirth (historical)—pop pl OR-9
Mirth Lake—lake MN-6
Miru-Ko FM-9
Miru-Kuchi FM-9
Miru-to MP-9
Miruu Passage MP-9
Miruu To MP-9
Miry Branch—stream (3) NC-3
Miry Branch—stream TN-4
Miry Brook—locale CT-1
Miry Brook—stream (2) CT-1
Miry Creek NE-7
Miry Creek—stream UT-8
Miry Creek—stream VA-3
Miry Dam Pond—lake CT-1
Miry Gut—gut NC-3
Miry Hole Branch—stream NC-3
Miry Place Canyon—valley NV-8
Miry Pond—lake DE-2
Miry Ridge—ridge TN-4
Miry Run—stream (3) NJ-2
Miry Run—stream (2) VA-3
Miry Swamp—swamp CT-1
Miry Wash—valley UT-8
Mis DE-2
Misac Creek—stream OR-9
Misaki Island PW-9
Misaki To PW-9
Misa Stream—stream AS-9
Miscauna Creek—stream MI-6

Miscauno Creek—*stream* ... WI-6
Miscauno Island—*island* ... WI-6
Miscauno Pond—*reservoir* ... WI-6
Mischel, George and Sons, Bldg—*hist pl* ... KY-4
Mischke, Charles, House—*hist pl* ... GA-3
Misch Lake—*reservoir* ... MI-6
Mischos Pond—*reservoir* ... WI-6
**Misco**—*pop pl* ... OH-6
Miscoe Brook—*stream* (3) ... MA-1
Miscoe Lake—*reservoir* ... MA-1
Miscoe Lake—*reservoir* ... RI-1
Miscoe Meadow—*swamp* ... MA-1
MISCO Grain Elevator—*hist pl* ... MT-8
Miscol—*locale* ... SD-7
*Miscol Ranch* ... SD-7
Miscowawbic Peak—*summit* ... MI-6
Miscus Pond—*lake* ... CT-1
Mise Cem—*cemetery* ... MO-7
Misels Chapel—*church* ... AR-4
Misemer Cem—*cemetery* ... MO-7
Misener Sch—*school* ... MI-6
**Misenheimer**—*pop pl* ... NC-3
**Misenheimer (RR name Misenheimer Springs)**—*pop pl* ... NC-3
Misenheimer Sch—*school* ... IL-6
Misenheimer Springs (RR name for Misenheimer)—*other* ... NC-3
Misenheimer Springs Station—*locale* ... NC-3
Misenhimer Draw—*valley* ... AZ-5
*Miser* ... TN-4
Miserable Canyon—*valley* ... NM-5
Miserable Cave—*cave* ... AL-4
Miserable Island—*island* ... IL-6
Miserable Lake—*lake* ... IL-6
Miserable Rsvr—*reservoir* ... WY-8
Miserable Springs—*spring* ... NM-5
Miser Canyon—*valley* ... MT-8
Misercordia Coll—*school* ... PA-2
Miser Creek—*stream* ... MT-8
Miser Creek—*stream* ... NC-3
Misere, Bayou—*stream* ... LA-4
Misere, Lake—*lake* ... LA-4
Misere Brook—*stream* ... ME-1
Miser Gulch—*valley* ... NV-8
Miser Hollow—*valley* ... MO-7
Miser Hollow—*valley* ... TN-4
Misericordia Home—*building* ... IL-6
Misericordia Hosp—*hospital* ... PA-2
Miser Post Office (historical)—*building* ... TN-4
Misers Chest Mine—*mine* ... NM-5
Miser Sch (historical)—*school* ... TN-4
Miser Spring—*spring* ... NV-8
Misers Run—*stream* ... OH-6
*Misers Station* ... TN-4
*Misers Station Post Office* ... TN-4
**Miser Station**—*pop pl* ... TN-4
*Misertown* ... PA-2
**Misertown**—*pop pl* ... PA-2
*Miserva Lake* ... IN-6
Miser Well—*well* ... NM-5
Miser Windmill—*locale* ... NM-5
Misery, Bayou—*gut* ... LA-4
Misery, Lake—*lake* ... LA-4
Misery, Lake—*lake* ... NY-2
Misery, Mount—*summit* ... CA-9
Misery, Mount—*summit* ... CT-1
Misery, Mount—*summit* (3) ... ME-1
Misery, Mount—*summit* (2) ... MA-1
Misery, Mount—*summit* ... MI-6
Misery, Mount—*summit* (5) ... NH-1
Misery, Mount—*summit* ... NY-2
Misery, Mount—*summit* ... OR-9
Misery, Mount—*summit* ... PA-2
Misery, Mount—*summit* ... RI-1
Misery, Mount—*summit* ... WA-9
Misery Bay—*bay* (3) ... MI-6
Misery Bay—*bay* ... PA-2
Misery Bay Sch—*school* ... MI-6
Misery Brook—*stream* ... CT-1
Misery Creek—*stream* ... AK-9
Misery Creek—*stream* (2) ... CA-9
Misery Creek—*stream* (2) ... MI-6
Misery Creek—*stream* ... MT-8
Misery Creek—*stream* (2) ... OR-9
Misery Creek—*stream* ... UT-8
*Misery Flat* ... OR-9
Misery Flat—*flat* ... OR-9
Misery Gore—*unorg* ... ME-1
*Misery Gutter* ... MA-1
Misery Hill—*summit* ... CT-1
Misery Hill—*summit* ... ME-1
Misery Hill—*summit* ... NH-1
Misery Island—*island* ... AK-9
Misery Island Reservation—*park* ... MA-1
Misery Knob—*summit* ... ME-1
Misery Lake—*lake* ... WA-9
Misery Ledge—*bar* ... ME-1
Misery Ledge—*bar* ... MA-1
*Misery Mountain* ... MI-6
Misery Mtn—*summit* ... MA-1
Misery Mtn—*summit* ... NY-2
Misery Mtn—*summit* ... NC-3
Misery Peak—*summit* ... WA-9
Misery Point—*cape* ... WA-9
Misery Pond—*reservoir* ... ME-1
Misery Ridge—*ridge* ... ME-1
Misery Ridge—*ridge* ... OR-9
Misery River—*stream* ... MI-6
Misery Rock—*rock* ... MA-1
Misery Shoal—*bar* ... MA-1
Misery Spring—*spring* ... AZ-5
Misery Spring Campground—*locale* ... WA-9
Misery Stream—*stream* ... ME-1
Misery (Township of)—*unorg* ... ME-1
Misery Trail—*trail* ... FL-3
Misery Well—*well* (2) ... AZ-5
Misfire Creek—*stream* ... ID-8
Misfit Creek—*stream* ... OR-9
Misfit Spring—*spring* ... OR-9
Misgen—*locale* ... VI-3
*Misgow* ... FM-9
**Mish**—*pop pl* ... MS-4
Mish, Henry, Barn—*hist pl* ... VA-3
Mishak Cem—*cemetery* ... OK-5
Mishak Lakes—*lake* ... CO-8
Misha Mokwa—*locale* ... WI-6
*Mishantatuck* ... RI-1
Mishap Creek—*stream* ... AK-9
Mishaum Ledge—*bar* ... MA-1
Mishaum Point—*cape* ... MA-1
**Mishaum Point**—*pop pl* ... MA-1
Mishawaka—*locale* ... CO-8
**Mishawaka**—*pop pl* ... IN-6
Mishawaka Club—*locale* ... PA-2
Mishawaka HS—*school* ... IN-6
Mishawaka Pilots Club Airp—*airport* ... IN-6
*Mishawum* ... MA-1
**Mishawum**—*pop pl* ... MA-1
Mishawum Lake—*reservoir* ... MA-1
Misheguk Mtn—*summit* ... AK-9
Mishe-Mokwa, Lake—*reservoir* ... NJ-2
*Mishemokwa Creek* ... MI-6
Mishe-Mokwa Dam—*dam* ... NJ-2
Mishevik Slough—*gut* ... AK-9
*Mishewaka* ... IN-6
Mish House—*hist pl* ... CA-9
**Mishicot**—*pop pl* ... WI-6
*Mishicott* ... WI-6
**Mishicot (Town of)**—*pop pl* ... WI-6
*Mishigan Lake* ... IN-6
Mishike Lake—*lake* ... MI-6
*Mi Shima* ... FM-9
*Mishi Shima* ... FM-9
Mishler—*locale* ... PA-2
**Mishler**—*pop pl* ... OH-6
**Mishler Corners**—*pop pl* ... PA-2
Mishler Ditch—*canal* ... IN-6
Mishler Landing Strip—*airport* ... IN-6
Mishler Theatre—*hist pl* ... PA-2
*Mishnic Pond* ... RI-1
*Mishnic Swamp* ... RI-1
Mishnock, Lake—*lake* ... RI-1
*Mishnock Pond* ... RI-1
Mishnock River—*stream* ... RI-1
Mishnock Swamp—*swamp* ... RI-1
Mishonagon Creek—*stream* ... WI-6
Mishonagon Swamp—*swamp* ... WI-6
*Mishonginivi* ... AZ-5
**Mishongnovi**—*pop pl* ... AZ-5
Mishuk Creek—*stream* ... AK-9
Mishula Tubba Prairie—*area* ... MS-4
Misionario Evangelico—*church* ... PR-3
Mision Noel—*church* ... PR-3
*Miskee Hill* ... MA-1
Miskell Mahoney Ditch—*canal* ... IN-6
*Miskiana Brook* ... RI-1
*Miskiania Brook* ... RI-1
*Miskianza Brook* ... RI-1
**Miskimon**—*pop pl* ... VA-3
*Miskin Bar* ... UT-8
Miski Run—*stream* ... MD-2
Miskita Lake—*lake* ... PA-2
Miskogineu Lake—*lake* ... MN-6
Mislatnah Creek—*stream* ... OR-9
Mislatnah Lookout (historical)—*locale* ... OR-9
Misling Island—*island* ... WI-6
Mismer Bay—*bay* ... MI-6
Misna Ridge—*ridge* ... WI-6
Misner Drain—*canal* ... MI-6
Misner Hollow—*valley* ... PA-2
Misoe Hill—*summit* ... MA-1
*Miso Meadow Pond* ... MA-1
*Miso Meadow Pond* ... RI-1
Mispah Cem—*cemetery* ... NC-3
Mispah Cem—*cemetery* ... VA-3
Mispah Ch—*church* ... SC-3
Mispah Ch—*church* ... VA-3
*Mispalling Creek* ... DE-2
*Mispelion Creek* ... DE-2
*Mispelon Creek* ... DE-2
*Mispening Creek* ... DE-2
*Mispeninge* ... DE-2
*Mispeninge Creek* ... DE-2
*Misperange River* ... DE-2
Mispillion Hundred—*civil* ... DE-2
**Mispillion Light**—*pop pl* ... DE-2
Mispillion Lighthouse and Beacon Tower—*hist pl* ... DE-2
Mispillion Marina—*harbor* ... DE-2
*Mispillion Neck* ... DE-2
Mispillion River—*stream* ... DE-2
Misplaced Lake—*lake* ... MN-6
Misquah Hills—*range* ... MN-6
Misquah Lake—*lake* ... MN-6
Misquakee Lake—*lake* ... IL-6
**Misquamicut**—*pop pl* ... RI-1
*Misquoc Hill* ... MA-1
*Misquoe Hill* ... MA-1
Missa—*locale* ... IL-6
*Missabe Junction* ... MN-6
Missabe Junction—*locale* ... MN-6
Missabe Mountain Mine—*mine* ... MN-6
Missabe Mountain (Township of)—*other* ... MN-6
Missak Bay—*bay* ... AK-9
*Missakianu* ... IA-7
**Missal**—*pop pl* ... IL-6
Missala—*locale* ... MS-4
Missala (historical)—*locale* ... AL-4
Missaukee, Lake—*lake* ... MI-6
**Missaukee (County)**—*pop pl* ... MI-6
Missaukee Junction—*locale* ... MI-6
**Missaukee Park**—*pop pl* ... MI-6
*Miss Barnes Brook* ... NH-1
Miss Bellows Falls Diner—*hist pl* ... VT-1
Missco Sch—*school* ... AR-4
Missed Spring—*spring* ... CA-9
*Misses Bass Landing* ... AL-4
**Missey**—*pop pl* ... MO-7
Missile Tank—*reservoir* ... AZ-5
Missile Tracking Station—*locale* ... UT-8
**Missile View**—*pop pl* ... CA-9
Missile 249 Dam—*dam* ... SD-7
Missile 249 Rsvr—*reservoir* ... SD-7
*Missing Canyon* ... UT-8
Missing Link Lake—*lake* ... MN-6
*Mission* ... WA-9
Mission—*locale* ... DE-2
Mission—*locale* ... MN-6
Mission—*locale* ... MT-8
Mission—*locale* ... NC-3
**Mission**—*pop pl* ... KS-7
**Mission**—*pop pl* ... MI-6
**Mission**—*pop pl* ... OR-9
**Mission**—*pop pl* ... SD-7
**Mission**—*pop pl* ... TX-5
Mission—*post sta* ... AZ-5
Mission—*post sta* ... CA-9
Mission—*uninc pl* (2) ... CA-9
**Mission, The**—*pop pl* ... MI-6
Mission Air Base—*military* ... TX-5
Mission Annex—*uninc pl* ... CA-9
Missionary—*locale* ... LA-4
Missionary—*locale* ... MS-4
**Missionary**—*pop pl* ... LA-4
**Missionary Acres**—*pop pl* ... MO-7
Missionary Alliance Ch—*church* ... GA-3
Missionary Alliance Ch—*church* ... MS-4
Missionary Assembly of God Ch—*church* ... FL-3
Missionary Baptist Ch—*church* ... AL-4
Missionary Baptist Ch—*church* ... MI-6
*Missionary Baptist Ch of Gravelly Springs* ... AL-4
Missionary Canal—*canal* ... ID-8
Missionary Cem—*cemetery* ... MS-4
Missionary Cem—*cemetery* ... OK-5
Missionary Ch—*church* (2) ... AL-4
Missionary Ch—*church* (3) ... AR-4
Missionary Ch—*church* (4) ... FL-3
Missionary Ch—*church* ... GA-3
Missionary Ch—*church* ... IN-6
Missionary Ch—*church* (2) ... KY-4
Missionary Ch—*church* (2) ... MI-6
Missionary Ch—*church* (2) ... MS-4
Missionary Ch—*church* ... MO-7
Missionary Ch—*church* (3) ... NC-3
Missionary Ch—*church* (4) ... OH-6
Missionary Ch—*church* ... OK-5
Missionary Ch—*church* ... PA-2
Missionary Ch—*church* (3) ... TN-4
Missionary Ch—*church* (3) ... TX-5
Missionary Ch—*church* (2) ... WV-2
Missionary Ch Number 2—*church* ... GA-3
*Missionary Creek* ... AL-4
Missionary Ferry—*locale* ... LA-4
Missionary Free Christian Ch—*church* ... IN-6
*Missionary Grove Baptist Ch* ... TN-4
Missionary Grove Ch—*church* ... AL-4
Missionary Grove Ch—*church* ... AR-4
Missionary Grove Ch—*church* ... TN-4
Missionary Indian Ch—*church* ... NY-2
Missionary Island—*island* ... OH-6
Missionary Lake—*lake* ... LA-4
Missionary Lake—*lake* ... MN-6
Missionary Mound Ch—*church* ... KY-4
Missionary Point—*cape* ... WI-6
Missionary Post Office (historical)—*building* ... MS-4
Missionary Range—*range* ... AK-9
Missionary Ridge—*locale* ... GA-3
Missionary Ridge—*ridge* ... CO-8
Missionary Ridge—*ridge* ... GA-3
Missionary Ridge—*ridge* (2) ... TN-4
Missionary Ridge Ch—*church* ... MO-7
Missionary Ridge Ch—*church* ... NC-3
Missionary Ridge Ch—*church* ... TN-4
Missionary Ridge Sch—*school* ... TN-4
Missionary Ridge Tunnel—*tunnel* ... TN-4
Missionary Society of the Methodist Episcopal Church—*hist pl* ... PR-3
Missionary Union Baptist Ch—*church* ... MS-4
Mission Ave Hist Dist—*hist pl* ... WA-9
Mission Ave Sch—*school* ... CA-9
Mission Ave Sch—*school* ... NM-5
Mission Bar—*bar* (2) ... OR-9
Mission Bautista Mexicana—*church* ... MS-4
Mission Bay—*bay* ... CA-9
Mission Bay—*bay* ... ND-7
Mission Bay—*bay* ... TX-5
Mission Bay Channel—*channel* ... CA-9
Mission Bay HS—*school* ... CA-9
*Mission Bay Lake* ... ND-7
Mission Bay Park—*park* ... CA-9
Mission B Canal—*canal* ... MT-8
**Mission Beach**—*pop pl* ... CA-9
**Mission Beach**—*pop pl* ... WA-9
Mission Beach Park—*park* ... CA-9
Mission Beach Roller Coaster—*hist pl* ... CA-9
Mission Beach Sch—*school* ... CA-9
Mission Bell Sch—*school* ... CA-9
Mission Bell Square (Shop Ctr)—*locale* ... FL-3
Mission Bend Public Use Area—*park* ... OK-5
Mission Bible Ch—*church* ... KS-7
Mission Bottom—*bend* ... MT-8
Mission Bottom—*bend* ... OR-9
*Mission Branch* ... MO-7
Mission Branch—*stream* ... MO-7
Mission Branch—*stream* ... NC-3
Mission Branch—*stream* ... OK-5
Mission Branch Sch—*school* ... MO-7
Mission Burial Park—*cemetery* (2) ... TX-5
Mission Buttes—*summit* ... MT-8
Mission Canyon—*valley* ... CA-9
Mission Canyon—*valley* ... MT-8
Mission Canyon—*valley* ... NV-8
Mission C Canal—*canal* ... MT-8
Mission (CCD)—*cens area* ... TX-5
Mission Cem—*cemetery* ... AR-4
Mission Cem—*cemetery* ... CA-9
Mission Cem—*cemetery* ... FL-3
Mission Cem—*cemetery* ... IA-7
Mission Cem—*cemetery* (2) ... KS-7
Mission Cem—*cemetery* (2) ... MN-6
Mission Cem—*cemetery* ... MS-4
Mission Cem—*cemetery* ... NE-7
Mission Cem—*cemetery* (2) ... OH-6
Mission Center Cem—*cemetery* ... MN-6
Mission Central HS—*school* ... CA-9
*Mission Centre* ... KS-7
*Mission Ch* ... MS-4
Mission Ch—*church* ... AL-4
Mission Ch—*church* (2) ... FL-3
Mission Ch—*church* ... GA-3
Mission Ch—*church* (3) ... KY-4
Mission Ch—*church* ... MD-2
Mission Ch—*church* ... MN-6
Mission Ch—*church* ... MS-4
Mission Ch—*church* ... MT-8
Mission Ch—*church* (4) ... NC-3
Mission Ch—*church* (3) ... OK-5
Mission Ch—*church* ... PA-2
Mission Ch—*church* ... SC-3
Mission Ch—*church* (2) ... TX-5
Mission Ch—*church* (2) ... WI-6
Mission Chapel—*church* ... IL-6
Mission Chapel—*church* ... LA-4
Mission Chapel—*church* (2) ... MO-7
Mission Chapel—*church* ... PA-2
Mission Chapel—*church* ... VT-1
Mission Chapel—*church* ... WI-6
Mission Chapel—*hist pl* ... MA-1
Mission Chapel Cem—*cemetery* ... IL-6
Mission Ch (historical)—*church* ... MO-7
Mission Ch (historical)—*church* ... TN-4
Mission Church—*hist pl* ... AK-9
Mission Church—*hist pl* ... MI-6
**Mission City**—*pop pl* ... FL-3
Mission City Annex—*post sta* ... CA-9
Mission Concepcion—*hist pl* ... TX-5
Mission Concepcion—*park* ... TX-5
*Mission Convenant Church* ... SD-7
*Mission Coulee* ... MT-8
Mission Coulee—*valley* (2) ... MT-8
Mission County Park—*park* ... TX-5
Mission Court—*hist pl* ... CA-9
Mission Cove—*bay* ... AK-9
Mission Covenant Cem—*cemetery* ... KS-7
Mission Covenant Cem—*cemetery* (3) ... MN-6
Mission Covenant Cem—*cemetery* ... WI-6
Mission Covenant Ch—*church* ... IA-7
Mission Covenant Ch—*church* ... KS-7
Mission Covenant Ch—*church* ... MI-6
Mission Covenant Ch—*church* (4) ... MN-6
Mission Covenant Ch—*church* ... MO-7
*Mission Creek* ... KS-7
*Mission Creek* ... WA-9
Mission Creek—*locale* ... MN-6
Mission Creek—*stream* (4) ... AK-9
Mission Creek—*stream* (6) ... CA-9
Mission Creek—*stream* (3) ... ID-8
Mission Creek—*stream* ... IL-6
Mission Creek—*stream* (4) ... KS-7
Mission Creek—*stream* (2) ... MI-6
Mission Creek—*stream* (4) ... MN-6
Mission Creek—*stream* ... MO-7
Mission Creek—*stream* (5) ... MT-8
Mission Creek*—*stream* ... NE-7
Mission Creek—*stream* ... NE-7
Mission Creek—*stream* (2) ... OK-5
Mission Creek—*stream* (2) ... OR-9
Mission Creek—*stream* (2) ... SD-7
Mission Creek—*stream* ... TX-5
Mission Creek—*stream* (7) ... WA-9
Mission Creek Cem—*cemetery* ... KS-7
Mission Creek Cem—*cemetery* ... MI-6
Mission Creek Cem—*cemetery* ... NE-7
Mission Creek Ch—*church* ... NE-7
Mission Creek Community Center—*locale* ... KS-7
Mission Creek Dam—*dam* ... OR-9
Mission Creek Dam and Acequia Site—*hist pl* ... TX-5
Mission Creek (historical)—*locale* ... KS-7
Mission Creek Rsvr—*reservoir* ... OR-9
Mission Creek Sch—*school* ... MT-8
**Mission Creek Township**—*pop pl* ... KS-7
Mission Creek (Township of)—*civ div* ... MN-6
Mission Dam—*dam* ... NC-3
Mission Dam—*dam* ... SD-7
Mission Dam and Fume Historic Site—*locale* ... CA-9
Mission de la Purisima Concepcion de Maria Santisima Site—*hist pl* ... CA-9
**Mission District**—*pop pl* ... CA-9
Mission Ditch—*canal* ... OR-9
Mission Ditch—*canal* ... WY-8
Mission Dolores—*church* ... CA-9
Mission Dolores—*hist pl* ... CA-9
Mission Dolores a Vista—*church* ... TX-5
Mission Espada—*church* ... TX-5
Mission Espada Cem—*cemetery* ... TX-5
Mission Espiritu Santo—*church* ... TX-5
Mission Falls—*falls* ... ID-8
Mission Falls—*falls* ... MT-8
Mission Farm—*locale* ... WV-2
**Mission Farms**—*pop pl* ... MN-6
**Missionfield**—*pop pl* ... IL-6
Missionfield Pond—*lake* ... IL-6
Mission Flats—*flat* ... ID-8
Mission Free Cem—*cemetery* ... ND-7
Mission Free Ch—*church* ... ND-7
Mission Garden Cem—*cemetery* ... NM-5
Mission Gas Field—*oilfield* ... TX-5
Mission Golf Course—*locale* ... SD-7
Mission Gorge—*valley* ... CA-9
**Mission (Government Indian Mission)**—*pop pl* ... OR-9
Mission Grove Ch—*church* ... AL-4
Mission Gulch—*valley* ... ID-8
Mission H Canal—*canal* ... MT-8
Mission-Herring Barn—*hist pl* ... KS-7
Mission Highlands—*locale* ... CA-9
Mission Highlands—*uninc pl* ... KS-7
**Mission Hill**—*pop pl* ... PA-2
**Mission Hill**—*pop pl* ... SD-7
Mission Hill—*summit* ... AK-9
Mission Hill—*summit* ... ID-8
Mission Hill—*summit* ... MI-6
Mission Hill—*summit* ... MT-8
Mission Hill—*summit* ... TX-5
Mission Hill Area Hist Dist—*hist pl* ... CA-9
Mission Hill Cem—*cemetery* ... MI-6
Mission Hill Ch—*church* ... MS-4
Mission Hill Ch—*church* ... NC-3
Mission Hill Hosp—*hospital* ... OK-5
Mission Hill JHS—*school* ... CA-9
**Mission Hills**—*pop pl* (2) ... CA-9
**Mission Hills**—*pop pl* ... IL-6
**Mission Hills**—*pop pl* ... KS-7
**Mission Hills**—*pop pl* ... TX-5
Mission Hills (census name for Lompoc North)—*CDP* ... CA-9
Mission Hills Country Club—*other* ... KS-7
Mission Hills Park—*park* ... CA-9
**Mission Hills (subdivision)**—*pop pl* ... AL-4
**Mission Hill Township**—*pop pl* ... SD-7
Mission Hollow—*valley* ... WV-2
Mission Home—*locale* ... VA-3
Mission Home Cem—*cemetery* ... VA-3
Mission Home Ch—*church* ... MO-7
Mission Home Ch—*church* ... NC-3
Mission Home Ch—*church* ... OK-5
Mission Hosp—*hospital* ... CA-9
Mission Hosp—*hospital* ... MT-8
Mission House—*hist pl* ... MA-1
Mission House—*hist pl* ... MI-6
Mission House Coll—*school* ... WI-6
Mission House Hist Dist—*hist pl* ... WI-6
Mission HS—*school* (2) ... CA-9
Missionhurst—*building* ... VA-3
Mission Indian Res—*reserve* ... CA-9
*Mission Ind Res* ... CA-9
Mission Inlet—*canal* ... TX-5
Mission Inn—*hist pl* ... CA-9
Mission Island—*island* ... AK-9
Mission Island (historical)—*island* ... SD-7
Mission JHS—*school* ... CA-9
Mission Junction—*locale* ... CA-9
Mission Lake—*bay* ... TX-5
Mission Lake—*lake* ... AK-9
Mission Lake—*lake* (2) ... MN-6
Mission Lake—*lake* ... MT-8
Mission Lake—*lake* ... OR-9
Mission Lake—*lake* (2) ... TX-5
Mission Lake—*lake* (2) ... WA-9
Mission Lake—*lake* (2) ... WI-6
Mission Lake—*reservoir* ... KS-7
Mission Lake—*reservoir* ... NC-3
Mission Lake—*reservoir* ... OR-9
Mission Lake—*reservoir* ... SD-7
Mission Lake—*swamp* ... MN-6
Mission Lake Camp—*locale* ... KS-7
Mission Lake Dam—*dam* ... KS-7
Mission Lands—*civil* ... CA-9
Mission Lands Of Santa Cruz—*civil* ... CA-9
Mission La Purisima—*civil* ... CA-9
Mission La Purisima Concepcion—*church* ... CA-9
Mission Lookout—*locale* ... MT-8
Mission Main Canal—*canal* ... TX-5
Mission Manor—*uninc pl* ... AZ-5
Mission Manor Sch—*school* ... AZ-5
Mission Manor Shop Ctr—*locale* ... AZ-5
Mission Mart Shop Ctr—*locale* ... KS-7
Mission Memorial Park (Cem)—*cemetery* ... CA-9
Mission Mine—*mine* ... AZ-5
**Mission Monterey (subdivision)**—*pop pl* (2) ... AZ-5
*Mission Mountain* ... MT-8
Mission Mountain—*ridge* ... CA-9
Mission Mount Bethel Ch—*church* ... AL-4
Mission Mtn—*summit* (2) ... ID-8
Mission Mtn—*summit* ... NC-3
Mission Mtn—*summit* ... OK-5
Mission Mtn—*summit* ... WA-9
Mission Nuestra Senora de los Dolores de los Ais Site—*hist pl* ... TX-5
Mission Nuestra Senora del Rosario—*locale* ... TX-5
Mission Number 11—*church* ... IN-6
**Mission Oaks**—*pop pl* ... TN-4
Mission Of Faith Ch—*church* ... IN-6
Mission of Las Cabreras—*locale* ... TX-5
Mission of Nombre de Dios and La Leche Shrine—*church* ... FL-3
Mission of San Gabriel—*civil* ... CA-9
Mission of San Juan del Puerto Archeol Site—*hist pl* ... FL-3
Mission Park—*park* (2) ... AZ-5
Mission Park—*park* ... CA-9
Mission Park—*park* ... WA-9
**Mission Park**—*pop pl* ... NM-5
Mission Park Sch—*school* ... CA-9
Mission Parkway—*hist pl* ... TX-5
Mission Pass—*gap* ... CA-9
Mission Peak—*summit* ... CA-9
Mission Peak—*summit* ... MT-8
Mission Peak—*summit* ... NV-8
Mission Peak—*summit* (2) ... WA-9
Mission Pine Basin—*basin* ... CA-9
Mission Pine Camp—*locale* ... CA-9
Mission Pine Trail—*trail* ... CA-9
Mission Point—*cape* ... CA-9
Mission Point—*cape* ... MI-6
Mission Point—*summit* ... CA-9
Mission Point Ch—*church* ... MO-7
Mission Point Ch—*church* ... TX-5
Mission Pond—*lake* ... GA-3
Mission Pump—*other* ... TX-5
Mission Rafael—*uninc pl* ... CA-9
Mission Ranch—*locale* (2) ... CA-9
Mission Ranch—*locale* ... MT-8
Mission Ranch—*locale* ... NE-7
Mission Range—*spring* ... MT-8
**Mission Ridge**—*pop pl* ... SD-7
Mission Ridge—*ridge* ... MT-8
Mission Ridge—*ridge* ... NH-1
Mission Ridge—*ridge* ... OK-5
Mission Ridge—*ridge* (2) ... WA-9
Mission Ridge—*ridge* ... WV-2
Mission Ridge—*uninc pl* ... GA-3
*Mission Ridge Baptist Ch* ... MS-4
Mission Ridge Baptist Ch—*church* ... TN-4
Mission Ridge Ch—*church* ... MS-4
Mission Ridge Ch—*church* (2) ... MO-7
Mission Ridge Ch—*church* ... TX-5
Mission Ridge Ch—*church* ... WV-2
Mission Ridge (historical)—*locale* ... SD-7
Mission Ridge Park—*park* ... AZ-5
Mission Ridge Sch—*school* (2) ... IL-6
Mission Ridge Sch (historical)—*school* ... MO-7
Mission Ridge Trail—*trail* ... WA-9
Mission Ridge Winter Sports Area—*locale* ... WA-9
Mission River—*stream* ... TX-5
Mission River Oil And Gas Field—*oilfield* ... TX-5
Mission Road Ch of God in Christ—*church* ... FL-3
Mission Road Foundation Sch—*school* ... TX-5
Mission Road Landing Strip—*airport* ... KS-7
Mission Rock Terminal—*other* ... CA-9
Mission Rsvr—*reservoir* ... CA-9
Mission Rsvr—*reservoir* ... MT-8
Mission San Buenaventura—*church* ... CA-9
Mission San Buenaventura and Mission Compound Site—*hist pl* ... CA-9
Mission San Carlos—*church* ... CA-9
Mission San Diego—*civil* ... CA-9
Mission San Diego de Alcala—*civil* ... CA-9
Mission San Diego de Alcala—*hist pl* ... CA-9
Mission San Fernando—*church* ... CA-9
Mission San Fernando Rey de Convento Bldg—*hist pl* ... CA-9
Mission San Francisco de la Espada—*church* ... TX-5
Mission San Francisco de la Espada—*hist pl* ... TX-5
Mission San Francisco De La Espada—*well* ... TX-5
Mission San Francisco de la Espada (Boundary Increase)—*hist pl* ... TX-5
Mission San Francisco Solano Vineyard—*other* ... CA-9
Mission San Gabriel Arrangel—*school* ... CA-9
Mission San Jose—*hist pl* ... CA-9
Mission San Jose—*uninc pl* ... CA-9
Mission San Jose de Guadalupe—*church* ... CA-9
**Mission San Jose District**—*pop pl* ... CA-9
Mission San Jose HS—*school* ... CA-9
Mission San Juan Bautista—*park* ... CA-9
Mission San Juan Capistrano—*hist pl* ... CA-9
Mission San Juan Capistrano—*hist pl* ... TX-5
Mission San Juan de Capistrano—*church* ... TX-5
Mission San Lorenzo de la Santa Cruz—*hist pl* ... TX-5
Mission San Luis Obispo de Tolosa—*church* ... CA-9
Mission San Luis Rey de Francia—*church* ... CA-9
Mission San Miguel—*hist pl* ... CA-9
Mission San Rafael—*civil* ... CA-9
Mission Santa Clara de Asis—*church* ... CA-9
Mission Santa Clara De Asis Historical Monmt—*park* ... CA-9
Mission Santa Ines—*church* ... CA-9
*Mission Santos Angeles de Guevavi* ... AZ-5
Missions Building—*other* ... IN-6
Mission Sch—*school* (2) ... CA-9
Mission Sch—*school* ... HI-9
Mission Sch—*school* ... KS-7
Mission Sch—*school* ... MD-2
Mission Sch—*school* ... SD-7
Mission Sch (historical)—*school* (2) ... AL-4
Mission Sioux Airp—*airport* ... SD-7
Mission Soledad—*locale* ... CA-9
Mission Spring—*spring* ... WA-9
**Mission Springs**—*pop pl* ... CA-9
**Mission Springs (Bible Camps)**—*pop pl* ... CA-9
Mission Springs Ch—*church* ... TX-5
**Mission Square**—*pop pl* ... VA-3
Mission Stadium—*other* ... TX-5
Missions Tailings Dam Number Two—*dam* ... AZ-5
Mission Street Park—*park* ... WA-9
Mission Sweet Mine—*mine* ... CA-9
Mission Tabernacle—*church* ... WV-2
Mission Tailings Dam Number One—*dam* ... AZ-5
Mission Tejas State Park—*park* ... TX-5
Mission Temple—*church* ... MO-7
**Mission Township**—*pop pl* (3) ... KS-7
**Mission Township**—*pop pl* ... ND-7
**Mission Township**—*pop pl* ... SD-7
**Mission (Township of)**—*pop pl* ... IL-6
**Mission (Township of)**—*pop pl* ... MN-6
Mission Trail—*trail* ... CA-9
Mission Union Sch—*school* ... CA-9
**Mission Valley**—*pop pl* (2) ... TX-5
Mission Valley—*valley* ... CA-9
Mission Valley—*valley* ... MT-8
Mission Valley Cem—*cemetery* ... TX-5
Mission Valley Country Club—*locale* ... FL-3
Mission Valley Gas Field—*oilfield* ... TX-5
Mission Valley Guest Ranch—*locale* ... TX-5
Mission Valley HS—*school* ... KS-7
Mission Valley Sch—*school* ... CA-9
Mission Valley Shop Ctr—*locale* ... CA-9
**Mission Valley (subdivison)**—*pop pl* (2) ... AZ-5
Mission Valley West Gas Field—*oilfield* ... TX-5
Mission Vieja (Site)—*locale* ... CA-9
*Mission Viejo* ... CO-8
**Mission Viejo**—*pop pl* ... CA-9
Mission Viejo Golf Club—*other* ... CA-9
Mission Viejo HS—*school* ... CA-9
Mission Viejo Or La Paz—*civil* ... CA-9
Mission View Cem—*cemetery* ... KS-7
Mission View Park—*park* ... CA-9
Mission View Sch—*school* ... AZ-5
Mission Wash—*stream* ... CA-9
Mission Well—*well* ... CA-9
Mission Well—*well* ... MT-8
Mission Wells—*well* ... CA-9
Mission Windmill—*locale* ... NM-5
**Mission Woods**—*pop pl* ... KS-7
Mission Zanja, The—*canal* ... CA-9
**Missisinewa (historical)**—*pop pl* ... IN-6
*Missisinewa River* ... IN-6
*Missiskouie* ... VT-1
Missisquoi Bay—*bay* ... VT-1
Missisquoi Bay Bridge—*bridge* ... VT-1
**Missisquoi (local name East Richford)**—*pop pl* ... VT-1
Missisquoi Natl Wildlife Ref—*park* ... VT-1
Missisquoi River—*stream* ... VT-1
Missisquoi Station—*locale* ... VT-1
*Mississackaway Creek* ... NJ-2
*Mississinawa River* ... IN-6
Mississinawa (Township of)—*civ div* ... OH-6
*Mississinaway River* ... IN-6
*Mississinewa* ... IN-6
Mississinewa Ch—*church* ... IN-6
Mississinewa Country Club—*other* ... IN-6
Mississinewa HS—*school* ... IN-6
Mississinewa Lake—*reservoir* ... IN-6
Mississinewa Lake Dam—*dam* ... IN-6
Mississinewa Memorial Cem—*cemetery* ... IN-6
*Mississinewa Reservoir* ... IN-6
Mississinewa River—*stream* ... IN-6
*Mississineway River* ... IN-6
*Mississippi Academy* ... MS-4
Mississippi Agricultural and Forestry Experiment Station—*locale* ... MS-4
*Mississippi Agricultural and Mechanical College* ... MS-4
Mississippi Baptist HS—*school* ... MS-4
*Mississippi Baptist Med Ctr* ... MS-4
Mississippi Bar—*bar* ... CA-9
Mississippi Bayou—*stream* (2) ... LA-4
Mississippi Bend—*bend* ... KY-4
Mississippi Canyon—*valley* ... NV-8
Mississippi Central Junction—*locale* ... MS-4
*Mississippi Central Normal School* ... MS-4
**Mississippi Choctaw Ind Res**—*pop pl* ... MS-4
**Mississippi City**—*pop pl* ... MS-4
Mississippi Coast Coliseum and Convention Center—*building* ... MS-4
Mississippi Coliseum—*building* ... MS-4
Mississippi Coll—*school* ... MS-4
*Mississippi Coll Coliseum* ... MS-4
Mississippi College Lake—*reservoir* ... MS-4
Mississippi Conservatory of Art and Expression (historical)—*school* ... MS-4
**Mississippi (County)**—*pop pl* ... AR-4
**Mississippi County**—*pop pl* ... MO-7
Mississippi County Airp—*airport* ... MO-7

Mississippi County Courthouse—*hist pl* AR-4
Mississippi County Jail—*hist pl* AR-4
Mississippi County Memorial Gardens—*cemetery* AR-4
Mississippi County Penal Farm—*other* AR-4
Mississippi Crafts Center—*building* MS-4
Mississippi Creek—*stream* (3) CA-9
Mississippi Creek—*stream* MN-6
*Mississippi Delta Junior College* MS-4
Mississippi Federation of Women's Clubs—*hist pl* MS-4
Mississippi Female Coll (historical)—*school* MS-4
Mississippi Flats—*flat* SD-7
Mississippi Governor's Mansion—*hist pl* MS-4
Mississippi Gulf Coast Junior Coll—*school* (2) MS-4
Mississippi Head—*cliff* OR-9
Mississippi Headwaters State For—*forest* MN-6
Mississippi Heights Acad (historical)—*school* MS-4
Mississippi Highway Patrol Lake Dam—*dam* MS-4
MISSISSIPPI III—*hist pl* OH-6
Mississippi Industrial Coll—*school* MS-4
Mississippi Industrial College Hist Dist—*hist pl* MS-4
*Mississippi Industrial Training Sch* MS-4
Mississippi Lake—*lake* MN-6
Mississippi Mine—*mine* MO-7
Mississippi No Name 1 Dam—*dam* MS-4
Mississippi No Name 116 Dam—*dam* MS-4
Mississippi No Name 140 Dam—*dam* MS-4
Mississippi No Name 152 Dam—*dam* MS-4
Mississippi No Name 156 Dam—*dam* MS-4
Mississippi No Name 157 Dam—*dam* MS-4
Mississippi No Name 158 Dam—*dam* MS-4
Mississippi No Name 159 Dam—*dam* MS-4
Mississippi No Name 161 Dam—*dam* MS-4
Mississippi No Name 162 Dam—*dam* MS-4
Mississippi No Name 163 Dam—*dam* MS-4
Mississippi No Name 171 Dam—*dam* MS-4
Mississippi No Name 173 Dam—*dam* MS-4
Mississippi No Name 183 Dam—*dam* MS-4
Mississippi No Name 186 Dam—*dam* MS-4
Mississippi No Name 199 Dam—*dam* MS-4
Mississippi No Name 217 Dam—*dam* MS-4
Mississippi No Name 219 Dam—*dam* MS-4
Mississippi No Name 220 Dam—*dam* MS-4
Mississippi No Name 222 Dam—*dam* MS-4
Mississippi No Name 223 Dam—*dam* MS-4
Mississippi No Name 224 Dam—*dam* MS-4
Mississippi No Name 226 Dam—*dam* MS-4
Mississippi No Name 228 Dam—*dam* MS-4
Mississippi No Name 24 Dam—*dam* MS-4
Mississippi No Name 30 Dam—*dam* MS-4
Mississippi No Name 34 Dam—*dam* MS-4
Mississippi No Name 35 Dam—*dam* MS-4
Mississippi No Name 43 Dam—*dam* MS-4
Mississippi No Name 5 Dam—*dam* MS-4
Mississippi No Name 53 Dam—*dam* MS-4
Mississippi No Name 55 Dam—*dam* MS-4
Mississippi No Name 58 Dam—*dam* MS-4
Mississippi No Name 59 Dam—*dam* MS-4
Mississippi No Name 6 Dam—*dam* MS-4
Mississippi No Name 65 Dam—*dam* MS-4
Mississippi No Name 68 Dam—*dam* MS-4
Mississippi No Name 7 Dam—*dam* MS-4
Mississippi No Name 75 Dam—*dam* MS-4
*Mississippi Normal College* MS-4
Mississippi Normal Coll (historical)—*school* MS-4
Mississippi Normal Institute (historical)—*school* MS-4
Mississippi Number One Mine—*mine* MN-6
Mississippi-Obion (CCD)—*cens area* TN-4
Mississippi-Obion Division—*civil* TN-4
Mississippi Palisades State Park—*park* IL-6
Mississippi Park—*park* MN-6
Mississippi Park—*park* TN-4
Mississippi Pond—*lake* (2) AL-4
Mississippi Power and Light Company Lake Dam—*dam* MS-4
Mississippi Power and Light Pond Dam—*dam* MS-4
Mississippi Research and Technology Park—*locale* MS-4
Mississippi River—*stream* AR-4
Mississippi River—*stream* IL-6
Mississippi River*—*stream* IA-7
Mississippi River—*stream* KY-4
Mississippi River—*stream* LA-4
Mississippi River—*stream* MN-6
Mississippi River—*stream* MS-4
Mississippi River—*stream* MO-7
Mississippi River—*stream* TN-4
Mississippi River—*stream* WI-6
Mississippi River Delta—*area* LA-4
*Mississippi River-Gulf Outlet* LA-4
Mississippi River-Gulf Outlet Canal—*canal* LA-4
*Mississippi River-Gulf Outlet Channel* LA-4
Mississippi River Lock Dam Number Eighteen—*dam* IA-7
Mississippi River Lock Dam Number Eleven—*dam* IA-7
Mississippi River Lock Dam Number Fifteen—*dam* IA-7
Mississippi River Lock Dam Number Fourteen—*dam* IA-7
Mississippi River Lock Dam Number Seventeen—*dam* IA-7
Mississippi River Lock Dam Number Sixteen—*dam* IA-7
Mississippi River Lock Dam Number Thirteen—*dam* IA-7
Mississippi Sandhill Crane Natl Wildlife Ref—*park* (2) MS-4
Mississippi Sch—*school* (2) MN-6
Mississippi Sch for the Blind—*school* MS-4
Mississippi Sch for the Deaf—*school* MS-4
Mississippi Sheriffs Boys Ranch—*locale* MS-4
Mississippi Slough—*stream* MO-7
Mississippi Sound—*bay* AL-4
Mississippi Sound—*bay* LA-4
Mississippi Sound—*bay* MS-4
Mississippi Springs—*spring* NV-8
Mississippi Springs (historical)—*locale* MS-4
Mississippi State—*post sta* MS-4
Mississippi State Capitol—*hist pl* MS-4
*Mississippi State College for W* MS-4
Mississippi State College Lake Dam—*dam* MS-4
Mississippi State Experimental Station—*locale* MS-4
Mississippi State Extension Lake Dam—*dam* MS-4
*Mississippi State Game and Fish Commission Calhoun County Refuge* MS-4
Mississippi State Hosp—*hospital* MS-4
*Mississippi State Mental Hosp* MS-4
Mississippi State Penitentiary—*building* MS-4
Mississippi State Univ—*school* MS-4
Mississippi State University School of Forest Resources—*school* MS-4
*Mississippi State Univ Experimental Forests* MS-4
Mississippi Synodical Coll (historical)—*school* MS-4
Mississippi Test Facility (NASA)—*building* MS-4
Mississippi Test Facility (NASA)—*other* MS-4
Mississippi Township—*civil* MO-7
Mississippi (Township of)—*fmr MCD* (3) AR-4
**Mississippi (Township of)**—*pop pl* IL-6
Mississippi Univ for Women—*school* MS-4
Mississippi Valley Fair Grounds—*other* IA-7
**Mississippi Valley State Univ**—*pop pl* MS-4
Mississippi Valley State Univ—*school* MS-4
*Mississippi Vocational Coll* MS-4
Mississippi Wash—*stream* AZ-5
Miss Lake—*lake* MN-6
Missler—*locale* KS-7
Missoo Gulch—*valley* CO-8
*Missou Creek* CO-8
**Missoula**—*pop pl* MT-8
Missoula Cem—*cemetery* MT-8
Missoula County Airport—*airport* MT-8
Missoula County Courthouse—*hist pl* MT-8
Missoula Creek—*stream* AK-9
Missoula Gulch—*valley* ID-8
Missoula Gulch—*valley* MT-8
Missoula Lake—*lake* MT-8
Missoula Mine—*mine* MT-8
*Missoula River* ID-8
*Missoula River* WA-9
Missoula Snow Bowl—*basin* MT-8
Missoula South—*CDP* MT-8
**Missoula Southwest**—*pop pl* MT-8
**Missoula West**—*pop pl* MT-8
Missouri, Kansas, and Texas RR Depot—*hist pl* MO-7
Missouri, Kansas and Texas RR Depot—*hist pl* MO-7
Missouri Ave Sch—*school* NM-5
Missouri Baptist Coll—*school* MO-7
Missouri Baptist Hosp—*hospital* (2) MO-7
Missouri Baptist Hospital Heliport—*airport* MO-7
Missouri Bar—*bar* (3) CA-9
Missouri Bar—*bar* OR-9
Missouri Basin—*basin* CO-8
Missouri Bench—*bench* MT-8
Missouri Bend—*bend* CA-9
Missouri Bend—*bend* OR-9
Missouri Bend Recreation Site—*park* OR-9
Missouri Bend School (abandoned)—*locale* OR-9
Missouri Bill Hill—*summit* AZ-5
Missouri Bill Tank—*reservoir* AZ-5
Missouri Botanical Garden—*park* MO-7
Missouri Botanical Garden Arboretum—*park* MO-7
Missouri Botanical Gardens—*hist pl* MO-7
Missouri Bottom—*bend* OR-9
**Missouri Branch**—*pop pl* WV-2
Missouri Branch—*stream* KY-4
Missouri Branch—*stream* MO-7
Missouri Branch—*stream* NC-3
Missouri Branch—*stream* WV-2
Missouri Buttes—*summit* WY-8
Missouri Buttes Lake—*lake* WY-8
Missouri Canyon—*valley* (3) CA-9
Missouri Canyon—*valley* CO-8
Missouri Cem—*cemetery* OK-5
Missouri Center—*locale* CO-8
Missouri Ch—*church* AR-4
Missouri Ch—*church* VA-3
Missouri Chute—*stream* MO-7
**Missouri City**—*pop pl* MO-7
**Missouri City**—*pop pl* TX-5
Missouri Conservation Department-Branson HQ—*building* MO-7
*Missouri Coteau* ND-7
Missouri Coulee—*valley* MT-8
*Missouri Creek* CO-8
*Missouri Creek* WA-9
Missouri Creek—*stream* AK-9
Missouri Creek—*stream* CA-9
Missouri Creek—*stream* (4) CO-8
Missouri Creek—*stream* ID-8
Missouri Creek—*stream* IL-6
Missouri Creek—*stream* MN-6
Missouri Creek—*stream* MO-7
Missouri Creek—*stream* OR-9
Missouri Creek—*stream* UT-8
Missouri Creek—*stream* WV-2
Missouri Creek—*stream* WI-6
Missouri Cutoff—*gap* MT-8
Missouri Delta Heliport—*airport* MO-7
Missouri Department of Conservation District Forester Office—*building* MO-7
Missouri Ditch—*canal* CO-8
Missouri Ditch—*canal* MT-8
Missouri Ditch—*canal* OH-6
Missouri Ditch No 4—*canal* MO-7
Missouri Falls—*falls* CO-8
Missouri Flat—*flat* ID-8
Missouri Flat—*flat* NV-8
Missouri Flat—*flat* (2) OR-9
Missouri Flat—*flat* WA-9
Missouri Flat—*locale* CA-9
Missouri Flat Creek—*stream* ID-8
Missouri Flat Creek—*stream* WA-9
**Missouri Flat (historical)**—*pop pl* OR-9
Missouri Flat Mine—*mine* CA-9
Missouri Flats—*flat* CO-8
Missouri Flats—*flat* MT-8
Missouri Flats—*flat* WA-9
Missouri Flat Sch—*school* CA-9
Missouri Flats Sch—*school* KS-7
Missouri Flat Well—*well* NV-8
Missouri Fork—*stream* (2) WV-2
Missouri Governor's Mansion—*hist pl* MO-7
Missouri Gulch—*valley* CA-9
Missouri Gulch—*valley* (4) CO-8
Missouri Gulch—*valley* (2) ID-8
Missouri Gulch—*valley* MT-8
Missouri Gulch—*valley* OR-9
Missouri Gulch Trail—*trail* CO-8
Missouri Harbor—*bay* WA-9
*Missouri Heights Reservoir* CO-8
Missouri Hill—*summit* (2) CO-8
Missouri Hollow—*valley* KY-4
Missouri Hollow—*valley* OR-9
Missouri Hollow Ch—*church* KY-4
Missouri John Spring—*spring* WY-8
Missouri-Kansas-Texas Company RR Station—*hist pl* TX-5
Missouri Key—*island* FL-3
Missouri Lake—*lake* CO-8
Missouri Lake—*lake* (2) MN-6
Missouri Lakes—*lake* CO-8
Missouri Landing—*locale* FL-3
Missouri Little Duck Key Channel—*channel* FL-3
Missouri Military Acad—*school* MO-7
Missouri Mine—*mine* CO-8
Missouri Mine—*mine* ID-8
Missouri Mine—*mine* MT-8
Missouri Mountains—*ridge* AR-4
Missouri Mtn—*summit* CO-8
Missouri Pacific Depot—*hist pl* (2) AR-4
Missouri Pacific Depot—*hist pl* (2) MO-7
Missouri Pacific Hosp—*hospital* MO-7
Missouri Park—*flat* CO-8
Missouri Park—*park* MO-7
**Missouri Park**—*pop pl* CO-8
Missouri Park Ditch—*canal* CO-8
Missouri Plaza Indian Ruins—*locale* NM-5
Missouri Pump Canal—*canal* MT-8
Missouri Ridge—*fmr MCD* NE-7
Missouri Ridge—*ridge* ID-8
Missouri Ridge—*ridge* OR-9
Missouri Ridge—*ridge* WA-9
**Missouri Ridge Township**—*pop pl* ND-7
Missouri River*—*stream* IA-7
Missouri River*—*stream* KS-7
Missouri River—*stream* MO-7
Missouri River—*stream* MT-8
Missouri River*—*stream* NE-7
Missouri River*—*stream* ND-7
Missouri River*—*stream* SD-7
Missouri River Township—*civil* MO-7
Missouri Run—*stream* WV-2
Missouri Sch for Blind—*school* MO-7
Missouri Sch of Mines (abandoned)—*school* MO-7
Missouri Sch of Mines (historical)—*school* MO-7
Missouri/Sedalia Trust Company—*hist pl* MO-7
Missouri Sister Island—*island* IL-6
Missouri Slope Grazing Association Number 1 Dam—*dam* SD-7
Missouri Slope Grazing Association Number 2 Dam—*dam* SD-7
Missouri Slough—*stream* AR-4
Missouri State Capitol Bldg and Grounds—*hist pl* MO-7
Missouri State Capitol Hist Dist—*hist pl* MO-7
Missouri State Highway Patrol HQ—*other* MO-7
Missouri State Teachers Association—*hist pl* MO-7
Missouri Theater—*hist pl* MO-7
Missouri Theater and Missouri Theater Bldg—*hist pl* MO-7
Missouri Township—*civil* MO-7
**Missouri Township**—*pop pl* MO-7
**Missouri Township**—*pop pl* ND-7
Missouri (Township of)—*fmr MCD* (3) AR-4
**Missouri (Township of)**—*pop pl* IL-6
Missouri Trachoma Hosp (abandoned)—*hospital* MO-7
**Missouri Training Center for Men**—*pop pl* MO-7
**Missouri Triangle**—*pop pl* CA-9
Missouri Tunnel—*tunnel* CO-8
Missouri United Methodist Church—*hist pl* MO-7
**Missouri Valley**—*pop pl* IA-7
Missouri Valley—*valley* WY-8
Missouri Valley Ch—*church* WY-8
Missouri Valley Coll—*school* MO-7
Missouri Valley Spraying Private Airfield—*airport* ND-7
Missouri Valley Trust Company Hist Dist—*hist pl* MO-7
Missouri Western Coll—*school* MO-7
Miss Thatchers Pond—*reservoir* MA-1
Missuori John Draw—*valley* WY-8
Missy Gap—*gap* GA-3
**Mist**—*pop pl* AR-4
**Mist**—*pop pl* OR-9
Mist, Mount—*summit* NH-1
Mistake Harbor—*bay* ME-1
Mistake Island—*island* ME-1
Mistake Lake—*lake* WY-8
Mistake Mine—*mine* AZ-5
Mistake Mine—*mine* CA-9
Mistaken Creek—*stream* KY-4
Mistaken Creek—*stream* MO-7
Mistake Peak—*summit* AZ-5
Mistake Point—*cape* CA-9
Mistake Tank—*reservoir* AZ-5
Mistake Tank—*reservoir* NM-5
Mist Cove—*bay* AK-9
Mist Creek—*stream* AK-9
Mist Creek—*stream* ID-8
Mist Creek—*stream* MT-8
Mist Creek—*stream* OR-9
Mist Creek—*stream* WA-9
Mist Creek—*stream* WY-8
Mist Creek Pass—*gap* WY-8
Mist Creek Trail—*trail* WY-8
Misteguay Creek—*stream* MI-6
Mister and Mrs Larry Lee Carter Natural Area—*park* TN-4
Misterfeldt Home Place—*hist pl* MS-4
Misterton—*locale* MS-4
Mist Falls—*falls* CA-9
Mist Falls—*falls* OR-9
Mist Harbor—*bay* AK-9
*Mistic* MA-1
Mist Island—*island* AK-9
Mist Lake—*lake* CA-9
Mist Lake—*lake* MN-6
*Mistletoe* MP-9
Mistletoe—*hist pl* MS-4
Mistletoe—*locale* KY-4
Mistletoe—*locale* OR-9
Mistletoe Cem—*cemetery* TX-5
Mistletoe Corners—*locale* GA-3
*Mistletoe Creek* TX-5
Mistletoe Creek—*stream* MN-6
Mistletoe Creek—*stream* NC-3
Mistletoe Gulch—*valley* NM-5
Mistletoe Lake—*lake* MN-6
Mistletoe Mine (Inactive)—*mine* CA-9
Mistletoe Oil Field—*oilfield* MS-4
Mistletoe Sch—*school* CA-9
Mistletoe State Park—*park* GA-3
Mistletoe Trail—*trail* MD-2
Mistletoe Villa—*hist pl* NC-3
Mistletow Canyon—*valley* ID-8
**Miston**—*pop pl* TN-4
Miston Baptist Ch—*church* TN-4
Miston (historical)—*locale* MS-4
Miston Post Office—*building* TN-4
Mistor Cem—*cemetery* MS-4
Mist Park—*flat* WA-9
Mistress Gray Bar—*bar* AL-4
Mistretta Park—*park* FL-3
Mistum Creek—*stream* WY-8
Mistwood Airp—*airport* MO-7
Misty Acres Ranch—*locale* CO-8
Misty Cove Marina—*locale* TN-4
**Misty Harbor**—*pop pl* AL-4
**Misty Hills Subdivision - Numbers 1-7**—*pop pl* UT-8
**Misty Hills Subdivision - Numbers 8-10**—*pop pl* UT-8
Misty Lake—*lake* (2) MI-6
Misty Meadows Airp—*airport* MO-7
**Misty Meadows Subdivision**—*pop pl* (3) UT-8
Mistymoon Lake—*lake* WY-8
Misty Mtn—*summit* AK-9
**Misty Pines**—*pop pl* AL-4
**Misty Ridge**—*pop pl* TN-4
Misty Vale—*hist pl* DE-2
Mitawan Creek—*stream* MN-6
Mitawan Lake—*lake* MN-6
MIT Camp—*locale* ME-1
*Mitcham* AL-4
Mitcham Branch—*stream* TX-5
**Mitchaw**—*pop pl* OH-6
Mitchburg Post Office (historical)—*building* TN-4
*Mitch Chapel* AL-4
*Mitchel Canyon* TX-5
Mitchel Canyon—*valley* NV-8
Mitchel Canyon—*valley* NM-5
Mitchel Cem—*cemetery* NM-5
Mitchel Cem—*cemetery* SC-3
Mitchel Coll—*school* NY-2
*Mitchel Creek* IN-6
*Mitchel Creek* MT-8
Mitchel Creek—*stream* IN-6
Mitchel Creek—*stream* MI-6
Mitchel Crest Cem—*cemetery* TN-4
Mitchel Drain—*canal* ID-8
Mitchel Grove Ch—*church* GA-3
Mitchel Grove Ch—*church* NC-3
**Mitchel Heights (subdivision)**—*pop pl* TN-4
Mitchel Hollow—*valley* TN-4
*Mitchell* AL-4
*Mitchell* NE-7
*Mitchell* PA-2
*Mitchell* VA-3
Mitchell—*dam* AL-4
Mitchell—*locale* AL-4
Mitchell—*locale* AR-4
Mitchell—*locale* CO-8
Mitchell—*locale* ID-8
Mitchell—*locale* IL-6
Mitchell—*locale* MN-6
Mitchell—*locale* MS-4
Mitchell—*locale* (2) OR-9
Mitchell—*locale* TX-5
Mitchell—*locale* WA-9
Mitchell—*locale* WV-2
**Mitchell**—*pop pl* AR-4
**Mitchell**—*pop pl* GA-3
**Mitchell**—*pop pl* IL-6
**Mitchell**—*pop pl* IN-6
**Mitchell**—*pop pl* IA-7
**Mitchell**—*pop pl* KS-7
**Mitchell**—*pop pl* (2) LA-4
**Mitchell**—*pop pl* MS-4
**Mitchell**—*pop pl* MO-7
**Mitchell**—*pop pl* NE-7
**Mitchell**—*pop pl* OR-9
**Mitchell**—*pop pl* SD-7
**Mitchell**—*pop pl* TN-4
Mitchell, Alexander, House—*hist pl* UT-8
Mitchell, Byron T., House—*hist pl* UT-8
Mitchell, Charles, House—*hist pl* OH-6
Mitchell, Charles T., House—*hist pl* MI-6
Mitchell, Crowell, House—*hist pl* SC-3
Mitchell, Gen. William, House—*hist pl* VA-3
Mitchell, Guy, House—*hist pl* TX-5
Mitchell, James, House—*hist pl* PA-2
Mitchell, Joseph, House—*hist pl* IN-6
Mitchell, Lake—*lake* FL-3
Mitchell, Lake—*lake* MI-6
Mitchell, Lake—*lake* MN-6
Mitchell, Lake—*lake* NY-2
Mitchell, Lake—*lake* SD-7
Mitchell, Lake—*reservoir* MS-4
Mitchell, Lake—*reservoir* SD-7
Mitchell, McKendree, House—*hist pl* SC-3
Mitchell, Mount—*summit* OR-9
Mitchell, Mount—*summit* WA-9
Mitchell, Randolph, House—*hist pl* OH-6
Mitchell, Richard H., House—*hist pl* OH-6
Mitchell, S. Weir, Sch—*hist pl* PA-2
Mitchell, William, House—*hist pl* NC-3
Mitchell Airp—*airport* TN-4
Mitchel Lake—*reservoir* MS-4
Mitchell And Gering Canal—*canal* NE-7
Mitchell And Long Ditch—*canal* WY-8
Mitchell Archeol Site—*hist pl* IL-6
Mitchell-Arnold House—*hist pl* RI-1
Mitchell Ave—*post sta* TX-5
Mitchell Ave—*uninc pl* TX-5
Mitchell Baptist Ch—*church* AL-4
Mitchell Bar—*bar* AL-4
Mitchell Bay—*bay* AK-9
Mitchell Bay—*bay* NY-2
Mitchell Bay—*bay* TX-5
Mitchell Bay—*bay* WA-9
Mitchell Bay—*swamp* NC-3
Mitchell Bayou—*stream* LA-4
Mitchell Bay Trail—*trail* AK-9
**Mitchell Beach**—*pop pl* FL-3
Mitchell Bend—*bend* (2) TN-4
Mitchell Bend—*bend* (2) TX-5
Mitchell Bend Cem—*cemetery* TX-5
Mitchel L Black Elem Sch—*school* FL-3
Mitchell Bldg—*hist pl* WI-6
Mitchell Bluff—*beach* MD-2
Mitchell Bluff—*cliff* FL-3
Mitchell Bluff—*cliff* TN-4
Mitchell Bluff—*cliff* VA-3
Mitchell Blvd Ch—*church* TX-5
Mitchell Blvd Sch—*school* TX-5
Mitchell Bottom—*bend* NE-7
*Mitchell Branch* TN-4
**Mitchell Branch**—*pop pl* WV-2
Mitchell Branch—*stream* AL-4
Mitchell Branch—*stream* (7) AR-4
Mitchell Branch—*stream* FL-3
Mitchell Branch—*stream* (2) GA-3
Mitchell Branch—*stream* IN-6
Mitchell Branch—*stream* (2) KY-4
Mitchell Branch—*stream* LA-4
Mitchell Branch—*stream* (3) MS-4
Mitchell Branch—*stream* (2) MO-7
Mitchell Branch—*stream* (3) NC-3
Mitchell Branch—*stream* SC-3
Mitchell Branch—*stream* (4) TN-4
Mitchell Branch—*stream* (5) TX-5
Mitchell Branch—*stream* (3) VA-3
Mitchell Branch—*stream* (2) WV-2
**Mitchell Branch Junction**—*pop pl* WV-2
Mitchell Bridge—*bridge* GA-3
Mitchell Brook—*stream* (4) ME-1
Mitchell Brook—*stream* (2) MA-1
Mitchell Brook—*stream* (2) NH-1
Mitchell Brook—*stream* VT-1
Mitchell Building-First State Bank Bldg—*hist pl* KY-4
Mitchell Butte—*summit* AZ-5
Mitchell Butte—*summit* OR-9
Mitchell Butte Hot Spring—*spring* OR-9
Mitchell Butte Lateral—*canal* OR-9
Mitchell Butte Wash—*valley* UT-8
Mitchell Cabin Spring—*spring* AZ-5
Mitchell Camp—*locale* CA-9
*Mitchell Canal* NE-7
Mitchell Canyon—*valley* (2) AZ-5
Mitchell Canyon—*valley* (3) CA-9
Mitchell Canyon—*valley* CO-8
Mitchell Canyon—*valley* MT-8
Mitchell Canyon—*valley* NV-8
Mitchell Canyon—*valley* NM-5
Mitchell Canyon—*valley* (2) TX-5
Mitchell Canyon—*valley* (2) UT-8
Mitchell Canyon Creek—*stream* TX-5
Mitchell Canyon Windmill—*locale* TX-5
Mitchell Cave—*cave* AL-4
Mitchell Caverns State Park—*park* CA-9
Mitchell (CCD)—*cens area* GA-3
Mitchell (CCD)—*cens area* OR-9
Mitchell Cem—*cemetery* (13) AL-4
Mitchell Cem—*cemetery* AR-4
Mitchell Cem—*cemetery* (3) FL-3
Mitchell Cem—*cemetery* (3) GA-3
Mitchell Cem—*cemetery* (5) IL-6
Mitchell Cem—*cemetery* (3) IN-6
Mitchell Cem—*cemetery* IA-7
Mitchell Cem—*cemetery* (3) KS-7
Mitchell Cem—*cemetery* (3) KY-4
Mitchell Cem—*cemetery* LA-4
Mitchell Cem—*cemetery* ME-1
Mitchell Cem—*cemetery* MN-6
Mitchell Cem—*cemetery* (9) MS-4
Mitchell Cem—*cemetery* (12) MO-7
Mitchell Cem—*cemetery* NE-7
Mitchell Cem—*cemetery* NY-2
Mitchell Cem—*cemetery* (3) NC-3
Mitchell Cem—*cemetery* OH-6
Mitchell Cem—*cemetery* OK-5
Mitchell Cem—*cemetery* OR-9
Mitchell Cem—*cemetery* (3) PA-2
Mitchell Cem—*cemetery* SC-3
Mitchell Cem—*cemetery* (8) TN-4
Mitchell Cem—*cemetery* (5) TX-5
Mitchell Cem—*cemetery* (3) VA-3
Mitchell Cem—*cemetery* (3) WV-2
Mitchell Cem—*cemetery* WI-6
*Mitchell Ch* AL-4
Mitchell Ch—*church* (2) LA-4
Mitchell Ch—*church* (2) NC-3
Mitchell Chapel—*church* AL-4
Mitchell Chapel—*church* GA-3
Mitchell Chapel—*church* (2) NC-3
Mitchell Chapel—*church* SC-3
Mitchell Chapel—*church* TN-4
Mitchell Chapel—*church* VA-3
Mitchell Ch (historical)—*church* AL-4
Mitchell Ch (historical)—*church* MO-7
Mitchell Coll—*school* CT-1
Mitchell Coll—*school* NC-3
Mitchell College Hist Dist—*hist pl* NC-3
Mitchell Community Center—*locale* NC-3
Mitchell Corner—*locale* AR-4
Mitchell Corner—*locale* CA-9
Mitchell Corner—*locale* (2) ME-1
**Mitchell Corner**—*pop pl* OR-9
Mitchell Corners—*locale* MN-6
*Mitchell Coulee* MT-8
Mitchell Coulee—*valley* MT-8
Mitchell County—*civil* KS-7
**Mitchell (County)**—*pop pl* GA-3
**Mitchell County**—*pop pl* NC-3
**Mitchell (County)**—*pop pl* TX-5
Mitchell County Courthouse—*hist pl* IA-7
Mitchell County Courthouse—*hist pl* KS-7
Mitchell County Courthouse—*hist pl* NC-3
Mitchell County Home—*building* IA-7
Mitchell Cove—*bay* ME-1
Mitchell Cove—*valley* NC-3
Mitchell Cove—*valley* TN-4
Mitchell Cove Branch—*stream* NC-3
Mitchell Cove Branch—*stream* TN-4
*Mitchell Creek* AL-4
*Mitchell Creek* CO-8
*Mitchell Creek* FL-3
*Mitchell Creek* MT-8
*Mitchell Creek* NE-7
*Mitchell Creek* OR-9
*Mitchell Creek* PA-2
*Mitchell Creek* UT-8
Mitchell Creek—*locale* PA-2
Mitchell Creek—*stream* (3) AL-4
Mitchell Creek—*stream* AK-9
Mitchell Creek—*stream* (2) AR-4
Mitchell Creek—*stream* (4) CA-9
Mitchell Creek—*stream* (2) CO-8
Mitchell Creek—*stream* (2) FL-3
Mitchell Creek—*stream* GA-3
Mitchell Creek—*stream* (2) ID-8
Mitchell Creek—*stream* IL-6
Mitchell Creek—*stream* IN-6
Mitchell Creek—*stream* (2) IA-7
Mitchell Creek—*stream* KY-4
Mitchell Creek—*stream* LA-4
Mitchell Creek—*stream* (5) MI-6
Mitchell Creek—*stream* (2) MS-4
Mitchell Creek—*stream* MO-7
Mitchell Creek—*stream* (3) MT-8
Mitchell Creek—*stream* (3) NV-8
Mitchell Creek—*stream* (3) NC-3
Mitchell Creek—*stream* (2) OK-5
Mitchell Creek—*stream* (6) OR-9
Mitchell Creek—*stream* (2) PA-2
Mitchell Creek—*stream* SC-3
Mitchell Creek—*stream* SD-7
Mitchell Creek—*stream* TN-4
Mitchell Creek—*stream* (8) TX-5
Mitchell Creek—*stream* VA-3
Mitchell Creek—*stream* (5) WA-9
Mitchell Creek—*stream* WY-8
Mitchell Creek Breaks—*range* WY-8
Mitchell Creek Canyon—*valley* NE-7
Mitchell Creek Ch—*church* TX-5
Mitchell Creek Park—*park* CA-9
Mitchell Creek Sch (historical)—*school* TN-4
Mitchell Crossing—*locale* TX-5
*Mitchell Cross Road* AL-4
Mitchell Crossroads—*locale* AL-4
Mitchell Crossroads—*locale* VA-3
Mitchell Cut—*channel* LA-4
Mitchell Dam—*dam* (4) AL-4
Mitchell Dam—*dam* NY-2
Mitchell Dam—*dam* SD-7
Mitchell Dam Number Six—*dam* NC-3
Mitchell Dam Number Three—*dam* TN-4
Mitchell Ditch—*canal* (2) CO-8
Mitchell Ditch—*canal* ID-8
Mitchell Ditch—*canal* IN-6
Mitchell Ditch—*canal* UT-8
Mitchell Ditch—*canal* WY-8
Mitchell Ditch No 1—*canal* WY-8
Mitchell Drain—*canal* CA-9
Mitchell Drain—*canal* NE-7
Mitchell Drain—*stream* MI-6
Mitchell Draw—*valley* CO-8
Mitchell Draw—*valley* NM-5
Mitchell Draw—*valley* SD-7
Mitchell Draw—*valley* TX-5
Mitchell Draw—*valley* WA-9
Mitchell Draw—*valley* (2) WY-8
*Mitchell Elementary School* AL-4
Mitchell Elem Sch—*school* IN-6
Mitchell Elem Sch—*school* KS-7
**Mitchell Estates**—*pop pl* DE-2
**Mitchell Estates Subdivision**—*pop pl* UT-8
Mitchell Falls—*falls* NC-3
Mitchell Field—*flat* CA-9
Mitchellfield Cem—*cemetery* NC-3
Mitchell Flat—*flat* WA-9
Mitchell Ford—*locale* AL-4
Mitchell Ford—*locale* TN-4
Mitchell Forks—*locale* GA-3
Mitchell Gap—*gap* AR-4
Mitchell Gap—*gap* GA-3
Mitchell Gap—*gap* (2) PA-2
Mitchell Gas Plant—*oilfield* TX-5
Mitchell Glen—*valley* WI-6
Mitchell Grove Ch—*church* (3) GA-3
Mitchell Guard Station—*locale* OR-9
Mitchell Gulch—*valley* CA-9
Mitchell Gulch—*valley* (2) CO-8
Mitchell Gulch—*valley* ID-8
Mitchell Gulch—*valley* (2) MT-8
Mitchell Hall—*hist pl* OK-5
Mitchell Hammock—*island* (2) FL-3
Mitchell Hammock—*island* LA-4
**Mitchell Heights**—*pop pl* WV-2
**Mitchell Hill**—*pop pl* KY-4
Mitchell Hill—*summit* AL-4
Mitchell Hill—*summit* AR-4
Mitchell Hill—*summit* CA-9
Mitchell Hill—*summit* CT-1
Mitchell Hill—*summit* KY-4
Mitchell Hill—*summit* (2) ME-1
Mitchell Hill—*summit* MA-1
Mitchell Hill—*summit* (2) NH-1
Mitchell Hill—*summit* PA-2
Mitchell Hill—*summit* WA-9
Mitchell Hill Cem—*cemetery* SC-3
Mitchell Hill Creek—*stream* VA-3
Mitchell Hill Road—*trail* NH-1
Mitchell Hist Dist—*hist pl* OH-6
Mitchell Historic Commercial District—*hist pl* SD-7
*Mitchell Hollow* TN-4
Mitchell Hollow—*stream* MO-7
Mitchell Hollow—*valley* (2) AL-4
Mitchell Hollow—*valley* AR-4
Mitchell Hollow—*valley* IN-6
Mitchell Hollow—*valley* MO-7
Mitchell Hollow—*valley* (2) NY-2
Mitchell Hollow—*valley* PA-2
Mitchell Hollow—*valley* (7) TN-4
Mitchell Hollow—*valley* TX-5
Mitchell Hollow—*valley* UT-8
Mitchell Hollow Well—*cave* TN-4
*Mitchell Home* NV-8

Mitchell Hotel—hist pl ID-8
Mitchell House—hist pl (3) AR-4
Mitchell House—hist pl ME-1
Mitchell House—hist pl MD-2
Mitchell House—hist pl TN-4
Mitchell HS—school IN-6
Mitchell Island LA-4
Mitchell Island—island FL-3
Mitchell Island—island GA-3
Mitchell Island—island LA-4
Mitchell Island—island MO-7
Mitchell Key LA-4
Mitchell Key—island LA-4
Mitchell Keys LA-4
Mitchell Knob—summit KY-4
Mitchell Knob—summit NC-3
Mitchell Knob—summit (2) TN-4
Mitchell Knob—summit VA-3
Mitchell Knob—summit WV-2
Mitchell Knoll—summit VT-1
Mitchell Lake IN-6
Mitchell Lake—lake CO-8
Mitchell Lake—lake (2) LA-4
Mitchell Lake—lake (7) MI-6
Mitchell Lake—lake (4) MN-6
Mitchell Lake—lake ND-7
Mitchell Lake—lake PA-2
Mitchell Lake—lake SD-7
Mitchell Lake—lake TN-4
Mitchell Lake—lake (2) TX-5
Mitchell Lake—lake WA-9
Mitchell Lake—lake WI-6
Mitchell Lake—reservoir (4) AL-4
Mitchell Lake—reservoir AR-4
Mitchell Lake—reservoir (2) KY-4
Mitchell Lake—reservoir LA-4
Mitchell Lake—reservoir SD-7
Mitchell Lake—reservoir TN-4
Mitchell Lake—reservoir (2) TX-5
Mitchell Lake Dam—dam AL-4
Mitchell Lake Dam—dam (3) MS-4
Mitchell Lake Dam—dam SD-7
Mitchell Lake Dam—dam TN-4
Mitchell Lake Dam Number One—dam TN-4
**Mitchell Lake Estates**—pop pl FL-3
Mitchell Lake Number One—reservoir TN-4
Mitchell Lake Number Three—reservoir TN-4
Mitchell Lakes—lake MI-6
Mitchell Lakes—swamp CO-8
Mitchell Landing—locale KY-4
Mitchell Landing—locale (2) NC-3
Mitchell Landing (historical)—locale NC-3
Mitchell Ledge—ridge ME-1
Mitchell Library—building AL-4
Mitchell Lick—summit NC-3
Mitchell Lick Fork—stream WV-2
Mitchell Lodge—locale AZ-5
Mitchell Lodge—locale NC-3
**Mitchell Manor**—pop pl MD-2
Mitchell Marsh—swamp ME-1
Mitchell Meadow—flat CA-9
Mitchell Memorial Highway Ch of Christ—church FL-3
Mitchell Memorial Library—building MS-4
Mitchell Memorial Sch—school MS-4
Mitchell Mesa—summit AZ-5
Mitchell Mesa—summit TX-5
Mitchell Mill—locale VA-3
**Mitchell Mill**—pop pl AR-4
**Mitchell Mill**—pop pl CA-9
Mitchell Mill Creek—stream FL-3
Mitchell Millpond—reservoir NC-3
Mitchell Millpond—reservoir VA-3
Mitchell Mills—locale PA-2
Mitchell Mine—mine (2) CA-9
Mitchell Mine—mine MO-7
Mitchell Mine—mine NV-8
Mitchell Mine (underground)—mine AL-4
Mitchell Monument—other OR-9
Mitchell Mtn NY-2
Mitchell Mtn—summit AL-4
Mitchell Mtn—summit CO-8
Mitchell Mtn—summit ME-1
Mitchell Mtn—summit MT-8
Mitchell Mtn—summit NY-2
Mitchell Mtn—summit (2) NC-3
Mitchell Mtn—summit OR-9
Mitchell Mtn—summit TX-5
Mitchell Mtn—summit VT-1
Mitchell Mtn—summit WA-9
Mitchell Mtn—summit WV-2
Mitchell Municipal Airp—airport SD-7
Mitchell Number 1 Lode Mine—mine SD-7
Mitchell Number 2 Lode Mine—mine SD-7
Mitchell Opera House—hist pl IN-6
Mitchell Park—flat MT-8
Mitchell Park—flat TX-5
Mitchell Park—park AZ-5
Mitchell Park—park CA-9
Mitchell Park—park CO-8
Mitchell Park—park CT-1
Mitchell Park—park IA-7
Mitchell Park—park MI-6
Mitchell Park—park MO-7
Mitchell Park—park WI-6
Mitchell Park—uninc pl PA-2
Mitchell Pass—gap NE-7
Mitchell Peak—summit AZ-5
Mitchell Peak—summit (2) CA-9
Mitchell Peak—summit TX-5
Mitchell Peak—summit WY-8
Mitchell Petroglyph Archeol Site—hist pl MO-7
Mitchell Pit—cave AL-4
Mitchell Place—locale CA-9
Mitchell Place—locale NM-5
Mitchell Place—locale TX-5
Mitchell Placer—mine CO-8
Mitchell Plain—plain IN-6
Mitchell Point TX-5
Mitchell Point—cape AK-9
Mitchell Point—cape AR-4
Mitchell Point—cape FL-3
Mitchell Point—cape (2) ME-1
Mitchell Point—cape NM-5
Mitchell Point—cape OR-9
Mitchell Point—cape TN-4
Mitchell Point—cliff WA-9
Mitchell Pond—lake AL-4
Mitchell Pond—lake CT-1
Mitchell Pond—lake GA-3
Mitchell Pond—lake LA-4
Mitchell Pond—lake ME-1
Mitchell Pond—lake (2) NH-1
Mitchell Pond—lake NY-2
Mitchell Pond—lake RI-1
Mitchell Pond—lake VT-1
Mitchell Pond—reservoir GA-3
Mitchell Pond—reservoir KS-7
Mitchell Pond—reservoir NC-3
Mitchell Pond Brook—stream NY-2
Mitchell Pond Dam—dam NC-3
Mitchell Pond Number Six—reservoir NC-3
Mitchell Ponds—lake (2) NY-2
Mitchell Ponds Mtn—summit NY-2
Mitchell Post Office (historical)—building MS-4
Mitchell Post Office (historical)—building TN-4
Mitchell Powerhouse and Dam—hist pl IA-7
Mitchell Quarry—mine TN-4
Mitchell Ranch—locale (3) CO-8
Mitchell Ranch—locale FL-3
Mitchell Ranch—locale ID-8
Mitchell Ranch—locale (2) MT-8
Mitchell Ranch—locale (2) NV-8
Mitchell Ranch—locale (2) NM-5
Mitchell Ranch—locale (6) TX-5
Mitchell Ranch—locale WY-8
Mitchell Ravine—valley CA-9
Mitchell Reservoir Creek NV-8
Mitchell-Reynolds Cem—cemetery MO-7
Mitchell Ridge—ridge AR-4
Mitchell Ridge—ridge NC-3
Mitchell Ridge—ridge OH-6
Mitchell Ridge—ridge OK-5
Mitchell Ridge—ridge OR-9
Mitchell Ridge—ridge TN-4
Mitchell Ridge—ridge WV-2
Mitchell River—stream FL-3
Mitchell River—stream MA-1
Mitchell River—stream NC-3
Mitchell River Ch—church NC-3
Mitchell River Island—swamp FL-3
Mitchell River Marshes—swamp MA-1
Mitchell Road Sch—school TN-4
Mitchell Rock—bar ME-1
Mitchell Rock—other AK-9
Mitchell Rock—pillar RI-1
Mitchell Rock—rock MA-1
Mitchell Rock—summit CA-9
Mitchell-Rountree House—hist pl WI-6
Mitchell (RR name for Mitchells)—other VA-3
Mitchell Run—stream KY-4
Mitchell Run—stream MD-2
Mitchell Run—stream OH-6
Mitchell Run—stream (2) PA-2
Mitchell Run—stream VA-3
Mitchell Run—stream (6) WV-2
Mitchells PA-2
Mitchells—locale PA-2
**Mitchells**—pop pl VA-3
Mitchells Bluff MS-4
Mitchells Bluff—cliff (2) TN-4
Mitchells Branch—stream VA-3
Mitchells Brook—stream CT-1
**Mitchellsburg**—pop pl KY-4
Mitchellsburg Knob—summit KY-4
Mitchell Sch—school AL-4
Mitchell Sch—school (3) AZ-5
Mitchell Sch—school AR-4
Mitchell Sch—school (3) CA-9
Mitchell Sch—school CO-8
Mitchell Sch—school CT-1
Mitchell Sch—school (2) FL-3
Mitchell Sch—school IL-6
Mitchell Sch—school KS-7
Mitchell Sch—school KY-4
Mitchell Sch—school LA-4
Mitchell Sch—school ME-1
Mitchell Sch—school (2) MA-1
Mitchell Sch—school (4) MI-6
Mitchell Sch—school MS-4
Mitchell Sch—school MT-8
Mitchell Sch—school NV-8
Mitchell Sch—school OK-5
Mitchell Sch—school PA-2
Mitchell Sch—school (2) SC-3
Mitchell Sch—school SD-7
Mitchell Sch—school TX 5
Mitchell Sch—school (3) WI-6
Mitchell Sch (abandoned)—school MO-7
Mitchell Sch (abandoned)—school PA-2
Mitchells Chapel—church MS-4
Mitchells Chapel—church (2) NC-3
Mitchells Chapel Baptist Church TN-4
Mitchells Ch (historical)—church MS-4
Mitchell Sch (historical)—school (3) AL-4
Mitchell Sch (historical)—school (2) PA-2
**Mitchells Corner**—pop pl CA-9
**Mitchells Corner**—pop pl MO-7
Mitchells Creek PA-2
Mitchells Creek SC-3
Mitchells Creek TN-4
Mitchells Creek—stream NY-2
Mitchells Crossroads AL-4
Mitchells Cross Roads MS-4
Mitchells Cut—gut TX-5
Mitchell Sea Ch—church SC-3
Mitchells Falls—falls MA-1
Mitchells Ferry (historical)—locale AL-4
Mitchell Shaft—mine CA-9
Mitchell-Shealy House—hist pl SC-3
Mitchells Hollow—valley UT-8
Mitchell-Shook House—hist pl PA-2
**Mitchell Siding**—pop pl NC-3
Mitchells Island SC-3
Mitchell Site—hist pl SD-7
Mitchells Knob TN-4
Mitchells Lake—lake LA-4
Mitchells Lake—reservoir GA-3
Mitchells Lake—reservoir NC-3
Mitchells Lake—reservoir SC-3
Mitchells Lake Dam—dam NC-3
Mitchells Landing TN-4
Mitchells Landing (historical)—locale AL-4
Mitchell Slough—gut AK-9
Mitchell Slough—lake MN-6
Mitchell Slough—stream CA-9
Mitchell Slough—stream MO-7
Mitchell Slough—stream WY-8
Mitchells Mill AL-4
Mitchells Mill MS-4
Mitchells Mill PA-2
Mitchells Mill—locale CA-9
Mitchells Mill—locale VA-3
Mitchells Mill (historical)—locale (2) MS-4
Mitchells Mill Post Office (historical)—building MS-4
Mitchells Mills PA-2
Mitchells Mtn—summit VA-3
Mitchells Nipple—summit WY-8
Mitchell Speedway—other IN-6
Mitchells Point TN-4
Mitchells Pond RI-1
Mitchells Pond—reservoir (2) NC-3
Mitchells Pond Dam—dam NC-3
Mitchells Pond Lower Dam—dam NC-3
Mitchells Presbyterian Church—hist pl VA-3
Mitchell Spring—spring (2) AZ-5
Mitchell Spring—spring MO-7
Mitchell Spring—spring (2) NV-8
Mitchell Spring—spring (2) OR-9
Mitchell Spring—spring (2) TN-4
Mitchell Spring—spring UT-8
Mitchell Spring—spring WA-9
Mitchell Spring—spring WY-8
Mitchell Spring Branch—stream AL-4
Mitchell Spring Branch—stream TN-4
Mitchell Spring Ch—church TN-4
Mitchell Springs—locale TN-4
Mitchell Springs Baptist Church TN-4
Mitchell Springs Ch—church AL-4
Mitchell Springs Ch—church MS-4
Mitchell Springs Sch (historical)—school TN-4
Mitchell Spur—locale MI-6
**Mitchells (RR name Mitchell)**—pop pl VA-3
Mitchells Run—stream KY-4
Mitchells Sch (historical)—school MS-4
**Mitchells Spur**—pop pl MI-6
Mitchells Station MS-4
**Mitchells Store**—pop pl VA-3
Mitchells Store P.O. (historical)—building MS-4
Mitchells Switch MS-4
Mitchell State Public Shooting Area—park SD-7
Mitchell Station AL-4
Mitchell Station MS-4
Mitchell Station—locale IA-7
Mitchell Store (historical)—locale AL-4
Mitchell Store (historical)—locale TN-4
Mitchells (Township of)—fmr MCD NC-3
**Mitchell Subdivision**—pop pl UT-8
Mitchellsville TN-4
**Mitchellsville**—pop pl IL-6
**Mitchellsville**—pop pl NY-2
Mitchellsville Creek—stream NY-2
Mitchellsville Post Office TN-4
Mitchell Swamp—stream NC-3
Mitchell Swamp—swamp SC-3
Mitchell Swamp Canal—canal NC-3
Mitchell Tank—reservoir (2) AZ-5
Mitchell Tank—reservoir NM-5
Mitchell Tank—reservoir TX-5
Mitchell-Tappan House—hist pl MN-6
Mitchelltown—locale AL-4
**Mitchell Town**—pop pl AL-4
**Mitchelltown**—pop pl VA-3
**Mitchell (Town of)**—pop pl WI-6
Mitchell Township—fmr MCD IA-7
**Mitchell Township**—pop pl (2) KS-7
**Mitchell Township**—pop pl SD-7
Mitchell (Township of)—fmr MCD AR-4
**Mitchell (Township of)**—pop pl MI-6
**Mitchell (Township of)**—pop pl MN-6
Mitchell Trail—trail (2) PA-2
Mitchelltree (Township of) IN-6
Mitchell Triangle—park OH-6
Mitchell Valley—valley VA-3
Mitchell Valley Cem—cemetery KS-7
Mitchell Valley Cem—cemetery NE-7
Mitchell Valley Ch—church VA-3
Mitchell Valley Sch—school NE-7
**Mitchell Village (subdivision)**—pop pl NC-3
Mitchellville IN-6
**Mitchellville**—pop pl AL-4
**Mitchellville**—pop pl AR-4
**Mitchellville**—pop pl IA-7
**Mitchellville**—pop pl MD-2
**Mitchellville**—pop pl MO-7
**Mitchellville**—pop pl SC-3
**Mitchellville**—pop pl TN-4
Mitchellville Ch—church MO-7
Mitchellville First Baptist Ch—church TN-4
Mitchellville Post Office—building TN-4
Mitchellville Sch (historical)—school MO-7
Mitchellville Sch (historical)—school TN-4
Mitchell Wash—stream AZ-5
Mitchell Well—well AZ-5
Mitchell Wilson Mill (historical)—locale TN-4
Mitchell Windmill—locale AZ-5
Mitchell Windmill—locale NM-5
Mitchell Windmill—locale (2) TX-5
Mitchell Windmills—locale CO-8
Mitchell Y-P Ranch—locale MT-8
Mitchell Zion Ch—church GA-3
Mitchel Memorial Hosp—hospital NH-1
Mitchel Mine—mine KY-4
Mitchel Mtn—summit ME-1
Mitchel Place—locale CO-8
Mitchel Range—range CA-9
Mitchels Falls—rapids MA-1
**Mitchels Fork**—pop pl NC-3
Mitchel Sink—basin FL-3
Mitchel Springs—spring NM-5
Mitchels Ranch—locale AK-9
Mitchels River NC-3
Mitchels Run PA-2
Mitcheltown—locale CT-1
Mitcheltree Hollow—valley PA-2
**Mitcheltree Township**—pop pl IN-6
Mitchel Windmill—locale NM-5
Mitchem Cem—cemetery WV-2
Mitchem Ditch—canal IN-6
Mitchem Sch (historical)—school TN-4
**Mitchener**—pop pl MS-4
**Mitchener**—pop pl NC-3
Mitcheners Crossroads NC-3
**Mitcheners Crossroads**—pop pl NC-3
Mitcher Creek—stream AK-9
Mitcherrer NC-3
Mitch Hill Spring—spring AR-4
Mitchie—locale IL-6
Mitchigan River MI-6
Mitchigan River—stream MI-6
**Mitchiner**—pop pl LA-4
Mitchiner Cem—cemetery NC-3
**Mitchiners Crossroads**—pop pl NC-3
Mitchiners Pond—reservoir NC-3
Mitchke Valley—valley TX-5
Mitchler Run—stream PA-2
Mitchner Ditch—canal IN-6
**Mitchner (historical)**—pop pl MS-4
Mitchners Crossroads NC-3
Mitchners Pond Dam—dam NC-3
Mitchs Canyon—valley UT-8
Mitchum Lake—reservoir AL-4
Mitchum Lake Dam—dam AL-4
Mitchum Ranch—locale NV-8
Mitchums Lake—reservoir NC-3
Miteathow—island FM-9
Mite Cove—bay AK-9
Miteeluug FM-9
Miteeluuq—summit FM-9
Miteenifeeng—cape FM-9
Mite Island—island AK-9
Mite Lake—lake MN-6
Mitelu' FM-9
Mitenifeng FM-9
Miter, The—summit CA-9
Mitethow FM-9
**Mitford**—pop pl SC-3
Mitheanoog—summit FM-9
Mitheno' FM-9
Mitigwaki, Lake—lake MI-6
Mitigwaki Creek—stream MI-6
Mitik Creek—stream AK-9
Mitikun—bar (2) FM-9
Mitikun Pukuan—bar FM-9
**Mitiwanga**—pop pl OH-6
Mitkof Island—island AK-9
Mit Lake—lake MN-6
Mitlak Mtn—summit AK-9
Mit-Le-Topik—other AK-9
Mitletukeruk—locale AK-9
Mitliktavik (Abandoned)—locale AK-9
Mitlon Boyd Catfish Pond Dam—dam MS-4
M.I.T. (Massachusetts Institute of Technology)—uninc pl MA-1
Mitmoen Lake—lake MN-6
Mitotes Canyon—valley CO-8
Mitotes Lake—reservoir CO-8
Mitouer Gulch MT-8
Mitover Gulch MT-8
Mitre, The—summit AK-9
Mitre Peak—summit CO-8
Mitre Peak—summit TX-5
Mitre Peak Camp—locale TX-5
Mitre Rock—pillar WA-9
Mitrofania—locale AK-9
Mitrofania Bay—bay AK-9
Mitrofania Harbor—bay AK-9
Mitrofania Island—island AK-9
Mitsu Shoal—bar FM-9
Mitt and Bar Canyon—valley NM-5
Mitt and Bar Ranch—locale NM-5
Mittelstedt Slough—gut SD-7
Mitten, Mount—summit NH-1
Mitten, The—summit NV-8
Mitten Butte—summit WY-8
Mitten Canyon—valley UT-8
Mitten Creek WY-8
Mitten Creek—stream AK-9
Mittendorf SC-3
Mitten Flow WA-9
Mitten Hill—summit AK-9
Mitten Hill—summit PA-2
Mitten Lake—lake LA-4
Mitten Lake—lake (2) MI-6
Mitten Lake—lake MN-6
Mitten Lake—lake MT-8
Mitten Lake—lake WI-6
Mitten Lakes LA-4
Mitten Ledge—bar ME-1
Mitten Mtn—summit MT-8
Mitten Peak AZ-5
Mitten Peak—summit AZ-5
Mitten Prong—stream WY-8
Mitten Rock—summit NM-5
Mitten Spring—spring OR-9
Mitten Springs—spring WY-8
**Mitterhofer**—pop pl WI-6
Mitternight Park—park AL-4
Mittersbaugh Gap PA-2
Mittie—locale TX-5
**Mittie**—pop pl LA-4
Mittigy Channel—channel VA-3
**Mittineague**—pop pl MA-1
Mittineague Park—park MA-1
Mittineaque MA-1
Mitt Lake—lake MN-6
Mittle Tank—reservoir NM-5
Mittletons Landing (historical)—locale MS-4
Mitton, Samuel Crowthers, House—hist pl UT-8
Mitton Peak—summit UT-8
Mittower Gulch—valley MT-8
Mitt Pond—lake NJ-2
Mittry Lake—reservoir AZ-5
Mittry Lake Ref—park AZ-5
Mitts Cem—cemetery (3) MO-7
Mitts Chapel—church AL-4
Mitts Chapel Ch AL-4
Mitts Creek—stream TN-4
Mitts Ref—park MS-4
Mitts Rsvr—reservoir UT-8
Mittvatsky House—hist pl IA-7
Mittye P Locke Elem Sch—school FL-3
**Mitylene**—pop pl AL-4
Mitz Branch—stream MO-7
Mitzie Creek—stream CA-9
Mitzi Rsvr—reservoir OR-9
Miuka Creek—stream AL-4
Miwok Beach—beach CA-9
Miwok Lake—lake CA-9
**Mi-Wuk Village**—pop pl CA-9
**Mix**—pop pl LA-4
Mix Branch—stream MS-4
Mix Cabin—locale ID-8
Mix Canyon—valley CA-9
Mix Cem—cemetery PA-2
Mix Creek—stream NY-2
Mix Creek—stream PA-2
Mixed Creek—stream IN-6
Mixed Grove Sch—school NE-7
Mixen Tank—reservoir NM-5
Mixer Cem—cemetery NY-2
Mixer Lake—lake MI-6
Mixer Pond—lake ME-1
Mixer Riffle—rapids OR-9
**Mixersville**—pop pl IN-6
Mixerville IN-6
**Mixerville**—pop pl IN-6
Mixes Baldy—summit MT-8
Mixes Food Creek—stream SD-7
Mix Hollow—valley PA-2
Mix Hollow Trail—trail PA-2
Mixie—locale TN-4
Mixie Flat—flat NV-8
Mixie Post Office (historical)—building TN-4
Mix Lake—lake CO-8
Mix Lake Campground—locale CO-8
Mixon—locale AR-4
Mixon—locale MS-4
Mixon—locale TX-5
Mixon Branch—stream LA-4
Mixon Canyon—valley CO-8
Mixon Cem—cemetery GA-3
Mixon Cem—cemetery LA-4
Mixon Cem—cemetery (4) MS-4
Mixon Ch—church LA-4
Mixon Chapel Cave—cave AL-4
Mixon Creek—bay NC-3
Mixon Creek—stream AR-4
Mixon Creek—stream MS-4
Mixon Creek—stream TX-5
Mixon Elem Sch—school MS-4
Mixon Gulch—valley MT-8
Mixon Lake—reservoir AL-4
Mixon Lakes—lake MS-4
Mixon-Mizelle Cem—cemetery MS-4
Mixons Creek TX-5
Mixons Creek—stream MS-4
Mixons Hammock—island GA-3
Mixons Mill MS-4
Mixon Springs Branch—stream AL-4
Mixons Sch (historical)—school AL-4
Mixon Store (historical)—locale MS-4
Mixon Tank—reservoir AZ-5
Mixonville—locale AL-4
Mixon Windmill—locale NM-5
Mix Run PA-2
Mix Run—locale PA-2
Mix Run—stream (2) PA-2
Mixsell, Jacob, House—hist pl PA-2
Mixsell Creek PA-2
**Mixson**—pop pl AL-4
Mixsons Crossroads AL-4
Mix Spring—spring SD-7
Mix Spring—spring WY-8
Mixter Sch—school MA-1
Mixter Sch—school MI-6
Mixtown—locale PA-2
Mixture Bayou—stream AR-4
Mixture Lake—lake AR-4
Mix-up Peak—summit WA-9
Mixup Spring—spring OR-9
**Mixville**—pop pl CT-1
**Mixville**—pop pl SC-3
Mixville Brook CT-1
Mixville Brook—stream CT-1
Mixville Pond—lake CT-1
Miyakma Range CA-9
Miyanenap—bar FM-9
Miyan To MP-9
Miyuka Creek AL-4
Mize—locale KY-4
**Mize**—pop pl GA-3
**Mize**—pop pl MS-4
Mize, Lake—lake FL-3
Mize Attendance Center—school MS-4
Mize Baptist Ch—church MS-4
Mize Branch—stream (2) KY-4
Mize Branch—stream TN-4
Mize Cem—cemetery AL-4
Mize Cem—cemetery FL-3
Mize Cem—cemetery IL-6
Mize Ch—church KY-4
Mize Dam—dam AL-4
Mize Hollow—valley MO-7
Mizell—locale GA-3
Mizell, Lake—lake FL-3
Mizell Bluff—cliff TN-4
Mizell Cave—cave TN-4
Mizell Cem—cemetery AL-4
Mizell Cem—cemetery LA-4
Mizell Cem—cemetery MO-7
Mizell Cem—cemetery (2) NC-3
Mizell Cem—cemetery TX-5
Mizell Creek—stream GA-3
Mizelle Creek—stream FL-3
**Mizell (historical)**—pop pl TN-4
Mizell Kiddie Kampus—school FL-3
Mizell Memorial Hosp—hospital AL-4
Mizell Post Office (historical)—building TN-4
Mizell Prairie—swamp GA-3
Mizells Plantation (historical)—locale AL-4
Mizell Spring—spring TN-4
Mize Lookout Tower—locale MS-4
Mize Methodist Ch—church MS-4
Mize Point—cape VA-3
Mizer Cem—cemetery MO-7
Mizer Ditch—canal ID-8
Mizer Draw—valley WY-8
**Mizers**—pop pl OH-6
Mizer Swamp—swamp TN-4
Mize Sch—school FL-3
Mize-Wadkins Cemetery AL-4
Mize Well—well NM-5
Mizner Drain—stream MI-6
Mizner Hollow—valley OH-6
Mizner Sch—school TX-5
Mizotas Kipuka—area HI-9
Mizpah—locale MT-8
Mizpah—locale NV-8
**Mizpah**—pop pl MN-6
**Mizpah**—pop pl NJ-2
Mizpah Baptist Ch—church KS-7
Mizpah Cem—cemetery CO-8
Mizpah Cem—cemetery IL-6
Mizpah Cem—cemetery IA-7
Mizpah Cem—cemetery SD-7
Mizpah Ch—church (5) GA-3
Mizpah Ch—church KS-7
Mizpah Ch—church MI-6
Mizpah Ch—church MS-4
Mizpah Ch—church (3) NC-3
Mizpah Ch—church PA-2
Mizpah Ch—church (2) SC-3
Mizpah Ch—church VA-3
Mizpah Creek—stream ID-8
Mizpah Creek—stream (2) MT-8
Mizpah Extension—mine NV-8
Mizpah Hill—summit NV-8
Mizpah Hotel—hist pl NV-8
Mizpah HS—school FM-9
Mizpah Mine—mine ID-8
Mizpah Mine—mine (3) NV-8
**Mizpah Park**—pop pl MI-6
Mizpah Peak—summit MT-8
Mizpah Point—summit NV-8
Mizpah Post Office (historical)—building MS-4
Mizpah Presbyterian Church of East Portland—hist pl OR-9
Mizpah-Pumpkin—cens area MT-8
Mizpah River MT-8
Mizpah Sch—school MT-8
Mizpah Sch—school NE-7
Mizpah Spring Shelter—locale NH-1
Mizpah Station (historical)—locale NV-8
Mizpah Well NV-8
Mizpah Well—well (2) NV-8
Mizzell Creek—stream AR-4
**Mizzelle**—pop pl NC-3
Mizzen Top—summit NY-2
Miz-zou-rye River KS-7
M J B Creek—stream WA-9
M J Brecht Elementary School PA-2
M J Brown Ditch—canal (2) IN-6
M J Carlisle Mall—locale PA-2
MJ Creek—stream AK-9
M J Fitzgerald Dam—dam AL-4
M Johnson Ranch—locale ND-7
M J Simmons Pond Dam—dam MS-4
Mkal FM-9
M.K. and T. Depot in Laverne—hist pl OK-5
M K and T School KS-7
M K Crossing—locale TX-5
M Kelley Number 1 Dam—dam SD-7
M K Ranch—locale CA-9
M K Ranch—locale CO-8
M K Tank—reservoir AZ-5
MKT Depot—hist pl TX-5
M K T Lake—reservoir MO-7
M K T Sch—school KS-7
M Kunner Grant—civil FL-3
M K Windmill—locale AZ-5
M'Ladies Mtn—summit AK-9
M'laiksini Yaina OR-9
M Lake—lake FL-3
M Lateral—canal CA-9
M L Blalock Dam—dam NC-3
M L Blalock Lake—reservoir NC-3
M L Coleman Ranch—locale WY-8
M Lee Ranch—locale NE-7
Mlengui, Toachel—channel PW-9
M L Husband Lake Dam—dam MS-4
M Line Creek—stream CA-9
M L King Park—park NC-3
M L Tillis Pond AL-4
M L Tillis Pond Dam—dam AL-4
M Lucille Reisz Elem Sch—school IN-6
Mlunguieinlass Passage PW-9
ML Windmill—locale AZ-5
M Lynn Bennion Sch—school UT-8
M'Mahon's OH-6
M Matthews Dam—dam SD-7
M-M Cabins—locale CO-8
M M Jones Dam—dam AL-4
M M Lake—lake WA-9
MM Mine—mine NV-8
M Mraz Dam—dam SD-7
M M Roberts Stadium—park MS-4
Mn Chavez Rsvr No 1—reservoir NM-5
Mn'iy FM-9
Mo—bar FM-9
Moaalele—summit HI-9
Moa Ave AZ-5
Moa Ave Settlement AZ-5
Moa Ave Spring (historical)—spring AZ-5
**Moab**—pop pl UT-8
Moab Baptist Ch—church UT-8
Moab Cabin—hist pl UT-8
Moab Canyon—valley UT-8
Moab Christian Center—church UT-8
Moab City Park UT-8
Moab Division—civil UT-8
Moab KOA—park UT-8
Moab LDS Church—hist pl UT-8
**Moab (Newman Lake Post Office)**—pop pl (2) WA-9
Moab Post Office—building UT-8
Moab Slickrock Bike Trail UT-8
Moab Slickrock Trail—trail UT-8
Moab Valley—bend UT-8
Moag Sch—school TX-5
Moah—locale MO-7
Moa Heiau—locale HI-9
Moak—cemetery MS-4
Moak Cem—cemetery MS-4
Moak Cove—valley CA-9
Moak Creek MS-4
Moak Creek Church MS-4
Moak Drain—stream MI-6
Moakea—civil HI-9
Moake Cem—cemetery IL-6
Moaks Creek—stream MS-4
Moaks Creek Ch—church MS-4
Moak Trail—trail CA-9
Moal, Dauen—gut FM-9
Moalepe Stream—stream HI-9
Moalii—civil HI-9
Moalol FM-9
Moana Hotel—hist pl HI-9
Moanalua—civil HI-9
Moanalua Gardens—other HI-9
Moanalua Golf Course—other HI-9
Moanalua Sch—school HI-9
Moanalua Stream—stream HI-9
Moanalulu—civil HI-9
Moana Ranch—locale AZ-5
Moana Tank—reservoir AZ-5
Moaning Caves—cave CA-9

*Moano* HI-9
*Moanualua* HI-9
Moanui—*civil* HI-9
Moanuiahea—*summit* HI-9
Moanui Stream—*stream* HI-9
**Moapa**—*pop pl* NV-8
Moapa Peak—*summit* NV-8
Moapa River Ind Res—*reserve* NV-8
Moapa Township—*inact MCD* NV-8
Moapa Valley—*valley* NV-8
Moap Lake—*lake* UT-8
Moar Cem—*cemetery* OR-9
**Moark**—*pop pl* AR-4
Mo-Ark Camp—*locale* MO-7
Moark Cem—*cemetery* AR-4
Moark Ditch—*canal* AR-4
Moark Ditch—*canal* MO-7
Moark Junction—*locale* UT-8
Moark Ridge—*ridge* AR-4
Moar Lake—*lake* OR-9
Moar Mound And Village—*hist pl* OH-6
Moarnamion Sch—*school* NY-2
Moat, The—*swamp* NY-2
Moat Brook—*stream* NH-1
Moat Creek—*stream* CA-9
Moates Bay—*swamp* AL-4
Moates Branch—*stream* GA-3
Moates Knob—*summit* GA-3
Moates Lake—*reservoir* AL-4
Moat Island—*island* NH-1
Moat Lake—*lake* CA-9
Moat Mountain Trail—*trail* NH-1
Moats—*locale* OH-6
**Moats**—*pop pl* WV-2
Moats, William, Farm—*hist pl* IL-6
Moats Cave—*cave* AL-4
Moats Cem—*cemetery* OH-6
Moats Hollow—*valley* (2) AL-4
Moats Hollow—*valley* WV-2
Moats Spring—*spring* AL-4
Moatstown—*locale* WV-2
**Moatsville**—*pop pl* WV-2
Moat Vly—*swamp* NY-2
*Moaula* HI-9
Moaula Falls—*falls* HI-9
Moaula Gulch—*valley* HI-9
Moaulaiki, Puu—*summit* HI-9
Moaulanui, Puu—*crater* HI-9
Moaula Ridge—*ridge* HI-9
Moaula Stream—*stream* HI-9
**Mobase**—*pop pl* WA-9
Mobbly Bay—*bay* FL-3
Mobbly Bayou—*gut* FL-3
Mob Branch—*stream* NC-3
Mobbs Ch (historical)—*church* AL-4
Mobbs Sch—*school* AL-4
Mob Creek—*stream* VA-3
**Mobeetie**—*pop pl* TX-5
Mobeetie Cem—*cemetery* TX-5
**Mobeetie (New Mobeetie)**—*pop pl* TX-5
Moberg Canyon—*valley* ID-8
Moberg Hill—*summit* WA-9
Moberg Lake—*lake* MN-6
Moberley Bottom—*flat* AL-4
Moberley Cem—*cemetery* AL-4
**Moberly**—*pop pl* IN-6
**Moberly**—*pop pl* KY-4
**Moberly**—*pop pl* MO-7
Moberly, John, House—*hist pl* KY-4
Moberly Country Club—*other* MO-7
Moberly Junior Coll—*school* MO-7
*Moberly Lake* MO-7
M O Best Park—*park* AZ-5
**Mobet Meadows (Trailer Park)**—*pop pl* IL-6
Mobey Lake—*lake* MI-6
Mobil Chemical Company—*facility* IL-6
Mobile—*locale* AZ-5
Mobile—*locale* GA-3
**Mobile**—*pop pl* AL-4
Mobile, Lake—*lake* FL-3
Mobile and Ohio RR Depot—*hist pl* IL-6
Mobile and Ohio RR Depot—*hist pl* MS-4
Mobile Bay—*bay* AL-4
*Mobile Bay Channel* AL-4
Mobile Bay Light—*locale* AL-4
Mobile Branch—*stream* AL-4
Mobile (CCD)—*cens area* AL-4
Mobile Channel—*canal* AL-4
Mobile Christian Sch—*school* AL-4
Mobile City Hall—*hist pl* AL-4
Mobile City Hosp—*hist pl* AL-4
**Mobile City Trailer Park (subdivision)**—*pop pl* NC-3
Mobile Coast Guard Base—*military* AL-4
Mobile Coll—*school* AL-4
Mobile Country Club—*other* AL-4
**Mobile County**—*pop pl* AL-4
Mobile County Farm (historical)—*locale* AL-4
Mobile County HS—*school* AL-4
Mobile County Training Sch—*school* AL-4
Mobile County Youth Center—*building* AL-4
Mobile Division—*civil* AL-4
Mobile Elem Sch—*school* AZ-5
**Mobile Gardens (subdivision)**—*pop pl* FL-3
**Mobile Gardens (trailer park)**—*pop pl* DE-2
Mobile Grayhound Park—*locale* AL-4
**Mobile Haven Estates**—*pop pl* FL-3
Mobile Haven Park—*locale* AZ-5
Mobile Heights Baptist Ch—*church* AL-4
**Mobile Heights (subdivision)**—*pop pl* AL-4
Mobile Highway Baptist Ch—*church* FL-3
Mobile Highway Ch—*church* FL-3
**Mobile Home Estates (subdivision)**—*pop pl* NC-3
Mobile Home Park—*uninc pl* FL-3
Mobile Infirmary—*hospital* AL-4
Mobile Island—*cape* MO-7
Mobile Junction—*locale* AL-4
**Mobile Manor (Trailer Park)**—*pop pl* FL-3
Mobile Memorial Gardens Cem—*cemetery* AL-4
Mobile Mennonite Ch—*church* AL-4
Mobile Mental Health Center—*hospital* AL-4
Mobile Mine—*mine* NV-8
Mobile Municipal Airp—*airport* AL-4
Mobile Municipal Auditorium—*building* AL-4
*Mobile Natl Cemetery* AL-4
Mobile Point—*cape* AL-4
Mobile Point Light—*locale* AL-4
Mobile Public Library—*building* AL-4
Mobile Ravine—*valley* CA-9
Mobile Rescue Mission—*church* AL-4
Mobile Revival Center—*church* AL-4
Mobile Ridge—*ridge* LA-4
Mobile River—*stream* AL-4
*Mobile River Channel* AL-4
Mobile RR Station—*building* AZ-5
Mobile Ship Channel—*channel* AL-4
Mobile Shrine of Memory Cem—*cemetery* AL-4
Mobile Swamp—*swamp* FL-3
Mobile - Tensaw Cut-off Channel—*canal* AL-4
Mobile Turning Basin—*canal* AL-4
Mobile Valley—*valley* AZ-5
Mobile Waterworks—*other* AL-4
Mobile Well—*well* AZ-5
Mobile Yacht Club—*other* AL-4
Mobil Oil Corporation—*facility* IL-6
Mobjack—*locale* VA-3
Mobjack Bay—*bay* VA-3
*Mobley* GA-3
Mobley—*locale* WV-2
Mobley, Col. Green G., House—*hist pl* AL-4
Mobley Bay—*swamp* GA-3
Mobley Bluff—*cliff* MO-7
Mobley Branch—*stream* GA-3
Mobley Branch—*stream* SC-3
Mobley Cem—*cemetery* AL-4
Mobley Cem—*cemetery* (3) GA-3
Mobley Cem—*cemetery* MS-4
Mobley Cem—*cemetery* SC-3
Mobley Cem—*cemetery* (2) TN-4
Mobley Cem—*cemetery* WV-2
*Mobley Creek* SC-3
Mobley Creek—*stream* AL-4
Mobley Creek—*stream* GA-3
Mobley Creek—*stream* SC-3
Mobley Creek Ch—*church* AL-4
Mobley Crossing—*locale* GA-3
Mobley Cut—*gap* TN-4
Mobley Dam—*dam* AL-4
**Mobley (historical)**—*pop pl* TN-4
Mobley Hollow—*valley* IN-6
Mobley Hollow—*valley* TN-4
Mobley Hollow—*valley* VA-3
Mobley hollow (historical)—*valley* TN-4
Mobley Hotel—*hist pl* TX-5
Mobley Lake—*lake* AR-4
Mobley Lake—*reservoir* AL-4
Mobley Landing (historical)—*locale* TN-4
Mobley Mill Creek—*stream* GA-3
Mobley Mtn—*summit* VA-3
Mobley Place—*locale* CO-8
Mobley Pond—*lake* (2) FL-3
Mobley Pond Ch—*church* GA-3
Mobley Post Office (historical)—*building* TN-4
Mobley Ridge—*ridge* TN-4
Mobley Rsvr—*reservoir* CO-8
Mobley Run—*stream* WV-2
Mobley Sch—*school* (2) MO-7
Mobleys Lake—*lake* GA-3
Mobleys Pond—*reservoir* GA-3
Mobley Spring—*spring* CA-9
Mobley Swamp—*swamp* GA-3
Moblo Lake—*lake* MI-6
Mobly Bayou—*gut* LA-4
Mob Neck—*cape* VA-3
Moboy Gulch—*valley* CA-9
Mobra—*locale* TN-4
*Mobray* TN-4
Mobray Lookout—*locale* WA-9
**Mobridge**—*pop pl* SD-7
Mobridge Airp (historical)—*airport* SD-7
Mobridge Auditorium—*hist pl* SD-7
Mobridge Catholic Ch (historical)—*church* SD-7
Mobridge Masonic Temple—*hist pl* SD-7
Mobridge Municipal Airp—*airport* SD-7
*Mobthug* FM-9
Moburg Lake—*lake* MN-6
**Moca**—*pop pl* PR-3
Mocabee Creek—*stream* KY-4
*Mocalvane Bay* FL-3
Mocam Springs—*spring* CA-9
Moca (Municipio)—*civil* PR-3
**Mocanaqua**—*pop pl* PA-2
Mocane—*locale* OK-5
Moca (Pueblo)—*fmr MCD* PR-3
**Mocarter**—*pop pl* MS-4
*Mocassin Creek* WI-6
Mocassin Gap—*gap* TN-4
Mocassin Post Office—*building* AZ-5
Moc-a-Tek Lake—*reservoir* PA-2
Moccasin—*gut* FL-3
Moccasin—*locale* CA-9
Moccasin—*locale* TN-4
**Moccasin**—*pop pl* AZ-5
**Moccasin**—*pop pl* CA-9
**Moccasin**—*pop pl* IL-6
**Moccasin**—*pop pl* MT-8
Moccasin Basin—*basin* WY-8
Moccasin Bay—*swamp* (2) FL-3
Moccasin Bayou—*gut* AL-4
Moccasin Bayou—*stream* AR-4
Moccasin Bayou—*stream* LA-4
Moccasin Bay Public Use Area—*park* ND-7
Moccasin Bend—*bend* OK-5
Moccasin Bend—*bend* TN-4
Moccasin Bend Archeol District—*hist pl* TN-4
Moccasin Bend Golf Course—*locale* TN-4
Moccasin Bend Gun Club—*locale* TN-4
*Moccasin Bend Mental Health Institute* TN-4
*Moccasin Bend Mental Hospital* TN-4
Moccasin Bend Psychiatric Hosp—*hospital* TN-4
Moccasin Bluff—*cliff* SC-3
Moccasin Bluff Sch (historical)—*school* TN-4
Moccasin Bluff Site—*hist pl* MI-6
*Moccasin Branch* FL-3
*Moccasin Branch* TN-4
Moccasin Branch—*stream* (6) AL-4
Moccasin Branch—*stream* (2) AR-4
Moccasin Branch—*stream* (4) FL-3
Moccasin Branch—*stream* (2) LA-4
Moccasin Branch—*stream* (2) NC-3
Moccasin Branch—*stream* SC-3
Moccasin Branch—*stream* (3) TN-4
Moccasin Branch—*stream* (2) TX-5
Moccasin Branch—*stream* VA-3
Moccasin Branch—*stream* WV-2
Moccasin Brook—*stream* MA-1
Moccasin Butte—*summit* MT-8
Moccasin Canal—*canal* NC-3
Moccasin Canyon—*valley* AZ-5
Moccasin Canyon—*valley* CO-8
Moccasin Cem—*cemetery* AR-4
Moccasin Ch—*church* NC-3
*Moccasin Creek* GA-3
*Moccasin Creek* LA-4
*Moccasin Creek* NC-3
*Moccasin Creek* WY-8
Moccasin Creek—*stream* (2) AL-4
Moccasin Creek—*stream* (6) AR-4
Moccasin Creek—*stream* (3) CA-9
Moccasin Creek—*stream* (5) FL-3
Moccasin Creek—*stream* (4) GA-3
Moccasin Creek—*stream* (2) ID-8
Moccasin Creek—*stream* IL-6
Moccasin Creek—*stream* (2) KY-4
Moccasin Creek—*stream* LA-4
Moccasin Creek—*stream* (3) MS-4
Moccasin Creek—*stream* MO-7
Moccasin Creek—*stream* (3) MT-8
Moccasin Creek—*stream* (7) NC-3
Moccasin Creek—*stream* ND-7
Moccasin Creek—*stream* OK-5
Moccasin Creek—*stream* SD-7
Moccasin Creek—*stream* (2) TN-4
Moccasin Creek—*stream* (5) TX-5
Moccasin Creek—*stream* WV-2
Moccasin Creek—*stream* WI-6
Moccasin Creek—*stream* (2) WY-8
Moccasin Creek Bay—*bay* ND-7
Moccasin Creek Cove—*bay* GA-3
Moccasin Draw—*valley* NM-5
*Moccasin Gap* AL-4
*Moccasin Gap* VA-3
Moccasin Gap—*gap* AR-4
Moccasin Gap—*gap* FL-3
Moccasin Gap—*gap* KY-4
Moccasin Gap—*gap* MO-7
Moccasin Gap—*gap* (2) NC-3
Moccasin Gap—*gap* (2) TN-4
Moccasin Gap—*gap* VA-3
Moccasin Gap—*locale* VA-3
Moccasin Gap Mine—*mine* TN-4
Moccasin Gap (RR name for Weber City)—*other* VA-3
Moccasin Gap Sch—*school* VA-3
Moccasin Head—*summit* CO-8
Moccasin Hollow—*valley* (2) AR-4
Moccasin Hollow—*valley* WV-2
Moccasin John Canyon—*valley* NM-5
Moccasin John Mtn—*summit* NM-5
Moccasin John Well—*well* NM-5
Moccasin Kill—*stream* NY-2
Moccasin Lake—*lake* (4) MI-6
Moccasin Lake—*lake* (2) MN-6
Moccasin Lake—*lake* (2) MT-8
Moccasin Lake—*lake* OR-9
Moccasin Lake—*lake* UT-8
Moccasin Lake—*lake* WA-9
Moccasin Lake—*lake* (3) WI-6
Moccasin Lake—*lake* WY-8
Moccasin Lake—*reservoir* UT-8
Moccasin Lake Dam—*dam* UT-8
Moccasin Landing—*locale* FL-3
Moccasin Mesa—*summit* CO-8
Moccasin Mill—*locale* VT-1
Moccasin Mound—*summit* FL-3
Moccasin Mountains—*summit* AZ-5
Moccasin Mtn—*summit* ID-8
Moccasin Mtn—*summit* NC-3
Moccasin Mtns—*range* UT-8
Moccasin Overlook—*locale* CO-8
Moccasin Path Trail—*trail* TN-4
Moccasin Peak—*summit* CA-9
Moccasin Peak—*summit* ID-8
Moccasin Point—*cape* MN-6
Moccasin Point—*cape* MS-4
Moccasin Point Public Use Area—*park* MS-4
Moccasin Pond—*lake* ME-1
Moccasin Pond—*lake* SC-3
Moccasin Pond—*lake* TX-5
Moccasin Pond—*swamp* FL-3
Moccasin Prairie—*flat* OR-9
Moccasin Ranch (Site)—*locale* CA-9
Moccasin Ridge—*ridge* MT-8
Moccasin Ridge—*ridge* VA-3
Moccasin Ridge Tunnel—*tunnel* VA-3
*Moccasin River* NC-3
Moccasin Rsvr—*reservoir* CA-9
Moccasin Run—*stream* NC-3
Moccasin Run—*stream* PA-2
Moccasin Sch—*school* KY-4
Moccasin Sch—*school* MI-6
Moccasin Sch (historical)—*school* MS-4
Moccasin Shoals—*bar* AL-4
Moccasin Siding—*locale* VA-3
Moccasin Slough—*gut* FL-3
Moccasin Slough—*stream* FL-3
Moccasin Slough—*stream* GA-3
Moccasin Slough—*swamp* FL-3
Moccasin Slough—*swamp* MS-4
Moccasin Spring—*spring* AZ-5
Moccasin Spring—*spring* TX-5
Moccasin Springs—*locale* MO-7
Moccasin State Wildlife Mngmt Area—*park* MN-6
*Moccasin Swamp* NC-3
Moccasin Swamp—*swamp* FL-3
Moccasin Tank—*reservoir* TX-5
Moccasin Terrace—*bench* UT-8
**Moccasin (Township of)**—*pop pl* IL-6
Moccasin Trail Canyon—*valley* UT-8
Moccasin Valley—*valley* VA-3
*Moccason Brook* MA-1
Moch—*island* FM-9
Mocham—*area* GU-9
*Mochaquo Mountain* TX-5
Mochelngel—*bay* PW-9
Mochenap—*channel* FM-9
Mochettaz Rsvr—*reservoir* OR-9
*Mocheu* FM-9
M & O Chevrolet Company—*hist pl* NC-3
*Mochler Ditch* IN-6
Moch (Municipality)—*civ div* FM-9
*Mochngod* FM-9
Mocho, Mount—*summit* CA-9
Mocho Camp—*locale* CA-9
Mocho Canyon—*valley* AZ-5
*Mochochaw* PW-9
Mocho Creek—*stream* CA-9
Mochom—*hist pl* GU-9
*Mochon* MH-9
**Mochon**—*pop pl* FM-9
Mochonap—*channel* FM-9
*Mochong* MH-9
Mochong—*hist pl* MH-9
Mochong—*slope* MH-9
Mochon Point—*cape* MH-9
*Mochon-saki* MH-9
Mocho Spring—*spring* AZ-5
Mochos Windmill—*locale* TX-5
Mocho Tank—*reservoir* AZ-5
*Moch-Ovi* AZ-5
Mocho Windmill—*locale* (3) TX-5
*Mochun Eparit* FM-9
*Mochun Mutikun* FM-9
*Mochun Nenom* FM-9
*Mochun Ochonap* FM-9
*Mochun Ochopenges* FM-9
*Mochun Onaf* FM-9
*Mochun Unigar* FM-9
*Mociac Mountain* AZ-5
*Mociac Wash* AZ-5
*Mociac Wash* UT-8
Mociac Well—*locale* AZ-5
*Mock* MT-8
Mock—*airport* NJ-2
Mock—*locale* CA-9
Mock—*locale* WA-9
Mock, John, House—*hist pl* OR-9
Mock, Randolf, Farm—*hist pl* KY-4
Mock Branch—*stream* GA-3
Mock Branch—*stream* (2) KY-4
Mock Branch—*stream* TX-5
Mock Cem—*cemetery* GA-3
Mock Cem—*cemetery* IN-6
Mock Cem—*cemetery* (2) MS-4
Mock Cem—*cemetery* NC-3
Mock Cigar Factory and House—*hist pl* MN-6
**Mock City**—*pop pl* WA-9
Mock Corner—*locale* MO-7
Mock Creek—*stream* IN-6
Mock Creek—*stream* PA-2
Mock Ditch—*canal* WY-8
Mock Ditch No 2—*canal* WY-8
*Mockeson* TN-4
Mockeson Branch—*stream* TN-4
Mockeson Post Office (historical)—*building* TN-4
Mock Gulch—*valley* WY-8
Mock Hill—*summit* CO-8
Mock Hollow—*valley* PA-2
Mockhorn Bay—*bay* VA-3
Mockhorn Channel—*channel* VA-3
Mockhorn Island—*island* VA-3
Mockhorn Point—*cape* VA-3
Mockingbird Canyon—*valley* CA-9
Mockingbird Canyon—*valley* NM-5
Mockingbird Creek—*stream* DE-2
Mockingbird Creek—*stream* MD-2
Mockingbird Draw—*valley* TX-5
Mockingbird Gap—*gap* NM-5
Mockingbird Gap Mine—*mine* NM-5
Mockingbird Gap Well—*well* NM-5
**Mockingbird Hill**—*pop pl* DE-2
**Mocking Bird Hill**—*pop pl* PA-2
**Mockingbird Hill**—*pop pl* TN-4
Mockingbird Hill—*summit* AZ-5
Mockingbird Hill—*summit* KY-4
Mockingbird Hill—*summit* MO-7
Mockingbird Hill—*summit* (2) TX-5
**Mockingbird Hills**—*pop pl* DE-2
Mockingbird Hills Lake—*reservoir* TN-4
Mockingbird Lake—*lake* GA-3
Mockingbird Lake—*reservoir* OK-5
Mockingbird Mine—*mine* AZ-5
Mocking Bird Mine—*mine* NV-8
Mockingbird Mountains—*summit* NM-5
Mockingbird Pass—*gap* AZ-5
*Mockingbird Pond* MD-2
Mockingbird Pond—*reservoir* MD-2
Mockingbird Ridge—*ridge* CA-9
Mockingbird Rsvr—*reservoir* CA-9
Mockingbird Spring—*spring* AZ-5
Mockingbird Spring—*spring* NV-8
**Mockingbird Valley**—*pop pl* KY-4
Mockingbird Wash—*stream* (2) AZ-5
Mockingbrid Lake—*lake* GA-3
Mocking Crow Mtn—*summit* TN-4
Mock Knob—*summit* VA-3
Mockley Point—*cape* MD-2
*Mocklin Canyon* NE-7
Mockmer Butte—*summit* ID-8
Mock Mill—*locale* VA-3
Mockonema—*locale* WA-9
Mock Roy Creek—*stream* KY-4
Mock Rsvr—*reservoir* CO-8
Mocks Bottom—*bend* OR-9
Mocks Branch—*stream* KY-4
Mocks Ch—*church* NC-3
Mocks Crest—*cliff* OR-9
Mocks Gulch—*valley* OR-9
Mock Spring—*spring* GA-3
**Mocksville**—*pop pl* NC-3
Mocksville Elem Sch—*school* NC-3
Mocksville Industrial Park—*locale* NC-3
Mocksville Lake—*reservoir* NC-3
Mocksville Lake Dam—*dam* NC-3
Mocksville MS—*school* NC-3
**Mocksville (subdivision)**—*pop pl* NC-3
Mocksville (Township of)—*fmr MCD* NC-3
Mock Tank—*reservoir* TX-5
Mock Well—*well* MT-8
Mock Well—*well* NM-5
Mock Windmill—*locale* NM-5
Mock Windmill—*locale* TX-5
**Moclips**—*pop pl* WA-9
Moclips Aloha Sch—*school* WA-9
Moclips River—*stream* WA-9
Moco Canyon—*valley* CA-9
Mococks Branch—*stream* NC-3
Mococo—*locale* CA-9
Mocogo Ranch—*locale* CA-9
*Mocoma Lake* PA-2
Moco Spring—*spring* OR-9
Moct—*locale* KY-4
Moctileme Creek—*stream* ID-8
Mocus Creek—*stream* ID-8
Mocus Point—*cliff* ID-8
**Modale**—*pop pl* IA-7
Modale Ditch—*canal* IA-7
Modarelli Mines—*mine* NV-8
*Modas Lake* TX-5
Mod Branch—*stream* WV-2
Mod Creek—*stream* KS-7
Modders Swamp—*swamp* MI-6
Moddersville—*locale* MI-6
Moddersville Lookout Tower—*locale* MI-6
**Mode**—*pop pl* IL-6
Mode Cem—*cemetery* AR-4
Model—*locale* TN-4
**Model**—*pop pl* CO-8
**Model Addition (subdivision)**—*pop pl* UT-8
Model A Tank—*reservoir* AZ-5
Model A Windmill—*locale* TX-5
Model (CCD)—*cens area* TN-4
**Model City**—*pop pl* NY-2
Model Cove—*bay* AK-9
Model Creek—*stream* AZ-5
Model Ditch—*canal* CO-8
Model Division—*civil* TN-4
Model Elem Sch—*school* IN-6
Model HS—*school* GA-3
Model Intake Canal—*canal* CO-8
Model Land Canal—*canal* FL-3
Model Land Company Hist Dist—*hist pl* FL-3
Model Landing (historical)—*locale* TN-4
Model Laundry—*hist pl* TX-5
Modell Cem—*cemetery* KS-7
**Modello**—*pop pl* FL-3
Modello Baptist Ch—*church* FL-3
Modello Wayside Park—*park* FL-3
*Modell Township* KS-7
Model Mine—*mine* CA-9
*Model Mountain* ID-8
*Model Mountain Lookout* ID-8
Modelo Canyon—*valley* CA-9
Modelo Peak—*summit* CA-9
Model Post Office (historical)—*building* TN-4
Model Rsvr—*reservoir* CO-8
Model Sch—*hist pl* MN-6
Model Sch—*school* WI-6
*Model School* TN-4
Model T Flat—*flat* FL-3
*Modeltown* NY-2
**Model Township**—*pop pl* ND-7
Model T Park—*flat* CO-8
Model Village—*uninc pl* PA-2
*Modena* CA-9
**Modena**—*pop pl* IL-6
**Modena**—*pop pl* MO-7
**Modena**—*pop pl* NY-2
**Modena**—*pop pl* PA-2
**Modena**—*pop pl* UT-8
**Modena**—*pop pl* WI-6
Modena—*unorg reg* SD-7
Modena Borough—*civil* PA-2
Modena Cem—*cemetery* NY-2
Modena Cem—*cemetery* TX-5
Modena Cem—*cemetery* UT-8
Modena Cem—*cemetery* WI-6
Modena Ch—*church* NC-3
Modena City Rsvr—*reservoir* UT-8
Modena Dam—*dam* UT-8
Modena Draw—*valley* UT-8
Modena Draw Dam—*dam* UT-8
Modena Draw Rsvr—*reservoir* UT-8
Modena Elem Sch—*hist pl* UT-8
**Modena Gardens**—*pop pl* NY-2
**Modena (RR name Paperville)**—*pop pl* PA-2
Modena Rsvr—*reservoir* UT-8
Modena Sch (abandoned)—*school* MO-7
Modena Station—*locale* PA-2
**Modena (Town of)**—*pop pl* WI-6
Modena Township—*civil* SD-7
*Modenos Pass* CO-8
Moder Archeol District—*hist pl* MO-7
Modern—*uninc pl* VA-3
Modern Diner—*hist pl* RI-1
Modern Manor—*other* OH-6
Modern News Bldg—*hist pl* AR-4
Modern Tool Company—*hist pl* PA-2
*Modern Woodmen of America Hall* SD-7
Modern Woodmen of America Hall (historical)—*building* SD-7
Moders Airp—*airport* MO-7
Mode-S Canyon—*valley* MT-8
Modes Island—*island* NC-3
Modesky Park—*park* FL-3
Modes Spring—*spring* NV-8
**Modest**—*pop pl* OH-6
Modest Creek—*stream* VA-3
**Modeste**—*pop pl* LA-4
Modest Lateral—*canal* AZ-5
**Modesto**—*pop pl* CA-9
**Modesto**—*pop pl* IL-6
**Modesto**—*pop pl* IN-6
Modesto Camp—*locale* CA-9
Modesto (CCD)—*cens area* CA-9
Modesto Christian Sch—*school* CA-9
**Modesto Colony**—*pop pl* CA-9
Modesto Creek—*stream* OR-9
*Modesto-Empire Junction* CA-9
Modesto Fork—*stream* CA-9
Modesto Gun Club—*other* CA-9
Modesto HS—*school* CA-9
Modesto Junior Coll—*school* CA-9
Modesto Lateral Number One—*canal* CA-9
Modesto Main Canal—*canal* CA-9
Modesto Rsvr—*reservoir* CA-9
Modesto State Hosp—*hospital* CA-9
**Modesto Terminal**—*pop pl* CA-9
Modesto Union Acad—*school* CA-9
Modest Saint Ch—*church* FL-3
*Modesttown* VA-3
**Modest Town**—*pop pl* VA-3
Modesty Creek—*stream* MT-8
Modesty Gulch—*valley* CA-9
*Modeville* PA-2
Modeville—*locale* OR-9
Modglin Cem—*cemetery* IL-6
*Modie Canyon* CA-9
Modin Creek—*stream* CA-9
Modine Sch—*school* IL-6
Modisette Creek—*stream* OK-5
**Modjeska**—*pop pl* CA-9
Modjeska Canyon—*valley* CA-9
Modjeska House—*hist pl* CA-9
Modjeska Park—*park* CA-9
Modjeska Peak—*summit* CA-9
Modjeska Rsvr—*reservoir* CA-9
*Modjon* FM-9
Modlin Branch—*stream* NC-3
Modlin Branch—*stream* SC-3
Modlin Creek—*stream* CO-8
Modlin Hollow—*valley* AR-4
Modoc—*locale* KY-4
Modoc—*locale* OH-6
Modoc—*locale* WV-2
**Modoc**—*pop pl* AR-4
**Modoc**—*pop pl* GA-3
**Modoc**—*pop pl* IL-6
**Modoc**—*pop pl* IN-6
**Modoc**—*pop pl* KS-7
**Modoc**—*pop pl* SC-3
*Modoc Basin* KS-7
Modoc Bethel Ch—*church* IN-6
Modoc Billy Creek—*stream* OR-9
Modoc Bottom (historical)—*flat* TN-4
Modoc Camp Area—*locale* SC-3
Modoc Cem—*cemetery* KS-7
Modoc Cem—*cemetery* TX-5
Modoc Ch—*church* OK-5
Modoc Ch—*church* TX-5
**Modoc (County)**—*pop pl* CA-9
Modoc Crater—*crater* CA-9
*Modoc Creek* ID-8
Modoc Creek—*stream* AK-9
Modoc Creek—*stream* CO-8
Modoc Creek—*stream* ID-8
Modoc Creek—*stream* MO-7
Modoc Creek—*stream* (2) OR-9
Modoc Creuasse—*basin* AR-4
Modoc Ditch—*canal* CA-9
Modoc Ditch—*canal* WY-8
*Modoc Gulch* CO-8
Modoc Hollow—*valley* TN-4
Modoc Incline—*mine* NM-5
Modock Sch—*school* NE-7
Modoc Landing—*locale* AR-4
Modoc Mill—*hist pl* CO-8
Modoc Mine—*mine* CA-9
Modoc Mine—*mine* NV-8
Modoc Mine—*mine* NM-5
Modoc Mines—*mine* CA-9
Modoc Mission Church and Cemetery—*hist pl* OK-5
*Modoc Mountain* OR-9
Modoc Mtn—*summit* AZ-5
Modoc Natl Wildlife Ref—*park* CA-9
Modoc Peak—*summit* CA-9
Modoc Peak—*summit* NV-8
Modoc Point—*cape* OR-9
**Modoc Point**—*pop pl* OR-9
Modoc Point Main Canal—*canal* OR-9
Modoc Post Office (historical)—*building* TN-4
Modoc Ridge—*cliff* OR-9
Modoc Ridge—*ridge* OR-9
Modoc Rim—*cliff* OR-9
Modoc Rock Shelter—*hist pl* IL-6
Modoc Rock Shelter Natl Historic Site—*park* IL-6
Modoc Run—*stream* OH-6
Modoc (Station)—*locale* IL-6
Modoc Tunnel—*tunnel* NM-5
Modoc Valley—*valley* MO-7
Modoc Valley—*valley* OK-5
*Modoge* FM-9
Modrall Sch (historical)—*school* MO-7
Modred Abyss—*valley* AZ-5
Mod Run—*stream* WV-2
Modum Cem—*cemetery* MN-6
*Mody Canyon* CA-9
Moe—*locale* NJ-2
Moe—*locale* SD-7
Moe, Bergetta, Bakery—*hist pl* MN-6
Moeauoa One-Two—*civil* HI-9
*Moe Ave* AZ-5
Moebes Pit Number One—*cave* AL-4
Moebes Pit Number Two—*cave* AL-4
Moe Cabin—*locale* CO-8
Moe Canyon—*valley* WA-9
Moe Cem—*cemetery* TN-4
Moe Cem—*cemetery* WI-6
Moe Ch—*church* WI-6
**Moecherville**—*pop pl* IL-6
Moeck, George F., House—*hist pl* OR-9
*Moe Coulee* WI-6
Moe Coulee—*valley* WI-6
Moe Creek—*stream* OR-9
Moeg—*cape* FM-9
Moega-a-uila—*other* AS-9
Moe Gulch—*valley* MT-8
*Moehavi* AZ-5
Moe Heights Cem—*cemetery* MN-6
*Moe Hill* WA-9
Moe Hill—*summit* WA-9
Moehler Hill—*summit* MT-8
M Oehlerking Dam—*dam* SD-7
Moehlman Bottoms—*bend* KS-7
Moehnke Cem—*cemetery* OR-9
*Moe Lake* MN-6
Moe Lake—*lake* ID-8
Moe Lake—*lake* (3) MN-6
Moelhman Slough—*lake* TX-5
Moellenberg Ranch—*locale* CO-8
Moellenbrocks—*locale* IL-6
Moeller Camp—*locale* FL-3
Moeller Cem—*cemetery* MO-7
Moeller Creek—*stream* CO-8
Moeller Ditch—*canal* WY-8
Moeller Ditch No 1—*canal* WY-8
Moeller House—*hist pl* TX-5
Moeller HS—*school* OH-6
Moeller Park—*park* MI-6
Moeller Park—*park* NE-7
Moellring, Frank, House—*hist pl* MO-7
Moeloa Falls—*falls* HI-9
Moe Mine—*mine* NM-5
*Moen* FM-9
*Moen Abi* AZ-5
*Moenave* AZ-5
**Moenave**—*pop pl* AZ-5
Moenave Canyon—*valley* AZ-5
Moen Cem—*cemetery* WI-6
*Moencopie* AZ-5
*Moencopie Wash* AZ-5
Moen Creek—*stream* WI-6
*Moen Insel* FM-9
*Moen Island* FM-9

Moenkapi AZ-5
Moenkedick Lake—lake MN-6
**Moenkopi**—pop pl AZ-5
Moenkopi Campground—locale UT-8
Moenkopi Canyon AZ-5
Moenkopi Creek AZ-5
Moenkopi Elem Sch—school AZ-5
Moenkopi Plateau—plain AZ-5
Moen Lake—lake (3) MN-6
Moen Lake—lake (2) WI-6
Moen (Municipality)—island FM-9
Moenn FM-9
Moenning Cem—cemetery WI-6
**Moenville**—pop pl SD-7
Moenville (historical)—locale SD-7
Moe Peak—summit ID-8
Moepitz Canyon—valley UT-8
Moe Ranch—locale NM-5
Moe Ridge—ridge WA-9
Moerke Lake WY-8
Moerke Reservoir WY-8
Moerle Corner NJ-2
Moerls Corner—locale NJ-2
Moe Sch—school SD-7
Moe Slough—lake SD-7
Moesner Lake—lake ND-7
Moesser Farm—hist pl KY-4
Moes Slough—lake AR-4
**Moe (Township of)**—pop pl MN-6
Moeur, W. A., House—hist pl AZ-5
Moeur Park—park AZ-5
**Moeville**—pop pl WI-6
Mofax Cem—cemetery NM-5
Mofeta—locale TX-5
Moffat TN-4
Moffat—locale AL-4
**Moffat**—pop pl (2) CO-8
**Moffat**—pop pl TX-5
Moffat, John S., House—hist pl WI-6
Moffat Bridge—bridge MT-8
Moffat Canal—canal UT-8
Moffat Cem—cemetery TX-5
Moffat Creek—stream WY-8
Moffat Drain—stream NE-7
Moffat Filter Plant—other CO-8
Moffat Gulch—valley CO-8
Moffat Mine—mine CO-8
Moffat Mine—mine MT-8
Moffat Oil Field—oilfield CO-8
Moffat Post Office TN-4
Moffat Road Assembly of God Ch—church AL-4
Moffat Road Ch—church AL-4
Moffat Road Ch of Christ—church AL-4
Moffat Rsvr—reservoir NV-8
Moffat Sch—school TX-5
Moffats Creek VA-3
**Moffats Creek (Newport)**—pop pl VA-3
Moffat Station TN-4
Moffat Station—hist pl CO-8
Moffat Station Post Office TN-4
Moffatt—locale TN-4
Moffatt Bluff—cliff AR-4
Moffatt Bridge—other MI-6
Moffatt Creek OR-9
Moffatt Creek VA-3
Moffatt Hill MA-1
Moffatt Hill—summit MA-1
Moffatt-Ladd House—hist pl NH-1
Moffatt Mine AL-4
Moffatt Sch (historical)—school AL-4
Moffatts Creek VA-3
Moffatts Creek—stream VA-3
Moffatts Station TN-4
**Moffatt (Township of)**—pop pl MI-6
Moffat Tunnel—tunnel CO-8
Moffet—locale AL-4
Moffet Bridge—bridge KS-7
Moffet Cem—cemetery AL-4
Moffet Cem—cemetery MS-4
Moffet Cem—cemetery TX-5
Moffet Creek CA-9
Moffet Creek—stream NE-7
Moffet Gulch—valley MT-8
Moffet Lagoon—bay AK-9
Moffet Meadow—swamp CO-8
Moffet Mtn—summit MT-8
Moffet Pass—gap NV-8
Moffet Point—cape AK-9
Moffets Ch—church OH-6
Moffet Sch—school AL-4
Moffet Sch—school PA-2
Moffet Slough—lake ND-7
Moffett IN-6
Moffett—locale VA-3
**Moffett**—pop pl AL-4
**Moffett**—pop pl OK-5
**Moffett**—pop pl TX-5
Moffett, Mount—summit AK-9
Moffett Bottom—flat OK-5
Moffett Cem—cemetery AR-4
Moffett Cem—cemetery IL-6
Moffett Cem—cemetery KY-4
Moffett Channel—channel CA-9
Moffett Creek—stream CA-9
Moffett Creek—stream ID-8
Moffett Creek—stream OR-9
Moffett Creek—stream VA-3
Moffett Falls—falls OR-9
Moffett Field Naval Air Station—military CA-9
Moffett Hollow—valley AR-4
Moffett Knob—summit WV-2
Moffett Lake—lake MS-4
Moffett Memorial Ch—church VA-3
Moffett Place Sch—school VA-3
Moffett Pond NY-2
Moffett Pond (historical)—lake TN-4
Moffett Public Use Area—park OK-5
Moffett-Ralston House—hist pl IN-6
Moffett Ranch—locale TX-5
Moffett Ranch—locale WY-8
Moffett School—locale IL-6
Moffett's Creek Schoolhouse—hist pl VA-3
**Moffetts Hot Springs**—pop pl WA-9
Moffett Springs—spring ID-8
Moffett Tunnel CO-8
Moffett West Oil Field—oilfield KS-7
Moffetville Cem—cemetery AL-4
Moffetville Ch—church AL-4
Moffit AR-4
**Moffit**—pop pl AR-4
**Moffit**—pop pl ND-7
Moffit, Mount—summit AK-9
Moffit Basin—basin UT-8
Moffit Butte—summit ND-7
Moffit Butte—summit OR-9
**Moffit Canyon**—pop pl MT-8
Moffit Canyon—valley AZ-5
Moffit Canyon—valley MT-8
Moffit Cem—cemetery ND-7
Moffit Cem—cemetery OH-6
Moffit Creath Cem—cemetery TX-5
Moffit Creek—stream UT-8
Moffit Grove Cem—cemetery IA-7
**Moffit Heights**—pop pl OH-6
Moffit Hill NC-3
Moffit Hollow—valley PA-2
Moffit Lake—lake NE-7
Moffit Lake—reservoir KY-4
Moffit Pass—gap UT-8
Moffit Peak—summit UT-8
Moffit Pond—lake NY-2
Moffit Settlement Hollow—valley NY-2
Moffits Grove—locale IA-7
Moffits Mill—locale AL-4
**Moffitsville**—pop pl NY-2
Moffitt—locale FL-3
**Moffitt**—pop pl IN-6
Moffit Table—summit OR-9
Moffit Tank—reservoir AZ-5
Moffitt Bend—bend TX-5
Moffitt Cem—cemetery (2) IN-6
Moffitt Creek NE-7
Moffitt Ditch IN-6
Moffitt Ditch—canal IN-6
Moffitt Ditch—canal OH-6
Moffitt Flat—flat NV-8
**Moffitt Heights**—pop pl OH-6
**Moffitt Hill**—pop pl NC-3
Moffitt Hill Sch—school MI-6
Moffitt Hollow—valley VT-1
Moffitt Island—island NY-2
Moffitt Mtn—summit NC-3
Moffitt Mtn—summit VT-1
Moffitt Ranch—locale CA-9
Moffitt Sch—school CA-9
Moffitt Sch—school OR-9
Moffitt Sch (abandoned)—school PA-2
**Moffitts Mills**—pop pl PA-2
Moffitts Pond—lake CT-1
Moffitt Spring—spring NV-8
Moffitt Spring—spring OR-9
**Moffitts Subdivision**—pop pl UT-8
**Moffitt Sterling**—pop pl PA-2
Moffittsville—locale NY-2
**Moffitty**—pop pl PA-2
Mofield Ridge—ridge KY-4
**Mofuba**—pop pl CA-9
Mog FM-9
Mog—other KY-4
Moga Butte—summit ND-7
**Mogadore**—pop pl OH-6
Mogadore Rsvr OH-6
Mogadore Rsvr—reservoir OH-6
Mogadore (Township of)—other OH-6
Mogak Creek—stream AK-9
Mogan Ridge—ridge IN-6
Mogans Lake—lake MI-6
Mogarts Beach—locale VA-3
Mogbeck Spring—spring UT-8
Mogck Slough State Public Shooting Area—park SD-7
Mogee PA-2
**Mogees (Mogeetown)**—pop pl PA-2
**Mogees Station**—pop pl PA-2
Mogee Tank—reservoir NM-5
Mogeetown PA-2
**Mogeetown**—pop pl PA-2
Moger Lagoon Natl Wildlife Mgt Area—park NE-7
Mogfog—area GU-9
Mogg Creek—stream ID-8
Mogg (Green River Station)—locale KY-4
Mogg Mtn—summit ID-8
Moghoweyik River—stream AK-9
Mogie Lake—lake MN-6
Mogil MP-9
Mogiri Channel MP-9
Mogiri Island—island MP-9
Mogiri Pass—channel MP-9
Mogiri-suido MP-9
Mogiri-to MP-9
Mogle Bridge—bridge NE-7
Mogler Cem—cemetery MO-7
Mogmog—island FM-9
Mogolel FM-9
Mogollon—locale NM-5
Mogollon Baldy Lookout Cabin—hist pl NM-5
Mogollon Baldy Peak—summit NM-5
Mogollon Canyon—valley NM-5
Mogollon Cem—cemetery NM-5
Mogollon Creek—stream NM-5
Mogollon Creek Trail (Pack)—trail NM-5
Mogollon Divide—ridge NM-5
Mogollon Escarpment AZ-5
**Mogollon (Ghost Town)**—pop pl NM-5
Mogollon Hist Dist—hist pl NM-5
Mogollon Mesa AZ-5
Mogollon Mesa—summit AZ-5
Mogollon Mountains AZ-5
Mogollon Mountains—other NM-5
Mogollon Plateau—plain AZ-5
Mogollon Pueblo—hist pl NM-5
Mogollon Rim—cliff AZ-5
Mogoolea—summit FM-9
Mogooleal FM-9
Mogoosh Tank—reservoir NM-5
Mogotas Arroyo—stream CO-8
Mogote—pillar NM-5
**Mogote**—pop pl CO-8
**Mogote**—pop pl PR-3
Mogote Artesian Well—well TX-5
Mogote Cem—cemetery CO-8
Mogote Ditch—canal CO-8
Mogote Hills—summit NM-5
Mogotes Hill—summit TX-5
M O'Grady Dam—dam SD-7
Mogridge Lake Dam—dam MS-4
Mogui Eye UT-8
Mogui Motel Campground—park UT-8
Mogui Window UT-8
Mogul—locale GA-3
Mogul—locale NV-8
Mogul Canyon CA-9
Mogul Canyon—valley CA-9
Mogul Canyon—valley NV-8
Mogul Creek—stream AK-9
Mogul Draw—valley AZ-5
Mogul Mine—mine CO-8
Mogul Mine—mine OR-9
Mogul Peak—summit CA-9
Mogul Ranch—locale TX-5
Mogul Sch (historical)—school MS-4
Mogul Tunnel—mine CO-8
Moguncoy Plantation MA-1
Moh, Mount—summit ID-8
Mohaba MS-4
**Mohall**—pop pl ND-7
Mohall Cem—cemetery ND-7
Mohall Lake—lake NE-7
Mohall Municipal Airp—airport ND-7
Mohan Cem MO-7
Mohan Run—stream PA-2
Mohansic Lake—lake NY-2
Mohansic State Park—park NY-2
**Mohat**—pop pl TX-5
Mohave CA-9
Mohave, Lake—reservoir AZ-5
Mohave, Lake—reservoir NV-8
Mohave Canyon—valley AZ-5
Mohave Canyon—valley CA-9
Mohave City AZ-5
**Mohave County**—pop pl AZ-5
Mohave County Airp AZ-5
Mohave County Airp—airport AZ-5
Mohave County Courthouse—building AZ-5
Mohave County Courthouse and Jail—hist pl AZ-5
Mohave County Fairgrounds—park AZ-5
Mohave County General Hospital Airfield—airport AZ-5
Mohave County Hosp—hist pl AZ-5
Mohave Creek AZ-5
Mohave Creek—stream MT-8
Mohave Crossing—locale AZ-5
Mohave Elementary School AZ-5
Mohave Generating Station—locale NV-8
Mohave HS—school AZ-5
Mohave Lateral—canal CA-9
Mohave Mine—mine AZ-5
Mohave Mountains CA-9
Mohave Mountains—range AZ-5
Mohave North (CCD)—cens area AZ-5
Mohave Peak—summit AZ-5
Mohave Point—cliff AZ-5
Mohave Range AZ-5
Mohave River CA-9
Mohave Rock—island AZ-5
Mohave Sch—school AZ-5
Mohave Springs—spring AZ-5
Mohave Springs Mesa—summit AZ-5
Mohave Tank—reservoir AZ-5
Mohave Tanks—reservoir AZ-5
Mohave Valley—basin NV-8
**Mohave Valley**—pop pl AZ-5
Mohave Valley—valley AZ-5
Mohave Valley Post Office—building AZ-5
Mohave Valley Sch—school AZ-5
Mohave Wash—stream (2) AZ-5
Mohave Wash—stream CA-9
Mohawk IL-6
Mohawk MO-7
Mohawk OH-6
Mohawk WV-2
Mohawk—locale AZ-5
Mohawk—locale FL-3
Mohawk—locale OK-5
**Mohawk**—pop pl CA-9
**Mohawk**—pop pl IN-6
**Mohawk**—pop pl MI-6
**Mohawk**—pop pl NY-2
**Mohawk**—pop pl NC-3
**Mohawk**—pop pl OH-6
**Mohawk**—pop pl OR-9
**Mohawk**—pop pl SC-3
**Mohawk**—pop pl TN-4
**Mohawk**—pop pl WV-2
Mohawk, Lake—reservoir MS-4
Mohawk, Lake—reservoir NJ-2
Mohawk, Lake—reservoir OH-6
Mohawk, Mount—summit NY-2
Mohawk Beach Estates Dam—dam MA-1
Mohawk Branch—stream WV-2
Mohawk Brook CT-1
Mohawk Brook—stream (2) MA-1
Mohawk Buddy Mine—mine CA-9
Mohawk Canal—canal AZ-5
Mohawk Canyon—valley AZ-5
Mohawk Canyon—valley (2) NV-8
Mohawk (CCD)—cens area TN-4
Mohawk Cem—cemetery VA-3
Mohawk Cem—cemetery WV-2
Mohawk Ch—church OH-6
Mohawk Club—locale PA-2
Mohawk Corner—locale MO-7
Mohawk Creek CA-9
Mohawk Creek—stream AZ-5
Mohawk Creek—stream CA-9
Mohawk Creek—stream VA-3
Mohawk Creek—stream WY-8
Mohawk Cross Road TN-4
Mohawk Crossroad—locale TN-4
Mohawk Cross Roads TN-4
Mohawk Dam—dam OH-6
Mohawk Division—civil TN-4
Mohawk Draw—valley TX-5
Mohawk Falls—falls PA-2
Mohawk Gap AZ-5
**Mohawk Gardens**—pop pl NY-2
Mohawk Golf Course—other NY-2
Mohawk Gulch—valley CO-8
Mohawk Gulch—valley ID-8
Mohawk Gulch—valley MT-8
Mohawk Hill—locale NY-2
Mohawk Hill—summit CA-9
Mohawk Inn AZ-5
Mohawk Interchange—crossing AZ-5
Mohawk Island NY-2
Mohawk Island—island ME-1
Mohawk Island—island NH-1
Mohawk Junction—locale OR-9
Mohawk Lake—lake CO-8
Mohawk Lake—lake MA-1
Mohawk Lake—lake MI-6
Mohawk Lake—lake OK-5
Mohawk Lake—lake UT-8
Mohawk Lake—reservoir OH-6
Mohawk Lake—reservoir TN-4
Mohawk Memorial Cem—cemetery NY-2
Mohawk Mica Prospect Mine—mine SD-7
Mohawk Mine—mine (4) AZ-5
Mohawk Mine—mine (3) CA-9
Mohawk Mine—mine CO-8
Mohawk Mine—mine MT-8
Mohawk Mine—mine (2) NV-8
Mohawk Mine—mine SD-7
Mohawk Mine—mine TX-5
Mohawk Mountain AZ-5
Mohawk Mountains AZ-5
Mohawk Mountains—range AZ-5
Mohawk Mtn—summit CT-1
Mohawk Papago Well Road (Jeep)—trail AZ-5
Mohawk Park—park IA-7
Mohawk Park—park OK-5
Mohawk Pass—gap AZ-5
Mohawk Pasture—flat NV-8
Mohawk Pathway Camp—locale NY-2
Mohawk Peak—summit AZ-5
Mohawk Pond—lake CT-1
Mohawk Pond—reservoir NJ-2
Mohawk Post—locale OR-9
Mohawk Post Office—building TN-4
Mohawk Range AZ-5
Mohawk Rapids—rapids ME-1
Mohawk Ravine—valley CA-9
Mohawk Ridge—ridge TN-4
Mohawk River—stream NH-1
Mohawk River—stream NY-2
Mohawk River—stream OR-9
Mohawk Roller Mill (historical)—locale TN-4
Mohawk Run—stream PA-2
Mohawks, Isle of the—island NY-2
Mohawk Sch—school (2) IL-6
Mohawk Sch—school KS-7
Mohawk Sch—school NH-1
Mohawk Sch—school NY-2
Mohawk Sch—school OH-6
Mohawk Sch (abandoned)—school PA-2
Mohawk Sch (historical)—school TN-4
Mohawksin, Lake—reservoir WI-6
Mohawk Spring—spring CA-9
Mohawk State For—forest CT-1
Mohawk State Park—park CT-1
Mohawk Stream—stream ME-1
Mohawk Swamp—swamp CT-1
Mohawk Tank—reservoir TX-5
**Mohawk (Town of)**—pop pl NY-2
Mohawk Trail—hist pl MA-1
Mohawk Trails Golf Course—locale PA-2
Mohawk Union HS—school OR-9
Mohawk Valley—valley AZ-5
Mohawk Valley—valley CA-9
Mohawk Valley—valley OR-9
Mohawk Valley—valley PA-2
Mohawk Valley—valley WI-6
Mohawk Valley Sch—hist pl AZ-5
Mohawk Valley Sch—school AZ-5
Mohawk Valley Technical Institute—school NY-2
**Mohawk View**—pop pl NY-2
**Mohawk Village**—pop pl OH-6
Mohawk Wash—stream (2) AZ-5
Mohawk Well—well WY-8
Mohawk 6.3 Lateral—canal AZ-5
Mohawk 6.9 Lateral—canal AZ-5
Mohawk 7.9 Lateral—canal AZ-5
Mohawk 8.5 Lateral—canal AZ-5
Mohawk 9.1 Lateral—canal AZ-5
Mohawk 9.8 Lateral—canal AZ-5
Mohaw Lake UT-8
Mohee, Lake—reservoir IN-6
Mohegan—locale RI-1
**Mohegan**—pop pl CT-1
**Mohegan**—pop pl WV-2
Mohegan, Lake—reservoir NY-2
Mohegan Bluffs—cliff RI-1
**Mohegan Bluffs**—pop pl RI-1
Mohegan Brook—stream CT-1
Mohegan Ch—church CT-1
**Mohegan Heights**—pop pl NY-2
Mohegan Hill—summit CT-1
**Mohegan (historical)**—pop pl MS-4
Mohegan Lake—lake (2) NY-2
**Mohegan Lake**—pop pl NY-2
Mohegan Outlet—stream NY-2
Mohegan Park—park CT-1
Mohegan Post Office (historical)—building MS-4
Mohegan River RI-1
Mohegan Sch—school CT-1
Mohemenco—other VA-3
Mohemnco VA-3
Mohepinoke, Mount—summit NJ-2
Mohiakea Gulch—valley HI-9
Mohican Canyon—valley NY-2
Mohican Ch—church OH-6
Mohican Creek—stream MT-8
Mohican Falls—falls PA-2
**Mohican Hills**—pop pl MD-2
Mohican Island—island NY-2
Mohican Lake—lake MI-6
Mohican Lake—lake NY-2
**Mohican Lake**—pop pl NY-2
Mohican River—stream OH-6
Mohican River Fishing Area—park OH-6
Mohican Sch—school LA-4
Mohican State For—forest OH-6
**Mohican (Township of)**—pop pl OH-6
Mohican Trail—trail NC-3
**Mohicanville**—pop pl OH-6
Mohicanville Dam—dam OH-6
Mohihi Falls—falls HI-9
Mohihi River HI-9
Mohihi Stream—stream HI-9
Mohlang, Liyang—cave MH-9
Mohlenoff Pond Dam—dam MS-4
Mohler—locale ID-8
Mohler—locale NE-7
Mohler—locale WA-9
**Mohler**—pop pl OR-9
Mohler, William E., House—hist pl WV-2
Mohler Cem—cemetery IA-7
Mohler Cem—cemetery TX-5
Mohler Ditch—canal IN-6
Mohler (historical)—locale SD-7
Mohler Lake—lake AK-9
Mohler Run—stream PA-2
Mohlers Ch—church (2) PA-2
Mohler Sch—school IL-6
Mohler-Union Cem—cemetery OH-6
Mohn Cem—cemetery KS-7
Mohney Lake—lake MI-6
Mohnike Cem—cemetery IA-7
Mohnshill PA-2
Mohns Hill—locale PA-2
**Mohnton**—pop pl PA-2
Mohnton Borough—civil PA-2
Mohnton Boy Scout Camp—locale PA-2
Moho—cape HI-9
Mohoba Ch—church MS-4
**Mohoba (historical)**—pop pl MS-4
Mohokea Iki—civil HI-9
Mohokea Nui—civil HI-9
Mohokea One-Two—civil HI-9
Moho Mtn—summit NV-8
Mohon Camp—locale AZ-5
Mohon Canyon—valley AZ-5
Mohone Peak AZ-5
Mohonk Lake—lake NY-2
**Mohonk Lake**—pop pl NY-2
**Mohonk Lake (Lake Mohonk Mountain House)**—pop pl NY-2
Mohon Mountains—range AZ-5
Mohon Peak—summit AZ-5
Mohon Spring—spring AZ-5
Mohon Tank—reservoir AZ-5
Mohopilo—civil HI-9
Mohorn Creek—stream AL-4
Mohouli Pond—lake HI-9
Mohr, Louis, Block—hist pl IN-6
Mohrbacher, Paul, House—hist pl MN-6
Mohr Canyon—valley WA-9
Mohr Cem—cemetery IN-6
Mohr Cem—cemetery OH-6
Mohr Cem—cemetery SD-7
Mohr Creek—stream MI-6
Mohr Ditch—canal IN-6
Mohrhardt Ridge—ridge CA-9
Mohris-Abschier House—hist pl TX-5
Mohrland—locale UT-8
Mohrland Mine—mine UT-8
Mohrland Sch—school CA-9
Mohrman-Jack-Evans House—hist pl OH-6
Mohrs Lake—lake IA-7
**Mohrsville**—pop pl PA-2
**Mohrtown**—pop pl WV-2
**Mohrweis**—pop pl WA-9
Mohts-ovi—cliff AZ-5
Mohuna Gulch—valley HI-9
Mohun Ch—church LA-4
Mohundro Cemetery MS-4
Moic, Lake—lake CA-9
Moiese—locale MT-8
Moiese A Canal—canal MT-8
Moiese A-30 Lateral—canal MT-8
Moiese Bible Ch—church MT-8
Moiese Camp—locale MT-8
Moiese Creek—stream MT-8
Moiese Hills—spring MT-8
Moiese Sch—school MT-8
Moiese Valley—basin MT-8
Moiese 30-13 Lateral—canal MT-8
Moikeha Canal—canal HI-9
Moiki Point—cape HI-9
Moila Golf Course—other MO-7
Moilan Lake—lake MN-6
Moiles Lake—lake MI-6
**Moiliili**—pop pl HI-9
Moiliili Japanese Sch—school HI-9
Moiliili Quarry (Athletic Field)—park HI-9
Moiliili Triangle—park HI-9
Moine Creek—stream IA-7
**Moingona**—pop pl IA-7
Moinui Point—cape HI-9
Moir PW-9
**Moira**—pop pl NY-2
Moira Lake—lake WA-9
Moira Rock—island AK-9
Moira Sound—bay AK-9
**Moira (Town of)**—pop pl NY-2
Moir Bldg—hist pl CA-9
Moir Park—park MN-6
Moisant Airport—post sta LA-4
Moise, Julius J., House—hist pl NM-5
Moise Ranch—locale NM-5
Moistown TX-5
Moivavi AZ-5
Moi Vaya AZ-5
**Moi Vaya**—pop pl AZ-5
Moiver Canal—canal CA-9
Moiwi HI-9
Moiwi Peak HI-9
Moiyaka Lake—lake MN-6
Moize Creek—stream TN-4
Mojada Blancas Tank—reservoir NM-5
Mojada Rsvr—reservoir TX-5
Mojado Well (Flowing)—well TX-5
Mojalaki Golf Course—other NH-1
**Mojave**—pop pl CA-9
Mojave City—locale AZ-5
Mojave County AZ-5
Mojave Desert CA-9
Mojave Desert—plain CA-9
Mojave East Park—park CA-9
**Mojave Heights**—pop pl CA-9
Mojave River—stream CA-9
Mojave River Forks Rsvr—reservoir CA-9
Mojave River Sink CA-9
Mojave River Wash—stream CA-9
Mojave State Fish Hatchery—other CA-9
Mojave Tank—reservoir CA-9
Mojave Valley AZ-5
Mojave Valley—valley (2) CA-9
Mojave West Park—park CA-9
Mojie River ID-8
Mojjokkarik MP-9
Mojohave Ridge—ridge AZ-5
Mo-John, Betsy, Cabin—hist pl OH-6
Mojonera Canyon—valley AZ-5
Mojonera Well—well AZ-5
Mojonnier—locale WA-9
**Mojosin**—pop pl NC-3
Mokaac Mtn—summit AZ-5
Mokaac Rsvr—reservoir AZ-5
Mokaac Spring—spring AZ-5
Mokaac Wash—arroyo AZ-5
Mokaac Wash—valley UT-8
Mokae—civil HI-9
Mokae—locale HI-9
Mokae Cove—bay HI-9
Mokae Landing—locale HI-9
Mokalusha MS-4
**Mokane**—pop pl MO-7
Mokane Bridge—other MO-7
Mokano—cape HI-9
**Mokaoku**—pop pl HI-9
Mokapoo Point HI-9
Mokapu Burial Area—hist pl HI-9
Mokapu (census name for Kaneohe)—CDP HI-9
Mokapu Island—island HI-9
Mokapu Peninsula—cape HI-9
Mokapu Point—cape HI-9
Mokapu Sch—school HI-9
Mokauea HI-9
Mokauea Island—island HI-9
Mokay Cave—cave TN-4
Mokay Hollow—valley TN-4
MoKeAk Mountain AZ-5
MoKeAk Wash AZ-5
Moke Branch—stream SC-3
Mokeehia HI-9
Mokeehia Island—island HI-9
Mokeler Creek—stream IL-6
Mokeley Hill—summit AL-4
Mokelumne Aqueduct—canal CA-9
Mokelumne City—locale CA-9
**Mokelumne Hill**—pop pl CA-9
Mokelumne Peak—summit CA-9
Mokelumne River CA-9
Mokelumne River—stream CA-9
Mokelumne River Campground—locale CA-9
Mokelumne River Fish Installation—other CA-9
Mokelumne Telons—ridge CA-9
Mokelumne Wilderness—area CA-9
**Mokena**—pop pl IL-6
Mo-Ke-ock Mountain AZ-5
Mo-Ke-ok Mountain AZ-5
Mo-Ke-ok Wash AZ-5
Moke Rock—other AK-9
Mokeromok Island—island MP-9
MoKersky Sch—school MI-6
Moki UT-8
Mokiac Mountain AZ-5
Mokiac Wash AZ-5
Mokiah Mountain AZ-5
Mokiah Wash AZ-5
Mokiah Wash UT-8
Moki Bar UT-8
Moki Caverns UT-8
Moki Dugway—locale UT-8
Moki Dugway—slope UT-8
Moki Dugway Overlook—locale UT-8
Mokie Indian Ruin—locale NM-5
Mokihana Bay—bay HI-9
Mokihana Stream—stream HI-9
Mokihana Valley—valley HI-9
Mokil Atoll—island FM-9
Mokil (Municipality)—island FM-9
Mokins Bay—bay ID-8
Mokins Bay Campground—locale ID-8
Mokins Creek—stream ID-8
Mokins Slough—gut ID-8
Mokio HI-9
Mokio—cape HI-9
Mo-Ki-ok Mountain AZ-5
Mo-Ki-Ok Wash AZ-5
Mokio Point—cape HI-9
Moki Spring—spring UT-8
Moki Stairs—other UT-8
Moki Tank—reservoir UT-8
Mokler Sch—school CA-9
Mok-Mok MP-9
Moko—locale AR-4
Mokohola HI-9
Mokohola Island—island HI-9
Mokokaemu PW-9
Mokokaemu Island PW-9
Mokokaemu To PW-9
Mokolea HI-9
Mokolea Island HI-9
Mokolea Point—cape (2) HI-9
Mokolea Rock—island HI-9
Mokolea Rock (State Bird Refuge)—island HI-9
Mokole Point HI-9
Mokolii HI-9
Mokolii Island (Chinamans Hat)—island HI-9
Mokoma PA-2
Mokoma Lake—reservoir PA-2
Mokomoke Mtns—range NV-8
Mokomoko Gulch—valley HI-9
Moko Mtn—summit OK-5
Mokota River FM-9
Mokouia Valley—valley HI-9
Mokowanis Cascade—falls MT-8
Mokowanis Lake—lake MT-8
Mokowanis River—stream MT-8
Mokowanis Shelter Cabin—locale MT-8
Mokst Butte—summit OR-9
Moku HI-9
**Moku**—pop pl HI-9
Mokuaaniwa HI-9
Mokuaeae—island HI-9
Mokuaeae Island HI-9
Mokuaia Island—island HI-9
Mokuaikaua Church—hist pl HI-9
Moku Akulikuli HI-9
Mokualai (Bird Refuge)—island HI-9
Mokualai Islet HI-9
Mokuami Island HI-9
Mokuapihi Point—cape HI-9
Mokuauia (Bird Refuge)—island HI-9
Mokuauia Island HI-9
Mokuaweowea Crater HI-9
Mokuaweoweo—crater HI-9
Mokuaweoweo Crater HI-9
Mokuchis—channel FM-9
Mokuhonu—island HI-9
Mokuhonua—civil HI-9
Mokuhooniki—island HI-9
Mokuia Point—cape HI-9

Mokuiki—*island* HI-9
*Mokulalai Island* HI-9
Mokulau—*island* HI-9
**Mokulau**—*pop pl* HI-9
Mokulau Landing—*locale* HI-9
Mokulehua Gulch—*valley* HI-9
Mokuleia—*civil* HI-9
**Mokuleia**—*pop pl* HI-9
Mokuleia Beach—*beach* HI-9
*Mokuleia Beach Lots* HI-9
Mokuleia Beach Park—*park* HI-9
Mokuleia For Res—*forest* HI-9
**Mokuleia (Mokuleia Beach Lots)**—*pop pl* HI-9
*Mokuleia Station* HI-9
Mokuleia Trail—*trail* HI-9
*Mokulua* HI-9
Mokulua Islands—*island* HI-9
Mokulua Islands (State Bird Refuge)—*island* HI-9
Mokumana Gulch—*valley* HI-9
Moku Manu—*island* HI-9
Mokumanu—*island* HI-9
*Mokumanu Island* HI-9
Mokunaia Point—*cape* HI-9
Mokunui—*island* HI-9
*Mokuoeo* HI-9
Mokuoeo Island—*island* HI-9
*Mokuohope Island* HI-9
Mokuohua Gulch—*valley* HI-9
Mokuokahailani Rock—*island* HI-9
*Mokuola* HI-9
*Mokuola Island* HI-9
*Moku o Lo'e* HI-9
*Moku o Loe Island* HI-9
Mokuone Stream—*stream* HI-9
Mokuone Valley—*valley* HI-9
*Mokuo Niki* HI-9
Mokuoniki—*civil* HI-9
*Mokuopihi* HI-9
*Mokuopuhi* HI-9
Mokupane Point—*cape* HI-9
Mokupapa—*civil* HI-9
Mokupapa Island—*island* HI-9
*Moku Papapa* HI-9
Mokupapapa—*island* HI-9
Mokupapa Point—*cape* HI-9
Mokupau Stream—*stream* HI-9
Mokupea Gulch—*valley* HI-9
Mokupipi Island—*island* HI-9
Mokupuku—*island* HI-9
*Mokupuku Island* HI-9
*Mokupu Point* HI-9
Mokupupu—*cape* (2) HI-9
*Moku Umeume* HI-9
*Mokuyo To* FM-9
**Molalla**—*pop pl* OR-9
Molalla (CCD)—*cens area* OR-9
Molalla Elem Sch—*school* OR-9
Molalla HS—*school* OR-9
Molalla MS—*school* OR-9
Molalla River—*stream* OR-9
Molalla Trail—*trail* OR-9
Moland—*locale* MN-6
**Moland**—*pop pl* MN-6
Moland Ch—*church* MN-6
Moland Ch—*church* WI-6
Molander Historic Site—*park* ND-7
Molander Park—*park* OH-6
Molander State Park—*park* ND-7
**Moland (Township of)**—*pop pl* MN-6
Molaneil Island—*island* FM-9
Molan (historical)—*locale* SD-7
Molan Sch—*school* SD-7
**Molan Township**—*pop pl* SD-7
Molar Creek—*stream* ID-8
Molar Sch—*school* MO-7
Molas Creek—*stream* CO-8
*Molas Divide* CO-8
Molash Creek—*stream* WI-6
Molas Lake—*reservoir* CO-8
Molas Mine—*mine* CO-8
Molas Park—*park* CO-8
Molas Pass—*gap* CO-8
Molasses Bayou—*gut* TX-5
Molasses Branch—*gut* FL-3
Molasses Corners—*locale* NY-2
*Molasses Creek* PA-2
Molasses Creek—*stream* CA-9
Molasses Creek—*stream* IN-6
Molasses Creek—*stream* NC-3
Molasses Creek—*stream* (3) PA-2
Molasses Creek—*stream* SC-3
Molasses Creek—*stream* TX-5
Molasses Gap—*gap* PA-2
Molasses Gap Trail—*trail* PA-2
Molasses Hill—*summit* PA-2
Molasses Hill—*summit* RI-1
Molasses Hollow—*valley* TX-5
Molasses Junction—*locale* FL-3
Molasses Key—*island* FL-3
Molasses Point—*cape* NY-2
Molasses Point Landing—*locale* TN-4
Molasses Pond—*lake* ME-1
Molasses Pond—*lake* MA-1
Molasses Reef—*bar* FL-3
Molasses Reef Channel—*channel* FL-3
Molasses Reef Light—*locale* FL-3
Molasses Reef Light 10—*locale* FL-3
Molasses River—*stream* MI-6
Molasses River Flooding Number Five—*reservoir* MI-6
Molasses River Flooding Number One—*reservoir* MI-6
Molasses River Flooding Number Three—*reservoir* MI-6
Molasses River Flooding Number Two—*reservoir* MI-6
Molasses Tank—*reservoir* NM-5
*Molawnquinteouk* PA-2
*Molawnquioteouk* PA-2
Molayses Spring (historical)—*spring* SD-7
Molazigan Island—*island* ME-1
Molbdenum Ridge—*ridge* AK-9
Molby Creek—*stream* OR-9
Mold—*locale* WA-9
Mold Cem—*cemetery* WA-9
Molde Lookout Tower—*locale* MN-6
Molden Creek—*stream* MS-4
Moldenhauer Hill—*summit* WI-6
Moldenhauer Lake—*lake* WI-6
Molden Hollow—*valley* VA-3
Molder Branch—*stream* AL-4
Molder Camp—*locale* GA-3
Molder Cem—*cemetery* TN-4
Molder (historical)—*locale* AL-4
Molder Hollow—*valley* AR-4
*Moldier Creek* MD-2
*Moldier Run* MD-2
Moldingroom Hollow—*valley* TN-4
**Mold (local name Sims Corner)**—*pop pl* WA-9
Moldon Plantation (historical)—*locale* MS-4
Moldoon Hill—*summit* CO-8
Moldy Lake—*lake* AK-9
Mole—*locale* TN-4
Mole Brook—*stream* WI-6
Mole Creek—*stream* IL-6
Moleen—*locale* NV-8
*Molegojok* PW-9
*Molegoyok* PW-9
Mole Grove Ch—*church* GA-3
Mole Harbor—*bay* AK-9
*Mole Hill* WV-2
Mole Hill—*summit* VA-3
Mole Hill Chapel—*church* WV-2
Molehu—*cape* HI-9
Moleka Stream—*stream* HI-9
Mole Lake—*lake* WI-6
**Mole Lake**—*pop pl* WI-6
Mole Lake Ind Res—*reserve* WI-6
Mole Mountian—*summit* WA-9
Mole Mtn—*summit* GA-3
Molen—*locale* UT-8
Molena—*locale* CA-9
**Molena**—*pop pl* GA-3
Molena-Castle Playground—*park* MI-6
Molen Cem—*cemetery* UT-8
Molen Ditch—*canal* UT-8
Molen Lake—*lake* LA-4
Molen Reef—*ridge* UT-8
Molen Seep Wash—*valley* (2) UT-8
*Molen Soap Wash* UT-8
*Molen Tank* UT-8
Molen Tanks—*reservoir* UT-8
*Moleo* MP-9
Mole Pier—*locale* CA-9
Moler Bayou—*stream* LA-4
Moler Crossroads—*locale* WV-2
Mole River—*stream* AK-9
*Molers* WV-2
**Molers**—*pop pl* WV-2
Moles Cave State Wildlife Area—*park* MO-7
Moles Cem—*cemetery* TN-4
Moles Cem—*cemetery* WV-2
Molessa County Park—*park* MI-6
Molesworth Creek—*stream* CA-9
Molesworth Mesa—*summit* TX-5
Molette Bend—*bend* AL-4
Molette Bend Sch—*school* AL-4
Molette Cem—*cemetery* AL-4
*Mol Heron Creek* MT-8
*Mol Heron Creek* WY-8
*Molherron Creek* MT-8
Molholm Sch—*school* CO-8
*Molii* HI-9
Molii Fishpond—*hist pl* HI-9
Moliili Field—*park* HI-9
Molii Pond—*lake* HI-9
Molilele, Heiau o—*locale* HI-9
*Molina* GA-3
**Molina**—*pop pl* CO-8
**Molina**—*pop pl* PR-3
Molina Basin—*basin* AZ-5
Molina Canyon—*valley* CA-9
Molina JHS—*school* TX-5
Molina Lateral—*canal* AZ-5
Molina Mine—*mine* CA-9
Molina Spring—*spring* AZ-5
Molina Spring—*spring* NM-5
*Molin Creek* ID-8
*Moline* PA-2
Moline—*locale* TX-5
Moline—*other* PA-2
**Moline**—*pop pl* IL-6
**Moline**—*pop pl* KS-7
**Moline**—*pop pl* MI-6
**Moline**—*pop pl* OH-6
Moline, Milburn and Stoddard Company—*hist pl* MN-6
**Moline Acres**—*pop pl* MO-7
Moline Cem—*cemetery* KS-7
Moline City Dam—*dam* KS-7
*Moline Corral* CA-9
*Moline Creek* ID-8
*Moline Creek* MO-7
Moline Hosp—*hospital* IL-6
Moline Pool—*lake* IL-6
Moline Rsvr—*reservoir* ID-8
Moline Sch—*school* ND-7
**Moline (Township of)**—*pop pl* IL-6
Moline Tunnel—*mine* CO-8
*Molinitos* AZ-5
Molino—*locale* CA-9
Molino—*locale* MS-4
Molino—*locale* MO-7
Molino—*locale* PA-2
**Molino**—*pop pl* FL-3
**Molino**—*pop pl* TN-4
Molino, Canada Del —*valley* CA-9
Molino Basin—*basin* AZ-5
Molino Basin Campground—*park* AZ-5
Molino Canyon—*valley* AZ-5
Molino Canyon—*valley* CO-8
Molino Canyon—*valley* NM-5
Molino Creek—*stream* CA-9
Molino Creek—*stream* TN-4
Molino Crossroads—*locale* FL-3
Molino Lodge Bldg—*hist pl* CA-9
Molino Peak—*summit* NM-5
Molino Post Office (historical)—*building* MS-4
Molino Post Office (historical)—*building* TN-4
Molinos—*civil* CA-9
Molino Sch—*school* FL-3
Molino Sch (historical)—*school* TN-4
Molino Spring—*spring* NM-5
Molino Tank, El—*reservoir* AZ-5
Molino Tower (fire tower)—*tower* FL-3
Molino Viejo Well—*well* NM-5
*Molinton* AZ-5
Moliter Lake—*swamp* MN-6
Moliter Mine—*mine* CA-9
Molitor Cem—*cemetery* WI-6
Molitor Spring—*spring* WA-9
**Molitor (Town of)**—*pop pl* WI-6
Mollahan Cem—*cemetery* WV-2
Mollalla River State Park—*park* OR-9
Mollar Lake—*lake* MN-6
Moll Canal—*canal* LA-4
Mollclark River—*stream* GA-3
*Moll Creek* KS-7
Moll Creek—*stream* VA-3
Moll Creek Ch—*church* VA-3
Moll Dyers Run—*stream* MD-2
Molle Hogans—*summit* UT-8
**Mollenauer**—*pop pl* PA-2
Mollendal—*locale* VI-3
Mollenhour Creek—*stream* OR-9
Mollenkamp Field—*airport* KS-7
Mollenkope Ditch—*canal* OH-6
Mollenkramer Reservoir Dam—*dam* IN-6
Mollenkramer Rsvr—*reservoir* IN-6
Mollens Hollow—*valley* UT-8
Mollen Well—*well* AZ-5
*Moller* HI-9
Moller Creek—*stream* IN-6
Moller House—*hist pl* MO-7
*Moller Island* HI-9
Moller Road Park—*park* IN-6
Moller Ski Trail—*trail* AK-9
Moller Spit—*bar* AK-9
*Molles Lake* MI-6
Molleson Canyon—*valley* NV-8
Molleson Gap—*gap* NV-8
Mollete Lake—*lake* WI-6
Molletes, Arroyo—*valley* TX-5
Mollet Park—*flat* MT-8
Molley Brook—*stream* CT-1
*Molley Creek* VA-3
Molleys Hollow—*valley* WV-2
*Molley's Nipple* UT-8
*Molleystown* PA-2
*Moll Fork* WV-2
Mollhead Creek—*stream* PA-2
Mollicy Bayou—*stream* LA-4
Mollidgewock Brook—*stream* NH-1
Mollidgewock Pond—*lake* ME-1
Mollie—*locale* NC-3
**Mollie**—*pop pl* AL-4
Mollie B Hoover Elem Sch—*school* IN-6
Mollie Branch—*stream* AL-4
Mollie Branch—*stream* GA-3
Mollie Branch—*stream* (2) NC-3
Mollie Branch—*stream* VA-3
Mollie Cove—*bay* ME-1
Mollie Davenport Mine—*mine* AZ-5
Mollie Dozier Chute—*stream* MO-7
Mollie Gap—*gap* NC-3
Mollie Gibson Canyon—*valley* CA-9
Mollie Gibson Mines—*mine* CA-9
Mollie Gibson Shaft—*mine* CO-8
Mollie Gulch—*valley* ID-8
Mollie Hollow—*valley* VA-3
Mollie Kathleen Mine—*mine* CO-8
Mollie Lake—*lake* MN-6
Mollie Lake—*lake* SD-7
Mollie Mtn—*summit* NC-3
*Mollie P. O.* MS-4
Mollie Point—*summit* ID-8
Mollie Ridge—*ridge* NC-3
Mollies Butt—*summit* TN-4
Mollies Creek—*stream* WI-6
Mollies Lake—*lake* ID-8
*Mollie's Nipple* UT-8
Mollies Nipple—*summit* AZ-5
Mollies Nipple—*summit* (5) UT-8
Mollies Nipple Well—*well* UT-8
Mollies Point—*cape* MD-2
Mollies Ridge—*ridge* TN-4
Mollies Ridge Shelter—*locale* TN-4
Mollie Swamp—*stream* NC-3
Mollini Mine—*mine* NV-8
*Molliockett Mountain* ME-1
Mollirene, Lake—*reservoir* SC-3
Mollison Hill—*summit* MA-1
Mollison Lake—*lake* MN-6
Mollison Lake—*lake* SD-7
Mollison Sch—*school* IL-6
**Mollison Townhouses**—*pop pl* CA-9
Moll Lake—*lake* MI-6
Mollman Creek—*stream* MT-8
Mollman Lakes—*lake* MT-8
Mollman Pass—*gap* MT-8
*Moll Ockett Mountain* ME-1
Mollohan Mill—*hist pl* WV-2
**Molloy**—*pop pl* AL-4
Molloy Bay—*bay* KY-4
Molloy Branch—*stream* KY-4
Molloy Cave—*cave* TN-4
Molloy Coll—*school* NY-2
Molloy Hollow—*valley* TN-4
Molloy HS—*school* NY-2
Molloy Post Office (historical)—*building* AL-4
Molloy Sch—*school* CT-1
Molloy Sch—*school* MA-1
Molloys Grove Ch—*church* NC-3
Moll Pond—*lake* MA-1
Moll Rsvr—*reservoir* CA-9
Molls Cove—*bay* MD-2
Molls Creek—*stream* MS-4
*Molls Pond* MA-1
**Moll Spur**—*pop pl* NE-7
**Molltown**—*pop pl* PA-2
Mollusk—*locale* VA-3
Mollusk Mine—*mine* CA-9
Mollusk Wash—*stream* CA-9
Molly, Lake—*lake* FL-3
Molly, Lake—*reservoir* IN-6
Molly, Mount—*summit* NH-1
Molly and Mable—*summit* CO-8
Molly Ann Brook—*stream* NJ-2
Molly Ann Draw—*valley* AZ-5
*Molly Anns Brook* NJ-2
Molly Ann Tank—*reservoir* AZ-5
Molly Bailey Windmill—*locale* TX-5
**Molly Barr Cove (subdivision)**—*pop pl* MS-4
Molly Bawn Mine—*mine* CO-8
Molly Booth Run—*stream* VA-3
Molly Branch—*stream* (2) AL-4
Molly Branch—*stream* KY-4
Molly Branch—*stream* (2) NC-3
Molly Branch—*stream* (3) SC-3
Molly Branch—*stream* TN-4
Molly Branch—*stream* WV-2
Molly Branch Sch—*school* KY-4
Molly Brown Campground—*locale* CO-8
Molly Cabin Branch—*stream* KY-4
Molly Camel Run—*stream* VA-3
Molly Clark Slough—*gut* TX-5
Molly Cove—*bay* MA-1
Molly Creek—*stream* AK-9
Molly Creek—*stream* AR-4
Molly Creek—*stream* ID-8
Molly Creek—*stream* MN-6
Molly Creek—*stream* MT-8
Molly Field Ch—*church* OK-5
Molly Field Hollow—*valley* OK-5
Molly Fork—*stream* NC-3
Molly Fork—*stream* WY-8
Molly Gap Creek—*stream* AR-4
Molly Gibson—*mine* UT-8
Molly Gibson Mine—*mine* OR-9
Molly Gulch—*valley* CO-8
Molly Gut—*gut* ME-1
Molly Hill Mine (abandoned)—*mine* OR-9
Molly Hollow—*valley* TN-4
Molly Horn Branch—*stream* MD-2
Molly Islands—*island* WY-8
*Molly Janns Brook* NJ-2
Molly Kincaid Branch—*stream* WV-2
Molly Lake—*lake* CO-8
Molly Lake—*lake* MI-6
Molly Lake—*lake* MN-6
Molly Lake—*lake* MT-8
Molly Logan Mine—*mine* WY-8
Mollyockett Mtn—*summit* ME-1
Molly Pond—*lake* VT-1
Mollys Branch—*stream* NC-3
Mollys Brook—*stream* MA-1
Mollys Brook—*stream* VT-1
Mollys Castle—*summit* UT-8
Mollys Cave—*cave* AL-4
Mollys Creek—*stream* VA-3
Mollys Creek—*stream* WV-2
Mollys Falls—*falls* VT-1
*Molly's Gut* NY-2
Mollys Head—*cape* ME-1
Mollys Hill—*summit* WV-2
Mollys Island—*island* MA-1
Mollys Knob—*summit* VA-3
Mollys Mtn—*summit* VA-3
*Mollys Nipple* UT-8
Mollys Nipple—*summit* ID-8
Mollys Nipple—*summit* (2) UT-8
Mollys Nipples—*summit* NV-8
Mollys Pond—*lake* VT-1
Mollys Rock Rec Area—*park* SC-3
Mollys Run—*stream* IN-6
Mollys Stocking—*ridge* UT-8
Molly Stark Hosp—*hospital* OH-6
Molly Stark Lake—*lake* MN-6
Molly Stark Mtn—*summit* VT-1
Molly Stark State For—*forest* VT-1
Molly Stark Trail—*trail* VT-1
*Molly Wheatens Run* NJ-2
*Molly Wheatons Creek* NJ-2
*Molly Wheatons Run* NJ-2
*Mollywocket Brook* NH-1
Molma Moulton Tank—*lake* NM-5
Moloaa—*civil* HI-9
Moloaa Bay—*bay* HI-9
Moloaa For Res—*forest* HI-9
Moloaa Stream—*stream* HI-9
*Moloai* FM-9
*Moloch Beach* OR-9
*Moloch Creek* OR-9
Moloc Smelter—*locale* MO-7
Molokai—*island* HI-9
Molokai Airp—*airport* HI-9
*Molokai Channel* HI-9
Molokai HS—*school* HI-9
Molokai Lighthouse—*locale* HI-9
Molokainuiahina Gulch—*valley* HI-9
Molokai Tunnel—*tunnel* HI-9
Molokini—*island* HI-9
*Molonitos* AZ-5
*Molouai* FM-9
*Molousi* FM-9
*Molove* FM-9
*Molowa* FM-9
*Molowe* FM-9
*Molower* FM-9
Molpus Cem—*cemetery* MS-4
Molpus Lumber Company Lake Dam—*dam* MS-4
Molpus Sch (historical)—*school* MS-4
Molsbee Cem—*cemetery* TX-5
Molskness Cem—*cemetery* SD-7
Molson—*locale* WA-9
Molson Hill—*summit* WA-9
Molson Lake—*lake* WA-9
Molstad Lake—*reservoir* SD-7
Molstad Lake Dam—*dam* SD-7
Molstad Village—*hist pl* SD-7
**Molt**—*pop pl* MT-8
Molten Bluff—*cliff* AR-4
Molten Spring—*spring* UT-8
Moltham Rsvr Five—*reservoir* OR-9
Moltham Rsvr Four—*reservoir* OR-9
Moltham Rsvr One—*reservoir* OR-9
Moltham Rsvr Three—*reservoir* OR-9
Moltham Rsvr Two—*reservoir* OR-9
Moltke—*locale* MI-6
Moltke Post Office (historical)—*building* TN-4
Moltkes Landing (historical)—*locale* TN-4
**Moltke (Township of)**—*pop pl* MI-6
**Moltke (Township of)**—*pop pl* MN-6
Molton Cem—*cemetery* KY-4
Molton Mine—*mine* MT-8
**Moltonville**—*pop pl* NC-3
Molty Smith Lake—*swamp* TX-5
*Moluaka* HI-9
Molumby Slough—*lake* SD-7
**Molunkus**—*pop pl* ME-1
Molunkus Lake—*lake* ME-1
Molunkus Stream—*stream* ME-1
Molunkus (Township of)—*unorg* ME-1
Molus—*locale* CA-9
**Molus**—*pop pl* KY-4
*Molusk* VA-3
Molver Island—*island* AK-9
*Molway* FM-9
Moly—*locale* NM-5
Molybdenite Creek—*stream* CA-9
Molybdenite Mtn—*summit* WA-9
Molybdenum Mtn—*summit* AK-9
**Molyneaux Corners**—*pop pl* NY-2
*Molyneaux Hill* PA-2
Molyneaux Ranch—*locale* NM-5
Molyneux Hill—*summit* PA-2
Moman Lake—*reservoir* AL-4
**Momauguin**—*pop pl* CT-1
Momauguin Beach—*beach* CT-1
*Momaw* AL-4
**Mombaccus**—*pop pl* NY-2
Mombaccus Creek—*stream* NY-2
Mombaccus Mtn—*summit* NY-2
Mombasha Lake—*reservoir* NY-2
Momb Lake—*lake* MN-6
**Momence**—*pop pl* IL-6
Momence Cem—*cemetery* IL-6
**Momence Township**—*pop pl* NE-7
**Momence (Township of)**—*pop pl* IL-6
*Momeneetown* OH-6
**Momeneetown**—*pop pl* OH-6
**Momeyer**—*pop pl* NC-3
**Momford Landing**—*pop pl* NC-3
*Momford Point* NC-3
*Mommie Teel Creek* NJ-2
*Mommytaw Creek* KS-7
Mommy Teel Creek—*stream* NJ-2
*Momon Lake* OR-9
Momo Park—*park* AZ-5
*Momo-Shima* FM-9
*Momo Sima* FM-9
*Momo To* FM-9
*Momotsuto To* MP-9
*Momotto-to* MP-9
Momoualoa—*civil* HI-9
*Momoualoa Gulch* HI-9
Momoualoa Gulch—*valley* HI-9
Mompano Dam—*dam* OR-9
Mompano Rsvr—*reservoir* OR-9
Momyer Creek—*stream* CA-9
*Mona* WV-2
Mona—*locale* WY-8
Mona—*other* WV-2
**Mona**—*pop pl* IA-7
**Mona**—*pop pl* MT-8
**Mona**—*pop pl* TN-4
**Mona**—*pop pl* UT-8
*Mona Beach* MI-6
**Monaca**—*pop pl* PA-2
Monaca Borough—*civil* PA-2
Mona Campground—*park* OR-9
*Monacan Town* VA-3
Monaca Rochester Bridge—*bridge* PA-2
Mona Cem—*cemetery* UT-8
Monachals Fork—*stream* IN-6
Monache Creek—*stream* CA-9
Monache HS—*school* CA-9
Monache Meadows—*flat* CA-9
Monache Mtn—*summit* CA-9
*Monachles Creek* IN-6
Monacillo (Barrio)—*fmr MCD* PR-3
Monacillo Urbano (Barrio)—*fmr MCD* PR-3
*Mona City Cemetery* UT-8
**Monaco**—*pop pl* CA-9
Monaco Sch—*school* CO-8
Monaco Street Parkway—*hist pl* CO-8
Mona Creek—*stream* OR-9
Mona Creek—*stream* UT-8
Mona Creek—*stream* WA-9
Monada—*locale* CA-9
**Monadale**—*pop pl* TX-5
Mona Dam—*dam* UT-8
Monadnock Amphitheater—*basin* AZ-5
Monadnock Block—*hist pl* IL-6
*Monadnock Canyon* AZ-5
Monadnock Mills—*hist pl* NH-1
Monadnock Mtn—*summit* NH-1
Monadnock Mtn—*summit* VT-1
*Monadnock Pond* NH-1
Monadnock Sunapee Trail—*trail* NH-1
Monadnock View Cem—*cemetery* NH-1
Monadox Point—*cape* VA-3
Mona Front Wildlife Mngmt Area—*park* UT-8
**Monaghan**—*pop pl* SC-3
Monaghan Cem—*cemetery* NY-2
Monaghan Creek—*stream* MI-6
Monaghan Creek—*stream* WA-9
Monaghan Dam—*dam* AL-4
Monaghan Lake—*reservoir* AL-4
Monaghan P O (historical)—*building* PA-2
Monaghan Point—*cape* MI-6
Monaghan Rapids—*rapids* WA-9
**Monaghan (Township of)**—*pop pl* PA-2
Monahan Bayou—*stream* LA-4
Monahan Canyon—*valley* OR-9
Monahan Cem—*cemetery* OH-6
Monahan Coal Mine—*locale* CO-8
**Monahan Corner**—*pop pl* NH-1
Monahan Creek—*stream* (2) AK-9
Monahan Creek—*stream* CA-9
Monahan Creek—*stream* CO-8
Monahan Creek—*stream* OR-9
Monahan Creek—*stream* WA-9
Monahan Draw—*valley* CO-8
Monahan Flat—*flat* AK-9
Monahan Gulch—*valley* CO-8
Monahan Homestead—*locale* CO-8
Monahan House—*hist pl* OR-9
Monahan Lake—*flat* OR-9
Monahan Lake—*lake* MI-6
Monahan Lake—*lake* WI-6
Monahan Lakes—*reservoir* CO-8
Monahan Lookout Tower—*locale* WI-6
Monahan Mtn—*summit* MT-8
Monahan Pond—*lake* NY-2
Monahan Ranch—*locale* NE-7
**Monahans**—*pop pl* TX-5
Monahans (CCD)—*cens area* TX-5
Monahan Sch—*school* IL-6
Monahan Sch—*school* MT-8
Monahans Draw—*valley* TX-5
Monahans Gasoline Plant—*oilfield* TX-5
*Monahan Slough* ND-7
Monahans Oil Field—*oilfield* TX-5
Monahan Spring—*spring* ID-8
Monahans Sand Hills State Park—*park* TX-5
Monahill Ch—*church* WV-2
Mona (historical)—*locale* AL-4
Mona (historical)—*locale* KS-7
*Monahon Creek* CA-9
**Mona Junction**—*pop pl* IA-7
**Mona Kay Heights**—*pop pl* KS-7
Mona Kay Heights—*uninc pl* KS-7
*Monakin* VA-3
*Mona Lake* CA-9
Mona Lake—*lake* MA-1
Mona Lake—*lake* MI-6
Mona Lake Park—*park* MI-6
Monalua Golf Course—*other* HI-9
Mona Mine—*mine* CO-8
**Monango**—*pop pl* ND-7
**Monango Crossing**—*pop pl* ND-7
Mona Park Sch—*school* CA-9
Mona Passage—*channel* PR-3
Mona Post Office (historical)—*building* AL-4
Monarat—*other* VA-3
Monarat Ch—*church* VA-3
Monarca Mine—*mine* ID-8
Monarcas Creek—*stream* NC-3
Monarch—*hist pl* MI-6
Monarch—*locale* AR-4
Monarch—*locale* UT-8
Monarch—*locale* VA-3
Monarch—*locale* WV-2
Monarch—*locale* WY-8
**Monarch**—*pop pl* CO-8
**Monarch**—*pop pl* FL-3
**Monarch**—*pop pl* KY-4
**Monarch**—*pop pl* MS-4
**Monarch**—*pop pl* MO-7
**Monarch**—*pop pl* MT-8
**Monarch**—*pop pl* PA-2
**Monarch**—*pop pl* SC-3
Monarch, Mount—*summit* AK-9
*Monarch-agate Pass* CO-8
**Monarch Bay**—*pop pl* CA-9
Monarch Canyon—*valley* CA-9
Monarch Canyon—*valley* MT-8
Monarch Canyon—*valley* NM-5
Monarch Canyon—*valley* UT-8
Monarch Cem—*cemetery* WY-8
Monarch (census name Monarch Mills)—*uninc pl* SC-3
Monarch Center for Exceptional Students—*school* FL-3
Monarch Creek—*stream* AK-9
Monarch Creek—*stream* CA-9
Monarch Creek—*stream* MI-6
Monarch Creek—*stream* (2) MT-8
Monarch Divide—*ridge* CA-9
Monarch Flat—*flat* CA-9
*Monarch Gulch* WA-9
Monarch Gulch—*valley* ID-8
**Monarch Hills Subdivision**—*pop pl* UT-8
Monarch Lake—*reservoir* CO-8
Monarch Lakes—*lake* CA-9
**Monarch (Leisenring No. 3)**—*pop pl* PA-2
Monarch Millpond—*lake* MI-6
Monarch Mills (census name for Monarch)—*CDP* (2) SC-3
Monarch Mine—*mine* (2) AZ-5
Monarch Mine—*mine* (2) CA-9
Monarch Mine—*mine* CO-8
Monarch Mine—*mine* (2) ID-8
Monarch Mine—*mine* MT-8
Monarch Mine—*mine* (3) NV-8
Monarch Mine—*mine* SD-7
Monarch Mine—*mine* TN-4
Monarch Mine—*mine* (2) UT-8
Monarch Mine—*mine* WA-9
Monarch Mtn—*summit* CA-9
Monarch Mtn—*summit* MT-8
Monarch-Neihart—*cens area* MT-8
Monarch No 4 Mine—*mine* CO-8
*Monarch Park* PA-2
*Monarch Pass* CO-8
Monarch Pass—*gap* CO-8
Monarch-Payne House—*hist pl* KY-4
Monarch Peak—*summit* CA-9
*Monarch Ranch* NV-8
Monarch-Rand Mine—*mine* CA-9
Monarch Ridge—*ridge* CO-8
Monarch Ridge—*ridge* UT-8
Monarch Sch—*school* MO-7
Monarch (Site)—*locale* NV-8
Monarch Slough—*gut* AK-9
Monarch Spring—*spring* CA-9
Monarch Station—*locale* MO-7
Monarch Wash—*stream* AZ-5
Monarch Well—*well* UT-8
**Monarda**—*pop pl* ME-1
Monark Ch—*church* MO-7
**Monark Springs**—*pop pl* MO-7
Monark Springs—*spring* MO-7
Mona RR Station—*locale* FL-3
Mona Rsvr—*reservoir* (2) UT-8
Mona Sch—*school* UT-8
Monasco Mtn—*summit* VA-3
Monasco Spring—*spring* CO-8
Monashka Bay—*bay* AK-9
Monashka Creek—*stream* AK-9
Monashka Mtn—*summit* AK-9
*Mona Shores* MI-6
Mona Shores HS—*school* MI-6
**Monaskon**—*pop pl* VA-3
Monasterio-Jacks Creek Rsvr—*reservoir* ID-8
Monasterio Ranch—*locale* ID-8
Monastery, The—*hist pl* PA-2
Monastery and Church of Saint Michael the Archangel—*hist pl* NJ-2
Monastery Brook—*stream* RI-1
Monastery Gap—*gap* VT-1
Monastery Mtn—*summit* VT-1
Monastery of Mary Immaculate—*church* NY-2
Monastery of Saint Clare—*church* IN-6
Monastery of the Exaltation of the Most Holy Cross—*church* FL-3
Monastery Of The Holy Ghost—*church* GA-3
Monastery of the Little Portion—*church* NY-2
Monastery of the Perpetual Rosary—*church* PA-2
Monastery of the Precious Blood—*hist pl* OR-9
Monastery of the Visitation—*church* OH-6
Monastery Run—*stream* PA-2
Monastery Spring—*spring* UT-8

Monatiquet Sch—school ..... MA-1
Monatiquot River ..... MA-1
Monatiquot River—stream ..... MA-1
Monatou Bay—bay ..... MI-6
**Mona (Township of)**—pop pl ..... IL-6
Mona View ..... MI-6
Mona View Cem—cemetery ..... MI-6
Monaview Sch—school ..... SC-3
**Monaville**—pop pl ..... IL-6
**Monaville**—pop pl ..... TX-5
**Monaville**—pop pl ..... WV-2
Monaville Cem—cemetery ..... TX-5
Mona Vista ..... MI-6
**Mona Vista**—pop pl ..... CA-9
Monazite Gulch—valley ..... ID-8
Mon Bijou—locale ..... VI-3
Mon Bluff—cliff ..... CA-9
**Monbo**—pop pl ..... NC-3
Mon Canyon—valley ..... CA-9
Monce Pond—lake ..... CT-1
Monchego Creek—stream ..... CO-8
Monchego Park—flat ..... CO-8
**Monches**—pop pl ..... WI-6
Moncisco Mesa—summit ..... NM-5
Moncisco Wash—stream ..... NM-5
**Moncks Corner**—pop pl ..... SC-3
Moncks Corner (CCD)—cens area ..... SC-3
Monckton Park ..... DE-2
**Moncla**—pop pl ..... LA-4
Moncleuse Bay—lake ..... LA-4
**Monclo**—pop pl ..... WV-2
**Monclova**—pop pl ..... OH-6
Monclova Ch—church ..... LA-4
Monclova Gardens ..... OH-6
**Monclova (Township of)**—pop pl ..... OH-6
Monclovia Cem—cemetery ..... IL-6
Monclovia Sch—school ..... IL-6
Moncove Lake—reservoir ..... WV-2
Moncreiffe Ridge—ridge ..... WY-8
Moncrief ..... GA-3
**Moncrief**—pop pl ..... GA-3
Moncrief Cem—cemetery ..... AL-4
Moncrief Cem—cemetery ..... OK-5
Moncrief Creek—stream ..... FL-3
Moncrief Creek—stream ..... LA-4
Moncrief Creek—stream ..... NY-2
Moncrieffe Ridge ..... WY-8
Moncrief Park—park ..... MS-4
Moncrief Ridge ..... WY-8
Moncrief Sch—school ..... FL-3
Moncrief Sch House (historical)—school ..... AL-4
Moncriefs Store—locale ..... GA-3
Moncuin Creek—stream ..... VA-3
Moncuin Pond—reservoir ..... VA-3
Moncure—locale ..... MS-4
**Moncure**—pop pl ..... NC-3
Moncure Corner—locale ..... VA-3
Moncure Creek—stream ..... MT-8
Moncure Sch—school ..... NC-3
Moncure Sch—school ..... VA-3
Moncur Sch—school ..... SD-7
Moncur Spring—spring ..... UT-8
Moncur Springs—spring ..... WY-8
Mondak Cem—cemetery ..... MT-8
MonDak Mobile Home Park—locale ..... AZ-5
**Mondamin**—pop pl ..... IA-7
**Mondamin Township**—pop pl ..... SD-7
Mondamon Farm—hist pl ..... DE-2
**Monday**—pop pl ..... VA-3
Monday, Cape—cape ..... ME-1
Monday Branch—stream ..... AL-4
Monday Branch—stream ..... KY-4
Monday Branch—stream ..... MO-7
Monday Branch—stream ..... SC-3
Monday Branch—stream ..... TN-4
Monday Camp—locale ..... ID-8
Monday Canyon—valley ..... UT-8
Monday Cem—cemetery ..... MS-4
Monday Cem—cemetery (2) ..... TN-4
Monday Cem—cemetery ..... TX-5
Monday Creek—gut ..... VA-3
Monday Creek—stream ..... AK-9
Monday Creek—stream ..... MT-8
Monday Creek—stream ..... OH-6
Monday Creek—stream ..... WY-8
Monday Creek Junction—locale ..... OH-6
Monday Creek (Township of)—civ div ..... OH-6
Monday Flat—flat ..... CA-9
Monday Gulch—valley (2) ..... ID-8
Monday Hill ..... MA-1
Monday Hollow—valley ..... TN-4
Monday Island ..... FM-9
Monday Island—island ..... TN-4
Monday Key—island ..... FL-3
Monday Lake—lake ..... LA-4
Monday Lake—lake ..... WI-6
Monday Lick Run—stream ..... WV-2
Monday Point—cape ..... TN-4
Mondays Creek—bay ..... MD-2
Mondays Landing ..... KY-4
Monday Spring—spring ..... AL-4
Mondeaux Creek—stream ..... WI-6
Mondeaux Dam—dam ..... WI-6
Mondeaux Dam Rec Area—hist pl ..... WI-6
Mondeaux Flowage—reservoir ..... WI-6
Mondeaux River—stream ..... WI-6
Mondel—locale ..... NM-5
Mondell—locale ..... MD-2
Mondell Hill—summit ..... WI-6
Monden Camp—locale ..... FL-3
Monden Creek—stream ..... FL-3
**Mon de Ville Condominium**—pop pl ..... UT-8
Mondl Creek—stream ..... WI-6
Mondle Sch—school ..... WY-8
Mondongo Island—island ..... FL-3
Mondongo Rocks—island ..... FL-3
Mondovi—locale ..... WA-9
**Mondovi**—pop pl ..... WI-6
**Mondovi (Town of)**—pop pl ..... WI-6
Mondragon Canyon—valley ..... NM-5
Mondragon Tank—reservoir ..... NM-5
**Mondray**—pop pl ..... KY-4
Mondress, Lake—lake ..... WA-9
Monds Island—island ..... NJ-2
Mondtony Siding (historical)—locale ..... KS-7
Monecato ..... KS-7
**Monee**—pop pl (2) ..... IL-6
**Moneek**—pop pl ..... IA-7
Monee Rsvr—reservoir ..... IL-6
**Monee (Township of)**—pop pl ..... IL-6
Monegan ..... MO-7
Monegar Ridge—ridge ..... CO-8
Monegaw Creek—stream ..... MO-7
**Monegaw Springs**—pop pl ..... MO-7
Monegaw Township—civil ..... MO-7
Monegraw Creek ..... MO-7
Monehan Creek—stream ..... MI-6
Moneka ..... KS-7
Moneka (historical)—locale ..... KS-7
Monell—locale ..... WY-8
**Monero**—pop pl ..... NM-5
Monero Mtn ..... NM-5
Monero Mtn—summit (2) ..... NM-5
**Monessen**—pop pl ..... PA-2
Monessen City—civil ..... PA-2
Monessen HS—school ..... PA-2
**Monessen (sta.)**—pop pl ..... PA-2
Monet—locale ..... FL-3
**Moneta**—pop pl ..... IA-7
**Moneta**—pop pl ..... VA-3
**Moneta**—pop pl ..... WY-8
Moneta—uninc pl ..... CA-9
Moneta Branch—hist pl ..... CA-9
Moneta Divide—ridge ..... WY-8
Moneta Draw—valley ..... WY-8
Moneta Hills—range ..... WY-8
Moneta Reservoir ..... WY-8
Moneto Creek—stream ..... TX-5
Monett—locale ..... KS-7
Monett—locale ..... OR-9
**Monett**—pop pl ..... MO-7
**Monetta**—pop pl ..... SC-3
Monetta (CCD)—cens area ..... SC-3
Monetta Ch—church ..... SC-3
Monett Airp—airport ..... MO-7
Monetta Sch—school ..... SC-3
Monett Big M Public Use Area ..... MO-7
Monette—locale ..... IA-7
**Monette**—pop pl ..... AR-4
**Monette Ferry**—pop pl ..... LA-4
Monette Hill—summit ..... WA-9
Monett Ferry—locale ..... LA-4
Monett Municipal Airp—airport ..... MO-7
Monett State Training Sch—school ..... MO-7
Monett Township—civil ..... MO-7
Monetuck Hill ..... CT-1
**Money**—pop pl ..... MS-4
Money Bay ..... NC-3
Money Bayou—gut ..... MS-4
**Money Bayou**—pop pl ..... FL-3
Money Bayou—stream ..... FL-3
Money Beach—beach ..... FL-3
Money Bean Hollow—valley ..... OK-5
Moneyboque Bay—bay ..... NY-2
Money Branch—stream ..... KY-4
Money Brook—stream ..... MA-1
Money Cave—cave ..... MO-7
Money Cem—cemetery ..... GA-3
Money Cem—cemetery ..... MI-6
Money Cem—cemetery ..... TX-5
Money Chapel—church ..... TX-5
Money Cliff—cliff ..... KY-4
Money Cove—bay ..... ME-1
**Money Creek**—pop pl ..... MN-6
Money Creek—stream ..... CA-9
Money Creek—stream ..... IL-6
Money Creek—stream ..... MD-2
Money Creek—stream (2) ..... MN-6
Money Creek—stream ..... WA-9
Money Creek Campground—locale ..... WA-9
Money Creek Cem—cemetery ..... MN-6
**Money Creek (Township of)**—pop pl ..... IL-6
**Money Creek (Township of)**—pop pl ..... MN-6
Money Farm—hist pl ..... KY-4
Moneyhan Branch ..... TN-4
Money Head—cape ..... MA-1
Money Hill—summit ..... IN-6
Money (historical)—locale ..... MS-4
Moneyhole Mtn—summit ..... NY-2
Money Hollow—valley ..... AL-4
Money Hollow—valley ..... IN-6
Moneyhollow Rock—bar ..... NY-2
Moneyhun Cem—cemetery ..... TN-4
Money Island—cape ..... NJ-2
Money Island—island ..... CT-1
Money Island—island ..... LA-4
Money Island island ..... ME-1
Money Island—island ..... NJ-2
Money Island—island ..... NY-2
Money Island—island (2) ..... NC-3
Money Island—island ..... PA-2
**Money Island**—pop pl ..... NJ-2
Money Island Bay—bay ..... NC-3
**Money Island Beach**—pop pl ..... NC-3
Money Island Swamp—stream ..... NC-3
Money Key ..... FL-3
Money Key—island (2) ..... FL-3
Money Key Channel—channel ..... FL-3
Money Knob—summit ..... AK-9
Money Lake—lake ..... WI-6
Money Landing (historical)—locale ..... MS-4
Money Ledge Hill—summit ..... NY-2
Moneymaker Lake—lake ..... ME-1
Money Marsh—swamp ..... DE-2
Money Metal Shaft—mine ..... AZ-5
Money Mtn—summit ..... AR-4
Moneypenney Run ..... WV-2
Moneypenny Creek—stream ..... PA-2
Money Point—cape ..... CT-1
Money Point—cape ..... ME-1
Money Point—cape ..... NC-3
Money Point—cape ..... VA-3
Money Point—cliff ..... NY-2
Money Point—uninc pl ..... VA-3
Money Pond—lake (2) ..... NY-2
Money Pond—lake ..... RI-1
Money Run—stream ..... WV-2
Money Sch—school ..... SD-7
Moneys Corner—locale ..... VA-3
Money Slough—gut ..... NC-3
Moneyslump Swamp ..... MD-2
Moneysmith Lake—lake ..... WA-9
Moneys Pond—reservoir ..... AL-4
Moneystump Swamp—swamp ..... MD-2
Money Swamp Pond—reservoir ..... RI-1
Money Windmill—locale ..... TX-5
Monford—locale ..... KY-4
**Monfort**—pop pl ..... CO-8
Monfort Acad—school ..... VA-3
Monfort Cemetery—hist pl ..... NY-2
Monfort Heights—CDP ..... OH-6
Monfort Island—island ..... GA-3
Monforton Sch—school ..... MT-8
Monfort Park—park ..... AZ-5
Monfort Sch—school ..... MI-6
Mong ..... PA-2
Mongahl ..... FM-9
Mongal ..... FM-9
Mongar Creek—stream ..... MT-8
Mongaup—locale ..... NY-2
Mongaup Creek—stream ..... NY-2
Mongaup Falls Rsvr—reservoir ..... NY-2
Mongaup Mtn—summit ..... NY-2
Mongaup Pond—lake ..... NY-2
Mongaup Pond Campsite—locale ..... NY-2
Mongaup River—stream ..... NY-2
Mongaup Station (historical)—locale ..... PA-2
**Mongaup Valley**—pop pl ..... NY-2
Mongaup Valley Cem—cemetery ..... NY-2
Mongaup Valley Ch—church ..... NY-2
Monger Ch—church ..... MO-7
Monger Creek—stream ..... AL-4
Monger Creek—stream ..... ID-8
Monger Creek—stream ..... NC-3
Monger Elem Sch—school ..... IN-6
Monger Hill—summit ..... AL-4
Monger Island—island ..... AL-4
Monger Lake—lake ..... AL-4
Monger Run—stream ..... VA-3
Mongers Landing (historical)—locale ..... AL-4
Mongle Spring—locale ..... VA-3
**Mongmong**—pop pl ..... GU-9
Mongmong-Toto-Maite (Election District)—fmr MCD ..... GU-9
**Mongo**—pop pl ..... IN-6
Mongo Creek—stream ..... MI-6
Mongola Windmill—locale ..... NM-5
Mongold Gap—gap ..... SC-3
Mongold Hollow—valley ..... VA-3
Mongo Reservoir Dam—dam ..... IN-6
Mongo Rsvr—reservoir ..... IN-6
Mongoulois, Lake—lake ..... LA-4
Mongrel Neck—cape ..... MD-2
Mongrel Ridge—ridge ..... OR-9
Mong Sch—school ..... IL-6
**Mongtown**—pop pl ..... PA-2
Mongue Meadow Brook—stream ..... MA-1
**Mongul**—pop pl ..... PA-2
Mongus Creek—stream ..... MS-4
Monhagen Brook—stream ..... NY-2
Monhagen Lake—lake ..... NY-2
**Monhegan**—pop pl ..... ME-1
Monhegan Harbor—bay ..... ME-1
Monhegan Island—island ..... ME-1
Monhegan Island Lighthouse and Quarters—hist pl ..... ME-1
Monhegan (Plantation of)—civ div ..... ME-1
Monheim Ranch—locale ..... SD-7
Monhollow Artificial Stone House—hist pl ..... OK-5
Monhonan Cove—bay ..... ME-1
Moniac—locale ..... GA-3
Monia Canyon—valley ..... NM-5
Moniac Cem—cemetery ..... GA-3
Moniac Ch—church ..... GA-3
Monia Cem—cemetery ..... NE-7
Monia Creek—stream ..... NM-5
Monia Creek—stream ..... TX-5
Moniaghan Creek—stream ..... WA-9
Moniak—island ..... MP-9
Moniak Island ..... MP-9
Monias, Arroyo—valley ..... TX-5
Monias Draw—valley ..... NM-5
Monias Windmill—locale ..... NM-5
Monia Tank—reservoir ..... NM-5
Monia Well—well ..... NM-5
Monica—locale ..... KY-4
**Monica**—pop pl (2) ..... IL-6
**Monica**—pop pl ..... TX-5
Monica Cabin—locale ..... NM-5
Monica Canyon—valley ..... NM-5
Monica Creek ..... CA-9
Monical Branch—stream ..... IN-6
Monical Cem—cemetery ..... IN-6
Monical Lake—reservoir ..... IN-6
Monical Lake Dam—dam ..... IN-6
Monica Saddle—gap ..... NM-5
Monick Branch—stream ..... KY-4
**Monico**—pop pl ..... WI-6
Monico Creek—stream ..... WI-6
**Monico (Town of)**—pop pl ..... WI-6
**Monida**—pop pl ..... MT-8
Monida Pass—gap ..... ID-8
Monida Pass—gap ..... MT-8
**Monie**—pop pl ..... MD-2
Monie Bay—bay ..... MD-2
Monie Creek—stream ..... MD-2
Monie Lake—lake ..... AK-9
Monie Marsh—swamp ..... MD-2
Monie Neck—cape ..... MD-2
Monie Point—cape ..... MD-2
Monie Swamp—stream ..... NC-3
Moniger Creek—stream ..... CO-8
**Moniger Heights (subdivision)**—pop pl ..... PA-2
Moniger Park—flat ..... CO-8
Monighan Canyon—valley ..... NM-5
Monighan Creek—stream ..... MN-6
Monighan Creek—stream ..... SD-7
Monigue Pond Dam—dam ..... MS-4
Monimoy ..... MA-1
Monin, Adam, House—hist pl ..... KY-4
**Moninger**—pop pl ..... PA-2
Moningers—locale ..... IA-7
Monique Spring—spring ..... CO-8
Mon Island—island ..... NC-3
Mon Island—island ..... VA-3
Monism Church ..... MS-4
Monison Drain—stream ..... MI-6
Monistique ..... MI-6
Monistique Lake ..... MI-6
**Moniteau**—pop pl ..... PA-2
Moniteau Ch—church ..... MO-7
Moniteau Chapel—church ..... MO-7
**Moniteau County**—pop pl ..... MO-7
Moniteau County Courthouse Square—hist pl ..... MO-7
Moniteau Creek—stream (2) ..... MO-7
Moniteau HS—school ..... PA-2
Moniteau Township—civil (2) ..... MO-7
Monitor ..... CA-9
Monitor—locale ..... KY-4
Monitor—locale ..... VA-3
**Monitor**—pop pl ..... IN-6
**Monitor**—pop pl ..... OR-9
**Monitor**—pop pl ..... WA-9
**Monitor**—pop pl (2) ..... WV-2
Monitor—uninc pl ..... NJ-2
Monitor, The—summit ..... NV-8
Monitor Butte—summit (2) ..... UT-8
Monitor Canyon—valley ..... NV-8
Monitor Ch—church ..... KS-7
Monitor Creek ..... CO-8
Monitor Creek—stream ..... CA-9
Monitor Creek—stream ..... CO-8
Monitor Creek—stream (2) ..... MT-8
Monitor Field—flat ..... NV-8
Monitor Flat—flat ..... CA-9
Monitor Gulch—valley (2) ..... CO-8
Monitor Hill—summit ..... OK-5
Monitor Hills—summit ..... NV-8
Monitor (historical)—locale ..... KS-7
Monitor House—hist pl ..... OH-6
Monitoring Station—locale ..... WA-9
Monitor Island—island ..... CA-9
**Monitor Junction**—pop pl ..... WV-2
Monitor Mesa—summit ..... CO-8
Monitor Mesa—summit ..... UT-8
Monitor Mesa Trail—trail ..... CO-8
Monitor Mill (Site)—locale ..... NV-8
Monitor Mine—mine ..... AZ-5
Monitor Mine—mine (2) ..... CA-9
Monitor Mine—mine ..... NV-8
Monitor Mine—mine ..... SD-7
Monitor Mine—mine ..... WA-9
Monitor Mine (historical)—mine ..... ID-8
Monitor Mines (historical)—mine ..... ID-8
Monitor Mtn—summit ..... MT-8
Monitor Pass—gap ..... CA-9
Monitor Peak—summit ..... CO-8
Monitor Peak—summit ..... MT-8
Monitor Peak—summit ..... NV-8
Monitor Point—cape ..... CA-9
Monitor Ranch—locale ..... NV-8
Monitor Range—range ..... NV-8
Monitor Ridge—ridge ..... WA-9
Monitor Rock—summit ..... CO-8
Monitor Sch—school ..... AR-4
Monitor Sch—school ..... IL-6
Monitor Sch—school ..... IN-6
Monitor Sch—school ..... MN-6
Monitor Sch—school ..... MO-7
Monitor Sch—school ..... OH-6
Monitor Sch—school ..... OR-9
Monitor Sch—school ..... SD-7
Monitor Shaft—mine ..... NV-8
Monitor Springs—spring ..... IN-6
**Monitor (sta.)**—pop pl ..... MI-6
**Monitor (Township of)**—pop pl ..... MI-6
Monitor Tunnel—tunnel ..... MT-8
Monitor Valley—basin ..... NV-8
Monitor Windmill—locale ..... NM-5
Monitor Windmill—locale ..... TX-5
Monjas Creek—stream ..... CA-9
Monjas Spring—spring ..... CA-9
Monjeau Lookout—hist pl ..... NM-5
Monjeau Peak—summit ..... NM-5
Monk ..... KY-4
Monk—other ..... VA-3
Monka Hill—summit ..... NY-2
Monk Blevens Ford (historical)—locale ..... TN-4
Monk Branch—stream ..... AL-4
Monk Branch—stream ..... MO-7
Monk Branch—stream ..... TN-4
Monk Branch—stream ..... VA-3
Monk Cem—cemetery ..... LA-4
Monk Cem—cemetery ..... TN-4
Monk Chapel—church ..... AL-4
Monk Creek ..... AL-4
Monk Creek—stream ..... AL-4
Monk Creek Rsvr—reservoir ..... AL-4
Monk Draw ..... AZ-5
Monk Draw—valley ..... AZ-5
Monker Creek—stream ..... MN-6
Monker Lake—lake ..... MN-6
Monkey Bay—swamp ..... SC-3
Monkey Bayou—stream ..... MS-4
Monkey Box—locale ..... FL-3
Monkey Branch—stream ..... AL-4
Monkey Branch—stream ..... NC-3
Monkey Business, Lake—lake ..... FL-3
Monkey Business Pond ..... FL-3
Monkey Canyon—valley ..... AZ-5
Monkey Cove—bay ..... AZ-5
Monkey Creek—stream ..... AL-4
Monkey Creek—stream (2) ..... CA-9
Monkey Creek—stream ..... CO-8
Monkey Creek—stream (2) ..... FL-3
Monkey Creek—stream ..... NV-8
Monkey Creek—stream ..... OK-5
Monkey Creek—stream ..... OR-9
Monkey Creek—stream ..... TX-5
Monkey Creek Ridge—ridge ..... CA-9
Monkey Face—summit ..... CO-8
Monkey Face Creek ..... CA-9
Monkeyface Creek—stream ..... CA-9
Monkeyface Falls—falls ..... CA-9
Monkey Flat Ridge—ridge ..... UT-8
Monkey Fork Dry Canyon—stream ..... UT-8
Monkey Gulch—valley ..... CA-9
Monkey Hill—summit (2) ..... CA-9
Monkey Hill—summit ..... WA-9
Monkey Hill—summit ..... WY-8
Monkey Hill Mine—mine ..... AR-4
Monkey Hole—bay ..... NV-8
Monkey Hollow—valley ..... PA-2
Monkey Hollow Ditch—canal ..... IN-6
Monkey Island ..... FM-9
Monkey Island—island ..... FL-3
Monkey Island—island ..... GA-3
Monkey Island—island ..... LA-4
Monkey Island—island ..... NC-3
Monkey Island—island ..... OK-5
Monkey Island Creek—stream ..... GA-3
Monkey Island Water Tank—tower ..... NC-3
Monkey Joe Key—island ..... FL-3
Monkey John Branch—stream ..... NC-3
Monkey John Swamp—swamp ..... SC-3
Monkey Jungle—park ..... FL-3
Monkey Lake ..... MN-6
Monkey Lake—lake ..... GA-3
Monkey Lode Mine—mine ..... SD-7
Monkey Lodge Hill—summit ..... MD-2
Monkey Mtn—summit ..... MO-7
Monkey Mtn—summit ..... NY-2
Monkey Point—cape ..... SC-3
Monkey Pond—lake ..... ME-1
Monkey Ranch Gulch—valley ..... OR-9
Monkey Rock—summit ..... AZ-5
Monkey Rock—summit ..... CA-9
**Monkey Run**—pop pl ..... AR-4
**Monkey Run**—pop pl ..... MO-7
Monkey Run—stream ..... IA-7
Monkey Run—stream ..... KS-7
Monkey Run—stream (2) ..... NY-2
Monkey Run—stream (2) ..... OH-6
Monkey Run—stream ..... OR-9
Monkey Run—stream ..... VA-3
Monkey Run Cem—cemetery ..... AR-4
Monkeys Eyebrow—locale ..... KY-4
Monkeys Head—summit ..... AZ-5
Monkey Slough—stream ..... TX-5
Monkey Spring—spring (3) ..... AZ-5
Monkey Springs ..... AZ-5
Monkey Tank—reservoir (2) ..... AZ-5
Monkeytown ..... RI-1
**Monkeytown**—pop pl ..... WV-2
Monkeywrench Creek—stream ..... OK-5
Monkey Wrench Wash—stream ..... NV-8
Monk Hill ..... MA-1
Monk Hollow—valley (3) ..... KY-4
Monkhouse Gulch—valley ..... SD-7
Monkins Hollow—valley ..... UT-8
Monk Lake—lake ..... MI-6
Monk Lake—reservoir ..... TX-5
Monkland—locale ..... OR-9
Monkland Ranch ..... OR-9
Monkman Ranch—locale ..... MT-8
Monk Memorial Ch—church ..... NC-3
Monk Pond—swamp ..... GA-3
Monk Ranch—locale ..... AZ-5
Monk Rock—pillar ..... CO-8
Monks—locale ..... NJ-2
Monks Bay—bay ..... MT-8
Monks Corner—cliff ..... TN-4
Monks Corner TVA Small Wild Area—park ..... TN-4
Monks Creek—stream ..... IA-7
Monks Creek—stream ..... KY-4
Monks Creek—stream ..... MD-2
Monks Crossing—locale ..... GA-3
**Monks Crossroads**—pop pl ..... NC-3
Monks Grove Ch—church ..... SC-3
Monks Hammock—locale ..... LA-4
Monks Hill—summit ..... ME-1
Monks Hill—summit ..... MA-1
Monks Hollow—valley (2) ..... PA-2
Monks Hollow—valley ..... UT-8
Monks Island—island ..... MD-2
Monks Island—island ..... NC-3
Monks Mill Bridge—bridge ..... AL-4
Monks Mound—summit ..... IL-6
Monks Pond—reservoir ..... NC-3
Monk Spring—spring ..... UT-8
Monk Spring Creek—stream ..... UT-8
Monks Ranch—locale ..... SD-7
Monks Run ..... AL-4
**Monkstown**—pop pl ..... TX-5
Monksville—uninc pl ..... NJ-2
Monk Tank—reservoir ..... AZ-5
Monk Tank—reservoir ..... NM-5
Monkton ..... VT-1
**Monkton**—pop pl ..... MD-2
**Monkton**—pop pl ..... VT-1
**Monkton Boro**—pop pl ..... VT-1
Monkton Borough ..... VT-1
Monkton Ch—church ..... VT-1
Monkton Pond ..... VT-1
Monktonridge—other ..... VT-1
**Monkton Ridge**—pop pl ..... VT-1
Monkton Town Hall—hist pl ..... VT-1
**Monkton (Town of)**—pop pl ..... VT-1
Monland Place Hist Dist—hist pl ..... GA-3
**Mon Louis**—pop pl ..... AL-4
Mon Louis Island—island ..... AL-4
Monlux Sch—school ..... CA-9
Monmouth ..... NJ-2
Monmouth—hist pl ..... MS-4
Monmouth—locale ..... AL-4
**Monmouth**—pop pl ..... CA-9
**Monmouth**—pop pl ..... IL-6
**Monmouth**—pop pl ..... IN-6
**Monmouth**—pop pl ..... IA-7
**Monmouth**—pop pl ..... KS-7
**Monmouth**—pop pl ..... ME-1
**Monmouth**—pop pl ..... OR-9
Monmouth Acad—school ..... ME-1
Monmouth Battlefield—hist pl ..... NJ-2
Monmouth Beach—airport ..... NJ-2
**Monmouth Beach**—pop pl ..... NJ-2
Monmouth Cem—cemetery ..... IA-7
Monmouth Cem—cemetery ..... KS-7
Monmouth Coll—school ..... NJ-2
Monmouth County—airport ..... NJ-2
**Monmouth County**—pop pl ..... NJ-2
Monmouth Courthouse ..... NJ-2
**Monmouth Heights**—pop pl ..... NJ-2
**Monmouth Heights at Manalapan**—pop pl ..... NJ-2
**Monmouth Heights at Marlboro**—pop pl ..... NJ-2
**Monmouth Hills**—pop pl ..... NJ-2
Monmouth-Independence (CCD)—cens area ..... OR-9
**Monmouth Junction**—pop pl ..... NJ-2
Monmouth Memorial Hosp—hospital ..... NJ-2
Monmouth Memorial Park—cemetery ..... NJ-2
Monmouth Park—park ..... NJ-2
Monmouth Park (Jockey Club)—uninc pl ..... NJ-2
Monmouth Park Sch—hist pl ..... NE-7
Monmouth Park Sch—school ..... NE-7
Monmouth Peak ..... OR-9
Monmouth Presbyterian Ch—church ..... TN-4
Monmouth Regional HS—school ..... NJ-2
Monmouth Reservoir ..... NJ-2
Monmouth Ridge—ridge ..... ME-1
Monmouth Ridge Cem—cemetery ..... ME-1
Monmouth Rsvr—reservoir ..... OR-9
**Monmouth (Town of)**—pop pl ..... ME-1
Monmouth Township—fmr MCD ..... IA-7
**Monmouth Township**—pop pl ..... KS-7
**Monmouth (Township of)**—pop pl ..... IL-6
Monnaie, Bayou—gut ..... LA-4
Monner Spring—spring ..... OR-9
Monnett—locale ..... OH-6
Monnett Cem—cemetery ..... OH-6
Monnett Chapel—church ..... OH-6
Monnett Dam—dam ..... CA-9
Monnett Elem Sch—school ..... IN-6
**Monnette (Monnett)**—pop pl ..... OH-6
Monnett Memorial M. E. Chapel—hist pl ..... OH-6
Monnier Sch—school ..... MI-6
**Monnie Springs**—pop pl ..... AR-4
Monnig JHS—school ..... TX-5
Monnish Memorial Baptist Church ..... AL-4
Monnonite Cem—cemetery ..... NE-7
Monnotti Creek ..... CA-9
**Mono**—pop pl ..... SC-3
Monoa ..... PA-2
Monoa ..... FM-9
Mono Adams Ranch—locale ..... NM-5
Mono Alamar Trail (Pack)—trail ..... CA-9
Mono Basin—basin ..... CA-9
Mono Bay ..... CA-9
Mono Bras Pond ..... CT-1
**Monocacy**—pop pl ..... PA-2
Monocacy Aqueduct—other ..... MD-2
Monocacy Ch—church ..... MD-2
Monocacy Creek—stream (2) ..... PA-2
Monocacy Hill—summit ..... PA-2
Monocacy Island—island ..... MD-2
Monocacy Natl Battlefield—hist pl ..... MD-2
Monocacy Natl Battlefield—park ..... MD-2
Monocacy Natural Resources Area—park ..... MD-2
Monocacy Park—park ..... PA-2
Monocacy River—stream ..... MD-2
Monocacy (RR name for Monocacy Station)—other ..... PA-2
Monocacy Sch—school ..... MD-2
Monocacy Sch—school ..... PA-2
Monocacy Site—hist pl ..... MD-2
Monocacy Station—locale ..... PA-2
**Monocacy Station (RR name Monocacy)**—pop pl ..... PA-2
Mono Camp—locale ..... CA-9
Mono Campground—locale ..... CA-9
Monocanock Island—island ..... PA-2
Monocco Mine—mine ..... UT-8
Mo-Nock-Nong ..... NY-2
Monocle Lake—lake ..... MI-6
Monocline, The—summit ..... NV-8
Monocline Canyon—valley ..... NV-8
Monocline Ridge—ridge ..... CA-9
Monocline Valley—valley ..... NV-8
Monocnoc, Lake—lake ..... MS-4
Monoco Mine—mine ..... CA-9
**Mono (County)**—pop pl ..... CA-9
Mono County Courthouse—hist pl ..... CA-9
Mono Crater ..... CA-9
Mono Craters—crater ..... CA-9
Mono Craters Tunnel—tunnel ..... CA-9
Mono Creek ..... CA-9
Mono Creek—stream (2) ..... CA-9
Mono Creek—stream ..... MT-8
Mono Creek Campground—locale ..... CA-9
Mono Creek Campground—locale ..... MT-8
Mono Crossing—locale ..... CA-9
Mono Diggings—locale ..... CA-9
Mono Divide—ridge ..... CA-9
Mono Dome—summit ..... CA-9
Monogahela Incline—trail ..... PA-2
Monogram—locale ..... NC-3
Monogram Creek—stream ..... WA-9
Monogram Lake—lake ..... WA-9
Monogram Lakes—lake ..... OR-9
Monogram Mesa—summit ..... CO-8
Monogram Mesa Rsvr—reservoir ..... CO-8
Monogram Mines—mine ..... CO-8
Monogram Square—hist pl ..... TX-5
Mono Gulch—valley ..... CA-9
Monohaa—locale ..... HI-9
Monohan ..... WA-9
Monohan—locale ..... WA-9
Monohan Mine ..... TN-4
Monohanset Island ..... MA-1
Monohansett Island—island ..... MA-1
Monohansett Rock—rock ..... MA-1
Monohen ..... WA-9
Monohon ..... WA-9
Monohon—locale ..... WA-9
Monohon Tunnel Mine—mine ..... OR-9
**Mono Hot Springs**—pop pl ..... CA-9
Mono Jim Peak—summit ..... CA-9
Monola—locale ..... CA-9
Mono Lake ..... CT-1
Mono Lake—lake ..... CA-9
**Mono Lake Post Office (historical)**—pop pl ..... CA-9
**Monolith (Cement Plant)**—pop pl ..... CA-9
Monolith Ditch—canal ..... WY-8
Monolith Goforth Ranch—locale ..... WY-8
Monolith Hunziker Ranch—locale ..... WY-8
Monolith Point—cape ..... AK-9
Monolith Ranch—locale ..... WY-8
Monolith Well No 1—well ..... WY-8
Monolith Well No 3—well ..... WY-8
Monolith Well No 5—well ..... WY-8
Monolith Well No 7—well ..... WY-8
Monomascoy Peninsula ..... MA-1
Mono Meadow—flat (2) ..... CA-9
Mono Meadow Trail—trail ..... CA-9
Monomee Pond ..... MA-1
Monomee Pond ..... NH-1
Monomentum Assonetense ..... MA-1
Mono Mills—locale ..... CA-9
Mono Mine—mine ..... CA-9
Monomomac Pond ..... MA-1
Monomonac, Lake—lake ..... NH-1
Monomonac, Lake—reservoir ..... MA-1
Monomonack Lake ..... MA-1
Monomonack Pond ..... MA-1
Monomonac Pond ..... NH-1
Monomonoc Pond ..... NH-1
Monomoscoy Peninsula ..... MA-1
**Monomoy**—pop pl ..... MA-1
Monomoy Beach—beach ..... MA-1
Monomoyet Island ..... MA-1
Monomoyet Point ..... MA-1
Monomoyett Island ..... MA-1
Monomoyett Point Monomoyit Point ..... MA-1
Monomoyick ..... MA-1
Monomoy Island—island ..... MA-1

Monomoy Island Dunes—range MA-1
Monomoyit Island MA-1
Monomoy Natl Wildlife Ref—park MA-1
Monomoy Point—cape MA-1
Monomoy Point Lighthouse—hist pl MA-1
Monomoy Shoals—bar (2) MA-1
Monomy Point MA-1
Monon FM-9
**Monon**—pop pl IN-6
**Monona**—pop pl IA-7
**Monona**—pop pl WI-6
Monona, Lake—lake WI-6
Monona Bay—bay WI-6
Monona Cem—cemetery IA-7
Monona County Courthouse—hist pl IA-7
Monona Flat—flat CA-9
Monona Grove HS—school WI-6
Monona Harrison Ditch—canal IA-7
Monona Township—fmr MCD IA-7
Monon Cem—cemetery IN-6
Monon Chapel—church IN-6
**Mononcue**—pop pl OH-6
Monon Ditch IN-6
Monon Ditch—canal IN-6
Monon Elem Sch—school IN-6
Monon Freight Depot—hist pl KY-4
**Monongah**—pop pl WV-2
**Monongahela**—pop pl PA-2
Monongahela Brook—stream NJ-2
Monongahela Cem—cemetery (3) PA-2
Monongahela City—civil PA-2
Monongahela City Bridge—bridge PA-2
Monongahela Creek—stream PA-2
Monongahela Incline—hist pl PA-2
Monongahela JHS—school NJ-2
Monongahela Junction—uninc pl PA-2
Monongahela Junction Station—building PA-2
Monongahela Location—locale MI-6
Monongahela Mine—mine MI-6
Monongahela River—stream PA-2
Monongahela River—stream WV-2
Monongahela River Lock And Dam Eight—dam PA-2
Monongahela River Lock And Dam Seven—dam PA-2
Monongahela River Locks And Dam Three—dam PA-2
Monongahela River Locks And Dam Two—dam PA-2
Monongahela River Pool Eight—reservoir PA-2
Monongahela River Pool Four—reservoir PA-2
Monongahela River Pool Seven—reservoir PA-2
Monongahela River Pool Three—reservoir PA-2
Monongahela River Pool Two—reservoir PA-2
**Monongahela (Township of)**—pop pl PA-2
Monongahela Valley Country Club—other PA-2
Monongalia Ch—church WV-2
**Monongalia (County)**—pop pl WV-2
Monongalia County Courthouse—hist pl WV-2
Mononghela City PA-2
Monong River IN-6
Monon Hill—summit CO-8
Monon Lake—lake OR-9
Monon Mine—mine CO-8
Mononomy Island MA-1
Monononack Lake MA-1
Mono North (CCD)—cens area CA-9
Monon River IN-6
**Monon (Township of)**—pop pl IN-6
Monoosmoc Brook MA-1
Monoosmoc Hills MA-1
Monoosnoc Brook—stream MA-1
Monoosnoc Hill MA-1
Monoosnoc Hills—summit MA-1
Monoosnock Brook MA-1
Monoosnock Country Club—locale MA-1
Monoosnoc Mountains MA-1
Monoosuck Hills MA-1
Mono Park—flat MT-8
Mono Park—park CA-9
Mono Pass—gap (2) CA-9
Monopoly Creek—stream AK-9
Monopoly Lake MO-7
Monopoly Marsh—swamp MO-7
Mono Pond—reservoir CT-1
**Monoquet**—pop pl IN-6
Monore Sch—school WA-9
Mono Rock CA-9
Mono Rock—summit CA-9
Mono Run—stream IN-6
Mono Sch—school CA-9
Mono South (CCD)—cens area CA-9
Monotis Creek—stream AK-9
Monotony Valley—basin NV-8
Mono Trail—trail CA-9
Monotti Creek—stream CA-9
Monotti Hill—summit CA-9
Mono Valley—basin CA-9
**Mono Village**—pop pl CA-9
**Monoville**—pop pl TN-4
Monoville Post Office—building TN-4
Monoville Sch (historical)—school TN-4
**Mono Vista**—pop pl CA-9
Mono Vista Spring—spring CA-9
Monowa FM-9
Monowe—locale FM-9
**Monowe**—pop pl FM-9
**Monowi**—pop pl NE-7
Monponset Lakes MA-1
Monponset Pond MA-1
**Monponsett**—pop pl MA-1
Monponsett Lakes MA-1
Monponsett Pond—lake MA-1
**Monponsett ( with PMSA's 1120 and 1200 )**—pop pl MA-1
Monrak River—stream AK-9
Monrak (Site)—locale AK-9
Monreal Ranch—locale CA-9
Monreal Well (dry)—well AZ-5
Monreath—hist pl NC-3
Monroe AL-4
Monroe MA-1
Monroe NJ-2
Monroe NC-3
Monroe PA-2
Monroe TN-4
Monroe VT-1
Monroe VA-3
Monroe—fmr MCD (2) NE-7
Monroe—locale CT-1
Monroe—locale NJ-2
Monroe—locale (2) OH-6
Monroe—locale (2) PA-2
Monroe—locale TX-5
**Monroe**—pop pl (2) AR-4
**Monroe**—pop pl CA-9
**Monroe**—pop pl FL-3
**Monroe**—pop pl GA-3
**Monroe**—pop pl (2) IN-6
**Monroe**—pop pl IA-7
**Monroe**—pop pl KY-4
**Monroe**—pop pl (2) LA-4
**Monroe**—pop pl ME-1
**Monroe**—pop pl MI-6
**Monroe**—pop pl (2) MS-4
**Monroe**—pop pl NE-7
**Monroe**—pop pl NH-1
**Monroe**—pop pl NJ-2
**Monroe**—pop pl NY-2
**Monroe**—pop pl NC-3
**Monroe**—pop pl OH-6
**Monroe**—pop pl OK-5
**Monroe**—pop pl OR-9
**Monroe**—pop pl PA-2
**Monroe**—pop pl SD-7
**Monroe**—pop pl TN-4
**Monroe**—pop pl UT-8
**Monroe**—pop pl VA-3
**Monroe**—pop pl WA-9
**Monroe**—pop pl WI-6
Monroe, Bessie, House—hist pl MA-1
Monroe, James, Family Home Site—hist pl VA-3
Monroe, James, Tomb—hist pl VA-3
Monroe, Lake—lake FL-3
Monroe, Lake—lake MT-8
Monroe, Lake—reservoir GA-3
Monroe, Lake—reservoir MS-4
Monroe, Lake—reservoir NC-3
Monroe, Lake—reservoir PA-2
Monroe, Mount—summit NH-1
Monroe, Point—cape WA-9
Monroe, Robert Nancy, House—hist pl NC-3
Monroe, The Calculator Company—facility SC-3
Monroe Acad—school AR-4
Monroe Acad—school GA-3
Monroe Academy AL-4
Monroe Airp—airport NC-3
Monroe and Barnes Rsvr—reservoir CO-8
Monroe and Walton Mills Hist Dist—hist pl GA-3
Monroe Ave Church TN-4
Monroe Ave Commercial Buildings—hist pl MI-6
Monroe Ave Elem Sch—school NC-3
Monroe Bank—hist pl OH-6
Monroe Bay—bay AK-9
Monroe Bay—bay VA-3
Monroe Bidwell Ditch—canal OH-6
Monroe Borough—civil PA-2
Monroe Branch—stream AL-4
Monroe Branch—stream KY-4
Monroe Branch—stream MS-4
Monroe Branch—stream SC-3
Monroe Branch—stream TN-4
Monroe Bridge—bridge VA-3
**Monroe Bridge**—pop pl MA-1
Monroe Bridge Dam Site MA-1
Monroe Brook—stream ME-1
Monroe Brook—stream MI-6
Monroe Brook—stream NH-1
Monroe-Brumfield Cem—cemetery MS-4
Monroe Butte—summit (2) ID-8
Monroe Canal—canal (2) FL-3
Monroe Canal—canal UT-8
Monroe Canyon AZ-5
Monroe Canyon—valley AZ-5
Monroe Canyon—valley (3) CA-9
Monroe Canyon—valley ID-8
Monroe Canyon—valley NE-7
Monroe Canyon—valley NV-8
Monroe Canyon Windmill—locale AZ-5
Monroe Carnegie Library—hist pl IN-6
Monroe (CCD)—cens area GA-3
Monroe (CCD)—cens area WA-9
Monroe-Cedar Knoll (Cedar Knolls) NJ-2
Monroe-Cedar Knolls NJ-2
Monroe Cem—cemetery CT-1
Monroe Cem—cemetery IN-6
Monroe Cem—cemetery (2) IA-7
Monroe Cem—cemetery KS-7
Monroe Cem—cemetery LA-4
Monroe Cem—cemetery MO-7
Monroe Cem—cemetery NE-7
Monroe Cem—cemetery (9) OH-6
Monroe Cem—cemetery OR-9
Monroe Cem—cemetery (3) TN-4
Monroe Cem—cemetery WV-2
Monroe Cemetery SD-7
Monroe Center—locale ME-1
Monroe Center—locale MI-6
**Monroe Center**—pop pl CT-1
**Monroe Center**—pop pl IL-6
**Monroe Center**—pop pl OH-6
**Monroe Center**—pop pl WI-6
Monroe Center Cem—cemetery MI-6
Monroe Center Cem—cemetery WI-6
Monroe Center Ch—church ME-1
Monroe Center Hist Dist—hist pl CT-1
Monroe Central High School IN-6
Monroe Central Junior-Senior HS—school IN-6
Monroe Ch—church AL-4
Monroe Ch—church IA-7
Monroe Ch—church (2) KY-4
Monroe Ch—church NE-7
Monroe Ch—church PA-2
Monroe Ch—church VA-3
Monroe Chapel—church OH-6
Monroe Chapel—church VA-3
Monroe Chapel (historical)—church MO-7
**Monroe City**—pop pl IL-6
**Monroe City**—pop pl IN-6
**Monroe City**—pop pl (2) MO-7
**Monroe City**—pop pl TX-5
Monroe City Cem—cemetery UT-8
Monroe City Creek—stream IL-6
Monroe City Hall—hist pl GA-3
Monroe City Hall—hist pl NC-3
Monroe City Hall—hist pl UT-8
Monroe City Hollow—valley IL-6
Monroe City Regional Airp—airport MO-7
Monroe Coll—school VA-3
Monroe Commercial Hist Dist—hist pl GA-3
Monroe Commerical District—hist pl WI-6
Monroe Community Coll—school NY-2
Monroe Corner NJ-2
Monroe Corner—locale VA-3
Monroe Corners NJ-2
**Monroe (corporate name for Monroeton)**—pop pl PA-2
Monroe Corrals—locale CA-9
Monroe Country Club and Golf Course—locale NC-3
**Monroe County**—pop pl AL-4
**Monroe (County)**—pop pl AR-4
**Monroe County**—pop pl FL-3
**Monroe (County)**—pop pl GA-3
**Monroe (County)**—pop pl IL-6
**Monroe County**—pop pl IN-6
**Monroe (County)**—pop pl KY-4
**Monroe (County)**—pop pl MI-6
**Monroe County**—pop pl MS-4
**Monroe County**—pop pl MO-7
**Monroe (County)**—pop pl NY-2
**Monroe (County)**—pop pl OH-6
**Monroe County**—pop pl PA-2
**Monroe County**—pop pl TN-4
**Monroe (County)**—pop pl WV-2
**Monroe (County)**—pop pl WI-6
Monroe County Airp—airport AL-4
Monroe County Airp—airport IN-6
Monroe County Airp—airport MS-4
Monroe County Airp—airport TN-4
Monroe County Community Coll—school MI-6
Monroe County Comservation Area—park IA-7
Monroe County Courthouse—building MS-4
Monroe County Courthouse—hist pl AR-4
Monroe County Courthouse—hist pl GA-3
Monroe County Courthouse—hist pl IN-6
Monroe County Courthouse—hist pl IA-7
Monroe County Courthouse—hist pl MS-4
Monroe County Courthouse—hist pl OH-6
Monroe County Courthouse—hist pl WI-6
Monroe County Farm (historical)—locale TN-4
Monroe County Flowage—reservoir WI-6
Monroe County Home—building KY-4
Monroe County Home—building MS-4
Monroe County Hosp—hospital AL-4
Monroe County HS—school AL-4
Monroe County Jail—hist pl AR-4
Monroe County Jail—hist pl MS-4
Monroe County Public Lake AL-4
Monroe County Public Lake Dam—dam AL-4
Monroe County Public Library—building FL-3
Monroe County Vocational Center—school TN-4
Monroe Court House MS-4
Monroe Creek VA-3
Monroe Creek—stream (2) CA-9
Monroe Creek—stream FL-3
Monroe Creek—stream (4) ID-8
Monroe Creek—stream MI-6
Monroe Creek—stream MN-6
Monroe Creek—stream MS-4
Monroe Creek—stream MT-8
Monroe Creek—stream NE-7
Monroe Creek—stream OH-6
Monroe Creek—stream (2) OR-9
Monroe Creek—stream (2) PA-2
Monroe Creek—stream TN-4
Monroe Creek—stream UT-8
Monroe Creek—stream VA-3
Monroe Creek—stream (2) WA-9
Monroe Creek—stream WY-8
Monroe-Crook House—hist pl TX-5
Monroe Crossroads—locale SC-3
Monroe Ditch—canal CO-8
Monroe Ditch—canal IN-6
Monroe Division—civil UT-8
Monroe Downtown Hist Dist—hist pl NC-3
Monroe Draft—valley WV-2
Monroe Drain—canal (2) MI-6
Monroe Elem Sch—school PA-2
Monroefield—locale OH-6
Monroe Field—park MN-6
Monroe Flat CA-9
Monroe Flat—flat CA-9
Monroe Franklin Sch—school PA-2
Monroe Furnace—locale PA-2
**Monroe Gardens**—pop pl VA-3
**Monroe Gardens Subdivision**—pop pl UT-8
Monroe Gas Field—area LA-4
Monroe Gas Field—oilfield LA-4
Monroe General Hosp—hospital FL-3
Monroe General Hosp—hospital WA-9
Monroe Golf Club—other NY-2
Monroe Golf Course—other WA-9
Monroe Green—park NM-5
Monroe Gulch—valley MT-8
Monroe Hall MA-1
**Monroe Hall**—pop pl VA-3
**Monroe Heights**—pop pl PA-2
Monroe Hill—summit NH-1
Monroe Hills Memorial Gardens—cemetery GA-3
Monroe (historical)—locale KS-7
Monroe (historical)—locale (2) MS-4
Monroe Hollow—valley AR-4
Monroe Hollow—valley (2) IN-6
Monroe Hollow—valley OH-6
Monroe Hollow—valley (2) TX-5
Monroe Hollow—valley WV-2
Monroe Homestead—locale CO-8
Monroe Hot Springs Resort—park UT-8
Monroe-Howell Cem—cemetery MS-4
Monroe HS—school AK-9
Monroe HS—school CA-9
Monroe HS—school GA-3
Monroe HS—school MN-6
Monroe HS—school NY-2
Monroe HS—school NC-3
Monroe HS—school VA-3
Monroe Inlet—bay NY-2
Monroe Island—island ME-1
Monroe JHS—school CA-9
Monroe JHS—school FL-3
Monroe JHS—school NM-5
Monroe JHS—school NY-2
Monroe JHS—school OH-6
Monroe JHS—school OK-5
Monroe JHS—school OR-9
Monroe JHS—school UT-8
Monroe JHS—school VA-3
Monroe Junction—locale WA-9
Monroe Junior Sch—school IA-7
Monroe Knob—summit WV-2
Monroe Lake—lake CA-9
Monroe Lake—lake FL-3
Monroe Lake—lake ID-8
Monroe Lake—lake ME-1
Monroe Lake—lake MI-6
Monroe Lake—lake NJ-2
Monroe Lake—lake WY-8
**Monroe Lake**—pop pl PA-2
Monroe Lake—reservoir IN-6
Monroe Lake—reservoir OH-6
Monroe Lake Dam—dam IN-6
Monroe Lake Dam—dam PA-2
Monroe Lake State Wildlife Area—park OH-6
Monroe Lateral—canal AZ-5
Monroe Law Office—hist pl VA-3
Monroe-Madison Sch—school NJ-2
Monroe (Magisterial District)—fmr MCD (2) VA-3
Monroe Mall—locale NC-3
**Monroe Manor**—pop pl IN-6
Monroe Meadows—flat CA-9
Monroe Meadows—flat UT-8
Monroe Memorial Park—cemetery MS-4
Monroe Memorial Park—cemetery WA-9
Monroe Methodist Episcopal Church—hist pl UT-8
Monroe Mill Pond—reservoir NC-3
**Monroe Mills**—pop pl OH-6
Monroe Mills (historical P.O.)—locale IN-6
Monroe Mine—mine ID-8
Monroe Mine—mine NV-8
Monroe Mine (underground)—mine AL-4
Monroe Missionary Station (historical)—locale MS-4
Monroe Mission Church MS-4
Monroe Mission (historical)—church MS-4
Monroe MS—school NC-3
Monroe Mtn—summit NC-3
Monroe Mtn—summit OK-5
Monroe Mynard Pond—reservoir AL-4
Monroe Mynard Pond Dam—dam AL-4
Monroe Oil Field—oilfield TX-5
Monroe Park—park FL-3
Monroe Park—park GA-3
Monroe Park—park IL-6
Monroe Park—park (2) IA-7
Monroe Park—park NJ-2
Monroe Park—park OR-9
Monroe Park—park UT-8
Monroe Park—park VA-3
Monroe Park—park WI-6
**Monroe Park**—pop pl DE-2
**Monroe Park**—pop pl NC-3
Monroe Park Hist Dist—hist pl VA-3
Monroe Peak—summit UT-8
Monroe Plantation—locale LA-4
Monroe Playground—park MI-6
Monroe Plaza—locale PA-2
Monroe Plaza Shop Ctr—locale NC-3
Monroe Point—cape AL-4
Monroe Point—cape MN-6
Monroe Ponds—lake NY-2
Monroe Post Office—building TN-4
Monroe Post Office—building UT-8
Monroe Prairie Creek—stream IN-6
Monroe Presbyterian Church—hist pl UT-8
Monroe Ranch—locale ND-7
Monroe Ranch—locale TX-5
Monroe Regional Airp—airport LA-4
Monroe Reservoir IN-6
Monroe Residential Hist Dist—hist pl NC-3
Monroe Ridge—ridge NJ-2
Monroe Ridge—ridge WV-2
Monroe Roads Cem—cemetery MI-6
Monroe Roughs—summit OR-9
Monroe (RR name for New Deal)—other TX-5
Monroe Rsvr—reservoir MT-8
Monroe Rsvr—reservoir WA-9
Monroe Run—stream MD-2
Monroe's MA-1
**Monroes**—pop pl MA-1
Monroe Sch—hist pl AZ-5
Monroe Sch—hist pl OH-6
Monroe Sch—school AL-4
Monroe Sch—school AZ-5
Monroe Sch—school (13) CA-9
Monroe Sch—school CT-1
Monroe Sch—school DC-2
Monroe Sch—school ID-8
Monroe Sch—school (7) IL-6
Monroe Sch—school (3) IA-7
Monroe Sch—school KS-7
Monroe Sch—school MA-1
Monroe Sch—school (6) MI-6
Monroe Sch—school (3) MN-6
Monroe Sch—school (2) NE-7
Monroe Sch—school (2) NC-3
Monroe Sch—school (6) OH-6
Monroe Sch—school (3) OK-5
Monroe Sch—school PA-2
Monroe Sch—school (2) SD-7
Monroe Sch—school TN-4
Monroe Sch—school (2) UT-8
Monroe Sch—school VA-3
Monroe Sch—school WA-9
Monroe Sch—school WV-2
Monroe Sch—school (3) WI-6
Monroe Sch (historical)—school MS-4
Monroe Sch (historical)—school (2) PA-2
Monroe Sch (historical)—school TN-4
Monroes Corner—locale FL-3
Monroe Senior HS AL-4
Monroe Shop Ctr—locale NC-3
Monroe Sink—basin KY-4
Monroe Southwest—CDP NY-2
Monroe Sporting Club Lake Dam—dam MS-4
Monroe Spring—spring OR-9
Monroe State For—forest MA-1
Monroe State Park—park VT-1
Monroe Station AL-4
Monroe Station—locale FL-3
Monroe Station (historical)—locale MS-4
Monroe Strand—swamp FL-3
Monroe Street—uninc pl TX-5
Monroe Street Apartments—hist pl GA-3
Monroe Street Bridge—hist pl WA-9
Monroe Street Commercial Buildings—hist pl OH-6
Monroe Street East Hist Dist—hist pl WV-2
Monroe Street Sch—school NY-2
Monroe Tank—reservoir TX-5
Monroe-Tener Mine—mine MN-6
**Monroeton**—pop pl AL-4
**Monroeton**—pop pl NC-3
**Monroeton**—pop pl PA-2
Monroeton (corporate name Monroe) PA-2
Monroeton Elem Sch—school NC-3
**Monroetown**—pop pl (2) NC-3
Monroe Townhall—building (2) IA-7
**Monroe (Town of)**—pop pl CT-1
**Monroe (Town of)**—pop pl ME-1
**Monroe (Town of)**—pop pl MA-1
**Monroe (Town of)**—pop pl NH-1
**Monroe (Town of)**—pop pl NY-2
**Monroe (Town of)**—pop pl (2) WI-6
Monroe Township—civil (3) MO-7
Monroe Township—civil SD-7
Monroe Township—fmr MCD (11) IA-7
**Monroe Township**—pop pl KS-7
**Monroe Township**—pop pl (3) MO-7
**Monroe Township**—pop pl NE-7
**Monroe Township**—pop pl ND-7
**Monroe Township**—pop pl SD-7
Monroe Township Cem—cemetery IA-7
Monroe Township Elem Sch—school PA-2
Monroe Township Hall-Opera House—hist pl OH-6
Monroe (Township of)—fmr MCD (2) AR-4
Monroe (Township of)—fmr MCD (2) NC-3
**Monroe (Township of)**—pop pl IL-6
**Monroe (Township of)**—pop pl (16) IN-6
**Monroe (Township of)**—pop pl (2) MI-6
**Monroe (Township of)**—pop pl MN-6
**Monroe (Township of)**—pop pl (2) NJ-2
**Monroe (Township of)**—pop pl (22) OH-6
**Monroe (Township of)**—pop pl (7) PA-2
Monroe Trimble Ditch—canal IN-6
Monroe Valley—basin CA-9
Monroe Valley—valley (2) PA-2
Monroe Valley Golf Course—locale PA-2
Monroe Valley Sch—school PA-2
Monroeville PA-2
**Monroeville**—pop pl AL-4
**Monroeville**—pop pl IN-6
**Monroeville**—pop pl NJ-2
**Monroeville**—pop pl (2) OH-6
Monroeville Acad—school AL-4
Monroeville (CCD)—cens area AL-4
Monroeville Cem—cemetery NJ-2
Monroeville Division—civil AL-4
Monroeville Grammar Sch (historical)—school AL-4
Monroeville Hills Shop Ctr—locale PA-2
Monroeville JHS—school AL-4
Monroeville Junior High School PA-2
Monroeville Mall—locale PA-2
Monroeville School PA-2
Monroeville Station NJ-2
**Monroeville (subdivision)**—pop pl PA-2
Monroeville Synogogue—church NJ-2
Monroe Well—well CO-8
Monroe Windmill—locale TX-5
Monroe-Woodbury Central HS—school NY-2
Monroney JHS—school OK-5
Monrovia AL-4
Monrovia—locale VA-3
**Monrovia**—pop pl AL-4
**Monrovia**—pop pl CA-9
**Monrovia**—pop pl IN-6
**Monrovia**—pop pl KS-7
**Monrovia**—pop pl MD-2
Monrovia—uninc pl KS-7
Monrovia Canyon—valley CA-9
Monrovia Cem—cemetery KS-7
Monrovia Ch—church VA-3
Monrovia Elem Sch—school IN-6
Monrovia Golf Course—other AL-4
Monrovia HS—school CA-9
Monrovia Junior-Senior HS—school IN-6
Monrovia Mountain Park—park CA-9
Monrovia MS—school AL-4
Monrovian Park—flat UT-8
Monrovian Park Campground—park UT-8
Monrovia Peak—summit CA-9
Monrovia Post Office (historical)—building AL-4
Mons—locale CA-9
Monsanto—locale CA-9
Monsanto—other IL-6
**Monsanto**—pop pl ID-8
**Monsanto (Chemical Plant)**—pop pl TN-4
Monsanto Company—facility IL-6
Monsanto Company—facility IA-7
Monsanto Company Upper Dam—dam MA-1
Monsanto Number Fifteen Dam—dam TN-4
Monsanto Number Fifteen Lake—reservoir TN-4
Monsanto Number Twelve Dam—dam TN-4
Monsanto Number Two Dam—dam TN-4
Monsanto Tailings Pond Number Five Dam—dam TN-4
Monsanto Tailings Pond Number Four—dam TN-4
Monsanto Tailings Pond Number Nine—dam TN-4
Monsanto Tailings Pond Number Ten—dam TN-4
Monsanto Tailings Pond Number Three Dam—dam TN-4
Monsapec—locale ME-1
Mons Creek—stream MN-6
Monse—locale WA-9
Monsees Cem—cemetery MO-7
Monserate—civil CA-9
Monserate Mtn—summit CA-9
Monserrate—locale (2) PR-3
**Monserrate**—pop pl (3) PR-3
**Monsey**—pop pl NY-2
**Monsey Heights**—pop pl NY-2
Monsey Lake—reservoir NY-2
Monsey Sch—school NY-2
Monsieur Giron's Confectionary—hist pl KY-4
Monsignor Bonner HS—school PA-2
Monsignor Edward Pace HS—school FL-3
Monsignor Ferrell HS—school NY-2
Mons Lake—lake MN-6
Monsod Bay—cove MA-1
Monsod Pond MA-1
Monson—locale CO-8
**Monson**—pop pl CA-9
**Monson**—pop pl ME-1
**Monson**—pop pl MA-1
**Monson**—pop pl WV-2
Monson Brook ME-1
Monson Canyon—valley ID-8
Monson Cem—cemetery ME-1
Monson Cem—cemetery MN-6
Monson (census name for Monson Center)—CDP MA-1
Monson Center MA-1
Monson Center (census name Monson)—other MA-1
Monson Chapel—church (2) IN-6
Monson Ditch—canal CA-9
Monson Flowage WI-6
Monson Flowage—reservoir WI-6
Monson Gulch—valley CO-8
Monson HS—school MA-1
Monson Island—island MN-6
Monson Junction—locale ME-1
Monson Lake—lake ME-1
Monson Lake—lake (4) MN-6
Monson Lake—reservoir WI-6
Monson Lake Ch—church MN-6
Monson Lake Flowage WI-6
Monson Lake Memorial State Park—park MN-6
Monson Lateral—canal ID-8
Monson Pond—lake (2) ME-1
Monson Pond—lake WI-6
Monson Rsvr—reservoir MA-1
Monson Sch—school ND-7
Monson State Wildlife Mngmt Areas—park MN-6
Monson Stream—stream ME-1
**Monson (Town of)**—pop pl ME-1
**Monson (Town of)**—pop pl MA-1
**Monson (Township of)**—pop pl MN-6
Monsoon Lake—lake AK-9
Monsoono Lake—lake AK-9
Mons Run—stream PA-2
Monster Rsvr—reservoir MT-8
Mont IL-6
Mont—locale KY-4
Mont—locale TX-5
**Mont**—pop pl IL-6
Montadale Sch—school TX-5
Montadon PA-2
Montage (ski area)—locale PA-2
Montagne Creek—stream WI-6
Montague—locale AL-4
Montague—locale FL-3
Montague—locale MT-8
Montague—locale OR-9
Montague—locale TN-4
Montague—locale VA-3
**Montague**—pop pl CA-9
**Montague**—pop pl MA-1
**Montague**—pop pl MI-6
**Montague**—pop pl MO-7
**Montague**—pop pl NJ-2
**Montague**—pop pl NC-3
**Montague**—pop pl OR-9
**Montague**—pop pl SC-3
**Montague**—pop pl TN-4
**Montague**—pop pl TX-5
**Montague**—pop pl VA-3
Montague, Henry, House—hist pl MI-6
Montague Butte—summit MT-8
Montague Canal MA-1
Montague Cave—cave AL-4
Montague (CCD)—cens area CA-9
Montague Cem—cemetery NC-3
Montague Cem—cemetery (2) TN-4
Montague Cem—cemetery VA-3
Montague Center Sch—school MA-1
Montague Centre MA-1
Montague Ch—church TX-5
**Montague City**—pop pl MA-1
**Montague (County)**—pop pl TX-5
Montague Creek WI-6
Montague Creek—stream MI-6
Montague Creek—stream TX-5
Montague Creek—stream VA-3
Montague Creek—stream WA-9
Montague Ditch—canal CA-9
**Montague Forest**—pop pl IL-6
Montague-Forestburg (CCD)—cens area TX-5
Montague-Grigg Cem TN-4
**Montague Hill**—pop pl MO-7
Montague Hill—summit VT-1
Montague Hills NC-3
Montague Hills—ridge NC-3
**Montague (historical)**—pop pl OR-9
Montague Hollow—valley MO-7
Montague Hollow—valley TX-5
Montague Island—island AK-9
Montague Lake—lake MI-6
Montague Lake—lake NJ-2
Montague Lake—reservoir TX-5
Montague Lakes—lake MI-6
Montague Landing—locale VA-3
Montague Memorial Plaque—other OR-9
Montague Mine—mine CA-9
Montague Mines (underground)—mine AL-4
Montague Mtn—summit AL-4
Montague Park—park TN-4
Montague Peak—summit AK-9
Montague Plain—flat MA-1
Montague Point—cape AK-9
Montague Post Office (historical)—building TN-4
Montague Power Canal Rsvr—reservoir MA-1
Montague-Rodgers—uninc pl MD-2
Montague Sch—school CA-9
Montague Sch—school MI-6
Montague Sch (historical)—school MS-4
Montague-Shipman Cemetery TN-4
Montague Spring—spring AZ-5
Montague State For—forest MA-1
**Montague Station**—pop pl MA-1
Montague Strait—channel AK-9
Montague Street Sch—school CA-9
Montague (Town of)—civil MA-1

**Montague (Town of)**—pop pl MA-1
**Montague (Town of)**—pop pl NY-2
**Montague (Township of)**—pop pl MI-6
**Montague (Township of)**—pop pl NJ-2
Montague Village (West Fort Hood)—CDP TX-5
Montague Well—well AZ-5
Montag Valley—valley TX-5
Montair ND-7
Montair—uninc pl CA-9
Mont Air Creek—stream VA-3
Montair Sch—school CA-9
**Montalba**—pop pl TX-5
Mont Alban MS-4
Montalban Ridge—ridge NH-1
Montalba-Tennessee Colony (CCD)—cens area TX-5
Montaldo Mountain PA-2
Monta Loma Sch—school CA-9
**Mont Alto**—pop pl PA-2
Mont Alto Borough—civil PA-2
Montalto Mtn—summit PA-2
Mont Alto State For—forest PA-2
Mont Alto State Park—park PA-2
Montalva, Sabana—plain PR-3
Montalva (Barrio)—fmr MCD PR-3
Montalvan Point—cape VI-3
Montalvin Manor—uninc pl CA-9
Montalvin Manor Sch—school CA-9
**Montalvo**—pop pl CA-9
Montalvo Cem—cemetery TX-5
Montana PA-2
Montana—locale AK-9
Montana—locale AR-4
Montana—locale NJ-2
**Montana**—pop pl CA-9
**Montana**—pop pl KS-7
**Montana**—pop pl WI-6
**Montana**—pop pl (3) PR-3
Montana Apartments—hist pl OH-6
Montana (Barrio)—fmr MCD PR-3
Montana Bible Institute—school MT-8
Montana Bill Creek—stream AK-9
Montana Canyon—valley ID-8
Montana Cem—cemetery KS-7
Montana Ch—church WV-2
Montana City—locale MT-8
Montana Creek—stream (8) AK-9
Montana Creek—stream CO-8
Montana Creek—stream (2) ID-8
Montana Creek—stream KS-7
Montana Creek—stream MI-6
Montana Creek—stream MT-8
Montana Creek—stream WA-9
Montana Creek—stream WY-8
Montana Creek (Montana)—other AK-9
Montana Creek Trail—trail AK-9
Montana Dam—dam AZ-5
Montana Deaf and Dumb Asylum—hist pl MT-8
Montana del Sur AZ-5
Montana De Oro State Park—park CA-9
Montana Ditch—canal MT-8
Montana Gulch—valley (2) AK-9
Montana Gulch—valley (3) MT-8
Montana Gulch Campground—locale MT-8
Montana Junction—uninc pl ID-8
Montana Lake—lake WI-6
Montana Lake—lake WY-8
Montana Mine—mine AZ-5
Montana Mine—mine CA-9
Montana Mine—mine (2) CO-8
Montana Mine—mine MT-8
Montana Mine—mine SD-7
Montana Mine—mine UT-8
Montana Mine—mine WA-9
**Montana Mines (Montana)**—pop pl WV-2
**Montana (Montana Mines Post Office)**—pop pl WV-2
Montana Morning Mine—mine MT-8
Montana Mtn—summit AZ-5
Montana Mtn—summit CO-8
Montana Mtns—range NV-8
Montana Park—park MT-8
Montana Peak—summit AK-9
Montana Peak—summit AZ-5
Montana Peak—summit ID-8
Montana Point—summit ID-8
Montanapolis Sch—school MT-8
**Montanapolis Springs**—pop pl MT-8
Montanapolis Springs—spring MT-8
Montana Premier Mine—mine MT-8
Montana Prince Mine—mine MT-8
Montana Ranch—locale AZ-5
**Montana Ranchos Subdivision**—pop pl UT-8
Montana Ridge—ridge ID-8
Montana Ridge—ridge WI-6
Montanas Aymamon—range PR-3
Montana School of Mines—mine MT-8
Montanas de Corozal—range PR-3
Montanas de Juan Gonzalez—range PR-3
Montanas de Uroyan—range PR-3
Montanas Guarionex—range PR-3
Montana Shaft—mine UT-8
Montana Silver Star Mine—mine MT-8
Montana Spring—spring OR-9
Montana Springs—spring ID-8
Montana State Capitol Bldg—hist pl MT-8
Montana State Coll—school MT-8
Montana State Hosp Galen Campus—hospital MT-8
Montana State Normal Sch—hist pl MT-8
Montana State Prison Ranch Number 2—locale MT-8
**Montana State T.b. Sanitarium**—pop pl (2) MT-8
Montana State Training Sch—school MT-8
Montana Street Sch—school AL-4
Montana Territorial and State Prison—hist pl MT-8
Montana Tonopah—mine NV-8
**Montana (Town of)**—pop pl WI-6
**Montana Township**—pop pl (2) KS-7
Montana Wash AZ-5
Montana Wash—stream AZ-5
Montana Wash—stream NV-8
Montana Windmill—locale TX-5
Montana-Yerington Mine—mine NV-8
**Montandon**—pop pl PA-2
Montandon Sand Dunes—summit PA-2
Montanez Adobe—hist pl CA-9
Montania, Lake—reservoir NC-3
Montanis, Lake—lake WI-6
Montano Flats—flat NM-5
Montano Ranch—locale AZ-5
Montano Ranch—locale (2) NM-5
Montano School (Abandoned)—locale NM-5
Montano Spring—spring NM-5
Montano Well—well NM-5
Montaqua—locale MT-8
Mont Aqua Hot Spring—locale MT-8
Montaque Island—island IL-6
**Montara**—pop pl CA-9
Montara Beach—beach CA-9
Montara Knob—summit CA-9
Montara Mtn—summit CA-9
**Montara (subdivision)**—pop pl (2) AZ-5
**Montario Point**—pop pl NY-2
Monta Sch—school MT-8
Montauk—hist pl IA-7
Montauk—locale MO-7
**Montauk**—pop pl NY-2
Montauk, Lake—lake NY-2
Montauk Air Force Station—military NY-2
Montauk Association Hist Dist—hist pl NY-2
**Montauk Beach**—pop pl NY-2
Montauk Bluff—cliff AK-9
Montauk Creek—stream AK-9
Montauk Downs Golf Club—other NY-2
**Montauk Estates**—pop pl NY-2
Montauk Gun Club—other NY-2
Montauk Harbor NY-2
Montauk Manor—hist pl NY-2
Montauk Point—cape NY-2
Montauk Point Lighthouse—hist pl NY-2
Montauk Springs—spring MO-7
Montauk State Historical Site—park IA-7
Montauk State Park—park MO-7
Montauk State Park Open Shelter—hist pl MO-7
Montauk State Public Hunting Area—locale MO-7
**Montauk Station**—pop pl NY-2
Montauk Tennis Auditorium—hist pl NY-2
Montauk Yacht Club—other NY-2
Montaup Number 3 Dam—dam MA-1
Montavallo Church AL-4
**Montavilla**—pop pl OR-9
Montavilla Park—park OR-9
**Monta Vista**—pop pl CA-9
**Monta Vista**—pop pl WA-9
Monta Vista Cem—cemetery VA-3
Monta Vista Sch—school CA-9
Montazona Mine—mine AZ-5
Montazona Pass—gap AZ-5
Montazuma IN-6
**Montbello**—pop pl CO-8
**Mont Belvieu**—pop pl TX-5
Mont Belvieu (CCD)—cens area TX-5
Mont Blanc—summit TX-5
**Montborne**—pop pl WA-9
Mont Branch—stream IN-6
**Montbrook**—pop pl FL-3
Mont Calm—hist pl VA-3
**Montcalm**—pop pl LA-4
**Montcalm**—pop pl WV-2
Montcalm, Lake—lake MI-6
**Montcalm (County)**—pop pl MI-6
Montcalm Hill—summit NH-1
Montcalm Lake—lake MI-6
Montcalm Playground—locale MI-6
Mont Calm P. O. AL-4
Montcalm Point—cape NY-2
Montcalm Sch—school NH-1
**Montcalm (Township of)**—pop pl MI-6
**Montcastle Hills (subdivision)**—pop pl TN-4
**Montchanin**—pop pl DE-2
Montchanin Hist Dist—hist pl DE-2
**Montchan (subdivision)**—pop pl DE-2
Mont Chateau State Park—park WV-2
Montcla—locale LA-4
Montclair CO-8
Mont Clair KY-4
Mont Clair NJ-2
**Montclair**—pop pl FL-3
**Montclair**—pop pl GA-3
**Montclair**—pop pl IN-6
**Montclair**—pop pl (2) KY-4
**Montclair**—pop pl NJ-2
Montclair, Lake—reservoir VA-3
Montclair Acad—school NJ-2
Montclair Annex Sch—school CO-8
Montclair Art Museum—hist pl NJ-2
Montclair Coll Prep Sch—school CA-9
**Montclair Colony**—pop pl NY-2
Montclaire IN-6
Montclair Elem Sch—school FL-3
Montclair Elem Sch—school NC-3
Montclaire Sch—school CA-9
Montclaire Sch—school NC-3
**Montclaire South (subdivision)**—pop pl NC-3
**Montclaire (subdivision)**—pop pl NC-3
Montclair Glen Camp—locale VT-1
Montclair Golf Club—other NJ-2
Montclair Golf Course—locale TN-4
Montclair Heights—locale NJ-2
Montclair Heights Station—building NJ-2
Montclair (historical)—locale ND-7
Montclair HS—school CA-9
Montclair Park—hist pl CO-8
Montclair Park—park CO-8
Montclair Playground—park CA-9
Montclair RR Station—hist pl NJ-2
Montclair Sch—school CA-9
Montclair Sch—school CO-8
Montclair Sch—school FL-3
Montclair Sch—school OR-9
Montclair Sch—school PA-2
Montclair Sch—school TX-5
Montclair Shop Ctr—locale TX-5
**Montclair South (subdivision)**—pop pl TN-4
Montclair State Coll—school NJ-2
Montclair Station—locale NJ-2
**Montclair (subdivision)**—pop pl CA-9
**Montclair (subdivision)**—pop pl MA-1
**Montclair (subdivision)**—pop pl (5) NC-3
**Montclair (subdivision)**—pop pl TN-4
**Montclair Terrace (subdivision)**—pop pl (2) AZ-5
**Montclair (Township of)**—pop pl NJ-2
Mont Clare IL-6
Montclare PA-2
Montclare SC-3
**Montclare**—pop pl DE-2
**Mont Clare**—pop pl PA-2
**Mont Clare**—pop pl SC-3
Montclare, Lake—lake IL-6
**Montcoal**—pop pl WV-2
**Montcrest**—pop pl TN-4
**Montdale**—pop pl PA-2
Mont Downing Sch—school WA-9
Monte CA-9
Monte—locale VI-3
Mont Eagle TN-4
**Monteagle**—pop pl TN-4
Monteagle Cem—cemetery TN-4
Monteagle Cove—valley TN-4
Monteagle Cove Branch—stream TN-4
Monteagle Falls—falls TN-4
Mont Eagle Post Office TN-4
Monteagle Post Office—building TN-4
Monteagle Saltpeter Cave TN-4
Monteagle Sch—school TN-4
Monteagle-South Pittsburg (CCD)—cens area TN-4
Monteagle-South Pittsburg Division—civil TN-4
Monteagle Sunday Sch Assembly Hist Dist—hist pl TN-4
**Monte Alto**—pop pl TX-5
Monte Alto Reservoir TX-5
Monte Alto Windmill—locale TX-5
**Monte Aplanado**—pop pl NM-5
Monte Arido Trail—trail CA-9
Monte Basin—basin NV-8
Monte Bay—bay VI-3
Monte Beach Park—park TX-5
Monte Belen Arroyo—stream (2) NM-5
Montebello—locale PA-2
Montebello—locale VA-3
**Montebello**—pop pl CA-9
**Montebello**—pop pl NY-2
**Montebello**—pop pl PR-3
Montebello, Lake—lake MD-2
Montebello Elem Sch—school MS-4
**Monte Bello Estates (subdivision)**—pop pl AL-4
**Monte Bello Estates Subdivision**—pop pl UT-8
Montebello Gardens—uninc pl CA-9
Montebello Gardens Sch—school CA-9
Montebello Hills—other CA-9
Montebello HS—school CA-9
Montebello JHS MS-4
Montebello Municipal Golf Course—other CA-9
**Montebello Park**—pop pl MD-2
Montebello Park Sch—school CA-9
Monte Bello Ridge—ridge CA-9
Montebello Sch—school AZ-5
Monte Bello Sch—school CA-9
Montebello Sch—school MD-2
Montebello Sch—school MS-4
Montebello State Park—park IL-6
**Montebello (Township of)**—pop pl IL-6
Montebrier—hist pl AL-4
Monte Calvario Cem—cemetery NM-5
Monte Camado—summit CO-8
Montecarlo—locale WV-2
**Monte Carlo**—pop pl PR-3
Monte Carlo—summit WA-9
**Monte Carlo Condominium Subdivision**—pop pl UT-8
Monte Carlo Creek—stream CA-9
**Monte Carlo Estates**—pop pl TN-4
Monte Carlo Gap—gap NM-5
Monte Carlo Interchange—crossing AZ-5
Monte Carlo Island—island AK-9
Monte Carlo Meadows—flat CA-9
Monte Carlo Mine—mine CO-8
Monte Carlo Mine—mine UT-8
Monte Casino Sch—school OK-5
**Monte Cassino Shrine**—pop pl IN-6
Montecello SC-3
**Montecello**—pop pl LA-4
Monte Christo—locale TX-5
Monte Christo Gas Field—oilfield TX-5
**Montecito**—pop pl CA-9
**Montecito**—pop pl NM-5
Montecito Apartments—hist pl CA-9
Montecito Country Club—other CA-9
Montecito Creek—stream CA-9
Montecito Memorial Park (Cemetery)—cemetery CA-9
Montecito Mobile Home Estates—locale AZ-5
Montecito Peak CA-9
Montecito Peak—summit CA-9
Montecito Sch—school CA-9
Montecito Sch for Girls—school CA-9
Montecitos Tank—reservoir NM-5
Monte Clare SC-3
Monte Creek—stream (2) CA-9
Monte Cristo—locale WA-9
**Monte Cristo**—pop pl OR-9
Monte Cristo—summit WA-9
Monte Cristo Campground—locale UT-8
**Monte Cristo Condo**—pop pl UT-8
Monte Cristo Cottage—hist pl CT-1
Monte Cristo Creek—stream (3) AK-9
Monte Cristo Creek—stream CA-9
Monte Cristo Creek—stream CO-8
Monte Cristo Forest Service Station UT-8
Monte Cristo Guard Station—locale UT-8
Monte Cristo Hotel—hist pl WA-9
Monte Cristo Island—island UT-8
Monte Cristo Lake—lake WA-9
Monte Cristo Mine—mine (3) AZ-5
Monte Cristo Mine—mine (3) CA-9
Monte Cristo Mine—mine ID-8
Monte Cristo Mine—mine (2) MT-8
Monte Cristo Mine—mine NV-8
Monte Cristo Mine—mine UT-8
Monte Cristo Mine—mine WY-8
Monte Cristo Mtns—range NV-8
Monte Cristo Peak—summit UT-8
Monte Cristo Peak—summit WA-9
Monte Cristo Range—range NV-8
Monte Cristo Range—range UT-8
Monte Cristo Range—range WA-9
Monte Cristo (Site)—locale CA-9
Monte Cristo (Site)—locale NV-8
Monte Cristo (site)—locale NV-8
Monte Cristo Spring—spring (2) NV-8
Monte Cristo Substation—locale AZ-5
Monte Cristo Valley—basin NV-8
Monte Crist Ranch—locale NV-8
Monte de la Brea—summit PR-3
Monte de la Expuma AZ-5
Monte de la Luz—summit PR-3
Monte Del Diablo—civil CA-9
Monte de Oro—summit CA-9
Monte de Oro Mine—mine (2) CA-9
Monte de Santa Ana—summit PR-3
Monte Diablo Creek CA-9
Monte El Gato—summit PR-3
Monte El Ojo—summit PR-3
Monte Encantado—summit PR-3
Monteer MO-7
Montefalco Sch—school MI-6
Monte Figueroa—summit PR-3
Montefiore Cem—cemetery NY-2
Montefiore Cem—cemetery PA-2
Montefiore Hosp—hospital NY-2
Montefiore Hosp—hospital PA-2
Montefiore Sanitarium—hospital NY-2
Montefiore Sch—school IL-6
Monteflore Cem—cemetery VA-3
**Monteflores**—pop pl PR-3
Montegail Pond—lake ME-1
Montegail Stream—stream ME-1
Monte Gardens Sch—school CA-9
Montego—post sta MD-2
Monte Grande—locale TX-5
Monte Grande—locale PR-3
**Monte Grande**—pop pl PR-3
Monte Grande—summit PR-3
Monte Grande (Barrio)—fmr MCD PR-3
Montegue Creek VA-3
Montegue Landing VA-3
Monte Guilarte—summit PR-3
**Montegut**—pop pl (2) LA-4
Montegut Oil and Gas Field—oilfield LA-4
Montegut Plantation House—hist pl LA-4
Monteigne—hist pl MS-4
Monte Iguina—summit PR-3
Monteith—locale GA-3
**Monteith**—pop pl IA-7
Monteith, Mark L. and Harriet E., House—hist pl IN-6
Monteith,Thomas and Walter, House—hist pl OR-9
Monteith Branch—stream NC-3
Monteith Camp—locale NC-3
Monteith Cove—valley NC-3
Monteith Hall—hist pl OH-6
Monteith Hist Dist—hist pl OR-9
**Monteith (historical)**—pop pl NC-3
Monteith Junction—locale MO-7
Monteith Ridge—ridge TN-4
Monteith Rock—pillar OR-9
Monteith Sch—school (3) MI-6
Monte Jayuya—other PR-3
Montel—locale MD-2
Monte Lake—lake AK-9
Monte Lake—lake NM-5
Monte Largo—summit NM-5
Monte Largo Tank—reservoir NM-5
Monte Las Pardas—summit PR-3
**Montell**—pop pl TX-5
Monte Llano—ridge PR-3
Monte Llano (Barrio)—fmr MCD (4) PR-3
Montell Creek—stream TX-5
**Montello**—pop pl NV-8
**Montello**—pop pl PA-2
**Montello**—pop pl WI-6
Montello, Lake—lake WI-6
Montello Air Strip NV-8
Montello Canyon NV-8
Montello Canyon—valley NV-8
Montello Corners—locale WI-6
Montello Creek—stream NV-8
Montello (historical)—locale NV-8
Montello JHS—school ME-1
Montello Landing Strip—airport NV-8
Montello Park MI-6
Montello Park Sch—school MI-6
Montello River WI-6
Montello River—stream WI-6
Montello Springs—spring NV-8
Montello Station (historical)—locale MA-1
**Montello (subdivision)**—pop pl MA-1
**Montello (Town of)**—pop pl WI-6
Montello Valley NV-8
Montello Well Number One—well NV-8
Montello Well Number Two—well NV-8
Montelores Bridge—bridge CO-8
Montemalaga Sch—school CA-9
Monte Maria Acad—school VA-3
Monte Mariquilla—summit PR-3
Monte Marqueno—summit PR-3
Monte Membrillo—summit PR-3
Monte Meta Cem—cemetery TX-5
Monte Mtn—summit NV-8
Monte Ne—hist pl AR-4
Monte Ne—locale AR-4
Monte Ne Branch—stream AR-4
Monte Negro—summit NM-5
Montenegro Spring—spring CA-9
Monte Negro Windmill—locale TX-5
**Monte Ne Shores**—pop pl AR-4
Monte Neva NV-8
Monte Neva Hot Springs—spring NV-8
**Monte Nido**—pop pl CA-9
Monte Nido Fire Station—locale CA-9
Monteocha—locale FL-3
Monteocha Creek—stream FL-3
Monteola—locale NY-2
Monteola—locale TX-5
Monte Palmero—summit PR-3
Monte Pond—reservoir AL-4
Monte Pond—reservoir MA-1
Monte Pond Dam—dam MA-1
Monte Prieto Ranch—locale NM-5
Monte Resaca—summit PR-3
Monterey MN-6
Monterey MS-4
Monterey NY-2
Monterey TN-4
Monterey—hist pl DE-2
Monterey—hist pl VA-3
Monterey—locale KY-4
Monterey—locale MO-7
Monterey—locale PA-2
Monterey—locale (2) TX-5
Monterey—mine UT-8
**Monterey**—pop pl AL-4
**Monterey**—pop pl AR-4
**Monterey**—pop pl CA-9
**Monterey**—pop pl IL-6
**Monterey**—pop pl IN-6
**Monterey**—pop pl IA-7
**Monterey**—pop pl KY-4
**Monterey**—pop pl LA-4
**Monterey**—pop pl MA-1
**Monterey**—pop pl MI-6
**Monterey**—pop pl MS-4
**Monterey**—pop pl NE-7
**Monterey**—pop pl NY-2
**Monterey**—pop pl (2) OH-6
**Monterey**—pop pl (3) PA-2
**Monterey**—pop pl TN-4
**Monterey**—pop pl VA-3
**Monterey**—pop pl WI-6
Monterey—uninc pl FL-3
Monterey, Lake—reservoir OH-6
Monterey Acad (historical)—school AL-4
Monterey Acres—uninc pl CA-9
**Monterey Addition (subdivision)**—pop pl UT-8
Monterey Ave Sch—school CA-9
Monterey Baptist Ch—church FL-3
Monterey Bay—bay CA-9
Monterey Bay Acad—school CA-9
**Monterey Bay Academy(Seventh Day Adventist Bdg Sch.)**—76pop pl CA-9
**Monterey Beach**—pop pl NJ-2
Monterey Bend—bend MS-4
Monterey Canyon—valley CA-9
Monterey (CCD)—cens area TN-4
Monterey Cem—cemetery AL-4
Monterey Cem—cemetery OH-6
Monterey Cem—cemetery TX-5
Monterey Cemetery MS-4
**Monterey Center**—pop pl MI-6
Monterey Ch—church AL-4
Monterey Ch—church MS-4
Monterey Ch of the Nazarene—church TN-4
Monterey City Hall—building TN-4
**Monterey (County)**—pop pl CA-9
Monterey Division—civil TN-4
Monterey Elem Sch—school IN-6
**Monterey Estates**—pop pl NY-2
**Monterey Farms (subdivision)**—pop pl DE-2
Monterey First Baptist Ch—church TN-4
Monterey Freewill Baptist Ch—church TN-4
**Monterey Heights**—pop pl AL-4
Monterey Highlands Sch—school CA-9
Monterey Hill—summit MA-1
Monterey Hills Sch—school CO-8
**Monterey Hills (subdivision)**—pop pl TN-4
Monterey Hist Dist—hist pl PA-2
Monterey Hotel—hist pl VA-3
Monterey HS—school TN-4
Monterey HS—school TX-5
Monterey Lake—lake AK-9
Monterey Lake—lake LA-4
Monterey Lake—lake TN-4
Monterey Lake—lake TX-5
Monterey Lake—reservoir TN-4
Monterey Lake Dam TN-4
Monterey Lake Dam Number One—dam TN-4
Monterey Lake Dam Number Two—dam TN-4
Monterey Lake Number One—reservoir TN-4
Monterey Lake Number Two—reservoir TN-4
Monterey (Magisterial District)—fmr MCD VA-3
Monterey Methodist Ch—church TN-4
Monterey Mine—mine AZ-5
Monterey Mine No 1—mine IL-6
Monterey Mtn—summit VA-3
Monterey-New Columbus (CCD)—cens area KY-4
Monterey Old Town Hist Dist—hist pl CA-9
Monterey Park—park AZ-5
Monterey Park—park WI-6
**Monterey Park**—pop pl CA-9
**Monterey Park**—pop pl NC-3
Monterey Park Sch—school AZ-5
Monterey Park Sch—school CA-9
**Monterey Park (subdivision)**—pop pl AL-4
Monterey Peak—summit PA-2
Monterey Peninsula Coll—school CA-9
Monterey Peninsula International Airp—airport CA-9
Monterey Place—hist pl AL-4
Monterey Point—cape CA-9
Monterey Post Office TN-4
Monterey Post Office—building TN-4
Monterey Post Office (historical)—building MS-4
Monterey Public Library—building TN-4
Monterey Road Sch—school CA-9
Monterey Sanitarium—hospital CA-9
Monterey Sch—school CA-9
Monterey Sch—school NM-5
Monterey Sch—school OH-6
Monterey Sch—school PA-2
Monterey Sch—school VA-3
Monterey Sch (historical)—school AL-4
Monterey Siding—locale IL-6
Monterey State Beach—park CA-9
**Monterey (Town of)**—pop pl MA-1
**Monterey (Township of)**—pop pl MI-6
**Monterey (Township of)**—pop pl OH-6
Monterey Village IL-6
Monterey Village IN-6
**Monterey Village**—pop pl IN-6
Monterey Village Shop Ctr—locale AZ-5
Monterey Vista Sch—school CA-9
Monterey Well—well NM-5
Monteria Lake—lake CA-9
Monterica Creek—stream OR-9
Monte Rico Ridge—ridge OR-9
**Monte Rio**—pop pl CA-9
Monte Rio Fire Trail—trail CA-9
Montero KS-7
Montero Rsvr—reservoir NV-8
**Monte Rosa**—pop pl CA-9
**Monterrey**—pop pl PR-3
Monterrey Artesian Well—well TX-5
Monterrey Banco Number 89—levee TX-5
Monterrey Park—park TX-5
Monterrey Tank—reservoir TX-5
**Monterrey Village**—pop pl MD-2
Monterrey Windmill—locale (2) TX-5
Monte Run—stream IN-6
**Monterville**—pop pl WV-2
**Monte-Sano**—pop pl AL-4
**Montesano**—pop pl CA-9
**Montesano**—pop pl WA-9
Monte Sano Baptist Ch—church AL-4
Monte Sano Bayou—stream LA-4
Monte Sano Center—locale LA-4
Monte Sano Ch—church AL-4
Monte Sano Elementary School AL-4
Monte Sano Mtn—summit AL-4
Monte Sano Post Office (historical)—building AL-4
Monte Sano Sch—school AL-4
Monte Sano Sch—school GA-3
Monte Sano State Park—park AL-4
Monte Santo FM-9
Monte Santo—post sta PR-3
Montes Creek—stream UT-8
Montes Creek Dam—dam UT-8
Montes Creek Rsvr—reservoir UT-8
Montes de Barina—summit PR-3
Montes de Caneja—summit PR-3
Montes de Hatillo—summit PR-3
Montes de San Patricio—summit PR-3
Monte Seco—other NM-5
Monte Sena Bayou LA-4
**Monte Sereno**—pop pl CA-9
Montes Hollow—valley UT-8
Monte Siesta Home—building TX-5
Monte-Sil Ch—church AL-4
Montesito Creek—stream NM-5
Montesito Sch—school NM-5
Montes La Toyosa—summit PR-3
Monte Spring—spring NV-8
Monte Springs—spring NV-8
Montessori Casa Dei Bambini—school FL-3
Montessori Childrens House—school (2) FL-3
Montessori Childrens House of Miami Lakes—school FL-3
Montessori Cooperative Early Sch—school FL-3
Montessori House—school FL-3
Montessori International Sch—school FL-3
Montessori Learning Center—school FL-3
Montessori Sch—school AL-4
Montessori Sch—school CA-9
Montessori Sch—school FL-3
Montessori Sch—school IL-6
Montessori Sch—school MA-1
Montessori Sch—school PA-2
Montessori Sch—school TX-5
Montessori Sch of Deerfield Beach—school FL-3
Montessori Sch of Fort Myers—school FL-3
Montessori Sch of Kendall—school FL-3
Montessori Sch of Miami Beach—school FL-3
Montessori Sch of Tallahassee—school FL-3
Montes Spring—spring AZ-5
Monte Swamp NC-3
**Monte Toyon**—pop pl CA-9
**Montevallo**—pop pl AL-4
**Montevallo**—pop pl MO-7
Montevallo Baptist Ch—church AL-4
Montevallo (CCD)—cens area AL-4
Montevallo Cem—cemetery AL-4
Montevallo Ch—church AL-4
Montevallo Division—civil AL-4
Montevallo Elem Sch—school AL-4
Montevallo HS—school AL-4
Montevallo Methodist Ch—church AL-4
Montevallo MS—school AL-4
Montevallo Number 1 Mine (underground)—mine AL-4
Montevallo Primary School AL-4
Montevallo Public Sch (historical)—school AL-4
**Montevallo Township**—pop pl MO-7
**Monte Verde**—pop pl NM-5
Monte Verde Sch—school CA-9
Monte Verde Windmill—locale TX-5
Monte Verita—summit ID-8
Montevideo—locale VA-3
**Montevideo**—pop pl GA-3
**Montevideo**—pop pl (2) MD-2
**Montevideo**—pop pl MN-6
Montevideo Carnegie Library—hist pl MN-6
**Montevideo (Montivedo)**—pop pl GA-3
Monteview—locale ID-8
Monteville WV-2
Monte Vista CA-9
Monte Vista WA-9
Monte Vista—hist pl PA-2
Monte Vista—hist pl VA-3
Monte Vista—locale CA-9
**Monte Vista**—pop pl AL-4
**Monte Vista**—pop pl CO-8
**Monte Vista**—pop pl FL-3
**Monte Vista**—pop pl MS-4
**Montevista**—pop pl MS-4
Monte Vista—post sta CA-9
Monte Vista Baptist Ch—church MS-4
Monte Vista Baptist Church TN-4
Monte Vista Canal—canal CO-8
Monte Vista Cem—cemetery CO-8
Montevista Cem—cemetery MS-4
Monte Vista Cem—cemetery TN-4
Monte Vista Ch—church NM-5
Monte Vista Ch—church SC-3
Monte Vista Ch—church TN-4
Monte Vista Ch—church VA-3
Montevista Ch—church VA-3
Monte Vista Christian Sch—school CA-9
**Monte Vista Estates**—pop pl CO-8
**Monte Vista Estates**—pop pl TN-4
Monte Vista Fire Station—hist pl NM-5
Monte Vista HS—school (2) CA-9
Monte Vista Lateral—canal CO-8
Monte Vista Lookout Cabin—hist pl AZ-5
Monte Vista Natl Wildlife Ref—park CO-8
Monte Vista Park—cemetery WV-2
Monte Vista Peak—summit AZ-5
Monte Vista Peak Lookout—tower AZ-5
Monte Vista Plantation House—hist pl LA-4
Montevista Post Office (historical)—building MS-4
Monte Vista Ranch—locale CA-9
Monte Vista Sch—hist pl NM-5
Monte Vista Sch—school AZ-5

Monte Vista Sch—*school* (9) CA-9
Monte Vista Sch—*school* NM-5
Monte Vista Sch—*school* UT-8
Monte Vista Sch—*school* VA-3
Montevista Sch (historical)—*school* MS-4
**Monte Vista Subdivision**—*pop pl* UT-8
*Monteviteo* GA-3
**Montevue**—*pop pl* VA-3
Montez Ditch—*canal* CO-8
Montez Rsvr—*reservoir* CO-8
Montezuma—*hist pl* VA-3
Montezuma—*locale* AZ-5
Montezuma—*locale* (3) CA-9
Montezuma—*locale* IL-6
Montezuma—*locale* NV-8
**Montezuma**—*pop pl* CO-8
**Montezuma**—*pop pl* GA-3
**Montezuma**—*pop pl* (2) IN-6
**Montezuma**—*pop pl* IA-7
**Montezuma**—*pop pl* KS-7
**Montezuma**—*pop pl* NM-5
**Montezuma**—*pop pl* NY-2
**Montezuma**—*pop pl* NC-3
**Montezuma**—*pop pl* OH-6
**Montezuma**—*pop pl* TN-4
**Montezuma**—*pop pl* VA-3
Montezuma, Lake—*lake* AZ-5
Montezuma Acad—*school* AL-4
Montezuma Airp—*airport* AZ-5
Montezuma and the Whizzers Mine—*mine* SD-7
Montezuma Bar—*bar* MS-4
Montezuma Bay—*bay* OH-6
Montezuma Bend—*bend* MS-4
Montezuma Bridge—*bridge* KY-4
Montezuma Camp—*locale* OK-5
Montezuma Canal—*canal* AZ-5
Montezuma Canyon—*valley* AZ-5
Montezuma Canyon—*valley* UT-8
Montezuma Castle Natl Monmt—*hist pl* AZ-5
Montezuma Castle Natl Monmt—*park* AZ-5
Montezuma Cave—*cave* AZ-5
Montezuma (CCD)—*cens area* GA-3
Montezuma Cem—*cemetery* NY-2
Montezuma Cem—*cemetery* OK-5
Montezuma Cem—*cemetery* TN-4
Montezuma Club—*other* CA-9
**Montezuma Creek**—*pop pl* UT-8
Montezuma Creek—*stream* CO-8
Montezuma Creek—*stream* ID-8
Montezuma Creek—*stream* OH-6
Montezuma Creek—*stream* OK-5
Montezuma Creek—*stream* UT-8
Montezuma Creek Overlook—*locale* UT-8
Montezuma Creek Sch—*school* UT-8
Montezuma Creek Trading Post—*locale* UT-8
Montezuma Cut-Off—*channel* MS-4
Montezuma Depot—*hist pl* GA-3
Montezuma Elem Sch—*school* IN-6
Montezuma Elem Sch—*school* KS-7
Montezuma Gap—*gap* NC-3
**Montezuma Gardens**—*pop pl* VA-3
*Montezuma Head* AZ-5
Montezuma Head—*summit* (2) AZ-5
Montezuma Hill—*summit* CA-9
Montezuma Hills—*range* CA-9
Montezuma (historical)—*locale* AL-4
Montezuma (historical)—*locale* SD-7
Montezuma Honor Camp—*locale* CA-9
Montezuma Hotel—*hist pl* AZ-5
Montezuma Hotel Complex—*hist pl* NM-5
Montezuma HS—*school* KS-7
Montezuma Island—*island* CA-9
Montezuma Junior High and Senior HS—*school* IN-6
Montezuma Lake—*lake* AZ-5
Montezuma Marsh—*swamp* NY-2
Montezuma Mesa—*summit* CO-8
Montezuma Mine—*mine* (2) AZ-5
Montezuma Mine—*mine* (3) CA-9
Montezuma Mine—*mine* CO-8
Montezuma Mine—*mine* KY-4
Montezuma Mine—*mine* NV-8
Montezuma Mine—*mine* UT-8
Montezuma Natl Wildlife Ref—*park* NY-2
Montezuma Pass—*gap* AZ-5
Montezuma Peak—*summit* (2) AZ-5
Montezuma Peak—*summit* CO-8
Montezuma Peak—*summit* NV-8
Montezuma Peak—*summit* UT-8
Montezuma Point—*cliff* AZ-5
Montezuma Post Office (historical)—*building* TN-4
Montezuma Ranch—*locale* AZ-5
Montezuma Range—*range* NV-8
Montezuma Ridge—*ridge* CA-9
Montezuma Sch—*school* AZ-5
Montezuma Sch—*school* (3) CA-9
Montezuma Sch—*school* NM-5
Montezumas Chair—*summit* AZ-5
Montezuma Sch (historical)—*school* TN-4
*Montezumas Head* AZ-5
Montezumas Head—*summit* AZ-5
Montezuma Sleeping—*summit* AZ-5
Montezuma Slough—*stream* CA-9
Montezuma Spring—*spring* NV-8
Montezuma Spring—*spring* OR-9
Montezuma Station—*locale* NY-2
**Montezuma Station**—*pop pl* IN-6
Montezuma Street Sch—*school* NM-5
Montezuma Tank—*reservoir* (2) AZ-5
Montezuma Towhead—*island* AR-4
**Montezuma (Town of)**—*pop pl* NY-2
**Montezuma Township**—*pop pl* KS-7
**Montezuma (Township of)**—*pop pl* IL-6
Montezuma Valley—*area* CO-8
Montezuma Valley—*basin* NV-8
Montezuma Valley—*valley* CA-9
Montezuma Valley Overlook—*locale* CO-8
Montezuma Well—*well* (2) AZ-5
Montezuma Well—*well* NM-5
Montezuma Wells—*locale* NV-8
Montfor Bridge—*bridge* NY-2
*Montford* NC-3
**Montford**—*pop pl* VA-3
Montford Area Hist Dist—*hist pl* NC-3
Montford Cove Ch—*church* NC-3
Montford Cove (Township of)—*fmr MCD* NC-3
Montford Creek—*stream* ID-8
Montford Hall—*hist pl* NC-3
**Montford Hills**—*pop pl* NC-3
Montford Lake Dam—*dam* MS-4
Montford Park—*park* NC-3
*Montford Point* NC-3
**Montford Point**—*pop pl* NC-3
Montford Sch—*school* MT-8
Montfort—*locale* TX-5
**Montfort**—*pop pl* WI-6
**Montfort Heights (subdivision)**—*pop pl* OH-6
Montfort Jones Memorial Hosp—*hospital* MS-4
**Montfort Junction**—*pop pl* WI-6
Montfort Seminary—*school* NY-2
Montgall Playground—*park* MO-7
*Montgomery* KS-7
*Montgomery* MS-4
*Montgomery* PA-2
*Montgomery* TN-4
Montgomery—*locale* CA-9
Montgomery—*locale* KY-4
Montgomery—*locale* MS-4
Montgomery—*locale* NJ-2
Montgomery—*locale* SC-3
Montgomery—*locale* VA-3
**Montgomery**—*pop pl* AL-4
**Montgomery**—*pop pl* GA-3
**Montgomery**—*pop pl* IL-6
**Montgomery**—*pop pl* IN-6
**Montgomery**—*pop pl* IA-7
**Montgomery**—*pop pl* LA-4
**Montgomery**—*pop pl* MA-1
**Montgomery**—*pop pl* MI-6
**Montgomery**—*pop pl* MN-6
**Montgomery**—*pop pl* MS-4
**Montgomery**—*pop pl* NY-2
**Montgomery**—*pop pl* OH-6
**Montgomery**—*pop pl* PA-2
**Montgomery**—*pop pl* (2) TN-4
**Montgomery**—*pop pl* TX-5
**Montgomery**—*pop pl* VT-1
**Montgomery**—*pop pl* WV-2
Montgomery, Dr. Thomas, House—*hist pl* KY-4
Montgomery, Gen. William, House—*hist pl* PA-2
Montgomery, I. T., House—*hist pl* MS-4
Montgomery, Mount—*summit* NV-8
Montgomery, Nathaniel, House—*hist pl* RI-1
Montgomery, Walter Scott, House—*hist pl* SC-3
Montgomery, William, House—*hist pl* KY-4
Montgomery Acad—*school* AL-4
Montgomery Airp—*airport* MS-4
Montgomery Archeol Site—*hist pl* MO-7
*Montgomery Area Vocational Center* AL-4
Montgomery Ave Hist Dist—*hist pl* KY-4
*Montgomery Baptist Church* MS-4
Montgomery Baptist Temple—*church* AL-4
Montgomery Bar—*bar* AL-4
Montgomery Bar Ravine—*valley* CA-9
Montgomery Basin—*basin* CA-9
Montgomery Bay—*bay* AK-9
Montgomery Bay—*bay* MI-6
Montgomery Bell Acad—*school* TN-4
Montgomery Bell Bridge—*bridge* TN-4
Montgomery Bell State Park—*park* TN-4
Montgomery Blair HS—*school* MD-2
Montgomery Borough—*civil* PA-2
Montgomery Boys Club—*building* AL-4
*Montgomery Branch* IN-6
Montgomery Branch—*stream* AR-4
Montgomery Branch—*stream* IN-6
Montgomery Branch—*stream* (2) KY-4
Montgomery Branch—*stream* TN-4
Montgomery Branch—*stream* TX-5
Montgomery Bridge—*bridge* GA-3
Montgomery Bridge—*bridge* KY-4
Montgomery Bridge—*bridge* OR-9
Montgomery Brook—*stream* NH-1
Montgomery Canyon—*valley* (2) CA-9
Montgomery Canyon—*valley* NV-8
Montgomery Canyon—*valley* WY-8
Montgomery Catholic HS—*school* AL-4
Montgomery (CCD)—*cens area* AL-4
Montgomery (CCD)—*cens area* GA-3
Montgomery (CCD)—*cens area* TX-5
Montgomery Cem—*cemetery* (3) AL-4
Montgomery Cem—*cemetery* GA-3
Montgomery Cem—*cemetery* (2) IL-6
Montgomery Cem—*cemetery* (2) IN-6
Montgomery Cem—*cemetery* (2) KS-7
Montgomery Cem—*cemetery* (5) KY-4
Montgomery Cem—*cemetery* (7) MS-4
Montgomery Cem—*cemetery* (2) MO-7
Montgomery Cem—*cemetery* (2) OH-6
Montgomery Cem—*cemetery* OR-9
Montgomery Cem—*cemetery* PA-2
Montgomery Cem—*cemetery* (8) TN-4
Montgomery Cem—*cemetery* (6) TX-5
Montgomery Cem—*cemetery* (2) VA-3
**Montgomery Center**—*pop pl* (2) VT-1
Montgomery Center Cem—*cemetery* MA-1
Montgomery Ch—*church* IL-6
Montgomery Ch—*church* KY-4
Montgomery Ch—*church* MA-1
Montgomery Ch—*church* MS-4
Montgomery Ch—*church* (2) MO-7
Montgomery Ch—*church* PA-2
Montgomery Ch—*church* VA-3
Montgomery Chapel—*church* (2) AR-4
Montgomery Chapel—*church* IN-6
Montgomery Chapel—*church* MD-2
Montgomery Chapel—*church* MS-4
*Montgomery Chapel God of Prophecy Ch* MS-4
*Montgomery Church* AL-4
Montgomery City—*locale* CA-9
**Montgomery City**—*pop pl* MO-7
Montgomery Coll—*school* MD-2
Montgomery Corner—*locale* GA-3
Montgomery Correctional Institute—*building* GA-3
Montgomery Country Club—*other* AL-4
Montgomery Country Day Sch—*school* PA-2
Montgomery County—*civil* KS-7
**Montgomery County**—*pop pl* AL-4
**Montgomery (County)**—*pop pl* AR-4
**Montgomery (County)**—*pop pl* GA-3
**Montgomery (County)**—*pop pl* IL-6
**Montgomery County**—*pop pl* IN-6
**Montgomery (County)**—*pop pl* KY-4
**Montgomery (County)**—*pop pl* MD-2
**Montgomery County**—*pop pl* MS-4
**Montgomery County**—*pop pl* MO-7
**Montgomery (County)**—*pop pl* NY-2
**Montgomery County**—*pop pl* NC-3
**Montgomery (County)**—*pop pl* OH-6
**Montgomery County**—*pop pl* PA-2
**Montgomery County**—*pop pl* TN-4
**Montgomery (County)**—*pop pl* TX-5
**Montgomery (County)**—*pop pl* VA-3
Montgomery County Airp—*airport* NC-3
Montgomery County Community Coll—*school* PA-2
Montgomery County Courthouse—*building* MS-4
Montgomery County Courthouse—*building* TN-4
Montgomery County Courthouse—*hist pl* AR-4
Montgomery County Courthouse—*hist pl* GA-3
Montgomery County Courthouse—*hist pl* IA-7
Montgomery County Courthouse—*hist pl* NC-3
Montgomery County Courthouse—*hist pl* OH-6
Montgomery County Courthouse Hist Dist—*hist pl* MD-2
Montgomery County General Hosp—*hospital* MD-2
*Montgomery County Geriatric and Rehabilitation Center* PA-2
Montgomery County Health Center—*hospital* AL-4
Montgomery County Home—*locale* TN-4
Montgomery County HS—*school* AL-4
Montgomery County Jail and Sheriff's Residence—*hist pl* IN-6
Montgomery County Park—*park* CA-9
Montgomery County Prison Farm—*locale* PA-2
Montgomery County State Lake—*reservoir* KS-7
Montgomery County State Lake Dam—*dam* KS-7
Montgomery County State Park—*park* KS-7
Montgomery County Vocational Technical Sch—*school* TN-4
Montgomery Court—*hist pl* CO-8
*Montgomery Court House* MD-2
Montgomery Covered Bridge—*hist pl* VT-1
*Montgomery Creek* CO-8
*Montgomery Creek* NC-3
*Montgomery Creek* TN-4
**Montgomery Creek**—*pop pl* CA-9
Montgomery Creek—*stream* AL-4
Montgomery Creek—*stream* AR-4
Montgomery Creek—*stream* (7) CA-9
Montgomery Creek—*stream* CO-8
Montgomery Creek—*stream* GA-3
Montgomery Creek—*stream* ID-8
Montgomery Creek—*stream* IN-6
Montgomery Creek—*stream* (2) IA-7
Montgomery Creek—*stream* (5) KY-4
Montgomery Creek—*stream* MI-6
Montgomery Creek—*stream* MO-7
Montgomery Creek—*stream* (3) OR-9
Montgomery Creek—*stream* PA-2
Montgomery Creek—*stream* SC-3
Montgomery Creek—*stream* (2) TX-5
Montgomery Creek—*stream* WI-6
Montgomery Creek Cave—*cave* AL-4
Montgomery Creek Rancheria (Indian Reservation)—*1 (1980)* CA-9
*Montgomery Dam* MA-1
Montgomery Dam—*dam* AL-4
Montgomery Dam—*dam* (2) PA-2
*Montgomery Ditch* IN-6
Montgomery Ditch—*canal* (3) IN-6
Montgomery Division—*civil* AL-4
Montgomery Draw—*valley* WY-8
Montgomery East Exchange Park—*park* AL-4
Montgomery East Industrial Park—*locale* AL-4
Montgomery East Plaza Shop Ctr—*locale* AL-4
**Montgomery East (subdivision)**—*pop pl* AL-4
Montgomery Elem Sch—*school* MS-4
Montgomery Elem Sch—*school* PA-2
**Montgomery Estates (subdivision)**—*pop pl* TN-4
**Montgomery Ferry**—*pop pl* (2) PA-2
Montgomery Flat—*flat* CA-9
Montgomery Flats—*flat* CO-8
Montgomery Fork—*stream* TN-4
Montgomery Furnace (historical)—*locale* TN-4
**Montgomery Gardens**—*pop pl* TX-5
Montgomery Glade—*flat* CA-9
Montgomery Golf Course—*locale* AL-4
Montgomery-Grand-Liberty Streets Hist Dist—*hist pl* NY-2
Montgomery Gulch—*valley* CA-9
Montgomery Gulch—*valley* CO-8
Montgomery Gulch—*valley* MT-8
Montgomery Gulch—*valley* WA-9
Montgomery Hall—*hist pl* MS-4
Montgomery Hall Park—*park* VA-3
**Montgomery Heights**—*pop pl* OH-6
**Montgomery Heights**—*pop pl* WV-2
Montgomery Heights Sch—*school* CA-9
**Montgomery Hill**—*pop pl* AL-4
Montgomery Hill—*summit* AR-4
Montgomery Hill—*summit* CA-9
Montgomery Hill—*summit* GA-3
Montgomery Hill—*summit* KY-4
Montgomery Hill—*summit* MT-8
Montgomery Hill—*summit* ND-7
Montgomery Hill Baptist Church—*hist pl* AL-4
Montgomery Hill Ch—*church* AL-4
Montgomery Hill Detention Home—*building* PA-2
*Montgomery Hill Landing* AL-4
Montgomery Hill Landing—*locale* AL-4
**Montgomery Hills**—*pop pl* MD-2
Montgomery Hills JHS—*school* MD-2
Montgomery (historical)—*locale* KS-7
**Montgomery (historical)**—*pop pl* TN-4
Montgomery Historic House Museum—*building* MS-4
Montgomery Hollow—*valley* MD-2
Montgomery Hollow—*valley* (2) MO-7
Montgomery Hollow—*valley* NY-2
Montgomery Hollow—*valley* (2) TN-4
Montgomery Hosp—*hospital* PA-2
Montgomery House—*hist pl* DE-2
Montgomery House—*hist pl* (2) KY-4
Montgomery House—*hist pl* MS-4
Montgomery House—*hist pl* PA-2
Montgomery HS—*school* AL-4
Montgomery HS—*school* MD-2
Montgomery Hunting Club Lake—*reservoir* AL-4
*Montgomery Industrial School* AL-4
Montgomery Infirmary (historical)—*hospital* AL-4
Montgomery Institute (historical)—*school* (2) AL-4
Montgomery International Speedway—*locale* AL-4
*Montgomery Island* AL-4
Montgomery Island—*island* AR-4
Montgomery Island (historical)—*island* PA-2
Montgomery-Janes-Whittaker House—*hist pl* AL-4
Montgomery JHS—*school* CA-9
**Montgomery Junction**—*pop pl* TN-4
Montgomery Junior Coll—*school* MD-2
Montgomery Knob—*summit* VA-3
**Montgomery Knolls**—*pop pl* (2) MD-2
Montgomery Knolls Sch—*school* MD-2
Montgomery Lake—*lake* AL-4
Montgomery Lake—*lake* FL-3
Montgomery Lake—*lake* LA-4
Montgomery Lake—*lake* MO-7
Montgomery Lake—*lake* NY-2
Montgomery Lake—*lake* ND-7
Montgomery Lake—*lake* (2) WI-6
Montgomery Lake—*reservoir* MS-4
Montgomery Lake—*reservoir* TX-5
*Montgomery Lake Dam* IN-6
Montgomery Lake Dam—*dam* AL-4
Montgomery Lake Dam—*dam* MS-4
Montgomery-Liman House—*hist pl* OK-5
Montgomery Locks And Dam—*dam* PA-2
Montgomery Lookout Tower—*tower* MS-4
Montgomery Mall—*locale* PA-2
Montgomery Mall Shop Ctr—*locale* AL-4
Montgomery Meadow—*flat* CA-9
Montgomery Memorial Methodist Ch—*church* MS-4
Montgomery Memorial Park—*cemetery* WV-2
Montgomery Mine—*mine* AR-4
Montgomery Mine—*mine* (2) ID-8
Montgomery Mine—*mine* NM-5
Montgomery Mtn—*summit* AR-4
Montgomery Mtn—*summit* ME-1
Montgomery Mtn—*summit* NV-8
Montgomery Number Three Spring—*spring* CA-9
Montgomery Number Two Spring—*spring* CA-9
Montgomery Opera House—*hist pl* MO-7
Montgomery Park—*flat* MT-8
Montgomery Park—*park* NJ-2
**Montgomery Park (subdivision)**—*pop pl* MS-4
Montgomery Pass—*gap* CO-8
Montgomery Pass—*gap* NV-8
Montgomery Peak—*summit* CA-9
Montgomery Pinetum—*park* CT-1
Montgomery Place—*hist pl* NY-2
Montgomery Place Landing (historical)—*locale* MS-4
Montgomery Point—*cape* AR-4
Montgomery Point—*cape* (2) ME-1
Montgomery Point—*cape* MI-6
Montgomery Pond—*lake* GA-3
Montgomery Pond—*reservoir* SC-3
Montgomery Post Office (historical)—*building* MS-4
Montgomery Potrero—*flat* CA-9
Montgomery Primitive Baptist Ch—*church* AL-4
Montgomery Public Library—*building* AL-4
Montgomery Public Library East Branch—*building* AL-4
*Montgomery Public School* AL-4
Montgomery Ranch—*locale* CA-9
Montgomery Ranch—*locale* FL-3
Montgomery Ranch—*locale* OR-9
Montgomery Ranch—*locale* (3) TX-5
Montgomery Rapids—*rapids* OR-9
Montgomery Recreation Center—*building* AL-4
Montgomery Ridge—*ridge* (3) CA-9
Montgomery Ridge—*ridge* WA-9
Montgomery Road Interchange—*crossing* AZ-5
Montgomery Ross Ditch—*canal* IN-6
Montgomery Rsvr—*reservoir* CO-8
Montgomery Run—*stream* (2) PA-2
Montgomery Run—*stream* VA-3
Montgomery Run—*stream* WV-2
Montgomery Saltbox Houses—*hist pl* OH-6
Montgomerys Cabin—*locale* NV-8
Montgomerys Cabin—*locale* OR-9
Montgomery Sch—*school* (3) CA-9
Montgomery Sch—*school* DC-2
Montgomery Sch—*school* IL-6
Montgomery Sch—*school* (2) MI-6
Montgomery Sch—*school* (2) MO-7
Montgomery Sch—*school* NJ-2
Montgomery Sch—*school* NM-5
Montgomery Sch—*school* TN-4
Montgomery Sch—*school* TX-5
Montgomery Sch (abandoned)—*school* PA-2
Montgomery Sch (historical)—*school* (2) AL-4
Montgomery Sch (historical)—*school* (3) MO-7
Montgomery Sch (historical)—*school* PA-2
*Montgomerys Ferry* PA-2
Montgomery-Shoshone Mine—*mine* NV-8
Montgomery Siding—*locale* TX-5
Montgomerys Lake—*reservoir* AL-4
Montgomery Slough—*gut* FL-3
Montgomery Slough—*gut* NC-3
Montgomery's Mill—*hist pl* KY-4
**Montgomerys Mill**—*pop pl* KY-4
Montgomerys Millpond—*reservoir* NC-3
Montgomery Spring—*spring* AR-4
Montgomery Spring—*spring* (3) CA-9
Montgomery Spring—*spring* CO-8
Montgomery Spring—*spring* MT-8
Montgomery Square—*locale* PA-2
**Montgomery Square**—*pop pl* MD-2
Montgomery Stadium—*locale* AZ-5
Montgomery State Fishing Lake—*park* KS-7
Montgomery Street-Columbus Circle Hist Dist—*hist pl* NY-2
Montgomery Street Sch—*hist pl* KY-4
Montgomery Substation—*locale* AZ-5
Montgomery Tank—*reservoir* NM-5
Montgomery Technical Institute—*school* NC-3
Montgomery Towhead—*island* AR-4
**Montgomery (Town of)**—*pop pl* MA-1
**Montgomery (Town of)**—*pop pl* NY-2
**Montgomery (Town of)**—*pop pl* VT-1
Montgomery Township—*civil* (2) MO-7
**Montgomery Township**—*pop pl* MO-7
Montgomery (Township of)—*fmr MCD* (2) AR-4
Montgomery (Township of)—*other* OH-6
**Montgomery (Township of)**—*pop pl* (2) IL-6
**Montgomery (Township of)**—*pop pl* (3) IN-6
**Montgomery (Township of)**—*pop pl* MN-6
**Montgomery (Township of)**—*pop pl* NJ-2
**Montgomery (Township of)**—*pop pl* (3) OH-6
**Montgomery (Township of)**—*pop pl* (3) PA-2
Montgomery Union Station and Trainshed—*hist pl* AL-4
Montgomery Unitarian Ch—*church* AL-4
Montgomery Village—*CDP* MD-2
Montgomery Village—*post sta* CA-9
*Montgomeryville* PA-2
Montgomeryville—*locale* WI-6
**Montgomeryville**—*pop pl* PA-2
Montgomeryville Airp—*airport* PA-2
Montgomeryville Ch—*church* PA-2
Montgomeryville Golf Course—*locale* PA-2
Montgomeryville Mall—*locale* PA-2
Montgomeryville (RR name for Adrian)—*other* PA-2
Montgomeryville Sch—*school* PA-2
Montgomeryville Station—*locale* PA-2
Montgomery Ward-Alabama Power Company Bldg—*hist pl* AL-4
Montgomery Ward Bldg—*hist pl* ID-8
Montgomery Ward Bldg—*hist pl* IN-6
Montgomery Ward Bldg—*hist pl* OK-5
Montgomery Ward Bldg—*hist pl* PA-2
Montgomery Ward Bldg—*hist pl* TX-5
Montgomery Ward & Company—*hist pl* OR-9
Montgomery Ward Company Complex—*hist pl* IL-6
Montgomery Water Filtration Plant—*building* AL-4
Montgomery-Wehrman Airp—*airport* MO-7
**Montgomery White Oak**—*pop pl* MD-2
Montgomery-Wilkins Cem—*cemetery* LA-4
Montgomery Windmill—*locale* TX-5
**Montgomery Woods**—*pop pl* DE-2
Montgomery Woods State Park—*park* CA-9
Montgomery Worsted Mills—*hist pl* NY-2
Montgomery Youth Facility—*building* AL-4
Montgomery Zoo—*locale* AL-4
Monthalia—*locale* TX-5
Monthalia Ch—*church* TX-5
Mont Helena—*locale* MS-4
Mont Helena Post Office (historical)—*building* MS-4
Montholia (historical)—*locale* MS-4
Monti—*locale* IA-7
*Monti Bay* NY-2
Monti Bay—*bay* AK-9
*Monticello* MO-7
*Monticello* TN-4
Monticello—*building* VA-3
Monticello—*hist pl* KY-4
Monticello—*hist pl* VA-3
Monticello—*locale* IA-7
Monticello—*locale* KY-4
Monticello—*other* NY-2
**Monticello**—*pop pl* AL-4
**Monticello**—*pop pl* AR-4
**Monticello**—*pop pl* FL-3
**Monticello**—*pop pl* GA-3
**Monticello**—*pop pl* IL-6
**Monticello**—*pop pl* IN-6
**Monticello**—*pop pl* IA-7
**Monticello**—*pop pl* KS-7
**Monticello**—*pop pl* (2) KY-4
**Monticello**—*pop pl* LA-4
**Monticello**—*pop pl* ME-1
**Monticello**—*pop pl* MN-6
**Monticello**—*pop pl* MS-4
**Monticello**—*pop pl* MO-7
**Monticello**—*pop pl* NM-5
**Monticello**—*pop pl* NY-2
**Monticello**—*pop pl* NC-3
**Monticello**—*pop pl* OH-6
**Monticello**—*pop pl* PA-2
**Monticello**—*pop pl* SC-3
**Monticello**—*pop pl* TN-4
**Monticello**—*pop pl* TX-5
**Monticello**—*pop pl* UT-8
**Monticello**—*pop pl* WI-6
Monticello, Lake—*reservoir* VA-3
Monticello And Sangamon Valley Railway Museum—*other* IL-6
Monticello Arcade—*hist pl* VA-3
Monticello Baptist Ch—*church* MS-4
Monticello Box—*gap* NM-5
Monticello Canyon—*valley* NM-5
Monticello (CCD)—*cens area* FL-3
Monticello (CCD)—*cens area* GA-3
Monticello (CCD)—*cens area* KY-4
Monticello Cem—*cemetery* CA-9
Monticello Cem—*cemetery* IL-6
Monticello Cem—*cemetery* KS-7
Monticello Cem—*cemetery* NM-5
Monticello Cem—*cemetery* WI-6
Monticello Ch—*church* AL-4
Monticello Ch—*church* GA-3
Monticello Ch—*church* KS-7
Monticello Ch—*church* KY-4
Monticello Ch—*church* NC-3
Monticello Ch—*church* TX-5
Monticello City Cem—*cemetery* UT-8
Monticello City Number One Dam—*dam* UT-8
Monticello City Number One Rsvr—*reservoir* UT-8
Monticello Community Ditch—*canal* NM-5
Monticello Dam—*dam* CA-9
Monticello Division—*civil* UT-8
Monticello Elem Sch—*school* KS-7
Monticello Elem Sch—*school* MS-4
Monticello Elem Sch—*school* NC-3
Monticello Farm—*locale* AR-4
Monticello Fire Control HQ (fire tower)—*tower* FL-3
Monticello First Baptist Ch—*church* MS-4
**Monticello Forest**—*pop pl* VA-3
Monticello Golf Club—*other* IL-6
Monticello Hist Dist—*hist pl* FL-3
**Monticello (historical)**—*pop pl* NC-3
Monticello Historic Commercial District—*hist pl* KY-4
Monticello HS—*hist pl* GA-3
Monticello HS—*school* MS-4
Monticello HS—*school* UT-8
Monticello JHS—*school* OH-6
Monticello JHS—*school* WA-9
Monticello Lake—*lake* UT-8
Monticello Lake Dam—*dam* UT-8
Monticello Med Ctr Heliport—*airport* WA-9
Monticello Memorial Park—*cemetery* VA-3
Monticello Methodist Church—*hist pl* SC-3
*Monticello Mills* PA-2
Monticello North Main Street Hist Dist—*hist pl* AR-4
Monticello Park—*park* TX-5
**Monticello Park**—*pop pl* VA-3
Monticello P.O. (historical)—*locale* AL-4
Monticello Point Archeol District—*hist pl* NM-5
Monticello Post Office—*building* UT-8
Monticello Raceway—*other* NY-2
*Monticello Reservoir* CA-9
Monticello Residence Sch—*school* CA-9
Monticello-Salem (CCD)—*cens area* SC-3
Monticello Sch—*school* CA-9
Monticello Sch—*school* ME-1
Monticello Sch—*school* MO-7
Monticello Sch—*school* NC-3
Monticello Sch—*school* UT-8
*Monticello's Meadow Branch* VA-3
Monticello Station—*locale* ME-1
Monticello Store and Post Office—*hist pl* SC-3
**Monticello (subdivision)**—*pop pl* NC-3
**Monticello (subdivision)**—*pop pl* TN-4
**Monticello (Thomas Jefferson Home)**—*pop pl* VA-3
**Monticello (Town of)**—*pop pl* ME-1
**Monticello (Town of)**—*pop pl* WI-6
**Monticello Township**—*pop pl* KS-7
**Monticello (Township of)**—*pop pl* IL-6
**Monticello (Township of)**—*pop pl* MN-6
Monticello United Methodist Ch—*church* MS-4
**Monticello Village**—*pop pl* VA-3
**Monticello Woods**—*pop pl* VA-3
**Monticello Woods (subdivision)**—*pop pl* NC-3
Monticito Sch—*school* CA-9
**Mont Ida**—*pop pl* KS-7
Mont Ida Cem—*cemetery* KS-7
Mont Ida Elem Sch—*school* KS-7
**Montier**—*pop pl* MO-7
Montier Township—*civil* MO-7
*Montieth* GA-3
*Montieth* IA-7
Montieth Ranch—*locale* NM-5
*Montieth Rock* OR-9
Montini Ranch—*locale* ID-8
*Montivedio* GA-3
Montivedio—*other* GA-3
Montivilla—*locale* FL-3
Montjoys Landing (historical)—*locale* MS-4
Montlake—*lake* TN-4
Montlake Bridge—*hist pl* WA-9
Montlake Cut—*channel* WA-9
Montlake Lookout Tower—*locale* TN-4
*Montlake Number Eight Mine* TN-4
Montlake Playground—*park* WA-9
Montlake Post Office (historical)—*building* TN-4
Montlake Public Shooting Center—*locale* TN-4
Montlake Sch—*school* WA-9
Mont La Salle Sch—*school* CA-9
Montlawn Memorial Park—*cemetery* NC-3
*Montllair* ND-7
Montlure Camp—*locale* AZ-5
Mont Milner Lake—*reservoir* (2) TN-4
Mont Milner Lake Dam—*dam* TN-4
**Montmorenci**—*pop pl* IN-6
**Montmorenci**—*pop pl* PA-2
**Montmorenci**—*pop pl* SC-3
Montmorenci Ch—*church* NC-3
Montmorenci Sch—*school* PA-2
*Mont Morency* PA-2
Montmorency Cem—*cemetery* MI-6
**Montmorency (County)**—*pop pl* MI-6
**Montmorency (Township of)**—*pop pl* IL-6
**Montmorency (Township of)**—*pop pl* MI-6
**Montoco**—*pop pl* KY-4
Montogomery, Lake—*lake* SD-7
*Montogomery High School* MS-4
Montogue Creek—*stream* MO-7
**Montoma**—*pop pl* NY-2
Montones (Barrio)—*fmr MCD* PR-3
**Montongo**—*pop pl* AR-4
Montonia, Lake—*lake* NC-3
*Montopolis* TX-5
**Montopolis**—*pop pl* TX-5
Montopolis Bridge—*bridge* TX-5
*Montora Mountain* CA-9
*Montora Point* CA-9
Montosa Basin—*basin* AZ-5
Montosa Camp—*locale* NM-5
Montosa Canyon—*valley* (2) AZ-5
Montosa Canyon—*valley* NM-5
Montosa Draw—*valley* NM-5
Montosa Mine—*mine* AZ-5
Montosa Mtn—*summit* NM-5
Montosa Tank—*reservoir* NM-5
Montoso, Cerro—*summit* AZ-5
Montoso (Barrio)—*fmr MCD* (2) PR-3
Montoso Peak—*summit* NM-5
Montoso Tank—*reservoir* NM-5
**Montour**—*pop pl* ID-8
**Montour**—*pop pl* IA-7
**Montour**—*pop pl* PA-2
Montour Ch—*church* PA-2
**Montour County**—*pop pl* PA-2
Montour Creek—*stream* PA-2
**Montour Falls**—*pop pl* NY-2
Montour Falls Hist Dist—*hist pl* NY-2
Montour Heights Country Club—*other* PA-2
Montour HS—*school* PA-2
Montour Joint Sch—*school* PA-2
Montour Junction—*other* PA-2
**Montour Junction**—*pop pl* PA-2

Moody Lake—reservoir AL-4
Moody Lake—reservoir NC-3
Moody Lake—reservoir TX-5
Moody Lake—swamp MI-6
Moody Lake Dam—dam (2) AL-4
Moody Landing—locale GA-3
Moody Lateral—canal IN-6
Moody Ledge—summit NH-1
Moody-Leon Ch—church TX-5
Moody Meadow—flat ID-8
Moody Meadows—flat CA-9
Moody Mill Creek—stream AL-4
Moody Mill Creek—stream NC-3
Moody Millpond—reservoir MS-4
Moody Moore Hollow—valley WV-2
**Moody Mountain**—pop pl ME-1
Moody Mtn—summit (4) ME-1
Moody Mtn—summit NV-8
Moody Mtn—summit (2) NH-1
Moody Mtn—summit NC-3
Moody Oil Field—oilfield TX-5
Moody Old River—lake AR-4
Moody Park—flat CO-8
Moody Park—park NH-1
Moody Park—park NJ-2
Moody Park—park TX-5
Moody Peak—summit NV-8
Moody Point—cape FL-3
Moody Point—cape ME-1
**Moody Point**—pop pl ME-1
Moody Point—summit AZ-5
Moody Pond PA-2
Moody Pond—lake FL-3
Moody Pond—lake (3) ME-1
Moody Pond—lake MA-1
Moody Pond—lake NH-1
Moody Pond—lake NY-2
Moody Prospect—mine TN-4
Moody Ranch—locale CA-9
Moody Ranch—locale TX-5
Moody Ridge—ridge (2) CA-9
Moody Road Park—park GA-3
Moody Run—stream IA-7
Moody Run—stream WV-2
Moodys AL-4
Moodys—locale OK-5
Moodys Branch AL-4
Moody Sch—school CT-1
Moody Sch—school ID-8
Moody Sch—school IL-6
Moody Sch—school KS-7
Moody Sch—school ME-1
Moody Sch—school (2) MA-1
Moody Sch—school MI-6
Moody Sch—school MN-6
Moody Sch—school NE-7
Moody Sch—school VA-3
**Moodys Chapel**—pop pl AL-4
Moodys Chapel Cem—cemetery AL-4
Moodys Chapel Church AL-4
Moody Sch (historical)—school AL-4
Moody Sch (historical)—school MO-7
Moody School (abandoned)—locale OR-9
Moodys Corner MA-1
Moodys Corner—locale VA-3
**Moodys Crossroads**—pop pl AL-4
Moodys Ferry (historical)—locale NC-3
Moodys Fork TN-4
Moodys Fork—stream TN-4
Moodys Fork - in part TN-4
Moodys Island—island TX-5
Moody (Site)—locale CA-9
Moodys Lake—lake MS-4
Moodys Lake—reservoir AL-4
Moodys Landing—locale MS-4
Moodys Landing Rec Area—park MS-4
Moody Slough—stream AL-4
Moodys Pass—gap TX-5
Moodys Point—cape NH-1
Moodys Pond MA-1
Moodys Pond—reservoir AL-4
Moody Spring NV-8
Moody Spring—spring AZ-5
Moody Spring—spring (2) CA-9
Moody Spring—spring MA-1
Moody Spring—spring NV-8
Moody Spring—spring (2) OR-9
Moody Spring—spring SC-3
Moody Springs KS-7
Moody Springs—spring CA-9
Moodys Run PA-2
Moodys Sch (historical)—school (2) AL-4
Moody Stamp—gap NC-3
Moody State Sch—school TX-5
Moody Station WA-9
Moody Swamp—swamp ID-8
Moody Tabernacle—church AL-4
Moody Tank—reservoir AZ-5
Moody Tank—reservoir NM-5
Moody Temple CME Ch—church AL-4
Moody-Tillman Cem—cemetery GA-3
Moody Top—summit NC-3
Moody Valley—valley NE-7
**Moodyville**—pop pl TN-4
Moodyville Baptist Ch—church TN-4
Moodyville Cem—cemetery KS-7
Moodyville (historical)—locale KS-7
Moodyville Post Office (historical)—building TN-4
Moodyville Sch (historical)—school TN-4
Moodyville Springs KS-7
Moody Wash—valley UT-8
**Mooers**—pop pl (2) NY-2
Mooers, Frederick Mitchell, House—hist pl CA-9
Mooers Camp Meeting Association—locale NY-2
**Mooers Forks**—pop pl NY-2
Mooers Lake—lake MN-6
**Mooers (Town of)**—pop pl NY-2
Moof FM-9
Moog Gulch—valley CO-8
Mooheau Park—park HI-9
Moohnton AL-4
Mooiki—civil (2) HI-9
M-O Oil Field—oilfield WY-8
Mook—locale KY-4
Mook Cem—cemetery WI-6
Mook Creek—stream TN-4
Mookini Heiau—hist pl HI-9
Mookini Heiau—locale HI-9
Mook Spring—spring TN-4
Moolack Beach—beach OR-9
Moolack Butte—summit OR-9
Moolack Creek—stream ID-8
Moolack Creek—stream (2) OR-9
Moolack Flat—flat OR-9
Moolack Lake—lake OR-9
Moolack Mtn—summit OR-9
Moolack Spring—spring WA-9
Moole Ditch—canal HI-9
Mo'olelo Pali HI-9
Moolelo Pali—cliff HI-9
Moole Stream—stream HI-9
Mooley Hollow Run—stream PA-2
**Mooleyville**—pop pl KY-4
Mooliuvaa Cove—bay AS-9
Mool Mool Spring—spring WA-9
Mooloa—civil (2) HI-9
Mooloa—summit HI-9
Mooloa Falls—falls HI-9
Moolock, Lake—lake WA-9
Moolock Creek—stream ID-8
Mooman Creek—stream VA-3
**Moomaw Corner**—pop pl NE-7
Moomaw Glacier—glacier CO-8
Moomoku—civil HI-9
Moomomi—bay HI-9
Moomomi—locale HI-9
Moomooiki Gulch—valley HI-9
Moomoonui Gulch—valley HI-9
Moomuku—civil HI-9
Moomuku Gulch—valley HI-9
Moon IL-6
Moon—locale KY-4
Moon—locale OK-5
Moon—locale SD-7
**Moon**—pop pl IL-6
**Moon**—pop pl MS-4
**Moon**—pop pl PA-2
**Moon**—pop pl VA-3
**Moon**—pop pl WI-6
Moon, Darius B., House—hist pl MI-6
Moon, D. R., Memorial Library—hist pl WI-6
Moon, Lake of the Fallen—lake CA-9
Moon, Owen, Farm—hist pl VT-1
Moon, Valley of the—basin AZ-5
Moona—locale WA-9
**Moonachie**—pop pl NJ-2
Moonachie Creek—stream NJ-2
Moonakis River MA-1
Moonakiss River Quastinet River MA-1
Moon Anchor Mine—mine AZ-5
Moon and Hamilton Drain—canal MI-6
Moon Barcley Ditch—canal IN-6
Moon Bay—bay MD-2
**Moon Beach**—pop pl NY-2
Moonbeam Island—island PA-2
Moonbeam Lake—lake MI-6
Moon Beem Mine—mine CO-8
Moon Block—hist pl NE-7
Moon Bluffs—cliff AR-4
Moon Bottom—bend AL-4
Moon Bottom—bend UT-8
Moon Branch—stream IN-6
Moon Branch—stream KS-7
Moon Branch—stream TN-4
Moon Branch—stream TX-5
Moon Branch Creek KS-7
Moon Brook—stream IN-6
Moon Brook—stream NY-2
Moon Brook—stream VT-1
Moon Brook Country Club—other NY-2
Moon Canyon—valley AZ-5
Moon Canyon—valley CA-9
Moon Canyon—valley (2) CO-8
Moon Canyon—valley NM-5
Moon Canyon—valley OR-9
Moon Canyon—valley UT-8
Moon Canyon—valley WA-9
Moon Cave—cave (2) AL-4
Moon Cem—cemetery (2) AL-4
Moon Cem—cemetery AR-4
Moon Cem—cemetery GA-3
Moon Cem—cemetery IN-6
Moon Cem—cemetery IA-7
Moon Cem—cemetery (2) KY-4
Moon Cem—cemetery MD-2
Moon Cem—cemetery MI-6
Moon Cem—cemetery OH-6
Moon Cem—cemetery TN-4
Moon Cem—cemetery TX-5
Moon Cem—cemetery VA-3
Moon Change Swamp—swamp GA-3
Moon Channel—channel NJ-2
Moon Channel—channel PA-2
Moon Chapel—church (2) MS-4
Moon Chapel (historical)—church MS-4
Moon Church AL-4
Moon Chute—lake AR-4
Moon Corner—locale VA-3
Moon Cove—bay AR-4
Moon Crater—crater AZ-5
Moon Creek—channel SC-3
Moon Creek—stream AK-9
Moon Creek—stream AZ-5
Moon Creek—stream CA-9
Moon Creek—stream CO-8
Moon Creek—stream (4) ID-8
Moon Creek—stream IL-6
Moon Creek—stream IN-6
Moon Creek—stream (2) IA-7
Moon Creek—stream KS-7
Moon Creek—stream MD-2
Moon Creek—stream MO-7
Moon Creek—stream (3) MT-8
Moon Creek—stream NE-7
Moon Creek—stream NC-3
Moon Creek—stream (5) OR-9
Moon Creek—stream TN-4
Moon Creek—stream VA-3
Moon Creek—stream (2) WA-9
Moon Creek—stream WI-6
Moon Creek—stream WY-8
Moon Creek Cem—cemetery OR-9
Moon Creek Sch—school MT-8
Moon Creek Sch—school NE-7
**Moon Crest**—pop pl PA-2
Mooncrest Ranch—locale WY-8
Moon Crest Sch—school PA-2
Moon Curve—locale TN-4
Moon Dam—dam OR-9
Moon Ditch—canal (3) IN-6
Moon-Dominick House—hist pl SC-3
Moon Drain—stream MI-6
Moon Draw—valley SD-7
Moondrop Lake—lake GA-3
**Moone**—pop pl IL-6
Moone Creek—stream WY-8
Moones Creek VA-3
Moone Spring—spring WY-8
Mooney (2) IN-6
Mooney—locale TN-4
Mooney, Edward, House—hist pl NY-2
Mooney, Mount—summit CA-9
Mooney, William C., House—hist pl OH-6
Mooney Ave Sch—school LA-4
Mooney Basin—basin NV-8
Mooney Basin Summit—gap NV-8
Mooney Basin Well—well NV-8
Mooney Bay—bay NY-2
Mooney Branch—stream (2) AL-4
Mooney Branch—stream GA-3
Mooney Branch—stream IL-6
Mooney Branch—stream MS-4
Mooney Branch—stream (2) MO-7
Mooney Branch—stream (2) NC-3
Mooney Branch—stream TN-4
Mooney Bridge—other MO-7
Mooney Canyon—valley AZ-5
Mooney Canyon—valley CA-9
Mooney Cem—cemetery AR-4
Mooney Cem—cemetery IL-6
Mooney Cem—cemetery KY-4
Mooney Cem—cemetery NC-3
Mooney Cem—cemetery TN-4
Mooney Coulee—valley MT-8
Mooney Creek—stream AL-4
Mooney Creek—stream IL-6
Mooney Creek—stream IA-7
Mooney Creek—stream KS-7
Mooney Creek—stream MS-4
Mooney Creek—stream MT-8
Mooney Creek—stream NE-7
Mooney Creek—stream WA-9
Mooney Ditch—canal IN-6
Mooney Draw—valley CO-8
Mooney Draw—valley (2) WY-8
Mooney Falls—falls AZ-5
**Mooney Flat**—pop pl CA-9
Mooney Gap—gap (3) NC-3
Mooney Gulch—valley CA-9
Mooney Gulf—valley NY-2
Mooneyham—locale TN-4
Mooneyham Branch—stream GA-3
Mooneyham Branch—stream (2) TN-4
Mooneyham (CCD)—cens area TN-4
Mooneyham Cem—cemetery (2) TN-4
Mooneyham Division—civil TN-4
Mooneyham Mine—mine TN-4
Mooneyham Mine (underground)—mine TN-4
Mooneyham Sch (historical)—school TN-4
Mooneyhan Branch TN-4
Mooney Harbor—bay FL-3
Mooney Harbor Key—island FL-3
Mooney Hills—summit CO-8
Mooney Hollow—valley IA-7
Mooney Hollow—valley (2) MO-7
Mooney Hollow—valley TN-4
Mooney Hollow Sch—school MO-7
Mooney Island—island CA-9
Mooney Island—island NH-1
Mooney JHS—school OH-6
Mooney Lake—lake MN-6
Mooney Lake—lake (2) TX-5
Mooney Mine (surface)—mine TN-4
Mooney Mtn—summit AZ-5
Mooney Mtn—summit OR-9
Mooney Pocket—basin IL-6
Mooney Point—cape FL-3
Mooney Pond—lake FL-3
Mooney Pond—lake NY-2
Mooney Pond—lake TX-5
Mooney Ranch—locale MT-8
Mooney Ridge—ridge CA-9
Mooney Ridge—ridge IA-7
Mooney's Bay NY-2
Mooney Sch—school IL-6
Mooney Sch—school WV-2
Mooneys Grove Park—park CA-9
Mooneys Island TN-4
Mooney's Lake MN-6
Mooneys Shoals—bar TN-4
Mooney Swamp—swamp WA-9
Mooney Tank—reservoir AZ-5
Mooney Township—civil MO-7
Mooney (Township of)—fmr MCD AR-4
Mooney Trail—trail AZ-5
Mooney 1 Dam—dam SD-7
Moonfalls—falls OR-9
Moon Fork Cottonwood Creek—stream CA-9
Moongael—locale FM-9
Moongael—summit FM-9
Moon Glade—flat CA-9
Moon Glow Lake—reservoir AL-4
Moon Glow Lake Dam—dam AL-4
Moon Grove Ch—church GA-3
Moon Gulch—valley CO-8
Moon Head—cliff MA-1
Moon Head Reach—channel TX-5
Moon Hill—summit AZ-5
Moon Hill—summit CO-8
Moon Hill—summit ID-8
Moon Hill—summit MA-1
Moon Hill—summit MI-6
Moon Hill—summit NY-2
Moon Hill—summit OR-9
Moon Hill—summit WA-9
Moon Hill—summit WV-2
Moon Hill Bridge—bridge CO-8
Moon Hill Sch—school CO-8
Moon (historical)—locale SD-7
**Moon (historical)**—pop pl TN-4
Moon Hollow—valley AL-4
Moon Hollow—valley IL-6
Moon Hollow—valley NY-2
Moon Hollow—valley OH-6
Moon Hollow—valley TN-4
Moon Hollow—valley VA-3
Moon Hollow Cave—cave AL-4
Moon Hollow Run—stream OH-6
Moonhull Canyon—valley NM-5
Moonhull Mtn—summit AR-4
Mooningham Branch—stream TN-4
Moon Island—island ME-1
Moon Island—island MA-1
Moon Island—island MI-6
Moon Island—island NC-3
Moon Island—island PA-2
Moon Island—island TN-4
Moon Island—island WA-9
Moon Island Canal—canal LA-4
Moon JHS—school OK-5
Moon Lake AR-4
Moon Lake MI-6
Moon Lake MN-6
Moon Lake MS-4
Moon Lake WI-6
Moon Lake—basin MS-4
Moon Lake—flat OR-9
Moon Lake—lake (3) AL-4
Moon Lake—lake (3) AK-9
Moon Lake—lake (4) AR-4
Moon Lake—lake (2) CA-9
Moon Lake—lake CO-8
Moon Lake—lake (3) FL-3
Moon Lake—lake IN-6
Moon Lake—lake (6) LA-4
Moon Lake—lake (13) MI-6
Moon Lake—lake (8) MN-6
Moon Lake—lake (6) MS-4
Moon Lake—lake (3) MT-8
Moon Lake—lake (2) NE-7
Moon Lake—lake (2) NY-2
Moon Lake—lake (2) ND-7
Moon Lake—lake (4) OR-9
Moon Lake—lake PA-2
Moon Lake—lake TN-4
Moon Lake—lake (2) TX-5
Moon Lake—lake WA-9
Moon Lake—lake (7) WI-6
Moon Lake—lake WY-8
Moon Lake—reservoir AL-4
Moon Lake—reservoir CA-9
Moon Lake—reservoir UT-8
Moon Lake—stream MS-4
Moon Lake—swamp MS-4
Moon Lake Bed—flat LA-4
Moon Lake Campground—locale UT-8
Moon Lake Canal—canal UT-8
Moon Lake Ch—church AL-4
Moon Lake Chapel—church AL-4
Moon Lake Dam—dam AL-4
Moon Lake Dam—dam UT-8
Moon Lake Drain—stream MI-6
Moon Lake Elem Sch—school FL-3
Moon Lake Group Site Campground—park UT-8
Moon Lake Guard Station UT-8
**Moon Lake (historical)**—pop pl MS-4
**Moon Lake Lodge**—pop pl UT-8
Moon Lake Marsh—swamp NE-7
**Moon Lake Resort**—pop pl UT-8
Moon Lakes—lake AR-4
Moon Lake Sch—school AL-4
Moon Lake Slough—stream AR-4
Moon Lake State Wildlife Mngmt Area—park ND-7
**Moon Lake Township**—pop pl ND-7
Moon Lake Trail—trail OR-9
Moon Lake Trail—trail WY-8
Moon Lake Village IL-6
Moon Landing (historical)—locale TN-4
Moonlick Spring No 1—spring CO-8
Moonlick Spring No 2—spring CO-8
Moonlight UT-8
Moonlight—locale KS-7
Moonlight—locale (2) VA-3
**Moonlight**—pop pl IN-6
Moonlight Bay—bay AK-9
Moonlight Bay—bay MO-7
Moonlight Bay—bay WI-6
Moonlight Bay Rsvr—reservoir AZ-5
Moonlight Brook—stream NH-1
Moonlight Canyon—valley CA-9
Moonlight Canyon—valley WA-9
Moonlight Ch—church AR-4
Moonlight Creek AZ-5
Moonlight Creek UT-8
Moonlight Creek—stream (3) AK-9
Moonlight Creek—stream CA-9
Moonlight Creek—stream ID-8
Moonlight Creek—stream (3) MT-8
Moonlight Dome—summit WA-9
Moonlight Gulch—valley CO-8
Moonlight Gulch—valley ID-8
Moonlight Lake—lake CA-9
Moonlight Lake—lake OR-9
Moonlight Lateral—canal CO-8
Moonlight Meadow—flat ID-8
Moonlight Mesa—summit CA-9
Moonlight Mine—mine ID-8
Moonlight Mine—mine MT-8
Moonlight Mine—mine (2) NV-8
Moonlight Mines—mine CA-9
Moonlight Mtn—summit ID-8
Moonlight Pass—gap CA-9
Moonlight Peak—summit CA-9
Moonlight Peak—summit MT-8
Moonlight Point—cape AK-9
Moonlight Sch—school KS-7
Moonlight State Beach—park CA-9
Moonlight Towers—hist pl TX-5
Moonlight Valley—valley CA-9
Moonlight Wash AZ-5
Moonlight Wash UT-8
Moon Meadow—flat OR-9
Moon Mesa—summit CO-8
Moon Mountain Sch—school AZ-5
Moon Mountain Shop Ctr—locale AZ-5
Moon Mtn—summit (2) AZ-5
Moon Mtn—summit MA-1
Moon Mtn—summit NM-5
Moon Mtn—summit NY-2
Moon Mtn—summit (3) OR-9
Moon Mtn—summit TX-5
Moon Mtn—summit VA-3
Moon Mtn—summit WA-9
**Moon Park Subdivision**—pop pl UT-8
Moon Pass—gap CO-8
Moon Pass—gap ID-8
Moon Peak—summit ID-8
Moon Peak—summit MT-8
Moon Point—cape TX-5
Moon Point—summit OR-9
Moon Pond—lake MA-1
Moon Pond—lake MN-6
Moon Pond—lake NY-2
Moon Pond Meadow MA-1
Moon Pond Meadow—flat MA-1
Moonponset Pond MA-1
Moonponsett Pond MA-1
Moon Post Office (historical)—building MS-4
Moon Post Office (historical)—building TN-4
Moon Prairie Guard Station—locale OR-9
Moon Ranch—locale (2) NM-5
Moon Ranch—locale OR-9
Moon Ranch—locale TX-5
Moonridge—locale CO-8
**Moonridge**—pop pl CA-9
Moon Ridge—ridge CA-9
Moon Ridge—ridge OH-6
Moon Ridge—ridge UT-8
Moon Ridge—ridge WI-6
Moon Ridge Canyon—valley UT-8
Moonridge Trail—trail WI-6
Moonrise Spring—spring OR-9
Moon River—stream GA-3
Moon River—stream NV-8
Moon River Basin Well—well NV-8
Moon River Spring—spring NV-8
Moon Rock—island CT-1
Moon Rock—summit AL-4
Moon Rsvr—reservoir OR-9
**Moon Run**—pop pl PA-2
Moon Run—stream (3) PA-2
Moons—locale GA-3
Moons—locale NY-2
**Moons**—pop pl TN-4
Moon Saddle—gap ID-8
Moon Savanna—swamp SC-3
Moons Bay MD-2
Moons Bend—bend CA-9
Moons Brook—stream ME-1
**Moons (Buena Vista)**—pop pl OH-6
Moons Camp—locale TX-5
Moon Sch—school CA-9
Moon Sch—school (3) IL-6
Moon Sch—school (2) MI-6
Moon Sch—school MS-4
Moon Sch—school NE-7
Moon Sch—school NY-2
Moons Chapel—church NC-3
Moons Chapel (historical)—church TN-4
**Moon Shadows**—pop pl TN-4
Moons Hill MA-1
Moonshine—locale IL-6
Moonshine Alley—valley OR-9
Moonshine Bay—bay FL-3
Moonshine Beach—beach MO-7
Moonshine Beach—locale MO-7
Moonshine Canyon UT-8
Moonshine Canyon—valley (2) AZ-5
Moonshine Canyon—valley CA-9
Moonshine Canyon—valley ID-8
Moonshine Canyon—valley (2) NV-8
Moonshine Canyon—valley NM-5
Moonshine Canyon—valley (2) OR-9
Moonshine Canyon—valley SD-7
Moonshine Canyon—valley (2) UT-8
Moonshine Canyon—valley WA-9
Moonshine Canyon—valley WY-8
Moonshine Caves—cave TN-4
Moonshine Ch—church PA-2
Moonshine County Park—park OR-9
Moonshine Creek—stream (3) AK-9
Moonshine Creek—stream AZ-5
Moonshine Creek—stream CA-9
Moonshine Creek—stream (5) ID-8
Moonshine Creek—stream MN-6
Moonshine Creek—stream NV-8
Moonshine Creek—stream (2) OR-9
Moonshine Ditch—canal OR-9
Moonshine Draw AZ-5
Moonshine Draw—valley AZ-5
Moonshine Draw—valley MT-8
Moonshine Draw—valley UT-8
Moonshine Draw—valley WY-8
Moonshine Falls—falls NY-2
Moonshine Field—area LA-4
Moonshine Gulch—valley (2) AZ-5
Moonshine Gulch—valley CO-8
Moonshine Gulch—valley ID-8
Moonshine Gulch—valley (3) MT-8
Moonshine Gulch—valley NV-8
Moonshine Gulch—valley (2) SD-7
Moonshine Gulch—valley (2) WY-8
**Moonshine Hill**—pop pl TX-5
Moonshine Hill—summit AZ-5
Moonshine Hill—summit MA-1
Moonshine Hole—cave TN-4
Moonshine Hollow—valley KY-4
Moonshine Hollow—valley (2) MO-7
Moonshine Hollow—valley PA-2
Moonshine Hollow—valley WI-6
Moonshine Island—flat GA-3
Moonshine Island—island FL-3
Moonshine Lake—lake MI-6
Moonshine Lake—lake (3) MN-6
Moonshine Lake—lake SD-7
Moonshine Lake—lake (2) WI-6
Moonshine Lakebed—flat MN-6
Moonshine Mountaink Pocamoonshine Mountain ME-1
Moonshine Mtn—summit ID-8
Moonshine Park—flat (2) AZ-5
Moonshine Park—flat CO-8
Moonshine Park—flat WY-8
Moonshine Peak—summit ID-8
Moonshine Peak—summit NV-8
Moonshine Peak—summit WY-8
Moonshine Pond—lake CA-9
Moonshine Pond—lake NH-1
Moonshine Pond—lake NY-2
Moonshine Rapids—rapids UT-8
Moonshine Ridge—ridge AZ-5
Moonshine Ridge—ridge GA-3
Moonshiners Cave—cave ID-8
Moonshiner Spring—spring AZ-5
Moonshine Run—stream IN-6
Moonshine Sch—school IL-6
Moonshine Spring NV-8
Moonshine Spring—spring (3) AZ-5
Moonshine Spring—spring (2) CA-9
Moonshine Spring—spring CO-8
Moonshine Spring—spring (4) ID-8
Moonshine Spring—spring MT-8
Moonshine Spring—spring (4) NV-8
Moonshine Spring—spring (5) OR-9
Moonshine Spring—spring SD-7
Moonshine Spring—spring UT-8
Moonshine Spring—spring WA-9
Moonshine Spring—spring (2) WY-8
Moonshine Spring Number Three—spring AZ-5
Moonshine Spring Number Two—spring AZ-5
Moonshine Springs—spring AZ-5
Moonshine Springs—spring NV-8
Moonshine Springs—spring WI-6
Moonshine Swamp—swamp RI-1
Moonshine Tank—reservoir (2) AZ-5
Moonshine Tanks—reservoir UT-8
**Moonshine (Township of)**—pop pl MN-6
Moonshine Wash—valley UT-8
Moonshine Water Hole UT-8
Moonshine Waterhole—lake UT-8
Moonshine Well—well (2) UT-8
Moonshine Woods—woods WA-9
Moon Shoal—bar MA-1
Moon Sinkhole Cave—cave AL-4
Moons Lake OR-9
Moons Lake—reservoir GA-3
Moon Slough—stream WA-9
Moons Mount Wharf—locale VA-3
Moons Point Cem—cemetery IL-6
Moon Spring—spring AL-4
Moon Spring Branch—stream AL-4
Moon Spring Cave—cave AL-4
Moon Springs—spring CA-9
Moon Springs Rsvr—reservoir CA-9
Moons Ranch SD-7
Moons Spring Branch AL-4
**Moonstone**—pop pl CA-9
Moonstone—summit WY-8
Moonstone Beach—beach CA-9
Moonstone Beach—locale RI-1
Moonstone Mtn—summit ID-8
Moonstone Rsvr—reservoir WY-8
**Moonstown**—pop pl PA-2
**Moon (subdivision), The**—pop pl AL-4
Moonsville IN-6
Moon Tank—reservoir (2) NM-5
Moon Tank—reservoir TX-5
Moontown—locale AL-4
Moontown Cem—cemetery MO-7
Moon Town Ch AL-4
Moontown Ch—church AL-4
**Moon (Township of)**—pop pl PA-2
Moon Township Senior HS—school PA-2
**Moon Valley**—pop pl WI-6
Moon Valley—valley AZ-5
Moon Valley Access Point—locale MO-7
**Moon Valley Canyon (subdivision)**—pop pl (2) AZ-5
Moon Valley Country Club—other AZ-5
Moon Valley HS—school AZ-5
Moon Valley Mobile Home Estates—locale AZ-5
Moon Valley Park—park AZ-5
Moon Valley Plaza Shop Ctr—locale AZ-5
Moon Viewing Island MH-9
**Moonville**—pop pl IN-6
**Moonville**—pop pl SC-3
Moonville—tunnel OH-6
Moonville Cem—cemetery IN-6
Moonville Creek—stream AZ-5
Moonwater Canyon—valley UT-8
Moonwater Point—cape UT-8
Moonwater Rapids—rapids UT-8
Moonwater Springs—spring UT-8
Moon Well—locale NM-5
Moon Well—well NM-5
Moon Windmill—locale NM-5
Moon Windmill—locale TX-5
Moony Creek AL-4
Mooquit Valley—valley SD-7
Moor—locale NV-8
Moorcastle Creek—stream ID-8
Moorcastle Springs—spring ID-8
Moorcraft WY-8
**Moorcroft**—pop pl WY-8
Moor Crossroads AL-4
Moordener Kill—stream NY-2
Moord Sch Number 2—school ND-7
Moord Sch Number 3—school ND-7
**Moord Township**—pop pl ND-7
Moore NC-3
Moore MH-9
Moore—locale AR-4
Moore—locale CA-9
Moore—locale CO-8
Moore—locale KY-4
Moore—locale LA-4
Moore—locale NJ-2
Moore—locale TX-5
Moore—locale WA-9
Moore—locale WV-2
**Moore**—pop pl CA-9
**Moore**—pop pl ID-8
**Moore**—pop pl IN-6
**Moore**—pop pl MT-8
**Moore**—pop pl OK-5
**Moore**—pop pl PA-2
**Moore**—pop pl SC-3
**Moore**—pop pl TX-5
**Moore**—pop pl UT-8
**Moore**—pop pl WV-2
Moore, Benjamin, Estate—hist pl NY-2
Moore, Benjamin C., Mill—hist pl NY-2
Moore, Capt. Thomas, House—hist pl PA-2
Moore, C. H., House—hist pl IL-6
Moore, Charles H., House—hist pl OH-6
Moore, Charles H./Sleeper, Albert E., House—hist pl MI-6
Moore, Clarence B., House—hist pl PA-2
Moore, D. D. T. Farmhouse—hist pl NY-2
Moore, Deacon John, House—hist pl CT-1
Moore, Dora, Elem Sch—hist pl CO-8
Moore, Dr. Volney L., House—hist pl WI-6
Moore, Edward and Ann, House—hist pl CT-1
Moore, Edward B., House—hist pl WA-9

Moores Island—*island* ... OR-9
**Moores Junction**—*pop pl* ... OH-6
Moore-Skillman Cem—*cemetery* ... IA-7
Moores Knob—*summit* ... NC-3
Moores Knob Trail—*trail* ... NC-3
*Moores Lake* ... MN-6
*Moores Lake* ... MS-4
Moores Lake—*lake* (2) ... AR-4
Moores Lake—*lake* ... ID-8
Moores Lake—*lake* ... MI-6
Moores Lake—*lake* ... MO-7
Moores Lake—*lake* ... TN-4
Moores Lake—*reservoir* ... AL-4
Moores Lake—*reservoir* ... DE-2
Moores Lake—*reservoir* ... ND-7
Moores Lake—*reservoir* ... TX-5
Moores Lake Creek—*stream* ... ID-8
Moores Lake Dam—*dam* ... AL-4
Moores Lake Dam—*dam* ... DE-2
**Moores Lake Development (subdivision)**—*pop pl* ... DE-2
*Moores Landing* ... AL-4
*Moores Landing* ... NY-2
Moores Landing—*locale* ... SC-3
Moores Landing (historical)—*locale* ... TN-4
Moore Slough—*stream* ... TX-5
**Moores Meadows (Moores Mill)**—*pop pl* ... NJ-2
Moores Memorial Cem—*cemetery* ... MS-4
Moores Mill—*locale* ... AL-4
Moores Mill—*locale* ... AR-4
Moores Mill—*locale* ... KY-4
Moores Mill—*locale* ... MD-2
**Moores Mill**—*pop pl* ... MS-4
**Moores Mill**—*pop pl* ... NJ-2
**Moores Mill**—*pop pl* ... NY-2
**Moores Mill**—*pop pl* ... VA-3
Moores Mill Access—*locale* ... MO-7
Moores Mill Ch—*church* ... AL-4
Moores Mill Creek—*stream* ... AL-4
Moores Mill Creek—*stream* ... FL-3
Moores Mill (historical)—*locale* ... AL-4
Moores Mill (historical)—*locale* (2) ... MS-4
Moores Millpond—*lake* ... SC-3
*Moores Mills* ... AL-4
Moores Mills Post Office (historical)—*building* ... AL-4
*Moores Mineral Spring* ... OR-9
Moores Park—*park* ... MI-6
Moores Park Sch—*school* ... MI-6
*Moores Point* ... ME-1
*Moore's Point* ... OH-6
Moores Point—*cape* ... MO-7
Moores Point—*cape* ... VA-3
*Moores Pond* ... DE-2
*Moores Pond* ... SC-3
Moores Pond—*lake* ... AL-4
Moores Pond—*lake* ... FL-3
Moores Pond—*lake* (2) ... ME-1
Moores Pond—*lake* ... NH-1
Moores Pond—*lake* ... NJ-2
Moores Pond—*lake* ... NY-2
Moores Pond—*reservoir* (2) ... AL-4
Moores Pond—*reservoir* ... MA-1
Moores Pond—*reservoir* ... NJ-2
Moores Pond—*reservoir* ... NC-3
Moores Pond Dam—*dam* ... NC-3
Moores Ponds—*reservoir* ... VT-1
Moores Post Office (historical)—*building* ... TN-4
Moores Prairie—*flat* ... CA-9
Moores Prairie Ch—*church* ... IL-6
Moores Prairie (Township of)—*civ div* ... IL-6
Moore Spring—*spring* ... AL-4
Moore Spring—*spring* ... AZ-5
Moore Spring—*spring* ... CO-8
Moore Spring—*spring* ... ID-8
Moore Spring—*spring* ... KY-4
Moore Spring—*spring* ... MT-8
Moore Spring—*spring* ... OR-9
Moore Spring—*spring* (4) ... TN-4
Moore Spring—*spring* ... TX-5
Moore Spring—*spring* ... WY-8
*Moore Spring Branch* ... NC-3
Moore Spring Branch—*stream* ... MS-4
Moore Spring Hills—*range* ... WY-8
Moore Springs—*spring* ... MT-8
Moore Springs—*spring* ... NV-8
Moore Springs—*spring* ... WY-8
Moore Springs Branch—*stream* ... NC-3
Moore Springs Cem—*cemetery* ... TX-5
Moore Spring Sch—*school* ... WY-8
*Moore Spring Shelter* ... NC-3
Moore Springs Shelter—*locale* ... NC-3
Moore Spring (Subtle Post Office)—*locale*. KY-4
Moore Square—*park* ... NC-3
Moore Square Hist Dist—*hist pl* ... NC-3
*Moores Ranch* ... KS-7
Moores Ranch—*locale* ... WY-8
Moores Ridge—*ridge* ... IN-6
Moores Ridge—*ridge* ... OR-9
Moores Ridge Ch—*church* ... IN-6
Moores Rock—*bar* ... ME-1
Moores RR Station (historical)—*locale* ... FL-3
Moores Run—*stream* (2) ... MD-2
Moores Run—*stream* (2) ... OH-6
Moores Run—*stream* ... PA-2
Moores Run—*stream* ... WV-2
Moores Run Cem—*cemetery* ... PA-2
Moores Run Fire Trail—*trail* ... PA-2
Moores Sch—*school* (2) ... KY-4
Moores Sch (historical)—*school* ... TN-4
*Moores School* ... TN-4
*Moores Schoolhouse* ... NC-3
**Moores School House**—*pop pl* ... NC-3
**Moores Siding (historical)**—*pop pl* ... IA-7
Moores Slough—*stream* ... AR-4
Moores Spring—*spring* ... AL-4
Moores Spring—*spring* ... AZ-5
Moores Spring—*spring* ... ID-8
Moores Spring—*spring* (2) ... OR-9
*Moores Springs* ... OR-9
Moores Springs—*locale* ... NC-3
*Moores Station* ... TX-5
Moores Station—*locale* ... ID-8
Moores Station—*locale* ... NV-8
Moores Station Buttes—*summit* ... NV-8
Moores Station Wash—*stream* ... NV-8
*Moores Store* ... VA-3
Moores Store—*locale* ... VA-3
Moores Summit—*gap* ... MA-1
Moores Swamp—*stream* (3) ... VA-3
Moores Swamp Ch—*church* ... VA-3
Moores Switch—*locale* ... TN-4
Moores Switch Lookout Tower—*locale* ... TN-4
**Moores Switch (subdivision)**—*pop pl* ... MO-7
Moore Station—*locale* ... PA-2
**Moore Station**—*pop pl* ... TX-5
**Moorestown**—*pop pl* ... IN-6
**Moorestown**—*pop pl* ... MI-6
**Moorestown**—*pop pl* ... NJ-2
**Moorestown**—*pop pl* ... PA-2
Moorestown Cem—*cemetery* ... MI-6
Moorestown Friends Sch & Meetinghouse—*hist pl* ... NJ-2
Moorestown HS—*school* ... NJ-2
Moorestown-Lenola—*CDP* ... NJ-2
Moorestown Swamp—*swamp* ... MI-6
**Moorestown (Township of)**—*pop pl* ... NJ-2
Moores Valley—*locale* ... AL-4
Moores Valley—*valley* ... OR-9
Moores Valley Cem—*cemetery* ... OR-9
*Mooresville* ... IN-6
Mooresville—*hist pl* ... AL-4
Mooresville—*locale* ... ME-1
Mooresville—*locale* ... OH-6
**Mooresville**—*pop pl* ... AL-4
**Mooresville**—*pop pl* ... IN-6
**Mooresville**—*pop pl* ... KY-4
**Mooresville**—*pop pl* ... MO-7
**Mooresville**—*pop pl* ... NC-3
**Mooresville**—*pop pl* ... PA-2
**Mooresville**—*pop pl* ... TN-4
**Mooresville**—*pop pl* ... TX-5
**Mooresville**—*pop pl* ... WV-2
*Mooresville Airport* ... NC-3
Mooresville-Belle Mina Sch—*school* ... AL-4
Mooresville Brook—*stream* ... ME-1
Mooresville (CCD)—*cens area* ... AL-4
Mooresville Cem—*cemetery* ... IN-6
Mooresville Ch—*church* ... MD-2
Mooresville Creek—*stream* ... TN-4
Mooresville Division—*civil* ... AL-4
Mooresville Friends Acad Bldg—*hist pl* ... IN-6
Mooresville Hist Dist—*hist pl* ... NC-3
Mooresville HS—*school* ... IN-6
Mooresville JHS—*school* ... NC-3
Mooresville Junction—*uninc pl* ... NC-3
Mooresville Plaza—*locale* ... NC-3
Mooresville Post Office—*building* ... AL-4
Mooresville Post Office (historical)—*building* ... TN-4
Mooresville Sch—*school* ... TN-4
Mooresville Senior HS—*school* ... NC-3
Mooresville Spring—*spring* ... AL-4
**Mooresville Township**—*pop pl* ... MO-7
*Moores Vineyard* ... IN-6
Moores Wall—*cliff* ... NC-3
Moore Swamp—*stream* ... NC-3
Moore Swamp—*swamp* ... IN-6
Moore Swamp—*swamp* ... NC-3
Moore Swamp Ch—*church* ... NC-3
Moore Tank—*reservoir* (4) ... AZ-5
Moore Tank—*reservoir* ... NM-5
Moore Tank—*reservoir* ... TX-5
Moore Tank Draw—*valley* ... TX-5
Moore Theatre and Hotel—*hist pl* ... WA-9
**Mooreton**—*pop pl* ... ND-7
Mooreton Town Hall—*building* ... ND-7
**Mooreton Township**—*pop pl* ... ND-7
*Mooretown* ... IN-6
*Mooretown* ... MS-4
*Mooretown* ... NC-3
*Mooretown* ... PA-2
*Mooretown* ... TN-4
*Mooretown* ... VT-1
Mooretown—*locale* ... VA-3
Mooretown—*other* ... OH-6
**Moore Town**—*pop pl* ... AL-4
**Mooretown**—*pop pl* ... NC-3
**Mooretown**—*pop pl* ... TN-4
Mooretown Ch—*church* ... PA-2
Moore Town Hall—*building* ... ND-7
Mooretown Post Office (historical)—*building* ... MS-4
Mooretown Ridge—*ridge* ... CA-9
Mooretown Sch—*school* ... LA-4
Mooretown Sch (historical)—*school* (2) ... TN-4
Moore Township—*civil* (2) ... MO-7
**Moore Township**—*pop pl* (2) ... KS-7
**Moore Township**—*pop pl* ... ND-7
**Moore Township**—*pop pl* (2) ... SD-7
Moore Township Elem Sch—*school* ... PA-2
Moore Township Hall—*building* ... SD-7
Moore Township (historical)—*civil* ... ND-7
**Moore (Township of)**—*pop pl* ... MI-6
**Moore (Township of)**—*pop pl* ... MN-6
**Moore (Township of)**—*pop pl* ... PA-2
Moore Tract—*civil* ... CA-9
Moore Trail—*trail* ... WV-2
Moore Tunnel—*tunnel* ... VA-3
Moore-Union Ch—*church* ... NC-3
Moore Union Ch—*church* ... NC-3
Mooreville—*locale* ... CT-1
**Mooreville**—*pop pl* ... MI-6
**Mooreville**—*pop pl* ... MS-4
Mooreville Cem—*cemetery* ... MI-6
Mooreville Cem—*cemetery* ... TX-5
**Mooreville (historical)**—*pop pl* ... IA-7
Mooreville Methodist Ch—*church* ... MS-4
Mooreville Ridge—*ridge* (2) ... CA-9
Mooreville Sch—*school* ... MS-4
Mooreville (site)—*locale* ... OR-9
Moore-Vinson Cem—*cemetery* ... IL-6
Moore-Ward Cobblestone House—*hist pl* .. NM-5
Moore Wash—*stream* ... AZ-5
Moore Watkins Oil Field—*oilfield* ... TX-5
Moore Well—*well* (3) ... AZ-5
Moore Well—*well* ... NV-8
Moore Well—*well* (5) ... NM-5
Moore Windmill—*locale* ... NM-5
Moore Windmill—*locale* (2) ... TX-5
Moore-Witt Ditch—*canal* ... CA-9
Moorewood—*locale* ... OK-5
Moorewood Pond—*lake* ... NC-3
Moore-Youse-Maxon House—*hist pl* ... IN-6
*Moorfield* ... IN-6
*Moorfield* ... NJ-2
Moor Field—*park* ... CA-9
*Moorfield Creek* ... NJ-2
Moor Green—*hist pl* ... VA-3
Moorhead—*locale* ... MT-8
Moorhead—*locale* ... PA-2
**Moorhead**—*pop pl* ... IA-7
**Moorhead**—*pop pl* ... MN-6
**Moorhead**—*pop pl* ... MS-4
Moorhead Airpark—*airport* ... PA-2
Moorhead Baptist Ch—*church* ... MS-4
Moorhead Bayou—*stream* (2) ... MS-4
Moorhead Canal—*canal* ... CA-9
*Moorhead Cem* ... MS-4
Moorhead Cem—*cemetery* ... MS-4
Moorhead Cem—*cemetery* ... NE-7
Moorhead Cem—*cemetery* ... PA-2
Moorhead Ch—*church* ... OH-6
Moorhead Creek—*stream* ... IA-7
Moorhead Drain—*canal* ... CA-9
Moorhead Elem Sch—*school* ... IN-6
Moorhead Elem Sch—*school* ... MS-4
Moorhead Gulch—*valley* ... CO-8
Moorhead (historical P.O.)—*locale* ... IA-7
Moorhead Hollow—*valley* ... TN-4
Moorhead Lagoon Dam—*dam* ... MS-4
*Moorhead Memorial Airpark* ... PA-2
Moorhead Memorial Gardens Cem—*cemetery* ... MN-6
Moorhead Memorial Park—*park* ... CO-8
Moorhead Methodist Ch—*church* ... MS-4
*Moorhead Mountain* ... ID-8
Moorhead Presbyterian Ch (historical)—*church* ... MS-4
*Moorheads* ... PA-2
**Moorhead (Township of)**—*pop pl* ... MN-6
**Moorheadville**—*pop pl* ... PA-2
Moor Hen Meadow—*flat* ... NV-8
Moor Hill—*summit* ... TN-4
Moorhouse Corner—*locale* ... NY-2
**Moorhouse (historical)**—*pop pl* ... OR-9
Moorhouse Ranch—*locale* ... NM-5
Moorhouse Ranch—*locale* ... TX-5
*Mooriesville* ... TN-4
Mooring—*locale* ... TX-5
Mooring—*locale* ... VA-3
**Mooring**—*pop pl* ... TN-4
Mooring Bayou—*gut* ... TN-4
Mooring Cem—*cemetery* ... AL-4
Mooring Cem—*cemetery* ... TN-4
Mooring Ch—*church* ... TN-4
Mooring Creek—*stream* ... TX-5
Mooring Landing—*locale* ... NC-3
*Mooring Methodist Ch* ... TN-4
Mooring Post Office (historical)—*building* .. TN-4
**Moorings**—*pop pl* ... VA-3
**Moorings, The**—*pop pl* ... FL-3
*Moorings Bay* ... FL-3
Moorings Bay—*lake* ... FL-3
Mooring Sch (historical)—*school* ... TN-4
Mooring Slough—*gut* ... TX-5
**Mooringsport**—*pop pl* ... LA-4
Moorings Presbyterian Ch—*church* ... FL-3
Moor Intercharge—*crossing* ... NV-8
Mooris Cem—*cemetery* ... IL-6
Mooris Cem—*cemetery* ... WV-2
*Moorland* ... OH-6
**Moorland**—*pop pl* ... IA-7
**Moorland**—*pop pl* ... KY-4
**Moorland**—*pop pl* ... MI-6
Moorland Cem—*cemetery* ... MI-6
*Moorland Creek* ... MS-4
Moorland Oil Field—*oilfield* ... MS-4
**Moorlands**—*pop pl* ... WA-9
**Moorland (Township of)**—*pop pl* ... MI-6
Moor-Lin Cabin Site—*locale* ... TN-4
**Moorman**—*pop pl* ... KY-4
**Moorman**—*pop pl* ... NE-7
**Moorman**—*pop pl* ... TN-4
Moorman Cem—*cemetery* ... AL-4
Moorman Cem—*cemetery* ... IA-7
Moorman Cem—*cemetery* ... VA-3
Moorman Creek—*stream* ... NY-2
Moorman Creek—*stream* ... TX-5
Moorman Ditch—*canal* ... IN-6
Moorman Hill—*summit* ... AL-4
Moormann, Bernard H., House—*hist pl* ... OH-6
Moorman Post Office (historical)—*building* ... TN-4
*Moorman Ranch* ... NV-8
Moorman Ranch Airp—*airport* ... NV-8
Moorman Ridge—*ridge* ... NV-8
Moorman Spring—*spring* ... NV-8
Moorman Spring (Hot)—*spring* ... NV-8
*Moormans River* ... VA-3
Moormans River—*stream* ... VA-3
Moormans River Overlook—*locale* ... VA-3
Moorman Valley—*valley* ... KY-4
Moor Park—*park* ... MN-6
**Moorpark**—*pop pl* ... CA-9
Moorpark (CCD)—*cens area* ... CA-9
Moorpark Coll—*school* ... CA-9
**Moorpark Home Acres**—*pop pl* ... CA-9
Moorpark Park—*park* (2) ... CA-9
Moors—*locale* ... MO-7
**Moors, The**—*pop pl* ... KY-4
*Moors Brook* ... MA-1
Moors Brook—*stream* ... ME-1
**Moors Camp, The**—*pop pl* ... KY-4
Moors Cem—*cemetery* ... DE-2
*Moors Creek* ... NJ-2
Moors Creek—*stream* ... AL-4
Moors Creek—*stream* ... MT-8
*Moorse Lake* ... MN-6
Moorse Pond Dam—*dam* ... MA-1
*Moorsfield* ... NJ-2
Moors Gap—*gap* ... NC-3
*Moors Lake* ... MN-6
Moors Memorial Chapel—*church* ... OH-6
Moors Mill—*locale* ... PA-2
Moors Mtn—*summit* ... MT-8
Moors Run—*stream* ... OH-6
*Moors Town* ... NJ-2
Moor Summit—*summit* ... NV-8
*Moorton* ... DE-2
Moosabec Reach—*channel* ... ME-1
Moosa Canyon—*valley* ... CA-9
Moosalamoo, Mount—*summit* ... VT-1
Moos Cem—*cemetery* ... ND-7
**Moose**—*pop pl* ... WY-8
Moose And Deer Pond—*lake* ... ME-1
*Mooseback Lake* ... NJ-2
*Mooseback Pond* ... NJ-2
Moose Basin—*basin* ... WY-8
Moose Basin Divide—*ridge* ... WY-8
Moose Bay—*bay* (3) ... MN-6
Moose Bog—*reservoir* ... ME-1
Moose Bog Brook—*stream* ... ME-1
Moose Bog Brook—*stream* ... NH-1
Moose Bog Brooke—*stream* ... ME-1
Moose Bog Camp—*locale* ... ME-1
Moose Bog Camp—*locale* ... NH-1
Moose Branch—*stream* ... NC-3
*Moose Brook* ... ME-1
*Moose Brook* ... NH-1
Moose Brook—*stream* (9) ... ME-1
Moose Brook—*stream* (2) ... MA-1
Moose Brook—*stream* ... MN-6
Moose Brook—*stream* (6) ... NH-1
Moose Brook Camp (historical)—*locale* ... ME-1
Moose Brook Islands—*island* ... ME-1
Moose Butte—*summit* ... ID-8
Moose Butte—*summit* ... MT-8
Moose Butte Creek—*stream* ... ID-8
Moose Camp—*locale* ... CA-9
Moose Camp (historical)—*locale* ... SD-7
Moosecamp Lake—*lake* ... MN-6
Moose Camp Spring—*spring* ... MT-8
Moose Can Gully—*valley* ... MT-8
Moose Canyon—*valley* ... OK-5
Moose Canyon—*valley* ... TX-5
Moose City—*locale* ... ID-8
Moose Coulee—*valley* ... MT-8
Moose Country Pond—*lake* ... MT-8
Moose Cove—*basin* ... NC-3
Moose Cove—*bay* (4) ... ME-1
*Moose Creek* ... ID-8
*Moose Creek* ... PA-2
Moose Creek—*locale* ... AK-9
**Moose Creek**—*pop pl* ... AK-9
Moose Creek—*stream* (13) ... AK-9
Moose Creek—*stream* (3) ... CO-8
Moose Creek—*stream* ... GA-3
Moose Creek—*stream* (17) ... ID-8
Moose Creek—*stream* ... IA-7
Moose Creek—*stream* (5) ... MN-6
Moose Creek—*stream* (21) ... MT-8
Moose Creek—*stream* (8) ... NY-2
Moose Creek—*stream* (2) ... OR-9
Moose Creek—*stream* ... PA-2
Moose Creek—*stream* ... TX-5
Moose Creek—*stream* ... WA-9
Moose Creek—*stream* ... WI-6
Moose Creek—*stream* (5) ... WY-8
Moose Creek Bluff—*summit* ... AK-9
Moose Creek Butte—*summit* ... ID-8
Moose Creek Buttes—*summit* ... ID-8
Moose Creek Campground—*locale* (2) ... MT-8
Moose Creek Falls—*falls* ... OR-9
Moose Creek Lake—*lake* ... AK-9
Moose Creek No 1—*stream* ... AK-9
Moose Creek No 2—*stream* ... AK-9
Moose Creek Plateau—*area* ... ID-8
Moose Creek Plateau—*plain* ... MT-8
Moose Creek Ranger Cabin No. 19—*hist pl* ... AK-9
Moose Creek Ranger Station—*locale* ... ID-8
Moose Creek Reservoir Dam—*dam* ... PA-2
Moose Creek Rsvr—*reservoir* ... PA-2
**Moose Creek (Township of)**—*pop pl* ... MN-6
Moose Draw—*valley* ... ID-8
Moose Draw—*valley* ... WY-8
Moose Ear Creek—*stream* ... WI-6
Moose Ear Lake—*lake* ... WI-6
*Mooseelauke Brook* ... NH-1
Moose Falls—*falls* ... NH-1
Moose Falls—*falls* ... WY-8
Moose Flat—*flat* ... WY-8
Moose Flat Campground—*locale* ... WY-8
Moose Gulch—*valley* ... AK-9
Moose Gulch—*valley* (3) ... MT-8
Moose Gulch—*valley* ... WY-8
Moosehead—*locale* ... PA-2
**Moosehead**—*pop pl* ... ME-1
Moosehead Bay—*bay* ... WY-8
Moosehead Creek—*stream* ... CA-9
*Moose Head Lake* ... MI-6
Moosehead Lake—*lake* ... AK-9
Moosehead Lake—*lake* ... ME-1
Moosehead Lake—*lake* ... MI-6
Moosehead Lake—*lake* ... MN-6
Moose Head Mtn—*summit* ... CO-8
Moosehead Mtn—*summit* ... NY-2
Moosehead Pond—*lake* ... NY-2
Moosehead Pond Outlet—*stream* ... NY-2
Moosehead Rack—*summit* ... AK-9
Moose Head Ranch—*locale* ... WY-8
Moosehead Rapids—*rapids* ... AK-9
Moosehead Rapids—*rapids* ... NY-2
Moosehead Trail—*trail* ... ME-1
**Mooseheart**—*pop pl* ... IL-6
Mooseheart Lake—*lake* ... IL-6
Mooseheart Mtn—*summit* ... AK-9
Moose Hill—*summit* (2) ... AK-9
Moose Hill—*summit* (2) ... CT-1
Moose Hill—*summit* (4) ... ME-1
Moose Hill—*summit* (2) ... MA-1
Moose Hill—*summit* (2) ... NH-1
Moose Hill—*summit* ... NY-2
Moose Hill—*summit* ... PA-2
Moose Hill Cem—*cemetery* ... ME-1
*Moosehillock Brook* ... NH-1
*Moose Hill Pond* ... CT-1
Moose Hill Pond—*lake* ... ME-1
Moose Hill Sch—*school* ... GA-3
Moosehorn—*locale* (2) ... ME-1
*Moose Horn Brook* ... MA-1
Moosehorn Brook—*stream* (3) ... CT-1
Moosehorn Brook—*stream* ... ME-1
Moosehorn Brook—*stream* ... MA-1
Moosehorn Campground—*locale* ... UT-8
Moosehorn Corner—*locale* ... RI-1
Moosehorn Creek—*stream* ... WY-8
Moosehorn Crossing—*locale* ... ME-1
Moosehorn Hill—*summit* ... CT-1
*Moose Horn Lake* ... MN-6
Moosehorn Lake—*lake* (2) ... AK-9
Moosehorn Lake—*lake* ... MN-6
Moosehorn Lake—*lake* ... UT-8
*Moosehorn Lake Campground* ... UT-8
Moose Horn Mine—*mine* ... MT-8
Moosehorn Mtn—*summit* ... VT-1
Moosehorn Natl Wildlife Ref—*park* ... ME-1
*Moose Horn Pond* ... MA-1
Moosehorn Pond—*lake* ... MA-1
Moosehorn Ridge—*ridge* ... AK-9
*Moosehorn River* ... MN-6
Moose Horn River—*stream* ... MN-6
Moosehorn Stream—*stream* (3) ... ME-1
Moose House—*hist pl* ... AR-4
*Moose Island* ... ME-1
Moose Island—*island* ... AK-9
Moose Island—*island* ... IL-6
Moose Island—*island* (6) ... ME-1
Moose Island—*island* ... MN-6
Moose Island—*island* ... NH-1
Moose Island—*island* (3) ... NY-2
Moose Island—*island* ... WY-8
Moose Jaw Creek—*stream* ... ID-8
Moose Jaw Creek—*stream* ... MT-8
Moose Jaw Meadow—*flat* ... ID-8
Moose Junction—*locale* ... WY-8
**Moose Junction**—*pop pl* ... WI-6
*Moose Lake* ... MI-6
*Moose Lake* ... MN-6
Moose Lake—*lake* (5) ... AK-9
Moose Lake—*lake* ... CA-9
Moose Lake—*lake* (4) ... ID-8
Moose Lake—*lake* (4) ... MI-6
Moose Lake—*lake* (27) ... MN-6
Moose Lake—*lake* (6) ... MT-8
Moose Lake—*lake* ... OR-9
Moose Lake—*lake* ... WA-9
Moose Lake—*lake* (7) ... WI-6
Moose Lake—*lake* (4) ... WY-8
**Moose Lake**—*pop pl* ... MN-6
Moose Lake—*reservoir* ... IL-6
Moose Lake—*reservoir* ... WV-2
Moose Lake Camp—*locale* ... MN-6
Moose Lake Cem—*cemetery* (2) ... MN-6
*Moose Lake Creek* ... MN-6
Moose Lake Creek—*stream* ... MN-6
Moose Lake Lookout Tower—*locale* ... MN-6
*Moose Lakes* ... WY-8
Moose Lakes—*lake* ... AK-9
Moose Lakes—*lake* ... MI-6
**Moose Lake (Township of)**—*pop pl* (3) ... MN-6
Moose Lake View County Club—*other* ... KY-4
Moose Ledge—*bar* ... ME-1
Mooseleuk Lake—*lake* ... ME-1
Mooseleuk Mtn—*summit* ... ME-1
Mooseleuk Stream—*stream* ... ME-1
Mooseleuk Tote Road—*trail* ... ME-1
*Mooselocmaguntic Lake* ... ME-1
Moose Lodge Pond—*reservoir* ... AL-4
**Mooselookmeguntic**—*pop pl* ... ME-1
*Mooselookmeguntick Lake* ... ME-1
Mooselookmeguntic Lake—*lake* ... ME-1
Moose Meadow—*flat* ... MT-8
Moose Meadow—*swamp* ... ME-1
Moose Meadow Brook—*stream* ... MA-1
Moose Meadow Brook—*stream* ... NH-1
Moose Meadow Brook Rsvr—*reservoir* ... MA-1
Moose Meadow Cem—*cemetery* ... CT-1
Moose Meadow Creek—*stream* ... ID-8
Moose Meadow Creek—*stream* ... MT-8
*Moose Meadows* ... MT-8
Moose Meadows—*flat* (3) ... ID-8
Moose Meadows—*flat* (4) ... MT-8
Moose Meadows—*flat* ... WY-8
Moose Meadow Sch—*school* ... CT-1
Moose Meadows Point—*summit* ... ID-8
Moose Mill Camp—*locale* ... ME-1
Moose Mine—*mine* ... CA-9
Moose Mine—*mine* ... CO-8
*Moose Mountain* ... MA-1
Moose Mountain—*ridge* ... NH-1
Moose Mountain Pond—*lake* ... NY-2
Moose Mountains—*summit* ... NH-1
Moose Mountain Slide—*cliff* ... WY-8
Moose Mtn—*summit* ... CO-8
Moose Mtn—*summit* (2) ... ID-8
Moose Mtn—*summit* (5) ... ME-1
Moose Mtn—*summit* (4) ... MN-6
Moose Mtn—*summit* (2) ... MT-8
Moose Mtn—*summit* (9) ... NY-2
Moose Mtn—*summit* ... OR-9
Moose Mtn—*summit* (2) ... WY-8
Moose Mtns—*range* ... ID-8
*Mooseneah Peak* ... UT-8
*Moose Neck* ... ME-1
Moose Neck—*cape* ... ME-1
Moose Oil Field—*oilfield* ... TX-5
Moosepac Pond—*reservoir* ... NJ-2
Moose Park—*flat* (4) ... MT-8
Moose Park—*park* ... CA-9
Moose Park—*park* ... MN-6
Moose Park—*park* ... UT-8
Moose Park—*park* ... WI-6
**Moose Park (Township of)**—*pop pl* ... MN-6
Moose Pass—*CDP* ... AK-9
Moose Pass—*gap* ... AK-9
Moose Pass—*gap* ... MT-8
Moose Pasture Lake—*lake* ... AK-9
Moose Pasture Pass—*gap* ... AK-9
Moose Peak—*summit* ... CA-9
Moose Peak—*summit* (2) ... MT-8
Moose Peak Trail—*trail* ... MT-8
Moose Plain—*bench* ... MA-1
Moose Point—*cape* ... AK-9
Moose Point—*cape* ... ME-1
Moose Point—*cape* ... MI-6
Moose Point—*cape* (2) ... MN-6
Moose Point—*summit* ... MN-6
Moose Point Shoal—*bar* ... AK-9
Moose Point State Park—*park* ... ME-1
*Moose Pond* ... ME-1
*Moose Pond* ... MA-1
Moose Pond—*lake* (15) ... ME-1
Moose Pond—*lake* (5) ... NH-1
Moose Pond—*lake* (6) ... NY-2
Moose Pond—*lake* ... WY-8
Moose Pond—*reservoir* ... ME-1
Moose Pond Brook—*stream* (2) ... ME-1
Moose Pond Brook—*stream* ... NH-1
Moose Pond Brook—*stream* ... NY-2
Moose Pond Club—*locale* ... NY-2
Moose Pond Mtn—*summit* ... NY-2
Moose Pond Stream—*stream* (2) ... ME-1
Moose Ranch Tank—*reservoir* ... AZ-5
Moose Range Park—*park* ... IL-6
Mooser Creek—*stream* ... OK-5
Moose Ridge—*ridge* ... ID-8
Moose Ridge—*ridge* ... ME-1
Moose Ridge—*ridge* ... MT-8
Moose Ridge—*ridge* ... OH-6
Moose Ridge—*ridge* ... OR-9
Moose Ridge Cem—*cemetery* ... OH-6
*Moose River* ... MN-6
Moose River—*bay* ... ME-1
**Moose River**—*pop pl* ... ME-1
**Moose River**—*pop pl* ... NY-2
Moose River—*stream* ... AK-9
Moose River—*stream* ... ME-1
Moose River—*stream* (4) ... MN-6
Moose River—*stream* ... NH-1
Moose River—*stream* ... NY-2
Moose River—*stream* ... VT-1
Moose River—*stream* (2) ... WI-6
Moose River Cem—*cemetery* (2) ... MN-6
Moose River Flowage—*stream* ... MN-6
Moose River Mtn—*summit* ... NY-2
Moose River Pool—*reservoir* ... MN-6
Moose River Sch—*school* ... ME-1
Moose River Site—*hist pl* ... AK-9
**Moose River (Town of)**—*pop pl* ... ME-1
**Moose River (Township of)**—*pop pl* ... MN-6
Moose Rock—*island* ... ME-1
Moose Rsvr—*reservoir* ... ID-8
Moose Rsvr—*reservoir* ... IL-6
Moose Run—*stream* (2) ... PA-2
*Mooses Creek* ... AL-4
Moose Snare Cove—*bay* ... ME-1
Moose Springs—*spring* ... WI-6
Mooses Tooth, The—*summit* ... AK-9
Moose Town—*locale* ... MT-8
**Moose (Township of)**—*pop pl* ... MN-6
**Mooseup Valley**—*pop pl* ... RI-1
Moose Valley—*valley* ... AK-9
Moose Well—*well* ... AZ-5
Moose Willow River Ditch—*canal* ... MN-6
Moosey Canyon—*valley* ... UT-8
Moosey Point—*cape* ... UT-8
*Mooshausick River* ... RI-1
*Mooshausic River* ... RI-1
*Mooshelock Brook* ... NH-1
**Moosic**—*pop pl* ... PA-2
Moosic Borough—*civil* ... PA-2
Moosic Industrial Park—*locale* ... PA-2
Moosic Lakes—*reservoir* ... PA-2
Moosic Mountains—*range* ... PA-2
Moosic Powder Works (historical)—*building* ... PA-2
Moosic Power Company Mills—*building* ... PA-2
Moosic Sch (abandoned)—*school* ... PA-2
Moosilauke, Mount—*summit* ... NH-1
Moosilauke Brook—*stream* ... NH-1
Moosilauke Camp—*locale* ... NH-1
Moosilauke Carriage Road—*trail* ... NH-1
Moosilauke Pond—*reservoir* ... NH-1
Moosman Bridge—*bridge* ... NE-7
Moosman Draw—*valley* ... UT-8
Moosman Rsvr—*reservoir* ... UT-8
Moosmoos Creek—*stream* ... OR-9
Moos Ranch—*locale* ... TX-5
Moos Sch—*school* ... IL-6
**Moosup**—*pop pl* ... CT-1
Moosup Pond—*lake* ... CT-1
Moosup River—*stream* ... CT-1
Moosup River—*stream* ... RI-1
Moosup River Site (RI-1153)—*hist pl* ... RI-1
*Moosup Valley* ... RI-1
**Moosup Valley**—*pop pl* ... RI-1
Moosup Valley Hist Dist—*hist pl* ... RI-1
Moos Windmill—*locale* ... TX-5
Moosy Brook—*stream* ... NY-2
Mooth Waters—*channel* ... CO-8
Moots Creek—*stream* ... IN-6
Moots Hollow—*valley* ... UT-8
Moots Run—*stream* ... OH-6
Moots Store—*locale* ... MO-7
*Mootz Creek* ... IN-6
Mootz Drain—*canal* ... CA-9
Mootz Lateral—*canal* ... CA-9
Moovalya Lake—*reservoir* ... AZ-5
Moovalya Lake—*reservoir* ... CA-9
*Mooyie River* ... ID-8
Mopac Field—*park* ... TX-5
Mopac Station—*hist pl* ... AR-4
Mopah Peaks—*summit* ... CA-9
Mopah Range—*range* ... CA-9
Mopah Spring—*spring* ... CA-9
*Mopan Creek* ... WA-9
Mopang Creek—*stream* ... WA-9
Mopang First Lake—*lake* ... ME-1
Mopang Lake—*lake* ... ME-1
Mopang Second Lake—*lake* ... ME-1
Mopang Stream—*stream* ... ME-1
**Mopeco**—*pop pl* ... CA-9
Moping Hollow—*valley* ... VA-3
Mopkins Lake—*lake* ... AR-4
Moppin Branch—*stream* ... MO-7
Moppin Cem—*cemetery* ... OK-5
Mopping Branch—*stream* ... MO-7
Mop Point—*cape* ... AK-9
Mop Run—*stream* ... IN-6
**Mopua**—*pop pl* ... HI-9
Mopung Hills—*summit* ... NV-8
Mopus Brook—*stream* ... CT-1
Mopus Brook—*stream* ... NY-2
Moqof—*cape* ... FM-9
**Moquah**—*pop pl* ... WI-6
Moquah Lake—*lake* ... WI-6
Moquah Lookout Tower—*locale* ... WI-6
Moquawkie Ind Res—*reserve* ... AK-9
Moquawkie (Tyonek)—*other* ... AK-9
*Moqueak Mountain* ... AZ-5
*Moqueak Wash* ... AZ-5
Moquet Creek—*stream* ... WA-9
*Moqui* ... AZ-5
**Moqui**—*pop pl* ... AZ-5
Moqui Bar—*bar* ... UT-8
Moqui Camp—*locale* ... AZ-5
*Moqui Canyon* ... UT-8
Moqui Canyon—*valley* ... CO-8
Moqui Canyon—*valley* ... UT-8
Moqui Draw—*valley* ... AZ-5
*Moquie Bar* ... UT-8
*Moquie Canyon* ... UT-8
Moqui Fork—*valley* ... UT-8
Moqui Jug Mine—*mine* ... CO-8
Moqui Lake—*lake* ... CO-8
Moqui Lookout Cabin—*hist pl* ... AZ-5

**Morgan Branch**—pop pl TN-4
Morgan Branch—stream (2) AL-4
Morgan Branch—stream (3) AR-4
Morgan Branch—stream (2) DE-2
Morgan Branch—stream FL-3
Morgan Branch—stream (2) GA-3
Morgan Branch—stream IA-7
Morgan Branch—stream (3) KY-4
Morgan Branch—stream (5) LA-4
Morgan Branch—stream (5) MS-4
Morgan Branch—stream (4) MO-7
Morgan Branch—stream (5) NC-3
Morgan Branch—stream (10) TN-4
Morgan Branch—stream WV-2
Morgan Branch Chapel—church TN-4
Morgan Bridge—bridge AL-4
Morgan Bridge—bridge GA-3
Morgan Bridge—bridge SC-3
Morgan Bridge—locale NY-2
Morgan Bridge—other IL-6
Morgan Brook—stream CT-1
Morgan Brook—stream ME-1
Morgan Brook—stream MA-1
Morgan Brook—stream VT-1
Morgan Brothers Dam—dam OR-9
Morgan Brothers Rsvr OR-9
Morganburg KY-4
Morganburgh AL-4
Morganburgh Post Office AL-4
Morgan Butte—summit AZ-5
Morgan Butte—summit (2) OR-9
Morgan Butte Spring—spring OR-9
Morgan Cabin—locale CO-8
Morgan Cabin Rsvr—reservoir CO-8
Morgan Camp—locale CO-8
Morgan Camp Run—stream WV-2
Morgan Canal—canal CA-9
Morgan Canal—canal LA-4
Morgan Canyon—valley AZ-5
Morgan Canyon—valley (3) CA-9
Morgan Canyon—valley CO-8
Morgan Canyon—valley ID-8
Morgan Canyon—valley NV-8
Morgan Canyon—valley (2) NM-5
Morgan Canyon—valley OR-9
Morgan Canyon—valley UT-8
Morgan Canyon—valley WY-8
Morgan Cave—cave AR-4
Morgan Cave—cave KY-4
Morgan Cave—cave TN-4
Morgan (CCD)—cens area GA-3
Morgan Cem—cemetery (2) AL-4
Morgan Cem—cemetery (6) AR-4
Morgan Cem—cemetery (3) CT-1
Morgan Cem—cemetery FL-3
Morgan Cem—cemetery (2) GA-3
Morgan Cem—cemetery (4) IL-6
Morgan Cem—cemetery (3) IN-6
Morgan Cem—cemetery (2) IA-7
Morgan Cem—cemetery (4) KY-4
Morgan Cem—cemetery LA-4
Morgan Cem—cemetery (3) MI-6
Morgan Cem—cemetery MN-6
Morgan Cem—cemetery (3) MS-4
Morgan Cem—cemetery (6) MO-7
Morgan Cem—cemetery MT-8
Morgan Cem—cemetery NJ-2
Morgan Cem—cemetery (5) NC-3
Morgan Cem—cemetery ND-7
Morgan Cem—cemetery OH-6
Morgan Cem—cemetery (2) OK-5
Morgan Cem—cemetery OR-9
Morgan Cem—cemetery (11) TN-4
Morgan Cem—cemetery (4) TX-5
Morgan Cem—cemetery (2) VA-3
Morgan Cem—cemetery (9) WV-2
**Morgan Center**—pop pl (2) OH-6
**Morgan Center**—pop pl VT-1
Morgan Ch—church AL-4
Morgan Ch—church IA-7
Morgan Ch—church OH-6
Morgan Ch—church VA-3
Morgan Channel—channel OR-9
Morgan Chapel—church (2) AL-4
Morgan Chapel—church CA-9
Morgan Chapel—church GA-3
Morgan Chapel—church KS-7
Morgan Chapel—church LA-4
Morgan Chapel—church MS-4
Morgan Chapel—church NC-3
Morgan Chapel—church OH-6
Morgan Chapel—church VA-3
Morgan Chapel—church (2) WV-2
**Morgan Chapel**—pop pl AL-4
Morgan Chapel and Graveyard—hist pl WV-2
Morgan Chapel Baptist Ch—church MS-4
Morgan Chapel Baptist Church AL-4
Morgan Chapel Cem—cemetery MS-4
Morgan Chapel Cem—cemetery TX-5
Morgan Chapel Christian Methodist Episcopal Ch—church MS-4
Morgan City UT-8
**Morgan City**—pop pl AL-4
**Morgan City**—pop pl LA-4
**Morgan City**—pop pl MS-4
Morgan City, Bayou—stream LA-4
Morgan City Baptist Ch—church MS-4
**Morgan City Beach**—pop pl LA-4
Morgan City City Hall and Courthouse—hist pl LA-4
Morgan City Hist Dist—hist pl LA-4
Morgan City Mine—mine AZ-5
Morgan City Wash—stream AZ-5
Morgan City Well—well AZ-5
**Morgan Corners**—pop pl (2) MI-6
**Morgan Corners**—pop pl NY-2
**Morgan Corners**—pop pl VT-1
Morgan Coulee—valley MT-8
Morgan Coulee—valley (2) WI-6
Morgan County—civil UT-8
**Morgan County**—pop pl AL-4
**Morgan (County)**—pop pl GA-3
**Morgan (County)**—pop pl IL-6
**Morgan County**—pop pl IN-6
**Morgan (County)**—pop pl KY-4
**Morgan County**—pop pl MO-7
**Morgan (County)**—pop pl OH-6
**Morgan County**—pop pl TN-4
**Morgan (County)**—pop pl WV-2
Morgan County Community Ch—church UT-8
Morgan County Courthouse—building AL-4
Morgan County Courthouse—hist pl IL-6
Morgan County Courthouse—hist pl KY-4
Morgan County Courthouse—hist pl MO-7
Morgan County High School AL-4
Morgan County High School TN-4
Morgan County Park—park OR-9
Morgan County Vocational Center—school TN-4
Morgan Court House TN-4
Morgan Cove—valley AL-4
Morgan Cove—valley NC-3
Morgan Covered Bridge—hist pl VT-1
Morgan Crater—crater ID-8
Morgan Creek MS-4
Morgan Creek MT-8
Morgan Creek TN-4
Morgan Creek TX-5
Morgan Creek—stream (6) AL-4
Morgan Creek—stream AK-9
Morgan Creek—stream (3) AR-4
Morgan Creek—stream (4) CA-9
Morgan Creek—stream CO-8
Morgan Creek—stream (4) ID-8
Morgan Creek—stream IL-6
Morgan Creek—stream (2) IN-6
Morgan Creek—stream IA-7
Morgan Creek—stream KS-7
Morgan Creek—stream (2) KY-4
Morgan Creek—stream (3) LA-4
Morgan Creek—stream (2) MD-2
Morgan Creek—stream (2) MI-6
Morgan Creek—stream MN-6
Morgan Creek—stream MS-4
Morgan Creek—stream (3) MT-8
Morgan Creek—stream NE-7
Morgan Creek—stream NV-8
Morgan Creek—stream NM-5
Morgan Creek—stream NY-2
Morgan Creek—stream (5) NC-3
Morgan Creek—stream OK-5
Morgan Creek—stream (10) OR-9
Morgan Creek—stream (2) PA-2
Morgan Creek—stream SC-3
Morgan Creek—stream (5) TN-4
Morgan Creek—stream (5) TX-5
Morgan Creek—stream (3) WA-9
Morgan Creek—stream (3) WI-6
Morgan Creek—stream WY-8
Morgan Creek Ch—church IN-6
Morgan Creek Falls—falls CO-8
**Morgan Creek Hills (subdivision)**—pop pl NC-3
Morgan Creek Oil Field—oilfield TX-5
Morgan Creek Park—park IA-7
Morgan Creek Post Office (historical)—building TN-4
Morgan Creek Pumping Station—other TX-5
Morgan Creek Rsvr—reservoir MT-8
Morgan Creek Rsvr No. 1—reservoir CO-8
Morgan Creek Sch—school MT-8
Morgan Creek Summit—summit ID-8
Morgan-Curtis House—hist pl AL-4
Morgan Cut—gap NC-3
Morgan Cut—gut NY-2
**Morgandale**—pop pl OH-6
Morgandale Sch—school WI-6
Morgan Dam—dam NC-3
Morgan Ditch IN-6
Morgan Drain—canal CO-8
Morgan Drain—canal MI-6
Morgan Drain—stream MI-6
Morgan Draw—valley KS-7
Morgan Draw—valley ND-7
Morgan Draw—valley WY-8
Morgan Draw Tank—reservoir AZ-5
Morgan-Duck Cem—cemetery MS-4
Morgan Eddy—rapids TX-5
Morgan Elem Sch—hist pl UT-8
Morgan Elem Sch—school IN-6
Morgan Elem Sch—school KS-7
Morgan Elem Sch—school NC-3
**Morgan Estates**—pop pl TN-4
Morgan Extension Ditch IN-6
Morgan Falls—falls WI-6
Morgan Falls Ch—church GA-3
Morgan Falls Dam—dam GA-3
Morgan Falls Sch—school GA-3
Morgan Farms Airp—airport KS-7
**Morgan Farms Subdivision**—pop pl UT-8
Morgan Ferry (historical)—locale MS-4
**Morganfield**—pop pl KY-4
Morganfield (CCD)—cens area KY-4
Morganfield Commercial District—hist pl KY-4
Morgan Field Park—park IL-6
Morgan Flat—flat AZ-5
Morgan Ford—locale NC-3
Morgan Ford—locale VA-3
Morgan Ford Bridge—bridge VA-3
Morgan Fork—stream (2) KY-4
Morgan Fork—stream MS-4
Morgan Fork—stream WV-2
Morgan Fork Chapel—church OH-6
Morgan Game and Fish Conservation Club Pond—reservoir CO-8
Morgan Gap—gap AL-4
Morgan Gap—gap TN-4
Morgan-Gold House—hist pl WV-2
Morgan-Gordon Cem—cemetery MS-4
Morgan Grove—locale WV-2
Morgan Grove Ch—church MS-4
Morgan Grove Sch—school MS-4
Morgan Gulch CO-8
Morgan Gulch—valley (2) CA-9
Morgan Gulch—valley (4) CO-8
Morgan Gulch—valley (2) MT-8
Morgan Harbor—bay LA-4
Morgan Harbor Pass—channel LA-4
Morgan-Hartman Cem—cemetery AL-4
**Morgan Heights**—pop pl (2) MO-7
**Morgan Heights**—pop pl NJ-2
**Morgan Heights**—pop pl WV-2
Morgan Heights Sanatorium—hospital MI-6
Morgan Heights Sch—school WV-2
**Morgan Heights (subdivision)**—pop pl NC-3
Morgan Hicks Lake Dam—dam MS-4
Morgan Hill CA-9
Morgan Hill—cliff IN-6
**Morgan Hill**—pop pl CA-9
**Morgan Hill**—pop pl NY-2
**Morgan Hill**—pop pl PA-2
Morgan Hill—summit AL-4
Morgan Hill—summit AZ-5
Morgan Hill—summit (2) CA-9
Morgan Hill—summit CT-1
Morgan Hill—summit IN-6
Morgan Hill—summit MT-8
Morgan Hill—summit NV-8
Morgan Hill—summit (2) NH-1
Morgan Hill—summit (2) NY-2
Morgan Hill—summit NC-3
Morgan Hill—summit (2) PA-2
Morgan Hill—summit TX-5
Morgan Hill—summit (2) VT-1
Morgan Hill—summit WA-9
Morgan Hill Cem—cemetery AR-4
Morgan Hill Cem—cemetery GA-3
Morgan Hill Ch—church NC-3
Morgan Hill Creek—stream NY-2
Morgan Hill Farm—hist pl MD-2
Morganhill (Morgan Hill) CA-9
**Morgan Hill (Morganhill)**—pop pl CA-9
**Morgan (historical)**—pop pl TN-4
Morgan Hole Creek—stream FL-3
Morgan Hollow—valley (2) AL-4
Morgan Hollow—valley (2) AR-4
Morgan Hollow—valley (4) KY-4
Morgan Hollow—valley (3) MO-7
Morgan Hollow—valley (2) NY-2
Morgan Hollow—valley OH-6
Morgan Hollow—valley (8) TN-4
Morgan Hollow—valley UT-8
Morgan Hollow—valley WV-2
Morgan Hollow—valley WI-6
Morgan Hollow Trail—trail PA-2
Morgan Hot Spring—spring CA-9
Morgan House—hist pl AZ-5
Morgan House—hist pl IN-6
Morgan House—hist pl NC-3
Morgan House—hist pl TN-4
Morgan HS—school CT-1
Morgan HS—school UT-8
Morgan HS Mechanical Arts Bldg—hist pl UT-8
Morgan Island—island (2) AK-9
Morgan Island—island DE-2
Morgan Island—island (2) FL-3
Morgan Island—island LA-4
Morgan Island—island NE-7
Morgan Island—island NY-2
Morgan Island—island NC-3
Morgan Island—island OR-9
Morgan Island—island SC-3
Morgan Island (historical)—island TN-4
Morgan Jones Canyon—valley ID-8
Morgan Jones Lake—reservoir MT-8
Morgan Key—island FL-3
Morgan Knob—summit VA-3
Morgan Lake CA-9
Morgan Lake NE-7
Morgan Lake—lake GA-3
Morgan Lake—lake ID-8
Morgan Lake—lake IN-6
Morgan Lake—lake (2) MI-6
Morgan Lake—lake (2) MN-6
Morgan Lake—lake MT-8
Morgan Lake—lake NE-7
Morgan Lake—lake NM-5
Morgan Lake—lake NY-2
Morgan Lake—lake OR-9
Morgan Lake—lake (3) TX-5
Morgan Lake—lake (3) WA-9
Morgan Lake—lake (2) WI-6
Morgan Lake—lake WY-8
Morgan Lake—reservoir (2) AL-4
Morgan Lake—reservoir GA-3
Morgan Lake—reservoir IN-6
Morgan Lake—reservoir MS-4
Morgan Lake—reservoir NM-5
Morgan Lake—reservoir (2) NC-3
Morgan Lake—reservoir OR-9
Morgan Lake—reservoir (2) TN-4
Morgan Lake Campground—locale WI-6
Morgan Lake Dam—dam IN-6
Morgan Lake Dam—dam (3) MS-4
Morgan Lake Dam—dam OR-9
Morgan Lake Dam—dam (2) TN-4
Morgan Lake Park—park AL-4
Morgan Lakes—lake MI-6
Morgan Lakeside Park—park TX-5
Morganland Ch—church PA-2
Morganland Chapel—church WV-2
Morgan Landing—locale FL-3
Morgan Landing—locale (2) OR-9
Morgan Landing—locale VA-3
Morgan Landing Access Area—park MS-4
Morgan-Lindsey Lakes—reservoir TX-5
Morgan Lower Range—channel OR-9
**Morgan Manor (subdivision)**—pop pl PA-2
Morgan Mansion—hist pl OH-6
Morgan Marsh—swamp WA-9
Morgan Marsh—swamp WI-6
Morgan Meadow—flat CA-9
Morgan Meadow—flat ID-8
Morgan Meadow—swamp ME-1
Morgan Meadows—flat CA-9
Morgan Memorial Ch—church SC-3
Morgan Memorial Ch—church WV-2
**Morgan Mill**—pop pl TX-5
Morgan Mill-Bluff Dale (CCD)—cens area TX-5
Morgan Mill Branch—stream MS-4
Morgan Mill Creek—stream NC-3
Morgan Millpond—lake FL-3
Morgan Mill (Ruins)—locale NV-8
Morgan Mills PA-2
Morgan Mill Stream—stream VA-3
Morgan Mine—mine AZ-5
Morgan Mine—mine CA-9
Morgan Mine—mine CO-8
Morgan Mine—mine NV-8
Morgan Mines—locale WV-2
Morgan Mines—mine NM-5
Morgan Mine (underground)—mine AL-4
Morgan Mine (underground)—mine TN-4
Morgan-Monroe State For IN-6
Morgan Monroe State For—forest IN-6
Morgan Mountain Spring—spring OR-9
Morgan Mountain Spring Number Two—spring OR-9
Morgan MS—school UT-8
Morgan Mtn AR-4
Morgan Mtn—summit AL-4
Morgan Mtn—summit AZ-5
Morgan Mtn—summit AR-4
Morgan Mtn—summit CA-9
Morgan Mtn—summit ID-8
Morgan Mtn—summit MT-8
Morgan Mtn—summit NY-2
Morgan Mtn—summit (2) NC-3
Morgan Mtn—summit OK-5
Morgan Mtn—summit (2) OR-9
Morgan Mtn—summit TX-5
Morgan Mtn—summit VT-1
Morgan Municipal Airp—airport UT-8
Morgan North—cens area UT-8
Morgan North Division—civil UT-8
Morgan Park IL-6
Morgan Park IN-6
Morgan Park MN-6
Morgan Park—park CT-1
Morgan Park—park MA-1
Morgan Park—park MN-6
Morgan Park—park NE-7
Morgan Park—park NY-2
Morgan Park—park OK-5
Morgan Park—park TN-4
Morgan Park—park (2) WI-6
**Morgan Park**—pop pl IN-6
**Morgan Park**—pop pl MN-6
Morgan Park Acad—school IL-6
Morgan Park HS—school IL-6
Morgan Pass MT-8
Morgan Pass—channel FL-3
Morgan Pass—gap CA-9
Morgan Pass—gap NV-8
Morgan Peak—summit CO-8
Morgan Peak—summit TX-5
Morgan Peak—summit VT-1
Morgan Place—locale FL-3
Morgan Place—locale ID-8
**Morgan Place**—pop pl OH-6
Morgan Playground—park LA-4
Morgan Point TX-5
Morgan Point—cape AK-9
Morgan Point—cape (2) AR-4
Morgan Point—cape CA-9
Morgan Point—cape (2) CT-1
Morgan Point—cape FL-3
Morgan Point—cape MD-2
Morgan Point—cape TN-4
Morgan Point—cape TX-5
Morgan Point—cliff AR-4
Morgan Point Bar—bar TN-4
Morgan Point Dikes—levee TN-4
Morgan Point Rec Area—park AR-4
Morgan Pond CT-1
Morgan Pond—bay (2) LA-4
Morgan Pond—dam AL-4
Morgan Pond—lake (2) FL-3
Morgan Pond—lake IL-6
Morgan Pond—lake MI-6
Morgan Pond—lake NH-1
Morgan Pond—lake NC-3
Morgan Pond—reservoir AL-4
Morgan Pond Dam—dam MS-4
Morgan Pond Rsvr—reservoir CT-1
Morgan Ponds—lake NC-3
Morgan Post Office—building UT-8
Morgan Post Office (historical)—building (2) TN-4
Morgan Ranch—locale MT-8
Morgan Ranch—locale NV-8
Morgan Ranch—locale NM-5
Morgan Ranch—locale OR-9
Morgan Ranch—locale TX-5
Morgan Ranch—locale UT-8
Morgan Ranch—locale WY-8
Morgan Rapids—rapids NY-2
Morganrath Lake WA-9
Morgan Ravine—valley CA-9
Morgan Ridge—ridge CA-9
Morgan Ridge—ridge (2) ID-8
Morgan Ridge—ridge OR-9
Morgan Ridge—ridge (2) TN-4
Morgan Ridge—ridge (2) WV-2
Morgan Ridge Cem—cemetery MO-7
Morgan River CT-1
Morgan River—gut FL-3
Morgan River—stream LA-4
Morgan River—stream SC-3
Morgan Road Sch—school NY-2
Morgan Rock—island CA-9
Morganroth Creek—stream WA-9
Morganroth Lake WA-9
Morgan Row—hist pl KY-4
Morgan Rsvr—reservoir CA-9
Morgan Rsvr—reservoir CO-8
Morgan Rsvr—reservoir (2) OR-9
Morgan Rsvr—reservoir WY-8
Morgan Run—locale OH-6
Morgan Run—locale PA-2
Morgan Run—stream MD-2
Morgan Run—stream (2) OH-6
Morgan Run—stream (2) PA-2
Morgan Run—stream VA-3
Morgan Run—stream (7) WV-2
Morgans MS-4
**Morgans**—pop pl MS-4
Morgans Alley—post sta ID-8
Morgans Bayou—stream LA-4
Morgans Branch VA-3
Morgans Branch—stream AL-4
Morgans Bridge—bridge GA-3
Morgans Buckhorn—summit OR-9
Morgansburg SD-7
Morgans Cem—cemetery SD-7
Morgan Sch—school CA-9
Morgan Sch—school CO-8
Morgan Sch—school DC-2
Morgan Sch—school FL-3
Morgan Sch—school (4) IL-6
Morgan Sch—school IN-6
Morgan Sch—school IA-7
Morgan Sch—school KY-4
Morgan Sch—school MI-6
Morgan Sch—school MO-7
Morgan Sch—school NC-3
Morgan Sch—school (3) OH-6
Morgan Sch—school SC-3
Morgan Sch—school SD-7
Morgan Sch—school (2) TN-4
Morgan Sch—school (2) UT-8
Morgan Sch—school WV-2
Morgan Sch—school (2) WI-6
Morgan Sch (abandoned)—school MO-7
Morgans Chapel AL-4
Morgans Chapel—church GA-3
Morgans Chapel—church NC-3
Morgans Chapel—church TN-4
Morgans Chapel—church VA-3
Morgans Chapel Church AL-4
Morgan Sch (historical)—school (2) AL-4
Morgan Sch (historical)—school MS-4
Morgan Sch (historical)—school MO-7
Morgan Sch (historical)—school NC-3
Morgan Sch (historical)—school (2) TN-4
Morgan Sch Number 86 IN-6
Morgans Corner PA-2
Morgans Corner—locale OK-5
**Morgans Corners**—pop pl NC-3
**Morgan's Corner (Spences Corner)**—pop pl NC-3
Morgans Creek TN-4
Morgans Creek—stream KY-4
Morgans Creek—stream NC-3
Morgans Creek Sch—school KY-4
Morgans Crossroad AL-4
Morgans Crossroads AL-4
**Morgans Crossroads**—pop pl AL-4
Morgans Dam—dam AL-4
Morgans Dock—locale TN-4
Morgans Ferry—locale AZ-5
Morgans Fork MS-4
Morgan's Gulch CO-8
Morgans Gulch—valley CO-8
Morgans Gulch—valley ID-8
Morgans Hill PA-2
**Morgans Hill**—pop pl PA-2
Morgans Shoal—bar IL-6
Morgans Homo Chitto MS-4
Morgans Knob VA-3
Morgans Lake NJ-2
Morgans Lake—reservoir MS-4
Morgans Lake Dam—dam MS-4
**Morgans Land**—pop pl PA-2
Morgans Landing—locale CA-9
Morgans Slough—gut CA-9
Morgans Slough—gut IL-6
Morgans Slough—stream AR-4
Morgans Memorial Ch—church NC-3
Morgans Mill TX-5
Morgan's Mill—hist pl NC-3
Morgans Mills—locale MS-4
Morgan South—cens area UT-8
Morgan South Division—civil UT-8
Morgans Pasture—flat ID-8
Morgans Peak TX-5
Morgan's Point AR-4
Morgan's Point CT-1
Morgans Point—cape (2) TX-5
**Morgan's Point**—pop pl TX-5
**Morgans Point**—pop pl TX-5
**Morgan's Point Resort**—pop pl TX-5
Morgans Pond—lake (2) GA-3
Morgans Pond—reservoir (2) AL-4
Morgans Pond—reservoir (3) NC-3
Morgans Pond—swamp MA-1
Morgans Pond Dam—dam NC-3
Morgan Spring—lake MI-6
Morgan Spring—spring (2) AZ-5
Morgan Spring—spring CA-9
Morgan Spring—spring MO-7
Morgan Spring—spring MT-8
Morgan Spring—spring (3) NV-8
Morgan Spring—spring (3) OR-9
Morgan Spring—spring TN-4
Morgan Spring Ch—church AR-4
Morgan Springs—locale CA-9
**Morgan Springs**—pop pl AL-4
**Morgan Springs**—pop pl TN-4
Morgan Springs—spring TN-4
Morgan Springs—spring TX-5
Morgan Springs Cem—cemetery TN-4
Morgan Springs Lookout Tower—locale AL-4
Morgan Springs Post Office (historical)—building AL-4
Morgan Springs Post Office (historical)—building TN-4
Morgan Springs Sch (historical)—school TN-4
Morgan Springs Well AZ-5
Morgan Spring Well—locale AZ-5
Morgans Run—other WV-2
**Morgans Run**—pop pl WV-2
Morgans Run—stream WV-2
Morgans Sch TN-4
Morgan's Shoal IL-6
Morgans Spring—spring FL-3
Morgans Station—building PA-2
Morgans Steep—cliff TN-4
**Morgans Store**—pop pl MS-4
Morgans Store (historical)—locale AL-4
Morgan State Coll—school MD-2
Morgan State For—forest TN-4
Morgan Street Hist Dist—hist pl KY-4
Morgan Summit—summit CA-9
Morgans Valley PA-2
Morgansville MD-2
**Morgansville**—pop pl OH-6
**Morgansville**—pop pl WV-2
Morgan Swamp—stream NC-3
Morgan Swamp—swamp MA-1
Morgan Swamp—swamp NC-3
Morgans Waterhole—lake ID-8
Morgans Well—well CA-9
Morgan Tabernacle—church AL-4
Morgan Table—bench MT-8
Morgan Tank—reservoir (4) AZ-5
Morgan Tank—reservoir (2) NM-5
Morgan Territory—area CA-9
Morgan Territory School (Abandoned)—locale CA-9
Morgantine, Lake—swamp LA-4
**Morganton**—pop pl AR-4
**Morganton**—pop pl GA-3
**Morganton**—pop pl NC-3
**Morganton**—pop pl TN-4
Morganton Baptist Ch—church TN-4
Morganton (CCD)—cens area GA-3
Morganton Cem—cemetery TN-4
Morganton Cumberland Presbyterian Ch (historical)—church TN-4
Morganton Downtown Hist Dist—hist pl NC-3
Morganton Ferry—locale TN-4
Morganton (historical)—locale MS-4
Morganton JHS—school NC-3
Morganton Junior Acad—school NC-3
Morganton-Lenoir Airp—airport NC-3
Morganton Plaza—locale NC-3
Morganton Point Rec Area—park GA-3
Morganton Post Office (historical)—building TN-4
Morganton Rec Area—park TN-4
Morganton Road Elem Sch—school NC-3
Morgantons Crossroads TN-4
Morganton (Township of)—fmr MCD NC-3
Morganton Watershed Dam—dam NC-3
Morganton Watershed Lake—reservoir NC-3
Morgantown IN-6
Morgantown TN-4
Morgantown—locale FL-3
Morgantown—locale VA-3
**Morgantown**—pop pl AZ-5
**Morgantown**—pop pl IN-6
**Morgantown**—pop pl KY-4
**Morgantown**—pop pl (2) MD-2
**Morgantown**—pop pl (3) MS-4
**Morgantown**—pop pl NC-3
**Morgantown**—pop pl (2) OH-6
**Morgantown**—pop pl PA-2
**Morgantown**—pop pl TN-4
**Morgantown**—pop pl WV-2
Morgantown Aero Corp Airp—airport PA-2
Morgantown Airp PA-2
Morgantown Baptist Ch—church MS-4
Morgantown (CCD)—cens area KY-4
Morgantown Cem—cemetery MS-4
Morgantown Elem Sch—school MS-4
Morgan Town Hall—building ND-7
Morgantown HS—school MS-4
Morgantown Interchange PA-2
Morgantown Lock—other WV-2
Morgantown MS—school MS-4
Morgantown Municipal Airport (W. L. Bill Hart Field)—airport WV-2
**Morgan (Town of)**—pop pl VT-1
**Morgan (Town of)**—pop pl WI-6
Morgantown Oil Field—oilfield (2) MS-4
Morgantown Sch—school KS-7
Morgantown Sch (historical)—school TN-4
Morgan Township—fmr MCD (5) IA-7
**Morgan Township**—pop pl KS-7
**Morgan Township**—pop pl MO-7
**Morgan Township**—pop pl ND-7
**Morgan Township**—pop pl SD-7
Morgan (Township of)—fmr MCD (4) AR-4
Morgan (Township of)—fmr MCD (2) NC-3
**Morgan (Township of)**—pop pl IL-6
**Morgan (Township of)**—pop pl (3) IN-6
**Morgan (Township of)**—pop pl MN-6
**Morgan (Township of)**—pop pl (6) OH-6
**Morgan (Township of)**—pop pl PA-2
Morgan Trail—trail CA-9
Morgan Trail Park—park IN-6
Morgan Upper Range—channel OR-9
Morgan Upper Range—channel WA-9
Morgan Valley—valley CA-9
Morgan Valley—valley GA-3
Morgan Valley—valley PA-2
Morgan Valley—valley UT-8
Morgan Valley Ch—church IA-7
Morgan Valley Run—stream PA-2
Morgan Valley Sch (historical)—school PA-2
**Morgan Village**—pop pl NJ-2
Morganville (2) AL-4
Morganville MS-4
Morganville—locale GA-3
**Morganville**—pop pl KS-7
**Morganville**—pop pl NJ-2
**Morganville**—pop pl NY-2
**Morganville**—pop pl OH-6
**Morganville**—pop pl PA-2
**Morganville**—pop pl TN-4
**Morganville**—pop pl WA-9
Morganville Cem—cemetery KS-7
Morganville Cem—cemetery NY-2
Morganville Ditch—canal CO-8
Morganville Elem Sch—school KS-7
Morganville Pottery Factory Site—hist pl NY-2
Morgan Wash AZ-5
Morgan Wash—stream (2) AZ-5
Morgan Well AZ-5
Morgan Well—well NM-5
Morgan-Wells House—hist pl IL-6
Morgan Windmill—locale NM-5
Morgan Windmill—locale (2) TX-5
Morganwood Camp—locale MS-4
Morgan Woods Elem Sch—school FL-3
**Morganza**—pop pl LA-4
**Morganza**—pop pl MD-2
**Morganza**—pop pl PA-2
Morganza Crevasse—valley LA-4
Morganza Dam—dam PA-2
Morganza Floodway—flat (2) LA-4
Morganza Landing—locale LA-4
Morganza Landing (historical)—locale MS-4
Morganza Rsvr—reservoir PA-2
Morganzia LA-4
Morganzia Crevasse LA-4
Morganzia Landing LA-4
Morgareidge Cem—cemetery WY-8
Morgareidge Ditch—canal WY-8
**Morgarts Beach**—pop pl VA-3
Morgenroth Lake WA-9
Morgenroth Lake—lake WA-9
Morgenson Springs—spring CA-9
**Morgan Station**—pop pl MD-2
**Morges**—pop pl OH-6
Morgeson Creek MI-6
Morg Hill—summit MO-7
**Morgin Valley (historical)**—pop pl IA-7
Morgloba, Lake—reservoir AL-4
**Morgnec**—pop pl MD-2
Morgridge Pond—lake ME-1
Morg Spring—spring OR-9
Morgue Fork—stream KY-4
**Morhain**—pop pl IA-7
Morhardt Sch—school MT-8
Morhead City MS—school NC-3
Moriah—locale IA-7
**Moriah**—pop pl AL-4
**Moriah**—pop pl IL-6
**Moriah**—pop pl NY-2
**Moriah**—pop pl NC-3

Morrill Brook—*stream* (4) VT-1
*Morrill Cave* TN-4
Morrill Cem—*cemetery* WI-6
*Morrill Creek* TN-4
Morrill Creek—*stream* MA-1
Morrill Fish Pond Branch—*stream* TX-5
Morrill Hall, Cornell Univ—*hist pl* NY-2
Morrill Hall, Univ of Nevada/
Reno—*hist pl* NV-8
Morrill Hill—*summit* ME-1
Morrill Hill—*summit* NH-1
Morrill-Lassonde House—*hist pl* NH-1
Morrill Ledges—*summit* ME-1
Morrill Memorial Library—*building* MA-1
Morrill Mtn—*summit* VT-1
Morrill Park—*park* TX-5
Morrill Pond—*lake* ME-1
Morrill Pond—*lake* (2) NH-1
**Morrills**—*pop pl* MA-1
Morrill Sch—*school* IL-6
Morrill Sch—*school* SD-7
Morrill Sch—*school* VT-1
**Morrills Corner**—*pop pl* ME-1
Morrill Slope Mine (underground)—*mine* AL-4
*Morrill Spring* TN-4
*Morrillton* AR-4
**Morrill (Town of)**—*pop pl* ME-1
**Morrill Township**—*pop pl* KS-7
**Morrill (Township of)**—*pop pl* MN-6
Morrill Trail—*trail* TN-4
*Morrils Cave* TN-4
**Morrilton**—*pop pl* AR-4
Morrilton Cutoff—*channel* AR-4
Morrilton Male and Female
College—*hist pl* AR-4
Morrilton RR Station—*hist pl* AR-4
**Morrin Subdivision**—*pop pl* UT-8
Morris—*locale* AR-4
Morris—*locale* IA-7
Morris—*locale* MS-4
Morris—*locale* NJ-2
Morris—*locale* WV-2
**Morris**—*pop pl* AL-4
**Morris**—*pop pl* CT-1
**Morris**—*pop pl* GA-3
**Morris**—*pop pl* IL-6
**Morris**—*pop pl* (2) IN-6
**Morris**—*pop pl* KS-7
**Morris**—*pop pl* LA-4
**Morris**—*pop pl* MN-6
**Morris**—*pop pl* MS-4
**Morris**—*pop pl* NY-2
**Morris**—*pop pl* OK-5
**Morris**—*pop pl* PA-2
Morris—*uninc pl* KS-7
Morris, Andrew James, House—*hist pl* UT-8
Morris, Anthony, House—*hist pl* PA-2
Morris, C. E., House—*hist pl* OH-6
Morris, Dr. William, Office and
House—*hist pl* KY-4
Morris, Fort—*fo* MA-1
Morris, Jim, Barn—*hist pl* AR-4
Morris, Joseph Henry, House—*hist pl* MS-4
Morris, Josie Bassett, Ranch
Complex—*hist pl* UT-8
Morris, Lake—*lake* AK-9
Morris, Lake—*lake* WI-6
Morris, Lake—*reservoir* KY-4
Morris, Lewis G., House—*hist pl* NY-2
Morris, Mount—*summit* NY-2
Morris, Mount—*summit* WI-6
Morris, Richard Vaughen, House—*hist pl* UT-8
Morris, Wright, Boyhood House—*hist pl* NE-7
Morris, W. W., House—*hist pl* TN-4
**Morris Acres**—*pop pl* SC-3
Morris Airp—*airport* PA-2
Morrisana Plantation (historical)—*locale* MS-4
Morris and Caple Tunnel—*mine* NV-8
**Morrisania**—*pop pl* NY-2
Morrisania Hosp—*hospital* NY-2
Morrisania Mesa—*summit* CO-8
Morris Arboretum—*park* PA-2
Morris Ave Hist Dist—*hist pl* AL-4
Morris Avenue-First Ave North Hist
Dist—*hist pl* AL-4
Morris Ave Sch—*school* CT-1
Morris-Baker Cem—*cemetery* OR-9
Morris Basin—*basin* NV-8
Morris Basin—*basin* OR-9
Morris Basin Spring—*spring* NV-8
Morris Bay—*basin* SC-3
Morris Bay—*bay* MI-6
Morris Bay—*bay* VA-3
Morris Bayou—*stream* LA-4
**Morris Beach**—*pop pl* NJ-2
Morris Bend—*bend* AR-4
Morris Bldg—*hist pl* KY-4
Morris Bluff—*cliff* MO-7
Morris Bluff—*cliff* TN-4
Morris Brake—*swamp* AR-4
*Morris Branch* WV-2
Morris Branch—*stream* (2) AL-4
Morris Branch—*stream* (2) AR-4
Morris Branch—*stream* (2) DE-2
Morris Branch—*stream* FL-3
Morris Branch—*stream* GA-3
Morris Branch—*stream* (3) KY-4
Morris Branch—*stream* LA-4
Morris Branch—*stream* MD-2
Morris Branch—*stream* MS-4
Morris Branch—*stream* MO-7
Morris Branch—*stream* (3) NC-3
Morris Branch—*stream* PA-2
Morris Branch—*stream* (2) SC-3
Morris Branch—*stream* (3) TN-4
Morris Branch—*stream* TX-5
Morris Branch—*stream* (3) VA-3
Morris Bridge—*bridge* AL-4
Morris Bridge—*bridge* FL-3
Morris Bridge—*bridge* ND-7
Morris Bridge—*bridge* OR-9
Morris Bridge—*bridge* VA-3
Morris Bridge (historical)—*bridge* TN-4
Morris Brook—*stream* NH-1
Morris Brook—*stream* NY-2
Morris Brooks Cave—*cave* AL-4
Morris Brown—*uninc pl* GA-3
Morris Brown Coll—*school* GA-3
Morrisburg Cem—*cemetery* IA-7
**Morrisburgh (historical)**—*pop pl* IA-7

Morris-Butler House—*hist pl* IN-6
Morris Butt—*summit* VA-3
Morris Butte—*summit* OR-9
Morris Camp—*locale* TX-5
Morris Canal—*canal* NJ-2
Morris Canal—*hist pl* NJ-2
Morris Canal (Abandoned)—*canal* NJ-2
Morris Canal Basin—*basin* NJ-2
Morris Canyon—*stream* OR-9
Morris Canyon—*valley* CA-9
Morris Canyon—*valley* ID-8
Morris Canyon—*valley* NM-5
Morris Canyon—*valley* OR-9
Morris Canyon—*valley* WA-9
Morris Canyon—*valley* WY-8
Morris Canyon Spring—*spring* ID-8
Morris Carnegie Library—*hist pl* MN-6
Morris Cave—*cave* AR-4
Morris Cave—*cave* IN-6
Morris Cave—*cave* TN-4
Morris (CCD)—*cens area* OK-5
*Morris Cem* MS-4
Morris Cem—*cemetery* (11) AL-4
Morris Cem—*cemetery* (3) AR-4
Morris Cem—*cemetery* CA-9
Morris Cem—*cemetery* (3) GA-3
Morris Cem—*cemetery* (3) IL-6
Morris Cem—*cemetery* IN-6
Morris Cem—*cemetery* KS-7
Morris Cem—*cemetery* (10) KY-4
Morris Cem—*cemetery* LA-4
Morris Cem—*cemetery* (3) MS-4
Morris Cem—*cemetery* (13) MO-7
Morris Cem—*cemetery* NM-5
Morris Cem—*cemetery* NC-3
Morris Cem—*cemetery* (3) OH-6
Morris Cem—*cemetery* (2) OK-5
Morris Cem—*cemetery* (2) PA-2
Morris Cem—*cemetery* SC-3
Morris Cem—*cemetery* (17) TN-4
Morris Cem—*cemetery* (5) TX-5
Morris Cem—*cemetery* VA-3
Morris Cem—*cemetery* (6) WV-2
Morris Center Cem—*cemetery* KS-7
Morris Ch—*church* IN-6
Morris Ch—*church* LA-4
Morris Ch—*church* NJ-2
Morris Ch—*church* OH-6
Morris Ch—*church* OK-5
Morris Chapel—*church* (2) AL-4
Morris Chapel—*church* AR-4
Morris Chapel—*church* GA-3
Morris Chapel—*church* (4) IN-6
Morris Chapel—*church* KY-4
Morris Chapel—*church* MI-6
Morris Chapel—*church* MS-4
Morris Chapel—*church* (2) MO-7
Morris Chapel—*church* (3) NC-3
Morris Chapel—*church* (4) OH-6
Morris Chapel—*church* (3) SC-3
Morris Chapel—*church* TN-4
Morris Chapel—*church* TX-5
Morris Chapel—*church* (2) WV-2
**Morris Chapel**—*pop pl* (2) TN-4
*Morris Chapel Baptist Ch* AL-4
Morris Chapel (CCD)—*cens area* AL-4
Morris Chapel (CCD)—*cens area* TN-4
Morris Chapel Cem—*cemetery* (2) AL-4
Morris Chapel Cem—*cemetery* IL-6
Morris Chapel Cem—*cemetery* OH-6
Morris Chapel Cem—*cemetery* TN-4
Morris Chapel Cem—*cemetery* (2) TX-5
Morris Chapel Division—*civil* AL-4
Morris Chapel Division—*civil* TN-4
*Morris Chapel Methodist Church* TN-4
*Morris Chapel Missionary Baptist Ch* MS-4
Morris Chapel Sch—*school* TN-4
Morris Chapel United Methodist
Ch—*church* AL-4
Morris Church—*locale* VA-3
Morris Coll—*school* SC-3
Morris Corner—*locale* ME-1
**Morris Corner**—*pop pl* MA-1
Morris Coulee—*valley* MT-8
Morris County—*civil* KS-7
**Morris County**—*pop pl* NJ-2
**Morris (County)**—*pop pl* TX-5
Morris County Courthouse—*hist pl* NJ-2
**Morris County Junction**—*pop pl* NJ-2
*Morris County Swamp* NJ-2
Morris Cove—*bay* CT-1
Morris Cove—*bay* NY-2
Morris Cove—*bay* WI-6
**Morris Cove**—*pop pl* CT-1
Morris Covington Pond Dam—*dam* MS-4
*Morris Creek* SD-7
*Morris Creek* TN-4
*Morris Creek* VA-3
*Morris Creek* WI-6
Morris Creek—*stream* (2) AK-9
Morris Creek—*stream* (2) CO-8
Morris Creek—*stream* CT-1
Morris Creek—*stream* GA-3
Morris Creek—*stream* (4) ID-8
Morris Creek—*stream* IL-6
Morris Creek—*stream* IN-6
Morris Creek—*stream* (2) KY-4
Morris Creek—*stream* MS-4
Morris Creek—*stream* (5) MT-8
Morris Creek—*stream* NV-8
Morris Creek—*stream* (4) NC-3
Morris Creek—*stream* ND-7
Morris Creek—*stream* OK-5
Morris Creek—*stream* (7) OR-9
Morris Creek—*stream* SC-3
Morris Creek—*stream* SD-7
Morris Creek—*stream* (2) TN-4
Morris Creek—*stream* (4) TX-5
Morris Creek—*stream* UT-8
Morris Creek—*stream* (2) VA-3
Morris Creek—*stream* (3) WV-2
Morris Creek Ch—*church* KY-4
Morris Creek Ch—*church* SC-3
Morris Creek Sch—*school* SD-7
*Morris Crossroad* AL-4
*Morris Cross Roads* PA-2
**Morris Crossroads**—*pop pl* AL-4
**Morris Crossroads**—*pop pl* PA-2
**Morrisdale**—*pop pl* PA-2
**Morrisdale**—*pop pl* VA-3

Morrisdale Dam—*dam* PA-2
Morris Dam—*dam* (2) CA-9
Morris Dam—*dam* TN-4
Morris Day Gap—*gap* AZ-5
Morris Dees Dam—*dam* AL-4
Morris Dees Lake Number Two—*reservoir* AL-4
Morris Dees Number 2 Dam—*dam* AL-4
Morris Ditch—*canal* IN-6
Morris Ditch—*canal* WY-8
Morris Drain—*canal* (2) MI-6
Morris Drain—*stream* MI-6
Morris Draw—*valley* (2) WY-8
*Morris Elem Sch* AL-4
Morris Elem Sch—*school* AL-4
Morris Elem Sch—*school* KS-7
Morris Elem Sch—*school* PA-2
Morris-Erickson County Park—*park* WI-6
Morris Estates—*locale* GA-3
**Morris Estates**—*pop pl* DE-2
Morrisett Chapel—*church* TN-4
*Morrisette Creek* AL-4
Morrisette Landing—*locale* AL-4
Morrisett Oil Field—*oilfield* TX-5
*Morrisetts Chapel* TN-4
*Morrisetts Chapel Baptist Ch* TN-4
Morrisey—*locale* WY-8
Morrisey Creek—*stream* ID-8
Morrisey Park Church
Campground—*locale* KY-4
Morrisey Well (Abandoned)—*well* NM-5
Morris Ferry Bridge—*bridge* TN-4
Morris Ferry Dock—*locale* TN-4
Morris Ferry (historical)—*crossing* TN-4
Morris Ferry (historical)—*locale* AL-4
Morris Field—*park* NM-5
Morris Field (historical)—*airport* NC-3
Morris Flat—*flat* CA-9
Morris Ford Bridge (historical)—*locale* MO-7
Morris Ford (historical)—*crossing* TN-4
**Morris Fork**—*pop pl* KY-4
**Morris Fork**—*pop pl* WV-2
Morris Fork—*stream* (2) KY-4
Morris Fork—*stream* (2) WV-2
Morris Fork Cem—*cemetery* KY-4
Morris Fork Ch—*church* WV-2
Morris-Franks Site—*hist pl* OH-6
*Morris Gap* TN-4
Morris Gap—*gap* GA-3
Morris Gap—*gap* KY-4
Morris Gap—*gap* (2) TN-4
Morris Gap—*gap* VA-3
**Morrisgap (historical)**—*pop pl* TN-4
*Morris Gap Post Office* TN-4
Morrisgap Post Office
(historical)—*building* TN-4
Morris Graves—*cemetery* GA-3
Morris Grove—*locale* TX-5
Morris Grove Ch—*church* VA-3
Morris Gulch—*valley* CO-8
Morris Hamilton Dam—*dam* SD-7
Morris Harvey Coll—*school* WV-2
**Morris Heights**—*pop pl* NY-2
Morris Heights Cem—*cemetery* OK-5
**Morris Heights (subdivision)**—*pop pl* AL-4
Morris Hill—*summit* KS-7
Morris Hill—*summit* KY-4
Morris Hill—*summit* (3) NY-2
Morris Hill—*summit* OR-9
Morris Hill—*summit* TX-5
Morris Hill—*summit* VA-3
Morris Hill—*summit* WY-8
*Morris Hill Baptist Church* TN-4
Morris Hill Cem—*cemetery* AL-4
Morris Hill Cem—*cemetery* ID-8
Morris Hill Cemetery Mausoleum—*hist pl* ID-8
*Morris Hill Ch* MS-4
*Morris Hill Ch* TN-4
Morris Hill Ch—*church* KY-4
Morris Hill Ch—*church* (2) MS-4
Morris Hill Ch—*church* TN-4
Morris Hill Ch—*church* VA-3
Morris Hill Ch (historical)—*church* AL-4
Morris Hill Full Gospel Pentecostal
Ch—*church* AL-4
*Morris Hills* IL-6
Morris Hill Sch—*school* NJ-2
Morris Hill Sch—*school* TN-4
Morris (historical)—*locale* PA-2
Morris Hollow—*valley* AL-4
Morris Hollow—*valley* (2) MO-7
Morris Hollow—*valley* (4) TN-4
Morris Hollow—*valley* TX-5
Morris Hollow—*valley* WV-2
Morris House—*hist pl* (2) AR-4
Morris House—*hist pl* CT-1
Morris House—*hist pl* OH-6
Morris HS—*school* NY-2
Morrish Sch—*school* MI-6
Morris HS Hist Dist—*hist pl* NY-2
Morris Industrial Sch for Indians
Dormitory—*hist pl* MN-6
Morris Institute—*school* AR-4
Morris Island—*cape* MA-1
Morris Island—*island* SC-3
Morris Island—*island* VA-3
Morris Island Creek—*stream* VA-3
Morris Island (historical)—*island* (2) TN-4
Morris Island Lighthouse—*hist pl* SC-3
Morris Island Marshes—*swamp* MA-1
Morris Jensen Dam—*dam* SD-7
Morris-Jumel Mansion—*hist pl* NY-2
Morris Junior Coll of Business—*school* FL-3
Morris Kennedy Mid Sch—*school* IL-6
*Morris Knob* VA-3
Morris Knob—*summit* VA-3
Morris K Udall Regional Park—*park* AZ-5
*Morris Lake* MN-6
Morris Lake—*lake* AL-4
Morris Lake—*lake* CA-9
Morris Lake—*lake* (2) FL-3
Morris Lake—*lake* LA-4
Morris Lake—*lake* (3) MI-6
Morris Lake—*lake* (2) MN-6
Morris Lake—*lake* NM-5
Morris Lake—*lake* SD-7
Morris Lake—*lake* WA-9
Morris Lake—*reservoir* LA-4
Morris Lake—*reservoir* NJ-2
Morris Lake—*reservoir* OK-5
Morris Lake—*reservoir* TN-4

Morris Lake Dam—*dam* MS-4
Morris Lake Dam—*dam* NJ-2
Morris Lake State Public Shooting
Area—*park* SD-7
Morris Landing—*locale* NC-3
*Morris Listons Land* DE-2
Morris Lookout Tower—*locale* TN-4
Morris Lookout Tower—*locale* WI-6
Morris Mansion and Mill—*hist pl* NJ-2
Morris Meadows—*flat* CA-9
Morris Meadows Camp—*locale* CA-9
Morris Memorial Baptist Ch—*church* TN-4
Morris Memorial Bldg—*hist pl* TN-4
Morris Memorial Ch—*church* NC-3
Morris Memorial Ch—*church* WV-2
Morris Memorial County Park—*park* IA-7
*Morris Mill* AL-4
Morris Mill—*locale* AL-4
Morris Mill—*locale* DE-2
Morris Mill (historical)—*locale* AL-4
Morris Mill (historical)—*locale* TN-4
*Morris Mill Pond* DE-2
Morris Millpond—*reservoir* DE-2
Morris Millpond Dam—*dam* DE-2
Morris Mine—*mine* CA-9
Morris Mine—*mine* MI-6
Morris Mine—*mine* MN-6
Morris Mine—*mine* MO-7
Morris Mine—*mine* OR-9
**Morris Mine**—*pop pl* FL-3
Morris Mine RR Station—*locale* FL-3
Morris Mine (underground)—*mine* AL-4
Morris-Moore House—*hist pl* TX-5
*Morris Mountain* WY-8
Morris Mtn—*summit* AL-4
Morris Mtn—*summit* KY-4
Morris Mtn—*summit* NC-3
Morris Neck—*cape* MD-2
Morris North Mine (surface)—*mine* AL-4
Morris' No. 41 Archeol District—*hist pl* NM-5
Morrison—*locale* CA-9
Morrison—*locale* LA-4
Morrison—*locale* MD-2
**Morrison**—*pop pl* CO-8
**Morrison**—*pop pl* IL-6
**Morrison**—*pop pl* IA-7
**Morrison**—*pop pl* MO-7
**Morrison**—*pop pl* OK-5
**Morrison**—*pop pl* SC-3
**Morrison**—*pop pl* TN-4
**Morrison**—*pop pl* VA-3
**Morrison**—*pop pl* WV-2
**Morrison**—*pop pl* WI-6
Morrison, Alfred W., House—*hist pl* MO-7
Morrison, Andrew J., Sch—*hist pl* PA-2
Morrison, Fort—*fo* MA-1
Morrison, Francis H., House—*hist pl* IN-6
Morrison, Jackson, House—*hist pl* GA-3
Morrison, Mount—*summit* CA-9
Morrison, Mount—*summit* CO-8
Morrison Bay—*bay* MN-6
Morrison Bayou—*gut* MI-6
Morrison Block (M. O'Connor Grocery
Wholesalers)—*hist pl* IN-6
Morrison Bluff—*cliff* FL-3
**Morrison Bluff**—*pop pl* AR-4
*Morrison Branch* WI-6
Morrison Branch—*stream* (2) GA-3
Morrison Branch—*stream* IL-6
Morrison Branch—*stream* (4) KY-4
Morrison Branch—*stream* ME-1
Morrison Branch—*stream* SC-3
Morrison Branch—*stream* TN-4
Morrison Branch—*stream* TX-5
Morrison Branch—*swamp* FL-3
Morrison Bridge—*bridge* NC-3
Morrison Bridge—*bridge* OR-9
Morrison Brook—*stream* (3) ME-1
Morrison Brook—*stream* MN-6
Morrison Brook—*stream* NY-2
Morrison Brook—*stream* VT-1
Morrison Brothers Dam—*dam* (2) AL-4
Morrison Brothers Lake—*reservoir* (2) AL-4
Morrison Cabin—*locale* CA-9
Morrison Camp—*locale* CA-9
Morrison-Campbell House—*hist pl* NC-3
Morrison Campground—*locale* GA-3
Morrison Campground—*locale* PA-2
Morrison Canal—*canal* LA-4
Morrison Canyon—*valley* CA-9
Morrison Canyon—*valley* (2) CO-8
Morrison Canyon—*valley* MT-8
Morrison Canyon—*valley* WA-9
Morrison Canyon—*valley* WY-8
Morrison Catfish Ponds Dam—*dam* MS-4
Morrison (CCD)—*cens area* TN-4
Morrison Cem—*cemetery* AL-4
Morrison Cem—*cemetery* AR-4
Morrison Cem—*cemetery* (3) IL-6
Morrison Cem—*cemetery* (3) IN-6
Morrison Cem—*cemetery* (2) IA-7
Morrison Cem—*cemetery* (2) KS-7
Morrison Cem—*cemetery* KY-4
Morrison Cem—*cemetery* LA-4
Morrison Cem—*cemetery* MI-6
Morrison Cem—*cemetery* (2) MS-4
Morrison Cem—*cemetery* (2) MO-7
Morrison Cem—*cemetery* NY-2
Morrison Cem—*cemetery* (3) OK-5
Morrison Cem—*cemetery* (3) PA-2
Morrison Cem—*cemetery* (5) TN-4
Morrison Cem—*cemetery* (2) VA-3
Morrison Cem—*cemetery* (2) WV-2
Morrison Ch—*church* GA-3
Morrison Ch—*church* MO-7
Morrison Ch—*church* NC-3
Morrison Ch—*church* TN-4
Morrison Ch—*church* WV-2
Morrison Channel—*channel* MI-6
Morrison Chapel—*church* AL-4
Morrison Chapel—*church* MS-4
Morrison Chapel—*church* WV-2
*Morrison Chapel Baptist Ch* MS-4
Morrison Chute—*stream* MO-7
**Morrison City**—*pop pl* TN-4
Morrison Cliff—*cliff* VA-3
Morrison Consolidated Ditch—*canal* CO-8
Morrison Corner—*locale* ME-1
Morrison Corners—*locale* PA-2
Morrison Coulee—*valley* MT-8

**Morrison (County)**—*pop pl* MN-6
Morrison County Courthouse—*hist pl* MN-6
Morrison Cove—*bay* (2) ME-1
Morrison Cove—*bay* NH-1
Morrison Cove—*valley* PA-2
*Morrison Creek* CO-8
*Morrison Creek* MI-6
*Morrison Creek* VA-3
*Morrison Creek* WY-8
Morrison Creek—*bend* FL-3
Morrison Creek—*locale* TN-4
Morrison Creek—*stream* AL-4
Morrison Creek—*stream* AZ-5
Morrison Creek—*stream* (5) CA-9
Morrison Creek—*stream* (4) CO-8
Morrison Creek—*stream* GA-3
Morrison Creek—*stream* IN-6
Morrison Creek—*stream* (4) MI-6
Morrison Creek—*stream* (2) MT-8
Morrison Creek—*stream* NC-3
Morrison Creek—*stream* OH-6
Morrison Creek—*stream* OR-9
Morrison Creek—*stream* (3) TN-4
Morrison Creek—*stream* (3) TX-5
Morrison Creek—*stream* WA-9
Morrison Creek—*stream* (3) WI-6
Morrison Creek Campground—*locale* WA-9
Morrison Creek Sch (historical)—*school* TN-4
Morrison Crossroad—*locale* AL-4
*Morrison Crossroads* AL-4
Morrison Cutoff—*channel* LA-4
Morrison Dam—*dam* ND-7
Morrison Dam—*dam* OR-9
*Morrison Depot* TN-4
Morrison Ditch—*canal* IN-6
Morrison Ditch—*canal* MT-8
Morrison Ditch Number One—*canal* IN-6
Morrison Ditch Number Two—*canal* IN-6
Morrison Divide Trail—*trail* CO-8
Morrison Division—*civil* TN-4
*Morrison Drain* MI-6
Morrison Drain—*canal* MI-6
Morrison Drain—*stream* MI-6
*Morrison Drop* GA-3
Morrison Eddy—*rapids* OR-9
*Morrison Elementary School* MS-4
Morrison Elem Sch—*school* KS-7
Morrison Elem Sch—*school* TN-4
**Morrison Estates**
**(subdivision)**—*pop pl* TN-4
**Morrison Falls**—*pop pl* TX-5
Morrison Farm and Store—*hist pl* TN-4
**Morrison Farms**—*pop pl* VA-3
*Morrison Field* NC-3
Morrison First Baptist Ch—*church* TN-4
Morrison Fish Hatchery—*locale* NC-3
Morrison Fork—*stream* WV-2
Morrison Grove Ch—*church* GA-3
Morrison Grove Ch—*church* VA-3
Morrison Grove Sch—*school* NC-3
Morrison Gulch—*valley* (5) CA-9
Morrison Gulch—*valley* (2) MT-8
Morrison Gulch—*valley* OR-9
Morrison Hammock—*island* FL-3
Morrison Heath—*swamp* ME-1
**Morrison Heights**—*pop pl* NY-2
Morrison Heights—*summit* ME-1
Morrison Heights Baptist Ch—*church* MS-4
Morrison Heights Ch—*church* MS-4
Morrison Hill—*summit* CT-1
Morrison Hill—*summit* FL-3
Morrison Hill—*summit* MT-8
Morrison Hill—*summit* NH-1
Morrison Hill—*summit* VT-1
Morrison Hill Ch—*church* TN-4
*Morrison Hill Christian Ch* TN-4
Morrison Hill Sch (abandoned)—*school* PA-2
Morrison Hist Dist—*hist pl* CO-8
Morrison (historical)—*locale* SD-7
**Morrison (historical)**—*pop pl* PA-2
Morrison Hole—*lake* MO-7
Morrison Hollow—*valley* IL-6
Morrison Hollow—*valley* KY-4
Morrison Hollow—*valley* MO-7
Morrison Hollow—*valley* (2) OH-6
Morrison Hollow—*valley* PA-2
Morrison Hollow—*valley* TN-4
**Morrison Home**—*pop pl* FL-3
Morrison House—*hist pl* AZ-5
Morrison House—*hist pl* OH-6
Morrison Island—*island* AR-4
Morrison Island—*island* FL-3
Morrison Island—*island* IN-6
Morrison-Kenyon Library—*hist pl* KY-4
Morrison Knoll—*summit* ME-1
*Morrison Lake* MI-6
*Morrison Lake* MN-6
Morrison Lake—*lake* AR-4
Morrison Lake—*lake* FL-3
Morrison Lake—*lake* IN-6
Morrison Lake—*lake* (4) MI-6
Morrison Lake—*lake* (4) MN-6
Morrison Lake—*lake* MT-8
Morrison Lake—*lake* NM-5
Morrison Lake—*lake* ND-7
Morrison Lake—*lake* OH-6
Morrison Lake—*lake* TX-5
Morrison Lake—*lake* WI-6
Morrison Lake—*reservoir* CO-8
Morrison Lake—*reservoir* KS-7
Morrison Landing—*locale* MO-7
Morrison Lodge—*hist pl* KY-4
Morrison Meadows—*flat* WY-8
Morrison Mine—*mine* CO-8
Morrison Mine—*mine* MN-6
Morrison Mine—*mine* UT-8
Morrison Mine (underground)—*mine* AL-4
Morrison Mock Elem Sch—*school* IN-6
Morrison-Mott House—*hist pl* NC-3
Morrison Mounds—*hist pl* MN-6
Morrison Mtn—*summit* OK-5
Morrison Observatory—*other* MO-7
Morrison Park—*flat* WY-8
Morrison Park—*park* IN-6
Morrison Park—*park* MN-6
Morrison Park—*park* (2) VA-3
Morrison Peak—*summit* MT-8
Morrison Plantation Smokehouse—*hist pl* AR-4
Morrison Playground—*park* MA-1
Morrison Point—*cape* ME-1

*Morrison Pond* ME-1
Morrison Pond—*lake* ME-1
Morrison Pond—*reservoir* IN-6
Morrison Pond Dam—*dam* IN-6
Morrison Pond Mtn—*summit* ME-1
Morrison Ponds—*lake* ME-1
Morrison Post Office—*building* TN-4
Morrison Ranch—*locale* (2) MT-8
Morrison Ranch—*locale* NV-8
Morrison Ranch—*locale* SD-7
Morrison Ranch—*locale* (3) TX-5
Morrison Ranch—*locale* (2) WY-8
Morrison Red Rocks Sch—*school* CO-8
Morrison Ridge—*ridge* (2) CA-9
Morrison Ridge—*ridge* ID-8
Morrison Ridge—*ridge* ME-1
Morrison Ridge—*ridge* TX-5
Morrison Ridge—*ridge* (2) WV-2
Morrison Ridge—*uninc pl* KS-7
Morrison Ridge Spring—*spring* ID-8
Morrison Rsvr—*reservoir* OR-9
*Morrison Run* PA-2
Morrison Run—*stream* KY-4
Morrison Run—*stream* (2) OH-6
Morrison Run—*stream* (4) PA-2
Morrison Run—*stream* WV-2
**Morrisons**—*pop pl* MD-2
**Morrisons**—*pop pl* OH-6
Morrison Sch—*school* AR-4
Morrison Sch—*school* CA-9
Morrison Sch—*school* IL-6
Morrison Sch—*school* (2) ME-1
Morrison Sch—*school* MA-1
Morrison Sch—*school* MS-4
Morrison Sch—*school* (2) OH-6
Morrison Sch—*school* OR-9
Morrison Sch—*school* PA-2
Morrison Sch—*school* TX-5
Morrison Sch—*school* VA-3
Morrison Sch (historical)—*school* PA-2
Morrison Schoolhouse—*hist pl* CO-8
*Morrisons Creek* AL-4
*Morrisons Creek* TN-4
Morrisons Creek—*stream* VA-3
*Morrisons Creek School* TN-4
*Morrison's Drop* GA-3
Morrisons Ferry (historical)—*locale* AL-4
Morrison Siphon Lateral—*canal* CA-9
Morrisons Lake—*reservoir* SC-3
*Morrisons Landing* MO-7
Morrison Slough—*channel* GA-3
Morrison Slough—*stream* CA-9
Morrison Spring—*spring* FL-3
Morrison Spring—*spring* NM-5
Morrison Spring—*spring* OR-9
Morrison Spring—*spring* TN-4
Morrison Spring Branch—*stream* IL-6
Morrison Spring Branch—*stream* NC-3
Morrison Spring Run—*stream* FL-3
Morrison Springs Branch—*stream* TX-5
**Morrison Springs**
**(subdivision)**—*pop pl* TN-4
*Morrison's Station* GA-3
**Morrisons Store**—*pop pl* NC-3
*Morrison Station* TN-4
Morrison Store (historical)—*locale* TN-4
Morrison Suspension Bridge—*hist pl* OK-5
Morrison Swamp—*swamp* WI-6
Morrison Tank—*reservoir* TX-5
Morrison Temple—*church* TN-4
Morrison Towhead—*island* MO-7
**Morrison (Town of)**—*pop pl* WI-6
**Morrison (Township of)**—*pop pl* MN-6
Morrison Trail—*trail* WY-8
Morrison Training Sch—*school* NC-3
Morrisonville—*locale* VA-3
**Morrisonville**—*pop pl* IL-6
**Morrisonville**—*pop pl* LA-4
**Morrisonville**—*pop pl* NY-2
**Morrisonville**—*pop pl* WI-6
Morrisonville Cem—*cemetery* IL-6
Morrison Well—*well* WY-8
Morrison Windmill—*locale* NM-5
Morrison Windmill—*locale* TX-5
Morris Park—*park* IA-7
Morris Park—*park* PA-2
Morris Park—*park* TN-4
Morris Park—*park* WV-2
**Morris Park**—*pop pl* NJ-2
**Morris Park**—*pop pl* (2) NY-2
**Morris Park**—*pop pl* WI-6
Morris Park Country Club—*other* IN-6
Morris Park Sch—*school* MN-6
Morris Park Sch—*school* NJ-2
**Morris Park (subdivision)**—*pop pl* NC-3
Morris Peak—*summit* (2) CA-9
**Morris Plains**—*pop pl* NJ-2
Morris Plains Station—*hist pl* NJ-2
Morris Plan (Central Union Bank)—*hist pl* IN-6
Morris Point—*cape* MN-6
*Morris Pond* DE-2
Morris Pond—*lake* FL-3
Morris Pond—*lake* GA-3
Morris Pond—*lake* NY-2
Morris Pond—*lake* UT-8
Morris Pond—*reservoir* AL-4
Morris Pond—*reservoir* GA-3
Morris Pond—*reservoir* (2) NC-3
Morris Pond—*reservoir* SC-3
Morris Pond—*swamp* TX-5
Morris Pond Dam—*dam* (2) NC-3
Morris Prong—*stream* MD-2
Morris Ranch—*locale* (2) CA-9
Morris Ranch—*locale* CO-8
Morris Ranch—*locale* (2) MT-8
Morris Ranch—*locale* (2) NE-7
Morris Ranch—*locale* NM-5
Morris Ranch—*locale* (2) TX-5
Morris Ranch—*locale* (3) UT-8
Morris Ranch Schoolhouse—*hist pl* TX-5
Morris Ravine—*valley* CA-9
Morris Reef—*bar* AK-9
*Morris Reservoir* TN-4
*Morris River* NJ-2
Morris Rodgers Creek—*stream* OR-9
Morris Rsvr—*reservoir* (2) CA-9
Morris Rsvr—*reservoir* (2) CO-8
Morris Rsvr—*reservoir* CT-1
Morris Rsvr—*reservoir* MT-8
Morris Rsvr—*reservoir* NY-2

Morris Rsvr—reservoir UT-8
Morris Run DE-2
**Morris Run**—pop pl PA-2
Morris Run—stream NC-3
Morris Run—stream (6) PA-2
Morris Run—stream (2) VA-3
Morris Run—stream (2) WV-2
Morris Run Ch—church WV-2
Morris Run Mine Dam Number Three—dam PA-2
Morris Run Rsvr—reservoir PA-2
Morris Run Trail—trail PA-2
Morriss Cem—cemetery AR-4
Morriss Cem—cemetery VA-3
Morris Sch—school (2) CA-9
Morris Sch—school IL-6
Morris Sch—school IA-7
Morris Sch—school (2) MA-1
Morris Sch—school (2) MI-6
Morris Sch—school MO-7
Morris Sch—school NE-7
Morris Sch—school NJ-2
Morris Sch—school NY-2
Morris Sch—school OH-6
Morris Sch—school (2) PA-2
Morris Sch—school TN-4
Morris Sch—school TX-5
Morris Sch—school VA-3
Morris Sch (abandoned)—school MO-7
Morris Sch (historical)—school AL-4
Morris Sch (historical)—school MS-4
Morris Sch (historical)—school PA-2
Morriss Creek—stream MO-7
Morriss Drain MI-6
Morrissette Cem—cemetery (2) AL-4
Morrissey Brook—stream CT-1
Morrissey Park—park IL-6
Morrissey Sch—school IL-6
Morris Shaft—mine NV-8
Morris Sheppard Dam (Possum Kingdom Dam)—dam TX-5
Morris Siding—uninc pl GA-3
Morris Slave Cem—cemetery TN-4
Morris Spring—spring (2) AL-4
Morris Spring—spring AR-4
Morris Spring—spring CA-9
Morris Spring—spring MI-6
Morris Spring—spring MT-8
Morris Spring—spring OR-9
Morris Spring—spring TN-4
Morris Store—locale VA-3
Morris Store (historical)—locale MS-4
Morris Street—uninc pl NJ-2
Morris Street Sch—school GA-3
Morris Street United Methodist Ch—church IN-6
Morris Swamp NJ-2
Morris Tank—reservoir (3) AZ-5
Morris Tank—reservoir TX-5
Morriston—locale MS-4
**Morriston**—pop pl AR-4
**Morriston**—pop pl FL-3
Morriston Baptist Church MS-4
Morriston Cem—cemetery MS-4
Morriston Ch—church MS-4
Morriston (historical)—locale AL-4
Morriston Post Office (historical)—building MS-4
Morriston Sch (historical)—school MS-4
Morristown IL-6
Morristown IN-6
Morristown NC-3
Morristown PA-2
Morristown—locale CA-9
Morristown—locale IL-6
Morristown—locale WV-2
**Morristown**—pop pl AZ-5
**Morristown**—pop pl IL-6
**Morristown**—pop pl IN-6
**Morristown**—pop pl (2) MN-6
**Morristown**—pop pl (2) NJ-2
**Morristown**—pop pl NY-2
**Morristown**—pop pl (2) OH-6
**Morristown**—pop pl SD-7
**Morristown**—pop pl TN-4
**Morristown**—pop pl VT-1
Morristown Baptist Church TN-4
Morristown Bay—bay NY-2
**Morristown (Castle Hot Springs (sta.))**—pop pl AZ-5
Morristown (CCD)—cens area TN-4
Morristown Cem TN-4
Morristown Cem—cemetery (2) IL-6
Morris Town Cem—cemetery TN-4
Morristown Center—locale NY-2
Morristown City Hall—building TN-4
Morris Town Coll—school TN-4
Morristown College Hist Dist—hist pl TN-4
Morristown Corners (local name for Morristown)—other VT-1
Morristown Dam—dam PA-2
Morristown District—hist pl NJ-2
Morristown Division—civil TN-4
Morristown East Lake—reservoir SD-7
Morristown Golf and Country Club—locale TN-4
Morristown Green—park NJ-2
Morristown-Hamblen County Hosp—hospital TN-4
Morristown High School East TN-4
Morristown Hist Dist—hist pl OH-6
Morristown Hist Dist (Boundary Increase)—hist pl NJ-2
Morristown HS—school NJ-2
Morristown Lake—reservoir SD-7
Morristown Lake Dam SD-7
Morristown Mall Shop Ctr—locale TN-4
Morristown Memorial Hospital—airport NJ-2
Morristown Municipal—airport NJ-2
Morristown Municipal Power House—building TN-4
Morristown Natl Historic Park—hist pl NJ-2
**Morris (Town of)**—pop pl CT-1
**Morris (Town of)**—pop pl NY-2
**Morris (Town of)**—pop pl WI-6
Morristown Overpass—crossing AZ-5
Morristown Plaza Shop Ctr—locale TN-4
Morristown Point—cape NY-2
Morristown Post Office—building TN-4
Morristown Ravine—valley CA-9
Morristown Reservoir NJ-2
Morristown Reservoir Dam—dam NJ-2
Morristown Ridge—ridge CA-9
Morristown RR Dam SD-7
Morristown Sch—school AZ-5
Morristown Schoolhouse—hist pl NY-2
Morristown Seventh Day Adventist Ch—church TN-4
Morris Township KS-7
Morris Township—civ div KS-7
Morris Township—civil PA-2
**Morris Township**—pop pl KS-7
**Morris Township**—pop pl (2) MO-7
**Morris Township**—pop pl ND-7
Morris Township No. 1—civ div KS-7
Morris Township No. 2—civ div KS-7
Morris Township No. 3—civ div KS-7
Morris Township No. 4—civ div KS-7
Morris Township No. 5—civ div KS-7
Morris Township No. 6—civ div KS-7
Morris Township No. 7—civ div KS-7
Morris Township No. 8—civ div KS-7
Morris Township No. 9—civ div KS-7
Morris (Township of)—fmr MCD AR-4
**Morris (Township of)**—pop pl IL-6
**Morris (Township of)**—pop pl MN-6
**Morris (Township of)**—pop pl NJ-2
**Morris (Township of)**—pop pl OH-6
**Morris (Township of)**—pop pl (5) PA-2
Morristown State Fish Hatchery—locale TN-4
**Morristown (Town of)**—pop pl NY-2
**Morristown (Town of)**—pop pl VT-1
**Morristown (Township of)**—pop pl MN-6
Morris Trail—trail PA-2
**Morrisvale**—pop pl WV-2
Morrisvale Sch—school WV-2
Morris Valley Ch—church KY-4
Morrisville—locale AL-4
Morrisville—locale OH-6
Morrisville—locale VA-3
**Morrisville**—pop pl MO-7
**Morrisville**—pop pl NJ-2
**Morrisville**—pop pl NY-2
**Morrisville**—pop pl NC-3
**Morrisville**—pop pl (2) PA-2
**Morrisville**—pop pl SC-3
**Morrisville**—pop pl VT-1
Morrisville Baptist Church AL-4
Morrisville Borough—civil PA-2
Morrisville Cem—cemetery AL-4
Morrisville Ch—church AL-4
Morrisville Hist Dist—hist pl VT-1
Morrisville (historical)—locale MS-4
**Morrisville (historical)**—pop pl AL-4
Morrisville Methodist Ch (historical)—church AL-4
Morrisville (Station)—locale MO-7
**Morrisville Station**—pop pl NY-2
Morrisville Swamp—swamp NY-2
Morris Well—locale NM-5
Morris Well—well (2) NM-5
Morris Williams Golf Course—other TX-5
Morris Windmill—locale AZ-5
Morris Windmill—locale TX-5
Morris Windmills—locale NM-5
Morrisy Coulee—valley MT-8
Morrisy Coulee Narrows—gap MT-8
Morrisy Coulee Spring—spring MT-8
Morrisy Creek—stream MI-6
Morrizon Cut Off LA-4
Morro Bay—bay CA-9
**Morro Bay**—pop pl CA-9
Morro Bay State Park—park CA-9
Morro Creek—stream CA-9
Morrocroft—hist pl NC-3
Morro Hill—summit (2) CA-9
**Morro Palisades**—pop pl CA-9
Morro Rock—summit CA-9
Morro Strand State Beach—park CA-9
Morro Tank—reservoir AZ-5
Morrow KS-7
Morrow—locale ID-8
**Morrow**—pop pl AR-4
**Morrow**—pop pl GA-3
**Morrow**—pop pl LA-4
**Morrow**—pop pl OH-6
Morrow, James, House—hist pl DE-2
Morrow, John, Elem Sch—hist pl PA-2
**Morrow Acres (subdivision)**—pop pl AL-4
Morrow Bluff—cliff TN-4
Morrow Branch—stream LA-4
Morrow Branch—stream MS-4
Morrow Branch—stream MO-7
Morrow Branch—stream (3) NC-3
Morrow Branch—stream TN-4
Morrow Branch—stream TX-5
Morrow Brook—stream ME-1
Morrow Brook—stream VT-1
Morrow Brothers Dam—dam OR-9
Morrow Cem—cemetery AL-4
Morrow Cem—cemetery (3) AR-4
Morrow Cem—cemetery GA-3
Morrow Cem—cemetery ID-8
Morrow Cem—cemetery KY-4
Morrow Cem—cemetery LA-4
Morrow Cem—cemetery (2) NC-3
Morrow Cem—cemetery (2) TN-4
Morrow Cem—cemetery (2) TX-5
Morrow Ch—church AL-4
Morrow Ch—church (2) AR-4
Morrow Chapel—church KY-4
Morrow Chapel Cem—cemetery TX-5
**Morrow (County)**—pop pl OH-6
**Morrow County**—pop pl OR-9
Morrow County Courthouse—hist pl OR-9
Morrow County Courthouse And Jail—hist pl OH-6
Morrow Cove—bay CA-9
Morrow Creek WY-8
Morrow Creek—stream CA-9
Morrow Creek—stream MI-6
Morrow Creek—stream NY-2
Morrow Creek—stream NC-3
Morrow Creek—stream SC-3
Morrow Elem Sch—school FL-3
Morrow Gap—gap AL-4
Morrow Gap—gap NC-3
Morrow Hall—hist pl AR-4
Morrow Hill—summit WA-9
Morrow Hill Ch—church TN-4
Morrow Hill Sch—school TN-4
Morrow Hollow—valley AL-4
Morrow Hollow—valley MO-7
Morrow Hollow—valley PA-2
Morrow Hollow—valley TN-4
Morrow House—hist pl KY-4
Morrow HS—school NJ-2
Morrow-Hudson House—hist pl AZ-5
Morrow Island—island CA-9
Morrow Island Farm—locale CA-9
Morrow Lake FL-3
Morrow Lake—lake FL-3
Morrow Lake—lake TX-5
Morrow Lake—lake WA-9
Morrow Lake—lake GU-9
Morrow Lake—reservoir MI-6
Morrow Lake—reservoir TN-4
Morrow Lake Dam—dam (2) MS-4
Morrow Lateral—canal IN-6
Morrow Meadow—flat OR-9
Morrow Meadow—flat WA-9
Morrow Memorial Cem—cemetery MS-4
Morrow Memorial Hosp—hospital FL-3
Morrow Mine—mine MN-6
Morrow Mines (underground)—mine AL-4
Morrow Mine (underground)—mine AL-4
Morrow Mountain State Park—park NC-3
Morrow Mtn—summit AL-4
Morrow Mtn—summit NC-3
Morrow-Overman-Fairley House—hist pl OH-6
Morrow Park—park NJ-2
Morrow Park—park WA-9
Morrow Plots, Univ of Illinois—hist pl IL-6
Morrow Point—cliff CO-8
Morrow Point Reservoir CO-8
Morrow Point Rsvr—reservoir CO-8
Morrow Ranch—locale ID-8
Morrow Ranch—locale NM-5
Morrow Ridge—ridge WA-9
Morrow Road—locale ME-1
Morrow Rock—bar AL-4
**Morrow (RR name Morrows)**—pop pl LA-4
Morrow Rsvr—reservoir ID-8
Morrow Sch PA-2
Morrow Sch—school CA-9
Morrow Sch—school IL-6
Morrow Sch—school KS-7
Morrow Sch—school PA-2
Morrow Sch—school TX-5
Morrows Chapel—church AL-4
Morrows Chapel—church NC-3
Morrows Chapel—church TX-5
Morrow Schools—school NJ-2
Morrows Corner—locale PA-2
**Morrows Grove**—pop pl AL-4
**Morrows (historical)**—pop pl NC-3
Morrows Landing (historical)—locale AL-4
Morrows Mill (historical)—locale AL-4
Morrow Spring—spring MO-7
Morrows (RR name for Morrow)—other LA-4
Morrow Station KS-7
Morrow Township—civil (2) MO-7
Morrow (Township of)—fmr MCD AR-4
Morrow Trail—trail CA-9
Morrow Valley Sch (historical)—school TN-4
**Morrowville**—pop pl KS-7
Morrowville Cem—cemetery KS-7
Morrow Well—well NM-5
Morrow Well—well OR-9
Morrow Windmill—locale NM-5
Morrs Ravine—valley CA-9
Morsay Creek OR-9
Morsay Creek—stream OR-9
**Morschels**—pop pl MO-7
Morsche Park—park IN-6
Morse OK-5
Morse—locale IL-6
Morse—locale OK-5
**Morse**—pop pl CA-9
**Morse**—pop pl IA-7
**Morse**—pop pl KS-7
**Morse**—pop pl LA-4
**Morse**—pop pl NY-2
**Morse**—pop pl NC-3
**Morse**—pop pl TX-5
**Morse**—pop pl WI-6
Morse, Amos, House—hist pl MA-1
Morse, Asa, Farm—hist pl NH-1
Morse, Capt. Thomas, Farm—hist pl NH-1
Morse, Charles Copeland, House—hist pl CA-9
Morse, Daniel, III, House—hist pl MA-1
Morse, Eli, Farm—hist pl NH-1
Morse, Eli, Sawmill Foundations—hist pl NH-1
Morse, Henry, House—hist pl MA-1
Morse, Moses, House—hist pl MA-1
Morse, Robert I., House—hist pl WA-9
Morse, Samuel F. B., Sch—hist pl PA-2
Morse Ave Elem Sch—school FL-3
Morse-Barber House—hist pl MA-1
Morse-Beidler Sch—school IL-6
Morse Bluff—cliff KY-4
**Morse Bluff**—pop pl NE-7
**Morse Bluff Township**—pop pl NE-7
Morse Bridge—hist pl ME-1
Morse Brook MA-1
Morse Brook—stream ME-1
Morse Brook—stream MA-1
Morse Brook—stream NH-1
Morse Brook—stream VT-1
Morse Camp—locale ME-1
Morse Canyon AZ-5
Morse Canyon—valley AZ-5
Morse Canyon—valley CA-9
Morse Canyon—valley NV-8
Morse Canyon—valley NM-5
Morse Canyon—valley UT-8
Morse Canyon—valley WA-9
Morse Canyon Campground—park AZ-5
Morse Cem—cemetery (2) IL-6
Morse Cem—cemetery IA-7
Morse Cem—cemetery (3) KY-4
Morse Cem—cemetery LA-4
Morse Cem—cemetery ME-1
Morse Cem—cemetery MA-1
Morse Cem—cemetery NY-2
Morse Cem—cemetery OK-5
Morse Cem—cemetery TX-5
Morse Cem—cemetery WI-6
Morse Chapel—church OH-6
Morse & Co. Office Bldg—hist pl ME-1
**Morse Corner**—pop pl MA-1
Morse Corners—locale ME-1
Morse Cove—bay AK-9
Morse Cove—bay (2) ME-1
Morse Covered Bridge—bridge ME-1
Morse Creek AZ-5
Morse Creek NJ-2
Morse Creek—stream CA-9
Morse Creek—stream ID-8
Morse Creek—stream KS-7
Morse Creek—stream NE-7
Morse Creek—stream NJ-2
Morse Creek—stream OR-9
Morse Creek—stream (2) WA-9
Morse Creek Campground—locale WA-9
Morse Creek Post Office (historical)—building TN-4
Morse Creek Sch (abandoned)—school SD-7
Morse Ditch IN-6
Morse Ditch—canal IN-6
Morse Drain—canal MI-6
Morse Elem Sch—school KS-7
Morse Flat—flat WA-9
Morse Glacier—glacier AK-9
Morse Gulch—valley OR-9
Morse Hill—summit AL-4
Morse Hill—summit KY-4
Morse Hill—summit ME-1
Morse Hill—summit (2) MA-1
Morse Hill—summit (2) NH-1
Morse Hill—summit NY-2
Morse Hill Cem—cemetery LA-4
Morse Hollow—valley VT-1
Morse Hosp—hospital MA-1
Morse House—hist pl MA-1
Morse House—hist pl OR-9
Morse House—hist pl WA-9
Morse HS—school CA-9
Morse HS—school ME-1
Morse Island WA-9
Morse Island—island IA-7
Morse Island—island ME-1
Morse Island Creek—channel SC-3
Morse Junction—locale TX-5
Morse Lake MI-6
Morse Lake MN-6
Morse Lake—lake IA-7
Morse Lake—lake (2) MI-6
Morse Lake—reservoir TX-5
Morse Lakes—reservoir NJ-2
Morse Lakes Dam—dam NJ-2
Morse Lake State Game Mngmt Area—park IA-7
Morse Lateral—canal WI-6
Morse Ledge—bar ME-1
Morse-Lewis Cem—cemetery OH-6
Morse-Libby Mansion—hist pl ME-1
Morse Lord Drain—stream MI-6
Morse Meadow Pond CT-1
Morse Meadow Pond—lake CT-1
Morsemere—locale NJ-2
**Morse Mill**—pop pl MO-7
**Morse Mill**—pop pl NY-2
Morse Mtn—summit CO-8
Morse Mtn—summit (2) ME-1
Morse Mtn—summit NH-1
Morse Mtn—summit (2) VT-1
Morse Neck ME-1
Morse Oil Field—oilfield OK-5
Morse Park—park CO-8
Morse Park—park CT-1
Morse Park—park MO-7
Morse Peak—summit AK-9
Morse Point—cape CA-9
Morse Point—cape ME-1
Morse Point—cape NC-3
Morse Point—cape VA-3
Morse Pond MD-2
Morse Pond MA-1
Morse Pond—lake CT-1
Morse Pond—lake ME-1
Morse Pond—lake (3) MA-1
Morse Pond—lake WI-6
Morse Pond—reservoir MA-1
Morse Pond—reservoir NC-3
Morse Pond Dam—dam MA-1
Morse Reservoir Dam—dam IN-6
Morse Reservoir Dam—dam MA-1
Morse Ridge—ridge KY-4
Morse River—stream ME-1
Morse Rock—other AK-9
Morse Rsvr—reservoir CT-1
Morse Rsvr—reservoir IN-6
Morse Rsvr—reservoir MA-1
Morse Run—stream PA-2
Morse Sch—school (2) CA-9
Morse Sch—school DC-2
Morse Sch—school IL-6
Morse Sch—school MA-1
Morse Sch—school (3) MI-6
Morse Sch—school (2) NY-2
Morse Sch—school WI-6
Morses Creek—stream NJ-2
Morses Creek—uninc pl NJ-2
Morses Gulch—valley CA-9
Morses Hill MA-1
Morse Shores—locale FL-3
Morse Shores Shop Ctrs—locale FL-3
Morse's Island MN-6
Morse-Skinner Ranch House—hist pl CA-9
Morses Lake—reservoir NC-3
Morses Lake Dam—dam NC-3
Morse's landing WI-6
**Morses Line**—pop pl VT-1
**Morses Mill**—pop pl VT-1
Morses Mill Pond—reservoir TX-5
**Morses Mills**—pop pl VT-1
Morses Mill Stream—stream NJ-2
Morses Pond—reservoir MA-1
Morses Pond Dam—dam MA-1
Morses Reservoir MA-1
Morse Street Sch—school ME-1
Morse-Tay-Leland-Hawes House—hist pl MA-1
Morsetown Brook—stream NJ-2
**Morse (Town of)**—pop pl WI-6
**Morse (Township of)**—pop pl (2) MN-6
**Morse Village**—pop pl MA-1
Morseville—locale MI-6
**Morseville**—pop pl (2) MA-1
Morseville Cem—cemetery NE-7
**Morseville (Plum River)**—pop pl IL-6
Morsey Community Center—locale MO-7
Morsingills Creek—stream GA-3
Morskoi Rock—other AK-9
Morsman (historical)—locale IA-7
Morsman Siding—locale SD-7
Morson's Row—hist pl VA-3
Morss Homestead/Federal City Homestead—hist pl NY-2
Morss Tannery (historical)—building PA-2
**Morsston**—pop pl NY-2
**Morstein**—pop pl PA-2
Morstons Mills MA-1
Mort—locale MN-6
Mort Adams Spring—spring ND-7
Mortandad Canyon—valley NM-5
Mortandad Creek—stream NM-5
Mortar, The MH-9
Mortar Branch—stream KY-4
Mortar Branch—stream VA-3
Mortar Creek ID-8
Mortar Creek—stream AL-4
Mortar Creek—stream AR-4
Mortar Creek—stream ID-8
Mortar Creek Cem—cemetery AR-4
Mortar Gulch CA-9
Mortar Point—cape OR-9
Mortar Prairie—flat OR-9
Mortar Run—stream IN-6
Mortarstone Bluff—cliff MT-8
Mort Elem Sch—school FL-3
Mortensen Canyon—valley (2) UT-8
Mortensen Creek—stream UT-8
Mortensen Ditch—canal CA-9
Mortensens AZ-5
Mortensens Lagoon—bay AK-9
Mortensen Spring—spring UT-8
Mortensen Wash AZ-5
Mortensen Wash—arroyo (2) AZ-5
Mortenson AZ-5
Mortenson Canyon—valley ID-8
Mortenson Lake—lake WY-8
Mortenson Wash AZ-5
Mortero Canyon—valley CA-9
Mortero Palms—locale CA-9
Morteros, Arroyo—stream TX-5
Morterson Wash AZ-5
Mortesen Canyon UT-8
Mortesen Spring UT-8
Mortgage Draw AZ-5
Mortgage Draw—arroyo AZ-5
Mortgage Spring—spring AZ-5
Mortgage Trust Ditch—canal IN-6
Mortimer TN-4
Mortimer—locale CO-8
Mortimer—locale IL-6
Mortimer—locale NY-2
Mortimer—locale NC-3
Mortimer Canyon—valley OR-9
Mortimer Canyon Dam—dam OR-9
Mortimer Canyon Rsvr—reservoir OR-9
Mortimer Creek—stream KS-7
Mortimer Flat—flat CA-9
Mortimer Gulch—valley MT-8
Mortimer (historical) IA-7
Mortimer (historical)—locale AL-4
Mortimer (historical)—locale KS-7
Mortimer Jordan High School AL-4
Mortimer Jordan Sch—school AL-4
Mortimer Lake Dam—dam MS-4
Mortimer L Schiff Boy Scout Reservation—park NJ-2
Mortimer Mine—mine ID-8
**Mortimer (North Findlay)**—pop pl OH-6
Mortimer Post Office (historical)—building TN-4
Mortimer Rec Area—locale NC-3
Mortimer Slough—lake SD-7
Mortimer Station—locale KY-4
Mortimer Valley—valley WI-6
Mortimer Work Center—locale NC-3
Mortimore Canyon—valley OR-9
**Mortiner Station**—pop pl KY-4
Mortin Sch—school VA-3
Mortiz Lake AZ-5
Mortland Island—island IL-6
Mortland Island State Fish And Waterfowl Man—park IL-6
Mortlock Island—island MP-9
Mortlock Islands—island FM-9
**Mortmar**—pop pl CA-9
Morton KS-7
Morton ND-7
Morton—fmr MCD NE-7
Morton—locale GA-3
Morton—locale ID-8
Morton—locale TX-5
Morton—locale UT-8
Morton—locale (2) WY-8
**Morton**—pop pl AR-4
**Morton**—pop pl IL-6
**Morton**—pop pl IN-6
**Morton**—pop pl MN-6
**Morton**—pop pl MS-4
**Morton**—pop pl MO-7
**Morton**—pop pl NY-2
**Morton**—pop pl PA-2
**Morton**—pop pl TX-5
**Morton**—pop pl WA-9
Morton, George W., House—hist pl TN-4
Morton, J. Sterling, HS East Auditorium—hist pl IL-6
Morton, Lake—lake FL-3
Morton, Lake—lake WA-9
Morton, Oliver P., House—hist pl IN-6
Morton, Samuel S., House—hist pl TN-4
Morton, Will, Tavern Stand—hist pl KY-4
Morton, William, House—hist pl KY-4
Morton Arboretum—park IL-6
Morton Ave Sch—school GA-3
Morton Bend—bend GA-3
Morton Bldg—hist pl GA-3
Morton Bluff—cliff TN-4
Morton Borough—civil PA-2
Morton Branch—stream KY-4
Morton Branch—stream (2) MO-7
Morton Branch—stream (2) TN-4
Morton Branch—stream TX-5
Morton Brook—stream ME-1
Morton Brothers Grocery—hist pl TX-5
Morton Butte—summit (2) OR-9
Morton Canyon—valley CA-9
Morton Canyon Wash—arroyo AZ-5
Morton (CCD)—cens area TX-5
Morton (CCD)—cens area WA-9
Morton Cem MS-4
Morton Cem—cemetery AR-4
Morton Cem—cemetery GA-3
Morton Cem—cemetery IL-6
Morton Cem—cemetery KY-4
Morton Cem—cemetery MA-1
Morton Cem—cemetery (2) MI-6
Morton Cem—cemetery MS-4
Morton Cem—cemetery ND-7
Morton Cem—cemetery OH-6
Morton Cem—cemetery OK-5
Morton Cem—cemetery (5) TN-4
Morton Cem—cemetery TX-5
Morton Cem—cemetery VA-3
Morton Ch—church NC-3
Morton Ch—church SC-3
Morton Chapel—church (2) AL-4
Morton Chapel—church GA-3
Morton Chapel—church IL-6
Morton Chapel—church TX-5
Morton Chapel Cem—cemetery AL-4
Morton Chapel Cem—cemetery MS-4
Morton Chapel Cem—cemetery TX-5
Morton Chapel (historical)—church MS-4
Morton Corner—locale WI-6
**Morton Corners**—pop pl (2) NY-2
Morton Corners Ch—church NY-2
Morton Coulee—valley MT-8
Morton Country Club—other TX-5
Morton County—civil KS-7
Morton County—civil ND-7
Morton County Fairgrounds—locale KS-7
Morton County Pumping Station—other KS-7
Morton County WPA Bridge—hist pl KS-7
Morton Creek WY-8
Morton Creek—stream AR-4
Morton Creek—stream CA-9
Morton Creek—stream NC-3
Morton Creek—stream (2) OR-9
Morton Creek—stream TX-5
Morton Creek—stream VA-3
Morton Dam—dam AZ-5
Morton Dam—dam TN-4
Morton Dam—reservoir TN-4
Morton Ditch—canal CO-8
Morton Ditch—canal MT-8
Morton Ditch—canal WY-8
Morton Drain MI-6
Morton Elem Sch—school (2) IN-6
Morton Elem Sch—school MS-4
Morton Elevator—locale TX-5
Morton Flat—flat CA-9
**Morton Fork**—pop pl NC-3
Morton F Plant Hosp—hospital FL-3
Morton Gap—gap TN-4
**Morton Grove**—pop pl IL-6
Morton Grove—woods CA-9
Morton Grove Sch—school IL-6
Morton Gulch—valley CA-9
Morton Hill—locale TN-4
Morton Hill—summit AL-4
Morton Hill—summit NE-7
Morton Hill—summit NY-2
Morton (historical)—locale AL-4
**Morton (historical)**—pop pl OR-9
Morton Hollow MO-7
Morton Hollow—valley (2) MO-7
Morton Hollow—valley TN-4
Morton Homestead—hist pl PA-2
Morton Hosp—hospital MA-1
Morton Hotel—hist pl NJ-2
Morton House—hist pl TX-5
Morton House—hist pl WV-2
Morton HS IN-6
Morton HS—school MA-1
Morton HS—school MS-4
Morton Island—island OR-9
Morton-James Public Library—hist pl NE-7
Morton JHS—school KY-4
Morton JHS—school MA-1
Morton JHS—school MS-4
Morton JHS—school OH-6
Morton Junior Coll—school IL-6
Morton Knob—summit TN-4
Morton Lake—lake CO-8
Morton Lake—lake WI-6
Morton Lake—reservoir AZ-5
Morton Lake—reservoir TN-4
Morton Ledge—bar ME-1
**Morton Manor (subdivision)**—pop pl NC-3
**Morton Meadows Subdivision**—pop pl UT-8
Morton Memorial Cem—cemetery MS-4
Morton Memorial Ch—church GA-3
Morton Memorial Library—hist pl NY-2
Morton Memorial Sch IN-6
Morton Memorial United Methodist Ch—church TN-4
Morton Methodist Episcopal Ch TN-4
**Morton Mills**—pop pl IA-7
Morton Mine—mine MN-6
Morton Mine—mine TX-5
**Morton (Morton Salt Plant)**—pop pl OH-6
Morton Mtn—summit NY-2
Morton Mtn—summit SC-3
Morton Natl Wildlife Ref—park NY-2
Morton Oil Field—other NM-5
Morton Overlook—locale TN-4
Morton Park IL-6
Morton Park—park (2) IL-6
Morton Park—park MA-1
Morton Park—park NE-7
Morton Park—park TX-5
Morton Pass—gap WY-8
Morton Peak—summit CA-9
Morton Pond—lake CT-1
Morton Pond—lake (2) MA-1
Morton Post Office (historical)—building AL-4
Morton Prospect—mine TN-4
Morton Ranch—locale CA-9
Morton Ranch—locale MT-8
Morton Ranch—locale (2) WY-8
Morton Ridge—ridge KY-4
Morton Ridge Ch—church OH-6
Morton Ridge Trail—trail CA-9

*Moswetusett* MA-1
*Mot* FM-9
*Mot* MP-9
**Mot**—*pop pl* LA-4
Mota—*locale* FM-9
Mota Bonita Windmill—*locale* TX-5
Mota Casa—*summit* TX-5
Mota Chica Windmill—*locale* TX-5
Mota Corpus Windmill—*locale* TX-5
Mota del Tacon Windmill—*locale* TX-5
Mota Huisache Windmill—*locale* TX-5
**Motala**—*pop pl* NE-7
Mota Mesquite Well (Windmill)—*locale* TX-5
Mota Negra—*summit* TX-5
Mota Negra Artesian Well—*well* TX-5
Motanic—*locale* OR-9
Motanic (historical)—*locale* OR-9
*Mo-Ta-Nucke* NY-2
Motaralla Windmill—*locale* TX-5
*Motarappu-to* MP-9
Mota Redonda Artesian Well—*well* TX-5
Mota Redonda Windmill—*locale* TX-5
*Motaruppu-To* MP-9
Motas Negras Windmill—*locale* TX-5
Mota Verde Artesian Well—*well* TX-5
**Motbridge**—*pop pl* SC-3
Mot Ch—*church* LA-4
Motch—*locale* TN-4
*Mote* NV-8
**Mote**—*pop pl* NV-8
Motegosu—*island* FM-9
Mote Interchange—*crossing* NV-8
Mote-Morris House—*hist pl* FL-3
Moten Cem—*cemetery* MS-4
Moten Ch—*church* AR-4
Moten Lake—*lake* TX-5
Moten Mtn—*summit* OK-5
Moten Sch—*school* DC-2
Mote Park—*park* OH-6
*Moterikku* MP-9
*Moterikku*—*island* MP-9
*Moterikku Island* MP-9
*Motes Branch* GA-3
Motes Cem—*cemetery* AL-4
Motes Cem—*cemetery* FL-3
Motes Chapel—*church* IL-6
*Motes Creek* IN-6
Motes Creek—*stream* NC-3
Moteshard Mtn—*summit* WV-2
Motes Hill—*summit* AL-4
Motes Hollow—*valley* AL-4
Mote Siding—*locale* NV-8
Motes Mill Creek—*stream* AL-4
Motes Point—*cape* FL-3
Mote Spring—*spring* OR-9
*Motes-Watson Cemetery* AL-4
*Motett Creek* OR-9
*Motett Spring* OR-9
Moth Bay—*bay* AK-9
Motheral, John, House—*hist pl* TN-4
Mother and Child, The—*pillar* UT-8
Mother and Child Turned to Stone—*locale* PW-9
Mother Bethel A.M.E. Church—*hist pl* PA-2
*Mother Brook* MA-1
Mother Brook—*stream* (2) MA-1
Mother Bunch Islands—*island* NY-2
Mother Bush Pond—*lake* ME-1
Mother Butler Memorial HS—*school* CA-9
Mother Butte—*summit* MT-8
Mother Cabrina Sch—*school* NY-2
Mother Cabrini Memorial Hosp—*hospital* NY-2
Mother Cabrini Orphanage—*other* CO-8
Mother Cabrini Shrine—*church* CO-8
Mother Cabrini Shrine—*other* NY-2
Mother Ch of God in Christ—*church* DE-2
Mother Church, The—*church* SC-3
*Mother Church of the Delta* MS-4
Mother Cline Slide—*cliff* CO-8
Mother Colony House—*building* CA-9
*Mother Creek* DE-2
Mother Creek—*stream* NY-2
Mother Dee Mine—*mine* CO-8
Mother Earth Lower Dam—*dam* NC-3
Mother Earth Upper—*reservoir* NC-3
Mother Earth Upper Dam—*dam* NC-3
Mother East Point—*cape* VI-3
Mother Featherlegs Cem—*cemetery* WY-8
Mother Frances Hosp—*hospital* TX-5
Mother Goose Glacier—*glacier* AK-9
Mother Goose Lake—*lake* AK-9
Mother Goose Nursery and Kindergarden—*school* FL-3
*Mother Griffin Creek* SC-3
Mother Grundy Peak—*summit* CA-9
Mother Grundy Truck Trail—*trail* CA-9
Mother Guerin HS—*school* IL-6
Mother Gut—*gut* VA-3
Mother Hubbard Canyon—*valley* AZ-5
Mother Hubbard Canyon—*valley* NM-5
Mother-in-Law Tank—*reservoir* TX-5
*Mother Kill* DE-2
*Motherkiln Creek* DE-2
Mother Lake—*fmr MCD* NE-7
Mother Lake—*lake* MN-6
Mother Lake—*lake* NE-7
Mother Lode Acres—*area* CA-9
Mother Lode Creek—*stream* OR-9
Mother Lode Hill—*summit* ID-8
Mother Lode Mine—*mine* AK-9
Mother Lode Mine—*mine* CA-9
Mother Lode Mine—*mine* (2) ID-8
Mother Lode Mine—*mine* NV-8
Mother Lode Trail—*trail* OR-9
Mother Lot Point—*cape* WI-6
Mother Mary Mission—*church* AL-4
Mother McAuley HS—*school* IL-6
Mother Miguel Mtn—*summit* CA-9
Mother Mtn—*summit* WA-9
Mother Myrick Mtn—*summit* VT-1
Mother Neff Ch—*church* TX-5
Mother Neff State Park—*park* TX-5
Mother of Christ Catholic Ch—*church* FL-3
Mother of Divine Grace Sch—*school* NY-2
Mother of Dolors Cem—*cemetery* IL-6
Mother Of God Cem—*cemetery* KY-4
Mother Of God Ch—*church* OH-6
Mother Of God Roman Catholic Church—*hist pl* KY-4
Mother of God Sch—*school* IL-6
Mother of Good Counsel Novitiate—*school* NY-2
Mother of Good Counsel Sch—*school* CA-9
Mother of Good Counsel Sch—*school* KY-4
Mother of Grace Ch—*church* LA-4
Mother of Perpetual Help Ch—*church* LA-4
Mother of Perpetual Help Ch—*church* VI-3
Mother of Perpetual Help Monastery—*church* NY-2
Mother Of Perpetual Help Shrine—*other* OH-6
Mother of Sorrows Cem—*cemetery* MN-6
Mother of Sorrows Ch—*church* NY-2
Mother of Sorrows Ch—*church* PA-2
Mother of Sorrows Sch—*school* CA-9
Mother Of Sorrows Sch—*school* OH-6
Mothers' and Daughters' Club House—*hist pl* NH-1
Mothers Branch—*stream* AL-4
*Mother'S Brook* MA-1
Mothers Canyon—*valley* AZ-5
*Mothers Creek* DE-2
Mothers Creek—*stream* OR-9
Mother Seton Catholic Ch—*church* FL-3
Mother Seton House—*hist pl* MD-2
Mothershed Branch—*stream* AL-4
Mothershed Cem—*cemetery* AL-4
Mothers Hill—*summit* CO-8
Mothers Home Ch—*church* GA-3
Mothers Home Ch—*church* KY-4
*Mothers Lake* NJ-2
*Mother Sousans Church* MS-4
*Mothers Shed Cem* AL-4
Mothers United Ch—*church* WV-2
Mother Superior Lake—*lake* CT-1
Mothers Well—*well* NM-5
Mother Thompson House—*hist pl* OH-6
**Mother Vineyard**—*pop pl* NC-3
Mother Waldron Playground—*park* HI-9
Mother Walker Falls—*falls* ME-1
Motherwell Airp—*airport* IN-6
Motherwood Point—*cape* AK-9
Mothiglam Bayou—*stream* LA-4
Moth Lake—*lake* MI-6
Moth Lake—*lake* MN-6
Moth Point—*cape* AK-9
Motichka Creek—*stream* MT-8
Motie, Joseph, House—*hist pl* IA-7
Motil Pond—*lake* CT-1
Motion—*locale* CA-9
Motion Creek—*stream* CA-9
Motion Picture Country House and Hosp—*hospital* CA-9
Motions, The—*bar* ME-1
*Mot Island* FM-9
*Motlap* MP-9
**Motleta**—*pop pl* NC-3
Motley—*locale* AL-4
Motley—*locale* KY-4
Motley—*locale* MO-7
**Motley**—*pop pl* MI-6
**Motley**—*pop pl* MN-6
**Motley**—*pop pl* TX-5
**Motley**—*pop pl* VA-3
*Motley Attendance Center* MS-4
Motley Branch—*stream* AL-4
Motley Branch—*stream* MO-7
Motley Branch—*stream* SC-3
Motley Branch—*stream* VA-3
*Motley Cem* TN-4
Motley Cem—*cemetery* MN-6
Motley Cem—*cemetery* MS-4
Motley Cem—*cemetery* (2) MO-7
Motley Cem—*cemetery* TN-4
Motley Cem—*cemetery* (2) TX-5
Motley Ch—*church* MS-4
**Motley (County)**—*pop pl* TX-5
Motley Creek—*stream* KY-4
*Motley Elementary School* MS-4
Motley Fork—*stream* (2) KY-4
Motley Gap—*gap* AR-4
Motley Island—*island* SD-7
Motley Lookout Tower—*locale* MN-6
*Motley Millpond* VA-3
Motley Oil Field—*oilfield* TX-5
Motley Pond—*lake* MA-1
Motley Ranch—*locale* SD-7
Motley Rsvr—*reservoir* OR-9
Motley Sch—*school* IL-6
Motley Sch—*school* MN-6
Motley Sch—*school* MS-4
Motley Sch—*school* MO-7
Motleys Chapel—*church* AR-4
Motley Sch (historical)—*school* TN-4
Motley Slough—*stream* MS-4
Motley Slough Bridge—*hist pl* MS-4
*Motley Slu* MS-4
Motleys Mill—*locale* VA-3
**Motley (Township of)**—*pop pl* MN-6
Motlou Creek—*stream* SC-3
Motlow Cave—*cave* TN-4
Motlow Cem—*cemetery* (2) TN-4
Motlow Cove—*valley* TN-4
Motlow Creek Ch—*church* SC-3
Motlow Hollow—*valley* TN-4
Motlow State Community Coll—*school* TN-4
*Motly Slough* MS-4
Motno Mesquite Artesian Well—*well* TX-5
*Moton Cemetery* MS-4
Moton Center—*school* FL-3
Moton Field (airport)—*airport* AL-4
Moton Hosp—*hospital* OK-5
Moton HS—*school* AL-4
Moton Sch—*school* LA-4
Moton Sch—*school* VA-3
Motonui Island—*island* FM-9
Motoqua—*locale* UT-8
Motor—*locale* (2) IA-7
Motorboat Lake—*lake* IN-6
*Motor Branch* VA-3
Motor Ch—*church* IA-7
Motor City—*locale* CA-9
Motor City Drag Strip—*other* MI-6
Motor Creek—*stream* ID-8
Motor Cross Race Track—*other* KS-7
Motor (historical)—*locale* KS-7
*Motor Island* NY-2
**Motor Junction**—*pop pl* CA-9
Motorman, The—*rock* UT-8
Motor Townsite—*hist pl* IA-7
**Motoron**—*pop pl* VA-3
Motsu Spoil Disposal Dike—*dam* NC-3
Mott—*locale* CA-9
Mott—*locale* FL-3
**Mott**—*pop pl* ND-7
Mottarns Mill—*locale* PA-2
Mottarville Cem—*cemetery* IL-6
Mott Ave Control House—*hist pl* NY-2
Mott Basin—*basin* OR-9
Mott Branch—*stream* TX-5
Mott Branch—*stream* VA-3
Mott Bottom—*flat* CO-8
*Mott Bridge* AL-4
Mott Camp—*locale* MI-6
Mott Camp—*locale* TX-5
Mott Canyon—*valley* NV-8
Mott Cem—*cemetery* IN-6
Mott Cem—*cemetery* MS-4
Mott Cem—*cemetery* (2) NY-2
Mott Cem—*cemetery* (2) TX-5
Mott Coulee—*valley* ND-7
Mott Cove—*bay* NY-2
Mott Cove—*valley* TN-4
Mott Cove Cave—*cave* TN-4
*Mott Creek* TX-5
Mott Creek—*stream* MO-7
Mott Creek—*stream* MT-8
Mott Creek—*stream* NJ-2
Mott Creek—*stream* NY-2
Mott Creek—*stream* (2) NC-3
Mott Creek—*stream* OK-5
Mott Creek—*stream* TX-5
Mott Creek—*stream* WA-9
Mott Ditch—*canal* IN-6
Mott Drain—*stream* MI-6
Motte, Isle la—*island* VT-1
Motte Canyon—*valley* CA-9
*Motte Channel* NC-3
Motter, John C., House—*hist pl* MD-2
Motte Reef—*bar* VT-1
Mottern Cem—*cemetery* (2) TN-4
Mottern Sch (abandoned)—*school* PA-2
**Motters**—*pop pl* MD-2
Mottet Creek—*stream* OR-9
Mottet Spring—*spring* OR-9
**Mott Haven**—*pop pl* NY-2
Mott Haven Hist Dist—*hist pl* NY-2
Mott Haven Junction—*uninc pl* NY-2
Mott Haven Yard—*locale* NY-2
Mott Hill—*summit* PA-2
Mott Hill Brook—*stream* CT-1
Mott Hill Hollow—*valley* PA-2
Mott Hollow—*valley* IL-6
Motthorn Saddle—*gap* ID-8
Mott House—*hist pl* GA-3
Mott HS—*school* MI-6
Motti Hill—*summit* KS-7
Mott Island—*island* MI-6
Mott Island—*island* OR-9
*Mott Lake* NY-2
Mott Lake—*lake* AR-4
Mott Lake—*lake* CA-9
Mott Lake—*lake* MI-6
Mott Lake—*lake* WI-6
Mott Lake—*reservoir* AL-4
Mott Lake—*reservoir* NC-3
Mott Lake Dam—*dam* AL-4
Mottley Sch—*school* MO-7
Mottman Bldg—*hist pl* WA-9
Mott Mine—*mine* CA-9
Mott Mine—*mine* MN-6
Mott Municipal Airp—*airport* ND-7
Motto Cem—*cemetery* IA-7
Motto River—*stream* VA-3
Motto Windmill—*locale* TX-5
*Mott Park* MI-6
Mott Park—*park* MI-6
Mott Point—*cape* NY-2
Mottram Lake—*reservoir* OH-6
Mott Road Sch—*school* NY-2
**Motts**—*pop pl* AL-4
Motts Basin—*bay* NY-2
Motts Branch—*stream* KY-4
Motts Bridge (historical)—*bridge* AL-4
Motts Brook—*stream* NY-2
Motts Cem—*cemetery* OH-6
Mott Sch—*school* MI-6
Mott Sch—*school* NJ-2
Mott Sch—*school* NY-2
Mott Sch—*school* PA-2
Mott Sch (abandoned)—*school* PA-2
Mott Sch and Second Street School—*hist pl* NJ-2
Motts Channel—*channel* NC-3
Mott Sch (historical)—*school* MO-7
Mott Sch Number 3—*school* IN-6
Motts Corner—*locale* NY-2
Motts Creek—*bay* NC-3
Motts Creek—*stream* MS-4
Motts Creek—*stream* NY-2
Motts Grove Ch—*church* NC-3
Motts Hill—*summit* NY-2
Motts Hollow—*valley* KY-4
*Motts Lake* WI-6
Motts Lick Creek—*stream* KY-4
Mott Slough—*stream* TX-5
Motts Park—*park* IN-6
*Motts Peak* AL-4
*Mott's Point* NY-2
Motts Point—*cape* NY-2
Mott Spring—*spring* AZ-5
Motts Run Hill—*summit* VA-3
Motts Run Rsvr—*reservoir* VA-3
*Motts Station* IN-6
**Mott Station**—*pop pl* IN-6
Mott Stream—*stream* ME-1
Mottsville—*locale* NV-8
Mottsville Cem—*cemetery* NV-8
Mott Swamp—*stream* NC-3
Mott Township—*fmr MCD* IA-7
**Mott Township**—*pop pl* ND-7
Mott Trail—*trail* OR-9
**Mottville**—*pop pl* MI-6
**Mottville**—*pop pl* NY-2
**Mottville (Township of)**—*pop pl* MI-6
Mott Watershed Dam—*dam* ND-7
Mott Windmill—*locale* TX-5
Mott Yard—*locale* NY-2
Motu Iloto Island—*island* FM-9
Motu Ituo Island—*island* FM-9
Motusaga Point—*cape* AS-9
Motusaga Ridge—*ridge* AS-9
Motu Wei Island—*island* FM-9
Motyka Lake—*lake* WI-6
*Motz Bank* PA-2
Mouatt Reef—*bar* WA-9
Moucha Sch—*school* MN-6
Mouchoir De L'Ourse, Bayou—*stream* LA-4
Moude Mountain Trail—*trail* OR-9
Moudess Creek—*stream* MT-8
*Moudges Corner* VA-3
Mouds Bottom—*flat* CO-8
Moudy Cem—*cemetery* MO-7
**Moudy Hill**—*pop pl* PA-2
Mouflon Reef—*bar* TX-5
*Mougers Landing* AL-4
Mougeys Lake—*lake* MI-6
Moughmer Point—*cliff* ID-8
Moughmer Ridge—*ridge* ID-8
Mouille Creek—*stream* MI-6
Mouille March—*swamp* MI-6
*Mouiller A'Yor* LA-4
Mouillere d Dehors —*lake* LA-4
*Mouiller Swamp* LA-4
Mouilliere, La —*swamp* LA-4
Moulas Mine—*mine* CA-9
Moulden Cem—*cemetery* TN-4
Moulden Cem—*cemetery* TX-5
Moulden Hollow—*valley* TN-4
Moulden Hollow Branch—*stream* TN-4
Moulden Sch—*school* IL-6
Moulder Cem—*cemetery* MS-4
Moulder Mtn—*summit* TN-4
*Moulder Oil Field* TX-5
*Moulders Chapel* TN-4
Moulder Sch (historical)—*school* TN-4
Moulders Sch (historical)—*school* TN-4
Moulding Creek—*stream* ID-8
Mouldin Mine (underground)—*mine* AL-4
Moulds Lodge—*locale* VT-1
Mouldy Pond—*lake* NY-2
*Mouldy Run* MD-2
Moules Lake—*lake* NY-2
Moulfon Creek—*stream* IA-7
*Moulier A'Yor* LA-4
*Mouliere Swamp* LA-4
Moulihan Cem—*cemetery* IL-6
Moulin Mtn—*summit* NY-2
Moul Sch (abandoned)—*school* PA-2
Moulsons Pond—*lake* CT-1
Moulstown—*locale* PA-2
Moulten Playground—*park* MA-1
Moulten Slough—*stream* AL-4
Moulten Slough Creek—*stream* FL-3
Moulthrop Brook—*stream* CT-1
Moulthrop Brook—*stream* CT-1
*Moulton* IL-6
**Moulton**—*pop pl* AL-4
**Moulton**—*pop pl* IA-7
**Moulton**—*pop pl* MT-8
**Moulton**—*pop pl* NC-3
**Moulton**—*pop pl* OH-6
**Moulton**—*pop pl* TX-5
Moulton Baptist Ch—*church* AL-4
**Moultonboro**—*pop pl* NH-1
*Moultonboro Falls* NH-1
Moultonborough Bay—*bay* NH-1
**Moultonborough Falls**—*pop pl* NH-1
Moultonborough Neck—*cape* NH-1
**Moultonborough (Town of)**—*pop pl* NH-1
Moulton Branch—*stream* AL-4
Moulton Brook—*stream* (2) ME-1
Moulton Brook—*stream* NH-1
Moulton (CCD)—*cens area* AL-4
Moulton (CCD)—*cens area* TX-5
Moulton Cem—*cemetery* IL-6
Moulton Cem—*cemetery* NE-7
Moulton Cem—*cemetery* NY-2
Moulton Ch of Christ—*church* AL-4
Moulton City Lake—*reservoir* AL-4
Moulton Creek—*stream* WY-8
*Moulton Dam* MA-1
Moulton Dam Dropped—*dam* MA-1
Moulton Distribution Rsvr—*reservoir* MT-8
Moulton Division—*civil* AL-4
Moulton Elem Sch—*school* AL-4
Moulton Falls—*falls* WA-9
**Moulton Heights**—*pop pl* AL-4
*Moulton Heights Elementary School* AL-4
Moulton Heights JHS—*school* AL-4
Moulton Heights Sch—*school* AL-4
Moulton Hill—*summit* ME-1
Moulton Hill—*summit* MA-1
Moulton Hill—*summit* NH-1
Moulton Hill Brook—*stream* NH-1
Moulton Hill Cem—*cemetery* MA-1
Moulton Hill Cem—*cemetery* NH-1
*Moulton HS* AL-4
*Moulton Intermediate Sch* AL-4
Moulton Lake—*lake* (2) MN-6
Moulton Lateral—*canal* CA-9
Moulton Ledge—*bar* ME-1
Moulton MS—*school* AL-4
Moulton Municipal Cem—*cemetery* AL-4
Moulton Pond—*lake* ME-1
Moulton Pond—*reservoir* MA-1
Moulton Post Office—*building* AL-4
Moulton Reservoir Number Two—*stream* MT-8
Moulton Ridge—*ridge* ME-1
Moulton Ridge—*ridge* NH-1
Moulton Rsvr—*reservoir* MT-8
Moulton Rsvr No 2—*reservoir* MT-8
Moulton Sch—*school* MO-7
Moultons Cove—*bay* NH-1
Moulton (Site)—*locale* ID-8
Moulton Speedway—*locale* AL-4
Moulton Spring—*spring* TN-4
**Moulton (Township of)**—*pop pl* MN-6
**Moulton (Township of)**—*pop pl* OH-6
Moulton Valley—*valley* AL-4
Moulton Valley—*valley* CO-8
**Moultonville**—*pop pl* NH-1
**Moultonville**—*pop pl* NC-3
**Moultonville (Moltonville)**—*pop pl* NC-3
Moultonville Sch—*school* IL-6
Moulton Water Plant—*building* AL-4
Moulton Weir—*dam* CA-9
Moulton-Yard Cem—*cemetery* NH-1
Moultray Cem—*cemetery* MO-7
Moultrie—*locale* FL-3
**Moultrie**—*pop pl* GA-3
**Moultrie**—*pop pl* OH-6
Moultrie, Lake—*reservoir* SC-3
Moultrie Baptist Ch—*church* FL-3
Moultrie (CCD)—*cens area* GA-3
Moultrie Cem—*cemetery* AL-4
Moultrie Ch—*church* FL-3
Moultrie Chapel—*church* OH-6
**Moultrie (County)**—*pop pl* IL-6
Moultrie Creek—*stream* FL-3
Moultrie Field—*bay* TN-4
Moultrie HS—*hist pl* GA-3
Moultrie HS—*school* SC-3
**Moultrie Junction**—*pop pl* FL-3
Moultrie Municipal Airp—*airport* GA-3
Moultries (historical)—*locale* AL-4
Moument Mine—*mine* MT-8
*Mouna Huararai* HI-9
*Mouna Kea* HI-9
*Mouna Koa* HI-9
*Mouna Roa* HI-9
Mounce Creek—*stream* NJ-2
Mounce Hollow—*valley* MO-7
Mounce Pond—*lake* MA-1
*Mounces Creek* NJ-2
*Mound* AR-4
Mound—*civil* KS-7
Mound—*locale* OH-6
**Mound**—*pop pl* LA-4
**Mound**—*pop pl* MN-6
**Mound**—*pop pl* ND-7
**Mound**—*pop pl* TX-5
Mound—*summit* CA-9
Mound—*uninc pl* WV-2
Mound, Lake of the—*lake* LA-4
Mound, The—*summit* FL-3
Mound, The—*summit* (4) IL-6
Mound, The—*summit* IN-6
Mound, The—*summit* KY-4
Mound, The—*summit* (2) MN-6
Mound, The—*summit* (5) MO-7
Mound, The—*summit* NV-8
Mound, The—*summit* OK-5
Mound, The—*summit* SC-3
Mound, The—*summit* (2) TN-4
Mound Bayou—*gut* AR-4
Mound Bayou—*gut* (6) LA-4
Mound Bayou—*lake* LA-4
**Mound Bayou**—*pop pl* MS-4
Mound Bayou—*stream* (4) MS-4
Mound Bayou Cem—*cemetery* AR-4
Mound Bayou Ch—*church* AR-4
Mound Bayou Ch (historical)—*church* MS-4
Mound Bayou Recreation Lake Dam—*dam* MS-4
Mound Bayou Sewage Lagoon Dam—*dam* MS-4
Mound Bluff—*cliff* MS-4
Mound Bogard—*summit* MO-7
Mound Bottom—*bend* TN-4
Mound Bottom—*hist pl* TN-4
**Mound Bottom (historical)**—*pop pl* TN-4
Mound Branch—*stream* KS-7
Mound Branch—*stream* MO-7
*Moundbuilders* OH-6
Mound Builders Fort (historical)—*locale* IN-6
Moundbuilders State Memorial—*park* OH-6
*Mound Canyon* AZ-5
*Mound Canyon* UT-8
Mound Cem—*cemetery* AR-4
Mound Cem—*cemetery* (3) IL-6
Mound Cem—*cemetery* (2) IN-6
Mound Cem—*cemetery* (2) IA-7
Mound Cem—*cemetery* (4) KS-7
Mound Cem—*cemetery* LA-4
Mound Cem—*cemetery* (3) MN-6
Mound Cem—*cemetery* MS-4
Mound Cem—*cemetery* (2) MO-7
Mound Cem—*cemetery* NE-7
Mound Cem—*cemetery* OH-6
Mound Cem—*cemetery* PA-2
Mound Cem—*cemetery* TX-5
Mound Cem—*cemetery* (3) WI-6
Mound Cemetery, The—*cemetery* TN-4
Mound Cemetery Mound—*hist pl* (2) OH-6
Mound Cemetery Site—*hist pl* MS-4
Mound Ch—*church* IL-6
Mound Ch—*church* MO-7
Mound Chapel—*church* (2) IL-6
Mound Chapel—*church* LA-4
Mound Chapel—*church* MO-7
Mound Chapel Cem—*cemetery* IL-6
Mound Ch (historical)—*church* MS-4
Mound City—*locale* AR-4
Mound City—*locale* TX-5
Mound City—*locale* UT-8
**Mound City**—*pop pl* IL-6
**Mound City**—*pop pl* KS-7
**Mound City**—*pop pl* (2) MS-4
**Mound City**—*pop pl* MO-7
**Mound City**—*pop pl* SD-7
**Mound City**—*pop pl* TX-5
Mound City Cem—*cemetery* SD-7
Mound City Church Cem—*cemetery* AR-4
Mound City Chute—*gut* AR-4
Mound City Civil War Naval Hosp—*hist pl* IL-6
Mound City (Election Precinct)—*fmr MCD* IL-6
Mound City Elem Sch—*school* KS-7
Mound City Group Natl Monmt—*hist pl* OH-6
Mound City Group Natl Monmt—*park* OH-6
Mound City Group Natl Monmt—*pillar* OH-6
Mound City Natl Cem—*cemetery* IL-6
Mound City Township—*civil* SD-7
**Mound City Township**—*pop pl* KS-7
Mound City (Township of)—*fmr MCD* AR-4
*Mound Creek* KS-7
*Mound Creek* TX-5
Mound Creek—*stream* KS-7
Mound Creek—*stream* (2) MN-6
Mound Creek—*stream* MS-4
Mound Creek—*stream* (2) MO-7
Mound Creek—*stream* TN-4
Mound Creek—*stream* (4) TX-5
Mound Creek—*stream* WI-6
Mound Creek Cem—*cemetery* KS-7
Mound Creek (historical)—*locale* KS-7
Mound Crevasse—*lake* MS-4
Mound Crossing—*locale* OH-6
Mound Ditch—*canal* AR-4
Mound Ditch—*canal* LA-4
Mound Field—*flat* TN-4
Mound Fort (historical)—*locale* UT-8
Mound Fort JHS—*school* UT-8
Mound Fort MS—*school* UT-8
Mound Grove—*locale* FL-3
Mound Grove—*locale* OK-5
Mound Grove Cem—*cemetery* IL-6
Mound Grove Cem—*cemetery* MO-7
Mound Grove Sch—*school* IL-6
**Mound Haven**—*pop pl* IN-6
Mound Hedren Ch—*church* LA-4
Mound Hill—*summit* AK-9
Mound Hill Archeol Site—*hist pl* KY-4
Mound Hill Cem—*cemetery* (2) OH-6
Mound Hill Ch—*church* OH-6
Moundhill Point—*cape* AK-9
**Mound (historical)**—*pop pl* OR-9
Mound House—*hist pl* OH-6
Mound House Site—*hist pl* IL-6
Mound House (Site)—*locale* NV-8
Mound Island—*island* AL-4
Mound Island—*island* IL-6
Mound JHS—*school* IL-6
Mound Key—*hist pl* FL-3
Mound Key—*island* (2) FL-3
*Mound Lake* FL-3
Mound Lake—*lake* AR-4
Mound Lake—*lake* (2) FL-3
Mound Lake—*lake* (2) IL-6
Mound Lake—*lake* (2) MN-6
Mound Lake—*lake* OR-9
Mound Lake—*lake* (2) TX-5
Mound Lake (reduced usage)—*lake* IL-6
Mound Landing—*locale* MS-4
Mound Lodge—*locale* LA-4
Mound Lookout Tower—*tower* FL-3
*Mound Meadow* MA-1
Mound Mtn—*summit* AZ-5
Mound Mtn—*summit* UT-8
Mound Olive Cem—*cemetery* OK-5
Mound Park—*park* OH-6
Mound Park Hosp—*hospital* FL-3
Mound Park Sch—*school* MI-6
*Mound Place* MS-4
Mound Place Lodge—*locale* AR-4
Mound Plantation—*locale* LA-4
Mound Plantation (historical)—*locale* MS-4
Mound Point—*cape* AK-9
Mound Point—*cape* LA-4
Mound Pond—*lake* AR-4
Mound Pond—*lake* TX-5
Mound Pond—*lake* UT-8
Mound Pond—*lake* WA-9
*Mound Prairie* WA-9
Mound Prairie—*locale* MN-6
Mound Prairie Cem—*cemetery* MN-6
Mound Prairie Cem—*cemetery* WI-6
Mound Prairie Ch—*church* MN-6
Mound Prairie Creek—*stream* MN-6
Mound Prairie Creek—*stream* TX-5
Mound Prairie Sch—*school* TX-5
Mound Prairie Sch—*school* WI-6
Mound Prairie Sch (historical)—*school* MO-7
Mound Prairie Township—*fmr MCD* IA-7
Mound Prairie (Township of)—*civ div* MN-6
*Mound Ridge* KS-7
**Moundridge**—*pop pl* KS-7
Mound Ridge—*ridge* WI-6
Mound Ridge Camp—*locale* MO-7
Moundridge HS—*school* KS-7
*Moundridge Landing Strip* KS-7
Moundridge Municipal Airfield—*airport* KS-7
Mound Ridge Sch—*school* OK-5
Mound Run—*stream* IN-6
Mound Run—*stream* WV-2
Mounds—*locale* UT-8
**Mounds**—*pop pl* (2) AR-4
**Mounds**—*pop pl* IL-6
**Mounds**—*pop pl* OK-5
Mounds, Cove of the—*cave* WI-6
Mounds, The—*summit* CA-9
Mounds, The—*summit* IN-6
Mounds Branch—*stream* WI-6
Mounds Cem—*cemetery* AR-4
Mounds Cem—*cemetery* IA-7
Mounds Cem—*cemetery* MO-7
Mounds Cem—*cemetery* OH-6
Mounds Ch—*church* IN-6
Mounds Ch—*church* LA-4
Mounds Ch—*church* MO-7
Mound Sch—*school* CA-9
Mound Sch—*school* (8) IL-6
Mound Sch—*school* IA-7
Mound Sch—*school* (2) KS-7
Mound Sch—*school* (3) MO-7
Mound Sch—*school* (2) OH-6
Mound Sch—*school* WV-2
Mound Sch (abandoned)—*school* MO-7
Mound Sch (historical)—*school* MS-4
Mound Sch (Primary Division)—*school* CA-9
*Mounds Creek* WI-6
Mounds Creek Ch—*church* WI-6
Mounds (Election Precinct)—*fmr MCD* IL-6
Mound Seminary Sch—*school* IL-6
Mounds Ford—*locale* AL-4
*Mounds Lake* OK-5
Mound Slough—*gut* AR-4
Mound Slough—*stream* KY-4
Mounds Park Hosp—*hospital* MN-6
Mounds Park JHS—*school* MN-6
Mounds Park Sch—*school* MN-6
Mounds Pond—*lake* FL-3
Mounds Pond—*reservoir* WI-6
Mounds Pool—*reservoir* FL-3
*Mound Spring* NV-8
Mound Spring—*reservoir* UT-8
Mound Spring—*spring* CA-9
Mound Spring—*spring* MI-6
Mound Spring—*spring* NV-8
Mound Springs—*spring* (2) NV-8
Mound Springs—*spring* NM-5
Mound Springs Creek—*stream* CA-9
Mound Springs Creek—*stream* MO-7
Mound Springs Park—*park* MN-6
Mound Springs Sch—*school* MO-7
Mounds Reef—*ridge* UT-8
Mounds Rsvr—*reservoir* UT-8
Mounds Sch (historical)—*school* MO-7
Mounds State Park—*hist pl* IN-6
Mounds State Park—*park* IN-6
*Mounds State Rec Area* IN-6
Mounds State Rec Area—*park* IN-6
Mound State Monmt—*park* AL-4

*Mound Station* ... IL-6
**Mound Station (corporate name for Timewell)**—pop pl ... IL-6
**Mound Station Timewell Post Office**—pop pl ... IL-6
Mound Street Sch—school ... WI-6
**Mounds View**—pop pl ... MN-6
Mounds View HS—school ... MN-6
**Moundsville**—pop pl ... OH-6
**Moundsville**—pop pl ... WV-2
Moundsville Golf Course—other ... WV-2
**Mound Township**—pop pl (3) ... KS-7
**Mound Township**—pop pl ... MO-7
**Mound Township**—pop pl ... ND-7
**Mound (Township of)**—pop pl (2) ... IL-6
**Mound (Township of)**—pop pl ... IN-6
**Mound (Township of)**—pop pl ... MN-6
Mound Valley—locale ... ID-8
**Mound Valley**—pop pl ... KS-7
Mound Valley—valley ... ID-8
Mound Valley—valley ... MO-7
Mound Valley—valley ... NV-8
Mound Valley Cem—cemetery ... KS-7
Mound Valley Cem—cemetery (2) ... OK-5
Mound Valley Ch—church ... OK-5
Mound Valley Elem Sch—school ... KS-7
Mound Valley Sch—school ... KS-7
Mound Valley Sch—school ... NV-8
Mound Valley Sch—school (3) ... OK-5
Mound Valley Sch—school ... WI-6
**Mound Valley Township**—pop pl ... KS-7
*Mound View* ... OH-6
Mound View Cem—cemetery ... OH-6
Mound View Rock—summit ... WI-6
Mound View Sch—school ... IL-6
Mound View Sch—school ... WI-6
*Moundville* ... KS-7
Moundville—hist pl ... AL-4
**Moundville**—pop pl ... AL-4
**Moundville**—pop pl ... MO-7
Moundville Baptist Ch—church ... AL-4
Moundville (CCD)—cens area ... AL-4
Moundville Ch—church ... WI-6
Moundville Division—civil ... AL-4
Moundville Elem Sch—school ... AL-4
Moundville Methodist Ch—church ... AL-4
Moundville Plantation House—hist pl ... LA-4
**Moundville (Town of)**—pop pl ... WI-6
**Moundville Township**—pop pl ... MO-7
*Mounger Cemetery* ... AL-4
Moungers Creek—stream ... MS-4
*Moungers Landing* ... AL-4
**Mounkes**—pop pl ... CA-9
Mounment Hill—summit ... WA-9
Mounment Springs—spring ... ID-8
Mounsey Ditch—canal ... IN-6
*Mount* ... AL-4
*Mount* ... AZ-5
*Mount* ... CO-8
*Mount* ... ME-1
*Mount* ... MA-1
*Mount* ... UT-8
Mount—locale ... NJ-2
Mount—locale ... UT-8
Mount—locale ... VA-3
Mount, Bethel Ch—church ... GA-3
Mount, Pleasant Cem—cemetery ... VT-1
Mount, The—hist pl ... MA-1
Mount, The—summit ... MA-1
Mount, The—summit ... RI-1
Mount, William Sydney, House—hist pl ... NY-2
*Mount Aadmalkon* ... PW-9
*Mount Aadmalkou* ... PW-9
*Mount Aadulkou* ... PW-9
Mount Aaran Ch—church ... AL-4
Mount Aaron Cem—cemetery ... MS-4
*Mount Aaron Ch* ... AL-4
Mount Aaron Ch—church ... MS-4
Mount Aaron Sch (historical)—school ... MS-4
*Mount Aawela* ... HI-9
Mount Abbey Ch—church ... LA-4
*Mount Abel* ... CA-9
Mount Abel Cem—cemetery ... AR-4
*Mount Aben* ... PW-9
Mount Able Cem—cemetery ... MS-4
Mount Able Ch—church ... MS-4
Mount Abnah Cem—cemetery ... NY-2
*Mount Abram* ... ME-1
Mount Abram Cem—cemetery ... ME-1
Mount Abram (Township of)—unorg ... ME-1
*Mount Abraums* ... CO-8
Mount Acadia Park—park ... CA-9
Mount Ada Baptist Ch (historical)—church ... AL-4
Mount Ada Ch—church ... FL-3
*Mount Adams* ... OH-6
Mount Adams—hist pl ... MD-2
**Mount Adams**—pop pl ... OH-6
Mount Adams Cem—cemetery ... WA-9
Mount Adams Golf and Country Club—other ... WA-9
Mount Adams Lake—lake ... WA-9
Mount Adams Public Sch—hist pl ... OH-6
Mount Adar Ch—church ... NC-3
*Mount Adeline* ... CA-9
Mount Adnah Cem—cemetery ... MA-1
Mount Adow Ch—church ... MO-7
*Mount Aeolus* ... CO-8
Mount Aeral Ch—church ... SC-3
Mount Aerial—locale ... KY-4
Mount Aerial Ch—church ... AL-4
Mount Aerial Sch (historical)—school ... MO-7
Mount Aerie Ch—church ... IN-6
Mount Aeriel Cem—cemetery ... MO-7
**Mount Aetna**—pop pl ... MD-2
**Mount Aetna**—pop pl ... PA-2
Mount Aetna Acad—school ... MD-2
Mount Aetna Ch—church ... IN-6
Mount Aetna Creek—stream ... MD-2
*Mount Agade* ... PW-9
*Mount Agassez* ... UT-8
Mount Agony Ch—church ... GA-3
*Mount Ahiakalio* ... HI-9
Mount Aid Ch—church ... AL-4
Mount Aide Ch (historical)—church ... MS-4
*Mount Ailol* ... PW-9
Mount Aily Ch—church ... GA-3
*Mountain* ... PA-2
Mountain—locale ... MO-7
Mountain—locale ... OR-9
Mountain—locale ... TX-5
Mountain—locale ... VI-3
**Mountain**—pop pl ... MD-2
**Mountain**—pop pl ... ND-7
**Mountain**—pop pl ... TX-5
**Mountain**—pop pl ... WV-2
**Mountain**—pop pl ... WI-6
Mountain, Lake—lake (2) ... CA-9
Mountain, Point of the—cliff (2) ... AZ-5
Mountain, The—summit ... GA-3
Mountain, The—summit ... ME-1
Mountain, The—summit ... MA-1
Mountain, The—summit ... TN-4
**Mountain Acres**—pop pl ... AL-4
**Mountainair**—pop pl ... NM-5
Mountain Air Camp—locale ... WA-9
Mountainair (CCD)—cens area ... NM-5
Mountainair Cem—cemetery ... NM-5
**Mountainaire**—pop pl ... AZ-5
**Mountain Aire Subdivision**—pop pl ... UT-8
Mountainair HS—school ... NM-5
Mountainair Municipal Auditorium—hist pl ... NM-5
**Mountain Air Park**—pop pl ... OR-9
Mountain Airpark Airport, The—airport ... WA-9
Mountainair Pumping Station—other ... NM-5
Mountainair Ranger Station—locale ... NM-5
**Mountain Ash**—pop pl ... KY-4
Mountain Ash Creek—stream ... WY-8
Mountain Ash Lake—lake ... MN-6
Mountain Ash Springs—spring ... OR-9
**Mountain Ave**—pop pl ... NJ-2
Mountain Ave Cave—cave ... PA-2
Mountain Ave Station—hist pl ... NJ-2
Mountain Ave Station—locale ... NJ-2
Mountain Bailey—summit ... OR-9
*Mountain Baldy* ... ID-8
*Mountain Baldy* ... MT-8
*Mountain Baptist Church* ... AL-4
**Mountain Base**—pop pl ... NH-1
Mountain Bayou Lake—reservoir ... LA-4
**Mountain Beach**—pop pl ... MI-6
Mountain Belle Mine—mine ... OR-9
Mountain Ben Lake—lake ... MT-8
Mountain Beulah Ch—church ... NC-3
Mountain Bloomery Forge (historical)—locale ... TN-4
**Mountainboro**—pop pl ... AL-4
Mountainboro (CCD)—cens area ... AL-4
Mountainboro Division—civil ... AL-4
Mountainboro Missionary Baptist Ch—church ... AL-4
Mountain Boy Gulch—valley ... CO-8
Mountain Boy Mine—mine ... CA-9
Mountain Boy Mine—mine ... ID-8
Mountain Boy Mine—mine ... NV-8
Mountain Boy Park—flat ... CO-8
Mountain Boy Range—summit ... NV-8
*Mountain Branch* ... GA-3
*Mountain Branch* ... PA-2
*Mountain Branch* ... VA-3
Mountain Branch—stream (2) ... AL-4
Mountain Branch—stream ... IL-6
Mountain Branch—stream ... KY-4
Mountain Branch—stream ... MD-2
Mountain Branch—stream (3) ... NC-3
Mountain Branch—stream ... PA-2
Mountain Branch—stream ... SC-3
Mountain Branch—stream ... TX-5
Mountain Branch—stream (4) ... VA-3
**Mountain Breeze Subdivision**—pop pl ... UT-8
*Mountain Brook* ... CT-1
*Mountain Brook* ... NH-1
*Mountain Brook* ... PA-2
*Mountain Brook* ... WI-6
Mountainbrook—locale ... GA-3
**Mountain Brook**—pop pl (2) ... AL-4
**Mountain Brook**—pop pl ... SC-3
Mountain Brook—stream (4) ... CT-1
Mountain Brook—stream (11) ... ME-1
Mountain Brook—stream (4) ... MA-1
Mountain Brook—stream (6) ... NH-1
Mountain Brook—stream ... NJ-2
Mountain Brook—stream (7) ... NY-2
Mountain Brook—stream (4) ... VT-1
Mountain Brook Baptist Ch—church ... AL-4
Mountain Brook Ch—church ... AL-4
Mountain Brook Country Club—other ... AL-4
Mountain Brook Elem Sch—school ... AL-4
Mountain Brook HS—school ... AL-4
Mountain Brook Lake—reservoir ... AL-4
Mountain Brook Pond—lake ... ME-1
Mountain Brook Ranch—locale ... CA-9
Mountain Brook Sch—school ... MT-8
Mountain Brook Sch—school ... WA-9
**Mountain Brook (subdivision)**—pop pl ... NC-3
**Mountainbrook (subdivision)**—pop pl ... NC-3
**Mountain Brook Village**—pop pl ... AL-4
**Mountainburg**—pop pl ... AR-4
Mountain Calvary Ch—church ... PA-2
Mountain Camp—locale ... NY-2
Mountain Canal—canal ... NC-3
Mountain Can Mine—mine ... MT-8
Mountain Canyon Mine—mine ... NM-5
Mountain Catcher Pond—lake ... ME-1
Mountain Cem—cemetery ... CA-9
Mountain Cem—cemetery ... GA-3
Mountain Cem—cemetery ... NJ-2
Mountain Cem—cemetery ... ND-7
Mountain Cem—cemetery ... PA-2
Mountain Cem—cemetery ... WV-2
**Mountain Center**—pop pl ... CA-9
*Mountain Ch* ... AL-4
Mountain Ch—church ... AL-4
Mountain Ch—church (2) ... PA-2
Mountain Ch—church ... SC-3
Mountain Ch—church ... VA-3
Mountain Ch—church ... WV-2
Mountain Chapel—church ... AL-4
Mountain Chapel—church ... KY-4
Mountain Chapel—church (2) ... PA-2
Mountain Chapel—church ... VA-3
Mountain Chapel—church ... WV-2
Mountain Chapel Calvary (historical)—church ... AL-4
*Mountain Chapel Ch* ... AL-4
Mountain Charlie Gulch—valley ... CA-9
**Mountain Chest**—pop pl ... AL-4
Mountain Chief Creek—stream ... CA-9
Mountain Chief Mine—mine ... CA-9
Mountain Chief Mine—mine (2) ... ID-8
Mountain Chief Mine—mine ... MT-8
Mountain Chief Mine—mine ... OR-9
Mountain Chief Tunnel—mine ... CA-9
*Mountain City* ... SD-7
Mountain City—locale ... TX-5
**Mountain City**—pop pl ... GA-3
**Mountain City**—pop pl ... NV-8
**Mountain City**—pop pl ... TN-4
*Mountain City Administrative Site* ... NV-8
Mountain City (CCD)—cens area ... TN-4
Mountain City District Ranger Office—locale ... NV-8
Mountain City Division—civil ... TN-4
Mountain City Elem Sch—school ... TN-4
Mountain City First Baptist Ch—church ... TN-4
Mountain City Post Office—building ... TN-4
Mountain City Ranger District—forest ... NV-8
Mountain City Ranger Station—locale ... NV-8
Mountain City Sch Number 1—school ... ND-7
Mountain City Sch Number 2—school ... ND-7
Mountain City Township—inact MCD ... NV-8
**Mountain Cove**—pop pl ... WV-2
*Mountain Creek* ... AL-4
*Mountain Creek* ... AR-4
*Mountain Creek* ... CA-9
*Mountain Creek* ... GA-3
*Mountain Creek* ... MT-8
*Mountain Creek* ... NC-3
*Mountain Creek* ... PA-2
*Mountain Creek* ... SC-3
**Mountain Creek**—pop pl ... AL-4
Mountain Creek—stream (5) ... AL-4
Mountain Creek—stream (5) ... AK-9
Mountain Creek—stream (2) ... AR-4
Mountain Creek—stream ... CA-9
Mountain Creek—stream ... CO-8
Mountain Creek—stream (10) ... GA-3
Mountain Creek—stream ... KS-7
Mountain Creek—stream ... MI-6
Mountain Creek—stream ... MS-4
Mountain Creek—stream ... MO-7
Mountain Creek—stream (2) ... MT-8
Mountain Creek—stream (11) ... NC-3
Mountain Creek—stream (3) ... OK-5
Mountain Creek—stream (3) ... OR-9
Mountain Creek—stream (2) ... PA-2
Mountain Creek—stream (6) ... SC-3
Mountain Creek—stream (2) ... TN-4
Mountain Creek—stream (7) ... TX-5
Mountain Creek—stream (3) ... VA-3
Mountain Creek—stream ... WV-2
Mountain Creek—stream (2) ... WY-8
Mountain Creek—uninc pl ... TX-5
*Mountain Creek Baptist Church* ... TN-4
Mountain Creek Cem—cemetery ... MS-4
Mountain Creek Cem—cemetery ... NC-3
Mountain Creek Cem—cemetery ... TX-5
Mountain Creek Ch—church ... AL-4
Mountain Creek Ch—church (3) ... GA-3
Mountain Creek Ch—church (3) ... NC-3
Mountain Creek Ch—church (3) ... SC-3
Mountain Creek Ch—church ... TN-4
Mountain Creek Ch (abandoned)—church ... MO-7
Mountain Creek Ch of Christ—church ... TN-4
*Mountain Creek Elementary School* ... TN-4
**Mountain Creek (historical)**—pop pl ... MS-4
*Mountain Creek Lake* ... AL-4
Mountain Creek Lake—reservoir ... NC-3
Mountain Creek Lake—reservoir ... TX-5
Mountain Creek Lake Dam—dam ... NC-3
Mountain Creek Post Office (historical)—building ... TN-4
Mountain Creek Power Plant—other ... TX-5
*Mountain Creek Primitive Baptist Church* ... TN-4
Mountain Creek Rsvr—reservoir ... TX-5
Mountain Creek Sch—school (2) ... NC-3
Mountain Creek Sch—school ... TN-4
Mountain Creek Sch (historical)—school ... MO-7
Mountain Creek (Township of)—fmr MCD ... NC-3
Mountain Creek Trail—trail ... WY-8
Mountain Crest—locale ... AR-4
Mountain Crest HS—school ... UT-8
**Mountain Crest Subdivision**—pop pl ... UT-8
Mountain Cube—summit ... NH-1
*Mountaindale* ... NY-2
**Mountaindale**—pop pl ... AL-4
**Mountaindale**—pop pl ... MD-2
**Mountaindale**—pop pl ... NY-2
**Mountain Dale**—pop pl ... NY-2
**Mountaindale**—pop pl ... OR-9
**Mountaindale**—pop pl ... PA-2
**Mountain Dale**—pop pl ... TN-4
**Mountaindale**—pop pl ... WV-2
Mountaindale Airstrip—airport ... OR-9
Mountain Dale Cem—cemetery ... MO-7
Mountaindale Ch—church ... OR-9
Mountaindale Ch—church ... WV-2
Mountain Dale Ch—church ... WV-2
*Mountaindale Pond* ... RI-1
Mountaindale Reservoir Dam—dam ... RI-1
Mountaindale Rsvr—reservoir ... RI-1
Mountaindale Sch—school ... OR-9
Mountaindale Sch—school ... TN-4
Mountain Dale Sch (abandoned)—school ... MO-7
Mountain Dale Sch (historical)—school ... PA-2
Mountaindale Station—locale ... MD-2
**Mountain Dale (subdivision)**—pop pl ... PA-2
Mountain Dell—basin ... UT-8
Mountain Dell—locale ... UT-8
Mountain Dell Canyon—valley ... UT-8
Mountain Dell Dam—dam ... UT-8
Mountain Dell Dam—hist pl ... UT-8
Mountain Dell Golf Course—other ... UT-8
Mountain Dell Mine—mine ... UT-8
**Mountain Dell Park Subdivision**—pop pl ... UT-8
Mountain Dell Rsvr—reservoir ... UT-8
Mountain Dimmick Pond—lake ... ME-1
Mountain District—hist pl ... NJ-2
*Mountain Eagle* ... PA-2
Mountain Eastman Trail—trail ... NH-1
Mountaineer Bend (historical)—bend ... ND-7
Mountaineer Ch—church ... WV-2
Mountaineer Creek—stream (2) ... CA-9
Mountaineer Creek—stream ... CO-8
Mountaineer Creek—stream ... WA-9
Mountaineer Glacier—glacier ... MT-8
Mountaineer Lake—lake ... MT-8
Mountaineer Mine—mine ... CA-9
Mountaineer Peak—summit ... MT-8
Mountaineers Pass—gap ... AK-9
Mountaineer Speedway—other ... WV-2
Mountain Empire (CCD)—cens area ... CA-9
Mountain Empire Union HS—school ... CA-9
Mountain End Lake—reservoir ... GA-3
**Mountain Estates Subdivision**—pop pl (2) ... UT-8
Mountain Falls—falls ... VA-3
Mountain Falls—locale ... VA-3
Mountain Farms Mall—locale ... MA-1
Mountain Flower Sch—school ... WV-2
Mountain Fork—locale ... AR-4
Mountain Fork—stream ... AL-4
Mountain Fork—stream (2) ... AR-4
Mountain Fork—stream (3) ... OK-5
Mountain Fork—stream ... TN-4
Mountain Fork—stream ... WV-2
Mountain Fork Ch—church (2) ... AL-4
Mountain Fork Ch—church ... OK-5
*Mountain Fork Little River* ... AR-4
*Mountain Fork Little River* ... OK-5
*Mountain Fork of Little River* ... AR-4
*Mountain Fork Of Little River* ... OK-5
*Mountain Fork of the Brazos River* ... TX-5
*Mountain Fork River* ... AR-4
*Mountain Fork River* ... OK-5
Mountain Fork Sch—school ... AL-4
Mountain Friendship Ch—church ... TN-4
*Mountain Gap* ... AR-4
Mountain Gap—locale ... AL-4
Mountain Gap—locale ... VA-3
Mountain Gap Ch—church ... GA-3
*Mountain Gap Elementary School* ... AL-4
**Mountain Gap Estates (subdivision)**—pop pl ... AL-4
Mountain Gap Sch—school ... AL-4
**Mountain Gate**—pop pl ... CA-9
Mountain Gate Cem—cemetery ... WV-2
Mountain Gate Mobile Home Park—locale ... AZ-5
Mountain Gate Tunnel—mine ... CA-9
Mountain Gilead Bethel Ch—church ... CO-8
**Mountain Glen**—pop pl ... IL-6
Mountain Glen—valley ... PA-2
Mountain Grange—locale ... PA-2
**Mountain Green**—pop pl ... PA-2
**Mountain Green**—pop pl ... UT-8
Mountain Green Cem—cemetery ... UT-8
Mountain Grove—hist pl ... VA-3
Mountain Grove—locale ... NC-3
Mountain Grove—locale ... VA-3
**Mountain Grove**—pop pl ... AL-4
**Mountain Grove**—pop pl ... AR-4
**Mountain Grove**—pop pl ... MO-7
**Mountain Grove**—pop pl ... PA-2
Mountain Grove—stream ... IN-6
*Mountain Grove Baptist Church* ... AL-4
Mountain Grove Branch—stream ... AL-4
Mountain Grove Cem—cemetery ... AL-4
Mountain Grove Cem—cemetery ... GA-3
Mountain Grove Cem—cemetery ... IN-6
Mountain Grove Cem—cemetery ... MO-7
Mountain Grove Cem—cemetery ... OK-5
Mountain Grove Ch—church (4) ... AL-4
Mountain Grove Ch—church (3) ... AR-4
Mountain Grove Ch—church (2) ... GA-3
Mountain Grove Ch—church (2) ... MO-7
Mountain Grove Ch—church (7) ... NC-3
Mountain Grove Ch—church ... OK-5
Mountain Grove Ch—church ... SC-3
Mountain Grove Ch—church (2) ... VA-3
Mountain Grove Chapel—church ... VA-3
Mountain Grove Memorial Airp—airport ... MO-7
Mountain Grove Sch—school ... AL-4
Mountain Grove Sch—school ... WV-2
Mountain Grove Sch (abandoned)—school ... MO-7
Mountain Grove Sch (abandoned)—school ... PA-2
Mountain Grove Sch (historical)—school ... TN-4
Mountain Grove Township—civil ... MO-7
Mountain Gulch—valley ... ID-8
Mountain Hall Sch—school ... AR-4
*Mountain Head* ... ME-1
Mountain Head—cape ... AK-9
Mountain Head—summit ... ME-1
Mountain Head Ch—church ... SD-7
**Mountain Heights (subdivision)**—pop pl ... AL-4
Mountain Heritage HS—school ... NC-3
Mountain High Chapel—church ... CO-8
Mountain Hill—locale ... GA-3
**Mountain Hill**—pop pl ... VA-3
Mountain Hill—summit ... LA-4
Mountain Hill—summit ... MD-2
Mountain Hill—summit ... MA-1
Mountain Hill—summit ... TN-4
Mountain Hill—summit ... VA-3
Mountain Hill Bogs—swamp ... MA-1
Mountain Hill Branch—stream ... GA-3
Mountain Hill Ch—church ... AL-4
Mountain Hill Ch—church ... SC-3
Mountain Hill Sch—school ... GA-3
**Mountain (historical)**—pop pl ... MS-4
**Mountain (historical)**—pop pl ... TN-4
Mountain Hole—bay ... AR-4
Mountain Hollow—valley ... VA-3
Mountain Home—hist pl ... WV-2
Mountain Home—locale ... CA-9
Mountain Home—locale ... NY-2
Mountain Home—locale (3) ... OR-9
Mountain Home—locale ... TX-5
Mountain Home—locale ... UT-8
Mountain Home—locale ... WA-9
Mountain Home—locale ... WV-2
**Mountain Home**—pop pl ... AL-4
**Mountain Home**—pop pl (2) ... AR-4
**Mountain Home**—pop pl ... ID-8
**Mountain Home**—pop pl ... NC-3
**Mountainhome**—pop pl ... PA-2
**Mountain Home**—pop pl ... TN-4
**Mountain Home**—pop pl ... WY-8
Mountain Home—summit ... UT-8
Mountain Home AFB—military ... ID-8
Mountain Home Air Force Base—other ... ID-8
Mountain Home Air Force Base Gunnery Range—other ... ID-8
Mountain Home Baptist Church—hist pl ... ID-8
*Mountain Home Baptist Mission* ... AL-4
Mountain Home Base—obs name ... ID-8
Mountain Home Camp—locale ... WA-9
Mountain Home Canyon—valley ... ID-8
Mountain Home Carnegie Library—hist pl ... ID-8
Mountain Home Cem—cemetery (2) ... AL-4
Mountain Home Cem—cemetery ... AR-4
Mountain Home Cem—cemetery (2) ... MI-6
Mountain Home Cem—cemetery (3) ... OK-5
Mountain Home Cem—cemetery (2) ... TN-4
Mountain Home Cem—cemetery ... TX-5
Mountain Home Ch—church (6) ... AL-4
Mountain Home Ch—church (2) ... AR-4
Mountain Home Ch—church ... MO-7
Mountain Home Ch—church ... NC-3
Mountain Home Ch—church ... TN-4
Mountain Home Ch—church (2) ... WV-2
Mountain Home Ch of Christ—church ... AL-4
Mountain Home Creek—stream ... CA-9
Mountain Home Draw—valley ... UT-8
Mountain Home Grange—locale ... ID-8
Mountain Home Grove—woods ... CA-9
**Mountain Home (historical)**—pop pl ... NC-3
Mountain Home Hotel—hist pl ... ID-8
Mountain Home Mine—mine ... NM-5
Mountain Home Missionary Ch—church ... TX-5
*Mountain Home Number 1 Ch* ... AL-4
**Mountain Home Park**—pop pl ... WA-9
Mountain Home Pass—gap ... UT-8
Mountain Home Peak—summit ... CA-9
Mountain Home Post Office—building ... TN-4
Mountain Home Post Office (historical)—building ... AL-4
Mountain Home Ranch—locale ... WY-8
*Mountain Home Range* ... UT-8
Mountain Home Range—range ... UT-8
Mountain Home (RR name for Mountainhome)—other ... PA-2
**Mountainhome (RR name Mountain Home)**—pop pl ... PA-2
Mountain Home Rsvr—reservoir ... CO-8
Mountain Home Rsvr—reservoir ... ID-8
*Mountain Home Sch* ... MO-7
Mountain Home Sch—school ... ID-8
Mountain Home Sch—school ... MO-7
Mountainhome Sch—school ... PA-2
Mountain Home Sch (historical)—school ... AL-4
Mountain Home School—locale ... AR-4
Mountain Home School (historical)—locale ... MO-7
Mountain Home Spring—spring (2) ... CA-9
Mountain Home Spring—spring (2) ... UT-8
Mountain Home Spring—spring ... WY-8
Mountain Home Spring Branch—stream ... AL-4
Mountain Home State Forest—locale ... CA-9
Mountain Home (Township of)—fmr MCD ... AR-4
Mountain Home (Veterans Administration Center)—hospital ... TN-4
**Mountain Home Village**—pop pl ... CA-9
Mountain Home Wash—hist pl ... UT-8
Mountain House—hist pl ... OH-6
Mountain House—locale (3) ... CA-9
Mountain House—locale ... ID-8
Mountain House—locale ... NY-2
**Mountain House**—pop pl ... CA-9
**Mountain House**—pop pl ... NY-2
Mountain House—summit ... MT-8
*Mountain House Creek* ... CA-9
Mountain House Creek—stream (3) ... CA-9
Mountain House Draw—valley ... MT-8
Mountain House (historical)—locale ... NV-8
**Mountain House (historical)**—pop pl ... OR-9
Mountain House Historic Site—locale ... MT-8
Mountain House Sch—school ... CA-9
Mountain House (Site)—locale ... HI-9
Mountain House Spring—spring ... MT-8
Mountain House Trail—trail ... HI-9
**Mountain Iron**—pop pl ... MN-6
Mountain Iron Mine—hist pl ... MN-6
Mountain Iron Mine—mine ... MN-6
Mountain Island—island ... KY-4
Mountain Island—island (2) ... NC-3
Mountain Island—island ... SC-3
**Mountain Island**—pop pl ... NC-3
Mountain Island Branch—stream ... NC-3
*Mountain Island Dam* ... NC-3
Mountain Island Lake—reservoir ... NC-3
Mountain Island Reservoir Dam—dam ... NC-3
*Mountain Island Rsvr* ... NC-3
Mountain Island Rsvr—reservoir ... NC-3
Mountain King Mine—mine ... AZ-5
Mountain King Mine—mine ... CA-9
Mountain King Mine—mine ... CO-8
Mountain King Mine—mine ... ID-8
Mountain King Mine—mine ... OR-9
Mountain King Mine (Abandoned)—mine ... CA-9
*Mountain Lake* ... CA-9
*Mountain Lake* ... CT-1
*Mountain Lake* ... NV-8
*Mountain Lake* ... PA-2
*Mountain Lake* ... SC-3
*Mountain Lake* ... UT-8
Mountain Lake—lake ... AK-9
Mountain Lake—lake (2) ... CA-9
Mountain Lake—lake ... CO-8
Mountain Lake—lake (2) ... FL-3
Mountain Lake—lake (3) ... MI-6
Mountain Lake—lake (2) ... MN-6
Mountain Lake—lake ... NJ-2
Mountain Lake—lake (4) ... NY-2
Mountain Lake—lake ... VA-3
Mountain Lake—lake ... WA-9
Mountain Lake—lake (3) ... WI-6
Mountain Lake—locale ... PA-2
Mountain Lake—locale ... VA-3
**Mountain Lake**—pop pl ... FL-3
**Mountain Lake**—pop pl ... MN-6
**Mountain Lake**—pop pl ... NJ-2
Mountain Lake—reservoir (2) ... AL-4
Mountain Lake—reservoir ... CO-8
Mountain Lake—reservoir (2) ... GA-3
Mountain Lake—reservoir ... MD-2
Mountain Lake—reservoir ... MA-1
Mountain Lake—reservoir ... MN-6
Mountain Lake—reservoir ... MO-7
Mountain Lake—reservoir (2) ... NH-1
Mountain Lake—reservoir (2) ... NJ-2
Mountain Lake—reservoir (2) ... NY-2
Mountain Lake—reservoir ... OK-5
Mountain Lake—reservoir (4) ... PA-2
Mountain Lake—reservoir (2) ... SC-3
Mountain Lake Brook—stream ... NJ-2
Mountain Lake Camp—locale ... OH-6
Mountain Lake Camp—locale ... PA-2
**Mountain Lake Camp**—pop pl ... NC-3
Mountain Lake Ch—church ... PA-2
**Mountain Lake Colony**—pop pl ... SC-3
*Mountain Lake Dam* ... PA-2
Mountain Lake Dam—dam ... AL-4
Mountain Lake Dam—dam ... MA-1
Mountain Lake Dam—dam (2) ... NJ-2
Mountain Lake Dam—dam (2) ... PA-2
**Mountain Lake Estates (subdivision)**—pop pl ... AL-4
*Mountain Lake-Lower Lake* ... PA-2
Mountain Lake Park—park ... CA-9
**Mountain Lake Park**—pop pl ... MD-2
Mountain Lake Park Hist Dist—hist pl ... MD-2
*Mountain Lake Reservoir* ... PA-2
Mountain Lake Resort Dam—dam ... AL-4
Mountain Lake Run—stream ... PA-2
Mountain Lakes—lake ... NY-2
Mountain Lakes—lake ... WI-6
**Mountain Lakes**—pop pl ... NJ-2
Mountain Lakes—reservoir ... SC-3
Mountain Lake Site—hist pl ... MN-6
Mountain Lake State Wildlife Mngmt Area—park ... MN-6
**Mountain Lake Station**—pop pl ... FL-3
Mountain Lakes Trail—trail ... OR-9
Mountain Lake (Township of)—civ div ... MN-6
**Mountain Lake View**—pop pl ... MD-2
Mountain Lake Wilderness Area—reserve ... OR-9
Mountain Lick Creek—stream ... PA-2
Mountain Lick Creek—stream ... WV-2
Mountain Lick Run—stream ... WV-2
Mountain Lily Mine—mine ... CA-9
Mountain Lion Canyon—valley (2) ... AZ-5
Mountain Lion Canyon—valley ... NV-8
Mountain Lion Canyon—valley ... NM-5
Mountain Lion Creek—stream ... CO-8
*Mountain Lion Mine* ... SD-7
Mountain Lion Mine—mine ... NV-8
Mountain Lion Mine—mine ... OR-9
Mountain Lion Spring—spring ... AZ-5
Mountain Lion Spring—spring ... CO-8
Mountain Lion Spring—spring (2) ... NV-8
Mountain Lion Spring—spring ... UT-8
Mountain Lion Spring Ridge—ridge ... UT-8
**Mountain Lodge**—pop pl (2) ... NY-2
Mountain Lookout Tower—locale ... WI-6
**Mountain Manor (subdivision)**—pop pl ... NC-3
Mountain Marys Grave—cemetery ... PA-2
*Mountain Meadow* ... AL-4
Mountain Meadow—flat (2) ... CA-9
Mountain Meadow—flat (2) ... ID-8
Mountain Meadow—flat ... MT-8
Mountain Meadow—flat ... UT-8
Mountain Meadow—locale ... AZ-5
Mountain Meadow Cem—cemetery ... SD-7
Mountain Meadow Creek—stream (2) ... ID-8
Mountain Meadow Farm—hist pl ... PA-2
Mountain Meadow (Historical Monument)—park ... UT-8
Mountain Meadow Lake—lake ... CA-9
*Mountain Meadow Massacre Historical Monument* ... UT-8
*Mountain Meadow Massacre Monument* ... UT-8
Mountain Meadow Mine—mine ... MT-8
Mountain Meadow Ranch—locale ... WY-8
*Mountain Meadows* ... UT-8
Mountain Meadows—flat (2) ... CA-9
Mountain Meadows—flat ... ID-8
Mountain Meadows—flat ... OR-9
Mountain Meadows—flat ... UT-8
Mountain Meadows—flat (2) ... WA-9
**Mountain Meadows**—pop pl ... TN-4
**Mountain Meadows Condominiums**—pop pl ... UT-8
Mountain Meadows Creek—stream ... CA-9
**Mountain Meadows Estates Subdivision Plat One**—pop pl ... UT-8
Mountain Meadows (historical)—locale ... SD-7
Mountain Meadows Historic Site—hist pl ... UT-8
Mountain Meadows I (historical)—locale ... SD-7
Mountain Meadows Lake—lake ... WA-9
Mountain Meadows Memorial Gardens—cemetery ... AZ-5
Mountain Meadows Rsvr—reservoir ... CA-9
Mountain Meadows Trail—trail ... OR-9
Mountain Meadow Trail—trail ... MT-8
**Mountain Men Estates (subdivision)**—pop pl ... UT-8
**Mountain Mesa**—pop pl ... CA-9
*Mountain Mills* ... PA-2
Mountain Mills Cem—cemetery ... AL-4
Mountain Mills (historical)—locale ... AL-4
Mountain Mills Lookout Tower—locale ... AL-4
Mountain Mills Methodist Episcopal Ch (historical)—church ... AL-4
*Mountain Mills P.O.* ... AL-4
Mountain Mills Ridge—ridge ... AL-4
Mountain Mine—mine (2) ... CA-9
Mountain Mine—mine ... MT-8
*Mountain Mirror* ... MA-1
Mountain Mission—church ... VA-3
**Mountain Mission**—pop pl ... WV-2
Mountain Mission Sch—school ... VA-3
Mountain Mud Pond—lake ... PA-2
*Mountain New Hope Church* ... AL-4
Mountain Oak Cem—cemetery ... MO-7
Mountain Oak Ch (historical)—church ... TN-4
Mountain Oak Creek—stream ... GA-3
Mountain Oak Sch—school ... TN-4
Mountain Oak Sch (abandoned)—school ... MO-7
**Mountain Oaks Estates Subdivision 1and2**—pop pl ... UT-8
Mountain Oak Spring—spring ... CA-9
*Mountain-of-the-Sun* ... UT-8
**Mountain Orchard Estates (subdivision)**—pop pl ... UT-8
Mountain Orchards Sch (abandoned)—school ... PA-2
Mountain Orphanage—school ... NC-3
**Mountain Page**—pop pl ... NC-3
*Mountain Palm Spring* ... CA-9
Mountain Palm Springs Area—area ... CA-9
Mountain Park—CDP ... FL-3
Mountain Park—CDP ... GA-3
Mountain Park—park ... CA-9
Mountain Park—park ... PA-2

**Mountain Park**—*pop pl* AL-4
**Mountain Park**—*pop pl* CO-8
**Mountain Park**—*pop pl* GA-3
**Mountain Park**—*pop pl* MA-1
**Mountain Park**—*pop pl* NM-5
**Mountain Park**—*pop pl* NC-3
**Mountain Park**—*pop pl* OK-5
Mountain Park—*post sta* GA-3
Mountain Park Cem—*cemetery* NC-3
Mountain Park Cem—*cemetery* OK-5
Mountain Park (Cemetery)—*cemetery* TX-5
Mountain Park Elem Sch—*school* NC-3
Mountain Park Golf Course—*other* CO-8
Mountain Park Picnic Area—*locale* VA-3
Mountain Park Rsvr—*reservoir* MA-1
**Mountain Park Subdivision (Plat A-F)**—*pop pl* UT-8
**Mountain Park Subdivision (Plat WB)**—*pop pl* UT-8
Mountain Pass—*gap* TX-5
**Mountain Pass**—*pop pl* CA-9
Mountain Pass Ch—*church* VA-3
Mountain Pass Creek—*stream* CA-9
Mountain Pasture Windmill—*locale* TX-5
Mountain Path—*trail* VA-3
Mountain Peak—*locale* TX-5
**Mountain Pine**—*pop pl* AR-4
Mountain Plains Ch—*church* VA-3
Mountain Plaza (Shop Ctr)—*locale* FL-3
Mountain Pocket Creek—*stream* MT-8
Mountain Point—*cape* (5) AK-9
Mountain Point—*cape* MD-2
**Mountain Point**—*pop pl* AK-9
*Mountain Pond* ME-1
*Mountain Pond* NH-1
Mountain Pond—*lake* (7) ME-1
Mountain Pond—*lake* (4) NH-1
Mountain Pond—*lake* NJ-2
Mountain Pond—*lake* (9) NY-2
Mountain Pond—*lake* PA-2
Mountain Pond—*reservoir* CT-1
Mountain Ponds—*lake* ME-1
Mountain Ponds—*lake* NY-2
Mountain Pond Stream—*stream* ME-1
Mountain Pond Stream—*stream* NY-2
Mountain Post Office (historical)—*building* MS-4
Mountain Prairie Ch—*church* IL-6
Mountain Quail Mine—*mine* CO-8
Mountain Queen Mine—*mine* CO-8
Mountain Queen Mine—*mine* MT-8
Mountain Ranch—*locale* CA-9
Mountain Ranch—*locale* OR-9
**Mountain Ranch**—*pop pl* CA-9
Mountain Ranch, The—*locale* AZ-5
Mountain Ranch Spring Number Two—*spring* SD-7
Mountain Ranch Trail Number Ten—*trail* AZ-5
*Mountain Range* UT-8
Mountain Rest—*cemetery* NC-3
Mountain Rest—*hist pl* MA-1
Mountain Rest—*locale* SC-3
Mountain Rest (CCD)—*cens area* SC-3
Mountain Rest Ch—*church* SC-3
Mountain Rest Guard Station—*locale* CA-9
Mountain Rest Lake—*reservoir* SC-3
Mountain Rest Sch—*school* SC-3
Mountain Rest Sch (historical)—*school* TN-4
**Mountain Ridge**—*pop pl* MO-7
Mountain Ridge—*ridge* TN-4
Mountain Ridge Cem—*cemetery* MS-4
Mountain Ridge Ch—*church* MS-4
Mountain Ridge Ch—*church* NC-3
Mountain Ridge Country Club—*other* NJ-2
Mountain Ridge Lake—*reservoir* NJ-2
Mountain Ridge RV Park—*park* UT-8
**Mountain Ridge (subdivision)**—*pop pl* TN-4
Mountain Road Ch—*church* (2) NC-3
Mountain Road Ch—*church* OH-6
**Mountain Road Estates (subdivision)**—*pop pl* UT-8
Mountain Road Hist Dist—*hist pl* VA-3
Mountain Rsvr—*reservoir* WY-8
*Mountain Run* PA-2
*Mountain Run* VA-3
Mountain Run—*stream* (2) NC-3
Mountain Run—*stream* (4) PA-2
Mountain Run—*stream* (7) VA-3
Mountain Run—*stream* (4) WV-2
Mountain Run Lake—*reservoir* VA-3
Mountain Sanitarium—*hospital* NC-3
Mountain Scene—*locale* GA-3
Mountain Sch—*school* (2) CA-9
Mountain Sch—*school* NC-3
Mountain Sch—*school* (3) PA-2
Mountain Sch—*school* SD-7
Mountain Sch—*school* VA-3
Mountain Sch (abandoned)—*school* (3) PA-2
Mountain Sch (historical)—*school* AL-4
Mountain Sch (historical)—*school* (3) PA-2
Mountain School (Abandoned)—*locale* CA-9
Mountains Community Hosp—*hospital* CA-9
Mountains Dam, The—*dam* NC-3
Mountain Sedgwick—*summit* NM-5
Mountain Shadow Lake—*reservoir* PA-2
Mountain Shadow Lake Dam—*dam* PA-2
Mountain Shadows Mobile Homes Park—*locale* AZ-5
Mountain Shadows Ranch—*locale* CA-9
Mountain Shadows Shop Ctr—*locale* UT-8
**Mountain Shadows Subdivision**—*pop pl* UT-8
Mountain Shaw—*summit* NH-1
Mountain Shaw Trail—*trail* NH-1
Mountain Sheep Canyon—*valley* (4) UT-8
Mountain Sheep Creek—*stream* OR-9
Mountain Sheep Dam—*dam* OR-9
Mountain Sheep Lake—*lake* WY-8
Mountain Sheep Mine—*mine* WA-9
Mountain Sheep Pass—*gap* UT-8
Mountain Sheep Point—*cape* CO-8
Mountain Sheep Rapids—*rapids* ID-8
Mountain Sheep Rapids—*rapids* OR-9
Mountain Sheep Spring—*spring* (2) AZ-5
Mountain Sheep Spring—*spring* NM-5
Mountain Sheep Wash—*valley* AZ-5
Mountain Shoals Plantation—*hist pl* SC-3
**Mountainside**—*pop pl* NJ-2
Mountainside Branch—*stream* NC-3
Mountainside Cem—*cemetery* OR-9
Mountainside Hosp—*hospital* NJ-2
Mountainside Mine—*mine* MT-8
Mountainside Park—*park* NJ-2
Mountain Side Sch—*school* MO-7
Mountainside Sch—*school* NJ-2
Mountainside Sch—*school* WI-6
Mountainside Spring—*spring* AZ-5
**Mountainside Subdivision**—*pop pl* UT-8
Mountain Side Tabernacle—*church* WV-2
Mountainside Theater—*locale* NC-3
Mountain Side Trail—*trail* VA-3
Mountain Side Trail—*trail* WV-2
Mountain Sink—*lake* FL-3
Mountains Lake, The—*reservoir* NC-3
Mountain Slough—*stream* AK-9
**Mountains Meadows Subdivision**—*pop pl* UT-8
*Mountains of Socorro* NM-5
**Mountain Spa**—*pop pl* UT-8
**Mountain Spring**—*pop pl* CA-9
Mountain Spring—*spring* AL-4
Mountain Spring—*spring* (7) AZ-5
Mountain Spring—*spring* (3) CA-9
Mountain Spring—*spring* (2) ID-8
Mountain Spring—*spring* (2) MT-8
Mountain Spring—*spring* (2) NV-8
Mountain Spring—*spring* (2) OR-9
Mountain Spring—*spring* (3) UT-8
Mountain Spring Camp—*locale* CA-9
*Mountain Spring Canyon* AZ-5
Mountain Spring Canyon—*valley* ID-8
Mountain Spring Cem—*cemetery* AR-4
Mountain Spring Cem—*cemetery* IN-6
*Mountain Spring Ch* AL-4
Mountain Spring Ch—*church* (3) AL-4
Mountain Spring Ch—*church* GA-3
Mountain Spring Ch—*church* (2) SC-3
*Mountain Spring Creek* CA-9
Mountain Spring Creek—*stream* CA-9
Mountain Spring Creek—*stream* CO-8
Mountain Spring Fork—*stream* UT-8
Mountain Spring Gap—*gap* KY-4
Mountain Spring (historical P.O.)—*locale* IN-6
Mountain Spring House—*locale* CA-9
Mountain Spring House Ridge—*ridge* CA-9
Mountain Spring Lake—*lake* NY-2
Mountain Spring Lake—*reservoir* PA-2
**Mountain Spring Lakes**—*pop pl* NJ-2
Mountain Spring Mine—*mine* CO-8
Mountain Spring Peak—*summit* UT-8
Mountain Spring Rsvr—*reservoir* UT-8
Mountain Spring Rsvr—*reservoir* WA-9
*Mountain Springs* AL-4
Mountain Springs—*locale* GA-3
Mountain Springs—*locale* PA-2
**Mountain Springs**—*pop pl* AR-4
**Mountain Springs**—*pop pl* NV-8
**Mountain Springs**—*pop pl* TX-5
Mountain Springs—*spring* AZ-5
Mountain Springs—*spring* NV-8
Mountain Springs—*spring* UT-8
Mountain Springs Airp—*airport* PA-2
*Mountain Springs Baptist Ch* AL-4
*Mountain Springs Baptist Church* TN-4
Mountain Springs Branch—*stream* NC-3
Mountain Springs Canyon—*valley* CA-9
Mountain Springs Cave—*cave* AL-4
Mountain Springs Cem—*cemetery* (2) AL-4
Mountain Springs Cem—*cemetery* AR-4
Mountain Springs Cemeteries—*cemetery* AL-4
Mountain Springs Ch—*church* (4) AL-4
Mountain Springs Ch—*church* (2) AR-4
Mountain Springs Ch—*church* (3) GA-3
Mountain Springs Ch—*church* (2) NC-3
Mountain Springs Ch—*church* SC-3
Mountain Springs Ch—*church* TN-4
Mountain Spring Sch—*school* AR-4
Mountain Spring Sch—*school* KY-4
Mountain Spring Sch (historical)—*school* AL-4
Mountain Springs Creek—*stream* CA-9
Mountain Springs Dam—*dam* PA-2
**Mountain Springs Estates (subdivision)**—*pop pl* AL-4
Mountain Springs Hotel—*hist pl* PA-2
Mountain Springs Lake—*lake* NJ-2
*Mountain Springs Lakes* NJ-2
Mountain Springs Mine—*mine* NV-8
Mountain Springs Ranch—*locale* WY-8
Mountain Springs Ranch Dam—*dam* OR-9
Mountain Springs Ranch Rsvr—*reservoir* OR-9
Mountain Springs Sch—*school* AR-4
Mountain Springs Sch—*school* SC-3
*Mountain Springs School* AL-4
Mountain Springs Summit—*summit* NV-8
Mountain Spring Wash—*stream* AZ-5
Mountain Spring Wash—*valley* UT-8
Mountain Spur—*locale* TN-4
**Mountain Star**—*pop pl* AL-4
Mountain State Christian Sch—*school* WV-2
Mountain State Coll—*school* WV-2
Mountain State HS—*school* WV-2
Mountain State Memorial Gardens—*cemetery* WV-2
Mountain States Childrens Home—*other* CO-8
Mountain States Telephone and Telegraph Company—*hist pl* MT-8
Mountain States Telephone and Telegraph Company Tower—*tower* AZ-5
Mountain Station—*hist pl* NJ-2
Mountain Station—*locale* NJ-2
Mountain Station Cem—*cemetery* OK-5
*Mountain Stream* CT-1
Mountain Stream—*stream* IN-6
Mountain Stream—*stream* MI-6
Mountain Street Rsvr—*reservoir* MA-1
Mountain Street Sch—*school* VT-1
*Mountainsville* PA-2
Mountain Swamp—*swamp* NY-2
Mountain Talc Mine—*mine* MT-8
Mountain Tank—*reservoir* AZ-5
Mountain Tank—*reservoir* (4) NM-5
Mountain Tank—*reservoir* TX-5
Mountain Tanks—*reservoir* NM-5
Mountain Tea Branch—*stream* NC-3
Mountain Tea Ridge—*ridge* IN-6
**Mountain Terrace Estates Subdivision**—*pop pl* UT-8
**Mountain Terrace Subdivision Number 1-4**—*pop pl* UT-8
Mountain Theater—*other* CA-9
*Mountaintop* PA-2
*Mountain Top* WV-2
Mountain Top—*locale* KY-4
Mountain Top—*locale* PA-2
Mountain Top—*locale* WA-9
**Mountain Top**—*pop pl* AR-4
**Mountain Top**—*pop pl* PA-2
Mountain Top—*summit* CA-9
Mountain Top Airp—*airport* PA-2
Mountain Top Ch—*church* AR-4
Mountain Top Ch—*church* TX-5
Mountain Top Ch—*church* VA-3
Mountain Top Chapel—*church* KY-4
Mountain Top Club—*locale* VT-1
**Mountain Top Estates**—*pop pl* PA-2
Mountain Top Gem Mine—*mine* NC-3
Mountain Top Junction—*locale* CA-9
Mountain Top Lake—*lake* VA-3
Mountain Top Mine—*mine* CO-8
Mountain Top Mine—*mine* NV-8
**Mountain Top Park Subdivision**—*pop pl* UT-8
Mountain Top Sch—*school* OR-9
Mountaintop Sch—*school* VA-3
Mountain Top Slope Mine (underground)—*mine* AL-4
Mountaintop Tank—*reservoir* AZ-5
Mountain Top Trail—*trail* VA-3
**Mountaintown**—*pop pl* GA-3
Mountaintown Ch—*church* GA-3
*Mountaintown Creek* GA-3
Mountaintown Creek—*stream* GA-3
Mountain Township—*civil* (2) MO-7
Mountain Township (historical)—*civil* SD-7
Mountain (Township of)—*fmr MCD* (11) AR-4
Mountain (Township of)—*fmr MCD* NC-3
**Mountain (Township of)**—*pop pl* IL-6
**Mountain Trace**—*pop pl* TN-4
*Mountain Trail* PA-2
Mountain Trail—*trail* VA-3
Mountain Trail Memorial Cem—*cemetery* WV-2
Mountain Trails Campground—*locale* VT-1
Mountain Tree Farm Center—*locale* WA-9
Mountain Tree Historic Site—*locale* ID-8
Mountain Tunnel—*tunnel* UT-8
Mountain Tunnel Ditch—*canal* UT-8
Mountain Union Cem—*cemetery* MS-4
Mountain Union Ch—*church* MS-4
Mountain Vale Memory Gardens—*cemetery* CO-8
Mountain Vale Ranch—*locale* CA-9
*Mountain Valley* MO-7
*Mountain Valley* TN-4
Mountain Valley—*locale* AR-4
Mountain Valley—*locale* KY-4
Mountain Valley—*locale* NC-3
Mountain Valley—*locale* VA-3
Mountain Valley—*valley* CA-9
Mountain Valley—*valley* NM-5
Mountain Valley Baptist Chapel (SBC)—*church* UT-8
Mountain Valley Cem—*cemetery* AR-4
Mountain Valley Cem—*cemetery* MO-7
Mountain Valley Cem—*cemetery* NM-5
Mountain Valley Cem—*cemetery* NC-3
Mountain Valley Ch—*church* (2) AR-4
Mountain Valley Ch—*church* CO-8
Mountain Valley Ch—*church* MO-7
Mountain Valley Ch—*church* (3) NC-3
Mountain Valley Ch—*church* (2) TN-4
Mountain Valley Ch—*church* (3) VA-3
Mountain Valley Ch—*church* (2) WV-2
Mountain Valley Ch of God—*church* UT-8
Mountain Valley (historical)—*locale* AL-4
Mountain Valley Lake—*reservoir* PA-2
**Mountain Valley Meadows Subdivision**—*pop pl* UT-8
Mountain Valley Mine (underground)—*mine* AL-4
**Mountain Valley Ranchettes (subdivision)**—*pop pl* UT-8
Mountain Valley Sch—*school* MO-7
Mountain Valley Sch—*school* TX-5
Mountain Valley Sch—*school* WA-9
**Mountain Valley Subdivision**—*pop pl* UT-8
*Mountain Valley Wash* UT-8
*Mountain View* ID-8
Mountain View—*hist pl* NC-3
Mountain View—*hist pl* (2) VA-3
Mountain View—*locale* AL-4
Mountain View—*locale* AK-9
Mountain View—*locale* AZ-5
Mountain View—*locale* CO-8
Mountainview—*locale* ME-1
Mountain View—*locale* TX-5
Mountain View—*locale* (3) VA-3
Mountain View—*locale* (2) WA-9
Mountain View—*locale* WV-2
**Mountain View**—*pop pl* AL-4
**Mountain View**—*pop pl* AK-9
**Mountain View**—*pop pl* AR-4
**Mountain View**—*pop pl* (3) CA-9
**Mountain View**—*pop pl* (3) CO-8
**Mountain View**—*pop pl* (2) GA-3
**Mountain View**—*pop pl* HI-9
**Mountain View**—*pop pl* MO-7
**Mountain View**—*pop pl* NJ-2
**Mountain View**—*pop pl* (2) NM-5
**Mountain View**—*pop pl* NY-2
**Mountain View**—*pop pl* (4) NC-3
**Mountain View**—*pop pl* OK-5
**Mountain View**—*pop pl* SC-3
**Mountain View**—*pop pl* (3) TN-4
**Mountain View**—*pop pl* TX-5
**Mountain View**—*pop pl* (3) VA-3
**Mountain View**—*pop pl* WA-9
**Mountain View**—*pop pl* WV-2
**Mountain View**—*pop pl* (2) WY-8
Mountain View—*uninc pl* AZ-5
Mountain View—*uninc pl* TN-4
Mountain View Access Point—*locale* GA-3
Mountain View Acres—*CDP* CA-9
**Mountain View Acres**—*pop pl* CO-8
**Mountain View Acres**—*pop pl* TN-4
Mountain View Acres Cem—*cemetery* NM-5
**Mountain View Acres (subdivision)**—*pop pl* PA-2
**Mountain View Addition (subdivision)**—*pop pl* TN-4
**Mountain View Addition (subdivision)**—*pop pl* UT-8
Mountain View Airp—*airport* MO-7
Mountain View Air Park—*airport* OR-9
Mountain View and Proctor Mine—*mine* CA-9
Mountain View Auto Court—*hist pl* UT-8
*Mountain View Baptist Ch* TN-4
Mountain View Baptist Ch—*church* MS-4
Mountain View Baptist Ch—*church* (2) TN-4
*Mountain View Baptist Church* AL-4
Mountain View Beach—*locale* WA-9
Mountain View Burial Park—*cemetery* VA-3
Mountain View Camp—*locale* AL-4
Mountain View Campground—*locale* CA-9
Mountain View Campground—*locale* (2) ID-8
Mountain View Campground—*park* UT-8
Mountain View Canyon—*valley* NV-8
Mountain View (CCD)—*cens area* OK-5
*Mountain View Cem* NM-5
Mountain View Cem—*cemetery* AL-4
Mountain View Cem—*cemetery* (4) AZ-5
Mountain View Cem—*cemetery* (4) AR-4
Mountain View Cem—*cemetery* (6) CA-9
Mountain View Cem—*cemetery* (5) CO-8
Mountain View Cem—*cemetery* (3) CT-1
Mountain View Cem—*cemetery* (4) ID-8
Mountain View Cem—*cemetery* (2) ME-1
Mountain View Cem—*cemetery* (2) MD-2
Mountainview Cem—*cemetery* MD-2
Mountain View Cem—*cemetery* MD-2
Mountain View Cem—*cemetery* (3) MA-1
Mountain View Cem—*cemetery* MI-6
Mountain View Cem—*cemetery* (2) MO-7
Mountain View Cem—*cemetery* (2) MT-8
Mountainview Cem—*cemetery* MT-8
Mountain View Cem—*cemetery* MT-8
Mountain View Cem—*cemetery* NV-8
Mountain View Cem—*cemetery* NH-1
Mountain View Cem—*cemetery* NJ-2
Mountain View Cem—*cemetery* (4) NM-5
Mountain View Cem—*cemetery* (3) NY-2
Mountain View Cem—*cemetery* ND-7
Mountain View Cem—*cemetery* OK-5
Mountain View Cem—*cemetery* (6) OR-9
Mountain View Cem—*cemetery* (2) PA-2
Mountain View Cem—*cemetery* (2) SC-3
Mountain View Cem—*cemetery* SD-7
Mountain View Cem—*cemetery* (6) TN-4
Mountain View Cem—*cemetery* TX-5
Mountain View Cem—*cemetery* (6) UT-8
Mountain View Cem—*cemetery* (5) VT-1
Mountain View Cem—*cemetery* (5) VA-3
Mountain View Cem—*cemetery* (6) WA-9
Mountain View Cem—*cemetery* (4) WV-2
Mountain View Cem—*cemetery* (2) WY-8
Mountain View Cemetery—*hist pl* MT-8
Mountain View (census name for Mountainview)—*CDP* HI-9
**Mountainview (census name Mountain View)**—*pop pl* HI-9
*Mountainview (Center Ossipee)* NH-1
Mountain View Ch—*church* (16) AL-4
Mountain View Ch—*church* (8) AR-4
Mountain View Ch—*church* (8) GA-3
Mountain View Ch—*church* IN-6
Mountain View Ch—*church* (3) MO-7
Mountain View Ch—*church* (18) NC-3
Mountain View Ch—*church* (6) OK-5
Mountain View Ch—*church* PA-2
Mountain View Ch—*church* (4) SC-3
Mountain View Ch—*church* (18) TN-4
Mountain View Ch—*church* (22) VA-3
Mountain View Ch—*church* (4) WV-2
Mountain View Ch (historical)—*church* AL-4
Mountain View Ch (historical)—*church* (2) TN-4
*Mountain View Christian Church* TN-4
Mountain View Community Hall—*locale* CO-8
Mountain View Community Hall—*locale* WY-8
Mountain View Country Club—*other* CA-9
Mountain View Country Club—*other* OH-6
Mountain View Creek—*stream* ID-8
Mountain View Creek—*stream* MT-8
Mountain View Creek—*stream* NV-8
Mountain View Creek—*stream* OR-9
Mountain View Crest—*ridge* CO-8
Mountain View Dock—*locale* TN-4
**Mountain View East**—*pop pl* NY-2
*Mountainview Elementary School* AL-4
*Mountain View Elementary School* TN-4
*Mountain View Elementary School* UT-8
Mountain View Elem Sch—*school* NC-3
Mountain View Elem Sch—*school* (2) PA-2
**Mountain View Estates**—*pop pl* MD-2
**Mountain View Estates**—*pop pl* TN-4
**Mountain View Estates**—*pop pl* (2) UT-8
**Mountain View Estates Numbers 23,24, 25,26**—*pop pl* UT-8
**Mountain View Estates (subdivision)**—*pop pl* AL-4
**Mountain View Estates (subdivision)**—*pop pl* (2) AZ-5
**Mountain View Estates (subdivision)**—*pop pl* NC-3
**Mountain View Estates (subdivision)**—*pop pl* PA-2
**Mountain View Estates Subdivision**—*pop pl* UT-8
Mountain View Farm—*hist pl* NH-1
Mountain View Golf Course—*locale* NC-3
Mountain View Guard Station—*locale* ID-8
Mountain View Gulch—*valley* MT-8
Mountain View (historical)—*locale* NC-3
Mountain View Hosp—*hospital* OR-9
Mountain View Hosp—*hospital* UT-8
*Mountain View Hospital* AL-4
Mountain View Hospital Heliport—*airport* UT-8
Mountain View Hotel—*hist pl* TN-4
Mountain View HS—*school* AZ-5
Mountain View HS—*school* OR-9
Mountain View HS—*school* UT-8
Mountain View JHS—*school* OR-9
Mountainview Junior Acad—*school* PA-2
Mountain View Lake—*lake* AL-4
Mountain View Lake—*lake* ID-8
Mountain View Lake—*lake* MT-8
Mountainview Lake—*lake* NH-1
Mountain View Lake—*lake* NY-2
Mountain View Lake—*reservoir* (2) AL-4
Mountain View Lake—*reservoir* TN-4
Mountain View Lake—*reservoir* VA-3
*Mountain View Lake Dam* AL-4
**Mountain View Lakes**—*pop pl* CO-8
Mountain View Lakes—*reservoir* CO-8
**Mountain View Meadows**—*pop pl* TN-4
**Mountain View Meadows (subdivision)**—*pop pl* (2) AZ-5
Mountain View Memorial Cem—*cemetery* AL-4
Mountain View Memorial Gardens—*cemetery* OR-9
*Mountain View Memorial Park* UT-8
Mountain View Memorial Park—*cemetery* PA-2
Mountain View Memorial Park—*cemetery* WV-2
Mountain View Memory Gardens—*cemetery* KY-4
Mountain View Memory Gardens—*cemetery* WV-2
*Mountain View Mine* NV-8
Mountain View Mine—*mine* (2) CA-9
Mountain View Mine—*mine* MT-8
Mountain View Mine—*mine* NV-8
Mountain View Mine—*mine* OR-9
Mountain View Mines—*mine* CA-9
Mountainview Mission—*church* NM-5
Mountain View Mobile Home Park—*locale* AZ-5
*Mountain View Oil Field* CA-9
**Mountain View Orchard Heights Subdivision**—*pop pl* UT-8
Mountain View Overpass—*crossing* AZ-5
Mountain View Park—*locale* MT-8
Mountain View Park—*park* (4) AZ-5
Mountain View Park—*park* (3) CA-9
Mountain View Park—*park* WA-9
**Mountainview Park**—*pop pl* ME-1
Mountain View Park Cem—*cemetery* GA-3
**Mountain View Park Condo**—*pop pl* UT-8
Mountain View Peak—*summit* CA-9
Mountain View Peak—*summit* ID-8
*Mountain View Pioneer Hosp* AZ-5
Mountain View Pioneer Hosp—*hospital* AZ-5
Mountain View Pond—*lake* (2) ME-1
Mountain View Recreation Center—*park* NC-3
*Mountain View Reservoir* CA-9
*Mountain View Sch* PA-2
Mountainview Sch—*school* AL-4
Mountain View Sch—*school* AZ-5
Mountain View Sch—*school* AR-4
Mountain View Sch—*school* (8) CA-9
Mountain View Sch—*school* (4) CO-8
Mountain View Sch—*school* GA-3
Mountain View Sch—*school* IA-7
Mountain View Sch—*school* KY-4
Mountain View Sch—*school* (8) MT-8
Mountainview Sch—*school* MT-8
Mountain View Sch—*school* (2) MT-8
Mountain View Sch—*school* NV-8
Mountain View Sch—*school* NM-5
Mountainview Sch—*school* NM-5
Mountain View Sch—*school* NC-3
Mountainview Sch—*school* NC-3
Mountain View Sch—*school* NC-3
Mountain View Sch—*school* (3) OR-9
Mountain View Sch—*school* (4) PA-2
Mountain View Sch—*school* (5) TN-4
Mountain View Sch—*school* (2) UT-8
Mountain View Sch—*school* (5) VA-3
Mountain View Sch—*school* (2) WA-9
Mountain View Sch—*school* (3) WV-2
Mountain View Sch—*school* WI-6
Mountainview Sch—*school* WY-8
Mountain View Sch (abandoned)—*school* PA-2
Mountain View Sch (historical)—*school* (2) AL-4
Mountain View Sch (historical)—*school* PA-2
Mountain View Sch (historical)—*school* (7) TN-4
Mountain View Sch Number 1—*school* ND-7
Mountain View Sch Number 2—*school* ND-7
Mountain View Sch Number 3—*school* ND-7
Mountain View Sch Number 4—*school* ND-7
*Mountain View School* UT-8
Mountain View School (Abandoned)—*locale* MO-7
Mountain View (Site)—*locale* NV-8
Mountain View Slough—*gut* CA-9
Mountain View Spring—*spring* ID-8
Mountain View Spring—*spring* NV-8
**Mountain View (subdivision)**—*pop pl* NC-3
**Mountain View (subdivision)**—*pop pl* PA-2
**Mountain View Subdivision**—*pop pl* UT-8
**Mountain View Subdivision #10, 11, 12, 13**—*pop pl* UT-8
Mountain View Tank—*reservoir* (2) AZ-5
**Mountain View Terrace**—*pop pl* TN-4
Mountain View Trailer Court—*locale* AZ-5
Mountain View Trailer Park—*park* (2) UT-8
Mountain View United Methodist Ch—*church* MT-8
*Mountain View United Methodist Church* TN-4
**Mountain Village**—*pop pl* AK-9
**Mountainville**—*pop pl* ME-1
**Mountainville**—*pop pl* NJ-2
**Mountainville**—*pop pl* NY-2
**Mountainville (historical)**—*pop pl* TN-4
Mountainville Post Office (historical)—*building* TN-4
Mountainville Shop Ctr—*locale* PA-2
**Mountainville (subdivision)**—*pop pl* PA-2
**Mountain Vista (subdivision)**—*pop pl* (2) AZ-5
Mountain Well—*locale* (2) NM-5
Mountain Well—*well* CA-9
Mountain Well—*well* NV-8
Mountain Well—*well* NM-5
Mountain Well—*well* OR-9
Mountain Well Camp—*locale* OR-9
Mountain Well Canyon—*valley* NV-8
Mountain Well (dry)—*well* AZ-5
Mountain Wells Trail—*trail* OR-9
**Mountain West Commercial Center**—*pop pl* UT-8
Mountainwest Mobile Home Campground—*park* UT-8
Mountain Wilderness Airpark—*airport* NC-3
Mountain Windmill—*locale* NM-5
Mountain Windmill—*locale* TX-5
Mountain Woods—*uninc pl* AL-4
Mountain Woods Lake Dam—*dam* AL-4
Mountain Woods Park—*uninc pl* AL-4
**Mountainwood (subdivision)**—*pop pl* TN-4
Mountainy Pond—*lake* ME-1
Mountain Zion Cem—*cemetery* OR-9
*Mount Air* KS-7
*Mountair* PA-2
*Mount Air* UT-8
Mount Air—*hist pl* MD-2
Mount Air—*locale* PA-2
**Mount Air**—*pop pl* OH-6
Mount Air Ch—*church* GA-3
Mount Air Ch—*church* MO-7
**Mount Aire**—*pop pl* UT-8
Mount Aire Canyon—*valley* UT-8
**Mount Air Estates Subdivision**—*pop pl* UT-8
Mount Airey Ch—*church* VA-3
Mount Airie—*locale* PA-2
Mountair Park—*park* CO-8
**Mountair Park Subdivision**—*pop pl* UT-8
*Mountairy* NJ-2
*Mount Airy* OH-6
*Mountairy* TN-4
Mount Airy—*hist pl* (2) MD-2
Mount Airy—*hist pl* VA-3
Mount Airy—*locale* NV-8
Mount Airy—*locale* (3) PA-2
Mount Airy—*locale* (2) TN-4
Mount Airy—*locale* (2) VA-3
Mount Airy—*other* PA-2
**Mount Airy**—*pop pl* GA-3
**Mount Airy**—*pop pl* LA-4
**Mount Airy**—*pop pl* MD-2
**Mount Airy**—*pop pl* MO-7
**Mount Airy**—*pop pl* NJ-2
**Mount Airy**—*pop pl* NY-2
**Mount Airy**—*pop pl* NC-3
**Mount Airy**—*pop pl* OH-6
**Mount Airy**—*pop pl* (3) PA-2
**Mount Airy**—*pop pl* TX-5
**Mount Airy**—*pop pl* VA-3
**Mount Airy**—*pop pl* WV-2
*Mount Airy Baptist Ch* MS-4
Mount Airy Cem—*cemetery* IL-6
Mount Airy Cem—*cemetery* (2) MS-4
Mount Airy Cem—*cemetery* MO-7
Mount Airy Cem—*cemetery* PA-2
Mount Airy Center—*locale* OH-6
*Mount Airy Ch* MS-4
Mount Airy Ch—*church* (9) GA-3
Mount Airy Ch—*church* (2) LA-4
Mount Airy Ch—*church* (3) MS-4
Mount Airy Ch—*church* MO-7
Mount Airy Ch—*church* (3) NC-3
Mount Airy Ch—*church* PA-2
Mount Airy Ch—*church* SC-3
Mount Airy Ch—*church* (2) TN-4
Mount Airy Ch—*church* TX-5
Mount Airy Ch—*church* (4) VA-3
Mount Airy Ch—*church* WV-2
*Mount Airy Church* AL-4
Mount Airy Cove—*bay* VA-3
Mount Airy Creek—*stream* GA-3
Mount Airy Dam—*dam* PA-2
Mount Airy Drift Fence—*other* WY-8
**Mount Airy Estates**—*pop pl* MD-2
Mount Airy For—*forest* OH-6
Mount Airy Hill—*summit* NY-2
Mount Airy Hist Dist—*hist pl* MD-2
Mount Airy Hist Dist—*hist pl* NC-3
Mount Airy Hist Dist—*hist pl* PA-2
Mount Airy HS—*school* NC-3
Mount Airy JHS—*school* NC-3
Mount Airy Lodge Ski Area—*locale* PA-2
Mount Airy Millpond—*reservoir* VA-3
Mount Airy Plantation (historical)—*locale* AL-4
Mountairy Post Office (historical)—*building* TN-4
*Mount Airy Range* NV-8
Mount Airy Sch—*school* IL-6
Mount Airy Sch—*school* KS-7
Mount Airy Sch—*school* MS-4
Mount Airy Sch—*school* PA-2
Mount Airy Sch—*school* TN-4
Mount Airy Sch—*school* (2) VA-3
Mount Airy Sch (historical)—*school* AL-4
Mount Airy Sch (historical)—*school* MS-4
Mount Airy Sch (historical)—*school* PA-2
Mount Airy Spring—*spring* NV-8
**Mount Airy Springs**—*pop pl* TN-4
Mount Airy Summit—*gap* NV-8
Mount Airy-Surry County Airp—*airport* NC-3
**Mount Airy Terrace**—*pop pl* PA-2
Mount Airy (Township of)—*fmr MCD* NC-3
Mount Airy Well—*well* WY-8
Mount Aix Trail—*trail* WA-9
*Mount Aiyon* PW-9
*Mount Akihi* HI-9
*Mount Alandar* MA-1
*Mount Alani* HI-9
*Mount Alban* MS-4
*Mount Alban Ridge* NH-1
Mount Alban Station (historical)—*locale* MS-4
Mount Albia Sch—*school* MO-7
Mount Albin Cem—*cemetery* MS-4
Mount Albin Ch—*church* MS-4
*Mount Albin Missionary Baptist Ch* MS-4
Mount Albion Cem—*cemetery* NY-2
Mount Aldrich Ch—*church* GA-3
Mount Alerno Novitiate—*church* IL-6
Mount Alexander Ch—*church* WV-2
Mount Alford Ch—*church* SC-3
*Mount Alice* CA-9
*Mount Alice* UT-8
Mount Allamuchy Camp—*locale* NJ-2
*Mount Allen* CA-9
**Mount Allen**—*pop pl* PA-2
Mount Allen Cem—*cemetery* KS-7
**Mount Allen Estates (subdivision)**—*pop pl* PA-2
Mount Allen Park—*park* PA-2
*Mount Almagre* CO-8
Mount Aloysius Junior Coll—*school* PA-2
Mount Alta Mine (Inactive)—*mine* CA-9
*Mount Alto* GA-3
*Mount Alto* PA-2
Mount Alto—*locale* VA-3
**Mount Alto**—*pop pl* WV-2
Mount Alto Ch—*church* GA-3
**Mount Alton**—*pop pl* PA-2

Mount Alto Park—*flat* CO-8
Mount Alvernia Acad—*school* MA-1
Mount Alvernia Coll—*school* MA-1
Mount Alvernia Seminary—*school* NY-2
**Mount Alverno**—*pop pl* PA-2
Mount Alverno Convent—*church* CA-9
Mount Alverno Sch—*school* OH-6
Mount Alverno Station—*building* PA-2
Mount Ambler—*summit* NC-3
*Mount Amiangal* PW-9
*Mount Anahola* HI-9
*Mount Anakeakua* HI-9
Mount Anderson Ch—*church* NC-3
Mount Andrew—*locale* AL-4
**Mount Andrew**—*pop pl* AL-4
Mount Andrew Cem—*cemetery* (2) AL-4
Mount Andrew Cem—*cemetery* SC-3
Mount Andrew Ch—*church* (2) AL-4
Mount Andrew Ch (historical)—*church* AL-4
Mount Andrews Cem—*cemetery* AL-4
Mount Andrews Mine—*mine* AK-9
*Mount Angel* OR-9
**Mount Angel**—*pop pl* OR-9
Mount Angel Abbey Cem—*cemetery* OR-9
Mount Angel (CCD)—*cens area* OR-9
Mount Angel Cem—*cemetery* OR-9
Mount Angeles Cem—*cemetery* WA-9
*Mount Ann* MA-1
Mount Anna Missionary Ch—*church* SC-3
*Mount Annie* NV-8
*Mount Annie Baptist Church* TN-4
Mount Annie Ch—*church* TN-4
Mount Annis Ch—*church* GA-3
Mount Ann Park—*park* MA-1
Mount Annville Cem—*cemetery* PA-2
Mount Anthony Country Club—*other* VT-1
Mount Antioch Ch—*church* TX-5
*Mount Antioch Church* AL-4
*Mount Antone* MT-8
Mountanye Sch—*school* NY-2
*Mount Aoleus* CO-8
*Mount Apetite* ME-1
*Mount Araat Church* AL-4
Mount Arab—*locale* NY-2
Mount Arab Lake—*lake* NY-2
Mount Arab Station—*locale* NY-2
Mount Araint Ch—*church* MS-4
Mount Arara Sch—*school* AL-4
*Mount Ararat* AL-4
*Mount Ararat* MA-1
Mount Ararat—*locale* TN-4
**Mount Ararat**—*pop pl* PA-2
Mount Ararat Cem—*cemetery* AL-4
Mount Ararat Cem—*cemetery* FL-3
Mount Ararat Cem—*cemetery* IA-7
Mount Ararat Cem—*cemetery* MS-4
Mount Ararat Cem—*cemetery* NY-2
Mount Ararat Cem—*cemetery* (4) TN-4
Mount Ararat Cemeterys—*cemetery* TN-4
Mount Ararat Ch—*church* (6) AL-4
Mount Ararat Ch—*church* AR-4
Mount Ararat Ch—*church* FL-3
Mount Ararat Ch—*church* (4) GA-3
Mount Ararat Ch—*church* (2) LA-4
Mount Ararat Ch—*church* MD-2
Mount Ararat Ch—*church* (4) MS-4
Mount Ararat Ch—*church* (2) MO-7
Mount Ararat Ch—*church* NC-3
Mount Ararat Ch—*church* SC-3
Mount Ararat Ch—*church* (4) TN-4
Mount Ararat Ch—*church* (4) VA-3
Mount Ararat Ch of Christ—*church* TN-4
Mount Ararat Cumberland Presbyterian Ch (historical)—*church* TN-4
*Mount Ararat Missionary Baptist Ch* MS-4
*Mount Ararat Missionary Baptist Ch* TN-4
Mount Ararat Missionary Baptist Ch—*church* MS-4
*Mount Ararat Primitive Baptist Ch* TN-4
Mount Ararat Sch—*school* ME-1
Mount Ararat Sch (historical)—*school* AL-4
Mount Ararat Sch (historical)—*school* (2) TN-4
Mount Ararat Spring—*spring* TN-4
Mount Arat Ch—*church* SC-3
Mount Arat Ch—*church* TX-5
Mount Arbor Ch—*church* GA-3
**Mount Area Estates (subdivision)**—*pop pl* TN-4
Mount Aria Ch—*church* MS-4
Mount Aria Ch—*church* WV-2
Mount Ariah Ch (historical)—*church* AL-4
Mount Arie Ch—*church* AL-4
Mount Ariel Ch—*church* NC-3
Mount Aries Sch (historical)—*school* TN-4
Mount Aris Ch—*church* WV-2
**Mount Arlington**—*pop pl* NJ-2
Mount Arlington Hist Dist—*hist pl* NJ-2
Mount Arlington Sch—*school* NJ-2
Mount Armenia Ch—*church* OH-6
Mount Arnon Ch (historical)—*church* TN-4
Mount Arnon Sch—*school* TN-4
*Mount Arrarat Baptist Ch* AL-4
Mount Arrat Baptist Ch—*church* AL-4
Mount Arrat Ch—*church* LA-4
Mount Arrat Ch—*church* MS-4
*Mount Arrie Ch* AL-4
*Mount Arubon* PW-9
*Mount Arumii* PW-9
*Mount Arurukoku* PW-9
*Mount Ary Baptist Ch* MS-4
Mount Ary Cem—*cemetery* MS-4
*Mount Ary Ch* MS-4
Mount Ary Ch—*church* (2) MS-4
Mount Asa Ch—*church* VA-3
Mount Asby Ch—*church* AR-4
Mount Ashland Trail—*trail* OR-9
Mount Asia Ch—*church* AL-4
Mount Assisi Acad—*school* IL-6
Mount Assisi Monastery—*church* PA-2
Mount Assissi Acad—*school* PA-2
**Mount Athena Condominium**—*pop pl* UT-8
**Mount Athena Subdivision**—*pop pl* UT-8
Mount Athen Ch—*church* SC-3
Mount Athos—*hist pl* VA-3
**Mount Athos (historical)**—*pop pl* VA-3
*Mount Auburn* KS-7
*Mount Auburn* OH-6
Mount Auburn—*locale* KY-4
**Mount Auburn**—*pop pl* IL-6
**Mount Auburn**—*pop pl* (3) IN-6
**Mount Auburn**—*pop pl* IA-7
**Mount Auburn**—*pop pl* OH-6
Mount Auburn Bridge—*bridge* IA-7
Mount Auburn Bridge Park—*park* IA-7
Mount Auburn Cem—*cemetery* (4) IL-6
Mount Auburn Cem—*cemetery* IN-6
Mount Auburn Cem—*cemetery* KS-7
Mount Auburn Cem—*cemetery* KY-4
Mount Auburn Cem—*cemetery* ME-1
Mount Auburn Cem—*cemetery* MD-2
Mount Auburn Cem—*cemetery* MA-1
Mount Auburn Cem—*cemetery* MN-6
Mount Auburn Cem—*cemetery* (2) MO-7
Mount Auburn Cem—*cemetery* NE-7
Mount Auburn Cem—*cemetery* OH-6
Mount Auburn Cem—*cemetery* SD-7
Mount Auburn Cem—*cemetery* TN-4
Mount Auburn Cemetery—*hist pl* MA-1
Mount Auburn Cemetery Reception House—*hist pl* MA-1
Mount Auburn Ch—*church* IN-6
Mount Auburn Ch—*church* MO-7
Mount Auburn Ch—*church* NC-3
Mount Auburn Ch—*church* TN-4
Mount Auburn Hist Dist—*hist pl* OH-6
Mount Auburn (historical P.O.)—*locale* MA-1
Mount Auburn Hosp—*hospital* MA-1
Mount Auburn Sch—*school* NC-3
Mount Auburn Sch—*school* TX-5
Mount Auburn Station (historical)—*locale* MA-1
**Mount Auburn (subdivision)**—*pop pl* MA-1
Mount Auburn (Township of)—*civ div* IL-6
Mount Audubon Trail—*trail* CO-8
Mount Augustine Novitiate—*school* OH-6
*Mount Aukum* CA-9
**Mount Aukum**—*pop pl* CA-9
Mount Aukum Sch—*school* CA-9
Mount Auragasak—*summit* PW-9
Mount Austin Cem—*cemetery* MS-4
Mount Austin Ch—*church* MS-4
Mount Avalon Trail—*trail* NH-1
Mount Aver Ch—*church* MS-4
Mount Avery Cem—*cemetery* GA-3
Mount Avery Cem—*cemetery* MS-4
*Mount Avery Ch* AL-4
Mount Avery Ch—*church* AL-4
Mount Avery Ch—*church* (3) MS-4
Mount Avon Cem—*cemetery* MI-6
Mount Ayr—*locale* KS-7
**Mount Ayr**—*pop pl* IN-6
**Mount Ayr**—*pop pl* IA-7
Mount Ayr Cem—*cemetery* KS-7
Mount Ayr Cem—*cemetery* MO-7
Mount Ayr Ch—*church* KS-7
Mount Ayre Ch—*church* MO-7
*Mount Ayr Game Area* IA-7
Mount Ayr JHS—*school* IN-6
Mount Ayr Sch—*school* KS-7
Mount Ayr Sch (historical)—*school* MO-7
Mount Ayr State Wildlife Area—*area* IA-7
**Mount Ayr Township**—*pop pl* KS-7
Mount Azure Cem—*cemetery* AL-4
Mount Azure Ch—*church* AL-4
*Mount Babuquiburi* AZ-5
Mount Bailey Trail—*trail* OR-9
**Mount Baker**—*pop pl* WA-9
Mount Baker Lodge—*locale* WA-9
Mount Baker Ridge Tunnel—*hist pl* WA-9
Mount Baker Theatre—*hist pl* WA-9
*Mount Bald* WA-9
*Mount Baldy* AZ-5
*Mount Baldy* CA-9
*Mount Baldy* OR-9
*Mount Baldy* TX-5
**Mount Baldy**—*pop pl* CA-9
Mount Baldy—*summit* (2) NM-5
Mount Baldy Guard Station—*locale* UT-8
Mount Baldy Log Pond—*reservoir* OR-9
Mount Baldy Log Pond Dam—*dam* OR-9
**Mount Baldy (Mt. Baldy)**—*pop pl* CA-9
Mount Baldy Notch—*gap* CA-9
*Mount Baldy Primitive Area* AZ-5
Mount Baldy Wilderness—*park* AZ-5
Mount Baldy-Wrightwood (CCD)—*cens area* CA-9
*Mount Bally* CA-9
*Mount Barlow* OR-9
*Mount Barrett* CO-8
*Mount Barton Elementary School* MS-4
Mount Barton Sch—*school* MS-4
*Mount Battux* ME-1
Mount Bayou—*stream* LA-4
Mount Beacon Incline Railway and Power House—*hist pl* NY-2
*Mount Beauchamp* AZ-5
*Mount Beauford* AZ-5
*Mount Beaula Ch* AL-4
Mount Beaula Ch—*church* NC-3
*Mount Beckwith* CO-8
Mount Beeser Ch—*church* FL-3
Mount Bemis Trail—*trail* NH-1
Mount Benedict Cem—*cemetery* MA-1
*Mount Ben Lomond* UT-8
Mount Bennnett Hills—*range* ID-8
Mount Berrain Ch—*church* FL-3
**Mount Berry**—*pop pl* GA-3
*Mount Berthoud* CO-8
*Mount Bessemer Ch* AL-4
Mount Bethany Cem—*cemetery* MS-4
Mount Bethany Ch—*church* MS-4
Mount Bethany Ch—*church* TN-4
Mount Bethany Ch—*church* TX-5
*Mount Bethel* AL-4
Mount Bethel—*locale* GA-3
Mount Bethel—*locale* NJ-2
Mount Bethel—*locale* TX-5
**Mount Bethel**—*pop pl* GA-3
**Mount Bethel**—*pop pl* NJ-2
**Mount Bethel**—*pop pl* PA-2
*Mount Bethel Baptist* TX-5
*Mount Bethel Baptist Ch* AL-4
*Mount Bethel Baptist Ch* MS-4
Mount Bethel Baptist Ch—*church* FL-3
Mount Bethel Baptist Ch—*church* (3) MS-4
Mount Bethel Baptist Ch—*church* TN-4
Mount Bethel Baptist Institutional Ch—*church* FL-3
Mount Bethel Baptist Meetinghouse—*hist pl* NJ-2
*Mount Bethel Cem* AL-4
Mount Bethel Cem—*cemetery* (2) AL-4
Mount Bethel Cem—*cemetery* NC-3
Mount Bethel Cem—*cemetery* (2) PA-2
Mount Bethel Cem—*cemetery* (2) TN-4
*Mount Bethel Cemetery* MS-4
*Mount Bethel Ch* AL-4
Mount Bethel Ch—*church* (4) AL-4
Mount Bethel Ch—*church* (3) AR-4
Mount Bethel Ch—*church* (5) FL-3
Mount Bethel Ch—*church* (4) GA-3
Mount Bethel Ch—*church* IN-6
Mount Bethel Ch—*church* KY-4
Mount Bethel Ch—*church* (5) LA-4
Mount Bethel Ch—*church* MD-2
Mount Bethel Ch—*church* MI-6
Mount Bethel Ch—*church* (5) MS-4
Mount Bethel Ch—*church* MO-7
Mount Bethel Ch—*church* (10) NC-3
Mount Bethel Ch—*church* OH-6
Mount Bethel Ch—*church* OK-5
Mount Bethel Ch—*church* (2) PA-2
Mount Bethel Ch—*church* (6) SC-3
Mount Bethel Ch—*church* (3) TN-4
Mount Bethel Ch—*church* (2) TX-5
Mount Bethel Ch—*church* (8) VA-3
Mount Bethel Ch (historical)—*church* TN-4
Mount Bethel Ch of Christ Holiness—*church* MS-4
Mount Bethel Church—*cemetery* GA-3
Mount Bethelehem Baptist Ch—*church* TN-4
Mount Bethel Methodist Church—*hist pl* NJ-2
Mount Bethel Number 2 Ch—*church* MS-4
Mount Bethel Recreation Center—*locale* VA-3
Mount Bethel Sch—*school* VA-3
Mount Bethel Youth Camp—*locale* AL-4
Mount Bethel Youth Camp—*locale* GA-3
*Mount Bethlehem Church* AL-4
Mount Bethlehem Primitive Baptist Ch—*church* FL-3
Mount Beulah—*locale* KY-4
**Mount Beulah**—*pop pl* SC-3
Mount Beulah Baptist Ch—*church* MS-4
Mount Beulah Cem—*cemetery* AR-4
Mount Beulah Cem—*cemetery* (2) GA-3
*Mount Beulah Ch* AL-4
Mount Beulah Ch—*church* AL-4
Mount Beulah Ch—*church* AR-4
Mount Beulah Ch—*church* FL-3
Mount Beulah Ch—*church* GA-3
Mount Beulah Ch—*church* KY-4
Mount Beulah Ch—*church* MD-2
Mount Beulah Ch—*church* (2) MS-4
Mount Beulah Ch—*church* NC-3
Mount Beulah Ch—*church* (2) SC-3
Mount Beulah Ch—*church* VA-3
Mount Beulah Ch (historical)—*church* MS-4
Mount Beulah Coll—*school* MS-4
Mount Beulah Hotel—*hist pl* NC-3
Mount Beulah Sch—*school* SC-3
Mount Beulah Sch—*school* WV-2
Mount Bidwell Sch—*school* CA-9
*Mount Bigelow* ME-1
*Mount Biliver* OR-9
*Mount Black* NC-3
*Mount Blain* CO-8
Mount Blair Cem—*cemetery* PA-2
*Mount Blanca* CO-8
Mount Blanca Well—*well* CO-8
**Mount Blanchard**—*pop pl* OH-6
*Mount Blanco* CA-9
Mount Blanco—*locale* OH-6
**Mount Blanco**—*pop pl* TX-5
**Mount Blanco**—*pop pl* VA-3
Mount Blessing Camp—*locale* PA-2
Mount Bliss Cem—*cemetery* MI-6
Mount Blue (historical P.O.)—*locale* MA-1
Mount Blue HS—*school* ME-1
Mount Blue Pond—*lake* ME-1
Mount Blue State Park—*park* ME-1
Mount Blue Stream—*stream* ME-1
**Mount Bolus (subdivision)**—*pop pl* NC-3
*Mount Bonneville* OR-9
*Mount Borah* ID-8
Mount Bowdoin Station (historical)—*locale* MA-1
**Mount Bowdoin (subdivision)**—*pop pl* MA-1
**Mount Braddock**—*pop pl* PA-2
Mount Bradley Trail—*trail* MT-8
Mount Branch—*stream* IL-6
Mount Branson Christian Ch—*church* MO-7
*Mount Breckenridge* CA-9
**Mount Briar**—*pop pl* MD-2
*Mount Brigham* UT-8
Mount Brighton Ski Area—*other* MI-6
*Mount Brior* MD-2
Mount Brokaw Sch—*school* KS-7
**Mount Brook**—*pop pl* WA-9
Mount Brown Fire Lookout—*hist pl* MT-8
*Mount Browning* NC-3
Mount Brown Lookout—*locale* MT-8
Mount Brown Lookout Trail—*trail* MT-8
Mount Bruin Ch—*church* MS-4
Mount Brundage Park—*park* CA-9
*Mount Bryant* MA-1
Mount Bryd Ch—*church* KY-4
Mount Buache—*summit* FM-9
*Mount Bucky* AL-4
*Mount Buford* AZ-5
Mount Bula Ch—*church* LA-4
**Mount Bullion**—*pop pl* CA-9
Mount Bushnell State Park—*park* CT-1
Mount Cabot Sch—*school* NH-1
Mount Cabot Trail—*trail* NH-1
Mount Caesar Sch—*school* NH-1
*Mount Callahan* NV-8
Mount Callahan Spring—*spring* CO-8
**Mount Calm**—*pop pl* TX-5
Mount Calm Cem—*cemetery* (2) TX-5
Mount Calm Ch—*church* LA-4
Mount Calm Sch—*school* LA-4
Mount Calm (Township of)—*fmr MCD* AR-4
Mount Calvaire Cem—*cemetery* NH-1
**Mount Calvary**—*pop pl* TX-5
**Mount Calvary**—*pop pl* WI-6
Mount Calvary Assembly of God Ch—*church* UT-8
*Mount Calvary Baptist Ch* AL-4
*Mount Calvary Baptist Ch* TN-4
Mount Calvary Baptist Ch—*church* (5) AL-4
Mount Calvary Baptist Ch—*church* (3) FL-3
Mount Calvary Baptist Ch—*church* IN-6
Mount Calvary Baptist Ch—*church* (2) MS-4
Mount Calvary Baptist Ch—*church* TN-4
*Mount Calvary Cem* OR-9
Mount Calvary Cem—*cemetery* (6) AL-4
Mount Calvary Cem—*cemetery* AR-4
Mount Calvary Cem—*cemetery* (2) CA-9
Mount Calvary Cem—*cemetery* CO-8
Mount Calvary Cem—*cemetery* FL-3
Mount Calvary Cem—*cemetery* ID-8
Mount Calvary Cem—*cemetery* (5) IL-6
Mount Calvary Cem—*cemetery* (7) IN-6
Mount Calvary Cem—*cemetery* (8) IA-7
Mount Calvary Cem—*cemetery* (16) KS-7
Mount Calvary Cem—*cemetery* (3) LA-4
Mount Calvary Cem—*cemetery* MD-2
Mount Calvary Cem—*cemetery* (9) MI-6
Mount Calvary Cem—*cemetery* (3) MN-6
Mount Calvary Cem—*cemetery* (3) MS-4
Mount Calvary Cem—*cemetery* (4) MO-7
Mount Calvary Cem—*cemetery* MT-8
Mount Calvary Cem—*cemetery* NE-7
Mount Calvary Cem—*cemetery* (5) NH-1
Mount Calvary Cem—*cemetery* (4) NJ-2
Mount Calvary Cem—*cemetery* (4) NM-5
Mount Calvary Cem—*cemetery* (5) NY-2
Mount Calvary Cem—*cemetery* ND-7
Mount Calvary Cem—*cemetery* (9) OH-6
Mount Calvary Cem—*cemetery* (2) OR-9
Mount Calvary Cem—*cemetery* (3) PA-2
Mount Calvary Cem—*cemetery* SD-7
Mount Calvary Cem—*cemetery* TN-4
Mount Calvary Cem—*cemetery* (4) TX-5
Mount Calvary Cem—*cemetery* UT-8
Mount Calvary Cem—*cemetery* (2) VT-1
Mount Calvary Cem—*cemetery* (3) VA-3
Mount Calvary Cem—*cemetery* (4) WV-2
Mount Calvary Cem—*cemetery* (2) WI-6
*Mount Calvary Ch* AL-4
Mount Calvary Ch—*church* (14) AL-4
Mount Calvary Ch—*church* (4) AR-4
Mount Calvary Ch—*church* (3) FL-3
Mount Calvary Ch—*church* (21) GA-3
Mount Calvary Ch—*church* (5) IN-6
Mount Calvary Ch—*church* (2) KY-4
Mount Calvary Ch—*church* (7) LA-4
Mount Calvary Ch—*church* (5) MD-2
Mount Calvary Ch—*church* MA-1
Mount Calvary Ch—*church* (8) MS-4
Mount Calvary Ch—*church* (5) MO-7
Mount Calvary Ch—*church* (3) NJ-2
Mount Calvary Ch—*church* (18) NC-3
Mount Calvary Ch—*church* (2) OH-6
Mount Calvary Ch—*church* (7) PA-2
Mount Calvary Ch—*church* (18) SC-3
Mount Calvary Ch—*church* (5) TN-4
Mount Calvary Ch—*church* (9) TX-5
Mount Calvary Ch—*church* (21) VA-3
Mount Calvary Ch—*church* WV-2
Mount Calvary Ch (abandoned)—*church* MO-7
Mount Calvary Chapel—*church* LA-4
Mount Calvary Ch (historical)—*church* AL-4
Mount Calvary Ch (historical)—*church* MO-7
Mount Calvary Episcopal Ch—*church* PA-2
Mount Calvary Lutheran Ch—*church* AL-4
*Mount Calvary Missionary Baptist Ch* AL-4
Mount Calvary Missionary Baptist Ch—*church* (2) FL-3
Mount Calvary Monastery—*church* CA-9
*Mount Calvary Presbyterian Ch* AL-4
Mount Calvary Primitive Baptist Ch—*church* AL-4
Mount Calvary Sch—*school* AL-4
Mount Calvary Sch—*school* IN-6
Mount Calvary Sch—*school* MD-2
Mount Calvary Sch—*school* MI-6
Mount Calvary Sch—*school* MO-7
Mount Calvary Sch—*school* OH-6
Mount Calvary Sch—*school* (2) WI-6
Mount Calvary Sch (abandoned)—*school* MO-7
Mount Calvary Station—*locale* NJ-2
Mount Calvary Temple Ch of God in Christ—*church* DE-2
Mount Calvary United Methodist Ch—*church* DE-2
Mount Calvert—*locale* MD-2
Mount Calvert Ch—*church* (2) NC-3
Mount Calvery Cem—*cemetery* KS-7
Mount Calvery Cem—*cemetery* MS-4
Mount Calvery Ch—*church* MS-4
*Mount Calvery Church* AL-4
Mount Calvery Sch (historical)—*school* AL-4
Mount Calvin Ch—*church* GA-3
*Mount Campbell Church* AL-4
Mount Camp Cem—*cemetery* MI-6
Mount Canaan Baptist Ch—*church* AL-4
Mount Canaan Baptist Ch—*church* (2) FL-3
Mount Canaan Baptist Ch—*church* TN-4
Mount Canaan Ch—*church* (8) AL-4
Mount Canaan Ch—*church* (2) AR-4
Mount Canaan Ch—*church* FL-3
Mount Canaan Ch—*church* KY-4
Mount Canaan Ch—*church* (2) LA-4
Mount Canaan Ch—*church* MS-4
Mount Canaan Ch—*church* SC-3
Mount Canaan Sch—*school* (2) AL-4
Mount Cana Ch—*church* VA-3
Mount Canana Ch—*church* AL-4
Mount Canary Company Log Pond—*reservoir* OR-9
Mount Caney Ch—*church* AR-4
Mount Canna Ch—*church* (2) MS-4
Mount Cannan Ch (historical)—*church* MS-4
Mount Cannon Ch—*church* MS-4
Mount Capers Cem—*cemetery* TX-5
*Mount Caramel* TX-5
*Mount Carbon* CO-8
**Mount Carbon**—*pop pl* IL-6
**Mount Carbon**—*pop pl* PA-2
**Mount Carbon**—*pop pl* WV-2
Mount Carbon Borough—*civil* PA-2
Mount Cardigan State Park—*park* NH-1
*Mount Cardwell* TN-4
Mount Carey Ch—*church* AL-4
Mount Carey Ch (historical)—*church* MS-4
*Mount Carmal Ch* AL-4
Mount Carman Cem—*cemetery* WV-2
Mount Carman Ch—*church* WV-2
Mount Carmel—*church* TX-5
Mount Carmel—*locale* FL-3
Mount Carmel—*locale* GA-3
Mount Carmel—*locale* KY-4
Mount Carmel—*locale* MD-2
Mount Carmel—*locale* NY-2
Mount Carmel—*locale* TN-4
**Mount Carmel**—*pop pl* (4) AL-4
**Mount Carmel**—*pop pl* AR-4
**Mount Carmel**—*pop pl* CT-1
**Mount Carmel**—*pop pl* IL-6
**Mount Carmel**—*pop pl* (2) IN-6
**Mount Carmel**—*pop pl* IA-7
**Mount Carmel**—*pop pl* KY-4
**Mount Carmel**—*pop pl* LA-4
**Mount Carmel**—*pop pl* MD-2
**Mount Carmel**—*pop pl* MS-4
**Mount Carmel**—*pop pl* NC-3
**Mount Carmel**—*pop pl* ND-7
**Mount Carmel**—*pop pl* (2) OH-6
**Mount Carmel**—*pop pl* (2) PA-2
**Mount Carmel**—*pop pl* SC-3
**Mount Carmel**—*pop pl* (6) TN-4
**Mount Carmel**—*pop pl* TX-5
**Mount Carmel**—*pop pl* UT-8
**Mount Carmel**—*pop pl* (2) VA-3
Mount Carmel—*uninc pl* NY-2
Mount Carmel Acad—*school* KS-7
Mount Carmel Acad (historical)—*school* TN-4
Mount Carmel A.M.E. Zion Campground—*hist pl* SC-3
*Mount Carmel Baptist Ch* AL-4
*Mount Carmel Baptist Ch* MS-4
Mount Carmel Baptist Ch—*church* (2) AL-4
Mount Carmel Baptist Ch—*church* (3) FL-3
Mount Carmel Baptist Ch—*church* IN-6
Mount Carmel Baptist Ch—*church* (2) MS-4
*Mount Carmel Baptist Church* TN-4
Mount Carmel Borough—*civil* PA-2
Mount Carmel Branch—*stream* SC-3
Mount Carmel Camp—*locale* MN-6
Mount Carmel Cave—*cave* IN-6
Mount Carmel (CCD)—*cens area* SC-3
Mount Carmel (CCD)—*cens area* TN-4
Mount Carmel Cem—*cemetery* (9) AL-4
Mount Carmel Cem—*cemetery* (2) AR-4
Mount Carmel Cem—*cemetery* CA-9
Mount Carmel Cem—*cemetery* CO-8
Mount Carmel Cem—*cemetery* FL-3
Mount Carmel Cem—*cemetery* (3) GA-3
Mount Carmel Cem—*cemetery* (5) IL-6
Mount Carmel Cem—*cemetery* (9) IN-6
Mount Carmel Cem—*cemetery* (2) IA-7
Mount Carmel Cem—*cemetery* (3) KS-7
Mount Carmel Cem—*cemetery* (4) KY-4
Mount Carmel Cem—*cemetery* (2) LA-4
Mount Carmel Cem—*cemetery* ME-1
Mount Carmel Cem—*cemetery* (2) MD-2
Mount Carmel Cem—*cemetery* MA-1
Mount Carmel Cem—*cemetery* (2) MI-6
Mount Carmel Cem—*cemetery* (3) MN-6
Mount Carmel Cem—*cemetery* (9) MS-4
Mount Carmel Cem—*cemetery* (6) MO-7
Mount Carmel Cem—*cemetery* (3) NE-7
Mount Carmel Cem—*cemetery* (3) NJ-2
Mount Carmel Cem—*cemetery* (6) NY-2
Mount Carmel Cem—*cemetery* (2) NC-3
Mount Carmel Cem—*cemetery* ND-7
Mount Carmel Cem—*cemetery* (5) OH-6
Mount Carmel Cem—*cemetery* (3) OK-5
Mount Carmel Cem—*cemetery* (12) PA-2
Mount Carmel Cem—*cemetery* (2) SC-3
Mount Carmel Cem—*cemetery* (14) TN-4
Mount Carmel Cem—*cemetery* (4) TX-5
Mount Carmel Cem—*cemetery* UT-8
Mount Carmel Cem—*cemetery* (2) VA-3
Mount Carmel Cem—*cemetery* WA-9
Mount Carmel Cem—*cemetery* (3) WV-2
*Mount Carmel Ch* AL-4
*Mount Carmel Ch* MS-4
Mount Carmel Ch—*church* (35) AL-4
Mount Carmel Ch—*church* (12) AR-4
Mount Carmel Ch—*church* (4) FL-3
Mount Carmel Ch—*church* (29) GA-3
Mount Carmel Ch—*church* (4) IL-6
Mount Carmel Ch—*church* (11) IN-6
Mount Carmel Ch—*church* (17) KY-4
Mount Carmel Ch—*church* (7) LA-4
Mount Carmel Ch—*church* (6) MD-2
Mount Carmel Ch—*church* MA-1
Mount Carmel Ch—*church* MN-6
Mount Carmel Ch—*church* (21) MS-4
Mount Carmel Ch—*church* (14) MO-7
Mount Carmel Ch—*church* NY-2
Mount Carmel Ch—*church* (34) NC-3
Mount Carmel Ch—*church* (15) OH-6
Mount Carmel Ch—*church* (2) OK-5
Mount Carmel Ch—*church* (7) PA-2
Mount Carmel Ch—*church* (17) SC-3
Mount Carmel Ch—*church* (28) TN-4
Mount Carmel Ch—*church* (5) TX-5
Mount Carmel Ch—*church* (22) VA-3
Mount Carmel Ch—*church* (13) WV-2
Mount Carmel Chapel—*church* NM-5
Mount Carmel Chapel—*church* TX-5
Mount Carmel Ch (historical)—*church* (3) AL-4
Mount Carmel Ch (historical)—*church* (4) MS-4
Mount Carmel Ch (historical)—*church* TN-4
*Mount Carmel Ch of Christ* AL-4
*Mount Carmel Ch of God* MS-4
Mount Carmel Ch of God in Christ—*church* KS-7
*Mount Carmel Congregational Methodist Ch* TN-4
Mount Carmel Convent—*church* IA-7
Mount Carmel Convent—*church* LA-4
Mount Carmel Creek—*stream* AR-4
Mount Carmel Creek Cem—*cemetery* AR-4
*Mount Carmel Cumberland Presbyterian Ch* TN-4
Mount Carmel Cumberland Presbyterian Ch (historical)—*church* TN-4
Mount Carmel Dam—*dam* ND-7
Mount Carmel Division—*civil* TN-4
Mount Carmel (Election Precinct)—*fmr MCD* IL-6
*Mount Carmel Elementary School* MS-4
*Mount Carmel Elementary School* TN-4
Mount Carmel Ferry—*locale* IL-6
Mount Carmel Hall—*school* NY-2
**Mount Carmel Heights**—*pop pl* OH-6
Mount Carmel Hist Dist—*hist pl* SC-3
Mount Carmel (historical)—*locale* AL-4
Mount Carmel (historical)—*locale* KS-7
**Mount Carmel (historical)**—*pop pl* TN-4
Mount Carmel Holy Temple—*church* NC-3
Mount Carmel Hosp—*hospital* KS-7
Mount Carmel Hosp—*hospital* OH-6
Mount Carmel Hosp—*hospital* WA-9
Mount Carmel HS—*school* CA-9
Mount Carmel HS—*school* CO-8
Mount Carmel HS—*school* MD-2
Mount Carmel HS—*school* NY-2
Mount Carmel Junction—*locale* PA-2
Mount Carmel Junction—*locale* UT-8
**Mount Carmel Junction (Alaska)**—*pop pl* PA-2
*Mount Carmel Junction Station* PA-2
Mount Carmel Library—*building* TN-4
Mount Carmel (Magisterial District)—*fmr MCD* VA-3
Mount Carmel Male and Female Acad (historical)—*school* MS-4
Mount Carmel Mercy Hosp—*hospital* MI-6
*Mount Carmel Methodist Church* AL-4
*Mount Carmel Methodist Church* MS-4
*Mount Carmel Methodist Church* TN-4
Mount Carmel Missionary Baptist Ch—*church* MS-4
*Mount Carmel Missionary Baptist Church* AL-4
Mount Carmel Monastery—*church* MD-2
Mount Carmel Monastery—*church* WV-2
Mount Carmel Number 2 Mine Station—*locale* PA-2
Mount Carmel Park—*park* TN-4
Mount Carmel Post Office—*building* TN-4
Mount Carmel Post Office (historical)—*building* MS-4
Mount Carmel Post Office (historical)—*building* TN-4
Mount Carmel Presbyterian Ch—*church* TN-4
Mount Carmel Presbyterian Ch (historical)—*church* MS-4
*Mount Carmel Presbyterian Church* MS-4
Mount Carmel Primitive Baptist Ch—*church* AL-4
Mount Carmel Ridge—*ridge* IN-6
Mount Carmel Ridge—*ridge* PA-2
Mount Carmel Ridge—*ridge* TN-4
Mount Carmel Ridge—*ridge* (2) WV-2
Mount Carmel Sch—*school* (2) AL-4
Mount Carmel Sch—*school* AZ-5
Mount Carmel Sch—*school* CA-9
Mount Carmel Sch—*school* CT-1
Mount Carmel Sch—*school* GA-3
Mount Carmel Sch—*school* (5) IL-6
Mount Carmel Sch—*school* IN-6
Mount Carmel Sch—*school* IA-7
Mount Carmel Sch—*school* (2) KY-4
Mount Carmel Sch—*school* (2) LA-4
Mount Carmel Sch—*school* MA-1
Mount Carmel Sch—*school* (2) MS-4
Mount Carmel Sch—*school* MO-7
Mount Carmel Sch—*school* (4) NJ-2
Mount Carmel Sch—*school* (6) NY-2
Mount Carmel Sch—*school* OH-6
Mount Carmel Sch—*school* (2) PA-2
Mount Carmel Sch—*school* (3) SC-3
Mount Carmel Sch—*school* (2) TN-4
Mount Carmel Sch—*school* (2) TX-5
Mount Carmel Sch—*school* MH-9
Mount Carmel Sch (abandoned)—*school* MO-7
Mount Carmel Sch (historical)—*school* AL-4
Mount Carmel Sch (historical)—*school* MS-4
Mount Carmel Sch (historical)—*school* (5) TN-4
Mount Carmel Seminary—*school* TX-5
Mount Carmel Shop Ctr—*locale* TN-4
Mount Carmel Springs Branch—*stream* AL-4
Mount Carmel Springs Branch—*stream* FL-3
Mount Carmel State For—*forest* VT-1
Mount Carmel Station—*locale* CT-1
**Mount Carmel Township**—*pop pl* ND-7
**Mount Carmel (Township of)**—*pop pl* PA-2
**Mount Carmel Trailer Park**—*pop pl* UT-8
*Mount Carmel United Methodist Church* TN-4
Mount Carmen Cem—*cemetery* AR-4
Mount Carmen Ch—*church* GA-3
*Mount Carmen Church* MS-4
Mount Carmer Ch—*church* VA-3
Mount Carmon Cem—*cemetery* MS-4
Mount Carmon Ch (historical)—*church* MS-4
Mount Carnel Ch—*church* AR-4
Mount Carney Cem—*cemetery* MS-4
Mount Carney Ch—*church* MO-7
Mount Caroline Livermore—*summit* CA-9
Mount Carrick—*locale* OH-6
**Mount Carrie**—*pop pl* FL-3
**Mount Carroll**—*pop pl* IL-6
Mount Carroll Ch—*church* VA-3
Mount Carroll Hist Dist—*hist pl* IL-6
Mount Carroll (Township of)—*civ div* IL-6
Mount Carry Ch—*church* GA-3
*Mount Carson* UT-8
*Mount Carson* WA-9
Mountcastle—*locale* VA-3
Mount Castle Ch—*church* WV-2
Mountcastle Methodist Ch (historical)—*church* TN-4
Mount Castle Sch (historical)—*school* AL-4
*Mount Catherine* UT-8
Mount Catherine Ch—*church* IL-6
Mount Cazy Cem—*cemetery* MS-4
Mount Cedar Ch—*church* SC-3
Mount Cedrum Cem—*cemetery* AL-4
Mount Celestial Ch—*church* MO-7
*Mount Celia* MT-8
Mount Cella Cem—*cemetery* LA-4
Mount Cello Ch—*church* FL-3
Mount Cem—*cemetery* AL-4
Mount Cem—*cemetery* IN-6
Mount Cem—*cemetery* ME-1
Mount Cem—*cemetery* MA-1
Mount Cem—*cemetery* MO-7
Mount Cem—*cemetery* TN-4
Mount Center Ch—*church* (2) MS-4
Mount Centre Ch—*church* MS-4
Mount Cephus Ch—*church* MS-4
Mount Ch—*church* IL-6
*Mount Chadwick* WA-9
Mount Chapel—*church* AL-4
Mount Chapel—*church* GA-3
Mount Chapel—*church* WV-2
Mount Chapel Cem—*cemetery* VA-3

Mount Chapel Ch ... AL-4
Mount Chapel Ch—church ... AR-4
Mount Chapel Ch—church ... KY-4
Mount Chapel Ch—church ... SC-3
Mount Chapman ... MT-8
Mount Chapman—summit ... NC-3
Mount Charity ... OR-9
Mount Charity Ch—church (2) ... MS-4
**Mount Charleston**—pop pl ... NV-8
Mount Charleston Natl Recreation Trail—trail ... NV-8
Mount Charleston North Trailhead—locale ... NV-8
**Mount Charron Estates (subdivision)**—pop pl ... AL-4
Mount Chase (Plantation of)—civ div ... ME-1
**Mount Chestnut**—pop pl ... PA-2
Mount Chestnut Cem—cemetery ... PA-2
**Mount Chestnut Springs**—pop pl ... PA-2
Mount Chocorura ... NH-1
Mount Chuai ... CA-9
Mount Church, The ... AL-4
Mount Church, The—church ... VA-3
Mount Churchill ... CA-9
Mount Cilla Ch—church ... GA-3
Mount Cille Springs Ch—church ... GA-3
Mount Cilley Trail—trail ... NH-1
Mount Claim Ch—church ... AR-4
**Mount Clair**—pop pl ... IL-6
Mount Clair Sch—school ... AL-4
Mount Clair Sch—school ... WV-2
Mount Clare—hist pl ... MD-2
**Mount Clare**—pop pl ... IL-6
**Mount Clare**—pop pl ... IA-7
**Mount Clare**—pop pl ... NE-7
**Mount Clare**—pop pl ... WV-2
Mount Clare—uninc pl ... MD-2
Mount Clarence King ... CO-8
Mount Clark Cem—cemetery ... IA-7
Mount Clear Ch—church ... AL-4
Mountclef Ridge—ridge ... CA-9
**Mountclef Village**—pop pl ... CA-9
**Mount Clemens**—pop pl ... MI-6
Mount Clemens South ... MI-6
**Mount Clemens Southeast**—pop pl ... MI-6
Mount Clement Ch—church ... SC-3
Mount Clendon Ch—church ... LA-4
Mount Cleveland ... CO-8
Mount Cleveland Baptist Ch—church ... AL-4
Mount Cliff Mine—mine ... MT-8
Mount Cliffty Trail—trail ... WA-9
**Mount Clifton**—pop pl ... VA-3
Mount Clifton Ch—church ... FL-3
Mount Clinton ... NH-1
Mount Clinton ... NY-2
**Mount Clinton**—pop pl ... VA-3
Mount Clinton Ch—church ... VA-3
Mount Clinton Trail—trail ... NH-1
**Mount Cobb**—pop pl ... PA-2
Mount Coland Cem—cemetery ... VA-3
Mount Collier Ch—church ... MD-2
Mount Collins ... NC-3
Mount Collins ... TN-4
Mount Collins—summit ... NC-3
Mount Collins Cem—cemetery ... PA-2
Mount Columbia ... CO-8
Mount Comfort—locale ... AR-4
**Mount Comfort**—pop pl ... IN-6
Mount Comfort Airfield—airport ... IN-6
Mount Comfort Baptist Ch—church ... MS-4
Mount Comfort Cem—cemetery ... MS-4
Mount Comfort Cem—cemetery (2) ... TN-4
Mount Comfort Cem—cemetery (3) ... TX-5
Mount Comfort Cem—cemetery ... VA-3
Mount Comfort Ch—church ... LA-4
Mount Comfort Ch—church ... MS-4
Mount Comfort Ch—church ... MO-7
Mount Comfort Ch—church ... TX-5
Mount Comfort Ch—church ... VA-3
Mount Comfort Post Office (historical)—building ... TN-4
Mount Comfort Sch (historical)—school ... MS-4
Mount Commodoe Ch—church ... GA-3
Mount Common Ch—church ... LA-4
Mount Common Church ... MS-4
Mount Coney Ch—church ... AL-4
Mount Copeland ... CO-8
Mount Coppin Square—park ... CA-9
Mount Corcoran ... CA-9
Mount Cornith Ch—church ... TX-5
Mount Corson ... UT-8
**Mount Cory**—pop pl ... OH-6
Mount Cove Ch—church ... TX-5
Mount Craig—summit ... NC-3
**Mount Crawford**—pop pl ... VA-3
**Mount Crawford (sta.) (North River)**—pop pl ... VA-3
Mount Creek ... SC-3
Mount Creek—stream ... MT-8
Mount Creek—stream ... VA-3
Mount Creek Ch—church ... TN-4
Mount Crescent ... NH-1
Mount Crest ... AR-4
Mount Crest—locale ... TN-4
Mount Crest Ch—church ... TN-4
**Mount Crested Butte**—pop pl ... CO-8
Mount Crest Sch (historical)—school ... TN-4
**Mount Croghan**—pop pl ... SC-3
Mount Croghan (CCD)—cens area ... SC-3
Mount Cross—locale ... VA-3
Mount Cross Camp—locale ... CA-9
**Mount Cuba**—pop pl ... DE-2
Mount Cuba Hist Dist—hist pl ... DE-2
Mount Culmen Ch—church ... PA-2
Mount Cumberland Cem—cemetery (2) ... TN-4
Mount Cumberland Ch—church ... TN-4
Mount Cumberland Sch (historical)—school ... TN-4
Mount Curlwood ... MI-6
Mount Custer Sch—school ... NE-7
Mount Cutler Sch—school ... ME-1
Mount Dale Sch—school ... MO-7
Mount Dallas—locale ... PA-2
Mount Daniel ... MA-1
**Mount Daniel**—pop pl ... VA-3
Mount Daniel Sch—school ... VA-3
Mount Davidson Sch—school ... VA-3
Mount Davis Airp—airport ... PA-2
Mount Davis Natural Area—area ... PA-2
Mount Davis Observation Tower—tower ... PA-2
Mount Davis Picnic Area—area ... PA-2
Mount Davis Recreational Camp—locale ... PA-2
Mount Day ... CA-9
Mount Deary Creek—stream ... ID-8
**Mount de Chantal**—pop pl ... WV-2
Mount de Chantal Acad—school ... WV-2
Mount de Chantal Visitation Acad—hist pl ... WV-2
Mount De Chantel—uninc pl ... WV-2
Mount Defiance—summit ... NY-2
Mount Defiance Trail—trail ... WA-9
Mount Delane Ch—church ... NC-3
Mount Delano ... UT-8
Mount Della Ch—church ... TN-4
**Mount Dell Subdivision**—pop pl ... UT-8
Mount Dempsy ... PA-2
Mount Dena Ch—church ... TX-5
Mount Denson—locale ... TN-4
Mount Denson Cem—cemetery ... TN-4
Mount Denson Cumberland Presbyterian Ch—church ... TN-4
**Mount De Sales**—pop pl ... MD-2
**Mount DeSales**—pop pl ... MD-2
Mount de Sales Acad—hist pl ... MD-2
Mount DeSales HS—school ... MD-2
Mount Desert ... ME-1
Mount Desert Island—island ... ME-1
Mount Desert Light Station—hist pl ... ME-1
Mount Desert Lookout Tower—locale ... WV-2
Mount Desert Narrows—channel ... ME-1
**Mount Desert (Somesville)**—pop pl ... ME-1
**Mount Desert (Town of)**—pop pl ... ME-1
Mount Devonshire Ch—church ... AR-4
Mount Dew Cem—cemetery ... VA-3
Mount Dexter ... MS-4
Mount Diablo ... NV-8
Mount Diablo ... OR-9
Mount Diablo Creek—stream ... CA-9
Mount Diablo HS—school ... CA-9
Mount Diablo Mine—mine ... CA-9
Mount Diablo Mine—mine ... NV-8
Mount Diablo State Park—park ... CA-9
Mount Dogas ... MH-9
Mount Dolaway Ch—church ... GA-3
**Mount Dora**—pop pl ... FL-3
**Mount Dora**—pop pl ... NM-5
Mount Dora (CCD)—cens area ... FL-3
Mount Dora HS—school ... FL-3
Mount Dora MS—school ... FL-3
Mount Dora Plaza (Shop Ctr)—locale ... FL-3
Mount Dora Public Library—building ... FL-3
Mount Dougal ... MA-1
Mount Dougal ... WY-8
Mount Dowell Ch—church ... SC-3
Mount Drewer ... MT-8
Mount Dumpling ... MA-1
Mount Dunlap ... PA-2
Mount Dyke Sch (abandoned)—school ... MO-7
Mount Eager Baptist Ch ... TN-4
Mount Eager Ch—church ... TN-4
Mount Eagle—locale ... VI-3
**Mount Eagle**—pop pl ... PA-2
Mount Eagle Ch—church ... MS-4
Mount Eagle Ch—church (2) ... VA-3
Mount Eagle Independent Baptist Ch—church ... IN-6
Mount Eagle Sch—school ... KY-4
Mount Eagle Sch—school ... VA-3
Mount Ealm Ch—church ... LA-4
Mount Eara Ch—church ... TX-5
Mount Earnest Cem—cemetery ... WV-2
Mount Earnest Ch—church ... WV-2
Mount Eary Ch—church ... WV-2
**Mount Eaton**—pop pl ... OH-6
Mount Eaton Ch—church ... TX-5
Mount Eba Lake—reservoir ... AL-4
Mount Ebal Ch—church ... IN-6
Mount Ebal Ch—church ... NC-3
Mount Ebal Ch—church ... SC-3
Mount Ebal Methodist Protestant Church—hist pl ... NC-3
Mount Ebel Ch—church ... GA-3
Mount Ebell Ch—church ... AL-4
Mount Ebell Ch—church ... GA-3
Mount Ebenezer Ch—church ... WV-2
Mount Ebiru-Mayahan ... PW-9
Mount Eble Cem—cemetery ... GA-3
Mount Ebron Ch—church ... AL-4
**Mount Echo**—pop pl (2) ... WV-2
Mount Echo Bible Institute—locale ... NY-2
Mount Echo Park—park ... OH-6
Mount Ed Ch—church ... VA-3
**Mount Eden**—pop pl ... CA-9
**Mount Eden**—pop pl ... KY-4
Mount Eden Cem—cemetery ... CA-9
Mount Eden Cem—cemetery ... IN-6
Mount Eden Cem—cemetery ... NY-2
Mount Eden Ch—church ... IN-6
Mount Eden Ch—church (3) ... KY-4
Mount Eden Ch—church ... PA-2
Mount Eden Creek—stream ... CA-9
Mount Eden HS—school ... CA-9
Mount Eden Ridge—ridge ... KY-4
Mount Eden Sch—school ... KY-4
Mount Eden Station—locale ... CA-9
**Mount Edgecombe**—pop pl ... AK-9
Mount Edgecumbe—uninc pl ... AK-9
Mount Edgecumbe Trail—trail ... AK-9
Mount Edie Ch—church ... MS-4
Mount Edin Ch ... MS-4
Mount Edwin Ch—church ... KY-4
Mount Efen Ch—church ... FL-3
Mount Eisenhower ... NH-1
Mount Elam Cem—cemetery (3) ... MS-4
Mount Elam Ch—church ... AL-4
Mount Elam Ch—church (2) ... MS-4
Mount Elam Ch—church (3) ... NC-3
Mount Elam Ch—church ... TX-5
Mount Elam Missionary Baptist Ch ... MS-4
Mount Elan Ch—church ... FL-3
Mount Eland Ch—church ... AL-4
Mount Elba—locale ... AR-4
Mount Elba Ch—church ... AR-4
Mount Elbert Ch—church ... VA-3
Mount Elbert Trail—trail ... CO-8
Mount Elden ... AZ-5
Mount Elden—uninc pl ... AZ-5
Mount Elden Little League Field—park ... AZ-5
Mount Elden Sch—school ... AZ-5
Mount Elem Ch—church ... MS-4
Mount Eleuwe ... HI-9
Mount Elgrim Ch—church ... NC-3
Mount Elim Baptist Ch ... TN-4
Mount Elim Ch—church ... TN-4
Mount Eliza—hist pl ... TX-5
Mount Elizabeth Ch—church ... MS-4
Mount Elizabeth Ch (historical)—church ... MO-7
Mount Ellemeham ... WA-9
Mount Ellen Creek—stream ... UT-8
Mount Elliott ... MI-6
Mount Elliott Cem—cemetery ... MI-6
Mount Elliott Spring—spring ... AZ-5
Mount Elliott Springs—locale ... VA-3
**Mount Ellis**—pop pl ... MT-8
Mount Ellis Acad—school ... MT-8
Mount Ellis Ch—church ... VA-3
Mount Elm Ch—church ... MS-4
Mount Elm Ch—church ... TX-5
Mount Elmira Ch—church ... KY-4
Mount Elohim Ch—church ... SC-3
Mount Elon Ch—church (3) ... SC-3
Mount Elsum ... PW-9
Mount Emblem Cem—cemetery ... IL-6
Mount Emerald and Capitol Additions Historic Residential District—hist pl ... NE-7
Mount Emily Creek—stream ... OR-9
Mount Emma—summit ... CA-9
Mount Emma Ridge—ridge ... CA-9
**Mount Emmons**—pop pl ... UT-8
Mount Emny ... OR-9
Mount Ena Ch—church ... GA-3
**Mount Energy**—pop pl ... NC-3
**Mount Energy (Energy)**—pop pl ... NC-3
Mount Energy Hist Dist—hist pl ... NC-3
Mount Enna Branch—stream ... GA-3
Mount Enna Ch—church ... GA-3
**Mount Enon**—pop pl ... FL-3
Mount Enon Cem—cemetery ... TX-5
Mount Enon Ch—church (2) ... AL-4
Mount Enon Ch—church (2) ... GA-3
Mount Enon Ch—church (2) ... SC-3
Mount Enon Ch—church ... TX-5
Mount Enon Ch (historical)—church ... AL-4
Mount Enon Church and Cemetery—hist pl ... GA-3
Mount Enon Sch—school ... MO-7
Mount Enterprise—locale ... TX-5
**Mount Enterprise**—pop pl ... TX-5
Mount Enterprise (CCD)—cens area ... TX-5
Mount Enterprise Ch—church ... TX-5
Mount Eoleus ... CO-8
Mount Eolus ... VT-1
Mount Ephraim ... MA-1
Mount Ephraim—locale ... MD-2
**Mount Ephraim**—pop pl ... NJ-2
**Mount Ephraim**—pop pl (2) ... OH-6
Mount Ephraim Ch—church ... NC-3
Mount Ephraim Ch—church ... OH-6
Mount Ephraim Ch—church ... VA-3
Mount Ephriam, Town of ... MA-1
Mount Equinox ... VT-1
Mount Era Cemetery ... AL-4
Mount Era Ch—church ... AL-4
Mount Era Methodist Ch ... AL-4
Mounterest Ranch—locale ... AZ-5
Mount Eria Ch—church ... MO-7
**Mount Erie**—pop pl ... IL-6
Mount Erie Cem—cemetery ... FL-3
Mount Erie Ch—church ... FL-3
Mount Erie Park—park ... WA-9
Mount Erie Sch—school ... WA-9
**Mount Erie (Township of)**—pop pl ... IL-6
Mount Erin Cem—cemetery ... MD-2
Mount Eron Sch (historical)—school ... MS-4
Mount Ester Ch (historical)—church ... AL-4
Mount Estes ... ID-8
Mount Esther ... CA-9
Mount Etekkueiku ... PW-9
Mount Etekkueiku—summit ... PW-9
Mount Ethel Ch—church ... GA-3
Mount Ethel Ch (historical)—church ... TN-4
**Mount Etna**—pop pl ... IN-6
**Mount Etna**—pop pl ... IA-7
**Mount Etna**—pop pl ... PA-2
Mount Etna Cem—cemetery ... IA-7
Mount Etna Ch—church ... IL-6
Mount Etna Ch—church ... IN-6
Mount Etna Park—park ... CA-9
Mount Etna Sch—school ... AR-4
Mount Etna Sch—school ... MO-7
Mount Etna State Rec Area—park ... IN-6
Mount Etta Ch—church ... TN-4
Mount Ettney Cem—cemetery ... OH-6
Mount Eunice Ch—church ... GA-3
Mount Eva Ch ... MS-4
Mount Eva Ch—church (2) ... MS-4
Mount Evans—summit ... CO-8
Mount Evans Elk Mngmt Area—park ... CO-8
Mount Evans Elk Mngmt HQ—locale ... CO-8
Mount Evans Shelter House—locale ... CO-8
Mount Evart Sch (historical)—school ... MO-7
**Mount Eve**—pop pl ... NY-2
Mount Evely ... ID-8
Mount Ever Ch—church ... MS-4
Mount Everest Ch—church ... AR-4
Mount Everet Cem—cemetery ... MS-4
Mount Everet Ch—church (2) ... MS-4
Mount Everett ... OH-6
Mount Everett Ch—church ... LA-4
Mount Everett Ch—church ... MO-7
Mount Everett Regional Sch—school ... MA-1
**Mount Evergreen**—pop pl ... TX-5
Mount Evergreen Cem ... MS-4
Mount Evergreen Cem—cemetery (2) ... IL-6
Mount Evergreen Cem—cemetery ... KS-7
Mount Evergreen Cem—cemetery ... MI-6
Mount Evergreen Cem—cemetery ... MS-4
Mount Evergreen Cem—cemetery ... NJ-2
Mount Evergreen Cem—cemetery ... TX-5
Mount Evergreen Ch—church ... MS-4
Mount Evergreen Ch—church ... VA-3
Mount Evergreen Ch (historical)—church ... MS-4
Mount Ever-Rest Memorial Park—cemetery ... MI-6
Mount Evia Ch—church ... MS-4
Mount Evon Ch—church ... MS-4
Mounte Wollaston ... MA-1
Mount Fadder ... ME-1
Mount Fagan Ranch—locale ... AZ-5
Mountfair—locale ... VA-3
Mount Fair Ch—church ... LA-4
Mount Fairview ... CO-8
Mount Fairview Ch—church ... MD-2
Mount Faith ... OR-9
Mount Fancy—locale ... VI-3
Mount Fanny Spring—spring ... OR-9
Mount Feake Cem—cemetery (2) ... MA-1
**Mount Fern**—pop pl ... NJ-2
Mount Fern Ch—church ... NJ-2
Mount Fernow ... WA-9
Mount Fernow Potholes—other ... WA-9
Mount Field Brook—stream ... NH-1
Mount Fields ... MT-8
Mount Figuration Ch—church ... SC-3
Mount Flat Ch—church ... AL-4
Mount Florence ... KS-7
**Mount Forest**—pop pl ... MI-6
Mount Forest Cem—cemetery ... IL-6
Mount Forest Cem—cemetery ... MI-6
Mount Forest Oil Field—other ... MI-6
Mount Forest Sch—school ... MI-6
Mount Forest (Township of)—civ div ... MI-6
**Mount Forest Trails**—pop pl ... OH-6
Mount Francis Trail Forty Eight—trail ... AZ-5
Mount Franklin Ch—church ... TX-5
**Mount Freedom**—pop pl ... MO-7
**Mount Freedom**—pop pl ... NJ-2
Mount Freedom Cem—cemetery ... NJ-2
Mount Freedom Ch—church ... KY-4
Mount Freedom Ch—church ... LA-4
Mount Freedom Hebrew Cem—cemetery ... NJ-2
Mount Fremont Lookout—locale ... WA-9
Mount Friendship Circuit Ch—church ... DE-2
Mount Friendship Sch—school ... DE-2
Mount Fritz ... MT-8
Mount Frizzell ... MA-1
Mount Gaarukadakku ... PW-9
Mount Gaarukagakku ... PW-9
Mount Gaines Mine—mine ... CA-9
Mount Gainor—locale ... TX-5
Mount Gale Ch—church ... AR-4
Mount Galilee Baptist Ch—church ... MS-4
Mount Galilee Ch—church ... GA-3
Mount Galilee Ch—church (3) ... MS-4
Mount Galilee Sch (historical)—school ... MS-4
**Mount Gallagher**—pop pl ... SC-3
Mount Gallant ... NC-3
Mount Gallard Ch—church ... AR-4
Mount Galled Ch—church ... NC-3
Mount Gallitzin Acad—school ... PA-2
**Mount Gallows**—pop pl ... NC-3
Mount Galogus ... PW-9
Mount Gamedo ... PW-9
Mount Gap Ch—church ... AR-4
Mount Garashiyoo ... PW-9
Mount Garfield ... MT-8
Mount Garfield Sch—school ... WV-2
Mount Garland—locale ... VA-3
**Mount Garmel**—pop pl ... MS-4
Mount Garner Cem—cemetery ... TN-4
Mount Garrison Cem—cemetery ... IN-6
**Mount Gay**—pop pl ... WV-2
**Mount Gayler**—pop pl ... AR-4
**Mount Gaylor**—pop pl ... AR-4
Mount Gay (RR name Gay)—uninc pl ... WV-2
Mount Gay-Shamrock—CDP ... WV-2
Mount Gazerine Ch—church ... VA-3
Mount Gazy Ch—church ... MS-4
Mount Genet ... AK-9
Mount George ... CO-8
**Mount George**—pop pl ... AR-4
Mount George Union Sch—school ... CA-9
Mount Gerizem Ch—church ... VA-3
Mount Gethsemane Ch—church ... VA-3
Mount Gibbes—summit ... NC-3
Mount Gibbs ... NC-3
Mount Gibraltar ... MT-8
Mount Gibson Ch—church ... MO-7
Mount Gideon Cem—cemetery ... MS-4
Mount Gideon Cem—cemetery ... TX-5
Mount Gideon Ch—church ... LA-4
Mount Gideon Ch—church ... NC-3
Mount Gideon Ch—church (2) ... TX-5
Mount Giea Ch—church ... VA-3
Mount Gilbert Cem—cemetery ... NC-3
Mount Gilbert Ch—church ... NC-3
Mount Gilboa Ch—church (2) ... KY-4
Mount Gilead—locale (3) ... KY-4
Mount Gilead—locale ... NC-3
**Mount Gilead**—pop pl (2) ... NC-3
**Mount Gilead**—pop pl ... OH-6
**Mount Gilead**—pop pl ... TN-4
Mount Gilead Baptist Ch ... AL-4
Mount Gilead Baptist Ch ... TN-4
Mount Gilead Baptist Ch—church ... TN-4
Mount Gilead Baptist Church ... MS-4
Mount Gilead Cem—cemetery (7) ... AL-4
Mount Gilead Cem—cemetery (2) ... GA-3
Mount Gilead Cem—cemetery ... IN-6
Mount Gilead Cem—cemetery ... IA-7
Mount Gilead Cem—cemetery ... KY-4
Mount Gilead Cem—cemetery ... MD-2
Mount Gilead Cem—cemetery (6) ... MS-4
Mount Gilead Cem—cemetery ... MO-7
Mount Gilead Cem—cemetery ... OH-6
Mount Gilead Cem—cemetery (3) ... TN-4
Mount Gilead Cem—cemetery ... VA-3
Mount Gilead Ch ... AL-4
Mount Gilead Ch ... MS-4
Mount Gilead Ch—church (17) ... AL-4
Mount Gilead Ch—church ... AR-4
Mount Gilead Ch—church (2) ... FL-3
Mount Gilead Ch—church (14) ... GA-3
Mount Gilead Ch—church (2) ... IL-6
Mount Gilead Ch—church (6) ... IN-6
Mount Gilead Ch—church (8) ... KY-4
Mount Gilead Ch—church ... LA-4
Mount Gilead Ch—church (6) ... MS-4
Mount Gilead Ch—church (7) ... MO-7
Mount Gilead Ch—church (10) ... NC-3
Mount Gilead Ch—church ... OH-6
Mount Gilead Ch—church (2) ... PA-2
Mount Gilead Ch—church (5) ... TN-4
Mount Gilead Ch—church ... TX-5
Mount Gilead Ch—church (5) ... VA-3
Mount Gilead Ch—church ... WV-2
Mount Gilead Ch (historical)—church ... AL-4
Mount Gilead Cumberland Presbyterian Ch ... TN-4
Mount Gilead Elem Sch—school ... NC-3
Mount Gilead (historical)—locale ... AL-4
Mount Gilead (historical)—locale ... KS-7
Mount Gilead (historical)—locale ... NC-3
**Mount Gilead (historical)**—pop pl ... TN-4
Mount Gilead Lakes—reservoir ... OH-6
Mount Gilead Lookout Tower—locale ... TN-4
Mount Gilead Methodist Church ... TN-4
Mount Gilead Post Office (historical)—building ... TN-4
Mount Gilead Primitive Baptist Ch ... MS-4
Mount Gilead Sch—school ... GA-3
Mount Gilead Sch—school ... IL-6
Mount Gilead Sch—school ... KY-4
Mount Gilead Sch (historical)—school (3) ... AL-4
Mount Gilead Sch (historical)—school (2) ... MO-7
Mount Gilead State Park—park ... OH-6
Mount Gilead (Township of)—fmr MCD ... NC-3
Mount Gilean Cem—cemetery ... AR-4
Mount Gilean Ch—church ... AR-4
Mount Gilgal Ch—church ... GA-3
Mount Gillard ... MS-4
Mount Gillard Baptist Church ... AL-4
Mount Gillard Cem—cemetery ... AL-4
Mount Gillard Cem—cemetery ... LA-4
Mount Gillard Ch—church ... AL-4
Mount Gillard Ch—church ... AR-4
Mount Gillard Ch—church (2) ... MS-4
Mount Gillard Sch—school ... KY-4
Mount Gillead Ch ... AL-4
Mount Gillead Ch—church ... AL-4
Mount Gilled Baptist Ch ... AL-4
Mount Gilled Cem—cemetery ... AL-4
Mount Gilliad Ch—church ... MS-4
Mount Gilliam Ch—church ... NC-3
Mount Gillian Cem—cemetery ... AR-4
Mount Gillian Cem—cemetery ... KS-7
Mount Gillian Cem—cemetery ... KY-4
Mount Gillian Cem—cemetery ... MS-4
Mount Gillian Ch—church ... KS-7
Mount Gillian Ch—church ... MS-4
Mount Gillian Ch—church ... MO-7
Mount Gillian Ch—church ... OK-5
Mount Gillian Ch—church ... VA-3
Mount Gillian New Site Ch—church ... VA-3
Mount Gilliard Cem—cemetery ... IN-6
Mount Gilliard Ch ... MS-4
Mount Gilliard Ch—church ... GA-3
Mount Gilliard Ch—church ... NC-3
Mount Gillie Ch—church ... MS-4
Mount Gillion Ch—church ... LA-4
Mount Gillion Church ... AL-4
**Mount Gillis**—pop pl ... AL-4
Mount Girl-Bradley Field—airport ... NC-3
Mount Giving Cem—cemetery ... MS-4
Mount Gladys ... WA-9
Mount Gleason Campground—locale ... CA-9
Mount Gleason JHS—school ... CA-9
Mount Glen Lakes—reservoir ... NJ-2
Mount Glenwood Cem—cemetery ... IL-6
Mount Glory Baptist Church ... MS-4
Mount Glory Cem—cemetery ... FL-3
Mount Glory Ch—church ... FL-3
Mount Glory Ch—church ... MS-4
Mount Glory Ridge—ridge ... NC-3
Mount Godfrey Ch—church ... AL-4
Mount Golda Cem—cemetery ... NY-2
Mount Goode ... CA-9
Mount Goode ... WA-9
Mount Gordon ... WV-2
Mount Gore ... VT-1
Mount Gospel Mission Ch (abandoned)—church ... PA-2
Mount Gospel Tabernacle—church ... PA-2
Mount Gossett Sch (historical)—school ... TN-4
**Mount Gould**—pop pl ... NC-3
Mount Gould Landing—locale ... NC-3
Mount Graham ... AZ-5
Mount Graham Golf Course—other ... AZ-5
Mount Graham Mill Site—locale ... AZ-5
Mount Graham Sawmill—locale ... AZ-5
Mount Grant ... NV-8
Mount Greek—stream ... OR-9
Mount Green Cem—cemetery ... MT-8
Mount Green Cem—cemetery ... NY-2
Mount Green Ch—church ... GA-3
Mount Greenwood ... IL-6
Mount Greenwood Cem—cemetery ... IL-6
Mount Greenwood Cem—cemetery ... PA-2
Mount Greenwood Park—park ... IL-6
Mount Greenwood Sch—school ... IL-6
Mount Gregory Sch—school ... MD-2
**Mount Gretna**—pop pl ... PA-2
Mount Gretna Borough—civil ... PA-2
**Mount Gretna Heights**—pop pl ... PA-2
Mount Greylock Ski Club—locale ... MA-1
Mount Greylock State Reservation—park ... MA-1
Mount Greylook Regional HS—school ... MA-1
Mount Grove Cem—cemetery ... CT-1
Mount Grove Ch—church (3) ... AL-4
Mount Grove Ch—church ... IL-6
Mount Grove Ch—church ... PA-2
Mount Grove Ch—church (2) ... SC-3
Mount Grove Ch—church (2) ... WV-2
Mount Grove Union Ch ... PA-2
Mount Gualo Rai ... MH-9
Mount Guillard Ch—church ... GA-3
Mount Gulian—hist pl ... NY-2
Mount Gulitel ... PW-9
Mount Gullion Ch—church ... LA-4
Mount Gurikeru-Yageru ... PW-9
Mount Guritoru ... PW-9
Mount Guyot ... NC-3
Mount Guyot ... TN-4
Mount Guyot—summit ... NC-3
Mount Hagan—summit ... OR-9
Mount Hagen ... OR-9
Mount Haid Ch—church ... WV-2
Mount Halepohaku ... HI-9
Mount Haley Ch—church ... MI-6
Mount Haley Drain—canal ... MI-6
**Mount Haley (Township of)**—pop pl ... MI-6
Mount Hall Sch—school ... ID-8
Mount Haloa ... HI-9
**Mount Hamill**—pop pl ... IA-7
Mount Hamilton ... NV-8
**Mount Hamilton (Lick Observatory)**—pop pl ... CA-9
Mount Hamilton Springs—spring ... CA-9
Mount Hammock—island ... FL-3
Mount Hanaula ... HI-9
Mount Hanlon ... CA-9
**Mount Hannah Lodge**—pop pl ... CA-9
Mount Haran Ch—church ... VA-3
Mount Harbin ... CA-9
Mount Hardison—summit ... NC-3
Mount Hardy ... NC-3
Mount Hardy—summit ... NC-3
Mount Harman Cem—cemetery ... OK-5
Mount Harmon—hist pl ... MD-2
Mount Harmon Cem—cemetery ... MS-4
Mount Harmon Cem—cemetery ... MO-7
Mount Harmon Ch ... AL-4
Mount Harmon Ch—church (2) ... AL-4
Mount Harmon Ch—church ... AR-4
Mount Harmon Ch—church ... MI-6
Mount Harmon Ch—church (2) ... MS-4
Mount Harmon Ch—church ... SC-3
Mount Harmon Ch—church (2) ... TN-4
Mount Harmon JHS—school ... UT-8
Mount Harmon Sch—school ... MO-7
Mount Harmon Sch (historical)—school ... MS-4
Mount Harmony—locale (3) ... TN-4
**Mount Harmony**—pop pl ... MD-2
**Mount Harmony**—pop pl ... TN-4
**Mount Harmony**—pop pl ... WV-2
Mount Harmony Baptist Ch ... TN-4
Mount Harmony Baptist Ch—church (2) ... TN-4
Mount Harmony Cem—cemetery ... IA-7
Mount Harmony Ch—church (2) ... AL-4
Mount Harmony Ch—church (2) ... AR-4
Mount Harmony Ch—church (3) ... GA-3
Mount Harmony Ch—church (5) ... NC-3
Mount Harmony Ch—church (2) ... SC-3
Mount Harmony Ch—church (5) ... TN-4
Mount Harmony Ch—church ... VA-3
Mount Harmony Ch—church ... WV-2
Mount Harmony Ch of Christ ... AL-4
Mount Harmony Free Will Baptist Ch ... AL-4
Mount Harmony Sch—school ... LA-4
Mount Harmony Sch—school ... TN-4
Mount Harmony Sch (historical)—school (2) ... TN-4
Mount Harmony Select Sch for Males and Females (historical)—school ... TN-4
Mount Harris—locale ... CO-8
Mount Harris Cem—cemetery ... SC-3
Mount Harris Ch—church ... SC-3
Mount Harwood ... CA-9
Mount Haupu ... HI-9
Mount Haven Ch—church ... NC-3
Mount Haven Sch—school ... TX-5
**Mounthaven Subdivision**—pop pl ... UT-8
Mount Hawley Cem—cemetery ... IL-6
Mount Hawley Country Club—other ... IL-6
Mount Hayes ... MD-2
Mount Hayes Cem—cemetery ... NH-1
Mount Hays ... MD-2
Mount Hazel Cem—cemetery ... MI-6
Mount Heaborn Ch—church ... IN-6
Mount Healthy ... PA-2
**Mount Healthy**—pop pl ... IN-6
**Mount Healthy**—pop pl ... OH-6
Mount Healthy Ch—church ... IN-6
**Mount Healthy Heights**—pop pl ... OH-6
Mount Healthy Post Office (historical)—building ... PA-2
Mount Healthy (Township of)—other ... OH-6
Mount Heaver I Ch—church ... MS-4
Mount Heaver II Ch—church ... MS-4
Mount Heaver Number 1 Ch ... MS-4
Mount Heber Cem—cemetery ... TN-4
Mount Hebo Air Force Station—military ... OR-9
Mount Hebo Campground—park ... OR-9
Mount Hebrew Ch—church ... AR-4
Mount Hebron—locale (2) ... AL-4
**Mount Hebron**—pop pl ... AL-4
**Mount Hebron**—pop pl ... CA-9
**Mount Hebron**—pop pl ... MD-2
Mount Hebron Baptist Ch ... AL-4
Mount Hebron Baptist Ch ... MS-4
Mount Hebron Baptist Ch—church (2) ... AL-4
Mount Hebron Camp Ground (historical)—locale ... TN-4
Mount Hebron Cem ... TN-4
Mount Hebron Cem—cemetery (7) ... AL-4
Mount Hebron Cem—cemetery (2) ... IN-6
Mount Hebron Cem—cemetery ... MD-2
Mount Hebron Cem—cemetery (3) ... MS-4
Mount Hebron Cem—cemetery (2) ... NJ-2
Mount Hebron Cem—cemetery ... SC-3
Mount Hebron Cem—cemetery ... TN-4
Mount Hebron Cem—cemetery ... VA-3
Mount Hebron Cem—cemetery ... WV-2
Mount Hebron Ch ... AL-4
Mount Hebron Ch ... MS-4
Mount Hebron Ch—church (15) ... AL-4
Mount Hebron Ch—church (4) ... AR-4
Mount Hebron Ch—church (2) ... GA-3
Mount Hebron Ch—church (3) ... IL-6
Mount Hebron Ch—church ... IN-6
Mount Hebron Ch—church (7) ... KY-4
Mount Hebron Ch—church ... LA-4
Mount Hebron Ch—church (6) ... MS-4
Mount Hebron Ch—church (5) ... NC-3
Mount Hebron Ch—church ... PA-2
Mount Hebron Ch—church (4) ... SC-3
Mount Hebron Ch—church (5) ... TN-4
Mount Hebron Ch—church ... TX-5
Mount Hebron Ch—church (3) ... VA-3
Mount Hebron Ch—church (3) ... WV-2
Mount Hebron Ch (historical)—church ... AL-4
Mount Hebron East Ch—church ... AL-4
Mount Hebron Freewill Baptist Ch (historical)—church ... AL-4
Mount Hebron Grammar Sch (historical)—school ... AL-4
Mount Hebron Methodist Ch ... MS-4
Mount Hebron Missionary Baptist Ch (historical)—church ... MS-4
**Mount Hebron Park**—pop pl ... VA-3
Mount Hebron Sch—school ... AL-4
Mount Hebron Sch—school ... IL-6
Mount Hebron Sch—school ... LA-4
Mount Hebron Sch—school ... NJ-2
Mount Hebron Sch—school ... WV-2
Mount Hebron Sch (historical)—school (2) ... AL-4
Mount Hebron Temperance Hall—hist pl ... SC-3
Mount Hebron West Ch—church ... AL-4
Mount Hebrow Ch—church ... IN-6
Mount Heeren Ch—church ... AL-4
Mount Height Cem—cemetery ... ME-1

**Mount Helen**—*pop pl* ... TN-4
Mount Helen Cem—*cemetery* ... TN-4
Mount Helen Ch—*church* ... GA-3
Mount Helen Ch—*church* ... TN-4
Mount Helen Childrens Home—*building* ... CA-9
Mount Helen Post Office (historical)—*building* ... TN-4
Mount Helens Ch—*church* ... MS-4
*Mount Helen United Baptist Church* ... TN-4
Mount Helix—*uninc pl* ... CA-9
Mount Helix Hosp—*hospital* ... CA-9
Mount Helix Rsvr—*reservoir* ... CA-9
Mount Helm Baptist Ch—*church* ... MS-4
Mount Helm Cem Number One—*cemetery* ... MS-4
Mount Helm Cem Number Two—*cemetery* ... MS-4
*Mount Helu* ... HI-9
*Mount Hendricks* ... CO-8
Mount Henry Lakes—*lake* ... MT-8
Mount Henry Trail—*trail* ... MT-8
*Mount Herman* ... KY-4
*Mount Herman* ... MD-2
*Mount Herman* ... NJ-2
*Mount Herman* ... WA-9
Mount Herman—*locale* ... GA-3
Mount Herman—*locale* ... NC-3
Mount Herman—*locale* ... TX-5
**Mount Herman**—*pop pl* ... KY-4
**Mount Herman**—*pop pl* ... MS-4
**Mount Herman**—*pop pl* ... NC-3
**Mount Herman**—*pop pl* ... OK-5
**Mount Herman**—*pop pl* ... PA-2
**Mount Herman**—*pop pl* (3) ... TN-4
*Mount Herman Baptist Church* ... TN-4
Mount Herman (CCD)—*cens area* ... KY-4
Mount Herman Cem—*cemetery* (2) ... AL-4
Mount Herman Cem—*cemetery* ... KS-7
Mount Herman Cem—*cemetery* ... MS-4
Mount Herman Cem—*cemetery* (2) ... OH-6
Mount Herman Cem—*cemetery* ... TN-4
Mount Herman Cem—*cemetery* ... VA-3
*Mount Herman Ch* ... NC-3
*Mount Herman Ch* ... TN-4
Mount Herman Ch—*church* (5) ... AL-4
Mount Herman Ch—*church* ... FL-3
Mount Herman Ch—*church* ... KY-4
Mount Herman Ch—*church* ... LA-4
Mount Herman Ch—*church* ... MS-4
Mount Herman Ch—*church* ... MO-7
Mount Herman Ch—*church* (10) ... NC-3
Mount Herman Ch—*church* (2) ... OH-6
Mount Herman Ch—*church* ... OK-5
Mount Herman Ch—*church* (2) ... PA-2
Mount Herman Ch—*church* (2) ... SC-3
Mount Herman Ch—*church* (5) ... TN-4
Mount Herman Ch—*church* ... TX-5
Mount Herman Ch—*church* (2) ... VA-3
Mount Herman Ch—*church* (2) ... WV-2
Mount Herman Ch (historical)—*church* ... AL-4
*Mount Herman Christian Methodist Episcopal Church* ... TN-4
Mount Herman Grange—*locale* ... CO-8
*Mount Herman Missionary Baptist Ch* ... AL-4
Mount Herman Missionary Baptist Ch—*church* ... MS-4
Mount Herman Sch—*school* ... FL-3
Mount Herman Sch—*school* ... SC-3
Mount Herman Sch—*school* ... TN-4
Mount Herman Sch (abandoned)—*school* ... MO-7
Mount Herman Sch (historical)—*school* (3) ... AL-4
Mount Herman Sch (historical)—*school* ... MO-7
Mount Herman Valley (CCD)—*cens area* ... AL-4
Mount Herman Valley Division—*civil* ... AL-4
Mount Hermel Ch—*church* ... AL-4
*Mount Hermon* ... CO-8
*Mount Hermon* ... NY-2
Mount Hermon—*church* ... DE-2
Mount Hermon—*locale* ... KY-4
Mount Hermon—*locale* ... MD-2
Mount Hermon—*locale* ... VA-3
**Mount Hermon**—*pop pl* ... CA-9
**Mount Hermon**—*pop pl* ... LA-4
**Mount Hermon**—*pop pl* ... MA-1
**Mount Hermon**—*pop pl* ... NJ-2
Mount Hermon Baptist Ch—*church* ... FL-3
*Mount Hermon Baptist Church* ... TN-4
Mount Hermon Cem—*cemetery* ... AR-4
Mount Hermon Cem—*cemetery* ... LA-4
Mount Hermon Cem—*cemetery* ... MA-1
Mount Hermon Cem—*cemetery* ... NY-2
Mount Hermon Cem—*cemetery* ... PA-2
*Mount Hermon Ch* ... AL-4
Mount Hermon Ch—*church* (2) ... AL-4
Mount Hermon Ch—*church* ... AR-4
Mount Hermon Ch—*church* ... GA-3
Mount Hermon Ch—*church* ... IN-6
Mount Hermon Ch—*church* (2) ... KY-4
Mount Hermon Ch—*church* ... MD-2
Mount Hermon Ch—*church* ... MS-4
Mount Hermon Ch—*church* (4) ... MO-7
Mount Hermon Ch—*church* (9) ... NC-3
Mount Hermon Ch—*church* ... OH-6
Mount Hermon Ch—*church* (5) ... SC-3
Mount Hermon Ch—*church* (3) ... TN-4
Mount Hermon Ch—*church* (10) ... VA-3
Mount Hermon Ch—*church* (5) ... WV-2
Mount Hermond Ch—*church* ... AL-4
Mount Hermon Female Seminary (historical)—*school* ... MS-4
*Mount Hermon Methodist Ch* ... NC-3
Mount Hermon Missionary Baptist Ch—*church* ... TN-4
Mount Hermon Sch—*school* (2) ... VA-3
Mount Hermon Sch (abandoned)—*school* ... MO-7
*Mount Hermon School* ... AL-4
**Mount Hermon (sta.)**—*pop pl* ... MA-1
**Mount Hermon Station**—*pop pl* ... MA-1
Mount Hermon (Township of)—*fmr MCD* ... NC-3
*Mount Hermon United Methodist Ch* ... TN-4
*Mount Herndon Church* ... MS-4
Mount Heron Ch—*church* ... MS-4
**Mount Heron**—*pop pl* ... VA-3
Mount Heron Ch—*church* ... TN-4
Mount Hersey—*locale* ... AR-4
Mount Hersey Cem—*cemetery* ... AR-4
Mount Hester—*locale* ... AL-4
Mount Hester Cem—*cemetery* ... AL-4
Mount Hester Ch—*church* ... AL-4
*Mount Hester Cumberland Presbyterian Ch* ... AL-4
Mount Hester Sch (historical)—*school* ... AL-4
Mount Hickory Acad (historical)—*school* ... AL-4
Mount Hickory Ch—*church* ... AL-4
Mount Higby Rsvr—*reservoir* ... CT-1
*Mount Higgins* ... WA-9
Mount High Cem—*cemetery* ... AL-4
Mount High Ch—*church* (3) ... AL-4
*Mount High Primitive Baptist Ch* ... AL-4
*Mount Hilead Church* ... AL-4
*Mount Hilgard* ... UT-8
**Mount Hillard**—*pop pl* ... AL-4
Mount Hillard Ch—*church* ... AL-4
Mount Hill Ch—*church* ... AL-4
Mount Hill Ch—*church* ... SC-3
*Mount Hillery Ch* ... AL-4
Mount Hillery Crossroads Ch—*church* ... AL-4
Mount Hilliard Ch—*church* (3) ... AL-4
*Mount Hill Missionary Ch* ... AL-4
*Mount Hilread Ch* ... AL-4
Mount Hinds—*summit* ... OK-5
Mount Hobart Ch—*church* ... WV-2
*Mount Hober Ch* ... AL-4
*Mount Hoffman* ... CA-9
*Mount Hokuula* ... HI-9
Mount Holder Ch—*church* ... GA-3
Mount Holdyke Coll—*school* ... MA-1
Mount Holiness Cem—*cemetery* ... NJ-2
*Mountholly* ... NJ-2
*Mount Holly* ... PA-2
Mount Holly—*airport* ... NJ-2
Mount Holly—*hist pl* ... MS-4
Mount Holly—*locale* ... OH-6
Mount Holly—*locale* ... SC-3
Mount Holly—*locale* ... VA-3
**Mount Holly**—*pop pl* ... AR-4
**Mount Holly**—*pop pl* ... MD-2
**Mount Holly**—*pop pl* ... NJ-2
**Mount Holly**—*pop pl* ... NC-3
**Mount Holly**—*pop pl* ... OH-6
**Mount Holly**—*pop pl* ... VT-1
Mount Holly Cem—*cemetery* ... AR-4
Mount Holly Cem—*cemetery* ... KY-4
Mount Holly Cem—*cemetery* ... LA-4
Mount Holly Cem—*cemetery* ... ME-1
Mount Holly Cem—*cemetery* ... NJ-2
Mount Holly Cem—*cemetery* ... OH-6
Mount Holly Cem—*cemetery* ... SC-3
Mount Holly Cem—*cemetery* ... TN-4
Mount Holly Cem—*cemetery* ... VA-3
Mount Holly Cemetery—*hist pl* ... AR-4
Mount Holly Ch—*church* ... AR-4
Mount Holly Ch—*church* ... KY-4
Mount Holly Ch—*church* (2) ... NC-3
Mount Holly Ch—*church* ... VA-3
Mount Holly Ch (historical)—*church* ... MS-4
Mount Holly Creek—*stream* ... VA-3
Mount Holly Hist Dist—*hist pl* ... NJ-2
Mount Holly Mausoleum—*hist pl* ... AR-4
Mount Holly Oil And Gas Field—*oilfield* ... AR-4
Mount Holly Park—*park* ... PA-2
Mount Holly Sch—*school* ... SC-3
Mount Holly Ski Area—*locale* ... UT-8
Mount Holly Speedway—*other* ... NJ-2
*Mount Holly Spring* ... PA-2
Mount Holly Spring Elem Sch—*school* ... PA-2
**Mount Holly Springs**—*pop pl* ... PA-2
Mount Holly Springs Borough—*civil* ... PA-2
Mount Holly Springs Cem—*cemetery* ... PA-2
Mount Holly Springs Lake—*reservoir* ... PA-2
Mount Holly Springs Rsvr—*reservoir* ... PA-2
**Mount Holly (Town of)**—*pop pl* ... VT-1
**Mount Holly (Township of)**—*pop pl* ... NJ-2
Mount Holmes Trail—*trail* ... WY-8
Mount Holston Ch—*church* ... TN-4
Mount Holston Sch (historical)—*school* ... TN-4
Mount Holy Ch—*church* ... OH-6
Mount Holy Ch—*church* ... VA-3
**Mount Home**—*pop pl* ... WV-2
*Mount Home Baptist Ch* ... AL-4
Mount Home Cem—*cemetery* ... MS-4
Mount Home Ch—*church* ... AL-4
Mount Home Ch—*church* ... GA-3
Mount Home Ch—*church* ... NC-3
Mount Homer—*locale* ... FL-3
Mount Homer Ch—*church* ... GA-3
**Mount Hood**—*pop pl* ... OR-9
Mount Hood Canal—*canal* ... OR-9
Mount Hood (CCD)—*cens area* ... OR-9
Mount Hood Ch—*church* ... MS-4
Mount Hood College Rsvr—*reservoir* ... OR-9
Mount Hood Community Coll—*school* ... OR-9
*Mount Hood Flat* ... OR-9
Mount Hood Flat—*flat* ... OR-9
Mount Hood Flat Sch—*school* ... OR-9
Mount Hood Golf Course—*locale* ... MA-1
Mount Hood Golf Course—*other* ... OR-9
**Mount Hood (historical)**—*pop pl* ... OR-9
Mount Hood Memorial Park—*park* ... MA-1
Mount Hood Natl For—*forest* ... OR-9
Mount Hood-Parkdale—*post sta* ... OR-9
*Mount Hood Primitive Area* ... OR-9
*Mount Hood Wild Area* ... OR-9
Mount Hood Wilderness Area—*area* ... OR-9
Mount Hood Wilderness Area—*reserve* ... OR-9
*Mount Hoolio* ... HI-9
*Mount Hope* ... AZ-5
*Mount Hope* ... KS-7
*Mounthope* ... NJ-2
*Mounthope* ... OR-9
*Mount Hope* ... PA-2
Mount Hope—*hist pl* ... MD-2
Mount Hope—*hist pl* ... MS-4
Mount Hope—*hist pl* ... SC-3
Mount Hope—*hist pl* ... VA-3
Mount Hope—*locale* ... CA-9
Mount Hope—*locale* ... MD-2
Mount Hope—*locale* ... MO-7
Mount Hope—*locale* ... NY-2
Mount Hope—*locale* (2) ... PA-2
Mount Hope—*locale* ... TN-4
Mount Hope—*locale* ... WA-9
Mount Hope—*locale* ... WV-2
**Mount Hope**—*pop pl* ... AL-4
**Mount Hope**—*pop pl* (2) ... CT-1
**Mount Hope**—*pop pl* ... KS-7
**Mount Hope**—*pop pl* ... NJ-2
**Mount Hope**—*pop pl* (2) ... NY-2
**Mount Hope**—*pop pl* ... OH-6
**Mount Hope**—*pop pl* (5) ... PA-2
**Mount Hope**—*pop pl* ... TN-4
**Mount Hope**—*pop pl* (4) ... WV-2
**Mount Hope**—*pop pl* ... WI-6
Mount Hope—*summit* ... RI-1
Mount Hope Athens Cem—*cemetery* ... IN-6
Mount Hope Ave Sch—*school* ... MI-6
Mount Hope Baptist Ch—*church* ... AL-4
Mount Hope Bay—*bay* ... MA-1
Mount Hope Bay—*bay* ... RI-1
Mount Hope Boulder Caves—*cave* ... PA-2
Mount Hope Branch—*stream* ... GA-3
Mount Hope Bridge—*hist pl* ... RI-1
Mount Hope Brook—*stream* ... NY-2
Mount Hope Camp—*locale* ... KY-4
Mount Hope (CCD)—*cens area* ... AL-4
Mount Hope Cem—*cemetery* (2) ... AL-4
Mount Hope Cem—*cemetery* (3) ... CA-9
Mount Hope Cem—*cemetery* (2) ... CT-1
Mount Hope Cem—*cemetery* ... GA-3
Mount Hope Cem—*cemetery* (12) ... IL-6
Mount Hope Cem—*cemetery* (5) ... IN-6
Mount Hope Cem—*cemetery* (8) ... IA-7
Mount Hope Cem—*cemetery* (17) ... KS-7
Mount Hope Cem—*cemetery* ... KY-4
Mount Hope Cem—*cemetery* (3) ... ME-1
Mount Hope Cem—*cemetery* (2) ... MD-2
Mount Hope Cem—*cemetery* (9) ... MA-1
Mount Hope Cem—*cemetery* (15) ... MI-6
Mount Hope Cem—*cemetery* (6) ... MN-6
Mount Hope Cem—*cemetery* (3) ... MS-4
Mount Hope Cem—*cemetery* (7) ... MO-7
Mount Hope Cem—*cemetery* (11) ... NE-7
Mount Hope Cem—*cemetery* (13) ... NY-2
Mount Hope Cem—*cemetery* (2) ... NC-3
Mount Hope Cem—*cemetery* (2) ... OH-6
Mount Hope Cem—*cemetery* (7) ... OK-5
Mount Hope Cem—*cemetery* (2) ... OR-9
Mount Hope Cem—*cemetery* (5) ... PA-2
Mount Hope Cem—*cemetery* (4) ... SD-7
Mount Hope Cem—*cemetery* (4) ... TN-4
Mount Hope Cem—*cemetery* (4) ... TX-5
Mount Hope Cem—*cemetery* (3) ... WA-9
Mount Hope Cem—*cemetery* (3) ... WV-2
Mount Hope Cem—*cemetery* (8) ... WI-6
Mount Hope Cem—*cemetery* (2) ... WY-8
Mount Hope Cemetery District—*hist pl* ... ME-1
Mount Hope Cemetery Mausoleum—*hist pl* ... SD-7
*Mount Hope Ch* ... AL-4
*Mount Hope Ch* ... TN-4
Mount Hope Ch—*church* (7) ... AL-4
Mount Hope Ch—*church* (3) ... AR-4
Mount Hope Ch—*church* ... FL-3
Mount Hope Ch—*church* (6) ... GA-3
Mount Hope Ch—*church* ... IL-6
Mount Hope Ch—*church* (3) ... IN-6
Mount Hope Ch—*church* (3) ... IA-7
Mount Hope Ch—*church* (2) ... KS-7
Mount Hope Ch—*church* (5) ... KY-4
Mount Hope Ch—*church* (3) ... LA-4
Mount Hope Ch—*church* (3) ... MD-2
Mount Hope Ch—*church* (4) ... MI-6
Mount Hope Ch—*church* (5) ... MS-4
Mount Hope Ch—*church* (6) ... MO-7
Mount Hope Ch—*church* (4) ... NC-3
Mount Hope Ch—*church* (6) ... OH-6
Mount Hope Ch—*church* (11) ... PA-2
Mount Hope Ch—*church* (3) ... SC-3
Mount Hope Ch—*church* (4) ... TN-4
Mount Hope Ch—*church* (4) ... TX-5
Mount Hope Ch—*church* (12) ... VA-3
Mount Hope Ch—*church* ... WA-9
Mount Hope Ch—*church* (5) ... WV-2
Mount Hope Chapel—*church* ... CT-1
Mount Hope Ch (historical)—*church* (2) ... AL-4
*Mount Hope Ch of Christ* ... MS-4
*Mount Hope Ch of Christ* ... TN-4
Mount Hope Christian Ch—*church* ... TN-4
Mount Hope Community Center—*locale* ... MO-7
**Mount Hope Corners**—*pop pl* ... WI-6
Mount Hope Creek—*stream* (2) ... GA-3
Mount Hope Division—*civil* ... AL-4
Mount Hope Elem Sch—*school* ... KS-7
Mount Hope Estate—*hist pl* ... PA-2
Mount Hope Farm—*hist pl* ... RI-1
*Mount Hope Freewill Baptist Church* ... AL-4
*Mount Hope High School* ... AL-4
Mount Hope (historical)—*locale* ... IA-7
**Mount Hope (historical)**—*pop pl* ... TN-4
Mount Hope Lake—*reservoir* ... NJ-2
Mount Hope Lake Dam—*dam* ... NJ-2
Mount Hope Memorial Garden—*cemetery* ... MI-6
Mount Hope Methodist Ch—*church* ... AL-4
Mount Hope Methodist Ch—*church* ... TN-4
Mount Hope Mine—*mine* ... CA-9
Mount Hope Mine—*mine* ... NJ-2
Mount Hope Mine (Inactive)—*mine* ... NV-8
Mount Hope Mineral Junction—*uninc pl* ... NJ-2
*Mount Hope Missionary Baptist Ch* ... AL-4
Mount Hope Park Cem—*cemetery* ... OH-6
Mount Hope Pet Cem—*cemetery* ... OH-6
Mount Hope Plantation House—*hist pl* ... LA-4
Mount Hope Point—*cape* ... RI-1
Mount Hope Pond—*reservoir* ... MA-1
Mount Hope Pond—*reservoir* ... NJ-2
Mount Hope Pond Dam—*dam* ... NJ-2
Mount Hope Post Office (historical)—*building* ... PA-2
Mount Hope Public Access—*park* ... IA-7
Mount Hope Ridge—*ridge* ... WI-6
Mount Hope River—*stream* ... CT-1
Mount Hope Sch—*school* ... AL-4
Mount Hope Sch—*school* (2) ... CO-8
Mount Hope Sch—*school* (2) ... IL-6
Mount Hope Sch—*school* (2) ... KS-7
Mount Hope Sch—*school* ... KY-4
Mount Hope Sch—*school* ... MD-2
Mount Hope Sch—*school* ... MA-1
Mount Hope Sch—*school* ... MI-6
Mount Hope Sch—*school* ... MN-6
Mount Hope Sch—*school* ... MO-7
Mount Hope Sch—*school* (6) ... NE-7
Mount Hope Sch—*school* ... NH-1
Mount Hope Sch—*school* (2) ... PA-2
Mount Hope Sch—*school* ... SD-7
Mount Hope Sch—*school* ... WV-2
Mount Hope Sch (abandoned)—*school* (3) ... MO-7
Mount Hope Sch (abandoned)—*school* ... PA-2
Mount Hope Sch (historical)—*school* (3) ... MO-7
Mount Hope Sch (historical)—*school* ... PA-2
Mount Hope Sch (historical)—*school* ... TN-4
Mount Hope School—*locale* ... NE-7
Mount Hope School (abandoned)—*locale* ... OR-9
Mount Hope School (Abandoned)—*locale* ... TX-5
Mount Hope Spring—*spring* ... NV-8
Mount Hope State Rec Area—*park* ... IN-6
Mount Hope Station (historical)—*locale* ... MA-1
**Mount Hope (subdivision)**—*pop pl* ... MA-1
Mount Hope Swamp—*stream* ... SC-3
Mount Hope Tank—*reservoir* ... AZ-5
**Mount Hope (Town of)**—*pop pl* ... NY-2
**Mount Hope (Town of)**—*pop pl* ... WI-6
**Mount Hope (Township of)**—*pop pl* ... IL-6
*Mount Hope Wash* ... AZ-5
Mount Hopewell Ch—*church* ... SC-3
*Mount Hopkins* ... MA-1
*Mount Hopkins* ... NY-2
Mount Horan Ch—*church* ... VA-3
Mount Horbem Ch—*church* ... FL-3
Mount Hor Ch—*church* ... SC-3
Mount Horeb—*locale* ... NJ-2
**Mount Horeb**—*pop pl* ... MS-4
**Mount Horeb**—*pop pl* ... TN-4
**Mount Horeb**—*pop pl* ... WI-6
Mount Horeb Baptist Ch—*church* ... IN-6
*Mount Horeb Baptist Church* ... MS-4
*Mount Horeb Baptist Church* ... TN-4
Mount Horeb Baptist Church—*hist pl* ... MO-7
Mount Horeb Cem—*cemetery* ... AR-4
Mount Horeb Cem—*cemetery* ... GA-3
Mount Horeb Cem—*cemetery* (3) ... MS-4
Mount Horeb Cem—*cemetery* (2) ... MO-7
Mount Horeb Cem—*cemetery* ... OH-6
Mount Horeb Cem—*cemetery* (2) ... TN-4
Mount Horeb Cem—*cemetery* ... TX-5
Mount Horeb Ch—*church* (3) ... AL-4
Mount Horeb Ch—*church* (2) ... FL-3
Mount Horeb Ch—*church* (4) ... GA-3
Mount Horeb Ch—*church* ... IL-6
Mount Horeb Ch—*church* ... IN-6
Mount Horeb Ch—*church* ... KY-4
Mount Horeb Ch—*church* (3) ... LA-4
Mount Horeb Ch—*church* (4) ... MS-4
Mount Horeb Ch—*church* (2) ... MO-7
Mount Horeb Ch—*church* ... NC-3
Mount Horeb Ch—*church* (2) ... SC-3
Mount Horeb Ch—*church* (2) ... TN-4
Mount Horeb Ch—*church* (3) ... TX-5
Mount Horeb Ch—*church* (11) ... VA-3
Mount Horeb Ch—*church* (2) ... WV-2
Mount Horeb Ch of God in Christ—*church* ... KS-7
Mount Horeb Drain—*canal* ... IN-6
Mount Horebe Ch—*church* ... TX-5
*Mount Horeb Methodist Ch* ... MS-4
Mount Horeb Missionary Baptist Ch—*church* ... MS-4
Mount Horeb Post Office (historical)—*building* ... TN-4
*Mount Horeb Presbyterian Church* ... TN-4
Mount Horeb Primitive Baptist Ch—*church* ... FL-3
Mount Horeb Sch (historical)—*school* ... MS-4
Mount Horeb Sch (historical)—*school* (2) ... TN-4
Mount Hored Sch (historical)—*school* ... AL-4
Mount Horem Ch—*church* ... MS-4
Mount Horne Ch—*church* ... FL-3
Mount Horton Ch—*church* ... MS-4
Mount Horum Ch—*church* ... GA-3
Mount Hosea Ch—*church* ... GA-3
Mount Hosey Cem—*cemetery* ... FL-3
Mount Hosey Ch—*church* ... FL-3
Mount Hosmer Park—*park* ... IA-7
**Mount Houmas**—*pop pl* ... LA-4
*Mount Hourp Church* ... AL-4
**Mount Houston**—*pop pl* ... TX-5
Mount Houston Sch—*school* ... TX-5
Mount Howard Gondola Lift—*locale* ... OR-9
*Mount Hozomeen* ... WA-9
Mount HS—*school* ... AL-4
*Mount Hualalai* ... HI-9
*Mount Hudson* ... TX-5
Mount Hulda—*locale* ... MO-7
Mount Hulda Ch—*church* ... MO-7
Mount Hulda Lookout Tower—*locale* ... MO-7
Mount Hulda State Wildfile Area—*park* ... MO-7
Mount Hull Ch—*church* ... MS-4
*Mount Humphrey* ... AZ-5
Mount Hunger—*summit* ... NY-2
Mount Hunger Sch—*school* ... VT-1
Mount Hunt Divide—*ridge* ... WY-8
*Mount Hutch* ... AZ-5
Mountian View Cem—*cemetery* ... OR-9
*Mount Ida* ... AR-4
*Mount Ida* ... KS-7
*Mount Ida* ... MS-4
*Mount Ida* ... PA-2
Mount Ida—*hist pl* ... TN-4
Mount Ida—*hist pl* ... VA-3
Mount Ida—*locale* ... AL-4
**Mount Ida**—*pop pl* ... AR-4
**Mount Ida**—*pop pl* ... VA-3
**Mount Ida**—*pop pl* ... WI-6
Mount Ida Baptist Ch—*church* ... AL-4
Mount Ida Cem—*cemetery* ... AR-4
Mount Ida Cem—*cemetery* ... NY-2
Mount Ida Ch—*church* (2) ... AL-4
Mount Ida Ch—*church* ... AR-4
Mount Ida Ch—*church* ... IA-7
**Mount Idaho**—*pop pl* ... ID-8
Mount Ida Junior Coll—*school* ... MA-1
Mount Ida Plantation (historical)—*locale* ... AL-4
**Mount Ida (subdivision)**—*pop pl* ... MA-1
**Mount Ida (Town of)**—*pop pl* ... WI-6
*Mount Idy Church* ... AL-4
*Mount Ili* ... HI-9
*Mount Iliahi* ... HI-9
Mount Independence—*hist pl* ... VT-1
**Mount Independence**—*pop pl* ... PA-2
Mountine, Bayou—*stream* ... LA-4
*Mount Inyo* ... CA-9
*Mount Io* ... HI-9
*Mount Iole* ... HI-9
*Mount Irwin* ... TX-5
Mount Irwin Cem—*cemetery* ... PA-2
Mount Isabel Cem—*cemetery* ... TN-4
Mount Isabel Ch—*church* ... TN-4
*Mount Isabell* ... WY-8
*Mount Isabell Baptist Ch* ... TN-4
*Mount Isabell Cemetery* ... TN-4
Mount Isiac Ch—*church* ... GA-3
Mount Israel Ch—*church* (2) ... AR-4
Mount Israel Ch—*church* ... MS-4
Mount Ivah Ch—*church* ... AL-4
*Mount Ivey Ch* ... AL-4
Mount Ivriah Sch—*school* ... MA-1
**Mount Ivy**—*pop pl* ... NY-2
Mount Ivy Churches—*church* ... VA-3
Mount Ivy Swamp—*swamp* ... NY-2
Mount Jacinto State Park—*park* ... CA-9
Mount Jack County Park—*park* ... PA-2
*Mount Jackson* ... IN-6
*Mount Jackson* ... OR-9
**Mount Jackson**—*pop pl* ... CA-9
**Mount Jackson**—*pop pl* ... IN-6
**Mount Jackson**—*pop pl* ... PA-2
**Mount Jackson**—*pop pl* ... VA-3
Mount Jackson Cem—*cemetery* ... IN-6
Mount Jackson Cem—*cemetery* ... PA-2
Mount Jackson Cem—*cemetery* ... VA-3
Mount Jackson Ch—*church* ... VA-3
Mount Jackson Island—*island* ... PA-2
*Mount Jackson Ridge* ... NV-8
Mount Jacob Cem—*cemetery* ... PA-2
*Mount Jefferson* ... MT-8
Mount Jefferson—*locale* ... AL-4
**Mount Jefferson**—*pop pl* ... OH-6
Mount Jefferson—*summit* ... NY-2
Mount Jefferson Ch—*church* ... NC-3
Mount Jefferson I.O.O.F. Cem—*cemetery* ... OR-9
Mount Jefferson JHS—*school* (2) ... ME-1
Mount Jefferson Lumber Company Airstrip—*airport* ... OR-9
Mount Jefferson Overlook—*locale* ... NC-3
*Mount Jefferson Primitive Area* ... OR-9
Mount Jefferson State Park—*park* ... NC-3
Mount Jefferson Wilderness Area—*reserve* ... OR-9
*Mount Jessie* ... NH-1
Mount Jessup Colliery—*building* ... PA-2
Mount Jesus Cem—*cemetery* ... KS-7
**Mount Jewett**—*pop pl* ... PA-2
Mount Jewett Borough—*civil* ... PA-2
Mount Jewett Elem Sch—*school* ... PA-2
**Mount Jordan Addition**—*pop pl* ... UT-8
Mount Jordan Ch—*church* ... MS-4
**Mount Jordan Meadows Subdivision**—*pop pl* ... UT-8
**Mount Jordan Mesa Subdivision**—*pop pl* ... UT-8
Mount Jordan MS—*school* ... UT-8
*Mount Joseph* ... UT-8
Mount Joshua Ch—*church* (2) ... SC-3
Mount Joy—*hist pl* ... PA-2
Mount Joy—*locale* ... DE-2
Mount Joy—*locale* ... IL-6
Mount Joy—*locale* ... TX-5
**Mount Joy**—*pop pl* ... IA-7
**Mount Joy**—*pop pl* ... NJ-2
**Mount Joy**—*pop pl* ... OH-6
**Mount Joy**—*pop pl* (3) ... PA-2
**Mount Joy**—*pop pl* ... TN-4
*Mount Joy Baptist Church* ... AL-4
*Mount Joy Baptist Church* ... TN-4
Mount Joy Borough—*civil* ... PA-2
Mount Joy Cave Number Five—*cave* ... PA-2
Mount Joy Cave Number One—*cave* ... PA-2
Mount Joy Cave Number Three—*cave* ... PA-2
Mount Joy Cem—*cemetery* ... AL-4
Mount Joy Cem—*cemetery* ... GA-3
Mount Joy Cem—*cemetery* ... IL-6
Mount Joy Cem—*cemetery* ... IA-7
Mount Joy Cem—*cemetery* ... MS-4
Mount Joy Cem—*cemetery* ... MO-7
Mount Joy Cem—*cemetery* ... PA-2
*Mountjoy Ch* ... PA-2
Mount Joy Ch—*church* (8) ... AL-4
Mount Joy Ch—*church* (3) ... AR-4
Mount Joy Ch—*church* ... IL-6
Mount Joy Ch—*church* ... MD-2
Mount Joy Ch—*church* ... MS-4
Mount Joy Ch—*church* ... MO-7
Mount Joy Ch—*church* ... NC-3
Mount Joy Ch—*church* (5) ... PA-2
Mount Joy Ch—*church* ... SC-3
Mount Joy Ch—*church* ... TN-4
Mount Joy Ch—*church* (2) ... VA-3
Mount Joy Ch—*church* ... WV-2
Mount Joy Church—*church* ... IN-6
Mount Joy Crossing—*locale* ... MS-4
Mount Joy Cumberland Presbyterian Ch (historical)—*church* ... MS-4
Mount Joy (historical P.O.)—*locale* ... IA-7
*Mount Joy Missionary Baptist Ch* ... AL-4
*Mount Joy Primitive Baptist Ch* ... AL-4
Mount Joy Sch—*school* ... IL-6
Mount Joy Sch (historical)—*school* ... MO-7
Mount Joy Sch (historical)—*school* ... PA-2
Mount Joy Sch (historical)—*school* ... TN-4
Mountjoy Store—*locale* ... VA-3
**Mount Joy (Township of)**—*pop pl* (2) ... PA-2
Mount Joy United Methodist Ch—*church* ... DE-2
Mount Judah Cem—*cemetery* ... NY-2
**Mount Judea**—*pop pl* ... AR-4
**Mount Juliet**—*pop pl* ... TN-4
Mount Juliet (CCD)—*cens area* ... TN-4
Mount Juliet Cem—*cemetery* ... TN-4
Mount Juliet Division—*civil* ... TN-4
Mount Juliet Elem Sch—*school* ... TN-4
Mount Juliet HS—*school* ... TN-4
Mount Juliet JHS—*school* ... TN-4
Mount Juliet Little League Park—*park* ... TN-4
Mount Juliet Training Sch (historical)—*school* ... TN-4
Mount Jupiter Trail—*trail* ... WA-9
*Mount Kaala* ... HI-9
*Mount Kabekobekushi* ... PW-9
*Mount Kali* ... HI-9
*Mount Kamanu* ... HI-9
*Mount Kamilianlul* ... PW-9
*Mount Kancamacus* ... NH-1
*Mount Kanepuu* ... HI-9
*Mount Kapaka* ... HI-9
*Mount Kapoki* ... HI-9
*Mount Kapu* ... HI-9
*Mount Kapuaa* ... HI-9
*Mount Kapuai* ... HI-9
*Mount Karukail* ... PW-9
Mount Katahdin (Township of)—*unorg* ... ME-1
*Mount Katteluel* ... PW-9
*Mount Kauhikoa* ... HI-9
*Mount Kaumakani* ... HI-9
*Mount Kaupakuhale* ... HI-9
*Mount Kearsarge North* ... NH-1
Mount Kearsarge State Park—*park* ... NH-1
Mount Kelley Cem—*cemetery* ... MI-6
Mount Kemble Home—*hist pl* ... NJ-2
Mount Kemble Lake—*reservoir* ... NJ-2
Mount Kemble Lake Dam—*dam* ... NJ-2
*Mount Kendrick* ... AZ-5
Mount Kenton Cem—*cemetery* ... KY-4
Mount Kenyon Sch—*school* ... LA-4
*Mount Kekee* ... HI-9
*Mount Keokeo* ... HI-9
*Mount Kephart* ... NC-3
*Mount Kephart* ... TN-4
Mount Kephart—*summit* ... NC-3
Mount Kineo Trail—*trail* ... NH-1
Mount Kingdom Ch—*church* ... LA-4
Mount Kingdom Ch (historical)—*church* ... MS-4
*Mount Kinneloa* ... CA-9
*Mount Kinsman* ... NH-1
Mount Kinsman Trail—*trail* ... NH-1
*Mount Kiowa* ... CO-8
**Mount Kisco**—*pop pl* ... NY-2
Mount Kisco Country Club—*other* ... NY-2
Mount Kisco (Town of)—*civ div* ... NY-2
Mount Knight—*summit* ... CA-9
*Mount Koali* ... HI-9
*Mount Kolekole* ... HI-9
*Mount Konochti* ... CA-9
*Mount Konokti* ... CA-9
Mount Koram Ch—*church* ... MS-4
*Mount Ktaadn* ... ME-1
*Mount Kukui* ... HI-9
*Mount Kuwale* ... HI-9
*Mount Lader Ch* ... MS-4
*Mount Lafayette* ... PA-2
Mount Laffee—*locale* ... PA-2
*Mount La Grange* ... MN-6
**Mount Laguna**—*pop pl* ... CA-9
Mount Laguna Sch—*school* ... CA-9
Mount Laguna United States Air Force Station—*military* ... CA-9
*Mount Lahikiola* ... HI-9
*Mount Lake* ... PA-2
Mount Lake—*lake* ... SC-3
Mount Lake—*reservoir* ... SC-3
**Mountlake Terrace**—*pop pl* ... WA-9
Mountlake Terrace HS—*school* ... WA-9
Mountlake Terrace Sch—*school* ... WA-9
Mount Laki Cem—*cemetery* ... OR-9
*Mount Lamark* ... CA-9
*Mount Lanaihale* ... HI-9
**Mount Landing**—*pop pl* ... VA-3
Mount Landing Creek—*stream* ... VA-3
Mount Langdon Shelter—*locale* ... NH-1
Mount Langham—*summit* ... IL-6
Mount Lasca Sch (historical)—*school* ... MO-7
*Mount Lassen* ... CA-9
Mount Lassen Trout Farm—*locale* ... CA-9
*Mount Lassic* ... CA-9
*Mount Lasso* ... MH-9
Mount Latham Cem—*cemetery* ... OH-6
Mount Laurel—*locale* ... VA-3
**Mount Laurel**—*pop pl* ... NJ-2
**Mount Laurel**—*pop pl* ... PA-2
Mount Laurel Cem—*cemetery* ... NJ-2
Mount Laurel Cem—*cemetery* ... PA-2
Mount Laurel Lake—*reservoir* ... NJ-2
Mount Laurel Lake Dam—*dam* ... NJ-2
Mount Laurel Park—*park* ... PA-2
Mount Laurel Sch—*school* ... VT-1
Mount Laurel State Park—*park* ... NJ-2
**Mount Laurel (Township of)**—*pop pl* ... NJ-2
Mount Lavergne Ch—*church* ... TN-4
Mount Lavergne Sch—*school* ... TN-4
Mount La View Sch—*school* ... TN-4
**Mount Lawn**—*pop pl* ... IN-6
Mount Lawn Brook—*stream* ... IN-6
Mount Lawn Cem—*cemetery* ... NC-3
Mount Lawn Cem—*cemetery* ... PA-2
Mount Lawn Cem—*cemetery* ... VA-3
Mountlawn Memorial Park—*cemetery* ... NC-3
*Mount Lawrance* ... OK-5
**Mount Lawrence**—*pop pl* ... LA-4
**Mount Lebannon Acres Subdivision**—*pop pl* ... UT-8
Mount Lebannon Baptist Ch—*church* ... TN-4
*Mount Lebanon* ... NH-1
Mount Lebanon—*locale* ... AL-4
Mount Lebanon—*locale* ... KY-4
Mount Lebanon—*locale* (2) ... TN-4
**Mount Lebanon**—*pop pl* ... LA-4
**Mount Lebanon**—*pop pl* ... NJ-2
**Mount Lebanon**—*pop pl* ... PA-2
**Mount Lebanon**—*pop pl* ... TN-4
Mount Lebanon Baptist Ch—*church* ... IN-6
*Mount Lebanon Baptist Church* ... AL-4
*Mount Lebanon Baptist Church* ... TN-4
Mount Lebanon Baptist Church—*hist pl* ... LA-4
Mount Lebanon Brook—*stream* ... MA-1
Mount Lebanon Cem—*cemetery* ... AL-4
Mount Lebanon Cem—*cemetery* ... IN-6
Mount Lebanon Cem—*cemetery* ... LA-4
Mount Lebanon Cem—*cemetery* (2) ... MO-7
Mount Lebanon Cem—*cemetery* (2) ... NJ-2
Mount Lebanon Cem—*cemetery* ... NY-2
Mount Lebanon Cem—*cemetery* ... OH-6
Mount Lebanon Cem—*cemetery* (3) ... PA-2
Mount Lebanon Cem—*cemetery* ... SC-3
Mount Lebanon Cem—*cemetery* (5) ... TN-4
Mount Lebanon Cem—*cemetery* ... VA-3
*Mount Lebanon Ch* ... AL-4
*Mount Lebanon Ch* ... TN-4
Mount Lebanon Ch—*church* (5) ... AL-4
Mount Lebanon Ch—*church* (2) ... AR-4
Mount Lebanon Ch—*church* ... DE-2
Mount Lebanon Ch—*church* (2) ... GA-3
Mount Lebanon Ch—*church* (6) ... IN-6
Mount Lebanon Ch—*church* (5) ... KY-4
Mount Lebanon Ch—*church* (2) ... LA-4
Mount Lebanon Ch—*church* ... MO-7
Mount Lebanon Ch—*church* (5) ... NC-3
Mount Lebanon Ch—*church* ... PA-2
Mount Lebanon Ch—*church* (6) ... SC-3
Mount Lebanon Ch—*church* (8) ... TN-4
Mount Lebanon Ch—*church* (3) ... TX-5
Mount Lebanon Ch—*church* (9) ... VA-3
Mount Lebanon Ch—*church* (3) ... WV-2

Mount Pleasant Powerplant—*other* ... UT-8
*Mount Pleasant Primitive Baptist Church* ... AL-4
Mount Pleasant Public Library—*hist pl* ... IA-7
Mount Pleasant Public Schools—*school* ... AR-4
Mount Pleasant Quarry—*mine* ... TN-4
Mount Pleasant Ridge—*ridge* ... IN-6
Mount Pleasant Rsvr—*reservoir* ... PA-2
*Mount Pleasant Sch* ... AL-4
*Mount Pleasant Sch* ... MO-7
Mount Pleasant Sch—*hist pl* ... MO-7
Mount Pleasant Sch—*school* (3) ... AL-4
Mount Pleasant Sch—*school* (2) ... AR-4
Mount Pleasant Sch—*school* ... CA-9
Mount Pleasant Sch—*school* ... CO-8
Mount Pleasant Sch—*school* ... FL-3
Mount Pleasant Sch—*school* ... GA-3
Mount Pleasant Sch—*school* (11) ... IL-6
Mount Pleasant Sch—*school* ... KS-7
Mount Pleasant Sch—*school* (2) ... KY-4
Mount Pleasant Sch—*school* ... LA-4
Mount Pleasant Sch—*school* (2) ... MA-1
Mount Pleasant Sch—*school* ... MI-6
Mount Pleasant Sch—*school* (6) ... MO-7
Mount Pleasant Sch—*school* (5) ... NE-7
Mount Pleasant Sch—*school* ... NH-1
Mount Pleasant Sch—*school* ... NJ-2
Mount Pleasant Sch—*school* ... NY-2
Mount Pleasant Sch—*school* ... OH-6
Mount Pleasant Sch—*school* ... OR-9
Mount Pleasant Sch—*school* (5) ... PA-2
Mount Pleasant Sch—*school* ... SD-7
Mount Pleasant Sch—*school* (6) ... TN-4
Mount Pleasant Sch—*school* (3) ... TX-5
Mount Pleasant Sch—*school* ... UT-8
Mount Pleasant Sch—*school* ... VT-1
Mount Pleasant Sch—*school* (3) ... VA-3
Mount Pleasant Sch—*school* ... WV-2
Mount Pleasant Sch—*school* ... WI-6
Mount Pleasant Sch (abandoned)—*school* (5) ... MO-7
Mount Pleasant Sch (abandoned)—*school* (8) ... PA-2
Mount Pleasant Sch (historical)—*school* (5) ... AL-4
Mount Pleasant Sch (historical)—*school* (4) ... MS-4
Mount Pleasant Sch (historical)—*school* (7) ... MO-7
Mount Pleasant Sch (historical)—*school* (2) ... PA-2
Mount Pleasant Sch (historical)—*school* (2) ... TN-4
Mount Pleasant Sch Number 32 (historical)—*school* ... SD-7
Mount Pleasant School (abandoned)—*locale* ... MO-7
Mount Pleasant Schoolhouse (abandoned)—*school* ... PA-2
Mount Pleasant-Scottdale Airp—*airport* ... PA-2
Mount Pleasant Ski Resort—*locale* ... PA-2
Mount Pleasant Spiritual Ch—*church* ... AL-4
**Mount Pleasant (sta.) (Mount Pleasant Cemetery)**—*pop pl* ... NY-2
Mount Pleasant State Public Shooting Area—*park* ... SD-7
Mount Pleasant Station (historical)—*locale* ... MA-1
**Mount Pleasant (Town of)**—*pop pl* ... NY-2
**Mount Pleasant (Town of)**—*pop pl* (2) . WI-6
Mount Pleasant Township—*civil* (4) ... MO-7
**Mount Pleasant Township**—*pop pl* (2) .. KS-7
**Mount Pleasant Township**—*pop pl* ... SD-7
Mount Pleasant (Township of)—*civ div* ... IL-6
Mount Pleasant (Township of)—*civ div* ... IN-6
Mount Pleasant (Township of)—*civ div* ... MN-6
Mount Pleasant (Township of)—*civ div* ... OH-6
Mount Pleasant (Township of)—*fmr MCD* (2) ... AR-4
**Mount Pleasant (Township of)**—*pop pl* (5) ... PA-2
Mount Pleasant Trail—*trail* ... NH-1
**Mount Pleasant (trailer park)**—*pop pl* . DE-2
Mount Pleasant United Methodist Ch—*church* ... DE-2
Mount Pleasant United Methodist Ch—*church* ... FL-3
*Mount Pleasant United Methodist Church* ... MS-4
Mount Pleasant Wharf (historical)—*locale* . NC-3
**Mount Plymouth**—*pop pl* ... FL-3
Mount Plymouth Ch—*church* ... DE-2
Mount Plymouth Lake—*lake* ... FL-3
**Mount Plymouth Lakes**—*pop pl* ... FL-3
**Mount Pocono**—*pop pl* ... PA-2
Mount Pocono Borough—*civil* ... PA-2
Mount Pocono Golf Course—*locale* ... PA-2
Mount Pocono Overlook—*locale* ... PA-2
*Mount Pohoula* ... HI-9
Mount Poland Ch—*church* ... KY-4
**Mount Polk**—*pop pl* ... AL-4
*Mount Pomeroy* ... MA-1
Mount Poole Ch—*church* ... VA-3
*Mount Porcupine* ... MI-6
*Mount Posgah* ... PA-2
*Mount Poso Oil Field* ... CA-9
Mount Powel Ch—*church* ... AL-4
*Mount Powell* ... MT-8
*Mount Powell Ch* ... AL-4
Mount Powell Sch (historical)—*school* ... AL-4
Mount Prairie Ch—*church* ... MO-7
Mount Prairie Ch—*church* ... TX-5
Mount Prairie Hollow—*valley* ... MO-7
Mount Precious Blood Sch—*school* ... NY-2
*Mount Preuss* ... ID-8
**Mount Princeton**—*pop pl* ... CO-8
Mount Princeton Hot Springs—*locale* ... CO-8
*Mount Prong* ... SC-3
Mount Prong Creek—*stream* ... SC-3
*Mount Prospect* ... IN-6
*Mount Prospect* ... MA-1
Mount Prospect—*hist pl* ... NC-3
**Mount Prospect**—*pop pl* ... IL-6
Mount Prospect Cem—*cemetery* ... ME-1
Mount Prospect Cem—*cemetery* (2) ... MA-1
Mount Prospect Cem—*cemetery* ... NJ-2
Mount Prospect Cem—*cemetery* ... NY-2
Mount Prospect Cem—*cemetery* ... SC-3
Mount Prospect Cem—*cemetery* ... TX-5
Mount Prospect Ch—*church* (2) ... AL-4
Mount Prospect Ch—*church* ... AR-4
Mount Prospect Ch—*church* ... GA-3
Mount Prospect Ch—*church* ... MD-2
Mount Prospect Ch—*church* ... MS-4
Mount Prospect Ch—*church* ... PA-2
Mount Prospect Ch—*church* (3) ... SC-3
Mount Prospect Ch—*church* ... TX-5
Mount Prospect Ch—*church* ... WV-2
Mount Prospect Country Club—*other* ... IL-6
*Mount Prospect Gardens* ... IL-6
Mount Prospect Sch—*school* ... TX-5
Mount Prospect Shop Ctr—*locale* ... IL-6
**Mount Prosper**—*pop pl* ... NY-2
*Mount Providence Baptist Ch* ... MS-4
Mount Providence Ch—*church* ... PA-2
Mount Psyam Cem—*cemetery* ... AR-4
**Mount Pulaski**—*pop pl* ... IL-6
Mount Pulaski Courthouse—*hist pl* ... IL-6
Mount Pulaski (Township of)—*civ div* ... IL-6
Mount Pullen Ch—*church* ... GA-3
*Mount Putnam* ... ID-8
*Mount Puualii* ... HI-9
*Mount Puukoa* ... HI-9
*Mount Quabbin* ... MA-1
Mount Raha Ch—*church* ... FL-3
Mountrail County—*civil* ... ND-7
Mountrail County Courthouse—*hist pl* ... ND-7
**Mountrail Township**—*pop pl* ... ND-7
**Mount Rainier**—*pop pl* ... MD-2
Mount Rainier (CCD)—*cens area* ... WA-9
Mount Rainier JHS—*school* ... MD-2
Mount Rainier Natl Park—*park* ... WA-9
Mount Rainier Ordnance Depot—*other* ... WA-9
Mount Rainier Sch—*school* ... MD-2
Mount Ramoth Ch—*church* ... AL-4
Mount Rascal—*summit* ... NY-2
*Mount Rasmussen* ... AK-9
Mount Rayburne—*summit* ... AZ-5
Mount Raymond Camp—*locale* ... CA-9
Mount Ray Trail—*trail* ... OR-9
**Mount Read**—*pop pl* ... NY-2
*Mount Red Owl* ... MT-8
Mount Regan Sch—*school* ... IL-6
*Mount Regis* ... NC-3
*Mount Remian* ... PW-9
**Mount Rena**—*pop pl* ... SC-3
Mount Rena Ch—*church* ... NC-3
Mount Renia Cem—*cemetery* ... AR-4
Mount Repose—*hist pl* ... MS-4
**Mount Repose**—*pop pl* ... OH-6
Mount Repose Cem—*cemetery* (2) ... ME-1
Mount Repose Cem—*cemetery* ... NY-2
Mount Repose Cem—*cemetery* ... WI-6
Mount Repose Ch—*church* ... OH-6
Mount Reserve Ch (historical)—*church* ... TN-4
Mount Rest Cem—*cemetery* (2) ... IL-6
Mount Rest Cem—*cemetery* (3) ... ME-1
Mount Rest Cem—*cemetery* ... MD-2
Mount Rest Cem—*cemetery* ... MI-6
Mount Rest Cem—*cemetery* ... NJ-2
Mount Ricca Sch (historical)—*school* ... MS-4
*Mount Richie* ... CO-8
Mount Richmond Cem—*cemetery* ... NY-2
Mount Ridge Ch—*church* ... GA-3
Mount Ridge Ch—*church* ... TX-5
*Mount Riga* ... CT-1
Mount Riga—*locale* ... NY-2
Mount Riga State Park—*park* ... CT-1
*Mount Rige Brook* ... CT-1
Mount Riley—*locale* ... NM-5
Mount Riley—*summit* ... NM-5
Mount Roberts Ch—*church* ... KY-4
Mount Roberts Trail—*trail* ... AK-9
*Mount Rock* ... PA-2
**Mount Rock**—*pop pl* (2) ... PA-2
**Mountrock**—*pop pl* ... PA-2
**Mount Rock**—*pop pl* ... PA-2
Mount Rock Cem—*cemetery* ... PA-2
Mount Rock Ch—*church* ... VA-3
Mount Rock Sch—*school* ... PA-2
Mount Rock Spring—*spring* ... PA-2
Mount Rock Spring Creek—*stream* ... PA-2
*Mount Roe Church* ... MS-4
Mount Roepstorff and Southgate Farm—*locale* ... VI-3
Mount Roe Sch (historical)—*school* ... MS-4
*Mount Rogers* ... MT-8
Mount Rogers Sch—*school* ... VA-3
Mount Rona Ch—*church* (2) ... SC-3
Mount Rona Sch—*school* ... SC-3
Mount Roosevelt State For—*forest* ... TN-4
*Mount Rosa Ch* ... AL-4
*Mount Rosalie* ... CO-8
Mount Rose—*locale* ... NC-3
**Mount Rose**—*pop pl* ... NJ-2
**Mount Rose**—*pop pl* ... NC-3
Mount Rose—*summit* ... OR-9
Mount Rosebrook Trail—*trail* ... NH-1
Mount Rose Campground—*locale* ... NV-8
Mount Rose Cem—*cemetery* ... PA-2
Mount Rose Cem—*cemetery* ... WV-2
Mount Rose Center Elem Sch (abandoned)—*school* ... PA-2
*Mount Rose Ch* ... AL-4
Mount Rose Ch—*church* ... AL-4
Mount Rose Ch—*church* (2) ... MS-4
Mount Rose Ch—*church* (3) ... TX-5
Mount Rose Elem Sch—*hist pl* ... NV-8
Mount Rose Elem Sch (abandoned)—*school* ... PA-2
Mount Rose Hosp—*hospital* ... MO-7
Mount Rose HS (historical)—*school* ... AL-4
Mount Rose JHS (abandoned)—*school* ... PA-2
Mount Rose Memorial Park—*park* ... MO-7
Mount Rose Sch—*school* ... MS-4
Mount Rose Sch—*school* ... MO-7
Mount Rose Sch—*school* ... NV-8
Mount Rose Sch—*school* ... ND-7
Mount Rose Sch (historical)—*school* ... MS-4
Mount Rose Substation—*locale* ... NV-8
Mount Rose Summit—*gap* ... NV-8
**Mount Rose Township**—*pop pl* ... ND-7
Mount Rose Trail—*trail* ... CA-9
Mount Rose Trail (Pack)—*trail* ... NV-8
Mount Rosies Ch—*church* ... MS-4
**Mount Ross**—*pop pl* ... NY-2
Mount Ross Ch—*church* ... AL-4
*Mount Roszell* ... AL-4
*Mount Roszell Post Office* ... AL-4
Mount Rouell Ch—*church* ... SC-3
*Mount Rouge* ... NY-2
*Mount Row Ch* ... AL-4
*Mount Royal* ... MN-6
Mount Royal—*hist pl* ... FL-3
**Mount Royal**—*pop pl* ... FL-3
**Mount Royal**—*pop pl* ... NJ-2
**Mount Royal**—*pop pl* ... PA-2
Mount Royal—*summit* ... NY-2
Mount Royal—*uninc pl* ... MD-2
Mount Royal Cem—*cemetery* ... PA-2
Mount Royal Mine—*mine* ... NM-5
Mount Royal Station—*hist pl* ... MD-2
Mount Royal Windmill—*locale* ... NM-5
*Mount Royce* ... CA-9
**Mount Rozell**—*pop pl* ... AL-4
Mount Rozell Post Office (historical)—*building* ... AL-4
Mount Rozell Sch—*school* ... AL-4
Mount Rubidoux Park—*park* ... CA-9
*Mount Ruger* ... MT-8
Mount Ruhama Ch—*church* ... NC-3
Mount Run—*stream* ... IN-6
Mount Run—*stream* ... PA-2
Mount Run—*stream* (2) ... WV-2
Mount Rupert Ch—*church* ... WV-2
Mount Rush—*locale* ... VA-3
Mount Rushmore—*unorg reg* ... SD-7
Mount Rushmore Memorial—*locale* ... SD-7
Mount Rushmore Natl Memorial—*hist pl* ... SD-7
Mount Rushmore Natl Memorial—*park* (2) ... SD-7
Mount Ruth Cove—*basin* ... OR-9
*Mounts* ... VA-3
**Mounts**—*pop pl* (2) ... IN-6
Mount Sacred Heart Convent—*church* ... CT-1
Mount Sacred Heart Schools—*school* ... TX-5
Mount Sainai Ch—*church* ... NC-3
*Mount Sainai Church* ... AL-4
Mount Saint Agnes Coll—*school* ... MD-2
Mount Saint Alphonsus Seminary—*school* . NY-2
Mount Saint Andrews (Home For Aged)—*building* ... NJ-2
Mount Saint Benedict Acad—*school* ... MN-6
Mount Saint Benedict Cem—*cemetery* ... CT-1
Mount Saint Bernard Seminary—*school* ... IA-7
Mount Saint Ch—*church* ... NC-3
Mount Saint Charles Ranch—*locale* ... WA-9
Mount Saint Clare Coll—*school* ... IA-7
Mount Saint Clements Coll—*school* ... MO-7
Mount Saint Florence Sch—*school* ... NY-2
Mount Saint Frances Lake—*reservoir* ... IN-6
Mount Saint Frances Lake Dam—*dam* ... IN-6
Mount Saint Francis—*church* ... CO-8
Mount Saint Francis Ch—*church* ... NY-2
Mount Saint Francis Chapel—*church* ... NY-2
Mount Saint Francis Convent—*church* ... IL-6
Mount Saint Francis Sch—*school* ... NJ-2
Mount Saint Francis Seminary—*school* ... IN-6
Mount Saint Gertrude Acad—*school* ... CO-8
*Mount Saint Helens Crater* ... WA-9
Mount Saint James—*uninc pl* ... MA-1
Mount Saint James Cem—*cemetery* ... CT-1
**Mount Saint John**—*pop pl* ... OH-6
Mount Saint Joseph—*post sta* ... OH-6
Mount Saint Joseph Acad—*school* ... VT-1
Mount Saint Joseph Acad (Maple Mount P O)—*school* ... KY-4
Mount Saint Joseph Cem—*cemetery* ... VT-1
Mount Saint Joseph Childrens Home—*building* ... IL-6
**Mount Saint Joseph College**—*pop pl* ... RI-1
Mount Saint Joseph Convent—*church* ... WV-2
Mount Saint Joseph Home—*building* ... IL-6
Mount Saint Josephs Acad—*school* ... MA-1
Mount Saint Josephs Acad—*school* ... NY-2
Mount Saint Joseph Sch—*school* ... CT-1
Mount Saint Josephs Coll—*school* ... MD-2
Mount Saint Josephs Convent—*school* ... OH-6
Mount Saint Josephs Convent Ch—*church* .. PA-2
Mount Saint Joseph Seminary—*church* ... CA-9
Mount Saint Lawrence Novitiate—*school* .. MA-1
Mount Saint Macrina Acad—*school* ... PA-2
Mount Saint Mark Cem—*cemetery* ... ND-7
Mount Saint Mary Acad—*school* ... AR-4
Mount Saint Mary Acad—*school* ... IL-6
Mount Saint Mary Cem—*cemetery* ... NV-8
Mount Saint Mary Coll—*school* ... NH-1
Mount Saint Marys Abbey—*church* ... MA-1
Mount Saint Marys Acad—*school* ... CA-9
Mount Saint Marys Acad—*school* ... MA-1
Mount Saint Marys Acad—*school* ... NJ-2
Mount Saint Marys Acad—*school* (2) ... NY-2
Mount Saint Marys Cem—*cemetery* ... MO-7
Mount Saint Marys Coll—*school* (2) ... CA-9
Mount Saint Marys Coll—*school* ... MD-2
Mount Saint Marys Hosp—*hospital* ... OH-6
Mount Saint Marys Sch—*school* ... NH-1
Mount Saint Marys Seminary—*church* ... OH-6
Mount Saint Marys Seminary—*school* ... NH-1
Mount Saint Michael Cem—*cemetery* ... WA-9
Mount Saint Michael Sch—*school* ... TX-5
Mount Saint Michael Scholasticate—*school* ... WA-9
Mount Saint Michaels Sch—*school* ... NY-2
Mount Saint Peters Cem—*cemetery* ... CT-1
*Mount Saint Vrain* ... CO-8
*Mount Salem* ... OR-9
Mount Salem—*locale* ... NJ-2
**Mount Salem**—*pop pl* ... KY-4
**Mount Salem**—*pop pl* ... NJ-2
*Mount Salem Baptist Ch* ... MS-4
Mount Salem Baptist Meetinghouse—*hist pl* ... VA-3
Mount Salem Cem—*cemetery* ... IN-6
Mount Salem Cem—*cemetery* ... LA-4
Mount Salem Cem—*cemetery* ... OH-6
*Mount Salem Ch* ... MS-4
Mount Salem Ch—*church* ... AR-4
Mount Salem Ch—*church* ... DE-2
Mount Salem Ch—*church* ... FL-3
Mount Salem Ch—*church* (3) ... GA-3
Mount Salem Ch—*church* ... KY-4
Mount Salem Ch—*church* ... LA-4
Mount Salem Ch—*church* (6) ... MS-4
Mount Salem Ch—*church* (6) ... MO-7
Mount Salem Ch—*church* ... NJ-2
Mount Salem Ch—*church* ... PA-2
Mount Salem Ch—*church* ... SC-3
Mount Salem Ch—*church* ... TX-5
Mount Salem Ch—*church* (5) ... VA-3
Mount Salem Ch—*church* ... WV-2
Mount Salem Ch (historical)—*church* ... MS-4
Mount Salem Methodist Ch—*church* ... DE-2
Mount Salem Methodist Episcopal Church—*hist pl* ... NJ-2
Mount Salem Sch—*school* ... MS-4
Mount Salem School (abandoned)—*locale* ... MO-7
Mount Salem United African Methodist Episcopal Ch—*church* ... DE-2
*Mount Salor* ... NV-8
*Mount Salus* ... MS-4
Mount Salus Christian Day Sch—*school* ... MS-4
Mount Salus Presbyterian Ch—*church* ... MS-4
Mount Samuel Ch—*church* ... MS-4
Mount San Antonio Junior Coll—*school* ... CA-9
**Mount San Antonio (Mount San Antonio Junior College)**—*pop pl* ... CA-9
*Mount San Georgiano* ... CA-9
*Mount San Gorgonia* ... CA-9
*Mount San Gorgonio* ... CA-9
*Mount Sanhedrin* ... CA-9
Mount San Jacinto State Park—*park* ... CA-9
Mount San Rafael Hosp—*hospital* ... CO-8
Mount Sarah Ch—*church* ... WV-2
Mount Sariah Ch—*church* ... LA-4
Mount Sarver Ball Field—*park* ... WV-2
Mount Savage—*locale* ... KY-4
**Mount Savage**—*pop pl* ... MD-2
Mount Savage Hist Dist—*hist pl* ... MD-2
Mount Savage Junction—*locale* ... MD-2
Mount Saviour Monastery—*church* ... NY-2
*Mount Sawtell* ... ID-8
*Mount Sayler* ... NV-8
Mounts Branch—*stream* ... OH-6
Mounts Cem—*cemetery* ... OH-6
Mounts Cem—*cemetery* ... VA-3
Mounts Cem—*cemetery* (3) ... WV-2
Mounts Cemeteries—*cemetery* ... WV-2
Mount Sch—*school* ... MI-6
Mount Sch—*school* ... TX-5
*Mount Scholastica Academy* ... KS-7
Mount Scilla Ch—*church* (2) ... AL-4
Mount Scilla Sch—*school* ... AL-4
*Mount Scillo Church* ... AL-4
**Mount Scott**—*pop pl* ... OK-5
Mount Scott—*summit* ... OK-5
Mount Scott Camp Grounds—*locale* ... OK-5
Mount Scott Cem—*cemetery* ... OK-5
Mount Scott Comache Mission—*church* ... OK-5
Mount Scott Creek—*stream* ... OR-9
**Mount Scott (historical)**—*pop pl* ... OR-9
Mount Scott Kiowa Mission—*church* ... OK-5
Mount Scott Park—*park* ... OR-9
Mount Scotts Boy—*summit* ... OK-5
Mount Scott Trail—*trail* ... OR-9
Mounts Creek—*stream* ... NY-2
Mounts Creek—*stream* ... PA-2
Mounts Creek—*stream* ... WA-9
Mounts Creek Lake—*lake* ... NY-2
Mounts Cross Roads Post Office (historical)—*building* ... TN-4
Mount Seal Ch—*church* ... SC-3
**Mount Selman**—*pop pl* ... TX-5
Mount Selman (CCD)—*cens area* ... TX-5
Mount Selman Speed Bowl—*other* ... TX-5
Mount Senario Coll—*school* ... WI-6
*Mount Seneca* ... VT-1
*Mount Seneca Howland* ... AZ-5
*Mount Senord Church* ... TX-5
Mount Senore Baptist Ch—*church* ... TX-5
Mount Sequoyah—*summit* ... NC-3
Mount Serene Cem—*cemetery* ... AL-4
*Mount Seven* ... CO-8
Mount Shade Church—*school* ... AL-4
*Mount Shader* ... NV-8
*Mount Shador* ... NV-8
Mount Shady Ch—*church* ... AL-4
Mount Shady Ch—*church* (2) ... GA-3
*Mount Shady Methodist Ch* ... AL-4
Mount Sharon—*locale* ... AL-4
Mount Sharon Cem—*cemetery* ... PA-2
Mount Sharon Cem—*cemetery* ... TN-4
*Mount Sharon Cemetery* ... AL-4
Mount Sharon Ch—*church* ... KY-4
Mount Sharon Ch—*church* ... LA-4
Mount Sharon Ch—*church* ... WV-2
Mount Sharon Cumberland Presbyterian Ch—*church* ... TN-4
**Mount Sharp**—*pop pl* ... TX-5
Mount Sharp Cem—*cemetery* ... TX-5
**Mount Shasta**—*pop pl* ... CA-9
Mount Shasta (CCD)—*cens area* ... CA-9
Mount Shasta Nursery—*other* ... CA-9
Mount Shasta Woods—*locale* ... CA-9
*Mount Shasty* ... OR-9
*Mount Shatterack* ... MA-1
*Mount Shavano* ... CO-8
Mount Shavery Ch—*church* ... AR-4
Mount Sheba Ch—*church* ... NC-3
Mount Sheba Ch (historical)—*church* ... AL-4
*Mount Sheep* ... SD-7
*Mount Shellrock* ... OR-9
Mount Shepherd Camp—*locale* ... NC-3
Mount Shepherd Ch—*church* ... NC-3
Mount Shepherd Pottery Site—*hist pl* ... NC-3
Mount Sheridan Trail—*trail* ... WY-8
*Mount Sherman* ... ID-8
Mount Sherman—*locale* ... AR-4
**Mount Sherman**—*pop pl* ... KY-4
Mount Sherman—*summit* ... OK-5
Mount Sherman Cem—*cemetery* ... AR-4
Mount Sherman Ch—*church* ... KY-4
*Mount Shideler* ... WY-8
Mount Shiloh Ch—*church* ... AL-4
Mount Shiloh Ch—*church* ... MS-4
Mount Shiloh Ch—*church* ... NC-3
Mount Shiloh Ch—*church* ... PA-2
Mount Shiloh Ch—*church* (2) ... VA-3
Mount Shinn Lake—*lake* ... CA-9
**Mount Shira**—*pop pl* ... MO-7
Mount Shira Elk River Public Access Area—*locale* ... MO-7
Mount Siani Ch—*church* ... MS-4
**Mount Sidney**—*pop pl* ... VA-3
Mount Sidney Cem—*cemetery* ... KS-7
**Mount Signal**—*pop pl* ... CA-9
Mount Signal Cem—*cemetery* ... AL-4
Mount Signal Ch—*church* ... AL-4
Mount Signal Drain—*canal* ... CA-9
Mount Signal Drain Four—*canal* ... CA-9
Mount Signal Drain One—*canal* ... CA-9
Mount Signal Drain One-A—*canal* ... CA-9
Mount Signal Drain Three—*canal* ... CA-9
Mount Signal Sch—*school* ... CA-9
Mount Si Golf Course—*other* ... WA-9
Mount Si HS—*school* ... WA-9
Mount Silah Ch—*church* ... AL-4
Mount Simon Baptist Ch (historical)—*church* ... AL-4
Mount Simon Park—*park* ... WI-6
Mount Sina Ch—*church* ... SC-3
Mount Sinai—*locale* ... OH-6
Mount Sinai—*locale* ... TN-4
**Mount Sinai**—*pop pl* (2) ... AL-4
**Mount Sinai**—*pop pl* ... IN-6
**Mount Sinai**—*pop pl* ... LA-4
**Mount Sinai**—*pop pl* ... NY-2
*Mount Sinai Baptist Ch* ... AL-4
*Mount Sinai Baptist Ch* ... MS-4
Mount Sinai Baptist Ch—*church* ... AL-4
Mount Sinai Baptist Ch—*church* ... FL-3
Mount Sinai Baptist Ch—*church* (2) ... MS-4
Mount Sinai Baptist Ch (historical)—*church* ... AL-4
*Mount Sinai Baptist Church* ... TN-4
*Mount Sinai Beach* ... NY-2
Mount Sinai Branch—*stream* ... FL-3
Mount Sinai Cem—*cemetery* (2) ... AL-4
Mount Sinai Cem—*cemetery* ... FL-3
Mount Sinai Cem—*cemetery* (2) ... GA-3
Mount Sinai Cem—*cemetery* ... IN-6
Mount Sinai Cem—*cemetery* ... ME-1
Mount Sinai Cem—*cemetery* ... MD-2
Mount Sinai Cem—*cemetery* ... MI-6
Mount Sinai Cem—*cemetery* (4) ... MS-4
Mount Sinai Cem—*cemetery* ... MO-7
Mount Sinai Cem—*cemetery* (2) ... NE-7
Mount Sinai Cem—*cemetery* (2) ... NJ-2
Mount Sinai Cem—*cemetery* ... NY-2
Mount Sinai Cem—*cemetery* ... NC-3
Mount Sinai Cem—*cemetery* ... PA-2
Mount Sinai Cem—*cemetery* ... SC-3
Mount Sinai Cem—*cemetery* (3) ... TN-4
Mount Sinai Cem—*cemetery* (2) ... TX-5
*Mount Sinai Ch* ... AL-4
Mount Sinai Ch—*church* (23) ... AL-4
Mount Sinai Ch—*church* (3) ... AR-4
Mount Sinai Ch—*church* (6) ... FL-3
Mount Sinai Ch—*church* (11) ... GA-3
Mount Sinai Ch—*church* (2) ... IN-6
Mount Sinai Ch—*church* ... KY-4
Mount Sinai Ch—*church* (4) ... LA-4
Mount Sinai Ch—*church* (11) ... MS-4
Mount Sinai Ch—*church* (4) ... MO-7
Mount Sinai Ch—*church* (13) ... NC-3
Mount Sinai Ch—*church* ... OH-6
Mount Sinai Ch—*church* (11) ... SC-3
Mount Sinai Ch—*church* (5) ... TN-4
Mount Sinai Ch—*church* ... TX-5
Mount Sinai Ch—*church* (14) ... VA-3
Mount Sinai Ch—*church* (2) ... WV-2
Mount Sinai Chapel—*church* ... MO-7
Mount Sinai Ch (historical)—*church* (2) ... AL-4
Mount Sinai Ch (historical)—*church* (2) ... TN-4
Mount Sinai Harbor—*bay* ... NY-2
*Mount Sinai Hosp* ... FL-3
Mount Sinai Hosp—*hospital* (2) ... CA-9
Mount Sinai Hosp—*hospital* ... CT-1
Mount Sinai Hosp—*hospital* ... FL-3
Mount Sinai Hosp—*hospital* ... IL-6
Mount Sinai Hosp—*hospital* ... MN-6
Mount Sinai Hosp—*hospital* ... NY-2
Mount Sinai House of Prayer—*church* ... FL-3
Mount Sinai Med Ctr—*hospital* ... FL-3
Mount Sinai Memorial Park—*cemetery* ... CA-9
Mount Sinai Memorial Park—*cemetery* ... FL-3
Mount Sinai Memorial Park—*cemetery* ... VA-3
Mount Sinai Missionary Baptist Ch—*church* ... AL-4
Mount Sinai Missionary Baptist Ch—*church* ... FL-3
Mount Sinai Number 1 Ch—*church* ... AL-4
Mount Sinai Prayer Temple—*church* ... FL-3
Mount Sinai Primitive Baptist Ch—*church* .. FL-3
Mount Sinai Ridge—*ridge* ... IN-6
Mount Sinai Ridge—*ridge* ... WV-2
Mount Sinai Sch—*school* ... GA-3
Mount Sinai Sch—*school* ... LA-4
Mount Sinai Sch—*school* ... NY-2
Mount Sinai Sch—*school* ... WV-2
Mount Sinai Sch (historical)—*school* ... PA-2
Mount Sinai Sch (historical)—*school* ... TN-4
Mount Sinai School (historical)—*locale* ... MO-7
Mount Sinai Seventh Day Adventist Ch—*church* ... FL-3
Mount Sinai Spiritual Ch—*church* ... AL-4
Mount Sinal Cem—*cemetery* ... AL-4
Mount Sinal Ch—*church* ... AR-4
Mount Sinal Ch—*church* (2) ... VA-3
*Mount Sinani* ... AL-4
Mount Sinia Cem—*cemetery* ... MS-4
*Mount Sinia Ch* ... AL-4
Mount Sinia Ch—*church* ... AL-4
*Mount Sinia Ch Number 1* ... AL-4
*Mount Sinyala* ... AZ-5
*Mount Sitgreaves* ... AZ-5
*Mount Sky High* ... RI-1
*Mount Smart* ... ID-8
Mounts Mills—*locale* ... NJ-2
**Mount Snow (Snow Mountain Inn)**—*pop pl* ... VT-1
Mount Solitude Cem—*cemetery* ... ME-1
*Mount Solomon* ... CA-9
**Mount Solon**—*pop pl* ... VA-3
Mount Solon Cem—*cemetery* ... WV-2
Mount Solon Ch—*church* ... VA-3
*Mount Spicket* ... MA-1
Mount Spiritual Gospel Ch—*church* ... AL-4
Mount Spokane (CCD)—*cens area* ... WA-9
Mount Spokane Fire Station—*locale* ... WA-9
Mount Spokane State Park—*park* ... WA-9
Mount Spokane West Airpark Airp—*airport* ... WA-9
Mount Spring—*spring* ... TN-4
Mount Spring Dam—*dam* ... PA-2
Mount Spring Lake—*reservoir* ... PA-2
*Mount Springs Ch* ... AL-4
Mount Springs Ch—*church* ... GA-3
Mount Spruce Sch (historical)—*school* ... PA-2
Mount Squires—*summit* ... NC-3
*Mounts Run* ... NJ-2
Mounts Run—*stream* ... IN-6
Mounts Run Ch—*church* ... IN-6
Mounts Sch—*school* ... IL-6
*Mount Stanley* ... AL-4
Mount Stanley Baptist Ch (historical)—*church* ... AL-4
Mount Stanley Sch (historical)—*school* ... AL-4
Mount Stanton Trail—*trail* ... NH-1
**Mount Star**—*pop pl* ... AL-4
*Mount Steel* ... WA-9
*Mount Stella* ... CO-8
*Mount Stephens* ... WY-8
Mount Stephens Ch—*church* ... GA-3
*Mount Sterling* ... NV-8
Mount Sterling—*locale* ... NC-3
Mount Sterling—*locale* ... UT-8
Mount Sterling—*other* ... OH-6
**Mount Sterling**—*pop pl* ... AL-4
**Mount Sterling**—*pop pl* ... IL-6
**Mount Sterling**—*pop pl* ... IN-6
**Mount Sterling**—*pop pl* ... IA-7
**Mount Sterling**—*pop pl* ... KY-4
**Mount Sterling**—*pop pl* ... MO-7
**Mount Sterling**—*pop pl* ... OH-6
**Mount Sterling**—*pop pl* ... PA-2
**Mount Sterling**—*pop pl* ... WI-6
Mount Sterling, Lake—*reservoir* ... IL-6
Mount Sterling Baptist Ch—*church* ... AL-4
Mount Sterling (CCD)—*cens area* ... KY-4
Mount Sterling Cem—*cemetery* (2) ... MO-7
Mount Sterling Cem—*cemetery* ... UT-8
Mount Sterling Ch—*church* ... IL-6
Mount Sterling Ch—*church* ... IN-6
Mount Sterling Ch—*church* ... KY-4
Mount Sterling Ch—*church* ... LA-4
Mount Sterling Ch—*church* ... TX-5
Mount Sterling Ch (abandoned)—*church* .. MO-7
Mount Sterling Commercial District—*hist pl* ... KY-4
Mount Sterling Commercial Hist Dist—*hist pl* ... IL-6
Mount Sterling Creek—*stream* ... NC-3
Mount Sterling Gap—*gap* ... NC-3
Mount Sterling Hist Dist—*hist pl* ... OH-6
**Mount Sterling (historical)**—*pop pl* ... TN-4
Mount Sterling Methodist Ch—*church* ... AL-4
Mount Sterling Methodist Church—*hist pl* ... AL-4
Mount Sterling Post Office (historical)—*building* ... TN-4
Mount Sterling Ridge—*ridge* ... NC-3
Mount Sterling Sch (abandoned)—*school* . MO-7
Mount Sterling (Township of)—*civ div* ... IL-6
Mount Stevens Cem—*cemetery* ... LA-4
Mount Stewart—*locale* ... VI-3
Mount St Francis (Seminary)—*facility* ... IN-6
Mount St Helen's Aero Ranch Airp—*airport* ... WA-9
Mount Stirling Ch—*church* ... VA-3
Mount St. Joseph Acad—*hist pl* ... CT-1
Mount St. Joseph Acad—*hist pl* ... KY-4
Mount St. Mary's Acad and Convent—*hist pl* ... CA-9
*Mount Stone* ... WA-9
*Mount Stoney African Methodist Episcopal Zion church* ... AL-4
Mount Stoney Ch—*church* ... AL-4
**Mount Storm**—*pop pl* ... WV-2
Mount Storm Ch (historical)—*church* ... TN-4
Mount Storm Lake—*reservoir* ... WV-2
Mount Storm Park—*park* ... OH-6
Mount Stratus—*summit* ... CO-8
Mount St. Scholastica Convent—*hist pl* ... KS-7
Mount St. Vincent—*uninc pl* ... NY-2
*Mount Success* ... NH-1
Mount Sugarloaf State Reservation—*park* ... MA-1
**Mount Sulphur**—*pop pl* ... TN-4
Mount Sulphur Cem—*cemetery* ... TN-4
Mount Sumac Ch—*church* ... GA-3
**Mount Summit**—*pop pl* ... IN-6
**Mount Summit**—*pop pl* ... OH-6
Mount Summit Cem—*cemetery* ... IL-6
Mount Summit Cem—*cemetery* ... IN-6
Mount Summit Ch—*church* ... OH-6
**Mount Sunapee**—*pop pl* ... NH-1
Mount Sunapee State Park—*park* ... NH-1
Mount Sunny Sch—*school* ... IL-6
Mount Supeal Sch—*school* ... LA-4
Mount Superior Ch—*church* ... AR-4
Mount Superior Ch—*church* (2) ... LA-4
Mount's Villa—*hist pl* ... LA-4
Mount Swamp—*swamp* ... VA-3
**Mount Sylvan**—*pop pl* ... TX-5
Mount Sylvan Acad for Boys (historical)—*school* ... MS-4
Mount Sylvan Ch—*church* ... NC-3
Mount Sylvia Ch—*church* ... TX-5
*Mount Tabequache* ... CO-8
Mount Taber Cem—*cemetery* ... MO-7
Mount Taber Ch—*church* (2) ... MO-7
Mount Taber Ch—*church* ... NC-3
Mount Taber Ch—*church* ... VA-3
Mount Taber Sch (historical)—*school* ... MO-7
Mount Table Cem—*cemetery* ... VA-3
*Mount Table Ch* ... AL-4
Mount Table Ch—*church* ... AR-4
Mount Tablor Cem—*cemetery* ... IN-6
*Mount Tabo Ch* ... AL-4
*Mount Tabor* ... IN-6
*Mount Tabor* ... MS-4
*Mount Tabor* ... NJ-2
*Mount Tabor* (2) ... SC-3
Mount Tabor—*locale* ... AL-4
Mount Tabor—*locale* ... AR-4
Mount Tabor—*locale* ... KY-4
Mount Tabor—*locale* ... NC-3
Mount Tabor—*locale* ... PA-2
Mount Tabor—*locale* ... SC-3
Mount Tabor—*locale* (2) ... TN-4
Mount Tabor—*locale* ... VA-3
Mount Tabor—*locale* ... WV-2
Mount Tabor—*locale* ... WI-6
**Mount Tabor**—*pop pl* ... AR-4
**Mount Tabor**—*pop pl* ... IN-6
**Mount Tabor**—*pop pl* ... NC-3
**Mount Tabor**—*pop pl* ... PA-2
**Mount Tabor**—*pop pl* ... VT-1
**Mount Tabor**—*pop pl* ... WV-2
Mount Tabor—*summit* ... MO-7

Mount Tabor African Methodist Episcopal Ch—*church* FL-3
Mount Tabor Annex—*school* OR-9
*Mount Tabor Baptist Ch* AL-4
Mount Tabor Baptist Ch—*church* AL-4
*Mount Tabor Baptist Church* TN-4
*Mount Tabor Brook* VT-1
Mount Tabor Brook—*stream* VT-1
Mount Tabor Camp—*locale* MN-6
Mount Tabor Cem—*cemetery* (5) AL-4
Mount Tabor Cem—*cemetery* AR-4
Mount Tabor Cem—*cemetery* FL-3
Mount Tabor Cem—*cemetery* IL-6
Mount Tabor Cem—*cemetery* (2) IN-6
Mount Tabor Cem—*cemetery* IA-7
Mount Tabor Cem—*cemetery* MD-2
Mount Tabor Cem—*cemetery* MS-4
Mount Tabor Cem—*cemetery* MO-7
Mount Tabor Cem—*cemetery* (4) OH-6
Mount Tabor Cem—*cemetery* (5) PA-2
Mount Tabor Cem—*cemetery* (3) TN-4
Mount Tabor Cem—*cemetery* (2) TX-5
Mount Tabor Cem—*cemetery* VT-1
Mount Tabor Cem—*cemetery* WA-9
Mount Tabor Cem—*cemetery* WV-2
Mount Tabor Cem—*cemetery* (2) WI-6
Mount Tabor Cemetary—*cemetery* AR-4
*Mount Tabor Ch* TN-4
Mount Tabor Ch—*church* (11) AL-4
Mount Tabor Ch—*church* (8) AR-4
Mount Tabor Ch—*church* (6) FL-3
Mount Tabor Ch—*church* (10) GA-3
Mount Tabor Ch—*church* (2) IL-6
Mount Tabor Ch—*church* (6) IN-6
Mount Tabor Ch—*church* IA-7
Mount Tabor Ch—*church* (6) KY-4
Mount Tabor Ch—*church* LA-4
Mount Tabor Ch—*church* (4) MD-2
Mount Tabor Ch—*church* (4) MS-4
Mount Tabor Ch—*church* (3) MO-7
Mount Tabor Ch—*church* (12) NC-3
Mount Tabor Ch—*church* (8) OH-6
Mount Tabor Ch—*church* (7) PA-2
Mount Tabor Ch—*church* (12) SC-3
Mount Tabor Ch—*church* (8) TN-4
Mount Tabor Ch—*church* (2) TX-5
Mount Tabor Ch—*church* (8) VA-3
Mount Tabor Ch—*church* (4) WV-2
Mount Tabor Ch (historical)—*church* MO-7
**Mount Tabor Church**—*pop pl* WV-2
Mount Tabor Church Cem—*cemetery* IN-6
Mount Tabor Churchs—*church* TN-4
Mount Tabor Community Ch (historical)—*church* TN-4
Mount Tabor Convent—*church* TX-5
*Mount Tabor Cumberland Presbyterian Ch* TN-4
**Mount Tabor (Gatton)**—*pop pl* KY-4
Mount Tabor Holiness Ch (historical)—*church* MS-4
Mount Tabor Hosp—*hospital* OR-9
Mount Tabor HS—*school* NC-3
Mount Tabor Lake—*reservoir* NJ-2
Mount Tabor Lake Dam—*dam* NJ-2
**Mount Tabor (local name for Tabor)**—*pop pl* NJ-2
Mount Tabor Lutheran Ch—*church* UT-8
Mount Tabor (Magisterial District)—*fmr MCD* VA-3
Mount Tabor Methodist Ch—*church* AL-4
Mount Tabor Missionary Baptist Ch—*church* (2) AL-4
Mount Tabor Oil Field—*oilfield* KS-7
Mount Tabor Park—*park* MO-7
Mount Tabor Park—*park* OR-9
Mount Tabor Pentecostal Ch—*church* TN-4
Mount Tabor Presbyterian Ch—*church* TN-4
Mount Tabor Ridge—*ridge* IN-6
Mount Tabor Sch—*school* FL-3
Mount Tabor Sch—*school* IL-6
Mount Tabor Sch—*school* IN-6
Mount Tabor Sch—*school* IA-7
Mount Tabor Sch—*school* LA-4
Mount Tabor Sch—*school* (2) MO-7
Mount Tabor Sch—*school* OR-9
Mount Tabor Sch—*school* SC-3
Mount Tabor Sch—*school* TN-4
Mount Tabor Sch (abandoned)—*school* MO-7
Mount Tabor Sch (historical)—*school* (5) AL-4
Mount Tabor Sch (historical)—*school* (2) MS-4
Mount Tabor Sch (historical)—*school* MO-7
Mount Tabor Sch (historical)—*school* TN-4
Mount Tabor Spring—*spring* TN-4
**Mount Tabor (sta.)**—*pop pl* NJ-2
**Mount Tabor (Town of)**—*pop pl* VT-1
*Mount Tabor United Methodist Church* AL-4
*Mount Tabour Church* MS-4
*Mount Tacoma* WA-9
*Mount Tadden* ME-1
Mount Tahoma HS—*school* WA-9
Mount Talley Cem—*cemetery* MS-4
Mount Talley Ch—*church* MS-4
*Mount Tamaire* PW-9
Mount Tamalpais Cem—*cemetery* CA-9
Mount Tamalpais Game Ref—*park* CA-9
Mount Tamalpais State Park—*park* CA-9
*Mount Tantalus* HI-9
Mount Tanya Ch—*church* MS-4
*MountTapochiyo* MH-9
*Mount Tapotchau* MH-9
*Mount Taylor* ID-8
Mount Teamor Cem—*cemetery* MS-4
Mount Teamor Ch—*church* MS-4
*Mount Tea Ridge* IN-6
*Mount Tebo Church* AL-4
*Mount Tecate* CA-9
*Mount Tekoa* MA-1
Mount Tell—*locale* WV-2
Mount Tema Ch—*church* SC-3
Mount Tema Ch—*church* TN-4
Mount Temah Chapel—*church* LA-4
Mount Teman Ch—*church* TN-4
Mount Temon Ch—*church* AL-4
Mount Temple Ch—*church* GA-3
Mount Temple Ch—*church* LA-4
Mount Tena Creek—*stream* MS-4
Mount Tena Creek—*stream* TN-4
Mount Tenjo Fortifications—*hist pl* GU-9
Mount Tepee Ch—*church* OK-5
*Mount Terrel* UT-8
*Mount Terrel Guard Station* UT-8
*Mount Terril* UT-8
Mount Terrill Guard Station—*locale* UT-8
*Mount Terryl* UT-8
Mount Terza Cem—*cemetery* MS-4
Mount Terza Ch—*church* MS-4
*Mount Terza Methodist Ch* MS-4
*Mount Teton* MT-8
Mount Thabor Cem—*cemetery* IL-6
*Mount Thompson* WA-9
*Mount Thomson* WY-8
Mount Tilla Ch—*church* GA-3
Mount Timpanogos Campground—*locale* UT-8
Mount Timpanogos Trail—*trail* UT-8
*Mount Tipo Pale* MH-9
*Mount Tipton Ch* TN-4
Mount Tipton Christian Methodist Episcopal Ch—*church* TN-4
**Mount Tirzah**—*pop pl* NC-3
*Mount Tirzah Baptist Ch* TN-4
Mount Tirzah Ch—*church* TN-4
Mount Tirzah Ch—*church* VA-3
Mount Tirzah Sch—*school* NC-3
Mount Tirzah (Township of)—*fmr MCD* NC-3
Mount Tiver Ch—*church* TX-5
Mount Tobin Mine—*mine* NV-8
Mount Toby State For—*forest* MA-1
**Mount Tom**—*pop pl* MA-1
Mount Tom Brook—*stream* NH-1
Mount Tom Cem—*cemetery* WI-6
Mount Tom Club Wildlife Marsh—*reservoir* RI-1
Mount Tom Club Wildlife Marsh Dam—*dam* RI-1
Mount Tom Creek—*stream* WA-9
*Mount Tom Park* MA-1
Mount Tom Park—*park* WI-6
Mount Tom Pond—*lake* CT-1
Mount Tom Range—*range* MA-1
Mount Tom Rock—*pillar* RI-1
Mount Tom Rsvr—*reservoir* MA-1
Mount Tom Shelter—*locale* WA-9
Mount Tom State Park—*park* CT-1
Mount Tom State Reservation—*park* (2) MA-1
Mount Tone (ski area)—*locale* PA-2
*Mount Toorup* CA-9
Mount Top—*locale* PA-2
Mount Toppin—*summit* NY-2
Mount Torment—*locale* WA-9
Mount Toro—*summit* CA-9
*Mount Torquemado* CA-9
Mount Torry Furnace—*locale* VA-3
Mount Trail Ch—*church* FL-3
Mount Tramp Ch—*church* LA-4
Mount Traveler Ch—*church* AL-4
Mount Tremont Trail—*trail* NH-1
**Mount Tremper**—*pop pl* NY-2
**Mount Tremper (The Corner)**—*pop pl* NY-2
Mount Trexler Ch—*church* PA-2
Mount Trial Primitive Baptist Ch—*church* FL-3
Mount Trinity Acad—*school* MA-1
Mount Triumphant Ch—*church* LA-4
Mount Triumph Baptist Ch—*church* AL-4
Mount Triumph Baptist Ch Number Two—*church* AL-4
Mount Triumph Ch—*church* LA-4
Mount Triumph Ch—*church* SC-3
Mount Trolly Ch—*church* SC-3
**Mount Troy**—*pop pl* PA-2
*Mount Trumbull* CA-9
Mount Trumbull—*locale* AZ-5
Mount Trumbull (historical P.O.)—*locale* AZ-5
**Mount Tucker Addition**—*pop pl* TN-4
Mount Tug—*summit* NY-2
Mount Tunnel Cem—*cemetery* PA-2
*Mount Tuns* PW-9
*Mount Turep* CA-9
Mount Tyler—*other* WV-2
*Mount Tyndall* CO-8
*Mount Uau* HI-9
*Mount Ukaopua* HI-9
**Mount Ulla**—*pop pl* NC-3
*Mount Ulla Elementary School* NC-3
Mount Ulla Sch—*school* NC-3
Mount Ulla (Township of)—*fmr MCD* NC-3
*Mount Uluong* PW-9
Mount Underwood Ch—*church* NC-3
Mount Unger Ch—*church* OH-6
Mount Unger Ridge—*ridge* OH-6
Mount Union—*locale* TX-5
**Mount Union**—*pop pl* AL-4
**Mount Union**—*pop pl* IA-7
**Mount Union**—*pop pl* KY-4
**Mount Union**—*pop pl* LA-4
**Mount Union**—*pop pl* OH-6
**Mount Union**—*pop pl* (2) PA-2
**Mount Union**—*pop pl* (2) TN-4
**Mount Union**—*pop pl* VA-3
Mount Union Airp—*airport* PA-2
Mount Union Area Junior Senior HS—*school* PA-2
*Mount Union Baptist Ch* MS-4
Mount Union Baptist Ch (historical)—*church* TN-4
*Mount Union Baptist Ch of Muldon* MS-4
*Mount Union Baptist Church* TN-4
Mount Union Borough—*civil* PA-2
Mount Union Cem—*cemetery* (2) AL-4
Mount Union Cem—*cemetery* IN-6
Mount Union Cem—*cemetery* IA-7
Mount Union Cem—*cemetery* NJ-2
Mount Union Cem—*cemetery* OR-9
Mount Union Cem—*cemetery* PA-2
Mount Union Cem—*cemetery* TN-4
Mount Union Cem—*cemetery* VT-1
Mount Union Ch—*church* AL-4
Mount Union Ch—*church* GA-3
Mount Union Ch—*church* IN-6
Mount Union Ch—*church* (6) KY-4
Mount Union Ch—*church* (2) LA-4
Mount Union Ch—*church* MD-2
Mount Union Ch—*church* MS-4
Mount Union Ch—*church* MO-7
Mount Union Ch—*church* (4) OH-6
Mount Union Ch—*church* (7) PA-2
Mount Union Ch—*church* (2) TN-4
Mount Union Ch—*church* TX-5
Mount Union Ch—*church* (2) VA-3
Mount Union Ch—*church* (11) WV-2
Mount Union Ch (historical)—*church* MO-7
Mount Union College District—*hist pl* OH-6
Mount Union Family Picnic Ground—*park* AZ-5
Mount Union Lookout Cabin—*hist pl* AZ-5
Mount Union Mine—*mine* AZ-5
Mount Union Missionary Baptist Ch—*church* MS-4
*Mount Union (Mount Union College)* OH-6
Mount Union No 5 Ch—*church* KY-4
Mount Union Rec Area—*park* AZ-5
Mount Union Ridge—*ridge* WV-2
Mount Union Rsvr—*reservoir* PA-2
Mount Union Sch—*school* AL-4
Mount Union Sch—*school* IL-6
Mount Union Sch—*school* KS-7
Mount Union Sch—*school* (2) KY-4
Mount Union Sch (abandoned)—*school* PA-2
Mount Union Sch (historical)—*school* MS-4
Mount Union Sch (historical)—*school* PA-2
Mount Union Sch (historical)—*school* (2) TN-4
*Mount Unkeshu* PW-9
**Mount Upton**—*pop pl* NY-2
*Mount Usher* CO-8
Mount Vale Ch—*church* TN-4
Mountvale Ch—*church* VA-3
Mount Vale Ch—*church* VA-3
Mount Valley—*locale* IA-7
Mount Valley—*locale* NC-3
Mount Valley Baptist Ch—*church* MS-4
Mount Valley Cem—*cemetery* AR-4
Mount Valley Ch—*church* AL-4
Mount Valley Ch—*church* MS-4
Mount Valley Ch—*church* (2) NC-3
Mount Valley Township—*fmr MCD* IA-7
*Mount Vancouver* OR-9
*Mount Van Dam* CA-9
*Mount Van de Whacker* NY-2
*Mount Van Hoevenburg* NY-2
Mount Van Hoevenburg Rec Area—*park* NY-2
*Mount Vaughn* RI-1
Mount Veeder Sch—*school* CA-9
*Mount Velma* NV-8
*Mount Venus Lakes* WA-9
Mount Vera Ridge—*ridge* AL-4
**Mount Verd**—*pop pl* TN-4
*Mount Verd Baptist Church* TN-4
Mount Verd Ch—*church* TN-4
Mount Verd Post Office (historical)—*building* TN-4
Mount Vernal Ch—*church* TN-4
*Mount Vernon* AL-4
*Mount Vernon* KS-7
*Mount Vernon* MA-1
*Mount Vernon* NH-1
*Mount Vernon* NC-3
*Mount Vernon* OH-6
*Mount Vernon* TN-4
Mount Vernon—*hist pl* NC-3
Mount Vernon—*hist pl* VA-3
Mount Vernon—*locale* AL-4
Mount Vernon—*locale* AR-4
Mount Vernon—*locale* GA-3
Mount Vernon—*locale* KS-7
Mount Vernon—*locale* NY-2
Mount Vernon—*locale* NC-3
Mount Vernon—*locale* (2) PA-2
Mount Vernon—*locale* (2) TN-4
Mount Vernon—*locale* VA-3
**Mount Vernon**—*pop pl* (4) AL-4
**Mount Vernon**—*pop pl* (2) AR-4
**Mount Vernon**—*pop pl* (2) GA-3
**Mount Vernon**—*pop pl* IL-6
**Mount Vernon**—*pop pl* (2) IN-6
**Mount Vernon**—*pop pl* IA-7
**Mount Vernon**—*pop pl* (2) KY-4
**Mount Vernon**—*pop pl* ME-1
**Mount Vernon**—*pop pl* MD-2
**Mount Vernon**—*pop pl* MI-6
**Mount Vernon**—*pop pl* (2) MS-4
**Mount Vernon**—*pop pl* MO-7
**Mount Vernon**—*pop pl* NE-7
**Mount Vernon**—*pop pl* NJ-2
**Mount Vernon**—*pop pl* (2) NY-2
**Mount Vernon**—*pop pl* NC-3
**Mount Vernon**—*pop pl* OH-6
**Mount Vernon**—*pop pl* OR-9
**Mount Vernon**—*pop pl* (3) PA-2
**Mount Vernon**—*pop pl* SD-7
**Mount Vernon**—*pop pl* (5) TN-4
**Mount Vernon**—*pop pl* TX-5
**Mount Vernon**—*pop pl* WA-9
**Mount Vernon**—*pop pl* (2) WV-2
**Mount Vernon**—*pop pl* WI-6
*Mount Vernon Academy* TN-4
*Mount Vernon African Methodist Episcopal Church* MS-4
Mount Vernon-Ailey (CCD)—*cens area* GA-3
Mount Vernon A.M.E. Church—*hist pl* KY-4
Mount Vernon Arsenal-Searcy Hosp Complex—*hist pl* AL-4
*Mount Vernon Avenue* OH-6
*Mount Vernon Baptist Ch* AL-4
*Mount Vernon Baptist Ch* TN-4
Mount Vernon Baptist Ch—*church* AL-4
Mount Vernon Baptist Ch—*church* IN-6
Mount Vernon Baptist Ch—*church* TN-4
Mount Vernon Baptist Ch—*church* TX-5
*Mount Vernon Baptist Church* MS-4
Mount Vernon Beach—*beach* MD-2
Mount Vernon Branch—*stream* MO-7
**Mount Vernon-Burlington (sta.)**—*pop pl* WA-9
Mount Vernon Camp—*locale* RI-1
Mount Vernon Canyon—*valley* CO-8
Mount Vernon (CCD)—*cens area* AL-4
Mount Vernon (CCD)—*cens area* KY-4
Mount Vernon (CCD)—*cens area* TX-5
Mount Vernon (CCD)—*cens area* WA-9
**Mount Vernon Cedars**—*pop pl* VA-3
*Mount Vernon Cem* MS-4
Mount Vernon Cem—*cemetery* (2) AL-4
Mount Vernon Cem—*cemetery* (2) AR-4
Mount Vernon Cem—*cemetery* CT-1
Mount Vernon Cem—*cemetery* GA-3
Mount Vernon Cem—*cemetery* (3) IL-6
Mount Vernon Cem—*cemetery* (2) IN-6
Mount Vernon Cem—*cemetery* (2) IA-7
Mount Vernon Cem—*cemetery* (5) KS-7
Mount Vernon Cem—*cemetery* (3) KY-4
Mount Vernon Cem—*cemetery* (2) MA-1
Mount Vernon Cem—*cemetery* MN-6
Mount Vernon Cem—*cemetery* (7) MS-4
Mount Vernon Cem—*cemetery* (2) MO-7
Mount Vernon Cem—*cemetery* NE-7
Mount Vernon Cem—*cemetery* (2) NY-2
Mount Vernon Cem—*cemetery* (3) OK-5
Mount Vernon Cem—*cemetery* OR-9
Mount Vernon Cem—*cemetery* (3) PA-2
Mount Vernon Cem—*cemetery* SC-3
Mount Vernon Cem—*cemetery* SD-7
Mount Vernon Cem—*cemetery* (6) TN-4
Mount Vernon Cem—*cemetery* (3) TX-5
Mount Vernon Cem—*cemetery* WV-2
Mount Vernon Cem—*cemetery* (4) WI-6
*Mount Vernon Ch* AL-4
*Mount Vernon Ch* TN-4
*Mount Vernon Ch* TX-5
Mount Vernon Ch—*church* (8) AL-4
Mount Vernon Ch—*church* (8) AR-4
Mount Vernon Ch—*church* FL-3
Mount Vernon Ch—*church* (20) GA-3
Mount Vernon Ch—*church* IL-6
Mount Vernon Ch—*church* IN-6
Mount Vernon Ch—*church* IA-7
Mount Vernon Ch—*church* (16) KY-4
Mount Vernon Ch—*church* (3) LA-4
Mount Vernon Ch—*church* MD-2
Mount Vernon Ch—*church* MN-6
Mount Vernon Ch—*church* (23) MS-4
Mount Vernon Ch—*church* (4) MO-7
Mount Vernon Ch—*church* NJ-2
Mount Vernon Ch—*church* (18) NC-3
Mount Vernon Ch—*church* (2) OH-6
Mount Vernon Ch—*church* OK-5
Mount Vernon Ch—*church* (2) PA-2
Mount Vernon Ch—*church* (9) SC-3
Mount Vernon Ch—*church* (17) TN-4
Mount Vernon Ch—*church* (2) TX-5
Mount Vernon Ch—*church* (13) VA-3
Mount Vernon Ch—*church* (8) WV-2
Mount Vernon Charity Tabernacle—*church* TN-4
Mount Vernon Ch (historical)—*church* MS-4
Mount Vernon Ch (historical)—*church* TN-4
Mount Vernon Ch Number 1—*church* LA-4
Mount Vernon Ch Number 2—*church* LA-4
*Mount Vernon Ch of Christ* TN-4
Mount Vernon Ch of God—*church* KS-7
Mount Vernon Ch of the Nazarene—*church* TN-4
Mount Vernon Church Cem—*cemetery* GA-3
**Mount Vernon Club Place**—*pop pl* CO-8
Mount Vernon Commercial District—*hist pl* KY-4
Mount Vernon Community Center—*locale* NE-7
Mount Vernon Community Hall—*building* CA-9
Mount Vernon Community Hall—*building* KS-7
Mount Vernon Community Hall—*locale* MO-7
**Mount Vernon Cove Condominium**—*pop pl* UT-8
Mount Vernon Creek—*stream* CO-8
Mount Vernon Creek—*stream* GA-3
Mount Vernon Creek—*stream* KY-4
Mount Vernon Creek—*stream* WI-6
Mount Vernon Crossing (historical)—*locale* AL-4
Mount Vernon Division—*civil* AL-4
Mount Vernon Drain—*stream* MI-6
Mount Vernon Elem Sch—*school* IN-6
Mount Vernon Elem Sch—*school* NC-3
**Mount Vernon Estates (subdivision)**—*pop pl* TN-4
**Mount Vernon Forest**—*pop pl* VA-3
*Mount Vernon Furnace* TN-4
Mount Vernon Gardens—*cemetery* TN-4
**Mount Vernon Gardens**—*pop pl* PA-2
Mount Vernon Goodwin Sch—*school* NC-3
Mount Vernon Grange—*locale* CA-9
**Mount Vernon Grove**—*pop pl* VA-3
Mount Vernon Gulch—*valley* CA-9
**Mount Vernon Hills**—*pop pl* VA-3
Mount Vernon (historical)—*locale* AL-4
**Mount Vernon (Historical Monument)**—*pop pl* VA-3
*Mount Vernon Hospital* AL-4
Mount Vernon Hot Springs—*spring* OR-9
Mount Vernon House—*hist pl* CO-8
Mount Vernon HS—*school* IN-6
Mount Vernon HS—*school* NY-2
Mount Vernon HS (historical)—*school* TN-4
Mount Vernon JHS—*school* CA-9
**Mount Vernon Junction**—*pop pl* IN-6
Mount Vernon Junior Coll and Seminary—*school* DC-2
Mount Vernon (Magisterial District)—*fmr MCD* VA-3
**Mount Vernon Manor**—*pop pl* VA-3
Mount Vernon Memorial Highway—*hist pl* DC-2
Mount Vernon Memorial Highway—*hist pl* VA-3
Mount Vernon Memorial Park (Cemetery)—*cemetery* CA-9
Mount Vernon Memorial Park (Cemetery)—*cemetery* IL-6
*Mount Vernon Methodist Ch* MS-4
Mount Vernon Methodist Ch—*church* (2) AL-4
Mount Vernon Methodist Ch—*church* MS-4
*Mount Vernon Methodist Church* TN-4
Mount Vernon Mine—*mine* (2) CA-9
*Mount Vernon Missionary Baptist Ch* MS-4
Mount Vernon MS—*school* IN-6
Mount Vernon Municipal Airp—*airport* IN-6
Mount Vernon Municipal Airp—*airport* MO-7
Mount Vernon Municipal Rsvr—*reservoir* TX-5
Mount Vernon-Outland Airp—*airport* IL-6
Mount Vernon Park—*park* IL-6
Mount Vernon Park—*park* PA-2
Mount Vernon Park—*park* TX-5
**Mount Vernon Park**—*pop pl* VA-3
**Mount Vernon Park (subdivision)**—*pop pl* MA-1
**Mount Vernon Park (subdivision)**—*pop pl* NC-3
Mount Vernon Place Hist Dist—*hist pl* MD-2
Mount Vernon Place Methodist Episcopal Ch—*church* DC-2
Mount Vernon Place United Methodist Church and Asbury House—*hist pl* MD-2
Mount Vernon P. O. (historical)—*locale* MS-4
Mount Vernon Presbyterian Ch (historical)—*church* TN-4
*Mount Vernon Primitive Baptist Ch* AL-4
*Mount Vernon Reservoir* IL-6
Mount Vernon Ridge—*ridge* TN-4
*Mount Vernon Sch* TN-4
Mount Vernon Sch—*school* AR-4
Mount Vernon Sch—*school* (4) CA-9
Mount Vernon Sch—*school* FL-3
Mount Vernon Sch—*school* GA-3
Mount Vernon Sch—*school* (6) IL-6
Mount Vernon Sch—*school* IA-7
Mount Vernon Sch—*school* MD-2
Mount Vernon Sch—*school* MI-6
Mount Vernon Sch—*school* MS-4
Mount Vernon Sch—*school* (2) MO-7
Mount Vernon Sch—*school* MT-8
Mount Vernon Sch—*school* OH-6
Mount Vernon Sch—*school* OR-9
Mount Vernon Sch—*school* (2) PA-2
Mount Vernon Sch—*school* SC-3
Mount Vernon Sch—*school* (2) TN-4
Mount Vernon Sch—*school* (3) VA-3
Mount Vernon Sch—*school* WV-2
Mount Vernon Sch—*school* WI-6
Mount Vernon Sch (abandoned)—*school* MO-7
Mount Vernon Sch (abandoned)—*school* (3) PA-2
Mount Vernon Sch (historical)—*school* (4) MS-4
Mount Vernon Sch (historical)—*school* MO-7
Mount Vernon Sch (historical)—*school* (5) TN-4
Mount Vernon School (Abandoned)—*locale* IA-7
Mount Vernon Shop Ctr—*locale* FL-3
**Mount Vernon Springs**—*pop pl* NC-3
Mount Vernon Springs Ch—*church* NC-3
Mount Vernon Springs Hist Dist—*hist pl* NC-3
Mount Vernon Square—*park* DC-2
**Mount Vernon Square Apartments**—*pop pl* VA-3
Mount Vernon State Game Farm—*park* IL-6
Mount Vernon State Hosp—*hospital* OH-6
**Mount Vernon (subdivision)**—*pop pl* NC-3
**Mount Vernon (subdivision)**—*pop pl* TN-4
Mount Vernon Tavern—*hist pl* RI-1
**Mount Vernon Terrace**—*pop pl* VA-3
Mount Vernon Towhead Island—*island* KY-4
**Mount Vernon (Town of)**—*pop pl* ME-1
Mount Vernon Township—*civil* MO-7
Mount Vernon Township—*fmr MCD* (2) IA-7
**Mount Vernon Township**—*pop pl* SD-7
Mount Vernon (Township of)—*civ div* IL-6
Mount Vernon (Township of)—*civ div* MN-6
Mount Vernon (Township of)—*fmr MCD* (3) AR-4
*Mount Vernon United Methodist Church* MS-4
**Mount Vernon Valley**—*pop pl* VA-3
Mount Vernon West—*uninc pl* NY-2
*Mount Vernon West Ch* AL-4
Mount Vernon Wharf—*locale* MD-2
**Mount Vernon Woods**—*pop pl* VA-3
Mount Vernon Woods Sch—*school* VA-3
Mount Vernon Yacht Club—*other* VA-3
Mount Veron Ch—*church* KY-4
**Mount Victor**—*pop pl* KY-4
Mount Victoria—*locale* MD-2
*Mount Victory* KY-4
Mount Victory—*locale* VI-3
**Mount Victory**—*pop pl* KY-4
**Mount Victory**—*pop pl* OH-6
Mount Victory (CCD)—*cens area* KY-4
Mount Victory Cem—*cemetery* TX-5
Mount Victory Ch—*church* IN-6
Mount Victory Ch—*church* (2) KY-4
Mount Victory Ch—*church* PA-2
Mount Victory Ch—*church* VA-3
Mount Victory Lookout Tower—*locale* KY-4
Mount Victory Sch—*school* (3) IL-6
Mount Vida Mine—*mine* UT-8
Mountview—*hist pl* TN-4
Mount View—*locale* AL-4
Mountview—*locale* MD-2
Mount View—*locale* OK-5
Mountview—*locale* WV-2
Mount View—*locale* WI-6
**Mount View**—*pop pl* AL-4
**Mount View**—*pop pl* CA-9
**Mount View**—*pop pl* NC-3
**Mountview**—*pop pl* OH-6
**Mount View**—*pop pl* OR-9
**Mount View**—*pop pl* RI-1
**Mount View**—*pop pl* SC-3
**Mount View**—*pop pl* (3) TN-4
**Mount View**—*pop pl* WA-9
**Mountview**—*pop pl* WV-2
Mount View Airfield (historical)—*airport* PA-2
*Mount View Airp* PA-2
Mount View Airp—*airport* PA-2
*Mount View Baptist Church* TN-4
Mount View Cem—*cemetery* (2) AR-4
Mount View Cem—*cemetery* (2) CA-9
Mount View Cem—*cemetery* CO-8
Mount View Cem—*cemetery* ME-1
Mount View Cem—*cemetery* MI-6
Mountview Cem—*cemetery* MT-8
Mount View Cem—*cemetery* NM-5
Mount View Cem—*cemetery* (4) NY-2
Mount View Cem—*cemetery* ND-7
Mount View Cem—*cemetery* OR-9
Mount View Cem—*cemetery* SC-3
Mount View Cem—*cemetery* TN-4
Mountview Cem—*cemetery* TX-5
Mount View Cem—*cemetery* (2) VA-3
Mount View Cem—*cemetery* WV-2
Mount View Ch—*church* (5) AL-4
Mount View Ch—*church* (3) AR-4
Mount View Ch—*church* (5) GA-3
Mount View Ch—*church* IL-6
Mount View Ch—*church* MS-4
Mount View Ch—*church* MO-7
Mountview Ch—*church* MO-7
Mount View Ch—*church* (11) NC-3
Mount View Ch—*church* SC-3
Mount View Ch—*church* (7) TN-4
Mountview Ch—*church* TN-4
Mount View Ch—*church* (5) TN-4
Mount View Ch—*church* TX-5
Mount View Ch—*church* (9) VA-3
Mount View Ch—*church* WV-2
**Mount View Gardens**—*pop pl* MD-2
Mount View Girls Sch—*school* CO-8
Mount View Golf Course—*locale* NC-3
Mount View (historical)—*locale* ND-7
Mount View Hosp—*hospital* NY-2
Mount View Hotel—*hist pl* CA-9
Mount View Memorial Park (Cemetery)—*cemetery* WA-9
*Mount View Missionary Baptist Ch* AL-4
Mount View Park Racetrack—*other* PA-2
Mount View Plantation (historical)—*locale* TN-4
Mount View Ranch—*locale* CA-9
Mountview Ridge—*ridge* TN-4
Mount View Sch—*school* AL-4
Mount View Sch—*school* (3) CA-9
Mount View Sch—*school* CO-8
Mountview Sch—*school* MA-1
Mount View Sch—*school* PA-2
Mount View Sch—*school* TN-4
Mountview Sch—*school* UT-8
Mount View Sch—*school* VA-3
Mount View Sch—*school* WV-2
Mount View Sch (abandoned)—*school* MO-7
Mountview Sch (historical)—*school* TN-4
Mount View Sch (historical)—*school* TN-4
**Mount View (subdivision)**—*pop pl* PA-2
**Mount View Subdivision**—*pop pl* UT-8
**Mount View Township**—*pop pl* ND-7
Mount Villa Ch—*church* LA-4
Mountville—*locale* OH-6
Mountville—*locale* VA-3
**Mountville**—*pop pl* GA-3
**Mountville**—*pop pl* MD-2
**Mountville**—*pop pl* PA-2
**Mountville**—*pop pl* SC-3
Mountville Borough—*civil* PA-2
Mountville Ch—*church* PA-2
Mountville Elem Sch—*school* PA-2
Mountville Lookout Tower—*locale* SC-3
Mountville Post Office (historical)—*building* PA-2
Mountville Sch—*school* PA-2
Mount Vincent Cem—*cemetery* TN-4
Mount Vincent Ch—*church* TN-4
Mount Vinco—*locale* VA-3
**Mount Vinson**—*pop pl* TN-4
Mount Vinson Cem—*cemetery* TN-4
Mount Vinson Ch—*church* TN-4
**Mount Vision**—*pop pl* NY-2
Mount Visit Ch—*church* SC-3
**Mountvista**—*pop pl* MD-2
Mount Vista (historical)—*locale* MS-4
**Mount Vista (historical)**—*pop pl* TN-4
Mount Vista Park—*park* WA-9
Mount Vista Post Office (historical)—*building* TN-4
**Mount Vista Subdivision**—*pop pl* UT-8
*Mount Waawaa* HI-9
Mount Wachusett Community Coll—*school* MA-1
Mount Wade Baptist Ch—*church* (2) MS-4
Mount Wade Ch—*church* (2) LA-4
Mount Wade Ch—*church* MS-4
Mount Wade Sch (historical)—*school* MS-4
*Mount Wado* AZ-5
*Mount Wait* MA-1
*Mount Waite* MA-1
**Mount Waldo**—*pop pl* ME-1
Mount Waldo Granite Works—*hist pl* ME-1
**Mount Waller**—*pop pl* MO-7
*Mount Wanalancet* NH-1
*Mount Warner* OR-9
Mount Washburn Spur Trail—*trail* WY-8
*Mount Washington* MA-1
*Mount Washington* MT-8
*Mount Washington* OH-6
Mount Washington—*locale* VI-3
**Mount Washington**—*pop pl* CA-9
**Mount Washington**—*pop pl* KY-4
**Mount Washington**—*pop pl* MD-2
**Mount Washington**—*pop pl* MA-1
**Mount Washington**—*pop pl* MO-7
**Mount Washington**—*pop pl* NH-1
**Mount Washington**—*pop pl* OH-6
**Mount Washington**—*pop pl* (3) PA-2
Mount Washington—*summit* NM-5
Mount Washington Boat Route—*locale* NH-1
Mount Washington Boat Route—*trail* NH-1
Mount Washington (CCD)—*cens area* KY-4
Mount Washington Cem—*cemetery* (2) KY-4
Mount Washington Cem—*cemetery* (2) MO-7
Mount Washington Cem—*cemetery* NY-2
Mount Washington Cem—*cemetery* OK-5
Mount Washington Cem—*cemetery* PA-2
Mount Washington Ch—*church* IN-6
Mount Washington Ch—*church* KY-4
Mount Washington Ch—*church* LA-4
Mount Washington Ch—*church* NY-2
Mount Washington Ch—*church* OH-6
Mount Washington Ch—*church* PA-2
Mount Washington Hotel—*hist pl* NH-1
Mount Washington Lookout Tower—*tower* MA-1
Mount Washington Overlook—*locale* PA-2
Mount Washington Park—*park* PA-2
Mount Washington P.O. (historical)—*building* MS-4
Mount Washington Sch—*school* CA-9
Mount Washington Sch—*school* KY-4
Mount Washington Sch—*school* MO-7
Mount Washington Sch—*school* OK-5
Mount Washington Sch—*school* VA-3
Mount Washington Sch—*school* WI-6
Mount Washington State For—*forest* MA-1
**Mount Washington (Town of)**—*pop pl* MA-1
Mount Washington Trail—*trail* WA-9
*Mount Washington Wild Area* OR-9
Mount Washington Wilderness Area—*area* OR-9
Mount Washington Wilderness Area—*reserve* OR-9
*Mount Waumbec* NH-1
*Mount Wawhalock Post Office* MS-4
Mount Webster Trail—*trail* NH-1
*Mount Weisner* AL-4
Mount Welcome—*locale* VI-3
**Mount Welcome**—*pop pl* (2) WV-2
Mount Welcome Ch—*church* WV-2
Mountwell Park—*park* NJ-2
*Mount Welsh* PA-2
Mount Wesley—*locale* TX-5
**Mount Wesley**—*pop pl* MD-2
Mount Wesley Cem—*cemetery* (2) TN-4

Mount Wesley Ch—church ... NC-3
Mount Wesley Ch—church (2) ... TN-4
Mount Wesley Ch—church ... WV-2
Mount Wesley Methodist Ch (historical)—church ... TN-4
Mount Wesley United Methodist Ch ... TN-4
**Mount Westley**—pop pl ... MD-2
Mount Wheeler ... NV-8
Mount Whitney—locale ... CA-9
Mount Whitney Ditch—canal ... CA-9
Mount Whitney Fish Hatchery—other ... CA-9
Mount Whitney HS—school ... CA-9
Mount Whitney Trail—trail ... CA-9
**Mount Whittier (West Ossipee)**—pop pl ... NH-1
Mount Wiesner ... ID-8
Mount Wilderness ... MI-6
Mount Wilkinson ... CO-8
Mount Wilkinson—locale ... GA-3
Mount Will Cem—cemetery ... ME-1
Mount William Ch—church ... MS-4
Mount William Pond—lake ... NH-1
**Mount Williams**—pop pl ... VA-3
Mount Williams Ch—church ... WV-2
Mount Williams Reservoir Dam—dam ... MA-1
Mount Williams Rsvr—reservoir ... MA-1
Mount Willie Ch—church (2) ... AR-4
**Mount Willing**—pop pl ... AL-4
**Mount Willing**—pop pl ... SC-3
Mount Willing Cem—cemetery ... AL-4
Mount Willing Cem—cemetery ... FL-3
Mount Willing Ch—church (2) ... AL-4
Mount Willing Lookout Tower—locale ... AL-4
Mount Willow Ch—church ... AR-4
Mount Wilson ... AL-4
Mount Wilson ... UT-8
Mount Wilson—locale ... MD-2
**Mount Wilson**—pop pl ... CA-9
**Mount Wilson**—pop pl ... PA-2
Mount Wilson Guest Ranch Airp—airport ... NV-8
**Mount Wilson (Mount Wilson State Hospital)**—pop pl ... MD-2
**Mount Wilson (Mt. Wilson Observatory)**—pop pl ... CA-9
Mount Wilson State Hosp—hospital ... MD-2
Mount Wilson Trail—trail ... CA-9
Mount Wilson Trail—trail ... OR-9
**Mount Winans**—pop pl ... MD-2
Mount Winfield ... CO-8
Mount Wing ... AZ-5
Mount Wittenburg ... CA-9
**Mount Wolf**—pop pl ... PA-2
Mount Wolf Borough—civil ... PA-2
Mount Wollaston ... MA-1
Mount Wollaston, Town of ... MA-1
Mount Wollaston Cem—cemetery ... MA-1
Mount Wood Cem—cemetery ... WV-2
Mount Woodland Ch—church ... VA-3
Mount Woodrow Ch—church ... TX-5
Mount Woodson ... CA-9
Mount Worner ... MA-1
Mount Wrangell Crater—crater ... AK-9
Mount Wright ... WA-9
Mount Yeckel—valley ... CO-8
Mounty Elam Ch—church ... NC-3
Mount Yonaguska—summit ... NC-3
Mounty Spring—spring ... MO-7
Mounty Spring Hollow—valley ... MO-7
Mount Yuma—summit ... CO-8
Mount Zeno Sch—school ... TN-4
**Mount Zephyr**—pop pl ... VA-3
Mount Zero Ch—church ... SC-3
Mountz House—hist pl ... IN-6
Mount Zineche Cem—cemetery ... AR-4
Mount Zinia Ch—church ... MS-4
Mount Zion ... AL-4
Mount Zion ... NC-3
Mount Zion ... TN-4
Mount Zion ... WA-9
Mount Zion—hist pl ... VA-3
Mount Zion—locale ... AL-4
Mount Zion—locale ... KY-4
Mount Zion—locale ... MS-4
Mount Zion—locale ... NC-3
Mount Zion—locale ... OH-6
Mount Zion—locale ... OK-5
Mount Zion—locale (3) ... PA-2
Mount Zion—locale (6) ... TN-4
Mount Zion—locale ... TX-5
Mount Zion—locale ... WV-2
**Mount Zion**—pop pl (2) ... AL-4
**Mount Zion**—pop pl ... AR-4
**Mount Zion**—pop pl ... GA-3
**Mount Zion**—pop pl ... IL-6
**Mount Zion**—pop pl ... IN-6
**Mount Zion**—pop pl ... IA-7
**Mount Zion**—pop pl (3) ... KY-4
**Mount Zion**—pop pl (2) ... LA-4
**Mount Zion**—pop pl (3) ... MD-2
**Mount Zion**—pop pl ... MS-4
**Mount Zion**—pop pl (2) ... MO-7
**Mount Zion**—pop pl ... NC-3
**Mount Zion**—pop pl (7) ... PA-2
**Mount Zion**—pop pl ... SC-3
**Mount Zion**—pop pl (2) ... TN-4
**Mount Zion**—pop pl ... TX-5
**Mount Zion**—pop pl ... VA-3
**Mount Zion**—pop pl ... WV-2
**Mount Zion**—pop pl ... WI-6
Mount Zion—school ... NC-3
Mount Zion African Methodist Episcopal Ch—church (2) ... DE-2
Mount Zion African Methodist Episcopal Ch—church ... FL-3
Mount Zion African United Methodist Protestant Ch—church ... DE-2
Mount Zion AME Ch—church ... AL-4
Mount Zion AME Ch (historical)—church ... AL-4
Mount Zion A.M.E. Church—hist pl ... FL-3
Mount Zion Assembly of God Ch ... AL-4
Mount Zion Baptist ... MS-4
Mount Zion Baptist Ch ... MS-4
Mount Zion Baptist Ch ... TN-4
Mount Zion Baptist Ch—church (6) ... AL-4
Mount Zion Baptist Ch—church ... DE-2
Mount Zion Baptist Ch—church ... KS-7
Mount Zion Baptist Ch—church (2) ... MS-4
Mount Zion Baptist Ch—church (4) ... TN-4
Mount Zion Baptist Ch (historical)—church ... AL-4
Mount Zion Baptist Church ... AL-4
Mount Zion Baptist Church—hist pl ... AL-4
Mount Zion Baptist Church—hist pl ... AR-4
Mount Zion Baptist Church—hist pl ... FL-3
Mount Zion Baptist Church—hist pl ... NC-3
Mount Zion Baptist Church—hist pl ... OH-6
Mount Zion Baptist Church—hist pl ... WV-2
Mount Zion Baptist Missionary Baptist Ch ... MS-4
Mount Zion Branch—stream ... GA-3
Mount Zion Branch—stream ... IN-6
Mount Zion Branch—stream ... IA-7
Mount Zion Branch—stream ... TN-4
Mount Zion Brick Church—hist pl ... NE-7
Mount Zion Campground—park ... IN-6
Mount Zion (CCD)—cens area ... GA-3
Mount Zion Cem ... MS-4
Mount Zion Cem—cemetery (33) ... AL-4
Mount Zion Cem—cemetery (17) ... AR-4
Mount Zion Cem—cemetery ... CA-9
Mount Zion Cem—cemetery ... DE-2
Mount Zion Cem—cemetery (6) ... FL-3
Mount Zion Cem—cemetery (9) ... GA-3
Mount Zion Cem—cemetery ... ID-8
Mount Zion Cem—cemetery (8) ... IL-6
Mount Zion Cem—cemetery (15) ... IN-6
Mount Zion Cem—cemetery (6) ... IA-7
Mount Zion Cem—cemetery (6) ... KS-7
Mount Zion Cem—cemetery (6) ... KY-4
Mount Zion Cem—cemetery (10) ... LA-4
Mount Zion Cem—cemetery (2) ... MD-2
Mount Zion Cem—cemetery (2) ... MA-1
Mount Zion Cem—cemetery ... MN-6
Mount Zion Cem—cemetery (32) ... MS-4
Mount Zion Cem—cemetery (21) ... MO-7
Mount Zion Cem—cemetery (5) ... NE-7
Mount Zion Cem—cemetery ... NJ-2
Mount Zion Cem—cemetery (2) ... NM-5
Mount Zion Cem—cemetery ... NY-2
Mount Zion Cem—cemetery ... NC-3
Mount Zion Cem—cemetery (18) ... OH-6
Mount Zion Cem—cemetery (9) ... OK-5
Mount Zion Cem—cemetery (14) ... PA-2
Mount Zion Cem—cemetery (5) ... SC-3
Mount Zion Cem—cemetery ... SD-7
Mount Zion Cem—cemetery (25) ... TN-4
Mount Zion Cem—cemetery (19) ... TX-5
Mount Zion Cem—cemetery (5) ... VA-3
Mount Zion Cem—cemetery ... WA-9
Mount Zion Cem—cemetery (5) ... WV-2
Mount Zion Cem—cemetery (4) ... WI-6
Mount Zion Cemetary—cemetery ... AR-4
Mount Zion Cemetery—hist pl ... DC-2
Mount Zion Cemeterys—cemetery ... GA-3
Mount Zion Center Ch—church ... MS-4
Mount Zion Ch ... AL-4
Mount Zion Ch ... MS-4
Mount Zion Ch ... MO-7
Mount Zion Ch ... PA-2
Mount Zion Ch—church (123) ... AL-4
Mount Zion Ch—church (59) ... AR-4
Mount Zion Ch—church (30) ... FL-3
Mount Zion Ch—church (129) ... GA-3
Mount Zion Ch—church (28) ... IL-6
Mount Zion Ch—church (38) ... IN-6
Mount Zion Ch—church (7) ... IA-7
Mount Zion Ch—church (4) ... KS-7
Mount Zion Ch—church (41) ... KY-4
Mount Zion Ch—church (42) ... LA-4
Mount Zion Ch—church (19) ... MD-2
Mount Zion Ch—church (3) ... MI-6
Mount Zion Ch—church (101) ... MS-4
Mount Zion Ch—church (45) ... MO-7
Mount Zion Ch—church (2) ... NE-7
Mount Zion Ch—church (10) ... NJ-2
Mount Zion Ch—church ... NM-5
Mount Zion Ch—church (2) ... NY-2
Mount Zion Ch—church (85) ... NC-3
Mount Zion Ch—church ... ND-7
Mount Zion Ch—church (32) ... OH-6
Mount Zion Ch—church (14) ... OK-5
Mount Zion Ch—church (38) ... PA-2
Mount Zion Ch—church (67) ... SC-3
Mount Zion Ch—church (69) ... TN-4
Mount Zion Ch—church (65) ... TX-5
Mount Zion Ch—church (64) ... VA-3
Mount Zion Ch—church (51) ... WV-2
Mount Zion Ch—church (2) ... WI-6
Mount Zion Ch (abandoned)—church ... MO-7
Mount Zion Ch (abandoned)—church ... PA-2
Mount Zion Chapel—church (2) ... AL-4
Mount Zion Ch (historical)—church (6) ... AL-4
Mount Zion Ch (historical)—church (9) ... MS-4
Mount Zion Ch (historical)—church (2) ... MO-7
Mount Zion Ch (historical)—church ... SD-7
Mount Zion Ch (historical)—church (5) ... TN-4
Mount Zion Ch Number 2 ... AL-4
Mount Zion Ch Number 5—church ... LA-4
Mount Zion Ch of Christ ... AL-4
Mount Zion Ch of Christ ... MS-4
Mount Zion Ch of Christ (historical)—church ... TN-4
Mount Zion Ch of Christ Holiness—church ... MS-4
Mount Zion Ch of God ... TN-4
Mount Zion Ch of God in Christ—church ... IN-6
Mount Zion Ch of God in Christ—church (2) ... MS-4
Mount Zion Christian Ch ... MS-4
Mount Zion Church ... DE-2
Mount Zion Church ... TN-4
Mount Zion Church—hist pl (2) ... TN-4
Mount Zion Church Cem—cemetery ... IN-6
Mount Zion Congregational Ch ... AL-4
Mount Zion Congregational Methodist Ch ... MS-4
**Mount Zion Corner**—pop pl ... IN-6
Mount Zion Covered Bridge—hist pl ... KY-4
Mount Zion Cumberland Presbyterian Ch ... AL-4
Mount Zion Cumberland Presbyterian Ch ... MS-4
Mount Zion Cumberland Presbyterian Ch (historical)—church ... AL-4
Mount Zion East Cemetery ... MS-4
Mount Zion East Ch—church ... GA-3
Mount Zion Freewill Baptist Ch ... AL-4
Mount Zion Freewill Baptist Ch—church ... AL-4
Mount Zion Freewill Baptist Ch—church ... TN-4
Mount Zion General Baptist Ch—church ... IN-6
Mount Zion-Hays Cem—cemetery ... PA-2
Mount Zion Heights ... PA-2
Mount Zion (historical)—locale (3) ... AL-4
Mount Zion (historical)—locale (2) ... MS-4
**Mount Zion (historical)**—pop pl ... MS-4
Mount Zion Hollow—valley ... TN-4
Mount Zion Holy Ch—church ... DE-2
Mount Zion Institute—school ... SC-3
Mount Zion JHS—school ... AL-4
Mount Zion Lookout—locale ... TX-5
**Mount Zion (Lothian Post Office)**—pop pl (2) ... MD-2
Mount Zion Lutheran Ch—church ... PA-2
Mount Zion Meetinghouse ... TN-4
Mount Zion Methodist Ch ... AL-4
Mount Zion Methodist Ch ... MS-4
Mount Zion Methodist Ch—church ... AL-4
Mount Zion Methodist Ch—church ... MS-4
Mount Zion Methodist Ch (historical)—church (2) ... AL-4
Mount Zion Methodist Ch (historical)—church ... MS-4
Mount Zion Methodist Ch (historical)—church ... TN-4
Mount Zion Methodist Church ... TN-4
Mount Zion Methodist Episcopal Church South—hist pl ... TN-4
Mount Zion Methodist Protestant Ch (historical)—church ... AL-4
Mount Zion Millpond—reservoir ... IN-6
Mount Zion Millpond Dam—dam ... IN-6
Mount Zion Mission—church ... LA-4
Mount Zion Missionary Baptist Ch ... AL-4
Mount Zion Missionary Baptist Ch ... MS-4
Mount Zion Missionary Baptist Ch—church ... FL-3
Mount Zion Missionary Baptist Ch—church (2) ... MS-4
Mount Zion Missionary Baptist Ch—church ... TN-4
Mount Zion Missionary Baptist Church—hist pl ... AR-4
Mount Zion Missionary Baptist Institutional Ch—church ... FL-3
Mount Zion Missionary Ch—church ... OH-6
Mount Zion Number 1 Baptist Ch—church ... MS-4
Mount Zion Number 2 Ch—church ... TX-5
Mount Zion Park—park ... MI-6
Mount Zion Park—park ... TX-5
Mount Zion Post Office ... TN-4
Mount Zion Presbyterian Ch (historical)—church ... MS-4
Mount Zion Presbyterian Church—hist pl ... OH-6
Mount Zion Primitive Baptist Ch ... AL-4
Mount Zion Primitive Baptist Ch—church (2) ... AL-4
Mount Zion Primitive Baptist Ch of Macon—church ... FL-3
Mount Zion Progressive Baptist Ch—church ... FL-3
Mount Zion Refuge Chapel—church ... NY-2
Mount Zion Ridge—ridge ... TN-4
Mount Zion Ridge—ridge ... WV-2
Mount Zion Sch ... AL-4
Mount Zion Sch—school (5) ... AL-4
Mount Zion Sch—school (2) ... AR-4
Mount Zion Sch—school (2) ... FL-3
Mount Zion Sch—school (5) ... IL-6
Mount Zion Sch—school ... IN-6
Mount Zion Sch—school ... KS-7
Mount Zion Sch—school (6) ... KY-4
Mount Zion Sch—school ... LA-4
Mount Zion Sch—school (2) ... MD-2
Mount Zion Sch—school (4) ... MS-4
Mount Zion Sch—school (5) ... MO-7
Mount Zion Sch—school (4) ... NE-7
Mount Zion Sch—school ... NC-3
Mount Zion Sch—school ... OH-6
Mount Zion Sch—school ... OK-5
Mount Zion Sch—school (2) ... PA-2
Mount Zion Sch—school (6) ... SC-3
Mount Zion Sch—school (2) ... TN-4
Mount Zion Sch—school (3) ... TX-5
Mount Zion Sch—school (2) ... VA-3
Mount Zion Sch—school (2) ... WV-2
Mount Zion Sch—school ... WI-6
Mount Zion Sch (abandoned)—school ... FL-3
Mount Zion Sch (abandoned)—school (6) ... MO-7
Mount Zion Sch (abandoned)—school ... PA-2
Mount Zion Sch (historical)—school (8) ... AL-4
Mount Zion Sch (historical)—school (6) ... MS-4
Mount Zion Sch (historical)—school (2) ... MO-7
Mount Zion Sch (historical)—school (8) ... TN-4
Mount Zion School—locale ... IL-6
Mount Zion School (historical)—locale ... MO-7
Mount Zion State For—forest ... CA-9
**Mount Zion (Township of)**—pop pl ... IL-6
Mount Zion Trail—trail ... TN-4
Mount Zion Trail—trail ... WA-9
Mount Zion Union Ch—church ... PA-2
Mount Zion United Ch of Christ—church ... PA-2
Mount Zion United Methodist Ch—church ... DE-2
Mount Zion United Methodist Ch—church ... PA-2
Mount Zion United Methodist Church ... AL-4
Mount Zion United Methodist Church ... TN-4
Mount Zion United Methodist Church—hist pl ... DC-2
Mount Zion United Methodist Church—hist pl ... NC-3
Mount Zion West Cemetery ... MS-4
Mount Zion West Ch—church ... GA-3
Mount Zion White Station Church ... MS-4
Mount Zircon Rsvr—reservoir ... ME-1
Mount Zircon Spring—spring ... ME-1
Mount Zoar—locale ... MD-2
Mount Zoar Ch—church ... AL-4
Mount Zoar Ch—church (2) ... MD-2
Mount Zoar Sch (historical)—school ... AL-4
Mount Zuba Ch—church ... GA-3
Mount Zura Baptist Ch—church ... FL-3
Mount Zwingli Ch—church ... OH-6
Moupin Butte ... OR-9
Mourberry ... TN-4
**Mourberry (Moberry)**—pop pl ... TN-4
Moures Landing ... AL-4
Mourey Cem—cemetery ... PA-2
Mourey Ditch—canal ... IN-6
Mourning Creek—stream ... MI-6
Mourning Dove Spring—spring ... UT-8
Mourning Kill—stream ... NY-2
Mourning Port Church—other ... AR-4
Mourning Valley Ch—church ... VA-3
Mourn Lake—lake ... TX-5
Moursund—locale ... TX-5
Moursville ... PA-2
Mous—locale ... AL-4
**Mousam Lake**—pop pl ... ME-1
Mousam Lake—reservoir ... ME-1
Mousam River—stream ... ME-1
Mouscochuck Creek ... RI-1
Mouse Branch—stream ... NC-3
Mouse Butte—summit ... MT-8
Mouse Canyon—valley ... MT-8
Mouse Coulee—valley ... MT-8
Mouse Creek ... TN-4
Mouse Creek—stream ... AK-9
Mouse Creek—stream ... IA-7
Mouse Creek—stream ... KS-7
Mouse Creek—stream ... MS-4
Mouse Creek—stream ... MO-7
Mouse Creek—stream ... NC-3
Mouse Creek—stream (2) ... OR-9
Mouse Creek—stream ... PA-2
Mouse Creek—stream (2) ... WA-9
Mouse Creek—stream ... WI-6
Mouse Creek Baptist Church ... TN-4
Mouse Creek Falls—falls ... NC-3
Mouse Creek Male and Female Acad (historical)—school ... TN-4
Mouse Creek Mill (historical)—locale ... TN-4
Mouse Creek Post Office ... TN-4
Mouse Creek Ridge—ridge ... TN-4
Mouse Creek Sch (historical)—school (3) ... TN-4
Mouse Creek Valley—valley ... TN-4
Mouse Fork—stream (2) ... WV-2
Mouse Harbor—bay ... NC-3
Mouse Harbor Bay ... NC-3
Mouse Harbor Ditch—canal ... NC-3
Mousehawk Butte—summit ... OR-9
Mouse Hill ... MA-1
Mouse Hollow—valley ... OK-5
Mouse Island ... ME-1
Mouse Island ... FM-9
Mouse Island—island ... CT-1
Mouse Island—island (8) ... ME-1
Mouse Island—island ... NH-1
Mouse Island—island ... OH-6
Mouse Island Reef—bar ... OH-6
Mouse Knob—summit ... NC-3
Mouse Knob Branch—stream ... NC-3
Mouse Lake—lake ... MI-6
Mouse Lake—lake ... MN-6
Mouse Lake—lake ... OR-9
Mouse Lake—lake ... WA-9
Mousel Sch—school ... NE-7
Mouse Meadow—flat ... NV-8
Mouse Mountain ... OR-9
Mouse Mtn—summit ... NC-3
Mouse Park—park ... TX-5
Mouse Pass—gap ... CA-9
Mouse Point—cape ... AK-9
Mouser—locale ... OK-5
Mouser Branch—stream ... KY-4
Mouser Cem—cemetery (2) ... MO-7
Mouser Creek—stream ... TX-5
Mouser Grain Elevator—hist pl ... OK-5
Mouse River ... ND-7
Mouse River Cem—cemetery ... ND-7
Mouse River Ch—church ... ND-7
Mouse River Park—park ... ND-7
Mouse River Sch Number 1—school ... ND-7
Mouse River Sch Number 2—school ... ND-7
Mouse River Sch Number 3—school ... ND-7
**Mouse River Township**—pop pl ... ND-7
Mouse Rock—bar ... CA-9
Mouser Place—locale ... NM-5
Mouser Ridge—ridge ... WV-2
Mouser Sch (abandoned)—school ... MO-7
Mouse Run—stream ... VA-3
Mouse Run—stream ... WV-2
Mouser Woodframe Grain Elevator/Collingwood Elevator—hist pl ... OK-5
Mouse Spring—spring ... CA-9
Mouse Spring—spring (2) ... OR-9
Mouses Tank Picnic Area—locale ... NV-8
Mouse Tail ... TN-4
Mousetail Eddy—rapids ... TN-4
**Mousetail (historical)**—pop pl ... TN-4
Mouse Tail Landing ... TN-4
Mousetail Landing—locale ... TN-4
Mousetail Landing State Park—park ... TN-4
Mouse Tail Post Office ... TN-4
Mousetail Post Office (historical)—building ... TN-4
Mousetail State Park ... TN-4
Mousetown—locale ... MD-2
Mouse Trap Butte—summit ... OR-9
Mouse Trap Rsvr—reservoir ... OR-9
Mouse Windmill—locale ... TX-5
Mousic Mountain ... PA-2
**Mousie**—pop pl ... KY-4
Mousie (CCD)—cens area ... KY-4
Mousley Brook—stream ... NH-1
Mousley Mtn—summit ... NH-1
Moussam—locale ... ME-1
Mousser Hall Ditch—canal ... WA-9
Moutainy Pond ... ME-1
Moutardier—locale ... KY-4
Mouth, The—bay ... PA-2
**Mouthcard**—pop pl ... KY-4
Mouth Hewassee Post Office ... TN-4
Mouth Hiwassee ... TN-4
Mouth of Bear River—area ... UT-8
Mouth of Blacklog Sch—school ... KY-4
Mouth of Branham Creek Sch—school ... KY-4
Mouth of Caney Fork Sch—school ... KY-4
Mouth of Coldwater (historical)—locale ... MS-4
Mouth of Cottonwood Windmill—locale ... NM-5
Mouth of Creek Island—island ... TN-4
Mouth of Daniel Sch—school ... KY-4
Mouth of Doe ... TN-4
Mouth of Doe Post Office ... TN-4
**Mouth of Hewassee (historical)**—pop pl ... TN-4
Mouth of Hickory Creek Campground—park ... TX-5
Mouth of Hiwassee Post Office ... TN-4
Mouth of Hollybush Sch—school ... KY-4
Mouth of Jackson Creek Landing (historical)—locale ... AL-4
Mouth Of Lacey Sch—school ... KY-4
Mouth of Laurel—locale ... VA-3
Mouth of Little River Post Office (historical)—building ... TN-4
Mouth of Long Branch Sch—school ... KY-4
Mouth of Meathouse Creek Sch—school ... KY-4
Mouth of Piney Hole—reservoir ... MO-7
Mouth of Richland Baptist Ch—church ... TN-4
Mouth of Richland Cem—cemetery ... TN-4
Mouth of Rio Grande—locale ... TX-5
Mouth of River Windmill—locale ... TX-5
Mouth of Sandy Landing (historical)—locale ... TN-4
Mouth of Seneca ... WV-2
**Mouth of Seneca**—pop pl ... WV-2
Mouth of Sipsey Landing (historical)—locale ... AL-4
Mouth of Tellico Post Office (historical)—building ... TN-4
Mouth of Terry Sch—school ... KY-4
Mouth of The Branch Landing—locale ... GA-3
Mouth of The Swamp Landing—locale ... GA-3
Mouth of the Yahara Archeol District—hist pl ... WI-6
Mouth of Turtle Hole Windmill—locale ... TX-5
Mouth of Wiley Sch—school ... KY-4
**Mouth of Wilson**—pop pl ... VA-3
Mouth of Wolf ... TN-4
Mouth of Wolf Post Office ... TN-4
Mouth of Yellow Creek Ford—locale ... TN-4
**Mouton**—pop pl ... LA-4
Mouton, Alexandre, House—hist pl ... LA-4
Mouton, Charles H., House—hist pl ... LA-4
Mouton Canal—canal ... LA-4
Mouton Cove Cem—cemetery ... LA-4
Moutray Cem—cemetery ... IL-6
Moutray Slough—stream ... IL-6
Mouweit Hill—summit ... RI-1
**Mouzon**—pop pl ... SC-3
Mouzon Lake—lake ... AL-4
Mouzon Sch—school ... SC-3
**Moval**—pop pl ... NE-7
Mova Windmill—locale ... TX-5
**Movella**—pop pl ... MS-4
Movella Assembly of God Church ... MS-4
Movella Cem—cemetery (2) ... MS-4
Movella Ch—church ... MS-4
**Movella (Mauvella)**—pop pl ... MS-4
Movella Missionary Baptist Ch—church ... MS-4
Move Over Lake Dam—dam ... IN-6
Moverick Lake ... NE-7
Moves Run—stream ... NC-3
**Movico**—pop pl ... AL-4
Movie Flat—flat ... CA-9
Movie Lake—lake ... AK-9
Movie Manor Landing Area—airport ... CO-8
Movie Mtn—summit ... TX-5
Movies, The—basin ... UT-8
Movie Stringer—stream ... CA-9
Movil Lake—lake ... MN-6
**Moville**—pop pl ... IA-7
Moville Township—fmr MCD ... IA-7
Moving Cloud Lake—lake ... WI-6
Moving Mtn—summit ... AK-9
Moving Star Hall—hist pl ... SC-3
Moving Wall Cave—cave ... AL-4
Movo Lake—lake ... WY-8
Movotny Cem—cemetery ... NE-7
**Mowata**—pop pl ... LA-4
Mowat Creek—stream ... ID-8
Mowat JHS—school ... FL-3
Mowato Ch—church ... LA-4
Mowatt (historical)—locale ... SD-7
Mowatt Memorial Ch—church ... MD-2
Mowberg Creek—stream ... WY-8
Mowbray—locale ... TN-4
Mowbray Ch—church ... TN-4
Mowbray Chapel—church ... MD-2
Mowbray Creek—stream ... ND-7
Mowbray Creek—stream ... TN-4
Mowbray Elementary School ... TN-4
Mowbray Number 18 Mine (surface)—mine ... TN-4
Mowbray Post Office (historical)—building ... TN-4
Mowbray Sch—school ... TN-4
Mowby Lake—lake ... MI-6
**Moweaqua**—pop pl ... IL-6
**Moweaqua (Township of)**—pop pl ... IL-6
Mowee ... HI-9
**Moween**—pop pl ... PA-2
Mowe Lake—lake ... MI-6
Mower ... NJ-2
Mower, George, House—hist pl ... SC-3
**Mower (County)**—pop pl ... MN-6
Mower Creek—stream ... WY-8
Mower Hill—summit ... NM-5
Mower House and Arcola Mill Site—hist pl ... MN-6
Mower Machine Flat—flat ... ND-7
Mower Pond ... RI-1
Mower Pond—lake ... ME-1
Mower Pond Dam—dam ... RI-1
Mower Rsvr—reservoir ... CO-8
Mowers—locale ... NJ-2
Mowers' Block—hist pl ... MA-1
Mowers Spring—spring ... ID-8
**Mowersville**—pop pl ... PA-2
Mowery Cem—cemetery ... IN-6
Mowery Creek ... MO-7
Mowery Lake—lake ... TX-5
Mowery Meadow—flat ... CA-9
Mowery Sch (historical)—school ... MO-7
Mowfield—hist pl ... NC-3
Mowglis Mtn—summit ... NH-1
Mowglis Trail—trail ... NH-1
Mowi ... HI-9
Mowich—locale ... OR-9
Mowich Butte—summit ... WA-9
Mowich Creek—stream ... ID-8
Mowich Creek—stream ... OR-9
Mowich Face—cliff ... WA-9
Mowich Illahee—locale ... WA-9
Mowich Lake—lake ... OR-9
Mowich Lake—lake ... WA-9
Mowich Lake Entrance—locale ... WA-9
Mowich Park—flat ... OR-9
Mowich River—stream ... WA-9
Mowich Spring—spring ... OR-9
Mowich Spring Butte—summit ... OR-9
Mowing Machine Coulee—valley ... MT-8
Mowing Machine Draw—valley ... WY-8
Mowing Machine Lake—lake ... TX-5
Mowing Machine Spring—spring ... AZ-5
Mowitch Basin—basin ... MT-8
Mowitch Creek ... ID-8
Mowitch Creek—stream ... ID-8
Mowitch Lake—lake ... WA-9
Mowitza Mine—mine ... UT-8
Mowitz Butte—summit ... CA-9
Mowitz Butte Tank—reservoir ... CA-9
Mowitz Creek—stream ... CA-9
Mow Lake—lake ... MN-6
Mowles Chapel—church ... WV-2
Mowls Gap—gap ... TN-4
Mowls Mill—locale ... TN-4
Mowna kaah ... HI-9
Mowna-Kaak ... HI-9
Mowna Roa ... HI-9
Mowna-Worrorar ... HI-9
Mowray Trail—trail ... PA-2
Mowrer Cem—cemetery ... IA-7
Mowrer Ditch—canal ... IN-6
Mowrey Ditch—canal ... IN-6
Mowrey Landing—locale ... OR-9
Mowrus Mills ... PA-2
Mowry—locale ... ID-8
Mowry—locale ... PA-2
**Mowry**—pop pl ... PA-2
Mowry, William, House—hist pl ... RI-1
Mowry Basin—basin ... WY-8
Mowry Basin Ditch—canal ... WY-8
Mowry Bluff Archeol Site—hist pl ... NE-7
Mowry Brook—stream ... MA-1
Mowry Brook—stream ... RI-1
Mowry Camp—locale ... CA-9
Mowry Canal—canal ... CA-9
Mowry Canal Number C-103—canal ... FL-3
Mowry Creek—stream ... CA-9
Mowry Creek—stream ... WY-8
Mowry Draw—valley ... WY-8
Mowry Gap—gap ... PA-2
Mowry Hill—summit ... NY-2
Mowry Landing—locale ... CA-9
Mowry Meadow—swamp ... RI-1
Mowry Meadow Brook ... RI-1
Mowry Mine—mine ... AZ-5
Mowry Mine—mine ... CA-9
Mowry Paine Brook—stream ... RI-1
Mowry Park—park ... PA-2
Mowry Peak—summit ... WY-8
Mowry Point—cape ... ME-1
Mowry Pond ... RI-1
Mowry Ranch—locale ... CA-9
Mowry Ranch—locale ... WY-8
Mowry Run—stream (2) ... PA-2
Mowry Run—stream ... WV-2
Mowry Run Trail—trail ... WV-2
Mowry Sch—school ... CA-9
Mowry Sch (abandoned)—school ... PA-2
Mowrys Corners—locale ... RI-1
Mowry Slough—gut ... CA-9
Mowrys Mills ... PA-2
Mowrys Point ... ME-1
Mowrys Run ... PA-2
**Mowrystown**—pop pl ... OH-6
Mowrystown Cem—cemetery ... OH-6
Mowry Wash—stream ... AZ-5
Mowry Well—well ... CA-9
Mows Butte—summit ... MT-8
Mow Spring—spring ... CO-8
Mow Spring Gulch—valley ... CO-8
Moxa—locale ... WY-8
Moxa Ditch—canal ... WY-8
**Moxahala**—pop pl ... OH-6
Moxahala Cem—cemetery ... OH-6
Moxahala Creek—stream ... OH-6
Moxahala Park—park ... OH-6
Moxahala Ridge—ridge ... OH-6
Mox Chehalis Creek—stream ... WA-9
Mox Chuck Slough—stream ... WA-9
Mox Chuck Truck Trail—trail ... WA-9
Mox Creek—stream ... ID-8
Mox Creek—stream ... WI-6
**Moxee City**—pop pl ... WA-9
Moxee Valley—valley ... WA-9
Moxham—locale ... KS-7
**Moxham**—pop pl ... PA-2
Moxham Mtn—summit ... NY-2
Moxham Point—cliff ... NY-2
Moxham Pond—lake ... NY-2
Moxie Bog—lake ... ME-1
Moxie Cove—bay ... ME-1
Moxie Falls—falls ... ME-1
Moxie Gore—unorg ... ME-1
Moxie Island—island ... MN-6
Moxie Mtn—summit ... ME-1
Moxie Pond—reservoir ... ME-1
Moxies Island ... MN-6
Moxie Stream—stream ... ME-1
Mox Lake—lake ... AK-9
Moxley ... KY-4
Moxley—locale ... KY-4
**Moxley**—pop pl ... GA-3
**Moxley**—pop pl ... NC-3
Moxley Branch—stream ... WV-2
Moxley Cem—cemetery ... GA-3
Moxley Cem—cemetery ... MO-7
Moxley Cem—cemetery ... OR-9
Moxley Corners—locale ... PA-2
Moxley Covered Bridge—hist pl ... VT-1
Moxley Farm—hist pl ... KY-4
Moxley (historical)—locale ... AL-4
Moxley Landing—locale ... KY-4
Moxleys Corner ... AL-4
Moxleys Crossroads ... AL-4
Moxlie Creek—stream ... WA-9
Mox Peaks—summit ... WA-9
Moxy Reef—bar ... ME-1
Moya Canyon—valley ... WY-8
**Moyal Anderson Subdivision**—pop pl ... UT-8
Moyamensing Prison—building ... PA-2
Moyano ... MH-9
Moya Spring—spring ... NM-5
**Moyd**—pop pl ... SC-3
Moye—locale ... GA-3
Moyea River ... ID-8
Moye Cem—cemetery (2) ... GA-3
Moyer—locale ... WY-8
**Moyer**—pop pl ... PA-2
Moyer, C. E., Nurseries Property—hist pl ... OR-9
Moyer, John M., House—hist pl ... OR-9

Moyer Airp—airport PA-2
Moyer Basin—basin ID-8
Moyer Branch—stream TN-4
Moyer Canyon—valley WA-9
Moyer Cem—cemetery IN-6
Moyer Cem—cemetery IA-7
Moyer Cem—cemetery MI-6
Moyer Cem—cemetery PA-2
Moyer Cem—cemetery TN-4
Moyer Cem—cemetery TX-5
Moyer Creek—stream ID-8
Moyer Creek—stream MI-6
Moyer Creek—stream NY-2
Moyer Dam—dam KS-7
Moyer Draw—valley WY-8
Moyer Gap—gap WV-2
Moyer Mine—mine WY-8
Moyer Peak—summit ID-8
Moyer Ranch—locale WY-8
Moyer Ridge—ridge PA-2
Moyer Road Sch—school VA-3
Moyer Run—stream (2) WV-2
Moyers—locale OK-5
Moyers—locale PA-2
Moyers—locale WV-2
Moyers Buildings—hist pl KY-4
Moyers Cem—cemetery IL-6
Moyers Cem—cemetery OK-5
Moyers Cem—cemetery (2) TN-4
Moyers Cem—cemetery VA-3
Moyers Cem—cemetery (2) WV-2
Moyer Sch—school KY-4
Moyer Sch—school MI-6
Moyers Church PA-2
Moyers Corners—locale NY-2
**Moyers Corners**—pop pl NY-2
Moyers Grove—locale PA-2
Moyers Lake—lake PA-2
Moyers Mill Run—stream PA-2
Moyer Springs—spring WY-8
Moyers Ridge—ridge TN-4
Moyers Run—stream WV-2
Moyers Store PA-2
**Moyer (Township of)**—pop pl MN-6
Moyes, William, Jr., House—hist pl UT-8
Moyes Ch—church NC-3
Moyeville Baptist Church AL-4
Moyeville Ch—church AL-4
Moyeville Church Cem—cemetery AL-4
Moyewood—locale NC-3
Moyie Falls—falls ID-8
Moyie Gulch—valley MT-8
Moyie Mountain ID-8
Moyie River—stream ID-8
Moyie Spring—spring MT-8
**Moyie Springs**—pop pl ID-8
Moyina—locale OR-9
Moyina Hill—summit OR-9
**Moylan**—pop pl PA-2
Moylan, Maj. Myles, House—hist pl CA-9
Moylan-Rose Valley (RR name for Moylan)—other PA-2
**Moylan-Rose Valley Station**—pop pl PA-2
**Moylan (RR name Moylan-Rose Valley)**—pop pl PA-2
Moylan Sch—school CT-1
**Moylan (Township of)**—pop pl MN-6
Moyle Cove—bay NY-2
Moyle Field—park KS-7
**Moyle Heights (subdivision)**—pop pl NC-3
Moyle Mine (underground)—mine AL-4
Moymer Cabin—locale UT-8
Moyne CO-8
Moyne—locale MT-8
Moyne Arroyo CO-8
Moynier Spring—spring UT-8
**Moyock**—pop pl NC-3
Moyock Cem—cemetery NC-3
Moyocke Creek NC-3
Moyock Elem Sch—school NC-3
Moyock Run NC-3
Moyock (Township of)—fmr MCD NC-3
Moys Cem—cemetery WA-9
Moyse Bldg—hist pl CA-9
Moysonec—hist pl VA-3
Moyumpse Island VA-3
Moyza Canyon—valley AZ-5
Moyza Ranch—locale AZ 5
Moyza Tank—reservoir AZ-5
Moyza Well—well AZ-5
Mozambique Point—cape LA-4
Mozambique Point Light—locale LA-4
Mozark Club—other MO-7
Mozark Mtn—summit WV-2
Mozart—locale (2) AR-4
Mozart—locale ID-8
Mozart—locale PA-2
**Mozart**—pop pl (2) WV-2
Mozart Mine—mine CO-8
Mozart Park—park IL-6
Mozart Sch—school IL-6
Moze Gulch—valley MT-8
Mozelle—locale KY-4
**Mozelle**—pop pl TX-5
Mozelle (CCD)—cens area KY-4
Moz En Udidan FM-9
Mozeppa PA-2
Mozer—locale WV-2
Mozette Creek—stream PA-2
**Mozier**—pop pl IL-6
Mozier Creek—stream ID-8
Mozier Hollow—valley IL-6
Mozier Hollow—valley TN-4
Mozier Island—island MO-7
**Mozier Landing**—pop pl IL-6
Mozier Mill Hollow—valley TN-4
Mozier Peak—summit ID-8
Mozingo Cem—cemetery (2) MS-4
Mozingo Creek—stream MO-7
Mozingo Sch (historical)—school MS-4
Mozingo Store (historical)—locale MS-4
Mozingo Valley Sch (historical)—school MO-7
Mozley Park—park GA-3
Mozo—locale TX-5
M Peterson Ranch—locale NE-7
M P Moore Pond Dam—dam (2) MS-4
M Pool—reservoir MI-6
M P Ranch—locale SD-7
M P Well—well NM-5
M-Q Ranch—locale FL-3
Mr. PA-2
M Ranch—locale CA-9
Mravlag Sch—school NJ-2
Mraz Brothers Dam—dam SD-7
Mrazek Pond—lake FL-3
Mraz Park—park IL-6
M R Branch—stream AR-4
Mreniu FM-9
M Rich—locale TX-5
Mrion Community Hosp—hospital FL-3
M R Ranch—locale AZ-5
Mrs Ardell Blankenship Dam—dam TN-4
Mrs Ardell Blankenship Lake—reservoir TN-4
Mrs A S Kyle Pond Dam—dam MS-4
Mrs B Carr—locale TX-5
Mrs Brown—locale TX-5
Mrs C Bradshaw—locale TX-5
Mrs Curtis Brawner Pond Dam—dam MS-4
Mrs Florine Ulmer Pond Dam—dam MS-4
Mrs Francis Fulkson Pond Dam—dam MS-4
Mrs Graham Lake Dam—dam MS-4
Mrs Harry Seay Pond Dam—dam MS-4
Mrs Jack Morman Pond Dam—dam MS-4
Mrs Jesse Cox Lake Dam—dam MS-4
Mrs Margaret Laird Pond Dam—dam MS-4
Mrs Pauline Taylor Pond Dam—dam MS-4
Mrs P Lancaster—locale TX-5
Mrs R E Payne Pond Dam—dam MS-4
Mrs Roland Stacy Lake Dam—dam MS-4
Mrs. Smiths Pond MA-1
Mrs S O Tharp Lake Dam—dam MS-4
Mrs T P Wilson Pond Dam—dam MS-4
Mrs Vaught Catfish Ponds Dam—dam MS-4
Mrs W G McGee Lake Dam—dam MS-4
Msas FM-9
M Schatz Number 1 Dam—dam (2) SD-7
M Schatz Number 2 Dam—dam SD-7
M Schremp Dam—dam SD-7
M Scism Number 1 Dam—dam SD-7
M S Creek—stream MT-8
M S Crockett Tank—reservoir NM-5
M S Davies Ranch—locale OR-9
Msgr McClancy Memorial HS—school NY-2
M S Hershey Med Ctr Helistop—airport PA-2
M-S Hill—summit WY-8
M S Johnson Pond Dam—dam MS-4
M Smith Dam—dam SD-7
M Solon Ditch IN-6
M S Thomas Bridge—bridge FL-3
M Street HS—hist pl DC-2
Mt. Airy PA-2
Mt. Airy Sch No. 27—hist pl DE-2
Mt. Airy Station—hist pl PA-2
MTA JHS—school TN-4
Mt. Albion Cemetery—hist pl NY-2
**Mt Angel**—pop pl OR-9
M Tarnavsky Ranch—locale ND-7
Mt. Ashland Ski Area—park OR-9
Mt. Assabet MA-1
Mt. Aventine Hist Dist—hist pl GA-3
Mt. Baldy Log Ponds—reservoir OR-9
Mt. Calm Branch AR-4
**Mt Carmel**—pop pl OR-9
Mt. Carmel Methodist Church—hist pl AR-4
Mt. Carmel Monastery—hist pl MD-2
Mt. Carmel Presbyterian Church—hist pl TN-4
Mt. Carmel Sch—school MA-1
Mt. Carmel Sch and Church—hist pl UT-8
MTD Industries (Plant)—facility OH-6
Mte Hormiga—summit PR-3
Mteultoachel—channel PW-9
Mt. Gilboa Chapel—hist pl MD-2
Mt. Gilead Baptist Church—hist pl KY-4
Mt. Healthy Public Sch—hist pl OH-6
Mt Holyoke College Lower Pond Dam—dam MA-1
Mt Holyoke College Upper Dam—dam MA-1
Mt. Hood Sch House—hist pl OR-9
Mt. Hope-Highland Hist Dist—hist pl NY-2
Mt. Horeb Earthworks, Unit A—hist pl KY-4
Mt. Horeb Presbyterian Church and Cemetery—hist pl NC-3
M Thybo Ranch—locale SD-7
Mt. Hygeia—hist pl RI-1
Mt Jackson Island PA-2
Mt Matade FM-9
Mt. McSauba Site—hist pl MI-6
Mt. Meridian Schoolhouse—hist pl VA-3
Mt. Moriah African Methodist Episcopal Church—hist pl MD-2
Mt. Moriah Baptist Church—hist pl KY-4
Mt. Nebo WV-2
Mt. Nebo—hist pl MD-2
Mt. Nebo Archeol District—hist pl OH-6
Mt. Olive Road Covered Bridge—hist pl OH-6
Mt. Olivet Methodist Church—hist pl KY-4
Mt. Pisgah A.M.E. Church—hist pl SC-3
Mt. Pisgah Baptist Church—hist pl SC-3
Mt. Pisgah Lutheran Church—hist pl IN-6
Mt. Pisgah Presbyterian Church—hist pl KY-4
Mt. Pisgah Regional Park—park OR-9
Mt. Pleasant—hist pl KY-4
Mt. Pleasant Baptist Church—hist pl KY-4
Mt. Pleasant Covered Bridge—hist pl PA-2
Mt. Pleasant Hist Dist—hist pl PA-2
Mt. Pleasant Presbyterian Church—hist pl OR-9
MT Ranch—locale AZ-5
Mt. Riga Lake CT-1
Mt. Sidney Sch—hist pl VA-3
Mt. Sinai Baptist Church—hist pl NC-3
Mt Skirgo Pond Dam—dam MA-1
Mt. Tabor Baptist Church—hist pl WV-2
M T Tank—reservoir NM-5
Mt. Torry Furnace—hist pl VA-3
Mtuftuf FM-9
Mt. Vernon Methodist Church—hist pl VA-3
Mt. Zion Church and Cemetery—hist pl TN-4
Mt. Zion Methodist Church—hist pl AR-4
Mt. Zion Presbyterian Church—hist pl AR-4
Mt. Zion Schoolhouse—hist pl VA-3
Mu NJ-2
Mu' FM-9
Muah Mtn—summit CA-9
Muanon—civil FM-9
**Muanon**—pop pl FM-9
Muav Canyon—valley AZ-5
Muav Caves—cave AZ-5
Muav Saddle—gap AZ-5
Mubby Creek—stream MS-4
Muberry Ch—church TN-4
Muberry Gap—gap TN-4
Mucalsea Mtn—summit ME-1
Muc-a-Muc Mine—mine CA-9
Mucarabones—CDP PR-3
Mucarabones (Barrio)—fmr MCD PR-3
Muce—locale FL-3
Muchachinock IA-7
Muchacho Spring—spring NV-8
Muchacho Tank—reservoir TX-5
Muchackinoc IA-7
muchakianock IA-7
Muchakinock Creek—stream IA-7
Muchakinock (historical)—locale IA-7
Mucha Koo Ave TX-5
Mucha Kooay Mountain TX-5
Mucha Koody Mountain TX-5
Mucha Kooga TX-5
Mucha Kowa Peak TX-5
Mucha Lake—lake AK-9
Muchattoes Lake—lake NY-2
Muchikinock Creek—stream IA-7
Muchinippi Ch—church OH-6
Muchinippi Creek—stream OH-6
Muchinippi Ditch OH-6
Muchnic, H. E., House—hist pl KS-7
Mucho MH-9
Mucho Grande Mine—mine CO-8
Muchos Canones —area AZ-5
Muchos Hombres Windmill—locale TX-5
Muchos Ojos Canyon—valley NM-5
Mucho Spring—spring CA-9
Muchot MH-9
Muchot, Puntan—cape MH-9
Much Water Creek—stream MT-8
Muck, The—flat NY-2
Muckafoonee Creek—stream GA-3
Muckalee Creek—stream GA-3
Muckaloochee Creek—stream GA-3
Muckaloon Creek—stream MS-4
Muck-a-Muck Creek—stream CA-9
Muckamuck Creek—stream WA-9
Muckamuck Hill—summit WA-9
Muckamuck Mtn—summit WA-9
Muckamuck Pass—gap WA-9
Muckamuck Trail—trail WA-9
Muckawanago Creek—stream CO-8
Muckawee Gulch—valley CA-9
Muckaysee Lake WI-6
Muck Branch—stream KY-4
Muck Cem—cemetery WV-2
**Muck City**—pop pl AL-4
Muck Creek—stream (2) AL-4
Muck Creek—stream GA-3
Muck Creek—stream NY-2
Muck Creek—stream WA-9
Muckenfuss Cem—cemetery SC-3
Muckenthaler House—hist pl CA-9
Mucker AR-4
Mucker Lake—lake MN-6
Muckey Lake—lake CO-8
Muckfau Bridge—bridge AL-4
Muck Forty Hole—channel MO-7
Muck Hollow—valley TN-4
Muckilteo WA-9
Muckinipates Creek—stream PA-2
Muckinipattis Creek PA-2
Muck Lake MN-6
Muck Lake—lake FL-3
Muck Lake—lake WA-9
Muck Lake—lake (3) WI-6
Muckland—locale MN-6
Muckleberry Pond—lake ME-1
Muckle Branch—stream (2) TN-4
Muckle Cove—valley NC-3
Muckle Lake—lake OR-9
Muckler Brook—stream VT-1
Muckleroy Cem—cemetery TX-5
Muckleroy Creek—stream AL-4
**Muckleshoot Ind Res**—pop pl WA-9
Muckleshoot Ind Res—reserve WA-9
Muckleshoot Prairie—flat WA-9
Muckles Ridge AL-4
Muckney Lake—lake OR-9
Muckow Creek MI-6
Muck Pond—lake FL-3
Mucksah Creek MI-6
Muckshaw Ponds—lake NJ-2
Muck Valley—valley CA-9
Muckwa Creek—stream MI-6
Muckwa Lake—lake (2) MN-6
Mucky Creek—stream MN-6
Mucky Flat—flat OR-9
Mucorrera Cem—cemetery TX-5
Mucorrera Creek—stream TX-5
Mud MI-6
Mud—locale WV-2
Mud Acre Sch—school IL-6
Mud Alke WI-6
Mudbaden—locale MN-6
Mudbaden Sulphur Springs Company—hist pl MN-6
Mudbank, The—other AK-9
Mudbank Cabin—locale AK-9
Mud Bank Mine—mine TN-4
Mud Bar—bar AL-4
Mud Basin—basin UT-8
Mud Basin—lake TN-4
Mud Basin Spring—spring UT-8
Mud Bat Fork Creek NC-3
Mud Bay ID-8
Mud Bay WA-9
Mud Bay WI-6
Mud Bay—bay (9) AK-9
Mud Bay—bay (3) FL-3
Mud Bay—bay LA-4
Mud Bay—bay MI-6
Mud Bay—bay (3) MN-6
Mud Bay—bay NY-2
Mud Bay—bay SC-3
Mud Bay—bay VA-3
Mud Bay—bay (3) WA-9
Mud Bay—bay WI-6
Mud Bay—lake LA-4
**Mud Bay**—pop pl AK-9
Mud Bay Gut—gut VA-3
Mud Bayou TX-5
Mud Bayou—bay (2) FL-3
Mud Bayou—gut LA-4
Mud Bayou—gut NE-7
Mud Bayou—stream LA-4
Mud Bayou—stream MO-7
Mud Bayou—stream TX-5
Mud Bayou—swamp MS-4
Mud Bay River—stream AK-9
Mud Bottom—locale TN-4
Mud Bottom Brook—stream RI-1
Mud Bottom Lake—lake FL-3
Mud Branch TN-4
Mud Branch—stream AL-4
Mud Branch—stream AR-4
Mud Branch—stream GA-3
Mud Branch—stream (2) IN-6
Mud Branch—stream (2) KY-4
Mud Branch—stream LA-4
Mud Branch—stream (3) MS-4
Mud Branch—stream (3) MO-7
Mud Branch—stream (2) NC-3
Mud Branch—stream (5) TN-4
Mud Branch—stream (2) TX-5
Mud Branch—stream VA-3
Mud Branch—stream WI-6
Mud Bridge—bridge MS-4
Mud Bridge—bridge TX-5
Mud Bridge—other IL-6
Mudbridge Ch—church GA-3
Mud Brook CT-1
Mud Brook—stream CT-1
Mud Brook—stream (15) ME-1
Mud Brook—stream MN-6
Mud Brook—stream (7) NY-2
Mud Brook—stream (2) OH-6
Mud Brook—stream RI-1
Mud Brook—stream (2) VT-1
Mud Brook—stream WI-6
Mudbrook Creek—stream OH-6
Mud Brook Flowage—lake ME-1
Mud Brook Trail—trail ME-1
**Mud Butte**—pop pl SD-7
Mud Butte—summit MT-8
Mud Butte—summit (4) SD-7
Mud Butte—summit WY-8
Mud Butte Dam—dam (2) SD-7
Mud Buttes—range ND-7
Mud Buttes—range SD-7
Mud Buttes—spring MT-8
Mud Butte Sch—school ND-7
Mud Butte Sch—school (2) SD-7
Mud Cabin Creek—stream ID-8
Mud Camp—locale KY-4
Mud Camp Cem—cemetery KY-4
Mud Camp Ch—church KY-4
Mud Camp Creek—stream KY-4
Mud Canal—canal FL-3
Mud Canyon NV-8
Mud Canyon—valley AK-9
Mud Canyon—valley CA-9
Mud Canyon—valley NM-5
Mud Canyon—valley TX-5
Mud Canyon—valley (2) UT-8
Mud Canyon Butte—summit UT-8
Mud Castle—locale NC-3
Mudcat Drain—canal MI-6
Mudcat Lake—lake GA-3
Mud Cat Tank—reservoir AZ-5
Mud Cave—cave (2) AL-4
Mud Cave—cave (2) MO-7
Mud Cave Hollow—valley MO-7
**Mud Center**—pop pl IN-6
Mud Channel Country Club—other MI-6
Mud Channel Creek—stream AK-9
Mud City NJ-2
Mud City Sch—school VT-1
Mud Coll—school PA-2
Mud Coll (historical)—school TN-4
Mud Coll Sch (historical)—school MO-7
Mud Corners Sch—school IL-6
Mud Cove ME-1
Mud Cove MA-1
Mud Cove—bay FL-3
Mud Cove—bay (5) ME-1
Mud Cove—bay MD-2
Mud Cove—bay NJ-2
Mud Cove—bay RI-1
Mud Cove Fishery—locale FL-3
Mud Creek AL-4
Mud Creek CA-9
Mud Creek GA-3
Mud Creek IN-6
Mud Creek KS-7
Mud Creek KY-4
Mud Creek MD-2
Mud Creek MA-1
Mud Creek MI-6
Mud Creek MN-6
Mudcreek MS-4
Mud Creek MT-8
Mud Creek NV-8
Mud Creek NY-2
Mud Creek NC-3
Mud Creek OH-6
Mud Creek OK-5
Mud Creek OR-9
Mud Creek SC-3
Mud Creek TN-4
Mud Creek VA-3
Mud Creek WA-9
Mud Creek WI-6
Mud Creek—channel GA-3
Mud Creek—gut (2) FL-3
Mud Creek—gut NY-2
Mud Creek—gut SC-3
Mud Creek—locale KS-7
Mud Creek—locale TN-4
**Mud Creek**—pop pl AL-4
**Mud Creek**—pop pl TN-4
Mud Creek—stream (21) AL-4
Mud Creek—stream (6) AK-9
Mud Creek—stream AZ-5
Mud Creek—stream (13) AR-4
Mud Creek—stream (13) CA-9
Mud Creek—stream (4) CO-8
Mud Creek—stream CT-1
Mud Creek—stream (6) FL-3
Mud Creek—stream (18) GA-3
Mud Creek—stream (13) ID-8
Mud Creek—stream (24) IL-6
Mud Creek—stream (25) IN-6
Mud Creek—stream (18) IA-7
Mud Creek—stream (20) KS-7
Mud Creek—stream (8) KY-4
Mud Creek—stream (3) LA-4
Mud Creek—stream (3) MD-2
Mud Creek—stream (2) MA-1
Mud Creek—stream (25) MI-6
Mud Creek—stream (12) MN-6
Mud Creek—stream (10) MS-4
Mud Creek—stream (12) MO-7
Mud Creek—stream (17) MT-8
Mud Creek—stream (7) NE-7
Mud Creek—stream NV-8
Mud Creek—stream (3) NJ-2
Mud Creek—stream (25) NY-2
Mud Creek—stream (5) NC-3
Mud Creek—stream (2) ND-7
Mud Creek—stream (8) OH-6
Mud Creek—stream (19) OK-5
Mud Creek—stream (18) OR-9
Mud Creek—stream (2) PA-2
Mud Creek—stream (6) SC-3
Mud Creek—stream (11) SD-7
Mud Creek—stream (25) TN-4
Mud Creek—stream (21) TX-5
Mud Creek—stream (4) UT-8
Mud Creek—stream (3) VT-1
Mud Creek—stream (5) VA-3
Mud Creek—stream (8) WA-9
Mud Creek—stream (22) WI-6
Mud Creek—stream (6) WY-8
Mud Creek Assembly Grounds—locale NC-3
Mud Creek Baptist Church TN-4
Mud Creek Bay—bay MN-6
Mud Creek Blowing Cave AL-4
Mud Creek Boat Dock—locale AL-4
Mud Creek Butte—summit CA-9
Mud Creek Campground—locale MT-8
Mud Creek Canal—canal WA-9
Mud Creek Canyon—hist pl CA-9
Mud Creek Canyon—valley CA-9
Mud Creek (CCD)—cens area AL-4
Mud Creek (CCD)—cens area KY-4
Mud Creek Cem—cemetery GA-3
Mud Creek Cem—cemetery TX-5
Mud Creek Ch—church AL-4
Mud Creek Ch—church (2) GA-3
Mud Creek Ch—church KY-4
Mud Creek Ch—church MS-4
Mud Creek Ch—church NC-3
Mud Creek Ch—church TN-4
Mud Creek Cove—bay FL-3
Mud Creek Dam—dam CA-9
Mud Creek Dam Number 15m-28-1—dam TN-4
Mud Creek Ditch—canal AK-9
Mud Creek Division—civil AL-4
Mud Creek Drain—canal MI-6
Mud Creek Drainage Ditch—canal MO-7
Mud Creek Falls—falls MT-8
Mud Creek Fisherman Access (proposed)—locale UT-8
Mud Creek Gap—gap KY-4
Mud Creek Harbor—bay WI-6
Mud Creek (historical)—locale AL-4
Mud Creek Lake—reservoir TN-4
Mud Creek Lookout Tower—locale KY-4
Mud Creek Methodist Ch—church TN-4
Mud Creek Missionary Baptist Ch MS-4
Mud Creek Point—cape NJ-2
Mud Creek Post Office AL-4
Mudcreek Post Office (historical)—building MS-4
Mud Creek Post Office (historical)—building TN-4
Mud Creek Public Shooting Area—park AL-4
Mud Creek Ridge—ridge (2) OR-9
Mud Creek Rim—cliff CA-9
Mud Creek Rsvr OR-9
Mud Creek Rsvr Number One—reservoir OR-9
Mud Creek Sch—school GA-3
Mud Creek Sch—school IL-6
Mud Creek Sch—school KS-7
Mud Creek Sch (historical)—school AL-4
Mud Creek Sch (historical)—school MS-4
Mud Creek Sch (historical)—school TN-4
Mud Creek School (historical)—locale MO-7
Mud Creek Shut-in—gap MO-7
Mud Creek Spring—spring AL-4
Mud Creek Spring—spring OR-9
Mud Creek State Waterfowl Area—park VT-1
Mud Creek Tank—reservoir TX-5
Mud Creek Valley Sch (historical)—school TN-4
Mud Creek Watershed Dam Fifteen—dam TN-4
Mud Creek Watershed Dam Five—dam TN-4
Mud Creek Watershed Dam Number Seventeen—dam TN-4
Mud Creek Watershed Lake Dam Nine—dam TN-4
Mud Creek Watershed Lake Fifteen—reservoir TN-4
Mud Creek Watershed Lake Five—reservoir TN-4
Mud Creek Watershed Lake Nine—reservoir TN-4
Mud Creek Watershed Lake Number Seventeen—reservoir TN-4
Mud Cut—gap TN-4
Mud Cut—gut TX-5
**Mud Cut**—pop pl NC-3
Mudcut Branch—stream NC-3
**Mudd**—pop pl KY-4
Mud Dauber Creek—stream TX-5
Mudd Cem—cemetery NC-3
Mudd Coll—school CA-9
Mudd Creek—stream (2) MT-8
Mudd Creek—stream TX-5
Mudd Creek Ridge—ridge MT-8
Mudderbach Tank—reservoir AZ-5
Mudder Kill—stream NY-2
Mudders Gulch—valley ID-8
Muddies, The—cove FL-3
**Muddig**—pop pl TX-5
Mud District No 2 Canal—canal WA-9
Mud Ditch—canal MO-7
Mud Ditch—canal NY-2
Mud Ditch—canal WI-6
Mudd Lake—lake FL-3
Mudd Lake—lake (2) MI-6
Mudd Lake—lake MT-8
Mudd Lake—lake NE-7
Mudd Lake—lake TX-5
Mudd Lake Drain—canal MI-6
Mudd Lake Extension Drain—stream MI-6
**Muddlety**—pop pl WV-2
Muddlety Creek—stream WV-2
Mud Dock—locale VT-1
Mud Dog Branch—stream SC-3
Mudd Pond—lake VT-1
Mud Draw—valley MT-8
Mud Draw—valley SD-7
Mud Draw Tank—reservoir TX-5
Mudd Sch—school MO-7
Mudd School (historical)—locale MO-7
Mudd's Grove—hist pl MO-7
Mudds Landing—locale IL-6
Mudds Marsh—swamp MD-2
Muddy—fmr MCD NE-7
**Muddy**—pop pl IL-6
Muddy, The NV-8
Muddy Basin—basin CO-8
Muddy Bay AK-9
Muddy Bay—bay FL-3
Muddy Bay—bay SC-3
Muddy Bayou LA-4
Muddy Bayou—canal LA-4
Muddy Bayou—gut AL-4
Muddy Bayou—gut MS-4
Muddy Bayou—stream AR-4
Muddy Bayou—stream (6) LA-4
Muddy Bayou—stream (5) MS-4
Muddy Bayou—swamp MI-6
Muddy Bayou Cem—cemetery MS-4
Muddy Bayou Church MS-4
Muddy Bench—bench WY-8
Muddy Boggy Creek—stream OK-5
Muddy Boggy River OK-5
Muddy Bottom Ditch—stream DE-2
Muddy Branch—stream (4) AL-4
Muddy Branch—stream (2) AR-4
Muddy Branch—stream DE-2
Muddy Branch—stream FL-3
Muddy Branch—stream (5) GA-3
Muddy Branch—stream (2) IN-6
Muddy Branch—stream (12) KY-4
Muddy Branch—stream (2) LA-4
Muddy Branch—stream MD-2
Muddy Branch—stream (3) MO-7
Muddy Branch—stream (5) NC-3
Muddy Branch—stream PA-2
Muddy Branch—stream SC-3
Muddy Branch—stream (20) TN-4
Muddy Branch—stream TX-5
Muddy Branch—stream VT-1
Muddy Branch—stream (7) VA-3
Muddy Branch Creek—stream IN-6
Muddy Branch Sch—school KY-4
Muddy Branch Sch (historical)—school AL-4
Muddy Bridge Branch—stream WV-2
Muddy Brook MA-1
Muddy Brook NH-1
Muddy Brook—lake MA-1
Muddy Brook—stream (6) CT-1
Muddy Brook—stream (3) ME-1
Muddy Brook—stream (7) MA-1
Muddy Brook—stream NH-1
Muddy Brook—stream (2) NJ-2
Muddy Brook—stream (3) NY-2
Muddy Brook—stream VT-1
Muddy Brook Pond MA-1
Muddy Brook Sch—school VT-1
Muddy Butte OR-9
Muddy Canyon WA-9
Muddy Canyon—arroyo AZ-5
Muddy Canyon—valley AZ-5
Muddy Canyon—valley CA-9
Muddy Canyon—valley NM-5
Muddy Canyon—valley OR-9
Muddy Canyon—valley UT-8
Muddy Cedar Creek—stream TX-5
Muddy Cem—cemetery MO-7
Muddy Corners—locale OH-6
Muddy Cove MA-1
Muddy Cove RI-1
Muddy Cove—bay (2) FL-3
Muddy Cove—bay NC-3
Muddy Cove—bay VA-3
Muddy Cove—cove (2) MA-1
Muddy Cove Brook—stream MA-1
Muddy Cove Marshes—swamp MA-1
Muddy Cove Pond—reservoir MA-1
Muddy Cove Pond Dam—dam MA-1
Muddy Creek AZ-5
Muddy Creek CO-8
Muddy Creek DE-2
Muddy Creek GA-3
Muddy Creek ID-8
Muddy Creek IN-6
Muddy Creek IA-7
Muddy Creek KY-4
Muddy Creek MD-2
Muddy Creek MN-6
Muddy Creek MS-4
Muddy Creek MO-7
Muddy Creek MT-8
Muddy Creek NV-8
Muddy Creek NJ-2
Muddy Creek NC-3
Muddy Creek OR-9
Muddy Creek PA-2
Muddy Creek SC-3
Muddy Creek TN-4
Muddy Creek TX-5
Muddy Creek UT-8
Muddy Creek VA-3
Muddy Creek WA-9
Muddy Creek WY-8
Muddy Creek—bay (3) MD-2
Muddy Creek—channel MD-2
**Muddy Creek**—pop pl NC-3
**Muddy Creek**—pop pl PA-2
Muddy Creek—stream (2) AL-4
Muddy Creek—stream (2) AK-9
Muddy Creek—stream AZ-5
Muddy Creek—stream (2) AR-4
Muddy Creek—stream (4) CA-9
Muddy Creek—stream (13) CO-8
Muddy Creek—stream (4) ID-8
Muddy Creek—stream (6) IL-6
Muddy Creek—stream IN-6
Muddy Creek—stream (2) IA-7
Muddy Creek—stream (4) KS-7

Mud Millpond—*reservoir* DE-2
Mud Millpond—*reservoir* MD-2
**Mud Mills**—*pop pl* NY-2
Mud Mills Stream—*stream* ME-1
*Mud Minnow Lake* WI-6
Mud Minnow Lake—*lake* WI-6
Mud Mountain Dam—*dam* WA-9
Mud Mountain Lake—*reservoir* WA-9
*Mud Mountain Rsvr* WA-9
*Mud Mtn* AZ-5
Mud Mtn—*summit* AZ-5
Mud Mtn—*summit* NM-5
Mud Mtn—*summit* WA-9
Mud Narrows—*gut* VA-3
Mudngerur—*summit* PW-9
Mudnoonguch—*island* FM-9
Mud Number One Tank—*reservoir* AZ-5
Mudobago—*bar* FM-9
Mudok Harbor—*harbor* FM-9
Mudokkumachin—*island* FM-9
Mudokolos—*island* FM-9
*Mudorom* PW-9
Mudos, Arroyo de los—*valley* TX-5
Mud Palisades—*cliff* CA-9
Mud Pass—*channel* LA-4
Mud Pass—*gap* WY-8
Mud Path Bay—*swamp* FL-3
Mud Peak—*summit* WY-8
Mud Pike Ch—*church* (2) IN-6
Mud Pine Creek—*stream* IN-6
Mud Pit—*basin* TX-5
Mud Point—*cape* FL-3
Mud Point—*cape* (2) LA-4
Mud Point—*cape* MD-2
Mud Point—*cape* TX-5
Mud Point—*cape* VT-1
Mud Point—*cape* VA-3
*Mud Pond* AL-4
*Mud Pond* CT-1
*Mud Pond* IN-6
*Mud Pond* MA-1
*Mud Pond* NH-1
*Mud Pond* NJ-2
*Mud Pond* NY-2
*Mud Pond* PA-2
*Mud Pond* VT-1
Mud Pond—*lake* AR-4
Mud Pond—*lake* CT-1
Mud Pond—*lake* (4) FL-3
Mud Pond—*lake* (69) ME-1
Mud Pond—*lake* (9) MA-1
Mud Pond—*lake* (2) MI-6
Mud Pond—*lake* (26) NH-1
Mud Pond—*lake* (3) NJ-2
Mud Pond—*lake* (70) NY-2
Mud Pond—*lake* (12) PA-2
Mud Pond—*lake* (24) VT-1
Mud Pond—*lake* VA-3
Mud Pond—*reservoir* MA-1
Mud Pond—*reservoir* NJ-2
Mud Pond—*reservoir* (5) PA-2
Mud Pond—*swamp* ME-1
Mud Pond—*swamp* (2) NY-2
*Mud Pond Brook* CT-1
Mud Pond Brook—*stream* (2) ME-1
Mud Pond Brook—*stream* (2) NY-2
Mud Pond Brook—*stream* VT-1
*Mud Pond Cove* RI-1
Mud Pond Creek—*stream* NY-2
*Mud Pond Dam* AL-4
Mud Pond Dam—*dam* NJ-2
Mud Pond Dam—*dam* PA-2
Mud Pond Gap—*gap* VA-3
Mud Pond Gap Trail—*trail* VA-3
Mud Pond Lake—*lake* NH-1
Mud Pond Mtn—*summit* (2) NY-2
Mud Pond Mtn—*summit* PA-2
Mud Pond Outlet—*stream* (2) NY-2
Mud Pond Ridge—*ridge* (2) ME-1
Mud Pond Ridge—*ridge* NH-1
Mud Pond Ridge—*ridge* PA-2
Mud Pond Run—*stream* (2) PA-2
*Mud Ponds* PA-2
Mud Ponds—*lake* ME-1
Mud Ponds—*lake* MA-1
Mud Ponds—*lake* NY-2
Mud Ponds—*lake* VT-1
Mud Pond Stream—*stream* ME-1
Mud Pond Swamp—*swamp* NY-2
Mud Portage Lake—*lake* MN-6
Mudport Basin—*lake* OH-6
Mud Pot—*well* WY-8
Mud Pot Waterhole—*lake* OR-9
*Mud Prairie* FL-3
Mud Prairie Lake—*lake* FL-3
*Mudpuppy Lake* OR-9
Mud Puppy Lake—*lake* OR-9
Mud Ridge—*ridge* OR-9
Mud Ridge—*ridge* UT-8
Mud Ridge Branch—*stream* KY-4
*Mud River* MN-6
*Mud River* NH-1
*Mud River* OH-6
*Mud River* TX-5
*Mud River* WI-6
Mud River—*channel* GA-3
Mud River—*gut* FL-3
Mud River—*stream* AK-9
Mud River—*stream* CT-1
Mud River—*stream* FL-3
Mud River—*stream* GA-3
Mud River—*stream* KY-4
Mud River—*stream* (2) MN-6
Mud River—*stream* WV-2
Mud River Covered Bridge—*hist pl* WV-2
Mud River Lookout Tower—*locale* MN-6
Mud River Mine Sch—*school* KY-4
Mud River Pool—*reservoir* MN-6
Mud River Spring—*spring* FL-3
Mud River Union Sch—*school* KY-4
Mud River Valley Sch—*school* KY-4
Mudro Lake—*lake* MN-6
Mud Rsvr—*reservoir* CO-8
Mud Rsvr—*reservoir* ID-8
Mud Rsvr—*reservoir* OR-9
*Mud Run* PA-2
Mud Run—*locale* PA-2
Mud Run—*stream* CA-9
Mud Run—*stream* (3) IL-6
Mud Run—*stream* (8) IN-6
Mud Run—*stream* (2) KY-4
Mud Run—*stream* (16) OH-6
Mud Run—*stream* (18) PA-2
Mud Run—*stream* (4) VA-3
Mud Run—*stream* (12) WV-2
Mud Run—*stream* WI-6
Mud Run Cem—*cemetery* (2) OH-6
Mud Run Ch—*church* WV-2
Mud Run Creek—*stream* PA-2
*Mud Run Dam* PA-2
Mud Run Dam—*dam* PA-2
Mud Run Mtn—*summit* VA-3
Mud Run Park—*park* OH-6
Mud Run Rsvr—*reservoir* MT-8
Mud Run Rsvr—*reservoir* PA-2
Mud Run Sch—*school* IL-6
Mud Run Swamp—*swamp* PA-2
Mud Rush Creek—*stream* AL-4
**Mudsand**—*pop pl* OK-5
Mud Sch—*school* WV-2
Mud Sch (historical)—*school* PA-2
Mud Schoolhouse Corners—*locale* NY-2
Mud Seep—*spring* AZ-5
Mud Seep—*spring* UT-8
Mud Seep Draw—*valley* TX-5
Mud Seep Tank—*reservoir* AZ-5
**Mud Settlement**—*pop pl* NY-2
Mudsill Spring—*spring* CO-8
Mudsink—*locale* TN-4
Mud Slash Sch—*school* KY-4
Mud Slide Cave—*cave* AL-4
Mudslide Creek—*stream* AK-9
*Mud Slough* OR-9
Mud Slough—*gut* (2) AR-4
Mud Slough—*gut* (3) CA-9
Mud Slough—*gut* (4) IL-6
Mud Slough—*gut* (2) KY-4
Mud Slough—*gut* LA-4
Mud Slough—*gut* MN-6
Mud Slough—*gut* MO-7
Mud Slough—*gut* OK-5
Mud Slough—*gut* (2) OR-9
Mud Slough—*lake* MN-6
Mud Slough—*stream* AR-4
Mud Slough—*stream* (3) CA-9
Mud Slough—*stream* FL-3
Mud Slough—*stream* ID-8
Mud Slough—*stream* (2) IL-6
Mud Slough—*stream* MO-7
Mud Slough—*stream* OK-5
Mud Slough—*stream* OR-9
Mud Slough—*stream* TN-4
Mud Slough Bypass—*canal* CA-9
Mud Slough Ditch—*canal* (2) AR-4
Mud Slough Ditch—*canal* MO-7
*Mudsock* IN-6
**Mudsock**—*pop pl* OH-6
Mud Sock Branch—*stream* KY-4
Mud Sock Cem—*cemetery* OH-6
**Mudsock (Sand Fork)**—*pop pl* OH-6
*Mud Spring* AZ-5
*Mud Spring* NV-8
*Mud Spring* NM-5
*Mud Spring* OR-9
*Mud Spring* WA-9
Mud Spring—*hist pl* UT-8
Mud Spring—*spring* (52) AZ-5
Mud Spring—*spring* (2) AR-4
Mud Spring—*spring* (28) CA-9
Mud Spring—*spring* (12) CO-8
Mud Spring—*spring* FL-3
Mud Spring—*spring* (16) ID-8
Mud Spring—*spring* (2) MO-7
Mud Spring—*spring* (13) MT-8
Mud Spring—*spring* (51) NV-8
Mud Spring—*spring* (9) NM-5
Mud Spring—*spring* (54) OR-9
Mud Spring—*spring* SD-7
Mud Spring—*spring* TN-4
Mud Spring—*spring* (6) TX-5
Mud Spring—*spring* (56) UT-8
Mud Spring—*spring* (8) WA-9
Mud Spring—*spring* (8) WY-8
Mud Spring Basin—*basin* NV-8
Mud Spring Bench—*bench* (2) UT-8
Mud Spring Branch—*stream* AL-4
Mud Spring Branch—*stream* TN-4
Mud Spring Butte—*summit* OR-9
Mud Spring Cabin—*locale* MT-8
Mud Spring Camp—*locale* OR-9
*Mud Spring Canyon* OR-9
Mud Spring Canyon—*valley* (6) AZ-5
Mud Spring Canyon—*valley* CO-8
Mud Spring Canyon—*valley* (2) ID-8
Mud Spring Canyon—*valley* (5) NV-8
Mud Spring Canyon—*valley* (3) NM-5
Mud Spring Canyon—*valley* OR-9
Mud Spring Canyon—*valley* (2) UT-8
Mud Spring Canyon—*valley* WA-9
Mud Spring Community Club—*locale* WA-9
Mud Spring Coulee—*valley* (2) MT-8
*Mud Spring Creek* CO-8
*Mud Spring Creek* MT-8
*Mud Spring Creek* OR-9
Mud Spring Creek—*stream* AZ-5
Mud Spring Creek—*stream* CA-9
Mud Spring Creek—*stream* CO-8
Mud Spring Creek—*stream* ID-8
Mud Spring Creek—*stream* MT-8
Mud Spring Creek—*stream* (2) NV-8
Mud Spring Creek—*stream* OR-9
Mud Spring Creek—*stream* TX-5
Mud Spring Creek—*stream* (2) UT-8
Mud Spring Creek—*stream* WY-8
*Mud Spring Draw* AZ-5
Mud Spring Draw—*valley* CO-8
Mud Spring Draw—*valley* TX-5
Mud Spring Draw—*valley* (3) UT-8
Mud Spring Draw—*valley* WY-8
Mud Spring (Dry)—*spring* CA-9
Mud Spring Flat—*flat* UT-8
Mud Spring Gap—*gap* CA-9
Mud Spring Gulch—*valley* CA-9
Mud Spring Gulch—*valley* CO-8
Mud Spring Gulch—*valley* (2) ID-8
Mud Spring Gulch—*valley* MT-8
Mud Spring Gulch—*valley* (2) NV-8
Mud Spring Hills—*summit* UT-8
*Mud Spring Hollow* UT-8
Mud Spring Hollow—*valley* AR-4
Mud Spring Hollow—*valley* (2) MO-7
Mud Spring Hollow—*valley* OK-5
Mud Spring Hollow—*valley* TN-4
Mud Spring Hollow—*valley* (4) UT-8
Mud Spring Hollow—*valley* WY-8
*Mud Spring Lake* IN-6
Mud Spring Mesa—*bench* NM-5
Mud Spring Mesa—*summit* (2) AZ-5
Mud Spring Mesa—*summit* NM-5
Mud Spring Mine—*mine* NV-8
Mud Spring Mine (Inactive)—*mine* NV-8
Mud Spring Mtn—*summit* (2) NM-5
Mud Spring Mtn—*summit* OR-9
Mud Spring Number One—*spring* NV-8
Mud Spring Number Two—*spring* NV-8
Mud Spring Pond—*lake* OR-9
Mud Spring Ranch—*locale* CO-8
Mud Spring Ridge—*ridge* (2) UT-8
Mud Spring Ridge—*ridge* WA-9
Mud Spring Rsvr—*reservoir* (2) CO-8
Mud Spring Rsvr—*reservoir* OR-9
Mud Spring Rsvr No 1—*reservoir* UT-8
Mud Spring Rsvr No 3—*reservoir* UT-8
*Mud Springs* ID-8
*Mud Springs* NV-8
Mud Springs—*locale* ID-8
Mud Springs—*locale* NV-8
Mud Springs—*other* NM-5
Mud Springs—*spring* (11) AZ-5
Mud Springs—*spring* (8) CA-9
Mud Springs—*spring* (2) CO-8
Mud Springs—*spring* (5) ID-8
Mud Springs—*spring* (6) MT-8
Mud Springs—*spring* NE-7
Mud Springs—*spring* (10) NV-8
Mud Springs—*spring* NM-5
Mud Springs—*spring* (5) OR-9
Mud Springs—*spring* (2) TX-5
Mud Springs—*spring* (6) UT-8
Mud Springs—*spring* (7) WY-8
Mud Springs—*stream* TX-5
Mud Spring (salt)—*spring* OR-9
*Mud Springs Basin* NV-8
Mud Springs Branch—*stream* WY-8
*Mud Springs Canyon* AZ-5
Mud Springs Canyon—*valley* (4) AZ-5
Mud Springs Canyon—*valley* (2) CA-9
Mud Springs Canyon—*valley* CO-8
Mud Springs Canyon—*valley* (2) NM-5
Mud Springs Canyon—*valley* OR-9
*Mud Springs Creek* AZ-5
*Mud Springs Creek* UT-8
Mud Springs Creek—*stream* CA-9
Mud Springs Creek—*stream* CO-8
Mud Springs Creek—*stream* (2) ID-8
Mud Springs Creek—*stream* (4) MT-8
Mud Springs Creek—*stream* NE-7
Mud Springs Creek—*stream* (3) OR-9
Mud Springs Draw—*valley* (2) AZ-5
Mud Springs Draw—*valley* (2) CO-8
Mud Springs Draw—*valley* NV-8
Mud Springs Draw—*valley* (2) NM-5
Mud Springs Draw—*valley* WY-8
Mud Springs Flats—*flat* WY-8
Mud Springs Gulch—*valley* (3) CO-8
Mud Springs Gulch—*valley* (2) OR-9
*Mud Springs Hills* UT-8
Mud Springs Hollow—*valley* MO-7
Mud Springs Knoll—*summit* AZ-5
Mud Springs Lake—*lake* WY-8
*Mud Springs Mesa* AZ-5
Mud Springs Mountains—*ridge* NM-5
Mud Springs Mtn—*summit* NM-5
Mud Springs Peaks—*ridge* NM-5
Mud Springs Plains—*plain* CA-9
Mud Springs Point—*cliff* UT-8
Mud Springs Pond—*reservoir* ID-8
Mud Springs Pony Express Station Site—*hist pl* NE-7
Mud Springs Pueblo—*hist pl* CO-8
Mud Springs Ranch—*locale* AZ-5
Mud Springs Ranch—*locale* NV-8
Mud Springs Ranch—*locale* NM-5
Mud Springs Ranch—*locale* WY-8
Mud Springs Ridge—*ridge* ID-8
Mud Springs Rsvr—*reservoir* ID-8
Mud Springs Rsvr—*reservoir* WY-8
Mud Springs Saddle—*gap* NV-8
Mud Springs Sch—*school* NE-7
Mud Springs Tank—*reservoir* AZ-5
Mud Springs Tank No 1—*reservoir* NM-5
Mud Springs Tank Number One—*reservoir* AZ-5
Mud Springs Tank Number Two—*reservoir* AZ-5
Mud Spring Station—*locale* NM-5
Mud Springs Trail Forty-nine—*trail* AZ-5
Mud Springs Underpass—*crossing* AZ-5
Mud Springs Valley—*valley* OR-9
*Mud Springs Wash* NV-8
Mud Springs Wash—*stream* AZ-5
Mud Springs Wash—*stream* (2) NV-8
Mud Spring Tank—*reservoir* (2) AZ-5
Mud Spring Tank—*reservoir* NM-5
Mud Spring Tank—*reservoir* TX-5
*Mud Spring Wash* UT-8
Mud Spring Wash—*stream* NV-8
Mud Spring Wash—*valley* NV-8
Mud Spring Wash—*valley* UT-8
Mud Spring Windmill—*locale* NM-5
Mud Spring Windmill—*locale* TX-5
*Mudstone Branch* DE-2
Mud Stream—*stream* ME-1
Mudsuck Branch—*stream* WV-2
Mud Suck Creek—*stream* TN-4
Mud Swamp—*stream* GA-3
Mud Swamp—*swamp* AL-4
Mud Swamp—*swamp* CA-9
Mud Swamp—*swamp* (5) FL-3
Mud Swamp—*swamp* (2) GA-3
Mud Swamp—*swamp* LA-4
Mud Swamp—*swamp* PA-2
Mud Tank—*reservoir* (20) AZ-5
Mud Tank—*reservoir* (4) NM-5
Mud Tank—*reservoir* (3) TX-5
*Mud Tank Draw* AZ-5
Mud Tank Number Two—*reservoir* AZ-5
Mud Tanks Draw—*valley* AZ-5
Mud Tanks Mesa—*summit* AZ-5
Mud Tanks Trail Fifty—*trail* AZ-5
Mud Tank Wash—*stream* AZ-5
**Mudtavern**—*pop pl* TN-4
Mud Tavern—*uninc pl* TN-4
Mud Tavern Creek—*stream* AL-4
Mud Tavern Hill—*summit* AL-4
Mud Thorofare—*channel* (2) NJ-2
*Mudtown* AL-4
**Mud Town**—*pop pl* MO-7
Mudtown—*uninc pl* VA-3
Mudtown Branch—*stream* AR-4
Mud Town Creek—*stream* MO-7
Mud Trough Spring—*spring* NV-8
Mud Tunnel—*tunnel* KY-4
Mud Tunnel—*tunnel* VA-3
Mud Tunnel Branch—*stream* TN-4
Mud Tunnel Hollow—*valley* TN-4
Mud Tunnel Hollow Mine—*mine* TN-4
Mud Turtle Pond—*lake* NH-1
Mud Turtle Spring—*spring* MT-8
*Mudunonguch* FM-9
*Mudurom* PW-9
**Mud Valley**—*pop pl* GA-3
Mud Valley—*valley* CA-9
Mud Valley Ch—*church* IL-6
Mudville—*locale* TN-4
**Mudville**—*pop pl* LA-4
**Mudville**—*pop pl* TX-5
Mud Volcano—*geyser* WY-8
Mud Wash—*stream* NV-8
Mud Water Canyon—*valley* UT-8
Mud Wells—*spring* NV-8
Mud Windmill—*locale* NV-8
*Mudy Creek* ID-8
Mudyutok River—*stream* AK-9
Muecke Cem—*cemetery* TN-4
Muehlsville—*locale* TX-5
Muela Creek—*stream* TX-5
Muela Mtn—*summit* TX-5
Muela Tank—*reservoir* TX-5
Muela Well—*well* TX-5
Muel Lake—*reservoir* OK-5
Muelle de Ponce—*locale* PR-3
Muellen Lake—*lake* WI-6
Mueller, Christ, House—*hist pl* OH-6
Mueller Archeol Site—*hist pl* MO-7
Mueller Brass Company—*facility* MS-4
Mueller Brewery—*hist pl* OH-6
Mueller Cabin—*locale* WY-8
Mueller Cem—*cemetery* IL-6
Mueller Cem—*cemetery* MN-6
Mueller Cem—*cemetery* SD-7
Mueller Cem—*cemetery* TN-4
Mueller Cem—*cemetery* TX-5
Mueller Christian Sch—*school* FL-3
Mueller Cove—*bay* AK-9
Mueller Creek—*stream* WA-9
Mueller Elem Sch—*school* KS-7
**Mueller Heights Subdivision**—*pop pl* UT-8
Mueller Hill Cem—*cemetery* IL-6
Mueller Homestead—*hist pl* SD-7
Mueller Lake—*lake* MN-6
Mueller Lake—*lake* OH-6
Mueller Lake—*lake* UT-8
Mueller Lake—*lake* WI-6
Mueller Lumber Company—*hist pl* IA-7
Mueller Mine—*mine* CA-9
Mueller Mtn—*summit* AK-9
Mueller Oil Field—*oilfield* TX-5
Mueller Park—*locale* WA-9
Mueller Park—*park* IL-6
*Mueller Park Campground* UT-8
Mueller Park JHS—*school* UT-8
Mueller Park Recreation Site—*park* UT-8
Mueller Ranch—*locale* NE-7
Mueller Ranch—*locale* WY-8
Muellers Camp—*locale* ID-8
Mueller Sch—*school* CA-9
Mueller Sch—*school* IL-6
Mueller-Schmidt House—*hist pl* KS-7
Mueller State Wildlife Mngmt Area—*park* MN-6
Muellersville—*locale* TX-5
**Mueller (Township of)**—*pop pl* MI-6
Mueller-Wright House—*hist pl* WI-6
Muench, Adolf, House—*hist pl* MN-6
Muench Island—*island* WI-6
*Muencovi* AZ-5
**Muenster**—*pop pl* TX-5
Muenster (CCD)—*cens area* TX-5
Muerlin Lake—*lake* MN-6
Muerta Island—*island* AK-9
Muerto, Canyon del—*valley* AZ-5
Muerto, Loma del—*summit* TX-5
Muerto Arroyo, El—*valley* TX-5
Muerto Camp—*locale* TX-5
Muerto Canyon—*valley* NM-5
*Muerto Creek* TX-5
Muerto Creek—*stream* (2) TX-5
Muerto Pens—*locale* TX-5
Muertos Canyon—*valley* CA-9
Muertos Canyon—*valley* NM-5
Muertos Canyon Windmill—*locale* NM-5
Muertos Creek—*stream* NM-5
Muerto Spring—*spring* NM-5
Muertos Windmill—*locale* TX-5
Muerto Windmill—*locale* (2) TX-5
Muery Cem—*cemetery* TX-5
Mueschkle Cem—*cemetery* TX-5
Muesch Ranch—*locale* NE-7
Muesebach Creek—*stream* TX-5
*Mueseback Creek* TX-5
Mueses Canyon Tank—*reservoir* NM-5
Muesial Creek—*stream* OR-9
Muesing Cem—*cemetery* IN-6
Muesing Creek—*stream* IN-6
Muessel Elem Sch—*school* IN-6
Muessel Grove Park—*park* IN-6
*Muesse School* IN-6
*Mueykava* AZ-5
Muff—*locale* PA-2
Muffin Arch—*arch* (2) UT-8
Muffin Butte—*summit* UT-8
Muffin Islands—*area* AK-9
*Muffittville* MO-7
**Muffittville**—*pop pl* MO-7
Muffle Lake—*lake* MI-6
Muffley Sch—*school* IL-6
Muffley Spring—*spring* PA-2
*Muga* FL-3
Mugai Channel—*channel* FM-9
*Mugerara Creek* TX-5
*Mugerera Creek* TX-5
*Mugerrara Creek* TX-5
Mugg Cem—*cemetery* TX-5
Mugge, Edward, House—*hist pl* TX-5
Mugget Hill—*summit* MA-1
*Muggett Hill* MA-1
Mugg-Ingels Ditch—*canal* IN-6
Muggins Creek—*stream* CA-9
Muggins Creek—*stream* MT-8
Muggins Flat—*flat* AZ-5
Muggins Flat—*flat* UT-8
Muggins Gap—*gap* MT-8
Muggins Gulch—*valley* (2) CO-8
Muggins Mesa—*bench* AZ-5
Muggins Mountains—*range* AZ-5
Muggins Peak—*summit* AZ-5
Muggins Placers Mine—*mine* AZ-5
Muggins Rsvr—*reservoir* AZ-5
**Mugginsville**—*pop pl* CA-9
Mugginsville Mtn—*summit* TX-5
Muggins Wash—*stream* AZ-5
*Mugglers Meadow* CA-9
Muggs Castle Tank—*reservoir* AZ-5
Muggun Creek—*stream* MI-6
Muggy Point—*summit* NM-5
Mug House—*locale* CO-8
Mugisitokiwik—*locale* AK-9
Mug Lake—*lake* (2) MN-6
Mugler Creek—*stream* CA-9
Muglers Meadow—*flat* CA-9
Mugmaar—*summit* FM-9
*Mugmar* FM-9
Mug Post Office (historical)—*building* TN-4
Mugser Run—*stream* PA-2
Mug Tank—*reservoir* AZ-5
Muguchig—*bar* FM-9
Mugu Lagoon—*bay* CA-9
Mugum Peak—*summit* AK-9
Mugu Peak—*summit* CA-9
*Mugurrewock* ME-1
Muguwilap—*bar* FM-9
Mugwump Lake—*lake* MN-6
Mugwump Lake—*lake* OR-9
Mugwump Spring—*spring* UT-8
Muhammads Islamic Temple—*church* IN-6
Muheenui—*summit* HI-9
Muheim House—*hist pl* AZ-5
*Muhlberger* KS-7
Muhle Creek—*stream* TX-5
Muhleman Run—*stream* OH-6
**Muhlenberg**—*pop pl* (2) PA-2
Muhlenberg—*uninc pl* NJ-2
Muhlenberg Coll—*school* PA-2
**Muhlenberg (County)**—*pop pl* KY-4
Muhlenberg County Courthouse—*hist pl* KY-4
Muhlenberg Elem Sch—*school* PA-2
Muhlenberg Med Ctr—*hospital* PA-2
**Muhlenberg Park**—*pop pl* PA-2
*Muhlenberg Sch* PA-2
Muhlenberg Sch—*hist pl* PA-2
Muhlenberg Station (abandoned)—*locale* PA-2
**Muhlenberg (Township of)**—*pop pl* OH-6
**Muhlenberg (Township of)**—*pop pl* PA-2
**Muhlenburg**—*pop pl* PA-2
Muhlenburg Hosp—*hospital* NJ-2
Muhlenfels Point—*cape* VI-3
*Muhley Point* UT-8
Muhr, Simon, Work Training Sch—*hist pl* PA-2
Muhr Sch—*school* PA-2
*Muhuagueitt Pond* RI-1
Muiel Dam—*dam* AL-4
Muiel Lake—*reservoir* AL-4
*Mui Island* MP-9
Muik Vaya—*area* AZ-5
Muil—*locale* TX-5
Muinick Hollow—*valley* AR-4
Muir—*locale* KY-4
Muir—*locale* MT-8
**Muir**—*pop pl* AR-4
**Muir**—*pop pl* (2) CA-9
**Muir**—*pop pl* MI-6
**Muir**—*pop pl* PA-2
Muir, David, House—*hist pl* UT-8
Muir, John, Branch—*hist pl* CA-9
Muir, Mount—*summit* AK-9
Muir, Mount—*summit* CA-9
Muir AAF Airp—*airport* PA-2
Muir Beach—*beach* CA-9
**Muir Beach**—*pop pl* CA-9
Muir Beach Archeol Site—*hist pl* CA-9
Muir Camp—*locale* CA-9
Muir Canyon—*valley* CA-9
Muir Cem—*cemetery* MO-7
Muir Church of Christ—*hist pl* MI-6
Muir Creek—*channel* MD-2
Muir Creek—*stream* ID-8
Muir Creek—*stream* MT-8
Muir Creek—*stream* (3) OR-9
Muir Creek Falls—*falls* OR-9
Muir Draw—*valley* NM-5
**Muirfield**—*pop pl* MO-7
Muir Glacier—*glacier* AK-9
Muir Gorge—*valley* CA-9
Muir Grove—*woods* CA-9
Muirhead—*locale* NJ-2
Muirheid Cem—*cemetery* IL-6
Muir House—*hist pl* KY-4
Muir Inlet—*bay* AK-9
Muir JHS—*school* (2) CA-9
Muir JHS—*school* WI-6
Muirkirk—*locale* MD-2
*Muir Lake* WI-6
Muir Lake—*lake* CA-9
Muir Lake—*lake* (2) IN-6
Muir Lake—*lake* MI-6
Muirlands JHS—*school* CA-9
**Muir Meadows Subdivision**—*pop pl* UT-8
Muir Memorial Park—*cemetery* WI-6
Muir Mine—*mine* CA-9
Muir Park—*park* WI-6
Muir Pass—*gap* CA-9
Muir Playground—*park* CA-9
Muir Point—*cape* AK-9
Muir Pond—*lake* NY-2
Muir Ponds—*reservoir* CO-8
Muir Ranch—*locale* NM-5
Muir Rapids—*rapids* OR-9
Muir Rsvr—*reservoir* OR-9
Muir Rsvr—*reservoir* WY-8
**Muirs**—*pop pl* MI-6
Muir Sch—*school* (7) CA-9
Muir Sch—*school* OH-6
Muir Sch—*school* UT-8
Muir Sch—*school* WA-9
Muir Sch—*school* WI-6
Muir Sch (abandoned)—*school* MO-7
Muirs Chapel—*church* NC-3
Muir Snowfield—*glacier* WA-9
Muir Spring—*spring* MT-8
Muir Spring—*spring* OR-9
Muir Springs—*spring* CO-8
Muir Tank—*lake* NM-5
Muir Trail Ranch—*locale* CA-9
Muir Woods Natl Monmt—*park* CA-9
*Muit* MP-9
*Muitekun* FM-9
*Muitekun Pass* FM-9
Muitikino—*bar* FM-9
*Mui-to* MP-9
Muitrikrik (not verified)—*island* MP-9
**Muitzeskill**—*pop pl* NY-2
Muitzes Kill—*stream* NY-2
Muitzes Kill Hist Dist—*hist pl* NY-2
Mujares Creek—*stream* TX-5
*Mujer Arroyo* TX-5
*Mujerero Creek* TX-5
Mujeres Camp—*locale* NM-5
Mujeres Well—*well* TX-5
Mujeres Windmill—*locale* TX-5
*Mujinkaarikku To* MP-9
Mujinkarikku—*island* MP-9
*Mujinkarikku-to* MP-9
*Mujinkarikku-to Island* MP-9
*Mujinkarikkuu Muginkarikku* MP-9
*Mujun* FM-9
Mukacharni Mtn—*summit* AK-9
Mukachiak Creek—*stream* AK-9
*Mukeru* PW-9
Mukewater Cem—*cemetery* TX-5
Mukewater Creek—*stream* TX-5
Mukialik—*locale* AK-9
*Mukil Island* MP-9
**Mukilteo**—*pop pl* WA-9
Mukilteo Light Station—*hist pl* WA-9
Mukilteo State Park—*park* WA-9
*Mukkaw Bay* WA-9
*Mukkuri* MP-9
Mukkuri—*island* MP-9
*Mukkuri-To* MP-9
Muklassa—*hist pl* AL-4
Mukluk Creek—*stream* (2) AK-9
Mukluk Slough—*stream* AK-9
Mukluktulik River—*stream* AK-9
Muklung Hills—*other* AK-9
Muklung River—*stream* AK-9
Muknuk River—*stream* AK-9
*Muko Jima* FM-9
Mukooda Lake—*lake* MN-6
*Mu-koon-tu-weap* AZ-5
*Mu-Koon'-Tu-Weap* UT-8
*Muko Shima* FM-9
Mukslulik Creek—*stream* AK-9
Mukuaiki Point—*cape* HI-9
Mukuksok Channel—*stream* AK-9
Mukuksok Point—*cape* AK-9
*Mukuntuweap* UT-8
*Mukuntuweap River* UT-8
*Mukwanago Lake* WI-6
Mukwa State Wildlife Area—*park* WI-6
**Mukwa (Town of)**—*pop pl* WI-6
**Mukwonago**—*pop pl* WI-6
Mukwonago Lake—*lake* WI-6
Mukwonago Park—*park* WI-6
Mukwonago River—*stream* WI-6
**Mukwonago (Town of)**—*pop pl* WI-6
Mula (Barrio)—*fmr MCD* PR-3
Mula Creek—*stream* TX-5
Mula Pasture—*flat* TX-5
Mulas (Barrio)—*fmr MCD* PR-3
Mulat—*locale* FL-3
Mula Tank—*reservoir* TX-5
Mulat Lookout Tower—*tower* FL-3
*Mulato* MH-9
Mulato Creek—*stream* TX-5
Mulato Dam—*dam* TX-5
Mulatos Well—*well* TX-5
Mulatto Bayou—*gut* LA-4
Mulatto Bayou—*stream* FL-3
Mulatto Bayou—*stream* MS-4
Mulatto Bayou Sch (historical)—*school* MS-4
Mulatto Bend Landing—*locale* LA-4
Mulatto Branch—*stream* (2) NC-3
Mulatto Canyon—*valley* NM-5
Mulatto Mtn—*summit* NC-3
Mulatto Run—*stream* VA-3
Mulatu—*basin* MH-9
*Mulawai Stream* HI-9
Mula Well (Flowing)—*well* TX-5
*Mulberry* KS-7
*Mulberry* MO-7
*Mulberry* WV-2
Mulberry—*CDP* SC-3
Mulberry—*locale* (2) AL-4
Mulberry—*locale* KY-4
Mulberry—*locale* MS-4
Mulberry—*locale* NC-3
**Mulberry**—*pop pl* AL-4
**Mulberry**—*pop pl* AR-4
**Mulberry**—*pop pl* FL-3
**Mulberry**—*pop pl* GA-3
**Mulberry**—*pop pl* IN-6
**Mulberry**—*pop pl* KS-7
**Mulberry**—*pop pl* LA-4
**Mulberry**—*pop pl* MI-6
**Mulberry**—*pop pl* MS-4
**Mulberry**—*pop pl* MO-7
**Mulberry**—*pop pl* NC-3
**Mulberry**—*pop pl* OH-6
**Mulberry**—*pop pl* TN-4
**Mulberry**—*pop pl* TX-5
**Mulberry Acres (subdivision)**—*pop pl* TN-4
Mulberry Baptist Ch—*church* NC-3
Mulberry Baptist Ch (historical)—*church* MS-4
*Mulberry Baptist Church* AL-4
Mulberry Bayou—*stream* LA-4
Mulberry Branch—*stream* AL-4
Mulberry Branch—*stream* (2) KY-4
Mulberry Branch—*stream* (3) NC-3
Mulberry Branch—*stream* (3) SC-3

Mullens Branch—stream (2) ... WV-2
Mullens Brook—stream ... CT-1
Mullens Camp—locale ... CA-9
Mullens Canyon—valley ... NV-8
Mullens Cem—cemetery ... LA-4
Mullens Cem—cemetery (3) ... MS-4
Mullens Cem—cemetery (2) ... WV-2
Mullen Sch—school ... IL-6
Mullen Sch—school ... NY-2
Mullen Sch—school ... WI-6
Mullens Cove ... ME-1
Mullens Cove—bay ... TN-4
Mullen's Cove—hist pl ... ME-1
Mullens Cove Checking Station—locale ... TN-4
Mullens Creek—stream ... IA-7
Mullens Creek—stream ... MT-8
Mullens Creek—stream ... TN-4
Mullens Cut—gap ... AZ-5
Mullens Gap—gap ... AR-4
Mullen Slough—stream ... AK-9
Mullens Pass ... NV-8
Mullens Pond—lake ... CT-1
Mullens Pond—reservoir ... NC-3
Mullens Pond Dam—dam ... NC-3
Mullen Spring—spring ... AZ-5
Mullen Spring—spring (3) ... OR-9
Mullens Ridge—ridge ... KY-4
Mullens Sch—school ... MS-4
Mullens Spring—spring ... CA-9
**Mullensville**—pop pl ... WV-2
Mullen Swamp—swamp ... PA-2
**Mullen Township**—pop pl ... NE-7
**Mullen Township**—pop pl ... SD-7
Mullenville ... KS-7
Mullen Wash—stream ... AZ-5
Mullen Well—well ... AZ-5
Mullen Wells ... AZ-5
**Muller**—pop pl ... AR-4
Muller, Daniel C., Carousel—hist pl ... OH-6
Muller, Mount—summit ... WA-9
Muller Basin Spring—spring ... OR-9
Muller Bay—bay ... VI-3
Muller Brook—stream ... NY-2
Muller Cem—cemetery ... OR-9
Muller Cem—cemetery ... TX-5
Muller Creek—stream ... AK-9
Muller Creek—stream ... CO-8
Muller Dam—dam ... NM-5
Muller Hill—summit ... NY-2
Muller Hollow—valley ... TN-4
Muller Hollow Branch—stream ... TN-4
Muller House—hist pl ... IL-6
Muller Key Channel Fishing Pier Lights—locale ... FL-3
Mullerleile Pond—lake ... OR-9
Muller Mtn—summit ... NV-8
Muller Park—park ... UT-8
Muller Pond—lake ... NY-2
Muller Ponds—reservoir ... OR-9
Muller Rsvr—reservoir ... OR-9
Mullers Barn Ridge—ridge ... SC-3
Mullers Big Lake—lake ... SC-3
Mullers Canyon—valley ... WA-9
Muller Sch—school ... CA-9
Muller Sch—school ... SD-7
Muller Sch (abandoned)—school ... PA-2
Mullers Little Lake—lake ... SC-3
Muller Spring—spring ... MT-8
Mullers Spring—spring ... AR-4
**Mullertown**—pop pl ... PA-2
Muller Well—well ... UT-8
Mullery Creek—stream ... MT-8
Mullery Island ... TX-5
Mullet ... MI-6
Mullet, Lake—reservoir ... TX-5
Mullet Bay—bay ... FL-3
Mullet Branch—stream ... KY-4
Mullet Brook—stream ... NY-2
Mullet Cove—bay ... LA-4
Mullet Cove—bay ... NC-3
Mullet Creek ... WI-6
Mullet Creek—channel ... VA-3
Mullet Creek—gut ... FL-3
Mullet Creek—stream (3) ... FL-3
Mullet Creek—stream ... NY-2
Mullet Creek—stream ... NC-3
Mullet Creek—stream ... SC-3
Mullet Creek Bay—bay ... NY-2
Mulletcunk River ... NJ-2
Mullet Gut—stream ... NC-3
Mullet Hall—locale ... SC-3
Mullet Island—island ... CA-9
Mullet Island—island ... TX-5
Mullet Key—hist pl ... FL-3
Mullet Key—island (2) ... FL-3
Mullet Key Bayou—bay ... FL-3
Mullet Key Channel—channel ... FL-3
Mullet Key Shoal—bar ... FL-3
Mullet Lake ... MI-6
Mullet Lake—lake (2) ... FL-3
Mullet Lake—lake ... MS-4
Mullet Lake—lake ... ND-7
Mullet Lake—lake ... WI-6
**Mullet Lake Park**—pop pl ... FL-3
Mullet Marsh—swamp ... WI-6
Mullet Point—cape ... AL-4
Mullet Point Park—park ... AL-4
Mullet Pond—lake ... FL-3
Mullet Pond—lake ... NC-3
Mullet River—stream ... WI-6
Mullet River State Wildlife Area—park ... WI-6
Mullet Run—stream ... DE-2
Mullet Run—stream ... NC-3
Mullet Run—stream ... OH-6
Mullet Shoal—bar (2) ... NC-3
Mullet Slough—gut ... FL-3
Mullett ... MI-6
Mullett Creek—stream ... MI-6
Mullett Island ... CA-9
Mullett Lake—lake ... MI-6
**Mullett Lake**—pop pl ... MI-6
Mullett River ... WI-6
**Mullett (Township of)**—pop pl ... MI-6
Mulley Point—cape ... UT-8
Mulleyville Pond—lake ... NY-2
Mulley Windmill—locale ... TX-5
Mull Glove Pit—cave ... AL-4
Mull Grove ... NC-3
Mull Grove Ch—church ... NC-3
Mull Grove (historical)—locale ... NC-3
Mullhall ... OK-5
**Mullica Hill**—pop pl ... NJ-2
Mullica Hill Pond—reservoir ... NJ-2
Mullican Branch—stream ... AL-4
Mullican Canyon—valley ... AZ-5
Mullicane Sch (abandoned)—school ... MO-7
Mullican Hollow—valley ... TN-4
Mullican Place Tank—reservoir ... AZ-5
Mullican Ranch—locale ... AZ-5
Mullican Spring—spring ... TN-4
Mullican Tank—reservoir ... AZ-5
Mullican Tank Number One—reservoir ... AZ-5
Mullican Tank Number Two—reservoir ... AZ-5
Mullica River—stream ... NJ-2
Mullicas River ... NJ-2
**Mullica (Township of)**—pop pl ... NJ-2
Mullicus Creek ... NJ-2
Mullicus River ... NJ-2
Mulligan—locale ... AR-4
Mulligan Airp—airport ... PA-2
Mulligan Brook—stream ... NY-2
Mulligan Butte—summit ... WA-9
Mulligan Canyon ... AZ-5
Mulligan Canyon—valley ... CO-8
Mulligan Canyon—valley ... NV-8
Mulligan Creek ... GA-3
Mulligan Creek—stream ... AK-9
Mulligan Creek—stream (2) ... ID-8
Mulligan Creek—stream (2) ... MI-6
Mulligan Creek—stream ... NY-2
Mulligan Creek—stream ... OR-9
Mulligan Creek—stream ... SC-3
Mulligan Creek—stream ... WI-6
Mulligan Ditch—canal ... IN-6
Mulligan Draw—valley ... WY-8
Mulligan Gap—gap ... AL-4
Mulligan Gap—gap ... NV-8
Mulligan Gulch—valley ... OR-9
Mulligan Hill—summit (2) ... CA-9
Mulligan Hill—summit ... PA-2
Mulligan Hole—bay ... WY-8
Mulligan Hollow—valley ... AR-4
Mulligan Hollow—valley ... PA-2
Mulligan Hump—summit ... ID-8
Mulligan JHS—school ... NY-2
Mulligan Lake—lake (2) ... MN-6
Mulligan Lake—lake ... WI-6
Mulligan Meadow—flat ... WA-9
Mulligan Park—flat ... WY-8
Mulligan Peak—summit ... AZ-5
Mulligan Plains—flat ... MI-6
Mulligan Ponds—lake ... NH-1
Mulligan Rsvr—reservoir (2) ... CO-8
Mulligan Run—stream ... PA-2
Mulligans Cem—cemetery ... IN-6
Mulligan Sch—school ... IL-6
Mulligans Hollow Park—park ... MI-6
Mulligan State Wildlife Mngmt Area—park ... MN-6
Mulligan Stew Canyon—valley ... OR-9
Mulligan Stream—stream ... ME-1
Mulligan Swamp—swamp ... MI-6
**Mulligan (Township of)**—pop pl ... MN-6
Mulligan Wash—valley ... UT-8
**Mulliken**—pop pl ... MI-6
Mullikin ... MD-2
Mullikin Brook—stream ... NH-1
Mullikin Cem—cemetery ... TN-4
Mullikin Hollow—valley ... MO-7
Mullikin Junction—locale ... KY-4
Mullikin Sch—school ... MD-2
**Mullin**—pop pl ... TX-5
**Mullin**—pop pl ... VA-3
Mullinaw Creek—stream ... TX-5
Mullinax Cem—cemetery ... MO-7
Mullinax Cem—cemetery ... SC-3
Mullinax Cove—valley ... NC-3
Mullinax Gap—gap ... NC-3
Mullinax Hollow—valley ... TN-4
Mullinax Mtn—summit ... GA-3
Mullinax Trail—trail ... NC-3
Mullin Bible Camp—school ... NC-3
Mullin Bog—swamp ... ME-1
Mullin Branch ... VA-3
Mullin Branch—stream ... KY-4
Mullin Branch—stream ... MO-7
Mullin Canyon—valley ... TX-5
Mullin Cem—cemetery ... KY-4
Mullin Cem—cemetery ... VA-3
Mullin Creek—stream ... MO-7
Mullin Creek—stream ... TX-5
Mulliner Ditch—canal ... IN-6
Mullin Hill—summit ... CT-1
Mullin Hill—summit ... NY-2
Mullin Hill—summit ... NC-3
Mullinix—locale ... MD-2
Mullinix Creek—stream ... NV-8
Mullinix Creek—stream ... OR-9
Mullin Lake—reservoir ... AL-4
Mullin Lake—reservoir ... GA-3
Mullin Lake Dam—dam ... AL-4
Mullin Pond—lake ... KY-4
Mullin-Priddy (CCD)—cens area ... TX-5
Mullin Ranch—locale ... CO-8
Mullin Ridge—ridge ... WI-6
Mullins—locale ... KY-4
**Mullins**—pop pl ... AL-4
**Mullins**—pop pl ... IL-6
**Mullins**—pop pl ... SC-3
**Mullins Addition (Blair Town)**—pop pl ... KY-4
Mullins Big Spring—spring ... AL-4
Mullins Bottom ... VA-3
Mullins Branch ... VA-3
Mullins Branch—stream (2) ... AL-4
Mullins Branch—stream (6) ... KY-4
Mullins Branch—stream ... TN-4
Mullins Branch—stream (2) ... VA-3
Mullins Branch—stream ... WV-2
Mullins (CCD)—cens area ... SC-3
Mullins Cem—cemetery ... AL-4
Mullins Cem—cemetery ... KY-4
Mullins Cem—cemetery ... MO-7
Mullins Cem—cemetery (5) ... TN-4
Mullins Cem—cemetery (2) ... TX-5
Mullins Cem—cemetery (9) ... VA-3
Mullins Cem—cemetery (7) ... WV-2
Mullins Cem (City View)—cemetery ... TN-4
Mullins Cemetery ... MS-4
Mullins Ch—church ... TN-4
Mullin Sch—school ... TX-5
Mullins Chapel—church (2) ... TN-4
Mullins Chapel Baptist Ch ... TN-4
Mullins Chapel (historical)—church ... TN-4
Mullins Chapel Sch (historical)—school ... TN-4
Mullin School (Abandoned)—locale ... MO-7
Mullins Coulee—valley ... MT-8
Mullins Cove ... TN-4
Mullins Cove Dock—locale ... TN-4
Mullins Creek ... TN-4
Mullins Creek—stream ... WA-9
Mullins Crossing—locale ... TX-5
Mullins Crossroads—locale ... NC-3
Mullins Ditch—canal ... MT-8
Mullins Ferry ... MS-4
Mullins Flow—channel ... NY-2
Mullins Ford Ch—church ... GA-3
Mullins Fork—stream (2) ... KY-4
Mullins Fork—stream ... VA-3
Mullins Gap—gap ... KY-4
Mullins Hollow—valley (2) ... KY-4
Mullins Hollow—valley ... MO-7
Mullins Hollow—valley (4) ... TN-4
Mullins Hollow—valley ... VA-3
Mullins Hollow—valley ... WV-2
Mullins Lake—dam ... AL-4
Mullins Lake—lake ... WI-6
Mullins Lake Dam—dam ... MS-4
Mullins Marsh Creek—stream ... NY-2
Mullins Mill Bridge—bridge ... TN-4
Mullins Mill (historical)—locale (2) ... TN-4
Mullins Mill P.O. (historical)—locale ... AL-4
Mullins Mtn—summit ... VA-3
Mullins-Nettleton Cem—cemetery ... MS-4
Mullins Old Mill ... TN-4
Mullins Point Chapel—church ... KY-4
Mullins Pond—reservoir ... VA-3
Mullins Post Office (historical)—building ... AL-4
Mullins Prairie—locale ... TX-5
Mullin Spring—spring ... AZ-5
Mullin Spring—spring ... ID-8
Mullin Spring—spring ... WA-9
Mullin Spring Gulch—valley ... WA-9
Mullins Ridge—ridge (2) ... VA-3
Mullins Sch—school ... KY-4
Mullins Sch—school ... OK-5
Mullins Sch (historical)—school ... AL-4
Mullins Sch (historical)—school ... MS-4
Mullins Sch (historical)—school (2) ... TN-4
Mullins School ... TN-4
Mullins Spring ... AL-4
Mullins-Stacy Cem—cemetery ... NC-3
Mullins Station Ch—church ... TN-4
Mullins Store (historical)—locale (3) ... MS-4
Mullins Tank—reservoir ... NM-5
**Mullinsville**—pop pl ... FL-3
Mullins Windmill—locale ... CO-8
**Mullins (Withers)**—pop pl ... KY-4
**Mullinville**—pop pl ... KS-7
Mullinville Elem Sch—school ... KS-7
Mullinville HS—school ... KS-7
Mullin Well—well ... NM-5
Mullis Bay—bay ... GA-3
Mullis Branch—stream ... AR-4
Mullis Cem—cemetery ... GA-3
**Mullis City**—pop pl ... FL-3
Mullis-Cole Cem—cemetery ... GA-3
Mullis Hollow—valley ... IN-6
Mullis Lake—lake ... NE-7
Mull Island—island ... NY-2
Mullison Creek—stream ... WY-8
Mullison Island—island ... WY-8
Mullison Park—flat ... WY-8
Mullis Ponds—lake ... GA-3
Mull Lake—lake ... AK-9
Mull Mountain—ridge ... GA-3
Mull Mtn—summit ... AL-4
Mullock Creek—stream ... FL-3
Mullock Gulch—valley ... CO-8
Mullon ... MT-8
Mullory Rsvr—reservoir ... MT-8
**Mulloy**—pop pl ... OR-9
**Mulloy**—pop pl ... TN-4
Mulloy Brook—stream ... ME-1
Mulloy Landing—locale ... FL-3
Mulloys ... TN-4
Mulloys Post Office (historical)—building ... TN-4
Mull Sch—school ... NC-3
Mulls Chapel—church (2) ... NC-3
Mulls Gap—gap ... PA-2
Mullu ... MP-9
Mullu Island ... MP-9
Mulmick Gulch—valley ... ID-8
Mulnix—locale ... LA-4
Mulno Cove—bay ... WA-9
Mulnolland Creek ... WA-9
Muloeloew—locale ... FM-9
Mulolou ... FM-9
Mulolow ... FM-9
Mulona—summit ... GU-9
Mulos Hills—range ... TX-5
Mulos Hills Ranch—locale ... TX-5
Mulpus Brook—stream ... MA-1
Mulrien House—hist pl ... NY-2
Mulro' ... FM-9
Mulroo ... FM-9
**Mulroq**—pop pl ... FM-9
Mulsonburg Sch—school ... PA-2
Mulstay Creek—stream ... CO-8
Multa Trina Ditch—canal ... CO-8
Multiple Mountain ... OR-9
Multiple Springs—spring ... OR-9
Multnomah ... OR-9
**Multnomah**—pop pl ... OR-9
Multnomah Channel—channel ... OR-9
Multnomah Civic Stadium—locale ... OR-9
Multnomah Coll—school ... OR-9
**Multnomah County**—pop pl ... OR-9
Multnomah County Courthouse—hist pl ... OR-9
Multnomah Creek—stream ... OR-9
Multnomah Falls—falls ... WA-9
Multnomah Falls—locale ... OR-9
Multnomah Falls Ban—bar ... OR-9
Multnomah Falls Lodge and Footpath—hist pl ... OR-9
Multnomah Falls Upper Range Channel—channel ... OR-9
Multnomah Hotel—hist pl ... OR-9
Multnomah Island ... OR-9
Multnomah Park Cem—cemetery ... OR-9
Multnomah Saint Sch—school ... CA-9
Multnomah Sch—school ... OR-9
Multnomah Sch of the Bible—school ... OR-9
Multnomah Slough ... OR-9
Multnomah Street School—valley ... CA-9
Multnumah River ... OR-9
**Multona Springs**—pop pl ... MS-4
Multona Springs Sch (historical)—school ... MS-4
Multorpor Butte ... OR-9
Multorpor Mtn—summit ... OR-9
Mulvale Baptist Church ... NC-3
Mulvale Ch—church ... NC-3
**Mulvane**—pop pl ... KS-7
Mulvane Cem—cemetery ... KS-7
Mulvane Creek—stream ... KS-7
Mulvane HS—school ... KS-7
Mulvaney Gulch—valley ... OR-9
Mulventon House—hist pl ... AZ-5
Mulvey—locale ... LA-4
Mulvey Gulch—valley ... MT-8
Mulvey Mercantile—hist pl ... OK-5
Mulvey Pond—swamp ... IN-6
Mulvey Sch—school ... NY-2
Mulville House—hist pl ... CT-1
Mulvinia Hill—summit ... MO-7
Mulvinia Lookout Tower—locale ... MO-7
Mulwee Branch—stream ... AL-4
Mulybys Island—island ... MN-6
Mulyn Creek—stream ... SC-3
Muma Creek—stream ... MI-6
Muma Lake—lake ... MN-6
Mumaw Hill—summit ... VA-3
Mumbauersville—locale ... PA-2
Mumblehead Top—summit ... NC-3
Mumbo Basin—basin ... CA-9
Mumbo Creek—stream ... CA-9
Mumbo Lake—lake ... CA-9
Mum Brook ... MA-1
Mumby Sch—school ... NE-7
**Mumford**—pop pl ... NY-2
**Mumford**—pop pl ... TX-5
Mumford, Silas Site (Tappan Site RI-705)—hist pl ... RI-1
Mumford, Sylvester, House—hist pl ... GA-3
Mumford Bar—bar ... CA-9
Mumford Bar Trail—trail ... CA-9
Mumford Basin—basin ... CA-9
Mumford Canyon—valley ... CA-9
Mumford Cem—cemetery ... KY-4
Mumford Cem—cemetery ... MO-7
Mumford Cem—cemetery ... OH-6
Mumford Cem—cemetery ... TX-5
Mumford Ch—church ... PA-2
Mumford Cove—bay ... CT-1
Mumford Creek—channel ... GA-3
Mumford Creek—stream ... WY-8
Mumford Hill—summit ... WA-9
Mumford Hills—range ... IN-6
Mumford HS—school ... MI-6
Mumford Lake—lake ... TX-5
Mumford Lateral—canal ... ID-8
Mumford Manor—locale ... DE-2
Mumford Meadow—flat ... CA-9
Mumford Peak—summit ... CA-9
Mumford Point—cape ... CT-1
Mumford Point—cape ... NC-3
Mumford Ranch—locale ... ID-8
Mumford Ridge—ridge ... WY-8
Mumford River—stream ... MA-1
Mumford River Rsvr—reservoir ... MA-1
Mumford Rsvr—reservoir ... UT-8
Mumford Rural Cem—cemetery ... NY-2
Mumford Sch—school ... IL-6
Mumford Sch—school ... IA-7
Mumford Sch—school ... NE-7
Mumfords Mill ... RI-1
Mumfort Islands—island ... VA-3
Mumik Lake—lake ... AK-9
Mumma, Jacob H. W., House—hist pl ... OH-6
Mumma Cem—cemetery ... MD-2
Mumma Cem—cemetery ... PA-2
Mumma Draw—valley ... WY-8
Mumma Ford—locale ... MD-2
**Mummasburg**—pop pl ... PA-2
Mummasburg Run—stream ... PA-2
Mummas Sch (abandoned)—school ... PA-2
Mummerts Ch—church ... PA-2
Mummet Island—island ... MP-9
**Mummle**—pop pl ... KY-4
Mumm Lake—lake ... MN-6
Mumms Bay—bay ... WI-6
Mummy, The—arch ... UT-8
Mummy, The—summit ... MT-8
Mummy Bay—bay ... AK-9
Mummy Cave—cave ... AZ-5
Mummy Cave—cave ... WY-8
Mummy Cave—hist pl ... WY-8
Mummy Cave Overlook—locale ... AZ-5
Mummy Cave Ruins—locale ... AZ-5
Mummy Cliff—cliff ... UT-8
Mummy House ... AZ-5
Mummy Island—island ... AK-9
Mummy Mountain Golf Course—other ... AZ-5
Mummy Mountain Observatory—building ... AZ-5
Mummy Mtn—summit ... AZ-5
Mummy Mtn—summit ... CO-8
Mummy Mtn—summit ... MI-6
Mummy Mtn—summit ... NV-8
Mummy Pass—gap ... CO-8
Mummy Pass Creek—stream ... CO-8
Mummy Pass Trail—trail ... CO-8
Mummy Range—range ... CO-8
Mummy Rocks—island ... WA-9
Mummys Cove—bay ... MD-2
Mummy Spring—spring ... NV-8
Mump Creek—stream ... AL-4
Mump Creek Reservior—reservoir ... AL-4
Mump Creek Reservoir Dam—dam ... AL-4
Mump Creek Rsvr ... AL-4
Mumper—locale ... NE-7
**Mumper Corner**—pop pl ... CO-8
Mumper Spring Trail—trail ... PA-2
Mumphry Ditch—canal ... LA-4
Mumpower Creek—stream ... VA-3
**Mumpower (Oak Grove)**—pop pl ... VA-3
Mumpumpey Hill—summit ... NE-7
Mumser Knob ... OH-6
Mum Spring—spring ... NM-5
Mumtrak (Goodnews Bay)—other ... AK-9
Mumtrak Hill—summit ... AK-9
Mumudul ... FM-9
Mumurs-va—well ... AZ-5
Mumut ... MP-9
M'un ... FM-9
Muncas Creek—stream ... MO-7
Muncaster Creek—stream ... AK-9
Muncaster Mtn—summit ... WA-9
Muncaster Sch—school ... WA-9
Muncey Creek—stream ... OR-9
Munch, Paul, House—hist pl ... MN-6
Munch Cem—cemetery ... VA-3
Munch Ditch—canal ... IN-6
Munchmeyers Cem—cemetery ... WV-2
Munch Post Office (historical)—building ... TN-4
Munch-Roos House—hist pl ... MN-6
**Munch (Township of)**—pop pl ... MN-6
Munchuk (historical P.O.)—locale ... IA-7
Munchy Branch—stream ... DE-2
Muncie ... KY-4
**Muncie**—pop pl ... IL-6
**Muncie**—pop pl ... IN-6
**Muncie**—pop pl ... KS-7
Muncie—uninc pl ... KS-7
Muncie Branch—stream ... KY-4
Muncie Cem—cemetery ... KS-7
Muncie Chapel—church ... MO-7
Muncie Creek ... IN-6
Muncie Creek—stream ... IN-6
Muncie Creek—stream ... KS-7
Muncie Draw—valley ... NM-5
Muncie Elem Sch—school ... KS-7
**Muncie (historical)**—pop pl ... TN-4
**Muncie Hollow**—pop pl ... OH-6
Muncie Hollow—valley ... AR-4
Muncie Knob—summit ... KY-4
Muncie Lake—lake ... IN-6
Muncie Lake—lake ... MI-6
Muncie Mall—locale ... IN-6
Muncie Prairie Ditch ... IN-6
Muncie Public Library—hist pl ... IN-6
Muncie Sch ... IN-6
Muncie Sch—school ... KS-7
Muncillia House (State Historical Memorial)—park ... FL-3
Muncipal Golf Course—locale ... NC-3
Munck Sch—school ... CA-9
Muncy ... KY-4
Muncy—locale ... TX-5
**Muncy**—pop pl ... PA-2
Muncy Borough—civil ... PA-2
Muncy Bottom ... PA-2
Muncy Branch—stream ... KY-4
Muncy Cem—cemetery ... PA-2
Muncy Cem—cemetery ... TX-5
Muncy Cove—bay ... ME-1
Muncy Creek—stream ... KY-4
Muncy Creek—stream ... NV-8
Muncy Creek Ch—church ... KY-4
Muncy Creek Sch—school ... KY-4
**Muncy Creek Township**—pop pl ... PA-2
**Muncy Creek (Township of)**—pop pl ... PA-2
Muncy Fork—stream ... KY-4
Muncy Hills—range ... PA-2
Muncy Hist Dist—hist pl ... PA-2
Muncy Industrial Home for Women—building ... PA-2
Muncy Point Trail—trail ... PA-2
Muncy Ranch—locale ... NM-5
Muncy Ranch HQ—locale ... NM-5
Muncy Rsvr—reservoir ... PA-2
Muncy Sch—school ... CA-9
Muncy Sch—school ... KY-4
Muncy Station—locale ... PA-2
Muncy Township—civil ... PA-2
**Muncy (Township of)**—pop pl ... PA-2
Muncy (Tracy)—locale ... OK-5
**Muncy (Tracy)**—pop pl ... OK-5
**Muncy Valley**—pop pl ... PA-2
Muncy Valley Ch—church ... WV-2
Muncy Valley Hosp—hospital ... PA-2
Muncy Windmill—locale ... TX-5
Mundale—locale ... NY-2
**Mundale**—pop pl ... MA-1
Mundal Hill—summit ... VT-1
Munday—locale ... WV-2
**Munday**—pop pl ... TX-5
Munday (CCD)—cens area ... TX-5
Munday Cem—cemetery ... MI-6
Munday Cem—cemetery ... VA-3
Munday Country Club—other ... TX-5
Munday Cove—valley ... NC-3
Munday Creek—stream ... AK-9
Munday House—hist pl ... NC-3
Munday Peak—summit ... AK-9
Mundays Landing ... KY-4
Munday's Landing—hist pl ... KY-4
Mund Cem—cemetery ... TX-5
Mundcho Lake—lake ... AK-9
**Mundelein**—pop pl ... IL-6
Mundelein Coll—school ... IL-6
Mundelein College Skyscraper Bldg—hist pl ... IL-6
Mundelein Ridge Estates ... IL-6
Mundell Cem—cemetery ... PA-2
Mundell Ch—church ... IN-6
Mundell Elem Sch—school ... IN-6
Mundell Hollow—valley ... PA-2
Munden ... MO-7
Munden—locale ... VA-3
**Munden**—pop pl ... KS-7
Munden Creek ... WA-9
Munden Creek—stream ... WA-9
Munden Hill—summit ... FL-3
Munden Park—park ... AL-4
**Munderf**—pop pl ... PA-2
Munderf Cem—cemetery ... PA-2
Munderf Trail—trail ... PA-2
Mundgi Flat—flat ... CA-9
Mund Hill—summit ... TX-5
Mundine Branch—stream ... NC-3
Mundine Branch—stream ... TX-5
Mundine Cem—cemetery ... TX-5
Mundinger Creek—stream ... IL-6
Munding Flat—flat ... MT-8
Munding Prospect—mine ... UT-8
Mund Lake—lake ... MN-6
Mundo—locale ... CA-9
Mundo, As—slope ... MH-9
**Mundorf**—pop pl ... OR-9
Mundorf Lake—reservoir ... NC-3
Mundorf Lake Dam—dam ... NC-3
**Mundo Vista**—pop pl ... NC-3
Munds Canyon—valley (2) ... AZ-5
Mund Sch—school ... IL-6
Munds Draw—valley ... AZ-5
Munds Mtn—summit ... AZ-5
Munds Park—flat ... AZ-5
**Munds Park**—pop pl ... AZ-5
Munds Park Interchange—crossing ... AZ-5
Munds Park Rest Area—locale ... AZ-5
Munds Park Substation—locale ... AZ-5
Munds Spring—spring ... AZ-5
Munds Tank—reservoir (3) ... AZ-5
Munds Tank Number One—reservoir ... AZ-5
Munds Tank Number Two—reservoir ... AZ-5
Munds Well—well ... AZ-5
Mundt, John, Bldg—hist pl ... SD-7
Mundt Creek—stream ... WA-9
Mundthag Lake—lake ... AK-9
Mundt Lake—reservoir (2) ... SD-7
Mundt Lake Dam ... SD-7
Mundus Cem—cemetery ... IL-6
Mundy Bayou—gut ... LA-4
Mundy Bayou—stream ... LA-4
Mundy Branch—stream ... AL-4
Mundy Branch—stream ... VA-3
Mundy Brook—stream ... PA-2
Mundy Cem—cemetery ... GA-3
Mundy Cem—cemetery ... MS-4
Mundy Ch—church ... LA-4
Mundy Chapel (historical)—church ... AL-4
Mundy Cove—valley ... NC-3
Mundy Creek—stream ... NC-3
Mundy Gap ... TX-5
Mundy Gap—gap ... TN-4
Mundy Hill—summit ... MA-1
Mundy Hollow—valley ... CT-1
Mundy Landing—locale ... MO-7
Mundy-McFarland House—hist pl ... LA-4
Mundy Point—locale ... VA-3
Mundy Point—summit ... AR-4
Mundy Run—stream ... OH-6
Mundys ... KY-4
**Mundys Corner**—pop pl ... PA-2
Mundys Gap—gap ... TX-5
Mundys Landing ... MO-7
Mundys Landing—locale ... KY-4
Mundys Mill—locale ... GA-3
Mundys Millpond—reservoir ... GA-3
Mundys Run—stream ... NC-3
Mundys Spring—spring ... TX-5
Mundy Station ... IN-6
**Mundy (Township of)**—pop pl ... MI-6
Munedowk Lake ... WI-6
Muneyaku-to ... MP-9
Muney Ch—church ... PA-2
**Munford**—pop pl ... AL-4
**Munford**—pop pl ... TN-4
Munford-Atoka (CCD)—cens area ... TN-4
Munford-Atoka Division—civil ... TN-4
Munford Baptist Ch—church ... TN-4
Munford Canyon ... CA-9
Munford (CCD)—cens area ... AL-4
Munford Ch of Christ—church ... TN-4
Munford City Hall—building ... TN-4
Munford City Park—park ... TN-4
Munford Division—civil ... AL-4
Munford Elem Sch—school ... TN-4
Munford HS—school ... AL-4
Munford HS—school ... TN-4
Munford Inn—hist pl ... KY-4
Munford Memorial Library—building ... TN-4
Munford Post Office—building ... TN-4
Munford Primary Sch (historical)—school ... TN-4
Munford Sch—school ... MI-6
Munford Station ... AL-4
Munford United Methodist Ch—church ... TN-4
**Munfordville**—pop pl ... KY-4
Munfordville Baptist Church—hist pl ... KY-4
Munfordville (CCD)—cens area ... KY-4
Munfordville Presbyterian Church and Green River Lodge No.88—hist pl ... KY-4
Munfordville Sch—hist pl ... KY-4
**Mungen**—pop pl ... OH-6
Munger—locale (2) ... IL-6
Munger—locale ... MO-7
Munger—locale ... TX-5
**Munger**—pop pl ... MI-6
**Munger**—pop pl ... MN-6
Munger—uninc pl ... KS-7
Munger, Darius Sales, House—hist pl ... KS-7
Munger Branch—stream ... TX-5
Munger Brook—stream ... CT-1
Munger Brook—stream ... NY-2
Munger Canyon—valley ... CO-8
Munger Cem—cemetery ... AL-4
Munger Cem—cemetery ... IN-6
Munger Cem—cemetery ... MI-6
Munger Cem—cemetery ... NY-2
Munger Creek—stream ... CO-8
Munger Creek—stream ... OR-9
Munger Gulch—valley ... CA-9
Munger Lake—lake ... WI-6
Munger Lake—reservoir ... KS-7
Munger Lakebed—flat ... MN-6
Munger Mtn—summit ... WY-8
Munger Place Hist Dist—hist pl ... TX-5
Mungers—locale ... MO-7
Mungers Butte—summit ... OR-9
Munger Sch—school ... KS-7
Munger Sch—school ... MI-6
Munger Sch—school ... MN-6
**Mungers Corners**—pop pl ... NY-2
Mungers Lake ... TN-4
Mungers Pond—reservoir ... TN-4
Mungers Pond Dam—dam ... TN-4
Munger Station—locale ... IL-6
Munger Street Cem—cemetery ... VT-1
Munger Tank—reservoir ... TX-5
Munger Terrace—hist pl ... MN-6
Mungerville—locale ... TX-5
**Mungo Corner**—pop pl ... MA-1
Mungo Creek ... PA-2
Mungos Corner ... MA-1
Munguuy—bay ... FM-9
Munguuy—locale ... FM-9
Munguy ... FM-9
Mungy Branch—stream ... MO-7
Mungy Sch—school ... MO-7
**Munhall**—pop pl ... PA-2
Munhall Borough—civil ... PA-2

Munhall Sch—school ... IL-6
Munhall Sch—school ... PA-2
**Munhall Terrace**—pop pl ... PA-2
Munice Cem—cemetery ... OK-5
**Munich**—pop pl ... ND-7
**Municipal Acres Subdivision**—pop pl ... UT-8
Municipal Airp—airport (2) ... MO-7
Municipal Airport—other ... NC-3
Municipal Asphalt Plant—hist pl ... NY-2
Municipal Athletic Park—park ... NC-3
Municipal Auditorium—building ... VA-3
Municipal Auditorium—hist pl (2) ... GA-3
Municipal Bldg—building ... NC-3
Municipal Bldg—hist pl ... AR-4
Municipal Bldg—hist pl ... CT-1
Municipal Bldg—hist pl ... IA-7
Municipal Bldg—hist pl ... ME-1
Municipal Bldg—hist pl ... MS-4
Municipal Bldg—hist pl (2) ... NY-2
Municipal Bldg—hist pl ... OH-6
Municipal Bldg—hist pl ... TN-4
Municipal Bldg—hist pl ... WV-2
Municipal Bldg and Central Fire Station, 340—hist pl ... PA-2
*Municipal Building* ... DC-2
Municipal Building—uninc pl ... NY-2
Municipal College Campus, Simmons Univ—hist pl ... KY-4
Municipal Courts Bldg—hist pl ... IL-6
Municipal Creek—stream ... IN-6
Municipal Ferry Pier—hist pl ... NY-2
Municipal Golf Course—other ... CA-9
Municipal Group Hist Dist—hist pl ... MA-1
Municipal Hosp—hospital ... VA-3
Municipal Island—island ... IA-7
**Municipality of Murrysville**—pop pl ... PA-2
Municipality of Murrysville Borough—civil ... PA-2
Municipal Lake—reservoir ... OK-5
Municipal Lighting and Waterworks Plant—hist pl ... NE-7
Municipal Light Plant—hist pl ... AZ-5
*Municipal Park* ... FL-3
Municipal Park—park ... CA-9
Municipal Park—park ... FL-3
Municipal Park—park ... IN-6
Municipal Park—park ... MI-6
Municipal Park Lake Number One—reservoir ... AL-4
Municipal Park Lake Number 1 Dam—dam ... AL-4
**Municipal Park Subdivision**—pop pl ... UT-8
Municipal Pier—hist pl ... IL-6
Municipal Pier—locale (3) ... CA-9
*Municipal Pond* ... MI-6
Municipal Rose Garden—park (2) ... CA-9
Municipal Sch—school ... UT-8
Municipal Square Sch—school ... NJ-2
Municipal Stadium—other ... OH-6
Municipal Stadium—stadium ... NE-7
Municipal Swimming Pool—hist pl ... TX-5
Municipal Trailer Park—uninc pl ... FL-3
Municipal Yacht Harbor—bay ... CA-9
**Munien**—pop pl ... FM-9
Munion Field—locale ... NJ-2
**Munising**—pop pl ... MI-6
*Munising Bay* ... MI-6
Munising Falls Creek—stream ... MI-6
Munising Junction—locale ... MI-6
**Munising (Township of)**—pop pl ... MI-6
Muniteate—island ... FM-9
**Munith**—pop pl ... MI-6
Munith Cem—cemetery ... MI-6
Munition—other ... WV-2
Munitions Bldg (historical)—building ... DC-2
Muniz—civil ... CA-9
Muniz Canyon—valley ... NM-5
Muniz Ranch—locale ... NM-5
Muniz Tank—reservoir ... NM-5
*Munjak* ... MP-9
Munjin Sch—school ... GA-3
Munjor—island ... MP-9
**Munjor**—pop pl ... KS-7
**Munjoy Hill**—pop pl ... ME-1
*Munjur* ... MP-9
Munk—locale ... KY-4
Munk Cem—cemetery ... AR-4
Munk Cem—cemetery ... OH-6
**Munk City**—pop pl ... AL-4
*Munker Creek* ... KS-7
Munker Island—island ... MN-6
**Munkers**—pop pl ... OR-9
Munkers Creek—stream ... KS-7
Munkers Ranch—locale ... OR-9
Munkers Spring—spring ... OR-9
Munkirs Cem—cemetery ... MO-7
Munk Lake—lake ... IN-6
*Munkre Creek* ... KS-7
Munkres Branch—stream ... MO-7
Munkres Pass—gap ... WY-8
Munkres Sch (historical)—school ... MO-7
**Munks Corners**—pop pl ... OH-6
Munks Crossroads—locale ... NC-3
Munkus Slope Mine (underground)—mine ... AL-4
*Mun Lakes* ... AL-4
Munley—locale ... OR-9
Munlin Cem—cemetery ... GA-3
Munlin Creek—gut ... FL-3
Munlin Island—island ... FL-3
Munn Brook—stream ... MA-1
Munn Camp—locale ... CA-9
Munn Cem—cemetery ... AR-4
Munn Cem—cemetery ... NC-3
Munn Cem—cemetery ... OH-6
Munn Dam—dam ... OR-9
Munnell Run—stream ... PA-2
Munnerlyn—locale ... GA-3
Munnerlyn Chapel—church ... LA-4
Munn Hollow—valley ... WI-6
Munnisunk Brook—stream ... CT-1
Munn Lake—lake ... MI-6
Munn Lake—lake ... NY-2
Munn Lake—lake ... WA-9
Munn Lake—reservoir ... NM-5
Munn Oil Field—oilfield ... TX-5
Munnomin Lake—lake ... WI-6
Munn Park—park ... FL-3
Munn Pond—lake ... NH-1
Munn Ranch—locale (2) ... TX-5
Munn Rsvr—reservoir ... OR-9
Munn Run—stream ... OH-6
Munns—locale ... NY-2
*Munns Bridge* ... AL-4
*Munns Brook* ... MA-1
Munn Sch—school ... MI-6
Munns Creek—stream ... IA-7
**Munns Ferry**—pop pl ... MA-1
Munn Spring—spring ... ID-8
Munn's Sch—hist pl ... KY-4
Munns Siding—locale ... SC-3
**Munnsville**—pop pl ... NY-2
Munnsville West Hill—summit ... NY-2
**Munntown**—pop pl ... PA-2
Munntown Cem—cemetery ... PA-2
Munn Well—well ... TX-5
Munnwyler Lake—lake (2) ... MN-6
Munny Sokol Park—park ... AL-4
Munoz Canyon—valley ... CO-8
Munoz Canyon—valley (3) ... NM-5
Munoz Creek—stream ... NM-5
**Munoz Grillo**—pop pl (2) ... PR-3
**Munoz Rivera**—pop pl (2) ... PR-3
Munoz Rivera (Barrio)—fmr MCD ... PR-3
Munoz Spring—spring ... NM-5
**Munoz Torruellas**—pop pl (2) ... PR-3
Munpuna—bar ... FM-9
**Munra**—pop pl ... OR-9
Munra Point—summit ... OR-9
Munro Cem—cemetery ... MI-6
Munro Creek—stream ... MT-8
*Munroe* ... CA-9
*Munroe* ... IL-6
**Munroe**—pop pl ... MA-1
Munroe, Horace, House—hist pl ... ME-1
Munroe, Ralph M., House—hist pl ... FL-3
Munroe Basin—lake ... OH-6
Munroe Brook—stream ... MA-1
Munroe Brook—stream ... VT-1
Munroe Cem—cemetery ... MA-1
Munroe Cem—cemetery ... NH-1
Munroe Cem—cemetery ... WI-6
Munroe Chapel—church ... MD-2
Munroe Creek—stream ... LA-4
Munroe Creek Ch—church ... LA-4
Munroe-Dunlap-Snow House—hist pl ... GA-3
**Munroe Falls**—pop pl ... OH-6
Munroe Falls (Township of)—other ... OH-6
Munroe-Goolsby House—hist pl ... GA-3
Munroe Gravity Canal—canal ... CO-8
Munroe Hill—summit ... MA-1
**Munroe (historical)**—pop pl ... NC-3
*Munroe Island* ... ME-1
*Munroe Lake* ... FL-3
Munroe Ranch—locale ... CO-8
Munroe Regional Med Ctr—hospital ... FL-3
Munroe Sch—school ... CO-8
Munroe Sch—school ... FL-3
Munroes Mill (historical)—locale ... AL-4
**Munroe Station**—pop pl ... MA-1
Munroe Tavern—building ... MA-1
Munro-Hawkins House—hist pl ... VT-1
Munro Lake—lake ... MI-6
Munro-M.A. Hanna Mining Company Office Bldg—hist pl ... MI-6
Munro Point—cape ... MI-6
Munro Rsvr—reservoir ... AZ-5
Munro Sch—school ... VA-3
**Munro (Township of)**—pop pl ... MI-6
Munro Windmill—locale ... TX-5
Munsatli Mountains—other ... AK-9
Munsatli Ridge—ridge ... AK-9
*Muns Brook* ... MA-1
*Muns Creek* ... OR-9
Muns Creek—stream ... OR-9
Munsel Creek—stream ... OR-9
Munsel Creek Park—park ... OR-9
Munsell—locale ... MO-7
Munsel Lake—lake ... OR-9
Munsel Landing County Park—park ... OR-9
Munsell Cem—cemetery ... IL-6
Munsell Cem—cemetery ... MA-1
Munsell Cem—cemetery ... MI-6
Munsell Hill—summit ... WA-9
Munsell Spring—spring ... MO-7
Munsen Canyon—valley ... CA-9
*Munsey* ... IN-6
*Munsey* ... TN-4
*Munsey Branch* ... WV-2
Munsey Cem—cemetery ... MO-7
Munsey Cem—cemetery ... VA-3
*Munsey Cove* ... ME-1
*Munsey Creek* ... OR-9
Munsey Creek—stream ... CO-8
Munsey Ditch—canal ... ID-8
Munsey Hollow—valley ... TN-4
Munsey Lake—flat ... OR-9
Munsey-Maple Hill Sch—school ... TN-4
Munsey Memorial United Methodist Ch—church ... TN-4
**Munsey Park**—pop pl ... NY-2
Munsey Ruby Stock Driveway—trail ... CO-8
Munsey Sch—school ... CA-9
Munseys Chapel—church ... VA-3
Munsey School (historical)—locale ... MO-7
Munsinger Gardens—park ... MN-6
Munsing Street Cem—cemetery ... MA-1
Munsley Cem—cemetery ... VA-3
*Munsod Pond* ... MA-1
Munson—locale ... FL-3
Munson—locale ... OR-9
Munson—locale ... TX-5
**Munson**—pop pl ... LA-4
**Munson**—pop pl ... MI-6
**Munson**—pop pl ... PA-2
**Munson**—pop pl ... WV-2
Munson, Judge Albert, House—hist pl ... OH-6
Munson, Lake—lake (2) ... FL-3
Munson Basin—basin ... CA-9
Munson Bldg—hist pl ... IA-7
Munson Brook—stream ... CT-1
Munson Brook—stream ... VT-1
Munson Cem—cemetery ... CT-1
Munson Cem—cemetery ... IL-6
Munson Cem—cemetery ... OH-6
Munson Cem—cemetery ... TX-5
Munson Center Sch—school ... IL-6
Munson Corners—locale ... NY-2
Munson Creek—stream (2) ... AK-9
Munson Creek—stream ... CA-9
Munson Creek—stream ... MS-4
Munson Creek—stream ... MT-8
Munson Creek—stream (2) ... NE-7
Munson Creek—stream (2) ... OR-9
Munson Creek—stream ... SD-7
Munson Creek—stream ... WA-9
Munson Creek County Park—park ... OR-9
Munson Ditch—canal ... IN-6
Munson Flat—flat ... VT-1
*Munson Flowage* ... WI-6
Munson Gulch—valley ... CO-8
Munson Hill—locale ... OH-6
**Munson Hill**—pop pl ... VA-3
Munson Hill—summit ... NY-2
**Munson (historical)**—pop pl ... MS-4
Munson Hollow—valley ... UT-8
Munson HS—school ... FL-3
Munson Island—island ... AK-9
Munson Island—island ... FL-3
Munson Island—island ... ME-1
**Munson Island**—pop pl ... FL-3
Munson Knob—summit ... OH-6
Munson Lake—lake ... ME-1
Munson Lake—lake ... MI-6
Munson Lake—lake ... MN-6
Munson Lake—lake ... TX-5
Munson Lake—swamp ... TX-5
Munson Lookout Tower—tower ... FL-3
Munson-McLellen (CCD)—cens area ... FL-3
*Munson Mill* ... PA-2
Munson Mine—mine ... CA-9
Munson Park—park ... TX-5
Munson Point—cape ... WA-9
Munson Point—summit ... OR-9
Munson Pond—lake ... NY-2
Munson Pond—reservoir ... NY-2
Munson Prairie—flat ... WA-9
Munson Ranch—locale ... CA-9
Munson Ranch—locale ... CO-8
Munson Rec Area—park ... FL-3
Munson Reservation—other ... NM-5
Munson Ridge—ridge ... OR-9
Munson Rips—rapids ... ME-1
**Munsons**—pop pl ... MO-7
Munson Sch—school ... IL-6
Munson Sch—school ... MI-6
Munson Sch—school (2) ... OH-6
Munsons Corner—locale ... NY-2
**Munsons Corners**—pop pl ... NY-2
*Munsons Crossing* ... MS-4
Munson Slough—stream ... FL-3
Munson Spring Branch—stream ... MD-2
Munson Springs—spring ... OR-9
Munson Tank—reservoir ... NM-5
**Munson (Township of)**—pop pl ... IL-6
**Munson (Township of)**—pop pl ... MN-6
**Munson (Township of)**—pop pl ... OH-6
Munson Valley—valley ... OR-9
Munson Valley Hist Dist—hist pl ... OR-9
Munson Valley Trail—trail ... OR-9
*Munsonville* ... AZ-5
*Munsonville* ... TX-5
**Munsonville**—pop pl ... NH-1
**Munsonville**—pop pl ... NY-2
Munson-Williams-Proctor Institute—school ... NY-2
Munson Windmill—locale ... NM-5
Munsow Meadow—flat ... CA-9
Mun Spring—spring ... OR-9
Munstel—locale ... IL-6
Munster—locale ... ND-7
Munster—locale ... VI-3
**Munster**—pop pl ... IL-6
**Munster**—pop pl ... IN-6
**Munster**—pop pl ... PA-2
**Munster**—pop pl ... SC-3
Munster HS—school ... IN-6
**Munster Township**—pop pl ... ND-7
**Munster (Township of)**—pop pl ... PA-2
*Munsungan Brook* ... ME-1
Munsungan Brook—stream ... ME-1
Munsungan-Chase Lake Thoroughfare Archeol District—hist pl ... ME-1
Munsungan Falls—falls ... ME-1
*Munsungan Lake* ... ME-1
Munsungan Lake—lake ... ME-1
Munsungan Lake Tote Road—trail ... ME-1
Munsungan Ridge—ridge ... ME-1
Munsungan Stream—stream ... ME-1
*Munsungun Brook* ... ME-1
*Munsungun Lake* ... ME-1
**Muntainbrook**—pop pl ... TN-4
Muntakai—locale ... FM-9
**Muntanna**—pop pl ... OH-6
Munter Lake—lake ... MN-6
**Munterville**—pop pl ... IA-7
Munterville (historical P.O.)—locale ... IA-7
Munt Gilead Sch (historical)—school ... TN-4
Munther Creek—stream ... AK-9
Munt Hill—summit ... NH-1
Munton Drain—canal ... MI-6
Muntz Drain—canal ... MI-6
Muntz Hollow—valley (2) ... AR-4
Muntz Run—stream ... OH-6
Muntz Run—stream ... PA-2
**Munuscong**—pop pl ... MI-6
Munuscong Channel—channel ... MI-6
Munuscong Island—island ... MI-6
Munuscong Lake—lake ... MI-6
Munuscong River—stream ... MI-6
Munuscong State For—forest ... MI-6
Munyan Cem—cemetery ... CT-1
Munyon—locale ... CA-9
Munyon Drain—canal ... CA-9
Munyon Island—island ... FL-3
Munyon Lateral—canal ... CA-9
Munyon Sch—school ... MT-8
Munz Canyon—valley ... CA-9
Munzer Lake—lake ... MN-6
Munzer Meadow—flat ... CA-9
Munz Lakes—lake ... CA-9
Munz Ranch—locale ... CA-9
Muolea—civil ... HI-9
**Muolea**—pop pl ... HI-9
Muolea Point—cape ... HI-9
Mu Point—cape ... AS-9
Mupu Sch—school ... CA-9
Murach Lake—lake ... ND-7
Muraco Sch—school ... MA-1
Murad—locale ... SC-3
Murado, Arroyo—stream ... CA-9
Mural Hill—summit ... AZ-5
Muralla Tank—reservoir ... TX-5
Muraski Sch—school ... OH-6
Murat—locale ... VA-3
Murat—locale ... WI-6
Murat Hills—uninc pl ... FL-3
Murat Point—cape ... FL-3
Muravief, Mount—summit ... AK-9
Muray Shoal—bar ... TX-5
Murbach Ditch—canal ... OH-6
Murbou Lake—lake ... WI-6
Murchie Mine—mine ... CA-9
Murchinson, Mount—summit ... AK-9
Murchinson Cem—cemetery ... TX-5
**Murchison**—pop pl ... NC-3
**Murchison**—pop pl ... TX-5
Murchison Branch—stream ... TX-5
Murchison Cem—cemetery ... AL-4
Murchison Ch—church ... NC-3
Murchison Chapel—church ... NC-3
Murchison Creek—stream ... TX-5
Murchison House—hist pl ... SC-3
Murchison (site)—locale ... SD-7
Murchison Street Sch—school ... CA-9
**Murchisontown**—pop pl ... NC-3
Murchison Windmill—locale ... TX-5
Murch Ridge—ridge ... ME-1
Murch Sch—school ... DC-2
Murckle Branch—stream ... AL-4
Murdale Gardens of Memory—cemetery ... IL-6
Murden Cove—bay ... WA-9
Murden Sch—school ... GA-3
Murdens Corner—locale ... VA-3
**Murden's Corner**—pop pl ... VA-3
Murder Bayou—gut ... LA-4
Murder Branch—stream ... KY-4
Murder Bridge Hill—summit ... NY-2
Murder Cove—bay ... AK-9
Murder Creek—stream ... AL-4
Murder Creek—stream ... AR-4
Murder Creek—stream ... FL-3
Murder Creek—stream ... GA-3
Murder Creek—stream ... MS-4
Murder Creek—stream ... NY-2
Murder Creek—stream ... OR-9
Murderer Gulch—valley ... OR-9
Murderers Bar—bar (2) ... CA-9
*Murderers Creek* ... NY-2
Murderers Creek—stream ... NY-2
Murderers Creek—stream ... OR-9
Murderers Creek Forest Service Station—locale ... OR-9
Murderers Creek Ranch—locale ... OR-9
*Murderers Grave* ... AZ-5
Murderers Gulch—valley (5) ... CA-9
Murder Hill—summit ... NY-2
Murder Hole—locale ... VA-3
Murder Hole, The—bend ... VA-3
Murder Hollow—valley ... WV-2
*Murder Kill Creek* ... DE-2
*Murderkill Hundred* ... DE-2
*Murder Kill Neck* ... DE-2
Murderkill Neck—cape ... DE-2
Murderkill River—stream ... DE-2
Murder Point—cape ... AL-4
Murder Point—cape ... AK-9
Murder Trail—trail ... VA-3
Murdicks Spring—spring ... ID-8
*Murdner's Creek* ... NY-2
Murdo—locale ... TX-5
**Murdo**—pop pl ... SD-7
Murdo Cem—cemetery ... SD-7
Murdoch, John, House—hist pl ... UT-8
Murdoch Cabin—locale ... WY-8
Murdoch Center—hospital ... NC-3
Murdoch Point—cape ... NY-2
**Murdochs Crossing**—pop pl ... NY-2
*Murdochs Sulfer Springs* ... AL-4
Murdock—locale ... UT-8
**Murdock**—pop pl ... FL-3
**Murdock**—pop pl ... IL-6
**Murdock**—pop pl ... IN-6
**Murdock**—pop pl ... KS-7
**Murdock**—pop pl ... MN-6
**Murdock**—pop pl ... NE-7
**Murdock**—pop pl ... OH-6
**Murdock**—pop pl ... PA-2
**Murdock**—pop pl ... WA-9
Murdock, Almira Lott, House—hist pl ... UT-8
Murdock, Jack M., House—hist pl ... UT-8
Murdock, John Riggs and Mae Bain, House—hist pl ... UT-8
Murdock, John Riggs and Wolfenden, Mary Ellen, House—hist pl ... UT-8
Murdock, Joseph S., House—hist pl ... UT-8
Murdock, Sabin S., House—hist pl ... MN-6
Murdock Basin—basin ... UT-8
Murdock Bayou—bay ... FL-3
Murdock Branch—stream ... PA-2
Murdock Branch—stream ... TN-4
Murdock Campground—locale ... ID-8
*Murdock Canal* ... UT-8
Murdock Cem—cemetery ... IL-6
Murdock Cem—cemetery ... KS-7
Murdock Cem—cemetery ... LA-4
Murdock Cem—cemetery ... MS-4
Murdock Cem—cemetery (3) ... OH-6
Murdock Cem—cemetery ... TN-4
Murdock Cem—cemetery ... TX-5
Murdock Cem—cemetery ... WV-2
Murdock Ch—church ... AL-4
Murdock Creek—stream ... ID-8
Murdock Creek—stream ... KS-7
Murdock Creek—stream ... MS-4
Murdock Creek—stream (2) ... OR-9
Murdock Creek—stream ... WA-9
Murdock Creek—stream ... WY-8
Murdock Crossing—locale ... MS-4
Murdock Crossing (Ford)—locale ... CA-9
Murdock Crossing Spring—spring ... CA-9
Murdock Eddy Lake—lake ... LA-4
Murdock Elem Sch—school ... AZ-5
Murdock Elem Sch—school ... IN-6
Murdock Elem Sch—school ... KS-7
Murdock Gulch—valley ... WA-9
Murdock Hill—summit ... CT-1
Murdock Hollow—valley (2) ... UT-8
Murdock HS—school ... MA-1
Murdock Lake—lake ... CA-9
Murdock Lake—lake ... WI-6
Murdock Lake—reservoir ... MS-4
Murdock Lake Dam—dam ... MS-4
Murdock Lakes—lake ... WA-9
Murdock McRaes Landing—locale ... GA-3
Murdock Mtn—summit ... NV-8
Murdock Mtn—summit ... NY-2
Murdock Mtn—summit ... UT-8
Murdock Neighborhood Center—locale ... AZ-5
Murdock Park—park ... IN-6
Murdock Peak—summit ... UT-8
Murdock Point—cape ... FL-3
Murdock Pond—reservoir ... AL-4
Murdock Pond—reservoir ... MA-1
Murdock Pond Dam—dam ... AL-4
Murdock Powerhouse—other ... UT-8
Murdock Pumping Station—other ... UT-8
*Murdock Reservoir* ... UT-8
Murdock Ridge—ridge ... GA-3
Murdock Rsvr—reservoir ... OR-9
Murdocks—locale ... VA-3
Murdock Sch—hist pl ... MA-1
Murdock Sch—school ... KS-7
*Murdocks Crossing* ... MS-4
Murdocks Eddy—bay ... MS-4
Murdocks Ferry (historical)—locale ... MS-4
Murdocks Point—cape ... NY-2
*Murdock Spring* ... NV-8
Murdock Spring—spring (2) ... NV-8
Murdock Spring—spring ... TN-4
Murdock Spring No 1—spring ... WA-9
Murdock Spring No 2—spring ... WA-9
Murdock Spring No 3—spring ... WA-9
Murdock Springs—spring ... NV-8
**Murdock Subdivision**—pop pl ... UT-8
**Murdocksville**—pop pl ... NC-3
**Murdocksville**—pop pl ... PA-2
**Murdock Township**—pop pl ... KS-7
**Murdock (Township of)**—pop pl ... IL-6
Murdock Well—well ... NM-5
Murdock Windmill—locale ... TX-5
**Murdock Woods**—pop pl ... NY-2
Murdo Dam—dam ... SD-7
Murdo Golf Course—locale ... SD-7
Murdo Island—island ... AK-9
Murdo Municipal Airp—airport ... SD-7
*Murdo Number 1 Dam* ... SD-7
Murdo Township—civil ... SD-7
Murdough Hill—summit ... NH-1
Murdough Hollow—valley ... AR-4
Murdy Sch—school ... CA-9
**Murdy Station**—pop pl ... IN-6
*Mureil Lake* ... NE-7
Murell Hollow—valley ... OK-5
**Muren**—pop pl ... IN-6
*Murf* ... TN-4
*Murffs* ... MS-4
Murfree Cem—cemetery ... TN-4
**Murfreesboro**—pop pl ... AR-4
**Murfreesboro**—pop pl ... NC-3
**Murfreesboro**—pop pl ... TN-4
Murfreesboro (CCD)—cens area ... TN-4
Murfreesboro Country Club—locale ... TN-4
Murfreesboro Division—civil ... TN-4
Murfreesboro Hist Dist—hist pl ... NC-3
Murfreesboro HS—school ... NC-3
Murfreesboro Municipal Airp—airport ... TN-4
Murfreesboro (Township of)—fmr MCD ... NC-3
*Murfreesborough* ... TN-4
Murfrees Fork—stream ... TN-4
Murhunt Park—park ... MN-6
Murhut Creek—stream ... WA-9
Murie, Lake—lake ... ND-7
Murie Creek—stream ... UT-8
Murie Islets—island ... AK-9
*Muriel* ... TX-5
Muriel—locale ... NE-7
Muriel—other ... TX-5
Muriel Branch—stream ... KY-4
Muriel Branch—stream ... TX-5
Muriel Lake—lake ... CA-9
Muriel Peak—summit ... CA-9
Muriel Sch—school ... HI-9
Murietta Canyon—valley ... CA-9
Murietta Divide—gap ... CA-9
**Murietta Farm**—pop pl ... CA-9
Murillo Banco Number One Hundred Thirty-four, El—levee ... TX-5
Murillo (Municipality)—civ div ... FM-9
Murilo Atoll—island ... FM-9
Murilo Island—island ... FM-9
Murk Bay—bay ... AK-9
Murk Branch—stream ... TN-4
**Murke**—pop pl ... WY-8
Murken Bench—bench ... CA-9
*Murken Butte* ... CA-9
Murken Lake—lake ... CA-9
Murkey Lake—lake ... WY-8
Murk Kui Wash—stream ... AZ-5
Murk Lake—lake ... MN-6
Murkland Ch—church ... NC-3
*Murky Lake* ... WY-8
Murl—locale ... KY-4
Murl Branch—stream ... AR-4
Murl Cem—cemetery ... KY-4
*Murle Island* ... MP-9
Murley Branch—stream ... MD-2
Murley Branch—stream ... MS-4
Murley Hollow—valley ... MO-7
Murley Run—stream ... MD-2
**Murlin Heights**—pop pl ... OH-6
Murlin Lake Drain—canal ... MI-6
Murmer Creek—stream ... IN-6
Murmur Creek—stream ... MN-6
Murmur Creek—stream ... NY-2
Murn—locale ... MT-8
Murnaham Cem—cemetery ... OH-6
Murnan Cem—cemetery ... IN-6
Murnen—locale ... WA-9
Muro Blanco—cliff ... CA-9
*Muroc* ... CA-9
**Muroc**—pop pl ... CA-9
*Murow Creek* ... SD-7
*Muro Y Cayucos* ... CA-9
**Murphey**—pop pl ... NC-3
Murphey, Dr. William E., House—hist pl ... AL-4
Murphey Cem—cemetery ... IL-6
Murphey Cem—cemetery (3) ... TN-4
Murphey Elem Sch—school ... NC-3
Murphey Flying Service Airp—airport ... MS-4
Murphey-Jennings House—hist pl ... MS-4
*Murphey Lake* ... MI-6
*Murphey Orphanage* ... DE-2
*Murpheys Bluff* ... AL-4
*Murpheys Chapel Methodist Church* ... AL-4
*Murphey School* ... AZ-5
*Murpheys Cove* ... TN-4
Murpheys Creek—stream ... NC-3
**Murpheyville**—pop pl ... VA-3
Murpheyville Cem—cemetery ... VA-3
Murphin Point—cliff ... OH-6
Murph Mill Creek—stream ... SC-3
*Murphree* ... AL-4
**Murphree**—pop pl ... AL-4
Murphree Branch—stream ... AL-4
Murphree Cem—cemetery ... AL-4
Murphree Cem—cemetery ... GA-3
Murphree Cem—cemetery ... TN-4
Murphree Creek—stream ... MS-4
Murphree Creek—stream ... WY-8
Murphree Eddy—rapids ... TN-4
Murphree Lake—reservoir (2) ... AL-4
Murphree Lake Dam—dam (2) ... AL-4
Murphree Park—park ... AL-4
**Murphree Place**—pop pl ... AL-4
**Murphreesboro (historical)**—pop pl ... MS-4
Murphreesboro P.O. (historical)—building ... MS-4
Murphreesboro Sch—school ... MS-4
*Murphrees Spur* ... MS-4
**Murphree Subdivision**—pop pl ... MS-4
*Murphrees Valley* ... AL-4
*Murphree Valley* (2) ... AL-4
Murphree Valley—valley ... AL-4
Murphree Valley P.O. (historical)—locale ... AL-4
*Murphreys Valley* ... AL-4
*Murphy* ... AL-4
*Murphy* ... CA-9
*Murphy* ... NC-3
Murphy—locale ... NE-7
Murphy—locale ... NJ-2
Murphy—locale ... OK-5
Murphy—locale ... OR-9
Murphy—locale ... SD-7
Murphy—locale ... VA-3
Murphy—locale ... WV-2
**Murphy**—pop pl ... AL-4
**Murphy**—pop pl ... GA-3
**Murphy**—pop pl ... ID-8
**Murphy**—pop pl (2) ... IA-7
**Murphy**—pop pl (2) ... MS-4
**Murphy**—pop pl ... MO-7
**Murphy**—pop pl ... NC-3
**Murphy**—pop pl ... TX-5
Murphy, Charles H., Sr., House—hist pl ... AR-4
Murphy, Daniel, Log House—hist pl ... OH-6
Murphy, Daniel F., House—hist pl ... ID-8
Murphy, D. J., House—hist pl ... CA-9
Murphy, Frank, Birthplace—hist pl ... MI-6
Murphy, George A., House—hist pl ... OK-5
Murphy, John T., House—hist pl ... MT-8
Murphy, Lake—lake ... FL-3
Murphy, Lake—lake ... OR-9
Murphy, Mrs. J. V., House—hist pl ... TX-5
Murphy, Patrick, House—hist pl ... CT-1
Murphy, Patrick, House—hist pl ... MS-4
Murphy, Samuel R., House—hist pl ... AL-4
Murphy, Stephen, House—hist pl ... KY-4
Murphy, Timothy, House—hist pl ... MI-6
Murphy, W. H., House—hist pl ... ID-8
Murphy, William, House—hist pl ... MA-1
Murphy, William J., House—hist pl ... AR-4
**Murphy Acres**—pop pl ... IL-6
Murphy Archeol Site—hist pl ... IN-6
Murphy Arm—canal ... IN-6
Murphy Arroyo—stream ... NM-5
Murphy Averette Dam—dam ... AL-4
Murphy Averette Lake—reservoir ... AL-4
Murphy Bar—bar ... OR-9
Murphy Bay—bay ... AK-9
Murphy Bay—bay ... ID-8
Murphy Bay—bay ... IL-6
Murphy Bay—bay ... MN-6
Murphy Bay—swamp ... NC-3
Murphy Bayou—stream ... LA-4
Murphy Bayou—stream ... MS-4
Murphy-Blair District—hist pl ... MO-7
Murphy Bldg—hist pl ... OK-5
Murphy Blvd Park—park ... MO-7
Murphy Bottom—bend ... GA-3
*Murphy Branch* ... MO-7
Murphy Branch—stream (2) ... AL-4
Murphy Branch—stream ... IA-7
Murphy Branch—stream (5) ... KY-4
Murphy Branch—stream (4) ... MS-4
Murphy Branch—stream ... MO-7
Murphy Branch—stream (2) ... NC-3
Murphy Branch—stream (4) ... TN-4
Murphy Branch—stream (3) ... TX-5
Murphy Branch—stream (2) ... WV-2
Murphy Brook—stream ... CT-1
Murphy Brook—stream ... ME-1
Murphy Brook—stream ... NY-2
Murphy Brook—stream (2) ... VT-1
Murphy Brothers Lake Dam—dam ... MS-4
Murphy Brothers Ranch—locale ... OR-9
Murphy-Burroughs House—hist pl ... FL-3
Murphy-Bush Cem—cemetery ... TN-4
Murphy Butte—summit ... MT-8
Murphy Cabin—locale ... CA-9
Murphy Cadler Park—park ... GA-3
Murphy Camp—locale ... OR-9
Murphy Camp Creek—stream ... OR-9
Murphy Canal—canal ... LA-4
Murphy Candler Sch—school ... GA-3
Murphy Canyon—valley ... AZ-5
Murphy Canyon—valley (5) ... CA-9
Murphy Canyon—valley ... MT-8
Murphy Canyon—valley ... NV-8
Murphy Canyon—valley ... OR-9
Murphy Canyon—valley ... WY-8
Murphy Cem—cemetery (2) ... AL-4
Murphy Cem—cemetery ... AR-4
Murphy Cem—cemetery (4) ... GA-3
Murphy Cem—cemetery ... IL-6
Murphy Cem—cemetery ... IN-6
Murphy Cem—cemetery ... IA-7
Murphy Cem—cemetery ... KS-7
Murphy Cem—cemetery (2) ... KY-4
Murphy Cem—cemetery ... LA-4
Murphy Cem—cemetery ... MD-2
Murphy Cem—cemetery ... MS-4
Murphy Cem—cemetery (3) ... MO-7
Murphy Cem—cemetery ... NE-7

Murphy Cem—cemetery (3) ... NC-3
Murphy Cem—cemetery (7) ... TN-4
Murphy Cem—cemetery (5) ... TX-5
Murphy Cem—cemetery ... VT-1
Murphy Cem—cemetery (3) ... WV-2
Murphy Ch ... TN-4
Murphy Ch—church ... IA-7
Murphy Chapel—church ... AL-4
Murphy Chapel—church ... AR-4
Murphy Chapel—church ... MS-4
Murphy Chapel—church ... NC-3
Murphy Chapel Ch ... AL-4
Murphy Chapel Freewill Ch ... AL-4
Murphy Chapel (historical)—church ... TN-4
**Murphy City**—pop pl ... MN-6
Murphy Collegiate Institute ... TN-4
Murphy Commerical Park—locale ... TN-4
**Murphy Corner**—pop pl (2) ... ME-1
**Murphy Corner**—pop pl ... WI-6
Murphy Corners—locale ... NY-2
Murphy Corral—locale ... OR-9
Murphy Coulee—stream ... MT-8
Murphy Coulee—valley (3) ... MT-8
Murphy Cove—bay ... AK-9
Murphy Cow Camp—locale ... NM-5
Murphy Creek ... AL-4
Murphy Creek ... FL-3
Murphy Creek ... ID-8
Murphy Creek ... MT-8
Murphy Creek—channel ... FL-3
Murphy Creek—stream ... AL-4
Murphy Creek—stream ... AK-9
Murphy Creek—stream ... AR-4
Murphy Creek—stream (6) ... CA-9
Murphy Creek—stream (2) ... CO-8
Murphy Creek—stream (2) ... GA-3
Murphy Creek—stream (4) ... ID-8
Murphy Creek—stream ... IL-6
Murphy Creek—stream ... KS-7
Murphy Creek—stream (2) ... KY-4
Murphy Creek—stream ... MI-6
Murphy Creek—stream (2) ... MN-6
Murphy Creek—stream (2) ... MS-4
Murphy Creek—stream (3) ... MO-7
Murphy Creek—stream (5) ... MT-8
Murphy Creek—stream ... NV-8
Murphy Creek—stream ... ND-7
Murphy Creek—stream (11) ... OR-9
Murphy Creek—stream ... SD-7
Murphy Creek—stream (2) ... TN-4
Murphy Creek—stream (4) ... TX-5
Murphy Creek—stream ... VA-3
Murphy Creek—stream (4) ... WA-9
Murphy Creek—stream ... WV-2
Murphy Creek—stream (2) ... WI-6
Murphy Creek—stream (3) ... WY-8
Murphy Creek Baptist Church ... MS-4
Murphy Creek Campground—locale ... WY-8
Murphy Creek Cem—cemetery ... MS-4
Murphy Creek Ch—church ... MS-4
Murphy Creek Ch—church ... WV-2
Murphy Crossing—locale ... CA-9
Murphy Crossroads ... AL-4
Murphy Cross Roads—locale ... AL-4
Murphy Dam—dam ... AL-4
Murphy Dam—dam ... OR-9
Murphy Dam—dam ... WI-6
Murphy Dam Flowage ... WI-6
Murphy Desert Ranch—locale ... CO-8
Murphy Ditch ... MT-8
Murphy Ditch—canal ... CO-8
Murphy Ditch—canal ... IA-7
Murphy Ditch—canal (2) ... MT-8
Murphy Ditch—canal ... SD-7
Murphy Ditch—canal (2) ... WY-8
Murphy Dome—summit ... AK-9
Murphy Dome (Air Force Station)—military ... AK-9
Murphy Dome Draw—valley ... WY-8
Murphy Dome Oil Field—oilfield ... WY-8
Murphy Drain—canal ... ID-8
Murphy Drain—stream ... MI-6
Murphy Draw—valley (3) ... WY-8
Murphy Elem Sch—school ... NC-3
Murphy Elem Sch—school ... OR-9
Murphy Falls—falls ... NC-3
Murphy Farm—locale ... MS-4
Murphy Ferry—locale ... MS-4
Murphy Flat ... CA-9
Murphy Flat—flat (4) ... CA-9
Murphy Flat—flat ... ID-8
Murphy Flat—flat ... MT-8
Murphy Flowage—reservoir ... WI-6
Murphy Ford—locale ... AL-4
Murphy Ford—locale ... KY-4
Murphy Fork ... TN-4
Murphyfork—locale ... KY-4
Murphy Fork—stream (2) ... KY-4
Murphy Fork—stream ... VA-3
Murphy Fork—stream ... WV-2
Murphy Gap—gap ... NV-8
Murphy Gap—gap ... NC-3
Murphy Gap Rsvr—reservoir ... NV-8
Murphy Gin Branch—stream (2) ... AL-4
Murphy Glades—flat (2) ... CA-9
Murphy Grove Ch—church ... VA-3
Murphy Guard Station—locale ... OR-9
Murphy Gulch—valley (2) ... CA-9
Murphy Gulch—valley ... CO-8
Murphy Gulch—valley ... ID-8
Murphy Gulch—valley (2) ... OR-9
Murphy Gulch—valley (2) ... WY-8
Murphy Gulch Ditch—canal ... WY-8
**Murphy Heights (subdivision)**—pop pl ... NC-3
Murphy Hill—summit ... AL-4
Murphy Hill—summit ... CA-9
Murphy Hill—summit ... FL-3
Murphy Hill—summit ... ME-1
Murphy Hill—summit ... MO-7
Murphy Hill—summit (2) ... NY-2
Murphy Hill—summit ... ND-7
Murphy Hill—summit ... OR-9
Murphy Hill—summit ... TN-4
Murphy Hill—summit ... WA-9
Murphy Hill—uninc pl ... TN-4
Murphy Hill Brook—stream ... NY-2
Murphy Hill Ch—church ... AL-4
**Murphy Hills**—pop pl ... TN-4
Murphy Hill Sch (historical)—school ... AL-4
Murphy Hill Tank—reservoir ... TX-5
Murphy (historical)—locale ... AL-4
Murphy Hogback—ridge ... UT-8
Murphy Hollow—valley (2) ... AR-4
Murphy Hollow—valley ... GA-3
Murphy Hollow—valley (2) ... MO-7
Murphy Hollow—valley ... OH-6
Murphy Hollow—valley ... PA-2
Murphy Hollow—valley (6) ... TN-4
Murphy Hollow—valley ... UT-8
Murphy Hollow Creek—stream ... GA-3
**Murphy Hot Springs**—pop pl ... ID-8
Murphy House—hist pl ... OK-5
Murphy House, The—hist pl ... AL-4
Murphy HS—hist pl ... AL-4
Murphy HS—school ... AL-4
Murphy HS—school (2) ... GA-3
Murphy HS—school ... NC-3
Murphy HS—school ... WI-6
Murphy Island ... NY-2
Murphy Island—island ... FL-3
Murphy Island—island ... MO-7
Murphy Island—island ... NE-7
Murphy Island—island ... SC-3
Murphy Islands—island ... NY-2
Murphy JHS—school ... MI-6
Murphy Johnson Tank—reservoir ... AZ-5
Murphy Junction—locale ... GA-3
**Murphy Junction**—pop pl ... NC-3
Murphy-Kemper-Cockburn Cem—cemetery ... AL-4
Murphy Lake ... MI-6
Murphy Lake ... MN-6
Murphy Lake ... OR-9
Murphy Lake ... WA-9
Murphy Lake—lake (2) ... AR-4
Murphy Lake—lake ... CA-9
Murphy Lake—lake ... CO-8
Murphy Lake—lake ... LA-4
Murphy Lake—lake (5) ... MI-6
Murphy Lake—lake (7) ... MN-6
Murphy Lake—lake ... MT-8
Murphy Lake—lake (3) ... NE-7
Murphy Lake—lake (2) ... NM-5
Murphy Lake—lake ... NY-2
Murphy Lake—lake ... WA-9
Murphy Lake—lake (6) ... WI-6
Murphy Lake—reservoir ... AL-4
Murphy Lake—reservoir ... GA-3
Murphy Lake—reservoir ... TX-5
Murphy Lake Ditch—canal ... AR-4
Murphy Lake Ranger Station—locale ... MT-8
Murphy Lakes—lake ... WA-9
Murphy Lakes—lake ... WY-8
Murphy Lakes—reservoir ... GA-3
Murphy Lake State Game Area—park ... MI-6
Murphy-Lamb House and Cemetery—hist pl ... NC-3
Murphy Landing (historical)—locale ... TN-4
Murphy (Magisterial District)—fmr MCD ... WV-2
Murphy Meadow—flat ... CA-9
Murphy Meadows—flat ... CA-9
Murphy Meadows—flat ... NV-8
Murphy Memorial Bridge—bridge ... CA-9
Murphy Memorial Hosp—hospital ... IA-7
Murphy Mill—locale ... TN-4
Murphy Mill Branch—stream ... AL-4
Murphy Millpond—reservoir ... AL-4
Murphy Mill Sch—school ... AL-4
Murphy Mine—mine ... MT-8
Murphy Mine—mine ... NV-8
Murphy Mine—mine ... TN-4
Murphy Mine—mine ... UT-8
Murphy Mine (underground)—mine ... AL-4
Murphy Mound Archeol Site—hist pl ... MO-7
Murphy Mtn—summit ... AL-4
Murphy Mtn—summit ... CA-9
Murphy Mtn—summit ... MN-6
Murphy Mtn—summit ... MT-8
Murphy Mtn—summit (2) ... OR-9
Murphy Mutual Canal—canal ... ID-8
Murphy Oil Field—oilfield ... KS-7
Murphy Oil Field—oilfield ... OK-5
Murphy Park—park ... AZ-5
Murphy Park—park ... AR-4
Murphy Park—park ... IN-6
Murphy Park—park ... IA-7
Murphy Park—park ... MI-6
Murphy Park—park ... MO-7
Murphy Park—park ... NY-2
Murphy Park—park ... TX-5
Murphy Park—park ... WI-6
Murphy Peak—summit ... AZ-5
Murphy Peak—summit ... CA-9
Murphy Peak—summit ... ID-8
Murphy Peak—summit ... MT-8
Murphy Place—locale ... CA-9
Murphy Place—locale ... NM-5
Murphy Point—cape ... CT-1
Murphy Point—cape ... ME-1
Murphy Point—cape ... MN-6
Murphy Point—cape ... UT-8
Murphy Point Overlook—locale ... UT-8
Murphy Pond—lake ... CA-9
Murphy Pond—lake ... KY-4
Murphy Pond—lake ... ME-1
Murphy Pond—lake ... MA-1
Murphy Pond—lake ... MO-7
Murphy Pond—lake ... NV-8
Murphy Pond—reservoir ... VA-3
Murphy Ponds—lake ... ME-1
Murphy Quaintance Ditch—canal ... MT-8
Murphy Ranch—locale (2) ... AZ-5
Murphy Ranch—locale (4) ... CA-9
Murphy Ranch—locale ... CO-8
Murphy Ranch—locale (4) ... MT-8
Murphy Ranch—locale ... NE-7
Murphy Ranch—locale (2) ... NV-8
Murphy Ranch—locale ... OR-9
Murphy Ranch—locale ... SD-7
Murphy Ranch—locale ... WY-8
Murphy Ranch Mtn—summit ... AZ-5
Murphy Ranch Sch—school ... CA-9
Murphy Range—range ... UT-8
Murphy Ridge—ridge ... AR-4
Murphy Ridge—ridge ... MN-6
Murphy Ridge—ridge ... NC-3
Murphy Ridge—ridge ... SD-7
Murphy Ridge—ridge ... UT-8
Murphy Ridge—ridge ... WY-8
Murphy Rim—cliff ... ID-8
Murphy River—stream ... MI-6
Murphy Road—locale ... ME-1
Murphy Road Annex—post sta ... CT-1
Murphy Rock—pillar ... CA-9
Murphy Rsvr—reservoir (2) ... CO-8
Murphy Rsvr—reservoir ... OR-9
Murphy Run—stream ... IN-6
Murphy Run—stream (2) ... MD-2
Murphy Run—stream ... WV-2
**Murphys**—pop pl ... CA-9
Murphys Bayou ... MS-4
Murphys Bluff—cliff ... AL-4
**Murphysboro**—pop pl ... IL-6
Murphysboro, Lake—reservoir ... IL-6
**Murphysboro (Township of)**—pop pl ... IL-6
Murphysburg—other ... OH-6
**Murphys Camp (historical)**—pop pl ... OR-9
Murphy Sch—school ... AZ-5
Murphy Sch—school (2) ... CA-9
Murphy Sch—school ... CT-1
Murphy Sch—school ... IL-6
Murphy Sch—school (2) ... KY-4
Murphy Sch—school (2) ... MA-1
Murphy Sch—school ... MI-6
Murphy Sch—school ... MN-6
Murphy Sch—school ... NE-7
Murphy Sch—school ... NC-3
Murphy Sch—school ... SD-7
Murphy Sch—school ... TN-4
Murphy Sch—school ... TX-5
Murphy Sch—school ... WV-2
Murphy Sch (abandoned)—school ... MO-7
Murphys Chapel—church ... AL-4
Murphys Chapel Cem—cemetery ... NM-5
Murphy Sch (historical)—school ... MS-4
Murphy Sch (historical)—school ... MO-7
Murphy Sch Number Two—school ... AZ-5
Murphy Sch Three—school ... AZ-5
**Murphys Corner**—pop pl ... AR-4
**Murphys Corner**—pop pl ... ME-1
**Murphy's Corner**—pop pl ... WA-9
**Murphys Corner**—pop pl ... WA-9
Murphys Corner Cem—cemetery ... ME-1
Murphys Cove—bay (2) ... FL-3
Murphys Creek ... TN-4
Murphys Creek ... TX-5
Murphys Creek—stream ... WI-6
Murphys Ferry (historical)—locale ... AL-4
Murphys Grammar Sch—hist pl ... CA-9
Murphy Sheep Sheds—locale ... MT-8
Murphy Shoal—bar ... NY-2
Murphys Hole—basin ... CO-8
Murphys Hole—bend ... WA-9
Murphys Hotel—hist pl ... CA-9
Murphy Siding—locale ... ID-8
**Murphy Siding**—pop pl ... PA-2
Murphys Island ... FL-3
Murphys Island ... MO-7
Murphys Lake—lake ... LA-4
Murphys Landing ... TN-4
Murphy Slough—bay ... TN-4
Murphy Slough—gut ... IL-6
Murphy Slough—stream (2) ... CA-9
Murphy Slough—stream ... ID-8
Murphys Lower Forge (historical)—locale ... TN-4
Murphys Mill (historical)—locale ... TN-4
Murphys Mill Historical Site—park ... AL-4
Murphys Millpond—reservoir ... VA-3
Murphys Point—cliff ... WA-9
Murphys Pond ... MA-1
Murphys Pond—reservoir ... NC-3
Murphys Ponds—reservoir ... FL-3
Murphy Spring—spring ... AL-4
Murphy Spring—spring (2) ... AZ-5
Murphy Spring—spring (2) ... CA-9
Murphy Spring—spring ... GA-3
Murphy Spring—spring (2) ... NV-8
Murphy Spring—spring ... OR-9
Murphy Spring—spring ... TN-4
Murphys Station ... AL-4
Murphy State Wildlife Mngmt Area—park ... MN-6
Murphy Station—locale ... AL-4
Murphys Upper Forge (historical)—locale ... TN-4
Murphys Valley ... AL-4
Murphysville—locale ... KY-4
Murphy Swamp—swamp ... MN-6
Murphy Swamp—swamp ... NE-7
Murphy Swamp—swamp ... NC-3
Murphys Well—well ... CA-9
Murphys Well—well ... NV-8
Murphy Table—summit ... NE-7
Murphy Tank—reservoir (2) ... AZ-5
Murphy Tank—reservoir (2) ... NM-5
Murphy Tank—reservoir ... TX-5
Murphy Top—summit ... GA-3
**Murphytown**—pop pl ... NC-3
**Murphytown**—pop pl ... WV-2
Murphy (Township of)—fmr MCD ... NC-3
Murphy Trail—trail ... CA-9
Murphy Trail and Bridge—hist pl ... UT-8
Murphy Varnish Works—hist pl ... NJ-2
Murphy Vly—swamp ... NY-2
Murphy Wash—stream ... AZ-5
Murphy Wash—stream (3) ... NV-8
Murphy Wash Administrative Site—locale ... NV-8
Murphy Waterhole—lake ... OR-9
Murphy Waterholes—lake ... OR-9
Murphy Well—locale ... AZ-5
Murphy Well—well (2) ... AZ-5
Murphy Well—well (2) ... CA-9
Murphy Well—well ... NV-8
Murrah Cem—cemetery ... AL-4
Murrah Chapel ... MS-4
Murrah Church ... MS-4
Murrah House—hist pl ... TX-5
Murrah HS—school ... MS-4
Murrah Ranch—locale ... TX-5
Murrahs Chapel—church ... MS-4
Murrah Windmill—locale (2) ... TX-5
Murray ... NY-2
Murray ... TX-5
Murray—locale ... AR-4
Murray—locale ... CA-9
Murray—locale ... CT-1
Murray—locale ... MN-6
Murray—locale ... ND-7
Murray—locale (2) ... PA-2
Murray—locale ... TX-5
Murray—locale ... WV-2
**Murray**—pop pl ... ID-8
**Murray**—pop pl ... IN-6
**Murray**—pop pl ... IA-7
**Murray**—pop pl ... KY-4
**Murray**—pop pl ... MT-8
**Murray**—pop pl ... NE-7
**Murray**—pop pl ... NY-2
**Murray**—pop pl ... SC-3
**Murray**—pop pl ... UT-8
Murray, Dr. John, Farm—hist pl ... KY-4
Murray, Frederick H., House—hist pl ... WA-9
Murray, George, House—hist pl ... UT-8
Murray, George, House—hist pl ... WI-6
Murray, Gov. William H., House—hist pl ... OK-5
Murray, James H., House—hist pl ... MI-6
Murray, Jonathan, House—hist pl ... CT-1
Murray, Lake—reservoir ... GA-3
Murray, Lake—reservoir ... OK-5
Murray, Lake—reservoir ... SC-3
Murray, Mount—summit ... MT-8
Murray, Thomas, House—hist pl ... IA-7
Murray, Thomas, House—hist pl ... PA-2
Murray Airp—airport ... KS-7
Murray Ave Sch—school ... NY-2
Murray Baptist Ch—church ... UT-8
Murray Basin—basin ... AZ-5
Murray Bay—bay ... MI-6
Murray Bayou—bay ... FL-3
Murray Bluff—summit ... IL-6
Murray Branch—stream (2) ... AL-4
Murray Branch—stream ... AR-4
Murray Branch—stream (2) ... GA-3
Murray Branch—stream ... IN-6
Murray Branch—stream (2) ... KY-4
Murray Branch—stream ... MD-2
Murray Branch—stream (2) ... MO-7
Murray Branch—stream (4) ... NC-3
Murray Branch—stream ... SC-3
Murray Branch—stream (6) ... TN-4
Murray Branch—stream (2) ... TX-5
Murray Branch Picnic Area—locale ... NC-3
Murray Branch Post Office—building ... UT-8
Murray Branch Sch—school ... SC-3
Murray Brook—stream (2) ... NY-2
**Murray Burton Acres Subdivision**—pop pl ... UT-8
Murray Butte ... OR-9
Murray Butte—summit ... SD-7
Murray Cabin—locale ... MT-8
Murray Canyon—other ... AK-9
Murray Canyon—valley (3) ... CA-9
Murray Canyon—valley ... NV-8
Murray Canyon Trail—trail ... MT-8
Murray (CCD)—cens area ... KY-4
Murray Cem ... MO-7
Murray Cem—cemetery ... IL-6
Murray Cem—cemetery ... IN-6
Murray Cem—cemetery (2) ... IA-7
Murray Cem—cemetery (2) ... KY-4
Murray Cem—cemetery ... MO-7
Murray Cem—cemetery (3) ... NY-2
Murray Cem—cemetery ... OR-9
Murray Cem—cemetery ... PA-2
Murray Cem—cemetery (3) ... TN-4
Murray Cem—cemetery (2) ... TX-5
Murray Cem—cemetery ... UT-8
Murray Cem—cemetery ... WV-2
Murray Ch—church ... AR-4
Murray Ch—church ... SC-3
Murray Ch—church ... TN-4
Murray Chapel—church ... AL-4
Murray Chapel Sch—school ... AR-4
**Murray City**—pop pl ... OH-6
Murray City Cemetery ... UT-8
**Murray Condominium**—pop pl ... UT-8
Murray Conservation Club—other ... IN-6
Murray Corners ... DE-2
**Murray Cottonwood Med Ctr Subdivision**—pop pl ... UT-8
Murray Coulee—valley (2) ... MT-8
**Murray (County)**—pop pl ... GA-3
**Murray (County)**—pop pl ... MN-6
**Murray (County)**—pop pl ... OK-5
Murray County Courthouse—hist pl ... GA-3
Murray County Courthouse—hist pl ... OK-5
Murray Courthouse—hist pl ... ID-8
Murray Cove—valley ... NC-3
Murray Creek ... MT-8
Murray Creek ... NV-8
Murray Creek ... TX-5
Murray Creek—stream (2) ... AK-9
Murray Creek—stream (3) ... AR-4
Murray Creek—stream ... CA-9
Murray Creek—stream ... FL-3
Murray Creek—stream ... GA-3
Murray Creek—stream (3) ... ID-8
Murray Creek—stream ... IA-7
Murray Creek—stream ... KS-7
Murray Creek—stream ... MN-6
Murray Creek—stream ... MS-4
Murray Creek—stream (3) ... MT-8
Murray Creek—stream ... NC-3
Murray Creek—stream ... OK-5
Murray Creek—stream (4) ... OR-9
Murray Creek—stream ... PA-2
Murray Creek—stream ... TN-4
Murray Creek—stream (2) ... WA-9
Murray Creek—stream (2) ... WI-6
Murray Creek—stream ... WY-8
Murray Creek Ditch—canal ... AR-4
Murray Creek Sch—school ... WI-6
Murray Creek Y-13a-1 Dam—dam ... MS-4
Murray Creek Y-13a-2 Dam—dam ... MS-4
Murray Creek Y-13a-4 Dam—dam ... MS-4
Murray Creek Y-13a-5 Dam—dam ... MS-4
Murraycross ... AL-4
**Murray Dale Subdivision**—pop pl ... UT-8
Murray Dam—dam ... OR-9
Murray Dam Site Public Use Area—park ... AR-4
Murray Ditch—canal ... ID-8
Murray Ditch—canal ... MT-8
Murray Ditch—canal ... OR-9
Murray Ditch—canal ... WY-8
Murray Drain—canal (3) ... MI-6
Murray Drain Number 17—canal ... ND-7
Murray Draw—valley ... CO-8
Murray Draw—valley ... ID-8
Murray Draw—valley ... WY-8
**Murray Estates**—pop pl ... TN-4
**Murray Estates (subdivision)**—pop pl ... DE-2
Murray Farm ... TX-5
Murray Field—flat ... OR-9
**Murrayfield**—pop pl ... VA-3
Murrayfield, Town of ... MA-1
Murrayfield Branch—stream ... VA-3
Murray Fire Control Station—locale ... CA-9
Murray Gap—gap ... NC-3
Murray Gap—gap (2) ... TN-4
Murray Gap—gap ... VA-3
Murray Gap Cem—cemetery ... NC-3
Murray-George House—hist pl ... WI-6
Murray Gilbert Slough—stream ... MT-8
Murraygill ... KS-7
**Murray Gill**—pop pl ... KS-7
**Murraygill**—pop pl ... KS-7
**Murray Grove**—pop pl ... NJ-2
Murray Gulch—valley ... AK-9
Murray Gulch—valley ... CA-9
Murray Gulch—valley ... OR-9
Murray Head—stream ... FL-3
**Murray Heights East Addition Subdivision**—pop pl ... UT-8
**Murray Heights Subdivision**—pop pl ... UT-8
Murray Hill ... TN-4
Murray Hill—hist pl ... NY-2
Murray Hill—locale ... GA-3
**Murray Hill**—pop pl ... FL-3
**Murray Hill**—pop pl ... KY-4
**Murray Hill**—pop pl ... NH-1
**Murray Hill**—pop pl ... NJ-2
**Murray Hill**—pop pl ... NY-2
Murray Hill—summit ... CA-9
Murray Hill—summit ... MI-6
Murray Hill—summit ... MT-8
Murray Hill—summit ... NY-2
Murray Hill—summit (2) ... OR-9
Murray Hill—summit ... VT-1
Murray Hill—uninc pl ... NY-2
Murray Hill Baptist Church Kindergarten—school ... FL-3
Murray Hill Canal—canal ... SC-3
Murray Hill Cem—cemetery ... OR-9
Murray Hill Ch—church ... OK-5
Murray Hill Elem Sch—school ... KS-7
**Murray Hill Gardens Subdivision**—pop pl ... UT-8
**Murray Hills**—pop pl ... GA-3
**Murray Hills**—pop pl ... MD-2
**Murray Hills**—pop pl ... TN-4
Murray Hill Sch—hist pl ... OH-6
Murray Hill Sch—school ... OH-6
Murray Hill Sch (abandoned)—school ... MO-7
Murray Hill Spring—spring ... OR-9
**Murray Hills (subdivision)**—pop pl ... NC-3
Murray Hill Station—hist pl ... NJ-2
Murray Hill Station—locale ... NJ-2
Murray Hill Station—locale ... NY-2
**Murray Hill (subdivision)**—pop pl ... FL-3
Murray Hill Summer Home District—hist pl ... NH-1
Murray Hill United Methodist Ch—church ... FL-3
Murray Hilton Lake—reservoir ... NC-3
Murray Hilton Lake Dam—dam ... NC-3
Murray (historical)—locale ... AL-4
Murray Hollow ... TN-4
Murray Hollow—valley ... KY-4
Murray Hollow—valley ... MO-7
Murray Hollow—valley ... NY-2
Murray Hollow—valley (2) ... TN-4
Murray Hollow—valley ... VT-1
Murray Hosp—hospital ... SC-3
Murray HS—school ... FL-3
Murray HS—school ... MI-6
Murray HS—school ... MN-6
Murray HS—school ... UT-8
Murray Island ... NY-2
Murray Island—island ... AK-9
Murray Island—island ... IA-7
Murray Island—island ... MT-8
Murray Isle—island ... NY-2
**Murray Isle**—pop pl ... NY-2
Murray JHS—school ... CA-9
Murray JHS—school ... GA-3
Murray JHS—school ... OR-9
**Murray Junction**—pop pl ... LA-4
Murray Key—island ... FL-3
Murray Knob—summit ... VA-3
Murray Lake ... WI-6
Murray Lake—lake ... AK-9
Murray Lake—lake ... CO-8
Murray Lake—lake (6) ... MI-6
Murray Lake—lake ... MN-6
Murray Lake—lake ... MT-8
Murray Lake—lake ... NE-7
Murray Lake—lake (2) ... WI-6
Murray Lake—lake (2) ... WY-8
Murray Lake—reservoir ... IN-6
Murray Lake—reservoir ... LA-4
Murray Lake—reservoir ... OK-5
Murray Lake—reservoir ... SD-7
Murray Lake—reservoir ... TN-4
Murray Lake Dam—dam ... IN-6
**Murray Lake Estates**—pop pl ... TN-4
Murray-Lake Hills—post sta ... TN-4
Murray Landing—locale ... SC-3
**Murray Lane Estates**—pop pl ... TN-4
Murray-Lasaine Sch—school ... SC-3
Murray Ledge—bar ... ME-1
Murray Lock and Dam—dam ... AR-4
Murray Manor Sch—school ... CA-9
**Murray Manor Subdivision**—pop pl ... UT-8
Murray Marsh ... DE-2
Murray Marsh Cove—bay ... DE-2
Murray Masonic Hall—hist pl ... ID-8
**Murray Meadows Subdivision**—pop pl ... UT-8
Murray Memorial Cem—cemetery ... MT-8
Murray Memorial Gardens—cemetery ... KY-4
Murray Memorial Gardens Cem—cemetery ... GA-3
Murray Mill Brook—stream ... NH-1
Murray Mine (underground)—mine (2) ... AL-4
Murray MS—school ... FL-3
Murray Number 4 Mine (underground)—mine ... AL-4
**Murray Oakes Subdivision**—pop pl ... UT-8
Murray Ohio Airp—airport ... TN-4
Murray Opening—flat ... CA-9
Murray Park—flat ... CO-8
Murray Park—flat ... UT-8
Murray Park—park ... CT-1
Murray Park—park ... FL-3
Murray Park—park ... OR-9
Murray Park—park ... TX-5
**Murray Park**—pop pl ... CA-9
**Murray Park Cove Subdivision**—pop pl ... UT-8
Murray Park Spring—spring ... UT-8
Murray Pasture—flat ... OR-9
Murray Peak ... OR-9
Murray Peak—summit ... ID-8
Murray Peak—summit ... OR-9
Murray Place—locale ... CO-8
Murray Place—locale ... MT-8
Murray Playground—park ... IL-6
Murray Point ... DE-2
Murray Point—cape ... FL-3
Murray Pond—lake ... FL-3
Murray Pond—reservoir ... GA-3
Murray Pond—reservoir ... PA-2
Murray Pond—reservoir ... SC-3
Murray Pond Dam—dam ... MA-1
Murray Ponds—lake ... CT-1
Murray Printing Company Dam—dam ... MA-1
Murray Ranch—locale ... MT-8
Murray Ranch—locale ... NM-5
Murray Ranch—locale ... ND-7
Murray Reynolds Falls—falls ... PA-2
Murray Ridge—ridge ... TN-4
Murray Road Sch—school ... MA-1
Murray Rock—bar ... ME-1
Murray Rsvr—reservoir ... CA-9
Murray Rsvr—reservoir ... CO-8
Murray Rsvr—reservoir (2) ... OR-9
Murray Rsvr—reservoir ... WY-8
Murray Run—stream ... KY-4
Murray Run—stream ... OH-6
Murray Run—stream (2) ... PA-2
Murray Run—stream ... VA-3
Murray Run—stream ... WV-2
Murray Saddle—gap ... OR-9
Murray Saint Sch—school ... KY-4
Murrays Baptist Church ... TN-4
Murrays Cabins—locale ... MI-6
Murrays Canyon—valley ... UT-8
Murrays Cem—cemetery ... UT-8
Murray Sch—school (2) ... CA-9
Murray Sch—school ... IL-6
Murray Sch—school ... KY-4
Murray Sch—school ... MI-6
Murray Sch—school ... NC-3
Murray Sch—school (2) ... SC-3
Murray Sch—school ... TN-4
Murray Sch—school ... VA-3
Murray Sch (abandoned)—school ... PA-2
Murrays Chapel ... TN-4
Murrays Chapel—church ... AL-4
**Murrays Chapel**—pop pl ... AL-4
Murray Sch (historical)—school ... AL-4
Murrays Corner—locale ... DE-2
**Murrays Corner**—pop pl ... NY-2
Murrays Corners ... DE-2
Murrays Crossroads—locale ... GA-3
**Murrays Development**—pop pl ... DE-2
Murrays Ford Bridge—bridge ... VA-3
**Murrays Haven (subdivision)**—pop pl ... DE-2
Murray's Hill ... MI-6
**Murrays Hill**—pop pl ... NC-3
Murrays Hill—summit ... UT-8
**Murray Siding**—pop pl ... MD-2
Murrays Inlet ... SC-3
Murrays Lake—lake ... AZ-5
**Murray's Lake**—pop pl ... GA-3
Murrays Lake—reservoir ... GA-3
Murrays Landing—locale ... WI-6
Murray Slough—stream ... IL-6
Murrays Mill ... NJ-2
Murray's Mill Hist Dist—hist pl ... NC-3
Murrays Mill (historical)—locale ... NC-3
Murrays Mill Lake—lake ... NC-3
Murrays Millpond—reservoir ... NC-3
Murrays Mill Pond—reservoir ... NC-3
Murrays Mill Pond Dam—dam ... NC-3
Murrays Pond—lake ... OR-9
Murrays Pond—reservoir ... NY-2
Murrays Pond—reservoir ... NC-3
Murrays Pond Dam—dam ... NC-3
Murray Spring—spring ... NV-8
Murray Spring—spring ... TN-4
Murray Spring—spring (2) ... UT-8
Murray Spring—spring ... WA-9
Murray Springs—spring ... UT-8
Murrays Run ... PA-2
Murrays Spring—spring ... UT-8
Murray State Childrens Center—building ... IL-6
Murray State Coll—school ... OK-5
Murray State Univ—school ... KY-4
Murray State Univ Historic Buildings—hist pl ... KY-4
Murray State Univ Historic Buildings, Addition: Main Library—hist pl ... KY-4
Murrays Temple Ch of God—church ... MS-4
**Murray Store**—pop pl ... TN-4
Murraysville—locale ... WV-2
**Murraysville**—pop pl ... NC-3
**Murraysville**—pop pl ... SC-3
Murraysville (RR name for Murrysville)—other ... PA-2
**Murraysville (RR name Murrayville)**—pop pl ... WV-2
Murray Swamp—stream ... SC-3
Murray Swamp—swamp ... MD-2
Murrays Wharf ... MD-2
Murray Tank—reservoir (2) ... AZ-5
Murray Tank—reservoir ... NM-5
Murray Temple CME Ch—church ... AL-4
Murray Theater—hist pl ... IN-6
**Murray Town**—pop pl ... NC-3
**Murraytown**—pop pl ... NC-3
**Murray (Town of)**—pop pl ... NY-2
Murray Township—civil ... MO-7
**Murray Township**—pop pl ... KS-7
Murray (Township of)—fmr MCD ... AR-4
**Murray (Township of)**—pop pl ... MN-6
Murray Trick Tank—reservoir ... AZ-5
**Murrayville**—pop pl ... GA-3
**Murrayville**—pop pl ... IL-6
Murrayville Baptist Church ... TN-4
Murrayville (CCD)—cens area ... GA-3
Murrayville Cem—cemetery ... TN-4
Murrayville Ch—church ... TN-4
Murrayville (Election Precinct)—fmr MCD ... IL-6

Murrayville (RR name for Murraysville)—*other* WV-2
Murray Wash—*stream* AZ-5
Murray Well—*well* (2) NM-5
Murray Wells—*other* NM-5
Murray West Well—*well* NM-5
Murray Wharf—*locale* MD-2
Murray White Canal—*canal* UT-8
Murr Branch—*stream* GA-3
Murr Branch—*stream* TN-4
Murr Ch—*church* TX-5
*Murr Creek* NC-3
Murr Creek—*stream* MT-8
*Murrel Inlet* SC-3
**Murrell**—*pop pl* PA-2
Murrell, Samuel, House—*hist pl* KY-4
Murrell Bench—*bench* TN-4
Murrell Branch—*stream* KY-4
Murrell Branch—*stream* MS-4
Murrell Canal—*canal* LA-4
Murrell Cem—*cemetery* AL-4
Murrell Cem—*cemetery* MO-7
Murrell Cem—*cemetery* (5) TN-4
Murrell Cem—*cemetery* TX-5
Murrell Creek—*stream* TN-4
Murrell Gap—*gap* KY-4
Murrell Hill—*summit* TN-4
Murrell Hill Lookout Tower—*locale* AL-4
Murrell Hollow—*valley* MO-7
Murrell Hollow—*valley* TN-4
Murrell Home—*hist pl* OK-5
Murrell Home Park—*park* OK-5
*Murrell Inlet* SC-3
*Murrell Mill* TN-4
Murrell Sch—*school* TN-4
Murrells Inlet—*bay* SC-3
**Murrells Inlet**—*pop pl* SC-3
Murrells Inlet Hist Dist—*hist pl* SC-3
*Murrells Landing* AL-4
Murrells Lodge—*locale* SC-3
*Murrell Town* TN-4
Murrelltown—*locale* TN-4
*Murrels Inlet* SC-3
Murren Hill—*summit* OH-6
Murre Rocks—*island* AK-9
Murrers Upper Meadow—*flat* CA-9
*Murrey Gap* TN-4
Murrey Pond—*lake* NY-2
Murrey Sch—*school* KY-4
Murrie Cem—*cemetery* IL-6
**Murrieta**—*pop pl* CA-9
Murrieta (CCD)—*cens area* CA-9
Murrieta Creek—*stream* CA-9
Murrieta Creek Archeol Area—*hist pl* CA-9
**Murrieta Hot Springs**—*pop pl* CA-9
*Murrietta* CA-9
Murril Branch—*stream* MO-7
Murrill Cem—*cemetery* MO-7
Murrill Gap—*gap* VA-3
Murrill Hill Ch—*church* WV-2
Murrill Landing—*locale* NC-3
Murrins Mines—*mine* PA-2
**Murrinsville**—*pop pl* PA-2
*Murrinville* PA-2
*Murrn Hill* OH-6
*Murrow Creek* WY-8
Murr Peak—*summit* MT-8
Murr Peak Trail—*trail* MT-8
Murr Ranch—*locale* CO-8
Murr Ranch—*locale* TX-5
Murr Sch (abandoned)—*school* MO-7
*Murru* FM-9
*Murry* NC-3
Murry—*locale* MS-4
Murry—*locale* WI-6
**Murry**—*pop pl* MO-7
*Murry Branch* TX-5
Murry Branch—*stream* LA-4
Murry Camp—*locale* CA-9
Murry Canyon—*valley* (2) NV-8
Murry Cem—*cemetery* MS-4
Murry Cem—*cemetery* (2) MO-7
*Murry Creek* CA-9
*Murry Creek* NV-8
*Murry Creek* OK-5
*Murry Creek* PA-2
Murry Creek—*stream* AL-4
Murry Creek—*stream* (2) CA-9
Murry Creek—*stream* CO-8
Murry Creek—*stream* (2) GA-3
Murry Creek—*stream* NV-8
Murry Creek—*stream* OK-5
Murry Creek—*stream* (2) OR-9
Murry Creek—*stream* WI-6
Murry Creek Camping Area—*locale* GA-3
Murrycross—*locale* AL-4
Murry Drain—*canal* MI-6
Murry Flat—*flat* CA-9
Murry Gulch—*valley* CA-9
*Murry Hill* OR-9
**Murry Hill**—*pop pl* PA-2
Murry Hill—*summit* CA-9
Murry Hill—*summit* CT-1
Murry Hill—*summit* MO-7
Murry Hill—*summit* OR-9
Murryhill—*uninc pl* TX-5
Murry Hill Park—*park* NC-3
Murry (historical)—*locale* MS-4
Murry Hollow—*valley* VA-3
Murry Lake—*lake* MI-6
Murry Landing—*locale* DE-2
Murry Memorial Cem—*cemetery* TX-5
Murry Mine (abandoned)—*mine* OR-9
Murry Park—*park* CA-9
Murry Pond—*reservoir* GA-3
Murry Ranch—*locale* MT-8
Murry Ranch—*locale* NE-7
Murry Rock—*pillar* NV-8
Murry Rogers Catfish Operation Dam—*dam* MS-4
Murry Rogers Catfish Ponds Dam—*dam* MS-4
Murry Sch—*school* MO-7
Murry Sch (abandoned)—*school* MO-7
Murry Site—*hist pl* PA-2
Murry Springs—*spring* AL-4
Murry Springs—*spring* NV-8
*Murry Spur* MS-4
**Murry Spur**—*pop pl* OK-5
Murry Spur Ch—*church* OK-5
Murry Summit—*gap* NV-8
**Murrysville**—*pop pl* PA-2
Murrysville Golf Course—*other* PA-2
*Murrysville (RR name Murraysville)* PA-2
Murry Tank—*reservoir* NM-5
**Murry (Town of)**—*pop pl* WI-6
Murry Treat Hollow—*valley* AR-4
Murry Well—*well* TX-5
*Murry Wharf* MD-2
Murschel House—*hist pl* OH-6
Mursh Run—*stream* OH-6
Murta—*locale* AR-4
*Murtagh Creek* OR-9
**Murtaugh**—*pop pl* ID-8
**Murtaugh**—*pop pl* MN-6
Murtaugh Creek—*stream* OR-9
Murtaugh Creek—*stream* TX-5
Murtaugh Lake—*reservoir* ID-8
Murtha, Charles, House and Brick Yard—*hist pl* SD-7
Murtha Sch (historical)—*school* SD-7
*Murther Creek* DE-2
*Murtherkill* DE-2
Murthum Sch—*school* MI-6
Murtland Field—*park* TN-4
Murtocks Hole—*basin* NM-5
*Murule-To* MP-9
*Murure* MP-9
*Murure-to* MP-9
*Muru'ru'* FM-9
*Muruu* FM-9
*Murval Bayou* TX-5
*Murvaul* TX-5
Murvaul, Lake—*reservoir* TX-5
Murvaul Creek—*stream* TX-5
*Murvaul Lake* TX-5
*Murvaul Reservoir* TX-5
*Murvauls Bayou* TX-5
Murwood Sch—*school* CA-9
*Murymere Falls* WA-9
*Musa* FL-3
*Musall Ditch* IN-6
*Muscackituck River* IN-6
*Muscadine* NC-3
**Muscadine**—*pop pl* AL-4
Muscadine Blowhole—*cave* TN-4
Muscadine Bower Sch (historical)—*school* MS-4
Muscadine Branch—*stream* (2) TX-5
Muscadine Cave—*cave* AL-4
Muscadine Ch—*church* AL-4
Muscadine Creek—*stream* AL-4
Muscadine Hollow—*valley* (2) TN-4
*Muscadine Junction* AL-4
**Muscadine Junction**—*pop pl* AL-4
Muscadine Mtn—*summit* AL-4
Muscadine Point—*cape* AL-4
*Muscallonge* MI-6
Muscallonge Bay—*bay* MI-6
*Muscalonge Bay* NY-2
*Muscalonge Creek* NY-2
Muscamoot Ridge—*island* MI-6
**Muscat**—*pop pl* CA-9
*Muscatatuck Creek* IN-6
Muscatatuck Natl Wildlife Ref—*park* IN-6
Muscatatuck River—*stream* IN-6
Muscatatuck State Hosp and Training Center—*hospital* IN-6
Muscatatuck State Park—*park* IN-6
Muscatatuck State Sch—*school* IN-6
Muscatel—*locale* CA-9
Muscatel Sch—*school* CA-9
Muscatel Windmill—*locale* TX-5
**Muscatine**—*pop pl* IA-7
Muscatine City Hall—*building* IA-7
Muscatine County Courthouse—*hist pl* IA-7
Muscatine County Home—*building* IA-7
Muscatine County Hosp—*hospital* IA-7
Muscatine Highway Bridge—*other* IL-6
Muscatine HS—*school* IA-7
Muscatine Island—*island* IA-7
Muscatine Island Pumping Station—*other* IA-7
Muscatine Municipal Electric Plant—*other* IA-7
**Muscatine Park Subdivision**—*pop pl* UT-8
Muscatine Slough—*stream* IA-7
Muscatine Township—*fmr MCD* IA-7
*Muscatutuck River* IN-6
Muscelini, Bayou—*gut* LA-4
*Muschaug Pond* RI-1
Muschel Sch—*school* NJ-2
Muschino Hollow—*valley* PA-2
**Muschopauge**—*pop pl* MA-1
Muschopauge Brook—*stream* MA-1
Muschopauge Pond—*reservoir* MA-1
Muschopauge Pond Dam—*dam* MA-1
Muscle, Bayou—*gut* LA-4
Muscle Bay—*lake* LA-4
*Muscle Bayou* LA-4
*Muscle Creek* AL-4
*Muscle Creek* MT-8
*Muscle Creek* TX-5
Muscle Hole—*bay* MD-2
Muscle Hole Point—*cape* MD-2
Muscle Lake—*lake* LA-4
*Muscle Point* MA-1
Muscle Ridge Channel—*channel* ME-1
Muscle Ridge Islands—*island* ME-1
*Muscle Shoal* RI-1
Muscle Shoal—*bar* ME-1
Muscle Shoals—*bar* AL-4
**Muscle Shoals**—*pop pl* AL-4
Muscle Shoals Airp—*airport* AL-4
Muscle Shoals Baptist Ch—*church* AL-4
Muscle Shoals Canal (historical)—*canal* AL-4
Muscle Shoals First Baptist Ch—*church* AL-4
*Muscle Shoals Forest Nursery* AL-4
Muscle Shoals Golf and Country Club—*other* AL-4
Muscle Shoals Headstart Sch—*school* AL-4
Muscle Shoals HS—*school* AL-4
Muscle Shoals Reservation—*other* AL-4
Muscle Shoals Sailing Club—*locale* AL-4
*Muscle Shoals Technical College* AL-4
Muscle Shoals Technical Institute—*school* AL-4
Muscle Shoals Vocational Sch—*school* AL-4
Musco Creek—*stream* MO-7
**Muscoda**—*pop pl* AL-4
**Muscoda**—*pop pl* WI-6
Muscoda Island—*island* WI-6
Muscoda JHS—*school* AL-4
Muscoda Mtn—*summit* AL-4
Muscoda Sch—*school* AL-4
**Muscoda (Town of)**—*pop pl* WI-6
Muscogee—*locale* FL-3
Muscogee—*other* GA-3
*Muscogee (County)* GA-3
Muscogee County Flatrock Park—*park* GA-3
Muscogee County Health Center—*hospital* GA-3
Muscogee Junction (Muscogee)—*uninc pl* GA-3
Muscogee Lake—*lake* FL-3
Muscogee Landing—*locale* FL-3
Muscogee Lookout Tower—*locale* GA-3
Muscogee Wharf—*locale* FL-3
*Musconetcong* NJ-2
Musconetcong, Lake—*reservoir* NJ-2
Musconetcong Country Club—*other* NJ-2
**Musconetcong Junction**—*pop pl* NJ-2
Musconetcong Mtn—*summit* NJ-2
Musconetcong River—*stream* NJ-2
Musconetcong State Park—*park* NJ-2
Musconetcong Valley—*valley* NJ-2
Musconetcong Valley Ch—*church* NJ-2
*Musconetcong Village* NJ-2
*Musconetgung River* NJ-2
**Muscongus**—*pop pl* ME-1
*Muscongus Bar* ME-1
Muscongus Bay—*bay* (2) ME-1
**Muscongus Bay**—*pop pl* ME-1
Muscongus Harbor—*bay* ME-1
*Muscongus Island* ME-1
*Muscongus Island Bar* ME-1
Muscongus Sound—*bay* ME-1
Muscoot Dam—*dam* NY-2
Muscooten Bay—*bay* IL-6
Muscoot River—*stream* NY-2
Muscoot Rsvr—*reservoir* NY-2
**Muscotah**—*pop pl* KS-7
Muscott Bridge—*bridge* OR-9
Muscott Creek—*stream* OR-9
Muscott Creek—*stream* WA-9
Muscott Sch—*school* CA-9
**Muscoy**—*pop pl* CA-9
Muscoy Sch—*school* CA-9
Muscrowe Branch—*stream* AL-4
Muscupiabe—*civil* CA-9
**Muse**—*pop pl* OK-5
**Muse**—*pop pl* PA-2
Muse Branch—*stream* KY-4
Muse Branch—*stream* TN-4
Muse Cem—*cemetery* LA-4
Muse Cem—*cemetery* (3) TN-4
Muse Cem—*cemetery* VA-3
Muse Ch—*church* TX-5
Muse Creek—*stream* AR-4
Muse Elem Sch—*school* PA-2
Muse Gap—*gap* TN-4
Muse Hollow—*valley* KY-4
Muse Hollow—*valley* TN-4
Muse Island—*island* AK-9
Muse Junction—*locale* PA-2
Musek Branch—*stream* TX-5
Muse Lake Dam—*dam* MS-4
**Musella**—*pop pl* GA-3
Musellmans Crossing—*locale* PA-2
*Musellunge Lake* WI-6
Musembeah Peak—*summit* WY-8
Muse Meadow—*flat* CA-9
Muse Mill (historical)—*locale* MS-4
Muse Mtn—*summit* AR-4
Muse Park—*park* TN-4
Muses Beach—*locale* VA-3
Muses Bottom—*bend* WV-2
**Muses Bottom**—*pop pl* WV-2
Muses Bridge—*bridge* SC-3
Muses Chapel—*church* KY-4
**Muses Mills**—*pop pl* KY-4
*Muse-Stephenson Cemetery* TN-4
Museum—*post sta* WY-8
Museum Canyon—*valley* CA-9
Museum Creek—*stream* KS-7
Museum-Grotto Residence—*hist pl* UT-8
Museum (historical)—*locale* KS-7
Museum Lake—*lake* MN-6
*Museum of American Art* NC-3
Museum of American Treasures—*building* CA-9
Museum of AM-Jewish History—*building* PA-2
Museum of Appalachia—*building* TN-4
Museum of Art—*building* PA-2
Museum of Art—*building* TX-5
Museum of Arts—*building* NY-2
Museum of Early Southern Decorative Arts—*building* NC-3
Museum of International Folk Art—*building* NM-5
Museum of Modern Art—*building* NY-2
Museum of Natural Science—*building* MS-4
Museum of Northern Arizona—*building* AZ-5
Museum of Science—*building* MA-1
Museum Of Science And Industry—*building* IL-6
Museum of the Albermarle—*building* NC-3
Museum of the Alphabet—*building* NC-3
Museum Of Transport—*building* MO-7
Museum Park—*park* IL-6
Museville—*locale* VA-3
**Museville**—*pop pl* OH-6
Museville Post Office (historical)—*building* AL-4
Musfeldt Cem—*cemetery* IA-7
Musgano Site—*hist pl* TX-5
Musgow—*cape* FM-9
Musgow—*locale* FM-9
Musgrave Branch—*stream* VA-3
Musgrave Canyon—*valley* TX-5
Musgrave Cem—*cemetery* IL-6
Musgrave Creek—*stream* TX-5
Musgrave Ditch—*canal* CO-8
Musgrave Hollow—*valley* MO-7
Musgrave Hollow—*valley* OH-6
Musgrave Lakes—*lake* MI-6
*Musgraves Creek* PA-2
**Musgraves Crossroads**—*pop pl* NC-3
Musgrove—*locale* TX-5
Musgrove Bay—*swamp* GA-3
Musgrove Block—*hist pl* MA-1
*Musgrove Canyon* NV-8
Musgrove Cem—*cemetery* AR-4
*Musgrove Ch* AL-4
Musgrove Chapel—*church* AL-4
*Musgrove Chapel Ch* AL-4
Musgrove Ch (historical)—*church* AL-4
Musgrove Country Club—*other* AL-4
Musgrove Creek—*stream* AL-4
Musgrove Creek—*stream* ID-8
Musgrove Creek—*stream* NV-8
Musgrove Creek—*stream* WA-9
Musgrove (historical)—*locale* AL-4
Musgrove Mine (Inactive)—*mine* ID-8
Musgrove Mine (underground)—*mine* AL-4
Musgrove Pratt Mine (underground)—*mine* AL-4
Musgrove's Mill Historic Battle Site—*hist pl* SC-3
Mushat Gilchrist Cem—*cemetery* AL-4
*Mushaug Pond* RI-1
Mushaway Peak—*summit* TX-5
Mushback Point—*cape* UT-8
Mush Bluff—*cliff* GA-3
Mush Campground—*locale* ID-8
*Mush Creek* WA-9
*Mush Creek* WY-8
Mush Creek—*stream* (2) AL-4
Mush Creek—*stream* SC-3
Mush Creek—*stream* SD-7
Mush Creek—*stream* TX-5
Mush Creek—*stream* WA-9
Mush Creek—*stream* WY-8
Mush Creek Ch—*church* SC-3
Mush Creek Oil Field—*oilfield* WY-8
Mush Creek Pumping Station—*other* WY-8
Mushgee Lake—*lake* MN-6
Mush Island—*island* NC-3
Mush Island Gut—*stream* NC-3
Mush Lake—*lake* AK-9
Mush Lake—*lake* MN-6
Mushman Hollow—*valley* MO-7
Mushmelon Creek—*stream* GA-3
Mush Mtn—*summit* NM-5
Mushoak Creek—*stream* CA-9
Mushotuba Creek—*stream* TX-5
Mush Paddle Hollow—*valley* MO-7
Mush Point—*cape* ID-8
Mush Pond Swamp—*swamp* VA-3
Mushpot, The—*flat* TN-4
Mushpots, The—*spring* WY-8
*Mushroom* WA-9
Mushroom Basin—*other* NM-5
Mushroom Cave—*cave* MO-7
Mushroom Corner—*locale* WA-9
Mushroom Creek—*stream* MT-8
**Mushroom Farms**—*pop pl* PA-2
Mushroom Gulch—*valley* CO-8
Mushroom Island—*island* AK-9
Mushroom Islets—*other* AK-9
Mushroom Mtn—*summit* MT-8
Mushroom Reef—*bar* AK-9
Mushroom Reef—*bar* AZ-5
Mushroom Rock—*bar* WA-9
Mushroom Rock—*locale* CA-9
Mushroom Rock—*pillar* (2) CA-9
Mushroom Run—*stream* WV-2
Mushroom Springs—*spring* UT-8
*Mush Run* OH-6
Mush Run—*stream* OH-6
Mushrush Cem—*cemetery* PA-2
Mush Saddle—*gap* ID-8
Mush Swamp—*stream* SC-3
Mushy Park—*swamp* CO-8
Music—*locale* KY-4
**Music Acres**—*pop pl* TN-4
Musical Fund Hall—*hist pl* PA-2
Music Bar—*bar* ID-8
Music Branch—*stream* (2) KY-4
Music Branch—*stream* VA-3
Music Camp—*locale* CA-9
*Music Canyon* AZ-5
Music Canyon—*valley* AZ-5
Music Canyon—*valley* NV-8
Music Canyon Spring—*spring* AZ-5
Music Cem—*cemetery* KY-4
Music Cem—*cemetery* (2) VA-3
*Music Cemetery* TN-4
Music Ch—*church* MO-7
Music Creek—*stream* CA-9
Music Creek—*stream* OR-9
Music Creek—*stream* WY-8
Music Fork—*stream* (2) KY-4
Music Hall—*hist pl* NJ-2
Music Hall—*hist pl* (2) NY-2
Music Hall Evangelical Lutheran Church—*hist pl* SC-3
**Music (historical)**—*pop pl* TN-4
**Musick**—*pop pl* WV-2
Musick Cem—*cemetery* IN-6
Musick Cem—*cemetery* TN-4
Musick Cem—*cemetery* (4) VA-3
Musick Cem—*cemetery* WV-2
Musick Chapel—*church* KY-4
*Musick Creek* VA-3
Musick Creek—*stream* CA-9
Musick Guard Station—*locale* CA-9
Musick Guard Station—*locale* OR-9
Musick Mine—*mine* OR-9
Musick Mtn—*summit* CA-9
Musick Sch—*school* CA-9
Musick Sch—*school* (2) IL-6
Musick Sch—*school* VA-3
**Musicks Ferry**—*pop pl* MO-7
Music Mesa—*summit* CO-8
Music Mountain—*hist pl* CT-1
Music Mountain—*ridge* AR-4
Music Mountain Mine—*mine* AZ-5
Music Mountain Oil Field—*oilfield* PA-2
Music Mountains—*range* AZ-5
Music Mtn—*summit* AZ-5
Music Mtn—*summit* CA-9
Music Mtn—*summit* CO-8
Music Mtn—*summit* CT-1
Music Mtn—*summit* TX-5
Music Pass—*gap* CO-8
Music Pass Creek—*stream* CO-8
Music Pass Trail—*trail* CO-8
Music Run—*stream* WV-2
Music Temple Bar (inundated)—*bar* UT-8
Music Temple (inundated)—*cave* UT-8
Music Valley—*basin* CA-9
*Musina Peak* UT-8
Musinea Administrative Site—*locale* UT-8
*Musinia Peak* UT-8
*Muskakituk River* IN-6
Muskallonge Lake—*lake* MI-6
Muskallonge Lake State Park—*park* MI-6
*Muskalonge Bay* NY-2
Muskalonge Cem—*cemetery* NY-2
*Muskalonge Creek* NY-2
*Muskalonge Lake* MI-6
*Muskalunge Lake* IN-6
*Muskeag Lake* MN-6
Muskedine—*locale* MS-4
Muskee Creek—*stream* NJ-2
Muskee Hill—*summit* NJ-2
*Muskeeket Island* MA-1
Muskeg—*locale* WI-6
*Muskegat Island* MA-1
Muskeg Bay—*bay* MN-6
Muskeg Creek—*stream* AK-9
Muskeg Creek—*stream* ID-8
Muskeg Creek—*stream* MN-6
Muskeg Creek—*stream* WI-6
Muskeget Channel—*channel* MA-1
Muskeget Island—*island* MA-1
Muskeget Rock—*rock* MA-1
Muskeg Lake—*lake* MI-6
Muskeg Lake—*lake* (4) MN-6
Muskeg Lake—*lake* WI-6
**Muskego**—*pop pl* WI-6
Muskego Bay—*bay* MN-6
Muskego Canal—*canal* WI-6
*Muskego Creek* WI-6
Muskego HS—*school* WI-6
*Muskego Lake* WI-6
Muskego Lake—*reservoir* WI-6
**Muskegon**—*pop pl* MI-6
**Muskegon**—*pop pl* MS-4
Muskegon Army Engine Plant—*other* MI-6
Muskegon Business Coll—*school* MI-6
Muskegon Community Coll—*school* MI-6
**Muskegon (County)**—*pop pl* MI-6
Muskegon County Airp—*airport* MI-6
Muskegon Creek—*stream* ID-8
Muskegon Creek—*stream* WA-9
**Muskegon Heights**—*pop pl* MI-6
Muskegon Hist Dist—*hist pl* MI-6
Muskegon Lake—*lake* MI-6
Muskegon Lake—*lake* WA-9
Muskegon Newaygo Drain—*canal* MI-6
*Muskegon River* MI-6
Muskegon River—*stream* MI-6
Muskegon State Game Area—*park* MI-6
Muskegon State Park—*park* MI-6
**Muskegon (Township of)**—*pop pl* MI-6
Muskegon YMCA Bldg—*hist pl* MI-6
Muskego Point—*cape* MN-6
**Muskego Township**—*pop pl* ND-7
*Muskejet Island* MA-1
Muskellunge Bay—*bay* NY-2
Muskellunge Creek—*stream* AK-9
Muskellunge Creek—*stream* NY-2
Muskellunge Creek—*stream* (5) WI-6
Muskellunge Lake—*lake* IN-6
Muskellunge Lake—*lake* (2) MI-6
Muskellunge Lake—*lake* (6) WI-6
Muskellunge Lookout Tower—*locale* WI-6
Muskellunge Point—*cape* NY-2
*Muskesih Lake* WI-6
Muskesin Lake—*lake* WI-6
*Musketaquid* MA-1
Musket Ball Canyon—*valley* NM-5
Musket Bay—*swamp* GA-3
Musket Brook—*stream* ME-1
Musketeep Lake—*lake* MI-6
*Musketeers Pas* FL-3
*Musketequid* MA-1
*Musketequid Plantation* MA-1
**Musket Hills**—*pop pl* VA-3
Musket Lake—*lake* WI-6
Musket Mtn—*summit* OK-5
Musketo Inlet—*channel* NC-3
*Musket Point* VA-3
Musketry Flats—*flat* OK-5
Musket Shot Springs (site)—*locale* UT-8
Muskgrave Creek—*stream* CA-9
*Muskgrove Canyon* NV-8
*Muskgrove Creek* NV-8
Musk Hog Canyon—*valley* (2) AZ-5
Musk Hog Canyon—*valley* TX-5
Musk Hog Canyon Spring—*spring* AZ-5
Muskhog Hollow—*valley* TX-5
Muskhog Mtn—*summit* AZ-5
Musk Hog Spring—*spring* (2) AZ-5
Muskhog Spring—*spring* AZ-5
Muskhog Spring—*spring* (3) TX-5
Muskhog Tank—*reservoir* AZ-5
Muskhog Water—*spring* AZ-5
Muskie Lake—*lake* ND-7
Muskie Lake—*lake* (2) WI-6
*Muskie Spring Lake* WI-6
Muskie Springs Lake—*lake* WI-6
Muskingum Brook—*stream* NJ-2
Muskingum Ch—*church* OH-6
Muskingum Coll—*school* OH-6
Muskingum College Campus Hist Dist—*hist pl* OH-6
**Muskingum (County)**—*pop pl* OH-6
Muskingum County Courthouse And Jail—*hist pl* OH-6
Muskingum Draw—*valley* TX-5
Muskingum Island—*island* WV-2
Muskingum River—*stream* OH-6
Muskingum River Lock No. 10 And Canal—*hist pl* OH-6
**Muskingum (Township of)**—*pop pl* (2) OH-6
Muskingum Valley Ch—*church* OH-6
Muskingum Watershed Conservancy District—*area* OH-6
Musko Branch—*stream* MO-7
Muskoda—*locale* MN-6
Muskoday, Lake—*lake* MI-6
Muskoday, Lake—*lake* NY-2
**Muskogee**—*pop pl* OK-5
Muskogee (CCD)—*cens area* OK-5
Muskogee Ch—*church* OK-5
Muskogee Country Club—*other* OK-5
**Muskogee (County)**—*pop pl* OK-5
Muskogee County Courthouse—*hist pl* OK-5
Muskogee HS—*school* OK-5
Muskogee Southwest (CCD)—*cens area* OK-5
*Muskogy* OK-5
Muskomee Bay—*bay* AK-9
*Muskonetcunk River* NJ-2
**Musk Ox**—*pop pl* AK-9
Muskrat Basin—*basin* WY-8
Muskrat Bay—*bay* IN-6
Muskrat Bay—*bay* MN-6
Muskrat Bay—*bay* NY-2
Muskrat Bayou—*gut* LA-4
Muskrat Bayou—*stream* LA-4
Muskrat Bluff—*cliff* VA-3
Muskrat Branch—*stream* NC-3
Muskrat Branch—*stream* VA-3
Muskrat Brook—*stream* NY-2
Muskrat Canyon—*valley* UT-8
Muskrat Canyon—*valley* WY-8
Muskrat Cave—*cave* AL-4
Muskrat Channel—*channel* MN-6
Muskrat Creek—*stream* AK-9
Muskrat Creek—*stream* GA-3
Muskrat Creek—*stream* MI-6
Muskrat Creek—*stream* (4) MT-8
Muskrat Creek—*stream* (2) NY-2
Muskrat Creek—*stream* NC-3
Muskrat Creek—*stream* ND-7
Muskrat Creek—*stream* (2) WI-6
Muskrat Creek—*stream* (2) WY-8
Muskrat Creek Trail—*trail* MT-8
Muskrat Ditch—*canal* CO-8
Muskrat Farm Lake—*lake* MI-6
*Muskrat Haven* DE-2
Muskrat Hollow—*valley* IA-7
Muskrat Hollow—*valley* OH-6
Muskrat Hollow—*valley* OK-5
Muskrat Junction State Wildlife Mngmt Area—*park* MN-6
*Muskrat Lake* MI-6
*Muskrat Lake* MN-6
Muskrat Lake—*lake* (2) AK-9
Muskrat Lake—*lake* CO-8
Muskrat Lake—*lake* ID-8
Muskrat Lake—*lake* IL-6
Muskrat Lake—*lake* IA-7
Muskrat Lake—*lake* (12) MI-6
Muskrat Lake—*lake* (7) MN-6
Muskrat Lake—*lake* MO-7
Muskrat Lake—*lake* OR-9
Muskrat Lake—*lake* (3) WA-9
Muskrat Lake—*lake* (2) WI-6
Muskrat Lake—*reservoir* MI-6
Muskrat Lake—*swamp* ND-7
Muskrat Lake—*swamp* WI-6
Muskrat Lake Cem—*cemetery* MI-6
Muskrat Lakes—*lake* CO-8
Muskrat Lakes—*lake* MI-6
Muskrat Mtn—*summit* OK-5
Muskrat Oil Field—*oilfield* WY-8
Muskrat Pass—*gap* MT-8
Muskrat Point—*cape* MI-6
Muskrat Pond—*lake* ID-8
Muskrat Pond—*lake* IN-6
Muskrat Pond—*lake* (2) ME-1
Muskrat Pond—*lake* (4) NY-2
Muskrat Pond—*lake* OR-9
Muskrat Ridge—*ridge* NC-3
Muskrat Rsvr—*reservoir* CO-8
Muskrat Run—*stream* (2) PA-2
Muskrat Run—*stream* WI-6
Muskrat Slough State Game Mngmt Area—*park* IA-7
Muskrat Spring—*spring* UT-8
Muskrat Spring—*spring* WY-8
Muskrat Springs Post Office (historical)—*building* TN-4
*Muskrattown* MD-2
**Muskwa Village**—*pop pl* AK-9
Musky Bay—*bay* (3) WI-6
Muslatt Mtn—*summit* CA-9
Muslin Creek—*stream* OR-9
*Musphilion Land* DE-2
**Musquabuck Park**—*pop pl* IN-6
Musquacook Deadwater—*channel* ME-1
Musquacook Mtn—*summit* ME-1
Musquacook Stream—*stream* ME-1
*Musquapog Pond* MA-1
Musquapsink Brook—*stream* NJ-2
Musquash Bay—*bay* ME-1
Musquash Brook—*stream* NH-1
Musquash Brook—*stream* NJ-2
Musquash Cove—*bay* ME-1
Musquashcut Brook—*stream* MA-1
*Musquashcut Harbor* MA-1
Musquashcut Pond—*lake* MA-1
*Musquashent Brook* MA-1
*Musquashent Pond* MA-1
*Musquashiat Brook* MA-1
*Musquashiat Pond* MA-1
*Musquashicut Brook* MA-1
*Musquashicut Pond* MA-1
Musquash Island—*island* ME-1
*Musquash Lake* ME-1
Musquash Lake—*lake* MN-6
Musquash Mtn—*summit* ME-1
*Musquashout Pond* MA-1
Musquash Point—*cape* ME-1
Musquash Pond—*lake* ME-1
*Musquash River* ME-1
*Musquash Stream* ME-1
*Musquatage Point* RI-1
*Musquataug Point* RI-1
Musque Lake—*lake* MI-6
Musquetaquid Pond—*reservoir* MA-1
Musquetaquid Pond Dam—*dam* MA-1
Musqueti Point—*cape* WA-9
*Musquetiquit Brook* RI-1
*Musquetohaug Brook* RI-1
*Musquetohauke Brook* RI-1
*Musquetopaug Brook* RI-1
*Musquillo* MP-9
*Musquillo Atoll* MP-9
*Musquillo Inseln* MP-9
*Musquito Brook* MA-1
*Musquito Lake* MS-4
*Musquito Point* VA-3
Musquiz Canyon—*valley* TX-5
Musquiz Creek—*stream* TX-5
Mussachuck Creek—*stream* RI-1
Mussacuma, Lake—*reservoir* MS-4
Mussacuna Creek—*stream* MS-4
Mussacunna Post Office (historical)—*building* MS-4
*Musse* MS-4
Mussel Bar—*bar* AR-4
Mussel Bayou—*stream* LA-4

Myers Gulch—*valley* (3) ... CO-8
Myers Gulch—*valley* ... OR-9
Myers Hall—*hist pl* ... OH-6
Myers-Hicks Place—*hist pl* ... MS-4
Myers Hill—*summit* ... MA-1
Myers Hill—*summit* ... NV-8
Myers Hill—*summit* ... NY-2
Myers Hill—*summit* ... PA-2
*Myers Hill Baptist Church* ... AL-4
Myers Hill Cem—*cemetery* ... AL-4
*Myers Hill Church* ... AL-4
Myers Hill Congregational Methodist Ch—*church* ... TN-4
Myers Hill Sch—*school* ... TN-4
Myers Hollow—*valley* (2) ... OH-6
Myers Hollow—*valley* ... PA-2
Myers Hollow—*valley* ... TN-4
Myers Hollow—*valley* ... VA-3
Myers House—*hist pl* ... WV-2
Myers HS—*school* ... MO-7
Myers Island—*island* ... OH-6
Myers Knob—*summit* ... OH-6
*Myers Lake* ... MI-6
*Myers Lake* ... OH-6
Myers Lake—*lake* ... IL-6
Myers Lake—*lake* ... LA-4
Myers Lake—*lake* (4) ... MI-6
Myers Lake—*lake* (2) ... MN-6
Myers Lake—*lake* ... MS-4
Myers Lake—*lake* ... SC-3
Myers Lake—*lake* ... SD-7
Myers Lake—*reservoir* ... MO-7
Myers Lake—*reservoir* ... NC-3
Myers Lake Dam—*dam* ... MS-4
Myers Lake Dam—*dam* ... NC-3
Myers Landing Field—*airport* ... SD-7
Myers Landing (historical)—*locale* ... AL-4
Myers-Masker House—*hist pl* ... NJ-2
Myers Meadow—*flat* ... OR-9
Myers Meadow Spring—*spring* ... OR-9
Myers Memorial Arena—*building* ... TX-5
Myers Memorial Baptist Ch—*church* ... AL-4
Myers Mesa—*summit* ... NM-5
Myers Mill (historical)—*locale* ... MS-4
Myers Mill (historical)—*locale* ... TN-4
*Myers' Mills* ... IL-6
Myers Mine—*locale* ... ID-8
Myers Mine—*mine* ... AZ-5
Myers Mound—*hist pl* ... TN-4
Myers Mtn—*summit* ... NV-8
Myers-Newhoff House—*hist pl* ... WI-6
Myers Number Two Lake—*reservoir* ... AL-4
Myers Number 2 Dam—*dam* ... AL-4
Myers Park—*park* ... FL-3
Myers Park—*park* ... NY-2
Myers Park—*park* ... OH-6
Myers Park—*park* ... OK-5
Myers Park Country Club—*locale* ... NC-3
Myers Park Hist Dist—*hist pl* ... NC-3
Myers Park HS—*school* ... NC-3
Myers Park Memorial Municipal Airp—*airport* ... MO-7
Myers Park Sch—*school* ... NC-3
**Myers Park (subdivision)**—*pop pl* ... NC-3
Myers Point—*cape* ... NY-2
Myers Pond—*lake* (2) ... CT-1
Myers Pond—*reservoir* ... NC-3
Myers Pond—*reservoir* ... SC-3
Myers Post Office (historical)—*building* ... TN-4
Myer Spring—*spring* ... CA-9
Myers Ranch—*locale* ... CA-9
Myers Ranch—*locale* ... MT-8
Myers Ranch—*locale* ... NV-8
Myers Ranch—*locale* ... ND-7
Myers Ranch—*locale* (2) ... WY-8
Myers Ridge—*ridge* ... KY-4
**Myers (RR name Ludlowville (sta.))**—*pop pl* ... NY-2
Myers Rsvr—*reservoir* ... CA-9
Myers Rsvr—*reservoir* ... OR-9
Myers Rsvr—*reservoir* ... WY-8
Myers Run—*stream* ... OH-6
Myers Run—*stream* ... PA-2
Myers Run—*stream* ... WV-2
Myers Sch—*hist pl* ... ID-8
Myers Sch—*school* ... CA-9
Myers Sch—*school* ... IL-6
Myers Sch—*school* ... IA-7
Myers Sch—*school* (3) ... MI-6
Myers Sch—*school* ... ND-7
Myers Sch—*school* ... OH-6
Myers Sch—*school* ... OK-5
Myers Sch—*school* (2) ... PA-2
Myers Sch—*school* ... TN-4
Myers Sch—*school* (2) ... VA-3
Myers Sch (abandoned)—*school* (3) ... PA-2
Myers Sch (historical)—*school* ... MO-7
Myers Sch (historical)—*school* ... PA-2
*Myers School* ... IN-6
Myers School—*locale* ... MI-6
Myers School (historical)—*locale* ... MO-7
Myers Sch Timbered Lodge (32BI401)—*hist pl* ... ND-7
Myers Siding—*locale* ... MT-8
Myers Spring—*spring* ... CO-8
Myers Spring—*spring* ... WY-8
Myers Spring Draw—*valley* ... WY-8
Myers Spring (inundated)—*spring* ... TN-4
*Myers Store* ... PA-2
Myers Store (historical)—*locale* ... TN-4
Myers Street Sch—*school* ... NC-3
*Myers Swamp* ... NY-2
Myers Swamp—*swamp* ... NY-2
Myers Tank—*reservoir* ... AZ-5
Myers Temple—*church* ... LA-4
**Myerstown**—*pop pl* (2) ... PA-2
**Myerstown**—*pop pl* ... WV-2
Myerstown Borough—*civil* ... PA-2
Myerstown Elem Sch—*school* ... PA-2
Myerstown Rsvr—*reservoir* ... PA-2
Myerstown Sch—*school* ... PA-2
**Myers Township**—*pop pl* ... MO-7
*Myers Valley* ... OR-9
Myers Valley—*valley* ... UT-8
Myers Valley (historical)—*locale* ... KS-7
*Myersville* ... IL-6
*Myersville* ... PA-2
Myersville—*locale* ... AR-4
Myersville—*locale* ... SD-7
Myersville—*locale* ... WY-8
**Myersville**—*pop pl* ... MD-2
**Myersville**—*pop pl* ... OH-6
Myersville Sch—*school* ... SC-3
Myersville Sch (historical)—*school* ... MO-7
*Myers West Ditch* ... IN-6
Myers West Ditch—*canal* ... IN-6
Myers-White House—*hist pl* ... NC-3
Myers Windmill—*locale* (3) ... NM-5
Myer Valley—*valley* ... CA-9
Myetta Ch—*church* ... MO-7
Myette Point—*cape* ... LA-4
Myette Point Ch—*church* ... LA-4
My Fathers House Ch—*church* ... AL-4
Myford Cem—*cemetery* ... LA-4
Myghapowit Mtn—*summit* ... AK-9
My Grandfather's House—*hist pl* ... TN-4
*My Hall Creek* ... GA-3
Myhr Creek—*stream* ... MN-6
Myhre, Jens, Round Barn—*hist pl* ... ND-7
Myhre Lake—*lake* ... MN-6
Myhre State Wildlife Mngmt Area—*swamp* ... MN-6
My Island—*island* ... MN-6
Mykawa—*locale* ... TX-5
Mykawa Oil Field—*oilfield* ... TX-5
Mykawa Road—*post sta* ... TX-5
Myklebust Lake—*lake* ... WI-6
Mykrantz Ranch—*locale* ... CA-9
Mykrantz Truck Trail—*trail* ... CA-9
My Lady's Manor—*hist pl* ... MD-2
My Ladys Manor Branch—*stream* ... MD-2
My Ladys Swamp—*stream* ... VA-3
My Lake—*lake* ... AK-9
My Lake—*lake* (2) ... MN-6
My Lake—*lake* ... MT-8
My Lake—*lake* ... WA-9
Mylan Ch—*church* ... TX-5
Mylburn Cem—*cemetery* ... WV-2
Myler Creek—*stream* ... UT-8
Myler Grove—*woods* ... UT-8
Myler House—*hist pl* ... AR-4
Myler Rsvr—*reservoir* ... CO-8
**Myles**—*pop pl* ... MS-4
Myles Creek—*stream* ... MT-8
Myles Knob—*summit* ... WV-2
Myles Lake Dam—*dam* ... MS-4
Myles Plantation (historical)—*locale* ... MS-4
Myles Post Office (historical)—*building* ... MS-4
*Myless Bridge* ... MA-1
Myles Standish Homestead—*locale* ... MA-1
Myles Standish State For—*forest* (2) ... MA-1
Myles Standish State Park—*park* ... MA-1
*Myles Station* ... MS-4
Mylet Ranch—*locale* ... WY-8
Mylin Corners—*locale* ... PA-2
**Mylith Park**—*pop pl* ... IL-6
Mylius Ditch—*canal* ... IN-6
**Mylo**—*pop pl* ... ND-7
Mylo Cem—*cemetery* ... ND-7
Mylo Park—*park* ... PA-2
*My Lord's Island* ... DC-2
Mylo Sch—*school* ... PA-2
*Mynard* ... AL-4
**Mynard**—*pop pl* ... NE-7
**Mynatt**—*pop pl* ... TN-4
Mynatt Cem—*cemetery* (3) ... TN-4
Mynatt Creek—*stream* ... OR-9
Mynatt Park—*park* ... TN-4
Mynatt Post Office (historical)—*building* ... TN-4
Mynatt Road Ch—*church* ... TN-4
Mynderse Acad—*school* ... NY-2
Mynderse-Frederick House—*hist pl* ... NY-2
Mynders Sch—*school* ... TN-4
Myndus—*locale* ... NM-5
Myndus—*locale* ... VA-3
Mynot—*locale* ... AL-4
Mynot Ch—*church* ... AL-4
*Mynot Ch of Christ* ... AL-4
Mynot Creek—*stream* ... CA-9
Mynot Hollow—*valley* ... AL-4
Mynot Ridge—*ridge* ... CA-9
Mynot Sch (historical)—*school* ... AL-4
Mynott Chapel Missionary Baptist Ch—*church* ... AL-4
Mynyard Lake—*lake* ... WI-6
Myobeach—*locale* ... PA-2
My Old Kentucky Home—*hist pl* ... KY-4
My Old Kentucky Home State Park—*park* ... KY-4
Myoma—*locale* ... CA-9
**Myoma**—*pop pl* ... PA-2
**Myonia**—*pop pl* ... PA-2
Myosotis Lake—*lake* ... NY-2
Myoukchuk Point—*cape* ... AK-9
Myra—*locale* ... KY-4
Myra—*locale* ... ME-1
Myra—*locale* ... ND-7
Myra—*locale* ... PA-2
Myra—*locale* ... WV-2
**Myra**—*pop pl* ... TX-5
**Myra**—*pop pl* ... WI-6
Myra, Lake—*lake* ... FL-3
Myra, Lake—*reservoir* ... NC-3
Myra and Coly Drain—*canal* ... MI-6
Myra Branch—*stream* ... KY-4
Myra Cem—*cemetery* ... LA-4
Myracle Cem—*cemetery* ... TN-4
Myra (historical)—*locale* ... KS-7
Myran Ditch—*canal* ... IN-6
Myra Station—*locale* ... KY-4
Myre Lake—*lake* ... WI-6
Myren—*locale* ... MI-6
Myres Bayside Park—*park* ... FL-3
Myres Cem—*cemetery* ... OH-6
Myres Chapel—*church* ... AR-4
Myre Slough State Game Mngmt Area—*park* ... IA-7
Myres Mine—*mine* ... AZ-5
Myre State Park—*park* ... MN-6
Myriad, Lake—*reservoir* ... TX-5
Myriad Creek—*stream* ... WY-8
Myriad Islands—*area* ... AK-9
Myria Knob—*summit* ... NC-3
Myric Creek—*stream* ... MS-4
Myrick—*locale* ... OR-9
**Myrick**—*pop pl* ... MS-4
**Myrick**—*pop pl* ... MO-7
**Myrick**—*pop pl* ... NC-3
Myrick, William and Martha, House—*hist pl* ... UT-8
Myrick Baptist Ch—*church* ... MS-4
Myrick Branch—*stream* ... TN-4
Myrick Canyon—*valley* ... CA-9
Myrick Cem—*cemetery* (2) ... MS-4
Myrick Ch—*church* ... KY-4
Myrick Chapel—*church* ... AL-4
*Myrick Chapel Ch* ... AL-4
Myrick Cove—*bay* ... ME-1
Myrick Cutoff—*trail* ... CA-9
Myrick Elem Sch—*school* ... MS-4
Myrick House—*hist pl* ... NC-3
Myrick Lake—*lake* ... WI-6
Myrick-Palmer House—*hist pl* ... MI-6
Myrick Park—*park* ... WI-6
*Myrick Pond* ... MA-1
Myrick Pond—*lake* ... ME-1
Myrick Pond—*reservoir* ... NC-3
Myrick Pond Dam—*dam* ... NC-3
Myrick Prairie—*flat* ... CA-9
Myrick Ridge—*ridge* ... ME-1
**Myricks**—*pop pl* ... MA-1
Myricks Bayou—*stream* ... LA-4
Myricks Branch—*stream* ... TX-5
Myrick Sch—*school* ... ME-1
Myrick Sch (historical)—*school* ... AL-4
**Myricks Corner**—*pop pl* ... CA-9
Myrick Siphon—*canal* ... CA-9
*Myricks Mill* ... MS-4
Myrick's Mill—*hist pl* ... GA-3
Myricks Mill—*locale* ... GA-3
Myricks Pond—*lake* ... MA-1
Myrick Spring—*spring* ... CA-9
*Myrick Station* ... MA-1
*Myrickville* ... ME-1
Myrick-Yeates-Vaughan House—*hist pl* ... NC-3
*Myrifield, Town of* ... MA-1
*Myrill Springs* ... TX-5
Myrkle Gut—*gut* ... DE-2
Myrland Ditch—*canal* ... IA-7
Myrland Sky Lodge—*building* ... WI-6
Myrleville—*locale* ... MS-4
Myrl Windmill—*locale* ... TX-5
**Myron**—*pop pl* ... AR-4
**Myron**—*pop pl* ... IL-6
Myron Cem—*cemetery* ... SD-7
Myron Cem—*cemetery* ... WI-6
Myron Creek—*stream* ... TN-4
Myron H Avery Peak—*summit* ... ME-1
Myron Kinney Brook—*stream* ... CT-1
Myron Lake—*lake* ... MT-8
Myron Park—*park* ... WI-6
Myron Pond—*reservoir* ... AZ-5
Myron Stratton Home—*other* ... CO-8
**Myron Township**—*pop pl* ... SD-7
Myrtal Branch—*stream* ... TX-5
Myrtice, Lake—*reservoir* ... GA-3
Myrtis—*locale* ... FL-3
Myrtis—*locale* ... LA-4
Myrtis Mill Creek—*stream* ... LA-4
Myrtis Mill Pond—*reservoir* ... LA-4
*Myrtle* ... AL-4
Myrtle—*locale* ... AR-4
Myrtle—*locale* ... GA-3
Myrtle—*locale* ... ID-8
Myrtle—*locale* ... TX-5
Myrtle—*locale* ... VA-3
**Myrtle**—*pop pl* ... IL-6
**Myrtle**—*pop pl* ... MN-6
**Myrtle**—*pop pl* ... MS-4
**Myrtle**—*pop pl* ... MO-7
**Myrtle**—*pop pl* ... PA-2
**Myrtle**—*pop pl* (2) ... WV-2
Myrtle, Lake—*lake* (5) ... FL-3
Myrtle, Lake—*lake* ... GA-3
Myrtle, Mount—*summit* ... AK-9
Myrtle Ann Mine—*mine* ... SD-7
Myrtle Arms Apartment Bldg—*hist pl* ... OR-9
*Myrtle Ave School* ... PA-2
Myrtle Bank—*hist pl* ... MS-4
Myrtle Bay—*bay* ... NC-3
Myrtle Bay—*swamp* ... FL-3
*Myrtle Bayou* ... LA-4
Myrtle Bayou—*stream* (2) ... LA-4
*Myrtle Beach* ... CT-1
**Myrtle Beach**—*pop pl* ... CT-1
**Myrtle Beach**—*pop pl* ... SC-3
Myrtle Beach Air Force Base—*mil airp* ... SC-3
Myrtle Beach (CCD)—*cens area* ... SC-3
Myrtle Beach State Park—*park* ... SC-3
Myrtle Branch—*stream* ... TX-5
Myrtle Brook—*stream* ... NY-2
Myrtle Butte—*summit* ... MT-8
Myrtle Butte—*summit* ... OR-9
*Myrtle Cem* ... TX-5
Myrtle Cem—*cemetery* (2) ... MS-4
Myrtle Cem—*cemetery* ... NE-7
Myrtle Cem—*cemetery* (2) ... NY-2
Myrtle Cem—*cemetery* (2) ... TX-5
Myrtle Chapel—*church* ... KY-4
*Myrtle City* ... SD-7
*Myrtle Creek* ... MT-8
*Myrtle Creek* ... TX-5
Myrtle Creek—*gut* ... FL-3
**Myrtle Creek**—*pop pl* ... OR-9
Myrtle Creek—*stream* (5) ... AK-9
Myrtle Creek—*stream* ... CA-9
Myrtle Creek—*stream* ... FL-3
Myrtle Creek—*stream* (5) ... ID-8
Myrtle Creek—*stream* ... MT-8
Myrtle Creek—*stream* ... NE-7
Myrtle Creek—*stream* (6) ... OR-9
Myrtle Creek—*stream* (5) ... TX-5
Myrtle Creek-Riddle (CCD)—*cens area* ... OR-9
Myrtle Creek Sch—*school* ... OR-9
**Myrtle Creek South (census name Tri City)**—*pop pl* ... OR-9
Myrtle Crest Memorial Gardens—*cemetery* ... OR-9
Myrtle Crest Sch—*school* ... OR-9
Myrtle Day Ch—*church* ... OK-5
Myrtle Ditch—*canal* ... NC-3
Myrtle Drain—*canal* ... CA-9
Myrtle Elem Sch—*school* ... PA-2
Myrtle Fern—*hist pl* ... IN-6
Myrtle Green Cem—*cemetery* ... NC-3
Myrtle Grove—*hist pl* ... MD-2
Myrtle Grove—*locale* ... AR-4
Myrtle Grove—*locale* ... GA-3
Myrtle Grove—*locale* ... NJ-2
**Myrtle Grove**—*pop pl* ... FL-3
**Myrtle Grove**—*pop pl* ... LA-4
**Myrtle Grove**—*pop pl* ... NC-3
Myrtle Grove—*uninc pl* ... LA-4
Myrtle Grove Annex—*school* ... FL-3
Myrtle Grove Baptist Ch—*church* ... FL-3
Myrtle Grove Campground—*park* ... OR-9
Myrtle Grove Cem—*cemetery* (2) ... LA-4
Myrtle Grove Cem—*cemetery* ... MS-4
Myrtle Grove Cem—*cemetery* ... NY-2
Myrtle Grove Ch—*church* ... NC-3
Myrtle Grove Elem Sch—*school* ... FL-3
**Myrtle Grove Junction**—*pop pl* ... NC-3
Myrtle Grove Memorial (Cemetery)—*cemetery* ... CA-9
Myrtle Grove Plantation—*hist pl* ... LA-4
**Myrtle Grove Plantation**—*pop pl* ... LA-4
Myrtle Grove Sch—*school* ... FL-3
Myrtle Grove Sound—*bay* ... NC-3
Myrtle Grove United Methodist Ch—*church* ... FL-3
Myrtle Grove Wildlife Mngmt Area—*park* ... MD-2
Myrtle Gulch—*valley* ... CA-9
Myrtle Gulch—*valley* ... OR-9
*Myrtle Hall Plantation* ... AL-4
**Myrtle Hall (subdivision)**—*pop pl* ... MS-4
Myrtle Head—*locale* ... NC-3
Myrtle Head Ch—*church* ... NC-3
Myrtlehead Ch—*church* ... TX-5
Myrtle Hill—*hist pl* ... KY-4
Myrtle Hill Cem—*cemetery* ... FL-3
Myrtle Hill Cem—*cemetery* (3) ... GA-3
Myrtle Hill Cem—*cemetery* ... OH-6
Myrtle Hill Cemetery—*hist pl* ... GA-3
Myrtle Hill Memorial Park—*cemetery* ... FL-3
Myrtle Hill Plantation House—*hist pl* ... LA-4
**Myrtle Hill (subdivision)**—*pop pl* ... NC-3
Myrtle (historical)—*locale* ... AL-4
Myrtle (historical)—*locale* ... KS-7
Myrtle Island—*island* ... NC-3
Myrtle Island—*island* ... OR-9
Myrtle Island—*island* ... VA-3
Myrtle Island—*locale* ... FL-3
**Myrtle Island**—*pop pl* ... SC-3
Myrtle Island Beach—*beach* ... VA-3
Myrtle Lake—*lake* ... AK-9
Myrtle Lake—*lake* ... AZ-5
Myrtle Lake—*lake* (3) ... FL-3
Myrtle Lake—*lake* ... ID-8
Myrtle Lake—*lake* ... MI-6
Myrtle Lake—*lake* (5) ... MN-6
Myrtle Lake—*lake* (4) ... WA-9
Myrtle Lake—*lake* (2) ... WI-6
Myrtle Lake—*lake* ... WY-8
Myrtle Lake Baptist Ch—*church* ... FL-3
Myrtle Lateral—*canal* ... CA-9
Myrtle Lawn—*hist pl* ... NC-3
Myrtle Lookout Tower—*locale* ... MS-4
Myrtle Marsh Gut—*stream* ... NC-3
Myrtle Marsh Point—*cape* ... NC-3
Myrtle Moor—*hist pl* ... SC-3
*Myrtle Mountain* ... ID-8
Myrtlene Branch—*stream* ... VA-3
Myrtle Park—*park* ... AZ-5
Myrtle Park Butte—*summit* ... WA-9
Myrtle Park Meadows—*flat* ... OR-9
Myrtle Peak—*summit* ... ID-8
Myrtle Pla Sch—*school* ... LA-4
Myrtle Point—*cape* ... ID-8
Myrtle Point—*cape* (2) ... MD-2
Myrtle Point—*cape* ... NC-3
Myrtle Point—*cape* ... WA-9
Myrtle Point—*cliff* ... AZ-5
**Myrtle Point**—*pop pl* ... OR-9
Myrtle Point—*summit* ... TN-4
Myrtle Point (CCD)—*cens area* ... OR-9
Myrtle Point Log Pond—*reservoir* ... OR-9
Myrtle Point Veneer Company Log Dam—*dam* ... OR-9
Myrtle Prairie—*flat* ... TX-5
**Myrtle Ridge**—*pop pl* ... SC-3
Myrtle Ridge—*ridge* ... OH-6
Myrtle Ridge Ch—*church* ... OH-6
Myrtle Rsvr—*reservoir* ... WY-8
Myrtle Sch—*school* ... IL-6
Myrtle Sch—*school* ... MS-4
Myrtle Sch—*school* ... NE-7
Myrtle Sch—*school* ... NC-3
Myrtle Slough—*gut* (2) ... FL-3
Myrtle Slough—*stream* (3) ... FL-3
*Myrtle Sound* ... NC-3
**Myrtle Sound**—*pop pl* ... NC-3
Myrtles Plantation—*hist pl* ... LA-4
Myrtle Spring—*spring* (2) ... OR-9
Myrtle Spring—*spring* ... TX-5
Myrtle Spring Ch—*church* ... TX-5
**Myrtle Springs**—*pop pl* ... TX-5
Myrtle Springs Branch—*stream* (2) ... TX-5
Myrtle Springs Cem—*cemetery* (3) ... TX-5
Myrtle Springs Ch—*church* ... GA-3
Myrtle Springs Ch—*church* (4) ... TX-5
Myrtle Springs Sch—*school* ... TX-5
*Myrtle Street Dam* ... MA-1
Myrtle Street Flats—*hist pl* ... CA-9
Myrtle Street Hist Dist—*hist pl* ... MS-4
Myrtle Street Sch—*hist pl* ... MA-1
Myrtle Street Sch—*school* ... MA-1
Myrtle Swamp—*stream* ... VA-3
Myrtle Tank—*reservoir* ... AZ-5
Myrtletown—*CDP* ... CA-9
Myrtle Township—*civil* (2) ... MO-7
**Myrtle Township**—*pop pl* ... NE-7
**Myrtle Township**—*pop pl* ... ND-7
Myrtle Trail—*trail* ... AZ-5
*Myrtletree Baptist Church* ... AL-4
Myrtletree Cem—*cemetery* ... AL-4
Myrtletree Ch—*church* ... AL-4
Myrtle Tree Ch—*church* ... OH-6
Myrtle Tree Sch (historical)—*school* ... MO-7
Myrtle Valley Ch—*church* ... WV-2
Myrtleville Post Office (historical)—*building* ... MS-4
Myrtle Wayside—*locale* ... OR-9
**Myrtlewood**—*pop pl* ... AL-4
Myrtlewood Campground—*park* ... OR-9
Myrtlewood Cem—*cemetery* ... AL-4
Myrtlewood Point—*cape* ... FL-3
Myrtlewood Sch—*school* ... AL-4
*Mys Arucenas* ... AK-9
Myse Cem—*cemetery* ... AR-4
Myser Gulch—*valley* ... CO-8
Myser Spring—*spring* ... CO-8
*Mys Kitovyy* ... AK-9
*Mys Polovinnoy* ... AK-9
Mysse Ranch—*locale* ... MT-8
*Mysterious Canyon* ... UT-8
Mysterious Creek—*stream* ... CA-9
Mysterious Creek—*stream* ... CO-8
Mysterious Lake—*lake* ... CO-8
Mysterious Valley—*valley* ... CA-9
Mystery, Mount—*summit* ... WA-9
Mystery, Mtn of—*summit* ... UT-8
Mystery Bay—*bay* ... WA-9
Mystery Campground—*locale* ... WA-9
*Mystery Canyon* ... UT-8
Mystery Canyon—*valley* ... UT-8
Mystery Canyon (inundated)—*valley* ... UT-8
Mystery Castle—*building* ... AZ-5
Mystery Cave—*cave* ... MT-8
Mystery Cave Number One—*cave* ... MN-6
Mystery Cave Number Two—*cave* ... MN-6
Mystery Creek—*stream* (5) ... AK-9
Mystery Creek—*stream* (2) ... ID-8
Mystery Creek—*stream* ... OR-9
Mystery Falls Cave—*cave* ... TN-4
Mystery Hill—*summit* ... NH-1
Mystery Hill—*summit* ... PA-2
Mystery Hills—*other* ... AK-9
Mystery Hills Rsvr—*reservoir* ... OR-9
*Mystery Island* ... MA-1
Mystery Lake—*lake* ... CA-9
Mystery Lake—*lake* ... ID-8
Mystery Lake—*lake* ... MI-6
Mystery Lake—*lake* ... MN-6
Mystery Lake—*lake* ... MT-8
Mystery Lake—*lake* (5) ... WI-6
Mystery Lake—*lake* ... WY-8
MYSTERY (log canoe)—*hist pl* ... MD-2
Mystery Mine—*mine* ... CA-9
*Mystery Mountain* ... WA-9
Mystery Mountains—*other* ... AK-9
Mystery Ridge—*ridge* ... NV-8
Mystery Ridge—*ridge* ... VA-3
Mystery Rock Pile Cave—*cave* ... AL-4
Mystery Spring—*spring* ... AZ-5
Mystery Spring—*spring* ... CA-9
Mystery Spring—*spring* ... MT-8
Mystery Spring—*spring* ... OR-9
Mystery Tank—*reservoir* ... TX-5
Mystery Valley—*basin* ... AZ-5
*Mystic* ... MA-1
Mystic—*locale* ... CA-9
Mystic—*locale* ... CO-8
Mystic—*locale* ... KY-4
Mystic—*locale* ... MO-7
Mystic—*locale* ... SD-7
**Mystic**—*pop pl* ... CT-1
**Mystic**—*pop pl* ... GA-3
**Mystic**—*pop pl* ... IA-7
**Mystic**—*pop pl* ... PA-2
Mystic, Lake—*lake* ... FL-3
Mystic, The—*stream* ... NH-1
Mystic Bayou Gas Field—*oilfield* ... LA-4
Mystic Bridge Hist Dist—*hist pl* ... CT-1
Mystic Canyon—*valley* (3) ... CA-9
Mystic Cave—*cave* ... AR-4
Mystic Caverns—*locale* ... TN-4
Mystic Ch—*church* ... LA-4
Mystic Creek—*stream* (2) ... AK-9
Mystic Creek—*stream* (2) ... OR-9
Mystic Crew Bayou—*stream* ... LA-4
Mystic Falls—*falls* ... WY-8
**Mystic Grove**—*pop pl* ... MA-1
Mystic Harbor—*bay* ... CT-1
Mystic (historical)—*locale* ... KS-7
*Mystic Island* ... CT-1
Mystic Island—*CDP* ... NJ-2
Mystic Island Lake—*lake* ... CO-8
**Mystic Islands**—*pop pl* ... NJ-2
Mystic Isle—*island* ... WY-8
Mystic Junction—*uninc pl* ... MA-1
*Mystick River* ... MA-1
Mystic Lake—*lake* ... CA-9
Mystic Lake—*lake* ... FL-3
Mystic Lake—*lake* ... MA-1
Mystic Lake—*lake* ... MI-6
Mystic Lake—*lake* (2) ... MT-8
Mystic Lake—*lake* ... OR-9
Mystic Lake—*lake* (2) ... WA-9
Mystic Lake—*reservoir* ... MT-8
Mystic Lake Ditch—*canal* ... MT-8
Mystic Lake Hydroelectric Plant—*other* ... MT-8
Mystic Lake Ranger Station—*locale* ... MT-8
Mystic Lakes—*lake* ... MA-1
Mystic Mall (Shop Ctr)—*locale* ... MA-1
**Mystic Mountain Subdivision**—*pop pl* ... UT-8
Mystic Mtn—*summit* ... AK-9
Mystic Mtn—*summit* ... MT-8
Mystic Oval Sch—*school* ... CT-1
**Mystic Park**—*pop pl* ... PA-2
Mystic Park (historical)—*park* ... MA-1
Mystic Pass—*gap* ... AK-9
*Mystic Pond* ... MA-1
Mystic Pond—*lake* ... MA-1
Mystic Reservoir Dam—*dam* ... IA-7
*Mystic River* ... MA-1
Mystic River—*stream* ... CT-1
Mystic River—*stream* ... MA-1
Mystic River Bridge—*bridge* ... MA-1
Mystic River Hist Dist—*hist pl* ... CT-1
Mystic River Marsh (historical)—*swamp* ... MA-1
Mystic River Reservation—*park* ... MA-1
Mystic Rsvr—*reservoir* ... CT-1
Mystic Rsvr—*reservoir* ... IA-7
Mystic Rsvr—*reservoir* ... MA-1
Mystic Sch—*school* ... MA-1
Mystic Seaport—*locale* ... CT-1
*Mystic Side, Town of* ... MA-1
Mystic Spring—*spring* ... AZ-5
Mystic Spring—*spring* ... NV-8
*Mystic Spring Plateau* ... AZ-5
Mystic Theatre—*hist pl* ... ND-7
Mystic Townsite Hist Dist—*hist pl* ... SD-7
**Mystic Valley**—*pop pl* ... TN-4
Mystic Wharf—*locale* ... MA-1
*Mys Tonkiy* ... AK-9
Myth Lake—*lake* (2) ... MN-6
Myth Shoal—*bar* ... LA-4
*Mytic River* ... MA-1
*Mytilene* ... AL-4
Myting Spring—*spring* ... WA-9
Mytoge Lake—*lake* ... UT-8
*Mytoge Mountain* ... UT-8
Mytoge Mtns—*summit* ... UT-8
**Myton**—*pop pl* ... UT-8
Myton Cem—*cemetery* ... UT-8
*Myton City Cemetery* ... UT-8
Myton City Rsvr—*reservoir* ... UT-8
Myton Pumping Station—*locale* ... UT-8
Myton Sch—*school* ... UT-8
Myton Sch (abandoned)—*school* ... PA-2
Myton Townsite Canal—*canal* ... UT-8
My Valley—*valley* ... CO-8
My Windmill—*locale* ... NM-5
M-Z Bar Ranch—*locale* ... AZ-5
M4 Ranch—*locale* ... UT-8

# N

*N* MH-9
N, Lateral (abandoned)—*canal* MT-8
Na—*island* FM-9
*Naa* FM-9
**Na-Ab-Tee Canyon (Trading Post)**—*pop pl* AZ-5
*Naaccu* FM-9
Naachpunkt Brook—*stream* NJ-2
*Naachpurkt Brook* NJ-2
*Naachtpunkt Brook* NJ-2
*Naago* MP-9
*Naago-To* MP-9
Na Ah Tee—*locale* AZ-5
*Naahtee Canyon* AZ-5
Na Ah Tee Canyon—*valley* AZ-5
Na Ah Tee Canyon Spring—*spring* AZ-5
Na Ah Tee Wash—*valley* AZ-5
*Naa Island* FM-9
*Naajibuen Island* MP-9
Naakai N Daachaahi Wash—*valley* AZ-5
Naakea—*cape* HI-9
Naal—*island* MP-9
Naalae Gulch—*valley* HI-9
Naalapa Falls—*falls* HI-9
**Naalehu**—*pop pl* HI-9
Naalehu Substation—*other* HI-9
*Naallo* MP-9
Naaman—*locale* DE-2
Naaman—*locale* TX-5
Naaman Creek—*stream* DE-2
Naaman Creek—*stream* PA-2
Naamans Bridge—*bridge* DE-2
*Naamans Corner* DE-2
*Naamans Creek* DE-2
*Naamans Creek* PA-2
**Naamans Gardens**—*pop pl* DE-2
*Naamans Hock* DE-2
**Naamans Manor**—*pop pl* DE-2
Naamans North Park—*park* DE-2
**Naamans Trailer Park**—*pop pl* DE-2
*Naamkeek* MA-1
*Naanin Island* MP-9
Naankotkot—*island* MP-9
Naans Branch—*stream* IN-6
*Naaotchi Island* MP-9
Naaotchi Island—*island* MP-9
*Naaotchi-To* MP-9
*Naarappu Island* MP-9
Naarappu Island—*island* MP-9
*Naarappu-To* MP-9
Naardueis Point—*cape* PW-9
*Naarigirikku* MP-9
*Naarigirikku Knox Islands* MP-9
*Naarigirikku-To* MP-9
*Na-a-tih Trading Post* AZ-5
*Na-at-tee Canyon* AZ-5
Naaukahihi—*cape* HI-9
Naausay Cem—*cemetery* IL-6
Naausay Ch—*church* IL-6
**Naausay (Township of)**—*pop pl* IL-6
Nabaksyalik Point—*cape* AK-9
Nabakyalik Point—*cape* AK-9
Nabangoyak Rock—*island* AK-9
**Nabb**—*pop pl* (2) IN-6
Nabb Cem—*cemetery* KY-4
*Nabbequannemue Island* RI-1
Nabb Radio Range Station—*other* IN-6
Nabbs Creek—*stream* MD-2
Nabby Cove—*bay* ME-1
Nabbys Lake—*lake* PA-2
Nab Cem—*cemetery* GA-3
Nab Drennen Dam Number 2—*dam* AL-4
Nab Drennen Dams—*dam* AL-4
Nab Drennen Lake Number 1—*reservoir* AL-4
Nab Drennen Lake Number 2—*reservoir* AL-4
Nabek Lake—*lake* MN-6
Nabers, Morrow and Sinnige, Bldg—*hist pl* AL-4
*Nabert Hollow* OH-6
**Nabesna**—*pop pl* AK-9
Nabesna Glacier—*glacier* AK-9
Nabesna Gold Mine Hist Dist—*hist pl* AK-9
Nabesna (Northway)—*other* AK-9
Nabesna River—*stream* AK-9
Nabesna Slough—*stream* AK-9
Nabesna Village—*locale* AK-9
Nabisco Cem—*cemetery* OK-5
Nable Bayou—*stream* LA-4
**Nabnasset**—*pop pl* MA-1
Nabnasset Lake Country Club—*locale* MA-1
Nabnasset Pond—*reservoir* MA-1
Nabnasset Pond Dam—*dam* MA-1
*Nabnassett Pond* MA-1
**Nabob**—*pop pl* WV-2
**Nabob**—*pop pl* WI-6
Nabob Creek—*stream* ID-8
Nabob Mine—*mine* CO-8
Nabob Mine—*mine* ID-8
*Nabo Chapel* MS-4
Nabon—*island* MP-9
*Na Bonchase Bayou* LA-4
Na Bonchasse, Bayou—*stream* LA-4
*Nabon Island* MP-9
Nabor Creek—*stream* CO-8
Nabor Creek—*stream* NM-5
*Nabors* AL-4
Nabors Branch—*stream* AL-4
*Nabors Brook* AL-4
Nabors Cem—*cemetery* AL-4
Nabors Creek—*stream* TX-5
Nabors Creek Cem—*cemetery* TX-5
Nabors (historical)—*locale* MS-4
Nabors Lake—*reservoir* TX-5
Nabors Pond—*reservoir* LA-4
Nabors Tank—*reservoir* NM-5
**Naborton**—*pop pl* LA-4
Nabotna Pond—*reservoir* IA-7
Nabotna Pond Park—*park* IA-7
Nabours Mtn—*summit* NM-5
Nabours Spring—*spring* NM-5
**Nabs Corner**—*pop pl* MA-1
Nacalina—*locale* TX-5
*Nacalula Falls* AL-4
*Naccalulah Falls* AL-4
**Nace**—*pop pl* VA-3
Nace Cem—*cemetery* OK-5
Nace Corner—*locale* OH-6
Nace Creek—*stream* WI-6
Nace (Neas), George, House—*hist pl* PA-2
Nace Run—*stream* OH-6
Nace Sch (abandoned)—*school* PA-2
Naces Corner—*locale* PA-2
**Nacetown**—*pop pl* PA-2
Naceville—*locale* PA-2
**Naceville**—*pop pl* OH-6
Nachalni Island—*island* AK-9
Nachalni Point—*cape* AK-9
*Nachalula Falls* AL-4
*Nachap* FM-9
*Nachchese River* WA-9
Nache Peak—*summit* NV-8
*Naches* AZ-5
**Naches**—*pop pl* WA-9
Naches And Cowiche Ditch—*canal* WA-9
*Naches Creek* LA-4
Naches Heights—*summit* WA-9
Naches Pass—*gap* WA-9
Naches Pass Campground—*locale* WA-9
Naches Peak—*summit* WA-9
Naches River—*stream* WA-9
*Nachess River* WA-9
Naches Trail—*trail* WA-9
Naches Valley HS—*school* WA-9
*Nachez River* TX-5
*Nachibaru* MP-9
Nachibaru—*island* MP-9
*Nachibaru-To* MP-9
*Nachikku* FM-9
Nachi Kulik—*summit* AZ-5
Nachiu—*well* FM-9
Nachman Sch—*school* LA-4
Nachralik Pass—*gap* AK-9
Nachter Butte—*summit* OR-9
Nachtman Draw—*valley* WY-8
Nachtman Rsvr—*reservoir* WY-8
Nachtman Sch—*school* WY-8
Nachtrab Ditch—*canal* OH-6
Nachu—*island* FM-9
**Nachusa**—*pop pl* IL-6
Nachusa House—*hist pl* IL-6
**Nachusa (Township of)**—*pop pl* IL-6
*Nacimento River* CA-9
Nacimiento—*locale* CA-9
Nacimiento, Lake—*reservoir* CA-9
Nacimiento Campground—*locale* NM-5
Nacimiento Creek—*stream* NM-5
Nacimiento Mine—*mine* NM-5
Nacimiento Peak—*summit* NM-5
Nacimiento Ranch—*locale* CA-9
*Nacimiento Reservoir* CA-9
Nacimiento River—*stream* CA-9
Nacional—*civil* CA-9
*Nackobamoma Creek* MS-4
Nacko Creek—*stream* CA-9
*Naclina* TX-5
Naclina—*locale* TX-5
Naco—*locale* WA-9
**Naco**—*pop pl* AZ-5
**Nacogdoches**—*pop pl* TX-5
Nacogdoches (CCD)—*cens area* TX-5
Nacogdoches Country Club—*other* TX-5
**Nacogdoches (County)**—*pop pl* TX-5
Naco Hills—*summit* AZ-5
*Nacoma Falls* MA-1
Naco-Mammoth Kill Site—*hist pl* AZ-5
Nacome—*other* TN-4
Nacome Camp—*locale* TN-4
Naconiche Creek—*stream* TX-5
*Nacoochee* GA-3
Nacoochee—*locale* GA-3
*Nacoochee Lake* GA-3
**Nacoochee Point Subdivision (subdivision)**—*pop pl* AL-4
Nacoochee Valley—*hist pl* GA-3
Nacoochee Valley—*valley* GA-3
Naco Post Office—*building* AZ-5
Nacora—*locale* NE-7
Nacote Creek—*stream* NJ-2
Nada—*other* KY-4
**Nada**—*pop pl* TX-5
**Nada**—*pop pl* UT-8
Nada Arches—*arch* KY-4
*Nadaburg* AZ-5
Nadaburg Sch—*school* AZ-5
Nada Cem—*cemetery* TX-5
Nada Lake—*lake* WA-9
Nada Lombard PO—*locale* KY-4
Nada Mine—*mine* MT-8
Nada Tunnel—*tunnel* KY-4
Nadawah—*locale* AL-4
Nadean Pond—*lake* ME-1
N A D Earle—*airport* NJ-2
**Nadeau**—*pop pl* CA-9
**Nadeau**—*pop pl* MI-6
**Nadeau**—*pop pl* TX-5
Nadeau, Lake—*lake* WA-9
Nadeau Creek—*stream* MI-6
Nadeau Mission (historical)—*church* MI-6
Nadeau Pond—*lake* ME-1
Nadeau Thoroughfare—*channel* ME-1
**Nadeau (Township of)**—*pop pl* MI-6
Nadeau Trail—*trail* CA-9
N A Degerstrom Yard Heliport—*airport* WA-9
Nadelos Campground—*locale* CA-9
Naden Creek—*stream* AK-9
Naderman Buttes—*summit* MT-8
Naderman Dam—*dam* MT-8
Naderman Ditch—*canal* MT-8
Na Des Bah Well—*locale* AZ-5
Nadezhda Islands—*area* AK-9
Nadik—*island* MP-9
*Nadikdi* MP-9
Nadikdik—*island* MP-9
Nadina Glacier—*glacier* AK-9
Nadina River—*stream* AK-9
**Nadine**—*pop pl* MO-7
**Nadine**—*pop pl* NM-5
**Nadine**—*pop pl* PA-2
Nadine, Lake—*lake* PA-2
Nadine Butte—*summit* (2) NV-8
Nadine Lake—*lake* PA-2
Nadine Lateral—*canal* ID-8
Nadir—*locale* VI-3
Nadir Lateral—*canal* ID-8
Nadjak Lake—*lake* WI-6
*Nadju* FM-9
Nadler Sch—*school* IL-6
*Nadon, Mount* FM-9
Nadoway Point—*cape* MI-6
**Nady**—*pop pl* AR-4
Nady Ch—*church* AR-4
Nady Hollow—*valley* PA-2
Nadzaheer Cove—*bay* AK-9
**Naef**—*pop pl* OR-9
Naegele Creek—*stream* TX-5
Naegele Springs—*spring* TX-5
Naegelin Canyon—*valley* AZ-5
Naegelin Rim—*cliff* AZ-5
Naegelin Rim Tank—*reservoir* AZ-5
Naegelin Spring—*spring* AZ-5
Naegelin Spring Canyon—*valley* AZ-5
Naegle Tank—*reservoir* AZ-5
Naegle Well—*well* AZ-5
Naegle Winery—*hist pl* UT-8
Naehu—*summit* HI-9
*Naehu Head* HI-9
*Naen* MP-9
Naen Island—*island* MP-9
Naenlap—*island* MP-9
*Naenlap Island* MP-9
*Naen-to* MP-9
Naerie Rock—*island* AK-9
Naeset, Jens, House—*hist pl* WI-6
*Na-ettee* AZ-5
Naf—*locale* ID-8
Nafan—*spring* FM-9
Nafanua Bank—*other* AS-9
Nafas Lake—*lake* NM-5
*Nafauach* FM-9
Nafauoch, Unun En—*cape* FM-9
*Nafauot* FM-9
NAFEC Atlantic City Airp—*airport* NJ-2
Naff—*locale* LA-4
Natt—*locale* VA-3
Naff Ridge—*ridge* WA-9
**Naffs**—*pop pl* VA-3
*Naffziger Creek* WY-8
*Nafolee* AL-4
Nafonong, Oror En—*locale* FM-9
*Naftan* MH-9
Naftan—*summit* MH-9
Naftan, I—*cape* MH-9
Naftan, Laderan I—*cliff* MH-9
Naftan, Puntan I—*cape* MH-9
*Naftan Cliffs* MH-9
*Naftan Island* MH-9
*Naftan Islet* MH-9
*Naftan Peak* MH-9
*Naftan Point* MH-9
Naftan Rock—*island* MH-9
Naftel—*locale* AL-4
*Nafutan* MH-9
*Nafutan-Misaki* MH-9
*Nafutan Mountain* MH-9
*Nafutan Point* MH-9
*Nafutan Rock* MH-9
*Nafutan-San* MH-9
Na-Gah Flat—*flat* UT-8
Nagahut Rocks—*island* AK-9
Nagai Island—*island* AK-9
Nagai Rocks—*bar* AK-9
Nagan—*area* GU-9
*Naganesu* MP-9
Naganesu—*island* MP-9
*Naganesu-To* MP-9
*Nagany* PA-2
Naga Point—*cape* AK-9
*Nagarekeai* PW-9
Nagasay Cove—*bay* AK-9
*Nagatain* MP-9
*Nagatain-To* MP-9
Nagawicka Lake—*reservoir* WI-6
Nageethluk River—*stream* AK-9
**Nageezi**—*pop pl* NM-5
Nageezi Dam—*dam* NM-5
*Nagek Lake* MI-6
Nagel Bros Ranch—*locale* TX-5
Nagel Brothers Dam—*dam* SD-7
Nagel Canyon—*valley* CA-9
**Nagel Corner (Belknap Corner)**—*pop pl* MI-6
Nagelin Cem—*cemetery* MO-7
*Nagelin Rim* AZ-5
Nagel Lake—*lake* (2) MN-6
Nagel Logging Camp—*locale* AZ-5
Nagel Rsvr—*reservoir* CA-9
Nagels Creek—*stream* MI-6
Naggara Creek—*stream* ID-8
Nagiller Ranch (historical)—*locale* AZ-5
Nagiller Tank—*reservoir* (3) AZ-5
Naginak Cove—*bay* AK-9
**Naginey**—*pop pl* PA-2
Nagishlamina River—*stream* AK-9
Naglatuk Hill—*summit* AK-9
Nagle, John, House—*hist pl* NJ-2
Nagle Creek—*stream* IA-7
Nagle Ditch—*canal* IN-6
Nagle Ditch—*canal* OH-6
Naglee Mtn—*summit* PA-2
Nagle Hall—*school* MA-1
**Nagle (historical)**—*pop pl* OR-9
Nagle Hollow—*valley* MO-7
Nagle Lake—*reservoir* TN-4
**Nagle Road**—*pop pl* PA-2
Nagles Crossing—*locale* AZ-5
Nagles Crossroad—*locale* PA-2
Nagle Site—*hist pl* OK-5
Nagle Spring—*spring* WY-8
Nagle-Warren Mansion—*hist pl* WY-8
Nagley Knob—*summit* PA-2
Nagogami Lodge—*locale* MO-7
Nagog Brook—*stream* MA-1
Nagog Hill—*summit* MA-1
Nagog Pond—*reservoir* MA-1
Nagog Pond Dam—*dam* MA-1
*Nagomina Creek* NV-8
Nagooltee Peak—*summit* NM-5
Nagos—*locale* MT-8
Nagosakchowik—*locale* AK-9
Nagosakchowik Slough—*stream* AK-9
Nagotligageivik Mtn—*summit* AK-9
Nagowee Ch—*church* OK-5
Nag Pond—*lake* RI-1
Nagrom—*locale* WA-9
**Nags Head**—*pop pl* NC-3
Nags Head Beach Cottages Hist Dist—*hist pl* NC-3
Nags Head Island—*island* NC-3
Nags Head Pier—*locale* NC-3
Nags Head (Township of)—*fmr MCD* NC-3
Nags Head Woods—*woods* NC-3
*Nags Pond* RI-1
**Naguabo**—*pop pl* PR-3
Naguabo (Municipio)—*civil* PR-3
Naguabo (Pueblo)—*fmr MCD* PR-3
*Naguag, Town of* MA-1
Naguag Sch—*school* MA-1
Naguchik—*lake* AK-9
Nagugun Creek—*stream* AK-9
Nagugun Lake—*lake* AK-9
Nagunt Mesa—*summit* UT-8
Nagwika Lake—*lake* KS-7
Nagyagat Mtn—*summit* AK-9
Naha—*beach* HI-9
Nuhu Buy—*buy* AK 9
Naha Gulch—*valley* HI-9
*Nahaha* HI-9
*Nahaha Hill* HI-9
Nahahum Canyon—*valley* WA-9
Nahaku Point—*cape* HI-9
Nahalah Ch—*church* NC-3
Naha Lake—*lake* WA-9
Nahaleokoo—*area* HI-9
*Nahamakanta Stream* ME-1
Nahanada Village Site—*hist pl* ME-1
Nahant—*locale* IA-7
Nahant—*locale* SD-7
**Nahant**—*pop pl* MA-1
Nahant Bay—*bay* MA-1
*Nahant Beach* MA-1
*Nahanteau, Town of* MA-1
Nahant Harbor—*bay* MA-1
*Nahanton, Town of* MA-1
Nahanton Hill—*summit* MA-1
Nahanton Street Swamp—*swamp* MA-1
*Nahant Rock* MA-1
Nahant Rock—*rock* MA-1
Nahant Sch—*school* SD-7
Nahant Townhall—*building* MA-1
**Nahant (Town of)**—*pop pl* MA-1
Naha River—*stream* AK-9
Nahatan Street Shop Ctr—*locale* MA-1
*Nahcheess River* WA-9
*Nah-cheeze River* WA-9
*Nahche Mountain* AZ-5
**Nahcotta**—*pop pl* WA-9
Nahcotta Channel—*channel* WA-9
*Nahculola Fal* AL-4
*Naheala* AL-4
*Nahe Lake* WA-9
Naheola—*locale* AL-4
Naheola Landing (historical)—*locale* AL-4
**Nahiku**—*pop pl* HI-9
Nahiku Homesteads—*civil* HI-9
Nahimana Lake—*lake* MN-6
Nahiwa Point—*cape* HI-9
Nahkapw—*island* FM-9
Nahku Bay—*bay* AK-9
Nahlap Island—*island* FM-9
Nahlos—*island* FM-9
**Nahma**—*pop pl* MI-6
Nahma Junction—*locale* MI-6
Nahmakanta Lake—*lake* ME-1
Nahmakanta Stream—*stream* ME-1
Nah Malek—*unknown* FM-9
**Nahma (Township of)**—*pop pl* MI-6
Nahna Orepeng—*summit* FM-9
Nahneke Mtn—*summit* ID-8
Nahnningi—*island* FM-9
*Nahnpwil* FM-9
Nahnsapwe, Dolen—*summit* FM-9
Nahoko—*cape* HI-9
Nahoko Gulch—*valley* HI-9
Naholoku—*civil* HI-9
Nahon—*locale* SD-7
*Nah Oon Kara* CO-8
Nahor—*locale* VA-3
Nahor Hill—*summit* NH-1
Nahpali—*island* FM-9
*Nahpali Island* FM-9
*Nah-po-pah Creek* UT-8
Nahri—*bar* FM-9
Nahri Dipwidipw—*bar* FM-9
Nahrwold Ditch—*canal* IN-6
Nahsukin Lake—*lake* MT-8
Nahsukin Mtn—*summit* MT-8
*Nah Supah Hot Spring* ID-8
Nahtik—*island* FM-9
Nahtuk Mtn—*summit* AK-9
Nahtuk River—*stream* AK-9
Nahtzillee Canyon—*valley* NM-5
Nahtzillee Dam—*dam* NM-5
Nahuina (Site)—*locale* HI-9
Nahuluhulu Point—*cape* HI-9
*Nahumaalo* HI-9
Nahumaalo Point—*cape* HI-9
*Nahum Keike* MA-1
Nahuna—*cape* HI-9
Nahunakueu—*cape* HI-9
Nahunga Creek—*stream* NC-3
**Nahunta**—*pop pl* GA-3
**Nahunta**—*pop pl* NC-3
Nahunta (CCD)—*cens area* GA-3
Nahunta Ch—*church* (2) NC-3
Nahunta Elem Sch—*school* NC-3
Nahunta Falls—*falls* WA-9
Nahunta Swamp—*stream* NC-3
Nahunta (Township of)—*fmr MCD* NC-3
*Nahwah Creek* ID-8
Nahwatzel Lake—*lake* WA-9
*Naiad Lake* WA-9
Naiad Queen Lode Mine—*mine* SD-7
Nail—*locale* AR-4
Nail Bed—*basin* IN-6
Nail Branch—*stream* AL-4
*Nail Canyon* AZ-5
Nail Canyon—*valley* AZ-5
Nail Cem—*cemetery* AR-4
Nail Cem—*cemetery* KY-4
Nail Cem—*cemetery* OK-5
*Nail Creek* GA-3
*Nail Creek* MS-4
Nail Creek—*stream* AZ-5
Nail Creek—*stream* IN-6
Nail Creek—*stream* MO-7
Nail Crook—*stroam* NY-2
Nail Creek—*stream* OK-5
Nail Creek—*stream* SD-7
Nail Creek—*stream* TN-4
Nail Creek—*stream* (2) TX-5
Nail Creek—*stream* WI-6
Nail Creek Branch—*stream* TN-4
Nail Creek Lake—*reservoir* SD-7
Naildriver—*mine* UT-8
Nailer Cem—*cemetery* MO-7
Nailers Pond—*lake* MD-2
Nail Factory Mtn—*summit* PA-2
Nail Gap—*gap* AL-4
*Nail Hill* TN-4
Nail Hill—*summit* TX-5
Nail Hollow—*valley* OH-6
Nailiakauea—*summit* HI-9
Nailiilihaele Stream—*stream* HI-9
Nailing Branch—*stream* TN-4
Nailing Cem—*cemetery* TN-4
*Nailix* OR-9
Nail Keg Creek—*stream* OR-9
Nail Keg Riffle—*rapids* OR-9
Naillon Branch—*stream* TN-4
**Naillon (historical)**—*pop pl* TN-4
Naillon Island—*island* TN-4
Naillon Post Office (historical)—*building* TN-4
*Naillon Station* TN-4
**Naillontown (historical)**—*pop pl* TN-4
*Nailon* TN-4
*Nailor Elementary School* MS-4
Nailor Sch—*school* MS-4
Nailors Rock—*summit* KY-4
Nail Point—*cape* MD-2
Nail Point—*cliff* AZ-5
Nail Ranch—*locale* AZ-5
Nail Ranch—*locale* TX-5
Nailrod Sch—*school* IL-6
Nail Run—*stream* WV-2
Nails Bayou—*gut* MS-4
*Nails Creek* NC-3
Nails Creek—*stream* (3) GA-3
Nails Creek—*stream* MS-4
Nails Creek—*stream* OR-9
Nails Creek—*stream* (3) TN-4
Nails Creek—*stream* TX-5
Nails Creek Cem—*cemetery* TN-4
Nails Creek Ch—*church* (2) GA-3
**Nails Creek (Jewelville)**—*pop pl* GA-3
Nails Creek State Park—*park* TX-5
*Nails Hill* TN-4
Nail Spring—*spring* (2) OR-9
Nail Spring—*spring* SC-3
Nail's Station—*hist pl* OK-5
*Nails Valley* KY-4
Nain—*locale* VA-3
Nain Ch—*church* WV-2
*Nain Island* MP-9
Naio, Moku—*island* HI-9
Naio Gulch—*valley* HI-9
Naird Ch (historical)—*church* MS-4
**Nairn**—*pop pl* LA-4
Nairn Cem—*cemetery* LA-4
Nairn Ditch—*canal* CO-8
*Nairobi* CA-9
**Naisbitt Acres (subdivision)**—*pop pl* UT-8
**Naisbitt Subdivision**—*pop pl* UT-8
*Na Island* FM-9
Naismith—*locale* MT-8
Naiwa (Apana 1)—*civil* HI-9
*Najaboke* MP-9
Najabwake—*island* MP-9
*Naja Island* MP-9
Najaj—*island* MP-9
Najaka Pond—*lake* PA-2
*Najbol* MP-9
*Najbol Island* MP-9
Najbwol—*island* MP-9
*Najibol* MP-9
*Najibuen Island* MP-9
Najibuen Island—*island* MP-9
*Najibuen-to* MP-9
Naji Point—*cliff* AZ-5
Najo Spring—*reservoir* AZ-5
*Najutak* MP-9
**Naka**—*pop pl* LA-4
Nakaaha—*cape* HI-9
Nakaaha—*civil* HI-9
Naka Gas Field—*oilfield* LA-4
*Nakaibito* NM-5
*Nakai Canyon* AZ-5
*Nakai Canyon* UT-8
*Nakai Creek* AZ-5
*Nakai Creek* UT-8
*Nakai Dome* UT-8
Nakailingak Creek—*stream* AK-9
*Nakai Mesa* AZ-5
*Nakai Mesa* UT-8
Nakai Peak—*summit* CO-8
Nakai Yazzie Spring—*spring* AZ-5
Nakakauila Stream—*stream* HI-9
Nakaktuk Lakes—*lake* AK-9
Nakalaloa Stream—*stream* HI-9
*Nakalele* HI-9
*Nakalele Head* HI-9
Nakalele Point—*cape* HI-9
Nakalilok Bay—*bay* AK-9
*Nakamo-Sho* PW-9
Nakaneej—*island* MP-9
*Nakano* PW-9
*Nakano Island* PW-9
*Nakano Sho* PW-9
Nakanukalolo Ridge—*ridge* HI-9
*Nakaohu* HI-9
Nakaohu—*civil* HI-9
Nakaohu Point—*cape* HI-9
*Nakap* FM-9
*Nakap-en-Parram* FM-9
*Nakap Island* FM-9
*Nakappu-To* FM-9
Na Ka Puaiakone—*stream* HI-9
Nakarna Mtn—*summit* ID-8
Nakat Bay—*bay* AK-9
*Nakate* FL-3
Nakat Harbor—*bay* AK-9
Nakat Inlet—*bay* AK-9
Nakat Lake—*lake* AK-9
Nakat Mtn—*summit* AK-9
Nakawaa—*area* HI-9
Nakchamik Island—*island* AK-9
Naked City Airstrip—*airport* IN-6
Naked Creek—*stream* (2) GA-3
Naked Creek—*stream* (5) NC-3
Naked Creek—*stream* SC-3
Naked Creek—*stream* (5) VA-3
Naked Creek Cem—*cemetery* VA-3
Naked Creek Ch—*church* VA-3
Naked Creek Overlook—*locale* VA-3
Naked Ground—*locale* NC-3
Naked Ground Branch—*stream* NC-3
Naked Island—*island* (2) AK-9
Naked Joe Bald—*summit* MO-7
Naked Joe Knob—*summit* AR-4
Naked Lady Airp—*airport* FL-3
Naked Mountain Branch—*stream* GA-3
Naked Mtn—*summit* PA-2
Naked Mtn—*summit* (2) VA-3
Naked Place—*swamp* FL-3
Naked Place Mtn—*summit* NC-3
Naked Ridge—*ridge* VA-3
Naked Run—*stream* NC-3

Nawaihulili Stream—stream HI-9
Nawaii Lake WI-6
Nawaikulua Point—cape HI-9
Nawaimaka Stream—stream HI-9
Nawaimaka Valley—valley HI-9
Nawakwa NJ-2
Nawakwa Lake—lake MI-6
Nawakwa Lake—lake MN-6
Nawakwa Trail—trail TN-4
Nawaowaeoalika HI-9
Nawawaeoaliko—summit HI-9
Nawiliwile Bay HI-9
Nawiliwili—civil HI-9
**Nawiliwili**—pop pl HI-9
Nawiliwili Bay—bay HI-9
Nawiliwili Light Station—locale HI-9
Nawiliwilior HI-9
Nawiliwili Stream—stream HI-9
Nawini—summit HI-9
Naw Inlet NC-3
Nawlombages ME-1
Nawney Creek—stream VA-3
Nawoj—island MP-9
Nawsett MA-1
Nawtawaket Creek—stream CA-9
Nawtawaket Mtn—summit CA-9
Nawt Vaya—locale AZ-5
Nawt Vaya Well—well AZ-5
Naxera—locale VA-3
Nayanquing Point—cape MI-6
Nayanquing Point Wildlife Area—park MI-6
Nayantovoy Creek NV-8
Naya Nuki Peak—summit MT-8
Nayasset MA-1
Nayat RI-1
**Nayatt**—pop pl RI-1
Nayatt Beach RI-1
Nayatt Point—cape RI-1
Nayatt Point Lighthouse—hist pl RI-1
**Nay Aug**—pop pl PA-2
Nay Aug Falls—falls PA-2
Nay Aug Gulch—valley ID-8
Nay Aug Park—park PA-2
Nay Aug Park Gorge—valley PA-2
Nay Brook—stream NY-2
Nay Canyon—valley UT-8
Nay Chapel—church WV-2
Nayer Sch—school TX-5
Naylon Canyon—valley UT-8
Naylor—locale LA-4
Naylor—locale MD-2
Naylor—locale WA-9
**Naylor**—pop pl AR-4
**Naylor**—pop pl GA-3
**Naylor**—pop pl MO-7
**Naylor**—pop pl OH-6
Naylor (CCD)—cens area GA-3
Naylor Cem—cemetery AR-4
Naylor Cem—cemetery (2) IL-6
Naylor Cem—cemetery KY-4
Naylor Cem—cemetery MO-7
Naylor Cem—cemetery NC-3
Naylor Cem—cemetery OH-6
Naylor Cem—cemetery OK-5
Naylor Cem—cemetery VA-3
Naylor Cem—cemetery (2) WV-2
Naylor Ch—church AR-4
Naylor Chapel—church MS-4
Naylor Corners—locale NY-2
Naylor Creek—stream KY-4
Naylor Creek—stream MO-7
Naylor Ditch—canal OH-6
Naylor Ditch—canal WY-8
**Naylor Gardens**—pop pl DC-2
Naylor House—hist pl IA-7
Naylor JHS—school AZ-5
Naylor Lake—lake CO-8
Naylor Pond—reservoir NC-3
Naylor Ridge—ridge KY-4
**Naylors Beach**—pop pl VA-3
Naylors Sch—school CT-1
Naylor Sch—school MO-7
Naylor School MS-4
Naylors Corner DE-2
Naylors Corners—locale DE-2
Naylors Point—cape VA-3
Naylors Run—stream PA-2
Naylors Run Dam—dam PA-2
Naylox Mtn—summit OR-9
Naylox Ridge OR-9
Naylox (site)—locale OR-9
**Nayon Heights Condominium**—pop pl UT-8
Nayor Knob—summit NC-3
Nayorurun River—stream AK-9
Nay Pond—lake NH-1
Naysses Bay—bay VA-3
Nay Spring—spring OR-9
**Naytahwaush**—pop pl MN-6
Nayuka River—stream AK-9
Nayzatch Cem—cemetery ND-7
Nazaire-Biron Bridge—bridge NH-1
Nazan Bay—bay AK-9
Nazanne Lake—lake WA-9
Nazarath (Orphanage)—uninc pl NC-3
Nazarea Galilee Ch—church AL-4
Nazare Cem—cemetery TX-5
Nazare Ch AL-4
Nazare Ch—church TX-5
Nazarene Acres Camp—locale IL-6
Nazarene Camp—locale (2) OK-5
Nazarene Campground—locale MI-6
Nazarene Cem—cemetery LA-4
Nazarene Cem—cemetery SC-3
Nazarene Cem—cemetery TN-4
Nazarene Ch MS-4
Nazarene Ch—church (2) AL-4
Nazarene Ch—church AR-4
Nazarene Ch—church (2) IL-6
Nazarene Ch—church IN-6
Nazarene Ch—church (2) LA-4
Nazarene Ch—church MI-6
Nazarene Ch—church MN-6
Nazarene Ch—church (3) MO-7
Nazarene Ch—church NM-5
Nazarene Ch—church OH-6
Nazarene Ch—church OK-5
Nazarene Ch—church SC-3
Nazarene Ch—church SD-7
Nazarene Ch—church (2) TN-4
Nazarene Ch—church WI-6
Nazarene Chapel—church OK-5
Nazarene Ch Camp AL-4
Nazarene Ch of Berry—church AL-4
Nazarene Church Camp Lake Dam—dam (2) AL-4
Nazarene Church Lake—reservoir AL-4
Nazarene Indian Mission—church OK-5
Nazarene Sch—school CA-9
Nazarene Sch—school FL-3
Nazarene Sch—school SC-3
Nazarene Seminary—school MO-7
Nazarene Seminary—school TX-5
Nazaren Primeith Ch—church AL-4
Nazareth—locale KY-4
Nazareth—locale VI-3
**Nazareth**—pop pl NC-3
**Nazareth**—pop pl PA-2
**Nazareth**—pop pl TX-5
Nazareth Acad—school IL-6
Nazareth Acad—school NY-2
Nazareth Acad—school OH-6
Nazareth Area JHS—school PA-2
Nazareth Area Senior HS—school PA-2
Nazareth Baptist Ch—church (2) AL-4
Nazareth Baptist Ch—church MS-4
Nazareth Bay—bay VI-3
Nazareth Borough—civil PA-2
Nazareth Catholic Sch—school AL-4
Nazareth Cem—cemetery (2) AL-4
Nazareth Cem—cemetery SD-7
Nazareth Cem—cemetery WV-2
Nazareth Cem—cemetery WI-6
Nazareth Ch—church (5) AL-4
Nazareth Ch—church (2) GA-3
Nazareth Ch—church MN-6
Nazareth Ch—church (2) MS-4
Nazareth Ch—church (2) NC-3
Nazareth Ch—church ND-7
Nazareth Ch—church OH-6
Nazareth Ch—church PA-2
Nazareth Ch—church (8) SC-3
Nazareth Ch—church (2) VA-3
Nazareth Coll—school MI-6
Nazareth Coll And Acad—school KY-4
**Nazareth College**—pop pl NY-2
Nazareth Coll of Rochester—school NY-2
Nazareth Convent—church MO-7
Nazareth Convent—school KS-7
Nazareth Convent and Acad—hist pl KS-7
Nazareth Hall—school MN-6
Nazareth Hall Sch—school NY-2
Nazareth Hall Tract—hist pl PA-2
Nazareth Hist Dist—hist pl PA-2
Nazareth Home for Boys—building MA-1
Nazareth Hosp—hospital PA-2
Nazareth Hospital—locale NM-5
Nazareth House—hist pl NY-2
Nazareth House for Boys—school CA-9
Nazareth HS—school NY-2
Nazareth Junction PA-2
Nazareth Lee Missionary Baptist Ch—church MS-4
Nazareth Mission—church KY-4
Nazareth (Nazareth College) MI-6
Nazareth of Galilee Ch—church AL-4
Nazareth Primitive Baptist Ch AL-4
Nazareth Rsvr—reservoir PA-2
Nazareth Sch—school IL-6
Nazareth Sch—school MA-1
Nazareth Sch—school SC-3
Nazareth Sch (historical)—school AL-4
Nazarre Lateral—canal ID-8
Naze Hollow—valley TN-4
Nazer Draw—valley UT-8
**Nazlini**—pop pl AZ-5
Nazlini Airp—airport AZ-5
Nazlini Canyon—valley AZ-5
Nazlini Creek AZ-5
Nazlini Creek—stream AZ-5
Nazlini Trading Post AZ-5
Nazlini Trading Post—locale AZ-5
**Nazlini (Trading Post)**—pop pl AZ-5
Nazlini Wash AZ-5
Nazlini Wash—stream AZ-5
Nazuruk Channel—stream AK-9
Nazworthy Sch—school IL-6
N Bar Lake—lake NM-5
N Bar Park—park NM-5
N Bar Ranch—locale MT-8
N Bar Ranch—locale NM-5
NB Clements JHS—school VA-3
NBC-TV Studios—other CA-9
N B Fields Lake Dam—dam AL-4
N B Gray Pond Dam—dam MS-4
NB Lateral—canal TX-5
N B Ranch—locale AZ-5
N Breowick Ranch—locale ND-7
N Canal—canal MT-8
N Canal—canal NV-8
N Canal—canal OR-9
NC Aquarium NC-3
NC Creek—stream AK-9
**N C Love Addition (subdivision)**—pop pl TN-4
NCNG Armory—building NC-3
NC Noname Eight-Hundred Forty—dam NC-3
NC Noname Eight-Hundred Forty-Seven—dam NC-3
NC Noname Eighty-One—dam NC-3
NC Noname Eighty-Two—dam NC-3
NC Noname Forty-Five—dam NC-3
NC Noname Forty-Four—dam NC-3
NC Noname Forty-Six—dam NC-3
NC Noname Forty-Three—dam NC-3
NC Noname One-Hundred Thirty-Nine—dam NC-3
NC Noname One-Hundred Twenty-Seven—dam NC-3
NC Noname One-Thousand Thirty-One—dam NC-3
NC Noname Sixty-Eight—dam NC-3
NC Noname Thirty-Eight—dam NC-3
NC Noname Thirty-Five—dam NC-3
NC Noname Thirty-Four—dam NC-3
NC Noname Thirty-Six—dam NC-3
NC Noname Two-Hundred Sixty—dam NC-3
NC Noname Two-Hundred Thirteen—dam NC-3
NC Noname Two-Hundred Thirty-Nine—dam NC-3
NCO Railway Depot—hist pl CA-9
N C S Beach—beach GU-9
N C State Port Authority—harbor NC-3
NC State University Farm Pond Number Two—reservoir NC-3
NC State University Farm Unit Number Two Dam—dam NC-3
NCSU Pond Number One—reservoir NC-3
NCSU Pond Number One Dam—dam NC-3
Ndishchii Naati—area AZ-5
N Drain—canal CA-9
Neabon FM-9
**Neabsco**—pop pl VA-3
Neabsco Ch—church VA-3
Neabsco Creek—stream VA-3
Neabsco (Magisterial District)—fmr MCD VA-3
Neace Ch MO-7
Neace Memorial Ch—church KY-4
Neacola River—stream AK-9
Neacoxie Creek—stream OR-9
**Nead**—pop pl IN-6
**Neadeauville**—pop pl ME-1
Nead Elem Sch—school IN-6
Nead Lake—lake ND-7
Neadmore—locale IL-6
Neaf Spring—spring UT-8
Neafus—locale KY-4
**Neafus**—pop pl KY-4
Neafus Peak—summit CA-9
Neafus Ranch—locale NM-5
Neagle Cem—cemetery KY-4
Neagle Creek—stream MT-8
Neagle Point—cape WA-9
Neagle Ranch—locale AZ-5
Neagle Ridge—ridge UT-8
Neaglin Rim AZ-5
Neah WA-9
Neah Bay—bay WA-9
**Neah Bay**—pop pl WA-9
**Neahkahnie Beach**—pop pl OR-9
Neahkahnie Creek OR-9
Neahkahnie Creek—stream OR-9
Neahkahnie Lake—reservoir OR-9
Neahkahnie Mtn—summit OR-9
**Neahkahnie (Neahkahnie Beach)**—pop pl OR-9
Neahkahnie Sch—school OR-9
**Neahr**—pop pl OR-9
Neah-Ta-Wanta Point—cape MI-6
Neahwa Park—park NY-2
Neakok Island—island AK-9
Neal—locale CA-9
Neal—locale (2) GA-3
Neal—locale IL-6
Neal—locale OK-5
Neal—locale WV-2
**Neal**—pop pl KS-7
Neal, Halbert F. and Grace, House—hist pl ID-8
Neal, Jairus, House—hist pl KS-7
Neal, James, House—hist pl NH-1
Neal, W. Scott, House—hist pl ID-8
Neal and Dixon's Warehouse—hist pl SC-3
Neal Ayers Gin Branch—stream AL-4
Neal Branch—stream GA-3
Neal Branch—stream (2) NC-3
Neal Branch—stream (2) SC-3
Neal Branch—stream (3) TN-4
Neal Bridge—bridge TN-4
Neal Brook—stream VT-1
Neal Butler Park—park AZ-5
Neal Butte—summit OR-9
Neal Cabe Dam—dam NC-3
Neal Cabe Lake—reservoir NC-3
Neal Cabin—locale AZ-5
Neal Camp Burn—area OR-9
Neal Canyon—valley AZ-5
Neal Canyon—valley ID-8
Neal Canyon—valley WA-9
Neal Cave—cave TN-4
Neal Cem—cemetery AR-4
Neal Cem—cemetery GA-3
Neal Cem—cemetery (4) IL-6
Neal Cem—cemetery KS-7
Neal Cem—cemetery (3) KY-4
Neal Cem—cemetery (2) LA-4
Neal Cem—cemetery (3) MS-4
Neal Cem—cemetery MO-7
Neal Cem—cemetery NC-3
Neal Cem—cemetery (2) OH-6
Neal Cem—cemetery OK-5
Neal Cem—cemetery (6) TN-4
Neal Cem—cemetery TX-5
Neal Cem—cemetery (3) WV-2
Neal Ch—church MI-6
Neal Chapel—church TN-4
Neal Chapel Cem—cemetery AL-4
Neal Chapel Cem—cemetery TN-4
Neal Clothing—hist pl OH-6
Neal Coulee—valley MT-8
Neal Cove—bay CA-9
Neal Creek NC-3
Neal Creek—gut NC-3
Neal Creek—stream AR-4
Neal Creek—stream CA-9
Neal Creek—stream MT-8
Neal Creek—stream (2) NC-3
Neal Creek—stream (2) OR-9
Neal Creek—stream SC-3
Neal Creek—stream TN-4
Neal Creek Lateral—canal OR-9
Neal Crossing—locale GA-3
Neal Dam—dam OR-9
Neal Dam—dam PA-2
Neale—locale LA-4
Neale—locale TX-5
**Neale**—pop pl PA-2
Neale, George, Jr., House—hist pl WV-2
Neale, William P., House—hist pl KY-4
Neale Branch—stream GA-3
Neale Branch—stream KY-4
Neale Cem—cemetery KY-4
Neale Cem—cemetery WV-2
Neale Mesa—summit AZ-5
Neale Oil Field—oilfield LA-4
**Neale Place**—pop pl MA-1
Neale Post Office (historical)—building PA-2
Nealer Ch—church GA-3
Neale Sch—school WV-2
Neale Sound—bay MD-2
Neale Sound Channel—channel MD-2
Nealey Creek—stream GA-3
Nealey Creek—stream WA-9
Nealey Creek Trail—trail WA-9
Nealeys—locale PA-2
Nealeys Corner—locale CA-9
Nealeys Corner—locale ME-1
Neal Ford (historical)—locale TN-4
Neal Gap—gap GA-3
Neal Gulf—valley GA-3
Neal-Hamblen House—hist pl KY-4
Neal Hill—summit NH-1
Neal Hill Cem—cemetery AL-4
Neal Hollow—valley (2) KY-4
Neal Hollow—valley TN-4
Neal Hollow—valley VA-3
Neal Hollow—valley WV-2
Neal House—hist pl KY-4
Neal House—hist pl TX-5
Neal Howard Creek—stream KY-4
Nealie Branch—stream KY-4
Neal Island—island WV-2
Neal JHS—school IL-6
Neal JHS—school NC-3
Neal Key—island FL-3
Neal Lake MS-4
Neal Lake—lake TX-5
Neal Lake—reservoir AL-4
Neal Lake—reservoir MS-4
Neal Lake—reservoir PA-2
Neal Landing—locale LA-4
Neal Landing—locale TN-4
Neal Lateral—canal WI-6
Neal Levee—levee IN-6
Neall Lake—lake CA-9
Neally Brook—stream ME-1
Neal Mill Bridge—bridge IN-6
Neal Mine (surface)—mine TN-4
**Nealmont**—pop pl PA-2
Neal Mountain Tank—reservoir AZ-5
Neal Mtn—summit AZ-5
Neal Mtn—summit AR-4
Neal Mtn—summit ME-1
Neal Mtn—summit OR-9
Neal Mtn—summit VA-3
Nealon Lateral—canal CA-9
Nealon Park—park CA-9
Nealon Sch (historical)—school TN-4
Neal Park—park FL-3
Neal Park—park NE-7
Neal Point—cape AK-9
Neal Pond—lake MO-7
Neal Pond—lake VT-1
Neal Pond—lake WV-2
Neal Pond—reservoir GA-3
Neal Pond—swamp MA-1
Neal Post Office (historical)—building TN-4
Neal Ranch—locale MT-8
Neal Ranch—locale NM-5
Neal Ranch—locale TX-5
Neal Rsvr—reservoir WY-8
Nealruk Mtn—summit AK-9
Neal Run—stream PA-2
Neal Run—stream VA-3
Neal Run—stream WV-2
Neals—locale FL-3
Neals Bay—bay LA-4
Neals Branch NJ-2
Neals Cem—cemetery MS-4
Neal Sch—school AL-4
Neal Sch—school GA-3
Neal Sch—school MI-6
Neals Chapel—church AL-4
Neals Chapel—church KY-4
Neals Chapel—church (2) MS-4
Neals Chapel Sch—school SC-3
Neal Sch (historical)—school AL-4
Neal Sch (historical)—school MS-4
Neals Corner—locale ME-1
Neals Corner—locale OH-6
Neals Corner—locale VA-3
Neals Cove—bay NH-1
Neals Creek MD-2
Neals Creek NC-3
Neals Creek—gut NC-3
Neals Creek—stream AL-4
Neals Creek—stream GA-3
Neals Creek—stream KY-4
Neals Creek—stream MO-7
Neals Creek—stream NC-3
Neals Creek—stream (2) SC-3
Neals Creek—stream VA-3
Neals Creek Cem—cemetery MO-7
Neals Creek Ch—church SC-3
Neals Ferry MS-4
Neals Flat—flat UT-8
Neals Folly OR-9
Neals Hill—slope OR-9
Neals Hill—summit VT-1
**Neals (historical)**—pop pl MS-4
Neal Shoals—rapids SC-3
Neals Lake—flat OR-9
Neals Landing—locale GA-3
Neal Sound MD-2
Neal Speers Dam—dam AL-4
Neal Speers Lake—reservoir AL-4
Neals Point—cape VA-3
Neals Pond MA-1
Neals Pond—reservoir AL-4
Neals Post Office (historical)—building MS-4
Neal Spring—spring (4) AZ-5
Neal Spring—spring TX-5
Neal Springs—locale AR-4
Neals Run—locale WV-2
Neals Run—stream (2) PA-2
Neals Sound MD-2
Neals Spring—spring CA-9
Neals Tank TX-5
Neals Tank—reservoir TX-5
Neal State Wildlife Mngmt Area—park MN-6
Neals Temple—church (2) FL-3
**Neals Valley**—pop pl TX-5
Nealsville NC-3
Neal Tank—mine AZ-5
Neal Tank—reservoir AZ-5
Neal Tank—reservoir NM-5
Neal Tank Number Two—reservoir AZ-5
Neal Thomas Sch—school TN-4
Neal Towhead—flat TN-4
Neal (Township of)—fmr MCD AR-4
Neal Valley—valley KY-4
Nealy Branch—stream AR-4
Nealy Branch—stream (2) KY-4
Nealy Branch—stream LA-4
Nealy Branch—stream TX-5
Nealy Branch Sch—school KY-4
Nealy Creek—stream MI-6
Nealy Gap—gap NC-3
Nealy Park—park TX-5
Nealy Ridge—locale VA-3
Nealy Ridge—ridge VA-3
Nealy Ridge Lookout Tower—locale VA-3
Nealy Run—stream KY-4
Nealy Well—well AZ-5
Neaman Gulch—valley CA-9
Neame—locale LA-4
Neamon Cem—cemetery LA-4
Neander Lake—lake MN-6
Neang—bar FM-9
Neanu, Unun En—bar FM-9
Neapach—well FM-9
**Neapolis**—pop pl OH-6
**Neapolis**—pop pl TN-4
Neapsico Creek VA-3
Near—well FM-9
Near Black Creek AL-4
Near Brook—stream IN-6
Near Creek—stream LA-4
Near Draw—valley CO-8
Near Draw Rsvr—reservoir CO-8
Near East Camp—locale CT-1
Near East Side Hist Dist—hist pl WI-6
Nearen Cem—cemetery AL-4
Nearest MS-4
Nearest Grave Cem—cemetery AL-4
Near Fork Sandsuck Creek—stream KY-4
Near Halfshot Cove—cave AL-4
Near Hollow—valley VA-3
Nearhouse Mine—mine AK-9
Nearing Drain—canal MI-6
Nearing Hill—summit FL-3
Nearing Run—stream PA-2
Near Island—island (2) AK-9
Near Island—island MI-6
Near Islands—island AK-9
Nearman—locale KS-7
Nearman Creek—stream KS-7
Nearman Station KS-7
Near North Hist Dist—hist pl IL-6
Near North Side IL-6
Near Northside Hist Dist—hist pl OH-6
Nearns Point—cape WA-9
Near Point—cape (2) AK-9
Near Point—summit AK-9
Near Pond—lake OR-9
Near Prong Rester Creek—stream MS-4
Near Ranch—locale CA-9
Near River Ch—church SC-3
Near the Cross Ch—church NC-3
Nearus Lagoon—swamp CA-9
Nearway Ridge—ridge VA-3
Nearway Run—stream WV-2
Near Westside Hist Dist—hist pl NY-2
Neary Mtn—summit MA-1
Neary-Rodriguez Adobe—hist pl CA-9
Nease Creek—stream OH-6
Nease Memorial Ch—church MI-6
Nease Settlement—locale OH-6
Nease Spring—spring TN-4
**Neason Hill**—pop pl PA-2
Neason Hill Elem Sch—school PA-2
Neasons Flat—flat CA-9
**Neasons Hill**—pop pl PA-2
Neatahwanta, Lake—lake NY-2
Neat Camp Creek NC-3
Neat Creek—stream FL-3
Neath—locale PA-2
Neathammer Creek—stream OR-9
Neathawk Cem—cemetery VA-3
Neatherlin Lateral—canal AZ-5
Neatherlin Ranch—locale NM-5
Neatherly Branch—stream TN-4
Neatherly Cem—cemetery TN-4
Neatherwood Park—park NM-5
Neathery, Sam, House—hist pl TX-5
Neathery Cem—cemetery (2) IL-6
Neathery Cem—cemetery TX-5
Neat Hollow—valley KY-4
Neatman Creek—stream NC-3
Neatmans Creek NC-3
Neaton Drain MI-6
Neaton Drain—stream MI-6
Neaton Sch—school MN-6
Neatsville—locale KY-4
Neauo FM-9
Neauo—CDP FM-9
Neauo—spring FM-9
Neaut FM-9
Neaut Canal FM-9
Neauwo FM-9
Neave—locale KY-4
Neaves Spring—spring AL-4
**Neave (Township of)**—pop pl OH-6
Neavill Cem—cemetery IN-6
**Neavill Grove**—pop pl IN-6
**Neavitt**—pop pl MD-2
Neawachang FM-9
Neawanna OR-9
Neawanna Creek—stream OR-9
**Neawanna Station**—pop pl OR-9
Nebadeer Pond MA-1
Nebagamon, Lake—lake WI-6
Nebagamon Creek—stream WI-6
Nebbletts Creek TX-5
Nebbons Hill—other PA-2
Nebdan—island MP-9
Nebeker Ranch—locale UT-8
Nebeker Spring—spring (2) UT-8
Nebel Coulee—valley MT-8
Nebelhorn—locale CA-9
Neberai FM-9
Neberen MP-9
Neberen Island MP-9
Neberen Island—island MP-9
Nebergall "Knoll Crest" Round Barn—hist pl IA-7
Neber Pond—lake CT-1
Nebinger, George W., Sch—hist pl PA-2
Nebinger Elem Sch PA-2
Nebinger Sch—school PA-2
Nebinger Sch (abandoned)—school PA-2
Nebish—locale MN-6
Nebish Lake—lake MN-6
Nebish Lake—lake WI-6
**Nebish (Township of)**—pop pl MN-6
Neble—locale WY-8
Neble Hill—summit WY-8
Neblets Landing—locale TN-4
Neblett Cem—cemetery TN-4
Neblett Cem—cemetery TX-5
Nebletts Creek—stream (2) TX-5
Nebletts Landing (historical)—locale MS-4
Nebletts Millpond—reservoir VA-3
Nebletts Mill Run—stream VA-3
Nebo IN-6
Nebo NJ-2
Nebo—locale AL-4
Nebo—locale AR-4
Nebo—locale CA-9
Nebo—locale GA-3
Nebo—locale KY-4
Nebo—locale LA-4
Nebo—locale OK-5
Nebo—locale PA-2
Nebo—locale VA-3
Nebo—locale (2) WV-2
**Nebo**—pop pl AR-4
**Nebo**—pop pl IL-6
**Nebo**—pop pl KY-4
**Nebo**—pop pl MO-7
**Nebo**—pop pl (2) NC-3
**Nebo**—pop pl PA-2
Nebo, Lake—lake NY-2
Nebo, Mount—summit AR-4
Nebo, Mount—summit CO-8
Nebo, Mount—summit CT-1
Nebo, Mount—summit (2) IN-6
Nebo, Mount—summit (3) MD-2
Nebo, Mount—summit (2) MA-1
Nebo, Mount—summit MN-6
Nebo, Mount—summit NM-5
Nebo, Mount—summit (2) NY-2
Nebo, Mount—summit OH-6
Nebo, Mount—summit OK-5
Nebo, Mount—summit (3) OR-9
Nebo, Mount—summit TN-4
Nebo, Mount—summit TX-5
Nebo, Mount—summit UT-8
Nebo, Mount—summit WI-6
Nebo Basin—basin UT-8
Nebo Basin Trail—trail UT-8
Nebo Basin Trail - in part UT-8
Nebo Bench—bench UT-8
Nebo Branch—stream TN-4
Nebo (CCD)—cens area KY-4
Nebo Cem—cemetery (3) AL-4
Nebo Cem—cemetery AR-4
Nebo Cem—cemetery GA-3
Nebo Cem—cemetery IN-6
Nebo Cem—cemetery (2) KY-4
Nebo Cem—cemetery LA-4
Nebo Cem—cemetery (3) MS-4
Nebo Cem—cemetery NC-3
Nebo Cem—cemetery ND-7
Nebo Cem—cemetery PA-2
Nebo Center—CDP CA-9
Nebo Ch AL-4
Nebo Ch MS-4
Nebo Ch TN-4
Nebo Ch—church (4) AL-4
Nebo Ch—church FL-3
Nebo Ch—church GA-3
Nebo Ch—church (5) MS-4
Nebo Ch—church MO-7
Nebo Ch—church (2) NC-3
Nebo Ch—church OH-6
Nebo Ch—church (3) PA-2
Nebo Ch—church (4) SC-3
Nebo Ch—church TN-4
Nebo Ch (historical)—church (2) AL-4
Nebo Ch of Christ—church TN-4
Nebo Church Cem—cemetery AL-4
Nebo Church Cem—cemetery NC-3
Nebo Creek—stream CA-9
Nebo Creek—stream CO-8
Nebo Creek—stream KS-7
Nebo Creek—stream OR-9
Nebo Creek—stream (2) UT-8
Nebo Cumberland Presbyterian Ch AL-4
Nebo Elem Sch—school NC-3
Nebogigig Lake MN-6
Nebo-Hemphill Oil Field—oilfield LA-4
Nebo Hill—summit AL-4
Nebo Hill—summit MO-7
Nebo Hill Archeol Site—hist pl MO-7
Nebo (historical)—locale AL-4
Nebo Island—island PA-2
Nebo Knob—summit GA-3
Nebo Knobs—summit TN-4
Nebo Lake—reservoir KS-7
Nebo Lake Dam—dam IN-6
Nebo Lateral—canal ID-8
Nebo Lookout—locale OR-9
Nebo Methodist Ch TN-4
Nebo Methodist Ch—church AL-4
Nebo Methodist Ch—church TN-4
Nebo Mtn—summit AL-4
Nebo Mtn—summit ME-1
Nebo Mtn—summit (2) TX-5
Nebo Peak Trail (Pack)—trail UT-8
Nebo Post Office (historical)—building AL-4
Nebo Presbyterian Church AL-4
Nebo Ridge—ridge IN-6
Nebo Rock—summit CA-9
Nebo Sch—school IL-6
Nebo Sch—school LA-4
Nebo Sch—school MO-7
Nebo Sch—school ND-7
Nebo Sch—school OK-5
Nebo Sch (abandoned)—school MO-7
Nebo Sch (historical)—school (3) AL-4
Nebo Sch (historical)—school SC-3
Nebo Sch (historical)—school TX-5
Nebo Springs, Mount—spring TN-4
Nebo State Fishing Lake and Wildlife Area—park KS-7
Nebo Store (historical)—building MS-4
Nebo Swamp—swamp PA-2
Nebot, Zaldo de, Residencia—hist pl PR-3
Neboth Ch (historical)—church TN-4
**Nebo Township**—pop pl ND-7
Nebo (Township of)—fmr MCD NC-3

Nebou—spring ... FM-9
Nebo United Methodist Church ... AL-4
**Neboville**—pop pl ... TN-4
Neboville Cem—cemetery ... TN-4
Neboville Post Office (historical)—building ... TN-4
Neboville Sch (historical)—school ... TN-4
Nebowa Camp—locale ... IA-7
Nebo Watershed Lake ... KS-7
Neboyias Water Well—well ... AZ-5
Nebraska—locale ... PA-2
**Nebraska**—pop pl ... IN-6
**Nebraska**—pop pl ... NC-3
**Nebraska**—pop pl ... PA-2
Nebraska Bar—bar ... MS-4
Nebraska Bay—bay ... MN-6
Nebraska Brook—stream ... NY-2
Nebraska Ch—church ... AL-4
Nebraska Christian HS—school ... NE-7
**Nebraska City**—pop pl ... NE-7
Nebraska City Hist Dist—hist pl ... NE-7
Nebraska City Junction ... IA-7
Nebraska Creek—stream ... ID-8
Nebraska Elem Sch—school ... IN-6
Nebraska Flat—flat ... WY-8
Nebraska Hill—summit ... CO-8
Nebraska Hollow—valley ... WI-6
Nebraska Landing—locale ... TN-4
Nebraska Loan and Trust Company Bldg—hist pl ... NE-7
Nebraska Notch—gap ... VT-1
Nebraska Point ... TN-4
Nebraska River ... NE-7
Nebraska Sch—school ... IL-6
Nebraska Sch—school ... WY-8
Nebraska State Capitol—hist pl ... NE-7
Nebraska State Teachers Coll—school ... NE-7
Nebraska Telephone Company Bldg—hist pl ... NE-7
Nebraska Township—fmr MCD ... IA-7
**Nebraska (Township of)**—pop pl ... IL-6
Nebraska Vocational Training Sch—school ... NE-7
Nebraska Wesleyan Univ—school ... NE-7
Nebrigs Hill—summit ... AL-4
Nebson Bay—bay ... AK-9
Nebula—locale ... GA-3
Nebunnom ... FM-9
Neby Shelter—locale ... WA-9
**Necaise**—pop pl ... MS-4
Necaise Cem—cemetery ... MS-4
Necaise Lake Dam—dam ... MS-4
Necaise Lookout Tower—tower ... MS-4
Necanacum ... OR-9
Necanacum River ... OR-9
Necanicum Guard Station—locale ... OR-9
**Necanicum (historical)**—pop pl ... OR-9
Necanicum Junction—locale ... OR-9
Necanicum Picnic Area—park ... OR-9
Necanicum River—stream ... OR-9
Necanknev Cliff ... MA-1
N E Canyon—valley ... ID-8
Necarney Creek—stream ... OR-9
Neccu ... FM-9
**Necedah**—pop pl ... WI-6
Necedah Bluff—summit ... WI-6
Necedah Lake—reservoir ... WI-6
Necedah Natl Wildlife Ref—park ... WI-6
**Necedah (Town of)**—pop pl ... WI-6
Necessary Cem—cemetery (2) ... VA-3
Necessary Creek—stream ... GA-3
Necessity—locale ... TX-5
Necessity, Lake—reservoir ... TX-5
Necessity Cove—bay ... AK-9
Necessity Ditch—canal ... IN-6
Necessity Rsvr—reservoir ... MT-8
Nechanic River ... NJ-2
Nechanitz—locale ... TX-5
Nechap—civil ... FM-9
**Nechap**—pop pl ... FM-9
Nechap Sch—school ... FM-9
**Neche**—pop pl ... ND-7
Neche Dam—dam ... ND-7
Nechelik Channel—channel ... AK-9
Necheriw—spring ... FM-9
**Neches**—pop pl ... TX-5
Neches Bluff Overlook—locale ... TX-5
Neches Canal ... TX-5
Neches Cem—cemetery ... TX-5
Neches Club—other ... TX-5
**Neches Indian Village**—pop pl ... TX-5
Neches Junction—uninc pl ... TX-5
Neches River ... TX-5
Neches River—stream ... TX-5
Neches River Settlement ... TX-5
**Neche Township**—pop pl ... ND-7
Nechewan—spring ... FM-9
Nechinam, Oror En—locale ... FM-9
Nechinapa, Oror En—locale ... FM-9
Nechireng—slope ... FM-9
**Nechocho**—pop pl ... FM-9
Nechocho, Unun En—bar ... FM-9
Necholas Run—stream ... WV-2
Nechonon—spring ... FM-9
Ne chu se chin ga ... KS-7
Ne Citra Oil And Gas Field—oilfield ... OK-5
Neck ... RI-1
Neck, The ... AL-4
Neck, The ... MA-1
Neck, The ... MS-4
neck, The ... NY-2
Neck, The—bench ... UT-8
Neck, The—cape ... MD-2
Neck, The—cape (2) ... MA-1
Neck, The—cape ... MS-4
Neck, The—cape ... NC-3
Neck, The—cape ... OR-9
Neck, The—cape ... PA-2
Neck, The—cape (2) ... SC-3
Neck, The—flat ... MS-4
Neck, The—gap ... TX-5
Neck, The—gap ... UT-8
Neck, The—island ... ME-1
Neck Branch—stream ... KY-4
Neck Branch Sch—school ... KY-4
**Neck City**—pop pl ... MO-7
Neck Creek—stream ... MA-1
Neck Creek—stream ... NY-2
Neck Creek—stream ... VA-3
**Necker**—pop pl ... MD-2
Necker Bay—bay ... AK-9
Necker Cem—cemetery ... TX-5
Necker Island—island ... HI-9
Necker Island Archeol District—hist pl ... HI-9
Necker Islands—area ... AK-9
Neck Hill—summit ... MA-1
Neck Island ... ME-1
Necklace Lakes—lake ... MT-8
Necklace Spring ... UT-8
Necklace Valley—valley ... WA-9
Neck Lake—lake (2) ... AK-9
Neck Lake—lake ... ID-8
Neck Meadow—flat ... CA-9
Neck Meetinghouse and Yard—hist pl ... MD-2
Neck of Land Cemetery—hist pl ... MA-1
Neck Of The Desert—plain ... UT-8
Neck Point—cape ... AK-9
Neck Point—cape ... MD-2
Neck Point—cape ... NY-2
Neck Point—cape ... WA-9
Neck Pond—lake ... MA-1
Neck Ranger Station—locale ... UT-8
Neck Ridge—ridge ... ME-1
Neck River—stream ... CT-1
Neckshorta Lake—lake ... AK-9
Neck Spring—spring ... UT-8
Necktie Basin—basin ... CA-9
Necktie Canyon—valley ... CA-9
Necktie River—stream ... MN-6
Neco—locale ... GA-3
Necomanchee River ... WA-9
**Necombtown**—pop pl ... NJ-2
Neconish, Lake—lake ... WI-6
Necons River—stream ... AK-9
Necot—locale ... IA-7
Necoxie Creek ... OR-9
N E Creek—stream ... ID-8
**Nectar**—pop pl ... AL-4
Nectar Covered Bridge—bridge ... AL-4
Nectar Covered Bridge—hist pl ... AL-4
Nectar Heights Ch—church ... AL-4
**Nectarine**—pop pl ... PA-2
Nectarine Lateral—canal ... CA-9
Nectar Lake—lake ... MN-6
Nectar Lateral—canal ... ID-8
Nectar Sch—school ... AL-4
Nector ... AL-4
Ned—locale ... KY-4
**Ned**—pop pl ... PA-2
**Neda**—pop pl ... WI-6
Neda Creek—stream ... WI-6
Nedaros Cem—cemetery ... ND-7
Ned Bees Point—cape ... NC-3
Ned Branch—stream (2) ... KY-4
Ned Branch—stream (2) ... NC-3
Ned Branch—stream ... TN-4
Ned Branch—stream ... TX-5
Ned Brown Preserve—park ... IL-6
Ned Creek—stream ... ID-8
Ned Creek—stream ... SC-3
Ned Dam—dam ... SC-3
Neddick, Cape—cape ... ME-1
Neddie Creek—stream ... NC-3
Neddie Knob—summit ... NC-3
Neddie Mountain—ridge ... NC-3
Neddie Mountain Ch—church ... NC-3
Neddy Branch—stream ... KY-4
Neddy Creek—stream ... TX-5
Neddy Fork—stream ... KY-4
Neddy Mtn—summit ... TN-4
Neddys Mtn ... TN-4
Neddys Spring—spring ... TN-4
**Nederland**—pop pl ... CO-8
**Nederland**—pop pl ... TX-5
Nederland Air Natl Guard Station—building ... TX-5
Nederland HS—school ... CO-8
Nederland Lake ... CO-8
Nedeshelu River ... PW-9
Ned Fork—stream ... KY-4
Ned Fork—stream ... OH-6
Ned Fork Sch—school ... KY-4
Ned Gap—gap ... NC-3
Ned Gulch—valley (2) ... CA-9
Nedham Hollow—valley ... AL-4
Ned Hill—summit ... WA-9
Ned Hill Trail—trail ... WA-9
Ned Hollow—valley ... AR-4
Ned Hollow—valley ... TN-4
Ned Hollow—valley ... VA-3
Nedigh Ditch—canal ... IN-6
Ned Island—island ... ME-1
Ned Lake—lake ... AZ-5
Ned Lake—lake ... AR-4
Ned Lake—lake ... FL-3
Ned Lake—lake ... MI-6
Ned Lake Creek—stream ... MI-6
Ned Lockard Pond Dam—dam ... MS-4
Ned Locklard Pond Dam—dam ... MS-4
Ned Mtn—summit ... CT-1
Ned Mtn—summit ... NC-3
Ned Mtn—summit ... TN-4
Nedodo ... FM-9
**Nedonna**—pop pl ... OR-9
**Nedonna Beach**—pop pl ... OR-9
Nedonna Creek—stream ... OR-9
Nedonna Lake—lake ... OR-9
Nedo Well—well ... TX-5
Ned Point—cape ... MA-1
Ned Point Light—hist pl ... MA-1
Ned Point Light—locale ... MA-1
Ned Pond—lake ... AK-9
Ned Pond—lake ... FL-3
Nedra Tank—reservoir ... NM-5
Ned Rock ... WA-9
**Nedrose Township**—pop pl ... ND-7
**Nedrow**—pop pl ... NY-2
Nedrow Cem—cemetery ... PA-2
Nedrow Homestead—locale ... CO-8
Ned Rsvr—reservoir ... UT-8
Ned Run—stream ... MD-2
Ned Run—stream ... WV-2
**Neds Branch**—pop pl ... WV-2
Neds Branch—stream ... KY-4
Neds Branch—stream (2) ... WV-2
Neds Creek—channel ... NY-2
Neds Creek—stream ... SC-3
Neds Creek—stream ... VA-3
Neds Ditch—swamp ... MA-1
Neds Fork—stream ... KY-4
Neds Fork Sch—school ... KY-4
Neds Gulch—valley ... CA-9
Neds Gulch—valley ... OR-9
Neds Gully—valley ... TX-5
Neds Hole Channel ... NY-2
Neds Hole Creek—channel ... NY-2
Neds Hollow—valley ... KY-4
Ned's Island ... ME-1
Neds Island—island ... MD-2
Neds Lake—lake ... AK-9
Neds Lake—lake ... MI-6
Neds Lake—lake ... MN-6
Neds Lick Gap—gap ... NC-3
Neds Meadow—swamp ... NY-2
Neds Mtn—summit ... WV-2
Neds Point ... MA-1
Neds Point—cape ... ME-1
Neds Point Light—locale ... MA-1
Neds Rock—island ... WA-9
Neds Run—stream ... WV-2
Ned Swamp—locale ... SC-3
Neds Well—well ... NM-5
Ned Tank—lake ... NM-5
Ned Tank—reservoir ... NM-5
Nedved Cem—cemetery ... SD-7
Nedved Sch—school ... SD-7
Nedville Ch—church ... TX-5
Ned Wesson Branch—stream ... SC-3
Neeah ... WA-9
Neeah Bay ... WA-9
Neeb Airp—airport ... PA-2
Neeben Lake ... MN-6
Neebish Island—island ... MI-6
Neecap ... FM-9
Neece Branch—stream ... MO-7
Neece Canyon—valley ... OR-9
Neece Cem—cemetery (2) ... TN-4
Neece Cem—cemetery ... VA-3
Neece Chapel—church ... KY-4
Neece Creek—stream ... VA-3
Neeces (corporate name Neeses) ... SC-3
Need—locale ... CA-9
Needed Tank—reservoir (2) ... AZ-5
Needels Sch (historical)—school ... MO-7
Nee De Mise Betoh—spring ... AZ-5
**Needful**—pop pl ... PA-2
Needful Ch—church ... GA-3
Needfull—locale ... OH-6
Needham—hist pl ... VA-3
**Needham**—pop pl ... AL-4
**Needham**—pop pl ... AR-4
**Needham**—pop pl ... GA-3
**Needham**—pop pl ... IN-6
**Needham**—pop pl ... MA-1
Needham, Lake—lake ... FL-3
Needham Alford Cem—cemetery ... MS-4
Needham Assembly of God Ch—church ... AL-4
Needham Booher Ditch—canal ... IN-6
Needham Branch—stream ... TN-4
Needham Brown Cem—cemetery ... SC-3
Needham Butte—summit ... OR-9
Needham Cem—cemetery ... IL-6
Needham Cem—cemetery ... IN-6
Needham Cem—cemetery ... KS-7
Needham Cem—cemetery ... MA-1
Needham Cem—cemetery ... MO-7
Needham Cem—cemetery ... TN-4
Needham Ch—church ... AR-4
Needham Ch—church ... IN-6
**Needham Corner**—pop pl ... MA-1
Needham Corner South Memorial Sch—school ... MA-1
Needham Creek—stream ... AL-4
Needham Creek—stream ... MS-4
Needham Creek—stream ... OR-9
Needham Creek—stream ... WA-9
Needham Cumberland Ch—church ... KY-4
Needham Cutoff—bend ... AR-4
Needham Ford (historical)—crossing ... TN-4
Needham Gulch—valley ... MT-8
Needham Gulch—valley ... OR-9
Needham-Hayes House—hist pl ... MN-6
**Needham Heights (subdivision)**—pop pl ... MA-1
Needham Hill—summit ... VT-1
Needham Hill—summit ... WA-9
Needham Hole Creek—gut ... NC-3
Needham Hollow—valley ... TN-4
Needham Hosp—hospital ... WA-9
Needham House—hist pl ... NH-1
Needham House—locale ... TX-5
Needham HS—school ... MA-1
**Needham Junction (subdivision)**—pop pl ... MA-1
Needham Lake ... IN-6
Needham Lake—lake ... IN-6
Needham Lateral—canal ... ID-8
Needham Marsh Branch—stream ... TX-5
Needham Mtn—summit ... CA-9
Needham Mtn—summit ... MT-8
Needham Pond—reservoir ... MA-1
Needham Rsvr—reservoir ... MA-1
Needham Rsvr—reservoir ... OR-9
Needhams Airp—airport ... TN-4
Needham Sch—school ... CA-9
Needham Sch—school ... CO-8
Needham Sch—school ... MA-1
Needhams Corner ... MA-1
Needhams Grove Ch—church ... NC-3
Needhams Island—island ... DE-2
Needhams Mtn—summit ... NC-3
Needham Station (historical)—locale ... MA-1
Needham Street Bridge—hist pl ... MA-1
Needham Townhall—building ... MA-1
**Needham (Town of)**—pop pl ... MA-1
**Needham (Township of)**—pop pl ... IN-6
Needham Well—well ... OR-9
Need Hill—summit ... IN-6
Needle, The ... AZ-5
needle, The ... WY-8
Needle, The—island ... AK-9
Needle, The—pillar (3) ... AZ-5
Needle, The—pillar ... WA-9
Needle, The—stream ... HI-9
Needle, The—summit ... UT-8
Needle, The—summit ... WY-8
Needle Boy Lake—lake ... MN-6
Needle Branch—stream ... MO-7
Needle Branch—stream ... OR-9
Needle Butte—pillar ... MT-8
Needle Butte—summit ... ID-8
Needle Butte Rsvr—reservoir ... MT-8
Needle Camp—locale ... CA-9
Needle Canyon—valley (2) ... AZ-5
Needle Creek—stream ... AK-9
Needle Creek—stream ... AZ-5
Needle Creek—stream (2) ... CO-8
Needle Creek—stream ... ID-8
Needle Creek—stream (2) ... MT-8
Needle Creek—stream (2) ... OR-9
Needle Creek—stream (2) ... TX-5
Needle Creek—stream (2) ... WA-9
Needle Creek—stream ... WI-6
Needle Creek—stream (3) ... WY-8
Needle Creek Ditch—canal ... CO-8
Needle Creek Flat—flat ... CO-8
Needle Creek Rsvr—reservoir ... CO-8
Needle Draw—valley ... WY-8
Needle Eye—pillar ... SD-7
Needle Eye Basin—bay ... TN-4
Needle Eye Canyon—valley ... UT-8
Needle Eye Creek ... KY-4
Needle Eye Mtn—summit ... AR-4
Needle Eye Point—cape ... UT-8
Needle Eye Tunnel—tunnel ... CO-8
Needle Eye Water—spring ... UT-8
Needle Falls—falls ... MT-8
Needle Fork—stream ... OR-9
Needle Grass Spring—spring ... CA-9
Needle Grove Ch—church ... TX-5
Needle Hardpan Rsvr—reservoir ... UT-8
Needle Island—island ... NY-2
Needle Island—island ... TX-5
Needle Lake—lake ... AK-9
Needle Lake—lake ... CA-9
Needle Lake—lake ... MN-6
Needle Mtn—summit ... AK-9
Needle Mtn—summit ... AZ-5
Needle Mtn—summit ... UT-8
Needle Mtns—range ... CO-8
Needle Mtns—range ... UT-8
Needle Mtns Peak Eight—summit ... CO-8
Needle Mtns Peak Eleven—summit ... CO-8
Needle Mtns Peak Fifteen—summit ... CO-8
Needle Mtns Peak Five—summit ... CO-8
Needle Mtns Peak Four—summit ... CO-8
Needle Mtns Peak Fourteen—summit ... CO-8
Needle Mtns Peak Nine—summit ... CO-8
Needle Mtns Peak One—summit ... CO-8
Needle Mtns Peak Seven—summit ... CO-8
Needle Mtns Peak Six—summit ... CO-8
Needle Mtns Peak Sixteen—summit ... CO-8
Needle Mtns Peak Ten—summit ... CO-8
Needle Mtns Peak Thirteen—summit ... CO-8
Needle Mtns Peak Three—summit ... CO-8
Needle Mtns Peak Two—summit ... CO-8
Needle Peak—summit (2) ... AK-9
Needle Peak—summit ... AZ-5
Needle Peak—summit (2) ... CA-9
Needle Peak—summit (2) ... ID-8
Needle Peak—summit ... MT-8
Needle Peak—summit ... NV-8
Needle Peak—summit (3) ... TX-5
Needle Peak—summit ... WA-9
Needle Peak—summit ... WY-8
Needle Pinnacle—pillar ... NM-5
Needle Point ... UT-8
Needle Point—cape (2) ... MI-6
Needle Point—cape ... SC-3
Needle Point—cape ... UT-8
Needle Point—cape ... WA-9
Needle Point—other ... TX-5
Needle Point—pillar ... TX-5
Needle Point—pillar ... UT-8
Needle Point—summit ... CA-9
Needle Point—summit ... MT-8
Needle Point—summit ... OR-9
Needle Point, The—summit ... TX-5
Needle Point Mtn—summit ... UT-8
Needle Point Spring—spring ... UT-8
Needle Range ... UT-8
Needle Ridge—ridge ... CO-8
Needle Rock—island ... AK-9
Needle Rock—island ... CA-9
Needle Rock—island ... OR-9
Needle Rock—pillar ... AL-4
Needle Rock—pillar ... AK-9
Needle Rock—pillar (3) ... CO-8
Needle Rock—pillar ... NV-8
Needle Rock—pillar (2) ... OR-9
Needle Rock—pillar ... TX-5
Needle Rock—pillar ... WA-9
Needle Rock—summit (2) ... AZ-5
Needle Rock—summit ... MT-8
Needle Rock—summit ... NV-8
Needle Rock—summit ... WY-8
Needle Rock Creek ... UT-8
Needlerock Creek—stream ... CA-9
Needle Rock Ditch—canal ... CO-8
Needle Rock Point—pillar ... CA-9
Needle Rocks—summit ... OR-9
Needle Rocks, The—pillar ... NV-8
Needle Rock Spring Camp—locale ... OR-9
Needle Rsvr—reservoir ... UT-8
Needle Rsvr—reservoir ... WY-8
Needles ... AZ-5
Needles—island ... CA-9
Needles—island ... OR-9
**Needles**—pop pl ... CA-9
**Needles**—pop pl ... MO-7
Needles—summit ... ID-8
Needles, The ... AZ-5
Needles, The—area ... UT-8
Needles, The—cliff ... WY-8
Needles, The—island ... OR-9
Needles, The—other ... NM-5
Needles, The—pillar ... AZ-5
Needles, The—pillar (2) ... CO-8
Needles, The—pillar ... ID-8
Needles, The—pillar ... MN-6
Needles, The—pillar ... MT-8
Needles, The—pillar ... OR-9
Needles, The—pillar ... SD-7
Needles, The—pillar (2) ... UT-8
Needles, The—pillar ... WA-9
Needles, The—ridge ... WA-9
Needles, The—summit ... CA-9
Needles, The—summit ... MT-8
Needles, The—summit ... NV-8
Needles, The—summit ... SD-7
Needles, The—summit ... UT-8
Needles, The—summit ... WY-8
Needles Campground ... UT-8
Needles Canyon, The—valley ... UT-8
Needles Cave—cave ... ID-8
Needles (CCD)—cens area ... CA-9
Needles Country ... UT-8
Needles Country, The—area ... UT-8
Needles Creek ... WY-8
Needles Creek—stream ... OH-6
Needles Eye ... AZ-5
Needles Eye—bend ... NY-2
Needles Eye—flat ... CA-9
Needles Eye—gap (2) ... AZ-5
Needles Eye—gap ... AR-4
Needles Eye—gap ... VT-1
Needles Eye—summit ... AZ-5
Needles Eye—summit ... NM-5
Needles Eye Butte—summit ... WY-8
Needles Eye Creek—stream ... SC-3
Needles Eye Mtn—summit ... AR-4
Needle Shop Brook—stream ... NH-1
Needles Outpost ... UT-8
Needles Outpost Campground—park ... UT-8
Needles Overlook ... UT-8
Needles Overlook, The—locale ... UT-8
Needle Spring—spring ... MT-8
Needles Ranger Station, The—locale ... UT-8
Needles Rec Area—park ... CA-9
Needles Spring—spring ... NV-8
Needles Summit—summit ... ID-8
Needles Trail—trail ... ID-8
Needleton—locale ... CO-8
Needleton Water Tank—other ... CO-8
Needle Trail—trail ... AZ-5
Needle Valley—valley ... AZ-5
Needmor ... AR-4
Needmore ... AL-4
Needmore ... IN-6
Needmore ... KY-4
Needmore ... MO-7
Needmore ... TN-4
Needmore—locale (2) ... AL-4
Needmore—locale ... AR-4
Needmore—locale ... GA-3
Needmore—locale (4) ... KY-4
Needmore—locale (2) ... NC-3
Needmore—locale ... OK-5
Needmore—locale ... TN-4
Needmore—locale (3) ... TX-5
Needmore—locale ... WV-2
**Needmore**—pop pl (3) ... AL-4
**Needmore**—pop pl ... AR-4
**Needmore**—pop pl ... FL-3
**Needmore**—pop pl ... GA-3
**Needmore**—pop pl (3) ... IN-6
**Needmore**—pop pl (3) ... KY-4
**Needmore**—pop pl ... MI-6
**Needmore**—pop pl (2) ... MO-7
**Needmore**—pop pl (2) ... NC-3
**Needmore**—pop pl (2) ... OH-6
**Needmore**—pop pl ... PA-2
**Needmore**—pop pl (4) ... TN-4
**Needmore**—pop pl ... TX-5
**Needmore**—pop pl ... VA-3
Needmore Branch—stream ... KY-4
Needmore Branch—stream ... NC-3
Needmore Branch—stream ... TN-4
Needmore (CCD)—cens area ... AL-4
Needmore Cem—cemetery ... AL-4
Needmore Cem—cemetery ... AR-4
Needmore Cem—cemetery ... GA-3
Needmore Cem—cemetery (2) ... KY-4
Needmore Cem—cemetery ... MS-4
Needmore Cem—cemetery ... SC-3
Needmore Cem—cemetery (2) ... TN-4
Needmore Cem—cemetery ... TX-5
Needmore Cemetery ... MO-7
Needmore Ch ... MO-7
Needmore Ch—church ... AL-4
Needmore Ch—church ... KY-4
Needmore Ch—church (2) ... MO-7
Needmore Ch—church (3) ... TN-4
Needmore Ch—church ... WV-2
Needmore Creek—stream ... TN-4
Needmore Creek—stream ... TX-5
Needmore Division—civil ... AL-4
Needmore Elem Sch—school ... IN-6
Needmore Hill—summit ... MO-7
Needmore Hill—summit ... TN-4
Needmore (historical)—locale ... AL-4
**Needmore (historical)**—pop pl ... IN-6
**Needmore (historical)**—pop pl ... MS-4
Needmore Hollow—valley ... KY-4
Needmore Hollow—valley ... MO-7
Needmore Mine (underground)—mine ... AL-4
Needmore Mission—church ... MO-7
Needmore Point—cape ... FL-3
Needmore Pond—lake ... FL-3
Needmore Post Office (historical)—building ... AL-4
Needmore Sch—school ... KY-4
Needmore Sch—school ... MO-7
Needmore Sch—school (2) ... NE-7
Needmore Sch—school (2) ... TN-4
Needmore Sch (historical)—school ... AL-4
Needmore Sch (historical)—school ... TN-4
Needmore Spring—spring ... AL-4
Needmore Tank—reservoir ... AZ-5
Needmore Tank—reservoir ... NM-5
Needmore Wash—stream ... AZ-5
Needs Creek—stream ... AR-4
Needs Creek Ch—church ... AR-4
Needstan Creek—stream ... VA-3
Need Tank—reservoir ... AZ-5
Needum Creek ... AL-4
**Needville**—pop pl ... TX-5
Needville (CCD)—cens area ... TX-5
Needville HS—school ... TX-5
Needville Oil Field—oilfield ... TX-5
Need Water Rsvr—reservoir ... WY-8
**Needwood**—pop pl ... VA-3
Needwood Cem—cemetery ... TX-5
Needwood Ch—church ... GA-3
**Needwood Estates**—pop pl ... MD-2
**Needy**—pop pl ... OR-9
Needy Creek ... TX-5
Needy Creek—stream ... GA-3
N'eef—locale ... FM-9
Neef, Frederick W., House—hist pl ... CO-8
Neefewuwimw ... FM-9
Neefsville ... PA-2
Neegronda Rsvr—reservoir ... CO-8
Neejeepojesuc Ponds ... MA-1
Neejer Hill—summit ... NY-2
Neekequaw Pond ... RI-1
Neekequawse Pond ... RI-1
Neel—locale ... OH-6
Neel—locale ... FM-9
**Neel**—pop pl ... AL-4
Neel Airp—airport ... KS-7
Neelands Cem—cemetery ... KS-7
Neel Branch ... AL-4
Neel Branch—stream ... VA-3
Neel Cem—cemetery ... GA-3
Neel Cem—cemetery ... TN-4
Neel Ch—church ... AL-4
Neel Chapel Cem—cemetery ... TN-4
Neel Creek ... MT-8
Neel Creek—stream ... AL-4
Neel Creek—stream ... GA-3
Neeld Ditch—canal ... IN-6
**Neeld Estates**—pop pl ... MD-2
Neele Branch—stream ... IA-7
Neel Elem Sch—school ... AL-4
**Neeley**—pop pl ... ID-8
**Neeley**—pop pl ... MI-6
Neeley Basin—basin ... UT-8
Neeley Branch—stream (2) ... AL-4
Neeley Branch—stream ... KY-4
Neeley Branch—stream ... MS-4
Neeley Cem—cemetery ... GA-3
Neeley Cem—cemetery ... ID-8
Neeley Cem—cemetery ... IN-6
Neeley Cem—cemetery ... MO-7
Neeley Cem—cemetery (2) ... TN-4
Neeley Cem—cemetery ... TX-5
Neeley Chapel—church ... MS-4
Neeley Cove—bay ... ID-8
Neeley Creek ... TN-4
Neeley Creek—stream ... AL-4
Neeley Creek—stream ... IA-7
Neeley Creek—stream ... TX-5
Neeley Ditch—canal ... UT-8
Neeley Hill—summit ... CA-9
Neeley Hollow—valley ... TN-4
Neeley Point—cape ... AL-4
Neeleys Chapel Ch—church ... AL-4
Neeleys Creek ... AL-4
Neeleys Ferry—locale ... KY-4
Neeley Valley—valley ... TN-4
**Neeleyville**—pop pl ... MO-7
Neeleyville Cem—cemetery ... MO-7
Neeleyville Ditch—canal ... MO-7
Neel Gap ... GA-3
Neel Hollow—valley ... UT-8
Neel Lee Gillis Bridge—bridge ... GA-3
Neelle Lake—lake ... CA-9
Neel Post Office (historical)—building ... AL-4
Neel Run—stream ... PA-2
Neels—locale ... UT-8
Neels Creek—stream ... GA-3
Neels Ferry—locale ... MS-4
Neels Gap—locale ... GA-3
Neels Rsvr No 2—reservoir ... UT-8
Neels Sch—school ... PA-2
Neelsville—locale ... MD-2
Neely ... ID-8
**Neely**—pop pl ... AL-4
**Neely**—pop pl ... MS-4
**Neely**—pop pl ... TN-4
Neely, Aaron, Sr., Mansion—hist pl ... WA-9
Neely, John, House—hist pl ... TN-4
Neely Arroyo—valley ... TX-5
Neely Baptist Ch—church ... MS-4
Neely Branch—stream ... AL-4
Neely Branch—stream (3) ... KY-4
Neely Branch—stream ... MS-4
Neely Branch—stream (2) ... TN-4
Neely Branch—stream ... WV-2
Neely Canyon ... TX-5
Neely Cave—cave ... TN-4
Neely Cem ... MS-4
Neely Cem ... TN-4
Neely Cem—cemetery (2) ... MS-4
Neely Cem—cemetery (4) ... TN-4
Neely Chapel—church ... TN-4
Neely Chapel Cem—cemetery ... TN-4
Neely Creek—stream ... AR-4
Neely Creek—stream ... IL-6
Neely Creek—stream ... MS-4
Neely Creek—stream ... OR-9
Neely Creek—stream ... TN-4
Neely Crossroads—locale ... TN-4
Neely Crossroads Ch of Christ—church ... TN-4
Neely Flat Cem—cemetery ... NE-7
Neely Gap—gap ... KY-4
Neely Gap Sch—school ... KY-4
Neely Henry Lake ... AL-4
Neely Hollow—valley ... AR-4
Neely Hollow—valley ... WV-2
Neely Island—island ... OH-6
Neely Landing ... MO-7
Neely Mine—mine ... TN-4
Neely Mtn—summit ... OK-5
Neely Mtn—summit ... OR-9
**Neely (New Neely)**—pop pl ... AR-4
Neely Plantation (historical)—locale ... MS-4
Neely Ranch—locale ... TX-5
Neelys ... MO-7
Neelys ... TN-4
**Neelys**—pop pl ... IL-6
Neelys Bend—bend ... TN-4
Neelys Bend Ch—church ... TN-4
Neelys Bend JHS—school ... TN-4
Neelys Bend Sch—school ... TN-4
Neelys Camp—locale ... MT-8
Neelys Cem—cemetery ... KY-4
Neely Sch—school ... MO-7
Neely Sch—school ... OH-6
Neely Sch—school ... SD-7
Neely Sch—school ... TN-4
Neelys Chapel Cemetery ... TN-4
Neelys Chapel (historical)—church ... TN-4
Neelys Schoolhouse (historical)—school ... PA-2
Neelys Creek—stream ... KY-4
Neelys Creek—stream ... MO-7
Neelys Creek—stream ... SC-3
Neelys Creek Ch—church ... KY-4
Neelys Creek Ch—church ... SC-3
Neelys Cross Roads ... TN-4

Neelys Cross Roads Sch (historical)—school TN-4
Neely-Sieber House—hist pl OH-6
Neely Site 41 RR 48—hist pl TX-5
Neelys Lake—lake AR-4
Neelys Lake—reservoir GA-3
**Neelys Landing**—pop pl MO-7
Neelys Mill TN-4
**Neelys (Neelys Landing)**—pop pl MO-7
Neelys Post Office (historical)—building TN-4
Neely Spring—spring AZ-5
Neely Spring Branch—stream TX-5
Neelysville—locale OH-6
Neelysville Sch—school OH-6
Neely Tank—reservoir TX-5
**Neelyton**—pop pl PA-2
Neelytown—locale NY-2
Neely Township—civil MO-7
**Neelyville**—pop pl MO-7
**Neelyville Post Office (Neely Station)**—pop pl IL-6
Neeman Sch—school SD-7
Neemas FM-9
Neemwonon FM-9
**Neenach**—pop pl CA-9
Neenach Sch—school CA-9
Neenach Substation—other CA-9
Neenah—locale AL-4
Neenah—locale VA-3
**Neenah**—pop pl WI-6
Neenah Channel—channel WI-6
Neenah Creek—stream WI-6
Neenah Lake—lake WI-6
Neenah Point—cape WI-6
**Neenah (Town of)**—pop pl WI-6
Neenan Mine—mine MT-8
Nee-Nee-Oke-Pi-Yah KS-7
Neenomw FM-9
Neenoshe Rsvr—reservoir CO-8
Nee Ozho River KS-7
Neepaulin, Lake—lake NJ-2
Neeper—locale MO-7
Neepiinomw FM-9
Neepikon Falls—falls MI-6
Neepwon FM-9
Neepwononog FM-9
Neer City Cem—cemetery OR-9
**Neer City (historical)**—pop pl OR-9
Neer City Sch—school OR-9
Neer Creek—stream OR-9
Neergaard Cem—cemetery TN-4
Neersville—locale VA-3
Neesaraw FM-9
Neese—locale GA-3
Neese, Elbert, House—hist pl WI-6
Neese, William, Sr., Homestead—hist pl TX-5
Neese Cem—cemetery (2) IL-6
Neese Cem—cemetery IN-6
Neese Ditch—canal IN-6
Neeseponsett Pond MA-1
Neesepogesuck Ponds MA-1
Neesepogesuck Ponds Wrights Ponds MA-1
Neeseponset Pond MA-1
Neeseponsett Pond—lake MA-1
Neese Ridge—ridge CA-9
**Neeses**—pop pl SC-3
Neeses (CCD)—cens area SC-3
Neese Sch (abandoned)—school MO-7
**Neeses (corporate name for Neeces)**—pop pl SC-3
Neeses Fire Tower—locale SC-3
Neeses Lake—lake SC-3
Neesh Lake—lake MN-6
Neeskah Rsvr—reservoir CO-8
Neeskara Sch—school WI-6
Neesmith School AL-4
Neesopah Rsvr—reservoir CO-8
Neessen, Chris, House—hist pl IA-7
Neet Bridge—hist pl IN-6
Neet Covered Bridge—bridge IN-6
Neet Lake—lake OR-9
Neets Bay—bay AK-9
Neets Creek—stream AK-9
Neets Lake—lake AK-9
Neetus Gulch—valley CA-9
Neetuutu FM-9
Neeves Creek—stream OR-9
Ne Ew—well FM-9
Neewen FM-9
Neewin Lake—lake MN-6
Neewoc FM-9
Neewoomas FM-9
Neeworoor FM-9
Neeye Mine—mine AZ-5
Neeyewut FM-9
Neezar Gut—gut NC-3
N'ef FM-9
Nefalil—locale FM-9
Nefalil, Foko—reef FM-9
Nefalil, Lulu—lagoon FM-9
Nefat—bar FM-9
Nefetin—spring FM-9
Neff—locale AZ-5
Neff—locale PA-2
Neff—locale VA-3
**Neff**—pop pl OK-5
Neff, Conrad, House—hist pl OH-6
Neff, Edward E., House—hist pl OH-6
Neff, Maj. John, Homestead—hist pl PA-2
Neff Apartments—hist pl OH-6
Neff Cem—cemetery IN-6
Neff Cem—cemetery KY-4
Neff Cem—cemetery MD-2
Neff Cem—cemetery OH-6
Neff Cem—cemetery PA-2
Neff Cem—cemetery VA-3
**Neff Corner**—pop pl IN-6
Neff Creek—stream ID-8
Neff Ditch—canal (2) IN-6
Neff Ditch—canal WY-8
Neff Elem Sch—school PA-2
Neff Fish Camp—camp FL-3
Neff Fork—stream WV-2
Neff Hill—summit CT-1
Neff Hill—summit NY-2
Neff HS—school CA-9
Neff Lake—lake CO-8
Neff Lake—lake FL-3
Neff Lake—lake MI-6
Neff Lake—lake MN-6
Neff Mtn—summit CO-8
Neff Park—flat WY-8
Neff Park—park CA-9
Neff Ranch—locale WA-9
Neff Ranch—locale WY-8
Neff Ridge—ridge OH-6
Neff Round Barn—hist pl PA-2
Neff Rsvr—reservoir UT-8
Neff Rsvr—reservoir (2) WY-8
Neff Run—stream MD-2
Neffs OK-5
Neffs—locale WV-2
**Neffs**—pop pl OH-6
**Neffs**—pop pl PA-2
Neffs Camp—locale CA-9
Neffs Canyon—valley UT-8
Neff Sch—school MI-6
Neff Sch (abandoned)—school PA-2
Neffs Dam—dam UT-8
Neffs Gulch—valley CO-8
Neffs Lake—lake IL-6
Neff's Mill Covered Bridge—hist pl PA-2
**Neffs Mills**—pop pl PA-2
Neffs Park—park PA-2
Neff Spring—spring CO-8
Neffs Reservoir UT-8
Neffs Rsvr—reservoir UT-8
Neffs Run—stream OH-6
Neffs Spring—spring (2) UT-8
Neffsville PA-2
**Neffsville**—pop pl PA-2
Neff Tavern Smokehouse—hist pl MO-7
Neff Train Stop (historical)—building TX-5
Nefin—summit FM-9
Nefin—well FM-9
Nefis—well FM-9
Nefonmourunong—spring FM-9
Nefor—bar FM-9
Nefou—spring FM-9
Nefou, Unun En—bar FM-9
Nefoundland Dike—levee UT-8
Nefounimos—spring FM-9
Nefoupuech—cape FM-9
Nefouto—spring FM-9
Nefouweis—bar FM-9
Nefsy Divide—ridge WY-8
Nefsy Draw—valley WY-8
Neftin—spring FM-9
Nefure Hollow—valley PA-2
**Negangards Corner**—pop pl IN-6
Negani Lake—lake WI-6
**Negaunee**—pop pl MI-6
Negaunee Cem—cemetery MI-6
Negaunee Lake—lake MI-6
Negaunee Mine—mine MI-6
Negaunee Sch—school MI-6
**Negaunee (Township of)**—pop pl MI-6
Negelin Rim AZ-5
Negely Dam—dam PA-2
Negilik Site—hist pl AK-9
Negisticook Creek WA-9
Negit Island—island CA-9
Negit Lake—lake CA-9
Neglar Spring—spring WV-2
Neglected Mine—mine CO-8
Neglected Mine—mine NM-5
Neglected Mine—mine WA-9
**Negley**—pop pl OH-6
**Negley**—pop pl TX-5
Negley Lookout Tower—locale TX-5
Negley Pond—reservoir PA-2
Negley Post Office—locale TX-5
Negley Ranch—locale WY-8
Neglie Creek—stream IN-6
Neglige Lake—lake MN-6
Neglin Rim AZ-5
Negly Park—park PA-2
Negotsena Creek—stream AK-9
Negra—locale NM-5
Negracka River KS-7
Negras Tank—reservoir TX-5
Negreet—locale LA-4
Negreet, Bayou—stream LA-4
Negreet Creek—stream LA-4
Negresse, Bay—lake LA-4
Negrita Tank, La—reservoir AZ-5
Negrito—locale PR-3
Negrito Creek—stream NM-5
Negrito Mtn—summit NM-5
Negrito Pasture Tank—reservoir NM-5
Negrito Spring—spring NM-5
Negrito Springs—spring NM-5
Negro, Arroyo—stream TX-5
Negro, Cerro—summit AZ-5
Negro, Mar—lake PR-3
Negro Abes—locale NV-8
Negro Andy Canyon—valley NM-5
Negro Arroyo—valley TX-5
Negro Arroyo Creek TX-5
Negro Baby Creek—stream WY-8
Negro Bar—bar CA-9
Negro Bar Channel—channel NY-2
Negro Bar Creek—stream CA-9
Negro Basin—basin CO-8
Negro Bay—bay AL-4
Negro Bay—bay NC-3
**Negro Bay**—pop pl VI-3
Negro Bayou—gut (2) LA-4
Negro Bayou—stream AL-4
Negro Bend—bend MO-7
Negro Bend—bend TN-4
Negro Bend—bend TX-5
Negro Bend—locale OK-5
Negro Bend Bluff—cliff MO-7
Negro Bend Spring—spring CA-9
Negro Ben Mtn—summit OR-9
Negro Ben Peak—summit AZ-5
Negro Ben Spring—spring AZ-5
Negro Bill Canyon—valley UT-8
Negro Bill Gulch ID-8
Negro Bill Gulch—valley ID-8
Negro Bill Point—cape AR-4
Negro Bill Spring—spring NM-5
Negro Bob Well—well NM-5
Negro Bottom—bend TN-4
Negro Boy Mine—mine CA-9
Negro Branch AL-4
Negro Branch—stream (4) AR-4
Negro Branch—stream (2) GA-3
Negro Branch—stream (3) KY-4
Negro Branch—stream NE-7
Negro Branch—stream OK-5
Negro Branch—stream SC-3
Negro Branch—stream (2) TN-4
Negro Branch—stream TX-5
Negro Branch—stream VA-3
Negro Branch—stream WV-2
Negro Brook ME-1
Negro Brook—stream CT-1
Negro Brook—stream ME-1
Negro Brook—stream (4) NY-2
Negro Brook—stream VT-1
Negro Brook Lakes ME-1
Negro Brown Canyon—valley OR-9
Negro Butte—summit CA-9
Negro Butte—summit WY-8
Negro Cabin Branch—stream KY-4
Negro Cabin Branch—stream LA-4
Negro Camp Branch—stream VA-3
Negro Camp Fork—stream KY-4
Negro Camp Gulch—valley CA-9
Negro Camp Island—island FL-3
Negro Camp Island—island GA-3
Negro Camp Mtn—summit CA-9
Negro Camp (Ruins)—locale CA-9
Negro Camp Run—stream WV-2
Negro Camp Spring—spring CA-9
Negro Canyon—valley (3) AZ-5
Negro Canyon—valley (2) CA-9
Negro Canyon—valley (2) CO-8
Negro Canyon—valley (7) NM-5
Negro Canyon—valley SD-7
Negro Church Branch—stream AL-4
Negro Clearing Trail—trail PA-2
Negro Coulee—valley MT-8
Negro Cove—bay FL-3
Negro Cove—bay MD-2
Negro Creek MI-6
Negro Creek OK-5
Negro Creek TX-5
Negro Creek WA-9
Negro Creek—bay NC-3
Negro Creek—stream (2) AL-4
Negro Creek—stream AK-9
Negro Creek—stream AR-4
Negro Creek—stream (4) CA-9
Negro Creek—stream (2) CO-8
Negro Creek—stream (3) ID-8
Negro Creek—stream (3) IL-6
Negro Creek—stream (2) IN-6
Negro Creek—stream IA-7
Negro Creek—stream (5) KS-7
Negro Creek—stream (4) KY-4
Negro Creek—stream (2) MI-6
Negro Creek—stream MO-7
Negro Creek—stream (2) NV-8
Negro Creek—stream NJ-2
Negro Creek—stream NY-2
Negro Creek—stream (2) NC-3
Negro Creek—stream OH-6
Negro Creek—stream (9) OK-5
Negro Creek—stream (3) OR-9
Negro Creek—stream (3) SD-7
Negro Creek—stream (2) TN-4
Negro Creek—stream (6) TX-5
Negro Creek—stream VA-3
Negro Creek—stream (3) WA-9
Negro Creek—stream (6) WY-8
Negro Creek Administrative Site—locale NV-8
Negro Creek Canyon—valley CA-9
Negro Creek Cem—cemetery KY-4
Negro Creek Oil Field—oilfield KS-7
Negro Creek Park—flat WY-8
Negro Creek Ranch—locale NV-8
Negro Creek Sch—school KY-4
Negro Creek Sch—school SD-7
Negro Crossing—locale TX-5
**Negro Crossroads**—pop pl MS-4
Negro Cut—gut FL-3
Negro Dan Hollow—valley UT-8
Negro Dan Spring—spring UT-8
Negro Den Creek—stream TN-4
Negro Den Hollow—valley VA-3
Negro Ditch—canal IN-6
Negro Draw—valley CO-8
Negro Draw—valley MT-8
Negro Draw—valley WY-8
Negro Ed—summit AZ-5
Negroedge Canyon—valley SD-7
Negro Ed Spring—spring AZ-5
Negro Field Branch—stream SC-3
Negro Flat—flat AZ-5
Negro Flat—flat OR-9
Negro Flat Tank—reservoir AZ-5
Negro Foot—locale VA-3
Negro Foot Bayou—stream LA-4
Negrofoot Branch—stream AL-4
Negro Fork OK-5
Negro Fork—stream KY-4
Negro Fork—stream SC-3
Negro Fork Rsvr—reservoir SC-3
Negro Fort FL-3
Negro Gap—gap PA-2
Negro Gap—gap TX-5
Negro George Draw—valley NV-8
Negro Glade Run PA-2
Negro Grave Hollow—valley TN-4
Negro Graveyard—cemetery AL-4
Negro Green Creek—stream ID-8
Negro Grove Hollow TN-4
Negro Gulch—valley (3) CA-9
Negro Gulch—valley (3) CO-8
Negro Gulch—valley ID-8
Negro Gulch—valley MT-8
Negro Gulch—valley OR-9
Negro Gulch—valley SD-7
Negro Gulch—valley WY-8
**Negro Gull (historical)**—pop pl TN-4
Negro Gully—valley TX-5
Negro Hammock—island LA-4
Negro Head ID-8
Negro Head—cape FL-3
Negro Head—cliff AK-9
Negrohead—summit (2) AZ-5
Negro Head—summit (2) CA-9
Negrohead—summit NM-5
Negrohead—summit TX-5
Negro Head—summit TX-5
Negrohead—summit TX-5
Negrohead, The (historical)—island AL-4
Negrohead Bluff—cliff TX-5
Negro Head Branch—stream GA-3
Negrohead Butte—summit (2) NM-5
**Negro Head Corner**—pop pl AR-4
Negrohead Creek CA-9
Negrohead Creek NC-3
Negrohead Creek—stream AK-9
Negrohead Fork—stream WY-8
Negrohead Lake—lake NE-7
Negrohead Lake—lake TX-5
Negrohead Mtn—summit AK-9
Negrohead Point—cape FL-3
Negrohead Point—cape NY-2
Negro Head Rapids—rapids ID-8
Negro Head Rapids—rapids WA-9
Negro Head Rock—pillar VA-3
Negro Head Slough—stream AR-4
Negro Head Spring—spring AZ-5
Negrohead Well—well NM-5
Negro Heel Bar—bar AL-4
Negroheel Butte—summit OR-9
Negro Heel Lake—lake WI-6
Negro Henry Canyon—valley AZ-5
Negro Henry Hollow—valley MO-7
Negro Hill—locale CA-9
Negro Hill—ridge AR-4
Negro Hill—summit (3) AR-4
Negro Hill—summit (3) CA-9
Negro Hill—summit CO-8
Negro Hill—summit (2) KY-4
Negro Hill—summit (2) ME-1
Negro Hill—summit MO-7
Negro Hill—summit NM-5
Negro Hill—summit (7) NY-2
Negro Hill—summit NC-3
Negro Hill—summit OK-5
Negro Hill—summit SD-7
Negro Hill—summit TN-4
Negro Hill—summit (2) TX-5
Negro Hill—summit WI-6
Negro Hill—summit (2) WY-8
Negro Hill Brook—stream CT-1
Negro Hill Ch—church AR-4
Negro Hills SD-7
Negro Hills—other OK-5
Negro Hollow—valley AL-4
Negro Hollow—valley IL-6
Negro Hollow—valley KS-7
Negro Hollow—valley (6) KY-4
Negro Hollow—valley MO-7
Negro Hollow—valley MT-8
Negro Hollow—valley (3) NY-2
Negro Hollow—valley OK-5
Negro Hollow—valley OR-9
Negro Hollow—valley (5) PA-2
Negro Hollow—valley (12) TN-4
Negro Hollow—valley (3) TX-5
Negro Hollow—valley (2) UT-8
Negro Hollow—valley (2) VA-3
Negro Hollow—valley WV-2
Negro Hollow Branch—stream TN-4
Negro Hollow Ch—church NY-2
Negro Hollow Run—stream PA-2
Negro Island ME-1
Negro Island—island DE-2
Negro Island—island (2) FL-3
Negro Island—island GA-3
Negro Island—island LA-4
Negro Island—island (3) ME-1
Negro Island—island MD-2
Negro Island—island TN-4
Negro Island Gut—stream MD-2
Negro Island Ledge—bar ME-1
Negro Jack Gulch—valley CA-9
Negro Jack Hill—summit CA-9
Negro Jack Point—cliff CA-9
Negro Jake Hollow—valley OK-5
Negro Jim Gulch ID-8
Negro Jim Gulch—valley ID-8
Negro Jim Hammock Bridge—bridge FL-3
Negro Jim Scrub—woods FL-3
Negro Joe Draw—valley WY-8
Negro Joe Ridge—ridge CA-9
Negro Jumpoff—cliff TN-4
Negro Knob—summit AZ-5
Negro Knob—summit AR-4
Negro Knob—summit KY-4
Negro Knob—summit OR-9
Negro Knob Trail—trail OR-9
Negro Lagoon—lake LA-4
Negro Lake—lake AL-4
Negro Lake—lake AK-9
Negro Lake—lake FL-3
Negro Lake—lake IL-6
Negro Lake—lake MN-6
Negro Lake—lake NE-7
Negro Lake—lake NY-2
Negro Lake—lake TX-5
Negro Lake—reservoir LA-4
Negro Lake—swamp NY-2
Negro Lake Run—stream SC-3
Negro Lakes—lake WI-6
Negro Ledge—bar MA-1
Negro Lick—stream IL-6
Negro Liza Wash—valley UT-8
Negro Mag Wash—valley UT-8
Negro Marsh—swamp NY-2
Negro Marsh—swamp TX-5
Negro Mesa—summit CO-8
Negro Mesa—summit NM-5
Negro Mine AL-4
Negro Mountain WA-9
Negro Mountain Cem—cemetery AL-4
Negro Mountain Cem—cemetery MD-2
Negro Mountain Ch—church MD-2
Negro Mtn PA-2
Negro Mtn—range MD-2
Negro Mtn—range PA-2
Negro Mtn—summit (3) AL-4
Negro Mtn—summit AR-4
Negro Mtn—summit CA-9
Negro Mtn—summit (2) MT-8
Negro Mtn—summit NC-3
Negro Mtn—summit OK-5
Negro Mtn—summit PA-2
Negro Mtn—summit (2) TN-4
Negro Park—flat CO-8
Negro Peak—summit CA-9
Negro Peak—summit ID-8
Negro Point MS-4
Negro Point—cape LA-4
Negro Point—cape ME-1
Negro Point—cape NY-2
Negro Point—cape VA-3
Negro Pond FL-3
Negro Pond NJ-2
Negro Pond NY-2
Negro Pond—lake FL-3
Negro Pond—lake MA-1
Negro Pond—lake VT-1
Negro Pond—reservoir PA-2
Negro Pond—swamp TX-5
Negro Pond Dam—dam PA-2
Negro Pond (historical)—lake AL-4
Negro Pond Lake PA-2
Negro Prong—stream NC-3
Negro Ravine—valley NV-8
Negro Ridge CA-9
Negro Ridge—ridge MS-4
Negro Ridge—ridge OR-9
Negro Ridge—ridge (6) TN-4
Negro Ridge—summit OR-9
Negro Ridge Mine—mine TN-4
Negro Rock—pillar OR-9
Negro Rock—summit OR-9
Negro Rock Canyon—valley OR-9
Negro Rock Rsvr—reservoir OR-9
Negrorow Branch—stream KY-4
Negro Rube Creek CA-9
Negro Run—stream NJ-2
Negro Run—stream (3) OH-6
Negro Run—stream PA-2
Negro Run—stream (3) VA-3
Negro Run—stream WV-2
Negro Run Ravine—valley CA-9
Negro Saddle Tank—reservoir NM-5
Negro Sam Slough—stream CA-9
Negro Sandy Creek—stream OK-5
Negro Sawmill Brook—stream RI-1
Negros (Barrio)—fmr MCD PR-3
Negro Shack Mine—mine NM-5
Negro Shanty Hollow—valley TN-4
**Negros Liberty Settlement**—pop pl TX-5
Negro Slough—gut WA-9
Negro Slough—lake MO-7
Negro Slough—stream AL-4
Negros Mine—mine MT-8
Negro Spring—spring (2) AZ-5
Negro Spring—spring CA-9
Negro Spring—spring CO-8
Negro Spring—spring OK-5
Negro Spring No 1—spring CO-8
Negro Spring No 2—spring CO-8
Negro Spring Salt Well—well IL-6
Negro Springs Camp (historical)—locale MO-7
Negro Tank AZ-5
Negro Tank—reservoir (2) AZ-5
Negro Tank—reservoir NM-5
Negro Tank—reservoir (2) TX-5
Negrotown Branch—stream TN-4
**Negrotown Knoll**—pop pl FL-3
Negrotown Marsh—swamp FL-3
Negro Valley CA-9
Negro Wash—stream AZ-5
Negro Well—well AZ-5
Negro Wool Ridge—ridge SD-7
Negukthlik River—stream AK-9
Neguntatogue Creek—stream NY-2
Negus Brook—stream VT-1
Negus Drain—canal MI-6
Negus Mtn—summit MA-1
Negus Playground—locale MA-1
Negus Run PA-2
Neh—unknown FM-9
Neh, Pilen—stream FM-9
**Nehalem**—pop pl OR-9
Nehalem Bay—bay OR-9
Nehalem Bay State Airp—airport OR-9
Nehalem Bay State Park—park OR-9
Nehalem Beach—beach OR-9
Nehalem (CCD)—cens area OR-9
**Nehalem Fall (historical)**—pop pl OR-9
Nehalem Falls—falls OR-9
Nehalem Falls Creek OR-9
Nehalem Fish Hatchery—other OR-9
Nehalem Junction—locale OR-9
Nehalem River—stream OR-9
Nehalem Spit—bar OR-9
Nehalem Valley—valley OR-9
Nehantic State For—forest CT-1
Nehasane—locale NY-2
Nehasane Lake—lake NY-2
Nehaunsey Branch NJ-2
Nehausey Brook NJ-2
Nehawoski Spring—spring OK-5
**Nehawka**—pop pl NE-7
Nehawka Flint Quarries—hist pl NE-7
Neheb—locale FL-3
Nehemoosha AL-4
Nehenta Bay—bay AK-9
Nehe Point—cape HI-9
Nehi FL-3
Ne Hi Canyon—valley CA-9
Nehi Creek—stream OR-9
Nehmabin Lake WI-6
Nehmer Lake—lake MI-6
Ne-hoi-al-pit-kwu WA-9
Nehonsey Brook—stream NJ-2
Nehouse Creek—stream CA-9
Nehr Canyon—valley CA-9
Nehring Cem—cemetery KS-7
Nehring Creek—stream KS-7
Nehring Sch (abandoned)—school ND-7
Nehrt Ditch—canal IN-6
Nehumkeag—locale ME-1
Nehumkeag Brook ME-1
Nehumkeag Pond—lake ME-1
Nehumkek MA-1
Nehu Playground—park HI-9
Nei FM-9
Neiamon FM-9
Neiam Sch—school PA-2
Ne-i-ash-i Point—cape MN-6
Neiber Draw—valley WY-8
Neiber Pulliam Station—locale WY-8
Neiber Swamp—swamp NY-2
**Neibert**—pop pl WV-2
Neibert-Fisk House—hist pl MS-4
Neiburr Sch—school IL-6
Neicy Slash—stream AR-4
Neiderer Airp—airport PA-2
Neiderworder Dam—dam SD-7
Neidig Ch—church PA-2
Neidigk Lake—lake TX-5
Neiding Park—park OH-6
Neiding Swamp—swamp NY-2
Neidlinger Cem—cemetery IN-6
**Neier**—pop pl MO-7
Neifert Creek—stream PA-2
Neifert Creek Dam—dam PA-2
Neifert Creek Impoundment—reservoir PA-2
Neiffer—locale PA-2
Neigebaur Sch—school MI-6
Neiger Sch (abandoned)—school MO-7
Neigharts Run PA-2
Neighbor Branch TN-4
Neighborhood Canyon—valley AZ-5
Neighborhood Cem—cemetery AZ-5
Neighborhood Ch—church AL-4
Neighborhood Ch—church FL-3
Neighborhood Ch—church NM-5
Neighborhood Chapel Ch of God—church AL-4
Neighborhood Ch of the Advent—church AL-4
Neighborhood Drain—canal MI-6
Neighborhood Gardens Apartments—hist pl MO-7
Neighborhood House—hist pl OR-9
Neighborhood House of Prayer Ch—church AL-4
Neighborhood Lakes—swamp FL-3
Neighborhoood Alliance Ch—church FL-3
Neighbor Lake—lake MI-6
Neighbor Mountain, The VA-3
Neighbor Mtn—summit VA-3
Neighbors—locale CA-9
Neighbors Branch—stream NC-3
Neighbors Branch—stream TN-4
Neighbors Cem—cemetery AR-4
Neighbors Creek TN-4
Neighbors Crossroads—locale SC-3
Neighbors Grove Ch—church NC-3
Neighbors Hollow—valley AL-4
**Neighbors Mill**—pop pl AL-4
Neighbor Spring—spring AZ-5
Neighbortown OH-6
Neighbor Trail—trail VA-3
Neigh Branch—stream MS-4
Neighorn Creek—stream MO-7
Neiglick Creek—stream OR-9
Neihardt, John G., Study—hist pl NE-7
**Neihart**—pop pl MT-8
Neihart Baldy—summit MT-8
Neihart Cem—cemetery IN-6
Neihart Cem—cemetery MT-8
Neihart Rsvr—reservoir MT-8
Neiharts PA-2
Neiis Creek NC-3
Neikiniaw FM-9
Neil—locale MS-4
Neil—locale TN-4
**Neil**—pop pl CA-9
Neil A Armstrong JHS—school PA-2
Neil A Armstrong MS—school PA-2
Neil Armstrong Elem Sch—school FL-3
Neil Armstrong JHS—school OR-9
Neil Armstrong Sch—school NY-2
Neil Bell Monmt—pillar WY-8
Neil Beyer Dam—dam OR-9
Neil Beyer Rsvr—reservoir OR-9
Neil Branch TN-4
Neil Branch—stream MS-4
Neil Branch—stream WV-2
Neil Butte—summit WY-8
Neil Canyon—valley OR-9
Neil Cem—cemetery MO-7
Neil Cem—cemetery (2) TN-4
Neil Church MS-4
Neil Corner—locale PA-2
Neil Creek AL-4
Neil Creek NY-2
Neil Creek—stream MT-8
Neil Creek—stream NV-8
Neil Creek—stream (5) OR-9
Neil Creek—stream UT-8
Neil Creek—stream WA-9
Neil Ditch—stream TN-4
Neild Ranch—locale MT-8
Neil Fisher Cave—cave IN-4
Neil Gap—gap NC-3
Neil Gap—gap TN-4
Neil Gap Branch—stream NC-3
Neil Hill—summit MS-4
Neil Hollow—valley KY-4
Neilhurst—locale FL-3
Neill—locale OK-5
Neil Lake—lake AK-9
Neil Lake—lake CA-9
Neil Lake—lake OR-9
Neil Lake—lake TX-5
Neil Lake—lake WY-8
Neill Archeol Site—hist pl MS-4
Neill Branch—stream TN-4
Neill Brothers Rsvr—reservoir CO-8
Neill Cem—cemetery KS-7
Neill Cem—cemetery TN-4
Neill-Cochran House—hist pl TX-5
Neill Creek MT-8
Neill Lake—swamp MN-6
Neill-Mauran House—hist pl PA-2
Neil Long House—building PA-2
Neill Point—cape WA-9
Neill Run—stream PA-2
Neills Bluff—cliff AR-4
Neillsburg PA-2
Neill Sch—school (2) MN-6
Neill Sch—school SD-7
Neills Coon Branch—stream NC-3
Neills Creek—stream NC-3
Neills Creek Ch—church NC-3
Neills Creek (Township of)—fmr MCD NC-3
**Neillsville**—pop pl WI-6
Neillsville Mounds—ridge WI-6
Neilltown—locale PA-2
Neilltown Creek—stream PA-2
Neil Lumpkin Lake Dam—dam MS-4
Neil Mine—mine TN-4
Neilon Creek—stream AR-4
Neil Page Pond Dam—dam MS-4
Neil Point—cape MN-6
Neil Ranch—locale ID-8

*Neskuetonga River* ... KS-7
*Neslen Canyon* ... UT-8
Nesley Ditch—*canal* ... OR-9
**Nesmith**—*pop pl* ... AL-4
**Ne Smith**—*pop pl* ... AL-4
**Nesmith**—*pop pl* ... OR-9
**Nesmith**—*pop pl* ... SC-3
Nesmith, Lake—*lake* ... OH-6
Nesmith (CCD)—*cens area* ... SC-3
Nesmith Cem—*cemetery* (2) ... AL-4
**Nesmith (historical)**—*pop pl* ... OR-9
**Nesmith Mills (historical)**—*pop pl* ... OR-9
Nesmith Point—*summit* ... OR-9
Nesmith Point Trail—*trail* ... OR-9
Nesmith Pond—*lake* ... GA-3
Nesmith Post Office (historical)—*building* ... AL-4
Nesmith Sch—*school* ... SC-3
Ne Smith Sch (historical)—*school* ... AL-4
Nesmith Sch Number 3 (historical)—*school* ... SD-7
Nesmuk, Mount—*summit* ... PA-2
*Nesochaque Creek* ... NJ-2
**Nesom**—*pop pl* ... LA-4
Nesom Cem—*cemetery* ... LA-4
Nesop—*bar* ... FM-9
Nesourdnahunk (Township of)—*unorg* ... ME-1
Nesowadnehunk Deadwater—*lake* ... ME-1
Nesowadnehunk Falls—*falls* ... ME-1
*Nesowadnehunk Lake* ... ME-1
Nesowadnehunk Lake—*reservoir* ... ME-1
Nesowadnehunk Stream—*stream* ... ME-1
Nesowaonehunk Field—*flat* ... ME-1
**Nespelem**—*pop pl* ... WA-9
Nespelem Bar—*bar* ... WA-9
Nespelem Con Mine—*mine* ... WA-9
Nespelem Rapids—*rapids* ... WA-9
Nespelem River—*stream* ... WA-9
NE Spring—*spring* ... AZ-5
**Nesquehoning**—*pop pl* ... PA-2
Nesquehoning Borough—*civil* ... PA-2
Nesquehoning Creek—*stream* ... PA-2
Nesquehoning Junction—*locale* ... PA-2
*Nesquehoning Junction Station* ... PA-2
Nesquehoning Mtn—*summit* ... PA-2
Nesquehoning 4th Hollow Dam—*dam* ... PA-2
Ness, Andres O., House—*hist pl* ... ND-7
Ness Airstrip—*airport* ... ND-7
Ness Cem—*cemetery* ... MN-6
Ness Cem—*cemetery* ... PA-2
Ness Ch—*church* (2) ... MN-6
Ness Ch—*church* (2) ... ND-7
Ness Chain Lake—*lake* ... SD-7
**Ness City**—*pop pl* ... KS-7
*Ness City Airfield* ... KS-7
Ness City Elem Sch—*school* ... KS-7
Ness City HS—*school* ... KS-7
Ness City Municipal Airp—*airport* ... KS-7
Ness County—*civil* ... KS-7
Ness County Bank—*hist pl* ... KS-7
Ness Creek—*stream* ... AK-9
Ness Creek—*stream* ... NC-3
Nesse Cem—*cemetery* ... IA-7
Nesselrood Cem—*cemetery* ... WV-2
Nesselrood Run—*stream* ... WV-2
Nesselrode, Mount—*summit* ... AK-9
Nesselrod Knob—*summit* ... WV-2
**Nessel (Township of)**—*pop pl* ... MN-6
**Nessen City**—*pop pl* ... MI-6
*Nesseponsett Pond* ... MA-1
**Nesser**—*pop pl* ... LA-4
Nesseth Lake—*lake* ... MN-6
Ness Lake—*lake* ... MN-6
Nessler Mine—*mine* ... CA-9
Nessler Point—*cape* ... ME-1
Nessly Chapel—*church* ... WV-2
Nesson Post Office (historical)—*building* ... ND-7
Nesson Valley—*unorg reg* ... ND-7
Ness Sch—*school* ... WA-9
**Ness Township**—*pop pl* ... ND-7
**Ness (Township of)**—*pop pl* ... MN-6
*Nest* ... VA-3
*Nest, The* ... PA-2
Nest Brook—*stream* ... IN-6
Nest Creek—*stream* ... MT-8
Nestepol Marsh—*swamp* ... NY-2
Nesterbank Ranch—*locale* ... WA-9
Nester Bluffs—*cliff* ... MN-6
Nester Branch—*stream* ... GA-3
*Nester Canyon* ... NM-5
Nester Canyon—*valley* ... NM-5
Nester Cem—*cemetery* ... VA-3
Nester Chapel—*church* ... MO-7
Nester Creek—*stream* ... KS-7
Nester Creek—*stream* ... MI-6
Nester Creek—*stream* ... MN-6
Nester Draw—*valley* ... NM-5
Nester House—*hist pl* ... NY-2
Nester Lake—*lake* ... MI-6
Nester Sch—*school* ... MO-7
Nesters Creek—*stream* ... MI-6
Nester Tank—*reservoir* ... NM-5
Nester Tank—*reservoir* (2) ... TX-5
**Nester (Township of)**—*pop pl* ... MI-6
Nesterville (historical)—*locale* ... AL-4
Nester Well—*locale* ... NM-5
Nester Well—*well* ... NM-5
Nester Well—*well* ... TX-5
**Nesthaven (subdivision)**—*pop pl* ... NC-3
Nesting—*locale* ... VA-3
Nest Island—*island* ... AK-9
Nest Keys—*island* ... FL-3
Nest Lake—*lake* ... AK-9
Nest Lake—*lake* (2) ... MN-6
Nestle Ave Sch—*school* ... CA-9
Nestle Cem—*cemetery* ... NY-2
Nestle Lake—*lake* ... WI-6
Nestle Sch—*school* ... NY-2
**Nestleway Acres (subdivision)**—*pop pl* ... NC-3
Nestlow—*locale* ... WV-2
Nestlow Branch—*stream* ... WV-2
**Nestoctin (historical)**—*pop pl* ... OR-9
Nestor—*locale* ... LA-4
**Nestor**—*pop pl* ... CA-9
Nestor, Mount—*summit* ... AZ-5
Nestor Canal—*canal* ... LA-4
Nestor Canyon—*valley* ... NM-5
Nestor Drain—*canal* ... MI-6
Nestor Hollow—*valley* ... PA-2
Nestoria—*locale* ... MI-6
Nestoria Creek—*stream* ... MI-6
Nestor Kivimaki Dam Number 1—*dam* ... SD-7
Nestor Lakes—*lake* ... MI-6
Nestor Peak—*summit* ... WA-9
Nestor Peak Trail—*trail* ... WA-9
*Nestors* ... AZ-5
Nestor Sch—*school* ... CA-9
Nestor Sch—*school* ... MI-6
**Nestorville**—*pop pl* ... WV-2
*Nestovial* ... MI-6
Nest Rock—*island* ... AK-9
Nest Run—*stream* (3) ... IN-6
Nestucca Bay—*bay* ... OR-9
Nestucca Grange Hall—*locale* ... OR-9
Nestucca River—*stream* ... OR-9
*Nestucca Spit* ... OR-9
Nestucca Spit State Park—*park* ... OR-9
*Nestuccas River* ... OR-9
Nestucca Union HS—*school* ... OR-9
*Nestuckles River* ... OR-9
*Nestuggah River* ... OR-9
*Nestugga River* ... OR-9
*Nestuoca Bay* ... OR-9
Nest Well—*well* ... AZ-5
Nesuftanga—*locale* ... AZ-5
*Nesuketonga River* ... KS-7
Nesuntabunt Mtn—*summit* ... ME-1
Net—*civil* ... FM-9
Net, Dolen—*summit* ... FM-9
N E Taconi Elem Sch—*school* ... MS-4
NE Tank—*reservoir* ... AZ-5
**Netarts**—*pop pl* ... OR-9
Netarts Bay—*bay* ... OR-9
Netarts Bay Campground—*park* ... OR-9
Netarts Spit—*bar* ... OR-9
**Netawaka**—*pop pl* ... KS-7
**Netawaka Township**—*pop pl* ... KS-7
Netawanap, Oror En—*locale* ... FM-9
Net Bayou—*gut* ... LA-4
*Net Beach* ... MH-9
*Net Cliffs* ... MH-9
**Netcong**—*pop pl* ... NJ-2
Neteler Cem—*cemetery* ... IL-6
*Netherland* ... KS-7
**Netherland**—*pop pl* ... TN-4
Netherland—*uninc pl* ... KY-4
Netherland Cem—*cemetery* ... TN-4
Netherland Ch—*church* ... TN-4
Netherland Heights Spring—*spring* ... TN-4
Netherland Inn and Complex—*hist pl* ... TN-4
Netherland Post Office (historical)—*building* ... TN-4
Netherland-Rice Cem—*cemetery* ... TN-4
Netherlands—*locale* ... MO-7
**Netherlands (historical)**—*pop pl* ... TN-4
Netherlands Legation Bldg—*building* ... DC-2
*Netherlands Station* ... TN-4
Nether Providence Elem Sch—*school* ... PA-2
Nether Providence MS—*school* ... PA-2
*Nether Providence Sch* ... PA-2
Nether Providence Township—*CDP* ... PA-2
**Nether Providence (Township of)**—*pop pl* ... PA-2
Nethers—*locale* ... VA-3
Netherton Sch (historical)—*school* ... MO-7
Netherwood—*locale* ... NY-2
**Netherwood**—*pop pl* ... NJ-2
Netherwood Sch—*school* ... NY-2
Netherwood Station—*hist pl* ... NJ-2
Netherwood Station—*locale* ... NJ-2
*Nethery Cemetery* ... TN-4
Nethery Ranch—*locale* ... TX-5
Nethkahati Creek—*stream* ... AK-9
Nethker Creek—*stream* ... ID-8
Nethker Lake—*lake* ... ID-8
Nethkin—*locale* ... WV-2
Nethkin Cem—*cemetery* ... WV-2
Nethkin Ch—*church* ... WV-2
Nethkin Hill—*summit* ... WV-2
Net Hole, The—*lake* ... NC-3
Netholzende Lake—*lake* ... AK-9
Netik—*spring* ... FM-9
Net Island—*island* ... MI-6
Netiw—*bar* ... FM-9
Netiw, Oror En—*locale* ... FM-9
*Net Lake* ... MN-6
Net Lake—*lake* (3) ... MN-6
Net Lake—*lake* ... WI-6
Netland Island—*island* ... AK-9
Netletna River—*stream* ... AK-9
Netley Branch—*stream* (2) ... KY-4
**Neton**—*pop pl* ... FM-9
Netonom—*well* ... FM-9
*Netop* ... OH-6
Netop Mtn—*summit* ... VT-1
Netouche Pas, Bayou—*gut* ... LA-4
*Netoutou* ... FM-9
*Netoutou Channel* ... FM-9
*Net River* ... MI-6
Net River—*stream* ... MI-6
Net River—*stream* ... MN-6
*Netsiland* ... NC-3
Nets Peak—*summit* ... NE-7
Net Spread Key—*island* ... FL-3
*Nett* ... FM-9
Nett, Lake—*reservoir* ... AL-4
Netta, Lake—*lake* ... MN-6
*Nettels School* ... KS-7
Netter Creek—*stream* ... OR-9
Netters Point—*summit* ... KY-4
Netterville Cem—*cemetery* ... MS-4
Netterville Landing Strip—*airport* ... MS-4
Netterville Sch—*school* ... MS-4
**Nettie**—*pop pl* ... WV-2
Nettie, Lake—*lake* ... FL-3
Nettie, Lake—*lake* ... MI-6
Nettie, Lake—*lake* ... ND-7
*Nettie Bald* ... NC-3
Nettie B Lake—*lake* ... WI-6
*Nettie Creek* ... IN-6
Nettie Creek—*stream* ... OR-9
Nettie Hartnett Elem Sch—*school* ... KS-7
Nettie Lee Roth HS—*school* ... OH-6
Nettie Patch—*gap* ... NC-3
Netties Canyon—*valley* ... UT-8
Netties Lake—*lake* ... WI-6
Nettiewynnt Lake Bed—*flat* ... MN-6
Nett Lake—*lake* ... MN-6
**Nett Lake**—*pop pl* ... MN-6
Nett Lake Ind Res—*other* ... MN-6
Nett Lake Petroglyphs Site—*hist pl* ... MN-6
Nett Lake Ranger Station—*locale* ... MN-6
Nett Lake River—*stream* ... MN-6
Nett Lake (Unorganized Territory of)—*unorg* (2) ... MN-6
Nettleboro—*locale* ... AL-4
Nettle Branch—*stream* (2) ... NC-3
Nettle Branch—*stream* ... VA-3
*Nettle Carrier Creek* ... TN-4
Nettlecarrier Creek—*stream* ... TN-4
Nettlecarrier Creek Cem—*cemetery* ... TN-4
**Nettle Carrier (historical)**—*pop pl* ... TN-4
Nettle Carrier Post Office (historical)—*building* ... TN-4
Nettle Cem—*cemetery* ... IN-6
Nettle Cove—*valley* ... NC-3
*Nettle Creek* ... IN-6
Nettle Creek—*locale* ... IL-6
Nettle Creek—*stream* ... CO-8
Nettle Creek—*stream* (2) ... ID-8
Nettle Creek—*stream* ... IL-6
Nettle Creek—*stream* (3) ... IN-6
Nettle Creek—*stream* ... NY-2
Nettle Creek—*stream* ... NC-3
Nettle Creek—*stream* (2) ... OH-6
Nettle Creek—*stream* ... OR-9
Nettle Creek—*stream* ... VA-3
Nettle Creek Bald—*summit* ... NC-3
Nettle Creek Cem—*cemetery* ... IN-6
Nettle Creek Cem—*cemetery* ... OH-6
Nettle Creek Ch—*church* ... IN-6
Nettle Creek Sch—*school* ... IL-6
*Nettle Creek (Township of)* ... IN-6
Nettle Creek (Township of)—*civ div* ... IL-6
Nettle Drain—*canal* ... CA-9
Nettle Hill—*locale* ... PA-2
Nettle Hill—*summit* ... PA-2
Nettle Hollow—*valley* ... KY-4
Nettle Hollow—*valley* ... TN-4
Nettle Hollow—*valley* ... VA-3
Nettlehorst Ditch—*canal* ... IN-6
Nettlehorst Sch—*school* ... IL-6
Nettle Island—*island* ... ME-1
*Nettle Knob* ... NC-3
Nettle Knob—*summit* (3) ... NC-3
Nettle Lake—*lake* ... OH-6
**Nettle Lake**—*pop pl* ... OH-6
Nettle Lake Ch—*church* ... OH-6
Nettle Lake Mound Group—*hist pl* ... OH-6
Nettle Lateral—*canal* ... CA-9
Nettle Mtn—*summit* ... VA-3
Nettle Mtn—*summit* ... WV-2
Nettle Patch, The—*area* ... VA-3
*Nettle Rash* ... MH-9
Nettleridge—*locale* ... VA-3
Nettle Ridge—*ridge* ... PA-2
Nettle Ridge—*ridge* ... VA-3
Nettle Ridge—*ridge* ... WV-2
Nettle Ridge Cem—*cemetery* ... FL-3
Nettle Ridge Trail—*trail* ... PA-2
Nettle Run—*canal* ... MI-6
Nettle Run—*stream* (2) ... WV-2
Nettles Bay—*basin* ... SC-3
Nettles Bluff—*cliff* ... MO-7
*Nettlesboro* ... AL-4
Nettles Branch—*stream* ... AL-4
Nettles Cem—*cemetery* (2) ... MS-4
Nettles Cem—*cemetery* ... TX-5
Nettle Sch—*school* ... MA-1
Nettles Chapel (historical)—*church* ... AL-4
Nettles Creek—*stream* ... TX-5
Nettles Creek—*stream* ... VA-3
Nettles Island—*island* ... FL-3
Nettle Spring—*spring* (2) ... CA-9
Nettle Spring—*spring* ... OR-9
Nettle Spring—*spring* ... UT-8
Nettle Spring Branch—*stream* ... VA-3
Nettles Store (historical)—*locale* ... AL-4
Nettle Tank—*reservoir* ... AZ-5
Nettleton—*locale* ... KS-7
Nettleton—*other* ... PA-2
**Nettleton**—*pop pl* ... AR-4
**Nettleton**—*pop pl* ... MS-4
**Nettleton**—*pop pl* ... MO-7
Nettleton Cem—*cemetery* ... MS-4
Nettleton Ch of Christ—*church* ... MS-4
Nettleton Gulch—*valley* ... ID-8
Nettleton House—*hist pl* ... NH-1
Nettleton HS—*school* ... MS-4
Nettleton Lake—*lake* ... WA-9
*Nettleton Lower Elem Sch* ... MS-4
Nettleton Presbyterian Ch—*church* ... MS-4
Nettleton Ranch—*locale* ... TX-5
Nettleton Sch—*school* ... MN-6
Nettleton (Township of)—*fmr MCD* ... AR-4
Nettleton United Methodist Ch—*church* ... MS-4
Nettleton Upper Elem Sch—*school* ... MS-4
Nettle Valley Cem—*cemetery* ... NY-2
Nettle Valley Creek—*stream* ... NY-2
Nett (Municipality)—*civ div* ... FM-9
Nett Ranch—*locale* ... MT-8
Nett River (Township of)—*other* ... MN-6
Netty—*locale* ... KY-4
*Netul River* ... OR-9
Netur—*bar* ... FM-9
Netutu—*channel* ... FM-9
Neubauer Ranch—*locale* ... NE-7
Neuberger, Mount—*summit* ... AK-9
**Neubert**—*pop pl* ... KY-4
**Neubert**—*pop pl* ... TN-4
Neubert Cem—*cemetery* ... TN-4
*Neubert Church* ... TN-4
Neubert Post Office—*locale* ... TN-4
Neubert Quarry—*mine* ... TN-4
*Neuberts* ... TN-4
Neubert Sch (historical)—*school* ... TN-4
Neubert Spring—*spring* ... OR-9
**Neubert Springs**—*pop pl* ... TN-4
*Neubert Station* ... TN-4
Neubert Sulphur Springs—*spring* ... TN-4
*Neucastle* ... DE-2
*Neuces River* ... TX-5
Neuchatel—*locale* ... KS-7
Neuchatle Township—*civil* ... KS-7
Neu Creek—*stream* ... IN-6
Neudeckers Mtn—*summit* ... IL-6
Neudorf Cem—*cemetery* ... SD-7
Neudorfer Ch—*church* ... MT-8
Neue Bay—*bay* ... HI-9
**Neuern**—*pop pl* ... WI-6
Neufeld—*locale* ... CA-9
Neufer Hollow—*valley* ... PA-2
Neu Field—*airport* ... KS-7
**Neuhardt**—*pop pl* ... AR-4
Neuhardt Coulee—*valley* ... MT-8
Neuharth Sch—*school* ... SD-7
Neuharth State Public Shooting Area—*park* ... SD-7
Neuhaus, C. L., House—*hist pl* ... TX-5
Neuhausen, Carl M., House—*hist pl* ... UT-8
*Neujahrs-Insel* ... MP-9
Neukech—*summit* ... FM-9
Neukom, Albert, House—*hist pl* ... OH-6
Neukons—*post sta* ... FL-3
Neum—*bar* ... FM-9
Neuman—*other* ... OH-6
Neuman Creek—*stream* ... NY-2
Neuman Drain—*canal* ... MI-6
Neuman Gap—*gap* ... OR-9
Neuman Lake—*reservoir* ... CO-8
Neumann Cem—*cemetery* ... IA-7
Neuman Neck—*cape* ... VA-3
Neumann HS—*school* ... NY-2
Neumann Island—*island* ... AK-9
Neumanns Airp—*airport* ... KS-7
Neumans Corners—*locale* ... NY-2
Neuman-Scott Ranch—*locale* ... SD-7
Neuner Lake—*lake* ... MN-6
**Neunert**—*pop pl* ... IL-6
Neunert Cem—*cemetery* ... IL-6
Neunlist Cem—*cemetery* ... IL-6
Neur—*summit* ... FM-9
**Neuralia**—*pop pl* ... CA-9
Neure—*bar* ... FM-9
*Neuremburg* ... PA-2
**Neureru**—*pop pl* ... WI-6
Neureu—*bar* ... FM-9
Neuri, Mochun—*channel* ... FM-9
*Neuri Durchfahrt* ... FM-9
Neurls Run—*stream* ... KY-4
*Neurui Pass* ... FM-9
*Neus* ... NC-3
Neusatz Cem—*cemetery* ... ND-7
Neusatz Cem—*cemetery* ... SD-7
Neuschwanger Rsvr—*reservoir* ... OR-9
Neuse—*locale* ... NC-3
*Neuseco Lake* ... NC-3
**Neuse Crossroads**—*pop pl* ... NC-3
**Neuse Forest**—*pop pl* ... NC-3
*Neuseoca Lake* ... NC-3
Neuseoca Lake—*reservoir* ... NC-3
Neuseoca Lake Dam—*dam* ... NC-3
Neuseoco Lake—*reservoir* ... NC-3
Neuse River—*stream* ... NC-3
Neuse River Cut-Off—*bend* ... NC-3
Neuse River Recreation Site—*park* ... NC-3
Neuse (Township of)—*fmr MCD* (2) ... NC-3
*Neusiok* ... NC-3
Neusiok Trail—*trail* ... NC-3
*Neuskahl Creek* ... WA-9
*Neuske Creek* ... WA-9
*Neustadt* ... PW-9
Neusteter Bldg—*hist pl* ... CO-8
*Neustuckles River* ... OR-9
*Neut* ... TX-5
*Neutaconkanot River* ... RI-1
Neutaconkanut Hill—*summit* ... RI-1
Neuter Fort—*locale* ... NY-2
Neutral—*locale* ... KS-7
Neutral Buoyancy Space Simulator—*hist pl* ... AL-4
*Neutral City* ... KS-7
Neutral Ditch—*canal* ... IL-6
Neutral Sch—*school* ... KS-7
*Neutral Strip* ... OK-5
Neutral Strip (historical)—*area* ... OK-5
Neutze Hill—*summit* ... TX-5
*Neuustooc* ... NC-3
*Neuvas Filipinas* ... FM-9
**Neuville**—*pop pl* ... TX-5
Neuville Cem—*cemetery* ... TX-5
Neuville Sch—*school* ... TX-5
*Neuvy* ... NJ-2
Neuweiler Brewery—*hist pl* ... PA-2
Neuwra—*spring* ... FM-9
Neuwsma Lake—*lake* ... ND-7
*Neva* ... ND-7
Neva—*locale* ... ID-8
Neva—*locale* ... KS-7
Neva—*locale* ... TN-4
**Neva**—*pop pl* ... WI-6
Neva, Lake—*lake* ... MI-6
Neva, Lake—*reservoir* ... GA-3
Neva, Mount—*summit* ... CO-8
Neva, Mount—*summit* ... NV-8
Neva Bay—*bay* ... AK-9
Neva (CCD)—*cens area* ... TN-4
**Neva Corners**—*pop pl* ... WI-6
Neva Cove—*bay* ... AK-9
Neva Creek—*stream* ... AK-9
Neva Creek—*stream* ... WY-8
Nevada—*locale* ... CA-9
Nevada—*locale* ... IL-6
Nevada—*locale* ... MS-4
**Nevada**—*pop pl* ... IN-6
**Nevada**—*pop pl* ... IA-7
**Nevada**—*pop pl* ... KY-4
**Nevada**—*pop pl* ... MO-7
**Nevada**—*pop pl* ... OH-6
**Nevada**—*pop pl* ... TX-5
Nevada, Sierra—*range* ... NV-8
**Nevada Addition (subdivision)**—*pop pl* ... UT-8
Nevada Ave Sch—*school* ... NY-2
Nevada Beach Forest Camp—*locale* ... NV-8
Nevada Bottom—*basin* ... CA-9
Nevada Brewery—*hist pl* ... CA-9
Nevada-California-Oregon Railway Co. General Office Bldg—*hist pl* ... CA-9
Nevada-California-Oregon Railway Passenger Station—*hist pl* ... OR-9
Nevada-California-Oregon RR Depot—*hist pl* ... NV-8
Nevada-California Power Company Substation and Auxiliary Power Bu—*hist pl* ... NV-8
Nevada Canal—*canal* ... OR-9
Nevada Canyon—*valley* ... NV-8
Nevada (CCD)—*cens area* ... TX-5
Nevada Cem—*cemetery* ... IL-6
Nevada Cem—*cemetery* ... OH-6
Nevada Center Sch—*school* ... MN-6
Nevada Central Mine—*mine* ... NV-8
*Nevada Cinnabar Mine* ... NV-8
Nevada City—*locale* ... MT-8
**Nevada City**—*pop pl* ... CA-9
Nevada City (CCD)—*cens area* ... CA-9
Nevada City Downtown Hist Dist—*hist pl* ... CA-9
Nevada City Firehouse No. 2—*hist pl* ... CA-9
Nevada Country Club—*other* ... MO-7
**Nevada (County)**—*pop pl* ... AR-4
**Nevada (County)**—*pop pl* ... CA-9
Nevada County Golf Course—*other* ... CA-9
Nevada Creek—*stream* (4) ... AK-9
Nevada Creek—*stream* (2) ... CA-9
Nevada Creek—*stream* ... ID-8
Nevada Creek—*stream* (2) ... MT-8
Nevada Creek—*stream* ... NV-8
*Nevada Creek Storage Project* ... MT-8
Nevada Denver Mine—*mine* ... NV-8
Nevada Department of Wildlife State HQ Heliport—*airport* ... NV-8
Nevada Ditch—*canal* ... CO-8
Nevada Dock—*locale* ... CA-9
Nevada Dominion Mine—*mine* ... NV-8
Nevada Eagle Mine—*mine* (2) ... NV-8
*Nevada Fall* ... CA-9
Nevada Fall—*falls* ... CA-9
Nevada Fish and Game Region III HQ Heliport—*airport* ... NV-8
Nevada Flyers Airp—*airport* ... NV-8
Nevada Girls Training Center—*building* ... NV-8
Nevada Governor Mansion—*building* ... NV-8
Nevada Governors Spring—*spring* ... NV-8
Nevada Gulch—*valley* ... CO-8
Nevada Gulch—*valley* ... ID-8
Nevada Gulch—*valley* ... NV-8
Nevada Gulch—*valley* ... OR-9
Nevada Gulch Sch—*school* ... SD-7
Nevada Hill—*summit* ... CO-8
Nevada Hill—*summit* ... NV-8
Nevada Hills Mine—*mine* ... NV-8
Nevada (historical)—*locale* ... KS-7
Nevada Hot Springs—*spring* ... NV-8
Nevada Lake—*reservoir* ... MT-8
Nevada Memorial Park—*cemetery* ... NV-8
Nevada Mica Mine—*mine* ... NV-8
**Nevada Mills**—*pop pl* ... IN-6
Nevada Mine—*mine* (3) ... NV-8
Nevada Mtn—*summit* ... MT-8
Nevada Municipal Airp—*airport* ... MO-7
Nevada Narrows—*gap* ... MT-8
Nevada Packard Mines—*mine* ... NV-8
Nevada Park—*park* ... WA-9
Nevada Point—*ridge* ... CA-9
Nevada Point Ridge—*ridge* ... CA-9
Nevada Point Trail—*trail* ... CA-9
Nevada Quicksilver Mine—*mine* ... NV-8
Nevada Rand Mine—*mine* ... NV-8
Nevada Royale Quarries—*mine* ... NV-8
Nevada Royale Quarry—*mine* ... NV-8
*Nevada Silica Sand Mine* ... NV-8
Nevada Southern Univ—*school* ... NV-8
Nevada State Capitol—*building* ... NV-8
Nevada State Capitol—*hist pl* ... NV-8
Nevada State Hosp—*hospital* ... NV-8
Nevada State Maximum Security Prison—*locale* ... NV-8
Nevada State Medium Security Prison—*locale* ... NV-8
Nevada State Printing Office—*hist pl* ... NV-8
Nevada Telephone Cove—*bay* ... NV-8
Nevada Test Site—*locale* ... NV-8
Nevada Test Site—*trail* ... NV-8
Nevada Test Site Area 1—*locale* ... NV-8
Nevada Test Site Area 10—*locale* ... NV-8
Nevada Test Site Area 11—*locale* ... NV-8
Nevada Test Site Area 12—*locale* ... NV-8
Nevada Test Site Area 14—*locale* ... NV-8
Nevada Test Site Area 15—*locale* ... NV-8
Nevada Test Site Area 18—*locale* ... NV-8
Nevada Test Site Area 2—*locale* ... NV-8
Nevada Test Site Area 3—*locale* ... NV-8
Nevada Test Site Area 4—*locale* ... NV-8
Nevada Test Site Area 400—*area* ... NV-8
Nevada Test Site Area 401—*locale* ... NV-8
Nevada Test Site Area 5—*locale* ... NV-8
Nevada Test Site Area 6—*locale* ... NV-8
Nevada Test Site Area 7—*locale* ... NV-8
Nevada Test Site Area 8—*locale* ... NV-8
Nevada Test Site Area 9—*locale* ... NV-8
Nevada Theatre—*hist pl* ... CA-9
Nevada Township—*fmr MCD* (2) ... IA-7
**Nevada Township**—*pop pl* ... KS-7
**Nevada (Township of)**—*pop pl* ... IL-6
**Nevada (Township of)**—*pop pl* ... MN-6
Nevada Valley—*valley* ... MT-8
Nevadaville—*locale* ... CO-8
Nevada Wild Horse Mngmt Area—*area* ... NV-8
Nevada Youth Training Center—*building* ... NV-8
Neva Division—*civil* ... TN-4
Nevadum—*locale* ... SC-3
**Nevadun**—*pop pl* ... SC-3
Neva Elem Sch—*school* ... TN-4
Nevahbe Ridge—*ridge* ... CA-9
Neva Island—*island* ... AK-9
Neva Lateral—*canal* ... ID-8
Neva Point—*cape* ... AK-9
Neva Post Office (historical)—*building* ... TN-4
Nevares Peak—*summit* ... CA-9
Nevares Springs—*spring* ... CA-9
Nevark—*locale* ... AR-4
*Neva Star* ... WI-6
Neva Strait—*channel* ... AK-9
**Neva (Town of)**—*pop pl* ... WI-6
Neva West Oil And Gas Field—*oilfield* ... TX-5
Neve Creek—*stream* ... WA-9
Neveda-California-Oregon Railway Locomotive House and Machine Sho—*hist pl* ... NV-8
Neve Glacier—*glacier* ... WA-9
Neveh Zedek Cem—*cemetery* ... OR-9
Nevel Chapel—*church* ... TN-4
*Nevel Chapel Baptist Ch* ... TN-4
Nevel Hollow—*valley* ... PA-2
*Nevells Bay* ... TN-4
*Nevells Bay Access Area* ... TN-4
*Nevells Creek* ... TN-4
Neveln Sch—*school* ... MN-6
Nevels Corners—*locale* ... WI-6
Nevelsville—*locale* ... KY-4
Nevens—*locale* ... NE-7
*Nevens Lake* ... MN-6
Nevens Lake—*lake* ... MN-6
Never Creek—*stream* ... ID-8
Never Fail Bay—*bay* ... MN-6
Neverfail Cem—*cemetery* ... TN-4
Neverfail Ch—*church* ... TN-4
**Neverfail (historical)**—*pop pl* ... TN-4
*Never Fail Lake* ... MS-4
Neverfail Ledge—*rock* ... MA-1
Never Fail Mine—*mine* ... NM-5
Neverfail Post Office (historical)—*building* ... TN-4
Never Fail Sch—*school* ... CO-8
Neverfail Sch (historical)—*school* ... TN-4
Nevergo Creek—*stream* ... OR-9
Never Go Dry Tank—*reservoir* ... AZ-5
N Evergreen Sch—*school* ... MI-6
Never Hole—*basin* ... AL-4
Never Laughs Mtn—*summit* ... MT-8
Nevermore Lake—*reservoir* ... ND-7
Never Mtn—*summit* ... NC-3
Never-Never Lake—*lake* ... AK-9
*Never No Summer Range* ... CO-8
Nevers Dam—*dam* ... MN-6
*Never Seet Coulee* ... MT-8
Nevershine—*summit* ... AZ-5
Nevershine Hollow—*valley* ... UT-8
*Never Sinck* ... NJ-2
*Neversink* ... NJ-2
**Neversink**—*pop pl* ... NY-2
**Neversink**—*pop pl* ... PA-2
Neversink Mtn—*summit* ... PA-2
Never Sink Pit—*cave* ... AL-4
Neversink Resort—*locale* ... CO-8
*Neversink River* ... NJ-2
Neversink River—*stream* ... NY-2
Neversink Rondout Aqueduct—*canal* ... NY-2
Neversink Rsvr—*reservoir* ... NY-2
Neversink Rsvr—*reservoir* ... PA-2
**Neversink (Town of)**—*pop pl* ... NY-2
**Neverson**—*pop pl* ... NC-3
Neverstill (site)—*locale* ... OR-9
*Never Summer Mountains, The* ... CO-8
Never Summer Mtns—*range* ... CO-8
*Never Summer Range* ... CO-8
*Neversunk* ... NJ-2
Neversweat Canyon—*valley* ... NV-8
Never Sweat Canyon—*valley* ... NV-8
Never Sweat Coulee—*valley* ... MT-8
Neversweat Creek—*stream* ... ID-8
Neversweat Creek—*stream* ... OK-5
Never Sweat Gulch—*valley* ... MT-8
Never Sweat Hills—*ridge* ... NV-8
Neversweat Peak—*summit* ... ID-8
Neversweat Ridge—*ridge* ... AZ-5
Neversweat Rsvr—*reservoir* ... CO-8
Neversweat Wash—*valley* ... UT-8
*Never Sweet Gulch* ... MT-8
Neversweet Gulch—*valley* ... CA-9
Nevertouch Pond—*lake* ... MA-1
*Neve Sincks* ... NJ-2
Neves Lake—*lake* ... WA-9
Neves Rsvr—*reservoir* ... WY-8
**Nevesville (Walden Post Office)**—*pop pl* ... VT-1
*Nevice Arroyo* ... TX-5
*Nevice Creek* ... TX-5
Nevidiskov Bay—*bay* ... AK-9
Nevidiskov Creek—*stream* ... AK-9
Nevidiskov River—*stream* ... AK-9
Nevil Cem—*cemetery* ... LA-4
Nevil Creek—*stream* ... NC-3
Nevill Bayou—*stream* ... TX-5
Nevill Cem—*cemetery* ... MS-4
Nevill Cem—*cemetery* ... TN-4
Nevill Cem—*cemetery* ... TX-5
Neville—*locale* ... MS-4
**Neville**—*pop pl* ... OH-6
Neville—*uninc pl* ... WV-2
Neville Airp—*airport* ... NC-3
Neville Bay—*bay* ... TN-4
Neville Bay Lake Access—*park* ... TN-4
Neville Canal—*canal* ... UT-8
Neville Cem—*cemetery* ... AL-4
Neville Cem—*cemetery* ... WI-6
*Neville Cemetery* ... TN-4
Neville Ch—*church* ... KS-7
Neville Chapel—*church* ... NC-3
Neville Creek—*stream* ... NC-3
Neville Creek—*stream* ... TN-4
Neville Creek—*stream* ... TX-5
Neville Creek Cem—*cemetery* ... TN-4
Neville Creek Ch—*church* ... TN-4
Neville House—*hist pl* ... AL-4
Neville House—*hist pl* ... NY-2
Neville House—*hist pl* ... PA-2
Neville HS—*hist pl* ... LA-4
Neville HS—*school* ... LA-4
Neville Island—*island* ... PA-2
Neville Island Bridge—*bridge* ... PA-2
Neville Island (Township name Neville)—*uninc pl* ... PA-2
Neville-Patterson-Lamkin House—*hist pl* ... KY-4
Neville Ranch—*locale* ... NM-5
*Neville Rapids* ... AZ-5
Neville Ridge—*ridge* ... WA-9
Neville Sch—*school* ... OH-6
Neville Sch—*school* ... SD-7
Neville Sch (historical)—*school* ... AL-4
Neville Spring—*spring* ... ID-8
Neville Spring—*spring* ... TX-5
Neville Township—*CDP* ... PA-2
**Neville (Township of)**—*pop pl* ... PA-2
Nevills Arch—*arch* ... UT-8
*Nevills Bayou* ... TX-5
Nevills Creek—*stream* ... GA-3
Nevills Creek Ch—*church* ... GA-3
Nevills Inscription (1940)—*other* ... UT-8
*Nevills Natural Arch* ... UT-8
*Nevills Prairie* ... TX-5
Nevills Rapids—*rapids* ... AZ-5
**Nevils**—*pop pl* ... GA-3
Nevils Bluff—*cliff* ... LA-4
Nevils Cem—*cemetery* ... LA-4
Nevils Ch—*church* ... TX-5
Nevils Pond—*reservoir* ... GA-3
Nevils-Stilson (CCD)—*cens area* ... GA-3
Nevin—*locale* ... CA-9
Nevin—*locale* ... KY-4
Nevin—*locale* ... NV-8
Nevin, Lake—*lake* ... KY-4

Newnansville Cem—cemetery FL-3
Newnansville Town Site—hist pl FL-3
Newnan Waterworks Lakes—reservoir GA-3
Newnata—pop pl AR-4
New Natl Aeronautical Space Administration Bldg—building DC-2
New Naugatuck Rsvr—reservoir CT-1
New Nazarene Ch—church LA-4
New Nazareth Ch—church AL-4
New Neely—locale AR-4
New Newsom Springs Cem—cemetery AL-4
New Nixon Sch—school SD-7
New North Almaden Mine—mine CA-9
New North Reformed Low Dutch Church—hist pl NJ-2
New Oak Grove Cem—cemetery MS-4
New Oak Grove Cem—cemetery NC-3
New Oak Grove Ch AL-4
New Oak Grove Ch—church AL-4
New Oak Grove Ch—church FL-3
New Oak Grove Ch—church (2) MS-4
New Oak Grove Missionary Baptist Ch AL-4
New Oakland Ch—church FL-3
New Oakland Ch—church MD-2
New Oakland City Lake IN-6
New Oakland City Lake Dam—reservoir IN-6
New Oakwood Cem—cemetery TX-5
New Oaky Bower Ch—church AL-4
New Oberlin—pop pl OK-5
Newoch—bar FM-9
New Offenburg—pop pl MO-7
New Ohio—locale NY-2
New Ohio Cem—cemetery NY-2
New Olathe Lake—reservoir KS-7
New Olathe Lake Dam—dam KS-7
Newold—pop pl KY-4
New Old River Lake—lake TX-5
New Olea Well—well AZ-5
New Olive Grove Ch—church SC-3
Newomas, Oror En—pop pl FM-9
Newonong—spring FM-9
Newonun—bar FM-9
New Opera House—hist pl NE-7
New Opera House—hist pl WV-2
New Oraibi—pop pl AZ-5
New Oran Cem—cemetery OH-6
New Orange Ch—church FL-3
New Oregon—locale IA-7
New Oregon—pop pl NY-2
New Oregon Ch—church AL-4
New Oregon Township—fmr MCD IA-7
New Oregon Township Cem—cemetery (2) IA-7
New Ore Mine—mine AZ-5
New Orleans—pop pl LA-4
New Orleans Acad—school LA-4
New Orleans Army Base—military LA-4
New Orleans Baptist Ch—church FL-3
New Orleans Baptist Christian Day Sch—school FL-3
New Orleans City Park Carousel and Pavilion—hist pl LA-4
New Orleans Coast Guard Base—military LA-4
New Orleans Cotton Exchange Bldg—hist pl LA-4
New Orleans Country Club—other LA-4
New Orleans Gulch—valley CA-9
New Orleans International Airp (Moisant Field)—airport LA-4
New Orleans Naval Air Station—military LA-4
New Orleans Naval Support Activity—military LA-4
New Orleans Theological Seminary—school LA-4
Neworor—summit FM-9
Newoses—tunnel FM-9
Newot—locale FM-9
New Otter Gap Trail—trail PA-2
New Otting Drain—stream MI-6
New Otto IN-6
New Otto—other IN-6
New Owen Cem—cemetery AR-4
New Owens Mine—mine CA-9
New Oxford—pop pl PA-2
New Oxford Borough—civil PA-2
New Pait Cem—cemetery NC-3
New Palatine—pop pl IL-6
New Palestine—pop pl IL-6
New Palestine—pop pl IN-6
New Palestine—pop pl OH-6
New Palestine Baptist Ch—church MS-4
New Palestine Cem—cemetery IN-6
New Palestine Ch—church MS-4
New Palestine Elem Sch—school IN-6
New Palestine HS—school IN-6
New Palmer Sch—school VT-1
Newpaltz NY-2
New Paltz—pop pl NY-2
New Paltz Cem—cemetery NY-2
New Paltz (Town of)—pop pl NY-2
New Panther Creek Ch—church KY-4
New Paradise Ch—church MS-4
New Paris—locale WI-6
New Paris—pop pl IN-6
New Paris—pop pl OH-6
New Paris—pop pl PA-2
New Paris Borough—civil PA-2
New Paris Central Sch—school PA-2
New Paris Covered Bridge—hist pl PA-2
New Paris Elem Sch—school IN-6
Newpark PA-2
New Park—pop pl PA-2
New Park Ave Sch—school CT-1
New Park Cem—cemetery GA-3
New Park Cem—cemetery TN-4
New Parkersburg Baptist Ch—church MS-4
New Park Well—well AZ-5
New Park Windmill—locale TX-5
New Parrot Home Ch—church NC-3
New Party Mine—mine NV-8
New Pass—channel (2) FL-3
New Pass—channel LA-4
New Pass—gap OR-9
New Pass—valley NV-8
New Pass Bay FL-3
New Pass (historical)—channel FL-3
New Pass Mine—mine NV-8
New Pass Mountains NV-8
New Pass Peak—summit NV-8
New Pass Range NV-8
New Pass Range—range NV-8
New Pass Summit—summit NV-8
New Pass Well—well NV-8
New Pasture Number Thirteen—flat KS-7
New Pasture Tank—reservoir AZ-5
New Pasture Well—well AZ-5
New Pasture Well—well NM-5
New Pasture Windmill—locale NM-5
New Pasture Windmill—locale TX-5
New Paterson NJ-2
New Paynetown Ch—church IN-6
New Peace and Harmony Ch—church MO-7
New Peach Orchard Mine—mine TN-4
New Peachtree Ch—church NC-3
New Pekin—pop pl IN-6
New Pence Lake—lake MO-7
New Pennington—pop pl IN-6
New Pennsylvania Cem—cemetery IN-6
New Pens Well—well TX-5
New Perth NJ-2
New Peter Lockett Tank—reservoir AZ-5
New Petersburg—pop pl OH-6
New Philadelphia CA-9
New Philadelphia TN-4
New Philadelphia—pop pl IL-6
New Philadelphia—pop pl IN-6
New Philadelphia—pop pl OH-6
New Philadelphia—pop pl PA-2
New Philadelphia Borough—civil PA-2
New Philadelphia Cem—cemetery IN-6
New Philadelphia Ch—church LA-4
New Philadelphia Ch—church NC-3
New Philadelphia Missionary Baptist Ch—church FL-3
New Philadelphia (Township of)—other OH-6
New Philippines FM-9
New Piasa Chautauqua Hist Dist—hist pl IL-6
New Picker Cem—cemetery MO-7
New Pickton Cem—cemetery TX-5
New Pierce—pop pl FL-3
New Pilgrim Baptist Ch—church UT-8
New Pilgrim Ch—church AL-4
New Pilgrim Ch—church MS-4
New Pilgrim Ch—church SC-3
New Pilgrim Sch (historical)—school MS-4
New Pilgrim Star Ch—church LA-4
New Pilot Ch—church TN-4
New Pilot Mine—mine MN-6
New Pine Creek—pop pl CA-9
New Pine Creek—pop pl OR-9
New Pine Creek Cem—cemetery OR-9
New Pine Grove Cem—cemetery CT-1
New Pine Grove Ch—church AL-4
New Pine Grove Ch—church (3) GA-3
New Pine Grove Ch—church MS-4
New Pine Hill Cem—cemetery LA-4
New Pine Landing—locale FL-3
New Piney Grove Ch—church AL-4
New Pink Draw—valley TX-5
New Pink Windmill—locale TX-5
New Pipeline Tub—well NM-5
New Piper—locale MO-7
New Pisgah Cem—cemetery MS-4
New Pisgah Ch—church MS-4
New Pisgah Ch—church SC-3
New Piti Sch—school GU-9
New Pittsburg KS-7
New Pittsburg—locale OH-6
New Pittsburg—pop pl IN-6
New Pittsburg—pop pl OH-6
New Pittsburgh KS-7
New Pittsburgh—pop pl OH-6
New Place Rsvr—reservoir OR-9
New Plantation MA-1
New Plantation by Concord MA-1
New Platte SD-7
New Pleasant Ch—church AL-4
New Pleasant Ch—church SC-3
New Pleasantdale Baptist Ch—church MS-4
New Pleasant Gap Ch—church TN-4
New Pleasant Grove Ch—church GA-3
New Pleasant Hill Cem—cemetery NE-7
New Pleasant Hill Ch MS-4
New Pleasant Point Ch—church KY-4
New Pleasant Ridge Ch—church TN-4
New Pleasant Valley Ch—church AL-4
New Pleasant View Ch—church LA-4
New Plimouth MA-1
New Plymouth—pop pl ID-8
New Plymouth—pop pl OH-6
New Plymouth Congregational Church—hist pl ID-8
New Plymouth Heights—pop pl OH-6
New Plymouth Sch—school ID-8
Newpoint IN-6
New Point NJ-2
New Point—locale GA-3
Newpoint—other GA-3
New Point—pop pl IN-6
New Point—pop pl MO-7
New Point—pop pl VA-3
New Point Baptist Church—hist pl NJ-2
New Point Ch—church GA-3
New Point Ch—church MS-4
New Point Ch—church TX-5
New Point Ch—church VA-3
New Point Comfort—cape VA-3
New Point Comfort—pop pl FL-3
New Point Comfort Lighthouse—hist pl VA-3
Newpoint (corporate name for New Point)—pop pl IN-6
New Point (Newpoint)—pop pl GA-3
New Point Sch—school VA-3
New Pond—lake CT-1
New Pond—lake KY-4
New Pond—lake MA-1
New Pond—lake NH-1
New Pond—lake (2) NY-2
New Pond—reservoir CT-1
New Pond—reservoir (2) MA-1
New Pond—reservoir (2) RI-1
New Pond Brook—stream NY-2
New Pond Ch—church GA-3
New Pond Creek—stream WA-9
New Pond Dam RI-1
New Pond Dam—dam (2) MA-1
New Pontotoc Cem—cemetery TX-5
New Pony Spring Well—well NV-8
New Pool Tank—reservoir TX-5
New Poplar Ch—church AL-4
New Poplar Mountain Ch—church VA-3
New Poplar Spring Ch—church GA-3
New Poplar Springs Ch—church (3) AL-4
New Porland NJ-2
New Port AL-4
New Port DE-2
Newport IL-6
Newport IN-6
Newport KS-7
Newport ND-7
Newport PA-2
New Port SC-3
Newport TN-4
Newport—CDP ME-1
Newport—locale AR-4
Newport—locale CA-9
Newport—locale GA-3
Newport—locale IL-6
Newport—locale (2) IA-7
Newport—locale MD-2
Newport—locale NJ-2
Newport—locale NY-2
Newport—locale PA-2
Newport—locale VA-3
Newport—locale WA-9
Newport—pop pl AR-4
Newport—pop pl DE-2
Newport—pop pl (2) FL-3
Newport—pop pl IN-6
Newport—pop pl IA-7
Newport—pop pl KY-4
Newport—pop pl ME-1
New Port—pop pl MD-2
Newport—pop pl MI-6
Newport—pop pl MN-6
Newport—pop pl (2) MS-4
Newport—pop pl MO-7
Newport—pop pl NE-7
Newport—pop pl NH-1
Newport—pop pl NJ-2
Newport—pop pl (3) NY-2
Newport—pop pl NC-3
Newport—pop pl (4) OH-6
Newport—pop pl OK-5
Newport—pop pl OR-9
Newport—pop pl (2) PA-2
Newport—pop pl RI-1
Newport—pop pl SC-3
Newport—pop pl TN-4
Newport—pop pl (2) TX-5
Newport—pop pl VT-1
Newport—pop pl (2) VA-3
Newport—pop pl WA-9
Newport—pop pl WV-2
Newport, Lake—lake OH-6
Newport, Lake—reservoir VA-3
Newport Acad (historical)—school TN-4
New Portage Junction—pop pl PA-2
Newport Apartments—hist pl ND-7
Newport Army Ammun Plant—military IN-6
Newport Artillery Company Armory—hist pl RI-1
New Port Ayre DE-2
Newport Bar—bar AL-4
Newport Bay MA-1
Newport Bay RI-1
Newport Bay—bay CA-9
Newport Bay—bay MD-2
Newport Bay—bay WI-6
Newport Beach RI-1
Newport Beach—beach CA-9
Newport Beach—pop pl CA-9
Newport Bight MA-1
Newport Bight RI-1
Newport Borough—civil PA-2
Newport Branch—stream MD-2
Newport Bridge—bridge FL-3
Newport Brook—stream NY-2
Newport Camp TN-4
Newport Casino—hist pl RI-1
Newport Caves—cave TN-4
Newport (CCD)—cens area KY-4
Newport (CCD)—cens area TN-4
Newport (CCD)—cens area WA-9
Newport Cem—cemetery CA-9
Newport Cem—cemetery MN-6
Newport Cem—cemetery MO-7
Newport Cem—cemetery NC-3
Newport Cem—cemetery PA-2
Newport Cem—cemetery (2) TN-4
Newport Cem—cemetery TX-5
Newport Cem—cemetery VA-3
Newport Cem—cemetery WA-9
Newport Center—pop pl PA-2
Newport Center—pop pl VT-1
Newport Center Cem—cemetery PA-2
Newport Centre PA-2
Newport Ch—church MS-4
Newport Ch—church MO-7
Newport Ch—church NC-3
Newport Ch—church WI-6
Newport Ch (historical)—church AL-4
Newport Coll—school VA-3
Newport Community Hosp Heliport—airport WA-9
Newport Compact (census name Newport)—pop pl NH-1
Newport County (in PMSA 2480, 6480)—pop pl RI-1
Newport Cove—bay ME-1
Newport Creek—stream MD-2
Newport Creek—stream PA-2
Newport Creek—stream WA-9
Newport Dam—dam TN-4
Newport Ditch—canal CO-8
Newport Ditch—canal WY-8
Newport Division—civil TN-4
Newport Downtown Hist Dist—hist pl NH-1
Newport East—pop pl RI-1
Newport Elem Sch—school IN-6
Newport Elem Sch—school NC-3
Newport Entrance—channel AK-9
Newport Ferry (historical)—locale AL-4
Newport First Baptist Ch—church TN-4
Newport Geophysical Observatory—other WA-9
Newport Harbor CA-9
Newport Harbor—bay RI-1
Newport Harbor HS—school CA-9
Newport Harbor Lighthouse—hist pl RI-1
Newport Haven Subdivision—pop pl UT-8
Newport Heights—pop pl CA-9
Newport Heights—pop pl DE-2
Newport Heights—pop pl OR-9
Newport Heights Condominium—pop pl UT-8
Newport Heights Sch—school CA-9
Newport Heights Subdivision—pop pl UT-8
Newport Hill—summit ID-8
Newport Hill—summit VA-3
Newport Hills—pop pl MD-2
Newport Hills—pop pl WA-9
Newport Hills Sch—school WA-9
Newport Hist Dist—hist pl RI-1
New Port (historical)—locale AL-4
Newport (historical)—locale (2) AL-4
Newport (historical)—pop pl MS-4
Newport Hotel and Restaurant—hist pl OK-5
Newport HS—school WA-9
Newport Industrial Complex—locale MS-4
Newport Island—island CA-9
Newport Island—uninc pl CA-9
Newport JHS—school MD-2
Newport Junction—locale TN-4
Newport Junction (RR name for Newport)—other ME-1
Newport Junior & Senior HS—hist pl AR-4
Newport Lake OH-6
Newport Lake—lake AR-4
Newport Lake—reservoir TN-4
New Portland NJ-2
New Portland—pop pl ME-1
New Portland Hill—summit ME-1
Newport Landing—locale AL-4
Newport Landing—locale NJ-2
Newport Landing (historical)—locale AL-4
Newport Landing (historical)—locale TN-4
New Portland Landing TN-4
New Portland (Town of)—pop pl ME-1
New Portland Wire Bridge—hist pl ME-1
Newport Lookout Tower—tower FL-3
Newport (Magisterial District)—fmr MCD VA-3
Newport Marsh—swamp DE-2
Newport Marsh—swamp MD-2
Newport Marshes—swamp NC-3
Newport Marsh Run—stream MD-2
Newport Meadows—lake NJ-2
Newport Mine—mine MI-6
Newport Mountain ME-1
Newport Municipal Airp—airport OR-9
Newport Naval Regional Med Ctr—military RI-1
Newport Neck—cape (2) MD-2
Newport Neck—cape NJ-2
Newport Neck—cape RI-1
Newport News Bar—bar VA-3
Newport News Channel—channel VA-3
Newport News City—civil (2) VA-3
Newport News Creek—stream VA-3
Newport News (ind. city)—pop pl VA-3
Newport News Middle Ground—bar VA-3
Newport News Middle Ground Light—locale VA-3
Newport News Point—cape NC-3
Newport News Point—cape VA-3
Newport Number Two TN-4
New Port Of Miami—pop pl FL-3
Newport Pass—channel TX-5
New Port Plaza (Shop Ctr)—locale FL-3
Newport P.O. AL-4
Newport Pond ME-1
Newport Pond—lake NY-2
Newport Post Office—building TN-4
Newport Rec Area—park VA-3
Newport Resort—locale TN-4
New Port Richey—pop pl FL-3
New Port Richey (CCD)—cens area FL-3
New Port Richey East—CDP FL-3
Newport River—stream NC-3
Newport River Park—park NC-3
Newport Rsvr—reservoir KY-4
Newport Rsvr—reservoir OR-9
Newport Rsvr—reservoir PA-2
Newport Run—stream MD-2
Newport Sch—school CA-9
Newport Sch—school IL-6
Newport Sch—school MN-6
Newport Sch—school MS-4
Newport Shoals—bar AL-4
Newport Shores—pop pl WA-9
New Portsmouth—locale NH-1
Newport Spring—spring FL-3
Newport State Airp—airport RI-1
Newport Station—locale FL-3
Newport Steam Factory—hist pl RI-1
Newport (subdivision)—pop pl PA-2
Newport Subdivision—pop pl UT-8
Newport (Town of)—pop pl ME-1
Newport (Town of)—pop pl NH-1
Newport (Town of)—pop pl NY-2
Newport (Town of)—pop pl VT-1
Newport (Town of)—pop pl WI-6
Newport Township—fmr MCD IA-7
Newport Township—pop pl MO-7
Newport Township—pop pl ND-7
Newport Township—pop pl SD-7
Newport (Township of)—fmr MCD NC-3
Newport (Township of)—pop pl IL-6
Newport (Township of)—pop pl OH-6
Newport (Township of)—pop pl PA-2
Newportville—pop pl PA-2
Newportville Terrace—pop pl PA-2
New Port Walter (Abandoned)—locale AK-9
New Post AZ-5
New Post KS-7
New Post—pop pl VA-3
New Post—pop pl WI-6
New Post Oak Cem—cemetery OK-5
New Post Oak Ch—church AL-4
New Post Office (historical)—building MS-4
New Potasi (historical)—locale AL-4
New Prague—pop pl MN-6
New Prairie Creek—stream IN-6
New Prairie HS—school IN-6
New Prairie JHS—school IN-6
New Prairie State Wildlife Mngmt Area—park MN-6
New Prairie Township—pop pl ND-7
New Prairie (Township of)—pop pl MN-6
New Preston—pop pl CT-1
New Preston Hill—summit CT-1
New Preston Hill Hist Dist—hist pl CT-1
New Preston-Marble Dale—pop pl CT-1
New Primary Sch—school SC-3
New Princeton—locale OH-6
New Princeton—locale OR-9
New Promised Land Cem—cemetery SC-3
New Promised Land Ch—church SC-3
New Prospect AL-4
New Prospect IN-6
New Prospect MS-4
New Prospect NJ-2
New Prospect PA-2
New Prospect—locale TX-5
New Prospect—pop pl (2) AL-4
New Prospect—pop pl SC-3
New Prospect—pop pl TN-4
New Prospect—pop pl TX-5
New Prospect—pop pl WI-6
New Prospect Baptist Ch AL-4
New Prospect Baptist Ch MS-4
New Prospect Baptist Ch TN-4
New Prospect Baptist Ch—church (2) AL-4
New Prospect Baptist Ch—church (2) MS-4
New Prospect Baptist Ch—church TN-4
New Prospect Cem MS-4
New Prospect Cem—cemetery (5) AL-4
New Prospect Cem—cemetery (5) MS-4
New Prospect Cem—cemetery (2) TN-4
New Prospect Cem—cemetery WI-6
New Prospect Ch AL-4
New Prospect Ch MS-4
New Prospect Ch TN-4
New Prospect Ch—church (20) AL-4
New Prospect Ch—church (3) AR-4
New Prospect Ch—church FL-3
New Prospect Ch—church (14) GA-3
New Prospect Ch—church (2) IL-6
New Prospect Ch—church (2) IN-6
New Prospect Ch—church (3) LA-4
New Prospect Ch—church (20) MS-4
New Prospect Ch—church (3) MO-7
New Prospect Ch—church NY-2
New Prospect Ch—church (5) NC-3
New Prospect Ch—church OK-5
New Prospect Ch—church (6) SC-3
New Prospect Ch—church (8) TN-4
New Prospect Ch—church (8) TX-5
New Prospect Ch—church (3) VA-3
New Prospect Ch—church (2) WV-2
New Prospect Ch (historical)—church AL-4
New Prospect Ch (historical)—church (4) MS-4
New Prospect Elem Sch—school TN-4
New Prospect (historical)—locale AL-4
New Prospect (historical)—locale MS-4
New Prospect (historical)—pop pl TN-4
New Prospect Mine—mine TN-4
New Prospect Mine (underground)—mine TN-4
New Prospect Missionary Baptist Ch—church MS-4
New Prospect Missionary Baptist Ch (historical)—church (2) AL-4
New Prospect Missionary Baptist Church TN-4
New Prospect Post OFfice (historical)—building TN-4
New Prospect Presbyterian Ch MS-4
New Prospect Primitive Baptist Ch AL-4
New Prospect Private Sch—school FL-3
New Prospects Camp—locale MS-4
New Prospect Sch—school (2) AL-4
New Prospect Sch—school FL-3
New Prospect Sch—school TN-4
New Prospect Sch (historical)—school MS-4
New Prospect Sch (historical)—school MO-7
New Prospect United Presbyterian Church TN-4
New Prosper Ch—church AR-4
New Prosperity Ch—church AR-4
New Prosperity Ch—church MS-4
New Prosperity Missionary Baptist Ch MS-4
New Providence IN-6
New Providence—locale NC-3
New Providence—locale TN-4
New Providence—other IL-6
New Providence—pop pl IN-6
New Providence—pop pl IA-7
New Providence—pop pl KY-4
New Providence—pop pl MS-4
New Providence—pop pl NJ-2
New Providence—pop pl PA-2
New Providence—pop pl TN-4
New Providence Baptist Ch MS-4
New Providence Baptist Ch TN-4
New Providence Baptist Ch—church AL-4
New Providence Baptist Ch—church MS-4
New Providence Baptist Ch—church TN-4
New Providence Cem—cemetery (2) AL-4
New Providence Cem—cemetery GA-3
New Providence Cem—cemetery IL-6
New Providence Cem—cemetery IN-6
New Providence Cem—cemetery IA-7
New Providence Cem—cemetery KY-4
New Providence Cem—cemetery (3) MS-4
New Providence Cem—cemetery MO-7
New Providence Cem—cemetery SC-3
New Providence Cem—cemetery (3) TN-4
New Providence Ch AL-4
New Providence Ch—church (8) AL-4
New Providence Ch—church (3) AR-4
New Providence Ch—church (8) GA-3
New Providence Ch—church (2) IL-6
New Providence Ch—church IN-6
New Providence Ch—church KY-4
New Providence Ch—church (5) MS-4
New Providence Ch—church (3) MO-7
New Providence Ch—church (2) NC-3
New Providence Ch—church (2) PA-2
New Providence Ch—church (2) SC-3
New Providence Ch—church (5) TN-4
New Providence Ch—church (2) TX-5
New Providence Ch—church VA-3
New Providence Ch of Christ TN-4
New Providence (historical)—locale MS-4
New Providence Meeting House (historical)—church MS-4
New Providence Missionary Baptist Ch—church FL-3
New Providence MS—school TN-4
New Providence P. O. (historical)—locale AL-4
New Providence Post Office—building TN-4
New Providence Post Office (historical)—building PA-2
New Providence Presbyterian Church—hist pl KY-4
New Providence Presbyterian Church—hist pl VA-3
New Providence Presbyterian Church, Academy, and Cemetery—hist pl TN-4
New Providence Primitive Baptist Church TN-4
New Providence Rec Area—park TN-4
New Providence Sch—school WI-6
New Providence Sch (historical)—school MS-4
New Providence Sch (historical)—school TN-4
New Providence School TN-4
New Providence Special Education Center—school TN-4
New Providence Station—locale NJ-2
New Provisor Ch—church GA-3
New Prue—pop pl OK-5
Newquacaw AL-4
New Quarry—pop pl VA-3
New Quarter Ch—church VA-3
New Quarters—locale LA-4
New Quarters Lake—swamp LA-4
New Queen Ch—church AL-4
New Quigley Canyon—valley UT-8
New Quincy Sch—school KS-7
New Rainbow Mine—mine ID-8
New Rall Dam—dam PA-2
New Ramah Ch—church LA-4
New Ramey Cem—cemetery TN-4
New Ramey Ch—church GA-3
New Ramireno Cem—cemetery TX-5
New Ranch Tank—reservoir AZ-5
New Range—range CA-9
New Rapids—rapids UT-8
New Raymer CO-8
New Raymer—pop pl CO-8
New Reading—pop pl OH-6
New Redden Cem—cemetery TN-4
New Redden Chapel Cem TN-4
New Redding IA-7
New Redford Oil Well (Dry)—well CA-9
New Red Hill Ch—church GA-3
New Redington OH-6
New Redland Ch—church GA-3
New Redmond Hotel—hist pl OR-9
New Red Steer Tank—reservoir NM-5
New Red Tank—reservoir TX-5
New Red Top Ch—church MO-7
New Reedy Creek Ch—church TN-4
New Rehoboth Ch—church VA-3
New Reigel OH-6
New Reliance SD-7
New Reliance—locale WA-9
New Resident Ch—church MS-4
New Resident Missionary Baptist Ch MS-4
New Retreat NJ-2
New Reveille Mine—mine NV-8
New Revelation Ch—church TX-5
New Reynolds Well—well TX-5
New Rhodes Cem—cemetery MI-6
New Richland—pop pl MN-6
New Richland—pop pl OH-6
New Richland Ch—church GA-3
New Richland Ch—church MO-7
New Richland (Township of)—civ div MN-6
New Richmond—pop pl IN-6
New Richmond—pop pl KY-4
New Richmond—pop pl MI-6
New Richmond—pop pl OH-6
New Richmond—pop pl PA-2
New Richmond—pop pl WV-2
New Richmond—pop pl WI-6
New Richmond Lake—lake MN-6
New Richmond Mine—mine MI-6
New Richmond News Bldg—hist pl WI-6
New Richmond Roller Mills Co.—hist pl WI-6
New Richmond Station—locale KY-4
New Richmond West Side Hist Dist—hist pl WI-6
New Riding Club—hist pl MA-1
New Riegel—pop pl OH-6
New Riegle OH-6
New Riffle—rapids OR-9
New Right Ch AL-4
New Rigolet Pass LA-4
New Rim Ditch—canal CA-9
New Ringgold—pop pl PA-2
New Ringgold Borough—civil PA-2
New Ringgold Gristmill—hist pl PA-2
New Rising Star School AL-4
New Rising Sun Ch—church LA-4
New River AL-4
Newriver AZ-5
New River CA-9
Newriver TN-4
New River—locale FL-3
New River—pop pl AZ-5
New River—pop pl TN-4
New River—pop pl VA-3
New River—stream AL-4
New River—stream AZ-5
New River—stream (3) CA-9
New River—stream (5) FL-3
New River—stream (2) GA-3
New River—stream LA-4
New River—stream MI-6
New River—stream NH-1
New River—stream (2) NC-3
New River—stream OR-9
New River—stream SC-3
New River—stream TN-4
New River—stream TX-5
New River—stream VA-3
New River—stream WV-2
New River—uninc pl FL-3
New River Air Station NC-3
New River Baptist Ch—church TN-4
New River Bay—bay AK-9
New River Bayou—bay FL-3
New River Canal—canal LA-4
New River (CCD)—cens area TN-4
New River Cem—cemetery MI-6
New River Cem—cemetery NC-3
New River Cem—cemetery VA-3
New River Ch AL-4
New River Ch—church AL-4
New River Ch—church (2) FL-3
New River Ch—church (3) GA-3
New River Ch—church LA-4
New River Ch—church (3) NC-3

**Newton**—*pop pl* TX-5
**Newton**—*pop pl* UT-8
**Newton**—*pop pl* WV-2
**Newton**—*pop pl* (2) WI-6
Newton, Charles, House—*hist pl* MA-1
Newton, George, House—*hist pl* MI-6
Newton, Judge Eben, House—*hist pl* OH-6
Newton, Lake—*reservoir* CA-9
Newton, Marvin, House—*hist pl* VT-1
Newton, William Walter, House—*hist pl* TX-5
Newton Acad (historical)—*school* AL-4
Newton-Allaire House—*hist pl* MI-6
Newton Ave Hist Dist—*hist pl* OH-6
Newton Bald—*summit* NC-3
Newton Bay—*basin* SC-3
Newton Bayou—*gut* AR-4
Newton Bend Bar—*bar* MS-4
Newton Booth Sch—*school* CA-9
*Newton Branch* IL-6
Newton Branch—*stream* IL-6
Newton Branch—*stream* IN-6
Newton Branch—*stream* KY-4
Newton Branch—*stream* NC-3
Newton Branch—*stream* TN-4
Newton Branch—*stream* (3) TX-5
Newton Branch West Cache Canal—*canal* UT-8
Newton Brook—*stream* ME-1
Newton Brook—*stream* (3) MA-1
Newton Brook—*stream* NH-1
Newton Brook—*stream* (2) NY-2
Newton Brook—*stream* VT-1
Newtonburg—*locale* WI-6
**Newtonburg**—*pop pl* PA-2
*Newtonburgh* WI-6
Newton Butte—*summit* AZ-5
Newton Cabin—*locale* OR-9
Newton Cabin—*locale* VT-1
Newton Cannon Cem—*cemetery* TN-4
Newton Canyon—*valley* AZ-5
Newton Canyon—*valley* (2) CA-9
Newton Canyon—*valley* TX-5
Newton Canyon—*valley* UT-8
Newton (CCD)—*cens area* GA-3
Newton (CCD)—*cens area* TX-5
Newton Cem—*cemetery* (2) AL-4
Newton Cem—*cemetery* (3) AR-4
Newton Cem—*cemetery* (2) IL-6
Newton Cem—*cemetery* (3) KY-4
Newton Cem—*cemetery* LA-4
Newton Cem—*cemetery* (2) MA-1
Newton Cem—*cemetery* (3) MO-7
Newton Cem—*cemetery* NJ-2
Newton Cem—*cemetery* (3) NY-2
Newton Cem—*cemetery* NC-3
Newton Cem—*cemetery* (2) OH-6
Newton Cem—*cemetery* PA-2
Newton Cem—*cemetery* SC-3
Newton Cem—*cemetery* (3) TN-4
Newton Cem—*cemetery* (2) TX-5
Newton Cem—*cemetery* UT-8
**Newton Center**—*pop pl* PA-2
**Newton Center (subdivision)**—*pop pl* MA-1
*Newton Centre* MA-1
*Newton Centre* PA-2
Newton Centre Station (historical)—*locale* MA-1
Newton Ch—*church* GA-3
Newton Ch—*church* MI-6
Newton Ch—*church* WI-6
Newton Chapel—*church* (2) AR-4
Newton Chapel—*church* IL-6
Newton Chapel—*church* MS-4
Newton Chapel—*church* OH-6
Newton Chevrolet Bldg—*hist pl* TN-4
Newton Ch of Christ—*church* MS-4
Newton Christian Ch—*church* MS-4
Newton Christian Sch—*school* IA-7
*Newton Church* AL-4
*Newton City* KS-7
Newton City-County Airp—*airport* KS-7
Newton City Hall—*building* MA-1
Newton City Hall—*building* MS-4
Newton City Lake—*reservoir* NC-3
Newton City Lake Dam—*dam* NC-3
Newton Clark Glacier—*glacier* OR-9
Newton Coll of the Sacred Heart—*school* MA-1
Newton Conover Airp—*airport* NC-3
Newton-Conover HS—*school* NC-3
Newton-Conover JHS—*school* NC-3
Newton-Conover MS—*school* NC-3
**Newton Corner**—*pop pl* MA-1
Newton Corners—*locale* IL-6
Newton Country Club—*locale* KS-7
**Newton (County)**—*pop pl* AR-4
**Newton (County)**—*pop pl* GA-3
**Newton County**—*pop pl* IN-6
**Newton County**—*pop pl* MS-4
**Newton County**—*pop pl* MO-7
**Newton (County)**—*pop pl* TX-5
Newton County Courthouse—*hist pl* GA-3
Newton County Courthouse—*hist pl* TX-5
*Newton Creek* CO-8
*Newton Creek* NJ-2
*Newton Creek* UT-8
**Newton Creek**—*pop pl* OR-9
Newton Creek—*stream* AL-4
Newton Creek—*stream* AK-9
Newton Creek—*stream* AR-4
Newton Creek—*stream* CA-9
Newton Creek—*stream* GA-3
Newton Creek—*stream* ID-8
Newton Creek—*stream* (2) MI-6
Newton Creek—*stream* NJ-2
Newton Creek—*stream* NC-3
Newton Creek—*stream* (3) OR-9
Newton Creek—*stream* TX-5
Newton Creek—*stream* UT-8
Newton Creek—*stream* VA-3
Newton Creek—*stream* WY-8
Newton Creek Campground—*locale* WY-8
Newton Dam—*dam* UT-8
Newton D. Baker Veterans Administration Center—*hospital* WV-2
*Newton Depot* MS-4
Newton Ditch—*canal* CO-8
Newton Ditch—*canal* IL-6
Newton Ditch—*canal* OH-6
Newton Drain—*stream* MI-6
Newton Draw—*valley* NM-5
Newton Draw—*valley* TX-5
Newton Draw—*valley* WY-8
Newton Drury Peak—*summit* CA-9
Newton Elem Sch—*school* MS-4
Newton Estates Sch—*school* GA-3
**Newton Factory**—*pop pl* GA-3
Newton Factory Cem—*cemetery* GA-3
Newton Falls—*falls* MN-6
**Newton Falls**—*pop pl* NY-2
**Newton Falls**—*pop pl* OH-6
Newton Falls Brook—*stream* NY-2
Newton Falls Covered Bridge—*hist pl* OH-6
Newton First Methodist Protestant Ch—*church* MS-4
Newton Flat Cem—*cemetery* AR-4
Newton Fork—*stream* SD-7
Newton Friends' Meetinghouse—*hist pl* NJ-2
**Newton Grove**—*pop pl* NC-3
Newton Grove Ch—*church* GA-3
Newton Grove (Township of)—*fmr MCD* NC-3
Newton Gulch—*valley* AK-9
Newton Gulch—*valley* (2) MT-8
**Newton Hamilton**—*pop pl* PA-2
Newton Hamilton Borough—*civil* PA-2
**Newton Heights**—*pop pl* NJ-2
**Newton Heights (subdivision)**—*pop pl* NC-3
Newton Highlands Hist Dist—*hist pl* MA-1
**Newton Highlands (subdivision)**—*pop pl* MA-1
*Newton Hill* ME-1
*Newton Hill* UT-8
Newton Hill—*summit* ME-1
Newton Hill—*summit* MA-1
Newton Hill—*summit* NY-2
Newton Hill—*summit* PA-2
Newton Hill—*summit* TN-4
Newton Hill—*summit* WY-8
Newton Hill Cem—*cemetery* PA-2
Newton Hill Quarry—*mine* TN-4
Newton Hills State Park—*park* SD-7
Newton (historical)—*civil* SD-7
Newton (historical)—*locale* SD-7
Newton Hollow—*valley* AR-4
Newton Hollow—*valley* VA-3
Newton Homestead—*hist pl* NY-2
**Newton Hook**—*pop pl* NY-2
Newton Hosp—*hospital* MS-4
*Newton Hospital* KS-7
Newton House—*hist pl* KY-4
Newton House—*hist pl* TX-5
Newton HS—*school* KS-7
Newton HS—*school* MA-1
Newton HS—*school* MS-4
Newton HS—*school* NJ-2
Newtonia—*locale* MS-4
**Newtonia**—*pop pl* MO-7
Newtonia Branch—*stream* MO-7
Newtonia Female Institute (historical)—*school* MS-4
Newtonia Institute for Boys (historical)—*school* MS-4
Newtonia Post Office (historical)—*building* MS-4
Newtonia Township—*civil* MO-7
Newton Island—*island* AR-4
Newton Island—*island* MA-1
Newton Island—*island* WI-6
Newton JHS—*school* CO-8
Newton Junction—*locale* PA-2
**Newton Junction**—*pop pl* NH-1
Newton Junior Coll—*school* MA-1
Newton-Kemp Houses—*hist pl* KY-4
Newton Lagoon Dam—*dam* MS-4
Newton Lake—*lake* AR-4
Newton Lake—*lake* FL-3
Newton Lake—*lake* (2) MI-6
Newton Lake—*lake* (2) MN-6
Newton Lake—*lake* NJ-2
Newton Lake—*lake* PA-2
Newton Lake—*lake* TX-5
Newton Lake—*lake* (2) WI-6
**Newton Lake**—*pop pl* PA-2
Newton Lake—*reservoir* GA-3
Newton Lake Park—*park* NJ-2
Newton Lakes—*reservoir* TX-5
Newton Lakes—*reservoir* WY-8
Newton Landing—*locale* AR-4
Newton Landing (historical)—*locale* MS-4
Newton Lookout Tower—*locale* MS-4
Newton Lower Falls Dam—*dam* MA-1
Newton Lower Falls Hist Dist—*hist pl* MA-1
**Newton Lower Falls (subdivision)**—*pop pl* MA-1
Newton Male and Female Coll (historical)—*school* MS-4
*Newton Meadow Pond* MA-1
Newton Memorial Hosp—*hospital* NY-2
Newton Memorial Hosp—*hospital* TX-5
Newton Memorial Sch—*school* MA-1
Newton Mesa—*summit* TX-5
Newton-Midland City (CCD)—*cens area* AL-4
Newton-Midland City Division—*civil* AL-4
Newton Mine—*mine* CA-9
Newton Mtn—*summit* MT-8
*Newton Neck* MD-2
**Newton (New Boston Junction)**—*pop pl* PA-2
Newton Observatory—*building* CA-9
Newton Oil Field—*oilfield* TX-5
Newton Park—*flat* SD-7
Newton Park—*park* AL-4
Newton Park—*park* MN-6
**Newton Park (subdivision)**—*pop pl* NC-3
**Newton Park (subdivision)**—*pop pl* VA-3
Newton Parrish Sch—*school* KY-4
*Newton Pass* LA-4
*Newton Peak* UT-8
Newton Peak—*summit* AK-9
Newton Point—*cape* KY-4
Newton Point—*cape* TX-5
Newton Pond—*reservoir* (2) AL-4
Newton Pond—*reservoir* MA-1
Newton Pond Dam—*dam* MA-1
Newton Post Office—*building* MA-1
Newton Post Office (historical)—*building* TN-4
Newton Presbyterian Ch—*church* MS-4
Newton Prospect—*mine* WY-8
Newton Public Library—*building* MS-4
Newton-Ramsom Sch—*school* PA-2
Newton Ranch—*locale* NE-7
Newton Ransom Elem Sch—*school* PA-2
Newton Reservoir—*hist pl* UT-8
Newton Reservoir Dam—*dam* MA-1
Newton Rock—*pillar* RI-1
Newton Rogers Cem—*cemetery* NC-3
Newton Rsvr—*reservoir* (2) MA-1
Newton Rsvr—*reservoir* MT-8
Newton Rsvr—*reservoir* NJ-2
Newton Rsvr—*reservoir* UT-8
Newton Run—*stream* NY-2
Newton Run—*stream* (2) PA-2
**Newtons Acres (subdivision)**—*pop pl* DE-2
Newton Sch—*school* (2) CA-9
Newton Sch—*school* CO-8
Newton Sch—*school* MD-2
Newton Sch—*school* MA-1
Newton Sch—*school* (3) MI-6
Newton Sch—*school* MO-7
Newton Sch—*school* MT-8
Newton Sch—*school* NC-3
Newton Sch—*school* OH-6
Newton Sch (abandoned)—*school* MO-7
Newton Sch (historical)—*school* (2) MO-7
Newton Sch (historical)—*school* TN-4
*Newton School* PA-2
Newtons Creek—*stream* KY-4
Newtons Creek Ch—*church* KY-4
Newtons Creek (historical)—*stream* VA-3
Newtons Crossroads—*locale* NC-3
Newtons Eddy—*bay* NY-2
Newtons Grove—*locale* IA-7
Newtons Hill—*summit* MA-1
**Newtons (historical)**—*pop pl* OR-9
Newtons Lake Dam—*dam* MS-4
Newtons Landing—*locale* TN-4
Newtons Mill Run—*stream* VA-3
Newton Smith Brook—*stream* MA-1
Newton South HS—*school* MA-1
Newton Speedway—*other* IA-7
Newtons Pond—*lake* VA-3
Newtons Pond—*reservoir* NC-3
Newtons Pond Dam—*dam* NC-3
Newton Spring—*spring* OR-9
Newton Spring—*spring* TN-4
Newton Spring—*spring* WY-8
*Newton Springs* AL-4
**Newton Springs**—*pop pl* AL-4
Newton Springs Ch—*church* AR-4
Newton Springs Ch—*church* KY-4
*Newton Station* IN-6
Newton Station—*building* PA-2
Newton Station—*locale* PA-2
**Newton Stewart**—*pop pl* IN-6
Newton-Stewart State Rec Area—*park* IN-6
Newton Street Railway Carbarn—*hist pl* MA-1
Newton Street Sch—*hist pl* MA-1
Newton Street Sch—*school* NJ-2
**Newton Subdivision**—*pop pl* UT-8
**Newtonsville**—*pop pl* OH-6
Newton Theological Institution Hist Dist—*hist pl* MA-1
Newton (Town of)—*civil* MA-1
**Newton (Town of)**—*pop pl* NH-1
**Newton (Town of)**—*pop pl* (2) WI-6
Newton Township—*civil* MO-7
Newton Township—*fmr MCD* (4) IA-7
**Newton Township**—*pop pl* KS-7
Newton Township Consolidated Sch—*school* PA-2
Newton (Township of)—*fmr MCD* AR-4
Newton (Township of)—*fmr MCD* NC-3
**Newton (Township of)**—*pop pl* IL-6
**Newton (Township of)**—*pop pl* IN-6
**Newton (Township of)**—*pop pl* (2) MI-6
**Newton (Township of)**—*pop pl* MN-6
**Newton (Township of)**—*pop pl* (5) OH-6
**Newton (Township of)**—*pop pl* PA-2
Newton Union Schoolhouse—*hist pl* NJ-2
Newton United Methodist Ch—*church* MS-4
Newton Upper Falls Dam—*dam* MA-1
Newton Upper Falls Hist Dist—*hist pl* MA-1
**Newton Upper Falls (subdivision)**—*pop pl* MA-1
Newton Valley—*valley* WI-6
*Newton Varnado Cemetery* MS-4
**Newton Village**—*pop pl* MD-2
Newtonville—*locale* IA-7
Newtonville—*locale* NJ-2
Newtonville—*locale* TX-5
**Newtonville**—*pop pl* AL-4
**Newtonville**—*pop pl* IN-6
**Newtonville**—*pop pl* NY-2
**Newtonville**—*pop pl* SC-3
Newtonville Cem—*cemetery* NJ-2
Newtonville Hist Dist—*hist pl* MA-1
**Newtonville (historical)**—*pop pl* MS-4
Newtonville Post Office—*hist pl* NY-2
Newtonville Sch—*school* AL-4
*Newtonville Station* MS-4
Newtonville Station Post Office (historical)—*building* MS-4
**Newtonville (subdivision)**—*pop pl* MA-1
Newton Vocational Sch—*school* MS-4
Newton Waterworks—*other* KS-7
Newton Well—*well* (2) NM-5
Newton-Wellesley Hosp—*hospital* MA-1
Newton West Church Hist Dist—*hist pl* MS-4
**Newton Woods**—*pop pl* DE-2
**Newton Woods**—*pop pl* VA-3
**Newtopia Acres Subdivision**—*pop pl* UT-8
*New Topsail Beach* NC-3
New Topsail Beach—*other* NC-3
New Topsail Inlet—*bay* NC-3
*New Town* AL-4
*Newtown* FL-3
*Newtown* IN-6
*New Town* KS-7
*Newtown* ME-1
*New Town* MD-2
*Newtown* MA-1
*Newtown* MS-4
*Newtown* NJ-2
*New Town* NC-3
*Newtown* OH-6
*Newtown* PA-2
*New Town* VA-3
Newtown—*locale* CA-9
Newtown—*locale* GA-3
New Town—*locale* GA-3
Newtown—*locale* ME-1
Newtown—*locale* MD-2
Newtown—*locale* NJ-2
New Town—*locale* OH-6
Newtown—*locale* (2) PA-2
Newtown—*locale* TN-4
Newtown—*locale* (4) VA-3
Newtown—*other* IL-6
Newtown—*other* OH-6
**New Town**—*pop pl* AL-4
**Newtown**—*pop pl* AR-4
**New Town**—*pop pl* AR-4
**Newtown**—*pop pl* (2) CA-9
**Newtown**—*pop pl* CT-1
**New Town**—*pop pl* GA-3
**Newtown**—*pop pl* GA-3
**Newtown**—*pop pl* IL-6
**Newtown**—*pop pl* IN-6
**Newtown**—*pop pl* KY-4
**Newtown**—*pop pl* (2) MD-2
**New Town**—*pop pl* MD-2
**Newtown**—*pop pl* MD-2
**Newtown**—*pop pl* MA-1
**New Town**—*pop pl* (2) MS-4
**Newtown**—*pop pl* MO-7
**Newtown**—*pop pl* (3) NY-2
**New Town**—*pop pl* (2) NC-3
**New Town**—*pop pl* ND-7
**Newtown**—*pop pl* (2) OH-6
**New Town**—*pop pl* PA-2
**Newtown**—*pop pl* (9) PA-2
**New Town**—*pop pl* SC-3
**New Town**—*pop pl* (3) TN-4
**Newtown**—*pop pl* (2) TN-4
**Newtown**—*pop pl* (4) VA-3
**Newtown**—*pop pl* (2) WV-2
Newtown Battlefield—*hist pl* NY-2
Newtown Battlefield Reservation—*park* NY-2
Newtown Bend—*bend* MS-4
Newtown Borough—*civil* PA-2
Newtown Branch—*stream* KY-4
New Town Branch—*stream* TN-4
Newtown Cem—*cemetery* IN-6
New Town Cem—*cemetery* MS-4
New Town Cem—*cemetery* NH-1
Newtown Cem—*cemetery* NC-3
New Town Cem—*cemetery* TN-4
Newtown Cem—*cemetery* TN-4
Newtown Ch—*church* GA-3
New Town Ch—*church* OK-5
New Town Ch—*church* SC-3
Newtown Ch—*church* TN-4
New Town Ch of Christ—*church* AL-4
Newtown Country Club—*other* CT-1
*Newtown Creek* MD-2
Newtown Creek—*stream* CA-9
Newtown Creek—*stream* ME-1
Newtown Creek—*stream* (2) NY-2
Newtown Creek—*stream* PA-2
Newtown Creek Bridge—*hist pl* PA-2
Newtown Dam—*dam* PA-2
*New Towne* MA-1
*New Towne, Town of* MA-1
*New Towneck* MD-2
New Town Elem Sch (historical)—*school* AL-4
Newtowne Mall—*locale* NC-3
New Towne South—*uninc pl* VA-3
Newtown Ferry (historical)—*locale* AL-4
Newtown Flat—*flat* CA-9
Newtown Flats—*flat* PA-2
Newtown Friends Meetinghouse and Cemetery—*hist pl* PA-2
**Newtown Heights**—*pop pl* PA-2
Newtown Heights—*uninc pl* FL-3
*Newtown Hill* ME-1
Newtown Hill—*summit* ME-1
Newtown Hill—*summit* MA-1
Newtown Hist Dist—*hist pl* PA-2
Newtown Hist Dist—*hist pl* (2) VA-3
Newtown Hist Dist (Boundary Increase)—*hist pl* PA-2
Newtown Hist Dist (Boundary Increase: North and South Exts)—*hist pl* PA-2
Newtown (historical)—*locale* (2) AL-4
Newtown (historical)—*locale* MS-4
**Newtown (historical)**—*pop pl* IA-7
**New Town (historical)**—*pop pl* MA-1
**New Town (historical)**—*pop pl* VA-3
Newtown Hollow—*valley* MO-7
Newtown HS—*school* NY-2
*Newtown JHS* PA-2
Newtown Landing (historical)—*locale* AL-4
Newtown (Magisterial District)—*fmr MCD* VA-3
Newtown Mine—*mine* CA-9
New Town Municipal Airp—*airport* ND-7
Newtown Neck—*cape* MD-2
Newtown Plains—*flat* NH-1
*Newtown Pond* MA-1
Newtown Post Office (historical)—*building* PA-2
Newtown Presbyterian Church—*hist pl* PA-2
New Town Public Use Area—*park* ND-7
Newtown Sch—*school* IL-6
New Town Sch—*school* SC-3
New Town Sch—*school* TX-5
**Newtown Square**—*pop pl* PA-2
**Newtown Square (Township name Newtown)**—*pop pl* PA-2
**New Town (subdivision)**—*pop pl* AL-4
**Newtown (Town of)**—*pop pl* CT-1
Newtown (Township of)—*other* OH-6
**Newtown (Township of)**—*pop pl* IL-6
**Newtown (Township of)**—*pop pl* (2) PA-2
Newtown Village Cem—*cemetery* CT-1
Newt Prong—*stream* TN-4
New Trace Creek Ch—*church* MO-7
New Trail Canyon—*valley* CA-9
New Trail Mine—*mine* CA-9
New Travel Ch—*church* MS-4
New Travelers Home Ch—*church* GA-3
New Travelers Rest Baptist Ch—*church* MS-4
**New Trenton**—*pop pl* IN-6
New Trenton Hill—*summit* IN-6
New Tribe Mission Lake Dam—*dam* MS-4
New Tribes Institute—*school* PA-2
New Tribes Mission—*church* MO-7
New Tribes Mission HQ—*church* FL-3
Newt Ridge—*ridge* NC-3
**New Trier**—*pop pl* MN-6
New Trier HS—*school* IL-6
**New Trier (Township of)**—*pop pl* IL-6
New Trinity Ch—*church* AL-4
New Trinity Ch—*church* SC-3
**New Tripoli**—*pop pl* PA-2
*New Troy* AL-4
**New Troy**—*pop pl* MI-6
New Troy Cem—*cemetery* AR-4
New Troy Cem—*cemetery* MI-6
*New True Light Baptist Ch* AL-4
New True Light Ch—*church* AL-4
New Truelight Ch—*church* (2) MS-4
**New Truxton**—*pop pl* MO-7
Newts Canyon—*valley* UT-8
Newtson Ditch—*canal* IN-6
Newts Waterhole—*lake* OR-9
New Tuck Cem—*cemetery* KY-4
**New Tucson**—*pop pl* AZ-5
New Tulsa—*locale* OK-5
**New Tulsa**—*pop pl* OK-5
*New Turkestan* AL-4
*New Turkestan Cemetery* AL-4
New Turkey Key—*island* FL-3
Newt Young Ditch—*canal* OR-9
*Newty Pond* MA-1
**New Ulm**—*pop pl* MN-6
**New Ulm**—*pop pl* TX-5
New Ulm Armory—*hist pl* MN-6
New Ulm Cem—*cemetery* TX-5
New Ulm Country Club—*other* MN-6
New Ulm Oil Company Service Station—*hist pl* MN-6
New Ulm Oil Field—*oilfield* TX-5
New Ulm Post Office—*hist pl* MN-6
*New Ulysses* KS-7
**New Underwood**—*pop pl* SD-7
New Underwood Dam—*dam* SD-7
**New Union**—*pop pl* MS-4
**New Union**—*pop pl* TN-4
*New Union Baptist Ch* AL-4
*New Union Baptist Church* TN-4
New Union Cem—*cemetery* AL-4
New Union Cem—*cemetery* IL-6
New Union Cem—*cemetery* MS-4
New Union Ch—*church* (4) AL-4
New Union Ch—*church* FL-3
New Union Ch—*church* (4) GA-3
New Union Ch—*church* (2) IN-6
New Union Ch—*church* KY-4
New Union Ch—*church* LA-4
New Union Ch—*church* MS-4
New Union Ch—*church* (2) NC-3
New Union Ch—*church* (5) TN-4
New Union Ch of Christ—*church* TN-4
New Union Congregational Methodist Ch—*church* AL-4
New Union Creek—*stream* LA-4
New Union Elem Sch—*school* TN-4
New Union Field Cem—*cemetery* NY-2
New Union Fork Ch—*church* TN-4
*New Union Grove Ch* AL-4
*New Union Holiness Ch* AL-4
New Union Methodist Ch (historical)—*church* TN-4
New Union Sch—*school* IL-6
New Union Sch—*school* (2) KS-7
New Union Sch (abandoned)—*school* PA-2
New Union Sch (historical)—*school* TN-4
**New Unionville**—*pop pl* IN-6
**New Upsala**—*pop pl* FL-3
**New Upton**—*pop pl* VA-3
New USGS Camp—*locale* HI-9
**New Utrecht**—*pop pl* NY-2
New Utrecht Reformed Church and Buildings—*hist pl* NY-2
*Newuwoma* FM-9
New Valewood Ditch—*canal* MS-4
**New Valley**—*pop pl* MD-2
New Valley Cem—*cemetery* TN-4
New Valley Ch—*church* TN-4
New Valley Grove Ch—*church* GA-3
New Valley Sch—*school* MD-2
New Veale Creek Cem—*cemetery* IN-6
**New Verda**—*pop pl* LA-4
New Verde Mines—*mine* CO-8
New Vermillion Ch—*church* IN-6
New Vermont Cem—*cemetery* NY-2
New Vernon—*locale* NY-2
**New Vernon**—*pop pl* NJ-2
**New Vernon**—*pop pl* PA-2
New Vernon Cem—*cemetery* NJ-2
New Vernon Cem—*cemetery* NY-2
New Vernon Ch—*church* AL-4
New Vernon Ch—*church* NC-3
New Vernon Ch—*church* VA-3
New Vernon Hist Dist—*hist pl* NJ-2
**New Vernon (Township of)**—*pop pl* PA-2
**New Victory**—*pop pl* TN-4
New Victory Baptist Ch—*church* TN-4
New Victory Cem—*cemetery* TN-4
New Victory Ch—*church* OK-5
New Victory United Methodist Ch—*church* TN-4
New Viele Chapel—*church* SC-3
**New Vienna**—*pop pl* IA-7
**New Vienna**—*pop pl* OH-6
New View Ch—*church* AR-4
New View Sch—*school* TN-4
*New Village* PA-2
**New Village**—*pop pl* CT-1
**New Village**—*pop pl* MA-1
**New Village**—*pop pl* NJ-2
New Village Ch—*church* NY-2
**New Village (subdivision)**—*pop pl* AL-4
**New Village (subdivision)**—*pop pl* PA-2
*Newville* MS-4
*Newville* PA-2
Newville—*locale* CA-9
Newville—*locale* ND-7
Newville—*locale* PA-2
Newville—*locale* VA-3
**Newville**—*pop pl* AL-4
**Newville**—*pop pl* IN-6
**Newville**—*pop pl* NY-2
**Newville**—*pop pl* OH-6
**Newville**—*pop pl* (3) PA-2
**Newville**—*pop pl* VA-3
**Newville**—*pop pl* WV-2
**Newville**—*pop pl* WI-6
Newville Baptist Ch—*church* AL-4
Newville Borough—*civil* PA-2
Newville Cem—*cemetery* AL-4
Newville Cem—*cemetery* PA-2
Newville Cem—*cemetery* WV-2
Newville Cem—*cemetery* WI-6
**Newville Center**—*pop pl* IN-6
Newville Ch—*church* OH-6
Newville Creek—*stream* NY-2
Newville HS—*school* AL-4
Newville (Magisterial District)—*fmr MCD* VA-3
Newville Sch—*school* SC-3
**Newville (Township of)**—*pop pl* IN-6
New Vine Ch—*church* KY-4
New Vine Ch—*church* (2) VA-3
New Vine Run Cem—*cemetery* KY-4
**New Vineyard**—*pop pl* ME-1
New Vineyard Basin—*basin* ME-1
New Vineyard Mountains—*summit* ME-1
**New Vineyard (Town of)**—*pop pl* ME-1
New Virgin Ch—*church* AL-4
*New Virginia* AZ-5
**New Virginia**—*pop pl* IL-6
**New Virginia**—*pop pl* IA-7
**New Virginia**—*pop pl* PA-2
New Virginia Cem—*cemetery* NE-7
New Virginia Ch—*church* NE-7
New Virginia Cove—*bay* VA-3
New Visher Rsvr—*reservoir* OR-9
New Vision Ch—*church* MO-7
**New Visitors Center**—*pop pl* NC-3
New Volunteer Mine—*mine* MI-6
*New Waco* KS-7
**New Wakefield**—*pop pl* AL-4
*New Wakefield P.O.* AL-4
**New Wales**—*pop pl* FL-3
New Wales RR Station (historical)—*locale* FL-3
New Wall Lake Dam—*dam* SD-7
New Walnut Grove Sch—*school* KY-4
New Wapping Cem—*cemetery* CT-1
New Warden Airp—*airport* WA-9
**New Washington**—*pop pl* IN-6
**New Washington**—*pop pl* OH-6
**New Washington**—*pop pl* PA-2
New Washington Borough—*civil* PA-2
New Washington Township (historical)—*civil* ND-7
**New Washoe City**—*pop pl* NV-8
*New Water* AZ-5
**New Waterford**—*pop pl* OH-6
New Water Line Camp—*locale* AZ-5
*New Water Mountains* AZ-5
New Water Mountains—*range* AZ-5
New Water Pass—*gap* AZ-5
New Water Spring—*spring* AZ-5
New Water Tank—*reservoir* (2) AZ-5
New Water Tanks—*reservoir* AZ-5
New Water Well—*well* (4) AZ-5
New Water Windmill—*locale* AZ-5
*New Watson* (2) IN-6
**New Waverly**—*pop pl* IN-6
**New Waverly**—*pop pl* TX-5
New Waverly (CCD)—*cens area* TX-5
New Wawayanda Lake—*reservoir* NJ-2
New Wawayanda Lake Dam—*dam* NJ-2
*Newway* OH-6
**Newway**—*pop pl* OH-6
**New Way**—*pop pl* OH-6
New Way Fellowship Baptist Ch—*church* FL-3
New Weber Ditch—*canal* CA-9
*New Weeping Willow Church* AL-4
*New Wehdem* TX-5
**New Wehdem**—*pop pl* TX-5
*New Welcome Baptist Church* AL-4
New Welcome Ch—*church* AL-4
New Well—*locale* (3) NM-5
New Well—*well* (6) AZ-5
New Well—*well* (32) NM-5
New Well—*well* (16) TX-5
New Well Canyon—*valley* (2) NM-5
New Well Canyon—*valley* (2) TX-5
New Well Draw—*valley* NM-5
New Well Hills—*summit* TX-5
**New Wells**—*pop pl* MO-7
New Wells—*well* NM-5
New Wells Lake—*reservoir* TX-5
New Wells Sch—*school* MO-7
New Well Windmill—*locale* (8) TX-5
New Well Windmill—*well* AZ-5
New West Cem—*cemetery* CT-1
New West Chapel—*church* TX-5
New West Greene—*locale* AL-4
New West Grove Cem—*cemetery* PA-2
New West Hollow—*valley* WV-2
**New Weston**—*pop pl* OH-6
New West Point Ch—*church* TN-4
*New West Point Freewill Baptist Ch* TN-4
New Westside Cem—*cemetery* MA-1
**New Westville**—*pop pl* OH-6
New Wharf—*locale* DE-2
**New Whiteland**—*pop pl* IN-6
New White Stone Baptist Ch—*church* MS-4
New Whitestone Ch (historical)—*church* MS-4
New Wildcat Windmill—*locale* TX-5
**New Willard**—*pop pl* TX-5
**New Wilmington**—*pop pl* PA-2
New Wilmington Borough—*civil* PA-2
**New Wilson**—*pop pl* IL-6
New Wilson Ch—*church* IN-6
New Wilton Rsvr—*reservoir* NH-1
**New Winchester**—*pop pl* IN-6
**New Winchester**—*pop pl* OH-6
New Winchester Cem—*cemetery* IN-6
New Windfall Shaft—*mine* NV-8
New Windmill—*locale* (4) AZ-5
New Windmill—*locale* CO-8
New Windmill—*locale* NE-7
New Windmill—*locale* (18) NM-5
New Windmill—*locale* (29) TX-5
New Windmills—*locale* TX-5
*New Windsor* CO-8
**New Windsor**—*pop pl* MD-2
**New Windsor**—*pop pl* NY-2
New Windsor Cantonment—*hist pl* NY-2
New Windsor Cem—*cemetery* IL-6
New Windsor (census name for New Windsor Center)—*CDP* NY-2
*New Windsor Center* NY-2
New Windsor Center (census name New Windsor)—*other* NY-2
*New Windsor (corporate name Windsor)* IL-6
New Windsor Oil Field—*oilfield* CO-8
New Windsor Sch—*school* NY-2
**New Windsor (Town of)**—*pop pl* NY-2
New Windsor West—*CDP* NY-2

**New Windsor (Windsor)**—pop pl ... IL-6
New Wine Township—fmr MCD ... IA-7
New Winsor (historical)—locale ... KS-7
New Wit Ch—church ... VA-3
New Witten ... SD-7
**New Witten**—pop pl ... SD-7
New Wolfpen Branch—stream ... VA-3
New Wood Creek—stream ... WI-6
New Wood River—stream ... WI-6
New Wood State Public Hunting Grounds—park ... WI-6
**New Woodstock**—pop pl ... NY-2
New Woodstock Elementary School ... AL-4
New Woodville (corporate name Woodville) ... OK-5
**New Woollam**—pop pl ... MO-7
**New Worcester (historical)**—pop pl ... MA-1
New Worke ... DE-2
New World—area ... TN-4
New World Acad—school ... FL-3
New World Gulch—valley ... MT-8
New World Learning Center—school ... FL-3
New World Park—park ... AZ-5
New World Temple—church ... NJ-2
New Wortham Lake—reservoir ... TX-5
**New Wren**—pop pl ... MS-4
New Wright Ch—church ... AL-4
New Wright Monmt—park ... AZ-5
New Wrights Chapel—church ... TN-4
New Yale Sch—school ... NE-7
New-Yau-Cau ... AL-4
New Yaucaw ... AL-4
New Yauger ... AL-4
New Year—locale ... MT-8
New Year Bar (inundated)—bar ... UT-8
New Year Bay ... CA-9
New Year Creek ... CA-9
New Year Creek—stream ... TX-5
New Year Gulch—valley ... AK-9
New Year Gulch—valley ... MT-8
New Year Island ... CA-9
New Year Island ... MP-9
New Year Islands—island ... AK-9
New Year Lake—lake ... NV-8
New Year Mine—mine ... AZ-5
New Year Mine—mine ... CA-9
New Year Mine—mine ... MT-8
New Year Mine—mine ... NV-8
New Year Peak—summit ... MT-8
New Years Cabin Spring—spring ... AZ-5
New Years Canyon—valley ... NV-8
New Years Cave—cave ... AL-4
New Years Creek—stream ... NC-3
New Years Creek—stream ... OH-6
New Years Lake—lake ... ID-8
New Years Mine—mine ... CA-9
New Years Point ... CA-9
New Yellow Spot Mine—mine ... CO-8
New York ... AL-4
New York ... IN-6
New York—fmr MCD ... NE-7
New York—locale ... FL-3
New York—locale ... KY-4
New York—locale ... TX-5
New York—mine ... UT-8
**New York**—pop pl ... IA-7
**New York**—pop pl ... MO-7
**New York**—pop pl ... NM-5
**New York**—pop pl ... NY-2
New York—uninc pl ... GA-3
New York, Westchester and Boston RR Administration Bldg—hist pl ... NY-2
New Yorka ... AL-4
New York Amsterdam News Bldg—hist pl ... NY-2
New York Athletic Club—other ... NY-2
New York Ave Ch—church ... TX-5
New York Ave JHS—school ... NY-2
New York Bar—bar (2) ... CA-9
New York Bar—flat ... WA-9
New York Basin—basin ... CO-8
New York Bay Cem—cemetery ... NJ-2
New York Belting and Packing Co.—hist pl ... CT-1
New York Block—hist pl ... WI-6
New York Botanical Gardens—hist pl ... NY-2
New York Branch—stream ... IA-7
New York Butte—summit ... CA-9
New York Canal—canal ... ID-8
New York Cancer Hosp—hist pl ... NY-2
New York Canyon ... NV-8
New York Canyon—valley (4) ... CA-9
New York Canyon—valley (7) ... NV-8
New York Cardiac Home—building ... NY-2
New York Cem—cemetery ... IA-7
New York Cem—cemetery (2) ... MS-4
New York Central Freight House—hist pl ... OH-6
New York Central Junction ... OH-6
New York Central Terminal—hist pl ... NY-2
New York City Community Coll—school ... NY-2
New York City Marble Cemetery—hist pl ... NY-2
New York Collection Canal—canal ... CO-8
New York Cotton Exchange—hist pl ... NY-2
New York (County) ... NY-2
New York County Lawyers Association Bldg—hist pl ... NY-2
New York Creek—stream (2) ... AK-9
New York Creek—stream (2) ... CA-9
New York Creek—stream (2) ... CO-8
New York Creek—stream ... MI-6
New York Creek—stream ... NE-7
New York Creek—stream ... TX-5
New York Elem Sch—school ... KS-7
New Yorker Hollow—valley ... MN-6
New York Executive Mansion—hist pl ... NY-2
New York Flat—swamp ... CA-9
New York & Greenwood Lake Junction—uninc pl ... NJ-2
New York Guild Home—building ... NY-2
New York Gulch ... CO-8
New York Gulch—valley ... AK-9
New York Gulch—valley (3) ... CA-9
New York Gulch—valley ... ID-8
New York Gulch—valley ... WA-9
New York Hill—summit ... CA-9
New York Hill—summit ... TX-5
**New York (historical)**—pop pl ... MS-4
**New York (historical)**—pop pl ... TN-4
New York Historical Society—building ... NY-2
New York Hosp—hospital (2) ... NY-2
New York Hotel—hist pl ... UT-8
New York Institute of Technology—school ... NY-2
New York Island—island ... MN-6
New York Island—island ... WA-9
New York Lake—lake ... CO-8
New York Life Bldg—hist pl ... MO-7
New York Life Bldg—hist pl ... NY-2
New York Marble Cemetery—hist pl ... NY-2
New York Medical Coll—school ... NY-2
New York Mill Acad—school ... NY-2
**New York Mills**—pop pl ... MN-6
**New York Mills**—pop pl ... NY-2
**New York Mills Gardens**—pop pl ... NY-2
New York Mine—mine (2) ... AZ-5
New York Mine—mine (3) ... CA-9
New York Mine—mine ... CO-8
New York Mine—mine ... ID-8
New York Mine—mine ... NV-8
New York Mine—mine ... OR-9
New York Mine—mine ... SD-7
New York Mining District—civil ... NV-8
New York Mountains—range ... CA-9
New York Mountain Trail—trail ... CO-8
New York Mtn—summit ... CO-8
New York Mtns—range ... NV-8
New York Mutual Life Insurance Company Bldg—hist pl ... PA-2
New York Natl Speedway—other ... NY-2
New York of the Pacific ... CA-9
New York Peak—summit ... CO-8
New York Peak—summit ... NV-8
New York Point—cape ... CA-9
New York Post Office (historical)—building ... MS-4
New York Post Office (historical)—building ... TN-4
New York Presbyterian Church—hist pl ... NY-2
New York Public Library—hist pl ... NY-2
New York Public Library, Hamilton Grange Branch—hist pl ... NY-2
New York Public Library, 115th Street Branch—hist pl ... NY-2
New York Public Library and Bryant Park—hist pl ... NY-2
New York Ranch Gulch—valley ... CA-9
New York Ranch Sch—school ... CA-9
New York Ravine—valley (2) ... CA-9
New York Sch—school ... MS-4
New York Sch (abandoned)—school ... MO-7
New York Sch For the Deaf—school ... NY-2
New York Sch (historical)—school ... MS-4
New York Sch of Applied Design—hist pl ... NY-2
New York Sch of Printing—school ... NY-2
New York Settlement ... ND-7
New York Shakespeare Festival Public Theater—hist pl ... NY-2
New York Shipyard—other ... NY-2
New York Slough—channel ... CA-9
New York Spring—spring ... NV-8
New York State Armory—hist pl ... NY-2
New York State Armory—hist pl (2) ... NY-2
New York State Canal ... NY-2
New York State Capitol—hist pl ... NY-2
New York State Court of Appeals Bldg—hist pl ... NY-2
New York State Department of Education Bldg—hist pl ... NY-2
New York State Fish Hatchery—other ... NY-2
New York State Milit Reservation—military ... NY-2
New York State Monmt—park ... MD-2
New York State Reservation—park ... NY-2
New York Stock Exchange—hist pl ... NY-2
New York Summit—summit ... ID-8
New York Tonopah—mine ... NV-8
**New York Township**—pop pl ... MO-7
New York Tunnel—mine ... UT-8
New York Univ—school (2) ... NY-2
New York Univ Coll of Engineering—school ... NY-2
New York Valley Ch—church ... KS-7
New York Yacht Club—hist pl ... NY-2
New Youka ... AL-4
New Yufala ... FL-3
New Zealand Ch—church ... NC-3
New Zealand Hill—summit ... NH-1
New Zeal Ch—church ... TN-4
New Zebulon Elem Sch—school ... NC-3
New Zion—locale ... KY-4
**New Zion**—pop pl ... KY-4
**New Zion**—pop pl ... SC-3
**New Zion**—pop pl (2) ... TN-4
New Zion Baptist Ch ... MS-4
New Zion Baptist Ch—church ... AL-4
New Zion Baptist Ch—church ... KS-7
New Zion Baptist Ch—church (5) ... MS-4
New Zion Baptist Ch—church ... UT-8
New Zion Baptist Church ... TN-4
New Zion Bethel Ch—church ... TX-5
New Zion Cem—cemetery (2) ... FL-3
New Zion Cem—cemetery ... IL-6
New Zion Cem—cemetery (3) ... LA-4
New Zion Cem—cemetery (14) ... MS-4
New Zion Cem—cemetery ... MO-7
New Zion Cem—cemetery ... NJ-2
New Zion Cem—cemetery ... OH-6
New Zion Cem—cemetery ... OK-5
New Zion Cem—cemetery ... SD-7
New Zion Cem—cemetery (4) ... TN-4
New Zion Cem—cemetery (2) ... TX-5
New Zion Ch—church (11) ... AL-4
New Zion Ch—church (4) ... AR-4
New Zion Ch—church (12) ... FL-3
New Zion Ch—church (10) ... GA-3
New Zion Ch—church (3) ... IL-6
New Zion Ch—church (3) ... IN-6
New Zion Ch—church ... IA-7
New Zion Ch—church (9) ... KY-4
New Zion Ch—church (21) ... LA-4
New Zion Ch—church (38) ... MS-4
New Zion Ch—church ... MO-7
New Zion Ch—church (8) ... NC-3
New Zion Ch—church (5) ... OH-6
New Zion Ch—church (2) ... OK-5
New Zion Ch—church (13) ... SC-3
New Zion Ch—church (7) ... TN-4
New Zion Ch—church (14) ... TX-5
New Zion Ch—church (4) ... VA-3
New Zion Ch—church (2) ... WV-2
New Zion Chapel—church ... OK-5
New Zion Ch (historical)—church (3) ... MS-4
New Zion Ch (historical)—church (2) ... TN-4
New Zion Ch of Christ ... MS-4
New Zion Creek—stream ... KY-4
New Zion Freewill Baptist Ch ... AL-4
New Zion Hill Cem—cemetery ... NC-3
New Zion Hill Ch—church ... AL-4
New Zion Hill Ch—church ... AR-4
New Zion Hill Ch—church ... GA-3
New Zion Hill Ch—church ... MS-4
New Zion Holiness Ch—church ... GA-3
New Zion Methodist—church ... MS-4
New Zion Missionary Baptist Ch ... AL-4
New Zion Missionary Baptist Ch ... MS-4
New Zion Missionary Baptist Ch—church ... AL-4
New Zion Missionary Baptist Ch—church ... FL-3
New Zion Primitive Baptist Ch—church ... FL-3
New Zion Sch—school ... LA-4
New Zion Sch—school ... MS-4
New Zion Sch—school (2) ... TN-4
New Zion Sch (abandoned)—school ... MO-7
New Zion Sch (historical)—school ... TN-4
New Zion Station—locale ... SC-3
New Zion Union Ch—church ... MS-4
New Zion Union Ch—church ... WV-2
New Zion United Methodist Ch—church ... DE-2
New Zion United Methodist Ch—church ... MS-4
New 24 Liberty Ch—church ... AR-4
Next—locale ... WV-2
Next Move Theatre—building ... MA-1
**Ney**—pop pl ... OH-6
Ney, Elisabet, Studio and Museum—hist pl ... TX-5
Neyami—locale ... GA-3
Ney Cave—cave ... TX-5
Ney Cem—cemetery ... IL-6
**Neydell**—pop pl ... MT-8
Neye Island—island ... GU-9
Neyezee Well—well ... AZ-5
Ney Hill—summit ... NY-2
Ney Hollow—valley ... TX-5
Neyland Cem—cemetery (2) ... TX-5
Neyland Creek—stream ... TX-5
Neyland Lake—lake (2) ... TX-5
Neyland Mine—mine ... TX-5
Neyland Stadium—park ... TN-4
**Neylandville**—pop pl ... TX-5
**Neyles**—pop pl ... SC-3
Neyog—other ... GU-9
Ney Post Office (historical)—building ... SD-7
Ney Springs Creek—stream ... CA-9
Ney Springs (Site)—locale ... CA-9
Nezinscot River—stream ... ME-1
Nez Perce—cens area (3) ... ID-8
**Nezperce**—pop pl ... ID-8
Nez Perce—summit ... WY-8
Nez Perce Camp—locale ... MT-8
Nez Perce County Farm—locale ... ID-8
Nezperce Creek ... MT-8
Nez Perce Creek—stream (2) ... ID-8
Nez Perce Creek—stream (2) ... MT-8
Nez Perce Creek—stream ... WA-9
Nez Perce Creek—stream ... WY-8
Nez Perce Ford—crossing ... WY-8
Nezperce Fork ... MT-8
Nez Perce Fork—stream ... MT-8
Nez Perce Fork Bitterroot River ... MT-8
Nez Perce Gulch—valley ... MT-8
Nez Perce Hollow—valley ... MT-8
Nezperce Indian War Historical Monmt—park ... ID-8
**Nez Perce Ind Res**—pop pl ... ID-8
Nez Perce Nat Hist Park (Spalding Area)—park ... ID-8
Nezperce Natl For—forest (2) ... ID-8
Nez Perce Natl Historical Park—hist pl ... ID-8
Nez Perce Natl Historical Park—park ... ID-8
Nez Perce Pass ... ID-8
Nez Perce Pass ... MT-8
Nez Perce Pass—gap ... ID-8
Nez Perce Pass—gap ... MT-8
Nez Perce Peak ... WY-8
Nez Perce Peak—summit ... ID-8
Nez Perce Reservation—hist pl ... OK-5
Nez Perce Ridge—ridge ... MT-8
Nez Perce Snake River Archeol District—hist pl ... ID-8
Nez Perce Snake River Archeol District—hist pl ... WA-9
Nez Perce Spring—spring ... ID-8
Nez Perce Trail—trail ... ID-8
Nezpique, Bayou—stream (2) ... LA-4
Nezqually Glacier ... WA-9
Nezqually River ... WA-9
Nez Spring—spring ... AZ-5
N-F Ditch—canal ... MT-8
N Five Spring—spring ... AZ-5
N F Lateral—canal ... TX-5
Ng ... PW-9
Ngabad ... PW-9
Ngabad Island ... PW-9
Ngabard ... PW-9
Ngabard Island ... PW-9
Ngabuked ... PW-9
Ngaburok ... PW-9
Ngachang—area ... GU-9
Ngad ... MP-9
Ngadarak ... PW-9
Ngadarak Reef ... PW-9
Ngadebechal—summit ... PW-9
Ngadeg ... PW-9
Ngadert ... PW-9
Ngadolog ... PW-9
Ngadolog Beach ... PW-9
Ngadpiseg ... PW-9
Ngaiabes ... PW-9
Ngain Island—island ... MP-9
Ngajange ... PW-9
Ngajangel ... PW-9
Ngak ... MP-9
Ngalap ... PW-9
Ngalard ... PW-9
Ngaldolok ... PW-9
Ngalu ... MP-9
Ngamalagel ... PW-9
Ngamalagel-Einfahrt ... PW-9
Ngamedu ... PW-9
Ngamegei Passage ... PW-9
Ngapsong Mongle ... PW-9
Ngaraard (County-equivalent)—civil ... PW-9
Ngaraard Elem Sch—school ... PW-9
Ngarabau ... PW-9
Ngarabekus ... PW-9
Ngarabelobang ... PW-9
Ngaradermang ... PW-9
Ngaragalbukl Rock ... PW-9
Ngaragatong River ... PW-9
Ngaragebukl ... PW-9
Ngaragumelbai ... PW-9
Ngarair—cape ... PW-9
Ngarakassoul ... PW-9
Ngarakeai ... PW-9
Ngarakis ... PW-9
Ngaramasag ... PW-9
Ngaramasag Bay ... PW-9
**Ngaramasch**—pop pl ... PW-9
Ngaramasech ... PW-9
Ngaramlungui ... PW-9
Ngaraod-Eikl ... PW-9
Ngaraod-Emel ... PW-9
Ngaraod Peaks ... PW-9
Ngarapalas Island ... PW-9
Ngarapelik ... PW-9
Ngarapelik Cape ... PW-9
Ngarapelik Point ... PW-9
Ngarard ... PW-9
Ngarasag Island ... PW-9
Ngarasog ... PW-9
Ngarasog Island ... PW-9
Ngara Tegetei ... PW-9
Ngarategetei Island ... PW-9
Ngarbaged ... PW-9
Ngarbagedesau ... PW-9
Ngarbaged Rengul ... PW-9
Ngarbau ... PW-9
Ngarbeched ... PW-9
Ngarchelong ... PW-9
Ngarchelong (County-equivalent)—civil ... PW-9
Ngardebotar ... PW-9
Ngarderar River ... PW-9
Ngarderartaog ... PW-9
Ngardis ... PW-9
Ngardk River ... PW-9
Ngardmau Bay—bay ... PW-9
Ngardmau (County-equivalent)—civil ... PW-9
Ngardmau Point ... PW-9
Ngardok Lake ... PW-9
Ngardok River ... PW-9
Ngardololok ... PW-9
Ngarduais ... PW-9
Ngarduais Island ... PW-9
Ngarebasuk Mountain ... PW-9
Ngarebesul ... PW-9
Ngareboku ... PW-9
Ngaregamai ... PW-9
Ngaregeu ... PW-9
Ngaregumelbai ... PW-9
Ngaregur ... PW-9
Ngarekai ... PW-9
Ngarekamais ... PW-9
Ngarekeai ... PW-9
Ngarekeklau ... PW-9
Ngarekeklau Island ... PW-9
Ngarekesauaol ... PW-9
Ngareklim ... PW-9
Ngarekobasang ... PW-9
Ngarekobasanga ... PW-9
Ngaremedin Point ... PW-9
Ngaremediu ... PW-9
Ngaremediu Head ... PW-9
Ngaremediu Peak ... PW-9
Ngaremediu Point ... PW-9
Ngaremedu Pass ... PW-9
Ngaremeskang ... PW-9
Ngaremetengel ... PW-9
Ngaremlengui ... PW-9
Ngaremlengui (County-equivalent)—civil ... PW-9
Ngarenedu ... PW-9
Ngarepekpus ... PW-9
Ngarepekpus Cape ... PW-9
Ngarevikl ... PW-9
Ngargol ... PW-9
Ngargol Insel ... PW-9
Ngargol Island ... PW-9
Ngarikul Channel ... PW-9
Ngariois ... PW-9
Ngariungs ... PW-9
Ngariungs Island ... PW-9
Ngariy—locale ... FM-9
Ngariynga ... PW-9
Ngarklim Island ... PW-9
Ngarmasag Bay ... PW-9
Ngarmid ... PW-9
Ngarmoked ... PW-9
Ngarmoked Island ... PW-9
Ngarngesang ... PW-9
Ngarongor ... PW-9
Ngarpaet-Durchfahrt ... PW-9
Ngarsmau Bucht ... PW-9
Ngarsul ... PW-9
Ngarsul Mountain ... PW-9
Ngarsung ... PW-9
Ngartabepeab Lagune ... PW-9
Ngaruak Mountain ... PW-9
Ngaruang ... PW-9
Ngaruangel ... PW-9
Ngaruangl Atoll ... PW-9
Ngaruangl Durchfahrt ... PW-9
Ngaruangl Island ... PW-9
Ngaruangl Island—island ... PW-9
Ngaruangl Passage ... PW-9
Ngaruangl Reef—bar ... PW-9
Ngaruangl Riff ... PW-9
Ngaruru Island ... PW-9
Ngasachang ... PW-9
Ngasaksao Pass ... PW-9
Ngasano ... FM-9
**Ngasano, Oror En**—pop pl ... FM-9
Ngasias ... PW-9
Ngatagalabad ... PW-9
Ngatbechuul, Bkul A—cape ... PW-9
Ngatbong ... PW-9
Ngategum ... PW-9
Ngategum Mountain ... PW-9
Ngategum Peak ... PW-9
Ngatelngal ... PW-9
Ngatemdung ... PW-9
Ngathaal—summit ... FM-9
Ngathaaw'—locale ... FM-9
Ngathal ... FM-9
Ngathaw ... FM-9
Ngatik Atoll—island ... FM-9
Ngatik Island—island ... FM-9
Ngatik (Municipality)—civ div ... FM-9
Ngatkip ... PW-9
Ngatmedug ... PW-9
Ngatmedug Island ... PW-9
**Ngatmel**—pop pl ... PW-9
Ngatpael Pass ... PW-9
Ngatpaet-Einfahrt ... PW-9
Ngatpaet Passage ... PW-9
Ngatpakui ... PW-9
Ngatpang ... PW-9
Ngatpang Bay ... PW-9
Ngatpang (County-equivalent)—civil ... PW-9
Ngatpang Elem Sch—school ... PW-9
Ngatpank ... PW-9
Ngatpast Passage ... PW-9
Ngatpokui ... PW-9
Ngatpokul ... PW-9
Ngaur ... PW-9
Ngcheangel—civil ... PW-9
Ngcheangel—island ... PW-9
Ngcheangel Uet—area ... PW-9
**Ngchemiangel**—pop pl (2) ... PW-9
Ngchemiangel, Debel A—bay ... PW-9
Ngchemiangel Sch—school ... PW-9
Ngchesar—civil ... PW-9
Ngchesar—locale ... PW-9
**Ngchesar**—pop pl ... PW-9
**Ngchesar (County-equivalent)**—pop pl ... PW-9
Ngchesar Municipality ... PW-9
**Ngchesechang**—pop pl ... PW-9
Ngchesuch, Omoachel Ra—stream ... PW-9
Ngchus—bay ... PW-9
Ngchus, Bkul A—cape ... PW-9
N G Creek—stream ... OR-9
N G Creek Rsvr—reservoir ... OR-9
Ngdorak River ... PW-9
Nge—island ... MP-9
Ngeanges—island ... PW-9
Ngeauar ... PW-9
Ngeaur ... PW-9
Ngeaur—civil ... PW-9
Ngeaur Municipal Office—building ... PW-9
Ngebad—island ... PW-9
Ngebard—bar ... PW-9
Ngebard, Bkul A—bar ... PW-9
Ngebard, Tochelir Ra—channel ... PW-9
Ngebedangel—island ... PW-9
Ngebedangel, Elechol Ra—beach ... PW-9
Ngebedanget, Bkul A—cape ... PW-9
Ngebedel—island ... PW-9
**Ngebei**—pop pl ... PW-9
Ngebokel ... PW-9
Ngebsong—bay ... PW-9
**Ngebuked**—pop pl ... PW-9
**Ngeburch**—pop pl (2) ... PW-9
Ngebureg ... PW-9
Ngedbaet, Toachel—channel ... PW-9
Ngedbang ... PW-9
Ngedbus—island ... PW-9
Ngedech—summit ... PW-9
Ngedechelabed, Rois—summit ... PW-9
Ngederak Riff ... PW-9
Ngederrak—bar ... PW-9
Ngedert—island ... PW-9
Ngedesakr—island ... PW-9
Ngedloch, Elechol Ra—beach ... PW-9
Ngedos ... PW-9
N Gee Grant (landgrant)—civil ... FL-3
Ngeil ... PW-9
Ngeil Island ... PW-9
Ngeit ... PW-9
Ngeiungel ... PW-9
Ngel, Toachel Ra—channel ... PW-9
Ngelab—bay ... PW-9
ngel Brook ... NJ-2
Ngelekulegel Reef ... PW-9
Ngellang—island ... PW-9
Ngell Channel ... PW-9
Ngell Durchfahrt ... PW-9
Ngell Einfahrt ... PW-9
Ngelsibel—island ... PW-9
Ngelsum—summit ... PW-9
Ngeluong—island ... PW-9
Ngeluul, Bkul A—cape ... PW-9
Ngem ... PW-9
Ngemai—bar ... PW-9
Ngemechii ... PW-9
Ngemeduu—summit ... PW-9
Ngemelachel ... PW-9
Ngemelachel—channel ... PW-9
Ngemelis Group ... PW-9
Ngemelis Insel ... PW-9
Ngemelis Islands ... PW-9
**Ngemerdang**—pop pl ... PW-9
Ngemewangel ... PW-9
Ngemlis—island ... PW-9
Ngemolei—island ... PW-9
Ngenge Island ... MP-9
Ngeour ... PW-9
Ngerael—bar ... PW-9
Ngerael, Bkul A—bar ... PW-9
Ngerael, Telebadel Ra—channel ... PW-9
Ngeraod—summit ... PW-9
Ngerard ... PW-9
Ngerasaka—slope ... PW-9
Ngerasech—island ... PW-9
Ngerbailiang—summit ... PW-9
**Ngerbau**—pop pl ... PW-9
Ngerbecharerong—summit ... PW-9
**Ngerbeched**—pop pl ... PW-9
Ngerbechetei—island ... PW-9
Ngerbekebekur ... PW-9
Ngerbelas ... PW-9
**Ngerbodel**—pop pl ... PW-9
Ngerbuit ... PW-9
Ngerchaol—island ... PW-9
**Ngerchebetan**—pop pl ... PW-9
Ngerchebukl—island ... PW-9
Ngerchelchuus—summit ... PW-9
Ngerchelngael—cape ... PW-9
Ngerchelong—civil ... PW-9
Ngerchelong Sch—school ... PW-9
**Ngercheluuk**—pop pl ... PW-9
**Ngerchemai**—pop pl ... PW-9
Ngerchetang—stream ... PW-9
Ngercheu—island ... PW-9
Ngerchong ... PW-9
Ngerdelolk ... PW-9
Ngerdelungch—summit ... PW-9
Ngerderar—stream ... PW-9
**Ngerderemang**—pop pl ... PW-9
Ngerdesiur—flat ... PW-9
Ngerdiluches—bar ... PW-9
Ngerdims, Elechol Ra—beach ... PW-9
**Ngerdiol**—pop pl ... PW-9
Ngerdis—cape ... PW-9
Ngerdmau—civil ... PW-9
Ngerdobotar—bay ... PW-9
Ngerdok—lake ... PW-9
Ngerdong River ... PW-9
Ngerdorch—stream ... PW-9
Ngerdorch, Taoch Ra—gut ... PW-9
Ngerduais—island ... PW-9
Ngerdways ... PW-9
Ngeream ... PW-9
Ngeream—island ... PW-9
Ngerebaduk—summit ... PW-9
Ngerebekus ... PW-9
Ngerebelang, Bkul A—cape ... PW-9
Ngerebelas—island ... PW-9
Ngerebelik—slope ... PW-9
Ngerebelik Point ... PW-9
Ngerebetei ... PW-9
Ngerebkus—cape ... PW-9
Ngerechong—island ... PW-9
Ngerechur—island ... PW-9
Ngeredekuu—stream ... PW-9
Ngeregong ... PW-9
Ngeregong Island ... PW-9
Ngerekebesang—island ... PW-9
**Ngerekebesang**—pop pl ... PW-9
Ngerekliangl—summit ... PW-9
Ngereklim—bar ... PW-9
**Ngereklmadel**—pop pl ... PW-9
Ngereksong—bay ... PW-9
Ngereksong—stream ... PW-9
Ngeremasech—bay ... PW-9
Ngeremasech, Taoch Ra—gut ... PW-9
Ngeremdiu—summit ... PW-9
Ngeremdiw Point ... PW-9
Ngeremduu—bay ... PW-9
**Ngeremecheluch**—pop pl ... PW-9
Ngeremediu ... PW-9
Ngeremekediu—island ... PW-9
Ngeremeleg ... PW-9
Ngeremeskang River ... PW-9
Ngeremlengui ... PW-9
Ngeremlengui—civil ... PW-9
Ngeremlenqui Elem Sch—school ... PW-9
Ngeresiuur River ... PW-9
Ngergeai ... PW-9
Ngergoi ... PW-9
Ngerhong ... PW-9
Ngeridebaol ... PW-9
Ngeridebaul—channel ... PW-9
Ngerikl, Elechol Ra—beach ... PW-9
Ngeriklreker—bar ... PW-9
Ngerikoek—summit ... PW-9
Ngerikui ... PW-9
Ngerikui Channel ... PW-9
Ngerikul Channel ... PW-9
Ngerikul Passage ... PW-9
Ngerikuul—bay ... PW-9
Ngerikuul—channel ... PW-9
Ngerikuul Bay ... PW-9
Ngerimel—stream ... PW-9
Ngerimid, Bkul A—bend ... PW-9
Ngeriois ... PW-9
Ngeriois, Elechol Ra—beach ... PW-9
Ngeritang—cape ... PW-9
Ngerithebaur Passage ... PW-9
Ngeriuch—cape ... PW-9
Ngeriungs—island (2) ... PW-9
Ngerkall—lake ... PW-9
**Ngerkeai**—pop pl ... PW-9
Ngerkeai Sch—school ... PW-9
Ngerkebeas, Bkul A—cape ... PW-9
Ngerkebuit—island ... PW-9
Ngerkeklau—island ... PW-9
**Ngerkeseuaol**—pop pl ... PW-9
Ngerkesewaol ... PW-9
**Ngerkesou**—pop pl ... PW-9
Ngerkeyai ... PW-9
Ngerkiulongel—bar ... PW-9
Ngermaech ... PW-9
Ngermalk—island ... PW-9
Ngermeaus—island ... PW-9
Ngermechaech—island ... PW-9
Ngermechau ... PW-9
**Ngermechau**—pop pl ... PW-9
**Ngermelech**—pop pl ... PW-9
Ngermelt—cave ... PW-9
Ngermerand—bay ... PW-9
Ngermerecherakl—cape ... PW-9
Ngermereues—cape ... PW-9
**Ngermeskang**—pop pl ... PW-9
Ngermeskang—stream ... PW-9
Ngermetang—bar ... PW-9
**Ngermetengel**—pop pl ... PW-9
Ngermeuangel—basin ... PW-9
Ngermeuangel—bay ... PW-9
**Ngermid**—pop pl ... PW-9
Ngermoked ... PW-9
Ngermoket—cape ... PW-9
**Ngerngesang**—pop pl ... PW-9
**Ngerngiil**—pop pl ... PW-9
Ngeroleamel—bay ... PW-9
**Ngersuul**—pop pl ... PW-9
Ngersuul, Olekull Ra—cemetery ... PW-9
Ngertachebeab—bay ... PW-9
Ngertachuel—bay ... PW-9
Ngertechiel—island ... PW-9
Ngertmel Reef ... PW-9
Ngertoel ... PW-9
Ngertoell—bar ... PW-9
Ngertuker—slope ... PW-9
Ngeruach—summit ... PW-9
Ngeruangel Passage ... PW-9
Ngeruangel Riff ... PW-9
Ngeruangl, Euchelel—channel ... PW-9
Ngerub, Rois—summit ... PW-9
**Ngerubesang**—pop pl ... PW-9
Ngeruchaech—summit ... PW-9
Ngerucheach ... PW-9
Ngeruchebtang ... PW-9
**Ngeruchob**—pop pl ... PW-9
Ngeruchubtang—island ... PW-9
Ngerudechong—cape ... PW-9

*Ngerudeong Point* ... PW-9
*Ngerugelbtang* ... PW-9
*Ngerugelbtang Island* ... PW-9
*Ngerugelptan Island* ... PW-9
*Ngeruiki* ... PW-9
**Ngeruikl**—*pop pl* ... PW-9
Ngeruikl, Taoch Ra—*gut* ... PW-9
Ngerukeuid—*island* ... PW-9
*Ngerukeuid Islands Wildlife Preserv* ... PW-9
Ngerukeuid Wildlife Reservation Area—*park* ... PW-9
*Ngerukewid* ... PW-9
*Ngerukewid Islands Wildlife Preserv* ... PW-9
Ngeruktabel—*island* ... PW-9
Ngerulaol—*summit* ... PW-9
*Ngeruliang Point* ... PW-9
**Ngeruling**—*pop pl* ... PW-9
*Ngerulkael* ... PW-9
Ngerulluang—*island* ... PW-9
**Ngeruluobel**—*pop pl* ... PW-9
*Ngerumekaol* ... PW-9
Ngerumekaul—*bay* ... PW-9
Ngerumetochel—*island* ... PW-9
*Ngerumetoel* ... PW-9
Ngerumtoi—*island* ... PW-9
Ngerunguikl—*summit* ... PW-9
Ngeruong—*summit* ... PW-9
*Ngerupesang* ... PW-9
Ngerur—*island* ... PW-9
**Ngerusar**—*pop pl* ... PW-9
Ngerusisech—*island* ... PW-9
Ngerutechei, Taoch Ra—*gut* ... PW-9
*Ngerutegel* ... PW-9
*Ngerutehei River* ... PW-9
Ngerutekill—*bay* ... PW-9
Ngerutoi—*island* ... PW-9
**Ngerutoi**—*pop pl* ... PW-9
*Ngeruwikl* ... PW-9
Ngerwaiu—*cape* ... PW-9
*Ngerwangel Passage* ... PW-9
*Ngerwangel Riff* ... PW-9
*Ngeryungs* ... PW-9
**Ngesang**—*pop pl* ... PW-9
Ngesang, Bkul A—*cape* ... PW-9
Ngesaol—*cape* ... PW-9
*Ngesar* ... PW-9
Ngesbokel—*island* ... PW-9
*Ngesebokl* ... PW-9
*Ngesebokul* ... PW-9
*Ngesebus* ... PW-9
*Ngesebus Island* ... PW-9
*Ngesenhong River* ... PW-9
*Ngeshbokul* ... PW-9
Ngesibang—*summit* ... PW-9
Ngesomel—*island* ... PW-9
Ngesuall—*island* ... PW-9
*Ngeswall* ... PW-9
*Ngeswall Island* ... PW-9
**Ngetbong**—*pop pl* ... PW-9
Ngetchulang—*summit* ... PW-9
Ngetchum—*summit* ... PW-9
Ngetechirur, Elechol Ra—*beach* ... PW-9
Ngeteklou—*island* ... PW-9
Ngetengchau—*island* ... PW-9
*Ngethil* ... PW-9
*Ngethil Island* ... PW-9
Ngetkebui—*swamp* ... PW-9
**Ngetkib**—*pop pl* ... PW-9
*Ngetkip* ... PW-9
Ngetkuml—*island* ... PW-9
*Ngetkurm* ... PW-9
Ngetmadei—*cape* ... PW-9
Ngetmeduch—*island* ... PW-9
Ngetmelabel—*bay* ... PW-9
Ngetmerchong—*summit* ... PW-9
Ngetmiich—*stream* ... PW-9
*Ngetngod* ... PW-9
Ngetngod—*bar* ... PW-9
Ngetpang—*civil* ... PW-9
Ngetpang—*stream* ... PW-9
**Ngeungel**—*pop pl* ... PW-9
*Nggasagang* ... PW-9
*Nggesar* ... PW-9
*Ngghesar* ... PW-9
*Nghesar* ... PW-9
*Nghesehang* ... PW-9
N G Horse Camp—*locale* ... OR-9
N Gibbs Ranch—*locale* ... TX-5
*Ngid* ... PW-9
*Ngidopie Reef* ... PW-9
*Ngidopie Riff* ... PW-9
*Ngid Passage* ... PW-9
Ngihneni—*summit* ... FM-9
*Ngiil Point* ... PW-9
Ngiit—*channel* ... PW-9
*Ngimes* ... PW-9
*Ngimis* ... PW-9
*Ngiri* ... FM-9
Ngirkiil—*stream* ... PW-9
*Ngirraruh* ... PW-9
Ngis—*island* ... PW-9
*Ngiwal* ... PW-9
Ngiwal (County-equivalent)—*civil* ... PW-9
Ngiwal Sch—*school* ... PW-9
Ngkael—*island* ... PW-9
**Ngkebeduul**—*pop pl* ... PW-9
**Ngkekau**—*pop pl* ... PW-9
*Ngkesiil* ... PW-9
Ngkesill—*island* ... PW-9
*Ng Kesill Island* ... PW-9
Ngkesiu—*summit* ... PW-9
Ngkesol—*bar* ... PW-9
Ngkesol, Bkul—*bar* ... PW-9
Ngkesol, Telebadel Ra—*channel* ... PW-9
Ngkesol, Toachel—*channel* ... PW-9
Ngkeuall—*island* ... PW-9
*Ngkewall* ... PW-9
**Nglas**—*pop pl* ... PW-9
Ngmal—*stream* ... PW-9
Ngmersau, Elechol Ra—*beach* ... PW-9
*Ngobasangel* ... PW-9
*Ngof* ... FM-9
**Ngolog**—*pop pl* ... FM-9
Ngolsang—*stream* ... PW-9
Ngongtaen—*locale* ... MP-9
Ngoof—*locale* ... FM-9
*Ngorsul* ... PW-9
*Ngorsum* ... PW-9
*Ngorungol Island* ... PW-9
*Ngorungor* ... PW-9
Ngos—*bar* ... PW-9
*Ngothugothu* ... PW-9
*Ngothugothu Island* ... PW-9
*Ngrategetei Island* ... PW-9
*Ngriel* ... PW-9
**Ngriil**—*pop pl* ... PW-9
Ngrikiil, Taoch—*gut* ... PW-9
*Ngril* ... PW-9
N G Taylor Memorial Ch—*church* ... TN-4
*Ngtkip* ... PW-9
*Nguchuth* ... FM-9
*Nguchuuth* ... FM-9
Ngulitel—*summit* ... PW-9
*Ngulokl* ... PW-9
Ngulu—*island* ... FM-9
Ngulu Anchorage—*harbor* ... FM-9
Ngulu Islands—*island* ... FM-9
Ngulu (Municipality)—*civ div* ... FM-9
*Nguritoi* ... PW-9
*Nguror Island* ... PW-9
*Ngurugei* ... PW-9
*Ngurugei Beach* ... PW-9
Nguruhei, Elechol Ra—*beach* ... PW-9
*Ngurukdapel Island* ... PW-9
*Nguruleang* ... PW-9
*Nguruloang Island* ... PW-9
Ngurungor—*island* ... PW-9
*Ngurur* ... PW-9
*Ngurur Island* ... PW-9
*Ngurusar* ... PW-9
*Ngurutoi* ... PW-9
N Hanna Ranch—*locale* ... NE-7
N Hildre Ranch—*locale* ... ND-7
N H Ridge—*ridge* ... WY-8
NH Tank—*reservoir* ... NM-5
Ni—*island* ... MP-9
Niabi Zoo—*park* ... IL-6
Niagara—*locale* ... KY-4
Niagara—*locale* ... OR-9
Niagara—*locale* ... VA-3
**Niagara**—*pop pl* ... NC-3
**Niagara**—*pop pl* ... ND-7
**Niagara**—*pop pl* ... PA-2
**Niagara**—*pop pl* ... WI-6
Niagara Ave Sch—*school* ... NY-2
Niagara Brook—*stream* ... NY-2
Niagara Camp—*hist pl* ... CA-9
Niagara Cave—*cave* ... MN-6
Niagara Cem—*cemetery* ... ND-7
Niagara Ch—*church* ... NC-3
**Niagara (County)**—*pop pl* ... NY-2
*Niagara Creek* ... OR-9
Niagara Creek—*stream* ... AK-9
Niagara Creek—*stream* ... AZ-5
Niagara Creek—*stream* (2) ... CA-9
Niagara Creek—*stream* ... ID-8
Niagara Creek—*stream* ... MO-7
Niagara Creek—*stream* ... NV-8
Niagara Creek—*stream* (2) ... OR-9
Niagara Dam—*dam* ... ND-7
Niagara Engine House—*hist pl* ... NY-2
Niagara Escarpment—*cliff* ... WI-6
Niagara Falls—*falls* ... NY-2
Niagara Falls—*falls* ... WV-2
**Niagara Falls**—*pop pl* ... NY-2
Niagara Falls AFB—*military* ... NY-2
Niagara Falls Country Club—*other* ... NY-2
Niagara Falls International Airport—*mil airp* ... NY-2
Niagara Falls Memorial Park—*park* ... NY-2
Niagara Falls Public Library—*hist pl* ... NY-2
Niagara Frontier Country Club—*other* ... NY-2
Niagara Gulch—*valley* ... CO-8
Niagara Gulch—*valley* ... ID-8
Niagara Gulch—*valley* ... NM-5
Niagara Island (historical)—*island* ... TN-4
**Niagara Junction**—*pop pl* ... NY-2
Niagara Mine—*mine* ... CA-9
Niagara Mtn—*summit* ... NY-2
Niagara Park—*park* ... PA-2
Niagara Peak—*summit* ... CO-8
Niagara Point—*summit* ... OR-9
Niagara Pond—*lake* ... PA-2
Niagara Power Plant Dam—*dam* ... VA-3
Niagara Reservation—*hist pl* ... NY-2
Niagara River—*stream* ... NY-2
Niagara Sch—*school* ... KY-4
Niagara Shaft (historical)—*mine* ... PA-2
Niagara Shoals—*rapids* ... TN-4
Niagara Spring—*spring* (2) ... NV-8
Niagara Springs—*spring* ... ID-8
Niagara Square—*park* ... NY-2
*Niagara Station* ... MA-1
Niagara Street Sch—*school* ... NY-2
Niagara Town—*CDP* ... NY-2
**Niagara (Town of)**—*pop pl* ... NY-2
**Niagara (Town of)**—*pop pl* ... WI-6
**Niagara Township**—*pop pl* ... ND-7
Niagara Tunnel—*tunnel* ... NM-5
Niagara Univ—*school* ... NY-2
Niagara-Wheatfield HS—*school* ... NY-2
*Niagora* ... OR-9
*Niagra Creek* ... NV-8
Niagra Creek—*stream* ... ID-8
Niahlek—*unknown* ... FM-9
Ni Ahwar—*unknown* ... FM-9
Niak Creek—*stream* ... AK-9
Niakogon Buttes—*other* ... AK-9
Niakogon Mtn—*summit* ... AK-9
Niaktuvik, Mount—*summit* ... AK-9
Niaktuvik Creek—*stream* ... AK-9
Niakuk Islands—*area* ... AK-9
**Niangua**—*pop pl* ... MO-7
Niangua, Lake—*reservoir* ... MO-7
Niangua Arm—*bay* ... MO-7
*Niangua City* ... MO-7
Niangua Hills—*other* ... MO-7
Niangua River—*stream* ... MO-7
Niangua Township—*civil* ... MO-7
*Niangura River* ... MO-7
Nianiau—*summit* ... HI-9
*Nianiau Mtn* ... HI-9
Nianque, Lake—*lake* ... NY-2
*Niantic* ... RI-1
Niantic—*locale* ... PA-2
**Niantic**—*pop pl* ... CT-1
**Niantic**—*pop pl* (2) ... IL-6
Niantic Bay—*bay* ... CT-1
*Niantic River* ... CT-1
Niantic River—*stream* ... CT-1
**Niantic (Township of)**—*pop pl* ... IL-6
Niarada—*locale* ... MT-8
Ni Aul—*locale* ... FM-9
Niaupala Fishpond—*lake* ... HI-9
*Niaur* ... PW-9
Niavi Wash—*stream* ... NV-8
Nia-Wanda Park—*park* ... NY-2
Niawiakum River—*stream* ... WA-9
Nibble—*locale* ... MT-8
Nibble Lake—*lake* ... MN-6
Nibbler Creek—*stream* ... ID-8
Nibbling Brook—*stream* ... CT-1
Nibbs Creek—*stream* ... ID-8
Nibbs Creek—*stream* ... VA-3
Nibbs Knob—*summit* ... CA-9
Nibbs Spring—*spring* ... ID-8
**Nibbyville**—*pop pl* ... IN-6
Nibin Lake—*lake* ... MN-6
Niblack (Aban'd)—*locale* ... AK-9
Niblack Anchorage—*bay* ... AK-9
Niblack Branch—*stream* ... TX-5
Niblack Chapel—*church* ... OK-5
Niblack Hollow—*stream* ... AK-9
Niblack Islands—*area* ... AK-9
Niblack Lake—*lake* ... AK-9
Niblack Levee—*levee* ... IN-6
Niblack Point—*cape* ... AK-9
Niblack Sch—*school* ... FL-3
*Niblells Bluff* ... LA-4
Niblett—*locale* ... LA-4
**Niblett Bluff**—*pop pl* ... LA-4
Niblett Canal—*canal* ... LA-4
Niblett Hollow—*valley* ... TN-4
Niblett Landing—*locale* ... MS-4
*Nibletts Bluff* ... LA-4
**Nibletts Bluff**—*pop pl* ... LA-4
*Nibletts Mill Run* ... VA-3
Nibletts Pond—*reservoir* ... AL-4
Nibley—*locale* ... UT-8
**Nibley**—*pop pl* ... OR-9
**Nibley**—*pop pl* ... UT-8
**Nibley (historical)**—*pop pl* ... OR-9
Nibley Park—*park* ... UT-8
Nibley Park Sch—*school* ... UT-8
Niblick Cem—*cemetery* ... IL-6
Niblick Draw—*valley* ... CO-8
Niblock—*locale* ... TX-5
Niblock Ditch—*canal* ... CO-8
Niblock-Yacovetta Terrace—*hist pl* ... CO-8
*Niblo Creek* ... MO-7
*Nibun* ... MP-9
Nibwung—*island* ... MP-9
Nicaboyne Lake—*lake* ... WI-6
Nicado Creek—*stream* ... MN-6
Nicado Lake—*lake* ... MN-6
*Nicahoyne Lake* ... WI-6
Nicanor—*locale* ... NC-3
Nicasio—*locale* ... CA-9
Nicasio (Black)—*civil* ... CA-9
Nicasio (Buckelew)—*civil* ... CA-9
Nicasio Creek—*stream* ... CA-9
Nicasio Dam—*dam* ... CA-9
Nicasio (Frink And Reynolds)—*civil* ... CA-9
Nicasio (Halleck)—*civil* ... CA-9
Nicasio Rsvr—*reservoir* ... CA-9
Nicasio Sch—*school* ... CA-9
Nicatou Island—*island* ... ME-1
Nicatous Club—*other* ... ME-1
Nicatous Lake—*lake* ... ME-1
Nicatous Stream—*stream* ... ME-1
Niccolls Creek—*stream* ... WA-9
Niccum Cem—*cemetery* ... IL-6
Niccum Hollow—*valley* ... AR-4
Niccum Rsvr—*reservoir* ... ND-7
*Nic do it soe* ... AZ-5
**Nice**—*pop pl* ... CA-9
Nice, Philip, House—*hist pl* ... MI-6
Nice Camp Campground—*locale* ... WA-9
Nice Chapel—*church* ... GA-3
Nice Creek—*stream* ... OR-9
Nice Hollow—*valley* ... PA-2
Nice Lake—*lake* ... WI-6
**Niceleytown**—*pop pl* ... VA-3
Nicely Branch—*stream* ... KY-4
Nicely Branch—*stream* (2) ... TN-4
Nicely Branch—*stream* ... VA-3
Nicely Gulch—*valley* ... MT-8
Nicely Run—*stream* ... PA-2
Nicely Sch—*school* ... PA-2
Nicelytown—*locale* ... VA-3
**Nicetown**—*pop pl* ... PA-2
Nicetown (Midvale)—*uninc pl* ... PA-2
Nicetown Sch—*school* ... PA-2
**Niceville**—*pop pl* (2) ... FL-3
Niceville Senior HS—*school* ... FL-3
Niceville-Valparaiso (CCD)—*cens area* ... FL-3
Nicewander Lake—*reservoir* ... IN-6
Nicewander Lake Dam—*dam* ... IN-6
**Nicewood**—*pop pl* ... VA-3
Nicey Branch—*stream* ... VA-3
Nicey Grove Ch—*church* ... NC-3
Nichawak Mtn—*summit* ... AK-9
Nichawak River—*stream* ... AK-9
Nichburg—*locale* ... AL-4
Nichburg JHS—*school* ... AL-4
Nichecronk Brook—*stream* ... PA-2
*Nichecronk Lake* ... PA-2
Nichecronk Pond—*lake* ... PA-2
Nichelini Winery—*hist pl* ... CA-9
Nichenthraw Mtn—*summit* ... AK-9
Nicherson-Tarbox House, Shed and Barn—*hist pl* ... MN-6
**Nichewaug**—*pop pl* ... MA-1
Nichewaug Cem—*cemetery* ... MA-1
*Nichewoag Plantation* ... MA-1
Nichiren Buddhist Temple—*church* ... UT-8
*Nichi Suido* ... FM-9
*Nichiyo To* ... FM-9
*Nichol* ... IA-7
Nichola—*locale* ... PA-2
Nichola (historical)—*locale* ... AL-4
Nicholai Sch—*school* ... NY-2
*Nichola Run* ... PA-2
Nicholas—*locale* ... LA-4
Nicholas—*locale* ... TX-5
Nicholas—*locale* ... VA-3
Nicholas—*locale* ... VI-3
Nicholas, Bayou—*gut* ... LA-4
Nicholas, Jacob, House—*hist pl* ... PA-2
Nicholas, Lake—*lake* ... AK-9
Nicholas Basin—*basin* ... MT-8
Nicholas Brook—*stream* ... NY-2
*Nicholas Canyon* ... CA-9
Nicholas Cem—*cemetery* ... OH-6
Nicholas Ch—*church* ... OH-6
*Nicholas Channel* ... NJ-2
**Nicholas (County)**—*pop pl* ... KY-4
**Nicholas (County)**—*pop pl* ... WV-2
Nicholas Creek—*stream* ... CA-9
Nicholas Creek—*stream* ... ID-8
Nicholas Creek—*stream* ... KS-7
Nicholas Creek—*stream* ... SC-3
Nicholas Creek—*stream* ... SD-7
Nicholas Creek—*stream* ... VA-3
*Nicholas Ditch* ... IN-6
Nicholas Drive Sch—*school* ... OH-6
Nicholas Fagan Memorial Cem—*cemetery* ... TX-5
Nicholas Flat—*flat* ... CA-9
Nicholas Hollow—*valley* ... WV-2
*Nicholas Lake* ... MN-6
Nicholas Lake—*lake* ... MI-6
Nicholas Lake—*lake* ... WA-9
Nicholas-Lang House—*hist pl* ... OR-9
Nicholas Lewis Plantation (historical)—*locale* ... AL-4
*Nicholas Mountain* ... MD-2
*Nicholas Point* ... NJ-2
Nicholas Point—*cape* ... NY-2
Nicholas Ridge—*ridge* ... MD-2
Nicholas Sch—*school* ... CA-9
Nicholas School Abandoned—*locale* ... NE-7
Nicholas Spring—*spring* ... MO-7
Nicholas Spring—*spring* ... NV-8
Nicholas Tank—*lake* ... NM-5
Nicholasville—*locale* (2) ... GA-3
**Nicholasville**—*pop pl* ... KY-4
Nicholasville (CCD)—*cens area* ... KY-4
Nicholasville Hist Dist—*hist pl* ... KY-4
Nicholas Wash—*stream* ... CO-8
Nichol Branch—*stream* ... SC-3
*Nichol Brook* ... MA-1
Nichol Cem—*cemetery* ... IL-6
Nichol Cem—*cemetery* ... TX-5
*Nichol Creek* ... MA-1
Nichol Creek—*stream* ... TN-4
Nichol Creek—*stream* ... WI-6
Nicholes Ranch—*locale* ... UT-8
Nichol Flat—*flat* ... ID-8
**Nichol Hills (subdivision)**—*pop pl* ... AL-4
Nicholi, Bayou—*gut* ... LA-4
**Nicholia**—*pop pl* ... ID-8
Nicholia Canyon—*valley* ... ID-8
Nicholia Creek—*stream* ... MT-8
Nicholias Canyon—*valley* ... CA-9
Nicholia Sch—*school* ... MT-8
*Nichol Lake* ... MN-6
Nichol Lake—*lake* ... NE-7
*Nichollia Creek* ... MT-8
Nicholl Park—*park* ... CA-9
Nicholl Pond—*bay* ... LA-4
**Nicholls**—*pop pl* ... GA-3
Nicholls Brook—*stream* ... NH-1
Nicholls (CCD)—*cens area* ... GA-3
Nicholls Cem—*cemetery* ... AL-4
Nicholls Cem—*cemetery* ... IA-7
Nicholls-Crook House—*hist pl* ... SC-3
Nicholls HS—*school* ... LA-4
Nicholls Knob—*summit* ... VA-3
Nicholls Mtn—*summit* ... WA-9
*Nicholls Point* ... VT-1
Nicholls Sch (abandoned)—*school* ... PA-2
Nicholls University (Francis T Nicholl)—*uninc pl* ... LA-4
**Nicholls Warm Springs**—*pop pl* ... CA-9
*Nichol Point* ... NY-2
*Nichols* ... ME-1
*Nichols* ... MI-6
*Nichols* ... MN-6
Nichols—*locale* ... CA-9
Nichols—*locale* ... CT-1
Nichols—*locale* ... FL-3
Nichols—*locale* ... KY-4
Nichols—*locale* ... MS-4
Nichols—*locale* ... MT-8
Nichols—*locale* ... NY-2
**Nichols**—*pop pl* ... IA-7
**Nichols**—*pop pl* ... KY-4
**Nichols**—*pop pl* ... MD-2
**Nichols**—*pop pl* ... MN-6
**Nichols**—*pop pl* ... MO-7
**Nichols**—*pop pl* ... NY-2
**Nichols**—*pop pl* ... SC-3
**Nichols**—*pop pl* ... WI-6
Nichols, Capt. John P., House—*hist pl* ... ME-1
Nichols, Daniel, Homestead—*hist pl* ... MA-1
Nichols, Edward, House—*hist pl* ... VA-3
Nichols, Eli, Farm—*hist pl* ... OH-6
Nichols, James, House—*hist pl* ... MA-1
Nichols, Jeremiah, Sch—*hist pl* ... PA-2
Nichols, Jerry, Tavern—*hist pl* ... MA-1
Nichols, J.L., House and Studio—*hist pl* ... IN-6
Nichols, John H., House—*hist pl* ... OH-6
Nichols, Lake—*lake* ... GA-3
Nichols, Oscar, House—*hist pl* ... IA-7
Nichols, Richard, House—*hist pl* ... MA-1
Nichols, Samuel, House—*hist pl* ... IA-7
Nichols, Walter, House—*hist pl* ... OH-6
Nichols, William Anzi, House—*hist pl* ... IA-7
Nichols Airp—*airport* ... PA-2
Nichols Arboretum—*park* ... MI-6
Nichols Ave Sch—*school* ... CT-1
Nichols Ave Sch—*school* ... DC-2
Nichols Bay—*bay* ... AK-9
*Nichols Branch* ... MS-4
*Nichols Branch* ... VA-3
Nichols Branch—*stream* (2) ... AL-4
Nichols Branch—*stream* ... AR-4
Nichols Branch—*stream* (3) ... KY-4
Nichols Branch—*stream* (3) ... MS-4
Nichols Branch—*stream* (2) ... MO-7
Nichols Branch—*stream* (2) ... NC-3
Nichols Branch—*stream* ... OR-9
Nichols Branch—*stream* (4) ... TN-4
Nichols Branch—*stream* ... TX-5
Nichols Brook—*stream* ... ME-1
Nichols Brook—*stream* (2) ... MA-1
Nichols Brook—*stream* ... NY-2
Nichols Brook—*stream* ... VT-1
Nichols Cabin—*locale* ... MO-7
Nichols Camp—*locale* ... OR-9
Nichols Canyon—*valley* (2) ... CA-9
Nichols Canyon—*valley* ... ID-8
Nichols Canyon—*valley* ... NM-5
Nichols Canyon—*valley* ... OR-9
Nichols Canyon—*valley* ... WY-8
Nichols Cem—*cemetery* (2) ... AL-4
Nichols Cem—*cemetery* (4) ... AR-4
Nichols Cem—*cemetery* ... FL-3
Nichols Cem—*cemetery* ... GA-3
Nichols Cem—*cemetery* ... IL-6
Nichols Cem—*cemetery* ... IN-6
Nichols Cem—*cemetery* ... IA-7
Nichols Cem—*cemetery* ... KS-7
Nichols Cem—*cemetery* (3) ... KY-4
Nichols Cem—*cemetery* (2) ... LA-4
Nichols Cem—*cemetery* ... ME-1
Nichols Cem—*cemetery* ... MS-4
Nichols Cem—*cemetery* (3) ... MO-7
Nichols Cem—*cemetery* (4) ... NY-2
Nichols Cem—*cemetery* ... OH-6
Nichols Cem—*cemetery* ... OR-9
Nichols Cem—*cemetery* ... SC-3
Nichols Cem—*cemetery* (6) ... TN-4
Nichols Cem—*cemetery* (2) ... TX-5
Nichols Cem—*cemetery* (2) ... VA-3
Nichols Channel—*channel* ... NJ-2
Nichols Chapel—*church* ... TN-4
Nichols Chapel African Methodist Episcopal Ch—*church* ... AL-4
Nichols Chapel AME Ch—*church* ... AL-4
Nichols Coll—*school* ... MA-1
**Nichols Corner**—*pop pl* ... RI-1
Nichols Corners—*locale* (2) ... NY-2
**Nichols Corners**—*pop pl* ... NY-2
Nichols Coulee—*valley* ... MT-8
Nichols Coulee Camp—*locale* ... MT-8
Nichols Cove Branch—*stream* ... NC-3
Nichols Cove Branch—*stream* ... TN-4
*Nichols Creek* ... MO-7
*Nichols Creek* ... MT-8
*Nichols Creek* ... WA-9
*Nichols Creek* ... WI-6
Nichols Creek—*stream* ... AL-4
Nichols Creek—*stream* ... AR-4
Nichols Creek—*stream* ... CO-8
Nichols Creek—*stream* ... FL-3
Nichols Creek—*stream* ... KS-7
Nichols Creek—*stream* (2) ... LA-4
Nichols Creek—*stream* ... MA-1
Nichols Creek—*stream* ... MS-4
Nichols Creek—*stream* (3) ... MO-7
Nichols Creek—*stream* (3) ... MT-8
Nichols Creek—*stream* (3) ... OR-9
Nichols Creek—*stream* ... SD-7
Nichols Creek—*stream* (3) ... TX-5
Nichols Creek—*stream* ... WI-6
Nichols Creek Ch—*church* ... TX-5
Nichols Creek State Wildlife Area—*park* ... WI-6
Nichols Dam—*dam* ... AL-4
Nichols Diggings—*mine* ... CA-9
Nichols Ditch—*canal* (2) ... MT-8
Nichols Ditch—*canal* ... WY-8
Nichols Drain—*canal* ... MI-6
Nichols Draw—*valley* ... CO-8
Nichols Family Cem—*cemetery* ... AL-4
Nichols Farm Cem—*cemetery* ... CT-1
Nichols Farms Hist Dist—*hist pl* ... CT-1
Nichols Fork—*stream* ... KY-4
Nichols Gap—*gap* ... AL-4
Nichols Gap—*gap* ... GA-3
Nichols Gap—*gap* ... OR-9
Nichols Gap—*gap* ... VA-3
Nichols Grove Cem—*cemetery* ... MO-7
Nichols Grove Ch—*church* ... MO-7
Nichols Gulch—*valley* ... ID-8
Nichols Hill—*summit* ... CT-1
Nichols Hill—*summit* ... KY-4
Nichols Hill—*summit* (2) ... MA-1
Nichols Hill—*summit* ... NH-1
Nichols Hill—*summit* ... NY-2
Nichols Hill—*summit* ... WA-9
Nichols Hill—*summit* ... WV-2
Nichols Hill Island—*island* ... NY-2
Nichols Hills—*other* ... AK-9
**Nichols Hills**—*pop pl* ... OK-5
Nichols Hills Sch—*school* ... OK-5
**Nichols (historical)**—*pop pl* (2) ... LA-4
**Nichols (historical)**—*pop pl* ... OR-9
Nichols Hollow—*valley* ... GA-3
Nichols Hollow—*valley* ... MO-7
Nichols Hollow—*valley* ... OK-5
Nichols Hollow—*valley* ... PA-2
Nichols Hollow—*valley* (2) ... TN-4
Nichols House—*hist pl* ... LA-4
Nichols House—*hist pl* ... MA-1
Nichols House—*hist pl* ... OR-9
Nichols House—*hist pl* ... VT-1
Nichols House Museum—*building* ... MA-1
Nichols Islands—*area* ... AK-9
Nichols JHS—*school* ... AL-4
Nichols JHS—*school* ... MS-4
Nichols-Jones Cem—*cemetery* ... SC-3
Nichols Knob—*summit* ... MO-7
Nichols Knob—*summit* (2) ... WV-2
Nichols Lake—*lake* ... AK-9
Nichols Lake—*lake* ... AR-4
Nichols Lake—*lake* ... FL-3
Nichols Lake—*lake* ... LA-4
Nichols Lake—*lake* (3) ... MI-6
Nichols Lake—*lake* ... MN-6
Nichols Lake—*lake* (2) ... WI-6
Nichols Lake—*reservoir* ... AL-4
Nichols Lake—*reservoir* ... KY-4
Nichols Lake—*reservoir* ... MO-7
Nichols Lake—*reservoir* ... NC-3
Nichols Lake—*reservoir* ... OK-5
Nichols Lake Dam—*dam* ... MS-4
Nichols Lake Dam—*dam* ... NC-3
Nichols Landing—*locale* ... AL-4
Nichols Landing Strip—*airport* ... LA-4
Nichols Lane Run—*stream* ... WV-2
Nichols Ledge—*bench* ... VT-1
Nichols Lookout Tower—*locale* ... SC-3
Nichols Lynchner Cave—*cave* ... PA-2
Nichols Memorial Library—*hist pl* ... NH-1
Nichols-Merritt Ditch—*canal* ... NV-8
Nichols Mill (historical)—*locale* ... AL-4
Nichols Mill (Site)—*locale* ... CA-9
Nichols Mound—*summit* ... IL-6
Nichols Mtn—*summit* ... AK-9
Nichols Mtn—*summit* ... AR-4
Nichols Mtn—*summit* (2) ... TN-4
Nichols Number 1 Dam—*dam* ... SD-7
Nichols Number 2 Dam—*dam* ... SD-7
Nichols Oil and Gas Field—*oilfield* ... KS-7
*Nicholson* ... OH-6
Nicholson—*locale* ... MI-6
Nicholson—*locale* ... ND-7
**Nicholson**—*pop pl* ... GA-3
**Nicholson**—*pop pl* ... KY-4
**Nicholson**—*pop pl* ... MI-6
**Nicholson**—*pop pl* ... MS-4
**Nicholson**—*pop pl* ... PA-2
Nicholson, Grace, Bldg—*hist pl* ... CA-9
Nicholson, James, House—*hist pl* ... OH-6
Nicholson, James, House—*hist pl* ... SC-3
Nicholson, Lake—*lake* ... SD-7
Nicholson, Sarah and Samuel, House—*hist pl* ... NJ-2
Nicholson Borough—*civil* ... PA-2
Nicholson Branch—*stream* ... GA-3
Nicholson Branch—*stream* (2) ... MS-4
Nicholson Branch—*stream* ... NJ-2
Nicholson Branch—*stream* ... TN-4
Nicholson Bridge—*bridge* ... GA-3
Nicholson Bridges—*bridge* ... SC-3
Nicholson (CCD)—*cens area* ... GA-3
Nicholson Cem—*cemetery* (2) ... AL-4
Nicholson Cem—*cemetery* ... AR-4
Nicholson Cem—*cemetery* ... GA-3
Nicholson Cem—*cemetery* (2) ... IN-6
Nicholson Cem—*cemetery* ... MO-7
Nicholson Cem—*cemetery* ... NY-2
Nicholson Cem—*cemetery* ... NC-3
Nicholson Cem—*cemetery* ... ND-7
Nicholson Cem—*cemetery* ... SC-3
Nicholson Cem—*cemetery* (4) ... TN-4
Nicholson Cem—*cemetery* (2) ... TX-5
Nicholson Chapel—*church* ... WV-2
Nicholson Coulee—*valley* ... MT-8
Nicholson Creek—*stream* ... IA-7
Nicholson Creek—*stream* (2) ... NC-3
Nicholson Creek—*stream* ... SC-3
Nicholson Creek—*stream* ... TX-5
Nicholson Creek—*stream* ... VA-3
Nicholson Creek—*stream* (2) ... WA-9
Nicholson Draw—*valley* ... WY-8
Nicholson Elem Sch—*school* ... MS-4
Nicholson Field—*airport* ... ND-7
Nicholson-Freeman Cem—*cemetery* ... FL-3
Nicholson Gap—*gap* ... AL-4
Nicholson Gap—*gap* ... GA-3
**Nicholson Heights**—*pop pl* ... TN-4
Nicholson Hill—*summit* ... PA-2
Nicholson (historical)—*locale* ... AL-4
Nicholson Hollow—*valley* ... VA-3
Nicholson Hollow Trail—*trail* ... VA-3
Nicholson House—*hist pl* ... AL-4
Nicholson House and Inn—*hist pl* ... PA-2
Nicholson Island—*island* ... PA-2
Nicholson Knob—*locale* ... VA-3
Nicholson Lake—*lake* ... AK-9
Nicholson Lake—*lake* ... CO-8
Nicholson Lake—*lake* ... WA-9
Nicholson Licklog Creek—*stream* ... NC-3
Nicholson Mine—*mine* ... MT-8
Nicholson Mtn—*summit* ... TN-4
Nicholson Point Park—*park* ... CA-9
Nicholson Pond—*lake* ... IN-6
Nicholson Prospects—*mine* ... TN-4
Nicholson Rocks—*area* ... AK-9
*Nicholson Run* ... PA-2
Nicholson Run—*stream* ... PA-2
Nicholson Run—*stream* ... VA-3
*Nicholson Sch* ... IN-6
Nicholson Sch—*school* ... IL-6
Nicholson Sch—*school* (2) ... IN-6
Nicholson Sch—*school* ... LA-4
*Nicholsons Chapel* ... AL-4
*Nicholson Sch Number 70* ... IN-6
Nicholson Sch of Bradenton—*school* ... FL-3
*Nicholson Sch 96* ... IN-6
*Nicholsons Creek* ... NC-3
Nicholson Spring—*spring* ... OR-9
Nicholson Springs—*spring* ... WY-8
**Nicholson Springs (historical)**—*pop pl* ... TN-4
*Nicholsons Run* ... PA-2
*Nicholsons Store* ... AL-4
**Nicholson (Township of)**—*pop pl* (2) ... PA-2
Nicholson Valley Ch—*church* ... IN-6
**Nicholson Village**—*pop pl* ... SC-3
*Nicholsonville* ... IN-6
*Nicholsonville* ... NC-3
Nicholsonville—*locale* ... GA-3
Nicholsonville Baptist Church—*hist pl* ... GA-3
Nichols Park—*park* ... CA-9
Nichols Park—*park* ... MO-7
Nichols Park—*park* ... NE-7
Nichols Park—*park* ... NJ-2
Nichols Park—*park* ... OK-5
Nichols Passage—*channel* ... AK-9
*Nichols Peak* ... CA-9
Nichols Peak—*summit* ... UT-8
*Nichols Point* ... NY-2
Nichols Point—*cape* ... AK-9
Nichols Point—*cape* ... MD-2
Nichols Point—*cape* ... MI-6
Nichols Point—*cape* ... NJ-2
Nichols Point—*cape* ... VT-1
Nichols Point—*cape* ... WI-6
Nichols Point—*summit* ... PA-2
Nichols Pointe Park—*park* ... MI-6
*Nichols Pond* ... ME-1
*Nichols Pond* ... VT-1
Nichols Pond—*lake* ... AL-4
Nichols Pond—*lake* ... CT-1
Nichols Pond—*lake* ... ME-1
Nichols Pond—*lake* ... MA-1
Nichols Pond—*lake* ... NY-2
Nichols Pond—*lake* ... VT-1
Nichols Pond—*reservoir* ... RI-1
Nichols Pond—*swamp* ... FL-3
Nichols Pond Dam—*dam* ... RI-1
Nichols Post Office (historical)—*building* ... TN-4
Nichol Spring—*spring* ... OR-9
Nichols Pump—*other* ... OR-9
Nichols Ranch—*locale* ... MT-8
Nichols Ranch—*locale* ... OR-9
Nichols Ranch—*locale* ... TX-5
Nichols Ranch—*locale* (3) ... WY-8

Nichols Rapids—locale ME-1
Nichols Reef—bar TN-4
Nichols Road Dam—dam MA-1
Nichols Rsvr—reservoir ID-8
Nichols Rsvr—reservoir NM-5
**Nichols Run**—pop pl NY-2
Nichols Run—stream IL-6
Nichols Run—stream NY-2
Nichols Run—stream NC-3
Nichols Run—stream PA-2
Nichols Run—stream VA-3
Nichols Sch—school CA-9
Nichols Sch—school (3) IL-6
Nichols Sch—school KS-7
Nichols Sch—school KY-4
Nichols Sch—school (2) MI-6
Nichols Sch—school MO-7
Nichols Sch—school (4) NY-2
Nichols Sch—school OH-6
Nichols Sch—school OK-5
Nichols Sch—school WI-6
Nichols Sch (historical)—school AL-4
Nichols Sch (historical)—school IA-7
Nichols Sch (historical)—school (2) TN-4
Nichols School (Abandoned)—locale MO-7
Nichols Shoals—bar AL-4
Nichols Shop Ctr—locale NC-3
**Nichols Shore Acres**—pop pl WI-6
Nichols Siding—uninc pl NY-2
Nichols Spit—bar AK-9
Nichols Spring—spring CA-9
Nichols Spring—spring ID-8
Nichols Spring—spring MO-7
Nichols Spring—spring NM-5
Nichols Spring—spring (2) OR-9
Nichols Spring Branch—stream AL-4
Nichols State Public Shooting Area—park SD-7
Nichols Station RI-1
Nichols-Sterner House—hist pl MA-1
Nichols Store (historical)—locale AL-4
**Nichols (Town of)**—pop pl NY-2
Nichols (Township of)—fmr MCD AR-4
Nichols (Township of)—other MN-6
Nicholsville GA-3
Nicholsville RI-1
Nicholsville—locale NY-2
**Nicholsville**—pop pl AL-4
**Nicholsville**—pop pl MI-6
**Nicholsville**—pop pl OH-6
Nicholsville Ch—church AL-4
**Nicholsville (historical)**—pop pl NC-3
Nichols Well—well AZ-5
Nichols Windmill—locale TX-5
**Nicholtown**—pop pl SC-3
**Nicholville**—pop pl NY-2
Nichomus Run—stream NJ-2
Nichovson Creek NC-3
Nicho Well—well TX-5
Nicicola Creek—stream OK-5
Niciper Creek—stream TX-5
Nick MS-4
Nick—locale KY-4
Nick, Lake—lake LA-4
Nick, Mount—summit AK-9
Nickaburr Creek—stream TX-5
**Nickajack**—pop pl GA-3
Nickajack Branch—stream TN-4
Nickajack Cave—cave TN-4
Nickajack Cove—valley GA-3
Nickajack Creek—stream GA-3
Nickajack Creek—stream NC-3
Nickajack Dam—dam TN-4
Nickajack Gap—gap (2) GA-3
Nickajack Gap—gap NC-3
Nickajack Lake—reservoir TN-4
Nickals Tank—reservoir AZ-5
Nick and Nora Tank—reservoir AZ-5
Nickatous Lake ME-1
Nickatous Stream ME-1
Nickawampus Creek—stream VA-3
Nick Barry Dam—dam OR-9
Nick Barry Spring—spring OR-9
Nick Bottom—bend NC-3
Nick Branch—stream KY-4
Nick Branch—stream MO-7
Nick Branch—stream NC-3
Nick Brown Creek—stream OK-5
Nick Creek NC-3
Nick Creek TN-4
Nick Creek—stream (2) ID-8
Nick Creek—stream (2) LA-4
Nick Creek—stream NY-2
Nick Creek—stream (2) NC-3
Nick Creek—stream PA-2
Nick Davis Cem—cemetery AL-4
Nick Dennery Lake Dam—dam MS-4
Nick Eaton Ridge—ridge OR-9
Nickel—locale LA-4
Nickel—locale TX-5
Nickel Bar Gulch—valley MT-8
**Nickelberry**—pop pl TX-5
Nickel Branch—stream KY-4
Nickel Canyon—valley CA-9
Nickel Canyon—valley WA-9
Nickel Cem—cemetery KS-7
**Nickel Creek**—pop pl TX-5
Nickel Creek—stream AK-9
Nickel Creek—stream CA-9
Nickel Creek—stream (2) ID-8
Nickel Creek—stream KS-7
Nickel Creek—stream MN-6
Nickel Creek—stream NV-8
Nickel Creek—stream OK-5
Nickel Creek—stream OR-9
Nickel Creek—stream TX-5
Nickel Creek—stream WA-9
Nickel Creek—stream WY-8
Nickel Creek Pocket—basin ID-8
Nickel Creek Rsvr—reservoir ID-8
Nickel Creek Shelter—locale WA-9
Nickel Creek Spring—spring ID-8
Nickel Creek Station—locale TX-5
Nickel Creek Table—summit ID-8
Nickeles Spring NM-5
Nickel (historical)—locale KS-7
Nickell—locale KY-4
Nickell, William, A., House—hist pl WI-6
Nickel Lake—lake (2) MN-6
Nickell Branch—stream (3) KY-4
Nickell Cove—valley KY-4
Nickell Fork—stream KY-4
Nickell Park—park MO-7
Nickell Point Rec Area—park KY-4
Nickells Cave—cave AR-4
Nickells Dam—dam TN-4
Nickells Lake—reservoir TN-4
Nickells Memorial Ch—church AR-4
Nickells Mill—locale WV-2
Nickellton—locale MO-7
Nickel Mine Brook—stream (2) CT-1
Nickel Mine Brook—stream MA-1
Nickel Mine Hill—summit MA-1
Nickel Mines—locale PA-2
Nickel Mines Mission—building PA-2
Nickel Mine Spring—spring KS-7
Nickel Mines Run—stream PA-2
Nickel Mtn—summit OR-9
**Nickel Plate**—pop pl MI-6
Nickelplate Mtn—summit ID-8
Nickel Plate Road Steam Locomotive No. 587—hist pl IN-6
Nickel Ridge—ridge KY-4
Nickel Ridge Ch—church KY-4
Nickel Row TN-4
Nickel Run—stream PA-2
Nickels Arcade—hist pl MI-6
Nickels Branch—stream TN-4
Nickels Branch—stream VA-3
Nickels Cem—cemetery VA-3
Nickel Scribner Ditch—canal WY-8
Nickelsen Creek—stream IN-6
Nickels Gin—locale TX-5
Nickel Shaft Mine—mine CO-8
Nickels Marsh—swamp WI-6
Nickels-Milam House—hist pl SC-3
Nickelson Cem—cemetery AR-4
Nickelson Creek—stream CO-8
Nickelson Lake CO-8
Nickelson Place—locale WY-8
Nickelson Well—locale NM-5
Nickels-Sortwell House—hist pl ME-1
Nickelsville GA-3
Nickelsville—locale GA-3
**Nickelsville**—pop pl VA-3
**Nickelsville (Big Sandy)**—pop pl GA-3
Nickeltown Branch—stream TN-4
Nickel Valley Run—stream OH-6
Nickelville GA-3
Nickelville PA-2
Nickelville—locale MO-7
Nickel Vly Brook—stream NY-2
Nickens Hollow—valley TN-4
**Nickerson**—pop pl KS-7
**Nickerson**—pop pl MN-6
**Nickerson**—pop pl (2) NE-7
Nickerson, Samuel, House—hist pl IL-6
Nickerson Beach—beach MA-1
Nickerson Brook—stream ME-1
Nickerson Cem—cemetery ME-1
Nickerson Cem—cemetery MO-7
Nickerson Coulee—valley MT-8
Nickerson Creek—stream MT-8
Nickerson Cutoff—canal UT-8
Nickerson Elem Sch—school KS-7
Nickerson Hill MA-1
Nickerson Hill—summit CT-1
Nickerson Hill—summit IN-6
Nickerson HS—school KS-7
Nickerson Island—island ME-1
Nickerson Lake—lake ME-1
Nickerson Ledge—bench NH-1
Nickerson Lookout Tower—locale MN-6
Nickerson Mansion—hist pl MA-1
Nickerson Mills—locale ME-1
Nickerson Mountains—ridge NH-1
Nickerson Neck MA-1
Nickerson Ranch (site)—locale CA-9
Nickerson School—locale MI-6
Nickersons Neck—cape MA-1
Nickerson State Forest Park—park MA-1
Nickerson State Park MA-1
**Nickerson Township**—pop pl NE-7
**Nickerson (Township of)**—pop pl MN-6
Nicke Sch—school MI-6
Nickeus Park—park ND-7
Nickey Lake—lake AR-4
Nick Gap—gap NC-3
Nicking House—hist pl IA-7
Nickjack—locale GA-3
Nick Lake—lake WI-6
Nickleberry—locale TX-5
Nickleberry Swamp VA-3
Nickleberry Swamp—stream VA-3
Nickle Creek KS-7
Nickle Creek—stream AK-9
Nickle Creek—stream WY-8
Nick Ledge—bar ME-1
Nickle-Martin-Rathbone Cem—cemetery AL-4
Nickles Canyon—valley WA-9
Nickle Sch—school MI-6
Nickles Chapel Cem—cemetery AR-4
Nickles Hollow—valley KY-4
Nickleson Branch—stream AR-4
Nickleson Creek—stream MS-4
Nickles Ranch—locale NM-5
Nicklesville GA-3
Nicklesville—locale GA-3
**Nickletown**—pop pl TN-4
Nickletown Cem—cemetery KS-7
Nickleville—locale GA-3
**Nickleville**—pop pl PA-2
Nicklewis Bar AL-4
Nick Lewis Bar—bar AL-4
Nicklin—locale CA-9
**Nicklin**—pop pl PA-2
Nicklin Ave Sch—school OH-6
Nicklund Creek—stream WA-9
Nicklwaite Creek—stream CA-9
Nick Mtn—summit CO-8
Nick Mtn—summit NY-2
Nick Myers Gulch CO-8
Nickol Creek—stream WA-9
Nickoli Lake—lake AK-9
Nickols Cem—cemetery LA-4
Nickol Sch—school MT-8
Nickols Creek—stream (2) TX-5
Nickols Crossing ND-7
Nickols Knob—summit CA-9
**Nickolson**—pop pl KY-4
Nickolson Branch—stream GA-3
Nickolson Cem—cemetery IN-6
Nickolson Creek—stream IL-6
Nickolson Creek—stream IA-7
Nickolson Lake—lake MN-6
Nickolson Spring Branch—stream TN-4
Nickols Ranch—locale MT-8
Nickols Well—well NM-5
Nickowitz Creek—stream CA-9
Nick Patterson Cem—cemetery TN-4
Nick Peak CO-8
Nick Peak—summit ID-8
Nick Pond—lake PA-2
Nick Post Office (historical)—building MS-4
Nick Preen Mines—mine MT-8
Nick Ray Draw—valley WY-8
Nick Reservoit—reservoir UT-8
Nicks AL-4
Nicks Bayou TX-5
Nicks Branch—stream MO-7
Nicks Cabin—locale UT-8
Nicks Camp Canyon—valley AZ-5
Nicks Cem—cemetery (2) MO-7
Nicks Cem—cemetery (2) TN-4
Nicks Coulee—valley MT-8
Nicks Cove—locale CA-9
Nicks Creek NC-3
Nicks Creek—locale TN-4
Nicks Creek—stream NY-2
Nicks Creek—stream NC-3
Nicks Creek—stream TN-4
Nicks Creek—stream VA-3
Nicks Creek Baptist Ch—church TN-4
Nicks Creek Cem—cemetery TN-4
Nicks Creek Ch—church NC-3
Nicks Creek Ch—church VA-3
Nicks Cut—channel TX-5
Nicks Flying Service Inc Airp—airport MS-4
Nicks Gulch—valley MT-8
Nicks Gut—channel ME-1
Nick's Hamburger Shop—hist pl SD-7
Nicks Hole FL-3
Nicks Hollow TN-4
Nicks Lake—lake FL-3
Nicks Lake—lake LA-4
Nicks Lake—lake NY-2
Nicks Lake—lake TX-5
Nicks Lake Gas Field—oilfield LA-4
Nicks Mate MA-1
Nicks Nest Branch—stream NC-3
Nickson Hill—summit KY-4
Nicks Point RI-1
Nicks Point—cape NY-2
Nicks Point—summit UT-8
Nicks Pond—lake (2) NY-2
Nicks Pond—lake UT-8
Nick Spring—spring CO-8
Nick Springs—locale AR-4
Nicks Ranch—locale TX-5
Nicks Rock—rock MA-1
Nicks Spring—spring CA-9
Nicks Spring—spring TN-4
Nicks Swamp—swamp PA-2
Nicks Tank—reservoir AZ-5
**Nicksville**—pop pl AZ-5
Nicks Well—well NV-8
**Nicktown**—pop pl PA-2
Nickville—locale GA-3
Nickwack Cem—cemetery LA-4
Nickwaket, Mount—summit VT-1
Nickwall—locale MT-8
Nickwall Creek—stream MT-8
Nickwall Dam—dam MT-8
Nick Welch Spring—spring CA-9
Nick Wynn Mtn—summit ID-8
Nicodemus—locale PA-2
**Nicodemus**—pop pl KS-7
Nicodemus Cem—cemetery ID-8
Nicodemus Cem—cemetery KS-7
Nicodemus Cem—cemetery PA-2
Nicodemus Community Ch—church AR-4
Nicodemus Hist Dist—hist pl KS-7
Nicodemus Slough—gut FL-3
**Nicodemus Township**—pop pl KS-7
Nicohn—locale ME-1
Nicojack GA-3
Nicojack Creek GA-3
Nicojack Post Office (historical)—building TN-4
Nicol MN-6
Nicol, Lake—reservoir AL-4
Nicola Creek—stream MT-8
Nicolai Cem—cemetery MN-6
Nicolai Mtn—summit OR-9
Nicolai Ridge—ridge OR-9
Nicolaisen Cem—cemetery SD-7
Nicolaisen Landing Field—airport SD-7
Nicolai Valley—valley WI-6
Nicola Ridge—ridge MT-8
Nicolar Island—island ME-1
Nicolas Canyon CA-9
Nicolas Cem—cemetery IN-6
Nicolas Duran De Chavez Grant—civil NM-5
Nicolas JHS—school CA-9
Nicolas Lake WA-9
Nicolas Ranch—locale WA-9
Nicolas Spring—spring NM-5
**Nicolaus**—pop pl CA-9
Nicolaus Cem—cemetery CA-9
Nicolay House—hist pl MO-7
Nicol Creek—stream MT-8
Nicol Drain—canal MI-6
Nicol Drain—stream MI-6
Nicolet, Lake—lake MI-6
Nicolet Bay—bay WI-6
Nicolet Creek—stream AK-9
Nicolet Creek—stream MN-6
Nicolet Lake—lake MN-6
Nicolet Natl For—forest WI-6
Nicolet Public Sch—hist pl WI-6
Nicolet Sch—school (3) WI-6
**Nicolette**—pop pl WV-2
**Nicoletti Drive**—pop pl UT-8
Nicolet Trail—trail MN-6
Nicolie Creek—stream AK-9
Nicolin ME-1
Nicolis Canyon OR-9
Nicoll, Caroline, House—hist pl CT-1
Nicoll Bay—bay NY-2
Nicoll Creek—stream OR-9
**Nicollet**—pop pl MN-6
Nicollet Bay—bay MN-6
Nicollet Cem—cemetery MN-6
**Nicollet (County)**—pop pl MN-6
Nicollet County Bank—hist pl MN-6
Nicollet Field—park MN-6
Nicollet Hotel—hist pl MN-6
Nicollet House Hotel—hist pl MN-6
Nicollet Island—ISLAND MN-6
Nicollet Landing—locale MN-6
Nicollet Park—park MN-6
**Nicollet (Township of)**—pop pl MN-6
Nicoll Lake—lake NM-5
Nicoll Point—cape (2) NY-2
Nicolls Canyon OR-9
Nicolls Peak—summit CA-9
Nicolls Point NY-2
Nicoll Spring—spring CA-9
Nicolls Ranch—locale SD-7
Nicols MN-6
Nicol's MN-6
Nicols—locale MN-6
Nicolson, William P., House—hist pl GA-3
Nicolson Cemetery OR-9
Nicol Table Mountain Ditch—canal WY-8
Nicol Tank—reservoir NM-5
**Nicolville**—pop pl MN-6
Nic-o-man-chie River WA-9
**Nicoma Park**—pop pl OK-5
Nicoma Park JHS—school OK-5
Nicomodes Gulch—valley CO-8
Niconza Ch—church IN-6
Niconzah, Lake—reservoir IN-6
Nico Park—park IL-6
Nicopolis Ch—church VA-3
Nicoson Cem—cemetery OR-9
Nicotoon Lake—lake FL-3
Nicut—locale OK-5
Nicut—locale WV-2
Nicut Run—stream WV-2
Nicy Grove Ch—church SC-3
Nida—locale WV-2
**Nida**—pop pl MS-4
**Nida**—pop pl OK-5
Nida Cem—cemetery (2) WV-2
Nid Aigle, Bayou—gut LA-4
Nida Point—cape OK-5
Nidaros Cem—cemetery SD-7
Nidaros Ch—church MN-6
Nidaros Ch—church SD-7
Nidarose Ch—church ND-7
**Nidaros (Township of)**—pop pl MN-6
Niday—locale VA-3
Niddokan—bar MP-9
Nidever Branch TN-4
Nidey Branch Cow Creek—stream OR-9
Nidifer Branch—stream TN-4
Nidifer Prospect—mine TN-4
Nidiffer Chapel—church TN-4
Nido Ranch—locale TX-5
Nido Tank—reservoir TX-5
Nido Windmill—locale TX-5
Niebauer Springs—spring WI-6
Nieber Spring—spring ID-8
Niebes, As—summit MH-9
Nieblas Sch—school CA-9
Niebuh Mine—mine NV-8
Niebuhr, John, Farmhouse—hist pl MN-6
Niebull Cem—cemetery WI-6
Niece Athletic Field—park TX-5
Niece Branch—stream WV-2
Niece Ch—church MO-7
Niece Tank—reservoir TX-5
Niedan Number 1 Dam—dam SD-7
Niedbala Dam MA-1
Niedermeier Sch—school MI-6
**Niederwald**—pop pl TX-5
Niederwald Cem—cemetery TX-5
Niehardt, Mount—summit CO-8
Nieholson Sch—school WI-6
Niehs Research Triangle Park Dam—dam NC-3
Nieiruk, Oror En—locale FM-9
Niej—island MP-9
Nieji MP-9
Nieji—island MP-9
Nieji Island MP-9
Niekerk Ch—church MI-6
Nieland Creek—stream CO-8
Nieland House—hist pl IA-7
Niel Creek—stream MT-8
Niel Creek—stream NV-8
Nielon Gulch—valley CA-9
Nielsburg—locale CA-9
Nielsen, Jens, House—hist pl UT-8
Nielsen, Niels, Fourteen-Side Barn Farm—hist pl ND-7
Nielsen Canyon—valley UT-8
Nielsen Cem—cemetery SD-7
Nielsen Coulee—valley MT-8
Nielsen Ditch—canal WY-8
Nielsen Lake—lake MN-6
Nielsen Number 1 Dam—dam SD-7
Nielsen Ranch—locale CO-8
Nielsen Ranch—locale WY-8
Nielsen Spring—spring WY-8
Nielson, Hans Peter, Gristmill—hist pl UT-8
Nielson, Jens, House—hist pl UT-8
Nielson, N. S., House—hist pl UT-8
Nielson Airstrip—airport OR-9
Nielson Canyon—valley OR-9
Nielson Ditch—canal ID-8
Nielson Ditch—canal (2) UT-8
**Nielson Estates Subdivision**—pop pl UT-8
Nielson Knoll—summit UT-8
Nielson Mine—mine CO-8
Nielson Place—locale CA-9
Nielson Pond—reservoir UT-8
Nielson Ranch—locale (3) CA-9
Nielson Ranch—locale MT-8
Nielson Rsvr—reservoir CO-8
Nielsons Peak—summit UT-8
**Nielson Subdivision**—pop pl UT-8
Nielson Wash NV-8
Niel Spring—spring UT-8
**Nielsville**—pop pl MN-6
Niemackl Lakes—lake MN-6
Niemada Lake—lake MN-6
Niemaki Lake MN-6
Niemakl Lake MN-6
Nieman Creek—stream IN-6
Nieman Creek—stream KS-7
Nieman Ditch IN-6
Nieman Ditch—canal NE-7
Nieman Elem Sch—school KS-7
Nieman Lake WI-6
Niemann Cem—cemetery TN-4
Niemann Elem Sch—school IN-6
Nieman Plaza—locale KS-7
Niemans Creek—stream MO-7
Niemela Gulch—valley CA-9
Niemes Sch—school CA-9
Niemi Camp—locale MN-6
Niemi Lake—lake MI-6
Niemi Number 1 Dam—dam SD-7
Niemi Number 2 Dam—dam SD-7
Niemi Number 3 Dam—dam SD-7
Niemi Number 4 Dam—dam SD-7
Niemi Number 5 Dam—dam SD-7
Niemi Ranch—locale NM-5
Niemno Ch—church GA-3
Niemonds Ch—church PA-2
Niemon Lake WI-6
Niemoth Ranch—locale (2) NE-7
Nienda TX-5
Niene Lake—lake WI-6
Nienie—civil (2) HI-9
Nienie Gulch—valley HI-9
Nier Cem—cemetery IN-6
Niergarth Sch—school MI-6
Niers Branch—stream KY-4
Niesky PA-2
Nies Mine—mine MT-8
Niespodziany Ditch—canal IN-6
Niesson Creek—stream WA-9
Nieswanders Fort—locale VA-3
**Niets Crest**—pop pl NY-2
Nieusma Dam—dam ND-7
Nieve, Canon—valley CO-8
Niewerth Bldg—hist pl IN-6
Niezer Dam—dam IN-6
Nif FM-9
Nifa (North Illinois Fair Association) IL-6
Niffer PA-2
Niffin Vly—swamp NY-2
Nifong Cem—cemetery IL-6
Nifty Rock—island CA-9
Nifu FM-9
Nigag Mtn—summit AK-9
Nigaktoviakvik Creek—stream AK-9
Nigaktukvik Creek—stream AK-9
Nigara Creek IN-6
Nigar Lake MI-6
Nigaruyaru—island FM-9
Nigatuk Creek—stream AK-9
Nig Bayou—stream TX-5
Nig Branch TN-4
Nigehus Point—cape AK-9
Niger Canyon CA-9
Niger Hill—summit PA-2
Nigeruk Creek—stream AK-9
Nig Field—flat TN-4
Nigger Abe Creek NV-8
Nigger Bar Creek CA-9
Nigger Bar Creek WA-9
Nigger Bay NC-3
Nigger Bend MO-7
Nigger Bend Bluff MO-7
Nigger Bend Spring CA-9
Nigger Ben Mountain OR-9
Nigger Brook ME-1
Nigger Brook Lakes ME-1
Nigger Camp Mountain CA-9
Nigger Canyon AZ-5
Nigger Canyon CA-9
Nigger Canyon NM-5
Nigger Cove MD-2
Nigger Creek AR-4
Nigger Creek CA-9
Nigger Creek CO-8
Nigger Creek ID-8
Nigger Creek IN-6
Nigger Creek MI-6
Nigger Creek NV-8
Nigger Creek NC-3
Nigger Creek OK-5
Nigger Creek OR-9
Nigger Creek SD-7
Nigger Creek TX-5
Nigger Creek WA-9
Nigger Creek WI-6
Nigger Creek WY-8
Nigger Ditch IN-6
Niggeredge Canyon SD-7
Nigger Flat OR-9
Niggerfoot Branch AL-4
Nigger Gap PA-2
Nigger George Draw NV-8
Nigger Gulch CA-9
Nigger Gulch CO-8
Nigger Gulch MT-8
Niggerhead AL-4
Nigger Head CA-9
Nigger Head ID-8
Niggerhead WA-9
Niggerhead Brook VT-1
Niggerhead Creek AK-9
Niggerhead Creek NC-3
Niggerhead Creek WA-9
Niggerhead Lake MI-6
Niggerhead Lake NE-7
Niggerhead Mtn VT-1
Niggerhead Point FL-3
Niggerhead Pond CT-1
Niggerhead Pond VT-1
Nigger Head Rapids ID-8
Nigger Heel Bar AL-4
Niggerheel Butte OR-9
Nigger Hill AR-4
Nigger Hill CA-9
Nigger Hill CO-8
Nigger Hill Ch AR-4
Nigger Hollow OR-9
Nigger Hollow PA-2
Nigger Island MD-2
Nigger Island MI-6
Nigger Island WA-9
Nigger Island Gut MD-2
Nigger Jack Creek OR-9
Nigger Jack Slough CA-9
Nigger Jim Hammock Bridge FL-3
Nigger Joe Ridge CA-9
Nigger Lake MI-6
Nigger Lake MN-6
Nigger Lake NY-2
Nigger Lake WA-9
Nigger Lake WI-6
Nigger Lakes WI-6
Nigger Lick IL-6
Nigger Mountain CA-9
Nigger Mountain MT-8
Nigger Mountain NC-3
Nigger Mountain WA-9
Nigger Point MI-6
Nigger Pond AL-4
Nigger Pond NJ-2
Nigger Pond NY-2
Nigger Pond WA-9
Nigger Ridge OR-9
Nigger Rube Creek CA-9
Nigger Run OK-5
Nigger Run PA-2
Nigger Run VA-3
Nigger Run Ravine CA-9
Nigger Sam Slough CA-9
Nigger Sawmill Brook RI-1
Nigger Shack Mine NM-5
Nigger Slough MO-7
Nigger Spring CA-9
Niggertown Knoll FL-3
Niggertown Marsh FL-3
Nigger Valley CA-9
Niggerville Creek CA-9
Nigger Wash AZ-5
Niggler Cem—cemetery MN-6
Niggletetwist Run—stream WV-2
Niggs Creek—stream TN-4
Niggs Creek Sch—school TN-4
Nigh—locale KY-4
Nigh Cem—cemetery MO-7
Nigh Chapel—church IL-6
Nigh Creek—stream MN-6
Nigh Creek—stream NY-2
Nighcut Hill—summit WV-2
Nigh Gap Run—stream WV-2
Nigh Lake MN-6
Nigh Lake—lake MN-6
Nigh Sch (historical)—school MO-7
Nighswander, Benjamin, House—hist pl IA-7
Nighswander Creek—stream OR-9
Nighswonger Cem—cemetery IL-6
Night Bayou TX-5
Nightcap—island ME-1
Nightcap Ledge—bar ME-1
Night Cap Peak—summit CA-9
Night Creek SD-7
Night Draw—valley WY-8
Nightengale Sch—school NY-2
Nighten Helser Coulee—valley MT-8
Nightgown Ridge—ridge UT-8
Nighthart Cem—cemetery IN-6
Night Hawk—locale MO-7
Night Hawk—mine AZ-5
**Nighthawk**—pop pl CO-8
**Nighthawk**—pop pl WA-9
Nighthawk Creek—stream MI-6
Nighthawk Hill—summit CO-8
Nighthawk Hill (historical)—locale DC-2
Nighthawk Hollow Brook—stream NH-1
Nighthawk Lake—lake MN-6
Nighthawk Mtn—summit ME-1
Night Hawk Spring—spring AZ-5
Nightingale AL-4
Nightingale CA-9
Nightingale—locale NV-8
**Nightingale**—pop pl CA-9
Nightingale Brook—stream CT-1
Nightingale Canyon—valley WA-9
Nightingale Cem—cemetery MA-1
Nightingale Gulch—valley CA-9
Nightingale Hall Rice Mill Chimney—hist pl SC-3
Nightingale Hosp—hospital TX-5
Nightingale JHS—school CA-9
Nightingale Mine—mine NV-8
Nightingale Mtns—range NV-8
Nightingale Plantation—locale SC-3
Nightingale Pond—lake MA-1
Nightingale Pond—reservoir CT-1
Nightingale Sch—school (3) CA-9
Nightingale Sch—school (2) IL-6
Nightingale Sch—school SD-7
**Nightingale Trailer Park**—pop pl VA-3
Night Lake—lake MN-6
Night Lake—lake WY-8
Nightmare, The—area FL-3
Nightmare Camp—locale WA-9
**Nightmute**—pop pl AK-9
Nigh Trap Tank—reservoir AZ-5
Nightshade Lakes—lake OR-9
Nightshoot Cem—cemetery MT-8
Nightshoot Coulee—valley MT-8
Night Trap Tank—reservoir AZ-5
Nighway Branch—stream KY-4
Nighway Branch—stream TN-4
Nighway Branch—stream VA-3
Nighway Branch—stream WV-2
Nigikmigoon River—stream AK-9
Nigikpalvgururvrak Creek—stream AK-9
Nigiktlik Creek—stream AK-9
Niginfew FM-9
Nigisaktuvik River—stream AK-9
Nigis Creek—stream NC-3
Niglaktak Lake—lake AK-9
Nigman Branch—stream MO-7
Nigs Pond—lake CT-1
**Nigton**—pop pl TX-5
Nigtun Lake—lake AK-9
Niguanak Ridge—ridge AK-9
Niguanak River—stream AK-9
Nigu Bluff—summit AK-9
Niguel—civil CA-9
Niguel Hill—summit CA-9
**Niguel Terrace**—pop pl CA-9
Nigu Hills—other AK-9
Nigu River—stream AK-9
Nig Well Number Two—well AZ-5
Nihareke—unknown FM-9
Nihart—locale SD-7
Nihart Siding SD-7
Nihart Spring—spring SD-7
Nihatisset River MA-1
Niheke—locale FM-9

**Nihil**—*pop pl* PA-2
Nihill Siding—*locale* MT-8
Nihizer Cem—*cemetery* OH-6
**Nihizertown**—*pop pl* KY-4
**Nihkaikes**—*pop pl* FM-9
Nihkaras—*locale* FM-9
Nih Kawad—*locale* FM-9
Nihkelekel—*swamp* FM-9
Nihkewe—*civil* FM-9
**Nihmesehl**—*pop pl* FM-9
**Nihmoak**—*pop pl* FM-9
Nihmwed—*unknown* FM-9
Nihmwerei—*unknown* FM-9
Nihoa—*civil* HI-9
Nihoa Gulch—*valley* (2) HI-9
Nihoa Island Archeol District—*hist pl* HI-9
*Nihomus Run* NJ-2
Nihon Go Gakko—*hist pl* (2) WA-9
Nihooawa Gulch—*valley* HI-9
Nihpaden Nahkapw—*bar* FM-9
Nihpatapat—*locale* FM-9
Nih Peina—*cliff* FM-9
Nihpit—*civil* FM-9
Nih Pwekil—*unknown* FM-9
Nih Pwongin—*locale* FM-9
Nihsein—*locale* FM-9
Nihsou—*locale* FM-9
Nihwel—*locale* FM-9
*Niibunku* MP-9
Niibunku—*island* MP-9
*Niibunku Island* MP-9
*Niibunku-to* MP-9
Niihau—*island* HI-9
Niihau (CCD)—*cens area* HI-9
*Niimaru* FM-9
Ni Imwinwer—*cape* FM-9
*Niinii-to* MP-9
*Niipe Cave* AL-4
*Ni Island* MP-9
Niitltoktalogi Mtn—*summit* AK-9
**Niiwa**—*pop pl* FM-9
**Nijmegen (subdivision)**—*pop pl* NC-3
Nijode Lakes—*lake* MI-6
*Nijon* FM-9
Nikabuna Lake—*lake* AK-9
Nikabuna Lakes—*area* AK-9
Nikadavna Creek—*stream* AK-9
Ni Kahng—*swamp* FM-9
Nikalap Island—*island* FM-9
Nike JHS—*school* MO-7
**Nikep**—*pop pl* MD-2
**Nikep (Pekin)**—*pop pl* MD-2
Nikesa Cem—*cemetery* ID-8
Nikesa Creek—*stream* ID-8
Ni Ketieu, Pilen—*stream* FM-9
Niki Lake—*lake* MN-6
*Nikishka* AK-9
Nikishka—*CDP* AK-9
*Nikishka Number One* AK-9
*Nikishka Number Two* AK-9
*Nikishki Bay* AK-9
Ni Kisinre—*unknown* FM-9
*Nikiska Bay* AK-9
*Nikiski* AK-9
**Nikiski**—*pop pl* (2) AK-9
Nikiski Bay—*bay* AK-9
*Nikiski Wharf* AK-9
Nikka Creek—*stream* WA-9
Niklason Lake—*lake* AK-9
Niklavik Creek—*stream* AK-9
Niknar Country Club—*locale* MS-4
Nikodym Cem—*cemetery* SD-7
Nikok River—*stream* AK-9
**Nikolai**—*pop pl* AK-9
Nikolai Bay—*bay* AK-9
Nikolai Butte—*summit* AK-9
Nikolai Cove—*bay* AK-9
Nikolai Creek—*stream* (2) AK-9
Nikolai Gulch—*valley* AK-9
Nikolai Lake—*lake* AK-9
Nikolai Mine—*mine* AK-9
Nikolai Pass—*gap* AK-9
Nikolai (Site)—*locale* AK-9
Nikolai Slough—*gut* AK-9
Nikolaus Eureka Mine—*mine* CA-9
**Nikolski**—*pop pl* AK-9
Nikolski ANV073—*reserve* AK-9
Nikolski Bay—*bay* AK-9
Nik-O-Mahs Camp—*locale* PA-2
*Nikomos Lake* CO-8
Nikonda Creek—*stream* AK-9
Nikonda Glacier—*glacier* AK-9
*Ni Kumi* FM-9
Nikwasi Indian Mound—*locale* NC-3
Nila Ch—*church* AL-4
*Nila Free Ch* AL-4
**Nilan**—*pop pl* PA-2
**Niland**—*pop pl* CA-9
Niland Chapel—*church* MS-4
Niland Lateral Five—*canal* CA-9
Niland Lateral Four—*canal* CA-9
Niland Lateral One—*canal* CA-9
Niland Lateral Three—*canal* CA-9
Niland Lateral Two—*canal* CA-9
Niland Ridge—*ridge* WI-6
Niland Spring—*spring* WY-8
**Nilan (Guyaux)**—*pop pl* PA-2
Nilan Rsvr—*reservoir* MT-8
Nila Sch—*school* AL-4
Nil Desperandum Gulch—*valley* AK-9
Nile—*locale* WV-2
**Nile**—*pop pl* MS-4
**Nile**—*pop pl* NY-2
**Nile**—*pop pl* TX-5
**Nile**—*pop pl* WA-9
Nile Brook—*stream* ME-1
Nile Canyon—*valley* CO-8
*Nile Church* MS-4
Nile Community Ch—*church* WA-9
Nile Creek—*stream* WA-9
Nile Ditch—*canal* (2) CO-8
Nile Ditch—*canal* (2) MI-6
Nile Drain—*canal* MI-6
Nilegan Dam—*dam* MI-6
Nile Inlet—*canal* CO-8
Nile Lake—*lake* WA-9
Nile Lateral—*canal* ID-8
Nile Point—*cape* AK-9
Nile Post Office (historical)—*building* MS-4
Nile Post Office (historical)—*building* TN-4
Nile Ridge Trail—*trail* WA-9
**Niler Spur**—*pop pl* MT-8
Nile Rsvr—*reservoir* CO-8
Niles—*locale* FL-3
Niles—*locale* MS-4
Niles—*locale* OK-5
**Niles**—*pop pl* IL-6
**Niles**—*pop pl* IA-7
**Niles**—*pop pl* KS-7
**Niles**—*pop pl* MI-6
**Niles**—*pop pl* MO-7
**Niles**—*pop pl* NY-2
**Niles**—*pop pl* ND-7
**Niles**—*pop pl* OH-6
**Niles**—*pop pl* PA-2
**Niles**—*pop pl* TX-5
Niles—*uninc pl* CA-9
Niles Bay—*bay* MN-6
Niles Beach—*beach* MA-1
**Niles Beach**—*pop pl* OH-6
Niles Brook—*stream* ME-1
Niles Cabin—*locale* CA-9
Niles Canyon—*valley* (3) CA-9
Niles Canyon—*valley* WA-9
Niles Car & Manufacturing Company Electric Railway Interurban Combine No. 21—*hist pl* OH-6
Niles Cem—*cemetery* IN-6
Niles Cem—*cemetery* MI-6
Niles Cem—*cemetery* (2) NY-2
Niles Cem—*cemetery* OK-5
Niles Cem—*cemetery* VT-1
*Niles Center* IL-6
Niles Center—*other* IL-6
*Niles Centre* IL-6
Nile Sch—*school* MO-7
Niles Channel—*channel* FL-3
Nile Sch (historical)—*school* MS-4
*Niles City* MS-4
Niles Coulee—*valley* MT-8
**Niles District**—*pop pl* CA-9
Niles Ditch—*canal* IN-6
Niles Farmhouse—*hist pl* NY-2
Niles Ferry—*locale* TN-4
*Niles Ferry Baptist Church* TN-4
Niles Ferry Ch—*church* TN-4
Niles Ferry Spring—*spring* TN-4
Niles Flat—*flat* CA-9
Niles Gulch—*valley* ID-8
Niles Gulch—*valley* MT-8
Niles Hill—*summit* PA-2
Niles Hollow—*valley* (3) PA-2
*Niles Island* TN-4
Niles Junction—*locale* OH-6
**Niles Junction**—*pop pl* CA-9
Niles-McGhee Cem—*cemetery* TN-4
Niles Park—*park* MS-4
Niles Park—*park* NJ-2
Niles Point—*cape* MN-6
*Niles Pond* MA-1
*Niles Pond* PA-2
Niles Pond—*lake* MA-1
Niles Post Office (historical)—*building* MS-4
Nile Spring—*spring* NV-8
Niles Ranch—*locale* CA-9
Niles Ranch—*locale* WY-8
Niles Rsvr—*reservoir* CA-9
Niles Sch—*school* CA-9
Niles Sch—*school* IL-6
Niles Sch—*school* MI-6
Niles Sch—*school* VT-1
Niles Shoals—*bar* TN-4
Niles Spring—*spring* CA-9
Niles Spring—*spring* MT-8
Niles Swamp—*swamp* RI-1
**Niles (Town of)**—*pop pl* NY-2
Niles Township—*fmr MCD* IA-7
**Niles (Township of)**—*pop pl* IL-6
**Niles (Township of)**—*pop pl* IN-6
**Niles (Township of)**—*pop pl* MI-6
Niles Trail—*trail* PA-2
Niles Union Cem—*cemetery* OH-6
**Niles Valley**—*pop pl* PA-2
Niles Valley Cem—*cemetery* PA-2
*Nilesville* KS-7
**Nilesville**—*pop pl* IA-7
Nilo Tample Country Club—*other* WA-9
**Nile (Township of)**—*pop pl* OH-6
Nilikluguk (Camp Site)—*locale* AK-9
Nilik River—*stream* AK-9
Nililak—*locale* AK-9
Nililak Point—*cape* AK-9
**Nililak (Variant: Nilak)**—*pop pl* AK-9
Niller Cem—*cemetery* MO-7
Nilles Corner—*locale* WA-9
Nillik—*locale* AK-9
*Nill Point* WA-9
Nilly Hollow—*valley* KY-4
*Nilon Reservoir* MT-8
Nilsen Creek—*stream* ID-8
Nilsen Ranch—*locale* NE-7
**Nilsen (Township of)**—*pop pl* MN-6
*Nilson Creek* ID-8
Nilson Lake—*lake* MN-6
Nilson Sch—*school* ND-7
Nilson Trail—*trail* WY-8
*Nils Sch* AL-4
Nilsson, Andrew, House—*hist pl* WA-9
*Nilul* FM-9
Nilunorat Hills—*other* AK-9
Nilus Brook—*stream* NH-1
**Nilwood**—*pop pl* IL-6
**Nilwood (Township of)**—*pop pl* IL-6
**Nimaar**—*pop pl* FM-9
*Nimal* FM-9
*Nimar* FM-9
*Nimaru* FM-9
*Nimberg* NE-7
Nimblewill—*locale* GA-3
Nimblewill Creek—*stream* GA-3
Nimblewill Gap—*gap* GA-3
Nim Branch—*stream* MS-4
**Nimburg**—*pop pl* NE-7
Nimburg Cem—*cemetery* NE-7
Nimbus—*locale* CA-9
Nimbus, Mount—*summit* CO-8
Nimbus Dam—*dam* CA-9
Nim City—*locale* NE-7
Nimenim Ridge—*ridge* NM-5
Nimerick Point—*cliff* CO-8
Ni Mesen Takai—*unknown* FM-9
Nimgil—*other* FM-9
Nimgun Creek—*stream* AK-9
Nimgun Lake—*lake* AK-9
Nimham, Lake—*lake* NY-2
Nimham Mount—*summit* NY-2
Nim Hollow—*valley* KY-4
Nimiir—*cape* FM-9
Nimikon Falls—*falls* MI-6
*Nimir* FM-9
*Nimishillen Creek* OH-6
**Nimishillen (Township of)**—*pop pl* OH-6
**Nimisila**—*pop pl* OH-6
Nimisila Creek—*stream* OH-6
Nimisila Rsvr—*reservoir* OH-6
Nimita Sch—*school* HI-9
**Nimitz**—*pop pl* WV-2
Nimitz—*uninc pl* TX-5
Nimitz Beach—*beach* HI-9
Nimitz Beach Park—*park* GU-9
Nimitz Hill—*summit* GU-9
Nimitz Hill Annex—*CDP* GU-9
Nimitz Hill Rsvr—*reservoir* GU-9
Nimitz JHS—*school* OK-5
Nimitz JHS—*school* TX-5
Nimitz Sch—*school* CA-9
Nimiuktuk River—*stream* AK-9
Nimkai Mtn—*summit* AK-9
*Nimme Lake* WA-9
*Nimmir* FM-9
Nimmo—*locale* VA-3
**Nimmo**—*pop pl* AR-4
Nimmo Cem—*cemetery* MO-7
Nimmo Cem—*cemetery* TN-4
Nimmo Draw—*valley* WY-8
Nimmo Hill—*summit* KY-4
**Nimmons**—*pop pl* AR-4
**Nimmons**—*pop pl* SC-3
Nimmons Bridge—*bridge* SC-3
**Nimmonsburg**—*pop pl* NY-2
Nimmons Cem—*cemetery* AR-4
Nimmons Cem—*cemetery* SC-3
Nimmo Ranch—*locale* WY-8
Nimmo Rsvr No 9—*reservoir* WY-8
*Nimms Hill* NH-1
Nimnicht Creek—*stream* IN-6
Ni Moangen Eni—*summit* FM-9
Nimocks House—*hist pl* NC-3
Nimocks House—*hist pl* OH-6
Nimon Lake—*lake* WI-6
Nimpal—*gut* FM-9
*Nimpoain* FM-9
*Nimpol* FM-9
*Nimpol-Einfahrt* FM-9
*Nimpol Entrance* FM-9
*Nimpomo* CA-9
*Nimporu-Ko* FM-9
Nim Ridge—*ridge* NC-3
*Nimrod* KS-7
Nimrod—*locale* (2) MT-8
Nimrod—*locale* TX-5
**Nimrod**—*pop pl* AR-4
**Nimrod**—*pop pl* MN-6
**Nimrod**—*pop pl* OR-9
**Nimrod**—*pop pl* TX-5
Nimrod Butte—*summit* OR-9
Nimrod Canyon—*valley* CA-9
Nimrod Cem—*cemetery* AR-4
Nimrod Creek—*stream* SC-3
Nimrod Dam—*dam* AR-4
Nimrod Hall—*locale* VA-3
Nimrod Hill—*summit* AK-9
Nimrod Lake—*reservoir* AR-4
Nimrod Lake—*reservoir* NY-2
Nimrod Peak—*summit* AK-9
Nimrod River County Park—*park* OR-9
*Nimrod Rsvr* AR-4
Nimrod State Game Mngmt Area—*park* AR-4
Nimrod State Wildlife Mngmt Area—*park* AR-4
Nimrod-Stephenson Memorial Cem—*cemetery* NC-3
Nimrod Tunnels—*tunnel* MT-8
**Nims**—*pop pl* NC-3
Nims, Rudolph, House—*hist pl* MI-6
Nims, William Reuben, House—*hist pl* MI-6
Nims Branch—*stream* KY-4
Nims Cem—*cemetery* MI-6
Nims Gulch—*valley* WA-9
Nimshew—*locale* CA-9
Nims Hill—*summit* NH-1
Nims JHS—*school* FL-3
Nims Lake—*reservoir* MO-7
Nims Sch—*school* MI-6
Nimue Lake—*lake* WA-9
*Nimuporu-Ko* FM-9
*Nimuporu-Kuchi* FM-9
*Nimur Islet* MP-9
*Nimuru To* MP-9
*Nimwur* MP-9
Nimwutik Creek—*stream* AK-9
*Nina* AL-4
Nina—*locale* KY-4
Nina—*locale* TN-4
Nina—*locale* WV-2
**Nina**—*pop pl* KY-4
*Nina Baptist Church* TN-4
Nina Ch—*church* TN-4
Nina Cove—*bay* AK-9
Ninagiak Island—*island* AK-9
Ninagiak River—*stream* AK-9
Nina Lake—*reservoir* OH-6
Nina Moose Lake—*lake* MN-6
Nina Moose River—*stream* MN-6
Nina-Ninos —*park* AZ-5
*Nina P.O.* AL-4
Nina Pond—*reservoir* AZ-5
**Nina Station**—*pop pl* LA-4
Ninaview—*locale* CO-8
Nina Well—*well* AZ-5
Ninchelser, Dr., House—*hist pl* OH-6
Nind—*locale* MO-7
Ninde—*locale* VA-3
Nindeidei—*unknown* FM-9
Nindol—*ridge* FM-9
Nindol—*summit* FM-9
Ninduwi—*unknown* FM-9
Nine, Dam—*dam* TX-5
Nine, Lake—*lake* MI-6
Nine, Lake—*lake* WI-6
**Nine Acre Corner**—*pop pl* (2) MA-1
Nineacre Island—*island* NH-1
Nine Acre Lake—*lake* MI-6
Nine Acre Mine—*mine* KY-4
Nine A M Lake—*lake* MN-6
Nine and a Half Mile Tank—*reservoir* AZ-5
Nine and Onehalf Mile Camp—*locale* HI-9
Nine-Bar Ranch—*locale* TX-5
Nine Bar W Ranch—*locale* WY-8
Nine Buck Butte—*summit* CA-9
Nine Canyon—*valley* WA-9
Nine Corner Lake—*lake* NY-2
Nine Creek—*stream* WA-9
Nine Dollar Gulch—*valley* OR-9
Nine Draw—*valley* TX-5
Nine Draw—*valley* WY-8
Nine Eagles State Park—*park* IA-7
Nine Foot Brook—*stream* RI-1
Ninefoot Canal—*canal* NC-3
Ninefoot Creek—*stream* WA-9
Ninefoot Knoll—*bar* MD-2
Ninefoot Rapids—*rapids* ID-8
Ninefoot Shoal—*bar* AK-9
Ninefoot Shoal—*bar* FL-3
Nine Foot Shoal—*bar* VA-3
Nine Foot Shoal—*bar* WI-6
Ninefoot Shoal Light—*locale* FL-3
**Nine Forks**—*pop pl* LA-4
Nine Forks Ch—*church* SC-3
Ninegar Creek—*stream* CO-8
Ninegar Rsvr—*reservoir* CO-8
*Ninegrets Pond* RI-1
*Ninegut Pond* RI-1
Nine Hearths—*hist pl* KY-4
Nine Hill—*summit* NV-8
Nine Hill, The—*summit* TX-5
Nine Hole—*basin* UT-8
Nine Hour Lake—*lake* WA-9
Nine Hundred Acre Lake—*lake* NM-5
Nine Hundred and Sixty Nine Creek—*stream* MT-8
Nine Hundred Sixteen Ranch—*locale* NM-5
Nine Hundred Windmill—*locale* TX-5
Nine-H-6 Hill—*summit* WY-8
Nine Island—*island* NH-1
*Nine Island Creek* AL-4
Nine-K Windmill—*locale* TX-5
Nine Lake—*lake* ND-7
Nine Lake Basin—*basin* CA-9
Nine Lot Dam—*dam* MA-1
Nine Meadow Brook—*stream* ME-1
Nine Meadow Ridge—*ridge* ME-1
Ninemeyer Campground—*locale* ID-8
Ninemeyer Creek—*stream* ID-8
Ninemeyer Spring—*spring* OR-9
*Nine Mile* TN-4
Ninemile—*area* AZ-5
Ninemile—*cliff* NV-8
Nine Mile—*locale* FL-3
Ninemile—*locale* MT-8
Ninemile—*locale* TN-4
**Nine Mile**—*pop pl* IN-6
**Nine Mile**—*pop pl* MI-6
**Nine-mile**—*pop pl* MT-8
**Nine Mile**—*pop pl* TN-4
Ninemile Bank—*bar* FL-3
Ninemile Basin—*basin* CO-8
Ninemile Basin—*basin* NV-8
Ninemile Bay—*bay* LA-4
Ninemile Bay—*bay* NV-8
Ninemile Bayou—*gut* LA-4
Ninemile Bayou Light—*locale* LA-4
Ninemile Beaver Creek—*stream* OK-5
Ninemile Bend—*locale* FL-3
Ninemile Bottom—*bend* UT-8
Ninemile Branch—*stream* AL-4
Ninemile Branch—*stream* FL-3
Ninemile Branch—*stream* GA-3
Ninemile Branch—*stream* TN-4
Ninemile Bridge—*bridge* VA-3
Ninemile Bridge—*locale* ME-1
Ninemile Bridge—*other* MI-6
Ninemile Brook—*stream* ME-1
Ninemile Cabin—*locale* (2) AK-9
Ninemile Camp—*locale* AK-9
Ninemile Camp—*locale* OR-9
Ninemile Camp—*locale* WA-9
Ninemile Canal—*canal* CO-8
Ninemile Canal—*canal* FL-3
Ninemile Canal—*canal* NE-7
*Ninemile Canyon* NE-7
*Nine Mile Canyon* NV-8
*Ninemile Canyon* OK-5
*Nine Mile Canyon* UT-8
*Nine Mile Canyon* WA-9
Ninemile Canyon—*valley* CA-9
Ninemile Canyon—*valley* (3) NV-8
Ninemile Canyon—*valley* UT-8
Ninemile Canyon—*valley* WA-9
Ninemile Canyon—*valley* WY-8
Ninemile Canyons—*valley* OK-5
Ninemile Cem—*cemetery* IL-6
Nine Mile Ch—*church* GA-3
Ninemile Ch—*church* IL-6
Ninemile Ch—*church* WV-2
Ninemile Channel—*channel* NE-7
Ninemile Community Hall—*building* MT-8
Ninemile Corner—*locale* CO-8
Nine Mile Corner—*locale* ND-7
**Ninemile Corner**—*pop pl* CO-8
Ninemile Corral—*locale* AZ-5
Ninemile Coulee—*valley* (3) MT-8
*Ninemile Creek* ID-8
*Nine Mile Creek* MT-8
*Nine Mile Creek* OH-6
*Nine Mile Creek* TN-4
*Nine Mile Creek* TX-5
*Nine Mile Creek* UT-8
*Nine Mile Creek* WA-9
*Ninemile Creek* WV-2
*Ninemile Creek* WI-6
Ninemile Creek—*stream* (4) AK-9
Ninemile Creek—*stream* (2) AZ-5
Ninemile Creek—*stream* AR-4
Ninemile Creek—*stream* (3) CA-9
Ninemile Creek—*stream* CO-8
Ninemile Creek—*stream* (4) FL-3
Ninemile Creek—*stream* GA-3
Ninemile Creek—*stream* (6) ID-8
Ninemile Creek—*stream* IL-6
Ninemile Creek—*stream* (3) IA-7
Ninemile Creek—*stream* (2) KS-7
Ninemile Creek—*stream* MI-6
Ninemile Creek—*stream* (3) MN-6
Ninemile Creek—*stream* MS-4
Ninemile Creek—*stream* (4) MT-8
Ninemile Creek—*stream* NE-7
Ninemile Creek—*stream* NM-5
Ninemile Creek—*stream* (5) NY-2
Nine Mile Creek—*stream* NC-3
Ninemile Creek—*stream* (5) OH-6
Ninemile Creek—*stream* (4) OK-5
Ninemile Creek—*stream* OR-9
Ninemile Creek—*stream* (2) SD-7
Ninemile Creek—*stream* TN-4
Ninemile Creek—*stream* (4) TX-5
Ninemile Creek—*stream* UT-8
Ninemile Creek—*stream* (7) WA-9
Ninemile Creek—*stream* (2) WV-2
Ninemile Creek—*stream* (5) WI-6
Ninemile Creek—*stream* (2) WY-8
Nine Mile Creek Aqueduct—*hist pl* NY-2
Nine Mile Creek Baptist Ch (historical)—*church* TN-4
Nine Mile Creek Post Office (historical)—*building* TN-4
Ninemile Creek State Shooting Area—*park* SD-7
Nine Mile Dam—*dam* AZ-5
Ninemile Dam—*dam* UT-8
Ninemile Deadwater—*channel* ME-1
Ninemile Ditch—*canal* WY-8
Ninemile Divide—*ridge* MT-8
Ninemile Draw—*valley* AZ-5
Ninemile Draw—*valley* CO-8
Ninemile Draw—*valley* SD-7
Ninemile Draw—*valley* (2) TX-5
Ninemile Draw—*valley* (2) WY-8
Nine Mile Falls—*falls* WA-9
Ninemile Falls—*falls* WA-9
**Nine Mile Falls**—*pop pl* WA-9
Ninemile Flat—*flat* TX-5
Ninemile Flat—*flat* WA-9
Ninemile Flats—*flat* CO-8
Ninemile Gap—*gap* CO-8
Nine Mile Gas Field—*oilfield* UT-8
Ninemile Gulch—*valley* NE-7
*Ninemile Hill* TX-5
Ninemile Hill—*summit* (4) CO-8
Ninemile Hill—*summit* MI-6
Ninemile Hill—*summit* MT-8
Ninemile Hill—*summit* (2) NE-7
Ninemile Hill—*summit* NM-5
Ninemile Hill—*summit* TN-4
Ninemile Hill—*summit* (3) TX-5
Ninemile Hill—*summit* (2) WI-6
Ninemile Hill—*summit* (2) WY-8
Nine Mile Hill—*summit* WY-8
Ninemile Hill—*summit* (3) WY-8
Ninemile Hills—*other* AK-9
Ninemile Hill Swamp—*swamp* MI-6
Ninemile Island—*island* AK-9
Ninemile Island—*island* IA-7
Ninemile Island—*island* PA-2
Ninemile Island—*island* WI-6
Ninemile Knoll—*summit* ID-8
Ninemile Knoll—*summit* UT-8
Ninemile Lake—*lake* AK-9
Ninemile Lake—*lake* (2) MI-6
Ninemile Lake—*lake* MN-6
Ninemile Lake—*lake* ND-7
Ninemile Lake—*lake* SD-7
Ninemile Lake—*lake* WY-8
Ninemile Lookout Tower—*locale* MT-8
Ninemile Mtn—*summit* AK-9
Ninemile Mtn—*summit* CO-8
Ninemile Mtn—*summit* (2) NV-8
Ninemile Mtn—*summit* OR-9
Ninemile Park—*flat* MT-8
Ninemile Peak—*summit* AZ-5
Ninemile Peak—*summit* NV-8
*Nine Mile Place* IN-6
**Nine Mile Place**—*pop pl* IN-6
Ninemile Point—*cape* (2) AK-9
Ninemile Point—*cape* CA-9
Ninemile Point—*cape* (2) FL-3
Ninemile Point—*cape* LA-4
Ninemile Point—*cape* (3) MI-6
Ninemile Point—*cape* MT-8
Ninemile Point—*cape* (2) NY-2
Ninemile Point—*cape* TX-5
Ninemile Point—*summit* NV-8
*Nine Mile Pond* MA-1
Ninemile Pond—*lake* FL-3
Ninemile Pond—*lake* MA-1
Nine Mile Post Office (historical)—*building* TN-4
Ninemile Prairie—*flat* MT-8
Nine-Mile Prairie—*hist pl* NE-7
Nine Mile Prairie Township—*civil* MO-7
Ninemile Ranch—*locale* AZ-5
Nine Mile Ranch—*locale* NV-8
Ninemile Ranch—*locale* NV-8
Ninemile Ranch—*locale* NM-5
Ninemile Ranch—*locale* TX-5
Ninemile Ranch—*locale* WY-8
Nine Mile Ranch (historical)—*locale* SD-7
Ninemile Ranger Station—*locale* MT-8
Ninemile Rapids—*rapids* WI-6
*Nine-Mile Reservoir* UT-8
Ninemile Ridge—*ridge* NV-8
Ninemile Ridge—*ridge* OR-9
Nine Mile Ridge—*ridge* TN-4
*Nine Mile River* MN-6
Ninemile River—*stream* AK-9
Ninemile Rock—*pillar* WY-8
Ninemile Rocks—*locale* NV-8
Ninemile Rsvr—*reservoir* (2) UT-8
Nine Mile Rsvr—*reservoir* WA-9
Ninemile Rsvr—*reservoir* WY-8
Ninemile (Ruins)—*locale* AK-9
*Nine Mile Run* IA-7
Ninemile Run—*stream* (4) PA-2
Ninemile Run—*stream* VA-3
*Nine Miles* HI-9
Ninemile Saddle—*gap* OR-9
Ninemile Sch—*school* KS-7
Ninemile Sch—*school* MN-6
Nine Mile Sch—*school* MT-8
Ninemile Sch—*school* ND-7
Ninemile Sch—*school* SD-7
Ninemile Seep—*spring* AZ-5
Ninemile Slough—*stream* AK-9
Ninemile Slough—*stream* OR-9
Ninemile Slough—*stream* WI-6
**Nine Miles (Ninemile Camp)**—*pop pl* HI-9
Ninemile Spring—*spring* CO-8
Ninemile Spring—*spring* OR-9
Ninemile Spring—*spring* TX-5
Ninemile Spring—*spring* (2) WY-8
Ninemile Springs—*spring* (2) NV-8
Ninemile Springs—*spring* WY-8
Ninemile Spur—*ridge* VA-3
*Nine Mile Station* AZ-5
Ninemile Summit—*summit* (2) NV-8
Ninemile Swamp—*swamp* (2) NY-2
Ninemile Swamp—*swamp* WI-6
Ninemile Tank—*reservoir* (2) AZ-5
Ninemile Tank—*reservoir* (3) TX-5
Nine Mile Township (historical)—*civil* SD-7
Ninemile Trail—*trail* WY-8
*Ninemile Valley* NE-7
*Nine Mile Valley* UT-8
Ninemile Valley—*valley* CO-8
Ninemile Wash—*stream* AZ-5
Ninemile Wash—*stream* CA-9
Ninemile Wash—*valley* UT-8
Ninemile Wash—*valley* WY-8
Ninemile Waterhole—*lake* TX-5
Ninemile Waterhole Draw—*valley* WY-8
Ninemile Well—*well* AZ-5
Ninemile Well—*well* NV-8
Ninemile Windmill—*locale* NM-5
Ninemile Windmill—*locale* TX-5
Ninemille Creek—*stream* OR-9
Nine O'Clock Run—*stream* PA-2
Nine Old Men Hunt Club—*other* CA-9
Nine Partners Cem—*cemetery* NY-2
Nine Partners Creek—*stream* PA-2
Nine Penny Branch—*stream* IN-6
*Nine Pin Branch* MD-2
Ninepin Branch—*stream* MD-2
*Ninepin Bridges Creek* MD-2
*Ninepin Creek* MD-2
Ninepin Swamp—*swamp* MD-2
Ninepipe Natl Wildlife Ref—*park* MT-8
Ninepipe Rsvr—*reservoir* MT-8
Ninepipe Substation—*other* MT-8
Nine Point Creek—*stream* OR-9
Nine Point Draw—*valley* TX-5
*Nine Points* PA-2
**Ninepoints**—*pop pl* PA-2
Nine Pup—*stream* AK-9
Nine Quarter Circle Ranch—*locale* MT-8
Niner Hill—*summit* OH-6
Nine Right Hollow—*valley* KY-4
**Nine Row**—*pop pl* PA-2
Nine R Ranch—*locale* TX-5
*Ninescah River Township* KS-7
*Ninescau River* KS-7
*Ninescau River Township* KS-7
Nine Section Windmill—*locale* TX-5
Nines Flat—*flat* WY-8
*Nine-Six Creek* SC-3
Nines Pond—*lake* PA-2
**Nine Springs**—*pop pl* WI-6
Nine Springs Creek—*stream* WI-6
Nine Springs Rsvr—*reservoir* CA-9
Nine Stream—*stream* WA-9
Nine Stream Shelter—*locale* WA-9
Nine Tank—*reservoir* AZ-5
Nine T Bar Creek—*stream* WY-8
Nineteen—*locale* KY-4
Nineteen, Lake—*lake* MI-6
Nineteen, Lake—*lake* WI-6
Nineteen Brook—*stream* NH-1
Nineteen Coulee—*valley* MT-8
Nineteen Creek—*stream* MT-8
Nineteen Creek—*stream* (2) WA-9
Nineteen Draw—*valley* TX-5
Nineteen Gulch—*valley* CO-8
Nineteen Gully—*valley* NY-2
Nineteen Hundred And Eight Cut Off—*bend* TX-5
Nineteen hundred and Eight Cut-off Lake—*lake* OK-5
Nineteen hundred and forty Cut-off Lake—*lake* AR-4
Nineteen hundred and sixteen Cut-off Lake—*lake* AR-4
Nineteen hundred and three Lateral N—*canal* MT-8
Nineteenhundred Eighteen Gulch—*valley* OR-9
Nineteenhundred Seventeen Gulch—*valley* OR-9
Nineteenhundred Sixteen Gulch—*valley* OR-9
Nineteen K Canal—*canal* MT-8
Nineteen Lake—*lake* (2) MI-6
Nineteen Mile—*locale* MT-8
Nineteenmile (Aban'd)—*locale* AK-9
Nineteenmile Bay—*bay* NH-1
Nineteenmile Brook—*stream* NH-1
Nineteenmile Camp—*locale* ID-8
Nineteenmile Creek—*stream* ID-8
Nineteenmile Creek—*stream* WA-9
Nineteen Mile Crossing—*locale* TX-5
Nineteen Mtn—*summit* ME-1
Nineteen Mtn—*summit* WA-9
Nineteen Oaks—*flat* CA-9
Nineteen R, Lateral—*canal* AZ-5
Nineteen R-37, Lateral—*canal* AZ-5
Nineteen R-37-24, Lateral—*canal* AZ-5
Nineteen ten Ridge—*summit* MT-8
Nineteenth Ave Baptist Ch—*church* MS-4
*Nineteenth Avenue* IL-6
Nineteenth Hill—*summit* MA-1
Nineteenth Pond—*lake* NY-2
*Nineteenth Siding* ND-7
Nineteenth Street Bridge—*bridge* PA-2
Nineteenth Street Ch of Christ—*church* AL-4
Nineteenth Street Park—*park* IA-7
Nineteenth Street Pentecostal Ch—*church* AL-4
Nineteen Windmill—*locale* TX-5
Nineth District Sch—*school* KY-4
Nine Thirty Two Creek—*stream* MI-6
Nineth Street Sch—*school* WI-6
**Nine Times**—*pop pl* SC-3
Nine Times Creek—*stream* SC-3
Nine Top Spring—*spring* OR-9
Nine Trough Spring—*spring* MT-8
Ninety—*locale* TX-5

Nixon Springs—lake WI-6
Nixons Ranch—locale AK-9
**Nixonton**—pop pl NC-3
Nixonton (Township of)—fmr MCD NC-3
**Nixon Township**—pop pl ND-7
**Nixon (Township of)**—pop pl IL-6
Nixonville AL-4
**Nixonville**—pop pl SC-3
Nixon Wildlife Mngmt Area—park UT-8
Nix P.O. AL-4
Nix Point—cape FL-3
Nix Sch—school AL-4
Nix Slough—bay TX-5
Nixs Mate MA-1
Nixson Hall—locale AL-4
Nixson JHS—school TX-5
Nix Towhead—island TN-4
Nix (Township of)—fmr MCD AR-4
**Nixville**—pop pl SC-3
Nixville P.O. AL-4
Nixville Sch—school SC-3
Niyghapak Point—cape AK-9
Niyiklik Creek—stream AK-9
Niykhapakhit Lake—lake AK-9
Niyrakpak Lagoon—lake AK-9
Nizhoni Point—cliff AZ-5
Nizina Glacier—glacier AK-9
Nizina Mtn—summit AK-9
Nizina River—stream AK-9
Nizki Cove—bay AK-9
Nizki Island—island AK-9
NI-11 Airp—airport NC-3
N K Cooper Special Education Center—school FL-3
Nkebeduul—stream PW-9
N Ketchum Ranch—locale SD-7
N Lateral—canal CA-9
N Latham Ranch—locale NM-5
N Lazy H Ranch—locale AZ-5
NI Tank—reservoir AZ-5
Nlul FM-9
Nluul—locale FM-9
N Main Drain—canal ID-8
N McDougal Ranch—locale CA-9
N Mouth Creek SD-7
N Mtn—summit ID-8
N Murray Ridge Cem—cemetery OH-6
N N A Cem—cemetery OH-6
N N Siding—locale KS-7
No Ache—swamp NC-3
No Ache Bay—bay NC-3
No Ache Island—island NC-3
Noack—locale TX-5
Noack Cem—cemetery TX-5
Noack Oil Field—oilfield TX-5
No Agua—locale NM-5
No Agua Peaks—summit NM-5
No Agua Tank—reservoir NM-5
Noah IN-6
Noah MS-4
Noah—locale AL-4
Noah—locale AZ-5
Noah—locale GA-3
Noah—locale TN-4
**Noah**—pop pl IN-6
Noah, Lake—lake OH-6
Noah Ark Ch—church GA-3
Noah Baptist Church AL-4
Noah Berkey Ditch IN-6
Noah Brake—swamp LA-4
Noah Branch FL-3
Noah Branch—stream GA-3
Noah Butte—summit OR-9
Noah Cem—cemetery AL-4
Noah Cem—cemetery LA-4
Noah Cem—cemetery OK-5
Noah Cem—cemetery OR-9
Noah Cem—cemetery TN-4
Noah Ch—church AL-4
Noah Chapel—church GA-3
Noah Chapel (historical)—church TN-4
Noah Creek IA-7
Noah Creek—stream IA-7
Noah Creek—stream (2) OR-9
Noah Draw—valley WY-8
Noah Dunkin Hollow—valley TN-4
Noah Eastman Pond—lake ME-1
Noah Fork—stream IN-4
Noah Fork Ch—church TN-4
Noah Gap—gap GA-3
Noah (historical)—locale MS-4
Noah Island—island FL-3
Noah Knob TN-4
Noah Knob—summit TN-4
Noah Lake—lake AK-9
Noah Lake—lake MI-6
Noahle—locale FM-9
Noah Mound—summit FL-3
Noah Mtn—summit NC-3
Noah Pirogue Trail—canal LA-4
Noah Pond—lake DE-2
Noah Post Office (historical)—building AL-4
Noah Post Office (historical)—building MS-4
Noah Post Office (historical)—building TN-4
Noah Ridge—ridge MD-2
**Noahs**—pop pl AR-4
Noahs Ark—summit AL-4
Noahs Ark—summit UT-8
Noahs Ark Airp—airport MO-7
Noahs Ark Ch—church GA-3
Noah's Ark Ch—church GA-3
Noahs Ark Ch—church (2) GA-3
Noahs Ark Christian Child Care Center—school FL-3
Noahs Ark Day Care and Kindergarten—school FL-3
Noahs Ark Sch—school FL-3
Noahs Chapel—church TN-4
Noah Sch (historical)—school TN-4
Noahs Fork TN-4
Noahs Fork Baptist Church TN-4
Noahs Glade—flat PA-2
Noah Sias Cem—cemetery WV-2
Noahs Marsh—swamp SC-3
Noahs Pond—lake ME-1
Noahs Rump—summit NY-2
Noahs Spring—spring TN-4
Noahs Spring Branch—stream KY-4
Noahs Spring Branch—stream TN-4
Noah Teter Hollow—valley WV-2
Noak, Mount—summit AK-9
Nooks Island—island VT-1
**Noall Subdivision**—pop pl UT-8
Noanat Brook MA-1
Noanet Brook—stream MA-1
Noanete Brook MA-1
Noanet Peak—summit MA-1
**Noank**—pop pl CT-1
Noank Hist Dist—hist pl CT-1
Noannet Pond—reservoir MA-1
Noannet Pond Dam—dam MA-1
Noark Camp—locale AR-4
**Noatak**—pop pl AK-9
Noatak ANV876—reserve AK-9
Noatak Canyon—valley AK-9
Noatak Natl Monmt—park AK-9
Noatak Natl Preserve—park AK-9
Noatak River—stream AK-9
Noatak River Delta—area AK-9
Noaukta Slough—stream AK-9
Nobadee Pond MA-1
Nobadeer Pond MA-1
Nobadeer Pond—lake MA-1
Nobadeer Valley—valley MA-1
No Bar Creek TN-4
N O Bar Mesa—summit AZ-5
N O Bar Mesa Tank—reservoir AZ-5
N O Bar Mesa Tank Number Two—reservoir AZ-5
N O Bar Ranch—locale AZ-5
**Nobart (historical)**—pop pl ND-7
Nobaska Point Light—locale MA-1
Nobbin Ridge—ridge TN-4
Nobby Creek—stream WA-9
Nobby Hill—summit NH-1
Nobby Island—island NY-2
Nob Crook Brook—stream CT-1
Nobe—locale WV-2
Nobe Branch—stream AL-4
Nobeck Dam—dam SD-7
Nobel Branch—stream MO-7
Nobel Canyon CA-9
Nobel Elem Sch—school IN-6
Nobel Hill Cem—cemetery FL-3
Nobel JHS—school CA-9
Nobel Lake CA-9
Nobel Sch—school IL-6
Nobels Millpond—reservoir NC-3
Nobels Millpond Dam—dam NC-3
Nober Cem—cemetery AR-4
Noberto Sandoval Canon NM-5
Noberto Sandoval Canon—valley NM-5
Nobe Young Creek—stream CA-9
Nobe Young Meadow—flat CA-9
Nob Hill—CDP SC-3
**Nob Hill**—pop pl CO-8
**Nob Hill**—pop pl (2) MD-2
Nob Hill—post sta FL-3
Nob Hill—summit (4) CA-9
Nob Hill—summit (2) MA-1
Nob Hill—summit OH-6
Nob Hill—summit WY-8
Nob Hill—uninc pl CA-9
**Nob Hill Addition (subdivision)**—pop pl UT-8
**Nob Hill Annex Subdivision**—pop pl UT-8
Nobhill Creek—stream AK-9
Nob Hill Elem Sch—school FL-3
Nob Hill Hist Dist—hist pl ID-8
Nob Hill Park—park TX-5
Nob Hill Ranch—locale TX-5
Nob Hill Sch—school WA-9
**Nob Hill (subdivision)**—pop pl NC-3
**Nobhill Subdivision**—pop pl UT-8
**Nob Hill Subdivision**—pop pl UT-8
Nob Hill Tank—reservoir TX-5
Nobil Cem—cemetery AL-4
Nobility—locale TX-5
Nobinson Windmill—locale NM-5
Nob Island—island WA-9
Noble CT-1
Noble KS-7
Noble OH-6
Noble—locale GA-3
Noble—locale KY-4
Noble—locale NV-8
Noble—locale WA-9
**Noble**—pop pl IL-6
**Noble**—pop pl IN-6
**Noble**—pop pl IA-7
**Noble**—pop pl LA-4
**Noble**—pop pl MO-7
**Noble**—pop pl OK-5
**Noble**—pop pl PA-2
**Noble**—pop pl TX-5
Noble, John Glover, House—hist pl CT-1
Noble, Jonathan, House—hist pl OH-6
Noble, Samuel, Monmt—hist pl AL-4
Noble and Greenough Sch—school MA-1
Noble And Tiffin Cem—cemetery OH-6
Noble Ave Sch—school CA-9
Noble Ave Sch—school MN-6
Noble Basin—basin ID-8
Noble Basin—basin WY-8
Noble Block—hist pl ME-1
Noble Bluff—cliff CA-9
**Nobleboro**—pop pl ME-1
**Nobleboro**—pop pl NY-2
Nobleboro Central Sch—school ME-1
**Nobleboro (Town of)**—pop pl ME-1
Nobleborough ME-1
Nobleborough—other ME-1
Noble Branch—stream KY-4
Noble Bridge—bridge PA-2
Noble Brook—stream ME-1
Noble Butte—summit CA-9
Noble Canal—canal ID-8
Noble Canyon—valley (2) CA-9
Noble Canyon Rsvr—reservoir OR-9
Noble (CCD)—cens area OK-5
Noble Cem—cemetery AL-4
Noble Cem—cemetery IA-7
Noble Cem—cemetery (2) KY-4
Noble Cem—cemetery (2) LA-4
Noble Cem—cemetery MO-7
Noble Cem—cemetery OH-6
Noble Cem—cemetery OK-5
Noble Cem—cemetery OR-9
Noble Cem—cemetery TX-5
Noble Cemeteries—cemetery KY-4
Noble Center Cem—cemetery IA-7
Noble Center Ch—church IA-7
Noble Ch—church WV-2
Noble Corner—locale NY-2
Noble Cottage—hist pl AL-4
**Noble County**—pop pl IN-6
**Noble (County)**—pop pl OH-6
**Noble (County)**—pop pl OK-5
Noble County Courthouse—hist pl IN-6
Noble County Courthouse—hist pl OK-5
Noble County Sheriff's House and Jail—hist pl IN-6
Noble Creek NV-8
Noble Creek TX-5
Noble Creek—stream (2) CA-9
Noble Creek—stream GA-3
Noble Creek—stream ID-8
Noble Creek—stream MT-8
Noble Creek—stream (4) OR-9
Noble Creek—stream TX-5
Noble Creek—stream (2) WA-9
Noble Ditch—canal MT-8
Noble Ditch—canal SD-7
Noble Drain—canal ID-8
Noble Draw Tank—reservoir AZ-5
Noble Fork—stream MT-8
Noble Furnace—locale VA-3
Noble Garden Spring—spring OR-9
Noble Gulch—valley ID-8
Noble Gulch—valley MT-8
Noble Hall—hist pl AL-4
Noble Hammock—island FL-3
Noble Hammock Canoe Trail—trail FL-3
**Noble Hill**—pop pl AL-4
Noble Hill—summit CT-1
Noble Hill—summit OR-9
Noble Hill—summit WA-9
Noble Hill Cem—cemetery AL-4
Noble Hill Ch—church AL-4
Noble Hill Ch—church MO-7
Noble Hill Missionary Baptist Ch AL-4
Noble Hill Sch—hist pl GA-3
**Noble Hills (subdivision)**—pop pl NC-3
Noble (historical)—locale KS-7
Noble (historical)—locale ND-7
Noble Hosp—hospital NY-2
Noble Hospital, The—hospital MA-1
Noble House—hist pl CT-1
Noble Institute (historical)—school AL-4
Noble Island—island ID-8
Noble JHS—school NC-3
Noble-Kendall House—hist pl IA-7
Noble Knob—summit WA-9
Nobleknob Camp—locale FL-3
Noble Lake—lake AR-4
Noble Lake—lake CA-9
Noble Lake—lake MI-6
Noble Lake—lake MT-8
Noble Lake—lake WA-9
Noble Lake—lake WI-6
**Noble Lake**—pop pl AR-4
**Noble Manor**—pop pl LA-4
Noble-McCaa-Butler House—hist pl AL-4
Noble Mica Mine—mine SD-7
Noble Mill—locale MD-2
Noble Mine—mine CA-9
Noble Mine—mine MT-8
Noble Mine—mine NV-8
Noble Mtn—summit AZ-5
Noble Mtn—summit NY-2
Noble Oil Field—oilfield OK-5
Noble Park—park ID-8
Noble Park—park KY-4
Noble Park—park OK-5
Noble Pass CA-9
Noble Pass—gap CA-9
Noble Peak—summit MT-8
Noble Point—cape TX-5
Noble Pond ME-1
Noble Pond—lake MI-6
Noble Pond—lake OR-9
Noble Ranch—locale CA-9
Noble Ranch—locale MT-8
Noble Ranch—locale OR-9
Noble Ranch—locale WY-8
Noble Ridge—ridge CA-9
Noble Ridge—ridge WY-8
Noble Road Sch—school OH-6
Noble Rsvr—reservoir MT-8
Noble Rsvr—reservoir OR-9
Noble Rsvr Number One—reservoir OR-9
**Nobles**—pop pl TN-4
Nobles—uninc pl FL-3
Nobles, Dr. A. B., House and McKendree Church—hist pl NC-3
**Noblesboro**—pop pl NY-2
Nobles Branch—stream GA-3
Nobles Cem—cemetery IN-6
Nobles Cem—cemetery NC-3
Nobles Ch—church NC-3
Noble Sch—school (2) CA-9
Noble Sch—school CT-1
Noble Sch—school IN-6
Noble Sch—school LA-4
Noble Sch—school (2) MI-6
Noble Sch—school NE-7
Noble Sch—school (3) OH-6
Noble Sch—school OK-5
Noble Sch—school PA-2
Nobles Chapel—church IN-6
Nobles Chapel—church NC-3
**Nobles Corner**—pop pl ME-1
**Nobles (County)**—pop pl MN-6
Nobles Crossing SD-7
Nobles Crossing—locale NC-3
Nobles Crossroads—locale NC-3
**Nobles Cross Roads**—pop pl NC-3
Nobles Ditch—canal MT-8
Nobles Dock—locale TN-4
Nobles East Windmill—locale TX-5
Nobles Emigrant Trail CA-9
Nobles Emigrant Trail—hist pl CA-9
Nobles Ferry (historical)—locale AL-4
Nobles Ford (historical)—locale SD-7
Nobles Gin Landing (historical)—locale AL-4
Nobles Hill—summit NY-2
Noble Shores—locale NY-2
Nobles House—park OR-9
Nobles Island—bar ME-1
Nobles Island—island NY-2
Nobles Lake—lake IA-7
Nobles Lake—reservoir SC-3
Nobles Lake Dam—dam MS-4
Nobles Lake State Wildlife Mngmt Area—park IA-7
Noble Slough—gut SC-3
Nobles Mill—locale NC-3
Nobles Mill (historical)—locale AL-4
Nobles Millpond—reservoir NC-3
Nobles Mill Pond Dam—dam NC-3
Nobles Pass—gap CA-9
Nobles Pond DE-2
Noble Spring—spring MT-8
Noble Spring—spring NV-8
Noble Spring—spring OR-9
Nobles Store (historical)—locale MS-4
Nobles Swamp—stream VA-3
Noble Stadium—park MS-4
**Noblestown**—pop pl PA-2
Nobles Trail CA-9
Noble Street Baptist Church AL-4
Noble Street Ch—church AL-4
Noblesville KS-7
**Noblesville**—pop pl IN-6
Noblesville HS—school IN-6
Noblesville JHS—school IN-6
**Noblesville (Township of)**—pop pl IN-6
Noblet Creek—stream GA-3
Noblet Drain—stream OH-6
**Nobleton**—pop pl FL-3
**Nobleton**—pop pl WI-6
Nobleton (historical)—locale IA-7
Nobletown—locale OK-5
Noble Township KS-7
Noble Township—civ div NE-7
Noble Township—civil MO-7
Noble Township—fmr MCD IA-7
**Noble Township**—pop pl (3) KS-7
**Noble Township**—pop pl ND-7
**Noble (Township of)**—pop pl IL-6
**Noble (Township of)**—pop pl (7) IN-6
**Noble (Township of)**—pop pl MI-6
**Noble (Township of)**—pop pl (3) OH-6
Noble Trail—trail CA-9
Noblett Creek UT-8
Noblett Creek—stream MO-7
Noblett Lake—reservoir MO-7
Noblett Lake Campground—locale MO-7
Nobletts Administrative Site—locale UT-8
Nobletts Cave—cave TN-4
Nobletts Creek—stream (2) UT-8
Nobletts Creek Trail—trail UT-8
Nobleville PA-2
Noble Well—well CA-9
Noble Well—well NV-8
Noblin Cem—cemetery MS-4
Noblin Cem—cemetery NC-3
Noblit Cem—cemetery TN-4
Noblitt Ditch—canal WY-8
Noblitt Falls IN-6
Noblitt Lake—reservoir IN-6
Noblitt Windmill—locale NM-5
Nob Mountain VA-3
Nobnocket MA-1
Nobob—locale KY-4
Nobob Creek—stream KY-4
Nobodeer Pond MA-1
Nobodeer POond MA-1
Nobodies Creek—stream AL-4
Nobody Station—locale NY-2
Noboken Lake—lake WI-6
No Bottom Cem—cemetery AR-4
No Bottom Lake—lake WI-6
No Bottom Pond MA-1
No Bottom Pond—lake (4) MA-1
No Bottom Pond—lake NH-1
No Bottom Pond—lake NY-2
No Bottom Pond—lake (2) RI-1
No Bottom Spring—spring KY-4
Nobrac—locale LA-4
Nobreechies Ridge—ridge NC-3
No Brook—stream IN-6
**Nobscot**—pop pl MA-1
Nobscot Hill—summit MA-1
Nobscott MA-1
Nobscott Shop Ctr—locale MA-1
Nobscusset Harbor—bay MA-1
Nobscusset Point—cape MA-1
Nobska Beach—beach (2) MA-1
**Nobska Beach**—pop pl MA-1
Nobska Bluff MA-1
Nobska Hill—summit MA-1
Nobska Lighthouse—locale MA-1
Nobska Point—cape MA-1
Nobska Point—cliff MA-1
Nobska Point Ledge—bar MA-1
Nobska Point Light Station—hist pl MA-1
Nobska Pond—lake MA-1
NOBSKA (steamship)—hist pl MD-2
Nobsquassitt MA-1
No Buck Creek—stream CO-8
No Business Branch—stream KY-4
No Business Branch—stream TN-4
No Business Canyon—valley ID-8
No Business Creek VA-3
No Business Creek—stream (4) AL-4
No Business Creek—stream GA-3
No Business Creek—stream (3) ID-8
No Business Creek—stream (2) IL-6
Nobusiness Creek—stream IN-6
No Business Creek—stream IA-7
No Business Creek—stream MT-8
No Business Creek—stream NC-3
No Business Creek—stream (3) TN-4
Nobusiness Creek—stream VA-3
Nobusiness Creek-historical mouth-384527N0855903W IN-6
No Business Creek - in part TN-4
No Business Hollow—valley TN-4
No Business Knob—summit NC-3
No Business Knob—summit TN-4
No Business Mtn—summit ID-8
No Business Mtn—summit NC-3
No Business Mtn—summit (2) VA-3
No Business Post Office (historical)—building AL-4
No Business Ridge—ridge TN-4
No Business Saddle—gap ID-8
No Business Sch—school TN-4
No Business Trail—trail TN-4
Nocam—locale VA-3
N-O Canyon—valley AZ-5
**Nocar**—pop pl NC-3
No Catchum Rsvr—reservoir OR-9
**Nocatee**—pop pl FL-3
Nocatee Elem Sch—school FL-3
Noccalula Ch of God—church AL-4
Noccalula Falls—falls AL-4
Noccalula Park—park AL-4
Noccalula Seminary (historical)—school AL-4
Noccona TX-5
Nocelly Gulch—valley ID-8
Nocentown DE-2
Noche Buena—civil (2) CA-9
Noche Buena Sch—school CA-9
Noche Buena Windmill—locale (2) TX-5
Noche Bueno (Windmill)—locale TX-5
Nochesitas Windmill—locale TX-5
Nochlega Point—cape AK-9
Nochonohonubbe Creek OK-5
**Nocho Park**—pop pl NC-3
Nocho Park Golf Course—locale NC-3
Nockamixon, Lake—reservoir PA-2
Nockamixon Cem—cemetery PA-2
Nockamixon Cliffs—cliff PA-2
Nockamixon Lake PA-2
Nockamixon State Park—park PA-2
Nockamixon State Park Dam—dam PA-2
**Nockamixon (Township of)**—pop pl PA-2
Nockenut—locale TX-5
Nockenut Cem—cemetery TX-5
Nock House—hist pl KY-4
Nocks Branch—stream VA-3
Nockum Hill—summit RI-1
**Nocona**—pop pl TX-5
Nocona, Lake—reservoir TX-5
Nocona (CCD)—cens area TX-5
Nocona North Spanish Fort Oil Field—oilfield TX-5
Nocona Siding—locale NC-3
Nocoroco—hist pl FL-3
Nocreek KY-4
No Creek—locale KY-4
**Nocreek**—pop pl KY-4
No Creek—stream AK-9
No Creek—stream KY-4
No Creek—stream MO-7
No Creek—stream MT-8
No Creek—stream NC-3
No Creek Ch—church NC-3
No Creek Sch (abandoned)—school MO-7
Noctor—locale KY-4
Nod—locale MS-4
**Nodaway**—pop pl IA-7
**Nodaway**—pop pl MO-7
Nodaway Cem—cemetery IA-7
Nodaway Cem—cemetery MO-7
**Nodaway County**—pop pl MO-7
Nodaway County Community Lake—reservoir MO-7
Nodaway County Courthouse—hist pl MO-7
Nodaway County Farm (abandoned)—locale MO-7
Nodaway Lake—reservoir IA-7
Nodaway Mills (historical P.O.)—locale IA-7
Nodaway Park—park IA-7
Nodaway River IA-7
Nodaway River VA-3
Nodaway River*—stream IA-7
Nodaway River—stream MO-7
Nodaway River Ditch—canal MO-7
Nodaway Township—civil (2) MO-7
Nodaway Township—fmr MCD (3) IA-7
**Nodaway Township**—pop pl MO-7
Nod Brook—stream CT-1
Nod Brook—stream MA-1
Noddin Sch—school CA-9
Noddle Heads—summit CO-8
Noddleman Island—island IA-7
Noddle's Island MA-1
Noddy Canyon—valley UT-8
NODDY (log canoe)—hist pl MD-2
Node—locale KY-4
Node—locale WY-8
**Nodena**—pop pl AR-4
Nodena Bend—bend TN-4
Nodena Cem—cemetery AR-4
Nodena Site—hist pl AR-4
Nodgrass Hill—summit TN-4
Nod Hill—summit CT-1
No Dice Lake—lake WA-9
**Nodine**—pop pl MN-6
Nodine Creek—stream OR-9
Nodman Canyon—valley AZ-5
Nododehon Lake—lake AK-9
No Doe Hunting Club—other MI-6
Nodoubt Peak—summit WA-9
Nodoway Point MI-6
Nodtinghan Ranch—locale MT-8
Nodule Point—cape WA-9
No Ear Bar—bend CA-9
Noe Canal—canal AZ-5
Noe Cem—cemetery KY-4
Noe Cem—cemetery VA-3
Noe Cem—cemetery WV-2
Noe Chapel—church (2) TN-4
Noecker Rsvr—reservoir CO-8
Noe Creek—stream AR-4
Noe Creek—stream ID-8
Noe Creek—stream SC-3
Noe Creek—stream TN-4
Noe Creek—stream WA-9
Noel MO-7
Noel—locale CO-8
Noel—locale LA-4
Noel—locale OK-5
Noel—locale VA-3
**Noel**—pop pl IA-7
**Noel**—pop pl MO-7
**Noel**—pop pl PA-2
Noelani Sch—school HI-9
Noel Bay—swamp SC-3
Noel Branch—stream NC-3
Noel Canal—canal LA-4
Noel Canyon—valley CA-9
Noel Cem—cemetery (2) AL-4
Noel Cem—cemetery IL-6
Noel Cem—cemetery KS-7
Noel Cem—cemetery LA-4
Noel Cem—cemetery MO-7
Noel Cem—cemetery WV-2
Noel Chapel—locale KY-4
Noel Chapel Sch—school KY-4
Noel Creek—stream MT-8
Noel Creek—stream (2) OR-9
Noel Ditch—canal OH-6
Noel Ditch—canal WY-8
**Noel Heights**—pop pl CA-9
Noel Hollow—valley OH-6
Noel Hotel—hist pl TN-4
Noeline Station—locale PA-2
Noel Island—island GA-3
Noelke—locale TX-5
Noelke Creek—stream TX-5
Noelke Draw—valley TX-5
Noelke Hill—summit TX-5
Noelke Oil Field—oilfield TX-5
Noelke Ranch—locale TX-5
Noelke Well—well TX-5
Noelke Windmill—locale TX-5
Noel Lake—lake WY-8
Noel Lake—reservoir IN-6
Noel Lake Dam—dam IN-6
Noelridge Park—park IA-7
Noelridge Sch—school IA-7
Noels Branch—stream VA-3
Noels Creek—stream PA-2
Noels Draw—valley CO-8
Noels Knoll—summit CA-9
Noel Slough—stream LA-4
Noels Pass—gut LA-4
Noel Spring—spring CA-9
Noel Spring Ridge—ridge CA-9
Noels Store—locale MO-7
Noe Mill (historical)—locale TN-4
No End Creek—stream IN-6
Noes Branch TN-4
Noes Chapel United Methodist Church TN-4
Noes Creek—stream NJ-2
Noes Ferry TN-4
Noes Ferry Post Office TN-4
Noe Stream—stream HI-9
Noeton Baptist Church TN-4
Noeton Ch—church TN-4
**Noeton (historical)**—pop pl TN-4
Noeton Post Office (historical)—building TN-4
**Noetown**—pop pl KY-4
Noe Valley—uninc pl CA-9
Noeville Branch—stream KY-4
No Exeter Cem—cemetery ME-1
**Noez**—pop pl PR-3
Nof FM-9
Nofat Mtn—summit NC-3
No Feed Creek—stream WY-8
Noffsinger Bridge—other MO-7
Noffsinger Cem—cemetery IL-6
Noffsinger Cem—cemetery IN-6
Noffsinger Cem—cemetery MO-7
Noffsinger Sch—school KS-7
No Fish Lake—lake MT-8
No Flesh Creek—stream SD-7
**Nofog (historical)**—pop pl OR-9
No Fork Of So Fork Of North Fabius River*—stream IA-7
Nofstger Rsvr—reservoir CO-8
Nofstger Zeigler Rsvr—reservoir CO-8
Noftzger-Adams House—hist pl IN-6
Nogadaneoda Lake—lake AK-9
Nogahabara Sand Dunes—area AK-9
Nogak Creek—stream AK-9
Nogal—locale AR-4
**Nogal**—pop pl NM-5
Nogal Arroyo—arroyo NM-5
Nogal Arroyo—stream NM-5
Nogal Canyon—valley (5) NM-5
Nogal Canyon Ranch—locale NM-5
Nogal Cem—cemetery NM-5
Nogal Creek—stream (2) NM-5
Nogal Draw—valley NM-5
Nogales MS-4
**Nogales**—pop pl AZ-5
Nogales Canyon—valley AZ-5
Nogales (CCD)—cens area AZ-5
Nogales Electric Light, Ice & Water Company Power House—hist pl AZ-5
Nogales HS—hist pl AZ-5
Nogales HS—school AZ-5
Nogales HS—school CA-9
Nogales International Airp—airport AZ-5
Nogales International Waste Water Treatment Plant—locale AZ-5
Nogales Ranch—locale TX-5
Nogales Sch—school TX-5
Nogales Spring AZ-5
Nogales Spring—spring AZ-5
Nogales Steam Laundry Bldg—hist pl AZ-5
Nogales Substation—locale AZ-5
Nogales Wash—stream AZ-5
Nogales Well—well TX-5
Nogalita Spring—spring NM-5
Nogalito Spring—spring AZ-5
Nogal Lake—lake NM-5
Nogal Lake Campground—locale NM-5
Nogal Peak—summit NM-5
Nogal Ranch—locale NM-5
Nogal Tank—reservoir NM-5
Nogalus—locale TX-5
Nogalus Fire Tower TX-5
Nogalus Lookout Station TX-5
Nogalus Lookout Tower—locale TX-5
**Nogalus (Nogalus Prairie)**—pop pl TX-5
Nogalus Prairie—other TX-5
Nogamut—locale AK-9
Nogan—locale MS-4
Nogate Creek—stream TX-5
No Gegro MS-4
Nogel Tank—reservoir TX-5
Noggin Head Branch—stream MS-4
Noggle Cem—cemetery PA-2
Noggle Creek—stream MT-8
Noggle Lake—lake MI-6
Noggle School—locale MI-6
Nogle Ch—church MO-7
Nogle Creek—stream OR-9
Nogle Sch (abandoned)—school MO-7
**Nogo**—pop pl AR-4
No Good Lake—lake AK-9
No Good Park—flat CO-8
No Good Tank—reservoir AZ-5
Nogo Sch—school AR-4

**Nogosek Township**—*pop pl* ND-7
Nogoyalna Slough—*gut* AK-9
No Grass Creek—*stream* MT-8
No Grease—*locale* NC-3
Nogrilenten, Lake—*lake* AK-9
No Grub Creek—*stream* AK-9
Noguchi Tunnel—*tunnel* HI-9
**Nogueras**—*pop pl* PR-3
Noharts Creek—*stream* KS-7
Noharts Creek—*stream* NE-7
**Nohead Bottom**—*pop pl* VA-3
No Head Branch—*stream* AL-4
No Head Branch—*stream* NC-3
No Head Hollow—*valley* AL-4
No Head Hollow Public Use Area—*park* OK-5
No Heart Butte—*summit* SD-7
No Heart Creek—*stream* SD-7
Nohili Point—*cape* HI-9
Nohiu—*bay* HI-9
*Nohle* (2) MT-8
Nohly—*locale* MT-8
Nohly Cem—*cemetery* MT-8
Nohly Lake—*lake* ND-7
Noho Creek—*stream* ID-8
Nohokomeen Glacier—*glacier* WA-9
Nohonaohae—*summit* HI-9
Nohonaohaeiki—*summit* HI-9
Nohorn Butte—*summit* OR-9
Nohorn Creek—*stream* OR-9
Nohorn Trail—*trail* OR-9
Nohr Cabin—*locale* WY-8
Nohrenberg Number 3 Dam—*dam* SD-7
Nohrgang Ranch—*locale* MT-8
Noh Springs—*spring* NV-8
*Noh-tin-oah Mountain* CA-9
Noiin—*cape* FM-9
Noio—*cape* HI-9
Noio Point—*cape* HI-9
Noipa Kam—*locale* AZ-5
Noipa Kam Hills—*summit* AZ-5
Noisette Creek—*stream* SC-3
*Noisey Creek* OR-9
Noisey Inlet—*bay* NY-2
Noisey Ridge—*ridge* NY-2
Noisy Branch—*stream* KY-4
Noisy Brook—*stream* ME-1
Noisy Brook—*stream* NM-5
*Noisy Creek* MT-8
Noisy Creek—*stream* (2) CA-9
Noisy Creek—*stream* (2) MT-8
Noisy Creek—*stream* (3) OR-9
Noisy Creek—*stream* TN-4
Noisy Creek—*stream* (2) WA-9
Noisy Creek—*stream* (2) WI-6
Noisy Creek Campground—*locale* WA-9
Noisy Creek Forest Camp—*locale* OR-9
Noisy Creek Notch Trail—*trail* MT-8
Noisy Islands—*island* AK-9
Noisy Lake—*lake* ID-8
Noisy Mtn—*summit* AK-9
Noisy Passage—*channel* AK-9
Noisy Point—*cape* MA-1
Noix Creek—*stream* MO-7
Noix Creek Cem—*cemetery* MO-7
Noix Creek Ch—*church* MO-7
No Jacket Creek—*bay* NC-3
Noji, Lake—*reservoir* IN-6
Nojoqui—*civil* CA-9
Nojoqui Creek—*stream* CA-9
Nojoqui Falls—*falls* CA-9
Nojoqui Falls Park—*park* CA-9
Nojoqui Summit—*summit* CA-9
Nokai Canyon—*valley* AZ-5
Nokai Canyon—*valley* UT-8
Nokai Creek—*stream* AZ-5
Nokai Creek—*stream* UT-8
Nokai Dome—*summit* UT-8
Nokai Mesa—*summit* AZ-5
Nokai Mesa—*summit* UT-8
Nokaito Bench—*bench* AZ-5
Nokaito Bench—*bench* UT-8
*Nokasippi Lake* MN-6
Nokasippi River—*stream* MN-6
*Nokay* MN-6
Nokay Lake—*civ div* MN-6
Nokay Lake—*lake* MN-6
*Nokay Sebie* MN-6
*Nokay Sibe* MN-6
Noker Mine Draw—*valley* WY-8
*Nokes Branch* TN-4
Nokes Cem—*cemetery* MO-7
**Nokes Heights (subdivision)**—*pop pl* TN-4
**Nokesville**—*pop pl* VA-3
Nokesville Truss Bridge—*hist pl* VA-3
Noketchee Creek—*stream* GA-3
No Ketchum Pond—*lake* NH-1
Nokhu Crags—*pillar* CO-8
Nokio Creek—*stream* MT-8
Nokispeta—*swamp* FM-9
Nokispetiw—*swamp* FM-9
*Nokkwaje* MP-9
*Nokkweie* MP-9
*Nokkweie Island* MP-9
Nokkweie Island (not verified)—*island* MP-9
Nokogamiut—*locale* AK-9
Nokogamiut Island—*island* AK-9
*Nokomis* MN-6
Nokomis—*locale* VA-3
**Nokomis**—*pop pl* AL-4
**Nokomis**—*pop pl* FL-3
**Nokomis**—*pop pl* IL-6
Nokomis, Lake—*lake* CO-8
Nokomis, Lake—*lake* MN-6
Nokomis, Lake—*lake* WI-6
Nokomis, Lake—*reservoir* IA-7
Nokomis, Lake—*reservoir* WI-6
Nokomis Baptist Ch—*church* AL-4
**Nokomis Beach**—*pop pl* FL-3
Nokomis Camp—*locale* MI-6
Nokomis Camp—*locale* NY-2
Nokomis Ch—*church* AL-4
Nokomis Ch—*church* FL-3
Nokomis Church Cem—*cemetery* AL-4
Nokomis Elem Sch—*school* FL-3
Nokomis Falls—*falls* MI-6
Nokomis Hollow—*valley* AR-4
Nokomis JHS—*school* MN-6
*Nokomis Lake* WI-6
Nokomis Lake—*lake* WI-6
Nokomis Pond—*lake* ME-1
Nokomis Sch—*school* CA-9
Nokomis Sch—*school* MI-6
Nokomis Sch—*school* MN-6
Nokomis Sch—*school* NY-2
Nokomis Sch—*school* WI-6
**Nokomis (Town of)**—*pop pl* WI-6
Nokomis Township—*fmr MCD* IA-7
**Nokomis (Township of)**—*pop pl* IL-6
No-Ko-Mos Lake—*lake* MI-6
Nokoni, Lake—*lake* CO-8
Nokotlek Point—*cape* AK-9
Nokotlek River—*stream* AK-9
Nokrot—*locale* AK-9
*Nola* VA-3
**Nola**—*pop pl* AR-4
**Nola**—*pop pl* MS-4
Nola Butte—*summit* CO-8
Nola Cem—*cemetery* CO-8
Nola Cem—*cemetery* WI-6
*Nolachuckey Elementary School* TN-4
*Nola Chuckey River* TN-4
*Nola Chucky* TN-4
Nola Chucky Post Office (historical)—*building* TN-4
*Nolachucky River* NC-3
*Nolachucky River* TN-4
*Nola Creek* WA-9
Nola Creek—*stream* WA-9
*Nolak* FM-9
No Lake Creek—*stream* AK-9
Nola Lateral—*canal* ID-8
Nolan—*locale* AK-9
Nolan—*locale* KS-7
Nolan—*locale* ND-7
**Nolan**—*pop pl* TX-5
**Nolan**—*pop pl* WV-2
Nolan, James N., House—*hist pl* TN-4
Nolan Bar—*bar* TN-4
Nolan Bayou—*gut* LA-4
Nolan Branch—*stream* (4) KY-4
Nolan Branch—*stream* TN-4
Nolan Branch—*stream* TX-5
Nolan Cabin—*locale* CA-9
Nolan Cem—*cemetery* IN-6
Nolan Cem—*cemetery* KY-4
Nolan Cem—*cemetery* MO-7
Nolan Cem—*cemetery* (2) TN-4
Nolan Cem—*cemetery* TX-5
Nolan Ch—*church* FL-3
**Nolan (County)**—*pop pl* TX-5
*Nolan Creek* AL-4
*Nolan Creek* MT-8
*Nolan Creek* WA-9
*Nolan Creek* WI-6
Nolan Creek—*stream* (2) AK-9
Nolan Creek—*stream* AZ-5
Nolan Creek—*stream* CA-9
Nolan Creek—*stream* CO-8
Nolan Creek—*stream* ID-8
Nolan Creek—*stream* NM-5
Nolan Creek—*stream* (2) TX-5
Nolan Creek—*stream* WA-9
Nolan Creek—*stream* WI-6
Nolan Creek Lake—*lake* AK-9
*Noland* NC-3
Noland—*locale* AR-4
Noland—*locale* CO-8
Noland—*locale* KY-4
**Noland**—*pop pl* AL-4
Nolandale—*uninc pl* AL-4
Nolan Davis Lake Dam Number One—*dam* AL-4
Noland Cabin—*locale* WY-8
Noland Cem—*cemetery* KY-4
Noland Cem—*cemetery* (2) MO-7
Noland Cem—*cemetery* NC-3
Noland Cem—*cemetery* OH-6
Noland Creek—*stream* AL-4
Noland Creek—*stream* KY-4
Noland Creek—*stream* (2) NC-3
Noland Divide—*ridge* NC-3
Noland Fashion Square—*locale* MO-7
*Noland Fork* IN-6
Noland Gap—*gap* NC-3
Noland Gulch—*valley* CA-9
Noland Gulch—*valley* CO-8
Noland Hill Sch—*school* MS-4
Noland Hollow—*valley* MO-7
Noland Hosp—*hospital* AL-4
Nolan Divide Lake—*reservoir* TX-5
Noland Mound (15-Ma-14)—*hist pl* KY-4
Noland Mtn—*summit* NC-3
Noland Plaza—*locale* MO-7
Noland Ridge—*ridge* WV-2
Noland Road Retail Center—*locale* MO-7
Noland Sch—*school* MO-7
Noland Sch (historical)—*school* AL-4
*Nolands Creek* KS-7
Nolands Ferry I Archeol Site (18FR17)—*hist pl* MD-2
Nolands Fork—*stream* IN-6
Nolands Island—*island* MD-2
Noland South Shop Ctr—*locale* MO-7
Nolands Point—*cape* MO-7
Nolands Point Seaplane Base—*airport* MO-7
Noland Spring—*spring* CO-8
*Nolands River* TX-5
Noland Store (historical)—*locale* AL-4
Nolands Trail—*trail* PA-2
Noland (Township of)—*fmr MCD* AR-4
Nolan-Edwards Oil Field—*oilfield* TX-5
Nolan Engle Drain—*stream* MI-6
Nolan Field—*park* CT-1
Nolan Field—*park* NC-3
Nolan Grant—*civil* CO-8
Nolan Hill—*summit* KS-7
**Nolan Hills**—*pop pl* AL-4
Nolan Hollow—*valley* AR-4
Nolan Hollow—*valley* KY-4
Nolan Hollow—*valley* TN-4
Nolan House—*hist pl* NM-5
Nolan Knob—*summit* AR-4
Nolan Lake—*lake* CO-8
Nolan Lake—*reservoir* ID-8
Nolan Lake—*reservoir* TN-4
Nolan Lake Dam—*dam* TN-4
Nolan Point—*cliff* AR-4
Nolan Ranch—*locale* (2) AZ-5
Nolan River—*stream* TX-5
Nolan River Country Club—*other* TX-5
Nolan River Park—*park* TX-5
Nolan Run—*stream* WV-2
Nolansburg Sch—*school* KY-4
**Nolansburg (Splint Post Office)**—*pop pl* KY-4
Nolan Sch—*school* CT-1
Nolan Sch—*school* MA-1
Nolan Sch—*school* MI-6
Nolan Sch—*school* NY-2
Nolan Sch—*school* TX-5
Nolan Sexton Dam—*dam* SD-7
Nolan Slough—*stream* OR-9
Nolans Point—*cape* NJ-2
Nolan Spring—*spring* TN-4
Nolan Tank—*reservoir* (2) AZ-5
Nolan Valley Ch—*church* TX-5
**Nolanville**—*pop pl* TX-5
Nolanville (historical)—*locale* AL-4
Nolan (Wiseman)—*other* AK-9
Nola Post Office (historical)—*building* TN-4
Nolar Spring—*spring* TN-4
Nolda Ranch—*locale* NM-5
Nolda Tank No 1—*reservoir* NM-5
Nolde Forest State Park—*park* PA-2
Nolden Creek—*stream* NC-3
Noldner Number 1 Dam—*dam* SD-7
*Nolechuckey Rive* TN-4
*Nolechucky River* NC-3
*Nole Hoe Creek* MS-4
Nolehoe Creek—*stream* MS-4
Nolen Blue Hole—*lake* MO-7
Nolen Cem—*cemetery* (2) AL-4
Nolen Cem—*cemetery* IN-6
Nolen Cem—*cemetery* TN-4
Nolenchec Creek—*stream* MI-6
Nolen Creek—*stream* NC-3
Nolen Dam—*dam* (2) AL-4
Nolen Davis Lake Dam Number Two—*dam* AL-4
Nolen Davis Lake Number One—*reservoir* AL-4
Nolen Davis Lake Number Two—*reservoir* AL-4
Nolen Draw—*valley* TX-5
Nolen Hollow—*valley* TN-4
Nolen Lake—*reservoir* (2) AL-4
Nolen Peak—*summit* NM-5
Nolen Pocket—*basin* WY-8
Nolen Sch—*school* AR-4
Nolen Sch—*school* MO-7
**Nolensville**—*pop pl* TN-4
*Nolensville Baptist Church* TN-4
Nolensville (CCD)—*cens area* TN-4
Nolensville Cem—*cemetery* TN-4
Nolensville Ch—*church* TN-4
Nolensville Division—*civil* TN-4
*Nolensville Elementary School* TN-4
Nolensville Post Office—*building* TN-4
Nolensville Sch—*school* TN-4
Noles Branch—*stream* AL-4
Noles Cem—*cemetery* GA-3
Noles Cem—*cemetery* TN-4
Nole Sch (historical)—*school* TN-4
**Noles Landing**—*pop pl* LA-4
Nolf Corners—*locale* PA-2
*Nolf Fun* PA-2
Nolf Run—*stream* PA-2
*Noli* AZ-5
*Nolia* AZ-5
Nolia—*locale* OK-5
**Nolia**—*pop pl* AZ-5
Nolia Cem—*cemetery* OK-5
Nolia Tank—*reservoir* AZ-5
Nolia Trail—*trail* OK-5
Nolic—*locale* AZ-5
Nolichuckey Elem Sch—*school* TN-4
Nolichucky Dam—*dam* TN-4
Nolichucky Golf Club—*locale* TN-4
**Nolichucky (historical)**—*pop pl* TN-4
Nolichucky River—*stream* NC-3
Nolichucky River—*stream* TN-4
Nolichucky River Trail—*trail* TN-4
Nolin—*locale* OR-9
**Nolin**—*pop pl* KY-4
Nolina Cove—*valley* CA-9
Nolina Wash—*stream* CA-9
Nolin Banking Company—*hist pl* KY-4
Nolin Cem—*cemetery* OR-9
Nolin Ch—*church* KY-4
*Nolin Creek* WY-8
Nolin Lake—*reservoir* AL-4
Nolin Lake—*reservoir* KY-4
Nolin Lake Estates—*locale* KY-4
*Nolin Reservoir* KY-4
Nolin Ridge—*ridge* TN-4
Nolin River—*stream* KY-4
*Nolin River Reservoir* KY-4
Nolins Landing (historical)—*locale* TN-4
Nolitna Creek—*stream* AK-9
Noll, Joseph, Chalkrock Barn—*hist pl* SD-7
Noll Airp—*airport* PA-2
Noll Branch—*stream* MO-7
Nollesemic Lake—*lake* ME-1
Nollesemic Stream—*stream* ME-1
Nolley Chapel—*church* TN-4
Nolley Oil Field—*oilfield* TX-5
Nolleytuby Creek—*stream* OK-5
*Noll Mountain* NV-8
Noll Sch—*school* IN-6
**Nollville**—*pop pl* WV-2
**Nolo**—*pop pl* PA-2
Nolo Sch—*school* IA-7
*Nolsemic Lake* ME-1
Nolt Cem—*cemetery* IN-6
**Nolte**—*pop pl* TX-5
Nolte Canal—*canal* TX-5
Nolte Dam—*dam* TX-5
Nolten Canyon—*valley* NM-5
Nolten Lake—*lake* MI-6
Noltie Creek—*stream* AL-4
**Noltimier Township**—*pop pl* ND-7
Nolting Pond—*lake* VA-3
Noltings—*locale* IL-6
*Noltke Creek* TX-5
*Noltke Hill* TX-5
**Nolton**—*pop pl* PA-2
Nolton Cem—*cemetery* PA-2
Nolton Creek—*stream* CA-9
Nolton Creek—*stream* TX-5
*Nolton Lake* MI-6
Nolton Point—*cape* AL-4
Nolton Ridge—*ridge* NC-3
Nolton (Site)—*locale* CA-9
Nolton Station—*locale* PA-2
*Noluck Lake* AK-9
*Noluk Lake* AK-9
Nolynn Ch—*church* KY-4
**Noma**—*pop pl* FL-3
Nomad Lake—*lake* MN-6
Nomad Lateral—*canal* ID-8
*Nomagua* MA-1
Nomahegan Brook—*stream* NJ-2
Nomahegan Park—*park* NJ-2
Noma Junction—*locale* FL-3
Noma Lake—*lake* MN-6
No Man Creek—*stream* (2) ID-8
No Man Creek—*stream* MT-8
No Man Creek—*stream* OR-9
Noman Creek—*stream* WA-9
*No Man Island* ME-1
No Man Lake—*lake* MT-8
*No Man Mesa* UT-8
No Man Mesa—*summit* UT-8
No Man Peak—*summit* MT-8
No Man Ridge—*ridge* MT-8
*No Mans Canyon* UT-8
No Mans Canyon—*valley* TX-5
No Mans Canyon—*valley* UT-8
*No Mans Creek* ID-8
No Mans Creek—*stream* AK-9
No Mans Creek—*stream* CA-9
No Mans Creek—*stream* ID-8
No Mans Creek—*stream* WI-6
No Mans Friend Creek—*gut* SC-3
No Mans Friend Pond—*lake* GA-3
No Mans Friend Reach—*channel* DE-2
No Man Shelter—*locale* OR-9
No Mans Island—*island* ME-1
No Mans Island—*island* NH-1
No Mans Island—*island* NJ-2
No-Mans Island—*island* UT-8
*No Mans Lake* WI-6
No Mans Lake—*lake* MI-6
No Mans Lake—*lake* MN-6
No Mans Lake—*lake* (3) WI-6
*No Mans Land* AZ-5
*No Mans Land* MA-1
*No Mans Land* OK-5
No Mans Land—*area* NM-5
No Mans Land—*island* ME-1
Nomans Land—*island* MA-1
No Mans Land (historical)—*summit* AZ-5
*No Mans Land Island* MA-1
No Mans Land Point—*cape* UT-8
No Mans Land Swamp—*swamp* CT-1
No Mans Ledge—*bar* MA-1
No Mans Mesa—*summit* CO-8
No Mans Mesa—*summit* (3) UT-8
No Mans Mtn—*summit* UT-8
No Mans Pass—*gap* WY-8
Nomans River—*stream* FL-3
Nomans Store (historical)—*locale* MS-4
Noman Towhead (inundated)—*island* AL-4
Nomaram—*bar* FM-9
**Nombre de Dios (historical)**—*pop pl* FL-3
**Nome**—*pop pl* AK-9
**Nome**—*pop pl* ND-7
**Nome**—*pop pl* TX-5
Nome Airp—*airport* AK-9
*Nome (Census Area)* AK-9
**Nome (Census Subarea)**—*pop pl* AK-9
Nome-China (CCD)—*cens area* TX-5
Nome Creek—*stream* AK-9
Nome Creek—*stream* MT-8
Nome Creek—*stream* OR-9
Nomeet Branch—*stream* TN-4
Nome Lackee Cem—*cemetery* CA-9
Nome Lackee Ind Res Monmt—*pillar* CA-9
*Nom En Sou* FM-9
Nomenuk—*bay* FM-9
Nome Oil Field—*oilfield* TX-5
Nome Park—*park* CO-8
Nome Peak—*summit* OR-9
Nome Point—*summit* MT-8
Nome River—*stream* AK-9
Nome Stake Creek—*stream* AK-9
Nomilo Fishpond—*lake* HI-9
Nomilu Valley—*valley* HI-9
Nomini—*locale* VA-3
Nomini Bay—*bay* VA-3
Nomini Bridge—*bridge* VA-3
Nomini Cliffs—*cliff* VA-3
Nomini Creek—*stream* VA-3
Nomini Grove—*locale* VA-3
Nom Inside Pond—*gut* LA-4
*Nominy Grove* VA-3
Nomisaram—*bay* FM-9
*Nomituck* FM-9
Nomland Dam—*dam* MT-8
Nommel Place—*locale* AZ-5
Nomna—*area* GU-9
Nomna Bay—*bay* GU-9
Nomna Bay Site—*hist pl* GU-9
Nomna Point—*cape* GU-9
No Moccasin Creek—*stream* SD-7
Nomofefin—*bay* FM-9
*Nomoi* FM-9
Nomoneas—*bar* FM-9
Nomoneas—*island* FM-9
*Nomon Nematon* FM-9
No More, Mount—*summit* NJ-2
*Nomos* FM-9
*Nomo Shima* FM-9
*No Mouth Creek* SD-7
No Mouth Creek—*stream* SD-7
Nom Outside Pond—*bay* LA-4
Noms Pass—*gut* LA-4
*Nomsusmuc* RI-1
Nomun Nepimwar—*bay* FM-9
Nomunsou—*bay* FM-9
*Nomunsow* FM-9
Nomur, Oror En—*locale* FM-9
Nomus—*bar* FM-9
Nomus—*swamp* FM-9
Nomwin Atoll—*island* FM-9
Nomwin Island—*island* FM-9
Nomwin (Municipality)—*civ div* FM-9
*Nomwoneyas* FM-9
**Non**—*pop pl* OK-5
*Nona* AL-4
Nona—*locale* MO-7
Nona—*locale* TX-5
Nona, Lake—*lake* FL-3
Nona, Lake—*lake* WI-6
*Nonaberg* TN-4
Nonaburg—*locale* TN-4
*Nonaburgh* TN-4
*Nonaburgh Post Office* TN-4
Nonaburg Post Office (historical)—*building* TN-4
*Nonacanicus Brook* MA-1
*Nonacauicus Brook* MA-1
*Nonacoicus Brook* MA-1
Nonacoicus Brook—*stream* MA-1
Nona Creek—*stream* WY-8
Nonada Hill—*summit* CA-9
*Nonaicoicus Brook* MA-1
Nonaicoicus Hill—*summit* MA-1
Nona Lake—*lake* WI-6
No Name—*locale* OH-6
Noname—*reservoir* (28) NC-3
No Name Bay—*bay* AK-9
No Name Brook—*stream* ME-1
Noname Canyon—*valley* CA-9
No Name Canyon—*valley* MT-8
No Name Canyon—*valley* NM-5
No Name Cem—*cemetery* OR-9
*No Name Cove* AZ-5
No Name Cove—*bay* AK-9
*No Name Creek* WA-9
No Name Creek—*stream* (2) AK-9
No Name Creek—*stream* AZ-5
No Name Creek—*stream* CA-9
No Name Creek—*stream* (5) CO-8
Noname Creek—*stream* CO-8
No Name Creek—*stream* CO-8
No Name Creek—*stream* (4) ID-8
No Name Creek—*stream* IN-6
No Name Creek—*stream* (2) MT-8
No Name Creek—*stream* OH-6
No Name Creek—*stream* (5) OR-9
No Name Creek—*stream* (2) WA-9
Noname Creek—*stream* (4) WA-9
No Name Creek—*stream* WI-6
No Name Creek—*stream* WY-8
No Name Draw—*valley* CO-8
No Name Flat—*flat* OR-9
No Name Gulch—*valley* (3) CO-8
No Name Gulch—*valley* ID-8
No Name Gulch—*valley* (2) MT-8
No Name Harbor—*harbor* FL-3
No Name Hills—*summit* TX-5
*No Name Island* AK-9
No Name Island—*island* AK-9
*Noname Key* FL-3
No Name Key—*island* FL-3
*No Name Lake* MI-6
*No Name Lake* WA-9
No Name Lake—*lake* AK-9
Noname Lake—*lake* CA-9
No Name Lake—*lake* CO-8
No Name Lake—*lake* MI-6
No Name Lake—*lake* MT-8
No Name Lake—*lake* WA-9
Noname Lake—*lake* WA-9
No Name Lake—*lake* (2) WA-9
No Name Lakes—*lake* WY-8
No Name Mesa—*summit* UT-8
No Name Peak—*summit* WA-9
No Name Pond—*lake* (2) ME-1
No-Name Rapids—*rapids* OR-9
No Name Ridge—*cape* CO-8
No Name Ridge—*ridge* WA-9
No Name Rsvr—*reservoir* AZ-5
No Name Rsvr—*reservoir* NV-8
No Name Rsvr—*reservoir* OR-9
No Name Rsvr—*reservoir* (2) WY-8
No Name Spring—*spring* AZ-5
No Name Spring—*spring* OR-9
No Name Springs—*spring* OR-9
Nonamesset Island—*island* MA-1
Nonamesset Point—*cape* MA-1
Nonamesset Shoal—*bar* MA-1
*Nonamessett* MA-1
*Nonamessett Island* MA-1
No Name Tank—*reservoir* (4) AZ-5
No Name Wash—*stream* AZ-5
No Name Wash Dam—*dam* AZ-5
No Name Well—*well* UT-8
Nona Mills Oil Field—*oilfield* TX-5
*Nonandem* MA-1
Nonans Peak—*summit* CO-8
Nonantum Hill—*summit* MA-1
**Nonantum (subdivision)**—*pop pl* MA-1
*Nonatuck Grist Mill* MA-1
*Nonatuck Lake* MA-1
Nonatum Mills—*locale* DE-2
**Nonaville**—*pop pl* TN-4
Nonaville Ch—*church* TN-4
Nonaville Post Office (historical)—*building* TN-4
Nonaville Sch (historical)—*school* TN-4
*Noncahnah Creek* TN-4
*Noncannah Creek* TN-4
Non Cem—*cemetery* OK-5
Nonchalanta (historical)—*locale* KS-7
Nonchalanta Sch—*school* KY-4
Nonconnah—*uninc pl* TN-4
Nonconnah Creek—*stream* TN-4
Nondaga Cem—*cemetery* NY-2
**Nondalton**—*pop pl* AK-9
None—*reservoir* MS-4
*No Negro* MS-4
Noneless Creek—*stream* AL-4
*Nonequasset Island* RI-1
Nonesuch—*locale* MI-6
**Nonesuch**—*pop pl* KY-4
*Nonesuch Brook* MA-1
Nonesuch Brook—*stream* ME-1
Nonesuch Cove—*bay* ME-1
Nonesuch Creek—*stream* DE-2
Nonesuch Point—*cape* ME-1
*None Such Pond* MA-1
Nonesuch Pond—*lake* MA-1
Nonesuch River—*stream* ME-1
Nonesuch Rocks—*ridge* AZ-5
Nonesuch Sch—*school* KY-4
Nonesuch Spring—*spring* AZ-5
Nonewaug River—*stream* CT-1
*Nongejokenen Island* MP-9
Nonio—*swamp* FM-9
*Nonkapenparam* FM-9
Nonnell—*locale* KY-4
**Nonnel (Tarma)**—*pop pl* KY-4
Nonnenmacher Bakery—*hist pl* AL-4
Nonnenmacher House—*hist pl* AL-4
*Nonnezoshi Biko* UT-8
*Nonnozoshi* UT-8
**Nonopahu**—*pop pl* HI-9
Nonopahu Ridge—*ridge* HI-9
Nonopahu Rsvr—*reservoir* HI-9
**Nonopahu Village**—*pop pl* HI-9
**Nonopapa**—*pop pl* HI-9
*Nono Peak* HI-9
Nonose Creek—*stream* OR-9
*Nonotuck* MA-1
Nonotuck, Mount—*summit* MA-1
*Nonotuck, Town of* MA-1
*Nonotuck City of Northampton* MA-1
*Nonotuck Lake* MA-1
Nonotuck Park—*park* MA-1
Nonou—*spring* FM-9
Nonou—*summit* HI-9
Nonou Bay—*bay* HI-9
Nonou For Res—*forest* HI-9
Nonoula—*crater* HI-9
Nonou Mtn—*summit* HI-9
*Nonou Ridge* HI-9
Nonpareil—*locale* OR-9
**Nonpareil**—*pop pl* NE-7
Nonpareil Mine—*mine* MT-8
Nonpariel Creek—*stream* MT-8
*Nonplus Hill* RI-1
*Nonquit* MA-1
Nonquit Pond—*lake* RI-1
Nonquit Pond—*reservoir* RI-1
Nonquit Pond Dam—*dam* RI-1
**Nonquitt**—*pop pl* MA-1
Non-School Vocational Education—*school* FL-3
*Nonset Brook* MA-1
Nonset Brook—*stream* MA-1
*Nontolemal Point* FM-9
Nonukan—*bar* FM-9
Nonuo—*bar* FM-9
Nonvalnuk River—*stream* AK-9
Nonvianuk Lake—*lake* AK-9
Nonvianuk River—*stream* AK-9
Nooday Mine—*mine* CA-9
**Noodle**—*pop pl* TX-5
Noodle Creek—*stream* TX-5
Noodle Lake—*lake* MN-6
Noodle Oil Field—*oilfield* TX-5
Noodles Lake—*lake* MI-6
Noodor Dome—*summit* AK-9
*Nooiksut* AK-9
**Noojinsville**—*pop pl* AL-4
Nook—*locale* PA-2
Nook, The—*bay* ME-1
Nook, The—*cove* MA-1
Nook, The—*hist pl* PA-2
Nook, The—*locale* MO-7
Nook, The—*ridge* OR-9
Nookachamps Creek—*stream* WA-9
*Nookagee Brook* MA-1
*Nookagee River* MA-1
Nookati Creek—*stream* AK-9
Nook Campground—*park* UT-8
Nook Canyon—*valley* UT-8
Nook Creek—*stream* (2) OR-9
Nook Farm and Woodland Street District—*hist pl* CT-1
Nook Hill—*summit* NJ-2
Nooks, The—*bend* NC-3
*Nooksachk* WA-9
*Nooksachk River* WA-9
*Nooksacht* WA-9
*Nooksacht River* WA-9
**Nooksack**—*pop pl* WA-9
Nooksack Camp—*locale* WA-9
Nooksack Cirque—*basin* WA-9
Nooksack Falls—*falls* WA-9
Nooksack Falls Hydroelectric Power Plant—*hist pl* WA-9
*Nooksack Glacier* WA-9
**Nooksack Ind Res**—*pop pl* WA-9
Nooksack Power Plant—*other* WA-9
Nooksack Ridge—*ridge* WA-9
*Nooksack River* WA-9
Nooksack River—*stream* WA-9
**Nooksack Salmon Hatchery**—*pop pl* WA-9
Nooksack Tower—*summit* WA-9
Nooksack Valley HS—*school* WA-9
*Nooksahk* WA-9
*Nooksahk River* WA-9
*Nooksak* WA-9
*Nooksak River* WA-9
Nooks Hill—*summit* CT-1
Nooksie Windmill—*locale* TX-5
*Noolik* AZ-5
*Noon* VA-3
Noon—*locale* WA-9
**Noon**—*pop pl* OR-9
Noon, A. S., Bldg—*hist pl* AZ-5
Noon, Philip, House—*hist pl* PA-2
Noonah Gulch—*valley* (2) CA-9
Noonan—*locale* TX-5
**Noonan**—*pop pl* ND-7
Noonan, Walter T., House—*hist pl* ND-7
Noonan Canyon—*valley* AZ-5
Noonan Cove—*cove* MA-1
Noonan Ditch—*canal* CO-8
Noonan-Norblad House—*hist pl* OR-9
Noonan Park—*park* MN-6
Noonan Park Dam—*dam* ND-7
Noonan Pond—*lake* GA-3
Noonan Ranch—*locale* CO-8
Noonan Sch—*school* MA-1
Noonan Sch—*school* TX-5
Noonan Springs—*spring* OR-9
**Noonan Township**—*pop pl* ND-7
Noonas Spring—*spring* CA-9
Noon Branch—*stream* PA-2
*Noon Camp* AZ-5
Noon Canyon—*valley* UT-8
Noon Canyon Butte—*summit* UT-8
Noonchester Mine—*mine* CA-9
Noon Creek—*stream* AZ-5
Noon Creek—*stream* (2) ID-8
Noon Creek—*stream* OR-9
Noon Creek Campground—*park* AZ-5
Noon Creek Picnic Grounds—*park* AZ-5
Noon Creek Ridge—*ridge* AZ-5

Noon Creek Spring—*spring* ... ID-8
Noon Creek Trail—*trail* ... AZ-5
Noonday—*locale* ... GA-3
Noonday—*locale* ... TX-5
**Noonday**—*pop pl* ... TX-5
Noonday Canyon—*valley* ... NM-5
Noonday Ch—*church* ... AL-4
Noonday Ch—*church* (3) ... GA-3
Noonday Creek—*stream* ... GA-3
Noonday Mine—*mine* ... CA-9
Noonday Mine—*mine* ... OR-9
Noonday Mine—*mine* ... UT-8
Noonday Peak—*summit* ... NM-5
Noonday Ridge—*ridge* ... OR-9
**Noone**—*pop pl* ... NH-1
Noonen Rsvr—*reservoir* ... CO-8
Nooner Cem—*cemetery* ... AR-4
*Nooner-Mitchell Cemetery* ... TN-4
Nooney, Lake—*lake* ... MT-8
Nooney, William , House—*hist pl* ... OH-6
Noon Hill—*summit* ... MA-1
Nooning Creek—*stream* ... CA-9
Nooning Creek—*stream* ... VA-3
Nooning Ground—*flat* ... CA-9
Nooning Ground (Site)—*locale* ... UT-8
Noon Lake—*lake* ... UT-8
Noon Mark—*summit* ... MT-8
Noonmark Mtn—*summit* ... NY-2
*Noon Mtn* ... MA-1
Noon Mtn—*summit* ... ME-1
Noon Notch—*gap* ... NY-2
Noon Peak—*summit* ... CA-9
Noon Peak—*summit* ... NH-1
Noon Point—*cape* (2) ... AK-9
Noon Point—*cliff* ... WY-8
Noon Rock—*pillar* ... NV-8
Noon Rock Canyon—*valley* ... UT-8
Noon Rock Peak—*summit* ... UT-8
Noon Rocks—*summit* ... WY-8
Noon Rsvr—*reservoir* ... OR-9
Noon Run—*stream* ... PA-2
Noon Tank—*reservoir* ... AZ-5
*Noontootla River* ... GA-3
Noontootla Ch—*church* ... GA-3
Noontootla Creek—*stream* ... GA-3
Noonuklook Mtn—*summit* ... AK-9
Noonville (site)—*locale* ... AZ-5
Nooravlooksmiut Island—*island* ... AK-9
Noordeloos—*locale* ... MI-6
Noordeloos Cem—*cemetery* ... MI-6
Noordmans State Wildlife Mngmt Area—*park* ... MN-6
*Noord Zee* ... MA-1
**Noorvik**—*pop pl* ... AK-9
**Nooseneck**—*pop pl* ... RI-1
*Nooseneck Hill* ... RI-1
Nooseneck Hill—*summit* ... RI-1
*Nooseneck Hill Brook* ... RI-1
Nooseneck River—*stream* ... RI-1
Nootas Hill—*summit* ... MA-1
Nootas Hill—*summit* ... RI-1
Nooteeming Lake—*reservoir* ... NY-2
Nootnagle Dam—*dam* ... OR-9
Nootnagle Rsvr—*reservoir* ... OR-9
*Nootsachk River* ... WA-9
*Nootsack River* ... WA-9
*Noowallo* ... FL-3
Nooya Lake—*lake* ... AK-9
Nopah Range—*ridge* ... CA-9
Nopal—*locale* (2) ... TX-5
Nopaleras Creek—*stream* ... TX-5
Nopal Ranch—*locale* ... TX-5
Nopal Well—*well* (2) ... TX-5
*Nopaquonomuss Swamp* ... RI-1
Nopeitiu—*bar* ... FM-9
**Nopeming**—*pop pl* ... MN-6
No Permit Tank—*reservoir* ... NM-5
Nopkins Mill Hist Dist—*hist pl* ... RI-1
No Point, Point—*cape* (3) ... MD-2
No Point, Point—*cape* ... NJ-2
No Point, Point—*cape* (2) ... WA-9
No Pole Cave—*cave* ... AL-4
Nopone Lookout Tower—*locale* ... GA-3
No Pone Ridge—*ridge* (2) ... TN-4
No Pone Valley—*valley* ... TN-4
Nopos—*spring* ... FM-9
Noposok—*spring* ... FM-9
N O P Park—*park* ... ID-8
Noppet, The—*summit* ... MA-1
*Nopque* ... MA-1
Noquebay, Lake—*lake* ... WI-6
*Noque Lake* ... WI-6
Noquez Mine—*mine* ... NV-8
**Noquochoke**—*pop pl* ... MA-1
Noquochoke Lake—*reservoir* ... MA-1
Noquochoke Lake Dam—*dam* ... MA-1
*Nora* ... IN-6
Nora—*locale* ... KY-4
Nora—*locale* ... WI-6
**Nora**—*pop pl* ... IL-6
**Nora**—*pop pl* ... IN-6
**Nora**—*pop pl* ... NE-7
**Nora**—*pop pl* ... SD-7
**Nora**—*pop pl* ... VA-3
Nora, Lake—*reservoir* ... SD-7
Nora Branch—*stream* ... IN-6
Nora Cem—*cemetery* ... IL-6
Nora Cem—*cemetery* ... MN-6
Nora Cem—*cemetery* ... NE-7
Nora Cem—*cemetery* ... SD-7
Nora Cem—*cemetery* ... WI-6
Nora Ch—*church* (2) ... MN-6
Nora Ch—*church* ... ND-7
Nora Creek—*stream* ... AK-9
Nora Creek—*stream* ... ID-8
*Noracy Pond* ... ME-1
*Nora Davis Elementary School* ... MS-4
Nora Davis Memorial Cem—*cemetery* ... MS-4
Nora Davis Sch—*school* ... MS-4
Norad Mill—*hist pl* ... MA-1
Nora Elem Sch—*school* ... IN-6
Nora Free Christian Church—*hist pl* ... MN-6
**Norager Acres Subdivision**—*pop pl* ... UT-8
**Norah**—*pop pl* ... LA-4
Nora (historical)—*locale* ... KS-7
Nora (historical)—*locale* ... SD-7
**Nora Junction**—*pop pl* ... IA-7
Norak Lake—*lake* ... AK-9
*Norala* ... AL-4
**Norala**—*pop pl* ... AL-4
Norala Junction—*locale* ... AL-4
Nora Lake—*lake* ... CA-9
Nora Lateral—*canal* ... ID-8
**Nora Lee Subdivision**—*pop pl* ... UT-8
Nora Lily Mine—*mine* ... CO-8
Noralto Sch—*school* ... CA-9
**Noralyn**—*pop pl* ... FL-3
Noralyn Mine Lake—*lake* ... FL-3
Noralyn RR Station—*locale* ... FL-3
Noranale Mtn—*summit* ... NY-2
**Noranda**—*pop pl* ... WA-9
Nora Plaza—*locale* ... IN-6
Nora Pond—*lake* ... OR-9
Nora Post Office (historical)—*building* ... SD-7
Nora Sch—*school* ... SD-7
Noras Cove—*bay* ... NC-3
Nora Smith Ch—*church* ... MS-4
**Nora Springs**—*pop pl* ... IA-7
*Nora Springs Junction* ... IA-7
Nora Springs-Rock Falls Sch—*school* ... IA-7
Nora State Wildlife Mngmt Area—*park* ... MN-6
Nora Town Hall—*building* ... ND-7
**Nora Township**—*pop pl* ... ND-7
Nora Township Dam—*dam* ... ND-7
**Nora (Township of)**—*pop pl* ... IL-6
**Nora (Township of)**—*pop pl* (2) ... MN-6
Norbacher Canyon—*valley* ... WY-8
**Norbeck**—*pop pl* ... MD-2
**Norbeck**—*pop pl* ... SD-7
Norbeck, Peter, Summer House—*hist pl* ... SD-7
*Norbeck Dam* ... SD-7
Norbeck Draw—*valley* ... SD-7
Norbeck JHS—*school* ... MD-2
Norbeck Lake—*reservoir* ... SD-7
Norbeck Pass—*gap* ... SD-7
Norbeck Sch—*school* ... SD-7
Norberg Creek—*stream* ... AK-9
*Norberg Lake* ... MN-6
Norberg Lake—*lake* ... ND-7
*Norbert* ... SD-7
Norbert—*locale* ... LA-4
Norbert Bonhorst Dam—*dam* ... SD-7
Norborg Lake—*lake* ... MN-6
**Norborne**—*pop pl* ... MO-7
Norborne Cem—*cemetery* ... WV-2
Norborne Drainage Ditch—*canal* ... MO-7
**Norbourne Estates**—*pop pl* ... KY-4
Norbridge Sch—*school* ... CA-9
Norburn Terrace—*hist pl* ... NC-3
Norburys Landing—*locale* ... NJ-2
Norby Creek—*stream* ... MI-6
Norby House—*hist pl* ... MT-8
Norby Lake—*lake* ... WI-6
Norby Sch—*school* ... MN-6
**Norcatur**—*pop pl* ... KS-7
Norcatur Cem—*cemetery* ... KS-7
Norcatur Elem Sch—*school* ... KS-7
Norclay Sch—*school* ... MO-7
**Norco**—*pop pl* ... CA-9
**Norco**—*pop pl* ... LA-4
Norco (CCD)—*cens area* ... CA-9
*Norco-Goodhope* ... LA-4
Norco HS—*school* ... CA-9
Norco JHS—*school* ... CA-9
Norconian, Lake—*lake* ... CA-9
*Norconks Pond* ... PA-2
Norco Oil and Gas Field—*oilfield* ... LA-4
Norco Sch—*school* ... CA-9
Norcrest Sch—*school* ... FL-3
Norcross—*locale* ... VA-3
**Norcross**—*pop pl* ... GA-3
**Norcross**—*pop pl* ... ME-1
**Norcross**—*pop pl* ... MN-6
Norcross, William, House—*hist pl* ... MN-6
Norcross Brook—*stream* ... ME-1
Norcross Brook—*stream* ... NH-1
Norcross Brothers Houses—*hist pl* ... MA-1
Norcross (CCD)—*cens area* ... GA-3
Norcross Cem—*cemetery* ... ME-1
Norcross Chapel—*church* ... GA-3
Norcross Creek—*stream* ... OR-9
Norcross Hill—*summit* ... MA-1
Norcross Hill Brook—*stream* ... MA-1
Norcross Hill Cem—*cemetery* ... MA-1
**Norcross Hills (subdivision)**—*pop pl* ... TN-4
Norcross Hist Dist—*hist pl* ... GA-3
Norcross Lake—*lake* ... MN-6
Norcross Mtn—*summit* ... ME-1
Norcross Number Four Dam—*dam* ... MA-1
Norcross Number Three Dam—*dam* ... MA-1
Norcross Number 2 Dam—*dam* ... MA-1
Norcross Point—*cape* ... ME-1
Norcross Point—*cape* ... MA-1
Norcross Point—*cape* ... NY-2
Norcross Pond—*lake* ... ME-1
Norcross Pond—*lake* ... NH-1
Norcross Pond Number Four—*reservoir* ... MA-1
Norcross Pond Number One—*reservoir* ... MA-1
Norcross Pond Number Three—*reservoir* ... MA-1
Norcross Pond Number Two—*reservoir* ... MA-1
Norcross Ponds—*reservoir* ... MA-1
Norcross Run—*stream* ... PA-2
Norcross Spring—*spring* ... OR-9
Norcross Wash—*stream* ... NM-5
Norcum HS—*school* ... VA-3
**Norcum Park**—*pop pl* ... VA-3
**Nord**—*pop pl* ... CA-9
Nordahl Coulee—*valley* ... MT-8
Nordale Park—*park* ... OH-6
Nordale Sch—*school* ... AK-9
Nordan Branch—*stream* ... AL-4
Nordang Coulee—*valley* ... MT-8
Nordby Lake—*lake* ... WA-9
*Nord Durchfahrt* ... FM-9
*Nord-Durchfahrt* ... MP-9
Nordeen Slough—*lake* ... MN-6
Nordell Canyon—*valley* ... ID-8
Nordell Dam—*dam* ... ND-7
Norden—*locale* ... NE-7
**Norden**—*pop pl* ... AR-4
**Norden**—*pop pl* ... CA-9
Norden, Lake—*lake* ... SD-7
Norden Cabin—*locale* ... MT-8
Norden Cem—*cemetery* ... MN-6
Norden Ch—*church* ... MN-6
Norden East Cem—*cemetery* ... NE-7
Norden Gulch—*valley* ... CA-9
Norden Post Office (historical)—*building* ... SD-7
Nordenskiold House—*locale* ... CO-8
**Norden Township**—*pop pl* ... ND-7
**Norden Township**—*pop pl* (2) ... SD-7
Norden Township (historical)—*civil* ... SD-7
**Norden (Township of)**—*pop pl* ... MN-6
Norden Trinity Ch—*church* ... WI-6
Norden West Cem—*cemetery* ... NE-7
Nordhaus, Robert, House—*hist pl* ... NM-5
**Nordheim**—*pop pl* ... TX-5
Nordheim—*uninc pl* ... WI-6
Nordheim Cem—*cemetery* ... TX-5
Nordheim Ch—*church* ... ND-7
Nordheimer Creek—*stream* ... CA-9
Nordheimer Flat—*flat* ... CA-9
Nordheimer Lake—*lake* ... CA-9
Nordheim Flying K Airpark—*airport* ... NJ-2
Nordheim Gas Field—*oilfield* ... TX-5
Nordhoff Peak—*summit* ... CA-9
Nordhoff Ridge—*ridge* ... CA-9
Nordhoff Union HS—*school* ... CA-9
Nordhoff Union Sch—*school* ... CA-9
Nordhouse Sch—*school* ... MI-6
Nordica Hill—*summit* ... NY-2
Nordica Homestead—*hist pl* ... ME-1
Nordic Hills Country Club—*other* ... IL-6
*Nordic Hollow* ... MO-7
Nordic Hollow—*valley* ... MO-7
**Nordick**—*pop pl* ... VA-3
**Nordick (Township of)**—*pop pl* ... MN-6
**Nordic Park**—*pop pl* ... IL-6
**Nordic Valley Estates Subdivision**—*pop pl* ... UT-8
Nordic Valley Ski Area—*locale* ... UT-8
Nordin Cem—*cemetery* ... AR-4
Nordin Ranch—*locale* ... UT-8
Nord Island—*island* ... AK-9
Nord Lake—*lake* ... MN-6
*Nordland* ... SD-7
Nordland—*locale* ... IA-7
Nordland—*locale* ... WA-9
Nordland Cem—*cemetery* ... MN-6
Nordland Cem—*cemetery* ... ND-7
Nordland Cem—*cemetery* ... SD-7
Nordland Ch—*church* ... MN-6
**Nordland Township**—*pop pl* ... SD-7
**Nordland (Township of)**—*pop pl* (2) ... MN-6
Nordman—*locale* ... ID-8
Nordman Ditch—*canal* ... IN-6
Nordman Lake—*lake* ... MI-6
Nordmanna Cem—*cemetery* ... ND-7
**Nordmont**—*pop pl* ... PA-2
Nordmont Camp—*locale* ... PA-2
**Nordmore Township**—*pop pl* ... ND-7
Nord Myr Park—*park* ... MN-6
Nordness—*locale* ... IA-7
Nordonia HS—*school* ... OH-6
*Nordost-Durchfahrt* ... MP-9
Nord Pass—*gap* ... WY-8
Nordrum Lake—*lake* ... WA-9
*Nord-Spitze* ... MP-9
Nords Ranch—*locale* ... AZ-5
Nordstrom Arroyo—*stream* ... NM-5
Nordstrom Dam—*dam* ... SD-7
Nordwall Canyon—*valley* ... WY-8
*Nordwest Riff* ... PW-9
*Nordwest-Spitze* ... MP-9
Nordyke—*locale* ... NV-8
Nordyke Creek—*stream* ... VA-3
Nordyke (historical P.O.)—*locale* ... IA-7
Nordyke Island—*island* ... AK-9
Nordyke Pass—*gap* ... NV-8
Nordyk (historical)—*locale* ... IA-7
Norea del Rincon—*area* ... NM-5
Noreast Lake—*lake* ... FL-3
Nored Ranch—*locale* ... TX-5
Noregate Shop Ctr—*locale* ... IN-6
Norells Bell Ranch—*locale* ... CO-8
Norenberg Sch—*school* ... ND-7
Noren Creek—*stream* ... MI-6
**Norene**—*pop pl* ... TN-4
Norene Sch—*school* ... TN-4
Noren Lake—*lake* ... MI-6
Nore Numedahl Ch—*church* ... ND-7
**Nore (Township of)**—*pop pl* ... MN-6
**Norfield**—*pop pl* ... MS-4
*Norfield Bethel Baptist Church* ... MS-4
Norfleet—*locale* ... KY-4
Norfleet—*locale* ... NC-3
**Norfleet**—*pop pl* ... FL-3
Norfleet Cem—*cemetery* ... KY-4
Norfleet Cem—*cemetery* ... NC-3
Norfleet Ch—*church* ... MO-7
Norfleet Hollow—*valley* ... TX-5
Norfleet Pond—*reservoir* ... VA-3
Norfleet Sch—*school* ... MO-7
Norfleets Ferry Site (historical)—*locale* ... NC-3
Norfleet Turner Dam—*dam* ... TN-4
Norfleet Turner Lake—*reservoir* ... TN-4
Norflick Shore—*beach* ... NC-3
Norfolk—*locale* ... CO-8
Norfolk—*locale* ... MS-4
Norfolk—*locale* ... ND-7
**Norfolk**—*pop pl* ... CT-1
**Norfolk**—*pop pl* ... MA-1
**Norfolk**—*pop pl* ... NE-7
**Norfolk**—*pop pl* ... NY-2
**Norfolk**—*pop pl* ... OK-5
Norfolk Acad—*hist pl* ... VA-3
Norfolk Acad—*school* ... VA-3
Norfolk Airp—*airport* ... VA-3
Norfolk and Western Freight Station—*hist pl* ... OH-6
Norfolk And Western Overlook—*locale* ... VA-3
Norfolk And Western RR Depot—*hist pl* ... OH-6
Norfolk Bay—*bay* ... MI-6
Norfolk Bayou—*gut* ... MS-4
*Norfolk Brook* ... CT-1
Norfolk Brook—*stream* ... CT-1
Norfolk Camp—*locale* ... VA-3
Norfolk (census name for Norfolk Center)—*CDP* ... NY-2
Norfolk Center (census name Norfolk)—*other* ... NY-2
Norfolk Ch—*church* ... KY-4
Norfolk Ch—*church* ... MS-4
Norfolk City—*civil* ... VA-3
Norfolk City Hall—*hist pl* ... VA-3
Norfolk Country Club—*other* ... CT-1
Norfolk Country Club House—*hist pl* ... CT-1
*Norfolk County* ... VA-3
Norfolk County Courthouse—*hist pl* ... MA-1
Norfolk County Hosp—*hospital* ... MA-1
**Norfolk County (in PMSA 1120,1200, 6060)**—*pop pl* ... MA-1
Norfolk County Jail—*building* ... MA-1
Norfolk Creek—*stream* ... IA-7
Norfolk Downs Shelter—*hist pl* ... CT-1
**Norfolk Downs (subdivision)**—*pop pl* ... MA-1
**Norfolk Gardens**—*pop pl* ... VA-3
Norfolk General Hosp—*hospital* ... VA-3
Norfolk General Hospital Airp—*airport* ... VA-3
**Norfolk Highlands**—*pop pl* ... VA-3
Norfolk Hist Dist—*hist pl* ... CT-1
Norfolk HS—*school* ... MA-1
**Norfolk (ind. city)**—*pop pl* ... VA-3
Norfolk International Airp—*airport* ... VA-3
Norfolk International Terminals—*locale* ... VA-3
Norfolk Junior Coll—*school* ... NE-7
*Norfolk Lake* ... AR-4
Norfolk Lake—*lake* ... MS-4
Norfolk Landing—*locale* ... MO-7
Norfolk Landing (historical)—*locale* ... MS-4
Norfolk Municipal Azalea Gardens—*area* ... VA-3
Norfolk Naval Air Station—*military* ... VA-3
Norfolk Naval Public Works Center—*military* ... VA-3
Norfolk Naval Shipyard—*military* ... VA-3
Norfolk Naval Station—*military* ... VA-3
Norfolk Naval Supply Center—*military* ... VA-3
Norfolk Post Office (historical)—*building* ... MS-4
*Norfolk Reservoir* ... VA-3
*Norfolk Revetment - in part* ... MS-4
Norfolk (RR name for New London)—*other* ... TX-5
Norfolk Rsvr—*reservoir* ... WY-8
Norfolk Sch—*school* ... MA-1
Norfolk Sch—*school* ... SD-7
Norfolk Sch District No 6 (abandoned)—*school* ... MO-7
Norfolk Southern Industrial Park—*locale* ... NC-3
Norfolk Star Revetment—*levee* ... MS-4
*Norfolk State College* ... VA-3
Norfolk State Hosp—*hospital* ... NE-7
*Norfolk State University* ... VA-3
Norfolk Street Hist Dist—*hist pl* ... MA-1
**Norfolk (Town of)**—*pop pl* ... CT-1
**Norfolk (Town of)**—*pop pl* ... MA-1
**Norfolk (Town of)**—*pop pl* ... NY-2
Norfolk Township—*civil* ... SD-7
**Norfolk (Township of)**—*pop pl* ... MN-6
**Norfolk & Western Junction**—*pop pl* ... OH-6
**Norfolk & Western Junction**—*pop pl* ... VA-3
Norfolk Yard—*other* ... VA-3
Norford Lake—*lake* ... VT-1
**Norfork**—*pop pl* ... AR-4
Norfork Country Club—*other* ... NE-7
Norfork Dam—*dam* ... AR-4
Norfork Lake—*reservoir* ... AR-4
Norfork Lake—*reservoir* ... MO-7
*Norfork Rsvr* ... AR-4
*Norfork Rsvr* ... MO-7
*Norge* ... ND-7
**Norge**—*pop pl* ... OK-5
**Norge**—*pop pl* ... VA-3
Norge Storage Site—*hist pl* ... AK-9
Norgrain Hill—*summit* ... WY-8
*Noria* ... AZ-5
Noria—*locale* ... KS-7
Noria—*locale* ... NM-5
Noria Bee Windmill—*locale* ... TX-5
Noria Bueno Windmill—*locale* ... TX-5
Noria Caliente Flowing Well (Hot)—*well* ... TX-5
Noriacitas Creek—*stream* ... TX-5
Noria Dan Windmill—*locale* ... TX-5
Noria de la Compania Well—*well* ... TX-5
Noria del Bordo Windmill—*locale* ... TX-5
Noria del Charro Windmill—*locale* ... TX-5
Noria de Llano Windmill—*locale* ... TX-5
Noria de Tomas Windmill—*locale* ... TX-5
Noria Honda Windmill—*locale* ... TX-5
Noria Maria Well (Windmill)—*locale* ... TX-5
Noria Nueva Artesian Well—*well* ... TX-5
Noria Richie Windmill—*locale* ... TX-5
Norias—*locale* ... TX-5
Norias Cem—*cemetery* ... TX-5
Norias HQ King Ranch—*locale* ... TX-5
Norias Sch—*school* ... TX-5
Noria Tank—*reservoir* ... TX-5
Noria Viejo Well—*well* ... TX-5
Noria Willie—*locale* ... TX-5
Norice Lake—*lake* ... UT-8
Noriega Home Sch—*school* ... CA-9
Noriegas Island—*island* ... FL-3
Norin Creek—*stream* ... MN-6
Norin Plaza—*uninc pl* ... FL-3
Noris—*locale* ... KY-4
Noris Ch—*church* ... KY-4
Nork Creek—*stream* ... OR-9
Norkes Chapel—*church* ... AR-4
Norkett Branch—*stream* ... NC-3
Norkirk Sch—*school* ... WA-9
Norkok Butte—*summit* ... WY-8
Norkok Creek—*stream* ... WY-8
Norkok Meadows—*flat* ... WY-8
Norkok Meadows Creek—*stream* ... WY-8
Norks Pit—*cave* ... AL-4
**Norlake**—*pop pl* ... CA-9
Norland—*CDP* ... FL-3
Norland—*locale* ... VA-3
**Norland**—*pop pl* ... ID-8
Norland Ch—*church* ... ME-1
Norland Ch—*church* ... MN-6
Norland Ch—*church* ... ND-7
Norland Ditch—*canal* ... CO-8
Norland Methodist Preschool—*school* ... FL-3
Norland MS—*school* ... FL-3
**Norland Park**—*pop pl* ... IN-6
Norlands, The—*hist pl* ... ME-1
Norland Sch—*school* ... FL-3
Norland Shop Ctr—*locale* ... PA-2
Norlex Shop Ctr—*locale* ... NC-3
*Norlic* ... AZ-5
**Norlina**—*pop pl* ... NC-3
Norlina MS—*school* ... NC-3
Norlin Quadrangle Hist Dist—*hist pl* ... CO-8
Norma—*locale* ... WI-6
**Norma**—*pop pl* ... IL-6
**Norma**—*pop pl* ... LA-4
**Norma**—*pop pl* ... NJ-2
**Norma**—*pop pl* ... ND-7
**Norma**—*pop pl* ... TN-4
Norma Baptist Ch—*church* ... TN-4
Norma Bay—*bay* ... AK-9
Norma Beach—*locale* ... WA-9
Norma (CCD)—*cens area* ... TN-4
Norma Creek—*stream* ... OR-9
Norma Division—*civil* ... TN-4
*Normahiggen Brook* ... NJ-2
Normain Heights Park—*park* ... IN-6
*Norma Jean Addition* ... IN-6
**Norma Jean Addition**—*pop pl* ... IN-6
Norma Jean Mine—*mine* ... CO-8
Norma Jean No. 2 Mine—*mine* ... CO-8
*Normal* ... PA-2
Normal—*locale* ... AL-4
Normal—*other* ... KY-4
Normal—*other* ... VA-3
**Normal**—*pop pl* ... IL-6
**Normal**—*pop pl* ... IN-6
**Normal**—*pop pl* ... KY-4
**Normal**—*pop pl* ... PA-2
Normal—*uninc pl* ... TN-4
*Norma Lake* ... WI-6
Norma Lake—*lake* ... WI-6
Normal Branch—*stream* ... AL-4
Normal Cem—*cemetery* ... AL-4
**Normal Heights**—*pop pl* ... CA-9
Normal Heights—*uninc pl* ... KY-4
Normal Hill Hist Dist—*hist pl* ... LA-4
Normal Industrial and Collegiate Institute (historical)—*school* ... AL-4
**Normal Institute**—*pop pl* ... MD-2
*Normal Junction* ... IL-6
Normal Junction—*locale* ... AZ-5
Normal Park—*park* ... NE-7
Normal Park Elem Sch—*school* ... TN-4
Normal Post Office (historical)—*building* ... AL-4
Normal Sch Hist Dist—*hist pl* ... MA-1
Normal Sch (historical)—*school* ... MO-7
**Normal Square**—*pop pl* ... PA-2
**Normal Township**—*pop pl* ... ND-7
**Normal (Township of)**—*pop pl* ... IL-6
**Normalville**—*pop pl* ... PA-2
Norma Mines—*mine* ... AZ-5
*Norman* ... TX-5
Norman—*locale* ... AL-4
Norman—*locale* ... CA-9
Norman—*locale* ... GA-3
Norman—*locale* ... IA-7
Norman—*locale* ... PA-2
Norman—*locale* ... VA-3
Norman—*locale* ... WA-9
**Norman**—*pop pl* ... AR-4
**Norman**—*pop pl* ... FL-3
**Norman**—*pop pl* ... GA-3
**Norman**—*pop pl* ... IN-6
**Norman**—*pop pl* ... NE-7
**Norman**—*pop pl* ... NC-3
**Norman**—*pop pl* ... ND-7
**Norman**—*pop pl* ... OK-5
**Norman**—*pop pl* ... WV-2
**Norman**—*pop pl* ... WI-6
Norman, Felix Grundy, House—*hist pl* ... AL-4
Norman, Lake—*reservoir* ... AL-4
Norman, Lake—*reservoir* ... NC-3
Norman, Ruskin C., Site (41 HY 86)—*hist pl* ... TX-5
Norman Apartment Bldg—*hist pl* ... IA-7
Norman Apartments—*hist pl* ... CO-8
Norman-Blanton Cem—*cemetery* ... NC-3
Norman Branch—*stream* ... AL-4
Norman Branch—*stream* ... IL-6
Norman Branch—*stream* ... KY-4
Norman Branch—*stream* (2) ... MO-7
Norman Branch—*stream* ... TN-4
Norman Branch—*stream* ... TX-5
Norman Bridge—*bridge* ... AL-4
Norman Bridge South Shop Ctr—*locale* ... AL-4
Norman Brook—*stream* ... CT-1
Norman Canal—*canal* (2) ... LA-4
Norman Canyon—*valley* ... NM-5
Norman Canyon—*valley* ... OR-9
Norman (CCD)—*cens area* ... OK-5
*Norman Cem* ... TN-4
Norman Cem—*cemetery* ... KS-7
Norman Cem—*cemetery* (2) ... KY-4
Norman Cem—*cemetery* (3) ... MS-4
Norman Cem—*cemetery* ... NE-7
Norman Cem—*cemetery* ... NC-3
Norman Cem—*cemetery* ... ND-7
Norman Cem—*cemetery* (3) ... OH-6
Norman Cem—*cemetery* (4) ... TN-4
Norman Cem—*cemetery* ... TX-5
Norman Cem—*cemetery* ... WV-2
Norman Ch—*church* ... MO-7
Norman Ch—*church* (2) ... ND-7
Norman Chapel—*church* ... TN-4
*Norman Chapel Ch* ... TN-4
Norman Chapel Sch (historical)—*school* (2) ... TN-4
Norman Clyde Glacier—*glacier* ... CA-9
Norman Clyde Peak—*summit* ... CA-9
**Norman (County)**—*pop pl* ... MN-6
Norman County Courthouse—*hist pl* ... MN-6
Norman Cove—*bay* ... MD-2
Norman Cove—*valley* ... TN-4
Norman Cove Creek—*stream* ... MD-2
Norman Creek—*stream* ... AL-4
Norman Creek—*stream* ... CO-8
Norman Creek—*stream* (2) ... GA-3
Norman Creek—*stream* ... MD-2
Norman Creek—*stream* ... MO-7
Norman Creek—*stream* ... MT-8
Norman Creek—*stream* ... OR-9
Norman Creek—*stream* ... TN-4
Norman Creek—*stream* ... WI-6
*Norman Crossing* ... TX-5
**Normanda**—*pop pl* ... IN-6
Normanda Cem—*cemetery* ... IN-6
*Normandale* ... MN-6
**Normandale**—*pop pl* ... IL-6
Normandale Baptist Ch—*church* ... AL-4
Normandale Methodist Ch—*church* ... AL-4
Normandale Park—*park* ... MN-6
Normandale Park—*park* ... OR-9
Normandale Playground—*park* ... CA-9
Normandale Shop Ctr—*locale* ... AL-4
**Normandale (subdivision)**—*pop pl* (2) ... AL-4
Norman Dam—*dam* ... AL-4
**Normandie**—*pop pl* ... NJ-2
Normandie Ave Sch—*school* ... CA-9
Normandie Golf Club—*other* ... MO-7
Normandie Shop Ctr—*locale* ... KS-7
Normandin JHS—*school* ... MA-1
Normandin Spring—*spring* ... OR-9
Normandy—*locale* ... KY-4
**Normandy**—*pop pl* ... FL-3
**Normandy**—*pop pl* ... IL-6
**Normandy**—*pop pl* ... MO-7
**Normandy**—*pop pl* ... PA-2
**Normandy**—*pop pl* ... TN-4
**Normandy**—*pop pl* ... TX-5
Normandy—*uninc pl* ... FL-3
**Normandy Addition**—*pop pl* ... IN-6
Normandy Baptist Temple Kindergarten—*school* ... FL-3
**Normandy Beach**—*pop pl* ... NJ-2
Normandy Brake—*swamp* ... LA-4
Normandy Ch—*church* ... FL-3
Normandy Dam—*dam* ... TN-4
Normandy Ditch—*canal* ... IL-6
Normandy Farms—*hist pl* ... OH-6
Normandy First Baptist Ch—*church* ... TN-4
Normandy Grange—*hist pl* ... NY-2
Normandy Harbor—*bay* ... NJ-2
**Normandy Harbor**—*pop pl* ... NJ-2
**Normandy Heights**—*pop pl* ... MD-2
**Normandy Heights**—*pop pl* ... OH-6
**Normandy Heights (subdivision)**—*pop pl* ... NC-3
*Normandy Hill* ... IL-6
Normandy Hist Dist—*hist pl* ... TN-4
Normandy HS—*school* ... MO-7
Normandy Isle—*island* ... FL-3
Normandy Isle—*uninc pl* ... FL-3
Normandy JHS—*school* ... MO-7
Normandy Lake—*reservoir* ... TN-4
Normandy Lane Plaza (Shop Ctr)—*locale* ... FL-3
Normandy Mall—*locale* ... FL-3
**Normandy Manor**—*pop pl* ... DE-2
Normandy Manor—*uninc pl* ... FL-3
**Normandy Mobile Homes Estates (subdivision)**—*pop pl* ... UT-8
Normandy Park—*park* ... TX-5
**Normandy Park**—*pop pl* ... LA-4
**Normandy Park**—*pop pl* ... WA-9
**Normandy Park Subdivision**—*pop pl* ... UT-8
Normandy Post Office—*building* ... TN-4
Normandy Sch—*school* (3) ... FL-3
Normandy Sch—*school* ... OH-6
Normandy Sch (abandoned)—*school* ... MO-7
Normandy Sch (historical)—*school* ... TN-4
Normandy Shop Ctr—*locale* ... MO-7
**Normandy Shores**—*pop pl* ... FL-3
Normandy Shores Golf Course—*locale* ... FL-3
Normandy Square (Shop Ctr)—*locale* ... FL-3
**Normandy Subdivision**—*pop pl* ... UT-8
Normandy Township—*civil* ... MO-7
Normandy United Methodist Ch—*church* ... TN-4
*Normandy Villa* ... IL-6
**Normandy Village**—*pop pl* ... FL-3
Normandy Village Elem Sch—*school* ... FL-3
Normandy Waterway—*channel* ... FL-3
Normane State Dam—*dam* ... SD-7
Norman Fann Farm Airp—*airport* ... MO-7
Norman Fountain Dam—*dam* ... AL-4
Norman Fountain Lake—*reservoir* ... AL-4
*Norman Fountain Pond* ... AL-4
**Normangee**—*pop pl* ... TX-5
Normangee (CCD)—*cens area* ... TX-5
Normangee Cem—*cemetery* ... TX-5
Normangee City Park—*park* ... TX-5
Normangee Lake—*reservoir* ... TX-5
Norman Grove Ch—*church* (2) ... GA-3
Norman Gulch—*valley* ... MT-8
Norman G Wilder Wildlife Area—*park* ... DE-2
Norman Hall Sch—*school* ... VA-3
**Norman Heights (subdivision)**—*pop pl* ... NC-3
Norman Hill—*summit* ... ME-1
Norman Hill—*summit* ... TX-5
Norman Hist Dist—*hist pl* ... OK-5
Norman Hollow—*valley* ... AR-4
Norman Hollow—*valley* ... KY-4
Norman Hollow—*valley* (2) ... TN-4
Norman Homestead—*locale* ... MT-8
Normania—*locale* ... MN-6
**Normania Township**—*pop pl* ... ND-7
**Normania (Township of)**—*pop pl* ... MN-6
Norman Island—*island* ... MN-6
Norman Johnson Lake Dam—*dam* ... MS-4
Norman King Mine—*mine* ... NM-5
Norman Lake—*lake* (2) ... IN-6
Norman Lake—*lake* ... MN-6
Norman Lake—*lake* ... ND-7
Norman Lake—*reservoir* ... TN-4
Norman Lake Dam—*dam* ... MS-4
Norman Lake Dam—*dam* ... TN-4
Norman Lakes—*lake* ... WY-8
Norman Landing—*locale* ... SC-3
Norman Mill (Site)—*locale* ... NV-8
Norman Mines—*mine* ... NV-8
Norman Mountain—*ridge* ... AL-4
Norman Mtn—*summit* ... MT-8
**Normanna**—*pop pl* ... TX-5
Normanna Cem—*cemetery* ... MN-6
Normanna Cem—*cemetery* ... TX-5
Normanna Gas Field—*oilfield* ... TX-5
**Normanna Township**—*pop pl* ... ND-7
**Normanna (Township of)**—*pop pl* ... MN-6
Norman No. 1 Oil Well Site—*hist pl* ... KS-7
Norman Number One Oil Well—*oilfield* ... KS-7
Norman Number 1 Dam—*dam* ... SD-7
Norman Nystrou Dam—*dam* ... SD-7
Norman Oil Field—*oilfield* ... OK-5
Norman Olson Lake—*reservoir* ... IN-6
Norman Olson Lake Dam—*dam* ... IN-6
Normanook—*locale* ... NJ-2
Normanook Lookout Tower—*locale* ... NJ-2
Norman Otto Hill—*summit* ... ND-7
Norman Park—*park* ... CA-9
**Norman Park**—*pop pl* ... GA-3
Norman Park (CCD)—*cens area* ... GA-3
Norman Pond—*lake* ... NY-2
Norman Pond Knob—*summit* ... TN-4
Norman Post Office (historical)—*building* ... AL-4
Norman Public Sch (historical)—*school* ... MS-4
Norman Research Park—*locale* ... OK-5
Norman Ridge—*ridge* ... NY-2
Norman Rock Bend—*bend* ... IN-6
Norman Rockwell Museum—*building* ... PA-2
Norman Rsvr—*reservoir* ... NE-7
Norman Run—*stream* ... OH-6

Norman Run—stream ... WV-2
**Normans**—pop pl ... MD-2
Normans Bridge—bridge ... VA-3
Norman Sch—school ... AR-4
Norman Sch—school ... CA-9
Norman Sch—school ... LA-4
Norman Sch—school (2) ... MO-7
Norman Sch—school ... NE-7
Norman Sch (historical)—school ... MO-7
Norman Sch (historical)—school ... SD-7
Norman Sch (historical)—school ... TN-4
*Norman Schilling Dam* ... SD-7
Norman Schillinstad Dam—dam ... SD-7
Norman Sch Number 1—school ... ND-7
Norman Sch Number 2—school ... ND-7
Norman Sch Number 3—school ... ND-7
*Normans Creek* ... TN-4
Normans Creek—bay ... MD-2
Normans Creek Marsh—swamp ... MD-2
**Norman's Crossing**—pop pl ... TX-5
Normanside Country Club—other ... NY-2
*Normans Inlet* ... NC-3
Norman Site—hist pl ... MS-4
Normans Kill—stream ... NY-2
Normans Lake—reservoir ... AL-4
Norman Smith Legion Beach—locale ... NC-3
Normans Point—cape ... MD-2
Norman Spring—spring (2) ... AZ-5
Norman Spring—spring ... MO-7
Norman Springs—spring ... CA-9
Norman's Retreat—hist pl ... MD-2
*Norman's Run* ... OH-6
Normans Store (historical)—locale ... TN-4
Normans Store Post Office (historical)—building ... TN-4
*Norman Station* ... IN-6
Normanstone Parkway—park ... DC-2
*Normansville* ... NC-3
**Normansville**—pop pl ... NY-2
*Normans Woe* ... MA-1
Normans Woe—cape ... MA-1
Normans Woe Cove—cove ... MA-1
Normans Woe Rock—rock ... MA-1
Norman Tank—reservoir ... NM-5
**Normantown**—pop pl ... GA-3
**Normantown**—pop pl ... IL-6
**Normantown**—pop pl ... WV-2
Norman Township—civil ... MO-7
**Norman Township**—pop pl ... ND-7
Norman Township (historical)—civil ... ND-7
**Norman (Township of)**—pop pl ... IL-6
**Norman (Township of)**—pop pl ... MI-6
**Norman (Township of)**—pop pl (2) ... MN-6
Norman Townsite Oil Field—oilfield ... OK-5
Norman Valley—valley ... WI-6
Norman Valley Bridge—bridge ... TX-5
Norman Valley Cem—cemetery ... TX-5
**Normanville**—pop pl ... NC-3
Normanville (historical)—locale ... KS-7
*Norman Woe Point* ... MA-1
Norma Post Office—building ... TN-4
Norma Sch—school ... TN-4
Norma Spring—spring ... UT-8
Norma Station—locale ... NJ-2
**Norma Township**—pop pl ... ND-7
*Norma Woe Rock* ... MA-1
Normen Cem—cemetery ... KY-4
Norment Cem—cemetery ... TN-4
**Normikemark Estates Subdivision**—pop pl ... UT-8
**Normira**—pop pl ... MD-2
Normon Trail Lake—lake ... IA-7
Normont Sch—school ... CA-9
Normoyle Park—park ... TX-5
Norna Spring—spring ... OR-9
Norn Hill—summit ... CA-9
Nornside Ch—church ... LA-4
Noroeste, Cerro—summit ... CA-9
Noroma Creek—stream ... OR-9
Noroneke Lake—lake ... CT-1
Noron (historical)—locale ... KS-7
No Rope Pit—cave ... AL-4
**Noroton**—pop pl ... CT-1
**Noroton Heights**—pop pl ... CT-1
Noroton Neck—cape ... CT-1
Noroton Point—cape ... CT-1
Noroton River—stream ... CT-1
**Norpak**—pop pl ... ND-7
*Norpaul* ... IL-6
**Norphlet**—pop pl ... AR-4
Norphlet (Township of)—fmr MCD ... AR-4
Norquist Lake—lake ... MN-6
Norrback Sch—school ... MA-1
Norred Cem—cemetery ... TX-5
Norred Creek—stream ... ND-7
Norreigo Point—cape ... FL-3
Norrel Island—flat ... AR-4
Norrell—locale ... MS-4
Norrell, Lake—reservoir ... AR-4
Norrell Branch—stream ... AL-4
Norrell Ditch—canal ... CO-8
**Norrell Junction**—pop pl ... AL-4
Norrell Plantation (historical)—locale ... MS-4
Norrell Post Office (historical)—building ... MS-4
Norrell Ranch—locale ... CO-8
Norrell Sch—school ... VA-3
Norrell Sink—basin ... AL-4
Norrell Spur—locale ... AR-4
*Norrell Station* ... MS-4
*Norreys Hole* ... MA-1
Norrias Club Pond—lake ... FL-3
Norrick—locale ... TX-5
**Norridge**—pop pl ... IL-6
**Norridgewock**—pop pl ... ME-1
Norridgewock Center (census name Norridgewock)—other ... ME-1
Norridgewock Free Public Library—hist pl ... ME-1
Norridgewock Lake—lake ... NY-2
**Norridgewock (Town of)**—pop pl ... ME-1
**Norrie**—pop pl ... CO-8
**Norrie**—pop pl ... MI-6
**Norrie**—pop pl ... WI-6
Norrie Brook—stream ... WI-6
**Norrie Heights**—pop pl ... NY-2
Norrie Lake—lake ... WI-6
Norrie Park—park ... MI-6
Norrie Point—cape ... NY-2
Norrie State Park—park ... NY-2
**Norrie (Town of)**—pop pl ... WI-6
**Norrington Crossroads**—pop pl ... NC-3
Norrington Sch—school ... NC-3
*Norris* ... IN-6
*Norris* ... WY-8
Norris—locale ... GA-3
Norris—locale ... OK-5
**Norris**—pop pl ... IL-6
**Norris**—pop pl ... MS-4
**Norris**—pop pl ... MO-7
**Norris**—pop pl ... MT-8
**Norris**—pop pl ... OH-6
**Norris**—pop pl ... SC-3
**Norris**—pop pl ... SD-7
**Norris**—pop pl (2) ... TN-4
Norris—uninc pl ... PA-2
Norris, F. M., House—hist pl ... IA-7
Norris, Frank, Cabin—hist pl ... CA-9
Norris, Jewett, Library—hist pl ... MO-7
Norris, Lake—lake ... FL-3
Norris, Madison, and Fishing Bridge Museums—hist pl ... WY-8
Norris, Mount—summit ... VT-1
Norris, Mount—summit ... WY-8
Norris, Senator George William, House—hist pl ... NE-7
Norris Aquatic Center—locale ... TN-4
*Norris Branch* ... IL-6
Norris Branch—stream ... AR-4
Norris Branch—stream ... KY-4
Norris Branch—stream (3) ... NC-3
Norris Branch—stream ... OH-6
Norris Branch Canal—canal ... LA-4
Norris Bridge—bridge ... AL-4
Norris Bridge—bridge ... VA-3
Norris Brook—stream ... ME-1
Norris Brook—stream ... MA-1
Norris Brook—stream ... NH-1
Norris Brook—stream ... PA-2
Norris Camp State Game Ref—park ... MN-6
Norris Canal—canal ... CA-9
Norris Canyon—valley ... MT-8
Norris (CCD)—cens area ... GA-3
Norris (CCD)—cens area ... TN-4
Norris Cem—cemetery (2) ... AL-4
Norris Cem—cemetery ... AR-4
Norris Cem—cemetery ... GA-3
Norris Cem—cemetery (2) ... KY-4
Norris Cem—cemetery ... LA-4
Norris Cem—cemetery (2) ... MO-7
Norris Cem—cemetery ... NE-7
Norris Cem—cemetery ... NY-2
Norris Cem—cemetery (3) ... NC-3
Norris Cem—cemetery (2) ... OH-6
Norris Cem—cemetery ... OK-5
Norris Cem—cemetery (2) ... SC-3
Norris Cem—cemetery ... SD-7
Norris Cem—cemetery (3) ... TN-4
Norris Cem—cemetery (2) ... TX-5
Norris Cem—cemetery (2) ... VA-3
Norris Cem—cemetery ... WV-2
Norris Chapel—church ... AR-4
Norris Chapel—church ... GA-3
Norris Chapel—church ... IN-6
**Norris Circle (subdivision)**—pop pl ... AL-4
**Norris City**—pop pl ... IL-6
Norris City Cem—cemetery ... PA-2
**Norris Corner**—pop pl ... MD-2
**Norris Corner**—pop pl ... MA-1
*Norris Creek* ... CA-9
*Norris Creek* ... MT-8
*Norris Creek* ... TN-4
*Norris Creek* ... TX-5
Norris Creek—stream (2) ... CA-9
Norris Creek—stream ... CO-8
Norris Creek—stream (2) ... GA-3
Norris Creek—stream ... MI-6
Norris Creek—stream ... MS-4
Norris Creek—stream (3) ... MO-7
Norris Creek—stream ... NC-3
Norris Creek—stream (2) ... OR-9
Norris Creek—stream ... SC-3
Norris Creek—stream ... TN-4
Norris Creek—stream ... TX-5
Norris Creek—stream ... WY-8
Norris Creek Post Office (historical)—building ... TN-4
Norris Cut—channel ... FL-3
Norris Dam—dam (2) ... TN-4
Norris Dam Cave—cave ... TN-4
*Norris Dam Marina* ... TN-4
Norris Dam State Park—park ... TN-4
Norris Dead River—stream ... FL-3
Norris District—hist pl ... TN-4
Norris Ditch—canal (2) ... CO-8
Norris Ditch—canal ... IN-6
Norris Divide—ridge ... WY-8
Norris Division—civil ... TN-4
Norris Elem Sch—school ... TN-4
**Norris Estates (subdivision)**—pop pl ... AL-4
Norris Evaporation Station (historical)—building ... TN-4
Norris Field—park ... TN-4
Norris Ford—locale ... TN-4
Norris Ford Covered Bridge—hist pl ... IN-6
Norris Forestry Research Area—forest ... TN-4
Norris Fork—stream ... NC-3
Norris Geyser Basin—basin ... WY-8
Norris Glacier—glacier ... AK-9
Norris Graves Ranch—locale ... WY-8
Norris Gulch—valley ... MT-8
**Norris (Harristown)**—pop pl ... IN-6
Norris Hill—ridge ... NH-1
Norris Hill—summit ... ME-1
Norris Hill—summit ... MN-6
Norris Hill Cem—cemetery ... AR-4
Norris Hill Ch—church ... LA-4
*Norris Hill Church* ... AL-4
Norris Hollow—valley (2) ... AR-4
Norris Hollow—valley ... KY-4
Norris Hollow—valley ... MO-7
Norris Hollow—valley ... WI-6
Norris Hot Springs—spring ... MT-8
Norris House—hist pl ... CA-9
Norris HS—school ... AL-4
Norris HS—school ... MI-6
Norris Island—island (2) ... ME-1
Norris Island—island ... MI-6
Norris Junction—locale ... AL-4
Norris Junction—locale ... WY-8
*Norris Lake* ... MI-6
Norris Lake—lake ... CA-9
Norris Lake—lake (2) ... MN-6
Norris Lake—lake ... NE-7
Norris Lake—reservoir (2) ... GA-3
Norris Lake—reservoir ... MS-4
Norris Lake—reservoir (2) ... TN-4
Norris Lake Dam—dam ... MS-4
*Norris Landing* ... MS-4
Norris Lateral—canal ... ID-8
Norris Lookout Tower—locale ... MN-6
Norris Memorial Gardens—cemetery ... TN-4
Norris Mill (historical)—locale ... TN-4
Norris MS—school ... TN-4
Norris Mtn—summit ... AK-9
Norris Mtn—summit ... MT-8
Norris Mtn—summit ... VT-1
Norris Municipal Park—park ... TN-4
Norris Museum—locale ... WY-8
Norris Museum/Norris Comfort Station—hist pl ... WY-8
Norris Number One Mine (underground)—mine ... TN-4
Norris Park—park ... NE-7
Norris Park—park ... TX-5
**Norris Park**—pop pl ... TN-4
Norris Pass—gap ... WY-8
Norris Peak—summit ... SD-7
Norris Point—cape (2) ... ME-1
*Norris Pond* ... ME-1
*Norris Pond* ... NC-3
*Norris Pond* ... PA-2
Norris Pond—lake ... MD-2
Norris Pond—lake ... NY-2
Norris Pond—lake ... OR-9
Norris Pond—reservoir (2) ... AL-4
Norris Pond—reservoir ... VA-3
Norris Post Office—building ... TN-4
Norris Post Office (historical)—building ... MS-4
Norris Post Office (historical)—building ... TN-4
Norris Prong—stream ... VA-3
Norris Ranch—locale ... CA-9
Norris Ranch—locale ... CO-8
Norris Ranch—locale ... NM-5
Norris Ranch—locale ... TX-5
Norris Ranger Station—locale ... WY-8
*Norris Reservoir* ... TN-4
Norris Run—stream ... MD-2
Norris Run—stream ... OH-6
Norris Run—stream ... VA-3
Norris Sch—school (2) ... CA-9
Norris Sch—school ... CT-1
Norris Sch—school ... KS-7
Norris Sch—school ... MI-6
Norris Sch—school ... SD-7
Norris Sch—school ... TN-4
Norris Sch—school ... TX-5
Norris Sch—school ... WV-2
Norris Sch—school ... WI-6
**Norris Siding**—pop pl ... IA-7
Norris Slough—stream ... WA-9
Norris Spring—spring ... MT-8
Norris Springs—spring ... MT-8
Norris Square—locale ... PA-2
Norris-Stirling House—hist pl ... MD-2
Norris Taku Ridge—ridge ... AK-9
Norris Tank—reservoir ... AZ-5
Norris Tank—reservoir ... NM-5
*Norristown* ... IN-6
Norristown—locale ... GA-3
Norristown—locale ... OH-6
**Norristown**—pop pl ... AR-4
**Norristown**—pop pl ... GA-3
**Norristown**—pop pl ... IN-6
**Norristown**—pop pl ... PA-2
Norristown Area HS—school ... PA-2
Norristown Borough—civil ... PA-2
Norristown Cem—cemetery ... AR-4
*Norristown Dam* ... PA-2
Norris Town For—forest ... TN-4
*Norristown Interchange* ... PA-2
Norristown Junction—locale ... GA-3
Norristown Mtn—summit ... AR-4
**Norris Township**—pop pl ... SD-7
Norristown State Hosp—hospital ... PA-2
**Norrisville**—pop pl ... MD-2
**Norrisville**—pop pl ... PA-2
*Norriton* ... PA-2
Norriton Ch—church ... PA-2
Norriton Square—locale ... PA-2
*Norritonville* ... PA-2
Norritonville—locale ... PA-2
Norr Lake—lake ... MI-6
Norrod Cem—cemetery ... TN-4
Norrod Hollow—valley ... TN-4
Norrod Mtn—summit ... TN-4
Norroway Brook—stream ... MA-1
Norroway Pond—lake ... MA-1
Norrie Guard Station—locale ... CO-8
Norrsken, Lake—reservoir ... NJ-2
Norrs Mine (underground)—mine ... AL-4
**Norse**—pop pl ... TX-5
Norse Butte—summit ... CA-9
Norse Gold Mine—mine ... TX-5
Norse Hill—summit ... TX-5
Norseland—locale ... MN-6
Norseland Cem—cemetery ... MN-6
Norseland Ch—church ... MN-6
Norseland General Store—hist pl ... MN-6
Norseland Sch—school ... MN-6
Norseman Lake—lake (2) ... AK-9
Norseman Sch—school ... CA-9
Norse Peak—summit ... WA-9
Norse Pond—lake ... ME-1
Norseth, Martin, House—hist pl ... MN-6
Norshor Junction—locale ... MN-6
**Norske**—pop pl ... WI-6
Norstedt Lake—lake ... MN-6
**Nortac**—pop pl ... MS-4
*NortA VAR Mud Creek* ... MN-6
Norte, Paso del—gap ... TX-5
Norte Del Rio HS—school ... CA-9
Norte Vista HS—school ... CA-9
Norte Well—well ... UT-8
Norte Windmill—locale (4) ... TX-5
*North* ... AL-4
*North* ... IL-6
*North* ... IN-6
*North* ... MA-1
*North* ... RI-1
*North* ... TX-5
*North* ... UT-8
North—locale ... VA-3
**North**—pop pl ... IN-6
**North**—pop pl ... SC-3
North—post sta ... AR-4
North—post sta ... CA-9
North—post sta ... PR-3
North—uninc pl ... KY-4
North—uninc pl ... MA-1
North—uninc pl (2) ... MS-4
North—uninc pl ... NJ-2
North—uninc pl ... NY-2
North—uninc pl ... NC-3
North—uninc pl (2) ... TN-4
North, Austin, House—hist pl ... MT-8
North, Benjamin D., House—hist pl ... NY-2
North, James, House—hist pl ... MO-7
North, John A., House—hist pl ... WV-2
North, Rsvr—reservoir ... IN-6
North, Townsend, House—hist pl ... MI-6
North Aberdeen Hist Dist—hist pl ... MS-4
North abeyta Creek—stream ... CO-8
North Abilene—locale ... TX-5
**North Abington**—pop pl ... MA-1
North Abington Depot—hist pl ... MA-1
North Abington Station (historical)—locale ... MA-1
**North Abington (Township of)**—pop pl ... PA-2
North Absaroka Wilderness—area ... WY-8
North Abutment Public Use Area—park (2) ... MS-4
North Accomack Sch—school ... VA-3
North Acorn Creek—stream ... CO-8
*North Acres Baptist Church* ... TN-4
North Acres Ch—church ... TN-4
North Acres Park—park ... WA-9
**North Acres (subdivision)**—pop pl ... TN-4
**North Acton**—pop pl ... MA-1
**North Adams**—pop pl ... MA-1
**North Adams**—pop pl (2) ... MI-6
North Adams Cem—cemetery ... NY-2
North Adams City Hall—building ... MA-1
North Adams Country Club—locale ... MA-1
North Adams Junction—uninc pl ... MA-1
North Adams Oil Field—other ... MI-6
North Adams (Town of)—civil ... MA-1
North Adolph Windmill—locale ... TX-5
North Adrian Sch—school ... MI-6
**North Afton**—pop pl ... NY-2
**North Agawam**—pop pl ... MA-1
North Aiken—uninc pl ... SC-3
North Aiken Ch—church ... SC-3
North Aiken Sch—school ... SC-3
North Ajo Peak—summit ... AZ-5
*North Akron* ... OH-6
**North Akron**—pop pl ... OH-6
North Alabama Bend (historical)—bend ... SD-7
North Alabama Childrens Home—building ... AL-4
North Alabama Horticulture Substation—locale ... AL-4
North Alabama Hosp—hospital ... AL-4
*North Alabama Junction* ... AL-4
North Alabama Junction—locale ... AL-4
North Alabama Presbyterian Camp—locale ... AL-4
North Alabama State Fair Park—park ... AL-4
North Alameda Sch—school ... CO-8
North Alamosa Ditch—canal ... CO-8
**North Albany**—pop pl ... OR-9
North Albany—uninc pl ... GA-3
North Albany (CCD)—cens area ... OR-9
North Albany Club—locale ... WY-8
North Albany Point—cape ... MI-6
North Albemarle—uninc pl ... NC-3
North Albemarle Sch—school ... NC-3
North Albemarle (Township of)—fmr MCD ... NC-3
North Alder Brook—stream ... VT-1
North Alder Creek—stream ... AZ-5
North Alder Creek—stream ... CA-9
North Alder Creek Tank—reservoir ... AZ-5
**North Alexander**—pop pl ... NY-2
North Alexandria (RR name for Brush Creek)—other ... TN-4
North Alfalfa (CCD)—cens area ... OK-5
**North Alfred**—pop pl ... ME-1
North Alkali Creek—stream ... OR-9
North Alkali Creek—stream ... WY-8
North Alkali Creek Siphon—canal ... OR-9
North Alkali Drain—canal ... ID-8
North Alkali Draw—valley ... WY-8
North Alkali Draw Rsvr—reservoir ... OR-9
North Alkali Lake—lake ... OR-9
*North Alkali Rsvr* ... OR-9
North Alkali Spring—spring ... OR-9
North Allegheny HS—school ... PA-2
North Allegheny Intermediate Sch—school ... PA-2
*North Allen Church* ... AL-4
**North Alliance**—pop pl ... OH-6
North Alligator Bayou—stream ... AR-4
North Allis Cem—cemetery ... MI-6
**North Allis (Township of)**—pop pl ... MI-6
North Almond—locale ... NY-2
North Almond Cem—cemetery ... WI-6
**North Almont**—pop pl ... ND-7
*North Alton* ... IL-6
**North Alton**—pop pl ... IL-6
North Aluk Hill—summit ... AK-9
North Alum Creek—stream ... AR-4
North Amarillo—uninc pl ... TX-5
North Amber Cem—cemetery ... MI-6
North Amber Sch—school ... MI-6
*North Ambo Channel* ... MP-9
North Amboy—locale ... NY-2
Northam Cem—cemetery ... VT-1
Northam Creek—stream ... VA-3
North Amelong Creek—stream ... MT-8
North American Ch—church ... IL-6
*North American Creek* ... MT-8
North American Mine—mine ... MN-6
North American Mine—mine ... WA-9
North American Rockwell Corporation—facility ... KY-4
North America Rockwell Corporation—facility ... OH-6
**North Amherst**—pop pl ... MA-1
North Amherst Cem—cemetery ... MA-1
North Amish Cem—cemetery ... IA-7
**North Amity**—pop pl ... ME-1
**North Amityville**—pop pl ... NY-2
Northam Memorial Chapel and Gallup Memorial Gateway—hist pl ... CT-1
Northam Narrows—gut ... VA-3
Northampton Ch—church ... NY-2
*Northampton* ... IN-6
*Northampton* ... NY-2
**Northampton**—pop pl (2) ... MD-2
**Northampton**—pop pl ... MA-1
**Northampton**—pop pl ... PA-2
**Northampton**—pop pl ... VA-3
Northampton, City of—civil ... MA-1
*Northampton, Town of* ... MA-1
Northampton Area JHS—school ... PA-2
Northampton Area Senior HS—school ... PA-2
Northampton Beach Campsite—locale ... NY-2
Northampton Borough—civil ... PA-2
Northampton Country Club—locale ... MA-1
Northampton Country Club—other (2) ... PA-2
**Northampton County**—pop pl ... NC-3
**Northampton County**—pop pl ... PA-2
**Northampton (County)**—pop pl ... VA-3
Northampton County Courthouse Hist Dist—hist pl ... VA-3
Northampton County Courthouse Square—hist pl ... NC-3
Northampton County Prison—building ... PA-2
Northampton Creek—stream ... SC-3
*Northampton Dam* ... PA-2
Northampton Dam—dam ... PA-2
Northampton Downtown Hist Dist—hist pl ... MA-1
Northampton Downtown Hist Dist (Boundary Increase)—hist pl ... MA-1
Northampton Fire Tower—locale ... SC-3
**Northampton Heights**—pop pl ... PA-2
Northampton High East—school ... NC-3
*Northampton High West* ... NC-3
**Northampton Hills**—pop pl ... PA-2
Northampton HS—school ... MA-1
Northampton HS—school ... VA-3
Northampton JHS—school ... MA-1
Northampton Memorial Shrine—cemetery ... PA-2
Northampton Park—park ... NY-2
Northampton Reservoir Lower Dam—dam ... MA-1
Northampton Reservoir Upper Dam—dam ... MA-1
*Northampton River* ... NJ-2
Northampton Rsvr (Lower)—reservoir ... MA-1
Northampton Rsvr Upper—reservoir ... MA-1
Northampton Sch—school ... OH-6
Northampton Sch for Girls—school ... MA-1
**Northampton (Town of)**—pop pl ... NY-2
*Northampton Township* ... KS-7
Northampton (Township of)—civ div ... OH-6
**Northampton (Township of)**—pop pl (2) ... PA-2
*Northampton Valley Golf Course* ... PA-2
**Northampton (Wildwood Lake)**—pop pl ... NY-2
Northam Road Park—park ... OH-6
*Northams Brook* ... MA-1
Northam Sch—school ... CA-9
Northam Sch—school ... NV-8
Northam Sch—school ... VT-1
*Northams Narrows* ... VA-3
Northan Cem—cemetery ... NC-3
North Anchorage—bay ... AK-9
*North Anclote* ... FL-3
North Anclote Key—island ... FL-3
*North Anderson* ... IN-6
**North Anderson**—pop pl ... IN-6
North Anderson—uninc pl ... SC-3
North Anderson Elem Sch—school ... IN-6
*North Andover* ... MA-1
**North Andover**—pop pl ... MA-1
**North Andover**—pop pl ... WI-6
*North Andover Center* ... MA-1
**North Andover Center**—pop pl ... MA-1
North Andover Center Hist Dist—hist pl ... MA-1
*North Andover Depot* ... MA-1
North Andover HS—school ... MA-1
North Andover Mall—locale ... MA-1
North Andover Plaza—locale ... MA-1
**North Andover (Town of)**—pop pl ... MA-1
**North Andrew Gardens (subdivision)**—pop pl ... FL-3
North Andrews Garden Elem Sch—school ... FL-3
North Andrews Gardens—CDP ... FL-3
**North Andrews Terrace**—pop pl ... FL-3
North and South Boat Lake—lake ... FL-3
North and South Trail—trail ... OR-9
North Angleton Oil Field—oilfield ... TX-5
North Angosta Well No 1—well ... NM-5
North Angosta Well No 2—well ... NM-5
North Anna—locale ... VA-3
North Anna Nuclear Power Plant—other ... VA-3
North Ann Arbor Street Hist Dist—hist pl ... MI-6
North Anna River—stream ... VA-3
**North Annex**—pop pl ... CA-9
North Annville Elem Sch—school ... PA-2
North Annville (Township of)—civ div ... PA-2
**North Anson**—pop pl ... ME-1
North Ant Basin—basin ... ID-8
North Ant Canyon—valley ... ID-8
North Antelope Canal—canal ... OR-9
North Antelope Creek—stream ... NE-7
North Antelope Creek—stream ... NV-8
North Antelope Creek—stream ... TX-5
North Antelope Creek—stream ... WY-8
North Antelope Flat—flat ... ID-8
*North Antelope Hills Oil Field* ... CA-9
North Antelope Park—flat ... CO-8
North Antelope Spring—spring ... ID-8
North Antelope Spring—spring ... SD-7
North Antelope Valley (CCD)—cens area ... CA-9
North Anthonys Nose—summit ... NM-5
North Anthracite Creek—stream ... CO-8
North Antioch Cem—cemetery ... MO-7
North Antioch Ch—church ... TX-5
North Antioch Oil Field—oilfield ... OK-5
North Apache Creek—stream ... CO-8
**North Apollo**—pop pl ... PA-2
North Apollo Borough—civil ... PA-2
North Apollo Elem Sch—school ... PA-2
North Appleton—locale ... ME-1
*North Appoquinimink River* ... DE-2
**North Arab**—pop pl ... AL-4
North Arapaho Peak—summit ... CO-8
North Archer City Oil Field—oilfield ... TX-5
**North Ardmore**—pop pl ... PA-2
**North Argyle**—pop pl ... NY-2
North Arkansas Christian Sch—school ... AR-4
North Arlington—other ... VA-3
**North Arlington**—pop pl ... NJ-2
North Arm—bay ... AK-9
North Arm—bay ... CA-9
North Arm—bay (2) ... MN-6
North Arm—bay (2) ... OR-9
North Arm—canal ... IN-6
North Arm—channel ... AK-9
North Arm—valley ... CA-9
North Arm Beck Ditch—canal ... IN-6
North Arm Campground—park ... UT-8
North Arm Community Center—locale ... IL-6
North Arm Creek—stream ... AK-9
*North Arm Great Salt Lake* ... UT-8
North Arm Hood Bay—bay ... AK-9
North Arm Hoonah Sound—channel ... AK-9
North Arm Lake Itasca—lake ... MN-6
North Arm Moira Sound—bay ... AK-9
North Arm Naknek Lake—lake ... AK-9
North Arm Nuka Bay—bay ... AK-9
North Arm Port Houghton—bay ... AK-9
North Arm Rice Creek—stream ... CA-9
**North Arms**—pop pl ... MI-6
North Arm Sand Arroyo Bay—bay ... MT-8
North Arm Three Arm Bay—bay ... AK-9
North Arm Trout Lake—lake ... MN-6
North Arndell Windmill—locale ... TX-5
**North Aronimink**—pop pl ... PA-2
North Aroostook (Unorganized Territory of)—other ... ME-1
North Arpin Ch—church ... WI-6
North Arrastre Creek—stream ... CO-8
North Arrowhead Lake—reservoir ... PA-2
North Arrowhead Lake Dam—dam ... PA-2
North Arundel Hosp—hospital ... MD-2
North Arvada JHS—school ... CO-8
North Asbury Park—locale ... NJ-2
**North Ashburnham**—pop pl ... MA-1
*North Ashburnham Station* ... MA-1
North Ash Ch of the Nazarene—church ... KS-7
*North Ash Creek* ... UT-8
North Ash Creek—stream ... UT-8
**North Asheboro**—pop pl ... NC-3
**North Asheboro (census name Balfours)**—pop pl ... NC-3
North Asheboro JHS—school ... NC-3
North Ashford—locale ... CT-1
North Ashford Brook—stream ... CT-1
North Ashford Cem—cemetery ... CT-1
North Ashley Creek—stream ... MO-7
North Aspen Sch—school ... MD-2
*North Assabeth River* ... MA-1
North Asylum Bay—bay ... WI-6
North Atelope Draw—valley ... WY-8
North Athens—uninc pl ... AL-4
North Athens Baptist Ch—church ... TN-4
North Athens Sch—school ... GA-3
**North Atlanta**—pop pl ... GA-3
*North Atlantic Ocean* ... ME-1
North Atlantic Street Hist Dist—hist pl ... TN-4
North Atoka (CCD)—cens area ... OK-5
**North Attleboro**—pop pl ... MA-1
North Attleboro HS—school ... MA-1
North Attleboro JHS—school ... MA-1
*North Attleborough* ... MA-1
North Attleborough Town Center Hist Dist—hist pl ... MA-1
**North Attleborough (Town of)**—pop pl ... MA-1
**North Atwood**—pop pl ... KS-7
North Atwood Oil Field—oilfield ... OK-5
*North Auburn* ... ME-1
*North Auburn* ... NE-7
North Auburn—CDP ... CA-9
**North Auburn**—pop pl ... AL-4
**North Auburn**—pop pl ... ME-1
**North Auburn**—pop pl ... OH-6
North Auburn Cem—cemetery ... ME-1
North Auburndale Cem—cemetery ... WI-6
**North Augusta**—pop pl ... ME-1
**North Augusta**—pop pl ... SC-3
**North Augusta Addition**—pop pl ... IN-6
North Augusta (CCD)—cens area ... SC-3
North Augusta Golf Club—other ... SC-3
**North Aurelius**—pop pl ... MI-6
North Aurelius Sch—school ... MI-6
North Aurora—cens area ... CO-8
**North Aurora**—pop pl ... IL-6
North Aurora Island—island ... IL-6
North Austin—uninc pl ... TX-5
North Ave Commerical District—hist pl ... NJ-2
North Ave Commerical Hist Dist—hist pl ... NJ-2
North Ave Congregational Church—hist pl ... MA-1
*Northaven* ... IN-6
Northaven—uninc pl ... TX-5
Northaven Elem Sch—school ... IN-6
Northaven Park—cemetery ... TX-5
North Avenue—uninc pl ... WI-6
**Northaven Woods (subdivision)**—pop pl ... MS-4
North Ave Presbyterian Church—hist pl ... GA-3
North Avery Creek—stream ... IA-7
North Ave Sch—school ... CA-9
North Ave Sch—school ... GA-3
North Ave Sch—school ... OH-6
North Ave Sch—school ... TX-5
North Ave Sch—school ... WV-2
North Ave Station—building ... PA-2
North Ave U Sch—school ... TX-5
North Avon—locale ... NY-2
**North Avon**—pop pl ... WA-9
**North Avondale**—pop pl ... CO-8
North Avondale Sch—school ... OH-6
North Babcock—uninc pl ... FL-3
**North Babylon**—pop pl ... NY-2
North Badger Creek—stream ... ID-8
North Badger Creek—stream ... MT-8
North Badger Creek—stream ... WY-8
North Badger-Elbow Creek Trail—trail ... MT-8
North Badger Lake—lake ... MN-6
**North Bailey**—pop pl ... NY-2
North Bainard Creek—stream ... CO-8
North Baird Glacier—glacier ... AK-9
North Baker Lake—lake ... MN-6
North Baker Sch—school ... OR-9
North Baker Windmill—locale ... NM-5

North Baker Windmills—locale NM-5
North Bald CA-9
North Bald TN-4
North Bald Cap—summit NH-1
North Bald Eagle Creek PA-2
North Baldface—summit NH-1
North Bald Mountain NV-8
North Bald Mountain Tank—reservoir AZ-5
North Bald Mtn—summit CO-8
North Baldwin—locale ME-1
**North Baldwin**—pop pl NY-2
North Baldy CO-8
North Baldy—summit NM-5
North Baldy—summit WA-9
North Baldy Lookout Tower—pillar WA-9
North Baldy Mtn—summit CO-8
**North Bal Harbor**—pop pl FL-3
North Ballard Ch—church KY-4
North Ballston Spa—CDP NY-2
**North Baltimore**—pop pl OH-6
North Baltimore Town Hall—hist pl OH-6
North Bancroft—locale ME-1
North Bancroft Oil Field—oilfield LA-4
North Bangor ME-1
**North Bangor**—pop pl ME-1
**North Bangor**—pop pl NY-2
**North Bangor**—pop pl PA-2
North Bangor Station (historical)—building PA-2
North Bank—bar FL-3
North Bank—levee MS-4
North Banks—bay FL-3
North Bank Sch—school PA-2
North Bank Siding—locale OK-5
North Banner Lake—lake WY-8
North Baptist Ch—church IN-6
North Baptist Ch (historical)—church AL-4
North Bar Bay—bay WY-8
North Barber Creek—stream CA-9
North Bar Canyon—valley NV-8
North Bar Coulee—valley MT-8
North Bar Creek—stream MT-8
North Barcus Creek—stream CO-8
North Bar Lake MI-6
North Bar Lake—lake MI-6
**North Barnaby**—pop pl MD-2
**North Barnesboro**—pop pl PA-2
North Barnhart Road Draw—canal WA-9
North Barnstead—locale NH-1
North Barrel Spring—spring WY-8
North Barrel Springs Draw—valley WY-8
**North Barringer (historical)**—pop pl NC-3
**North Barrington**—pop pl IL-6
North Barry Rsvr—reservoir OR-9
North Bartlett Creek—stream WY-8
North Barton—locale NY-2
North Barton Gulch—valley CO-8
North Base—military CA-9
North Basin—basin ID-8
North Basin—basin ME-1
North Basin—basin MD-2
North Basin—basin UT-8
North Basin—basin WA-9
North Basin—bay NJ-2
North Basin—reservoir CA-9
North Basin Tank—reservoir AZ-5
North Basin Well—well NM-5
**North Bassett**—pop pl VA-3
North Bass Island—island OH-6
North Bass Island—other OH-6
North Bass Lake WI-6
North Bass Lake—lake (2) WI-6
North Bates Creek—stream WY-8
North Batesville Baptist Ch—church MS-4
North Bates Windmill—locale TX-5
North Bath ME-1
**North Bath**—pop pl ME-1
**North Baton Rouge**—pop pl LA-4
North Battle Creek—stream CO-8
North Battle Creek—stream WY-8
North Battle Creek Rsvr—reservoir CA-9
North Battle Mtn—summit NV-8
North Baxter—locale WY-8
North Baxter Basin—basin WY-8
North Bay CA-9
North Bay FL-3
North Bay TX-5
North Bay VA-3
North Bay—bay (2) AK-9
North Bay—bay AZ-5
North Bay—bay (2) CA-9
North Bay—bay CT-1
North Bay—bay FL-3
North Bay—bay (2) ME-1
North Bay—bay MA-1
North Bay—bay (4) MI-6
North Bay—bay (2) MN-6
North Bay—bay (7) NY-2
North Bay—bay (2) NC-3
North Bay—bay OK-5
North Bay—bay SD-7
North Bay—bay UT-8
North Bay—bay VA-3
North Bay—bay (4) WA-9
North Bay—bay WI-6
**North Bay**—pop pl NY-2
**North Bay**—pop pl (2) WI-6
North Bay—post sta MS-4
North Bay—reservoir UT-8
North Bay—swamp NY-2
**North Bay City**—pop pl MI-6
North Bay City Oil Field—oilfield TX-5
North Bay Community Ch—church FL-3
North Bay Dam—dam ND-7
North Bay Elem Sch—school MS-4
North Bay Houghton Lake—lake MI-6
North Bay Island—island FL-3
North Baylor Creek—stream TX-5
North Bayou MS-4
North Bayou—bay MI-6
North Bayou—gut (2) MS-4
North Bayou—stream (2) AR-4
North Bayou—stream (2) LA-4
North Bayou—stream MS-4
North Bayou Blue—stream TX-5
North Bayou Cocodrie Oil Field—oilfield LA-4
North Bayou Rapides Sch—school LA-4
North Bay Park (historical)—park FL-3
North Bay Point FL-3
North Bay Sch—school MI-6
**North Bay Shore**—pop pl NY-2
North Bayshore Park—park (2) FL-3
North Bay Shore Rec Area—park WI-6
North Bayside (CCD)—cens area OR-9
North Bay Stream—stream NY-2
North Bay View Park—uninc pl CA-9
**North Bay Village**—pop pl FL-3
North Bay Vista Park—park FL-3
North Beach OR-9
North Beach PW-9
North Beach—beach FL-3
North Beach—beach ID-8
North Beach—beach OR-9
North Beach—beach (2) WA-9
North Beach—locale OH-6
**North Beach**—pop pl CA-9
**North Beach**—pop pl MD-2
**North Beach**—pop pl NH-1
**North Beach**—pop pl NJ-2
**North Beach**—pop pl NY-2
**North Beach**—pop pl OR-9
**North Beach**—pop pl TX-5
North Beach Campground—locale CA-9
North Beach (CCD)—cens area WA-9
North Beach Community Hosp—hospital FL-3
**North Beach Haven**—pop pl NJ-2
North Beach Park—park MI-6
North Beach Park—park MO-7
**North Beach Park**—pop pl MD-2
North Beach Peninsula—cape WA-9
North Beach Plaza (Shop Ctr)—locale FL-3
North Beach Sch—school FL-3
North Beach Sch—school WA-9
North Beach Sch—school WI-6
North Beach State Park—park ID-8
North Beacon Mtn—summit NY-2
North Beall Windmill—locale TX-5
North Bear Branch—stream FL-3
North Bear Canyon Spring—spring MT-8
North Bear Creek CO-8
North Bear Creek KS-7
North Bear Creek PA-2
North Bear Creek—stream CO-8
North Bear Creek—stream IA-7
North Bear Creek—stream KS-7
North Bear Creek—stream WI-6
North Bear Creek—stream (3) WY-8
North Bear Lake—lake FL-3
North Bear Mtn—summit WY-8
North Beaver Brook—stream CO-8
North Beaver (CCD)—cens area OK-5
North Beaver Ch—church NC-3
North Beaver Creek CA-9
North Beaver Creek OR-9
North Beaver Creek WI-6
North Beaver Creek—stream (4) CO-8
North Beaver Creek—stream IA-7
North Beaver Creek—stream KS-7
North Beaver Creek—stream OR-9
North Beaver Creek—stream SD-7
North Beaver Creek—stream (3) WY-8
North Beaver Creek Ch—church WI-6
North Beaverdam Creek GA-3
North Beaverdam Lake—lake ME-1
North Beaver Dams Sch—school NY-2
North Beaver Mesa—summit UT-8
North Beaver (Township of)—civ div PA-2
North Beck Ditch—canal IN-6
North Becket MA-1
North Becket, Town of MA-1
North Becket Village Hist Dist—hist pl MA-1
North Beck Mine—mine UT-8
North Bedford Ch—church VA-3
North Bedias Creek—stream TX-5
North Bedke Spring—spring UT-8
North Beebe Spring—spring WA-9
North Bee Creek—stream OK-5
North Beede Rsvr—reservoir OR-9
North Bee House Creek—stream TX-5
**North Bel Air (subdivision)**—pop pl MD-2
**North Belgrade**—pop pl ME-1
**North Belgrade Station**—pop pl ME-1
North Bellcow Creek—stream OK-5
**North Belle Isle**—pop pl NY-2
North Bellevernon PA-2
**North Belle Vernon**—pop pl PA-2
North Belle Vernon Borough—civil PA-2
**North Belleville**—pop pl IN-6
North Belleville Mill Pond RI-1
**North Bellevue**—pop pl IA-7
**North Bell (Grange Hall)**—pop pl MI-6
**North Bellingham**—pop pl MA-1
North Bellingham Cem—cemetery MA-1
North Bellingham Sch—school WA-9
**North Bellmore**—pop pl NY-2
**North Bellport**—pop pl NY-2
North Bell Sch—school MI-6
**North Belmont**—pop pl NC-3
North Belmont (Belmont Junction)—CDP NC-3
North Belmont Elem Sch—school NC-3
North Beloit—uninc pl WI-6
**North Belridge**—pop pl CA-9
North Belridge Oil Field CA-9
North Belt—post sta TX-5
Northbelt Homesites IL-6
**North Belton**—pop pl SC-3
North Belton Cem—cemetery TX-5
North Beltrami (Unorganized Territory of)—unorg MN-6
North Bench—bench ID-8
North Bench—bench MT-8
North Bench—bench UT-8
North Bench Community Hall—locale MT-8
North Bend OR-9
North Bend—bend VA-3
North Bend—locale PA-2
North Bend—locale WV-2
Northbend—other WA-9
**North Bend**—pop pl LA-4
**North Bend**—pop pl MD-2
**North Bend**—pop pl MS-4
**North Bend**—pop pl NE-7
**North Bend**—pop pl OH-6
**North Bend**—pop pl OR-9
**North Bend**—pop pl WA-9
**North Bend**—pop pl WI-6
North Bend Air Force Station—military OR-9
North Bend Bottom—bend KY-4
North Bend Canal—canal LA-4
North Bend Carnegie Library—hist pl NE-7
North Bend Cem—cemetery IN-6
North Bend Cem—cemetery LA-4
North Bend Cem—cemetery (2) MS-4
North Bend Ch—church IA-7
North Bend Ch—church MS-4
North Bend Ch—church NC-3
North Bend Ch—church OH-6
North Bend Cutoff Ditch—canal NE-7
North Bend Lower Range Channel—channel OR-9
North Bend Municipal Airp—airport OR-9
**North Bend (Northbend)**—pop pl WA-9
North Bend Public Use Area—park VA-3
North Bend Range Channel—channel OR-9
North Bend Rec Area—park SD-7
North Bend Sch—school IL-6
North Bend Sch—school NY-2
North Bend State Park—park WV-2
**North Bend (Town of)**—pop pl WI-6
**North Bend (Township of)**—pop pl IN-6
North Bend Upper Range Channel—channel OR-9
North Benedict Windmill—locale TX-5
North Bennett Ch—church TX-5
North Bennett Creek—stream TX-5
North Bennett Creek—stream WY-8
North Bennett Well—well TX-5
**North Bennington**—pop pl VT-1
North Bennington Depot—hist pl VT-1
North Bennington Hist Dist—hist pl VT-1
North Bennington Rsvr—reservoir VT-1
North Benson Ch—church KY-4
North Benson Creek—stream KY-4
North Benton—locale MN-6
**North Benton**—pop pl OH-6
North Benton (CCD)—cens area OR-9
**North Benton (sta.)**—pop pl OH-6
**North Benton Station**—pop pl OH-6
North Benton Township—civil (2) MO-7
**North Bergen**—pop pl NJ-2
**North Bergen**—pop pl NY-2
North Bergen (Township of)—civ div NJ-2
North Bergen Yards—locale NJ-2
**North Berkeley**—pop pl WV-2
North Berkeley—uninc pl CA-9
**North Berkeley (North Berkeley Springs)**—pop pl WV-2
North Berkeley Springs—other WV-2
North Berlin Cem—cemetery OH-6
**North Bernardston**—pop pl MA-1
**North Berne**—pop pl OH-6
**North Berwick**—pop pl ME-1
North Berwick Center (census name North Berwick)—other ME-1
**North Berwick (Town of)**—pop pl ME-1
North Berwick Woolen Mill—hist pl ME-1
North Bessemer—locale MI-6
**North Bessemer**—pop pl PA-2
North Bessemer Sch—school MI-6
North Bessemer Yards—locale PA-2
**North Bethel**—pop pl ME-1
North Bethel Cem—cemetery MO-7
North Bethel Oil Field—oilfield OK-5
North Bethel Sch—school OK-5
North Bethel Sch (historical)—school MO-7
North Bethesda—CDP MD-2
North Bethesda JHS—school MD-2
**North Bethlehem**—pop pl NY-2
North Bethlehem (Township of)—civ div PA-2
North Beverly Cemeterys—cemetery MA-1
**North Beverly (subdivision)**—pop pl MA-1
North Bibb Ch—church AL-4
North Big Blue Creek—stream TX-5
North Big Creek—stream (2) AR-4
North Big Creek—stream IA-7
North Big Creek—stream KS-7
North Bight—bay (2) AK-9
North Big Island Oil Field—oilfield LA-4
North Biglow Lake—lake MT-8
North Big Rock (Township of)—fmr MCD AR-4
North Big Saddle Point—cape AZ-5
North Big Saddle Trick Tank—reservoir AZ-5
North Big Springs Rsvr—reservoir ID-8
**North Billerica**—pop pl MA-1
North Billings—unorg reg ND-7
**North Biloxi**—pop pl MS-4
North Biloxi Library—building MS-4
North Bingen—locale AK-4
**North Bingham**—pop pl PA-2
North Bingham Cem—cemetery PA-2
North Bingham Creek—stream TX-5
North Birch Creek—stream MT-8
North Bird Creek—stream OK-5
North Bird Island—island TX-5
Northbird Peak—summit AK-9
**North Birmingham**—pop pl AL-4
North Birmingham Baptist Ch—church AL-4
North Birmingham Ch of Christ—church AL-4
North Birmingham Ch of the Nazarene—church AL-4
North Birmingham Golf Course AL-4
North Birmingham Park—park AL-4
North Birmingham Presbyterian Ch—church AL-4
North Birmingham Sch—school AL-4
North Bishop Tank—reservoir AZ-5
North Bitch Creek—stream WY-8
North Bitch Creek Trail—trail WY-8
North Bitterswash Creek—stream NC-3
North Black Banks NY-2
North Black Banks Hassock—island NY-2
North Black Bay Oil and Gas Field—oilfield LA-4
North Blackbird Creek*—stream IA-7
North Blackbird Creek—stream MO-7
North Blackbird Creek—stream NE-7
North Blackfish Bayou—stream AR-4
North Blackjack Creek—stream MO-7
North Black Mountain Ch—church NC-3
North Black Rocks—summit UT-8
North Blacksnake ME-1
North Blacktail Butte—summit ID-8
**North Blandford**—pop pl MA-1
North Blandford Brook MA-1
North Blanford Cem—cemetery MA-1
North Blanket Creek OR-9
**North Blendon**—pop pl MI-6
**North Blenheim**—pop pl NY-2
North Blenheim Hist Dist—hist pl NY-2
North Blind Creek—gut FL-3
North Block—summit UT-8
North Bloomfield—locale CT-1
**North Bloomfield**—pop pl CA-9
**North Bloomfield**—pop pl NY-2
**North Bloomfield**—pop pl OH-6
North Bloomfield Sch—hist pl NY-2
North Bloomfield (Township of)—civ div OH-6
North Bloom Lateral—canal CA-9
North Blow Down Tank—reservoir AZ-5
North Blowout Rsvr—reservoir ID-8
North Blue Cem—cemetery NE-7
North Blue Earth Ch—church MN-6
North Blue Flats—flat UT-8
North Blue Hill—locale ME-1
North Blue Hole—lake MS-4
North Blue Lake—lake MI-6
North Blue Lake Group—lake OR-9
North Bluff WA-9
North Bluff—cliff AR-4
North Bluff—cliff WA-9
North Bluff—fmr MCD NE-7
North Bluff—summit WI-6
North Bluff Creek MN-6
North Bluff Creek—stream IN-6
North Bluff Point—cape NC-3
North Blvd Sch—school NJ-2
North Blye Tank—reservoir AZ-5
North Boat Ditch—canal AR-4
North Boat Lake—lake FL-3
North Boggy Creek OK-5
North Boggy Creek—stream OK-5
North Boggy Creek—stream TX-5
North Boggy Creek—stream WY-8
North Bogus Jim Creek—stream SD-7
North Bolton—locale NY-2
North Bombsite Windmill—locale TX-5
North Bonanza Mine—mine NV-8
North Bonfield Branch—stream IL-6
North Bonfield Brook IL-6
North Bon Homme State Public Shooting Area—park SD-7
North Bonita Canyon—valley AZ-5
North Bonito Prairie Tank—reservoir AZ-5
North Bonner Well—locale NM-5
North Bonnet Pond—lake FL-3
**North Bonneville**—pop pl WA-9
North Bonneville Archeol District—hist pl WA-9
**North Bonneville Subdivision**—pop pl UT-8
North Boomerang Extension—canal CO-8
North Boone Creek—stream WY-8
North Boone HS—school IL-6
**North Boonville**—pop pl MO-7
North Boothbay ME-1
**North Boothe**—pop pl AR-4
North Bootlegger Picnic Area—park MT-8
North Boquet Mtn—summit NY-2
Northboro MA-1
Northboro VT-1
**Northboro**—pop pl IA-7
Northboro Elem Sch—school FL-3
Northboro (RR name for Northborough)—other MA-1
Northboro (RR name for North Thetford)—other VT-1
Northboro Station VT-1
**Northborough**—pop pl MA-1
Northborough Center—other MA-1
Northborough (Northborough Center) RR name:Northboro—32CDP MA-1
Northborough Reservoir Dam—dam MA-1
Northborough Rsvr—reservoir MA-1
Northborough Town Hall—hist pl MA-1
**Northborough (Town of)**—pop pl MA-1
North Boscawen NH-1
North Bosque River TX-5
North Bosque River—stream TX-5
**North Boston**—pop pl NY-2
North Bottle Hollow Dam—dam UT-8
North Bottleneck Ravine MH-9
North Bouie Ch—church TX-5
North Boulder CO-8
North Boulder Creek CO-8
North Boulder Creek—stream CO-8
North Boulder Creek—stream ID-8
North Boulder Creek—stream OR-9
North Boulder Farmers Ditch—canal CO-8
North Boulder Park—park CO-8
North Boulder Ridge—ridge WA-9
North Boulder Spring—spring UT-8
North Boundary Butte Oil Field—oilfield UT-8
North Boundary Tank—reservoir AZ-5
North Boundary Trail—trail CO-8
North Boundary Trail—trail MT-8
Northbound Creek—stream ID-8
Northbound Lake—lake ID-8
North Bouquet Mountain NY-2
North Boxelder Creek—stream SD-7
North Boyer Gulch—valley NM-5
North Boylston—locale NY-2
North Boyne River MI-6
**North Braddock**—pop pl PA-2
North Braddock Borough—civil PA-2
**North Bradford**—pop pl ME-1
North Bradford Cem—cemetery ME-1
North Bradford Sch—school ME-1
**North Bradley**—pop pl MI-6
North Brae Sch—school CA-9
**North Brainerd (subdivision)**—pop pl TN-4
North Braman Oil Field—oilfield OK-5
North Branch IL-6
Northbranch KS-7
North Branch ME-1
North Branch MD-2
North Branch MA-1
North Branch MI-6
North Branch MN-6
North Branch MT-8
North Branch NV-8
Northbranch NJ-2
North Branch NY-2
North Branch OH-6
North Branch PA-2
North Branch WV-2
North Branch—canal MI-6
North Branch—fmr MCD NE-7
North Branch—gut CA-9
North Branch—lake NY-2
**North Branch**—pop pl IA-7
**North Branch**—pop pl KS-7
**Northbranch**—pop pl KS-7
**North Branch**—pop pl KY-4
**North Branch**—pop pl MD-2
**North Branch**—pop pl MI-6
**North Branch**—pop pl MN-6
**North Branch**—pop pl NH-1
**North Branch**—pop pl NJ-2
**North Branch**—pop pl NY-2
**North Branch**—pop pl WI-6
North Branch—stream IN-6
North Branch—stream KS-7
North Branch—stream NH-1
North Branch—stream NC-3
North Branch—stream WV-2
North Branch Absecon Creek—stream NJ-2
North Branch Adams Creek—stream LA-4
North Branch Akeley Run—stream PA-2
North Branch Alder Stream—stream ME-1
North Branch American Colony Canal—canal CA-9
North Branch Amos Palmer Drain—stream MI-6
North Branch Anderson Creek—stream MI-6
North Branch Appomattox River VA-3
North Branch Aquashicola Creek PA-2
North Branch Arnold Creek—stream IN-6
North Branch Ashwaubenon Creek—stream WI-6
North Branch Au Sable River—stream MI-6
North Branch Bad River MI-6
North Branch Ball Mountain Brook—stream VT-1
North Branch Bark River—stream MI-6
North Branch Bart Creek—stream MI-6
North Branch Basket Creek—stream NY-2
North Branch Battle River—stream MN-6
North Branch Bear Creek LA-4
North Branch Bear Creek—stream MI-6
North Branch Bear Creek—stream PA-2
North Branch Beaver Brook—stream WI-6
North Branch Beaver Creek—stream PA-2
North Branch Beaver Creek—stream WI-6
North Branch Beaverdam Creek—stream NJ-2
North Branch Belle River—stream MI-6
North Branch Ben Davis Creek—stream IN-6
North Branch Bennett Creek—stream MD-2
North Branch Bermudian Creek—stream PA-2
North Branch Big Blue River NE-7
North Branch Big Blue River—stream NE-7
North Branch Big Marsh Drain—stream MI-6
North Branch Big Mineral Creek—stream TX-5
North Branch Big Ox Creek—stream IN-6
North Branch Big Swamp Creek—stream MT-8
North Branch Big Timber Creek—stream NJ-2
North Branch Birch River—stream ME-1
North Branch Black Cat Brook—stream ME-1
North Branch Black Creek—stream NY-2
North Branch Blacklick Creek—stream PA-2
North Branch Black River MI-6
North Branch Black River—stream (2) MI-6
North Branch Black River—stream NY-2
North Branch Black River—stream VT-1
North Branch Black Valley—valley WI-6
North Branch Blackwater River—stream ME-1
North Branch Blackwater River—stream WV-2
North Branch Boardman River—stream MI-6
North Branch Boquet River—stream NY-2
North Branch Bowline Creek—stream ND-7
North Branch Bowman Creek—stream PA-2
North Branch Box Butte Creek—stream NE-7
North Branch Boxelder Creek—stream CO-8
North Branch Boxelder Creek—stream WY-8
North Branch Boyne River—stream MI-6
North Branch Brady Run—stream PA-2
North Branch Brassua Stream—stream ME-1
North Branch Brayley Brook—stream ME-1
North Branch Brick Kiln Branch—stream VA-3
North Branch Brook RI-1
North Branch Brook—stream MA-1
North Branch Brown Brook—stream CT-1
North Branch Browns Run—stream PA-2
North Branch Brushy Canyon—valley CA-9
North Branch Brushy Creek—stream TX-5
North Branch Buffalo Creek—stream PA-2
North Branch Bulkley Creek NY-2
North Branch Bull Valley UT-8
North Branch Bull Valley Creek UT-8
North Branch Bunnell Brook—stream CT-1
North Branch-Burlington Cem—cemetery MI-6
North Branch Burnt Mill Creek—stream FL-3
North Branch Caesar Creek—stream OH-6
North Branch Calkins Creek—stream PA-2
North Branch Callicoon Creek—stream NY-2
North Branch Calvin Run—stream PA-2
North Branch Camp—locale ME-1
North Branch Campbell Brook—stream ME-1
North Branch Camp Creek—stream NE-7
North Branch Camp Kettle Creek—stream OR-9
North Branch Canal—canal IL-6
North Branch Canal—canal WA-9
North Branch Cane Creek SC-3
North Branch Caney Creek—stream TX-5
North Branch Cantapeta Creek—stream ND-7
North Branch Cantepeta Creek ND-7
North Branch Carp River—stream MI-6
North Branch Carry Brook—stream ME-1
North Branch Carrying Place Stream—stream ME-1
North Branch Cascade River—stream MN-6
North Branch Casselman River—stream MD-2
North Branch Cass River—stream MI-6
North Branch Cave Gulch—valley WY-8
North Branch Cedar Creek—stream CO-8
North Branch Cedar Creek—stream KY-4
North Branch Cedar Creek—stream MI-6
North Branch Cedar Creek—stream WY-8
North Branch Cedar River—stream (2) MI-6
North Branch Cem—cemetery IN-6
North Branch Cem—cemetery IA-7
North Branch Cem—cemetery VT-1
North Branch Cem—cemetery (2) WI-6
North Branch Ch—church NE-7
North Branch Ch—church PA-2
North Branch Chanarambie Creek—stream MN-6
North Branch Chanta Peta Creek ND-7
North Branch Chase Stream—stream ME-1
North Branch Cherry Run—stream PA-2
North Branch Chicago River—stream IL-6
North Branch Chico Creek—stream CO-8
North Branch Chippewa River—stream (2) MI-6
North Branch Chopawamsic Creek—stream VA-3
North Branch Chub Creek—stream MN-6
North Branch Clear Creek—stream NY-2
North Branch Clear Creek—stream ND-7
North Branch Cleveland Canal—canal UT-8
North Branch Clifty Creek—stream IN-6
North Branch Clinton River—stream MI-6
North Branch Coal Run—stream OH-6
North Branch Cobb Creek—stream SD-7
North Branch Cobscook River ME-1
North Branch Cold River—stream VT-1
North Branch Cole Creek—stream MI-6
North Branch Cole Creek—stream PA-2
North Branch Colegrove Brook—stream PA-2
North Branch Cone Creek—stream MI-6
North Branch Conemaugh River PA-2
North Branch Conewango Creek—stream NY-2
North Branch Conjelos River—stream CO-8
North Branch Cooper River—stream NJ-2
North Branch Copper Creek—stream WI-6
North Branch CormoraA VAR Cormant River MN-6
North Branch Cormorant River MN-6
North Branch Corn Wash AZ-5
North Branch Corrumpa Creek—stream NM-5
North Branch Cottonwood Creek - in part NV-8
North Branch Cove Creek—stream OR-9
North Branch Cowanesque River—stream PA-2
North Branch Cowanshannock Creek—stream PA-2
North Branch Cozine Creek—stream OR-9
North Branch Crabgrass Creek—stream FL-3
North Branch Crane Creek—stream SC-3
North Branch Crawfish River—stream WI-6
North Branch Creek—stream MI-6
North Branch Creek—stream UT-8
North Branch Crockery Creek—stream MI-6
North Branch Crooked Creek—stream NE-7
North Branch Crooked Creek—stream WY-8
North Branch Cross Creek—stream OH-6
North Branch Cross Creek—stream TN-4
North Branch Crow Creek—stream IL-6
North Branch Crow Creek—stream WY-8
North Branch Crow River MN-6
North Branch Cucumber Run—stream PA-2
North Branch Cummings Creek—stream NY-2
North Branch Cypress Creek—stream LA-4
North Branch Dead River—stream ME-1
North Branch Deerfield River VT-1
North Branch Deerfield River—stream VT-1
North Branch Denton Creek—stream MI-6
NorthBranch Depot NJ-2
Northbranch Depot NJ-2
North Branch Depot—locale NJ-2
North Branch Devil River MI-6
North Branch Devils River—stream MI-6
North Branch Dicks Brook—stream NJ-2
North Branch Dicks Creek—stream OH-6
North Branch Double Springs Creek—stream OK-5
North Branch Douglas Creek—stream WI-6
North Branch Drain—canal MI-6
North Branch Dry Creek MT-8
North Branch Dry Creek—stream SD-7
North Branch Duck Creek—stream WI-6
North Branch Dudley Brook—stream ME-1
North Branch Eagle Creek—stream NE-7
North Branch Eagle Creek—stream OH-6
North Branch Echo Brook—stream ME-1
North Branch Ed Stone Branch—stream WV-2
North Branch Elk Creek—stream VA-3
North Branch Elk Creek—stream WI-6
North Branch Elkhart River—stream IN-6
North Branch Elkhorn Creek WV-2
North Branch Elkhorn River NE-7
North Branch Elk River—stream IA-7
North Branch Elm Creek KS-7
North Branch Elm Creek—stream OK-5
North Branch Elm River—stream ND-7
North Branch Elvoy Creek WI-6
North Branch Embarass River WI-6
North Branch Embarrass River—stream WI-6
North Branch Fall Creek—stream OR-9
North Branch Fall River Canal—canal ID-8
North Branch Fancy Creek KS-7
North Branch Fellows Creek—stream MI-6
North Branch Fish Creek—stream NY-2
North Branch Fishing Creek—stream MD-2
North Branch Fishpot Run—stream PA-2
North Branch Fish River AL-4
North Branch Five Creek—stream KS-7
North Branch Flint River—stream MI-6
North Branch Flower Creek—stream MI-6
North Branch Ford River—stream MI-6
North Branch Forest River—stream ND-7
North Branch Forest River Number 1 Dam—dam ND-7
North Branch Forest River Number 3 Dam—dam ND-7
North Branch Forest River Number 5 Dam—dam ND-7
North Branch Forest River Number 6 Dam—dam ND-7
North Branch Forked River—stream NJ-2
North Branch Fourmile Creek—stream AL-4
North Branch Fourmile Run—stream PA-2
North Branch Fox Brook—stream ME-1
North Branch French Creek - in part PA-2
North Branch Gale River—stream NH-1
North Branch Garner Creek ND-7
North Branch Garrison Creek—stream IN-6
North Branch Genesee Creek—stream WI-6
North Branch Gilbert Creek—stream WI-6
North Branch Glazier Brook—stream ME-1
North Branch Glendening Creek—stream NY-2
North Branch Gold Creek—stream MI-6
North Branch Goose River—stream ND-7
North Branch Grant Creek—stream IN-6
North Branch Grass River—stream NY-2
North Branch Great Chazy River—stream NY-2
North Branch Grindstone Creek—stream NY-2
North Branch Grindstone River—stream MN-6
North Branch Gulf Stream NY-2
North Branch Hackberry Creek—stream KS-7
North Branch Hackberry Creek—stream TX-5
North Branch Hamlin Brook—stream CT-1
North Branch Harbor Brook—stream CT-1
North Branch Harvey Creek WI-6
North Branch Harvey Creek—stream WI-6
North Branch Hasting Creek—stream TX-5

*North Branch Hefty Creek* ... WI-6
*North Branch Held Creek* ... MI-6
North Branch Hemlock Creek—*stream* ... NY-2
North Branch Hemlock Creek—*stream* (2) ... PA-2
North Branch Herman Creek—*stream* ... WA-9
North Branch Hickory Creek—*stream* ... KS-7
North Branch Hickory Creek—*stream* ... MI-6
*North Branch High Line Canal* ... AZ-5
North Branch Highline Canal—*canal* ... AZ-5
North Branch Hodge Run—*stream* ... PA-2
North Branch Hog Creek—*stream* ... MI-6
North Branch Holcomb Creek—*stream* ... MI-6
North Branch Holdens Creek—*stream* ... VA-3
North Branch Holmes Creek—*stream* ... WI-6
North Branch Honey Creek—*stream* ... WI-6
North Branch Hoosic River—*stream* ... MA-1
North Branch Hoosic River—*stream* ... VT-1
North Branch Hoosic River Rsvr—*reservoir* ... MA-1
North Branch Horne Brook—*stream* ... NH-1
*North Branch Housatonic River* ... MA-1
North Branch Hurricane Creek—*stream* ... MS-4
North Branch Hursey Ditch—*canal* ... IN-6
North Branch Independence Creek—*stream* ... KS-7
North Branch Independent Canal—*canal* ... ID-8
North Branch Indian Creek—*stream* ... NE-7
North Branch Indian Creek—*stream* ... NY-2
North Branch Indian Creek—*stream* ... OH-6
North Branch Indian Creek—*stream* ... PA-2
North Branch Indian Creek—*stream* ... VA-3
North Branch Indian Run—*stream* (2) ... PA-2
North Branch Iron River—*stream* ... MI-6
North Branch Island Canal—*canal* ... CA-9
North Branch Island Run—*stream* ... PA-2
North Branch Jacobs Brook—*stream* ... NH-1
North Branch Jennings Run—*stream* ... MD-2
North Branch Jennings Run—*stream* ... PA-2
North Branch J-N Creek—*stream* ... OK-5
North Branch Johns River—*stream* ... ME-1
North Branch Jones Falls—*stream* ... MD-2
*North Branch Jordan Creek* ... IN-6
North Branch Jordan Creek—*stream* ... MO-7
North Branch Kalamazoo River—*stream* ... MI-6
*North Branch Kawkawlin River* ... MI-6
North Branch Kawkawlin River—*stream* ... MI-6
North Branch King Creek—*stream* ... MS-4
North Branch Kings Creek—*stream* ... KS-7
North Branch Kishwaukee River—*stream* ... IL-6
North Branch Kisiwa Creek—*stream* ... KS-7
North Branch Knapp Creek—*stream* ... MT-8
*North Branch Knapps Creek - in part* ... PA-2
North Branch Knights Creek—*stream* ... WI-6
North Branch Kochville and Frankenlust Drain—*stream* ... MI-6
North Branch Kokosing River—*stream* ... OH-6
North Branch Kokosing River Lake—*reservoir* ... OH-6
North Branch Lake—*lake* ... NY-2
North Branch Lakes—*lake* ... MI-6
North Branch Lamoille River—*stream* ... VT-1
North Branch Larry Creek—*stream* ... IL-6
*North Branch Larrys Creek* ... IL-6
*North Branch Laurel Run* ... PA-2
North Branch Laurel Run—*stream* ... MD-2
*North Branch Laurel Run - in part* ... PA-2
North Branch Legionville Run—*stream* ... PA-2
*North Branch Levitt Creek* ... WI-6
*North Branch Levitts Creek* ... WI-6
North Branch Ley Creek—*stream* ... NY-2
North Branch Limbocker Drain—*canal* ... MI-6
North Branch Lincoln River—*stream* ... MI-6
North Branch Linton Creek—*stream* ... MI-6
North Branch Little Aughwick Creek—*stream* ... PA-2
North Branch Little Bear Creek—*stream* ... WI-6
North Branch Little Bear Creek—*stream* ... WY-8
North Branch Little Black Creek—*stream* ... NY-2
North Branch Little Conemaugh River—*stream* ... PA-2
North Branch Little Elk River—*stream* ... WI-6
*North Branch Little Fork River* ... MN-6
North Branch Little Heart River—*stream* ... ND-7
North Branch Little Hunting Creek—*stream* ... VA-3
*North Branch Little Medicine River* ... WY-8
North Branch Little Musquash Stream—*stream* ... ME-1
North Branch Little Pigeon River—*stream* ... MI-6
North Branch Little River—*stream* ... ME-1
North Branch Little River—*stream* ... WI-6
North Branch Little Salmon River—*stream* ... NY-2
North Branch Little Sulphur Creek—*stream* ... CA-9
North Branch Little Walnut River—*stream* ... KS-7
North Branch Little Wolf River—*stream* ... WI-6
North Branch Lizard Creek—*stream* ... IA-7
North Branch Lulbegrud Creek—*stream* ... KY-4
North Branch Macatawa River—*stream* ... MI-6
North Branch Macon Creek—*stream* ... MI-6
*North Branch Macon River* ... MI-6
*North Branch Mad River* ... NH-1
North Branch Mad River—*stream* ... NY-2
North Branch Maggie Creek—*stream* ... NV-8
North Branch Magowah Creek—*stream* ... MS-4
North Branch Mahantango Creek—*stream* ... PA-2
North Branch Manhan River—*stream* ... MA-1
North Branch Manistee River—*stream* ... MI-6
North Branch Manitowoc River—*stream* ... WI-6
North Branch Margaret Creek—*stream* ... OH-6
North Branch Marie DeLarme Creek—*stream* ... OH-6
*North Branch Marsh River* ... ME-1
North Branch Marsh River—*stream* ... ME-1
*North Branch Marsh Stream* ... ME-1
North Branch Marsh Stream—*stream* ... ME-1
North Branch Marten Creek—*stream* ... MT-8
North Branch McDonald Creek—*stream* ... WI-6
North Branch McKee Creek—*stream* ... IL-6
North Branch Medicine Lodge River—*stream* ... KS-7
North Branch Meduxnekeag River—*stream* ... ME-1
North Branch Meduxnekeag Stream—*stream* ... ME-1
North Branch Mehoopany Creek—*stream* ... PA-2
North Branch Menominee Creek—*stream* ... WI-6
North Branch Meshoppen Creek—*stream* ... PA-2
*North Branch Metedeconk* ... NJ-2
North Branch Metedeconk River—*stream* ... NJ-2
North Branch Middlebury River—*stream* ... VT-1
North Branch Middle Creek—*stream* ... PA-2
North Branch Middle Fork Owl Creek—*stream* ... WY-8
*North Branch Middle Fork Pole Creek* ... WY-8
North Branch Middle Fork Williams River—*stream* ... WV-2
North Branch Middle Fork Zumbro River—*stream* ... MN-6
North Branch Middle Lodgepole Creek—*stream* ... WY-8
North Branch Middle Loup River—*stream* ... NE-7
North Branch Milakokia River—*stream* ... MI-6
North Branch Mill Creek—*stream* ... MI-6
North Branch Mill Creek—*stream* (2) ... NY-2
North Branch Millers River—*stream* ... MA-1
North Branch Millers River—*stream* ... NH-1
North Branch Mill River—*stream* ... MA-1
North Branch Milwaukee River—*stream* ... WI-6
*North Branch Mineral Creek* ... TX-5
North Branch Miner Creek—*stream* ... MT-8
North Branch Mira Creek—*stream* ... NE-7
*North Branch Miry Creek* ... NE-7
North Branch Miscauno Creek—*stream* ... WI-6
North Branch Misery River—*stream* ... MI-6
North Branch Misery Stream—*stream* ... ME-1
North Branch Mission Creek—*stream* ... KS-7
North Branch Missisquoi River—*stream* ... VT-1
North Branch Mohawk River—*stream* ... NH-1
North Branch Montgomery Creek—*stream* ... PA-2
North Branch Moordener Kill—*stream* ... NY-2
*North Branch Moose Creek* ... PA-2
North Branch Moose River—*stream* ... NY-2
North Branch Mosquito Creek—*stream* ... CA-9
North Branch Mountain Brook—*stream* ... NY-2
North Branch Mount Lebanon Brook—*stream* ... MA-1
North Branch Mount Misery Brook—*stream* ... NJ-2
North Branch Mowry Brook—*stream* ... MA-1
North Branch Mtn—*summit* ... NY-2
North Branch Mud Creek—*stream* ... NE-7
North Branch Muddy Creek—*stream* ... OH-6
North Branch Muddy Creek—*stream* ... PA-2
North Branch Mud Run—*stream* ... PA-2
North Branch Murphy Creek—*stream* ... MI-6
North Branch Neshaminy Creek—*stream* ... PA-2
North Branch Neshobe River—*stream* ... VT-1
*North Branch Net River* ... MI-6
Northbranch Newport Creek—*stream* ... PA-2
North Branch Newton Brook—*stream* ... NH-1
North Branch Newton Creek—*stream* ... NJ-2
North Branch Newtown Creek—*stream* ... NY-2
North Branch Nibbs Creek—*stream* ... VA-3
North Branch Nippersink Creek—*stream* (2) ... IL-6
North Branch Nippersink Creek—*stream* ... WI-6
North Branch Norris Glacier—*glacier* ... AK-9
North Branch North Fork Elk River—*stream* ... CA-9
North Branch North Fork Stillaguamish River—*stream* ... WA-9
*North Branch North Fork Watonwan River* ... MN-6
North Branch North River—*stream* ... IA-7
North Branch Nulhegan River—*stream* ... VT-1
North Branch Oak Creek—*stream* ... TX-5
*North Branch Oconto River* ... WI-6
North Branch Oconto River—*stream* ... WI-6
*North Branch Of Kokosing Lake* ... OH-6
*North Branch Of Kokosing Reservoir* ... OH-6
*North Branch of Mill River* ... MA-1
*North Branch Of Pensauken Creek* ... NJ-2
*North Branch of Smith Creek* ... NV-8
*North Branch Of Sunrise River* ... MN-6
*North Branch of the Pawtuxet River* ... RI-1
*North Branch Of The sunrise River* ... MN-6
North Branch Ogontz River—*stream* ... MI-6
North Branch Oilspring Run—*stream* ... OH-6
North Branch Olamon Stream—*stream* ... ME-1
North Branch Old Mans Creek—*stream* ... IA-7
North Branch Oleander Canal—*canal* ... CA-9
North Branch Oliverian Brook—*stream* ... NH-1
North Branch Onancock Creek—*stream* ... VA-3
North Branch O'Neill Creek—*stream* ... WI-6
North Branch Orrs Creek—*stream* ... MI-6
North Branch Ottauquechee River—*stream* ... VT-1
*North Branch Ottawa River* ... MI-6
*North Branch Ottawa River* ... OH-6
*North Branch Otter Brook* ... NH-1
*North Branch Otter Creek* ... IN-6
North Branch Otter Creek—*stream* (2) ... IL-6
North Branch Otter Creek—*stream* ... IN-6
North Branch Otter Creek—*stream* ... KS-7
North Branch Otter Creek—*stream* ... MI-6
North Branch Otter Creek Bridge—*hist pl* ... KS-7
North Branch Otter River—*stream* ... MI-6
North Branch Owl Creek—*stream* ... CA-9
North Branch Paint River—*stream* ... MI-6
*North Branch Papillion Creek* ... NE-7
North Branch Park—*park* (2) ... MA-1
North Branch Park—*park* ... NJ-2
North Branch Park Gulch—*valley* ... CO-8
North Branch Park River—*stream* ... CT-1
North Branch Park River—*stream* ... ND-7
North Branch Patapsco River—*stream* ... MD-2
North Branch Paul Stream—*stream* ... VT-1
North Branch Pawpaw Creek—*stream* ... TN-4
North Branch Paw Paw River—*stream* ... MI-6
North Branch Pawtuxet River—*cape* ... RI-1
North Branch Peapack Brook—*stream* ... NJ-2
North Branch Pebble Creek—*stream* ... NE-7
North Branch Pelican River—*stream* ... WI-6
North Branch Pemebonwon River—*stream* ... WI-6
North Branch Pennsauken Creek—*stream* ... NJ-2
North Branch Penobscot River—*stream* ... ME-1
North Branch Pensaukee River—*stream* ... WI-6
*North Branch Pensauken Creek* ... NJ-2
North Branch Pentwater River—*stream* ... MI-6
North Branch Perley Brook—*stream* ... ME-1
North Branch Peshtigo Brook—*stream* ... WI-6
North Branch Peshtigo River—*stream* ... WI-6
North Branch Phelps Creek—*stream* ... KY-4
North Branch Phillips Creek—*stream* ... NY-2
North Branch Piedmont Creek—*stream* ... CA-9
North Branch Pigeon Creek—*stream* ... PA-2
North Branch Pigeon River—*stream* ... WI-6
North Branch Pike River—*stream* ... WI-6
North Branch Pine Creek—*stream* ... SD-7
North Branch Pine Creek—*stream* (2) ... WI-6
*North Branch Pine River* ... MI-6
North Branch Pine River—*stream* (3) ... MI-6
North Branch Pine River—*stream* (2) ... WI-6
North Branch Pipestone Creek—*stream* ... MN-6
North Branch Platte River—*stream* ... MI-6
*North Branch Pleasant River* ... ME-1
North Branch Pleasant Run—*stream* ... IN-6
North Branch Plum Bottom Creek—*stream* ... NY-2
North Branch Plum Creek—*stream* ... PA-2
North Branch Point Of Rocks Creek—*stream* ... NE-7
North Branch Pootatuck River—*stream* ... CT-1
North Branch Popple River—*stream* ... WI-6
North Branch Portage River—*stream* ... OH-6
North Branch Portfield Creek—*stream* ... CA-9
North Branch Potomac River—*stream* ... MD-2
North Branch Potomac River—*stream* ... WV-2
North Branch Prairie River—*stream* ... WI-6
North Branch Presque Isle Stream—*stream* ... ME-1
North Branch Pretty Run—*stream* ... OH-6
North Branch Quartermaster Creek—*stream* ... OK-5
*North Branch Queens Branch* ... OR-9
North Branch Quemahoning Creek—*stream* ... PA-2
North Branch Ranch Creek—*stream* ... OK-5
North Branch Rancocas Creek—*stream* ... NJ-2
*North Branch Rapide De Femme* ... ME-1
North Branch Rapid River—*stream* ... MN-6
North Branch Raritan River—*stream* ... NJ-2
North Branch Rice Creek—*stream* ... MI-6
North Branch Right Fork Garden Creek—*stream* ... VA-3
North Branch Ripley Creek—*stream* ... IN-6
North Branch River—*stream* ... NH-1
North Branch Robinsons Run—*stream* ... PA-2
North Branch Rock Creek—*stream* ... KS-7
North Branch Rock Creek—*stream* ... MD-2
North Branch Rock Run—*stream* ... PA-2
North Branch Rocky Brook—*stream* ... ME-1
North Branch Rolfe Brook—*stream* ... ME-1
*North Branch Root River* ... MN-6
North Branch Root River—*stream* ... MN-6
North Branch Ross Inlet—*stream* ... ME-1
North Branch Rough Run—*stream* ... PA-2
North Branch Rowdy Creek—*stream* ... TX-5
*North Branch Royal River* ... ME-1
*North Branch Run* ... PA-2
*North Branch Rush River* ... MN-6
North Branch Rush River—*stream* ... MN-6
North Branch Russell Brook—*stream* ... ME-1
*North Branch Salmon Brook* ... CT-1
*North Branch Salmon River* ... CT-1
North Branch Salmon River—*stream* ... NY-2
North Branch Salt Creek—*stream* ... NE-7
North Branch Salt Creek—*stream* ... OH-6
North Branch Salt River—*stream* ... MI-6
*North Branch Sand Creek* ... KS-7
North Branch Sand Creek—*stream* ... CA-9
*North Branch Sand Mountain* ... PA-2
*North Branch Sandy Creek* ... NY-2
North Branch Sandy Creek—*stream* ... MI-6
North Branch Sandy Creek—*stream* ... NY-2
North Branch Sandy River—*stream* ... VA-3
North Branch Santa Cruz Wash—*stream* ... AZ-5
North Branch Saquache Creek—*stream* ... CO-8
North Branch Saranac River—*stream* ... NY-2
*North Branch Saugatuck River* ... CT-1
North Branch Sawmill Run—*stream* ... NY-2
North Branch Sch—*school* ... MA-1
North Branch Sch—*school* ... VT-1
North Branch Settlement Branch—*stream* ... TX-5
North Branch Shamokin Creek—*stream* ... PA-2
*North Branch Sharpe Creek* ... KS-7
North Branch Sharps Creek—*stream* ... KS-7
North Branch Shier Drain—*canal* ... MI-6
North Branch Shingle Shanty Brook—*stream* ... NY-2
North Branch Silver Brook—*stream* ... MA-1
North Branch Silver Springs Creek—*stream* ... WY-8
North Branch Simpson Creek—*stream* ... VA-3
*North Branch Sioux Creek* ... WI-6
North Branch Slapneck Creek—*stream* ... MI-6
North Branch Slater Creek—*stream* ... MT-8
North Branch Slater Creek—*stream* ... WY-8
North Branch Slide Creek—*stream* ... NY-2
North Branch Slippery Rock Creek—*stream* ... PA-2
North Branch Smith Creek—*stream* ... FL-3
North Branch Snake Creek—*stream* ... NE-7
North Branch Snook Kill—*stream* ... NY-2
North Branch Snowy Creek—*stream* ... WV-2
North Branch Soper Brook—*stream* ... ME-1
North Branch South Branch Kishwaukee River—*stream* ... IL-6
*North Branch South Fork Beaver Creek* ... CO-8
*North Branch South Fork Beaver Creek* ... KS-7
North Branch South Fork Bens Creek—*stream* ... PA-2
North Branch South Fork Ogden River—*stream* ... UT-8
North Branch South Fork Panther Creek—*stream* ... KY-4
North Branch South Fork Pine Creek—*stream* ... PA-2
North Branch Spillman Creek—*stream* ... KS-7
North Branch Spoon Shop Brook—*stream* ... CT-1
North Branch Spring Brook—*stream* ... MI-6
*North Branch Spring Creek* ... PA-2
North Branch Spring Creek—*stream* ... VA-3
North Branch Spruce Brook—*stream* ... ME-1
North Branch Squaconning Creek—*stream* ... MI-6
North Branch Squankum Brook—*stream* ... NJ-2
North Branch State Creek—*stream* ... KS-7
North Branch Stearns Brook—*stream* ... ME-1
North Branch Stearns Brook—*stream* ... NH-1
North Branch Straight Run—*stream* ... PA-2
North Branch Sturgeon River—*stream* ... MI-6
North Branch Stutts Creek—*stream* ... MI-6
North Branch Suamico River—*stream* ... WI-6
North Branch Sucker Brook—*stream* ... VT-1
North Branch Sugar Creek—*stream* ... PA-2
North Branch Sugar River—*stream* ... NH-1
North Branch Sugar River—*stream* ... NY-2
North Branch Sugar Run—*stream* (2) ... PA-2
North Branch Sunrise River—*stream* ... MN-6
North Branch Swan Creek—*stream* ... MI-6
North Branch Swanson Creek—*stream* ... OR-9
North Branch Swift Creek—*stream* ... GA-3
North Branch Swift River—*stream* ... MA-1
North Branch Sycamore Creek—*stream* ... OH-6
North Branch Symmes Creek—*stream* ... OH-6
*North Branch Tenmile Creek* ... MI-6
*North branch Tenmile Creek* ... OH-6
North Branch Tenmile Creek—*stream* ... WI-6
North Branch Thoroughfare Brook—*stream* ... ME-1
*North Branch Thoroughfare Stream* ... ME-1
North Branch Three Brooks—*stream* ... ME-1
North Branch Thunder Bay River—*stream* ... MI-6
North Branch Timber Creek—*stream* ... NE-7
North Branch Timber Swamp Brook—*stream* ... NJ-2
North Branch Tobacco River—*stream* ... MI-6
*North Branch Toms River* ... NJ-2
North Branch Towanda Creek—*stream* ... PA-2
North Branch Townline Creek—*stream* ... MI-6
North Branch (Township of)—*civ div* ... MI-6
North Branch (Township of)—*civ div* ... MN-6
**North Branch (Township of)**—*pop pl* ... PA-2
North Branch Tracy Run—*stream* ... PA-2
North Branch Trail—*trail* ... VA-3
North Branch Trempealeau River—*stream* ... WI-6
North Branch Tributary Park—*park* ... MA-1
North Branch Trimble Glacier—*glacier* ... AK-9
North Branch Trout Brook—*stream* ... ME-1
North Branch Trout Brook—*stream* ... NY-2
North Branch Tule River—*stream* ... CA-9
North Branch Tupper Creek—*stream* ... WI-6
North Branch Turkey Creek—*stream* ... IN-6
North Branch Turkey River—*stream* ... IA-7
North Branch Turtle Creek—*stream* ... NE-7
North Branch Turtle Creek—*stream* ... OH-6
North Branch Turtle River—*stream* ... ND-7
*North Branch Tuscarora Creek* ... NY-2
North Branch Tuscarora Creek—*stream* ... NY-2
North Branch Twin Creek—*stream* ... MI-6
North Branch Two Hearted River—*stream* ... MI-6
North Branch Two Lick Creek—*stream* ... PA-2
North Branch Twomile Brook—*stream* ... ME-1
*North Branch Two Rivers* ... MN-6
North Branch Two Rivers—*stream* ... MN-6
North Branch Ulcohatchee Creek—*stream* ... GA-3
North Branch Upper Ammonoosuc River—*stream* ... NH-1
North Branch Upper Iowa River—*stream* ... MN-6
North Branch Upper Morgan Run—*stream* ... PA-2
North Branch Van Campen Creek—*stream* ... NY-2
North Branch Verdigre Creek—*stream* ... NE-7
North Branch Verdigris River—*stream* ... KS-7
North Branch Vickery Brook—*stream* ... ME-1
North Branch Volga River—*stream* ... IA-7
North Branch Wadleigh Brook—*stream* ... ME-1
North Branch Wakarusa River—*stream* ... KS-7
North Branch Wallace Run—*stream* ... PA-2
*North Branch Wallis Run* ... PA-2
North Branch Ward Creek—*stream* ... CA-9
North Branch Ward Creek—*stream* ... LA-4
North Branch Warehouse Creek—*stream* ... AK-9
North Branch Warren Canal—*canal* ... UT-8
North Branch Washington Colony Canal—*canal* ... CA-9
North Branch Water Gap Wash—*valley* ... WY-8
*North Branchwatonwan River* ... MN-6
North Branch Wedde Creek—*stream* ... WI-6
North Branch Weeping Water Creek—*stream* ... NE-7
North Branch Wells River—*stream* ... VT-1
*North Branch West Branch Escanaba River* ... MI-6
North Branch West Branch Sacandaga River—*stream* ... NY-2
North Branch West Branch Saugatuck River—*stream* ... CT-1
North Branch West Fork Big Blue River—*stream* ... NE-7
North Branch West Nodaway River—*stream* ... IA-7
North Branch West Papillion Creek—*stream* ... NE-7
North Branch West Twin Brook—*stream* ... ME-1
North Branch West Weber Canal—*canal* ... UT-8
North Branch Whippany River—*stream* ... NJ-2
North Branch Whistle Creek—*stream* ... WY-8
North Branch White Bear Creek—*stream* ... MT-8
North Branch White Creek—*stream* ... MI-6
North Branch Whiteface River—*stream* ... MN-6
North Branch White River—*stream* ... MI-6
North Branch White Rock Creek—*stream* ... KS-7
North Branch Whitney Brook—*stream* ... ME-1
North Branch Who Who Creek—*stream* ... CA-9
North Branch Wildcat Creek—*stream* ... SC-3
North Branch Wilford Canal—*canal* ... ID-8
North Branch Wilhite Creek—*stream* ... MS-4
North Branch Willow Creek—*stream* ... CA-9
North Branch Willow Creek—*stream* ... MI-6
North Branch Willow Creek—*stream* ... PA-2
North Branch Willow Run—*stream* ... MI-6
North Branch Wilson Canal—*canal* ... UT-8
North Branch Wilson Creek—*stream* ... WI-6
North Branch Wilsons Creek—*stream* ... MO-7
North Branch Winooski River—*stream* ... VT-1
North Branch Wiscoy Creek—*stream* ... NY-2
North Branch Wolf Creek—*stream* ... IN-6
North Branch Wolf Creek—*stream* ... NY-2
North Branch Wolf Creek—*stream* ... OH-6
North Branch Wolf Run—*stream* ... WV-2
North Branch Wood Stream—*stream* ... ME-1
North Branch Wreck Pond Brook—*stream* ... NJ-2
North Branch Wyalusing Creek—*stream* ... PA-2
North Branch Yellow Medicine River—*stream* ... MN-6
North Branch Zion Ch—*church* ... NE-7
*North Branch Zuleger Creek* ... MN-6
**North Branford**—*pop pl* ... CT-1
North Branford HS—*school* ... CT-1
**North Branford (Town of)**—*pop pl* ... CT-1
North Breakwater Lighthouse—*locale* ... MI-6
**North Brentwood**—*pop pl* ... MD-2
North Brentwood Sch—*school* ... MD-2
North Breton Brook—*stream* ... VT-1
North Breton Sch—*school* ... VT-1
**North Brevard**—*pop pl* ... NC-3
North Brevard Public Library—*building* ... FL-3
*North Brewer* ... ME-1
**North Brewer**—*pop pl* ... ME-1
*North Brewster* ... OH-6
**North Brewster**—*pop pl* ... OH-6
*North Brewster Island* ... MA-1
*North Brewton Baptist Church* ... AL-4
North Brewton Ch—*church* ... AL-4
*North Brewton Elementary School* ... AL-4
North Brewton Sch—*school* ... AL-4
*North Bridge* ... MA-1
North Bridge—*bridge* ... FL-3
North Bridge—*bridge* ... ME-1
**Northbridge**—*pop pl* ... MA-1
Northbridge—*uninc pl* ... SC-3
**Northbridge (census name Northbridge Compact)**—*pop pl* ... MA-1
**Northbridge Center**—*pop pl* ... MA-1
*Northbridge Centre* ... MA-1
Northbridge Ch—*church* ... SC-3
Northbridge Compact (census name Northbridge)—*other* ... MA-1
North Bridge Cove—*bay* ... TX-5
Northbridge HS—*school* ... MA-1
*North Bridgeport* ... CT-1
North Bridger Creek—*stream* ... WY-8
North Bridges Creek—*stream* ... MO-7
North Bridge Terrace—*uninc pl* ... SC-3
**Northbridge (Town of)**—*pop pl* ... MA-1
North Bridge Visitor Center—*building* ... MA-1
*North Bridgewater* ... MA-1
**North Bridgewater**—*pop pl* ... NY-2
*North Bridgewater, Town of* ... MA-1
North Bridgewater Brook—*stream* ... VT-1
North Bridgewater Cem—*cemetery* ... VT-1
North Bridgewater Ch—*church* ... OH-6
**North Bridgton**—*pop pl* ... ME-1
**North Brighton (subdivision)**—*pop pl* ... MA-1
**North Brinkley**—*pop pl* ... AR-4
North Brinton Cem—*cemetery* ... MI-6
**North Bristol**—*pop pl* ... OH-6
**North Bristol**—*pop pl* ... WI-6
North Bristol—*uninc pl* ... MA-1
North Bristol—*uninc pl* ... VA-3
North Bristol Cem—*cemetery* ... WI-6
North Bristol Sch—*school* ... WI-6
*North Britain Brook* ... VT-1
*North Brittain Brook* ... VT-1
*North Brnch* ... PA-2
**North Broadalbin**—*pop pl* ... NY-2
*North Broad River* ... GA-3
North Broad Street—*uninc pl* ... PA-2
North Broad Street Hist Dist—*hist pl* ... GA-3
North Broad Street Hist Dist—*hist pl* ... NY-2
North Broad Street Mansion District—*hist pl* ... PA-2
North Broad Street Residential Hist Dist—*hist pl* ... GA-3
North Broadway—*uninc pl* ... TX-5
North Broadway Hist Dist—*hist pl* ... MS-4
North Broadway Hist Dist—*hist pl* ... OH-6
North Broadway Park—*park* ... MN-6
North Broadway Sch—*school* ... KS-7
North Broadway-Short Street Hist Dist—*hist pl* ... KY-4
North Broadway Street Hist Dist—*hist pl* ... WI-6
*North Brokenback Creek* ... WY-8
*North Brook* ... CT-1
*North Brook* ... MA-1
*North Brook* ... VT-1
Northbrook—*locale* ... PA-2
**Northbrook**—*pop pl* ... IL-6
**Northbrook**—*pop pl* ... OH-6
**Northbrook**—*pop pl* ... TN-4
North Brook—*stream* (2) ... CT-1
North Brook—*stream* (4) ... ME-1
North Brook—*stream* (4) ... MA-1
North Brook—*stream* ... MN-6
North Brook—*stream* ... NH-1
North Brook—*stream* (3) ... NY-2
North Brook—*stream* ... PA-2
North Brook—*stream* (2) ... VT-1
Northbrook Ch—*church* ... MI-6
North Brook Ch—*church* ... NC-3
North Brook Country Club—*other* ... WI-6
*North Brook Elementary School* ... NC-3
**Northbrook Estates**—*pop pl* ... MD-2
**North Brookfield**—*pop pl* ... MA-1
**North Brookfield**—*pop pl* ... NY-2
North Brookfield Center—*CDP* ... MA-1
*North Brookfield Centre* ... MA-1
North Brookfield HS—*school* ... MA-1
North Brookfield (Town of)—*civil* ... MA-1
North Brook Golf Course—*other* ... MI-6
**Northbrook Hills**—*pop pl* ... PA-2
Northbrook Hist Dist—*hist pl* ... PA-2
**North Brook (historical)**—*pop pl* ... NC-3
*Northbrook Knolls* ... IL-6
**North Brooklin**—*pop pl* ... ME-1
**North Brookline**—*pop pl* ... NH-1
North Brook North Nepaug Brook—*stream* ... CT-1
Northbrook Park—*park* ... IL-6
Northbrook Plaza Shop Ctr—*locale* ... AL-4
North Brook Ridge—*ridge* ... ME-1
Northbrook Sch—*school* ... MI-6
North Brook Sch No 1—*school* ... NC-3
North Brook Sch No 2—*school* ... NC-3
North Brook Sch No 3—*school* ... NC-3
Northbrook Shop Ctr—*locale* ... IN-6
Northbrook Shop Ctr—*locale* ... ND-7
North Brooks Slough—*lake* ... ND-7
**North Brook (subdivision)**—*pop pl* ... TN-4
North Brooksville—*CDP* ... FL-3
**North Brooksville**—*pop pl* ... ME-1
North Brook (Township of)—*fmr MCD* ... NC-3
**Northbrook West**—*pop pl* ... IL-6
North Broons Canyon—*valley* ... UT-8
North Brother—*island* ... CT-1
North Brother—*summit* ... ME-1
North Brother Island—*island* ... NY-2
North Brothers Airp—*airport* ... IN-6
North Broward County Park—*park* ... FL-3
North Broward Day Sch—*school* ... FL-3
North Broward Hosp—*hospital* ... FL-3
North Browington Sch—*school* ... VT-1
*North Brown Creek* ... TX-5
North Brownie Creek—*stream* ... UT-8
North Browns Cem—*cemetery* ... TX-5
North Brown Sch—*school* ... KS-7
*North Browns Creek* ... TX-5
**North Brown Township**—*pop pl* ... KS-7
North Bruce Ch—*church* ... MI-6
North Bruff Creek—*stream* ... CO-8
*North Brunner Canyon* ... AZ-5
North Bruno Canyon—*valley* ... AZ-5
North Bruno Tank—*reservoir* ... AZ-5
**North Brunswick**—*pop pl* ... GA-3
**North Brunswick**—*pop pl* ... NJ-2
*North Brunswick Township* ... NJ-2
**North Brunswick (Township of)**—*pop pl* ... NJ-2
*North Brush Creek* ... CO-8
North Brush Creek—*stream* ... CO-8
North Brush Creek—*stream* (2) ... WY-8
North Brushy Creek—*stream* ... AR-4
North Brushy Creek—*stream* ... MO-7
North Brushy Creek—*stream* ... NE-7
North Brushy Creek—*stream* ... OK-5
North Brushy Windmill—*locale* ... TX-5
*North Bruster Island* ... MA-1
**North Bryant Township**—*pop pl* ... SD-7
North Buck Creek—*stream* ... WI-6
North Buck Creek—*stream* ... WY-8
North Buck Creek Cove—*bay* ... MO-7
North Buckeye Oil Field—*other* ... MI-6
**North Buckfield**—*pop pl* ... ME-1
North Buckhorn Well—*well* ... NM-5
North Buckley Lake—*lake* ... MN-6
North Buck Shoals (Township of)—*fmr MCD* ... NC-3
North Buckskin Creek—*stream* ... VA-3
**North Bucksport**—*pop pl* ... ME-1
North Bucks Trail Canyon—*valley* ... NV-8
North Buck Tank—*reservoir* ... AZ-5
**North Buena Vista**—*pop pl* ... IA-7
North Buena Vista (CCD)—*cens area* ... GA-3
North Buena Vista Historical Site—*other* ... PA-2
North Buena Vista Sch—*school* ... CO-8
**North Buffalo**—*pop pl* ... PA-2
North Buffalo—*unorg reg* ... SD-7
North Buffalo Ch—*church* ... PA-2
North Buffalo Chapel—*church* ... NC-3
North Buffalo Creek—*stream* ... NC-3
North Buffalo Creek—*stream* ... SD-7
North Buffalo Creek—*stream* ... VA-3
North Buffalo Creek—*stream* ... WY-8
North Buffalo Elem Sch—*school* ... PA-2
North Buffalo Fork—*stream* ... WY-8
North Buffalo Prairie Sch—*school* ... IL-6
*North Buffalo River* ... WI-6
**North Buffalo (Township of)**—*pop pl* ... PA-2
North Bull Creek—*stream* ... AZ-5
North Bull Creek—*stream* ... SD-7
North Bull Creek Tank—*reservoir* ... AZ-5
*North Bull River* ... MT-8
North Bully Creek—*stream* ... OR-9
North Buncombe HS—*school* ... NC-3
North Bunk Clay Well—*locale* ... NM-5
North Bunker Hill Sch—*school* ... OH-6
*North Burg Island* ... NY-2
North Burial Ground—*cemetery* ... MA-1
North Burial Ground—*hist pl* ... MA-1
North Burial Ground—*hist pl* ... RI-1
North Burke—*locale* ... NY-2
North Burke—*unorg reg* ... ND-7
North Burkett Windmill—*locale* ... TX-5
*North Burlington* ... VT-1
North Burlington—*uninc pl* ... NC-3
North Burned Timber Mtn—*summit* ... NM-5
North Burnett Island—*island* ... AK-9
North Burno Mtn—*summit* ... CO-8
North Burns Cem—*cemetery* ... OK-5
North Burn Spring—*spring* ... AZ-5
North Burnt Fork Creek—*stream* ... MT-8
North Burnt Timber Creek—*stream* ... CO-8
North Burris Island—*island* ... NC-3
North Burritt Cem—*cemetery* ... IL-6
North Burro Peak—*summit* ... UT-8
*Northbury* ... CT-1
**Northbush**—*pop pl* ... NY-2
**North Bush**—*pop pl* ... NY-2
**North Butler**—*pop pl* ... PA-2
North Butler Ch—*church* ... PA-2
North Butte—*summit* (2) ... AZ-5
North Butte—*summit* ... CA-9
North Butte—*summit* (2) ... ID-8
North Butte—*summit* ... NM-5
North Butte—*summit* (3) ... OR-9
North Butte—*summit* ... UT-8
North Butte—*summit* ... WA-9
North Butte—*summit* (2) ... WY-8
North Butte Cem—*cemetery* ... CA-9
*North Butte Creek* ... ND-7
North Butte Creek—*stream* ... CO-8
North Butte Creek—*stream* ... MT-8
North Butte Creek—*stream* ... ND-7
North Buzan Canyon—*valley* ... NM-5
North Buzzard Roost Mesa Tank—*reservoir* ... AZ-5
Northby Creek—*stream* ... MN-6
North Bynum Creek—*stream* ... MS-4
North Bypass Ditch—*canal* ... CA-9
**North Byron**—*pop pl* ... MI-6
North Byron Cem—*cemetery* ... NY-2
North Cabin Creek—*stream* ... MT-8
North Cabin Creek—*stream* ... WY-8
North Cache JHS—*school* ... UT-8
*North Cache Middle School* ... UT-8
North Cactus Windmill—*locale* ... TX-5
North Caddo Community Sch—*school* ... LA-4
North Caddo HS—*school* ... LA-4
**North Cadillac**—*pop pl* ... MI-6
North Cadron Ridge—*ridge* ... AR-4
North Caineville Mesa—*summit* ... UT-8
North Caineville Reef—*ridge* ... UT-8
**North Cairo**—*pop pl* ... IL-6
**North Calais**—*pop pl* ... VT-1
North Calais Sch—*school* ... VT-1
*North Caldwell* ... NJ-2
North Caldwell—*locale* ... WV-2
North Caldwell Hist Dist—*hist pl* ... ID-8
North Caldwell Sch—*school* ... NJ-2
**North Caldwell (Township of)**—*pop pl* ... NJ-2
North Calimus Spring—*spring* ... OR-9
North Callahan Creek—*stream* ... ID-8
North Callahan Creek—*stream* ... MT-8
North Calvary Baptist Ch—*church* ... MS-4
North Calvary Tabernacle—*church* ... LA-4
North Cambridge—*locale* ... NY-2
**North Cambridge**—*pop pl* ... VT-1
**North Cambridge (subdivision)**—*pop pl* ... MA-1
**North Camelia Acres**—*pop pl* ... VA-3
**North Camellia Acres**—*pop pl* ... VA-3
North Cameron—*locale* ... NY-2
North Camp—*locale* ... NM-5

North Creek Ch—*church* NC-3
North Creek Ch—*church* TX-5
North Creek Chapel—*church* PA-2
North Creek Dam—*dam* UT-8
North Creek Draw—*valley* TX-5
North Creek Draw—*valley* UT-8
North Creek Pass—*gap* UT-8
Northcreek Plaza Shop Ctr—*locale* AL-4
North Creek Recreation Site—*park* UT-8
North Creek RR Station Complex—*hist pl* NY-2
North Creek Rsvr—*reservoir* CO-8
North Creek Rsvr—*reservoir* NY-2
North Creek Rsvr—*reservoir* OR-9
North Creek Rsvr—*reservoir* UT-8
North Creek School—*locale* WA-9
North Creek Spring—*spring* (2) NV-8
North Creek Trail—*trail* CO-8
North Creek Truck Trail—*trail* WA-9
North Creek Windmill—*locale* (2) NM-5
North Creek Windmill—*locale* TX-5
North Creighton Sch—*school* SD-7
*Northcrest* IN-6
**Northcrest**—*pop pl* CA-9
**North Crest**—*pop pl* FL-3
**Northcrest**—*pop pl* IN-6
**Northcrest**—*pop pl* TX-5
Northcrest Baptist Ch—*church* MS-4
**Northcrest Estates**—*pop pl* TX-5
**North Crest Manor (subdivision)**—*pop pl* UT-8
North Crestone Campground—*locale* CO-8
North Crestone Creek—*stream* CO-8
North Crestone Ditch—*canal* CO-8
North Crestone Lake—*lake* CO-8
Northcrest Park—*park* TX-5
**North Crest Park Condominium**—*pop pl* UT-8
Northcrest Sch—*school* IL-6
**Northcrest (subdivision)**—*pop pl* AL-4
**Northcrest (subdivision)**—*pop pl* DE-2
**Northcrest Subdivision**—*pop pl* UT-8
North Crillon Glacier—*glacier* AK-9
North Criner Creek—*stream* OK-5
North Crockett Community Center—*locale* TX-5
*Northcroft Mountain* WA-9
North Croghan—*locale* NY-2
North Croghan Crossing—*locale* NY-2
**North Cromwell**—*pop pl* CT-1
*North Cronin Creek* OR-9
North Crooked Brook—*stream* ME-1
North Crooked Creek—*stream* OH-6
North Crooked Lake—*lake* MI-6
Northcross Cem—*cemetery* MS-4
North Cross Creek—*stream* (2) TN-4
**North Crossett**—*pop pl* AR-4
*North Cross Lake* MN-6
North Cross Ranch—*locale* WY-8
**North Crossroads**—*pop pl* MS-4
North Cross Roads Cem—*cemetery* MS-4
North Cross Sch—*school* VA-3
**North Crossville Addition**—*pop pl* TN-4
**North Crosswicks**—*pop pl* NJ-2
North Croton Creek—*stream* TX-5
North Crow Community House—*locale* MT-8
North Crow Creek—*stream* MT-8
North Crow Creek—*stream* WY-8
North Crow Creek Campground—*locale* MT-8
North Crow Creek Canyon—*valley* MT-8
North Crow Diversion Rsvr—*reservoir* WY-8
North Crowley Oil and Gas Field—*oilfield* LA-4
North Crow Sch—*school* WY-8
**North Crows Nest**—*pop pl* IN-6
North Crow Windmill—*locale* TX-5
North Crystal Lake—*lake* FL-3
**North Cuba**—*pop pl* NY-2
**North Cucamonga**—*pop pl* CA-9
North Cumberland Elem Sch—*school* TN-4
North Cummings Lake—*lake* WI-6
North Curtis Canyon—*valley* NM-5
North Curtis Creek—*stream* WY-8
North Curtis Ranch—*locale* TX-5
**North Cushing**—*pop pl* ME-1
North Custer—*cens area* MT-8
Northcut Bay—*bay* MI-6
Northcut Branch—*stream* MO-7
North Cut Ditch—*canal* MO-7
North Cutler—*locale* ME-1
*Northcuts Cove Sch* TN-4
Northcutt—*locale* GA-3
Northcutt—*locale* KY-4
Northcutt, H. B., House—*hist pl* TN-4
Northcutt Branch—*stream* (2) TN-4
Northcutt Cave—*cave* TN-4
Northcutt Cem—*cemetery* KY-4
Northcutt Cem—*cemetery* TN-4
*Northcutt Cove School* TN-4
Northcutt House—*hist pl* TX-5
Northcutt Plantation—*hist pl* TN-4
Northcutt Post Office (historical)—*building* AL-4
*Northcutt Sch* TN-4
Northcutt Sch—*school* TX-5
**Northcutts Cove**—*pop pl* TN-4
Northcutts Cove—*valley* TN-4
Northcutts Cove Cem—*cemetery* TN-4
Northcutts Cove Ch—*church* TN-4
Northcutts Cove Chapel—*hist pl* TN-4
*Northcutts Cove Ch of Christ* TN-4
Northcutts Cove Sch—*school* TN-4
North Cypress Creek—*stream* AR-4
North Cypress Creek—*stream* TX-5
North Cypress Lake—*reservoir* MS-4
North Dade Bible Ch—*church* FL-3
North Dade Ch—*church* GA-3
North Dade Christian Sch—*school* FL-3
North Dade Community Ch—*church* FL-3
*North Dade Country Club* FL-3
North Dade Detention Center—*locale* FL-3
North Dade Health Center—*locale* FL-3
North Dade JHS—*school* FL-3
North Dade JHS Park—*school* FL-3
North Dade Optimists Club Park—*park* FL-3
North Dade Regional Acad—*school* (2) FL-3
North Dade Sch—*school* GA-3
North Dadeville—*locale* AL-4
North Dakota Agriculture Coll—*school* ND-7
North Dakota Cem—*cemetery* WI-6
North Dakota Fisheries Mngmt Area—*park* ND-7
North Dakota Sch of Forestry—*school* ND-7
North Dakota State Univ District—*hist pl* ND-7
*North Dakota State University* ND-7
*Northdale* MN-6
Northdale—*locale* CO-8
**Northdale**—*pop pl* MN-6
Northdale—*post sta* FL-3
Northdale Ch—*church* NC-3
Northdale Park—*park* PA-2
Northdale Sch—*school* LA-4
Northdale Sch—*school* MN-6
North Dallas—*uninc pl* TX-5
North Dallas HS—*school* TX-5
North Dallas (RR name for Dallesport)—*other* WA-9
*North Dalles* WA-9
Northdalles Station—*locale* WA-9
*North Dallison* WV-2
*North Dam* MA-1
*North Dam* SD-7
North Dam—*dam* MT-8
North Dam—*dam* SD-7
North Dam—*dam* WA-9
North Dam Canyon—*valley* NM-5
North Dam Tailings Pond—*reservoir* AZ-5
**North Dana (historical)**—*pop pl* MA-1
**North Dansville (Town of)**—*pop pl* NY-2
North Danvers Ch—*church* IL-6
**North Danville**—*pop pl* NH-1
**North Danville**—*pop pl* VT-1
North Dardanelle—*locale* AR-4
**North Darien**—*pop pl* NY-2
**North Dartmouth**—*pop pl* MA-1
North Dartmouth Mall (Shop Ctr)—*locale* MA-1
North Davidson HS—*school* NC-3
North Davidson JHS—*school* NC-3
*North Davidson Senior HS* NC-3
North Davie JHS—*school* NC-3
North Daviess Junior-Senior HS—*school* IN-6
North Davis—*cens area* UT-8
North Davis Creek—*stream* OR-9
North Davis Creek Campground—*park* OR-9
North Davis Division—*civil* UT-8
*North Davis Junior High School* UT-8
North Davis Millpond Branch—*stream* MD-2
North Davis Sch—*school* CA-9
North Dawes Glacier—*glacier* AK-9
North Daye Hill—*locale* AL-4
*North Dayton* OH-6
**North Dayton**—*pop pl* TN-4
North Dayton Oil Field—*oilfield* TX-5
North Deadman Canyon—*valley* CO-8
North Deadman Creek—*stream* WA-9
North Deadman Gulch—*valley* CO-8
North Deadman Gulch—*valley* ID-8
**North Deale**—*pop pl* MD-2
North Dearborn HS—*school* IN-6
North Dease Lake—*lake* MI-6
North Decatur—*locale* GA-3
North Decatur Ch—*church* GA-3
North Deception Lake—*lake* AK-9
North Deckard Mountain—*ridge* AR-4
North Deckard Mtn—*summit* AR-4
North Decker Creek—*stream* CO-8
North Deep Creek—*stream* CA-9
North Deep Creek—*stream* NC-3
North Deep Lake Oil and Gas Field—*oilfield* LA-4
North Deep Red Ch—*church* OK-5
North Deepwater Creek—*stream* MO-7
North Deer Creek—*stream* MO-7
North Deer Creek—*stream* OK-5
North Deer Creek—*stream* PA-2
North Deer Creek—*stream* SD-7
North Deer Creek—*stream* WY-8
North Deerfield Cem—*cemetery* WI-6
**North Deering**—*pop pl* ME-1
North Deer Island—*island* TX-5
North Deer Isle—*locale* ME-1
North Deer Mountain Trail—*trail* CO-8
North Deerskin Lake—*lake* MI-6
North De Lamar Pit—*mine* ID-8
North De Land—*CDP* FL-3
North Delaney Lake—*lake* CO-8
North Delaware Ch—*church* OH-6
**North Delphi**—*pop pl* IN-6
**North Delta**—*pop pl* CO-8
North Delta Canal—*canal* CO-8
**North Dennis**—*pop pl* MA-1
**North Dennis**—*pop pl* NJ-2
*North Dennisville* NJ-2
North Depoe Bay Creek—*stream* OR-9
North Depoe Bay Creek Rsvr—*reservoir* OR-9
North De Quincy Oil Field—*oilfield* LA-4
**North Derby**—*pop pl* VT-1
North Derby Gulch—*valley* MT-8
**North Des Arc**—*pop pl* MO-7
North Desert Waterhole—*spring* OR-9
North Desert Waterhole Number Nineteen—*reservoir* OR-9
North Desert Waterhole Number Thirty-Two—*reservoir* OR-9
**North Detroit Township**—*pop pl* SD-7
North Devon Sch—*school* MT-8
North Dewey—*unorg reg* SD-7
North Dewey Sch—*school* WI-6
**North Dexter**—*pop pl* ME-1
North Diamond Community Hall—*building* KS-7
*North Diamond Gulch* UT-8
North Dibble Oil Field—*oilfield* OK-5
North Dickey Peak—*summit* OR-9
**North Dighton**—*pop pl* MA-1
**North Dinuba**—*pop pl* CA-9
North Dirt Tank—*reservoir* NM-5
North Ditch—*canal* CA-9
North Ditch—*canal* CO-8
North Ditch—*canal* NM-5
North Ditch—*canal* (6) UT-8
North Ditch—*canal* VA-3
North Ditch—*canal* WI-6
North Ditch—*stream* WY-8
North Divide Draw—*valley* WY-8
North Divide Lake—*lake* CA-9
North Division HS—*school* IL-6
North Division HS—*school* WI-6
North Dixie Ditch—*canal* OR-9
North Dixie Lake—*lake* OR-9
North Dixie Plaza Shop Ctr—*locale* FL-3
North Dixmond—*locale* ME-1
**North Dixmont**—*pop pl* ME-1
*North Dixon* IL-6
North Dixon Creek—*stream* MT-8
North Dobbyn Creek—*stream* CA-9
North Dock—*locale* NY-2
North Dock (Marina)—*locale* NM-5
North Dodgeville Ch—*church* WI-6
North Dokegood Creek—*stream* TX-5
North Dome—*pillar* CA-9
North Dome—*ridge* CA-9
North Dome—*summit* AK-9
North Dome—*summit* CA-9
North Dome—*summit* NY-2
North Dome Trail—*trail* CA-9
North Donkey Creek Oil Field—*oilfield* WY-8
North Dora Oil Field—*oilfield* TX-5
North Dorchester—*locale* NH-1
**North Dorr**—*pop pl* MI-6
**North Dorset**—*pop pl* VT-1
North Dotson Gillins Ditch—*canal* UT-8
North Double Barrel Creek—*stream* FL-3
North Double Creek—*stream* AL-4
North Double Creek—*stream* NC-3
North Double Dam—*dam* AZ-5
North Doublehead—*summit* NH-1
North Double R Creek—*stream* SD-7
North Double Tanks—*reservoir* TX-5
*North Douglas* MN-6
North Dover Cem—*cemetery* MI-6
North Dover Ch—*church* OH-6
North Dovre Ch—*church* ND-7
North Downey—*uninc pl* CA-9
North Dragon Creek—*stream* UT-8
North Drain—*canal* AZ-5
North Drain—*canal* ID-8
North Drain—*canal* WA-9
North Drain—*stream* NC-3
North Drainage Canal—*canal* CA-9
North Drain Ditch—*canal* NM-5
North Draw—*valley* (2) CO-8
North Draw—*valley* NE-7
North Draw—*valley* NM-5
North Draw—*valley* (7) WY-8
North Draw Rsvr—*reservoir* NE-7
*North Drews Canal* OR-9
North Drew Tank—*reservoir* NM-5
North Drip Rsvr—*reservoir* OR-9
North Drisco Shoal—*bar* MI-6
North Druid Hills—*CDP* GA-3
North Drum Oil Field—*oilfield* OK-5
North Dry Creek—*fmr MCD* NE-7
North Dry Creek—*stream* MS-4
North Dry Creek—*stream* NE-7
North Dry Creek—*stream* NM-5
North Dry Creek—*stream* WY-8
North Dry Creek Ditch—*canal* NE-7
North Dryden Cem—*cemetery* MI-6
North Dry Fork—*stream* CO-8
North Dry Lake State Public Shooting Area—*park* SD-7
*North Dry Sac Creek* MO-7
North Dry Sac River—*stream* MO-7
North Dublin—*uninc pl* GA-3
North Duchesne—*cens area* UT-8
North Duchesne Division—*civil* UT-8
North Duck Creek—*stream* OK-5
North Duck Creek—*stream* WY-8
North Dumpling—*island* NY-2
North Dunbar Dam—*dam* CO-8
North Dunbury (historical P.O.)—*locale* MA-1
North Duncan Branch—*stream* TN-4
North Dunedin Ch—*church* FL-3
North Dunn Canyon—*valley* MT-8
North Duplin Elem Sch—*school* NC-3
North Duplin Sch—*school* NC-3
**North Dupo**—*pop pl* IL-6
North Dupo Ch—*church* IL-6
North Durham—*uninc pl* NC-3
North Durham-Duke Park District—*hist pl* NC-3
North Durham Sch—*school* NC-3
North Dutch John Well—*well* NV-8
North Dutchman Tank—*reservoir* TX-5
**North Duxbury**—*pop pl* MA-1
**North Duxbury**—*pop pl* VT-1
*North Duxbury Station* MA-1
North Dyer Creek—*stream* CO-8
North Dyke Cem—*cemetery* OH-6
**North Eagle Butte**—*pop pl* SD-7
North Eagle Cem—*cemetery* MI-6
North Eaglenest Mtn—*summit* NC-3
North Eagle Sch (abandoned)—*school* MO-7
North Eagle Trail—*trail* NM-5
North Earlsboro Oil Field—*oilfield* OK-5
*Northeast* MD-2
*Northeast* MO-7
**North East**—*pop pl* MD-2
**North East**—*pop pl* PA-2
Northeast—*post sta* MI-6
Northeast—*post sta* OK-5
Northeast—*uninc pl* AZ-5
Northeast—*uninc pl* LA-4
Northeast—*uninc pl* TN-4
Northeast—*uninc pl* TX-5
Northeast Acad—*school* NC-3
Northeast Aitkin (Unorganized Territory of)—*unorg* MN-6
Northeast Alabama Agricultural Sch (historical)—*school* AL-4
Northeast Alabama Regional Med Ctr—*hospital* AL-4
Northeast Alabama State Junior Coll—*school* AL-4
Northeast Antioch Oil Field—*oilfield* OK-5
Northeast Arm Mummy Bay—*bay* AK-9
Northeast Arm Uganik Bay—*bay* AK-9
Northeast Athletic Field—*park* MN-6
Northeast Baptist Ch—*church* (2) FL-3
Northeast Baptist Ch—*church* IN-6
Northeast Baptist Hosp—*hospital* TX-5
Northeast Bay—*bay* AK-9
North East Beaver County Sch—*school* PA-2
Northeast Bebee Oil And Gas Field—*oilfield* OK-5
Northeast Bight—*bay* AK-9
Northeast Bluff—*cliff* AK-9
Northeast Bluff—*cliff* ME-1
Northeast Boatright Tank—*reservoir* TX-5
Northeast Bon Homme—*unorg reg* SD-7
North East Borough—*civil* PA-2
Northeast Bowl—*basin* CO-8
Northeast Bradford HS—*school* PA-2
*Northeast Branch* NC-3
Northeast Branch—*stream* NY-2
Northeast Branch Anacostia River—*stream* MD-2
Northeast Branch Fishing Creek—*stream* MD-2
Northeast Branch Harris Creek—*stream* MD-2
*North East Branch of Amite River* LA-4
*North East Branch Of Amite River* MS-4
*Northeast Branch of Perkiomen Creek* PA-2
*Northeast Branch Penobscot River* ME-1
*North East Branch Perkiomen Creek* PA-2
Northeast Branch Sarah Creek—*stream* VA-3
Northeast Branch Western Branch Patuxent Riv—*stream* MD-2
Northeast Brazos (CCD)—*cens area* TX-5
Northeast Brook—*stream* ME-1
Northeast Burying Ground—*cemetery* CT-1
Northeast Butterly Oil Field—*oilfield* OK-5
Northeast Byars Oil Field—*oilfield* OK-5
Northeast Cape—*cape* AK-9
**Northeast Cape**—*pop pl* AK-9
*North East Cape Fear River* NC-3
Northeast Cape Fear River—*stream* NC-3
**North East Carry**—*pop pl* ME-1
Northeast Carry (Township of)—*unorg* ME-1
Northeast (CCD)—*cens area* TX-5
Northeast Cem—*cemetery* (2) MA-1
**Northeast Center**—*pop pl* NY-2
*Northeast Ch* IN-6
Northeast Ch—*church* (2) NC-3
Northeast Chapel—*church* NC-3
Northeast Chaves (CCD)—*cens area* NM-5
Northeast Cheyenne Valley Oil Field—*oilfield* OK-5
Northeast Ch of Christ—*church* DE-2
Northeast Ch of Christ—*church* IN-6
Northeast Christian Day Sch—*school* PA-2
Northeast Civit Oil Field—*oilfield* OK-5
Northeast Closman Workings—*mine* TN-4
Northeast Cobb (CCD)—*cens area* GA-3
Northeast Comanche (CCD)—*cens area* OK-5
Northeast Community HS—*school* IA-7
Northeast Congregation Jehovahs Witnesses—*church* KS-7
Northeast Corson—*unorg reg* SD-7
Northeast Cove—*bay* AK-9
Northeast Cove—*bay* (5) ME-1
Northeast Cove—*bay* MD-2
*Northeast Creek* MD-2
*Northeast Creek* PA-2
*North East Creek* VA-3
Northeast Creek—*stream* AK-9
North East Creek—*stream* CO-8
Northeast Creek—*stream* ME-1
Northeast Creek—*stream* MD-2
North East Creek—*stream* MD-2
Northeast Creek—*stream* (2) NC-3
North East Creek—*stream* PA-2
Northeast Creek—*stream* (2) VA-3
Northeast Crescent Oil Field—*oilfield* OK-5
Northeast Criner Oil Field—*oilfield* OK-5
Northeast Crossroads Oil Field—*oilfield* OK-5
Northeast Davis Oil Field—*oilfield* OK-5
Northeast Dibble Oil Field—*oilfield* OK-5
Northeast Ditch—*canal* VA-3
*Northeast D McCormick Park* AZ-5
Northeast Drain—*canal* CA-9
Northeast Dubois HS—*school* IN-6
Northeast Edmond Gas And Oil Field—*oilfield* OK-5
Northeast Elem Sch—*school* IN-6
Northeast Elem Sch—*school* TN-4
Northeast Ellis (CCD)—*cens area* OK-5
Northeast Emmons—*unorg reg* ND-7
Northeast Entrance—*locale* MT-8
Northeast Entrance Station—*hist pl* MT-8
*Northeastern* MI-6
Northeastern A M College—*post sta* OK-5
Northeastern Bible Institute—*school* NJ-2
Northeastern Cem—*cemetery* NC-3
Northeastern Hosp—*hospital* PA-2
Northeastern Hotel—*hist pl* MN-6
Northeastern HS—*school* MI-6
Northeastern HS—*school* NC-3
Northeastern HS—*school* OH-6
Northeastern HS—*school* PA-2
Northeastern JHS—*school* MA-1
Northeastern JHS—*school* MI-6
Northeastern MS—*school* OH-6
Northeastern Oklahoma A and M Junior Coll—*school* OK-5
Northeastern Sch—*school* OH-6
Northeastern State Coll—*school* OK-5
Northeastern Univ Edwards Laboratory—*school* MA-1
Northeastern Univ Suburban Campus—*school* MA-1
Northeast Fall River—*unorg reg* SD-7
*North East Federal Penitentiary* PA-2
Northeast Federal Penitentiary—*locale* PA-2
Northeast Florida State Hosp—*hospital* (2) FL-3
Northeast Florida State Hospital—*school* FL-3
Northeast Fork Blackwater Creek—*stream* VA-3
Northeast Fork Carros Creek—*stream* NM-5
Northeast Fork Kahiltna Glacier—*glacier* AK-9
Northeast Fork Rock Creek—*stream* OR-9
Northeast Fork Toddy Draw—*valley* WY-8
Northeast Gainesville Residential District—*hist pl* FL-3
Northeast Gibbon Spur Oil Field—*oilfield* OK-5
Northeast Gibson Oil Field—*oilfield* LA-4
Northeast Glades (CCD)—*cens area* FL-3
Northeast Grave—*rock* MA-1
Northeast Gregory—*unorg reg* SD-7
**North Eastham**—*pop pl* MA-1
Northeast Harbor—*bay* (2) AK-9
Northeast Harbor—*bay* (2) ME-1
**Northeast Harbor**—*pop pl* ME-1
Northeast Harris (CCD)—*cens area* TX-5
Northeast Head—*cape* FL-3
**Northeast Heights**—*pop pl* MD-2
Northeast Heights—*uninc pl* NM-5
Northeast Heights Ch of Christ—*church* KS-7
**Northeast Henrietta**—*pop pl* NY-2
Northeast Hill—*summit* ME-1
Northeast HS—*school* AR-4
Northeast HS—*school* (2) FL-3
Northeast HS—*school* KS-7
Northeast HS—*school* MD-2
Northeast HS—*school* MO-7
Northeast HS—*school* NE-7
Northeast HS—*school* OK-5
Northeast HS—*school* PA-2
Northeast HS—*school* TN-4
North East HS (abandoned)—*school* PA-2
North East Iowa Garden of Memories—*cemetery* IA-7
Northeast Island—*island* MD-2
Northeast Islands—*island* FM-9
Northeast Itasca (Unorganized Territory of)—*unorg* MN-6
Northeast Jefferson—*cens area* CO-8
Northeast JHS—*school* CT-1
Northeast JHS—*school* KS-7
Northeast JHS—*school* (2) MI-6
Northeast JHS—*school* MN-6
Northeast JHS—*school* MO-7
Northeast JHS—*school* (2) NC-3
Northeast JHS—*school* OK-5
Northeast JHS—*school* (2) PA-2
Northeast Jones HS—*school* MS-4
North East Junction—*locale* NY-2
North East Junior-Senior HS—*school* PA-2
*Northeast Lake* IN-6
Northeast Lake—*lake* WI-6
Northeast Lake—*reservoir* IA-7
Northeast Lake—*reservoir* OK-5
Northeast Lake Dam—*dam* IA-7
Northeast Lancaster Township Hist Dist—*hist pl* PA-2
Northeast Lateral Watershed Number Five—*reservoir* TX-5
Northeast Lateral Watershed Number Four—*reservoir* TX-5
Northeast Lateral Watershed Number One—*reservoir* TX-5
Northeast Lateral Watershed Number Six—*reservoir* TX-5
Northeast Lateral Watershed Number Two—*reservoir* TX-5
*Northeast Lauderdale Elem Sch* MS-4
Northeast Lauderdale JHS—*school* MS-4
Northeast Lauderville HS—*school* MS-4
Northeast Ledge—*bar* (2) ME-1
Northeast Lincoln (CCD)—*cens area* OK-5
Northeast Lonsdale Mine—*mine* TN-4
North East Louisiana State Coll—*school* LA-4
Northeast Louisiana Univ—*post sta* LA-4
Northeast Lyman—*unorg reg* SD-7
**Northeast Madison (Township of)**—*pop pl* PA-2
Northeast Manual Training Sch—*hist pl* PA-2
Northeast Marin (CCD)—*cens area* CA-9
Northeast Marion Township—*civil* MO-7
Northeast Mchenry—*unorg reg* ND-7
Northeast Middlefield Sch—*school* OH-6
Northeast Mississippi Ch of God and Christ—*church* MS-4
*Northeast Mississippi Hospital* MS-4
Northeast Mississippi Junior Coll—*school* MS-4
Northeast Mississippi Museum—*building* MS-4
Northeast Missouri State Univ—*school* MO-7
Northeast Modesto—*uninc pl* CA-9
Northeast Morgan County Water Treatment Plant—*building* AL-4
Northeast Mtn—*summit* VT-1
Northeast Nahola Oil Field—*oilfield* OK-5
Northeast Neighborhood Park—*park* PA-2
Northeast Nellie, Lake—*lake* FL-3
*North East of Davisville* RI-1
**North Easton**—*pop pl* MA-1
**North Easton**—*pop pl* NY-2
North Easton Hist Dist—*hist pl* MA-1
North Easton RR Station—*hist pl* MA-1
Northeast Park—*park* FL-3
Northeast Park—*park* (2) IL-6
Northeast Park—*park* NY-2
North East Park Baptist Ch—*church* FL-3
Northeast Park Hill Well—*well* TX-5
*Northeast Pass* FM-9
*North East Pass* MP-9
Northeast Pass—*channel* LA-4
Northeast Pass—*channel* (2) MP-9
Northeast Passage—*channel* ME-1
Northeast Passage—*channel* MP-9
Northeast Peak—*summit* VA-3
Northeast Pennington—*unorg reg* SD-7
*Northeast Philadelphia Airport* PA-2
Northeast Piscataquis (Unorganized Territory of)—*unorg* ME-1
North East Plaza—*locale* NC-3
Northeast Plaza Shop Ctr—*locale* FL-3
Northeast Plaza Shop Ctr—*locale* VA-3
Northeast Plus Ultra Mine—*mine* NV-8
*North East Point* FM-9
Northeast Point—*cape* (2) AK-9
Northeast Point—*cape* GA-3
Northeast Point—*cape* (5) ME-1
Northeast Point—*cape* RI-1
Northeast Point—*cape* SC-3
Northeast Point—*cape* MP-9
Northeast Point Ledges—*bar* ME-1
Northeast Point Reef—*bar* ME-1
Northeast Pond—*lake* (2) ME-1
Northeast Pond—*lake* MA-1
Northeast Pond—*lake* NH-1
Northeast Pond—*lake* NC-3
Northeast Pond Ledge—*bar* ME-1
Northeast Pontotoc (CCD)—*cens area* OK-5
Northeast Preserve Park—*park* TX-5
Northeast Prong—*bay* NC-3
Northeast Prong—*stream* NC-3
Northeast Pueblo—*cens area* CO-8
Northeast (Quadrant)—*fmr MCD* DC-2
Northeast Recreation Center—*park* TN-4
Northeast Red White and Blue Windmill—*locale* TX-5
Northeast Residential Hist Dist—*hist pl* KY-4
*Northeast River* MD-2
North East River—*stream* MD-2
Northeast Riverside Sch—*school* SD-7
Northeast Roberts Branch Mine—*mine* TN-4
Northeast Rocks—*island* AK-9
Northeast Rockwall (CCD)—*cens area* TX-5
Northeast Rome Cem—*cemetery* OH-6
*Northeast Roseau River* MN-6
Northeast Rosedale Oil Field—*oilfield* OK-5
*Northeast Sch* IN-6
Northeast Sch—*school* CT-1
Northeast Sch—*school* GA-3
Northeast Sch—*school* (2) IL-6
Northeast Sch—*school* KS-7
Northeast Sch—*school* (2) LA-4
North East Sch—*school* MA-1
Northeast Sch—*school* MA-1
Northeast Sch—*school* (4) MI-6
Northeast Sch—*school* NE-7
Northeast Sch—*school* NJ-2
Northeast Sch—*school* NM-5
Northeast Sch—*school* (3) NY-2
Northeast Sch—*school* OK-5
Northeast Sch—*school* VT-1
Northeast Seamen Tank—*reservoir* TX-5
Northeast Senior HS—*school* NC-3
Northeast Shawnee Oil Field—*oilfield* OK-5
Northeast Shop Ctr—*locale* FL-3
North East Shop Ctr—*locale* FL-3
Northeast Somerset (Unorganized Territory of)—*unorg* ME-1
Northeast Spring—*spring* ID-8
Northeast Station Post Office—*building* AZ-5
Northeast St. Louis (Unorganized Territory of)—*unorg* MN-6
**Northeast (subdivision)**—*pop pl* PA-2
Northeast Sunflower Windmill—*locale* TX-5
**Northeast Tacoma**—*pop pl* WA-9
Northeast Tank—*reservoir* (2) AZ-5
Northeast Tank—*reservoir* (2) NM-5
Northeast Tarrant (CCD)—*cens area* TX-5
Northeast Tiffin Hist Dist—*hist pl* OH-6
**North East (Town of)**—*pop pl* NY-2
*North East Township* IN-6
**Northeast Township**—*pop pl* IN-6
**Northeast (Township of)**—*pop pl* IL-6
**North East (Township of)**—*pop pl* PA-2
Northeast Truck Center Airp—*airport* PA-2
Northeast Umatilla (CCD)—*cens area* OR-9
Northeast Verden Oil Field—*oilfield* OK-5
Northeast Village—*uninc pl* PA-2
Northeast Washita (CCD)—*cens area* OK-5
North Eastway Park—*park* IN-6
Northeast Well—*well* NM-5
Northeast Wharton (CCD)—*cens area* TX-5
Northeast Wilson (CCD)—*cens area* TN-4
Northeast Wilson Division—*civil* TN-4
Northeast Windmill—*locale* (4) NM-5
Northeast Windmill—*locale* (2) TX-5
North Eastwood Christian Ch—*church* IN-6
North Eastwood Shop Ctr—*locale* IN-6
Northeast Yakima (CCD)—*cens area* WA-9
Northeast Yeager Tank—*reservoir* TX-5
**North Eaton**—*pop pl* OH-6
North Eddington Cem—*cemetery* ME-1
North Eddy Creek—*stream* MI-6
North Eden Canyon—*valley* UT-8
**North Edgecomb**—*pop pl* ME-1
North Edgecomb Cem—*cemetery* ME-1
North Edgecombe HS—*school* NC-3
North Edge Dairy—*hist pl* MT-8
Northedge Sch—*school* NY-2
**North Edinburg**—*pop pl* PA-2
**North Edison**—*pop pl* NJ-2
*North Edisto River* SC-3
North Edisto River—*stream* SC-3
North Edisto Sch—*school* SC-3
North Edmeston—*locale* NY-2
**North Edwards**—*pop pl* CA-9
North Effington Ch—*church* MN-6
**North Egremont**—*pop pl* MA-1
North Eighth Ave City Park—*park* AL-4
North Eight Tank—*reservoir* AZ-5
**Northeim**—*pop pl* WI-6
**North Elba**—*pop pl* NY-2
North Elba Cem—*cemetery* NY-2
**North Elba (Town of)**—*pop pl* NY-2
**North Elberton**—*pop pl* GA-3
North El Dorado (CCD)—*cens area* CA-9
**North Eldred**—*pop pl* PA-2
North Eldridge Well—*well* NV-8
*North Elementary School* UT-8
*North Elem Sch* NC-3
North Elem Sch—*school* FL-3
North Elem Sch—*school* (4) IN-6
North Elem Sch—*school* KS-7
North Elem Sch—*school* TN-4
North Elizabeth—*uninc pl* NJ-2
North Elk Cow Camp—*locale* CO-8
North Elk Creek—*stream* (2) CO-8
North Elk Creek—*stream* KS-7
North Elkhorn Creek—*stream* KY-4
North Elkhorn Creek—*stream* MO-7
North Elkhorn Creek—*stream* WY-8
North Elkhorn Township—*civil* MO-7
**North Elkin**—*pop pl* NC-3
North Elkin Elem Sch—*school* NC-3
**North Elkin (Elkin Valley)**—*pop pl* NC-3
North Elkins Draw—*valley* TX-5
North Elkins Tank—*reservoir* TX-5
North Elk Ridge—*ridge* UT-8
North Elk Run—*stream* PA-2
*North Ellsworth* ME-1
**North Ellsworth**—*pop pl* ME-1
North Ellsworth Cem—*cemetery* ME-1
North Elm—*locale* TX-5
North Elm Cem—*cemetery* KS-7
North Elm Creek—*stream* IA-7
North Elm Creek—*stream* (2) KS-7
North Elm Creek—*stream* OK-5
North Elm Creek—*stream* (3) TX-5
**North Elmore**—*pop pl* AL-4
**North Elsinore**—*pop pl* CA-9
North Elsmere Sch—*school* NE-7
North Elton Gas Field—*oilfield* LA-4
North Emanuel Bend—*bend* FL-3
North Emblem Rsvr—*reservoir* WY-8
North Embleton Coulee—*valley* MT-8
North Emerson Lake—*lake* CA-9
North Emory Creek—*stream* MO-7
North Empire Creek—*stream* CO-8
**North Emporia**—*pop pl* VA-3
*North End* CT-1
*North End* MI-6
North End—*bay* WA-9
**North End**—*pop pl* NY-2
North End—*uninc pl* CO-8
North End—*uninc pl* PA-2
Northend Ball Park—*park* TN-4
*North End Branch* VA-3
North End Branch—*stream* VA-3
North End Bridge—*bridge* MA-1

North End Cem—*cemetery* ... CT-1
North End Cem—*cemetery* ... GA-3
North End Cem—*cemetery* ... NY-2
North End Cem—*cemetery* (2) ... VT-1
North End Dam—*dam* ... AZ-5
North End Dam—*dam* ... CA-9
North End Dam Tank—*reservoir* ... AZ-5
North End Field—*park* ... CT-1
North End Hist Dist—*hist pl* ... CO-8
North End Hist Dist—*hist pl* ... RI-1
North End Hist Dist—*hist pl* ... VA-3
North End Historic Residential District—*hist pl* ... AZ-5
North End Indian Well—*well* ... ID-8
*North End of Black Number One Beach* ... MH-9
North End Park—*flat* ... TX-5
North End Park—*park* ... CT-1
North End Park—*park* ... IL-6
North End Park—*park* ... MN-6
North End Park—*park* ... TN-4
North End Point—*cape* ... VA-3
Northend Point—*cape* ... VA-3
North End Rsvr—*reservoir* ... WA-9
Northend Sch—*school* ... CT-1
North End Sch—*school* ... MD-2
North End Sch—*school* ... MO-7
North End Sch—*school* ... NJ-2
North End Sch—*school* (3) ... NC-3
North End Sch—*school* ... PA-2
North End Shop Ctr—*locale* ... PA-2
**North End (subdivision)**—*pop pl* (2) ... MA-1
**North End Subdivision**—*pop pl* ... UT-8
North End Trail (Pack)—*trail* ... NM-5
North End Tub—*well* ... TX-5
**North Englewood**—*pop pl* ... MD-2
North Englewood Playground—*park* ... MD-2
**North English**—*pop pl* ... IA-7
North English River—*stream* ... IA-7
**North Enid**—*pop pl* ... OK-5
**North Enid (Billings Junction)**—*pop pl* ... OK-5
North Enoree River—*stream* ... SC-3
**North Enosburg**—*pop pl* ... VT-1
North Ensley Cem—*cemetery* ... MI-6
*North Entrance* ... PW-9
North Entrance—*channel* ... AK-9
North Entrance Indian Well—*well* ... ID-8
*North Entrance Kita* ... PW-9
*North Entrance Monument Canyon* ... CO-8
North Entrance Rock—*bar* ... CA-9
North Entrance Yellowstone Natl Park—*locale* ... MT-8
North Eolus—*summit* ... CO-8
North Ephraim Ditch—*canal* ... UT-8
North Epping—*locale* ... NH-1
**North Epworth**—*pop pl* ... MI-6
North Erickson Lake—*lake* ... UT-8
Northerly Island—*island* ... AK-9
Northerly Island—*island* ... IL-6
Northern—*locale* ... KY-4
Northern—*uninc pl* ... MD-2
Northern Area Sch (abandoned)—*school* ... PA-2
Northern Arizona Normal Sch Hist Dist—*hist pl* ... AZ-5
Northern Arizona University—*other* ... AZ-5
Northern Bay—*bay* ... ME-1
**Northern Beach**—*pop pl* ... IN-6
Northern Bedford County HS—*school* ... PA-2
Northern Belle Mine—*mine* ... NV-8
Northern Block—*hist pl* ... WI-6
Northern Block and Supply Company—*other* ... MI-6
Northern Brake—*swamp* ... AR-4
Northern Branch—*stream* ... AL-4
*Northern Branch Turtle River* ... ND-7
Northern Brewery—*hist pl* ... MI-6
Northern California Youth Center—*other* ... CA-9
Northern Cambria HS—*school* ... PA-2
Northern Canal—*canal* ... MA-1
Northern Canal—*canal* ... UT-8
Northern Canal Head Gates Dam—*dam* ... MA-1
Northern Cem—*cemetery* ... MN-6
Northern Cem—*cemetery* ... TN-4
Northern Center Univ Of Kentucky—*school* ... KY-4
Northern Ch—*church* ... MD-2
Northern Ch—*church* ... TN-4
Northern Cheyenne—*cens area* (2) ... MT-8
**Northern Cheyenne Ind Res**—*pop pl* ... MT-8
Northern Cochise Community Hosp—*hospital* ... AZ-5
Northern Colorado Power Company Substation—*hist pl* ... CO-8
Northern Crags—*cliff* ... WA-9
Northern Creek—*stream* ... AR-4
Northern Ditch—*canal* ... KY-4
Northern Essex Community Coll—*school* ... MA-1
Northern Glades—*flat* ... OR-9
Northern Gospel Mission—*church* ... MN-6
Northern Gun Club—*other* ... CA-9
*Northern Heights* ... MO-7
**Northern Heights**—*pop pl* ... MO-7
Northern Heights Ch—*church* ... MI-6
Northern Heights HS—*school* ... KS-7
Northern Heights Park—*park* ... MN-6
Northern Highland State For—*forest* ... WI-6
Northern Hill Ch—*church* ... OH-6
**Northern Hills**—*pop pl* ... AZ-5
**Northern Hills**—*pop pl* ... KS-7
**Northern Hills**—*pop pl* ... TN-4
Northern Hills Baptist Ch—*church* ... KS-7
Northern Hills Ch of God—*church* ... FL-3
Northern Hills Sch—*school* ... KS-7
Northern Hills Sch—*school* ... NE-7
**Northern Hills Subdivision**—*pop pl* ... UT-8
Northern Hollow—*valley* ... KY-4
Northern Home for Children—*building* ... PA-2
Northern HS—*school* (3) ... MI-6
Northern HS—*school* ... NC-3
Northern Illinois Univ—*school* ... IL-6
Northern Indiana Gas and Electric Company Bldg—*hist pl* ... IN-6
Northern Inlet—*stream* ... ME-1
Northern Island—*island* ... ME-1
Northern Islands (Municipality)—*civil* ... MH-9
Northern JHS—*school* ... NC-3
Northern Joint HS—*school* ... PA-2
Northern Kentucky Industrial Foundation—*facility* ... KY-4
Northern Lake—*lake* ... MN-6
*Northern Landing Strip* ... KS-7
Northern Landing Strip—*airport* ... KS-7
Northern Lebanon HS—*school* ... PA-2
Northern Lehigh JHS—*school* ... PA-2
Northern Lehigh Senior HS—*school* ... PA-2
Northern Liberties Hist Dist—*hist pl* ... PA-2
Northern Liberties Hosp—*hospital* ... PA-2
Northern Life Tower—*hist pl* ... WA-9
Northern Light Lake—*lake* ... MN-6
Northern Light Sch (historical)—*school* ... IA-7
Northern Lights Masonic Lodge—*hist pl* ... ND-7
Northern Lights Memorial Cem—*cemetery* ... AK-9
Northern Lights Mine—*mine* ... NV-8
Northern Loop Trail—*trail* ... WA-9
Northern (Magisterial District)—*fmr MCD* (2) ... WV-2
**Northern Maine Junction**—*pop pl* ... ME-1
Northern Maine Regional Airp at Presque Isle—*airport* ... ME-1
**Northern Meadows**—*pop pl* ... IN-6
Northern Methodist Ch—*church* ... AL-4
Northern Michigan Asylum—*hist pl* ... MI-6
Northern Michigan Coll—*school* ... MI-6
Northern Michigan Sanitorium—*hospital* ... MI-6
Northern Mine—*mine* ... AZ-5
Northern Montana Coll—*school* ... MT-8
Northernmost Mines—*mine* ... AL-4
Northern Nash HS—*school* ... NC-3
Northern Natl Bank—*hist pl* ... PA-2
Northern Neck—*cape* ... ME-1
**Northern Ohio**—*pop pl* ... AR-4
Northern Oklahoma Junior Coll—*school* ... OK-5
Northern Ordance Plant—*other* ... MN-6
**Northern Pacific Crossing**—*pop pl* ... ND-7
Northern Pacific Depot—*hist pl* (3) ... MN-6
Northern Pacific Depot and Freight House—*hist pl* ... ND-7
Northern Pacific Hosp—*hospital* ... MN-6
Northern Pacific Office Bldg—*hist pl* ... WA-9
Northern Pacific Passenger Depot—*hist pl* ... MN-6
Northern Pacific Railway Company Como Shops Hist Dist—*hist pl* ... MN-6
Northern Pacific Railway Depot—*hist pl* ... ID-8
Northern Pacific Railway Depot—*hist pl* ... MN-6
Northern Pacific Railway Depot—*hist pl* (2) ... ND-7
Northern Pacific RR Completion Site, 1883—*hist pl* ... MT-8
Northern Pacific RR Depot—*hist pl* ... MT-8
Northern Pacific RR Settling Tanks—*hist pl* ... MT-8
Northern Pacific Rsvr—*reservoir* ... MT-8
Northern Pacific Warehouse—*hist pl* ... MT-8
Northern Parkway Sch—*school* ... NY-2
Northern Pass—*channel* ... FL-3
Northern Petrochemical Company—*facility* ... IL-6
Northern Petrochemical Company (Lemont)—*facility* ... IL-6
Northern Petrochemical Corporation—*facility* ... IL-6
Northern Pike Elem Sch—*school* ... PA-2
Northern Pine Ch—*church* ... MN-6
Northern Pond—*bay* ... NC-3
Northern Pond—*lake* ... ME-1
Northern Potter Sch—*school* ... PA-2
Northern Prairie—*flat* ... OR-9
Northern Prong Saint Jerome Creek—*bay* ... MD-2
Northern Ridge—*ridge* ... KY-4
Northern River Street Hist Dist—*hist pl* ... NY-2
Northerns Airport—*park* ... KS-7
Northern Saving Fund and Safe Deposit Company—*hist pl* ... PA-2
Northern Sch—*school* ... KY-4
Northern Sch—*school* ... MN-6
Northern Sch—*school* ... OH-6
Northern Sch (abandoned)—*school* ... PA-2
*Northerns Chapel Baptist Church* ... TN-4
*Northerns Church* ... TN-4
Northern Seminary—*school* ... IL-6
Northern Simmons Pond—*lake* ... MA-1
Northern Spring—*spring* ... AL-4
Northern Spy—*mine* ... UT-8
Northerns Sch (historical)—*school* ... TN-4
Northern State Coll—*school* ... SD-7
Northern State Hosp—*hospital* ... WA-9
Northern Stream—*stream* ... ME-1
Northern Tier Childrens Home—*building* ... PA-2
**Northern (Township of)**—*pop pl* ... IL-6
**Northern (Township of)**—*pop pl* ... MN-6
Northern Triangles—*bar* ... ME-1
Northern Valley HS—*school* ... KS-7
Northern Valley Regional HS—*school* ... NJ-2
Northern Village Shop Ctr—*locale* ... AZ-5
Northern Virginia Community Coll (Manass—*school* ... VA-3
Northern Virginia Facility—*post sta* ... VA-3
Northern Virginia Police Acad—*school* ... VA-3
Northern Wisconsin Training Sch—*school* ... WI-6
Norther Slough—*gut* ... CA-9
North Escalante Canyon Outstanding Natural Area—*area* ... UT-8
*North Escanaba* ... MI-6
**North Escanaba (sta.)**—*pop pl* ... MI-6
**North Escanaba (subdivision)**—*pop pl* ... MI-6
North Esperance Oil Field—*oilfield* ... MS-4
North Esplanade Hist Dist—*hist pl* ... KS-7
North Essex Cem—*cemetery* ... IL-6
**North Essington**—*pop pl* ... PA-2
North Estates Lake—*reservoir* ... IN-6
North Estes Windmill—*locale* (2) ... TX-5
**North Etowah**—*pop pl* ... TN-4
North Etowah Baptist Ch—*church* ... TN-4
North Etowah Sch (historical)—*school* ... TN-4
North Eugene HS—*school* ... OR-9
**North Evans**—*pop pl* ... NY-2
North Evans Cem—*cemetery* ... MO-7
North Evans Windmill—*locale* ... TX-5
North Everetts Sch—*school* ... NC-3
Northe Windmill—*locale* ... TX-5
North Extension Canal—*canal* ... ID-8
North Extension Drain—*stream* ... MI-6
Northey Gulch—*valley* ... MT-8
Northey Hill—*summit* ... NH-1
Northey Point—*uninc pl* ... MA-1
North Fabius Creek—*stream* ... IA-7
North Fabius River*—*stream* ... IA-7
North Fabius River—*stream* ... MO-7
*North Fahang Valley* ... MH-9
**North Fairfax**—*pop pl* ... VT-1
North Fairfield—*locale* ... ME-1
**North Fairfield**—*pop pl* ... OH-6
**North Fairhaven**—*pop pl* ... MA-1
**North Fair Haven**—*pop pl* ... NY-2
**North Fairlington**—*pop pl* ... VA-3
North Fairmont—*uninc pl* ... WV-2
North Fairmount Sch—*school* ... OH-6
North Fair Oaks—*CDP* ... CA-9
North Fairview Cem—*cemetery* ... IA-7
North Fairview Mtn—*summit* ... OR-9
North Fairview Run—*stream* ... IN-6
North Fairview Sch—*school* ... IL-6
North Fairview Sch—*school* ... OK-5
North Fairview Sch (historical)—*school* ... MO-7
North Falcon Creek—*stream* ... TX-5
North Fall Canyon—*valley* ... AZ-5
*North Fall Creek* ... WY-8
**North Falmouth**—*pop pl* ... ME-1
**North Falmouth**—*pop pl* ... MA-1
North Falmouth Sch—*school* ... MA-1
**North Falmouth Station**—*pop pl* ... MA-1
*North Falmouth Village* ... MA-1
*North Fanaganam Valley* ... MH-9
North Fanif Elem Sch—*school* ... FM-9
North Fannin Gas Field—*oilfield* ... TX-5
North Farallon—*island* ... CA-9
**North Farmington**—*pop pl* ... MI-6
North Farmington Cem—*cemetery* ... MI-6
*North Farmington (census name Quakertown North)* ... MI-6
North Farmington Ditch—*canal* ... NM-5
North Farmington HS—*school* ... MI-6
North Farmington Junction—*locale* ... UT-8
**North Farms**—*pop pl* ... MA-1
North Farms Lakes—*lake* ... ID-8
North Farms Rsvr—*reservoir* ... CT-1
*North Farra Brook* ... CT-1
North Farrars Brook—*stream* ... CT-1
North F A Windmill—*locale* ... TX-5
North Fayette—*locale* ... ME-1
**North Fayette (Township of)**—*pop pl* ... PA-2
**North Fayston**—*pop pl* ... VT-1
North Feeder Canal—*canal* ... FL-3
**North Feesburg**—*pop pl* ... OH-6
**North Fenton**—*pop pl* ... NY-2
**North Ferrisburg**—*pop pl* ... VT-1
North Ferrisburg Station—*locale* ... VT-1
North Ferry Cem—*cemetery* ... MI-6
North Ferry Point—*cape* ... MD-2
*Northfield* ... KS-7
*Northfield* ... NH-1
*Northfield* ... ND-7
North Field—*airport* ... MH-9
Northfield—*locale* ... IA-7
Northfield—*locale* ... KY-4
Northfield—*locale* ... ME-1
Northfield—*locale* ... MI-6
**Northfield**—*pop pl* ... CT-1
**Northfield**—*pop pl* ... IL-6
**Northfield**—*pop pl* ... IN-6
**Northfield**—*pop pl* ... KY-4
**Northfield**—*pop pl* ... MA-1
**Northfield**—*pop pl* ... MI-6
**Northfield**—*pop pl* ... MN-6
**Northfield**—*pop pl* ... NH-1
**Northfield**—*pop pl* (2) ... NJ-2
**Northfield**—*pop pl* ... NY-2
**Northfield**—*pop pl* ... OH-6
**Northfield**—*pop pl* ... TX-5
**Northfield**—*pop pl* ... VT-1
**Northfield**—*pop pl* ... WI-6
North Field—*swamp* ... GA-3
Northfield Brook—*stream* ... CT-1
Northfield Brook Dam—*dam* ... CT-1
North Field Canyon—*valley* ... AZ-5
Northfield Cem—*cemetery* ... CT-1
Northfield Cem—*cemetery* ... VA-3
Northfield (census name for Northfield Center)—*CDP* ... MA-1
**Northfield Center**—*pop pl* ... OH-6
**Northfield Center**—*pop pl* ... VT-1
Northfield Center (census name Northfield)—*other* ... MA-1
Northfield Center Sch—*school* ... MA-1
Northfield Center (Township of)—*civ div* ... OH-6
Northfield Community Ch—*church* ... IN-6
Northfield Court Shop Ctr—*locale* ... TN-4
**Northfield Falls**—*pop pl* ... VT-1
Northfield Falls Covered Bridge—*hist pl* ... VT-1
**Northfield Farms**—*pop pl* ... MA-1
*Northfield Gulf* ... VT-1
*Northfield High School* ... IN-6
*Northfield Hill* ... CT-1
*Northfield Hills* ... MI-6
Northfield Hist Dist—*hist pl* ... MN-6
Northfield Junior-Senior HS—*school* ... IN-6
Northfield-Macedonia Cem—*cemetery* ... OH-6
Northfield Main Street Hist Dist—*hist pl* ... MA-1
Northfield Mountain Reservoir Dam—*dam* ... MA-1
Northfield Mountains—*range* ... VT-1
Northfield-Mount Hermon Sch—*school* ... MA-1
Northfield Mtn—*summit* ... MA-1
Northfield Park—*park* ... IL-6
Northfield Park—*park* ... OH-6
**Northfield (P.O.)**—*pop pl* ... OH-6
Northfield Pond—*lake* ... CT-1
Northfield Rsvr—*reservoir* ... MA-1
**Northfields**—*pop pl* ... VA-3
Northfield Sch—*school* ... ME-1
Northfield Sch—*school* ... MI-6
Northfield Sch—*school* ... OH-6
Northfield School Upper Reservoir Dam—*dam* ... MA-1
**Northfields (subdivision)**—*pop pl* ... NC-3
Northfield State For—*forest* ... MA-1
Northfield Station—*locale* ... NH-1
Northfield Townhall—*building* ... MA-1
**Northfield (Town of)**—*pop pl* ... ME-1
**Northfield (Town of)**—*pop pl* ... MA-1
**Northfield (Town of)**—*pop pl* ... NH-1
**Northfield (Town of)**—*pop pl* ... VT-1
**Northfield (Town of)**—*pop pl* ... WI-6
**Northfield Township**—*pop pl* ... ND-7
Northfield (Township of)—*other* ... OH-6
**Northfield (Township of)**—*pop pl* ... IL-6
**Northfield (Township of)**—*pop pl* ... MI-6
**Northfield (Township of)**—*pop pl* ... MN-6
Northfield Union Church—*hist pl* ... NH-1
*Northfield Village* ... IN-6
*Northfield Village* ... MA-1
**Northfield Village**—*pop pl* ... IN-6
**Northfield Woods**—*pop pl* ... IL-6
**North Fillmore**—*pop pl* ... CA-9
**North Findlay (Mortimer)**—*pop pl* ... OH-6
North Finger Island—*island* ... WA-9
North First Street Hist Dist—*hist pl* ... WI-6
North Fish Creek—*stream* ... TX-5
North Fish Creek—*stream* ... WI-6
North Fishers Reef Gas Field—*oilfield* ... TX-5
North Fish Lake—*lake* ... WI-6
North Fishtail Bay—*bay* ... MI-6
North Fitsum Summit—*summit* ... ID-8
North Fitts Oil Field—*oilfield* ... OK-5
North Five Windmill—*locale* ... TX-5
North Flanders Brook—*stream* ... CT-1
North Flat—*flat* ... NM-5
North Flat—*flat* ... PA-2
North Flat—*flat* (2) ... UT-8
North Flat—*other* ... AK-9
North Flat Cem—*cemetery* ... PA-2
North Flat Creek—*stream* ... MO-7
North Flat Creek—*stream* ... TX-5
North Flat River—*stream* ... NC-3
North Flat Spring—*spring* ... OR-9
North Flat Tank—*reservoir* ... TX-5
North Flat Top—*summit* ... WY-8
*North Flint* ... MI-6
North Flint Creek—*stream* ... AR-4
North Flint Sch—*school* ... IL-6
North Floater Ditch—*canal* ... WI-6
North Floodway—*basin* ... TX-5
**North Florence**—*pop pl* ... AL-4
North Florence Park—*park* ... AL-4
North Florida Christian Sch—*school* ... FL-3
North Florida Evaluation and Treatment Center—*hospital* ... FL-3
North Florida Evaluation and Treatment Center—*school* ... FL-3
North Florida Heights Ch—*church* ... FL-3
North Florida Junior Coll—*school* ... FL-3
North Florida Junior College Library—*building* ... FL-3
North Florida Juvenile Detention Center—*school* ... FL-3
North Florida Regional Hosp—*hospital* ... FL-3
North Floyd Windmill—*locale* ... TX-5
**North Fogelsville**—*pop pl* ... PA-2
**North Fogelsville (Hunktown)**—*pop pl* ... PA-2
**North Folk Village**—*pop pl* ... OH-6
**North Fond du Lac**—*pop pl* ... WI-6
*North Foose Creek* ... CO-8
North Fooses Creek—*stream* ... CO-8
*North For* ... WY-8
**Northford**—*pop pl* ... CT-1
Northford Cem—*cemetery* ... CT-1
Northford Post Office (historical)—*building* ... TN-4
**North Fordyce**—*pop pl* ... AR-4
North Foreland—*cape* ... AK-9
**North Forest Acres**—*pop pl* ... NY-2
North Forest Beach—*uninc pl* ... SC-3
North Forest Cem—*cemetery* ... PA-2
**North Forest Hills (subdivision)**—*pop pl* ... NC-3
North Forest JHS—*school* ... NY-2
**North Forestville**—*pop pl* ... MD-2
North Forest Well—*well* ... NM-5
*North Fork* ... AR-4
*North Fork* ... CA-9
*North Fork* ... CO-8
*North Fork* ... GA-3
*North Fork* ... HI-9
*North Fork* ... IL-6
*North Fork* ... IN-6
*North Fork* ... KS-7
*North Fork* ... MD-2
*North Fork* ... MN-6
*North Fork* ... NE-7
*North Fork* ... NV-8
*North Fork* ... NC-3
*North Fork* ... OH-6
*North Fork* ... OK-5
*North Fork* ... OR-9
*North Fork* ... PA-2
*North Fork* ... UT-8
*North Fork* ... WA-9
*North Fork* ... WV 2
*North Fork* ... WY-8
North Fork—*fmr MCD* ... NE-7
North Fork—*locale* ... MT-8
North Fork—*locale* ... OR-9
North Fork—*locale* ... PA-2
North Fork—*locale* ... TN-4
North Fork—*locale* ... VA-3
**North Fork**—*pop pl* ... CA-9
**North Fork**—*pop pl* ... ID-8
**North Fork**—*pop pl* ... MO-7
**North Fork**—*pop pl* ... NV-8
**North Fork**—*pop pl* ... NC-3
**Northfork**—*pop pl* ... WV-2
North Fork—*stream* ... AK-9
North Fork—*stream* ... CA-9
North Fork—*stream* ... MO-7
North Fork—*stream* ... WV-2
North Fork—*stream* ... WY-8
North Fork Aarons Creek—*stream* ... VA-3
North Fork Abbott Creek—*stream* ... OR-9
North Fork Abercrombie Creek—*stream* ... OR-9
North Fork Adams Creek—*stream* ... CA-9
North Fork Agate Creek—*stream* ... CO-8
North Fork Ah Pah Creek—*stream* ... CA-9
*North Fork Ahtanum Creek* ... WA-9
North Fork Ahtanum Creek—*stream* ... WA-9
North Fork Airp—*airport* ... CO-8
North Fork Alamito Creek—*stream* ... TX-5
North Fork Albion River—*stream* ... CA-9
North Fork Alder Canyon—*valley* ... CA-9
*North Fork Alder Creek* ... CA-9
*North Fork Alder Creek* ... ID-8
North Fork Alder Creek—*stream* (2) ... CA-9
North Fork Alder Creek—*stream* ... ID-8
*North Fork Alkali Creek* ... ND-7
North Fork Alkali Creek—*stream* ... CO-8
North Fork Alkali Creek—*stream* ... ID-8
North Fork Alkali Creek—*stream* (2) ... MT-8
North Fork Alkali Creek—*stream* ... WY-8
North Fork Allen Creek—*stream* ... MT-8
North Fork Alligator Creek—*stream* ... FL-3
North Fork Allison Creek—*stream* ... NV-8
North Fork Alsea River—*stream* ... OR-9
North Fork Amazon Hollow—*valley* ... UT-8
North Fork American Crow Creek—*stream* ... SD-7
*North Fork American Fork* ... MT-8
North Fork American Fork—*stream* ... MT-8
North Fork American River—*stream* ... CA-9
North Fork Ames Branch—*stream* ... WI-6
North Fork Anchor River—*stream* ... AK-9
*North Fork Anderson Creek* ... CA-9
North Fork Anderson Creek—*stream* ... OR-9
North Fork Anderson Creek—*stream* ... WY-8
North Fork Angel Creek—*stream* ... NV-8
North Fork Aniakchak River—*stream* ... AK-9
North Fork Animas River—*stream* ... CO-8
*North Fork Antelope Creek* ... ID-8
North Fork Antelope Creek—*stream* ... CA-9
North Fork Antelope Creek—*stream* ... WY-8
North Fork Anthony Campground—*park* ... OR-9
North Fork Anthony Creek—*stream* ... OR-9
North Fork Anthony Creek—*stream* ... WV-2
North Fork Apishapa River—*stream* ... CO-8
*North Fork Applegate* ... OR-9
North Fork Arikaree River—*stream* ... CO-8
*North Fork Arkansas Creek* ... ID-8
*North Fork Arkansas Creek* ... WA-9
North Fork Arrastra Creek—*stream* ... MT-8
North Fork Arroyo Chico—*stream* ... NM-5
North Fork Arroyo Conejo—*stream* ... CA-9
North Fork Arroyo Leon—*stream* ... NM-5
North Fork Arroyo Salada—*stream* ... CA-9
*North Fork Ash Creek* ... OR-9
*North Fork Ash Creek* ... UT-8
North Fork Ash Creek—*stream* ... AZ-5
North Fork Ash Creek—*stream* ... MT-8
North Fork Ash Creek—*stream* ... OR-9
*North Fork Ashley Creek* ... UT-8
North Fork Ashley Creek—*stream* ... UT-8
*North Fork Asotin Creek* ... WA-9
North Fork Asotin Creek—*stream* ... WA-9
North Fork Augur Creek—*stream* ... OR-9
North Fork Avery Creek—*stream* ... ID-8
North Fork Bachelor Creek—*stream* ... MT-8
North Fork Backbone Creek—*stream* ... CA-9
North Fork Back Creek—*stream* ... VA-3
North Fork Bacon Creek—*stream* ... ID-8
North Fork Bad Axe River—*stream* ... WI-6
*North Fork Badger Creek* ... ID-8
*North Fork Badger Creek* ... WY-8
North Fork Badger Creek—*stream* ... CA-9
North Fork Badger Creek—*stream* ... ID-8
North Fork Bad River—*stream* ... SD-7
North Fork Bairs Creek—*stream* ... CA-9
North Fork Baker Canyon—*valley* ... UT-8
North Fork Baker Creek—*stream* ... AK-9
North Fork Baker Creek—*stream* ... NV-8
North Fork Baker Creek—*stream* ... WA-9
North Fork Baker Gulch—*valley* ... ID-8
North Fork Baking Powder Creek—*stream* ... MT-8
North Fork Ballenger Draw—*valley* ... WY-8
*North Fork Balleus Creek* ... NC-3
*North Fork Baptist Ch* ... TN-4
North Fork Baptist Ch—*church* ... TN-4
*North Fork Barber Creek* ... MT-8
North Fork Barnett Creek—*stream* ... KY-4
North Fork Baron Creek—*stream* ... ID-8
North Fork Barrett Canyon—*valley* ... CA-9
North Fork Barrett Canyon—*valley* ... NV-8
North Fork Barron Creek—*stream* ... OR-9
North Fork Bartlett Creek—*stream* ... CA-9
North Fork Basin—*basin* ... MT-8
North Fork Basin Creek—*stream* ... TN-4
North Fork Battle Creek—*stream* ... CA-9
North Fork Battle Creek—*stream* ... NV-8
North Fork Battle Creek—*stream* ... UT-8
North Fork Batts Creek—*stream* ... MO-7
*North Fork Bayou Pierre* ... MS-4
North Fork Beaerdam Creek—*stream* ... KY-4
*North Fork Bean Blossom Creek* ... IN-6
North Fork Beanblossom Creek—*stream* ... IN-6
North Fork Bean Creek—*stream* ... ID-8
North Fork Bean Creek—*stream* ... OR-9
North Fork Bear Canyon—*valley* ... CO-8
*North Fork Bear Creek* ... AL-4
*North Fork Bear Creek* ... CA-9
*North Fork Bear Creek* ... ID-8
*North Fork Bear Creek* ... IL-6
*North Fork Boar Crook* ... MT-8
*North Fork Bear Creek* ... OR-9
North Fork Bear Creek—*stream* (4) ... CA-9
North Fork Bear Creek—*stream* ... CO-8
North Fork Bear Creek—*stream* (2) ... ID-8
North Fork Bear Creek—*stream* ... MN-6
North Fork Bear Creek—*stream* ... MS-4
North Fork Bear Creek—*stream* (3) ... MT-8
North Fork Bear Creek—*stream* ... OR-9
North Fork Bear Creek—*stream* ... TN-4
North Fork Bear Creek—*stream* (2) ... WA-9
North Fork Bear Creek—*stream* (2) ... WY-8
North Fork Bear Gulch—*valley* ... MT-8
North Fork Bear Gulch—*valley* ... SD-7
North Fork Bear Gulch—*valley* ... WY-8
North Fork Bear Wallow Creek—*stream* ... AZ-5
North Fork Beason Creek—*stream* ... TN-4
*North Fork Beauchamp Creek* ... MT-8
*North Fork Beaver Creek* ... CO-8
*North Fork Beaver Creek* ... KS-7
*North Fork Beaver Creek* ... TN-4
North Fork Beaver Creek—*stream* ... MO-7
North Fork Beaver Creek—*stream* (2) ... MT-8
North Fork Beaver Creek—*stream* (3) ... OR-9
North Fork Beaver Creek—*stream* ... WA-9
North Fork Beaver Creek—*stream* ... WV-2
North Fork Beaver Creek—*stream* ... WI-6
North Fork Beaverdam Creek—*stream* ... MT-8
North Fork Beaver Dam Creek—*stream* ... SD-7
North Fork Bee Bayou—*stream* ... AR-4
North Fork Beech Creek—*stream* ... NC-3
North Fork Beech Creek—*stream* (2) ... PA-2
North Fork Beech Creek—*stream* ... TN-4
*North Fork Beef river* ... WI-6
North Fork Beegum Creek—*stream* ... CA-9
North Fork Beeman Branch—*stream* ... MO-7
North Fork Belly River—*stream* ... MT-8
North Fork Belly River Trail—*trail* ... MT-8
North Fork Bennetts Run—*stream* ... VA-3
North Fork Bens Creek—*stream* ... PA-2
North Fork Benton Creek—*stream* ... ID-8
North Fork Berea Creek—*stream* ... NE-7
North Fork Berry Creek—*stream* ... NV-8
North Fork Berry Creek—*stream* ... OR-9
North Fork Berry Creek—*stream* ... WA-9
North Fork Bieberstedt Creek—*stream* ... OR-9
North Fork Bieler Run—*stream* ... PA-2
North Fork Big Bear Creek—*stream* ... UT-8
North Fork Big Bear Hollow—*valley* ... UT-8
North Fork Big Beaver Creek—*stream* ... TN-4
*North Fork Big Blue River* ... NE-7
*North Fork Big Branch* ... WV-2
North Fork Big Brook—*stream* ... ME-1
North Fork Big Brook—*stream* ... NH-1
North Fork Big Butte Creek—*stream* ... OR-9
North Fork Big Canyon—*valley* ... NM-5
North Fork Big Clear Creek—*stream* ... WV-2
North Fork Big Coulee Creek—*stream* ... MT-8
*North Fork Big Creek* ... KS-7
North Fork Big Creek—*stream* ... CA-9
North Fork Big Creek—*stream* ... CO-8
North Fork Big Creek—*stream* (3) ... ID-8
North Fork Big Creek—*stream* (2) ... KS-7
North Fork Big Creek—*stream* ... KY-4
North Fork Big Creek—*stream* ... MT-8
North Fork Big Creek—*stream* (2) ... NV-8
North Fork Big Creek—*stream* (2) ... WV-2
North Fork Big Creek—*stream* ... WY-8
North Fork Big Elk Creek—*stream* ... MT-8
North Fork Big Flat Creek—*stream* ... CA-9
*North Fork Big Graham Creek* ... IN-6
North Fork Big Gulch—*valley* ... CO-8
*North Fork Big Hat Creek* ... ID-8
North Fork Big Hole River—*stream* ... MT-8
North Fork Big Lost River—*stream* ... ID-8
*North Fork Big Muddy Creek* ... MT-8
*North Fork Big Nemaha River* ... NE-7
North Fork Big Nemaha River—*stream* ... NE-7
*North Fork Big Otter River* ... VA-3
North Fork Big Pine Creek—*stream* ... CA-9
North Fork Big Pine Creek—*stream* ... NC-3
North Fork Big River—*stream* (2) ... AK-9
North Fork Big River—*stream* ... CA-9
North Fork Big Run Trail—*trail* ... WV-2
North Fork Big Saline Bayou—*stream* ... LA-4
North Fork Big Sewickley Creek—*stream* ... PA-2
North Fork Big Sheep Creek—*stream* ... OR-9
North Fork Big Smoky Creek—*stream* ... ID-8
North Fork Big Sur River—*stream* ... CA-9
North Fork Big Thompson River—*stream* ... CO-8
*North Fork Big Walnut Creek* ... IN-6
North Fork Big Wash—*stream* ... NV-8
North Fork Big Willow Creek—*stream* ... NC-3
North Fork Big Wood River—*stream* ... ID-8
North Fork Birch Creek—*stream* ... AK-9
North Fork Birch Creek—*stream* ... CA-9
North Fork Birch Creek—*stream* ... ID-8
North Fork Birch Creek—*stream* ... MT-8
North Fork Birch Creek—*stream* (4) ... UT-8
North Fork Bird Creek—*stream* ... CA-9
North Fork Birdwood Creek—*stream* ... NE-7
North Fork Bishop Creek—*stream* ... CA-9
*North Fork Bitch Creek* ... WY-8
*North Fork Bitter Creek* ... WY-8
North Fork Black Birch Canyon—*valley* ... UT-8
North Fork Black Canyon—*valley* ... AZ-5
North Fork Black Creek—*stream* ... FL-3
North Fork Blackfoot River—*stream* ... MT-8
North Fork Black Hawk Creek—*stream* ... IA-7
*North Fork Black River* ... AZ-5
*North Fork Black River* ... MI-6
North Fork Black River—*stream* ... AZ-5
North Fork Blacktail Creek—*stream* ... SD-7
North Fork Black Valley Creek—*stream* ... MO-7
North Fork Black Vermillion River—*stream* ... KS-7
*North Fork Black Warrior River* ... AL-4
North Fork Blackwater River—*stream* ... MO-7
North Fork Blackwater River—*stream* ... VA-3
North Fork Blackwater River—*stream* ... WV-2
North Fork Blackwater Swamp—*stream* ... VA-3
North Fork Black Wolf Creek—*stream* ... CO-8
North Fork Blackwood Creek—*stream* ... CA-9
North Fork Blair Creek—*stream* ... NC-3
North Fork Blake Creek—*stream* ... WI-6
North Fork Blakely Creek—*stream* ... AR-4
North Fork Blanchard Creek—*stream* ... MT-8
North Fork Blanchard Creek—*stream* ... WA-9
North Fork Blind Indian Creek—*stream* ... AZ-5
North Fork Blood River—*stream* ... TN-4
North Fork Blood River Drainage Ditch—*canal* ... TN-4
North Fork Bloom Creek—*stream* ... MT-8
North Fork Bloomington Creek—*stream* ... ID-8
North Fork Blue Branch—*stream* ... MO-7
North Fork Blue Canyon—*valley* ... NM-5
North Fork Blue Creek—*stream* ... CA-9
North Fork Blue Creek—*stream* (3) ... TN-4
*NORTH Fork Blue River* ... NE-7
North Fork Bluewater Creek—*stream* ... MT-8
North Fork Bluff Creek—*stream* ... CA-9
North Fork Bob Creek—*stream* ... WI-6
North Fork Bogachiel River—*stream* ... WA-9
North Fork Bogard Creek—*stream* ... TN-4
North Fork Boise Creek—*stream* ... CA-9
North Fork Boise River—*stream* ... ID-8
North Fork Bonanza Creek—*stream* ... AK-9
North Fork Bonanza Creek—*stream* ... MT-8
North Fork Bonita Canyon—*valley* ... NV-8
*North Fork Bonita Creek* ... AZ-5
North Fork Boquet River—*stream* ... NY-2
North Fork Borrego Palm Canyon—*valley* ... CA-9
*North Fork Bosque River* ... TX-5
North Fork Bottom Creek—*stream* ... OR-9
*North Fork Boulder Creek* ... CO-8
North Fork Boulder Creek—*stream* ... MT-8
North Fork Boulder Creek—*stream* (2) ... OR-9
North Fork Boulder Creek—*stream* (2) ... WA-9
North Fork Boulder Creek—*stream* ... WY-8
*North Fork Bouquet River* ... NY-2
North Fork Bowers Creek—*stream* ... MT-8
North Fork Bowery Creek—*stream* ... ID-8
North Fork Box Creek—*stream* ... MT-8
North Fork Box Creek—*stream* ... UT-8
North Fork Box Creek—*stream* ... WY-8
North Fork Brackett Creek—*stream* ... MT-8
North Fork Bradbury Brook—*stream* ... MN-6
North Fork Bradfield River—*stream* ... AK-9
North Fork Brady Canyon—*valley* ... AZ-5
*North Fork Branch* ... TN-4
North Fork Bratten Spring Creek—*stream* ... MO-7
North Fork Breitenbush River—*stream* ... OR-9
North Fork Bremner River—*stream* ... AK-9

North Fork Brewster Creek—stream....MT-8
North Fork Bridge—bridge....ID-8
North Fork Bridge Creek—stream (2)....OR-9
North Fork Bridge Creek—stream....WA-9
North Fork Bridger Creek—stream....MT-8
North Fork Brim Creek—stream....WA-9
North Fork Briscoe Creek—stream....CA-9
North Fork Bristow Creek—stream....MT-8
North Fork Broad River—stream....GA-3
North Fork Broad Run—stream....VA-3
North Fork Brokenback Creek....WY-8
North Fork Brook....MN-6
North Fork Brouilletts Creek....IL-6
North Fork Brownie Creek—stream....OR-9
North Fork Brownlee Creek—stream....ID-8
North Fork Bruce Creek—stream....WA-9
North Fork Brush Creek....CO-8
North Fork Brush Creek—stream....ID-8
North Fork Brush Creek—stream....WV-2
North Fork Brush Fork—stream....OH-6
North Fork Brushy Creek—stream....TX-5
North Fork Brushy Creek—stream....WA-9
North Fork Buck Creek....IN-6
North Fork Buck Creek—stream....MO-7
North Fork Buck Creek—stream....NM-5
North Fork Buck Creek—stream (2)....OR-9
North Fork Buck Creek—stream....TX-5
North Fork Buckeye Creek—stream (2)....CA-9
North Fork Buckhorn Creek—stream....ID-8
North Fork Buckland River—stream....AK-9
North Fork Buckskin Creek—stream....OH-6
North Fork Bud Kimball Creek—stream....WY-8
North Fork Buffalo Creek....MS-4
North Fork Buffalo Creek....NV-8
North Fork Buffalo Creek....WY-8
North Fork Buffalo Creek—stream....MO-7
North Fork Buffalo Creek—stream....MT-8
North Fork Buffalo Creek—stream....NV-8
North Fork Buffalo Creek—stream....OH-6
North Fork Buffalo Creek—stream (2)....TX-5
North Fork Buffalo Creek—stream....WV-2
North Fork Buffalo Creek—stream (2)....WY-8
North Fork Buffalo Creek Rsvr—reservoir....TX-5
North Fork Buffalo River....MS-4
North Fork Buffalo River—stream....TN-4
North Fork Buffalo River—stream....VA-3
North Fork Buffalo River—stream....WI-6
North Fork Bull Creek—stream....KY-4
North Fork Bull Creek—stream (2)....MT-8
North Fork Bull Creek—stream....ND-7
North Fork Bull Creek—stream....TX-5
North Fork Bullfrog Creek—stream....UT-8
North Fork Bull Lake Creek—stream....WY-8
North Fork Bull River—stream....MT-8
North Fork Bull Run Creek....OR-9
North Fork Bull Run Creek....TN-4
North Fork Bullrun Creek—stream....TN-4
North Fork Bull Run River—stream....OR-9
North Fork Bullskin Run—stream....WV-2
North Fork Bully Creek—stream....OR-9
North Fork Burdeck Creek—stream....CO-8
North Fork Burger Creek—stream....MT-8
North Fork Burnett Creek—stream....IN-6
North Fork Burns Creek....ID-8
North Fork Burns Creek—stream....MT-8
North Fork Burnt River—stream....OR-9
North Fork Bustahatchee Creek—stream....GA-3
North Fork Butte Creek—stream....MT-8
North Fork Butte Creek—stream....OR-9
North Fork Butte Creek—stream....WY-8
North Fork Butter Creek....OR-9
North Fork Byron Creek—stream....OR-9
North Fork Cabin—locale....MT-8
North Fork Cabin Creek—stream....CO-8
North Fork Cabin Creek—stream....ID-8
North Fork Cabin Creek—stream....MT-8
North Fork Cabin Creek—stream (2)....NV-8
North Fork Cabin Creek—stream....OR-9
North Fork Cabin Fork—stream....ID-8
North Fork Cable Creek—stream....OR-9
North Fork Cache Creek....MT-8
North Fork Cache Creek—stream....CA-9
North Fork Cache Creek—stream....MT-8
North Fork Cache La Poudre River—stream....CO-8
North Fork Cadron Creek....AR-4
North Fork Cadron Creek—stream....AR-4
North Fork Calapooia River—stream....OR-9
North Fork Calapooya Creek—stream....OR-9
North Fork Calaveras River—stream....CA-9
North Fork Calawah River—stream....WA-9
North Fork Calf Creek—stream....CA-9
North Fork California Creek—stream....NV-8
North Fork Calispel Creek....WA-9
North Fork Calispell Creek....WA-9
North Fork Calispell Creek—stream....WA-9
North Fork Callis Creek—stream....ID-8
North Fork Cameron Creek—stream....MT-8
North Fork Camp—locale....CA-9
North Fork Camp—locale (2)....WA-9
North Fork Campbell Creek—stream....AK-9
North Fork Camp Creek—stream....CA-9
North Fork Camp Creek—stream....GA-3
North Fork Camp Creek—stream....ID-8
North Fork Camp Creek—stream....NV-8
North Fork Camp Creek—stream....TX-5
North Fork Campground—locale (2)....CA-9
North Fork Campground—locale....CO-8
North Fork Campground—locale (2)....ID-8
North Fork Campground—locale....MO-7
North Fork Campground—locale (2)....WA-9
North Fork Campground—locale....WY-8
North Fork Camp Rader Run—stream....VA-3
North Fork Canada del Agua—stream....NM-5
North Fork Canadian River....OK-5
North Fork Canadian River—stream....CO-8
North Fork Canal—canal....CA-9
North Fork Caney Creek—stream....AL-4
North Fork Cannon Ball River....ND-7
North Fork Canoe Creek—stream....CA-9
North Fork Canoe Creek—stream....KY-4
North Fork Canyon—valley (2)....AZ-5
North Fork Canyon—valley....TX-5
North Fork Canyon—valley (2)....WY-8
North Fork Canyon Creek—stream....AK-9
North Fork Canyon Creek—stream....CA-9
North Fork Canyon Creek—stream (2)....ID-8
North Fork Canyon Creek—stream (3)....MT-8
North Fork Canyon Creek—stream....NV-8
North Fork Canyon Creek—stream (2)....WA-9
North Fork Canyon Creek—stream....WY-8
North Fork Cape Creek—stream....OR-9
North Fork Cape Winn Creek—stream....NV-8
North Fork Carnero Creek—stream....CO-8
North Fork Carp River....MI-6
North Fork Carrol Creek—stream....MT-8
North Fork Carrol Creek—stream....OR-9
North Fork Cascade Creek—stream....OR-9
North Fork Cascade River—stream....WA-9
North Fork Casper Creek—stream....WY-8
North Fork Castle Canyon—valley....AZ-5
North Fork Castle Creek....OR-9
North Fork Castle Creek—stream....CA-9
North Fork Castle Creek—stream....ID-8
North Fork Castle Creek—stream....OR-9
North Fork Castle Creek—stream....SD-7
North Fork Castle Wash—valley....UT-8
North Fork Catawba Creek—stream....VA-3
North Fork Catawba River—stream....NC-3
North Fork Cat Creek—stream....CO-8
North Fork Cat Creek—stream....NV-8
North Fork Catfish Creek....IA-7
North Fork Catfish Creek—stream....IA-7
North Fork Catherine Creek—stream....OR-9
North Fork Catoctin Creek—stream....VA-3
North Fork Catron Wash—stream....NM-5
North Fork Cattail Creek—stream....NC-3
North Fork Cattle Creek—stream....CO-8
North Fork Cave—cave....TN-4
North Fork Cedar Creek—stream....AL-4
North Fork Cedar Creek—stream....CA-9
North Fork Cedar Creek—stream (2)....CO-8
North Fork Cedar Creek—stream....KY-4
North Fork Cedar Creek—stream (3)....MT-8
North Fork Cedar Creek—stream....NM-5
North Fork Cedar Creek—stream....ND-7
North Fork Cedar Creek—stream (3)....OR-9
North Fork Cedar Creek—stream....TN-4
North Fork Cedar Creek—stream....TX-5
North Fork Cedar Creek—stream....WA-9
North Fork Cedar River—stream (2)....WA-9
North Fork Cedar Wash—stream....NV-8
North Fork Cellar Springs Creek—stream....AZ-5
North Fork Cem—cemetery....CA-9
North Fork Cem—cemetery....NE-7
North Fork Cem—cemetery....OK-5
North Fork Cement Creek—stream....CO-8
North Fork Central Canyon—valley....NV-8
North Fork Ch—church....IL-6
North Fork Ch—church (2)....NC-3
North Fork Ch—church....OH-6
North Fork Ch—church....OK-5
North Fork Ch—church....SC-3
North Fork Ch—church (2)....TN-4
North Fork Ch—church (4)....VA-3
North Fork Ch—church (5)....WV-2
North Fork Chalk Creek—stream....CO-8
North Fork Chalk Creek—stream....UT-8
North Fork Chambers Creek—stream....NC-3
North Fork Chambers Creek—stream....TX-5
North Fork Chamokane Creek—stream....WA-9
North Fork Champion Creek—stream....TX-5
North Fork Chandalar River—stream....AK-9
North Fork Chaparral Creek—stream....WA-9
North Fork Chappel Fork—stream....PA-2
North Fork Charrette Creek—stream....MO-7
North Fork Chatterdown Creek—stream....CA-9
North Fork Chattooga River....NC-3
North Fork Chatworth Creek—stream....CA-9
North Fork Cheaha Creek....AL-4
North Fork Chena River—stream....AK-9
North Fork Cheney Creek—stream....CO-8
North Fork Cherokee Creek—stream....TX-5
North Fork Cherry Creek....ID-8
North Fork Cherry Creek—stream....CA-9
North Fork Cherry Creek—stream....ID-8
North Fork Cherry Creek—stream (2)....MT-8
North Fork Cherry Creek—stream....OR-9
North Fork Cherry Creek—stream....WA-9
North Fork Cherry Creek—stream....WY-8
North Fork Cherry River—stream....WV-2
North Fork Chestnut Creek....VA-3
North Fork Chetco River—stream....OR-9
North Fork Chevelon Canyon....AZ-5
North Fork Chevelon Canyon (historical)—valley....AZ-5
North Fork Chewelah Creek—stream....WA-9
North Fork Chiatovich Creek—stream....NV-8
North Fork Chickadee Creek—stream....WA-9
North Fork Chief River—stream....WI-6
North Fork Chikaskia River—stream....KS-7
North Fork Chilcoot Creek—stream....OR-9
North Fork Chilli Creek—stream....MS-4
North Fork Chimney Rock Canyon—valley....UT-8
North Fork China Gulch—valley....CA-9
North Fork Chloride Canyon—valley....UT-8
North Fork Chocktoot Creek—stream....OR-9
North Fork Chokecherry Creek—stream....NV-8
North Fork Christie Creek—stream....ID-8
North Fork Chukar Creek—stream....ID-8
North Fork Cienega Creek—stream....TX-5
North Fork Cienegita Canyon—valley....NM-5
North Fork Cimarroncito Creek—stream....NM-5
North Fork Cimarron River—stream....CO-8
North Fork Cimarron River—stream....KS-7
North Fork Cispus River—stream....WA-9
North Fork Citico Creek—stream....TN-4
North Fork Citico Trail—trail....TN-4
North Fork City Creek—stream (2)....UT-8
North Fork Clackamas River—stream....OR-9
North Fork Clam River—stream....WI-6
North Fork Clanton Creek—stream....IA-7
North Fork Clark Canyon—valley....NM-5
North Fork Clark Creek—stream....CA-9
North Fork Clark Creek—stream....ND-7
North Fork Clark Creek—stream....OR-9
North Fork Clark Fork—stream....ID-8
North Fork Clarks Fork Creek—stream....OR-9
North Fork Clarkson Creek....UT-8
North Fork Clark Wash—stream....AZ-5
North Fork Clatskanie River—stream....OR-9
North Fork Claybank Creek....MO-7
North Fork Claybank Creek—stream....MO-7
North Fork Clear Creek—stream (2)....CA-9
North Fork Clear Creek—stream....CO-8
North Fork Clear Creek—stream....ID-8
North Fork Clear Creek—stream....IL-6
North Fork Clear Creek—stream....MO-7
North Fork Clear Creek—stream....MT-8
North Fork Clear Creek—stream....NV-8
North Fork Clear Creek—stream....OK-5
North Fork Clear Creek—stream....TN-4
North Fork Clear Creek—stream....UT-8
North Fork Clear Creek—stream....WA-9
North Fork Clearwater River—stream....ID-8
North Fork Cleve Creek—stream....NV-8
North Fork Clicks Creek—stream....CA-9
North Fork Cliff Creek—stream....OR-9
North Fork Clinch River—stream....TN-4
North Fork Clinch River—stream (2)....VA-3
North Fork Clover Creek—stream....MT-8
North Fork Clover Creek—stream....WA-9
North Fork Clugston Creek—stream....WA-9
North Fork Coal Bank Creek—stream....MT-8
North Fork Coal Creek—stream....IN-6
North Fork Coal Draw—valley....WY-8
North Fork Coal Fork—stream....UT-8
North Fork Coal Gulch—valley....MT-8
North Fork Coal Gulch—valley....WY-8
North Fork Coalpit Run—stream....PA-2
North Fork Coal Wash—valley....UT-8
North Fork Cochino Bayou—stream....TX-5
North Fork Coeur d'Alene River—stream....ID-8
North Fork Coffee Creek—stream....CA-9
North Fork Cogswell Creek—stream....OR-9
North Fork Cold Creek—stream....ID-8
North Fork Cold Creek—stream....MT-8
North Fork Cold Creek—stream....NV-8
North Fork Cold Spring Creek—stream....OR-9
North Fork Cold Springs Canyon—valley....OR-9
North Fork Cole Branch—stream....KY-4
North Fork Coles Creek—stream....MS-4
North Fork Collier Creek—stream....OR-9
North Fork Colockum Creek—stream....WA-9
North Fork Colony Creek—stream....TX-5
North Fork Community Center—locale....MT-8
North Fork Compton Creek—stream....OH-6
North Fork Conejos River—stream....CO-8
North Fork Cone Rock Draw—valley....CO-8
North Fork Conley Creek—stream....CA-9
North Fork Cook Creek—stream....OR-9
North Fork Cooks Creek—stream....MT-8
North Fork Coon Creek—stream....CO-8
North Fork Coon Creek—stream....TN-4
North Fork Cooper Creek—stream....WY-8
North Fork Cooper Forks—stream....AZ-5
North Fork Coos River....OR-9
North Fork Copeland Creek—stream....OR-9
North Fork Coppei Creek—stream....WA-9
North Fork Copper Creek—stream....KY-4
North Fork Copper Creek—stream....MT-8
North Fork Copper River—stream....WI-6
North Fork Coquille River—stream....OR-9
North Fork Corbin Creek—stream....CA-9
North Fork Corn Creek....AZ-5
North Fork Corn Creek—stream....UT-8
North Fork Corner Canyon—valley....UT-8
North Fork Corn Wash....AZ-5
North Fork Corral Canyon—valley....NM-5
North Fork Corral Creek—stream (2)....MT-8
North Fork Corral Creek—stream....OR-9
North Fork Cosumnes River—stream....CA-9
North Fork Cottaneva Creek—stream....CA-9
North Fork Cotton Creek—stream....KS-7
North Fork Cotton Creek—stream....MT-8
North Fork Cotton Creek—stream....OK-5
North Fork Cottonwood Canyon—valley....NV-8
North Fork Cottonwood Creek....CA-9
North Fork Cottonwood Creek....MT-8
North Fork Cottonwood Creek—stream (4)....CA-9
North Fork Cottonwood Creek—stream....CO-8
North Fork Cottonwood Creek—stream (2)....ID-8
North Fork Cottonwood Creek—stream (10)....MT-8
North Fork Cottonwood Creek—stream (2)....NV-8
North Fork Cottonwood Creek—stream....OR-9
North Fork Cottonwood Creek—stream (2)....UT-8
North Fork Cottonwood Creek—stream (5)....WY-8
North Fork Cottonwood Draw—valley....WY-8
North Fork Cottonwood River....KS-7
North Fork Couer d'Alene River....ID-8
North Fork Cougar Creek—stream....ID-8
North Fork Country Club—other....NY-2
North Fork Country Club—other....PA-2
North Fork Countryman Creek—stream....MT-8
North Fork County Park—park....OR-9
North Fork Courtneys Creek—stream....MT-8
North Fork Cove Creek....UT-8
North Fork Cove Creek—stream....ID-8
North Fork Cove Creek—stream....NC-3
North Fork Cow Bayou....TX-5
North Fork Cow Cabin Creek—stream....MT-8
North Fork Cow Camp—locale....OR-9
North Fork Cow Creek—stream....ID-8
North Fork Cow Creek—stream....MT-8
North Fork Cow Creek—stream....NV-8
North Fork Cow Creek—stream....NC-3
North Fork Cow Creek—stream....WA-9
North Fork Coweeta Creek—stream....NC-3
North Fork Cowiche Creek—stream....WA-9
North Fork Cowikee Creek—stream....AL-4
North Fork Cox Creek—stream....IL-6
North Fork Cox Creek—stream....OR-9
North Fork Crabtree Creek—stream....MD-2
North Fork Cracker Box Creek—stream....MT-8
North Fork Cranberry River—stream....WV-2
North Fork Crandall Creek—stream....WY-8
North Fork Crane Creek—stream....OR-9
North Fork Crazy Creek—stream....AK-9
North Fork Crazy Woman Creek—stream....WY-8
North Fork Creek....CA-9
North Fork Creek....CO-8
North Fork Creek....ID-8
North Fork Creek....MO-7
North Fork Creek....MT-8
North Fork Creek....NE-7
North Fork Creek....NV-8
North Fork Creek....OK-5
North Fork Creek....OR-9
North Fork Creek....PA-2
North Fork Creek....TN-4
North Fork Creek....WA-9
North Fork Creek—stream....AL-4
North Fork Creek—stream....CA-9
North Fork Creek—stream....ID-8
Northfork Creek—stream....ND-7
North Fork Creek—stream....OR-9
North Fork Creek—stream (2)....TN-4
North Fork Creek—stream....TX-5
North Fork Creek—stream....WA-9
North Fork Crescent River—stream....AK-9
North Fork Cronin Creek—stream....OR-9
North Fork Crooked Creek....IL-6
North Fork Crooked Creek—stream....AL-4
North Fork Crooked Creek—stream....CA-9
North Fork Crooked Creek—stream....MN-6
North Fork Crooked Creek—stream (2)....MO-7
North Fork Crooked Creek—stream....MT-8
North Fork Crooked Creek—stream....NC-3
North Fork Crooked Creek—stream....OR-9
North Fork Crooked Creek—stream (2)....TN-4
North Fork Crooked Creek—stream....TX-5
North Fork Crooked Creek—stream....WA-9
North Fork Crooked Creek—stream....WY-8
North Fork Crooked Draw—valley....WY-8
North Fork Crooked River—stream....GA-3
North Fork Crooked River—stream....OR-9
North Fork Cross Creek....TN-4
North Fork Cross Creek—stream....PA-2
North Fork Crossing Forest Camp—locale....OR-9
North Fork Crow Creek....WY-8
North Fork Crow Creek—stream....UT-8
North Fork Crow Creek—stream....WY-8
North Fork Crow River—stream....MN-6
North Fork Crum Canyon—valley....WA-9
North Fork Crystal Creek—stream....OR-9
North Fork Crystal Creek—stream....WY-8
North Fork Crystal River—stream....CO-8
North Fork Cub Creek—stream....TN-4
North Fork Cuivre River—stream....MO-7
North Fork Culebra Creek....CO-8
North Fork Cuneo Creek—stream....CA-9
North Fork Cunningham Creek—stream....VA-3
North Fork Curley Creek—stream....WA-9
North Fork Currant Creek—stream....WA-9
North Fork Curreys Fork....KY-4
North Fork Currys Fork—stream....KY-4
North Fork Cut Bank Creek—stream....MT-8
North Fork Cypress Bayou—stream....AR-4
North Fork Cypress Creek—stream....AL-4
North Fork Cypress Creek—stream....TX-5
North Fork Dabbs Creek—stream....TN-4
North Fork Dagislakhna Creek—stream....AK-9
North Fork Dahl Creek—stream....OR-9
North Fork Dairy Creek—stream....WA-9
North Fork Daisy Dean Creek—stream....MT-8
North Fork Dakota Creek—stream....WA-9
North Fork Dale Creek—stream....MT-8
North Fork Daly Creek—stream....OR-9
North Fork Dam—dam (2)....CA-9
North Fork Dam—dam....NM-5
North Fork Dam—dam....NC-3
North Fork Dam—dam (4)....OR-9
North Fork Dam—dam (2)....PA-2
North Fork Daniels Creek—stream....ID-8
North Fork Darby Creek—stream....WY-8
North Fork Date Creek—stream....AZ-5
North Fork Davis Creek—stream....CA-9
North Fork Davis Creek—stream....MT-8
North Fork Davis Gulch....CO-8
North Fork Davis Gulch—valley....CO-8
North Fork Day Creek—stream....WA-9
North Fork Dead Boy Creek—stream....MT-8
North Fork Dead Horse Creek—stream....WY-8
North Fork Deadman Creek—stream....AZ-5
North Fork Deadman Creek—stream (2)....MT-8
North Fork Deadman Creek—stream....WA-9
North Fork Deadman Creek—stream....WY-8
North Fork Deadman Gulch....WA-9
North Fork Deadwood Creek—stream....OR-9
North Fork Deaf Smith Canyon—valley....UT-8
North Fork Dearborn River....MT-8
North Fork Dear Creek....CA-9
North Fork Deardorff Creek—stream....OR-9
North Fork Deep Creek—stream....AK-9
North Fork Deep Creek—stream....CA-9
North Fork Deep Creek—stream....CO-8
North Fork Deep Creek—stream....ID-8
North Fork Deep Creek—stream (5)....MT-8
North Fork Deep Creek—stream....NV-8
North Fork Deep Creek—stream (2)....OR-9
North Fork Deep Creek—stream (3)....UT-8
North Fork Deep Creek—stream (3)....WA-9
North Fork Deer Canyon Creek—stream....MT-8
North Fork Deer Creek....CA-9
North Fork Deer Creek....MT-8
North Fork Deer Creek—stream....CA-9
North Fork Deer Creek—stream (3)....CO-8
North Fork Deer Creek—stream (5)....ID-8
North Fork Deer Creek—stream (2)....MT-8
North Fork Deer Creek—stream....NV-8
North Fork Deer Creek—stream....OH-6
North Fork Deer Creek—stream (3)....OR-9
North Fork Deer Creek—stream....TN-4
North Fork Deer Creek—stream....UT-8
North Fork Deer Creek—stream....WA-9
North Fork Deer Creek—stream....WY-8
North Fork Deering Creek....NV-8
North Fork Deer River....TN-4
North Fork Deer River—stream....AL-4
North Fork DeGarmo Canyon—valley....OR-9
North Fork DeHaven Creek—stream....CA-9
North Fork Del Puerto Creek—stream....CA-9
North Fork Dempsey Creek—stream....MT-8
North Fork Dempsey Creek—stream....WY-8
North Fork Dennett Creek—stream....ID-8
North Fork Denny Creek—stream....CO-8
North Fork Derby Creek—stream....CO-8
North Fork Desolation Creek—stream....OR-9
North Fork Devils Canyon—valley....MT-8
North Fork Devils Creek—stream....NM-5
North Fork Devils Creek—stream....WA-9
North Fork Devils Gulch—valley....CA-9
North Fork Diamond Creek—stream....AZ-5
North Fork Diamond Creek—stream....CA-9
North Fork Diamond Creek—stream....OR-9
North Fork Diamond Gulch....UT-8
North Fork Dibble Creek—stream....CA-9
North Fork Dick Creek—stream....WY-8
North Fork Dicks Creek—stream....ID-8
North Fork Dillon Creek—stream....CA-9
North Fork Dismal Creek—stream....OR-9
North Fork Dismal River—stream....NE-7
North Fork Ditch—canal....CA-9
North Fork Ditch—canal (2)....CO-8
North Fork Ditch—canal....OR-9
North Fork Ditch—canal....WY-8
North Fork Ditch Creek—stream....CA-9
North Fork Ditch Creek—stream....WY-8
North Fork Ditch No 1—canal....WY-8
North Fork Ditch No 2—canal (2)....WY-8
North Fork Ditch No 5—canal....WY-8
North Fork Diversion Canal—canal....WY-8
North Fork Diversion Dam—dam....OR-9
North Fork Diversion Rsvr—reservoir....OR-9
North Fork Divide Creek—stream (2)....MT-8
North Fork Dixie Creek—stream....OR-9
North Fork Dodge Creek—stream....MT-8
North Fork Dog Coulee—valley....MT-8
North Fork Dog Creek—stream....CA-9
North Fork Dog Slaughter Creek—stream....KY-4
North Fork D'Olive Creek—stream....AL-4
North Fork Dollar Creek—stream....ID-8
North Fork Donahoe Creek—stream....TX-5
North Fork Doolittle Fork Creek—stream....MT-8
North Fork Double Branch—stream....GA-3
North Fork Double Canyon—valley....CA-9
North Fork Double Creek—stream (2)....OK-5
North Fork Double Mountain Fork Brazos River—stream....TX-5
North Fork Douglas Canyon—valley....AZ-5
North Fork Douglas Creek—stream....MT-8
North Fork Drake Branch—stream....TN-4
North Fork Draw—valley....WY-8
North Fork Driftwood Creek—stream....KS-7
North Fork Driftwood Creek—stream....NE-7
North Fork Dry Beaver Creek—stream....WY-8
North Fork Dry Branch—stream....IN-6
North Fork Dry Cottonwood Creek—stream....MT-8
North Fork Dry Creek....WA-9
North Fork Dry Creek—stream....AL-4
North Fork Dry Creek—stream....AR-4
North Fork Dry Creek—stream (3)....CA-9
North Fork Dry Creek—stream....MO-7
North Fork Dry Creek—stream (2)....MT-8
North Fork Dry Creek—stream....NM-5
North Fork Dry Creek—stream....OK-5
North Fork Dry Creek—stream (2)....OR-9
North Fork Dry Creek—stream (2)....TX-5
North Fork Dry Creek—stream....UT-8
North Fork Dry Creek—stream (2)....WA-9
North Fork Dry Creek—stream (2)....WY-8
North Fork Dry Creek Trail—trail....CO-8
North Fork Dryden Creek—stream....KY-4
North Fork Dry Fork—stream....AR-4
North Fork Dry Fork—stream....UT-8
North Fork Dry Fork Cheyenne River—stream (2)....WY-8
North Fork Dry Fork Marias River—stream....MT-8
North Fork Dry Gulch—valley....MT-8
North Fork Dry Gulch Canal—canal....UT-8
North Fork Dry Piney Creek—stream....WY-8
North Fork Dry Run—stream....VA-3
North Fork Dry Valley Creek—stream....NV-8
North Fork Dry Willow Creek—stream....CO-8
North Fork Duchesne River - in part....UT-8
North Fork Duck Creek....NC-3
North Fork Duck Creek—stream....CA-9
North Fork Duck Creek—stream....ID-8
North Fork Duck Creek—stream (2)....MT-8
North Fork Duck Creek—stream (2)....WY-8
North Fork Duck River....TN-4
North Fork Dugout Coulee—valley....MT-8
North Fork Duncan Creek—stream....KY-4
North Fork Dunkard Fork—stream....PA-2
North Fork Dunn Creek—stream....CA-9
North Fork Dunn Creek—stream....OR-9
North Fork Dupuyer Creek—stream....MT-8
North Fork Durham Creek—stream....OR-9
North Fork Durse Canyon—valley....UT-8
North Fork Dutch John Creek—stream....NV-8
North Fork Dye Creek—stream....CA-9
North Fork Eagle Creek—stream (2)....CA-9
North Fork Eagle Creek—stream (2)....ID-8
North Fork Eagle Creek—stream (2)....MT-8
North Fork Eagle Creek—stream....OR-9
North Fork Eagle Creek—stream....TN-4
North Fork Earley Creek—stream....WY-8
North Fork East Branch Pemigewasset River—stream....NH-1
North Fork East Creek—stream....CA-9
North Fork East Creek—stream....VT-1
North Fork East Fork Black River—stream....AZ-5
North Fork East Fork Chandalar River—stream....AK-9
North Fork East Fork Clear Creek—stream....CA-9
North Fork East Fork Hayfork Creek—stream....CA-9
North Fork East Fork Kaskaskia River—stream....IL-6
North Fork East Fork La Moine River—stream....IL-6
North Fork East Fork Rock Creek—stream....OR-9
North Fork East Lee Canyon—valley....NV-8
North Fork East Redwater Creek—stream....MT-8
North Fork East River....AZ-5
North Fork East River—stream....ID-8
North Fork East Squaw Creek—stream....NV-8
North Fork Eau Claire River—stream....WI-6
North Fork Ecola Creek—stream....OR-9
North Fork Edisto River—stream....SC-3
North Fork Edwards Creek—stream....MT-8
North Fork Eel River....IN-6
North Fork Eel River—stream....CA-9
North Fork Eightmile Canyon—valley....CO-8
North Fork Eightmile Canyon—valley....ID-8
North Fork Eightmile Creek—stream (3)....MT-8
North Fork Elbow Creek—stream....MT-8
North Fork Elder Creek—stream....CA-9
North Fork Elk Creek....CA-9
North Fork Elk Creek....ID-8
North Fork Elk Creek....OR-9
North Fork Elk Creek....WI-6
North Fork Elk Creek....WY-8
North Fork Elk Creek—stream (2)....CA-9
North Fork Elk Creek—stream....CO-8
North Fork Elk Creek—stream (2)....ID-8
North Fork Elk Creek—stream (6)....MT-8
North Fork Elk Creek—stream (2)....OR-9
North Fork Elk Creek—stream....WA-9
North Fork Elk Creek—stream (3)....WY-8
North Fork Elkhead Creek—stream....CO-8
North Fork Elkhorn Creek....KY-4
North Fork Elkhorn Creek....WV-2
North Fork Elkhorn Creek—stream (2)....ID-8
North Fork Elkhorn Creek—stream....WV-2
North Fork Elkhorn River—stream (2)....NE-7
North Fork Elk River....CA-9
North Fork Elk River—stream....CA-9
North Fork Elk River—stream....OR-9
North Fork Ellejoy Creek—stream....TN-4
North Fork Elliott Creek—stream....CO-8
North Fork Ellison Branch—stream....NC-3
North Fork Elm Creek—stream....MN-6
North Fork Elm Creek—stream....OK-5
North Fork Elmore Creek—stream....TN-4
North Fork Elochoman River—stream....WA-9
North Fork Embarras River—stream....IL-6
North Fork Embarrass River....IL-6
North Fork Emerson Creek—stream....CA-9
North Fork Encampment River—stream....WY-8
North Fork English River....IA-7
North Fork Entiat River—stream....WA-9
North Fork Escalante Creek—stream....CO-8
**North Fork Estates Subdivision**—pop pl....UT-8
North Fork Estes Creek—stream....SD-7
North Fork Evers Creek—stream....MT-8
North Fork Everson Creek—stream....MT-8
North Fork Ewing Creek—stream....TN-4
North Fork Extension Ditch—canal....CA-9
North Fork Fairchild Creek—stream....WA-9
North Fork Fall Branch—stream....TN-4
North Fork Fall Creek....OR-9
North Fork Fall Creek—stream....CO-8
North Fork Fall Creek—stream....IN-6
North Fork Fall Creek—stream....OR-9
North Fork Fall Creek—stream....SC-3
North Fork Fall Creek—stream....WY-8
North Fork Falling River....VA-3
North Fork Falls—falls....MT-8
North Fork Falls—falls....OR-9
North Fork Falls—falls....WA-9
North Fork Falls—falls (2)....WY-8
North Fork Falls Creek—stream....WA-9
North Fork Fan Creek—stream....MT-8
North Fork Fan Creek—stream....WY-8
North Fork Fancy Creek—stream....KS-7
North Fork Feather River—stream....CA-9
North Fork Feliz Creek—stream....CA-9
North Fork Fence Creek—stream....MT-8
North Fork Fence Creek—stream....WY-8
North Fork Fiddler Creek....WY-8
North Fork Fiddler Creek—stream....WY-8
North Fork Fifteenmile Creek—stream....WY-8
North Fork Fine Gold Creek—stream....CA-9
North Fork Finney Creek—stream....MO-7
North Fork Fir Creek—stream....MT-8
North Fork Fire Gulch—valley....MT-8
North Fork First Broad Creek—stream....NC-3
North Fork First Creek—stream....MT-8
North Fork First Hay Creek—stream....MT-8
North Fork Fish Canyon—valley....CA-9
North Fork Fish Creek....UT-8
North Fork Fish Creek....WY-8
North Fork Fish Creek—stream....CA-9
North Fork Fish Creek—stream (3)....CO-8
North Fork Fish Creek—stream (2)....ID-8
North Fork Fish Creek—stream....MT-8
North Fork Fish Creek—stream....OR-9
North Fork Fish Creek—stream....TX-5
North Fork Fish Creek—stream....WA-9
North Fork Fish Creek—stream (3)....WY-8
North Fork Fish Creek Wash—stream....CA-9
North Fork Fish Draw—valley....SD-7
North Fork Fisherman Creek—stream....WY-8
North Fork Fishhawk Creek....OR-9
North Fork Fishhawk Creek—stream....OR-9
North Fork Fishing Creek—stream....WV-2
North Fork Fitsum Creek—stream....ID-8
North Fork Fitzhugh Creek—stream....CA-9
North Fork Fitzsimmons Creek—stream....MT-8
North Fork Fitzum Creek....ID-8
North Fork Fivemile Creek—stream (3)....MT-8
North Fork Fivemile Creek—stream....OR-9
North Fork Fivemile Gulch—valley....CA-9
North Fork Five Springs Creek....WY-8
North Fork Flambeau....WI-6
North Fork Flat Creek....AL-4
North Fork Flat Creek—stream....NV-8
North Fork Flat Creek—stream....NC-3
North Fork Flat Creek—stream....TN-4
North Fork Flathead Creek—stream....MT-8
North Fork Flathead River—stream....MT-8
North Fork Flat Willow Creek....MT-8
North Fork Flatwillow Creek—stream....MT-8
North Fork Flint Creek—stream....MT-8
North Fork Flint River - in part....TN-4
North Fork Floras Creek—stream....OR-9
North Fork Floyd River—stream....IA-7
North Fork Floyds Fork—stream....KY-4
North Fork Ford Creek—stream....MT-8
North Fork Forked Deer River—stream (2)....TN-4
North Fork Forman Ravine—valley....CA-9
North Fork Forrester Creek—stream....KS-7
North Fork Fortification Creek—stream....CO-8
North Fork Fortune Creek—stream....WA-9
North Fork Fortymile River—stream....AK-9
North Fork Foster Creek—stream....MT-8
North Fork Foster Creek—stream....OR-9
North Fork Foundation Creek—stream....WA-9
North Fork Fourbit Creek—stream....OR-9
North Fork Fourche a Renault—stream....MO-7
North Fork Fourche Creek—stream....MO-7
North Fork Fourchette Creek—stream....MT-8
North Fork Four Dam....UT-8
North Fork Four Lakes Creek—stream....MT-8
North Fork Fourmile Creek—stream (2)....MT-8
North Fork Fourmile Creek—stream (2)....WY-8
North Fork Fourteen Mile Creek....MT-8
North Fork Fourth Gulch—valley....ID-8
North Fork Fowkes Canyon Creek—stream....WY-8
North Fork Fox Creek—stream....AK-9
North Fork Fox Creek—stream (2)....MT-8
North Fork Frazier Creek—stream....MT-8
North Fork Freeman Creek—stream....MT-8
North Fork French Broad River—stream....NC-3
North Fork French Creek....CO-8
North Fork French Creek—stream....CA-9
North Fork French Creek—stream....CO-8
North Fork French Creek—stream....ID-8

North Fork French Creek—*stream*............SD-7
North Fork Frenchman Creek—*stream*.......CO-8
*North Fork Frenchman River*......................CO-8
North Fork Freshwater Creek—*stream*......AK-9
*North Fork Fresno River*...........................CA-9
North Fork Frisco Creek—*stream*..............OK-5
North Fork Fritz Creek—*stream*................ID-8
*North Fork Frog Creek*..............................NV-8
North Fork Frog Creek—*stream*................NV-8
North Fork Fryingpan River—*stream*.........CO-8
North Fork Fuller Creek—*stream*..............CA-9
North Fork Gales Creek—*stream*...............OR-9
North Fork Galice Creek—*stream*..............OR-9
North Fork Game Creek—*stream*...............WY-8
North Fork Gap—*gap*...............................WV-2
North Fork Garcia River—*stream*..............CA-9
North Fork Garden Creek—*stream*.............NV-8
North Fork Garner Creek—*stream*..............ND-7
North Fork Gate Creek—*stream* (2)...........OR-9
*North Fork Gato Creek*..............................CO-8
North Fork Gauley River—*stream*..............WV-2
North Fork Geary Creek—*stream*...............CO-8
*North Fork Gentry Branch*..........................TN-4
North Fork Gentry Creek—*stream*.............TN-4
North Fork George River—*stream*..............AK-9
North Fork Gettings Creek—*stream*...........OR-9
*North Fork Gibson Jack Creek*....................ID-8
North Fork Gilbert Creek—*stream*.............MT-8
North Fork Gilbert Creek—*stream*.............UT-8
North Fork Gills Creek—*stream*................VA-3
North Fork Glen Aiken Creek—*stream*.......OR-9
North Fork Glenn Creek—*stream*...............MT-8
North Fork Glover Creek—*stream*..............ID-8
North Fork Goat Creek—*stream*................ID-8
North Fork Goble Creek—*stream*...............WA-9
North Fork Goetz Creek—*stream*..............WY-8
North Fork Goetze Creek—*stream*.............WY-8
North Fork Gold Creek—*stream*.................OR-9
North Fork Gold Creek—*stream* (3)............WA-9
North Fork Gold Fork River—*stream*..........ID-8
North Fork Goldsborough Creek—*stream*...WA-9
North Fork Goodale Coulee—*valley*...........MT-8
*North Fork Good Luck Creek*......................MT-8
North Fork Good Luck Creek—*stream*........MT-8
North Fork Goodpaster River—*stream*........AK-9
North Fork Goodwin Canyon—*valley*.........AZ-5
*North Fork Goose Creek*............................VA-3
North Fork Goose Creek—*stream* (2).........VA-3
North Fork Goose Creek—*stream*..............WA-9
*North Fork Goose River*............................ND-7
North Fork Goosmus Creek—*stream*..........WA-9
North Fork Gordon Creek—*stream*............CA-9
North Fork Gordon Creek—*stream*............OH-6
North Fork Gordon Creek—*stream*............OR-9
North Fork Gordon Creek—*stream*............UT-8
North Fork Grace Creek—*stream*..............CO-8
North Fork Graham Creek—*stream*............IN-6
North Fork Gramm Creek—*stream*.............WY-8
North Fork Grand Central River—*stream*....AK-9
North Fork Grand River—*stream*...............ND-7
North Fork Grand River—*stream*...............SD-7
*North Fork Granite Creek*..........................MT-8
North Fork Granite Creek—*stream*............ID-8
North Fork Granite Creek—*stream* (2).......WA-9
North Fork Granite Creek—*stream*............WY-8
North Fork Grapevine Creek—*stream*........MT-8
North Fork Grapevine Creek—*stream*........TX-5
North Fork Grassy Creek—*stream*.............KY-4
North Fork Grassy Creek—*stream*.............NC-3
North Fork Grave Creek—*stream*..............WV-2
North Fork Gravel Creek—*stream*.............OR-9
North Fork Gray Canyon—*valley*...............WA-9
North Fork Gray Creek—*stream*...............CA-9
North Fork Gray Creek—*stream*...............NV-8
North Fork Grays Creek—*stream*..............ID-8
North Fork Greasewood Creek—*stream*.....CO-8
North Fork Greasewood Creek—*stream*.....MT-8
North Fork Greasy Creek—*stream*.............VA-3
North Fork Great Miami River—*stream*......OH-6
North Fork Greely Creek—*stream*.............OR-9
North Fork Green Creek—*stream*..............MT-8
North Fork Greenhorn Creek—*stream*........MT-8
*North Fork Greenleaf Creek*.......................CO-8
*North Fork Green Mountain Canon Creek - in part*.............................................NV-8
North Fork Green Point Creek—*stream*......OR-9
North Fork Green River—*stream*..............WA-9
North Fork Green Run—*stream*................DE-2
North Fork Green Run—*stream*................MD-2
North Fork Green Timber Creek—*stream*....OR-9
*North Fork Greenwood Valley*....................MO-7
North Fork Griffin Creek—*stream*.............OR-9
North Fork Grindstone Creek—*stream*.......MO-7
North Fork Griswold Creek—*stream*..........CA-9
North Fork Grizzly Creek—*stream*.............CA-9
North Fork Groundhog Creek—*stream*........OR-9
*North Fork Grouse Creek*..........................UT-8
North Fork Grouse Creek—*stream* (2)........ID-8
North Fork Grove Creek—*stream* (2)..........MT-8
North Fork Guadalupe River—*stream*.........TX-5
North Fork Gualala River—*stream*.............CA-9
North Fork Guard Station—*locale*.............MT-8
North Fork Guard Station—*locale*.............NV-8
North Fork Guard Station—*locale*.............OR-9
North Fork Guard Station—*locale* (3).........WA-9
North Fork Guard Station No. 1142—*hist pl*.......................................WA-9
North Fork Guess Fork—*stream*...............VA-3
North Fork Guinns Creek—*stream*............MO-7
North Fork Gulch—*valley*........................CA-9
North Fork Gumboot Creek—*stream*..........OR-9
North Fork Gunnison River—*stream*..........CO-8
*North Fork Hackberry Creek*......................KS-7
North Fork Haddow Creek—*stream*...........MT-8
North Fork Hadley Creek—*stream*............IL-6
North Fork Halfway Coulee—*valley*...........MT-8
*North Fork Hall Creek*...............................WA-9
North Fork Hall Creek—*stream*................CA-9
North Fork Hall Creek—*stream*................WA-9
North Fork Hall Creek—*stream*................WY-8
North Fork Halls Gulch—*valley*.................CA-9
*North Fork Hanaupah Canyon*....................CA-9
North Fork Hanaupah Canyon—*valley*.......CA-9
North Fork Hancock Branch—*stream*.........NH-1
*North Fork Hangman Creek*.......................ID-8
*North Fork Hangman Creek*.......................WA-9
North Fork Hannahs Fork—*stream*............ID-8
North Fork Hanson Creek—*stream*............NV-8
North Fork Hardesty Creek—*stream*..........UT-8
North Fork Hardware River—*stream*..........VA-3
North Fork Hardy Creek—*stream*..............CA-9
North Fork Harmon Creek—*stream*............TN-4
*North Fork Haron Creek*.............................VA-3
North Fork Harris Creek—*stream*..............TN-4
North Fork Harrison Creek—*stream*...........AK-9
North Fork Harvey Creek—*stream* (2).........WA-9
*North Fork Hat Creek*................................ID-8
North Fork Hat Creek—*stream*.................ID-8
North Fork Hawk Branch—*stream*..............NC-3
North Fork Hawley Creek—*stream*.............MT-8
North Fork Hay Creek—*stream*.................MT-8
North Fork Hay Creek—*stream* (3)............WY-8
North Fork Hayden Creek—*stream*............ID-8
North Fork Hayes Creek—*stream* (2).........MT-8
North Fork Hay Hollow—*valley*................NM-5
North Fork Haystack Creek—*stream*..........ID-8
North Fork Haywood Creek—*stream*..........TN-4
North Fork Hayworth Creek—*stream*.........CA-9
North Fork Hazel Creek—*stream*..............CA-9
North Fork Helen Creek—*stream*..............MT-8
North Fork Hell Canyon—*valley*................UT-8
North Fork Hell Roaring Creek—*stream*......MT-8
North Fork Hemlock Creek—*stream*...........MT-8
North Fork Hemlock Creek—*stream*...........WI-6
North Fork Hensley Creek—*stream*............CA-9
North Fork Henson Creek—*stream*............CO-8
North Fork Herder Creek—*stream*.............NV-8
North Fork Hess Creek—*stream*................AK-9
North Fork Hickory Creek—*stream*............VA-3
North Fork High Creek—*stream*...............UT-8
North Fork Highwood Creek—*stream*.........MT-8
North Fork Hilgard Creek—*stream*............MT-8
North Fork Hill Creek—*stream*.................OR-9
North Fork Hill Creek—*stream*.................TX-5
North Fork Hinch Creek—*stream*..............MT-8
North Fork Hinkle Creek—*stream*..............OR-9
North Fork Hist Dist—*hist pl*....................CO-8
**North Fork (historical)**—*pop pl*..............MS-4
North Fork Hog Canyon—*valley*...............UT-8
North Fork Hollow—*valley*........................MO-7
North Fork Holly Creek—*stream*...............OK-5
North Fork Holmes Creek—*stream*............UT-8
North Fork Holston River—*stream*............TN-4
North Fork Holston River—*stream*............VA-3
North Fork Honey Creek—*stream*..............IN-6
North Fork Honey Creek—*stream*..............TN-4
North Fork Hooper Canyon—*valley*...........UT-8
North Fork Hoover Creek—*stream*.............MT-8
*North Fork Horse Canyon*..........................UT-8
North Fork Horse Canyon—*valley*.............NV-8
North Fork Horse Canyon—*valley*.............UT-8
North Fork Horse Creek—*stream*..............CO-8
North Fork Horse Creek—*stream* (4)..........MT-8
North Fork Horse Creek—*stream*..............NM-5
North Fork Horse Creek—*stream*..............TX-5
North Fork Horse Creek—*stream* (2)..........WY-8
North Fork Horsefall Canyon—*valley*.........AZ-5
North Fork Horsefly Creek—*stream*...........CO-8
North Fork Horse Range Creek—*stream*......CA-9
North Fork Horseshoe Creek—*stream*........ID-8
North Fork Hot Springs Creek—*stream*.......AK-9
North Fork Hot Springs Creek—*stream*.......MT-8
North Fork Howard Creek—*stream*............MT-8
North Fork Howell Creek—*stream*.............MO-7
*North Fork Hubbard Creek*.........................TX-5
North Fork Hubbard Creek—*stream*...........OR-9
North Fork Huckleberry Creek—*stream*.......WA-9
North Fork Hughes Creek—*stream*............CA-9
North Fork Hughes Creek—*stream*............ID-8
North Fork Hughes River—*stream*.............WV-2
*North Fork Humboldt River*........................NV-8
North Fork Humboldt River—*stream*..........NV-8
*North Fork Hungry Creek*...........................ID-8
*North Fork Hunt Creek*..............................ID-8
North Fork Hunt Creek—*stream*...............WA-9
North Fork Hunter Creek—*stream*.............OR-9
North Fork Hunter Creek—*stream*.............WA-9
North Fork Hu-Pwi Wash—*stream*.............NV-8
North Fork Hurricane Creek—*stream* (2)......AL-4
North Fork Hurricane Creek—*stream*..........KY-4
North Fork Hurricane Creek—*stream*..........TN-4
North Fork Huslia River—*stream*..............AK-9
North Fork Hyde Canyon—*valley*..............ID-8
North Fork Hyndman Creek—*stream*..........ID-8
North Fork Illinois Bayou—*stream*............AR-4
North Fork Imnaha River—*stream*.............OR-9
North Fork Independence Creek—*stream*....TX-5
North Fork Indian Canyon—*valley*.............NM-5
North Fork Indian Canyon—*valley*.............UT-8
North Fork Indian Coulee—*valley*..............MT-8
*North Fork Indian Creek*............................ID-8
*North Fork Indian Creek*............................MT-8
North Fork Indian Creek—*stream*.............CA-9
North Fork Indian Creek—*stream* (2).........ID-8
North Fork Indian Creek—*stream*.............IL-6
North Fork Indian Creek—*stream*.............KY-4
North Fork Indian Creek—*stream* (3).........MT-8
North Fork Indian Creek—*stream*.............NV-8
North Fork Indian Creek—*stream*.............OH-6
North Fork Indian Creek—*stream* (3).........OR-9
North Fork Indian Creek—*stream*.............TX-5
North Fork Indian Creek—*stream*.............UT-8
North Fork Indian Creek—*stream* (2).........WY-8
North Fork Indian Creek Dam—*dam*..........OR-9
*North Fork Indian Creek Rsvr*.....................OR-9
North Fork Indian Mission—*church*............CA-9
North Fork Indian River—*stream*..............AK-9
North Fork Indian Run—*stream*................OH-6
North Fork Indian Valley—*valley*...............CA-9
North Fork Indigo Creek—*stream*..............OR-9
North Fork Inman Creek—*stream*.............ID-8
North Fork Innoko River—*stream*.............AK-9
North Fork Ira Canyon—*valley*..................NM-5
North Fork Iron Creek—*stream*................ID-8
North Fork Iron Creek—*stream*................OR-9
North Fork Irwin Canyon—*valley*...............NV-8
North Fork Island—*island*........................AK-9
North Fork Issaquah Creek—*stream*..........WA-9
North Fork Italian Creek—*stream*.............NV-8
North Fork Ivy Creek—*stream*..................NC-3
North Fork Jackass Creek—*stream*............CA-9
North Fork Jack Canyon—*valley*...............CO-8
North Fork Jack Fork Creek—*stream*..........OK-5
*North Fork Jacks Creek*.............................NV-8
*North Fork Jacks Fork*...............................MO-7
North Fork Jackson Creek—*stream*...........CA-9
North Fork Jackson Creek—*stream*...........MT-8
North Fork Jackson Creek—*stream*...........NV-8
North Fork Jacobsen Gulch—*valley*...........OR-9
*North Fork Jacobson Gulch*........................OR-9
North Fork Jakes Creek—*stream*..............NV-8
North Fork James Creek—*stream*.............CA-9
North Fork Jaycox Creek—*stream*.............NY-2
North Fork Jennings Creek—*stream*...........TN-4
North Fork Jenny Branch—*stream*............LA-4
North Fork Jim Coulee—*valley*..................MT-8
North Fork Jim Creek—*stream*................OR-9
*North Fork Jocko River*.............................MT-8
North Fork Joe Creek—*stream*.................ID-8
North Fork Joe Ney Slough—*stream*..........OR-9
North Fork Joe Wright Creek—*stream*........CO-8
North Fork John Creek—*stream*...............WA-9
North Fork John Day Campground—*park*....OR-9
North Fork John Day River—*stream*..........OR-9
North Fork John Evans Canyon—*valley*.......ID-8
North Fork Johnny Gulch—*valley*..............MT-8
*North Fork Johns Creek*.............................OH-6
*North Fork Johns Creek*.............................WA-9
North Fork Johnson Creek—*stream*...........NE-7
North Fork Johns River—*stream*...............WA-9
North Fork Johnston Creek—*stream* (2)......OR-9
North Fork Jonca Creek—*stream*..............MO-7
North Fork Jones Creek—*stream*..............AK-9
North Fork Jones Creek—*stream*..............MO-7
North Fork Jones Creek—*stream*..............NC-3
*North Fork Jordan Creek*...........................MO-7
North Fork Jordan Creek—*stream*.............IN-6
North Fork Juan Creek—*stream*...............CA-9
North Fork Juda Branch—*stream*..............WI-6
North Fork Jump River—*stream*...............WI-6
North Fork Juncal Creek—*stream*.............CA-9
North Fork Juniper Canyon—*valley*............OR-9
*North Fork Kahnah Creek*..........................CO-8
North Fork Kalama River—*stream*.............WA-9
North Fork Kalamazoo Creek—*stream*........NV-8
North Fork Kanaka Creek—*stream*............CA-9
North Fork Kane Canyon—*valley*...............UT-8
North Fork Kannah Creek—*stream*............CO-8
North Fork Kanosh Canyon—*valley*............UT-8
North Fork Kashwitna River—*stream*..........AK-9
North Fork Kaukonahua Stream—*stream*....HI-9
North Fork Kaunakakai Gulch—*valley*.........HI-9
North Fork Kaweah River—*stream*.............CA-9
North Fork Kays Creek—*stream*................UT-8
North Fork Keeler Creek—*stream*.............MT-8
North Fork Kelly Creek—*stream*...............ID-8
North Fork Kelly Creek—*stream*...............NV-8
North Fork Kelsey Creek—*stream*.............CA-9
North Fork Kennally Creek—*stream*...........ID-8
*North Fork Kennedy Creek*.........................MT-8
North Fork Kent Creek—*stream*...............IL-6
North Fork Kentucky River—*stream*...........KY-4
North Fork Keren Neff Ditch—*canal*...........IN-6
North Fork Kiagna River—*stream*..............AK-9
North Fork Kid Creek—*stream*.................CA-9
North Fork Kilchis River—*stream*..............OR-9
*North Fork Kimberling Creek*......................VA-3
North Fork Kimberling Creek—*stream*.........VA-3
North Fork King Creek—*stream*...............OR-9
North Fork King Creek—*stream*...............WY-8
North Fork Kingsbury Gulch—*valley*..........CA-9
North Fork Kings Creek—*stream*..............PA-2
North Fork Kings Creek—*stream*..............WV-2
*North Fork Kings River*.............................CA-9
North Fork Kings River—*stream* (2)...........CA-9
North Fork Kintla Creek—*stream*..............MT-8
North Fork Kiowa Creek—*stream*.............OK-5
North Fork Kiowa Creek—*stream*.............TX-5
North Fork Kirkwood Creek—*stream*..........MT-8
North Fork Kirtley Creek—*stream*.............ID-8
North Fork Kisaralik River—*stream*...........AK-9
North Fork Kiutuestia Creek—*stream*.........GA-3
North Fork Klaskanine River—*stream*.........OR-9
North Fork Klopton Creek—*stream*............ID-8
North Fork Knobs—*range*.........................VA-3
North Fork Knobs—*ridge*..........................TN-4
North Fork Koger Creek—*stream*..............KY-4
North Fork Kougarok River—*stream*...........AK-9
North Fork Koyukuk River—*stream*............AK-9
North Fork Kraut Creek—*stream*..............OH-6
North Fork Kuskokwim River—*stream*.........AK-9
North Fork Kusshi Creek—*stream*.............WA-9
North Fork Kuzitrin River—*stream*.............AK-9
*North Fork Labrea Creek*...........................CA-9
North Fork La Brea Creek—*stream*............CA-9
North Fork Lacamas Creek—*stream*..........WA-9
North Fork Ladder Creek—*stream*............CO-8
North Fork La Guide Creek—*stream*..........CO-8
*North Fork La Guarde Creek*.......................CO-8
*North Fork Lake*.......................................TX-5
North Fork Lake—*lake*.............................AK-9
North Fork Lake—*lake*.............................ID-8
North Fork Lake—*lake*.............................MT-8
North Fork Lake—*lake*.............................NM-5
North Fork Lake—*lake*.............................WY-8
North Fork Lake—*reservoir*.......................CA-9
North Fork Lake—*reservoir*.......................VA-3
North Fork Lake Canyon—*valley*...............UT-8
North Fork Lake Creek—*stream*...............CO-8
North Fork Lake Creek—*stream*...............KS-7
North Fork Lake Creek—*stream*...............OR-9
North Fork Lake Creek—*stream*...............TX-5
North Fork Lake Fork—*stream*..................ID-8
North Fork Lake Fork—*stream*..................IL-6
North Fork Lakes—*area*............................AK-9
North Fork Lamarck Creek—*stream*...........CA-9
North Fork Lame Johnny Creek—*stream*......SD-7
North Fork Lancel Creek—*stream*.............CA-9
North Fork Lander Creek—*stream*.............WY-8
North Fork Las Cruces Arroyo—*stream*.......NM-5
*North Fork latah Creek*..............................ID-8
*North Fork latah Creek*..............................WA-9
North Fork Laurel Creek—*stream*..............NC-3
North Fork Lavaca River—*stream*..............TX-5
*North Fork Lava Creek*...............................ID-8
North Fork Lava Creek—*stream*................ID-8
North Fork Lawson Creek—*stream*............ID-8
North Fork Leatherwood Creek—*stream*......TN-4
North Fork Lee Creek—*stream*..................MT-8
North Fork Lee Creek—*stream*..................WV-2
North Fork Leeds Creek—*stream*..............WY-8
North Fork Left Fork Hurricane Creek—*stream*.......................................KY-4
North Fork Left Fork Proctor Creek—*stream*.......................................WV-2
*North Fork Leigh Creek*.............................ID-8
*North Fork Leion River*..............................TX-5
North Fork Lena Creek—*stream*...............MT-8
North Fork Leonard Creek—*stream*...........NV-8
North Fork Leon River—*stream*.................TX-5
*North Fork Lewis Creek*..............................IN-6
North Fork Lewis Creek—*stream*...............CA-9
North Fork Libby Creek—*stream*...............WA-9
North Fork Lick Creek—*stream*.................ID-8
North Fork Lick Creek—*stream*.................MT-8
North Fork Lick Creek—*stream* (3)............TN-4
North Fork Licking River—*stream* (2).........KY-4
North Fork Licking River—*stream*..............OH-6
North Fork Lightning Creek—*stream*..........ID-8
North Fork Lightning Creek—*stream*..........OR-9
*North Fork Limber Jim Creek*......................OR-9
North Fork Limber Jim Creek—*stream*........OR-9
*North Fork Lime Creek*...............................CO-8
North Fork Lime Creek—*stream*................ID-8
North Fork Limekiln Creek—*stream*...........UT-8
North Fork Lincoln Creek—*stream*.............WA-9
North Fork Lindsay Creek—*stream*............NV-8
North Fork Linganore Creek—*stream*.........MD-2
North Fork Linn Creek—*stream*.................MO-7
North Fork Lion Coulee—*stream*...............MT-8
North Fork Lisk Creek—*stream*.................MT-8
North Fork Little Arkansas River—*stream*...KS-7
North Fork Little Backbone Creek—*stream*.......................................CA-9
North Fork Little Badger Creek—*stream*.....MT-8
North Fork Little Barren Creek—*stream*......MO-7
North Fork Little Bayou San Miguel—*stream*.....................................LA-4
North Fork Little Beaver Creek—*stream* (2)......................................................OH-6
North Fork Little Beaver Creek—*stream*.....PA-2
*North Fork Little Beaver River*....................OH-6
*North Fork Little Beaver River*....................PA-2
*North Fork Little Belt Creek*.......................MT-8
North Fork Little Belt Creek—*stream*.........MT-8
*North Fork Little Blue River*........................IN-6
*North Fork Little Blue River*........................NE-7
North Fork Little Boulder Creek—*stream*....WA-9
North Fork Little Boulder River—*stream*......MT-8
North Fork Little Butte Creek—*stream*.......OR-9
North Fork Little Butte Creek Forest Camp—*locale*......................................OR-9
North Fork Little Cacapon River—*stream*....WV-2
North Fork Little Canyon Creek—*stream*....WY-8
North Fork Little Chestnut Creek—*stream*..VA-3
North Fork Little Copeland Creek—*stream*.......................................OR-9
North Fork Little Copper Creek—*stream*.....ID-8
North Fork Little Cow Creek—*stream*.........CA-9
North Fork Little Coyote Creek—*stream*.....NM-5
North Fork Little Creek—*stream*...............AL-4
North Fork Little Creek—*stream*...............MT-8
North Fork Little Deep Creek—*stream*.......WA-9
North Fork Little Dry Creek—*stream*.........CA-9
*North Fork Little Elk Creek*.........................MT-8
North Fork Little Fruin Creek—*stream*.......OR-9
North Fork Little Gooseberry Creek—*stream*.......................................WY-8
North Fork Little Green Creek—*stream*......TX-5
North Fork Little Henderson Creek—*stream*.......................................CO-8
North Fork Little Hoquiam River—*stream*...WA-9
North Fork Little Humboldt River—*stream*..NV-8
*North Fork Little Joe Creek*........................MT-8
North Fork Little Joe Creek—*stream*..........MT-8
North Fork Little Laramie River—*stream*....WY-8
North Fork Little Maquoketa River—*stream*.......................................IA-7
*North Fork Little Mazarn Creek*...................AR-4
North Fork Little McKittrick Draw—*valley*..NM-5
North Fork Little Medicine Bow River—*stream*.......................................WY-8
North Fork Little Miami River—*stream*.......OH-6
North Fork Little Mill Creek—*stream*.........CA-9
*North Fork Little Missouri River*..................WY-8
North Fork Little Missouri River—*stream*...WY-8
North Fork Little Mud Creek—*stream*........GA-3
North Fork Little Muddy Creek—*stream*.....WY-8
*North Fork Little Naches River*...................WA-9
North Fork Little Naches River—*stream*.....WA-9
North Fork Little Nemaha River—*stream*.....NE-7
*North Fork Little OA VAR Little Otter Creek*..VA-3
*North Fork Little Osage Creek*....................KS-7
North Fork Little Osage River—*stream*.......KS-7
*North Fork Little Otter Creek*......................VA-3
North Fork Little Pagosa Creek—*stream*.....CO-8
*North Fork Little Pend Oreille River*.............WA-9
North Fork Little Peoples Creek—*stream*....MT-8
*North Fork Little Pigeon Creek*....................IN-6
North Fork Little Pigeon Creek—*stream*.....IN-6
North Fork Little Pipestone Creek—*stream*.......................................MT-8
North Fork Little Prickly Pear Creek—*stream*.......................................MT-8
*North Fork Little River*...............................SC-3
North Fork Little River—*stream*...............GA-3
North Fork Little River—*stream*...............KY-4
North Fork Little River—*stream*...............NC-3
North Fork Little River—*stream*...............OK-5
North Fork Little River—*stream* (2)...........VA-3
North Fork Little Salt Creek—*stream*.........UT-8
North Fork Little Scrubgrass Creek—*stream*.......................................PA-2
North Fork Little Snake River—*stream*.......CO-8
North Fork Little Snake River—*stream*.......WY-8
North Fork Little Squaw Creek—*stream*.....ID-8
North Fork Little Sugar Creek—*stream*......KS-7
North Fork Little Thompson River—*stream*.......................................CO-8
North Fork Little Thompson River—*stream*.......................................MT-8
North Fork Little Timber Creek—*stream*.....ID-8
North Fork Little Timber Creek—*stream*.....MT-8
North Fork Little Wichita River—*stream*.....TX-5
*North Fork Little Willow Creek*....................UT-8
North Fork Little Willow Creek—*stream*.....OR-9
North Fork Little Wind River—*stream*........WY-8
*North Fork Llano River*..............................TX-5
North Fork Lobe Bremner Glacier—*glacier*..AK-9
North Fork Lobster Creek—*stream*............OR-9
North Fork Locate Creek—*stream*.............MT-8
North Fork Lockwood Creek—*stream*.........CA-9
North Fork Lodge Grass Canyon—*valley*.....MT-8
*North Fork Lodgepole Creek*.......................WY-8
North Fork Lodgepole Creek—*stream*........MT-8
North Fork Logan Creek—*stream*..............CA-9
North Fork Logy Creek—*stream*...............WA-9
*North Fork Lone Pine Creek*.......................CO-8
North Fork Lone Pine Creek—*stream*.........CA-9
North Fork Lone Ranch Creek—*stream*.......WA-9
North Fork Lone Tree Creek—*stream*.........CA-9
North Fork Lone Tree Creek—*stream*.........MT-8
North Fork Lone Tree Creek—*stream*.........WY-8
North Fork Lone Tree Gulch—*valley*..........WY-8
North Fork Long Branch—*stream*..............TN-4
North Fork Long Canyon—*valley*...............AZ-5
North Fork Long Canyon—*valley* (2)..........CA-9
North Fork Long Canyon—*valley*...............NV-8
North Fork Long Creek—*stream*................IA-7
North Fork Long Creek—*stream*................OK-5
North Fork Long Run—*stream*..................WV-2
North Fork Los Banos Creek—*stream*.........CA-9
North Fork Los Burros Creek—*stream*........CA-9
North Fork Los Pinos River—*stream*..........CO-8
North Fork Lost Boy Creek—*stream*...........MT-8
*North Fork Lost Creek*...............................MO-7
North Fork Lost Creek—*stream*................CO-8
North Fork Lost Creek—*stream* (2)...........MT-8
*North Fork Lost River*................................IN-6
North Fork Lost River—*stream*.................IN-6
North Fork Lost Trail Creek—*stream*.........CO-8
North Fork Lou Creek—*stream*.................CO-8
*North Fork Loup River*...............................NE-7
North Fork Louse Creek—*stream*..............OR-9
North Fork Lousignont Creek—*stream*........OR-9
North Fork Lower Keechi Creek—*stream*.....TX-5
North Fork Lower Willow Creek—*stream*.....MT-8
North Fork Loxahatchee River—*stream*.......FL-3
North Fork Lubken Creek—*stream*............CA-9
*North Fork Lubkin Creek*............................CA-9
North Fork Luffenholtz Creek—*stream*........CA-9
North Fork Luman Creek—*stream*.............WY-8
North Fork Lunice Creek—*stream*.............WV-2
North Fork Lynch Creek—*stream*..............TX-5
North Fork Lyons Creek—*stream*..............MT-8
North Fork Lytle Creek—*stream*................CA-9
North Fork Macks Creek—*stream* (2).........ID-8
North Fork Mad Creek—*stream*................CO-8
North Fork Madden Brook—*stream*...........VT-1
North Fork Mad River—*stream*.................CA-9
North Fork Maggie Creek—*stream*............ID-8
North Fork Maggodee Creek—*stream*........VA-3
*North Fork Maggotty Creek*.........................VA-3
North Fork (Magisterial District)—*fmr MCD*..................................VA-3
North Fork (Magisterial District)—*fmr MCD*..................................WV-2
North Fork Mahogany Creek—*stream*........ID-8
North Fork Maiden Creek—*stream*............MT-8
North Fork Main Creek—*stream*................WI-6
North Fork Malheur Campground—*park*.....OR-9
North Fork Malheur River—*stream*............OR-9
North Fork Mammoth Creek—*stream*.........MT-8
North Fork Manastash Creek—*stream*........WA-9
North Fork Manatee River—*stream*............FL-3
*North Fork Mancos River*...........................CO-8
North Fork Manor Creek—*stream*.............WA-9
North Fork Manti Canyon—*valley*..............UT-8
*North Fork Maple Canyon*..........................ID-8
North Fork Maple Creek—*stream*.............CA-9
North Fork Maquoketa River—*stream*.........IA-7
North Fork Marrowbone Creek—*stream*......TN-4
North Fork Marsh Coulee—*valley*..............MT-8
*North Fork Marsh Creek*.............................ID-8
North Fork Marsh Creek—*stream*.............MT-8
North Fork Mary Ann Creek—*stream*.........WA-9
North Fork Marys Creek—*stream*..............TX-5
*North Fork Massie Creek*............................OH-6
North Fork Massies Creek—*stream*............OH-6
North Fork Matilija Creek—*stream*............CA-9
North Fork Mattole River—*stream*.............CA-9
North Fork Mauvaise Terre Creek—*stream*...IL-6
*North Fork Maverick Canyon - in part*...........NV-8
North Fork McAfee Creek—*stream*............CA-9
North Fork McCann Branch—*stream*..........TN-4
North Fork McCowan Creek—*stream*..........TN-4
North Fork McCoy Creek—*stream*.............CA-9
North Fork McDonald Creek—*stream* (2).....MT-8
North Fork McDowell Creek—*stream*..........OR-9
North Fork McGrady Creek—*stream*...........KY-4
North Fork McGuire Creek—*stream*...........MT-8
North Fork McGuire Creek—*stream*...........OH-6
North Fork McKay Creek—*stream*.............MT-8
North Fork McKay Creek—*stream*.............OR-9
North Fork McKim Creek—*stream*.............ID-8
North Fork McKittricks Branch—*stream*.......VA-3
North Fork McLean Brook—*stream*............ME-1
North Fork Meacham Creek—*stream*.........OR-9
North Fork Meadow—*flat*..........................OR-9
*North Fork Meadow Creek*..........................WA-9
North Fork Meadow Creek—*stream*...........ID-8
North Fork Meadow Creek—*stream*...........MT-8
North Fork Meadow Creek—*stream*...........UT-8
North Fork Meadow Creek—*stream*...........WA-9
North Fork Meadows—*flat*........................CA-9
North Fork Meadows—*flat*........................WY-8
North Fork Meadows Trail—*trail*................CA-9
*North Fork Medicine Creek*.........................SD-7
North Fork Medicine Creek—*stream*..........SD-7
North Fork Meetinghouse Canyon—*valley*...UT-8
*North Fork Mehoopany Creek*......................PA-2
*North Fork Mehoppany Creek*......................PA-2
North Fork Melton Mill Branch—*stream*......TN-4
North Fork Memorial Cem—*cemetery*.........WV-2
*North Fork Merced River*............................CA-9
North Fork Merced River—*stream*.............CA-9
North Fork Mesa Creek—*stream*..............CO-8
*North Fork Methow River*...........................WA-9
North Fork Mexican Creek—*stream*...........CO-8
*North Fork Miami River*..............................OH-6
North Fork Miami River—*stream*...............FL-3
North Fork Mica Creek—*stream*................ID-8
North Fork Michigan River—*stream*...........CO-8
North Fork Middle Beaver Creek—*stream*...WY-8
North Fork Middle Boone Creek—*stream*....WY-8
North Fork Middle Boulder Creek—*stream*.......................................CO-8
North Fork Middle Cottonwood Creek—*stream*.......................................CO-8
*North Fork Middle Creek*............................CA-9
North Fork Middle Creek—*stream*.............CO-8
North Fork Middle Creek—*stream*.............NV-8
North Fork Middle Fabius River—*stream*....MO-7
North Fork Middle Fork Eel River—*stream*.CA-9
North Fork Middle Fork Grassy Creek—*stream*.......................................KY-4
*North Fork Middle Fork Hat Creek*...............ID-8
*North Fork Middle Fork Mokelumne River*.....CA-9
North Fork Middle Fork Tule River—*stream*.......................................CA-9
North Fork Middle Fork Walnut Creek—*stream*.......................................KS-7
North Fork Middle Fork Willamette River—*stream*.......................................OR-9
North Fork Middle Grave Creek—*stream*....WV-2
North Fork Middle Ladder Creek—*stream*...KS-7
North Fork Middle River—*stream*...............FL-3
North Fork Miles Creek—*stream*................MT-8
North Fork Milkhouse Creek—*stream*.........NV-8
*North Fork Milk River*................................MT-8
North Fork Milk River—*stream*..................MT-8
*North Fork Mill Creek*................................MT-8
*North Fork Mill Creek*................................OR-9
North Fork Mill Creek—*stream* (5)............CA-9
North Fork Mill Creek—*stream*.................ID-8
North Fork Mill Creek—*stream*.................KS-7
North Fork Mill Creek—*stream*.................LA-4
North Fork Mill Creek—*stream*.................MI-6
North Fork Mill Creek—*stream*.................NV-8
North Fork Mill Creek—*stream*.................OH-6
North Fork Mill Creek—*stream* (4)............OR-9
North Fork Mill Creek—*stream*.................PA-2
North Fork Mill Creek—*stream*.................TN-4
North Fork Mill Creek—*stream* (2)............UT-8
North Fork Mill Creek—*stream* (3)............WA-9
North Fork Mill Creek—*stream*.................WY-8
North Fork Miller Creek—*stream*...............MT-8
North Fork Miller Creek—*stream*...............WY-8
North Fork Millsap Creek—*stream*.............CO-8
North Fork Mills River—*stream*..................NC-3
*North Fork Mine*........................................OR-9
North Fork Mine—*mine*.............................CA-9
North Fork Mineral Canyon—*valley*............UT-8
North Fork Mineral Creek—*stream*.............NM-5
North Fork Mineral Creek—*stream*.............OR-9
North Fork Mineral Creek—*stream*.............WA-9
North Fork Miner Creek—*stream*...............WY-8
North Fork Mingo Creek—*stream*..............CA-9
North Fork Minneosa Creek—*stream*..........NM-5
*North Fork Minnesota Creek*.......................CO-8
North Fork Mission Creek—*stream*............CA-9
North Fork Mission Creek—*stream* (2)........MT-8
North Fork Missouri Ditch—*canal*..............MT-8
*North Fork Mitchell River*............................NC-3
*North Fork Moccasin Creek*.........................GA-3
North Fork Moccasin Creek—*stream*..........GA-3
North Fork Moccasin Creek—*stream*..........VA-3
North Fork Moclips River—*stream*..............WA-9
North Fork Mohawk River—*stream*............OR-9
North Fork Mokelumne River—*stream*........CA-9
*North Fork Mokins Creek*............................ID-8
*North Fork Molalla River*.............................OR-9
North Fork Molalla River—*stream*..............OR-9
North Fork Mono Creek—*stream*...............CA-9
North Fork Montana Creek—*stream*...........AK-9
North Fork Montgomery Creek—*stream*......CA-9
North Fork Montgomery Fork—*stream*........TN-4
North Fork Montgomery Gulch—*valley*.......MT-8
North Fork Montour Run—*stream*..............PA-2
North Fork Monumental Creek—*stream*......ID-8
North Fork Monument Creek—*stream*........MT-8
North Fork Moormans River—*stream*..........VA-3
North Fork Moose Creek—*stream*.............AK-9
North Fork Moose Creek—*stream*.............ID-8
North Fork Moose Creek—*stream*.............MT-8
North Fork Moquitch Canyon—*valley*.........AZ-5
North Fork Moran Creek—*stream*..............WY-8
North Fork Moreau River—*stream*.............SD-7
North Fork Morgan Creek—*stream*............ID-8
North Fork Morgan Creek—*stream*............TX-5
North Fork Morrison Creek—*stream*...........CO-8
North Fork Mosquito Creek—*stream*..........AK-9
North Fork Mosquito Creek—*stream*..........NV-8
North Fork Mosquito Creek—*stream*..........WY-8
North Fork Moss Agate Creek—*stream*.......SD-7
North Fork Moss Agate Creek—*stream*.......WY-8
*North Fork Mountain*..................................WY-8
North Fork Mountain—*ridge*......................WV-2
North Fork Mountain Creek—*stream*..........NC-3
North Fork Mountain Creek—*stream*..........WV-2
North Fork Mountain Lookout Tower—*locale*....................................WV-2
North Fork Mtn—*summit*..........................CA-9
North Fork Mud Creek—*stream*...............GA-3
North Fork Mud Creek—*stream*...............ID-8
North Fork Mud Creek—*stream*...............MT-8
North Fork Mud Creek—*stream* (2)...........TN-4
North Fork Mud Creek—*stream*...............WA-9
North Fork Mud Creek—*stream*...............WY-8
North Fork Mud Creek Spring—*spring*........WA-9
*North Fork Muddy Creek*............................NC-3
*North Fork Muddy Creek*............................UT-8
*North Fork Muddy Creek*............................WY-8
North Fork Muddy Creek—*stream*............KY-4
North Fork Muddy Creek—*stream*............MD-2
North Fork Muddy Creek—*stream*............MT-8
North Fork Muddy Creek—*stream*............UT-8
North Fork Muddy Creek—*stream*............WY-8
North Fork Muddy Creek Marsh—*swamp*....MD-2
North Fork Mud River—*stream*.................CA-9
North Fork Mud Spring Wash—*valley*.........UT-8
North Fork Mule Canyon—*valley*...............UT-8
*North Fork Mullen Creek*............................WY-8
North Fork Muncy Creek—*stream*.............NV-8
North Fork Munger Creek—*stream*............OR-9
North Fork Murphy Creek—*stream*...........WY-8
North Fork Murray Creek—*stream*.............CA-9
North Fork Murr Creek—*stream*...............MT-8
*North Fork Muscatat*..................................IN-6
*North Fork Muscatatuck Creek*....................IN-6
*North Fork Muscatatuck River*.....................IN-6
*North Fork Muscatatus Creek*......................IN-6
North Fork Mush Creek—*stream*...............WY-8
*North Fork Musselshell Creek*.....................ID-8
North Fork Musselshell River—*stream*........MT-8
North Fork Mustang Creek—*stream*..........CO-8
North Fork Mustang Creek—*stream* (3)......TX-5
North Fork Myers Creek—*stream*..............OR-9
*North Fork Naches River*............................WA-9
North Fork Naked Creek—*stream*..............VA-3
North Fork Nancy Creek—*stream*..............GA-3
North Fork Narrows Creek—*stream*...........ID-8
North Fork Naselle River—*stream*..............WA-9
North Fork Navarro River—*stream*.............CA-9
North Fork Necanicum River—*stream*.........OR-9
North Fork Negrito Creek—*stream*............NM-5
North Fork Negro Creek—*stream*..............NV-8
North Fork Nehalem River—*stream*............OR-9
North Fork Neils Creek—*stream*...............TX-5
*North Fork Nemaha River*...........................NE-7

North Fork Newaukum River—stream ... WA-9
North Fork New River ... CA-9
North Fork New River—stream ... FL-3
North Fork New River—stream ... NC-3
North Fork Nichols Branch—stream ... MO-7
North Fork Nigger Creek ... WA-9
North Fork Nile Creek—stream ... WA-9
North Fork Ninemile Creek—stream ... WY-8
North Fork Ninnescah River—stream ... KS-7
North Fork Nolin River—stream ... KY-4
North Fork Nooksack River—stream ... WA-9
North Fork North Anna River ... VA-3
North Fork North Benson Creek—stream ... KY-4
North Fork North Bosque River—stream ... TX-5
North Fork North Branch Lamoille River—stream ... VT-1
North Fork North Buffalo Creek—stream ... WY-8
North Fork North Clifty Creek—stream ... AR-4
North Fork North Creek—stream (2) ... UT-8
North Fork North Creston Creek—stream ... CO-8
North Fork North Cross Creek—stream ... TN-4
North Fork North Dry Creek—stream ... WY-8
North Fork North Elk Creek—stream ... CO-8
North Fork North Fabius River—stream ... MO-7
North Fork North Fork American River—stream ... CA-9
North Fork North Fork Gate Creek—stream ... OR-9
North Fork North Fork Klaskanine River—stream ... OR-9
North Fork North Fork Navarro River—stream ... CA-9
North Fork North Fork Trask River—stream ... OR-9
North Fork North Platte River—stream ... CO-8
North Fork North Powder River—stream ... OR-9
North Fork North River - in part ... MO-7
North Fork North Salt Creek—stream ... CA-9
North Fork Norton Creek—stream ... OR-9
North Fork Nosoni Creek—stream ... CA-9
North Fork Notchy Creek—stream ... TN-4
North Fork Nottoway River—stream ... VA-3
North Fork Noyo River—stream ... CA-9
North Fork Nuluk River—stream ... AK-9
North Fork Number Five Dam ... UT-8
North Fork Number One Dam ... UT-8
North Fork Number Six Dam ... UT-8
North Fork Number Two Dam ... UT-8
North Fork O ... NE-7
North Fork Oak Canyon—valley ... AZ-5
North Fork Oak Canyon—valley ... CA-9
North Fork Oak Creek—stream ... CA-9
North Fork Oak Creek—stream ... WA-9
North Fork Oat Creek—stream ... CA-9
North Fork Obia Creek ... ID-8
North Fork Obion River—stream ... TN-4
North Fork O'Brien Coulee ... MT-8
North Fork O'Brien Creek—stream ... MT-8
North Fork O'Brien Creek—stream ... WA-9
North Fork Observation Point—locale ... WY-8
North Fork Ocla Draw—valley ... WY-8
North Fork Oconee Rver ... GA-3
North Fork Of Big Blue River ... NE-7
North Fork Of Canadian River ... OK-5
North Fork of Cannon Ball River ... ND-7
North Fork of Cowiche River ... WA-9
North Fork of Diamond Creek ... CA-9
North Fork of Double Mo ... TX-5
North Fork of Double Mountain Fork Brazos River ... TX-5
North Fork of Dry Run ... VA-3
North Fork of East Fork Bitterroot River ... MT-8
North Fork of East Fork Black River ... AZ-5
North Fork of Eel River ... CA-9
North Fork of Flathead River ... MT-8
North Fork of Fresno River ... CA-9
North Fork of Grand River ... AZ-5
North Fork of Grand River ... CA-9
North Fork Of Grand River ... CO-8
North Fork of Grand River ... NV-8
North Fork of Grand River ... UT-8
North Fork of Hogan Creek ... IN-6
North Fork of Horse Range Creek ... CA-9
North Fork of Kaweah River ... CA-9
North Fork of La Brea Creek ... CA-9
North Fork Of Lewis River ... WA-9
North Fork of Lost Horse Creek ... MT-8
North Fork Of Miami River ... OH-6
North Fork of Middle Fork American River—stream ... CA-9
North Fork of Middle Fork Cosumnes River ... CA-9
North Fork of Middle Fork Eel River ... CA-9
North Fork Of Minam River ... OR-9
North Fork of Montezuma ... UT-8
North Fork of Muddy Creek ... UT-8
North Fork of North Fork ... CA-9
North Fork of North Fork American River ... CA-9
North Fork of North Fork of Yuba River ... CA-9
North Fork of North Fork Yuba River ... CA-9
North Fork of North River ... MO-7
North Fork of North Yuba River ... CA-9
North Fork of Popo Agie river ... WY-8
North Fork of Potomac River ... WV-2
North Fork of Redwater Creek ... WY-8
North Fork of Silent Canyon ... NV-8
North Fork of Skalkaho Creek ... MT-8
North Fork of Solomon River ... KS-7
North Fork of South Branch of Potomac River ... WV-2
North Fork of the Flathead River ... MT-8
North Fork of the Grand River ... ND-7
North Fork Of The Red River ... OK-5
North Fork of the Red River ... TX-5
North Fork Of The Republican River ... CO-8
North Fork of the South Fork of Stillwater River ... MT-8
North Fork of the Yachats Bridge—hist pl ... OR-9
North Fork of the Yuba River ... CA-9
North Fork of Thompson ... CO-8
North Fork of Tuolumne River ... CA-9
North Fork of Wailua River ... HI-9
North Fork of White River ... AZ-5
North Fork of White River ... AR-4
North Fork of White River ... MO-7
North Fork of Willow Creek ... MT-8
North Fork of Willow Creek ... OR-9
North Fork Ogden River—stream ... UT-8
North Fork Ogeechee River ... GA-3
North Fork Ogeechee River—stream ... GA-3
North Fork Ogilvy Ditch—canal ... CO-8
North Fork Oil Field—oilfield ... WY-8
North Fork Ojitos Canyon—valley ... NM-5
North Fork Okeson Draw—valley ... WY-8
North Fork Old Man Creek ... IA-7
North Fork Oldtown Creek—stream ... KY-4
North Fork Olmstead Creek—stream ... WY-8
North Fork Onancock Creek ... VA-3
North Fork One Eye Creek—stream ... CA-9
North Fork Ophir Creek—stream ... MT-8
North Fork Oregon Creek—stream ... CA-9
North Fork Orestimba Creek—stream ... CA-9
North Fork Otis Canyon—valley ... CA-9
North Fork Otter Creek ... VA-3
North Fork Otter Creek—stream ... AK-9
North Fork Otter Creek—stream ... MT-8
North Fork Otter Creek—stream ... WY-8
North Fork Otter River ... VA-3
North Fork Ouachita River—stream ... AR-4
North Fork Outlaw Creek—stream ... WA-9
North Fork Overton Wash—stream ... NV-8
North Fork Owen Creek ... OR-9
North Fork Owens Creek—stream ... CA-9
North Fork Owens Creek—stream ... OR-9
North Fork Owing Creek ... OR-9
North Fork Owings Creek—stream ... MT-8
North Fork Owl Creek ... WY-8
North Fork Owl Creek—stream ... WY-8
North Fork Owyhee River—stream ... ID-8
North Fork Owyhee River—stream ... OR-9
North Fork Oxford Creek—stream ... TN-4
North Fork Ozan Creek—stream ... AR-4
North Fork (P—stream ... OR-9
North Fork Pacheco Creek—stream ... CA-9
North Fork Packsaddle Creek—stream ... ID-8
North Fork Pacoima Canyon—valley ... CA-9
North Fork Paine Creek—stream ... WA-9
North Fork Paint Creek—stream ... OH-6
North Fork Painter Creek—stream ... TN-4
North Fork Paint River—stream ... AK-9
North Fork Palisades Creek—stream ... ID-8
North Fork Palix River—stream ... WA-9
North Fork Palm Wash—stream ... CA-9
North Fork Palomas Creek—stream ... NM-5
North Fork Palomino Canyon—valley ... AZ-5
North Fork Palo Pinto Creek ... TX-5
North Fork Palouse River—stream ... ID-8
North Fork Panther Creek ... TN-4
North Fork Panther Creek—stream ... AL-4
North Fork Panther Creek—stream ... AR-4
North Fork Panther Creek—stream ... KY-4
North Fork Panther Creek—stream (2) ... OR-9
North Fork Papoose Creek—stream ... CA-9
North Fork Paradise Canyon—valley ... UT-8
North Fork Paris Creek—stream ... WA-9
North Fork Park—park ... UT-8
North Fork Park Creek ... CA-9
North Fork Park Creek ... UT-8
North Fork Park Creek—stream ... OR-9
North Fork Parker Creek—stream ... AZ-5
North Fork Parker Creek—stream ... CA-9
North Fork Parker Creek—stream ... VA-3
North Fork Parmenter Creek—stream ... MT-8
North Fork Parsnip Creek—stream ... MT-8
North Fork Partridge Creek—stream ... ID-8
North Fork Pass Creek ... WY-8
North Fork Pass Creek—stream ... CO-8
North Fork Pass Creek—stream ... ID-8
North Fork Pass Creek—stream ... MT-8
North Fork Pass Creek—stream ... OR-9
North Fork Pass Creek—stream ... WA-9
North Fork Pass Creek—stream ... WY-8
North Fork Pasture—flat ... KS-7
North Fork Patterson Creek—stream ... CA-9
North Fork Patterson Creek—stream ... MO-7
North Fork Patterson Creek—stream ... WV-2
North Fork Payette River ... ID-8
North Fork Payette River—stream ... ID-8
North Fork Peachtree Creek—stream ... GA-3
North Fork Peak—summit ... WY-8
North Fork Pea Ridge Creek—stream ... MO-7
North Fork Pearl Creek—stream ... ID-8
North Fork Pebble Creek ... ID-8
North Fork Pebble Creek—stream ... ID-8
North Fork Pedee Creek—stream ... OR-9
North Fork Pelton Creek—stream ... WY-8
North Fork Pemberton Branch ... DE-2
North Fork Pennel Creek ... MT-8
North Fork Pens—locale ... TX-5
North Fork Perkins Fork—stream ... WA-9
North Fork Perry Aiken Creek—stream ... CA-9
North Fork Persian Ditch—canal ... CA-9
North Fork Peters Gulch—valley ... ID-8
North Fork Peumansen Creek ... VA-3
North Fork Phelps Brook—stream ... UT-8
North Fork Phillips Canyon—valley ... WY-8
North Fork Philpot Creek—stream ... CA-9
North Fork Pickett Creek—stream ... WY-8
North Fork Picnic Area—locale ... WY-8
North Fork Picnic Ground—locale ... CO-8
North Fork Pico Creek—stream ... CA-9
North Fork Piedra Blanca Creek—stream ... CA-9
North Fork Pierre River ... ID-8
North Fork Pierre River ... WY-8
North Fork Pierre's River ... ID-8
North Fork Pigeon Creek ... PA-2
North Fork Pigeon Roost Creek—stream ... TN-4
North Fork Pinchot Creek ... MT-8
North Fork Pine Creek ... NV-8
North Fork Pine Creek ... UT-8
North Fork Pine Creek—stream ... CA-9
North Fork Pine Creek—stream (3) ... ID-8
North Fork Pine Creek—stream ... IN-6
North Fork Pine Creek—stream ... MT-8
North Fork Pine Creek—stream ... NV-8
North Fork Pine Creek—stream ... OR-9
North Fork Pine Creek—stream (2) ... PA-2
North Fork Pine Creek—stream ... TN-4
North Fork Pine Creek—stream ... UT-8
North Fork Pine Creek—stream (2) ... WA-9
North Fork Pine Hollow Creek—stream ... WY-8
North Fork Pine Tree Canyon—valley ... CA-9
North Fork Pine Tree Canyon—valley ... NM-5
North Fork Piney Creek ... TN-4
North Fork Piney River—stream ... CO-8
North Fork Piney River—stream ... VA-3
North Fork Pinnacle—summit ... AR-4
North Fork Pin Oak Creek—stream ... TX-5
North Fork Pioneer Creek—stream ... AK-9
North Fork Pioneer Creek—stream ... MT-8
North Fork Pipestem Canyon ... AZ-5
North Fork Pismire Wash—valley ... UT-8
North Fork Pistol Creek—stream ... UT-8
North Fork Pistol River—stream ... OR-9
North Fork Pitman Creek ... KY-4
North Fork Pit River—stream ... CA-9
North Fork Placid Creek—stream ... MT-8
North Fork Pleasant Creek—stream ... UT-8
North Fork Plum Creek—stream ... CA-9
North Fork Plum Creek—stream ... NE-7
North Fork Plum River—stream ... IL-6
North Fork Pocatello Creek—stream ... ID-8
North Fork Pocket Creek—stream ... MT-8
North Fork Pointers Creek—stream ... MO-7
North Fork Poker Jim Creek—stream ... MT-8
North Fork Pole Creek ... MT-8
North Fork Pole Creek ... WY-8
North Fork Pole Creek—stream ... CO-8
North Fork Pole Creek—stream ... MT-8
North Fork Pole Gulch ... OR-9
North Fork Pomme de Terre River—stream ... MO-7
North Fork Ponderosa Canyon—valley ... UT-8
North Fork Poor House Creek—stream ... VA-3
North Fork Poorman Creek ... MT-8
North Fork Poplar River ... WI-6
North Fork Popo Agie River ... WY-8
North Fork Popple River—stream ... WI-6
North Fork Popular River ... WI-6
North Fork Porcupine Creek—stream (2) ... MT-8
North Fork Porphyry Creek—stream ... ID-8
North Fork Porter Creek—stream ... WA-9
North Fork Porterfield Creek—stream ... AK-9
North Fork Post Office (historical)—building ... TN-4
North Fork Potato Creek—stream ... WA-9
North Fork Potomac River ... WV-2
North Fork Pottawatomie Creek ... KS-7
North Fork Potts Creek—stream ... WV-2
North Fork Poudre Campground—locale ... CO-8
North Fork Pound River—stream ... VA-3
North Fork Powder River—stream ... WY-8
North Fork Powder Wash—valley ... CO-8
North Fork Powder Wash—valley ... WY-8
North Fork Powell Creek—stream ... PA-2
North Fork Powell River—stream ... VA-3
North Fork Prairie Creek—stream ... IN-6
North Fork Prairie Dog Creek—stream (2) ... KS-7
North Fork Prairie Dog Creek—stream ... ND-7
North Fork Pratt Creek—stream ... NV-8
North Fork Preacher Creek—stream ... AK-9
North Fork Prestons Fork ... IN-6
North Fork Price Branch—stream ... TN-4
North Fork Prospect Creek—stream ... UT-8
North Fork Prosser Creek—stream ... CA-9
North Fork Provo River—stream (2) ... UT-8
North Fork Pryor Cove Branch—stream ... TN-4
North Fork Pugh Canyon—valley ... UT-8
North Fork Pumpkin Draw—valley ... WY-8
North Fork Purgatoire River—stream ... CO-8
North Fork Quartz Creek—stream ... AK-9
North Fork Quartz Creek—stream ... MT-8
North Fork Quartz Creek—stream (2) ... OR-9
North Fork Quealy Creek—stream ... WY-8
North Fork Queen Creek—stream ... ID-8
North Fork Queens Creek—stream ... OR-9
North Fork Quinault River—stream ... WA-9
North Fork Quitchupah Creek—stream ... UT-8
North Fork R ... OR-9
North Fork Rabbit Creek—stream ... CO-8
North Fork Rabbit Creek—stream ... ID-8
North Fork Raccoon Creek—stream ... IL-6
North Fork Racetrack Creek—stream ... MT-8
North Fork Raft River—stream ... WA-9
North Fork Rainbow Creek—stream ... WA-9
North Fork Rainey Creek—stream ... ID-8
North Fork Rainy Creek ... ID-8
North Fork Rainy Creek—stream ... AK-9
North Fork Rainy Creek—stream ... SD-7
North Fork Ramelli Creek—stream ... CA-9
North Fork Ramey Creek ... ID-8
North Fork Ramshorn Creek—stream ... CA-9
North Fork Ramshorn Creek—stream ... MT-8
North Fork Ranch—locale ... NV-8
North Fork Ranch Creek—stream ... CO-8
North Fork Rancheria Creek—stream ... CA-9
North Fork Range ... ID-8
North Fork Range—range ... ID-8
North Fork Ranger Station—locale ... CO-8
North Fork Ranger Station—locale ... ID-8
North Fork Ranger Station—locale ... OR-9
North Fork Ranger Station—locale (2) ... WA-9
North Fork Rapid Creek—stream ... CO-8
North Fork Rapid Creek—stream ... ID-8
North Fork Rapid Creek—stream ... SD-7
North Fork Rapid River ... MN-6
North Fork Rapid River—stream ... WA-9
North Fork Rapier Mill Creek—stream ... NC-3
North Fork Raton Creek—stream ... CO-8
North Fork Rattlesnake Creek—stream ... CA-9
North Fork Rattlesnake Creek—stream (2) ... ID-8
North Fork Rattlesnake Creek—stream ... NC-3
North Fork Rattlesnake Creek—stream ... OH-6
North Fork Rattlesnake Creek—stream ... WA-9
North Fork Raven Creek—stream ... KY-4
North Fork Rawah Creek—stream ... CO-8
North Fork Ray Creek—stream ... MT-8
North Fork Red Bank Creek ... TX-5
North Fork Red Bank Creek—stream ... CA-9
North Fork Redbank Creek—stream ... PA-2
North Fork Red Bud Creek—stream ... MS-4
North Fork Red Butte Creek—stream ... UT-8
North Fork Red Canyon—valley ... UT-8
North Fork Red Cap Creek—stream ... CA-9
North Fork Reddies River—stream ... NC-3
North Fork Red Fork Powder River—stream ... WY-8
North Fork Red Mountain ... CA-9
North Fork Red River ... KY-4
North Fork Red River—stream ... OK-5
North Fork Red River—stream ... TX-5
North Fork Red Rock Creek ... MT-8
North Fork Red Run—stream ... WV-2
North Fork Redwood Creek—stream (2) ... CA-9
North Fork Reed Canyon—valley ... ID-8
North Fork Reed Creek ... VA-3
North Fork Reeds Creek—stream ... ID-8
North Fork Reese Creek—stream ... OR-9
North Fork Rei River ... OK-5
North Fork Rei River ... TX-5
North Fork Reno Creek—stream ... MT-8
North Fork Republican River—stream ... CO-8
North Fork Republican River—stream ... NE-7
North Fork Reservoir ... CA-9
North Fork Rex Creek—stream ... AK-9
North Fork Richardson Creek—stream ... VA-3
North Fork Richland Creek—stream ... IL-6
North Fork Richwood Run—stream ... WV-2
North Fork Rickard Coulee—valley ... MT-8
North Fork Ridge—ridge ... OR-9
North Fork Ridge—ridge ... UT-8
North Fork Riley Creek—stream ... OR-9
North Fork Rio de los Pinos—stream ... CO-8
North Fork Rio la Casa—stream ... NM-5
North Fork Rio Quemado—stream ... NM-5
North Fork Riordan Creek—stream ... ID-8
North Fork Rio Ruidoso—stream ... NM-5
North Fork Rio Virgin ... UT-8
North Fork Rivanna River—stream ... VA-3
North Fork River ... MN-6
North Fork River ... NC-3
North Fork River ... VA-3
North Fork River ... WV-2
North Fork River—stream ... AR-4
North Fork River—stream ... MO-7
North Fork River Run—stream ... WV-2
North Fork Roanoke River—stream ... VA-3
North Fork Robbers Roost Canyon—valley ... UT-8
North Fork Robie Creek—stream ... ID-8
North Fork Robinson Creek ... ID-8
North Fork Robinson Creek—stream ... ID-8
North Fork Robinson Wash—stream ... AZ-5
North Fork Rock Branch—stream ... TN-4
North Fork Rock Canyon—valley ... AZ-5
North Fork Rock Canyon—valley (2) ... UT-8
North Fork Rock Creek ... NV-8
North Fork Rock Creek ... OR-9
North Fork Rock Creek ... WY-8
North Fork Rock Creek—stream ... AZ-5
North Fork Rock Creek—stream ... CA-9
North Fork Rock Creek—stream ... CO-8
North Fork Rock Creek—stream ... ID-8
North Fork Rock Creek—stream (3) ... MT-8
North Fork Rock Creek—stream ... NE-7
North Fork Rock Creek—stream ... NC-3
North Fork Rock Creek—stream (6) ... OR-9
North Fork Rock Creek—stream ... TN-4
North Fork Rock Creek—stream ... TX-5
North Fork Rock Creek—stream ... WA-9
North Fork Rock Creek—stream ... WY-8
North Fork Rock Spring Canyon—valley ... OR-9
North Fork Rock Springs Creek—stream ... MT-8
North Fork Rocky Creek ... TX-5
North Fork Rocky Gulch—stream ... OR-9
North Fork Rodent Creek—stream ... WY-8
North Fork Rogers Creek—stream ... WA-9
North Fork Rolling ... KY-4
North Fork Rolling Fork ... KY-4
North Fork Roney Creek—stream ... WY-8
North Fork Roseau ... MN-6
North Fork Rosebud Creek—stream ... MT-8
North Fork Rose Creek—stream ... KS-7
North Fork Ross Creek—stream ... MT-8
North Fork Ross Fork—stream ... ID-8
North Fork Rotten Grass Canyon—valley ... MT-8
North Fork Rough and Ready Creek—stream ... OR-9
North Fork Rough Creek—stream ... CO-8
North Fork Rough Creek—stream ... MT-8
North Fork Rough River—stream ... KY-4
**Northfork (RR name North Fork)**—pop pl ... WV-2
North Fork Rsvr—reservoir ... NC-3
North Fork Rsvr—reservoir (4) ... OR-9
North Fork Rsvr—reservoir (2) ... PA-2
North Fork Ruby Creek—stream ... OR-9
North Fork Ruby Creek—stream ... WA-9
North Fork Rucker Canyon—valley ... AZ-5
North Fork Ruckles Creek—stream ... OR-9
North Fork Running Water Draw—valley ... TX-5
North Fork Running Wolf Creek—stream ... MT-8
North Fork Rush Creek—stream ... TX-5
North Fork Rushing Creek ... TN-4
North Fork Rush River ... MN-6
North Fork Russell Creek ... KY-4
North Fork Ruth Glacier—glacier ... AK-9
North Fork Rye Creek—stream ... MT-8
North Fork Ryegrass Creek ... OR-9
North Fork Sac Branch—stream ... KS-7
North Fork Sacramento River—stream ... CA-9
North Fork Sagebrush Creek—stream ... CO-8
North Fork Sage Creek ... MT-8
North Fork Sage Creek—stream (2) ... ID-8
North Fork Sage Creek—stream (3) ... MT-8
North Fork Sage Creek—stream ... UT-8
North Fork Sage Creek—stream ... WY-8
North Fork Sage Hen Creek—stream ... MT-8
North Fork Saguache Creek—stream ... CO-8
North Fork Saint Charles Creek—stream ... ID-8
North Fork Saint Joe River—stream ... ID-8
North Fork Saint Lucie River—stream ... FL-3
North Fork Saint Lucie River Aquatic Res—park ... FL-3
North Fork Saint Peter Creek—stream ... WA-9
North Fork Salado Creek—stream ... NM-5
North Fork Salcha River—stream ... AK-9
North Fork Saline River—stream (2) ... AR-4
North Fork Saline River—stream ... IL-6
North Fork Saline River—stream (2) ... KS-7
North Fork Sally Queen Creek—stream ... NC-3
North Fork Salmonberry Creek—stream ... OR-9
North Fork Salmonberry River—stream ... OR-9
North Fork Salmon Creek—stream ... WA-9
North Fork Salmon Falls Creek—stream ... ID-8
North Fork Salmon Falls Creek—stream ... NV-8
North Fork Salmon Falls River ... NV-8
North Fork Salmon River—stream ... CA-9
North Fork Salmon River—stream ... ID-8
North Fork Salmon River—stream ... WA-9
North Fork Salt Creek—stream ... CA-9
North Fork Salt Creek—stream ... CO-8
North Fork Salt Creek—stream ... IL-6
North Fork Salt Creek—stream ... IN-6
North Fork Salt Prong Hubbard Creek ... TX-5
North Fork Salt Prong Hubbard Creek—stream ... TX-5
North Fork Salt River ... AZ-5
North Fork Salt River ... MI-6
North Fork Salt River ... MO-7
North Fork Salt River—stream ... MO-7
North Fork Saluda River ... SC-3
North Fork San Antonio River—stream ... CA-9
North Fork Sand Arroyo—stream ... CO-8
North Fork Sand Creek—stream ... CA-9
North Fork Sand Creek—stream ... CO-8
North Fork Sand Creek—stream ... ID-8
North Fork Sand Creek—stream (3) ... MT-8
North Fork Sandrock Canyon—valley ... ID-8
North Fork Sand Run—stream ... MD-2
North Fork Sand Springs Arroyo—stream ... NM-5
North Fork Sand Wash ... CO-8
North Fork Sand Wash—valley ... CO-8
North Fork Sandy Creek—stream ... AL-4
North Fork San Fernando Creek—stream ... TX-5
North Fork Sanford Creek ... UT-8
North Fork San Gabriel River ... CA-9
North Fork San Gabriel River—stream ... CA-9
North Fork San Gabriel River—stream ... TX-5
North Fork San Jacinto River—stream ... CA-9
North Fork San Joaquin River ... CA-9
North Fork San Joaquin River—stream ... CA-9
North Fork San Jose Creek—stream ... CA-9
North Fork San Miguel Creek—stream ... LA-4
North Fork San Onofre Canyon—valley ... CA-9
North Fork San Pedro Creek—stream ... CA-9
North Fork San Pedro Creek—stream ... TX-5
North Fork Sanpoil River—stream ... WA-9
North Fork San Simeon Creek—stream ... CA-9
North Fork Santa Ana Creek—stream ... CA-9
North Fork Santa Anita Canyon—valley ... CA-9
North Fork Santiam River ... OR-9
North Fork Sappa Creek ... KS-7
North Fork Sappa Creek—stream ... KS-7
North Fork Sauk River—stream ... WA-9
North Fork Savery Creek—stream ... WY-8
North Fork Saw Creek—stream ... TN-4
North Fork Sawmill Canyon—valley (2) ... NV-8
North Fork Sawyer Creek—stream ... NC-3
North Fork Sayles Creek—stream ... WY-8
North Fork Scanty Branch—stream ... TN-4
North Fork Sch—school ... FL-3
North Fork Sch—school ... IL-6
North Fork Sch—school ... KY-4
North Fork Sch—school ... MN-6
North Fork Sch—school ... MT-8
North Fork Sch—school ... WV-2
North Fork Sch (historical)—school ... TN-4
North Fork Sch Number 1—school ... ND-7
North Fork Sch Number 2—school ... ND-7
North Fork School (Abandoned)—locale ... CA-9
North Fork Schooner Gulch—valley ... CA-9
North Fork Scorpion Creek—stream ... CA-9
North Fork Scotish Creek ... CA-9
North Fork Scott Creek—stream ... NC-3
North Fork Second Creek ... NC-3
North Fork Second Creek—stream (2) ... MT-8
North Fork Sekiu River—stream ... WA-9
North Fork Serpentine River—stream ... AK-9
North Fork Sevenmile Creek—stream ... CO-8
North Fork Sevenmile Creek—stream ... MT-8
North Fork Seventeenmile Creek—stream ... MT-8
North Fork Shale Creek—stream ... OR-9
North Fork Shannon Canyon—valley ... CA-9
North Fork Sharp Hollow—valley ... AZ-5
North Fork Shawnee Creek—stream ... IN-6
North Fork Shearer Creek—stream ... CO-8
North Fork Sheats Creek ... TN-4
North Fork Sheeds Creek—stream ... TN-4
North Fork Sheep Canyon—valley ... ID-8
North Fork Sheep Coulee—valley ... MT-8
North Fork Sheep Creek ... ID-8
North Fork Sheep Creek—stream (4) ... ID-8
North Fork Sheep Creek—stream (4) ... MT-8
North Fork Sheep Creek—stream ... NV-8
North Fork Sheep Creek—stream ... UT-8
North Fork Sheep Creek—stream (2) ... WY-8
North Fork Sheephead Creek—stream ... MT-8
North Fork Shelby Creek—stream ... IL-6
North Fork Shell Creek—stream ... WY-8
North Fork Shelton Creek ... WA-9
North Fork Shenandoah River—stream ... VA-3
North Fork Sherman Creek—stream ... WA-9
North Fork Sheyenne River—stream ... ND-7
North Fork Shields Creek—stream ... CA-9
North Fork Ship Creek—stream ... AK-9
North Fork Shoal Creek—stream ... IL-6
North Fork Shoals—bar ... TN-4
North Fork Shoal (Siuslaw River)—bar ... OR-9
North Fork Short Creek—stream ... OH-6
North Fork Short Creek—stream ... WV-2
North Fork Shoshone Creek—stream ... ID-8
North Fork Shoshone River—stream ... WY-8
North Fork Shotgun Creek—stream ... CA-9
North Fork Siding ... MT-8
North Fork Siletz River—stream ... OR-9
North Fork Sill Branch—stream ... TN-4
North Fork Silver Butte Creek—stream ... MT-8
North Fork Silver Creek ... WY-8
North Fork Silver Creek—stream ... ID-8
North Fork Silver Creek—stream ... NV-8
North Fork Silver Creek—stream (3) ... OR-9
North Fork Silver Creek—stream ... WA-9
North Fork Silver Creek—stream ... WY-8
North Fork Silver Falls Creek—stream ... UT-8
North Fork Simcoe Creek—stream ... WA-9
North Fork Simmons Creek—stream ... ID-8
North Fork Simms Creek—stream ... MT-8
North Fork Simpson Creek—stream ... OR-9
North Fork Singer Creek—stream ... CA-9
North Fork Sinker Creek—stream ... ID-8
North Fork Sioux Pass Creek—stream ... MT-8
North Fork Sitkum River—stream ... WA-9
North Fork Siuslaw Campground—park ... OR-9
North Fork Siuslaw River—stream (2) ... OR-9
North Fork Siwash Creek—stream ... WA-9
North Fork Six-bit Creek—stream ... ID-8
North Fork Six Creek—stream ... ND-7
North Fork Sixes River—stream ... OR-9
North Fork Sixmile Canyon—valley ... UT-8
North Fork Sixmile Creek—stream (2) ... MT-8
North Fork Sixmile Creek—stream ... UT-8
North Fork Sixmile Run—stream ... PA-2
North Fork Skagit River—stream ... WA-9
North Fork Skeenah Creek—stream ... NC-3
North Fork Skinner Creek—stream ... WI-6
North Fork Skokomish River—stream ... WA-9
North Fork Skookumchuck Creek—stream ... ID-8
North Fork Skookumchuck Creek—stream ... WA-9
North Fork Skookum Creek—stream ... WA-9
North Fork Skull Creek—stream (2) ... NV-8
North Fork Skykomish River—stream ... WA-9
North Fork Slate Creek—stream ... CA-9
North Fork Slate Creek—stream ... ID-8
North Fork Slate Creek—stream ... WY-8
North Fork Sleeman Creek—stream ... MT-8
North Fork Smackover Creek—stream ... AR-4
North Fork Smith Creek ... NV-8
North Fork Smith Creek—stream (2) ... ID-8
North Fork Smith Creek—stream ... MT-8
North Fork Smith Creek—stream ... NV-8
North Fork Smith Creek—stream ... NC-3
North Fork Smith Creek—stream ... ND-7
North Fork Smith Creek—stream ... TX-5
North Fork Smith Creek—stream ... UT-8
North Fork Smith River ... OR-9
North Fork Smith River—stream ... CA-9
North Fork Smith River—stream ... MT-8
North Fork Smith River—stream (2) ... OR-9
North Fork Smith River—stream ... VA-3
North Fork Smiths Fork—stream ... WY-8
North Fork Smoky Creek—stream ... CA-9
North Fork Smoky Hill River—stream ... CO-8
North Fork Smoky Hill River—stream ... KS-7
North Fork Snag Creek—stream ... WA-9
North Fork Snake Creek—stream ... SD-7
North Fork Snake Creek Canal—canal ... FL-3
North Fork Snake River ... ID-8
North Fork Snake River—stream ... AK-9
North Fork Snake River—stream ... CO-8
North Fork Snoqualmie River—stream ... WA-9
North Fork Snow Creek—stream ... NV-8
North Fork Snowshoe Canyon—valley ... WY-8
North Fork Soctish Creek—stream ... CA-9
North Fork Soldier Creek—stream ... CA-9
North Fork Soldier Creek—stream (2) ... ID-8
North Fork Soldier Creek—stream ... KY-4
North Fork Soldier Creek—stream ... NE-7
North Fork Soldier Creek—stream ... UT-8
North Fork Soleduck River—stream ... WA-9
North Fork Soleduck River Trail—trail ... WA-9
North Fork Solomon River—stream ... KS-7
North Fork Somerset Creek—stream ... KY-4
North Fork Sorrel Horse Creek—stream ... MT-8
North Fork Soup Creek—stream ... OR-9
North Fork South Arkansas River—stream ... CO-8
North Fork South Beaver Creek—stream ... IA-7
North Fork South Boone Creek—stream ... WY-8
North Fork South Branch Potomac River ... VA-3
North Fork South Branch Potomac River ... WV-2
North Fork South Branch Potomac River—stream ... WV-2
North Fork South Creek—stream ... MT-8
North Fork South Creek—stream (3) ... UT-8
North Fork South Fabius River—stream ... MO-7
North Fork South Fork Bear Creek—stream ... WY-8
North Fork South Fork Chambers Creek—stream ... TX-5
North Fork South Fork Crooked Creek—stream ... WA-9
North Fork South Fork Noyo River—stream ... CA-9
North Fork South Fork Ouachita River—stream ... AR-4
North Fork South Fork Sultan River—stream ... WA-9
North Fork South Fork Tacoma Creek—stream ... WA-9
North Fork South Fork Wildcat Creek ... IN-6
North Fork South Loup River—stream ... NE-7
North Fork South Piney Creek ... WY-8
North Fork South Piney Creek—stream ... WY-8
North Fork South Platte River—stream ... CO-8
North Fork South Toe River ... NC-3
North Fork South Zapata Creek—stream ... CO-8
North Fork Spanish Creek—stream ... CA-9
North Fork Spanish Creek—stream ... MT-8
North Fork Specimen Creek—stream ... MT-8
North Fork Spencer Creek—stream ... OR-9
North Fork Spirit River—stream ... WI-6
North Fork Split Creek—stream ... ID-8
North Fork Spotted Dog Creek—stream ... MT-8
North Fork Sprague River—stream ... OR-9
North Fork Spread Creek—stream ... WY-8
North Fork Spring—spring ... AZ-5
North Fork Spring Branch Creek—stream ... ID-8
North Fork Spring Canyon—valley ... CO-8
North Fork Spring Creek ... CO-8
North Fork Spring Creek ... IL-6
North Fork Spring Creek ... IN-6
North Fork Spring Creek ... MO-7
North Fork Spring Creek ... WY-8
North Fork Spring Creek—stream ... IN-6
North Fork Spring Creek—stream ... MO-7
North Fork Spring Creek—stream (3) ... MT-8
North Fork Spring Creek—stream ... OR-9
North Fork Spring Creek—stream ... WY-8
North Fork Spring Gulch—valley ... CA-9
North Fork Spring River—stream ... MO-7
North Fork Springs—spring ... MO-7
North Fork Spruce Creek—stream ... ID-8
North Fork Spy Run—stream ... VA-3
North Fork Squaw Creek—stream ... AZ-5
North Fork Squaw Creek—stream (2) ... CA-9
North Fork Squaw Creek—stream (3) ... ID-8
North Fork Squaw Creek—stream ... MT-8
North Fork Squaw Creek—stream ... NV-8
North Fork Squaw Creek—stream (2) ... OR-9
North Fork Squaw Creek—stream ... WA-9
North Fork Squaw Creek Rsvr—reservoir ... OR-9
North Fork Squirrel Creek—stream ... MT-8
North Fork Squirrel Creek—stream ... WY-8
North Fork Squirrel River—stream ... AK-9
North Fork Staley Creek—stream ... OR-9
North Fork Stanislaus River—stream ... CA-9
North Fork Star Creek—stream ... ID-8
North Fork Steel Creek—stream ... ID-8
North Fork Steelhead Creek—stream ... OR-9
North Fork Steephollow Creek—stream ... CA-9
North Fork Steiner Creek—stream ... NV-8
North Fork Stell Creek—stream ... OR-9
North Fork Steppes Creek—stream ... TX-5
North Fork Stevenson Creek—stream ... CA-9
North Fork Stewart Creek—stream ... OR-9
North Fork Stewarts Creek—stream ... VA-3
North Fork Stickney Creek—stream ... MT-8
North Fork Stillaguamish River—stream ... WA-9
North Fork Stillwater River—stream ... OH-6
North Fork Stillwell Creek—stream ... WV-2
North Fork Stinking River—stream ... VA-3
North Fork Stoddard Creek—stream ... ID-8

North Fork Stoner Creek—*stream* WY-8
North Fork Stony Creek—*stream* (2) CA-9
North Fork Stony Creek—*stream* TN-4
North Fork Stony Creek—*stream* VA-3
North Fork Storm Creek—*stream* ID-8
*North Fork Stotts Creek* IN-6
North Fork Stovall Creek—*stream* VA-3
North Fork Straight Canyon—*valley* NV-8
North Fork Straight Creek—*stream* PA-2
North Fork Stranger Creek—*stream* KS-7
North Fork Stranger Creek—*stream* WA-9
North Fork Strawberry Creek—*stream* WY-8
North Fork Street Creek—*stream* OR-9
North Fork String Creek—*stream* CA-9
North Fork Strongs Creek—*stream* CA-9
North Fork Stump Creek—*stream* ID-8
**North Fork (subdivision)**—*pop pl* NC-3
North Fork Sublett Creek—*stream* ID-8
*North Fork Sugar Creek* KS-7
*North Fork Sugar Creek* KY-4
North Fork Sugar Creek—*stream* ID-8
North Fork Sugar Creek—*stream* KY-4
North Fork Sugar Creek—*stream* OH-6
North Fork Sugar Creek—*stream* TN-4
North Fork Suggs Creek—*stream* TN-4
North Fork Sulatna River—*stream* AK-9
North Fork Sullivan Creek—*stream* MT-8
North Fork Sullivan Creek—*stream* WA-9
*North Fork Sulman Creek* OR-9
*North Fork Sulphur Creek* SD-7
North Fork Sulphur Creek—*stream* ID-8
North Fork Sulphur Creek—*stream* WY-8
North Fork Summit—*summit* PA-2
North Fork Summit Creek—*stream* OR-9
North Fork Sundance Creek—*stream* WY-8
*North Fork Sunday Creek* MT-8
North Fork Sun Hill Creek—*stream* GA-3
North Fork Sun River—*stream* MT-8
North Fork Surprise Creek—*stream* MT-8
*North Fork Sur River* CA-9
North Fork Suwannee River—*stream* GA-3
North Fork Swamp—*swamp* WA-9
North Fork Swampy Creek—*stream* WA-9
North Fork Swan Creek—*stream* NE-7
North Fork Swannanoa River—*stream* NC-3
North Fork Swan River—*stream* AK-9
North Fork Swan River—*stream* CO-8
North Fork Swasey Creek—*stream* UT-8
North Fork Swayze Creek—*stream* OR-9
North Fork Sweeney Creek—*stream* MT-8
North Fork Sweet Grass Creek—*stream* MT-8
North Fork Sweetwater Creek—*stream* MT-8
North Fork Sweetwater River—*stream* CA-9
North Fork Swens Canyon—*valley* UT-8
North Fork Swensons Canyon—*valley* UT-8
North Fork Swift Creek—*stream* CA-9
North Fork Swift Creek—*stream* WY-8
North Fork Swift River—*stream* AK-9
*North Fork Sybille Creek* WY-8
North Fork Sycamore Creek—*stream* CA-9
North Fork Sycamore Creek—*stream* NM-5
North Fork Sycamore Creek—*stream* TN-4
North Fork Tabeguache Creek—*stream* CO-8
North Fork Talala Creek—*stream* OK-5
North Fork Taneum Creek—*stream* WA-9
North Fork Taneum Trail—*trail* WA-9
North Fork Tangascootack Creek—*stream* PA-2
North Fork Tank—*reservoir* (2) AZ-5
North Fork Tanunak River—*stream* AK-9
North Fork Tanyard Branch—*stream* MD-2
*North Fork Tar Creek* CA-9
North Fork Tar Creek—*stream* CA-9
North Fork Tar River—*stream* NC-3
*North Fork Tarryall Creek* CO-8
North Fork Taylor Bayou—*stream* TX-5
North Fork Taylor Creek—*stream* FL-3
North Fork Taylor Creek—*stream* MT-8
North Fork Taylor Creek—*stream* UT-8
North Fork Taylor Creek—*stream* WA-9
North Fork Taylor Creek Well—*well* MT-8
North Fork Teal Creek—*stream* OR-9
North Fork Teanaway River—*stream* WA-9
*North Fork Tellico River* TN-4
*North Fork Tenmile Creek* CO-8
*North Fork Tenmile Creek* KY-4
North Fork Ten Mile Creek—*stream* KY-4
North Fork Tenmile Creek—*stream* WY-8
North Fork Ten Mile River—*stream* CA-9
North Fork Tennessee Creek—*stream* NM-5
North Fork Tepee Creek—*stream* MT-8
North Fork Tesuque Creek—*stream* NM-5
North Fork Teton Creek—*stream* WY-8
*north Fork Teton River* ID-8
*North Fork Teton River* WY-8
North Fork Teton River—*stream* MT-8
North Fork Texas Creek—*stream* AK-9
North Fork Texas Creek—*stream* (2) CO-8
North Fork Texas Creek—*stream* WA-9
North Fork Thirteenmile Creek—*stream* MT-8
North Fork Thirtyfive Mile Creek—*stream* WA-9
North Fork Thistle Creek—*stream* UT-8
*North Fork Thompson Creek* MT-8
*North Fork Thompson Creek* WY-8
North Fork Thompson Creek—*stream* ID-8
*North Fork Thompson River* CO-8
North Fork Thorn Creek—*stream* ID-8
North Fork Thornton River—*stream* VA-3
North Fork Thrashers Creek—*stream* VA-3
North Fork Three Bar Creek—*stream* MT-8
North Fork Three Creeks—*stream* (2) UT-8
North Fork Three Forks—*valley* UT-8
North Fork Threemile Creek—*stream* MT-8
North Fork Threemile Creek—*stream* UT-8
North Fork Threemile Creek—*stream* WA-9
North Fork Threemile Creek Well—*well* MT-8
North Fork Thumb River—*stream* AK-9
North Fork Thunder River—*stream* WI-6
North Fork Ticaboo Creek—*stream* UT-8
North Fork Tieton River—*stream* WA-9
North Fork Tieton Trail—*trail* WA-9
North Fork Tillatoba Creek—*stream* MS-4
North Fork Tillicum Creek—*stream* WA-9
North Fork Tilton River—*stream* WA-9
North Fork Timber Swamp Brook—*stream* NJ-2
*North Fork Tincup Creek* ID-8
North Fork Tlikakila River—*stream* AK-9
*North Fork Toats Coulee Creek* WA-9
North Fork Toats Coulee Creek—*stream* WA-9
North Fork Toats Creek Trail—*trail* WA-9
North Fork Tolt River—*stream* WA-9
North Fork Tolt Watershed—*area* WA-9
North Fork Tomahawk Creek—*stream* AR-4
*North Fork Tombeal Creek* ID-8
North Fork Tom Beall Creek—*stream* ID-8
*North Fork Tom Bell Creek* ID-8
North Fork Tombs Run—*stream* PA-2
*North Fork Tom Creek* TN-4
North Fork Tom Folley Creek—*stream* OR-9
North Fork Tomlinson Run—*stream* WV-2
North Fork Tom Neal Creek—*stream* CA-9
North Fork Toms Creek—*stream* TN-4
North Fork Toponce Creek—*stream* ID-8
North Fork Toppenish Creek—*stream* WA-9
North Fork Touchet River—*stream* WA-9
North Fork Toutle River—*stream* WA-9
North Fork Tower Creek—*stream* ID-8
Northfork Township—*civ div* ND-7
North Fork Township—*fmr MCD* IA-7
**North Fork Township**—*pop pl* MO-7
North Fork (Township of)—*fmr MCD* (2) AR-4
North Fork (Township of)—*fmr MCD* (2) NC-3
**North Fork (Township of)**—*pop pl* IL-6
**North Fork (Township of)**—*pop pl* MN-6
North Fork Trace Branch—*stream* AL-4
North Fork Trace Fork—*stream* WV-2
North Fork Trail—*trail* CO-8
North Fork Trail—*trail* ID-8
North Fork Trail—*trail* OR-9
North Fork Trail—*trail* (2) PA-2
North Fork Trail—*trail* (2) WA-9
North Fork Trail—*trail* WY-8
North Fork Trail Canyon—*valley* CA-9
North Fork Trail Creek—*stream* (3) MT-8
North Fork Trail Creek—*stream* WY-8
North Fork Trail (pack)—*trail* MT-8
North Fork Trail (Pack)—*trail* NM-5
*North Fork Trammel Creek* KY-4
North Fork Trammell Creek—*stream* KY-4
North Fork Trap Creek—*stream* ID-8
North Fork Trapper Creek—*stream* MT-8
North Fork Trask River—*stream* OR-9
North Fork Travis Creek—*stream* MT-8
North Fork Trestle—*other* GA-3
North Fork Trinchera Creek—*stream* CO-8
North Fork Trinity Creek—*stream* ID-8
North Fork Trinity River—*stream* CA-9
North Fork Triplett Creek—*stream* KY-4
North Fork Trout Creek—*stream* (2) MT-8
North Fork Trout Creek—*stream* NV-8
North Fork Trout Creek—*stream* (2) OR-9
North Fork Trout Creek—*stream* (2) WA-9
North Fork Trout Creek—*stream* WY-8
North Fork Trout Lake Creek—*stream* WA-9
North Fork Troy Canyon—*valley* NV-8
North Fork Trujillo Creek—*stream* CO-8
North Fork Tucker Creek—*stream* MT-8
North Fork Tucker Creek—*stream* NC-3
North Fork Tularosa Canyon—*valley* NM-5
North Fork Tule Creek—*stream* MT-8
North Fork Tule River—*stream* CA-9
North Fork Tumalo Creek—*stream* OR-9
North Fork Tuolumne River—*stream* CA-9
North Fork Turkeycock Creek—*stream* VA-3
*North Fork Turkey Creek* CO-8
*North Fork Turkey Creek* NC-3
North Fork Turkey Creek—*stream* KY-4
North Fork Turkey Creek—*stream* MO-7
North Fork Turkey Creek—*stream* NE-7
North Fork Turkey Creek—*stream* TN-4
North Fork Turkey Creek—*stream* TX-5
North Fork Tuskeegee Creek—*stream* NC-3
*North Fork Twelvemile Creek* SD-7
North Fork Twelvemile Creek—*stream* OR-9
North Fork Twelvemile Creek—*stream* SC-3
North Fork Twelvemile Creek—*stream* SD-7
*North Fork Twentymile Creek* WA-9
North Fork Twentymile Creek—*stream* ID-8
North Fork Twentymile Draw—*valley* WY-8
North Fork Twin Creek—*stream* KY-4
North Fork Twin Creek—*stream* NV-8
North Fork Twin Creek—*stream* WY-8
*North Fork Twisp River* WA-9
North Fork Twisp River—*stream* WA-9
*North Fork Two Leggin Creek* MT-8
North Fork Two Leggins Creek—*stream* MT-8
North Fork Two Tree Creek—*stream* MT-8
North Fork Tye River—*stream* VA-3
North Fork Tyson Creek—*stream* ID-8
*North Fork Uinta River* UT-8
North Fork Uinta River—*stream* UT-8
North Fork Umatilla River—*stream* OR-9
North Fork Unalakleet River—*stream* AK-9
North Fork Union Creek—*stream* NE-7
North Fork Union Creek—*stream* WA-9
North Fork Urraca Creek—*stream* NM-5
North Fork V—*flat* NV-8
North Fork Valentine Creek—*stream* OR-9
North Fork Valley—*valley* ID-8
North Fork Valley—*valley* TN-4
North Fork Valley Creek—*stream* (2) MT-8
North Fork Valley Creek—*stream* TX-5
North Fork Valley Ditch—*canal* WY-8
North Fork Valley Of Fire Wash—*stream* NV-8
North Fork Verdure Creek—*stream* UT-8
North Fork Vermejo River—*stream* CO-8
North Fork Vermejo River—*stream* NM-5
*North Fork Vermilion Creek* WY-8
North Fork Vermilion River—*stream* (2) IL-6
North Fork Vermillion Creek—*stream* WY-8
**North Fork Village**—*pop pl* OH-6
North Fork Virgin River—*stream* UT-8
North Fork Waddle Creek—*stream* MT-8
North Fork Waddle Creek—*stream* WY-8
North Fork Wade Creek—*stream* OR-9
North Fork Wages Creek—*stream* CA-9
North Fork Wahoo Creek—*stream* NE-7
North Fork Wailua River—*stream* HI-9
*North Fork Wailua Stream* HI-9
North Fork Walker Basin Creek—*stream* CA-9
North Fork Walker Creek—*stream* CA-9
North Fork Walker Creek—*stream* OR-9
North Fork Wallace Creek—*stream* CO-8
North Fork Wallace River—*stream* WA-9
North Fork Walla Walla River—*stream* OR-9
North Fork Wall Creek—*stream* MT-8
North Fork Wall Creek—*stream* OR-9
North Fork Wallowa Creek—*stream* OR-9
North Fork Walnut Canyon—*valley* NM-5
*North Fork Walnut Creek* AZ-5
North Fork Walnut Creek—*stream* AZ-5
North Fork Walnut Creek—*stream* IA-7
North Fork Walnut Creek—*stream* KS-7
North Fork Walnut Creek—*stream* (2) OK-5
North Fork War Canyon—*valley* NV-8
North Fork Ward Branch—*stream* MO-7
North Fork Warm Spring Creek—*stream* MT-8
North Fork Warm Springs Creek—*stream* MT-8
North Fork Warm Springs Creek—*stream* OR-9
North Fork Watab River—*stream* MN-6
North Fork Water Canyon—*valley* NM-5
*North Fork Watonwan River* MN-6
North Fork Watonwan River—*stream* MN-6
North Fork Webb Creek—*stream* MO-7
*North Fork Webber Creek* ID-8
North Fork Webber Creek—*stream* ID-8
*North Fork Weber Creek* ID-8
North Fork Weber Creek—*stream* CA-9
North Fork Weber River—*stream* UT-8
North Fork Well—*well* AZ-5
North Fork Well—*well* NV-8
North Fork Wenaha River—*stream* OR-9
North Fork Wenaha River—*stream* WA-9
North Fork Wenas Creek—*stream* WA-9
North Fork West Branch Laramie River—*stream* CO-8
North Fork West Branch Wynoochee River—*stream* WA-9
North Fork West Camp Creek—*stream* OR-9
North Fork West Creek—*stream* CO-8
North Fork West Creek—*stream* PA-2
North Fork West Fork Gallating River—*stream* MT-8
*North Fork West Fork Mancos River* CO-8
*North Fork West Fsork Fish Creek* MT-8
North Fork West Indian Creek—*stream* CO-8
North Fork West Mancos River—*stream* CO-8
North Fork West Pass Creek—*stream* WY-8
North Fork West Tennessee Creek—*stream* CO-8
North Fork West Virginia Fork Dunkard Creek—*stream* WV-2
North Fork Whale Creek—*stream* WA-9
*North Fork Whalehead Creek* OR-9
North Fork Whetstone Creek—*stream* MT-8
North Fork Whetstone Creek—*stream* SD-7
North Fork Whetstone River—*stream* SD-7
North Fork Whippoorwill Creek—*stream* KY-4
North Fork Whiskers Draw—*valley* UT-8
North Fork Whiskey Dick Creek—*stream* WA-9
North Fork Whisky Creek—*stream* OR-9
*North Fork Whisky Dick Creek* WA-9
*North Fork Whit* MO-7
*North Fork Whitebird Creek* ID-8
North Fork White Bird Creek—*stream* ID-8
North Fork Whitehawk Creek—*stream* ID-8
North Fork White Oak Creek—*stream* AR-4
North Fork White Oak Creek—*stream* OH-6
*North Fork White River* AZ-5
*North Fork White River* AR-4
*North Fork White River* IN-6
*North Fork White River* WA-9
North Fork White River—*stream* AK-9
North Fork White River—*stream* AZ-5
North Fork White River—*stream* CO-8
North Fork White Rock Coulee—*valley* MT-8
North Fork Whitetail Creek—*stream* (2) MT-8
*North Fork Whitewater River* CA-9
North Fork Whitewater River—*stream* CA-9
North Fork Whitewater River—*stream* MN-6
North Fork Whitman Coulee—*valley* MT-8
North Fork Whittlesey Creek—*stream* WI-6
*North Fork Wigwam Creek* MT-8
North Fork Wigwam Creek—*stream* MT-8
North Fork Wildcat Canyon—*valley* NV-8
*North Fork Wild Cat Creek* KS-7
North Fork Wildcat Creek—*stream* CA-9
North Fork Wildcat Creek—*stream* (2) KS-7
North Fork Wildcat Creek—*stream* WY-8
North Fork Wild Horse Canyon—*valley* NM-5
*North Fork Wild Horse Creek* WY-8
North Fork Willame Creek—*stream* WA-9
North Fork Williams Creek—*stream* ID-8
North Fork Williams Creek—*stream* NV-8
North Fork Williams Creek—*stream* WA-9
North Fork Willis Canyon—*valley* AZ-5
North Fork Willis Canyon—*valley* UT-8
North Fork Willoughby Creek—*stream* MT-8
North Fork Willow Canyon—*valley* CA-9
*North Fork Willow Creek* CA-9
*North Fork Willow Creek* WY-8
North Fork Willow Creek—*stream* (6) CA-9
North Fork Willow Creek—*stream* (3) ID-8
North Fork Willow Creek—*stream* (7) MT-8
North Fork Willow Creek—*stream* (4) NV-8
North Fork Willow Creek—*stream* (4) OR-9
North Fork Willow Creek—*stream* TX-5
North Fork Willow Creek—*stream* UT-8
North Fork Willow Creek—*stream* WA-9
North Fork Willow Creek—*stream* (2) WY-8
North Fork Willow Creek Canyon—*valley* UT-8
North Fork Willow River—*stream* MN-6
*North Fork Wills Creek* OH-6
North Fork Wills Creek—*stream* OH-6
North Fork Wilson Creek—*stream* CO-8
North Fork Wilson Creek—*stream* OR-9
North Fork Wilson Creek—*stream* WA-9
*North Fork Wilson River* OR-9
North Fork Wilson River—*stream* OR-9
North Fork Winberry Creek—*stream* OR-9
North Fork Wind Creek—*stream* OR-9
North Fork Wind Creek—*stream* WY-8
*North Fork Wind River* WY-8
*North Fork Wolf Creek* OR-9
North Fork Wolf Creek—*stream* CA-9
North Fork Wolf Creek—*stream* GA-3
North Fork Wolf Creek—*stream* OK-5
North Fork Wolf Creek—*stream* (2) OR-9
North Fork Wolf Creek—*stream* VA-3
North Fork Wolf Creek—*stream* WA-9
North Fork Wolf Fang Creek—*stream* ID-8
North Fork Wolf River—*stream* KS-7
North Fork Wolf River—*stream* TN-4
North Fork Wood Creek—*stream* OR-9
*North Fork Woodmon Creek* CA-9
North Fork Woods Gulch Creek—*stream* MT-8
North Fork Woody Canyon—*valley* NV-8
*North Fork Woody Creek* MT-8
North Fork Woody Creek—*stream* MT-8
North Fork Wooley Creek—*stream* CA-9
*North Fork Woolf Den Canyon* UT-8
*North Fork Wounded Man Creek* MT-8
North Fork Wounded Man Creek—*stream* MT-8
North Fork Wreck Creek—*stream* WA-9
North Fork Wyatte Creek—*stream* WY-8
North Fork Yachats River—*stream* OR-9
North Fork Yager Creek—*stream* CA-9
North Fork Yancey Branch—*stream* AL-4
North Fork Yancey Creek—*stream* TX-5
North Fork Yantarni Creek—*stream* AK-9
North Fork Yatama Creek—*stream* WA-9
North Fork Yellow Bank River—*stream* MN-6
North Fork Yellow Bank River—*stream* SD-7
North Fork Yellow Creek—*stream* (2) OH-6
North Fork Yellowleaf Creek—*stream* AL-4
*North Fork Yellow Medicine River* MN-6
North Fork Yellow River—*stream* IA-7
North Fork Yellow River—*stream* WI-6
North Fork Yellowstone River—*stream* WY-8
*North Fork Yuba River* CA-9
North Fork Zumbro River—*stream* MN-6
North Forrest Attendance Center—*school* MS-4
North Fort Hood—*military* TX-5
**North Fort Lewis (Fort Lewis North Post)**—*pop pl* WA-9
**North Fort Myers**—*pop pl* FL-3
North Fort Myers (CCD)—*cens area* FL-3
North Fort Myers First Baptist Church Sch—*school* FL-3
North Fort Myers HS—*school* FL-3
**North Fort Polk**—*pop pl* LA-4
**North Fort Riley**—*pop pl* KS-7
North Fort Worth—*uninc pl* TX-5
**North Foster**—*pop pl* RI-1
North Foster Gulch—*valley* CO-8
North Fourmile Creek—*stream* OR-9
North Fourmile Creek—*stream* WY-8
North Fourmile Tank—*reservoir* TX-5
North Fourteen Ditch—*canal* NM-5
North Fourteen Tank—*reservoir* AZ-5
North Fowl Lake—*lake* MN-6
**North Foxboro**—*pop pl* MA-1
*North Foxborough* MA-1
North Fox Canyon Creek—*stream* OR-9
North Fox Creek—*stream* IA-7
North Fox Creek—*stream* OK-5
North Fox Island—*island* MI-6
North Fox Well (flowing)—*well* NV-8
North Fraction Run—*stream* IL-6
*North Framingham* MA-1
North Francitas Oil Field—*oilfield* TX-5
**North Frankfort**—*pop pl* NY-2
North Franklin—*locale* CT-1
North Franklin—*locale* NY-2
*North Franklin Elementary School* PA-2
North Franklin Mtn—*summit* TX-5
*North Franklin Peak* TX-5
North Franklin Sch—*school* (2) OH-6
**North Franklin Township**—*pop pl* NE-7
**North Franklin (Township of)**—*pop pl* PA-2
North Franklin Township Sch—*school* PA-2
North Franklin (Unorganized Territory of)—*unorg* ME-1
North Franks Canyon—*valley* UT-8
North Frasier Branch—*stream* AL-4
**North Fredericktown**—*pop pl* PA-2
*North Fredricktown* PA-2
North Freeborn Ch—*church* MN-6
**North Freedom**—*pop pl* PA-2
**North Freedom**—*pop pl* WI-6
North Freedom Ch—*church* IL-6
North Freedom Sch—*school* SD-7
North Freeman Sch—*school* ME-1
North Freeny Oil Field—*oilfield* OK-5
North Freeport Cem—*cemetery* ME-1
North Freewoods Oil Field—*oilfield* MS-4
*North French Creek* CO-8
North French Creek—*stream* WY-8
North Frenchman Coulee—*valley* MT-8
North Frenchman Creek—*stream* NY-2
North Friendship Ch—*church* IN-6
North Friends Station Mine—*mine* TN-4
North Fritz Island—*island* MO-7
North Front Street Commercial District—*hist pl* MN-6
**North Fryeburg**—*pop pl* ME-1
*North Frying Pan Creek* MT-8
North Furlong Creek—*stream* NV-8
North Furlong Lake—*lake* NV-8
*North Furnace Hill* PA-2
*North Gaber Creek* MO-7
North Gables Hosp—*hospital* FL-3
*North Gabori* MO-7
North Gabouri Creek—*stream* MO-7
*North Gadsden* AL-4
North Gadsden Baptist Ch—*church* AL-4
North Gadsden Freewill Baptist Ch—*church* AL-4
North Gadsden Park—*park* AL-4
North Gadsden United Methodist Ch—*church* AL-4
**North Gage**—*pop pl* NY-2
North Gaines Creek—*stream* OK-5
**North Gainesville**—*pop pl* FL-3
**North Gainesville**—*pop pl* NY-2
North Gallagher Flowage—*reservoir* WI-6
North Gallegos Well—*well* NM-5
North Gallia HS—*school* OH-6
North Galloway Township—*civil* MO-7
*North Galveston* (2) IN-6
**North Galway**—*pop pl* NY-2
North Gammon Prong—*stream* WY-8
North Gap—*channel* MI-6
North Gap—*gap* CA-9
North Gap—*locale* VA-3
North Gap Creek—*stream* MT-8
North Gap Lake—*lake* WY-8
North Garber Creek—*stream* CO-8
**North Garden**—*pop pl* VA-3
**North Gardena**—*pop pl* CA-9
North Gardendale Ch—*church* AL-4
**North Garden (P.O.) (Cross Roads)**—*pop pl* VA-3
North Gardens Oil Field—*oilfield* MS-4
**North Garden (sta.) (North Garden Depot)**—*pop pl* VA-3
North Gardner Mtn—*summit* WA-9
North Garfield—*cens area* MT-8
North Garfield (CCD)—*cens area* OK-5
*North Gargathy Creek* VA-3
North Garner Intermediate Sch—*school* NC-3
North Garnerville Sch—*school* NY-2
North Gasconades Creek—*stream* TX-5
North Gastonia—*locale* NC-3
North Gaston Senior HS—*school* NC-3
*Northgate* IL-6
North Gate—*gap* CA-9
North Gate—*locale* CA-9
Northgate—*locale* CO-8
**North Gate**—*pop pl* DC-2
**North Gate**—*pop pl* IN-6
**Northgate**—*pop pl* MI-6
**Northgate**—*pop pl* ND-7
**Northgate**—*pop pl* (2) SC-3
**Northgate**—*pop pl* TX-5
Northgate—*post sta* TX-5
Northgate—*uninc pl* CA-9
Northgate—*uninc pl* NC-3
Northgate—*uninc pl* WA-9
Northgate Baptist Sch—*school* FL-3
North Gate Canyon—*valley* WY-8
Northgate Center—*locale* KS-7
North Gate Ch—*church* MD-2
North Gate Ch—*church* MI-6
Northgate Crossing Shop Ctr—*locale* TN-4
Northgate Dam—*dam* ND-7
North Gate Hall—*hist pl* CA-9
Northgate JHS—*school* MO-7
Northgate JHS—*school* PA-2
Northgate Mall—*locale* TN-4
Northgate Mall Shop Ctr—*locale* TN-4
Northgate Park—*park* MO-7
Northgate Park—*park* NC-3
Northgate Park—*park* OH-6
Northgate Peaks—*summit* UT-8
Northgate Plaza—*locale* NC-3
Northgate Plaza (Shop Ctr)—*locale* FL-3
Northgate Plaza (Shop Ctr)—*locale* NC-3
Northgate Plaza (Shop Ctr)—*locale* PA-2
Northgate Plaza Shop Ctr—*locale* TN-4
Northgate Plaza (Shop Ctr)—*locale* UT-8
**North Gates**—*pop pl* NY-2
Northgate Sch—*school* MI-6
Northgate Sch—*school* MN-6
Northgate Shop Ctr—*locale* (4) AL-4
Northgate Shop Ctr—*locale* AZ-5
Northgate Shop Ctr—*locale* (5) FL-3
Northgate Shop Ctr—*locale* KS-7
Northgate Shop Ctr—*locale* MA-1
Northgate Shop Ctr—*locale* (2) MS-4
Northgate Shop Ctr—*locale* NY-2
North Gate Shop Ctr—*locale* PA-2
Northgate Shop Ctr—*locale* SD-7
Northgate Shop Ctr—*locale* (2) TN-4
Northgate Shop Ctr—*locale* WA-9
Northgate Shop Ctr—*other* IN-6
Northgate Site—*hist pl* TX-5
**North Gate (subdivision)**—*pop pl* AL-4
**Northgate (subdivision)**—*pop pl* (2) MS-4
**Northgate Subdivision**—*pop pl* UT-8
*Northgate Village* IN-6
North Gate Well—*well* AZ-5
North Gatlin Creek—*stream* TX-5
North Gatlin Street Ch of Christ—*church* MS-4
North Gautier Baptist Ch—*church* MS-4
North Gawley Ridge—*ridge* OR-9
North Gayton Ch—*church* VA-3
North Geneva Cem—*cemetery* WI-6
North Geneva Hist Dist—*hist pl* IL-6
**North Georgetown**—*pop pl* OH-6
**North Georgetown (reduced usage)**—*pop pl* TX-5
North Georgia Coll—*school* GA-3
North Georgia Coll Farm—*school* GA-3
North Georgia Mine—*mine* AZ-5
North Georgia Vocational Sch—*school* GA-3
**North Germantown**—*pop pl* NY-2
North Germany Cem—*cemetery* MN-6
North Germany (Township of)—*civ div* MN-6
North Getaway Coulee—*valley* MT-8
North Gettysburg Shop Ctr—*locale* PA-2
North Ghent—*locale* PA-2
*North Gibson Post Office* TN-4
North Gila Drain—*canal* AZ-5
North Gila East Main Canal—*canal* AZ-5
North Gila Main Canal—*canal* AZ-5
North Gila Valley—*valley* AZ-5
*North Gildford* MT-8
North Gill Creek—*stream* CO-8
North Gillespie Windmill—*locale* NM-5
*North Girard* PA-2
North Girard—*other* PA-2
*North Glacier Lake* WA-9
North Glade—*flat* CA-9
North Glade—*locale* MD-2
North Glade Cem—*cemetery* MD-2
North Glade Cove—*bay* MD-2
North Glade Park—*park* FL-3
North Glade Run—*stream* MD-2
North Glade Sch—*school* FL-3
Northglade Sch—*school* MI-6
North Glass Butte Rsvr—*reservoir* OR-9
North Glass Butte Rsvr Number Two—*reservoir* OR-9
North Glen Ch—*church* MD-2
North Glencoe Baptist Ch—*church* AL-4
**North Glendale**—*pop pl* CA-9
North Glendale Sch—*school* MO-7
**North Glen Ellyn**—*pop pl* IL-6
**North Glen Estates**—*pop pl* TN-4
*North Glen Hills* MD-2
**Northglenn**—*pop pl* CO-8
North Glen Sch—*school* MD-2
North Glenside—*other* PA-2
North Glenside Sch—*school* PA-2
**Northglen (subdivision)**—*pop pl* NC-3
**North Glenwood**—*pop pl* CT-1
North Glory Hole—*bay* GA-3
North Goat Windmill—*locale* NM-5
North Goddard Creek—*stream* CA-9
North Goens Creek—*stream* TX-5
*North Gold Creek* ID-8
North Gold Creek—*stream* ID-8
North Gold Creek—*stream* MT-8
North Golden Lake—*lake* ND-7
North Golden Valley—*unorg reg* ND-7
North Goldsmith Lake—*swamp* MN-6
North Golf Course—*other* AZ-5
North Golondrinas Ditch—*canal* NM-5
North Gooding Canal—*canal* ID-8
North Gooding Main Canal—*canal* ID-8
North Goodland Ch—*church* MI-6
North Gooseberry Island—*island* MA-1
North Gorge Campground—*locale* WA-9
North Gorge Canyon—*valley* UT-8
**North Gorham**—*pop pl* ME-1
North Gorham Cem—*cemetery* ME-1
North Goshen—*locale* CT-1
North Goucher Creek—*stream* SC-3
North Gouge Eye Well—*well* NV-8
North Gouverneur—*locale* NY-2
North Gouverneur Cem—*cemetery* NY-2
North Gouverneur Ch—*church* NY-2
North Government Island—*island* MI-6
North Grade Elem Sch—*school* FL-3
North Grade Sch—*school* NE-7
**North Grafton**—*pop pl* MA-1
North Graham Sch—*school* NC-3
North Graham Shoal—*bar* MI-6
North Granada Ditch—*canal* CO-8
North Granby—*locale* CT-1
North Grand Cane Oil and Gas Field—*oilfield* LA-4
North Grand Ch—*church* ND-7
North Grand Forks—*locale* ND-7
North Grand Rapids—*other* MI-6
North Granite Creek—*stream* WA-9
**North Grantham**—*pop pl* NH-1
North Grant Lake—*lake* WI-6
**North Granville**—*pop pl* NY-2
North Granville Sch—*school* NC-3
North Grape Creek—*stream* TX-5
North Grasshopper Lake—*lake* FL-3
North Grass Lake Sch—*school* MN-6
North Grassy Mountain Rsvr—*reservoir* OR-9
**North Gray**—*pop pl* ME-1
North Gray Rocks—*summit* CA-9
North Gray Rsvr—*reservoir* CO-8
North Graysport Public Use Area—*park* MS-4
North Greasewood Creek—*stream* WY-8
**North Great River**—*pop pl* NY-2
**North Greece**—*pop pl* NY-2
North Greenbriar Creek—*stream* TX-5
North Greenbush Sch—*school* NY-2
**North Greenbush (Town of)**—*pop pl* NY-2
North Greene HS—*school* TN-4
North Greene Sch—*school* NC-3
North Greene Township—*civil* MO-7
**North Greenfield**—*pop pl* NY-2
**North Greenfield**—*pop pl* OH-6
North Greenfield Cem—*cemetery* OH-6
North Greenleaf Creek—*stream* CO-8
North Green Mine—*mine* IL-6
North Green Sedge—*swamp* NY-2
North Green Street-Bouchelle Street Hist Dist—*hist pl* NC-3
**North Green (subdivision)**—*pop pl* NC-3
North Green (Township of)—*fmr MCD* MO-7
**North Greenville**—*pop pl* MS-4
North Greenville—*uninc pl* SC-3
North Greenville Junior Coll—*school* SC-3
**North Greenwich**—*pop pl* CT-1
**North Greenwich**—*pop pl* NY-2
North Greenwood—*CDP* SC-3
North Greenwood Baptist Ch—*church* MS-4
North Greenwood Sch—*school* SD-7
**North Greer**—*pop pl* SC-3
North Gregg Well—*well* NM-5
North Gresham Sch—*school* OR-9
North Griffith Well—*well* NM-5
North Grimms—*locale* WI-6
North Grizzly Bend Creek—*stream* CA-9
North Grizzly Creek—*stream* ID-8
North Groesbeck—*locale* TX-5
North Groesbeck Creek—*stream* TX-5
*North Grosvenordale* CT-1
**North Grosvenor Dale**—*pop pl* CT-1
North Grosvenor Dale Pond—*reservoir* CT-1
*North Groton* MA-1
**North Groton**—*pop pl* NH-1
North Groton Cem—*cemetery* NH-1
*North Grouse Creek* UT-8
North Grove—*locale* IA-7
**North Grove**—*pop pl* IN-6
North Grove—*woods* (2) CA-9
**North Grove Addition (subdivision)**—*pop pl* SD-7
North Grove Cem—*cemetery* IN-6
North Grove Cem—*cemetery* (2) IA-7
North Grove Cem—*cemetery* MI-6
North Grove Cem—*cemetery* OH-6
North Grove Ch—*church* MN-6
North Grove Creek—*stream* TX-5
North Grove Sch—*school* IL-6
North Grove Sch—*school* MI-6
North Grove Sch—*school* MO-7
North Grove Shop Ctr—*locale* PA-2
Northgrove Shopping Center—*locale* FL-3
North Grove Street Hist Dist—*hist pl* NY-2
North Grundy (Magisterial District)—*fmr MCD* VA-3
North Guadalupe River—*stream* TX-5
North Guam—*locale* NM-5
North Guard—*summit* CA-9
North Guard Creek—*stream* CA-9
North Guardian Angel—*summit* UT-8
North Guardian Glacier—*glacier* WA-9
North Guard Lake—*lake* CA-9
**North Guilford**—*pop pl* CT-1
**North Guilford**—*pop pl* ME-1
North Guilford Corners—*locale* NY-2
*North Gulch* UT-8
North Gulch—*valley* (2) CA-9
North Gulch—*valley* (3) CO-8
North Gulch—*valley* ID-8
North Gulch—*valley* UT-8
North Gulfport (census name for West Gulfport)—*CDP* MS-4
*North Gull Island* MI-6
North Gully—*stream* NY-2
North Gully—*valley* NY-2
Northgutts Store (historical)—*locale* AL-4
North Gwinnett HS—*school* GA-3
North Gypsum Creek—*stream* KS-7
North Hackberry Draw—*valley* NM-5
North Hackberry Mine—*mine* AZ-5
North Hackberry Tank—*reservoir* TX-5
**North Hackensack**—*pop pl* NJ-2
**North Hadley**—*pop pl* MA-1
North Hadley Cem—*cemetery* MA-1
*North Halawa Gulch* HI-9

North Halawa Stream—*stream* HI-9
**North Haledon**—*pop pl* NJ-2
North Halfmoon Creek—*stream* CO-8
North Halfmoon Lakes—*lake* CO-8
**North Halifax**—*pop pl* VA-3
North Hall—*valley* UT-8
North Hall, Univ of Wisconsin—*hist pl* WI-6
North Hall-River Falls State Normal Sch—*hist pl* WI-6
North Hall Sch—*school* GA-3
*North Hambey Creek* NC-3
North Hamby Creek—*stream* NC-3
North Hamden Sch—*school* NY-2
North Hamilton—*uninc pl* PA-2
North Hamilton Elem Sch—*school* FL-3
North Hamilton Oil And Gas Field—*other* MI-6
**North Hamlet**—*pop pl* NC-3
**North Hamlin**—*pop pl* NY-2
North Hamma Hamma River Bridge—*hist pl* WA-9
North Hammock Canyon—*valley* NM-5
*North Hammond* IN-6
North Hammond—*locale* NY-2
North Hammond Brook—*stream* ME-1
North Hammond Brook—*stream* NH-1
*North Hampton* IN-6
**North Hampton**—*pop pl* IL-6
**North Hampton**—*pop pl* MD-2
**North Hampton**—*pop pl* NH-1
**North Hampton**—*pop pl* OH-6
**North Hampton**—*pop pl* VA-3
**Northhampton Acres**—*pop pl* TN-4
**North Hampton Center**—*pop pl* NH-1
**North Hampton (Town of)**—*pop pl* NH-1
North Hanaford Creek—*stream* WA-9
**North Hancock**—*pop pl* MA-1
**North Hannibal**—*pop pl* NY-2
North Hanover—*locale* IL-6
**North Hanover**—*pop pl* MA-1
North Hanover (historical P.O.)—*locale* MA-1
North Hanover HS—*school* MA-1
**North Hanover (Township of)**—*pop pl* NJ-2
North Hansel Mtns—*range* ID-8
North Hansel Mtns—*range* UT-8
North Hansen Fisk Ditch—*canal* CA-9
*North Hanson* MA-1
**North Hanson**—*pop pl* MA-1
North Hanson (historical P.O.)—*locale* MA-1
North Hanson Station (historical)—*locale* MA-1
North Harbor—*bay* NJ-2
North Harbor—*bay* VT-1
**North Harbor**—*pop pl* IN-6
**North Harbor (subdivision)**—*pop pl* NC-3
North Harding—*unorg reg* SD-7
North Harding (CCD)—*cens area* NM-5
North Hardscrabble Creek—*stream* CO-8
North Hardscrabble Mtn—*summit* CO-8
North Harford Ch—*church* MD-2
North Harford HS—*school* MD-2
North Harkins Well—*well* MT-8
**North Harlowe**—*pop pl* NC-3
North Harmony—*cemetery* NY-2
North Harmony Ch—*church* NY-2
**North Harmony (Town of)**—*pop pl* NY-2
North Harnett Sch—*school* NC-3
North Harney River—*stream* FL-3
North Harper Creek—*stream* NC-3
North Harper Lake—*lake* WI-6
**North Harpersfield**—*pop pl* NY-2
**North Harpswell**—*pop pl* ME-1
North Harris Channel—*channel* FL-3
North Harris Creek—*stream* OK-5
North Harrison Lake—*reservoir* IN-6
North Harrison Mine—*mine* MN-6
North Harrison (Township of)—*fmr MCD* AR-4
North Harter Ch—*church* IL-6
**North Hartland**—*pop pl* NY-2
North Hartland Dam—*dam* VT-1
**North Hartland (Evarts Station)**—*pop pl* VT-1
*North Hartland Lake* VT-1
North Hartland Rsvr—*reservoir* VT-1
**North Hartsville**—*pop pl* SC-3
North Hartsville (CCD)—*cens area* SC-3
*North Harvey* IL-6
**North Harwich**—*pop pl* MA-1
North Harwich Station—*building* MA-1
North Haskell Creek—*stream* NV-8
North Hatch Canyon—*valley* UT-8
**North Hatfield**—*pop pl* MA-1
North Hather Creek—*stream* AK-9
North Haven—*CDP* CT-1
**North Haven**—*pop pl* CT-1
**North Haven**—*pop pl* ME-1
**North Haven**—*pop pl* MS-4
**North Haven**—*pop pl* NY-2
North Haven Peninsula—*cape* NY-2
**North Haven (subdivision)**—*pop pl* AL-4
**North Haven (subdivision)**—*pop pl* NC-3
**North Haven (subdivision)**—*pop pl* TN-4
**North Haven (Town of)**—*pop pl* ME-1
**North Haverhill**—*pop pl* NH-1
*North Havre* MT-8
North Havre Community Hall—*locale* MT-8
North Hawthorne—*uninc pl* NJ-2
North Hawthorne Station—*locale* NJ-2
**North Hayden**—*pop pl* IN-6
North Hayes Gas Field—*oilfield* LA-4
North Haynes Lake—*lake* MN-6
North Hazard—*uninc pl* KY-4
North Hazlehurst Attendance Center—*school* MS-4
North Head—*cape* (2) AK-9
North Head—*cliff* AK-9
North Head—*cliff* MA-1
North Head—*cliff* WA-9
North Head Lighthouse—*locale* CA-9
North Head Lighthouse—*locale* WA-9
North Head Long Pond—*lake* MA-1
*North Head of Hummock* MA-1
*North Head of Long Pond* MA-1
North Healy Draw—*valley* WY-8
**North Heath**—*pop pl* MA-1
North Heather Creek—*stream* WY-8
**North Hebron**—*pop pl* NY-2
North Heglar Canyon—*valley* ID-8
North Hegman Lake—*lake* MN-6
North Heidelberg—*locale* PA-2
North Heidelberg Ch—*church* PA-2
**North Heidelberg (Township of)**—*pop pl* PA-2
North Height Park—*park* TX-5
North Heights—*uninc pl* AR-4
North Heights—*uninc pl* TX-5
North Heights Ch of Christ—*church* AR-4
North Heights Christian Ch—*church* KS-7
North Heights Sch—*school* (2) AR-4
North Heights Sch—*school* MN-6
North Heights Sch—*school* TX-5
**North Heights Subdivision**—*pop pl* UT-8
North Height Tabernacle—*church* TX-5
*North Hell Creek Spring* NV-8
North Hell Creek Spring—*spring* NV-8
North Helmer Lake—*lake* MI-6
North Helms Creek—*stream* TX-5
North Helmville Canal—*canal* MT-8
North Hemlock Lake—*lake* MT-8
North Hemlock Lake—*reservoir* IN-6
North Hempstead Country Club—*other* NY-2
**North Hempstead (Town of)**—*pop pl* NY-2
**North Henderson**—*pop pl* IL-6
**North Henderson**—*pop pl* NC-3
North Henderson (census name for Henderson North)—*CDP* NC-3
North Henderson Creek—*stream* IL-6
North Henderson (Township of)—*civ div* IL-6
North Henderson Well—*well* TX-5
North Hennepin State Coll—*school* MN-6
North Henry Lee Rsvr—*reservoir* CO-8
**North Hermon**—*pop pl* ME-1
**North Hero**—*pop pl* VT-1
North Hero Island—*island* VT-1
North Hero Sch—*school* VT-1
North Hero State Park—*park* VT-1
North Hero Station—*locale* VT-1
**North Hero (Town of)**—*pop pl* VT-1
**North Hero (Township of)**—*pop pl* MN-6
North Hialeah Baptist Ch—*church* FL-3
North Hialeah Baptist Kindergarten—*school* FL-3
North Hialeah Sch—*school* FL-3
*North Hibbing* MN-6
North Hickory Cem—*cemetery* MI-6
North Hickory Creek—*stream* TX-5
North Hidalgo (CCD)—*cens area* NM-5
North Hidden Lake—*lake* MT-8
*North Highland* IN-6
**North Highland**—*pop pl* IN-6
**North Highland**—*pop pl* NY-2
North Highland—*post sta* GA-3
North Highland Baptist Ch—*church* (2) AL-4
North Highland Cem—*cemetery* NY-2
North Highland Cem—*cemetery* OK-5
North Highland Park—*park* AL-4
**North Highlands**—*pop pl* AL-4
**North Highlands**—*pop pl* CA-9
**North Highlands**—*pop pl* GA-3
**North Highlands**—*pop pl* (2) LA-4
North Highlands Air Natl Guard—*military* CA-9
**North Highlands Beach**—*pop pl* NJ-2
North Highlands Ch—*church* AL-4
North Highlands Ch—*church* LA-4
North Highland Sch—*school* OR-9
*North Highlands Elementary School* AL-4
North Highlands Lake Dam—*dam* AL-4
North Highland Spring—*spring* OR-9
North Highlands Sch—*school* LA-4
North Highlands Sch—*school* OK-5
North Highline Lateral Canal—*canal* AZ-5
*North High School* KS-7
*North High School* PA-2
*North High Shoals* GA-3
**North High Shoals**—*pop pl* GA-3
North High Street Hist Dist—*hist pl* MA-1
North Highway—*channel* MI-6
North High Windmill—*locale* TX-5
*North Hill* OH-6
North Hill—*CDP* WA-9
**North Hill**—*pop pl* ME-1
**North Hill**—*pop pl* WV-2
North Hill—*summit* AK-9
North Hill—*summit* (2) CA-9
North Hill—*summit* ME-1
North Hill—*summit* MD-2
North Hill—*summit* (2) MA-1
North Hill—*summit* NV-8
North Hill—*summit* NH-1
North Hill—*summit* (5) NY-2
North Hill—*summit* UT-8
North Hill—*summit* (2) VT-1
North Hill Cem—*cemetery* IA-7
North Hill Cem—*cemetery* PA-2
North Hill Cem—*cemetery* VT-1
North Hill Ch—*church* TX-5
North Hill Hist Dist—*hist pl* OH-6
North Hill Marsh—*reservoir* MA-1
North Hill Marsh Dam—*dam* MA-1
North Hill Mine—*mine* ID-8
North Hill Plaza (Shop Ctr)—*locale* MA-1
North Hill Preservation District—*hist pl* FL-3
*North Hills* OH-6
**North Hills**—*pop pl* DE-2
**North Hills**—*pop pl* IL-6
**North Hills**—*pop pl* NY-2
**North Hills**—*pop pl* (3) PA-2
**North Hills**—*pop pl* TN-4
**North Hills**—*pop pl* WV-2
North Hills—*post sta* SC-3
North Hills—*range* UT-8
North Hills—*summit* UT-8
North Hill Sch—*school* IA-7
North Hill Sch—*school* MI-6
North Hill Sch—*school* NH-1
North Hill Sch—*school* NY-2
North Hill Sch—*school* ND-7
North Hills Christian Ch—*church* AL-4
North Hills Commerce Center—*locale* NC-3
North Hills Country Club—*other* AR-4
North Hills Country Club—*other* NY-2
North Hills Country Club—*other* PA-2
**North Hillsdale**—*pop pl* NY-2
**North Hillsdale Subdivision**—*pop pl* UT-8
North Hills Elem Sch—*school* PA-2
**North Hills Estates**—*pop pl* OH-6
**North Hills Estates (subdivision)**—*pop pl* (2) NC-3
**North Hills Estates Subdivision**—*pop pl* UT-8
*North Hills Industrial Park* NC-3
*North Hills JHS* PA-2
North Hills JHS—*school* PA-2
North Hills Memorial Gardens—*cemetery* AR-4
North Hills Municipal Golf Course—*locale* PA-2
North Hills Park—*park* MO-7
North Hills Park—*park* NC-3
*North Hills Sch* PA-2
North Hills Sch—*school* OH-6
North Hills Sch—*school* PA-2
North Hills Senior HS—*school* PA-2
North Hills Shop Ctr—*locale* MS-4
**North Hills Sligo Park**—*pop pl* MD-2
**North Hills (subdivision)**—*pop pl* AL-4
**North Hills (subdivision)**—*pop pl* (2) NC-3
**North Hills (subdivision)**—*pop pl* TN-4
**North Hills Subdivision**—*pop pl* UT-8
North Hills (subdivision)—*post sta* NC-3
**North Hills Terrace (subdivision)**—*pop pl* NC-3
North Hilmar Cem—*cemetery* CA-9
North Hilo (CCD)—*cens area* HI-9
North Hi-Mount Sch—*school* TX-5
**North Hinsdale**—*pop pl* NH-1
North (historical)—*locale* AL-4
North Hixon Well—*well* CO-8
North Hixson Ch of Christ—*church* TN-4
North Hixson Ch of God—*church* TN-4
**North Hodge**—*pop pl* LA-4
North Hodges Sch—*school* SC-3
*North Hogan* IN-6
North Hogan Creek—*stream* IN-6
North Hog Canyon—*valley* NV-8
North Hog Creek—*stream* AR-4
**North Holderness**—*pop pl* NH-1
North Holderness Freewill Baptist Church-Holderness Historical Society Bldg—*hist pl* NH-1
North Holding Pasture Well—*locale* NM-5
North Hole—*basin* AZ-5
North Hole—*gut* FL-3
North Hole—*valley* CO-8
North Hole Spring—*spring* AZ-5
North Hole Spring—*spring* NM-5
North Holiday Creek—*stream* VA-3
**North Holladay Subdivision**—*pop pl* UT-8
North Holland—*other* MI-6
North Holland Cem—*cemetery* MI-6
North Holley Tank—*reservoir* TX-5
**North Hollis**—*pop pl* ME-1
*North Hollow* UT-8
North Hollow—*locale* CT-1
North Hollow—*valley* CO-8
North Hollow—*valley* (2) KY-4
North Hollow—*valley* (4) MO-7
North Hollow—*valley* NY-2
North Hollow—*valley* PA-2
North Hollow—*valley* TN-4
North Hollow—*valley* (3) UT-8
North Hollow—*valley* VA-3
North Hollow—*valley* WV-2
North Hollow Cem—*cemetery* (2) VT-1
North Hollow Creek—*stream* NM-5
North Hollow Sch—*school* WI-6
North Hollow Sch (abandoned)—*school* PA-2
North Hollow Wildlife Mngmt Area—*park* UT-8
North Holly Branch—*stream* AR-4
*North Holly Creek* OK-5
North Holly Creek—*stream* (2) OK-5
**North Hollywood**—*pop pl* CA-9
North Hollywood Branch—*hist pl* CA-9
North Hollywood HS—*school* CA-9
North Hollywood Park—*park* CA-9
**North Holston**—*pop pl* VA-3
North Holston Ch—*church* VA-3
North Home Creek—*stream* MT-8
North Home Draw—*valley* (2) NM-5
North Home Lake—*lake* NM-5
North Home Mines—*mine* MT-8
North Homestead Tank—*reservoir* NM-5
**North Homestead Township**—*pop pl* KS-7
North Hominy Creek—*stream* NC-3
North Honcut Creek—*stream* CA-9
North Honey Island Flowage—*reservoir* WI-6
North Honey Run—*stream* IN-6
*North Honeysuckle Lake* MI-6
North Hoodoo Well—*well* AZ-5
North Hooper—*locale* IL-6
*North Hoopeston* IL-6
**North Hoosick**—*pop pl* NY-2
North Hoosier Creek—*stream* IA-7
North Hope Corner—*locale* ME-1
North Hope Creek—*stream* CO-8
North Hopewell Ch—*church* MS-4
**North Hopewell (Township of)**—*pop pl* PA-2
North Hopkins Sch—*school* (2) TX-5
North Hopkins-Sulphur Bluff (CCD)—*cens area* TX-5
**North Hornell**—*pop pl* NY-2
North Hornell Sch—*school* NY-2
North Hornet Creek—*stream* ID-8
North Hornet Mine—*mine* ID-8
North Horn Lake—*lake* TN-4
North Horn Mtn—*summit* UT-8
North Horse Creek—*stream* CO-8
North Horse Creek—*stream* (2) WY-8
North Horse Creek Lateral—*canal* NE-7
North Horse Creek Lateral—*canal* WY-8
North Horse Flat Tank—*reservoir* AZ-5
North Horseshoe Creek—*stream* (2) WY-8
North Horseshoe Island—*island* FL-3
North Horsethief Canyon—*valley* MT-8
North Hosp—*hospital* OH-6
North House Windmill—*locale* TX-5
North Houston—*locale* TX-5
**North Houston**—*pop pl* OH-6
**North Houston Heights**—*pop pl* TX-5
North Howard Sch—*school* MN-6
**North Howell**—*pop pl* OR-9
North Howell Sch—*school* OR-9
North Howland Cove—*bay* AZ-5
North HQ Tank—*reservoir* AZ-5
North HQ Wash—*stream* AZ-5
North HS—*hist pl* OH-6
North HS—*school* (3) CA-9
North HS—*school* CO-8
North HS—*school* IN-6
North HS—*school* (2) IA-7
North HS—*school* MA-1
North HS—*school* (2) MN-6
North HS—*school* NE-7
North HS—*school* (3) NY-2
North HS—*school* NC-3
North HS—*school* (4) OH-6
North HS—*school* TN-4
North HS—*school* (2) WI-6
*North Hubbard Creek* TX-5
North Hubbell Well—*well* NM-5
North Huckleberry Island—*island* NY-2
**North Hudson**—*pop pl* NY-2
**North Hudson**—*pop pl* WI-6
North Hudson Cem—*cemetery* NY-2
North Hudson Falls—*CDP* NY-2
North Hudson Hosp—*hospital* NJ-2
North Hudson Park—*park* NJ-2
**North Hudson (Town of)**—*pop pl* NY-2
North Hudson Yacht Club—*other* NJ-2
**North Hughes**—*pop pl* AR-4
North Hughes—*unorg reg* SD-7
North Hughes Canyon—*valley* UT-8
North Hume Sch—*school* IL-6
North Hungry Creek—*stream* CA-9
North Hungry Creek—*stream* OR-9
North Hunt Creek—*stream* CO-8
North Hunt Creek Ditch—*canal* CO-8
North Hunterdon Regional Sch—*school* NJ-2
*North Hunting Creek* NC-3
**North Huntingdon**—*pop pl* PA-2
North Huntingdon Township HS—*school* PA-2
**North Huntingdon (Township of)**—*pop pl* PA-2
*North Huntsville Baptist Church* AL-4
North Huntsville Chapel, The—*church* AL-4
North Huntsville Community Center—*building* AL-4
**North Hurley (Trailer Park)**—*pop pl* NM-5
**North Huron**—*pop pl* NY-2
North Huron JHS—*school* CO-8
**Northhurst (subdivision)**—*pop pl* DE-2
North Hutchinson Island—*island* FL-3
*North Hyco Creek* NC-3
North Hyde—*unorg reg* SD-7
**North Hyde Park**—*pop pl* NC-3
**North Hyde Park**—*pop pl* VT-1
North Idaho Childrens Home—*locale* ID-8
North Idaho Indian Agency—*locale* ID-8
*Northiem* WI-6
*North Ike Tank* AZ-5
**North Ilion**—*pop pl* NY-2
Northilla Beach—*beach* WA-9
North Illinois Fair Association—*other* IL-6
North Illinois Sch—*school* SD-7
North Immanuel Cem—*cemetery* MN-6
North Inarajan Site—*hist pl* GU-9
**North Indianapolis**—*pop pl* IN-6
North Indian Canyon—*valley* NM-5
North Indian Cem—*cemetery* OK-5
*North Indian Creek* MT-8
*North Indian Creek* OR-9
*North Indian Creek* SD-7
North Indian Creek—*stream* ID-8
North Indian Creek—*stream* (2) MO-7
North Indian Creek—*stream* NV-8
North Indian Creek—*stream* SD-7
North Indian Creek—*stream* TN-4
North Indian Creek Pass—*gap* WY-8
North Indian Field—*island* FL-3
**North Indian Head Estates**—*pop pl* MD-2
North Indian Run—*stream* WV-2
North Indian Tank—*reservoir* NM-5
North Industrial Park—*locale* TN-4
**North Industry**—*pop pl* OH-6
North Inglewood—*uninc pl* CA-9
Northington Branch—*stream* AL-4
Northington Cem—*cemetery* (2) KY-4
*Northington Elementary School* AL-4
*Northington General Hospital* AL-4
Northington Lake—*lake* TX-5
Northington Sch—*school* AL-4
North Inian Pass—*channel* AK-9
*North Inlet* OR-9
North Inlet—*bay* SC-3
North Inlet—*gut* VA-3
North Inlet—*lake* ME-1
North Inlet—*stream* CO-8
North Inlet—*stream* NH-1
North Inlet—*stream* NY-2
North Inlet Trail—*trail* CO-8
North Intake Ditch—*canal* HI-9
**North Inverness**—*pop pl* FL-3
North Inverness Junction—*locale* FL-3
North Iredell HS—*school* NC-3
North Iron Gate Tank—*reservoir* AZ-5
North Ironwood—*locale* MI-6
North Ironwood Creek—*stream* SD-7
**North Irvine**—*pop pl* KY-4
North Irving Ch—*church* MI-6
**North Irwin**—*pop pl* PA-2
North Irwin Borough—*civil* PA-2
North Isanti Ch—*church* MN-6
*North Island* FM-9
North Island—*island* (5) AK-9
North Island—*island* CA-9
North Island—*island* FL-3
North Island—*island* LA-4
North Island—*island* (2) MI-6
North Island—*island* OR-9
North Island—*island* SC-3
North Island—*island* FM-9
North Island—*island* MH-9
North Island—*island* MP-9
North Island—*locale* LA-4
North Island Canal—*canal* LA-4
North Island Lake—*lake* MN-6
North Island Naval Air Station—*military* CA-9
North Islands—*island* LA-4
*North Isleborough* ME-1
*North Islesboro* ME-1
**North Islesboro**—*pop pl* ME-1
North Jackard Well—*well* NM-5
North Jack Creek—*stream* OK-5
North Jack Creek—*stream* SD-7
*North Jackfork Creek* OK-5
North Jackfork Creek—*stream* OK-5
**North Jackson**—*pop pl* OH-6
**North Jackson**—*pop pl* PA-2
North Jackson Baptist Ch—*church* MS-4
North Jackson Baptist Ch—*church* TN-4
North Jackson Cem—*cemetery* PA-2
North Jackson Ditch—*canal* OH-6
North Jackson Elem Sch—*school* MS-4
North Jackson Hosp—*hospital* AL-4
North Jackson Sch—*school* GA-3
*North Jackson School* PA-2
North Jackson State Public Shooting Area—*park* SD-7
North Jackson Station—*locale* OH-6
North Jackson Street Ch of Christ—*church* MS-4
North Jacksonville Baptist Ch—*church* FL-3
North Jacksonville Oil Field—*oilfield* TX-5
North Jacktar Hollow—*valley* MO-7
*North Jacobson Gulch* OR-9
North James Windmill—*locale* TX-5
**North Jamul**—*pop pl* CA-9
**North Jasper**—*pop pl* NY-2
North Jasper Cem—*cemetery* NY-2
North Jasper Ch—*church* AL-4
**North Java**—*pop pl* NY-2
North Java Lake—*lake* MN-6
North Java Station—*locale* NY-2
North Jay—*locale* NY-2
**North Jay**—*pop pl* ME-1
North Jay Cem—*cemetery* NY-2
North Jay Grange Store—*hist pl* ME-1
North Jay Peak—*summit* VT-1
*North Jeddito Wash* AZ-5
North Jefferson—*locale* MO-7
**North Jefferson**—*pop pl* ME-1
**North Jefferson**—*pop pl* TX-5
North Jefferson Ave Hist Dist—*hist pl* MI-6
North Jefferson Creek—*stream* MT-8
North Jefferson Sch—*school* WV-2
North Jenny Lake Junction—*locale* WY-8
North Jenny Ledge—*bar* ME-1
North Jerico—*uninc pl* VA-3
North Jersey Country Club—*other* NJ-2
North Jersey Facility—*post sta* NJ-2
North Jersey Training Sch—*school* NJ-2
North Jetty—*cliff* CA-9
North Jetty—*dam* CA-9
North Jetty—*dam* FL-3
North Jetty—*dam* (3) OR-9
North Jetty—*dam* (2) TX-5
North Jetty—*locale* TX-5
North Jetty—*locale* (2) WA-9
North Jetty Light—*locale* NJ-2
North Jetty Light—*other* DE-2
North Jetty Nehalem Bay—*dam* OR-9
North Jetty Tillamook Bay—*dam* OR-9
North JHS—*school* AZ-5
North JHS—*school* CA-9
North JHS—*school* (2) CO-8
North JHS—*school* ID-8
North JHS—*school* IL-6
North JHS—*school* IA-7
North JHS—*school* (3) MA-1
North JHS—*school* MI-6
North JHS—*school* MN-6
North JHS—*school* MO-7
North JHS—*school* (2) NY-2
North JHS—*school* SC-3
North JHS—*school* SD-7
North JHS—*school* (2) TN-4
North JHS—*school* TX-5
North JHS—*school* WA-9
North Jim Hogg (CCD)—*cens area* TX-5
North Jocko Peak—*summit* MT-8
North Jog Well—*well* TX-5
**North Johns**—*pop pl* AL-4
North Johns (CCD)—*cens area* AL-4
North Johns Division—*civil* AL-4
**North Johns (Johns)**—*pop pl* AL-4
North Johns Mine (underground)—*mine* AL-4
**North Johnson City**—*pop pl* TN-4
North Johnson Oil Field—*other* IL-6
North Johnson Well—*well* TX-5
North Johnston HS—*school* NC-3
North Johnstown Cem—*cemetery* WI-6
North Jonesboro Sch—*school* GA-3
North Jones Canyon—*valley* NM-5
North Jones Prairie—*flat* OR-9
North Jones Trail—*trail* OR-9
North Jones Trail (jeep)—*trail* OR-9
North Jordan Canal—*canal* UT-8
*North Jordan Creek* MO-7
North Jr HS—*school* NY-2
**North Judson**—*pop pl* IN-6
North Jump Creek—*stream* ID-8
**North Junction**—*pop pl* CO-8
**North Junction**—*pop pl* MS-4
North Junction—*uninc pl* MD-2
**North Junction (Davidson)**—*pop pl* (2) OR-9
**North Juniata**—*pop pl* MI-6
North Junipers—*range* ID-8
North Juniper Wash—*valley* UT-8
North Jupiter Narrows—*gut* FL-3
North Justiceburg Oil Field—*oilfield* TX-5
North Kaibab Trail—*trail* AZ-5
North Kaigani Harbor—*bay* AK-9
*North Kalabera Cliffs* MH-9
North Kane Spring—*spring* UT-8
*North Kannah Creek* CO-8
**North Kannapolis**—*pop pl* NC-3
**North Kansas City**—*pop pl* MO-7
North Kansas City Hospital Heliport—*airport* MO-7
North Karako Bay—*bay* LA-4
*North Kaukinehua* HI-9
North Kearny Sch—*school* KS-7
North Keesler Tank—*reservoir* AZ-5
North Kelly Canyon—*valley* NM-5
North Kelly Windmill—*locale* TX-5
North Kelsey Peak—*summit* CA-9
North Kemmerer—*obs name* WY-8
*North Kenai* AK-9
**North Kenai**—*pop pl* AK-9
**North Kenilworth**—*pop pl* MD-2
*North Kenova* OH-6
**North Kensington**—*pop pl* MD-2
North Kent—*locale* CT-1
North Kent Brook—*stream* CT-1
North Kent Ch—*church* MI-6
North Kenyon—*locale* ID-8
*North Kenyon Lake* MI-6
North Kern Hosp—*hospital* CA-9
*North Key* FL-3
North Key—*island* FL-3
Northkey Harbor—*bay* FL-3
**North Key Largo Beach**—*pop pl* FL-3
North Keys—*island* FL-3
North Keys—*locale* MD-2
North Keystone Mine—*mine* CA-9
North Key West Spring—*spring* NV-8
North Kickapoo Creek—*stream* IL-6
North Kidney Butte—*summit* NV-8
North Kight Tank—*reservoir* NM-5
*North Kill Creek* PA-2
Northkill Creek—*stream* PA-2
North Killdeer Mtn—*summit* ND-7
Northkill Path—*trail* PA-2
North Kingman—*locale* OH-6
North Kings Canyon—*valley* NV-8
North King Sch—*school* SD-7
North Kingston Cem—*cemetery* IL-6
North Kingston Cem—*cemetery* MN-6
North Kingston Oil Field—*oilfield* MS-4
*North Kingstown* RI-1
North Kingstown Emergency Operations Pad (airport)—*airport* RI-1
**North Kingstown (local name Wickford)**—*pop pl* RI-1
**North Kingstown (Town of)**—*pop pl* RI-1
**North Kingsville**—*pop pl* OH-6
North Kingsville (Township of)—*other* OH-6
North King Well—*well* NM-5
North Kinnikinick Tank—*reservoir* AZ-5
North Kinnikinnick Creek—*stream* IL-6
North Kirby Coulee—*valley* MT-8
North Kirby Sch—*school* VT-1
North Kirkwood—*locale* GA-3
North Kissimmee Baptist Ch—*church* FL-3
North Kitsap HS—*school* WA-9
North Kittikaski Branch—*stream* AL-4
North Kiwanis Park—*park* MI-6
North Klawatti Glacier—*glacier* WA-9
North Knappie Canyon—*valley* SD-7
North Knob—*summit* KY-4
North Knob—*summit* NC-3
North Knob—*summit* PA-2
North Knob Creek—*stream* TN-4
*North Knob Creek - in part* TN-4
North Knobs (Township of)—*fmr MCD* NC-3
North Knoll Spring—*spring* UT-8
North Knox Central Elem Sch—*school* IN-6
North Knox East Elementary and JHS—*school* IN-6
North Knox HS—*school* IN-6
**North Knoxville**—*pop pl* TN-4
North Knoxville Baptist Ch—*church* TN-4
North Knoxville Oil Field—*oilfield* MS-4
North Knox Vocational Center—*school* TN-4
North Knox West Elem Sch—*school* IN-6
North Koffer Hollow—*valley* MO-7
North Kohala (CCD)—*cens area* HI-9
North Kolomin Lake—*lake* AK-9
**North Komelik**—*pop pl* AZ-5
North Kona (CCD)—*cens area* HI-9
North Kona Water System—*canal* HI-9
North Kootenai Lake—*lake* MT-8
**North Kortright**—*pop pl* NY-2
North Kuparuk State—*other* AK-9
North Kurtz Spring—*spring* ID-8
North Kuykendall Draw—*valley* NM-5
North K Windmill—*locale* NM-5
North La Barge Gas And Oil Field—*oilfield* WY-8
**North La Crosse**—*pop pl* WI-6
North La Crosse—*uninc pl* WI-6
North Lacy Creek—*stream* TX-5
*North Ladder Creek* CO-8
*North Ladder Creek* KS-7
North Ladue River—*stream* AK-9
North Lagoon—*lake* MP-9
North Lagrange Oil Field—*oilfield* MS-4
*North Lagua Point* MH-9
North Laguna Tank—*reservoir* AZ-5
North Laidlaw Butte—*summit* ID-8
**North La Junta**—*pop pl* CO-8
*North Lake* ID-8
*North Lake* IN-6
*North Lake* MA-1
*North Lake* MI-6
*North Lake* OR-9
*North Lake* WI-6
North Lake—*bay* LA-4
North Lake—*lake* AK-9
North Lake—*lake* AR-4
North Lake—*lake* (2) CA-9
North Lake—*lake* CO-8
North Lake—*lake* (5) FL-3
North Lake—*lake* GA-3
North Lake—*lake* (2) ID-8
North Lake—*lake* IN-6
North Lake—*lake* LA-4
North Lake—*lake* ME-1
North Lake—*lake* (13) MI-6
North Lake—*lake* (6) MN-6
North Lake—*lake* MS-4
North Lake—*lake* NE-7
North Lake—*lake* (3) NM-5
North Lake—*lake* NY-2
North Lake—*lake* (2) ND-7
North Lake—*lake* (2) OR-9
North Lake—*lake* PA-2
North Lake—*lake* (2) TX-5
North Lake—*lake* UT-8
North Lake—*lake* (4) WA-9
North Lake—*lake* (7) WI-6
North Lake—*lake* WY-8
North Lake—*other* TX-5
**Northlake**—*pop pl* IL-6
**North Lake**—*pop pl* (4) MI-6
**Northlake**—*pop pl* TX-5
**North Lake**—*pop pl* WA-9
**North Lake**—*pop pl* WI-6
Northlake—*post sta* GA-3
North Lake—*post sta* TX-5
North Lake—*reservoir* AL-4
North Lake—*reservoir* CA-9
North Lake—*reservoir* CO-8
North Lake—*reservoir* NM-5
North Lake—*reservoir* (2) NY-2
North Lake—*reservoir* NC-3
North Lake—*reservoir* ND-7
North Lake—*reservoir* OR-9
North Lake—*reservoir* PA-2
North Lake—*reservoir* (3) TX-5
North Lake—*reservoir* UT-8
North Lake Canal—*canal* ID-8
North Lake Canyon—*valley* NM-5

North Lake Canyon—valley ... UT-8
North Lake Canyon—valley ... WY-8
North Lake Cem—cemetery ... MI-6
North Lake (corporate and RR name Northlake) ... IL-6
North Lake Country Club—locale ... NC-3
North Lake Creek—stream ... CO-8
North Lake Dam—dam ... NC-3
North Lake Dam—dam ... PA-2
North Lake Ditch—canal ... IL-6
North Lake Estates Lake Dam—dam ... IN-6
**North Lake (historical)**—pop pl ... OR-9
North Lakeland Sch—school ... FL-3
North Lake Lucille Oil Field—oilfield ... MS-4
North Lake Manor ... IL-6
North Lake Mary Oil Field—oilfield ... MS-4
North Lake Metigoshe ... ND-7
North Lake Number One ... MI-6
North Lake Okahumpka—lake ... FL-3
North Lake Oscar—lake ... MN-6
North Lake Park—park ... MI-6
North Lake Park—park ... OH-6
North Lake Park—park ... TX-5
**North Lake Park**—pop pl ... AL-4
**North Lakeport**—pop pl ... MI-6
North Lakes—lake ... MI-6
North Lakes—lake ... MT-8
North Lakes—lake ... OR-9
North Lake Sch—school ... WA-9
North Lake Sch Number 4—school ... ND-7
North Lake Shoal—bar ... FL-3
Northlake Square (Shop Ctr)—locale ... FL-3
North Lake State Wildlife Mngmt Area—park ... ID-8
North Lake Talmadge—lake ... FL-3
North Lake Trail—trail ... CO-8
North Lake Valley Well Number One—well ... NV-8
North Lake Valley Well Number Three—well ... NV-8
North Lake Valley Well Number Two—well ... NV-8
**North Lakeville**—pop pl ... MA-1
North Lakeville Sch—school ... MA-1
North Lakeville Station (historical)—locale ... MA-1
North Lake Wales—lake ... FL-3
North Lake Windmill—locale ... NM-5
North Lakewood Sch—school ... CO-8
North Lamartine Cem—cemetery ... WI-6
North Lambert Rsvr—reservoir ... ID-8
**North Lamoine**—pop pl ... ME-1
North Lamoose Creek—stream ... MT-8
North LaMoure Ch—church ... ND-7
NOrth Lancaster ... MA-1
**North Lancaster**—pop pl ... MA-1
**North Lancaster (Town of)**—pop pl ... WI-6
Northland ... OH-6
Northland—hist pl ... MN-6
Northland—locale ... MI-6
**Northland**—pop pl ... KY-4
**Northland**—pop pl ... WI-6
Northland Cem—cemetery ... ND-7
Northland Center—post sta ... MI-6
Northland Ch—church ... MI-6
Northland Christian Ch—church ... KS-7
Northland Coll—school ... WI-6
Northland Community Ch—church ... FL-3
Northland Corners—locale ... MO-7
Northland Country Club—other ... MN-6
Northland Glacier—glacier ... AK-9
Northland Golf Club—other ... MO-7
**North Landgrove**—pop pl ... VT-1
North Landing ... IN-6
North Landing—locale ... CA-9
North Landing—locale ... NY-2
North Landing—locale ... VA-3
North Landing River—stream ... NC-3
North Landing River—stream ... VA-3
Northland Memorial Park—cemetery ... WI-6
Northland Pioneer Coll—school ... AZ-5
Northland Shop Ctr—locale ... KS-7
Northland Shop Ctr—locale ... MI-6
Northland Shop Ctr—locale ... MO-7
Northland Town Hall—building ... ND-7
**Northland Township**—pop pl ... ND-7
**Northland (Township of)**—pop pl (2) ... MN-6
North Lang Lake—lake ... WI-6
North Lansing ... MI-6
**North Lansing**—pop pl ... NY-2
North Lansing Cem—cemetery ... NY-2
North Lansing Gas Field—oilfield ... TX-5
North Lansing Historic Commercial District—hist pl ... MI-6
North Lapile Creek—stream ... AR-4
North Lapwai—locale ... ID-8
North Laramie Canal—canal ... WY-8
North Laramie Ditch No 3—canal ... WY-8
North Laramie River—stream ... WY-8
North Larchmont—other ... NY-2
**North Larchmont**—pop pl ... PA-2
North Largoeta Well—well ... NM-5
North Larkum Canyon—valley ... AZ-5
North Larney Creek ... MT-8
North Larsen Canyon—valley ... CO-8
North La Sal Mountain ... UT-8
North Last Chance Creek—stream ... UT-8
North Las Vagas Public Safety Building Helispot—airport ... NV-8
**North Las Vegas**—pop pl ... NV-8
North Las Vegas Air Terminal—airport (2) ... NV-8
North Las Vegas Regional Park—park ... NV-8
North Las Vegas Township—inact MCD ... NV-8
North Lateral ... CO-8
North Lateral—canal ... CO-8
North Lateral—canal ... SD-7
North Lateral—canal ... TX-5
North Lateral Bench Canal—canal ... WY-8
North Lateral C Canal—canal ... UT-8
North Lateral Lake Fork Canal—canal ... UT-8
North Lateral Marysville Canal—canal ... ID-8
**North Lauderdale**—pop pl ... FL-3
North Lauderdale Christian Sch—school ... FL-3
North Lauderdale Elem Sch—school ... FL-3
North Lauderdale Square (Shop Ctr)—locale ... FL-3
North Laulau Beach ... MH-9
North Laulau Point ... MH-9
North Laurel—CDP ... MD-2
North Laurel Ch—church ... NC-3
North Laurel Elem Sch—school ... DE-2
**North Laurel Park**—pop pl ... MD-2
North Laurel Shop Ctr—locale ... MS-4
North Laurinburg Elem Sch—school ... NC-3
North Laveta Creek ... CO-8
North La Veta Pass—gap ... CO-8
North Lawn Cem—cemetery ... IN-6
North Lawn Cem—cemetery ... IA-7
North Lawn Cem—cemetery ... MI-6
Northlawn Cem—cemetery ... MO-7
Northlawn Cem—cemetery ... NC-3
North Lawn Cem—cemetery ... OH-6
North Lawn Elem Sch—school ... KS-7
Northlawn Memorial Cem—cemetery ... TX-5
**North Lawrence**—pop pl ... NY-2
**North Lawrence**—pop pl ... OH-6
North Lawrence—unorg reg ... SD-7
North Lawrence Ch—church ... OH-6
North Lawrence-Monroe Street Hist Dist—hist pl ... AL-4
North Layton JHS—school ... UT-8
North Lead Lake—reservoir ... NV-8
**North Lebanon**—pop pl ... ME-1
North Lebanon (Township of)—fmr MCD ... AR-4
**North Lebanon (Township of)**—pop pl ... PA-2
North Ledge—bar ... AK-9
North Ledge—bar ... ME-1
North Ledge—other ... AK-9
North Ledge—rock ... MA-1
North Lee Canyon—valley ... NV-8
North Leeds—locale ... ME-1
**North Leeds**—pop pl ... WI-6
North Lee Elem Sch ... TN-4
North Lee Sch—school ... TN-4
North Left Fork ... UT-8
North Leigh Canal—canal ... ID-8
North Leigh Creek—stream ... ID-8
North Leigh Creek—stream ... WY-8
North Leigh Creek Trail—trail ... WY-8
North Lemmerhirt Lake—lake ... MN-6
**North Lemmon**—pop pl ... ND-7
North Lemmon Lake—lake ... ND-7
North Lemmon Lake State Game Mngmt Area—park ... ND-7
North Lemmon Sch—school ... ND-7
**North Lemmon Township**—pop pl ... ND-7
North Lemon Lake Dam—dam ... ND-7
North Lenoir Fire District—civil ... NC-3
North Lenoir Fire Station—building ... NC-3
North Lenoir HS—school ... NC-3
**North Leominster (subdivision)**—pop pl ... MA-1
North Leopard Creek—stream ... NC-3
**North Leroy**—pop pl ... NY-2
North Leslie—locale ... MI-6
North Le Valley Sch—school ... MI-6
**North Leverett**—pop pl ... MA-1
**North Lewisburg**—pop pl ... OH-6
North Lewis Center—building ... AZ-5
**North Lewiston**—pop pl ... ID-8
North Lewisville (Old Town)—uninc pl ... AR-4
North Lexa—locale ... AR-4
North Lexington—locale ... NY-2
**North Lexington**—pop pl ... MA-1
North Lexington—uninc pl ... KY-4
Northley MS—school ... PA-2
North Liberty—locale ... TN-4
**North Liberty**—pop pl ... IN-6
**North Liberty**—pop pl ... IA-7
**North Liberty**—pop pl ... OH-6
**North Liberty**—pop pl ... PA-2
North Liberty Cem—cemetery ... IA-7
North Liberty Cem—cemetery ... PA-2
North Liberty Ch ... IN-6
North Liberty Ch—church ... TX-5
North Liberty Christian Ch—church ... IN-6
North Liberty Sch—school ... IL-6
North Liberty Sch—school ... IN-6
North Liberty Sch—school ... IA-7
North Liberty Sch (historical)—school ... TN-4
North Liberty (Township of)—fmr MCD ... NC-3
**North Libertyville Estates (Liberty Estates)**—pop pl ... IL-6
**North Lilbourn**—pop pl ... MO-7
North Lilly Creek—stream ... TX-5
North Lily Shaft—mine ... UT-8
**North Lima**—pop pl ... OH-6
North Lima Ch—church ... OH-6
North Lima Ch—church ... WI-6
North Lime Creek—stream ... CO-8
North Lime Lake—lake ... AK-9
North Limestone Commercial District—hist pl ... KY-4
North Limestone Sch—school ... IL-6
**North Limington**—pop pl ... ME-1
**North Lincoln**—pop pl ... ME-1
North Lincoln Cem—cemetery ... MN-6
North Lincoln Ch—church ... MI-6
North Lincoln Hill Elem Sch—school ... PA-2
North Lincoln Hospital Heliport—airport ... OR-9
North Lincoln Sch—school ... MI-6
North Lincoln Sch—school ... SD-7
**North Lindenhurst**—pop pl ... NY-2
North Linden Sch—school ... OH-6
North Lindsay Ridge Oil Field—oilfield ... OK-5
North Lindstrom Lake—lake ... MN-6
Northline—locale ... WI-6
Northline Creek ... MT-8
Northline Creek ... WY-8
North Line Creek—stream ... MT-8
North Line Creek—stream ... WY-8
North Line Island—island ... NY-2
Northline Sch—school ... TX-5
Northline Shop Ctr—locale ... TX-5
**Northline Terrace**—pop pl ... TX-5
North Line Well—well ... NM-5
**North Linkhorn Park**—pop pl ... VA-3
North Linn Creek—stream ... MO-7
North Linn HS—school ... IA-7
North Linn Tank—reservoir ... NM-5
North Linn Township—civil ... MO-7
North Linson Creek—stream ... OK-5
**North Linthicum**—pop pl ... MD-2
North Lisbon Sch—school ... WI-6
North Lisbon Windmill—locale ... NM-5
**North Litchfield**—pop pl ... ME-1
**North Litchfield**—pop pl ... NY-2
**North Litchfield Beach**—pop pl ... SC-3
North Litchfield (Township of)—civ div ... IL-6
North Lito Sink ... MH-9
North Little Barren Creek ... MO-7
North Little Black Creek ... MS-4
North Little Creek—stream ... AR-4
North Little Creek—stream ... MO-7
North Little Hunting Creek—stream ... NC-3
North Little Kincaid Creek—stream ... KY-4
North Little Lake—lake ... IN-6
North Little Pigeon Creek ... IN-6
**North Little Rock**—pop pl ... AR-4
North Little Rock City Hall—hist pl ... AR-4
North Little Rock Post Office—hist pl ... AR-4
North Little Springs—spring ... NV-8
North Littleton—locale ... NH-1
**North Littleton**—pop pl ... MA-1
North Littleton Cem—cemetery ... NH-1
North Liveoak Draw—valley ... TX-5
North Liveoak Windmill—locale ... TX-5
**North Livermore**—pop pl ... ME-1
North Lizard Creek ... IA-7
North Llano Draw—valley ... TX-5
North Llano River—stream ... TX-5
North Lobe Creek—stream ... CO-8
North Lodge Pole Creek ... WY-8
North Lodgepole Creek—stream ... WY-8
North Lodgepole Ditch—canal ... WY-8
**North Logan**—pop pl ... UT-8
North Logan Benson Canal—canal ... UT-8
North Logan (CCD)—cens area ... OK-5
North Logan Creek—stream ... NE-7
**North Logan (historical)**—pop pl ... OR-9
North Logan House Creek—stream ... NV-8
North Logan Peak ... UT-8
North Logan Rsvr—reservoir ... WY-8
North Logan Sch—school ... KY-4
North Logan Sch—school ... OR-9
North Loggerhead Rsvr—reservoir ... OR-9
North Loi Island ... MP-9
North Loma Linda—uninc pl ... CA-9
**North Loma Township**—pop pl ... ND-7
North Londo Lake ... MI-6
**North Londonderry**—pop pl ... NH-1
**North Londonderry (Township of)**—pop pl ... PA-2
North London Mill—locale ... CO-8
North London Mine—mine ... CO-8
North Lone Elm Sch—school ... KS-7
North Lone Jack Rsvr—reservoir ... CO-8
North Lone Lake—lake ... ID-8
North Lone Pine Creek—stream ... CO-8
North Lone Pine Trail—trail ... CO-8
North Long Beach—CDP ... MS-4
**North Long Beach**—pop pl ... CA-9
North Long Beach (Lakewood (sta.))—uninc pl ... CA-9
**North Long Branch**—pop pl ... NJ-2
North Long Canyon—valley ... CA-9
North Long Creek ... KS-7
North Long Creek ... OK-5
North Long Creek—stream (2) ... OK-5
North Long Dry Creek—stream ... TX-5
North Long Lake—lake ... MN-6
North Long Point—cape ... UT-8
North Long Street-Park Ave Hist Dist—hist pl ... NC-3
North Lookout—summit ... PA-2
North Lookout Rsvr—reservoir ... ID-8
North Loon Lake Ch—church ... NY-2
North Loon Mtn—summit ... ID-8
**North Loop**—pop pl ... TX-5
North Loop Sch—school ... TX-5
North Los Angeles ... CA-9
North Los Tanos Tank—reservoir ... NM-5
North Lost Creek—stream ... UT-8
North Lost Hollow—valley ... UT-8
North Lost Horse Creek—stream ... MT-8
North Lothair Sch—school ... MT-8
North Loudon County MS ... TN-4
**North Loup**—pop pl ... NE-7
North Loup Dam—dam ... NE-7
North Loup River—stream ... NE-7
**North Loup Township**—pop pl ... NE-7
North Love Ch—church ... IL-6
**North Lovell**—pop pl ... ME-1
North Lovell Peak—summit ... NV-8
North Love Mesa Bench—bench ... CO-8
North Lowell—locale ... WI-6
North Lowell Sch—school ... SD-7
North Lowe Pasture—flat ... KS-7
North Lowndes Ch—church ... AL-4
North Loxa Sch—school ... IL-6
**North Lubec**—pop pl ... ME-1
North Luby Oil Field—oilfield ... TX-5
North Lucerne Valley—valley ... CA-9
North Lucy—locale ... NM-5
North Lumber Canyon—valley ... NM-5
**North Lumberton**—pop pl ... MS-4
North Lumberton—uninc pl ... NC-3
North Lump ... FL-3
North Lutheran Cem—cemetery ... NE-7
North Lyman Creek ... WY-8
**North Lyme**—pop pl ... CT-1
**North Lynbrook**—pop pl ... NY-2
North Lynch Oil Field—other ... NM-5
North Lyndeborough Cem—cemetery ... NH-1
North Lyndon ... ME-1
**North Lyndon**—pop pl ... ME-1
**North Lynnwood**—pop pl ... WA-9
North Macedon—locale ... NY-2
North Mackford Sch—school ... WI-6
North Macon Cemetery ... NC-3
North Macon Creek ... MI-6
North Madill Oil Field—oilfield ... OK-5
North Madison ... IN-6
**North Madison**—pop pl ... CT-1
**North Madison**—pop pl ... IN-6
**North Madison**—pop pl ... OH-6
North Madison—uninc pl ... WI-6
North Madison Ave Ch of Christ—church ... KS-7
North Madison Cem—cemetery ... IA-7
North Madison Cem—cemetery ... OH-6
North Madison Ch—church ... IN-6
North Madison Elem Sch—school ... IN-6
North Maginnis Creek—stream ... MT-8
North (Magisterial District)—fmr MCD ... WV-2
North Magutex Oil Field—oilfield ... TX-5
North Mahanoy Creek—stream ... PA-2
North Mahaska Junior Senior HS—school ... IA-7
North Mahogany Rsvr—reservoir ... NV-8
**North Mahoning (Township of)**—pop pl ... PA-2
North Maided Ch—church ... NC-3
North Main Ave Hist Dist—hist pl ... NC-3
North Main Canal—canal (2) ... CA-9
North Main Canal—canal ... CO-8
North Main Ch—church ... VA-3
North Main-North Adams Hist Dist—hist pl ... KY-4
North Main-North Detroit Street Hist Dist—hist pl ... OH-6
North Main Shop Ctr—locale ... KS-7
North Main Shop Ctr—locale ... MA-1
North Main Street Baptist Ch—church ... FL-3
North Main Street Hist Dist—hist pl ... AL-4
North Main Street Hist Dist—hist pl ... GA-3
North Main Street Hist Dist—hist pl (3) ... KY-4
North Main Street Hist Dist—hist pl ... MO-7
North Main Street Hist Dist—hist pl (2) ... NY-2
North Main Street Hist Dist—hist pl ... NC-3
North Main Street Hist Dist—hist pl ... TN-4
North Main Street Hist Dist—hist pl ... WI-6
North Main Street Sch—school ... NY-2
North Maljamar Oil Field—other ... NM-5
North Mam Creek ... CO-8
**North Mammoth**—pop pl ... AZ-5
North Mamm Peak—summit ... CO-8
North Mam Peak ... CO-8
**North Manchester**—pop pl ... IN-6
North Manchester Covered Bridge—hist pl ... IN-6
North Manchester Planning and Band Saw Mill (J.A. Browne Co.Mill)—hist pl ... IN-6
North Maney Ave Hist Dist—hist pl ... TN-4
North Mangrove Point ... FL-3
North Manhattan (Site)—locale ... NV-8
**North Manheim (Township of)**—pop pl ... PA-2
North Manistique Lake—lake ... MI-6
**North Manitou**—pop pl ... MI-6
North Manitou Island—island ... MI-6
North Manitou Island School—locale ... MI-6
North Manitou Shoal Light—locale ... MI-6
North Manitou Shoals—bar ... MI-6
**North Mankato**—pop pl ... MN-6
North Mankato Public Sch—hist pl ... MN-6
**North Manlius**—pop pl ... NY-2
**North Manor**—pop pl ... PA-2
North Mansion and Tenant House—hist pl ... NY-2
North Manursing Island—island ... NY-2
North Maple Canyon—valley ... UT-8
North Maple Lake—lake ... MN-6
North Maple Ridge Cem—cemetery ... IL-6
North Maple Ridge Ch—church ... MN-6
North Marais River—stream ... ND-7
North Marble Gulch—valley ... OR-9
North Marble Island—island ... AK-9
North Marbletown Ch—church ... NY-2
North Marcellon Ch—church ... WI-6
North Mare Pasture Windmill—locale ... WY-8
North Mariaville—locale ... ME-1
**North Marion**—pop pl ... IN-6
North Marion Ch—church ... ND-7
North Marion HS—school ... FL-3
North Marion Junior High School ... OR-9
North Marion Sch—school ... FL-3
North Marion Union HS—school ... OR-9
North Markel Windmill—locale ... NM-5
North Market—locale ... MA-1
North Market Hist Dist—hist pl ... OH-6
North Market Park—park ... IA-7
North Markham Oil Field—oilfield ... TX-5
North Maroon Peak—summit ... CO-8
North Marshall—summit ... VA-3
North Marshall (CCD)—cens area ... OK-5
North Marshall Ch—church ... KY-4
North Marshall HS—school ... KY-4
**North Marshfield**—pop pl ... MA-1
North Marshfield (historical P.O.)—locale ... MA-1
North Marsh Lake—lake ... NE-7
North Marston Filtration Plant—other ... CO-8
North Martha Washington Ditch—canal ... VA-3
North Martinton Ditch—canal ... IL-6
North Martinton Ditch No 2—canal ... IL-6
North Marty Well—well ... SD-7
North Maryland—locale ... LA-4
North Marysville—CDP ... WA-9
North Mason Oil Field—oilfield ... TX-5
North Mason Oil Field—other ... NM-5
**North Massapequa**—pop pl ... NY-2
North Massena Ch—church ... IA-7
**North Matewan**—pop pl ... WV-2
North Matthieu Lake—lake ... OR-9
North Maumee Bay—bay ... MI-6
North Maumee Bay Archeol District—hist pl ... MI-6
North Maxie Canyon—valley ... UT-8
North May Creek—stream ... CO-8
North Mayfair Park—park ... IL-6
North Mayo River ... VA-3
North Mayo River—stream ... NC-3
North Mayo River—stream ... VA-3
**North McAlester**—pop pl ... OK-5
North McAlester Cem—cemetery ... OK-5
North McCabe Lake—lake ... CO-8
North Mc Callum Oil Field—oilfield ... CO-8
North McClellan Creek—stream ... TX-5
**North McCloud**—pop pl ... CA-9
North McComb Baptist Ch—church ... MS-4
North Mccone—cens area ... MT-8
North McCurtain (CCD)—cens area ... OK-5
North McElroy Cave—cave ... TN-4
North McElroy Lateral—canal ... ID-8
North McGregor ... IA-7
North McKechnie Meadow—flat ... WY-8
**North McKees Rocks**—pop pl ... PA-2
North McKees Rocks Station—building ... PA-2
North Mckenzie—unorg reg ... ND-7
North McKittrick Canyon—valley ... NM-5
North McKittrick Canyon—valley ... TX-5
North McMillan Creek—stream ... NY-2
North McNally Canal—canal ... CA-9
North McNary—locale ... WA-9
North McSwain Mine—mine ... CA-9
North McWillie Oil Field—oilfield ... OK-5
North Meade—unorg reg ... SD-7
North Mead Lake County Park—park ... WI-6
North Meadow—flat ... CA-9
North Meadow—flat ... NY-2
North Meadow—swamp ... NY-2
North Meadow Brook ... MA-1
North Meadow Brook—stream ... NY-2
**North Meadowbrook Terrace**—pop pl ... FL-3
North Meadow Camp—locale ... ID-8
North Meadow Creek—stream ... CA-9
North Meadow Creek—stream ... ID-8
North Meadow Creek—stream ... MT-8
North Meadow Creek—stream ... WA-9
North Meadow Creek Camp—locale ... WY-8
North Meadow Creek Oil Field—oilfield ... WY-8
North Meadow Island—island ... NY-2
North Meadow Lake—lake ... AK-9
North Meadow Pond ... MA-1
North Meadows—flat ... MA-1
**North Meadows**—pop pl ... ME-1
North Meadows Dike—levee ... CT-1
North Mead Sch—school ... CA-9
North Mechumps Creek ... VA-3
North Mecklenburg HS—school ... NC-3
North Med Ctr—hospital ... NY-2
North Medicine Creek ... SD-7
North Medicine Creek—stream ... WA-9
North Meeteetse Creek—stream ... WY-8
North Meherrin River—stream ... VA-3
**North Mehoopany**—pop pl ... PA-2
North Memorial Cem—cemetery ... WI-6
North Memorial Hosp—hospital ... MN-6
North Memphis Street Hist Dist—hist pl ... MS-4
**North Menomonie**—pop pl ... WI-6
North Menomonie—uninc pl ... WI-6
North Mentor Ch—church ... OH-6
North Mentor Sch—school ... OH-6
North Mercer JHS—school ... WA-9
North Merchantville—uninc pl ... NJ-2
North Meridian Street Hist Dist—hist pl ... IN-6
**North Merrick**—pop pl ... NY-2
North Merritt Island—post sta ... FL-3
**North Merrydale**—pop pl ... LA-4
North Mesa ... WY-8
North Mesa—summit ... AZ-5
North Mesa—summit ... CO-8
North Mesa—summit (3) ... NM-5
North Mesa—summit ... TX-5
North Mesa Canyon Windmill—locale ... CO-8
North Mesa Community Hall—locale ... CO-8
North Mesa Sch—school ... CO-8
North Mesa Tank—reservoir ... AZ-5
North Mesa Windmill—locale ... CO-8
North Mesquite Creek—stream (2) ... TX-5
North Metcalfe Sch—school ... KY-4
**North Miami**—pop pl ... FL-3
**North Miami**—pop pl ... OK-5
**North Miami Beach**—pop pl ... FL-3
North Miami Beach Presbyterian Preschool—school ... FL-3
North Miami Beach Senior HS—school ... FL-3
North Miami Community Center—locale ... FL-3
North Miami Consolidated Elem Sch—school ... IN-6
North Miami Early Childhood Sch—school ... FL-3
North Miami General Hosp—hospital ... FL-3
North Miami HS—school ... IN-6
North Miami JHS—school ... FL-3
North Miami Med Ctr—hospital ... FL-3
North Miami Sch—school ... FL-3
North Miami Senior HS—school ... FL-3
**North Mianus**—pop pl ... CT-1
North Michigan Ave Hist Dist—hist pl ... MI-6
North Mickey Ridge—ridge ... CA-9
North Middle Alkali Sch—school ... SD-7
**North Middleboro**—pop pl ... MA-1
North Middleborough (historical P.O.)—locale ... MA-1
North Middle Branch ... MN-6
North Middle Branch Zumbro River ... MN-6
North Middle Butte—summit ... WY-8
North Middle Creek—stream ... CO-8
North Middle Mtn—summit ... CO-8
North Middlesex Regional HS—school ... MA-1
North Middleton Drain—canal ... ID-8
North Middleton Oil Field—oilfield ... OK-5
North Middleton Park—park ... PA-2
**North Middleton (Township of)**—pop pl ... PA-2
**North Middletown**—pop pl ... KY-4
North Middletown (CCD)—cens area ... KY-4
North Middle Well—well ... NM-5
**North Milford**—pop pl ... MA-1
North Milford Hist Dist—hist pl ... DE-2
North Military Hill—summit ... MI-6
North Mill ... NM-5
North Mill Camp—locale ... WY-8
North Mill Campground—park ... UT-8
North Mill Creek ... LA-4
North Mill Creek ... MT-8
North Mill Creek ... VA-3
North Mill Creek—stream ... AR-4
North Mill Creek—stream ... CA-9
North Mill Creek—stream ... IL-6
North Mill Creek—stream ... TX-5
North Mill Creek—stream ... WV-2
North Mill Creek Ch—church ... WV-2
**North Milledgeville**—pop pl ... GA-3
North Miller Creek—stream ... CA-9
North Miller Creek—stream ... MT-8
North Miller Creek—stream ... WY-8
North Millick Spring—spring ... NV-8
North Mill Pond—lake ... NH-1
North Mills—locale ... IA-7
**North Mills**—pop pl ... PA-2
North Mill Sch—school ... MI-6
North Mills River Rec Area—locale ... NC-3
North Mills River Recreation Site ... NC-3
North Mill Well—well ... AZ-5
**North Milton**—pop pl ... NY-2
North Milton Cem—cemetery ... NY-2
North Milton Sch—school ... WI-6
North Milwaukee—uninc pl ... WI-6
North Minam Guard Station—locale ... OR-9
North Minam Meadows—flat ... OR-9
North Minam River—stream ... OR-9
North Minam Trail—trail ... OR-9
North Mine Canyon Spring—spring ... CA-9
North Mineral Cem—cemetery ... IA-7
North Mineral Creek ... TX-5
North Mineral Creek—stream ... TX-5
North Miners Coulee ... MT-8
North Mineshas Island ... MI-6
North Mine Spring—spring ... AZ-5
North Mingus Trail Number One Hundred Six—trail ... AZ-5
**North Minister**—pop pl ... DE-2
Northminster Ch—church ... VA-3
Northminster Ch—church ... MI-6
Northminster Ch—church ... NY-2
Northminster Ch—church ... VA-3
Northminster Presbyterian Ch—church ... TN-4
North Mississippi Med Ctr—hospital ... MS-4
North Mississippi Retardation Center—hospital ... MS-4
North Mississippi Worship Center—church ... MS-4
**North Mitchell**—pop pl ... MN-6
**North Mitchell Heights**—pop pl ... WV-2
North Mizell Windmill—locale ... NM-5
North Moat Mtn—summit ... NH-1
**North Mobile**—pop pl ... AL-4
North Mobile Free Holiness Ch—church ... AL-4
North Moccasin Mountains—spring ... MT-8
North Modesto—uninc pl ... CA-9
North Mokelumne River—stream ... CA-9
North Momb Lake—lake ... MN-6
North Monahans Oil Field—oilfield ... TX-5
North Monistique Lake ... MI-6
North Moniteau Township—civil ... MO-7
**North Monmouth**—pop pl ... ME-1
North Monoosnoc Hill—summit ... MA-1
North Monroe—locale ... ME-1
**North Monroe**—pop pl ... LA-4
North Monroe Ch—church ... NH-1
**North Monroeville**—pop pl ... OH-6
**North Monson**—pop pl ... MA-1
**Northmont**—pop pl ... NJ-2
**Northmont**—pop pl ... PA-2
North Montana State Fairground—locale ... MT-8
North Monteo Area Technical Sch—school ... PA-2
**Northmont Estates (subdivision)**—pop pl ... TN-4
**North Montgomery**—pop pl ... AL-4
North Montgomery Baptist Ch—church ... AL-4
Northmont HS—school ... OH-6
North Monticello Point—cape ... NM-5
**North Montpelier**—pop pl ... VT-1
Northmont Sch—school ... CA-9
North Montville Ch—church ... ME-1
North Monument Creek—stream ... CO-8
North Moody Creek—stream ... ID-8
**Northmoor**—pop pl (2) ... MO-7
**Northmoor**—pop pl ... OH-6
Northmoor Country Club—other ... IL-6
North Moordener Kill ... NY-2
North Moore Sch—school ... NC-3
Northmoor Golf Course—other ... IL-6
North Moran Bay—bay ... WY-8
North Moran Creek—stream ... WY-8
**Northmore**—pop pl ... IL-6
North Moreau Creek—stream ... MO-7
North Moreau River ... MO-7
Northmore Elem Sch—school ... FL-3
Northmore Heights ... IL-6
**North Moreland**—pop pl ... OH-6
**Northmoreland (Township of)**—pop pl ... PA-2
**North Morenci**—pop pl ... MI-6
North Moreno Creek—stream ... NM-5
Northmore Park—park ... NV-8
North Morgan Canal—canal ... UT-8
North Morgan Cem—cemetery ... UT-8
North Morgan Island ... FL-3
North Morgan Township—civil ... MO-7
North Morris Tank—reservoir ... NM-5
North Morton Baptist Ch—church ... MS-4
North Morton Cem—cemetery ... MS-4
North Mosier Spring—spring ... NV-8
North Mosley Canyon—valley ... NM-5
North Mosquito Creek—stream ... FL-3
North Mosquito Creek—stream ... GA-3
North Motto Windmill—locale ... TX-5
North Mound—summit ... WI-6
**North Mounds**—pop pl ... IL-6
North Mountain ... ID-8
North Mountain ... ME-1
North Mountain—locale ... PA-2
North Mountain—locale ... VA-3
**North Mountain**—pop pl ... WV-2
North Mountain Flood Detention Dam Number Three—dam ... AZ-5
North Mountain Flood Detention Dam Number Two A—dam ... AZ-5
North Mountain Hosp—hospital ... AZ 5
North Mountain Lookout—locale ... CA-9
North Mountain Park—park ... AZ-5
North Mountains ... VA-3
North Mountains ... WV-2
North Mountain Trail—trail (5) ... VA-3
North Mountain Trail—trail (2) ... WV-2
North Mountain Windmill—locale ... TX-5
North Mount Carmel Sch—school ... IA-7
North Mount Hope Sch—school ... OH-6
North Mount Marshall ... VA-3
North Mount Olive Ch—church ... MS-4
North Mount Pleasant ... MS-4
North Mount Pleasant Ch—church ... GA-3
North Mount Putnam ... ID-8
North Mount Seward ... NY-2
**North Mount Vernon**—pop pl ... OH-6
**North Mount Vernon**—pop pl ... VA-3
North Mouse Creek—stream ... TN-4
North Mouth Arolik River—stream ... AK-9
North Mowich Glacier—glacier ... WA-9
North Mowich River—stream ... WA-9
North MS ... TN-4
North MS—school ... MA-1
North MS—school ... TN-4
North MS—school ... TX-5
North Mtn ... PA-2
North Mtn ... VA-3
North Mtn ... WV-2
North Mtn—summit ... AK-9
North Mtn—summit (3) ... AZ-5
North Mtn—summit ... AR-4
North Mtn—summit (2) ... CA-9
North Mtn—summit (2) ... CO-8
North Mtn—summit ... MA-1
North Mtn—summit ... NH-1
North Mtn—summit ... NY-2
North Mtn—summit ... OK-5
North Mtn—summit ... OR-9
North Mtn—summit ... PA-2
North Mtn—summit ... TN-4
North Mtn—summit (2) ... TX-5
North Mtn—summit (3) ... VA-3
North Mtn—summit ... WA-9

**Northport**—*pop pl* MI-6
**Northport**—*pop pl* NE-7
**Northport**—*pop pl* NY-2
**Northport**—*pop pl* TN-4
**Northport**—*pop pl* WA-9
**Northport**—*pop pl* (2) WI-6
North Portal—*tunnel* (2) CA-9
North Port Arthur—*uninc pl* TX-5
Northport Baptist Ch—*church* AL-4
Northport Baptist Ch—*church* TN-4
Northport Basin—*bay* NY-2
Northport Bay—*bay* MI-6
Northport Bay—*bay* NY-2
**North Port Byron**—*pop pl* NY-2
*Northport Camp Ground* ME-1
Northport Canal—*canal* NE-7
North Port (CCD)—*cens area* FL-3
North Port Center (Shop Ctr)—*locale* FL-3
*North Port Charlotte* FL-3
**North Port Charlotte**—*pop pl* FL-3
Northport Ch of Christ—*church* AL-4
Northport Ch of God—*church* AL-4
Northport Ch of the Nazarene—*church* AL-4
Northport Community Center—*building* AL-4
Northport Corners Shop Ctr—*locale* AL-4
North Port Elem Sch—*school* FL-3
Northport Elem Sch (historical)—*school* AL-4
North Porter Sch—*school* MI-6
Northport First United Methodist Ch—*church* AL-4
Northport Gulch—*valley* CA-9
Northport Harbor—*bay* NY-2
Northport Hist Dist—*hist pl* AL-4
North Port (historical)—*locale* AL-4
Northport HS—*school* NY-2
*Northport Irrigation Canal* NE-7
Northport JHS—*school* AL-4
North Portland—*locale* OR-9
North Portland Harbor—*channel* OR-9
North Portland (Industrial Area)—*uninc pl* OR-9
Northport Library—*building* AL-4
Northport Main Street Park—*park* AL-4
Northport Mall (Shop Ctr)—*locale* ND-7
Northport MS—*school* FL-3
North Port Neches Oil And Gas Field—*oilfield* TX-5
**North Port Norris**—*pop pl* NJ-2
**North Port (North Port Charlotte)**—*pop pl* FL-3
Northport Park—*park* MI-6
Northport Park—*park* MN-6
Northport Point—*cape* MI-6
**Northport Point**—*pop pl* MI-6
**Northport (RR name Old Northport)**—*pop pl* NY-2
Northport Rural Cem—*cemetery* NY-2
Northport Sch—*hist pl* WA-9
Northport Sch—*school* MN-6
Northport Sch—*school* WA-9
Northport Sch (historical)—*school* TN-4
Northport Sewage Treatment Plant—*building* AL-4
Northport (sta.)—*other* NY-2
**Northport (Town of)**—*pop pl* ME-1
Northport Veterans Hosp—*hospital* NY-2
North Port Village (Shop Ctr)—*locale* FL-3
*North Posey County School* IN-6
North Posey JHS—*school* IN-6
North Posey Senior HS—*school* IN-6
North Post—*post sta* VA-3
North Post Creek—*stream* CA-9
North Potato Creek—*stream* NC-3
North Potato Creek—*stream* TN-4
North Pothole—*reservoir* NM-5
**North Potomac**—*pop pl* MD-2
North Potrock Run—*stream* WV-2
North Potts Creek—*stream* NC-3
North Poudre Ditch—*canal* CO-8
**North Powder**—*pop pl* OR-9
*North Powder Lakes* OR-9
North Powder Pond Number One—*lake* OR-9
North Powder Pond Number Two—*lake* OR-9
North Powder River—*stream* OR-9
North Powder Valley—*basin* OR-9
North Powell Creek—*stream* OH-6
North Powellhurst Sch—*school* OR-9
North Power Lateral—*canal* ID-8
**North Pownal**—*pop pl* ME-1
**North Pownal**—*pop pl* VT-1
North Prairie—*flat* IL-6
North Prairie—*flat* OR-9
North Prairie—*lake* FL-3
North Prairie—*locale* TX-5
**North Prairie**—*pop pl* MN-6
**North Prairie**—*pop pl* WI-6
North Prairie Cem—*cemetery* (2) IL-6
North Prairie Cem—*cemetery* IA-7
North Prairie Cem—*cemetery* ND-7
North Prairie Cem—*cemetery* WI-6
North Prairie Ch—*church* IL-6
North Prairie Ch—*church* IA-7
North Prairie Ch—*church* MN-6
North Prairie Ch—*church* (3) ND-7
North Prairie Creek—*stream* TX-5
North Prairie Lee Park—*park* MO-7
North Prairie Sch—*school* (2) IL-6
North Prairie Sch—*school* MO-7
**North Prairie Township**—*pop pl* ND-7
*North Precinct of Cambridge, Town of* MA-1
North Presbyterian Church—*hist pl* IA-7
North Presbyterian Church—*hist pl* NE-7
North Presbyterian Church—*hist pl* OH-6
**North Prescott**—*pop pl* MA-1
North Presley Windmill—*locale* NM-5
North Preston Ch—*church* SD-7
**North Princeton**—*pop pl* NJ-2
North Privo Windmill—*locale* NM-5
North Promontory Mtns—*range* UT-8
*North Promontory Range* ID-8
*North Promontory Range* UT-8
*North Prong* NC-3
*North Prong* PA-2
*North Prong* TN-4
North Prong—*stream* DE-2
North Prong—*stream* PA-2
North Prong Alafia River—*stream* FL-3
North Prong Alligator Creek—*stream* FL-3
North Prong Anderson Creek—*stream* NC-3
*North Prong Antelope Creek* NE-7
*North Prong Antelope Creek* WY-8
North Prong Arkansas Creek—*stream* WY-8
North Prong Atascosa River—*stream* TX-5
North Prong Barren Fork—*stream* TN-4
North Prong Bay River—*stream* NC-3
North Prong Bays Fork—*stream* KY-4
North Prong Beaverdam Creek—*stream* MO-7
North Prong Beaverdam Creek—*stream* VA-3
North Prong Big Bear Creek—*stream* SC-3
North Prong Bilderback Creek—*stream* WY-8
*North Prong Blackburns Fork* TN-4
North Prong Black Coulee—*valley* MT-8
North Prong Box Elder Draw—*valley* WY-8
North Prong Brown Camp Branch—*stream* TN-4
North Prong Brush Creek—*stream* AR-4
North Prong Buckhorn Creek—*stream* VA-3
North Prong Buckner Creek—*stream* VA-3
North Prong Buffalo Creek—*stream* NC-3
North Prong Bullhead Creek—*stream* TX-5
North Prong Camp Creek—*stream* SC-3
North Prong Cane Creek—*stream* MO-7
North Prong Canoochee Creek—*stream* GA-3
North Prong Castleman Run—*stream* WV-2
North Prong Cedar Bluff Creek—*stream* MO-7
North Prong Ch—*church* FL-3
North Prong Chinners Swamp—*stream* SC-3
North Prong Circle Seven Creek—*stream* NM-5
North Prong Clark Creek—*stream* NC-3
North Prong Clear Fork—*stream* TN-4
*North Prong Clear Fork Creek* TN-4
North Prong Coal Creek—*stream* MT-8
North Prong College Creek—*stream* GA-3
*North Prong Colomokee Creek* GA-3
North Prong Cottonwood Creek—*stream* WY-8
North Prong Cox Creek—*stream* AL-4
*North Prong Creek* SC-3
North Prong Creek—*stream* TX-5
North Prong Cypress Creek—*stream* TX-5
North Prong Davis Creek—*stream* VA-3
North Prong Dead Horse Creek—*stream* WY-8
North Prong Deadman Creek—*stream* WY-8
North Prong Double Branch—*stream* FL-3
North Prong Double Branch—*stream* TN-4
North Prong Dry Fork Powder River—*stream* WY-8
North Prong Ellijay Creek—*stream* NC-3
North Prong Fishdam Creek—*stream* TN-4
North Prong Flat Fork—*stream* TN-4
*North Prong Flat Fork Branch* TN-4
North Prong Glade Creek—*stream* NC-3
North Prong Goose Pond Bayou—*stream* LA-4
*North Prong Gut Creek* AR-4
North Prong Hannahs Creek—*stream* NC-3
North Prong Hay Creek—*stream* MT-8
North Prong Hayden Creek—*stream* CO-8
North Prong Hords Creek—*stream* TX-5
North Prong Horse Creek—*stream* TN-4
North Prong Horse Creek—*stream* TX-5
North Prong Indian Camp Creek—*stream* KY-4
North Prong Irish Hollow—*valley* IL-6
North Prong Jacks Fork—*stream* MO-7
*North Prong Jacks Fork River* MO-7
North Prong Jernigan Creek—*stream* TX-5
North Prong Kolomoki Creek—*stream* GA-3
North Prong Leatherwood Creek—*stream* MO-7
North Prong Left Fork Soque River—*stream* GA-3
North Prong Leonard Pond Run—*stream* MD-2
North Prong Leoncita Creek—*stream* TX-5
North Prong Lewis Fork—*stream* NC-3
*North Prong Lewis Fork Creek* NC-3
North Prong Little Black River—*stream* MO-7
North Prong Little Pine Creek—*stream* NC-3
North Prong Little Red River—*stream* TX-5
North Prong Little Rock Creek—*stream* TN-4
North Prong Little Thunder Creek—*stream* WY-8
North Prong Long Draw—*valley* NM-5
North Prong Long Lick Creek—*stream* KY-4
North Prong Lostland Run—*stream* MD-2
North Prong Maple Creek—*stream* OR-9
North Prong Marler Creek—*stream* TX-5
North Prong Medina River—*stream* TX-5
North Prong Meridian Creek—*stream* TX-5
North Prong Michael Hollow—*valley* IL-6
North Prong Middle Creek—*stream* AR-4
North Prong Miller Creek—*stream* WV-2
North Prong Mud Bayou—*stream* TX-5
North Prong Muddy Creek—*stream* MS-4
*North Prong Mukewater Creek* TX-5
North Prong of Belle Isle Bayou—*stream* LA-4
North Prong of Grand Bayou—*stream* LA-4
*North Prong Of Ogeechee Creek* GA-3
North Prong of Schooner Bayou—*stream* LA-4
North Prong Otter Creek—*stream* FL-3
North Prong Pecan Bayou—*stream* TX-5
North Prong Poor Fork—*stream* TN-4
North Prong Pumpkin Creek—*stream* WY-8
North Prong Red Creek—*stream* WY-8
North Prong Reeds Creek—*stream* AR-4
North Prong Richland Creek—*stream* NC-3
*North Prong Roaring River* NC-3
North Prong Rock Creek—*stream* NC-3
*North Prong Saint Marys River* FL-3
*North Prong Saint Marys River* GA-3
North Prong Saint Marys River—*stream* FL-3
North Prong Saint Marys River—*stream* GA-3
North Prong Saint Sebastian River—*stream* FL-3
*North Prong Sand Mountain* PA-2
*North Prong Sandy Creek* TX-5
*North Prong Sebastian Creek* FL-3
North Prong Shade Creek—*stream* MT-8
North Prong Shell Creek—*stream* WY-8
North Prong Shining Creek—*stream* NC-3
North Prong Smith River—*stream* VA-3
North Prong Soldier Creek—*stream* WY-8
North Prong South Antelope Creek—*stream* NE-7
North Prong South Antelope Creek—*stream* WY-8
North Prong South Fork Mitchell River—*stream* NC-3
North Prong S R Creek—*stream* WY-8
North Prong Steep Creek—*stream* AL-4
North Prong Stewman Creek—*stream* TN-4
North Prong Stinking Quarter Creek—*stream* NC-3
North Prong Stotts Creek—*stream* IN-6
North Prong Sumac Creek—*stream* GA-3
North Prong Swift Creek—*stream* SC-3
North Prong Tauler Creek—*stream* AL-4
North Prong Taylors Creek—*stream* AL-4
North Prong Tenmile Creek—*stream* FL-3
*North Prong Thickhead Mountain* PA-2
North Prong Thick Mountain—*cape* PA-2
North Prong Turkey Creek—*stream* NC-3
*North Prong Wetappo Creek* FL-3
North Prong Whaley Creek—*stream* AR-4
North Prong White Oak River—*stream* NC-3
North Prong Whitmeyer Creek—*stream* WY-8
North Prong Wicomico River—*stream* MD-2
North Prong Wild Horse Creek—*stream* (2) WY-8
North Prong Williams Creek—*stream* GA-3
North Prong Willow Creek—*stream* WY-8
North Prong Wright Creek—*stream* NC-3
*North Prong Wrights Creek* NC-3
North Prospect Ch—*church* MI-6
North Prosser—*locale* WA-9
**North Prosser**—*pop pl* WA-9
North Providence—*CDP* RI-1
North Providence Sch—*school* SC-3
**North Providence (Town of)**—*pop pl* RI-1
North Prudhoe State 1—*well* AK-9
North Pruitt Sch—*school* NM-5
**North Pugh (subdivision)**—*pop pl* NC-3
North Pulaski (census name Pulaski North)—*other* VA-3
North Pumping Station—*locale* IN-6
North Purchase Cem—*cemetery* MA-1
North Purchase Street Cem—*cemetery* MA-1
North Pushmataha (CCD)—*cens area* OK-5
*North Putman Peak* ID-8
*North Putnam Mountain* ID-8
*north Putnam Peak* ID-8
**North Puyallup**—*pop pl* WA-9
*North Puyallup Glacier* WA-9
North Puyallup River—*stream* WA-9
North Quadra Mtn—*summit* AK-9
North Quail Creek—*stream* OR-9
North Quail Creek Rsvr—*reservoir* OR-9
North Quartz Creek—*stream* CO-8
North Quidnessett—*locale* RI-1
*North Quincy* MA-1
**North Quincy**—*pop pl* IL-6
**North Quincy (subdivision)**—*pop pl* MA-1
North Quiver Ditch—*canal* IL-6
North Raber Sch—*school* MI-6
North Rabon Creek—*stream* SC-3
North Raccoon River—*stream* IA-7
North Race—*channel* NY-2
North Race Street Hist Dist—*hist pl* KY-4
**North Radcliffe**—*pop pl* PA-2
North Raeford—*other* NC-3
North Ragland Tank—*reservoir* NM-5
North Rago Oil Field—*oilfield* CO-8
North Rahway—*uninc pl* NJ-2
North Rahway Station—*locale* NJ-2
North Raker—*summit* ID-8
**North Raleigh**—*pop pl* NC-3
North Raleigh Cem—*cemetery* MS-4
North Raleigh Chapel—*church* NC-3
North Rampart Spring—*spring* CO-8
North Ramp Creek—*stream* IN-6
North Ranch—*locale* NV-8
*North Ranch II* AZ-5
North Ranchito Sch—*school* CA-9
**North Randall**—*pop pl* OH-6
North Randall (CCD)—*cens area* TX-5
**North Randall Township**—*pop pl* KS-7
**North Randolph**—*pop pl* MA-1
**North Randolph**—*pop pl* VT-1
North Rand Sch—*school* IL-6
North Range—*range* WI-6
North Rankin Creek—*stream* WY-8
North Rapid Shop Ctr—*locale* SD-7
North Rapid Stage Station (historical)—*locale* SD-7
North Rattlesnake Butte—*summit* CO-8
North Rattlesnake Canyon—*valley* NM-5
North Rattlesnake Creek—*stream* CA-9
North Ravenswood—*uninc pl* WV-2
North Ravine—*valley* CA-9
North Rawah Peak—*summit* CO-8
North Raymond—*locale* ME-1
North Rayne Oil and Gas Field—*oilfield* LA-4
*North Raynham* MA-1
North Raynham—*CDP* MA-1
North Rays Fork—*stream* KY-4
North Reach—*channel* NJ-2
North Readfield—*locale* WI-6
North Reading—*locale* NY-2
**North Reading**—*pop pl* MA-1
**North Reading**—*pop pl* PA-2
North Reading Ch—*church* MI-6
North Reading HS—*school* MA-1
North Reading JHS—*school* MA-1
North Reading Rehabilitation Center—*building* MA-1
**North Reading (Town of)**—*pop pl* MA-1
North Rec Area—*locale* UT-8
North Recreation Center—*park* GA-3
North Red Bank Baptist Ch—*church* TN-4
North Red Creek—*stream* AZ-5
North Red Creek—*stream* CO-8
North Red Hill—*summit* AZ-5
**North Redington Beach**—*pop pl* FL-3
North Red Iron Lake—*lake* SD-7
**North Redlands**—*pop pl* CA-9
North Red Mtn—*summit* CA-9
North Redondo Beach—*uninc pl* CA-9
North Red Owl Sch—*school* SD-7
*North Red River* MN-6
North Red River (Township of)—*civ div* MN-6
North Red Springs Oil Field—*oilfield* OK-5
North Red Tank—*reservoir* NM-5
North Redwater Creek—*stream* WY-8
North Red Well—*well* TX-5
**North Red Wing**—*pop pl* WI-6
**North Redwood**—*pop pl* MN-6
North Redwood Industrial Park—*locale* UT-8
North Reelfoot Creek—*stream* TN-4
North Reese Creek—*stream* TX-5
North Reeves Tank—*reservoir* TX-5
North Reformed Church—*hist pl* NJ-2
North Regional Park—*park* FL-3
**North Rehoboth**—*pop pl* MA-1
North Reiradon Hill—*summit* CO-8
North Reno Elem Sch—*school* KS-7
North Reservoir Dam—*dam* MA-1
North Reynolds Creek—*stream* OR-9
North Rhine Peak—*summit* AK-9
North Rice Lake—*lake* WI-6
North Richard Tank—*reservoir* NM-5
North Richeau Creek—*stream* WY-8
*North Rich Elementery School* UT-8
North Riche Oil and Gas Field—*oilfield* LA-4
North Rich HS—*school* UT-8
**North Richland**—*pop pl* WA-9
**North Richland Hills**—*pop pl* TX-5
North Richland Sch—*school* TX-5
North Richmond—*locale* OH-6
**North Richmond**—*pop pl* CA-9
**North Richmond**—*pop pl* NH-1
North Richmond Ch—*church* PA-2
**North Rich Township**—*pop pl* KS-7
*North Ridge* WI-6
**Northridge**—*pop pl* CA-9
**North Ridge**—*pop pl* DE-2
**North Ridge**—*pop pl* KY-4
**North Ridge**—*pop pl* NY-2
**Northridge**—*pop pl* (2) OH-6
North Ridge—*ridge* AL-4
North Ridge—*ridge* (4) CA-9
North Ridge—*ridge* CO-8
North Ridge—*ridge* (2) ME-1
North Ridge—*ridge* (2) OH-6
North Ridge—*ridge* (2) TN-4
North Ridge—*ridge* VT-1
North Ridge—*ridge* VA-3
North Ridge—*ridge* WA-9
North Ridge—*ridge* (3) WI-6
North Ridge—*ridge* (2) WY-8
North Ridge—*summit* MA-1
North Ridge—*summit* NV-8
Northridge—*uninc pl* CO-8
North Ridge Cem—*cemetery* ME-1
North Ridge Cem—*cemetery* NY-2
North Ridge Cem—*cemetery* WI-6
Northridge Ch—*church* (2) TX-5
Northridge Convenience Center—*locale* KS-7
North Ridge Country Club—*locale* NC-3
Northridge Country Club—*other* CA-9
North Ridge Elem Sch—*school* NC-3
Northridge Friends Ch—*church* KS-7
Northridge General Hosp—*hospital* FL-3
**Northridge Heights**—*pop pl* MT-8
**Northridge Heights Condominium**—*pop pl* UT-8
Northridge HS—*school* IN-6
Northridge HS—*school* OH-6
Northridge JHS—*school* CA-9
North Ridge JHS—*school* IL-6
North Ridge Lower Dam—*dam* NC-3
**Northridge Manor**—*pop pl* MD-2
Northridge Military Acad—*school* CA-9
Northridge (North Los Angeles)—*uninc pl* CA-9
Northridge Park—*park* TX-5
Northridge Sch—*school* CA-9
North Ridge Sch—*school* IL-6
North Ridge Sch—*school* NY-2
Northridge Sch—*school* ND-7
Northridge Sch—*school* (2) OH-6
Northridge Sch—*school* UT-8
North Ridge Sch—*school* WI-6
North Ridge Shop Ctr—*locale* FL-3
Northridge Shop Ctr—*locale* KS-7
North Ridge Shop Ctr—*locale* TN-4
**North Ridge (subdivision)**—*pop pl* NC-3
**Northridge (subdivision)**—*pop pl* NC-3
**Northridge Subdivision**—*pop pl* UT-8
**North Ridge Subdivision**—*pop pl* UT-8
North Ridge Trail—*trail* WA-9
North Ridge Upper Dam—*dam* NC-3
**North Ridge Village**—*pop pl* IN-6
**North Ridgeville**—*pop pl* (2) OH-6
North Ridgeville City Hall—*hist pl* OH-6
**North Ridgeway**—*pop pl* NY-2
North Rienzi Ch of Christ—*church* MS-4
North Rigby Canal—*canal* ID-8
North Riggs Canyon—*valley* WA-9
*North Right Fork* UT-8
North Rigolets—*gut* MS-4
North Rigolets Island—*island* MS-4
North Riley Oil Field—*oilfield* TX-5
North Rim—*cliff* CO-8
North Rim—*rock* AZ-5
North Rim Entrance Station—*locale* AZ-5
**North Rim (Grand Canyon Lodge)**—*pop pl* AZ-5
North Rim Inn—*locale* AZ-5
North Rim Lookout Tower—*tower* AZ-5
North Rim Ranger Station—*locale* CO-8
North Rim Tank—*reservoir* AZ-5
North Rim Tank—*reservoir* NM-5
North Rincon Oil And Gas Field—*oilfield* TX-5
North Ringsaker Cem—*cemetery* ND-7
North Ripley Baptist Ch—*church* MS-4
North Ripple Hollow—*valley* IL-6
*North River* FL-3
*North River* MA-1
*North River* NJ-2
*North River* OH-6
*North River* VA-3
North River—*channel* GA-3
North River—*locale* IA-7
North River—*locale* MO-7
**North River**—*pop pl* NY-2
**North River**—*pop pl* NC-3
**North River**—*pop pl* ND-7
North River—*stream* AL-4
North River—*stream* AK-9
North River—*stream* FL-3
North River—*stream* GA-3
North River—*stream* IA-7
North River—*stream* MD-2
North River—*stream* (3) MA-1
North River—*stream* MI-6
North River—*stream* MN-6
North River—*stream* MO-7
North River—*stream* NH-1
North River—*stream* (2) NC-3
North River—*stream* TN-4
North River—*stream* (3) VA-3
North River—*stream* WA-9
North River—*stream* WV-2
North River Campground—*locale* VA-3
North River Canal (abandoned)—*canal* NE-7
North River Canal (abandoned)—*canal* NE-7
North River (CCD)—*cens area* AL-4
North River (CCD)—*cens area* TX-5
North River (CCD)—*cens area* WA-9
North River Cem—*cemetery* MA-1
North River Ch—*church* (2) IA-7
North River Channel—*channel* NC-3
North River Consolidated Sch—*school* WA-9
North River Corner—*locale* NC-3
North River Country Club—*locale* AL-4
**North River Country Club Estates (subdivision)**—*pop pl* AL-4
*North Riverdale* OH-6
North River Divide—*ridge* WA-9
North River Division—*civil* AL-4
North River Gap—*gap* VA-3
North River Gorge Trail—*trail* VA-3
North River (historical P.O.)—*locale* IA-7
North River HS—*hist pl* VA-3
North River JHS—*school* VA-3
*North River Lake* NH-1
North River (Magisterial District)—*fmr MCD* (2) VA-3
North River Marsh—*swamp* MA-1
North River Marsh—*swamp* NC-3
North River Marshes—*swamp* MA-1
**North River Mills**—*pop pl* WV-2
*North River Mountain* NY-2
North River Mountains—*summit* NY-2
North River (Mount Crawford Station)—*locale* VA-3
North River Mtn—*summit* WV-2
North River Number 1 Mine (underground)—*mine* AL-4
North River Park Ch—*church* AL-4
North River Picnic Area—*locale* VA-3
North River Point—*cape* FL-3
North River Point—*cape* NC-3
North River Pond—*reservoir* NH-1
North River Rec Area—*park* TN-4
North River Road Cem—*cemetery* ME-1
North River Rsvr—*reservoir* MA-1
North River Sch—*school* MO-7
North River School (Abandoned)—*locale* (2) IA-7
North River Shores—*CDP* FL-3
**North River Shores**—*pop pl* FL-3
**North River Shores (subdivision)**—*pop pl* AL-4
*North Riverside* TN-4
**North Riverside**—*pop pl* IL-6
**North Riverside**—*pop pl* TN-4
*North Riverside Junior High School* TN-4
North Riverside Park—*park* KS-7
North Riverside Sch—*school* NE-7
North Riverside Sch (historical)—*school* SD-7
North Riverside Township—*civil* SD-7
North River Slope—*flat* WY-8
North River Stone Schoolhouse—*hist pl* IA-7
North River Thorofare—*channel* NC-3
North River Township—*civil* MO-7
*North River Water Supply Dam* AL-4
North River Yacht Club—*locale* AL-4
**North Riviera (subdivision)**—*pop pl* AL-4
North Road Cem—*cemetery* (2) ME-1
North Roberts Island—*island* FL-3
North Robertson Fork Creek—*stream* TN-4
North Robertson Sch—*school* TN-4
North Robinson Lateral—*canal* ID-8
**North Robinson (RR name Robinson)**—*pop pl* OH-6
**North Roby**—*pop pl* TX-5
North Roby Ch—*church* TX-5
*North Rochester* NH-1
**North Rochester**—*pop pl* MA-1
**North Rochester**—*pop pl* PA-2
**North Rochester (Hayes Station)**—*pop pl* NH-1
North Rochester (historical P.O.)—*locale* MA-1
North Rock—*bar* AK-9
North Rock—*bar* WA-9
North Rock—*island* CA-9
North Rock—*island* ME-1
North Rock—*island* MI-6
North Rock—*island* NC-3
North Rock—*island* OR-9
North Rock—*other* AK-9
North Rock—*pillar* CO-8
North Rock—*rock* MA-1
North Rock—*summit* WA-9
North Rock Creek—*stream* (2) CO-8
North Rock Creek—*stream* WY-8
North Rock Creek Sch—*school* OK-5
North Rockdale (CCD)—*cens area* GA-3
North Rock Draw—*valley* TX-5
North Rockford Sch—*school* MN-6
North Rock Hill—*CDP* SC-3
North Rockhouse Mtn—*summit* MA-1
North Rockhouse Ridge—*ridge* NC-3
North Rock Light—*locale* FL-3
North Rocks—*area* AK-9
North Rock Sch—*school* IL-6
North Rock Springs Table—*summit* NV-8
North Rock Tank—*reservoir* TX-5
**North Rockville Centre**—*pop pl* NY-2
*North Rockwood Baptist Church* TN-4
North Rockwood Ch—*church* TN-4
North Rockwood Sch—*school* OR-9
North Rocky Arroyo—*stream* NM-5
North Rocky Creek—*stream* TX-5
North Rocky Mount—*uninc pl* NC-3
North Rocky Point—*cape* FL-3
North Rocky River Prong—*stream* NC-3
North Rocky Tank—*reservoir* NM-5
**North Rodessa**—*pop pl* LA-4
North Roebuck Sch—*school* AL-4
North Rogers Street Hist Dist—*hist pl* TX-5
North Rolette—*unorg reg* ND-7
**North Rolleston**—*pop pl* VA-3
North Rolling Creek—*stream* CO-8
North Rolling Fork—*stream* KY-4
North Rolling Fork Ch—*church* KY-4
North Rome—*locale* PA-2
North Rome Cem—*cemetery* MI-6
North Rome Ch—*church* MI-6
North Romero Tank—*reservoir* TX-5
North Rome Sch—*school* GA-3
**Northrop**—*pop pl* MN-6
Northrop, Julia Carter, House—*hist pl* OH-6
Northrop Coll—*school* MN-6
Northrop Ditch No 5—*canal* WY-8
Northrop Ditch No 7—*canal* WY-8
Northrop Institute of Technology—*school* CA-9
Northrop Sch—*school* (3) MN-6
Northrop Trail—*trail* MA-1
North Rosary Lake—*lake* OR-9
**North Roscoe Township**—*pop pl* KS-7
**North Rose**—*pop pl* NY-2
North Roseau (Unorganized Territory of)—*unorg* MN-6
North Roseburg—*post sta* OR-9
North Roslyn—*other* NY-2
North Roslyn Sch—*school* NY-2
North Roswell—*uninc pl* GA-3
North Rothwell Lake—*lake* MN-6
*North Rothwell Slough* MN-6
North Round Pond—*lake* NH-1
North Round Prairie Cem—*cemetery* MN-6
North Route Of Old Nez Perce Trail—*trail* MT-8
North Rover Oil Field—*oilfield* OK-5
North Rowan HS—*school* NC-3
*North Rowan MS* NC-3
North Rowan Primary Sch—*school* NC-3
North Roxboro (RR name Longhurst)—*uninc pl* NC-3
**North Royalton**—*pop pl* OH-6
**North Royalton**—*pop pl* VT-1
North Roy Creek—*stream* OR-9
North Rsvr—*reservoir* CA-9
North Rsvr—*reservoir* MA-1
North Rsvr—*reservoir* OH-6
North Rsvr—*reservoir* (2) OR-9
North Rsvr—*reservoir* WY-8
North Ruby Valley Sch—*school* NV-8
North Ruckels Branch—*stream* NJ-2
North Rudy Canal—*canal* ID-8
North Ruin Creek—*stream* KY-4
North Rumsey Creek—*stream* TX-5
*North Run* PA-2
North Run—*stream* NJ-2
North Run—*stream* (3) PA-2
North Run—*stream* VA-3
North Run—*stream* WV-2
North Run Ch—*church* VA-3
**North Run Hills**—*pop pl* VA-3
*North Run - in part* PA-2
North Running Brook—*stream* CT-1
North Running Valley Ch—*church* WI-6
North Run Trail—*trail* PA-2
North Runway—*other* GU-9
Northrup—*locale* NJ-2
Northrup—*locale* TX-5
Northrup—*locale* WA-9
Northrup, Stephen, House—*hist pl* RI-1
Northrup Canyon—*valley* NM-5
Northrup Canyon—*valley* WA-9
Northrup Cem—*cemetery* MO-7
Northrup Cem—*cemetery* WI-6
Northrup Ch—*church* KY-4
Northrup Chapel—*church* MS-4
Northrup Corners—*locale* NY-2
Northrup Creek—*stream* NY-2
Northrup Creek—*stream* OR-9
Northrup Creek—*stream* WA-9
**Northrup Rupert**—*pop pl* VT-1
Northrup Falls—*falls* TN-4
Northrup Gulch—*valley* CO-8
Northrup Lake—*lake* NY-2
Northrup Lake—*lake* WA-9
Northrup Park—*park* KS-7
Northrup Ranch—*locale* (2) ND-7
Northrup Sch—*school* CA-9
Northrups Corners—*locale* NY-2
Northrup Street Cem—*cemetery* NY-2
Northrup Street Sch—*school* NY-2
**North Rural Branch**—*pop pl* AR-4
North Rural Sch—*school* SD-7
North Rush—*locale* NY-2
*North Rush Creek* CO-8
North Rush Creek—*stream* CO-8
North Rushford Cem—*cemetery* WI-6
North Rushing Creek—*stream* TN-4
North Rush River Peace Ch—*church* WI-6
North Rushville—*fmr MCD* NE-7
**North Ruskin**—*pop pl* FL-3
North Rusk (rusk State Hospital)—*uninc pl* TX-5
North Russell—*locale* NY-2
*North Russell Cave* AL-4
North Russell Cem—*cemetery* NY-2
North Russell Mine—*mine* MN-6
North Russellville Baptist Ch—*church* AL-4
North Russian Creek—*stream* CA-9
**North Rutland**—*pop pl* MA-1
North Ryder Peak—*summit* CO-8
*North Saboo Lake* ME-1
**North Sacramento**—*pop pl* CA-9
North Saddle Lake—*lake* AK-9
North Saddle Mtn—*summit* AZ-5
North Saddle Peak—*summit* CO-8
**North Sagamore Heights**—*pop pl* OH-6
North Sage Spring Creek Oil Field—*oilfield* WY-8
*North Saginaw* MI-6
North Saint Charles Canyon—*valley* CO-8
*North Saint Charles River* CO-8
North Saint Charles River—*stream* CO-8
North Saint Johns Cem—*cemetery* MN-6
North Saint Nicholas Lake—*lake* TX-5
**North Saint Paul**—*pop pl* MN-6
North Saint Paul Cem—*cemetery* WI-6
North Saint Vrain Creek—*stream* CO-8
North Salado Creek—*stream* TX-5
North Salado Windmill—*locale* NM-5
North Salem—*locale* TX-5
**North Salem**—*pop pl* IN-6
**North Salem**—*pop pl* MO-7
**North Salem**—*pop pl* NH-1
**North Salem**—*pop pl* NY-2
**North Salem**—*pop pl* OH-6
North Salem Ch—*church* GA-3
North Salem Ch—*church* IN-6
North Salem Ch—*church* OH-6
North Salem Ch—*church* PA-2
North Salem Dam—*dam* NM-5
North Salem Sch—*school* IN-6
North Salem Sch—*school* NH-1
North Salem Senior HS—*school* OR-9
**North Salem (subdivision)**—*pop pl* MA-1
North Salem Town Hall—*hist pl* NY-2
**North Salem (Town of)**—*pop pl* NY-2

**North Salem Township**—pop pl ... MO-7
North Salinas HS—school ... CA-9
North Salina Street Hist Dist—hist pl ... NY-2
North Saline Lake Oil Field—oilfield ... LA-4
North Salmon Creek ... WA-9
North Salmon Creek Beach—beach ... CA-9
North Salt Canyon—valley ... CO-8
North Salt Canyon—valley ... NM-5
North Salt Creek—stream ... CA-9
North Salt Creek—stream ... IN-6
North Salt Creek—stream ... KS-7
North Salt Creek Windmill—locale ... TX-5
North Salt Lagoon—lake ... AK-9
North Salt Lake—lake ... ND-7
**North Salt Lake**—pop pl ... UT-8
North Salt Lake Industrial Park—locale ... UT-8
North Salt Lake State Game Mngmt Area—park ... ND-7
North Salt Wash—valley ... UT-8
North Saluda Creek ... SC-3
North Saluda River ... SC-3
North Saluda River—stream ... SC-3
North Saluda Rsvr—reservoir ... SC-3
North Sam Gabriel Dam—dam ... TX-5
North Samish River ... WA-9
North Samoa ... CA-9
North Samples Well—well ... NM-5
North Sampson Well—well ... TX-5
North San Antonio Sch—school ... CA-9
**North Sanbornton**—pop pl ... NH-1
North Sanchez Tank—reservoir ... NM-5
North Sand Branch—stream ... WV-2
North Sand Canyon—valley ... NM-5
North Sand Creek ... SD-7
North Sand Creek—stream (2) ... CO-8
North Sand Creek—stream ... MT-8
North Sand Creek—stream ... SD-7
North Sand Creek—stream ... WY-8
North Sand Draw Unit—other ... WY-8
North Sand Hills—range ... CO-8
North Sandhills Tank—reservoir ... NM-5
**North San Diego**—pop pl ... CA-9
North Sand Lake—lake ... MI-6
North Sand Mountain HS—school ... AL-4
North Sandusky Street Hist Dist—hist pl ... OH-6
**North Sandwich**—pop pl ... NH-1
North Sandwich Meeting House—hist pl ... NH-1
North Sandy—locale ... PA-2
North Sandy Branch—stream ... OK-5
North Sandy Draw—valley ... WY-8
North Sandy Run ... PA-2
**North Sanford**—pop pl ... NY-2
North Sangamon Ch—church ... IL-6
North Sangamon United Presbyterian Church—hist pl ... IL-6
North San Joaquin Main Canal—canal ... CA-9
**North San Juan**—pop pl ... CA-9
North San Pedro—CDP ... TX-5
North Sanpete HS—school ... UT-8
North Sanpete MS—school ... UT-8
North San Pitch Canyon—valley ... UT-8
North Santa Clara Creek—stream ... CO-8
North Santa Creek ... AL-4
**North Santa Maria**—pop pl ... CA-9
**North Santee**—pop pl ... SC-3
North Santee Bay—bay ... SC-3
North Santee River—stream ... SC-3
**North Santiam**—pop pl ... OR-9
North Santiam River—stream ... OR-9
**North Santian**—pop pl ... OR-9
**North San Ysidro**—pop pl ... NM-5
North Sarasota—CDP ... FL-3
North Sartin Draw—valley ... MT-8
North Sashabaw Sch—school ... MI-6
**North Saugus**—pop pl ... MA-1
North Sauty Creek—stream ... AL-4
North Sauty Creek Bar—bar ... AL-4
North Sauty Wildlife Ref—park ... AL-4
North Savannah—uninc pl ... GA-3
North Sawba Cem—cemetery ... AR-4
North Sawmill Canyon—valley ... NM-5
North Sawmill Creek—stream ... MT-8
North Sawtooth Mtn—summit ... WY-8
North Scalp Creek—stream ... SD-7
North Scappoose Creek—stream ... OR-9
North Scarboro ... ME-1
**North Scarborough**—pop pl ... ME-1
North Scatterwood Lake—lake ... SD-7
North Sch—hist pl ... ME-1
North Sch—school ... AZ-5
North Sch—school ... AR-4
North Sch—school (3) ... CA-9
North Sch—school ... CO-8
North Sch—school (2) ... CT-1
North Sch—school ... GA-3
North Sch—school (11) ... IL-6
North Sch—school (3) ... IA-7
North Sch—school (3) ... KS-7
North Sch—school ... KY-4
North Sch—school (2) ... LA-4
North Sch—school (6) ... MA-1
North Sch—school (5) ... MI-6
North Sch—school (2) ... MN-6
North Sch—school ... MO-7
North Sch—school ... MT-8
North Sch—school (4) ... NE-7
North Sch—school ... NJ-2
North Sch—school (2) ... NY-2
North Sch—school (3) ... NC-3
North Sch—school (6) ... OH-6
North Sch—school ... OK-5
North Sch—school (6) ... TX-5
North Sch—school ... UT-8
North Sch—school (2) ... VA-3
North Sch—school (2) ... WI-6
North Schelling Windmill—locale ... NM-5
North Schell Peak—summit ... NV-8
North Schneider Ditch—canal ... CO-8
North Sch No 135—school ... NE-7
North Sch No 165—school ... NE-7
North Sch No 28—school ... NE-7
North Sch No 92—school ... NE-7
North Sch No 93—school ... NE-7
**North Schodack**—pop pl ... NY-2
North Scholls ... OR-9
North School ... KS-7
North School Creek Spring—spring ... NV-8
North School Section Lake—lake ... MN-6
North School Section Rsvr—reservoir ... WY-8
North School Section Well—well (2) ... NM-5

North Schuylkill Junior Senior HS—school ... PA-2
North Scituate ... MA-1
**North Scituate**—pop pl ... MA-1
**North Scituate**—pop pl ... RI-1
North Scituate Beach—beach ... MA-1
North Scituate (historical P.O.)—locale ... MA-1
North Scituate Horseshoe Dam ... RI-1
North Scituate Station (historical)—locale ... MA-1
North Scott Ch—church ... IN-6
**North Scottdale**—pop pl ... PA-2
North Scott Lake ... MI-6
North Scott Lake—lake ... MI-6
North Scotty Creek—stream ... OR-9
North Scranton—uninc pl ... PA-2
North Scranton HS—school ... PA-2
**North Scriba**—pop pl ... NY-2
**North Sea**—pop pl ... NY-2
North Sea Bird Ravine ... MH-9
North Sea Cem—cemetery ... NY-2
**North Seadrift**—pop pl ... TX-5
**North Seaford**—pop pl ... NY-2
**North Seaford Heights**—pop pl ... DE-2
North Sea Harbor—bay ... NY-2
North Seal Beach—uninc pl ... CA-9
North Searight Oil Field—oilfield ... OK-5
**North Searsmont**—pop pl ... ME-1
**North Searsport**—pop pl ... ME-1
**North Sebago**—pop pl ... ME-1
North Seco Canyon—valley ... NM-5
North Seco Creek—stream ... NM-5
North Second Creek ... NC-3
North Seco Spring—spring ... NM-5
North Seco Well—well ... NM-5
**North Sedgwick**—pop pl ... ME-1
**North Seekonk**—pop pl ... MA-1
North Seekonk Sch—school ... MA-1
North Sefton Sch—school ... IL-6
North Selah—CDP ... WA-9
North Selkirk Lake—lake ... MI-6
North Selma—uninc pl ... AL-4
North Selma Cem—cemetery ... CA-9
North Senator Tank—reservoir ... AZ-5
North Settlement—locale ... NY-2
North Settlement Cem—cemetery (2) ... NY-2
North Seven Rivers—stream ... NM-5
North Seventh Street Historic Residential District—hist pl ... CO-8
North Seventh Street Sch—school ... TX-5
North Severn Creek—stream ... KY-4
North Sevier HS—school ... UT-8
North Sevier MS—school ... UT-8
**North Seward Township**—pop pl ... KS-7
**North Sewickley**—pop pl ... PA-2
**North Sewickley (Township of)**—pop pl ... PA-2
Norths Fork Neffs Canyon—valley ... UT-8
North Shade Ch—church ... MI-6
North Shade Drain—canal ... MI-6
North Shade Sch—school ... MI-6
**North Shade (Township of)**—pop pl ... MI-6
**North Shadow Mountain Estates**—pop pl ... UT-8
**North Shadydale**—pop pl ... TX-5
North Shady Lake—lake ... MN-6
North Shaft—mine ... CA-9
**North Shafter**—pop pl ... CA-9
**North Shafter (Myricks Corner)**—pop pl ... CA-9
**North Shaftsbury**—pop pl ... VT-1
**North Shapleigh**—pop pl ... ME-1
North Sharon Cem—cemetery ... WI-6
North Sharon Ch—church ... MI-6
North Shaser Creek—stream ... WA-9
North Shaser Trail—trail ... WA-9
North Shattuck Lake—lake ... WI-6
North Sheba Crater—crater ... AZ-5
North Sheep Mtn—summit (2) ... CO-8
North Sheep Mtn—summit ... WY-8
North Sheffield ... OH-6
North Sheie Cem—cemetery ... MN-6
North Shelby Cem—cemetery ... NY-2
North Shelby HS—school ... MO-7
**North Sheldon**—pop pl ... NY-2
**North Sheldon**—pop pl ... VT-1
North Sheldon Gulch—valley ... WY-8
North Sheldon South Concord Ditch—canal ... IL-6
North Shell Creek—stream ... NE-7
North Shell Rock Cem—cemetery ... IA-7
North Shelton Rock—summit ... TX-5
North Shenango Ch—church ... PA-2
North Shenango Sch—school ... PA-2
**North Shenango (Township of)**—pop pl ... PA-2
North Shepherd—uninc pl ... TX-5
North Sherburne—locale ... VT-1
North Sheridan—unorg reg ... ND-7
**North Sherman**—pop pl ... TX-5
**North Sherman Junction**—pop pl ... TX-5
North Sherwood Cem—cemetery ... MI-6
North Sherwood Draw—valley ... WY-8
**North Sherwood Forest**—pop pl ... MD-2
North Shilling Hist Dist—hist pl ... ID-8
North Shinnery Windmill—locale (2) ... TX-5
**Northshire**—pop pl ... DE-2
**Northshire**—pop pl ... MD-2
North Shirkshire Cem—cemetery ... MA-1
**North Shirley**—pop pl ... MA-1
North Shirttail Canyon—valley ... CA-9
North Shoal—bar ... ME-1
North Shoal—bar ... MD-2
North Shoal—bar ... NJ-2
North Shoal Creek—stream ... NC-3
North Shongaloo Oil Field—oilfield ... LA-4
North Shop Ctr—locale ... KS-7
**North Shore**—pop pl (2) ... CA-9
**North Shore**—pop pl ... FL-3
**North Shore**—pop pl ... IL-6
**North Shore**—pop pl ... LA-4
**North Shore**—pop pl ... MD-2
**North Shore**—pop pl ... MN-6
**North Shore**—pop pl ... NE-7
**North Shore**—pop pl ... SD-7
**North Shore**—pop pl ... TX-5
**North Shore**—pop pl ... WI-6
North Shore—post sta ... WI-6
**North Shore Acres**—pop pl ... TX-5
North Shore Art Association—building ... MA-1
North Shore Bay—bay ... LA-4
North Shore Beach—beach ... NY-2

**North Shore Beach**—pop pl ... LA-4
**North Shore Beach**—pop pl ... NY-2
North Shore Campground—locale ... CA-9
North Shore Campground—locale ... ID-8
North Shore Campground—locale ... LA-4
Northshore Cem—cemetery ... IL-6
North Shore Ch ... TN-4
North Shore Ch—church ... IL-6
Northshore Ch—church ... TN-4
North Shore Ch—church ... TX-5
North Shore Channel—canal ... IL-6
North Shore Channel—channel ... LA-4
North Shore Chapel—church ... LA-4
North Shore Chapel—church ... MN-6
North Shore Country Club—other ... MI-6
Northshore Country Club—other ... MO-7
North Shore Country Club—other ... WI-6
**Northshore Development (subdivision)**—pop pl ... SD-7
**Northshore Estates**—pop pl ... TN-4
**Northshore Hills (subdivision)**—pop pl ... TN-4
North Shore Hosp—hospital ... FL-3
North Shore Hosp—hospital ... NY-2
North Shore Hosp—hospital ... TX-5
North Shore HS—school ... FL-3
North Shore HS—school ... NY-2
North Shore HS—school ... TX-5
North Shore JHS—school ... NY-2
North Shore Junction—uninc pl ... FL-3
Northshore Lake—reservoir ... NC-3
Northshore Lake Dam—dam ... NC-3
**North Shoreland**—pop pl ... IL-6
North Shore Marina—locale ... CA-9
North Shore Med Ctr—hospital ... FL-3
North Shore Memory Garden—cemetery ... MI-6
North Shore Open Space Park—park ... FL-3
North Shore Park—park ... FL-3
Northshore Park—park ... TX-5
North Shore Picnic Ground—park ... ID-8
Northshore Plaza (Shop Ctr)—locale ... FL-3
North Shore Rec Area—park ... SD-7
**North Shores**—pop pl (4) ... DE-2
**North Shores**—pop pl ... MI-6
**North Shores Addition (subdivision)**—pop pl ... DE-2
North Shore Sanitary District Tower—hist pl ... IL-6
North Shore Sch—school ... CA-9
North Shore Sch—school (2) ... FL-3
North Shore Sch—school ... IL-6
North Shore Sch—school ... MA-1
North Shore Sch—school (3) ... MI-6
North Shore Sch—school ... TX-5
North Shores Child Care Center—school ... FL-3
Northshore Shop Ctr—locale ... FL-3
North Shore Shop Ctr—locale ... MA-1
North Shore Shopping Plaza—locale ... FL-3
North Shores JHS—school ... MI-6
**North Shore (subdivision)**—pop pl (2) ... NC-3
North Shore Trace—other ... IL-6
**Northshore Woods**—pop pl ... TN-4
North Shoshone Canal—canal ... ID-8
North Shoshone Peak—summit ... NV-8
North Shotgun Coulee—valley ... MT-8
North Shreveport ... LA-4
**North Shreveport**—pop pl ... LA-4
**North Shrewsbury**—pop pl ... VT-1
North Shrewsbury River ... NJ-2
North Shubuta Oil Field—oilfield ... MS-4
North Shugart Oil Field—other ... NM-5
North Shyster Creek—stream ... NV-8
North Sibley Cem—cemetery ... IA-7
North Sibley Well—well ... NM-5
North Side ... IA-7
North Side ... MI-6
Northside ... MN-6
North Side ... OH-6
North Side—locale ... LA-4
Northside—other ... OH-6
**Northside**—pop pl ... AL-4
**Northside**—pop pl ... MA-1
**Northside**—pop pl ... NC-3
**North Side**—pop pl ... NC-3
**North Side**—pop pl ... OH-6
**North Side**—pop pl ... OR-9
**North Side**—pop pl ... PA-2
**North Side**—pop pl ... TN-4
**Northside**—pop pl ... TX-5
**Northside**—pop pl ... VA-3
**North Side**—pop pl ... VI-3
North Side—post sta ... FL-3
Northside—post sta ... FL-3
Northside—post sta (2) ... ID-8
Northside—uninc pl ... FL-3
North Side—uninc pl ... GA-3
Northside—uninc pl ... NY-2
Northside—uninc pl ... OK-5
Northside—uninc pl ... VA-3
Northside—uninc pl ... WI-6
Northside Acres—locale ... AL-4
Northside Alliance—church ... FL-3
Northside Assembly of God Ch—church ... AL-4
Northside Assembly of God Ch—church (3) ... FL-3
Northside Athletic Complex—other ... TX-5
North Side Baptist Ch ... AL-4
Northside Baptist Ch ... MS-4
Northside Baptist Ch ... TN-4
Northside Baptist Ch—church (8) ... AL-4
Northside Baptist Ch—church (7) ... FL-3
Northside Baptist Ch—church ... IN-6
Northside Baptist Ch—church (3) ... MS-4
Northside Baptist Ch—church ... TN-4
Northside Bible Ch—church ... AL-4
North Side Canal—canal ... AZ-5
North Side Canal—canal ... CA-9
North Side Canal—canal ... OR-9
North Side Canal—canal ... TX-5
North Side Canal Company Slaughter House—hist pl ... ID-8
Northside Cem—cemetery ... AL-4
North Side Cem—cemetery ... GA-3
Northside Cem—cemetery ... MA-1
Northside Cem—cemetery ... MI-6
North Side Cem—cemetery ... MI-6
Northside Cem—cemetery ... MS-4
Northside Cem—cemetery ... OK-5
North Side Cem—cemetery ... PA-2
North Side Cem—cemetery ... TX-5
North Side Cem—cemetery ... WI-6

Northside (Census Subdistrict)—cens area ... VI-3
North Side Center ... NC-3
Northside Ch ... IN-6
North Side Ch—church ... AL-4
Northside Ch—church (3) ... AL-4
North Side Ch—church ... AL-4
Northside Ch—church (2) ... AL-4
Northside Ch—church (3) ... FL-3
Northside Ch—church (6) ... GA-3
North Side Ch—church ... GA-3
Northside Ch—church (2) ... IN-6
North Side Ch—church ... IN-6
Northside Ch—church ... KY-4
North Side Ch—church ... KY-4
Northside Ch—church ... LA-4
Northside Ch—church (4) ... MS-4
Northside Ch—church ... MO-7
North Side Ch—church ... MO-7
Northside Ch—church ... NY-2
Northside Ch—church (3) ... NC-3
North Side Ch—church ... NC-3
North Side Ch—church ... OH-6
North Side Ch—church ... OK-5
Northside Ch—church ... SC-3
Northside Ch—church (7) ... TN-4
North Side Ch—church ... TX-5
Northside Ch—church (2) ... TX-5
North Side Ch—church ... TX-5
Northside Ch—church ... TX-5
North Side Ch—church ... VA-3
Northside Chapel—church ... AR-4
Northside Chapel—church ... NC-3
Northside Chapel—church ... VA-3
Northside Ch of Christ ... MS-4
Northside Ch of Christ ... TN-4
Northside Ch of Christ—church (2) ... AL-4
Northside Ch of Christ—church (2) ... FL-3
Northside Ch of Christ—church (2) ... KS-7
Northside Ch of Christ—church ... TN-4
Northside Ch of God—church ... DE-2
Northside Ch of the Nazarene—church ... AL-4
Northside Ch of the Nazarene—church ... MS-4
Northside Christian Acad—school ... FL-3
Northside Christian Ch ... TN-4
Northside Christian Ch—church ... FL-3
Northside Christian Ch—church ... MS-4
Northside Christian Day Care—school ... FL-3
Northside Christian Schools—school ... FL-3
Northside Community Mental Health Center—hospital ... FL-3
North Side Consolidated Sch—school ... TX-5
Northside Ditch—canal ... WY-8
North Side Draw—valley ... WY-8
Northside East Sch—school ... PA-2
Northside Elementary School ... MS-4
North Side Elementary School ... TN-4
Northside Elem Sch ... PA-2
Northside Elem Sch—school ... AL-4
North Side Elem Sch—school ... IN-6
Northside Elem Sch—school ... IN-6
North Side Elem Sch—school (2) ... IN-6
Northside Elem Sch—school ... KS-7
Northside Elem Sch—school ... PA-2
**Northside Estates (subdivision)**—pop pl ... TN-4
North Side Fargo Builder's Residential Hist Dist—hist pl ... ND-7
North Side Fargo High Style Residential Hist Dist—hist pl ... ND-7
Northside Fire Department—building ... AR-4
**Northside Gardens (subdivision)**—pop pl ... NC-3
North Side Hist Dist—hist pl ... IL-6
Northside Hist Dist—hist pl ... IN-6
Northside Hist Dist—hist pl ... MA-1
Northside Hist Dist—hist pl ... NY-2
Northside Hist Dist (Boundary Increase)—hist pl ... IN-6
Northside Historic Residential District—hist pl ... KY-4
Northside Hosp ... TN-4
North Side Hosp—hospital ... OH-6
North Side Hosp—hospital ... TN-4
Northside HS ... AL-4
Northside HS ... IN-6
Northside HS—school ... AL-4
North Side HS—school ... AR-4
Northside HS—school (2) ... GA-3
North Side HS—school ... IN-6
Northside HS—school ... IN-6
North Side HS—school ... TN-4
North Side HS—school ... TX-5
Northside HS—school ... VA-3
North Side JHS ... TN-4
Northside JHS—school ... GA-3
North Side JHS—school ... IN-6
Northside JHS—school ... NY-2
Northside JHS—school ... SC-3
Northside JHS—school ... TN-4
North Side JHS—school ... TN-4
North Side JHS—school ... TX-5
Northside JHS—school ... VA-3
North Side Main Canal—canal ... ID-8
Northside Mall—locale ... FL-3
Northside Mall Shop Ctr—locale ... AL-4
Northside Methodist Acad—school ... AL-4
Northside Mission—church ... AR-4
North Side Mission—church ... TN-4
Northside Mission Ch—church ... SC-3
North Side Mountains ... AZ-5
Northside MS ... TN-4
Northside MS—school ... SC-3
North Side New Era Baptist Ch—church ... IN-6
Northside Park—park ... CA-9
North Side Park—park (2) ... IL-6
North Side Park—park ... MI-6
Northside Park—park ... MN-6
Northside Park—park (2) ... MS-4
Northside Park—park ... MT-8
Northside Park—park ... NE-7
Northside Park—park ... NC-3
Northside Park—park ... SD-7
North Side Park—park ... TX-5
Northside Park—park ... TX-5
Northside Park—park ... WI-6
Northside Park Ch—church ... GA-3
Northside-Pearl Sch—school ... MS-4
North Side Pine Tank—reservoir ... NM-5
Northside Playground—park ... MI-6
Northside Plaza Shop Ctr—locale ... AL-4

Northside Plaza (Shop Ctr)—locale ... FL-3
Northside Residential Hist Dist (Boundary Increase)—hist pl ... KY-4
Northside Ridge—ridge ... PA-2
Northside Rsvr—reservoir ... CO-8
North Side Rsvr—reservoir ... CO-8
Northside Rsvr—reservoir ... ID-8
Northside Rsvr—reservoir ... NY-2
Northside Sch ... AL-4
Northside Sch—hist pl ... MT-8
Northside Sch—school ... AL-4
North Side Sch—school ... AL-4
Northside Sch—school ... AR-4
North Side Sch—school ... AR-4
Northside Sch—school ... AR-4
North Side Sch—school ... AR-4
North Side Sch—school ... CA-9
North Side Sch—school ... CO-8
North Side Sch—school ... FL-3
Northside Sch—school (11) ... GA-3
North Side Sch—school (2) ... ID-8
North Side Sch—school (3) ... IL-6
North Side Sch—school ... KS-7
Northside Sch—school (2) ... KY-4
Northside Sch—school ... LA-4
North Side Sch—school ... LA-4
Northside Sch—school ... LA-4
Northside Sch—school ... MI-6
North Side Sch—school (2) ... MN-6
Northside Sch—school (3) ... MS-4
North Side Sch—school ... MS-4
Northside Sch—school ... MT-8
North Side Sch—school ... MT-8
Northside Sch—school ... NE-7
North Side Sch—school (4) ... NY-2
Northside Sch—school (2) ... NY-2
Northside Sch—school (3) ... NC-3
North Side Sch—school ... OH-6
Northside Sch—school ... OK-5
North Side Sch—school (2) ... PA-2
Northside Sch—school ... PA-2
Northside Sch—school (3) ... SC-3
Northside Sch—school ... TN-4
North Side Sch—school ... TN-4
Northside Sch—school ... TN-4
North Side Sch—school (2) ... TX-5
Northside Sch—school (2) ... TX-5
North Side Sch—school ... TX-5
Northside Sch—school ... TX-5
Northside Sch—school (2) ... VA-3
North Side Sch—school (2) ... WY-8
Northside School ... KS-7
North Side School—locale ... IL-6
Northside Shop Ctr—locale (2) ... FL-3
Northside Shop Ctr—locale (2) ... MS-4
Northside Shop Ctr—locale ... NC-3
North Side Shop Ctr—locale ... NC-3
Northsides HS—school ... VA-3
Northside Slough—stream ... ID-8
North Side Spring—spring ... OR-9
Northside Springs—spring ... ID-8
**Northside (subdivision)**—pop pl (3) ... NC-3
North Side Trail—trail ... CA-9
Northside United Methodist Church—hist pl ... OH-6
Northside United Presbyterian—hist pl ... TN-4
Northside United Presbyterian Ch—church ... TN-4
Northside Village Hist Dist—hist pl ... MA-1
Northside West Sch—school ... PA-2
North Siding—locale ... NM-5
North Sidney—locale ... ME-1
North Sidney Ch—church ... MI-6
North Silent Canyon—valley ... NV-8
North Silsbee Oil Field—oilfield ... TX-5
North Silver Creek Ch—church ... MS-4
North Silver Creek Youth Camp—locale ... OR-9
North Silver Dam ... MA-1
North Silver King Mine—mine ... NV-8
North Silver Lake—lake ... MN-6
North Silver Lake Dam—dam ... MA-1
North Silver Lake Rsvr—reservoir ... MA-1
North Simms Creek—stream ... TX-5
North Simon Creek—stream ... OK-5
North Sink—basin ... UT-8
North Sink Cave—cave ... AL-4
North Sinker Flat—flat ... ID-8
North Sioux—unorg reg ... ND-7
**North Sioux City**—pop pl ... SD-7
North Siouxon Creek—stream ... WA-9
North Sippo Park—park ... OH-6
North Sister ... OR-9
North Sister—summit ... OR-9
North Sister Creek—stream (2) ... OR-9
North Sister Island—island ... FL-3
North Sister Knob—summit ... VA-3
North Sisters ... OR-9
North Siuslaw (CCD)—cens area ... OR-9
North Siwash—summit ... ID-8
North Sixmile Canyon—valley ... NV-8
North Sixmile Canyon Spring—spring ... NV-8
North Sixmile Draw—valley ... TX-5
North Sixmile Wash—stream ... NV-8
North Six-shooter Campground ... UT-8
North Six-Shooter Peak ... UT-8
North Sixshooter Peak—summit ... UT-8
North Six Tank—reservoir ... AZ-5
North Sixth Street Cem—cemetery ... IA-7
North Skinner Creek—stream ... ID-8
North Skookum Lake—lake ... WA-9
North Skookum Peak ... WA-9
North Skull Cliffs ... MH-9
North Skull Creek—stream ... UT-8
North Skunk River—stream ... IA-7
**North Skyline View (subdivision)**—pop pl ... PA-2
Norths Landing—locale ... IN-6
North Slaterville Canal—canal ... UT-8
North Slaughter Canyon—valley ... NM-5
North Slick Creek—stream ... MT-8
North Slick Creek—stream ... SD-7
North Slick Rock Tank—reservoir ... AZ-5
North Slide—trail ... NH-1
**North Slidell**—pop pl ... LA-4
North Slide Peak—summit ... CA-9
North Sloan Well—well ... NM-5
**North Slope (Borough)**—pop pl ... AK-9
North Slope Ridge—ridge ... NC-3
North Slough—stream ... CA-9
North Slough—stream ... ID-8
North Slough—stream ... OR-9

North Slough Mariposa Creek—gut ... CA-9
North Sly Park Creek—stream ... CA-9
North Smithfield ... PA-2
**North Smithfield Estates (Greenleas Heights)**—pop pl ... AL-4
**North Smithfield (Town of)**—pop pl ... RI-1
North Smith Fork ... WY-8
North Smith Fork Gunnison River—stream ... CO-8
North Smith Run—stream ... PA-2
**North Smithtown**—pop pl ... NY-2
North Smoky Hill Flowage—reservoir ... WI-6
North Snap Creek ... MT-8
North Snohomish Lake—lake ... AK-9
North Snow Park ... ID-8
North Snow Peak—summit ... ID-8
North Snyder Rsvr—reservoir ... WY-8
North Sobol—locale ... OK-5
**North Soddy**—pop pl ... TN-4
North Soldier Creek—stream ... WY-8
**North Somers**—pop pl ... CT-1
North Somerset (Unorganized Territory of)—other ... ME-1
North Somerville ... MA-1
North Sommerville—uninc pl ... MA-1
North Sound Creek—stream ... FL-3
North South Branch Mountain ... ME-1
North South Canal—canal ... DE-2
North-South Canyon ... NV-8
North South Creek—stream ... UT-8
North-South Reach—channel ... GA-3
North South Trail—trail ... WV-2
North-South Window ... UT-8
North Spanish Creek ... CO-8
North Speck Oil Field—oilfield ... TX-5
North Spectacle Butte—summit ... WA-9
North Spectacle Pond—lake ... CT-1
North Spectacle Pond—lake ... MA-1
**North Spencer**—pop pl ... MA-1
**North Spencer**—pop pl ... NY-2
North Spink Sch—school ... SD-7
North Spirit Lake—lake ... WI-6
North Spit—bar (2) ... AK-9
North Spit—bar ... CA-9
North Spit—bar (2) ... OR-9
North Spit—cape ... AK-9
North Spivey Cave—cave ... TN-4
North Split Tank—reservoir ... AZ-5
North Spring—locale ... WV-2
North Spring—spring (3) ... AZ-5
North Spring—spring ... CA-9
North Spring—spring (12) ... NV-8
North Spring—spring ... NM-5
North Spring—spring (2) ... OR-9
North Spring—spring (2) ... SD-7
North Spring—spring ... TN-4
North Spring—spring ... TX-5
North Spring—spring (10) ... UT-8
North Spring Branch—stream ... IA-7
North Spring Branch—stream ... PA-2
North Spring Branch—stream ... WV-2
**North Springbrook**—pop pl ... MD-2
North Spring Cabin—locale ... UT-8
North Spring Canyon—valley ... NV-8
North Spring Canyon—valley (2) ... NM-5
North Spring Canyon—valley ... UT-8
North Spring Creek ... AL-4
North Spring Creek—stream (2) ... MO-7
North Spring Creek—stream ... TX-5
North Spring Creek—stream (3) ... WY-8
North Spring Creek Lake—lake ... WY-8
North Spring Draw—valley ... WY-8
North Springfield—CDP ... OR-9
**North Springfield**—pop pl ... PA-2
**North Springfield**—pop pl ... VT-1
**North Springfield**—pop pl ... VA-3
North Springfield Baptist Ch—church ... TN-4
North Springfield Lake ... VT-1
**North Springfield (RR name Springfield (sta.))**—pop pl ... PA-2
North Springfield Rsvr—reservoir ... VT-1
North Springfield Sch—school ... VA-3
North Spring Lake—lake ... FL-3
North Spring Point—cape ... NV-8
North Spring Pond ... FL-3
North Spring Post Office ... TN-4
North Spring River—stream ... NM-5
North Spring Rsvr—reservoir ... UT-8
**North Springs**—pop pl ... TN-4
North Springs—post sta ... GA-3
North Springs—spring ... NV-8
North Springs—spring ... UT-8
North Springs Post Office (historical)—building ... TN-4
North Springs Sch (historical)—school ... TN-4
North Springville Sch—school ... WI-6
North Spring Wash—valley ... UT-8
North Spruce Creek—stream ... CO-8
Northspur—locale ... CA-9
North Spur Valley—valley ... TX-5
North Spy Windmill—locale ... NM-5
North Square Lake Oil Field—other ... NM-5
North Squaw Tip—summit ... OR-9
North Squirrel Springs Canyon—valley ... NM-5
North Staatsburg Creek—stream ... NY-2
North Stacey Cem—cemetery ... MT-8
North Stacey Sch—school ... MT-8
North Stacey Spring—spring ... MT-8
North Stamford ... CT-1
**North Stamford**—pop pl ... CT-1
North Stamford Rsvr—reservoir ... CT-1
North Stanchfield Lake—lake ... MN-6
North Standard—mine ... UT-8
North Stang Lake—lake ... MN-6
North Stanley—unorg reg ... SD-7
North Stanly HS—school ... NC-3
North Stanton—locale ... VA-3
North Star ... PA-2
North Star—fmr MCD ... NE-7
North Star—locale ... CA-9
North Star—locale ... MN-6
North Star—locale ... PA-2
North Star—locale ... WI-6
North Star—locale ... VI-3
North Star—mine ... NV-8
North Star—mine ... UT-8
Northstar—other ... MI-6
**North Star**—pop pl ... DE-2
**North Star**—pop pl ... MI-6
**North Star**—pop pl ... NE-7

**North Star**—pop pl ... OH-6
**North Star Addition**—pop pl ... DE-2
North Star Baptist Ch—church ... AL-4
North Star Basin—basin ... CA-9
North Star Basin—basin ... NM-5
North Star Butte—summit ... ID-8
North Star Butte—summit ... ND-7
North Star Camp—locale ... MI-6
North Star Canyon—valley ... NM-5
North Star Cem—cemetery ... AR-4
North Star Cem—cemetery ... IN-6
North Star Cem—cemetery ... KS-7
North Star Cem—cemetery ... MI-6
North Star Cem—cemetery (3) ... MN-6
North Star Central Shaft—mine ... CA-9
North Star Ch—church ... LA-4
North Star Ch—church ... MN-6
North Star Ch—church ... MO-7
North Star Ch—church ... OK-5
North Star Country Club—other ... MI-6
North Star Creek ... OR-9
North Star Creek—stream ... AK-9
North Star Creek—stream (2) ... ID-8
North Star Creek—stream (2) ... WA-9
North Star Dam—dam ... ND-7
North Star Ditch—canal ... AK-9
North Star Grange—locale ... WA-9
North Star Gulch—stream ... OR-9
North Star Gulch—valley (2) ... ID-8
**North Star Hills**—pop pl ... TX-5
North Star Hollow—valley ... AR-4
North Star Hollow—valley ... WI-6
North Star Island—island ... AK-9
North Starks Oil Field—oilfield ... LA-4
North Starkville Sch—school ... CO-8
North Star Lake—lake ... ID-8
North Star Lake—lake ... MN-6
North Star Lake—lake ... UT-8
North Star Mall Shop Ctr—locale ... TX-5
North Star Meadows—flat ... ID-8
North Star Mesa—ridge ... NM-5
North Star Mine—mine (2) ... AZ-5
North Star Mine—mine (6) ... CA-9
North Star Mine—mine (3) ... CO-8
North Star Mine—mine (3) ... ID-8
North Star Mine—mine ... MN-6
North Star Mine—mine ... MT-8
North Star Mine—mine ... NV-8
North Star Mine—mine (2) ... NM-5
North Star Mine—mine ... OR-9
North Star Mine—mine ... SD-7
North Star Mine—mine ... UT-8
North Star Mine (Inactive)—mine ... NM-5
North Star Mtn ... WA-9
North Star Mtn—summit ... CO-8
North Star Mtn—summit ... WA-9
**North Star (Northstar)**—pop pl ... MI-6
North Star Peak—summit ... AZ-5
North Star Prospect—mine ... WY-8
North Star Ranch—locale ... ID-8
North Star Sch—school (3) ... IL-6
North Star Sch—school ... IA-7
North Star Sch—school ... KS-7
North Star Sch—school (2) ... MN-6
North Star Sch—school (3) ... MO-7
North Star Sch—school ... MT-8
North Star Sch—school (6) ... NE-7
North Star Sch—school ... PA-2
North Star Sch—school (5) ... SD-7
North Star Sch—school ... TX-5
North Star Sch—school (2) ... WI-6
North Star Sch—school ... WY-8
North Star Sch (abandoned)—school ... PA-2
North Star Sch (historical)—school ... MO-7
North Star Sch Number 4—school ... ND-7
North Star Shop Ctr—locale ... KS-7
North Star Shopping Plaza—locale ... FL-3
North Star Spring—spring ... NY-2
North Star Tank ... NM-5
North Star Tank—reservoir (2) ... NM-5
**North Star Township**—pop pl ... ND-7
**North Star (Township of)**—pop pl ... MI-6
**North Star (Township of)**—pop pl (2) ... MN-6
North Star Tunnel—mine ... NV-8
North Star Wash—stream ... AZ-5
North Star Well—well ... AZ-5
North State Dam—dam ... NC-3
North State Drain—canal ... MI-6
North State Lake—reservoir ... NC-3
North State Orchard Pond Number One—reservoir ... NC-3
North State Orchard Pond Number One Dam—dam ... NC-3
North State Orchard Pond Number Two—reservoir ... NC-3
North State Orchard Pond Number Two Dam—dam ... NC-3
**North State Orchards**—pop pl ... NC-3
North State Road Drain—stream ... MI-6
North Stauffer Creek—stream ... ID-8
North Steely Creek—stream ... CA-9
North Steer Draw—valley ... WY-8
North Stelton—locale ... NJ-2
North Stephens Oil And Gas Field—oilfield ... AR-4
**North Stephentown**—pop pl ... NY-2
North Sterling—locale ... NY-2
**North Sterling**—pop pl ... CT-1
North Sterling Canal—canal ... CO-8
North Sterling Inlet Canal ... CO-8
North Sterling Lateral No. 10—canal ... CO-8
North Sterling Lateral No. 12—canal ... CO-8
North Sterling Lateral No. 17—canal ... CO-8
North Sterling Lateral No. 19—canal ... CO-8
North Sterling Lateral No 40—canal ... CO-8
North Sterling Lateral No 42—canal ... CO-8
North Sterling Lateral No 44—canal ... CO-8
North Sterling Lateral No 46—canal ... CO-8
North Sterling Lateral No 47—canal ... CO-8
North Sterling Lateral No 52—canal ... CO-8
North Sterling Lateral No 52 B—canal ... CO-8
North Sterling Lateral No. 8—canal ... CO-8
North Sterling No. 22 Lateral—canal ... CO-8
North Sterling No 25 Lateral—canal ... CO-8
North Sterling Outlet Canal—canal ... CO-8
North Sterling Rsvr—reservoir ... CO-8
North Steuben Ch—church ... NY-2
North Stewart Elem Sch—school ... TN-4
North Stillwater Creek—stream ... OK-5
North Stinking Water Creek—stream ... WY-8
North Stink Lake State Public Shooting Area—park ... SD-7
North Stirrup Run—stream ... MD-2
North Stockbridge Cem—cemetery ... MI-6
**North Stockholm**—pop pl ... NY-2
North Stocking Lake—lake ... MN-6
North Stokes HS—school ... NC-3
**North Stonington**—pop pl ... CT-1
**North Stonington (Town of)**—pop pl ... CT-1
North Stonington Village Hist Dist—hist pl ... CT-1
North Store Shop Ctr—locale ... FL-3
North Storrie Inlet Canal—canal ... NM-5
**North Stoughton**—pop pl ... MA-1
North Stoughton Station (historical)—locale ... MA-1
North Stover Mtn—summit ... CA-9
**North St. Paul**—pop pl ... MN-6
**North Strabane (Township of)**—pop pl ... PA-2
North Strange Island—island ... GA-3
**North Stratford**—pop pl ... NH-1
North Stream—stream ... NH-1
North Street—locale ... MI-6
North Street Cem—cemetery ... OH-6
North Street Cem—cemetery ... VT-1
North Street Ch—church ... ME-1
North Street Ch—church ... MI-6
North Street Ch—church ... PA-2
North Street Ch of Christ—church ... FL-3
North Street-East Street Hist Dist—hist pl ... GA-3
North Street Hist Dist—hist pl ... WV-2
North Street Road Cem—cemetery ... NY-2
North Street Sch—school ... CT-1
North Street Sch—school ... LA-4
North Street Sch—school ... MA-1
North Street Sch—school ... NY-2
North Street Sch—school ... OH-6
North Strevell Creek—stream ... MT-8
North String Irrigation Ditch—canal ... UT-8
North Strool Sch—school ... SD-7
**North Stuttgart**—pop pl ... AR-4
North Sublette Meadow Spring—spring ... WY-8
North Suck Creek—stream ... TN-4
**North Sudbury**—pop pl ... MA-1
North Sudbury Cem—cemetery ... MA-1
North Sugar Creek—stream ... GA-3
North Sugar Creek—stream (2) ... KS-7
North Sugar Creek—stream ... MO-7
North Sugar Creek Township—civil ... MO-7
North Sugarloaf ... MA-1
North Sugarloaf—summit ... NH-1
North Sugar Loaf Hill ... MA-1
North Sugarloaf Island—island ... ME-1
North Sugarloaf Mtn—summit ... MA-1
North Sugarville Rsvr—reservoir ... UT-8
North Sulger—locale ... PA-2
**North Sullivan**—pop pl ... ME-1
North Sulphur Canyon—valley ... ID-8
North Sulphur Draw—valley ... WY-8
North Sulphur River—stream ... TX-5
North Sulphur Spring—spring ... UT-8
North Summerour Well—well ... TX-5
**North Summerville**—pop pl ... SC-3
North Summit HS—school ... UT-8
North Summit Mount Jefferson—summit ... NV-8
North Summit MS—school ... UT-8
North Summit Ridge—ridge ... UT-8
North Summit Sch—school ... UT-8
North Sump ... NV-8
North Sumter HS—school ... AL-4
North Sumter Intermediate Sch—school ... FL-3
North Sumter Primary Sch—school ... FL-3
North Sumter Sch ... AL-4
North Sunday Creek—stream ... MT-8
North Sunday Sch—school ... MT-8
**North Sunderland**—pop pl ... MA-1
North Sunderland Cem—cemetery ... MA-1
North Sunflower County Hosp—hospital ... MS-4
North Sunnyside Oil Field—oilfield ... MS-4
North Sun Oil Field—oilfield ... TX-5
North Supply Creek—stream ... CO-8
North Supply Ditch—canal ... MT-8
North Surry HS—school ... NC-3
North Survey Sch—school ... WI-6
**North Sutton**—pop pl ... NH-1
North Swag—basin ... UT-8
North Swale—valley ... UT-8
North Swamp Creek—stream ... MT-8
**North Swansea**—pop pl ... MA-1
North Swansey ... MA-1
**North Swanzey**—pop pl ... NH-1
North Swargart Drain—canal ... MI-6
North Swede Ch—church ... MO-7
North Sweetwater Baptist Ch—church ... TN-4
North Swiftcurrent Glacier—glacier ... MT-8
North Sybille Canyon—valley ... WY-8
North Sybille Creek—stream ... WY-8
North Sycamore Branch—stream (2) ... MO-7
North Sycamore Ch—church ... MO-7
North Sycamore Creek ... MO-7
North Sycamore Creek—stream ... AZ-5
North Sycamore Mesa Tank—lake ... NM-5
North Sylamore Creek ... AR-4
North Sylamore Creek—stream ... AR-4
North Syracuse—fmr MCD ... NE-7
**North Syracuse**—pop pl ... NY-2
North Syracuse Interchange—other ... NY-2
North Tablan Valley ... MH-9
North Table Creek—stream ... NE-7
North Table Mesa ... WY-8
North Table Mountain Infiltration Plant—other ... CO-8
North Table Mountain Rsvr—reservoir ... UT-8
North Table Mtn—summit ... CA-9
North Table Mtn—summit ... CO-8
North Table Mtn—summit (2) ... OR-9
North Table Mtn—summit ... WY-8
North Table Ravine ... MH-9
North Table Rock Creek—stream ... TX-5
North Tacoma Christian Ch—church ... IN-6
North Tahoma Glacier ... WA-9
North Tailholt Tank—reservoir ... AZ-5
**North Takoma Park**—pop pl ... MD-2
**North Talladega**—pop pl ... AL-4
North Tallahassee Creek—stream ... CO-8
North Talmadge, Lake—lake ... FL-3
North Tamarind Sch—school ... CA-9
**North Tampa Heights (subdivision)**—pop pl ... FL-3
North Tank ... AZ-5
North Tank—lake ... NM-5
North Tank—reservoir (28) ... AZ-5
North Tank—reservoir (22) ... NM-5
North Tank—reservoir (11) ... TX-5
North Tanks—reservoir ... TX-5
North Tank Well—well ... AZ-5
North Tank Windmill—locale ... TX-5
North Tanner Canyon—valley ... CO-8
North Tarboro Sch—school ... NC-3
North Tarryall Creek—stream ... CO-8
North Tarryall Peak—summit ... CO-8
**North Tarrytown**—pop pl ... NY-2
North Taunton Baptist Church—hist pl ... MA-1
North Taunton Ch—church ... MA-1
North Taylor Canyon—valley ... AZ-5
North Taylor Creek—stream ... CO-8
North Taylor Creek—stream ... NE-7
North Taylor Spring—spring ... NV-8
**North Tazewell**—pop pl ... VA-3
North Teal Lake—lake ... WA-9
North Technical Education Center—school ... FL-3
North Telegraph Creek—stream ... MT-8
North Telephone Canyon—valley ... TX-5
North Temperance Creek—stream ... OR-9
North Temperance Lake—lake ... MN-6
North Temple—church ... TX-5
North Temple Creek—stream ... WY-8
North Temple Plaza ... UT-8
North Temple Shop Ctr—locale ... UT-8
**North Temple Street Subdivision**—pop pl ... UT-8
North Temple Wash—valley ... UT-8
North Tenmile Ch—church ... PA-2
North Tenmile Creek—stream ... CO-8
North Tenmile Creek—stream ... MI-6
North Tenmile Creek—stream ... OH-6
North Tenmile Lake—lake ... MN-6
North Tenmile Lake—lake ... OR-9
North Tent Mtn—summit ... UT-8
North Teoctalia Creek ... MS-4
North Tepetate Oil and Gas Field—oilfield ... LA-4
North Terminal Interchange—other ... AR-4
North Terrace Park—park ... IL-6
North Terrace Park—park ... MO-7
North Terrace Sch—school ... CA-9
**North Terre Haute**—pop pl ... IN-6
North Terry Draw—valley ... WY-8
North Terry Road Shop Ctr—locale ... MS-4
**North Tewksbury**—pop pl ... MA-1
**North Texarkana**—pop pl ... TX-5
North Texas Creek—stream ... CO-8
North Texas Hill Canyon—valley ... NM-5
**North Texas (North Texas University)**—pop pl ... TX-5
North Texas State Coll—school ... TX-5
North Texas State College Golf Course—other ... TX-5
**North Thetford**—pop pl ... VT-1
North Thimble Island—island ... VA-3
North Third Street Hist Dist—hist pl ... WI-6
North Thirtythree Mile Rsvr—reservoir ... WY-8
North Thomas Canyon—valley ... CO-8
North Thomas Canyon—valley ... NM-5
North Thompson Canyon—valley ... SD-7
North Thompson Canyon—valley ... WY-8
North Thompson Ch—church ... GA-3
North Thompson Creek—stream ... CO-8
North Thompson Creek—stream ... MT-8
North Thompson Creek—stream ... WY-8
**North Thompsonville**—pop pl ... CT-1
North Three Forks Creek—stream ... WY-8
North Three Island Creek—stream ... CO-8
North Three Links Lakes—lake ... ID-8
North Thurston—locale ... NY-2
North Thurston Ditch—canal ... IN-6
North Thurston HS—school ... WA-9
North Tidwell Sch (historical)—school ... TN-4
North Tiger River ... SC-3
North Timber Cave—cave ... AL-4
North Timber Creek ... KS-7
North Timber Creek—stream ... IA-7
North Timber Peak—summit ... NV-8
North Timp Point—cliff ... AZ-5
North Tinian ... MH-9
North Tioga Gas Plant—oilfield ... ND-7
North Tioga Oil and Gas Field—oilfield ... ND-7
**North Tipalao**—pop pl ... GU-9
North Tippah Creek—stream ... MS-4
North Tippah Watershed LT-6a-1 Dam—dam ... MS-4
North Tippah Watershed LT-6a-14 Dam—dam ... MS-4
North Tippah Watershed LT-6a-2 Dam—dam ... MS-4
**North Tisbury**—pop pl ... MA-1
North Tisdale Oil Field—oilfield ... WY-8
**North Tiverton**—pop pl ... RI-1
North Tobacco Garden State Game Mngmt Area—park ... ND-7
North Tobiason Lake ... ND-7
North Toe River—stream ... NC-3
North Toiyabe Peak—summit ... NV-8
**North Tomah**—pop pl ... WI-6
North Tomah Sch—school ... WI-6
North Toms Prairie Ch—church ... IL-6
**North Tonawanda**—pop pl ... NY-2
North Tongass Highway—CDP ... AK-9
North Tongue River—stream ... WY-8
North Tongue River Campground—locale ... WY-8
North Tonk Branch—stream ... TX-5
North Tonk Creek—stream ... TX-5
**North Topeka**—pop pl ... KS-7
North Topeka—uninc pl ... KS-7
North Topeka Avenue-10th Street Hist Dist—hist pl ... KS-7
North Topeka Baptist Ch—church ... KS-7
North Topeka Wesleyan Ch—church ... KS-7
North Topsail Shores—beach ... NC-3
North Torrance—uninc pl ... CA-9
North Torrey Lae—lake ... OR-9
North Totem Lake—lake ... MT-8
North Touchee Run—stream ... PA-2
North Toutle Glacier ... WA-9
North Towanda—locale ... PA-2
**North Towanda (Township of)**—pop pl ... PA-2
North Tower—locale ... MI-6
North Tower Center Light—locale ... WA-9
**North Tower Forest (subdivision)**—pop pl ... TN-4
Northtown ... IL-6
Northtown ... MN-6
**Northtown**—pop pl ... KY-4
Northtown—post sta ... NY-2
North Townline Flowage—reservoir ... WI-6
North Town Mall—locale ... MO-7
**Northtown Plaza**—pop pl ... NY-2
Northtown Plaza Shop Ctr—locale ... NY-2
Northtown Plaza Shop Ctr—locale ... TN-4
Northtown Plaza Shop Ctr—locale ... TX-5
**North Town Plaza (subdivision)**—pop pl ... MS-4
North Townsand Windmill—locale ... NM-5
North Township—civil ... KS-7
**North Township**—pop pl (2) ... KS-7
**North Township**—pop pl ... MO-7
**North (Township of)**—pop pl (2) ... IN-6
**North (Township of)**—pop pl ... MN-6
**North (Township of)**—pop pl ... OH-6
Northtown Shop Ctr—locale ... MO-7
Northtown Square (Shop Ctr)—locale (2) ... FL-3
Northtown Village Shop Ctr—locale ... MS-4
North Tracy Ave Hist Dist—hist pl ... MT-8
North Tracy Canyon—valley ... CO-8
North Tracys Well—well ... AZ-5
North Tragedy Creek—stream ... CA-9
North Trail—trail ... FL-3
North Trail—trail ... UT-8
North Trail Canyon—valley ... UT-8
North Trail Creek—stream ... OR-9
North Trapper Creek—stream ... WY-8
North Trapper Peak—summit ... MT-8
North Trap Tank—reservoir ... NM-5
North Trap Windmill—locale ... TX-5
North Traveler Mtn—summit ... ME-1
North Travelstead Windmill—locale ... TX-5
North Treasure—cens area ... MT-8
North Tremble ... MH-9
North Trembling Beach ... MH-9
North Trembling Point ... MH-9
North Trenholm—CDP ... SC-3
North Trenton Park—park ... NJ-2
North Trescott—locale ... ME-1
North Triangle Pond ... MA-1
North Trick Lake—lake ... AK-9
North Trigo Peaks—summit ... AZ-5
North Trinity Cem—cemetery ... SD-7
North Trinity Ch—church ... ND-7
North Trinity Mtn—summit ... CA-9
North Tripp—unorg reg ... SD-7
North Trough ... AZ-5
North Trough Spring—spring ... UT-8
North Trout Creek—stream ... MT-8
**North Troy**—pop pl ... VT-1
North Truchas Peak—summit ... NM-5
North Truckee Drain—canal ... NV-8
North Truckee Irrigation Ditch—canal ... NV-8
**North Truro**—pop pl ... MA-1
North Truro Air Force Station—military ... MA-1
North Truro Station (historical)—building ... MA-1
North Tule Creek ... TX-5
North Tule Draw—valley ... TX-5
North Tulsa (CCD)—cens area ... OK-5
**North Tunbridge**—pop pl ... VT-1
North Tunica (census name for Tunica North)—CDP ... MS-4
North Tunnel Mine—mine ... ID-8
North Tupawek Bayou—stream ... LA-4
North Turkey Creek—stream ... CO-8
North Turkey Creek—stream ... IA-7
North Turkey Creek—stream ... NC-3
North Turkey Creek—stream ... OK-5
North Turkey Creek—stream (2) ... TX-5
North Turkeyfoot Creek—stream ... OH-6
**North Turlock**—pop pl ... CA-9
**North Turner**—pop pl ... ME-1
North Turner Ditch—canal ... CA-9
North Turner Mtn—summit ... ME-1
North Turtle Bayou Gas Field—oilfield ... LA-4
North Turtle Lake—lake ... MN-6
North Turtle Lake—lake ... WI-6
North Turtle River—stream ... MN-6
North Tuskaloosa ... AL-4
North Twentymile Meadows—flat ... WA-9
North Twentymile Peak—summit ... WA-9
North Twentymile Peak Trail—trail ... WA-9
North Twilight Peak—summit ... CO-8
North Twin ... MI-6
**North Twin**—pop pl ... ME-1
North Twin—summit ... AK-9
North Twin—summit ... WA-9
North Twin Bay—bay ... AK-9
North Twin Brook—stream ... ME-1
North Twin Cone Peak—summit ... CO-8
North Twin Creek ... NV-8
North Twin Creek—stream ... AK-9
North Twin Creek—stream (3) ... CO-8
North Twin Creek—stream (2) ... ID-8
North Twin Creek—stream ... TX-5
North Twin Creek—stream ... UT-8
North Twin Creek—stream (3) ... WY-8
North Twin Flat Mtn—summit ... UT-8
North Twin Glacier—glacier ... AK-9
North Twin Gulch—valley ... CA-9
North Twin Hollow—valley (2) ... UT-8
North Twin Hollows ... UT-8
North Twin Island—island ... WI-6
North Twin Lake ... MI-6
North Twin Lake ... MN-6
North Twin Lake ... WI-6
North Twin Lake—lake (2) ... FL-3
North Twin Lake—lake ... IN-6
North Twin Lake—lake ... ME-1
North Twin Lake—lake (3) ... MI-6
North Twin Lake—lake (7) ... MN-6
North Twin Lake—lake (3) ... NE-7
North Twin Lake—lake ... OR-9
North Twin Lake—lake ... WA-9
North Twin Lake—lake (3) ... WI-6
North Twin Lake—lake ... WY-8
North Twin Lake—reservoir ... IA-7
North Twin Lake Campground—park ... OR-9
North Twin Lakes—lake ... WY-8
North Twin Lakes Sch—school ... FL-3
North Twin Mtn—summit ... ME-1
North Twin Mtn—summit ... NH-1
North Twin Peak—summit ... AK-9
North Twin Peak—summit ... UT-8
North Twin Ridge—ridge ... ME-1
North Twin River—stream ... NV-8
North Twin Trail—trail ... NH-1
North Twin Wash—stream ... NM-5
North Twin Well—well ... WY-8
North Twin Windmills—locale ... NM-5
North Twistwood Creek—stream ... MS-4
North Twitchell Point—cape ... MT-8
North Two Lakes—lake ... WI-6
North Two Ocean Creek—stream ... WY-8
North Two River—stream ... MN-6
North Two Rivers ... MO-7
North Two Troughs Tank—reservoir ... AZ-5
North Tyger River—stream ... SC-3
**Northumberland**—pop pl ... NH-1
**Northumberland**—pop pl ... NY-2
**Northumberland**—pop pl ... PA-2
Northumberland Apartments—hist pl ... DC-2
Northumberland Borough—civil ... PA-2
Northumberland Canyon ... NV-8
Northumberland Cave—cave ... NV-8
**Northumberland County**—pop pl ... PA-2
**Northumberland (County)**—pop pl ... VA-3
Northumberland County Airp—airport ... PA-2
Northumberland County Courthouse—hist pl ... PA-2
Northumberland Hist Dist—hist pl ... PA-2
Northumberland HS—school ... VA-3
Northumberland Memorial Park—cemetery ... PA-2
Northumberland Mine—mine ... NV-8
Northumberland Pass—gap ... NV-8
Northumberland Sch—school ... PA-2
**Northumberland (Town of)**—pop pl ... NH-1
**Northumberland (Town of)**—pop pl ... NY-2
North Umpqua (CCD)—cens area ... OR-9
North Umpqua River—stream ... OR-9
North Umpqua Rsvr ... OR-9
**North Umpqua Village (historical)**—pop pl ... OR-9
**North Underhill**—pop pl ... VT-1
North Underhill Cem—cemetery ... VT-1
North Union—locale ... ME-1
**North Union**—pop pl ... IN-6
North Union Baptist Church ... MS-4
North Union Canal—canal ... UT-8
North Union Cem—cemetery (4) ... IN-6
North Union Cem—cemetery (2) ... MS-4
North Union Cem—cemetery ... OH-6
North Union Cem—cemetery ... PA-2
North Union Cem—cemetery ... TN-4
North Union Ch—church (3) ... IN-6
North Union Ch—church (2) ... MS-4
North Union Ch—church ... OH-6
North Union Ch—church (2) ... PA-2
North Union Ch—church ... TN-4
North Union Chapel Cem—cemetery ... TN-4
North Union Cumberland Presbyterian Ch ... TN-4
**North Union (historical)**—pop pl ... MS-4
North Union Lake—lake ... MN-6
North Union Methodist Church ... MS-4
North Union Sch—school (2) ... IL-6
North Union Sch—school ... ME-1
North Union Sch (historical)—school ... MS-4
North Union Sch (historical)—school ... PA-2
North Union School ... MS-4
North Union Shaker Site—hist pl ... OH-6
North Union Street Hist Dist—hist pl ... NC-3
**North Uniontown**—pop pl ... OH-6
North Union (Township of)—fmr MCD ... AR-4
**North Union (Township of)**—pop pl (2) ... PA-2
North Unit Diversion Dam—dam ... OR-9
North United Methodist Ch—church ... IN-6
North Unit Main Canal—canal ... OR-9
North Unity ... MI-6
**North Unity**—pop pl ... MI-6
North Unity Ch—church ... ND-7
North University—locale ... MI-6
North Univ Sch—school ... MI-6
**Northup**—pop pl ... OH-6
Northup Cem—cemetery ... NY-2
Northup Chapel ... MS-4
Northup Creek—stream ... MT-8
Northup Creek—stream ... TX-5
Northup Lumber Camp—locale ... CO-8
Northup Run—stream ... OH-6
North Upton Cem—cemetery ... IA-7
North Urbana—locale ... NY-2
North Ute Canyon—valley ... CO-8
North Ute Creek ... CO-8
**North Utica (corporate name for Utica)**—pop pl ... IL-6
North Utoy Creek—stream ... GA-3
North Uvalde—uninc pl ... TX-5
**North Uxbridge**—pop pl ... MA-1
North Uxbridge Sch—hist pl ... MA-1
North Vaiden HS—school ... MS-4
**Northvale**—pop pl ... NJ-2
North Vallejos Creek—stream ... CO-8
Northvalle Neuvy ... NJ-2
North Valley ... NV-8
North Valley ... NY-2
North Valley—area ... CA-9
North Valley—basin (2) ... NE-7
North Valley—basin ... NV-8
North Valley—CDP ... NM-5
North Valley—fmr MCD ... NE-7
North Valley—valley ... TX-5
North Valley—valley ... UT-8
**North Valley Acres (subdivision)**—pop pl ... AL-4
North Valley Ch—church ... WI-6
**North Valley City**—pop pl ... ND-7
North Valley Creek—stream ... CA-9
North Valley Hills—range ... PA-2
North Valley Mound Wasteway—canal ... ID-8
North Valley Prong—stream ... TX-5
North Valley Sch—school (2) ... NE-7
**North Valley Stream**—pop pl ... NY-2
North Valley View Lake—reservoir ... AL-4
North Valley View Lake Dam—dam ... AL-4
**North Valliant**—pop pl ... OK-5
**North Vandergrift**—pop pl ... PA-2
North Vandergrift Elem Sch—school ... PA-2
North Vandergrift-Pleasant View—CDP ... PA-2
North Van Etten Ch—church ... NY-2
**North Vassalboro**—pop pl ... ME-1
North Vellin Oil Field—oilfield ... LA-4
North Venice ... IL-6
**North Venice**—pop pl ... IL-6
North Vermillion High School—school ... IN-6
North Vermillion HS—school ... IN-6
**North Vernon**—pop pl ... IN-6
**North Vernon**—pop pl ... VT-1
North Vernon Airp—airport ... IN-6
North Vernon City ... IN-6
North Versailles—CDP ... PA-2
**North Versailles (Township of)**—pop pl ... PA-2
North Veta Creek ... CO-8
North Victoria Canal—canal ... CA-9
**North Victory**—pop pl ... NY-2
North Victory Cem—cemetery ... MI-6
North Victory Cem—cemetery ... VT-1
**North Vidor**—pop pl ... TX-5
North Vienna Ch—church ... ME-1
Northview—CDP ... OH-6
North View—locale ... UT-8
North View—locale ... VA-3
**Northview**—pop pl ... MO-7
**North View**—pop pl ... NC-3
**Northview**—pop pl ... NC-3
**North View**—pop pl ... WV-2
Northview Airp ... PA-2
North View Airp—airport ... PA-2
Northview Assembly of God Church ... MS-4
North View Cem—cemetery ... GA-3
Northview Cem—cemetery (2) ... GA-3
Northview Cem—cemetery ... IN-6
Northview Cem—cemetery ... MI-6
North View Cem—cemetery ... OH-6
Northview Cem—cemetery ... TX-5
Northview Cem—cemetery ... WV-2
North View Ch—church ... KY-4
Northview Ch—church ... MS-4
North View Ch—church ... NC-3
Northview Ch—church ... VA-3
North View Ch—church ... VA-3
Northview Ch of the Brethren—church ... IN-6
Northview Country Club—other ... KS-7
Northview Elem Sch—school ... IN-6
North View Elem Sch—school ... IN-6
Northview Elem Sch—school ... KS-7
Northview Grange—locale ... ID-8
Northview Heights Elem Sch—school ... PA-2
North View Hill—summit ... MO-7
**North View Hills**—pop pl ... PA-2
Northview HS—school ... AL-4
Northview HS—school ... CA-9
Northview HS—school ... MI-6
Northview JHS—school ... CA-9
Northview JHS—school ... IN-6
Northview JHS—school ... MI-6
Northview Park—park ... IA-7
Northview Park—park (2) ... MN-6
Northview Plaza—locale ... NC-3
Northview Sch—school ... IL-6
Northview Sch—school ... MN-6
Northview Sch—school ... NC-3
Northview Sch—school ... OH-6
North View Sch—school ... TX-5
North View Sch—school ... WV-2
Northview Sch—school ... WI-6
Northview Shop Ctr—locale ... IN-6
**Northview (subdivision)**—pop pl ... NC-3
Northview Village Shop Ctr—locale ... MS-4
North Viking Cem—cemetery ... ND-7
**North Viking Township**—pop pl ... ND-7
North Village ... MA-1
**North Village**—pop pl (3) ... MA-1
**North Village**—pop pl ... NH-1
**North Village**—pop pl ... OK-5
North Village Cem—cemetery ... MA-1
North Village Green—park ... NY-2
North Village Hist Dist—hist pl ... MA-1
North Village Shop Ctr—locale ... TX-5
Northville ... MA-1
Northville ... NH-1
Northville—locale ... CT-1
Northville—locale ... IA-7
**Northville**—pop pl ... IL-6
**Northville**—pop pl ... MA-1
**Northville**—pop pl (2) ... MI-6
**Northville**—pop pl ... NJ-2
**Northville**—pop pl (2) ... NY-2
**Northville**—pop pl ... OH-6
**Northville**—pop pl ... SD-7
Northville Cem—cemetery ... CT-1
Northville Cem—cemetery ... IL-6
Northville Cem—cemetery ... PA-2
Northville Downs—other ... MI-6
Northville Gas Storage Field—other ... MI-6
Northville Golf Course—other ... MI-6
Northville Hist Dist—hist pl ... MI-6
**Northville (historical)**—pop pl ... MA-1
Northville (historical P.O.)—locale ... IA-7
Northville Lake Placid Trail—trail ... NY-2
Northville Post Office ... TN-4
Northville Rsvr—reservoir ... NY-2
Northville State Hosp—hospital ... MI-6
**Northville Township**—pop pl ... SD-7
**Northville (Township of)**—pop pl ... IL-6
**Northville (Township of)**—pop pl ... MI-6
**North Vineland**—pop pl ... NJ-2
**North Vinemont**—pop pl ... AL-4
**North Virginia Beach**—pop pl ... VA-3
North Virginia Community Coll—school ... VA-3
North Vly—stream ... NY-2
North Volney—locale ... NY-2
**Northvue**—pop pl ... PA-2
North Waco JHS—school ... TX-5
North Waco Sch—school ... TX-5
**North Wade**—pop pl ... ME-1
North Waiehu Stream—stream ... HI-9
North Wailua Ditch—canal ... HI-9
**North Wakefield**—pop pl ... NH-1
**North Waldoboro**—pop pl ... ME-1
**North Wales**—pop pl ... PA-2
North Wales Borough—civil ... PA-2
North Wales Elem Sch—school ... PA-2
North Walker Canyon—valley ... UT-8
North Wallace Canyon—valley ... CA-9
North Walnut Creek ... KS-7
North Walnut Creek ... OK-5
North Walnut Creek—stream (3) ... IA-7
North Walnut Creek—stream ... KS-7
North Walnut Lake ... MN-6
**North Walpole**—pop pl ... NH-1
North Walrus Peak—summit ... AK-9
**North Walter**—pop pl ... AL-4

North Waltham—uninc pl ... MA-1
North Walworth Sch—school ... WI-6
North Wamac Sch—school ... IL-6
**North Wantagh**—pop pl ... NY-2
Northward Annex Sch—school ... TX-5
North Ward Canyon—valley ... AZ-5
**North Wardell**—pop pl ... MO-7
North Wardsboro ... VT-1
North Wardsboro (local name for Wardsboro)—other ... VT-1
North Ward Sch—school (2) ... FL-3
North Ward Sch—school ... MO-7
North Ward Sch—school (4) ... NE-7
North Ward Sch—school ... OH-6
Northward Sch—school ... TX-5
North Ward Sch—school (4) ... TX-5
North Ward Sch (abandoned)—school ... PA-2
North Warm Spring Creek ... WY-8
North Warner Viewpoint—summit ... OR-9
North Warren ... OH-6
**North Warren**—pop pl ... ME-1
**North Warren**—pop pl ... PA-2
North Warren Ch (historical)—church ... PA-2
North Warren HS—school ... NC-3
North Warrenton Ch—church ... NC-3
North Waseca Ch—church ... MN-6
North Wash ... UT-8
North Wash—stream ... CA-9
North Wash—valley ... UT-8
**North Washington**—pop pl ... IA-7
**North Washington**—pop pl (2) ... PA-2
North Washington Ave Workers' House—hist pl ... NC-3
North Washington Cem—cemetery ... IA-7
North Washington District—hist pl ... GA-3
**North Washington Heights**—pop pl ... CO-8
North Washington Lake—lake ... ND-7
North Washington Oil Field—oilfield ... OK-5
North Washington Sch—school ... PA-2
North Washington (Unorganized Territory of)—unorg ... ME-1
Northwater—lake ... FL-3
**North Waterboro**—pop pl ... ME-1
North Water Canyon—valley ... NM-5
Northwater Creek—stream ... CO-8
**North Wateree**—pop pl ... SC-3
**North Waterford**—pop pl ... ME-1
North Waterford Congregational Church—hist pl ... ME-1
**North Water Gap**—pop pl ... PA-2
North Water Hollow—valley ... UT-8
North Waterloo Cem—cemetery ... MI-6
North Waterloo Gas And Oil Field—oilfield ... OK-5
Northwater Spring—spring ... AZ-5
North Water Spring—spring (2) ... AZ-5
North Water Spring—spring ... ID-8
North Watertown Cem—cemetery ... NY-2
North Watertown Cem—cemetery ... OH-6
North Water Well—well ... AZ-5
**North Watson**—pop pl ... MN-6
North Watson Creek—stream ... OK-5
North Watuppa Pond—lake ... MA-1
North Wauchula Elem Sch—school ... FL-3
North Waugh Creek—stream ... CO-8
**North Waverly**—pop pl ... NY-2
**North Wawona**—pop pl ... CA-9
**Northway**—pop pl ... AK-9
**Northway**—pop pl ... CO-8
Northway ANV882—reserve ... AK-9
Northway Cem—cemetery ... KS-7
Northway Ch—church ... IN-6
Northway Ch—church ... PA-2
Northway Ch—church ... TX-5
Northway Elem Sch—school ... PA-2
Northway Exposition Center—building ... TX-5
**Northway Indian Village**—pop pl ... AK-9
Northway Junction—locale ... AK-9
Northway Motel—locale ... AK-9
**North Wayne**—pop pl ... ME-1
North Wayne Hist Dist—hist pl ... PA-2
North Waynesburg ... PA-2
**North Waynesburg**—pop pl ... PA-2
North Wayne Sch—school ... MI-6
Northway Plaza—post sta ... WI-6
Northway Plaza (Shop Ctr)—locale (2) ... FL-3
Northway Plaza Shop Ctr—locale ... NY-2
Northway School ... PA-2
Northway Village (native name Northway)—CDP ... AK-9
North Wea Creek—stream ... KS-7
North Weaning Windmill—locale ... TX-5
**North Weare**—pop pl ... NH-1
North Weare Cem—cemetery ... MI-6
North Weber Street-Wahsatch Ave Historic Residential District—hist pl ... CO-8
**North Webster**—pop pl ... IN-6
North Webster Elem Sch—school ... IN-6
North Webster JHS—school ... IN-6
North Webster Village Pond Dam—dam ... MA-1
North Weedsport—locale ... NY-2
**North Weems**—pop pl ... VA-3
**North Weissport**—pop pl ... PA-2
North Welch Ch—church ... WV-2
North Well—locale ... AZ-5
North Well—locale (3) ... NM-5
North Well—well (6) ... AZ-5
North Well—well ... CO-8
North Well—well (2) ... NV-8
North Well—well (28) ... NM-5
North Well—well (7) ... TX-5
North Well—well ... WY-8
North Well Canyon—valley ... NM-5
North Wellfleet ... MA-1
**North Wellham**—pop pl ... MD-2
North Wells Street Hist Dist—hist pl ... IL-6
North Wellville—locale ... VA-3
North Welsh Gas Field—oilfield ... LA-4
**North Welton**—pop pl ... IA-7
Northwest ... IA-7
North West ... MS-4
North West ... NC-3
Northwest ... OH-6
Northwest—locale ... VA-3
**Northwest**—pop pl ... FL-3
**Northwest**—pop pl ... NE-7
**Northwest**—pop pl ... NC-3
**North West**—pop pl ... NC-3
**Northwest**—pop pl ... PA-2
Northwest—post sta ... IA-7
Northwest—uninc pl ... AZ-5
Northwest—uninc pl ... OK-5
Northwest—uninc pl ... TX-5
Northwest, The—ridge ... MA-1
Northwest Acad—school ... MS-4
**Northwest Acres**—pop pl ... TN-4
Northwest Airstrip—airport ... NC-3
Northwest Aitkin (Unorganized Territory of)—unorg ... MN-6
North West Alabama Crippled Childrens Clinic—hospital ... AL-4
Northwest Alabama Junior Coll—school ... AL-4
Northwest Alabama State Junior Coll—school ... AL-4
Northwest Alabama State Technical Coll ... AL-4
Northwest Alabama State Trade Sch—school ... AL-4
Northwest Anchorage—bay ... CA-9
Northwest and XY Company Trading Post Sites—hist pl ... WI-6
Northwest Angle Inlet—BAY ... MN-6
Northwest Angle State For—forest ... MN-6
Northwest Angle (Unorganized Territory of)—unorg ... MN-6
Northwest Antelope Tank—reservoir ... TX-5
**Northwest Arctic (Borough)**—pop pl ... AK-9
Northwest Arctic (Census Subarea)—cens area ... AK-9
Northwest Area Park—park ... TX-5
Northwest Arm Castle Bay—bay ... AK-9
Northwest Arm of Death Valley ... CA-9
Northwest Aroostook (Unorganized Territory of)—unorg ... ME-1
Northwest Assembly of God Ch—church ... IN-6
Northwest Baptist Ch—church (2) ... FL-3
Northwest Baptist Ch—church ... IN-6
Northwest Basin—basin ... ME-1
Northwest Basin Trail—trail ... ME-1
Northwest Bay—bay ... AK-9
Northwest Bay—bay ... NY-2
North West Bay—bay ... NY-2
Northwest Bay Brook—stream ... NY-2
Northwest Bearden Oil Field—oilfield ... OK-5
Northwest Bell (CCD)—cens area ... TX-5
Northwest Bench Ditch—canal ... UT-8
Northwest Benton (CCD)—cens area ... WA-9
Northwest Bethel—locale ... ME-1
Northwest Bible Coll—school ... ND-7
Northwest Bluff—cliff ... MS-4
Northwest Bluff—cliff ... NY-2
Northwest Boatright Tank—reservoir ... TX-5
Northwest Bon Homme—unorg reg ... SD-7
Northwest Boundary Tank—reservoir ... AZ-5
Northwest Boys Club—locale ... FL-3
Northwest Bradley Oil Field—oilfield ... OK-5
Northwest Branch ... DE-2
North West Branch ... NC-3
Northwest Branch ... PA-2
North West Branch Amite River ... LA-4
North West Branch Amite River ... MS-4
Northwest Branch Anacostia River—stream ... MD-2
Northwest Branch Back River—stream ... VA-3
Northwest Branch Big Papillion Creek—stream ... NE-7
Northwest Branch Cana Var tepeta Creek ... ND-7
Northwest Branch Cantapeta Creek—stream ... ND-7
Northwest Branch Davis-Weber Canal—canal ... UT-8
Northwest Branch Harris Creek—stream ... MD-2
Northwest Branch McGowers Creek ... MS-4
Northwest Branch Montegail Stream—stream ... ME-1
Northwest Branch Oil and Gas Field—oilfield ... LA-4
Northwest Branch Papillion Creek*—stream ... NE-7
Northwest Branch Park—park ... MD-2
Northwest Branch Perkiomen Creek ... PA-2
Northwest Branch Pleasant River ... ME-1
Northwest Branch Saint John River—stream ... ME-1
Northwest Branch Sarah Creek—stream ... VA-3
Northwest Branch Severn River—stream ... VA-3
North West Brook Eight Mile River ... CT-1
Northwest Canal—canal ... VA-3
North West Cape ... FM-9
Northwest Cape—cape ... AK-9
Northwest Cape—cape ... CA-9
Northwest Cape—cape ... FL-3
Northwest Cape Light 4—locale ... FL-3
Northwest Cem—cemetery (2) ... CT-1
Northwest Cem—cemetery (2) ... MA-1
Northwest Cem—cemetery ... OK-5
Northwest Cem—cemetery ... VA-3
Northwest (Census Subdistrict)—cens area ... VI-3
Northwest Ch ... IN-6
Northwest Ch—church ... NC-3
Northwest Ch—church ... OK-5
Northwest Ch—church ... TX-5
Northwest Ch—church ... VA-3
North West Chadron—fmr MCD ... NE-7
North West Channel ... MS-4
Northwest Channel—channel (3) ... FL-3
Northwest Chaves (CCD)—cens area ... NM-5
Northwest Cherry Sch—school ... NE-7
**North Westchester**—pop pl ... CT-1
Northwest Ch of Christ—church ... MS-4
Northwest Ch of God—church ... KS-7
Northwest Ch of God—church ... TN-4
Northwest Christian Acad—school ... FL-3
Northwest Christian Ch—church ... FL-3
Northwest Christian Coll—school ... OR-9
Northwest Christian Sch—school ... WA-9
Northwest Clackamas (CCD)—cens area ... OR-9
Northwest Classen HS—school ... OK-5
Northwest Clearview Oil And Gas Field—oilfield ... OK-5
Northwest Coll—school ... WA-9
Northwest Comanche (CCD)—cens area ... OK-5
Northwest Company Post—hist pl ... MN-6
Northwest Coon Creek Gas And Oil Field—oilfield ... OK-5
Northwest Corner Light—locale ... AK-9
**Northwest Corners**—pop pl ... NY-2
Northwest Cornwall Cem—cemetery ... VT-1
Northwest Cove ... ME-1
Northwest Cove—bay (5) ... ME-1
Northwest Cove—cove ... MA-1
Northwest Creek—stream ... NY-2
Northwest Creek—stream (2) ... NC-3
Northwest Dade (CCD)—cens area ... FL-3
Northwest Dam—dam ... CO-8
Northwest Davenport Savings Bank—hist pl ... IA-7
Northwest Davenport Turner Society Hall—hist pl ... IA-7
Northwest Del Rio Park—park ... AZ-5
North West Dome—summit ... AZ-5
Northwest Dora Oil Field—oilfield ... TX-5
Northwest Dover Heights—uninc pl ... DE-2
Northwest Drain—canal ... AZ-5
Northwest Drain—canal (2) ... MI-6
Northwest Draw—valley ... WY-8
**Northwest Duxbury**—pop pl ... MA-1
Northwest Earlsboro Oil Field—oilfield ... OK-5
Northwest Eddy Oil Field—oilfield ... OK-5
North West Eileen State No 1—well ... AK-9
Northwest Elem Sch—school (2) ... FL-3
Northwest Elem Sch—school (2) ... IN-6
Northwest Elem Sch—school ... KS-7
Northwest Elem Sch—school ... NC-3
Northwest Elem Sch—school (2) ... PA-2
Northwest Elem Sch—school ... TN-4
Northwest Ellis (CCD)—cens area ... OK-5
Northwestern ... MI-6
**North Western**—pop pl ... NY-2
Northwestern Baptist Church ... TN-4
Northwestern Ch—church ... IN-6
Northwestern Ch—church ... TN-4
Northwestern Coll—school ... WI-6
Northwestern Community Schools—school ... IL-6
Northwestern Company—other ... AR-4
Northwestern Elem Sch—school (2) ... PA-2
Northwestern Fiord—valley ... AK-9
Northwestern Glacier ... AK-9
Northwestern Glacier—glacier ... AK-9
Northwestern Hawaiian Islands—island ... HI-9
Northwestern High School ... IN-6
Northwestern Hosp—hospital ... MN-6
Northwestern Hotel—hist pl ... IA-7
Northwestern HS ... PA-2
Northwestern HS—school (2) ... FL-3
Northwestern HS—school ... IL-6
Northwestern HS—school ... LA-4
Northwestern HS—school ... MD-2
Northwestern HS—school (2) ... MI-6
North Western HS—school ... OH-6
Northwestern HS—school ... OH-6
Northwestern Improvement Company Store—hist pl ... WA-9
Northwestern JHS—school ... PA-2
Northwestern Junior-Senior HS—school ... IN-6
Northwestern Knitting Company Factory—hist pl ... MN-6
Northwestern Lagoon ... AK-9
Northwestern Lagoon—bay ... AK-9
Northwestern Lake ... MN-6
Northwestern Lake—lake (2) ... MI-6
Northwestern Lake—lake ... MT-8
Northwestern Lake—lake ... ND-7
Northwestern Lake—reservoir ... WA-9
Northwestern Lehigh Junior-Senior HS—school ... PA-2
Northwestern Lutheran Acad—school ... SD-7
Northwestern Michigan Coll—school ... MI-6
Northwestern Military—school ... WI-6
Northwestern MS ... PA-2
Northwestern (Northwestern State College)—uninc pl ... LA-4
Northwestern Sch—school ... GA-3
Northwestern Sch—school (2) ... MI-6
Northwestern Sch—school ... PA-2
Northwestern Sch—school ... VT-1
Northwestern Sch—school ... VA-3
Northwestern Sch of Law—school ... OR-9
Northwestern Senior HS—school ... PA-2
Northwestern State Coll—school ... LA-4
Northwestern State Coll—school ... OK-5
Northwestern Table—summit ... WY-8
Northwestern Union Sch ... PA-2
Northwestern Univ—school (2) ... IL-6
North Western Univ (historical)—school ... IN-6
Northwestern Woods—woods ... IL-6
Northwest Escambia (CCD)—cens area ... FL-3
Northwest Evansville Oil Field—oilfield ... OK-5
**North Westfield**—pop pl ... MA-1
Northwest Flathead Community Hall—building ... MT-8
Northwest Flint Creek Oil Field—oilfield ... OK-5
Northwest Florida State Hosp—hospital ... FL-3
Northwest Fork ... FL-3
Northwest Fork Alligator River—stream ... NC-3
Northwest Fork Boons Creek—stream ... TX-5
Northwest Fork Bridge ... DE-2
Northwest Fork Hundred—civil ... DE-2
Northwest Fork Loxahatchee River ... FL-3
Northwest Fork Nanticoke River ... DE-2
Northwest Fork Nanticoke River ... MD-2
North West Fork of Jupiter River ... FL-3
Northwest Fork of Nanticoke ... DE-2
Northwest Fork Point Creek—stream ... TX-5
Northwest Fork Ruth Glacier—glacier ... AK-9
Northwest Fork Thirtymile Creek—stream ... MT-8
Northwest Garrett Oil And Gas Field—oilfield ... OK-5
Northwest Gas Division Elizabethtown Gas—airport ... NJ-2
Northwest Gate—channel ... FL-3
Northwest General Hosp—hospital ... TN-4
Northwest Georgia Experimental Station—other ... GA-3
Northwest Grange—locale ... WA-9
Northwest Grayson (CCD)—cens area ... TX-5
Northwest Greer (CCD)—cens area ... OK-5
Northwest Gutter—gut ... MA-1
Northwest Hancock (Unorganized Territory of)—unorg ... ME-1
Northwest Harbor—bay ... AK-9
Northwest Harbor—bay ... CA-9
Northwest Harbor—bay ... ME-1
Northwest Harbor—bay ... NY-2
Northwest Harbor—CDP ... NY-2
Northwest Harbor—harbor ... ME-1
Northwest Harbor—harbor ... MD-2
Northwest Harborcreek—CDP ... PA-2
Northwest Harris (CCD)—cens area ... TX-5
Northwest Hartley (CCD)—cens area ... TX-5
Northwest Head—summit ... ME-1
Northwest Hebrew Cem—cemetery ... MI-6
Northwest Heights Baptist Ch—church ... KS-7
Northwest Helicopters Heliport—airport ... WA-9
Northwest Highlands ... IL-6
North West Hill ... MA-1
Northwest Hill—summit ... MA-1
Northwest Hills Ch—church ... MS-4
**Northwest Hills (subdivision)**—pop pl ... MS-4
Northwest Hobart Well—well ... NM-5
Northwest Holbert Well—well ... NM-5
North West Horse Mountain ... UT-8
Northwest Hosp—hospital ... AZ-5
Northwest Hosp—hospital ... FL-3
Northwest Hosp—hospital ... IL-6
Northwest HS ... IN-6
Northwest HS—school ... IN-6
Northwest HS—school ... MI-6
Northwest HS—school (2) ... NC-3
Northwest HS—school (2) ... OH-6
Northwest HS—school ... TN-4
Northwest HS—school ... TX-5
Northwest Inlet—stream (2) ... ME-1
Northwest Intermediate Sch—school ... UT-8
Northwest Island—island ... LA-4
Northwest Island—island ... WA-9
Northwest Jackson—unorg reg ... SD-7
Northwest Jackson (CCD)—cens area ... OR-9
Northwest Jack Williams Bay—bay ... LA-4
Northwest JHS ... NC-3
Northwest JHS—school ... KS-7
Northwest JHS—school (2) ... MI-6
Northwest JHS—school ... MS-4
Northwest JHS—school (2) ... NC-3
Northwest JHS—school ... PA-2
Northwest JHS—school ... TN-4
Northwest JHS—school ... WA-9
Northwest Jones—unorg reg ... SD-7
Northwest Josephine (CCD)—cens area ... OR-9
Northwest Junior College—uninc pl ... MS-4
Northwest Junior High School ... UT-8
Northwest Kansas Area Vocational-Technical Sch—school ... KS-7
Northwest Kansas Vocational School ... KS-7
Northwest Keys—island ... FL-3
Northwest Kildare Oil And Gas Field—oilfield ... OK-5
Northwest Koochiching (Unorganized Territory of)—unorg ... MN-6
Northwest Lake—lake ... MI-6
Northwest Lake—lake ... TX-5
northwest Lake Nellie ... FL-3
**Northwest Landing**—pop pl ... NY-2
North-West Laurel Elem Sch—school ... DE-2
Northwest Laurens Sch—school ... GA-3
Northwest Ledge—bar (2) ... ME-1
Northwest Ledges ... ME-1
Northwest Lincoln (CCD)—cens area ... OK-5
Northwest Lonsdale Mine—mine ... TN-4
Northwest Louisiana State Sch—school ... LA-4
Northwest Main Canal—canal ... CA-9
**Northwest Manor**—pop pl ... IN-6
Northwest Marble Mine—mine ... WA-9
Northwest Marietta Hist Dist—hist pl ... GA-3
Northwest Marin (CCD)—cens area ... CA-9
Northwest Marion Township—civil ... MO-7
Northwest Mcintosh—unorg reg ... ND-7
Northwest McWhorter Tank—reservoir ... TX-5
Northwest Meadow Lake—lake ... NE-7
Northwest Middle School ... TN-4
**North Westminster**—pop pl ... VT-1
Northwest Mississippi Junior Coll—school ... MS-4
Northwest Mississippi Regional Med Ctr—hospital ... MS-4
Northwest Missouri State Univ—school ... MO-7
Northwest Nazarene Coll—school ... ID-8
Northwest Newnan Residential Hist Dist—hist pl ... GA-3
Northwest Noble Oil Field—oilfield ... OK-5
North West North Dakota Girl Scout Camp—locale ... ND-7
Northwest of Zeeland Drain—canal ... MI-6
Northwest Oil Field—oilfield ... OK-5
Northwest Oil Field—oilfield ... TX-5
Northwest Okemah Oil And Gas Field—oilfield ... OK-5
Northwest Osage (CCD)—cens area ... OK-5
Northwest Oshtemo Ch—church ... MI-6
Northwest Palacine Oil Field—oilfield ... OK-5
Northwest Park ... AZ-5
Northwest Park—park ... CA-9
Northwest Park—park ... IL-6
Northwest Park—park ... IA-7
Northwest Park—park ... MI-6
Northwest Park—park ... NY-2
Northwest Park—park ... TX-5
Northwest Park—park ... UT-8
**Northwest Park**—pop pl (3) ... MD-2
Northwest Pass—channel ... WA-9
Northwest Passage—channel ... MP-9
Northwest Peak—summit ... MT-8
Northwest Peak—summit ... WY-8
Northwest Piscataquis (Unorganized Territory of)—unorg ... ME-1
Northwest Pittsburg (CCD)—cens area ... OK-5
North West Plaza ... PA-2
Northwest Plaza—post sta ... MO-7
Northwest Plaza Shop Ctr—locale ... IN-6
Northwest Plaza Shop Ctr—other ... IN-6
Northwest Point—cape (2) ... AK-9
Northwest Point—cape ... FL-3
Northwest Point—cape ... ME-1
Northwest Point—cape ... MD-2
Northwest Point—cape ... NY-2
Northwest Point—cape ... NC-3
Northwest Point—cape ... RI-1
Northwest Point—hist pl ... MN-6
**North West Point**—pop pl ... GA-3
Northwest Point—range ... MP-9
Northwest Point Island—island ... NJ-2
Northwest Pond—lake (3) ... ME-1
Northwest Pontotoc (CCD)—cens area ... OK-5
Northwest Pool—reservoir ... MN-6
North Westport ... MA-1
North Westport (historical P.O.)—locale ... MA-1
Northwest Powder Rsvr—reservoir ... WY-8
Northwest Prong Newport River—stream ... NC-3
Northwest Prong of Nanticoke ... DE-2
Northwest (Quadrant)—fmr MCD ... DC-2
Northwest Rankin Attendance Center—school ... MS-4
Northwest Reach—channel ... NJ-2
Northwest Red White and Blue Windmill—locale ... TX-5
Northwest Reef ... PW-9
Northwest Regional Hosp—hospital ... FL-3
Northwest Ridge Road—trail ... ME-1
Northwest River—stream ... ME-1
Northwest River—stream ... NC-3
Northwest River—stream ... VA-3
Northwest River Marsh Wildlife Area—area ... NC-3
Northwest Rock—island (2) ... OR-9
Northwest Rocks—island ... FL-3
Northwest Rockwall (CCD)—cens area ... TX-5
Northwest Roseau (Unorganized Territory of)—unorg ... MN-6
Northwest Rsvr—reservoir ... TX-5
Northwest Rsvr—reservoir ... UT-8
Northwest Sch ... PA-2
Northwest Sch—school ... AL-4
Northwest Sch—school (2) ... CT-1
Northwest Sch—school ... GA-3
Northwest Sch—school ... IL-6
Northwest Sch—school ... LA-4
Northwest Sch—school ... MA-1
Northwest Sch—school (2) ... MI-6
Northwest Sch—school ... MO-7
Northwest Sch—school (2) ... NY-2
Northwest Sch—school ... NC-3
Northwest Sch—school ... OK-5
Northwest Sch—school (2) ... TX-5
Northwest Sch (historical)—school ... MS-4
Northwest Seamen Tank—reservoir ... TX-5
Northwest Senior HS—school ... NC-3
Northwest Sheldon Dome Oil Field—oilfield ... WY-8
Northwest Shop Ctr—locale ... MI-6
Northwest Shop Ctr—locale ... MS-4
Northwest Shop Ctr—locale ... MO-7
North Westside (CCD)—cens area ... FL-3
Northwest Slip—harbor ... CA-9
Northwest Slope—unorg reg ... ND-7
Northwest Somerset (Unorganized Territory of)—unorg ... ME-1
Northwest Station Post Office—building ... AZ-5
Northwest St. Louis (Unorganized Territory of)—unorg ... MN-6
Northwest Stockbridge Community Ch—church ... MI-6
North West Street Ch of Christ—church ... IN-6
Northwest Stutsman—unorg reg ... ND-7
**Northwest (subdivision)**—pop pl ... PA-2
Northwest Sulphur Oil Field—oilfield ... OK-5
Northwest Sumatra Oil Field—oilfield ... MT-8
Northwest Tampa Ch of Christ—church ... FL-3
Northwest Tank ... AZ-5
Northwest Tank—reservoir ... AZ-5
Northwest Tank—reservoir ... CO-8
Northwest Tank—reservoir (3) ... NM-5
Northwest Tennessee Mental Health Center—hospital ... TN-4
Northwest Texas Hosp—hospital ... TX-5
Northwest Town Hall—building ... ND-7
North West Township ... IN-6
Northwest Township—civil ... MO-7
**Northwest Township**—pop pl ... IN-6
**Northwest Township**—pop pl (2) ... ND-7
Northwest (Township of)—fmr MCD ... AR-4
Northwest (Township of)—fmr MCD ... NC-3
**Northwest (Township of)**—pop pl ... OH-6
Northwest Umatilla (CCD)—cens area ... OR-9
Northwest United Ch—church ... IL-6
Northwest Venice Ch—church ... MI-6
Northwest Village Shop Ctr—locale ... AZ-5
Northwest Wanette Oil Field—oilfield ... OK-5
Northwest Washita (CCD)—cens area ... OK-5
North Westway Park—park ... IN-6
North Westway Park Airp—airport ... IN-6
Northwest Well—well ... AZ-5
Northwest Well—well (3) ... NM-5
Northwest Well—well ... TX-5
Northwest Well Field—well ... FL-3
Northwest Windmill—locale ... NE-7
Northwest Windmill—locale (4) ... NM-5
Northwest Windmill—locale (3) ... TX-5
Northwest Windthorst Oil Field—oilfield ... TX-5
Northwest Woods—woods ... NY-2
Northwest Yakima (CCD)—cens area ... WA-9
Northwest Yeager Tank—reservoir ... TX-5
Northwest Yellowstone—cens area ... MT-8
Northwest Yeocomico River—stream ... VA-3
Northwest York Hist Dist—hist pl ... PA-2
**North Weymouth (subdivision)**—pop pl ... MA-1
North Whale Pass—CDP ... AK-9
North Wharton ... PA-2
North Whatley Windmill—locale ... TX-5
North Wheeler—locale ... MI-6
North Wheeler Rec Area—park ... SD-7
North Wheeling Hist Dist—hist pl ... WV-2
North Whidbey (CCD)—cens area ... WA-9
North Whidbey JHS—school ... WA-9
North Whitakers Sch—school ... NC-3
North Whitakers (Township of)—fmr MCD ... NC-3
North White Bear Coulee ... MT-8
North White Creek ... CO-8
North White Deer Ridge—ridge ... PA-2
**North Whitefield**—pop pl ... ME-1
North Whitehall ... PA-2
North Whitehall School ... PA-2
**North Whitehall (Township of)**—pop pl ... PA-2
North Whitehorse Rsvr—reservoir ... OR-9
North White HS—school ... IN-6
North White Lake ... NY-2
North White Oak Creek—stream ... TN-4
North White Oak Sch—school ... IA-7
North Whiteoak Sch—school ... MO-7
North White Peak—summit ... CO-8
**North White Plains**—pop pl ... NY-2
North White Plains (P.O.)—uninc pl ... NY-2
North White River Ch—church ... IN-6
North Whiteside Ch—church ... NC-3
North Whitey Coulee—valley ... MT-8
North Whitfield (CCD)—cens area ... GA-3
North Whitfield HS—school ... GA-3
North Whitmore Point Pond—reservoir ... AZ-5
North Whittenburg Windmill—locale ... TX-5
**North Whittier**—pop pl ... CA-9
**North Whittier Heights**—pop pl ... CA-9
North Whittier Sch—school ... CA-9
North Wichita—uninc pl ... KS-7
North Wichita River—stream ... TX-5
North Wicked Creek—stream ... AR-4
North Wickiup Campground—park ... OR-9
**North Wilbraham**—pop pl ... MA-1
North Wildcat Creek—stream ... IA-7
North Wildcat Creek—stream ... UT-8
North Wilder Lake—lake ... MN-6
North Wilderness Run—stream ... VA-3
North Wild Horse Campground—locale ... NV-8
North Wild Horse Creek—stream ... NV-8
North Wild Rice Cem—cemetery ... MN-6
**North Wildwood**—pop pl ... NJ-2
**North Wilkesboro**—pop pl ... NC-3
North Wilkesboro Elem Sch—school ... NC-3
North Wilkesboro Speedway—locale ... NC-3
North Wilkesboro (Township of)—fmr MCD ... NC-3
North Wilkesboro Womens Club—building ... NC-3
**North Williams**—pop pl ... MI-6
North Williams Ranch—locale ... NM-5
North Williams Windmill—locale ... TX-5
**North Williston**—pop pl ... VT-1
North Willow Canyon—valley ... UT-8
North Willow Creek—stream (2) ... CO-8
North Willow Creek—stream ... ID-8
North Willow Creek—stream (3) ... MT-8
North Willow Creek—stream ... OR-9
North Willow Creek—stream ... TX-5
North Willow Creek—stream ... UT-8
North Willow Creek—stream (2) ... WY-8
North Willow Grove Sch—school ... PA-2
North Willow Lake—lake ... UT-8
North Willow Spring—spring ... OR-9
North Willow Spring—spring ... UT-8
North Willow Springs—spring ... ID-8
North Willow Springs—spring ... UT-8
North Willow Springs Creek—stream ... ID-8
North Wilmer Run ... PA-2
**North Wilmington**—pop pl ... CA-9
**North Wilmington**—pop pl ... MA-1
North Wilmot—locale ... NH-1
**North Wilmurt**—pop pl ... NY-2
North Wilna—locale ... NY-2
North Wilson—summit ... OR-9
North Wilson Coulee—valley ... MT-8
North Wilson Creek—stream ... ID-8
North Wilson Rsvr—reservoir ... OR-9
North Wilsons Creek ... MO-7
North Wilson Windmill—locale ... TX-5
North Wilton—locale ... CT-1
North Windfohr And Brown Camp No 1—locale ... NM-5
**North Windham**—pop pl ... CT-1
**North Windham**—pop pl ... ME-1
**North Windham**—pop pl ... VT-1
North Windmill—locale ... CO-8
North Windmill—locale ... NE-7
North Windmill—locale (27) ... NM-5
North Windmill—locale ... SC-3
North Windmill—locale (47) ... TX-5
North Windmill—summit ... TX-5
North Windmill Draw—valley ... WY-8
North Windmills—locale ... NM-5
North Windmills—locale ... TX-5
North Windmill Well—well ... NM-5
North Window—arch ... UT-8
North Window—gap ... AZ-5
**North Windsor**—pop pl ... ME-1
North Windsor Cem—cemetery ... NY-2
North Windsor Ch—church ... WI-6
North Windsor Sch—school ... WI-6
North Windy Sch—school ... KS-7
North Winegar Canyon—valley ... WA-9
**North Winfield**—pop pl ... NY-2
North Winfield Creek—stream ... NY-2
North Winkle Windmill—locale ... NM-5
North Winneshiek Community Sch—school ... IA-7
North Winona Baptist Ch—church ... MS-4
North Winona Ch—church ... IN-6
**North Winston**—pop pl ... NC-3
North Winter Haven—CDP ... FL-3
North Winters Windmill—locale ... TX-5
North Winyah Heights—uninc pl ... SC-3
North Wisconsin Lumber Company Office—hist pl ... WI-6
North Witch Canyon—valley ... AZ-5
North Witmer Run—stream ... PA-2
**North Woburn**—pop pl ... MA-1
**North Woburn Junction**—pop pl ... MA-1
**North Wolcott**—pop pl ... NY-2
**North Wolcott**—pop pl ... VT-1
North Wolcott Cem—cemetery ... NY-2
North Wolf Canyon—valley ... WY-8
North Wolf Creek—stream ... MT-8
North Wolf Creek—stream ... OR-9
North Wolf Creek—stream ... SD-7
North Wolf Creek - in part ... PA-2
**North Wolfeboro**—pop pl ... NH-1
North Wolf River ... KS-7
Northwood (3) ... IN-6
Northwood—locale ... CA-9
Northwood—locale ... WA-9
**Northwood**—pop pl ... DE-2
**Northwood**—pop pl (2) ... FL-3
**Northwood**—pop pl ... IN-6
**Northwood**—pop pl ... IA-7
**Northwood**—pop pl ... MI-6
**Northwood**—pop pl ... NH-1
**Northwood**—pop pl (2) ... NJ-2
**Northwood**—pop pl ... NY-2
**Northwood**—pop pl ... ND-7
**Northwood**—pop pl (3) ... OH-6
**Northwood**—pop pl ... PA-2
Northwood—post sta ... IN-6
Northwood—uninc pl ... FL-3
Northwood—uninc pl ... MD-2
Northwood, Lake—reservoir ... MO-7
**Northwood Acres**—pop pl ... MO-7
Northwood Airp—airport ... MO-7
**North Woodbury**—pop pl ... CT-1
**North Woodbury**—pop pl ... NJ-2
**North Woodbury**—pop pl ... OH-6
**North Woodbury (Township of)**—pop pl ... PA-2
Northwood Camp—locale ... MI-6
North Wood Canyon—valley ... WY-8
Northwood Cem—cemetery ... ND-7
Northwood Cem—cemetery (2) ... OH-6

Number 2 Shaft—*mine* NY-2
Number 2 Store Hollow—*valley* WV-2
Number 2 Tunnel—*tunnel* WV-2
Number 20, Dam—*dam* (2) TX-5
Number 20, Lock—*other* NY-2
Number 20A, Dam—*dam* TX-5
Number 21, Dam—*dam* (2) TX-5
Number 21 Ch—*church* WV-2
Number 22, Dam—*dam* (2) TX-5
Number 22 Ch—*church* WV-2
Number 23, Dam—*dam* TX-5
Number 24, Dam—*dam* TX-5
Number 24, Lock—*other* NY-2
Number 25, Dam—*dam* TX-5
Number 25, Lock—*other* NY-2
Number 26, Dam—*dam* TX-5
Number 26 Ditch—*canal* AR-4
Number 26H, Dam—*dam* TX-5
Number 27, Drain—*canal* ND-7
Number 28, Dam—*dam* TX-5
Number 28, Drain—*canal* ND-7
Number 29, Dam—*dam* TX-5
Number 3, Dam—*dam* ND-7
Number 3, Dam—*dam* (7) TX-5
Number 3, Lock—*other* (3) NY-2
Number 3 Canyon—*valley* WA-9
*Number 3 Dam* PA-2
Number 3 Forebay Rsvr—*reservoir* MA-1
Number 3 Mine—*mine* MT-8
Number 3 Shaft—*mine* NY-2
*Number 3 Township School* NC-3
Number 3 Tunnel—*tunnel* WV-2
Number 30, Dam—*dam* TX-5
Number 30, Lock—*other* NY-2
Number 31, Dam—*dam* TX-5
Number 32, Dam—*dam* TX-5
Number 320, Dam—*dam* ND-7
Number 326, Dam—*dam* ND-7
Number 33, Dam—*dam* TX-5
Number 332, Dam—*dam* ND-7
Number 34, Dam—*dam* TX-5
Number 35, Dam—*dam* TX-5
Number 357, Dam—*dam* ND-7
Number 37, Dam—*dam* TX-5
Number 38—*locale* PA-2
Number 38, Dam—*dam* TX-5
Number 39, Dam—*dam* TX-5
Number 39, Drain—*canal* (2) ND-7
Number 4, Dam—*dam* MT-8
Number 4, Dam—*dam* ND-7
Number 4, Dam—*dam* (6) TX-5
Number 4, Drain—*canal* ND-7
Number 4, Lock—*other* (3) NY-2
Number 4, Trail—*trail* NY-2
Number 4A, Dam—*dam* ND-7
Number 4A, Dam—*dam* TX-5
Number 4 A, Trail—*trail* NY-2
*Number 4 Dam* PA-2
Number 4 Hook and Ladder Company—*hist pl* TX-5
Number 4 Mine—*mine* MT-8
Number 4 Reservoir Dam—*dam* MA-1
Number 40, Dam—*dam* TX-5
Number 41, Dam—*dam* TX-5
Number 42, Dam—*dam* TX-5
Number 44, Dam—*dam* TX-5
Number 45, Dam—*dam* TX-5
Number 46, Dam—*dam* TX-5
Number 47, Dam—*dam* TX-5
Number 48, Dam—*dam* TX-5
Number 49, Dam—*dam* TX-5
Number 5, Dam—*dam* (7) TX-5
Number 5, Lock—*other* (3) NY-2
Number 5, Trail—*trail* NY-2
Number 5 Canyon—*valley* WA-9
Number 5 Hill—*mine* AR-4
Number 5 Mine—*mine* WA-9
Number 5 Sch—*school* PA-2
Number 51, Dam—*dam* TX-5
Number 52, Dam—*dam* TX-5
Number 53, Dam—*dam* TX-5
Number 54, Dam—*dam* TX-5
Number 55, Dam—*dam* TX-5
**Number 56**—*pop pl* PA-2
Number 56, Dam—*dam* TX-5
Number 57, Dam—*dam* (2) TX-5
Number 58, Dam—*dam* TX-5
Number 59, Dam—*dam* (2) TX-5
Number 6, Dam—*dam* MT-8
Number 6, Dam—*dam* (2) ND-7
Number 6, Dam—*dam* (4) TX-5
Number 6, Lock—*other* (3) NY-2
Number 6A, Dam—*dam* TX-5
Number 6 Canyon—*valley* WA-9
Number 60, Dam—*dam* TX-5
Number 61, Dam—*dam* TX-5
Number 62, Dam—*dam* TX-5
Number 63, Dam—*dam* TX-5
Number 7, Dam—*dam* (5) TX-5
Number 7, Lock—*other* (2) NY-2
Number 7A, Dam—*dam* ND-7
Number 7 Ch—*church* WV-2
*Number 7 Dam* PA-2
Number 7 Hill—*summit* WV-2
Number 7 Junction—*locale* PA-2
Number 7 Mine—*mine* WA-9
Number 7 Sch—*school* NY-2
Number 72, Dam—*dam* TX-5
Number 74, Dam—*dam* TX-5
Number 76, Dam—*dam* TX-5
*Number 77* IN-6
Number 77, Dam—*dam* TX-5
Number 8, Dam—*dam* ND-7
Number 8, Dam—*dam* (4) TX-5
Number 8, Lock—*other* (3) NY-2
Number 8 Mine—*mine* WA-9
Number 83, Dam—*dam* ND-7
Number 84, Dam—*dam* ND-7
Number 87, Dam—*dam* ND-7
Number 89, Dam—*dam* TX-5
Number 9, Dam—*dam* (2) TX-5
Number 9, Lock—*other* NY-2
Number 9, Trail—*trail* NY-2
Number 9A, Dam—*dam* TX-5
Number 9B, Dam—*dam* TX-5
Number 9C, Dam—*dam* TX-5
Number 9 Hill—*summit* WA-9
Number 9 Mine—*mine* WA-9
Number 9 Sch—*school* VT-1
Number 92, Dam—*dam* TX-5
Number 93, Dam—*dam* TX-5
Number 94, Dam—*dam* TX-5
Number 96, Dam—*dam* ND-7
Number 97, Dam—*dam* TX-5
Number 98, Dam—*dam* TX-5
Number 98A, Dam—*dam* TX-5
Number 99, Dam—*dam* TX-5
*Numchenugmawis* ME-1
*Numdia* PA-2
Numdul—*locale* FM-9
**Numedal (Township of)**—*pop pl* MN-6
*Numenun* FM-9
Numeral Rock—*summit* CT-1
Numer Hollow—*valley* PA-2
Numero Uno Windmill—*locale* TX-5
Numertia Plantation—*hist pl* SC-3
**Numidia**—*pop pl* PA-2
Numidia Airp—*airport* PA-2
**Numila**—*pop pl* HI-9
Nu Mine—*mine* CO-8
**NuMine**—*pop pl* PA-2
**Nu Mine**—*pop pl* PA-2
*Num-mel-be-le-sas-pom* CA-9
Nummet, The—*flat* MA-1
Nummy, Lake—*reservoir* NJ-2
Nummy Island—*island* NJ-2
Nummy Island Creek—*gut* NJ-2
*Nummys Island* NJ-2
**Nummytown**—*pop pl* NJ-2
*Nummytown Mill Pond* NJ-2
*Numnum* FM-9
Numnung—*locale* FM-9
*Numphia Lake* WI-6
Nums Channel—*channel* NY-2
Nums Marsh—*swamp* NY-2
*Numumung* FM-9
Numurus Island—*island* FM-9
Nunabiklu Slough—*gut* AK-9
Nunachik Pass—*gut* AK-9
**Nunachuak**—*pop pl* AK-9
Nunachuak Creek—*stream* AK-9
**Nunachuk**—*pop pl* AK-9
Nuna Creek—*stream* AK-9
Nunakak Camp—*locale* AK-9
Nunaka Valley—*uninc pl* AK-9
Nunakitsu Island—*island* FM-9
Nunakogok River—*stream* AK-9
Nunaktuk Island—*island* AK-9
Nunally Dam—*dam* AL-4
Nunamaker Pond—*lake* OR-9
Nunamaker Spring—*spring* OR-9
Nunamiut (Abandoned)—*locale* AK-9
Nunamuit Mtn—*summit* AK-9
**Nunapitchuk**—*pop pl* AK-9
**Nunapitchuk(Included In Akolmiut) ANV885**—*pop pl* AK-9
**Nunapitsinchak**—*pop pl* AK-9
Nuna Ridge—*ridge* NC-3
Nuna Slough—*gut* AK-9
Nunatak, The—*summit* AK-9
Nunatak Chalet—*locale* AK-9
Nunatak Cove—*bay* AK-9
Nunatak Fiord—*bay* AK-9
Nunathloogagamiutbingoi Dunes—*beach* AK-9
Nunathloogagamiut (Summer Camp)—*locale* AK-9
Nunavachak Bay—*bay* AK-9
Nunavachak Lake—*lake* AK-9
Nunavakanukakslak Lake—*lake* AK-9
Nunavakanuk Lake—*lake* AK-9
Nunavak Bay—*bay* AK-9
Nunavakpak Lake—*lake* AK-9
Nunavaugaluk, Lake—*lake* AK-9
Nunavaugaluk Lake—*lake* AK-9
Nunaviksak Creek—*stream* AK-9
Nunavulnuk River—*stream* AK-9
Nunda—*locale* OH-6
**Nunda**—*pop pl* NY-2
**Nunda**—*pop pl* SD-7
Nunda Branch—*stream* NC-3
Nunda Rod and Gun Club—*other* NY-2
Nunda Rsvr—*reservoir* NY-2
Nunda Sch—*school* NE-7
**Nunda (Town of)**—*pop pl* NY-2
**Nunda Township**—*pop pl* SD-7
Nunda Township Hall—*building* SD-7
**Nunda (Township of)**—*pop pl* IL-6
**Nunda (Township of)**—*pop pl* MI-6
**Nunda (Township of)**—*pop pl* MN-6
Nunemaker Coulee—*valley* MT-8
Nunemaker Ditch—*canal* IN-6
Nunemaker Hill—*summit* MT-8
*Nuner Hollow* PA-2
*Nuner School* IN-6
Nunes Ranch—*locale* CA-9
**Nunez**—*pop pl* GA-3
**Nunez**—*pop pl* LA-4
Nunez Canyon—*valley* (2) CA-9
Nunez Ferry (historical)—*locale* AL-4
Nunez Post Office (historical)—*building* AL-4
Nunez Ranch—*locale* NM-5
Nunez Ranch—*locale* TX-5
*Nunez Spring* CA-9
Nungatak River—*stream* AK-9
Nunge Brook—*stream* VT-1
Nungee Brook—*stream* MA-1
Nungee Swamp—*swamp* MA-1
Nun Hollow—*valley* TN-4
Nun Hollow Mine—*mine* TN-4
**Nunica**—*pop pl* MI-6
Nunica Cem—*cemetery* MI-6
Nunica Post Office (historical)—*building* AL-4
*Nunih Waiyha* MS-4
*Nunis Ferry* AL-4
Nunivachak Island—*island* AK-9
Nunivak Bar—*bar* AK-9
Nunivak Island—*island* AK-9
Nunivak Slough—*stream* AK-9
*Nunketes Pond* MA-1
*Nunket Pond* MA-1
Nunkets Pond—*lake* MA-1
Nun Lake—*reservoir* CA-9
**Nunley**—*pop pl* AR-4
Nunley Cem—*cemetery* AR-4
Nunley Cem—*cemetery* (2) MS-4
Nunley Cem—*cemetery* MO-7
Nunley Hollow—*valley* (2) TN-4
Nunley Hollow—*valley* WV-2
Nunley Mtn—*summit* TN-4
Nunley Number 1 Mine (surface)—*mine* TN-4
Nunley Sch—*school* TN-4
Nunleys Cove—*valley* TN-4
Nunleys Cove Ch—*church* TN-4
Nunleys Cove Creek—*stream* TN-4
Nunly Mountain—*ridge* WV-2
Nun Mine—*mine* NV-8
Nun Mtn—*summit* AK-9
Nunn—*locale* KY-4
**Nunn**—*pop pl* CO-8
Nunn, Mount—*summit* CA-9
Nunnally Branch—*stream* AL-4
Nunnally Cem—*cemetery* MS-4
Nunnally Creek—*stream* MS-4
Nunnally Ford—*locale* AL-4
*Nunnaly Lake* AL-4
*Nunnamessett Island* MA-1
Nunnary Branch—*stream* KY-4
Nunn Brake (historical)—*swamp* LA-4
Nunn Branch—*stream* AL-4
Nunn Branch—*stream* KY-4
Nunn Cem—*cemetery* (2) FL-3
Nunn Cem—*cemetery* GA-3
Nunn Cem—*cemetery* IL-6
Nunn Cem—*cemetery* (3) KY-4
Nunn Cem—*cemetery* MO-7
Nunn Cem—*cemetery* (2) NC-3
Nunn Cem—*cemetery* TN-4
Nunn Cem—*cemetery* WV-2
*Nunn Creek* MI-6
Nunn Creek—*stream* CO-8
Nunn Creek—*stream* VA-3
Nunn Creek Basin—*basin* CO-8
Nunn Drain—*canal* MI-6
Nunnelee—*locale* TX-5
**Nunnelly**—*pop pl* TN-4
Nunnelly Mines—*mine* TN-4
Nunnelly Post Office—*building* TN-4
Nunnelly Sch (historical)—*school* TN-4
*Nunne-poag* MA-1
*Nunnepog* MA-1
Nunnepog (historical)—*locale* MA-1
**Nunnery**—*pop pl* PA-2
*Nunnery Cem* MS-4
Nunnery Cem—*cemetery* MS-4
Nunnery Lake Dam—*dam* MS-4
Nunnery Point—*cape* NY-2
Nunnery Store (historical)—*locale* (2) MS-4
Nunn Hill—*summit* TX-5
Nunn Hollow—*valley* TN-4
Nunn House—*hist pl* TX-5
Nunnley Branch—*stream* AL-4
Nunnley Ford Cem—*cemetery* TN-4
Nunn Mtn—*summit* NC-3
Nunn Oil Field—*oilfield* KS-7
Nunn Power Plant—*hist pl* UT-8
Nunn Ranch—*locale* NE-7
Nunn Ranch—*locale* (4) NM-5
Nunn Ranch—*locale* WY-8
Nunns—*locale* UT-8
Nunns Canyon—*valley* CA-9
Nunns Creek—*stream* MI-6
Nunns Iron Spring—*spring* CA-9
*Nunns Mill* AL-4
Nunns Mtn—*summit* VA-3
Nunn Spring—*spring* AL-4
Nunn Store—*locale* AL-4
Nunn Tank—*reservoir* AZ-5
Nunn Tank—*reservoir* TX-5
Nunn-Wheeler Cem—*cemetery* GA-3
*Nunpaug* MA-1
*Nunpauket* MA-1
*Nunpog* MA-1
*Nunpol Einfahrt* FM-9
Nunsatuk River—*stream* AK-9
Nuns Cove—*valley* TN-4
*Nuns Creek* MI-6
Nun's Green—*hist pl* MD-2
Nuns of the Battlefield Monmt—*park* DC-2
Nuntley Mine—*mine* NV-8
Nuntragut Slough—*stream* AK-9
Nunu, Banaderon—*basin* MH-9
Nunuluiki—*civil* HI-9
Nunulunui—*civil* HI-9
Nununyi Mound and Village Site—*hist pl* NC-3
Nunup—*well* FM-9
Nunvotchuk Lake—*lake* AK-9
Nuok Spit—*cape* AK-9
Nupenkinas—*bar* FM-9
Nuphar Lake—*lake* WY-8
**Nuremberg**—*pop pl* (2) PA-2
Nuremberg Cem—*cemetery* PA-2
*Nuremburg* PA-2
Nurenbern Ditch—*canal* IN-6
Nurey (historical)—*locale* SD-7
**Nuriva**—*pop pl* WV-2
**Nurmi Isles**—*pop pl* FL-3
Nurnberger Sch—*school* MI-6
Nurney—*locale* VA-3
Nurneysville—*locale* VA-3
Nurse Brook—*stream* MA-1
Nurse Cem—*cemetery* OH-6
Nurse Chapel—*church* SC-3
Nurse Creek—*stream* OR-9
Nurse Draw—*valley* WY-8
Nurse Lagoon—*bay* AK-9
Nurse Mtn—*summit* VT-1
Nurse Nursery Sch—*school* PA-2
*Nursery* WV-2
**Nursery**—*pop pl* TX-5
Nursery—*uninc pl* OK-5
Nursery Cem—*cemetery* TX-5
Nursery Creek—*stream* MT-8
Nursery Draw—*valley* SD-7
*Nursery Heights* WV-2
Nursery Hill—*summit* FL-3
Nursery Hill—*summit* SC-3
*Nursery Pond* MA-1
Nursery Site, RI-273—*hist pl* RI-1
Nurse Sch—*school* MO-7
Nurses Lakes—*lake* MT-8
Nurse Slough—*gut* CA-9
Nursey Gulch—*valley* CA-9
Nurukomarot Channel—*channel* AK-9
Nurusse—*summit* AZ-5
Nus, August, Polygonal Barn—*hist pl* IA-7
Nusbaum Chemical Plant—*building* PA-2
Nusbaum Farms Rsvr—*reservoir* OR-9
Nus Cem—*cemetery* TX-5
**Nushagak**—*pop pl* AK-9
Nushagak Bay—*bay* AK-9
Nushagak Hills—*other* AK-9
Nushagak Peninsula—*cape* AK-9
Nushagak Point—*cape* AK-9
Nushagak River—*stream* AK-9
Nushka Lake—*lake* MN-6
Nushka Lookout Tower—*locale* MN-6
Nushkolik Mtn—*summit* AK-9
Nushralutak Creek—*stream* AK-9
*Nuska Lake* MN-6
Nuskealik Lake—*lake* AK-9
*Nuss* WV-2
Nussbaum Spring—*spring* CO-8
Nuss Lake—*lake* OR-9
Nuss Oil Field—*oilfield* KS-7
Nussom Knob—*summit* TN-4
Nuss Ranch—*locale* CA-9
*Nustoc* NC-3
**Nutall Rise**—*pop pl* FL-3
**Nutal Rise**—*pop pl* FL-3
Nut Bank—*locale* MS-4
Nutbank Post Office (historical)—*building* MS-4
Nut Basin—*basin* ID-8
Nut Basin Lake—*lake* ID-8
Nut Branch—*stream* VA-3
Nut Brook—*stream* IN-6
Nutbush—*locale* VA-3
**Nutbush**—*pop pl* TN-4
Nutbush Bridge Campground—*locale* NC-3
Nutbush (CCD)—*cens area* TN-4
Nutbush Ch—*church* (2) NC-3
Nutbush Creek—*stream* NC-3
Nutbush Creek—*stream* VA-3
Nutbush Division—*civil* TN-4
*Nutbush Indian Fortification* AL-4
Nutbush Plantation (historical)—*locale* AL-4
Nutbush Post Office (historical)—*building* TN-4
Nutbush Sch—*school* NC-3
Nutbush Sch (historical)—*school* TN-4
Nutbush (Township of)—*fmr MCD* NC-3
Nut Creek—*stream* GA-3
Nut Creek—*stream* ID-8
Nut Creek—*stream* WY-8
*Nut Dam* AZ-5
Nute Cem—*cemetery* NY-2
*Nutenhook* NY-2
Nute Ridge—*ridge* NH-1
Nute Ridge Sch—*school* NH-1
Nute Slough—*stream* OR-9
*Nutes Slough* OR-9
*Nut Fall Canyon* AZ-5
Nutgrass Dike—*dam* NV-8
Nut Grove—*hist pl* NY-2
Nuthatch Creek—*stream* MI-6
Nuthatch Lake—*lake* AK-9
Nuthatch Lake—*lake* MN-6
Nuthatch Lake—*lake* WY-8
Nut Hill—*summit* ID-8
Nutirwik Creek—*stream* AK-9
Nut Island—*cliff* MA-1
Nut Island—*island* AK-9
*Nut Islet* MA-1
Nutkwa Falls—*falls* AK-9
Nutkwa Inlet—*bay* AK-9
Nutkwa Lagoon—*lake* AK-9
Nutkwa Point—*cape* AK-9
Nut Lake—*lake* WI-6
**Nutley**—*pop pl* NJ-2
Nutley HS—*school* NJ-2
Nutley Reach—*channel* NJ-2
Nutley Station—*locale* NJ-2
**Nutley Township**—*pop pl* SD-7
**Nutley (Township of)**—*pop pl* NJ-2
Nutling Pond—*lake* ME-1
Nutmeg Creek—*stream* (2) CA-9
Nutmeg Drain—*canal* CA-9
Nutmeg Flat—*flat* ID-8
Nutmeg Glen—*valley* CA-9
Nutmeg Gulch—*valley* AK-9
Nutmeg Gulch—*valley* CA-9
Nutmeg Lateral—*canal* CA-9
Nutmeg Mine—*mine* CA-9
Nutmeg Spring—*spring* CA-9
Nutmoyuk Creek—*stream* AK-9
Nut Mtn—*summit* NV-8
Nutone Plant—*facility* OH-6
Nut Pine Hills—*summit* UT-8
Nut Pine Spring—*spring* MT-8
**Nut Plains**—*pop pl* CT-1
Nut Plains Cem—*cemetery* CT-1
Nutras Creek—*stream* CO-8
**Nutree West Subdivision**—*pop pl* UT-8
Nutria—*locale* CO-8
Nutria—*locale* WY-8
Nutria Campground—*locale* NM-5
Nutria Canyon—*valley* NM-5
Nutria Ditch—*canal* WY-8
Nutria Diversion Reservior—*reservoir* NM-5
Nutria Road Draw—*valley* NM-5
Nutria Rsvr No 2—*reservoir* NM-5
Nutria Rsvr No 3—*reservoir* NM-5
Nutria Rsvr No 4—*reservoir* NM-5
*Nutrias* NM-5
Nutrias—*locale* NM-5
Nutrias Canyon—*valley* NM-5
Nutria Spring—*spring* (2) NM-5
**Nutrioso**—*pop pl* AZ-5
Nutrioso Creek—*stream* AZ-5
Nutrioso Dam—*dam* AZ-5
Nutrioso Rsvr—*reservoir* AZ-5
Nut Rsvr—*reservoir* OR-9
Nut Run—*stream* IN-6
Nutson Number 1 Dam—*dam* AL-4
Nutson Number 2 Dam—*dam* AL-4
Nutson Number 3 Dam—*dam* AL-4
Nut Spring—*spring* NV-8
Nut Swamp Brook—*stream* NJ-2
Nutt—*locale* NM-5
Nutt, Mount—*summit* AZ-5
Nuttal—*locale* PA-2
Nuttall—*locale* VA-3
*Nuttall Canyon* AZ-5
Nuttall Canyon—*valley* AZ-5
*Nuttalls* PA-2
Nuttall Station—*locale* WV-2
*Nuttallville* PA-2
Nutt Brook—*stream* NY-2
Nutt Cem—*cemetery* IN-6
Nutt Cem—*cemetery* MS-4
Nutt Cem—*cemetery* TN-4
Nutt Coulee—*valley* MT-8
*Nuttenhook* NY-2
Nutten Hook—*cape* NY-2
**Nutter**—*pop pl* NH-1
*Nutter Canyon* UT-8
Nutter Canyon Oil Field—*oilfield* UT-8
Nutter Cem—*cemetery* (2) IN-6
Nutter Cem—*cemetery* ME-1
Nutter Cem—*cemetery* MO-7
Nutter Cem—*cemetery* VA-3
Nutter Cem—*cemetery* (3) WV-2
Nutter Corner—*locale* ME-1
Nutter Cove—*bay* ME-1
*Nutter Creek* OK-5
Nutter Creek—*stream* IN-6
Nutter Ditch—*canal* IN-6
Nutter Draw—*valley* MT-8
**Nutter Farm**—*pop pl* WV-2
**Nutter Farm (Nutters Farm)**—*pop pl* WV-2
Nutter Fork—*stream* (2) WV-2
Nutter Fork Ch—*church* WV-2
**Nutter Fort**—*pop pl* WV-2
Nutter Fort-stonewood—*uninc pl* WV-2
Nutter Lake—*lake* CA-9
Nutter Memorial Park—*park* MT-8
*Nutter Mountain* VA-3
*Nutter Point* ME-1
Nutter Point—*cape* ME-1
Nutter Pond—*lake* ME-1
Nutter Pond—*reservoir* AZ-5
Nutter Rsvr—*reservoir* AZ-5
Nutter Run—*stream* (2) WV-2
Nutter-Rymes House—*hist pl* NH-1
Nutters Canyon—*valley* UT-8
Nutters Cathedral Peak—*summit* MT-8
Nutter Sch—*school* MO-7
Nutters Corral—*locale* UT-8
Nutters Farm—*other* WV-2
Nutters Hole—*basin* UT-8
Nutters Hole—*bend* UT-8
Nutters Mtn—*summit* VA-3
Nutters Neck—*cape* MD-2
*Nutter's Point* ME-1
Nutters Point—*cape* NH-1
Nutters Rock—*summit* UT-8
Nutters Spring—*spring* UT-8
Nutter Tank—*reservoir* AZ-5
*Nutterville* WI-6
Nutterville—*locale* WV-2
**Nutterville**—*pop pl* WI-6
Nutter Well—*well* MT-8
*Nutt Hollow* TN-4
Nutt Hollow—*valley* IA-7
Nutting, John C., House—*hist pl* MN-6
*Nutting Brook* MA-1
Nutting Brook—*stream* VT-1
Nutting Cem—*cemetery* IA-7
Nutting Corners—*locale* VT-1
Nutting Creek—*stream* IA-7
Nutting Draw—*valley* WY-8
Nutting Hall—*hist pl* PA-2
Nutting Hill—*summit* (2) MA-1
Nutting Homestead, The—*hist pl* ME-1
Nutting Lake—*lake* MA-1
**Nutting Lake**—*pop pl* MA-1
Nutting Ledge—*bench* ME-1
Nutting Rental—*hist pl* MT-8
**Nuttings Beach**—*pop pl* NH-1
*Nuttings Lake* MA-1
*Nuttings Pond* MA-1
Nutting Stream—*stream* MA-1
*Nuttle Canyon* AZ-5
Nuttle Cem—*cemetery* IL-6
*Nuttles Canyon* AZ-5
Nuttles Rocks—*pillar* PA-2
*Nutt Mountain* AZ-5
Nutt Mtn—*summit* NM-5
Nutt Park—*park* WI-6
Nutt Pond—*lake* NH-1
Nutt Prospect—*mine* TN-4
Nutt Ranch—*locale* TX-5
*Nuttras Creek* CO-8
Nut Tree—*post sta* CA-9
Nuttree Branch—*stream* VA-3
Nutts—*locale* AR-4
Nutts Chapel—*church* AR-4
Nutts Corners—*locale* PA-2
*Nutts Pond* NH-1
Nutt Spring—*spring* NM-5
Nutts Shop (historical)—*locale* MS-4
Nuttsville—*locale* VA-3
*Nutty Combe Township* KS-7
Nutuvukti Lake—*lake* AK-9
*Nut Valley* PA-2
Nutwell—*locale* MD-2
Nut Windmill—*locale* NM-5
Nutwood—*hist pl* GA-3
**Nutwood**—*pop pl* IL-6
**Nutwood**—*pop pl* IN-6
**Nutwood**—*pop pl* OH-6
Nutwood Place—*hist pl* OH-6
Nutwood Site—*hist pl* IL-6
Nutzotin Mountains—*range* AK-9
Nuu—*civil* HI-9
Nuu—*locale* HI-9
Nuuanu—*civil* HI-9
Nuuanu Pali—*cliff* HI-9
Nuuanu Petroglyph Complex—*hist pl* HI-9
Nuuanu Sch—*school* HI-9
Nuuanu Stream—*stream* HI-9
Nuuanu Valley—*valley* HI-9
Nuuanu Valley Park—*park* HI-9
Nuu Bay—*bay* HI-9
Nuuiti Rock—*island* AS-9
*Nuukan* FM-9
*Nuukanap* FM-9
*Nuu Landing* HI-9
Nuu Landing—*locale* HI-9
*Nuulolo* HI-9
Nuuolemaa Cove—*bay* AS-9
Nuuoleniu Cove—*cape* AS-9
Nuuomanu Rock—*island* AS-9
Nuuoosegi Cove—*bay* AS-9
Nuuooti Cove—*bay* AS-9
Nuuosina Rock—*island* AS-9
*Nuupia Fishpond* HI-9
Nuupia Pond—*lake* HI-9
Nuupule Rock—*island* AS-9
Nuusetoga Island—*island* AS-9
Nuusilaelae Island—*island* AS-9
Nuu Stream—*stream* AS-9
Nuutai Rock—*island* AS-9
Nuutavana Rock—*island* AS-9
Nuutele Island—*island* AS-9
Nuutele Rocks—*island* AS-9
Nuutoga Point—*cape* AS-9
Nuutoga Stream—*stream* AS-9
Nuututai Point—*cape* AS-9
Nuututai Rock—*island* AS-9
**Nu'uuli**—*pop pl* AS-9
**Nuuuli**—*pop pl* AS-9
Nuvagapak Lagoon—*bay* AK-9
Nuvagapak Point—*cape* AK-9
Nuvakwewtaqa—*hist pl* AZ-5
*Nuvat-i-kyan-bi* AZ-5
Nuview Sch—*school* CA-9
Nuvugalak Point—*cape* AK-9
**Nuway**—*pop pl* TX-5
Nu-Wray Inn—*hist pl* NC-3
Nuwuk—*locale* AK-9
Nuwuk Lake—*lake* AK-9
Nuyaka—*locale* OK-5
Nuyaka Cem—*cemetery* OK-5
Nuyaka Creek—*stream* OK-5
*Nuyaka Mission* OK-5
Nuyaka Mission—*hist pl* OK-5
Nuyaka Mission Ch—*church* OK-5
Nuyakuk Lake—*lake* AK-9
Nuyakuk River—*stream* AK-9
Nuziamundcho Lake—*lake* AK-9
Nuziamund Lake—*lake* AK-9
Nuzum, Godfrey, Barn—*hist pl* KS-7
Nuzum Cem—*cemetery* WV-2
**Nuzums**—*pop pl* WV-2
N Vansickel Dam—*dam* SD-7
Nvortulermiut Summer Camp—*locale* AK-9
Nwaja—*island* MP-9
N W International Dam—*dam* NC-3
N W Spring—*spring* ID-8
N X Bar Ranch—*locale* WY-8
**Nyac**—*pop pl* AK-9
NYA Camp—*locale* IL-6
*Nyack* KS-7
**Nyack**—*pop pl* MT-8
**Nyack**—*pop pl* NY-2
Nyack Creek—*stream* MT-8
Nyack Lakes—*lake* MT-8
Nyack Missionary Coll—*school* NY-2
Nyack Mtn—*summit* MT-8
Nyack Ranger Station—*locale* MT-8
Nyack Ranger Station Barn and Fire Cache—*hist pl* MT-8
Nyac Storage Bldg—*building* AK-9
**Nyala**—*pop pl* NV-8
*Nya Sweirges Elf* DE-2
*Nyaur* PW-9
Nyberg—*locale* CO-8
Nyberg Creek—*stream* OR-9
Nyberg Island—*island* MN-6
Nyborg Pond—*reservoir* AZ-5
Nyce Cabin—*locale* AZ-5
Nyce Farm—*hist pl* PA-2
Nyce Lake—*lake* AZ-5
Nyce Lake—*reservoir* PA-2
Nyctea Hills—*summit* AK-9
Nydeck Cem—*cemetery* TN-4
Nydegger Run—*stream* MD-2
Nydiver Lakes—*lake* CA-9
Nye—*locale* MT-8
Nye—*locale* OR-9
Nye—*locale* TX-5
Nye—*locale* WV-2
**Nye**—*pop pl* OR-9
**Nye**—*pop pl* WI-6
Nye, Clark, House—*hist pl* WI-6
Nye, Gov. James W., Mansion—*hist pl* NV-8
Nye, James, House—*hist pl* ID-8
Nye Beach—*beach* OR-9
Nye Block—*hist pl* VT-1
Nye Bog—*lake* ME-1
Nye Bog—*swamp* MA-1
Nye Bog Reservoir Dam—*dam* MA-1
Nye Bog Rsvr—*reservoir* MA-1
Nye Branch—*stream* PA-2
Nye Brook—*stream* (2) MA-1
Nye Canyon—*valley* (2) NV-8
Nye Cem—*cemetery* IN-6
Nye Cem—*cemetery* MT-8
Nye Cem—*cemetery* NC-3
Nye Cem—*cemetery* OH-6
Nye Chapel—*church* IL-6
Nye Chapel—*church* IN-6
Nye County—*civil* NV-8
*Nye County Airport* NV-8
Nye County Courthouse—*hist pl* NV-8
Nye County Mercantile Company Bldg—*hist pl* NV-8
Nye Cove—*bay* VA-3
Nye Creek—*stream* (3) CA-9
Nye Creek—*stream* (3) MT-8
Nye Creek—*stream* (5) OR-9
Nye Creek—*stream* WA-9
Nye Creek—*stream* WI-6
Nye Drain—*stream* MI-6
Nye Family House—*building* MA-1
Nye-Holman State For—*forest* CT-1
Nye House—*hist pl* NE-7
Nye Lake—*lake* AK-9
Nye Ledge—*rock* MA-1
Nye Meadows—*flat* CA-9
Nye Mine—*mine* NV-8
*Nye Mountain* MA-1
Nye Mtn—*summit* NY-2
*Nye Neck* MA-1
Nye Park—*park* FL-3
Nye Pond—*lake* (2) MA-1
Nye Pond Dam Number One—*dam* NC-3
Nye Pond Number One—*reservoir* NC-3
Nye Post Office (historical)—*building* TN-4
Nye Ranch—*locale* OR-9
Nye Ridge—*ridge* MO-7
*Nye River* VA-3
*Nyerwi Ki* AZ-5
Nye Sch—*school* MT-8
Nye Sch—*school* TX-5
**Nyes Corner**—*pop pl* ME-1
*Nyes Ledge* MA-1
Nyes Neck—*cape* (2) MA-1
*Nyes Point* MA-1
Nyes Point—*cape* MA-1
*Nyes Pond* MA-1

Nye Spring—*spring* .......... CA-9
Nye Spring—*spring* .......... OR-9
Nyes Swamp—*swamp* .......... VT-1
**Nyesville**—*pop pl* .......... IN-6
**Nyesville**—*pop pl* .......... PA-2
Nye Valley Sch—*school* .......... WV-2
Nygaard Duckpond Dam—*dam* .......... SD-7
Nygaard Leaky Dam—*dam* .......... SD-7
Nygaard Slough—*lake* .......... ND-7
Nygaard Trout Dam—*dam* .......... SD-7
Nygren Dam—*dam* .......... ND-7
Nygren Rsvr—*reservoir* .......... OR-9
Nyhart—*locale* .......... MO-7
Nyhart Ditch—*canal* .......... MT-8
**Nyland**—*pop pl* .......... CA-9
Nylanda Ch—*church* .......... MN-6
**Nyland Acres**—*pop pl* .......... CA-9
Nylanden Creek—*stream* .......... WY-8
Nylen And Gillespie Ranch—*locale* .......... WY-8
Nylon Peak—*summit* .......... WY-8
**Nyman**—*pop pl* .......... IA-7
Nyman, John, House—*hist pl* .......... MI-6
Nyman Lake—*reservoir* .......... KS-7
Nyman Lake Dam—*dam* .......... KS-7
Nyman Peninsula—*cape* .......... AK-9
*Nymans Cave* .......... AL-4
Nyman Spit—*bar* .......... AK-9
*Nymore* .......... MN-6
Nymore Cem—*cemetery* .......... MN-6
**Nymph**—*pop pl* .......... AL-4
Nymphia Lake—*lake* .......... WI-6
*Nymphia Pond* .......... WI-6
Nymph Lake—*lake* .......... CO-8
Nymph Lake—*lake* .......... WY-8
Nyona Lake—*lake* .......... IN-6
**Nyona Lake**—*pop pl* .......... IN-6
Nyota—*locale* .......... AL-4
Nyota Mine (surface)—*mine* .......... AL-4
Nyota Mine (underground)—*mine* .......... AL-4
Nyphaea Lake—*lake* .......... MT-8
Nyqist Coulee—*valley* .......... MN-6
Nyra (historical)—*locale* .......... KS-7
*Ny River* .......... VA-3
Nyroca Flats State Wildlife Mngmt Area—*park* .......... MN-6
NYS Armory—*hist pl* .......... NY-2
Nyskoga Cem—*cemetery* .......... MN-6
Nyson—*other* .......... GA-3
**Nyssa**—*pop pl* .......... MO-7
**Nyssa**—*pop pl* .......... OR-9
Nyssa (CCD)—*cens area* .......... OR-9
Nyssa Cem—*cemetery* .......... OR-9
Nyssa Drain—*canal* .......... OR-9
**Nyssa Heights**—*pop pl* .......... OR-9
Nyssens Lake—*lake* .......... MN-6
**Nysted**—*pop pl* .......... NE-7
Nystrom, Mount—*summit* .......... CO-8
Nystrom Mount—*summit* .......... WY-8
Nystrom Pond State—*reservoir* .......... CT-1
Nystrom Sch—*school* .......... CA-9
Nyswonger Mesa—*summit* .......... CO-8
Nyswonger Trail—*trail* .......... CO-8

# O

Oa FM-9
Oa—locale AS-9
**Oacoma**—pop pl SD-7
Oacoma Cem—cemetery SD-7
**Oacoma Township**—pop pl SD-7
Oaf Ranch ND-7
Oa Hafen FM-9
**Oahe**—pop pl SD-7
Oahe, Lake—reservoir ND-7
Oahe, Lake—reservoir SD-7
Oahe Chapel—hist pl SD-7
Oahe Dam—dam SD-7
Oahe Dam Reservoir ND-7
Oahe Damsite SD-7
Oahe Hills Country Club—locale SD-7
Oahe (historical)—locale SD-7
Oahe Mission (historical)—locale SD-7
Oahe Mission Rec Area—park SD-7
Oahe Post Office (historical)—building SD-7
Oahe Reservoir ND-7
Oahe 101 Orton School SD-7
O-A Hill—summit OR-9
Oahnke Airp—airport IN-6
Oahu—island HI-9
Oahu Country Club—other HI-9
Oahu Island—island NY-2
Oahu-Koolau HI-9
Oahu Point—cape HI-9
Oahu Prison—other HI-9
Oahu Railway and Land Company Right-of-Way—hist pl HI-9
Oaiwai—area HI-9
Oak (2) IN-6
Oak MI-6
Oak—cape NY-2
Oak—fmr MCD NE-7
Oak—locale IL-6
Oak—locale MI-6
Oak—locale OH-6
**Oak**—pop pl AL-4
**Oak**—pop pl FL-3
**Oak**—pop pl MO-7
**Oak**—pop pl NE-7
**Oak**—pop pl VA-3
Oak Acad—school GA-3
Oakachickan (historical)—locale MS-4
Oakachoy Covered Bridge—bridge AL-4
Oakachoy Creek—stream AL-4
**Oak Acres**—pop pl MD-2
**Oak Acres**—pop pl WV-2
Oak Acres Ch—church TN-4
**Oak Acres (subdivision)**—pop pl DE-2
**Oakahalla**—pop pl AL-4
Oakahatta Creek MS-4
Oakahay Creek MS-4
**Oakalla**—pop pl TX-5
Oakalla Covered Bridge—bridge IN-6
Oakalla Lake—reservoir IN-6
Oak Alley—locale LA-4
Oak Alley Plantation—hist pl LA-4
Oak Alley Plantation—locale LA-4
Oakander Drain—canal OR-9
Oak Arbor Sch—school MI-6
Oak Arbor Sch (historical)—school MO-7
Oakatazza Creek AL-4
**Oak at Wasatch Place Subdivision**—pop pl UT-8
Oak Ave Park—park FL-3
Oak Ave Playground—park CA-9
Oak Ave Sch—school (3) CA-9
Oak Ave Sch—school IL-6
Oak Ballroom—hist pl NE-7
Oak Bar—bar CA-9
Oak Barry Ch (historical)—church MS-4
Oak Basin—basin (2) UT-8
Oak Basin Canyon—valley UT-8
Oak Basin Draw—valley UT-8
Oak Bay—bay WA-9
Oak Bay (CCD)—cens area WA-9
Oak Bayou—gut (2) LA-4
Oak Bayou—gut TX-5
Oak Bayou—stream AL-4
Oak Bayou—stream AR-4
Oak Bayou—stream LA-4
Oak Bayou—stream MS-4
Oak Bay Park—park WA-9
**Oak Beach**—pop pl NY-2
Oak Beach County Park—locale MI-6
Oak Belt Trail—trail UT-8
Oak Bend—bend MS-4
Oak Bend Ch—church AR-4
Oak Bend Landing (historical)—locale MS-4
Oak Bend Upper Bar—bar MS-4
Oakbin Pond—lake GA-3
Oak Bluff AL-4
Oak Bluff—cliff MI-6
Oak Bluff—cliff TX-5
**Oakbluff**—pop pl LA-4
Oak Bluff Bayou—gut LA-4
Oak Bluff Memorial Park—park TX-5
**Oak Bluffs**—pop pl MA-1
Oak Bluff Sch (historical)—school AL-4
Oak Bluffs Ferry Slip Light—locale MA-1
Oak Bluffs Harbor—lake MA-1
Oak Bluffs North Breakwater Light—locale MA-1
**Oak Bluffs (Town of)**—pop pl MA-1
Oak Bluff (Township of)—fmr MCD AR-4
**Oakboro**—pop pl NC-3
Oakboro Cem—cemetery NC-3
Oakboro Sch—school NC-3
Oak Bottom—bend CA-9
Oak Bottom—bend UT-8
Oakbottom—locale PA-2
**Oak Bottom**—pop pl CA-9
Oak Bottom Campground—locale CA-9
Oak Bottom F S Station—locale CA-9
**Oakbourne**—pop pl PA-2
Oak Bowen Ch—church GA-3
Oak Bower AR-4
Oak Bower Ch—church AL-4
Oak Bower Ch—church (2) AR-4
Oakbowery AL-4
Oak Bowery—locale AL-4
Oak Bowery—locale MS-4
**Oak Bowery**—pop pl AL-4
Oak Bowery Cem—cemetery (3) AL-4
Oak Bowery Cemetery MS-4
Oak Bowery Ch—church (3) AL-4
Oak Bowery Ch—church AR-4
Oakbowery Ch—church MS-4
Oak Bowery Ch of Christ AL-4
Oak Bowery Female Institute (historical)—school AL-4
**Oak Bowery Heights (subdivision)**—pop pl AL-4
**Oak Bowery (historical)**—pop pl MS-4
Oak Bowery Methodist Church AL-4
Oak Bowery Missionary Baptist Church AL-4
Oak Bowery Primitive Baptist Church AL-4
Oak Bowery Sch (historical)—school MS-4
Oak Bowrey Ch—church AL-4
Oak Branch—stream FL-3
Oak Branch—stream IL-6
Oak Branch—stream KY-4
Oak Branch—stream (2) NC-3
Oak Branch—stream (3) TX-5
Oak Branch—stream WV-2
Oak Branch Ch—church TX-5
Oak Bridge—bridge NC-3
Oakbrook—locale OR-9
**Oak Brook**—pop pl IL-6
**Oakbrook**—pop pl NY-2
**Oakbrook**—pop pl PA-2
**Oakbrook**—pop pl WA-9
Oak Brook—stream (2) ME-1
Oakbrook Golf Course—locale PA-2
Oakbrook Plaza (Shop Ctr)—locale FL-3
Oakbrook Sch—school IL-6
Oakbrook Sch—school PA-2
Oakbrook Square (Shop Ctr)—post sta FL-3
**Oakbrook Terrace**—pop pl IL-6
Oak Brush Hill—summit CO-8
Oakbrush Ridge—ridge CO-8
Oakbur Junction—locale PA-2
**Oakbury**—pop pl MN-6
Oak Butte—summit AZ-5
Oak Cane Branch—stream GA-3
Oak Canon TX-5
Oak Canyon WY-8
Oak Canyon—stream WY-8
Oak Canyon—valley (4) AZ-5
Oak Canyon—valley (8) CA-9
Oak Canyon—valley NV-8
Oak Canyon—valley (7) NM-5
Oak Canyon—valley OR-9
Oak Canyon—valley TX-5
Oak Canyon—valley (4) UT-8
Oak Canyon Oil Field CA-9
Oak Canyon Tank—reservoir AZ-5
Oak Canyon Tank—reservoir NM-5
Oak Cave—cave AL-4
Oak Cem—cemetery AR-4
Oak Cem—cemetery IL-6
Oak Cem—cemetery ME-1
Oak Cem—cemetery MO-7
Oak Cem—cemetery NE-7
Oak Cem—cemetery PA-2
Oak Cem—cemetery TX-5
Oak Center—locale MN-6
**Oak Center**—pop pl WI-6
Oak Center Sch—school WI-6
Oak Center Shop Ctr—locale MS-4
Oak Ch—church AR-4
Oak Ch—church OH-6
Oak Chapel—church (2) GA-3
Oak Chapel—church IN-6
Oak Chapel—church MD-2
Oak Chapel—church (2) MO-7
Oak Chapel—church NC-3
Oak Chapel—church OK-5
Oak Chapel—church VA-3
Oak Chapel, The—church SC-3
Oak Chapel Cem—cemetery GA-3
Oak Chapel Sch—school IL-6
Oakchappo Creek MS-4
Oakchappo River AL-4
Oak Chewalla Creek—stream MS-4
Oakchia—locale AL-4
Oakchia Fire Tower (historical)—tower AL-4
Oakchia Landing (historical)—locale AL-4
Oakchia West Landing AL-4
Oakchi East Landing AL-4
Oakchihoola Branch AL-4
Oakchi Landing East (historical)—locale AL-4
Oakchi Landing West AL-4
Oakchinawa Creek AL-4
Oakchoys Old Town AL-4
**Oak City**—pop pl NC-3
**Oak City**—pop pl TN-4
**Oak City**—pop pl UT-8
Oak City Assembly of God Ch—church FL-3
Oak City Cem—cemetery GA-3
Oak City Cem—cemetery UT-8
Oak Cliff—locale TX-5
**Oak Cliff**—pop pl TX-5
Oak Cliff Cem—cemetery CT-1
Oak Cliff Cem—cemetery TX-5
Oak Cliff Country Club—other TX-5
Oak Cliff Lake—reservoir NC-3
Oak Cliff Lake Dam—dam NC-3
**Oakcliff Park Subdivision**—pop pl UT-8
**Oakcliff Park Subdivision Two**—pop pl UT-8
**Oakcliff Villas (subdivision)**—pop pl MS-4
Oak Corner—locale SC-3
**Oak Corner**—pop pl VA-3
Oak Corral—locale AZ-5
**Oak Court**—pop pl MD-2
Oak Cove—bay CA-9
Oak Cove—bay NC-3
Oak Cove—bay TX-5
Oak Cove—valley CA-9
Oak Cove Bridge—bridge TX-5
Oak Cove Creek CA-9
Oak Cove Creek—stream CA-9
Oak Cove Point—cape NC-3
Oak Creek AZ-5
Oak Creek CA-9
Oak Creek KS-7
Oak Creek NE-7
Oak Creek ND-7
Oak Creek OK-5
Oak Creek TX-5
Oak Creek WY-8
Oak Creek—bay MD-2
Oak Creek—locale AZ-5
**Oak Creek**—pop pl CO-8
**Oak Creek**—pop pl UT-8
**Oak Creek**—pop pl WI-6
Oak Creek—stream AL-4
Oak Creek—stream (13) AZ-5
Oak Creek—stream AR-4
Oak Creek—stream (7) CA-9
Oak Creek—stream (6) CO-8
Oak Creek—stream (5) FL-3
Oak Creek—stream IL-6
Oak Creek—stream (8) KS-7
Oak Creek—stream MN-6
Oak Creek—stream (12) NE-7
Oak Creek—stream NV-8
Oak Creek—stream (3) NM-5
Oak Creek—stream (2) NY-2
Oak Creek—stream (3) ND-7
Oak Creek—stream (3) OK-5
Oak Creek—stream (6) OR-9
Oak Creek—stream (4) SD-7
Oak Creek—stream (4) TX-5
Oak Creek—stream (7) UT-8
Oak Creek—stream (2) WA-9
Oak Creek—stream WV-2
Oak Creek—stream WI-6
Oak Creek—stream (3) WY-8
Oak Creek Airport AZ-5
Oak Creek Basin—basin WY-8
Oak Creek Bench—bench UT-8
Oak Creek Camp—locale CA-9
Oak Creek Campground UT-8
Oak Creek Campground—park UT-8
Oak Creek Canyon—valley AZ-5
Oak Creek Canyon—valley CA-9
Oak Creek Canyon—valley NV-8
Oak Creek Canyon—valley (2) UT-8
Oak Creek Canyon Natural Area—park AZ-5
Oak Creek Cem—cemetery FL-3
Oak Creek Cem—cemetery KS-7
Oak Creek Cem—cemetery (2) NE-7
Oak Creek Cem—cemetery ND-7
Oak Creek Cem—cemetery OR-9
Oak Creek Cem—cemetery WI-6
Oak Creek Ch—church KS-7
Oak Creek Ch—church TX-5
Oak Creek Ch—church WI-6
Oak Creek Dam—dam AZ-5
Oak Creek Dam—dam UT-8
Oak Creek Ditch—canal AZ-5
Oak Creek Ditch—canal AR-4
Oak Creek Ditch—canal CO-8
**Oak Creek Estates (subdivision)**—pop pl UT-8
**Oakcreek Estates Subdivision**—pop pl UT-8
Oak Creek Forest Camp—locale UT-8
**Oak Creek Hills Subdivision**—pop pl UT-8
Oak Creek Hist Dist—hist pl UT-8
**Oak Creek (historical)**—pop pl OR-9
Oak Creek Irrigation Canal—hist pl UT-8
Oak Creek Islands—island FL-3
Oak Creek JHS—school WI-6
Oak Creek Marsh—swamp FL-3
Oak Creek Mountain—locale AZ-5
Oak Creek Pass—gap CA-9
Oak Creek Picnic Grounds—locale CO-8
Oak Creek Point—summit UT-8
Oak Creek Ranch—locale (2) AZ-5
Oak Creek Ranger Station—building UT-8
**Oak Creek Residental Area**—pop pl UT-8
Oak Creek Ridge—ridge (2) UT-8
Oak Creek Rsvr—reservoir CO-8
Oak Creek Rsvr—reservoir TX-5
Oak Creek Rsvr—reservoir UT-8
Oak Creek Sch—school AZ-5
Oak Creek Sch—school (2) KS-7
Oak Creek Sch—school NE-7
Oak Creek Sch—school OH-6
Oak Creek Sch—school OR-9
Oak Creek Sinks—basin UT-8
Oak Creek Spring—spring AZ-5
Oak Creek Spring—spring NV-8
**Oak Creek (subdivision)**—pop pl MS-4
Oak Creek Tank—reservoir (2) AZ-5
Oak Creek (Town of)—other WI-6
Oak Creek Township—civ div NE-7
**Oak Creek Township**—pop pl (2) NE-7
**Oak Creek Township**—pop pl ND-7
Oak Creek Valley—valley OR-9
Oak Creek Vista Campground—park AZ-5
Oak Creek Well—well AZ-5
Oak Creek Wildlife Rec Area Hdqrs—park WA-9
**Oak Crest**—pop pl FL-3
**Oakcrest**—pop pl IN-6
**Oak Crest**—pop pl MD-2
**Oak Crest**—pop pl NC-3
**Oakcrest**—pop pl (2) VA-3
Oakcrest—post sta FL-3
Oakcrest Baptist Ch—church FL-3
Oakcrest Camp—locale TX-5
Oakcrest Camp—locale UT-8
Oakcrest Ch—church FL-3
Oak Crest Country Club—other IL-6
Oakcrest Country Club—other MD-2
Oakcrest Elem Sch—school FL-3
**Oakcrest Estates Subdivision**—pop pl UT-8
Oak Crest Farm Dam—dam OR-9
Oak Crest Farm Rsvr—reservoir OR-9
Oak Crest JHS—school CA-9
Oak Crest JHS—school TX-5
Oak Crest Manor Nursing Home—hospital TX-5
Oak Crest Park—park TX-5
**Oak Crest Park Addition Subdivision**—pop pl UT-8
Oak Crest RR Station—locale FL-3
Oakcrest Sch—school FL-3
Oak Crest Sch—school IL-6
Oak Crest Sch—school OK-5
**Oak Crest (subdivision)**—pop pl NC-3
**Oakcrest (subdivision)**—pop pl NC-3
**Oakcrest Subdivision**—pop pl (2) UT-8
**Oakcrest Towers**—pop pl MD-2
**Oak Crossing**—pop pl AL-4
Oak Dain Creek—stream TN-4
Oak Dain Sch—school TN-4
Oakdale IL-6
Oakdale IN-6
Oakdale MI-6
Oakdale MS-4
Oakdale OH-6
Oakdale WV-2
Oak Dale WI-6
Oakdale—CDP SC-3
Oakdale—hist pl PA-2
Oakdale—locale AL-4
Oakdale—locale DE-2
Oakdale—locale FL-3
Oakdale—locale KY-4
Oakdale—locale PA-2
Oakdale—locale TN-4
Oakdale—locale (2) TX-5
Oakdale—locale VA-3
**Oakdale**—pop pl AL-4
**Oakdale**—pop pl CA-9
**Oakdale**—pop pl CT-1
**Oakdale**—pop pl GA-3
**Oakdale**—pop pl IL-6
**Oakdale**—pop pl (2) IN-6
**Oakdale**—pop pl IA-7
**Oakdale**—pop pl (2) KY-4
**Oakdale**—pop pl (2) LA-4
**Oakdale**—pop pl ME-1
**Oakdale**—pop pl MD-2
**Oakdale**—pop pl (3) MA-1
**Oakdale**—pop pl MN-6
**Oakdale**—pop pl NE-7
**Oakdale**—pop pl NJ-2
**Oakdale**—pop pl (2) NY-2
**Oakdale**—pop pl (4) NC-3
**Oakdale**—pop pl ND-7
**Oakdale**—pop pl (3) OH-6
**Oakdale**—pop pl OR-9
**Oakdale**—pop pl (2) PA-2
**Oak Dale**—pop pl SC-3
**Oakdale**—pop pl (3) TN-4
**Oak Dale**—pop pl TN-4
**Oakdale**—pop pl TN-4
**Oakdale**—pop pl TX-5
**Oak Dale**—pop pl TX-5
**Oakdale**—pop pl WV-2
**Oakdale**—pop pl WI-6
Oakdale—uninc pl GA-3
Oakdale—uninc pl NY-2
**Oakdale Acres**—pop pl AL-4
Oakdale AHP Airp—airport PA-2
Oakdale Baptist Ch—church (2) AL-4
Oakdale Baptist Church MS-4
Oak Dale Baptist Church TN-4
Oakdale Borough—civil PA-2
Oak Dale Branch—stream MO-7
Oakdale Canyon—valley (2) CA-9
Oakdale (CCD)—cens area CA-9
Oakdale (CCD)—cens area KY-4
Oakdale (CCD)—cens area TN-4
Oakdale Cem—cemetery AL-4
Oakdale Cem—cemetery (2) FL-3
Oakdale Cem—cemetery (2) IL-6
Oakdale Cem—cemetery IN-6
Oakdale Cem—cemetery (3) IA-7
Oakdale Cem—cemetery (2) KS-7
Oakdale Cem—cemetery KY-4
Oakdale Cem—cemetery LA-4
Oakdale Cem—cemetery (2) ME-1
Oakdale Cem—cemetery (2) MA-1
Oakdale Cem—cemetery MI-6
Oakdale Cem—cemetery MN-6
Oakdale Cem—cemetery (3) MS-4
Oakdale Cem—cemetery MO-7
Oak Dale Cem—cemetery MO-7
Oakdale Cem—cemetery MO-7
Oakdale Cem—cemetery (2) NE-7
Oakdale Cem—cemetery (5) NC-3
Oakdale Cem—cemetery ND-7
Oakdale Cem—cemetery (4) OH-6
Oakdale Cem—cemetery (5) OK-5
Oakdale Cem—cemetery (2) PA-2
Oak Dale Cem—cemetery TX-5
Oakdale Cem—cemetery WV-2
Oakdale Cem—cemetery WI-6
Oak Dale Ch AL-4
Oakdale Ch—church (2) AL-4
Oakdale Ch—church AR-4
Oak Dale Ch—church FL-3
Oakdale Ch—church GA-3
Oak Dale Ch—church (2) GA-3
Oakdale Ch—church IL-6
Oakdale Ch—church IA-7
Oakdale Ch—church KY-4
Oakdale Ch—church (4) MS-4
Oakdale Ch—church MO-7
Oak Dale Ch—church (2) MO-7
Oakdale Ch—church (6) NC-3
Oak Dale Ch—church NC-3
Oakdale Ch—church OH-6
Oakdale Ch—church (4) OK-5
Oakdale Ch—church (2) PA-2
Oakdale Ch—church SC-3
Oak Dale Ch—church SC-3
Oakdale Ch—church (2) SC-3
Oakdale Ch—church (4) TN-4
Oak Dale Ch—church TX-5
Oakdale Ch—church (2) TX-5
Oak Dale Ch—church (2) VA-3
Oakdale Ch—church WV-2
Oakdale Ch (historical)—church MO-7
Oakdale Community Hall—locale OK-5
Oakdale Cotton Mill Village—hist pl NC-3
Oak Dale Cross Roads—locale NC-3
Oakdale Dam—dam IN-6
Oakdale District—hist pl KY-4
Oak Dale Ditch—canal CO-8
Oakdale Division—civil TN-4
Oakdale Elementary School AL-4
Oakdale Elem Sch—school IN-6
Oakdale Elem Sch—school KS-7
Oakdale Elem Sch—school NC-3
**Oakdale Farms**—pop pl VA-3
**Oakdale Farms (subdivision)**—pop pl NC-3
Oakdale First Baptist Ch—church TN-4
**Oakdale Forest (subdivision)**—pop pl NC-3
Oakdale Free Holiness Ch—church OK-5
Oakdale Gas And Oil Field—oilfield OK-5
Oakdale Heights Sch—school CA-9
Oakdale Hollow—valley OH-6
Oakdale HS—school TN-4
Oakdale Junction TN-4
Oak Dale Landing—locale LA-4
Oakdale Lateral—canal CA-9
**Oakdale Manor**—pop pl CT-1
**Oakdale Manor**—pop pl PA-2
Oakdale Memorial Park (Cemetery)—cemetery CA-9
Oakdale Methodist Ch—church AL-4
Oakdale Missionary Baptist Ch—church AL-4
Oakdale North Main Canal—canal CA-9
Oakdale Nursing Home—hospital AR-4
Oakdale Park—park IL-6
Oakdale Park—park IA-7
Oakdale Park—park KS-7
Oakdale Park—park WV-2
**Oakdale Park (subdivision)**—pop pl MS-4
Oakdale Playground—park FL-3
Oakdale Pond—lake CT-1
Oakdale Post Office—building TN-4
Oakdale Post Office (historical)—building TN-4
Oakdale Primitive Baptist Ch—church AL-4
Oak Dale Sch TN-4
Oakdale Sch—school (2) AL-4
Oakdale Sch—school AR-4
Oakdale Sch—school (4) CA-9
Oakdale Sch—school (5) IL-6
Oak Dale Sch—school IL-6
Oakdale Sch—school (3) IL-6
Oakdale Sch—school IA-7
Oakdale Sch—school KS-7
Oakdale Sch—school KY-4
Oakdale Sch—school MI-6
Oakdale Sch—school (3) MN-6
Oakdale Sch—school (3) MO-7
Oak Dale Sch—school MO-7
Oakdale Sch—school NE-7
Oakdale Sch—school NC-3
Oakdale Sch—school (2) OH-6
Oak Dale Sch—school OK-5
Oakdale Sch—school OK-5
Oakdale Sch—school (2) PA-2
Oakdale Sch—school SC-3
Oakdale Sch—school (2) SD-7
Oakdale Sch—school (2) TN-4
Oakdale Sch—school UT-8
Oakdale Sch—school WV-2
Oakdale Sch—school (3) WI-6
Oak Dale Sch (abandoned)—school MO-7
Oakdale Sch (abandoned)—school (2) PA-2
Oak Dale Sch (historical)—school AL-4
Oakdale Sch (historical)—school AL-4
Oak Dale Sch (historical)—school MO-7
Oakdale Sch (historical)—school MO-7
Oakdale Sch (historical)—school (2) TN-4
Oakdale School (historical)—locale MO-7
Oakdale Sch 8—school IA-7
Oakdale South Main Canal—canal CA-9
**Oakdale (sta.)**—pop pl GA-3
Oakdale Station NY-2
Oakdale Station—locale PA-2
**Oakdale (subdivision)**—pop pl AL-4
**Oak Dale (subdivision)**—pop pl AL-4
**Oakdale (subdivision)**—pop pl MA-1
**Oakdale (subdivision)**—pop pl (3) NC-3
**Oakdale (subdivision)**—pop pl TN-4
**Oakdale Subdivision**—pop pl (2) UT-8
Oakdale Tank—reservoir AZ-5
Oakdale Town & Country Park—park NC-3
**Oakdale (Town of)**—pop pl WI-6
Oak Dale Township—fmr MCD IA-7
**Oakdale Township**—pop pl NE-7
**Oakdale (Township of)**—pop pl IL-6
Oakdale United Methodist Ch—church AL-4
**Oakdale Village**—pop pl MA-1
**Oakdale Woods**—pop pl IL-6
Oakdale Yard—locale OH-6
Oak Dam—dam AZ-5
Oakdam (historical P.O.)—locale IN-6
Oak Dell—hist pl NJ-2
Oak Dell Ch—church MO-7
Oak Dell Sch (historical)—school PA-2
Oakden Canyon—valley ID-8
Oakdene—hist pl VA-3
Oakdene Place—hist pl GA-3
Oak Ditch—canal OH-6
Oak Ditch—canal TX-5
Oak Donnick Club House—locale AR-4
Oak Donnick Floodway—flat AR-4
Oak Donnick Gage—locale AR-4
Oak Drain—canal CA-9
Oak Draw—valley AZ-5
Oak Draw—valley CO-8
Oak Draw—valley TX-5
Oak Draw—valley UT-8
Oak Draw Water Well—well AZ-5
Oak Drive Ch—church AL-4
Oak Drive Sch—school NY-2
**Oak Drive (subdivision)**—pop pl DE-2
Oakel DE-2
Oakenwald Sch—school IL-6
**Oakeola (Horntown)**—pop pl PA-2
Oakerman Butte—summit OR-9
Oakerman Spring OR-9
Oaker Spring—spring AZ-5
Oakes LA-4
Oakes—locale NY-2
**Oakes**—pop pl ND-7
Oakes, Edward, House—hist pl MA-1
Oakes Bog—swamp ME-1
Oakes Cem—cemetery AR-4
Oakes Cem—cemetery KS-7
Oakes Cem—cemetery (2) TN-4
Oakes Cem—cemetery TX-5
Oakes Chapel—church AL-4
Oakes Chapel Ch AL-4
Oakes City ND-7
Oakes Corner—locale ME-1
Oakes Cove—bay MA-1
Oakes Creek—stream WA-9
**Oakesdale**—pop pl WA-9
Oakesdale Cem—cemetery WA-9
Oakes Ditch—canal CA-9
Oakes Estate—hist pl NJ-2
Oakes Golf Club—locale ND-7
Oakes Gulf—valley NH-1
Oakes Gulf Trail—trail NH-1
Oakes Hill—summit NY-2
Oakes Hollow—valley AL-4
Oakes Hotel Bldg—hist pl TX-5
Oakes Interchange—crossing ND-7
Oakes Junction ND-7
Oakes Knob—summit NC-3
Oakes Municipal Airp—airport ND-7
Oakes Natl Bank Block—hist pl ND-7
Oakes Nubble—summit ME-1
**Oakeson Villa Subdivision**—pop pl UT-8
Oakes Peak—summit WA-9
Oakes Pond—lake FL-3
Oakes Reservoir MA-1
Oakes Sch—school PA-2
Oakes Swamp—swamp PA-2
Oakes Tank—reservoir AZ-5
Oakes View Cem—cemetery ND-7
Oakes-Wood House—hist pl IA-7
Oakey Bay—locale SC-3
Oakey Branch—stream LA-4
Oakey Creek—stream GA-3
Oakey Grove Cem—cemetery NC-3
Oakey Grove Ch—church AL-4
Oakey Grove Ch—church GA-3
Oakey Grove Ch—church (2) NC-3
Oakey Knob—summit NC-3
Oakey Mountain Ch—church GA-3
Oakey Mtn—summit AL-4

Oakey Mtn—summit (5) GA-3
Oakey Point Cem—cemetery SC-3
Oakey Pond—swamp FL-3
Oakey Ridge—ridge TX-5
Oakey Ridge Church AL-4
Oakeys Brook—stream NJ-2
Oakey Streak Methodist Episcopal Church—hist pl AL-4
Oakey Swamp—stream SC-3
Oakey Top—summit GA-3
Oakey Woods Creek—stream MS-4
Oak Farm MS-4
Oak Farm (historical P.O.)—locale IN-6
**Oakfield**—pop pl GA-3
**Oakfield**—pop pl IA-7
**Oakfield**—pop pl ME-1
**Oakfield**—pop pl NY-2
**Oakfield**—pop pl (2) OH-6
**Oakfield**—pop pl TN-4
**Oakfield**—pop pl WI-6
Oakfield-Alabama Cem—cemetery NY-2
Oakfield Baptist Church TN-4
Oakfield Cem—cemetery IA-7
Oakfield Cem—cemetery ME-1
Oakfield Cem—cemetery MI-6
Oakfield Cem—cemetery NY-2
**Oakfield Center**—pop pl MI-6
Oakfield Ch—church MI-6
Oakfield Ch—church TN-4
Oakfield Hills—summit ME-1
Oakfield Post Office—building TN-4
Oakfield Rod and Gun Club—other NY-2
Oakfield Sch—school IL-6
Oakfield Sch (abandoned)—school MO-7
Oakfield Sch (historical)—school TN-4
Oakfield Station—hist pl ME-1
**Oakfield (Town of)**—pop pl ME-1
**Oakfield (Town of)**—pop pl NY-2
**Oakfield (Town of)**—pop pl WI-6
Oakfield Township—fmr MCD IA-7
**Oakfield (Township of)**—pop pl MI-6
Oak Flat CA-9
Oak Flat—flat (2) AZ-5
Oak Flat—flat (27) CA-9
Oak Flat—flat NV-8
Oak Flat—flat (4) OR-9
Oak Flat—flat (3) UT-8
Oak Flat—flat WA-9
Oak Flat—locale (2) TX-5
**Oak Flat**—pop pl TX-5
**Oak Flat**—pop pl WV-2
Oak Flat Campground—locale (2) CA-9
Oak Flat Campground—park AZ-5
Oak Flat Canyon—valley CA-9
Oak Flat Creek—stream (2) CA-9
Oak Flat Creek—stream OR-9
Oak Flat Creek—stream UT-8
Oak Flat Gulch—valley CA-9
Oak Flat (historical)—locale SD-7
Oak Flat Lookout—locale CA-9
Oak Flat Lookout—locale OR-9
Oak Flat Peak—summit CA-9
Oak Flat Ranch—locale CA-9
Oak Flats—flat (3) CA-9
Oak Flats—flat (2) OR-9
Oak Flats Branch—stream TN-4
Oak Flats Cem—cemetery OR-9
Oak Flat Sch—school PA-2
Oak Flat Spring—spring (2) AZ-5
Oak Flat Spring—spring CA-9
Oak Flats Ranch—locale CA-9
Oak Flat Tank—reservoir AZ-5
**Oakford**—pop pl IL-6
**Oakford**—pop pl IN-6
**Oakford**—pop pl PA-2
Oakford (Election Precinct)—fmr MCD IL-6
Oakford Lake—reservoir NJ-2
Oakford Lake Dam—dam NJ-2
Oakford Park—park PA-2
Oakford Pumping Station—locale PA-2
Oakford Sch—school WI-6
Oakforest IN-6
Oak Forest—locale KY-4
Oak Forest—locale NC-3
Oak Forest—locale (2) VA-3
**Oak Forest**—pop pl (2) AR-4
**Oak Forest**—pop pl IL-6
**Oak Forest**—pop pl IN-6
**Oak Forest**—pop pl LA-4
**Oak Forest**—pop pl MD-2
**Oak Forest**—pop pl NC-3
**Oak Forest**—pop pl PA-2
**Oak Forest**—pop pl TX-5
Oak Forest—post sta TX-5
Oak Forest—uninc pl SC-3
Oak Forest Acad—school LA-4
Oak Forest Baptist Ch—church MS-4
Oak Forest Cem—cemetery AR-4
Oak Forest Cem—cemetery MI-6
Oak Forest Cem—cemetery MS-4
Oak Forest Cem—cemetery (2) MO-7
Oak Forest Cem—cemetery NC-3
Oak Forest Ch—church AL-4
Oak Forest Ch—church IN-6
Oak Forest Ch—church (4) KY-4
Oak Forest Ch—church LA-4
Oak Forest Ch—church (3) MO-7
Oak Forest Ch—church (4) NC-3
Oak Forest Ch—church WV-2
Oak Forest Elementary School MS-4
**Oak Forest Estates (subdivision)**—pop pl DE-2
**Oak Forest Estates (subdivision)**—pop pl NC-3
Oak Forest (historical)—locale MS-4
Oak Forest Hosp—hospital IL-6
Oak Forest Memorial Gardens—cemetery TN-4
Oak Forest Park—park TX-5
Oak Forest Parkway—park TX-5
**Oak Forest (Roary)**—pop pl KY-4
Oak Forest Sanatorium—hospital WI-6
Oak Forest Sch—school (2) IL-6
Oak Forest Sch—school MS-4
Oak Forest Sch—school TX-5
Oak Forest Sch (historical)—school MS-4
Oak Forest Sch (historical)—school PA-2
**Oak Forest (subdivision)**—pop pl NC-3
**Oakforest (subdivision)**—pop pl NC-3
**Oak Forest Subdivision One**—pop pl UT-8
**Oak Forest Subdivision Two**—pop pl UT-8
Oak Forest (Township of)—fmr MCD AR-4
**Oak Forest (trailer park)**—pop pl DE-2
Oak Fork Campground—park OR-9
**Oak Forrest (subdivision)**—pop pl MS-4
Oakfuskee Bridge AL-4
Oakfuskee Council House (historical)—locale AL-4
Oakfuskee Creek AL-4
Oakfuskee (historical)—locale AL-4
Oakfuskee P.O. (historical)—locale AL-4
Oak Glade Ch—church OK-5
Oak Glen—hist pl RI-1
Oak Glen—locale CA-9
**Oak Glen**—pop pl CA-9
**Oakglen**—pop pl IL-6
**Oak Glen**—pop pl (2) NJ-2
Oak Glen Cem—cemetery NY-2
Oak Glen Conservation Camp—locale CA-9
Oak Glen Creek—stream CA-9
Oak Glen Divide Trail (Pack)—trail CA-9
Oak Glen Lake—reservoir IL-6
Oak Glenn Cem—cemetery TN-4
Oak Glenn Ch—church VA-3
Oak Glenn Union Cem—cemetery TN-4
Oak Glenn Union Ch (historical)—church TN-4
Oak Glen Nursing Home—hospital IL-6
Oakglen (Oak Glen) IL-6
Oak Glen (Oakglen) IL-6
**Oak Glen Park**—pop pl TX-5
Oak Glen Peak CA-9
Oak Glen Peak—summit CA-9
Oak Glens—area UT-8
Oak Glen Sch—school PA-2
Oak Glen Sch (historical)—school TN-4
Oak Glen State Wildlife Mngmt Area—park MN-6
Oak-Griner Baptist Ch—church FL-3
Oak-Griner Ch—church FL-3
Oak Griner Christian Sch—school FL-3
Oakgrove AL-4
Oakgrove DE-2
Oak Grove KY-4
Oakgrove MA-1
Oak Grove MS-4
Oak Grove NC-3
Oak Grove OK-5
Oak Grove OR-9
Oakgrove PA-2
Oakgrove TN-4
Oak Grove VA-3
Oak Grove WI-6
Oak Grove—CDP SC-3
Oak Grove—hist pl MD-2
Oak Grove—hist pl MS-4
Oak Grove—hist pl NC-3
Oak Grove—hist pl SC-3
Oak Grove—locale (6) AL-4
Oak Grove—locale AZ-5
Oak Grove—locale (5) AR-4
Oak Grove—locale (2) CA-9
Oak Grove—locale DE-2
Oak Grove—locale (2) FL-3
Oak Grove—locale (5) GA-3
Oak Grove—locale IA-7
Oak Grove—locale KY-4
Oak Grove—locale MD-2
Oak Grove—locale (3) MS-4
Oak Grove—locale NJ-2
Oak Grove—locale NM-5
Oak Grove—locale (3) NC-3
Oakgrove—locale NC-3
Oak Grove—locale OK-5
Oak Grove—locale OR-9
Oak Grove—locale (4) PA-2
Oakgrove—locale SC-3
Oak Grove—locale SC-3
Oak Grove—locale (11) TN-4
Oak Grove—locale (6) TX-5
Oak Grove—locale (4) VA-3
Oak Grove—locale (2) WV-2
**Oak Grove**—pop pl (7) AL-4
**Oak Grove**—pop pl (3) AR-4
**Oakgrove**—pop pl AR-4
**Oak Grove**—pop pl (3) AR-4
**Oakgrove**—pop pl AR-4
**Oak Grove**—pop pl (2) CA-9
**Oak Grove**—pop pl CO-8
**Oak Grove**—pop pl DE-2
**Oak Grove**—pop pl (4) FL-3
**Oak Grove**—pop pl (3) GA-3
**Oak Grove**—pop pl (2) IL-6
**Oak Grove**—pop pl (3) IN-6
**Oak Grove**—pop pl (6) LA-4
**Oak Grove**—pop pl (5) MI-6
**Oak Grove**—pop pl (2) MS-4
**Oak Grove**—pop pl (3) MO-7
**Oak Grove**—pop pl (3) NC-3
**Oakgrove**—pop pl NC-3
**Oak Grove**—pop pl (3) NC-3
**Oak Grove**—pop pl OH-6
**Oakgrove**—pop pl OH-6
**Oak Grove**—pop pl (3) OK-5
**Oak Grove**—pop pl (2) OR-9
**Oakgrove**—pop pl PA-2
**Oak Grove**—pop pl (2) PA-2
**Oakgrove**—pop pl PA-2
**Oak Grove**—pop pl PA-2
**Oak Grove**—pop pl (4) SC-3
**Oak Grove**—pop pl (10) TN-4
**Oakgrove**—pop pl TN-4
**Oak Grove**—pop pl (9) TN-4
**Oak Grove**—pop pl (2) TX-5
**Oak Grove**—pop pl (4) VA-3
**Oak Grove**—pop pl WI-6
Oak Grove—post sta GA-3
Oak Grove—uninc pl CA-9
Oak Grove—uninc pl DE-2
Oak Grove—woods CA-9
Oak Grove Academy MS-4
Oak Grove Acad (historical)—school (2) TN-4
Oak Grove Airfield NC-3
Oak Grove AME Church AL-4
Oak Grove Attendance Center—school MS-4
Oak Grove Baptist Ch TN-4
Oak Grove Baptist Ch—church (7) TN-4
Oak Grove Baptist Ch (historical)—church (2) TN-4
Oak Grove Baptist Church AL-4
Oak Grove Baptist Church MS-4
Oak Grove Branch—stream FL-3
Oak Grove Branch—stream GA-3
Oak Grove Bridge—bridge FL-3
Oak Grove Butte—summit OR-9
Oak Grove Butterfield Stage Station—hist pl CA-9
Oak Grove Campground—park UT-8
Oak Grove Canyon—valley (2) AZ-5
Oak Grove Canyon—valley CA-9
Oakgrove Canyon—valley CA-9
Oak Grove (CCD)—cens area GA-3
Oak Grove Cem AL-4
Oak Grove Cem TN-4
Oak Grove Cem—cemetery (16) AL-4
Oak Grove Cem—cemetery (19) AR-4
Oakgrove Cem—cemetery AR-4
Oak Grove Cem—cemetery AR-4
Oak Grove Cem—cemetery (2) CA-9
Oak Grove Cem—cemetery CT-1
Oak Grove Cem—cemetery (4) FL-3
Oak Grove Cem—cemetery (15) GA-3
Oak Grove Cem—cemetery (11) IL-6
Oak Grove Cem—cemetery (10) IN-6
Oak Grove Cem—cemetery (8) IA-7
Oak Grove Cem—cemetery (4) KS-7
Oak Grove Cem—cemetery (10) KY-4
Oak Grove Cem—cemetery (4) LA-4
Oak Grove Cem—cemetery (4) ME-1
Oak Grove Cem—cemetery MD-2
Oak Grove Cem—cemetery (9) MA-1
Oak Grove Cem—cemetery (16) MI-6
Oak Grove Cem—cemetery (12) MN-6
Oak Grove Cem—cemetery (28) MS-4
Oak Grove Cem—cemetery (17) MO-7
Oak Grove Cem—cemetery (2) NE-7
Oak Grove Cem—cemetery NJ-2
Oak Grove Cem—cemetery (2) NY-2
Oak Grove Cem—cemetery (8) NC-3
Oak Grove Cem—cemetery ND-7
Oak Grove Cem—cemetery (12) OH-6
Oak Grove Cem—cemetery (9) OK-5
Oak Grove Cem—cemetery OR-9
Oak Grove Cem—cemetery (6) PA-2
Oak Grove Cem—cemetery (2) SC-3
Oak Grove Cem—cemetery (21) TN-4
Oakgrove Cem—cemetery TN-4
Oak Grove Cem—cemetery (6) TN-4
Oak Grove Cem—cemetery (10) TX-5
Oak Grove Cem—cemetery (4) VA-3
Oak Grove Cem—cemetery (5) WV-2
Oak Grove Cem—cemetery (11) WI-6
Oak Grove Cemetery—hist pl (2) MA-1
Oak Grove Cemeterys—cemetery GA-3
Oak Grove Center Sch—school WI-6
Oak Grove Ch AL-4
Oak Grove Ch MS-4
Oak Grove Ch MO-7
Oakgrove Ch PA-2
Oak Grove Ch TN-4
Oak Grove Ch—church (77) AL-4
Oak Grove Ch—church (29) AR-4
Oakgrove Ch—church AR-4
Oak Grove Ch—church (6) AR-4
Oak Grove Ch—church (19) FL-3
Oak Grove Ch—church (12) GA-3
Oakgrove Ch—church GA-3
Oak Grove Ch—church (18) GA-3
Oakgrove Ch—church GA-3
Oak Grove Ch—church (36) GA-3
Oak Grove Ch—church (16) IL-6
Oak Grove Ch—church (20) IN-6
Oak Grove Ch—church (4) IA-7
Oak Grove Ch—church (30) KY-4
Oak Grove Ch—church (8) LA-4
Oakgrove Ch—church LA-4
Oak Grove Ch—church (13) LA-4
Oak Grove Ch—church (3) MD-2
Oak Grove Ch—church (2) MI-6
Oak Grove Ch—church MN-6
Oak Grove Ch—church (67) MS-4
Oak Grove Ch—church (27) MO-7
Oak Grove Ch—church NJ-2
Oak Grove Ch—church (71) NC-3
Oak Grove Ch—church (9) OH-6
Oak Grove Ch—church (9) OK-5
Oakgrove Ch—church OK-5
Oak Grove Ch—church (12) PA-2
Oak Grove Ch—church (23) SC-3
Oak Grove Ch—church (46) TN-4
Oak Grove Ch—church (23) TX-5
Oak Grove Ch—church (45) VA-3
Oak Grove Ch—church (15) WV-2
Oak Grove Ch (abandoned)—church MO-7
Oakgrove Ch (abandoned)—church PA-2
Oak Grove Chapel—church (2) MO-7
Oak Grove Chapel—church WV-2
Oak Grove Ch (historical)—church (4) AL-4
Oak Grove Ch (historical)—church (4) MS-4
Oak Grove Ch (historical)—church PA-2
Oak Grove Ch (historical)—church (6) TN-4
Oak Grove Ch No 2—church GA-3
Oak Grove Ch of Christ AL-4
Oak Grove Ch of Christ MS-4
Oak Grove Ch of Christ TN-4
Oak Grove Ch of Christ—church (3) TN-4
Oak Grove Ch of God—church FL-3
Oak Grove Church—locale AR-4
Oak Grove Church (abandoned)—building MO-7
Oak Grove CME Ch AL-4
Oak Grove Community Hall—building FL-3
Oak Grove Communtiy Hall (abandoned)—locale MO-7
**Oak Grove (corporate name for Oakgrove)**—pop pl AR-4
Oakgrove (corporate name Oak Grove) AR-4
Oak Grove Country Club—other TX-5
Oakgrove Creek GA-3
Oak Grove Creek—stream KY-4
Oak Grove Creek—stream NM-5
Oak Grove Crossroads School TN-4
Oak Grove Cumberland Presbyterian Ch TN-4
Oak Grove Cumberland Presbyterian Ch—church TN-4
Oak Grove Ditch—canal OR-9
Oak Grove East Sch (abandoned)—school MO-7
Oakgrove Elem Sch TN-4
Oak Grove Elem Sch—school KS-7
Oak Grove Elem Sch—school NC-3
Oak Grove Elem Sch—school (2) TN-4
**Oak Grove Estates**—pop pl AL-4
Oak Grove Fork Clackamas River—stream OR-9
Oak Grove Friends Ch—church IA-7
Oak Grove Friends Church TN-4
**Oak Grove Heights**—pop pl AR-4
**Oak Grove Heights**—pop pl MO-7
**Oak Grove Heights**—pop pl TN-4
Oak Grove (historical)—locale (2) AL-4
Oak Grove (historical)—locale MS-4
**Oak Grove (historical)**—pop pl MS-4
Oak Grove Holf Airp—airport NC-3
Oak Grove HS—school CA-9
Oak Grove HS—school ND-7
**Oak Grove Inn**—pop pl NC-3
Oak Grove Institute MS-4
Oak Grove Island—island GA-3
Oak Grove JHS—school FL-3
Oak Grove Lake—reservoir SC-3
Oak Grove Line Sch (historical)—school MS-4
Oak Grove Lookout Tower—locale AL-4
Oak Grove Memorial Ch—church LA-4
Oak Grove Memorial Gardens—cemetery MS-4
Oak Grove Memorial Gardens—cemetery NC-3
Oak Grove Memorial Park—cemetery TX-5
Oak Grove Methodist Church AL-4
Oak Grove Methodist Church MS-4
Oak Grove Methodist Church TN-4
Oak Grove Methodist Church—hist pl TN-4
Oak Grove Mine Lake—reservoir AL-4
Oak Grove Mine Lake Dam—dam AL-4
Oak Grove Mine (underground)—mine (2) AL-4
Oak Grove Mission—church AR-4
Oak Grove Missionary Baptist Church AL-4
Oak Grove Missionary Baptist Church MS-4
Oak Grove MS—school FL-3
Oak Grove Mtn—summit CO-8
Oak Grove Mtn—summit TN-4
Oak Grove Number 26 Sch (historical)—school AL-4
Oak Grove Number 29 Sch (historical)—school AL-4
Oak Grove Number 34 Sch (historical)—school AL-4
Oak Grove Park—other (2) IL-6
Oak Grove Park—park CA-9
Oak Grove Park—park FL-3
Oak Grove Park—park ND-7
Oak Grove Park—park TN-4
Oak Grove Park—park TX-5
**Oak Grove Park (subdivision)**—pop pl MS-4
Oak Grove Pentecostal Church AL-4
Oakgrove Picnic Area—locale MI-6
Oak Grove Post Office TN-4
Oak Grove Post Office (historical)—building AL-4
Oak Grove Post Office (historical)—building MS-4
Oakgrove Post Office (historical)—building (2) TN-4
Oak Grove Primitive Baptist Church AL-4
Oak Grove Primitive Baptist Church MS-4
Oak Grove Ranger Station—locale CA-9
Oak Grove Ranger Station—locale OR-9
Oak Grove Rec Area—park UT-8
Oak Grove Resort—locale MI-6
Oak Grove Ridge—ridge KY-4
Oak Grove Ridge—ridge LA-4
Oak Grove Ridge—ridge WV-2
**Oak Grove (RR name Thompsonville)**—pop pl KY-4
Oak Grove Safety Rest Area—locale OR-9
Oak Grove Sch MS-4
Oak Grove Sch TN-4
Oak Grove Sch—school (9) AL-4
Oak Grove Sch—school (7) AR-4
Oak Grove Sch—school CA-9
Oakgrove Sch—school CA-9
Oak Grove Sch—school (3) CA-9
Oak Grove Sch—school DE-2
Oak Grove Sch—school (5) FL-3
Oak Grove Sch—school (2) GA-3
Oak Grove Sch—school (22) IL-6
Oak Grove Sch—school (6) KS-7
Oak Grove Sch—school (5) KY-4
Oak Grove Sch—school LA-4
Oak Grove Sch—school MD-2
Oak Grove Sch—school MA-1
Oak Grove Sch—school (4) MI-6
Oak Grove Sch—school (5) MN-6
Oak Grove Sch—school (6) MS-4
Oak Grove Sch—school (23) MO-7
Oak Grove Sch—school (5) NC-3
Oak Grove Sch—school (2) OH-6
Oak Grove Sch—school (4) OK-5
Oak Grove Sch—school (4) OR-9
Oakgrove Sch—school PA-2
Oak Grove Sch—school (7) PA-2
Oak Grove Sch—school SC-3
Oakgrove Sch—school SC-3
Oak Grove Sch—school (11) SC-3
Oak Grove Sch—school (10) TN-4
Oak Grove Sch—school (4) TX-5
Oak Grove Sch—school (8) VA-3
Oak Grove Sch—school (3) WV-2
Oak Grove Sch—school (12) WI-6
Oak Grove Sch (abandoned)—school (11) MO-7
Oakgrove Sch (abandoned)—school MO-7
Oakgrove Sch (abandoned)—school PA-2
Oak Grove Sch (abandoned)—school (13) PA-2
Oak Grove Sch Annex—school VA-3
Oak Grove Sch (historical)—school (18) AL-4
Oak Grove Sch (historical)—school (16) MS-4
Oak Grove Sch (historical)—school (11) MO-7
Oakgrove Sch (historical)—school PA-2
Oak Grove Sch (historical)—school (3) PA-2
Oak Grove Sch (historical)—school (29) TN-4
Oakgrove Sch (historical)—school TN-4
Oak Grove Sch (historical)—school TN-4
Oak Grove School—locale MI-6
Oak Grove School—locale OK-5
Oak Grove School (Aban'd)—locale CA-9
Oak Grove School (Abandoned)—locale GA-3
Oak Grove School (abandoned)—locale MO-7
Oak Grove School (Abandoned)—locale MO-7
Oak Grove School (Abandoned)—locale TX-5
Oak Grove School (historical)—locale (7) MO-7
Oak Grove Schoolhouse—hist pl OR-9
Oak Grove Second Ch—church AL-4
Oak Grove Seminary—school ME-1
Oak Grove Shool (historical)—school MS-4
Oak Grove Spring—spring AZ-5
Oak Grove Stage Station Historical Marker—other CA-9
Oak Grove State Game Area—park MI-6
Oak Grove State Park—park IA-7
**Oak Grove (subdivision)**—pop pl AL-4
**Oak Grove (subdivision)**—pop pl MA-1
**Oak Grove (subdivision)**—pop pl (2) NC-3
Oak Grove Substation—locale MD-2
Oak Grove Tank—reservoir (3) AZ-5
**Oak Grove (Thompsonville Station)**—pop pl KY-4
Oak Grove Tower (fire tower)—tower FL-3
**Oak Grove (Town of)**—pop pl (3) WI-6
Oak Grove (Township of)—fmr MCD AR-4
Oak Grove (Township of)—fmr MCD NC-3
**Oak Grove (Township of)**—pop pl IN-6
**Oak Grove (Township of)**—pop pl MN-6
Oak Grove Trail—trail UT-8
**Oak Grove (Trailer Court)**—pop pl IL-6
Oak Grove Truck Trail—trail CA-9
Oak Grove Union Sch—school CA-9
Oak Grove Union Sch—school PA-2
Oak Grove United Methodist Ch—church MS-4
Oak Grove United Pentecostal Ch MS-4
Oak Grove Valley—valley CA-9
**Oak Grove Village**—pop pl MA-1
Oak Grove West Sch—school IL-6
Oak Grove 6th Sch—school TN-4
Oak Gulch—valley CA-9
Oak Gulch—valley CO-8
Oak Gulch—valley ND-7
Oak Gulch—valley OR-9
Oak Gulch—valley SD-7
**Oak Gulch Township**—pop pl SD-7
Oak Habor—uninc pl FL-3
Oak Hall—hist pl LA-4
Oak Hall—hist pl TN-4
Oak Hall—locale VA-3
**Oakhall**—pop pl MI-6
**Oak Hall**—pop pl PA-2
**Oak Hall**—pop pl WI-6
Oak Hall Bend—bend CA-9
Oak Hall Cem—cemetery WI-6
Oak Hall Ch—church VA-3
Oak Hall Hist Dist—hist pl PA-2
Oak Hall Mills PA-2
Oak Hall Sch—school PA-2
Oak Hall Sch (historical)—school TN-4
Oakham—hist pl TN-4
**Oakham**—pop pl MA-1
Oakham Center Cem—cemetery MA-1
Oakham Centre MA-1
Oak Hammock—island FL-3
Oak Hammock—island MD-2
Oak Hammock—island NC-3
**Oak Hampton**—pop pl TN-4
Oakham State For—forest MA-1
**Oakham (Town of)**—pop pl MA-1
Oak Harbor—bay WA-9
**Oak Harbor**—pop pl FL-3
**Oak Harbor**—pop pl OH-6
**Oak Harbor**—pop pl WA-9
Oak Harbor Air Park Airp—airport WA-9
Oak Harbor Ch—church OH-6
Oak Harbor HS—school WA-9
Oak Harbor JHS—school WA-9
Oak Harbor Sch—school WA-9
**Oakhaven**—pop pl AR-4
Oakhaven—uninc pl TN-4
**Oak Haven Acres**—pop pl TN-4
Oak Haven Acres Dock—locale TN-4
Oak Haven Cem—cemetery MO-7
Oakhaven Cem—cemetery NC-3
Oakhaven Ch—church TN-4
Oak Haven Heights Ch—church TX-5
Oak Haven Home—building TX-5
Oakhaven HS—school TN-4
Oakhaven Park—park TN-4
Oakhaven Park—park TX-5
**Oakhaven Park Subdivision**—pop pl UT-8
**Oak Haven (subdivision)**—pop pl FL-3
**Oakhaven Village Subdivision**—pop pl UT-8
Oak Head—cliff WA-9
Oak Head—summit MA-1
Oak Head—swamp FL-3
Oak Head Drain—stream GA-3
Oak Heights Ch—church AL-4
Oak Heights Sch—school OR-9
Oakherst Place Concrete Block District—hist pl MO-7
Oak Hill AL-4
Oakhill (2) KS-7
Oak Hill ME-1
Oak Hill MS-4
Oak Hill NJ-2
Oak Hill OR-9
Oak Hill PA-2
Oakhill TN-4
Oak Hill—hist pl KY-4
Oakhill—hist pl MI-6
Oak Hill—hist pl NY-2
Oak Hill—hist pl OH-6
Oak Hill—hist pl (4) VA-3
Oak Hill—island DE-2
Oak Hill—locale (2) AR-4
Oak Hill—locale (3) GA-3
Oak Hill—locale ME-1
Oakhill—locale MO-7
Oak Hill—locale NY-2
Oak Hill—locale OH-6
Oak Hill—locale OK-5
Oak Hill—locale PA-2
Oak Hill—locale (7) TN-4
Oak Hill—locale (2) TX-5
Oak Hill—locale (2) VA-3
Oak Hill—locale (3) WV-2
**Oak Hill**—pop pl AL-4
**Oakhill**—pop pl AL-4
**Oak Hill**—pop pl AL-4
**Oak Hill**—pop pl DE-2
**Oak Hill**—pop pl (2) FL-3
**Oak Hill**—pop pl IL-6
**Oak Hill**—pop pl IN-6
**Oak Hill**—pop pl KS-7
**Oak Hill**—pop pl (2) KY-4
**Oak Hill**—pop pl (3) ME-1
**Oak Hill**—pop pl MI-6
**Oakhill**—pop pl MN-6
**Oak Hill**—pop pl MS-4
**Oak Hill**—pop pl MO-7
**Oak Hill**—pop pl (3) NJ-2
**Oak Hill**—pop pl NY-2
**Oak Hill**—pop pl (6) NC-3
**Oak Hill**—pop pl OH-6
**Oak Hill**—pop pl (5) PA-2
**Oak Hill**—pop pl SC-3
**Oak Hill**—pop pl (6) TN-4
**Oak Hill**—pop pl (2) TX-5
**Oak Hill**—pop pl (4) VA-3
**Oak Hill**—pop pl WV-2
**Oak Hill**—pop pl WI-6
Oak Hill—ridge MA-1
Oak Hill—ridge NH-1
Oak Hill—summit AL-4
Oak Hill—summit (4) AZ-5
Oak Hill—summit (3) CO-8
Oak Hill—summit (29) ME-1
Oak Hill—summit MD-2
Oak Hill—summit (12) MA-1
Oak Hill—summit MI-6
Oak Hill—summit (14) NH-1
Oak Hill—summit (18) NY-2
Oak Hill—summit (2) OR-9
Oak Hill—summit (8) PA-2
Oak Hill—summit (2) RI-1
Oak Hill—summit TN-4
Oak Hill—summit TX-5
Oak Hill—summit (9) VT-1
Oak Hill—summit VA-3
Oak Hill—summit WA-9
Oak Hill—summit WV-2
Oak Hill Acad—school MS-4
Oak Hill Airstrip—airport OR-9
Oak Hill Baptist Ch TN-4
Oak Hill Baptist Ch—church FL-3
Oak Hill Baptist Ch—church TN-4
Oak Hill Baptist Church AL-4
Oak Hill Baptist Church MS-4
Oak Hill Baptist Church of Christ MS-4
Oak Hill Baptist of Christ MS-4
Oak Hill Branch—stream AL-4
Oak Hill Branch—stream MS-4
Oak Hill Branch—stream TN-4
Oakhill Breaker (historical)—building PA-2
Oak Hill Brook—stream MA-1
Oak Hill Cem—cemetery (2) AL-4
Oakhill Cem—cemetery AL-4
Oak Hill Cem—cemetery (7) AL-4
Oak Hill Cem—cemetery (3) AR-4
Oak Hill Cem—cemetery (2) CA-9
Oak Hill Cem—cemetery CT-1
Oak Hill Cem—cemetery DC-2
Oak Hill Cem—cemetery (5) FL-3
Oak Hill Cem—cemetery (5) GA-3
Oak Hill Cem—cemetery (12) IL-6
Oak Hill Cem—cemetery (8) IN-6
Oakhill Cem—cemetery IA-7
Oak Hill Cem—cemetery (9) IA-7
Oakhill Cem—cemetery IA-7
Oak Hill Cem—cemetery (9) IA-7
Oak Hill Cem—cemetery (10) KS-7
Oak Hill Cem—cemetery KY-4
Oak Hill Cem—cemetery LA-4
Oak Hill Cem—cemetery (6) ME-1
Oak Hill Cem—cemetery MD-2
Oak Hill Cem—cemetery (4) MA-1
Oak Hill Cem—cemetery (6) MI-6
Oakhill Cem—cemetery MI-6
Oak Hill Cem—cemetery MI-6
Oak Hill Cem—cemetery (14) MN-6
Oak Hill Cem—cemetery (5) MS-4
Oak Hill Cem—cemetery (6) MO-7
Oak Hill Cem—cemetery NE-7
Oak Hill Cem—cemetery NH-1
Oak Hill Cem—cemetery NJ-2
Oak Hill Cem—cemetery (8) NY-2
Oak Hill Cem—cemetery (4) OH-6
Oak Hill Cem—cemetery (3) OK-5
Oak Hill Cem—cemetery OR-9
Oak Hill Cem—cemetery (8) PA-2
Oak Hill Cem—cemetery (12) TN-4
Oak Hill Cem—cemetery (10) TX-5
Oak Hill Cem—cemetery (2) VT-1
Oak Hill Cem—cemetery (5) VA-3
Oak Hill Cem—cemetery (3) WV-2
Oak Hill Cem—cemetery (17) WI-6
Oak Hill Cemetery AL-4
Oak Hill Cemetery—hist pl AL-4
Oak Hill Cemetery Chapel—hist pl DC-2
Oakhill Ch AL-4
Oak Hill Ch—church (5) AL-4
Oakhill Ch—church AL-4
Oak Hill Ch—church (3) AL-4
Oak Hill Ch—church (5) AR-4
Oak Hill Ch—church (3) FL-3
Oak Hill Ch—church (10) GA-3
Oak Hill Ch—church (2) IL-6
Oak Hill Ch—church IN-6
Oak Hill Ch—church IA-7
Oak Hill Ch—church (5) KY-4
Oak Hill Ch—church (3) LA-4
Oak Hill Ch—church MD-2
Oak Hill Ch—church (11) MS-4
Oak Hill Ch—church (6) MO-7
Oak Hill Ch—church (2) NY-2
Oak Hill Ch—church (3) NC-3
Oak Hill Ch—church (2) OK-5
Oak Hill Ch—church PA-2
Oak Hill Ch—church (3) SC-3
Oak Hill Ch—church (11) TN-4
Oak Hill Ch—church (5) TX-5
Oak Hill Ch—church (6) VA-3
Oakhill Chapel AL-4
Oak Hill Chapel—church ME-1
Oak Hill Ch (historical)—church MS-4
Oak Hill Ch (historical)—church MO-7
Oak Hill Ch of Christ (historical)—church AL-4
Oak Hill Ch of the Nazarene—church FL-3
Oak Hill Christian Sch (historical)—school MS-4
Oak Hill Cliff—cliff ME-1
Oakhill Colliery (historical)—mine PA-2
Oak Hill Community Hosp—hospital FL-3
Oak Hill Conservation Club—other IN-6
Oak Hill Corner—locale VA-3

Oaklane Sch—school IL-6
Oak Lane Sch—school NC-3
Oaklane Station—building PA-2
**Oak Lane Subdivision**—pop pl UT-8
Oaklasausa Creek AL-4
Oaklasausa Sandy Creek AL-4
Oak Lateral—canal CA-9
Oaklawn IL-6
Oak Lawn LA-4
Oaklawn RI-1
Oak Lawn—hist pl MD-2
Oak Lawn—hist pl NC-3
Oak Lawn—hist pl VA-3
Oaklawn—locale (2) GA-3
Oaklawn—locale MS-4
Oaklawn—locale OR-9
**Oak Lawn**—pop pl AL-4
**Oak Lawn**—pop pl IL-6
**Oaklawn**—pop pl KS-7
**Oaklawn**—pop pl (2) LA-4
**Oaklawn**—pop pl MD-2
**Oaklawn**—pop pl MI-6
**Oaklawn**—pop pl RI-1
**Oaklawn**—pop pl TN-4
Oak Lawn—post sta (2) TX-5
Oaklawn—uninc pl AR-4
**Oaklawn Addition (subdivision)**—pop pl TN-4
Oaklawn Baptist Church TN-4
**Oaklawn Beechwood**—pop pl MI-6
Oaklawn Bridge and Waiting Station—hist pl CA-9
Oaklawn Canal—canal LA-4
Oaklawn Cem—cemetery AL-4
Oak Lawn Cem—cemetery AL-4
Oaklawn Cem—cemetery (4) AR-4
Oaklawn Cem—cemetery CT-1
Oaklawn Cem—cemetery (2) FL-3
Oak Lawn Cem—cemetery FL-3
Oaklawn Cem—cemetery FL-3
Oak Lawn Cem—cemetery GA-3
Oak Lawn Cem—cemetery (4) IL-6
Oaklawn Cem—cemetery (2) IN-6
Oak Lawn Cem—cemetery IN-6
Oak Lawn Cem—cemetery (2) IA-7
Oaklawn Cem—cemetery IA-7
Oak Lawn Cem—cemetery (2) IA-7
Oaklawn Cem—cemetery KS-7
Oaklawn Cem—cemetery LA-4
Oaklawn Cem—cemetery ME-1
Oaklawn Cem—cemetery MD-2
Oaklawn Cem—cemetery (2) MI-6
Oak Lawn Cem—cemetery MI-6
Oaklawn Cem—cemetery MI-6
Oak Lawn Cem—cemetery (2) MN-6
Oaklawn Cem—cemetery (2) MS-4
Oak Lawn Cem—cemetery MS-4
Oaklawn Cem—cemetery MO-7
Oak Lawn Cem—cemetery MO-7
Oaklawn Cem—cemetery (2) MO-7
Oaklawn Cem—cemetery NJ-2
Oak Lawn Cem—cemetery NY-2
Oaklawn Cem—cemetery (2) NY-2
Oak Lawn Cem—cemetery NC-3
Oaklawn Cem—cemetery NC-3
Oak Lawn Cem—cemetery ND-7
Oak Lawn Cem—cemetery OH-6
Oaklawn Cem—cemetery OH-6
Oaklawn Cem—cemetery (3) OK-5
Oak Lawn Cem—cemetery (2) PA-2
Oaklawn Cem—cemetery PA-2
Oak Lawn Cem—cemetery PA-2
Oaklawn Cem—cemetery TN-4
Oak Lawn Cem—cemetery (2) TX-5
Oaklawn Cem—cemetery (3) TX-5
Oaklawn Cem—cemetery VA-3
Oak Lawn Cem—cemetery VA-3
Oaklawn Cem—cemetery WI-6
Oak Lawn Cem—cemetery WI-6
Oaklawn Ch—church AR-4
Oak Lawn Ch—church GA-3
Oak Lawn Ch—church IA-7
Oaklawn Ch—church MI-6
Oak Lawn Ch—church NC-3
Oaklawn Ch—church (3) TN-4
Oaklawn Ch—church (3) TX-5
Oak Lawn Community Center—locale OK-5
Oaklawn Elem Sch—school IN-6
Oaklawn Elem Sch—school KS-7
Oaklawn Elem Sch—school NC-3
Oaklawn Farm—hist pl IL-6
Oaklawn Freewill Baptist Ch TN-4
**Oak Lawn (historical)**—pop pl NC-3
**Oaklawn (historical)**—pop pl OR-9
Oak Lawn HS—school IL-6
Oaklawn Manor—hist pl LA-4
Oaklawn Memorial Cem—cemetery TN-4
Oaklawn Memorial Ch—church GA-3
Oaklawn Memorial Gardens—cemetery NC-3
Oaklawn Memorial Gardens Cem—cemetery IN-6
Oaklawn Memorial Park—cemetery FL-3
Oaklawn Memorial Park—cemetery MS-4
Oaklawn Memorial Park—cemetery (2) TX-5
Oaklawn Memorial Park—cemetery (2) WV-2
Oak Lawn Memorial Park (cemetery)—cemetery OR-9
Oak Lawn Memory Gardens—cemetery VA-3
Oak Lawn Methodist Episcopal Church, South—hist pl TX-5
Oak Lawn Park—cemetery MS-4
Oak Lawn Park—park MI-6
Oaklawn Pet Cem—cemetery FL-3
Oaklawn Place Baptist Ch—church KS-7
Oaklawn Plantation—hist pl LA-4
Oak Lawn Plantation (historical)—locale AL-4
Oaklawn Prison Camp—locale SC-3
Oaklawn Racetrack—other AR-4
Oaklawn Sch—school AR-4
Oaklawn Sch—school IL-6
Oaklawn Sch—school LA-4
Oaklawn Sch—school NC-3
Oaklawn Sch—school TX-5
Oak Lawn Sch—school TX-5
Oaklawn Sch—school TX-5
Oak Lawn Sch—school WI-6
Oaklawn Sch—school WI-6
Oak Lawn Sch—school WI-6
Oaklawn Sch—school WI-6
Oaklawn School IN-6
Oak Lawn School (abandoned)—locale WI-6
**Oak Lawn (subdivision)**—pop pl NC-3
**Oaklawn (subdivision)**—pop pl TN-4
Oaklawn Terrace IN-6
**Oak Lawn (Township of)**—pop pl MN-6
Oak Lawn Village Hist Dist—hist pl RI-1
**Oak Leaf**—pop pl TX-5
Oakleaf Airfield—airport SD-7
Oak Leaf Bayou—gut AL-4
Oak Leaf Cem—cemetery MN-6
Oak Leaf Ch—church MS-4
Oak Leaf Country Club—other IL-6
Oak Leaf Grange Hall—locale MN-6
Oak Leaf Lake MI-6
Oakleaf Lake—lake MN-6
Oak Leaf Mine (underground)—mine AL-4
Oak Leaf Park—park MN-6
Oakleaf Park—uninc pl VA-3
Oak Leaf Sch—school IL-6
**Oak Leaf (subdivision)**—pop pl AL-4
**Oakleaf Subdivision**—pop pl UT-8
Oakle Bend—bend FL-3
Oak Ledge—bench VT-1
Oak Ledge—ridge ME-1
Oakledge Camp—locale FL-3
Oak Ledge Camp—locale ME-1
Oaklee River—stream AK-9
Oakleigh—hist pl AL-4
Oakleigh—locale MD-2
**Oakleigh**—pop pl PA-2
Oakleigh Cove—bay MD-2
Oakleigh Estates—uninc pl AL-4
**Oakleigh Estates (subdivision)**—pop pl AL-4
**Oakleigh Estates (subdivision)**—pop pl TN-4
**Oakleigh Forest**—pop pl MD-2
Oakleigh Garden Hist Dist—hist pl AL-4
Oakleigh JHS—school MI-6
**Oakleigh Manor**—pop pl MD-2
Oakleigh Mtn—summit MO-7
Oakleigh Sch—school MI-6
**Oaklette**—pop pl VA-3
Oak Level—locale AL-4
Oak Level—locale GA-3
Oak Level—locale VA-3
**Oak Level**—pop pl AL-4
**Oaklevel**—pop pl AL-4
**Oak Level**—pop pl AL-4
**Oak Level**—pop pl KY-4
**Oaklevel**—pop pl VA-3
**Oak Level**—pop pl VA-3
Oak Level Acad (historical)—school AL-4
Oak Level Branch—stream KY-4
Oak Level Cem—cemetery KY-4
Oak Level Cem—cemetery NC-3
Oak Level Ch—church AL-4
Oak Level Ch—church GA-3
Oak Level Ch—church (6) NC-3
Oak Level Ch—church (2) VA-3
Oak Level Heights Baptist Chruch—church FL-3
Oak Level (Township of)—fmr MCD NC-3
Oakley KY-4
Oakley OH-6
Oakley—hist pl TN-4
Oakley—hist pl VA-3
Oakley—locale AL-4
Oakley—locale DE-2
Oakley—locale KY-4
Oakley—locale LA-4
Oakley—locale PA-2
Oakley—locale VA-3
**Oakley**—pop pl CA-9
**Oakley**—pop pl ID-8
**Oakley**—pop pl IL-6
**Oakley**—pop pl IN-6
**Oakley**—pop pl IA-7
**Oakley**—pop pl KS-7
**Oakley**—pop pl (2) LA-4
**Oakley**—pop pl MD-2
**Oakley**—pop pl MI-6
**Oakley**—pop pl MS-4
**Oakley**—pop pl (2) NC-3
**Oakley**—pop pl OH-6
**Oakley**—pop pl SC-3
**Oakley**—pop pl TN-4
**Oakley**—pop pl UT-8
**Oakley**—pop pl VA-3
**Oakley**—pop pl WI-6
Oakley, George D., House—hist pl HI-9
Oakley, John, House—hist pl NY-2
Oakley, Violet, Studio—hist pl PA-2
Oakley Branch—stream IL-6
Oakley Branch—stream (3) TN-4
Oakley Branch—stream WI-6
Oakley Brick Ch—church IL-6
Oakley Canal—canal CA-9
Oakley Canyon—valley NV-8
Oakley Cave Branch—stream KY-4
Oakley Cem—cemetery KS-7
Oakley Cem—cemetery (2) KY-4
Oakley Cem—cemetery PA-2
Oakley Cem—cemetery (2) TN-4
Oakley Cem—cemetery UT-8
Oakley Ch—church AL-4
Oakley Ch—church LA-4
Oakley Ch—church MO-7
Oakley Ch—church NC-3
Oakley Ch—church PA-2
Oakley Ch—church VA-3
Oakley Chapel—church AR-4
Oakley Ch (historical)—church AL-4
Oakley Corners—locale NY-2
Oakley Corners State For—forest NY-2
Oakley Country Club—locale MA-1
Oakley Creek—stream KS-7
Oakley Creek—stream KY-4
Oakley Dam—dam ID-8
Oakley Depot SC-3
Oakley Ditch—canal IN-6
Oakley Draw—valley WY-8
Oakley Eide Number 1 Dam—dam SD-7
Oakley Eide Number 2 Dam—dam SD-7
Oakley Eide Number 3 Dam—dam SD-7
Oakley Elem Sch—school KS-7
Oakley Elem Sch—school NC-3
Oakley Gas Field—oilfield LA-4
Oakley Hall Sch—school SC-3
Oakley Hist Dist—hist pl ID-8
Oakley Hollow—valley KY-4
Oakley Hollow—valley MO-7
Oakley Hollow—valley TN-4
Oakley Home Ch—church KY-4
Oakley HS—school KS-7
Oakley JHS—school MS-4
Oakley Lake Dam—dam MS-4
Oakley Landing—locale LA-4
Oakley Landing—locale VA-3
Oakley Lookout—locale SC-3
Oakley Mill Branch—stream TN-4
Oakley Municipal Airp—airport KS-7
**Oakley (Oakley Training School)**—pop pl MS-4
Oakley Park—park IL-6
Oakley Park—park OH-6
**Oakley Park**—pop pl MI-6
Oakley-Parker Ditch—canal MT-8
Oakley Park Sch—school MI-6
**Oakley Park Subdivision**—pop pl UT-8
Oakley Plantation House—hist pl LA-4
Oakley Playground—park OH-6
Oakley Post Office (historical)—building MS-4
Oakley Post Office (historical)—building TN-4
Oakley Ranch—locale CA-9
Oakley Ranch—locale CO-8
Oakley Ranch—locale WY-8
Oakley Ridge—ridge NC-3
Oakley Sch—school CA-9
Oakley Sch—school WI-6
Oakley Springs Branch—stream AL-4
Oakley Square—locale OH-6
Oakley State Farm (historical)—locale MS-4
Oakley Street Park—park NC-3
**Oakley Subdivision North**—pop pl UT-8
**Oakley Subdivision South**—pop pl UT-8
**Oakley Township**—pop pl KS-7
**Oakley (Township of)**—pop pl IL-6
Oakley Training Sch—school MS-4
Oaklimetal (historical)—locale MS-4
Oaklimeter Creek—stream MS-4
Oaklimeter Watershed LT-8-12 Dam—dam MS-4
Oaklimeter Watershed LT 8-14 Dam—dam MS-4
Oaklimeter Watershed LT 8-16 Dam—dam MS-4
Oaklimeter Watershed LT-8-21 Dam—dam MS-4
Oaklimeter Watershed LT-8-35 Dam—dam MS-4
Oaklimeter Watershed LT 8-4—dam MS-4
Oaklimeter Watershed LT 8-5 Dam—dam MS-4
Oaklimeter Watershed LT 8-6 Dam—dam MS-4
Oakljmeter Creek MS-4
Oak Lodge—hist pl CT-1
Oak Lodge Ch—church OK-5
Oak Log Bayou—stream (2) AR-4
Oaklog Creek—stream AL-4
Oaklog Creek—stream KY-4
Oaklog Gap—gap NC-3
Oak Log Slough—gut AL-4
Oak Lookout Tower—locale MO-7
**Oaklyn**—pop pl NJ-2
**Oaklyn**—pop pl PA-2
**Oaklyn**—pop pl TN-4
Oaklyn Elem Sch—school PA-2
**Oaklyn Manor**—pop pl MD-2
Oak Lynn PA-2
**Oakman**—pop pl AL-4
**Oakman**—pop pl GA-3
**Oakman**—pop pl OK-5
Oakman (CCD)—cens area AL-4
Oakman Cem—cemetery AL-4
Oakman Cem—cemetery OK-5
Oakman Ch—church SC-3
Oakman Ch of Christ—church AL-4
Oakman Ch of God—church AL-4
Oakman Division—civil AL-4
Oakman Drift Mine (underground)—mine AL-4
Oakman Elem Sch—school AL-4
Oakman First Baptist Ch—church AL-4
**Oakman (historical)**—pop pl TN-4
Oakman HS—school AL-4
Oakman Methodist Ch—church AL-4
Oakman Mine AL-4
Oakman Mine (underground)—mine (2) AL-4
Oakman Number 2 Mine (surface)—mine AL-4
**Oak Manor**—pop pl LA-4
**Oak Manor**—pop pl PA-2
Oak Manor Sch—school CA-9
Oakman Pond—lake MA-1
Oakman Post Office—building AL-4
Oakman Sch—school (2) MI-6
Oakman Tunnel—tunnel TN-4
Oak Meadow Country Club—other MO-7
**Oak Meadows**—pop pl IL-6
Oak Meadows Park—park IL-6
Oak Meadows Park—park TX-5
**Oak Meadows (trailer park)**—pop pl DE-2
Oak Mesa—summit CO-8
Oak Mesa Mine—mine CA-9
Oak Mesa Reservoir CO-8
Oak Mill—locale NE-7
Oak Mill Hill—summit MS-4
**Oak Mills**—pop pl KS-7
Oak Mills Bend—bend KS-7
**Oakmont**—pop pl CA-9
**Oakmont**—pop pl MD-2
**Oakmont**—pop pl MO-7
**Oakmont**—pop pl (2) PA-2
**Oakmont**—pop pl (2) WV-2
Oakmont—uninc pl PA-2
**Oakmont Acres Subdivision**—pop pl UT-8
Oakmont Baptist Ch—church NC-3
Oakmont Borough—civil PA-2
Oakmont Cem—cemetery (2) PA-2
Oakmont Cem—cemetery TN-4
Oakmont Christian Ch—church AL-4
Oakmont Country Club—other CA-9
Oakmont Country Club Hist Dist—hist pl PA-2
Oakmont East Golf Course PA-2
Oakmont Elementary School TN-4
Oakmont Elem Sch—school PA-2
Oakmont Golf Course—other PA-2
Oakmont Heights Golf Course—other PA-2
Oakmont HS—school CA-9
Oakmont Memorial Park—cemetery CA-9
Oakmont Park—park AL-4
Oakmont Park—park OR-9
**Oakmont Park**—pop pl PA-2
Oakmont Presbyterian Ch—church AL-4
Oakmont Professional Plaza—building NC-3
Oakmont Regional HS—school MA-1
Oakmont Sch—school CA-9
Oakmont Sch—school FL-3
Oakmont Sch—school (2) TN-4
Oakmont School PA-2
**Oakmont (subdivision)**—pop pl DE-2
**Oakmont (subdivision)**—pop pl NC-3
**Oakmont (subdivision)**—pop pl PA-2
**Oakmont (subdivision)**—pop pl TN-4
Oakmont United Methodist Ch—church AL-4
Oakmont-Verona Cem—cemetery PA-2
Oakmoor—hist pl KY-4
Oakmoore Golf Course—other CA-9
Oak Moss Creek—stream CA-9
Oak Mound Bayou—gut LA-4
Oak Mound Cem—cemetery CA-9
Oak Mound Cem—cemetery (2) IL-6
Oak Mound Cem—cemetery MO-7
Oak Mound Cem—cemetery WI-6
Oak Mound Sch—school MN-6
Oak Mound Sch (abandoned)—school MO-7
Oak Mound School (abandoned)—locale MO-7
Oak Mound School (historical)—locale MO-7
Oak Mountain—locale (2) GA-3
Oak Mountain—ridge AL-4
Oak Mountain—ridge AR-4
Oak Mountain Acad—school GA-3
Oak Mountain Branch—stream VA-3
Oak Mountain Ch—church AL-4
**Oak Mountain (Cleola)**—pop pl GA-3
Oak Mountain Estates AL-4
Oak Mountain Lake—reservoir AL-4
Oak Mountain Lake Dam Number One—dam AL-4
Oak Mountain Lake Dam Number Two—dam AL-4
Oak Mountain New Lake Dam—dam AL-4
Oak Mountain Old Lake Dam—dam AL-4
Oak Mountain Public Lake AL-4
Oak Mountain Spring—spring GA-3
Oak Mountain State Park—park AL-4
Oak Mountain Tunnel—tunnel AL-4
Oakmount State Park AL-4
**Oakmount (subdivision)**—pop pl NC-3
Oak Mtn AL-4
Oak Mtn NY-2
Oak Mtn NC-3
Oak Mtn—summit (2) AL-4
Oak Mtn—summit AR-4
Oak Mtn—summit (5) CA-9
Oak Mtn—summit GA-3
Oak Mtn—summit (2) ME-1
Oak Mtn—summit MO-7
Oak Mtn—summit NH-1
Oak Mtn—summit (2) NY-2
Oak Mtn—summit NC-3
Oak Mtn—summit OR-9
Oakmuglee Creek AL-4
Oakmulgee—locale AL-4
Oakmulgee Creek—stream AL-4
Oak Mulgee Meeting House (historical)—church AL-4
Oakmulgee Post Office (historical)—building AL-4
Oakmulgee Wildlife Mngmt Area—park AL-4
Oak Narrows—channel MN-6
Oak Neck Beach—beach NY-2
Oak Neck Cem—cemetery MA-1
Oak Neck Creek—gut NY-2
Oak Neck Point—cape NY-2
Oaknolia—locale LA-4
Oaknoxaby River AL-4
Oak n' Spruce Village—park MA-1
Oakochappa River AL-4
Oakochappa River MS-4
Oakohay Cem—cemetery MS-4
Oakohay Creek—stream MS-4
Oak Opening Creek—stream CA-9
Oak Openings Park—park OH-6
Oak Orchard—locale NY-2
**Oak Orchard**—pop pl DE-2
**Oak Orchard**—pop pl (2) MD-2
**Oak Orchard**—pop pl NY-2
**Oak Orchard**—pop pl WI-6
Oak Orchard Beach—locale NY-2
Oak Orchard Cem—cemetery NY-2
Oak Orchard Creek—stream NY-2
Oak Orchard Creek State Game Ref—park NY-2
Oak Orchard Swamp—swamp NY-2
**Oak Orchard West (trailer park)**—pop pl DE-2
Oak Park IA-7
Oak Park MI-6
Oak Park MN-6
Oak Park—locale FL-3
Oakpark—locale VA-3
Oak Park—locale VA-3
Oak Park—locale WI-6
Oak Park—park AL-4
Oak Park—park (4) CA-9
Oak Park—park FL-3
Oak Park—park IA-7
Oak Park—park KS-7
Oak Park—park (3) MI-6
Oak Park—park (2) MO-7
Oak Park—park NE-7
Oak Park—park ND-7
**Oak Park**—pop pl (2) AL-4
**Oak Park**—pop pl AR-4
**Oak Park**—pop pl (2) CA-9
**Oak Park**—pop pl FL-3
**Oak Park**—pop pl GA-3
**Oak Park**—pop pl IL-6
**Oak Park**—pop pl IN-6
**Oak Park**—pop pl (2) MD-2
**Oak Park**—pop pl (2) MI-6
**Oak Park**—pop pl (2) MN-6
**Oak Park**—pop pl (2) NC-3
**Oak Park**—pop pl OH-6
**Oak Park**—pop pl OR-9
**Oak Park**—pop pl (2) PA-2
**Oak Park**—pop pl TN-4
**Oak Park**—pop pl TX-5
**Oak Park**—pop pl WA-9
**Oak Park**—pop pl WV-2
Oak Park—post sta NC-3
Oak Park—uninc pl AR-4
Oak Park—uninc pl LA-4
Oak Park—uninc pl TN-4
Oak Park Acad—school IA-7
Oak Park Baptist Ch—church (3) AL-4
Oak Park Baptist Ch—church FL-3
Oak Park Baptist Ch—church IN-6
Oak Park (CCD)—cens area GA-3
Oak Park Cem—cemetery CA-9
Oak Park Cem—cemetery FL-3
Oak Park Cem—cemetery GA-3
Oak Park Cem—cemetery (2) IN-6
Oak Park Cem—cemetery MN-6
Oak Park Cem—cemetery OK-5
Oak Park Cem—cemetery PA-2
Oak Park Cem—cemetery TX-5
Oak Park Ch—church FL-3
Oak Park Ch—church GA-3
Oak Park Ch—church IN-6
Oak Park Ch—church (4) MN-6
Oak Park Ch—church TX-5
Oak Park Community Hosp—hospital CA-9
Oak Park Country Club—other IL-6
Oak Park Elementary School MS-4
Oakpark Elem Sch—school FL-3
Oak Park Elem Sch—school FL-3
Oak Park Elem Sch—school PA-2
**Oak Park Estates**—pop pl TN-4
**Oak Park Estates (subdivision)**—pop pl SD-7
Oak Park Golf Club—locale PA-2
**Oak Park Heights**—pop pl MN-6
Oak Park Heights Sch—school MN-6
**Oak Park (historical)**—pop pl OR-9
Oak Park Hosp—hospital CA-9
Oak Park Hosp—hospital IL-6
Oak Park HS—school MO-7
Oak Park Junior High School DE-2
Oak Park Lookout Tower—locale GA-3
Oak Park Middle School AL-4
Oak Park Playground—park AL-4
Oak Park Playground—park CA-9
Oak Park Plaza (Shop Ctr)—locale FL-3
Oak Park Presbyterian Ch—church AL-4
Oak Park Reservoir UT-8
Oak Park Sch—school (2) AL-4
Oak Park Sch—school AR-4
Oak Park Sch—school (2) CA-9
Oak Park Sch—school FL-3
Oak Park Sch—school IL-6
Oak Park Sch—school IA-7
Oak Park Sch—school (2) LA-4
Oak Park Sch—school (2) MI-6
Oak Park Sch—school MS-4
Oak Park Sch—school (2) OK-5
Oak Park Sch—school TX-5
Oak Park Sch—school (3) WI-6
Oak Park Shop Ctr—locale AL-4
Oak Park Shop Ctr—locale KS-7
Oak Park Shop Ctr—locale ND-7
**Oak Park (subdivision)**—pop pl AL-4
**Oak Park (subdivision)**—pop pl NC-3
**Oak Park (subdivision)**—pop pl TN-4
**Oak Park (Township of)**—pop pl IL-6
**Oak Park (Township of)**—pop pl MN-6
**Oak Park Trailer Camp**—pop pl PA-2
Oak Park (Ventura County)—park CA-9
Oak Patch Lake—lake WA-9
Oak Patch Spring—spring UT-8
Oak Patch Wash—valley UT-8
Oak Peak—summit NM-5
Oak Pint Campground—locale IL-6
Oak Place Hosp—hospital TX-5
Oakplain TN-4
**Oakplain**—pop pl TN-4
Oak Plain Cem—cemetery MI-6
Oak Plain Cem—cemetery (2) MS-4
Oakplain Post Office (historical)—building TN-4
Oak Plain Presbyterian Church—hist pl NC-3
**Oak Plains**—pop pl TN-4
Oak Plains Ch—church NC-3
Oak Plaza Shop Ctr—locale MS-4
Oak Plaza (Shop Ctr)—locale NC-3
Oak Plaza Shop Ctr—locale TN-4
Oakpoint NY-2
Oakpoint OH-6
Oak Point—cape CT-1
Oak Point—cape (7) ME-1
Oak Point—cape MD-2
Oak Point—cape MI-6
Oak Point—cape (2) MN-6
Oak Point—cape (3) NY-2
Oak Point—cape WI-6
Oak Point—cliff LA-4
**Oak Point**—pop pl LA-4
**Oak Point**—pop pl MI-6
**Oak Point**—pop pl NY-2
**Oak Point**—pop pl TX-5
**Oak Point**—pop pl WA-9
Oak Point—summit CA-9
Oak Point—summit PA-2
Oak Point—uninc pl NY-2
**Oak Point Acres (subdivision)**—pop pl DE-2
Oak Point Cem—cemetery IA-7
Oak Point Creek—stream OR-9
Oak Point (historical)—locale SD-7
**Oak Point (historical)**—pop pl TN-4
Oak Point (historical P.O.)—locale IA-7
Oak Point Lake—lake MI-6
Oak Point Meadow—swamp ME-1
Oak Point Post Office (historical)—building TN-4
Oak Point Sch—school DE-2
Oak Point Sch—school VA-3
Oak Point Sch (abandoned)—school MO-7
Oak Point Sch (historical)—school TN-4
Oak Point Yard—locale NY-2
Oak Pond—lake DE-2
Oak Pond—lake (2) FL-3
Oak Pond—lake GA-3
Oak Pond—lake (2) ME-1
Oak Pond—lake NC-3
Oak Pond Branch—stream GA-3
Oak Port MI-6
**Oakport (Township of)**—pop pl MN-6
Oak Post Office IN-6
Oak Ranch—locale AZ-5
Oak Ranch—locale CA-9
Oak Ranch Creek—stream OR-9
Oak Ranch Pit—mine OR-9
Oak Ravine—valley CA-9
Oak Rest Cem—cemetery TX-5
Oak Ridge AL-4
Oak Ridge (2) AZ-5
Oak Ridge ME-1
Oak Ridge MI-6
Oakridge PA-2
Oak Ridge—CDP FL-3
Oakridge—hist pl VA-3
Oak Ridge—locale (2) KY-4
Oakridge—locale MN-6
Oak Ridge—locale MO-7
Oak Ridge—locale NJ-2
Oak Ridge—locale NC-3
Oak Ridge—locale PA-2
Oakridge—locale TN-4
Oak Ridge—locale TX-5
Oak Ridge—locale VA-3
Oakridge—locale WI-6
**Oak Ridge**—pop pl (2) AL-4
**Oakridge**—pop pl CO-8
**Oak Ridge**—pop pl FL-3
**Oak Ridge**—pop pl IL-6
**Oak Ridge**—pop pl KY-4
**Oak Ridge**—pop pl LA-4
**Oak Ridge**—pop pl ME-1
**Oak Ridge**—pop pl MD-2
**Oak Ridge**—pop pl MI-6
**Oak Ridge**—pop pl MN-6
**Oak Ridge**—pop pl MS-4
**Oak Ridge**—pop pl (3) MO-7
**Oak Ridge**—pop pl NJ-2
**Oak Ridge**—pop pl NY-2
**Oak Ridge**—pop pl NC-3
**Oak Ridge**—pop pl OH-6
**Oakridge**—pop pl (2) OK-5
**Oak Ridge**—pop pl OK-5
**Oakridge**—pop pl OR-9
**Oak Ridge**—pop pl PA-2
**Oakridge**—pop pl PA-2
**Oak Ridge**—pop pl (2) SC-3
**Oak Ridge**—pop pl TN-4
**Oak Ridge**—pop pl (4) TX-5
**Oak Ridge**—pop pl VA-3
**Oak Ridge**—pop pl WV-2
**Oakridge**—pop pl WI-6
Oak Ridge—ridge AL-4
Oak Ridge—ridge AR-4
Oak Ridge—ridge (12) CA-9
Oak Ridge—ridge (2) CO-8
Oak Ridge—ridge GA-3
Oak Ridge—ridge (2) IN-6
Oak Ridge—ridge KY-4
Oak Ridge—ridge (3) ME-1
Oak Ridge—ridge (2) MN-6
Oak Ridge—ridge MS-4
Oak Ridge—ridge MO-7
Oak Ridge—ridge NH-1
Oak Ridge—ridge (3) NY-2
Oak Ridge—ridge (2) NC-3
Oak Ridge—ridge (3) OR-9
Oak Ridge—ridge (3) PA-2
Oak Ridge—ridge UT-8
Oak Ridge—ridge VA-3
Oak Ridge—ridge (5) WI-6
Oakridge—uninc pl CA-9
Oakridge—uninc pl VA-3
Oak Ridge—uninc pl WV-2
**Oak Ridge Acres (subdivision)**—pop pl UT-8
Oak Ridge Airpark—airport TN-4
Oak Ridge Apartments—hist pl IL-6
Oak Ridge Associated University Hosp—hospital TN-4
Oak Ridge Baptist Ch—church FL-3
Oak Ridge Baptist Church AL-4
Oak Ridge Bay—swamp SC-3
Oak Ridge Branch LA-4
Oak Ridge Camp—locale CT-1
Oak Ridge Campground—locale VA-3
Oak Ridge Camping Area—park IN-6
Oak Ridge (CCD)—cens area GA-3
Oakridge (CCD)—cens area OR-9
Oak Ridge (CCD)—cens area (2) TN-4
Oak Ridge Cem—cemetery (2) AL-4
Oak Ridge Cem—cemetery (3) AR-4
Oak Ridge Cem—cemetery (6) FL-3
Oak Ridge Cem—cemetery GA-3
Oak Ridge Cem—cemetery (8) IL-6
Oak Ridge Cem—cemetery (4) IN-6
Oak Ridge Cem—cemetery (4) IA-7
Oak Ridge Cem—cemetery LA-4
Oak Ridge Cem—cemetery (2) MA-1
Oak Ridge Cem—cemetery (2) MI-6
Oakridge Cem—cemetery MI-6
Oak Ridge Cem—cemetery (2) MI-6
Oak Ridge Cem—cemetery (2) MN-6
Oak Ridge Cem—cemetery MS-4
Oakridge Cem—cemetery MS-4
Oak Ridge Cem—cemetery (2) MS-4
Oak Ridge Cem—cemetery (5) MO-7
Oak Ridge Cem—cemetery NE-7
Oak Ridge Cem—cemetery (3) NY-2
Oak Ridge Cem—cemetery (2) NC-3
Oak Ridge Cem—cemetery (2) OH-6
Oak Ridge Cem—cemetery (3) OK-5
Oakridge Cem—cemetery OR-9
Oak Ridge Cem—cemetery (2) PA-2
Oak Ridge Cem—cemetery SC-3
Oak Ridge Cem—cemetery SD-7
Oak Ridge Cem—cemetery TN-4
Oak Ridge Cem—cemetery VA-3
Oak Ridge Cem—cemetery (5) WI-6
Oak Ridge Ch MS-4
Oakridge Ch TN-4
Oak Ridge Ch—church (5) AL-4
Oak Ridge Ch—church (2) AR-4
Oak Ridge Ch—church (4) GA-3
Oak Ridge Ch—church (3) IN-6
Oak Ridge Ch—church (5) KY-4
Oak Ridge Ch—church (3) LA-4
Oak Ridge Ch—church (2) MN-6
Oak Ridge Ch—church (10) MS-4
Oak Ridge Ch—church (9) MO-7
Oakridge Ch—church MO-7
Oak Ridge Ch—church (10) NC-3
Oak Ridge Ch—church OH-6
Oak Ridge Ch—church (3) OK-5
Oak Ridge Ch—church SC-3

Oak Ridge Ch—church TN-4
Oak Ridge Ch—church (3) TX-5
Oak Ridge Ch—church (4) VA-3
Oak Ridge Ch—church WV-2
Oak Ridge Ch—church WI-6
Oak Ridge Ch of Christ MS-4
Oakridge Christian Ch—church MS-4
Oak Ridge Church (historical)—locale MO-7
Oak Ridge Civic Center—building TN-4
Oak Ridge Country Club—other MN-6
Oak Ridge Country Club—other NJ-2
**Oakridge Country Club Estates Subdivision A**—pop pl UT-8
**Oakridge Country Club Estates Subdivision A-W**—pop pl UT-8
**Oakridge Country Club Estates Subdivision Three**—pop pl UT-8
Oak Ridge Creek MN-6
Oak Ridge Division—civil (2) TN-4
Oak Ridge Elem Sch—school NC-3
**Oakridge Estates**—pop pl VA-3
Oakridge Estates—uninc pl VA-3
**Oakridge Estates (subdivision)**—pop pl MS-4
**Oakridge Farms Subdivision**—pop pl UT-8
Oak Ridge Fire Tower—locale WI-6
Oak Ridge First Baptist Ch—church TN-4
Oak Ridge Golf and Country Club—locale TN-4
Oak Ridge Golf Club—other CA-9
Oak Ridge Golf Course—other MI-6
Oak Ridge Hall Sch (historical)—school MS-4
Oak Ridge Health Care Center—hospital TN-4
**Oakridge Heights Subdivision**—pop pl UT-8
**Oakridge Highlands Subdivision**—pop pl UT-8
**Oak Ridge (historical)**—pop pl MS-4
Oak Ridge HS—school FL-3
Oakridge HS—school MI-6
Oak Ridge HS—school TN-4
Oakridge JHS—school MI-6
Oak Ridge Lake NJ-2
Oak Ridge Lake—lake OR-9
Oak Ridge Lake—lake WI-6
Oak Ridge Lake—reservoir NJ-2
**Oak Ridge Lake (Woodstock)**—pop pl NJ-2
Oak Ridge Lookout Tower—locale MS-4
**Oakridge Manor (subdivision)**—pop pl UT-8
Oak Ridge Memorial Cem—cemetery NC-3
Oak Ridge Memorial Park—cemetery TN-4
Oak Ridge Memory Gardens—cemetery MO-7
Oak Ridge Military Acad Hist Dist—hist pl NC-3
Oak Ridge Municipal Marina—locale TN-4
Oak Ridge Municipal Park—park TN-4
**Oak Ridge North**—pop pl TX-5
Oakridge Oil Field CA-9
Oak Ridge Park MI-6
**Oak Ridge Park**—pop pl AL-4
**Oak Ridge Park**—pop pl LA-4
**Oak Ridge Park**—pop pl NC-3
Oak Ridge Park Ditch—canal CO-8
Oak Ridge Park School—locale MI-6
**Oak Ridge Park (subdivision)**—pop pl FL-3
Oak Ridge Picnic Ground—locale UT-8
**Oakridge Place Subdivision**—pop pl UT-8
Oak Ridge Plantation (historical)—locale MS-4
Oak Ridge Plaza (Shop Ctr)—locale FL-3
Oak Ridge Post Office—building TN-4
Oak Ridge Presbyterian Church MS-4
Oak Ridge Primitive Baptist Church MS-4
Oak Ridge Public Use Area—park KS-7
Oak Ridge Quarry—mine CA-9
Oak Ridge Rec Area—park OK-5
Oak Ridge Reservoir Dam—dam NJ-2
Oak Ridge RR Overpass—hist pl VA-3
Oakridge RR Station—locale FL-3
Oak Ridge Rsvr—reservoir NJ-2
Oakridge Sanitarium—hospital TX-5
Oak Ridge Sch AL-4
Oak Ridge Sch—school AL-4
Oak Ridge Sch—school AR-4
Oak Ridge Sch—school CA-9
Oak Ridge Sch—school FL-3
Oakridge Sch—school FL-3
Oakridge Sch—school (2) IL-6
Oak Ridge Sch—school (9) IL-6
Oak Ridge Sch—school KS-7
Oak Ridge Sch—school (4) KY-4
Oakridge Sch—school MI-6
Oak Ridge Sch—school (6) MO-7
Oak Ridge Sch—school NC-3
Oak Ridge Sch—school (2) OK-5
Oakridge Sch—school OK-5
Oakridge Sch—school OR-9
Oak Ridge Sch—school (2) SC-3
Oakridge Sch—school SC-3
Oak Ridge Sch—school (2) TX-5
Oakridge Sch—school UT-8
Oak Ridge Sch—school VA-3
Oak Ridge Sch—school WV-2
Oak Ridge Sch—school (3) WI-6
Oak Ridge Sch (abandoned)—school (8) MO-7
Oak Ridge Sch (historical)—school AL-4
Oak Ridge Sch (historical)—school (8) MS-4
Oak Ridge Sch (historical)—school (6) MO-7
Oakridge Sch (historical)—school TN-4
Oak Ridge School MS-4
Oak Ridge School (Abandoned)—locale MO-7
Oak Ridge School (historical)—locale MO-7
Oak Ridge Shop Ctr—locale TN-4
Oak Ridge Spring—spring UT-8
Oakridge State Airp—airport OR-9
Oak Ridge State Wildlife Mngmt Area—park MN-6
**Oak Ridge (subdivision)**—pop pl AL-4
**Oakridge (subdivision)**—pop pl MS-4
**Oak Ridge (subdivision)**—pop pl (2) NC-3
Oak Ridge Terrace Subdivision UT-8
**Oakridge Terrace Subdivision**—pop pl UT-8
Oak Ridge (Township of)—fmr MCD NC-3
Oak Ridge Trail—trail (4) PA-2
**Oakridge (Trailer Park)**—pop pl NY-2
**Oakridge Village Condominium**—pop pl UT-8
**Oakridge Village Subdivision**—pop pl UT-8
Oak Ridge Wash—valley AZ-5
Oak Ridge Yacht Club—locale TN-4
Oak Road Sch—school PA-2
Oak Rock—rock MA-1
Oak Rock County Park—park OR-9
Oak Rock Island Park—park OR-9
Oak Row—locale VA-3
Oak Rsvr—reservoir CO-8
Oakrum Ch—church VA-3
Oak Run CA-9
**Oak Run**—pop pl CA-9
**Oak Run**—pop pl IL-6
Oak Run—stream (2) IN-6
Oak Run—stream (2) OH-6
Oak Run—stream PA-2
Oak Run Creek—stream CA-9
**Oak Run (Township of)**—pop pl OH-6
Oakryn—locale PA-2
Oaks—locale KY-4
Oaks—locale LA-4
Oaks—locale MD-2
Oaks—locale MS-4
Oaks—locale NC-3
Oaks—locale TX-5
Oaks—other KY-4
**Oaks**—pop pl CA-9
**Oaks**—pop pl (2) KY-4
**Oaks**—pop pl MO-7
**Oaks**—pop pl OK-5
**Oaks**—pop pl OR-9
**Oaks**—pop pl PA-2
Oaks—uninc pl TX-5
Oaks, Lake Of The—reservoir KS-7
Oaks, The—area CA-9
Oaks, The—hist pl AL-4
Oaks, The—hist pl CA-9
Oaks, The—hist pl LA-4
Oaks, The—hist pl MS-4
Oaks, The—hist pl (2) SC-3
Oaks, The—hist pl VA-3
Oaks, The—locale DE-2
Oaks, The—locale (2) OR-9
Oaks, The—locale VA-3
**Oaks, The**—pop pl (3) CA-9
**Oaks, The**—pop pl MD-2
**Oaks, The**—pop pl VA-3
Oak Saint Yards—locale KY-4
Oaks and Reese Mine—mine CA-9
**Oaks at Mutton Hollow Subdivision, The**—pop pl UT-8
Oaksaukee Creek AL-4
Oaks Bay—bay LA-4
Oaks Bayou—gut LA-4
Oaks Bog—swamp ME-1
Oaks Bog Brook—stream ME-1
Oaks Camp, The OR-9
Oaks Canal—canal LA-4
Oaks Cave—cave TN-4
Oaks Cem—cemetery (2) OK-5
Oaks Cem—cemetery (2) TN-4
Oaks Cem—cemetery (2) TX-5
Oaks Cem—cemetery WI-6
Oaks Ch—church IA-7
Oaks Ch—church SC-3
Oak Sch—school (3) IL-6
Oak Sch—school MI-6
Oak Sch—school WI-6
Oak Sch (abandoned)—school MO-7
Oaks Chapel—church AL-4
Oaks Chapel Cem—cemetery TN-4
Oaks Chapel (historical)—church TN-4
Oak Sch of Learning—school FL-3
Oak School (Abandoned)—locale TX-5
Oaks Corner—locale MN-6
**Oaks Corners**—pop pl NY-2
Oaks Country Club—locale MS-4
Oaks Country Club—other OK-5
Oaks Country Club—other TX-5
Oaks Country Club, The—other KY-4
Oaks Creek SC-3
Oaks Creek—gut SC-3
Oaks Creek—stream NY-2
Oaks Creek—stream TX-5
Oaks Dam—dam PA-2
Oaks Drain—canal MI-6
Oaks Elementary School PA-2
Oaks Ferry (historical)—locale NC-3
**Oaks (Glenburnie Gardens)**—pop pl NC-3
Oaks Golf Course—other IA-7
Oak Shade—locale VA-3
**Oak Shade**—pop pl NJ-2
**Oakshade**—pop pl OH-6
**Oak Shade**—pop pl PA-2
**Oakshade**—pop pl VA-3
Oakshade Cem—cemetery IA-7
Oak Shade Ch—church TX-5
Oak Shade Ch—church (2) VA-3
Oak Shade Fire Tower—locale TX-5
**Oak Shade (Oakshade)**—pop pl OH-6
**Oak Shade Park**—pop pl MI-6
Oak Shade Post Office (historical)—building PA-2
**Oak Shades**—pop pl NJ-2
Oak Shade Sch—school MO-7
Oaks Hill—summit AR-4
**Oakshire Manor**—pop pl LA-4
Oaks Hotel—hist pl LA-4
Oakside—locale MO-7
Oakside Cem—cemetery FL-3
Oakside Cem—cemetery MN-6
Oakside Ch—church GA-3
Oakside Sch—school NY-2
Oakside Sch—school WI-6
Oaks II—hist pl MD-2
**Oaks II, The**—pop pl NC-3
Oaks Island—island SC-3
Oaks Knob—summit NC-3
Oaks Lake—lake MN-6
Oak Slope—slope CA-9
Oak Slush Creek—stream MS-4
Oaks Mall—locale FL-3
Oaks Mesa—summit NM-5
**Oaksmith Acres (subdivision)**—pop pl NC-3
Oaks Neck—cape ME-1
Oaks Overlook, The—locale VA-3
Oaks Park—flat UT-8
Oaks Park Campground—park UT-8
Oaks Park Dam—dam UT-8
Oaks Park Rsvr—reservoir UT-8
Oaks Picnic Area—locale CA-9
Oaks Plantation (historical), The—locale AL-4
Oaks Plaza (Shop Ctr)—locale FL-3
Oaks Pond—lake ME-1
Oaks Post Office (historical)—building MS-4
Oak Spring AZ-5
Oak Spring UT-8
Oak Spring—locale IA-7
Oak Spring—spring (29) AZ-5
Oak Spring—spring (5) CA-9
Oak Spring—spring MO-7
Oak Spring—spring (4) NV-8
Oak Spring—spring (7) NM-5
Oak Spring—spring (2) PA-2
Oak Spring—spring (3) TX-5
Oak Spring—spring (16) UT-8
Oak Spring—spring (3) WA-9
Oak Spring Branch—stream MO-7
Oak Spring Butte—summit NV-8
Oak Spring Canyon AZ-5
Oak Spring Canyon UT-8
Oak Spring Canyon—valley (3) AZ-5
Oak Spring Canyon—valley (2) CA-9
Oak Spring Canyon—valley (2) UT-8
Oak Spring Cem—cemetery PA-2
Oak Spring Ch—church NC-3
Oak Spring Ch—church SC-3
Oak Spring Church MS-4
Oak Spring Creek—stream NM-5
Oak Spring Creek—stream UT-8
Oak Spring Draw AZ-5
Oak Spring Draw—valley AZ-5
Oak Spring Draw Tank—reservoir AZ-5
Oak Spring Flat UT-8
Oak Spring Flat—flat UT-8
Oak Spring Hollow—valley (3) UT-8
Oak Spring Number Two—spring AZ-5
Oak Spring Ranch—locale CA-9
Oak Spring Ranch—locale UT-8
Oak Springs—locale AZ-5
**Oak Springs**—pop pl OR-9
Oak Springs—spring AZ-5
Oak Springs—spring CO-8
Oak Springs—spring NM-5
Oak Springs—spring TN-4
Oak Springs—spring (4) UT-8
Oak Springs Canyon—valley AZ-5
Oak Springs Canyon—valley (2) NM-5
Oak Springs Canyon—valley UT-8
Oak Springs Cem—cemetery MS-4
Oak Springs Ch—church MS-4
Oak Springs Ch—church NC-3
Oak Spring Sch—school SC-3
Oak Springs Creek—stream OR-9
Oak Springs Flat—flat UT-8
Oak Springs Hollow—valley UT-8
**Oak Springs (Oak Ridge)**—pop pl AZ-5
Oak Springs Ranch—locale CA-9
Oak Springs Rsvr—reservoir CA-9
Oak Springs Sch—school TX-5
Oak Springs Sch (historical)—school TN-4
Oak Springs Summit—gap NV-8
Oak Springs Tank—reservoir NM-5
Oak Spring Tank—reservoir (2) AZ-5
Oak Spring Trail (Pack)—trail CA-9
Oak Spring Valley—valley AZ-5
Oak Spring Valley—valley UT-8
Oak Spring Wash—stream NV-8
Oak Spring Wash—stream NM-5
Oak Spring Wash—valley AZ-5
**Oak Spring Woods**—pop pl IL-6
Oak Square Park—park MS-4
Oak Square Sch—hist pl MA-1
Oak Square Sch—school MA-1
Oaks Ranch—locale NM-5
Oaks Reef—bar ME-1
Oaks Ridge Golf Course—other WA-9
Oaks (RR name for Oak Park)—other MN-6
Oaks Run—stream MD-2
Oaks Sch—school (3) PA-2
Oaks Sch—school TN-4
Oaks School, The—school CA-9
**Oaks (subdivision), The**—pop pl (4) NC-3
**Oaks Subdivision, The**—pop pl UT-8
Oak Station Ch—church AL-4
Oak Stream—stream ME-1
Oak Street MN-6
Oak Street Baptist Ch—church AL-4
Oak Street Baptist Ch—church (3) TN-4
Oak Street JHS—school IA-7
Oak Street Sch—hist pl ME-1
Oak Street Sch—school AZ-5
Oak Street Sch—school CA-9
Oak Street Sch—school IL-6
Oak Street Sch—school (2) NY-2
Oak Street Sch—school (3) OH-6
Oaks Tunnel—mine NM-5
**Oak Summit**—pop pl MD-2
**Oak Summit**—pop pl NY-2
**Oak Summit**—pop pl PA-2
Oak Summit Sch—school NC-3
Oak Summit Sch (historical)—school MO-7
Oaksville SD-7
**Oaksville**—pop pl NY-2
Oak Swamp—swamp MA-1
Oak Swamp Brook—stream MA-1
Oak Swamp Creek—stream MS-4
Oak Swamp Reservoir Dam—dam RI-1
Oak Swamp Rsvr—reservoir RI-1
Oak Swamp Stream MA-1
**Oaks West (subdivision)**—pop pl NC-3
Oaks Windmill—locale CO-8
Oak Tank—reservoir (8) AZ-5
Oak Tank—reservoir NM-5
Oaktarsarsey Creek AL-4
Oaktasasi—stream AL-4
Oaktasasi Creek AL-4
Oak-tau-hau-zau-see Creek AL-4
Oak-taw Sar-seg Creek AL-4
Oaktazaza Creek AL-4
**Oak Terrace**—pop pl FL-3
**Oak Terrace**—pop pl ME-1
**Oak Terrace**—pop pl MN-6
Oak Terrace Country Club—bridge PA-2
Oak Terrace JHS—school LA-4
Oak Terrace Sch—school IL-6
Oak Terrace Sch—school SC-3
Oak Thicket Ranch—locale AZ-5
Oak Thicket Spring—spring AZ-5
**Oakthorpe**—pop pl OH-6
Oaktibbee Creek MS-4
Oaktibbeehaw River MS-4
Oak-tib-be Haw Creek MS-4
Oaktibee Creek MS-4
Oaktomie Post Office (historical)—building MS-4
Oakton—locale GA-3
Oakton—locale WV-2
**Oakton**—pop pl IL-6
**Oakton**—pop pl IA-7
**Oakton**—pop pl KY-4
**Oakton**—pop pl MO-7
**Oakton**—pop pl NC-3
**Oakton**—pop pl VA-3
Oakton Gables—hist pl IL-6
Oakton HS—school VA-3
Oakton Park—park IL-6
Oakton Rsvr—reservoir PA-2
Oakton Sch—school (3) IL-6
Oakton Sch—school VA-3
Oakton Township SD-7
Oak Top—hist pl TN-4
**Oaktown**—pop pl IN-6
Oak Township—fmr MCD IA-7
**Oak Township**—pop pl KS-7
**Oak (Township of)**—pop pl MN-6
Oak Tree—locale PA-2
Oaktree—locale VA-3
**Oak Tree**—pop pl NJ-2
**Oaktree**—pop pl VA-3
Oak Tree Acad—school FL-3
**Oaktree Apartments**—pop pl DE-2
Oak Tree Canyon—valley AZ-5
Oak Tree Cem—cemetery MA-1
Oak Tree Cottage—hist pl AL-4
**Oak Tree Crossroads**—pop pl IN-6
Oak Tree Dam—dam PA-2
Oak Tree Falls—falls NY-2
**Oaktree Hollow**—pop pl PA-2
Oak Tree Lake—reservoir PA-2
Oak Tree Landing—locale AL-4
Oaktree Plaza (Shop Ctr)—locale FL-3
Oak Tree Plaza (Shop Ctr)—locale FL-3
Oak Tree Sch—school NJ-2
Oak Tree Spring—spring CA-9
**Oak Tree (subdivision)**—pop pl TN-4
Oak Tree Windmill—well AZ-5
Oak Trough Tank—reservoir AZ-5
Oaktupa Creek AL-4
Oak Tuppa Creek MS-4
Oakum Cem—cemetery MN-6
Oakum Creek—stream VA-3
Oak Union Ch—church VA-3
Oakvale MS-4
Oakvale—locale MO-7
Oakvale—locale NY-2
**Oak Vale**—pop pl MS-4
**Oakvale**—pop pl SC-3
**Oakvale**—pop pl WV-2
**Oakvale Blvd**—pop pl PA-2
Oak Vale Cem—cemetery OK-5
Oak Vale Ch—church MS-4
Oakvale Ch—church (2) WV-2
Oakvale Methodist Ch MS-4
Oakvale (RR name for Oak Vale)—other MS-4
**Oak Vale (RR name Oakvale)**—pop pl MS-4
Oakvale Sch—school CA-9
Oakvale Sch (historical)—school MS-4
**Oakvale (subdivision)**—pop pl TN-4
Oak Valley—basin UT-8
Oak Valley—locale CA-9
Oak Valley—locale RI-1
**Oak Valley**—pop pl CA-9
**Oak Valley**—pop pl KS-7
**Oak Valley**—pop pl NJ-2
**Oak Valley**—pop pl TX-5
**Oak Valley**—pop pl VA-3
Oak Valley—valley CA-9
Oak Valley—valley NE-7
Oak Valley—valley WI-6
Oak Valley Cem—cemetery AR-4
Oak Valley Cem—cemetery IL-6
Oak Valley Cem—cemetery KS-7
Oak Valley Cem—cemetery MS-4
Oak Valley Ch—church (3) AL-4
Oak Valley Ch—church AR-4
Oak Valley Ch—church (2) IL-6
Oak Valley Ch—church KY-4
Oak Valley Ch—church MS-4
Oak Valley Ch—church OK-5
Oak Valley Ch—church TN-4
Oak Valley Ch—church (2) TX-5
Oak Valley Christian Church MS-4
Oak Valley Creek—stream (2) CA-9
**Oak Valley Estates**—pop pl VA-3
Oak Valley Guard Station—locale CA-9
Oak Valley (historical)—locale AL-4
Oak Valley Landing—locale MS-4
Oak Valley Sch—school IL-6
Oak Valley Sch—school (2) NE-7
Oak Valley Sch Number 1—school ND-7
Oak Valley Sch Number 2—school ND-7
**Oak Valley Township**—pop pl KS-7
**Oak Valley Township**—pop pl ND-7
**Oak Valley (Township of)**—pop pl MN-6
Oakview TN-4
Oakview—hist pl MS-4
Oakview—locale (2) TN-4
**Oak View**—pop pl CA-9
**Oakview**—pop pl MD-2
**Oak View**—pop pl MD-2
**Oakview**—pop pl MO-7
**Oakview**—pop pl NJ-2
**Oakview**—pop pl NC-3
**Oakview**—pop pl OH-6
**Oakview**—pop pl PA-2
**Oak View**—pop pl TN-4
**Oak View**—pop pl VA-3
Oakview Cem—cemetery AL-4
Oak View Cem—cemetery CO-8
Oak View Cem—cemetery GA-3
Oakview Cem—cemetery (2) GA-3
Oakview Cem—cemetery IL-6
Oak View Cem—cemetery IA-7
Oakview Cem—cemetery MI-6
Oak View Cem—cemetery (2) MN-6
Oakview Cem—cemetery NY-2
Oak View Cem—cemetery OK-5
Oakview Cem—cemetery OK-5
Oak View Cem—cemetery TN-4
Oakview Cem—cemetery TX-5
Oak View Cem—cemetery VA-3
Oakview Ch—church AR-4
Oakview Ch—church GA-3
Oak View Ch—church GA-3
Oakview Ch—church MI-6
Oak View Ch—church MS-4
Oak View Ch—church NC-3
Oakview Ch—church (2) NC-3
Oak View Ch—church NC-3
Oak View Ch—church PA-2
Oak View Ch—church TN-4
Oakview Ch—church TN-4
Oak View Ch—church VA-3
Oakview Ch—church VA-3
Oakview Christian Ch—church KS-7
Oak View Community Center—building TN-4
Oak View Country Club—other IL-6
Oakview Cumberland Presbyterian Ch (historical)—church TN-4
**Oak View Estates Subdivision**—pop pl UT-8
**Oakview Estates Subdivision Numbers 2,3 & 4**—pop pl UT-8
**Oakview Estates Subdivision #1**—pop pl UT-8
Oak View Farm—locale AR-4
**Oakview Heights (Barger Hill)**—pop pl WV-2
Oakview Heights Mission—church WV-2
**Oakview (historical)**—pop pl TN-4
Oakview JHS—school IL-6
Oakview Memorial Gardens—cemetery AL-4
Oakview Memorial Park—park TN-4
Oak View Memorial Park (Cemetery)—cemetery CA-9
**Oakview Park**—pop pl PA-2
Oakview Recreation Park—park TN-4
Oakview Sch—school CA-9
Oakview Sch—school KY-4
Oakview Sch—school MD-2
Oakview Sch—school (3) MI-6
Oakview Sch—school MO-7
Oakview Sch—school (2) NJ-2
Oakview Sch—school NY-2
Oakview Sch—school NC-3
Oakview Sch—school (2) OH-6
Oak View Sch—school TN-4
Oak View Sch—school VA-3
Oakview Sch—school WA-9
Oakview Sch—school WI-6
Oak View Sch—school WI-6
Oakview Sch (historical)—school (3) TN-4
**Oakview (subdivision)**—pop pl NC-3
Oak View Union Sch—school CA-9
Oak Village—locale TX-5
**Oak Village**—pop pl AL-4
**Oak Village**—pop pl CA-9
Oak Villa Sch—school SC-3
Oak Villa Sch (historical)—school AL-4
Oakville NC-3
Oakville PA-2
Oakville—locale GA-3
Oakville—locale (2) MD-2
Oakville—locale NJ-2
Oakville—locale NY-2
Oakville—locale NC-3
Oakville—locale OR-9
**Oakville**—pop pl (2) AL-4
**Oakville**—pop pl CA-9
**Oakville**—pop pl CT-1
**Oakville**—pop pl IN-6
**Oakville**—pop pl IA-7
**Oakville**—pop pl KY-4
**Oakville**—pop pl LA-4
**Oakville**—pop pl MI-6
**Oakville**—pop pl (2) MO-7
**Oakville**—pop pl (2) PA-2
**Oakville**—pop pl TN-4
**Oakville**—pop pl TX-5
**Oakville**—pop pl (2) VA-3
**Oakville**—pop pl WA-9
Oakville (CCD)—cens area WA-9
Oakville Cem—cemetery OR-9
Oakville Ch—church AL-4
Oakville Ch—church MO-7
Oakville Drain—stream MI-6
Oakville Gas Field—oilfield TX-5
Oakville Memorial Hosp—hospital TN-4
Oakville Pond—lake AL-4
Oakville Pond Branch—stream AL-4
Oakville Post Office (historical)—building AL-4
**Oakville (Red Oak)**—pop pl KY-4
Oakville Road Sch—school OH-6
Oakville Sch—school IL-6
Oakville Sch—school MO-7
Oakville Sch—school ND-7
Oakville Sch—school OR-9
Oakville Sch—school PA-2
Oakville Sch—school (2) SC-3
Oakville Sch—school WV-2
Oakville Spring—spring AL-4
Oakville Town Hall—building ND-7
**Oakville Township**—pop pl ND-7
Oakville-Wilcox Gas Field—oilfield TX-5
**Oakvista Park (subdivision)**—pop pl UT-8
Oak Wash—stream AZ-5
Oak Wash—stream NM-5
**Oakway**—pop pl SC-3
Oakway (CCD)—cens area SC-3
Oakway Ch—church SC-3
Oakway Golf Course—other OR-9
**Oak Way Subdivision**—pop pl UT-8
Oak Well—well NM-5
Oak Well Canyon—valley NV-8
Oak Well Hollow—valley NV-8
Oak Wells—locale AZ-5
Oak Well Spring—spring NV-8
Oakwide Picnic Area—park CA-9
Oakwide Sch—school TX-5
Oakwillow—locale NC-3
Oakwinds Dam—dam NC-3
Oakwinds Lake—reservoir NC-3
Oakwold Plantation House—hist pl LA-4
Oakwood AL-4
Oakwood FL-3
Oakwood IL-6
Oakwood (2) MI-6
Oakwood MO-7
Oakwood—hist pl MS-4
Oakwood—hist pl MO-7
Oakwood—hist pl NJ-2
Oakwood—hist pl OH-6
Oakwood—hist pl SC-3
Oakwood—hist pl UT-8
Oakwood—locale ME-1
Oakwood—locale VA-3
**Oakwood**—pop pl (3) AL-4
**Oakwood**—pop pl GA-3
**Oakwood**—pop pl (2) IL-6
**Oakwood**—pop pl (2) IN-6
**Oakwood**—pop pl IA-7
**Oakwood**—pop pl (2) MD-2
**Oakwood**—pop pl (3) MI-6
**Oakwood**—pop pl (2) MO-7
**Oakwood**—pop pl NJ-2
**Oakwood**—pop pl (2) NY-2
**Oakwood**—pop pl NC-3
**Oakwood**—pop pl ND-7
**Oakwood**—pop pl (3) OH-6
**Oakwood**—pop pl OK-5
**Oakwood**—pop pl SC-3
**Oakwood**—pop pl (2) TN-4
**Oakwood**—pop pl TX-5
**Oakwood**—pop pl (4) VA-3
**Oakwood**—pop pl (2) WV-2
**Oakwood**—pop pl (2) WI-6
Oakwood—post sta LA-4
Oakwood—uninc pl CA-9
Oakwood—uninc pl TN-4
Oakwood—uninc pl WI-6
Oakwood, Lake—lake SD-7
Oakwood Acres Dam TN-4
Oakwood Acres Lake—reservoir TN-4
**Oakwood Acres (subdivision)**—pop pl (2) NC-3
**Oakwood Acres Subdivision**—pop pl UT-8
Oakwood Ave Ch—church NJ-2
Oakwood Ave Sch—school NJ-2
Oakwood Baptist Church TN-4
Oakwood Bayou—stream AR-4
Oakwood Beach—beach NY-2
**Oakwood Beach**—pop pl NJ-2
**Oakwood Beach**—pop pl NY-2
Oakwood Bottoms—flat IL-6
Oakwood Branch MS-4
Oakwood Branch—stream MS-4
Oakwood Cave—cave AL-4
Oakwood (CCD)—cens area GA-3
Oakwood (CCD)—cens area TX-5
Oak Wood Cem AL-4
Oak Wood Cem NC-3
Oakwood Cem—cemetery (4) AL-4
Oak Wood Cem—cemetery AL-4
Oakwood Cem—cemetery (3) AL-4
Oakwood Cem—cemetery (2) AR-4
Oakwood Cem—cemetery CA-9
Oak Wood Cem—cemetery CA-9
Oakwood Cem—cemetery FL-3
Oakwood Cem—cemetery GA-3
Oak Wood Cem—cemetery IL-6
Oakwood Cem—cemetery (13) IL-6
Oakwood Cem—cemetery IN-6
Oakwood Cem—cemetery (12) IA-7
Oakwood Cem—cemetery (3) KS-7
Oakwood Cem—cemetery KY-4
Oakwood Cem—cemetery LA-4
Oakwood Cem—cemetery (18) MI-6
Oakwood Cem—cemetery (9) MN-6
Oakwood Cem—cemetery (2) MS-4
Oakwood Cem—cemetery MO-7
Oakwood Cem—cemetery (9) NY-2
Oakwood Cem—cemetery (9) NC-3
Oakwood Cem—cemetery ND-7
Oak Wood Cem—cemetery ND-7
Oakwood Cem—cemetery OH-6
Oak Wood Cem—cemetery OH-6
Oakwood Cem—cemetery (3) OH-6
Oakwood Cem—cemetery (4) OK-5
Oakwood Cem—cemetery (3) PA-2
Oakwood Cem—cemetery SC-3
Oakwood Cem—cemetery SD-7
Oakwood Cem—cemetery (2) TN-4
Oakwood Cem—cemetery (15) TX-5
Oak Wood Cem—cemetery TX-5
Oakwood Cem—cemetery (2) TX-5
Oakwood Cem—cemetery (10) VA-3
Oak Wood Cem—cemetery WA-9
Oakwood Cem—cemetery (2) WV-2
Oakwood Cem—cemetery (9) WI-6
Oakwood Cemetery—hist pl NY-2
Oakwood Cemetery Chapel—hist pl MI-6
Oakwood Cemetery Mausoleum—hist pl MI-6
Oakwood (census name for New Castle West)—CDP PA-2
Oakwood Ch—church AR-4
Oakwood Ch—church IL-6
Oakwood Ch—church KY-4
Oakwood Ch—church MN-6
Oak Wood Ch—church MO-7
Oakwood Ch—church MO-7
Oakwood Ch—church NY-2
Oakwood Ch—church NC-3
Oakwood Ch—church OH-6
Oakwood Ch—church (4) TN-4
Oakwood Ch—church TX-5
Oakwood Ch—church (2) VA-3
Oakwood Chapel—church KY-4
Oakwood Coll—school AL-4
Oakwood Coll Acad—school AL-4
**Oakwood Commons**—pop pl IN-6
Oakwood Country Club—other AZ-5
Oak Wood Creek MS-4
Oakwood Dome Oil Field—oilfield TX-5
Oakwood Elementary School TN-4
**Oak Wood Estates**—pop pl TN-4
**Oakwood Estates Subdivisio**—pop pl UT-8
**Oakwood Estates (subdivision)**—pop pl AL-4
**Oakwood Estates (subdivision)**—pop pl MS-4
**Oakwood Estates (subdivision)**—pop pl NC-3
Oakwood Estates Subdivision Mini Park—park AZ-5
Oakwood Estates Subdivision Water Retention Basin—reservoir AZ-5
**Oakwood Estates (Valley Mills)**—pop pl WV-2
Oakwood Forest VA-3
**Oakwood Forest**—pop pl VA-3
Oakwood Golf Club—other MO-7
Oakwood Golf Club—other (2) OH-6
Oakwood Golf Course—other MI-6
Oakwood Heights MI-6

**Oakwood Heights**—*pop pl* IL-6
Oakwood Heights—*uninc pl* NY-2
**Oakwood Heights Station**—*pop pl* NY-2
**Oak Wood Heights Subdivision**—*pop pl* UT-8
**Oakwood Hills**—*pop pl* DE-2
**Oakwood Hills**—*pop pl* IL-6
Oakwood Hills Golf Course—*other* WI-6
Oakwood Hist Dist—*hist pl* (2) NC-3
Oakwood Hist Dist (Boundary Increase)—*hist pl* NC-3
Oakwood Hist Dist (Boundary Increase II)—*hist pl* NC-3
Oakwood (historical)—*locale* KS-7
Oakwood (historical)—*locale* SD-7
Oakwood Home—*locale* WI-6
Oakwood HS—*school* (2) OH-6
Oakwood JHS—*school* MI-6
Oakwood JHS—*school* NC-3
*Oakwood Junction* MI-6
*Oakwood Junior College* AL-4
*Oakwood Knolls* IL-6
**Oakwood Knolls**—*pop pl* MD-2
*Oakwood Lake* SD-7
Oakwood Lake—*reservoir* KY-4
Oakwood Lake—*reservoir* NJ-2
Oakwood Lake—*reservoir* WV-2
Oakwood Lakes—*lake* SD-7
**Oakwood Lakes**—*pop pl* NJ-2
Oakwood Lakes State Park—*park* SD-7
Oakwood Landing—*locale* LA-4
Oakwood Landing (historical)—*locale* MS-4
*Oakwood Manor* IN-6
**Oakwood Manor**—*pop pl* MO-7
Oakwood Memorial Gardens—*cemetery* VA-3
Oakwood Memorial Park—*park* IL-6
Oakwood Mtn—*summit* AL-4
**Oakwood (Oakwood Lakes)**—*pop pl* NJ-2
Oakwood Oil Field—*oilfield* TX-5
Oakwood Park—*park* NC-3
Oakwood Park—*park* OH-6
**Oakwood Park**—*pop pl* IN-6
**Oakwood Park**—*pop pl* MO-7
**Oakwood Park**—*pop pl* NJ-2
Oakwood Park—*uninc pl* PA-2
Oakwood Park Ch—*church* NC-3
**Oakwood Park Condo**—*pop pl* UT-8
**Oakwood Park (subdivision)**—*pop pl* PA-2
Oakwood Playground—*park* CA-9
Oakwood Plaza Shop Ctr—*locale* MS-4
Oakwood Point—*cape* WI-6
*Oakwood Post Office* TN-4
Oakwood Post Office (historical)—*building* TN-4
**Oakwoods**—*pop pl* NC-3
Oakwood Sanitarium—*hospital* OH-6
Oakwoods Cem—*cemetery* IL-6
Oak Woods Ch—*church* KY-4
Oak Woods Ch—*church* ME-1
Oakwood Sch—*school* CA-9
Oakwood Sch—*school* (5) IL-6
Oakwood Sch—*school* (2) MN-6
Oakwood Sch—*school* (2) NY-2
Oakwood Sch—*school* NC-3
Oakwood Sch—*school* (2) OH-6
Oakwood Sch—*school* (2) PA-2
Oakwood Sch—*school* SD-7
Oakwood Sch—*school* (2) TN-4
Oakwood Sch—*school* UT-8
Oakwood Sch—*school* VA-3
Oakwood Sch—*school* WA-9
Oakwood Sch—*school* (4) WI-6
Oak Wood Sch (historical)—*school* AL-4
Oakwood Sch (historical)—*school* TN-4
Oakwoods Country Club—*locale* NC-3
*Oakwoods Creek* MS-4
Oakwood Seminary (historical)—*school* TN-4
Oakwood Shop Ctr—*locale* AL-4
Oakwood Shop Ctr—*locale* NC-3
**Oakwood Shores**—*pop pl* IL-6
**Oakwood Shores**—*pop pl* IN-6
**Oak Wood Shores**—*pop pl* MI-6
**Oak Woods (subdivision)**—*pop pl* NC-3
**Oakwoods Subdivision, The**—*pop pl* UT-8
Oakwood Station—*locale* IA-7
**Oakwood Station (historical)**—*pop pl* IA-7
**Oakwood (subdivision)**—*pop pl* AL-4
**Oakwood (subdivision)**—*pop pl* NC-3
**Oakwood (subdivision)**—*pop pl* TN-4
**Oakwood (subdivision)**—*pop pl* VA-3
**Oakwood Subdivision Blocks 1and3**—*pop pl* UT-8
**Oakwood Subdivision Block Two**—*pop pl* UT-8
*Oakwood Township* ND-7
**Oakwood Township**—*pop pl* ND-7
**Oakwood Township**—*pop pl* SD-7
Oakwood (Township of)—*other* OH-6
**Oakwood (Township of)**—*pop pl* IL-6
**Oakwood (Township of)**—*pop pl* MN-6
Oakwood Training Center—*building* KY-4
Oakwood United Methodist Ch—*church* TN-4
Oakwood Valley—*valley* CA-9
**Oakwood Villa**—*pop pl* FL-3
**Oakwood Village**—*pop pl* OH-6
Oakwood Village Shop Ctr—*locale* AL-4
Oakwood Village Shop Ctr—*locale* UT-8
Oakwood Zion Cem—*cemetery* SD-7
**Oakworth**—*pop pl* AL-4
Oaky—*locale* GA-3
Oaky Bower Ch—*church* AL-4
Oaky Creek—*stream* MS-4
**Oaky Grove**—*pop pl* AL-4
*Oaky Grove Baptist Church* AL-4
Oaky Grove Cem—*cemetery* AL-4
*Oaky Grove Ch* AL-4
Oaky Grove Ch—*church* AL-4
Oaky Grove Ch—*church* GA-3
Oaky Heads—*swamp* FL-3
Oaky Ridge Ch—*church* AL-4
Oaky Sinks—*lake* GA-3
Oaky Streak—*locale* AL-4
Oaky Streak Cem—*cemetery* AL-4
Oaky Streak Ch—*church* AL-4
*Oaky Streak Methodist Ch* AL-4
Oaky Swamp—*swamp* NC-3
Oaky Woods Creek—*stream* AL-4
Oaky Woods Creek—*stream* GA-3
Oakzanita Peak—*summit* CA-9
Oakzanita Springs Campground—*locale* CA-9
O A Lake—*lake* OR-9
OA Lateral—*canal* OR-9
Oalesby Hole—*basin* TX-5
*Oalhout Ditch* IN-6
Oalii Cove—*bay* AS-9
**Oalmer Park (Seipsville)**—*pop pl* PA-2
Oalolo Ditch—*canal* HI-9
Oalos—*stream* FM-9
*Oalos River* FM-9
Oan—*island* FM-9
*Oanapuka* HI-9
Oanapuka—*summit* HI-9
O and C Froholm Ranch—*locale* ND-7
O and C Junction—*locale* NC-3
O and F Palmas Grant—*civil* FL-3
*O and S Chapel* TN-4
*O and S Chapel United Methodist Ch* TN-4
O and W Rapids—*rapids* TN-4
O and W Rsvr—*reservoir* PA-2
Oanica (historical)—*locale* KS-7
Oanui Stream—*stream* HI-9
Oao—*island* FM-9
Oar Creek—*stream* OR-9
Oard Drain—*canal* MI-6
Oard Flat—*flat* OR-9
Oard Spring—*spring* OR-9
Oare—*civil* FM-9
Oaring Cove—*bay* AK-9
Oar Island—*island* ME-1
**Oark**—*pop pl* AR-4
Oar Lake—*lake* (2) MN-6
Oarlock Island—*island* AK-9
*Oarmoar* FM-9
Oaroahrlap—*cape* FM-9
Oar Reservation—*reserve* AL-4
Oar Run—*stream* IN-6
Oars Ferry (historical)—*crossing* TN-4
Oarweed Cove—*bay* ME-1
Oasis—*locale* CA-9
Oasis—*locale* GA-3
Oasis—*locale* IA-7
Oasis—*locale* NM-5
Oasis—*other* TX-5
**Oasis**—*pop pl* CA-9
**Oasis**—*pop pl* MO-7
**Oasis**—*pop pl* NV-8
**Oasis**—*pop pl* NM-5
**Oasis**—*pop pl* UT-8
Oasis—*uninc pl* TX-5
Oasis, The—*other* AK-9
Oasis Bluff—*cliff* MO-7
Oasis Butte—*summit* OR-9
Oasis Campground—*park* UT-8
Oasis Canal—*canal* UT-8
Oasis Canal—*canal* WY-8
Oasis Cem—*cemetery* IA-7
Oasis Cem—*cemetery* UT-8
Oasis Cem—*cemetery* WI-6
Oasis Community Park—*park* AZ-5
Oasis Creek—*stream* CO-8
Oasis Creek—*stream* OR-9
Oasis Creek—*stream* TX-5
Oasis Ditch—*canal* CO-8
Oasis Ditch—*canal* WY-8
Oasis Divide—*gap* NV-8
Oasis Drain—*canal* CA-9
Oasis Faith Chapel Ch—*church* AL-4
Oasis Glacier—*glacier* AK-9
Oasis Gulch—*valley* MT-8
**Oasis (historical)**—*pop pl* MO-7
**Oasis (historical)**—*pop pl* OR-9
Oasis Interchange—*crossing* NV-8
Oasis Lake—*lake* MO-7
Oasis Lake—*reservoir* TX-5
Oasis Lakes—*lake* MT-8
*Oasis Landing* MS-4
Oasis Lateral—*canal* (2) CA-9
Oasis Mine—*mine* NV-8
Oasis Mtn—*summit* NV-8
Oasis of Mara—*spring* CA-9
Oasis Park—*uninc pl* AZ-5
Oasis Pond—*swamp* MT-8
Oasis Post Office (historical)—*building* AL-4
Oasis Ranch—*locale* AZ-5
Oasis Ranch—*locale* NM-5
Oasis Ranch—*locale* TX-5
Oasis Ranch—*locale* WY-8
Oasis Sch—*school* (2) CA-9
Oasis Spring—*spring* CA-9
Oasis Spring—*spring* (2) OR-9
Oasis Spring—*spring* WA-9
Oasis Spring Creek—*stream* WY-8
*Oasis Station* CA-9
**Oasis (Town of)**—*pop pl* WI-6
Oasis Valley—*valley* NV-8
Oasis Well—*well* WY-8
Oastler Castle—*summit* UT-8
Oastler Mtn—*summit* AK-9
Oastler Pass—*gap* AK-9
Oastler Shelter—*locale* MT-8
Oatbed Creek—*stream* SC-3
Oatbed Island—*island* SC-3
Oat Butte—*summit* OR-9
Oat Canyon—*valley* (2) CA-9
Oat Canyon—*valley* (2) NM-5
Oat Canyon—*valley* WY-8
Oat Creek—*stream* (5) CA-9
Oat Creek—*stream* OR-9
Oat Creek—*stream* SD-7
Oat Creek—*stream* WY-8
Oat Drain—*canal* CA-9
*Oates* SC-3
**Oates**—*pop pl* MO-7
Oates, John A., House—*hist pl* NC-3
Oates, Livingston, Farm—*hist pl* NC-3
Oates Branch—*stream* AL-4
Oates Branch—*stream* TX-5
Oates Cem—*cemetery* TN-4
Oates Creek—*stream* NC-3
*Oates Cross Roads* AL-4
Oates Island—*island* TN-4
Oates Island Post Office (historical)—*building* TN-4
Oates Lookout Tower—*locale* MO-7
Oates Post Office (historical)—*building* AL-4
**Oates Prairie**—*pop pl* TX-5
Oates Pumping Station—*other* TX-5
Oates-Reynolds Memorial Bldg—*hist pl* AL-4
Oates Sch—*school* TX-5
Oateston—*locale* AL-4
Oat Field Branch—*stream* KY-4
Oatfield Cave—*cave* AL-4
Oatfield Hill—*summit* OR-9
Oat Gap—*gap* CA-9
Oat Gulch—*valley* CA-9
Oat Hill—*summit* (5) CA-9
Oat Hill Extension Mine—*mine* CA-9
Oat Hill Mine—*mine* CA-9
Oat Hills—*other* CA-9
Oat Hills—*range* (3) CA-9
Oat Hills—*ridge* CA-9
Oat Hills Tunnel—*tunnel* CA-9
*Oathout Ditch* IN-6
Oathout Ditch—*canal* IN-6
Oaties Hollow—*valley* TX-5
Oatil Cem—*cemetery* NM-5
Oatka—*locale* NY-2
Oatka Cem—*cemetery* NY-2
*Oatka Creek* NY-2
Oatka Creek—*stream* NY-2
Oatka Creek Park—*park* NY-2
Oat Knob—*summit* CA-9
Oat Knob Canyon—*valley* CA-9
Oat Lake—*lake* CO-8
*Oatland* ND-7
**Oatland**—*pop pl* SC-3
Oatland Creek—*stream* GA-3
Oatland Creek—*stream* SC-3
Oatland Island—*island* GA-3
Oatlands—*hist pl* VA-3
Oatlands—*locale* VA-3
Oatlands Hist Dist—*hist pl* VA-3
Oat Lateral—*canal* CA-9
Oatly Lake—*lake* MI-6
**Oatman**—*pop pl* AZ-5
Oatman, Earl, House—*hist pl* WA-9
Oatman Creek—*stream* TX-5
Oatman Creek Ch—*church* TX-5
Oatman Flat—*flat* AZ-5
Oatman Flat—*flat* OR-9
Oatman Grave—*cemetery* AZ-5
*Oatman Lake* OR-9
Oatman Lake—*lake* MI-6
Oatman Lake—*lake* OR-9
Oatman Mtn—*summit* AZ-5
Oatman Post Office—*building* AZ-5
Oatman Ranch—*locale* NE-7
Oatman Southern Mine—*mine* AZ-5
Oatman Spring—*spring* SD-7
Oatman Syndicate Mine—*mine* AZ-5
Oatmeal—*locale* TX-5
Oatmeal Creek—*stream* TX-5
Oatmeal Lake—*lake* WI-6
*Oat Mtn* CA-9
Oat Mtn—*summit* (4) CA-9
*Oa-to* MP-9
*Oat Point* MI-6
Oat Ridge—*ridge* (2) CA-9
**Oats**—*pop pl* KY-4
**Oats**—*pop pl* SC-3
Oats Canyon—*valley* OK-5
Oats Ch—*church* SC-3
Oats Creek—*stream* AR-4
Oats Hole—*swamp* SC-3
*Oats Island* TN-4
Oats Park Sch—*school* NV-8
Oatspatch Hollow—*valley* KY-4
Oat Spring—*spring* AZ-5
Oats Run—*stream* IN-6
Oats Run—*stream* WV-2
**Oatsville**—*pop pl* IN-6
Oats Well—*well* TX-5
Oats Windmill—*locale* TX-5
*Oat Tank* AZ-5
Oat Tank—*reservoir* NM-5
Oat Valley—*basin* (2) CA-9
Oat Valley—*valley* CA-9
Oat Valley Creek—*stream* CA-9
*Oatville* IN-6
**Oatville**—*pop pl* KS-7
Oatville Elem Sch—*school* KS-7
Oatville Evangelical Methodist Ch—*church* KS-7
*Oaunoar* FM-9
**Oautoga Bluff**—*pop pl* IL-6
Oaxley Branch—*stream* TX-5
*Obadasa Lake* WI-6
Obadash Lake—*lake* WI-6
**Obadiah**—*pop pl* MS-4
Obadiah Cove—*valley* NC-3
Obadiah Gap—*gap* NC-3
Obadiah Post Office (historical)—*building* MS-4
*Oban* KS-7
Oban—*locale* CA-9
*Oban Creek* CO-8
Obanion Branch—*stream* LA-4
O'Banion Canyon—*valley* NV-8
O'Banion Gun Club—*other* CA-9
O'Banion Spring—*spring* NV-8
O'Bannon—*locale* KY-4
O'Bannon Cem—*cemetery* MO-7
O'Bannon Creek—*stream* MO-7
O'Bannon Creek—*stream* OH-6
O Bannon Field—*park* NM-5
O'Bannon Homestead—*hist pl* MO-7
O'Bannon Sch—*school* MS-4
**Obar**—*pop pl* NM-5
O Bar A Ranch—*locale* MT-8
O'Bara Sch—*school* NE-7
O'Bar Branch—*stream* AL-4
Obar Branch—*stream* TN-4
Obar Cem—*cemetery* NM-5
Obar Creek—*stream* TX-5
O'Bar Gap—*gap* AL-4
Obar Hill—*summit* TX-5
O Bar O Canyon—*valley* AZ-5
O Bar O Canyon—*valley* NM-5
O Bar O Mtn—*summit* NM-5
O Bar O Peak—*summit* NM-5
O-Bar-O Ranch—*locale* AZ-5
O Bar O Ranch—*locale* NM-5
O Bar O Ranch—*locale* TX-5
O Bar O Spring—*spring* NM-5
O Bar O Tank—*reservoir* AZ-5
O'Barr Lookout Tower—*locale* GA-3
Obar Spring—*spring* TN-4
*Obaysh River* IN-6
O B Draw—*valley* AZ-5
Obear Park—*park* MA-1
*Obed* TN-4
Obed—*locale* IL-6
Obed Creek—*stream* SC-3
Obed Heights—*summit* CT-1
Obed Heights Rsvr—*reservoir* CT-1
Obed (historical)—*locale* AL-4
Obed Junction—*locale* TN-4
Obed Magee Cem—*cemetery* MS-4
Obed Meadow—*swamp* AZ-5
Obed Post Office (historical)—*building* TN-4
Obed River—*stream* TN-4
**Obed River Estates**—*pop pl* TN-4
*Obed Rsvr* CT-1
Obeds Rock—*island* ME-1
*Obedstown* TN-4
Obed Wild and Scenic River—*park* TN-4
Obee House—*hist pl* IL-6
*Obeejan* MH-9
**Obeeville**—*pop pl* KS-7
Obe Fields Spring—*spring* CA-9
*O-be-good Lake* MN-6
*O-be-gwod Lake* MN-6
Obe Lee Cave—*cave* TN-4
Obe Lee Hollow—*valley* TN-4
Obelgoner Cem—*cemetery* TX-5
Obelisk—*locale* PA-2
Obelisk—*pillar* CA-9
Obelisk Lake—*lake* CA-9
*Obel Island* MP-9
Obella—*island* MP-9
*Obella Island* MP-9
Obenchain Cem—*cemetery* VA-3
Obenchain Dam—*dam* OR-9
Obenchain Draw—*valley* CO-8
Obenchain Mtn—*summit* OR-9
Obenchain Ranch—*locale* OR-9
Obenchain Rsvr—*reservoir* OR-9
Oben Creek—*stream* CO-8
Obendoffers Creek—*stream* PA-2
Obenhoff Creek—*stream* MI-6
Obenhoff Lake—*lake* MI-6
**Ober**—*pop pl* IN-6
Oberammergau, Mount—*summit* AR-4
Ober Creek—*stream* AK-9
Oberding Mine—*mine* CO-8
Ober Ditch—*canal* IN-6
*Oberg* NE-7
Oberg Brothers Dam—*dam* OR-9
Oberg Creek—*stream* WY-8
Oberg Lake—*lake* MN-6
Oberg Pass—*gap* WY-8
Oberg Ranch—*locale* SD-7
Oberg Ranch—*locale* WY-8
*Oberg Rsvr* OR-9
Oberg Rsvr—*reservoir* OR-9
Oberg Sch (abandoned)—*school* MO-7
Oberhaltzer Ditch—*canal* IN-6
Oberhaus Creek—*stream* OH-6
Ober Hill—*summit* VT-1
Oberhoffer, Emil J., House—*hist pl* MN-6
Oberholtzer Cem—*cemetery* PA-2
Oberkampf Ranch—*locale* TX-5
Oberle Sch—*school* IL-6
Oberlin—*locale* MI-6
Oberlin—*locale* OK-5
**Oberlin**—*pop pl* KS-7
**Oberlin**—*pop pl* LA-4
**Oberlin**—*pop pl* OH-6
**Oberlin**—*pop pl* PA-2
Oberlin, Mount—*summit* MT-8
**Oberlin Beach**—*pop pl* OH-6
Oberlin Coll—*school* OH-6
Oberlin College—*hist pl* OH-6
Oberlin Elem Sch—*school* KS-7
Oberlin Falls—*falls* MT-8
Oberlin Ferry—*locale* OK-5
**Oberlin Gardens**—*pop pl* PA-2
Oberlin Lake—*lake* IN-6
Oberlin Lake—*lake* OK-5
Oberlin Lake—*lake* WI-6
Oberlin Lake Shore And Michigan Southern Station—*hist pl* OH-6
Oberlin Municipal Airp—*airport* KS-7
Oberlin Park—*park* MN-6
*Oberlin Peak* MT-8
Oberlin Ridge—*summit* AK-9
Oberlin Rsvr—*reservoir* OH-6
Oberlin-Sappa State Park—*park* KS-7
**Oberlin Township**—*pop pl* KS-7
Oberly Crossing—*locale* TX-5
Oberman Park—*park* AR-4
Oberman Rsvr—*reservoir* OR-9
Obermayer, Mount—*summit* MT-8
Obermayer Lake—*reservoir* MT-8
*Ober Mtn* VT-1
**Obernburg**—*pop pl* NY-2
Obernoi Point—*cape* AK-9
Obernolte Spring—*spring* OR-9
*Obernouse Creek* OH-6
**Oberon**—*pop pl* ND-7
Oberon JHS—*school* CO-8
Oberon Lakes—*reservoir* CO-8
**Oberon Township**—*pop pl* ND-7
Oberry—*locale* GA-3
Oberry Bar—*bar* GA-3
O'Berry Canal—*canal* UT-8
O'Berry Cem—*cemetery* GA-3
Oberry Ch—*church* VA-3
*Oberry Lake* FL-3
O'Berry Lake—*lake* FL-3
O'Berry Training Sch—*school* NC-3
Ober Sch—*school* PA-2
Oberson Run—*stream* PA-2
Oberst, Lake—*reservoir* NJ-2
**Obert**—*pop pl* NE-7
Obert Cem—*cemetery* NE-7
Obert C Tanner Amphitheater—*basin* UT-8
*Obert Height Pond* CT-1
*Obert Heights Pond* CT-1
Oberthier Cem—*cemetery* TX-5
Obert Homestead—*locale* WY-8
Oberts Ditch—*stream* IN-6
*Oberweis Post Office* ND-7
Obes Branch—*stream* TN-4
Obes Branch—*stream* WV-2
Obes Glen—*valley* NY-2
Obes Thorofare—*channel* NJ-2
Obeth Cem—*cemetery* NC-3
**Obetz**—*pop pl* OH-6
Obetz Highway—*channel* MI-6
Obe Worthen Mesa—*summit* NM-5
Obey City—*locale* TN-4
Obey River—*stream* TN-4
Obey River Rec Area—*park* TN-4
Obeys Creek—*stream* VA-3
*Obeys River* TN-4
*Obhanan Ridgeway Branch* NJ-2
*Obhonan Branch* NJ-2
*Obhonan Brook* NJ-2
Obhonan Ridgeway Branch—*stream* NJ-2
*Obi* FM-9
Obi—*locale* NY-2
Obia Cabin—*locale* ID-8
*Obia Creek* ID-8
Obia Creek—*stream* ID-8
*Obiam* MH-9
*Obiamu* MH-9
*Obiamu-Misaki* MH-9
*Obiamu Point* MH-9
Obiaque Water Hole—*lake* OR-9
Obi Canyon—*valley* AZ-5
*Obid* NC-3
*Obid Creek* NC-3
Obids—*locale* NC-3
Obids Creek—*stream* NC-3
Obids (Township of)—*fmr MCD* NC-3
Obie—*locale* CA-9
*Obie Dillock Pass* OR-9
**Obie Junction**—*pop pl* CA-9
Obie Mill Cave—*cave* TN-4
*Obie Mill Spring* TN-4
Obie Mound—*summit* KY-4
Obies Chapel—*church* NC-3
Obi Hill—*summit* TX-5
Obi Hollow—*valley* OK-5
*Obiil* PW-9
*Obi Islands* FM-9
*Obijan* MH-9
*Obioati* MP-9
**Obion**—*pop pl* TN-4
Obion Ch—*church* (3) KY-4
Obion Chapel—*church* (3) TN-4
Obion Chapel Cem—*cemetery* TN-4
*Obion Church* TN-4
**Obion County**—*pop pl* TN-4
Obion County Central Sch—*school* TN-4
Obion County Courthouse—*building* TN-4
Obion County Home (historical)—*building* TN-4
*Obion Creek* KY-4
Obion Creek—*stream* KY-4
Obion Lake (historical)—*lake* TN-4
Obion Mounds—*hist pl* TN-4
Obion Post Office—*building* TN-4
*Obion River* TN-4
Obion River—*stream* TN-4
Obion River Drainage Canal—*canal* TN-4
Obion Sch—*school* TN-4
Obion Square Shop Ctr—*locale* TN-4
Obion-Tamm Revetment—*levee* TN-4
Obion-Troy (CCD)—*cens area* TN-4
Obion-Troy Division—*civil* TN-4
Obi Point—*cliff* AZ-5
*Obire* MP-9
*Obire-to* MP-9
Obis Tank—*reservoir* TX-5
Obis Well—*well* TX-5
*Obit-ko-ke-chee Kanyon* UT-8
*Obi To* FM-9
*Objam Point* MH-9
Objibway Lake—*lake* MN-6
O'Black Pond—*lake* OR-9
Oblaron Creek—*stream* AK-9
Oblate Coll—*school* MA-1
Oblate Fathers Novitiate—*church* IL-6
Oblate Fathers Novitiate—*church* NH-1
Oblate Gas Field—*oilfield* TX-5
Oblate Park—*park* TX-5
OB Lateral—*canal* OR-9
Oblate Southwest Coll—*school* TX-5
*Oble* MP-9
O'Blenis House—*hist pl* NJ-2
O'Blennis Lake—*lake* IN-6
*Obligation* MD-2
Obligation—*hist pl* MD-2
Oblivion (historical)—*locale* SD-7
OBlock Canyon—*valley* NM-5
**Oblong**—*pop pl* IL-6
Oblong Friends Meetinghouse—*hist pl* NY-2
Oblong Lake—*lake* IL-6
**Oblong (Township of)**—*pop pl* IL-6
Obney Run—*stream* PA-2
*Oboen* FM-9
*Obold* PA-2
Obold—*other* PA-2
O'Boyle Point—*cape* IL-6
O B Perry Corners—*locale* PA-2
Obregon—*locale* CA-9
Obregon—*locale* TX-5
Obregon Park—*park* CA-9
**Obrero**—*pop pl* (2) PR-3
O'Brian Canal—*canal* CO-8
O'Brian Creek—*stream* WA-9
O'Brian Creek—*stream* WY-8
O'Brian Ditch—*canal* IN-6
*O'Brian Gap* GA-3
*Obrian Hollow* PA-2
O'Brian Hollow—*valley* PA-2
*O'Brian Lake* NE-7
*O'brian Lake* WI-6
*O'Brian Run* IL-6
O'Brian Tank—*reservoir* NM-5
O'Brien—*locale* CA-9
O'Brien—*locale* IA-7
O'Brien—*locale* KS-7
Obrien—*locale* WA-9
**O'Brien**—*pop pl* FL-3
**O'Brien**—*pop pl* OR-9
**O'Brien**—*pop pl* TX-5
**Obrien**—*pop pl* WV-2
O'Brien, Lake—*lake* MI-6
O'Brien, Mathew, House—*hist pl* AZ-5
O'Brien, William, House—*hist pl* MT-8
O'Brien, William Thomas, House—*hist pl* NC-3
O'Brien Airp—*airport* PA-2
O'Brien Branch—*stream* KY-4
O'Brien Brook—*stream* NY-2
O'Brien Brook—*stream* VT-1
O'Brien Canyon—*valley* NE-7
O'Brien Cem—*cemetery* IL-6
O'Brien Cem—*cemetery* IN-6
O'Brien Cem—*cemetery* MS-4
O'Brien Cem—*cemetery* OH-6
O'Brien Corners—*locale* NY-2
O'Brien Coulee—*valley* MT-8
O'Brien Coulee—*valley* ND-7
O'Brien County Courthouse—*hist pl* IA-7
O'Brien County Home—*locale* IA-7
*Obrien Creek* MS-4
*O'Brien Creek* WV-2
O'Brien Creek—*stream* (6) AK-9
O'Brien Creek—*stream* IN-6
O'Brien Creek—*stream* (2) MN-6
O'brien Creek—*stream* MS-4
O'Brien Creek—*stream* (4) MT-8
O'Brien Creek—*stream* NV-8
O'Brien Creek—*stream* ND-7
O'Brien Creek—*stream* (5) OR-9
O'Brien Creek—*stream* (3) WA-9
O'Brien Creek—*stream* WY-8
O'Brien Creek Inlet—*bay* CA-9
O'Brien Ditch—*canal* IN-6
Obrien Ditch—*canal* IN-6
O'Brien Ditch—*canal* IN-6
O'Brien Drain—*canal* MI-6
O'Brien Electric Priming Company—*hist pl* IN-6
O'Brien Fork—*stream* (3) WV-2
O'Brien General Store and Post Office—*hist pl* NY-2
O'Brien Gulch—*valley* AZ-5
O'Brien Gulch—*valley* CO-8
O'Brien Gulch—*valley* (2) ID-8
O'Brien Hill—*summit* CA-9
O'Brien Hill—*summit* PA-2
O'Brien Hollow—*valley* PA-2
O'Brien HS—*school* MI-6
O'Brien Lake—*lake* CA-9
O'Brien Lake—*lake* FL-3
O'Brien Lake—*lake* IN-6
O'Brien Lake—*lake* (2) MI-6
O'Brien Lake—*lake* (3) MN-6
O'Brien Lake—*lake* MT-8
O Brien Lake—*lake* NE-7
O'Brien Lake—*lake* ND-7
O'Brien Lake—*lake* WA-9
O'Brien Lake—*lake* WI-6
O'Brien Lake—*swamp* NE-7
O'Brien Lateral—*canal* CA-9
O'Brien Lookout Tower—*locale* MN-6
O'Brien Mine—*mine* AZ-5
O'Brien Mine—*mine* MT-8
O'Brien Mtn—*summit* CA-9
O'Brien Mtn—*summit* MT-8
O'Brien Park—*flat* MT-8
Obrien Park—*park* IN-6
O'Brien Park—*park* TN-4
O'Brien Playground—*park* MI-6
O'Brien Point—*cape* VT-1
O'Brien Pond—*reservoir* MI-6
O'Brien Ranch—*locale* NM-5
O'Brien Ranch—*locale* ND-7
O'Brien Run—*stream* IL-6
O'Briens and Gatts Forge (historical)—*locale* TN-4
O'Brien Sch—*school* AR-4
O'brien Sch—*school* CT-1
O Brien Sch—*school* IL-6
O'Brien Sch—*school* NJ-2
O'Brien Sch—*school* (2) WI-6
*Obrien School* IN-6
**O'Briens Corner**—*pop pl* MA-1
Obriens Corner JHS—*school* MA-1
O'Briens Creek—*stream* MI-6
*O'Briens Fork* WV-2
O'Briens Knob—*summit* NV-8
O'Brien Spring—*spring* CA-9
O'Brien Spring—*spring* OR-9
O'Brien Spring—*spring* (2) WY-8
O'Brien Springs—*spring* WI-6
*O'Briens School* TN-4
**O'Brien (Township of)**—*pop pl* MN-6
O'Brion—*locale* WV-2
O'Brion Branch—*stream* KY-4
O'Brion Ch—*church* WV-2
O'Brion Creek—*stream* WV-2
O'Brion Ridge—*ridge* KY-4
Obrist Cem—*cemetery* OR-9
O'Bryan Cem—*cemetery* IL-6
Obryan Cem—*cemetery* KY-4
O'Bryan Cem—*cemetery* MO-7
O'Bryan Creek—*stream* MT-8
O'Bryan Gap—*gap* GA-3
O'Bryan Landing—*locale* MO-7
O'Bryan Ridge—*ridge* MO-7
O'Bryan Ridge Archeol District—*hist pl* MO-7
O'Bryant Branch—*stream* AR-4
*O'Bryant Ditch* OR-9
O'Bryan Towhead—*other* MO-7
O'Bryan Windmill—*locale* NM-5
Obscurity Lake—*lake* WA-9
Obsechki Island—*island* AK-9
*Observation* AZ-5
Observation Berryfield Campground—*locale* WA-9
Observation Bluff—*summit* KS-7
Observation Gap—*gap* OR-9
Observation Island—*island* (2) AK-9
Observation Island—*island* FL-3
Observation Knob—*summit* TN-4
Observation Knoll—*summit* UT-8
Observation Mtn—*summit* AK-9
Observation Park—*park* MO-7
Observation Park—*park* TN-4
Observation Pass—*gap* MT-8
*Observation Peak* UT-8
Observation Peak—*summit* AK-9
Observation Peak—*summit* (2) CA-9
Observation Peak—*summit* ID-8
Observation Peak—*summit* OR-9
Observation Peak—*summit* WA-9
Observation Peak—*summit* (2) WY-8
Observation Peak Trail—*trail* WA-9
*Observation Plateau* AZ-5
Observation Point—*cape* (2) AK-9
Observation Point—*cape* MT-8
Observation Point—*summit* MT-8
Observation Point—*summit* TN-4
Observation Point—*summit* UT-8
Observation Rock—*island* AK-9
Observation Rock—*summit* UT-8
Observation Rock—*summit* WA-9
Observation Shoal—*bar* FL-3

O'Connor, Cornelius, House—hist pl NE-7
O'Connor, Thomas M., House—hist pl TX-5
O'Connor Branch—stream PA-2
O'Connor Branch—stream WI-6
O'Connor Canyon—valley WA-9
O'Connor Cem—cemetery TN-4
O'Connor Cem—cemetery TX-5
O'Connor Ch—church TN-4
O'Connor Ch of Christ TN-4
O'Connor Creek—stream AK-9
O'Connor Creek—stream (2) WA-9
O'Connor Ditch—canal IN-6
O'Connor Ditch—canal MT-8
O'connor Drain—stream MI-6
O'Connor Gulch—valley CA-9
O'Connor Hosp—hospital CA-9
O'Connor House—hist pl ND-7
O'Connor Lake—lake MI-6
O'Connor Lakes—lake CA-9
**O'Connor Landing**—pop pl OH-6
O'Connor Landing Strip—airport MO-7
**O'Connor Point**—pop pl OH-6
O'Connor-Proctor Bldg—hist pl TX-5
O'Connor Ranch—locale CA-9
O'Connor Ranch—locale MT-8
O'Connor Rsvr—reservoir OR-9
O'Connor Run—stream PA-2
**O'connors**—pop pl TN-4
O'Connor Sch—school CA-9
O'Connor Sch—school IA-7
O'Connors Flat—flat CA-9
O'Connor Spring—spring OR-9
O'Connors Puddle Dam—dam OR-9
O'Connors Puddle Rsvr—reservoir OR-9
O'Connor Trail—trail PA-2
**Ocono Lufty**—pop pl NC-3
**Oconomowoc**—pop pl WI-6
Oconomowoc City Hall—hist pl WI-6
Oconomowoc Depot—hist pl WI-6
**Oconomowoc Lake**—pop pl WI-6
Oconomowoc Lake—reservoir WI-6
**Oconomowoc Lake South**—pop pl WI-6
Oconomowoc River—stream WI-6
**Oconomowoc (Town of)**—pop pl WI-6
**Oconto**—pop pl NE-7
**Oconto**—pop pl WI-6
Oconto City Park—park WI-6
**Oconto (County)**—pop pl WI-6
Oconto County Courthouse—hist pl WI-6
**Oconto Falls**—pop pl WI-6
**Oconto Falls (Town of)**—pop pl WI-6
Oconto Main Post Office—hist pl WI-6
Oconto Marsh State Game Ref—park WI-6
Oconto River WI-6
Oconto River—stream WI-6
Oconto Site—hist pl WI-6
**Oconto (Town of)**—pop pl WI-6
**Ocoonita**—pop pl VA-3
Ocopilco Creek GA-3
Ocopla Baptist Ch—church MS-4
Ocosochis FL-3
**Ocosta**—pop pl WA-9
Ocotillo CA-9
Ocotillo—locale AZ-5
**Ocotillo**—pop pl AZ-5
**Ocotillo**—pop pl CA-9
Ocotillo Badlands—area CA-9
Ocotillo Branch Library—building AZ-5
Ocotillo Flat—flat CA-9
Ocotillo Hills—range NM-5
Ocotillo Interchange—crossing AZ-5
Ocotillo Mine Group—mine AZ-5
Ocotillo Power Plant—building AZ-5
Ocotillo Sch—school AZ-5
Ocotillo Siding (reduced usage)—locale TX-5
Ocotillo Siding (reduced usage)—park TX-5
Ocotillo Tank—reservoir (2) AZ-5
Ocotillo Tank—reservoir (2) TX-5
Ocotillo Well—well (2) TX-5
**Ocotillo Wells**—pop pl CA-9
O Counting Dam—dam SD-7
O-cow-ocuh-hat-che Creek AL-4
Ocoya—locale IL-6
Ocoya Sch—school IL-6
**Ocqueoc**—pop pl MI-6
Ocqueoc Cem—cemetery MI-6
Ocqueoc Falls—falls MI-6
Ocqueoc Lake—lake MI-6
Ocqueoc River—stream MI-6
**Ocqueoc (Township of)**—pop pl MI-6
Ocquionis Creek—stream NY-2
Ocquittunk, Lake—reservoir NJ-2
**Ocracoke**—pop pl NC-3
Ocracoke Inlet—channel NC-3
Ocracoke Island—island NC-3
Ocracoke Island Airp—airport NC-3
Ocracoke Light House—locale NC-3
Ocracoke Light Station—hist pl NC-3
Ocracoke (Township of)—fmr MCD NC-3
Ocran—locale VA-3
Ocran Ch—church VA-3
Ocre AL-4
Ocre Grove Ch—church NC-3
Ocre Point RI-1
**Octa**—pop pl MO-7
**Octa**—pop pl OH-6
Octagon—locale AL-4
**Octagon**—pop pl IN-6
Octagon, The—hist pl DC-2
Octagon, The—hist pl NY-2
Octagon, The—hist pl OH-6
Octagonal Schoolhouse—hist pl DE-2
Octagonal Schoolhouse—hist pl NY-2
Octagonal School House—park DE-2
Octagon Barn, Otter Township—hist pl IA-7
Octagon Barn, Polk Township—hist pl IA-7
Octagon Barn, Richland Township—hist pl IA-7
Octagon Bldg—hist pl CA-9
Octagon Butte—summit AZ-5
Octagon Cem—cemetery AL-4
Octagon Church AL-4
Octagon Cottage—hist pl KY-4
Octagon Hall—hist pl KY-4
Octagon House—building DC-2
Octagon House—hist pl CT-1
Octagon House—hist pl GA-3
Octagon House—hist pl IL-6
Octagon House—hist pl (2) MA-1
Octagon House—hist pl SC-3
Octagon House—hist pl (2) WI-6
Octagon Round Barn, Indian Creek Township—hist pl IA-7
Octagon State Memorial—park OH-6
Octagon Station—locale AL-4
Octagon Stone Schoolhouse—hist pl PA-2
Octahatchee—locale FL-3
Octahatechee, Lake—reservoir FL-3
Octain Creek—stream IN-6
Octave—locale AZ-5
Octave Mine—mine AZ-5
Octave Pass—channel LA-4
Octave Pass—gut LA-4
Octave Pass North—channel LA-4
Octave Pond—bay LA-4
Octave Spring—spring PA-2
**Octavia**—pop pl NE-7
**Octavia**—pop pl OK-5
Octavia Ch—church AL-4
Octavia Ch—church KY-4
Octavio Sch—school TX-5
October Creek—stream ID-8
October Mine—mine NV-8
October Mountain State For—forest MA-1
October Mtn—summit MA-1
Octol—locale CA-9
Octonia Stone—hist pl VA-3
Octopus, Mount—summit WA-9
Octopus Creek—stream MT-8
Octopus Lake—lake AK-9
Octopus Lake—lake MN-6
Octopus Mine—mine NV-8
Octorara Ch—church PA-2
Octorara Farm—hist pl MD-2
Octoraro PA-2
**Octoraro**—pop pl MD-2
Octoraro Ch PA-2
Octoraro Creek—stream MD-2
Octoraro Creek—stream PA-2
Octoraro Dam PA-2
Octoraro Lake—reservoir PA-2
Octoraro Pines—locale PA-2
Octoraro Post Office (historical)—building PA-2
Odair—locale WA-9
Oda-Jima FM-9
Odajima Suido FM-9
Odakota Mtn—summit SD-7
Odalen Ch—church ND-7
Odalmelech—hist pl PW-9
Odam Cem—cemetery TN-4
Odamsville NC-3
**Odanah**—pop pl WI-6
Odanah Cem—cemetery WI-6
Odanah Ch—church WI-6
Odana Hills Golf Course—other WI-6
Odana Sch—school WI-6
O'Daniel Cem—cemetery GA-3
O'Daniel Cem—cemetery KY-4
Odart Cienega—flat AZ-5
Odart Mtn—summit AZ-5
Odart Ranch—locale AZ-5
**Odaville**—pop pl WV-2
O'Day Butte—summit MT-8
O'day Lake—lake WI-6
O D C Oil Field—oilfield TX-5
Odd IN-6
**Odd**—pop pl WV-2
Odden Cem—cemetery SD-7
Odd Fellow Cem—cemetery IN-6
Odd Fellow Female Coll (historical)—school TN-4
Odd Fellows and Confederate Cemetery—hist pl MS-4
Odd Fellows and Rebekah Home for Children—locale TX-5
Odd Fellows and Rebekahs Home—building TX-5
Odd Fellows Bldg—hist pl CA-9
Odd Fellows Bldg—hist pl (2) KY-4
Odd Fellows Bldg—hist pl MA-1
Odd Fellows Bldg—hist pl NV-8
Odd Fellows Bldg—hist pl OR-9
Odd Fellows Bldg—hist pl SD-7
Odd Fellows Bldg and Auditorium—hist pl GA-3
Odd Fellows Block—hist pl ME-1
Odd Fellows Block—hist pl ND-7
Odd Fellows Cem PA-2
Odd Fellows Cem—cemetery AL-4
Oddfellows Cem—cemetery AR-4
Odd Fellows Cem—cemetery CA-9
Oddfellows Cem—cemetery CA-9
Odd Fellows Cem—cemetery (8) IN-6
Odd Fellows Cem—cemetery IA-7
Odd Fellows Cem—cemetery (3) KY-4
Odd Fellows Cem—cemetery (2) MS-4
Odd Fellows Cem—cemetery (2) NC-3
Odd Fellows Cem—cemetery PA-2
Odd Fellows Cem—cemetery TN-4
Odd Fellows Cem—cemetery TX-5
Odd Fellows Cem—cemetery VA-3
Odd Fellows Cem—cemetery WY-8
Odd Fellows' Cemetery Mound—hist pl OH-6
Odd Fellows Hall—building MA-1
Odd Fellows Hall—hist pl (3) CA-9
Odd Fellows Hall—hist pl ID-8
Odd Fellows Hall—hist pl (2) IA-7
Odd Fellows Hall—hist pl KY-4
Odd Fellows Hall—hist pl MD-2
Odd Fellows' Hall—hist pl MA-1
Odd Fellows Hall—hist pl MA-1
Odd Fellow's Hall—hist pl MA-1
Odd Fellows Hall—hist pl NY-2
Odd Fellows Hall—hist pl (2) OH-6
Oddfellow's Hall—hist pl RI-1
Odd Fellows Hall—hist pl UT-8
Odd Fellows Hall—hist pl WY-8
**Odd Fellows Hall**—pop pl TN-4
Odd Fellows Hall Post Office (historical)—building TN-4
Odd Fellows High Male Sch (historical)—school MS-4
Odd Fellows High Sierra Park—park CA-9
Oddfellows Home—hist pl AZ-5
Odd Fellows' Home—hist pl MA-1
Odd Fellows Home—other IN-6
Odd Fellows Home District—hist pl MO-7
Odd Fellows' Home for Orphans, Indigent and Aged—hist pl OH-6
Oddfellows House—hist pl AK-9
Odd Fellows Lodge—hist pl MD-2
Odd Fellows Lodge—hist pl NC-3
Odd Fellows Orphans Home—building PA-2
**Odd Fellows Park**—pop pl CA-9
Oddfellows-Peterson Park—park AZ-5
Odd Fellows-Rebekah Hall—hist pl ME-1
Odd Fellows Rest Cemetery—hist pl LA-4
Odd Fellows Temple—hist pl CA-9
Odd Fellows Temple—hist pl KY-4
Odd Fellows Temple—hist pl OH-6
Oddie Bar—bend CA-9
Odd Lake—lake WI-6
Oddle, Mount—summit NV-8
Oddot MH-9
Odd Run—stream IN-6
Odds—locale KY-4
Odds—locale TX-5
Oddum Hill MS-4
Oddville—locale KY-4
Oddville Ch—church KY-4
O'Dea Cem—cemetery KS-7
O'Dea House—hist pl MD-2
O'Dear Cem—cemetery TN-4
Odear Cove—valley NC-3
Odear Creek NC-3
ODear Creek—stream NC-3
O'Dear Knob—summit NC-3
**Odebolt**—pop pl IA-7
Odebolt Cem—cemetery IA-7
Odebolt Creek—stream IA-7
Odee (historical)—locale KS-7
Odeen Island MI-6
**Odee Township**—pop pl KS-7
Ode Everage Sch—school KY-4
Odegaard Valley WI-6
Odegard Bog—swamp MN-6
Ode Hollow—valley AR-4
Odeima Lake—lake MN-6
Odekirk Cem—cemetery WI-6
Odekirk Spring—spring UT-8
Ode Lake—reservoir IN-6
Odell—locale AR-4
Odell—locale NY-2
Odell—locale NC-3
Odell—locale WV-2
**Odell**—pop pl IL-6
**Odell**—pop pl IN-6
**Odell**—pop pl NE-7
**Odell**—pop pl OH-6
**Odell**—pop pl OR-9
**Odell**—pop pl PA-2
**Odell**—pop pl TX-5
**Odell Acres (subdivision)**—pop pl UT-8
Odell Barrier Dam—dam MS-4
Odell Branch—stream IA-7
Odell Branch—stream TX-5
Odell Butte—summit OR-9
Odell Canal—canal CA-9
Odell (CCD)—cens area OR-9
O'Dell Cem—cemetery MN-6
O Dell Cem—cemetery MS-4
Odell Cem—cemetery (2) MO-7
Odell Cem—cemetery NE-7
Odell Cem—cemetery OR-9
O'Dell Cem—cemetery TN-4
Odell Cem—cemetery TX-5
Odell Cem—cemetery VA-3
Odell Cem—cemetery WV-2
O Dell Ch—church MS-4
Odell Ch—church MO-7
Odell Ch—church NC-3
Odell Ch—church TX-5
Odell Creek MT-8
O'Dell Creek—stream (2) MT-8
Odell Creek—stream (2) MT-8
Odell Creek—stream OH-6
Odell Creek—stream (3) OR-9
Odell Creek—stream TN-4
Odell Creek—stream (2) TX-5
Odell Creek Campground—park OR-9
Odell Dam—dam AZ-5
Odell Drain—canal MI-6
Odell Fork—stream WV-2
Odell High School NC-3
Odell Hill—summit NY-2
Odell (historical)—locale SD-7
**Odell (historical)**—pop pl ND-7
Odell Hollow—valley MO-7
Odell House—hist pl NY-2
O'Dell House—hist pl TN-4
O'Dell Island—island MN-6
Odell Islands—island NY-2
Odell Knob—summit WV-2
Odell Knob Ch—church WV-2
Odell Lake—lake CA-9
ODell Lake—lake MS-4
Odell Lake—lake MT-8
Odell Lake—lake NY-2
Odell Lake—lake OH-6
Odell Lake—lake OR-9
**Odell Lake**—pop pl OR-9
Odell Lake—reservoir AZ-5
O'Dell Lake Dam—dam AL-4
Odell Lateral OR-9
Odell-Locke-Randolph Cotton Mill—hist pl NC-3
Odell Meadows—swamp MT-8
Odell Mtn—summit MT-8
Odell Mtn—summit NV-8
Odell Pasture—flat OR-9
Odell Pond—lake MI-6
Odell Pond—reservoir NC-3
Odell Pond Dam—dam NC-3
Odell Ridge—ridge NC-3
Odell Rsvr OR-9
O'Dell Rsvr—reservoir MT-8
Odell Sch—school NC-3
Odell Sch—school WV-2
O'Dell Sch (historical)—school TN-4
Odell Spring OR-9
Odell Spring—spring OK-5
Odell Spring—spring OR-9
O'Dell Spring—spring TN-4
Odell Spring Branch—stream WV-2
O'Dell Tank—reservoir AZ-5
Odell Tank—reservoir NM-5
Odell Town—locale WV-2
Odell Township KS-7
Odell (Township of)—fmr MCD NH-1
**Odell (Township of)**—pop pl IL-6
Odell Well—well AZ-5
Odell Well—well NM-5
O'Dell Windmill—locale MT-8
Odelville Sch—school MI-6
**Odem**—pop pl TX-5
Odema Cem—cemetery OK-5
Odem Island—island TX-5
Odem Oil Field—oilfield TX-5
Odems Chapel—church TN-4
Odems Chapel United Pentecostal Ch TN-4
Odem Sch (historical)—school TN-4
**Odemville (historical)**—pop pl TN-4
Odemville Post Office (historical)—building TN-4
Oden—locale ID-8
**Oden**—pop pl AR-4
**Oden**—pop pl MI-6
Oden, Dr. Hezekiah, House—hist pl TN-4
Odena FL-3
Odena—locale AL-4
Odena—locale FL-3
Odena Fire Tower—tower FL-3
Odena Landing—locale FL-3
Odena Mill AL-4
Odena Tower (fire tower)—tower FL-3
Odenbach Bay—bay SD-7
Oden Bay—bay ID-8
**Odenburg**—pop pl LA-4
Oden Cem—cemetery MS-4
Oden Ch—church TX-5
Odencranze Table—summit NE-7
Oden Gap—gap AL-4
Odenheim AL-4
Oden Island—island MI-6
Oden Lake—lake LA-4
Oden Mill AL-4
Oden Mill—locale NC-3
Oden Ranch—locale OR-9
**Oden Ridge**—pop pl AL-4
Oden Ridge Cemetery AL-4
Oden Ridge Sch (historical)—school AL-4
Oden Run—stream MD-2
**Odens Bend**—pop pl TN-4
Oden Sch (historical)—school AL-4
Oden School ID-8
Oden School (historical)—locale ID-8
Odense—locale KS-7
Odense Cem—cemetery KS-7
Odens Mill (historical)—locale AL-4
**Odenthal**—pop pl PA-2
Odenthal Ranch—locale ND-7
**Odenton**—pop pl MD-2
**Odenton Gardens**—pop pl MD-2
Odenville TN-4
**Odenville**—pop pl AL-4
Odenville Industrial Park—locale AL-4
Odenwelder—uninc pl PA-2
**Odenweldertown (subdivision)**—pop pl PA-2
Odenweller, F. F.-James P. and Nettie Morey House—hist pl IA-7
Odeon Theater—hist pl MN-6
Oder Coulee—valley MT-8
Oder Run KY-4
Odesa, Lake—lake IA-7
Odesangel PW-9
Odessa—locale GA-3
Odessa—locale NE-7
Odessa—locale WV-2
**Odessa**—pop pl DE-2
**Odessa**—pop pl FL-3
**Odessa**—pop pl MN-6
**Odessa**—pop pl MO-7
**Odessa**—pop pl NY-2
**Odessa**—pop pl TX-5
**Odessa**—pop pl WA-9
Odessa Briggs Pond Dam—dam MS-4
Odessa Canyon—valley CA-9
Odessa (CCD)—cens area TX-5
Odessa (CCD)—cens area WA-9
Odessa Cem—cemetery MO-7
Odessa Cem—cemetery (2) ND-7
Odessa Cem—cemetery SD-7
Odessa Cem—cemetery WA-9
Odessa Ch—church FL-3
Odessa Ch—church KS-7
Odessa Ch—church OK-5
Odessa Coll—school TX-5
Odessa Country Club—other TX-5
**Odessa Creek**—pop pl OR-9
Odessa Creek—stream OR-9
**Odessadale**—pop pl GA-3
**Odessa Heights**—pop pl DE-2
Odessa Hist Dist—hist pl DE-2
Odessa Hist Dist (Boundary Increase)—hist pl DE-2
Odessa (historical)—locale KS-7
Odessa (historical)—locale ND-7
Odessa (historical)—locale SD-7
**Odessa (historical)**—pop pl OR-9
Odessa Jail—hist pl MN-6
Odessa Kilpatric Sch—school TX-5
Odessa Lake—lake CO-8
Odessa Lakes—lake MI-6
Odessa Meteor Crater—crater TX-5
Odessa Muni Airp—airport WA-9
Odessa Number 1 State Public Shooting Area—park SD-7
Odessa Number 2 State Public Shooting Area—park SD-7
Odessa Oil Field—oilfield KS-7
Odessa Sch—school SD-7
Odessa Sch Number 1—school ND-7
Odessa Sch Number 2—school ND-7
Odessa Sch Number 3—school ND-7
Odessa Spring—spring (2) OR-9
Odessa Township—civil (3) SD-7
**Odessa Township**—pop pl (2) KS-7
**Odessa Township**—pop pl NE-7
**Odessa Township**—pop pl (2) ND-7
**Odessa Township**—pop pl SD-7
**Odessa (Township of)**—pop pl MI-6
**Odessa (Township of)**—pop pl MN-6
Odessey Cave—cave AL-4
Odess Lake Dam—dam AL-4
Odet Run KY-4
Odetta—locale OK-5
O'Dette Drain—canal MI-6
Odette Drain—stream MI-6
Odett Run—stream KY-4
Odey Run—stream WV-2
Odgen—locale IL-6
Odgen Bay Refuge UT-8
Odgen Ditch TX-5
Odgensburg WI-6
Odgers Creek—stream NV-8
Odgers Ind Res NV-8
**Odgers Location**—pop pl MI-6
Odgers Ranch—locale NV-8
Odgers Ranch Ind Res NV-8
Odgers Ranch Ind Res—reserve NV-8
Odgers Well—well NV-8
Od House Creek—stream GA-3
Odia MP-9
Odiak Channel—channel AK-9
Odiak Slough—bay AK-9
Odie Branch—stream MO-7
Odie Sherrer Dam—dam AL-4
Odie Sherrer Lake AL-4
Odiilsau PW-9
Odile MP-9
Odillsau PW-9
Odin—locale PA-2
**Odin**—pop pl IL-6
**Odin**—pop pl KS-7
**Odin**—pop pl MN-6
**Odin**—pop pl MO-7
Odin Falls—falls OR-9
Odingsell River—stream GA-3
Odin Hollow—valley PA-2
Odin Hoxie Trail—trail PA-2
Odin Oil Field—oilfield KS-7
Odin Oil Field—other IL-6
**Odin Township**—pop pl ND-7
**Odin (Township of)**—pop pl IL-6
**Odin (Township of)**—pop pl MN-6
Odiorne Hill—summit NH-1
Odiorne Pond—lake NH-1
Odiornes Point—cape NH-1
Odis Crossroads—locale GA-3
Odis's Head ME-1
Odja FM-9
Odland Dam—dam ND-7
Odlaw—locale TX-5
Odle Cem—cemetery TN-4
Odle Corners—locale PA-2
**Odle Corners**—pop pl PA-2
Odle Hollow—valley TN-4
Odle Mtn—summit SC-3
Odle Ranch—locale AZ-5
Odlin County Park—park WA-9
Odlum Sch—school MI-6
O D Mize Lake Dam—dam MS-4
Ododikossi Lake—lake MN-6
Odofer Drain—canal MI-6
Odom—locale TX-5
**Odom**—pop pl AL-4
Odom, Frank, House—hist pl TX-5
Odom, Lake—lake FL-3
Odom Bay—swamp NC-3
Odom Bend School TN-4
Odom Branch—stream (2) AL-4
Odom Branch—stream TN-4
Odom Cem—cemetery AL-4
Odom Cem—cemetery (2) GA-3
Odom Cem—cemetery LA-4
Odom Cem—cemetery (2) MS-4
Odom Cem—cemetery SC-3
Odom Cem—cemetery TN-4
Odom Cem—cemetery (2) TX-5
Odom Ch—church MO-7
Odom Chapel TN-4
Odom Chapel—church NC-3
Odom Creek AL-4
Odom Creek—stream AL-4
Odom Creek—stream CA-9
Odom Creek—stream (2) GA-3
Odom Creek—stream (3) LA-4
Odom Crossroads—locale AL-4
Odom Hill—summit MS-4
Odom Hill—summit TX-5
Odom Hollow TX-5
Odom Hollow—valley (3) TN-4
Odom Hollow—valley TX-5
Odom Lake Dam—dam MS-4
Odom Lake Swamp TX-5
Odom Memorial Ch—church AL-4
Odom Mill (historical)—locale MS-4
Odom Point—summit AR-4
Odom Pond—reservoir NC-3
Odom Pond—reservoir SC-3
Odom Pond—swamp TX-5
Odom Ranch—locale TX-5
Odoms Bend—bend TN-4
Odoms Bend Access Area—park TN-4
Odoms Bend Sch—school TN-4
Odoms Cem—cemetery MS-4
Odom Sch—school LA-4
Odom Sch (historical)—school AL-4
Odom School MO-7
Odoms Lake Dam—dam MS-4
Odoms Mill Pond AL-4
Odoms Mine (underground)—mine AL-4
Odom State Prison Farm—locale NC-3
Odom Trout Lake—reservoir TN-4
Odom Trout Lake Dam—dam TN-4
Odom Windmill—locale TX-5
**Odon**—pop pl IN-6
O'Donald Bend AR-4
O'Donald Bend Community AR-4
O'Donald Creek—stream SD-7
O'Donald Golf Course—other CA-9
O'Donald Lake—lake MN-6
Odon Cem—cemetery LA-4
O'Donel House and Farm—hist pl PA-2
O'Donel Trail—trail PA-2
O'Donely Cem—cemetery KY-4
O'Donnally Cemetery TN-4
O'Donnel Creek—stream AK-9
O'Donnell—locale PA-2
O'Donnell—locale WY-8
**O'Donnell**—pop pl TX-5
O'Donnell, I. D., House—hist pl MT-8
O'Donnell, Lake—reservoir (2) TN-4
O'Donnel Landing AR-4
Odonnell Bend AR-4
O'Donnell Bend—locale AR-4
O'Donnell Bldg—hist pl IN-6
O'Donnell Canyon AZ-5
O'Donnell Canyon—valley AZ-5
O'Donnell (CCD)—cens area TX-5
ODonnell Cem—cemetery TX-5
O'Donnell Creek—stream AK-9
O'Donnell Creek—stream ID-8
O'Donnell Creek—stream PA-2
Odonnell Heights—uninc pl MD-2
O'Donnell Lake—lake MN-6
O'Donnell Lateral—canal CA-9
O'Donnell Mtn—summit MT-8
O'Donnell Place—locale TX-5
O'Donnell Run—stream PA-2
O'Donnell Sch—school NY-2
O Donnell Sch—school SD-7
O'Donnell Spring—spring NV-8
**O'donnell Spur**—pop pl WY-8
O'Donnel Ranch—locale WY-8
O'Donniley Cem—cemetery TN-4
O'Donoghue Sch—school NC-3
O'Donohue, C. A., House—hist pl NY-2
Odor Creek—stream AK-9
Odou Patterson Dam—dam SD-7
O'Dowd Lake—lake MN-6
Odra—locale LA-4
O Drageset Number 1 Dam—dam SD-7
O Drageset Number 2 Dam—dam SD-7
O Drageset Number 3 Dam—dam SD-7
O Drain—canal CA-9
O D Ranch—locale NM-5
Odricks Corner—locale VA-3
O D Ridge—ridge AZ-5
O'Driscoll Spring—spring UT-8
Odsen FM-9
Odshiapofa (historical)—locale AL-4
Odulund Island—island FL-3
**Odum**—pop pl GA-3
Odum Bayou—stream MS-4
Odum Branch—stream TN-4
Odum (CCD)—cens area GA-3
Odum Childrens Home—building GA-3
Odum Dam Number 1 AL-4
Odum Gap—gap AL-4
Odum Grove Ch—church GA-3
Odum Hill MS-4
Odum Hill Sch (historical)—school MS-4
**Odum (historical)**—pop pl TN-4
Odum Lake—reservoir GA-3
Odum Lake Number 1—reservoir AL-4
Odum Memorial Church AL-4
Odum Park—park OK-5
Odum Point—summit AL-4
Odum Post Office (historical)—building TN-4
Odums Mill Dam—dam AL-4
Odums Mill Pond—reservoir AL-4
Odum Spur—locale IL-6
Odum Trail—trail AL-4
O D Well—well NM-5
Odyssey Learning Center—school FL-3
Odyssey Peak—summit WY-8
Odzen FM-9
Oea Bay—bay HI-9
Oehler Cem—cemetery WI-6
Oehler Springs—spring TN-4
**Oehlmann Park**—pop pl CO-8
Oehlman Sch—school IA-7
Oehlrichs SD-7
Oehm, Lake—reservoir CO-8
Oehmen Branch—stream TN-4
Oeila Lake ND-7
Oeldorf Building/Wetherell's Jewelers—hist pl WV-2
Oele Fransens Creek DE-2
Oelhafen Creek—stream WI-6
**Oella**—pop pl MD-2
Oella Hist Dist—hist pl MD-2
**Oelrichs**—pop pl SD-7
Oelsen Ditch—canal CO-8
**Oelwein**—pop pl IA-7
Oelwein, Lake—lake IA-7
Oelwein HS—school IA-7
Oelwein JHS—school IA-7
Oems Free Gift Ch—church AR-4
**Oenaville**—pop pl TX-5
Oeneis, Mount—summit WY-8
Oerke Enterprises Airp—airport MO-7
**Oermann**—pop pl MO-7
Oerns Creek—stream AK-9
Oertel Mine—mine MT-8
Oesapimsuck Brook RI-1
Oescataupa River MS-4
O E Sch—school NY-2
Oeshboekel PW-9
Oeshbokul Island PW-9
Oe Spring—spring ID-8
OE Spring—spring WY-8
Oeste Park—park CA-9
Oesterle Lake—lake WI-6
Oest Mine—mine NV-8
Oestreicher Hill—summit ND-7
Oetterer Cem—cemetery MO-7
**Oetters**—pop pl MO-7
Oettiker Creek—stream MT-8
Oettiker Creek Trail—trail MT-8
Oetting Cem—cemetery MO-7
Oetting Ch—church MO-7
Oetting School (Abandoned)—locale MO-7
Oettle Bridge—bridge CA-9
Ofahoma—locale MS-4
**O'Fallon**—pop pl IL-6
**O'Fallon**—pop pl MO-7
O'Fallon Creek—stream MT-8
O'Fallon Park—park CO-8
O'Fallon Park—park MO-7
O'Fallons—locale NE-7
**Ofallons**—pop pl NE-7
O'Fallons Bluff—hist pl NE-7
O'Fallon Township—civil MO-7
**O'Fallon (Township of)**—pop pl IL-6
O'Farre Lake—lake MO-7
O'Farrel Gulch—valley OR-9
O'Farrell—locale TX-5
O'Farrell, John A., House—hist pl ID-8
O'Farrell Hollow—valley VA-3
O'Farrell JHS—school CA-9
O'Farrell Lookout—locale WA-9
O'Farrill Gulch—valley CA-9
OFDBA Dam Number 60-13—dam TN-4
OFDBA Dam Number 60-6—dam TN-4
OFDBA Dam Number 86-95-2—dam TN-4
OFDBA Lake Site Number 60-13—reservoir TN-4
OFDBA Lake Site Number 60-6—reservoir TN-4

OFDBA Lake Site Number 86-95-2—*reservoir* ... TN-4
OFDBA Little Cypress Creek Lake Number—*reservoir* ... TN-4
OFDBA Number 86-2 Dam—*dam* ... TN-4
*OFDBA Site Number 87-1* ... TN-4
OFDBA Spring Creek Site Number 105a-1 Dam—*dam* ... TN-4
OFDBA 87-3 Dam—*dam* ... TN-4
OFDBA 87-3 Lake—*reservoir* ... TN-4
Ofelia—*locale* ... AL-4
Ofer Basin—*valley* ... UT-8
Ofer Mine—*mine* ... UT-8
O'Ferrell Cem—*cemetery* ... TN-4
Offard Hollow—*valley* ... WV-2
*Offatt Bayou* ... TX-5
Offatts Bayou—*gut* ... TX-5
Offatt Spring—*spring* ... OR-9
Off Davis Hollow—*valley* ... MO-7
Off Ditch—*canal* ... IN-6
Offenbacher Gulch—*valley* ... OR-9
Offenbacher Point—*cape* ... OR-9
Offenhauser Insurance Bldg—*hist pl* ... TX-5
**Offerle**—*pop pl* ... KS-7
**Offerman**—*pop pl* ... GA-3
Offerman Cem—*cemetery* ... GA-3
Offerman Sch—*school* ... IL-6
Offer Ranch—*locale* ... TX-5
Offers Lake—*lake* ... WI-6
Office and Banking House of West Feliciana RR—*hist pl* ... MS-4
Office Bldg and U.S. Light-House Depot Complex—*hist pl* ... NY-2
Office Bridge—*hist pl* ... OR-9
Office Creek—*stream* ... TX-5
**Office Hall**—*pop pl* ... VA-3
Office of Personnel Mngmt Bldg—*building* ... DC-2
Office of the Register—*hist pl* ... NY-2
Officer—*locale* ... CO-8
Officer—*locale* ... UT-8
Officer Branch—*stream* ... TN-4
Officer Canyon—*valley* ... CO-8
Officer Cave—*cave* ... TN-4
Officer Creek—*stream* ... OR-9
Officer Knob—*summit* ... TN-4
Officer Orchard Ridge—*ridge* ... TN-4
*Officer Rsvr* ... OR-9
Officers Ch—*church* ... TN-4
**Officers Chapel**—*pop pl* ... TN-4
Officers Dam—*dam* ... OR-9
Officers Gulch—*valley* ... CO-8
Officers Gulch Pond—*lake* ... CO-8
Officers Lake—*lake* ... MS-4
Officer Spring—*spring* ... ID-8
Officer Spring—*spring* ... OR-9
Officer Springs—*spring* ... OR-9
Officer's Quarters—*hist pl* ... AZ-5
Officer's Quarters—*hist pl* ... OK-5
Officers Row, Fort Vancouver Barracks—*hist pl* ... WA-9
Officers Rsvr—*reservoir* ... OR-9
Officers Run—*stream* ... PA-2
Official Dog Town—*locale* ... OK-5
Offield Branch (historical)—*stream* ... TN-4
Offield Canyon—*valley* ... WA-9
Offield Creek—*stream* ... AK-9
Offield Creek—*stream* ... IN-6
Offield Creek—*stream* ... OR-9
Offield Landing—*locale* ... WA-9
Offield Mtn—*summit* ... CA-9
Offield Mtn—*summit* ... CO-8
Offield Place—*locale* ... CO-8
Offield Rsvr—*reservoir* ... CO-8
Offield Saddle—*gap* ... CA-9
Offielo Nursing Home—*other* ... CO-8
Offie Run—*stream* ... WV-2
Off Island—*island* ... NC-3
Offnear Lake—*lake* ... MI-6
Off Rock—*island* ... CA-9
Off Rock—*rock* ... MA-1
**Offset**—*pop pl* ... TN-4
*Offset Creek* ... PA-2
Offset Gulch—*valley* ... ID-8
*Offset Knob* ... PA-2
Offset Mine—*mine* ... MO-7
*Offset Nob* ... PA 2
Offset Sch (historical)—*school* ... TN-4
Offshore Reefs Archeol District—*hist pl* ... FL-3
Off Slough—*stream* ... UT-8
Off Spring—*spring* ... UT-8
Off-the-Neck Hist Dist—*hist pl* ... ME-1
*Off Trinidad Head* ... CA-9
*Offut* ... TN-4
Offut Cave—*cave* ... TN-4
Offutt—*locale* ... TN-4
**Offutt**—*pop pl* ... KY-4
**Offutt**—*pop pl* ... MD-2
Offutt Acres Airp—*airport* ... PA-2
Offutt AFB—*military* ... NE-7
Offutt Air Force Base East—*CDP* ... NE-7
Offutt Air Force Base West—*CDP* ... NE-7
Offutt-Cole Tavern—*hist pl* ... KY-4
Offutt Covered Bridge—*hist pl* ... IN-6
Offutt Field—*other* ... PA-2
Offutt Island—*island* ... MD-2
Offutt Lake—*lake* ... WA-9
Offutt Lake—*locale* ... WA-9
Offutt Landing—*locale* ... AR-4
Offutt Landing—*locale* ... MS-4
Offutt Post Office (historical)—*building* ... TN-4
*Offutts* ... TN-4
Offutts Shoals—*bar* ... TN-4
**Offutt Village**—*pop pl* ... VA-3
Ofield Cem—*cemetery* ... OK-5
Of Isles, Lake—*lake* ... CT-1
Ofoko—*spring* ... FM-9
*Ofsam* ... MH-9
**Ofu**—*pop pl* ... AS-9
Ofu (County of)—*civ div* ... AS-9
Ofu Island—*island* ... AS-9
*Ogachen Creek* ... WA-9
Ogados Lake—*reservoir* ... TX-5
*Ogalala Peak* ... CO-8
*Ogalalla* ... KY-4
*Ogalalla* ... NE-7
Ogalalla Lodge—*locale* ... CO-8
Ogalalla Peak—*summit* ... CO-8
**Ogallah**—*pop pl* ... KS-7
Ogallah Cem—*cemetery* ... KS-7
*Ogallah Creek* ... KS-7
Ogallah Oil Field—*oilfield* ... KS-7
**Ogallah Township**—*pop pl* ... KS-7
**Ogallala**—*pop pl* ... NE-7
Ogallala, Lake—*reservoir* ... TN-4
Ogallala Cem—*cemetery* ... NE-7
Ogallala Contry Club—*other* ... NE-7
Ogallala Gulch—*valley* ... NE-7
Ogallala Lake—*lake* ... NE-7
Ogallala Windmill—*locale* ... TX-5
*Ogamaw* ... AR-4
Ogan Cem—*cemetery* ... TX-5
Ogangen Island—*island* ... AK-9
Ogan Hollow—*valley* ... AR-4
Ogan Ranch—*locale* ... CA-9
*Oganse* ... OH-6
O'Gara Bay—*bay* ... ID-8
Ogard Point—*cape* ... MN-6
Ogaromtoc Lake—*lake* ... CA-9
Ogasan—*area* ... GU-9
**Ogborn**—*pop pl* (2) ... MO-7
Ogburn—*locale* ... TX-5
Ogburn—*locale* ... VA-3
Ogburn, Henry, House—*hist pl* ... KY-4
Ogburn, William, House—*hist pl* ... IA-7
Ogburn Branch—*stream* ... NC-3
Ogburn Cem—*cemetery* ... NC-3
Ogburn Chapel—*church* ... TN-4
Ogburn Crossroads—*locale* ... NC-3
Ogburn Inwood Cem—*cemetery* ... CA-9
Ogburn Park—*park* ... TN-4
Ogburns Crossroads—*locale* ... NC-3
**Ogburn Station**—*pop pl* ... NC-3
Ogburntown—*uninc pl* ... NC-3
Ogchul Island—*island* ... AK-9
*Ogden* ... KY-4
*Ogden* ... WV-2
Ogden—*locale* ... MO-7
Ogden—*locale* ... NJ-2
Ogden—*locale* ... NC-3
Ogden—*locale* ... OH-6
Ogden—*locale* ... TN-4
Ogden—*locale* (3) ... TX-5
**Ogden**—*pop pl* ... AR-4
**Ogden**—*pop pl* ... IL-6
**Ogden**—*pop pl* ... IN-6
**Ogden**—*pop pl* ... IA-7
**Ogden**—*pop pl* ... KS-7
**Ogden**—*pop pl* ... MI-6
**Ogden**—*pop pl* ... NC-3
**Ogden**—*pop pl* ... PA-2
**Ogden**—*pop pl* ... SC-3
**Ogden**—*pop pl* ... UT-8
**Ogden**—*pop pl* ... WV-2
Ogden—*uninc pl* ... NY-2
Ogden, David, House—*hist pl* ... CT-1
Ogden, Lake—*lake* ... MI-6
Ogden, Mount—*summit* ... AK-9
Ogden, Mount—*summit* (2) ... UT-8
Ogden, Point—*cape* ... FL-3
Ogden Ave Sch—*school* ... IL-6
*Ogden Baptist Church* ... MS-4
*Ogden Baptist Church* ... TN-4
Ogden Bay—*bay* ... UT-8
Ogden Bayou—*swamp* ... FL-3
Ogden Bayou Oil Field—*oilfield* ... MS-4
Ogden Bay Refuge HQ—*locale* ... UT-8
Ogden Bay Waterfowl Mngmt Area—*park* ... UT-8
Ogden Bend—*bend* ... CA-9
Ogden Branch—*stream* ... IL-6
Ogden Branch—*stream* ... KY-4
Ogden Branch—*stream* ... MS-4
Ogden Brigham Canal—*canal* ... UT-8
Ogden Brook—*stream* ... CT-1
Ogden Buddhist Ch—*church* ... UT-8
Ogden Canyon—*valley* ... UT-8
Ogden Canyon Conduit—*canal* ... UT-8
Ogden Canyon Tunnel—*tunnel* ... UT-8
**Ogden Canyon Wildwood Estates Subdivision**—*pop pl* ... UT-8
Ogden Cem—*cemetery* ... AR-4
Ogden Cem—*cemetery* ... FL-3
Ogden Cem—*cemetery* ... IL-6
Ogden Cem—*cemetery* ... IN-6
Ogden Cem—*cemetery* ... IA-7
Ogden Cem—*cemetery* ... KS-7
Ogden Cem—*cemetery* ... MS-4
Ogden Cem—*cemetery* ... OH-6
Ogden Cemeteries—*cemetery* ... LA-4
Ogden Center—*locale* ... UT-8
**Ogden Center**—*pop pl* ... MI-6
**Ogden Center**—*pop pl* ... NY-2
Ogden Center Ch—*church* ... MI-6
Ogden Ch—*church* ... AR-4
Ogden Ch—*church* ... MS-4
Ogden Ch—*church* ... NY-2
Ogden Ch—*church* ... NC-3
Ogden Ch—*church* ... TN-4
Ogden Ch—*church* ... VA-3
*Ogden City* ... UT-8
Ogden City Cem—*cemetery* ... UT-8
Ogden City Mall (Shop Ctr)—*locale* ... UT-8
Ogden Commercial and Industrial Park Plat A—*locale* ... UT-8
Ogden Commercial and Industrial Park Plat C—*locale* ... UT-8
Ogden Commercial and Industrial Park Plat D—*locale* ... UT-8
Ogden Commerical and Industrial Park Plat B—*locale* ... UT-8
*Ogden Community* ... TX-5
Ogden Creek—*stream* ... AR-4
Ogden Creek—*stream* ... CO-8
Ogden Creek—*stream* ... NJ-2
Ogden Creek—*stream* ... WY-8
*Ogden Dam* ... AL-4
Ogden Ditch—*canal* ... TX-5
Ogden Division—*civil* ... UT-8
**Ogden Dunes**—*pop pl* ... IN-6
Ogden Elem Sch—*school* ... KS-7
Ogden Elem Sch—*school* ... NC-3
Ogden-Fettie Site—*hist pl* ... IL-6
Ogden Gap Sch—*school* ... KY-4
Ogden Golf and Country Club—*other* ... UT-8
Ogden Gun Club—*other* ... UT-8
**Ogden Heights Subdivision**—*pop pl* ... UT-8
Ogden Hill—*summit* ... KS-7
Ogden House—*hist pl* ... IA-7
Ogden House—*hist pl* ... PA-2
Ogden HS—*hist pl* ... UT-8
Ogden HS—*school* ... UT-8
Ogden Island—*island* ... IN-6
Ogden Island—*island* ... NY-2
Ogden Lake—*reservoir* ... AL-4
Ogden Lake—*reservoir* ... FL-3
*Ogden Landing* ... KY-4
Ogden Meadows—*uninc pl* ... WA-9
Ogden Mill Cem—*cemetery* ... GA-3
*Ogden Mine* ... NJ-2
Ogden Mounds—*other* ... IL-6
Ogden Mtn—*summit* ... MT-8
Ogden Municipal Airp—*airport* ... UT-8
Ogden Norton Drain—*canal* ... MI-6
*Ogden Park* ... IL-6
Ogden Park—*park* ... IL-6
**Ogden Park**—*pop pl* ... PA-2
Ogden Park—*uninc pl* ... LA-4
Ogden Passage—*channel* ... AK-9
*Ogden Peak* ... UT-8
Ogden Point—*cape* (2) ... ME-1
Ogden Pond—*lake* ... FL-3
Ogden Pond—*lake* ... NY-2
Ogden Post Office—*building* ... UT-8
Ogden Post Office (historical)—*building* ... TN-4
Ogden Ranch—*locale* ... MT-8
*Ogden Refuge HQ* ... UT-8
Ogden Rescue Mission—*church* ... UT-8
Ogden River—*stream* ... UT-8
Ogden Run—*stream* ... OH-6
*Ogdensberg* ... NY-2
*Ogdensburg* ... KS-7
**Ogdensburg**—*pop pl* ... NJ-2
**Ogdensburg**—*pop pl* ... NY-2
**Ogdensburg**—*pop pl* ... PA-2
**Ogdensburg**—*pop pl* ... WI-6
Ogdensburg Cem—*cemetery* ... MI-6
Ogdensburg Cem—*cemetery* ... WI-6
Ogdensburg Ch—*church* ... MI-6
Ogdensburg Country Club—*locale* ... NY-2
*Ogdensburgh* ... KS-7
*Ogdensburgh* ... PA-2
Ogdensburg International Airp—*airport* ... NY-2
Ogdensburg Pond—*reservoir* ... WI-6
Ogdensburg-Prescott International Bridge—*bridge* ... NY-2
Ogdens Cave—*cave* ... VA-3
Ogden Sch—*school* ... IL-6
Ogden Sch—*school* ... IA-7
Ogden Sch—*school* ... NY-2
Ogden Sch—*school* ... NC-3
Ogden Sch—*school* (2) ... TX-5
Ogden Sch—*school* ... VA-3
Ogden Sch (abandoned)—*school* ... MO-7
Ogdens Creek—*stream* ... NJ-2
*Ogden's Landing* ... KY-4
Ogden Slip—*gut* ... IL-6
*Ogdens River* ... NV-8
**Ogden Sugar Spur**—*pop pl* ... UT-8
**Ogden Sugar Works**—*pop pl* ... UT-8
**Ogden Sugar Works Junction**—*pop pl* ... UT-8
*Ogdensville Post Office* ... TN-4
**Ogden (Town of)**—*pop pl* ... NY-2
**Ogden Township**—*pop pl* ... KS-7
**Ogden (Township of)**—*pop pl* ... IL-6
**Ogden (Township of)**—*pop pl* ... MI-6
Ogden Union Depot—*hist pl* ... UT-8
Ogden Valley—*cens area* ... UT-8
Ogden Valley—*valley* ... UT-8
Ogden Valley Canal—*canal* ... UT-8
Ogden Valley Division—*civil* ... UT-8
Ogden/Weber Municipal Bldg—*hist pl* ... UT-8
Ogden Well—*well* ... UT-8
Ogdonia—*locale* ... PA-2
Ogdonia Clubhouse—*locale* ... PA-2
Ogdonia Creek—*stream* ... PA-2
Oge—*locale* ... AS-9
Ogechie Lake—*lake* ... MN-6
Ogeden Cem—*cemetery* ... KY-4
Ogeechee—*locale* ... GA-3
Ogeechee—*locale* ... OK-5
Ogeechee Branch Ch—*church* ... GA-3
Ogeechee Ch—*church* (3) ... GA-3
Ogeechee Creek—*stream* ... GA-3
Ogeechee Creek—*stream* ... OK-5
*Ogeechee River* ... GA-3
Ogeechee River—*stream* ... GA-3
**Ogeechee Road**—*pop pl* ... GA-3
Ogeechee Run—*stream* ... GA-3
**Ogeecheeton**—*pop pl* ... GA-3
Ogee (historical)—*locale* ... AL-4
Ogeese Creek—*stream* ... KS-7
Ogefao—*locale* ... AS-9
Ogegasa Point—*cape* ... AS-9
Ogegase—*locale* ... AS-9
*Ogelesby* ... OK-5
Ogels Road Canyon—*valley* ... TX-5
**Ogema**—*pop pl* ... MN-6
**Ogema**—*pop pl* ... WI-6
Ogema Cem—*cemetery* (2) ... MN-6
Ogema Lake—*lake* ... MN-6
Ogema Millpond—*reservoir* ... WI-6
Ogema Springs State Wildlife Mngmt Area—*park* ... MN-6
**Ogema (Town of)**—*pop pl* ... WI-6
**Ogema (Township of)**—*pop pl* ... MN-6
**Ogemaw**—*pop pl* ... AR-4
Ogemaw, Lake—*reservoir* ... MI-6
**Ogemaw (County)**—*pop pl* ... MI-6
Ogemaw Creek—*stream* (2) ... MI-6
Ogemaw Lake—*lake* ... MI-6
**Ogemaw Springs**—*pop pl* ... MI-6
Ogemaw State For—*forest* ... MI-6
Ogemaw Swamp—*swamp* ... MI-6
**Ogemaw (Township of)**—*pop pl* ... MI-6
**Oger**—*pop pl* ... VA-3
Ogetu Ridge—*ridge* ... AS-9
Ogg—*locale* ... TX-5
*Oggawame* ... MA-1
Ogg Creek—*stream* ... OH-6
Ogg Drain—*canal* ... MI-6
Ogg Hollow—*valley* ... OH-6
Ogg Sch—*school* ... IA-7
Ogg Sch—*school* ... MO-7
Ogg Tank—*reservoir* ... NM-5
Ogier Point—*cape* ... ME-1
**Ogiil**—*pop pl* ... PW-9
Ogilbie Cem—*cemetery* ... AR-4
Ogilby—*locale* ... CA-9
Ogilby Canyon—*valley* ... CA-9
Ogilby Hills—*range* ... CA-9
Ogilivie Cem—*cemetery* (2) ... TN-4
**Ogilvie**—*pop pl* ... MN-6
Ogilvie, Mount—*summit* ... AK-9
Ogilvie, William, House—*hist pl* ... TN-4
Ogilvie Cem—*cemetery* ... FL-3
Ogilvie Coulee—*valley* ... MT-8
Ogilvie Creek—*stream* ... NV-8
Ogilvie Gulch—*valley* ... MT-8
Ogilvie Sch—*school* ... IL-6
Ogilvie Sch—*school* ... MI-6
Ogilvie Watertower—*hist pl* ... MN-6
Ogilvie Well—*well* ... AZ-5
**Ogilville**—*pop pl* ... IN-6
Ogilville Ch—*church* ... IN-6
Ogilville Sch—*school* ... IN-6
Ogilvy Ditch—*canal* ... CO-8
Ogilvy Ranch—*locale* ... CA-9
Ogima Falls—*falls* ... MI-6
Ogimakwe Falls—*falls* ... MI-6
*Ogimakwe Lake* ... MI-6
Ogishkemuncie Lake—*lake* ... MN-6
*Ogishki Muncie Lake* ... MN-6
Ogive Glacier—*glacier* ... AK-9
Ogive Mtn—*summit* ... AK-9
*Ogiwal* ... PW-9
*Ogiwaru* ... PW-9
*Ogiwaru Point* ... PW-9
Oglala—*locale* ... SD-7
Oglala Dam—*dam* ... SD-7
Oglala Lake—*reservoir* ... SD-7
Oglala Natl Grassland—*park* ... NE-7
Oglala Pass—*channel* ... AK-9
*Oglala Peak* ... CO-8
Oglala Point—*cape* ... AK-9
Oglala Sch—*school* (2) ... SD-7
Oglala-Sioux Sundance Arena—*locale* ... SD-7
Ogle—*locale* ... IL-6
Ogle—*locale* ... KY-4
Ogle—*locale* ... PA-2
Ogle, Bud, Farm—*hist pl* ... TN-4
Ogle, Joseph, House—*hist pl* ... TX-5
Oglebay Hall—*hist pl* ... WV-2
Oglebay Mansion Museum—*hist pl* ... WV-2
Oglebay Park—*park* ... WV-2
Ogle Branch—*stream* ... NC-3
Ogle Branch—*stream* ... VA-3
Ogleby Creek—*stream* ... FL-3
Ogle Cave—*cave* ... NM-5
Ogle Cem—*cemetery* ... OH-6
Ogle Chapel—*church* (2) ... TN-4
**Ogle (County)**—*pop pl* ... IL-6
Ogle County Courthouse—*hist pl* ... IL-6
Ogle Creek—*stream* ... NC-3
Ogle Creek—*stream* ... OR-9
Ogle Creek—*stream* ... VA-3
Ogle Creek—*stream* ... WA-9
Ogle Ditch—*canal* ... IN-6
Ogle Flat—*flat* ... NM-5
Ogle Gap—*gap* ... NC-3
Ogle Grove Cem—*cemetery* ... MO-7
Ogle Hollow—*valley* ... TN-4
Ogle JHS—*school* ... MD-2
Ogle Knob—*summit* ... NC-3
Ogle Lake—*lake* ... MN-6
Ogle Lake—*lake* ... WI-6
Ogle Lake—*reservoir* ... IN-6
Ogle Lake Dam—*dam* ... IN-6
*Ogle Meadow* ... NC-3
Ogle Meadows—*flat* ... NC-3
Ogle Mountain Mine—*mine* ... OR-9
Ogle Ridge—*ridge* ... NC-3
**Ogles**—*pop pl* ... IL-6
**Ogles**—*pop pl* ... TX-5
Oglesby—*locale* ... GA-3
**Oglesby**—*pop pl* ... IL-6
**Oglesby**—*pop pl* ... OK-5
**Oglesby**—*pop pl* ... TX-5
Oglesby—*uninc pl* ... TN-4
Oglesby Branch—*stream* ... VA-3
Oglesby (CCD)—*cens area* ... TX-5
Oglesby Cem—*cemetery* ... KY-4
Oglesby Cem—*cemetery* ... OK-5
Oglesby Cem—*cemetery* ... TX-5
Oglesby Cem—*cemetery* ... VA-3
Oglesby-Conrad—*hist pl* ... KY-4
*Oglesby Creek* ... FL-3
Oglesby Creek—*stream* ... OR-9
Oglesby Hill—*summit* ... KY-4
Oglesby Pond—*reservoir* ... GA-3
Oglesby Ranch—*locale* ... TX-5
Oglesby Sch—*school* ... IL-6
Ogles Cem—*cemetery* ... TN-4
Ogle Sch—*school* ... IL-6
Ogle Sch (historical)—*school* ... MO-7
Ogles Creek—*stream* ... IL-6
Ogles Hill—*summit* ... MO-7
Ogles Mtn—*summit* ... OK-5
Ogle Spring Branch—*stream* ... TN-4
Ogles Ridge Ch—*church* ... OH-6
**Oglesville**—*pop pl* ... MO-7
**Oglethorpe**—*pop pl* (2) ... GA-3
Oglethorpe, Mount—*summit* ... GA-3
Oglethorpe Ave Hist Dist—*hist pl* ... GA-3
*Oglethorpe Bay* ... GA-3
Oglethorpe Bay—*bay* ... GA-3
Oglethorpe Bluff—*cliff* ... GA-3
Oglethorpe Branch—*stream* ... GA-3
Oglethorpe (CCD)—*cens area* ... GA-3
Oglethorpe Ch—*church* ... GA-3
**Oglethorpe (County)**—*pop pl* ... GA-3
Oglethorpe Memorial Gardens—*cemetery* ... GA-3
**Oglethorpe Park**—*pop pl* ... GA-3
Oglethorpe Univ—*school* ... GA-3
*Ogleton* ... DE-2
Ogleton, Lake—*bay* ... MD-2
*Ogleton Lake* ... MD-2
**Ogletown**—*pop pl* ... DE-2
**Ogletown**—*pop pl* ... PA-2
Ogletown MS—*school* ... DE-2
**Ogle (Township of)**—*pop pl* ... PA-2
Ogletree, Lake—*reservoir* ... AL-4
Ogletree Branch—*stream* ... AL-4
Ogletree Cem—*cemetery* (2) ... GA-3
Ogletree Creek—*stream* ... AL-4
Ogletree Creek—*stream* ... MI-6
Ogletree Gap—*gap* ... TX-5
Ogletree Island—*island* ... AL-4
Ogletree Number Two Dam—*dam* ... AL-4
Ogletree Outing Club Dam—*dam* ... AL-4
Ogletree Outing Club Lake—*reservoir* ... AL-4
Ogletree Park—*park* ... AL-4
Ogletree Plaza Shop Ctr—*locale* ... AL-4
Ogletree Woods—*uninc pl* ... GA-3
Ogle Well—*well* ... AZ-5
Ogliuga Island—*island* ... AK-9
Ogliuga Pass—*channel* ... AK-9
Oglodak Island—*island* ... AK-9
*Ogomanaw* ... FM-9
*Ogontz* ... OH-6
*Ogontz* ... PA-2
Ogontz—*locale* ... ME-1
Ogontz—*locale* ... MI-6
**Ogontz**—*pop pl* ... OH-6
**Ogontz**—*pop pl* ... PA-2
Ogontz Bay—*bay* ... MI-6
Ogontz Brook—*stream* ... NH-1
**Ogontz Campus (Penn State College)**—*pop pl* ... PA-2
Ogontz Cem—*cemetery* ... MI-6
Ogontz Center—*locale* ... PA-2
Ogontz Lake—*lake* ... NH-1
Ogontz River—*stream* ... MI-6
*Ogontz School* ... PA-2
Ogontz White Mountain Camp—*locale* ... NH-1
O'Gorman HS—*school* ... SD-7
Ogo Station—*locale* ... CA-9
Ogotoruk Creek—*stream* ... AK-9
Ogotoruk Valley—*basin* ... AK-9
O'Grady Canyon—*valley* ... AZ-5
O'Grain Ranch—*locale* ... UT-8
Ogre, The—*summit* ... ID-8
Ogre Creek—*stream* ... OR-9
Ogreeta—*locale* ... NC-3
*Ogren* ... ME-1
Ogren—*locale* ... ME-1
Ogren Lake—*lake* ... MN-6
*Ogreta* ... NC-3
*Ogretta* ... NC-3
Ogriveg River—*stream* ... AK-9
Ogsachak—*locale* ... AK-9
Ogsachak Creek—*stream* ... AK-9
Ogsachak Mtn—*summit* ... AK-9
*Ogso Achugau* ... MH-9
*Ogso Dogas* ... MH-9
*Ogso Gualo Rai* ... MH-9
*Ogso Laulau* ... MH-9
*Ogso Tagpochau* ... MH-9
*Ogso Talofofo* ... MH-9
*Ogso Tipo Pale* ... MH-9
Ogstad Cem—*cemetery* ... SD-7
O G Steele Pond—*lake* ... FL-3
O'Guin Cem—*cemetery* ... TN-4
O'Guin Hollow—*valley* (2) ... TN-4
O'Guinn Cem—*cemetery* ... TN-4
O'Guinn Creek—*stream* ... TX-5
*Oguirrh Mountains* ... UT-8
Ogulin Canyon—*valley* ... CA-9
**Ogunquit**—*pop pl* ... ME-1
Ogunquit Beach—*beach* ... ME-1
Ogunquit Country Club—*other* ... ME-1
Ogunquit Memorial Library—*hist pl* ... ME-1
Ogunquit River—*stream* ... ME-1
**Ogunquit (Town of)**—*pop pl* ... ME-1
Oguohaydok Ridge—*ridge* ... AK-9
*Ohaca Cabins* ... AZ-5
O'Haco Cabins—*locale* ... AZ-5
O'Haco Lookout Tower—*tower* ... AZ-5
O'Haco Tank—*reservoir* (3) ... AZ-5
Ohai Point—*cape* (2) ... HI-9
O'Hair Park—*park* ... MI-6
O'Hair Spring—*spring* ... CO-8
Ohaiula Beach—*beach* ... HI-9
Ohaiula Ridge—*ridge* ... HI-9
Ohaiula Valley—*valley* ... HI-9
O'Hallaren Park—*park* ... IL-6
O'Hallihan Spring—*spring* ... OR-9
O'Halon Coulee—*valley* ... MT-8
Ohanapecosh Campground—*locale* ... WA-9
Ohanapecosh Glacier—*glacier* ... WA-9
Ohanapecosh Hot Springs—*spring* ... WA-9
Ohanapecosh Park—*flat* ... WA-9
Ohanapecosh River—*stream* ... WA-9
Ohanaula Gulch—*valley* ... HI-9
O'Hanlon Bldg—*hist pl* ... NC-3
*O'Hanlon Community Center* ... MS-4
O'Hanlon Coulee—*valley* (2) ... MT-8
*O'Hanna Creek* ... OR-9
O'Hara, John, House—*hist pl* ... PA-2
O'Hara Bros Ranch—*locale* ... MT-8
O'Hara Campground—*locale* ... ID-8
O'Hara Canyon—*valley* ... CA-9
O Hara Cem—*cemetery* ... IL-6
O'Hara Cem—*cemetery* ... KY-4
O'Hara Corners—*locale* ... NY-2
O'Hara Creek—*stream* ... ID-8
O'Hara Creek—*stream* ... WI-6
O'Hara Ditch—*canal* (2) ... IN-6
Ohara Elem Sch—*school* ... PA-2
O'Hara House—*hist pl* ... ID-8
O'Hara HS—*school* ... NY-2
*O'Hara JHS* ... PA-2
O Hara Key—*island* ... FL-3
O'Hara Oil Field—*oilfield* ... KS-7
O'Hara Point—*summit* ... ID-8
O'Hara Ranch—*locale* ... NE-7
O'Hara Saddle—*gap* ... ID-8
O'Hara Sch—*school* ... IL-6
O'Haras Peak—*summit* ... NV-8
O'Hara Spring—*spring* ... NV-8
**O'Hara (Township of)**—*pop pl* ... PA-2
O'Hara Youth Camp—*locale* ... ID-8
O'Hard Creek—*stream* ... OR-9
O'Hare Airport(Chicago O'Hare International Airport)—*other* ... IL-6
O'Hare Creek—*stream* ... WA-9
O'Hare Ditch—*canal* ... NE-7
O'Hare Point—*cape* ... SC-3
O'Harrel Canyon—*valley* ... CA-9
O'Harrel Canyon Creek—*stream* ... CA-9
O'Harrow Drain—*stream* ... MI-6
O'Harrow Oil Field—*oilfield* ... TX-5
Ohar Sholom Cem—*cemetery* ... PA-2
**Ohatchee**—*pop pl* ... AL-4
Ohatchee Baptist Ch (historical)—*church* ... AL-4
Ohatchee (CCD)—*cens area* ... AL-4
Ohatchee Cem—*cemetery* ... AL-4
*Ohatchee Ch* ... AL-4
Ohatchee Ch—*church* (2) ... AL-4
*Ohatchee Ch Number 2* ... AL-4
**Ohatchee (corporate name for Ohatchie)**—*pop pl* ... AL-4
Ohatchee Creek—*stream* ... AL-4
Ohatchee Division—*civil* ... AL-4
Ohatchee HS—*school* ... AL-4
*Ohatchee Missionary Baptist Church* ... AL-4
Ohatchee Mountains—*range* ... AL-4
Ohatchee Number 2 Cem—*cemetery* ... AL-4
Ohatchee United Methodist Ch—*church* ... AL-4
*Ohatchie* ... AL-4
*Ohatchie (corporate name Ohatchee)* ... AL-4
*Ohatchie Creek* ... AL-4
**Ohathlockhouchy (historical)**—*pop pl* ... FL-3
O Haugen Ranch—*locale* ... ND-7
O'Haver Cem—*cemetery* ... TN-4
O'Haver Hill—*summit* ... WY-8
O'Haver Lake—*lake* ... CO-8
O'Haver Peak—*summit* ... WY-8
O'Havers Chapel (historical)—*church* ... TN-4
Ohayo Mtn—*summit* ... NY-2
Oh-be-joyful Creek—*stream* ... CO-8
Oh-be-joyful Pass—*gap* ... CO-8
Oh-be-joyful Peak—*summit* ... CO-8
Oh Boy Forest Camp—*locale* ... OR-9
*O'Hearn Creek* ... MT-8
O'Hearn Creek—*stream* ... MT-8
Oheb Sholem Cem—*cemetery* ... NJ-2
*O Heim Ditch* ... IN-6
*Ohelo Peak* ... HI-9
O. Henry JHS—*school* ... TX-5
O Henry JHS—*school* ... TX-5
O'Henry Museum—*building* ... TX-5
**O Henry Oaks (subdivision)**—*pop pl* ... NC-3
*Ohent* ... ND-7
Oheo Gulch—*valley* ... HI-9
*Oheo Stream* ... HI-9
O'Hern HS—*school* ... NY-2
O'Hern Oil Field—*oilfield* ... TX-5
Ohey Sholem Cem—*cemetery* ... PA-2
Ohey Sholum Cem—*cemetery* ... PA-2
Ohia—*summit* ... HI-9
Ohia Ai Gulch—*valley* ... HI-9
Ohia Gulch—*valley* (2) ... HI-9
Ohiahuea Stream—*stream* ... HI-9
Ohialele—*summit* ... HI-9
Ohia Mill—*locale* ... HI-9
Ohianui—*area* ... HI-9
Ohiapili—*locale* ... HI-9
Ohia Spring—*spring* ... HI-9
Ohia Stream—*stream* ... HI-9
Ohiki—*civil* ... HI-9
Ohiki Bay—*bay* ... HI-9
Ohiki-lolo—*beach* ... HI-9
Ohikilolo—*civil* ... HI-9
Ohikilolo Beach Park—*park* ... HI-9
*Ohimish Lake* ... WI-6
*Ohimis Lake* ... WI-6
*Ohio* ... IL-6
*Ohio* ... KY-4
*Ohio* ... OH-6
*Ohio* ... PA-2
*Ohio* ... WV-2
Ohio—*fmr MCD* ... NE-7
Ohio—*locale* ... IA-7
Ohio—*locale* ... MO-7
Ohio—*locale* ... TX-5
**Ohio**—*pop pl* ... CO-8
**Ohio**—*pop pl* ... IL-6
**Ohio**—*pop pl* ... NY-2
Ohio, Falls of the—*falls* ... KY-4
Ohio Agricultural Experiment Station—*other* ... OH-6
Ohio And Erie Canal—*hist pl* ... OH-6
Ohio and Erie Canal Deep Lock—*hist pl* ... OH-6
Ohio Asylum for the Blind—*hist pl* ... OH-6
Ohio Ave Sch—*school* ... OH-6
Ohio Bahia Honda Channel—*channel* ... FL-3
Ohio Bar—*bar* ... AL-4
Ohio Bell Henderson-Endicott Exchange Bldg—*hist pl* ... OH-6
Ohio Branch—*stream* ... MD-2
Ohio Brook—*stream* ... ME-1
Ohio Brook—*stream* ... MA-1
Ohio Brush Creek—*stream* ... OH-6
Ohio Camp—*locale* ... WY-8
**Ohio Camp**—*pop pl* ... MT-8
Ohio Canal—*canal* ... OH-6
Ohio Canal Groundbreaking Site—*hist pl* ... OH-6
Ohio Canyon—*valley* ... CO-8
Ohio Canyon—*valley* ... NV-8
Ohio Caverns—*locale* ... OH-6
Ohio Cem—*cemetery* ... MN-6
Ohio Cem—*cemetery* ... MO-7
Ohio Center (historical)—*locale* ... KS-7
Ohio Ch—*church* (2) ... IA-7
Ohio Chapel—*church* (2) ... IL-6
Ohio Chapel—*church* ... IN-6
*Ohio City* ... CO-8
*Ohio City* ... KS-7
**Ohio City**—*pop pl* ... OH-6
Ohio City Preservation District—*hist pl* ... OH-6
Ohio-Colorado Smelting and Refining Company Smokestack—*hist pl* ... CO-8
Ohio Company (historical)—*locale* ... KS-7
Ohio Company Land Office—*hist pl* ... OH-6
**Ohio County**—*pop pl* ... IN-6
**Ohio (County)**—*pop pl* ... KY-4
**Ohio (County)**—*pop pl* ... WV-2
Ohio County Elementary-MS—*school* ... IN-6
Ohio Creek—*stream* (5) ... AK-9
Ohio Creek—*stream* ... CA-9
Ohio Creek—*stream* (2) ... CO-8
Ohio Creek—*stream* ... MT-8
Ohio Creek—*stream* ... VA-3
Ohio Department of Natural Resources—*other* ... OH-6
Ohio Draw—*valley* (2) ... WY-8
Ohio Exposition Center—*building* ... OH-6
*Ohio Falls* ... IN-6
Ohio Farm Bureau Federation Offices—*hist pl* ... OH-6
Ohio Ferro Alloys Corporation—*facility* ... OH-6
Ohio Furnace—*locale* ... OH-6
Ohio Gorge—*valley* (2) ... NY-2
Ohio Grove Cem—*cemetery* ... IL-6
Ohio Grove Grange—*locale* ... IL-6
Ohio Grove Sch—*school* ... IL-6
**Ohio Grove (Township of)**—*pop pl* ... IL-6
Ohio Gulch—*valley* (2) ... CO-8
Ohio Gulch—*valley* ... ID-8

Ohio Gulch—valley (2) MT-8
Ohio Gulch—valley NV-8
Ohio Hill—summit CA-9
Ohio Hill—summit VT-1
Ohio (historical)—locale KS-7
Ohio (historical P.O.)—locale IA-7
Ohio Hosp For Epileptics Stone Water Towers—hist pl OH-6
Ohio Institution for the Education of the Deaf and Dumb—hist pl OH-6
Ohio Island—island ME-1
Ohio Island (historical)—island AL-4
*Ohio Junction* (2) OH-6
Ohio Key—island FL-3
Ohio Lake—lake GA-3
Ohio Lantern Company—hist pl OH-6
Ohio Lode Mine—mine MT-8
Ohio Mechanical Institute—school OH-6
Ohio Mine—mine CO-8
Ohio Mine—mine MI-6
Ohio Mine—mine NM-5
Ohio Mine (historical)—mine ID-8
Ohio Mines—mine MT-8
Ohio Missouri Channel—channel FL-3
Ohio Natl Bank—hist pl OH-6
Ohio Natl Guard Armory—hist pl OH-6
Ohio Natl Guard Armory—military OH-6
Ohio Northern Univ—school OH-6
Ohio N U—school OH-6
Ohio One-Ohio Edison—hist pl OH-6
Ohio Pass—gap CO-8
Ohio Peak—summit (2) CO-8
*Ohiopehelle* PA-2
*Ohiopile* PA-2
Ohio Power Company—hist pl OH-6
*Ohio Pyle* PA-2
**Ohiopyle**—pop pl PA-2
Ohiopyle Borough—civil PA-2
Ohiopyle Cave—cave PA-2
Ohiopyle Falls—falls PA-2
Ohiopyle Gorge—valley PA-2
Ohio Pyle (RR name for Ohiopyle)—other PA-2
**Ohiopyle (RR name Ohio Pyle)**—pop pl PA-2
Ohiopyle State Park—park PA-2
Ohio Ravine—valley CA-9
Ohio River—stream IL-6
Ohio River—stream IN-6
Ohio River—stream KY-4
Ohio River—stream OH-6
Ohio River—stream PA-2
Ohio River—stream WV-2
Ohio River Lock and Dam No. 31 Grounds and Buildings—hist pl KY-4
Ohio River Pool—reservoir KY-4
Ohio Riverside Hist Dist (Boundary Increase)—hist pl KY-4
Ohio Rock—other AK-9
Ohio Sch—school IL-6
Ohio Sch—school (2) NY-2
Ohio Sch—school PA-2
Ohio Sch—school SD-7
Ohio Shoal—bar FL-3
Ohio Side—cliff MT-8
Ohio Soldiers' And Sailors' Home—hist pl OH-6
Ohio Soldiers And Sailors Home—other OH-6
Ohio Spring—spring NV-8
Ohio Stadium—hist pl OH-6
Ohio State Arsenal—hist pl OH-6
Ohio Statehouse—hist pl OH-6
Ohio State Normal College At Kent—hist pl OH-6
Ohio State Penitentary—building OH-6
Ohio State Penitentiary Junction City Branch—other OH-6
Ohio State Reformatory—hist pl OH-6
Ohio State Univ—school OH-6
Ohio State Univ Extension—school OH-6
Ohio Street Park—park IL-6
Ohio Theatre—hist pl (3) OH-6
Ohio Tonopah—mine NV-8
Ohio Townhall—building KS-7
**Ohio (Town of)**—pop pl NY-2
Ohio Township—CDP PA-2
Ohio Township—civil MO-7
Ohio Township—fmr MCD IA-7
**Ohio Township**—pop pl (5) KS-7
**Ohio Township**—pop pl SD-7
Ohio Township Elem Sch—school PA-2
Ohio (Township of)—civil PA-2
**Ohio (Township of)**—pop pl IL-6
**Ohio (Township of)**—pop pl (4) IN-6
**Ohio (Township of)**—pop pl (3) OH-6
**Ohio (Township of)**—pop pl PA-2
Ohio Tunnel—mine CO-8
Ohio Univ—school OH-6
Ohio Univ Campus Green Hist Dist—hist pl OH-6
Ohio Univ (Lancaster Branch)—school OH-6
Ohio Univ Portsmouth Branch—school OH-6
Ohio Valley—valley CA-9
Ohio Valley Ch—church (2) KY-4
Ohio Valley Clay Company—hist pl OH-6
Ohio Valley Coll—school WV-2
Ohio Valley General Hosp—hospital PA-2
Ohio Valley Hosp—hospital OH-6
Ohio Valley Institute Camp—park IN-6
Ohio Valley Speedway—other WV-2
**Ohioview**—pop pl PA-2
Ohio View Public Golf Course—locale PA-2
**Ohioville**—pop pl NY-2
**Ohioville**—pop pl PA-2
Ohioville Borough—civil PA-2
Ohioville Cem—cemetery MI-6
Ohioville Sch—school MI-6
Ohioville Sch—school PA-2
**Ohiowa**—pop pl NE-7
Ohiowa Cem—cemetery NE-7
Ohio Wesleyan Univ—school OH-6
Ohio Wesleyan Univ Student Observatory—hist pl OH-6
Ohio Windmill—locale TX-5
Ohisa Creek—stream NY-2
Ohison Mtn—summit AK-9
Ohiva Windmill—locale TX-5
**Ohl**—pop pl PA-2
Ohl Cem—cemetery OH-6
Ohlendorf Cem—cemetery TX-5
Ohler Branch—stream IN-6
Ohler Branch—stream KY-4
Ohler Ditch—canal IN-6
Ohler Gulch—valley CO-8
Ohlers Island—island WA-9
**Ohley**—pop pl WV-2
Ohl JHS—school OH-6
**Ohlman**—pop pl IL-6
Ohlman Cem—cemetery IL-6
Ohlman Ch—church MO-7
Ohlman-Shannon House—hist pl SD-7
Ohlone Junior Coll—school CA-9
Ohlones Cem—cemetery CA-9
Ohlones Sch—school CA-9
Ohlsrud Lake—lake MN-6
**Ohlton**—pop pl OH-6
**Ohltown**—pop pl OH-6
Ohm—locale CA-9
**Ohm**—pop pl WA-9
Ohm, John, House—hist pl CA-9
Ohman Creek—stream CA-9
Ohman Falls—falls AK-9
Ohman Lake—lake CO-8
Ohman Ranch—locale WY-8
Ohmar Drain—canal CA-9
Ohmar Lateral—canal CA-9
Ohmer, Nicholas, House—hist pl OH-6
Ohmer Creek—stream AK-9
Ohmer Creek Campground—locale AK-9
Ohmer Drain—canal MI-6
Ohmer Mtn—summit NY-2
*Ohmer Park* OH-6
Ohmer Park Ch—church OH-6
Ohmer Slough—gut AK-9
Ohme Sch—school NE-7
Ohmigod Rapids—rapids TN-4
Ohms Lake—lake IN-6
Ohm Spring—spring OR-9
*Ohns* WV-2
Ohnstad Cem—cemetery ND-7
*Ohoe Gulch* HI-9
**Ohogamiut**—pop pl AK-9
Ohogamiut ANV886—reserve AK-9
*Ohohia* HI-9
**Ohoopee**—pop pl GA-3
Ohoopee Ch—church GA-3
Ohoopee River—stream GA-3
**Ohop**—pop pl WA-9
Ohop Creek—stream WA-9
Ohop Lake—lake WA-9
Ohop Valley—valley WA-9
Oho Tank—reservoir NM-5
Ohovah Ch—church NC-3
Oho Windmill—locale NM-5
Ohrbach Arena—building NJ-2
Ohrback Lake—lake NY-2
Ohr Drain—canal MI-6
Oh Ridge—ridge CA-9
Ohrt, Frederick, House—hist pl HI-9
Ohtig Lake—lake AK-9
*Ohulehule* HI-9
*Ohulehule Peak* HI-9
Ohulelua Ridge—ridge HI-9
Ohuta Park—park MN-6
Ohwa—civil FM-9
Ohwa, Pilen—stream FM-9
Ohwiler Ridge—ridge CO-8
O H Williams Lake—reservoir AL-4
O H Williams Lake Dam—dam AL-4
Oiamoi—locale HI-9
*Oiel* FM-9
Oii—bar FM-9
*Oiiko-to* MP-9
*Oi Jima* FM-9
*Oikeirman Branch* KS-7
*Oike Tank* AZ-5
*Oikierman Branch* KS-7
**Oikull**—pop pl PW-9
**Oil**—pop pl KY-4
Oiland Ch—church MN-6
Oil Bay—bay AK-9
Oil Branch—stream KY-4
Oil Branch—stream (2) LA-4
Oil Branch—stream (3) OK-5
Oil Branch—stream TX-5
Oil Butte—summit WY-8
Oil Camp Creek—stream SC-3
Oilcan Ranch—locale WY-8
Oil Canyon—valley (5) CA-9
Oil Canyon—valley WY-8
*Oil Center* IL-6
Oil Center—locale CA-9
Oil Center—locale IL-6
Oil Center—locale KY-4
**Oil Center**—pop pl NM-5
**Oil Center**—pop pl OK-5
Oil Center—uninc pl LA-4
Oil City—locale CA-9
Oil City—locale KY-4
Oil City—locale MO-7
Oil City—locale (2) OK-5
Oil City—locale TX-5
Oil City—locale WA-9
**Oil City**—pop pl LA-4
**Oil City**—pop pl MI-6
**Oil City**—pop pl MS-4
**Oil City**—pop pl NM-5
**Oil City**—pop pl (2) PA-2
**Oil City**—pop pl WI-6
Oil City City—civil PA-2
Oil City JHS—school PA-2
Oil City Ranch—locale WY-8
Oil City Senior HS—school PA-2
Oil City Speedway—locale AL-4
Oil City Well—well NM-5
*Oil Creek* IN-6
*Oil Creek* MS-4
*Oil Creek* NY-2
Oil Creek—stream (2) AK-9
Oil Creek—stream (5) CA-9
Oil Creek—stream CO-8
Oil Creek—stream (2) IN-6
Oil Creek—stream MO-7
Oil Creek—stream NY-2
Oil Creek—stream (4) OK-5
Oil Creek—stream (4) PA-2
Oil Creek—stream TX-5
Oil Creek—stream VA-3
Oil Creek—stream WV-2
Oil Creek—stream WY-8
Oil Creek—uninc pl PA-2
Oil Creek Chapel—church PA-2
Oil Creek Ditch—canal CO-8
*Oil Creek Lake* PA-2
Oil Creek Ridge—ridge CA-9
Oil Creek State Park—park PA-2
**Oil Creek (Township of)**—pop pl PA-2
**Oilcreek (Township of)**—pop pl PA-2
**Oildale**—pop pl CA-9
Oildom—locale TX-5
Oil Drain—canal UT-8
Oil Draw—valley WY-8
Oiler Canyon—valley CA-9
Oiler Ditch—canal CA-9
Oiler Draw—valley WY-8
Oiler Peak—summit CA-9
Oiler Rsvr—reservoir WY-8
**Oilfield**—pop pl IL-6
Oil Field Ch—church (2) LA-4
Oilfields—locale CA-9
Oil Field Sch—school LA-4
Oil Field Windmill—locale TX-5
Oil Fork—stream KY-4
Oil Grove—locale IL-6
**Oil Hill**—pop pl KS-7
Oil Hill—summit KS-7
Oil Hill Elem Sch—school KS-7
Oil Hills—oilfield MT-8
Oil Hollow—valley OH-6
Oil Hollow—valley TN-4
Oil Hollow—valley UT-8
Oil House Branch—stream TN-4
Oili Puu—summit HI-9
**Oil Junction**—pop pl CA-9
Oilla—locale TX-5
*Oil Lake* MT-8
Oil Lake—lake AK-9
Oilles Creek—bay NC-3
Oil Mill Branch—stream (2) NC-3
Oil Mill Brook—stream (2) CT-1
Oil Mill Hollow—valley OH-6
Oil Mill Lake—reservoir TX-5
*Oilmill Run* PA-2
**Oilmont**—pop pl MT-8
*Oil Mountain* CO-8
Oil Mtn—summit (2) WY-8
Oilouch—island PW-9
Oilowai Gulch—valley HI-9
Oil Platform A—other AK-9
Oil Platform Anna—other AK-9
Oil Platform Baker—other AK-9
Oil Platform Bruce—other AK-9
Oil Platform C—other AK-9
Oil Platform Dolly Varden—other AK-9
Oil Platform Granite Point—other AK-9
Oil Platform Grayling—other AK-9
Oil Platform King—other AK-9
Oil Platform Mono—other AK-9
Oil Platform Spark—other AK-9
Oil Platform Trading Bay—other AK-9
Oil Point—cape AK-9
Oil Reef—bar AK-9
Oil Ridge—ridge CA-9
Oil Ridge—ridge (2) WV-2
Oil Ridge Ch—church WV-2
Oil Rock Run—stream WV-2
Oil Rock Sch—school WV-2
*Oil Run* PA-2
Oil Sand Canyon—valley UT-8
Oil Seep Bar (inundated)—bar UT-8
Oil Seeps—spring PA-2
**Oil Spring**—pop pl OH-6
Oil Spring—spring NV-8
Oil Spring—spring TN-4
Oil Spring Branch—stream KY-4
Oilspring Branch—stream OH-6
Oil Spring Cem—cemetery OK-5
Oil Spring Creek—stream IA-7
Oil Spring Mtn—summit CO-8
Oilspring Run—stream OH-6
Oil Spring Run—stream WV-2
Oil Springs—locale KY-4
Oil Springs—locale TX-5
**Oil Springs**—pop pl KY-4
**Oil Springs**—pop pl WY-8
Oil Springs—spring NV-8
Oil Springs Branch—stream TX-5
Oil Springs (CCD)—cens area KY-4
Oil Springs Cem—cemetery OK-5
Oil Springs Ch—church KY-4
Oil Springs Creek—stream WY-8
Oil Springs Ind Res—reserve NY-2
Oil Springs Oil and Gas Field—oilfield UT-8
Oil Springs Oil Field Discovery Well—hist pl TX-5
Oilton—locale KY-4
**Oilton**—pop pl OK-5
**Oilton**—pop pl TX-5
**Oil (Township of)**—pop pl IN-6
**Oil Trough**—pop pl AR-4
*Oil Trough Bottom* AR-4
Oil Trough Ferry—locale AR-4
Oil Trough (Township of)—fmr MCD AR-4
Oil Valley—locale KY-4
Oil Valley—valley PA-2
Oilville—locale VA-3
Oil Well Bench—bench (2) UT-8
Oilwell Branch—stream AL-4
Oil Well Branch—stream (4) KY-4
Oil Well Branch—stream OK-5
Oilwell Branch—stream TN-4
Oil Well Branch—stream TX-5
Oil Well Branch—stream WV-2
Oil Well Bridge—bridge AL-4
Oil Well Camp—locale CO-8
Oil Well Canyon—valley AZ-5
Oil Well Canyon—valley (4) CA-9
Oil Well Canyon—valley (2) TX-5
Oil Well Creek—stream CO-8
Oil Well Creek—stream TX-5
Oil Well Dam—dam NM-5
Oil Well Dam Number 1—dam SD-7
Oil Well Dam Number 2—dam SD-7
Oil Well Dome—summit UT-8
Oil Well Draw—valley UT-8
Oil Well Flat—flat UT-8
Oil Well Gulch—valley CO-8
Oil Well Hill—summit MT-8
Oil Well Hill—summit TN-4
*Oil Well Hills* OK-5
Oil Well Hole—basin KY-4
*Oil Well Hole Trail* PA-2
*Oil Well Hollow* TN-4
Oil Well Hollow—valley AR-4
Oil Well Hollow—valley (3) KY-4
Oil Well Hollow—valley NY-2
Oil Well Hollow—valley OK-5
Oil Well Hollow—valley (2) PA-2
Oilwell Hollow—valley TN-4
Oil Well Hollow—valley TN-4
Oil Well Hollow—valley WV-2
Oil Well Lake (historical)—lake TX-5
Oil Well Landing—locale AL-4
Oil Well Mtn—summit CO-8
Oil Well Pond—swamp TX-5
Oil Well Ranch—locale TX-5
Oil Well Rsvr—reservoir MT-8
Oil Well Spring—spring MS-4
Oil Well Spring—spring OR-9
Oil Well Spring—spring TX-5
Oil Wells Tank—reservoir TX-5
Oil Well Tank—reservoir AZ-5
Oil Well Tank—reservoir (2) TX-5
Oil Well Windmill—locale (5) NM-5
Oil Well Windmill—locale (23) TX-5
Oil Windmill—locale TX-5
Oily Lake—lake AK-9
Oimadelchesuch—island PW-9
Oimaderuul—beach PW-9
Oimaderuul—island PW-9
*Oimadorakoshoku* PW-9
Oiman Island—island FM-9
*Oimateiuul* PW-9
Oimo Grande Tank—reservoir TX-5
Oin—bar FM-9
**Oine**—pop pl NC-3
Oiner Lake—lake LA-4
Oio Gulch—valley HI-9
Oio Stream—stream HI-9
*Oiro Island* PW-9
*Oirou* PW-9
Oitab—island PW-9
Oite Island—island FM-9
*Oithlakutchi* FL-3
*Oith-le-ti-kee Creek* AL-4
Oit Ihuk—locale AZ-5
*O-Iwa* FM-9
Oiyer Spring—spring CA-9
*Ojai* FM-9
Ojai—civil CA-9
**Ojai**—pop pl CA-9
Ojai Country Club—other CA-9
Ojai Valley—valley CA-9
Ojai Valley Sch—school CA-9
*Ojal* FM-9
**Ojala**—pop pl CA-9
Ojala, Herman, Homestead—hist pl ID-8
Ojalla Bridge—bridge OR-9
Ojalla Creek—stream OR-9
O J Andy Lake Dam—dam MS-4
Ojanpera Sch—school MN-6
Oja Number 1 Dam—dam SD-7
Oja Number 2 Dam—dam SD-7
**Ojata (historical)**—pop pl ND-7
Ojeda Canyon—valley CA-9
Ojeda Park—park TX-5
Ojedo—locale IA-7
Ojero Mine (historical)—mine AZ-5
O Jewett Dam—dam SD-7
O J Fleming Lake—reservoir NC-3
O J Fleming Lake Dam—dam NC-3
O-J-I, Mount—summit ME-1
**Ojibwa**—pop pl WI-6
Ojibwa Courier Press Bldg—hist pl WI-6
Ojibwa Golf Club—other WI-6
Ojibwa Sch—school MI-6
Ojibwa State Park—park WI-6
**Ojibwa Subdivision**—pop pl TN-4
**Ojibwa (Town of)**—pop pl WI-6
Ojibway—locale MI-6
Ojibway, Lake—lake MI-6
Ojibway, Mount—summit MI-6
Ojibway Campground—locale MN-6
Ojibway Creek—stream WA-9
Ojibway Island—island MI-6
Ojibway Knoll—summit WA-9
Ojibway Lake—lake (2) MN-6
Ojibway Peak—summit MT-8
*Ojier Point* ME-1
Ojita—locale NM-5
Ojita Tank—reservoir TX-5
Ojito—locale NM-5
**Ojito**—pop pl NM-5
Ojito Adentro—spring TX-5
Ojito Banadero—spring CO-8
Ojito Camp—locale (2) NM-5
Ojito Canyon—valley (2) NM-5
Ojito Carrizo—spring NM-5
Ojito Chico—stream NM-5
Ojito Creek—stream (2) CO-8
Ojito de las Cienaguitas—spring NM-5
Ojito de las Tortolitas—spring NM-5
Ojito del Comanche—spring NM-5
Ojito del Quemado—spring NM-5
Ojito Encindso—spring NM-5
Ojito Escondido—spring NM-5
Ojito Escondido Canyon—valley NM-5
Ojito Jarosite—spring NM-5
Ojito Maes Spring—spring NM-5
Ojito Palo Duro—spring NM-5
Ojito Peak—summit CO-8
Ojito Ranch—locale NM-5
Ojitos, Canada—valley NM-5
Ojito Sastras—spring NM-5
Ojitos Canyon—valley (4) NM-5
Ojitos Cuates Draw—valley NM-5
Ojitos de los Gatos—spring NM-5
Ojitos Draw—valley NM-5
Ojito Seco—spring NM-5
Ojitos Frios Creek—stream NM-5
**Ojitos Frios (Gabaldon PO)**—pop pl NM-5
Ojitos Frios Ranch—locale NM-5
Ojito Soldados—spring NM-5
Ojito Spring—spring (2) NM-5
Ojitos Spring—spring NM-5
Ojito Tank—reservoir NM-5
Ojito Well—well NM-5
*.OjJaluij* MP-9
Ojo Abajenos—spring NM-5
Ojo Acebuche—spring TX-5
Ojo Agua Zarca—spring TX-5
Ojo Alamito—spring TX-5
Ojo Alamo—spring NM-5
Ojo Amarillo Canyon—valley NM-5
Ojo Atascoso—spring NM-5
Ojo Azabache—spring NM-5
Ojo Blanco Spring—spring AZ-5
Ojo Bonito—spring TX-5
Ojo Bonito Canyon—valley NM-5
Ojo Bonito Cem—cemetery NM-5
Ojo Bonito Tank—reservoir AZ-5
**Ojo Caliente**—pop pl (2) NM-5
Ojo Caliente—spring NM-5
Ojo Caliente Cem—cemetery NM-5
Ojo Caliente Grant—civil NM-5
Ojo Caliente Mineral Springs—hist pl NM-5
Ojo Caliente Rsvr—reservoir NM-5
Ojo Caliente Sch—school NM-5
Ojo Canoa—spring NM-5
Ojo Canoa—spring TX-5
Ojo Canyon—valley NM-5
Ojo Carrizo—spring TX-5
Ojo Chamisa—spring NM-5
**Ojo de Agua**—pop pl PR-3
Ojo De Agua, Arroyo—stream CA-9
Ojo de Agua Creek—stream TX-5
Ojo De Agua De La Coche—civil CA-9
Ojo de Alamo—spring NM-5
Ojo de Alamo Arroyo—stream CO-8
Ojo de Amado—spring NM-5
Ojo de Angua—locale TX-5
*Ojo de Casa Spring* AZ-5
Ojo de Gutierrez—spring NM-5
Ojo de la Cabra—spring NM-5
Ojo de la Cobra—spring NM-5
Ojo de la Gallina—spring NM-5
Ojo de la Mosca—spring NM-5
Ojo de la Parida—spring NM-5
Ojo de las Canas—spring NM-5
Ojo de las Gallinas—spring NM-5
Ojo de las Primallas—spring NM-5
Ojo de las Yeguas—spring (2) NM-5
Ojo de la Vaca—spring NM-5
Ojo Del Borrego—civil NM-5
Ojo del Chopo—spring NM-5
Ojo del Coyote—spring NM-5
Ojo del Dado—spring NM-5
Ojo Del Espiritu Santo—civil NM-5
Ojo del Gallo—spring NM-5
Ojo del Hijinio—spring NM-5
Ojo del Indio—spring NM-5
Ojo de Llano—spring NM-5
*Ojo de los Coyot* AZ-5
Ojo de los Indias—spring NM-5
Ojo de Los Jaramillos—spring NM-5
Ojo del Oso—spring NM-5
Ojo del Padre—spring NM-5
Ojo del Padre—stream NM-5
Ojo del Rancho del Medio—spring NM-5
Ojo del Rancho de Lopez—spring NM-5
Ojo de Maiz—spring NM-5
Ojo De Maiz Creek—stream NM-5
Ojo De San Jose—civil NM-5
Ojo De Santa Rosa—spring NM-5
Ojo Encino—spring NM-5
Ojo Encino Mesa—summit NM-5
Ojo Encino Trailer Sch—school NM-5
Ojo Escondido Spring—spring TX-5
Ojo Estaliando—spring NM-5
Ojo Eugenio—spring NM-5
**Ojo Feliz**—pop pl NM-5
Ojo Frio—spring (2) NM-5
Ojo Gato Spring—spring AZ-5
Ojo Grande—spring NM-5
Ojo Hallado Draw—valley NM-5
Ojo Hedionda—spring NM-5
Ojo Huelos—spring NM-5
Ojo Indian Ruins—locale NM-5
Ojo Jarido—spring NM-5
Ojo Jedeondilla—spring NM-5
Ojo la Casa—spring NM-5
Ojo La Jara—spring NM-5
Ojo Lemita—spring NM-5
Ojo los Caso—spring NM-5
Ojo los Rechuelos—spring NM-5
Ojo Marquez—spring NM-5
Ojo Mexicano—spring TX-5
Ojo Mines—mine CO-8
Ojo Navajo—spring NM-5
Ojo Negro—spring CO-8
Ojo Negro—spring NM-5
Ojo Negro Canyon—valley CO-8
Ojo Negro Creek—stream NM-5
Ojo Palo Blanco—spring NM-5
Ojo Piedra—spring NM-5
Ojo Pueblo (Ruins)—locale NM-5
Ojo Pueblo Windmill—locale NM-5
Ojo Redondo—spring (2) NM-5
Ojo Redondo Canyon—valley NM-5
*Ojos* AZ-5
Ojo Saladito—spring NM-5
Ojo San Mateo—spring NM-5
**Ojo Sarco**—pop pl NM-5
Ojo Sarco—spring NM-5
Ojo Sarco Canyon—valley NM-5
Ojo Sarco Los Alamos Tract—civil NM-5
Ojos Canyon—valley NM-5
Ojo Socorro—spring NM-5
Ojo Tank—reservoir NM-5
Ojo Tecolote Springs—spring NM-5
Ojo Ternera—spring NM-5
Ojo Verde Rsvr—reservoir CO-8
O J Turner Third Lake Dam—dam MS-4
**Ojuelas**—pop pl TX-5
**Ojus**—pop pl FL-3
Ojus Elem Sch—school FL-3
Ojus Park—park FL-3
Ojus Sch—school FL-3
**O. K.**—pop pl KY-4
Oka—locale WV-2
**Oka**—pop pl MT-8
**Okabena**—pop pl MN-6
Okabena Creek—stream MN-6
Okabena Lake—reservoir MN-6
*Oka Chambala River* MS-4
Okachickima Creek—stream MS-4
Okaga Lake—lake MT-8
Okahanikan Cove—bay MD-2
Okahanikan Point—cape MD-2
Okahatta Canal—canal MS-4
Okahatta Creek—stream MS-4
Okahay Baptist Ch (historical)—church MS-4
Okahola—locale MS-4
Okahola Baptist Ch—church MS-4
**Okahta Talaia (historical)**—pop pl MS-4
**Oka Hullo (historical)**—pop pl MS-4
*Okahumkee Lake* FL-3
**Okahumpka**—pop pl FL-3
Okahumpka, Lake—lake FL-3
**Okahumpka (historical)**—pop pl FL-3
Okahumpka Plaza—locale FL-3
Okahumpka Swamp—swamp FL-3
Oka Kapassa (historical)—locale AL-4
**Oka Kapassa (historical)**—pop pl MS-4
*Okakatta Creek* MS-4
Okak Bend—bend AK-9
*Okala* HI-9
Okala Island—island HI-9
Okalee Channel—channel AK-9
Okalee River—stream AK-9
Okalee Spit—bar AK-9
*Okalibbe* MS-4
Okalik Lake—lake AK-9
Okalla Lake Dam—dam IN-6
**Okalla Station**—pop pl IN-6
*Okaloacodchee Slough* FL-3
Okaloacoochee Branch—gut FL-3
Okaloacoochee Slough—lake FL-3
Okaloacoochee Slough—swamp FL-3
*Okalocknee River* FL-3
**Okalona**—pop pl TN-4
Okalona Cem—cemetery TN-4
Okalona Ch—church KY-4
Okalona United Methodist Ch—church TN-4
Okaloo—locale FL-3
Okaloosa—locale LA-4
**Okaloosa County**—pop pl FL-3
Okaloosa Island—CDP FL-3
Okaloosa-Watson Coll—school FL-3
*Okalopasaw River* MS-4
*Okalusa Creek* MS-4
*Okamanpedan Lake* IA-7
*Okamanpedan Lake* MN-6
Okamanpeedam State Park—park IA-7
Okamanpeedan Lake—lake MN-6
Okamanpeedan Lake—reservoir IA-7
*Okamanpeeden Lake* IA-7
*Okamanpeeden Lake* MN-6
*Okamanpidan Lake* IA-7
*Okamanpidan Lake* MN-6
OK Anderson Dam—dam SD-7
O'Kane Bldg—hist pl OR-9
Okane Island—island AR-4
Okanela Lodge—locale CO-8
O'Kane Market and O'Kane Bldg—hist pl NY-2
*Okannatie Creek* MS-4
Okannatie Creek—stream MS-4
**Okanogan**—pop pl WA-9
Okanogan (CCD)—cens area WA-9
Okanogan Cem—cemetery WA-9
**Okanogan County**—pop pl WA-9
Okanogan Creek—stream OR-9
Okanogan Legion Airp—airport WA-9
Okanogan Project: Conconully Resevoir Dam—hist pl WA-9
Okanogan River—stream WA-9
*Okanogon Natl For* WA-9
Okanogon Natl For—forest WA-9
Okanola Sch—school SC-3
Okapilco Ch—church GA-3
Okapilco Creek—stream GA-3
Okapilco Sch—school GA-3
Okara Lakes—lake NY-2
**Okarche**—pop pl OK-5
Okarche-Cashion (CCD)—cens area OK-5
Okarche Cem—cemetery OK-5
Oka Run—stream IN-6
Oka Siding—locale MT-8
Okat—locale FM-9
Okat, Finol—summit FM-9
Okat, Infal—stream FM-9
Okat, Molsron—harbor FM-9
*Oka Teebehaw Creek* MS-4
Okatee Bluff—cliff SC-3
Okatee Club—locale SC-3
Okatee River—stream SC-3
*Okati* MS-4
Okatibbee Creek—stream MS-4
*Okatibbee Creek Reservoir* MS-4
Okatibbee Dam—dam MS-4
*Okatibbee Game Mngmt Area* MS-4
Okatibbee (historical)—locale MS-4
Okatibbee Lake—reservoir MS-4
Okatibbee State Wildlife Area—park MS-4
Okatibbee Water Park—park MS-4
*Okatie* SC-3
Okatie—locale SC-3
*Oka Toma Creek* MS-4
Okatoma Creek—stream MS-4
*Okatoma Post Office* MS-4
*Okatoma River* MS-4
*Okatomy* MS-4
**Okaton**—pop pl SD-7
*Okatona Creek* MS-4
**Okaton Township**—pop pl SD-7
Okatuppa—locale AL-4
Okatuppa Creek—stream AL-4
Okatuppa Creek—stream MS-4
Okatuppa Creek Public Use Area—park AL-4
*Oka Tuppah Creek* AL-4
*Okau* FM-9
**Okauchee**—pop pl WI-6
Okauchee House—hist pl WI-6
Okauchee Lake—CDP WI-6
Okauchee Lake—reservoir WI-6
*Okaw* FM-9
**Okawahathako (historical)**—pop pl FL-3
Okaw Center Ch—church IL-6
Okaw (historical)—locale KS-7
*Okaw River* IL-6
**Okaw (Township of)**—pop pl IL-6
**Okawville**—pop pl IL-6
Okawville Cem—cemetery IL-6
**Okawville (Township of)**—pop pl IL-6
Okay—locale AR-4
**Okay**—pop pl OK-5
Okay Ch—church NE-7
**Okay Junction**—pop pl AR-4
Okay Sch—school NE-7
Okay Sch—school OK-5
O K Bar Ranch—locale NM-5

OK Bend—*bend* AR-4
OK Bend—*bend* MS-4
O K Braune—*locale* TX-5
OK Butte—*summit* OR-9
Ok Canyon—*valley* NM-5
O K Ch—*church* OK-5
*Okchai* AL-4
*Okchanya* AL-4
*Okchayi Creek* AL-4
Okchayi (historical)—*locale* AL-4
Okchayudshi (historical)—*locale* AL-4
*Okchinwa Creek* AL-4
Ok Creek—*stream* AK-9
OK Creek—*stream* OR-9
OK Creek—*stream* WI-6
OK Creek—*stream* WY-8
Ok Ditch—*canal* AZ-5
**Okeafenoke Swamp (historical)**—*pop pl* FL-3
Okeag Cem—*cemetery* WI-6
**O'Kean**—*pop pl* AR-4
**Okeana**—*pop pl* OH-6
O'Kean (Township of)—*fmr MCD* AR-4
*Okechobee* FL-3
*Oke-choy-atte* AL-4
*Oke Chukma* MS-4
Oke Doke Lake—*lake* UT-8
**Okee**—*pop pl* WI-6
Okee Bay—*bay* AK-9
**Okeechobee**—*pop pl* FL-3
Okeechobee, Lake—*lake* FL-3
Okeechobee Adult Education Center—*school* FL-3
Okeechobee Battlefield—*hist pl* FL-3
Okeechobee (CCD)—*cens area* FL-3
**Okeechobee County**—*pop pl* FL-3
*Okeechobee Cross-Florida Waterway* FL-3
Okeechobee Farm Labor Supply Center—*other* FL-3
Okeechobee HS—*school* FL-3
Okeechobee Metrorail Station—*locale* FL-3
Okeechobee Plaza (Shop Ctr)—*locale* FL-3
Okeechobee Rehabilitation Facility—*school* FL-3
Okeechobee South Elem Sch—*school* FL-3
Okeechobee Waterway—*channel* FL-3
Okeechobee 5th/6th Grade Center—*school* FL-3
O'Keefe, Point—*cape* MI-6
Okeefe Cem—*cemetery* LA-4
O'Keefe-Clark Boarding House—*hist pl* MS-4
O'Keefe Creek—*stream* ID-8
O'Keefe Creek—*stream* (2) MT-8
O'Keefe Creek—*stream* OR-9
O'Keefe Creek—*stream* WI-6
O'Keefe Field (airport)—*airport* MS-4
Okeefe Hills—*other* AK-9
O'Keefe HS—*school* GA-3
O'Keefe Lake—*reservoir* TX-5
O'Keefe Meadow—*flat* OR-9
O'Keefe Mtn—*summit* NY-2
*Okeefenokee* GA-3
O'Keefe Pond—*lake* NY-2
O'Keefe Ranch—*locale* OR-9
O'Keefe Rsvr—*reservoir* (2) OR-9
O'Keefe Rsvr Number Four—*reservoir* OR-9
O'Keefe Rsvr Number Six—*reservoir* OR-9
O'Keefe Sch—*school* IL-6
O'Keefe Sch—*school* MA-1
*O'Keefe's Island* FM-9
O'Keefe's Island—*hist pl* FM-9
O'Keefe Spring—*spring* AZ-5
O'Keefe Spring—*spring* OR-9
O'Keefe Springs—*spring* OR-9
O'Keefe Tank—*reservoir* AZ-5
O'Keefe Waterhole—*reservoir* OR-9
Okeeheelee Park—*park* FL-3
Okeelala Creek—*stream* MS-4
Okeelanta—*locale* FL-3
Okeelanta Station RR Station—*locale* FL-3
Okeena Park—*park* TN-4
*O'Keene* OK-5
**Okeene**—*pop pl* OK-5
Okeene (CCD)—*cens area* OK-5
Okeene Flour Mill—*hist pl* OK-5
Okee Point—*cape* AK-9
*Okeetee* SC-3
**Okeetee**—*pop pl* SC-3
Okeetuck Creek—*stream* GA-3
**Okeewemee**—*pop pl* NC-3
*Okefenoke* GA-3
**Okefenokee**—*pop pl* GA-3
*Okefenokee Canal* GA-3
Okefenokee Ch—*church* GA-3
Okefenokee Church Camp—*locale* GA-3
Okefenokee Fairgrounds—*locale* GA-3
Okefenokee Natl Wildlife Ref—*park* GA-3
Okefenokee Slough—*stream* FL-3
*Okefenokee Swamp* FL-3
Okefenokee Swamp—*swamp* GA-3
*Okefinokee* GA-3
*Okehumpkee* FL-3
Okelberry Pass—*gap* UT-8
O. K. Elem Sch—*school* KS-7
O'Kelley Cem—*cemetery* NC-3
*O'Kelley Creek* OR-9
Okell Hill—*summit* CA-9
*O'Kelly Cem* NC-3
O'Kelly Cem—*cemetery* TN-4
O'Kelly Creek—*stream* OR-9
O'Kelly's Chapel—*hist pl* NC-3
**Okema**—*pop pl* KY-4
**Okemah**—*pop pl* OK-5
Okemah (CCD)—*cens area* OK-5
Okemah Lake—*reservoir* OK-5
Okemah Oil Field—*oilfield* OK-5
Okemah Park—*park* AZ-5
Okemo Mountain Ski Area—*other* VT-1
*Okemo Mtn* VT-1
**Okemos**—*pop pl* MI-6
Okemos HS—*school* MI-6
Okemos Sch—*school* MI-6
Okemos South Ch—*church* MI-6
Okemos Station—*locale* MI-6
Okemo State For—*forest* VT-1
Okenok Neck—*cape* NY-2
*Oker* TX-5
Oker Drain—*canal* MI-6
Okerduul—*island* PW-9
Okerlund Campground—*park* UT-8
Okerlund Draw—*valley* UT-8
Okerokovik River—*stream* AK-9
Oke Rsvr—*reservoir* OR-9
**Okesa**—*pop pl* OK-5
*Okesan* DE-2
*Oke-see-sebo River* KS-7
*Okeshion* DE-2
*Okesian* DE-2
Okeson Draw—*valley* WY-8
*Okession* DE-2
**Okete**—*pop pl* MO-7
*Oketee* SC-3
*Oketeeochene Creek* AL-4
*O-ke-teyoc-en-ne Creek* AL-4
**Oketo**—*pop pl* KS-7
Oketo Cem—*cemetery* KS-7
**Oketol**—*pop pl* PW-9
Oketo Lake—*lake* MN-6
Oketo Park—*park* IL-6
**Oketo Township**—*pop pl* KS-7
Okey Branch—*stream* MS-4
Okey Ch—*church* OH-6
*Okey Woods Creek* MS-4
Okfauchavuk Slough—*gut* AK-9
O K Furnace (historical)—*locale* TN-4
Okfuskee—*locale* OK-5
Okfuskee Cem—*cemetery* OK-5
Okfuskee Ch—*church* OK-5
**Okfuskee (County)**—*pop pl* OK-5
Okfuskee County Courthouse—*hist pl* OK-5
Okgok—*slope* MH-9
Ok Gulch—*valley* ID-8
Ok Gulch—*valley* OR-9
*Okibarames Cape* PW-9
Okie Draw—*valley* WY-8
Okie Pasture—*flat* WY-8
Okie Tank—*reservoir* AZ-5
**Okietown**—*pop pl* OR-9
Okie Trail—*trail* WY-8
Okie Well—*well* AZ-5
Okie Windmill—*locale* TX-5
*Okihumpy* FL-3
Okikak Mtn—*summit* AK-9
O King Ranch—*locale* NE-7
*Okino Iwa* MH-9
Okino Reef—*bar* MH-9
*Okino Rock* MH-9
*Okino-sho* MH-9
Okiokilepe Pond—*hist pl* HI-9
Okiokiolepe Pond—*lake* HI-9
Okiotak Creek—*stream* AK-9
Okiotak Peak—*summit* AK-9
Okiron Cem—*cemetery* MI-6
*Okisk* NC-3
**Okisko**—*pop pl* NC-3
Okko—*island* FM-9
Oklahoma—*locale* KY-4
Oklahoma—*locale* MD-2
**Oklahoma**—*pop pl* MS-4
**Oklahoma**—*pop pl* NY-2
**Oklahoma**—*pop pl* OH-6
**Oklahoma**—*pop pl* (2) PA-2
**Oklahoma**—*pop pl* TX-5
Oklahoma, New Mexico and Pacific RR Depot—*hist pl* OK-5
Oklahoma Baptist Univ—*school* OK-5
**Oklahoma Beach**—*pop pl* NY-2
Oklahoma Borough—*civil* PA-2
Oklahoma Branch—*stream* TN-4
Oklahoma Cem—*cemetery* TN-4
Oklahoma Cem—*cemetery* TX-5
Oklahoma Ch—*church* MS-4
Oklahoma Ch—*church* MO-7
Oklahoma Childrens Center—*building* OK-5
Oklahoma Christian Coll—*school* OK-5
**Oklahoma City**—*pop pl* OK-5
Oklahoma City Air Force Station—*military* OK-5
Oklahoma City (CCD)—*cens area* OK-5
Oklahoma City Country Club—*other* OK-5
Oklahoma City Discovery Well—*hist pl* OK-5
Oklahoma City Univ—*hist pl* OK-5
Oklahoma City Univ—*school* OK-5
Oklahoma College Of Liberal Arts—*uninc pl* OK-5
Oklahoma Coll for Liberal Arts—*school* OK-5
**Oklahoma (County)**—*pop pl* OK-5
Oklahoma County Home for Girls—*hist pl* OK-5
Oklahoma Ditch No. 1—*canal* CO-8
Oklahoma Draw—*valley* TX-5
Oklahoma Elem Sch—*school* PA-2
Oklahoma Flat—*flat* AZ-5
Oklahoma Flat—*flat* CA-9
Oklahoma Flat—*flat* CO-8
Oklahoma Flat—*locale* TX-5
Oklahoma Flat Draw—*valley* AZ-5
Oklahoma Forest Camp—*locale* WA-9
Oklahoma Gas and Electric Company Bldg—*hist pl* OK-5
Oklahoma Gulch—*valley* WA-9
Oklahoma Gulf—*valley* NY-2
Oklahoma Hardware Bldg—*hist pl* OK-5
**Oklahoma Heights**—*pop pl* MA-1
Oklahoma High Top—*summit* OK-5
**Oklahoma Hill**—*pop pl* OR-9
Oklahoma Hill—*summit* IL-6
**Oklahoma Hills**—*pop pl* OK-5
Oklahoma (historical)—*locale* KS-7
Oklahoma Historic Reservation Area—*reserve* OK-5
Oklahoma Lane—*locale* TX-5
Oklahoma Lane Community Center—*locale* TX-5
Oklahoma Military Acad—*school* OK-5
Oklahoma Mine—*mine* AZ-5
Oklahoma Natural Gas Company Bldg—*hist pl* OK-5
Oklahoma No 2 Ditch—*canal* CO-8
*Oklahoma Panhandle* OK-5
Oklahoma Panhandle—*area* OK-5
Oklahoma Peak—*summit* OK-5
Oklahoma Presbyterian College—*hist pl* OK-5
Oklahoma Publishing Company Bldg—*hist pl* OK-5
Oklahoma Racetrack—*other* NY-2
Oklahoma Rsvr—*reservoir* CO-8
Oklahoma Sch—*school* CA-9
Oklahoma Sch—*school* CO-8
Oklahoma Sch—*school* OK-5
Oklahoma Sch—*school* TX-5
Oklahoma Sch—*school* WV-2
Oklahoma Sch—*school* WI-6
Oklahoma Sch (abandoned)—*school* (2) MO-7
Oklahoma Sch (historical)—*school* AL-4
Oklahoma Sch (historical)—*school* MO-7
Oklahoma State Bank Bldg—*hist pl* OK-5
Oklahoma State Capitol—*building* OK-5
Oklahoma State Capitol—*hist pl* OK-5
Oklahoma State Penitentiary (McLeod Honor Farm)—*building* OK-5
Oklahoma State Tech.—*post sta* OK-5
Oklahoma State Technical—*school* OK-5
Oklahoma State Univ—*school* OK-5
Oklahoma State University Engineering Camp—*locale* CO-8
Oklahoma State Univ Experimental Farm—*school* OK-5
Oklahoma Trail—*trail* WA-9
Oklahoma University Biological Station—*other* OK-5
Oklahoma Yards—*locale* TX-5
Oklahoma 15 Interchange—*other* OK-5
Oklahome Ch—*church* GA-3
Okland Ch—*church* TX-5
OK Landing—*locale* LA-4
Okland Sch—*school* MO-7
**Oklaunion**—*pop pl* TX-5
*Oklawaha* FL-3
**Oklawaha**—*pop pl* FL-3
Oklawaha Bridge Baptist Ch—*church* FL-3
Oklawaha River—*stream* FL-3
**Oklawaha (RR name Ocklawaha)**—*pop pl* FL-3
**Oklee**—*pop pl* MN-6
Oklee Racetrack—*other* MN-6
Okley Cave Branch—*stream* KY-4
Okley Cem—*cemetery* OK-5
*Oklocknee* FL-3
*Oklocknee Bay* FL-3
*Oklocknee River* FL-3
*Oklocknee River* GA-3
OK Lode Mine—*mine* (2) SD-7
*Oklolimeter Creek* MS-4
OK Mine—*mine* AZ-5
Ok Mine—*mine* CA-9
OK Mine—*mine* CO-8
O K Mine—*mine* CO-8
OK Mine—*mine* NV-8
O K Mine—*mine* NM-5
OK Mine—*mine* UT-8
O K Missionary Baptist Ch—*church* TN-4
Okmok Caldera—*basin* AK-9
**Okmulgee**—*pop pl* OK-5
Okmulgee Black Hosp—*hist pl* OK-5
Okmulgee (CCD)—*cens area* OK-5
Okmulgee Cem—*cemetery* OK-5
Okmulgee Country Club—*other* OK-5
**Okmulgee (County)**—*pop pl* OK-5
Okmulgee County Courthouse—*hist pl* OK-5
Okmulgee Creek—*stream* OK-5
Okmulgee Lake—*reservoir* OK-5
Okmulgee Public Library—*hist pl* OK-5
Okmulgee State Game Mngmt Area—*park* OK-5
Okmulgee Waterworks—*locale* OK-5
*Okmulkee* OK-5
*Okmulkee Creek* OK-5
OK Notch—*gap* AZ-5
OK Number 2 Lode Mine—*mine* SD-7
OK Number 4 Lode Mine—*mine* SD-7
**Okoboji**—*pop pl* IA-7
Okoboji Golf Course—*other* IA-7
Okoboji Lake—*lake* IA-7
Okoboji Township—*fmr MCD* IA-7
Okobojo—*locale* SD-7
Okobojo, Lake—*reservoir* SD-7
Okobojo Cem—*cemetery* SD-7
Okobojo Creek—*stream* SD-7
Okobojo Creek Rec Area—*park* SD-7
Okobojo Dam—*dam* SD-7
*Okobojo Lake* SD-7
*Okobojo Lake Dam* SD-7
Okobojo Rec Area—*park* SD-7
Okobojo Sch—*school* SD-7
Okobojo Township—*civil* SD-7
Oko Bojou Islands (historical)—*island* SD-7
**Okoe**—*pop pl* HI-9
Okoe Bay—*bay* HI-9
Okoee—*locale* OK-5
Okoe One-Two—*civil* HI-9
*Okohay Cemetery* MS-4
*Okohola* HI-9
*Okohola Hill* HI-9
*Okoii* HI-9
Okoklik Lake—*lake* AK-9
Okokmilaga River—*stream* AK-9
Okok Point—*locale* AK-9
Okok River—*stream* AK-9
*Okolalah Creek* MS-4
Okole Gulch—*valley* HI-9
Okoli—*summit* HI-9
*Okoloacoochee* FL-3
*Okolona* TN-4
Okolona—*hist pl* DE-2
Okolona—*locale* (2) TN-4
**Okolona**—*pop pl* AR-4
**Okolona**—*pop pl* KY-4
**Okolona**—*pop pl* MS-4
**Okolona**—*pop pl* OH-6
*Okolona Baptist Church* AL-4
Okolona Cem—*cemetery* AR-4
Okolona Ch—*church* (3) AL-4
*Okolona Christian Church* MS-4
Okolona Community Hosp—*hospital* MS-4
Okolona Elem Sch—*school* MS-4
**Okolona Estates**—*pop pl* TN-4
Okolona Female Acad (historical)—*school* MS-4
Okolona Female Coll (historical)—*school* MS-4
Okolona Female Institute (historical)—*school* MS-4
Okolona First Baptist Ch—*church* MS-4
Okolona First United Methodist Ch—*church* MS-4
Okolona HS—*school* MS-4
Okolona Industrial Sch (historical)—*school* MS-4
Okolona Lookout Tower—*locale* AR-4
Okolona Male Acad (historical)—*school* MS-4
Okolona Male and Female Acad (historical)—*school* MS-4
Okolona Post Office (historical)—*building* TN-4
Okolona Presbyterian Ch—*church* MS-4
*Okolona School* AL-4
Okolona United Methodist Ch—*church* TN-4
Okolona Vocational Technical Center—*school* MS-4
**Okome**—*pop pl* PA-2
Okome Cem—*cemetery* PA-2
Okomo Camp—*locale* AL-4
Okonagun Creek—*stream* AK-9
Okonatie Watershed UT-25-1 Dam—*dam* MS-4
Okonatie Watershed UT-25-2 Dam—*dam* MS-4
Okoni (historical)—*locale* AL-4
Okonite Wire & Cable Company—*facility* KY-4
Okonoka, Lake—*lake* MI-6
Okonoko—*locale* WV-2
Okonoko Ch—*church* WV-2
*Okoradegusu* PW-9
*Okoradegusu To* PW-9
Okorb Island—*island* MN-6
*Okoreppu Island* MP-9
Okotak Creek—*stream* AK-9
Okpikruak River—*stream* AK-9
Okpiksak River—*stream* AK-9
Okpiksugruk Creek—*stream* AK-9
Okpilak Glacier—*glacier* AK-9
Okpilak Lake—*lake* AK-9
Okpilak River—*stream* AK-9
Okpilatok Bluff—*cliff* AK-9
Okpirourak Creek—*stream* AK-9
O K Pocket—*lake* MS-4
Okra—*locale* TN-4
**Okra**—*pop pl* TX-5
Okracoke Fire Hall—*locale* NC-3
Okracoke Post Office—*locale* NC-3
Okracoke Sheriffs Office—*locale* NC-3
OK Ranch—*locale* AZ-5
OK Ranch—*locale* ND-7
Okra Post Office (historical)—*building* TN-4
**Okreek**—*pop pl* SD-7
Okroknakpak Lakes—*lake* AK-9
Okrurat Creek—*stream* AK-9
Okry Creek—*stream* TX-5
OK Sch—*school* KY-4
O K Sch—*school* NE-7
O K Sch—*school* OK-5
OK Sch (historical)—*school* MO-7
O K Sch (historical)—*school* (2) TN-4
Oksenof Beach—*beach* AK-9
Oksenof Point—*cape* AK-9
Okshokwewhik Pass—*gut* AK-9
Oksik Channel—*stream* AK-9
Oksik Creek—*stream* AK-9
O K Slip Brook—*stream* NY-2
O K Slip Pond—*lake* NY-2
*Okso' Takpochau* MH-9
Oksotalik Creek—*stream* AK-9
Oksrukuyik—*locale* AK-9
Okstukuk Hills—*other* AK-9
Okstukuk Lake—*lake* AK-9
**Oktaha**—*pop pl* OK-5
Oktaha Cem—*cemetery* OK-5
Oktaha Sch—*hist pl* OK-5
*Oktahatki* FL-3
**Oktahatko (historical)**—*pop pl* FL-3
OK Tank—*reservoir* AZ-5
**Oktibbeha**—*pop pl* MS-4
Oktibbeha Airp—*airport* MS-4
**Oktibbeha County**—*pop pl* MS-4
Oktibbeha County Courthouse—*building* MS-4
Oktibbeha County Heritage Museum—*building* MS-4
Oktibbeha County Hosp—*hospital* MS-4
Oktibbeha County Lake—*reservoir* MS-4
Oktibbeha County Lake Dam—*dam* MS-4
*Oktibbeha Creek* MS-4
**Oktibbeha Gardens (subdivision)**—*pop pl* MS-4
**Oktibbeha (historical)**—*pop pl* MS-4
Oktibbeha Memorial Gardens—*cemetery* MS-4
*Oktibbeh Creek* MS-4
*Oktibee Creek* MS-4
**Oktoc**—*pop pl* MS-4
Oktoc Creek—*stream* MS-4
Ok Truck Barn—*building* OR-9
O & K Tunnel—*tunnel* KY-4
Okumiak, Mount—*summit* AK-9
*Okumpka* FL-3
Okwakee Creek—*stream* AL-4
Okwakee Creek—*stream* MS-4
Okwakee Lake—*reservoir* AL-4
Ok-wa-nessett Camp—*locale* RI-1
Okwega Pass—*stream* AK-9
OK Well—*well* AZ-5
Ok Windmill—*locale* NM-5
O K Windmill—*locale* TX-5
OK Woods Point—*cape* FL-3
*Ola* FM-9
Ola—*locale* GA-3
Ola—*locale* NV-8
Ola—*locale* NC-3
Ola—*locale* SD-7
Ola—*locale* TX-5
**Ola**—*pop pl* AR-4
**Ola**—*pop pl* ID-8
**Ola**—*pop pl* MI-6
Ola, Lake—*lake* FL-3
Ola, Lake—*reservoir* AL-4
*Olaa* (2) HI-9
Olaa—*civil* HI-9
Olaa Dispensary—*hospital* HI-9
Olaa Flume Spring—*spring* HI-9
*Olaa Forest Park Res* HI-9
Olaa Forest Park Res—*park* HI-9
Olaa For Res—*forest* HI-9
Olaa Reservation Homesteads—*civil* HI-9
Olaa Reservation Lots—*civil* HI-9
Olaa Summer Lots—*civil* HI-9
Ola Beach—*locale* FL-3
Ola Ch—*church* MI-6
Ola-dale, Lake—*reservoir* AR-4
Olaf—*locale* IA-7
**Olaf**—*pop pl* VA-3
Olaf, Lake—*lake* (2) MN-6
Olaf Canyon—*valley* UT-8
Olaf Community Center—*locale* MT-8
Olaf Knolls—*summit* AZ-5
*Olaf Lake* MN-6
Olaf Lake—*lake* AK-9
Olaf Seim Mine—*mine* SD-7
Olafs Pond—*reservoir* UT-8
Ola (historical)—*locale* SD-7
Olah Lookout Tower—*locale* MS-4
*Olai Hill* HI-9
Olaine Lake—*lake* CA-9
*Olalee Creek* WA-9
*Olalee Meadow* WA-9
Olalla—*locale* OR-9
**Olalla**—*pop pl* WA-9
Olalla Barrier Rsvr—*reservoir* OR-9
Olalla Bay—*bay* WA-9
*Olalla Creek* OR-9
Olalla Creek—*stream* (2) OR-9
Olalla Creek—*stream* WA-9
Olalla Rsvr—*reservoir* OR-9
Olalla Rsvr City Park—*park* OR-9
Olalla Sch—*school* WA-9
Olalla Slough—*stream* OR-9
Olalla Valley—*valley* WA-9
Olalla Valley Golf Course—*other* OR-9
*Olallie* OR-9
Olallie Butte—*summit* OR-9
Olallie Butte Guard Station—*locale* OR-9
*Olallie Creek* OR-9
Olallie Creek—*stream* (3) OR-9
Olallie Creek—*stream* (4) WA-9
Olallie Forest Camp—*locale* OR-9
Olallie Guard Station—*locale* OR-9
Olallie Lake—*lake* OR-9
Olallie Lake—*lake* (2) WA-9
Olallie Meadow—*flat* OR-9
Olallie Meadow—*flat* WA-9
Olallie Meadows—*flat* OR-9
Olallie Mtn—*summit* OR-9
Olallie Peninsula Campground—*park* OR-9
*Olallie Slough* OR-9
Olallie Trail—*trail* OR-9
*Olamana Ridge* HI-9
Olamar, Lake—*lake* OK-5
**Olamon**—*pop pl* ME-1
Olamon Island—*island* (2) ME-1
Olamon Pond—*lake* ME-1
Olamon Stream—*stream* ME-1
Ola Mountain—*ridge* AR-4
*Olamwe* FM-9
*Olan* FM-9
Olana—*hist pl* NY-2
**Olancha**—*pop pl* CA-9
Olancha Creek—*stream* CA-9
Olancha Pass—*gap* CA-9
Olancha Peak—*summit* CA-9
Olancha Siding—*locale* CA-9
Oland Ch—*church* MO-7
O L And Ema Hicks Lake—*reservoir* AL-4
O L And Ema Hicks Lake Dam—*dam* AL-4
Olander Lake—*lake* MN-6
O Lane Ranch—*locale* NE-7
Olan Ferguson Bridge—*bridge* FL-3
*Olang* FM-9
*Olanta* ND-7
**Olanta**—*pop pl* PA-2
**Olanta**—*pop pl* SC-3
Olanta (CCD)—*cens area* SC-3
**Olar**—*pop pl* SC-3
Olar (CCD)—*cens area* SC-3
O Larson Ranch—*locale* ND-7
Ola Sch—*school* GA-3
Ola Sch—*school* MI-6
Olas Tank—*reservoir* NM-5
O Lateral—*canal* CA-9
**Olathe**—*pop pl* CO-8
**Olathe**—*pop pl* KS-7
Olathe Cem—*cemetery* CO-8
Olathe Lake—*reservoir* KS-7
Olathe North HS—*school* KS-7
Olathe Rsvr No 1—*reservoir* CO-8
Olathe Rsvr No 2—*reservoir* CO-8
**Olathe Township**—*pop pl* KS-7
**Olathia**—*pop pl* MO-7
Olaton—*locale* KY-4
**Ola Township**—*pop pl* SD-7
Ola Township (historical)—*civil* SD-7
Ola Valley—*valley* ID-8
*Olava P.o.* CO-8
Olaville Post Office (historical)—*building* AL-4
*Olay Butte* OR-9
*Olay Flat* UT-8
Olberg—*locale* AZ-5
Olberg Trading Post—*building* AZ-5
Olbrich Park—*park* WI-6
Olcott—*locale* CA-9
Olcott—*locale* KS-7
Olcott—*locale* KY-4
Olcott—*locale* TX-5
**Olcott**—*pop pl* NY-2
**Olcott**—*pop pl* WV-2
Olcott, Frances A., House—*hist pl* UT-8
Olcott Cem—*cemetery* IN-6
*Olcott Creek* OR-9
Olcott Hill—*summit* NY-2
Olcott Lake—*lake* MI-6
Olcott Park—*park* MN-6
Olcott Post Office (historical)—*building* TN-4
Olcott Sch—*school* NY-2
Old, The, Hotel—*hist pl* OH-6
Old Aadalen Cem—*cemetery* ND-7
Old Aalii Pump Station—*other* HI-9
Old Abe Lake—*reservoir* WI-6
Old Abe Mines—*mine* NM-5
Old Aberdeen Road Ch of Christ—*church* MS-4
Old Abreu Lodge—*locale* NM-5
Old Academy Cem—*cemetery* NC-3
Old Academy Park—*park* IN-6
Old A.C.L. Union Depot—*hist pl* FL-3
Oldacre Hollow—*valley* AL-4
Old Acton Cem—*cemetery* AL-4
Old Ada Cem—*cemetery* OK-5
Old Ada Dam—*dam* WV-2
**Old Adamsboro**—*pop pl* IN-6
Old Ada Sch—*school* SD-7
Old Administration Building, Fresno City College—*hist pl* CA-9
**Old Adobe**—*pop pl* CA-9
Old Adobe, The—*locale* CA-9
Old Adobe Barn—*hist pl* CA-9
Old Adobe Patio—*hist pl* AZ-5
Old Adobe Sch—*school* CA-9
Old Advance Ch—*church* MS-4
Old Aenon Ch—*church* TN-4
Old Aetna Furnace (historical)—*locale* TN-4
Old Aetna Furnace (40HI148)—*hist pl* TN-4
*Old Agency* MS-4
Old Agency Cem—*cemetery* OR-9
Old Agency Ranger Station—*locale* CO-8
Old Ahern Ditch—*canal* HI-9
*Old Ahrens Ditch* HI-9
Old Airport Community—*uninc pl* GA-3
Oldaker Cem—*cemetery* WV-2
Oldaker State Wildlife Area—*park* OH-6
Old Akron Post Office—*hist pl* OH-6
**Old Alabam**—*pop pl* AR-4
Old Alamo Mine Camp—*locale* AZ-5
Old Albany Cem—*cemetery* MA-1
Old Albany Post Road—*hist pl* NY-2
Old Albany Schoolhouse—*hist pl* KS-7
Old Albert Lake—*lake* AK-9
**Old Albertville**—*pop pl* WI-6
Old Albertville Cem—*cemetery* AL-4
Old Albuquerque (Old Town)—*uninc pl* NM-5
Old Alexander House—*hist pl* AR-4
Old Alexandria Ch—*church* MO-7
Old Algerita Cem—*cemetery* TX-5
Old Algerita Hotel—*hist pl* TX-5
Old Algoma (historical)—*locale* MS-4
*Old Algon Station* AL-4
Old Allamakee County Courthouse—*hist pl* IA-7
Old Allegany County Courthouse—*hist pl* NY-2
Old Allegheny Rows Hist Dist—*hist pl* PA-2
Old Allen—*uninc pl* KY-4
Old Allens Ferry—*locale* AR-4
Old Allison—*locale* OK-5
Old Allison Ranch Mine—*mine* CA-9
Old Allridge Place (historical)—*locale* UT-8
Old Alpine Tunnel—*tunnel* CO-8
Old Altizer Ranch—*locale* TX-5
Old Altman Ranch—*locale* WY-8
Old Alton Bridge—*hist pl* TX-5
Old Alton Ch—*church* TX-5
Old American Mine—*mine* CA-9
Old Americus—*locale* MS-4
Old Ames Cem—*cemetery* TN-4
Old Amherst Freight Depot—*hist pl* OH-6
**Old Anderafski**—*pop pl* AK-9
Old Anderson Ch—*church* GA-3
Old Andreafsky—*locale* AK-9
Old Andrew Ch—*church* VA-3
Old Anglan Cem—*cemetery* TX-5
Old Annapolis Cem—*cemetery* OH-6
Old Antelope Windmill—*locale* TX-5
Old Anthony Rock—*bar* ME-1
Old Antioch—*locale* TN-4
*Old Antioch Cem* AL-4
Old Antioch Cem—*cemetery* AL-4
Old Antioch Cem—*cemetery* (3) MS-4
Old Antioch Cem—*cemetery* SC-3
Old Antioch Cem—*cemetery* TN-4
Old Antioch Cem—*cemetery* WV-2
*Old Antioch Ch* AL-4
Old Antioch Ch—*church* AL-4
Old Antioch Ch—*church* MS-4
Old Antioch Ch (historical)—*church* MS-4
Old Antioch Ch (historical)—*church* TN-4
Old Antioch Sch—*school* TN-4
Old Antioch Sch (historical)—*school* TN-4
*Old Appleton (corporate name Appleton)* MO-7
Old Aquilla Cem—*cemetery* AL-4
Old Araz Stage Depot—*locale* CA-9
Old Arbor Mount Zion Ch—*church* MS-4
Old Arcadia Cem—*cemetery* KS-7
Old Arcadia Cem—*cemetery* TX-5
Old Arizona Catchment—*reservoir* AZ-5
Old Arkansas City HS—*hist pl* KS-7
Old Ark Ch—*church* SC-3
Old Armijo Sch—*hist pl* NM-5
Old Armory—*hist pl* ND-7
Old Armunger Cabin—*locale* OR-9
Old Arnold Creek—*stream* TX-5
Old Arthur—*locale* WV-2
Old Asbury Cem—*cemetery* AL-4
Old Asbury Methodist Church—*hist pl* DE-2
Old Ascension Cem—*cemetery* SD-7
Old Ash Cem—*cemetery* MS-4
**Old Ashippun** *pop pl* WI-6
Old Ashland Post Office—*hist pl* WI-6
Old Ashley Cem—*cemetery* MO-7
Old Ashton Hist Dist—*hist pl* RI-1
Old Ashton (historical)—*locale* SD-7
Old Aspermont Highway Windmill—*locale* TX-5
Old Athens—*locale* LA-4
Old Athens, Alabama Main Post Office—*hist pl* AL-4
Old Atkinson Crossing—*locale* AL-4
Old Atkinson Dam Site—*locale* MI-6
Old Atoka County Courthouse—*hist pl* OK-5
Old Atoka State Bank—*hist pl* OK-5
Old Attlebury Hill—*summit* NY-2
Old Atway Cem—*cemetery* MS-4
Old Auburn Hist Dist—*hist pl* CA-9
Old Auburn (historical)—*locale* MS-4
Old Auburn Rsvr—*reservoir* OR-9
Old Augusta—*locale* MS-4
Old Augusta Ch—*church* AL-4
Old Augusta (historical)—*locale* AL-4
Old Augusta Historic Site—*hist pl* MS-4
*Old Augusta School* AL-4
Old Au Sable River—*stream* MI-6
Old Austen House—*building* NY-2
**Old Austin**—*pop pl* AR-4
Old Automobile Tank—*reservoir* AZ-5
Old Auxvasse Ch—*church* MO-7
Old Avera—*locale* MS-4
Old Avery Cem—*cemetery* GA-3
Old Backs House—*hist pl* CA-9
Old Backus—*hist pl* MN-6
*Old Bacon Cemetery* TX-5
Old Badger Mills—*locale* WI-6
Old Bailey House—*hist pl* HI-9
Old Bailey Place—*locale* CA-9
Old Baker Cabin—*locale* CA-9
Old Baker County Courthouse—*hist pl* FL-3
*Old Baker Settlement* IN-6
Old Bakery—*hist pl* TX-5
Old Bald—*summit* NC-3
Old Bald Creek—*stream* NC-3
Old Baldface—*summit* ME-1

Old Field Ch—church GA-3
Old Field Ch—church MD-2
Oldfield Ch—church NC-3
Old Field Ch—church NC-3
Old Field Ch—church SC-3
Old Field Church AL-4
Old Field Club—other NY-2
Oldfield Creek NC-3
Old Field Creek—stream CT-1
Oldfield Creek—stream FL-3
Old Field Creek—stream GA-3
Old Field Creek—stream (2) MS-4
Old Field Creek—stream (4) NC-3
Oldfield Creek—stream SC-3
Oldfield Creek—stream (2) VA-3
Oldfield Fork—stream KY-4
Old Field Fork—stream (2) WV-2
Old Field Fork Cem—cemetery WV-2
Oldfield Gap—gap (2) NC-3
Old Field Hollow—valley MO-7
Oldfield Hollow—valley OH-6
Oldfield Hollow—valley TN-4
Old Field Hollow—valley TN-4
Old Field JHS—school NY-2
Old Field Joyner—flat GA-3
Old Field Lake—lake SC-3
Old Field Mountain—ridge WV-2
Old Field Mtn—summit SC-3
Oldfield Park—park TN-4
Old Field Point MS-4
Oldfield Point—cape MD-2
Old Field Point—cape MD-2
Old Field Point—cape MA-1
Old Field Point—cape NY-2
Old Field Point—cape (3) NC-3
Oldfield Pond—lake (2) FL-3
Oldfield Ridge—ridge OH-6
Old Fields—pop pl WV-2
Old Fields Cem—cemetery KY-4
Oldfield Sch—school CT-1
Oldfield Sch—school MD-2
Old Field Sch—school (2) SC-3
Oldfield Sch—school WV-2
Old Fields Creek—stream NC-3
Old Field South—pop pl NY-2
Old Fields Place—pop pl TN-4
Old Fields Place Branch—stream TN-4
Oldfields (Township of)—fmr MCD NC-3
Old Fields (Township of)—fmr MCD NC-3
Old Field Swamp—swamp NC-3
Oldfield Top—summit NC-3
Old Field Town FL-3
Oldfield Township—civil MO-7
Old Finch Ranch—locale AZ-5
Old Finds Bight—bay FL-3
Old Finnish Lutheran Church—hist pl SD-7
Old Fire Engine House—hist pl ME-1
Old Fire House—hist pl DE-2
Old Fire House No. 4—hist pl MI-6
Old Fireside Mine—mine UT-8
Old First Cem—cemetery MA-1
Old First Church—hist pl NY-2
Old First Church—hist pl OH-6
Old First Natl Bank Bldg—hist pl OR-9
Old First Natl Bank of Prineville, and Foster and Hyde Store—hist pl OR-9
Old First Parish Cem—cemetery MA-1
Old First Presbyterian Church—hist pl DE-2
Old First Presbyterian Church—hist pl NJ-2
Old First Presbyterian Church of Wilmington—hist pl DE-2
Old Fisher Ranch—locale WY-8
Old Fishing Pond—lake ME-1
Old Five Mile Presbyterian Church AL-4
Old Flag Windmill—locale TX-5
Old Flat Creek Cem TN-4
Old Flat Creek Cem—cemetery (2) TN-4
Old Flat Creek Ch—church TN-4
Old Flat Lick—pop pl KY-4
Old Flatonia—locale TX-5
Old Flatonia Cem—cemetery TX-5
Old Flat Top—summit MT-8
Old Flat Top—summit TX-5
Old Flatwood Ch—church AL-4
Old Fletcher Cemetery MS-4
Old Fletcher Well—well NM-5
Old Flight Line Trail (Jeep)—trail CA-9
Old Florence Cem—cemetery AL-4
Old Florey Park—park TX-5
Old Fly, The—lake NY-2
Old Fly, The—stream NY-2
Old Folks Flat Campground—park UT-8
Old Folks Home—building TX-5
Old Fonda Rsvr—reservoir NY-2
Old Foot Ridge—ridge MO-7
Old Forbestown—locale CA-9
Old Ford—pop pl NC-3
Old Ford Dairy—hist pl DE-2
Old Ford Dairy (Boundary Increase)—hist pl DE-2
Old Ford Place—locale MT-8
Old Ford Swamp—stream NC-3
Old Fordyce Post Office—hist pl AR-4
Old Forest Camp (site)—locale OR-9
Old Forest City Shaft—mine PA-2
Old Forester Tank—reservoir AZ-5
Old Forester Well—well AZ-5
Old Forge—pop pl NY-2
Old Forge—pop pl (3) PA-2
Old Forge Borough—civil PA-2
Old Forge Branch—stream DE-2
Old Forge Breaker (historical)—building PA-2
Old Forge Cem—cemetery PA-2
Old Forge Cem—cemetery VA-3
Old Forge Farm—hist pl MD-2
Old Forge Lake—reservoir NJ-2
Old Forge Number 2 Shaft—mine PA-2
Old Forge Picnic Area—area PA-2
Old Forge Pond—reservoir VA-3
Old Forge Rec Area—park TN-4
Old Forge Sch—school NY-2
Old Forge Sch—school PA-2
Old Forge Village—pop pl NJ-2
Old Fork WV-2
Old Fork—stream WV-2
Old Fork Cem—cemetery GA-3
Old Forked Oak Cem—cemetery MS-4
Old Forked Slough—stream AR-4
Old Fork Tank—reservoir NM-5
Old Fort AZ-5
Old Fort TN-4
Old Fort—hist pl MO-7
Old Fort—locale ID-8
Old Fort—locale PA-2
Old Fort—locale WV-2
Old Fort—pop pl NC-3
Old Fort—pop pl OH-6
Oldfort—pop pl TN-4
Old Fort Anahuac—locale TX-5
Old Fort Argyle Site—hist pl GA-3
Old Fort Bayou—stream MS-4
Old Fort Beauregard Ruins—locale LA-4
Old Fort Bent—locale CO-8
Old Fort Bliss—hist pl TX-5
Old Fort Blunt Ferry TN-4
Old Fort Bonneville Site—locale WY-8
Old Fort Bowie AZ-5
Old Fort Brady—hist pl MI-6
Old Fort Cem—cemetery NH-1
Old Fort Cem—cemetery NY-2
Old Fort Cem—cemetery SC-3
Old Fort Cem—cemetery TN-4
Old Fort Cem—cemetery TX-5
Old Fort Ch—church SC-3
Old Fort Church—hist pl DE-2
Old Fort Clagget—locale MT-8
Old Fort Creek—stream TN-4
Old Fort Crittenden AZ-5
Oldfort Defiance Park—park OH-6
Old Fort Dorchester—locale SC-3
Old Fort Drummond—locale MI-6
Old Fort Duchesne—locale UT-8
Old Fort Elem Sch—school NC-3
Old Fort Garland Military Reservation—other CO-8
Old Fort Harmony (historical)—locale UT-8
Old Fort Harrod State Park—park KY-4
Old Fort Hays—park KS-7
Old Fort Hays Museum—locale KS-7
Old Fort (historical)—locale NC-3
Old Fort Historical Monument, The—park AZ-5
Old Fort House—hist pl MS-4
Old Fort House—hist pl NY-2
Old Fort Jim—locale CA-9
Old Fort Jim Historical Marker—park CA-9
Old Fort King George—locale GA-3
Old Fort Lake—lake WA-9
Old Fort (LA 1869)—hist pl NM-5
Old Fort Loudon TN-4
Old Fort Lyon—locale CO-8
Old Fort Lyons—locale CO-8
Old Fort Madison Site—hist pl IA-7
Old Fort Mann KS-7
Old Fort Mason AZ-5
Old Fort Massachusetts—locale MS-4
Old Fort Mtn—summit NY-2
Old Fort Niagara—hist pl NY-2
Old Fort Niagara—locale NY-2
Old Fort Park—park FL-3
Old Fort Park—park NY-2
Old Fort Park—park TX-5
Old Fort Pena Colorada (reduced usage)—locale TX-5
Old Fort Pierce UT-8
Old Fort Pierre Sch—hist pl SD-7
Old Fort Point—cape ME-1
Old Fort Pond—lake NY-2
Oldfort Post Office—building TN-4
Old Fort Public Use Area—park MS-4
Old Fort Randall Cem—cemetery SD-7
Old Fort Ransom, Site of—locale ND-7
Old Fort Reno (site)—locale AZ-5
Old Fort Saint Marks (site)—locale FL-3
Old Fort San Jacinto—locale TX-5
Old Fort School TN-4
Old Fort Scott (historical)—locale KS-7
Old Fort Shaw—locale MT-8
Old Fort Sisseton (historical)—locale SD-7
Old Fort Stoddard Mount Vernon Landing—locale AL-4
Old Fort Sully Site (39HU52)—hist pl SD-7
Old Fort Sumner Cem—cemetery NM-5
Old Fort Tejon—locale CA-9
Old Fort Thomas Cem—cemetery AZ-5
Old Fort Townsend State Park—park WA-9
Old Fort (Township of)—fmr MCD NC-3
Old Fort Towson Cem—cemetery OK-5
Old Fort Towson Historic Site—locale OK-5
Old Fort Tyson AZ-5
Old Fort Tyson—locale AZ-5
Old Fort Vasquez—locale CO-8
Old Fort Wilkins—locale MI-6
Old Fort Winnebago Cem—cemetery WI-6
Old Fosters Ferry Road Ch of God—church AL-4
Old Fouke Cem—cemetery TX-5
Old Foundary Hill Cem—cemetery TN-4
Old Foundry Cem—cemetery TX-5
Old Foundry Hill Ch—church TN-4
Old Fountain Head Cem—cemetery TN-4
Old Fountain Head Ch (historical)—church TN-4
Old Fountain Trail—trail WY-8
Old Four Corners CA-9
Oldframe—pop pl PA-2
Old Frame—pop pl PA-2
Old Francis Ranch—locale WY-8
Old Frankfort Cemetery AL-4
Old Frankfort City Jail—hist pl KS-7
Old Frankfort Stone HS—hist pl IN-6
Old Franklin Ch—church IN-6
Old Franklin Ditch—canal MO-7
Old Franks Creek—stream AK-9
Old Franks Lake—lake AK-9
Old Frazier Place—locale WY-8
Old Fredonia—locale MO-7
Old Fredonia Cem—cemetery MS-4
Old Fred's Islands ME-1
Old Freedom Cem—cemetery NC-3
Old Freedom Creek—stream AR-4
Old Freeman Tank—reservoir AZ-5
Old Freesoil Sch—school MI-6
Old Freitag Place—locale TX-5
Old Fremont—pop pl TN-4
Old French Cem—cemetery IN-6
Old French Cem—cemetery MS-4
Old French Fort (historical)—military MS-4
Old Frenchtown Wharf—locale MD-2
Old Fresno Water Tower—hist pl CA-9
Old Friends Cem—cemetery ME-1
Old Friends Church Cem—cemetery IN-6
Old Friendship Baptist Ch—church TN-4
Old Friendship Cem AL-4
Old Friendship Cem—cemetery AL-4
Old Friendship Cem—cemetery KY-4
Old Friendship Cem—cemetery (3) MS-4
Old Friendship Cem—cemetery (2) TN-4
Old Friendship Cemetery FL-3
Old Friendship Ch—church IN-6
Old Friendship Ch—church (2) KY-4
Old Friendship Ch—church TN-4
Old Friendship Ch (historical)—church MS-4
Old Friendship Church MS-4
Old Friendship Sch—school TN-4
Old Frio County Jail—hist pl TX-5
Old Frisco Mining Town UT-8
Old Frizzell Ranch—locale OR-9
Old Frontenac—pop pl MN-6
Old Frontenac Hist Dist—hist pl MN-6
Old Fruita School House Historical Site UT-8
Old Frye Cem—cemetery ME-1
Old Fulton Cem—cemetery MI-6
Old Fundamental Ch—church IN-6
Old Furnace MA-1
Old Furnace—locale DE-2
Old Furnace—pop pl MA-1
Old Furnace—pop pl PA-2
Old Furnace Ch—church WV-2
Old Furnace Mill DE-2
Old Furnace Sch (historical)—school TN-4
Old Furnace (Shirley Mine Station)—pop pl (2) PA-2
Old Furnace State Park—park CT-1
Old Fussell Cemetery TN-4
Old Gailee Ch—church SC-3
Old Gaissert Homeplace—hist pl GA-3
Old Gallilee Cem—cemetery MS-4
Old Galloway Ridge—ridge CA-9
Old Galveston Customhouse—hist pl TX-5
Old Garcia Ranch—locale NM-5
Old Garden Beach—beach MA-1
Old Garfield Sch—hist pl OR-9
Old Gauley—pop pl WV-2
Old Gay Hill Ch—church TX-5
Old George Mtn—summit CA-9
Old Georgetown City Hall—hist pl WA-9
Old Georgetown Estates—pop pl MD-2
Old Georgetown (historical)—pop pl MS-4
Old Georgetown HS—hist pl TX-5
Old German-American State Bank—hist pl KS-7
Old German Brethren Ch—church OR-9
Old German Cem—cemetery AL-4
Old German Cem—cemetery GA-3
Old German Cem—cemetery IA-7
Old German Cem—cemetery MN-6
Old German Cem—cemetery (2) MO-7
Old German Cem—cemetery (2) OH-6
Old German Ch—church (5) IN-6
Old German Ch—church MI-6
Old German Ch—church OH-6
Old German Consulate—hist pl WA-9
Old Germantown—locale MD-2
Old Germantown Acad And Headmasters' Houses—hist pl PA-2
Old Germfask Cem—cemetery MI-6
Old Geyser Creek—stream MT-8
Old Gib Mtn—summit WA-9
Old Gibson Ch—church TN-4
Old Gibson Primitive Baptist Ch TN-4
Old Gibson Sawmill (site)—locale AZ-5
Old Gibson Wells TN-4
Old Gifford Ditch IN-6
Old Gilchrist—pop pl IL-6
Old Gilgal Cem—cemetery SC-3
Old Gillespie Lake—reservoir IL-6
Old Gillsburg Cem—cemetery MS-4
Old Gilpin Sch—school TX-5
Old Gilreath—pop pl NC-3
Old Gilroy—pop pl CA-9
Old Gin Branch—stream AL-4
Old Ginns Settlement Cemetery AL-4
Old Gists Creek Cem—cemetery TN-4
Old Glade Spring—pop pl VA-3
Old Glade Swamp—swamp AL-4
Old Glady Branch—stream AL-4
Old Glenrock Cem—cemetery NE-7
Old Globe Hollow—valley OH-6
Old Glory—locale AZ-5
Old Glory—pop pl TN-4
Old Glory—pop pl TX-5
Old Glory Beach—pop pl MD-2
Old Glory Canyon—valley AZ-5
Old Glory Cem—cemetery TX-5
Old Glory Creek—stream AK-9
Old Glory Mine—mine (3) MT-8
Old Glory Mine—mine OR-9
Old Glory Mtn—summit OK-5
Old Glory Oil Field—oilfield TX-5
Old Glory Spring—spring AZ-5
Old Golden—locale ID-8
Old Gold Mine Trail—trail ME-1
Old Gooch Cem—cemetery TX-5
Old Goodfield Cem—cemetery TN-4
Old Good Hope Cem—cemetery AL-4
Old Good Hope Cem—cemetery ID-8
Old Good Hope Cem—cemetery (2) MS-4
Old Goodnight Tank—reservoir TX-5
Old Goose Creek—stream SC-3
Old Goose Egg Ranchhouse ( Ruins)—locale WY-8
Old Goose Lake—swamp IL-6
Old Goose Pond—lake TX-5
Old Gore—locale OH-6
Old Goree Cem—cemetery TX-5
Old Goshen Cem—cemetery IN-6
Old Goshen Center (historical)—locale AL-4
Old Goshenhoppen Ch—church PA-2
Old Goshen Site—hist pl UT-8
Old Goss School (historical)—locale MO-7
Old Gothic Barns—hist pl OH-6
Old Goucher College Buildings—hist pl MD-2
Old Government Trail—trail NM-5
Old Governor's Mansion—hist pl AZ-5
Old Governor's Mansion—hist pl GA-3
Old Governor's Mansion—hist pl KY-4
Old Governor's Mansion—hist pl OH-6
Old Grace Cem—cemetery NY-2
Old Grafton County Courthouse—hist pl NH-1
Old Graham Homestead—locale OR-9
Old Graham Windmill—locale NM-5
Old Grandad Tank—reservoir AZ-5
Old Grand Bayou—channel LA-4
Old Grand Canyon Tank—reservoir AZ-5
Old Grand Glaise—pop pl AR-4
Old Grandin Library—hist pl NJ-2
Old Grand Pierre Ch—church IL-6
Old Grand River Cem—cemetery SD-7
Old Grapevine Well—well TX-5
Old Grassy Ch—church KY-4
Old Grassy Lake—lake FL-3
Old Grassy Lake—lake OK-5
Old Gravel Hill Cem—cemetery MS-4
Old Gravesend Cemetery—hist pl NY-2
Old Graveyard, The—cemetery IL-6
Old Graveyard Memorial Park—cemetery TN-4
Old Graveyard Slough—stream TN-4
Old Grayback CA-9
Old Gray Cem—cemetery TN-4
Old Grays Cem—cemetery AL-4
Old Grays Mill Cem—cemetery TN-4
Old Grays Millpond—reservoir VA-3
Old Greenboro Cem—cemetery MS-4
Old Green Burney Camp—locale CA-9
Old Green Cem AL-4
Old Green Creek Ch—church VA-3
Old Green Island Club—locale NC-3
Old Greenleafton Cem—cemetery MN-6
Old Green Oak Sch—school AL-4
Old Greenville Cem—cemetery MO-7
Old Greenville Ch—church FL-3
Old Greenville Rec Area—park MO-7
Old Greenwich—pop pl CT-1
Old Greenwich Ch—church NJ-2
Old Greenwood Cem—cemetery MS-4
Old Greenwood HS—hist pl SC-3
Old Griffin Cem—cemetery TN-4
Old Grist Mill—hist pl ME-1
Old Grist Mill—locale IL-6
Old Grist Mill—locale MA-1
Old Grist Mill Pond—lake MA-1
Old Grist Mill Pond Dam—dam MA-1
Old Grolier Club—hist pl NY-2
Old Grouch Top—summit AK-9
Old Ground Gut—stream MD-2
Old Ground Marsh—swamp MD-2
Old Grounds Cem—cemetery TX-5
Old Grove—locale FL-3
Old Grove Ch—church SC-3
Old Grove Ch—church TN-4
Old Grove Church AL-4
Old Groves Memorial Cem—cemetery VA-3
Old Groves Sch—school TX-5
Old Guaranty Bank Bldg—hist pl LA-4
Old Guard Locks Dam—dam MA-1
Old Guard Peak—summit WA-9
Old Guernsey Ranch—locale WY-8
Old Guides Cem—cemetery KY-4
Old Guilford Sch—school MD-2
Old Gulch—valley CA-9
Old Gum Point Ch—church AR-4
Old Gum Springs Cem—cemetery MS-4
Old Gum Tree—pop pl PA-2
Old Gun—pop pl VA-3
Old Gussettville Cem—cemetery TX-5
Old Gustavus Cem—cemetery OH-6
Old Hachita—pop pl NM-5
Old Hack Point—cape MD-2
Old Hackworth Cem—cemetery OH-6
Old Hadley Cem—cemetery MA-1
Old Hailes Cem—cemetery MS-4
Old Haines Place—locale CO-8
Old Halfway—locale NJ-2
Old Halfway—pop pl IN-6
Old Hall Cem—cemetery TN-4
Old Hall Landing—locale VA-3
Old Halltown Cem—cemetery GA-3
Old Halter and Flick Ranch—locale WY-8
Oldham VA-3
Oldham—locale KY-4
Oldham—locale TN-4
Oldham—locale TX-5
Oldham—pop pl MS-4
Oldham—pop pl MO-7
Oldham—pop pl SD-7
Oldham—pop pl TX-5
Oldham Acres—pop pl KY-4
Oldham Ave Hist Dist—hist pl TX-5
Oldham Bottoms—bend CO-8
Oldham Branch—stream KY-4
Oldham Branch—stream TX-5
Oldham Brook NJ-2
Oldham Cem—cemetery AL-4
Oldham Cem—cemetery MS-4
Oldham Cem—cemetery MO-7
Oldham Cem—cemetery SD-7
Oldham Cem—cemetery TX-5
Oldham Ch—church TX-5
Oldham Chapel—church AL-4
Oldham Chapel Ch AL-4
Oldham (County)—pop pl KY-4
Oldham (County)—pop pl TX-5
Oldham Creek—stream AL-4
Oldham Creek—stream OR-9
Oldham Creek—stream TN-4
Old Hamer Cem MS-4
Oldham Hollow—valley MS-4
Old Hamilton MS-4
Old Hamilton—pop pl MS-4
Old Hamilton Cem—cemetery SC-3
Old Hamilton County Jail—hist pl FL-3
Old Hamilton Works—other MO-7
Oldham Lake Lower Dam—dam NC-3
Oldham Lake One—reservoir NC-3
Oldham Lake Two—reservoir NC-3
Oldham Lake Upper Dam—dam NC-3
Oldham Methodist Church—hist pl SD-7
Old Hammock Creek—stream NC-3
Old Hammock Hill—summit FL-3
Old Hammond Road Ditch—canal LA-4
Old Hammondtown Sch—school MA-1
Oldham Oil Field—oilfield TX-5
Oldham Park—flat AZ-5
Oldham Pines—pop pl MA-1
Oldham Plantation—hist pl KY-4
Oldham Pond—lake MA-1
Oldham Pond—reservoir NJ-2
Oldham Pond Dam—dam NJ-2
Old Hampton—post sta VA-3
Oldham Run—stream VA-3
Oldham Run—stream WV-2
Oldhams—locale VA-3
Oldham Sch—school AR-4
Oldham Sch—school MA-1
Oldham Sch—school MO-7
Oldhams Chapel AL-4
Oldham Sch (historical)—school MS-4
Oldhams Lake—lake NC-3
Oldham Village—pop pl MA-1
Old Hancock County Buildings—hist pl ME-1
Old Handleman Bldg—hist pl LA-4
Old Hannastown, Site of—hist pl PA-2
Old Hanover Cem—cemetery MO-7
Old Hanson Canal—canal LA-4
Old Harbor MA-1
Old Harbor RI-1
Old Harbor—bay ME-1
Old Harbor—bay MA-1
Old Harbor—harbor RI-1
Old Harbor—pop pl AK-9
Old Harbor—pop pl MA-1
Old Harbor—pop pl RI-1
Old Harbor, The RI-1
Old Harbor Creek—stream MA-1
Old Harbor Hist Dist—hist pl RI-1
Old Harbor Island—bar LA-4
Old Harbor Island Shoal LA-4
Old Harbor Keys LA-4
Old Harbor Landing—locale RI-1
Old Harbor Life Saving Museum—building MA-1
Old Harbor Light—locale AK-9
Old Harbor Plaza (Shop Ctr)—locale FL-3
Old Harbor Point—cape RI-1
Old Harbor Pond—bay ME-1
Old Harbor U.S. Life Saving Station—hist pl MA-1
Old Harder Cem—cemetery TN-4
Old Hardesty—hist pl OK-5
Old Hardin Cem—cemetery TX-5
Old Hardshell Ch—church AR-4
Old Hardy Cem—cemetery MS-4
Old Hardy County Courthouse—hist pl WV-2
Old Harmon Cave—cave TN-4
Old Harmony—pop pl AL-4
Old Harmony Branch—stream AL-4
Old Harmony Cem MS-4
Old Harmony Cem—cemetery (3) AL-4
Old Harmony Cem—cemetery WV-2
Old Harmony Ch—church (3) AL-4
Old Harmony Ch—church AR-4
Old Harmony Ch (historical)—church MS-4
Old Harmony Mission Site—locale MO-7
Old Harris Creek Cem—cemetery OH-6
Old Harrison County Courthouse—hist pl IA-7
Old Harry Bayou—gut LA-4
Old Harry Rock—rock MA-1
Old Harry Swamp VA-3
Old Harvard Yard—hist pl MA-1
Old Hat Burnout—area TX-5
Old Hatchbend Cem—cemetery FL-3
Old Hatch Creek—stream NJ-2
Old Hatchery Creek—stream OR-9
Old Hatchery Lake—lake WA-9
Old Hatchet Ranch—locale NM-5
Old Hat Creek Stage Station—locale WY-8
Old Hattiesburg HS—hist pl MS-4
Old Haulover—gut NC-3
Old Haulover—stream NC-3
Old Haulover Canal—hist pl FL-3
Old Hauser Spring TN-4
Old Hauser Spring Branch TN-4
Old Havron Cem—cemetery TN-4
Old Havron Chapel Cem TN-4
Old Hawaiian Canoe Sheds—locale HI-9
Old Hawaiian Trail—trail HI-9
Old Hawley Ranch—locale MT-8
Old Hayes Cem—cemetery TN-4
Old Haymaker Place—locale WY-8
Old Haynesville Cem—cemetery LA-4
Old Hay Ranch—locale NV-8
Old Hazelrun Cem—cemetery MO-7
Old Hazelwood Cem—cemetery KY-4
Old Head Reef—bar CT-1
Old Heard Cem—cemetery MS-4
Old Hebbronville Cem—cemetery TX-5
Old Hebron Cem—cemetery MS-4
Old Hebron Cem—cemetery NE-7
Old Hebron Ch—church KY-4
Oldhe Fork—stream WV-2
Old Heidelberg Apartments—hist pl PA-2
Old Heises Pond—reservoir SC-3
Old Helena Cem—cemetery WI-6
Old Hell Bar—bar AL-4
Old Hell Bight—channel GA-3
Old Heller Ranch—locale NV-8
Old Hell Lake—lake GA-3
Old Hen—bar NY-2
Old Henderson Cem—cemetery MI-6
Old Hendry Cem—cemetery GA-3
Old Henley Place—locale FL-3
Old Henry—bar ME-1
Old Henryville Cem—cemetery TN-4
Old Hephzibah Cem—cemetery TN-4
Old Hephzibah Ch—church SC-3
Old Hepsibah Cem MS-4
Old Herbert Cem—cemetery MS-4
Old Herbron Cem—cemetery IN-6
Old Hibben Tank—reservoir AZ-5
Old Hickory TN-4
Old Hickory—hist pl LA-4
Old Hickory—locale AR-4
Old Hickory—pop pl TN-4
Old Hickory Acad—school TN-4
Old Hickory Beach Park—park TN-4
Old Hickory Brook—stream RI-1
Old Hickory Cem—cemetery AR-4
Old Hickory Cem—cemetery IN-6
Old Hickory Church MS-4
Old Hickory Creek—stream IL-6
Old Hickory Dam—dam (3) TN-4
Old Hickory Dam—reservoir TN-4
Old Hickory Flat Cem—cemetery MS-4
Old Hickory Golf Club—locale TN-4
Old Hickory Golf Club—other WI-6
Old Hickory Hist Dist—hist pl TN-4
Old Hickory (historical)—locale MS-4
Old Hickory Lake—reservoir (2) TN-4
Old Hickory Mall Shop Ctr—locale TN-4
Old Hickory Methodist Church—hist pl TN-4
Old Hickory Mine—mine UT-8
Old Hickory Point Cem—cemetery MO-7
Old Hickory Post Office (historical)—building PA-2
Old Hickory Reservoir TN-4
Old Hickory Sch (historical)—school MS-4
Old Hickory (Township of)—fmr MCD AR-4
Old Hickory Well—well AZ-5
Old Hicks Chapel—church AL-4
Old Hidalgo Courthouse and Buildings—hist pl TX-5
Old Hidalgo Sch—hist pl TX-5
Old Higgins Farm Windmill—hist pl MA-1
Old Higgins Windmill—locale MA-1
Old High Hill Cem—cemetery TX-5
Old Highland Business District—hist pl CO-8
Old Highland Lakes Estate Observation Tower—locale MI-6
Old Highway Eighty-Six Park—park MO-7
Old Highway Eighty-Six Public Use Area—locale MO-7
Old Highway Rsvr—reservoir NV-8
Old Highway 25 Recreation Areas—park AR-4
Old Highway 90 Missionary Baptist Ch—church AL-4
Old Hilger Camp—locale MI-6
Old Hill—pop pl IN-6
Old Hill Bay—bay NC-3
Old Hill Cem—cemetery TN-4
Old Hill Cem—cemetery TX-5
Old Hill Place Bridge—hist pl MS-4
Old Hills Chapel Ch (historical)—church TN-4
Old Hillsdale Cem—cemetery WI-6
Old Hillside Cem—cemetery CA-9
Old Hill (subdivision)—pop pl MA-1
Old Hilltown—pop pl CA-9
Old Hilton Hotel—hist pl NM-5
Old Historic Cem—cemetery KY-4
Old HK Ranch—locale WY-8
Old Hoffer Hill Ch—church OH-6
Old Hogan Tank—reservoir NM-5
Old Hog Wallow Lake—reservoir AL-4
Old Hokie House, The—building MA-1
Old Hollow Creek TX-5
Old Hollow Estates (subdivision)—pop pl NC-3
Old Holt Cem—cemetery TN-4
Old Home Branch—stream KY-4
Old Home Cem—cemetery KS-7
Old Home Cem—cemetery LA-4
Old Home Ch—church IL-6
Old Home Ch—church TX-5
Old Home Creek CO-8
Old Home Draw—valley TX-5
Old Home Ranch—locale AZ-5
Old Homer Village Hist Dist—hist pl NY-2
Old Homestead—hist pl MS-4
Old Homestead—hist pl PA-2
Old Homestead—pop pl CO-8
Old Homestead Ranch, The—locale NE-7
Old Hometown—uninc pl TN-4
Old Homochitto River—gut MS-4
Old Hook Cem—cemetery NJ-2
Old Hoopes Sch—hist pl PA-2
Old Hoosier Theatre—hist pl IN-6
Old Hoover Place Site (22HO502)—hist pl MS-4
Old Hope Cem—cemetery TN-4
Old Hope Station Ch—church SC-3
Old Hopewell Cem—cemetery GA-3
Old Hopewell Cem—cemetery (2) IN-6
Old Hopewell Cem—cemetery MS-4
Old Hopewell Cem—cemetery NC-3
Old Hopewell Cem—cemetery TX-5
Old Hopewell Ch—church TN-4
Old Hopkins Mine—mine AZ-5
Old Hopland—pop pl CA-9
Old Horner Place—locale NM-5
Old Horry County Courthouse—hist pl SC-3
Old Horse Ledge—bar ME-1
Old Horse Pasture Well—well NM-5
Old Horseshoe Canyon—valley AZ-5
Old Horseshoe Canyon—valley NM-5
Old Horse Springs—locale NM-5
Old Hose House—hist pl MA-1
Old Hose House No. 4—hist pl IN-6
Old Hospital—hist pl WI-6
Old Hospital Point—cape MA-1
Old Hotchkiss Road Jeep Trail—trail OR-9
Old Hotel—hist pl VA-3
Old Houlka—pop pl MS-4
Old Houlka Normal Boarding Sch (historical)—school MS-4
Old Houlka Sch (historical)—school MS-4
Old Hound Ridge—ridge PA-2
Old House—pop pl SC-3
Old House, The—hist pl NY-2
Old House Bay (Carolina Bay)—swamp NC-3
Old House Beach—beach NC-3
Oldhouse Branch—stream KY-4
Old House Branch—stream KY-4
Oldhouse Branch—stream (3) KY-4
Old House Branch—stream (2) KY-4
Oldhouse Branch—stream (2) KY-4
Old House Branch—stream KY-4
Oldhouse Branch—stream (2) KY-4
Old House Branch—stream (2) KY-4
Oldhouse Branch—stream (2) KY-4
Old House Branch—stream (2) KY-4
Oldhouse Branch—stream (5) KY-4
Old House Branch—stream KY-4
Oldhouse Branch—stream KY-4
Old House Branch—stream (2) KY-4
Old House Branch—stream (3) NC-3
Oldhouse Branch—stream TN-4
Old House Branch—stream TN-4
Oldhouse Branch—stream VA-3
Old House Branch—stream VA-3
Oldhouse Branch—stream (2) VA-3
Old House Branch—stream WV-2
Oldhouse Branch—stream WV-2
Old House Branch—stream WV-2
Oldhouse Branch—stream WV-2
Old House Branch—stream WV-2
Oldhouse Branch—stream (5) WV-2
Old House Branch—stream WV-2
Oldhouse Branch—stream WV-2
Old House Canyon—valley NV-8
Old House Channel—channel NC-3
Oldhouse Cove—bay ME-1
Old House Cove—bay MD-2

Old House Cove—bay NC-3
Old House Cove—cape MD-2
Old House Cove—cove MA-1
Old House Creek—channel SC-3
Old House Creek—gut VA-3
Oldhouse Creek—stream CA-9
Old House Creek—stream CO-8
Oldhouse Creek—stream GA-3
Old House Creek—stream KY-4
Oldhouse Creek—stream KY-4
Old House Creek—stream MD-2
Old House Creek—stream (2) NC-3
Old House Creek—stream OR-9
Old House Creek—stream (3) SC-3
Oldhouse Creek—stream VA-3
Old House Ditch—canal WY-8
Old House Fork—stream KY-4
Old House Fork—stream VA-3
Old House Gap—gap NC-3
Oldhouse Hollow WV-2
Old House Hollow—valley AR-4
Old House Hollow—valley (3) KY-4
Old House Hollow—valley (2) MO-7
Old House Hollow—valley VA-3
Old House Hollow—valley WV-2
Old House Junction MA-1
Old House Knob—summit WV-2
Old House Landing—locale MD-2
Oldhouse Landing—locale VA-3
Old House Place—locale TX-5
Old House Plantation—hist pl SC-3
Old House Plantation and Commissary (Boundary Increase)—hist pl SC-3
Old House Point—cape ME-1
Old House Point—cape (2) MD-2
Old House Pond—lake MA-1
Old House Pond—lake NC-3
Old Houser Cem—cemetery NY-2
Old House Run—stream (3) WV-2
Old House Slough NC-3
Old House Slough—gut TX-5
Old House Trail—trail PA-2
Old House Windmill—locale (3) TX-5
Old Houston Cem—cemetery AL-4
Old Houston Ferry Crossing AL-4
Old Houston Natl Bank—hist pl TX-5
Old Houston Place—locale TX-5
Old HQ—hist pl AZ-5
Old HQ Lake—lake MI-6
Old HQ Tank—reservoir TX-5
Old HQ Windmill—locale (6) TX-5
Old HQ Windmills—locale TX-5
Old Huckleberry Trail—trail PA-2
Old Hudsonville MS-4
Old Hughes Cem—cemetery TX-5
Old Hugh Fontenberry Cemetery MS-4
Old Hulbert Place—locale CA-9
Old Hull Mill (historical)—locale TN-4
Old Humbolt Diggings—locale OR-9
Old Hump Channel—channel ME-1
Old Hump Ledge—bar ME-1
Old Hump Ridge—ridge VA-3
Old Hundred WV-2
**Old Hundred**—pop pl NC-3
Old Hundred Cem—cemetery NC-3
Old Hundred Mine—mine CO-8
Old Hundred Sch—school NC-3
Old Huntington Cem—cemetery OR-9
Old Huron Cem—cemetery KS-7
Old Hurricane Branch NJ-2
Old Hurricane Brook—stream NJ-2
Old Hurricane Hill—summit VT-1
Old Hyde County Courthouse—hist pl SD-7
Old Hyde Park Village (Shop Ctr)—locale FL-3
Old Hyndman Peak—summit ID-8
Old Ibex Pass—gap CA-9
Old Ice Pond—reservoir NY-2
Old Idaho Stage Road—trail NV-8
Old Idaho State Penitentiary—hist pl ID-8
Old Iditarod Trail (Winter Trail)—trail AK-9
Old Iliamna—locale AK-9
Old Immaculate Conception Cemetery, The—cemetery PA-2
Old Immanuel Cem—cemetery NE-7
Old Indiana County Courthouse—hist pl PA-2
Old Indiana County Jail and Sheriff's Office—hist pl PA-2
Old Indian Agency—hist pl WA-9
Old Indian Agency House—hist pl WI-6
Old Indian Bayou—gut AR-4
Old Indian Cave—cave WY-8
Old Indian Cem AL-4
Old Indian Cem—cemetery LA-4
Old Indian Cem—cemetery MT-8
Old Indian Cem—cemetery OK-5
Old Indian Cem—cemetery TN-4
Old Indian Cemetery MO-7
Old Indian Ch—church MA-1
Old Indian Ch (historical)—church SD-7
Old Indian Church SD-7
Old Indian Creek Cem—cemetery IN-6
Old Indian Draw—valley NM-5
Old Indian Field KY-4
Old Indian Fort—locale CT-1
Old Indian Fort (site)—locale AZ-5
Old Indian Lead Mine—mine MO-7
Old Indian Mtn—summit SC-3
Old Indian Point—cape WI-6
Old Indian Spring—spring UT-8
Old Indian Trail—trail PA-2
Old Indian Trail—trail WY-8
Old Indian Village—locale NM-5
Old Ingram, Lake—reservoir TX-5
Olding Tunnel—tunnel HI-9
Old Inland Waterway NC-3
Old Inlet NJ-2
Old Inlet NC-3
Old Inlet—bay FL-3
Old Inlet Beach—beach DE-2
Old Inlet Marsh DE-2
Old Inlet Point—cape DE-2
Old Inn, The—hist pl MD-2
Old Inspiration Point—summit CA-9
Old Intracoastal Waterway—channel LA-4
Old Intracoastal Waterway—channel TX-5
Old Ireland Cem—cemetery AL-4
Old Irish Cem—cemetery MI-6
Old Ironbell Ch—church VA-3
Old Iron Bridge—bridge AL-4
Old Iron Bridge—bridge TX-5
Old Iron Bridge—other IL-6
Old Iron County Courthouse—hist pl WI-6
Old Iron Furnace—locale (2) VA-3
Old Iron Furnace—other MO-7
Old Iron Furnace (historical)—locale AL-4
Old Iron Mtn—summit CA-9
Old Ironsides MA-1
Old Ironsides County Park—park CA-9
Old Ironsides Mine (historical)—mine SD-7
Old Iron Town UT-8
Old Irontown—hist pl UT-8
Old Irontown—locale UT-8
Old Iroquois County Courthouse—hist pl IL-6
Old Isaacs Place—locale NM-5
Old Ish Ditch—canal CO-8
Old Island—island SC-3
Old Island Cem—cemetery LA-4
Old Island Landing—locale AL-4
Old Isle of Wight Courthouse—hist pl VA-3
Oldis Ranch—locale ND-7
Old Ivy Baptist Ch—church TX-5
Old Ivy Ch TX-5
Old Ivy Ch—church GA-3
Old Jack Mine—mine MO-7
Old Jacks Creek Primitive Baptist Church TN-4
Old Jackson Protection Levee—levee LA-4
Old Jackson Ranch—locale NM-5
Old Jackson Road—trail NH-1
Old Jacksonville Free Public Library—hist pl FL-3
Old Jacob Boone Cem—cemetery MS-4
Old Jacoby Creek Sch—hist pl CA-9
Old Jail—hist pl AL-4
Old Jail—hist pl GA-3
Old Jail—hist pl IA-7
Old Jail—hist pl MA-1
Old Jail—hist pl TN-4
Old Jail Lake—lake LA-4
Old Jail Lake—lake MS-4
Old Jamestown Reservoir Dam—dam TN-4
Old Jamestown Rsvr—reservoir TN-4
Old Japan Cem—cemetery MO-7
Old Jarales Ditch—canal NM-5
Old Jardine Juniper—locale UT-8
Old Jefferson—locale TN-4
Old Jefferson Parish Courthouse—hist pl LA-4
Old Jeffersonville Hist Dist—hist pl IN-6
Old Jeff Mine—mine SD-7
Old Jennings Cem—cemetery MI-6
Old Jenny Lind AR-4
**Old Jenny Lind**—pop pl AR-4
Old Jericho Cem—cemetery TN-4
Old Jerusalem Cem—cemetery MS-4
Old Jerusalem Cem—cemetery TX-5
Old Jerusalem Ch—church AR-4
Old Jerusalem Ch—church FL-3
Old Jerusalem Ch—church (2) MS-4
Old Jewish Cem—cemetery CT-1
Old Jim Mine—mine KY-4
Old Jims Lake—flat OR-9
Old Jims Open—flat OR-9
Old Job—locale VT-1
Old Joe—hist pl AR-4
**Old Joe**—pop pl AR-4
**Old Joe**—pop pl SC-3
Old Joe Creek—stream AL-4
Old Joerger Ranch—locale CA-9
Old John Lake—lake AK-9
Old John Mtn—summit AK-9
Old Johnson Cabin—locale OR-9
Old Johnson Cem—cemetery MS-4
Old Johnson Mill—locale OR-9
Old Johnson Place—locale WY-8
Old Johnson Sch—school SD-7
Old Johnsonville Sch—school SC-3
Old Johnson Well—well TX-5
Old Johnston Cem—cemetery OH-6
Old John Tank—reservoir TX-5
Old Jonah Ch—church TN-4
Old Jonah Mine—mine AZ-5
**Old Jonesboro**—pop pl AL-4
Old Jonesboro Cem—cemetery TN-4
Old Jonesboro Elem Sch (historical)—school AL-4
Old Jones Ranch—locale NM-5
Old Joppa Site—hist pl MD-2
Old Judson Cem—cemetery AL-4
Old Judy Church—hist pl WV-2
Old Juel Ranch—locale WY-8
Old Julie Branch—stream MS-4
Old Junction—uninc pl PA-2
Old Junction City HS—hist pl KS-7
Old Junction School—locale TX-5
Old Junction Wash—stream AZ-5
Old Juniper UT-8
Old Kagley Ch—church TN-4
Old Kagleys Ch TN-4
Old Kaguyak Bay—bay AK-9
Old Kaibab Trail—trail AZ-5
Old Kaibito Boarding Sch—school AZ-5
Old Kaintuck Guest Ranch—locale MT-8
Old Kamp Place—locale WY-8
Old K and E Canal IN-6
**Old Kane**—pop pl IL-6
Old Kaskaskia—locale IL-6
Old Kaskaskia Village—hist pl IL-6
Old Kaw Mission—hist pl KS-7
Old Keanae Landing—locale HI-9
Old Kehres Pond—lake MO-7
Old Kelick Rock—rock MA-1
Old Kelly Homestead—locale MT-8
Old Kelly Mill—locale OR-9
Old Kelly Place—locale WY-8
Old Kelsey Point—cape CT-1
Old Kendleton Cem—cemetery TX-5
Old Kenna Cem—cemetery NM-5
Old Kennedy Cabin—locale OR-9
Old Kennett Meetinghouse—church PA-2
Old Kennett Meetinghouse—hist pl PA-2
Old Kentuck—hist pl NJ-2
Old Kentucky Home Sch—school KY-4
Old Kentucky Ordnance Works (Abandoned)—other KY-4
Old Kentucky Tavern—hist pl KY-4
Old Ketchum Cem—cemetery OK-5
Old Kilbourne Cem—cemetery OH-6
Old Kilgore Millpond—reservoir SC-3
Old King David Mine—mine UT-8
Old King Ditch—canal WY-8
Old Kings Grove Cem—cemetery SC-3
Old Kings Highway—trail NH-1
Old King's Highway Hist Dist—hist pl MA-1
Old Kings Lake MO-7
Old Kings Lake Creek—stream MO-7
Old Kingsport—uninc pl TN-4
Old Kingsport Cem—cemetery TN-4
Old Kingsport Presbyterian Church—hist pl TN-4
**Old Kingston**—pop pl AL-4
Old Kingston Cem—cemetery AL-4
Old Kingston Ch—church AL-4
Old Kinkler—locale TX-5
Old Kinniconick Bed—stream KY-4
Old Kinser Church of God TN-4
Old Kinsley Cem—cemetery KS-7
Old Kiokee Ch—church GA-3
Old Kisatchie Cem—cemetery LA-4
Old Kiwanis Park—park TN-4
Old Knob—summit VT-1
Old Knob—summit VA-3
Old Knobbs Springs Cem—cemetery TX-5
Old Knob Creek—stream KY-4
Old Knob Creek—stream TN-4
Old Knob Creek Cem—cemetery TN-4
Old Knobs Springs Cem TX-5
Old Knoll Homestead—locale MT-8
Old Knoxville City Hall—hist pl TN-4
Old Kos Ranch—locale WY-8
Old Krieger Cem—cemetery IL-6
Old Kuhl Ranch—locale MT-8
Old Kvichak—other AK-9
Old Kymulga Ferry (historical)—locale AL-4
Old La Cinta Windmill—locale NM-5
Old Laclede Gas and Light Company Bldg—hist pl MO-7
Old Lade Run—stream OH-6
Old Ladies Creek—stream AK-9
Old Ladore Sch—hist pl CO-8
Old Lady Beam Hill—summit NE-7
Old Lady Canyon—valley WA-9
Old Lady Lake—bay LA-4
Old Lafayette City Hall—hist pl LA-4
**Old Lafitte**—pop pl LA-4
Old La Grange Schoolhouse—hist pl CA-9
Old Laird Ranch—locale MT-8
Old Lake IN-6
Old Lake—lake FL-3
Old Lake—lake LA-4
Old Lake—lake NM-5
Old Lake—reservoir AL-4
Old Lake—reservoir (2) IN-6
Old Lake—reservoir MT-8
Old Lake—reservoir (2) TX-5
Old Lake Davenport FL-3
Old Lake Park Dam—dam MS-4
Old Lakeport Cem—cemetery AR-4
Old Laketown Canyon—valley UT-8
Old Lake Windmill—locale TX-5
Old Lamar Cem—cemetery MS-4
Old Lamberton Canal—canal ID-8
Oldland Cow Camp—locale CO-8
Old Landen Point—cape MD-2
Oldland Gulch—valley CO-8
Old Landing—locale (2) DE-2
Old Landing—locale FL-3
Old Landing—locale GA-3
Old Landing—locale KY-4
Old Landing—locale NC-3
Old Landing (historical)—locale MS-4
Old Landing (historical)—locale NC-3
Old Landing Point—cape VA-3
**Old Landing Woods**—pop pl DE-2
Old Landmark Ch—church GA-3
Old Land Mark House of Prayer—church IN-6
Old Land Mark House of Prayer Brighter Day Number Three IN-6
Old Land Office Bldg—hist pl TX-5
Old Land Place—locale FL-3
Old Lane Prairie Cem—cemetery TX-5
Old Langley Cem—cemetery SC-3
Old Lantern Well—well CO-8
Old Laodicea Cemetery MS-4
Old Laodicea Primitive Baptist Ch (historical)—church MS-4
Old La Paz—hist pl AZ-5
Old Lapile—locale AR-4
Old Larissa TX-5
**Old Larissa**—pop pl TX-5
Old Larsen Mine—mine UT-8
Old LaSal UT-8
Old La Sal—locale UT-8
Old Lasea Ch—church TN-4
Old Lassen Trail—trail CA-9
Old Las S Windmill—locale TX-5
Old Las Vegas Post Office—hist pl NM-5
Old Laundry Mill—locale MO-7
**Old Laurel**—pop pl TX-5
Old Laurel Ch TN-4
Old Laurel Creek Cem—cemetery TN-4
Old Laury Dam—dam PA-2
Old La Veta Cem—cemetery CO-8
Old Lawrence City Hall—hist pl KS-7
Old Lawrence City Library—hist pl KS-7
Old Lawrence County Jail—hist pl OH-6
**Old Lawron**—pop pl TN-4
Old Lawson Ferry (historical)—locale AL-4
**Old Lawton**—pop pl TN-4
Old Lawtonville Cem—cemetery SC-3
Old LDS Tithing/Paris Post Bldg—hist pl ID-8
Old Leak Ferry—locale NC-3
Old Lease Hollow—valley KY-4
**Old Leavenworth**—pop pl WA-9
Old Leavenworth Cem—cemetery IN-6
Old Leavenworth Cem—cemetery CT-1
**Old Lebanon**—pop pl WI-6
Old Lebanon Ch—church (2) AL-4
Old Lebanon Ch—church MS-4
Old Leeville Cem—cemetery MS-4
Old LeFebre Ranch—locale NM-5
Old Lehigh Cem—cemetery OK-5
Old Lehigh County Courthouse—hist pl PA-2
Old Lehrton Bridge—bridge MS-4
Old Lenox College—hist pl IA-7
Old Leonard Cem—cemetery MA-1
Old Letdown Point—summit TX-5
Old Leupp AZ-5
**Old Leupp**—pop pl AZ-5
Old Leupp Trading Post—locale AZ-5
Old Lewisburg Reservoir TN-4
Old Lewisville Cem—cemetery AR-4
Old Lexington—locale AR-4
Old Lexington Ch—church SC-3
Old Liberty—locale VA-3
Old Liberty Cem AL-4
Old Liberty Cem—cemetery (2) AL-4
Old Liberty Cem—cemetery (3) AR-4
Old Liberty Cem—cemetery IN-6
Old Liberty Cem—cemetery KY-4
Old Liberty Cem—cemetery (2) MO-7
Old Liberty Cemetery MS-4
Old Liberty Ch GA-3
Old Liberty Ch—church (2) AR-4
Old Liberty Ch—church GA-3
Old Liberty Ch—church KY-4
Old Liberty Ch—church MD-2
Old Liberty Ch—church MS-4
Old Liberty Ch—church MO-7
Old Liberty Ch—church NC-3
Old Liberty Ch—church SC-3
Old Liberty Ch (historical)—church TN-4
Old Liberty Church AL-4
Old Liberty Hill Cem—cemetery (2) AL-4
Old Liberty Hill Cem—cemetery GA-3
Old Liberty Hill Ch—church AL-4
Old Library Bldg—hist pl AZ-5
Old Library Bldg—hist pl KY-4
Old Library Bldg—hist pl TN-4
Old Lick Creek—stream KY-4
Oldlick Creek—stream WV-2
Old Lick Gap—gap KY-4
Oldlick Run—stream WV-2
Old Lighthouse—locale CA-9
Old Lighthouse—locale MI-6
Old Lighthouse—locale OH-6
Old Lightsey Cem—cemetery MS-4
Old Likely Mill—locale CA-9
Old Likely Mill (Site)—locale CA-9
Old Lillian (historical)—locale MS-4
Old Limber Pine—locale UT-8
Old Limestone Church Spring—spring AL-4
Old Limestone Tank—reservoir AZ-5
Old Lincoln Sch—school IL-6
Old Line—locale PA-2
Old Line Cemetery AL-4
Old Line Ch—church AL-4
Old Line Creek AL-4
Old Line Ditch—canal MD-2
Old Line Post Office (historical)—building PA-2
Old Linn County Jail—hist pl KS-7
**Old Linn Creek**—pop pl MO-7
Old Linton Cem—cemetery IN-6
Old Lion Cem—cemetery AL-4
Old Little Tallahatchie River—stream MS-4
Old Live Oak Cem—cemetery LA-4
Old Live Oak City Hall—hist pl FL-3
Old Livery Stable—hist pl CO-8
Old Lock and Dam B (historical)—dam TN-4
Old Lock and Dam Number Eight (historical)—dam TN-4
Old Lock and Dam Number Five (historical)—dam TN-4
Old Lock and Dam Number Four (historical)—dam TN-4
Old Lock and Dam Number Seven (historical)—dam TN-4
Old Lock and Dam Number Six (historical)—dam TN-4
Old Lock and Dam Number Three (historical)—dam TN-4
Old Lock and Dam (submerged)—dam MO-7
Old Locke Road Path—trail NH-1
Old Lock Four AL-4
Old Lock Number Eight AL-4
Old Lock Number Eleven AL-4
Old Lock Number Fifteen AL-4
Old Lock Number Five (historical)—locale AL-4
Old Lock Number Fourteen AL-4
Old Lock Number Nine AL-4
Old Lock Number Seven AL-4
Old Lock Number Sixteen AL-4
Old Lock Number Ten (historical)—locale AL-4
Old Lock Number Thirteen AL-4
Old Lock Number Three AL-4
Old Lock Number Two AL-4
Old Lock Number 1—dam AL-4
Old Lock One Cut-Off—channel AL-4
Old Lock Pump House, Chesapeake and Delaware Canal—hist pl MD-2
Old Lock Three AL-4
Old Lock Three Access Area—park TN-4
Old Lock 15 Public Use Area—park AL-4
Old Lock 16 Public Use Area—park AL-4
Old Loco Well—well NM-5
Old Lodge Creek SD-7
Old Logan County Courthouse—hist pl KS-7
Old Log Cabin—hist pl NE-7
Old Log Church—hist pl KY-4
Old Loggers Path—trail PA-2
Old Logging Camp Rsvr—reservoir CO-8
Old Log Landing—locale GA-3
Old Log Post Office—hist pl OH-6
Old Log Spring—spring TX-5
Old Logway Canyon—valley UT-8
Old Loka Cem—cemetery UT-8
Old London—locale TX-5
Old London Bridge—bridge VA-3
Old Lone Star Brewery—hist pl TX-5
Old Lone Star Brewery (Boundary Increase)—hist pl TX-5
Old Long A Siding—locale ME-1
Old Longbotham Place—locale NM-5
Old Lonon Mtn—summit AR-4
Old Loogootee Sch—school IL-6
Old Lookout Cem—cemetery GA-3
Old Loramie Valley Cem—cemetery OH-6
Old Lost Creek—stream AK-9
Old Lost Well—well TX-5
Old Lot Mine—mine CO-8
Old Louisiana Governor's Mansion—hist pl LA-4
Old Louisiana State Capitol—hist pl LA-4
Old Louisville Residential District—hist pl KY-4
Old Louisville Residential District (Boundary Increase)—hist pl KY-4
Old Lout Mine—mine CO-8
Old Love Cem—cemetery MS-4
Old Lower Thorofare—channel NJ-2
Old L Seven Ranch—locale TX-5
Old LSU Site—hist pl LA-4
Old Ludlow (historical)—locale MS-4
Old Lund Ditch—canal MT-8
Old Lusk Cem—cemetery AL-4
Old Lusk Tabernacle—church AL-4
Old Lutheran Cem—cemetery OH-6
Old Lutheran Cem—cemetery TN-4
Old Lutheran Cemetery—park NC-3
Old Lutheran Parsonage—hist pl NY-2
**Old Lycoming (Township of)**—pop pl PA-2
Old Lyford HS—hist pl TX-5
**Old Lyme**—pop pl CT-1
Old Lyme Country Club—other CT-1
Old Lyme Hist Dist—hist pl CT-1
**Old Lyme Shores**—pop pl CT-1
**Old Lyme (Town of)**—pop pl CT-1
Old Lynch Cem—cemetery AL-4
Old Macedonia Cem MS-4
Old Macedonia Cem—cemetery GA-3
Old Macedonia Cem—cemetery KY-4
Old Macedonia Cem—cemetery MS-4
Old Macedonia Cem—cemetery NC-3
Old Macedonia Ch—church AL-4
Old Macedonia Ch—church LA-4
Old Macedonia Ch—church SC-3
Old Macedonia Ch (historical)—church MS-4
Old Macedonia Sch (historical)—school TN-4
Old Mac Intyre Furnace—locale NY-2
Old Mackeys Creek Cem—cemetery MS-4
Old Mackies Creek Ch (historical)—church MS-4
Old Mackinac Point—cape MI-6
Old Mac Mtn—summit TN-4
Old Macon Library—hist pl GA-3
Old Macoupin Creek—gut IL-6
Old Maddox Sch—school NM-5
Old Madera Mine—mine AZ-5
Old Madison TN-4
**Old Madison**—pop pl SC-3
Old Madison Ch—church MS-4
Old Madison County Courthouse—hist pl NY-2
Old Madison Powerhouse—other MT-8
Old Madisonville (historical)—locale MS-4
Old Maeystown Creek—stream IL-6
Old Magalloway Trail—trail ME-1
Old Magee Cem—cemetery LA-4
Old Magnolia Church MS-4
Old Mahoning County Courthouse—hist pl OH-6
Old Maid Canyon—valley NM-5
Old Maid Canyon—valley WA-9
Old Maid Cemetery MS-4
Old Maid Coulee—valley WA-9
Old Maid Creek OR-9
Old Maid Creek—stream ID-8
Old Maid Flat—flat OR-9
Old Maid Fork KS-7
Old Maid Gulch—valley WY-8
Old Maid Mine—mine CO-8
Old Maid Mtn—summit WA-9
Old Maid Pool—lake KS-7
Old Maid Rock—pillar ME-1
Old Maids Basin—basin OR-9
Old Maids Bloomers UT-8
Old Maids Bluff—cliff WI-6
Old Maids Brook—stream NH-1
Old Maids Canyon—valley OR-9
Old Maids Clearing, The—flat ID-8
Old Maids Coulee—valley MT-8
Old Maids Creek—stream MO-7
Old Maids Creek—stream OR-9
Old Maids Draw—valley WY-8
Old Maids Fork—stream KS-7
Old Maid's Orchard Mound—hist pl OH-6
Old Maid Spring—spring TX-5
Old Maid Spring—spring WY-8
Old Maids Spring—spring OR-9
Old Mail Station—locale AZ-5
Old Mail Trail—trail AZ-5
Old Mail Trail—trail PA-2
Old Main—hist pl IL-6
Old Main—hist pl IA-7
Old Main—hist pl PA-2
Old Main—hist pl SD-7
Old Main—hist pl VA-3
Old Main—hist pl WA-9
Old Main—hist pl WY-8
Old Main—school PA-2
Old Main, Almira College—hist pl IL-6
Old Main, Augustana Acad—hist pl SD-7
Old Main, Augustana College—hist pl IL-6
Old Main, Bethany College—hist pl WV-2
Old Main, California State College—hist pl PA-2
Old Main, Dr. Martin Luther College—hist pl MN-6
Old Main, Goethean Hall, and Diagnothian Hall—hist pl PA-2
Old Main, Knox College—hist pl IL-6
Old Main, Macalester College—hist pl MN-6
Old Main, Mankato State Teachers College—hist pl MN-6
Old Main, Marshall Univ—hist pl WV-2
Old Main, Nebraska Wesleyan Univ—hist pl NE-7
Old Main, Pembroke State Univ—hist pl NC-3
Old Main, St. Olaf College—hist pl MN-6
Old Main, Suomi College—hist pl MI-6
Old Main, Univ of Arizona—hist pl AZ-5
Old Main, Univ of Arkansas—hist pl AR-4
Old Main, Utah State Univ—hist pl UT-8
Old Main, Western Washington State College—hist pl WA-9
Old Main and Chemistry Bldg—hist pl PA-2
Old Main and Church Street Hist Dist—hist pl AL-4
Old Main and Science Buildings—hist pl UT-8
Old Main Bldg—hist pl IL-6
Old Main-Gustavus Adolphus College—hist pl MN-6
Old Main Hist Dist—hist pl IA-7
Old Main Street Cem—cemetery CT-1
Old Main Street Cem—cemetery NH-1
Old Main Street Hist Dist—hist pl WI-6
Old Malcum—locale MS-4
Old Mamalahoa Trail—trail HI-9
Old Mammoth—uninc pl CA-9
Old Mammoth Mine AZ-5
Old Mammoth Mine—mine CA-9
Old Mammoth Mine—summit AZ-5
Old Man—bar ME-1
Old Man—island ME-1
Old Man—rock MA-1
Old Manassa Cem—cemetery CO-8
Old Man Camp—locale OR-9
Old Man Campground—locale CA-9
Old Man Canyon—valley (2) CA-9
Old Man Canyon—valley ID-8
Old Man Canyon—valley NV-8
Old Man Creek IA-7
Oldman Creek NJ-2
Oldman Creek—gut NJ-2
Old Man Creek—gut SC-3
Old Man Creek—stream (4) AK-9
Old Man Creek—stream (3) ID-8
Old Man Creek—stream MD-2
Old Man Creek—stream (2) OR-9
Oldman Creek—stream WA-9
Oldman Creek Meadow—swamp NJ-2
Old Man Dancing Butte—summit ND-7
Old Manderfield Ditch—canal UT-8
Old Man Manhattan Gulch—valley NV-8
Old Man Hext Windmill—locale NM-5
Old Man Island—island NY-2
Old Man Lake—lake (2) AK-9
Old Man Lake—lake ID-8
Oldman Lake—lake MI-6
Oldman Lake—lake MT-8
Old Man Lead—stream SC-3
Old Man Ledge—bar ME-1
Old Manlius Sch—school IL-6
Old Man McMullen Pond—lake CT-1
Old Man Meadows—flat ID-8
Oldman Mill (historical)—locale TN-4
Old Man Mountain CO-8
Old Man Mountain NH-1
Old Man Mountain—ridge CA-9
Oldman Mtn—summit AZ-5
Old Man Mtn—summit (2) CA-9
Old Man Mtn—summit CO-8
Oldman Mtn—summit CO-8
Old Man of the Hills—summit MT-8
Old Man of the Mountain NH-1
Old Man of the Mountain UT-8
Old Man of the Mtn—summit NV-8
**Old Manor**—pop pl NJ-2
Old Manor Baptist Ch—church KS-7
Oldman Point NJ-2
Old Man Point—cliff ID-8
Oldman Ranch—locale WY-8
Old Man Ridge—ridge CA-9
Old Man Ridge—ridge ID-8
Old Man Riffle—rapids OR-9
Old Man Rock—pillar CA-9
Old Man Rock—pillar OR-9
Old Man Rocks—island AK-9
Old Man Run—stream WV-2
Oldmans—locale NJ-2
Oldmans Bay—bay AK-9
Old Mans Bay—bay NY-2
Old Mans Canyon—valley NV-8
Old Mans Cove—cave OH-6
Old Manscill Cem—cemetery AL-4
Old Mans Creek—stream CO-8
Old Mans Creek—stream IA-7
Oldmans Creek—stream NJ-2
Old Mans Creek Bridge IA-7
Old Manse—hist pl MA-1
Old Manse (North Bridge)—building MA-1
Old Mansford Bridge (historical)—bridge TN-4
Old Mans Gulch—valley CO-8
Old Mans Harbor NY-2
Old Man Shoal—bar MA-1
Old Mansion—hist pl VA-3
Old Mans Lagoon—bay AK-9
Old Man's Mountain NH-1
Old Mans Nose—cliff IN-6
Oldmans Point—cape NJ-2
Old Man Spring UT-8
Old Man Spring—spring NV-8
Old Man Spring—spring UT-8
Old Man Spring—spring WY-8
Old Man Springs Creek—stream CA-9
Old Mans Run—stream KY-4
Old Mans Slough—gut AK-9
**Oldmans (Township of)**—pop pl NJ-2
Oldman Tanque—spring AZ-5
Old Man Windmill—locale NM-5
Old Maple Grove Ch (historical)—church TN-4
Old Maplesville Cem—cemetery AL-4
Old Maplesville (historical)—locale AL-4
Old Marble AR-4
**Old Marco Junction**—pop pl FL-3
Old Marietta Cem—cemetery AL-4
Old Marina Canal—canal DE-2
Old Marine Hosp—hist pl SC-3
Old Marion Cem—cemetery KY-4
Old Marion Cem—cemetery MS-4
Old Marion Cem—cemetery OH-6
Old Marion County Courthouse—hist pl GA-3
Old Marissa IL-6
**Old Marissa**—pop pl IL-6
Old Market—hist pl GA-3
Old Market Bldg—hist pl SC-3
Old Market Bridge (historical)—bridge MS-4
Old Market Hist Dist—hist pl NE-7
Old Market House—building MA-1
Old Market House—hist pl IL-6
Old Market House Museum—hist pl TX-5
Old Mark Twain Sch—school MO-7
Old Marlborough Cem—cemetery CT-1
Old Marley Landing—locale MS-4
Old Marr Ranch—locale CA-9
Oldmars FL-3
Old Mars Cem—cemetery AL-4
Old Marshall Academy Spring—spring TN-4
Old Marsh Cem—cemetery VT-1
Old Mars Hill Cem—cemetery AL-4
Old Mars Hill Cem—cemetery PA-2
Old Mars Hill Cem—cemetery TN-4
Old Marsh Pond—lake CT-1
Old Marsh Pond—lake VT-1
Old Martin Cook Cem TN-4
Old Martin Mill Place—locale AR-4
Old Martin Pond SC-3
Old Martinsburg Cem—cemetery NY-2
Old Martins Creek Cem—cemetery NC-3
Old Martins Creek Ch—church NC-3
Old Mary Magdalene Ch—church LA-4
Old Marysville Road—trail WY-8
Old Mascoutah Cem—cemetery IL-6
Old Mason Cem—cemetery IL-6

**Old Port**—pop pl ... PA-2
Old Port Columbus Airport Control Tower—hist pl ... OH-6
Old Porter Ranch—locale ... NV-8
Old Portland Mine—mine ... ID-8
Old Port Sch (abandoned)—school ... PA-2
**Old Post Estates (subdivision)**—pop pl ... UT-8
Old Post House—hist pl ... TN-4
Old Post Oak Cem—cemetery ... OK-5
Old Post Office—hist pl ... AR-4
Old Post Office—hist pl ... CA-9
Old Post Office—hist pl ... IA-7
Old Post Office—hist pl ... LA-4
Old Post Office—hist pl (2) ... ME-1
Old Post Office—hist pl ... NH-1
Old Post Office—hist pl ... NM-5
Old Post Office—hist pl (2) ... NY-2
Old Post Office—hist pl ... TN-4
Old Post Office—post sta ... MO-7
Old Post Office and Clock Tower—hist pl ... DC-2
Old Post Office and Customshouse—hist pl ... FL-3
Old Post Office And Federal Bldg—hist pl ... OH-6
Old Post Office Bldg—hist pl (2) ... MA-1
Old Post Office Bldg—hist pl ... TN-4
Old Post Office Bldg and Customhouse—hist pl ... AR-4
Old Post Office Block—hist pl ... NH-1
Old Post Office Tower—park ... DC-2
Old Post Office Tower (Shop Ctr)—locale ... DC-2
Old Post Ofice—hist pl ... DE-2
Old Post Sanitarium—hist pl ... TX-5
Old Potawatomi Ind Res (historical)—reserve ... KS-7
Old Potters Place—locale ... WY-8
Old Pottinger Cem—cemetery ... IN-6
Old Pottstown Hist Dist—hist pl ... PA-2
*Old Powellton* ... VA-3
Old Powhatan Ch—church ... VA-3
Old Prairie Cem—cemetery ... MO-7
Old Prairie Creek—stream ... AR-4
Old Prairie duPont Creek—stream ... IL-6
Old Prairie Swamp—swamp ... IN-6
Old Pratts—locale ... VA-3
Old Prentice Distillery—hist pl ... KY-4
Old Presbyterian Cem—cemetery ... KY-4
Old Presbyterian Cem—cemetery ... MS-4
Old Presbyterian Cem—cemetery ... MO-7
Old Presbyterian Cem—cemetery ... NJ-2
Old Presbyterian Cem—cemetery ... OH-6
Old Presbyterian Church—hist pl ... AZ-5
Old Presbyterian Church—hist pl ... SC-3
Old Presbyterian Theological Seminary—hist pl ... KY-4
Old Presque Isle Lighthouse—hist pl ... MI-6
Old Preston Cem—cemetery ... KY-4
Old Prewitte Cem—cemetery ... AL-4
Old Price Mine—mine ... NM-5
Old Price Ranch—locale ... NM-5
Old Priest Grade—slope ... CA-9
*Old Prince Cemetery* ... TN-4
Old Prince Edward County Clerk's Office—hist pl ... VA-3
Old Prince Place Spring—spring ... AL-4
Old Princeton—locale ... IL-6
Old Prison Cem—cemetery ... TX-5
Old Probst Church—hist pl ... WV-2
Old Prophet Cem—cemetery ... IN-6
Old Proprietor—bar ... ME-1
Old Prospect Cem—cemetery ... AL-4
Old Prospect Cem—cemetery ... IN-6
Old Prospect Cem—cemetery ... TN-4
Old Prospect Cem—cemetery ... TX-5
Old Prospect Ch—church ... TX-5
*Old Prospect Number 2 Church* ... MS-4
Old Protestant Cem—cemetery ... NY-2
*Old Providence Baptist Church* ... AL-4
Old Providence Cem—cemetery ... AL-4
Old Providence Cem—cemetery ... GA-3
Old Providence Cem—cemetery ... MS-4
Old Providence Cem—cemetery ... MO-7
Old Providence Cem—cemetery ... TX-5
Old Providence Ch—church ... AL-4
Old Providence Ch—church ... FL-3
Old Providence Ch—church ... SC-3
Old Providence Ch—church ... TX-5
Old Providence Ch—church ... VA-3
Old Providence Presybterian Church—hist pl ... VA-3
Old Providence Stone Church—hist pl ... VA-3
**Old Providence (subdivision)**—pop pl ... NC-3
Old Pruit Ranch—locale ... NM-5
Old Public Library—hist pl ... MA-1
Old Public Safety Bldg—hist pl ... WA-9
Old Pumping Station Dam—dam ... MA-1
Old Purdy New Cem—cemetery ... TN-4
Old Purity Cem—cemetery ... SC-3
Old Quaker Burial Ground—cemetery ... NY-2
Old Quaker Cem—cemetery ... MA-1
Old Quaker Cem—cemetery ... NY-2
Old Quaker Cem—cemetery (3) ... OH-6
Old Quaker Cem—cemetery ... SC-3
Old Quaker Cem—cemetery ... VT-1
Old Quaker Cem—cemetery ... WV-2
Old Quaker Cem (Historical)—cemetery ... PA-2
Old Quaker Ch—church ... PA-2
Old Quaker Meetinghouse—church ... MA-1
Old Quaker Meetinghouse—hist pl ... NY-2
**Old Quaker Meetinghouse**—pop pl ... MA-1
Old Quaker Mine—mine ... NV-8
Old Quaker Rsvr—reservoir ... WY-8
Old Quarantine Pier Light—locale ... FL-3
Old Queen City Cem—cemetery ... IA-7
Old Queen's—hist pl ... NJ-2
Old Quigley Canyon—valley ... UT-8
*Old Quijotoa Well* ... AZ-5
Old Quijotoa Well—well ... AZ-5
Old Quincy Reservoir Dam—dam ... MA-1
Old Quincy Rsvr—reservoir ... MA-1
Old Quitman Cem—cemetery ... MO-7
Old Raccoon Furnace—locale ... KY-4
*Old Race Bridge* ... MD-2
Old Rag Mtn—summit ... VA-3
Old Rag Shelter—locale ... VA-3
Old Rag View Overlook—locale ... VA-3
Old Raleigh Cem—cemetery ... TX-5
Old Ramage Pond—lake ... UT-8
Old Ramah Cem—cemetery ... AL-4
Old Rambler Hill—summit ... UT-8
Old Ram Lake—lake ... WY-8
Old Rampart—locale ... AK-9
Old Ramp Trail—trail ... PA-2
Old Ramsay Camp—locale ... NH-1
Old Ranch—locale ... NM-5
Old Ranch—locale (2) ... TX-5
Old Ranch, The—locale ... TX-5
Old Ranch Canyon—valley ... NM-5
Old Ranch Canyon—valley ... TX-5
Old Ranch Cem—cemetery ... TX-5
Old Ranch Draw—valley ... TX-5
Old Ranch Knoll—summit ... NM-5
Old Ranch Spring—spring ... AZ-5
Old Ranch Spring—spring ... TX-5
Old Ranch Well—well ... AZ-5
Old Ranch Well—well ... NM-5
Old Ranch Well—well ... TX-5
Old Ranch Windmill—locale ... NM-5
Old Ranch Windmill—locale (4) ... TX-5
Old Randolph Cem—cemetery ... TN-4
Old Randolph County Courthouse—hist pl ... AR-4
**Old Rand Rock (reduced usage)**—pop pl ... TX-5
Old Rang Mtn—summit ... NY-2
Old Rankin Cem—cemetery ... MS-4
Old Raotireno Cem—cemetery ... TX-5
Old Raspberry Cem—cemetery ... AL-4
Old Rasson Spring—spring ... AL-4
Old Rattlesnake Tank—reservoir ... TX-5
Old Raystown Dam—dam ... PA-2
Old Reagan County Courthouse—hist pl ... TX-5
Old Rectory—hist pl ... VA-3
Old Red Bluff—summit ... TX-5
Old Redden Cem—cemetery ... TN-4
*Old Redden Chapel Cem* ... TN-4
Old Redford—post sta ... MI-6
Old Redford Cem—cemetery ... MO-7
Old Red Hill Cem—cemetery (2) ... TN-4
Old Red Lake Trail State Wildlife Mngmt—park ... MN-6
Old Red Mill—hist pl ... VT-1
Old Red Mill and Mill House—hist pl ... VT-1
Old Red Mill and Mill House (Boundary Increase)—hist pl ... VT-1
Old Red Mine—mine ... OR-9
Old Redoak Cem—cemetery ... OH-6
Old Red River—stream ... LA-4
Old Red River Cem—cemetery ... LA-4
Old Red Rock Cem—cemetery ... TX-5
Old Red Rock Place—locale ... CA-9
Old Red Sch—school ... MI-6
Old Red Sch—school ... VT-1
Old Red Spring—spring ... NY-2
Old Red Star—locale ... MS-4
Old Red Top Ch—church ... MO-7
Old Redtop Windmill—locale ... TX-5
Old Reed Place—locale ... TX-5
Old Reedy Creek Cem—cemetery ... GA-3
Old Reformed Cem—cemetery ... OH-6
Old Refuge Cem—cemetery ... MS-4
Old Regular Ch—church ... VA-3
Old Rehobeth Cem—cemetery ... TX-5
Old Reliable Ditch—canal ... WY-8
Old Republican Ch—church ... TN-4
Old Requa—hist pl ... CA-9
*Old Reservoir* ... PA-2
Old Retreat—locale ... SC-3
Old Retreat Ch—church ... SC-3
Old Retrop—locale ... OK-5
Old Revolutionary War Cem—cemetery ... VT-1
Old Reyno Ch—church ... AR-4
Old Reynolds Cem—cemetery ... AL-4
Old Rhodes Bank—bar ... FL-3
Old Rhodes Channel—channel ... FL-3
Old Rhodes Key—island ... FL-3
Old Rhodes Point—cape ... FL-3
Old Richmond Ch—church (2) ... NC-3
Old Richmond County Courthouse—hist pl ... GA-3
Old Richmond Creek—stream ... NC-3
*Old Richmond Elementary School* ... NC-3
Old Richmond Hist Dist—hist pl ... IN-6
Old Richmond Mine—mine ... MI-6
Old Richmond Sch—school ... NC-3
Old Richmond (Township of)—fmr MCD ... NC-3
Old Rim Ditch—canal ... CA-9
Old Rimrock Sch—school ... MT-8
Old Rinezi (historical)—locale ... MS-4
**Old Ripley**—pop pl ... IL-6
Old Ripley Cem—cemetery ... WV-2
Old Ripley Oil Field—other ... IL-6
**Old Ripley (Township of)**—pop pl ... IL-6
Old Ripsey Mine—mine ... AZ-5
Old Ritch Cem—cemetery ... GA-3
Old Rito Well—well ... NM-5
*Old River* ... LA-4
*Old River* ... MS-4
Old River—bay ... FL-3
Old River—bend ... AR-4
Old River—channel ... FL-3
Old River—channel ... IL-6
Old River—channel (2) ... TX-5
Old River—gut ... AL-4
Old River—gut (2) ... AR-4
Old River—gut ... GA-3
Old River—gut ... IL-6
Old River—gut (2) ... MS-4
Old River—gut ... TX-5
Old River—lake ... AR-4
Old River—lake ... GA-3
Old River—lake (2) ... LA-4
Old River—lake ... MO-7
Old River—lake (2) ... SC-3
Old River—lake ... TX-5
**Old River**—pop pl ... CA-9
Old River—stream (5) ... AR-4
Old River—stream (2) ... CA-9
Old River—stream ... FL-3
Old River—stream ... GA-3
Old River—stream ... IL-6
Old River—stream ... IN-6
Old River—stream (10) ... LA-4
Old River—stream (2) ... MS-4
Old River—stream ... MO-7
Old River—stream ... NH-1
Old River—stream ... SC-3
Old River—stream ... TN-4
Old River—stream (6) ... TX-5
Old River—stream ... WA-9
Old River—swamp ... AR-4
Old River Bay—bay ... LA-4
Old River Bayou—stream ... TX-5
Old River Bed—stream (2) ... UT-8
Old River Bridge—hist pl ... AR-4
Old River Camp—locale ... IL-6
Old River (CCD)—cens area ... TX-5
Old River Ch—church ... LA-4
*Old River Channel* ... TX-5
Old River Channel—channel (2) ... TX-5
Old River Channel—channel ... UT-8
Old River Channel—gut ... CA-9
Old River Channel Jordan River—gut ... UT-8
Old River Chute—channel ... MS-4
Old River Chute—gut ... MS-4
Old River Chute—lake ... LA-4
**Old River Community**—pop pl ... TX-5
Old River Control Structure—other ... LA-4
Old River Cove—bay ... TX-5
Old River Cutoff—channel ... TX-5
Old River Cutoff—lake ... MS-4
Old River Drain—stream ... TX-5
Old River Hollow—valley ... MO-7
Old River-Hoosier Creek Dam—dam ... LA-4
Old River Island—flat ... AR-4
Old River Island—island ... AR-4
Old River Island—island ... IL-6
Old River Island—island ... LA-4
Old River Island—island ... TX-5
Old River Island Lake—lake ... AR-4
*Old River Lake* ... AR-4
*Old River Lake* ... TX-5
Old River Lake—lake (11) ... AR-4
Old River Lake—lake ... IL-6
Old River Lake—lake (2) ... LA-4
Old River Lake—lake (6) ... MS-4
Old River Lake—lake (2) ... SC-3
Old River Lake—lake ... TN-4
Old River Lake—lake (5) ... TX-5
Old River Lakes—lake (3) ... TX-5
Old River Lock—dam ... LA-4
Old River Pass—channel ... TX-5
Old River Pond—lake ... IL-6
Oldriver Red River—stream ... LA-4
*Old River Run* ... MI-6
Old River Run—stream ... MS-4
Old River Run—stream ... TN-4
Old River Sch—school ... CA-9
Old Riverside Hutterite Colony—hist pl ... SD-7
Old River Slough—gut ... AR-4
Old River Slough—gut ... LA-4
**Old River Terrace**—pop pl ... TX-5
Old River (Township of)—fmr MCD ... AR-4
Old Riverview Hist Dist—hist pl ... CA-9
**Old River-Winfree**—pop pl ... TX-5
Old Roach—locale ... CO-8
*Old Road, The* ... AL-4
Old Road Bay—bay ... MD-2
Old Road Branch—stream ... TN-4
Old Road Camp Spring—spring ... OR-9
Old Road Ch—church ... PA-2
Old Road Fork—stream ... KY-4
Old Road Gap—gap ... NC-3
Old Road Hollow—valley (2) ... VA-3
Old Roadhouse Lake—lake ... AK-9
Old Road Ridge—ridge ... NC-3
Old Road Ridge—ridge ... TN-4
Old Road Run—stream (2) ... WV-2
Oldroad Run—stream ... WV-2
Old Road Tank—reservoir ... AZ-5
Old Road Tank—reservoir ... NM-5
Old Roanoke County Courthouse—hist pl ... VA-3
Old Roberts Cem—cemetery ... AL-4
Old Robertson Ranch—locale ... AZ-5
Old Robins Branch—stream ... NJ-2
Old Robinson Cem—cemetery ... AL-4
Old Robinson Cem—cemetery ... NC-3
Old Robinson Road—hist pl ... MS-4
Old Roby Cem—cemetery ... MS-4
Old Rochester Regional HS—school ... MA-1
Old Rochester Regional JHS—school ... MA-1
**Old Rock**—pop pl ... KS-7
**Old Rock**—pop pl ... MO-7
Old Rock Ch—church ... TX-5
Old Rockford Cem—cemetery ... AL-4
Old Rock Hill Cem—cemetery (2) ... TX-5
Old Rock Hill Tunnel (historical)—tunnel ... PA-2
Old Rock House—building ... SC-3
Old Rock House—hist pl ... GA-3
Old Rock House—hist pl ... MO-7
Old Rock House—locale ... AZ-5
Old Rock Landing Cem—cemetery ... CT-1
Old Rockport Bridge—hist pl ... AR-4
Old Rockport Hutterite Colony—hist pl ... SD-7
Old Rock Ranch—locale ... NM-5
Old Rock Run Cem—cemetery ... OH-6
Old Rock Saloon—hist pl ... TX-5
Old Rock Sch—hist pl (2) ... WI-6
Old Rock Sch—school ... IL-6
Old Rock Sch—school ... TX-5
Old Rock Spring Ch—church ... LA-4
Old Rock Spring Ch—church ... NC-3
Old Rock Springs—spring ... TX-5
Old Rock Springs Cem—cemetery (2) ... AL-4
Old Rock Tank—reservoir ... TX-5
Old Rockville HS and East Sch—hist pl ... CT-1
*Old Rocky* ... WY-8
Old Rocky Baptist Ch (historical)—church ... TN-4
Old Rocky Branch Cem—cemetery ... AL-4
Old Rocky Branch Cem—cemetery ... MS-4
Old Rocky Creek—stream ... TX-5
Old Rocky Ford—locale ... TN-4
Old Rocky Hill Ch—church ... KY-4
Old Rocky Hill Sch—school (2) ... KY-4
Old Rocky Knob—summit ... GA-3
*Old Rocky Mount Cem* ... AL-4
Old Rocky Mount Cem—cemetery ... AL-4
Old Rocky Mtn—summit ... NC-3
Old Rocky River Cem—cemetery ... SC-3
Old Rodney Presbyterian Ch—church ... MS-4
Old Roll Dam—dam ... ME-1
*Old Rollenson Sound* ... NC-3
Old Rollinson Channel—channel ... NC-3
Old Roman Catholic Cathedral—hist pl ... MD-2
Old Rome Cem—cemetery ... AR-4
Old Romerly Marsh Channel—stream ... GA-3
Old Romine Cem—cemetery ... AL-4
Old Romney Grade—trail ... WV-2
Old Root Narrows—gut ... VA-3
Old Rose Hill Cem—cemetery ... MS-4
Old Rose Hill Sch—school ... IA-7
Old Rose Tree Tavern—hist pl ... PA-2
Old Rotation—hist pl ... AL-4
Old Roughy—ridge ... NC-3
Old Round Ch—church ... VT-1
Old Roundhill Cem—cemetery ... PA-2
**Old Round Rock**—pop pl ... TX-5
Old Roundtop—summit ... NY-2
Old Round Top—summit ... PA-2
Old Rountree Lake—lake ... GA-3
Old Rowe School—reservoir ... SC-3
Old Rowsburg Cem—cemetery ... OH-6
Old Royal—locale ... WA-9
Old RR Grade Pond Dam—dam ... AL-4
Old RR Savings and Loan Bldg—hist pl ... KS-7
Old RR Station—hist pl ... OH-6
Old R Spring—spring ... AZ-5
Old Rsvr—reservoir ... IL-6
Old Rsvr—reservoir ... MA-1
Old Rsvr—reservoir ... TX-5
Old Ruby Cem—cemetery ... MS-4
Old Ruddell Hill Cem—cemetery ... AR-4
Old Ruff Cem—cemetery ... IL-6
Old Run—stream (2) ... IN-6
Old Runnels Cem—cemetery ... TX-5
Old Runnymede Church—hist pl ... KS-7
Old Ruskin Ch—church ... GA-3
Old Russell County Courthouse—hist pl ... VA-3
Old Russel Mine—mine ... MT-8
Old Russelville Cem—cemetery ... OH-6
Old Rutledge Cem—cemetery ... IL-6
Old Ryan Farm—hist pl ... NJ-2
Olds—locale ... WA-9
**Olds**—pop pl ... IA-7
**Olds**—pop pl ... NC-3
Olds, Alonzo W., House—hist pl ... MI-6
Olds, Mount—summit ... CA-9
Old Sabine River Channel—stream ... TX-5
Old Sabino Camp—locale ... NM-5
Old Sacramento Hist Dist—hist pl ... CA-9
*Old Saddleback* ... CA-9
**Old Safford (historical)**—pop pl ... TN-4
Old Sag, The—swamp ... AR-4
*Olds Agency* ... MS-4
Old Saint Aloysius Cem—cemetery ... MD-2
Old Saint Bridgets Cem—cemetery ... MO-7
Old Saint Catherine Creek—stream ... MS-4
Old Saint Charles Cem—cemetery ... MI-6
Old Saint Francis Cem—cemetery ... AL-4
Old Saint George Cem—cemetery ... MO-7
Old Saint James Cem—cemetery ... NY-2
Old Saint James Cem—cemetery ... OH-6
Old Saint James Ch—church ... LA-4
Old Saint John Ch—church ... AL-4
Old Saint John Ch—church ... MS-4
Old Saint Johns Cem—cemetery ... VA-3
Old Saint Johns County Jail—hist pl ... FL-3
Old Saint Joseph Cem—cemetery ... KS-7
Old Saint Joseph Cem—cemetery ... LA-4
Old Saint Joseph Cem—cemetery ... ND-7
Old Saint Joseph Ch—church ... MD-2
Old Saint Josephs Cem—cemetery ... CT-1
Old Saint Josephs Cem—cemetery ... MD-2
Old Saint Josephs Cem—cemetery ... NH-1
Old Saint Josephs Cem—cemetery ... NY-2
**Old Saint Louis**—pop pl ... IN-6
Old Saint Louis Cem—cemetery ... IN-6
Old Saint Luke's Hosp—hist pl ... FL-3
Old Saint Marcus Cem—cemetery ... MO-7
Old Saint Martins Ch—church ... MD-2
**Old Saint Marys**—pop pl ... TX-5
Old Saint Marys Cem—cemetery ... IL-6
Old Saint Marys Cem—cemetery ... MN-6
Old Saint Marys Cem—cemetery ... NJ-2
Old Saint Marys Cem—cemetery ... NY-2
Old Saint Marys Cem—cemetery (2) ... OH-6
Old Saint Marys Cem—cemetery ... WI-6
Old Saint Marys Ch—church ... FL-3
Old Saint Matthews Ch—church ... VA-3
Old Saint Nicholas Chapel—church ... MN-6
Old Saint Ottos Cem—cemetery ... SD-7
Old Saint Paul Cem—cemetery ... LA-4
Old Saint Paul Cem—cemetery ... SD-7
Old Saint Paul Cem—cemetery ... TN-4
Old Saint Paul Ch—church ... AR-4
Old Saint Pauls Ch—church ... NC-3
Old Saint Peter Cem—cemetery ... MS-4
*Old Saint Peter Missionary Baptist Church* ... MS-4
Old Saint Stephens Cem—cemetery ... AL-4
Old Saint Stephens (historical)—locale ... AL-4
Old Saint Thomas Sch (abandoned)—school ... MO-7
Old Saint Williams Cem—cemetery ... MA-1
Old Salem—locale ... NC-3
Old Salem—locale ... TX-5
**Old Salem**—pop pl ... TN-4
*Old Salem Baptist Church* ... AL-4
*Old Salem Baptist Church* ... TN-4
*Old Salem Cem* ... AL-4
*Old Salem Cem* ... MS-4
Old Salem Cem—cemetery (3) ... AL-4
Old Salem Cem—cemetery ... AR-4
Old Salem Cem—cemetery (2) ... GA-3
Old Salem Cem—cemetery ... IL-6
Old Salem Cem—cemetery (2) ... KY-4
Old Salem Cem—cemetery (5) ... MS-4
Old Salem Cem—cemetery ... MO-7
Old Salem Cem—cemetery ... NE-7
Old Salem Cem—cemetery ... NC-3
Old Salem Cem—cemetery (2) ... OH-6
Old Salem Cem—cemetery ... PA-2
Old Salem Cem—cemetery (4) ... TN-4
Old Salem Cem—cemetery ... TX-5
Old Salem Cem—cemetery ... VA-3
*Old Salem Ch* ... AL-4
*Old Salem Ch* ... TN-4
Old Salem Ch—church (5) ... AL-4
Old Salem Ch—church ... IL-6
Old Salem Ch—church ... IN-6
Old Salem Ch—church (7) ... KY-4
Old Salem Ch—church (2) ... MO-7
Old Salem Ch—church (2) ... NC-3
Old Salem Ch—church ... PA-2
Old Salem Ch—church (3) ... TN-4
Old Salem Ch—church ... TX-5
Old Salem Ch—church (2) ... VA-3
**Old Salem Chautauqua**—pop pl ... IL-6
Old Salem Ch (historical)—church ... AL-4
*Old Salem Church* ... MS-4
Old Salem Church and Cemetery—hist pl ... MD-2
Old Salem Hist Dist—hist pl ... NC-3
**Old Salem (Salem)**—pop pl ... TX-5
Old Salem Sch—school ... MS-4
Old Salem Sch (abandoned)—school ... MO-7
Old Salem Sch (historical)—school ... MS-4
*Old Salem School* ... TN-4
**Old Salem (subdivision)**—pop pl ... NC-3
**Old Salem Village**—pop pl ... MD-2
Old Salinas River—gut ... CA-9
Old Saline Bayou—gut ... LA-4
Old Saline Cem—cemetery ... AR-4
Old Saline Ch—church ... LA-4
Old Salmon Village—locale ... AK-9
Old Saltillo Ch—church ... TX-5
Old Saltillo Road Ch—church ... MS-4
Old Salt Works—hist pl ... OK-5
Old Salt Works Lake—lake ... TX-5
Old Sam Hollow—valley ... TN-4
Old Sam Mine—mine ... ID-8
*Old Sam Moore Tank* ... AZ-5
Old Sampson Windmill—locale ... TX-5
*Old Sams Pond* ... NJ-2
**Old Samuel**—pop pl ... AL-4
Old San Antonio Hosp—hist pl ... CA-9
Old Sanders Cem—cemetery ... TX-5
Old Sandhill Ch—church ... MS-4
Old San Diego—uninc pl ... CA-9
Old Sand Prairie Cem—cemetery ... IL-6
*Old Sand Springs Church* ... AL-4
Old Sand Well—well ... NM-5
Olds and Whipple Pond—lake ... CT-1
Old Sandy Cem—cemetery ... PA-2
Old Sandy Tank—reservoir ... NM-5
Old San Felipe Cem—cemetery ... TX-5
Old San Francisco Hist Dist—hist pl ... TX-5
Old San Joaquin Ranch—locale ... TX-5
Old San Juan—post sta ... PR-3
Old San Juan First Spanish Capitol 1598—other ... NM-5
Old San Patricio Cem—cemetery ... TX-5
Old Santa Elena—locale ... TX-5
Old Santa Fe RR Depot—hist pl ... KS-7
*Old Santa Fe Trail* ... KS-7
Old Santa Fe Trail—trail ... CO-8
Old Santa Fe Trail—trail (2) ... NM-5
Old Santa Fe Windmill—locale ... TX-5
Old Santa Rita Springs—spring ... NM-5
Old Santa Rosa Catholic Church and Cemetery—hist pl ... CA-9
Old Santa Susana Stage Road—hist pl ... CA-9
Old Santee Canal—canal ... SC-3
Old Sapello Cem—cemetery ... NM-5
*Old Saratoga* ... NY-2
Old Sardis Cem—cemetery (2) ... AL-4
Old Sardis Cem—cemetery ... LA-4
*Old Sardis Ch* ... MS-4
Old Sardis Ch—church (3) ... AL-4
*Old Sarepta Baptist Ch* ... MS-4
Old Sargent Cem—cemetery ... ND-7
*Old Sasco Ruins* ... AZ-5
Old Saugatuck—locale ... MI-6
Old Saulich—locale ... AK-9
Old Savanna—plain ... NC-3
Old Savonoski Site—hist pl ... AK-9
Old Savoy Cem—cemetery ... MS-4
Old Saw—bar ... MA-1
*Old Sawmill Hollow* ... TN-4
Old Sawmill Hollow—valley ... TN-4
Old Sawmill Spring—spring ... AZ-5
Old Sawmill Spring—spring ... NM-5
**Old Saybrook**—pop pl ... CT-1
**Old Saybrook Center (census name Old Saybrook)**—pop pl ... CT-1
Old Saybrook South Green—hist pl ... CT-1
**Old Saybrook (Town of)**—pop pl ... CT-1
Old Scab Mtn—summit ... WA-9
Old Scantum—bar ... ME-1
Old S C Ditch—canal ... CO-8
Old Scenic Ch—church ... MN-6
Old Schaeffer Camp—locale ... CA-9
Old Schaeffer Mill—locale ... CA-9
Old Sch House—hist pl ... FL-3
Old School Ch—church ... KY-4
Old School Ch—church ... TX-5
Old School Ch—church ... VA-3
Old School Ch (abandoned)—church ... MO-7
Old School Hill Cem—cemetery ... TX-5
Old Schoolhouse—hist pl ... ME-1
*Old Schoolhouse Branch* ... WV-2
Old Schoolhouse Branch—stream ... AL-4
Old Schoolhouse Bridge—hist pl ... VT-1
Old Schoolhouse Gulch—valley ... MT-8
Old Schoolhouse Hollow—valley (2) ... MO-7
Old Schoolhouse Spring—spring ... OR-9
Old School Presbyterian Ch—church ... AL-4
Old Sch Privy—hist pl ... OH-6
Old Schracktown Cem—cemetery ... PA-2
Old Schwamb Mill—hist pl ... MA-1
Olds Club—locale ... PA-2
Old Scooba Cem—cemetery ... MS-4
**Old Scooba (historical)**—pop pl ... MS-4
Old Scotch Cem—cemetery ... NY-2
Old Scotch Church—hist pl ... OR-9
Old Scotchtown Cem—cemetery ... NY-2
*Old Scotland* ... AL-4
Old Scotland Ch—church ... AL-4
Old Scots Cem—cemetery ... NJ-2
Old Scott Cem—cemetery ... IL-6
Old Scott Cem—cemetery ... OH-6
Old Scott County Jail—hist pl ... TN-4
Old Scott Ranch—locale ... NV-8
Old Scott Tank—reservoir ... AZ-5
Olds Cove—bay ... VA-3
*Old Scraggy* ... MT-8
Old Scraggy Peak—summit ... MT-8
Olds Creek—stream ... CA-9
Olds Creek—stream ... TX-5
Olds Creek—stream ... WA-9
Old Scroggie Pond—lake ... CT-1
Olds Ditch—canal ... IN-6
Old Sea Cem—cemetery ... MS-4
Old Sebago Beach—beach ... NY-2
Old Sebastian Cem—cemetery ... FL-3
Old Sebbas Ranch—locale ... CA-9
Old Seceder Cem—cemetery ... PA-2
Old Second Mesa Sch (site)—school ... AZ-5
Old Second Natl Bank—hist pl ... IL-6
Old Sedgwick County Courthouse—hist pl ... KS-7
Old Self Creek Ch—church ... MS-4
Old Sellers Cem—cemetery ... AL-4
Old Sell Lake Cem—cemetery ... MN-6
Old Selma Road Park—park ... AL-4
Old Seminary Bldg—hist pl ... GA-3
Old Senatobia Canal—canal ... MS-4
Old Senator Mill (historical)—locale ... AZ-5
Old Senator Mine—mine ... CA-9
Old Sergeant—pillar ... RI-1
Old Sergeant Cem—cemetery ... IN-6
Old Settler Mine—mine ... CO-8
Old Settlers' Association Park and Rhodham Bonnifield House—hist pl ... IA-7
Old Settlers Cem—cemetery ... IL-6
Old Settlers Cem—cemetery ... IN-6
Old Settlers Cem—cemetery (2) ... MA-1
Old Settlers Cem—cemetery ... NE-7
Old Settlers Graves—cemetery ... MA-1
Old Settlers Irrigation Ditch—canal ... OK-5
Old Settler's Irrigation Ditch—hist pl ... OK-5
Old Settlers Park—park ... IA-7
Old Settlers Park—park ... TX-5
Old Settlers Park—park (2) ... WI-6
Old Settlers Rest Cem—cemetery ... WI-6
Old Settlers Slough—stream ... OR-9
Old Settlers Spring—spring ... IL-6
Old Settler Tunnel—mine ... CO-8
Old Seventynine Tank—reservoir ... AZ-5
Olds Ferry (site)—locale ... ID-8
Old Shade Furnace—locale ... PA-2
Old Shady Grove Baptist Ch (historical)—church ... TX-5
Old Shady Grove Cem—cemetery ... LA-4
Old Shady Grove Cem—cemetery (2) ... MS-4
Old Shady Grove Cem—cemetery ... NC-3
Old Shady Grove Cem—cemetery ... TX-5
Old Shady Grove Ch—church (2) ... AL-4
Old Shady Grove Sch (historical)—school ... TX-5
Old Shallotte—locale ... NC-3
Old Shannon Cem—cemetery ... TN-4
Old Sharon Baptist Ch (historical)—church ... MS-4
Old Sharon Cem—cemetery ... GA-3
Old Sharon Cem—cemetery ... MS-4
Old Sharon Ch (historical)—church ... MS-4
Old Sharp Sch (historical)—school ... MS-4
Old Sharron Cem—cemetery ... AL-4
*Old Shatter* ... NC-3
**Old Shawneetown**—pop pl ... IL-6
Old Sheep Knob—summit ... NC-3
**Old Sheffield**—pop pl ... PA-2
Old She Hollow—valley ... KY-4
Old Shelby Cem—cemetery ... AL-4
Old Shelby Ch—church ... MS-4
*Old Shelby Iron Works Cem* ... AL-4
Old Shelbyville City Cem—cemetery ... TN-4
Old Shell Beach—locale ... LA-4
*Old Shell Road Elementary School* ... AL-4
Old Shell Road Sch—school ... AL-4
Old Shelton Cem—cemetery ... IN-6
Old Shephard Farm—hist pl ... MA-1
Old Shepherd Cem—cemetery ... AL-4
Old Shepherd Pond—reservoir ... MA-1
Old Shepherd Pond Dam—dam ... MA-1
Old Sheridan Mine—mine ... WA-9
Old Sherman Public Library—hist pl ... TX-5
Old Shiloh Cem—cemetery (2) ... AL-4
Old Shiloh Cem—cemetery ... AR-4
Old Shiloh Cem—cemetery ... FL-3
Old Shiloh Cem—cemetery ... GA-3
Old Shiloh Cem—cemetery (2) ... IL-6
Old Shiloh Cem—cemetery ... MD-2
Old Shiloh Cem—cemetery ... MS-4
*Old Shiloh Church* ... AL-4
Old Shiloh Church Cem—cemetery ... AL-4
Old Shincracker—summit ... VT-1
Old Shingle Mill—locale ... ME-1
Old Shinoak Springs—spring ... TX-5
Old Ship AME Zion Ch—church ... AL-4
Old Shipbuilder's Hist Dist—hist pl ... MA-1
Old Ship Ch—church ... AL-4
Old Ship Ch—church ... MA-1
Old Ship Channel—channel ... DE-2
Old Ship Meetinghouse—hist pl ... MA-1
Old Ship Street Hist Dist—hist pl ... MA-1
Old Shoal Creek Dam—dam ... TN-4
*Old Shoal Ford Cemetery* ... AL-4
Old Shoe Branch—stream ... IN-6
**Old Shongaloo**—pop pl ... LA-4
Old Shongaloo Ch—church ... LA-4
**Old Shongopavi (site)**—pop pl (2) ... AZ-5
Old Shooting Creek Ch—church ... NC-3
Old Shop Branch—stream ... WV-2
Old Shop Hollow—valley ... TN-4
Old Shop Tower—locale ... VA-3
Old Short Mine—mine ... MO-7
Old Shot Tower—building ... IA-7
**Old Side**—pop pl ... PA-2
Old Side Cem—cemetery ... AL-4
Old Side Cem—cemetery ... WV-2
*Old Sides Cem* ... AL-4
*Oldsides Church* ... AL-4
Old Sidney Holmes Sch—school ... ME-1
Old Silas Rock—bar ... NY-2
Old Siloam Ch—church ... NC-3
**Old Silver Beach**—pop pl ... MA-1
Old Silver Brook—locale ... PA-2
Old Silver Creek Cem—cemetery ... OH-6
Old Silver Creek Ch—church ... MS-4
Old Sipsey Mine (underground)—mine ... AL-4
Old Sisseton Indian Agency—locale ... SD-7
*Old Sister Island* ... FM-9
Old Sitka Rocks—area ... AK-9
Old Sitka (Ruins)—locale ... AK-9
Old Sitka Site—hist pl ... AK-9
Old Situk Creek—stream ... AK-9
Old Sixth Ward Hist Dist—hist pl ... TX-5
Old Sixty Hill—summit ... VT-1
Old Sixty Sch—school ... KS-7
Old Ski Hill—summit ... CA-9
Old Skinnersville—locale ... NC-3
Old Skipanon Creek—stream ... OR-9
Old Skunk—rock ... MA-1
Old Skwentna Road House (Site)—locale ... AK-9
*Old Slab Fork* ... WV-2
Old Slab Fork—stream ... WV-2
Old Slag Camp—locale ... NH-1
Old Slagle Cem—cemetery ... TN-4
*Olds Lake* ... FL-3
Olds Lake—lake ... MN-6
Old Slater Mill—hist pl ... RI-1
Old Slaughter Creek—stream ... DE-2

Old Slave Mart—*hist pl* SC-3
Old Sled Trail—*trail* CA-9
Old Slinkard Cem—*cemetery* IN-6
*Olds Lode Mine* SD-7
Old Slough—*gut* NC-3
Old Slough—*gut* OK-5
Old Slough Landing (historical)—*locale* TN-4
Old Slow and Easy Landing—*locale* OR-9
*Oldsman Creek* NJ-2
**Oldsmar**—*pop pl* FL-3
Oldsmar Elem Sch—*school* FL-3
Old Smedley Cem—*cemetery* IN-6
Old Smelter (historical)—*locale* SD-7
Old Smelter Well—*well* UT-8
Olds Mill (historical)—*locale* TN-4
Old Smith Cem—*cemetery* OH-6
Old Smithdale—*locale* MS-4
Old Smith Ditch—*canal* WY-8
Old Smith Ferry—*locale* NC-3
*Old Smith Hollow* TN-4
Old Smith Mine—*mine* AZ-5
Old Smokey Mtn—*summit* AZ-5
Old Smokey Ski Hill Park—*park* MN-6
Old Smoky Ch—*church* NC-3
Olds Mtn—*summit* AK-9
Old Smugglers Face—*rock* VT-1
Old Smyrna Cem—*cemetery* AR-4
Old Smyrna Cem—*cemetery* GA-3
**Old Snead**—*pop pl* AL-4
Old Sneedsboro—*locale* NC-3
*Old Snow Hill* AL-4
Old Snow Hill Cem—*cemetery* AL-4
Old Snowy—*summit* AK-9
Old Snowy Mtn—*summit* WA-9
Old Sny—*gut* IL-6
Old Sny Public Use Area—*park* IL-6
Old Soaker—*island* ME-1
Old Soldier River Ditch—*canal* IA-7
Old Soldiers Cem—*cemetery* AL-4
Old Soldiers Cem—*cemetery* AR-4
Old Soldiers Cem—*cemetery* MN-6
*Old Soldiers Graveyard* AL-4
**Old Somerset**—*pop pl* VA-3
**Old Sopori School**—*pop pl* AZ-5
Old Souenlovie Cem—*cemetery* MS-4
*Old South* MA-1
Old Southampton Cem—*cemetery* NY-2
Old South Cem—*cemetery* CT-1
Old South Cem—*cemetery* IN-6
Old South Cem—*cemetery* (4) MA-1
Old South Ch—*church* ME-1
Old South Ch—*church* MA-1
Old South Ch—*church* NJ-2
Old South Ch—*church* OH-6
Old South Church—*hist pl* OH-6
Old South Church in Boston—*hist pl* MA-1
Old Southeast Church—*hist pl* NY-2
Old Southeast Town Hall—*hist pl* NY-2
Old South Haven Ch—*church* NY-2
Old South Hill Cem—*cemetery* CT-1
Old South Meeting House—*building* MA-1
Old South Meetinghouse—*church* MA-1
Old South Meetinghouse—*hist pl* MA-1
Old South Norwalk Rsvr—*reservoir* CT-1
Old South Union Church—*hist pl* MA-1
Old South Windmill—*locale* NM-5
Old South Windmill—*locale* TX-5
Old Sow—*bar* NY-2
Old Sow—*rock* MA-1
Old Sow Island—*island* PA-2
Old Sow Rock—*pillar* RI-1
*Old Spain* MA-1
**Old Spain**—*pop pl* MA-1
Old Spanish Bridge—*other* GU-9
Old Spanish Cave—*cave* MO-7
Old Spanish Corral—*locale* CA-9
*Old Spanish Fort* AL-4
Old Spanish Fort—*hist pl* MS-4
Old Spanish Fort Archeol Site—*hist pl* MO-7
Old Spanish Fort Cem—*cemetery* MS-4
Old Spanish Lake Lowlands—*flat* LA-4
Old Spanish Mine (Inactive)—*mine* UT-8
Old Spanish Mission—*locale* GA-3
Old Spanish Monastery—*hist pl* FL-3
Old Spanish Oven—*other* GU-9
Old Spanish Pass—*channel* LA-4
Old Spanish Trail—*hist pl* UT-8
Old Spanish Trail—*trail* CA-9
Old Spanish Trail—*trail* NV-8
Old Spanish Trail—*trail* (2) TX-5
**Old Sparta**—*pop pl* AL-4
**Old Sparta**—*pop pl* NC-3
Old Sparta Cem—*cemetery* MO-7
Old Sparta Cem—*cemetery* TN-4
*Old Speckle Mountain* ME-1
Old Speck Mtn—*summit* ME-1
Old Spink Colony—*hist pl* SD-7
Old Spirit Rock—*rock* MA-1
Old Spiro Lake—*reservoir* OK-5
*Old Splatterfoot Mountain* VT-1
Olds Point—*cape* VA-3
Old Spring—*spring* TN-4
Old Spring—*spring* WA-9
Old Spring Branch—*stream* (2) AL-4
Old Spring Branch—*stream* MS-4
Old Springbrook Cem—*cemetery* IA-7
Old Spring Cem—*cemetery* IN-6
Old Spring Cottage Ch (historical)—*church* MS-4
Old Spring Creek Ditch—*canal* WY-8
Old Springfield Cem—*cemetery* NY-2
Old Springfield Ch—*church* OH-6
Old Springfield I.O.O.F. Cem—*cemetery* OR-9
**Old Spring Hill**—*pop pl* AL-4
Old Spring Hill Cem—*cemetery* FL-3
Old Spring Hill Cem—*cemetery* MS-4
Old Spring Hill Ch—*church* MS-4
Old Spring Hill Memorial Ch—*church* AL-4
**Old Spring Hope**—*pop pl* NC-3
Old Spring Ridge Cem—*cemetery* LA-4
Old Spring Tavern—*hist pl* WI-6
*Old Springville* TN-4
**Old Springville**—*pop pl* TN-4
Old Squaw, The—*rock* MT-8
Old Squaw Lake—*lake* CA-9
Old Squaw Lake—*lake* MN-6
Old Squaw Skin Landing—*locale* MI-6
Olds River—*stream* AK-9
Olds Sch—*school* NC-3
Olds Slough—*stream* TX-5
*Old Stafford Forge* NJ-2
Old Stafford Street Cem—*cemetery* CT-1
Old Stagecoach Inn—*building* TX-5
Old Stagecoach Stop—*hist pl* MO-7
Old Stage Line Monmt—*park* IL-6
Old Stage Route—*trail* CA-9
Old Stage Stand—*locale* TX-5
Old Stage Station—*locale* AZ-5
Old Stage Station—*locale* CO-8
Old Stage Station—*locale* NM-5
Old Stage Station—*locale* (2) UT-8
Old Stage Station (historical)—*locale* OR-9
Old Stage Station (ruins)—*locale* NV-8
Old Stage Station (site)—*locale* WY-8
Old Stage Trail—*trail* VT-1
Old Stanback Ferry—*locale* NC-3
Old Standard Hollow—*valley* TN-4
Old Stand Cem—*cemetery* AL-4
Old Stand Spring Branch—*stream* AL-4
Old Stanford Wood Camp—*locale* CA-9
Olds Tank—*reservoir* TX-5
Old St. Anne's Church—*hist pl* DE-2
Old St. Anthony's Catholic Church—*hist pl* TX-5
**Old Stanton**—*pop pl* PA-2
Old Stapleton Ranch—*locale* NM-5
Old Star Fort (Site)—*locale* SC-3
Old Star Sch (abandoned)—*school* PA-2
Old State Bank—*hist pl* IN-6
Old State Boundary Historical Marker—*park* NV-8
Old State Bridge—*bridge* CO-8
*Old State Canal* AL-4
Old State Canal—*canal* NC-3
Old State Capitol—*building* UT-8
Old State Capitol—*hist pl* GA-3
Old State Capitol—*hist pl* IL-6
Old State Capitol—*hist pl* MS-4
Old State Cem—*cemetery* IL-6
Old State Cem—*cemetery* SC-3
Old State Ditch—*canal* UT-8
Old State Hospital Cem—*cemetery* IL-6
Old State Hospital Cem—*cemetery* NY-2
Old State House—*building* MA-1
Old State House—*building* TN-4
Old Statehouse—*hist pl* AR-4
Old Statehouse—*hist pl* DE-2
Old Statehouse—*hist pl* KY-4
Old Statehouse—*hist pl* MA-1
Old Statehouse Hist Dist—*hist pl* KY-4
Old State Line Cem—*cemetery* MS-4
Old State Mutual Bldg—*hist pl* MA-1
Old State Prison Bldg—*hist pl* GA-3
Old State Road Ch—*church* WV-2
Old State Road Trail—*trail* PA-2
**Old Station**—*pop pl* CA-9
Old Station Cem—*cemetery* NC-3
Old Station Gap—*gap* NC-3
**Old Station (Post Office)**—*pop pl* CA-9
**Old Stephensburg**—*pop pl* KY-4
Old Stephenson Ranch—*locale* OR-9
Old Sterrett Cem—*cemetery* AL-4
*Old Stevenson Ranch* OR-9
Old Stewarts Landing (historical)—*locale* TN-4
Old St. Helena Parish Jail—*hist pl* LA-4
Old Stickney Lake—*reservoir* SD-7
Old Stickney Lake State Public Shooting Area—*park* SD-7
Old Still Hollow—*valley* MO-7
Old Still Hollow—*valley* VA-3
Old Stillhouse Hollow—*valley* MO-7
Old Stillhouse Spring—*spring* MO-7
Old St. John's Church—*hist pl* OH-6
**Old St. Louis**—*pop pl* IN-6
Old St. Luke's Episcopal Church—*hist pl* TX-5
Old St. Mary's Catholic Parish House—*hist pl* SD-7
Old St. Mary's Church—*hist pl* WI-6
Old St. Mary's Church, Sch and Rectory—*hist pl* OH-6
Old St. Nicholas Russian Orthodox Church—*hist pl* AK-9
Old Stockholm Cem—*cemetery* WI-6
Old Stock Rsvr—*reservoir* CO-8
Old Stockton Cem—*cemetery* KS-7
Old Stockton Well—*well* NV-8
Old Stone Arch, Natl Road—*hist pl* IL-6
Old Stone Arch Bridge—*hist pl* IL-6
Old Stone Barracks—*hist pl* NY-2
Old Stone Blacksmith Shop—*hist pl* VT-1
Old Stone Bridge—*bridge* TN-4
Old Stone Cem—*cemetery* MS-4
Old Stone Cem—*cemetery* OH-6
Old Stone Ch—*church* CT-1
Old Stone Ch—*church* (2) IA-7
Old Stone Ch—*church* KY-4
Old Stone Ch—*church* NY-2
Old Stone Ch—*church* OH-6
Old Stone Ch—*church* PA-2
Old Stone Ch—*church* SC-3
Old Stone Ch—*church* (2) VA-3
Old Stone Ch (historical)—*church* TN-4
Old Stone Church—*hist pl* MA-1
Old Stone Church—*hist pl* MO-7
Old Stone Church—*hist pl* NJ-2
Old Stone Church—*hist pl* OH-6
Old Stone Church—*hist pl* VA-3
Old Stone Church—*hist pl* WV-2
Old Stone Church and Cemetery—*hist pl* SC-3
Old Stone Church Cem—*cemetery* NJ-2
Old Stone Church Cem—*cemetery* SC-3
Old Stone Church Tower—*tower* TN-4
Old Stone Dock, The—*locale* MA-1
Old Stone Fort—*hist pl* TN-4
Old Stone Fort—*locale* CO-8
Old Stone Fort—*locale* NY-2
Old Stone Fort (historical)—*locale* TN-4
Old Stone Fort State Park—*park* TN-4
Old Stone Gate of Chicago Union Stockyards—*hist pl* IL-6
Old Stone Hill Hist Dist—*hist pl* MO-7
Old Stone Hotel—*hist pl* IL-6
Old Stone House—*building* PA-2
Old Stone House—*building* WV-2
Old Stone House—*hist pl* DC-2
Old Stone House—*hist pl* OR-9
Old Stone House—*hist pl* SC-3
Old Stone House—*hist pl* VT-1
Old Stone House—*hist pl* (2) VA-3
Old Stone House—*hist pl* (2) WV-2
Old Stone House—*locale* NC-3
**Old Stone (House Estates)**—*pop pl* IN-6
Old Stone Inn—*hist pl* KY-4
Old Stone Mill Brook—*stream* CT-1
Old Stone Road Ch—*church* VA-3
Old Stone Sch—*school* NY-2
Old Stone Schoolhouse Cem—*cemetery* OH-6
Old Stone Tavern—*building* MA-1
Old Stone Tavern—*hist pl* DE-2
Old Stone Tavern—*hist pl* KY-4
Old Stone Tavern—*hist pl* VA-3
Old Stone Tavern—*hist pl* WV-2
Old Stone Tavern—*park* DE-2
Old Stone Warehouse—*hist pl* NY-2
**Old Stonington**—*pop pl* IL-6
Old Stonington Cem—*cemetery* IL-6
Old Stonington Ch—*church* IL-6
Old Stonybrook Ch—*church* PA-2
Old Stony Creek Dam—*dam* NC-3
Old Store Bayou—*bay* FL-3
Old Stormy—*summit* ID-8
Old Stormy—*summit* MT-8
Old stovall Cem—*cemetery* TN-4
Old Stove Bend—*bend* TX-5
Old Stove Dam—*dam* MT-8
Old Stover Cem—*cemetery* MO-7
Olds Tower—*building* MI-6
Olds (Township of)—*fmr MCD* NC-3
Old St. Patrick's Cathedral Complex—*hist pl* NY-2
Old St. Patrick's Church—*hist pl* MO-7
Old St. Patrick's Church—*hist pl* OH-6
Old St. Paul's Methodist Episcopal Church—*hist pl* DE-2
Old St. Peter's Church—*hist pl* NY-2
**Old Straitsville**—*pop pl* OH-6
Old Strangers Home Baptist Ch—*church* MS-4
Old Stratfield Cem—*cemetery* CT-1
Old Stream—*stream* ME-1
Old Stream Branch—*stream* KY-4
*Old Stream Furnace Branch* KY-4
Old Stronach Cem—*cemetery* MI-6
Old St. Stephens Site—*hist pl* AL-4
Old St. Teresa's Catholic Church—*hist pl* GA-3
Old Stump Lake—*bay* LA-4
**Old Sturbridge Village**—*pop pl* MA-1
Old Sturgis Cem—*cemetery* MS-4
Old St. Wenceslaus Catholic Parish House—*hist pl* SD-7
**Old Success**—*pop pl* MO-7
Old Sugar Creek—*gut* MO-7
Old Sugar Creek Cem—*cemetery* IN-6
Old Sugar Hill Cem—*cemetery* NY-2
Old Sugarland Run—*stream* VA-3
**Old Sugar Loaf (subdivision)**—*pop pl* PA-2
Old Sugar Mill of Koloa—*hist pl* HI-9
Old Sugar Pine Guard Station—*locale* CA-9
*Old Suggsville* AL-4
Old Sulphur Springs Sch—*school* AL-4
Old Summit Springs—*spring* AZ-5
Old Sumner Cem—*cemetery* GA-3
Old Sump—*bar* MA-1
Old Sunflower Ch—*church* AL-4
Old Sun Glacier—*glacier* MT-8
Old Superior Mine—*mine* MI-6
Old Supply Trail—*trail* PA-2
Old Susan Mine—*mine* UT-8
Old Suslota—*locale* AK-9
Old Sussex County Courthouse—*hist pl* DE-2
*Old Sutherland Springs* TX-5
Old Sutton HS—*hist pl* WV-2
*Old Suwanee* GA-3
Old Suwanee Ch—*church* GA-3
*Old Suwany Town* FL-3
Oldsville Cem—*cemetery* NY-2
Old Swafford Cem—*cemetery* TN-4
Old Swale Marsh—*swamp* NY-2
Old Swamp River—*stream* MA-1
Old Swan Pond Ditch—*canal* IN-6
Old Sweat Bank—*bar* FL-3
Old Swede Mine—*mine* CA-9
*Old Swedes Church* DE-2
Old Swede's House—*hist pl* PA-2
Old Swedish Cem—*cemetery* IA-7
Old Swedish Ch—*church* IA-7
Old Sweet Canaan Cem—*cemetery* LA-4
Old Sweet Springs—*hist pl* WV-2
**Old Sweetwater**—*pop pl* TN-4
Old Sweetwater Baptist Ch—*church* TN-4
Old Sweetwater Cem—*cemetery* MS-4
Old Sweetwater Cem—*cemetery* TN-4
Old Sweetwater Ch—*church* SC-3
Old Swim Beach—*beach* NV-8
Old Swimmin Hole Lake—*reservoir* IN-6
Old Swoyer Well—*well* NM-5
Old Sycamore—*locale* VA-3
Old Sykes Spring—*spring* TN-4
Old Symarna Ch—*church* SC-3
Old Synagogue—*hist pl* WI-6
Old Synnes Ranch—*locale* MT-8
Old Tabernacle Cem—*cemetery* AL-4
Old Tabernacle Cem—*cemetery* MS-4
Old Tabernacle Cem—*cemetery* SC-3
Old Tabernacle Ch—*church* AL-4
*Old Tabernacle Methodist Ch* AL-4
Old Tacoma—*locale* WA-9
Old Tailor Cem—*cemetery* KS-7
Old Tajos Ranch—*locale* TX-5
Old Talbott Tavern—*hist pl* KY-4
Old Tampa Bay—*bay* FL-3
Old Tank—*reservoir* (2) AZ-5
Old Tank—*reservoir* NM-5
Old Tank—*reservoir* (2) TX-5
Old Tank Canyon—*valley* TX-5
*Old Tanner Trail* AZ-5
Old Tannery Brook—*stream* CT-1
Old Tanyard Cem—*cemetery* AL-4
**Old Tappan**—*pop pl* NJ-2
Old Tar Landing—*locale* MS-4
Old Tar Paper Shack Lake—*lake* MS-4
Old Tarrant Ch—*church* TX-5
Old Tarrytown Road Sch—*school* NY-2
Old Tar Trail—*trail* PA-2
Old Tatham Sch—*school* MA-1
Old Tavern—*hist pl* CA-9
Old Tavern—*hist pl* ME-1
Old Tavern—*locale* VA-3
Old Taylor Branch—*stream* NC-3
Old Taylor County Courthouse and Jail—*hist pl* TX-5
Old Taylor Hill Cem—*cemetery* MS-4
Old Taylor Lake—*lake* WI-6
Old Taylor Landing (historical)—*locale* AL-4
Old Taylorsville—*locale* MS-4
Old Taylor Tank Dam—*dam* AZ-5
Old Teakettle Creek—*channel* GA-3
Old Teegarden Cem—*cemetery* OH-6
Old Tejana Well—*well* NM-5
Old Telegraph Station (ruins)—*locale* NV-8
Old Telos Tote Road—*trail* ME-1
*Old Temple* TN-4
Old Tenant Pond—*reservoir* SC-3
Old Ten Mile Cem (historical)—*cemetery* TN-4
Old Tenmile Creek—*stream* TX-5
*Old Ten Mine* TN-4
Old Tennent Ch—*church* NJ-2
Old Tennessee Cem—*cemetery* LA-4
Old Tennessee Mine—*mine* TN-4
Old Terminal—*locale* TX-5
Old Terrell City Lake—*reservoir* TX-5
*Old Territorial Legislative Hall* IN-6
**Old Texas**—*pop pl* AL-4
Old Texas Cem—*cemetery* AR-4
Old Texas Cem—*cemetery* IL-6
Old Textile Hall—*hist pl* SC-3
Old Thickety Ch—*church* NC-3
Old Third District Courthouse—*hist pl* MA-1
Old Thomas Cem—*cemetery* FL-3
Old Thompson-Centrell Cem—*cemetery* AL-4
Old Thorne Ranch—*locale* MT-8
Old Thunder Slough—*gut* MT-8
Old Tikaboo Spring—*spring* NV-8
Old Tilden Mine—*mine* MI-6
Old Timber Lake—*reservoir* IN-6
Old Timber Lake Dam—*dam* IN-6
Old Timbers Campground—*locale* CO-8
Old Timbers Lodge—*park* IN-6
Old Tim Creek—*stream* MT-8
Old Tim Creek Trail—*trail* MT-8
Old Time Ch—*church* TN-4
Old Time Chapel—*church* KY-4
Old Timer Canyon—*valley* CA-9
Oldtimer Canyon—*valley* NM-5
Old Timer Creek—*stream* ID-8
Old Timer Mine—*mine* NV-8
Old Timer Mtn—*summit* ID-8
Old Timers Mine—*mine* NV-8
Old Tindells Ferry (historical)—*locale* AL-4
Old Tioga Camp—*locale* OR-9
Old Tippecanoe Main Street Hist Dist—*hist pl* OH-6
Old Tippins Cem—*cemetery* GA-3
Old Tipton Well—*well* NM-5
**Old Tip Town**—*pop pl* IN-6
Old Tishomingo County Courthouse—*hist pl* MS-4
Old Tubin Place—*locale* WY-8
Old Toboggan Run Rocks—*cliff* PA-2
Old Toccoa Ch—*church* GA-3
Old Toll Gate Site (historical)—*building* DC-2
Old Toll House—*locale* PA-2
Old Tom Bayou—*bay* FL-3
Old Tombstone—*hist pl* VA-3
Old Tom Creek—*stream* AK-9
Old Tom Creek—*stream* IL-6
Old Tom Mtn—*summit* ID-8
Old Tom Ridge—*ridge* OH-6
Old Tom Rock—*bar* ME-1
*Old Toms Cove* VA-3
Old Topanga Canyon—*valley* CA-9
Old Topsail Creek—*stream* NC-3
*Old Topsail Inlet* NC-3
Old Toroda—*locale* WA-9
Old Tourist Trail—*trail* CO-8
Old Tower Two—*hist pl* OK-5
*Oldtown* AL-4
*Old Town* FL-3
*Oldtown* IN-6
*Oldtown* ME-1
*Old Town* MD-2
*Old Town* MA-1
*Old Town* SC-3
*Old Town* TN-4
*Oldtown* VA-3
Old Town—*hist pl* TN-4
Old Town—*locale* CA-9
Old Town—*locale* GA-3
Old Town—*locale* IA-7
Oldtown—*locale* KY-4
Old Town—*locale* MD-2
Old Town—*locale* NC-3
Old Town—*locale* SC-3
Old Town—*locale* TN-4
Old Town—*locale* WA-9
**Old Town**—*pop pl* (2) AL-4
**Old Town**—*pop pl* AR-4
**Old Town**—*pop pl* CA-9
**Old Town**—*pop pl* FL-3
**Old Town**—*pop pl* ID-8
**Oldtown**—*pop pl* ID-8
**Oldtown**—*pop pl* IL-6
**Old Town**—*pop pl* IN-6
**Oldtown**—*pop pl* IN-6
**Old Town**—*pop pl* ME-1
**Oldtown**—*pop pl* MD-2
**Oldtown**—*pop pl* MA-1
**Old Town**—*pop pl* MO-7
**Old Town**—*pop pl* NM-5
**Old Town**—*pop pl* NC-3
**Old Town**—*pop pl* OH-6
**Oldtown**—*pop pl* OH-6
**Old Town**—*pop pl* OR-9
**Old Town**—*pop pl* SC-3
**Oldtown**—*pop pl* TN-4
**Oldtown**—*pop pl* VA-3
Old Town—*uninc pl* NY-2
Old Town Acres—*uninc pl* SC-3
Old Town Bay—*bay* LA-4
Old Town Bend—*bend* AR-4
Old Town Bend—*bend* MS-4
Oldtown Bend Revetment—*levee* AR-4
Oldtown Branch—*stream* FL-3
Old Town Branch—*stream* KY-4
Oldtown Branch—*stream* MD-2
Old Town Branch—*stream* MO-7
Oldtown Branch—*stream* TN-4
Old Town Bridge—*bridge* MA-1
Old Town Bridge—*hist pl* MA-1
Old Town Bridge—*hist pl* TN-4
Old Town Bridge—*other* NM-5
Old Town Cem—*cemetery* (2) AL-4
Old Town Cem—*cemetery* CO-8
Old Town Cem—*cemetery* FL-3
Oldtown Cem—*cemetery* IN-6
Old Town Cem—*cemetery* (2) IN-6
Old Town Cem—*cemetery* IA-7
Old Town Cem—*cemetery* MA-1
Old Town Cem—*cemetery* MS-4
Old Town Cem—*cemetery* MO-7
Old Town Cem—*cemetery* (4) NH-1
Oldtown Cem—*cemetery* NY-2
Oldtown Cem—*cemetery* OH-6
Old Town Cem—*cemetery* OH-6
Old Town Cem—*cemetery* TN-4
Old Town Cem—*cemetery* TX-5
Oldtown Cem—*cemetery* TX-5
*Old Town Cemetery* OR-9
*Old Town Ch* AL-4
Old Town Ch—*church* AL-4
Old Town Ch—*church* AR-4
Oldtown Ch—*church* IL-6
Old Town Ch—*church* MS-4
Oldtown Ch—*church* OH-6
*Oldtown Church* TN-4
Old Town Club—*locale* NC-3
*Old Town Country Club* NC-3
Oldtown Covered Bridge—*hist pl* KY-4
*Old Town Creek* AL-4
*Old Town Creek* MS-4
*Old Town Creek* NC-3
Old Town Creek—*stream* (6) AL-4
Old Town Creek—*stream* FL-3
Oldtown Creek—*stream* KY-4
Oldtown Creek—*stream* (4) OH-6
Oldtown Creek—*stream* SC-3
Old Town Creek—*stream* (2) TN-4
Old Town Creek—*stream* VA-3
Oldtown Creek—*stream* VA-3
Oldtown Creek—*stream* WV-2
Old Town Creek Ch—*church* (2) AL-4
Old Town Creek Sch (historical)—*school* TN-4
Old Town Creek Watershed Dam Number 24—*dam* AL-4
Old Town Creek Watershed Dam Number 25—*dam* AL-4
Old Town Creek Watershed Dam Number 26—*dam* AL-4
Old Town Creek Watershed Dam Number 31—*dam* AL-4
Old Town Creek Watershed Dam Number 32—*dam* AL-4
Old Town Creek Watershed Dam Number 37—*dam* AL-4
Old Town Creek Watershed Lake Number Thirty-one—*reservoir* AL-4
Old Town Creek Watershed Lake Number Thirty seven *reservoir* AL-4
Old Town Creek Watershed Lake Number Thirty-two—*reservoir* AL-4
Old Town Creek Watershed Lake Number 24—*reservoir* AL-4
Old Town Creek Watershed Lake Number 25—*reservoir* AL-4
Old Town Creek Watershed Lake Number 26—*reservoir* AL-4
Old Town Dam—*dam* SD-7
Old Towne—*post sta* CA-9
Old Towne Lake—*lake* NC-3
*Old Town Elementary School* NC-3
Old Towne Village Shop Ctr—*locale* FL-3
Old Town Farm—*hist pl* MA-1
Oldtown Flats—*locale* OH-6
Old Town Fort Collins—*hist pl* CO-8
Old Town Friends' Meetinghouse—*hist pl*. MD-2
Old Town Green Hist Dist—*hist pl* NY-2
Old Town Hall—*building* DE-2
Old Town Hall—*hist pl* (2) CT-1
Old Town Hall—*hist pl* DE-2
Old Town Hall—*hist pl* (2) MA-1
Old Town Hall Commercial Hist Dist—*hist pl* DE-2
Old Town Hall Hist Dist—*hist pl* MA-1
Old Town Hall Hist Dist—*hist pl* NY-2
Old Town Hammock—*island* FL-3
*Old Town Harbor* MA-1
**Old Town Harbor (subdivision)**—*pop pl* NC-3
Old Town Hill—*summit* MA-1
Old Town Hist Dist—*hist pl* (2) AL-4
Old Town Hist Dist—*hist pl* KY-4
Old Town Hist Dist—*hist pl* MO-7
Old Town Hist Dist—*hist pl* PA-2
Old Town (historical)—*locale* MS-4
**Old Town (historical)**—*pop pl* TN-4
Old Town House—*hist pl* MA-1
Old Town Lake—*lake* AR-4
Old Town Lake—*lake* TX-5
*Old Town Landing* SC-3
Old Town Landing—*locale* ME-1
Oldtown Landing—*locale* NC-3
**Old Town Landing**—*pop pl* MA-1
Old Town (Magisterial District)—*fmr MCD* . VA-3
Old Town Mine—*mine* CO-8
Old Town Mtn—*summit* WA-9
Old Town Neck—*cape* VA-3
*Old Town:Oldtown* MA-1
Old Town Overlook—*locale* MS-4
Old Town Plantation—*hist pl* NC-3
Old Town Plaza—*locale* NM-5
Old Town P.O. (historical)—*locale* AL-4
Old Town Point Wharf—*locale* MD-2
Old Town Pond—*lake* NY-2
*Oldtown Post Office* TN-4
Old Town Post Office (historical)—*building* TN-4
Old Town Public Use Area—*locale* KS-7
Old Town Residential Hist Dist—*hist pl* NM-5
Old Town Ridge—*ridge* AR-4
Oldtown Run—*stream* (2) OH-6
Oldtown Run—*stream* PA-2
Old Town Run—*stream* PA-2
**Old Town San Diego**—*pop pl* CA-9
Old Town San Diego Hist Dist—*hist pl* CA-9
Old Town San Diego State Historical Park—*park* CA-9
Old Town Sch—*school* FL-3
Old Town Sch—*school* NM-5
Old Town Sch—*school* NC-3
Oldtown Sch (historical)—*school* PA-2
Oldtown Sch (historical)—*school* TN-4
*Old Town School* TN-4
Old Township Ditch—*canal* IA-7
Old Town Shop Ctr—*locale* AL-4
Old Town Shop Ctr—*locale* (2) NC-3
Old Town (Site)—*locale* MT-8
Old Town Spring—*spring* VA-3
**Old Town Station**—*pop pl* NY-2
**Old Town (subdivision)**—*pop pl* AL-4
Old Town (Township of)—*fmr MCD* NC-3
**Oldtown (Township of)**—*pop pl* IL-6
Old Town Trading Post—*locale* OK-5
Old Town Triangle Hist Dist—*hist pl* IL-6
Old Town-Tuskahoma Cem—*cemetery* OK-5
Old Town Windmill—*locale* TX-5
Old Toxaway Ch—*church* NC-3
Old Trace Branch—*stream* (2) KY-4
Old Trace Creek—*stream* KY-4
Old Trace Park—*park* MS-4
Old Trail Point—*cliff* MT-8
Old Trail Ridge—*ridge* NC-3
Old Trails Bridge—*hist pl* AZ-5
Old Trails Highway Interchange—*crossing* AZ-5
Old Trails Park—*park* AZ-5
Old Trails (site)—*locale* AZ-5
*Oldtrap* NC-3
**Old Trap**—*pop pl* NC-3
**Old Trap**—*pop pl* VA-3
*Old Trap Bay* NC-3
Old Trap Island—*island* TN-4
Old Tree Island—*island* VA-3
Old Tree Swamp—*stream* NC-3
Old Trinity Cem—*cemetery* AL-4
Old Trinity Cem—*cemetery* AR-4
Old Trinity Cem—*cemetery* MD-2
Old Trinity Cem—*cemetery* ND-7
Old Trinity Cem—*cemetery* TX-5
**Old Tripoli**—*pop pl* IA-7
Old Triumph Mine—*mine* ID-8
Old Trolley Square—*locale* MA-1
**Old Trower**—*pop pl* VA-3
Old Troy Cem—*cemetery* TX-5
Old Troy Hosp—*hist pl* NY-2
Old Troy Park—*park* NJ-2
Old Tubac Schoolhouse—*hist pl* AZ-5
Old Tucson—*locale* AZ-5
Old Tulosa Ranch Site—*locale* TX-5
Old Tuloso Sch—*school* NM-5
Old Tunnel Mine—*mine* TN-4
Old Turkey Run Cem—*cemetery* IN-6
Old Turkey Windmill—*locale* TX-5
Old Turk Mtn—*summit* ME-1
Old Turnley Cem—*cemetery* TN-4
Old Turtle Creek—*gut* NJ-2
Old Turtle Point—*cape* NJ-2
Old Turtle Reach—*channel* NJ-2
Old Turtle Thorofare—*channel* NJ-2
Old Tuscaloosa County Jail—*hist pl* AL-4
Old Two Guns Ruin—*locale* AZ-5
Old Tyonek—*locale* AK-9
Old Tyonek Creek—*stream* AK-9
*Old Tyrone* MS-4
Old Ty Ty Ch—*church* GA-3
*Old Union* TN-4
Old Union—*locale* (2) TX-5
**Old Union**—*pop pl* AR-4
**Old Union**—*pop pl* MS-4
**Old Union**—*pop pl* (2) TX-5
*Old Union Baptist Church* AL-4
*Old Union Baptist Church* MS-4
Old Union Branch—*stream* AL-4
*Old Union Cem* TN-4
Old Union Cem—*cemetery* (4) AL-4
Old Union Cem—*cemetery* (4) AR-4
Old Union Cem—*cemetery* (2) GA-3
Old Union Cem—*cemetery* IL-6
Old Union Cem—*cemetery* (6) IN-6
Old Union Cem—*cemetery* (2) KY-4
Old Union Cem—*cemetery* (6) MS-4
Old Union Cem—*cemetery* (3) MO-7
Old Union Cem—*cemetery* OH-6
Old Union Cem—*cemetery* (2) PA-2
Old Union Cem—*cemetery* SC-3
Old Union Cem—*cemetery* (2) TN-4
Old Union Cem—*cemetery* (3) TX-5
*Old Union Ch* AL-4
*Old Union Ch* MS-4
Old Union Ch—*church* (8) AL-4
Old Union Ch—*church* (5) AR-4
Old Union Ch—*church* (2) GA-3
Old Union Ch—*church* (3) IL-6
Old Union Ch—*church* (6) IN-6
Old Union Ch—*church* (3) KY-4
Old Union Ch—*church* (2) LA-4
Old Union Ch—*church* (2) MS-4
Old Union Ch—*church* (2) MO-7
Old Union Ch—*church* (2) NC-3
Old Union Ch—*church* (2) PA-2
Old Union Ch—*church* (7) TN-4
Old Union Ch—*church* (3) TX-5
Old Union Ch (historical)—*church* MS-4
*Old Union Ch of Christ* TN-4
Old Union Church—*locale* DE-2
Old Union Church Cem—*cemetery* IN-6
Old Union County Courthouse—*hist pl* GA-3
Old Union County Courthouse—*hist pl* PA-2
Old Union Cumberland Presbyterian Ch—*church* TN-4
Old Union Depot—*hist pl* KS-7
Old Union Grove Cem—*cemetery* GA-3
Old Union Grove Cem—*cemetery* TN-4
*Old Union Grove Ch* TX-5
Old Union Grove Ch—*church* AL-4
Old Union Hill Cem—*cemetery* TX-5
Old Union Meetinghouse—*hist pl* ME-1
Old Union Methodist Church—*hist pl* DE-2
**Old Union (Poer)**—*pop pl* TX-5
*Old Union Sch* AL-4
Old Union Sch—*hist pl* (2) OH-6
Old Union Sch—*school* AL-4
Old Union Sch—*school* IL-6
Old Union Sch (historical)—*school* MS-4
Old United Methodist Cem—*cemetery* MO-7
Old Unity Cem—*cemetery* IN-6
Old Univ Library—*hist pl* NE-7
Old Urban Cemetery—*hist pl* PR-3
Old Uribano —*locale* TX-5
Old Ursuline Convent—*hist pl* LA-4
Old U.S. Courthouse and Post Office—*hist pl* KY-4

Olney Flat—*flat* WA-9
Olney Flat Drain—*canal* WA-9
Olney G S—*locale* OR-9
Olney (historical)—*locale* KS-7
Olney (historical)—*locale* MS-4
Olney HS—*hist pl* PA-2
Olney HS—*school* PA-2
Olney Lake—*lake* MI-6
Olney Lake—*lake* WA-9
Olney Lateral—*canal* CO-8
**Olney Mills**—*pop pl* MD-2
Olney Oil Field—*oilfield* TX-5
Olney Pass—*gap* WA-9
Olney Pond—*reservoir* RI-1
Olney Pond Dam—*dam* RI-1
Olney Recreation Center—*building* PA-2
Olney Run—*stream* OH-6
Olney Sch—*school* OH-6
Olney Sch—*school* PA-2
Olney Siding—*locale* UT-8
*Olneys Pond* RI-1
Olney Spring—*spring* WA-9
**Olney Springs**—*pop pl* CO-8
Olney Springs Cem—*cemetery* CO-8
Olney Springs Rsvr—*reservoir* CO-8
Olney Spring Water Supply—*well* CO-8
**Olney Square**—*pop pl* MD-2
**Olney (Township of)**—*pop pl* IL-6
**Olney (Township of)**—*pop pl* MN-6
*Olneyville* RI-1
**Olneyville**—*pop pl* RI-1
Olney Wasteway—*canal* CO-8
Olney Well Draw—*valley* AZ-5
Olney Well Draw—*valley* NM-5
Olngeuaol—*island* PW-9
*Olngewaol* PW-9
Olngooseenuk Mtn—*summit* AK-9
*Oloalu* HI-9
Oloava Crater—*crater* AS-9
*Olobetapel Inseln* PW-9
*Olobetapel Lagoon* PW-9
Olo Canyon—*valley* AZ-5
Oloewa—*civil* HI-9
Olofson Ridge—*ridge* CA-9
**Oloh**—*pop pl* MS-4
Oloh Baptist Ch—*church* MS-4
Oloh Cem—*cemetery* MS-4
Olokele Canyon—*valley* HI-9
Olokele Ditch—*canal* HI-9
Olokele River—*stream* HI-9
Olokele Trail—*trail* HI-9
*Oloku* HI-9
Olokui—*summit* HI-9
*Olokui Mtn* HI-9
*Ololian* PW-9
**Olomana**—*pop pl* HI-9
Olomana—*summit* HI-9
Olomana Golf Course—*other* HI-9
*Olomana Peak* HI-9
Olomana Ridge—*ridge* HI-9
Olomana Stream—*stream* HI-9
Olomanu Crater—*crater* AS-9
Olomatimu Crater—*crater* AS-9
Olo Mesa—*summit* AZ-5
Olomoana Mtn—*summit* AS-9
Olompali—*civil* CA-9
Olo Mtn—*summit* WA-9
Olopawa—*summit* HI-9
*Olopolis* KS-7
Olopua—*summit* HI-9
Olo Ridge—*ridge* AS-9
Olor Lake—*lake* MT-8
**Olosega**—*pop pl* AS-9
Olosega (County of)—*civ div* AS-9
Olosega Island—*island* AS-9
Olosega-Manu'a—*post sta* AS-9
*Olot* MP-9
Olotafatafa Ridge—*ridge* AS-9
Olotania Crater—*crater* AS-9
Olotele Mtn—*summit* AS-9
Olotina Point—*cape* AS-9
O'Loughlin Drain—*stream* MI-6
O'Loughlin Ranch—*locale* MT-8
O'Loughlin Sch—*school* MT-8
Oloupena—*beach* HI-9
Oloupena Falls—*falls* HI-9
Olovalu Crater—*crater* AS-9
*Olowalia* HI-9
Olowalu—*civil* HI-9
**Olowalu**—*pop pl* HI-9
Olowalu Ditch—*canal* HI-9
Olowalu Shaft (Well)—*well* HI-9
Olowalu Stream—*stream* HI-9
Olowalu Wharf—*locale* HI-9
**Olpe**—*pop pl* KS-7
Olpe City Dam—*dam* KS-7
Olpe City Lake—*reservoir* KS-7
Olpe Elem Sch—*school* KS-7
Olpe HS—*school* KS-7
Olpe JHS—*school* KS-7
Olpin, Joseph, House—*hist pl* UT-8
Ol Point—*cape* ME-1
Olquin Well—*well* NM-5
Olsacheltang—*summit* PW-9
**Olsburg**—*pop pl* KS-7
Olsburg Cem—*cemetery* KS-7
Olsen—*locale* ID-8
Olsen, Ben, House—*hist pl* WA-9
Olsen, Elias B., Ranch—*hist pl* SD-7
Olsen, Hans Peter, House—*hist pl* UT-8
Olsen, Mount—*summit* CA-9
Olsen Basin—*basin* WY-8
Olsen Bay—*bay* AK-9
Olsen Bench—*bench* UT-8
Olsen Canyon—*valley* CA-9
Olsen Canyon—*valley* NV-8
Olsen Canyon—*valley* (3) UT-8
Olsen Canyon—*valley* WA-9
Olsen Cem—*cemetery* SD-7
Olsen Corral—*summit* UT-8
Olsen Cove—*bay* AK-9
Olsen Creek—*stream* (4) CA-9
Olsen Creek—*stream* ID-8
Olsen Creek—*stream* MT-8
Olsen Creek—*stream* (2) OR-9
Olsen Creek—*stream* (2) WA-9
Olsen Creek—*stream* WY-8
Olsen Crossing—*locale* CA-9
Olsen Dam—*dam* SD-7
Olsen Dam—*dam* UT-8
Olsen Ditch—*canal* MT-8
Olsen Ditch—*canal* WY-8
Olsen Draw—*valley* (2) WY-8
Olsen Gulch—*valley* OR-9
Olsen Hill—*summit* MI-6
Olsen Hill—*summit* MT-8
Olsen (historical)—*locale* SD-7
Olsen Hollow—*valley* UT-8
**Olsen Homes (subdivision)**—*pop pl* NC-3
Olsen Island—*island* AK-9
Olsen JHS—*school* FL-3
*Olsen Lake* CO-8
Olsen Lake—*lake* CO-8
Olsen Lake—*lake* FL-3
Olsen Lake—*lake* UT-8
Olsen Meadows—*flat* CA-9
Olsen Mine—*mine* CA-9
Olsen Park Sch—*school* TX-5
*Olsen Peak* MT-8
Olsen Petroglyphs—*hist pl* CA-9
Olsen Ranch—*locale* (2) MT-8
Olsen Ranch—*locale* UT-8
Olsen Ranch—*locale* (2) WY-8
Olsen Rsvr—*reservoir* UT-8
*Olsen Ruby Creek Ditch* MT-8
Olsen Sch—*school* ND-7
Olsen Slough—*gut* ND-7
Olsen Slough—*lake* UT-8
Olsen Spring—*spring* (2) UT-8
Olsens Spring—*spring* UT-8
**Olsen Subdivision Number Two**—*pop pl* UT-8
Olsen Wash—*stream* AZ-5
Olso—*locale* FL-3
Olso Ch—*church* TX-5
Olso Lake—*lake* MN-6
Olson—*locale* MI-6
Olson—*locale* OR-9
Olson, Floyd B., House—*hist pl* MN-6
Olson, Joseph and Anna, Farm—*hist pl* TX-5
Olson, Lake—*lake* MN-6
Olson, Lewis, Log House—*hist pl* SD-7
Olson, Louis and Ellen, House—*hist pl* WA-9
Olson, Mount—*summit* WA-9
Olson, Oscar, House—*hist pl* MN-6
Olson Aerodrome—*airport* KS-7
*Olson Bay* MN-6
Olson Bay—*bay* (2) MN-6
Olson Bridge—*hist pl* SD-7
Olson Cabin—*locale* WY-8
*Olson Canyon* AZ-5
Olson Cem—*cemetery* CA-9
Olson Cem—*cemetery* CO-8
Olson Cem—*cemetery* ID-8
Olson Cem—*cemetery* IL-6
Olson Cem—*cemetery* (2) IA-7
Olson Cem—*cemetery* KS-7
Olson Cem—*cemetery* ND-7
Olson Cem—*cemetery* SD-7
Olson Cem—*cemetery* (2) WI-6
Olson Coulee—*valley* (2) MT-8
Olson Coulee—*valley* WI-6
Olson Creek—*stream* AK-9
Olson Creek—*stream* (4) ID-8
Olson Creek—*stream* (4) MI-6
Olson Creek—*stream* (4) MT-8
Olson Creek—*stream* OR-9
Olson Creek—*stream* (2) SD-7
Olson Creek—*stream* (3) WA-9
Olson Creek—*stream* WY-8
Olson Creek (historical)—*stream* SD-7
Olson Dam—*dam* (2) ND-7
Olson Dam*—*dam* ND-7
Olson Ditch—*canal* MT-8
Olson Drain—*canal* ID-8
Olson Draw—*valley* SD-7
Olson Draw—*valley* (2) WY-8
Olson Field—*airport* KS-7
Olson Grove—*woods* CA-9
Olson Gulch—*valley* ID-8
Olson Gulch—*valley* (2) MT-8
Olson-Hanson Farm—*hist pl* TX-5
Olson Hill—*summit* WA-9
Olson Homestead—*locale* MT-8
Olson JHS—*school* MN-6
*Olson Lake* MI-6
Olson Lake—*lake* AK-9
Olson Lake—*lake* MI-6
Olson Lake—*lake* (9) MN-6
Olson Lake—*lake* (2) ND-7
Olson Lake—*lake* (2) WA-9
Olson Lake—*lake* (2) WI-6
Olson Lateral—*canal* ID-8
Olson Lookout Tower—*locale* WV-2
Olson Meadows—*flat* OR-9
Olson Meadow Spring—*spring* NV-8
Olson Memorial Park—*park* IL-6
Olson Mine—*mine* ID-8
Olson Mound Group—*hist pl* WI-6
Olson Mtn—*summit* CA-9
Olson Mtn—*summit* (2) MT-8
Olson Mtn—*summit* OR-9
Olson Natl Wildlife Ref—*park* ND-7
Olson-Nelson Farm—*hist pl* TX-5
Olson Number 1 Dam—*dam* SD-7
Olson Number 2 Dam—*dam* SD-7
Olson Number 3 Dam—*dam* SD-7
Olson Oil Field—*oilfield* TX-5
Olson Park—*flat* MT-8
Olson Park—*park* IL-6
Olson Park—*park* MI-6
Olson Park—*park* SD-7
Olson Peak—*summit* (4) MT-8
Olson Peak—*summit* WA-9
Olson Place—*locale* CO-8
Olson Place—*locale* MT-8
Olson Pond—*lake* CA-9
Olson Pond—*reservoir* AL-4
Olson Pond—*reservoir* ID-8
Olson Private Airstrip—*airport* ND-7
Olson Ranch—*locale* (2) MT-8
Olson Ranch—*locale* NE-7
Olson Ranch—*locale* (2) ND-7
Olson Ranch—*locale* (2) SD-7
Olson Ranch—*locale* (2) WY-8
Olson Ranches Number 1 Dam—*dam* SD-7
Olson Ranches Number 10 Dam—*dam* SD-7
Olson Ranches Number 2 Dam—*dam* SD-7
Olson Ranches Number 5 Dam—*dam* SD-7
Olson Ranches Number 7 Dam—*dam* SD-7
Olson Ridge—*ridge* CO-8
Olson Rsvr—*reservoir* MT-8
Olson Russell Number 2 Dam—*dam* SD-7
Olsons Bay—*bay* WI-6
Olsons Brook—*stream* CT-1
Olson Sch—*school* (2) IL-6
Olson Sch—*school* MI-6
Olson Sch—*school* MN-6
Olson Sch—*school* NE-7
Olson Sch—*school* (2) SD-7
Olsons Lake—*lake* AK-9
Olson Slough—*lake* ND-7
Olson Spring—*spring* (2) MT-8
Olson Spring—*spring* WA-9
Olson Spring—*spring* WY-8
Olson Springs—*spring* WY-8
Olson Spur—*locale* WA-9
**Olson Township**—*pop pl* ND-7
Olson Valley—*valley* WI-6
**Olsonville**—*pop pl* SD-7
Olson Well—*well* AZ-5
Olson Well—*well* WY-8
Olso Square (Shop Ctr)—*locale* FL-3
Olsson, Captain Bror W., House—*hist pl* OR-9
Olssons Pond—*reservoir* VA-3
Olstad Ranch—*locale* ND-7
**Olszeski**—*pop pl* OH-6
**Olszeski Town**—*pop pl* OH-6
*Olterukel* PW-9
Olterukl—*island* PW-9
Oltman Sch—*school* MN-6
**Olton**—*pop pl* TX-5
Olton (CCD)—*cens area* TX-5
Olton Cem—*cemetery* TX-5
Olton Country Club—*other* TX-5
Olton Pumping Station—*other* TX-5
*Olualu* HI-9
Oluf Draw—*valley* WY-8
Oluf Rsvr—*reservoir* WY-8
*Oluksakel* PW-9
Olumagwilute River—*stream* AK-9
*Oluman Creek* WA-9
Olumpic Mountains—*range* WA-9
Olund Lake—*lake* MI-6
**Olustee**—*pop pl* AL-4
**Olustee**—*pop pl* (2) FL-3
**Olustee**—*pop pl* OK-5
Olustee Battlefield—*hist pl* FL-3
Olustee Battlefield State Monmt—*park* FL-3
Olustee Creek—*stream* AL-4
Olustee Creek—*stream* (2) FL-3
Olustee Experimental For—*forest* FL-3
Olustee Tower—*tower* FL-3
Olusty Creek (historical)—*locale* AL-4
Olutsee Cem—*cemetery* OK-5
**Olvey**—*pop pl* AR-4
Olvey Cem—*cemetery* AR-4
Olvey Cem—*cemetery* IN-6
Olvey Ch—*church* AR-4
Olvey (Township of)—*fmr MCD* AR-4
Olvida Penas—*hist pl* CA-9
Olvis Cem—*cemetery* MS-4
Olvis Grove Ch—*church* MS-4
Olwell Sch (historical)—*school* MO-7
**Olwen Heights**—*pop pl* PA-2
OL Windmill—*locale* TX-5
Olympia—*locale* MO-7
**Olympia**—*pop pl* CA-9
**Olympia**—*pop pl* KY-4
**Olympia**—*pop pl* NC-3
**Olympia**—*pop pl* SC-3
**Olympia**—*pop pl* WA-9
Olympia—*uninc pl* WA-9
Olympia, Lake—*lake* FL-3
Olympia, Lake—*reservoir* GA-3
Olympia, The—*hist pl* MO-7
Olympia Airp—*airport* WA-9
Olympia Bar—*bar* UT-8
Olympia (CCD)—*cens area* WA-9
Olympia Cem—*cemetery* SC-3
Olympia Creek—*stream* AK-9
Olympia East (CCD)—*cens area* WA-9
**Olympia Fields**—*pop pl* IL-6
Olympia Fields Country Club—*other* IL-6
**Olympia Gardens**—*pop pl* IL-6
**Olympia Heights**—*pop pl* FL-3
Olympia Heights Ch—*church* FL-3
Olympia Heights Elem Sch—*school* FL-3
Olympia Heights Shop Ctr—*locale* FL-3
Olympia Heights United Methodist Day Care—*school* FL-3
Olympia Junior Acad—*school* WA-9
Olympia Lakes—*lake* NJ-2
Olympia Marsh—*swamp* WA-9
*Olympia Mills* SC-3
Olympia Mine—*mine* NV-8
Olympia Mine—*mine* SD-7
Olympia Natl Bank—*hist pl* WA-9
**Olympian Village**—*pop pl* MO-7
**Olympia (Olympia Mills)**—*pop pl* SC-3
Olympia Park—*park* IL-6
Olympia Park—*park* PA-2
Olympia Park—*park* TX-5
Olympia Public Library—*hist pl* WA-9
Olympia Sch—*school* (2) CA-9
Olympia Shoal—*bar* WA-9
Olympia Spa Country Club—*locale* AL-4
Olympia Springs—*locale* KY-4
Olympia Stadium—*locale* MI-6
Olympia State For—*forest* KY-4
Olympia Substation—*other* WA-9
Olympia Theater and Office Bldg—*hist pl* FL-3
Olympia Water Supply—*other* WA-9
Olympia Well—*well* NM-5
Olympia West (CCD)—*cens area* WA-9
Olympic—*uninc pl* CA-9
Olympic Arena—*other* NY-2
Olympic Bobsled Run—*other* NY-2
Olympic (CCD)—*cens area* WA-9
Olympic Club Saloon—*hist pl* WA-9
Olympic Coll—*school* WA-9
Olympic Golf Club—*other* CA-9
*Olympic Heights* FL-3
*Olympic Heights* WA-9
Olympic Hills Sch—*school* WA-9
Olympic Hotel—*hist pl* WA-9
Olympic Hot Springs—*locale* WA-9
Olympic HS—*school* NC-3
Olympic Landing—*locale* LA-4
Olympic Memorial Garden Cem—*cemetery* WA-9
Olympic Memorial Hosp—*hospital* WA-9
Olympic Mountians—*range* WA-9
Olympic Natl For—*forest* WA-9
Olympic Natl Park—*park* WA-9
Olympic Natl Park HQ—*locale* WA-9
Olympic Park—*park* NJ-2
Olympic Power Plant—*other* WA-9
Olympic Sch—*school* CA-9
Olympic Sch—*school* WA-9
Olympic Shore—*locale* WA-9
Olympic Ski Jump—*other* NY-2
Olympic Stadium—*other* WA-9
*Olympic Terrace* IL-6
*Olympic Valley* CA-9
**Olympic Valley (Squaw Valley)**—*pop pl* CA-9
**Olympic View**—*pop pl* WA-9
Olympic View Sch—*school* (2) WA-9
*Olympic Village* IL-6
**Olympic Woods (subdivision)**—*pop pl* NC-3
Olympie Creek—*stream* AK-9
*Olympus* VT-1
Olympus—*locale* IA-7
**Olympus**—*pop pl* VT-1
Olympus, Mount—*summit* (2) CA-9
Olympus, Mount—*summit* CO-8
Olympus, Mount—*summit* HI-9
Olympus, Mount—*summit* KY-4
Olympus, Mount—*summit* UT-8
Olympus, Mount—*summit* VT-1
Olympus, Mount—*summit* WA-9
Olympus Cem—*cemetery* OK-5
Olympus Cem—*cemetery* TX-5
Olympus Dam—*dam* CO-8
Olympus Dam—*dam* PA-2
Olympus Guard Station—*locale* WA-9
**Olympus Heights**—*pop pl* CO-8
**Olympus Heights Subdivision**—*pop pl* UT-8
**Olympus Heights (subdivision)**—*pop pl* UT-8
Olympus Hills Shop Ctr—*locale* UT-8
Olympus HS—*school* UT-8
Olympus JHS—*school* UT-8
*Olympus Lake* PA-2
Olympus Lake—*lake* NY-2
Olympus Mine—*mine* CA-9
*Olympus Peak* HI-9
Olympus Pond—*reservoir* PA-2
Olympus Pool—*lake* VT-1
Olympus Post Office (historical)—*building* TN-4
**Olympus Shadows Estates Subdivision**—*pop pl* UT-8
Olympus Tunnel—*tunnel* CO-8
**Olympus View Heights**—*pop pl* UT-8
Olympus View Hosp—*hospital* UT-8
**Olympus View Subdivision**—*pop pl* UT-8
**Olyphant**—*pop pl* AR-4
**Olyphant**—*pop pl* PA-2
Olyphant Borough—*civil* PA-2
Olyphant HS—*school* PA-2
Olyphant Number Three Dam—*dam* PA-2
*Olyphant Number Three Reservoir* PA-2
Olyphant Number Two Dam—*dam* PA-2
*Olyphant Number Two Reservoir* PA-2
Olyphant Number Two Shaft—*mine* PA-2
Olyphant Rsvr No 1—*reservoir* PA-2
Olyphant Rsvr No 2—*reservoir* PA-2
Olyphant Rsvr No 3—*reservoir* PA-2
Olyphic—*locale* NC-3
Olyphic Post Office—*locale* NC-3
Oma—*locale* MS-4
**Oma**—*pop pl* (2) AR-4
Oma, Finol—*summit* FM-9
Oma Blanca—*summit* NM-5
Oma Cem—*cemetery* AR-4
Oma Ch—*church* WV-2
Omaday Lake—*lake* MN-6
Omadi—*fmr MCD* NE-7
**Omage**—*pop pl* AR-4
*Omager Creek* CA-9
Omaha—*locale* AL-4
Omaha—*locale* KY-4
Omaha—*locale* MO-7
Omaha—*locale* VA-3
**Omaha**—*pop pl* AR-4
**Omaha**—*pop pl* GA-3
**Omaha**—*pop pl* IL-6
**Omaha**—*pop pl* KY-4
**Omaha**—*pop pl* NE-7
**Omaha**—*pop pl* TX-5
Omaha Beach—*beach* IA-7
Omaha Bend—*bend* IA-7
Omaha Bend—*bend* NE-7
Omaha (CCD)—*cens area* GA-3
Omaha Country Club—*other* NE-7
Omaha Creek—*stream* ID-8
Omaha Creek—*stream* NE-7
Omaha Creek—*stream* SD-7
Omaha Creek Ditch—*canal* NE-7
**Omaha (Crikett)**—*pop pl* AR-4
Omaha Depot—*hist pl* MN-6
Omaha HS—*hist pl* NE-7
**Omaha Ind Res**—*pop pl* NE-7
Omaha Ind Res—*reserve* IA-7
Omaha Mine—*mine* WY-8
Omaha Natl Bank Bldg—*hist pl* NE-7
Omaha Oil And Gas Field—*other* IL-6
Omaha Point—*cape* IA-7
Omaha Public Library—*hist pl* NE-7
Omaha Quartermaster Depot Hist Dist—*hist pl* NE-7
Omaha Springs—*locale* GA-3
**Omaha Township**—*pop pl* NE-7
Omaha (Township of)—*fmr MCD* AR-4
**Omaha (Township of)**—*pop pl* IL-6
Omaha Tribal Cem—*cemetery* NE-7
Omaha Valley Cem—*cemetery* NE-7
*O'Mahoney Lake* UT-8
*Omahundra Millpond* VA-3
*Omahundra Run* VA-3
**Omak**—*pop pl* WA-9
Omak Airp—*airport* WA-9
Omak (CCD)—*cens area* WA-9
Omak Creek—*stream* WA-9
Omak Lake—*lake* WA-9
Omak Memorial Cem—*cemetery* WA-9
*Omak Mountains* WA-9
Omak Mtn—*summit* WA-9
Omakstalia Point—*cape* AK-9
**Omal**—*pop pl* OH-6
O'Maley Sch—*school* MA-1
Omalik Creek—*stream* AK-9
Omalik Hill—*summit* AK-9
Omalik Lagoon—*bay* AK-9
Omalik River—*stream* AK-9
O'Malley Brook—*stream* NY-2
Omalley Cem—*cemetery* MO-7
O'Malley Ditch—*canal* IN-6
O'Malley Draw—*valley* WY-8
O'Malley Lake—*lake* AK-9
O'Malley Peak—*summit* AK-9
O'Malley River—*stream* AK-9
Omaluruk Creek—*stream* AK-9
Oman Ranch—*locale* WA-9
Oman Ranch Airp—*airport* UT-8
Omans—*locale* WA-9
Omans Creek—*stream* MI-6
Omans Ranch—*locale* UT-8
**Omao**—*pop pl* HI-9
Omao Gulch—*valley* HI-9
Omao Homesteads—*civil* HI-9
Omaokoili—*summit* HI-9
Omaopio—*civil* HI-9
Omaopio Homesteads—*other* HI-9
Omao Rsvr—*reservoir* HI-9
Omao Stream—*stream* (2) HI-9
Omao Valley—*valley* HI-9
Oma Park—*park* WI-6
**Omapio**—*pop pl* HI-9
*Omar* MS-4
*Omar* WV-2
Omar—*locale* DE-2
Omar—*locale* IL-6
Omar—*locale* NV-8
Omar—*locale* OH-6
**Omar**—*pop pl* NY-2
**Omar**—*pop pl* WV-2
O'Mara Creek—*stream* WY-8
Omara Gulch—*valley* WY-8
Omar Cave—*cave* AL-4
Omar Cem—*cemetery* NY-2
Omar Cem—*cemetery* OH-6
Omar Chapel—*hist pl* OH-6
Omar Creek—*stream* (2) AK-9
Omar Creek—*stream* WI-6
Omard Cem—*cemetery* MI-6
Omard Ch—*church* MI-6
Omard Drain—*canal* MI-6
Omar Gause Sch—*school* WA-9
Omar Gibson Vocational-Technical Sch—*school* MO-7
Omar (historical)—*locale* AL-4
*Omar Mill Branch* DE-2
Omar Mtn—*summit* MT-8
Omar N Bradley Airp—*airport* MO-7
Omar Neff Ditch—*canal* IN-6
*Omar P.O.* AL-4
Omar Post Office (historical)—*building* TN-4
Omar River—*stream* AK-9
*Omarsville* KY-4
O'Mary Cem—*cemetery* AL-4
Omary Lake—*reservoir* NJ-2
Oma Sch—*school* OK-5
**Oma (Town of)**—*pop pl* WI-6
*Omau Stream* HI-9
Omaya Ranch—*locale* CA-9
Ombelim Channel—*channel* MP-9
Ombelim Island—*island* MP-9
*Ombelim Pass* MP-9
*Ombelim-Sand* MP-9
*Ombe Range* NV-8
Ombey—*locale* UT-8
*Ombiririen-suido* MP-9
*Ombiririen-to* MP-9
*Ombit-o-pah Creek* UT-8
O M Ch—*church* OK-5
*OMCO* NV-8
OMCO Mine—*mine* NV-8
Omco Wash—*stream* NV-8
OM Creek—*stream* TX-5
*Ome* MO-7
Omeara Point—*cape* WA-9
*Omebael* PW-9
Omechedecheraol Mesang—*island* PW-9
Omeduaol—*island* PW-9
Omega—*locale* (2) AR-4
Omega—*locale* CO-8
Omega—*locale* ID-8
Omega—*locale* KY-4
Omega—*locale* LA-4
Omega—*locale* NM-5
Omega—*locale* VA-3
**Omega**—*pop pl* AL-4
**Omega**—*pop pl* CA-9
**Omega**—*pop pl* GA-3
**Omega**—*pop pl* IL-6
**Omega**—*pop pl* IN-6
**Omega**—*pop pl* LA-4
**Omega**—*pop pl* MS-4
**Omega**—*pop pl* OH-6
**Omega**—*pop pl* OK-5
Omega (CCD)—*cens area* GA-3
Omega Cem—*cemetery* GA-3
Omega Cem—*cemetery* OH-6
Omega Cem—*cemetery* OK-5
Omega Ch—*church* AL-4
Omega Ch—*church* AR-4
Omega Ch—*church* IN-6
Omega Chapter of the Chi Phi Fraternity—*hist pl* GA-3
Omega Creek—*stream* AK-9
Omega Diggings—*locale* CA-9
Omega Gulch—*valley* AK-9
Omega (historical)—*locale* AL-4
**Omega (historical)**—*pop pl* TN-4
Omega Island—*island* AK-9
Omega Lake—*lake* MN-6
Omega Lake—*lake* MT-8
Omega Landing (historical)—*locale* (2) MS-4
Omega Mine—*mine* AZ-5
Omega Mine—*mine* (2) CA-9
Omega Mine—*mine* CO-8
Omega Mine (historical)—*mine* SD-7
Omega Mine (underground)—*mine* AL-4
Omega Point—*cape* AK-9
Omega Pond—*lake* RI-1
Omega Pond—*reservoir* RI-1
Omega Pond Dam—*dam* RI-1
Omega Post Office (historical)—*building* TN-4
Omega Sch—*school* SC-3
Omega Township—*fmr MCD* IA-7
Omega (Township of)—*fmr MCD* AR-4
**Omega (Township of)**—*pop pl* IL-6
*Omekang* PW-9
Omelaktavik, Lake—*lake* AK-9
Omelek—*island* MP-9
*Omelek Island* MP-9
Omelochel—*island* PW-9
O'Melveny Sch—*school* CA-9
**Omemee**—*pop pl* ND-7
O-Me-Mee Lake—*lake* MN-6
**Omen**—*pop pl* TX-5
**Omena**—*pop pl* MI-6
Omena Bay—*bay* MI-6
*Omena Lake* MI-6
Omena Lake—*lake* (2) MI-6
Omena Point—*cape* MI-6
*Omenee* ND-7
Omen Lake—*lake* MN-6
Omenoku Point—*cape* CA-9
Omen Road Bay—*bay* TX-5
O'Men Village Site—*hist pl* CA-9
Omer—*locale* KY-4
Omer—*locale* MO-7
**Omer**—*pop pl* MI-6
Omera Meadow—*flat* WY-8
Omera Spring—*spring* WY-8
Omer Branch—*stream* MO-7
Omer Cem—*cemetery* MO-7
Omer Ch—*church* GA-3
Omer Lake—*lake* WI-6
Omer Plains—*flat* MI-6
Omer/Pound House—*hist pl* KY-4
*Omesiochel* PW-9
Omete Creek—*stream* MO-7
Ometochel—*summit* PW-9
*Ometochl* PW-9
*Ometubei River* PW-9
Omeys Slough—*gut* IL-6
O & M Facilities Heliport—*airport* WA-9
O. M. H. Airp—*airport* WA-9
Omholt Cem—*cemetery* MT-8
Omi—*locale* NY-2
Omiaktalik, Lake—*lake* AK-9
Omicron Hill—*summit* AK-9
Omidkill—*cape* PW-9
Omie Cem—*cemetery* ND-7
Omikmak Creek—*stream* AK-9
Omikmuktusuk River—*stream* AK-9
Omikviorok River—*stream* AK-9
Omilak—*locale* AK-9
Omilak Creek—*stream* AK-9
Omilak Mtn—*summit* AK-9
Omild Slough—*lake* ND-7
Omill—*locale* ID-8
*Omin* FM-9
Omio (historical)—*locale* KS-7
Omiotl—*summit* PW-9
Omira—*locale* CA-9
Omiscol, Lake—*reservoir* VA-3
*O M Iwan Dam* SD-7
Omleblochel, Rois—*summit* PW-9
Omlee—*locale* NM-5
Ommaney, Cape—*cape* AK-9
Ommaney Bay—*bay* AK-9
Ommaney Peak—*summit* AK-9
*Ommelanden Park* DE-2
Ommelander Park—*park* DE-2
*Omnia* KS-7
**Omnia Township**—*pop pl* KS-7
OMNI International of Miami (Shop Ctr)—*locale* FL-3
Omni Plaza—*post sta* FL-3
Omni Range Radio Facility—*tower* AZ-5
*Omobodo River* PW-9
*Omobod River* PW-9
Omochumnes—*civil* CA-9
Omodes—*channel* PW-9
Omoe—*summit* HI-9
*Omoe Peak* HI-9
Omogar Creek—*stream* CA-9
Omohundra Millpond—*reservoir* VA-3
Omohundra Run—*stream* VA-3
Omohundro Hollow—*valley* TN-4
Omohundro Water Filtration Complex District—*hist pl* TN-4
*Omoi* HI-9
Omokaa—*civil* HI-9
Omokaa Bay—*bay* HI-9
Omo Mine—*mine* CA-9
*Omoobod River* PW-9
**Omo Ranch**—*pop pl* CA-9
Omp—*unknown* FM-9
Omphghent Sch—*school* IL-6
**Omphghent (Township of)**—*pop pl* IL-6
Omphus Ridge—*ridge* NC-3
Ompompanoosuc River—*stream* VT-1
Omps—*locale* WV-2
Omro—*locale* NY-2
**Omro**—*pop pl* WI-6
Omro Cem—*cemetery* WI-6
Omro HS, Annex and Webster Manual Training Sch—*hist pl* WI-6
Omro Junction Cem—*cemetery* WI-6
Omro State Wildlife Mngmt Area—*park* MN-6
**Omro (Town of)**—*pop pl* WI-6
**Omro (Township of)**—*pop pl* MN-6
Omro Union Cem—*cemetery* WI-6
Omruchel, Bkul A—*cape* PW-9
O. M. Scott & Sons (Plant)—*facility* OH-6
Omsrud Lake—*lake* MN-6
Omstead Spring—*spring* CO-8
Omstott Creek—*stream* CA-9
Omualdo, Cerro—*summit* CA-9
Omuchel—*bar* PW-9
Omus—*locale* CA-9
*Omusee* AL-4
Omusee Creek—*stream* AL-4
Omusee Creek Public Use Area—*park* AL-4
Omusee Post Office (historical)—*building* AL-4
*Omussee Creek* AL-4
Omussee Creek Sewage Treatment Plant—*locale* AL-4
*On* FM-9
*Ona* FM-9
Ona—*locale* OR-9
**Ona**—*pop pl* FL-3
**Ona**—*pop pl* WV-2

Ona, Lake—*lake* MI-6
Ona Beach—*beach* OR-9
Ona Beach State Park—*park* OR-9
*Onaf* FM-9
Onaf—*island* FM-9
**Onaga**—*pop pl* KS-7
Onaga Airp—*airport* KS-7
Onaga Cem—*cemetery* KS-7
Onaga Elem Sch—*school* KS-7
Onaga HS—*school* KS-7
Onagon Lake—*lake* MN-6
Onahan Sch—*school* IL-6
Onahu Creek—*stream* CO-8
Onahu Creek Trail—*trail* CO-8
**Onaka**—*pop pl* SD-7
Onaker Sch—*school* NH-1
**Onalaska**—*pop pl* TX-5
**Onalaska**—*pop pl* WA-9
**Onalaska**—*pop pl* WI-6
Onalaska, Lake—*reservoir* WI-6
Onalaska Lookout—*locale* TX-5
**Onalaska (Town of)**—*pop pl* WI-6
Onamac Point—*cape* WA-9
**Onamia**—*pop pl* MN-6
Onamia, Lake—*reservoir* MN-6
Onamia Municipal Hall—*hist pl* MN-6
**Onamia (Township of)**—*pop pl* MN-6
*Onamoe* FM-9
*Onamue Island* FM-9
*Onan* FM-9
Onan—*locale* VA-3
Onan, As—*slope* MH-9
O'Nan Bend—*bend* KY-4
**Onancock**—*pop pl* VA-3
Onancock Cem—*cemetery* VA-3
Onancock Creek—*stream* VA-3
*Onancock River* VA-3
Onandaga Falls—*falls* PA-2
Onanei—*bar* FM-9
*Onao Island* FM-9
**Onapa**—*pop pl* OK-5
Onapa Lake—*reservoir* OK-5
*Onapuka* HI-9
Onaqui—*locale* UT-8
Onaqui Division—*civil* UT-8
*Onaqui Mountain Range* UT-8
*Onaqui Mountains* UT-8
Onaqui Mtns—*range* UT-8
*Onaqui Range* UT-8
Onaram—*island* FM-9
Onareng, Unun En—*bar* FM-9
**Onarga**—*pop pl* IL-6
**Onarga (Township of)**—*pop pl* IL-6
Onari Island—*island* FM-9
Onari (Municipality)—*civ div* FM-9
Onas—*island* FM 9
Onativia—*locale* NY-2
On-a-Tree Cem—*cemetery* SD-7
On-a-Tree Ch—*church* SD-7
*Onau* FM-9
Onau—*civil* HI-9
Onava—*locale* NM-5
Onawa—*locale* ME-1
**Onawa**—*pop pl* IA-7
Onawa, Lake—*lake* ME-1
Onawa Junction—*locale* IA-7
Onawa Public Library—*hist pl* IA-7
Onawasa Creek—*stream* NY-2
**Onaway**—*pop pl* ID-8
**Onaway**—*pop pl* MI-6
Onaway Island—*island* WI-6
*Onaway Lake* ME-1
Onaway Sch—*school* OH-6
Onaway State Park—*park* MI-6
Onberg—*locale* PA-2
*Onbirien To* MP-9
*Onbiririen Suido* MP-9
*Onbiririen To* MP-9
**Onchiota**—*pop pl* NY-2
Oncio Pond—*lake* NY-2
Oncle John, Cypriere a—*swamp* LA-4
*Oncocus River* NJ-2
Onda—*locale* AR-4
Ondaig Island—*island* WI-6
Ondassagon Sch—*school* WI-6
**Ondawa**—*pop pl* NY-2
Ondawa, Lake—*reservoir* PA-2
Onderdonk, Horatio Gates, House—*hist pl* NY-2
Onderdonk, Isaac, House—*hist pl* NJ-2
Onderdonk Lake—*lake* NY-2
Onderdunk Lake—*lake* TX-5
Ondessonk Camp—*locale* IL-6
on Ditch, An—*canal* CO-8
One, Lake—*lake* AK-9
One, Lake—*lake* AZ-5
One, Lake—*lake* CA-9
One, Lake—*lake* LA-4
One, Lake—*lake* MI-6
One, Lake—*lake* MN-6
One, Lake—*lake* (3) WI-6
One, Lake—*reservoir* MN-6
One, Lake No—*reservoir* (2) AR-4
One, Well—*well* NV-8
One-A, Lateral—*canal* NV-8
One Accorn Ch—*church* VA-3
One Acre Lake—*lake* MN-6
*Oneal* WV-2
O'Neal—*locale* AL-4
O'Neal—*locale* AR-4
O Neal—*locale* GA-3
O'Neal—*locale* VA-3
**Oneal**—*pop pl* AL-4
**O'Neal**—*pop pl* SC-3
O'Neal, George, House—*hist pl* KY-4
O'Neal, James, House—*hist pl* KY-4
O'Neal, Lewis, Tavern—*hist pl* KY-4
O'Neal Branch—*stream* MS-4
O'Neal Branch—*stream* TN-4
O'Neal Bridge—*bridge* AL-4
*O'Neal Brook* MN-6
O'Neal Canyon—*valley* CA-9
*O'Neal Cem* TN-4
O'Neal Cem—*cemetery* (3) AL-4
O'Neal Cem—*cemetery* GA-3
O'Neal Cem—*cemetery* IL-6
O'Neal Cem—*cemetery* IN-6
O'Neal Cem—*cemetery* (4) MS-4
O'Neal Cem—*cemetery* NC-3
O'Neal Cem—*cemetery* (3) TN-4
Oneal Cem—*cemetery* TX-5
O'Neal Cem—*cemetery* TX-5
O'Neal Ch—*church* AL-4
O'Neal Ch—*church* SC-3
*O'Neal Ch of Christ* AL-4
*O'neal Creek* CO-8
O'Neal Creek—*stream* AR-4
O'Neal Creek—*stream* CO-8
O'Neal Creek—*stream* MI-6
O'Neal Creek—*stream* TX-5
O'Neal Harbor—*bay* AL-4
O'Neal Hill—*summit* CO-8
O'Neal Hill—*summit* OK-5
O'Neal Hollow—*valley* TN-4
One Alii Park—*park* HI-9
O'Neal Island—*island* WA-9
O'Neal Jackson Lake Dam—*dam* MS-4
O'Neal Lake—*lake* MI-6
O'Neal Lake—*lake* MS-4
O'Neal Lake—*lake* SD-7
O'Neal Lake—*reservoir* MO-7
O'Neal Lake—*reservoir* TN-4
O'Neal Lake Dam—*dam* MS-4
O'Neal Lake Dam—*dam* TN-4
*O'Neall Brook* MN-6
O'Neall Cem—*cemetery* IN-6
O'Neall Ditch—*canal* IN-6
O'Neal Lookout Tower—*locale* AL-4
O'Neal Oil Field—*oilfield* (2) TX-5
O'Neal Park—*flat* CO-8
O'Neal Park—*park* AZ-5
O'Neal Peak—*summit* NV-8
O'Neal Point—*cape* AL-4
O'Neal Point—*cape* MS-4
O'Neal Post Office (historical)—*building* AL-4
O'Neal Ranch—*locale* CA-9
ONeal Ranch—*locale* NM-5
O'Neal Rsvr—*reservoir* OR-9
**O'Neals**—*pop pl* CA-9
*O'Neals Branch* NJ-2
*O'Neal Sch* TN-4
O'Neal Sch—*school* AR-4
O'Neal Sch—*school* MO-7
Oneal Sch—*school* TN-4
O'Neal Sch (historical)—*school* AL-4
O'Neal Sch (historical)—*school* TN-4
*O'Neals Creek* MS-4
O'Neals Creek Landing—*locale* MS-4
O'Neals Crossroads—*locale* GA-3
O'Neals Landing—*locale* TN-4
O'Neal Slough—*gut* CA-9
O'Neals Meadow—*flat* CA-9
O'Neal Spring—*spring* CO-8
O'Neals Springs—*spring* CA-9
O'Neals Township—*civil* NC-3
*O'Neal Switch* MS-4
O'Neal Tank—*reservoir* NM-5
*Onean* FM-9
One Arm Creek—*stream* TX-5
One Arroyo—*stream* NM-5
Oneatta Point—*cape* OR-9
Oneawa Hills—*summit* HI-9
One Bee Camp—*locale* CA-9
One Buck Lake—*lake* WI-6
One Cabin Creek—*stream* WY-8
Onecho Cem—*cemetery* WA-9
Onecho Ch—*church* WA-9
Onecho Post Office (historical)—*building* TN-4
Oneck—*cape* NY-2
Oneck Drain—*stream* NY-2
**Oneco**—*pop pl* CT-1
**Oneco**—*pop pl* FL-3
**Oneco**—*pop pl* IL-6
Oneco Cem—*cemetery* IL-6
Oneco Elem Sch—*school* FL-3
Oneco Pond—*reservoir* CT-1
Oneco Square Shop Ctr—*locale* FL-3
**Oneco (Township of)**—*pop pl* IL-6
One Cottonwood Canyon—*valley* AZ-5
One Creek—*stream* (2) MT-8
One Creek—*stream* (2) OK-5
One Creek, Lake—*stream* WI-6
One Creek Cem—*cemetery* OK-5
One Creek Trail—*trail* OK-5
*Oneday* FM-9
One Doe Spring—*spring* OR-9
One-Eighty Windmill—*locale* NM-5
O'Neel, Mount—*summit* AK-9
O'Neel-Blackburn House—*hist pl* AR-4
O'Neel Cem—*cemetery* AR-4
One Eleven Detention Dam—*dam* AZ-5
One Eye Canyon—*valley* UT-8
*One Eye Creek* TX-5
One Eye Creek—*stream* CA-9
One Eye Creek—*stream* (2) TX-5
One Eyed Creek—*stream* CA-9
Oneeyed Flat—*flat* CA-9
Onega—*locale* MN-6
*Onega Lake* MN-6
Onega Lake—*lake* MI-6
**Onego**—*pop pl* WV-2
*One Haul Bay* AK-9
*Onehehee* HI-9
One Hole Spring—*spring* CA-9
One Horn Basin—*basin* MT-8
One Horn Canyon—*valley* AZ-5
One Horn Canyon—*valley* NM-5
One Horn Mtn—*summit* TX-5
One Horn Tank—*reservoir* AZ-5
One Horse Canyon—*valley* UT-8
One Horse Creek—*stream* CA-9
One Horse Creek—*stream* MT-8
One Horse Creek—*stream* OK-5
One Horse Gap—*gap* IL-6
One Horse Ridge—*ridge* CA-9
Onehorse Slough—*stream* OR-9
One Horse Spring—*spring* CA-9
One Horse Store—*locale* AR-4
**One Horse Town (historical)**—*pop pl* OR-9
One Hospital Trust Airp—*airport* RI-1
One Hour Rsvr—*reservoir* ID-8
*One Hundred Acre Cove* RI-1
One Hundred Acre Meadow—*flat* MT-8
Onehundred Acre Prairie—*area* CA-9
One Hundred Acre Slough—*gut* MN-6
One Hundred Acre Waterhole—*lake* HI-9
One Hundred and Fifty-five Canal—*canal* CA-9
One Hundred and Fortytwo Mile Creek—*stream* KS-7
One Hundred And Ninetyfive Broadway Corporation Helistop—*airport* NJ-2
One-hundred-and-one Ranch—*hist pl* OK-5
One Hundred And One Ranch—*locale* CA-9
**One Hundred and One Ranch**—*pop pl* MO-7
One Hundred and One Spring—*spring* AZ-5
*One Hundred and Ten Mile Creek* KS-7
One Hundred And Twenty Canal—*canal* CA-9
One Hundred And Two Ranch—*locale* WY-8
One Hundred and Two River—*stream* MO-7
One Hundred Dollar Mine—*mine* CA-9
One Hundred Eighteenth Street Sch—*school* CA-9
One Hundred Eighty-sixth Street Sch—*school* CA-9
One Hundred Eighty Three Mile Airp—*airport* AZ-5
One Hundred Eleven Ranch—*locale* AZ-5
One Hundred Eleventh Street Sch—*school* CA-9
One Hundred F Cem—*cemetery* NM-5
One Hundred Fifty Sixth Street Sch—*school* CA-9
One Hundred Fifty Third Street Sch—*school* CA-9
One Hundred Five, Tank—*reservoir* AZ-5
*One Hundred Forty-two Mile Creek* KS-7
*One Hundred Fourty-seventh Street* IL-6
Onehundred Mile Grove Cem—*cemetery* WI-6
One Hundred Mile Swamp—*swamp* MN-6
One Hundred Ninth Street Sch—*school* CA-9
One Hundred One Ch—*church* AR-4
OneHundredOne Mine—*mine* CA-9
**One Hundred Palms**—*pop pl* CA-9
Onehundred Ranch—*locale* NM-5
One Hundred Ranch—*locale* NM-5
One Hundred Second Street Sch—*school* CA-9
One Hundred Seventh Street Sch—*school* CA-9
One Hundred Sixteenth Street Sch—*school* CA-9
One Hundred Sixty Acre Draw—*valley* TX-5
**One Hundred Sixty-third Street**—*pop pl* FL-3
One Hundred Spring Plain—*flat* WY-8
One Hundred Thirteen, Tank—*reservoir* AZ-5
One Hundred Thirty Eighth—*post sta* NY-2
One Hundred Thirty Fifth Street Sch—*school* CA-9
One Hundred Thirty-Ninth Street Sch—*school* CA-9
One Hundred Three Mesa—*summit* AZ-5
One Hundred Twelth Street Sch—*school* CA-9
One Hundred Twenty-Second Street Sch—*school* CA-9
One Hunt Creek—*stream* WY-8
*Onoida* ID 8
*Oneida* KS-7
*Oneida* NY-2
Oneida—*locale* LA-4
Oneida—*locale* OH-6
Oneida—*locale* OK-5
Oneida—*locale* WA-9
**Oneida**—*pop pl* AR-4
**Oneida**—*pop pl* IL-6
**Oneida**—*pop pl* IA-7
**Oneida**—*pop pl* KS-7
**Oneida**—*pop pl* KY-4
**Oneida**—*pop pl* NY-2
**Oneida**—*pop pl* OH-6
**Oneida**—*pop pl* (2) PA-2
**Oneida**—*pop pl* TN-4
**Oneida**—*pop pl* (2) WI-6
Oneida, Lake—*reservoir* PA-2
Oneida, Mount—*summit* NY-2
Oneida Branch—*stream* VA-3
**Oneida Castle**—*pop pl* NY-2
Oneida (CCD)—*cens area* KY-4
Oneida (CCD)—*cens area* TN-4
Oneida Cem—*cemetery* IL-6
Oneida Cem—*cemetery* IA-7
Oneida Ch—*church* WI-6
Oneida City Rsvr—*reservoir* NY-2
Oneida Community Cem—*cemetery* NY-2
Oneida Community Mansion House—*hist pl* NY-2
**Oneida Corners**—*pop pl* NY-2
**Oneida (County)**—*pop pl* NY-2
**Oneida (County)**—*pop pl* WI-6
Oneida County Airp—*airport* NY-2
Oneida County Courthouse—*hist pl* ID-8
Oneida County Courthouse—*hist pl* WI-6
Oneida Creek—*stream* CA-9
Oneida Creek—*stream* NY-2
Oneida Division—*civil* TN-4
Oneida Falls—*falls* PA-2
Oneida First Baptist Ch—*church* TN-4
Oneida Golf Course—*other* WI-6
Oneida HS—*school* TN-4
**Oneida Ind Res**—*pop pl* WI-6
Oneida Junction—*locale* PA-2
Oneida Lake—*lake* CA-9
Oneida Lake—*lake* MI-6
Oneida Lake—*lake* NY-2
Oneida Lake—*lake* WI-6
**Oneida Lake Beach East**—*pop pl* NY-2
**Oneida Lake Beach West**—*pop pl* NY-2
Oneida Lake Ch—*church* NY-2
*Oneidal Lake* CA-9
Oneida Lookout Tower—*locale* KY-4
Oneida Mine—*mine* CA-9
Oneida Mine Station—*locale* PA-2
Oneida Mining Company Dam—*dam* PA-2
Oneida Narrows—*valley* ID-8
Oneida Narrows Rsvr—*reservoir* ID-8
Oneida River—*stream* NY-2
Oneida Rock—*bar* AK-9
Oneidas, Isle of the—*island* NY-2
Oneida Sch—*school* CO-8
Oneida Sch—*school* NY-2
Oneida Sch—*school* OH-6
Oneida Shores County Park—*park* NY-2
Oneida Stake Acad—*hist pl* ID-8
Oneida Station—*locale* ID-8
Oneida Street Station—*hist pl* WI-6
**Oneida Subdivision**—*pop pl* TN-4
**Oneida (Town of)**—*pop pl* WI-6
Oneida Township—*fmr MCD* (2) IA-7
**Oneida Township**—*pop pl* NE-7
**Oneida Township**—*pop pl* SD-7
Oneida Township Hall—*building* SD-7
**Oneida (Township of)**—*pop pl* MI-6
**Oneida (Township of)**—*pop pl* PA-2
**Oneida Valley**—*pop pl* NY-2
*O'Neil* OK-5
O'Neil—*locale* MI-6
O'Neil—*locale* MS-4
O'Neil—*locale* OR-9
**O'Neil**—*pop pl* FL-3
**O'neil**—*pop pl* WV-2
O'Neil, Mount (Baldy)—*summit* WA-9
O'Neil Basin—*basin* NV-8
O'Neil Branch—*stream* TN-4
O'Neil Bridge—*bridge* MS-4
*O'Neil Brook* MN-6
O'Neil Brook—*stream* MA-1
O Neil Butte—*summit* OR-9
*O'Neil Canyon* CA-9
*O'Neil Canyon* NV-8
O'Neil Canyon—*valley* CA-9
O'Neil Cem—*cemetery* TN-4
**O'Neil Corners**—*pop pl* OR-9
O'Neil Coulee—*valley* MT-8
*O'Neil Creek* MT-8
O'Neil Creek—*stream* (2) CA-9
O'Neil Creek—*stream* ID-8
O'Neil Creek—*stream* MI-6
O'Neil Creek—*stream* MS-4
Oneil Creek—*stream* MO-7
O'Neil Creek—*stream* MT-8
O'Neil Creek—*stream* NV-8
O'Neil Creek—*stream* ND-7
O'Neil Creek—*stream* OR-9
O Neil Creek—*stream* OR-9
O'Neil Creek—*stream* OR-9
O'Neil Creek—*stream* (2) WA-9
O'Neil Creek—*stream* WI-6
O'Neil Creek Campground—*locale* CA-9
O'Neil Creek Cem—*cemetery* WI-6
O'Neil Creek Flowage Number One—*lake* WI-6
O'Neil Creek Flowage Number Two—*reservoir* WI-6
O'Neil Creek Flowage Trail—*trail* WI-6
O'Neil Creek Shelter—*locale* WA-9
O'Neil Ditch—*canal* CA-9
O'Neil Ditch—*canal* CO-8
O'Neil Ditch—*canal* WY-8
O Neil Draw—*valley* NE-7
O'Neil Flow—*swamp* NY-2
O'Neil Gap—*gap* WV-2
O'Neil Glade—*flat* CA-9
O'Neil Gulch—*valley* UT-8
O'Neil Hill—*summit* MA-1
*O'Neil Hills* AZ-5
*O'Neil Hot Springs* OR-9
*O'Neil Island* AL-4
O'Noil Island—*island* AK 9
O'Neil Knob—*summit* WV-2
*O'Neill* CA-9
**O'Neill**—*pop pl* IA-7
**O'Neill**—*pop pl* NE-7
**O'Neill**—*pop pl* WV-2
O'Neill, Buckey, Cabin—*hist pl* AZ-5
O'Neil Lake—*lake* (2) MI-6
O'Neil Lake—*lake* WA-9
O'Neil Lake—*reservoir* MS-4
O'Neil Landing—*locale* NM-5
O'Neill Branch—*stream* IL-6
O'Neill Brook—*stream* MN-6
O'Neill Brothers Bldg—*hist pl* ID-8
O'Neill Butte—*summit* AZ-5
O'Neill Butte—*summit* OR-9
O'Neill Cem—*cemetery* NY-2
Oneill Cem—*cemetery* TX-5
O'Neill Crater—*crater* AZ-5
O'Neill Creek—*stream* MT-8
O'Neill Creek—*stream* WI-6
O'Neill Dam—*dam* CA-9
O'Neill Forebay—*reservoir* CA-9
O'Neill Gulch—*valley* ID-8
O'Neill Hill—*summit* ID-8
*O'Neill Hills* AZ-5
O'Neill Hills—*summit* AZ-5
Oneill Holland Ditch—*canal* CO-8
O'Neill Island—*island* MD-2
O'Neill Island Marsh—*swamp* MD-2
O'Neill Lake—*reservoir* CA-9
O'Neill Pass—*gap* AZ-5
*O'Neill Point* AZ-5
O'Neill Ranch—*locale* (2) CA-9
O'Neill Sch—*school* CA-9
O'Neill Sch—*school* NY-2
O'Neills Grave—*cemetery* AZ-5
O'Neill Site—*hist pl* MI-6
*O'Neills Point* MN-6
O'Neill Spring—*spring* AZ-5
O'Neill Spring (historical)—*spring* AZ-5
**O'Neill Subdivision**—*pop pl* UT-8
*O'Neil Mountains* NV-8
O'Neil Park—*park* CA-9
O'Neil Pass—*gap* AZ-5
O'Neil Pass—*gap* SD-7
O'Neil Pass—*gap* WA-9
O'Neil Peak—*summit* WA-9
O'Neil Place—*locale* CA-9
O'Neil Point—*cape* MN-6
O'Neil Point—*cape* NY-2
O'Neil Point—*cape* UT-8
O'Neil Ranch—*locale* NV-8
O'Neil Ridge—*ridge* CA-9
O'Neil Ridge—*ridge* WI-6
O'Neil Rsvr—*reservoir* CA-9
*O'Neils* MS-4
O'Neil Sch—*school* KS-7
O'Neil Sch—*school* MI-6
O'Neil Sch—*school* (2) SD-7
O'Neil School (Abandoned)—*locale* IL-6
*O'Neils Creek* NV-8
*O'Neils Hills* AZ-5
O'Neils Point—*cape* MN-6
*Oneil Spring* AZ-5
O'Neil Spring—*spring* AZ-5
O'Neil Spring—*spring* OR-9
O Neil Spring—*spring* OR-9
O'Neil Swamp—*swamp* MI-6
O'Neil Tank—*reservoir* AZ-5
**O'Neil Township**—*pop pl* SD-7
O'Neil Valley—*valley* NE-7
O'Neil Well—*well* NM-5
One Island Bay—*cove* FL-3
One Island Ch—*church* LA-4
*One Island Lake* MN-6
One Island Lake—*lake* MN-6
Onekahakaha Park—*park* HI-9
Oneka Lake—*lake* MN-6
**Onekama**—*pop pl* MI-6
Onekama Cem—*cemetery* (2) MI-6
Onekama Junction—*locale* MI-6
**Onekama (Township of)**—*pop pl* MI-6
Oneka (Township of)—*other* MN-6
*One Lake* MN-6
One Lake—*lake* WA-9
*One Leap Lake* MN-6
*One Leg Creek* OH-6
O'Nello Lake—*lake* FL-3
Oneloa Bay—*bay* HI-9
One Loaf Lake—*lake* MN-6
One Lung Windmill—*locale* TX-5
Onemak—*island* MP-9
Onemak East Passage—*channel* MP-9
*Onemak Island* MP-9
Onemak West Passage—*channel* MP-9
One Man Butte—*summit* ID-8
One Man Lake—*lake* WI-6
One Man Pit—*cave* AL-4
*One Mile* PA-2
One Mile—*locale* AZ-5
Onemile Bay—*swamp* FL-3
*One Mile Bayou* MS-4
Onemile Bayou—*gut* LA-4
Onemile Bayou—*stream* AL-4
Onemile Bayou—*stream* (2) LA-4
Onemile Bayou—*stream* (2) MS-4
Onemile Bluff—*cliff* WI-6
One Mile Branch—*stream* AR-4
Onemile Branch—*stream* GA-3
Onemile Branch—*stream* KY-4
Onemile Branch—*stream* TN-4
One Mile Branch—*stream* TX-5
Onemile Bridge—*bridge* CA-9
Onemile Brook—*stream* ME-1
One Mile Brook—*stream* NH-1
Onemile Camp—*locale* CA-9
Onemile Campground—*locale* CO-8
Onemile Cattle Trail—*trail* CO-8
*One Mile Creek* VA-3
*One Mile Creek* WI-6
*Onemile Creek* WY-8
Onemile Creek—*stream* AK-9
Onemile Creek—*stream* CA-9
Onemile Creek—*stream* CO-8
Onemile Creek—*stream* ID-8
Onemile Creek—*stream* KS-7
Onemile Creek—*stream* NY-2
Onemile Creek—*stream* ND-7
Onemile Creek—*stream* TN-4
Onomilo Crook stroam TX 5
Onemile Creek—*stream* UT-8
Onemile Creek—*stream* WA-9
Onemile Creek—*stream* (2) WV-2
Onemile Creek—*stream* (2) WI-6
Onemile Creek—*stream* (5) WY-8
Onemile Cut—*bend* GA-3
Onemile Draw—*valley* WY-8
*One Mile Guard Station* UT-8
Onemile Guard Station—*locale* UT-8
Onemile Island—*island* WI-6
*One Mile Lake* MS-4
*Onemile Lake* WI-6
Onemile Lake—*lake* CA-9
Onemile Lake—*lake* MI-6
Onemile Lake—*lake* MN-6
Onemile Lake—*lake* MS-4
Onemile Lake—*lake* TX-5
One Mile Lake—*lake* WI-6
*One Mile Point* FL-3
One Mile Pond—*lake* CO-8
Onemile Pond—*lake* MT-8
Onemile Race Creek—*stream* IL-6
*One Mile Reservoir* WY-8
Onemile Run—*stream* PA-2
Onemile Run—*stream* VA-3
Onemile Run—*stream* WV-2
Onemile Run Trail—*trail* VA-3
Onemile Spring—*spring* AZ-5
Onemile Spring—*spring* (2) NV-8
Onemile Tank—*reservoir* TX-5
One Mile Tanks—*reservoir* AZ-5
Onemile Trail—*trail* CO-8
Onemile Trail—*trail* NH-1
One-Million-Liter Test Sphere—*hist pl* MD-2
Onemo—*locale* VA-3
One Montgomery Plaza Airp—*airport* PA-2
One More Day Tank—*reservoir* AZ-5
One Mtn—*summit* AZ-5
One'ness Ch—*church* TX-5
*Oneness Church* MO-7
**Onenoa**—*pop pl* AS-9
*Onensheg Run* PA-2
*Onenshey Run* PA-2
Oneo Bay—*bay* HI-9
One O'Clock—*summit* UT-8
One O'Clock Lake—*reservoir* OR-9
*One Of Wilder Lakes* MN-6
Oneohilo Gulch—*valley* HI-9
Oneonelilii Point—*cape* AS-9
Oneoneloa—*locale* AS-9
Oneonta—*locale* OR-9
**Oneonta**—*pop pl* AL-4
**Oneonta**—*pop pl* KY-4
**Oneonta**—*pop pl* NY-2
Oneonta (CCD)—*cens area* AL-4
Oneonta Cem—*cemetery* LA-4
Oneonta Ch—*church* LA-4
Oneonta Ch of Christ—*church* AL-4
Oneonta Creek—*stream* NY-2
Oneonta Creek—*stream* OR-9
Oneonta Division—*civil* AL-4
Oneonta Elem Sch—*school* AL-4
Oneonta Falls—*falls* OR-9
*Oneonta Grammar Sch* AL-4
Oneonta (historical)—*locale* KS-7
Oneonta HS—*school* AL-4
Oneonta Lake—*lake* WI-6
Oneonta Methodist Ch—*church* AL-4
Oneonta Sch—*school* (2) CA-9
Oneonta Slough—*gut* CA-9
**Oneonta (Town of)**—*pop pl* NY-2
*Oneonto* AL-4
One-O-One Creek—*stream* ND-7
Oneopaewa Valley—*valley* HI-9
Oneop (Municipality)—*island* FM-9
*Oneota* (2) MN-6
**Oneota**—*pop pl* MN-6
Oneota Cem—*cemetery* MN-6
Oneota Park—*park* IA-7
*Oneota River* IA-7
**Oneota Township**—*pop pl* SD-7
Oneota Township (historical)—*civil* SD-7
One Oxford Center—*building* PA-2
Onepennee Cem—*cemetery* WA-9
One Pine Lake—*lake* MN-6
Onequa Sch—*school* UT-8
One Reef—*bar* WA-9
Oneroad Bethel Ch—*church* SD-7
Oneroad Lake—*lake* SD-7
One Road Sch (historical)—*school* SD-7
**One Road Township**—*pop pl* SD-7
One Seventy Windmill—*locale* NM-5
One Shoe Lake—*lake* WI-6
One Shot Gap—*gap* AK-9
One Shot Lake—*lake* ID-8
One Spoon Campground (historical)—*locale* ID-8
One Spoon Way (historical)—*trail* ID-8
**One Spot**—*pop pl* MD-2
Onesquethaw Cem—*cemetery* NY-2
Onesquethaw Creek—*stream* NY-2
**Onesquethaw (Tarrytown)**—*pop pl* NY-2
Onesquethaw Valley Hist Dist—*hist pl* NY-2
One Stack Brook—*stream* NH-1
Onesto Hotel—*hist pl* OH-6
Onestone Lake—*lake* AK-9
One Stone Lake—*lake* WI-6
One Suerte—*civil* CA-9
Oneta—*locale* OK-5
One Tank—*reservoir* NM-5
One Tank Spring—*spring* NV-8
Oneta Sch—*school* OK-5
One Thirty North Eighth Bldg—*hist pl* IL-6
One Thousand Acre Bog—*swamp* ME-1
One Thousand Acre Heath—*flat* ME-1
One Thousand Eight Hundred Eighty One Ditch—*canal* CA-9
One Thousand Marshes—*swamp* NC-3
One Thousand Nine Hundred Five Mine—*mine* NV-8
One Thousand One Hundred Ranch—*locale* NV-8
One Thousand One Hundred Seventeen Mtn—*summit* NM-5
One Thousand One Hundred Twenty Ranch—*locale* MT-8
*One Thousand Palms Canyon* CA-9
One Time Cave—*cave* PA-2
One Toe Lake—*lake* MN-6
Ono Too Ridgo ridgo AZ 5
*One Too Many Creek* WA-9
One Too Many Creek—*stream* WA-9
Oneto Ranch—*locale* CA-9
One Tree Island—*island* MN-6
One Tree Peak—*summit* NM-5
Onetree Rock—*island* AK-9
One Trough Canyon—*valley* OR-9
One Trough Spring—*spring* OR-9
Onetto Spring—*spring* AZ-5
*One Two Many Creek* WA-9
**Oneula Beach**—*pop pl* HI-9
One V Well—*well* AZ-5
One Way Cave—*cave* AL-4
One Way Ch—*church* NC-3
Oneway Hill—*summit* MI-6
One Way Pass—*gap* AZ-5
*One Wheel* NV-8
One Wheel Canyon—*valley* NV-8
One Windmill Well—*well* AZ-5
Oney—*other* OK-5
Oney Branch—*stream* KY-4
Oney Cem—*cemetery* WV-2
Oney Gap—*gap* WV-2
**Oney Gap**—*pop pl* WV-2
Oney Sch—*school* OK-5
Oney Tank—*reservoir* (2) NM-5
**Ong**—*pop pl* NE-7
**Ong**—*pop pl* NJ-2
Ongael—*island* PW-9
*Ongakemmy Pond* MA-1
Ongalkereel—*bay* PW-9
Ong Cem—*cemetery* NE-7
Ong Cem—*cemetery* OK-5
Ongeluluul—*hist pl* PW-9
Ongelunge—*channel* PW-9
Ongetkatel—*island* PW-9
**Ongeuidel**—*pop pl* PW-9
*Ong Hat* NJ-2
Ongie, Lake—*lake* MI-6
Ongingiang—*island* PW-9
Ongivinuck River—*stream* AK-9
Ongivinuk Lake—*lake* AK-9
Ongo—*locale* MO-7
*Ongo Island* FM-9
Ongoke River—*stream* AK-9
Ongorakvik River—*stream* AK-9
Ongoveyuk Lagoon—*lake* AK-9
Ongoveyuk River—*stream* AK-9
Ong Run—*stream* NJ-2
*Ongs* NJ-2
Ong's, Jim, Market—*hist pl* AZ-5
*Ongs Hat* NJ-2
*Ongs Run* NJ-2
Ongutvak Mtn—*summit* AK-9
Ongw—*island* MP-9
Ong Yut Geong Wholesale Market—*hist pl* AZ-5
*Onhson Siding* SD-7
**Onia**—*pop pl* AR-4
Oniad, Lake—*lake* NY-2
**Oniad Lake**—*pop pl* NY-2
**Onida**—*pop pl* SD-7
Onida Municipal Airp—*airport* SD-7
Onida Township—*civil* SD-7
*O'NIEL Brook* MA-1
O'Niel Creek—*stream* MI-6
Oniel Park—*park* AZ-5
Oniga Creek—*stream* AK-9
**Onigum**—*pop pl* MN-6
Onikinalu—*bay* HI-9
Onikipuka Ridge—*ridge* HI-9
*Onimaaku* MP-9
*Onimaari To* MP-9
Onimak Island—*island* MP-9

Onimaku-to MP-9
Onimish Lake—lake WI-6
Onimitchi Island MP-9
Onimitchi Island—island MP-9
Oninaen—island MP-9
Oninayan MP-9
Oninayan-To MP-9
Onini Gulch—valley HI-9
Oninuk—island FM-9
Onion, Bayou—stream LA-4
Onion Bay—bay AK-9
Onion Bayou—stream (2) LA-4
Onion Bayou—stream TX-5
Onion Bed Branch—stream NC-3
Onion Bed Ridge TN-4
Onionbed Ridge—ridge TN-4
Onion Blade Branch—stream KY-4
Onion Branch—stream MO-7
Onion Branch—stream (2) TX-5
Onion Brook—stream CT-1
Onion Butte—summit CA-9
Onion Camp—locale CA-9
Onion Camp—locale OR-9
Onion Cliff—cliff NC-3
Onion Cliff Falls—falls NC-3
Onion Creek IA-7
Onion Creek KS-7
Onion Creek MT-8
Onion Creek—locale TX-5
**Onion Creek**—pop pl WA-9
Onion Creek—stream AZ-5
Onion Creek—stream (3) AR-4
Onion Creek—stream (7) CA-9
Onion Creek—stream CO-8
Onion Creek—stream ID-8
Onion Creek—stream (2) IL-6
Onion Creek—stream (2) IA-7
Onion Creek—stream (4) KS-7
Onion Creek—stream (4) MI-6
Onion Creek—stream (2) MT-8
Onion Creek—stream (2) OK-5
Onion Creek—stream (5) OR-9
Onion Creek—stream TN-4
Onion Creek—stream (8) TX-5
Onion Creek—stream UT-8
Onion Creek—stream (3) WA-9
Onion Creek—stream WY-8
Onion Creek Campground—locale CA-9
Onion Creek Lodge—locale TX-5
Onion Creek Rapids—rapids UT-8
Onion Creek Ridge—ridge CA-9
Onion Creek Sch—school TX-5
Onion Creek Sch—school WA-9
Onion Creek Trail—trail OR-9
Onion Drain MI-6
Onion Drain—canal MI-6
Onion Falls—falls NC-3
Onion Farm Island—island FL-3
Onion Flat—flat (2) CA-9
Onion Flat—flat OR-9
Onion Flat—flat TX-5
Onion Flats—flat OR-9
Onion Flats—flat WY-8
Onion Flats Seep—spring UT-8
Onion Gulch—valley (3) OR-9
Onion Gulch—valley WY-8
Onion Gulch Meadow—flat OR-9
Onion Hill—summit CO-8
Onion Hill—summit IL-6
Onion Hill—summit LA-4
Onion Hill—summit ME-1
Onion Hill—summit NY-2
Onion Hollow—valley AR-4
Onion Hollow—valley (3) MO-7
Onion Key Bay—bay FL-3
Onion Knoll—summit OR-9
Onion Lake—lake (2) CA-9
Onion Lake—lake LA-4
Onion Lake—lake MN-6
Onion Lake—lake NV-8
Onion Lakes—lake CO-8
Onion Meadow—flat (2) CA-9
Onion Meadow Peak—summit CA-9
Onion Meadows—flat WY-8
Onion Mountain Overlook—locale VA-3
Onion Mtn OR-9
Onion Mtn—summit AZ-5
Onion Mtn—summit CA-9
Onion Mtn—summit CT-1
Onion Mtn—summit NC-3
Onion Mtn—summit OR-9
Onion Mtn—summit VA-3
Onion Mtn—summit WA-9
Onion Park—flat MT-8
Onion Patch Branch—stream KY-4
Onion Patch Gulch—valley CA-9
Onion Peak—summit OR-9
Onionpen Hollow—valley KY-4
Onion Portage—other AK-9
Onion Portage Archeol District—hist pl AK-9
Onion Prairie Ch—church IL-6
Onion Ridge—ridge CO-8
Onion Ridge—ridge WA-9
Onion River VT-1
Onion River WI-6
Onion River—stream MN-6
Onion River—stream NY-2
Onion River—stream (2) WI-6
Onion River Flouring Mill/Grist Mill—hist pl WI-6
Onion Rock—bar OR-9
Onion Run—stream OH-6
Onion Run—stream PA-2
Onion Saddle—gap AZ-5
Onion Sch—school IL-6
Onion Spring—spring (2) AZ-5
Onion Spring—spring CO-8
Onion Spring—spring NM-5
Onion Spring—spring (3) OR-9
Onion Spring—spring (2) TX-5
Onion Spring Meadow—flat CA-9
Onion Springs—spring (2) CA-9
Onion Springs—spring OR-9
Onion Springs—spring WY-8
Onion Springs Mountain OR-9
Onionta Lake WI-6
Onion Top—summit TX-5
**Oniontown**—pop pl (2) NY-2
**Oniontown**—pop pl PA-2
Onion Valley—basin CA-9
Onion Valley—flat CA-9
Onion Valley—valley (2) CA-9
Onion Valley—valley CO-8
Onion Valley—valley ID-8
Onion Valley Creek—stream CA-9
Onion Valley Rsvr—reservoir CA-9
Onion Valley Rsvr—reservoir NV-8
Onion Valley (Site)—locale CA-9
Onion Valley Spring Two—civil CA-9
Onion Valley Spring 2—spring CA-9
Onion Valley Trail (historical)—trail ID-8
Oniotto—island MP-9
Oniotto Island MP-9
Oniotto-to MP-9
Onip FM-9
Onip—CDP FM-9
Onip Olip FM-9
Oniskethau Creek NY-2
On Island MP-9
On Island—island MP-9
On It Creek—stream CA-9
Onitona lake WI-6
Oniu Stream—stream HI-9
Oniwish Lake WI-6
Onjebonge Pond—lake NY-2
Onkanikon Cove MD-2
Onkatema Island MA-1
Onkatonka Island MA-1
Onkeowne Beach—beach MI-6
Onklat Creek—stream AK-9
**Onks**—pop pl TN-4
Onks Cem—cemetery TN-4
Onland Lake—lake WI-6
**Onley**—pop pl VA-3
Onley Point—cape VA-3
**Onleys Station**—pop pl NY-2
Online Cave—cave AL-4
Online Pit—cave AL-4
**Only**—pop pl TN-4
Only Bar—bar MS-4
Only (CCD)—cens area TN-4
Only Chance Ditch—canal WY-8
Only Division—civil TN-4
Only Post Office—building TN-4
Only Saltpeter Cave—cave TN-4
Only Sch (historical)—school TN-4
Only Way Ch—church OK-5
Onmak MP-9
Onmak East Pass MP-9
Onmak Island MP-9
Onmugot FM-9
Onmugot Pass FM-9
Onna FM-9
Onna Island FM-9
Onna Jima FM-9
**Onnalinda**—pop pl PA-2
Onnang—island FM-9
Onnap—summit FM-9
Onnaram FM-9
Onnaram Island FM-9
Onna-Shima FM-9
Onnela Sch—school MI-6
Onno—bar FM-9
Onnogoc FM-9
Onnuteschuik Creek—stream AK-9
Ono AL-4
Ono—locale KY-4
**Ono**—pop pl (2) CA-9
**Ono**—pop pl PA-2
**Ono**—pop pl WI-6
Ono—valley GU-9
Ono, Point—cape AL-4
Onofre CA-9
Onofre Tank—reservoir NM-5
Onofutuk—bar FM-9
Ono Island—island AL-4
Ono Island—island FM-9
Onoit—swamp FM-9
Onokkochun—cape FM-9
Onokon—bar FM-9
Onolavik Lake—lake AK-9
Onomea—civil HI-9
**Onomea**—pop pl HI-9
Onomea Bay—bay HI-9
Onomue—island FM-9
Ono (Municipality)—civ div FM-9
**Onondaga**—pop pl MI-6
Onondaga, Mount—summit NY-2
**Onondaga Castle**—pop pl NY-2
Onondaga Cave—cave MO-7
Onondaga Central Sch—school NY-2
Onondaga Community Coll—school NY-2
Onondaga Country Club—other NY-2
**Onondaga (County)**—pop pl NY-2
Onondaga County Savings Bank Bldg—hist pl NY-2
Onondaga County War Memorial—hist pl NY-2
Onondaga Creek—stream NY-2
Onondaga Creek Flood Control Dam—dam NY-2
**Onondaga Hill**—pop pl NY-2
Onondaga Indian Sch—school NY-2
Onondaga Ind Res—592 (1980) NY-2
Onondaga Lake—lake NY-2
Onondaga Mine—mine NV-8
**Onondaga (Onondaga Hill)**—pop pl NY-2
Onondaga Park—park NY-2
Onondaga Road Sch—school NY-2
Onondagas, Isle of the—island NY-2
Onondaga Sanitarium—hospital NY-2
**Onondaga (Town of)**—pop pl NY-2
**Onondaga (Township of)**—pop pl MI-6
Onondaga Valley Acad—school NY-2
Onondaga Valley Cem—cemetery NY-2
**Onongoch**—pop pl FM-9
Onongot FM-9
Onongoru PW-9
Ononicoa HI-9
Ononwa Station—locale IA-7
Onopalani Gulch—valley HI-9
Onopen—bar FM-9
Onora, Lake—lake FL-3
Onora Park Lake MI-6
Ono Ridge—ridge (2) KY-4
Onosop—bar FM-9
Onota—locale MI-6
Onota Brook—stream MA-1
Onota Creek—stream WA-9
Ono'Ta Lake MA-1
Onota Lake—reservoir MA-1
Onota Lake Dam—dam MA-1
**Onota (Township of)**—pop pl MI-6
Onoto—locale WV-2
Onouli One-Two—civil HI-9
Onoun—bar FM-9
Onoville—locale NY-2
Onowa Creek—stream ID-8
Onset AR-4
**Onset**—pop pl MA-1
Onset Bay—bay MA-1
Onset (historical P.O.)—locale MA-1
Onset Island—island MA-1
Onset (sta.) (RR name for East Wareham)—other MA-1
**Onset Station**—pop pl MA-1
Onslow—locale WA-9
**Onslow**—pop pl IA-7
Onslow Acad—school NC-3
Onslow Bay—bay NC-3
Onslow Beach—beach NC-3
**Onslow County**—pop pl NC-3
Onslow County Recreation Park—park NC-3
**Onslow Gardens (subdivision)**—pop pl NC-3
Onslow Island—island AK-9
Onslow Island—island GA-3
Onslow Mall Shop Ctr—locale NC-3
Onslow Memorial Park—cemetery NC-3
Onslow Park—park TX-5
Onslow Point—cape AK-9
**Onspaugh Corners**—pop pl PA-2
Onstad Lake—lake MN-6
**Onstad (Township of)**—pop pl MN-6
**Onsted**—pop pl MI-6
Onsted State Wildlife Mngmt—park MI-6
Onstot Canyon—valley NE-7
Onstot Cem—cemetery TX-5
Onstott Branch—stream TX-5
Onstott Cem—cemetery TX-5
Onstott Ch—church IL-6
Ontario IA-7
Ontario—locale IL-6
Ontario—locale KS-7
Ontario—locale OK-5
Ontario—locale VA-3
**Ontario**—pop pl CA-9
**Ontario**—pop pl IN-6
**Ontario**—pop pl IA-7
**Ontario**—pop pl NY-2
**Ontario**—pop pl OH-6
**Ontario**—pop pl OR-9
**Ontario**—pop pl PA-2
**Ontario**—pop pl WI-6
Ontario—unorg reg SD-7
Ontario, Lake—lake NY-2
Ontario, Lake—lake ND-7
**Ontario Beach**—pop pl NY-2
Ontario Canyon—valley UT-8
Ontario (CCD)—cens area CA-9
Ontario (CCD)—cens area OR-9
**Ontario Center**—pop pl NY-2
Ontario Christian HS—school CA-9
Ontario Colliery (historical)—mine PA-2
**Ontario (County)**—pop pl NY-2
Ontario Creek—stream MT-8
Ontario Drain Tunnel—tunnel UT-8
Ontario Golf Course—other NY-2
**Ontario Heights**—pop pl OR-9
Ontario Heights Ch—church OR-9
Ontario Hosp—hospital CA-9
Ontario Hot Springs—spring CA-9
Ontario International Airp—airport CA-9
Ontario Island—island OR-9
Ontario Millpond—lake IN-6
Ontario Millpond Dam—dam IN-6
Ontario Mine—mine CO-8
Ontario Mine—mine ID-8
Ontario Mine—mine MT-8
Ontario Mine—mine NM-5
Ontario Motor Speedway—other CA-9
Ontario Municipal Airp—airport OR-9
Ontario No 1 Shaft—mine UT-8
Ontario Nyssa Canal—canal OR-9
**Ontario On the Lake**—pop pl NY-2
Ontario Peak—summit CA-9
Ontario Peak Trail—trail CA-9
Ontario Ridge—ridge UT-8
Ontario Sch—school OH-6
Ontario Sch—school SD-7
Ontario Schools Administration Bldg—building CA-9
Ontario Shaft No 2—mine UT-8
Ontario State Bank Block—hist pl CA-9
Ontario Street—post sta IL-6
**Ontario Subdivision**—pop pl UT-8
**Ontario (Town of)**—pop pl NY-2
Ontario Township—civil SD-7
**Ontario Township**—pop pl ND-7
**Ontario (Township of)**—pop pl IL-6
Ontario-Upland Sewage Disposal—other CA-9
**Ontarioville**—pop pl IL-6
Ontelaunee—locale PA-2
Ontelaunee Creek—stream PA-2
Ontelaunee Lake—reservoir PA-2
Ontelaunee Park—park PA-2
**Ontelaunee (Township of)**—pop pl PA-2
**Onteo Beach**—pop pl NY-2
Onteora Central Sch—school NY-2
Onteora Lake—lake NY-2
Onteora Mtn—summit NY-2
**Onteora Park**—pop pl NY-2
Onteora Pond—reservoir NY-2
Onteora Scout Reservoir—locale NY-2
On the Move for Christ Ch of God—church FL-3
On The Rim Waterhold—reservoir OR-9
Ontiora Mountain NY-2
Ontiora Park NY-2
Ontiveros Cem—cemetery CA-9
**Onton**—pop pl KY-4
**Ontonagon**—pop pl MI-6
**Ontonagon (County)**—pop pl MI-6
Ontonagon County Courthouse—hist pl MI-6
Ontonagon Ind Res—reserve MI-6
Ontonagon Lighthouse—hist pl MI-6
Ontonagon River MI-6
Ontonagon River—stream MI-6
Ontonagon River—stream WI-6
**Ontonagon (Township of)**—pop pl MI-6
Onton Cem—cemetery KY-4
Ontop Mine—mine CA-9
Ontset Island MA-1
**Ontwa (Township of)**—pop pl MI-6
Onugot FM-9
Onumak MP-9
Onupuku—island FM-9
**Onvil**—pop pl NC-3
Onville NC-3
Onville-Thickety Creek—locale NC-3
Onvy Hollow—valley TN-4
Onward—locale TN-4
**Onward**—pop pl IN-6
**Onward**—pop pl MS-4
Onward Ch—church MO-7
Onward Post Office (historical)—building (2) TN-4
Onward Seminary (historical)—school TN-4
Onwata Hollow—valley AR-4
Onwata Mine—mine AR-4
Onway Lake—lake NH-1
**Onway Lake**—pop pl NH-1
Onwentsia Club—other IL-6
Onwot Island MP-9
**Onycha**—pop pl AL-4
Onyx—locale AR-4
**Onyx**—pop pl CA-9
Onyx Bridge—arch AZ-5
Onyx Cave AL-4
Onyx Cave—cave AL-4
Onyx Cave—cave AR-4
Onyx Cave—cave (7) MO-7
Onyx Cave—cave PA-2
Onyx Cave—cave SD-7
Onyx Cave Picnic Area—locale MO-7
Onyx Cavern AL-4
Onyx Hill—summit VA-3
Onyx Mine—mine (3) CA-9
Onyx Peak—summit CA-9
Onyx Ranch—locale CA-9
Onyx Spring—spring CA-9
Onyx Summit—gap CA-9
Onyx Tank—reservoir AZ-5
Oo MP-9
Oo, Puu—summit HI-9
Ooa—summit HI-9
Ooahilla Peak CA-9
Ooa Island—island MP-9
Ooawa Kilika Gulch—valley HI-9
Ooc FM-9
Oochee Creek—stream (2) GA-3
Oochuse Bay FL-3
00 Cold Spring OR-9
Ooia Fishpond—lake HI-9
Ooia Pond HI-9
Ooiki Falls—falls HI-9
Ookala—civil HI-9
**Ookala**—pop pl HI-9
Ookala Trail—trail HI-9
Oo-Kut AZ-5
Oolagah OK-5
**Oolagah (corporate name for Oologah)**—pop pl OK-5
Oolagah-Talala (CCD)—cens area OK-5
Oolah Mtn—summit AK-9
Oolah Pass—gap AK-9
Oolahpuk Mtn—summit AK-9
Oolah Valley—valley AK-9
Oolamakapehu Gulch—valley HI-9
Oolamnagavik River—stream AK-9
Oolamushak Hill—summit AK-9
Oolenoe River SC-3
Oolenoy Ch—church SC-3
Oolenoy River—stream SC-3
Ooley Cem—cemetery TN-4
Ooley Sch—school IL-6
Oolite—locale KY-4
**Oolite**—pop pl FL-3
Oolite RR Station—locale FL-3
**Oolitic**—pop pl IN-6
Oolitic JHS—school IN-6
Oolka, Lake—lake FL-3
**Oologah**—pop pl OK-5
Oologah Bank—hist pl OK-5
Oologah Cem—cemetery OK-5
Oologah (corporate name Oolagah) OK-5
Oologah Dam—dam OK-5
Oologah Lake—reservoir OK-5
Oologah Oil Field—oilfield OK-5
Oologah Pump—hist pl OK-5
Oologah Reservoir OK-5
Oologah Sch—school OK-5
Ooltawah TN-4
Ooltera Creek—stream TN-4
**Ooltewah**—pop pl TN-4
Ooltewah (CCD)—cens area TN-4
Ooltewah Cem—cemetery TN-4
Ooltewah Ch (historical)—church TN-4
Ooltewah Division—civil TN-4
Ooltewah Elem Sch—school TN-4
Ooltewah HS—school TN-4
Ooltewah Lookout Tower—locale TN-4
Ooltewah MS—school TN-4
Oouaili—summit HI-9
Ooma Homesteads—civil HI-9
Oomano Point—cape HI-9
Ooma One HI-9
Ooma One—civil HI-9
Ooma Two—civil HI-9
Oomebuaol PW-9
Oomeyaluk Bay—bay AK-9
Oompaul Creek—stream ID-8
Oomyousik Point—cape AK-9
Oona Lake—lake AK-9
Oon Bogue Creek MS-4
Oongalambingoi Dunes—beach AK-9
Oongayuk Hill—summit AK-9
Oopulee Falls HI-9
Oopulele Falls—falls HI-9
Oopuola Point—cape HI-9
Oopuola Stream—stream HI-9
Oorakur Island PW-9
Oosechee AL-4
Oo-se-oo-chee AL-4
Oostana TN-4
**Oostanaula**—pop pl GA-3
Oostanaula Ch—church (2) GA-3
Oostanaula Church TN-4
Oostanaula Creek—stream TN-4
Oostanaula River—stream GA-3
Oostanaula Valley—valley TN-4
**Oostburg**—pop pl WI-6
Oostburg Cem—cemetery WI-6
Oosterneck Creek—stream TN-4
OO Tank—reservoir AZ-5
Ooten Cem—cemetery (2) WV-2
Ooten Creek—stream NC-3
Ooten Fork—stream WV-2
Ooten Lake—lake MS-4
Oothcalooga Creek GA-3
Oothkalooga Creek GA-3
Oothkalooga Ch—church GA-3
Oothkalooga Creek—stream GA-3
**Oot Park**—pop pl NY-2
Oow FM-9
Oowah, Lake—reservoir UT-8
Oowah Campground—park UT-8
Oowala—locale OK-5
Oowala Cem—cemetery OK-5
Ooynik Point—cape AK-9
Oozley Branch—stream WV-2
Oozy Flats—other AK-9
Opaekaa Falls—falls HI-9
Opaekaa Road Bridge—hist pl HI-9
Opaekaa Stream—stream HI-9
Opae Kalaole Falls—falls HI-9
Opaeloa—summit HI-9
Opaeloa Peak HI-9
Opaepilau Gulch—valley HI-9
Opaeula Camp Three—locale HI-9
**Opaeula Camp 3**—pop pl HI-9
Opaeula Ditch Tunnel—tunnel HI-9
Opaeula Gulch HI-9
Opaeula Number 2 Reservoir HI-9
Opaeula Rsvr—reservoir HI-9
Opaeula Stream HI-9
Opaeula Stream—stream HI-9
Opaeula Two Rsvr—reservoir HI-9
Opagyarak River—stream AK-9
Opah—locale OK-5
Opahwah Butte CA-9
Opaikaa Falls HI-9
Opaikaa Stream HI-9
Opakalua Gulch—valley HI-9
Opal—locale AR-4
Opal—locale MO-7
Opal—locale WV-2
**Opal**—pop pl (2) AR-4
**Opal**—pop pl SD-7
**Opal**—pop pl VA-3
**Opal**—pop pl WI-6
**Opal**—pop pl WY-8
Opal, Lake—lake (2) FL-3
Opalair Rsvr—reservoir CO-8
Opal Bench—bench WY-8
Opal Butte—summit OR-9
Opal Canyon OR-9
Opal Canyon—valley CA-9
Opal Cem—cemetery TX-5
Opal Ch—church VA-3
Opal City—locale OR-9
**Opal Cliffs**—pop pl CA-9
Opal Creek—stream CA-9
Opal Creek—stream (3) ID-8
Opal Creek—stream (3) OR-9
Opal Creek—stream WY-8
Opal Dam—dam SD-7
Opalene Ditch—canal ID-8
Opalene Gulch—valley ID-8
Opalene Sch—school ID-8
Opalescent River—stream NY-2
Opal Hill—summit CA-9
Opal (historical)—locale SD-7
Opal Lake—lake CO-8
Opal Lake—lake ID-8
Opal Lake—lake (2) MI-6
Opal Lake—lake (2) OR-9
Opal Lake—lake (2) WA-9
Opal Lake Campground—park OR-9
Opal Mine—mine CA-9
Opal Mine Draw—valley OR-9
Opal Mountains NV-8
Opal Mtn—summit CA-9
Opal Mtn—summit ID-8
Opal Mtn—summit NV-8
Opal Mtn—summit OR-9
**Opa-Locka**—pop pl FL-3
Opa-locka Bank—hist pl FL-3
Opa-Locka Community Correctional Center—building FL-3
Opa-Locka Company Administration Bldg—hist pl FL-3
**Opa-locka (corporate name for Opa locka)**—pop pl FL-3
Opa locka (corporate name Opa-locka) FL-3
Opa-Locka Elem Sch—school FL-3
Opa-locka North—CDP FL-3
Opa-Locka RR Station—hist pl FL-3
Opa Locka Sch—school FL-3
Opal Post Office (historical)—building AL-4
Opal Spring—spring ID-8
Opal Spring—spring (2) NV-8
Opal Spring—spring OR-9
Opal Springs—locale OR-9
Opal Springs—spring WY-8
Opal Valley—basin OR-9
Opana—civil (2) HI-9
Opana Gulch—valley HI-9
Opana Point—cape (2) HI-9
Opana Stream HI-9
Opano HI-9
Opansoitak AZ-5
Opapee Creek—stream CA-9
Opasni Point—cape AK-9
Opasoitac AZ-5
Opa Spring—spring NE-7
Opatrny Village Site—hist pl OH-6
Opau Bay—bay HI-9
O P Creek—stream ID-8
Opdahl Cem—cemetery (2) MN-6
Opdahl (historical)—locale SD-7
Opdahl Sch—school MN-6
Opdahl Slough State Public Shooting Area—park SD-7
**Opdahl Township**—pop pl SD-7
Opdal Cem—cemetery MN-6
Opdal Ch—church MN-6
**Opdyke**—pop pl IL-6
**Opdyke**—pop pl TX-5
Opdyke, Sylvester, House—hist pl MI-6
Opdyke Cem—cemetery IL-6
Opdyke Cow Camp—locale CA-9
Opdyke Hill—summit CA-9
Opdyke Sch—school IL-6
**Opdyke West**—pop pl TX-5
Opea—civil HI-9
Opeala Gulch—valley HI-9
Opea-Peleau Homesteads—civil HI-9
Opeccon Creek VA-3
Opeccon Creek WV-2
Opechee Bay—bay NH-1
Opechee Island—island ME-1
Opechee Park—park NH-1
Opechee Peak—summit VA-3
Opeckan Creek WV-2
Opeckon Creek VA-3
Opeckon Creek WV-2
Opeckon River VA-3
Opeckon River WV-2
Opeekhan Creek VA-3
Opeekhan Creek WV-2
Opekiska—locale WV-2
Opekiska Lock and Dam—dam WV-2
Opel, John, House—hist pl IN-6
Opel Blane Lake Dam—dam MS-4
Opelika—locale TX-5
**Opelika**—pop pl AL-4
Opelika City Lake AL-4
Opelika Gas Field—oilfield TX-5
Opelika HS—school AL-4
Opelika JHS—school AL-4
Opelikan AL-4
Opelika Public Sch (historical)—school AL-4
Opelika State Technical Sch—school AL-4
Opelike Female Institute (historical)—school AL-4
**Opelousas**—pop pl LA-4
Opelousas Bay—swamp LA-4
Opelousas City Hall—hist pl LA-4
Opelousas Oil and Gas Field—oilfield LA-4
Opelu Gulch—valley HI-9
Open A—flat UT-8
Open A Canyon—valley UT-8
Open Acres Baptist Ch—church AL-4
**Open Acres (subdivision)**—pop pl AL-4
Open A Diamond Ditch—canal CO-8
Open Air—uninc pl FL-3
Open Air Ch—church TX-5
Open Air Chapel—church WY-8
Open Air Sch—school FL-3
Open Air Sch—school NJ-2
Openaka Lake—reservoir NJ-2
Openaka Lake Dam—dam NJ-2
Open A Ranch—locale WY-8
Open Bay—bay AK-9
Open Bay—bay WA-9
Open Bay—swamp SC-3
Open Bayou—stream LA-4
Open Bible Baptist Ch—church FL-3
Open Bible Ch—church (3) IL-6
Open Bible Church, The—church MI-6
Open Bible Coll—school IA-7
Open Bible Gospel Tabernacle—church FL-3
Open Bible Mennonite Brethren Ch—church KS-7
Open Bible Tabernacle—church FL-3
Open Bible Tabernacle—church GA-3
Open Bight—bay AK-9
Open Bottom Creek—stream TX-5
Open Brake—lake AR-4
Open Brake—swamp LA-4
Open Branch—stream FL-3
Open Branch—stream NC-3
Open Brook—stream PA-2
Open Canyon—valley ID-8
Open Canyon—valley (2) WY-8
Open Canyon Trail—trail WY-8
Open Creek—stream (2) AK-9
Open Creek—stream (2) FL-3
Open Creek—stream (3) GA-3
Open Creek—stream ID-8
Open Creek—stream MT-8
Open Creek—stream WY-8
Open Diamond Tank Number One NM-5
Open Door, The—pillar WY-8
Open Door Baptist Ch—church (2) FL-3
Open Door Baptist Ch—church MS-4
Open Door Baptist Ch—church TN-4
Open Door Baptist Ch—church UT-8
Open Door Cemetery IN-4
Open Door Ch TN-4
Open Door Ch—church (3) AL-4
Open Door Ch—church GA-3
Open Door Ch—church MS-4
Open Door Ch—church NE-7
Open Door Ch—church (2) NC-3
Open Door Ch—church OH-6
Open Door Ch—church OK-5
Open Door Ch—church SC-3
Open Door Ch—church (2) TX-5
Open Door Chapel—church OH-6
Open-Door Chapel—church TN-4
Open Door Childrens Home—building KY-4
Open Door Childrens Home—other KY-4
Open Door Mennonite Ch—church MS-4
Open Door Sch—school FL-3
Open Door Sch—school TN-4
Open Door Union Ch—church TN-4
Open Draw—valley (2) AZ-5
Open Draw—valley CO-8
Open Draw—valley OR-9
Open Draw Spring—spring AZ-5
Open Draw Tank—reservoir (2) AZ-5
Open Fork VA-3
Open Fork—stream (9) KY-4
Open Fork—stream VA-3
Open Fork—stream (4) WV-2
Open Fork—stream WY-8
Open Fork Ch—church KY-4
Open Fork Ch—church VA-3
**Open Fork Junction**—pop pl WV-2
Open Fork Point Creek—stream KY-4
Open Fork Sch—school KY-4
Open Gap—gap MS-4
**Open Gates**—pop pl KY-4
Open Grounds—plain NC-3
Open Gulch—valley CO-8
Open Hammock—island FL-3
Open Hollow—valley AR-4
Open Hollow—valley MO-7
Open Hollow—valley (3) TX-5
Open Hollow—valley (2) WV-2

Open Hollow Gulch—*valley* NM-5
Opening, The—*flat* NC-3
Opening (historical), The—*flat* NC-3
Opening Pond—*lake* MA-1
Opening Pond—*lake* SC-3
*Open Lake* AR-4
Open Lake—*lake* AR-4
Open Lake—*lake* FL-3
Open Lake—*lake* (2) LA-4
Open Lake—*lake* TN-4
Open Lakes—*lake* TX-5
Openlander Drain—*canal* MI-6
Open Meadow Brook—*stream* VT-1
**Open Meadows**—*pop pl* NY-2
Open Meadows Cem—*cemetery* NY-2
Open Meadows Ch—*church* NY-2
Open Mouth Bayou—*stream* LA-4
Openmouth Branch—*stream* WV-2
Open Park—*flat* MT-8
Open Pit Mine—*mine* NV-8
*Open Pond* FL-3
Open Pond—*flat* KY-4
Open Pond—*lake* (2) AL-4
Open Pond—*lake* (9) FL-3
Open Pond—*lake* GA-3
Open Pond—*lake* IL-6
Open Pond—*lake* KY-4
Open Pond—*lake* TN-4
Open Pond Ch—*church* FL-3
Open Pond Lookout Tower—*locale* AL-4
*Open Pond Post Office* AL-4
Open Pond Rec Area—*park* AL-4
Open Ridge—*ridge* CA-9
Open Ridge—*ridge* NC-3
Open Ridge Draw—*valley* UT-8
*Open Road* AL-4
Open Run—*stream* PA-2
**Open Sands**—*pop pl* FL-3
Open Slough—*gut* LA-4
Open Spring—*spring* UT-8
Open Spring Canyon—*valley* NV-8
Open Swamp Bayou—*stream* LA-4
Open Tank—*reservoir* TX-5
Open Tank Windmill—*locale* TX-5
Open Triangle Tee Ranch—*locale* OR-9
Open Valley—*valley* OR-9
Open Valley Waterhole—*spring* OR-9
Open Valley Waterhole Number Three—*lake* OR-9
Open View Sch—*school* WI-6
Open Way Ch—*church* KS-7
Openwood Country Club—*locale* MS-4
Openwood Plantation Lake Dam—*dam* MS-4
**Openwood Plantation (subdivision)**—*pop pl* MS-4
*Open Wood Pond* PA-2
Open Woods Pond—*reservoir* PA-2
Open Woods Pond Dam—*dam* PA-2
*Opequan Creek* VA-3
*Opequan Creek* WV-2
Opequon—*locale* VA-3
Opequon Country Club—*other* WV-2
Opequon Creek—*stream* VA-3
Opequon Creek—*stream* WV-2
Opequon (Magisterial District)—*fmr MCD* VA-3
Opequon (Magisterial District)—*fmr MCD* WV-2
*Opequon River* VA-3
*Opequon River* WV-2
Opequon Sch—*school* WV-2
Opera Block—*hist pl* OK-5
Opera Block House—*hist pl* MN-6
Opera Box Mine—*mine* CO-8
Opera Hall Block—*hist pl* WI-6
Opera House—*hist pl* NE-7
Opera House and Yates Bookshop Bldg—*hist pl* KY-4
Opera House Block—*hist pl* IA-7
Opera House Block/Central Block Bldg—*hist pl* CO-8
Opera House Hollow—*valley* WV-2
Opergard Creek—*stream* WI-6
Operl Island—*island* AK-9
Opex—*mine* UT-8
Opez Spring—*spring* NM-5
O P Fox Dam—*dam* NC-3
Opha Post Office (historical)—*building* TN-4
**Opheim**—*pop pl* IL-6
**Opheim**—*pop pl* MT-8
Opheim Air Force Station—*military* MT-8
Opheim Port of Entry United States Custom—*locale* MT-8
Ophelia—*locale* VA-3
Ophelia, Lac—*lake* LA-4
Ophelia, Lake—*reservoir* NY-2
Ophelia Creek—*stream* AK-9
*Ophelia Hill Memorial High School* AL-4
**Ophelia (historical)**—*pop pl* MS-4
Ophelia Post Office (historical)—*building* MS-4
Ophelia S Hill Elem Sch—*school* AL-4
**Ophiem**—*pop pl* IL-6
O P Hill—*summit* VT-1
*Ophir* MT-8
Ophir—*locale* AL-4
Ophir—*locale* GA-3
Ophir—*locale* KS-7
Ophir—*locale* KY-4
Ophir—*locale* OR-9
**Ophir**—*pop pl* AK-9
**Ophir**—*pop pl* CA-9
**Ophir**—*pop pl* CO-8
**Ophir**—*pop pl* NC-3
**Ophir**—*pop pl* UT-8
Ophir, Mount—*summit* CA-9
Ophir Beach—*beach* OR-9
Ophir Canal—*canal* CA-9
Ophir Canyon—*valley* UT-8
Ophir Cave—*cave* MT-8
Ophir Creek—*stream* (6) AK-9
Ophir Creek—*stream* CO-8
Ophir Creek—*stream* ID-8
Ophir Creek—*stream* MT-8
Ophir Creek—*stream* (2) NV-8
Ophir Creek—*stream* UT-8
Ophir Creek Campground—*locale* CO-8
Ophir Gulch—*valley* AZ-5
Ophir Gulch—*valley* ID-8
Ophir Hill—*summit* CA-9
Ophir Hill—*summit* NV-8
*Ophir Lakes* CO-8
**Ophir Loop**—*pop pl* CO-8
Ophir Loop Sch—*school* CO-8
Ophir Loop Tram—*other* CO-8
Ophir Mill Historical Marker—*park* NV-8
Ophir Mine—*mine* AK-9
Ophir Mine—*mine* (3) CA-9
Ophir Mine—*mine* (2) CO-8
Ophir Mine—*mine* (2) NV-8
Ophir Mine—*mine* (2) OR-9
Ophir Mtn—*summit* CA-9
Ophir Mtn—*summit* CO-8
Ophir Mtn—*summit* OR-9
Ophir Needles—*pillar* CO-8
Ophir Park—*park* IL-6
Ophir Pass—*gap* CO-8
*Ophir Peak* CO-8
Ophir Post Office—*locale* CO-8
Ophir Ravine—*valley* NV-8
Ophir Rest Area—*park* OR-9
Ophir (Ruins)—*locale* NV-8
Ophir Sch—*school* CA-9
Ophir Sch—*school* MT-8
Ophir Shaft—*mine* NV-8
*Ophir Station* CO-8
Ophir Town Hall—*hist pl* UT-8
Ophir (Township of)—*fmr MCD* NC-3
**Ophir (Township of)**—*pop pl* IL-6
Ophir Tunnel—*mine* CO-8
Ophir Wash—*stream* NV-8
*Opickhon Creek* VA-3
*Opicon Creek* VA-3
Opie—*locale* VA-3
*Opie Dildock Pass* OR-9
Opie Dilldock Pass—*gap* OR-9
Opies Landing—*locale* GA-3
Opihihali One—*civil* HI-9
Opihihali Two—*civil* HI-9
*Opihihau* HI-9
**Opihikao**—*pop pl* HI-9
Opihikao Homesteads—*civil* HI-9
Opihilala—*civil* HI-9
Opihilala Gulch—*valley* HI-9
Opihinehe—*cape* HI-9
Opihipau Hukiaa—*civil* HI-9
Opihi Rock—*island* HI-9
*Opikoula* HI-9
Opikoula Point—*cape* HI-9
*Opillaka* AL-4
*O'Pine* AL-4
Opine—*locale* (2) AL-4
O'Pine Ch—*church* AL-4
Opine Community House—*building* AL-4
*O Pine Lake* MS-4
Opine Lake—*reservoir* AL-4
O'Pines, Lake—*lake* OH-6
O'Pine Sch (historical)—*school* AL-4
O Pines Lake—*reservoir* MS-4
Opine Timber Company Dam—*dam* AL-4
*Opintlocco Creek* AL-4
Opintlocco Creek—*stream* AL-4
*Opintloco Creek* AL-4
O Pipe—*canal* OR-9
Opitz Lake—*lake* SD-7
Opium Glade Ridge—*ridge* CA-9
Oplin—*locale* TX-5
**Oplin**—*pop pl* TX-5
Opoi—*area* HI-9
**Opole**—*pop pl* MN-6
**Opolis**—*pop pl* KS-7
*Opolu* HI-9
*Oponays Town* FL-3
Oponee Memorial Gardens—*cemetery* SC-3
**Oponys Town (historical)**—*pop pl* FL-3
*Opookta Creek* MS-4
Opop—*area* GU-9
Oporto Post Office (historical)—*building* SD-7
Opo Run—*stream* IN-6
*Oposssum Valley* AL-4
Opossum—*locale* TN-4
*Opossum Bayou* MS-4
Opossum Bayou—*gut* LA-4
Opossum Bayou—*stream* LA-4
Opossum Bayou Cut-Off—*bend* MS-4
Opossum Bend—*bend* KY-4
O'Possum Bight Bar—*bar* AL-4
Opossum Branch—*stream* (3) AL-4
Opossum Branch—*stream* AR-4
Opossum Branch—*stream* GA-3
Opossum Branch—*stream* IN-6
Opossum Branch—*stream* (3) KY-4
Opossum Branch—*stream* MO-7
Opossum Branch—*stream* SC-3
Opossum Branch—*stream* (3) TN-4
Opossum Branch—*stream* TX-5
Opossum Branch—*stream* (2) VA-3
Opossum Brook—*stream* PA-2
Opossum Camp—*locale* FL-3
Opossum Chute—*channel* LA-4
*Opossum Creek* AL-4
*Opossum Creek* AR-4
*Opossum Creek* OK-5
*Opossum Creek* TN-4
*Opossum Creek* VA-3
Opossum Creek—*stream* (2) AL-4
Opossum Creek—*stream* AR-4
Opossum Creek—*stream* (3) GA-3
Opossum Creek—*stream* (5) IL-6
Opossum Creek—*stream* (2) IN-6
Opossum Creek—*stream* IA-7
Opossum Creek—*stream* (2) KS-7
Opossum Creek—*stream* (4) KY-4
Opossum Creek—*stream* (7) MO-7
Opossum Creek—*stream* OH-6
Opossum Creek—*stream* (6) OK-5
Opossum Creek—*stream* (2) PA-2
Opossum Creek—*stream* SC-3
Opossum Creek—*stream* (4) TN-4
Opossum Creek—*stream* (4) TX-5
Opossum Creek—*stream* (3) VA-3
Opossum Creek—*stream* WV-2
Opossum Creek Ford—*locale* TN-4
**Opossum Creek Pines**—*pop pl* TN-4
Opossum Creek Res—*park* OH-6
Opossum Creek Sch (abandoned)—*school* MO-7
*Opossum Creek Shoals* TN-4
Opossum Fork—*stream* AR-4
*Opossum Gap* TN-4
Opossum Gap—*gap* WV-2
Opossum Gap Fork—*stream* WV-2
Opossum Hill—*summit* MD-2
Opossum Hill—*summit* TX-5
Opossum Hill Sch (abandoned)—*school* PA-2
Opossum Hill Tank—*reservoir* TX-5
Opossum Hill Union Ch—*church* PA-2
**Opossum (historical)**—*pop pl* TN-4
*Opossum Hollow* TN-4
Opossum Hollow—*valley* (4) AL-4
Opossum Hollow—*valley* AR-4
Opossum Hollow—*valley* IL-6
Opossum Hollow—*valley* (3) IN-6
Opossum Hollow—*valley* (2) KS-7
Opossum Hollow—*valley* (3) KY-4
Opossum Hollow—*valley* (4) MO-7
Opossum Hollow—*valley* (6) OH-6
Opossum Hollow—*valley* PA-2
Opossum Hollow—*valley* SD-7
Opossum Hollow—*valley* (6) TN-4
Opossum Hollow—*valley* (4) TX-5
Opossum Hollow—*valley* (2) VA-3
Opossum Hollow—*valley* (4) WV-2
Opossum Island—*island* FL-3
Opossum Island—*island* MD-2
Opossum Island—*island* TN-4
Opossum Key—*island* FL-3
Opossum Lake—*lake* PA-2
Opossum Lake—*reservoir* GA-3
Opossum Lake—*reservoir* PA-2
Opossum Lake Dam—*dam* PA-2
*Opossum Paw Hollow* TN-4
Opossum Point—*cape* GA-3
Opossum Point—*cape* LA-4
Opossum Point—*cape* SC-3
Opossum Point Cem—*cemetery* SC-3
Opossum Point Lake—*lake* GA-3
Opossum Point Landing—*locale* SC-3
Opossum Post Office (historical)—*building* TN-4
Opossum Quarter Creek—*stream* VA-3
Opossum Rock Baptist Ch—*church* TN-4
Opossum Rock Sch—*school* TN-4
Opossum Run—*stream* (3) IN-6
Opossum Run—*stream* KY-4
Opossum Run—*stream* (8) OH-6
Opossum Run—*stream* (3) PA-2
Opossum Shoals—*bar* TN-4
Opossum Strut Hollow—*valley* KY-4
Opossum Swamp—*stream* NC-3
Opossum Trial Ridge—*ridge* IN-6
Opossum Trot Branch—*stream* (2) KY-4
Opossum Trot Cem—*cemetery* MS-4
Opossum Trot Ch—*church* TX-5
Opossum Trot Trail—*trail* IL-6
*Opossum Valley* TN-4
Opossum Valley—*valley* (2) AL-4
Opossum Valley—*valley* TN-4
Opossum Valley Cave—*cave* AL-4
Opossum Walk Creek—*stream* AR-4
Opp—*locale* PA-2
**Opp**—*pop pl* AL-4
*Oppanaugue* RI-1
*Oppasum Valley* AL-4
Opp (CCD)—*cens area* AL-4
Opp Cem—*cemetery* TX-5
Opp City Hall—*building* AL-4
Opp Cottage—*hist pl* AL-4
Opp Country Club—*locale* AL-4
Opp Division—*civil* AL-4
Oppedahl State Game Mngmt Area—*park* IA-7
Oppegaard Lake—*lake* MN-6
*Oppeldtsville* PA-2
*Oppello* AR-4
**Oppelo**—*pop pl* AR-4
Oppelo Ch—*church* AR-4
*Oppeltsville* PA-2
**Oppenheim**—*pop pl* NY-2
**Oppenheimer**—*pop pl* PA-2
Oppenheimer Canyon—*valley* TX-5
Oppenheimer House—*hist pl* PR-3
Oppenheimer Run—*stream* PA-2
Oppenheim Park—*park* NY-2
**Oppenheim (Town of)**—*pop pl* NY-2
**Opperman**—*pop pl* OH-6
Opperman Lake—*lake* MN-6
Opperman Pass—*gap* PA-2
*Oppermans Cave* PA-2
Oppermans Corner—*locale* PA-2
Opp Fishing Club Dam—*dam* AL-4
Opp Fishing Club Lake—*reservoir* AL-4
Opp HS—*school* AL-4
*Oppie Dildock pass* OR-9
Oppio Park—*park* NV-8
Opp MS—*school* AL-4
*Opponenauhock* RI-1
*Opportunity* TX-5
**Opportunity**—*pop pl* MT-8
**Opportunity**—*pop pl* NE-7
**Opportunity**—*pop pl* WA-9
Opportunity Center Sch—*school* KY-4
Opportunity Center Sch—*school* TX-5
**Opportunity Farms**—*pop pl* MO-7
Opportunity Hall Special Sch—*school* AZ-5
Opportunity Heights—*uninc pl* OK-5
Opportunity Sch—*school* CO-8
Opportunity Sch—*school* SC-3
Opportunity School—*locale* CO-8
Opposite Creek—*stream* ID-8
Opposite Joe Baker Canyon—*valley* CO-8
Opposition Cem—*cemetery* AR-4
Opposition Creek—*stream* AR-4
Opposition Creek—*stream* CO-8
Opposition House—*hist pl* MA-1
Opposition Sch—*school* IA-7
*Oppossum Creek* OH-6
*Oppossum Creek* PA-2
*Oppossum Creek* TN-4
Oppossum Creek—*stream* MS-4
Oppossum Creek Ripple (historical)—*rapids* TN-4
Oppossum Fork—*stream* TN-4
*Oppossum Hollow* TN-4
Oppossum Hollow—*valley* TN-4
Oppossum Hollow—*valley* (2) VA-3
Oppossum Neck Cem—*cemetery* MS-4
Oppossum Run—*stream* OH-6
Oppossum Springs Shoals—*bar* TN-4
Opposum Creek—*stream* IL-6
Opposum Trot—*valley* TN-4
Opp Public Library—*building* AL-4
Opp Sch—*school* MO-7
Opp Spring—*spring* TX-5
**Oppy**—*pop pl* KY-4
Oppy Cem—*cemetery* OH-6
Oppy South Oil Field—*oilfield* KS-7
O P Rockwell Ranch—*locale* UT-8
Ops—*locale* ND-7
**Opstead**—*pop pl* MN-6
Opstead Ch—*church* MN-6
**Ops Township**—*pop pl* ND-7
**Optic**—*pop pl* NE-7
**Optima**—*pop pl* OK-5
Optima Dam—*dam* OK-5
Optima Grain Elevator—*hist pl* OK-5
Optima Lake—*reservoir* OK-5
*Optima Rsvr* OK-5
Optimist Boys Camp—*locale* LA-4
Optimist Camp—*locale* TX-5
Optimist Club Camp—*locale* OH-6
Optimist Club Lake—*reservoir* TN-4
Optimist Club Lake Dam—*dam* TN-4
Optimist Field—*park* GA-3
Optimist Lake—*reservoir* AL-4
Optimist Lake Dam—*dam* AL-4
Optimist Park—*flat* WY-8
Optimist Park—*park* AL-4
Optimist Park—*park* FL-3
Optimist Park—*park* IL-6
Optimist Park—*park* MS-4
Optimist Park—*park* (3) NC-3
Optimist Park—*park* OK-5
Optimist Ponds—*lake* TX-5
Optimists Home for Boys—*building* CA-9
Optimo—*locale* NM-5
**Optimo**—*pop pl* CA-9
**Optimus**—*pop pl* AR-4
Optimus Cem—*cemetery* AR-4
**Option**—*pop pl* PA-2
Option Post Office (historical)—*building* PA-2
Opuhano—*cape* HI-9
Opun—*locale* FM-9
Opunaha Gulch—*valley* HI-9
Opuntia Draw—*valley* NM-5
Opuohina—*cape* HI-9
Opyan—*beach* MH-9
Opyan, Laderan—*cliff* MH-9
Opyan, Puntan—*cape* MH-9
Opyan, Puntan Unai—*cape* MH-9
Opyan, Unai—*beach* MH-9
*Oquachton Creek* PA-2
*Oquafanoka* GA-3
**Oquaga**—*pop pl* NY-2
*Oquaga Creek* PA-2
Oquaga Creek—*stream* NY-2
Oquaga Lake—*lake* NY-2
**Oquaga Lake**—*pop pl* NY-2
*Oquartins Creek* PA-2
**Oquawka**—*pop pl* IL-6
Oquawka State Wildlife Ref—*park* IL-6
**Oquawka (Township of)**—*pop pl* IL-6
Oquawka Wagon Bridge—*hist pl* IL-6
Oquenoc Sch—*school* NY-2
Oquer Canyon—*valley* AZ-5
Oquer Lake—*lake* AZ-5
Oquer Point—*cliff* AZ-5
Oquer Spring—*spring* AZ-5
Oquina Creek—*stream* GA-3
O'Quin Cem—*cemetery* VA-3
O'Quinn—*locale* TX-5
O'Quinn Branch—*stream* TX-5
O'Quinn Cem—*cemetery* GA-3
O'Quinn Cem—*cemetery* MS-4
O'Quinn Cem—*cemetery* VA-3
O'Quinn Ch—*church* GA-3
O'Quinn Meadow—*flat* CA-9
O'Quinn Park—*park* FL-3
O'Quinn Pond—*lake* GA-3
**Oquirlane Subdivision**—*pop pl* UT-8
**Oquirrh Estates Subdivision**—*pop pl* UT-8
Oquirrh Hills MS—*school* UT-8
**Oquirrh Hills Office Building Condo**—*pop pl* UT-8
Oquirrh Hills Sch—*school* UT-8
**Oquirrh Hills Subdivision**—*pop pl* UT-8
**Oquirrh Hills Subdivision 2-4**—*pop pl* UT-8
**Oquirrh Hills Subdivision 5, 6, 8 and 9**—*pop pl* UT-8
*Oquirrh Mountain Range* UT-8
Oquirrh Mtns—*range* UT-8
*Oquirrh Range* UT-8
Oquirrh Sch—*school* UT-8
**Oquirrh Shadows Subdivision**—*pop pl* UT-8
**Oquirrh View Subdivision**—*pop pl* UT-8
*Oquirton* PA-2
*Oquiston Creek* PA-2
**Oquossoc**—*pop pl* ME-1
Oquossoc Angling Association—*other* ME-1
*Oquossoc Lake* ME-1
Oquossoc Log Church—*hist pl* ME-1
*Or* FM-9
**Or**—*pop pl* FM-9
*Ora* IL-6
Ora—*locale* CA-9
Ora—*locale* TX-5
**Ora**—*pop pl* IN-6
**Ora**—*pop pl* MS-4
**Ora**—*pop pl* NC-3
**Ora**—*pop pl* SC-3
Ora Acres Airp—*airport* AZ-5
Ora Arm—*canal* IN-6
Ora Baptist Ch—*church* MS-4
Ora B Cave—*cave* AL-4
*Orabi* AZ-5
Ora Cem—*cemetery* IN-6
Ora Cem—*cemetery* MS-4
Orachel—*island* PW-9
**Oracle**—*pop pl* AZ-5
Oracle Elem Sch—*school* AZ-5
**Oracle Foot Hill Estates**—*pop pl* AZ-5
**Oracle Foothills Estates**—*pop pl* AZ-5
Oracle Hill—*summit* AZ-5
Oracle Junction—*locale* AZ-5
Oracle Microwave Station—*tower* AZ-5
Oracle Mine—*mine* AK-9
Oracle Mines—*mine* AK-9
Oracle MS—*school* AZ-5
Oracle Mtn—*summit* AK-9
Oracle Park—*park* AZ-5
Oracle Place Shop Ctr—*locale* AZ-5
Oracle Ranger Station—*locale* AZ-5
Oracle Ridge—*ridge* AZ-5
Oracle Ridge Plaza Shop Ctr—*locale* AZ-5
Oracle Substation—*locale* AZ-5
Oracle Turbine Station—*locale* AZ-5
Ora Creek—*stream* OR-9
**Oradell**—*pop pl* NJ-2
Oradell Reservoir Dam—*dam* NJ-2
Oradell Rsvr—*reservoir* NJ-2
Oradell Station—*hist pl* NJ-2
Ora Ellington Sch—*school* OK-5
O'Rafferty HS—*school* MI-6
**Orafino**—*pop pl* NE-7
Orafino Cem—*cemetery* NE-7
*Ora Grande Creek* ID-8
Ora Grande Mine—*mine* CA-9
*Orahal* PW-9
Ora Hanna Spring—*spring* NV-8
Orahood Airstrip—*airport* CO-8
*Oraiba* AZ-5
*Oraibi* (2) AZ-5
Oraibi Butte—*summit* AZ-5
Oraibi Community Bldg—*building* AZ-5
Oraibi Day Sch—*school* AZ-5
*Oraibi Mesa* AZ-5
Oraibi Mesa—*summit* AZ-5
Oraibi Post Office—*building* AZ-5
*Oraibi Wash* AZ-5
Oraibi Wash—*arroyo* AZ-5
Orak—*island* PW-9
Orakibad—*bar* PW-9
*Orakura Island* PW-9
*Orakuru* PW-9
*Orakuru To* PW-9
**Oral**—*pop pl* SD-7
**Oral**—*pop pl* TN-4
**Oralabor**—*pop pl* IA-7
Oralabor Cem—*cemetery* IA-7
Ora Lake—*lake* CA-9
Oral Baptist Ch—*church* TN-4
*Oral Baptist Church* MS-4
Oral Cem—*cemetery* (2) MS-4
Oral Cem—*cemetery* TN-4
Oral Ch—*church* MS-4
**Oral Lake**—*pop pl* WV-2
Oral Oaks—*locale* VA-3
Oral Post Office (historical)—*building* TN-4
Oral Roberts Univ—*school* OK-5
Ora Mathews Canyon—*valley* CO-8
**Oramel**—*pop pl* NY-2
*Ora Mill* NC-3
**Ora Mill**—*pop pl* NC-3
Ora Mine—*mine* NV-8
Ora Mine—*mine* NM-5
Or Ami Synagogue—*church* PA-2
Oran—*locale* TX-5
**Oran**—*pop pl* IA-7
**Oran**—*pop pl* MO-7
**Oran**—*pop pl* NY-2
**Oran**—*pop pl* OH-6
Oranda—*locale* VA-3
*Orange* IN-6
*Orange* NJ-2
*Orange* ND-7
Orange—*CDP* CT-1
Orange—*locale* FL-3
Orange—*locale* GA-3
Orange—*locale* IL-6
Orange—*locale* MS-4
Orange—*locale* MO-7
Orange—*locale* OH-6
**Orange**—*pop pl* AL-4
**Orange**—*pop pl* CA-9
**Orange**—*pop pl* CT-1
**Orange**—*pop pl* IN-6
**Orange**—*pop pl* IA-7
**Orange**—*pop pl* MA-1
**Orange**—*pop pl* MS-4
**Orange**—*pop pl* NH-1
**Orange**—*pop pl* NJ-2
**Orange**—*pop pl* NM-5
**Orange**—*pop pl* NC-3
**Orange**—*pop pl* (2) OH-6
**Orange**—*pop pl* PA-2
**Orange**—*pop pl* TX-5
**Orange**—*pop pl* VT-1
**Orange**—*pop pl* VA-3
Orange, Lake—*lake* FL-3
Orange, Lake—*reservoir* NC-3
Orange, Lake—*reservoir* VA-3
Orange Air Natl Guard Communication Station—*building* CT-1
Orange-Alamance Lake—*reservoir* NC-3
Orange-Alamance Lake Dam—*dam* NC-3
Orange Ave Ch—*church* FL-3
Orange Ave Junction—*locale* CA-9
Orange Ave (Shop Ctr)—*locale* FL-3
Orange Ave Station—*locale* NJ-2
Orange Basin—*basin* NH-1
Orange Bayou—*gut* LA-4
*Orange Beach* MH-9
**Orange Beach**—*pop pl* AL-4
Orange Beach Marina—*locale* AL-4
Orange Beach Presbyterian Ch—*church* AL-4
*Orange Becah* PW-9
Orange Bend—*locale* FL-3
**Orange Blossom**—*pop pl* FL-3
Orange Blossom—*uninc pl* FL-3
Orange Blossom Center (Shop Ctr)—*locale* FL-3
**Orange Blossom Gardens**—*pop pl* FL-3
**Orange Blossom Hills**—*pop pl* FL-3
Orange Blossom Hills South—*locale* FL-3
Orange Blossom Mall—*locale* FL-3
Orange Blossom Mine—*mine* (2) CA-9
Orange Blossom Mine—*mine* CO-8
Orange Blossom Wash—*stream* CA-9
*Orange Bluff* FL-3
Orange Bluff—*cliff* FL-3
Orange Bowl (Burdine Stadium)—*locale* FL-3
Orange Branch—*stream* AL-4
Orange Branch—*stream* FL-3
Orange Branch—*stream* TX-5
Orange Brook—*stream* NH-1
Orange Brook—*stream* VT-1
Orange Brook Golf Course—*locale* FL-3
Orange Brook Sch—*school* FL-3
**Orangeburg**—*pop pl* KY-4
**Orangeburg**—*pop pl* NY-2
**Orangeburg**—*pop pl* OH-6
**Orangeburg**—*pop pl* SC-3
Orangeburg (CCD)—*cens area* SC-3
**Orangeburg (County)**—*pop pl* SC-3
Orangeburg County Fair Main Exhibit Bldg—*hist pl* SC-3
Orangeburg County Jail—*hist pl* SC-3
Orangeburg Downtown Hist Dist—*hist pl* SC-3
Orangeburg Natl Fish Hatchery—*other* SC-3
Orangeburg Post Office (historical)—*building* MS-4
Orangeburg Spring—*spring* ID-8
Orangeburg West (CCD)—*cens area* SC-3
Orange Butte—*summit* AZ-5
Orange-Cameron County Club House—*locale* LA-4
*Orange Canyon Creek* OR-9
Orange (CCD)—*cens area* TX-5
Orange Cem—*cemetery* (2) AL-4
Orange Cem—*cemetery* FL-3
Orange Cem—*cemetery* IN-6
Orange Cem—*cemetery* (2) IA-7
Orange Cem—*cemetery* KY-4
Orange Cem—*cemetery* (2) OH-6
Orange Cem—*cemetery* WI-6
Orange (census name for Orange Center)—*CDP* MA-1
*Orange Center* IA-7
Orange Center—*uninc pl* CA-9
Orange Center Cem—*cemetery* CT-1
Orange Center Cem—*cemetery* VT-1
Orange Center (census name Orange)—*other* MA-1
Orange Center Elem Sch—*school* FL-3
Orange Center Sch—*school* CA-9
*Orange Centre* MA-1
Orange Ch—*church* AL-4
Orange Ch—*church* (2) FL-3
Orange Ch—*church* GA-3
Orange Ch—*church* LA-4
Orange Ch—*church* NC-3
Orange Chapel—*church* AR-4
Orange Chapel—*church* IL-6
Orange Chapel—*church* (2) NC-3
Orange Chapel—*church* OH-6
Orange Ch (historical)—*church* MS-4
Orange Christian Sch—*school* FL-3
**Orange City**—*pop pl* FL-3
**Orange City**—*pop pl* IA-7
Orange City Elem Sch—*school* FL-3
**Orange City Hills**—*pop pl* FL-3
Orange City HS—*school* IA-7
Orange City Lookout Tower—*tower* FL-3
Orange City Plaza (Shop Ctr)—*locale* FL-3
Orange City Slough—*stream* IA-7
**Orange City (sta.)**—*pop pl* FL-3
Orange Cliffs—*cliff* UT-8
Orange Coast Coll—*school* CA-9
Orange Common Cem—*cemetery* NH-1
**Orange (County)**—*pop pl* CA-9
**Orange County**—*pop pl* FL-3
**Orange County**—*pop pl* IN-6
**Orange (County)**—*pop pl* NY-2
**Orange County**—*pop pl* NC-3
**Orange (County)**—*pop pl* TX-5
**Orange County**—*pop pl* VT-1
**Orange (County)**—*pop pl* VA-3
Orange County Courthouse—*hist pl* CA-9
Orange County Courthouse—*hist pl* IN-6
Orange County Courthouse—*hist pl* VA-3
Orange County Plaza Shop Ctr—*locale* CA-9
**Orange Cove**—*pop pl* CA-9
Orange Cove (CCD)—*cens area* CA-9
Orange Cove Santa Fe Railway Depot—*hist pl* CA-9
*Orange Creek* AL-4
Orange Creek—*stream* FL-3
Orange Creek—*stream* OH-6
Orange Creek—*stream* OR-9
*Orange Creek Camp* FL-3
*Orange Creek Camp Lake* FL-3
Orange Creek Camp Lake—*lake* FL-3
Orange Creek Ch—*church* FL-3
Orange Creek Methodist Ch—*church* FL-3
Orange Crossroads Ch—*church* NC-3
**Orangedale**—*pop pl* (2) FL-3
**Orangedale**—*pop pl* TX-5
Orangedale Sch—*school* AZ-5
Orange Drain—*canal* CA-9
Orange Drain—*stream* FL-3
**Orange Factory**—*pop pl* NC-3
Orange Fair Shop Ctr—*locale* CA-9
**Orangefield**—*pop pl* TX-5
Orange Flat—*flat* CA-9
Orange Free Public Library—*hist pl* NJ-2
Orange Glacier—*glacier* AK-9
Orange Glen—*post sta* CA-9
Orange Glen HS—*school* CA-9
Orange Glen Sch—*school* CA-9
Orangegrove—*locale* VI-3
**Orange Grove**—*pop pl* (2) MS-4
**Orange Grove**—*pop pl* NC-3
**Orange Grove**—*pop pl* TX-5
Orange Grove, The (Shop Ctr)—*locale* FL-3
Orange Grove Branch—*gut* FL-3
Orange Grove Canal—*canal* TX-5
Orange Grove Cem—*cemetery* IL-6
Orange Grove Cem—*cemetery* (2) LA-4
Orange Grove Cem—*cemetery* MS-4
Orange Grove Cem—*cemetery* SC-3
Orange Grove Ch—*church* GA-3
Orange Grove Ch—*church* KY-4
Orange Grove Ch—*church* NC-3
Orange Grove Ch—*church* (2) SC-3
Orange Grove Ch—*church* (2) VA-3
Orange Grove Court—*hist pl* CA-9
Orangegrove Creek—*stream* SC-3
**Orange Grove Estates**—*pop pl* AZ-5
Orange Grove Estates—*uninc pl* SC-3
*Orange Grove High School* MS-4
Orange Grove Independent Baptist Ch—*church* IN-6
Orange Grove Interchange—*crossing* AZ-5
Orange Grove Island—*island* FL-3
Orange Grove JHS—*school* AZ-5
Orange Grove Lake—*lake* FL-3
Orange Grove Oil and Gas Field—*oilfield* LA-4
**Orange Grove Plantation**—*pop pl* LA-4
Orange Grove Plantation House—*hist pl* LA-4
Orange Grove Post Office (historical)—*building* MS-4
Orange Grove-Sandia (CCD)—*cens area* TX-5
Orange Grove Sch—*school* (3) CA-9
Orange Grove Sch—*school* (2) FL-3

Orlando Junior Coll—school FL-3
Orlando Lake—reservoir PA-2
Orlando Naval Hospital—military FL-3
Orlando Naval Training Center—military FL-3
**Orlando Park**—pop pl MI-6
Orlando Plaza (Shop Ctr)—locale FL-3
Orlando Promotional Center (Shop Ctr)—locale FL-3
Orlando Public Library—building FL-3
Orlando Public Library, Eastland—building FL-3
Orlando Public Library, Fort Gatlin—building FL-3
Orlando Public Library, Kissimmee Branch—building FL-3
Orlando Public Library, Northgate—building FL-3
Orlando Ranch—locale FL-3
Orlando Regional Med Ctr—hospital FL-3
Orlando Rsvr No 2—reservoir CO-8
Orlando Tower (fire tower)—tower FL-3
**Orlando Township**—pop pl KS-7
Orlando Vocational/Technical Center—school FL-3
Orlando Worship Center—church FL-3
**Orland Park**—pop pl IL-6
Orland Park Cem—cemetery IL-6
Orland Park Ch—church IL-6
Orland Park Sch—school IL-6
Orland River—stream ME-1
**Orland (Town of)**—pop pl ME-1
**Orland Township**—pop pl SD-7
**Orland (Township of)**—pop pl IL-6
Orla Tank—lake TX-5
Orla Windmill—locale TX-5
Orlea Cem—cemetery IN-6
Orlean—locale (2) VA-3
Orlean Cem—cemetery VA-3
Orlean Ch—church VA-3
*Orleans* KS-7
*Orleans* VT-1
Orleans—locale IL-6
Orleans—locale OR-9
**Orleans**—pop pl CA-9
**Orleans**—pop pl IN-6
**Orleans**—pop pl (2) IA-7
**Orleans**—pop pl MA-1
**Orleans**—pop pl MI-6
**Orleans**—pop pl MN-6
**Orleans**—pop pl NE-7
**Orleans**—pop pl NY-2
**Orleans**—pop pl NC-3
**Orleans**—pop pl VT-1
Orleans Airp—airport IN-6
*Orleans Beach* MA-1
Orleans Beach—beach IA-7
Orleans Beach—beach MA-1
Orleans Cem—cemetery IA-7
Orleans Cem—cemetery MA-1
Orleans Cem—cemetery NY-2
Orleans Cem—cemetery OR-9
Orleans Ch—church (2) IA-7
Orleans Cheese Factory—building IA-7
Orleans Corners—other NY-2
**Orleans (County)**—pop pl NY-2
**Orleans County**—pop pl VT-1
Orleans County Courthouse and Jail Complex—hist pl VT-1
Orleans County Courthouse Hist Dist—hist pl NY-2
**Orleans Cross Roads**—pop pl WV-2
Orleans Elem Sch—school IN-6
**Orleans Estates (subdivision)**—pop pl TN-4
*Orleans Factory* MA-1
Orleans Flat—locale CA-9
**Orleans Four Corners**—pop pl NY-2
**Orleans Four Corners (Orleans Corners)**—pop pl NY-2
Orleans Hill—summit NV-8
Orleans (historical)—locale KS-7
Orleans (historical)—locale SD-7
Orleans (historical P.O.)—locale IA-7
Orleans HS—school IN-6
**Orleans Junction**—pop pl LA-4
*Orleans Lake Dam* IN-6
*Orleans Mills* MA-1
Orleans Mtn—summit CA-9
Orleans Outfall Canal—canal LA-4
**Orleans Parish**—pop pl LA-4
Orleans Park—park LA-4
**Orleans Road (Orleans Cross Roads)**—pop pl WV-2
Orleans Road Station—locale WV-2
Orleans Sch—school SD-7
Orleans Shop Ctr—locale MA-1
Orleans Shopping Plaza—locale MA-1
Orleans Springs (historical)—spring IN-6
Orleans State Fish Hatchery—locale IA-7
Orleans State Park—park IA-7
Orleans Swamp—swamp NY-2
*Orleans Terrace* IL-6
**Orleans (Town of)**—pop pl MA-1
**Orleans (Town of)**—pop pl NY-2
Orleans Township—fmr MCD IA-7
**Orleans Township**—pop pl NE-7
**Orleans (Township of)**—pop pl IN-6
**Orleans (Township of)**—pop pl MI-6
Orleans Trail Public Use Area—park MO-7
Orleans U. S. Life Saving Station (historical)—locale MA-1
*Orleans Village* MA-1
**Orleans Village**—pop pl VA-3
Orleans Water Works Reservoir Dam—dam IN-6
Orleans Water Works Rsvr—reservoir IN-6
Orlena—locale TX-5
Orlena Ch—church WV-2
**Orlien Township**—pop pl ND-7
**Orlinda**—pop pl TN-4
Orlinda Baptist Ch—church TN-4
Orlinda (CCD)—cens area TN-4
Orlinda Cem—cemetery TN-4
Orlinda Division—civil TN-4
Orlinda Post Office—building TN-4
**Orlovista**—pop pl FL-3
Orlo Vista Elem Sch—school FL-3
**Orma**—pop pl WV-2
Ormall Tank—reservoir AZ-5
Orman-Adams House—hist pl CO-8
Orman Cem—cemetery AL-4
*Orman Cemetery* MS-4
Orman Creek—stream IA-7
Orman Creek—stream TX-5
Ormand—locale CA-9
**Ormandale**—pop pl CO-8
Ormandale Sch—school CA-9
Orman Dam—dam SD-7
Ormand Hall Creek—stream SC-3
Ormand Park—park MI-6
Ormand Point—cliff UT-8
Ormand Sch—school MS-4
Ormans Cem—cemetery MS-4
Orman Sch—school SD-7
Orman Spring—spring OR-9
Ormanville—locale IA-7
Ormanville Cem—cemetery IA-7
**Ormas**—pop pl IN-6
Orme—locale MD-2
**Orme**—pop pl TN-4
Orme—uninc pl TX-5
Orme Cem—cemetery AL-4
Ormed—island MP-9
*Ormed Island* MP-9
Orme Ditch—canal IN-6
Ormega—locale CO-8
*Orme Island* MA-1
Orme Mountain Cem—cemetery TN-4
Orme Mountain Sch—school TN-4
Orme Mtn—summit TN-4
Orme Park—park AZ-5
Orme Pit Number One—cave TN-4
Orme Pit Number Two—cave TN-4
Orme Post Office (historical)—building TN-4
Orme Ranch Airstrip—airport AZ-5
Ormes Cem—cemetery IN-6
Ormes Cem—cemetery TN-4
Orme Sch—school MD-2
Ormes Chapel—church TN-4
Orme Sch (historical)—school TN-4
Ormes Lake—lake MI-6
Ormes Peak—summit CO-8
Orme Spring—spring UT-8
Ormes Store Post Office (historical)—building TN-4
Ormes Substation—locale AZ-5
Ormewood—locale GA-3
Ormigas Windmill—locale TX-5
Ormiston Corners—locale NY-2
Ormiston Point—summit CO-8
Ormiston Point Stock Driveway—trail CO-8
*Ormond* FL-3
*Ormond* PA-2
Ormond—locale NJ-2
Ormond—other FL-3
**Ormond**—pop pl LA-4
**Ormond**—pop pl VA-3
Ormond Beach—beach CA-9
**Ormond Beach**—pop pl FL-3
Ormond Beach (CCD)—cens area FL-3
Ormond Beach Elem Sch—school FL-3
Ormond Beach First Christian Ch—church FL-3
Ormond Beach JHS—school FL-3
Ormond Beach Mall—locale FL-3
Ormond Beach Memorial Hosp—hospital FL-3
Ormond Beach Public Library—building FL-3
Ormond Beach Union Ch—church FL-3
**Ormond-by-the-Sea**—pop pl FL-3
Ormond By The Sea (census for Ormond By-The-Sea)—CDP FL-3
Ormond By-The-Sea (census name Ormond By-The-Sea)—other FL-3
**Ormonde**—pop pl IL-6
Ormonde Apartment Bldg—hist pl OR-9
Ormond Hotel—hist pl FL-3
Ormond Plaza (Shop Ctr)—locale FL-3
Ormonds Island—island MN-6
Ormonds (Township of)—fmr MCD NC-3
**Ormondsville**—pop pl NC-3
Ormond Tomb State Park—park FL-3
**Ormrod**—pop pl PA-2
Ormrod, George, House—hist pl PA-2
*Ormsbee Pond* NY-2
Ormsbee Pond—lake NY-2
Ormsby—locale WI-6
**Ormsby**—pop pl MN-6
**Ormsby**—pop pl PA-2
*Ormsby Bottom* IN-6
Ormsby County Farm—locale NV-8
Ormsby Draw—valley (2) WY-8
Ormsby Heights Ch—church KY-4
Ormsby Hill Sch—school VT-1
Ormsby-Kelly House—hist pl IA-7
Ormsby Lake—reservoir NC-3
Ormsby-Laughlin Textile Companies Mill—hist pl NY-2
Ormsby Oil Field—oilfield PA-2
Ormsby Park—park AZ-5
Ormsby Pond—reservoir WI-6
Ormsby-Rosser House—hist pl NV-8
Ormsby Sch—school MI-6
Ormsby Sch (historical)—school MO-7
Ormsbys Summit—summit PA-2
Ormsby Village State Reservation—other KY-4
Orms Knob—summit KY-4
Ormuul—summit PW-9
Orna Villa—hist pl GA-3
Ornbaun Creek—stream (2) CA-9
Ornbaun Springs—spring CA-9
Ornbaun Springs Cem—cemetery CA-9
Ornbaun Valley—basin CA-9
Orndoff—locale WV-2
Orndoff Ch—church WV-2
Orndorff Cem—cemetery IN-6
Orndorff Ranch—locale NM-5
Ornduff Cem—cemetery VA-3
Orne, Sarah, House—hist pl MA-1
Orne Covered Bridge—hist pl VT-1
*Orne Island* MA-1
Orne Mtn—summit NH-1
Ornen Rock—pillar VI-3
Orners Corner—locale PA-2
Orner Slough—swamp ND-7
Ornes Hill—summit MA-1
*Ornes Island* MA-1
Orne Swamp—swamp MA-1
Orneville Cem—cemetery ME-1
Orneville Sch—school ME-1
Orneville (Township of)—other ME-1
Orneville (Township of)—unorg ME-1
Orneys Place Pond—lake AL-4
*Ornocor Bay* AL-4
Ornoname 10 Dam—other OR-9
Ornoname 11 Dam—other OR-9
Ornoname 12 Dam—other OR-9
Ornoname 13 Dam—other OR-9
Ornoname 14 Dam—other OR-9
Ornoname 15 Dam—other OR-9
Ornoname 16 Dam—other OR-9
Ornoname 17 Dam—other OR-9
Ornoname 18 Dam—other OR-9
Ornoname 2 Dam—other OR-9
Ornoname 21 Dam—other OR-9
Ornoname 22 Dam—other OR-9
Ornoname 24 Dam—dam OR-9
Ornoname 24 Rsvr—reservoir OR-9
Ornoname 3 Dam—other OR-9
Ornoname 4 Dam—other OR-9
Ornoname 5 Dam—other OR-9
Ornoname 7 Dam—other OR-9
Ornoname 8 Dam—other OR-9
Ornoname 9 Dam—other OR-9
Orno Peak—summit CO-8
*Oro* AZ-5
Oro—locale CO-8
Oro—spring FM-9
Oro, Canada del —valley AZ-5
Oro, Lago del—reservoir AZ-5
Oro Amigo Mine—mine NV-8
O'Roark Ch—church KY-4
O'Roarke Draft—valley VA-3
Oro Bay—bay WA-9
Oro Belle Mine—mine AZ-5
*Oro Blanco* AZ-5
**Oro Blanco**—pop pl AZ-5
Oro Blanco Dam—dam AZ-5
Oro Blanco Mine—mine AZ-5
*Oro Blanco Mountains* AZ-5
Oro Blanco Ranch—locale AZ-5
Oro Blanco Rsvr—reservoir AZ-5
Oro Blanco Wash—stream AZ-5
Oroch—bar FM-9
Oro Ch—church SC-3
Orocopia Canyon—valley CA-9
Orocopia Mountains—range CA-9
**Orocovis**—pop pl PR-3
Orocovis (Barrio)—fmr MCD PR-3
Orocovis (Municipio)—civil PR-3
Orocovis (Pueblo)—fmr MCD PR-3
*Oro Creek* CA-9
**Orodell**—pop pl CO-8
**Orodell (historical)**—pop pl OR-9
*Oro Del Plata Mine* CA-9
Oro del Rey Mine—mine UT-8
*Orofield* PA-2
Oro Fino—locale CA-9
**Orofino**—pop pl ID-8
Orofino Campground—locale MT-8
Oro Fino Canyon—valley (3) CA-9
Orofino Canyon—valley NV-8
Oro Fino Creek—stream AK-9
Oro Fino Creek—stream CA-9
Orofino Creek—stream ID-8
Orofino Creek—stream MT-8
Orofino Creek Point—cliff ID-8
Orofino Gulch—valley CA-9
Oro Fino Gulch—valley ID-8
Orofino Gulch—valley MT-8
Oro Fino Gulch—valley MT-8
Orofino Gulch—valley (2) OR-9
Orofino Hist Dist—hist pl ID-8
Oro Fino (historical)—mine SD-7
Orofino HS—school ID-8
Oro Fino Mine—mine AZ-5
Orofino Mine—mine AZ-5
Oro Fino Mine—mine CA-9
Oro Fino Mine—mine CO-8
Oro Fino Mine—mine ID-8
Oro Fino Mine—mine NV-8
Orofino Mine—mine (3) OR-9
Orofino Mtn—summit MT-8
*Oro Fino River* ID-8
Orofino Tank—reservoir AZ-5
Orofino Wash—stream AZ-5
Orofino Wash Well—well AZ-5
Orofino Windmill—locale AZ-5
Oro Flame Mine—mine AZ-5
Oroflame Mine—mine CA-9
*Oroflamme Canyon* CA-9
*Oroflamme Mountains* CA-9
Orognen Canyon—valley CA-9
**Oro Grande**—pop pl CA-9
**Orogrande**—pop pl ID-8
**Orogrande**—pop pl NM-5
Orogrande Aqueduct—canal NM-5
Orogrande Camp—locale ID-8
Oro Grande Canyon—valley CA-9
*Orogrande Creek* ID-8
Oro Grande Creek—stream AK-9
Orogrande Creek—stream ID-8
Orogrande Frisco Mine—mine ID-8
Oro Grande Mine—mine (2) AZ-5
Oro Grande Mine—mine CA-9
Orogrande Range Camp—locale NM-5
Oro Grande Sch—school CA-9
Orogrande Summit—summit ID-8
Oro Grande Wash—stream CA-9
Oro Gulch—valley CO-8
*Oroh* AZ-5
**Orohondo**—pop pl SD-7
Oro Hondo Mine—mine SD-7
**Oroleve**—pop pl CA-9
Oroleve Creek—stream CA-9
Oro Loma—locale CA-9
Oro Loma Sch—school CA-9
*Orolong* PW-9
Oroluk Anchorage—harbor FM-9
Oroluk Island—island FM-9
Oroluk Lagoon—bay FM-9
Oroluk (Municipality)—civ div FM-9
Oromange Island—island FM-9
*Oromed* MP-9
Oro Mine—mine CA-9
Oro Mine, El—mine AZ-5
Oro Mine (historical)—mine ID-8
Oro Monte Mine—mine NV-8
Oro Mtn—summit ID-8
Orona, Cerro—summit TX-5
**Orondo**—pop pl WA-9
Orondo Canyon—valley CA-9
Orondo Community Cem—cemetery WA-9
Orondo Mine—mine CA-9
Orondo Sch—school WA-9
Orongan, Unun En—bar FM-9
Oronikowaktalik Rock—island AK-9
**Orono**—pop pl ME-1
**Orono**—pop pl MN-6
Orono Cem—cemetery MN-6
**Orono Center**—pop pl ME-1
Oronoco—locale VA-3
**Oronoco**—pop pl MN-6
Oronoco Ch—church VA-3
Oronoco Sch—hist pl MN-6
Oronoco State Park—park MN-6
**Oronoco (Township of)**—pop pl MN-6
Orono Country Club—other MN-6
**Oronogo**—pop pl MO-7
Orono (historical)—locale AL-4
Orono HS—school MN-6
Orono Island—island (2) ME-1
*Oronoke* CT-1
**Oronoke**—pop pl CT-1
Oronoko Ch—church MI-6
**Oronoko (Township of)**—pop pl MI-6
Orono Lake—reservoir MN-6
Orono Main Street Hist Dist—hist pl ME-1
Orono Mine (underground)—mine AL-4
Orono Point—cape MN-6
Oronoque—locale CT-1
**Oronoque**—pop pl KS-7
Oronoque Cem—cemetery KS-7
Oro Northwest Oil Field—oilfield KS-7
**Orono (Town of)**—pop pl ME-1
Orono Township—fmr MCD IA-7
Oron Thompson Dam—dam OR-9
Oron Thompson Rsvr—reservoir OR-9
Oronto Bay—bay WI-6
Oronto Creek—stream WI-6
Oro Oil Field—oilfield KS-7
Orophi Mountains—summit AZ-5
Oro Plata Mine—mine (2) CA-9
Oro Plata Mine—mine NV-8
Oro Plata Mine—mine UT-8
Oro Point—cape AL-4
*Oropushakari To* PW-9
*Oropusharakaru To* PW-9
*Oropushhaka* PW-9
Oro Quay Peak—summit NM-5
O RO Ranch—locale AZ-5
*Oror En Fansafak* FM-9
*Oror En Fasafang* FM-9
*Oror En Faup* FM-9
*Oror En Nafenong* FM-9
*Oror En Nameis* FM-9
*Oror En Napinom* FM-9
*Oror En Napitu* FM-9
*Oror En Nemuan* FM-9
*Oror En Nenon* FM-9
*Oror En Neomas* FM-9
*Oror En Nepiepi* FM-9
*Oror En Nepinom* FM-9
*Oror En Newomas* FM-9
*Oror En Ngesano* FM-9
*Oror En Nukanap* FM-9
*Oror En Rusin* FM-9
*Oror En Unulou* FM-9
*Oror En Ununou* FM-9
*Oror Enurusin* FM-9
*Oror En Wone* FM-9
*Oror En Wonei* FM-9
*Ororian* PW-9
*O'Rorke Lake* MI-6
*Ororu* FM-9
*Ororumakku Island* PW-9
*Ororumakku To* PW-9
Orosco Ridge—ridge CA-9
Orosco Truck Trail—trail CA-9
Orosi—CDP CA-9
Orosi Branch Library—hist pl CA-9
Orosi-Cutler (CCD)—cens area CA-9
Orosi (sta.) (East Orosi)—CDP CA-9
Oro (site)—locale AZ-5
Oro Southeast Oil Field—oilfield KS-7
Oros Well—well AZ-5
Orote Field—hist pl GU-9
Orote Historical Complex—hist pl GU-9
Orote Island—island GU-9
Orote Peninsula—cape GU-9
Orote Point—summit GU-9
Orote Powerplant—other GU-9
*Oroto To* MP-9
*Orotto-to* MP-9
O'Rouick Spring—spring OR-9
O'Rourke Bay—bay ID-8
O'Rourke Canal—canal LA-4
O'Rourke Lake—lake MI-6
O'Rourkes Blue Hole—lake MO-7
**Orovada**—pop pl NV-8
**Oro Valley**—pop pl AZ-5
Oro Valley Country Club Golf Course—other AZ-5
**Oroville**—pop pl CA-9
**Oroville**—pop pl WA-9
Oroville, Lake—reservoir CA-9
Oroville (CCD)—cens area CA-9
Oroville (CCD)—cens area WA-9
Oroville Cem—cemetery CA-9
Oroville Chinese Temple—hist pl CA-9
Oroville Commercial District (old)—hist pl CA-9
Oroville Dam—dam CA-9
Oroville Gun Club—other CA-9
**Oroville Junction (Tres Vias)**—pop pl CA-9
Oroville (site)—locale AZ-5
Oroville Wildlife Area—park CA-9
Oroville Wyandotte Canal—canal CA-9
Oro Wash—stream CA-9
Oro Windmill—locale NM-5
Orowoc Creek—stream NY-2
Orowoc Lake—lake NY-2
*Orowoo* FM-9
Orozimbo—locale TX-5
**Orpha**—pop pl WY-8
Orphanage Branch—stream SC-3
Orphanage Cem—cemetery TX-5
Orphan Annie Rock—pillar NM-5
Orphan Annie Tank—reservoir NM-5
Orphan Annie Well—well NM-5
Orphan Boy Mine—mine AZ-5
Orphan Boy Mine—mine CO-8
Orphan Boy Mine—mine NV-8
Orphan Butte—summit CO-8
Orphan Butte—summit OR-9
Orphan Canyon—valley NM-5
Orphan Creek—stream (2) AK-9
Orphan Creek—stream MS-4
Orphan Creek—stream MT-8
Orphan Creek—stream OR-9
Orphan Hill—summit NM-5
Orphan Hill—summit TX-5
Orphan Mine—mine AZ-5
Orphan Point—cliff ID-8
Orphan Ridge—ridge TN-4
Orphan Rsvr—reservoir NV-8
Orphans Cem—cemetery GA-3
Orphans Creek—stream AL-4
Orphans Home—building TX-5
Orphans Home Lake—reservoir TN-4
Orphan Spring—spring CO-8
Orphans Sch—school KY-4
Orpheum Theater—hist pl AZ-5
Orpheum Theater and Office Bldg—hist pl KS-7
Orpheum Theatre—hist pl LA-4
Orpheum Theatre—hist pl SD-7
Orpheum Theatre—hist pl TN-4
Orpheum Theatre—hist pl UT-8
Orpheum Theatre and Site—hist pl IA-7
**Orpheum Village**—pop pl HI-9
**Orpheus**—pop pl OH-6
Orr—locale CO-8
Orr—locale KY-4
Orr—locale MI-6
Orr—locale WV-2
**Orr**—pop pl MN-6
**Orr**—pop pl ND-7
**Orr**—pop pl OK-5
**Orr**—pop pl SC-3
**Orr**—pop pl TX-5
**Orr**—pop pl WV-2
**Orr**—pop pl WY-8
Orr, Dr. Samuel Marshall, House—hist pl SC-3
Orr, Nathaniel, House and Orchard—hist pl WA-9
Orr, William, House—hist pl IN-6
Orrak—beach PW-9
Orr Bay—bay MN-6
Orr Branch—stream AL-4
Orr Branch—stream KY-4
Orr Branch—stream (2) NC-3
Orr Branch—stream TN-4
Orr Brook—stream ME-1
Orr Canyon—valley CO-8
Orr Canyon—valley NM-5
Orr Cem—cemetery AL-4
Orr Cem—cemetery GA-3
Orr Cem—cemetery IN-6
Orr Cem—cemetery KY-4
Orr Cem—cemetery (4) NC-3
Orr Cem—cemetery OK-5
Orr Cem—cemetery TN-4
Orr Cem—cemetery VA-3
Orr Coulee—valley MT-8
Orr Cove—bay ME-1
*Orr Creek* MI-6
Orr Creek—stream AL-4
Orr Creek—stream CA-9
Orr Creek—stream MI-6
Orr Creek—stream MS-4
Orr Creek—stream MT-8
Orr Creek—stream OR-9
Orr Creek—stream (3) WA-9
Orr Creek Dam—dam CA-9
Orr Ditch—canal NV-8
Orr Ditch—canal OH-6
Orrell House—hist pl AL-4
Orrenmaa Sch—school CA-9
Orr Estates Lake—reservoir AL-4
Orr Estates Pond—reservoir AL-4
**Orr Estates (subdivision)**—pop pl AL-4
Orrey, Mount—summit NY-2
Orr Gulch—valley WY-8
Orr-Herl Mound and Village Site—hist pl IL-6
Orr Hill—summit (2) NY-2
Orr Hill Sch (historical)—school PA-2
Orr HS—school IL-6
**Orrick**—pop pl MO-7
Orrick Cem—cemetery VA-3
Orrick Township—civil MO-7
Orridge Sch—school NC-3
Orrie Walker Flat—flat CO-8
**Orrin**—pop pl ND-7
**Orrington**—pop pl ME-1
**Orrington Center**—pop pl ME-1
Orrington Corner—other ME-1
*Orrington Great Pond* ME-1
Orrington Sch—school IL-6
**Orrington (Town of)**—pop pl ME-1
Orr Iron Company—hist pl IN-6
Orris—locale CA-9
Orris, Adam, House—hist pl PA-2
*Orr Island* ME-1
Orr Island—island AK-9
Orris Pond—lake OR-9
Orris Sch—school PA-2
Orrix Creek—stream VA-3
Orr JHS—school NV-8
Orr Lake—lake CA-9
Orr Lake—lake IN-6
Orr Lake—lake WI-6
Orr Mill—CDP SC-3
Orr Mill Park—park SC-3
Orr-Moore Sch—school MI-6
Orr Mtn—summit CA-9
Orrock—locale MN-6
Orrock, Rev. John, House—hist pl MA-1
Orrock Ch—church MN-6
**Orrock (Township of)**—pop pl MN-6
Orr Park—park OH-6
Orr-Patterson Family Cem—cemetery MS-4
Orr Peak—summit CA-9
Orr Ranch—locale CO-8
Orr Ranch—locale MT-8
Orr Ranch—locale (2) NE-7
Orr Ranch—locale UT-8
Orr Ranch—locale WY-8
Orr Ridge—ridge ME-1
Orr Ridge—ridge UT-8
*Orrs* CA-9
Orrs—locale TN-4
Orrs—locale TX-5
**Orrs**—pop pl GA-3
**Orrs**—pop pl SC-3
Orrsburg—locale MO-7
Orrs Ch—church GA-3
Orrs Ch—church SC-3
Orr Sch—hist pl AR-4
Orr Sch—school (2) AR-4
Orr Sch—school CA-9
Orr Sch—school DC-2
Orr Sch—school MI-6
Orr Sch—school MT-8
Orr Sch—school TX-5
Orr Sch—school WI-6
Orr Sch (abandoned)—school PA-2
Orrs Chapel—church TN-4
Orr Sch (historical)—school AL-4
**Orrs Corner**—pop pl OR-9
Orrs Corners—locale NY-2
*Orrs Cove* ME-1
Orrs Cove—bay ME-1
*Orrs Creek* MI-6
Orrs Creek—stream (2) CA-9
Orrs Creek—stream MI-6
*Orrs Ditch* IN-6
*Orrs Factory* AL-4
Orrs Gin (historical)—locale AL-4
Orrs Hill—summit ME-1
*Orr's Island* ME-1
Orrs Island—island ME-1
Orrs Island—island TN-4
**Orrs Island**—pop pl ME-1
Orrs Lake—reservoir AL-4
Orrs Lake Dam—dam AL-4
Orr Slough—gut TN-4
*Orrs Mill* AL-4
**Orrs Mill**—pop pl NY-2
Orrs Mill Creek—stream SC-3
Orrs Mtn—summit WV-2
Orrs Point—cape MI-6
Orrs Pond—lake GA-3
Orrs Pond—reservoir MA-1
Orrs Pond Dam—dam MA-1
Orr Spring—spring AZ-5
Orr Spring—spring NC-3
Orr Spring Canyon—valley CA-9
Orr Springs—spring ID-8
Orr Springs—spring UT-8
Orrs Run—stream WV-2
Orrs Sch—school GA-3
*Orrs Spring Branch* TN-4
**Orrs Springs**—pop pl CA-9
**Orrstown**—pop pl PA-2
Orrstown Borough—civil PA-2
Orrstown Elem Sch—school PA-2
*Orrsville* MS-4
Orr Swamp—swamp SC-3
Orr Tank—reservoir AZ-5
**Orrtanna**—pop pl PA-2
**Orrton**—pop pl PA-2
Orr Trap Corral—locale AZ-5
Orr Trap Tank—reservoir AZ-5
**Orrum**—pop pl NC-3
Orrum HS—school NC-3
Orrum (Township of)—fmr MCD NC-3
Orrville—locale AL-4
Orrville—locale MO-7
**Orrville**—pop pl AL-4
**Orrville**—pop pl IN-6
**Orrville**—pop pl OH-6
**Orrville**—pop pl PA-2
**Orrville**—pop pl SC-3
Orrville (CCD)—cens area AL-4
Orrville Cem—cemetery AL-4
Orrville Cem—cemetery IN-6
Orrville Cem—cemetery SC-3
Orrville Ch—church SC-3
Orrville Ditch—canal OH-6
Orrville Division—civil AL-4
Orrville Hills—range IN-6
*Orrville Junction* OH-6
**Orrville (Orville)**—pop pl AL-4
Orr Well—well TX-5
Orsa—locale CO-8
Orschell Overlook—locale IN-6
Orsemus—locale KS-7
Orser Creek—stream ID-8
Orser Drain—canal MI-6
Orsinger Park—park TX-5
Orsino—locale FL-3
Orsino Creek—stream WA-9
Orsman—locale GA-3
Orson—locale IA-7
**Orson**—pop pl PA-2
Orson Bedground—flat UT-8
Orson Bog—swamp ME-1
Orson Brook—stream ME-1
Orson Cem—cemetery PA-2
Orson Ch—church PA-2
Orson Coulee—stream MT-8
**Orson Ellis Subdivision**—pop pl UT-8
Orson Island—island ME-1
Orson Pond—reservoir PA-2
Orson Pond Dam—dam PA-2
Orson Run—stream PA-2
Orsons Pond—lake UT-8
Orston—uninc pl NJ-2
O Rsvr—reservoir OR-9
Ort—locale TX-5
Ort Creek—stream CA-9
Ortega—locale (2) CA-9
**Ortega**—pop pl FL-3
Ortega Bridge—bridge FL-3
Ortega Canyon—valley NM-5
*Ortega Creek* AZ-5
Ortega Creek—stream CA-9
Ortega Creek—stream NM-5
Ortega Draw—valley AZ-5
Ortega Elem Sch—school FL-3
**Ortega Farms**—pop pl FL-3
**Ortega Forest**—pop pl FL-3
Ortega Hill—summit (2) CA-9
Ortega Hills—summit FL-3
Ortega Hills—uninc pl FL-3
Ortega Kindergarten—school FL-3
*Ortega Lake* AZ-5
Ortega Lake—lake AZ-5
Ortega Mesa—summit NM-5
Ortega Mountains—other NM-5
Ortega Mtn—summit AZ-5
Ortega Ranch—locale NM-5
Ortega River—stream FL-3
Ortega Sch—school (4) CA-9

Ortega Sch—school ... TX-5
Ortega Sink—basin ... AZ-5
Ortega Spring—spring ... AZ-5
Ortega Spring—spring ... CA-9
Ortegas Ranch—locale ... AZ-5
Ortega Tank—reservoir (2) ... AZ-5
Ortega Tank—reservoir ... NM-5
**Ortega Terrace**—pop pl ... FL-3
Ortega Village Square (Shop Ctr)—locale ... FL-3
Ortega Wash ... AZ-5
Ortega Well—well ... AZ-5
Ortega Windmills—locale ... NM-5
Ortego Cem—cemetery ... LA-4
Ortell Creek—stream ... WA-9
Ortello Cem—cemetery ... NE-7
Ortello Chapel—church ... NE-7
Ortello Sch—school ... NE-7
Ortello Valley—basin ... NE-7
**Orten**—pop pl ... NC-3
Orten Creek—stream ... AR-4
Orter Hollow—valley ... MO-7
Orth—locale ... MN-6
Orth, John, House—hist pl ... OR-9
Orth, Lake—reservoir ... CA-9
Orth Cem—cemetery ... IL-6
Orth Cem—cemetery ... TX-5
Ort-Heeb Farm—hist pl ... KY-4
**Orthell Township**—pop pl ... ND-7
Orthel Township—fmr MCD ... IA-7
Orth House—hist pl ... IL-6
Orthmer Creek—stream ... AK-9
Orthodontic Strip—airport ... IN-6
Orthodox Ch—church ... KY-4
Orthodox Ch of Saint Stephen (OCA)—church ... FL-3
Orthodox Meetinghouse—hist pl ... PA-2
Ortho (historical P.O.)—locale ... IA-7
Orth Oil Field—oilfield ... KS-7
Orthopedic Hosp—hospital ... NY-2
Orth West Oil Field—oilfield ... KS-7
**Ortiga**—pop pl ... PR-3
Ortiga Creek—stream ... NM-5
Ortigalita Creek—stream ... CA-9
Ortigalita Peak—summit ... CA-9
Ortigalita Ridge—ridge ... CA-9
Ortigalito Creek ... CA-9
Ortigalito Peak ... CA-9
Ortigalito Ridge ... CA-9
Ortiga Ranch—locale ... NM-5
**Orting**—pop pl ... WA-9
Orting Cem—cemetery ... WA-9
Orting Lake—lake ... WA-9
**Ortin Heights**—pop pl ... WV-2
Ortiz—locale ... KY-4
**Ortiz**—pop pl ... CO-8
**Ortiz**—pop pl ... MO-7
**Ortiz**—pop pl (2) ... PR-3
Ortiz (Barrio)—fmr MCD ... PR-3
Ortiz Canyon—valley ... NM-5
Ortiz Cem—cemetery ... CO-8
Ortiz Ditch—canal ... NM-5
Ortiz House—hist pl ... AZ-5
Ortiz Mesa ... NM-5
Ortiz Mine—civil (2) ... NM-5
Ortiz Mine—mine ... NM-5
Ortiz Mountains—other ... NM-5
Ortiz Mtn—summit ... NM-5
Ortiz Peak—summit ... NM-5
Ortiz Ranch—locale ... NM-5
Ortiz Sch—school ... CO-8
Ortiz Siding—locale ... AL-4
Ortiz Spring—spring ... NM-5
Ortiz Tank—reservoir (3) ... NM-5
Ortiz Well—well ... NM-5
Ortiz Windmill—locale ... TX-5
Ortleib Lake—reservoir ... IN-6
Ortley ... NJ-2
Ortley—locale ... OR-9
**Ortley**—pop pl ... SD-7
**Ortley Beach**—pop pl ... NJ-2
**Ortley Beach (Ortley)**—pop pl ... NJ-2
Ortley Cem—cemetery ... SD-7
Ortley Cove—bay ... NJ-2
**Ortley Terrace**—pop pl ... NJ-2
**Ortley Township**—pop pl ... SD-7
Ortman Lake—lake ... MN-6
Ortman Landing Strip—airport ... SD-7
Ortner Drain—canal (2) ... MI-6
Ortners Pond—lake ... CT-1
Ortolani Number 2 Dam—dam ... MA-1
Ortolani Number 3 Dam—dam ... MA-1
Ortolani Rsvr—reservoir ... MA-1
Orton ... UT-8
Orton—locale ... AR-4
Orton—locale ... WV-2
**Orton**—pop pl ... IA-7
**Orton**—pop pl ... SD-7
Orton, Charles W., House—hist pl ... WA-9
Orton, Mount—summit ... CO-8
Ortona—locale ... FL-3
**Ortona**—pop pl ... FL-3
Ortona Cem—cemetery ... FL-3
Ortona Ch—church ... FL-3
Ortona Elem Sch—school ... FL-3
Ortona Lock—other ... FL-3
Orton Branch—stream ... NC-3
Orton Bridge (covered)—bridge ... OR-9
Orton Creek—stream ... CA-9
Orton Creek—stream ... NC-3
Orton Creek Bridge—bridge ... NC-3
Orton Flat—flat ... SD-7
Orton Gulch—valley ... CA-9
Orton Gully—valley ... TX-5
**Orton Hill (reduced usage)**—pop pl ... TX-5
Orton (historical)—locale ... SD-7
Orton Island—island ... MO-7
Orton Lake—lake ... AK-9
Orton Lake—reservoir ... TX-5
Orton Memorial Laboratory—hist pl ... OH-6
Orton Memorial Monmt—pillar ... OH-6
Orton Park—hist pl ... WI-6
Orton Park—park ... WI-6
Orton Park Hist Dist—hist pl ... WI-6
Orton Plantation—hist pl ... NC-3
Orton Plantation—locale ... NC-3
Orton Point—cape ... NC-3
Orton Pond—reservoir ... NC-3
Orton Ranch—locale ... AK-9
Orton Ranch—locale (2) ... WY-8
Ortons ... NC-3
Orton Sch—school ... MI-6
Orton Sch—school ... SD-7
Orton Spring—spring ... TN-4
**Orton (Township of)**—pop pl ... MN-6
Ortonville—locale ... CA-9
**Ortonville**—pop pl ... IA-7
**Ortonville**—pop pl ... MI-6
**Ortonville**—pop pl ... MN-6
Ortonville Commercial Hist Dist—hist pl ... MN-6
Ortonville Free Library—hist pl ... MN-6
Ortonville Mill—hist pl ... MI-6
Ortonville State Rec Area—park ... MI-6
**Ortonville (Township of)**—pop pl ... MN-6
Oruallubei ... PW-9
Orubebbu Island ... MP-9
Orudeerusao ... PW-9
Oruk ... MP-9
**Orukei**—pop pl ... PW-9
Oruko—swamp ... FM-9
Orukon Reef ... PW-9
Oruktalik Entrance—channel ... AK-9
Oruktalik Lagoon—bay ... AK-9
Orukuizu ... PW-9
Orukuizu Island ... PW-9
**Orull**—pop pl ... PW-9
Orulong ... PW-9
**Orum**—pop pl ... NE-7
**Orum**—pop pl ... SC-3
Orum Creek—stream ... AK-9
Orums Cem—cemetery ... WV-2
Oruregiru ... PW-9
Oruregiru Island ... PW-9
Oruregoru To ... PW-9
Orutorukkuru ... PW-9
Orutorukkuru—island ... PW-9
Orva—locale ... WI-6
Orvil—locale ... TX-5
**Orvilla**—pop pl ... PA-2
Orville—fmr MCD ... NE-7
Orville—locale ... KY-4
Orville—locale ... OR-9
Orville—locale ... PA-2
**Orville**—pop pl ... PA-2
**Orville**—pop pl ... WV-2
Orville, Lake—reservoir ... CA-9
Orville, Mount—summit ... AK-9
Orville Beach Memorial Manual Training Sch—hist pl ... WI-6
Orville Cave—cave ... AL-4
Orville Cem—cemetery ... MT-8
Orville Draw—valley ... WY-8
**Orville (historical)**—pop pl ... NC-3
Orville Platt HS—school ... CT-1
Orville Sch—school ... MI-6
Orville Wright Boys Sch—school ... KS-7
Orville Wright JHS—school ... CA-9
Orville Wright Sch—school (2) ... CA-9
**Orvil (Township of)**—pop pl ... IL-6
Orvil Windmill—locale ... TX-5
Orvin—locale ... ID-8
Orvin Fire Tower ... AL-4
Orvin Lookout Tower—tower ... AL-4
**Orvisburg**—pop pl ... MS-4
Orvisburg Cem—cemetery ... MS-4
Orvisburg Lake—reservoir ... MS-4
Orvisburg Lake Dam—dam ... MS-4
Orvis Cem—cemetery ... IL-6
Orvis Dam—dam ... CA-9
Orvis Evans, Mount—summit ... MT-8
Orvis Hill—summit ... NY-2
Orvis Hot Spring—spring ... CO-8
Orvis Road Hist Dist—hist pl ... MA-1
**Orviston**—pop pl (2) ... PA-2
Orwell—locale ... KS-7
Orwell—locale ... PA-2
**Orwell**—pop pl ... NY-2
**Orwell**—pop pl ... OH-6
**Orwell**—pop pl ... VT-1
Orwell Bridge—locale ... KS-7
Orwell Cem—cemetery ... PA-2
Orwell City ... KS-7
Orwell Creek—stream ... NY-2
Orwell Dam—dam ... MN-6
Orwell Lake—reservoir ... MN-6
Orwell Mine—mine ... MN-6
Orwell Reservoir ... MN-6
Orwell Site—hist pl ... MN-6
Orwell Site—hist pl ... VT-1
Orwell State Wildlife Mngmt Area—park ... MN-6
**Orwell (Town of)**—pop pl ... NY-2
**Orwell (Town of)**—pop pl ... VT-1
**Orwell (Township of)**—pop pl ... MN-6
**Orwell (Township of)**—pop pl ... OH-6
**Orwell (Township of)**—pop pl ... PA-2
Orwell Valley Cem—cemetery ... PA-2
Orwig—locale ... PA-2
Orwig Creek—stream ... WA-9
Orwig Hump—summit ... WA-9
Orwig Lake ... WI-6
**Orwigsburg**—pop pl ... PA-2
Orwigsburg Borough—civil ... PA-2
Orwigsburg Rsvr—reservoir ... PA-2
**Orwin**—pop pl ... PA-2
Orwin, Jessie, House—hist pl ... UT-8
O R Windmill—locale ... NM-5
Orwood—locale ... CA-9
Orwood—locale ... MS-4
Orwood Acad (historical)—school ... MS-4
Orwood Post Office (historical)—building ... MS-4
Orwood Sch—school ... MS-4
Orwood Tract—civil ... CA-9
Orworth (historical)—locale ... KS-7
O'Ryan Knob—summit ... TN-4
**Orysa**—pop pl ... TN-4
Orysa Post Office (historical)—building ... TN-4
Oryza ... TN-4
Orzaba Reef—bar ... AK-9
Orzinski Bay—bay ... AK-9
Osa ... MP-9
Osa—locale ... MO-7
Osa, Mesa de la—summit ... AZ-5
Osa, Rancho—locale ... AZ-5
Osa Ch—church ... MO-7
Osachees ... FL-3
Osa Creek ... TX-5
Osa Creek—stream ... CA-9
Osaga ... KS-7
Osage ... KS-7
Osage—fmr MCD ... NE-7
Osage—locale ... NJ-2
Osage—locale ... TX-5
**Osage**—pop pl ... AR-4
**Osage**—pop pl ... IL-6
**Osage**—pop pl ... IA-7
**Osage**—pop pl ... MN-6
**Osage**—pop pl ... OK-5
**Osage**—pop pl ... TN-4
**Osage**—pop pl ... WV-2
**Osage**—pop pl ... WY-8
Osage Agency—hist pl ... OK-5
Osage Ave Sch—school ... CA-9
Osage Bank of Fairfax—hist pl ... OK-5
Osage Bar—bar ... AL-4
**Osage Beach**—pop pl ... MO-7
**Osage Bend**—pop pl ... MO-7
Osage Bend Sch—school ... MO-7
Osage Bluff—locale ... MO-7
Osage Bluff Ferry (historical)—locale ... MO-7
Osage Bluff Public Use Area—locale ... MO-7
Osage Bluff Sch (abandoned)—school ... MO-7
Osage Canal—canal ... CA-9
Osage Cem—cemetery ... IL-6
Osage Cem—cemetery (2) ... KS-7
Osage Cem—cemetery ... MN-6
Osage Cem—cemetery ... NJ-2
Osage Cem—cemetery (2) ... OK-5
Osage Cem—cemetery (2) ... TX-5
Osage Center Sch—school ... IL-6
Osage Centre ... KS-7
Osage Ch—church ... KS-7
Osage Ch—church ... OH-6
Osage Ch—church ... OK-5
Osage City—other ... OK-5
**Osage City**—pop pl ... KS-7
**Osage City**—pop pl ... MO-7
Osage City Cem—cemetery ... MO-7
Osage City Country Club—other ... KS-7
Osage City Dam—dam ... KS-7
Osage City Elem Sch—school ... KS-7
Osage City HS—school ... KS-7
Osage City Municipal Airp—airport ... KS-7
Osage City Oil Field—oilfield ... OK-5
Osage City Rsvr—reservoir ... KS-7
Osage Country Club—locale ... MO-7
Osage County—civil ... KS-7
**Osage County**—pop pl ... MO-7
**Osage (County)**—pop pl ... OK-5
Osage County Courthouse—hist pl ... OK-5
Osage County Lake—reservoir ... KS-7
Osage County State Lake Dam—dam ... KS-7
Osage County State Park—park ... KS-7
Osage Creek ... AL-4
Osage Creek ... OK-5
Osage Creek—stream (2) ... AR-4
Osage Creek—stream ... KS-7
Osage Creek—stream (3) ... OK-5
Osage Creek Bridge—hist pl ... AR-4
Osage Cuestas—summit ... KS-7
Osage Drain—canal ... CA-9
Osage Fork Gasconade River—stream ... MO-7
Osage Fork State For—forest ... MO-7
Osage Gardens Cem—cemetery ... OK-5
Osage Heights ... MO-7
**Osage Heights**—pop pl ... MO-7
Osage Hill ... MO-7
Osage Hill—summit (2) ... OK-5
**Osage Hills**—pop pl ... MO-7
Osage Hills—range ... OK-5
Osage Hills Country Club—other ... OK-5
Osage Hills Estates—uninc pl ... OK-5
Osage Hills Sch—school ... OK-5
Osage Hills State Park—park ... OK-5
Osage Hollow—valley ... OK-5
Osage Hominy Oil Field—oilfield ... OK-5
**Osage Ind Res**—pop pl ... OK-5
Osage Junction—locale ... OK-5
Osage Lake—lake ... FL-3
Osage Lake—reservoir ... MO-7
Osage Lake—reservoir ... NC-3
Osage Lake—reservoir ... OK-5
Osage Lake Dam—dam ... NC-3
Osage Landing ... AL-4
Osage Lateral—canal ... CA-9
Osage Mills—locale ... AR-4
Osage Mills Dam—hist pl ... AR-4
Osage Mission ... KS-7
Osage Mound—summit ... OK-5
Osage Mtn—summit ... NC-3
Osage Oil Field—oilfield ... TX-5
Osage Oil Field—oilfield ... WY-8
**Osage (Osage City)**—pop pl ... MO-7
**Osage (Osage City)**—pop pl ... OK-5
Osage Park—park ... KS-7
Osage Plains ... KS-7
Osage Plaza—locale ... MO-7
Osage Plaza (Shop Ctr)—locale ... MO-7
Osage Point Park—park ... OK-5
Osage Res—reserve ... OK-5
Osage Reservoir ... KS-7
Osage River ... KS-7
Osage River ... MO-7
Osage River—stream ... MO-7
Osage Sch—school ... KS-7
Osage Sch—school ... MO-7
Osage Sch—school ... NJ-2
Osage Sch—school ... OK-5
Osage Sch—school ... TX-5
Osage Sch (abandoned)—school ... MO-7
Osage Sch (historical)—school ... MO-7
Osage Sch (historical)—school ... TN-4
Osage School—locale ... OK-5
Osage Spring—spring ... AR-4
Osage Spring Park—park ... IA-7
Osage State Fishing Lake—park ... KS-7
Osage-Tavern State Wildlife Area—park ... MO-7
Osage Township—civil (8) ... MO-7
Osage Township—fmr MCD ... IA-7
**Osage Township**—pop pl (5) ... KS-7
**Osage Township**—pop pl (3) ... MO-7
Osage (Township of)—fmr MCD (3) ... AR-4
**Osage (Township of)**—pop pl ... IL-6
**Osage (Township of)**—pop pl ... MN-6
Osage Valley Sch—school ... KS-7
Osage Village Shop Ctr—locale ... MO-7
Osage Woodyard Landing—locale ... AL-4
**Osago Township**—pop pl ... ND-7
Osahatchee ... GA-3
Osahatchee Creek ... GA-3
Osahatchi Creek ... GA-3
Osahatchie ... GA-3
Osaka—locale ... AL-4
**Osaka**—pop pl ... VA-3
Osaka Ch—church ... AL-4
Osaka Sch—school ... VA-3
**Osakis**—pop pl ... MN-6
Osakis, Lake—lake ... MT-8
Osakis, Lake—reservoir ... MN-6
Osakis Milling Company—hist pl ... MN-6
Osakis State Wildlife Mngmt Area—park ... MN-6
**Osakis (Township of)**—pop pl ... MN-6
Osakura ... FM-9
Osa Meadows—flat ... CA-9
Osan—island ... FM-9
**Osanippa**—pop pl ... AL-4
Osanippa Ch—church ... AL-4
Osanippa Creek—stream ... AL-4
Osanippo Creek ... AL-4
Osapa Chitto ... MS-4
Osar Creek—stream ... AK-9
Osar Lake—lake ... AK-9
Osar Stream—stream ... AK-9
Osas Ponderosa Airp—airport ... PA-2
Osata—well ... FM-9
Osa Tank, La—reservoir ... AZ-5
Osauge Ave Sch—school ... CT-1
Osa Wash, La—stream ... AZ-5
**Osawatomie**—pop pl ... KS-7
Osawatomie Cem—cemetery ... KS-7
Osawatomie City Dam—dam ... KS-7
Osawatomie HS—school ... KS-7
Osawatomie Lake—reservoir ... KS-7
Osawatomie-Paola Airport ... KS-7
Osawatomie-Paola Municipal Airp—airport ... KS-7
**Osawatomie Township**—pop pl ... KS-7
Osawattamie ... KS-7
Osawke ... KS-7
Osawkee ... KS-7
Osawkie ... KS-7
Osawkie Township ... KS-7
Osbeck, Ernst, House—hist pl ... MN-6
**Osbernville**—pop pl ... IL-6
Osbiston Shaft—mine ... NV-8
Osborn ... IN-6
Osborn ... OH-6
Osborn ... PA-2
Osborn—fmr MCD ... NE-7
Osborn—locale ... PA-2
**Osborn**—pop pl ... AL-4
**Osborn**—pop pl ... GA-3
**Osborn**—pop pl ... IL-6
**Osborn**—pop pl ... IN-6
**Osborn**—pop pl ... KY-4
**Osborn**—pop pl ... MS-4
**Osborn**—pop pl (2) ... MO-7
**Osborn**—pop pl ... SC-3
**Osborn**—pop pl ... TN-4
Osborn—post sta ... AZ-5
Osborn, Benjamin, House—hist pl ... MA-1
Osborn, Charles S., House—hist pl ... OH-6
Osborn, Garret K., House and Barn—hist pl ... NJ-2
Osborn, Lake—lake ... WI-6
Osborn, Mount—summit ... AK-9
Osborn Bay Lake—lake ... WA-9
Osborn Bluff—cliff ... MO-7
Osborn Branch ... VA-3
Osborn Branch—stream ... AL-4
Osborn Branch—stream ... FL-3
Osborn Branch—stream (2) ... KY-4
Osborn Branch—stream ... SC-3
Osborn Brook ... CT-1
Osborn Brook—stream ... NY-2
Osborn Butte ... ID-8
Osborn Cem—cemetery ... AL-4
Osborn Cem—cemetery ... AR-4
Osborn Cem—cemetery ... GA-3
Osborn Cem—cemetery ... IN-6
Osborn Cem—cemetery (2) ... MO-7
Osborn Cem—cemetery ... NE-7
Osborn Cem—cemetery ... TN-4
Osborn Cem—cemetery ... VA-3
Osborn Ch—church ... MI-6
Osborn Ch—church ... MO-7
Osborn Ch—church ... SC-3
Osborn Corner—locale ... WA-9
**Osborn Corners**—pop pl ... OH-6
Osborn Creek—stream (2) ... AL-4
Osborn Creek—stream ... AK-9
Osborn Creek—stream ... KY-4
Osborn Creek—stream (2) ... NC-3
Osborn Creek—stream (2) ... OR-9
Osborn Creek Drain—canal ... MI-6
Osborn Crossing—locale ... MO-7
Osborn Culver Pond—lake ... PA-2
Osborndale State Park—park ... CT-1
Osborn Ditch ... IN-6
Osborn Ditch—canal (2) ... IN-6
Osborn Drain—canal ... MI-6
Osborne ... CT-1
Osborne ... ID-8
Osborne ... MD-2
Osborne ... MS-4
Osborne—locale ... IA-7
Osborne—locale ... MD-2
**Osborne**—pop pl ... KS-7
**Osborne**—pop pl ... NC-3
**Osborne**—pop pl ... PA-2
**Osborne**—pop pl ... WV-2
Osborne, Jessie, House—hist pl ... ID-8
Osborne, John, House—hist pl ... CT-1
Osborne, Lake—lake ... FL-3
Osborne Bay—swamp ... FL-3
Osborne Bend Ridge—ridge ... KY-4
Osborne Borough—civil ... PA-2
Osborne Branch—stream (3) ... KY-4
Osborne Branch—stream ... NC-3
Osborne Branch—stream ... PA-2
Osborne Bridge—bridge ... ID-8
Osborne Bridge—bridge ... KS-7
Osborne Bridge (historical)—other ... MO-7
Osborne Butte—summit ... ID-8
Osborne Canal—canal ... KS-7
Osborne Canyon—valley ... CA-9
Osborne Canyon—valley ... OR-9
Osborne Cem—cemetery ... IN-6
Osborne Cem—cemetery ... KS-7
Osborne Cem—cemetery (2) ... KY-4
Osborne Cem—cemetery (2) ... MS-4
Osborne Cem—cemetery (3) ... NC-3
Osborne Cem—cemetery ... OH-6
Osborne Cem—cemetery ... TN-4
Osborne Cem—cemetery (7) ... VA-3
Osborne Cem—cemetery ... WV-2
Osborne Ch—church ... NC-3
Osborne Chapel—church ... VA-3
Osborne City ... KS-7
Osborne Community Center—building ... KS-7
Osborne Corner—locale ... WA-9
Osborne County—civil ... KS-7
Osborne Cove—valley ... NC-3
Osborne Creek ... NY-2
**Osborne Creek**—pop pl ... MS-4
Osborne Creek—stream ... CA-9
Osborne Creek—stream ... IA-7
Osborne Creek—stream ... MS-4
Osborne Creek—stream ... MT-8
Osborne Creek—stream ... NY-2
Osborne Creek—stream ... OR-9
Osborne Creek—stream ... WV-2
Osborne Creek Baptist Church ... MS-4
Osborne Creek Ch—church ... MS-4
Osborne Creek Dam—dam ... OR-9
Osborne Creek School ... MS-4
Osbornedale—hist pl ... CT-1
Osborne Dam—dam ... AL-4
Osborne Diversion Dam—dam ... KS-7
Osborne Drain—canal ... MI-6
Osborne Draw—valley ... WY-8
Osborne Elem Sch—school ... PA-2
Osborne Ford—locale ... TN-4
Osborne Fork—stream ... KY-4
Osborne Fork—stream ... WV-2
Osborne Hill—summit ... CA-9
Osborne Hill—summit ... CT-1
Osborne Hill—summit (2) ... NY-2
Osborne Hill—summit ... PA-2
Osborne Hill Sch—school ... NY-2
Osborne Hollow ... NY-2
Osborne Hollow—valley ... AR-4
Osborne Hollow—valley ... KY-4
Osborne Hollow—valley (2) ... VA-3
Osborne House—hist pl ... NY-2
Osborne Island ... NJ-2
Osborne Island—island ... NJ-2
Osborne Knob—locale ... NC-3
Osborne Lake—lake ... NE-7
Osborne Lake—reservoir (2) ... AL-4
Osborne Lake Dam—dam ... AL-4
Osborne Lakes—lake ... IN-6
Osborne Lakes—lake ... WA-9
Osborne Memorial Ch—church ... NC-3
Osborne Mountain Overlook—locale ... NC-3
Osborne Mountian—summit ... WA-9
Osborne Mountian Trail—trail ... WA-9
Osborne Mtn—summit ... NC-3
Osborne Mtn—summit ... SC-3
Osborne Mtn—summit ... VA-3
Osborne Municipal Airp—airport ... KS-7
Osborne Number 2 Dam—dam ... SD-7
Osborne Number 3 Dam—dam ... SD-7
Osborne Park—park ... FL-3
Osborne Place—locale ... WY-8
Osborne Pond ... NJ-2
Osborne Pond—lake ... MA-1
Osborne Pond—reservoir ... NJ-2
Osborne Public Carnegie Library—hist pl ... KS-7
Osborne Ranch—locale ... NM-5
Osborne Ridge—ridge ... CA-9
Osborne Ridge—ridge (2) ... VA-3
Osborne Rsvr—reservoir ... OR-9
Osborne Rsvr—reservoir ... WY-8
Osborne Run—stream ... OH-6
Osborne Run—stream ... WV-2
Osborne Sch—hist pl ... OH-6
Osborne Sch—school ... GA-3
Osborne Sch—school ... TX-5
**Osbornes Chapel**—pop pl ... VA-3
Osborne Sch (historical)—school ... MS-4
Osborne Sch (historical)—school ... MO-7
Osborne Shop Ctr—locale ... TN-4
Osbornes Landing ... DE-2
Osbornes Mill—locale ... WV-2
**Osbornes Mills**—pop pl ... NJ-2
**Osbornes Mills**—pop pl ... WV-2
Osborne Spring ... AZ-5
Osborne Spring—spring ... IN-6
Osborne Spring—spring ... OR-9
Osborne Spring—spring ... WY-8
Osborne Springs—spring ... ID-8
Osborne Springs—spring ... NV-8
Osborne Spring Wash—stream ... AZ-5
Osborne Tank—reservoir (2) ... AZ-5
Osborne Township ... KS-7
**Osborne Township**—pop pl ... KS-7
**Osborne (Township of)**—pop pl ... MN-6
Osborne Tunnel—tunnel ... CA-9
Osborn-Evergreen Cem—cemetery ... MO-7
Osborne Wash—stream ... AZ-5
Osborne Well—locale ... NM-5
Osborne Well—well (2) ... AZ-5
Osborne Well—well ... WY-8
Osborne Well Number Two—well ... AZ-5
Osborn Gap—gap ... KY-4
Osborn Gap—gap ... VA-3
Osborn Gulch—valley ... ID-8
Osborn Hill—summit ... CA-9
Osborn Hill—summit ... CT-1
Osborn Hill Cem—cemetery ... AL-4
Osborn Hill Sch—school ... CT-1
Osborn Hollow—valley ... KY-4
Osborn Hollow—valley ... MO-7
Osborn Hotel—hist pl ... OR-9
Osborn House—hist pl ... MA-1
Osborn HS—school ... MI-6
Osborn Island—island ... NJ-2
Osborn Lake ... AL-4
Osborn Lake ... MS-4
Osborn Lake ... WI-6
Osborn Lake—lake (3) ... MI-6
Osborn Lake—lake ... MO-7
Osborn Lake—lake ... NY-2
Osborn Lake Dam—dam ... MS-4
Osborn Landing—locale ... VA-3
**Osborn Landing**—pop pl ... IN-6
Osborn Manning Ditch—canal ... IN-6
Osborn Memorial Home—building ... NY-2
Osborn Mill Pond ... NJ-2
Osborn Mills—locale ... NJ-2
Osborn Mtn—summit ... WY-8
Osborn Park—park ... AZ-5
Osborn Park—park ... IA-7
Osborn Park—park ... MI-6
Osborn Park—park ... OH-6
Osborn Point—cape ... AR-4
Osborn Point—cliff ... WA-9
Osborn Pond ... MA-1
Osborn Pond—lake ... OR-9
Osborn Pond—reservoir ... NJ-2
Osborn Post Office (historical)—building ... AL-4
Osborn Post Office (historical)—building ... TN-4
Osborn Prairie Ch—church ... IN-6
Osborn Prison Farm—other ... CT-1
Osborn Ranch—locale ... NM-5
Osborn Ranch—locale (3) ... WY-8
Osborn Rock—locale ... VA-3
Osborn Rsvr—reservoir ... CO-8
Osborn Rsvr No 1—reservoir ... CO-8
Osborn Rsvr No 2—reservoir ... CO-8
Osborn Sch—school ... CA-9
Osborn Sch—school ... MA-1
Osborn Sch—school ... MI-6
Osborn Sch—school ... NY-2
Osborn Sch—school ... OH-6
Osborn Sch—school ... WI-6
Osborns Gap—locale ... VA-3
Osborn Site—hist pl ... IN-6
Osborn Site—hist pl ... TX-5
Osborns Lake Dam—dam ... MS-4
Osborn Spring ... ID-8
Osborn Spring—spring ... MT-8
Osborn Spring Wash ... AZ-5
Osborns Springs ... NV-8
**Osborns Store**—pop pl ... VA-3
Osborn State Farm—locale ... OH-6
Osborn Station—locale ... CA-9
Osborn Street Sch—hist pl ... MA-1
**Osbornsville**—pop pl ... NJ-2
**Osbornsville (Sky Manor)**—pop pl ... NJ-2
**Osborn (Town of)**—pop pl ... ME-1
**Osborn (Town of)**—pop pl ... WI-6
Osborn Township—civil ... KS-7
**Osborn Township**—pop pl ... ND-7
Osborn Village ... NC-3
Osbornville—locale ... NC-3
Osborn Well ... AZ-5
Osborn Well—well ... NM-5
Osbourne—locale ... IA-7
Osbourne—uninc pl ... CA-9
Osbourne Bridge (reduced usage)—locale ... NY-2
Osbourne Creek—stream ... CO-8
Osbrook Point ... CT-1
Osburger Gulch—valley ... CA-9
Osburn ... AL-4
Osburn ... OH-6
Os-Burn ... PA-2
**Osburn**—pop pl ... ID-8
**Osburn**—pop pl ... PA-2
Osburn Branch—stream ... KY-4
Osburn Branch—stream ... MS-4
Osburn Branch—stream ... TX-5
Osburn Canyon—valley ... WA-9
Osburn Cem—cemetery ... AL-4
Osburn Cem—cemetery ... AR-4
Osburn Cem—cemetery ... GA-3
Osburn Cem—cemetery ... TN-4
Osburn Cem—cemetery ... WV-2
Osburn Creek—stream ... AR-4
Osburn Dam—dam ... OR-9
Osburn Drain—canal ... MI-6
Osburn Draw—valley ... TX-5
Osburn Field—airport ... OR-9
Osburn Hill—summit ... NH-1
Osburn House—hist pl ... KY-4
Osburn Mound—summit ... MO-7
Osburn Rsvr—reservoir ... OR-9
Osburn Run ... PA-2
Osburn Sch—school ... GA-3
Osburn Sch—school ... MA-1
Osburn Sch—school ... NH-1
Osburns Stand (historical)—locale ... MS-4
Osburn-Watson Cem ... TN-4
Osburn Willis Cem—cemetery ... LA-4
Osby Cem—cemetery ... MS-4
Oscabe Point—cape ... MI-6
Oscaleta Lake—lake ... NY-2
Oscaloosa—locale ... KY-4
Oscar ... MI-6
Oscar ... MP-9
Oscar—locale ... OK-5
Oscar—locale ... PA-2
Oscar—locale ... TX-5
Oscar—locale ... WV-2
**Oscar**—pop pl ... KY-4
**Oscar**—pop pl ... LA-4
**Oscar**—pop pl ... MO-7
Oscar, Lake—lake (2) ... MN-6
Oscar, Mount—summit ... NH-1
Oscar Bottoms—bend ... KY-4
Oscar Cem—cemetery ... OK-5
Oscar Ch—church ... KY-4
Oscar Cobb Dam—dam ... AL-4
Oscar Cobb Lake—reservoir ... AL-4
Oscar Creek—stream ... OR-9
Oscar Dam No. 4429—dam ... OR-9
Oscar Dead River—lake ... MS-4
Oscar Diess Dam—dam ... SD-7
Oscar Hollow—valley ... MO-7
Oscar Island—island ... AK-9
Oscar-Jenny Lake—lake ... WI-6
Oscar Lake ... WI-6
Oscar Lake—lake ... AK-9
Oscar Lakebed—flat ... MN-6
Oscar Lake Ch—church ... MN-6
Oscar McGuffs Mine (underground)—mine ... AL-4
Oscar Meyer Spring—spring ... CA-9
Oscar Oil Field—oilfield ... OK-5
Oscar Orwick Dam—dam ... SD-7
Oscar Pool Windmill—locale ... NM-5
Oscar Preschool/Edu-Care—school ... FL-3
Oscar Right Hollow—valley ... KY-4
Oscar Rische Dam—dam ... SD-7
Oscar Rsvr Number 4429—reservoir ... OR-9
Oscars Bay—bay ... NY-2
Oscars Cabin—locale ... AK-9
Oscar Scherer State Park—park ... FL-3
Oscars Cove—bay ... TX-5
Oscars Gulch—stream ... WA-9
Oscarson Sch—school ... UT-8

*Otakooche Creek* MS-4
O Tank—*reservoir* TX-5
*Ota Pass* FM-9
*Otapasso Creek* MS-4
Otas—*uninc pl* KY-4
*Ota-Shima* FM-9
*Otashima Suido* FM-9
*Otasima Suido* FM-9
Otatso Creek—*stream* MT-8
Otatso Lake—*lake* MT-8
Otatsy, Lake—*lake* MT-8
**Otay**—*pop pl* CA-9
Otay (Domingues)—*civil* CA-9
Otay (Dominguez)—*civil* CA-9
Otay (Estudillo)—*civil* CA-9
Otay Mesa—*summit* CA-9
Otay Mesa—*uninc pl* CA-9
Otay Mountain Truck Trail—*trail* CA-9
Otay Mtn—*summit* CA-9
Otay Ranch—*locale* CA-9
*Otay Reservoir* CA-9
Otay River—*stream* CA-9
Otay Valley—*valley* CA-9
*Otcha* FM-9
*Otdia Island* MP-9
*Otdia Islands* MP-9
**Ote**—*pop pl* KY-4
O Teaford Ranch—*locale* NE-7
**Oteen**—*pop pl* NC-3
Oteen Veterans Administration Hosp Hist Dist—*hist pl* NC-3
*Otego* KS-7
*Otego* NY-2
Otego—*locale* KS-7
**Otego**—*pop pl* NY-2
Otego Ch—*church* NY-2
Otego Creek—*stream* NY-2
**Otego (Town of)**—*pop pl* NY-2
**Otego (Township of)**—*pop pl* IL-6
Otelia Ch—*church* PA-2
**Oteneagen (Township of)**—*pop pl* MN-6
Otero—*locale* AZ-5
Otero Canal—*canal* CO-8
Otero Canyon—*valley* AZ-5
Otero Canyon—*valley* NM-5
**Otero (County)**—*pop pl* NM-5
*Otero Creek* AZ-5
Otero Drain—*canal* NM-5
Otero Junior Coll—*school* CO-8
Otero Land Grant—*civil* AZ-5
Otero Lateral—*canal* NM-5
Otero Mesa—*summit* (2) NM-5
Otero Ranch—*locale* NM-5
Otero Spring—*spring* AZ-5
Otero Store—*locale* NM-5
Otero Tank—*reservoir* AZ-5
Otes—*locale* TN-4
*Otesgo Lake* MI-6
Otes Post Office (historical)—*building* TN-4
Otes United Methodist Ch—*church* TN-4
Otetiana Point—*cape* NY-2
Otey—*locale* TX-5
**Otey**—*pop pl* VA-3
Otey, William Madison, House—*hist pl* AL-4
Otey Chapel—*church* TN-4
Otey Island—*island* CA-9
Otey Memorial Parish Ch—*church* TN-4
Otey Mill Spring—*spring* TN-4
Oteyokwa Lake—*lake* PA-2
Oteyokwa Lake Dam—*dam* PA-2
Otey (Ramsey State Prison Farm)—*building* TX-5
**Oteys Sierra Village**—*pop pl* CA-9
Otey View—*summit* TN-4
Otgen Drain—*canal* MI-6
O T Gilbert Pond Dam—*dam* MS-4
*Otharp Lake* MT-8
O'The Hills, Lake—*lake* MI-6
O' The Hills, Lake—*reservoir* MS-4
**Othello**—*pop pl* NJ-2
**Othello**—*pop pl* NC-3
**Othello**—*pop pl* WA-9
Othello Air Force Station—*locale* WA-9
Othello Air Force Station—*other* WA-9
Othello (CCD)—*cens area* WA-9
Othello Cem—*cemetery* MN-6
**Othello (historical)**—*pop pl* OR-9
Othello Muni Airp—*airport* WA-9
Othello Post Office (historical)—*building* TN-4
Othello Sch—*school* SC-3
Othello Sch—*school* WA-9
Other—*locale* GA-3
Other Windmill—*locale* TX-5
O' the Woods, Lake—*lake* OH-6
Othma—*locale* VA-3
Otho—*locale* AL-4
**Otho**—*pop pl* IA-7
**Otho**—*pop pl* MS-4
Otho Branch—*stream* AL-4
Otho Cem—*cemetery* IA-7
Otho Post Office (historical)—*building* AL-4
Othorp Lake—*lake* MT-8
O Thorp Ranch—*locale* ND-7
Otho Township—*fmr MCD* IA-7
Otia—*locale* KY-4
Otila Basin—*basin* MT-8
Otila Creek—*stream* MT-8
Otipalin (historical)—*locale* AL-4
Oti Park—*flat* MT-8
Oti Point—*cape* AS-9
Otirgon Creek—*stream* AK-9
*Otis* CA-9
*Otis* TN-4
Otis—*locale* FL-3
Otis—*locale* ME-1
Otis—*locale* WI-6
**Otis**—*pop pl* CO-8
**Otis**—*pop pl* IN-6
**Otis**—*pop pl* IA-7
**Otis**—*pop pl* KS-7
**Otis**—*pop pl* LA-4
**Otis**—*pop pl* MA-1
**Otis**—*pop pl* MO-7
**Otis**—*pop pl* NM-5
**Otis**—*pop pl* (2) NY-2
**Otis**—*pop pl* OR-9
Otis, (First) Harrison Gray, House—*hist pl* MA-1
Otis, Lake—*lake* AK-9
Otis, Lake—*lake* FL-3
Otis, (Second) Harrison Gray, House—*hist pl* MA-1
Otis AFB—*military* MA-1
Otis Air Natl Guard Base—*building* MA-1
Otis-Albert Oil and Gas Field—*oilfield* KS-7
Otis Barfield Dam—*dam* AL-4
*Otis Barfield Lake* AL-4
*Otis Barfield Lake Dam* AL-4
Otis Basin—*basin* OR-9
Otis-Bison MS—*school* KS-7
Otis-Bison Primary Sch—*school* (2) KS-7
Otis-Boyle Ditch—*canal* IN-6
Otis Brook—*stream* NY-2
Otis Canyon—*valley* (2) CA-9
Otis Center—*other* MA-1
Otis Chalk—*locale* TX-5
**Otisco**—*pop pl* IN-6
**Otisco**—*pop pl* MN-6
**Otisco**—*pop pl* NY-2
Otisco Cem—*cemetery* MI-6
Otisco Lake—*reservoir* NY-2
Otisco-Lemond Cem—*cemetery* MN-6
Otis Company Mill No. 1—*hist pl* MA-1
**Otisco (Town of)**—*pop pl* NY-2
**Otisco (Township of)**—*pop pl* MI-6
**Otisco (Township of)**—*pop pl* MN-6
**Otisco Valley**—*pop pl* NY-2
Otisco Valley—*valley* NY-2
Otisco Valley Cem—*cemetery* NY-2
Otis Cove—*bay* ME-1
Otis Cove—*bay* NC-3
Otis Creek—*stream* KS-7
Otis Creek—*stream* (3) MT-8
Otis Creek—*stream* (2) NY-2
Otis Creek—*stream* OR-9
Otis Creek Rsvr—*reservoir* KS-7
Otis Ditch—*canal* IN-6
Otis E Brown Elem Sch—*school* IN-6
Otis Elevator Company—*facility* IN-6
Otis Elevator Company Bldg—*hist pl* OR-9
Otis Falls—*falls* MA-1
*Otisfield* ME-1
**Otisfield**—*pop pl* ME-1
Otisfield Cove—*bay* ME-1
**Otisfield Gore**—*pop pl* ME-1
**Otisfield (Town of)**—*pop pl* ME-1
Otis German Shop Ctr—*locale* FL-3
*Otis Gorge* CO-8
Otis Grove Cem—*cemetery* IA-7
**Otis Hill**—*pop pl* ME-1
Otis Hill—*summit* (2) MA-1
Otis Hill—*summit* NH-1
Otis (historical)—*locale* MS-4
Otis Hosp—*hist pl* OH-6
Otis House—*hist pl* AZ-5
**Otis Junction**—*pop pl* OR-9
*Otis Lake* WI-6
Otis Lake—*lake* MI-6
Otis Lake—*lake* MT-8
Otis Lake—*lake* ND-7
Otis Ledge—*bench* NY-2
Otis Memorial Sch—*school* MA-1
Otis Mtn—*summit* MT-8
Otis Mtn—*summit* NY-2
Otis Mtn—*summit* OR-9
**Otis Orchards**—*pop pl* WA-9
Otis Orchards-East Farms—*CDP* WA-9
**Otis (Otis Center)**—*pop pl* MA-1
Otis Park—*park* IN-6
Otis Peak—*summit* CO-8
Otis Point—*cape* ME-1
Otis Pratt Brook—*stream* MA-1
Otis Reservoir Dam—*dam* MA-1
Otis Ridge—*ridge* MA-1
Otis Ridge—*ridge* TX-5
Otis Ridge Ski Area—*locale* MA-1
Otis Rsvr—*reservoir* MA-1
*Otis Rsvr Brook* MA-1
Otis Sch—*school* IL-6
Otis Sch—*school* OH-6
Otis Sch—*school* OR-9
Otis Sch—*school* WI-6
Otis Sch (historical)—*school* TN-4
Otis Spring—*spring* CA-9
Otis Spring—*spring* OR-9
**Otis (Town of)**—*pop pl* ME-1
**Otis (Town of)**—*pop pl* MA-1
**Otis Township**—*pop pl* ND-7
Otisville—*locale* MN-6
**Otisville**—*pop pl* MI-6
**Otisville**—*pop pl* NY-2
Otisville Cem—*cemetery* MI-6
Otisville (historical P.O.)—*locale* (2) IA-7
Otis Wait Brook—*stream* MA-1
*Otis Woodland Reservoir* MA-1
Otis Wright Ranch—*locale* WY-8
*Otken Elementary School* MS-4
Otken Sch—*school* MS-4
Otkriti Bay—*bay* AK-9
Otkurak Creek—*stream* AK-9
*Otler Creek* MI-6
Otlershagen Prospect Mine—*mine* SD-7
**Otley**—*pop pl* IA-7
Otmeloi Island—*island* AK-9
Otmeloi Light—*locale* AK-9
Otmeloi Point—*cape* AK-9
**Oto**—*pop pl* IA-7
Oto Cem—*cemetery* IA-7
Oto Ch—*church* MO-7
*Otoclaffah Creek* MS-4
Otoe—*locale* OK-5
**Otoe**—*pop pl* NE-7
Otoe County Courthouse—*hist pl* NE-7
Otoe Creek—*stream* (2) NE-7
Otoe Creek—*stream* (2) OK-5
Otoe-Missouria Cem—*cemetery* OK-5
Otoe-Missouria Indian Agency—*locale* OK-5
Otoe Post Office (historical)—*building* MS-4
Otoe Public Use Area—*park* KS-7
*Otoko* FM-9
*Otoko Jima* FM-9
Otokomi Lake—*lake* MT-8
Otokomi Mtn—*summit* MT-8
*Otokoochee Creek* MS-4
*Otoko Shima* FM-9
*Otoman Zardusht Hanish* AZ-5
Otonawanda, Lake—*reservoir* CO-8
O'Took Creek—*stream* WA-9
O'Took Prairie—*flat* WA-9
**O'Toole**—*pop pl* WV-2
O'Toole Cem—*cemetery* NY-2
O'Toole Creek—*stream* NV-8
O'Toole Creek—*stream* WA-9
O'Toole Lake—*lake* WA-9
O'Toole Mtn—*summit* WA-9
O'Toole Ranch—*locale* NV-8
O'toole Ranch Airp—*airport* NV-8
O'Toole Rsvr—*reservoir* OR-9
O'Toole Sch—*school* IL-6
O'Toole Sch—*school* WI-6
O'Toole Spring—*spring* OR-9
Oto P.O. (historical)—*locale* AL-4
OTO Ranch—*locale* MT-8
Oto Ridge—*ridge* MO-7
*Otorii Island* MP-9
*Ototo Jima* FM-9
*Ototo-Shima* FM-9
Oto Township—*fmr MCD* IA-7
Otoucalofa Ch—*church* MS-4
Otoucalofa Creek—*stream* MS-4
Otoucalofa Creek Canal—*canal* MS-4
*Otoukalofa Creek* MS-4
Otowi—*locale* NM-5
Otowi Hist Dist—*hist pl* NM-5
Otowi Mesa—*bench* NM-5
Otowi Ruins—*locale* NM-5
O T Princes Landing—*locale* AL-4
Otranto—*locale* IA-7
**Otranto**—*pop pl* IA-7
**Otranto**—*pop pl* (2) SC-3
Otranto Park—*park* IA-7
Otranto Plantation—*hist pl* SC-3
Otranto Township—*fmr MCD* IA-7
Otrey Lake—*lake* MN-6
Otrey State Wildlife Mngmt Area—*park* MN-6
**Otrey (Township of)**—*pop pl* MN-6
Otrubistoi Point—*cape* AK-9
**Otsdawa**—*pop pl* NY-2
Otsdawa Creek—*stream* NY-2
Otsdawa Creek Site—*hist pl* NY-2
**Otsego**—*pop pl* MI-6
**Otsego**—*pop pl* MN-6
**Otsego**—*pop pl* (2) OH-6
**Otsego**—*pop pl* WV-2
**Otsego**—*pop pl* WI-6
Otsego Cem—*cemetery* OH-6
**Otsego Center**—*pop pl* IN-6
Otsego Center Cem—*cemetery* IN-6
**Otsego (County)**—*pop pl* MI-6
**Otsego (County)**—*pop pl* NY-2
Otsego County Courthouse—*hist pl* NY-2
Otsego County Park—*park* MI-6
Otsego Dam—*dam* MI-6
Otsego Lake—*lake* MI-6
Otsego Lake—*lake* NY-2
**Otsego Lake**—*pop pl* MI-6
Otsego Lake Cem—*cemetery* MI-6
Otsego Lake Resort—*locale* MI-6
Otsego Lake State Park—*park* MI-6
**Otsego Lake (Township of)**—*pop pl* MI-6
Otsogo Sch school OII-6
**Otsego (Town of)**—*pop pl* NY-2
**Otsego (Town of)**—*pop pl* WI-6
**Otsego (Township of)**—*pop pl* IN-6
**Otsego (Township of)**—*pop pl* MI-6
**Otsego (Township of)**—*pop pl* MN-6
**Otselic**—*pop pl* NY-2
**Otselic Center**—*pop pl* NY-2
*Otselic Creek* NY-2
Otselic Creek—*stream* NY-2
Otselic River—*stream* NY-2
**Otselic (Town of)**—*pop pl* NY-2
*Otsgaragee Cavern* NY-2
*Otside* SC-3
Otsikita Lake—*lake* MI-6
Otso Point—*cape* WA-9
*Otsquaga Creek* NY-2
Otsquago Creek—*stream* NY-2
Otstoia Island—*island* AK-9
Ott—*locale* AR-4
Ott—*locale* MO-7
Ott, Charles J. and Alvina, House—*hist pl* TX-5
Ott, John George, House—*hist pl* WI-6
Ott, S. I., House—*hist pl* TX-5
Ott, Will, House—*hist pl* WI-6
*Otta* FM-9
*Otta Island* FM-9
*Otta Jima* FM-9
*Otta Jima Suido* FM-9
*Ottakai* FM-9
Ottanola—*locale* NC-3
Ottanola Gap—*gap* NC-3
*Otta Pass* FM-9
*Otta Passage* FM-9
*Otta Quechee River* VT-1
*Ottaqueeche River* VT-1
Ottari Sanitarium—*hist pl* NC-3
Ottarnic Pond—*lake* NH-1
*Otta-S* FM-9
Ottauquechee River—*stream* VT-1
Ottawa—*locale* KY-4
Ottawa—*locale* MI-6
Ottawa—*locale* OK-5
Ottawa—*locale* PA-2
**Ottawa**—*pop pl* IL-6
**Ottawa**—*pop pl* (2) IA-7
**Ottawa**—*pop pl* KS-7
**Ottawa**—*pop pl* MN-6
**Ottawa**—*pop pl* OH-6
**Ottawa**—*pop pl* WV-2
**Ottawa**—*pop pl* WI-6
Ottawa, Lake—*lake* MI-6
Ottawa Ave Cem—*cemetery* IL-6
*Ottawa Bay* MI-6
Ottawa Beach—*beach* MI-6
**Ottawa Beach**—*pop pl* MI-6
Ottawa Boy Scott Camp—*locale* MI-6
Ottawa Canyon—*valley* IL-6
Ottawa Cem—*cemetery* IA-7
Ottawa Cem—*cemetery* MN-6
Ottawa Cem—*cemetery* WI-6
**Ottawa Center**—*pop pl* MI-6
Ottawa Center Chapel—*church* MI-6
Ottawa Ch—*church* MI-6
Ottawa Ch—*church* ND-7
*Ottawa City* OH-6
Ottawa County—*civil* KS-7
**Ottawa (County)**—*pop pl* MI-6
**Ottawa (County)**—*pop pl* OH-6
**Ottawa (County)**—*pop pl* OK-5
Ottawa County Courthouse—*hist pl* OH-6
Ottawa County State Lake Dam—*dam* KS-7
Ottawa County State Park—*park* KS-7
Ottawa County Youth Home—*building* MI-6
*Ottawa Creek* KS-7
Ottawa Creek—*stream* KS-7
Ottawa Creek—*stream* MI-6
Ottawa Creek—*stream* (2) OH-6
Ottawa Ditch—*canal* CO-8
Ottawa Gulch—*valley* MT-8
Ottawa Gun Club—*other* MI-6
**Ottawa Hills**—*pop pl* OH-6
Ottawa Hills HS—*school* MI-6
Ottawa Hills (Township of)—*other* OH-6
Ottawa (historical)—*locale* ND-7
Ottawa House—*hist pl* WI-6
Ottawa HS—*school* KS-7
Ottawa Indian Ch—*church* OK-5
Ottawa JHS—*school* MI-6
Ottawa Junction—*locale* KS-7
*Ottawa Lake* MI-6
Ottawa Lake—*lake* MI-6
Ottawa Lake—*lake* WI-6
**Ottawa Lake**—*pop pl* MI-6
Ottawa Lakebed—*flat* MI-6
Ottawa Lake Outlet—*stream* MI-6
Ottawa Lake Rec Area—*park* WI-6
Ottawa Library—*hist pl* KS-7
Ottawa Municipal Airp—*airport* KS-7
Ottawanah—*summit* NV-8
Ottawa Natl For—*forest* MI-6
Ottawa Natl Wildlife Ref—*park* OH-6
Ottawa Park—*park* MI-6
Ottawa Park—*park* OH-6
Ottawa Park Cem—*cemetery* MI-6
*Ottawa Point* MI-6
*Ottawa River* MI-6
*Ottawa River* OH-6
Ottawa River—*stream* MI-6
Ottawa River—*stream* (2) OH-6
Ottawa River Ch—*church* OH-6
Ottawa River HS—*school* OH-6
Ottawa Sch—*school* IA-7
Ottawa Sch—*school* KY-4
Ottawa Spring—*spring* NV-8
Ottawa State Fishing Lake and Wildlife Area—*park* KS-7
Ottawa State Wildlife Mngmt Area—*park* MN-6
**Ottawa Township**—*pop pl* (2) KS-7
Ottawa Township Hall—*hist pl* MN-6
Ottawa (Township of)—*other* OH-6
**Ottawa (Township of)**—*pop pl* IL-6
**Ottawa (Township of)**—*pop pl* MN-6
**Ottawa (Township of)**—*pop pl* OH-6
Ottawa Trail Woods North—*woods* IL-6
Ottawa Trail Woods South—*woods* IL-6
Ottawa Univ—*school* KS-7
Ottawa Valley Hosp—*hospital* OH-6
Ottawa Waterworks Bldg—*hist pl* OH-6
Ottaway Drain—*canal* MI-6
Ottaway Hollow—*valley* MO-7
Ottaway Valley—*valley* AK-9
Ott Bay—*bay* AK-9
Ott Cave—*cave* AR-4
Ott Cem—*cemetery* KS-7
Ott Cem—*cemetery* LA-4
Ott Cem—*cemetery* MI-6
Ott Cem—*cemetery* MO-7
Ott Cem—*cemetery* OK-5
Ott Cem—*cemetery* PA-2
Ott Cem—*cemetery* WV-2
Ott Cow Camp—*locale* OR-9
*Ott Creek* NV-8
Ott Creek—*stream* AR-4
Ott Creek—*stream* NV-8
Otte, Dennis, Round Barn—*hist pl* IL-6
Otten Branch—*stream* MO-7
Ottendorfer Public Library and Stuyvesant Polyclinic Hosp—*hist pl* NY-2
Otten Gulch—*valley* CO-8
**Ottenheim**—*pop pl* KY-4
Ottenheim Sch—*school* KY-4
Otten Memorial Airp—*airport* MO-7
Ottens Basin—*basin* NJ-2
Ottens Canal—*canal* NJ-2
*Ottens Cove* NC-3
Ottens Harbor—*bay* NJ-2
**Ottention (historical)**—*pop pl* ND-7
*Otter* ME-1
*Otter* WV-2
Otter—*locale* AK-9
Otter—*locale* MT-8
**Otter**—*pop pl* OH-6
Otter, Peaks of—*summit* VA-3
Otter Arm—*ridge* VA-3
Otter Bar—*bar* CA-9
Otter Bay—*bay* IA-7
Otter Bay—*bay* NY-2
Otter Bay—*swamp* FL-3
Otter Bay—*swamp* GA-3
Otter Bayou—*channel* LA-4
Otter Bayou—*gut* AL-4
Otter Bayou—*gut* AR-4
Otter Bayou—*gut* LA-4
Otter Bayou—*stream* (2) LA-4
Otter Bayou—*stream* MS-4
Otterbein—*locale* OH-6
**Otterbein**—*pop pl* CA-9
**Otterbein**—*pop pl* IN-6
**Otterbein**—*pop pl* OH-6
**Otterbein**—*pop pl* PA-2
Otterbein Cem—*cemetery* IL-6
Otterbein Cem—*cemetery* NE-7
Otterbein Cem—*cemetery* (2) OH-6
*Otterbein Ch* IN-6
Otterbein Ch—*church* IL-6
Otterbein Ch—*church* (5) IN-6
Otterbein Ch—*church* IA-7
Otterbein Ch—*church* KS-7
Otterbein Ch—*church* (2) OH-6
Otterbein Ch—*church* (2) PA-2
Otterbein Ch—*church* (3) WV-2
Otterbein Chapel—*church* (2) MO-7
Otterbein Chapel—*church* OH-6
Otterbein Chapel—*church* VA-3
Otterbein Church—*hist pl* MD-2
Otterbein Coll—*school* OH-6
Otterbein Ditch—*canal* IN-6
Otterbein Elem Sch—*school* IN-6
Otterbein Mausoleum—*hist pl* OH-6
Otterbein-Shaker Cem—*cemetery* OH-6
Otterbein United Methodist Ch—*church* IN-6
Otterbein United Methodist Ch—*church* KS-7
Otterbein United Methodist Ch—*church* TN-4
Otterbem Ch—*church* MO-7
Otterbien Cem—*cemetery* IA-7
Otterbien Home—*post sta* OH-6
Otter Bight—*bay* AK-9
Otterbin Ch—*church* OH-6
*Otterbine* OH-6
Otter Bluff—*cliff* TN-4
Otter Bluff Sch—*school* IL-6
Otter Bog—*swamp* ME-1
Otter Bog Mtn—*summit* ME-1
Otterbourne (historical)—*locale* KS-7
*Otter Branch* NH-1
Otter Branch—*stream* (2) AL-4
Otter Branch—*stream* FL-3
Otter Branch—*stream* GA-3
Otter Branch—*stream* (2) IL-6
Otter Branch—*stream* (2) KY-4
Otter Branch—*stream* MS-4
Otter Branch—*stream* NC-3
Otter Branch—*stream* PA-2
Otter Branch—*stream* WV-2
Otter Branch Ch—*church* WV-2
*Otter Brook* MA-1
*Otter Brook* MN-6
*Otter Brook* NH-1
Otter Brook—*stream* (13) ME-1
Otter Brook—*stream* MA-1
Otter Brook—*stream* (5) NH-1
Otter Brook—*stream* NJ-2
Otter Brook—*stream* (3) NY-2
Otter Brook—*stream* VT-1
Otter Brook Bog—*swamp* ME-1
*Otterburn* MI-6
Otterburn Cem—*cemetery* IL-6
Otterburn Marsh—*swamp* VA-3
Otterburn Sch—*school* VA-3
Otter Butte—*summit* ID-8
Otter Buttes—*summit* ID-8
Otter Camp—*locale* FL-3
Otter Camp (historical)—*locale* ME-1
Otter Cem—*cemetery* WV-2
Otter Chain Ponds—*lake* ME-1
Otter Cliff—*cliff* ME-1
*Otter Cove* ME-1
Otter Cove—*bay* (2) AK-9
Otter Cove—*bay* (2) ME-1
Otter Cove—*bay* NH-1
*Otter Cove Creek* ME-1
**Otter Cove Estates**—*pop pl* CT-1
*Otter Creek* IL-6
*Otter Creek* IN-6
*Otter Creek* IA-7
*Otter Creek* KS-7
*Otter Creek* ME-1
*Otter Creek* MT-8
*Otter Creek* PA-2
*Otter Creek* SD-7
*Ottercreek* TN-4
*Otter Creek* WV-2
*Otter Creek* WI-6
*Otter Creek* WY-8
Otter Creek—*bay* NC-3
Otter Creek—*bay* VI-3
Otter Creek—*channel* MD-2
Otter Creek—*channel* SC-3
Otter Creek—*gut* FL-3
Otter Creek—*locale* GA-3
Otter Creek—*locale* IA-7
Otter Creek—*locale* ND-7
Otter Creek—*park* KY-4
**Otter Creek**—*pop pl* FL-3
**Otter Creek**—*pop pl* ME-1
**Otter Creek**—*pop pl* MN-6
**Otter Creek**—*pop pl* NY-2
**Otter Creek**—*pop pl* TN-4
Otter Creek—*stream* AL-4
Otter Creek—*stream* (7) AK-9
Otter Creek—*stream* (6) AR-4
Otter Creek—*stream* CA-9
Otter Creek—*stream* CO-8
Otter Creek—*stream* (9) FL-3
Otter Creek—*stream* (5) GA-3
Otter Creek—*stream* (6) ID-8
Otter Creek—*stream* (9) IL-6
Otter Creek—*stream* (7) IN-6
Otter Creek—*stream* (11) IA-7
Otter Creek*—*stream* IA-7
Otter Creek—*stream* (5) IA-7
Otter Creek—*stream* (13) KS-7
Otter Creek—*stream* (9) KY-4
Otter Creek—*stream* LA-4
Otter Creek—*stream* ME-1
Otter Creek—*stream* (5) MI-6
Otter Creek—*stream* (6) MN-6
Otter Creek—*stream* (6) MO-7
Otter Creek—*stream* (6) MT-8
Otter Creek—*stream* (4) NE-7
Otter Creek—*stream* NJ-2
Otter Creek—*stream* (8) NY-2
Otter Creek—*stream* (5) NC-3
Otter Creek—*stream* (3) ND-7
Otter Creek—*stream* (2) OH-6
Otter Creek—*stream* (9) OK-5
Otter Creek—*stream* (6) OR-9
Otter Creek—*stream* (3) PA-2
Otter Creek—*stream* (2) SC-3
Otter Creek—*stream* (5) TN-4
Otter Creek—*stream* (2) TX-5
Otter Creek—*stream* (2) UT-8
Otter Creek—*stream* VT-1
Otter Creek—*stream* (3) VA-3
Otter Creek—*stream* (6) WA-9
Otter Creek—*stream* (4) WV-2
Otter Creek—*stream* (14) WI-6
Otter Creek—*stream* (3) WY-8
Otter Creek Archaeol Site (44FR31)—*hist pl* VA-3
Otter Creek Archeol Site—*hist pl* OK-5
Otter Creek Campground—*park* UT-8
Otter Creek Cem—*cemetery* IN-6
Otter Creek Cem—*cemetery* IA-7
Otter Creek Cem—*cemetery* KY-4
Otter Creek Cem—*cemetery* MO-7
Otter Creek Cem—*cemetery* NY-2
Otter Creek Cem—*cemetery* ND-7
Otter Creek Cem—*cemetery* (3) WI-6
Otter Creek Ch—*church* (2) FL-3
Otter Creek Ch—*church* (3) IN-6
Otter Creek Ch—*church* (3) KY-4
Otter Creek Ch—*church* (2) NC-3
Otter Creek Ch—*church* OK-5
Otter Creek Ch—*church* TN-4
Otter Creek Ch—*church* WI-6
Otter Creek County Ditch—*canal* IA-7
*Otter Creek Cove* ME-1
Otter Creek Dam—*dam* UT-8
Otter Creek Flats Overlook—*locale* VA-3
Otter Creek JHS—*school* IN-6
Otter Creek Junction—*locale* TN-4
**Otter Creek Junction**—*pop pl* IN-6
Otter Creek Marsh State Wildlife Ref—*park* IA-7
*Otter Creek Point* ME-1
Ottercreek Post Office (historical)—*building* TN-4
Otter Creek Rec Area—*park* KS-7
Otter Creek Rec Area—*park* VA-3
Otter Creek Rsvr—*reservoir* UT-8
*Otter Creek Sch* IN-6
Otter Creek Sch—*school* IL-6
Otter Creek Sch—*school* (2) KY-4
Otter Creek Sch—*school* (2) MT-8
Otter Creek Sch—*school* WV-2
Otter Creek Sch—*school* (2) WI-6
Otter Creek Sch (historical)—*school* MO-7
Otter Creek Spring—*spring* UT-8
Otter Creek State Fishery Area—*park* WI-6
Otter Creek State Park—*park* UT-8
Otter Creek State Public Hunting Grounds—*park* WI-6
Otter Creek State Wildlife Mngmt Area—*park* KS-7
Otter Creek Swamp—*swamp* FL-3
**Otter Creek (Town of)**—*pop pl* (2) WI-6
Otter Creek Township—*fmr MCD* (5) IA-7
**Otter Creek Township**—*pop pl* KS-7
**Otter Creek Township**—*pop pl* NE-7
**Otter Creek Township**—*pop pl* ND-7
**Otter Creek (Township of)**—*pop pl* (2) IL-6
**Otter Creek (Township of)**—*pop pl* (2) IN-6
**Otter Creek (Township of)**—*pop pl* PA-2
Otter Creek Trail—*trail* WV-2
Otter Creek Vee—*cape* WY-8
Otter Creek Wildlife Area—*park* IA-7
Otter Crest—*ridge* OR-9
Otter Crest Rest Area—*area* OR-9
Otter Crest State Park—*park* OR-9
*Otter Crest Wayside* OR-9
Otterdale Branch—*stream* VA-3
Otterdale Mill—*locale* MD-2
Otterdam Swamp—*stream* (2) VA-3
Otterdin Ch—*church* WV-2
Otter Drain—*stream* FL-3
Otter Falls—*falls* WA-9
Otter Fork—*stream* TN-4
Otter Fork—*stream* WV-2
Otter Fork Licking River—*stream* OH-6
Otter Gap—*gap* NC-3
Otter Gap—*gap* PA-2
Otter Gap Ch—*church* KY-4
Otter Gap Trail—*trail* PA-2
Otter Hill—*locale* VA-3
Otter Hole—*bay* NC-3
Otter Hole—*valley* WV-2
Otter Hole Branch—*stream* GA-3
Otter Hollow—*valley* OK-5
Otterholt Cem—*cemetery* WI-6
Otter Hook—*locale* NY-2
Otter House Bluff—*cliff* VA-3
Ottering Shelton Chapel—*church* TN-4
*Otter Island* AL-4
*Otter Island* ME-1
*Otter Island* SC-3
Otter Island—*island* AK-9
Otter Island—*island* (2) IA-7
Otter Island—*island* (5) ME-1
Otter Island—*island* MD-2
Otter Island—*island* NH-1
Otter Island—*island* OH-6
Otter Island—*island* (2) WI-6
Otter Island Ledge—*bar* (2) ME-1
Otter Island Passage—*channel* ME-1
Otter Islands—*island* SC-3
Otter Key—*island* (2) FL-3
Otter Kill—*locale* NY-2
Otter Kill—*stream* NY-2
Otter Kill Golf and Country Club—*other* NY-2
Otterkill Trail—*trail* MN-6
Otter Knobs—*summit* NC-3
*Otter Lake* MN-6
*Otter Lake* MS-4
*Otter Lake* OR-9
*Otter Lake* WI-6
Otter Lake—*lake* (8) AK-9
Otter Lake—*lake* (4) AR-4
Otter Lake—*lake* CA-9
Otter Lake—*lake* FL-3
Otter Lake—*lake* GA-3
Otter Lake—*lake* IL-6
Otter Lake—*lake* IN-6
Otter Lake—*lake* LA-4
Otter Lake—*lake* (2) ME-1
Otter Lake—*lake* (12) MI-6
Otter Lake—*lake* (15) MN-6
Otter Lake—*lake* (3) MS-4
Otter Lake—*lake* (2) MT-8
Otter Lake—*lake* NE-7
Otter Lake—*lake* NH-1
Otter Lake—*lake* (5) NY-2
Otter Lake—*lake* OR-9
Otter Lake—*lake* (2) SC-3
Otter Lake—*lake* SD-7
Otter Lake—*lake* TX-5
Otter Lake—*lake* (2) UT-8
Otter Lake—*lake* (4) WA-9
Otter Lake—*lake* (10) WI-6
Otter Lake—*lake* WY-8
**Otter Lake**—*pop pl* IN-6
**Otter Lake**—*pop pl* (2) MI-6
**Otter Lake**—*pop pl* NY-2
Otter Lake—*reservoir* IL-6
Otter Lake—*reservoir* PA-2
Otter Lake—*reservoir* TN-4
Otter Lake—*reservoir* VA-3
Otter Lake—*reservoir* WI-6

Otter Lake Bayou—stream ... MS-4
Otter Lake Dam—dam ... TN-4
Otter Lake Firetower—locale ... ME-1
Otter Lake (historical)—lake ... MS-4
Otter Lake Lookout Tower—locale ... MI-6
Otter Lake Oil Field—oilfield ... MS-4
Otter Lake Outlet—stream ... NY-2
Otter Lake Rec Area—park ... WI-6
Otterlick Community Ch—church ... WV-2
Otterlick Run—stream ... WV-2
Otter (Magisterial District)—fmr MCD (2) ... WV-2
Otterman Cem—cemetery ... IA-7
Otter Massacre Site—locale ... ID-8
Otter Mound—island ... FL-3
Otter Mtn—summit ... CO-8
Otter Mtn—summit ... MT-8
Otter Mtn—summit ... NC-3
Otternick Pond ... NH-1
Otter Park—park ... KY-4
Otter Peak—summit ... ID-8
Otter Point ... ME-1
Otter Point—cape ... AK-9
Otter Point—cape (4) ... ME-1
Otter Point—cape ... MD-2
Otter Point—cape ... NY-2
Otter Point—cape ... OR-9
**Otter Point**—pop pl ... MD-2
Otter Point Cliffs ... ME-1
Otter Point Creek—stream ... MD-2
Otter Point Wayside—locale ... OR-9
Otter Pond ... MA-1
Otter Pond ... NH-1
Otter Pond—lake ... AK-9
Otter Pond—lake ... AR-4
Otter Pond—lake (3) ... FL-3
Otter Pond—lake ... GA-3
Otter Pond—lake (3) ... IL-6
Otter Pond—lake ... IN-6
Otter Pond—lake ... KY-4
Otter Pond—lake (16) ... ME-1
Otter Pond—lake (2) ... MD-2
Otter Pond—lake ... MA-1
Otter Pond—lake ... MS-4
Otter Pond—lake ... MO-7
Otter Pond—lake (2) ... NH-1
Otter Pond—lake ... NJ-2
Otter Pond—lake (9) ... NY-2
Otter Pond—lake (2) ... TN-4
Otter Pond—lake ... WI-6
Otter Pond—locale ... KY-4
Otter Pond—reservoir ... AL-4
Otter Pond—reservoir ... MA-1
Otter Pond Branch—stream ... MD-2
Otter Pond Brook ... MA-1
Otter Pond Camps—locale ... ME-1
Otter Pond Cove—bay ... ME-1
Otter Pond Ditch—canal ... IL-6
Otter Pond Mtn—summit ... ME-1
Otter Pond Point—cape ... NC-3
Otter Ponds—lake ... FL-3
Otter Ponds—lake (2) ... ME-1
Otter Ponds—lake ... NY-2
Otter Pond Stream—stream ... ME-1
Otter Rack Branch—stream ... NC-3
Otter Rapids Dam—dam ... WI-6
Otter Ridge—ridge ... ID-8
Otter River ... MA-1
Otter River ... VA-3
Otter River—locale ... VA-3
**Otter River**—pop pl ... MA-1
Otter River—stream ... MA-1
Otter River—stream ... MI-6
Otter River—stream ... MN-6
Otter River Dam—dam ... MA-1
Otter River Rsvr—reservoir ... MA-1
Otter River Sch—school ... VA-3
Otter River State For—forest ... MA-1
Otter Robe Coulee—valley ... MT-8
Otter Rock ... OR-9
Otter Rock—island ... OR-9
**Otter Rock**—pop pl ... OR-9
Otter Rocks—island ... CT-1
Otter Rock Shoal—bar ... ME-1
Otter (RR name for Ivydale)—other ... WV-2
Otter Rsvr—reservoir ... ID-8
Otter Run ... WV-2
Otter Run—stream ... MA-1
Otter Run—stream (2) ... OH-6
Otter Run—stream ... PA-2
Otter Run—stream (2) ... WV-2
Otter Sch—school ... IL-6
Ottersdale—locale ... MD-2
Otters Hump Trail ... MT-8
Otters Hump Trail—trail ... MT-8
Otter Sink Camp—locale ... FL-3
Otter Slide Bay—swamp ... NC-3
Otterslide Branch—stream ... SC-3
Otter Slide Branch—stream ... VA-3
Otter Slide Creek—stream ... ID-8
Otterslide Creek—stream ... WV-2
Otter Slide Hollow—valley ... MO-7
Otter Slide Rapids—rapids ... WI-6
Otterslide Run—stream ... OH-6
Otter Slough—gut ... AR-4
Otter Slough—gut ... FL-3
Otter Slough—gut ... MO-7
Otter Slough—gut ... TN-4
Otter Slough—stream ... IA-7
Otter Slough—swamp ... FL-3
Otter Slough Ditch—canal (2) ... MO-7
Otter Slough State Wildlife Mngmt Area—park ... MO-7
Otterson Cem—cemetery ... IL-6
Otterson Creek—stream ... ID-8
Otterson Ditch—canal ... WY-8
Otter Spring—spring ... OR-9
Otter Spring Creek ... KS-7
Otter Springs—spring ... FL-3
Otter Springs—spring (2) ... ID-8
Otter Springs—spring ... WI-6
Otter Springs Creek—stream ... KS-7
Otter's River ... MA-1
Otter Strait—channel ... AK-9
Otter Stream—stream ... ME-1
**Ottertail**—pop pl ... MN-6
Otter Tail Cem—cemetery ... MN-6
Otter Tail (corporate name Ottertail) ... MN-6
**Otter Tail (County)**—pop pl ... MN-6
Otter Tail County Courthouse—hist pl ... MN-6
Ottertail Creek—stream (2) ... AK-9
Otter Tail Creek—stream ... ND-7
Ottertail Creek—stream ... WI-6
Otter Tail Lake—lake ... MN-6
Ottertail Lake—lake ... OR-9
Ottertail Point—cape ... MN-6
Ottertail Ridge—ridge ... AK-9
Otter Tail River—stream ... MN-6
Otter Tail Spring ... WI-6
Ottertail Springs—spring ... WI-6
**Ottertail (Township of)**—pop pl ... MN-6
Otter Township—fmr MCD ... IA-7
**Otter Township**—pop pl ... KS-7
Otter (Township of)—fmr MCD ... AR-4
Ottertrack Lake—lake ... MN-6
Ottervale Ch—church ... WI-6
Otter Valley Sch—school ... OK-5
**Otter Village**—pop pl ... IN-6
Otter Village Cem—cemetery ... IN-6
Otterville ... IN-6
Otterville—locale ... VA-3
**Otterville**—pop pl ... IL-6
**Otterville**—pop pl ... IA-7
**Otterville**—pop pl ... MO-7
**Otterville**—pop pl ... NH-1
Otterville Cem—cemetery ... IA-7
Otterville Ch—church ... TN-4
Otterville Ch—church ... WV-2
Otterville Post Office (historical)—building ... TN-4
Otterville Township—civil ... MO-7
Otterwood Ch—church ... VA-3
Ottery—locale ... AL-4
Ottery Ch—church ... MO-7
Ottery Creek—stream ... AL-4
Ottery Creek—stream ... MO-7
Ottes Creek ... IN-6
Ottesen, Hans, House—hist pl ... UT-8
Ottesen Spring—spring ... MT-8
Otteson Bluff—summit ... WI-6
Otteson Tank—reservoir ... AZ-5
**Ott Estates Subdivision**—pop pl ... UT-8
Ott Fork—stream (2) ... PA-2
Ott Hill—summit ... PA-2
Ott Hollow—valley ... AR-4
Ottilie, Lake—lake ... PA-2
**Ottine**—pop pl ... TX-5
Otting, Lake—lake ... FL-3
**Ottinger**—pop pl ... TN-4
Ottinger, Henry, House—hist pl ... NC-3
Ottinger Cem—cemetery ... TN-4
Ottinger Creek—stream ... TN-4
Ottinger Hall—hist pl ... UT-8
Ottinger Post Office (historical)—building ... TN-4
Ottinger Sch (historical)—school ... TN-4
Ottinger Shelton Chapel—church ... TN-4
Ottinger Springs—spring ... TN-4
Ottis Burrow Dam—dam ... AL-4
Ottis Creek ... TN-4
Ottis Ditch—canal ... IN-6
Ottis Garner Lake Dam—dam ... MS-4
Ottis Orchards ... WA-9
Ottis Post Office (historical)—building ... AL-4
Ottis Robertson Lake Dam—dam ... MS-4
Ottiwell Sch—school ... MA-1
Ott Lake—lake ... AZ-5
Ott Lake—lake ... MN-6
Ott Lake—reservoir ... NC-3
Ott Lake Dam—dam ... MS-4
Ott Lake Dam—dam ... NC-3
Ott Landing Strip—airport ... SD-7
Ottley—uninc pl ... GA-3
Ottley Gulch—valley ... CA-9
**Ottman Corners**—pop pl ... WI-6
Ottman Lake—lake ... WI-6
**Ott Meadows**—pop pl ... NY-2
Ottmers Ranch—locale ... TX-5
Ottmuller Sch—school ... IL-6
Otto—locale ... AR-4
Otto—locale ... KS-7
Otto—locale ... NM-5
Otto—locale ... PA-2
Otto—locale ... WV-2
Otto—locale ... WY-8
**Otto**—pop pl ... IL-6
**Otto**—pop pl ... IN-6
**Otto**—pop pl ... MN-6
**Otto**—pop pl ... MO-7
**Otto**—pop pl ... NY-2
**Otto**—pop pl ... NC-3
**Otto**—pop pl ... PA-2
**Otto**—pop pl ... TX-5
**Otto**—pop pl ... WY-8
Otto, Bodo, House—hist pl ... NJ-2
Otto, Lake—reservoir ... OH-6
Otto and Offer Cem—cemetery ... TX-5
Otto Bayou—gut ... LA-4
**Otto Berger Addition (subdivision)**—pop pl ... UT-8
Ottobine—locale ... VA-3
Ottobine Cem—cemetery ... OH-6
Ottobine Sch—school ... VA-3
Otto Boye Flat—flat ... OR-9
Otto Cem—cemetery ... IL-6
Otto Cem—cemetery ... MI-6
Otto Cem—cemetery ... NM-5
Otto Creek—stream ... CO-8
Otto Creek—stream ... ID-8
Otto Creek—stream (2) ... WY-8
Otto Dietterle Dam—dam ... SD-7
Otto Drain—stream ... MI-6
Otto Draw—valley ... NM-5
Otto-Eldred HS—school ... PA-2
Otto Elem Sch—school ... NC-3
Otto Ericson Dam Number 1—dam ... SD-7
Ottofy (historical)—locale ... ND-7
Ottofy Lake—lake ... ND-7
Otto Gulch—valley ... CO-8
Otto (historical)—locale (2) ... SD-7
Otto House—hist pl ... TX-5
Otto JHS—school ... MI-6
Ottokee—locale ... OH-6
**Ottokee**—pop pl ... OH-6
Otto Lake ... MN-6
Otto Lake—lake ... AK-9
Otto Lake—lake ... AR-4
Otto Lake—lake (2) ... MN-6
Otto Lakes—lake ... MN-6
Otto Lasley Spring—spring ... MO-7
Otto Lumber Camp—locale ... WY-8
Otto Mall—post sta ... IL-6
**Ottoman**—pop pl ... VA-3
Ottoman Amphitheater—basin ... AZ-5
Ottoman Wharf—locale ... VA-3
Otto Mills—locale ... NY-2
Otto Mine—mine ... CA-9
Otto Oil Field—oilfield ... TX-5
Otto Post Office (historical)—building ... TN-4
Otto Ranch—locale ... WY-8
Otto Run—stream (2) ... PA-2
Otto Sch—school (2) ... IL-6
Otto Sch—school ... KS-7
Otto Sch—school ... MI-6
Otto Sch—school ... NE-7
Otto Schmidt Dam—dam ... SD-7
Ottosee, Lake—reservoir ... TN-4
**Ottosen**—pop pl ... IA-7
Ottos Lake—lake ... MN-6
Ottoson Basin—basin ... UT-8
Ottoson Creek—stream ... UT-8
Otto Spur (historical)—locale ... MO-7
Ottos Rsvr—reservoir ... UT-8
Ottos Wells—well ... NM-5
Otto Tank—reservoir ... AZ-5
Otto Tank—reservoir ... NM-5
**Otto (Town of)**—pop pl ... NY-2
Otto Township ... KS-7
**Otto (Township of)**—pop pl ... IL-6
**Otto (Township of)**—pop pl ... MI-6
**Otto (Township of)**—pop pl ... MN-6
**Otto (Township of)**—pop pl ... PA-2
Ottoville ... MO-7
**Ottoville**—pop pl ... IL-6
**Ottoville**—pop pl ... MO-7
**Ottoville**—pop pl ... OH-6
Otto Wansley Lake Dam—dam ... MS-4
Ottoway Creek—stream ... CA-9
Ottoway Park—park ... NY-2
Ottoway Peak—summit ... CA-9
Ottown ... PA-2
**Ottown**—pop pl ... PA-2
Ott Point—cape ... FL-3
Ott Ranch—locale ... UT-8
Ott Rsvr—reservoir ... CO-8
Ott Run—stream ... PA-2
Otts ... PA-2
Ott's Assay Office—hist pl ... CA-9
Otts Basin—basin ... ID-8
Otts Canyon—valley ... UT-8
Ott Sch—school ... MI-6
Ott Sch—school ... MO-7
Ott Sch—school ... PA-2
Otts Chapel—church ... DE-2
Ott's Chapel—hist pl ... DE-2
Otts Creek—stream ... VA-3
Ott Shoals—rapids ... SC-3
Otts Park—park ... WI-6
**Ottsville**—pop pl ... PA-2
**Ott Town**—pop pl ... PA-2
Ottum Ranch—locale ... MT-8
**Ottumwa**—pop pl ... IA-7
**Ottumwa**—pop pl ... KS-7
**Ottumwa**—pop pl ... SD-7
Ottumwa Cem—cemetery ... IA-7
Ottumwa City Hall—building ... IA-7
Ottumwa Dam—dam ... SD-7
Ottumwa Ditch—canal ... AK-9
Ottumwa Heights Coll—school ... IA-7
Ottumwa HS—school ... IA-7
Ottumwa Industrial Airp—airport ... IA-7
**Ottumwa Junction**—pop pl ... IA-7
Ottumwa Lake—reservoir ... SD-7
Ottumwa Park Campground—park ... IA-7
Ottumwa Public Library—hist pl ... IA-7
**Ottumwa Township**—pop pl ... KS-7
**Ottusville**—pop pl ... KY-4
**Ottville**—pop pl ... IL-6
**Ottway**—pop pl ... TN-4
Ottway Elem Sch—school ... TN-4
Ottway Post Office (historical)—building ... TN-4
Ottway School ... TN-4
Ottway United Methodist Ch—church ... TN-4
O'Tuckalofa Baptist Church ... MS-4
O'Tuckalofa Sch (historical)—school ... MS-4
Otuk Creek—stream ... AK-9
Otuspasso Brook ... MS-4
**Otway**—pop pl ... NC-3
**Otway**—pop pl ... OH-6
Otway Covered Bridge—hist pl ... OH-6
Otwell—hist pl ... MD-2
**Otwell**—pop pl ... AR-4
**Otwell**—pop pl ... IN-6
Otwell Cem—cemetery ... IN-6
Otwell Creek ... MD-2
Otwell Elem Sch—school ... IN-6
Otwell Holiness Camp—park ... IN-6
Otwin Spring—spring ... OR-9
Otzenberger House—hist pl ... MO-7
Ou ... FM-9
Ou, Mauna—summit ... HI-9
Ouabache ... IN-6
Ouabache State Park—park ... IN-6
Ouabache State Rec Area ... IN-6
Ouabouskigou ... IN-6
Ouachita ... LA-4
**Ouachita**—pop pl ... AR-4
Ouachita, Lake—reservoir ... AR-4
Ouachita Baptist Univ—school ... AR-4
Ouachita Cem—cemetery ... AR-4
Ouachita Ch—church ... AR-4
Ouachita Ch—church ... LA-4
**Ouachita City**—pop pl ... LA-4
Ouachita College—uninc pl ... AR-4
**Ouachita (County)**—pop pl ... AR-4
Ouachita Creek—stream ... AR-4
Ouachita HS—school ... AR-4
**Ouachita (Ouachita City)**—pop pl ... LA-4
**Ouachita Parish**—pop pl ... LA-4
Ouachita Parish HS—hist pl ... LA-4
Ouachita Pinnacle—summit ... AR-4
Ouachita River—stream ... AR-4
Ouachita River—stream ... LA-4
Ouachita River Lock and Dam No. 8—hist pl ... AR-4
Ouachita (Township of)—fmr MCD (4) ... AR-4
**Ouachita Training Center**—pop pl ... OK-5
Ouachita Valley Sch—school ... LA-4
Ouaintance Ranch—locale ... CO-8
Ouallamet River ... OR-9
Oua Luck Butte ... OR-9
Ouang—stream ... PW-9
Ouap ... FM-9
**Ouaquaga**—pop pl ... NY-2
Ouaquaga Creek—stream ... NY-2
Oubache ... IN-6
Oubash ... IN-6
Oubask ... IN-6
**Oubre**—pop pl ... LA-4
Oucchanya ... AL-4
Ouchis—bar ... FM-9
Ouchklune Range—other ... AK-9
O U Creek—stream ... CO-8
Oudin Hill—summit ... WY-8
Ouelette Bridge—bridge ... MA-1
Ouellete ... ME-1
Ouellette—locale ... ME-1
Ouellette Brook—stream (3) ... ME-1
Ouellette Farm—locale ... ME-1
Ouest, Bayou de l'—gut ... LA-4
Ouff Lake—lake ... MN-6
Ough—locale ... NE-7
Ough Cem—cemetery ... NE-7
Oughoughton Creek—stream ... PA-2
Oughquoghton Creek ... PA-2
Ough Reef—bar ... WA-9
Oughton, Jack, House—hist pl ... ID-8
Oughton, John R., House—hist pl ... IL-6
Ough Township—civ div ... NE-7
Ouhi—civil ... HI-9
Ouhi Stream—stream ... HI-9
Ouiatenon Blockhouse—building ... IN-6
Ouigley Crossing ... UT-8
Ouiski Bayou—stream ... LA-4
**Ouita**—pop pl ... AR-4
Ouitumkis ... AL-4
Ouivett Cem—cemetery ... MA-1
Oukote Brook ... MA-1
Oulagisket—hist pl ... NY-2
Oulau ... FM-9
Ouleout, Mount—summit ... CT-1
Ouleout Ch—church ... NY-2
Ouleout Creek—stream (2) ... NY-2
Ouleout Lake—reservoir ... CT-1
Ouleout Sch—school ... NY-2
Ouleout Valley Cem—cemetery ... NY-2
Oulette Brook ... ME-1
Ouli—civil ... HI-9
Ouli Gulch—valley ... HI-9
Ouli Mountain ... HI-9
Oulton Point—cape ... CA-9
**Oulu**—pop pl ... WI-6
Oulu Cem—cemetery ... WI-6
Oulu Ch—church (2) ... WI-6
Oulu Sch—school ... WI-6
Ouluska Pass—gap ... NY-2
**Oulu (Town of)**—pop pl ... WI-6
Oulux Butte ... OR-9
Oumalik Lakes—lake ... AK-9
Oumalik River—stream ... AK-9
Oumalik Test Well—well ... AK-9
Oumengernger ... PW-9
Oumiamiak ... IN-6
Oumiamiouek ... IN-6
Oumoar—locale ... FM-9
Oumol ... FM-9
Oun—bar (2) ... FM-9
Ounce River—stream ... WI-6
Oundland Lake ... WI-6
Ounechen—cape ... FM-9
Ounnubaug River ... MA-1
Ounnubbage River ... MA-1
Ounse River ... WI-6
Ourand, Mount—summit ... AK-9
**Ouray**—pop pl ... CO-8
**Ouray**—pop pl ... UT-8
Ouray, Mount—summit ... CO-8
Ouray City Hall and Walsh Library—hist pl ... CO-8
Ouray Creek—stream ... CO-8
Ouray Hist Dist—hist pl ... CO-8
Ouray Lake—lake ... UT-8
Ouray Memorial Cem—cemetery ... CO-8
Ouray Mountain ... CO-8
Ouray Natl Waterfowl Refuge ... UT-8
Ouray Natl Wildlife Ref—park ... UT-8
Ouray Park—flat ... UT-8
Ouray Park Canal—canal ... UT-8
Ouray Peak ... CO-8
Ouray Peak—summit ... CO-8
Ouray School Canal—canal ... UT-8
Ouray Spring—spring ... CO-8
Ouray Valley Canal—canal ... UT-8
Our Carter (historical)—locale ... KS-7
Our Cave—cave ... AL-4
Our Ch—church ... OK-5
Our Creek—stream (4) ... AK-9
Our Creek—stream ... ID-8
Our Fathers House—locale ... MD-2
Our Home Ch—church ... MS-4
Our Home Universalist Cem—cemetery ... MS-4
Our Home Universalist Church ... MS-4
Our House—hist pl ... OH-6
Our House—locale ... CA-9
Our House Dam—dam ... CA-9
Our Lady, Queen of Heaven Church—hist pl ... ID-8
Our Lady and Saint Rose Elem Sch—school ... KS-7
Our Lady Ch—church ... GA-3
Our Lady Chapel—church ... LA-4
Our Lady Chapel—church ... WI-6
Our Lady Help of Christians Hist Dist—hist pl ... MA-1
Our Lady Help of Christians Sch—school ... CA-9
Our Lady Help of Christians Sch—school ... MI-6
Our Lady Help of Christians Sch—school ... NJ-2
Our Lady Of Angels Cem—cemetery (2) ... NY-2
Our Lady of Angels Ch—church ... NY-2
Our Lady Of Angels Ch—church ... VA-3
Our Lady of Angels Coll—school ... PA-2
Our Lady of Angels Sch—school ... CA-9
Our Lady of Angels Sch—school ... TX-5
Our Lady of Angels Seminary—school ... IL-6
Our Lady of Arizona—cliff ... AZ-5
Our Lady of Arizona (historical)—cliff ... AZ-5
Our Lady of Assumption Catholic Ch—church ... FL-3
Our Lady of Assumption Ch—church ... TX-5
Our Lady of Assumption Sch—school ... CA-9
Our Lady of Assumption Sch—school ... PA-2
Our Lady of Assumption Sch—school ... TX-5
Our Lady of Belen Cem—cemetery ... NM-5
Our Lady of Bellefonte Hosp—hospital ... KY-4
Our Lady of Bethlehem Acad—school ... IL-6
Our Lady Of Bethlehem Convent—church ... OH-6
Our Lady of Calvary Sch—school ... PA-2
Our Lady of Charity Sch—school ... PA-2
Our Lady of Charity Sch—school ... WI-6
Our Lady Of Cincinnati Coll—school ... OH-6
Our Lady Of Consolation Sch—school ... PA-2
Our Lady Of Czechowski Cem—cemetery ... MA-1
Our Lady of Czestochowa Ch—church ... MO-7
Our Lady of Czestochowa Polish Natl Shrine—church ... PA-2
Our Lady of Fatima Catholic Ch—church ... MS-4
Our Lady of Fatima Ch—church ... AL-4
Our Lady Of Fatima Ch—church ... CT-1
Our Lady of Fatima Ch—church ... DE-2
Our Lady of Fatima Ch—church ... MA-1
Our Lady Of Fatima Ch—church ... MN-6
Our Lady of Fatima Ch—church ... NM-5
Our Lady of Fatima Ch—church ... NY-2
Our Lady Of Fatima Ch—church ... OH-6
Our Lady Of Fatima Chapel—church (2) ... PA-2
Our Lady of Fatima Elem Sch—school ... MS-4
Our Lady of Fatima Nursery Sch—school ... FL-3
Our Lady of Fatima Sch—school ... AL-4
Our Lady of Fatima Sch—school (4) ... CA-9
Our Lady of Fatima Sch—school ... CO-8
Our Lady of Fatima Sch—school ... DE-2
Our Lady of Fatima Sch—school ... MO-7
Our Lady of Fatima Sch—school ... NJ-2
Our Lady of Fatima Sch—school (2) ... NY-2
Our Lady of Fatima Sch—school ... PA-2
Our Lady Of Fatima Sch—school ... PA-2
Our Lady of Fatima Sch—school ... TX-5
Our Lady Of Fatima Sch—school ... WA-9
Our Lady of Fatima Sch—school ... WV-2
Our Lady of Fatima Shrine—church ... NY-2
Our Lady Of Fatima Shrine—other ... OH-6
Our Lady of Fatina Ch—church ... KY-4
Our Lady of Good Council Cem—cemetery ... IA-7
Our Lady of Good Council Ch—church ... SD-7
Our Lady of Good Council Sch—school ... HI-9
Our Lady of Good Counsel Ch—church (2) ... NY-2
Our Lady of Good Counsel HS—school ... MD-2
Our Lady of Good Counsel Sch—school ... IL-6
Our Lady of Good Counsel Sch—school (2) ... MI-6
Our Lady of Good Counsel Sch—school (2) ... NY-2
Our Lady Of Good Counsel Sch—school ... VA-3
Our Lady of Good Hope Old Roman Catholic Ch—church ... FL-3
Our Lady Of Grace Cem—cemetery ... PA-2
Our Lady of Grace Ch—church ... MA-1
Our Lady of Grace Monastery—church ... CT-1
Our Lady of Grace Sch—school (3) ... CA-9
Our Lady Of Grace Sch—school ... CT-1
Our Lady of Grace Sch—school ... IL-6
Our Lady of Grace Sch—school (3) ... IN-6
Our Lady of Grace Sch—school (2) ... MI-6
Our Lady of Grace Sch—school ... MN-6
Our Lady of Grace Sch—school ... NJ-2
Our Lady of Grace Sch—school (4) ... NY-2
Our Lady Of Grace Sch—school (2) ... PA-2
Our Lady of Grace Sch—school ... TX-5
Our Lady of Guadaloupe Church—hist pl ... AZ-5
Our Lady of Guadalupe—church ... UT-8
Our Lady of Guadalupe Acad—school ... CA-9
Our Lady of Guadalupe Cem—cemetery ... TX-5
Our Lady of Guadalupe Ch—church ... KS-7
Our Lady of Guadalupe Ch—church ... NM-5
Our Lady of Guadalupe Ch—church ... NC-3
Our Lady of Guadalupe Ch—church ... TX-5
Our Lady of Guadalupe Convent—church ... TX-5
Our Lady of Guadalupe Mission—church ... AZ-5
Our Lady of Guadalupe Roman Catholic Ch—church ... KS-7
Our Lady of Guadalupe (Rose Hill) Sch—school ... CA-9
Our Lady of Guadalupe Sch—school ... AZ-5
Our Lady of Guadalupe Sch—school (2) ... CA-9
Our Lady of Guadalupe Sch—school ... FL-3
Our Lady of Guadalupe Sch—school ... IL-6
Our Lady of Guadalupe Sch—school ... KS-7
Our Lady of Guadalupe Sch—school ... NY-2
Our Lady of Guadalupe Sch—school ... TX-5
Our Lady of Heaven Sch—school ... MI-6
Our Lady of Help Cem—cemetery ... MO-7
Our Lady of Help Sch—school ... MO-7
Our Lady of Holy Cross Coll—school ... LA-4
Our Lady of Hope Cem—cemetery ... MI-6
Our Lady of Hope Sch—school ... IL-6
Our Lady of Hope Sch—school ... MD-2
Our Lady of Hope Sch—school ... NY-2
Our Lady of Hope Seminary—school ... NY-2
Our Lady of Humility Sch—school ... IL-6
Our Lady of Hungary Sch—school ... IL-6
Our Lady of Hungary Sch—school ... IN-6
Our Lady of Knock Sch—school ... IL-6
Our Lady of Lakes Catholic Ch—church ... FL-3
Our Lady Of LaSalette Seminary—school ... CT-1
Our Lady of LaSalette Seminary—school ... MA-1
Our Lady of Las Vegas Sch—school ... NV-8
Our Lady of Limerick Catholic Church—hist pl ... ID-8
Our Lady Of Lords Sch—school ... OH-6
Our Lady Of Loreto Sch—school ... PA-2
Our Lady of Loretta Ch—church ... WI-6
Our Lady of Loretto Ch—church ... OH-6
Our Lady of Loretto HS—school ... CA-9
Our Lady of Loretto Sch—school ... CA-9
Our Lady of Loretto Sch—school ... MI-6
Our Lady of Loretto Sch—school ... NY-2
Our Lady of Lourdes Acad—school ... AZ-5
Our Lady of Lourdes Camp—locale ... NY-2
Our Lady of Lourdes Catholic Cem—cemetery ... OR-9
Our Lady of Lourdes Catholic Ch—church ... AL-4
Our Lady of Lourdes Catholic Ch—church (2) ... TN-4
Our Lady of Lourdes Catholic Ch—church ... UT-8
Our Lady Of Lourdes Cem—cemetery ... IA-7
Our Lady of Lourdes Cem—cemetery ... LA-4
Our Lady of Lourdes Cem—cemetery ... MN-6
Our Lady Of Lourdes Cem—cemetery ... NE-7
Our Lady Of Lourdes Cem—cemetery ... PA-2
Our Lady of Lourdes Ch—church (2) ... FL-3
Our Lady Of Lourdes Ch—church ... IA-7
Our Lady of Lourdes Ch—church ... ND-7
Our Lady Of Lourdes Ch—church ... OH-6
Our Lady of Lourdes Ch—church ... PA-2
Our Lady of Lourdes Ch—church ... VA-3
Our Lady of Lourdes Church—hist pl ... TX-5
Our Lady of Lourdes Grotto—hist pl ... NM-5
Our Lady of Lourdes Hospital—airport ... NJ-2
Our Lady of Lourdes Hospital—school ... NJ-2
Our lady of Lourdes HS—school ... PA-2
Our Lady of Lourdes Mission—church ... AZ-5
Our Lady of Lourdes Mission—church ... SD-7
Our Lady of Lourdes Roman Catholic Ch—church ... IN-6
Our Lady of Lourdes Sch—school ... AL-4
Our Lady of Lourdes Sch—school (3) ... CA-9
Our Lady of Lourdes Sch—school (2) ... FL-3
Our Lady of Lourdes Sch—school ... IL-6
Our Lady of Lourdes Sch—school ... IN-6
Our Lady of Lourdes Sch—school ... KY-4
Our Lady Of Lourdes Sch—school ... KY-4
Our Lady of Lourdes Sch—school ... LA-4
Our Lady of Lourdes Sch—school ... MD-2
Our Lady of Lourdes Sch—school ... MA-1
Our Lady of Lourdes Sch—school ... MI-6
Our Lady of Lourdes Sch—school ... MN-6
Our Lady of Lourdes Sch—school ... MS-4
Our Lady of Lourdes Sch—school (2) ... MO-7
Our Lady Of Lourdes Sch—school ... NE-7
Our Lady of Lourdes Sch—school ... NJ-2
Our Lady of Lourdes Sch—school (7) ... NY-2
Our Lady of Lourdes Sch—school ... NC-3
Our Lady of Lourdes Sch—school ... PA-2
Our Lady of Lourdes Sch—school ... TX-5
Our Lady of Mercy Acad—school ... NY-2
Our Lady of Mercy Cem—cemetery ... FL-3
Our Lady of Mercy Cem—cemetery ... LA-4
Our Lady Of Mercy Cem—cemetery ... PA-2
Our Lady of Mercy Cem—cemetery ... TX-5
Our Lady of Mercy Ch—church ... FL-3
Our Lady of Mercy Ch—church ... MS-4
Our Lady of Mercy Ch—church ... NY-2
Our Lady Of Mercy Ch—church ... OH-6
Our Lady Of Mercy Ch—church ... PA-2
Our Lady of Mercy Chapel—hist pl ... NJ-2
Our Lady of Mercy HS—hist pl ... OH-6
Our Lady of Mercy HS—school ... MI-6
Our Lady of Mercy HS—school ... NY-2
Our Lady of Mercy Sch—school ... AL-4
Our Lady of Mercy Sch—school (2) ... CA-9
Our Lady of Mercy Sch—school ... CT-1
Our Lady of Mercy Sch—school ... IL-6
Our Lady of Mercy Sch—school ... LA-4
Our Lady of Mercy Sch—school ... MA-1
Our Lady of Mercy Sch—school ... NJ-2
Our Lady of Mercy Sch—school (2) ... NY-2
Our Lady of Mercy Sch—school ... TX-5
Our Lady of Mount Carmel Catholic Church—hist pl ... AZ-5
Our Lady of Mount Carmel Catholic Church—hist pl ... ME-1
Our Lady of Mount Carmel Cem—cemetery ... IA-7
Our Lady Of Mount Carmel Cem—cemetery ... IA-7
Our Lady Of Mount Carmel Cem—cemetery (2) ... PA-2
Our Lady of Mount Carmel Ch—church ... IA-7
Our Lady of Mount Carmel Ch—church ... MI-6
Our Lady of Mount Carmel Ch—church ... NM-5
Our Lady of Mount Carmel Ch—church ... NY-2
Our Lady Of Mount Carmel Ch—church ... OH-6
Our Lady of Mount Carmel Ch—church (2) ... TX-5
Our Lady of Mount Carmel Church—hist pl ... OH-6
Our Lady of Mount Carmel Hosp—hospital ... TX-5
Our Lady of Mount Carmel Monastary—church ... NM-5
Our Lady of Mount Carmel Sch—school ... AZ-5
Our Lady of Mount Carmel Sch—school ... IN-6
Our Lady of Mount Carmel Sch—school ... KY-4
Our Lady of Mount Carmel Sch—school ... MA-1
Our Lady of Mount Carmel Sch—school ... NJ-2
Our Lady of Mount Carmel Sch—school ... NY-2
Our Lady of Mount Carmel Sch—school ... OH-6
Our Lady Of Mount Carmel Sch—school ... OH-6
Our Lady of Mount Carmel Sch—school ... OH-6
Our Lady of Mount Carmel Sch—school ... PA-2
Our Lady of Mt. Carmel Church—hist pl ... NM-5
Our Lady Of Nazareth Sch—school ... VA-3
Our Lady of Peace Cathedral—hist pl ... HI-9
Our Lady of Peace Hosp—hospital ... KY-4
Our Lady of Peace Sch—school ... CA-9
Our Lady of Peace Sch—school (2) ... NJ-2
Our Lady of Peace Sch—school (3) ... NY-2
Our Lady Of Peace Sch—school (2) ... OH-6
Our Lady Of Peace Sch—school ... PA-2
Our Lady of Peace Sch—school ... WV-2
Our Lady of Perpetual Help Catholic Ch—church ... TN-4
Our Lady of Perpetual Help Catholic Church & Cemetery—hist pl ... NE-7
Our Lady of Perpetual Help Cem—cemetery ... SD-7
Our Lady of Perpetual Help Ch—church (2) ... FL-3
Our Lady of Perpetual Help Ch—church (2) ... KS-7
Our Lady of Perpetual Help Ch—church ... WI-6
Our Lady of Perpetual Help Church—hist pl ... AR-4
Our Lady of Perpetual Help Sch—school ... AZ-5
Our Lady of Perpetual Help Sch—school (4) ... CA-9
Our Lady of Perpetual Help Sch—school ... DC-2
Our Lady of Perpetual Help Sch—school ... FL-3
Our Lady of Perpetual Help Sch—school ... HI-9
Our Lady of Perpetual Help Sch—school (2) ... IN-6
Our Lady of Perpetual Help Sch—school ... KS-7
Our Lady of Perpetual Help Sch—school (2) ... NY-2
Our Lady Of perpetual Help Sch—school ... NY-2
Our Lady of Perpetual Help Sch—school ... NY-2
Our Lady Of Perpetual Help Sch—school ... OH-6
Our Lady of Perpetual Help Sch—school ... OH-6
Our Lady Of Perpetual Help Sch—school ... OH-6
Our Lady Of Perpetual Help Sch—school ... PA-2
Our Lady of Perpetual Help Sch—school ... PA-2

Owens Ford ... TN-4
Owens Gap—gap ... AL-4
Owens Gap—gap ... NC-3
Owens Gulch—valley ... ID-8
**Owens Hill**—pop pl ... OH-6
Owens Hill—summit ... GA-3
Owens Hill—summit ... TN-4
Owens Hollow—valley ... AR-4
Owens Hollow—valley ... KY-4
Owens Hollow—valley ... MS-4
Owens Hollow—valley (2) ... MO-7
Owens Hollow—valley (2) ... TN-4
Owens Hollow—valley ... UT-8
Owens Hollow—valley ... WV-2
Owens Hollw ... KY-4
Owens-Illinois Glass Company—facility ... GA-3
Owens Island—island ... GA-3
Owens Island—island ... KY-4
Owens Junior High School ... AL-4
Owens Knob—summit ... KY-4
Owens Knob—summit ... MO-7
Owens Knob—summit ... NC-3
Owens Lake ... FL-3
Owens Lake ... MI-6
Owens Lake—flat ... CA-9
Owens Lake—lake ... AR-4
Owens Lake—lake (2) ... FL-3
Owens Lake—lake ... LA-4
Owens Lake—lake ... MI-6
Owens Lake—lake ... TX-5
Owens Lake—lake ... WA-9
Owens Lake—reservoir ... AL-4
Owens Lake—reservoir ... NC-3
Owens Lake Dam—dam ... NC-3
Owens Landing—locale ... AL-4
Owens Landing—locale ... TN-4
Owens Landing—locale ... VA-3
Owens Lookout Tower—locale ... MI-6
Owens Marsh—swamp ... WA-9
Owens Meadow—flat ... WA-9
Owens Meadow Hollow—valley ... UT-8
Owens Mill (historical)—locale (2) ... AL-4
Owens Mills—locale ... NY-2
Owens Mills (historical)—locale ... TN-4
Owens Mine—mine ... AZ-5
Owens Mine—mine ... CA-9
Owens Mine—mine ... CO-8
Owens Mound—summit ... OH-6
Owens Mountain—ridge ... AL-4
Owens Mtn—summit (2) ... AR-4
Owens Mtn—summit ... CA-9
Owens Mtn—summit ... NV-8
Owens Peak—summit ... CA-9
Owens Point—summit ... CA-9
Owens Pond ... FL-3
Owens Pond—lake (2) ... FL-3
Owens Pond—lake ... VA-3
Owens Pond—reservoir ... AL-4
Owens Prairie Cem—cemetery ... OK-5
Owens Prairie Ch—church ... OK-5
Owen Spring—spring ... OR-9
Owen Spring—spring ... UT-8
Owen Spring Branch—stream ... TN-4
Owens Ranch—locale (2) ... NM-5
Owens Ranch—locale (3) ... TX-5
Owens Ranch—locale ... WY-8
Owens Ravine—valley ... CA-9
Owens Ridge—ridge ... AK-9
Owens River—stream ... CA-9
Owens River Canal—canal ... CA-9
Owens River Gorge—valley ... CA-9
Owens River Ranch—locale ... CA-9
Owens Rock—pillar ... WI-6
Owens (RR name for Kanawha City)—other ... WV-2
Owens Rsvr—reservoir ... CA-9
Owens Rsvr—reservoir ... CO-8
Owens Rsvr—reservoir ... ID-8
Owens Run—stream ... PA-2
Owens Sch—school (3) ... AL-4
Owens Sch—school (2) ... IL-6
Owens Sch—school (2) ... KY-4
Owens Sch—school ... MI-6
Owens Sch—school ... MO-7
Owens Sch—school ... WV-2
Owens Sch (abandoned)—school ... PA-2
Owens Sch (historical)—school ... TN-4
Owens School Park—park ... AL-4
**Owens Siding**—pop pl ... IL-6
Owens Site (22TU512)—hist pl ... MS-4
Owens Slough—stream ... KY-4
Owens Slough—stream ... TN-4
Owens Spring—spring ... FL-3
Owens Spring—spring ... ID-8
Owens Spring—spring ... KY-4
Owens Spring—spring ... MO-7
Owens Spring—spring ... NV-8
Owens Spring—spring ... OR-9
Owens Spring Branch ... TN-4
Owens Spring Branch—stream ... TN-4
Owens Spring Camp Ground (historical)—locale ... AL-4
Owens Spring Cem—cemetery ... AL-4
Owens Spring Methodist Ch (historical)—church ... AL-4
Owens State For—forest ... DE-2
Owens Station Sch (historical)—school ... TN-4
Owens Store ... DE-2
Owen Stadium—other ... OK-5
Owens Tank—reservoir (2) ... AZ-5
Owens Tank—reservoir ... TX-5
Owens Tanyard ... AL-4
Owen State Forest ... IN-6
Owen Station Sch (abandoned)—school ... MO-7
Owens-Thomas House—hist pl ... GA-3
**Owens (Township of)**—pop pl ... MN-6
Owens Tract State For ... DE-2
Owens-Tyer Cemetery ... TX-5
Owens United Methodist Church ... TN-4
Owens Valley—basin ... KY-4
Owens Valley—valley ... CA-9
Owens Valley—valley ... WI-6
Owens Valley Ranch—locale ... CA-9
Owensville (2) ... MD-2
Owensville—locale ... TX-5
Owensville—locale ... VA-3
**Owensville**—pop pl ... AR-4
**Owensville**—pop pl ... IN-6
**Owensville**—pop pl ... MO-7
**Owensville**—pop pl (2) ... OH-6
Owensville Cem—cemetery ... TX-5
Owensville Lake—reservoir ... OH-6
Owensville Public Sch—school ... IN-6
Owensville Sch—school ... OH-6
**Owens Wells**—pop pl ... MS-4
Owens Windmill—locale ... TX-5
Owen Tank—reservoir ... TX-5
Owen Tanyard ... AL-4
Owenton—locale ... VA-3
**Owenton**—pop pl ... AL-4
**Owenton**—pop pl ... KY-4
Owenton (CCD)—cens area ... KY-4
**Owentown**—pop pl ... TX-5
Owentown—uninc pl ... AL-4
Owen Township—fmr MCD ... IA-7
Owen (Township of)—fmr MCD (4) ... AR-4
**Owen (Township of)**—pop pl ... IL-6
**Owen (Township of)**—pop pl (4) ... IN-6
Owen Valley ... CA-9
Owen Valley Community HS—school ... IN-6
Owen Valley MS—school ... IN-6
**Owenyo**—pop pl ... CA-9
Owhat River—stream ... AK-9
Owhi Creek—stream ... WA-9
Owhi Flat—flat ... WA-9
Owhigh Lakes—lake ... WA-9
Owhi Lake—lake ... WA-9
Owhyee River ... OR-9
Owing Butte ... OR-9
Owing Creek ... OR-9
**Owings**—pop pl ... MD-2
**Owings**—pop pl ... SC-3
**Owings**—pop pl ... WV-2
Owings, Col. Thomas Deye, House—hist pl ... KY-4
Owings, John Calvin, House—hist pl ... SC-3
**Owings Beach**—pop pl ... MD-2
Owings Cem—cemetery ... GA-3
Owings Cem—cemetery ... MO-7
Owings Cliffs—cliff ... MD-2
Owings Creek ... OR-9
Owings Creek—stream ... MT-8
Owings Creek—stream ... OR-9
**Owings Mills**—pop pl ... MD-2
Owings Mills Sch—school ... MD-2
Owings Upper Mill—hist pl ... MD-2
**Owingsville**—pop pl ... KY-4
Owingsville (CCD)—cens area ... KY-4
Owingsville Commercial District and Courthouse Square—hist pl ... KY-4
Owingsville Commercial District and Courthouse Square (Boundary Increase)—hist pl ... KY-4
Owinip—spring ... FM-9
Owinza—locale ... ID-8
Owinza Butte—summit ... ID-8
Owinza Butte Lake—lake ... ID-8
O-Wi-Yu-Kuts Creek—stream ... CO-8
O-Wi-Yu-Kuts Creek—stream ... UT-8
O-Wi-Yu-Kuts Draw—valley ... CO-8
O-Wi-Yu-Kuts Draw—valley ... UT-8
O-Wi-Yu-Kuts Flats—flat ... CO-8
O-Wi-Yu-Kuts Flats—flat ... UT-8
O-wi-yu-kuts Mtns—range ... CO-8
O-Wi-Yu-Kuts Mtns—range ... UT-8
O-Wi-Yu-Kuts Spring—spring ... CO-8
Owl—locale ... CA-9
**Owl**—pop pl ... AZ-5
Owl, The—summit ... ME-1
Owl Bay—swamp ... GA-3
Owl Bayou—stream ... LA-4
Owl Blacksmith Shop—hist pl ... OK-5
Owl Box Canyon—valley ... AZ-5
Owl Branch ... SC-3
Owl Branch—stream ... IL-6
Owl Branch—stream ... IN-6
Owl Branch—stream ... KY-4
Owl Branch—stream ... MD-2
Owl Branch—stream ... MO-7
Owl Branch—stream ... NC-3
Owl Branch—stream ... SC-3
Owl Branch—stream (3) ... TN-4
Owl Bridge—other ... UT-8
Owl Brook—stream ... NH-1
Owl Butte—summit ... SD-7
Owl Cabin Way—trail ... OR-9
Owl Camp—locale ... CO-8
Owlcamp Branch—stream ... NC-3
Owl Camp Windmill—locale ... CO-8
Owl Canal—canal ... ID-8
Owl Canyon—locale ... CO-8
Owl Canyon—valley (2) ... AZ-5
Owl Canyon—valley (2) ... CA-9
Owl Canyon—valley (2) ... CO-8
Owl Canyon—valley (3) ... NM-5
Owl Canyon—valley ... OR-9
Owl Canyon—valley ... WY-8
Owl Cave—cave ... NM-5
Owl Cem—cemetery ... NC-3
Owl City—locale ... TN-4
**Owl City**—pop pl ... TN-4
Owl Creek ... NE-7
Owl Creek ... OH-6
Owl Creek ... WY-8
Owl Creek—gut ... AL-4
Owl Creek—locale ... TX-5
**Owl Creek**—pop pl ... TN-4
Owl Creek—stream (3) ... AL-4
Owl Creek—stream (2) ... AK-9
Owl Creek—stream ... AZ-5
Owl Creek—stream (5) ... AR-4
Owl Creek—stream (11) ... CA-9
Owl Creek—stream (5) ... CO-8
Owl Creek—stream (3) ... FL-3
Owl Creek—stream (2) ... GA-3
Owl Creek—stream (6) ... ID-8
Owl Creek—stream (2) ... IL-6
Owl Creek—stream (7) ... IN-6
Owl Creek—stream (7) ... KS-7
Owl Creek—stream (2) ... KY-4
Owl Creek—stream ... LA-4
Owl Creek—stream ... MI-6
Owl Creek—stream (4) ... MS-4
Owl Creek—stream (17) ... MO-7
Owl Creek—stream (6) ... MT-8
Owl Creek—stream (2) ... NE-7
Owl Creek—stream ... NV-8
Owl Creek—stream ... NM-5
Owl Creek—stream ... NY-2
Owl Creek—stream ... NC-3
Owl Creek—stream (6) ... OH-6
Owl Creek—stream (7) ... OK-5
Owl Creek—stream (10) ... OR-9
Owl Creek—stream (3) ... PA-2
Owl Creek—stream (2) ... SD-7
Owl Creek—stream (3) ... TN-4
Owl Creek—stream (6) ... TX-5
Owl Creek—stream (2) ... UT-8
Owl Creek—stream (2) ... VA-3
Owl Creek—stream (7) ... WA-9
Owl Creek—stream (2) ... WV-2
Owl Creek—stream ... WI-6
Owl Creek—stream (9) ... WY-8
Owl Creek Bay—swamp ... FL-3
Owl Creek Campground—locale ... WA-9
Owl Creek Cem—cemetery ... KS-7
Owl Creek Cem—cemetery ... OH-6
Owl Creek Ch—church ... NC-3
Owl Creek Ch—church (3) ... OH-6
Owl Creek Ch—church ... OK-5
Owl Creek Country Club—other ... KY-4
Owl Creek Gap—gap ... GA-3
Owl Creek Gap—gap ... NC-3
Owl Creek Hot Springs—spring ... ID-8
Owl Creek Meadow—swamp ... OR-9
Owl Creek Mountain ... WY-8
Owl Creek Mountains—summit ... TX-5
Owl Creek Mtns—range ... WY-8
Owl Creek Oil Field—oilfield ... KS-7
Owl Creek Pass—gap ... CO-8
Owl Creek Range ... WY-8
Owl Creek Rsvr—reservoir ... CO-8
Owl Creek Sch—school ... NE-7
Owl Creek Sch—school ... PA-2
Owl Creek Sch—school ... SD-7
Owl Creek Site—hist pl ... MS-4
Owl Creek Spur Trail—trail ... WA-9
Owl Creek Township—civil ... KS-7
Owl Creek Trail—trail ... CA-9
Owl Creek Trail—trail ... WY-8
Owl Creek Trail (pack)—trail ... OR-9
Owl Ditch—canal ... CO-8
Owl Draw—valley ... NM-5
Owl Draw—valley ... TX-5
Owl Draw—valley ... UT-8
Owlett Green—locale ... TX-5
Owley Ch—church ... AR-4
Owl Fork—stream ... WV-2
Owl Gap—gap ... GA-3
Owl Gap CCC Camp (abandoned)—locale ... PA-2
Owl Gap Trail—trail ... PA-2
Owl Gulch—valley ... AK-9
Owl Gulch—valley (2) ... CA-9
Owl Gulch—valley (4) ... CO-8
Owl Gulch—valley ... WY-8
Owl Hammock—island ... FL-3
Owl Hat Point—summit ... AZ-5
Owlhead—locale ... AZ-5
Owl Head—summit ... AZ-5
Owl Head—summit ... PA-2
Owl Head Buttes—summit ... AZ-5
Owl Head Canyon—valley ... MT-8
Owl Head Dam—dam ... AZ-5
Owlhead Mtn—summit ... NH-1
Owlhead Ridge ... PA-2
Owl Hill—summit ... AL-4
Owl Hill—summit ... MA-1
Owl Hill Post Office (historical)—building ... TN-4
Owl Hills—other ... AK-9
Owl Hills—range ... WY-8
Owl Hills—summit ... TX-5
Owl Hill Sch—school ... WV-2
Owl Hill Well Number 1 (oil)—oilfield ... NV-8
Owl Hole—gap ... PA-2
Owl Hole Gap—gap ... TN-4
Owl Hole Springs—spring ... CA-9
Owl Hollow—basin ... GA-3
Owl Hollow—locale ... PA-2
**Owlhollow**—pop pl ... TN-4
Owl Hollow—valley (3) ... AL-4
Owl Hollow—valley (4) ... AR-4
Owl Hollow—valley ... GA-3
Owl Hollow—valley (3) ... IN-6
Owl Hollow—valley (3) ... KY-4
Owl Hollow—valley ... NC-3
Owl Hollow—valley (2) ... OH-6
Owl Hollow—valley ... OR-9
Owl Hollow—valley (3) ... PA-2
Owl Hollow—valley (21) ... TN-4
Owl Hollow—valley (7) ... TX-5
Owl Hollow—valley ... VA-3
Owl Hollow—valley ... WV-2
Owl Hollow Branch—stream ... KY-4
Owl Hollow Branch—stream (2) ... TN-4
Owl Hollow Bridge (historical)—bridge ... TN-4
Owl Hollow Cem—cemetery ... TN-4
Owl Hollow Ch—church ... TN-4
Owl Hollow Creek—stream ... TN-4
Owl Hollow Mill (historical)—locale ... TN-4
Owl Hollow Mine—mine ... OR-9
Owl Hollow Sch (abandoned)—school ... PA-2
Owl Hollow Sch (historical)—school ... TN-4
Owl Hollow Trail—trail ... PA-2
Owl Hoot—locale ... TN-4
Owl Hoot Windmill—locale ... AZ-5
Owl Island—island ... AK-9
Owl Kill—stream ... NY-2
Owl Knob—summit ... NC-3
Owl Knob Hollow—valley ... WV-2
Owl Lake ... NY-2
Owl Lake—flat ... CA-9
Owl Lake—lake ... AK-9
Owl Lake—lake ... CA-9
Owl Lake—lake (3) ... MI-6
Owl Lake—lake (2) ... MN-6
Owl Lake—lake ... SD-7
Owl Lake—lake (2) ... WI-6
Owl Lake (historical)—lake ... IA-7
Owl Landing—locale ... FL-3
Owl Mine—mine (3) ... CA-9
Owl Mine—mine ... NM-5
Owl Mine—mine ... OR-9
Owl Mountain and Domestic Supply and Mason Ditch—canal ... CO-8
Owl Mountain Ditch—canal ... CO-8
Owl Mountian—summit ... WA-9
Owl Mtn—summit ... CA-9
Owl Mtn—summit ... CO-8
Owl Mtn—summit ... GA-3
Owl Mtn—summit ... ME-1
Owl Mtn—summit ... OK-5
Owl Mtn—summit ... WA-9
Owl Nest—summit ... AZ-5
Owl Nest Canyon—valley ... AZ-5
Owl Pate—summit ... NY-2
Owl Pate Pond—summit ... NY-2
Owl Peak—summit ... CA-9
Owl Peak—summit (2) ... MT-8
Owl Peak—summit ... WY-8
Owl Pen Hollow—valley ... TN-4
Owl Point—cape ... MD-2
Owl Pond—lake ... ME-1
Owl Pond—lake ... MA-1
Owl Pond—lake (4) ... NY-2
Owl Pond Brook—stream ... ME-1
Owl Ridge—ridge ... CO-8
Owl Ridge—ridge ... OR-9
Owl Ridge—ridge ... TN-4
Owl River ... SD-7
Owl Rock—pillar ... UT-8
Owl Rock—summit ... AZ-5
Owl Rock Ch—church ... GA-3
Owl Rocks—cliff ... AZ-5
Owl Roost Gap—gap ... TN-4
Owl Run—stream (2) ... PA-2
Owl Run—stream ... VA-3
Owl Run—stream (3) ... WV-2
Owls Bend—bend ... MO-7
Owl's Bend Site (23SH10)—hist pl ... MO-7
Owls Cap—summit ... AZ-5
Owls Cliff—cliff ... NH-1
Owls Creek ... TN-4
Owls Head ... PA-2
Owls Head—cape ... ME-1
Owls Head—cape ... NH-1
Owls Head—cliff ... ME-1
**Owls Head**—pop pl ... ME-1
**Owls Head**—pop pl ... NY-2
Owls Head—ridge ... NH-1
Owls Head—summit ... CA-9
Owls Head—summit ... IL-6
Owls Head—summit (3) ... ME-1
Owlshead—summit ... NH-1
Owls Head—summit ... NH-1
Owls Head—summit (4) ... NY-2
Owls Head—summit ... PA-2
Owls Head—summit (2) ... VT-1
Owlshead—summit (2) ... WV-2
Owls Head—valley ... FL-3
Owls Head Bay—bay ... ME-1
Owls Head Bay—bay ... VT-1
Owlshead Canyon—valley ... CA-9
Owls Head Harbor—bay ... ME-1
Owls Head Hill—summit ... WI-6
Owl's Head Hist Dist—hist pl ... IA-7
Owls Head Ledge—bar ... ME-1
Owls Head Light Station—hist pl ... ME-1
Owls Head Lookout—summit ... NY-2
Owlshead Mountains—range ... CA-9
Owls Head Mtn—summit (2) ... NY-2
Owlshead Mtn—summit ... VT-1
Owls Head Mtn—summit ... VT-1
Owlshead Mtn—summit ... VT-1
Owls Head Park—park ... NY-2
Owls Head Pinnacle—summit ... NY-2
Owls Head Pond—lake (2) ... NY-2
Owls Head Pond Outlet—stream ... NY-2
Owls Head Range—ridge ... NY-2
Owlshead Run ... WV-2
**Owls Head (Town of)**—pop pl ... ME-1
Owls Hill—summit ... NH-1
Owl's Nest—hist pl ... NY-2
**Owls Nest**—pop pl ... DE-2
**Owls Nest**—pop pl ... NY-2
**Owls Nest**—pop pl ... PA-2
Owlsnest Branch—stream ... KY-4
Owls Nest Canyon—valley ... TX-5
**Owls Nest Estates**—pop pl ... DE-2
Owls Nest Field—park ... NJ-2
Owls Nest Mtn—summit ... AZ-5
Owls Nest Park—park ... OH-6
Owls Nest Sch—school ... IL-6
**Owls Nest (subdivision)**—pop pl ... NC-3
Owl Spring—spring (3) ... AZ-5
Owl Spring—spring ... CO-8
Owl Spring—spring (2) ... NV-8
Owl Spring—spring (2) ... NM-5
Owl Spring—spring ... OR-9
Owl Spring—spring ... UT-8
Owl Spring Mesa—summit ... AZ-5
Owl Springs—spring ... NM-5
Owl Spring Valley—valley ... AZ-5
Owls Roost ... AL-4
Owls Roost, The—locale ... ME-1
Owlsville—locale ... NY-2
Owl Swamp—swamp ... MA-1
Owl Swamp—swamp ... NY-2
Owls Window—arch ... KY-4
Owl Tank—reservoir (2) ... AZ-5
Owl Tank—reservoir ... NM-5
Owl Tank—reservoir (2) ... TX-5
Owl Tank Canyon—valley ... NM-5
Owl Tanks—reservoir ... TX-5
Owltown—locale ... GA-3
Owltown—locale ... NC-3
Owltown—locale ... PA-2
Owltown Creek—stream ... GA-3
Owltown Gap—gap ... GA-3
Owltown Mtn—summit ... GA-3
Owl Valley ... AL-4
Owl Valley—valley ... AZ-5
Owl Village—locale ... AK-9
Owlville Creek—stream ... NY-2
Owlville Sch—school ... NY-2
Owl Wash—stream (2) ... AZ-5
Owl Water Spring—spring ... NM-5
Owl Well—well ... AZ-5
Ownbey Cem—cemetery ... MO-7
Ownbey Lake—lake ... MO-7
Ownby, John, Cabin—hist pl ... TN-4
Ownby, Jordan C., Stadium—hist pl ... TX-5
Ownby Cem—cemetery (2) ... TN-4
Ownby Hollow—valley ... TN-4
Ownby Well—well ... NM-5
Owneby Creek—stream ... NC-3
Owner Gap Creek ... OR-9
Owner Gap Creek—stream ... OR-9
Owner Run—stream ... IN-6
Owners Mutual Canal—canal ... ID-8
Ownes Cem—cemetery ... TN-4
Ownsby Lake—reservoir ... TX-5
O' Woods, Lake—reservoir ... WV-2
**Owosso**—pop pl ... MI-6
Owosso Country Club—other ... MI-6
Owosso Drain—canal ... MI-6
Owosso Junction ... MI-6
Owosso Speedway—other ... MI-6
**Owosso (Township of)**—pop pl ... MI-6
Owpel—cape ... FM-9
OW Point—summit ... AZ-5
OW Ranch—locale ... AZ-5
OW Ranch—locale ... MT-8
Owre, Dr. Oscar, House—hist pl ... MN-6
O W Reservoir ... PA-2
Owsley—locale ... KY-4
Owsley—locale ... MO-7
**Owsley**—pop pl ... IL-6
Owsley, Gov. William, House—hist pl ... KY-4
Owsley Bridge—bridge ... ID-8
Owsley Canal—canal ... ID-8
Owsley Canyon—valley ... OR-9
Owsley Cem—cemetery ... KY-4
Owsley Cem—cemetery ... WA-9
**Owsley (County)**—pop pl ... KY-4
Owsley Creek ... OR-9
Owsley Creek—stream ... OR-9
Owsley Fork—stream ... KY-4
Owsley Hogback—summit ... OR-9
Owsley Sch—school ... KS-7
Owsley Sch—school ... OK-5
Owsley Slough—stream ... MT-8
Owsley Wells—well ... ID-8
Owsley Windmill—locale ... NM-5
O W Tank—reservoir ... NM-5
Owunnegunset Hill—summit ... CT-1
**Owyhee**—pop pl ... ID-8
**Owyhee**—pop pl ... NV-8
**Owyhee**—pop pl ... OR-9
Owyhee, Lake—reservoir ... OR-9
Owyhee Airp—airport ... NV-8
Owyhee Bench—bench (2) ... OR-9
Owyhee Bluffs—cliff ... NV-8
Owyhee Breaks—summit ... OR-9
Owyhee Butte—summit ... OR-9
Owyhee Butte Rsvr—reservoir ... OR-9
Owyhee Butte Well—well ... OR-9
Owyhee Camp—locale ... NV-8
Owyhee Canal ... OR-9
Owyhee Canal—canal ... OR-9
Owyhee Canyon—valley (2) ... OR-9
Owyhee (CCD)—cens area ... OR-9
Owyhee Cem—cemetery ... OR-9
**Owyhee Corners**—pop pl ... OR-9
Owyhee County Courthouse—hist pl ... ID-8
Owyhee Dam—dam ... OR-9
Owyhee Dam Park—park ... OR-9
Owyhee Ditch—canal ... OR-9
Owyhee Heights—locale ... ID-8
Owyhee Lake ... OR-9
Owyhee Mountains—range (2) ... OR-9
Owyhee Mtns—range ... ID-8
Owyhee North Canal ... OR-9
Owyhee Range ... ID-8
Owyhee Range ... OR-9
Owyhee Ridge—ridge ... OR-9
Owyhee Rim Rsvr—reservoir ... OR-9
Owyhee River—stream ... ID-8
Owyhee River—stream ... NV-8
Owyhee River—stream ... OR-9
Owyhee River Cave—cave ... OR-9
Owyhee Rsvr ... OR-9
Owyhee Rsvr Number Four—reservoir ... NV-8
Owyhee Rsvr State Airp—airport ... OR-9
Owyhee Rsvr 3—reservoir ... NV-8
Owyhee Sch—school ... ID-8
Owyhee Siphon—canal ... OR-9
Owyhee South Canal ... OR-9
Owyhee Spring—spring ... OR-9
Owyhee Spring Rsvr—reservoir ... OR-9
Owyhee Well—well ... AZ-5
Owyhigh Lakes ... WA-9
Ox ... WV-2
Oxadak Mtn—summit ... AK-9
Oxalis—locale ... CA-9
Oxalis Drain—canal ... CA-9
Oxalis Lateral—canal ... CA-9
Oxana ... AL-4
**Oxanna**—pop pl ... AL-4
Oxarart Dam—dam ... MT-8
Oxberry—locale ... MS-4
Oxberry Bayou—gut ... MS-4
Oxberry Cem—cemetery ... MS-4
**Oxbo**—pop pl ... WI-6
Oxbo Creek—stream ... WI-6
Oxbo Lake ... WI-6
Oxbo Lake—lake ... WI-6
Ox Bone Slough—gut ... AR-4
**Oxboro**—pop pl ... MN-6
Oxboro Lake—lake ... MN-6
Ox Bottom—basin ... FL-3
Ox Bow ... MA-1
Oxbow ... WI-6
Oxbow—bend ... ID-8
Oxbow—bend ... IA-7
Ox Bow—bend ... ME-1
Oxbow—bend (2) ... NY-2
Oxbow—locale ... WV-2
**Oxbow**—pop pl ... ME-1
**Oxbow**—pop pl (3) ... MI-6
**Oxbow**—pop pl ... NY-2
**Oxbow**—pop pl ... ND-7
**Oxbow**—pop pl ... OR-9
Oxbow—summit ... PA-2
Oxbow, The—bend (5) ... ME-1
Ox Bow, The—bend ... MA-1
Oxbow, The—bend ... MI-6
Oxbow, The—bend ... MT-8
Oxbow, The—bend ... NH-1
Oxbow, The—bend ... OR-9
Oxbow, The—bend ... VT-1
Oxbow, The—bend ... WI-6
Ox Bow, The—cliff ... VT-1
Oxbow, The—lake ... MA-1
Oxbow, The—locale ... NH-1
Oxbow, The—other ... CA-9
Oxbow, The—stream ... MA-1
Ox Bow, The—summit ... VT-1
Oxbow Airstrip—airport ... OR-9
Oxbow Archeol District—hist pl ... MI-6
Oxbow Basin—basin ... OR-9
Oxbow Bayou—stream ... MS-4
Ox Bow Bend ... PA-2
Oxbow Bend—bend ... AL-4
Oxbow Bend—bend ... AR-4
Oxbow Bend—bend ... ID-8
Oxbow Bend—bend ... IN-6
Oxbow Bend—bend ... MS-4
Oxbow Bend—bend ... MT-8
Oxbow Bend—bend (2) ... PA-2
Oxbow Bend—bend ... WY-8
Oxbow Bend—island ... WY-8
Oxbow Bridge—bridge ... CA-9
Oxbow Brook ... MA-1
Oxbow Brook—stream (2) ... ME-1
Oxbow Brook—stream ... MA-1
Oxbow Butte—summit ... OR-9
Oxbow Cem—cemetery ... ME-1
Oxbow Cem—cemetery ... NE-7
Oxbow Cem—cemetery ... VT-1
Oxbow Cem—cemetery ... WI-6
Oxbow County Park—park ... OR-9
Oxbow Creek ... GA-3
Oxbow Creek ... TX-5
Oxbow Creek—stream (2) ... ID-8
Oxbow Creek—stream ... MI-6
Oxbow Creek—stream ... MT-8
Oxbow Creek—stream ... NE-7
Oxbow Creek—stream ... OR-9
Oxbow Creek—stream ... PA-2
Oxbow Creek—stream ... TX-5
Oxbow Creek—stream ... WA-9
Oxbow Creek—stream ... WY-8
Oxbow Cut—channel ... NH-1
Oxbow Cut -Off—bend ... MS-4
Oxbow Dam—dam (2) ... OR-9
**Oxbow (Dam Construction Area)**—pop pl ... OR-9
Oxbow Dam Site ... OR-9
Oxbow Gulch—valley ... AZ-5
Oxbow Hill—summit ... AZ-5
Oxbow Hist Dist—hist pl ... VT-1
Oxbow Hollow—valley ... NY-2
Oxbow Hollow—valley (2) ... PA-2
Oxbow Hollow Trail—trail ... PA-2
Oxbow HS—school ... VT-1
Oxbow Inlet—stream ... PA-2
Oxbow Lake ... MI-6
Oxbow Lake ... WI-6
Oxbow Lake—lake ... AK-9
Oxbow Lake—lake (2) ... AR-4
Oxbow Lake—lake (5) ... MI-6
Oxbow Lake—lake (4) ... MN-6
Oxbow Lake—lake ... MS-4
Oxbow Lake—lake ... NY-2
Oxbow Lake—lake ... PA-2
Oxbow Lake—lake (2) ... WI-6
Oxbow Lake—reservoir ... TX-5
Oxbow Lake Ch—church ... MI-6
Oxbow Mine—mine ... AZ-5
Oxbow Mountain—ridge ... AR-4
Oxbow Mountain Tank—reservoir ... AZ-5
Oxbow Mtn—summit ... AZ-5
Oxbow Mtn—summit ... ME-1
Oxbow Mtn—summit ... NY-2
Oxbow Natl Wildlife Ref—park ... MA-1
**Oxbow Park**—pop pl ... MI-6
Oxbow (Plantation of)—civ div ... ME-1
Oxbow Pond—lake ... NH-1
Oxbow Pond—lake ... WI-6
Ox Bow Ranch—locale ... FL-3
Oxbow Ranch—locale ... MT-8
Oxbow Ranch—locale ... OR-9
Oxbow Ranch—locale ... TX-5
Oxbow Ranch Dam—dam ... OR-9
Oxbow Ranch Landing Strip—airport ... OR-9
Oxbow Rapids—rapids ... WI-6
Oxbow Rsvr—reservoir ... OR-9
Oxbow Run—stream ... OH-6
Oxbow Saddle—gap ... ID-8
Oxbow Sch—school (2) ... MI-6
Oxbow Sch—school ... NE-7
Oxbow Sch—school ... OR-9
Oxbow Sch (abandoned)—school ... PA-2
Oxbows Landing (historical)—locale ... MS-4
Oxbow Slough—gut ... ID-8
Oxbow Slough—gut ... IL-6
Oxbow Spring—spring ... AZ-5
Oxbow Spring—spring ... ID-8
Oxbow Spring—spring (2) ... OR-9
Oxbow Tank—reservoir (4) ... AZ-5
Oxbow (Township of)—unorg ... ME-1
Ox Bow Trail Number One Hundred Sixty Three—trail ... AZ-5
Oxbow Trap Canyon—valley ... TX-5
Oxbow Well—well ... CO-8
Ox Branch—stream ... MS-4
Ox Branch—stream ... TX-5
Ox Brook—stream (3) ... NH-1
Oxbrook Stream—stream ... ME-1
Ox Camp Lake—lake ... MN-6
Ox Canyon—valley (2) ... NM-5
Ox Canyon Mine—mine ... NM-5
Ox Canyon Trail—trail ... NM-5
Oxcart Coulee ... MT-8
Ox Clove—valley ... NY-2
Ox Corral Creek—stream ... NV-8
Ox Corral Spring—spring ... NV-8
Ox Cove—bay ... ME-1
Ox Creek—stream ... MI-6
Ox Creek—stream ... MN-6
Ox Creek—stream ... MT-8
Ox Creek—stream ... NY-2
Ox Creek—stream ... NC-3
Ox Creek—stream ... ND-7
Ox Creek—stream ... TX-5
Ox Creek—stream (2) ... WI-6
Ox Creek Ch—church ... NC-3
Ox Creek Ch—church ... ND-7
Ox Creek Natl Wildlife Ref—park ... ND-7
Ox Ditch—canal ... IN-6
Oxear Cove—valley ... NC-3
Oxen—mine ... UT-8
Oxen Bayou—gut ... TX-5
Oxen Creek ... MD-2
Oxendine Bayou—stream ... IN-6
Oxendine Cem—cemetery ... NC-3
Oxendine Draw—valley ... CA-9
Oxen Hollow—valley ... TN-4
Ox Field—island ... FL-3
Oxfoot Bank—bar ... FL-3
Oxford ... PA-2

# P

*P* RI-1
Paa—*civil* HI-9
Pa Aalii Pump Station—*other* HI-9
*Paaheihei Koli Koli Creek* HI-9
Paaiki Valley—*valley* HI-9
*Paakahi* HI-9
Paakahi Point—*cape* HI-9
*Paakai Point* HI-9
Paakai Point—*cape* HI-9
*Paakea* HI-9
Paakea—*civil* HI-9
Paakea Gulch—*valley* HI-9
Paakeal—*island* FM-9
*Paakea Stream* HI-9
Paakikii—*cape* HI-9
Paako—*cape* HI-9
Pa-ako Ruins—*locale* NM-5
*Paalaa* HI-9
Paalaa Kai—*civil* HI-9
Paalaa Uka—*civil* HI-9
Paalaea—*civil* HI-9
Paalalea—*island* HI-9
Paanene Spring—*spring* HI-9
Paaoao Bay—*bay* HI-9
Paaoao Point—*cape* HI-9
Paao One-Six—*civil* HI-9
Paapala Cove—*bay* AS-9
P'aaramach—*cape* FM-9
P'aaramach—*gut* FM-9
Paarda Hook—*cape* NY-2
Paasan—*summit* GU-9
*Paasch Lake* WI-6
Paasch Lake—*lake* WI-6
Paasch Ranch—*locale* ND-7
*Paata* FM-9
Paato—*island* MP-9
Paauau Gulch—*valley* HI-9
Paauau One—*civil* HI-9
Paauau Two—*civil* HI-9
Paauhau—*civil* HI-9
**Paauhau**—*pop pl* HI-9
*Paauhau Gulch* HI-9
Paauhau Landing—*locale* HI-9
**Paauhau Mauka**—*pop pl* HI-9
Paauhau-Paauilo (CCD)—*cens area* HI-9
Paauilo—*civil* HI-9
**Paauilo**—*pop pl* HI-9
*Paauilo Gulch* HI-9
Paauilo Gulch—*valley* HI-9
Paauilo Homesteads—*civil* HI-9
*Paauilo Stream* HI-9
**Paavola**—*pop pl* MI-6
Paavola Creek—*stream* MN-6
*Pabama Lake* MI-6
Pabasco Tank—*reservoir* AZ-5
Pabawena Ditch—*canal* ID-8
**Pabco**—*pop pl* LA-4
Pabco—*uninc pl* CA-9
Pablano Tank—*reservoir* AZ-5
Pable Creek—*stream* WA-9
Pablito Tank—*reservoir* NM-5
Pablito Windmill—*locale* TX-5
**Pablo**—*pop pl* MT-8
Pablo, Mount—*summit* MT-8
Pablo, Sierra—*summit* CA-9
Pablo A Canal—*canal* MT-8
*Pablo Beach* FL-3
Pablo Blanco Windmill—*locale* TX-5
Pablo Canyon—*valley* AZ-5
Pablo Canyon—*valley* NV-8
Pablo Canyon Ranch—*locale* NV-8
Pablo Creek—*stream* FL-3
Pablo Creek—*stream* ID-8
Pablo Creek—*stream* WA-9
Pablo Feeder Canal—*canal* MT-8
Pablo Granpera Grant—*civil* FL-3
Pablo Island—*island* MT-8
Pablo Keys—*locale* FL-3
Pablo Montoya Grant—*civil* NM-5
Pablo Natl Wildlife Ref—*park* MT-8
Pablo Plaza (Shop Ctr)—*locale* FL-3
Pablo Point—*summit* CA-9
Pablo Ranch—*locale* MT-8
Pablo Rapids—*rapids* MT-8
Pablo Rosette Grant—*civil* FL-3
Pablo Rsvr—*reservoir* MT-8
Pablos Charco Rsvr—*reservoir* AZ-5
Pablo Sena Ranch—*locale* NM-5
Pablos Grove Park—*park* TX-5
Pablo Spring—*spring* CO-8
Pablos Windmill—*locale* NM-5
Pablo Tank—*reservoir* AZ-5
Pablo 10A Canal—*canal* MT-8
Pablo 13A Canal—*canal* MT-8
Pablo 31 A Canal—*canal* (2) MT-8
Pablo 31 A 07 Canal—*canal* (2) MT-8
Pablo 37Aa Canal—*canal* MT-8
Pablo 37A Canal—*canal* MT-8
Pablo 37A4 Canal—*canal* MT-8
Pablo 50A Canal—*canal* MT-8
Pablo 53A Canal—*canal* MT-8
Pablo 7oA Canal—*canal* MT-8
Pablo 71A Canal—*canal* MT-8
Pablo 73A14 Ditch—*canal* MT-8
Pablo 73A4 Ditch—*canal* MT-8
Pablo 73A5 Ditch—*canal* MT-8
Pabodie, Professor William, House—*hist pl* OH-6
Pabor Lake—*lake* FL-3
Pabrico—*locale* CA-9
Pabst—*locale* GA-3
Pabst, Frederick, House—*hist pl* WI-6
Pabst Bay—*bay* MI-6
Pabst Blue Ribbon Airp—*airport* PA-2
Pabst Brewery Saloon—*hist pl* WI-6
Pabst-Howe Ranch—*locale* CO-8
Pabst Peak—*summit* WY-8
Pabst Theater—*hist pl* WI-6
*Pacahantas* TN-4
Paca House and Garden—*hist pl* MD-2
Pacama—*locale* NY-2
*Pacana* AL-4
*Pacana Talache* AL-4
P A Canyon—*valley* NM-5
Pacard Run—*stream* PA-2
Paca Sch—*school* (2) MD-2
Paca Street Firehouse—*hist pl* MD-2
*Pacaussett Pond* CT-1
Paccini Lake—*lake* MN-6
**Pace**—*pop pl* FL-3
**Pace**—*pop pl* GA-3
**Pace**—*pop pl* LA-4
**Pace**—*pop pl* MS-4
Pace Airp—*airport* IN-6
Pace Assembly of God Ch—*church* FL-3
Pace Bend—*bend* TN-4
Pace Bend—*bend* TX-5
Pace Bluff—*cliff* TN-4
*Pace Branch* MS-4
Pace Branch—*stream* (2) KY-4
Pace Branch—*stream* NC-3
Pace Branch—*stream* TN-4
Pace Bridge—*bridge* SC-3
Pace Canyon—*valley* (2) UT-8
Pace (CCD)—*cens area* FL-3
Pace Cem—*cemetery* AL-4
Pace Cem—*cemetery* (2) KY-4
Pace Cem—*cemetery* MS-4
Pace Cem—*cemetery* MO-7
Pace Cem—*cemetery* NC-3
Pace Cem—*cemetery* (4) TN-4
Pace Cem—*cemetery* (4) TX-5
Pace Cem—*cemetery* VA-3
Pace Center Sch—*school* MS-4
Pace Ch—*church* MS-4
Pace City—*locale* AR-4
Pace City Oil And Gas Field—*oilfield* AR-4
Pace Coll—*school* NY-2
Pace Creek—*stream* AL-4
Pace Creek—*stream* AZ-5
Pace Creek—*stream* GA-3
Pace Creek—*stream* NM-5
Pace Creek—*stream* (2) TX-5
Pace Creek—*stream* UT-8
Pace Crossroads—*locale* NC-3
Pace Dam—*dam* UT-8
Pace Draw—*valley* UT-8
Pace East Number One Subdivision Mini Park—*park* AZ-5
Pace East Number One Subdivision Water Retention Basin—*reservoir* AZ-5
Pace Elem Sch—*school* MS-4
Pace Flat—*flat* CA-9
Pace Ford—*crossing* TN-4
Paceful Hill Cem—*cemetery* WA-9
Pace Gap—*gap* TN-4
Pace Hill—*ridge* AL-4
Pace Hill—*summit* TX-5
**Pace (historical)**—*pop pl* TN-4
Pace Hollow—*valley* MO-7
Pace Hollow—*valley* (2) TN-4
Pace Hollow—*valley* (2) UT-8
Pace HS—*school* (2) FL-3
Pace Independent Private School/Citrus County—*school* FL-3
Pace-King House—*hist pl* VA-3
Pace Knoll—*summit* UT-8
Pace Lake—*lake* FL-3
Pace Lake—*lake* LA-4
Pace Lake—*lake* MN-6
Pace Lake—*lake* UT-8
Pace Lake—*reservoir* AL-4
Pacelli HS—*school* WI-6
Pacelli Sch—*school* OH-6
Pace Lookout Tower—*tower* FL-3
Pacemaker—*airport* NJ-2
Pace McDonald Site—*hist pl* TX-5
*Pace Mill Creek* MS-4
Pace Mill Creek—*stream* FL-3
Pace MS—*school* FL-3
*Pacenche Creek* AL-4
*Pacentha Creek* AL-4
Pace Park—*park* FL-3
**Pace Park**—*pop pl* CA-9
Pace Picnic Islands—*island* FL-3
Pace Point—*cape* TN-4
Pace Point—*cape* TX-5
Pace Pond—*reservoir* UT-8
Pacer—*locale* CA-9
Pace Ranch—*locale* AZ-5
Pace Ranch—*locale* CO-8
Pacer Coulee—*valley* MT-8
Pace Ridge—*ridge* TN-4
Pacer Lake—*lake* UT-8
Pacer Lake—*reservoir* UT-8
Pacer Lake Reservoir Dam—*dam* UT-8
Pace (RR name for Paces)—*other* VA-3
Pacers Gap—*gap* VA-3
Pacer Stadium—*park* TN-4
Pace Rsvr—*reservoir* UT-8
Paces—*locale* VA-3
Paces Bayou—*stream* MS-4
Paces Branch—*stream* AL-4
Paces Branch—*stream* SC-3
Pace Sch—*school* CA-9
Pace Sch—*school* LA-4
Paces Chapel—*church* TX-5
Paces Creek—*stream* KY-4
Paces Creek—*stream* TX-5
Paces Creek Sch—*school* KY-4
*Pacesetter Park* IL-6
Pace Shanty Branch—*stream* TN-4
Paces Hollow—*valley* UT-8
Paces Island—*island* TN-4
Paces Landing—*locale* FL-3
Paces Landing East—*locale* AL-4
Paces Landing West—*locale* AL-4
Pace Spring—*spring* AZ-5
Pace Spring—*spring* NV-8
Pace Spring—*spring* UT-8
**Paces (RR name Pace)**—*pop pl* VA-3
Paces Trace Branch—*stream* KY-4
*Pacet Channel* FL-3
Pacet Channel—*channel* FL-3
*Pacet Key* FL-3
Pacetown—*locale* MO-7
Pacewell Draw—*valley* UT-8
*Pacha* FM-9
*Pachaca Spring* CA-9
Pachalka Spring—*spring* CA-9
*Pachanca Spring* CA-9
Pachangan, Oror En—*locale* FM-9
*Pachapa Spring* CA-9
Pachappa—*locale* CA-9
Pachappa Hill—*summit* CA-9
Pachappa Sch—*school* CA-9
*Pachauca Spring* CA-9
Pachaud Lateral—*canal* CA-9
Pachaug—*locale* CT-1
Pachaug Cem—*cemetery* CT-1
Pachaug Pond—*reservoir* CT-1
Pachaug River—*stream* CT-1
Pachaug State For—*forest* CT-1
Pacheca Cem—*cemetery* CO-8
**Pacheco**—*pop pl* CA-9
Pacheco, Don Fernando, Adobe—*hist pl* CA-9
Pacheco Banco Number 117—*levee* TX-5
Pacheco Bluff—*cliff* NM-5
Pacheco Canyon—*valley* CA-9
Pacheco Canyon—*valley* CO-8
Pacheco Canyon—*valley* NM-5
Pacheco Cem—*cemetery* (2) NM-5
*Pacheco Creek* CA-9
Pacheco Creek—*stream* (2) CA-9
Pacheco Grant—*civil* NM-5
Pacheco Hill—*summit* CA-9
Pacheco Lake—*lake* (2) NM-5
Pacheco Lake—*reservoir* CA-9
Pacheco Mine—*mine* NM-5
Pacheco Pass—*gap* CA-9
Pacheco Peak—*summit* CA-9
Pacheco Ranch—*locale* NM-5
Pacheco Ranger Station—*locale* CA-9
Pacheco Sch—*school* (5) CA-9
Pacheco Spring—*spring* CO-8
Pacheco Spring—*spring* NM-5
Pacheco Tank—*reservoir* NM-5
**Pacheco Village**—*pop pl* NM-5
Pacheco Wash—*stream* AZ-5
Pacheco Well—*well* NM-5
Pache Ditch—*canal* CO-8
Pachelo Ranch—*locale* AZ-5
Pacheta Creek—*stream* AZ-5
Pacheta Dam—*dam* AZ-5
Pacheta Lake—*reservoir* AZ-5
Pacheta Lake Campground—*park* AZ-5
Pachet Brook—*stream* RI-1
*Pachet Brook Pond* RI-1
*Pachet Brook Reservoir* RI-1
*Pachete Creek* AZ-5
*Pacheto Creek* AZ-5
Pache Trail—*trail* CO-8
*Pachet Reservoir* RI-1
**Pachin Mills**—*pop pl* NY-2
Pachitla—*locale* GA-3
Pachitla Cem—*cemetery* GA-3
Pachitla Ch—*church* GA-3
Pachitla Creek—*stream* GA-3
**Pachitta**—*pop pl* GA-3
Pachoango, Lake—*reservoir* NJ-2
Pachoango Dam—*dam* NJ-2
*Pachoquelin* PA-2
Pachta Farm Airp—*airport* KS-7
Pachta Windmill—*locale* NM-5
**Pachuta**—*pop pl* MS-4
Pachuta Cem—*cemetery* MS-4
Pachuta Creek—*stream* MS-4
Pachuta Oil Field—*oilfield* MS-4
Pacies Branch—*stream* KY-4
*Pacific* MP-9
**Pacific**—*pop pl* CA-9
**Pacific**—*pop pl* MO-7
**Pacific**—*pop pl* WA-9
Pacific—*uninc pl* CA-9
**Pacifica**—*pop pl* CA-9
Pacific and Idaho Northern RR Depot—*hist pl* ID-8
Pacific Ave Hist Dist—*hist pl* CA-9
Pacific Ave Hist Dist—*hist pl* WA-9
Pacific Ave Sch—*school* CA-9
Pacific Ave Sch—*school* NY-2
**Pacific Beach**—*pop pl* CA-9
**Pacific Beach**—*pop pl* WA-9
Pacific Beach JHS—*school* CA-9
Pacific Beach Naval Facility—*military* WA-9
Pacific Beach Park—*park* CA-9
Pacific Beach Sch—*school* CA-9
Pacific Beach (Siding)—*locale* CA-9
Pacific Brewing and Malting Company—*hist pl* WA-9
Pacific Brook—*stream* VT-1
Pacific Butte—*summit* WY-8
Pacific Canyon—*valley* AZ-5
Pacific Cem—*cemetery* MO-7
Pacific Cem—*cemetery* WI-6
Pacific Christian Coll—*school* CA-9
Pacific City—*locale* IA-7
**Pacific City**—*pop pl* OR-9
Pacific City State Airp—*airport* OR-9
Pacific Coast Club—*hist pl* CA-9
Pacific Coast Company House No. 75—*hist pl* WA-9
Pacific Coast Equestrian Research Farm—*other* CA-9
Pacific Coast Railway Company Grain Warehouse—*hist pl* CA-9
Pacific Coll—*school* CA-9
Pacific Communities Hospital Heliport—*airport* OR-9
Pacific Cooperative Poultry Producers Egg-Taking Station—*hist pl* OR-9
**Pacific County**—*pop pl* WA-9
Pacific County Courthouse—*hist pl* WA-9
Pacific Creek—*stream* CA-9
Pacific Creek—*stream* CO-8
Pacific Creek—*stream* MT-8
Pacific Creek—*stream* OR-9
Pacific Creek—*stream* (2) WY-8
Pacific Crest Natl Scenic Trail—*trail* (4) CA-9
Pacific Crest Natl Scenic Trail—*trail* OR-9
Pacific Crest Natl Scenic Trail—*trail* WA-9
Pacific Crest Natl Scenic Trail (Pack)—*trail* (2) CA-9
Pacific Crest Trail—*trail* WA-9
Pacific Curios Antiques—*hist pl* OH-6
Pacific Desk Bldg—*hist pl* NM-5
Pacific Drive Sch—*school* CA-9
Pacific Electric Railway Company Depot—*hist pl* CA-9
Pacific Electric Railway Company Substation No. 8—*hist pl* CA-9
Pacific Electric Sub-Station No. 14—*hist pl* CA-9
Pacific Express Stable—*hist pl* CO-8
**Pacific Gardens**—*pop pl* CA-9
Pacific Gas and Electric Company Substation J—*hist pl* CA-9
Pacific Gas & Electric Company Bldg—*hist pl* CA-9
**Pacific Grange Hall**—*pop pl* OR-9
**Pacific Grove**—*pop pl* CA-9
**Pacific Grove Acres**—*pop pl* CA-9
Pacific Grove HS—*school* CA-9
**Pacific Grove Subdivision**—*pop pl* UT-8
**Pacific Heights**—*pop pl* HI-9
Pacific Heights Sch—*school* (2) CA-9
**Pacific (historical)**—*pop pl* TN-4
Pacific Hosp—*hospital* CA-9
**Pacific House (Pacific)**—*pop pl* CA-9
Pacific HS—*school* (2) CA-9
*Pacific Islands* MP-9
Pacific Islands, Trust Territory of the—*civil* MP-9
Pacific Junction—*locale* MT-8
**Pacific Junction**—*pop pl* IA-7
Pacific Junction—*uninc pl* OK-5
Pacific Lake—*lake* WA-9
Pacific Livestock Company Ditch—*canal* (2) OR-9
Pacific Lodge Boys Home—*locale* CA-9
Pacific Lutheran Univ—*school* WA-9
**Pacific Manor**—*pop pl* (2) CA-9
Pacific Matchless Mine—*mine* NV-8
Pacific Mesa—*summit* CA-9
*Pacific Mills Lake* SC-3
Pacific Mine—*mine* AZ-5
Pacific Mine—*mine* (3) CA-9
Pacific Mine—*mine* ID-8
Pacific Mine—*mine* MT-8
Pacific Mine—*mine* NV-8
Pacific Mine—*mine* NM-5
Pacific Mine—*mine* UT-8
Pacific Missile Range—*other* CA-9
Pacific Missile Range Facility—*military* HI-9
Pacific Mobile Manor—*locale* AZ-5
*Pacific Mountain* CA-9
Pacific Mutual Mines—*mine* WA-9
Pacific Natl Bank Bldg—*hist pl* WA-9
Pacific Oaks Sch—*school* CA-9
Pacific Ocean—*sea* CA-9
Pacific Ocean—*sea* HI-9
Pacific Ocean—*sea* OR-9
Pacific Ocean—*sea* GU-9
Pacifico Mtn—*summit* CA-9
**Pacific Palisades**—*pop pl* CA-9
**Pacific Palisades**—*pop pl* HI-9
**Pacific Palisades**—*pop pl* OR-9
Pacific Park—*locale* WA-9
Pacific Park—*park* CA-9
Pacific Park—*park* SC-3
Pacific Park—*park* TX-5
Pacific Passage—*channel* CA-9
Pacific Peak—*summit* CO-8
Pacific Placer Rsvr—*reservoir* CA-9
Pacific Plywood Corporation Dam—*dam* OR-9
Pacific Plywood Corporation Log Pond—*reservoir* OR-9
Pacific Plywood Dam—*dam* OR-9
Pacific Plywood Log Pond—*reservoir* OR-9
Pacific Point—*summit* CA-9
Pacific Point—*summit* WA-9
Pacific Post Office (historical)—*building* TN-4
Pacific Press Bldg—*hist pl* CA-9
Pacific Ranch—*locale* CA-9
Pacific Ranger Station—*locale* CA-9
Pacific Reef—*bar* FL-3
Pacific Reef Channel—*channel* FL-3
Pacific Reef Lighthouse—*locale* FL-3
Pacific Ridge—*ridge* CA-9
Pacific Ridge Forest Service Station—*locale* CA-9
*Pacific Ridge Guard Station* CA-9
Pacific Sch—*school* (2) CA-9
Pacific Sch—*school* WI-6
Pacific Slab Mine—*mine* CA-9
Pacific Slope—*ridge* NM-5
Pacific Springs—*spring* WY-8
Pacific State Hosp—*hospital* CA-9
Pacific States Univ—*school* CA-9
Pacific Sunset Memorial Park Cem—*cemetery* OR-9
Pacific Telephone and Telegraph Bldg—*hist pl* WA-9
**Pacific (Town of)**—*pop pl* WI-6
Pacific Tunnel—*mine* NV-8
Pacific Tunnel—*tunnel* CA-9
Pacific Union Coll—*school* CA-9
*Pacific Union College* CA-9
Pacific Union Sch—*school* CA-9
Pacific Union Sch—*school* IL-6
Pacific Univ—*school* OR-9
Pacific Valley—*basin* CA-9
Pacific Valley Sch—*school* CA-9
Pacific View Memorial Park (Cemetery)—*cemetery* CA-9
Pacific View Sch—*school* CA-9
**Pacific Villas**—*pop pl* CA-9
Pacifie Road Ch—*church* TX-5
*Pacinimo* AZ-5
Pacio—*locale* TX-5
Pacio Post Office (historical)—*building* AL-4
**Pack**—*pop pl* MO-7
*Packachog Hill* MA-1
*Packachoog Hill* MA-1
*Packackoag Hill* MA-1
*Packana* AL-4
Packanack Brook—*stream* NJ-2
**Packanack Lake**—*pop pl* NJ-2
Packanack Lake—*reservoir* NJ-2
Packanack Lake Dam—*dam* NJ-2
Packanack Mtn—*summit* (2) NJ-2
Packanack Sch—*school* NJ-2
Pack and Lacey Crossing—*locale* MT-8
Packard—*locale* IA-7
Packard—*locale* KY-4
Packard—*locale* WA-9
Packard—*locale* WI-6
**Packard**—*pop pl* MI-6
Packard, James Ward, House—*hist pl* OH-6
Packard, Moses, House—*hist pl* MA-1
Packard Brook—*stream* (2) ME-1
Packard Brook—*stream* MA-1
Packard Canyon—*valley* UT-8
Packard Cem—*cemetery* MO-7
Packard Creek—*stream* IA-7
Packard Creek—*stream* (3) OR-9
Packard Creek—*stream* UT-8
Packard Creek—*stream* WA-9
Packard Creek—*stream* WI-6
Packard Creek Trail—*trail* OR-9
Packard Dam—*dam* MA-1
Packard-Doubler House—*hist pl* OH-6
Packard Drain—*stream* MI-6
Packard Electric Division (General Motors Corp.)—*facility* MS-4
Packard Elem Sch—*school* AZ-5
Packard Flat—*flat* NV-8
Packard Gospel Center—*church* MI-6
Packard Gulch—*valley* CO-8
Packard Gulch—*valley* (2) OR-9
**Packard Heights**—*pop pl* MA-1
Packard Hill—*summit* (2) ME-1
Packard Hill—*summit* MA-1
Packard JHS—*school* NY-2
Packard Lake—*lake* ME-1
Packard Lake—*lake* UT-8
Packard Landing—*locale* ME-1
Packard Ledge—*bar* ME-1
Packard Library—*hist pl* CA-9
Packard Mesa—*summit* AZ-5
Packard Mine—*mine* NV-8
Packard Motor Corporation Bldg—*hist pl* PA-2
Packard Mtn—*summit* MA-1
Packard Park—*park* IN-6
Packard Park—*park* MI-6
Packard Park—*park* OH-6
Packard Peak—*summit* UT-8
Packard Point—*cape* ME-1
Packard Point—*cape* MI-6
Packard Pond—*lake* MA-1
Packard Pond—*reservoir* MA-1
Packard Pond Dam—*dam* MA-1
Packard Ranch—*locale* AZ-5
Packard Ranch—*locale* NE-7
Packard Reservoir—*swamp* CO-8
Packard Ridge—*ridge* (2) CA-9
Packard Rocks—*pillar* RI-1
Packard Run—*stream* IN-6
*Packards* AZ-5
Packards—*locale* ME-1
Packards Bend—*locale* AL-4
Packards Bend Sch (historical)—*school* AL-4
Packard Sch—*school* MI-6
Packard (Site)—*locale* NV-8
*Packards Mountain* MA-1
Packard Spring—*spring* AZ-5
Packard Springs (Township of)—*fmr MCD* AR-4
Packard Stadium (baseball)—*locale* AZ-5
Packards Trail—*trail* ME-1
*Packardsville* MA-1
Packard Tank—*reservoir* AZ-5
Packard Trail Nmber Sixty Six—*trail* AZ-5
Packard Trail Tank—*reservoir* AZ-5
**Packardville**—*pop pl* MA-1
Packard Wash—*stream* AZ-5
Packard Wash—*stream* NV-8
Packard Well—*well* CA-9
Pack Basin—*basin* CO-8
Packbox Creek—*stream* ID-8
Packbox Pass—*gap* ID-8
Packbox Pass—*gap* MT-8
Pack Branch—*stream* (2) KY-4
Pack Branch—*stream* SC-3
Pack Branch—*stream* WV-2
Pack Cem—*cemetery* MS-4
Pack Ch—*church* (2) KY-4
Pack Creek—*stream* AK-9
Pack Creek—*stream* GA-3
Pack Creek—*stream* (4) ID-8
Pack Creek—*stream* UT-8
Pack Creek—*stream* WA-9
Pack Creek Picnic Area—*park* UT-8
Pack Demonstration For—*forest* NY-2
Packeka Creek—*stream* CA-9
*Packemit* MA-1
Packer—*locale* AZ-5
Packer—*locale* CT-1
Packer, Alonzo Hamilton, House—*hist pl* AZ-5
Packer, Asa, Mansion—*hist pl* PA-2
Packer, Harry, Mansion—*hist pl* PA-2
Packer Basin—*basin* NV-8
Packer Basin Creek—*stream* ID-8
Packer Bog—*swamp* NH-1
Packer Branch—*stream* LA-4
Packer Branch—*stream* MO-7
Packer Brook—*stream* (2) NH-1
Packer Butte—*summit* ID-8
Packer Canyon—*valley* NV-8
Packer Cem—*cemetery* CT-1
Packer Cem—*cemetery* (2) VT-1
**Packer Corner**—*pop pl* VT-1
Packer Creek—*stream* CA-9
Packer Creek—*stream* (3) ID-8
Packer Creek—*stream* MI-6
Packer Creek—*stream* MT-8
Packer Creek—*stream* OH-6
Packer Creek—*stream* WA-9
Packer Creek—*stream* WY-8
Packer Ditch—*canal* CO-8
Packer Ditch—*canal* WY-8
Packer Fork—*stream* PA-2
Packer Gulch—*valley* (2) CA-9
Packer Gulch—*valley* (2) CO-8
Packer Gulch—*valley* (2) ID-8
Packer Gulch—*valley* MT-8
Packer House—*hist pl* NJ-2
Packer Island—*island* CA-9
*Packer John Creek* ID-8
Packer John Mtn—*summit* ID-8
Packer Johns Cabin State Park—*park* ID-8
*Packer Lake* WI-6
Packer Lake—*lake* (2) CA-9
Packer Lake—*lake* MN-6
Packer Lake—*reservoir* WY-8
Packer Lake Lodge—*locale* CA-9
*Packer Landing* AL-4
Packer-Mason Cem—*cemetery* NY-2
Packer Meadows—*flat* (2) ID-8
Packer Memorial Chapel—*hist pl* PA-2
Packer Mtn—*summit* VT-1
**Packer Place Subdivision**—*pop pl* UT-8
Packers—*uninc pl* KS-7
Packers Bay—*bay* CA-9
Packers Camp—*locale* KS-7
Packer Sch—*school* PA-2
Packer Sch—*school* VT-1
Packers Creek—*stream* (3) AK-9
Packers Creek—*stream* (2) CA-9
Packers Creek—*stream* ID-8
Packers Creek—*stream* OR-9
Packers Creek Lake—*lake* AK-9
Packers Falls—*falls* NH-1
Packers Falls Bridge—*bridge* NH-1
*Packers Ford Run* PA-2
Packers Gap—*gap* CO-8
*Packers Gulch* MT-8
Packers Gulch—*valley* CA-9
Packers Gulch—*valley* ID-8
Packers Gulch—*valley* MT-8
Packers Gulch—*valley* (2) OR-9
Packers Hill—*summit* KS-7
Packers Island—*island* NJ-2
Packers Island—*island* PA-2
Packer's Natl Bank Bldg—*hist pl* NE-7
Packers Path—*trail* PA-2
Packers Peak—*summit* CA-9

Packers Point—*cape* AK-9
Packers Pond—*reservoir* NY-2
Packer Spring—*spring* ID-8
Packers Roost—*locale* MT-8
Packers Run—*stream* PA-2
Packers Spit—*bar* AK-9
Packers Trail—*trail* NM-5
Packers Valley—*valley* CA-9
*Packersville* PA-2
Packer Swamp—*swamp* LA-4
Packer Tank—*reservoir* AZ-5
**Packerton**—*pop pl* IN-6
**Packerton**—*pop pl* PA-2
Packerton Cem—*cemetery* PA-2
Packerton Junction—*locale* PA-2
*Packertown* IN-6
**Packertown (Packerton)**—*pop pl* IN-6
**Packer (Township of)**—*pop pl* PA-2
Packer Trail—*trail* PA-2
**Packerville**—*pop pl* CT-1
**Packery**—*pop pl* TX-5
Packery Channel—*channel* TX-5
Packery Channel Park—*park* TX-5
*Packeto Creek* AZ-5
Packet Rock—*island* VI-3
Packet Rock—*rock* MA-1
Packett Hollow—*valley* MO-7
Pack Forest Lake—*lake* NY-2
Pack Fork—*stream* (2) WV-2
Pack Gap—*gap* NC-3
Pack Gulch—*valley* AK-9
Pack Gulch—*valley* MT-8
Pack Hill Ridge—*ridge* NC-3
Pack Hollow—*valley* TN-4
Pack Hook Spring—*spring* ID-8
Pack Horse Creek—*stream* ID-8
Packhorse Creek—*stream* PA-2
*Pack Horse Mtn* PA-2
Packhorse Mtn—*summit* PA-2
*Pack Horse Run* PA-2
Packingham Lake—*lake* NE-7
Packingham Slough—*stream* FL-3
*Packing Horse Creek* AZ-5
Packing Horse Creek—*stream* AZ-5
Packing House Cave—*cave* MO-7
Packing House Corner—*locale* DE-2
Packinghouse Creek—*stream* IA-7
Pack Island—*island* TN-4
Pack Lake—*lake* AK-9
Packlets Creek—*stream* WV-2
**Packlynn Subdivision**—*pop pl* UT-8
**Packman**—*pop pl* IN-6
Pack Monadnock Mtn—*summit* NH-1
*Pack Mountain* SC-3
Pack Mtn—*summit* (2) GA-3
Pack Mtn—*summit* NC-3
Pack Mtn—*summit* OK-5
Packnett Cem—*cemetery* MS-4
Packout Cave—*cave* AL-4
Pack Rat Canyon—*valley* NV-8
Pack Rat Cave—*cave* AL-4
Packrat Gorge—*valley* WA-9
Pack Rat Hill—*summit* AZ-5
Packrat Lake—*lake* ID-8
Packrat Mtn—*summit* MT-8
Packrat Peak—*summit* ID-8
Pack Rat Spring—*spring* AZ-5
Pack Rat Spring—*spring* OR-9
Pack Rat Well—*well* AZ-5
Pack River—*stream* ID-8
Pack River Cem—*cemetery* ID-8
Pack River Flats—*flat* ID-8
*Pack River School* ID-8
Pack Sack Creek—*stream* AK-9
Pack Sack Lookout—*locale* WA-9
*Packsack Peak* ID-8
Packsack Point—*cliff* ID-8
*Packsaddle* TX-5
Pack Saddle—*gap* NC-3
Packsaddle—*locale* PA-2
Pack Saddle, The—*other* UT-8
Packsaddle Basin—*basin* ID-8
Pack Saddle Bridge—*bridge* OK-5
Packsaddle Bridge—*hist pl* PA-2
Packsaddle Butte—*summit* ID-8
Packsaddle Butte—*summit* MT-8
Packsaddle Campground—*locale* (2) ID-8
Packsaddle Campground—*park* AZ-5
Packsaddle Canyon—*valley* CA-9
Packsaddle Canyon—*valley* (4) NM-5
Packsaddle Canyon—*valley* OR-9
Packsaddle Canyon—*valley* WY-8
Packsaddle Cave—*cave* CA-9
*Pack Saddle Creek* AR-4
*Packsaddle Creek* ID-8
*Packsaddle Creek* OR-9
Packsaddle Creek—*stream* AR-4
Packsaddle Creek—*stream* (3) CA-9
Packsaddle Creek—*stream* (5) ID-8
Packsaddle Creek—*stream* MT-8
Packsaddle Creek—*stream* (4) OR-9
Packsaddle Creek—*stream* (2) WY-8
Packsaddle Gap—*gap* OR-9
Packsaddle Grove—*woods* CA-9
Packsaddle Gulch—*valley* AK-9
Pack Saddle Gulch—*valley* UT-8
Packsaddle Hill—*summit* TX-5
Packsaddle Island—*summit* AK-9
Packsaddle Lake—*lake* CA-9
Packsaddle Lake—*lake* (2) ID-8
Packsaddle Lake—*reservoir* OK-5
Packsaddle Meadow—*flat* CA-9
Packsaddle Mine—*mine* ID-8
Packsaddle Mountain Trail—*trail* OR-9
Packsaddle Mtn—*summit* (2) AZ-5
Packsaddle Mtn—*summit* ID-8
Packsaddle Mtn—*summit* (3) OR-9
Packsaddle Mtn—*summit* (2) TX-5
Packsaddle Pass—*gap* WY-8
Packsaddle Peak—*summit* MT-8
Packsaddle Ridge—*ridge* CA-9
Pack Saddle Ridge—*ridge* WV-2
Packsaddle Ridge—*ridge* WY-8
Packsaddle Rsvr—*reservoir* ID-8
Packsaddle Rsvr—*reservoir* OR-9
Pack Saddle Run—*stream* WV-2
Packsaddle Spring—*spring* ID-8
Packsaddle Spring—*spring* NV-8
Packsaddle Spring—*spring* (5) OR-9
*Pack Saddle Springs* OR-9
Packsaddle Tank—*reservoir* AZ-5
Packsaddle Trail—*trail* OR-9
Packsaddle Well—*well* ID-8
**Packs Branch**—*pop pl* WV-2
Packs Branch—*stream* (2) WV-2
Pack Sch (abandoned)—*school* MO-7
Pack Sch (historical)—*school* TN-4
Packs Creek—*stream* NC-3
Packs Gap—*gap* NC-3
Packs Knob—*summit* WV-2
Packs Mtn—*summit* WV-2
Pack Springs—*spring* UT-8
Packs The Hat Creek—*stream* MT-8
Packstring Creek—*stream* WY-8
**Packsville**—*pop pl* WV-2
Packton—*locale* LA-4
Pack Top—*summit* NC-3
Packus Airp—*airport* PA-2
**Packwaukee**—*pop pl* WI-6
Packwaukee Island—*island* WI-6
**Packwaukee (Town of)**—*pop pl* WI-6
Packway JHS—*school* FL-3
**Packwood**—*pop pl* IA-7
**Packwood**—*pop pl* WA-9
Packwood Airp—*airport* WA-9
Packwood Branch—*stream* IN-6
Packwood Canal—*canal* CA-9
Packwood Canyon—*valley* AZ-5
Packwood Cem—*cemetery* MO-7
**Packwood Corners**—*pop pl* NY-2
Packwood Creek—*stream* (3) CA-9
Packwood Creek—*stream* TX-5
Packwood Creek—*stream* WA-9
Packwood Ditch—*canal* CA-9
Packwood Ditch—*canal* OR-9
Packwood Flat—*flat* (2) CA-9
Packwood Glacier—*glacier* WA-9
Packwood House-American Hotel—*hist pl* PA-2
Packwood Lake—*lake* AK-9
Packwood Lake—*lake* MS-4
Packwood Lake—*lake* MO-7
Packwood Lake—*lake* WA-9
Packwood Lake Trail—*trail* WA-9
Packwood Mtn—*summit* AZ-5
*Packwood Peak* AZ-5
Packwood Place—*locale* FL-3
*Packwood Saddle* WA-9
Packwood Saddle—*gap* WA-9
Packwood Sch—*school* CA-9
Packwood Springs—*spring* AZ-5
Packwood Valley—*valley* CA-9
Packy Spring—*spring* CA-9
Pacobo Mine (underground)—*mine* AL-4
Pacock Brook—*stream* NJ-2
**Pacoima**—*pop pl* CA-9
Pacoima Canyon—*valley* CA-9
Pacoima Dam—*dam* CA-9
Pacoima Diversion Channel—*canal* CA-9
Pacoima JHS—*school* CA-9
Pacoima Memorial Hosp—*hospital* CA-9
Pacoima Rsvr—*reservoir* CA-9
Pacoima Sch—*school* CA-9
Pacoima Spreading Grounds—*basin* CA-9
Pacoima Wash—*stream* CA-9
Paco Lake—*lake* MN-6
**Pacolet**—*pop pl* SC-3
Pacolet (CCD)—*cens area* SC-3
*Pacolet Mill* SC-3
**Pacolet Mills**—*pop pl* SC-3
**Pacolet Park**—*pop pl* SC-3
Pacolet River—*stream* SC-3
Pacolet Road Ch—*church* SC-3
**Pacolet Valley**—*pop pl* NC-3
Pacolson Lake—*lake* FL-3
Pa Cove—*bay* AS-9
Pacquereau Bay—*bay* VI-3
Pactola Dam—*dam* SD-7
Pactola (historical)—*locale* SD-7
Pactola Rsvr—*reservoir* SD-7
Pactola Sch—*school* SD-7
Pactola Township (historical)—*civil* SD-7
Pactolian Gulch—*valley* ID-8
Pactolus—*locale* NV-8
Pactolus—*locale* TN-4
**Pactolus**—*pop pl* CO-8
**Pactolus**—*pop pl* KY-4
**Pactolus**—*pop pl* NC-3
Pactolus Ch—*church* TN-4
Pactolus Elem Sch—*school* NC-3
Pactolus Hills—*summit* NV-8
Pactolus Sch (historical)—*school* TN-4
Pactolus (Township of)—*fmr MCD* NC-3
*Pa-cu-ay* UT-8
*Pacummohquah* MA-1
*Pacummohquah Head* MA-1
Pacwawong Lake—*lake* WI-6
Pacwawong Spring—*spring* WI-6
**Pad**—*pop pl* WV-2
*Pada* FM-9
Padalower Spring—*spring* SD-7
*Padan-Aram* MA-1
Padanaram—*locale* OH-6
Padanaram Breakwater—*dam* MA-1
Padanaram Breakwater Light—*locale* MA-1
Padanaram Brook—*stream* CT-1
Padanaram Cem—*cemetery* OH-6
Padanaram Rsvr—*reservoir* CT-1
**Padanaram Village**—*pop pl* MA-1
Padanaram Village Hist Dist—*hist pl* MA-1
*Padan Creek* PA-2
Padan Sch—*school* CA-9
Padarahra—*unknown* FM-9
Pad Branch—*stream* KY-4
Padden, Lake—*lake* WA-9
Padden Creek—*stream* WA-9
Paddens Creek (historical)—*stream* PA-2
Paddison Drain—*stream* MI-6
**Paddison Hills**—*pop pl* OH-6
Paddison Ranch Buildings—*hist pl* CA-9
Paddison Sch—*school* CA-9
Paddison Square—*post sta* CA-9
Paddit Well—*well* AZ-5
Paddle Branch—*stream* NC-3
Paddle Creek—*stream* AK-9
Paddle Creek—*stream* CA-9
Paddle Creek—*stream* IN-6
Paddle Creek—*stream* KY-4
Paddle Creek—*stream* OH-6
Paddle Creek—*stream* TN-4
Paddle Creek—*stream* WV-2
Paddle Cross Lake—*lake* NM-5
*Paddlefords* NY-2
**Paddlefords**—*pop pl* NY-2
*Paddlefords Brook* NY-2
Paddle Lake—*lake* (2) AK-9
Paddle Lake—*lake* MN-6
Paddle Mtn—*summit* AK-9
Paddle Run—*stream* WV-2
Paddletown Cem—*cemetery* PA-2
*Paddock* MA-1
Paddock—*locale* (2) NE-7
Paddock—*locale* WA-9
Paddock—*other* MN-6
Paddock, Algernon S., House—*hist pl* NE-7
Paddock, Augustus, House—*hist pl* MI-6
Paddock Arcade—*hist pl* NY-2
Paddock-Bethel Cem—*cemetery* MN-6
Paddock Bldg—*hist pl* NY-2
Paddock Butte—*summit* OR-9
Paddock Camp—*park* OR-9
Paddock Cem—*cemetery* MA-1
Paddock Ch—*church* NE-7
Paddock Creek—*stream* IL-6
Paddock Creek—*stream* ND-7
Paddock Ditch—*canal* MT-8
*Paddock Gap* AL-4
Paddock Hill—*summit* VT-1
Paddock Hotel—*hist pl* NE-7
Paddock Lake—*lake* WI-6
**Paddock Lake**—*pop pl* WI-6
Paddock Lake Sch—*school* WI-6
Paddock Lane Sch—*school* NE-7
Paddock Mall—*locale* FL-3
Paddock Mansion—*hist pl* NY-2
Paddock Park—*park* TX-5
Paddock Ranch—*locale* AZ-5
Paddock Rock—*rock* MA-1
Paddock Rsvr—*reservoir* ID-8
Paddock Run—*stream* IN-6
Paddock Sch—*school* CO-8
Paddock Sch—*school* IL-6
Paddock Sch Number 12 (historical)—*school* SD-7
Paddock School (Abandoned)—*locale* CA-9
*Paddocks Island* MA-1
Paddock Slough—*stream* IL-6
Paddock South Oil Field—*other* NM-5
Paddocks Pond—*lake* MA-1
Paddock Spring—*spring* AZ-5
**Paddock Township**—*pop pl* (2) NE-7
**Paddock (Township of)**—*pop pl* MN-6
Paddock Valley Rsvr—*reservoir* ID-8
Paddock Viaduct—*hist pl* TX-5
Paddock Well—*well* AZ-5
Paddock Woods—*woods* IL-6
**Paddon**—*pop pl* CA-9
*Padds Creek* NC-3
Padds Run—*stream* WV-2
Paddy Bar—*bar* NJ-2
Paddy Bay—*bay* AK-9
Paddy Bay—*bay* LA-4
Paddy Bee Tree Run—*stream* VA-3
Paddy Biddle Cove—*bay* MD-2
Paddy Bluff—*cliff* KY-4
Paddy Branch—*stream* MO-7
Paddy Branch—*stream* TX-5
Paddy Branch—*stream* (2) WV-2
Paddy Brown Brook—*stream* NY-2
Paddy Butte—*summit* AZ-5
Paddy Cienega—*flat* AZ-5
Paddy Creek—*stream* (2) AZ-5
Paddy Creek—*stream* CA-9
Paddy Creek—*stream* ID-8
Paddy Creek—*stream* IL-6
Paddy Creek—*stream* KS-7
Paddy Creek—*stream* ME-1
Paddy Creek—*stream* MT-8
Paddy Creek—*stream* (2) NC-3
Paddy Creek—*stream* OH-6
Paddy Creek—*stream* OR-9
Paddy Creek—*stream* WV-2
Paddy Creek Dam—*dam* NC-3
Paddy Fay Creek—*stream* MT-8
Paddy Flat—*flat* ID-8
Paddy Flat Campground—*locale* ID-8
Paddy Flat Forest Service Station—*locale* ID-8
Paddy Flat Lake Fork Trail—*trail* ID-8
Paddy Flat Summit—*summit* ID-8
Paddy Fork Tank—*reservoir* AZ-5
*Paddy Foy Creek* MT-8
Paddy Gap—*gap* VA-3
Paddy-Go-Easy Pass—*gap* WA-9
**Paddy Hill**—*pop pl* NY-2
Paddy Hill—*summit* MA-1
Paddy Hill—*summit* NY-2
Paddy Hill Creek—*stream* NY-2
Paddy Hole—*lake* KY-4
Paddy Island—*island* IL-6
Paddy Knob—*summit* VA-3
Paddy Knob—*summit* WV-2
Paddy Lake—*reservoir* ID-8
Paddy Lick—*stream* VA-3
Paddy Lots Springs—*spring* OR-9
Paddy Lynch Windmill—*locale* AZ-5
Paddy Marsh State Wildlife Mngmt Are—*park* MN-6
Paddy Meadow Brook—*stream* ME-1
*Paddy Mtn* PA-2
Paddy Mtn—*summit* NY-2
Paddy Mtn—*summit* NC-3
Paddy Mtn—*summit* PA-2
Paddy Mtn—*summit* VA-3
Paddy Mtn—*summit* WV-2
*Paddy Piddle Cove* MD-2
*Paddy Piddles Cove* MD-2
Paddy Point—*cape* AK-9
Paddy Point—*cape* NY-2
Paddy Pond—*lake* NY-2
Paddy Ridge Sch—*school* IL-6
Paddy Run—*stream* KY-4
Paddy Run—*stream* (3) PA-2
Paddy Run—*stream* VA-3
Paddy Run—*stream* (3) WV-2
Paddys Branch—*stream* NC-3
Paddys Branch—*stream* TN-4
Paddy Sch (historical)—*school* MO-7
*Paddys Creek* NC-3
Paddys Creek—*stream* KY-4
Paddys Creek—*stream* MI-6
Paddys Creek Dam—*dam* NC-3
Paddys Delight Creek—*stream* NC-3
Paddys Hole—*other* NM-5
Paddys Knob—*summit* TN-4
Paddys Lake—*reservoir* OR-9
Paddys Meadow—*flat* OR-9
*Paddys Mountain* PA-2
Paddys Pride Mine—*mine* CA-9
Paddy Spring—*spring* OR-9
*Paddy Squash Island* NY-2
Paddys River—*stream* AZ-5
Paddys River Two hundred ninety three Trail—*trail* AZ-5
*Paddys Run* IN-6
*Paddy's Run* OH-6
Paddys Run—*stream* KY-4
Paddys Run—*stream* MT-8
Paddys Run—*stream* OH-6
Paddys Run—*stream* WV-2
*Paddys Thorofare* NJ-2
Paddys Valley—*valley* OR-9
Paddy Thorofare—*channel* NJ-2
Paddytown—*locale* PA-2
Paddytown Hollow—*valley* PA-2
Padelford—*locale* NY-2
Padelford Brook—*stream* NY-2
*Padelfords* NY-2
*Padelfords Brook* NY-2
Padelford Wash—*stream* AZ-5
**Paden**—*pop pl* MS-4
**Paden**—*pop pl* OK-5
Padena—*locale* GA-3
Padena Cem—*cemetery* GA-3
*Padenall* GA-3
Paden (CCD)—*cens area* OK-5
Paden Ch—*church* AL-4
**Paden City**—*pop pl* WV-2
Paden Corner—*locale* DE-2
Paden Creek—*stream* PA-2
Paden Drain—*canal* CA-9
Paden Fork—*stream* WV-2
Paden Fork Chapel—*church* WV-2
Paden HS—*school* MS-4
Paden Island—*island* WV-2
Paden Lake—*reservoir* OK-5
Paden Oil Field—*oilfield* KS-7
Paden Overlook Area—*park* MS-4
*Padens* MS-4
**Paderborn**—*pop pl* IL-6
Paderewski Sch—*school* IL-6
PAD Factory, The—*hist pl* NY-2
Padfield Branch—*stream* MO-7
Pad Fork—*stream* (2) WV-2
*Pad-gee-ligau Creek* AL-4
Padget Branch—*stream* LA-4
Padget Brook—*stream* NY-2
Padget Camp—*locale* FL-3
Padget Camp (abandoned)—*locale* FL-3
Padget Cem—*cemetery* TN-4
*Padget Creek* MT-8
Padget Creek—*stream* ID-8
*Padget Landing* SC-3
*Padgets Creek* SC-3
Padgett—*locale* NC-3
**Padgett**—*pop pl* SC-3
**Padgett**—*pop pl* TX-5
Padgett Bay—*swamp* FL-3
Padgett Bay—*swamp* GA-3
Padgett Bluff—*cliff* OK-5
Padgett Branch—*stream* AL-4
Padgett Branch—*stream* FL-3
Padgett Branch—*stream* KY-4
Padgett Branch—*stream* MS-4
Padgett Branch—*stream* NC-3
*Padgett Cem* TN-4
Padgett Cem—*cemetery* FL-3
Padgett Cem—*cemetery* GA-3
Padgett Cem—*cemetery* SC-3
Padgett Cem—*cemetery* TN-4
Padgett Cem—*cemetery* (2) TX-5
Padgett Cove—*valley* NC-3
*Padgett Creek* MT-8
Padgett Creek—*stream* FL-3
Padgett Ditch—*canal* IN-6
Padgett Falls—*falls* GA-3
Padgett Hammock—*island* FL-3
Padgett Hill—*summit* AR-4
Padgett (historical)—*locale* AL-4
Padgett Hollow—*valley* TX-5
Padgett Island—*island* AR-4
Padgett Island—*island* FL-3
Padgett Knob—*summit* TN-4
*Padgett Lake* MN-6
Padgett Lake—*lake* (2) FL-3
Padgett Landing—*locale* SC-3
Padgett Mill—*locale* TN-4
Padgett Oil Field—*oilfield* KS-7
**Padgetts**—*pop pl* SC-3
Padgett Sch—*school* FL-3
Padgetts Creek—*stream* NJ-2
Padgetts Creek—*stream* SC-3
Padgett's Creek Baptist Church—*hist pl* SC-3
Padgetts Creek Cem—*cemetery* SC-3
Padgetts Creek Ch—*church* SC-3
Padgetts Lake—*lake* GA-3
Padgett Spring Branch—*stream* FL-3
Padgett Temple—*church* NY-2
*Padgitt* TX-5
**Padilla**—*pop pl* PR-3
Padilla (Barrio)—*fmr MCD* PR-3
Padilla Bay—*bay* WA-9
Padilla Canyon—*valley* NM-5
Padilla Cem—*cemetery* NM-5
Padilla Creek—*stream* TX-5
Padilla Mesa—*summit* AZ-5
Padilla Mine—*mine* NM-5
Padilla Ranch—*locale* (5) NM-5
Padilla Spring—*spring* NM-5
Padilla Tank—*reservoir* AZ-5
Padilla Tank—*reservoir* (2) NM-5
Padilla Well—*well* (2) NM-5
Padilla Windmill—*locale* CO-8
Padilla Windmill—*locale* NM-5
*Padillo Creek* TX-5
Pad Island—*island* AK-9
Padlock—*locale* FL-3
Padlock Cem—*cemetery* GA-3
Padlock Cow Camp—*locale* WY-8
Padlock Lookout Tower—*locale* NY-2
Padlock Mine—*mine* CA-9
Padlock Ranch—*locale* MT-8
Padlock Ranch—*locale* WY-8
Padlock Rim—*cliff* WY-8
**Pado**—*pop pl* GU-9
*Padoncah River* KS-7
**Padonia**—*pop pl* KS-7
**Padonia**—*pop pl* MD-2
**Padonia Township**—*pop pl* KS-7
Padora (historical P.O.)—*locale* IN-6
*Padouca River* KS-7
Padre Alejos Artesian Well—*well* TX-5
Padre Alonzo Trail—*trail* NM-5
Padre Barona Creek—*stream* CA-9
Padre Bay—*bay* UT-8
Padre Bayou—*gut* LA-4
Padre Canyon—*valley* AZ-5
Padre Canyon—*valley* NM-5
Padre Canyon—*valley* TX-5
Padre Canyon—*valley* UT-8
Padre Creek—*stream* UT-8
Padre Francisco Garces Historical Monmt—*park* CA-9
Padre Island—*island* TX-5
Padre Island Natl Seashore—*park* TX-5
Padre Juan, Arroyo Del—*stream* CA-9
Padre Juan Canyon—*valley* CA-9
Padre Juanito Artesian Well—*well* TX-5
Padre Juanito Trap—*summit* TX-5
Padre Madre Mine—*mine* CA-9
*Padre Mariano Creek* TX-5
Padre Palomo Park—*park* GU-9
Padre Park—*park* TX-5
Padre Point—*cape* UT-8
Padre Rsvr—*reservoir* AZ-5
Padres Butte—*summit* UT-8
Padres Mesa—*summit* AZ-5
Padre Spring Creek—*stream* NM-5
Padre Spring Ranch—*locale* NM-5
Padre Tank—*reservoir* AZ-5
Padre Tank—*reservoir* UT-8
Padrone Hill—*summit* TX-5
Padrones Canyon—*valley* CA-9
Padrones Pasture—*flat* TX-5
Padrones Spring—*spring* CA-9
Padrones Well—*well* TX-5
**Padroni**—*pop pl* CO-8
Pads Branch—*stream* KY-4
Pads Creek—*stream* VA-3
Pads Fork—*stream* KY-4
**Padua**—*pop pl* IL-6
**Padua**—*pop pl* MN-6
**Padua**—*pop pl* OH-6
Padua Acad—*school* DE-2
Padua Hills Theater—*building* CA-9
Padua HS—*school* NY-2
Padua HS—*school* OH-6
Padua State Wildlife Mngmt Area—*park* MN-6
Paduca Breaks—*area* NM-5
**Paducah**—*pop pl* KY-4
**Paducah**—*pop pl* TX-5
Paducah and Illinois Fishing Camp—*other* IL-6
**Paducah and Illinois Junction (P&I Jct.)**—*pop pl* KY-4
Paducah (CCD)—*cens area* KY-4
Paducah Downtown Commercial District—*hist pl* KY-4
Paducah Downtown Commercial District (Boundary Increase)—*hist pl* KY-4
**Paducah (historical)**—*pop pl* MS-4
*Paducah Junction* TN-4
Paducah Market House District—*hist pl* KY-4
Paducah North (CCD)—*cens area* TX-5
Paducah Plant, Energy Research And Development Administration—*other* KY-4
Paducah South (CCD)—*cens area* TX-5
Paducah Tilghman HS—*school* KY-4
Paducah Towhead—*island* KY-4
Paducah Well Ch—*church* MS-4
Paduca Oil Field—*other* NM-5
*Paduliaes Point* PW-9
Padus—*locale* WI-6
Padus Lookout Tower—*locale* WI-6
*Padwisha* CA-9
Pad Wo'o Tank—*reservoir* AZ-5
Pady Gap—*gap* NC-3
Paea—*cape* HI-9
Paeahu—*civil* HI-9
*Paealui* HI-9
Paecheco Ranch—*locale* NM-5
Pae Gulch—*valley* HI-9
Paehala—*civil* HI-9
Paenapalaua Gulch—*valley* HI-9
Paeohe—*civil* HI-9
Paeohe Stream—*stream* HI-9
**Paeonian Springs**—*pop pl* VA-3
Paeoopu Pool—*lake* HI-9
Paepaemoana Point—*cape* HI-9
Paepke, Henry, House—*hist pl* WI-6
Paerdegat Basin—*bay* NY-2
Paerdegat Park—*park* NY-2
*Paesta Creek* TX-5
Paewa—*bay* HI-9
Pafallaya (historical)—*locale* AL-4
Paff Cem—*cemetery* AL-4
Paff Clearing—*locale* WA-9
Pafford Crossing—*locale* TX-5
Pafford Landing (historical)—*locale* TN-4
Paffords Branch—*stream* TN-4
Pagachao—*area* GU-9
Pagachao Creek—*stream* GU-9
*Pagahrit* UT-8
Pagai—*locale* AS-9
Pagaitua Point—*cape* AS-9
Pagami Creek—*stream* MN-6
Pagami Lake—*lake* MN-6
Pagan, Mount—*summit* MH-9
Pagan Cem—*cemetery* (2) MN-6
*Pagan Creek* DE-2
*Pagan Creek* VA-3
Pagan Creek Dike—*hist pl* DE-2
Pagan-Fletcher House—*hist pl* NY-2
*Pagan Insel* MH-9
*Pagan Island* MH-9
Pagan Island—*island* MH-9
Pagan Point—*cape* MD-2
Pagan River—*stream* VA-3
*Pagan-San* MH-9
Pagan Site, 41 LK 58—*hist pl* TX-5
*Pagan-To* MH-9
*Pagaon* MH-9
*Pagara* MH-9
Pagari—*locale* ID-8
Pagari Bridge—*bridge* ID-8
*Pagasus Airport* PA-2
Pagat—*other* GU-9
Pagatatua Ridge—*ridge* AS-9
Pagat Point—*summit* GU-9
Pagat Site—*hist pl* GU-9
*Page* KY-4
Page—*hist pl* KY-4
Page—*locale* NM-5
Page—*locale* NY-2
Page—*locale* OK-5
Page—*locale* OR-9
Page—*locale* VA-3
Page—*locale* WA-9
**Page**—*pop pl* AZ-5
**Page**—*pop pl* ID-8
**Page**—*pop pl* IN-6
**Page**—*pop pl* MN-6
**Page**—*pop pl* NE-7
**Page**—*pop pl* ND-7
**Page**—*pop pl* VA-3
**Page**—*pop pl* WV-2
Page, Daniel R. and Sophia G., House—*hist pl* UT-8
Page, H. P., House—*hist pl* MA-1
Page, Judge C. H., House—*hist pl* OR-9
Page, Lake—*reservoir* VA-3
Page, Louis, Archeol Site—*hist pl* TX-5
Page, Nathaniel, House—*hist pl* MA-1
Page, Paul D., House—*hist pl* TX-5
Page, Thomas D., House—*hist pl* MA-1
Page, Thomas Nelson, House—*hist pl* DC-2
Page, William House—*hist pl* KY-4
Page Airp—*airport* WA-9
Page and Corwin Mine—*mine* NV-8
Pageant Creek—*stream* MN-6
Pageant Lake—*lake* MN-6
Page Ave Ch—*church* MI-6
Page Bayou—*stream* LA-4
Page-Bell House—*hist pl* KY-4
Page Bench—*bench* UT-8
Page Blvd Police Station—*hist pl* MO-7
Page Branch—*stream* (2) AL-4
Page Branch—*stream* (2) GA-3
Page Branch—*stream* KY-4
Page Branch—*stream* MS-4
Page Branch—*stream* (2) MO-7
Page Branch—*stream* TN-4
Page Branch—*stream* VA-3
Page Bridge—*bridge* AL-4
Page Bridge—*other* IL-6
*Page Brook* MA-1
**Page Brook**—*pop pl* NY-2
Page Brook—*stream* (2) ME-1
Page Brook—*stream* MA-1
Page Brook—*stream* NH-1
Page Brook—*stream* (4) NY-2
Page Brook—*stream* VT-1
Page Brook—*stream* VA-3
Page Brothers Bldg—*hist pl* IL-6
Page Canal—*canal* UT-8
Page Canyon—*valley* WA-9
Page Cem—*cemetery* AR-4
Page Cem—*cemetery* GA-3
Page Cem—*cemetery* KS-7
Page Cem—*cemetery* (2) KY-4
Page Cem—*cemetery* (2) ME-1
Page Cem—*cemetery* (3) MS-4
Page Cem—*cemetery* (3) MO-7
Page Cem—*cemetery* (3) NC-3
Page Cem—*cemetery* ND-7
Page Cem—*cemetery* OK-5
Page Cem—*cemetery* SC-3
Page Cem—*cemetery* (3) TN-4
Page Cem—*cemetery* (2) TX-5
Page Cem—*cemetery* (2) VA-3
Page Center—*locale* IA-7
*Page Centre* IA-7
Page Ch—*church* GA-3
Page Ch—*church* LA-4
Page Chapel—*church* MS-4
Page Chapel—*church* NC-3
Page City—*locale* MO-7
**Page City**—*pop pl* KS-7
Page City Sch—*school* MO-7
Page Clearing—*island* FL-3
**Page (County)**—*pop pl* VA-3
Page County Courthouse—*hist pl* IA-7
Page County Courthouse—*hist pl* VA-3
*Page Creek* NC-3
*Page Creek* WA-9
Page Creek—*stream* (2) AL-4
Page Creek—*stream* FL-3
Page Creek—*stream* KS-7
Page Creek—*stream* KY-4
Page Creek—*stream* (2) MI-6
Page Creek—*stream* (2) MS-4
Page Creek—*stream* MT-8
Page Creek—*stream* NV-8
Page Creek—*stream* (2) OR-9
Page Creek—*stream* SC-3
Page Creek—*stream* (2) TX-5
Page Creek—*stream* VA-3
Page Creek—*stream* (2) WA-9
Page Creek—*stream* WI-6
Page Creek Guard Station—*locale* OR-9
**Pagedale**—*pop pl* MO-7
Page Dam—*dam* OR-9
Page Ditch—*canal* IN-6
Page Draw—*valley* WY-8
Page Elem Sch—*school* AZ-5
**Page Estates Subdivision**—*pop pl* UT-8
Page Field—*park* FL-3
Page Field (Airport)—*airport* FL-3
Page Flat—*flat* AZ-5
Page Flat—*flat* CA-9
Page Flat—*flat* WY-8
Page Flat Draw—*valley* WY-8
Page Flat Tank—*reservoir* AZ-5
Page Fork—*stream* UT-8
*Page Grove Church* MS-4
Page Gulch—*valley* CA-9
Page Gulch—*valley* MT-8
Page Heights Baptist Ch—*church* TN-4
Page Hill—*summit* (2) ME-1
Page Hill—*summit* (7) NH-1
Page Hill—*summit* (2) NY-2
Page Hill—*summit* VT-1
Page Hill Cem—*cemetery* VT-1

**Page Hollow**—pop pl VA-3
Page Hollow—valley AR-4
Page Hollow—valley MO-7
Page Hollow—valley (2) PA-2
Page Hollow—valley TN-4
Page Hollow—valley VA-3
Page HS—school AZ-5
Page HS—school NC-3
Page HS—school OK-5
Page Island—island RI-1
Page Island—island SC-3
Page-Jackson Sch—school WV-2
Page JHS—school MI-6
Page JHS—school TX-5
Page Knob—summit MO-7
Page Lake NC-3
Page Lake—lake FL-3
Page Lake—lake LA-4
Page Lake—lake MI-6
Page Lake—lake MN-6
Page Lake—lake MT-8
Page Lake—lake SC-3
Page Lake—reservoir PA-2
Page Lake Dam—dam (3) MS-4
Page Lake Dam—dam PA-2
**Pageland**—pop pl SC-3
Pageland (CCD)—cens area SC-3
Pagel Cem—cemetery TX-5
Page Lot Brook—stream CT-1
Pagel Settlement Cem—cemetery (2) TX-5
Pagels Sch—school CT-1
Page Maintenance Yard—other AZ-5
Page Manor OH-6
**Page Manor**—pop pl OH-6
Page Manor Schools—school OH-6
Page Meadows—flat CA-9
Page Military Acad—school CA-9
Page Mill Pond—lake WA-9
Page Mill (site)—locale CA-9
Page Mine—mine ID-8
**Page (Monk)**—pop pl VA-3
Page Mtn—summit AK-9
Page Mtn—summit CA-9
Page Mtn—summit GA-3
Page Mtn—summit (2) ME-1
Page Mtn—summit NY-2
Page Mtn—summit OR-9
Page Mtn—summit VA-3
Page Municipal Airp—airport AZ-5
Page Oil And Gas Field—oilfield TX-5
Page Park—park CT-1
Page Park—park TX-5
**Page Park**—pop pl FL-3
Page Park Sch—school IL-6
Page Peaks—summit CA-9
Page Place—locale OR-9
Page Place Rsvr—reservoir OR-9
Page Point—cape VT-1
Page Point—summit UT-8
Page Pond—lake FL-3
Page Pond—lake ME-1
Page Pond—lake MD-2
Page Pond—lake NH-1
Page Pond—lake NY-2
Page Pond—lake VT-1
Page Pond—lake WA-9
Page Pond Brook—stream NY-2
Page Pond Hill—summit NY-2
Page Ranch—locale AZ-5
Page Ranch—locale NM-5
Page Ranch—locale (2) TX-5
Page Ranch—locale UT-8
Page Ranch—locale WY-8
Page Randall Brook—stream NH-1
Pagerie, Smith, Site—hist pl NY-2
Page Rock—island ME-1
Page (RR name for Calvin)—other KY-4
Page Rsvr—reservoir OR-9
Page Run—stream PA-2
Page Run—stream VA-3
**Pages Beach**—pop pl MA-1
Pages Branch—stream TN-4
Pages Brook—stream MA-1
Page Sch—school CA-9
Page Sch—school IA-7
Page Sch—school KY-4
Page Sch—school (2) MA-1
Page Sch—school MN-6
Page Sch—school OK-5
Page Sch—school OR-9
Page Sch—school PA-2
Page Sch—school SD-7
Page Sch—school UT-8
Page Sch—school VA-3
Pages Corner—locale NH-1
Pages Corner—locale NJ-2
**Pages Corner**—pop pl NH-1
**Pages Corner**—pop pl NY-2
**Pages Corner**—pop pl VT-1
Pages Corners—locale PA-2
Pages Cove—bay CT-1
Pages Creek—stream AL-4
Pages Creek—stream NC-3
Pages Creek—stream SC-3
Pages (historical)—locale MS-4
Page Site (15LO1)—hist pl KY-4
Pages Lake NJ-2
Pages Lake—lake NC-3
Pages Lake—reservoir NC-3
Pages Lake—reservoir TN-4
Pages Lake Dam—dam NC-3
Pages Lane Shop Ctr—locale UT-8
Pages Mill Ch—church NC-3
Pages Millpond—reservoir CT-1
Pages Millpond—reservoir SC-3
Pages Mine (underground)—mine AL-4
Page Soddy—hist pl OK-5
Pages Old Ferry (historical)—locale AL-4
Pages on Sculmore MS-4
Pages Point—cape ME-1
Pages Pond PA-2
Page Spring—spring AL-4
Page Spring—spring AZ-5
Page Spring Branch—stream AL-4
**Page Springs**—pop pl AZ-5
Page Springs—spring NV-8
Page Springs—spring OR-9
Page Springs State Fish Cultural Station—locale AZ-5
Pages Rock Light—other VA-3
Pages Run—stream NJ-2
Pages Slough—bay WI-6
Pages Store—locale NM-5
Pages Swamp—swamp MD-2
**Page Subdivision**—pop pl MS-4
Page Substation—locale AZ-5
Paget—locale OH-6
Page Tank AZ-5
Paget Branch—stream NC-3
Paget Canyon—valley OR-9
Paget Creek—stream MT-8
Paget House and Heigold House Facade—hist pl KY-4
**Pageton**—pop pl WV-2
Pageton (historical)—locale KS-7
Pagetown OH-6
Pagetown—other OH-6
**Pagetown**—pop pl OH-6
Pagetown Cem—cemetery OH-6
**Page Township**—pop pl ND-7
**Page (Township of)**—pop pl MN-6
Page-Trowbridge Experimental Ranch—other AZ-5
Paget Rsvr Number Four—reservoir MT-8
Paget Rsvr Number One—reservoir MT-8
Paget Rsvr Number Three—reservoir MT-8
Paget Rsvr Number Two—reservoir MT-8
Paget Spring Number Four—spring MT-8
Paget Spring Number One—spring MT-8
Paget Spring Number Three—spring MT-8
Paget Spring Number Two—spring MT-8
Pagett Bay—swamp NC-3
Pagett Branch—stream FL-3
**Pagetts Corner**—pop pl MD-2
Page Valley—valley PA-2
Page Valley—valley VA-3
Page-Vawter House—hist pl WV-2
**Pageville**—pop pl OH-6
**Pageville**—pop pl PA-2
Pageville Ch—church TX-5
Pageville Sch—school MT-8
Page-Walker Hotel—hist pl NC-3
Page Wash—stream AZ-5
Page Water Storage Tank—reservoir AZ-5
Page Well—well MT-8
Pagge Creek—stream CA-9
Paggen Lake—lake MN-6
Paggett Cem—cemetery TN-4
Paggi, Michael, House—hist pl TX-5
Paghahacking DE-2
Pagie, Lake—lake LA-4
Pagilak River—stream AK-9
Pagil Gulch—valley MT-8
Pagin Cem—cemetery IA-7
Pagliarulo (Siding)—locale CA-9
Pago—area GU-9
Pago Bay—bay GU-9
Pago Channel—channel GU-9
Pagoda—hist pl PA-2
Pagoda—locale CO-8
Pagoda—pillar UT-8
**Pagoda**—pop pl TX-5
Pagoda Creek—stream CO-8
Pagoda Creek—stream ID-8
Pagoda Creek—stream MT-8
Pagoda Creek—stream WY-8
Pagoda Lake—lake CO-8
Pagoda Lake—lake MN-6
Pagoda Mall—locale AZ-5
Pagoda Mountain AZ-5
Pagoda Mtn—summit CO-8
Pagoda Mtn—summit MT-8
Pagoda Peak—summit CO-8
Pagoda Rock—pillar NM-5
Pagoda Tank—reservoir NM-5
Pagon MH-9
**Pago Pago**—pop pl AS-9
Pago Pago Harbor—bay AS-9
Pago Pago International Airp—airport AS-9
Pago Pago Samoa—post sta AS-9
Pago Point—summit GU-9
Pago Reef (Coral)—bar GU-9
Pago River—stream GU-9
**Pagosa**—pop pl CO-8
Pagosa Creek NM-5
Pagosa Creek—stream CO-8
**Pagosa Junction**—pop pl CO-8
Pagosa Peak—summit CO-8
**Pagosa Springs**—pop pl CO-8
Pagosa Springs Job Corps—locale CO-8
Pago Stream—stream AS-9
**Paguate**—pop pl NM-5
Paguate Purchase—civil NM-5
Paguate Rsvr—reservoir NM-5
Paguay CA-9
Paguekwash Point—cliff AZ-5
Pague Tank—reservoir NM-5
Pague Well—well NM-5
Paguna Arm—bay AK-9
Pagunon—ridge GU-9
Pagura Reef—bar FM-9
Paha—locale WA-9
Pahabe KS-7
Paha Cem—cemetery WA-9
Pahackqualong PA-2
Paha Coulee—valley WA-9
Pahaha HI-9
Pahaha Creek WA-9
**Pahala**—pop pl HI-9
Pahale Stream—stream HI-9
**Pahapesto Township**—pop pl SD-7
Pahaqualing PA-2
Pahaqualong PA-2
Pahaquarry—locale NJ-2
Pahaquarry Flat—flat NJ-2
**Pahaquarry (Township of)**—pop pl NJ-2
Paha Sapa SD-7
**Pahaska**—pop pl WY-8
Pahaska Campground—locale WY-8
Pahaska Tepee WY-8
Pahaska Tepee—hist pl WY-8
**Pahaska Tepee**—pop pl WY-8
Pahauqu Point—cape HI-9
Pa-Hay-Okee Lookout Tower—tower FL-3
Pah Canyon—valley NV-8
Pahcease Canal—canal UT-8
Pahcoon Flat—flat UT-8
Pahcoon Spring—spring UT-8
Pahcoon Springs Wash UT-8
Pahcoon Spring Wash—valley UT-8
Pahd—cape FM-9
Paheehee HI-9
Paheehee Hill HI-9
Paheehee Ridge HI-9
Paheehee Ridge—ridge HI-9
Paheehee Stream—stream HI-9
Pah Ga Ne A Campground—locale UT-8
Pah-gun-a-quint Creek UT-8
Pah-har-be KS-7
Pahihi Gulch—valley HI-9
Pahina—locale FM-9
Pahina—unknown FM-9
Pahina, Dolen—summit FM-9
Pahinahina—civil HI-9
Pahiomu Fishpond—lake HI-9
Pahipahialua—civil HI-9
Pahipahialua Gulch—valley HI-9
Pahl, Henry, House—hist pl IA-7
Pahlap—locale FM-9
Pahlil—ridge FM-9
Pahlone Peak—summit CO-8
Pahnaiau—locale FM-9
Pahnais—unknown FM-9
Pahnak Pwetepwet—bar FM-9
Pahn Apara—valley FM-9
Pahnasang—locale FM-9
**Pahnaul**—pop pl FM-9
Pahn Dau—gut FM-9
Pahn Diadi—locale FM-9
Pahn Dieinuh—cape FM-9
Pahn Dolente—ridge FM-9
Pahn Dolen Wenik—cliff FM-9
Pahn Dollap—unknown FM-9
Pahn Eken Lewetik—swamp FM-9
Pahneir Lap—unknown FM-9
Pahnepensepel—unknown FM-9
Pahngin, Pilen—stream FM-9
Pahnial—unknown FM-9
Pahniepw, Dolen—summit FM-9
Pahnihwi—unknown FM-9
Pahnihwi, Pilen—stream FM-9
Pahn Imwindol—locale FM-9
**Pahnios**—pop pl FM-9
Pahni Riviere KS-7
Pahnisou—locale FM-9
Pahn Kalang—locale FM-9
Pahn Kehnpwil—unknown FM-9
Pahn Kiemen Seu—bar FM-9
Pahnkios—unknown FM-9
Pahn Kipar—locale FM-9
Pahn Kupwuriso—cliff FM-9
Pahn Lepindong—locale FM-9
Pahn Loang—unknown FM-9
Pahn Mador—unknown FM-9
Pahn Malen Uht—plain FM-9
Pahn Mudok, Dauen—bay FM-9
Pahn Mwahnd—bar FM-9
Pahn Nihkehke—bar FM-9
Pahn Nihpit—summit FM-9
Pahn Nin Seitamw—cliff FM-9
Pahn Pahini FM-9
Pahnpalesed—bar FM-9
Pahnpar—ridge FM-9
Pahn Parahdok—locale FM-9
Pahnpe—unknown FM-9
Pahnpei—locale FM-9
**Pahn Peikapw**—pop pl FM-9
Pahn Pohtamw—unknown FM-9
Pahn Rahk—unknown FM-9
Pahnseiuh, Dauen—gut FM-9
Pahn Sekeren—locale FM-9
Pahn Sile—unknown FM-9
Pahnsille FM-9
Pahn Sounmall, Dauen—gut FM-9
**Pahn Tehlap**—pop pl FM-9
Pahntipwe—locale FM-9
**Pahntorong**—pop pl FM-9
Pahnwasank—island FM-9
Paho, Lake—reservoir MO-7
Pahoa—area HI-9
Pahoa—beach HI-9
Pahoa—civil (2) HI-9
**Pahoa**—pop pl HI-9
Pahoa Beach—beach HI-9
Pahoa-Kalapana (CCD)—cens area HI-9
Pahoehoe—civil HI-9
Pahoehoe Creek HI-9
Pahoehoe One—civil HI-9
Pahoehoe One-Four—civil HI-9
Pahoehoe One-Three—civil HI-9
Pahoehoe Stream—stream HI-9
Pahoehoe Two—civil HI-9
Pahoehoka HI-9
Pahoka Camp Lake—reservoir IN-6
Pahoka Camp Lake Dam—dam IN-6
Pahoka Creek—stream IN-6
**Pahokee**—pop pl FL-3
Pahokee Elem Sch—school FL-3
Pahokee Junior-Senior HS—school FL-3
Pahokee State Park—park FL-3
Paholei HI-9
Paholo HI-9
Paholoi HI-9
**Paholoi**—pop pl HI-9
Pahonu Point—cape HI-9
Pahpago MH-9
Pah Rah Mtn—summit NV-8
Pah Rah Range—range NV-8
Pahranagat HS—school NV-8
Pahranagat Natl Wildlife Ref—park NV-8
Pahranagat Range NV-8
Pahranagat Range—range NV-8
Pahranagat Valley—valley NV-8
Pahranagat Valley Sch—school NV-8
Pahranagat Wash—stream NV-8
Pahrea Creek UT-8
Pahreah Canyon AZ-5
Pahreah Canyon UT-8
Pahreah Creek UT-8
Pahreah Hollow UT-8
Pahreah Plateau AZ-5
Pahreah River AZ-5
Pahrea River AZ-5
Pah-rim CA-9
Pah-rimp CA-9
Pahrimp Valley NV-8
Pah-rim Valley NV-8
Pah River—stream AK-9
Pah River Flats—flat AK-9
Pahroc Canyon—valley NV-8
Pahrock Valley NV-8
Pahroc Range NV-8
Pahroc Range—range NV-8
Pahroc Spring—spring NV-8
Pahroc Summit NV-8
Pahroc Summit Pass—gap NV-8
Pahroc Valley NV-8
Pahroc Valley—basin NV-8
Pahron Creek—stream AK-9
Pah-Roose River AZ-5
Pah-roos River UT-8
**Pahrump**—pop pl NV-8
Pah-Rum Peak—summit NV-8
Pahrump Ranch—locale NV-8
Pahrump Township—inact MCD NV-8
Pahrump Valley—valley CA-9
Pahrump Valley—valley NV-8
Pahsimeroi Mtns—range ID-8
Pahsimeroi River—stream ID-8
Pahsimeroi Valley—valley ID-8
Pahsupp Mtn—summit NV-8
Pah Tempe Springs UT-8
Pahualoo—summit HI-9
Pahuamimi—lava HI-9
Pahuk—hist pl NE-7
Pahukauila Gulch—valley HI-9
Pahukini Heiau—hist pl HI-9
Pahuolona—summit HI-9
Pahu Point—cape HI-9
Pah-ute CA-9
Pahute Canyon AZ-5
Pah-ute Creek CA-9
Pahute Creek NV-8
Pahute Mesa—summit NV-8
Pahute Mesa Airstrip—airport NV-8
Pahute Peak CA-9
Pahute Peak NV-8
Pah Ute Range NV-8
Pahute Ridge NV-8
Pahvan Butte UT-8
Pahvan Range UT-8
Pah Vant Butte UT-8
Pahvant Butte—summit UT-8
Pahvant Guard Station—locale UT-8
Pa'hvant Mtn—summit UT-8
Pahvant Plateau UT-8
Pahvant Range—range UT-8
Pahvant Sch—school UT-8
Pahvant Valley—valley UT-8
Pahvan Valley UT-8
Pahvent Butte UT-8
Pahvent Range UT-8
Pahvent Valley UT-8
**Paia**—pop pl HI-9
Paia Bay—bay HI-9
Paiahaa Bay HI-9
Paiahaa Bay—bay HI-9
Paiakuli Rsvr (Aban'd)—reservoir HI-9
Paia Sch—school HI-9
**Paicines**—pop pl CA-9
Paicines Ranch—locale CA-9
Paicpouc Cove—bay GU-9
Paicpouc Point—cape GU-9
Paidi, Dauen—bay FM-9
Paieke—locale FM-9
Paiele HI-9
Paies—civil FM-9
Paies—locale FM-9
Paies—unknown FM-9
Paige—locale CA-9
Paige—locale VA-3
**Paige**—pop pl TX-5
Paige, David R., House—hist pl OH-6
Paige Bar—bar CA-9
Paige Bayou—stream MS-4
Paige Bend TX-5
Paige Branch—stream TN-4
Paige Canyon—valley AZ-5
Paige Cem—cemetery MI-6
Paige Cem—cemetery NY-2
Paige Cem—cemetery TN-4
Paige Creek—stream AZ-5
Paige-DeCrow-Weir House—hist pl TX-5
Paige Draw—valley NM-5
Paige Flat—flat TX-5
Paige Flat—flat UT-8
Paige Grove Ch—church MS-4
Paige Lake—lake MS-4
Paige Meadow CA-9
Paige Motor Car Co. Bldg—hist pl CA-9
Paige Pond FL-3
Paige Ranch—locale (2) CO-8
Paige Ridge—ridge WA-9
Paige Run—stream PA-2
Paige Sch—school NY-2
Paige Soube—stream CA-9
**Paige (subdivision)**—pop pl NC-3
Paigeville Canal—canal MT-8
Paige Well—well AZ-5
Paihaaloa—civil HI-9
Paihi Gulch—valley HI-9
Pai Island—island HI-9
Paiko Peninsula—cape HI-9
Paikuahiwi—area HI-9
Pailet Canal—canal LA-4
Pailey Creek—stream MS-4
Pailin Creek—stream NC-3
Pailing Creek—stream TX-5
Pailleen Queue Pond—bay LA-4
Paillet House—hist pl TX-5
Pailo—locale TN-4
Pailoa Bay—bay HI-9
Pailoa Point—cape HI-9
Pailolo Channel HI-9
Pailolo Channel—channel HI-9
Pailolo Passage HI-9
Pailo Post Office (historical)—building TN-4
**Pail Shop Corners**—pop pl NY-2
Paiment Ditch—canal MT-8
Paimiut—locale AK-9
**Paimiut**—pop pl AK-9
Paimiut ANV891—reserve AK-9
Paimiut Hills—other AK-9
Paimiut Portage—trail AK-9
Paimiut Slough—stream AK-9
Paimu Stream HI-9
Pain, Bayou—stream LA-4
Paina—cape HI-9
Pain Branch—stream TX-5
**Paincourtville**—pop pl LA-4
Pain Creek AL-4
**Paine**—pop pl PA-2
Paine, H. A., House—hist pl MN-6
Paine, Robert Treat, Jr. House—hist pl MA-1
Paine, Thomas, Cottage—hist pl NY-2
Paine, Timothy, House—hist pl MA-1
Paine AFB Outer Marker—other WA-9
Paine Art Center and Arboretum—hist pl WI-6
Paine Bank—hist pl MI-6
Paine Bottom—valley CA-9
Paine Branch—stream TN-4
Paine Brook—stream (3) ME-1
Paine Brook—stream NH-1
Paine Brook—stream RI-1
Paine Brook—stream VT-1
Paine Cem—cemetery MA-1
Paine Cem—cemetery MS-4
Paine Cem—cemetery NY-2
Paine Cem—cemetery TN-4
Paine Ch—church MS-4
Paine Chapel—church LA-4
Paine Chapel—church MS-4
Paine Chapel Cem—cemetery MS-4
Paine Chapel Sch—school MS-4
Paine Coll—school GA-3
Paine Corner—locale ME-1
Paine Creek ID-8
Paine Creek OR-9
Paine Creek—stream ID-8
Paine Creek—stream MA-1
Paine Creek—stream OH-6
Paine Creek—stream OR-9
Paine Creek—stream TN-4
Paine Creek—stream WA-9
Paine Crossing—locale OH-6
Paine Draw—valley TX-5
Paine Estate—hist pl MA-1
Paine Field Air Force Base—military WA-9
Paine Gulch—valley MT-8
Paine Gulch—valley NV-8
Paine High School MS-4
Paine Hill—summit CT-1
Paine Hill—summit ME-1
Paine Hill—summit PA-2
Paine Hollow—valley TN-4
Paine House—building NC-3
Paine House—hist pl IL-6
Paine House—hist pl RI-1
Paine Knob NC-3
Paine Knob—summit KY-4
Paine Lake CA-9
Paine Lake—lake (2) MN-6
Paine Lake—lake MS-4
Paine Lake—lake NY-2
Paine Lateral—canal ID-8
Paine Lumber Company Hist Dist—hist pl WI-6
Paine Memorial United Methodist Church MS-4
Paine Mtn—summit NC-3
Paine Mtn—summit VT-1
Paine Neighborhood Hist Dist—hist pl ME-1
Paine Pond RI-1
Paine Pond—lake ME-1
Paine Pond—lake MN-6
Paine Pond—reservoir CT-1
Paine Pond Dam—dam MS-4
Paine Ridge—ridge CO-8
Paine Run—stream OH-6
Paine Run—stream VA-3
Paine Run Rockshelter—hist pl VA-3
Paines—locale MI-6
Paines Branch—stream FL-3
Paine Sch—school CA-9
Paine Sch—school (2) MA-1
Paines Chapel—church TN-4
Paines Chapel African Methodist Episcopal Ch—church MS-4
Paines Chapel Missionary Baptist Ch MS-4
Paine School TN-4
Paines Corner—locale NY-2
**Paines Corner**—pop pl ME-1
Paines Creek MA-1
Paines Creek—stream NY-2
Paines Creek—stream WI-6
**Painesdale**—pop pl MI-6
Paine Shaft Mine (underground)—mine AL-4
**Paines Hollow**—pop pl NY-2
Paines Island—island PA-2
Paines Island—island WI-6
Paines Knob—summit WV-2
Paines Mtn—summit CO-8
Paines Point IL-6
Paines Point VA-3
Paines Point—other IL-6
Paine Spring—locale TN-4
Paine Spring—spring MT-8
Paine Spring—spring NV-8
Paines Summit—ridge PA-2
**Painesville**—pop pl OH-6
Painesville Chapel—hist pl WI-6
Painesville City Hall—hist pl OH-6
**Painesville Northeast**—pop pl OH-6
**Painesville on-the-Lake**—pop pl OH-6
**Painesville on the Lake (Township Park)**—pop pl OH-6
**Painesville Southwest**—pop pl OH-6
**Painesville (Township of)**—pop pl OH-6
Paine Swamp—swamp MA-1
Paine (Township of)—other OH-6
Paineville—locale VA-3
**Paineville**—pop pl IL-6
Paine Well—well NV-8
Pain Flat CA-9
Pain Fort (historical)—locale NC-3
Paingakmeut—locale AK-9
Pain Gulch MT-8
Pain in the Back Canyon—valley AZ-5
Painiu Stream—stream HI-9
Painorouyun Slough—stream AK-9
Pains Bay—bay NC-3
Pain School TN-4
Pains Creek AL-4
Pains Creek—stream NC-3
Pains Point—cape NC-3
**Paint**—pop pl PA-2
Paint Bank—locale VA-3
Paint Bank Branch—stream (2) VA-3
Paint Bank Gap—gap GA-3
Paint Bank Natl Fish Hatchery—other VA-3
Paint Bearden Branch—stream SC-3
Paintbed Brook—stream NY-2
Paint Borough—civil PA-2
Paint Branch—stream MD-2
Paint Branch—stream TN-4
Paint Branch—stream WV-2
**Paint Branch Estates**—pop pl MD-2
**Paint Branch Farm**—pop pl MD-2
**Paint Branch Farms**—pop pl MD-2
Paint Branch Park—park MD-2
Paint Brook—stream MA-1
Paintbrush Canyon—valley NV-8
Paintbrush Canyon—valley WY-8
Paintbrush Canyon Trail—trail WY-8
Paintbrush Divide—ridge WY-8
Paintbrush Divide Trail—trail WY-8
Paintbrush Rsvr—reservoir WY-8
Paint Canyon ID-8
Paint Canyon—valley ID-8
Paint Canyon Tank—reservoir TX-5
Paint Cliff—cliff KY-4
**Paint Cliff**—pop pl KY-4
Paint Cliff Ch—church KY-4
Paint Creek AL-4
Paint Creek TX-5
Paint Creek—locale PA-2
Paint Creek—locale TX-5
**Paint Creek**—pop pl MI-6
Paint Creek—stream AL-4
Paint Creek—stream CO-8
Paint Creek—stream ID-8
Paint Creek—stream IL-6
Paint Creek—stream IN-6
Paint Creek—stream (2) IA-7
Paint Creek—stream (2) KS-7
Paint Creek—stream (3) KY-4
Paint Creek—stream (3) MI-6
Paint Creek—stream (2) MT-8
Paint Creek—stream (4) OH-6
Paint Creek—stream OR-9
Paint Creek—stream (2) PA-2
Paint Creek—stream TN-4
Paint Creek—stream (7) TX-5
Paint Creek—stream VA-3
Paint Creek—stream WV-2
Paint Creek—stream WI-6
Paint Creek—stream WY-8
Paint Creek Archeol Site—hist pl KS-7
Paint Creek Campground—locale TN-4
Paint Creek (CCD)—cens area KY-4
Paint Creek Cem—cemetery MI-6
Paint Creek Cem—cemetery TX-5
Paint Creek Ch—church IN-6
Paint Creek Ch—church KS-7
Paint Creek Ch—church KY-4
Paint Creek Corge (historical)—locale TN-4
Paint Creek Country Club—other MI-6
Paint Creek Drain—stream MI-6
Paint Creek Junction—uninc pl WV-2
Paint Creek Lake—reservoir OH-6
Paint Creek Ranch—locale TX-5
Paint Creek Rec Area—park TN-4
Paint Creek Rsvr OH-6
Paint Creek Sch—school WY-8
Paint Creek Township—fmr MCD IA-7
Paint Creek Trail—trail MT-8
Paint Creek Trail—trail TN-4
Paint Creek Windmill—locale TX-5
Paint Crossing—locale TX-5
Paint Dam (abandoned)—locale MI-6
Painted Bluff—cliff AL-4
Painted Bluff—cliff TX-5
Painted Bluffs—summit AZ-5
Painted Canyon MT-8
Painted Canyon NV-8
Painted Canyon—valley CA-9
Painted Canyon—valley CO-8
Painted Canyon—valley MT-8
Painted Canyon—valley ND-7
Painted Canyon—valley OR-9
Painted Canyon—valley TX-5
Painted Canyon Overlook—locale ND-7
Painted Canyon Rsvr—reservoir OR-9
Painted Cave—cave CA-9
Painted Cave—hist pl CA-9
Painted Cave Ranch—locale AZ-5
Painted Cliffs—cliff AZ-5
Painted Desert—plain AZ-5
Painted Desert Inn—hist pl (2) AZ-5
Painted Desert Interchange—crossing AZ-5
Painted Desert Petroglyphs and Ruins Archeol District—hist pl AZ-5
Painted Desert Vista Picnic Area—park AZ-5
Painted Dunes—locale CA-9
Painted Gorge—valley CA-9
Painted Grotto—hist pl NM-5
Painted Hill—summit CA-9
Painted Hill—summit (2) MT-8
Painted Hill Quarry—mine CA-9
Painted Hill RV Park—park UT-8
Painted Hills—summit OR-9
Painted Hills Dam—dam NM-5
Painted Hills Dam—dam OR-9
Painted Hills Lake—reservoir IN-6
Painted Hills Lake Dam—dam IN-6
Painted Hills Mine—mine NV-8
Painted Hills Rsvr—reservoir OR-9
Painted Hills State Park—park OR-9
Painted Hill Trail—trail CA-9
Painted Kiva House—locale CO-8
Painted Lady—summit CA-9
Painted Lake—lake MT-8
Painted Mtn—summit AK-9
Painted Mtn—summit WA-9
Painted Peak—summit AK-9
Painted Point—summit NV-8
**Painted Post**—pop pl NY-2
Painted Post Ranch—locale CO-8
Painted Potholes—basin UT-8
Painted Riffle—rapids OR-9
Painted Robe Creek—stream MT-8
Painted Robe Tunnel—tunnel MT-8
Painted Rock—island OR-9
Painted Rock—pillar (3) CA-9
Painted Rock—pillar UT-8
Painted Rock—summit (2) CA-9
Painted Rock, The—rock MT-8
Painted Rock Campground—locale CA-9
Painted Rock Canyon—valley NM-5
Painted Rock Canyon—valley UT-8
Painted Rock Creek—stream OR-9
Painted Rock Dam—dam AZ-5

**Palestine**—*pop pl* ... AR-4
**Palestine**—*pop pl* ... IL-6
**Palestine**—*pop pl* (2) ... IN-6
**Palestine**—*pop pl* (3) ... MS-4
**Palestine**—*pop pl* ... NC-3
**Palestine**—*pop pl* ... OH-6
**Palestine**—*pop pl* (2) ... TN-4
**Palestine**—*pop pl* ... TX-5
**Palestine**—*pop pl* (2) ... WV-2
Palestine, Lake—*reservoir* ... TX-5
*Palestine Baptist Church* ... MS-4
*Palestine Baptist Churh* ... TN-4
Palestine Branch—*stream* ... IN-6
Palestine Carnegie Library—*hist pl* ... TX-5
Palestine (CCD)—*cens area* ... TX-5
Palestine Cem—*cemetery* ... AL-4
Palestine Cem—*cemetery* (4) ... AR-4
Palestine Cem—*cemetery* (3) ... IN-6
Palestine Cem—*cemetery* ... KY-4
Palestine Cem—*cemetery* ... LA-4
Palestine Cem—*cemetery* (8) ... MS-4
Palestine Cem—*cemetery* ... MO-7
Palestine Cem—*cemetery* ... OH-6
Palestine Cem—*cemetery* (6) ... TN-4
*Palestine Ch* ... IN-6
Palestine Ch—*church* (6) ... AL-4
Palestine Ch—*church* (7) ... AR-4
Palestine Ch—*church* (5) ... IL-6
Palestine Ch—*church* (3) ... IN-6
Palestine Ch—*church* ... IA-7
Palestine Ch—*church* (6) ... KY-4
Palestine Ch—*church* (3) ... LA-4
Palestine Ch—*church* (22) ... MS-4
Palestine Ch—*church* ... NE-7
Palestine Ch—*church* ... NJ-2
Palestine Ch—*church* (2) ... NC-3
Palestine Ch—*church* (2) ... OH-6
Palestine Ch—*church* ... OK-5
Palestine Ch—*church* (2) ... PA-2
Palestine Ch—*church* (5) ... TN-4
Palestine Ch—*church* (3) ... TX-5
Palestine Ch—*church* (3) ... VA-3
Palestine Ch—*church* ... WV-2
Palestine Ch (historical)—*church* (3) ... MS-4
Palestine Ch (historical)—*church* (2) ... TN-4
Palestine Creek—*stream* ... IA-7
Palestine Cumberland Presbyterian Ch—*church* ... TN-4
Palestine Cumberland Presbyterian Ch (historical)—*church* ... MS-4
**Palestine (Darden)**—*pop pl* ... TX-5
Palestine (Election Precinct)—*fmr MCD* ... IL-6
Palestine Evangelical Lutheran Church—*hist pl* ... SD-7
Palestine (historical)—*locale* ... AL-4
Palestine (historical)—*locale* ... MS-4
**Palestine (historical)**—*pop pl* ... IA-7
**Palestine (historical)**—*pop pl* ... TN-4
Palestine (historical P.O.)—*locale* ... IA-7
Palestine Hollow—*valley* ... AL-4
Palestine HS—*hist pl* ... TX-5
Palestine Lake—*lake* ... FL-3
Palestine Lake—*lake* ... IN-6
Palestine Lake Dam—*dam* ... IN-6
Palestine Methodist Ch (historical)—*church* ... AL-4
*Palestine Methodist Church* ... MS-4
*Palestine Methodist Church* ... TN-4
*Palestine Missionary Baptist Church* ... MS-4
Palestine Mtn—*summit* ... TN-4
Palestine No 1 Cem—*cemetery* ... IL-6
Palestine No 2 Cem—*cemetery* ... IL-6
Palestine Post Office (historical)—*building* ... TN-4
*Palestine Primitive Baptist Church* ... MS-4
*Palestine Sch* ... MS-4
Palestine Sch—*school* ... AR-4
Palestine Sch—*school* (2) ... IL-6
Palestine Sch—*school* ... IA-7
Palestine Sch—*school* ... KY-4
Palestine Sch—*school* ... MS-4
Palestine Sch—*school* ... TX-5
Palestine Sch—*school* ... WI-6
Palestine Sch (historical)—*school* ... AL-4
Palestine Sch (historical)—*school* (4) ... MS-4
Palestine Sch (historical)—*school* ... PA-2
Palestine Sch (historical)—*school* ... TN-4
Palestine State Fish Hatchery—*other* ... WV-2
Palestine Township—*civil* ... MO-7
Palestine Township—*fmr MCD* ... IA-7
**Palestine Township**—*pop pl* ... KS-7
Palestine (Township of)—*fmr MCD* ... AR-4
**Palestine (Township of)**—*pop pl* ... IL-6
*Palestine United Methodist Church* ... MS-4
Paleta Windmill—*locale* ... TX-5
*Paletiu* ... FM-9
**Paletown**—*pop pl* ... PA-2
*Palette-Bennion Ditch* ... WY-8
Palette Ranch—*locale* ... WY-8
Palette Ranch No 1—*locale* ... WY-8
Palette Ranch No 2—*locale* ... WY-8
*Palette-Rennion Ditch* ... WY-8
*Paley Cemetery* ... AL-4
Paley Creek—*stream* ... OK-5
Paley Hill—*summit* ... AL-4
Paley Hill—*summit* ... KY-4
Paliaalii—*locale* ... HI-9
Paliais—*locale* ... FM-9
Pali Akamoa Gulch—*valley* ... HI-9
Paliakoae Gulch—*valley* ... HI-9
Paliamano—*cliff* ... HI-9
Palianihi—*cliff* ... HI-9
Palianihi Point—*cape* ... HI-9
Paliapailong—*civil* ... FM-9
*Paliapeilong* ... FM-9
Paliau—*island* ... FM-9
*Palie* ... MH-9
*Palieidsch* ... FM-9
*Palieij* ... FM-9
Pali Eleele—*summit* ... HI-9
Paliemo Valley—*valley* ... HI-9
*Palientopata* ... FM-9
Pali Golf Course—*other* ... HI-9
Palihae Gulch—*valley* ... HI-9
Pali Haukeuke—*cliff* ... HI-9
*Pali Hooukapapa* ... HI-9
Palihooukapapa—*locale* ... HI-9
Pali'i—*slope* ... MH-9
Palii Hill—*summit* ... GU-9
*Pali Kaholo* ... HI-9
*Palikalao* ... FM-9
*Palikalao River* ... FM-9
*Palikalau* ... FM-9
*Pali Kea* ... HI-9
Palikea—*summit* (5) ... HI-9
*Palikea Mtn* ... HI-9
*Palikea Peak* ... HI-9
Palikea Ridge—*ridge* ... HI-9
Palikea Stream—*stream* (2) ... HI-9
Palikea Trail—*trail* ... HI-9
Palikir—*civil* ... FM-9
Palikir, Dolen—*summit* ... FM-9
*Palikir Einfahrt* ... FM-9
*Palikir-Hafen* ... FM-9
Palikir Passage—*channel* ... FM-9
*Palikoae* ... HI-9
Pali Koae—*cape* ... HI-9
Paliku Cabin—*locale* ... HI-9
Paliku Point—*cape* ... HI-9
Palima—*civil* ... HI-9
Palima Point—*cape* ... HI-9
Palimuku—*cliff* ... HI-9
*Palington Dam* ... PA-2
**Palin (historical)**—*pop pl* ... TN-4
Palin Pond—*lake* ... ME-1
*Pali o Kaeo* ... HI-9
*Palipahn Wei* ... FM-9
Palipohn Wei—*civil* ... FM-9
*Palisada* ... NE-7
**Palisade**—*pop pl* ... CO-8
**Palisade**—*pop pl* ... MN-6
**Palisade**—*pop pl* (2) ... NE-7
**Palisade**—*pop pl* ... NV-8
**Palisade**—*pop pl* ... NJ-2
Palisade, The—*cliff* ... CO-8
Palisade Basin—*basin* ... CA-9
Palisade Boat Club—*other* ... NY-2
Palisade Butte—*summit* ... MT-8
Palisade Campground—*locale* ... CO-8
Palisade Campground—*locale* ... UT-8
Palisade Campground—*park* ... UT-8
Palisade Canyon—*valley* ... AZ-5
Palisade Canyon—*valley* ... NV-8
Palisade Cem—*cemetery* ... NE-7
Palisade Cliffs—*cliff* ... AK-9
Palisade Creek—*stream* ... AZ-5
Palisade Creek—*stream* (2) ... CA-9
Palisade Creek—*stream* ... MN-6
Palisade Creek—*stream* (3) ... MT-8
Palisade Crest—*summit* ... CA-9
Palisade Falls Picnic Area—*locale* ... MT-8
Palisade Glacier—*glacier* ... CA-9
Palisade Head—*summit* ... MN-6
Palisade (historical)—*locale* ... SD-7
Palisade Island—*island* ... AK-9
*Palisadel* ... MN-6
Palisade Lagoon—*bay* ... AK-9
Palisade Lake—*lake* ... CA-9
Palisade Lake—*lake* ... MT-8
Palisade Lake—*lake* ... UT-8
Palisade Lake—*reservoir* ... UT-8
Palisade Lake Dam—*dam* ... UT-8
*Palisade Lakes* ... ID-8
Palisade Lakes—*lake* ... CA-9
Palisade Lakes—*lake* ... CO-8
Palisade Meadows—*flat* ... CO-8
Palisade Mesa—*summit* ... NV-8
Palisade Mine—*mine* ... CA-9
Palisade Mine—*mine* ... ID-8
Palisade Mines—*mine* ... CO-8
Palisade Mtn—*summit* ... CO-8
Palisade Mtn—*summit* (2) ... MT-8
*Palisade Park* ... NJ-2
*Palisade Peak* ... ID-8
Palisade Peak—*summit* ... AK-9
Palisade Point—*cape* ... AK-9
Palisade Point—*cape* ... OR-9
Palisade Point—*cliff* ... CO-8
Palisade Ranger Station—*locale* ... AZ-5
Palisade Rock—*pillar* ... AZ-5
Palisade Rocks—*summit* ... OR-9
Palisade Rsvr No. 1—*reservoir* ... CO-8
Palisade Rsvr No. 3—*reservoir* ... CO-8
*Palisades* ... CO-8
Palisades—*cliff* ... NY-2
Palisades—*cliff* (2) ... OR-9
Palisades—*cliff* ... TN-4
Palisades—*cliff* ... WA-9
Palisades—*locale* ... IL-6
Palisades—*locale* ... KY-4
Palisades—*locale* ... WA-9
**Palisades**—*pop pl* ... ID-8
**Palisades**—*pop pl* ... MO-7
**Palisades**—*pop pl* ... NY-2
Palisades—*post sta* ... DC-2
*Palisades, The* ... UT-8
Palisades, The—*cliff* ... AK-9
Palisades, The—*cliff* ... MI-6
Palisades, The—*cliff* ... NJ-2
Palisades, The—*cliff* ... OR-9
Palisades, The—*cliff* ... SD-7
Palisades, The—*cliff* (2) ... TX-5
Palisades, The—*cliff* ... VT-1
Palisades, The—*cliff* ... WA-9
Palisades, The—*cliff* (2) ... WY-8
**Palisades, The**—*pop pl* ... DC-2
Palisades, The—*range* ... CA-9
Palisades, The—*range* ... WY-8
Palisades, The—*summit* ... WA-9
Palisades Bench—*beach* ... ID-8
Palisades Cem—*cemetery* ... NJ-2
Palisades Ch—*church* ... MN-6
Palisades Corner—*locale* ... ID-8
Palisades Country Club—*other* ... IL-6
Palisades Creek—*stream* ... AZ-5
Palisades Creek—*stream* ... ID-8
Palisades Creek Campground—*locale* ... ID-8
Palisades Dam—*dam* ... ID-8
**Palisades del Rey**—*pop pl* ... CA-9
Palisades Ditch—*canal* ... CO-8
Palisades Falls—*falls* ... MT-8
Palisades General Hospital—*airport* ... NJ-2
*Palisades Head* ... MN-6
Palisades Interstate Park—*hist pl* ... NJ-2
Palisades Interstate Park—*hist pl* ... NY-2
Palisades Interstate Park—*park* ... NY-2
Palisades Junior-Senior HS—*school* ... PA-2
Palisades-Kepler State Park—*park* ... IA-7
*Palisades Memorial Park* ... UT-8
Palisades Nuclear Power Plant—*facility* ... MI-6
*Palisades of Fish Creek Canyon* ... AZ-5
Palisades of the Desert—*cliff* ... AZ-5
Palisades Park—*park* (2) ... CA-9
Palisades Park—*park* ... MD-2
**Palisades Park**—*pop pl* ... MI-6
**Palisades Park**—*pop pl* ... NJ-2
Palisades Peak—*summit* ... ID-8
*Palisades Point* ... OR-9
Palisades Point—*cape* ... AK-9
Palisades Point—*cape* ... CA-9
Palisade Spring—*spring* ... AZ-5
Palisades Rec Area—*park* ... SD-7
Palisades Rsvr—*reservoir* ... CA-9
Palisades Rsvr—*reservoir* ... ID-8
Palisades Rsvr—*reservoir* ... WY-8
*Palisades Sch* ... PA-2
Palisades Sch—*school* (2) ... CA-9
Palisades Sch—*school* ... HI-9
Palisades Sch—*school* ... IL-6
Palisades Sch—*school* ... OR-9
Palisades State Park—*park* ... NJ-2
Palisades State Park—*park* ... NY-2
**Palisades (subdivision)**—*pop pl* ... TN-4
Palisade State Boating Park—*park* ... UT-8
*Palisade State Park* ... UT-8
Palisades Viewpoint—*locale* ... WA-9
**Palisade Township**—*pop pl* ... SD-7
Palisado Ave Hist Dist—*hist pl* ... CT-1
Palisado Cem—*cemetery* ... CT-1
Pali Spring—*spring* ... HI-9
**Palito Blanco**—*pop pl* ... TX-5
Palito Blanco Arroyo—*valley* ... TX-5
Palito Blanco Windmill—*locale* ... TX-5
Paliuli—*cape* ... HI-9
Paliuli—*cliff* ... HI-9
*Palix River* ... WA-9
Palix River—*stream* ... WA-9
Paliza Campground—*canal* ... NM-5
Paliza Canyon—*valley* ... NM-5
Palk Hollow—*valley* ... OH-6
Palko Cem—*cemetery* ... TN-4
Pallardy Lake—*lake* ... MO-7
Pallas—*locale* ... PA-2
**Pallas**—*pop pl* ... UT-8
Pallay Bldg—*hist pl* ... OR-9
Pallbearers Cem—*cemetery* ... GA-3
*Palledu* ... FM-9
Pallen Lake—*lake* ... WI-6
Palleocus Cave—*cave* ... AL-4
Pallesen Ranch—*locale* ... WY-8
Pallett Creek—*stream* ... CA-9
Pallette Cem—*cemetery* ... TN-4
Pallette Lake—*lake* ... WI-6
Pallett Mtn—*summit* ... CA-9
**Pallett (Saint Andrews Priory)**—*pop pl* ... CA-9
Pallisades, The—*cliff* ... WA-9
*Pallmall* ... TN-4
**Pall Mall**—*pop pl* ... TN-4
Pall Mall Playground—*park* ... MD-2
*Pallmall Post Office* ... TN-4
Pall Mall Post Office—*building* ... TN-4
*Pallopels Island* ... NY-2
Pallot Park—*park* ... FL-3
Pallotti Coll—*school* ... MD-2
Pallotti HS—*school* ... MD-2
**Palls**—*pop pl* ... VA-3
Pallsades, The—*ridge* ... CA-9
Palluche Canyon—*valley* ... NM-5
*Palluche Draw* ... NM-5
*Palluche Wash* ... NM-5
Palluche Wash—*stream* ... NM-5
**Palm**—*pop pl* ... FL-3
**Palm**—*pop pl* ... PA-2
Palm, Lake—*lake* ... FL-3
Palma—*locale* ... NM-5
Palma—*locale* ... PA-2
**Palma**—*pop pl* ... KY-4
Palma Banco Number 25—*levee* ... TX-5
Palma Bay—*bay* ... AK-9
Palma Canyon—*valley* ... TX-5
**Palma Ceia**—*pop pl* ... FL-3
Palma Ceia Acad—*school* ... FL-3
Palma Ceia Christian Ch—*church* ... FL-3
Palma Ceia Sch—*school* ... CA-9
Palma Ceia Spring—*spring* ... FL-3
Palma Ceia United Methodist Day Sch—*school* ... FL-3
Palma Ciea Playground—*park* ... FL-3
**Palm Acres**—*pop pl* ... FL-3
Palma Escrita (Barrio)—*fmr MCD* ... PR-3
Palmaghatt Kill—*stream* ... NY-2
Palma Hill—*summit* ... NM-5
Palm Aire—*post sta* ... FL-3
Palm Aire Country Club—*locale* ... FL-3
Palm-Aire Shop Ctr—*locale* ... FL-3
Palma Lane Park—*park* ... IL-6
Palma Mesa—*summit* ... NM-5
Palma Park—*park* ... AZ-5
Palmar (Barrio)—*fmr MCD* ... PR-3
Palmarejo—*CDP* ... PR-3
**Palmarejo**—*pop pl* (4) ... PR-3
Palmarejo (Barrio)—*fmr MCD* (3) ... PR-3
**Palmaritas (subdivision)**—*pop pl* (2) ... AZ-5
Palmarito (Barrio)—*fmr MCD* ... PR-3
*Palmas* ... CA-9
Palmas—*CDP* (2) ... PR-3
Palmas, Loma de las—*summit* ... TX-5
Palmas Altas (Barrio)—*fmr MCD* ... PR-3
Palmas (Barrio)—*fmr MCD* (4) ... PR-3
Palmas Canyon—*valley* ... TX-5
Palmas del Sol (trailer park)—*locale* ... AZ-5
**Palmas del Sol (trailer park)**—*pop pl* ... AZ-5
**Palma Sola**—*pop pl* ... FL-3
**Palma Sola**—*pop pl* ... PR-3
Palma Sola Bay—*bay* ... FL-3
Palma Sola Ch—*church* ... FL-3
Palma Sola Creek—*stream* ... FL-3
Palma Sola Elem Sch—*school* ... FL-3
**Palma Sola Park**—*pop pl* ... FL-3
*Palma Sola Point* ... FL-3
*Palma Sola Sound* ... FL-3
**Palmas Royale (subdivision)**—*pop pl* (2) ... AZ-5
Palmas Well—*well* ... TX-5
Palma Tank—*reservoir* ... TX-5
Palmateer Creek—*stream* ... OR-9
Palmateer Meadows—*flat* ... OR-9
Palmatier Hollow—*valley* ... PA-2
Palmatier Trail—*trail* ... PA-2
Palmatree Island—*island* ... MS-4
Palm Ave Exceptional Child Center—*school* ... FL-3
Palm Ave Sch—*school* ... CA-9
Palm Ave Sch—*school* ... OH-6
Palma Windmill—*locale* ... TX-5
*Palm Bay* ... FL-3
Palm Bay—*bay* (2) ... FL-3
**Palm Bay**—*pop pl* ... FL-3
Palm Bay (CCD)—*cens area* ... FL-3
Palm Bay Elem Sch—*school* ... FL-3
Palm Bay HS—*school* ... FL-3
Palm Bay Plaza (Shop Ctr)—*locale* ... FL-3
Palm Bay Shop Ctr—*locale* ... FL-3
*Palm Beach* ... TX-5
Palm Beach—*beach* ... CA-9
**Palm Beach**—*pop pl* ... CA-9
**Palm Beach**—*pop pl* ... FL-3
**Palm Beach**—*pop pl* ... IL-6
Palm Beach Atlantic Coll—*school* ... FL-3
Palm Beach Atlantic College, E C Blomeyer Library—*building* ... FL-3
Palm Beach Christian Acad—*school* ... FL-3
Palm Beach Christian Schools—*school* ... FL-3
**Palm Beach County**—*pop pl* ... FL-3
Palm Beach County Public Library, Del-Trail Branch—*building* ... FL-3
Palm Beach County Public Library, Mid-County Branch—*building* ... FL-3
Palm Beach County Public Library, North-County Branch—*building* ... FL-3
Palm Beach County Public Library, Okeechobee Blvd Branch—*building* ... FL-3
Palm Beach County Public Library, Palm Beach Gardens Branch—*building* ... FL-3
Palm Beach Daily News Bldg—*hist pl* ... FL-3
Palm Beach Day Sch—*school* ... FL-3
**Palm Beach Farms**—*pop pl* ... FL-3
**Palm Beach Gardens**—*pop pl* ... FL-3
Palm Beach Gardens Community Hosp—*hospital* ... FL-3
Palm Beach Gardens Elem Sch—*school* ... FL-3
Palm Beach Gardens HS—*school* ... FL-3
Palm Beach International Airp—*airport* ... FL-3
**Palm Beach Isles (subdivision)**—*pop pl* ... FL-3
Palm Beach Junior Coll—*school* ... FL-3
Palm Beach Lakes—*uninc pl* ... FL-3
Palm Beach Mall—*locale* ... FL-3
Palm Beach Market Place (Shop Ctr)—*locale* ... FL-3
Palm Beach Memorial Park—*cemetery* ... FL-3
Palm Beach Park—*park* ... CA-9
Palm Beach Pines State Rec Area—*park* ... FL-3
Palm Beach Public Sch—*school* ... FL-3
Palm Beach Raceway—*locale* ... FL-3
**Palm Beach Shores**—*pop pl* ... FL-3
Palm Beach Winter Club—*hist pl* ... FL-3
Palm Bowl Grove—*woods* ... CA-9
Palm Branch—*stream* ... TN-4
Palmbrook Country Club Golf Course—*other* ... AZ-5
Palmburg Sch Number 1—*school* ... ND-7
*Palm Canyon* ... CA-9
Palm Canyon—*valley* ... AZ-5
Palm Canyon—*valley* ... CA-9
Palm Canyon Wash—*stream* (2) ... CA-9
*Palm Cem* ... FL-3
Palm Cem—*cemetery* ... FL-3
Palm Cem—*cemetery* ... MN-6
Palm Cem—*cemetery* ... TX-5
Palm Chapel—*church* ... FL-3
Palm Circle Hist Dist—*hist pl* ... HI-9
**Palm City**—*pop pl* (2) ... CA-9
**Palm City**—*pop pl* ... FL-3
Palm City Elem Sch—*school* ... FL-3
Palm Coast—*CDP* ... FL-3
Palm Coast Plaza (Shop Ctr)—*locale* ... FL-3
Palm Cottage—*hist pl* ... FL-3
Palm Cove Beach Sch—*school* ... FL-3
Palm Creek—*stream* ... GA-3
Palm Crest Sch—*school* ... CA-9
Palmcroft Sch—*school* ... AZ-5
Palmdale—*locale* ... MN-6
**Palmdale**—*pop pl* ... CA-9
**Palmdale**—*pop pl* ... FL-3
**Palmdale**—*pop pl* ... PA-2
Palmdale, Lake—*reservoir* ... CA-9
Palmdale Cem—*cemetery* ... CA-9
Palmdale Ditch—*canal* ... CA-9
Palmdale East—*CDP* ... CA-9
Palmdale HS—*school* ... CA-9
*Palmdale Lake* ... CA-9
Palmdale Lookout Tower (fire tower)—*tower* ... FL-3
Palmdale Production Flight/Test Installation—*airport* ... CA-9
*Palmdale Reservoir* ... CA-9
Palmdale Sch—*school* ... AZ-5
Palmdale Sch—*school* ... CA-9
Palm Day Sch—*school* ... FL-3
**Palm Desert**—*pop pl* ... CA-9
Palm Drain—*canal* ... CA-9
Palm Drive Shopping Plaza—*locale* ... FL-3
*Palmer* ... AL-4
*Palmer* ... MS-4
*Palmer* ... SD-7
Palmer—*CDP* ... PR-3
Palmer—*locale* ... IA-7
Palmer—*locale* ... KY-4
Palmer—*locale* ... MN-6
Palmer—*locale* ... WA-9
Palmer—*locale* ... WV-2
**Palmer**—*pop pl* ... AK-9
**Palmer**—*pop pl* (2) ... AR-4
**Palmer**—*pop pl* ... IL-6
**Palmer**—*pop pl* ... IN-6
**Palmer**—*pop pl* ... IA-7
**Palmer**—*pop pl* ... KS-7
**Palmer**—*pop pl* ... MA-1
**Palmer**—*pop pl* ... MI-6
**Palmer**—*pop pl* ... MO-7
**Palmer**—*pop pl* ... NE-7
**Palmer**—*pop pl* ... NY-2
**Palmer**—*pop pl* (2) ... PA-2
**Palmer**—*pop pl* ... TN-4
**Palmer**—*pop pl* ... TX-5
**Palmer**—*pop pl* ... VA-3
Palmer—*post sta* ... PA-2
Palmer, Albert, House—*hist pl* ... MI-6
Palmer, Amos, House—*hist pl* ... PA-2
Palmer, B. J., House—*hist pl* ... IA-7
Palmer, Charles, House—*hist pl* ... MI-6
Palmer, Col. Gustavius A., House—*hist pl* ... IL-6
Palmer, Edward Albert, Memorial Chapel and Autry House—*hist pl* ... TX-5
Palmer, Gen. Joseph B., House—*hist pl* ... TN-4
Palmer, Hezekiah, House—*hist pl* ... CT-1
Palmer, Isaac, House—*hist pl* ... CT-1
Palmer, John, House—*hist pl* ... OR-9
Palmer, John Denham, House—*hist pl* ... FL-3
Palmer, Judge Augustus C., House—*hist pl* ... CA-9
Palmer, Judge Peter L. House—*hist pl* ... CO-8
Palmer, Lake—*lake* ... FL-3
Palmer, Minnie Hill, House—*hist pl* ... CA-9
Palmer, Mount—*summit* ... AK-9
Palmer, Mount—*summit* ... CA-9
Palmer, O. K., House—*hist pl* ... WA-9
Palmer, Thomas H., House—*hist pl* ... VT-1
Palmer, W. E., House—*hist pl* ... TN-4
Palmer Acad at Bardmoor—*school* ... FL-3
Palmer Airp—*airport* ... MO-7
Palmer Bay—*bay* ... WI-6
*Palmer Bayou* ... MI-6
Palmer Bayou—*stream* ... AR-4
Palmer Bayou—*stream* ... MI-6
Palmer Bayou—*stream* ... TX-5
Palmer Branch—*stream* ... AL-4
Palmer Branch—*stream* ... FL-3
Palmer Branch—*stream* ... GA-3
Palmer Branch—*stream* (2) ... NC-3
Palmer Branch—*stream* ... SC-3
Palmer Branch—*stream* (4) ... TN-4
Palmer Branch—*stream* ... TX-5
Palmer Branch Drain—*canal* ... MI-6
*Palmer Brook* ... MA-1
Palmer Brook—*stream* ... CT-1
Palmer Brook—*stream* (4) ... ME-1
Palmer Brook—*stream* (2) ... MA-1
Palmer Brook—*stream* (2) ... NH-1
Palmer Brook—*stream* (2) ... NY-2
Palmer Brook Dam—*dam* ... MA-1
Palmer Brook Rsvr—*reservoir* ... MA-1
Palmer Brook Swamp—*swamp* ... NY-2
Palmer Brother's Octagons—*hist pl* ... WI-6
Palmer Burial Ground—*cemetery* ... PA-2
Palmer Butte—*summit* ... ID-8
Palmer Butte—*summit* ... OR-9
Palmer Camp Branch—*stream* ... NC-3
*Palmer Canyon* ... CO-8
Palmer Canyon—*valley* (4) ... CA-9
Palmer Canyon—*valley* ... ID-8
Palmer Canyon—*valley* ... NM-5
Palmer Canyon—*valley* ... UT-8
Palmer Canyon—*valley* ... WA-9
Palmer Canyon—*valley* (2) ... WY-8
Palmer Cave—*cave* ... CA-9
Palmer (CCD)—*cens area* ... TN-4
*Palmer Cem* ... AL-4
Palmer Cem—*cemetery* (4) ... AL-4
Palmer Cem—*cemetery* ... GA-3
Palmer Cem—*cemetery* (3) ... IL-6
Palmer Cem—*cemetery* ... IA-7
Palmer Cem—*cemetery* ... KY-4
Palmer Cem—*cemetery* ... ME-1
Palmer Cem—*cemetery* ... MA-1
Palmer Cem—*cemetery* ... MI-6
Palmer Cem—*cemetery* (3) ... MS-4
Palmer Cem—*cemetery* (4) ... MO-7
Palmer Cem—*cemetery* (3) ... NY-2
Palmer Cem—*cemetery* (3) ... NC-3
Palmer Cem—*cemetery* (3) ... OH-6
Palmer Cem—*cemetery* (2) ... OK-5
Palmer Cem—*cemetery* ... SC-3
Palmer Cem—*cemetery* (3) ... TN-4
Palmer Cem—*cemetery* ... TX-5
Palmer Cem—*cemetery* ... WV-2
Palmer (census name for Palmer Center)—*CDP* ... MA-1
**Palmer Center**—*pop pl* ... MA-1
Palmer Center Cem—*cemetery* ... MA-1
Palmer Center (census name Palmer)—*other* ... MA-1
*Palmer Centre* ... MA-1
Palmer Ch—*church* ... AL-4
Palmer Ch—*church* ... LA-4
Palmer Ch—*church* ... MS-4
Palmer Ch—*church* ... NC-3
Palmer Ch—*church* ... OH-6
Palmer Ch—*church* ... VA-3
Palmer Chapel—*church* ... NC-3
Palmer Chapel Sch—*school* ... TN-4
Palmer City Cem—*cemetery* ... TN-4
Palmer Coll—*school* ... SC-3
Palmer Corner—*locale* ... VT-1
Palmer Cove—*bay* ... CT-1
Palmer Cove—*bay* ... VA-3
Palmer Cove—*cove* ... MA-1
*Palmer Creek* ... CO-8
**Palmer Creek**—*pop pl* ... CA-9
Palmer Creek—*stream* (4) ... AK-9
Palmer Creek—*stream* (5) ... CA-9
Palmer Creek—*stream* ... GA-3
Palmer Creek—*stream* (2) ... ID-8
Palmer Creek—*stream* ... IL-6
Palmer Creek—*stream* ... IA-7
Palmer Creek—*stream* ... KS-7
Palmer Creek—*stream* (2) ... MI-6
Palmer Creek—*stream* ... MN-6
Palmer Creek—*stream* ... MS-4
Palmer Creek—*stream* (2) ... MO-7
Palmer Creek—*stream* ... MT-8
Palmer Creek—*stream* ... NE-7
Palmer Creek—*stream* (2) ... NY-2
Palmer Creek—*stream* ... NC-3
Palmer Creek—*stream* (6) ... OR-9
Palmer Creek—*stream* (2) ... SD-7
Palmer Creek—*stream* ... TN-4
Palmer Creek—*stream* ... TX-5
Palmer Creek—*stream* (3) ... WA-9
Palmer Creek—*stream* ... WI-6
Palmer Creek—*stream* ... WY-8
Palmer Creek Campground—*park* ... MS-4
Palmer Creek Trail—*trail* ... NC-3
Palmer Crossroads—*locale* ... VA-3
Palmerdale (CCD)—*cens area* ... AL-4
Palmerdale Ch—*church* ... AL-4
Palmerdale Division—*civil* ... AL-4
*Palmerdale Elementary School* ... AL-4
**Palmerdale (Palmers)**—*pop pl* ... AL-4
**Palmerdale (Palmers Station)**—*pop pl* ... AL-4
Palmerdale Sch—*school* ... AL-4
Palmer Dam—*dam* ... OR-9
Palmer Dam—*dam* ... PA-2
Palmer Deadwater—*swamp* ... ME-1
*Palmer Depot* ... MA-1
Palmer Depot—*hist pl* ... AK-9
Palmer Ditch—*canal* ... IN-6
Palmer Ditch—*canal* ... MT-8
Palmer Division—*civil* ... TN-4
Palmer Drain—*canal* ... CA-9
Palmer Draw—*valley* ... SD-7
Palmer Draw—*valley* (2) ... WY-8
Palmer Elem Sch—*school* ... IN-6
Palmer Elem Sch—*school* ... TN-4
Palmer Field—*park* ... CT-1
*Palmer Fire Dist Number 1 Upper Dam* ... MA-1
Palmer Fire Sch—*school* ... NC-3
Palmer Fire Tower—*tower* ... TN-4
Palmer Flats—*flat* ... CA-9
Palmer Flats—*flat* ... MT-8
Palmer Ford Bridge—*bridge* ... NC-3
Palmer Glacier—*glacier* ... OR-9
Palmer Grove Ch—*church* ... GA-3
Palmer Gulch—*valley* ... CA-9
Palmer Gulch—*valley* (5) ... CO-8
Palmer Gulch—*valley* ... WA-9
Palmer Hall—*hist pl* ... CO-8
**Palmer Heights**—*pop pl* ... PA-2
Palmer Hill—*summit* (2) ... ME-1
Palmer Hill—*summit* ... MA-1
Palmer Hill—*summit* ... NH-1
Palmer Hill—*summit* (4) ... NY-2
**Palmer (historical)**—*pop pl* (2) ... OR-9
*Palmer Hollow* ... TN-4
Palmer Hollow—*valley* (2) ... AR-4
Palmer Hollow—*valley* ... NY-2
Palmer Hollow—*valley* (2) ... TN-4
Palmer Home—*hist pl* ... DE-2
Palmer House—*hist pl* ... AR-4
Palmer House—*hist pl* ... FL-3
Palmer House—*hist pl* ... OH-6
Palmer House—*hist pl* ... OR-9
Palmer House—*locale* ... MD-2
Palmer House Hotel—*hist pl* ... MN-6
Palmer HS—*school* ... CO-8
Palmer HS—*school* ... MA-1
Palmer Institute—*school* ... MI-6
Palmer Island—*island* ... ME-1
Palmer Island—*island* ... MA-1
Palmer Island—*island* ... NC-3
Palmer Island Light Station—*hist pl* ... MA-1
Palmerita Ranch—*locale* ... AZ-5
Palmerito, Lake—*lake* ... FL-3
*Palmer Junction* ... OR-9
Palmer Junction—*locale* ... OR-9
Palmer Junction—*locale* ... WA-9
Palmer Junction Sch—*school* ... OR-9
Palmer Junior Coll—*school* ... IA-7
Palmer Lake—*lake* ... AR-4
Palmer Lake—*lake* ... CO-8
Palmer Lake—*lake* ... FL-3
Palmer Lake—*lake* ... LA-4
Palmer Lake—*lake* (7) ... MI-6
Palmer Lake—*lake* (2) ... MN-6
Palmer Lake—*lake* (2) ... NE-7
Palmer Lake—*lake* ... NJ-2
Palmer Lake—*lake* (2) ... NY-2
Palmer Lake—*lake* ... OR-9
Palmer Lake—*lake* ... SC-3
Palmer Lake—*lake* (4) ... TX-5
Palmer Lake—*lake* (3) ... WA-9
Palmer Lake—*lake* (2) ... WI-6
Palmer Lake—*lake* ... WY-8
**Palmer Lake**—*pop pl* (2) ... CO-8
Palmer Lake—*reservoir* ... CO-8
Palmer Lake Creek—*stream* ... NY-2
Palmer Lake Park—*park* ... MN-6
Palmer Lake Sch—*school* ... MN-6
Palmer Lake Trail—*trail* ... WY-8
Palmer Landing—*locale* ... LA-4
Palmer Lateral—*canal* ... CA-9
Palmer Lateral—*canal* ... NM-5
Palmer Ledge—*bench* ... NY-2
Palmer Ledge—*rock* ... MA-1
Palmer-Marsh House—*hist pl* ... NC-3
Palmer Meadow—*swamp* ... ME-1
Palmer Memorial Center for Crippled Children—*hospital* ... TN-4
Palmer Memorial Ch—*church* ... KY-4
Palmer Memorial Institute Hist Dist—*hist pl* ... NC-3
Palmer Mesa—*summit* ... CO-8
Palmer Mill Brook—*stream* ... MA-1
*Palmer Mine* ... PA-2
Palmer Mine—*mine* ... AZ-5
Palmer Mine—*mine* ... MN-6
Palmer Mine—*mine* ... TN-4
*Palmer Missionary Baptist Church* ... MS-4
Palmer Monroe Park—*park* ... FL-3
Palmer Mountain Tunnel—*tunnel* ... WA-9
*Palmer Mtn* ... CA-9
Palmer Mtn—*summit* ... CA-9
Palmer Mtn—*summit* ... ME-1
Palmer Mtn—*summit* ... MT-8
Palmer Mtn—*summit* ... NC-3
Palmer Mtn—*summit* ... OH-6
Palmer Mtn—*summit* ... OR-9
Palmer Mtn—*summit* (2) ... WA-9
Palmer-Northrup House—*hist pl* ... RI-1
Palmer Park—*locale* ... PA-2
Palmer Park—*park* ... AZ-5
Palmer Park—*park* ... CA-9
Palmer Park—*park* ... CO-8
Palmer Park—*park* ... IL-6
Palmer Park—*park* ... LA-4
Palmer Park—*park* (3) ... MI-6
Palmer Park—*park* ... PA-2
Palmer Park—*park* ... WI-6
**Palmer Park**—*pop pl* ... DE-2
**Palmer Park**—*pop pl* ... MD-2
Palmer Park Apartment Bldg Hist Dist—*hist pl* ... MI-6
Palmer Park Mall—*locale* ... PA-2
Palmer Park Sch—*school* ... MD-2
Palmer Peak—*summit* ... CO-8
Palmer Peak—*summit* (2) ... OR-9
Palmer Peak—*summit* ... WY-8
Palmer Pearson Number 1 Dam—*dam* ... SD-7

Palmer Pearson Number 2 Dam—*dam* SD-7
Palmer-Perkins House—*hist pl* FL-3
Palmer-Perkins House (Boundary Increase)—*hist pl* FL-3
Palmer Point—*cape* MA-1
Palmer Point—*cape* VA-3
Palmer Point Marina—*other* VA-3
Palmer Pond—*lake* (2) CT-1
Palmer Pond—*lake* ME-1
Palmer Pond—*lake* (2) MA-1
Palmer Pond—*lake* NH-1
Palmer Pond—*lake* (2) NY-2
Palmer Pond—*lake* WA-9
Palmer Pond—*reservoir* PA-2
Palmer Ponds Dam—*dam* MS-4
Palmer Post Office—*building* TN-4
Palmer Post Office (historical)—*building* MS-4
Palmer Pumping Station—*other* PA-2
Palmer Ranch—*locale* AZ-5
Palmer Ranch—*locale* CO-8
Palmer Ranch—*locale* MT-8
Palmer Ranch—*locale* NE-7
Palmer Ranch—*locale* NV-8
Palmer Ranch—*locale* TX-5
Palmer Ranch—*locale* UT-8
Palmer Ranch—*locale* WY-8
Palmer Reservoir Upper Dam—*dam* MA-1
Palmer Ridge—*ridge* CA-9
Palmer Ridge—*ridge* NY-2
Palmer Ridge—*ridge* WA-9
*Palmer River* MA-1
*Palmer River* RI-1
Palmer River—*stream* MA-1
Palmer River—*stream* RI-1
Palmer River Cem—*cemetery* MA-1
Palmer River Sch—*school* MA-1
Palmer (RR name for Palmers Crossing)—*other* MS-4
Palmer RR Station—*locale* FL-3
*Palmer Rsvr* OR-9
Palmer Rsvr—*reservoir* CO-8
Palmer Rsvr—*reservoir* MA-1
Palmer Rsvr—*reservoir* (2) OR-9
Palmer Rsvr—*reservoir* WY-8
Palmer Run—*stream* PA-2
*Palmers* AL-4
Palmers—*locale* MD-2
Palmers—*locale* MN-6
**Palmers**—*pop pl* PA-2
**Palmers**—*pop pl* WA-9
*Palmers Beach* MA-1
Palmers Branch—*stream* LA-4
*Palmers Brook* MA-1
Palmers Cabin—*locale* NH-1
Palmers Cem—*cemetery* AL-4
Palmer Sch—*school* AL-4
Palmer Sch—*school* CO-8
Palmer Sch—*school* FL-3
Palmer Sch—*school* (4) IL-6
Palmer Sch—*school* (2) IA-7
Palmer Sch—*school* LA-4
Palmer Sch—*school* ME-1
Palmer Sch—*school* MA-1
Palmer Sch—*school* (5) MI-6
Palmer Sch—*school* MS-4
Palmer Sch—*school* NY-2
Palmer Sch—*school* ND-7
Palmer Sch—*school* PA-2
Palmer Sch—*school* (2) SD-7
Palmer Sch—*school* (2) WI-6
Palmers Chapel—*church* NC-3
*Palmers Chapel School* TN-4
Palmer School (historical)—*locale* MO-7
**Palmers Corner**—*pop pl* MD-2
*Palmers Cove* CT-1
*Palmers Cove* MA-1
Palmers Cove—*bay* VA-3
**Palmers Crossing**—*pop pl* MS-4
Palmers Crossing (RR name Palmer)—*CDP* MS-4
Palmers Crossroads—*locale* VA-3
**Palmers Crossroads**—*pop pl* AL-4
Palmers Grove Ch—*church* NC-3
Palmers Grove Sch—*school* NC-3
Palmers Hall Sch (historical)—*school* MS-4
Palmer Shelter—*locale* TN-4
**Palmers Hill**—*pop pl* CT-1
Palmer Siding—*locale* WA-9
*Palmers Island* MA-1
Palmer Site—*hist pl* NE-7
Palmers Lake—*reservoir* AL-4
Palmers Lake—*reservoir* CO-8
Palmer Slough—*gut* AK-9
Palmer Slough—*gut* MO-7
Palmer Slough—*stream* FL-3
Palmers Mill (historical)—*locale* PA-2
*Palmers (Palmerdale)* AL-4
Palmers Point—*cape* CA-9
Palmers Point—*cape* MI-6
Palmers Point—*cape* VA-3
Palmers Pond—*lake* CT-1
Palmers Pond—*lake* (2) NY-2
Palmers Pond—*reservoir* GA-3
Palmers Prairie Ch—*church* IN-6
Palmer Spring—*spring* AZ-5
Palmer Spring—*spring* CA-9
Palmer Spring—*spring* CO-8
Palmer Spring—*spring* GA-3
Palmer Spring—*spring* ID-8
Palmer Spring—*spring* NY-2
Palmer Spring—*spring* ND-7
Palmer Spring—*spring* (3) OR-9
Palmer Spring—*spring* TX-5
Palmer Springs—*locale* VA-3
Palmer Springs—*spring* ID-8
Palmer Springs (Magisterial District)—*fmr MCD* VA-3
Palmer Square—*park* IL-6
Palmer Square—*post sta* NJ-2
*Palmer'S River* MA-1
*Palmers Springs* MS-4
Palmer Stadium—*building* NJ-2
*Palmer State Park* MA-1
*Palmer Station* MS-4
Palmer Stream—*stream* ME-1
**Palmer Subdivision**—*pop pl* SC-3
**Palmersville**—*pop pl* TN-4
Palmersville (CCD)—*cens area* TN-4
Palmersville Cem—*cemetery* TN-4
Palmersville Division—*civil* TN-4
Palmersville Elem Sch—*school* TN-4
Palmersville Missionary Baptist Ch—*church* TN-4
Palmersville Post Office—*building* TN-4
Palmersville Primitive Baptist Ch—*church* TN-4
Palmer Tank—*reservoir* (2) NM-5
Palmer Tank—*reservoir* TX-5
Palmer-Taylor Mound—*summit* FL-3
*Palmerton* PA-2
**Palmerton**—*pop pl* IN-6
**Palmerton**—*pop pl* (2) PA-2
Palmerton Area HS—*school* PA-2
Palmerton Borough—*civil* PA-2
Palmerton Ditch—*canal* CO-8
Palmerton East Station—*locale* PA-2
**Palmerton East (subdivision)**—*pop pl* PA-2
Palmerton Park—*park* OR-9
Palmerton (reduced usage)—*locale* IL-6
*Palmer Town* CT-1
**Palmertown**—*pop pl* CT-1
**Palmertown**—*pop pl* PA-2
Palmertown Cem—*cemetery* CT-1
Palmertown Mtn—*summit* NY-2
**Palmer (Town of)**—*pop pl* MA-1
Palmertown Range—*range* NY-2
**Palmer Township**—*pop pl* ND-7
Palmer Township Elem Sch—*school* PA-2
**Palmer (Township of)**—*pop pl* MN-6
**Palmer (Township of)**—*pop pl* (2) OH-6
**Palmer (Township of)**—*pop pl* PA-2
Palmer Trail—*trail* CO-8
Palmer Village-Napier Lake Airp—*airport* TN-4
Palmerville—*locale* NY-2
**Palmerville**—*pop pl* NC-3
**Palmerville**—*pop pl* SC-3
Palmer Wash—*stream* AZ-5
Palmer Way Sch—*school* CA-9
Palmer Well—*well* AZ-5
Palmer Woods Hist Dist—*hist pl* MI-6
**Palmeryville**—*pop pl* NC-3
Palmetal—*locale* TX-5
Palmeto Ch—*church* NC-3
Palmetta Lake—*lake* LA-4
Palmetto—*locale* CA-9
Palmetto—*locale* GA-3
Palmetto—*locale* LA-4
Palmetto—*locale* MD-2
Palmetto—*locale* MO-7
Palmetto—*locale* SC-3
Palmetto—*locale* TX-5
Palmetto—*locale* VA-3
**Palmetto**—*pop pl* AL-4
**Palmetto**—*pop pl* FL-3
**Palmetto**—*pop pl* GA-3
**Palmetto**—*pop pl* LA-4
**Palmetto**—*pop pl* MS-4
**Palmetto**—*pop pl* TN-4
Palmetto—*uninc pl* TX-5
Palmetto Baptist Ch—*church* FL-3
Palmetto Baptist Ch—*church* MS-4
*Palmetto Bay* SC-3
Palmetto Bayou—*gut* LA-4
Palmetto Bayou—*stream* (3) LA-4
Palmetto Bayou Oil and Gas Field—*oilfield* LA-4
**Palmetto Beach**—*pop pl* AL-4
Palmetto Bend—*bend* TX-5
Palmetto Bldg—*hist pl* SC-3
Palmetto Bluff—*cliff* FL-3
**Palmetto Bluff**—*pop pl* SC-3
Palmetto Branch—*stream* (3) FL-3
Palmetto Branch—*stream* GA-3
Palmetto Branch—*stream* (2) LA-4
Palmetto Branch—*stream* (2) NC-3
Palmetto By Pass Shop Ctr—*locale* FL-3
Palmetto (CCD)—*cens area* FL-3
Palmetto (CCD)—*cens area* GA-3
Palmetto Cem—*cemetery* GA-3
Palmetto Cem—*cemetery* LA-4
Palmetto Cem—*cemetery* (2) MS-4
Palmetto Cem—*cemetery* (2) SC-3
Palmetto Cem—*cemetery* TN-4
Palmetto Ch—*church* AR-4
Palmetto Ch—*church* MS-4
Palmetto Ch—*church* NC-3
Palmetto Ch—*church* (2) SC-3
Palmetto Christian Acad—*school* FL-3
*Palmetto City* KS-7
*Palmetto Community Ch* MS-4
Palmetto Community Covenant Preschool—*school* FL-3
Palmetto Compress and Warehouse Company Bldg—*hist pl* SC-3
Palmetto Country Club—*other* LA-4
Palmetto Court—*hist pl* CA-9
*Palmetto Creek* AL-4
*Palmetto Creek* GA-3
Palmetto Creek—*stream* AL-4
Palmetto Creek—*stream* CA-9
Palmetto Creek—*stream* FL-3
Palmetto Creek—*stream* GA-3
Palmetto Creek—*stream* LA-4
Palmetto Creek—*stream* TX-5
Palmetto Drain—*canal* CA-9
Palmetto Elem Sch—*school* (4) FL-3
Palmetto Estates—*CDP* FL-3
**Palmetto Estates (subdivision)**—*pop pl* MS-4
Palmetto Farm—*hist pl* TN-4
Palmetto Flats—*flat* MS-4
**Palmetto Fort**—*pop pl* SC-3
Palmetto General Hosp—*hospital* FL-3
Palmetto Golf Club—*other* SC-3
Palmetto Golf Course—*locale* FL-3
Palmetto Gulch—*valley* CO-8
Palmetto Gulch—*valley* WY-8
Palmetto Head—*stream* FL-3
Palmetto Hist Dist—*hist pl* FL-3
Palmetto (historical)—*locale* KS-7
Palmetto (historical)—*locale* NV-8
Palmetto Hollow—*valley* TX-5
*Palmetto Home* MS-4
Palmetto Home Landing (historical)—*locale* MS-4
Palmetto HS—*school* FL-3
Palmetto HS—*school* SC-3
*Palmetto Island* FL-3
*Palmetto Island* NC-3
Palmetto Island—*island* (2) FL-3
Palmetto Island—*island* (3) GA-3
Palmetto Island—*island* LA-4
Palmetto JHS—*school* FL-3
Palmetto Junction (railroad junction)—*locale* FL-3
*Palmetto Key* FL-3
Palmetto Lake—*lake* FL-3
Palmetto Lake—*lake* MS-4
Palmetto Lake—*reservoir* NC-3
Palmetto Lake Lower Dam—*dam* NC-3
Palmetto Lake Upper Dam—*dam* NC-3
Palmetto Landing—*locale* FL-3
Palmetto Lateral—*canal* CA-9
*Palmetto Methodist Church* MS-4
Palmetto Mine—*mine* NV-8
Palmetto Mtn—*summit* NV-8
Palmetto Mtns—*range* NV-8
Palmetto Park—*locale* TX-5
Palmetto Park—*park* GA-3
*Palmetto Peak* NV-8
Palmetto Plantation (historical)—*locale* MS-4
**Palmetto Plaza**—*pop pl* SC-3
Palmetto Plaza (Shop Ctr)—*locale* (2) FL-3
Palmetto Point—*cape* (3) FL-3
Palmetto Point—*cape* GA-3
Palmetto Point—*cape* MS-4
Palmetto Point—*cape* NC-3
Palmetto Point—*cape* SC-3
Palmetto Point—*cape* TX-5
Palmetto Pond—*lake* GA-3
Palmetto Post Office (historical)—*building* TN-4
Palmetto Race Track—*other* SC-3
Palmetto Revetment—*levee* MS-4
Palmettos Brake—*flat* LA-4
Palmetto Sch—*school* AL-4
Palmetto Sch—*school* CA-9
Palmetto Sch—*school* FL-3
Palmetto Sch—*school* LA-4
Palmetto Sch—*school* SC-3
Palmetto Sch (historical)—*school* AL-4
Palmetto Sch (historical)—*school* MS-4
Palmetto Senior HS—*school* FL-3
Palmetto Slough—*stream* LA-4
Palmetto South Ch—*church* GA-3
Palmetto State Park—*park* TX-5
Palmetto Street Baptist Ch—*church* AL-4
Palmetto Swamp—*stream* NC-3
Palmetto Swamp—*stream* SC-3
Palmetto Village (Shop Ctr)—*locale* FL-3
Palmetto Wash—*stream* NV-8
Palm Gardens Mobile Home Manor—*locale* AZ-5
Palm Glen Shop Ctr—*locale* AZ-5
*Palmgrove* IA-7
Palm Grove—*locale* CA-9
Palm Grove—*locale* IA-7
Palm Grove—*locale* TX-5
Palm Grove Ch—*church* FL-3
**Palm Grove Colony (subdivision)**—*pop pl* FL-3
Palm Grove Sch—*school* TX-5
Palm Grove Shop Ctr—*locale* AZ-5
*Palm Harbor* FL-3
**Palm Harbor**—*pop pl* FL-3
**Palm Harbor**—*pop pl* TX-5
*Palm Harbor Bay* FL-3
Palm Harbor Elem Sch—*school* FL-3
Palm Harbor Hosp—*hospital* CA-9
Palm Harbor JHS—*school* FL-3
Palm Harbor MS—*school* FL-3
Palm Harbour Montessori Sch—*school* FL-3
Palm Heights Park—*park* TX-5
Palm Hill—*summit* CA-9
Palm (historical)—*locale* SD-7
**Palmhurst**—*pop pl* TX-5
Palmich Canyon—*valley* WA-9
Palmichie Sch—*school* MS-4
*Palmick Canyon* WA-9
Palmilla Draw—*valley* NM-5
*Palm Island* FL-3
Palm Island—*island* (6) FL-3
Palmital Well North Windmill—*locale* TX-5
Palmital Well South Windmill—*locale* TX-5
Palmiter and Phelps Drain—*canal* MI-6
Palmitere Lake—*lake* MI-6
Palmito Hill—*summit* TX-5
Palmito Hill Battlefield—*locale* TX-5
Palmito Ranch—*locale* TX-5
Palmito Well—*well* TX-5
Palm JHS—*school* CA-9
Palm Johnson Shopping Plaza—*locale* FL-3
*Palm key* FL-3
Palm Key—*island* FL-3
Palm Lake—*lake* AZ-5
Palm Lake—*lake* WA-9
Palm Lake—*locale* WA-9
Palm Lake—*reservoir* GA-3
Palm Lake Christian Ch—*church* FL-3
**Palm Lake Park (subdivision)**—*pop pl* FL-3
Palm Lakes Elem Sch—*school* FL-3
Palm Lakes Golf Course—*other* CA-9
Palm Lakes Park—*park* FL-3
Palm Lakes Plaza (Shop Ctr)—*locale* FL-3
Palm Lakes Village (trailer park)—*locale* AZ-5
**Palm Lakes Village (trailer park)**—*pop pl* AZ-5
Palmland Park—*park* FL-3
Palm Lane Sch—*school* AZ-5
Palm Lane Sch—*school* CA-9
Palm Lateral—*canal* CA-9
Palm Lateral—*canal* ID-8
Palm Memorial Cem—*cemetery* FL-3
Palm Mesa—*summit* CA-9
Palmo—*locale* CA-9
**Palmo**—*pop pl* FL-3
Palm Olive Park—*park* MN-6
Palmona Park—*locale* FL-3
Pal Moore Meadow—*flat* WA-9
Palmore Branch—*stream* KY-4
Palmore Cem—*cemetery* TN-4
Palmore Hollow—*valley* TN-4
Palm Park—*park* CA-9
Palm Playground—*park* TX-5
Palm Plaza (Shop Ctr)—*locale* (7) FL-3
Palm Plaza (Shop Ctr)—*post sta* FL-3
Palm Point—*cape* AK-9
Palm Point—*cape* FL-3
Palmquist Creek—*stream* WA-9
Palmquist Sch—*school* CA-9
Palm Ranch—*locale* TX-5
Palm Ranch—*locale* (2) WY-8
*Palm River* FL-3
**Palm River**—*pop pl* FL-3
Palm River—*stream* FL-3
Palm River-Clair Mel—*CDP* FL-3
Palm River-East Tampa (CCD)—*cens area* FL-3
**Palm River Estates**—*pop pl* FL-3
Palm River Plaza (Shop Ctr)—*locale* FL-3
Palm River Sch—*school* FL-3
**Palm River Shores (subdivision)**—*pop pl* FL-3
Palms—*locale* MI-6
**Palms**—*pop pl* CA-9
Palms, Francis, Bldg and State Theater—*hist pl* MI-6
Palms, Francis, Bldg & State Theater—*hist pl* MI-6
Palms, Isle of—*island* FL-3
Palms, The—*hist pl* MI-6
Palms Book State Park—*park* MI-6
Palm Sch—*school* (3) CA-9
Palm Sch—*school* IL-6
Palm Sch—*school* TX-5
Palms Creek—*stream* MI-6
**Palm Shadows**—*pop pl* FL-3
Palm Shadows Mobile Home Park—*locale* AZ-5
**Palm Shores**—*pop pl* FL-3
Palms JHS—*school* CA-9
Palms Memorial Gardens—*cemetery* GA-3
Palms Memorial Park—*cemetery* FL-3
Palms Memorial Park Gardens—*cemetery* FL-3
Palms Mine—*mine* MI-6
Palms of Carrollwood (Shop Ctr)—*locale* FL-3
Palms of Pasadena Hosp—*hospital* FL-3
Palms Park—*park* CA-9
Palms Plaza, The (Shop Ctr)—*locale* FL-3
Palms Presbyterian Ch—*church* FL-3
Palm Spring—*spring* (2) CA-9
**Palm Spring Manor**—*pop pl* DE-2
*Palm Springs* GA-3
**Palm Springs**—*pop pl* AZ-5
**Palm Springs**—*pop pl* CA-9
**Palm Springs**—*pop pl* (2) FL-3
Palm Springs—*spring* FL-3
Palm Springs Baptist Ch—*church* FL-3
Palm Springs Baptist Sch—*school* FL-3
Palm Springs (CCD)—*cens area* CA-9
Palm Springs Ch—*church* FL-3
*Palm Springs Creek* GA-3
Palm Springs District Cem—*cemetery* CA-9
Palm Springs Drive Baptist Ch—*church* FL-3
Palm Springs Elem Sch—*school* FL-3
**Palm Springs Estates**—*pop pl* FL-3
Palm Springs General Hosp—*hospital* FL-3
Palm Springs JHS—*school* FL-3
**Palm Springs Manor**—*pop pl* DE-2
Palm Springs Mile Shop Ctr—*locale* FL-3
Palm Springs Municipal Airp—*airport* CA-9
**Palm Springs North**—*pop pl* FL-3
Palm Springs North Park—*park* FL-3
Palm Springs Plaza (Shop Ctr)—*locale* FL-3
Palm Springs Presbyterian Kindergarten—*school* FL-3
Palm Springs Sch—*school* FL-3
Palm Springs Station—*locale* CA-9
Palm Springs Village (Shop Ctr)—*locale* FL-3
Palms Sch—*school* (2) CA-9
Palms Sch—*school* (2) MI-6
Palms Shop Ctr—*locale* TX-5
Palms Trailer Park—*locale* AZ-5
Palmtown Sch (abandoned)—*school* PA-2
Palm Tract—*civil* CA-9
Palm Tree Ch—*church* NC-3
Palmtree Ch—*church* NC-3
Palm Tree Ch—*church* VA-3
Palm Tree Head—*summit* FL-3
Palmtree Hill—*summit* TX-5
Palmtree Islands—*area* AK-9
Palmtree Wash—*stream* AZ-5
**Palm Valley**—*pop pl* FL-3
**Palm Valley**—*pop pl* TX-5
Palm Valley Bridge—*bridge* FL-3
Palm Valley Ch—*church* TX-5
**Palm Valley Landing**—*pop pl* FL-3
Palm Valley Sch—*school* CA-9
Palm Valley Stormwater Channel—*canal* CA-9
**Palm View**—*pop pl* FL-3
**Palmview**—*pop pl* TX-5
Palmview Elem Sch—*school* (2) FL-3
Palmview Hosp—*hospital* FL-3
Palm View Peak—*summit* CA-9
Palm View Sch—*school* (2) CA-9
Palm View Sch—*school* FL-3
*Palm Village* CA-9
**Palm Village**—*pop pl* TX-5
Palm Village—*uninc pl* FL-3
Palm Village Shop Ctr—*locale* AZ-5
Palmville Cem—*cemetery* MN-6
Palmville Ch—*church* MN-6
**Palmville (Township of)**—*pop pl* MN-6
Palm Vista Sch—*school* CA-9
Palm Wash—*stream* CA-9
**Palm Wells**—*pop pl* CA-9
*Palmyra* IN-6
*Palmyra* KS-7
Palmyra—*locale* AL-4
Palmyra—*locale* AR-4
Palmyra—*locale* NJ-2
**Palmyra**—*pop pl* AL-4
**Palmyra**—*pop pl* GA-3
**Palmyra**—*pop pl* (2) IL-6
**Palmyra**—*pop pl* IN-6
**Palmyra**—*pop pl* IA-7
**Palmyra**—*pop pl* ME-1
**Palmyra**—*pop pl* MI-6
**Palmyra**—*pop pl* MO-7
**Palmyra**—*pop pl* NE-7
**Palmyra**—*pop pl* NJ-2
**Palmyra**—*pop pl* NY-2
**Palmyra**—*pop pl* NC-3
**Palmyra**—*pop pl* (2) OH-6
**Palmyra**—*pop pl* PA-2
**Palmyra**—*pop pl* TN-4
**Palmyra**—*pop pl* UT-8
**Palmyra**—*pop pl* (2) VA-3
**Palmyra**—*pop pl* WI-6
Palmyra, Lake—*reservoir* GA-3
Palmyra Bend—*bend* MS-4
Palmyra Borough—*civil* PA-2
Palmyra Campground—*locale* UT-8
Palmyra Cem—*cemetery* GA-3
Palmyra Cem—*cemetery* IN-6
Palmyra Cem—*cemetery* NE-7
Palmyra Cem—*cemetery* NC-3
Palmyra Cem—*cemetery* OH-6
Palmyra Center Hotel—*hist pl* OH-6
Palmyra Ch—*church* AL-4
Palmyra Ch—*church* GA-3
Palmyra Ch—*church* KS-7
Palmyra Ch—*church* MN-6
Palmyra Ch—*church* (2) NC-3
Palmyra Ch—*church* VA-3
Palmyra Chute—*stream* MS-4
Palmyra Consolidated Sch—*school* ME-1
Palmyra (historical)—*locale* MS-4
Palmyra Island Number One Hundred Six—*area* MS-4
Palmyra Lake—*lake* IN-6
Palmyra Lake—*lake* LA-4
Palmyra Lake—*lake* MS-4
Palmyra Lake—*reservoir* OH-6
Palmyra (Magisterial District)—*fmr MCD* VA-3
Palmyra Methodist Episcopal Church—*hist pl* IA-7
Palmyra Mine—*mine* CO-8
Palmyra MS—*school* PA-2
Palmyra Peak—*summit* CO-8
Palmyra Post Office—*building* TN-4
Palmyra Sch—*school* CA-9
Palmyra Sch—*school* GA-3
Palmyra Sch—*school* IL-6
Palmyra Sch—*school* VA-3
Palmyra Sch (historical)—*school* TN-4
Palmyra Senior HS—*school* PA-2
Palmyra-Shiloh (CCD)—*cens area* TN-4
Palmyra-Shiloh Division—*civil* TN-4
Palmyra Shop Ctr—*locale* PA-2
Palmyra Springs—*spring* GA-3
Palmyra (sta.) (RR name for Diamond)—*other* OH-6
Palmyra Station—*locale* NC-3
**Palmyra (Town of)**—*pop pl* ME-1
**Palmyra (Town of)**—*pop pl* NY-2
**Palmyra (Town of)**—*pop pl* WI-6
Palmyra Township—*fmr MCD* IA-7
**Palmyra Township**—*pop pl* KS-7
**Palmyra Township**—*pop pl* SD-7
Palmyra Township Hall—*building* SD-7
Palmyra (Township of)—*fmr MCD* NC-3
**Palmyra (Township of)**—*pop pl* IL-6
**Palmyra (Township of)**—*pop pl* IN-6
**Palmyra (Township of)**—*pop pl* MI-6
**Palmyra (Township of)**—*pop pl* MN-6
**Palmyra (Township of)**—*pop pl* OH-6
**Palmyra (Township of)**—*pop pl* (2) PA-2
Palmyre Ch—*church* NC-3
Palnez Acad—*school* FL-3
**Palo**—*pop pl* IA-7
**Palo**—*pop pl* MI-6
**Palo**—*pop pl* MN-6
Palo, Bayou—*gut* LA-4
*Palo Alto* (2) NC-3
*Palo Alto* TX-5
Palo Alto—*locale* TX-5
Palo Alto—*locale* VA-3
**Palo Alto**—*pop pl* CA-9
**Palo Alto**—*pop pl* LA-4
**Palo Alto**—*pop pl* MS-4
**Palo Alto**—*pop pl* (2) PA-2
**Palo Alto**—*pop pl* PR-3
Palo Alto, Arroyo—*valley* TX-5
Palo Alto Acad (historical)—*school* MS-4
Palo Alto Battlefield—*hist pl* TX-5
Palo Alto Battlefield Natl Historic Site—*park* TX-5
Palo Alto Borough—*civil* PA-2
Palo Alto Cem—*cemetery* (2) LA-4
Palo Alto Cem—*cemetery* MS-4
Palo Alto Ch—*church* IA-7
Palo Alto Ch—*church* (2) MS-4
Palo Alto Community Coll—*school* TX-5
Palo Alto County Hosp—*hospital* IA-7
Palo Alto Creek—*stream* CO-8
Palo Alto Creek—*stream* (2) TX-5
**Palo Alto Heights**—*pop pl* TX-5
Palo Alto Hill—*summit* CA-9
Palo Alto Hill—*summit* NV-8
Palo Alto Hills Golf and Country Club—*other* CA-9
Palo Alto HS—*school* CA-9
Palo Alto Key—*island* FL-3
Palo Alto Landing—*locale* MS-4
Palo Alto Military Acad—*school* CA-9
*Palo Alto Missionary Baptist Church* MS-4
Palo Alto Municipal Golf Course—*other* CA-9
Palo Alto Park—*park* TX-5
Palo Alto Plantation—*hist pl* LA-4
Palo Alto Plantation—*hist pl* NC-3
Palo Alto Ranch—*locale* AZ-5
Palo Alto Sch—*school* TX-5
Palo Alto Spring—*spring* NV-8
Palo Alto Stock Farm Horse Barn—*hist pl* CA-9
Palo Alto Terrace Park—*park* TX-5
Palo Alto Township—*fmr MCD* IA-7
Palo Alto Wells—*well* NV-8
Palo Amarillo Creek—*stream* TX-5
Palo Amarillo Ranch—*locale* NM-5
Palo Amarillo Windmill—*locale* TX-5
Paloa MS—*school* KS-7
Palobla Creek—*stream* TX-5
**Palo Blanco**—*pop pl* PR-3
Palo Blanco, Arroyo—*valley* (2) TX-5
Palo Blanco Ch—*church* NM-5
*Palo Blanco Creek* TX-5
Palo Blanco Creek—*stream* NM-5
Palo Blanco Creek—*stream* (3) TX-5
Palo Blanco Mtn—*summit* NM-5
Palo Blanco Oil Field—*oilfield* TX-5
Palo Blanco Spring—*spring* (2) NM-5
Palo Blanco Tank—*reservoir* (4) TX-5
Palo Blanco Windmill—*locale* (4) TX-5
Palo Canyon—*valley* NM-5
**Palo Cedro**—*pop pl* CA-9
Palo Cem—*cemetery* IA-7
Palo Cem—*cemetery* NE-7
Palo Christi Sch—*school* AZ-5
Palociento Creek—*stream* NM-5
Palo Colorado Canyon—*valley* CA-9
Palo Colorado Sch—*school* CA-9
Palo Comado Canyon—*valley* CA-9
Palo Corona—*summit* CA-9
Palo Corona Ranch—*locale* (2) CA-9
Palo Creek—*stream* MN-6
**Paloduro**—*pop pl* TX-5
Palo Duro Canyon—*valley* NM-5
Palo Duro Canyon—*valley* TX-5
Palo Duro Cem—*cemetery* TX-5
Palo Duro Ch—*church* TX-5
Palo Duro Club Lake—*reservoir* TX-5
*Paloduro Creek* OK-5
*Palo Duro Creek* TX-5
Palo Duro Creek—*stream* CO-8
Palo Duro Creek—*stream* OK-5
Palo Duro Creek—*stream* (2) TX-5
Palo Duro Pen (41AM5)—*hist pl* TX-5
Palo Duro Shelter (41AM6)—*hist pl* TX-5
Palo Duroso—*other* NM-5
Palo Duroso—*valley* NM-5
Palo Duroso Canyon—*valley* NM-5
Palo Duro State Park—*park* TX-5
Palo Duto HS—*school* TX-5
Palo Encebado Canyon—*valley* NM-5
Palo Encebado Peak—*summit* NM-5
Palo Escrito Peak—*summit* CA-9
Palo Ferro Ranch—*locale* AZ-5
Palo Fiero Tank—*reservoir* AZ-5
Palo Flechado Pass—*gap* NM-5
Palo Gaucho Bayou—*stream* TX-5
Palo Hincaco, Correo—*building* PR-3
Palo Hincado—*post sta* PR-3
Palo Hincado (Barrio)—*fmr MCD* PR-3
Palo Hueco Creek—*stream* TX-5
Palolo—*civil* HI-9
Palolo, Lae—*cape* HI-9
Palo Lobo Windmill—*locale* TX-5
Palolo Homesteads—*civil* HI-9
Palolo Sch—*school* HI-9
Palolo Stream—*stream* HI-9
Palolo Valley—*valley* HI-9
Paloma—*locale* TX-5
**Paloma**—*pop pl* CA-9
**Paloma**—*pop pl* IL-6
**Paloma**—*pop pl* LA-4
**Paloma**—*pop pl* PR-3
Paloma, Canada de la —*valley* AZ-5
Paloma, Mount—*summit* ID-8
Paloma Canyon Prospect—*locale* NM-5
Paloma Cem—*cemetery* IL-6
Paloma Creek—*stream* (2) CA-9
Paloma Creek—*stream* ID-8
Paloma Draw—*valley* TX-5
*Paloma Key* FL-3
*Paloma Key Bank* FL-3
*Paloma Key Banks* FL-3
Paloma Meadows—*flat* CA-9
Paloma Mtn—*summit* CA-9
*Paloma Oil Field* CA-9
*Paloma Oil Refinery* CA-9
**Paloma Park**—*pop pl* FL-3
Paloma Pass—*channel* AK-9
Paloma Prospect—*mine* AZ-5
**Palomar**—*pop pl* PR-3
Paloma Ranch Landing Field—*airport* AZ-5
Paloma Ravine—*valley* CA-9
Palo Marcado Well—*well* TX-5
Palomar Coll—*school* CA-9
Palomar Divide Truck Trail—*trail* CA-9
**Palomares**—*pop pl* CA-9
Palomares, Ygnacio, Adobe—*hist pl* CA-9
Palomares Cem—*cemetery* CA-9
Palomares Creek—*stream* CA-9
Palomares HS—*school* CA-9
Palomares JHS—*school* CA-9
Palomares Park—*park* CA-9
Palomares Sch—*school* CA-9
Paloma Ridge—*ridge* CA-9
Palomar-Julian (CCD)—*cens area* CA-9
Palomar Memorial Hosp—*hospital* CA-9
**Palomar Mountain (post Office)**—*pop pl* CA-9
Palomar Mountain State Park—*park* CA-9
*Palomar Mtn* CA-9
Palomar Mtn—*summit* CA-9
Palomar Observatory—*other* CA-9
Palomar Park—*flat* CA-9
Palomar Park—*park* CA-9
Palomar Sch—*school* CA-9
Palo Marsh County Park—*park* IA-7
Palomas—*locale* AZ-5
Palomas—*locale* NM-5
**Palomas**—*pop pl* (2) PR-3
Palomas, Arroyo—*valley* TX-5
Palomas (Barrio)—*fmr MCD* PR-3
Palomas Canyon—*valley* CA-9
Paloma Sch—*school* CA-9
Palomas Community Ditch—*canal* (2) NM-5
Palomas Creek—*stream* NM-5
Palomas Drain—*canal* CA-9
Palomas Draw Retention Dam No 7—*dam* NM-5
Palomas Draw Retention Dam No 8—*dam* NM-5
Palomas Gap Creek—*stream* NM-5
Palomas Hills—*ridge* NM-5
Palomas Mesa—*summit* NM-5
Palomas Moonshine Spring—*spring* NM-5
*Palomas Mountains* AZ-5
Palomas Mountains—*range* AZ-5
Palomas Pasture—*flat* TX-5
Palomas Peak—*summit* NM-5
Palomas Plain—*plain* AZ-5
Paloma Spring—*spring* AZ-5
Palomas Ranch—*locale* CA-9
Palomas Ranch—*locale* (2) TX-5
Palomas Spring—*spring* AZ-5
Palomas Tank—*reservoir* AZ-5
Palomas Tank—*reservoir* TX-5
Palomas Trail—*trail* NM-5
Palomas Wash—*stream* AZ-5
Palomas Well (Windmill)—*locale* TX-5
Palomas Windmill—*locale* (4) TX-5
Paloma Valley—*basin* CA-9
Paloma Wash—*stream* AZ-5
Paloma Well—*well* AZ-5
Palominas—*locale* AZ-5
Palominas Elem Sch—*school* AZ-5
Palominas Post Office—*building* AZ-5
Pal O Mine Ranch—*locale* CA-9
Palomino Airp—*airport* NV-8
Palomino Bench—*bench* NV-8

Palomino Buttes—*summit* ... OR-9
Palomino Canyon—*valley* ... AZ-5
Palomino Creek—*stream* ... OR-9
Palomino Creek Rsvr—*reservoir* ... OR-9
Palomino Draw—*valley* ... AZ-5
**Palomino Farms**—*pop pl* ... PA-2
Palomino Grade—*locale* ... OR-9
Palomino Hills—*summit* ... OR-9
Palomino Lake—*flat* ... OR-9
Palomino Lake—*lake* ... AZ-5
Palomino Lake—*lake* ... OR-9
Palomino Mtn—*summit* ... AZ-5
Palomino Mtn—*summit* ... CO-8
Palomino Mtn—*summit* ... OR-9
Palomino Peak—*summit* ... AZ-5
Palomino Ridge—*ridge* ... NV-8
Palomino Rim—*cliff* ... OR-9
Palomino Rim Rsvr—*reservoir* ... OR-9
Palomino Sch—*school* ... AZ-5
Palomino Tank—*reservoir* (2) ... AZ-5
Palomino Well—*well* ... NV-8
Palomo, As—*slope* ... MH-9
*Palomo Place* ... MH-9
Palomos Windmill—*locale* ... TX-5
Palomo Tank—*reservoir* ... TX-5
Palonas Gap—*gap* ... NM-5
Paloni Mtn—*summit* ... CA-9
Palookaville (Site)—*locale* ... MT-8
*Palo Paloduro Creek* ... TX-5
*Palopato* ... NC-3
**Palopato**—*pop pl* ... NC-3
*Palopel Island* ... NY-2
Palo Pinto—*locale* ... MO-7
**Palopinto**—*pop pl* ... MO-7
**Palo Pinto**—*pop pl* ... TX-5
**Palo Pinto (County)**—*pop pl* ... TX-5
Palo Pinto County Jail—*hist pl* ... TX-5
Palo Pinto Creek—*stream* ... TX-5
Palo Pinto Creek Rsvr—*reservoir* ... TX-5
Palo Pinto Mountains—*range* ... TX-5
Palo Pinto-Santo (CCD)—*cens area* ... TX-5
Palo Pinto Tank—*reservoir* ... TX-5
Palo Prado Interchange—*crossing* ... AZ-5
*Palo Prieto* ... CA-9
*Palo Prieto Canon* ... CA-9
*Palo Prieto Canyon* ... CA-9
Palo Prieto Canyon—*valley* ... CA-9
Palo Prieto Pass—*gap* ... CA-9
Palo Ranch (reduced usage)—*locale* ... MT-8
**Paloro**—*pop pl* ... CA-9
Palos—*locale* ... AL-4
Palos—*locale* ... OH-6
Palos—*locale* ... VA-3
Palos, Arroyo los—*valley* ... TX-5
Palos Blancos, Canada De Los —*valley* ... CA-9
Palos Blancos (Barrio)—*fmr MCD* ... PR-3
Palos Colorados Creek—*stream* ... CA-9
Palos Country Club—*other* ... IL-6
Palos Covered Bridge—*hist pl* ... OH-6
Palo Seco—*CDP* ... PR-3
**Palo Seco**—*pop pl* ... PR-3
Palo Seco (Barrio)—*fmr MCD* (2) ... PR-3
Palo Seco Creek—*stream* ... CA-9
**Palos Gardens**—*pop pl* ... IL-6
**Palos Heights**—*pop pl* ... IL-6
Palos Heights Sch—*school* ... IL-6
**Palos Hills**—*pop pl* ... IL-6
Palos Island—*island* ... LA-4
Palos Number 2 Mine (underground)—*mine* ... AL-4
Palos Number 3 Mine (underground)—*mine* ... AL-4
**Palos Park**—*pop pl* ... IL-6
Palos Park Sch—*school* ... IL-6
Palos Park Woods—*woods* ... IL-6
Palos Sch—*school* ... IL-6
**Palos (Township of)**—*pop pl* ... IL-6
**Palos Verde Estates Subdivision**—*pop pl* ... UT-8
**Palos Verdes**—*pop pl* ... CO-8
Palos Verdes (CCD)—*cens area* ... CA-9
Palos Verdes Country Club—*other* ... CA-9
**Palos Verdes Estates**—*pop pl* ... CA-9
Palos Verdes Hills—*range* ... CA-9
Palos Verdes HS—*school* ... CA-9
*Palos Verdes Peninsula* ... CA-9
**Palos Verdes Peninsula**—*pop pl* ... CA-9
Palos Verdes Peninsula—*uninc pl* ... CA-9
Palos Verdes Point—*cape* ... CA-9
Palos Verdes Rsvr—*reservoir* ... CA-9
*Palos Westgate* ... IL-6
Palos West Sch—*school* ... IL-6
Palotti Novitiate—*church* ... WI-6
Palourde, Bayou—*gut* ... LA-4
Palourde, Lake—*lake* (2) ... LA-4
**Palouse**—*pop pl* ... WA-9
Palouse Canyon Archaeol District—*hist pl* ... WA-9
Palouse Creek—*stream* ... OR-9
Palouse Empire Fairgrounds—*locale* ... WA-9
**Palouse Falk**—*pop pl* ... WA-9
**Palouse Falls**—*pop pl* ... WA-9
Palouse Falls Rec Area—*park* ... WA-9
Palouse Gulch—*valley* ... MT-8
Palouse Main Street Hist Dist—*hist pl* ... WA-9
Palouse Range—*range* ... ID-8
Palouse River—*stream* ... ID-8
Palouse River—*stream* ... WA-9
**Palo Verde**—*pop pl* ... AZ-5
**Palo Verde**—*pop pl* ... CA-9
Palo Verde Branch Library—*building* ... AZ-5
Palo Verde Camp—*locale* ... AZ-5
Palo Verde Canyon—*valley* ... CA-9
Palo Verde (CCD)—*cens area* ... CA-9
Palo Verde Cem—*cemetery* ... CA-9
Palo Verde Coll—*school* ... CA-9
Palo Verde County Park—*park* ... CA-9
Palo Verde Dam—*dam* ... AZ-5
Palo Verde Dam—*dam* ... CA-9
*Palo Verde Drain* ... CA-9
Palo Verde Drain—*canal* ... CA-9
Palo Verde Hills—*summit* ... AZ-5
Palo Verde Hosp—*hospital* ... CA-9
Palo Verde HS—*school* ... AZ-5
Palo Verde Intake—*gut* ... CA-9
Palo Verde Intake—*locale* ... AZ-5
Palo Verde Interchange—*crossing* ... AZ-5
*Palo Verde Lagoon* ... CA-9
Palo Verde Lagoon—*gut* ... CA-9
Palo Verde Mesa—*summit* ... CA-9
Palo Verde Mine—*mine* (2) ... AZ-5
**Palo Verde Mobile Home and Recreational Vehicle Park**—*pop pl* ... AZ-5
Palo Verde Mobile Manor—*locale* ... AZ-5
Palo Verde Mountains—*range* ... CA-9
Palo Verde Mountains—*ridge* ... AZ-5
Palo Verde Nuclear Generating Station—*locale* ... AZ-5
Palo Verde Overpass—*crossing* ... AZ-5
Palo Verde Park—*park* (3) ... AZ-5
Palo Verde Peak—*summit* ... CA-9
Palo Verde Picnic Area and Campground—*park* ... AZ-5
Palo Verde Plaza Shop Ctr—*locale* ... AZ-5
Palo Verde Ranch—*locale* ... AZ-5
Palo Verde Ranger Station—*locale* ... CA-9
Palo Verde Recreation Site 147—*park* ... AZ-5
Palo Verde Sch—*school* (2) ... AZ-5
Palo Verde Sch—*school* (2) ... CA-9
Palo Verde Spring—*spring* ... CA-9
**Palo Verde Stand**—*pop pl* ... AZ-5
Palo Verde Substation—*locale* ... AZ-5
Palo Verde Tank—*reservoir* (3) ... AZ-5
Palo Verde Valley—*valley* ... CA-9
Palo Verde Wash—*stream* ... AZ-5
Palo Verde Wash—*stream* ... CA-9
Palo Vista—*post sta* ... CA-9
*Palpais Point* ... AZ-5
Pal Ranch—*locale* ... WY-8
*Palsaliga Creek* ... AL-4
Palser Run—*stream* ... WV-2
*Palsgrove* ... IL-6
**Palsgrove**—*pop pl* ... IL-6
*Pals Lake* ... MI-6
Pals Lake—*reservoir* ... TN-4
Pals Lake Dam—*dam* ... TN-4
Palsor Knob—*summit* ... WV-2
Pal Spring—*spring* ... TX-5
**Palsville**—*pop pl* ... IA-7
Paltenghe Ranch—*locale* ... NM-5
*Paludura Creek* ... CO-8
Palugvik Archeol District—*hist pl* ... AK-9
Palugvik Creek—*stream* ... AK-9
Palumbo, J. C., Fruit Company Packing Warehouse Bldg—*hist pl* ... ID-8
Palumbo Playground—*park* ... PA-2
Palunak Dam—*dam* ... ND-7
*Palusha Bayou* ... MS-4
*Palusha Creek* ... MS-4
Palusha Creek Canal—*canal* ... MS-4
Palusrik, Infal—*stream* ... FM-9
Paluxy—*locale* ... TX-5
*Paluxy Creek* ... TX-5
Paluxy Oil Pool—*oilfield* ... MS-4
Paluxy River—*stream* ... TX-5
*Pamadumcook Lake* ... ME-1
**Pam Anne Estates**—*pop pl* ... IL-6
*Pamanset River* ... MA-1
*Pamansit River* ... MA-1
Pamas Creek—*stream* ... ID-8
Pambo Tank—*reservoir* ... AZ-5
Pamburn Creek—*stream* ... MT-8
Pameacha Pond—*lake* ... CT-1
*Pamedemcook Lake* ... ME-1
*Pamedumcook Lake* ... ME-1
Pamela, Lake—*lake* ... FL-3
**Pamela Heights**—*pop pl* ... TX-5
Pamela Park—*park* ... IL-6
Pamela Park—*park* ... MN-6
Pamelia Center—*locale* ... NY-2
Pamelia Creek—*stream* ... OR-9
Pamelia Four Corners—*locale* ... NY-2
Pamelia Lake—*lake* ... OR-9
Pamelia Lake Trail—*trail* ... OR-9
**Pamelia (Town of)**—*pop pl* ... NY-2
Pamely Cem—*cemetery* ... NY-2
Pamena Gap—*gap* ... CO-8
Pamena Windmill—*locale* ... CO-8
*Pamet* ... MA-1
Pamet Harbor—*harbor* ... MA-1
Pamet Hollow—*valley* ... MA-1
Pamet River—*stream* ... MA-1
Pamet River Marshes—*swamp* ... MA-1
Pamet River U. S. Life Saving Station (historical)—*locale* ... MA-1
Pamichtuk Lake—*lake* ... AK-9
Pamige Ranch—*locale* ... CO-8
Pamilla Creek—*stream* ... NM-5
Pamilla Spring—*spring* ... NM-5
Pamilla Windmill—*locale* ... NM-5
Pam Lake—*reservoir* ... AL-4
*Pamlicae Farme* ... NJ-2
**Pamlico**—*pop pl* ... NC-3
**Pamlico**—*pop pl* ... VA-3
**Pamlico Beach**—*pop pl* ... NC-3
Pamlico Canyon—*valley* ... NV-8
Pamlico Chapel—*church* ... NC-3
**Pamlico County**—*pop pl* ... NC-3
Pamlico County Airp—*airport* ... NC-3
Pamlico Creek—*stream* ... NC-3
Pamlico HS—*school* ... NC-3
Pamlico Mines—*mine* ... NV-8
*Pamlico Point* ... NC-3
Pamlico Point—*cape* ... NC-3
Pamlico Race Track—*locale* ... NC-3
Pamlico River—*stream* ... NC-3
**Pamlico Shores (subdivision)**—*pop pl* ... NC-3
Pamlico (site)—*locale* ... NV-8
Pamlico Sound—*bay* ... NC-3
Pammel Creek—*stream* ... WI-6
Pammel State Park—*park* ... IA-7
Pamola—*summit* ... ME-1
Pamola Pond—*lake* ... ME-1
Pamona Sch—*school* (2) ... CO-8
Pamona View Town Hall—*building* ... ND-7
Pamoranas Artesian Well—*well* ... TX-5
Pamorana Windmill—*locale* ... TX-5
Pamo Valley—*valley* ... CA-9
Pampa—*locale* ... VA-3
Pampa—*locale* ... WA-9
**Pampa**—*pop pl* ... TX-5
Pampa (CCD)—*cens area* ... TX-5
Pampa Country Club—*other* ... TX-5
Pampa East (CCD)—*cens area* ... TX-5
Pampa Peak—*summit* ... CA-9
Pampa Plant—*other* ... TX-5
Pampa Pond—*lake* ... WA-9
Pampas Drain—*canal* ... CA-9
Pampas Lateral—*canal* ... CA-9
Pampatike Landing—*locale* ... VA-3
Pampell-Day House—*hist pl* ... TX-5
Pamperin Park—*park* ... WI-6
*Pampet River* ... MA-1
Pampins Pond—*lake* ... OR-9
*Pamplico* ... NC-3
**Pamplico**—*pop pl* ... SC-3
Pamplico (CCD)—*cens area* ... SC-3
**Pamplin**—*pop pl* ... VA-3
Pamplin Cem—*cemetery* ... TN-4
*Pamplin City* ... VA-3
**Pamplin City (corporate name for Pamplin)**—*pop pl* ... VA-3
*Pamplin (corporate name Pamplin City)* ... VA-3
Pamplin Creek—*stream* ... TX-5
Pamplin Hills—*range* ... ND-7
Pamplin Pipe Factory—*hist pl* ... VA-3
Pamplins Pond—*reservoir* ... OR-9
Pamplins Pond—*reservoir* ... VA-3
Pamrapo—*uninc pl* ... NJ-2
*Pamrepau* ... NJ-2
Pams Cove—*bay* ... FL-3
P A Mtn—*summit* ... NM-5
Pamuk Imwintiati—*island* ... FM-9
*Pamunkey* ... MD-2
Pamunkey Ch—*church* (2) ... VA-3
*Pamunkey Creek* ... MD-2
Pamunkey Creek—*stream* ... VA-3
**Pamunkey Ind Res**—*pop pl* ... VA-3
Pamunkey Ind Res Archaeol District—*hist pl* ... VA-3
Pamunkey River—*stream* ... VA-3
Pamunkey River Bridge—*bridge* ... VA-3
*Pamunky* ... MD-2
*Pamunky Creek* ... MD-2
*Pamunky River* ... VA-3
*Pamunsend Creek* ... VA-3
**Pan**—*pop pl* ... OH-6
Pan, The—*area* ... TN-4
**Pana**—*pop pl* ... AL-4
**Pana**—*pop pl* ... IL-6
Pana, Lake—*reservoir* ... IL-6
**Panaca**—*pop pl* ... NV-8
Panaca Flat—*flat* ... NV-8
Panaca Hills—*summit* ... NV-8
Panaca Ridge—*ridge* ... UT-8
Panaca Spring—*spring* ... NV-8
Panaca Summit—*gap* ... NV-8
Panaca Township—*inact MCD* ... NV-8
**Panacea**—*pop pl* ... FL-3
**Panacea Park**—*pop pl* ... FL-3
Panacea Springs—*spring* ... NC-3
Panacea United Methodist Ch—*church* ... FL-3
**Panacoochee Retreats**—*pop pl* ... FL-3
Panaewa—*civil* ... HI-9
**Panaewa**—*pop pl* ... HI-9
Panaewa For Res—*forest* ... HI-9
Panahaha Fishpond—*lake* ... HI-9
*Panahahe Fishpond* ... HI-9
Panaihs—*locale* ... FM-9
Panakanic—*locale* ... WA-9
Panakanic Prairie—*flat* ... WA-9
Panakaninc—*locale* ... WA-9
Panakauahi Gulch—*valley* ... HI-9
Panales, Arroyo—*valley* ... TX-5
Panales Arroyo —*valley* ... TX-5
Panalto Well—*well* ... TX-5
*Panama* ... CA-9
Panama—*locale* ... KY-4
Panama—*locale* ... NV-8
**Panama**—*pop pl* ... CA-9
**Panama**—*pop pl* ... IL-6
**Panama**—*pop pl* ... IN-6
**Panama**—*pop pl* ... IA-7
**Panama**—*pop pl* ... MO-7
**Panama**—*pop pl* ... NE-7
**Panama**—*pop pl* ... NY-2
**Panama**—*pop pl* ... OK-5
Panama-Bokoshe (CCD)—*cens area* ... OK-5
Panama Canal—*canal* ... FL-3
Panama Canal—*canal* ... LA-4
Panama Canal—*canal* ... NM-5
Panama Canyon—*valley* ... WA-9
Panama Cem—*cemetery* ... NE-7
Panama Ch—*church* ... AL-4
**Panama City**—*pop pl* ... FL-3
Panama City-Bay County Airp—*airport* ... FL-3
*Panama City Beach* ... FL-3
**Panama City Beach**—*pop pl* ... FL-3
Panama City Beaches (CCD)—*cens area* ... FL-3
Panama City Beach Shop Ctr—*locale* ... FL-3
Panama City (CCD)—*cens area* ... FL-3
Panama City Mall—*locale* ... FL-3
Panama City Marine Institute—*school* ... FL-3
Panama City Seventh-Day Adventist Sch—*school* ... FL-3
Panama Creek—*stream* ... MT-8
Panama Creek—*stream* ... TX-5
Panama Ditch—*canal* ... OR-9
**Panama Heights**—*pop pl* ... FL-3
Panama Hotel—*hist pl* ... CA-9
*Panamaker Creek* ... WA-9
Panamaker Creek—*stream* ... WA-9
Panama Lake—*lake* ... FL-3
Panama Lake—*reservoir* ... IL-6
Panama Legation Bldg—*building* ... DC-2
Panama Martin Tank—*reservoir* ... NM-5
Panama Mine—*mine* ... NV-8
Panama Mine—*mine* ... WA-9
*Panama Missionary Baptist Ch* ... AL-4
**Panama Park**—*pop pl* ... FL-3
Panama Plaza (Shop Ctr)—*locale* ... FL-3
Panama Point—*cape* ... LA-4
Panama Ranch—*locale* ... NM-5
Panama Rocks—*cliff* ... NY-2
Panamaroff Creek—*stream* ... AK-9
Panama Rsvr No. 1—*reservoir* ... CO-8
Panama Sch—*school* ... CA-9
Panama Sch—*school* ... FL-3
Panama Sch—*school* ... KY-4
Panama Sch—*school* ... MO-7
Panama Slough—*stream* ... CA-9
Panama Station (RR name for North Clymer)—*locale* ... NY-2
Panama Tank—*reservoir* ... NM-5
Panama Well—*well* ... NV-8
Pan Am Building (Airport)—*airport* ... NY-2
Pan American C.M.A. Church—*hist pl* ... NJ-2
Pan American Coll—*school* ... TX-5
Pan American Hosp—*hospital* ... FL-3
Pan American Institute—*school* (2) ... FL-3
Pan American Mine—*mine* ... NV-8
Pan American Park—*park* ... CA-9
Pan American Playground—*park* ... TX-5
Pan American Sch—*school* ... TX-5
Pan American Seaplane Base and Terminal Bldg—*hist pl* ... FL-3
Pan-American State Park—*park* ... FL-3
*Pan American Union* ... DC-2
Panameta Point—*cliff* ... AZ-5
Panameta Terrace—*bench* ... AZ-5
Panamint—*locale* ... CA-9
Panamint Butte—*summit* ... CA-9
Panamint Canyon—*valley* ... CA-9
*Panamint Mountains* ... CA-9
Panamint Pass—*gap* ... CA-9
Panamint Range—*range* ... CA-9
Panamint Springs—*locale* ... CA-9
Panamint Valley—*valley* ... CA-9
Panamoka, Lake—*lake* ... NY-2
**Panarama City**—*pop pl* ... KY-4
*Panasoffkee* ... FL-3
Panasoffkee, Lake—*lake* ... FL-3
Panasoffkee (RR name for Lake Panasoffkee)—*other* ... FL-3
*Panasofkee* ... FL-3
**Pana (Township of)**—*pop pl* ... IL-6
Panau Iki—*civil* ... HI-9
Panau Nui—*civil* ... HI-9
Panawatt Springs—*spring* ... CA-9
*Panbow Island* ... KY-4
Panbowl—*area* ... KY-4
Panbowl Branch—*stream* ... KY-4
Panbowl Ch—*church* ... KY-4
Panbowl Lake—*reservoir* ... KY-4
Pan Branch—*stream* ... AR-4
Pan Branch—*stream* ... SC-3
Pancake—*locale* ... TX-5
Pancake—*locale* ... WV-2
**Pancake**—*pop pl* ... PA-2
Pancake Branch—*stream* ... NC-3
Pancake Cem—*cemetery* ... MO-7
Pancake Cem—*cemetery* ... OH-6
Pancake Creek—*stream* (2) ... MN-6
Pancake Creek—*stream* ... OH-6
Pancake Creek—*stream* ... OR-9
Pancake Draw—*valley* ... NM-5
Pancake Falls—*falls* ... MN-6
Pancake Flats—*flat* ... PA-2
Pancake Ground—*harbor* ... MA-1
Pancake Hollow—*valley* ... IL-6
*Pancake Island* ... MN-6
Pancake Island—*island* ... MN-6
Pancake Island—*island* ... SD-7
Pancake Island—*island* ... TX-5
*Pancake Islands* ... RI-1
Pancake Lake—*lake* (3) ... MN-6
*Pancake Mill* ... PA-2
*Pancake Point* ... WA-9
Pancake Point—*cape* ... MD-2
Pancake Point—*cape* ... WA-9
Pancake Range—*range* ... NV-8
Pancake Ravine—*valley* ... CA-9
Pancake Rock—*island* ... AK-9
Pancake Shoal—*bar* ... NY-2
Pancake Summit—*gap* ... NV-8
Pancake Valley—*valley* ... NE-7
Pancho Canyon—*valley* ... CA-9
Pancho Canyon—*valley* ... CO-8
Pancho Canyon—*valley* (2) ... NM-5
Pancho Creek—*stream* ... FL-3
Pancho Lake—*lake* ... ID-8
Pancho Rico Creek—*stream* ... CA-9
Pancho Rico Valley—*valley* ... CA-9
Pancho Spring—*reservoir* ... AZ-5
Pancho Spring—*spring* (2) ... AZ-5
Pancho Tank—*reservoir* ... AZ-5
Pancho Tank—*reservoir* ... TX-5
Pancho Villa State Park—*park* ... NM-5
**Panchoville**—*pop pl* ... LA-4
Panchuela Creek—*stream* ... NM-5
Panchuela Ranger Station—*locale* ... NM-5
Panchuela West—*area* ... NM-5
Panchuela West Cabin—*locale* ... NM-5
Panco—*locale* ... KY-4
Pancoast—*locale* ... NJ-2
Pancoast—*locale* ... PA-2
Pancoast, Lake—*lake* ... FL-3
**Pancoastburg**—*pop pl* ... OH-6
*Pancoastburgh* ... OH-6
Pancoast Creek—*stream* ... PA-2
Pancoast Mill Pond—*reservoir* ... NJ-2
Pancoast Mill Pond Dam—*dam* ... NJ-2
*Pancoast Mills* ... OH-6
Pancoast Shaft—*mine* ... PA-2
*Pancoasts Mill* ... NJ-2
Panco Branch—*stream* ... KY-4
Pancore Lake—*lake* ... MN-6
Pancras—*locale* ... GA-3
**Pancras**—*pop pl* ... GA-3
Pancrazi House—*hist pl* ... AZ-5
Pancrazi Lateral—*canal* ... AZ-5
Pan Creek—*stream* ... AL-4
Pan Creek—*stream* ... KS-7
Pan Creek—*stream* ... OR-9
Pan Creek Ch—*church* ... AL-4
P and A Deptford—*airport* ... NJ-2
Pandale—*locale* ... TX-5
Pan Dam—*dam* ... AZ-5
*Pandanus Cliffs* ... MH-9
Pandanus Place (Shop Ctr)—*locale* ... FL-3
Pandapas Pond—*reservoir* ... VA-3
P and E Junction—*locale* ... AZ-5
Pandella Landing—*locale* ... MS-4
*Pander Creek* ... NC-3
P and E Ridge—*ridge* ... WA-9
*Pando* ... WV-2
Pando—*locale* ... CO-8
Pando Canyon—*valley* ... CO-8
Pando Cem—*cemetery* ... GA-3
Pando Creek—*stream* ... CO-8
*Pando Juverno* ... WV-2
*Pandora* ... PA-2
Pandora—*locale* ... AL-4
Pandora—*locale* ... CO-8
Pandora—*locale* ... TN-4
Pandora—*locale* ... WA-9
**Pandora**—*pop pl* ... OH-6
**Pandora**—*pop pl* ... PA-2
**Pandora**—*pop pl* ... TX-5
Pandora Lake—*lake* ... LA-4
Pandora Mill—*locale* ... CO-8
Pandora Mine—*mine* ... CO-8
Pandora Mine—*mine* ... NV-8
Pandora Mtn—*summit* ... MT-8
Pandora Post Office (historical)—*building* ... MS-4
Pandora Post Office (historical)—*building* ... TN-4
Pandora Prospects—*mine* ... TN-4
P and p Spring—*spring* ... OR-9
**P and W Patch**—*pop pl* ... PA-2
*Pandy Lake* ... CA-9
Paneenee Pali—*cliff* ... HI-9
Pane (historical)—*locale* ... AL-4
Panek Block—*hist pl* ... OH-6
Panel Branch—*stream* ... NC-3
Panel Hill—*summit* ... VT-1
Panel Hill Cem—*cemetery* ... VT-1
*Panemuk* ... FM-9
*Pa-ne-ne-tah* ... KS-7
*Pane Peak* ... HI-9
*Pane P.O.* ... AL-4
Pane Post Office (historical)—*building* ... TN-4
**Paneras**—*pop pl* ... GA-3
Pan Fork (Summer Camp)—*locale* ... TX-5
Pan Gap—*gap* ... TN-4
**Pan Gap**—*pop pl* ... TN-4
Pan Gap Branch—*stream* ... TN-4
Pan Gap Dam—*dam* ... TN-4
Pan Gap Lake—*reservoir* ... TN-4
Pangborn, J. L., House—*hist pl* ... WI-6
Pangborn Field Airp—*airport* ... WA-9
Pangborn Field (Airport)—*airport* ... WA-9
Pangborn-Herndon Memorial Site—*hist pl* ... WA-9
Pangborn Park—*park* ... MD-2
Pangbron Sch—*school* ... MI-6
**Pangburn**—*pop pl* ... AR-4
Pangburn, Stephen, House—*hist pl* ... NY-2
Pangburn Corners—*locale* ... NY-2
Pangburn Hollow—*valley* ... PA-2
Pangi Lake—*lake* ... MN-6
Pangle Cem—*cemetery* ... TX-5
Pangletown Ridge—*ridge* ... VA-3
Panguingue Creek—*stream* ... AK-9
*Panguipa Creek* ... NV-8
**Panguitch**—*pop pl* ... UT-8
*Panguitch Airport* ... UT-8
Panguitch Canal—*canal* ... UT-8
*Panguitch Canon* ... UT-8
Panguitch Carnegie Library—*hist pl* ... UT-8
Panguitch City Cem—*cemetery* ... UT-8
Panguitch Creek—*stream* ... UT-8
Panguitch Division—*civil* ... UT-8
Panguitch Fish Hatchery—*locale* ... UT-8
*Panguitch Gulch* ... UT-8
Panguitch HS MS—*school* ... UT-8
Panguitch KOA—*park* ... UT-8
Panguitch Lake—*lake* ... UT-8
Panguitch Lake—*reservoir* ... UT-8
Panguitch Lake Dam—*dam* ... UT-8
Panguitch Lake North Campground—*park* ... UT-8
**Panguitch Lake Resort**—*pop pl* ... UT-8
Panguitch Lake South Campground—*park* ... UT-8
Panguitch Municipal Airp—*airport* ... UT-8
Panguitch Post Office—*building* ... UT-8
Panguitch Sch—*school* ... UT-8
*Pangvitch* ... UT-8
*Panhandle* ... OK-5
Panhandle—*area* ... KY-4
Panhandle—*cape* ... AL-4
Panhandle—*locale* ... AL-4
Panhandle—*locale* ... GA-3
Panhandle—*locale* ... KY-4
Panhandle—*locale* ... OH-6
Panhandle—*locale* ... PA-2
Panhandle—*locale* ... TX-5
Panhandle—*park* ... CA-9
**Panhandle**—*pop pl* ... NE-7
**Panhandle**—*pop pl* ... TX-5
Panhandle, The—*flat* ... CA-9
Panhandle Bayou—*gut* ... LA-4
Panhandle Branch—*stream* ... NC-3
Panhandle Branch—*stream* ... TN-4
Panhandle (CCD)—*cens area* ... GA-3
Panhandle (CCD)—*cens area* ... TX-5
Panhandle Cem—*cemetery* ... AL-4
**Panhandle Corners**—*pop pl* ... OH-6
*Panhandle Creek* ... TN-4
Panhandle Creek—*stream* ... CA-9
Panhandle Creek—*stream* ... CO-8
Panhandle Creek—*stream* ... VA-3
Panhandle Gap—*gap* ... WA-9
Panhandle Hills—*range* ... CA-9
Panhandle Island—*island* ... AK-9
Panhandle Key—*island* ... FL-3
Panhandle Lake—*lake* ... CA-9
Panhandle Lake—*lake* ... MN-6
Panhandle Lake—*lake* (3) ... WA-9
*Panhandle Mill Pond* ... WA-9
*Panhandle of Oklahoma* ... OK-5
Panhandle Park—*park* ... MI-6
Panhandle Point—*cape* ... MD-2
*Pan Handle Sch* ... TN-4
Panhandle Sch—*school* ... TN-4
Panhandle Sch (historical)—*school* ... AL-4
Panhandle Sch (historical)—*school* ... NC-3
Panhandle Sch (historical)—*school* (2) ... TN-4
Panhandle State Coll—*school* ... OK-5
Panhandle State Coll Farm—*school* ... OK-5
Panhandle Trail—*trail* ... MD-2
**Panhandle Village**—*pop pl* ... ID-8
Panhandle Windmill—*locale* ... TX-5
Panhat Point—*cape* ... AK-9
*Panian Hafen* ... FM-9
*Panian Island* ... FM-9
Paniau—*summit* ... HI-9
*Paniau Peak* ... HI-9
**Panic**—*pop pl* ... PA-2
Panic Ch—*church* ... PA-2
Panic Creek—*stream* ... AK-9
Panic Field Windmill—*locale* ... TX-5
Panier—*locale* ... VA-3
Panikpiak Creek—*stream* ... AK-9
*Panina Butte* ... OR-9
Panipou, Lae o—*cape* ... HI-9
*Pani Riviere* ... KS-7
*Panitiu* ... FM-9
Panitiw—*civil* ... FM-9
*Panitiw Kumi* ... FM-9
*Panitu* ... FM-9
Panjab Campground—*locale* ... WA-9
Panjab Creek—*stream* ... WA-9
*Pankapog Brook* ... MA-1
*Panker Pond* ... MA-1
**Pankey**—*pop pl* ... AR-4
*Pankey Addition* ... AR-4
Pankey Basin—*basin* ... OR-9
Pankey Branch—*stream* ... IL-6
Pankey Branch—*stream* ... MO-7
*Pankey Branch - in part* ... MO-7
Pankey Cem—*cemetery* ... MO-7
Pankey Creek—*stream* ... LA-4
Pankey Lake—*lake* ... OR-9
Pankey Mesa—*bench* ... NM-5
Pankey Park Cem—*cemetery* ... OR-9
Pankey Pond Ditch—*canal* ... IL-6
Pankey Rsvr—*reservoir* ... OR-9
*Pankeys Peak* ... CO-8
Pankey Springs—*spring* (2) ... OR-9
**Pankeyville**—*pop pl* ... IL-6
Pankof Breaker—*bay* ... AK-9
Pankov—*locale* ... AR-4
Pankratz Cem—*cemetery* ... KS-7
Panky Creek—*stream* ... TX-5
Panky Mine—*mine* ... NM-5
Pan Lake—*lake* (2) ... MI-6
Pan Lake—*lake* ... MN-6
*Panley* ... KY-4
Pan Motor Company Office and Sheet Metal Works—*hist pl* ... MN-6
Pannama Island—*island* ... FL-3
**Panna Maria**—*pop pl* ... TX-5
Panna Maria Creek—*stream* ... TX-5
Panna Maria Hist Dist—*hist pl* ... TX-5
*Pannaway Manor* ... NH-1
**Pannaway Manor**—*pop pl* ... NH-1
*Pannel Branch* ... TN-4
*Pannel Creek* ... AL-4
Pannell—*locale* ... GA-3
**Pannell**—*pop pl* ... MS-4
Pannell Branch—*stream* ... TN-4
Pannell Cave—*cave* ... AL-4
Pannell Cem—*cemetery* ... AL-4
Pannell Creek—*stream* ... AL-4
Pannell Hollow—*valley* ... AL-4
Pannell Hollow—*valley* ... AR-4
Pannell Post Office (historical)—*building* ... MS-4
Pannell Ranch—*locale* ... WY-8
Pannell Ridge—*ridge* ... TN-4
Pan Nepodk—*summit* ... AZ-5
*Pannill Fork* ... VA-3
**Pannill Fork**—*pop pl* ... VA-3
Panning Gulch—*valley* ... OR-9
Panno Place—*locale* ... NH-1
*Pannoquacut Pond* ... RI-1
Panochas, Canada De Las —*valley* ... CA-9
Panoche—*locale* ... CA-9
*Panoche Creek* ... AZ-5
*Panoche Creek* ... CA-9
Panoche Creek—*stream* ... CA-9
Panoche De San Juan Y Los Carrisali—*civil* ... CA-9
Panoche Hills—*other* ... CA-9
Panoche Junction—*locale* ... CA-9
Panoche Mtn—*summit* ... CA-9
Panoche Pass—*gap* ... CA-9
Panoche Sch—*school* ... CA-9
Panoche Substation—*other* ... CA-9
Panoche Valley—*valley* ... CA-9
*Panochita Creek* ... CA-9
Panochita Hill—*summit* ... CA-9
*Panochita Valley* ... CA-9
*Panola* ... MS-4
Panola—*locale* ... GA-3
Panola—*locale* ... KY-4
Panola—*locale* ... MI-6
**Panola**—*pop pl* (2) ... AL-4
**Panola**—*pop pl* ... IL-6
**Panola**—*pop pl* (2) ... LA-4
**Panola**—*pop pl* ... OK-5
**Panola**—*pop pl* ... SC-3
**Panola**—*pop pl* ... TX-5
Panola—*uninc pl* ... SC-3
Panola Bar—*bar* ... LA-4
Panola Bayou—*stream* ... LA-4
Panola Brake—*swamp* ... LA-4
Panola Branch—*stream* ... SC-3
Panola Cem—*cemetery* ... LA-4
Panola Cem—*cemetery* ... MN-6
*Panola Ch* ... AL-4
Panola Ch—*church* ... AL-4
Panola Ch—*church* ... AR-4
Panola Ch—*church* ... TX-5
Panola Country Club—*locale* ... MS-4
**Panola County**—*pop pl* ... MS-4
**Panola (County)**—*pop pl* ... TX-5
Panola County Airp—*airport* ... MS-4
Panola County Courthouse—*building* (2) ... MS-4
Panola County Jail—*hist pl* ... TX-5
Panola-Geiger (CCD)—*cens area* ... AL-4
Panola-Geiger Division—*civil* ... AL-4
**Panola Heights (subdivision)**—*pop pl* ... NC-3
Panola HS and Gymnasium—*hist pl* ... OK-5
Panola Industrial District—*facility* ... GA-3
Panola Junior Coll—*school* ... TX-5
Panola Mission—*church* ... TX-5
Panola Mtn—*summit* ... GA-3
Panola Quitman Floodway—*canal* ... MS-4
Panola Shoals—*bar* ... GA-3
*Panola Station* ... IL-6
**Panola (Township of)**—*pop pl* ... IL-6
**Panola Village**—*pop pl* ... SC-3
*Panole* ... SC-3
*Panolo School* ... AL-4
Panoluukia—*civil* ... HI-9
Panoma—*locale* ... OK-5
*Pa Noname Number Sixty-Five Dam* ... PA-2
*Pa Noname Number 14* ... PA-2
*Pa Noname Number 151* ... PA-2
*Pa Noname Number 42* ... PA-2
*Pa Noname 137* ... PA-2
*Pa Noname 149* ... PA-2
*Pa Noname 150* ... PA-2
*Pa Noname 67* ... PA-2
**Panora**—*pop pl* ... IA-7
Panora-Linden HS—*hist pl* ... IA-7
Panorama—*locale* ... VA-3
Panorama—*post sta* ... NY-2
**Panorama Acres (subdivision)**—*pop pl* ... UT-8
**Panorama Apartments Condominium**—*pop pl* ... UT-8
Panorama Baptist Sch—*school* ... CA-9

*Papaula* ... HI-9
Papaula Point—cape ... HI-9
Papauluana—civil ... HI-9
*Papau Peak* ... HI-9
*Papau Point* ... HI-9
Papausi Stream—stream ... AS-9
*Papau Valley* ... MH-9
Papaw—locale ... TN-4
Papawai Point—cape ... HI-9
Papaw Bayou—stream ... LA-4
Papaw Branch—stream ... KY-4
Papaw Cove—valley ... TN-4
Papaw Ferry (historical)—locale ... TN-4
Papaw Hollow—valley ... MO-7
Papa Willie Creek—stream ... AK-9
Papaw Lake—lake ... LA-4
Papaw Ridge—locale ... TN-4
Papaw Ridge Ch (historical)—church ... TN-4
Papaw Run—stream ... WV-2
Papaya Hammock—island ... FL-3
*Papcahesing* ... PA-2
Pape Cave—cave ... TX-5
Pape Cem—cemetery ... PA-2
Pape Ch—church ... MO-7
Pape Haffner Ditch—canal ... IN-6
Pape Place—locale ... CA-9
*Paper* ... NC-3
Paper Cabin Ridge—ridge ... CA-9
Paper House—building ... MA-1
Paperjack Creek—stream ... WI-6
Paper Maker Hunt Club—other ... SC-3
Paper Mill—locale ... PA-2
Paper Mill Brook—stream ... CT-1
**Paper Mill Corners**—pop pl ... NY-2
Paper Mill Creek—stream ... TX-5
Paper Mill Creek—stream ... VA-3
*Paper Mill Dam* ... PA-2
Papermill Hollow Airp—airport ... PA-2
Papermill Pond—lake (2) ... CT-1
Paper Mill Pond—lake ... CT-1
Papermill Pond—lake ... MD-2
Paper Mill Pond—reservoir (2) ... PA-2
Paper Mill Rsvr—reservoir ... MN-6
*Paper Mills* ... GA-3
*Paper Mills* ... MA-1
Paper Mills—locale ... PA-2
**Paper Mill Village**—pop pl (2) ... MA-1
**Paper Mill Village**—pop pl ... VT-1
Paper Rock—cape ... CT-1
Paper Run—stream ... IN-6
Papersack Canyon—valley ... OR-9
Paper Sch—school ... WI-6
Papers Lake—lake ... NM-5
Paper Spring—spring ... OR-9
Papers Wash—stream ... NM-5
*Papertown* ... PA-2
**Papertown**—pop pl ... AL-4
Papertown Ch—church ... AL-4
*Paperville* ... PA-2
**Paperville**—pop pl ... PA-2
**Paperville**—pop pl ... TN-4
Paperville Creek—stream ... TN-4
Paperville Knobs—ridge ... TN-4
Paperville Knobs—ridge ... VA-3
Paperville Post Office (historical)—building ... TN-4
Paperville (RR name for Modena)—other ... PA-2
Paperville Sch (historical)—school ... TN-4
**Papeton**—pop pl ... CO-8
Pape Valley—valley ... WI-6
Pap Huddlestons Sch (historical)—school ... TN-4
Papigak Creek—stream ... AK-9
Papiha Point—cape (2) ... HI-9
Papik Mtn—summit (2) ... AK-9
**Papillion**—pop pl ... NE-7
Papillion Cem—cemetery ... NE-7
Papillion Creek—stream ... NE-7
Papillion-Lavista—post sta ... NE-7
Papillion No. 2—fmr MCD ... NE-7
**Papin**—pop pl ... MI-6
**Papin**—pop pl ... MO-7
Papine—cape ... HI-9
**Papineau**—pop pl ... IL-6
Papineau Grave—cemetery ... NM-5
**Papineau (Township of)**—pop pl ... IL-6
**Papinsville**—pop pl ... MO-7
Papio Gulch—valley ... HI-9
Papiok, Mount—summit ... AK-9
Papka (Site)—locale ... AK-9
Papkee Lake—lake ... WI-6
Papke Hill—summit ... TX-5
Papkes Landing—locale ... AK-9
Papohaku Beach—beach ... HI-9
Papohaku Gulch—valley ... HI-9
Papohaku Park—park ... HI-9
*Papoi* ... HI-9
Papoia Island (State Bird Refuge)—island ... HI-9
Papoose—pillar ... CO-8
Papoose—summit ... MT-8
Papoose Basin—basin ... CO-8
Papoose Branch—stream ... NJ-2
Papoose Canyon—valley ... CO-8
Papoose Canyon—valley ... NV-8
Papoose Canyon—valley (2) ... UT-8
Papoose Canyon Oil Field—oilfield ... CO-8
Papoose Cavern—cave ... ID-8
Papoose Cove—bay ... AK-9
*Papoose Creek* ... CO-8
*Papoose Creek* ... MT-8
Papoose Creek—stream ... AK-9
Papoose Creek—stream (4) ... CA-9
Papoose Creek—stream (3) ... CO-8
Papoose Creek—stream (8) ... ID-8
Papoose Creek—stream ... IN-6
Papoose Creek—stream ... IA-7
Papoose Creek—stream ... MN-6
Papoose Creek—stream (4) ... MT-8
Papoose Creek—stream (3) ... OR-9
Papoose Creek—stream ... TX-5
Papoose Creek—stream ... UT-8
Papoose Creek—stream ... WA-9
Papoose Creek—stream (3) ... WI-6
Papoose Creek—stream (2) ... WY-8
Papoose Ditch—canal ... MT-8
Papoose Draw—valley ... TX-5
Papoose Flat—flat ... CA-9
Papoose Gulch—valley ... MT-8
Papoose Hill—summit ... CA-9
Papoose Hill—summit ... OK-5
Papoose Island—island ... ID-8
Papoose Island—island ... ME-1
Papoose Island—island ... NY-2
*Papoose Lake* ... MA-1
*Papoose Lake* ... MI-6
*Papoose Lake* ... UT-8
Papoose Lake—lake (2) ... CA-9
Papoose Lake—lake (2) ... CO-8
Papoose Lake—lake (3) ... ID-8
Papoose Lake—lake ... IL-6
Papoose Lake—lake (3) ... MI-6
Papoose Lake—lake (3) ... MN-6
Papoose Lake—lake ... NV-8
Papoose Lake—lake ... NY-2
Papoose Lake—lake (2) ... OR-9
Papoose Lake—lake (3) ... WI-6
Papoose Lake—reservoir ... NV-8
Papoose Lake—reservoir ... NJ-2
Papoose Lake—reservoir ... UT-8
Papoose Lake Dam—dam ... UT-8
Papoose Lakes—lake ... ID-8
Papoose Lakes—lake ... OR-9
Papoose Ledge—bench ... CT-1
Papoose Meadows—flat ... CA-9
Papoose Mtn—summit ... CO-8
Papoose Mtn—summit ... ID-8
Papoose Oil Field—oilfield ... OK-5
Papoose Park—park ... IA-7
Papoose Peak—summit ... CA-9
Papoose Peak—summit ... CO-8
Papoose Peak—summit ... ID-8
*Papoose Pond* ... ME-1
Papoose Pond—lake (2) ... ME-1
Papoose Range—ridge ... NV-8
Papoose Saddle—gap (2) ... ID-8
Papoose Spring—spring ... NV-8
Papoose Spring—spring ... UT-8
Papoose Trail—trail ... WY-8
Papoose Twins—lake ... AK-9
Pappans Plaza—locale ... PA-2
Pappapau Butte—summit ... WY-8
Pappapau Creek—stream ... WY-8
Pappapau Ditch—canal ... WY-8
Pappas, Theodore, A., House—hist pl ... MO-7
Pappas Creek—stream ... MT-8
Pappas Place—locale ... MT-8
Pappas Plaza (Shop Ctr)—locale ... FL-3
Pappenfort Cem—cemetery ... MO-7
Pappin Cem—cemetery ... OK-5
**Pappio**—pop pl ... NE-7
Pappis Pond—reservoir ... NV-8
*Pappoose Creek* ... WY-8
*Pappoose Lake* ... MN-6
*Pappoose Peak* ... ID-8
Papp Park—park ... MI-6
Papps Rsvr—reservoir ... MT-8
Pappy Jack Spring—spring ... GA-3
Pappys Corral Spring—spring ... NV-8
Pappys Creek—stream ... GA-3
Pappys Pasture—area ... UT-8
Pappys Pasture—flat ... UT-8
Paps, The—summit ... AK-9
Paps Branch—stream ... TN-4
Papscanee Creek—stream ... NY-2
Papscanee Island—flat ... NY-2
Paps Gulch—valley ... CA-9
Paps Hill—summit ... LA-4
Pap Slough—gut ... MN-6
Paps Mtn—summit ... ID-8
Paps Slough—gut ... AR-4
Papst Drain—canal ... MI-6
Papuaa—bay ... HI-9
Papuaa—civil ... HI-9
Papuaa Gulch—valley ... HI-9
Papuaa Ridge—ridge ... HI-9
Papuaa Rsvr—reservoir ... HI-9
Papuaa Stream—stream ... HI-9
Papua Gulch—valley ... HI-9
Papunawai Hills—summit ... HI-9
*Papys Bayou* ... FL-3
Papys Point—cape ... FL-3
*Paqay Pond* ... MA-1
*Paquaback Brook* ... RI-1
Paqua Creek—stream ... WA-9
*Paquantuck River* ... RI-1
Paqua Pond—lake ... MA-1
*Paquatannock* ... CT-1
*Paquatannock Cove* ... CT-1
Paqueno Tank—reservoir ... AZ-5
*Paquequash Point* ... AZ-5
Paquet, Bayou—stream ... LA-4
Paquet Gulch—valley ... OR-9
*Paquet Lake* ... MN-6
Paquet Lake—lake ... MN-6
*Paquette Canyon* ... AZ-5
*Paquette Lake* ... WI-6
Paquette Lake—lake ... MI-6
Paquette Sch—school ... ME-1
*Paquiac* ... NC-3
Paquin Creek—stream ... MI-6
Paquin Lake—lake ... MI-6
Paquita—locale ... NM-5
*Paquiwoc* ... NC-3
Paquiwock—area ... NC-3
Paraboo Campground—locale ... UT-8
**Parabueyon**—pop pl (2) ... PR-3
**Parachute**—pop pl ... CO-8
Parachute Canyon—valley ... NV-8
Parachute Creek—stream ... CO-8
Parachute Creek—stream ... ID-8
Parachute Ditch—canal ... CO-8
Parachute Hill—summit ... ID-8
Parachute Jump—hist pl ... NY-2
Parachute Key—island ... FL-3
Parachute Lake—lake ... ID-8
Parachute Meadow—flat ... WA-9
Parachute Ridge—ridge ... ID-8
Paraclifta Monument—other ... AR-4
Paraclifta (Township of)—fmr MCD ... AR-4
Para Creek—stream ... WA-9
Parada, Mesa—summit ... AZ-5
Parada de Senal Fulminante—locale ... PR-3
**Parada de Senal Fulminante**—pop pl ... PR-3
Parada de Senal Irizarry—locale ... PR-3
**Parada de Senal Irizarry**—pop pl ... PR-3
*Parada Hook* ... NY-2
Parade—locale ... SD-7
Parade, The—locale ... MO-7
Parade, The—PARK ... MN-6
Parade, The—park ... NY-2
*Parade Creek* ... SD-7
*Paradee Creek* ... SD-7
Parade Hill Cem—cemetery ... CT-1
Parade of Elephants—pillar ... UT-8
Parade Rest Ranch—locale ... MT-8
Paradesia Point—cape ... MI-6
*Paradice Lake* ... NJ-2
Paradie Branch—stream ... MD-2
*Paradijs Udden* ... DE-2
Paradine Creek—stream ... MI-6
**Paradis**—pop pl ... LA-4
Paradis Canal—canal ... LA-4
Paradis Creek—stream ... SD-7
*Paradise* ... ID-8
*Paradise* ... MO-7
Paradise—locale ... AK-9
Paradise—locale ... AR-4
Paradise—locale ... FL-3
Paradise—locale ... IA-7
Paradise—locale ... NJ-2
Paradise—locale ... NY-2
Paradise—locale ... OR-9
Paradise—locale ... PA-2
Paradise—locale ... WA-9
Paradise—locale ... WY-8
Paradise—locale ... VI-3
**Paradise**—pop pl ... AZ-5
**Paradise**—pop pl (2) ... CA-9
**Paradise**—pop pl ... GA-3
**Paradise**—pop pl ... IL-6
**Paradise**—pop pl ... IN-6
**Paradise**—pop pl ... KS-7
**Paradise**—pop pl ... KY-4
**Paradise**—pop pl ... LA-4
**Paradise**—pop pl ... MD-2
**Paradise**—pop pl ... MI-6
**Paradise**—pop pl ... MO-7
**Paradise**—pop pl ... MT-8
**Paradise**—pop pl ... NV-8
**Paradise**—pop pl ... OH-6
**Paradise**—pop pl (2) ... PA-2
**Paradise**—pop pl ... TX-5
**Paradise**—pop pl ... UT-8
**Paradise**—pop pl ... WV-2
Paradise—summit ... UT-8
Paradise, Lake—lake ... AR-4
Paradise, Lake—lake ... MI-6
Paradise, Lake—lake ... MS-4
Paradise, Lake—lake ... NY-2
Paradise, Lake—reservoir ... AL-4
Paradise, Lake—reservoir ... GA-3
Paradise, Lake—reservoir ... IL-6
Paradise Acre Lake—reservoir ... IN-6
**Paradise Acres (subdivision)**—pop pl (2) ... AZ-5
**Paradise Acres (subdivision)**—pop pl ... UT-8
Paradise Air Ranch Airp—airport ... WA-9
Paradise Alley—valley ... WY-8
Paradise Baptist Ch—church ... KS-7
Paradise Bar—bar ... OR-9
Paradise Basin—basin (2) ... CO-8
Paradise Basin—basin ... ID-8
Paradise Basin—basin ... WY-8
*Paradise Bay* ... FL-3
Paradise Bay—bay ... AR-4
Paradise Bay—bay ... CA-9
Paradise Bay—bay ... NJ-2
Paradise Bay—bay ... VT-1
**Paradise Bay**—pop pl ... FL-3
Paradise Bayou—gut ... AR-4
Paradise Beach—beach ... MN-6
Paradise Beach—beach ... PA-2
Paradise Beach—locale ... NY-2
**Paradise Beach**—pop pl ... FL-3
**Paradise Beach**—pop pl ... MD-2
Paradise Bench—bench ... UT-8
Paradise Bottom—bend ... KY-4
Paradise Brook—stream ... RI-1
Paradise Butte—summit ... AZ-5
Paradise Cabin—locale ... ID-8
Paradise Camp—locale ... CA-9
Paradise Campground—locale ... CA-9
Paradise Campground—locale ... ID-8
Paradise Campground—locale ... UT-8
Paradise Canal—canal ... MT-8
Paradise Canal—canal ... UT-8
*Paradise Canyon* ... UT-8
Paradise Canyon—valley (3) ... AZ-5
Paradise Canyon—valley (5) ... CA-9
Paradise Canyon—valley ... NV-8
Paradise Canyon—valley (3) ... NM-5
Paradise Canyon—valley (2) ... OR-9
Paradise Canyon—valley (5) ... UT-8
Paradise Canyon—valley ... WY-8
Paradise Canyon Mine—mine ... AZ-5
Paradise Canyon Sch—school ... CA-9
Paradise Cave—cave ... CA-9
**Paradise Cay**—pop pl ... CA-9
Paradise (CCD)—cens area ... CA-9
Paradise Cem—cemetery ... AZ-5
Paradise Cem—cemetery (2) ... IL-6
Paradise Cem—cemetery ... MS-4
Paradise Cem—cemetery ... MO-7
Paradise Cem—cemetery (3) ... OK-5
Paradise Cem—cemetery ... OR-9
Paradise Cem—cemetery (2) ... PA-2
Paradise Cem—cemetery (2) ... TX-5
Paradise Cem—cemetery ... UT-8
Paradise Ch—church ... AL-4
Paradise Ch—church (6) ... AR-4
Paradise Ch—church ... GA-3
Paradise Ch—church (2) ... IL-6
Paradise Ch—church (2) ... KY-4
Paradise Ch—church ... LA-4
Paradise Ch—church (3) ... MD-2
Paradise Ch—church (3) ... MS-4
Paradise Ch—church ... NC-3
Paradise Ch—church ... OH-6
Paradise Ch—church ... OK-5
Paradise Ch—church (7) ... PA-2
Paradise Ch—church ... SC-3
Paradise Ch—church (4) ... TX-5
Paradise Ch—church ... VA-3
Paradise Chape Sch—school ... IL-6
Paradise Christian Sch—school ... FL-3
*Paradise Cienega* ... AZ-5
**Paradise City**—pop pl ... AZ-5
Paradise Coulee—valley ... WI-6
Paradise County Park—park ... CA-9
Paradise Cove—bay ... AK-9
Paradise Cove—bay (4) ... CA-9
Paradise Cove—bay ... TX-5
Paradise Cove—bay (2) ... WA-9
Paradise Cove—locale ... WA-9
Paradise Cove Campground—locale ... CA-9
*Paradise Crag* ... CA-9
Paradise Craggy—summit ... CA-9
*Paradise Creek* ... ID-8
Paradise Creek—stream (3) ... AK-9
Paradise Creek—stream ... AZ-5
Paradise Creek—stream (6) ... CA-9
Paradise Creek—stream (2) ... CO-8
Paradise Creek—stream (10) ... ID-8
Paradise Creek—stream ... IA-7
Paradise Creek—stream ... KS-7
Paradise Creek—stream ... MT-8
Paradise Creek—stream ... NC-3
Paradise Creek—stream (8) ... OR-9
Paradise Creek—stream (2) ... PA-2
Paradise Creek—stream ... TX-5
Paradise Creek—stream (3) ... UT-8
Paradise Creek—stream ... VA-3
Paradise Creek—stream (4) ... WA-9
Paradise Creek—stream ... WI-6
Paradise Creek—stream (4) ... WY-8
Paradise Creek Forest Camp—locale ... WA-9
Paradise Crossing—locale ... PA-2
Paradise Cut—gut ... CA-9
Paradise Dam—dam ... CA-9
Paradise Ditch—canal ... WY-8
Paradise Draw—valley ... TX-5
Paradise Draw—valley ... UT-8
Paradise Dry Canyon—valley ... UT-8
Paradise (Election Precinct)—fmr MCD ... IL-6
Paradise Elem Sch—school ... KS-7
Paradise Elem Sch—school ... PA-2
Paradise Falls—falls ... PA-2
Paradise Falls—falls ... WA-9
**Paradise Falls**—pop pl ... PA-2
Paradise Farm—hist pl ... IA-7
Paradise Flat—flat (2) ... CA-9
Paradise Flat—flat (2) ... ID-8
Paradise Flats—flat ... ND-7
Paradise Flats—flat ... UT-8
Paradise Flats—flat ... WA-9
Paradise Flats—other ... AK-9
Paradise Flats Cem—cemetery ... WA-9
Paradise Fork Sethkokna River—stream ... AK-9
Paradise Furnace—locale ... PA-2
Paradise Gap—gap ... NV-8
Paradise Gas Field—oilfield ... TX-5
Paradise Glacier Caves—cave ... WA-9
Paradise Glaciers—glacier ... WA-9
**Paradise Green**—pop pl ... CT-1
Paradise Grove Family Park—park ... AZ-5
Paradise Grove Trailer Park—locale ... AZ-5
Paradise Guard Station—locale ... ID-8
Paradise Guard Station—locale ... UT-8
Paradise Gulch—valley ... CO-8
Paradise Gulch—valley ... MT-8
Paradise Gulch—valley ... SD-7
Paradise Hill—gap ... NV-8
Paradise Hill—locale (2) ... NY-2
**Paradise Hill**—pop pl ... NV-8
**Paradise Hill**—pop pl ... OH-6
**Paradise Hill**—pop pl ... OK-5
**Paradise Hill**—pop pl ... WA-9
Paradise Hill—summit ... AK-9
Paradise Hill—summit (2) ... ME-1
Paradise Hill—summit ... MA-1
Paradise Hill—summit ... VA-3
Paradise Hills—locale ... KY-4
**Paradise Hills**—pop pl ... CO-8
**Paradise Hills**—pop pl ... NM-5
Paradise Hills—range ... WA-9
Paradise Hills—uninc pl ... CA-9
Paradise Hills Park—park ... AZ-5
Paradise Hills Park—park ... CA-9
Paradise Hills Sch—school ... CA-9
Paradise Hills Shop Ctr—locale ... AZ-5
**Paradise Hills Subdivision**—pop pl (2) ... UT-8
*Paradise Hill Summit* ... NV-8
**Paradise (historical)**—pop pl ... OR-9
Paradise Hollow—valley ... MA-1
Paradise Hollow—valley ... TN-4
**Paradise Hot Springs**—pop pl ... ID-8
Paradise Inn—hist pl ... WA-9
**Paradise Inn**—pop pl ... WA-9
Paradise Island—island (4) ... FL-3
Paradise Island—island ... MN-6
Paradise Island—island ... NH-1
Paradise Island—island ... NY-2
Paradise Island—island ... NC-3
Paradise Island—island ... OH-6
Paradise Island—island ... SC-3
Paradise Island—island (3) ... WI-6
**Paradise Junction**—pop pl ... KY-4
Paradise Key—island (3) ... FL-3
Paradise Knolls Golf Course—other ... CA-9
*Paradise Lake* ... MI-6
*Paradise Lake* ... NJ-2
*Paradise Lake* ... WY-8
Paradise Lake—lake ... AK-9
Paradise Lake—lake (2) ... CA-9
Paradise Lake—lake ... CO-8
Paradise Lake—lake (2) ... FL-3
Paradise Lake—lake (2) ... ID-8
Paradise Lake—lake ... KY-4
Paradise Lake—lake (3) ... MI-6
Paradise Lake—lake (2) ... MN-6
Paradise Lake—lake ... MT-8
Paradise Lake—lake (2) ... NY-2
Paradise Lake—lake ... OR-9
Paradise Lake—lake ... WA-9
Paradise Lake—lake (2) ... WI-6
Paradise Lake—lake (2) ... WY-8
Paradise Lake—reservoir ... AL-4
Paradise Lake—reservoir ... GA-3
Paradise Lake—reservoir (2) ... IN-6
Paradise Lake—reservoir ... KS-7
Paradise Lake—reservoir ... MA-1
Paradise Lake—reservoir (2) ... MO-7
Paradise Lake—reservoir (2) ... TN-4
Paradise Lake—reservoir ... VA-3
Paradise Lake Dam—dam ... AL-4
Paradise Lake Dam—dam ... MA-1
Paradise Lake Dam—dam (2) ... TN-4
Paradise Lake (Old Lewisburg Reservoir)—reservoir ... TN-4
*Paradise Lakes* ... WA-9
Paradise Lakes—area ... AK-9
Paradise Lakes—lake ... CO-8
Paradise Lakes—lake ... WA-9
Paradise Lakes—lake ... WY-8
**Paradise Lakes**—pop pl ... IN-6
**Paradise Lakes**—pop pl ... NJ-2
Paradise Lakes—reservoir ... GA-3
Paradise Lakes—reservoir ... IN-6
Paradise Landing—locale (2) ... AR-4
Paradise Lodge—locale ... AR-4
Paradise Lodge—locale ... MT-8
Paradise Manor—hist pl ... MD-2
**Paradise Manor**—pop pl ... LA-4
Paradise Meadow—flat ... WA-9
Paradise Meadow—swamp ... ND-7
*Paradise Memorial Cemetery* ... FL-3
Paradise Memorial Gardens—cemetery ... AZ-5
Paradise Memorial Park—cemetery ... CA-9
Paradise Mine—mine ... CO-8
Paradise Mine—mine (2) ... NV-8
Paradise Mine—mine ... OR-9
Paradise Mtn—summit ... CA-9
Paradise Mtn—summit ... NV-8
Paradise Mtn—summit ... OR-9
Paradise Mtn—summit ... TX-5
Paradise Mtns—range ... UT-8
Paradise North Mobile Home Park—locale ... AZ-5
**Paradise Palms**—pop pl ... FL-3
**Paradise Palms**—pop pl ... NV-8
Paradise Palms Trailer Resorts—locale ... AZ-5
Paradise Park—basin ... MT-8
Paradise Park—flat (2) ... AZ-5
Paradise Park—flat (2) ... CO-8
Paradise Park—flat ... NM-5
Paradise Park—flat ... UT-8
Paradise Park—flat ... WA-9
Paradise Park—park ... AZ-5
Paradise Park—park ... CA-9
Paradise Park—park ... GA-3
Paradise Park—park ... NV-8
Paradise Park—park ... PA-2
**Paradise Park**—pop pl ... CA-9
**Paradise Park**—pop pl ... FL-3
**Paradise Park**—pop pl (2) ... GA-3
**Paradise Park**—pop pl ... OR-9
*Paradise Park Campground* ... UT-8
Paradise Park Dam—dam ... UT-8
Paradise Park Hist Dist—hist pl ... GA-3
Paradise Park Rsvr—reservoir ... UT-8
Paradise Park Shelter—locale ... OR-9
**Paradise Park (subdivision)**—pop pl ... NC-3
**Paradise Park Subdivision**—pop pl ... UT-8
Paradise Park Trail—trail ... OR-9
Paradise Park Youth Camp—park ... AZ-5
Paradise Pass—gap ... AK-9
Paradise Peak—summit ... AK-9
Paradise Peak—summit (2) ... CA-9
Paradise Peak—summit ... ID-8
Paradise Peak—summit (2) ... NV-8
Paradise Peak—summit ... UT-8
Paradise Peak—summit ... WA-9
Paradise Peak Mine—mine ... NV-8
*Paradise Point* ... DE-2
Paradise Point—cape ... CA-9
Paradise Point—cape (3) ... FL-3
Paradise Point—cape ... ID-8
Paradise Point—cape ... ME-1
Paradise Point—cape ... MT-8
Paradise Point—cape ... NV-8
Paradise Point—cape (3) ... NY-2
Paradise Point—cape ... NC-3
Paradise Point—cape ... OK-5
Paradise Point—cape ... SC-3
Paradise Point—cape ... TX-5
Paradise Point—cape (2) ... WA-9
Paradise Point—locale ... NC-3
Paradise Point—other ... IN-6
**Paradise Point**—pop pl ... FL-3
**Paradise Point**—pop pl ... NC-3
Paradise Point—summit ... ID-8
Paradise Point Dam—dam ... NC-3
Paradise Point Lake—reservoir ... NC-3
Paradise Point Public Use Area—park ... KS-7
Paradise Point Rec Area—locale ... MO-7
**Paradise Points**—pop pl ... AL-4
**Paradise Point (subdivision)**—pop pl ... MS-4
Paradise Pond—lake ... MA-1
Paradise Pond—reservoir ... MA-1
Paradise Pond Dam—dam ... MA-1
**Paradise Port (subdivision)**—pop pl ... FL-3
Paradise Post Office (historical)—building ... PA-2
Paradise Prairie Sch—school ... IL-6
Paradise Protectory—school ... PA-2
Paradise Ranch—locale (2) ... CA-9
Paradise Ranch—locale ... OR-9
Paradise Ranch—locale ... UT-8
Paradise Ranch—locale ... WY-8
Paradise Range—range ... CA-9
Paradise Range—range ... NV-8
Paradise Rec Area—locale ... MT-8
Paradise Rec Area—park ... OR-9
Paradise Ridge—ridge ... AZ-5
Paradise Ridge—ridge (2) ... CA-9
Paradise Ridge—ridge ... ID-8
Paradise Ridge—ridge ... OR-9
Paradise Ridge—ridge ... TN-4
Paradise Ridge—ridge ... WA-9
Paradise Ridge—ridge ... WY-8
Paradise River—stream ... WA-9
Paradise Rocks—pillar ... RI-1
Paradise Rsvr—reservoir ... UT-8
Paradise Run—stream ... PA-2
Paradise Sch—hist pl ... RI-1
Paradise Sch—school (2) ... IL-6
Paradise Sch—school ... LA-4
Paradise Sch—school ... MI-6
Paradise Sch—school ... NV-8
Paradise Sch—school ... NY-2
Paradise Sch—school ... PA-2
Paradise Sch—school (2) ... TX-5
Paradise Sch—school ... WI-6
Paradise Sch (historical)—school ... PA-2
Paradise Shadows Mobile Home Park—locale ... AZ-5
**Paradise Shores**—pop pl ... AL-4
**Paradise Shores**—pop pl ... FL-3
Paradise (site)—locale ... NV-8
*Paradise Spring* ... UT-8
Paradise Spring—spring (2) ... AZ-5
Paradise Spring—spring ... CA-9
Paradise Spring—spring ... ID-8
Paradise Spring—spring ... NV-8
Paradise Spring—spring (4) ... UT-8
Paradise Spring—spring ... WA-9
**Paradise Springs**—pop pl ... CA-9
Paradise Tank—reservoir ... AZ-5
Paradise Tanks—reservoir ... AZ-5
Paradise Tithing Office—hist pl ... UT-8
Paradise Tower—locale ... MI-6
Paradise Township—civil ... PA-2
Paradise Township—fmr MCD ... IA-7
**Paradise Township**—pop pl ... KS-7
**Paradise Township**—pop pl ... ND-7
**Paradise (Township of)**—pop pl ... IL-6
**Paradise (Township of)**—pop pl ... MI-6
**Paradise (Township of)**—pop pl (3) ... PA-2
Paradise Trail—trail ... CA-9
Paradise Trail—trail ... OR-9
Paradise Trail—trail ... WA-9
Paradise Valley—basin (3) ... CA-9
Paradise Valley—basin ... NV-8
Paradise Valley—basin ... UT-8
Paradise Valley—basin ... WA-9
Paradise Valley—flat (2) ... CA-9
**Paradise Valley**—pop pl ... AZ-5
**Paradise Valley**—pop pl ... GA-3
**Paradise Valley**—pop pl (2) ... NV-8
**Paradise Valley**—pop pl ... PA-2
**Paradise Valley**—pop pl ... WY-8
Paradise Valley—valley ... AK-9
Paradise Valley—valley (2) ... AZ-5
Paradise Valley—valley (8) ... CA-9
Paradise Valley—valley (4) ... ID-8
Paradise Valley—valley ... MN-6
Paradise Valley—valley ... MO-7
Paradise Valley—valley ... MT-8
Paradise Valley—valley (2) ... NV-8
Paradise Valley—valley ... TX-5
Paradise Valley—valley (4) ... WA-9
Paradise Valley—valley ... WI-6
Paradise Valley—valley (2) ... WY-8
Paradise Valley Canal—canal ... MT-8
Paradise Valley Cem—cemetery ... ID-8
Paradise Valley Ch—church ... OK-5
Paradise Valley Community Hall—locale ... MT-8
Paradise Valley Community House—locale ... WY-8
Paradise Valley Country Club—locale ... NV-8
Paradise Valley Country Club—other ... AZ-5
Paradise Valley Country Club—other ... WY-8
Paradise Valley Country Club—school ... CO-8
Paradise Valley County Park—park ... NV-8
Paradise Valley Day Sch—school ... CA-9
Paradise Valley HS—school ... AZ-5
Paradise Valley Lake—lake ... UT-8
Paradise Valley Lake—reservoir ... WI-6
Paradise Valley Mall—locale ... AZ-5
**Paradise Valley Miranda (subdivision)**—pop pl (2) ... AZ-5
**Paradise Valley Mobilhome Park**—pop pl ... AZ-5
**Paradise Valley Oasis (subdivision)**—pop pl (2) ... AZ-5
Paradise Valley Park—park ... AZ-5
Paradise Valley Park Golf Course—other ... AZ-5
Paradise Valley Racquet Club—other ... AZ-5
Paradise Valley Sch—school ... AZ-5
Paradise Valley Sch—school ... NE-7
Paradise Valley Sch (historical)—school ... MS-4
Paradise Valley Substation—locale ... AZ-5
Paradise Valley Township—inact MCD ... NV-8
Paradise Valley Trail—trail ... AK-9
**Paradise View**—pop pl ... OK-5
Paradise View Mobile Home Park—locale ... AZ-5
**Paradise Village North II (subdivision)**—pop pl (2) ... AZ-5
Paradise Village Shop Ctr—locale ... AZ-5
Paradise Vista Park—park ... NV-8
Paradise Well—well ... AZ-5
Paradise Well (Old Stage Station)—locale ... NV-8
Paradis Oil and Gas Field—oilfield ... LA-4
Paradis Peak—summit ... WA-9
Paradis Pond—lake ... MT-8
*Paradize Creek* ... PA-2
**Paradox**—pop pl ... CO-8
**Paradox**—pop pl ... NY-2
Paradox Bay—bay ... NY-2
Paradox Cem—cemetery ... CO-8
Paradox Creek—stream ... NY-2
Paradox Lake—lake ... NY-2
Paradox Road—trail ... CO-8
Paradox Sch—school ... CO-8
Paradox Valley—basin ... CO-8
*Parago Island* ... MP-9
Paragon—locale ... AL-4
Paragon—locale ... KY-4
Paragon—locale ... MT-8
**Paragon**—pop pl ... IN-6
**Paragonah**—pop pl ... UT-8
Paragonah Cem—cemetery ... UT-8
Paragon Bridge—bridge ... IN-6
Paragon Brook—stream ... NY-2
Paragon Cem—cemetery ... AL-4
Paragon Cem—cemetery ... NE-7
Paragon Ch (historical)—church ... AL-4
Paragon Country Club—other ... NJ-2
Paragon Ditch—canal ... CA-9
Paragon Elem Sch—school ... IN-6
**Paragon Estates**—pop pl ... CO-8
Paragon Gulch—valley ... ID-8
*Paragon Lake* ... NY-2
Paragon Lake—lake ... ID-8
Paragon Lake—lake ... OR-9
Paragon Lake—reservoir ... IN-6
Paragon Lake Dam—dam ... IN-6
Paragon Mills—uninc pl ... TN-4
Paragon Mills Sch—school ... TN-4
Paragon Mine—mine ... AZ-5
Paragon Mine—mine ... CA-9
Paragon Park—park ... MA-1
Paragon Sch (historical)—school ... AL-4
Paragon School—locale ... CO-8
*Paragoona* ... UT-8
*Paragoonah* ... UT-8
**Paragould**—pop pl ... AR-4
**Paragould Junction**—pop pl ... AR-4
Parah Ch—church ... SC-3
*Parah Church* ... AL-4
**Paraiso**—pop pl (3) ... PR-3

Paraiso Springs—*spring* CA-9
**Paraje (Casa Blanca P O)**—*pop pl* NM-5
Paraje De Sanches—*civil* CA-9
Paraje Irrigation Ditch—*canal* NM-5
Paraje Mesa—*summit* NM-5
Paraje Well—*well* NM-5
Para Lake—*lake* WA-9
Paralda Ditch—*canal* WY-8
Paralde Spring—*spring* NV-8
Parallel—*locale* OK-5
Parallel Arch—*arch* UT-8
Parallel Canyon—*valley* AZ-5
Parallel Creek—*stream* AK-9
Parallel Creek—*stream* ID-8
Parallel Creek—*stream* OR-9
Parallel Draw—*valley* WY-8
Parallel (historical)—*locale* KS-7
Parallel Plaza—*locale* KS-7
Parallet Spring—*spring* OR-9
**Paraloma**—*pop pl* AR-4
**Paralta**—*pop pl* IA-7
Paralysis Point—*cape* AK-9
*Paralyze Canyon* CA-9
Paralyze Canyon—*valley* CA-9
*Param* FM-9
Paramae Gulch—*valley* CA-9
Paramanof Bay—*bay* AK-9
Paramanof Mtn—*summit* AK-9
*Parames* NJ-2
*Param Island* FM-9
Param (Municipality)—*civ div* FM-9
Paramore Crater—*crater* AZ-5
**Paramore Farm (subdivision)**—*pop pl* NC-3
Paramore Hill—*locale* GA-3
*Paramore's Beach* VA-3
Paramore Spring—*spring* UT-8
Paramount—*CDP* MD-2
Paramount—*locale* AL-4
**Paramount**—*pop pl* CA-9
**Paramount**—*pop pl* KY-4
**Paramount**—*pop pl* MD-2
Paramount Canyon—*valley* NM-5
Paramount Ch (US-M962/Benndale/
1947)—*church* MS-4
Paramount Die Casting
Company—*facility* MI-6
Paramount HS—*school* AL-4
Paramount HS—*school* CA-9
Paramount JHS—*school* CA-9
Paramount Lake—*lake* OH-6
**Paramount Manor**—*pop pl* MD-2
Paramount Mine—*mine* CA-9
Paramount Mine (underground)—*mine* AL-4
Paramount Park—*park* CO-8
Paramount Park—*park* TX-5
**Paramount Park**—*pop pl* SC-3
**Paramount Park Subdivision**—*pop pl* UT-8
Paramount Sch—*school* CA-9
Paramount Spring—*spring* CA-9
Paramount Studios—*other* CA-9
Paramount Studios Complex—*hist pl* NY-2
Paramount Terrace Sch—*school* TX-5
Paramount Theater—*hist pl* CO-8
Paramount Theater—*hist pl* MN-6
Paramount Theater—*hist pl* TX-5
Paramount Theater Bldg—*hist pl* IA-7
Paramount Theatre—*hist pl* CA-9
Paramount Theatre—*hist pl* IL-6
Paramount Theatre—*hist pl* KY-4
Paramount Theatre—*hist pl* OR-9
Paramount Theatre—*hist pl* TX-5
Paramount Theatre—*hist pl* WA-9
Paramount Theatre and Office
Bldg—*hist pl* TN-4
Paramount Theatre Bldg—*hist pl* FL-3
Paramount Valley—*valley* NE-7
Paramount Valley Sch—*school* NE-7
Paramount Wash—*stream* CA-9
Paramour Creek—*stream* OH-6
**Paramus**—*pop pl* NJ-2
Paramus HS—*school* NJ-2
Paramus Park—*park* NJ-2
Paramus Reformed Church Hist
Dist—*hist pl* NJ-2
*Paran* AL-4
*Paran* FM-9
Paran—*locale* AL-4
Paran, Lake—*lake* VT-1
Paran Cem—*cemetery* TN-4
Paran Ch—*church* FL-3
Paran Creek—*stream* VT-1
Parang, Ununen—*bar* FM-9
Parang Island—*island* FM-9
*Paran Primitive Baptist Church* AL-4
*Paran United Methodist Church* TN-4
*Parao Island* MP-9
Parao Island—*island* MP-9
Parapet Brook—*stream* NH-1
*Parapet Creek* MT-8
Paraplane Cove—*bay* VA-3
Para Point—*cape* AK-9
Para Ranch—*locale* AZ-5
Parashant Canyon—*valley* AZ-5
*Parashant Wash* AZ-5
Parashant Wash—*arroyo* AZ-5
Parashant Well—*locale* AZ-5
*Parashont Canyon* AZ-5
Parashont Canyon—*valley* AZ-5
Parashont Point—*cliff* AZ-5
*Parashont Wash* AZ-5
Parasol—*locale* VI-3
Parasol Bayou—*stream* LA-4
Parasol Butte—*summit* OR-9
Parau—*locale* FM-9
Parau, Pilapen—*stream* FM-9
Paravigini Dam—*dam* AL-4
Paraviginis Lake—*reservoir* AL-4
*Parawa Creek* OR-9
Para Wash—*stream* CA-9
Parayne Hill—*summit* CA-9
*Parazo Canyon* CA-9
*Parbon Gulf* AL-4
Pa-Rc And D-105 Dam—*dam* PA-2
**Parcelas Falu**—*pop pl* (2) PR-3
Parcelas Penuelas—*CDP* PR-3
**Parcelas Penuelas**—*pop pl* PR-3
Parcell—*locale* PA-2
Parcell Lakes—*lake* MI-6
Parcell Salisbury Cem—*cemetery* MO-7
Parcell Sch—*school* MI-6
**Parcells Corner**—*pop pl* NY-2
Parcell Spring—*spring* UT-8
Parcel Post—*post sta* CA-9
Parcel Post—*post sta* (2) CT-1
Parcel Post—*post sta* (3) NY-2
Parcel Post—*post sta* OH-6
Parcel Post—*post sta* (2) PA-2
Parcel Post Annex—*post sta* (2) OH-6
Parcel Post Annex—*post sta* RI-1
Parce Mtn—*summit* NY-2
Parce Pond—*lake* NY-2
Parchaby Tump—*island* VA-3
Parch Corn Bay—*bay* NC-3
Parch Corn Creek—*stream* (2) TN-4
Parchcorn Hollow—*valley* TN-4
Parchcorn Hollow Branch—*stream* TN-4
Parchcorn Ridge—*ridge* TN-4
Parched Corn Bar—*bar* AL-4
Parched Corn Bay—*bay* NC-3
*Parched Corn Creek* TN-4
Parched Corn Creek—*stream* KY-4
Parched Corn Hollow—*valley* MO-7
Parched Corn Point—*cape* NC-3
Parcher Drain—*stream* MI-6
Parchers Camp—*locale* CA-9
Parches Cove—*basin* AL-4
Parchester Village—*uninc pl* CA-9
Parch Landing—*locale* FL-3
**Parchman**—*pop pl* MS-4
Parchman Cem—*cemetery* TN-4
Parchman Place Site—*hist pl* MS-4
Parchman Pond—*lake* FL-3
Parchman Post Office—*building* MS-4
Parchman (State Penitentiary)—*building* MS-4
*Parchment* WV-2
**Parchment**—*pop pl* MI-6
Parchment Chapel—*church* WV-2
Parchment Creek—*stream* WV-2
Parchment North Sch—*school* MI-6
Parchment Valley—*locale* WV-2
Parch Pond—*lake* NY-2
*Parcipany* NJ-2
*Parcipany Brook* NJ-2
*Parcipponog* NJ-2
*Parco* WY-8
**Parcoal**—*pop pl* WV-2
Parco Ditch—*canal* WY-8
Parco Hist Dist—*hist pl* WY-8
Parco Mines—*mine* UT-8
Parc Perdu, Bayou—*stream* LA-4
Parc-Way Assembly of God Ch—*church* IN-6
Parda, Sierra—*summit* TX-5
*Parda Hook* NY-2
Pardais Coulee—*valley* MT-8
Pardaloe Creek—*stream* CA-9
Pardaloe Peak—*summit* CA-9
*Pardalo Peak* CA-9
Pardee—*locale* CA-9
Pardee—*locale* ID-8
Pardee—*locale* PA-2
**Pardee**—*pop pl* PA-2
**Pardee**—*pop pl* VA-3
**Pardee**—*pop pl* WV-2
Pardee, George, House—*hist pl* MI-6
Pardee, Israel Platt, Mansion—*hist pl* PA-2
Pardee Camp—*locale* MT-8
Pardee Corner—*locale* ID-8
Pardee Creek—*stream* CA-9
Pardee Creek—*stream* MT-8
Pardee Creek—*stream* WI-6
Pardee Dam—*dam* CA-9
Pardee (historical)—*locale* KS-7
Pardee Hollow—*valley* NY-2
Pardee House—*hist pl* CA-9
Pardee Island—*island* MI-6
Pardee Lake—*lake* MI-6
Pardee Lake—*lake* WI-6
Pardee Memorial Hosp—*hospital* NC-3
Pardee Park—*park* MI-6
Pardee Point—*cliff* TN-4
Pardee Reservoir Rec Area—*park* CA-9
Pardee Rsvr—*reservoir* CA-9
Pardee Sch—*school* KS-7
Pardee Sch—*school* (2) MI-6
Pardee Sch—*school* NY-2
Pardee Sch (historical)—*school* PA-2
Pardees Ponds—*lake* NY-2
Pardee Spring—*spring* OR-9
**Pardeesville**—*pop pl* PA-2
Pardee Tunnel—*tunnel* CA-9
**Pardeeville**—*pop pl* WI-6
Pardeeville Corners—*locale* NY-2
Pardeeville Presbyterian Church—*hist pl* WI-6
Pardner Canyon—*valley* UT-8
Pardnership Tank—*reservoir* AZ-5
Pardnership Windmill—*locale* TX-5
Pardo—*locale* NV-8
Pardo, Cerro—*summit* TX-5
**Pardoe**—*pop pl* PA-2
Pardoe Lake—*lake* CA-9
Pardon Branch—*stream* TN-4
Pardon Hills—*summit* LA-4
Pardon Island—*island* FL-3
Pardon Slough—*gut* FL-3
Pardo Point—*cape* NY-2
Pardue Camp—*locale* (2) TX-5
Pardue Cem—*cemetery* (2) TN-4
Pardue Elevator—*locale* MT-8
Pardue (historical)—*locale* MS-4
*Pardue Lake* CA-9
Pardue Lake—*lake* AL-4
Pardue Lake—*reservoir* AL-4
Pardue Lake Dam—*dam* AL-4
Pardue Mill—*locale* GA-3
Pardue Sch—*school* (2) LA-4
*Pardues Landing* TN-4
Pardue Tabernacle—*church* GA-3
Pardus—*locale* PA-2
Pardus Creek—*stream* ID-8
Pardy Lake—*lake* MI-6
Pardy Pond—*lake* MI-6
Parea Butte—*summit* WY-8
*Parea Gulch* WY-8
Parea Mesa—*summit* NM-5
Parea Spring—*spring* WY-8
Paredon, Arroyo—*stream* CA-9
Parees Island—*island* ID-8
Parejo Hill—*summit* CA-9
*Parem* FM-9
Parem—*island* FM-9
Paremkep—*civil* FM-9
Paremore Camp—*locale* FL-3
Parempei—*island* FM-9
Parem Sch—*school* FM-9
Pareners Branch—*stream* FL-3
Parent—*locale* ME-1
Parent—*locale* MN-6
Parent Bay—*bay* MI-6
*Parent Creek* MI-6
*Parent Creek* NE-7
Parent Creek—*stream* MI-6
Parent Drain—*stream* MI-6
*Parent Harbor* MI-6
*Parent Lake* MN-6
Parent Lake—*lake* MI-6
Parent Lake—*lake* MN-6
*Parent River* MN-6
Parent Sch—*school* CA-9
Parent Slu—*stream* WI-6
Pare Sch—*school* MI-6
Paret, Dolen—*summit* FM-9
Paret Fire Tower—*locale* MS-4
Parett Fletcher Branch—*stream* VA-3
Parfel Park—*flat* CO-8
**Par Four Subdivision**—*pop pl* UT-8
Parfreys Glen—*valley* WI-6
Parfreys Glen Creek—*stream* WI-6
**Parfreyville**—*pop pl* WI-6
Pargey Creek—*stream* NJ-2
Pargin Mtn—*summit* CO-8
Pargney Sch—*school* PA-2
Pargon Ditch—*canal* AK-9
Pargon River—*stream* AK-9
**Parguera**—*pop pl* PR-3
Parguera (Barrio)—*fmr MCD* PR-3
Pargut Run—*stream* WV-2
**Parham**—*pop pl* MS-4
**Parham**—*pop pl* (2) TN-4
Parham Branch—*stream* FL-3
Parham Bridge Park—*park* MS-4
Parham Cem—*cemetery* GA-3
Parham Cem—*cemetery* (5) TN-4
Parham Chapel—*church* (2) TN-4
Parham Creek—*stream* VA-3
Parham Gap—*gap* TN-4
Parham Hosp—*hospital* NC-3
Parham Point—*cape* VA-3
Parham Post Office (historical)—*building* TN-4
Parhams—*locale* GA-3
**Parhams**—*pop pl* LA-4
Parhams Ch—*church* LA-4
Parham Sch—*school* AR-4
Parham Sch—*school* TN-4
*Parhams Chapel Methodist Episcopal Church* TN-4
Parhams Landing—*locale* AL-4
Parhams Mill (historical)—*locale* TN-4
Parham Spring—*spring* GA-3
Parham Springs—*spring* GA-3
Parham Springs Creek—*stream* GA-3
Paria Amphitheater—*valley* UT-8
Paria Canyon—*valley* AZ-5
Paria Canyon—*valley* UT-8
Paria Canyon Primitive Area—*area* UT-8
*Paria Canyon-Vermillion Cliffs Wilderness
Area* UT-8
*Paria Creek* UT-8
Paria Hollow—*valley* UT-8
Paria (Pahreah)—*locale* UT-8
Paria Plateau—*plain* AZ-5
Paria Point—*cape* UT-8
Paria Ranger Station—*locale* UT-8
*Pa-ria River* AZ-5
Paria River—*stream* AZ-5
Paria River—*stream* UT-8
*Paria Trailhead* UT-8
Paria View—*locale* UT-8
*Parida Creek* CA-9
*Parida Creek* TX-5
Parida Island—*island* AK-9
Parida Island Reef—*bar* AK-9
*Paridise* PA-2
Paridise Spring—*spring* UT-8
Paridise Valley Golf Course—*locale* NC-3
*Parie* MH-9
Pariette Bench—*bench* UT-8
Pariette Draw—*valley* UT-8
Pariette East Dike Dam—*dam* UT-8
Pariette East Dike Rsvr—*reservoir* UT-8
Pariette Flood Control Dam—*dam* UT-8
Pariette Flood Control Rsvr—*reservoir* UT-8
Pariette Mine—*mine* UT-8
Pariette Waterfowl Habitat Mngmt
Area—*park* UT-8
Parika Lake—*lake* CO-8
Parika Peak—*summit* CO-8
*Parikarao* FM-9
Parika Trail—*trail* CO-8
*Parikiiru San* FM-9
*Parikiiru Suido* FM-9
*Pariki River* KS-7
*Parikiru* FM-9
*Parington Creek* CA-9
*Paris* AL-4
*Paris* CA-9
*Paris* MS-4
Paris—*locale* CA-9
Paris—*locale* NH-1
Paris—*locale* OH-6
Paris—*locale* VA-3
**Paris**—*pop pl* AR-4
**Paris**—*pop pl* ID-8
**Paris**—*pop pl* IL-6
**Paris**—*pop pl* IN-6
**Paris**—*pop pl* (2) IA-7
**Paris**—*pop pl* KY-4
**Paris**—*pop pl* ME-1
**Paris**—*pop pl* MD-2
**Paris**—*pop pl* MI-6
**Paris**—*pop pl* MS-4
**Paris**—*pop pl* MO-7
**Paris**—*pop pl* NY-2
**Paris**—*pop pl* OH-6
**Paris**—*pop pl* OR-9
**Paris**—*pop pl* PA-2
**Paris**—*pop pl* SC-3
**Paris**—*pop pl* TN-4
**Paris**—*pop pl* TX-5
**Paris**—*pop pl* WI-6
Paris, Joseph, House—*hist pl* WA-9
Paris Archeol Site—*hist pl* WA-9
Paris Baptist Ch—*church* MS-4
Paris (Barrio)—*fmr MCD* PR-3
Paris Branch—*stream* MO-7
Paris Branch—*stream* NC-3
Paris Branch—*stream* TN-4
Paris Bridge—*bridge* SC-3
Paris Canyon—*valley* ID-8
*Paris Canyon Basin* ID-8
*Paris Canyon Creek* ID-8
Paris (CCD)—*cens area* KY-4
Paris (CCD)—*cens area* TN-4
Paris (CCD)—*cens area* TX-5
Paris Cem—*cemetery* GA-3
Paris Cem—*cemetery* IL-6
Paris Cem—*cemetery* IN-6
Paris Cem—*cemetery* IA-7
Paris Cem—*cemetery* (2) KY-4
Paris Cem—*cemetery* MS-4
Paris Cem—*cemetery* WI-6
Paris Cemetery—*hist pl* ID-8
Paris Cemetery Gatehouse—*hist pl* KY-4
Paris Ch—*church* MI-6
Paris City Hall—*building* TN-4
Paris Commercial Hist Dist—*hist pl* TN-4
Paris Commercial Hist Dist—*hist pl* TX-5
Paris Country Club—*other* TX-5
Paris Courthouse Square Hist
Dist—*hist pl* KY-4
Paris Creek—*stream* AK-9
Paris Creek—*stream* CO-8
Paris Creek—*stream* ID-8
Paris Creek—*stream* MI-6
Paris Creek—*stream* NV-8
Paris Creek—*stream* NM-5
Paris Creek—*stream* WA-9
**Paris Crossing**—*pop pl* IN-6
Paris Dainwood Draw—*valley* NM-5
Paris Dam—*dam* OR-9
Paris Ditch—*canal* IN-6
Paris Division—*civil* TN-4
Paris Drag Strip—*other* TX-5
Paris Drain—*canal* MI-6
Paris Elks Lodge No. 812 Bldg—*hist pl* IL-6
Paris First Baptist Ch—*church* TN-4
Paris Flat—*flat* ID-8
Paris Fork Ch—*church* MO-7
Paris Gap—*gap* NC-3
Paris Golf and Country Club—*locale* TN-4
Paris Grove Ch—*church* MS-4
*Parish* FL-3
Parish—*locale* GA-3
Parish—*locale* WV-2
**Parish**—*pop pl* NY-2
Parish Aerodrome Airp—*airport* TN-4
Parish Bridge—*bridge* AL-4
Parish Cabin Campground—*park* OR-9
Parish Camp—*locale* CA-9
Parish Camp Saddle Dam—*dam* CA-9
Parish Cem—*cemetery* IL-6
Parish Cem—*cemetery* MA-1
Parish Cem—*cemetery* (2) MO-7
Parish Cem—*cemetery* NY-2
Parish Cem—*cemetery* OH-6
Parish Cem—*cemetery* TX-5
Parish Cem—*cemetery* VT-1
Parish Center—*locale* NY-2
*Parish Court* VA-3
*Parish Creek* NY-2
Parish Creek—*bay* MD-2
Parish Creek—*stream* WA-9
Parish Drain—*stream* MI-6
Parisher Well—*well* NM-5
Parish Farm—*locale* LA-4
Parishfield—*locale* MI-6
Parish Flat—*flat* NY-2
Parish Fork—*stream* WV-2
Parish Grove (Township of)—*civ div* IN-6
Parish Hill—*summit* CT-1
*Parish Hill Creek* VA-3
**Parish Hills (subdivision)**—*pop pl* AL-4
*Parish Hollow* TN-4
*Paris Hill* ME-1
Paris Hill—*summit* CO-8
Paris Hill—*summit* ME-1
Paris Hill Hist Dist—*hist pl* ME-1
Paris Hills—*range* KY-4
Parish Island—*island* IL-6
Paris (historical)—*locale* KS-7
Paris (historical)—*locale* NC-3
Paris (historical)—*locale* SD-7
**Paris (historical)**—*pop pl* IA-7
**Paris (historical)**—*pop pl* NC-3
**Paris (historical)**—*pop pl* OR-9
Parish Lake—*gut* LA-4
Parish Lake—*lake* AR-4
Parish Lake—*lake* FL-3
Parish Lake—*lake* LA-4
Parish Lake—*lake* MI-6
Parish Lake—*lake* MS-4
Parish Lake—*lake* OR-9
Parish Lake Bayou—*gut* MS-4
Parish Lake Dam—*dam* (2) MS-4
Parish Mtn—*summit* VA-3
Parish of the Resurrection—*church* DE-2
Paris Hollow—*valley* GA-3
Paris Hollow—*valley* TN-4
*Parish Pond* MA-1
Parish Pond—*lake* FL-3
Parish Pond—*lake* MD-2
Parish Ranch—*locale* NM-5
Parish Rocks—*cliff* OH-6
Parish Run—*stream* VA-3
Paris HS—*school* KY-4
Parish Sch—*school* KS-7
Parish Sch—*school* VT-1
Parish Sch (historical)—*school* TN-4
Parishs Landing (historical)—*locale* MS-4
Parishs Store (historical)—*locale* AL-4
**Parish (subdivision)**—*pop pl* AL-4
**Parish (Town of)**—*pop pl* NY-2
Parish Trade Sch—*school* LA-4
**Parishville**—*pop pl* NY-2
**Parishville Center**—*pop pl* NY-2
Parishville-Hopkinton Sch—*school* NY-2
**Parishville (Town of)**—*pop pl* NY-2
Paris Ice Cave—*cave* ID-8
*Paris Island* SC-3
Paris Island—*island* GA-3
Paris Junior Coll—*school* TX-5
Paris Lake—*reservoir* GA-3
Paris Landing—*locale* TN-4
Paris Landing Marina—*locale* TN-4
Paris Landing Post Office
(historical)—*building* TN-4
Paris Landing State Park—*park* TN-4
Paris Lateral—*canal* ID-8
*Paris-Loraine* CA-9
Paris Lumber Company Bldg—*hist pl* ID-8
Paris Memorial Cem—*cemetery* TN-4
Paris Memorial Gardens—*cemetery* IL-6
Paris Mill—*locale* CO-8
Paris Millpond—*swamp* NC-3
Paris Mine—*mine* CO-8
Paris Mine—*mine* TN-4
Paris Mountain Country Club—*other* SC-3
Paris Mountain State Park—*park* SC-3
Paris Mtn—*summit* (2) GA-3
Paris Mtn—*summit* SC-3
Paris Mtn—*summit* VA-3
Paris Normal Sch (historical)—*school* MS-4
Paris Park—*park* KS-7
Paris Peak—*summit* ID-8
Paris Photo Studio—*hist pl* ID-8
**Paris (Piedmont Park)**—*pop pl* SC-3
Paris Pond—*lake* CT-1
Paris Post Office—*building* TN-4
Paris Public Sch—*hist pl* ID-8
Paris Ranch—*locale* NV-8
Paris RR Depot—*hist pl* KY-4
Paris Rsvr—*reservoir* AR-4
Paris Rsvr—*reservoir* (2) OR-9
Paris Run—*stream* PA-2
Parissawampitts Canyon—*valley* AZ-5
Parissawampitts Point—*cliff* AZ-5
Parissawampitts Spring—*spring* AZ-5
Paris Sch—*school* CO-8
Paris Sch—*school* IN-6
Paris Sch—*school* SD-7
Paris Sch—*school* WI-6
Paris Shop Ctr—*locale* TN-4
Paris Spring—*spring* ID-8
Paris Spring—*spring* NV-8
Paris Spring—*spring* OR-9
Paris Spring Number Five—*spring* NV-8
*Paris Spring Number One* NV-8
**Paris Springs**—*pop pl* MO-7
Paris Springs Ch—*church* MO-7
Paris Square Shop Ctr—*locale* TN-4
Paris (sta.) (Paris Crossing)—*other* IN-6
**Paris Station**—*pop pl* NY-2
**Paris (Town of)**—*pop pl* ME-1
**Paris (Town of)**—*pop pl* NY-2
**Paris (Town of)**—*pop pl* (2) WI-6
Paris Township—*fmr MCD* IA-7
**Paris Township**—*pop pl* KS-7
**Paris Township**—*pop pl* ND-7
*Paris (Township of)* MI-6
**Paris (Township of)**—*pop pl* IL-6
**Paris (Township of)**—*pop pl* MI-6
**Paris (Township of)**—*pop pl* (3) OH-6
Paris Valley—*basin* CA-9
**Paris Villa**—*pop pl* DE-2
Parisville—*locale* MI-6
Paris Woolen Mill—*hist pl* OR-9
Parita Ch—*church* TX-5
Parita Creek—*stream* TX-5
*Paritan Creek* MT-8
Pariyaaru—*bay* MH-9
*Pariyapairon* FM-9
*Pariyu To* PW-9
Parizek Pond—*reservoir* CT-1
*Park* AZ-5
*Park* IN-6
*Park* MI-6
*Park* ND-7
*Park* TN-4
Park—*flat* OR-9
Park—*locale* CO-8
Park—*locale* ID-8
Park—*locale* KY-4
Park—*locale* TX-5
Park—*locale* VA-3
Park—*locale* WA-9
Park—*other* MO-7
Park—*park* NC-3
**Park**—*pop pl* FL-3
**Park**—*pop pl* IN-6
**Park**—*pop pl* KS-7
**Park**—*pop pl* TN-4
**Park**—*pop pl* WA-9
Park—*uninc pl* CA-9
Park—*uninc pl* NJ-2
Park—*uninc pl* PA-2
Park—*uninc pl* VA-3
Park, Arroyo—*park* TX-5
Park, David, House—*hist pl* MN-6
Park, James, House—*hist pl* TN-4
Park, Jonathan, House—*hist pl* OH-6
Park, Lake—*lake* FL-3
Park, Lake—*lake* OH-6
Park, Lake—*reservoir* TX-5
Park, Point—*cape* TN-4
*Park, The* UT-8
Park, The—*flat* (3) AZ-5
Park, The—*flat* (2) MT-8
Park, The—*flat* NV-8
Park, The—*flat* NM-5
Park, The—*flat* OR-9
Park, The—*flat* TX-5
Park, The—*flat* (2) UT-8
Park, The—*flat* WY-8
Park, The—*locale* NM-5
Park, The (Shop Ctr)—*locale* FL-3
**Park Addition**—*pop pl* WV-2
Parkade Plaza—*locale* MO-7
Parkade Sch—*school* MO-7
*Park Airport* KS-7
Park and Bandstand—*hist pl* AL-4
Park and Bull Slough—*canal* NV-8
Park and Lemon Canal—*canal* ID-8
Park Apartments—*hist pl* CA-9
Parka Peak—*summit* AK-9
Parkard Creek Campground—*park* OR-9
Park Ave—*post sta* FL-3
Park Ave—*post sta* NJ-2
Park Ave—*valley* UT-8
Park Ave Baptist Ch—*church* (2) FL-3
Park Ave Baptist Church—*hist pl* OH-6
Park Ave Baptist Sch—*school* FL-3
Park Ave Bridge—*hist pl* AZ-5
Park Ave Ch—*church* (2) GA-3
Park Ave Ch—*church* KY-4
Park Ave Ch—*church* NC-3
Park Ave Ch—*church* TN-4
Park Ave Hist Dist—*hist pl* FL-3
Park Ave Hosp—*hospital* CO-8
Park Ave Hosp—*hospital* NY-2
Park Ave Houses—*hist pl* NY-2
Park Ave Interchange—*crossing* AZ-5
*Park Ave Middle School* TN-4
Park Ave Sch—*school* AR-4
Park Ave Sch—*school* CA-9
Park Ave Sch—*school* (2) CT-1
Park Ave Sch—*school* IA-7
Park Ave Sch—*school* KY-4
Park Ave Sch—*school* MA-1
Park Ave Sch—*school* NJ-2
Park Ave Sch—*school* (4) NY-2
Park Ave Sch—*school* (2) TN-4
Park Ave Sch—*school* VA-3
Park Ave Sch—*school* WA-9
**Park Ave Subdivision**—*pop pl* UT-8
**Park Away Mobile Home
Park**—*pop pl* PA-2
Park Bake Oven Trail—*trail* PA-2
*Park Bend* TN-4
Park Bldg—*hist pl* MA-1
Park Blvd Ch—*church* IL-6
Park Branch—*stream* MO-7
Park Branch Canal—*canal* MT-8
Park Brook—*stream* NY-2
Park Brook Sch—*school* MN-6
Parkburg—*locale* TN-4
*Parkburg Baptist Church* TN-4
Parkburg Ch—*church* TN-4
Park Butte—*summit* ID-8
Park Butte—*summit* OR-9
Park Butte—*summit* WA-9
Park Butte Lookout—*hist pl* WA-9
Park Campground—*locale* WA-9
Park Camp Spring—*spring* SD-7
*Park Canyon* ID-8
Park Canyon—*valley* AZ-5
Park Canyon—*valley* CA-9
Park Canyon—*valley* CO-8
Park Canyon—*valley* ID-8
Park Canyon—*valley* MT-8
Park Canyon—*valley* (3) NV-8
Park Canyon—*valley* (2) NM-5
Park Canyon—*valley* (3) UT-8
*Park Canyon Creek* UT-8
Park Canyon (site)—*locale* NV-8
Park Canyon Spring—*spring* NV-8
*Park Cem* AR-4
Park Cem—*cemetery* AR-4
Park Cem—*cemetery* CT-1
Park Cem—*cemetery* (2) IN-6
Park Cem—*cemetery* IA-7
Park Cem—*cemetery* (3) KS-7
Park Cem—*cemetery* MI-6
Park Cem—*cemetery* (3) MO-7
Park Cem—*cemetery* NE-7
Park Cem—*cemetery* NH-1
Park Cem—*cemetery* (2) NY-2
Park Cem—*cemetery* ND-7
Park Cem—*cemetery* OH-6
Park Cem—*cemetery* PA-2
Park Cem—*cemetery* (2) TN-4
Park Cem—*cemetery* TX-5
Park Cem—*cemetery* UT-8
**Park Center**—*pop pl* CO-8
Park Center Ch—*church* (2) ND-7
Park Center Lateral—*canal* CO-8
Park Center Pitch—*canal* CO-8
Park Center Sch—*school* NE-7
Park Central—*uninc pl* CA-9
Park Central Plaza (Shop Ctr)—*locale* FL-3
Park Central Shop Ctr—*locale* AZ-5
Park Central Square—*park* MO-7
**Park Central Subdivision**—*pop pl* UT-8
Park Ch—*church* FL-3
Park Ch—*church* KS-7
Park Ch—*church* NE-7
Park Ch—*church* NC-3
Park Channel—*channel* FL-3
Park Chapel—*church* VA-3
**Parkchester**—*pop pl* GA-3
**Parkchester**—*pop pl* NY-2
**Parkchester**—*pop pl* PA-2
Park Church—*hist pl* NY-2
Park Circle—*locale* CA-9
Park Circle—*locale* NY-2
Park Circle—*park* SC-3
Park Circle Ch—*church* SC-3
**Park Cities**—*pop pl* TX-5
Park Cities Ch—*church* TX-5
Park Cities Filtration Plant—*other* TX-5
Park City—*locale* CO-8
Park City—*locale* MT-8
**Park City**—*pop pl* AL-4
**Park City**—*pop pl* FL-3
**Park City**—*pop pl* GA-3
**Park City**—*pop pl* IL-6
**Park City**—*pop pl* KS-7
**Park City**—*pop pl* KY-4
**Park City**—*pop pl* MT-8
**Park City**—*pop pl* (2) TN-4
**Park City**—*pop pl* UT-8
Park City Baptist Ch—*church* UT-8
Park City Cem—*cemetery* CO-8
Park City Cem—*cemetery* UT-8
Park City Ch—*church* AL-4
Park City Ch—*church* FL-3
Park City Ch of God—*church* TN-4
Park City Community Church—*hist pl* UT-8
Park City Consolidated—*mine* UT-8
Park City Division—*civil* UT-8
**Park City (Glasgow Junction)**—*pop pl* KY-4
**Park City Heights**—*pop pl* TN-4
Park City Hist Dist—*hist pl* MI-6
Park City Hosp—*hospital* CT-1
Park City HS—*school* UT-8
Park City JHS—*hist pl* TN-4
Park City Lowry Sch—*school* TN-4
Park City Main Street Hist Dist—*hist pl* UT-8
Park City Miner's Hosp—*hist pl* UT-8
Park City Mines—*mine* MO-7
Park City Post Office—*building* UT-8
Park City Sch (historical)—*school* TN-4
Park City Shop Ctr—*locale* TN-4

Park City Ski Area—locale UT-8
Park City Ski Area Heliport—airport UT-8
Park City West Ski Area—locale UT-8
Park Cliffs—cliff WA-9
Park Coll—school MO-7
Park Coll Sch—school IL-6
Park Community Ch—church NJ-2
Park Community Hosp—hospital MI-6
Park Cone—summit CO-8
Park Coulee—valley MT-8
Park Country Club—other NY-2
Park County Courthouse and Jail—hist pl CO-8
**Park Courts**—pop pl AL-4
Park Cove TN-4
Park Creek CA-9
Park Creek CO-8
Park Creek MT-8
Park Creek OR-9
Park Creek—bay MD-2
Park Creek—stream AK-9
Park Creek—stream (4) AZ-5
Park Creek—stream AR-4
Park Creek—stream CA-9
Park Creek—stream (8) CO-8
Park Creek—stream (7) ID-8
Park Creek—stream IN-6
Park Creek—stream (13) MT-8
Park Creek—stream NV-8
Park Creek—stream (2) NY-2
Park Creek—stream (2) NC-3
Park Creek—stream (7) OR-9
Park Creek—stream PA-2
Park Creek—stream (2) SC-3
Park Creek—stream (2) SD-7
Park Creek—stream UT-8
Park Creek—stream (3) WA-9
Park Creek—stream (2) WI-6
Park Creek—stream (4) WY-8
Park Creek Cabins—locale AZ-5
Park Creek Campground—locale CO-8
Park Creek Campground—locale (2) ID-8
Park Creek Lateral—canal CO-8
Park Creek Meadow—flat WY-8
Park Creek Pass—gap WA-9
Park Creek Recreation Site—park OR-9
Park Creek Ridge—ridge WA-9
Park Creek Rsvr—reservoir CO-8
Park Creek Tank—reservoir AZ-5
Park Creek Trail—trail MT-8
Park Creek Trail—trail WA-9
**Park Crest**—pop pl PA-2
**Park Crest Subdivision**—pop pl UT-8
**Parkcrest Subdivision**—pop pl UT-8
Parkcrest Village MO-7
Park Crest Village Center—locale UT-8
Parkcrest Village Shop Ctr—other MO-7
Parkdale MO-7
Parkdale (2) OH-6
Parkdale—locale CO-8
Parkdale—locale MN-6
Parkdale—locale NJ-2
**Parkdale**—pop pl AL-4
**Parkdale**—pop pl AR-4
**Parkdale**—pop pl MI-6
**Parkdale**—pop pl (2) MO-7
**Parkdale**—pop pl OR-9
Parkdale—uninc pl (2) TX-5
Parkdale (CCD)—cens area OR-9
Parkdale Cem—cemetery TX-5
Parkdale Cemeteries—cemetery AR-4
Parkdale Cemetery OR-9
Parkdale Ch—church AL-4
Parkdale Cold Spring—spring OR-9
**Parkdale Junction**—pop pl CO-8
Parkdale Park—park MI-6
Parkdale Plaza—locale TX-5
Parkdale Ranger Station—hist pl OR-9
Parkdale Sch—school KS-7
Parkdale Sch—school MI-6
Parkdale Sch—school NY-2
Parkdale Sch—school TX-5
Parkdale Siding—locale CO-8
**Parkdale (subdivision)**—pop pl MS-4
**Parkdale Subdivision**—pop pl UT-8
Park De La Cruz—park CA-9
Park Department, Division of Playgrounds—hist pl WA-9
Park Ditch—canal (5) CO-8
Park Ditch—canal (2) WY-8
Park Ditch No 1—canal WY-8
Park Dota Plantation—locale LA-4
Park Drain—canal NM-5
Park Draw—valley (2) WY-8
Park Drive Ch—church TX-5
Park Drive United Pentecostal Ch—church MS-4
Parke PA-2
Parke—locale PA-2
Park East—locale KS-7
**Park East**—pop pl KS-7
Park East Synagogue, Congregation Zichron Ephraim—hist pl NY-2
Parke Canyon—valley ID-8
Parke Ch—church MN-6
**Parke County**—pop pl IN-6
Parke Creek—stream MT-8
Parke Creek—stream WA-9
Parke-Davis and Company Pharmaceutical Company Plant—hist pl MI-6
Parke-Davis Research Laboratory—hist pl MI-6
Parke Knob—summit GA-3
Parke Lake—lake MI-6
Park Elem Sch—hist pl MN-6
Park Elem Sch—school AZ-5
Park Elem Sch—school (3) IN-6
Park Elem Sch—school (7) KS-7
Park Elem Sch—school (3) PA-2
Parkell Creek—stream AL-4
Parke-Moore House—hist pl KY-4
Parken Fork—stream WY-8
Parke Peak—summit MT-8
Parker IN-6
Parker KS-7
Parker MS-4
Parker—locale (2) AL-4
Parker—locale IL-6
Parker—locale MT-8
Parker—locale NJ-2
Parker—locale NY-2
Parker—locale NC-3
Parker—locale OK-5
Parker—locale OR-9
Parker—locale TN-4
Parker—locale TX-5
Parker—locale VA-3
**Parker**—pop pl AZ-5
**Parker**—pop pl CO-8
**Parker**—pop pl FL-3
**Parker**—pop pl ID-8
**Parker**—pop pl KS-7
**Parker**—pop pl NH-1
**Parker**—pop pl NC-3
**Parker**—pop pl OK-5
**Parker**—pop pl PA-2
**Parker**—pop pl SD-7
**Parker**—pop pl TN-4
**Parker**—pop pl (2) TX-5
**Parker**—pop pl WA-9
Parker, Arthur M., House—hist pl MI-6
Parker, Capt. Nathaniel, Red House—hist pl MA-1
Parker, Charles, House—hist pl NY-2
Parker, C. W., Four-Row Park Carousel—hist pl OR-9
Parker, Dwight T., Public Library—hist pl WI-6
Parker, Francis, House—hist pl NC-3
Parker, James, House—hist pl MA-1
Parker, John, House—hist pl ID-8
Parker, John, Tavern—hist pl NJ-2
Parker, John P., House—hist pl OH-6
Parker, John W., House—hist pl TX-5
Parker, Joseph, House—hist pl MA-1
Parker, Joseph William, Farm—hist pl UT-8
Parker, Lake—lake (2) FL-3
Parker, Lake—lake VT-1
Parker, Martin Van Buren, House—hist pl KS-7
Parker, Milton, House—hist pl TX-5
Parker, Moses, House—hist pl OR-9
Parker, Mount—summit AK-9
Parker, Mount—summit NH-1
Parker, Quanah, Star House—hist pl OK-5
Parker, Samuel, House—hist pl MA-1
Parker, Stillman, House—hist pl MA-1
Parker, Thomas A., House—hist pl MI-6
Parker, William, House—hist pl MA-1
Parker and Dunstan Hardware/Dr. E. D. Lewis Bldg—hist pl MI-6
Parker and Joyner Mill (historical)—locale MS-4
Parker and Sampson Ditch—stream DE-2
Parker and Weeter Block—hist pl UT-8
Parker Arroyo—stream NM-5
Parker Assembly of God Ch—church FL-3
Parker Ave Sch—school MA-1
Parker Aviation Heliport—airport MA-1
Parker Basin—basin CO-8
Parker Basin School—locale CO-8
Parker Bay—bay MD-2
Parker Bay—swamp FL-3
Parker Bayou FL-3
Parker Bayou LA-4
Parker Bayou—bay FL-3
Parker Bayou—gut (2) MS-4
Parker Bayou—stream LA-4
Parker Bayou—stream MS-4
Parker Bay Tumps—island MD-2
Parker Bell Cem—cemetery AL-4
Parker Bennet Sch—school KY-4
Parker Bldg—hist pl MN-6
Parker Bluff—cliff TN-4
Parker Bluffs—cliff CA-9
Parker Bog Brook—stream ME-1
Parker Bog Ponds—lake ME-1
Parker-Boydston Cem—cemetery AR-4
Parker-Bradshaw House—hist pl TX-5
Parker Branch TX-5
Parker Branch—stream (7) AL-4
Parker Branch—stream (2) AR-4
Parker Branch—stream DE-2
Parker Branch—stream (3) FL-3
Parker Branch—stream (4) GA-3
Parker Branch—stream IL-6
Parker Branch—stream (3) KY-4
Parker Branch—stream (3) LA-4
Parker Branch—stream MD-2
Parker Branch—stream (6) MS-4
Parker Branch—stream (5) MO-7
Parker Branch—stream (5) NC-3
Parker Branch—stream (2) SC-3
Parker Branch—stream (10) TN-4
Parker Branch—stream (5) TX-5
Parker Branch—stream (2) VA-3
Parker Branch—stream (2) WV-2
Parker Bridge—bridge (2) AL-4
Parker Bridge—bridge CT-1
Parker Bridge—bridge FL-3
Parker Bridge—bridge MS-4
Parker Bridge—bridge NE-7
Parker Bridge—bridge NC-3
Parker Bridge—bridge TN-4
Parker Bridge (historical)—bridge TN-4
Parker Brook—stream ME-1
Parker Brook—stream (2) MA-1
Parker Brook—stream NJ-2
Parker Brook—stream NY-2
Parker-Bryson Hist Dist—hist pl TN-4
Parker Butte—ridge OR-9
Parker Butte—summit MT-8
Parker Butte—summit NV-8
Parker Butte—summit WA-9
Parker Cabin—locale MT-8
Parker Cabin Hollow—valley NY-2
Parker Cabin Mtn—summit NY-2
Parker Camp—locale CA-9
Parker Camp—locale TX-5
Parker Camp—locale VT-1
Parker Camp Trail—trail CA-9
Parker Canyon—valley (2) AZ-5
Parker Canyon—valley (3) CA-9
Parker Canyon—valley MT-8
Parker Canyon—valley NV-8
Parker Canyon—valley OR-9
Parker Canyon—valley (2) UT-8
Parker Canyon Dam—dam AZ-5
Parker Canyon Lake—reservoir AZ-5
Parker Canyon Lake Rec Area AZ-5
Parker Canyon Sch—school AZ-5
Parker Canyon Trail—trail UT-8
Parker Carson Stolport—airport NV-8
Parker Cave—cave AL-4
Parker (CCD)—cens area AZ-5
Parker Cem—cemetery (3) AL-4
Parker Cem—cemetery (3) AR-4
Parker Cem—cemetery CO-8
Parker Cem—cemetery (2) CT-1
Parker Cem—cemetery (5) GA-3
Parker Cem—cemetery IL-6
Parker Cem—cemetery (3) KS-7
Parker Cem—cemetery (4) KY-4
Parker Cem—cemetery (4) LA-4
Parker Cem—cemetery ME-1
Parker Cem—cemetery MD-2
Parker Cem—cemetery MA-1
Parker Cem—cemetery MI-6
Parker Cem—cemetery MN-6
Parker Cem—cemetery (9) MS-4
Parker Cem—cemetery (6) MO-7
Parker Cem—cemetery NE-7
Parker Cem—cemetery (2) NY-2
Parker Cem—cemetery (2) NC-3
Parker Cem—cemetery (3) OH-6
Parker Cem—cemetery OK-5
Parker Cem—cemetery (3) SC-3
Parker Cem—cemetery (20) TN-4
Parker Cem—cemetery (11) TX-5
Parker Cem—cemetery VT-1
Parker Cem—cemetery VA-3
Parker Cem—cemetery (2) WV-2
Parker Center—locale MO-7
Parker Ch AL-4
Parker Ch—church FL-3
Parker Ch—church NC-3
Parker Ch—church OK-5
Parker Chapel—church (2) AL-4
Parker Chapel—church MS-4
Parker Chapel—church NC-3
Parker Chapel—church TN-4
Parker Chapel—church TX-5
Parker Chapel—church VA-3
Parker Chapel Cem—cemetery KY-4
Parker Chapel Ch AL-4
Parker Chapel (historical)—church TN-4
Parker Chapel Missionary Baptist Ch AL-4
Parker Chapel Sch—school TN-4
Parker Church Cem—cemetery AL-4
Parker City—civil PA-2
**Parker City**—pop pl IN-6
Parker City (corporate name Parker) PA-2
Parker City Dam—Dam KS-7
Parker City Hall—building AZ-5
Parker Cook Hollow—valley NY-2
Parker Corners—locale NY-2
Parker Corners—locale PA-2
**Parker (corporate name for Parker City)**—pop pl PA-2
**Parker (County)**—pop pl TX-5
Parker County Courthouse—hist pl TX-5
Parker Courthouse—locale GA-3
Parker Cove—bay (2) ME-1
Parker Cove—bay NJ-2
Parker Covered Bridge—hist pl OH-6
Parker Creek AL-4
Parker Creek CA-9
Parker Creek GA-3
Parker Creek NY-2
Parker Creek—bay MD-2
Parker Creek—canal NC-3
Parker Creek—locale MD-2
**Parker Creek**—pop pl AZ-5
Parker Creek—stream (3) AL-4
Parker Creek—stream AK-9
Parker Creek—stream AZ-5
Parker Creek—stream (2) AR-4
Parker Creek—stream (7) CA-9
Parker Creek—stream (2) ID-8
Parker Creek—stream IL-6
Parker Creek—stream MD-2
Parker Creek—stream (3) MI-6
Parker Creek—stream (5) MS-4
Parker Creek—stream MO-7
Parker Creek—stream (4) MT-8
Parker Creek—stream (4) NC-3
Parker Creek—stream OK-5
Parker Creek—stream (14) OR-9
Parker Creek—stream SC-3
Parker Creek—stream SD-7
Parker Creek—stream (2) TN-4
Parker Creek—stream (11) TX-5
Parker Creek—stream VA-3
Parker Creek—stream (2) WA-9
Parker Creek—stream WV-2
Parker Creek—stream (3) WI-6
Parker Creek Ch—church TN-4
Parker Creek Experiment Station—locale AZ-5
Parker Creek Public Use Area—park AR-4
Parker Creek State Public Fishing Area—park WI-6
**Parker Crossroads**—pop pl SC-3
**Parker Crossroads**—pop pl TN-4
Parker Crossroads Sch (historical)—school TN-4
**Parkerdale**—pop pl IN-6
Parker Dam—dam AZ-5
Parker Dam—dam CA-9
Parker Dam—dam PA-2
Parker Dam—dam TN-4
**Parker Dam**—pop pl CA-9
Parker Dam Reservoir AZ-5
Parker Dam Reservoir CA-9
Parker Dam State Park—park PA-2
Parker Dam State Park Family Cabin District—hist pl PA-2
Parker Dam State Park-Octagonal Lodge—hist pl PA-2
Parker Dam State Park-Parker Dam District—hist pl PA-2
Parker Ditch OH-6
Parker Ditch—canal (2) IN-6
Parker Ditch—canal OR-9
Parker Ditch—canal TN-4
Parker Ditch—canal WY-8
Parker Drain—canal (2) MI-6
Parker Drain—stream MI-6
Parker Draw—valley AZ-5
Parker Draw—valley (2) WY-8
Parker Eastes Ditch—canal IN-6
Parker Elem Sch—school FL-3
Parker Elem Sch—school (2) IN-6
Parker Elem Sch—school KS-7
Parker Elem Sch—school PA-2
Parker Extension—canal MI-6
Parker Farmhouse—hist pl NY-2
Parker Farms Country Club—other CT-1
Parker Farms Sch—school CT-1
Parker Ferry (historical)—locale AL-4
Parker Field—locale VA-3
Parker Field—park MS-4
Parker Field—park NY-2
Parker Field (airport)—airport AL-4
Parker Flats—bar ME-1
Parker Flats—flat CA-9
Parker Flats—flat MA-1
Parkerford PA-2
Parker Ford—locale AR-4
Parker Ford—locale TN-4
**Parker Ford**—pop pl PA-2
Parker Ford (historical)—locale AL-4
Parker Fork—stream WV-2
Parker Gap—gap AL-4
Parker Gap—gap KY-4
Parker Gap—gap NC-3
Parker Gap—gap (2) TN-4
Parker Gap Branch—stream TN-4
Parker Gap Ch—church TN-4
Parker-Gray HS—school VA-3
Parker Group—area AK-9
Parker Grove Cem—cemetery AL-4
Parker Grove Ch—church AL-4
Parker Grove Ch—church GA-3
Parker Grove Ch—church NC-3
Parker Grove Ch—church TX-5
Parker Gulch—valley ID-8
Parker Gulch—valley WY-8
Parker Gulch Drain—canal ID-8
Parker Hammock—island FL-3
Parker Hammocks—island FL-3
Parker Head—cape ME-1
Parker Head—cliff ME-1
**Parker Head**—pop pl ME-1
Parker Head—summit ME-1
Parker Head Creek—stream ME-1
Parker Head Swamp—swamp ME-1
**Parker Heights**—pop pl AL-4
Parker Heights Grange—locale WA-9
Parker Heights Park—park IL-6
Parker Heights Sch—school WA-9
Parker-Hickman Farm Hist Dist—hist pl AR-4
Parker-Highland Cem—cemetery KS-7
Parker High Point—summit AL-4
**Parker Hill**—pop pl NH-1
**Parker Hill**—pop pl TN-4
Parker Hill—summit AR-4
Parker Hill—summit CT-1
Parker Hill—summit (3) ME-1
Parker Hill—summit (5) MA-1
Parker Hill—summit (4) NH-1
Parker Hill—summit (2) NY-2
Parker Hill—summit PA-2
Parker Hill—summit (2) TN-4
Parker Hill—summit (2) VT-1
Parker Hill—summit WV-2
Parker Hill—uninc pl MA-1
Parker Hill Cem—cemetery CT-1
Parker Hill Ch—church GA-3
Parker Hill Ch—church TN-4
Parker Hills NC-3
Parker Hills—summit OR-9
Parker Hill Sch (historical)—school TN-4
Parker (historical)—locale KS-7
**Parker (historical)**—pop pl (2) OR-9
Parker Hole—lake SC-3
Parker Hollow—valley AL-4
Parker Hollow—valley AR-4
Parker Hollow—valley (5) MO-7
Parker Hollow—valley NY-2
Parker Hollow—valley (5) PA-2
Parker Hollow—valley (6) TN-4
Parker Hollow—valley (2) UT-8
Parker Hollow—valley WV-2
Parker Hollow Creek—stream TX-5
Parker Hollow Rsvr—reservoir UT-8
Parker Hollow Trail—trail PA-2
Parker Horn—bay WA-9
Parker Hosp—hospital AZ-5
Parker House—hist pl CT-1
Parker House—hist pl IA-7
Parker House—hist pl MA-1
Parker HS—school AZ-5
Parker HS—school FL-3
Parker HS—school (2) IL-6
Parker HS—school NY-2
Parker HS—school SC-3
Parker-Hutchinson Farm—hist pl CT-1
Parker Ridge—ridge MT-8
Parker Island—island AL-4
Parker Island—island FL-3
Parker Island—island ME-1
Parker Island—island NE-7
Parker Island—island NH-1
Parker Island—island (2) NJ-2
Parker Island—island SC-3
Parker Island—island SD-7
Parker Island—island VA-3
Parker Island—locale FL-3
Parker Islands NJ-2
Parker Jail—hist pl AZ-5
Parker JHS—school NC-3
Parker JHS—school TX-5
Parker Junction—locale CA-9
Parker Knob—summit (2) NC-3
Parker Knoll—summit UT-8
Parker Lake FL-3
Parker Lake MI-6
Parker Lake PA-2
Parker Lake SD-7
Parker Lake WI-6
Parker Lake—lake AK-9
Parker Lake—lake CA-9
Parker Lake—lake CO-8
Parker Lake—lake FL-3
Parker Lake—lake ID-8
Parker Lake—lake MT-8
Parker Lake—lake (2) TX-5
Parker Lake—lake UT-8
Parker Lake—lake WA-9
Parker Lake—lake (4) WI-6
**Parker Lake**—pop pl MO-7
Parker Lake—reservoir (2) IN-6
Parker Lake—reservoir NJ-2
Parker Lake—reservoir NM-5
Parker Lake—reservoir TN-4
Parker Lake—swamp MI-6
Parker Lake Dam—dam (2) IN-6
Parker Lake Dam—dam (4) MS-4
Parker Lake Dam Number Two—dam NC-3
Parker Lake Number Two—reservoir NC-3
Parker Lakes—lake CA-9
Parker Lakes—lake IL-6
Parker Lakes—reservoir AL-4
Parker Lakes—reservoir SC-3
Parker Lakes Dam—dam MS-4
Parker Landing TN-4
Parker Landing—locale MS-4
Parker Landing—locale MO-7
Parker Landing—locale NC-3
Parker Landing—locale VA-3
Parker Landing (inundated)—locale AL-4
Parker Landing Light—locale WA-9
Parker Lateral—canal CA-9
Parker Lateral—canal ID-8
Parker Ledge—bench NH-1
Parker Ledge—cliff SC-3
Parker Lookout—locale MS-4
Parker Lumber Company Complex—hist pl TX-5
Parker Marsh VA-3
Parker Mathis Sch—school GA-3
Parker Meadow—flat (2) CA-9
Parker Meadow—flat OR-9
Parker Meadow—swamp OR-9
Parker Meadow Brook—stream ME-1
Parker Meadow Creek—stream CA-9
Parker Meadows—flat OR-9
Parker Meadows Forest Camp—locale OR-9
Parker Meadow Stock Driveway—trail CA-9
Parker Memorial Baptist Ch—church AL-4
Parker Memorial Baptist Church—hist pl AL-4
Parker Memorial Cem—cemetery TX-5
Parker Memorial Church AL-4
Parker Mesa—summit AZ-5
Parker Mesa—summit CA-9
Parker Mesa Windmill—locale AZ-5
Parker Mill—locale ID-8
Parker Millbrook Sch—school MA-1
Parker Mill Complex—hist pl MI-6
Parker Mill (historical)—locale MS-4
Parker Mill Pond MD-2
Parker Mills Bogs—swamp MA-1
Parker Mills Pond—reservoir MA-1
Parker Mills Pond Dam—dam MA-1
Parker Mills Station (historical)—locale MA-1
Parker Mine AL-4
Parker Mine TN-4
Parker Mine—mine AL-4
Parker Mine—mine (3) ID-8
Parker Mine (underground)—mine (2) AL-4
Parker Moore Cem—cemetery IN-6
Parker Moore Creek—stream MD-2
Parker Mountain Camp—locale NH-1
Parker Mtn—summit AL-4
Parker Mtn—summit (3) AR-4
Parker Mtn—summit CA-9
Parker Mtn—summit CT-1
Parker Mtn—summit (2) ID-8
Parker Mtn—summit KY-4
Parker Mtn—summit (2) NH-1
Parker Mtn—summit NY-2
Parker Mtn—summit (2) NC-3
Parker Mtn—summit OK-5
Parker Mtn—summit OR-9
Parker Mtn—summit UT-8
Parker Mtn—summit VA-3
Parker Mtn—summit WA-9
Parker Mtn—summit WV-2
Parker Municipal Airp—airport AZ-5
Parker Neck MD-2
Parker Neck—bay GA-3
Parker Neck—cape VA-3
Parker Number One Tank—reservoir AZ-5
Parker Oil Field—oilfield TX-5
Parker Park—park TN-4
Parker Pass—gap AK-9
Parker Pass—gap AZ-5
Parker Pass—gap (2) CA-9
Parker Pass—gap ID-8
Parker Pass Creek—stream CA-9
Parker Pass Lake—lake CA-9
Parker Peak—summit (2) CA-9
Parker Peak—summit ID-8
Parker Peak—summit SD-7
Parker Peak—summit WY-8
Parker Peak Grove—woods CA-9
Parker Place—locale OR-9
Parker Plaza (Shop Ctr)—locale FL-3
Parker Plaza Shop Ctr—locale FL-3
Parker Point—cape AK-9
Parker Point—cape FL-3
Parker Point—cape (3) ME-1
Parker Point—cape MT-8
Parker Pond ME-1
Parker Pond VT-1
Parker Pond—lake (2) FL-3
Parker Pond—lake (7) ME-1
Parker Pond—lake MD-2
Parker Pond—lake MA-1
Parker Pond—lake (2) NH-1
Parker Pond—lake NY-2
Parker Pond—lake NC-3
Parker Pond—reservoir CT-1
Parker Pond—reservoir MA-1
Parker Pond Brook—stream NH-1
Parker Pond Dam—dam MA-1
Parker Pond Dam—dam (2) MS-4
Parker Post Office—building AZ-5
Parker Post Office (historical)—building TN-4
Parker Private Sch (abandoned)—school TX-5
Parker Prong Badger Creek—stream WY-8
Parker Ranch—locale (2) AZ-5
Parker Ranch—locale FL-3
Parker Ranch—locale HI-9
Parker Ranch—locale ID-8
Parker Ranch—locale MT-8
Parker Ranch—locale NV-8
Parker Ranch—locale (3) NM-5
Parker Ranch—locale UT-8
Parker Ranch—locale WY-8
Parker Ranch House—hist pl WY-8
Parker Range UT-8
Parker Reef—bar WA-9
Parker Reservoir Dam—dam MA-1
Parker Reservoirs—reservoir NV-8
Parker-Reynolds House—hist pl AL-4
Parker Ridge—ridge AR-4
Parker Ridge—ridge CO-8
Parker Ridge Cem—cemetery TX-5
Parker River MA-1
Parker River—stream MA-1
Parker River Dam—dam MA-1
Parker River Dam At Central Street—dam MA-1
Parker River Marshes—swamp MA-1
Parker River Natl Wildlife Ref—park MA-1
Parker River Rsvr—reservoir MA-1
Parker Road Bog Dam—dam MA-1
Parker Road Pond—reservoir MA-1
Parker Rock—bar NY-2
Parker Rodeo Grounds—park AZ-5
Parker Rsvr—reservoir MA-1
Parker Rsvr—reservoir (2) OR-9
Parker Run—stream IL-6
Parker Run—stream KY-4
Parker Run—stream NJ-2
Parker Run—stream OH-6
Parker Run—stream PA-2
Parker Run—stream (2) VA-3
Parker Run—stream (3) WV-2
Parkers—locale GA-3
Parkers—locale ME-1
Parkers—locale NY-2
**Parkers**—pop pl AR-4
**Parkers**—pop pl TN-4
Parkers—uninc pl FL-3
Parker-Salem Cem—cemetery MS-4
Parkers Bay MD-2
Parkers Bayou MS-4
Parkers Bayou Landing (historical)—locale MS-4
Parkers Bend (historical)—bend ND-7
Parkers Bluff—cliff GA-3
Parkers Branch MS-4
Parkers Branch—stream KY-4
Parkers Branch—stream VA-3
Parkers Brook CT-1
Parkersburg—locale MS-4
Parkersburg—locale OK-5
Parkersburg—locale OR-9
**Parkersburg**—pop pl GA-3
**Parkersburg**—pop pl IL-6
**Parkersburg**—pop pl IN-6
**Parkersburg**—pop pl IA-7
**Parkersburg**—pop pl NC-3
**Parkersburg**—pop pl WV-2
Parkersburg Cem—cemetery OK-5
Parkersburg Cemetery OR-9
Parkersburg (Magisterial District)—fmr MCD WV-2
Parkersburg Oil Field—other IL-6
Parkersburg Post Office (historical)—building MS-4
Parkersburg Sch (historical)—school MS-4
Parkersburg School (Abandoned)—locale OK-5
Parkersburg Women's Club—hist pl WV-2
Parkers (CCD)—cens area GA-3
Parker Sch AL-4
Parkers Ch—church GA-3
Parker Sch—school AL-4
Parker Sch—school AR-4
Parker Sch—school (3) CA-9
Parker Sch—school GA-3
Parker Sch—school HI-9
Parker Sch—school (2) IL-6
Parker Sch—school IA-7
Parker Sch—school (2) KS-7
Parker Sch—school KY-4
Parker Sch—school (4) MA-1
Parker Sch—school (4) MI-6
Parker Sch—school MO-7
Parker Sch—school MT-8
Parker Sch—school NH-1
Parker Sch—school (2) NJ-2
Parker Sch—school (2) NC-3
Parker Sch—school OH-6
Parker Sch—school OR-9
Parker Sch—school (2) SC-3
Parker Sch—school SD-7
Parker Sch—school (2) TX-5
Parker Sch—school WA-9
Parker Sch—school WV-2
Parker Sch (abandoned)—school MO-7
Parker Sch (abandoned)—school PA-2
Parkers Chapel TN-4
Parkers Chapel—church AL-4
Parkers Chapel—church GA-3
Parkers Chapel—church MS-4
Parkers Chapel—church NC-3
Parkers Chapel—church OK-5
Parkers Chapel—church TN-4
**Parkers Chapel**—pop pl AR-4
Parkers Chapel F W B Ch—church NC-3
Parkers Chapel (historical)—church MS-4
Parkers Chapel Sch—school AR-4
Parkers Chapel Sch—school (2) TN-4
Parker Sch (historical)—school AL-4
Parker Sch (historical)—school MS-4
Parker Sch (historical)—school TN-4
Parker School IN-6
Parker School MS-4
Parker School Number 56 IN-6
Parkers Corner—locale AR-4
**Parkers Corners**—pop pl MI-6
**Parkers Corners**—pop pl NY-2
**Parkers Corners**—pop pl PA-2
Parker Scothan Drain—canal MI-6
Parkers Cove NJ-2
Parkers Creek MS-4
Parkers Creek NC-3
Parkers Creek VA-3
Parkers Creek—stream KS-7
Parkers Creek—stream (2) MS-4
Parkers Creek—stream (2) NJ-2
Parkers Creek—stream (3) NC-3
Parkers Creek—stream (2) TX-5
Parkers Creek—stream VA-3
Parkers Creek Branch—stream NJ-2
Parkers Cross Road AL-4
Parkers Crossroads TN-4
**Parkers Crossroads**—pop pl AL-4
**Parker's Cross Roads**—pop pl TN-4
Parkers Cross Road Sch (historical)—school AL-4
Parkers Ferry AL-4

Parks Corner Windmill—*locale* TX-5
Park Scottsdale Shop Ctr—*locale* AZ-5
Parks Cove—*bay* FL-3
Parks Cove—*bay* NY-2
Parks Covered Bridge—*hist pl* OH-6
Parks Covered Bridge—*hist pl* TN-4
Parks Creek—*stream* (2) AK-9
Parks Creek—*stream* CA-9
Parks Creek—*stream* FL-3
Parks Creek—*stream* (2) GA-3
Parks Creek—*stream* (5) ID-8
Parks Creek—*stream* (2) MI-6
Parks Creek—*stream* MO-7
Parks Creek—*stream* NY-2
Parks Creek—*stream* NC-3
Parks Creek—*stream* (2) PA-2
Parks Creek—*stream* TN-4
Parks Creek—*stream* TX-5
Parks Creek—*stream* VA-3
Parks Creek—*stream* WA-9
Parks Crossroad—*locale* PA-2
**Parks Crossroads**—*pop pl* NC-3
Parksdale—*CDP* CA-9
**Parksdale**—*pop pl* MO-7
Parks Ditch—*canal* MD-2
Parks Drain—*canal* (2) MI-6
Parks Drain—*stream* MI-6
Parks Duck Dam—*dam* SD-7
Park Sealevel Hosp—*hospital* NC-3
*Parks Elementary School* MS-4
Park Settlement—*locale* TN-4
Parks Ferry (historical)—*locale* TN-4
*Parks Fort* KS-7
Parks Gap—*gap* GA-3
Parks Gap—*gap* TN-4
Parks Gap Prospect—*mine* TN-4
Parks Grove Ch—*church* GA-3
Parks Grove Ch—*church* NC-3
Park Sheridan Plaza (Shop Ctr)—*locale* FL-3
Parks Hill—*summit* CA-9
Parks Hill—*summit* CO-8
Parks Hill—*summit* OK-5
Parks Hill—*summit* PA-2
Parks Hills—*range* ND-7
Parks Hollow—*valley* AL-4
Parks Hollow—*valley* AR-4
Parks Hollow—*valley* (2) MO-7
Parks Hollow—*valley* OH-6
Parks Hollow—*valley* TN-4
Parks Hollow—*valley* WV-2
Park Shop Ctr—*locale* NC-3
Park Shop Ctr—*locale* OH-6
**Park Shore**—*pop pl* TN-4
**Parkshore Estates**—*pop pl* TN-4
Park Shore Resort—*locale* MI-6
*Parkside* IN-6
Parkside—*locale* DE-2
Parkside—*locale* PA-2
**Parkside**—*pop pl* IN-6
**Parkside**—*pop pl* KY-4
**Parkside**—*pop pl* MD-2
**Parkside**—*pop pl* (2) NJ-2
**Parkside**—*pop pl* (2) NY-2
**Parkside**—*pop pl* PA-2
**Parkside**—*pop pl* PR-3
Parkside—*uninc pl* CA-9
Parkside—*uninc pl* FL-3
Parkside Airp—*airport* WA-9
Parkside Borough—*civil* PA-2
Parkside Campground—*locale* MT-8
Parkside Community Ch—*church* VA-3
**Parkside Courts**—*pop pl* PA-2
Parkside East Hist Dist—*hist pl* NY-2
Parkside Elem Sch—*school* (4) IN-6
Parkside Elem Sch—*school* UT-8
**Parkside Estates**—*pop pl* MD-2
Parkside Hist Dist—*hist pl* CT-1
Parkside Hist Dist—*hist pl* PA-2
Parkside HS—*school* MI-6
Parkside JHS—*school* NH-1
Parkside JHS—*school* NY-2
Parkside JHS—*school* VA-3
**Parkside Manor**—*pop pl* LA-4
Parkside Manor—*uninc pl* PA-2
Parkside Manor Nursing Home—*building* WA-9
Parkside Plaza Shop Ctr—*locale* MS-4
Parkside Recovery Center—*hospital* UT-8
Parkside Sch—*school* (7) CA-9
Parkside Sch—*school* (2) IL-6
Parkside Sch—*school* MD-2
Parkside Sch—*school* MI-6
Parkside Sch—*school* NJ-2
Parkside Sch—*school* (2) NY-2
Parkside Sch—*school* OK-5
Parkside Sch—*school* PA-2
**Parkside (subdivision)**—*pop pl* AL-4
**Parkside (subdivision)**—*pop pl* (2) AZ-5
**Parkside Subdivision**—*pop pl* UT-8
Parkside West Hist Dist—*hist pl* NY-2
*Park Siding* MI-6
Park Siding—*locale* ME-1
Park Siding—*uninc pl* CA-9
Parks Interchange—*crossing* AZ-5
Parks Island—*island* TN-4
Park Site Boat Ramp—*locale* KY-4
Park Site 36La96—*hist pl* PA-2
Parks Lake—*lake* FL-3
Parks Lake—*lake* MI-6
Parks Lake—*lake* MN-6
Parks Lake—*reservoir* AZ-5
Parks Lake—*reservoir* MS-4
Parks Lake—*reservoir* NC-3
Parks Lake—*reservoir* TX-5
Parks Lake Dam—*dam* (2) MS-4
Parks Lake Dam—*dam* NC-3
Parks Lake Rsvr—*reservoir* OR-9
Parks Landing (historical)—*locale* AL-4
Parks-Lead Siding—*locale* CA-9
Parks Lewisville Canal—*canal* ID-8
**Parksley**—*pop pl* VA-3
**Park Slope**—*pop pl* NY-2
Park Slope Hist Dist—*hist pl* NY-2
Park Slough (historical)—*lake* SD-7
**Parks (Maine)**—*pop pl* AZ-5
Parks Memorial Cem—*cemetery* IN-6
Parks Mill—*locale* GA-3
Parks Mill—*locale* SC-3
Parks Mill—*locale* VA-3
Parks Mill (historical)—*locale* (2) TN-4
Parks Millpond—*reservoir* GA-3
Parks Mill (Ruin)—*locale* TX-5
**Parks Mills**—*pop pl* OH-6
Park Smith Lake—*reservoir* KS-7
Parks Mtn—*summit* GA-3
Parks Mtn—*summit* NC-3
Parks Mtn—*summit* TX-5
*Park's Neck* MD-2
Parks Neck—*cape* MD-2
Parks Oil Field—*oilfield* TX-5
Parks Pasture—*flat* UT-8
*Parks Peak* CA-9
Parks Peak—*summit* (2) ID-8
Parks Peak Trail—*trail* ID-8
Parks-Penn Oil Field—*oilfield* TX-5
*Parks Place* MS-4
Parks Place—*hist pl* TN-4
**Parksplace**—*pop pl* MS-4
**Parks Place (historical)**—*pop pl* MS-4
Parksplace Post Office (historical)—*building* MS-4
Parks Plantation (historical)—*locale* MS-4
*Parks Pond* CT-1
*Parks Pond* NH-1
Parks Pond—*lake* CT-1
Parks Pond—*lake* ME-1
Parks Pond Bluff—*cliff* ME-1
Parks Pond Brook—*stream* CT-1
Parks Pond Brook—*stream* ME-1
*Park Spring* ID-8
**Park Spring**—*pop pl* NC-3
Park Spring—*spring* (2) AZ-5
Park Spring—*spring* MO-7
Park Spring—*spring* NM-5
Park Spring—*spring* SD-7
Park Spring—*spring* UT-8
Park Spring—*spring* WA-9
Park Spring Lake—*reservoir* NC-3
Park Springs—*locale* NM-5
**Park Springs**—*pop pl* TX-5
Park Springs Ch—*church* TX-5
Park Square—*park* MA-1
Park Square Hist Dist—*hist pl* MA-1
Park Square Hist Dist—*hist pl* NY-2
*Parks Quarries* PA-2
Parks Ranch—*locale* NM-5
Parks-Reagan House—*hist pl* AR-4
Parks Ridge—*ridge* GA-3
Parks Ridge—*ridge* (2) IN-6
Parks Ridge—*ridge* (2) KY-4
Parks Ridge—*ridge* NC-3
Parks Ridge Ch—*church* KY-4
Parks Rsvr—*reservoir* OR-9
Parks Run—*stream* PA-2
Parks Sch—*school* (2) IL-6
Parks Sch—*school* (2) KY-4
Parks Sch—*school* MS-4
Parks Sch—*school* MO-7
Parks Sch—*school* TN-4
Parks Sch—*school* TX-5
Parks Sch (historical)—*school* MS-4
Parks Sch (historical)—*school* TN-4
Parks Siding—*locale* MI-6
*Parks's Neck* MD-2
*Parks Spring* TN-4
Parks Spring—*spring* OR-9
**Parks Store**—*pop pl* TN-4
Parks Store (historical)—*locale* MS-4
**Parks Subdivision**—*pop pl* UT-8
Park Station—*locale* NY-2
**Park Station**—*pop pl* TN-4
**Parkston**—*pop pl* NY-2
**Parkston**—*pop pl* SD-7
Parkston Cem—*cemetery* SD-7
Parkston Country Club—*locale* SD-7
**Parkstone (subdivision)**—*pop pl* NC-3
Parkston Municipal Airp—*airport* SD-7
**Parkstown**—*pop pl* NC-3
**Parkstown**—*pop pl* (2) PA-2
Parks Township—*civ div* NE-7
Parks (Township of)—*fmr MCD* (2) AR-4
**Parks (Township of)**—*pop pl* PA-2
Park Street—*uninc pl* MA-1
Park Street Cem—*cemetery* (2) MA-1
Park Street Ch—*church* MA-1
Park Street District—*hist pl* MA-1
Park Street Firehouse—*hist pl* MA-1
Park Street Hist Dist—*hist pl* WI-6
Park Street Historic Commercial District—*hist pl* CA-9
Park Street Methodist Ch—*church* AL-4
Park Street Park—*park* MN-6
Park Street Row—*hist pl* ME-1
Park Street RR Station—*hist pl* MA-1
Park Street Sch—*school* GA-3
Park Street Sch—*school* MD-2
Park Street Sch—*school* MA-1
Park Street Sch—*school* MI-6
Park Street Sch—*school* (2) NY-2
Park Street Sch—*school* VT-1
Park Street Station (historical)—*locale* MA-1
Parks (Uyak)—*other* AK-9
Parks Valley—*valley* CA-9
Parks Valley—*valley* WV-2
*Parksville* PA-2
Parksville—*locale* GA-3
**Parksville**—*pop pl* KY-4
**Parksville**—*pop pl* NY-2
**Parksville**—*pop pl* SC-3
**Parksville**—*pop pl* TN-4
Parksville Beach—*beach* TN-4
Parksville Boat Ramp—*locale* TN-4
Parksville (CCD)—*cens area* SC-3
Parksville (CCD)—*cens area* TN-4
Parksville Ch—*church* GA-3
Parksville Division—*civil* TN-4
**Parksville (historical)**—*pop pl* IA-7
Parksville Knob—*summit* KY-4
Parksville Lake—*reservoir* TN-4
Parksville Lake Rec Area—*park* TN-4
Parksville Post Office (historical)—*building* TN-4
Parksville Sch—*school* NY-2
Parksville Sch (historical)—*school* TN-4
Parks Windmill—*locale* NM-5
Park Tank—*reservoir* (7) AZ-5
Park Tank—*reservoir* (3) NM-5
**Park Terrace**—*pop pl* NY-2
**Park Terrace**—*pop pl* NC-3
**Park Terrace**—*pop pl* UT-8
Park Terrace—*uninc pl* NV-8
Park Terrace Ch—*church* NY-2
Park Terrace Cumberland Presbyterian Ch—*church* AL-4
Park Terrace Sch—*school* NY-2
Park Terrace Sch—*school* PA-2
Park Terrace Shop Ctr—*locale* TN-4
Park Theatre—*hist pl* CO-8
**Parkton**—*pop pl* MD-2
**Parkton**—*pop pl* NC-3
Parkton Hotel—*hist pl* MD-2
Parkton K-12 Sch—*school* NC-3
Parkton Lookout Tower—*tower* NC-3
Parkton (Township of)—*fmr MCD* NC-3
*Parktown* ND-7
Parktown—*locale* NC-3
**Parktowne**—*pop pl* MD-2
**Parktown Estates**—*pop pl* PA-2
Parktown (historical)—*locale* ND-7
**Park Township**—*pop pl* KS-7
**Park Township**—*pop pl* ND-7
**Park Township**—*pop pl* SD-7
Park Township (historical)—*civil* (2) ND-7
**Park (Township of)**—*pop pl* (2) MI-6
**Park (Township of)**—*pop pl* MN-6
Park Trail—*trail* OR-9
Park Trap Windmill—*locale* TX-5
Park Tudor Sch—*school* IN-6
*Parkus Creek* TX-5
Parkvale—*locale* PA-2
**Parkvale Subdivision**—*pop pl* UT-8
Park Valley—*area* UT-8
**Park Valley**—*pop pl* UT-8
Park Valley—*valley* AZ-5
Park Valley—*valley* NE-7
Park Valley Cem—*cemetery* NE-7
Park Valley Cem—*cemetery* UT-8
Park Valley Sch—*school* TX-5
Park Valley Sch—*school* UT-8
*Parkview* IN-6
*Parkview* OH-6
*Parkview* PA-2
Park View—*CDP* IA-7
Parkview—*CDP* VA-3
**Park View**—*pop pl* DC-2
**Parkview**—*pop pl* IN-6
**Parkview**—*pop pl* IA-7
**Parkview**—*pop pl* MD-2
**Parkview**—*pop pl* NE-7
**Park View**—*pop pl* NM-5
**Parkview**—*pop pl* OH-6
**Park View**—*pop pl* PA-2
**Parkview**—*pop pl* PA-2
**Parkview**—*pop pl* TN-4
**Parkview**—*pop pl* VA-3
**Park View**—*pop pl* VA-3
**Parkview**—*pop pl* WV-2
**Park View**—*pop pl* WV-2
**Parkview**—*pop pl* WV-2
Park View—*post sta* MN-6
Park View—*post sta* NC-3
Parkview—*uninc pl* OK-5
Parkview—*uninc pl* (2) VA-3
Park View—*uninc pl* VA-3
Parkview Baptist Ch—*church* (3) FL-3
Parkview Baptist Ch—*church* KS-7
Parkview Baptist Ch—*church* (5) MS-4
Parkview Baptist Ch—*church* (2) TN-4
Parkview Cabins—*locale* MI-6
Parkview Campground—*locale* CO-8
Park View Cem—*cemetery* CA-9
Parkview Cem—*cemetery* ID-8
Parkview Cem—*cemetery* IL-6
Parkview Cem—*cemetery* IN-6
Parkview Cem—*cemetery* KS-7
Parkview Cem—*cemetery* MO-7
Parkview Cem—*cemetery* NE-7
Parkview Cem—*cemetery* NY-2
Parkview Cem—*cemetery* WI-6
Parkview Ch—*church* AL-4
Parkview Ch—*church* (2) FL-3
Parkview Ch—*church* IL-6
Parkview Ch—*church* (2) LA-4
Parkview Ch—*church* MS-4
Parkview Ch—*church* NC-3
Parkview Ch—*church* PA-2
Park View Ch—*church* PA-2
Park View Ch—*church* SC-3
Parkview Ch—*church* TX-5
Parkview Ch—*church* VA-3
Parkview Ch of God—*church* AL-4
Parkview Ch of God—*church* MS-4
Parkview Ch of the Nazarene—*church* AL-4
Parkview Community Ditch—*hist pl* NM-5
Parkview Creek—*stream* CO-8
Parkview Ditch—*canal* CO-8
Park View Ditch—*canal* NM-5
**Parkview East (subdivision)**—*pop pl* NC-3
*Parkview Elementary School* AL-4
*Parkview Elementary School* TN-4
Parkview Elem Sch—*school* FL-3
Parkview Elem Sch—*school* (2) IN-6
Parkview Elem Sch—*school* MS-4
**Parkview Estates**—*pop pl* MD-2
**Parkview Estates**—*pop pl* TX-5
**Parkview Estates (subdivision)**—*pop pl* AL-4
**Parkview Estates (subdivision)**—*pop pl* (2) AZ-5
**Park View Estates Subdivision**—*pop pl* UT-8
**Parkview Gardens**—*pop pl* MD-2
**Parkview Gardens**—*pop pl* PA-2
Parkview General Hosp—*hospital* TX-5
Parkview Golf Course—*other* IL-6
Park View Guest House—*hist pl* LA-4
**Park View Heights**—*pop pl* IN-6
**Parkview Heights**—*pop pl* OH-6
**Park View Heights**—*pop pl* PA-2
Parkview Heights Ch—*church* OH-6
**Park View Heights (subdivision)**—*pop pl* NC-3
Parkview Hill—*summit* WY-8
**Parkview Hills**—*pop pl* VA-3
Parkview Hist Dist—*hist pl* MO-7
Park View Hist Dist—*hist pl* VA-3
Parkview Hosp—*hospital* CA-9
Parkview Hosp—*hospital* CO-8
Parkview Hosp—*hospital* IN-6
Parkview Hosp—*hospital* PA-2
Parkview Hosp—*hospital* TX-5
*Parkview Hospital* AZ-5
*Parkview Hospital* TN-4
Park View Hosptial—*hospital* OK-5
Park View Hotel—*hist pl* CA-9
Parkview HS—*school* AR-4
Parkview HS—*school* MO-7
Park View HS—*school* VA-3
Parkview Intermediate Sch—*school* IN-6
Park View Island—*island* FL-3
Parkview JHS—*school* IL-6
Parkview JHS—*school* (2) IN-6
Parkview JHS—*school* MN-6
Parkview JHS—*school* TX-5
Parkview Junior High B-7 Bldg—*building* IN-6
Parkview Lake—*reservoir* IN-6
Parkview Lake Dam—*dam* IN-6
*Parkview Learning Center* AL-4
Parkview Memorial Cem—*cemetery* MI-6
Park View Memorial Gardens—*cemetery* MO-7
Parkview Memorial Gardens—*cemetery* WV-2
Parkview Memorial Hosp—*hospital* ME-1
**Parkview Mesa (subdivision)**—*pop pl* (2) AZ-5
Parkview Mtn—*summit* CO-8
**Parkview North (subdivision)**—*pop pl* (2) AZ-5
Parkview Park—*park* AZ-5
Parkview Park—*park* IL-6
Parkview Plaza—*locale* PA-2
Parkview Plaza Shop Ctr—*locale* AL-4
Park View Sch—*school* CA-9
Parkview Sch—*school* (3) CA-9
Parkview Sch—*school* CO-8
Park View Sch—*school* DC-2
Parkview Sch—*school* FL-3
Parkview Sch—*school* (5) IL-6
Parkview Sch—*school* LA-4
Parkview Sch—*school* MA-1
Parkview Sch—*school* MI-6
Parkview Sch—*school* (4) MN-6
Parkview Sch—*school* MO-7
Parkview Sch—*school* (2) NJ-2
Parkview Sch—*school* (2) NM-5
Park View Sch—*school* NY-2
Parkview Sch—*school* NC-3
Parkview Sch—*school* (2) OH-6
Park View Sch—*school* OK-5
Parkview Sch—*school* OK-5
Parkview Sch—*school* (2) TN-4
Parkview Sch—*school* (3) UT-8
Parkview Sch—*school* (2) VA-3
Park View Sch—*school* WV-2
Parkview Sch—*school* (2) WI-6
Park View Sch—*school* WI-6
Park View Sch (abandoned)—*school* MO-7
*Park View School Number 81* IN-6
Parkview Shop Ctr—*locale* (2) AL-4
Parkview Shop Ctr—*locale* NC-3
Park View Shop Ctr—*locale* NC-3
Parkview Shop Ctr—*locale* TN-4
**Parkview (subdivision)**—*pop pl* AL-4
**Park View (subdivision)**—*pop pl* FL-3
**Parkview (subdivision)**—*pop pl* MS-4
**Parkview (subdivision)**—*pop pl* TN-4
**Park View Subdivision**—*pop pl* UT-8
*Parkview Terrace* MI-6
Park View Trail—*trail* WV-2
**Parkview Trailer Court**—*pop pl* UT-8
**Parkview Village Mobile Home and Recreational Vehicle Park**—*pop pl* AZ-5
**Park Village**—*pop pl* CA-9
**Park Village**—*pop pl* NJ-2
**Park Village**—*pop pl* NY-2
**Park Village**—*pop pl* TX-5
**Park Village (Death Valley Natl Monument Hq.)**—*pop pl* CA-9
Park Village Plaza—*locale* PA-2
Park Village Sch—*school* NV-8
Park Village Shop Ctr—*locale* FL-3
**Park Village (subdivision)**—*pop pl* PA-2
**Park Village (subdivision)**—*pop pl* TN-4
*Parkville* CT-1
*Parkville* IN-6
Parkville—*locale* (2) CO-8
Parkville—*locale* NJ-2
**Parkville**—*pop pl* IL-6
**Parkville**—*pop pl* MD-2
**Parkville**—*pop pl* MI-6
**Parkville**—*pop pl* MN-6
**Parkville**—*pop pl* MO-7
**Parkville**—*pop pl* NY-2
**Parkville**—*pop pl* NC-3
**Parkville**—*pop pl* PA-2
**Parkville**—*pop pl* PR-3
Parkville Bend—*bend* KS-7
Parkville Cem—*cemetery* CA-9
Parkville Cem—*cemetery* MI-6
Parkville Ch—*church* IN-6
**Parkville Heights**—*pop pl* MD-2
Parkville Heights Shop Ctr—*locale* MO-7
Parkville (historical)—*locale* AL-4
Parkville Sch—*school* CA-9
Parkville (Township of)—*fmr MCD* NC-3
Park Vista Sch—*school* LA-4
Park Wash—*valley* UT-8
*Park Waste* UT-8
**Parkwater**—*pop pl* WA-9
*Parkway* IL-6
*Parkway* MO-7
**Parkway**—*pop pl* CA-9
**Parkway**—*pop pl* MO-7
Parkway—*uninc pl* NY-2
Parkway Assembly of God Ch—*church* AL-4
Parkway Baptist Ch—*church* (3) FL-3
Parkway Baptist Ch—*church* (7) MS-4
*Parkway Baptist Church* TN-4
Parkway Baptist Wee Care Center—*school* FL-3
Parkway Branch Mobile Public Library—*building* AL-4
Parkway Campground—*park* IA-7
Parkway Cem—*cemetery* MS-4
Parkway Cem—*cemetery* MO-7
Parkway Center—*locale* UT-8
**Parkway Center**—*pop pl* PA-2
Parkway Ch—*church* AL-4
Parkway Ch—*church* (4) FL-3
Parkway Ch—*church* KY-4
Parkway Ch—*church* NJ-2
Parkway Ch—*church* NC-3
Parkway Ch—*church* SC-3
Parkway Ch—*church* (3) TN-4
Parkway Ch—*church* VA-3
*Parkway Ch of God* AL-4
Parkway Ch of God—*church* FL-3
Parkway City Mall Shop Ctr—*locale* AL-4
Parkway Congregational Methodist Ch—*church* AL-4
Parkway Ditch—*canal* CO-8
Parkway East Huffman Shop Ctr—*locale* AL-4
*Parkway Elementary School* NC-3
**Parkway Estates**—*pop pl* AL-4
**Parkway Estates**—*pop pl* CA-9
**Parkway Estates**—*pop pl* TN-4
**Parkway Estates**—*pop pl* VA-3
**Parkway Forest**—*pop pl* NC-3
Parkway Heights United Methodist Ch—*church* MS-4
**Parkway Hills**—*pop pl* IN-6
Parkway Hosp—*hospital* NY-2
Parkway Hosp—*hospital* TX-5
Parkway JHS—*school* CA-9
Parkway JHS—*school* FL-3
Parkway JHS—*school* IN-6
Parkway JHS—*school* TN-4
*Parkway Junction* MN-6
**Parkway Manor**—*pop pl* NJ-2
**Park Way Manor**—*pop pl* PA-2
**Parkway Manor**—*pop pl* PA-2
Parkway Manor Elem Sch—*school* PA-2
Parkway Oaks Sch—*school* NY-2
**Parkway Pines**—*pop pl* NJ-2
Parkway Plaza—*locale* KS-7
Parkway Plaza Shop Ctr—*locale* AL-4
Parkway Plaza (Shop Ctr)—*locale* (2) FL-3
Parkway Plaza Shop Ctr—*locale* MS-4
Parkway Plaza Shop Ctr—*locale* NC-3
Parkway Plaza Shop Ctr—*locale* (2) TN-4
Parkway Presbyterian Ch—*church* AL-4
Parkway-Sacramento South—*CDP* CA-9
*Parkway Sch* IN-6
Parkway Sch—*school* (4) CA-9
Parkway Sch—*school* CT-1
Parkway Sch—*school* (2) FL-3
Parkway Sch—*school* (2) MD-2
Parkway Sch—*school* MI-6
Parkway Sch—*school* NJ-2
Parkway Sch—*school* (4) NY-2
Parkway Sch—*school* NC-3
Parkway Sch—*school* OH-6
Parkway Sch—*school* SD-7
Parkway Sch—*school* (2) WA-9
Parkway Sch—*school* (3) WI-6
Parkway Shop Ctr—*locale* (2) AL-4
Parkway Shop Ctr—*locale* FL-3
Park-way Shop Ctr—*locale* MO-7
Parkway Shop Ctr—*locale* (2) MO-7
Parkway Shop Ctr—*locale* NC-3
Parkway Shop Ctr—*locale* PA-2
Parkway Shop Ctr—*locale* TN-4
Parkway Special Sch—*school* AZ-5
**Parkway (subdivision)**—*pop pl* MS-4
**Parkway (subdivision)**—*pop pl* NC-3
**Parkway Subdivision One**—*pop pl* UT-8
**Parkway Subdivision Two and Three**—*pop pl* UT-8
**Parkway Terrace**—*pop pl* WV-2
**Parkway Village**—*pop pl* KY-4
**Parkway Village**—*pop pl* NJ-2
Parkway Village—*post sta* TN-4
Parkway Village Ch—*church* TN-4
Park Well—*well* (3) AZ-5
Park West—*park* AL-4
Park Western Place Sch—*school* CA-9
**Park West Estates Subdivision**—*pop pl* UT-8
Park West Hosp—*hospital* NY-2
Park West Hosp—*hospital* TN-4
*Park West Med Ctr* TN-4
*Parkwest Ski Area* UT-8
Park West Ski Area Heliport—*airport* UT-8
Park Wheeler Corner—*locale* OK-5
Parkwin Ave Methodist Ch—*church* AL-4
Parkwin Congregational Holiness Ch—*church* AL-4
Park Windmill—*locale* (3) TX-5
*Parkwood* IL-6
Parkwood—*CDP* CA-9
Parkwood—*CDP* WA-9
**Parkwood**—*pop pl* AL-4
**Parkwood**—*pop pl* DE-2
**Parkwood**—*pop pl* GA-3
**Parkwood**—*pop pl* IN-6
**Parkwood**—*pop pl* KY-4
**Parkwood**—*pop pl* MD-2
**Parkwood**—*pop pl* (2) NC-3
**Parkwood**—*pop pl* PA-2
**Parkwood**—*pop pl* TX-5
**Parkwood**—*pop pl* VA-3
Parkwood—*post sta* NC-3
**Parkwood Beach**—*pop pl* MA-1
Parkwood Branch—*stream* NC-3
Parkwood Cem—*cemetery* MD-2
Parkwood Ch—*church* AL-4
Parkwood Ch—*church* FL-3
Parkwood Ch—*church* MD-2
Parkwood Ch—*church* (3) NC-3
Parkwood Ch—*church* TN-4
*Parkwood Elementary School* AL-4
Parkwood Elem Sch—*school* IN-6
**Parkwood Estates**—*pop pl* TX-5
**Parkwood Estates**—*pop pl* VA-3
Parkwood Estates—*uninc pl* SC-3
**Parkwood Estates Condominium**—*pop pl* UT-8
**Parkwood Estates (subdivision)**—*pop pl* AL-4
**Parkwood Estates (subdivision)**—*pop pl* NC-3
**Parkwood Estates (subdivision)**—*pop pl* UT-8
**Parkwood (Hallison)**—*pop pl* NC-3
Parkwood Heights Park—*park* FL-3
Parkwood Heights Sch—*school* FL-3
*Parkwood High School* NC-3
Parkwood JHS—*school* OH-6
Parkwood Lake—*reservoir* NC-3
Parkwood Lake Dam—*dam* NC-3
**Parkwood Lake (subdivision)**—*pop pl* NC-3
Parkwood Mall—*locale* NC-3
Parkwood Mine (underground)—*mine* AL-4
Parkwood Park—*park* KS-7
Parkwood Park—*park* MI-6
Parkwood Park—*park* TX-5
Parkwood Playground—*park* MI-6
Parkwood Plaza (Shop Ctr)—*locale* FL-3
Parkwood Recreation Center—*building* AL-4
Parkwood Sch—*school* AL-4
Parkwood Sch—*school* GA-3
Parkwood Sch—*school* MD-2
Parkwood Sch—*school* (3) MI-6
Parkwood Sch—*school* (3) NC-3
Parkwood Sch—*school* OH-6
**Parkwood (subdivision)**—*pop pl* (3) AL-4
**Parkwood (subdivision)**—*pop pl* (2) AZ-5
**Parkwood (subdivision)**—*pop pl* (2) NC-3
**Park Wood (subdivision)**—*pop pl* NC-3
**Park Wood Subdivision**—*pop pl* UT-8
*Parkwood Village* IL-6
**Park Wynne Estates**—*pop pl* PA-2
**Park Yarn**—*pop pl* NC-3
Park '66' (Shop Ctr)—*locale* FL-3
**Parlange**—*pop pl* LA-4
Parlange Plantation House—*hist pl* LA-4
Parle, Lac Qui—*reservoir* MN-6
Parlemee Lake—*lake* MI-6
**Parler**—*pop pl* SC-3
*Parler Cross Roads* SC-3
*Parlers* SC-3
**Parlers**—*pop pl* SC-3
**Parlersville**—*pop pl* SC-3
Parlersville Ch—*church* SC-3
**Parlett**—*pop pl* OH-6
Parlett House—*hist pl* TN-4
*Parletts Run* VA-3
Parley—*locale* UT-8
Parley Black Lake—*lake* LA-4
Parley Canyon—*valley* UT-8
Parley Hollow—*valley* UT-8
Parley Lake—*lake* (2) MN-6
Parleys Canyon—*valley* (2) UT-8
Parleys Creek—*stream* UT-8
Parleys Fork Red Butte Creek—*stream* UT-8
Parleys Park—*flat* UT-8
*Parleys Park Elementary School* UT-8
Parleys Park Sch—*school* UT-8
Parleys Summit—*summit* UT-8
*Parley Street* NY-2
Parliament—*locale* OR-9
**Parliament**—*pop pl* VA-3
Parliament Place Sch—*school* NY-2
**Parlier**—*pop pl* CA-9
Parlier-Del Rey (CCD)—*cens area* CA-9
*Parlier Street* NY-2
*Parli Island* OR-9
**Parlin**—*pop pl* CO-8
**Parlin**—*pop pl* NJ-2
*Parlin Brook* ME-1
Parlin Brook—*stream* ME-1
Parlin Creek—*stream* CA-9
Parlin Flats—*flat* CO-8
Parlin Fork Conservation Camp—*locale* CA-9
Parlin Hill—*summit* ME-1
Parlin JHS—*school* MA-1
Parlin Mtn—*summit* ME-1
Parlin Pond—*lake* ME-1
Parlin Pond (Township of)—*unorg* ME-1
Parlin Stream—*stream* ME-1
*Parlners Creek* PA-2
Parlor Grove Ch—*church* KY-4
Parlor Point—*cape* MD-2
*Parlor Street* NY-2
Parlow Cem—*cemetery* TN-4
*Parlow Creek* MS-4
Parma—*locale* AR-4
Parma—*locale* CO-8
**Parma**—*pop pl* CO-8
**Parma**—*pop pl* ID-8
**Parma**—*pop pl* MI-6
**Parma**—*pop pl* MO-7
**Parma**—*pop pl* OH-6
Parma Canal—*canal* ID-8
Parma Cem—*cemetery* ID-8
Parma Cem—*cemetery* MO-7
**Parma Center**—*pop pl* NY-2
**Parma Center (Parma)**—*pop pl* NY-2
*Parmach* FM-9
*Parmacheene Lake* ME-1
Parmachenee Club—*other* ME-1
Parmachenee Lake—*lake* ME-1
Parmachenee (Township of)—*unorg* ME-1
**Parma Corners**—*pop pl* NY-2
Parmadale Orphanage—*building* OH-6
Parma Drain—*canal* CO-8
Parma Drain—*stream* ID-8
**Parma Heights**—*pop pl* OH-6
Parmakian Gulch—*valley* CO-8
Parmalee—*locale* FL-3
Parmalee and Shoemaker Ditch—*canal* CO-8
Parmalee and Shoemaker Ditch No 3—*canal* CO-8
Parmalee Bridge—*other* MI-6
Parmalee Brook—*stream* CT-1
Parmalee Creek—*stream* MI-6
Parmalee Gulch—*valley* CO-8
Parmalee Gulch Park—*park* CO-8
Parmalee Point—*cape* NC-3
Parmalee Sch—*school* CO-8
Parman Ranch—*locale* CA-9
Parman Rsvr—*reservoir* (2) NV-8
Parman Sch—*school* TN-4
Parman Spring—*spring* NV-8
Parma Park Sch—*school* OH-6
Parmar Run—*stream* WV-2
Par-Mar Valley Country Club—*locale* SD-7
*Parma (sta.)* OH-6
**Parma (Town of)**—*pop pl* NY-2
**Parma (Township of)**—*pop pl* MI-6
Parmatown Shop Ctr—*locale* OH-6
Parma Union Cem—*cemetery* NY-2
Parm Cem—*cemetery* TN-4
**Parmele**—*pop pl* (2) NC-3
**Parmelee**—*pop pl* MI-6
**Parmelee**—*pop pl* SD-7
Parmelee Ave Sch—*school* CA-9
Parmelee Dam—*dam* SD-7
Parmelee House—*hist pl* OH-6
Parmelee Park—*park* MI-6
Parmelee Sch—*school* OK-5
**Parmele Isles (subdivision)**—*pop pl* NC-3

*Parmelia Creek* OR-9
*Parmelia Lake* OR-9
Parmentar Creek—*stream* IA-7
Parmenter Brook—*stream* RI-1
Parmenter Cem—*cemetery* NE-7
Parmenter Creek—*stream* MT-8
Parmenter Creek—*stream* WA-9
Parmenter Memorial Hall—*hist pl* KS-7
Parmenter Mtn—*summit* MT-8
Parmenter Park—*park* CA-9
Parmenter Sch—*school* (2) MA-1
Parmer Cem—*cemetery* MI-6
Parmer Cem—*cemetery* NC-3
Parmer Cem—*cemetery* WV-2
**Parmer (County)**—*pop pl* TX-5
Parmer Creek—*stream* LA-4
Parmer Mtn—*summit* NC-3
Parmer Ranch—*locale* NM-5
Parmer Sch—*school* TN-4
Parmers Creek—*stream* LA-4
Parmerton—*locale* TX-5
Parmer Well—*well* NM-5
Parmeter Cem—*cemetery* ME-1
Parmeter Cem—*cemetery* NY-2
Parmeter Pond—*lake* NY-2
Parmeter Ranch—*locale* CA-9
**Par Metta Crest**—*pop pl* WV-2
Parmicha Creek—*stream* MS-4
Parmlee Canyon—*valley* WY-8
Parmley, J. W., House—*hist pl* SD-7
Parmley, Lake—*reservoir* SD-7
Parmley Hollow—*valley* MO-7
Parmley Hollow—*valley* TN-4
Parmley Land Office—*hist pl* SD-7
Parmley Sch—*school* KY-4
Parmleys Grove Ch—*church* KY-4
Parmleysville—*locale* KY-4
Parmleysville Sch—*school* KY-4
Parm Lick Pond—*reservoir* TN-4
Parmly Billings Memorial Library—*hist pl* MT-8
Parna (historical P.O.)—*locale* IA-7
Parnall Sch—*school* MI-6
**Parnassus**—*pop pl* PA-2
**Parnassus**—*pop pl* VA-3
Parnassus, Mount—*summit* CO-8
Parnassus Ch—*church* SC-3
Parnassus Hill—*summit* OH-6
Parn Cem—*cemetery* AR-4
Parnel Canyon—*valley* CA-9
*Parnel Knob* PA-2
Parnell—*locale* AL-4
Parnell—*locale* IL-6
Parnell—*locale* KS-7
Parnell—*locale* KY-4
Parnell—*locale* MI-6
Parnell—*locale* WI-6
**Parnell**—*pop pl* AR-4
**Parnell**—*pop pl* IA-7
**Parnell**—*pop pl* MO-7
**Parnell**—*pop pl* TX-5
Parnell Branch—*stream* DE-2
Parnell Branch—*stream* TN-4
Parnell Cem—*cemetery* AL-4
Parnell Cem—*cemetery* AR-4
Parnell Cem—*cemetery* NC-3
Parnell Cem—*cemetery* (2) SC-3
Parnell Cem—*cemetery* WV-2
Parnell Ch—*church* KY-4
*Parnell Church* AL-4
Parnell Creek—*stream* IA-7
Parnell Creek—*stream* MS-4
Parnell Dam—*dam* AL-4
Parnell Esker—*ridge* WI-6
Parnell Fish Hatchery (historical), Mount—*park* PA-2
Parnell Knob—*summit* PA-2
Parnell Observation Tower—*locale* WI-6
Parnell Oil Field—*other* IL-6
Parnell Park—*park* MO-7
Parnell Park—*park* OH-6
Parnell Sch—*school* CA-9
Parnell Sch—*school* NE-7
Parnells Pond—*reservoir* AL-4
Parnell Springs—*spring* AR-4
**Parnell Township**—*pop pl* KS-7
**Parnell Township**—*pop pl* SD-7
**Parnell (Township of)**—*pop pl* (2) MN-6
*Parnham Bridges Park* MS-4
Parobe P Turvin Grant—*civil* FL-3
Parochial Bade Oil Field—*oilfield* TX-5
Parody Draw—*valley* WY-8
Parola Canyon—*valley* CA-9
**Parole**—*pop pl* MD-2
Paroli Spring—*spring* CA-9
**Paron**—*pop pl* AR-4
Paron Cem—*cemetery* LA-4
Paron Ch—*church* AL-4
Paron Ch—*church* GA-3
Paron Ch—*church* LA-4
Paron Ch—*church* TN-4
Paron Ch—*church* TX-5
Paroni Spring—*spring* NV-8
**Paront**—*pop pl* FL-3
Paroquet—*locale* AR-4
Paroquet Bluff—*cliff* AR-4
Paro Sch—*school* MI-6
*Parovan* UT-8
**Parowan**—*pop pl* UT-8
Parowan Airp—*airport* UT-8
Parowan Canyon—*valley* (2) UT-8
Parowan Canyon Wash—*stream* UT-8
Parowan City Cem—*cemetery* UT-8
Parowan Creek—*stream* UT-8
Parowan Division—*civil* UT-8
Parowan Front Wildlife Mngmt Area—*park* UT-8
Parowan Gap—*gap* UT-8
Parowan Gap Petroglyphs—*hist pl* UT-8
Parowan Gap Petroglyphs—*other* UT-8
Parowan HS—*school* UT-8
Parowan Meetinghouse—*hist pl* UT-8
Parowan Post Office—*building* UT-8
Parowan Sch—*school* UT-8
Parowan Valley—*basin* UT-8
Parpala Ranch—*locale* WA-9
Par Pond—*reservoir* SC-3
Parquasito Verde Park —*park* AZ-5
**Parque**—*pop pl* PR-3
Parque Atletico Ildefonso Sola Morals—*park* PR-3
Parque Atletico Ovidio Rodriquez—*park* PR-3
Parque Barbosa—*park* PR-3
Parque Ceremonial de Indigena Caguana—*park* PR-3
Parque Creek—*stream* WY-8
Parque Creek Trail—*trail* WY-8
Parque de Bombas de Ponce—*hist pl* PR-3
Parque de Colon—*park* PR-3
Parque Doctor Jose N Gandara—*park* PR-3
Parque Isidoro Garcia—*park* PR-3
Parque Jesus Pinero—*park* PR-3
Parque La Merced—*park* PR-3
Parque Montaner—*park* PR-3
Parque Munoz Rivera—*park* PR-3
Parque Santiago Iglesias Pantin—*park* PR-3
Parque Sixto Escobar—*park* PR-3
Parque Suau—*park* PR-3
Parque Venado—*flat* NM-5
**Parque Vista Estates (subdivision)**—*pop pl* (2) AZ-5
Parr—*locale* VA-3
**Parr**—*pop pl* IN-6
**Parr**—*pop pl* SC-3
Parr, Calvin W., House—*hist pl* GA-3
Parr, Charles Henry, House—*hist pl* IA-7
Parra, Miguel, Adobe—*hist pl* CA-9
Parra Bayou—*stream* LA-4
Parrack Grove Ch—*church* MO-7
Parragon—*locale* TN-4
*Parragons* TN-4
**Parral**—*pop pl* OH-6
Parra Lake—*lake* TX-5
Parramore—*locale* FL-3
Parramore Beach—*beach* VA-3
Parramore Creek—*stream* CA-9
Parramore Creek—*stream* GA-3
Parramore Island—*island* VA-3
Parramore Prairie—*swamp* FL-3
Parramore Springs—*locale* CA-9
Parran—*locale* MD-2
**Parran**—*pop pl* NV-8
Parrans Chapel—*church* TN-4
*Parrans Chapel Baptist Ch* TN-4
Parras Canyon—*valley* CO-8
**Parras Plaza**—*pop pl* CO-8
Parras Spring—*spring* NM-5
Parra Tank—*reservoir* AZ-5
Parra Tank—*reservoir* TX-5
Parr Branch—*stream* AR-4
Parr Branch—*stream* GA-3
Parr Cem—*cemetery* IA-7
Parr Cem—*cemetery* (2) TN-4
Parr Cem—*cemetery* VA-3
Parr Creek—*stream* MT-8
Parr Ditch—*canal* IN-6
Parren Creek—*stream* MI-6
*Parrers Run* PA-2
Parrett Crossing—*locale* GA-3
Parrette Well—*well* AZ-5
Parrett Mtn—*summit* OR-9
Parr Field (airport)—*airport* TN-4
Parr Hollow—*valley* IN-6
Parriera Drain—*canal* CA-9
Parrilla Creek—*stream* TX-5
Parrilla Creek North—*stream* TX-5
Parrilla Creek South—*stream* TX-5
Parrilla Tank—*reservoir* TX-5
Parrill Run—*stream* WV-2
Parriott Cem—*cemetery* MS-4
Parriott Mesa—*summit* UT-8
Parris Branch—*stream* NC-3
Parris Branch—*stream* TN-4
Parris Brook—*stream* RI-1
Parris Brook Historic and Archeol District—*hist pl* RI-1
Parris Cem—*cemetery* NC-3
Parris Cem—*cemetery* OK-5
Parris Cem—*cemetery* TN-4
Parris Ch—*church* OK-5
Parris Chapel—*church* VA-3
Parris Creek—*stream* NC-3
Parris Grove Ch—*church* GA-3
*Parrish* MS-4
Parrish—*locale* CO-8
**Parrish**—*pop pl* AL-4
**Parrish**—*pop pl* FL-3
**Parrish**—*pop pl* IL-6
**Parrish**—*pop pl* PA-2
**Parrish**—*pop pl* WI-6
**Parrish Addition**—*pop pl* IL-6
Parrish Airp—*airport* IN-6
Parrish Bay—*swamp* FL-3
Parrish Branch—*stream* (2) AL-4
Parrish Branch—*stream* FL-3
Parrish Branch—*stream* IA-7
Parrish Branch—*stream* TN-4
Parrish Bridge—*other* MO-7
Parrish (CCD)—*cens area* AL-4
Parrish (CCD)—*cens area* FL-3
Parrish Cem—*cemetery* FL-3
Parrish Cem—*cemetery* IL-6
Parrish Cem—*cemetery* IN-6
Parrish Cem—*cemetery* KY-4
Parrish Cem—*cemetery* MS-4
Parrish Cem—*cemetery* NY-2
Parrish Cem—*cemetery* NC-3
Parrish Cem—*cemetery* (3) TN-4
Parrish Cem—*cemetery* (2) TX-5
Parrish Cem—*cemetery* WV-2
Parrish Cem—*cemetery* WI-6
Parrish Ch—*church* NC-3
Parrish Chapel—*church* (2) KY-4
Parrish Chapel—*church* NC-3
Parrish Chapel—*church* TN-4
*Parrish Chapel Baptist Ch* TN-4
**Parrish Court**—*pop pl* VA-3
*Parrish Creek* FL-3
Parrish Creek—*stream* AZ-5
Parrish Creek—*stream* FL-3
Parrish Creek—*stream* NY-2
Parrish Creek—*stream* NC-3
Parrish Creek—*stream* (2) OR-9
Parrish Creek—*stream* UT-8
Parrish Creek Research Center—*locale* UT-8
Parrish Ditch—*canal* IN-6
Parrish Division—*civil* AL-4
Parrish Drift Mine (underground)—*mine* AL-4
Parrish Elem Sch—*school* AL-4
Parrish Farm—*locale* NM-5
Parrish Gap—*gap* OR-9
**Parrish Gap**—*pop pl* NC-3
**Parrish Heights Subdivision**—*pop pl* UT-8
Parrish Henderson Cem—*cemetery* MS-4
*Parrish Hill* CT-1
Parrish Hill Ch—*church* VA-3
Parrish Hill Creek—*stream* VA-3
Parrish Hollow—*valley* MO-7
Parrish Hollow—*valley* TN-4
Parrish Homestead—*locale* CO-8
Parrish HS—*school* (2) AL-4
Parris Hill—*summit* VT-1
Parrish JHS—*school* OR-9
**Parrish Junction**—*pop pl* WI-6
Parrish Lake—*reservoir* NC-3
Parrish Lake Dam—*dam* NC-3
Parrish Park (county park)—*park* FL-3
**Parrish Park Subdivision**—*pop pl* UT-8
Parrish Peak—*summit* WA-9
Parrish Place—*hist pl* KY-4
Parrish Pond—*lake* AL-4
Parrish Pond—*lake* FL-3
Parrish Pond—*reservoir* AL-4
Parrish Pond—*reservoir* GA-3
Parrish Run—*stream* WV-2
Parrish Sch—*school* MS-4
*Parrish School* TN-4
Parrish Spring—*spring* MT-8
Parrish Spring Number Two—*spring* MT-8
**Parrish (Town of)**—*pop pl* WI-6
Parris Island—*island* SC-3
Parris Island Drydock and Commanding Generals House—*hist pl* SC-3
Parris Island Marine Corps Recruit Depot—*military* SC-3
Parris Island (Military Reservation)—*military* SC-3
Parris Island Spit—*bar* SC-3
Parris Lake—*lake* IL-6
Parrita Well—*well* TX-5
Parrita Windmill—*locale* TX-5
Parrit Cove—*bay* ME-1
Parrit Point—*cape* ME-1
*Parritt Cove* ME-1
*Parritt Point* ME-1
Parr-Jones Cem—*cemetery* IN-6
Parr Lateral—*canal* CA-9
Parron Gulch—*valley* CO-8
Parroquia del Espiritu Santo y San Patricio—*hist pl* PR-3
Parrot—*locale* ME-1
Parrot Bench—*bench* MT-8
Parrot Branch—*stream* KY-4
Parrot Branch—*stream* VA-3
Parrot Ch—*church* TN-4
Parrot Creek—*channel* SC-3
Parrot Creek—*stream* FL-3
Parrot Creek—*stream* ID-8
Parrot Creek—*stream* MT-8
Parrot Ditch—*canal* MT-8
Parrot Flat—*flat* MT-8
Parrot Homestead—*locale* CO-8
*Parrot Island* VA-3
Parrot Island—*island* AK-9
Parrot Jungle—*park* FL-3
Parrot Lake—*lake* AK-9
Parrot Lake—*lake* ID-8
Parrot (Letter Box)—*locale* KY-4
*Parrot Mesa* UT-8
*Parrot Peak* CO-8
Parrot Peak—*summit* NV-8
Parrot Point—*cape* AK-9
Parrot Point—*cape* ME-1
Parrot Point—*locale* SC-3
Parrot Point Creek—*stream* SC-3
Parrot Rock—*island* AK-9
**Parrots**—*pop pl* NC-3
*Parrots Creek* SC-3
Parrots Ferry Bridge—*locale* CA-9
Parrot Spring—*spring* NM-5
Parrot Spring Sulphur—*spring* CA-9
*Parrotsville* IN-6
Parrotsville Elem Sch—*school* TN-4
Parrotsville Post office—*building* TN-4
Parrotsville Seminary (historical)—*school* TN-4
Parrot Swamp—*stream* NC-3
*Parrott* CO-8
Parrott—*locale* OH-6
**Parrott**—*pop pl* GA-3
**Parrott**—*pop pl* VA-3
Parrott, Moses, House—*hist pl* OR-9
Parrott Branch—*stream* VA-3
Parrott Caves—*cave* TN-4
Parrott (CCD)—*cens area* GA-3
Parrott Cem—*cemetery* AR-4
Parrott Cem—*cemetery* LA-4
Parrott Cem—*cemetery* OK-5
Parrott Cem—*cemetery* (2) TN-4
Parrott Creek—*stream* CO-8
Parrott Creek—*stream* (2) OR-9
Parrott Crossing—*locale* WA-9
Parrotte Spring—*spring* NV-8
*Parrott Flat* MT-8
**Parrott Fork**—*pop pl* NC-3
Parrott Hall—*hist pl* NY-2
Parrott Hollow—*valley* KY-4
Parrott Insurance Bldg—*hist pl* GA-3
Parrott Island—*island* VA-3
Parrott Lake—*lake* AR-4
Parrott Landing—*locale* CA-9
Parrott Marshall Cem—*cemetery* OH-6
Parrott Peak—*summit* CO-8
Parrott Point—*cape* MD-2
Parrott Point—*cape* MI-6
Parrott Sch—*school* IL-6
Parrott Sch—*school* MI-6
*Parrotts Chapel* TN-4
Parrotts Chapel Cem—*cemetery* TN-4
Parrott Sch (historical)—*school* TN-4
Parrotts Creek—*stream* VA-3
**Parrottsville**—*pop pl* TN-4
Parrottsville Cave—*cave* TN-4
Parrottsville (CCD)—*cens area* TN-4
Parrottsville Division—*civil* TN-4
Parrottsville United Methodist Ch—*church* TN-4
Parrotts Wharf—*locale* MD-2
Parr Sch—*school* CO-8
Parr Sch—*school* TX-5
Parr Sch (historical)—*school* TN-4
Parr Shoals Dam—*dam* SC-3
**Parrs Mill**—*pop pl* PA-2
Parr's Mill Covered Bridge No. 10—*hist pl* PA-2
Parrs Pond—*reservoir* AL-4
Parr Spring Run—*stream* WV-2
Parrs Ridge—*ridge* (2) MD-2
**Parrsville**—*pop pl* MD-2
Parry—*locale* TN-4
**Parry**—*pop pl* NJ-2
Parry, John E., House—*hist pl* NY-2
Parry Cem—*cemetery* OH-6
Parry Center—*building* OR-9
Parry Creek—*stream* CO-8
Parry House—*hist pl* NY-2
*Parry Island* MP-9
Parry Lake—*lake* AK-9
*Parry Park* CO-8
Parry Peak—*summit* (2) CO-8
Parry Peak Campground—*locale* CO-8
*Parry's Island* MP-9
*Parrys Mill Creek* MS-4
Parry Spring—*spring* CA-9
**Parryville**—*pop pl* PA-2
Parryville Borough—*civil* PA-2
Parryville Lake—*reservoir* PA-2
Parryville Station—*locale* PA-2
*Parsee Hill* AZ-5
Parsell Cem—*cemetery* MO-7
Parsell Cem—*cemetery* NY-2
Parsell Ranch—*locale* MT-8
Parsell Sch—*school* MI-6
Parse Mackey Ridge—*ridge* MO-7
Parsenn Creek—*stream* CO-8
**Parshall**—*pop pl* CO-8
**Parshall**—*pop pl* ND-7
**Parshallburg (Havana)**—*pop pl* MI-6
Parshall Hosp—*hospital* NY-2
**Parshall Township**—*pop pl* ND-7
**Parshallville**—*pop pl* MI-6
Parshas—*locale* AK-9
Parshas Bay—*bay* AK-9
Parshas Point—*cape* AK-9
**Parshley**—*pop pl* MO-7
*Parshvanath Mountain* OR-9
Parsimmon Branch—*stream* NC-3
**Parsippany**—*pop pl* NJ-2
Parsippany, Lake—*reservoir* NJ-2
Parsippany Ch—*church* NJ-2
Parsippany (sta.)—*uninc pl* NJ-2
Parsippany-Troy Hills Township—*CDP* NJ-2
**Parsippany-Troy Hills (Township of)**—*pop pl* NJ-2
**Parsley**—*pop pl* WV-2
Parsley Bar—*bar* CA-9
Parsley Bar Crossing—*locale* CA-9
Parsley Bar Trail—*trail* CA-9
Parsley Big Branch—*stream* WV-2
**Parsley Bottom**—*pop pl* WV-2
Parsley Cem—*cemetery* (2) AR-4
Parsley Cem—*cemetery* IA-7
Parsley Cem—*cemetery* KY-4
Parsley Cem—*cemetery* MO-7
Parsley Cem—*cemetery* WV-2
Parsley Creek—*stream* OK-5
Parsley Creek—*stream* OR-9
Parsley Crossing—*locale* TX-5
Parsley Hollow—*valley* AR-4
Parsley Rsvr—*reservoir* AR-4
Parsleys Creek—*stream* VA-3
Parsleys Millpond—*reservoir* VA-3
Parslow Park—*park* MI-6
Parsner Creek—*stream* WV-2
*Parsnip Creek* OR-9
Parsnip Creek—*stream* CA-9
Parsnip Creek—*stream* MT-8
Parsnip Creek—*stream* (4) OR-9
Parsnip Creek Diversion Dam—*dam* OR-9
Parsnip Creek Diversion Rsvr—*reservoir* OR-9
Parsnip Creek Wash—*stream* NV-8
Parsnip Dam—*dam* OR-9
Parsnip Flat—*flat* CO-8
Parsnip Lake—*lake* MN-6
Parsnip Lakes—*lake* OR-9
*Parsnip Mountain* NV-8
Parsnip Mtn—*summit* MT-8
Parsnip Peak—*summit* NV-8
Parsnip Peak—*summit* OR-9
Parsnip Rsvr—*reservoir* OR-9
Parsnip Spring—*spring* AZ-5
Parsnip Spring—*spring* (2) NV-8
Parsnip Springs—*spring* CA-9
Parsnip Springs—*spring* OR-9
Parsnip Swamp—*swamp* WA-9
Parsnip Wash—*stream* NV-8
Parso Lake—*lake* MN-6
*Parson* PA-2
Parson, Dr. John, Cabin Complex—*hist pl* UT-8
**Parsonage**—*pop pl* VA-3
Parsonage, The—*hist pl* MA-1
*Parsonage Branch* NJ-2
Parsonage Branch—*stream* AL-4
Parsonage Brook—*stream* MA-1
Parsonage Cem—*cemetery* AL-4
Parsonage Cem—*cemetery* LA-4
Parsonage Chapel United Methodist Ch (historical)—*church* AL-4
Parsonage Corner—*locale* ME-1
Parsonage Cove—*bay* NY-2
Parsonage Creek—*gut* SC-3
Parsonage Creek—*stream* NY-2
Parsonage Hill—*summit* (2) ME-1
Parsonage Hill—*summit* MA-1
Parsonage Hill—*summit* (3) NH-1
Parsonage Hollow—*valley* TN-4
Parsonage Island—*island* NY-2
Parsonage Point—*cape* NY-2
Parsonage Run—*stream* NJ-2
Parson and Scoville Bldg—*hist pl* IN-6
Parson Bald—*summit* NC-3
Parson Bald—*summit* TN-4
Parson Branch—*stream* NC-3
Parson Branch—*stream* TN-4
Parson Branch—*stream* VA-3
*Parson Brook* CT-1
Parson Brothers Pond—*reservoir* NC-3
Parson Brothers Pond Dam—*dam* NC-3
Parson Canyon—*valley* NM-5
Parson Cem—*cemetery* IN-6
Parson Cem—*cemetery* IA-7
Parson Cem—*cemetery* MS-4
Parson Cem—*cemetery* (2) MO-7
Parson Ch—*church* TN-4
Parson City Spring—*spring* UT-8
*Parson Creek* ME-1
*Parson Creek* MD-2
Parson Creek—*stream* MO-7
Parson Creek—*stream* MT-8
Parson Creek—*stream* VA-3
Parson Creek—*stream* WA-9
Parson Creek Ch (historical)—*church* MO-7
Parson Creek Township—*civil* MO-7
Parson Dam—*dam* AL-4
Parson Drain—*canal* MI-6
Parson Draw—*valley* WY-8
Parson Falls—*falls* NY-2
Parson Falls Creek—*stream* AK-9
**Parson Farms**—*pop pl* NY-2
*Parsonfield* ME-1
**Parsonfield**—*pop pl* ME-1
Parsonfield (Town of)—*civ div* ME-1
Parson Gap—*gap* VA-3
Parson Grove Ch—*church* NC-3
Parson Grove Sch—*school* NC-3
Parson Gulch—*valley* MT-8
Parson High Top—*summit* TN-4
Parson Hill—*summit* AR-4
Parson Hill Cem—*cemetery* MS-4
Parson Hill Ch—*church* (2) MS-4
*Parson Hollow* TN-4
*Parson Island* FL-3
*Parson Island* MD-2
Parson Island—*island* MD-2
Parson Lake—*lake* CO-8
Parson Landing—*locale* ME-1
Parson Lead—*ridge* TN-4
Parson Mill—*locale* NY-2
*Parson Mountain* SC-3
Parson Open Mine (underground)—*mine* AL-4
Parson Pit—*cave* AL-4
Parson Point—*cape* DE-2
Parson Point—*cape* TN-4
Parson Ranch—*locale* CA-9
Parson Rapids—*rapids* (2) WA-9
Parson Rock—*pillar* CA-9
Parson Rsvr—*reservoir* ID-8
Parson Run—*stream* PA-2
Parsons—*locale* AL-4
Parsons—*locale* MS-4
**Parsons**—*pop pl* ID-8
**Parsons**—*pop pl* KS-7
**Parsons**—*pop pl* MO-7
**Parsons**—*pop pl* PA-2
**Parsons**—*pop pl* TN-4
**Parsons**—*pop pl* WV-2
Parsons, C. H., House—*hist pl* MS-4
Parsons, Edward, House—*hist pl* MA-1
Parsons, Josiah K., Homestead—*hist pl* ME-1
Parsons, Lake—*reservoir* KS-7
Parsons, Marion, House—*hist pl* ME-1
Parsons, Samuel, House—*hist pl* CT-1
Parsons, Stephen, House—*hist pl* ME-1
*Parsons, Town of* MA-1
*Parsons Bald* TN-4
Parsons Beach—*beach* ME-1
**Parsons Beach**—*pop pl* NY-2
Parsons Bend—*bend* TN-4
Parsons Block and Hall—*hist pl* MN-6
Parsons Branch—*stream* (3) KY-4
Parsons Branch—*stream* MO-7
Parsons Branch—*stream* NC-3
Parsons Branch—*stream* TN-4
Parsons Bridge—*bridge* MT-8
Parsons Brook—*stream* ME-1
Parsons Brook—*stream* MA-1
**Parsonsburg**—*pop pl* MD-2
Parsons Canyon—*valley* AZ-5
Parsons Canyon—*valley* (2) CA-9
Parsons Canyon—*valley* WA-9
Parsons Canyon—*valley* WY-8
Parsons (CCD)—*cens area* TN-4
Parsons Cem—*cemetery* AL-4
Parsons Cem—*cemetery* FL-3
Parsons Cem—*cemetery* KY-4
Parsons Cem—*cemetery* ME-1
Parsons Cem—*cemetery* MS-4
Parsons Cem—*cemetery* (3) MO-7
Parsons Cem—*cemetery* (2) TN-4
Parsons Cem—*cemetery* (4) VA-3
Parsons Cem—*cemetery* (6) WV-2
Parson Sch—*school* MA-1
Parson Sch—*school* NE-7
*Parsons City* KS-7
Parsons Coll—*school* IA-7
Parsons Coll (historical)—*school* TN-4
Parsons Country Club—*other* KS-7
Parsons Cow Camp—*locale* CO-8
*Parson's Creek* MD-2
*Parsons Creek* MO-7
*Parsons Creek* TN-4
Parsons Creek—*stream* (2) CA-9
Parsons Creek—*stream* GA-3
Parsons Creek—*stream* ID-8
Parsons Creek—*stream* KS-7
Parsons Creek—*stream* KY-4
Parsons Creek—*stream* ME-1
Parsons Creek—*stream* MD-2
Parsons Creek—*stream* NC-3
Parsons Creek—*stream* (2) OR-9
Parsons Creek—*stream* WI-6
Parsons Creek—*stream* WY-8
Parsons Creek Neck—*cape* MD-2
*Parsons Crossroads* NC-3
Parsons Dam—*dam* KS-7
Parsons Ditch—*canal* CA-9
Parsons Division—*civil* TN-4
Parsons Draw—*valley* CO-8
Parsons Elem Sch—*school* TN-4
**Parsonsfield**—*pop pl* ME-1
Parsonsfield Seminary—*hist pl* ME-1
Parsonsfield Seminary—*school* ME-1
Parsons Filled Arch Bridge—*hist pl* KS-7
Parsons First Baptist Ch—*church* TN-4
*Parsons Flats* TN-4
Parsons Grove—*locale* AZ-5
**Parsons Grove Church**—*pop pl* NC-3
Parsons Hill—*summit* MA-1
Parsons Hill Ch—*church* AR-4
Parsons Hill Ch—*church* PA-2
*Parsons Hill School* PA-2
Parsons (historical)—*locale* AL-4
Parsons Hollow—*valley* TN-4
Parsons Hollow—*valley* VA-3
Parsons Hollow—*valley* WV-2
Parsons Homestead—*hist pl* NH-1
Parsons Hosp—*hospital* NY-2
Parsons-Howell Cem—*cemetery* NC-3
Parsons HS—*school* KS-7
Parsons HS (historical)—*school* TN-4
Parsons Island—*island* MD-2
Parsons Island—*island* VA-3
Parsons JHS—*school* KS-7
Parsons JHS—*school* TN-4
Parsons Knob—*summit* NY-2
Parsons Lake—*lake* ID-8
Parsons Lake—*lake* MI-6
*Parsons Landing* TN-4
Parsons Landing—*beach* CA-9
Parsons Memorial Lodge—*hist pl* CA-9
Parsons Mill (historical)—*locale* TN-4
*Parsons Mill Pond* VT-1
Parsons Mine (underground)—*mine* AL-4
Parson Smith Tree—*hist pl* WA-9
Parsons Mountain Lake—*reservoir* SC-3
Parsons Mtn—*summit* SC-3
Parsons Pass—*channel* SD-7
*Parsons Peak* AK-9
Parsons Peak—*summit* CA-9
*Parsons Pentecostal Church* TN-4
**Parsons Place Subdivision, The**—*pop pl* UT-8
*Parsons Pond* VT-1
Parsons Pond—*lake* (2) MA-1
Parsons Pond—*lake* NY-2
Parsons Pond—*reservoir* NJ-2
Parsons Post Office—*building* TN-4
Parson Spring—*spring* CA-9
Parson Springs—*spring* NV-8
Parsons Ranch—*locale* CA-9
Parsons Ranch—*locale* CO-8
Parsons Ranch—*locale* MT-8
Parsons Ranch—*locale* (2) NM-5
Parsons Ranch—*locale* WY-8
Parsons Ridge—*ridge* WV-2
Parsons Rsvr—*reservoir* CO-8
Parsons Run—*stream* (2) PA-2
Parsons Run—*stream* WV-2
Parsons Saint Sch—*school* FL-3
Parsons Sch—*school* (2) CA-9
Parsons Sch—*school* IL-6
Parsons Sch—*school* IN-6
Parsons Sch—*school* (2) KS-7
Parsons Sch—*school* KY-4
Parsons Sch—*school* ME-1
Parsons Sch—*school* MI-6
Parsons Sch—*school* NJ-2
Parsons Sch—*school* NY-2
Parsons Sch—*school* (2) VT-1
Parsons Sch—*school* WV-2
Parsons Siding—*locale* VA-3
*Parsons Slough* TX-5
Parsons Slough—*stream* MT-8
Parsons Slough—*stream* TX-5
Parsons Spring—*spring* AZ-5
Parsons Spring—*spring* ID-8
Parsons Spring—*spring* MO-7
Parsons Spring—*spring* OR-9
Parsons Spring—*spring* UT-8
Parsons State Hosp—*hospital* KS-7
Parsons Station—*locale* PA-2
Parsons Street Sch—*school* MA-1
Parsons Studio and Casino—*hist pl* NH-1
Parsons Tank—*reservoir* AZ-5
Parsons-Taylor House—*hist pl* PA-2
Parsons United Methodist Ch—*church* TN-4
Parsons Village Square (Shop Ctr)—*locale* FL-3
**Parsonsville**—*pop pl* PA-2
Parsons Well—*well* CA-9
*Parsonville* PA-2
Parsonville—*locale* MD-2
Parsonville—*locale* NC-3
**Parsonville**—*pop pl* NJ-2
**Parsonville**—*pop pl* (2) PA-2
Parson Wright Branch—*stream* FL-3
Partain—*locale* AR-4
Partain Cem—*cemetery* IL-6
Partain Cem—*cemetery* TX-5
Part Brook—*stream* IN-6
Part Creek—*stream* OR-9
**Partee**—*pop pl* AR-4
**Partee**—*pop pl* MS-4
Partee, Hiram, House—*hist pl* TX-5
Partee Sch—*school* AR-4
**Partello**—*pop pl* MI-6
**Partello Corners**—*pop pl* NY-2
Partello Road Ch—*church* MI-6
Parten Sch—*school* TX-5
**Parthena (Ywca Camp)**—*pop pl* OK-5
Parthenia Cem—*cemetery* MS-4
Parthenia Chapel—*church* TN-4
Parthenia Street Sch—*school* CA-9
*Parthenia United Methodist Ch* TN-4
Parthenon—*building* TN-4
**Parthenon**—*pop pl* AR-4
Parthenon, The—*hist pl* TN-4
Par Three Golf Club—*other* IL-6
Partin Branch—*stream* KY-4
Partin Butte—*summit* OR-9
Partin Canal—*canal* FL-3
Partin Cem—*cemetery* (2) GA-3
Partin Cem—*cemetery* (4) KY-4
Partin Cem—*cemetery* NC-3
Partin Cem—*cemetery* (2) TN-4
Partin Creek—*stream* AK-9
Partin Gap—*gap* NC-3
*Parting Beach* RI-1
Parting Brook—*stream* CT-1
Parting Brook—*stream* NH-1
Parting Creek—*stream* VA-3
Parting of the Ways—*hist pl* WY-8
Parting Springs—*locale* WV-2
Partington Creek—*stream* CA-9
Partington Point—*cape* CA-9
Partington Ridge—*ridge* CA-9
Parting Ways Archeol District—*hist pl* MA-1
Parting Ways Cem—*cemetery* MA-1
Partins Pond—*reservoir* NC-3
Partins Pond Dam—*dam* NC-3
Partin Spring—*spring* OR-9
Partin Spring—*spring* TN-4
Partin Spring Cave—*cave* TN-4
*Partinville* TN-4

Partinville Post Office (historical)—building TN-4
Partiridge Island—island ME-1
Part Island—island FL-3
Partition Arch—arch UT-8
Partition Cove—bay AK-9
Partition Tank—reservoir TX-5
Partition Well—well NM-5
Partition Windmill—locale (3) TX-5
Partlett Mountains—range CA-9
Partlow—locale NY-2
Partlow—locale VA-3
Partlow Branch—stream TN-4
Partlow Cem—cemetery IL-6
Partlow Cem—cemetery KS-7
Partlow Dam Lower AL-4
Partlow Dam Upper AL-4
Partlow Hollow—valley MO-7
Partlow Lake—lake NY-2
Partlow Lake Lower—reservoir AL-4
Partlow Lake Upper—reservoir AL-4
Partlow Milldam—lake NY-2
Partlow Mtn—summit NY-2
Partlow Pond—lake NY-2
Partlow State School and Hosp—hospital AL-4
Partman Branch—stream MS-4
Partman Cem—cemetery MS-4
Partner Mine—mine AK-9
Partners Creek—stream PA-2
Partnership Rsvr—reservoir MT-8
Partnership Tank—reservoir (2) AZ-5
Partnership Well—locale NM-5
Partnership Well—well (2) AZ-5
Partnership Well—well NM-5
Partnership Windmill—locale NM-5
Partnership Windmill—locale TX-5
Partof Point—cape AK-9
Partofshikof Island—island AK-9
Part of the Shears DE-2
Parton Branch—stream AL-4
Parton Branch—stream TN-4
Parton Cem—cemetery TN-4
Parton Creek—stream OR-9
Parton Drain—canal WA-9
Parton Hollow—valley AR-4
**Partoun**—pop pl UT-8
Partridge AL-4
Partridge—locale KY-4
**Partridge**—pop pl KS-7
**Partridge**—pop pl MI-6
Partridge, Jabez, Homestead—hist pl MA-1
Partridge, John, House—hist pl MA-1
Partridge, Point—cape WA-9
Partridge Bank—bar WA-9
Partridge Bay MN-6
Partridge Bay—bay MI-6
Partridge Bayou—stream LA-4
Partridge Beach RI-1
Partridge Branch—stream VA-3
Partridge Brook—stream (3) ME-1
Partridge Brook—stream NH-1
Partridge Brook Flowage—lake ME-1
Partridge Canyon AZ-5
Partridge Canyon—valley UT-8
Partridge Cem—cemetery ME-1
Partridge Cem—cemetery MS-4
Partridge Cem—cemetery (2) NY-2
Partridge Cem—cemetery TX-5
Partridge Cove—bay (2) ME-1
Partridge Cow Camp—locale MT-8
Partridge Creek AL-4
Partridge Creek AZ-5
Partridge Creek VA-3
Partridge Creek—stream AL-4
Partridge Creek—stream AZ-5
Partridge Creek—stream (3) ID-8
Partridge Creek—stream (2) IL-6
Partridge Creek—stream MI-6
Partridge Creek—stream (3) MN-6
Partridge Creek—stream MT-8
Partridge Creek—stream NC-3
Partridge Creek—stream OR-9
Partridge Creek—stream SC-3
Partridge Creek—stream TX-5
Partridge Creek—stream VA-3
Partridge Creek—stream WI-6
Partridge Creek Lake—lake ID-8
Partridge Crop Flowage—reservoir WI-6
Partridge Crop Lake—lake (2) WI-6
Partridge Crossing AL-4
**Partridge Crossroads**—pop pl AL-4
Partridge Falls—falls MN-6
Partridgefield MA-1
Partridgefield, Town of MA-1
Partridge Gap—gap NC-3
Partridge Gap Ridge—ridge NC-3
Partridge Gulch—valley MT-8
Partridge Harbor—bay NY-2
Partridge Hill IL-6
Partridge Hill—summit ME-1
Partridge Hill—summit SC-3
Partridge Hill Cem—cemetery SC-3
Partridge (historical)—locale AZ-5
**Partridge (historical)**—pop pl AZ-5
Partridge Island ME-1
Partridge Island—island (3) ME-1
Partridge Island—island MI-6
Partridge Island—island NY-2
Partridge Island Cem—cemetery NY-2
Partridge Lake MI-6
Partridge Lake MN-6
Partridge Lake—lake (2) MI-6
Partridge Lake—lake (2) MN-6
Partridge Lake—lake NH-1
Partridge Lake—lake (3) WI-6
**Partridge Lake**—pop pl NH-1
Partridge Lakes MN-6
Partridge Landing—locale VA-3
Partridge Lumber Company Lake Dam—dam MS-4
Partridge Mountain Research Natural Area—area UT-8
Partridge Mtn—summit NY-2
Partridge Mtn—summit UT-8
Partridge Peak—summit ME-1
**Partridge Place**—pop pl MD-2
Partridge Point—cape MI-6
Partridge Point—cape MN-6
Partridge Pond—lake (2) ME-1
Partridge Pond—lake NY-2
Partridge Pond—reservoir MA-1
Partridge Ridge—ridge UT-8
Partridge River MN-6
Partridge River—stream (2) MN-6
Partridge Run Game Mngmt Area—park NY-2
Partridge Sch—school CA-9
Partridge Sch—school VA-3
Partridge Spring—spring TN-4
Partridge Town AL-4
Partridge Township Hall—hist pl MN-6
**Partridge (Township of)**—pop pl IL-6
**Partridge (Township of)**—pop pl MN-6
**Partridgeville**—pop pl (2) MA-1
Partridgeville (historical)—locale MA-1
Partridgeville Pond—reservoir MA-1
Partridgeville Pond Dam—dam MA-1
Partridge Wash AZ-5
Partwood Crossing—locale TX-5
Party Cape—cape AK-9
Party Hill—summit NY-2
Party Lake—lake MN-6
Party Trail—trail NY-2
Paruna Ch—church OK-5
Paruna Community Hall—locale OK-5
Pa-Ru'Nu-Weap UT-8
Parunuweap Canyon—valley UT-8
Parunuweap River UT-8
Parurugan-To MP-9
Par Value Lakes—lake CA-9
Par Valve Lake CA-9
Parvas Mine (underground)—mine AL-4
Parvin—locale OK-5
Parvin—locale TX-5
Parvin—locale WA-9
**Parvin**—pop pl KY-4
**Parvin**—pop pl PA-2
Parvin Branch—stream NJ-2
Parvin Branch—stream TX-5
Parvin Bridge—hist pl OR-9
Parvin Cem—cemetery OK-5
Parvin Gulch—valley CO-8
Parvin Lake—lake CO-8
Parvin Lake—reservoir CO-8
Parvin Lake—reservoir NJ-2
Parvin Lake Dam—dam NJ-2
Parvin Lateral—canal AZ-5
Parvins Branch NJ-2
Parvin State Park—park NJ-2
Pary Drain—canal MI-6
Pas—bar FM-9
Pasa—island FM-9
Pasadees Key—island FL-3
Pasa del Medio—channel PR-3
Pasadena NJ-2
Pasadena OH-6
**Pasadena**—pop pl CA-9
**Pasadena**—pop pl FL-3
**Pasadena**—pop pl MD-2
**Pasadena**—pop pl TX-5
Pasadena, Lake—lake FL-3
Pasadena Apartments—hist pl MI-6
Pasadena Baptist Ch—church FL-3
Pasadena Bay Shore Hosp—hospital TX-5
Pasadena Camp—locale (2) CA-9
Pasadena (CCD)—cens area CA-9
Pasadena (CCD)—cens area TX-5
Pasadena City Coll—school CA-9
Pasadena Civic Center District—hist pl CA-9
Pasadena Coll—school CA-9
Pasadena Continuation HS—school CA-9
Pasadena Fish and Wildlife Mngmt Area—park NJ-2
Pasadena Glen—valley CA-9
**Pasadena Hills**—pop pl MO-7
Pasadena Home—building CA-9
Pasadena Hosp—hospital CA-9
Pasadena HS—school CA-9
**Pasadena Junction**—pop pl CA-9
Pasadena Lake—lake FL-3
Pasadena Lake Elem Sch—school FL-3
Pasadena Little Theater—building TX-5
Pasadena Mine—mine CA-9
Pasadena Mine—mine ID-8
Pasadena Mtn—summit CA-9
Pasadena Oaks Shop Ctr—locale TX-5
**Pasadena Park**—pop pl MO-7
**Pasadena Park**—pop pl WA-9
Pasadona Park Sch—school WA 9
Pasadena Peak—summit CA-9
Pasadena Playhouse—hist pl CA-9
Pasadena Plaza Shop Ctr—locale TX-5
Pasadena Sch—school FL-3
Pasadena Sch—school NY-2
Pasadena Shop Ctr—locale FL-3
Pasadena Shores—locale FL-3
Pasadena Valley—basin ID-8
Pasadena Valley Sch—school ID-8
**Pasadena (Wheatland)**—pop pl NJ-2
Pasadera Mtn—summit AZ-5
Pasadizo Artesian Well—well TX-5
Pasagshak Bay—bay AK-9
Pasagshak Point—cape AK-9
Pasaick River NJ-2
Pasaik River NJ-2
Pasaje Cucaracha—channel PR-3
Pasaje de Margarita—channel PR-3
Pasaje de San Juan—channel PR-3
Pasaje de Vieques—channel PR-3
Pasaje Medio Mundo—channel PR-3
Pasajero Farm—locale CA-9
Pas a Loutre LA-4
Pasamano River—stream GU-9
Pasamonte Lake—lake NM-5
Pasamonte Ranch—locale NM-5
Pasa Robles Well—well AZ-5
**Pasatiempo**—pop pl CA-9
Pasaunt Mountain WA-9
Pasawena Spring ID-8
Pasayson River WA-9
Pasayten Airstrip Guard Station—locale WA-9
Pasayten Cabin—locale WA-9
Pasayten Peak—summit WA-9
Pasayten River—stream WA-9
Pasayton River WA-9
Pasbehegh, Lake—reservoir VA-3
Pascac Brook NJ-2
Pascac Brook NY-2
Pascack NJ-2
Pascack Brook—stream NJ-2
Pascack Brook—stream NY-2
Pascack Brook County Park—park NJ-2
Pascack Cem—cemetery NJ-2
Pascack Valley Regional HS—school NJ-2
**Pascagoula**—pop pl MS-4
Pascagoula Bay—bay MS-4
Pascagoula Bayou—stream LA-4
Pascagoula Beach Park and Rec Area—park MS-4
Pascagoula Canal—canal LA-4
Pascagoula Central Fire Station No. 1—hist pl MS-4
Pascagoula Channel—channel MS-4
Pascagoula City Hall—building MS-4
Pascagoula HS—school MS-4
Pascagoula JHS—school MS-4
Pascagoula Library—building MS-4
Pascagoula River—stream MS-4
**Pascagoula River Estates**—pop pl MS-4
Pascagoula River Front Park—park MS-4
Pascagoula River Game Mngmt Area MS-4
Pascagoula River State Wildlife Mngmt Area—park MS-4
Pascagoula Vocational Technical Training Center—school MS-4
Pascal—locale KY-4
Pascal Bldg—hist pl LA-4
Pascal Cem—cemetery AR-4
Pascal Ch—church AL-4
Pascal Creek—stream SD-7
Pascal Island (historical)—island SD-7
Pascall Ch—church GA-3
Pascal Sch (historical)—school TN-4
Pascals Island (historical)—island SD-7
Pascamanset River MA-1
Pasca Oocooloo River MS-4
Pascatowa ME-1
Pascatowal ME-1
Pascatowal River NH-1
Pascatowa River NH-1
Pascattowaie ME-1
Pascattowaie River NH-1
Pascattoway ME-1
Pascattoway River NH-1
Pascaul Rsvr OR-9
Pascault Row—hist pl MD-2
Paschal Hollow—valley AR-4
Paschal HS—school TX-5
**Paschall**—pop pl NC-3
**Paschall**—pop pl TN-4
Paschall—uninc pl PA-2
Paschall Cem—cemetery TN-4
Paschall Cem—cemetery TX-5
Paschall Ch—church NC-3
Paschall Ranch—locale NM-5
Paschal Pond—reservoir AL-4
Paschal Pond Dam—dam AL-4
Paschal Shaft—mine NM-5
Paschalville PA-2
Paschal-Womble House—hist pl NC-3
Pasche—locale TX-5
Paschen Lake WI-6
Paschen Park—park IL-6
Pasch Island—island MN-6
Pasco—locale FL-3
Pasco—locale GA-3
**Pasco**—pop pl OH-6
**Pasco**—pop pl WA-9
**Pascoag**—pop pl RI-1
Pascoag Reservoir Upper Dam—dam RI-1
Pascoag River—stream RI-1
Pascoag Rsvr—reservoir RI-1
Pascoay River RI-1
Pasco Canyon—valley NV-8
Pasco Carnegie Library—hist pl WA-9
Pasco (CCD)—cens area WA-9
Pascock Brook NJ-2
Pascock Brook NY-2
Pasco Coulee—valley MT-8
**Pasco County**—pop pl FL-3
Pasco Creek—stream (2) AK-9
Pasco Davis Dam—dam AL-4
Pascoe Lake—lake MN-6
Pasco Elem Sch—school FL-3
Pasco-Hernando Community Coll—school FL-3
Pasco HS—school FL-3
Pasco JHS—school FL-3
Pasco-Kennewick Bridge—hist pl WA-9
Pasco Kindergarten—school WA-9
**Pascola**—pop pl MO-7
Pascola Township—civil MO-7
Pascomanset River MA-1
Pascommattos Pond RI-1
Pasco North (CCD)—cens area WA-9
Pasconuquis Cove RI-1
Pasco Packing Company Lake—lake FL-3
Pasco Pass—gap AK-9
Pasco Plaza (Shop Ctr)—locale (2) FL-3
Pasco Pumping Station Lateral Canal—canal WA-9
Pasco Robles CA-9
**Pasco West (Riverview)**—pop pl WA-9
Pascual Arroyo—stream NM-5
Pascual Draw—valley NM-5
Pascualilla Banco No 132—levee TX-5
Pascual Rsvr—reservoir OR-9
**Pascua Yaqui Indian Village**—pop pl AZ-5
Pascua-Yaqui Reservation AZ-5
Pasedena Valley ID-8
Paseo Bridge—other MO-7
Paseo del Rey Sch—school CA-9
Paseo de Susana Park—park GU-9
Paseo HS—school MO-7
Paseo Victor Rojas—hist pl PR-3
Paseur Lake Dam—dam MS-4
Pasfallaya AL-4
Pasfield Park—park IL-6
**Pasha**—pop pl ND-7
Pashan Cem—cemetery IN-6
Pashan Sch—school IN-6
Pashawsey Lake MI-6
Pashiahai MH-9
Pash Island MN-6
Pashketaneset Island MA-1
Pashley Sch—school NY-2
Pashlo Creek MS-4
Pashok Drain—canal MI-6
Pashua Peak—summit MT-8
Pashubbe Creek—stream OK-5
Pashyah MH-9
Pasipuchammuck Cove Creek RI-1
Paskack NJ-2
Paskamanset River—stream MA-1
Paskamansett River MA-1
Paska Okla River MS-4
Pask Cem—cemetery MS-4
Paskell Pond (historical)—lake TN-4
**Paskenta**—pop pl CA-9
Paskenta Cem—cemetery CA-9
**Paskert**—pop pl VA-3
Paskett Canyon—valley UT-8
Paskett Spring—spring UT-8
Paskitchannesset MA-1
Paskomanset River MA-1
Pasko Park—park CA-9
Paskuisset Brook RI-1
**Pasley**—pop pl MO-7
**Pasley**—pop pl NC-3
Pasley Airp—airport MO-7
Pasley Cove—valley NC-3
Pasley Sch (abandoned)—school MO-7
Pasley Shoals—bar GA-3
Pasleys Ridge—ridge NC-3
Pasman Cem—cemetery LA-4
P. A. Smith Hotel—hist pl TX-5
Pasmore Creek MI-6
Paso, Arroyo Del—stream CA-9
Paso, Canon—valley CO-8
Paso Colorado Crossing—locale TX-5
Paso Corvinas—channel TX-5
Paso De Bartolo (Guirado)—civil CA-9
Paso De Bartolo (McFarland)—civil CA-9
Paso De Bartolo (McFarland and Downey)—civil CA-9
Paso De Bartolo (Pico)—civil CA-9
Paso De Bartolo (Sepulveda)—civil CA-9
Paso del Norte—gap NM-5
Paso De Robles—civil CA-9
Pasola Mtn—summit OR-9
Paso Los Flacos Well—well TX-5
Pason Dam Draw AZ-5
Paso Palma (Barrio)—fmr MCD PR-3
Paso Picacho Campground—locale CA-9
Paso Point—cape AK-9
Paso Real—locale TX-5
**Paso Robles**—pop pl CA-9
Paso Robles (CCD)—cens area CA-9
Paso Robles (corporate name El Paso de Robles) CA-9
Paso Robles Creek—stream AK-9
Paso Robles Creek—stream CA-9
**Paso Seco**—pop pl PR-3
Paso Slough CA-9
Paso Spring—spring NV-8
Pasour Mountain—ridge NC-3
Paso Verde Crossing—locale TX-5
Paspagola River MS-4
Paspatansy Creek VA-3
Paspotansie Creek VA-3
**Pasqua**—pop pl AL-4
Pasquagola Riv MS-4
Pasquahanza Creek—stream MD-2
Pasquahanza Pond MD-2
Pasqual CA-9
Pasqual Tank—reservoir NM-5
Pasquanahommaus Neck MA-1
Pasquaney Bay—bay NH-1
Pasqua Yaqui Ind Res—reserve AZ-5
Pasque Island—island MA-1
Pasquenese Island MA-1
Pasqueset Brook RI-1
Pasquini Canyon—valley CA-9
Pasquiset Brook—stream RI-1
Pasquiset Pond—lake RI-1
**Pasquo**—pop pl TN-4
Pasquotank—locale NC-3
**Pasquotank County**—pop pl NC-3
Pasquotank County Courthouse—building NC-3
Pasquotank River—stream NC-3
Pasquotank Sch—school NC-3
Pass, The PA-2
Pass, The—gap UT-8
Pass, The—valley MT-8
Pass Abel—channel LA-4
Passa Cavallo TX-5
**Passaconaway**—pop pl NH-1
Passaconaway, Mount—summit NH-1
Passaconaway Cutoff Trail—trail NH-1
Passaconaway Lodge—locale NH-1
Passaconaway Point—cape ME-1
Passaconaway Trail—trail NH-1
Passaconway ME-1
Passaconway Pond ME-1
Passadena Ave Sch—school CA-9
**Passadumkeag**—pop pl ME-1
Passadumkeag Mountains ME-1
Passadumkeag Mtn—summit ME-1
Passadumkeag River—stream ME-1
**Passadumkeag (Town of)**—pop pl ME-1
Passagasawakeag River ME-1
Passagassawakeag, Lake—lake ME-1
Passagassawakeag Bay ME-1
Passagassawakeag River—stream ME-1
Passagassawaukeag ME-1
Passagassawaukeag River ME-1
Passage, The—channel NC-3
Passage, The—channel FM-9
Passage Canal—bay AK-9
Passage Creek NV-8
Passage Creek UT-8
Passage Creek WA-9
Passage Creek—stream MT-8
Passage Creek—stream VA-3
Passage Creek—stream WY-8
Passage Creek For Trail—trail VA-3
Passage Gulf—valley NY-2
Passage Island—island (3) AK-9
Passage Island—island MI-6
Passage Islands—area AK-9
Passage Key—island FL-3
Passage Key Inlet—bay FL-3
Passage Key Natl Wildlife Ref—park FL-3
Passage Point—cape (3) AK-9
Passage Rock—other (2) AK-9
Pass A Grille FL-3
Pass-a-Grille Beach—beach FL-3
Pass-a-Grille Beach—uninc pl FL-3
Pass-A-Grille Beach Community Ch—church FL-3
Pass-A-Grille Channel—channel FL-3
Pass-A-Grille North Channel—channel FL-3
Pass-A-Grille South FL-3
Pass-A-Grille South Channel—channel FL-3
**Passaic**—pop pl MO-7
**Passaic**—pop pl NJ-2
**Passaic County**—pop pl NJ-2
Passaic County Vocational Sch—school NJ-2
Passaic Falls—falls NJ-2
Passaic Junction—locale NJ-2
Passaick River NJ-2
Passaic Machine Works-Watts, Campbell & Company—hist pl NJ-2
Passaic Park—uninc pl NJ-2
Passaic River—airport NJ-2
Passaic River—stream NJ-2
Passaic River Park—park NJ-2
Passaic Station—locale NJ-2
**Passaic (Township of)**—pop pl NJ-2
Passaic Valley HS—school NJ-2
Pass a Jean—channel LA-4
Pass a l'Outre LA-4
Pass a Loutre—channel LA-4
Pass a Loutre State Water Fowl Mngmt Area—park LA-4
Pass Alto CA-9
Passamada Quoda ME-1
Passamagamet Falls—falls ME-1
Passamagamet Lake—lake ME-1
Passamagmoc ME-1
Passamagmoc Falls ME-1
Passamagormac ME-1
Passamagormac Falls ME-1
Passamaquoddy Bay—bay ME-1
Passamari Ditch—canal MT-8
Passapae Landing—locale MD-2
Passapatanzy—locale VA-3
Passapatanzy Creek VA-3
Passapatanzy Creek—stream VA-3
Passaqua Playground—park MA-1
Passaquassawakeag River ME-1
Pass aux Huitres AL-4
Passavant Hosp—hospital PA-2
Passavant Hospital Airp—airport PA-2
Passavant House—hist pl PA-2
Passavant Memorial Homes—cemetery PA-2
Pass Barre—channel LA-4
Pass Branch—stream MO-7
Pass Butte—summit WA-9
Pass Canyon UT-8
Pass Canyon—valley (5) UT-8
Pass Canyon Spring—spring UT-8
Pass Cave—cave AL-4
Pass Cem—cemetery MS-4
Pass Cem—cemetery TN-4
Pass Chalon LA-4
Pass Channel—channel TX-5
**Pass Christian**—pop pl MS-4
Pass Christian City Hall—building MS-4
Pass Christian Coll (historical)—school MS-4
Pass Christian Elem Sch—school MS-4
Pass Christian HS—school MS-4
**Pass Christian Isles (subdivision)**—pop pl MS-4
Pass Christian Library—building MS-4
Pass Christian Lighthouse—locale MS-4
Pass Christian MS—school MS-4
Passconkquis Cove RI-1
Passconuquis Cove RI-1
Pass Creek GA-3
Pass Creek ID-8
Pass Creek MT-8
Pass Creek WA-9
Pass Creek WY-8
Pass Creek—stream (7) AK-9
Pass Creek—stream (3) CA-9
Pass Creek—stream (8) CO-8
Pass Creek—stream (8) ID-8
Pass Creek—stream MI-6
Pass Creek—stream (9) MT-8
Pass Creek—stream NE-7
Pass Creek—stream NV-8
Pass Creek—stream (4) OR-9
Pass Creek—stream (3) SD-7
Pass Creek—stream (2) TX-5
Pass Creek—stream (3) UT-8
Pass Creek—stream (9) WA-9
Pass Creek—stream (9) WY-8
Pass Creek Basin—basin SD-7
Pass Creek Basin—basin WY-8
Pass Creek Canyon—valley (2) WY-8
Pass Creek County Park—park OR-9
Pass Creek Guard Station—locale CA-9
Pass Creek Lake—lake CO-8
Pass Creek Lake—lake ID-8
Pass Creek Lake—reservoir CO-8
Pass Creek Lakes ID-8
Pass Creek Pass—gap CO-8
Pass Creek Pass—gap WA-9
Pass Creek Sch—hist pl MT-8
Pass Creek Sch—school MT-8
Pass Creek Shelter—locale OR-9
Pass Creek Snowshoe Cabin—hist pl MT-8
Pass Creek Spring—spring ID-8
Pass Creek State Wayside—locale OR-9
Pass Creek Summit—summit ID-8
Pass Creek Trail—trail OR-9
Pass Creek Well—well SD-7
**Passcut**—pop pl AL-4
Pass des Illes—gut LA-4
Pass de Wharf—gut (2) LA-4
Pass Du Bois—gut LA-4
Passe a Loutre LA-4
Passena MS-4
Passena Mill MS-4
Passenger and Baggage Car No. 4639—hist pl PA-2
Passenger Branch—stream KY-4
Passenger Coach No. 3556—hist pl PA-2
Passenger Creek—stream TN-4
Passenger Day Coach No. 8177—hist pl PA-2
Passenger Fork—stream WV-2
Passenger Lake—lake MN-6
Passenger Locomotive No. 1223—hist pl PA-2
Passenger Locomotive No. 1737—hist pl PA-2
Passenger Locomotive No. 460—hist pl PA-2
Passenger Locomotive No. 7002—hist pl PA-2
Passenger Swamp—stream VA-3
Passeonkquis Cove—bay RI-1
**Passer**—pop pl PA-2
Passerdyke Creek—stream MD-2
Pass Fernandez—channel LA-4
Pass Fork—stream (2) AK-9
Pass Grille FL-3
Pass Gulch—valley OR-9
Passhikhanneset Island MA-1
Passing—locale VA-3
Passino Sch—school MI-6
Passionate Spring—spring CA-9
Passionist Fathers Seminary—school MO-7
Passions Spring Cave—cave TN-4
Pass Island—island AK-9
Pass Key—island (2) FL-3
Pass La Graisse—gut (3) LA-4
Pass Lake—lake AK-9
Pass Lake—lake CO-8
Pass Lake—lake MI-6
Pass Lake—lake MT-8
Pass Lake—lake UT-8
Pass Lake—lake (2) WA-9
Pass Lake—lake (3) WY-8
Pass Lake—reservoir ID-8
Pass Lake—swamp ND-7
Pass Lakes—lake ND-7
Pass la Poule—channel LA-4
Pass Lateral—canal ID-8
Passless Creek—stream AK-9
Pass Machac Light—hist pl LA-4
Pass Manchac—stream LA-4
Pass Marianne—channel MS-4
Passmore PA-2
**Passmore**—pop pl PA-2
Passmore, Mansel, House—hist pl PA-2
Passmore Branch—stream (2) NC-3
Passmore Cem—cemetery AR-4
Passmore Cem—cemetery GA-3
Passmore Cem—cemetery IA-7
Passmore Cem—cemetery OK-5
Passmore Creek—gut VA-3
Passmore Creek—stream MI-6
Passmore Ditch—canal IN-6
Passmore Gulch—valley MT-8
Passmore House—hist pl AR-4
Passmore Knob—summit NC-3
Passmore Lake—lake AR-4
Passmore Run—stream PA-2
Passmore Springs—spring MI-6
Pass Mountain Overlook—locale VA-3
Pass Mountains AZ-5
Pass Mountain Shelter—locale VA-3
Pass Mountain Trail—trail VA-3
Pass Mtn AZ-5
Pass Mtn—summit AK-9
Pass Mtn—summit AZ-5
Pass Mtn—summit VA-3
Pass No Pass—gap WA-9
**Passo**—pop pl MO-7
Passo Caballo TX-5
Passo Cabello TX-5
Passoit Lake—lake LA-4
Passolt House—hist pl MI-6
**Passover**—pop pl MO-7
Passover Cem—cemetery MO-7
Passover Ch—church MO-7
Pass Peak—summit WY-8
**Passport**—pop pl IL-6
**Passport Township**—pop pl ND-7
Pass Quitman LA-4
Pass Reservoir Number Two WY-8
Pass Rigaud LA-4
Pass Rsvr—reservoir UT-8
Pass Rsvr—reservoir (2) WY-8
Pass Run—stream VA-3
Pass Spring—spring MT-8
Pass Spring Creek CO-8
**Pass Station**—pop pl FL-3
Pass Tank—reservoir (2) AZ-5
Pass Tank—reservoir NM-5
Pass Tante Phine—gut LA-4
Pass Tit Francois—gut LA-4
Pass Trail—trail WA-9
**Passumpsic**—pop pl VT-1
Passumpsic River—stream VT-1
Passwater Cem—cemetery IL-6
Passwaters Cross Road DE-2
Pass Wilson—channel LA-4
Passyunk Square—park PA-2
Pastack Brook NJ-2
Pastack Brook NY-2
Past Creek—stream OR-9
Paste Creek—stream OR-9
Pastel Cem—cemetery AR-4
Paster Reed Brake—stream MS-4
Pasteur Institute—school TX-5
Pasteur JHS—school CA-9
Pasteur JHS—school NY-2
Pasteur Park—park IL-6
Pasteur Sch—school CA-9
Pasteur Sch—school IL-6
Pasteur Sch—school MA-1
Pasteur Sch—school MI-6
Pasteur Sch—school OH-6
Pastillito—locale PR-3
**Pastillo**—pop pl (2) PR-3
**Pastillo Cana**—pop pl PR-3
**Pastime Park**—pop pl NY-2
Pasto (Barrio)—fmr MCD (4) PR-3
Pastohk—locale AK-9
Pastol Bay—bay AK-9
Pastol Bay Light—locale AK-9
Pastoliak River—stream AK-9
Pastolik River—stream AK-9
Pastolik River Lights—locale AK-9
Pastora Peak—summit AZ-5
Pastora Spring—spring TX-5
Pastoren Creek—stream TX-5
Pastore Tank—reservoir AZ-5
Pastoria—locale AR-4
Pastoria—locale VA-3
Pastoria Creek—stream CA-9
Pastoria De Las Borregas—civil CA-9
Pastoria Sch—school AR-4
Pastoria Siphon—canal CA-9
Pastoria (Township of)—fmr MCD AR-4
Pastorino Canyon—valley NV-8
Pastorium, Dexter Ave Baptist Church—hist pl AL-4
Pastorius Park—park PA-2
Pastorius Rsvr—reservoir CO-8
Pastorius Sch—school PA-2
Pastor Point—cape MD-2
Pastos—CDP PR-3

**Pasto Viejo**—pop pl ... PR-3
Pasto Viejo (Barrio)—fmr MCD ... PR-3
Pa Stream—stream ... HI-9
Pastry Ridge—ridge ... UT-8
Pastry Windmill—locale ... TX-5
Pastura—locale ... TX-5
**Pastura**—pop pl ... NM-5
Pasture, The—flat ... ID-8
Pasture, The—flat (2) ... UT-8
Pasture Across the Lane Windmill—locale ... TX-5
Pasture Bottom Creek—stream ... NC-3
Pasture Branch—stream (2) ... KY-4
Pasture Branch—stream (2) ... MS-4
Pasture Branch—stream ... NC-3
Pasture Branch—stream ... SC-3
Pasture Branch—stream ... TX-5
Pasture Branch Swamp—swamp ... NC-3
Pasture Brook ... MA-1
Pasture Brook—stream ... ME-1
Pasture Canyon ... NM-5
Pasture Canyon—valley (2) ... AZ-5
Pasture Canyon—valley (3) ... NM-5
Pasture Canyon—valley (4) ... UT-8
Pasture Canyon—valley ... WY-8
Pasture Canyon Dam—dam ... AZ-5
Pasture Canyon Rsvr—reservoir ... AZ-5
Pasture Canyon Well—well ... NM-5
Pasture Cave—cave ... AL-4
Pasture Cove—bay ... ME-1
Pasture Creek—bay (2) ... NC-3
Pasture Creek—stream ... AL-4
Pasture Creek—stream (3) ... CO-8
Pasture Creek—stream (3) ... ID-8
Pasture Creek—stream (4) ... MT-8
Pasture Creek—stream (3) ... NC-3
Pasture Creek—stream (2) ... OR-9
Pasture Creek—stream ... WY-8
Pasture Draw ... TX-5
Pasture Draw—valley ... MT-8
Pasture Fence Bayou—stream ... MS-4
Pasture Fence Mtn—summit ... VA-3
Pasture Fence Point—cape ... FL-3
Pasture Five Charco—reservoir ... AZ-5
Pasture Green Ch—church ... LA-4
Pasture Gulch—valley ... CA-9
Pasture Gulch—valley (2) ... CO-8
Pasture Gulch—valley ... MT-8
Pasture Gut—stream ... NC-3
Pasture Hill—summit ... MA-1
Pasture Hill—summit ... NY-2
Pasture Hollow—valley ... NM-5
Pasture Lake—lake ... MT-8
Pasture Lake—lake ... NM-5
Pasture Mill Camp—locale ... WY-8
Pasture Mtn—summit ... NC-3
Pasture Neck—cape ... VA-3
Pasture No 1 Windmill—locale ... CO-8
Pasture Number Eight—flat ... KS-7
Pasture Number Eighteen—flat ... KS-7
Pasture Number Eleven—flat ... KS-7
Pasture Number Five—flat ... KS-7
Pasture Number Forty—flat ... KS-7
Pasture Number Fortyeight—flat ... KS-7
Pasture Number Fortyfour—flat ... KS-7
Pasture Number Fortynine—flat ... KS-7
Pasture Number Fortyone—flat ... KS-7
Pasture Number Fortyseven—flat ... KS-7
Pasture Number Fortythree—flat ... KS-7
Pasture Number Four—flat ... KS-7
Pasture Number Nine—flat ... KS-7
Pasture Number Nineteen—flat ... KS-7
Pasture Number Seven—flat ... KS-7
Pasture Number Seventeen—flat ... KS-7
Pasture Number Six—flat ... KS-7
Pasture Number Sixteen—flat ... KS-7
Pasture Number Ten—flat ... KS-7
Pasture Number Thirty—flat ... KS-7
Pasture Number Thirtyeight—flat ... KS-7
Pasture Number Thirtyfive—flat ... KS-7
Pasture Number Thirtyfour—flat ... KS-7
Pasture Number Thirtynine—flat ... KS-7
Pasture Number Thirtyone—flat ... KS-7
Pasture Number Thirtyseven—flat ... KS-7
Pasture Number Thirtysix—flat ... KS-7
Pasture Number Thirtythree—flat ... KS-7
Pasture Number Three—flat ... KS-7
Pasture Number Three Tank—reservoir ... AZ-5
Pasture Number Twelve—flat ... KS-7
Pasture Number Twenty—flat ... KS-7
Pasture Number Twentyeight—flat ... KS-7
Pasture Number Twentyfive—flat ... KS-7
Pasture Number Twentyfour—flat ... KS-7
Pasture Number Twentynine—flat ... KS-7
Pasture Number Twentyone—flat ... KS-7
Pasture Number Twentysix—flat ... KS-7
Pasture Number Twentythree—flat ... KS-7
Pasture Number Twentytwo—flat ... KS-7
Pasture Park—flat ... WY-8
Pasture Point—cape (2) ... DE-2
Pasture Point—cape (3) ... NC-3
Pasture Point—cape ... UT-8
Pasture Point Canyon—valley ... UT-8
Pasture Point Cove—bay ... DE-2
Pasture Pond—lake ... FL-3
Pasture Pond—lake ... MA-1
Pasture Pond—swamp ... TX-5
Pasture Pond Branch—stream ... NC-3
Pasture Ridge—ridge ... ID-8
Pasture Ridge—ridge ... ME-1
Pasture Run Marsh—swamp ... MD-2
Pastures Hist Dist—hist pl ... NY-2
Pastures (Magisterial District)—fmr MCD ... VA-3
Pasture Spring ... AZ-5
Pasture Spring—spring (2) ... AZ-5
Pasture Spring—spring ... OR-9
Pasture Tank—reservoir (8) ... AZ-5
Pasture Tank—reservoir ... NM-5
Pasture Tank Number One—reservoir (2) ... AZ-5
Pasture Three Tank—reservoir ... AZ-5
Pasture Three Tanks ... AZ-5
Pasture Wash—stream ... AZ-5
Pasture Wash—valley ... UT-8
Pasture Wash Ranger Station—locale ... AZ-5
Pasture Wash Tank—reservoir ... AZ-5
Pasture Well—well (2) ... AZ-5
Pasture Well—well ... NV-8
Pasture Well—well ... TX-5
Pasture Windmill No 2—locale ... CO-8
Pasture 7A Well—well ... MT-8
Pastuxet Cove ... RI-1
Pasuk—bar ... FM-9
Pasumscut River ... ME-1
Pasup Spring—spring ... WY-8
Pasuuween'—cape ... FM-9
Pasuza Gun Club—other ... CA-9
Pat—locale ... MS-4
**Pat**—pop pl ... NC-3
Pata—island ... FM-9
**Pata**—pop pl ... FM-9
Pataconk Brook ... CT-1
Pataconk Lake ... CT-1
Pataconk Reservoir ... CT-1
Pat Adolf Dam ... MS-4
Pataganset Lake ... CT-1
Patagansett Lake ... CT-1
patagansett River ... CT-1
**Patagonia**—pop pl ... AZ-5
**Patagonia**—pop pl ... PA-2
**Patagonia**—pop pl ... PR-3
Patagonia (CCD)—cens area ... AZ-5
Patagonia Lake—lake ... AZ-5
Patagonia Lake State Park—park ... AZ-5
Patagonia Mountains—summit ... AZ-5
Patagonia Ranger Station—locale ... AZ-5
Patagonia-Sonoita Creek Sanctuary ... AZ-5
Patagonia Union HS—school ... AZ-5
Pataguanset Brook ... CT-1
Pataguanset Lake ... CT-1
Pataguanset River ... CT-1
Pataguonset Lake ... CT-1
Pataha—locale ... WA-9
**Pataha**—pop pl (2) ... WA-9
Pataha Campground—locale ... WA-9
**Pataha City**—pop pl ... WA-9
Pataha Creek ... WA-9
Pataha Creek—stream ... OR-9
Pataha Creek—stream ... WA-9
Pataha Flat—flat ... WA-9
Pataha Flat Cem—cemetery ... WA-9
Pataha Valley—valley ... WA-9
Pataha Valley Grange—locale ... WA-9
Pat Alexander Ridge—ridge ... KY-4
Pataloma Mine—mine ... MT-8
Pat and Mike Springs—spring ... NV-8
Patanjali Lake ... OR-9
**Patapsco**—pop pl (2) ... MD-2
Patapsco HS—school ... MD-2
Patapsco Neck Sch—school ... MD-2
Patapsco River ... MD-2
Patapsco River—stream ... MD-2
Patapsco River Neck—cape ... MD-2
Patapsco State Park—park ... MD-2
Pataquanset River ... CT-1
Patasa, Bayou—stream ... LA-4
**Pataskala**—pop pl ... OH-6
Pataskala Banking Company—hist pl ... OH-6
Pataskala Elem Sch—hist pl ... OH-6
Pataskala Jail—hist pl ... OH-6
Pataskala Presbyterian Church—hist pl ... OH-6
Pataskala Town Hall—hist pl ... OH-6
Pataskala (Township of)—other ... OH-6
Pataskala United Methodist
Church—hist pl ... OH-6
Patasquash Island ... NY-2
Patassa, Bayou—stream ... LA-4
Patassa, Lac—lake ... LA-4
Patata—uninc pl ... CA-9
Patato Windmill—locale ... TX-5
**Pataukunk**—pop pl ... NY-2
Pataula Creek—stream ... GA-3
Pataula Creek Public Use Area—park ... GA-3
Patawa Creek—stream ... OR-9
Patawatama Creek ... OH-6
Pat Bay—bay ... LA-4
Pat Bayle State For—forest ... MN-6
Pat Bayou—stream ... LA-4
Pat Branch—stream ... MS-4
Pat Branch—stream ... NC-3
Pat Brennan Creek—stream ... ID-8
Pat Brown Spring—spring ... NV-8
Pat Burn—area ... CA-9
Pat Canyon—valley (2) ... CO-8
Pat Canyon—valley ... ID-8
Pat Canyon—valley ... NV-8
Pat Canyon—valley ... OK-5
Pat Canyon Rsvr—reservoir ... CO-8
Pat Carroll Park—flat ... UT-8
Pat Cem—cemetery ... CA-9
**Patch**—pop pl ... CA-9
Patch Beach—beach ... MA-1
Patch Brook—stream ... MA-1
Patch Brook—stream ... NH-1
Patch Brook—stream ... VT-1
Patch Canal—canal (2) ... ID-8
Patch Cem—cemetery ... MI-6
Patch Coulee—valley ... MT-8
Patch Creek—stream ... MS-4
Patchell Run ... PA-2
Patchell Trail—trail ... PA-2
Patchel Run—uninc pl ... PA-2
Patchen Creek—stream ... WA-9
Patchen Hill—summit ... NY-2
Patchen Lake—lake ... MN-6
Patchen Run—stream ... PA-2
Patchen Sch—school ... MI-6
Patcher Run ... PA-2
Patcher Run—stream ... PA-2
Patches Canyon—valley ... CO-8
Patches Windmill—locale ... CO-8
Patchet Creek—stream ... NC-3
Patchett House—hist pl ... NY-2
**Patch Grove**—pop pl ... WI-6
Patch Grove Cem—cemetery ... WI-6
**Patch Grove (Town of)**—pop pl ... WI-6
Patch Gulch—valley ... OR-9
Patch Hill—summit (2) ... NH-1
Patch Hill—summit ... VT-1
Patch Hollow—valley ... TN-4
**Patchin**—pop pl ... NY-2
Patchin—uninc pl ... NY-2
**Patchin (Boston Center)**—pop pl ... NY-2
Patching Lake—lake ... AK-9
Patchin Run—stream ... PA-2
Patchin Swamp—swamp ... NY-2
**Patchinville**—pop pl ... NY-2
**Patchinville**—pop pl ... PA-2
Patch Island—island ... OR-9
Patch Meadow Brook—stream ... MA-1
Patch Mountain Cem—cemetery ... ME-1
Patch Mtn—summit ... ME-1
**Patchogue**—pop pl ... NY-2
Patchogue Bay—bay ... NY-2
Patchogue Cem—cemetery ... NY-2
Patchogue Creek ... NY-2
**Patchogue Highlands**—pop pl ... NY-2
Patchogue HS—school ... NY-2
Patchogue River—stream ... CT-1
Patchogue River—stream ... NY-2
Patch Pond ... VT-1
Patch Pond—lake ... VT-1
Patch Pond—reservoir ... MA-1
Patch Reservoir Dam—dam ... MA-1
Patch Rsvr—reservoir ... MA-1
Patch Skin Buttes—ridge ... SD-7
Patch Tank—reservoir ... AZ-5
Patchtop Mtn—summit ... MT-8
Patchuta Creek ... MS-4
Pat Cienega—flat ... AZ-5
Patcong Creek—stream ... NJ-2
Patcong Lake—reservoir ... NJ-2
Pat Creek—stream (3) ... AK-9
Pat Creek—stream ... AZ-5
Pat Creek—stream (2) ... CO-8
Pat Creek—stream ... KS-7
Pat Creek—stream (2) ... OR-9
Pat Creek—stream ... WA-9
Pat Dick Hill—summit ... TX-5
Pat Draw—valley ... WY-8
Pat Duffy Hollow—valley ... KY-4
Pat Duke Tank—reservoir ... AZ-5
**Pate**—pop pl ... AL-4
**Pate**—pop pl ... IN-6
Pate, Samuel, House—hist pl ... KY-4
Pate Bay—swamp ... FL-3
Pate Bayou—stream ... MS-4
Pate Bend—bend ... TX-5
Pate Branch—stream ... AR-4
Pate Branch—stream ... FL-3
Pate Branch—stream ... LA-4
Pate Branch—stream ... MS-4
Pate Cem—cemetery ... AL-4
Pate Cem—cemetery ... AR-4
Pate Cem—cemetery ... CA-9
Pate Cem—cemetery ... FL-3
Pate Cem—cemetery ... GA-3
Pate Cem—cemetery ... IL-6
Pate Cem—cemetery ... IN-6
Pate Cem—cemetery ... KY-4
Pate Cem—cemetery ... MS-4
Pate Cem—cemetery ... MO-7
Pate Cem—cemetery (3) ... NC-3
Pate Cem—cemetery ... SC-3
Pate Cem—cemetery ... TN-4
Pate Cem—cemetery ... TX-5
Pate Cem—cemetery ... VA-3
Pate Cem—cemetery ... WV-2
Pate Chapel—church ... IL-6
Patech Lake ... MI-6
Pate Creek ... GA-3
Pate Creek—stream ... AL-4
Pate Creek—stream ... AR-4
Pate Creek—stream ... LA-4
Pate Creek—stream (2) ... NC-3
Pate Ditch—canal ... WY-8
Patee, John, House—hist pl ... MO-7
Patee Park—park ... MO-7
Pate-Gardner Cem—cemetery ... MS-4
**Pate Hill**—pop pl ... TN-4
Pate Hollow—valley ... IN-6
Pate Lake—lake ... FL-3
Pate Lake—lake ... OR-9
Pate Lake—reservoir ... NC-3
Pate Lake Dam—dam ... NC-3
Patel Branch—stream ... TN-4
Patella Gin (historical)—locale ... AL-4
Patelzick Creek—stream ... ID-8
Patemas Creek—stream ... WA-9
Pate Mine (underground)—mine ... AL-4
Pate Mtn—summit ... AL-4
Pate Mtn—summit ... AR-4
Pate Neck—cape ... NC-3
Patent—locale ... NY-2
Patent Creek—stream ... CO-8
Patent Creek—stream ... MI-6
Patent Creek—stream ... MS-4
Patent Creek—stream ... WA-9
Patent Gate Township—civ div ... ND-7
Patent Line Mtn—summit ... NY-2
Pate Pond ... FL-3
Pate Pond—reservoir ... AL-4
Pate Pond—reservoir ... NC-3
Pate Pond—reservoir ... SC-3
Pate Pond—swamp ... FL-3
Pater Noster HS—school ... CA-9
**Pateros**—pop pl ... WA-9
Pateros, Lake—reservoir ... WA-9
Paterson ... NC-3
Paterson—locale ... WA-9
**Paterson**—pop pl ... NJ-2
Paterson, John M., Sch—hist pl ... PA-2
Paterson, William A., Factory
Complex—hist pl ... MI-6
Paterson Camp—locale ... NJ-2
Paterson Cem—cemetery ... MO-7
Paterson Creek ... CA-9
Paterson Creek—stream ... AL-4
Paterson Creek—stream ... OR-9
Paterson Field—park ... AL-4
Paterson Ford—locale ... MO-7
Paterson House—hist pl ... AL-4
Paterson Is ... MP-9
Paterson Junction—locale ... OR-9
Paterson Ridge—ridge ... WA-9
Paterson Run ... OH-6
Paterson Run ... PA-2
Paterson Sch—school ... AL-4
Paterson Sch—school ... CT-1
Patersons Corner—locale ... VA-3
Patersons Creek ... WV-2
Paterson Spring—spring ... AZ-5
Paterson Spring—spring ... PA-2
Paterson Station—locale ... NJ-2
Paterson Terrace Brook ... NJ-2
Patersonville—locale ... FL-3
Patersonville Cemetery—locale ... FL-3
Pates ... MS-4
**Pates**—pop pl ... NC-3
Pates Branch—stream ... GA-3
Pates Bridge (historical)—bridge ... AL-4
Pate Sch—school ... GA-3
Pate Sch—school ... SC-3
Pates Chapel—church ... AL-4
Pates Creek—stream ... AL-4
Pates Creek—stream ... GA-3
Pates Ford Dock—locale ... TN-4
Pates Ford (historical)—crossing ... TN-4
Pates Ford Marina ... TN-4
Pates Hill ... TN-4
Pates Hill Post Office
(historical)—building ... TN-4
Pates Island ... AL-4
Pates Lake—reservoir ... AL-4
Pates Lake Number Two—reservoir ... NC-3
Pates Lake Number Two Dam—dam ... NC-3
Pates Landing (historical)—locale ... AL-4
Pates Mill Branch—stream ... SC-3
Pate Spring—spring ... AZ-5
Pate Stadium—park ... NC-3
Pates Temple Cem—cemetery ... MS-4
Patesville—locale ... KY-4
Patesville (CCD)—cens area ... KY-4
**Patetown**—pop pl ... NC-3
Pate Valley—basin ... CA-9
Pateville—locale ... GA-3
Pate Well—well ... NM-5
Pate Windmill—locale ... NM-5
Patex Pond—reservoir ... NJ-2
Patex Pond Dam—dam ... NJ-2
Pat Flat—flat ... WV-2
Pat Ford Creek ... CA-9
Pat Ford Creek—stream ... CA-9
Pat Gibson Lake Dam—dam ... MS-4
Pat Gulch—valley ... MT-8
Path—locale ... PA-2
Pat Hale Lake ... MI-6
Pat Harrison Waterway Lake Dam—dam
(2) ... MS-4
Pathfinder Canal ... NE-7
Pathfinder Dam—dam ... WY-8
Pathfinder Dam—hist pl ... WY-8
Pathfinder Island—island ... NY-2
Pathfinder Mine—mine ... CA-9
Pathfinder Mtn—summit ... WY-8
Pathfinder Natl Wildlife Ref—park (2) ... WY-8
Pathfinder Rsvr—reservoir ... WY-8
**Pathfinder Spur**—pop pl ... SD-7
**Pathfork**—pop pl ... KY-4
Path Fork—stream ... KY-4
Pathic Lake—lake ... MI-6
Pat Hills—summit ... AZ-5
**Pathkiller Cove**—pop pl ... AL-4
Path Lake—lake ... MN-6
Pat Hollow—valley ... AR-4
Pat Hollow—valley ... ID-8
Pat Hollow—valley ... MO-7
Path Ridge—ridge ... VA-3
Path Run—stream ... IN-6
Pat Hughes Creek—stream ... ID-8
Pat Hughes Tank—reservoir ... AZ-5
Path Valley—valley (2) ... PA-2
Path Valley Cem—cemetery ... PA-2
Path Valley Mountain ... PA-2
Pathway Baptist Ch—church ... AL-4
Pathway Baptist Ch—church ... IN-6
Pathway Christian Sch—school ... FL-3
Pathway Sch—school ... PA-2
Patica ... FL-3
Paticho Lake—reservoir ... AZ-5
Patience—locale ... PA-2
Patience, Mount—summit ... NH-1
Patience, Point—cape ... MD-2
Patience Island—island ... RI-1
Patient, Lake—lake ... FL-3
Patiente Island ... RI-1
**Patillas**—pop pl ... PR-3
Patillas (Municipio)—civil ... PR-3
Patillas (Pueblo)—fmr MCD ... PR-3
Patill Canyon—valley ... OR-9
Patillo—locale ... GA-3
Patillo—locale ... TX-5
Patillo Ch—church ... NC-3
Patilo ... TX-5
**Patilo**—pop pl ... TX-5
**Patin**—pop pl (2) ... LA-4
Patin Dyke Slough—stream ... LA-4
Patins ... LA-4
**Patins**—pop pl ... LA-4
Patio—locale ... AZ-5
Patio del Moro—hist pl ... CA-9
Patio Ranch—locale ... TX-5
Patio Springs—spring ... UT-8
**Patio Springs (subdivision)**—pop pl ... UT-8
Pati Point—cape ... GU-9
Pat Island—island ... MD-2
Patit—locale ... WA-9
Patit Creek ... WA-9
Patit Creek—stream ... WA-9
Patitos Pasture—flat ... TX-5
Patjens Lakes—lake ... OR-9
Patjens Lakes Trail—trail ... OR-9
Pat Keyes Canyon—valley ... CA-9
Pat Keyes Spring—spring ... CA-9
Pat Keyes Trail—trail ... CA-9
Pat Knob—summit ... NC-3
Pat Knoll—summit ... AZ-5
Pat Knoll Guard Station—locale ... AZ-5
Pat Lake ... MI-6
Pat Lake—lake (2) ... MN-6
Pat Lake—lake ... MT-8
Pat Lake—lake ... WI-6
Pat Lake Bayou—stream ... LA-4
Pat Layne Memorial Bridge—bridge ... TN-4
Pat Le Doux Creek—stream ... NM-5
Pat Maloy Ravine—valley ... CA-9
**Patman**—pop pl ... TX-5
Pat Mann Dam—dam ... TN-4
Pat Mann Lake—reservoir ... TN-4
Patman Well—well ... NM-5
Pat Maynard Cem—cemetery ... WV-2
Pat Mayse Lake—reservoir ... TX-5
Pat McDonald Lake Dam—dam ... MS-4
Pat Mesa—summit ... AZ-5
Pat Miller Hill—summit ... TX-5
Pat M Neff JHS—school ... TX-5
Pat Morris Camp—locale ... CA-9
Pat Morris Spring—spring ... CA-9
Patmos—locale ... GA-3
**Patmos**—pop pl ... AR-4
**Patmos**—pop pl ... MS-4
**Patmos**—pop pl ... OH-6
Patmos Baptist Church ... TN-4
Patmos Cem—cemetery ... AR-4
Patmos Ch—church ... AR-4
Patmos Ch—church (2) ... VA-3
Patmos Chapel—locale ... TN-4
Patmos Chapel (historical)—church ... TN-4
Patmos Chapel Seventh Day Adventist
Ch—church ... FL-3
Patmos Head—summit ... UT-8
Patmos (historical)—locale ... MA-1
Patmos Mountain ... UT-8
Patmos Post Office (historical)—building ... MS-4
Patmos Ridge—ridge ... UT-8
Patmos Sch—school ... AR-4
Patmos Sch (historical)—school ... TN-4
Pat Mtn—summit ... AZ-5
Pat Mullen Mtn—summit ... AZ-5
Pat Mullen Spring—spring ... AZ-5
Pat Murphy Bridge—bridge ... TX-5
Patmus Ch—church ... FL-3
Patna—locale ... VA-3
Patnude, Charles, House—hist pl ... WA-9
Pato Caballo, Lake—lake ... LA-4
Pato Canyon—valley ... CA-9
Pato Creek ... TX-5
Pato Creek—stream ... TX-5
Pat O'Hara Basin—basin ... WY-8
Pat O'Hara Creek—stream ... WY-8
Pat O'Hara Mtn—summit ... WY-8
Pat O'Hara Peak—summit ... WY-8
Pat O'Hare Creek ... WY-8
Pat O'Harra Creek ... WY-8
**Patoka**—pop pl ... AR-4
**Patoka**—pop pl ... IL-6
**Patoka**—pop pl ... IN-6
Patoka Access Area—locale ... IL-6
Patoka Ch—church ... IN-6
Patoka East Oil Field—other ... IL-6
Patoka Island—island ... IN-6
Patoka Lake—reservoir ... IN-6
Patoka Lake Dam—dam ... IN-6
Patoka Oil Field—other ... IL-6
Patoka River—stream ... IN-6
Patoka Sch—school ... IL-6
Patoka Sch—school ... IN-6
Patoka South Oil Field—other ... IL-6
Patoka State Fish and Wildlife
Area—park ... IN-6
**Patoka (Township of)**—pop pl ... IL-6
**Patoka (Township of)**—pop pl (4) ... IN-6
Patoker Archeol Site—hist pl ... KY-4
Patoker Branch—stream ... KY-4
Patokwa Site (FS-5, LA-96)—hist pl ... NM-5
Pat Ollarra Creek ... WY-8
Paton—locale ... KS-7
**Paton**—pop pl ... IA-7
Patona Bay—reservoir ... IN-6
Patona Cem—cemetery ... MS-4
Paton Cem—cemetery ... IA-7
Paton Creek—stream ... NC-3
Paton Island—island ... MD-2
Paton Point—cape ... NC-3
Paton Sch—school ... MA-1
Patons Corner—locale ... MI-6
Paton Township—fmr MCD ... IA-7
Patos, Laguna de los—lake ... TX-5
Patos Cem—cemetery ... NM-5
Patos Creek—stream ... NM-5
**Patosi**—pop pl ... MS-4
Patos Island—island ... WA-9
Patos Island Light Station—hist pl ... WA-9
Patos Lake—lake ... NM-5
Patos Light—other ... WA-9
Patos Mountains ... NM-5
Patos Mountain Trail—trail ... NM-5
Patos Mtn—summit ... NM-5
Patos Spring—spring ... NM-5
Patos Windmill—locale ... NM-5
Patos Windmill—locale ... TX-5
Patout, Bayou—gut ... LA-4
Patout Canal—canal ... LA-4
**Patoutville**—pop pl ... LA-4
Patowmack Island—island ... VA-3
Pat Pond—lake (2) ... NY-2
Pat Post Office (historical)—building ... MS-4
Patrero Creek ... CA-9
Patrey Branch—stream ... TN-4
Patrey Hollow—valley ... TN-4
Patria—locale ... NY-2
Patriarch Tree—locale ... CA-9
**Patrich**—pop pl ... TX-5
**Patricia**—pop pl ... SD-7
**Patricia**—pop pl ... TX-5
Patricia, Lake—lake ... CO-8
Patricia, Lake—lake ... FL-3
Patricia, Lake—reservoir ... AR-4
Patricia, Lake—reservoir ... SC-3
Patricia Artesian Well—well ... TX-5
Patricia Bight—bay ... AK-9
Patricia Cay—island ... VI-3
Patricia Creek—stream ... AK-9
Patricia Creek—stream ... OR-9
Patricia Island—island ... OK-5
Patricia Lake—lake ... CA-9
Patricia Lake—lake ... MI-6
Patricia Lake—lake ... WI-6
PATRICIA (log canoe)—hist pl ... MD-2
Patrician Acad—school ... AL-4
Patrician Manor—uninc pl ... VA-3
Patricia Point—cape ... AK-9
Patricias Center for Learning—school ... FL-3
Patricio Island—island ... FL-3
Patricio Lake—lake ... TX-5
Patricio Pasture—flat ... TX-5
Patricio Shoal—bar ... FL-3
Patricio Windmill—locale (2) ... TX-5
Patrick—locale ... AR-4
Patrick—locale ... KY-4
Patrick—locale ... MS-4
**Patrick**—pop pl ... NV-8
**Patrick**—pop pl ... SC-3
**Patrick**—pop pl (2) ... TX-5
Patrick, Canal (historical)—canal ... AZ-5
Patrick, Lake—lake ... GA-3
Patrick, Lake—reservoir ... AL-4
Patrick, Marshall T., House—hist pl ... TX-5
Patrick, Woodson and Margaret,
House—hist pl ... TX-5
Patrick AFB—military ... FL-3
Patrick Air Force Base North—CDP ... FL-3
Patrick Air Force Base South—CDP ... FL-3
Patrick Annex Mine—mine ... MN-6
Patrick Bay—swamp ... GA-3
Patrick Bayou—gut ... LA-4
Patrick Bayou—stream ... TX-5
Patrick Branch—stream ... AR-4
Patrick Branch—stream ... GA-3
Patrick Branch—stream (6) ... KY-4
Patrick Branch—stream ... SC-3
Patrick Branch—stream ... TN-4
Patrick Brook—stream ... ME-1
Patrick Brook—stream ... VT-1
Patrick Butte—summit ... ID-8
Patrick (CCD)—cens area ... SC-3
Patrick Cem—cemetery ... AL-4
Patrick Cem—cemetery ... CA-9
Patrick Cem—cemetery (2) ... GA-3
Patrick Cem—cemetery (2) ... IN-6
Patrick Cem—cemetery (3) ... KY-4
Patrick Cem—cemetery ... MS-4
Patrick Cem—cemetery ... MO-7
Patrick Cem—cemetery ... NC-3
Patrick Cem—cemetery ... OK-5
Patrick Cem—cemetery ... SC-3
Patrick Cem—cemetery (2) ... TN-4
Patrick Cem—cemetery ... TX-5
Patrick Ch—church ... LA-4
Patrick Ch—church ... MS-4
Patrick Ch—church ... NC-3
Patrick Ch—church ... SC-3
**Patrick (County)**—pop pl ... VA-3
Patrick County Courthouse—hist pl ... VA-3
**Patrick Creek**—pop pl ... CA-9
Patrick Creek—stream ... AL-4
Patrick Creek—stream (2) ... CA-9
Patrick Creek—stream ... ID-8
Patrick Creek—stream ... LA-4
Patrick Creek—stream ... MS-4
Patrick Creek—stream (2) ... MT-8
Patrick Creek—stream (3) ... OR-9
Patrick Creek—stream ... TX-5
Patrick Creek—stream ... WV-2
Patrick Creek—stream ... WY-8
Patrick Creek Ch—church ... WV-2
Patrick Creek Guard Station—other ... CA-9
Patrick Dean Grant—civil ... FL-3
Patrick Ditch—canal ... IN-6
Patrick Ditch—canal ... OH-6
Patrick Drain ... MI-6
Patrick Drain—canal ... MI-6
Patrick Drain—canal ... NV-8
Patrick Drain—stream ... MI-6
Patrick Draw—valley ... WY-8
Patrick Draw Oil Field—oilfield ... WY-8
Patrick Gap—gap ... AL-4
Patrick Gap—gap ... GA-3
Patrick Gass, Mount—summit ... MT-8
Patrick-Gass Lake ... WA-9
Patrick Gomer Park—park ... CA-9
Patrick Gulch—valley ... OR-9
**Patrick Henry Heights**—pop pl ... VA-3
Patrick Henry Hosp—hospital ... VA-3
Patrick Henry HS—school ... CA-9
Patrick Henry HS—school (2) ... VA-3
Patrick Henry International Airp—airport ... VA-3
Patrick Henry JHS—school ... OH-6
Patrick Henry JHS—school ... SD-7
Patrick Henry JHS—school ... TX-5
Patrick Henry (Magisterial District)—fmr MCD
(2) ... VA-3
Patrick Henry Monmt—park ... VA-3
Patrick Henry's Birthplace Archeol
Site—hist pl ... VA-3
Patrick Henry Sch—school (4) ... CA-9
Patrick Henry Sch—school ... MD-2
Patrick Henry Sch—school ... OK-5
Patrick Henry Sch—school (4) ... VA-3
Patrick Henry State Junior Coll—school ... AL-4
Patrick Hollow—valley ... KY-4
Patrick Hollow—valley ... MO-7
Patrick Hollow—valley (2) ... VA-3
Patrick Lake ... CO-8
Patrick Lake—lake ... ME-1
Patrick Lake—lake ... MI-6
Patrick Lake—lake ... WI-6
Patrick Lake Dam—dam ... MS-4
**Patrick Landing**—pop pl ... MI-6
Patrick Lookout Tower—locale ... SC-3
Patrick Lower Branch, Canal
(historical)—canal ... AZ-5
Patrick Meadow—flat ... OR-9
Patrick Meadows—flat ... NC-3
Patrick Memorial Gardens—cemetery ... VA-3
Patrick Mine—mine ... MN-6
Patrick Mtn—summit ... AL-4
Patrick Mtn—summit ... AR-4
Patrick Mtn—summit ... ME-1
Patrick Mtn—summit ... OR-9
**Patrick Park**—pop pl ... AZ-5
Patrick Pierce Park—park ... ND-7
Patrick Place—locale ... UT-8
Patrick Plaza (Shop Ctr)—locale ... FL-3
Patrick Point—cape ... VI-3
Patrick Pond—lake ... AZ-5
Patrick Pond—reservoir ... GA-3
Patrick Rancheria—hist pl ... CA-9
Patrick Ranch House—hist pl ... CA-9
Patrick Reservoir ... CO-8
Patrick Ridge—ridge ... MT-8
Patrick Rsvr—reservoir ... CA-9
Patrick Run—stream (2) ... PA-2
Patricks Basin—basin ... MT-8
Patricks Bridge—bridge ... MS-4
**Patricksburg**—pop pl ... IN-6
**Patricksburg**—pop pl ... PA-2
Patricksburg Elem Sch—school ... IN-6
Patrick Sch—school ... IL-6
Patrick Sch—school ... MI-6
Patrick Sch—school ... OR-9
Patrick Sch (historical)—school ... MS-4
**Patricks Corner**—pop pl ... NJ-2
**Patricks Corners**—pop pl ... NJ-2
Patricks Creek—stream ... VA-3
Patricks Fish Camp—locale ... AL-4
Patricks Knob—summit ... MT-8
Patricks Lakes—reservoir ... GA-3
Patricks Landing—locale ... MD-2
Patricks Peak—summit ... WV-2
Patricks Plaza Shop Ctr—locale ... NC-3
Patricks Point ... CA-9

Patton Cove—*valley* (2) NC-3
*Patton Creek* OR-9
Patton Creek—*stream* (2) AL-4
Patton Creek—*stream* IL-6
Patton Creek—*stream* (2) MS-4
Patton Creek—*stream* NE-7
Patton Creek—*stream* NM-5
Patton Creek—*stream* PA-2
Patton Creek—*stream* (2) TN-4
Patton Creek—*stream* (3) TX-5
Patton Creek—*stream* WA-9
Patton Creek Bridge—*bridge* AL-4
Patton Creek Dam—*dam* AL-4
Patton Dam—*dam* IN-6
Patton Elem Sch—*school* PA-2
Patton Family Graves—*cemetery* TX-5
Patton Farm—*hist pl* NC-3
Patton Ferry (historical)—*locale* AL-4
*Patton Fork* AL-4
Patton Fork—*stream* (2) KY-4
Patton Gulch—*valley* MT-8
**Patton Hill**—*pop pl* IN-6
Patton Hill—*summit* AL-4
Patton Hill—*summit* IN-6
Patton Hill—*summit* ME-1
Patton Hill—*summit* NY-2
Patton Hill—*summit* WA-9
Patton Hill Cem—*cemetery* AL-4
*Patton Hill Church* AL-4
Patton Hill Fire Tower—*locale* AL-4
Patton Hollow—*valley* AL-4
Patton Hollow—*valley* IN-6
Patton Hollow—*valley* (2) MO-7
Patton Hollow—*valley* (4) TN-4
*Pattonia* MS-4
Patton Island—*island* AL-4
Patton Island—*island* AK-9
*Patton Junction* (2) AL-4
**Patton Junction**—*pop pl* MO-7
Patton Knob—*summit* TN-4
Patton Knob—*summit* WV-2
Patton Lake—*lake* AR-4
Patton Lake—*lake* LA-4
Patton Lake—*lake* NE-7
Patton Lake—*lake* TX-5
**Patton Lake**—*pop pl* IN-6
Patton Lake—*reservoir* AL-4
Patton Lake—*reservoir* (2) IN-6
Patton Lake—*reservoir* MS-4
Patton Lake Dam—*dam* AL-4
Patton Lake Dam—*dam* IN-6
Patton Lake Drain—*stream* LA-4
Patton Lane Park—*park* MS-4
Patton Mansion—*hist pl* VA-3
*Patton Masonic Sch* PA-2
Patton Meadow—*reservoir* OR-9
Patton Memorial Cem—*cemetery* KY-4
Patton Memorial Park—*park* MI-6
Patton Mill—*locale* CA-9
Patton Mill (historical)—*locale* TN-4
Patton Mine—*mine* TN-4
Patton Mine (underground)—*mine* AL-4
Patton Mine (underground)—*mine* TN-4
**Patton Mountain Estates (subdivision)**—*pop pl* NC-3
Patton Mtn—*summit* (2) NC-3
*Pattonna Cemetery* MS-4
*Patton Number 13 Mine* AL-4
Patton Number 3 Slope Mine (underground)—*mine* AL-4
Patton Park—*park* IL-6
Patton Park—*park* MA-1
Patton Park—*park* OR-9
**Patton Park (subdivision)**—*pop pl* NC-3
**Patton (Patton Junction)**—*pop pl* AL-4
**Patton (Patton State Hospital)**—*pop pl* CA-9
Patton Peak—*summit* CA-9
**Patton Place (subdivision)**—*pop pl* AL-4
**Patton Place (subdivision)**—*pop pl* MS-4
Patton Plaza Shop Ctr—*locale* MS-4
Patton Pond—*lake* TN-4
Patton Post Office (historical)—*building* AL-4
Patton Post Office (historical)—*building* TN-4
Patton Ranch—*locale* CO-8
Patton Ranch—*locale* TX-5
Patton River—*stream* AK-9
Patton Rsvr—*reservoir* UT-8
Patton Run—*stream* (6) OH-6
Patton Run—*stream* (2) PA-2
Patton Run—*stream* WV-2
**Pattonsburg**—*pop pl* IL-6
**Pattonsburg**—*pop pl* MO-7
Pattonsburg Lake—*reservoir* MO-7
*Patton Sch* AL-4
Patton Sch—*school* CA-9
Patton Sch—*school* (3) IL-6
Patton Sch—*school* KY-4
Patton Sch—*school* MI-6
Patton Sch—*school* MO-7
Patton Sch—*school* NC-3
Patton Sch—*school* PA-2
Patton Sch—*school* (2) TN-4
*Pattons Chapel Church* TN-4
Pattons Chapel Elem Sch—*school* AL-4
Patton Sch (historical)—*school* TN-4
Pattons Creek—*stream* KY-4
Pattons Ferry (historical)—*locale* MS-4
*Pattons Hill* AL-4
Patton-Simmons Cem—*cemetery* TN-4
*Pattons Island* AL-4
Pattons Lake—*reservoir* AL-4
*Pattons Mill* AL-4
Pattons Mill (historical)—*locale* AL-4
Pattons Pond—*lake* TX-5
Patton Spring—*spring* AZ-5
Patton Spring—*spring* (2) CO-8
Patton Spring—*spring* MT-8
Patton Spring—*spring* OR-9
Patton Spring Draw—*valley* AZ-5
Patton Springs—*spring* TX-5
Patton Spring Sch (historical)—*school* MS-4
Patton Springs Sch—*school* TX-5
Pattons Ridge—*locale* NC-3
Pattons Store (historical)—*locale* MS-4
Patton Stadium—*other* SC-3
Patton State Hosp—*hospital* CA-9
*Pattonsville* PA-2
**Pattonsville**—*pop pl* OH-6
**Pattonsville**—*pop pl* VA-3
Pattonsville Branch—*stream* VA-3
Pattonsville Ch—*church* OH-6
Patton Tank—*reservoir* TX-5
Patton Top—*summit* GA-3
Patton Township—*other* PA-2
**Patton (Township of)**—*pop pl* IL-6
**Patton (Township of)**—*pop pl* PA-2
Patton Valley—*valley* OR-9
**Patton Village (West Patton Village)**—*pop pl* CA-9
*Pattonville* MA-1
*Pattonville* PA-2
Pattonville—*locale* PA-2
**Pattonville**—*pop pl* AR-4
**Pattonville**—*pop pl* MO-7
**Pattonville**—*pop pl* PA-2
**Pattonville**—*pop pl* TX-5
**Pattonville (Pattonsville)**—*pop pl* OH-6
Pat Town—*locale* VA-3
Patts Branch—*stream* MS-4
Pattsville—*locale* AR-4
Pattsville Cem—*cemetery* AR-4
Pat Tuck Mine—*mine* CA-9
**Patty**—*pop pl* TN-4
Patty Branch—*stream* KY-4
Patty Branch—*stream* TN-4
**Patty Cannon Estates (subdivision)**—*pop pl* DE-2
Patty Cem—*cemetery* IL-6
Patty Cem—*cemetery* NC-3
Patty Cem—*cemetery* TN-4
Patty Chapel Cem—*cemetery* NC-3
Patty Creek—*stream* KY-4
Patty Creek—*stream* MI-6
Patty Creek—*stream* OH-6
Patty Creek—*stream* TN-4
Patty Field—*airport* KS-7
Patty Hollow—*valley* AL-4
Patty Hollow—*valley* KY-4
Patty Hollow—*valley* TN-4
Patty Jewett Municipal Golf Course—*other* CO-8
Patty Lot Hill—*summit* ME-1
Pattymocus Butte—*summit* CA-9
Patty Post Office (historical)—*building* TN-4
Patty Ridge Trail—*trail* TN-4
Pattys Branch—*stream* MD-2
Pattys Fork—*stream* NJ-2
Pattys Garden Ridge—*ridge* IN-6
Patty Sink—*basin* FL-3
Pattys Island—*island* FL-3
Pattys Pond—*lake* MA-1
Patty Spring—*spring* AR-4
Pattys Shoals—*rapids* TN-4
**Pattytown**—*pop pl* OH-6
Patty Wiggins Branch—*stream* FL-3
*Patuiset* MA-1
*Patuisett* MA-1
**Patuisset**—*pop pl* MA-1
*Patuissett* MA-1
Patupatu Ridge—*ridge* AS-9
Patuxent—*locale* MD-2
**Patuxent**—*pop pl* MD-2
**Patuxent Beach**—*pop pl* MD-2
Patuxent Ch—*church* MD-2
Patuxent Institution—*other* MD-2
**Patuxent Park**—*pop pl* MD-2
Patuxent River—*stream* MD-2
Patuxent River Air Test Center—*area* MD-2
Patuxent River Naval Air Test Center—*military* MD-2
Patuxent River Watershed Park—*park* MD-2
*Patuxet* MA-1
*Patuxit* MA-1
Pat Well—*well* (2) NM-5
Pat Williams Spring—*spring* AZ-5
Pat Willis Draw—*valley* UT-8
Patwin Indian Site—*hist pl* CA-9
*Patwisha* CA-9
Paty Fishing Camp—*locale* AL-4
Paty Hollow—*valley* MO-7
Pat Yore Flat—*flat* CA-9
Paty Pond—*lake* MO-7
Paty Spring—*spring* MO-7
**Patzau**—*pop pl* WI-6
Pau, Mount—*summit* CO-8
Pauahi—*civil* HI-9
Pauahi—*locale* HI-9
Pauahi Crater—*crater* HI-9
Pauahi Gulch—*valley* HI-9
*Paualaia* HI-9
Paualaia Point—*cape* HI-9
*Pauao Peak* HI-9
Paua Ridge—*ridge* HI-9
Paua Valley—*valley* HI-9
Pauba—*civil* CA-9
Pauba Valley—*valley* CA-9
*Paucamac Pond* RI-1
*Paucamet Pond* RI-1
Paucatuck Brook—*stream* MA-1
**Paucatuck (historical)**—*pop pl* MA-1
Pauchaug Brook—*stream* MA-1
Pauchaug Brook—*stream* NH-1
Pauchaug Meadow—*bench* MA-1
Pauekolu—*cape* HI-9
Paueono—*cape* HI-9
*Paugatchet River* RI-1
*Paugeamapauge Pond* RI-1
*Paugecachuke River* RI-1
Paugel Creek—*stream* WI-6
Paugh Ridge—*ridge* WV-2
Paughs Cem—*cemetery* MD-2
Paugnut Forest Administration Bldg—*hist pl* CT-1
Paugnut State For—*forest* CT-1
Paugus, Mount—*summit* NH-1
Paugus Bay—*bay* NH-1
Paugus Brook—*stream* NH-1
Paugus Mill—*locale* NH-1
Paugussett State For—*forest* CT-1
Paugwaunk Ch—*church* CT-1
Pau Island—*island* FM-9
Pauitue Well—*well* AZ-5
Paukaa—*civil* HI-9
**Paukaa**—*pop pl* HI-9
Paukaa Point—*cape* HI-9
Paukauila Stream—*stream* HI-9
**Paukotuk**—*pop pl* WI-6
**Paukukalo**—*pop pl* HI-9
Paukukalo—*swamp* HI-9
Paukupau—*bay* HI-9
**Paul**—*pop pl* AL-4
**Paul**—*pop pl* ID-8
**Paul**—*pop pl* MS-4
**Paul**—*pop pl* NE-7
Paul, Allen, House—*hist pl* TX-5
Paul, Bayou—*stream* LA-4
Paul, Denton J., Water Tank—*hist pl* ID-8
Paul, Lake—*lake* AK-9
Paul, Lake—*lake* MI-6
Paul, Mount—*summit* (2) NJ-2
Paul, Peter, House—*hist pl* VA-3
**Paula**—*pop pl* TX-5
Paula, Lake—*reservoir* TX-5
Paula Creek—*stream* OK-5
**Paula Heights**—*pop pl* TN-4
**Paula (historical)**—*pop pl* MS-4
Paul Airp (private)—*airport* PA-2
Paulaluk River—*stream* AK-9
Paulana River—*stream* GU-9
Paularino Channel—*canal* CA-9
Paularino Sch—*school* CA-9
**Paulas Corners**—*pop pl* NJ-2
Paul Ashers Branch—*stream* KY-4
Paulas Pit—*cave* PA-2
Paula Spring—*spring* CO-8
Paulas Ridge—*ridge* OH-6
Paula Tank—*reservoir* (2) TX-5
Paulauka—*bay* HI-9
Paul Baddour Pond Dam—*dam* MS-4
Paul Battles Catfish Ponds Dam—*dam* MS-4
*Paul Bayou* AL-4
*Paul Bayou Creek* AL-4
Paul Berry Dam—*dam* SD-7
Paul Bight—*bay* AK-9
Paul B. Johnson State Park—*park* MS-4
Paul Bldg—*hist pl* TX-5
Paul Branch—*gut* FL-3
Paul Branch—*stream* FL-3
Paul Branch—*stream* TN-4
Paul Branch Sch (historical)—*school* AL-4
Paul Braswell Catfish Ponds Dam—*dam* MS-4
*Paul Brook* MA-1
Paul Brook—*stream* NH-1
Paul Brook—*stream* NY-2
Paul Brook—*stream* PA-2
Paul B Stephens Exceptional Student Education Center—*school* FL-3
Paul Bunyan Campground—*locale* MT-8
Paul Bunyan Punch Bowl—*reservoir* MI-6
Paul Bunyan Rifle and Sportsmens Club—*other* WA-9
Paul Bunyans Cabin—*summit* MT-8
Paul Bunyans Potty—*arch* UT-8
Paul Bunyans Stump—*summit* WA-9
Paul Bunyan State For—*forest* MN-6
*Paul Bunyans Wood Pile* UT-8
Paul Bunyans Woodpile—*woods* UT-8
*Paul Bunyan Woodpile* UT-8
Paul Bunyon Camp—*locale* MI-6
Paul Canyon—*valley* NM-5
Paulcell Place—*locale* AZ-5
Paul Cem—*cemetery* GA-3
Paul Cem—*cemetery* ID-8
Paul Cem—*cemetery* (2) IL-6
Paul Cem—*cemetery* (2) LA-4
Paul Cem—*cemetery* ME-1
Paul Cem—*cemetery* MO-7
Paul Cem—*cemetery* TN-4
Paul Ch—*church* AL-4
Paul Ch—*church* TX-5
Paul Chapel—*church* TN-4
Paul Childress Junior Lake—*reservoir* AL-4
Paul Childress Junior Lake Dam—*dam* AL-4
Paul Childress Lake—*reservoir* AL-4
Paul Childress Lake Dam—*dam* AL-4
Paul Cove—*bay* MD-2
Paul Creek—*stream* AL-4
Paul Creek—*stream* AK-9
Paul Creek—*stream* (2) GA-3
Paul Creek—*stream* IL-6
Paul Creek—*stream* IA-7
Paul Creek—*stream* (2) MT-8
Paul Creek—*stream* NY-2
Paul Creek—*stream* (2) OR-9
Paul Creek—*stream* VA-3
Paul Creek—*stream* WA-9
Paul Creek—*stream* WY-8
Paul Cundall Ranch—*locale* WY-8
**Paulden**—*pop pl* AZ-5
Paulding—*locale* NJ-2
**Paulding**—*pop pl* MI-6
**Paulding**—*pop pl* MS-4
**Paulding**—*pop pl* MO-7
**Paulding**—*pop pl* OH-6
Paulding Cem—*cemetery* MS-4
**Paulding (County)**—*pop pl* GA-3
**Paulding (County)**—*pop pl* OH-6
Paulding County Carnegie Library—*hist pl* OH-6
Paulding County Courthouse—*hist pl* GA-3
Paulding County Courthouse—*hist pl* OH-6
Paulding Creek—*stream* MI-6
Paulding Post Office—*building* MS-4
**Paulding (Township of)**—*pop pl* OH-6
**Pauldingville**—*pop pl* MO-7
Pauldingville Cem—*cemetery* MO-7
Pauldo Branch—*stream* TN-4
Paul Draw—*valley* WY-8
Paul Dresser Bridge—*bridge* IN-6
*Paulett* TN-4
**Paulette**—*pop pl* MS-4
**Paulette**—*pop pl* TN-4
Paulette Brook—*stream* ME-1
Paulette Lookout Tower—*locale* MS-4
Paulette Post Office (historical)—*building* MS-4
Paulette Sch (historical)—*school* TN-4
**Pauley**—*pop pl* KY-4
Pauley Apartments—*hist pl* AZ-5
Pauley Cem—*cemetery* AR-4
Pauley Cem—*cemetery* KY-4
Pauley Cem—*cemetery* (3) WV-2
Pauley Ch—*church* WV-2
Pauley Creek—*stream* CA-9
Pauley Gap—*gap* KY-4
Pauley Hollow—*valley* KY-4
Pauley Hollow—*valley* WV-2
Pauley Lake—*lake* MN-6
Pauley (Pauley Addition)—*uninc pl* KY-4
Pauley Sch—*school* KY-4
Pauley Sch—*school* MO-7
Paul Family Complex—*hist pl* KY-4
Paul F Boston JHS—*school* IN-6
Paul Felder Ch—*church* TX-5
*Paul Flats* PA-2
Paul Gamiels Hill Coast Guard 171—*locale* NC-3
*Paul G. Blazer Dam* KY-4
*Paul Gulch* CA-9
Paul Gulch—*valley* CA-9
Paul Hall, Muskingum College—*hist pl* OH-6
Paul H Barrett Lake Dam—*dam* MS-4
Paul-Helen Bldg—*hist pl* IA-7
Paul Henry Sch—*school* NM-5
Paul Herring Lake—*reservoir* MO-7
Paul Hill—*summit* MA-1
Paul Hill—*summit* NH-1
Paul (historical P.O.)—*locale* IA-7
*Paul Hollow* MO-7
Paul Hollow—*valley* PA-2
Paul Horton Memorial Ch—*church* TX-5
Pauli Ch—*church* MN-6
Pauli Dam—*dam* SD-7
Pauliluc Bay—*bay* GU-9
Pauliluc River—*stream* GU-9
Paulina—*locale* OR-9
**Paulina**—*pop pl* LA-4
**Paulina**—*pop pl* NJ-2
**Paulina**—*pop pl* PR-3
Paulina, Lake—*reservoir* CA-9
Paulina Basin—*basin* OR-9
Paulina Branch—*stream* KY-4
Paulina Butte—*summit* (2) OR-9
*Paulina Creek* OR-9
Paulina Creek—*stream* AK-9
Paulina Creek—*stream* (2) OR-9
Paulina Creek Falls—*falls* OR-9
**Paulina Hills**—*pop pl* MO-7
Paulina (historical)—*locale* OR-9
Paulina Island—*island* AK-9
Paulina Lake—*lake* OR-9
Paulina Lake—*reservoir* NJ-2
Paulina Lake Campground—*park* OR-9
Paulina Lake Dam—*dam* NJ-2
Paulina Lake Guard Station—*hist pl* OR-9
Paulina Marsh—*swamp* OR-9
Paulina Mountains—*range* OR-9
Paulina Peak—*summit* OR-9
Paulina Peak Trail—*trail* OR-9
Paulina Prairie—*flat* OR-9
Paulina Rsvr—*reservoir* OR-9
Paulina Spring—*spring* OR-9
Paulina Valley—*valley* OR-9
Pauline—*locale* ID-8
Pauline—*locale* IL-6
Pauline—*locale* TX-5
**Pauline**—*pop pl* KS-7
**Pauline**—*pop pl* NE-7
**Pauline**—*pop pl* SC-3
**Pauline**—*pop pl* TX-5
Pauline—*uninc pl* KS-7
Pauline, Lake—*lake* MI-6
Pauline, Lake—*reservoir* AR-4
Pauline, Lake—*reservoir* TX-5
Pauline Bar—*bar* AL-4
Pauline Canyon—*valley* AZ-5
Pauline (CCD)—*cens area* SC-3
Pauline Cem—*cemetery* MO-7
Pauline Central Elem Sch—*school* KS-7
Pauline Ch—*church* GA-3
*Pauline Creek* OR-9
Pauline Creek—*stream* AK-9
Pauline Creek—*stream* CO-8
Pauline Creek—*stream* (2) MT-8
Pauline Creek—*stream* SC-3
Pauline Fletcher Camp—*locale* AL-4
Pauline Home—*building* OH-6
Pauline Island—*island* FL-3
Pauline Jones Elem Sch—*school* NC-3
*Pauline Lake* OR-9
Pauline Lake—*lake* MN-6
Pauline Lakes—*lake* AK-9
Pauline Mine—*mine* AZ-5
Pauline Mine—*mine* NV-8
*Pauline Mountains* OR-9
Pauline Sch—*school* SC-3
Pauline South MS—*school* KS-7
*Pauline Valley* OR-9
Pauline Well—*well* AZ-5
*Pauling Chapel* PA-2
*Paulin Kill* NJ-2
**Paulins Kill**—*pop pl* NJ-2
Paulins Kill—*stream* NJ-2
Paulins Kill Dam—*dam* NJ-2
Paulins Kill Lake—*reservoir* NJ-2
Pauli Pond—*swamp* TX-5
Paul Island—*island* AK-9
Paul Island—*island* FL-3
Paul Islands—*island* MI-6
Paulison-Christie House—*hist pl* NJ-2
Paul JHS—*school* DC-2
Paul John Brook—*stream* VT-1
Paul Jones Spring—*spring* ID-8
Paul J. Rainey Wildlife Ref and Game Preserve—*park* LA-4
*Paul J. Rainey Wildlife Sanctuary* LA-4
Paul Junction—*locale* TX-5
Paulk—*locale* GA-3
Paulk Cem—*cemetery* (2) AL-4
Paulk Cem—*cemetery* (5) GA-3
Paul Kennedy Number 1 Dam—*dam* AL-4
Paul Kennedy Number 2 Dam—*dam* AL-4
Paul Kennedy Number 3 Dam—*dam* AL-4
Paul Kennedy Number 4 Dam—*dam* AL-4
Paul Kennedy Number 5 Dam—*dam* AL-4
Paulk Hill—*summit* CT-1
Paulk Hill Brook—*stream* CT-1
Paulk Lake—*reservoir* AL-4
Paulk Lakes—*lake* GA-3
Paulk Landing—*locale* GA-3
*Paulk Pond* AL-4
Paulk Pond Dam—*dam* AL-4
Paulks Cem—*cemetery* GA-3
Paulks Mill Bridge—*bridge* TN-4
Paulks Pond—*lake* GA-3
Paulk Spring—*spring* TN-4
Paull, Alfred, House—*hist pl* MA-1
Paull, Harry and Louisiana Beall, Mansion—*hist pl* WV-2
*Paul Lake* MN-6
Paul Lake—*lake* AK-9
Paul Lake—*lake* MN-6
Paul Lake—*lake* UT-8
Paul Lake—*lake* WI-6
Paul Laurence Dunbar—*post sta* OH-6
Paull Brook—*stream* MA-1
Paull Creek—*stream* WA-9
Paul Levine Park—*park* AL-4
**Paullina**—*pop pl* IA-7
Paull Ranch—*locale* CA-9
Paullus Cem—*cemetery* MO-7
Paullus Sch (abandoned)—*school* MO-7
Paul Marsh Dam—*dam* AL-4
Paul-McArthur Ditch Number One—*canal* MT-8
Paul McGill Lake Dam—*dam* MS-4
Paul Meek Library—*building* TN-4
*Paul M Grist Park Lake* AL-4
Paul M Grist State Park—*park* AL-4
Paul Mine—*mine* OH-6
Paul Moore Island—*island* TX-5
Paul Moore Tank—*reservoir* AZ-5
Paul Mtn—*summit* AR-4
Paul Mtn—*summit* MT-8
Paul Mtn—*summit* TX-5
Paul Mtn—*summit* VA-3
Paul Mtn—*summit* WA-9
Paulmyer Creek—*stream* SD-7
Pauloff Harbor—*bay* AK-9
Pauloff Harbor ANV892—*reserve* AK-9
Paul Peak—*summit* ID-8
Paul Peak—*summit* WA-9
Paul Peak Trail—*trail* WA-9
Paul Point—*cape* MD-2
Paul Point—*cape* MA-1
Paul Pond—*bay* LA-4
Paul Pond—*lake* FL-3
Paul Quinn Coll—*school* TX-5
Paul Revere Capture Site—*locale* MA-1
Paul Revere Community Center—*building* WI-6
Paul Revere House—*building* MA-1
Paul Revere Mall—*park* MA-1
Paul Revere Park—*park* MA-1
Paul Revere Sch—*school* CA-9
Paul Rigsby Dam—*dam* AL-4
Paul Road Sch—*school* NY-2
Paul Roberts Lake Dam—*dam* MS-4
Paul Rsvr—*reservoir* ID-8
Paul Rsvr—*reservoir* MT-8
Paul Rsvr—*reservoir* WY-8
*Pauls* AR-4
*Pauls* ME-1
Pauls—*locale* ME-1
**Pauls**—*pop pl* AR-4
Pauls Arroyo—*stream* CO-8
Paul Saylor Elem Sch—*school* IN-6
Pauls Bay—*bay* AK-9
*Pauls Bayou* AL-4
Pauls Bluff—*cliff* ME-1
**Paulsboro**—*pop pl* NJ-2
Paulsboro Refinery—*airport* NJ-2
Pauls Branch—*stream* AL-4
Pauls Branch Ch—*church* VA-3
Paul's Bridge—*hist pl* MA-1
*Pauls Brook* PA-2
Pauls Camp Canyon—*valley* NV-8
Pauls Camp Spring—*spring* NV-8
Pauls Canyon—*valley* NM-5
Pauls Canyon—*valley* UT-8
Pauls Cem—*cemetery* LA-4
*Pauls Chapel* TN-4
Pauls Chapel—*church* IN-6
Pauls Chapel—*church* (2) MS-4
Pauls Chapel—*church* NC-3
Pauls Chapel Cem—*cemetery* MS-4
Pauls Chapel (historical)—*church* MS-4
*Pauls Chapel Methodist Ch* MS-4
Pauls Chapel Sch (historical)—*school* TN-4
Pauls Ch (historical)—*church* MS-4
Pauls Corner—*locale* ME-1
Pauls Corner—*locale* MD-2
*Pauls Creek* CA-9
Pauls Creek—*stream* AL-4
Pauls Creek—*stream* AK-9
Pauls Creek—*stream* CA-9
Pauls Creek—*stream* MN-6
Pauls Creek—*stream* NC-3
Pauls Creek—*stream* TX-5
Pauls Creek—*stream* (2) VA-3
Pauls Creek Ch—*church* VA-3
**Pauls Crossing**—*pop pl* NC-3
Pauls Crossroads—*locale* VA-3
**Pauls Cross Roads**—*pop pl* VA-3
Pauls Ditch—*stream* NC-3
Paul Seifer Ranch—*locale* NE-7
Paulsell—*locale* CA-9
Paulsell Extension—*canal* CA-9
Paulsell Lateral—*canal* CA-9
**Paulsen**—*pop pl* KY-4
Paulsen, Peter J., House—*hist pl* IA-7
**Paulsen Acres Subdivision**—*pop pl* UT-8
Paulsen Creek—*stream* ND-7
Paulsen Lake—*lake* WI-6
Paul Sevenich Boy Scout Camp—*locale* WA-9
*Pauls Gap* NC-3
Pauls Gulch—*valley* ID-8
**Pauls Hill**—*pop pl* AL-4
Pauls Hole—*basin* UT-8
Paulsin Basin—*basin* UT-8
Pauls Irrigation Dam—*dam* SD-7
Pauls Island—*island* CA-9
Pauls Island—*island* FL-3
*Pauls Lake* TX-5
Pauls Lake—*lake* AK-9
Pauls Lake—*lake* LA-4
Pauls Lake—*lake* OH-6
Pauls Lake—*lake* WA-9
Pauls Lake—*lake* WI-6
Pauls Landing—*locale* MS-4
Pauls Meadow—*area* UT-8
**Paul Smiths**—*pop pl* NY-2
Paul Smiths Coll—*school* (2) NY-2
**Paul Smiths Easy Street**—*pop pl* NY-2
Paulson—*locale* ND-7
Paulson, John E. and Christina, House—*hist pl* OR-9
Paulson Branch—*stream* WY-8
Paulson Creek—*stream* AK-9
Paulson Creek—*stream* MN-6
Paulson Dam—*dam* ND-7
Paulson Hill—*summit* WY-8
Paulson Hollow—*valley* WI-6
Paulson House—*hist pl* MI-6
*Paulson Lake* MN-6
Paulson Lake—*lake* (2) MI-6
Paulson Lake—*lake* MN-6
Paulson Lake—*lake* ND-7
Paulson Lake—*lake* WI-6
Paulson Northeast Oil Field—*oilfield* KS-7
Paulson Playground—*park* PA-2
Paulson Ranch—*locale* SD-7
**Paulson Township**—*pop pl* ND-7
Paulson Wash—*valley* UT-8
Paul S Owensby Lake Dam Number 2—*dam* AL-4
Paul S Owensby Lake Number Two—*reservoir* AL-4
Pauls Peak—*summit* VT-1
Pauls Pit—*cave* AL-4
*Pauls Point* MA-1
Pauls Point—*cape* CA-9
Pauls Point—*cape* TN-4
Pauls Pond—*reservoir* NY-2
Paul Spring—*spring* SD-7
Paul Spring Branch—*stream* VA-3
Paul Springs—*spring* NM-5
**Paul Spur**—*pop pl* AZ-5
*Paul S. Rainey Wildlife Refuge And Game Preserve* LA-4
*Pauls Ranch Corner* ME-1
Pauls Sch—*school* PA-2
Pauls Sch—*school* WI-6
Pauls Slough—*gut* LA-4
Pauls Slough—*lake* ND-7
Pauls Slough—*stream* WA-9
Pauls Store—*locale* TX-5
Pauls Stumps—*locale* MS-4
**Pauls Switch**—*pop pl* AR-4
Paul State For—*forest* VA-3
Paul State Wildlife Mngmt Area—*park* MN-6
Paul Stevens Trail—*trail* OK-5
Paul Stream—*stream* VT-1
Paul Stream Pond—*lake* VT-1
**Paul Subdivision**—*pop pl* (2) UT-8
Pauls Union Ch—*church* TX-5
**Pauls Valley**—*pop pl* OK-5
Pauls Valley (CCD)—*cens area* OK-5
Pauls Valley Hist Dist—*hist pl* OK-5
Pauls Valley Lake—*reservoir* OK-5
Pauls Valley Oil Field—*oilfield* OK-5
Pauls Valley State Sch—*school* OK-5
Paul Tank—*reservoir* AZ-5
Paul Tank—*reservoir* NM-5
Paul Thorton Lake Dam—*dam* MS-4
**Paulton**—*pop pl* IL-6
**Paulton**—*pop pl* PA-2
Paultown Cem—*cemetery* MO-7
Paul Trier Ditch—*canal* IN-6
*Paul Truitt Memorial Baptist Church* MS-4
Pault Sch—*school* SD-7
Paul Turney Ranch—*locale* TX-5
*Paulus Hook* NJ-2
Paulus Hook Hist Dist—*hist pl* NJ-2
Paulus Hook Hist Dist (Boundary Increase)—*hist pl* NJ-2
Paul Washington Indian Cem—*cemetery* OR-9
Paul Weildy Lake Dam—*dam* MS-4
Paul Well—*well* OR-9
Paul Windle Municipal Field—*airport* KS-7
Paul Wise Hill—*summit* NY-2
Pauly Branch—*stream* VA-3
Pauly Ditch—*canal* MT-8
Paul Young Creek—*stream* AK-9
Paul Young Dam—*dam* SD-7
Paulys Lake—*lake* WI-6
Paulys Pond Park—*park* MN-6
Pauly Springs—*spring* MT-8
Pauma—*civil* CA-9
Pauma Creek—*stream* CA-9
**Pauma Ind Res**—*pop pl* CA-9
**Paumalu**—*pop pl* HI-9
Paumalu Gulch—*valley* HI-9
Paumalu Stream—*stream* HI-9
Paumanok Sch—*school* NY-2
Pauma Sch—*school* CA-9
**Pauma Valley**—*pop pl* CA-9
Pauma Valley—*valley* CA-9
Pauma Valley (CCD)—*cens area* CA-9
Pauma Valley Cem—*cemetery* CA-9
Pauma Valley Sch—*school* CA-9
Paumaville Country Club—*other* CA-9
*Paumoho Camp* HI-9
*Paumond Send Creek* VA-3
Paunagaktuk Bluff—*cliff* AK-9
Paunau—*civil* HI-9
Paunch Mtn—*summit* ID-8
*Pauness lake* MN-6
Paunnacussing Creek—*stream* PA-2
*Paunpeck Creek* NJ-2
Paunpeck Creek—*stream* NJ-2
*Paunsagunt Plateau* UT-8
Paunsaugunt Plateau—*plateau* UT-8
Paun Sch—*school* MI-6
Pauoa—*civil* HI-9
Pauoa Bay—*bay* HI-9
Pauoa Flats—*flat* HI-9
Pauoa Sch—*school* HI-9
Pauoa Stream—*stream* HI-9
Pauoheohe—*summit* HI-9
Pauonuakea—*island* HI-9
Paup—*locale* AR-4
Paupac Creek—*stream* WA-9
**Paupack**—*pop pl* PA-2
Paupack, Lake—*reservoir* PA-2
Paupackan Lake—*reservoir* PA-2
Paupack Cem—*cemetery* PA-2
Paupack Ch—*church* PA-2
*Paupack School* PA-2
**Paupack (Township of)**—*pop pl* PA-2
Paupau—*summit* HI-9
Paupau Ditch—*canal* HI-9
*Paupau Point* HI-9
Paup Cem—*cemetery* AR-4
Pauper Cem—*cemetery* AL-4
Pauper Cem—*cemetery* KY-4
Pauper Cem—*cemetery* (2) TN-4
Pauper Cem—*cemetery* VA-3
Paupers Cem—*cemetery* MS-4
Paupers Dream Mine—*mine* MT-8
Paupores—*locale* MN-6
*Pauquin Creek* MI-6

Paurop ... FM-9
Paurop Island ... FM-9
Pausacaco Pond—reservoir ... RI-1
Paustian, Henry, House—hist pl ... IA-7
Pauteon Otero-Martinez—hist pl ... PR-3
Pautipaug Cem—cemetery ... CT-1
Pautipaug Hill—summit ... CT-1
Pauto Lake—lake ... WI-6
Pautz Lake—lake ... WI-6
**Pauwalu**—pop pl ... HI-9
Pauwalu Harbor—bay ... HI-9
Pauwalu Point—cape ... HI-9
Pauwela—civil ... HI-9
**Pauwela**—pop pl ... HI-9
Pauwela Gulch—valley ... HI-9
Pauwela-Kuiaha ... HI-9
Pauwela (Kuiaha)—CDP ... HI-9
Pauwela Point—cape ... HI-9
Pauwela Rsvr—reservoir ... HI-9
Pauzen Island ... MP-9
Pauzen Island—island ... MP-9
**Pavaiai**—pop pl ... AS-9
Pavalak Natl Forest Campground—locale ... NV-8
Pavant Butte ... UT-8
Pavant Mountain Range ... UT-8
Pavant Mountains ... UT-8
Pavant Plateau ... UT-8
Pavant Range ... UT-8
Pavant Ranger Station—locale ... UT-8
Pavant Valley ... UT-8
Pavatt Cem—cemetery ... TN-4
Pavatt Landing—locale ... TN-4
Pavatt Sch (historical)—school ... TN-4
Pavatts Landing ... TN-4
Pavelgrit Lake—lake ... MN-6
Pavelka Cem—cemetery ... TX-5
Pavelka Farmstead—hist pl ... NE-7
Pavelko State Wildlife Mngmt
Area—park ... MN-6
Pavell Island—island ... TX-5
Paveloff Creek—stream ... AK-9
Pavement Hill—summit ... CT-1
Pavey Draw—valley ... WY-8
Pavey Oil Field—oilfield ... TX-5
**Pavia**—pop pl ... PA-2
Pavia Run—stream ... PA-2
**Pavilion**—pop pl ... NY-2
Pavilion, The—locale ... NC-3
Pavilion Beach—beach ... MA-1
Pavilion Center—locale ... NY-2
Pavilion Dome—summit ... CA-9
Pavilion (historical)—locale ... KS-7
Pavilion Key Light 10—locale ... FL-3
Pavilion Shop Ctr—locale ... FL-3
Pavilion Springs—spring ... OK-5
**Pavilion (sta.)**—pop pl ... MI-6
**Pavilion (Town of)**—pop pl ... NY-2
**Pavilion (Township of)**—pop pl ... MI-6
Pavillion—locale ... MI-6
**Pavillion**—pop pl ... IL-6
**Pavillion**—pop pl ... WY-8
Pavillion at Highland Oaks, The—locale ... NC-3
Pavillion Butte—summit ... WY-8
Pavillion Center—locale ... MI-6
Pavillion Drain—canal ... WY-8
Pavillion Drain—stream ... WY-8
Pavillion Key—island ... FL-3
Pavillion Main Lateral—canal ... WY-8
Pavillion Point—cliff ... CO-8
Pavillion Ridge—ridge ... WY-8
Pavis Creek ... SC-3
Pavits Spring—spring ... NV-8
Pavlas Lake—lake ... WI-6
Pavlik Lakes—reservoir ... IA-7
Pavlof—locale ... AK-9
Pavlof Bay—bay ... AK-9
Pavlof Harbor—bay (2) ... AK-9
Pavlof Islands—island ... AK-9
Pavlof Lake—lake ... AK-9
Pavlof River—stream ... AK-9
Pavlof Sister—summit ... AK-9
Pavlof Volcano—summit ... AK-9
Pavlok Mine—mine ... NV-8
Pavlovic Corner—locale ... MI-6
Pavmetown Cem—cemetery ... TX-5
**Pavo**—pop pl ... GA-3
Pavoatuck Cem—cemetery ... MA-1
Pavo-Barwick (CCD)—cens area ... GA 3
Pavo Kug (historical)—locale ... AZ-5
Pavo Kug Wash ... AZ-5
Pavo Kug Wash—stream ... AZ-5
Pavolic Corner ... MI-6
Pavo Mesa—summit ... NM-5
Pavo Mine—mine ... NM-5
**Pavonia**—pop pl ... NJ-2
**Pavonia**—pop pl ... OH-6
Pavonia Junction—uninc pl ... NJ-2
Pavo Tank—reservoir (2) ... TX-5
**Pawaa**—pop pl ... HI-9
Pawahkee Creek ... WA-9
Pawai Crater—crater ... HI-9
Pawaina—locale ... HI-9
Pawamack Pond ... RI-1
Paw Cape—cape ... AK-9
**Pawcatuck**—pop pl ... CT-1
Pawcatuck Bay ... RI-1
Pawcatuck Point—cape ... CT-1
Pawcatuck River—reservoir (2) ... RI-1
Pawcatuck River—stream ... CT-1
Pawcatuck River—stream ... RI-1
Pawcatuck Rock—summit ... CT-1
Pawchasset River ... RI-1
**Paw Creek**—pop pl ... NC-3
Paw Creek—stream ... NC-3
**Paw Creek (RR name Thrift)**—pop pl ... NC-3
Paw Creek Sch—school ... NC-3
**Pawelekville**—pop pl ... TX-5
Paweo—cape ... HI-9
Paweo Point ... HI-9
**Pawheen**—pop pl ... AR-4
Pawheen Ch—church ... AR-4
Pawheen Sch—school ... AR-4
Paw Hole—reservoir ... AZ-5
**Pawhuska**—pop pl ... OK-5
Pawhuska, Lake—reservoir ... OK-5
Pawhuska (CCD)—cens area ... OK-5
Pawhuska Cem—cemetery ... OK-5
Pawhuska Downtown Hist Dist—hist pl ... OK-5
Pawhuska Lake ... OK-5
Pawili—area ... HI-9
Pawili—civil ... HI-9
Paw Lake—lake ... MI-6
Pawlak Field—park ... OH-6
**Pawlet**—pop pl ... VT-1
**Pawlet (Town of)**—pop pl ... VT-1
Pawley Canyon—valley ... CO-8
Pawley Creek ... CA-9
Pawley Creek—stream ... KY-4
Pawley Inlet ... SC-3
Pawley Island ... SC-3
Pawleys Creek—stream ... SC-3
Pawleys Inlet—bay ... SC-3
Pawleys Island—island ... SC-3
**Pawleys Island**—pop pl ... SC-3
Pawleys Island Creek—gut ... SC-3
Pawleys Island Hist Dist—hist pl ... SC-3
Pawleys Swamp—swamp ... SC-3
**Pawling**—pop pl ... NY-2
Pawling, Isaac, House—hist pl ... PA-2
Pawling Center ... NY-2
Pawling Chapel—church ... PA-2
Pawling Mtn—summit ... NY-2
Pawling Rsvr—reservoir ... NY-2
Pawling Sanitorium—hospital ... NY-2
**Pawling Station**—pop pl ... PA-2
Pawling Station P O ... NY-2
Pawlingstown ... NY-2
**Pawling (Town of)**—pop pl ... NY-2
Pawlins Kill ... NJ-2
Pawmet River ... MA-1
Pawnce Creek ... KS-7
Pawnee ... KS-7
Pawnee ... NE-7
Pawnee—fmr MCD ... NE-7
Pawnee—locale ... LA-4
Pawnee—locale ... MO-7
Pawnee—locale ... OH-6
**Pawnee**—pop pl ... IL-6
**Pawnee**—pop pl ... OK-5
**Pawnee**—pop pl ... TX-5
Pawnee Acres Community Hall—building ... KS-7
Pawnee Ave Ch of God—church ... KS-7
Pawnee Bill Museum State Park—park ... OK-5
Pawnee Buttes—summit ... CO-8
Pawnee Canal—canal ... CO-8
Pawnee (CCD)—cens area ... OK-5
Pawnee Cem—cemetery ... TX-5
**Pawnee City**—pop pl ... NE-7
Pawnee County—civil ... KS-7
**Pawnee (County)**—pop pl ... OK-5
Pawnee County Courthouse—hist pl ... OK-5
Pawnee Creek ... KS-7
Pawnee Creek—stream ... CO-8
Pawnee Creek—stream (2) ... KS-7
Pawnee Creek—stream ... MT-8
Pawnee Creek—stream (3) ... NE-7
Pawnee Creek—stream ... OK-5
Pawnee Ditch—canal ... CO-8
Pawnee Elem Sch—school ... KS-7
Pawnee Flats—flat ... KS-7
Pawnee Gulch—valley ... CO-8
Pawnee Gulch—valley ... MT-8
Pawnee Gulch—valley ... OR-9
**Pawnee Heights**—pop pl ... AL-4
Pawnee Heights HS—school ... KS-7
Pawnee Heights West Elem Sch—school ... KS-7
Pawnee Hills—range ... CO-8
Pawnee (historical)—locale ... KS-7
Pawnee Hollow—valley ... MO-7
Pawnee Indian Agency—hist pl ... OK-5
Pawnee Indian Village—park ... KS-7
Pawnee Indian Village Site—hist pl ... KS-7
Pawnee Inlet No 1—stream ... CO-8
Pawnee Inlet No 2—stream ... CO-8
Pawnee Junction—locale ... IL-6
Pawnee Lake—lake ... CO-8
Pawnee Lake—lake ... OR-9
Pawnee Lake—reservoir ... NE-7
Pawnee Lake—reservoir ... OK-5
Pawnee Lake Campground—locale ... CO-8
Pawnee Mine—mine ... CA-9
Pawnee Mission and Burnt Village Archeol
Site—hist pl ... NE-7
Pawnee Mound—summit ... KS-7
Pawnee Natl Grasslands Research
Center—locale ... CO-8
Pawnee-on-the-Reserve ... KS-7
Pawnee Park—park ... IL-6
Pawnee Park—park ... NE-7
Pawnee Pass—gap (2) ... CO-8
Pawnee Pass Trail—trail ... CO-8
**Pawnee (Pawnee Heights)**—pop pl ... AL-4
Pawnee Peak—summit ... CO-8
Pawnee Plaza Mall—locale ... KS-7
Pawnee Point—cliff ... KS-7
Pawnee River ... KS-7
Pawnee River—stream ... KS-7
Pawnee River Tributary Bridge—hist pl ... KS-7
Pawnee Rock—hist pl ... KS-7
**Pawnee Rock**—pop pl ... KS-7
Pawnee Rock Cem—cemetery ... KS-7
Pawnee Rock Elem Sch—school ... KS-7
Pawnee Rock JHS—school ... KS-7
Pawnee Rock Oil Field—oilfield ... KS-7
Pawnee Rock State Monument ... KS-7
Pawnee Rock State Park—park ... KS-7
**Pawnee Rock Township**—pop pl ... KS-7
Pawnee Rsvr—reservoir ... AL-4
Pawnee Slough—stream ... NE-7
Pawnee Springs Ranch—locale ... NE-7
**Pawnee Station**—pop pl ... KS-7
Pawnee Township—civil ... MO-7
**Pawnee Township**—pop pl (3) ... KS-7
**Pawnee (Township of)**—pop pl ... IL-6
Pawnee Valley—valley ... CO-8
Pawnee Valley (historical)—locale ... KS-7
Pawnee Valley Sch—school ... CO-8
Pawnee Village—locale ... NE-7
Pawner Sch—school ... PA-2
Pawnett ... MA-1
Pawn Rock—rock ... MA-1
Pawn Run—stream ... MD-2
Pawn (site)—locale ... OR-9
Pawona Witu—hist pl ... CA-9
Pawpaw ... TN-4
Paw Paw—locale ... MO-7
Paw Paw—locale ... OK-5
**Paw Paw**—pop pl ... IL-6
**Paw Paw**—pop pl ... KY-4
**Paw Paw**—pop pl ... MI-6
**Paw Paw**—pop pl (2) ... WV-2
Paw Paw Bayou—stream ... LA-4
Paw Paw Bayou—stream ... TX-5
Paw Paw Bldg—hist pl ... MD-2
Paw Paw Bottom—bend ... OK-5
Paw Paw Brake—swamp ... AR-4
Paw Paw Branch ... TX-5
Paw Paw Branch—stream ... DE-2
Pawpaw Branch—stream (2) ... KY-4
Paw Paw Branch—stream ... KY-4
Paw Paw Branch—stream ... WV-2
Pawpaw Cem—cemetery ... MS-4
Pawpaw Cem—cemetery (2) ... OH-6
Paw Paw Ch—church ... IN-6
Pawpaw Ch—church ... MS-4
PawPaw Ch—church ... OH-6
Pawpaw Ch—church ... TN-4
Paw Paw Chapel—church ... OK-5
Paw Paw Chute—gut ... MS-4
Paw Paw Chute—stream ... LA-4
Paw Paw City Hall—hist pl ... MI-6
Pawpaw (corporate and RR name Paw Paw) ... IL-6
Pawpaw Cove—bay ... MD-2
Paw Paw Cove—stream ... KY-4
Paw Paw Creek ... KS-7
Paw Paw Creek ... LA-4
Paw Paw Creek ... NC-3
Paw Paw Creek ... TN-4
Paw Paw Creek ... TX-5
Pawpaw Creek ... VA-3
Paw Paw Creek—stream ... IN-6
Pawpaw Creek—stream ... KS-7
Paw Paw Creek—stream ... KS-7
Pawpaw Creek—stream (3) ... KY-4
Pawpaw Creek—stream ... MD-2
Paw Paw Creek—stream ... MO-7
Pawpaw Creek—stream ... NC-3
Paw Paw Creek—stream ... NC-3
Pawpaw Creek—stream ... NC-3
PawPaw Creek—stream (2) ... OH-6
Pawpaw Creek—stream ... OK-5
Pawpaw Creek—stream (2) ... TN-4
Pawpaw Creek—stream (2) ... TX-5
Pawpaw Creek—stream (2) ... VA-3
Paw Paw Creek—stream ... WV-2
Paw Paw Creek Bridge No. 52—hist pl ... IN-6
Paw Paw Ford Post Office ... TN-4
Pawpaw Gap—gap ... VA-3
Pawpaw Hollow—bay ... MD-2
Pawpaw Hollow—valley ... AR-4
Pawpaw Hollow—valley ... KY-4
Paw Paw Hollow—valley (2) ... TN-4
Paw Paw Hollow Ch—church ... TN-4
Paw Paw Island ... TN-4
Paw Paw Island—island ... LA-4
Paw Paw Island Shoals—bar ... TN-4
Paw Paw Key ... FL-3
Paw Paw Lake—lake (3) ... MI-6
Paw Paw Lake—lake ... OH-6
**Paw Paw Lake**—pop pl ... MI-6
Paw Paw Landing—locale ... MS-4
Paw Paw (Magisterial District)—fmr MCD ... WV-2
Paw Paw Mound—summit ... FL-3
Paw Paw Pit—cave ... TN-4
Pawpaw Plains—locale ... TN-4
Paw Paw Point ... MD-2
Pawpaw Point—cape ... MD-2
Pawpaw Post Office (historical)—building ... TN-4
Paw Paw Ridge—ridge ... NC-3
Paw Paw Ridge—ridge ... WV-2
Paw Paw River ... MI-6
Pawpaw River ... SC-3
Paw Paw River—stream ... MI-6
Paw Paw Run—stream ... IL-6
Pawpaw Run—stream ... OH-6
Pawpaw Run—stream ... PA-2
Pawpaw Run—stream ... WV-2
Paw Paw Sch—school ... KY-4
Paw Paw Sch (historical)—school ... TN-4
Paw Paw Slough—gut ... AR-4
**Paw Paw Township**—pop pl ... KS-7
**Paw Paw (Township of)**—pop pl ... IL-6
**Paw Paw (Township of)**—pop pl ... IN-6
**Paw Paw (Township of)**—pop pl ... MI-6
Paw Paw Woods—woods ... IL-6
Pawpoesit ... MA-1
Pawpoesit Bay ... MA-1
Paw Point—cape ... MI-6
Paw Ridge Landing ... NC-3
Pawson Sch—school ... IL-6
Paws Pocket—basin ... AZ-5
Paws Water—lake ... ID-8
Pawticfaw Baptist Ch (historical)—church ... MS-4
Pawticfaw Cem—cemetery ... MS-4
Pawticfaw Creek—stream ... MS-4
Pawticfaw Post Office
(historical)—building ... MS-4
Pawticfow Creek ... MS-4
Pawtigfa Church ... MS-4
Pawtigfaw Cemetery ... MS-4
Pawtuckaway, Mount—summit ... NH-1
Pawtuckaway Lake ... NH-1
Pawtuckaway Mountains—summit ... NH-1
Pawtuckaway Pond—reservoir ... NH-1
Pawtuckaway Ponds ... NH-1
Pawtuckaway River—stream ... NH-1
Pawtuckaway State Reservation—park ... NH-1
Pawtucket ... MA-1
**Pawtucket**—pop pl ... RI-1
Pawtucket, Town of ... MA-1
Pawtucket Armory—hist pl ... RI-1
Pawtucket Canal—canal ... MA-1
Pawtucket Canal Rsvr—reservoir ... MA-1
Pawtucket City Hall—hist pl ... RI-1
Pawtucket Congregational Church—hist pl ... RI-1
Pawtucket Dam—dam ... MA-1
Pawtucket Elks Lodge Bldg—hist pl ... RI-1
Pawtucket Falls—falls ... MA-1
Pawtucket Gatehouse—building ... MA-1
Pawtucket Merrimac Canal ... MA-1
Pawtucket Post Office—hist pl ... RI-1
Pawtucket Reservoir Dam—dam ... RI-1
Pawtucket River ... MA-1
Pawtucket River ... RI-1
Pawtucket Rsvr ... RI-1
Pawtucket Rsvr—reservoir ... RI-1
Pawtucket Sch—school ... MA-1
Pawtuckett Elementary School ... NC-3
Pawtuckett Golf Course—locale ... NC-3
Pawtucket Times Bldg—hist pl ... RI-1
Pawtucketville Memorial Sch—school ... MA-1
**Pawtucketville (subdivision)**—pop pl ... MA-1
Pawtucketville Technological
Institute—school ... MA-1
Pawtucket West HS—hist pl ... RI-1
**Pawtuxet**—pop pl ... RI-1
Pawtuxet Cove—bay ... RI-1
Pawtuxet Long Neck ... RI-1
Pawtuxet Neck—cape ... RI-1
Pawtuxet River ... RI-1
Pawtuxet River—reservoir (3) ... RI-1
Pawtuxet River—stream ... RI-1
Pawtuxet River-South Branch—reservoir ... RI-1
Pawtuxet Village Hist Dist—hist pl ... RI-1
Paw Wah Kee Gulch ... WA-9
Paw Wah Pond—lake ... MA-1
**Pax**—pop pl ... WV-2
Pax Cem—cemetery ... WV-2
**Paxico**—pop pl ... KS-7
Paxines ... PA-2
**Paxinos**—pop pl ... PA-2
Paxinosa Elem Sch—school ... PA-2
Paxinosa Heights ... PA-2
Paxinosa Ridge ... PA-2
**Paxinosa (subdivision)**—pop pl ... PA-2
Paxman—mine ... UT-8
Pax Mtn—summit ... SC-3
Paxon—uninc pl ... FL-3
Paxon Hollow Golf Club—other ... PA-2
Paxon Hollow High School ... PA-2
Paxon Hollow JHS—school ... PA-2
Paxon Shop Ctr—locale ... FL-3
Paxon Township ... KS-7
Paxon Township—civil ... KS-7
Paxson—locale ... AK-9
Paxson, Edgar, House—hist pl ... MT-8
Paxson, Isaiah, Farm—hist pl ... PA-2
Paxson (historical)—locale ... KS-7
Paxson Lake—lake ... AK-9
Paxson Mtn—summit ... AK-9
Paxson Sch—school ... MT-8
Paxson Sch—school ... PA-2
Paxsons Corner ... PA-2
Paxsons Island ... PA-2
**Paxtang**—pop pl ... PA-2
Paxtang Borough—civil ... PA-2
Paxtang Cem—cemetery ... PA-2
**Paxtang Manor**—pop pl ... PA-2
**Paxtang Manor (subdivision)**—pop pl ... PA-2
Paxtaug ... PA-2
Paxton ... PA-2
Paxton—locale ... CA-9
Paxton—locale ... GA-3
Paxton—locale ... KS-7
Paxton—locale ... KY-4
Paxton—locale ... MI-6
Paxton—locale ... OR-9
Paxton—locale ... SD-7
Paxton—locale ... TX-5
Paxton—locale ... WA-9
**Paxton**—pop pl ... FL-3
**Paxton**—pop pl ... IL-6
**Paxton**—pop pl ... IN-6
**Paxton**—pop pl ... MA-1
**Paxton**—pop pl ... NE-7
**Paxton**—pop pl ... PA-2
**Paxton**—pop pl ... WV-2
Paxton, Lake—lake ... FL-3
Paxton, Lake—lake ... GA-3
**Paxton Acres (subdivision)**—pop pl ... PA-2
Paxton Brake—swamp ... MS-4
Paxton Branch—stream (2) ... VA-3
Paxton Canal—canal ... NE-7
Paxton Cem—cemetery ... KY-4
Paxton Cem—cemetery ... MS-4
Paxton Cem—cemetery ... MO-7
Paxton Cem—cemetery ... NE-7
Paxton Cem—cemetery (2) ... WV-2
Paxton Center Schools—school ... MA-1
Paxton Centre ... MA-1
Paxton Ch—church ... PA-2
Paxton Ch—church ... SD-7
Paxton Chapel—church ... VA-3
Paxton Ch (historical)—church ... MS-4
Paxton Creek—stream (2) ... NC-3
Paxton Creek—stream ... PA-2
Paxton Creek—stream ... WY-8
Paxton-Darlington (CCD)—cens area ... FL-3
Paxton First Schoolhouse—hist pl ... IL-6
Paxton Hershey Canal—canal ... NE-7
Paxton Hill—summit ... VA-3
Paxton Hollow—valley ... AR-4
**Paxton Hollow Estates
(subdivision)**—pop pl ... PA-2
Paxton HS—school (2) ... FL-3
**Paxtonia**—pop pl ... PA-2
Paxtonia Sch—school ... PA-2
Paxton JHS—school ... FL-3
Paxton Knob—summit ... AR-4
**Paxton (Mahantango)**—pop pl ... PA-2
Paxton Meadows—flat ... OR-9
Paxton Millpond—reservoir ... SC-3
Paxton Park—park ... CA-9
Paxton Park—park ... KY-4
Paxton Peak—summit ... VA-3
Paxton Place—hist pl ... VA-3
Paxton Place—locale ... AZ-5
Paxton Point—cape ... VA-3
Paxton Ranch—locale ... CA-9
Paxton Ridge—ridge ... WV-2
Paxton Rsvr—reservoir ... CO-8
Paxton Run—stream ... PA-2
Paxton Sch (historical)—school ... MS-4
Paxton Siding—locale ... NM-5
Paxtons Landing (historical)—locale ... MS-4
Paxton Spring—spring ... NM-5
Paxton Springs—locale ... NM-5
**Paxton Springs**—pop pl ... NM-5
Paxton Tank—reservoir ... NM-5
**Paxton (Town of)**—pop pl ... MA-1
**Paxton Township**—pop pl ... KS-7
**Paxton (Township of)**—pop pl ... MN-6
**Paxton (Township of)**—pop pl ... OH-6
**Paxtonville**—pop pl ... PA-2
Paxtonville Cave—cave ... PA-2
Paxton Water Tower and Pump
House—hist pl ... IL-6
Paxton Well—locale ... NM-5
**Paxville**—pop pl ... SC-3
Paxville (CCD)—cens area ... SC-3
Paya Lake—lake ... WI-6
Payan Canyon—valley ... CO-8
Payapae ... MH-9
Payapai—slope ... MH-9
Paya Point—cliff ... AZ-5
Pay Branch ... TN-4
Pay Canyon Rsvr—reservoir ... OR-9
Paycomo Windmill—locale ... TX-5
Pay Day Number One Mine—mine ... CA-9
Payden Run—stream ... OH-6
Pay Dirt Spring—spring ... AZ-5
**Paydown**—pop pl ... MO-7
Paydown Club—other ... MO-7
Paydown Ford (historical)—locale ... MO-7
Paydown Gasconade River Public
Access—locale ... MO-7
Paydown Sch (abandoned)—school ... MO-7
Paydown Springs—spring ... MO-7
Paye Creek—stream ... WA-9
Paye Pond ... PA-2
**Payette**—pop pl ... ID-8
Payette City Hall and Courthouse—hist pl ... ID-8
**Payette Heights**—pop pl ... ID-8
**Payette Junction**—pop pl ... OR-9
Payette Lake—lake ... ID-8
Payette Natl For—forest ... ID-8
Payette Peak—summit ... ID-8
Payette River ... ID-8
Payette River—stream ... ID-8
Paygan ... MH-9
Paylof Harbor (Pauloff Harbor)—other ... AK-9
Paylons Creek—stream ... MS-4
Paymaster Canyon—valley ... AZ-5
Paymaster Canyon—valley (2) ... NV-8
Paymaster Dam—dam ... AZ-5
Paymaster Gulch—valley ... ID-8
Paymaster Gulch—valley ... MT-8
**Paymaster Landing**—pop pl ... CA-9
Paymaster Mine—mine (3) ... AZ-5
Paymaster Mine—mine (4) ... CA-9
Paymaster Mine—mine (2) ... CO-8
Paymaster Mine—mine ... ID-8
Paymaster Mine—mine ... MT-8
Paymaster Mine—mine (3) ... NV-8
Paymaster Mine—mine ... NM-5
Paymaster Mine Shaft—mine ... UT-8
Paymaster Ridge—ridge ... NV-8
Paymaster Spring—spring ... AZ-5
Paymaster Tank—reservoir ... AZ-5
Paymaster Wash—stream ... AZ-5
**Payment**—pop pl ... MI-6
Payment Cem—cemetery ... MI-6
Payment Lake—lake ... WI-6
Payne ... KY-4
Payne—fmr MCD ... NE-7
Payne—locale ... AR-4
Payne—locale ... CA-9
Payne—locale ... CO-8
Payne—locale ... GA-3
Payne—locale ... ID-8
Payne—locale ... KY-4
Payne—locale ... OK-5
Payne—locale ... TX-5
Payne—locale (2) ... VA-3
**Payne**—pop pl ... GA-3
**Payne**—pop pl ... IA-7
**Payne**—pop pl ... MN-6
**Payne**—pop pl ... OH-6
Payne, Asa, House—hist pl ... KY-4
Payne, Charles, House—hist pl ... RI-1
Payne, Daniel, House—hist pl ... CT-1
Payne, Gen. John, House—hist pl ... KY-4
Payne, Henry, House—hist pl ... KY-4
Payne, Lewis, House—hist pl ... KY-4
Payne, M. S., House—hist pl ... TX-5
Payne, O. E., House—hist pl ... IA-7
Payne, Theodore F., House—hist pl ... CA-9
Payne Airp—airport ... MS-4
Payne Ave Baptist Ch—church ... TN-4
Payne Avenue ... MN-6
**Payne Beach**—pop pl ... NY-2
Payne Bed Mine (underground)—mine ... AL-4
Payne Bend—bend ... AL-4
Payne Bend Post Office
(historical)—building ... AL-4
Payne Branch—stream ... AL-4
Payne Branch—stream ... AR-4
Payne Branch—stream ... GA-3
Payne Branch—stream ... IN-6
Payne Branch—stream ... KY-4
Payne Branch—stream (2) ... MO-7
Payne Branch—stream (3) ... NC-3
Payne Branch—stream ... SC-3
Payne Branch—stream (3) ... TN-4
Payne Branch—stream (2) ... TX-5
Payne Branch—stream (2) ... VA-3
Payne Branch—stream (3) ... WV-2
Payne Bridge—bridge ... TN-4
Payne Brook—stream (2) ... NY-2
Payne Brook—stream ... VT-1
Payne Cabin—locale ... ID-8
Payne Camp—locale ... MT-8
Payne Canal—canal ... UT-8
Payne Canyon—valley ... CA-9
Payne Canyon—valley ... CO-8
Payne Canyon—valley ... NM-5
Payne Canyon—valley ... OR-9
Payne Canyon—valley ... SD-7
Payne Cem ... TN-4
Payne Cem—cemetery (2) ... AL-4
Payne Cem—cemetery ... AR-4
Payne Cem—cemetery ... DC-2
Payne Cem—cemetery (3) ... GA-3
Payne Cem—cemetery (4) ... IL-6
Payne Cem—cemetery ... IN-6
Payne Cem—cemetery ... IA-7
Payne Cem—cemetery (2) ... KY-4
Payne Cem—cemetery ... LA-4
Payne Cem—cemetery ... MI-6
Payne Cem—cemetery (2) ... MS-4
Payne Cem—cemetery (6) ... MO-7
Payne Cem—cemetery (4) ... NC-3
Payne Cem—cemetery ... OK-5
Payne Cem—cemetery (6) ... TN-4
Payne Cem—cemetery ... TX-5
Payne Cem—cemetery (3) ... VA-3
Payne Cem—cemetery (4) ... WV-2
Payne Ch ... AL-4
Payne Ch—church ... MD-2
Payne Ch—church (2) ... MS-4
Payne Ch—church ... TX-5
Payne Ch—church ... VA-3
Payne Chapel—church ... AL-4
Payne Chapel—church ... GA-3
Payne Chapel—church (2) ... NC-3
Payne Chapel—church ... WV-2
Payne Chapel AME Ch—church ... AL-4
Payne Chapel Cem ... AL-4
Payne Chapel Cem—cemetery ... AL-4
Payne Chapel Cem—cemetery ... MS-4
Payne Chapel (historical)—church ... TN-4
Payne Chapel Methodist Ch
(historical)—church (2) ... AL-4
Payne Cliffs—cliff ... OR-9
Payne Corner ... VA-3
**Payne (County)**—pop pl ... OK-5
Payne County Courthouse—hist pl ... OK-5
Payne Cove ... TN-4
**Payne Cove**—pop pl ... TN-4
Payne Cove—valley (2) ... TN-4
Payne Cove Sch—school ... TN-4
Payne-Craig House—hist pl ... WI-6
Payne Creek ... OR-9
Payne Creek ... TN-4
Payne Creek—bay ... FL-3
Payne Creek—stream (2) ... AL-4
Payne Creek—stream (2) ... AR-4
Payne Creek—stream ... CA-9
Payne Creek—stream ... CO-8
Payne Creek—stream ... FL-3
Payne Creek—stream (3) ... GA-3
Payne Creek—stream (4) ... ID-8
Payne Creek—stream ... KS-7
Payne Creek—stream ... KY-4
Payne Creek—stream (2) ... MI-6
Payne Creek—stream ... MT-8
Payne Creek—stream ... NE-7
Payne Creek—stream ... NC-3
Payne Creek—stream (4) ... OR-9
Payne Creek—stream ... TX-5
Payne Creek—stream (2) ... VA-3
Payne Creek Ch—church ... FL-3
Payne Creek Ch—church ... VA-3
Payne Creek Rsvr—reservoir ... ID-8
Payne Creek Trail—trail ... CO-8
Payne-Desha House—hist pl ... KY-4
Payne Ditch—canal ... IN-6
Payne Ditch—canal ... MD-2
Payne Draw—valley ... NM-5
Payne Elementary School ... AL-4
Payne Elem Sch—school ... KS-7
Payne Ferry (historical)—locale ... AL-4
Payne Field Airp—airport ... UT-8
Payne Flat—flat ... CA-9
Payne Flat—flat ... TX-5
Payne Ford—locale ... MO-7
Payne Ford Cem—cemetery ... TN-4
Payne Gap—gap (3) ... GA-3
Payne Gap—gap ... NC-3
Payne Gap—gap (2) ... TN-4
Payne Gap—gap ... TX-5
**Payne Gap**—pop pl ... KY-4
**Payne Gap (Upper Fishpond)**—pop pl ... KY-4
Payne-Gentry House—hist pl ... MO-7
Payne Gulch—valley ... CO-8
Payne Hill—summit ... NY-2
Payne Hill—summit ... TN-4
Payne Hill—summit ... TX-5
Payne Hills—summit ... TX-5
Payne Hollow—valley ... AR-4
Payne Hollow—valley ... IN-6
Payne Hollow—valley (3) ... KY-4
Payne Hollow—valley ... MO-7
Payne Hollow—valley ... OH-6
Payne Hollow—valley ... OK-5
Payne Hollow—valley ... TN-4
Payne Hollow—valley ... WA-9
Payne Hollow—valley (2) ... WV-2
Payne Homestead—locale ... MT-8
Payne House—hist pl (2) ... KY-4
Payne Island (historical)—island ... TN-4
Payne Junction ... IA-7
Payne Knob—summit ... GA-3
Payne Knob—summit (2) ... WV-2
Payne Lake ... MI-6
Payne Lake ... MS-4
Payne Lake ... PA-2
Payne Lake—dam ... AL-4
Payne Lake—lake ... CA-9
Payne Lake—lake ... FL-3
Payne Lake—lake (2) ... MI-6
Payne Lake—lake (2) ... NY-2
Payne Lake—lake ... TX-5
Payne Lake—lake ... WI-6
Payne Lake—reservoir (2) ... AL-4
Payne Lake—reservoir ... TN-4
Payne Lake Dam—dam ... TN-4
Payne Lake Eastside Campground—park ... AL-4
Payne Lake (historical)—lake ... TN-4
Payne Lake Lookout Tower ... AL-4
Payne Lake Rec Area ... AL-4
Payne Lake Westside Campground—park ... AL-4
Payne Lateral—canal ... ID-8
Payne Ledge—cliff ... ME-1
Payne Lookout Tower—tower ... AL-4
Payne Mesa—summit (2) ... CO-8
Payne Mill—hist pl ... KY-4
Payne Mine—mine ... CA-9
Payne Mine—mine ... UT-8
Payne Mine—mine ... WA-9
Payne Mtn—summit ... AR-4
Payne Mtn—summit (2) ... GA-3
Payne Mtn—summit (2) ... NY-2
Payne Mtn—summit ... NC-3
Payne Mtn—summit ... TX-5
Payne Number 1 Mine
(underground)—mine ... TN-4
Payne Oil Field—oilfield ... OK-5
Payne Opening Mine
(underground)—mine ... AL-4
Payne Park—park ... FL-3
Payne Park—park ... NY-2
Payne Peak—summit ... CA-9
Payne Place—locale ... CA-9
Payne Place—locale ... NM-5
Payne Place Cem—cemetery ... PA-2
Payne Placer—mine ... OR-9
Payne Point—cape ... MD-2
Payne Point—cape ... WI-6
Payne Pond ... FL-3

Peach Mountain ... VA-3
Peach Mountain Cem—cemetery ... OH-6
Peach Mountain Ch—church ... OH-6
Peach Mtn—summit ... MI-6
Peach Mtn—summit ... OH-6
Peach Mtn—summit ... TX-5
Peach Orchard ... PA-2
Peach Orchard—locale ... KY-4
**Peach Orchard**—pop pl ... AR-4
**Peach Orchard**—pop pl ... FL-3
**Peach Orchard**—pop pl ... GA-3
**Peach Orchard**—pop pl ... MO-7
**Peach Orchard**—pop pl ... TN-4
Peach Orchard, The—locale ... PA-2
Peach Orchard, The—locale ... WY-8
Peach Orchard Bluff—locale ... AR-4
Peach Orchard Branch—stream (4) ... KY-4
Peachorchard Branch—stream ... KY-4
Peach Orchard Branch—stream ... SC-3
Peachorchard Branch—stream ... WV-2
Peach Orchard Branch—stream ... WV-2
Peach Orchard Brook—stream ... NJ-2
Peach Orchard Cove ... MD-2
Peachorchard Cove—bay ... MD-2
Peach Orchard Cove—valley ... TN-4
Peach Orchard Creek ... MD-2
Peachorchard Creek—stream ... MD-2
Peach Orchard Creek—stream ... MI-6
Peach Orchard Creek—stream ... MO-7
Peach Orchard Creek—stream ... NC-3
Peach Orchard Draw—valley ... NM-5
Peach Orchard Flat—flat ... WY-8
Peach Orchard Gap—gap (2) ... TN-4
Peach Orchard Gap—gap ... VA-3
Peach Orchard Gut—gut ... VA-3
**Peach Orchard Heights**—pop pl ... MD-2
Peach Orchard Hill ... MA-1
Peach Orchard Hill—summit ... AL-4
Peach Orchard Hill—summit (2) ... KY-4
Peach Orchard Hill—summit ... MA-1
Peach Orchard Hill—summit ... OH-6
Peach Orchard Hollow—valley (2) ... KY-4
Peach Orchard Hollow—valley ... MO-7
Peach Orchard Hollow—valley ... PA-2
Peach Orchard Hollow—valley (2) ... TN-4
Peach Orchard Knob—summit (2) ... KY-4
Peach Orchard Mine—mine ... TN-4
Peach Orchard Mtn—summit ... SC-3
Peach Orchard Mtn—summit ... TN-4
Peach Orchard Mtn—summit ... VA-3
Peachorchard Point ... VA-3
Peach Orchard Point—cape ... NY-2
Peach Orchard Point—cape ... OH-6
Peachorchard Point—cape ... VA-3
Peach Orchard Point—cliff ... CO-8
Peach Orchard Ridge—ridge ... AL-4
Peach Orchard Ridge—ridge (2) ... KY-4
Peach Orchard Ridge—ridge ... TN-4
Peach Orchard Ridge—ridge ... WV-2
Peach Orchard Sch—school ... KY-4
Peach Orchard Spring ... AZ-5
Peach Orchard Spring—spring ... AZ-5
Peach Orchard Tank—reservoir ... TX-5
Peach Orchard (Township of)—civ div ... IL-6
Peach Orchard Trail—trail ... WV-2
Peach Orchard Windmill—locale ... NM-5
Peach Peak—summit ... NV-8
Peach Plains Sch—school ... MI-6
Peach Point ... MA-1
Peach Point—cape ... MD-2
Peach Pond—lake ... DE-2
Peach Pond—lake ... TX-5
Peach Post Office (historical)—building ... TN-4
Peach Pu—locale ... AZ-5
Peach Queen Camp—locale ... AL-4
Peach Ridge ... PA-2
Peach Ridge—ridge ... LA-4
Peach Ridge—ridge ... OH-6
Peach Ridge—ridge ... PA-2
Peach Ridge—ridge ... TX-5
Peach Ridge—ridge ... VA-3
Peach Ridge—ridge ... WV-2
Peach Run—stream ... MD-2
Peach Run—stream ... VA-3
Peachs Point—cape ... MA-1
Peach Spring ... AZ-5
Peach Spring—spring (4) ... AZ-5
Peach Spring—spring ... NV-8
Peach Spring—spring ... NM-5
Peach Spring Canyon—valley ... NM-5
**Peach Springs**—pop pl ... AZ-5
Peach Springs—spring ... AZ-5
Peach Springs Airp—airport ... AZ-5
Peach Springs Canyon—valley ... AZ-5
Peach Springs Post Office—building ... AZ-5
Peach Springs RR Station—building ... AZ-5
Peach Springs Wash—stream ... AZ-5
Peachstone Camp Hollow—valley ... TN-4
Peachstone Gulch—valley ... CA-9
Peachstone Shoals—bar ... GA-3
Peach Street Ch—church ... NC-3
Peach Tank—reservoir (2) ... AZ-5
Peachton—locale ... CA-9
**Peachtree**—pop pl ... NC-3
Peachtree, Lake—reservoir ... GA-3
Peachtree Bald ... NC-3
Peachtree Bar—bar ... CA-9
Peachtree Canal—canal ... GA-3
Peachtree Canyon—valley (2) ... CA-9
Peachtree Canyon—valley ... NM-5
Peachtree Center—uninc pl ... GA-3
Peachtree Ch—church ... MO-7
Peachtree Ch—church (2) ... NC-3
Peach Tree Ch—church ... TX-5
Peachtree Christian Church—hist pl ... GA-3
Peach Tree Church ... MS-4
Peach Tree City ... GA-3
**Peachtree City**—pop pl ... GA-3
**Peach Tree Condominium**—pop pl ... UT-8
Peachtree Corners—post sta ... GA-3
Peachtree Creek ... NC-3
Peachtree Creek—stream ... AL-4
Peach Tree Creek—stream ... CA-9
Peachtree Creek—stream ... GA-3
Peach Tree Creek—stream ... MS-4
Peachtree Creek—stream (2) ... NC-3
Peachtree Creek—stream ... TX-5
Peachtree Creek—stream ... WV-2
Peachtree Crossing—locale ... CA-9
Peachtree Crossing—locale ... OK-5
Peachtree Elem Sch—school ... NC-3
Peachtree Flat—flat ... CA-9
Peachtree Fork—stream ... KY-4
Peachtree Fork—stream ... MO-7
Peachtree Gap—gap ... NC-3
Peachtree Gap—gap ... TN-4
Peachtree Golf Course—other ... GA-3
Peachtree Heights Park—hist pl ... GA-3
Peachtree Highlands Hist Dist—hist pl ... GA-3
Peachtree Hills Country Club—locale ... NC-3
**Peach Tree Hills (subdivision)**—pop pl ... AL-4
Peach Tree Hollow—valley ... KY-4
Peachtree Hollow—valley ... PA-2
Peachtree Island—island ... LA-4
Peach Tree Island—island ... MS-4
Peachtree Lake—lake ... AR-4
Peachtree Lake—lake ... GA-3
Peachtree Lake—lake ... SC-3
Peachtree Landing—locale ... NC-3
Peachtree Landing—locale ... SC-3
Peachtree Point—cape ... MD-2
Peachtree Point—cape ... VA-3
Peach Tree Point—cliff ... TX-5
Peach Tree Point Lake—lake ... TX-5
Peach Tree Ridge—ridge ... FL-3
Peach Tree Ridge—ridge ... MO-7
Peachtree Ridge—ridge ... WV-2
Peachtree Road Ch—church (2) ... GA-3
Peachtree Run—stream ... WV-2
Peachtree Slope Mine (underground)—mine ... AL-4
Peachtree Southern Railway Station—hist pl ... GA-3
Peach Tree Spring—spring ... AZ-5
Peach Tree Spring—spring (2) ... CA-9
Peach Tree Springs—spring ... CA-9
**Peach Tree Subdivision**—pop pl ... UT-8
Peach Tree Tank—reservoir (3) ... AZ-5
Peachtree Treatment Plant—building ... NC-3
Peachtree Valley—valley ... CA-9
Peach Tree Village—locale ... TX-5
Peach Tree Village Cem—cemetery ... TX-5
Peachuhaley ... MS-4
**Peach Valley**—pop pl ... SC-3
Peach Valley—valley ... CO-8
Peach Valley Ch—church ... TN-4
Peach Valley Dam No 1—dam ... CO-8
Peachville Mtn—summit ... AZ-5
Peachville Tank—reservoir ... AZ-5
Peachville Wash—stream ... AZ-5
Peach Wash—stream ... AZ-5
**Peachwood**—pop pl ... MD-2
**Peachwood Estates Subdivision**—pop pl ... UT-8
**Peachwood Subdivision**—pop pl ... UT-8
Peachy Canyon—valley (2) ... CA-9
Peachys Creek—stream ... CA-9
Peacock—locale ... AL-4
Peacock—locale ... VA-3
**Peacock**—pop pl ... MI-6
**Peacock**—pop pl ... TX-5
Peacock Apartments—hist pl ... IN-6
Peacock Bald—summit ... MO-7
Peacock Branch—stream ... AL-4
Peacock Branch—stream ... FL-3
Peacock Branch—stream ... KY-4
Peacock Branch—stream ... NC-3
Peacock Branch—stream ... TN-4
Peacock Brook—stream ... NH-1
Peacock Brook—stream ... NY-2
Peacock Canyon—valley ... AZ-5
Peacock Canyon—valley ... CA-9
Peacock Canyon—valley ... NV-8
Peacock Canyon—valley ... NM-5
Peacock Canyon—valley ... TX-5
Peacock Cave—cave ... AL-4
Peacock Cave—cave ... WV-2
Peacock Cem—cemetery ... MI-6
Peacock Cem—cemetery ... MS-4
Peacock Cem—cemetery ... NJ-2
Peacock Cem—cemetery ... TN-4
Peacock Coal Mine—mine ... CO-8
Peacock Corners—locale ... NY-2
**Peacock Corners**—pop pl ... MD-2
Peacock Creek ... TX-5
Peacock Creek—stream ... AK-9
Peacock Creek—stream (2) ... CA-9
Peacock Creek—stream ... GA-3
Peacock Creek—stream ... MT-8
Peacock Creek—stream ... OR-9
Peacock Creek—stream (3) ... TX-5
Peacock Creek Trail—trail ... MT-8
Peacock Crossing—locale ... NC-3
Peacock Crossroads—locale ... NC-3
Peacock Ditch—canal ... MI-6
Peacock Ditch—stream ... GA-3
Peacock Drain—canal ... MI-6
Peacock Draw—valley ... NM-5
Peacock Field—flat ... TN-4
Peacock Flat—flat ... HI-9
Peacock Flat Trail—trail ... HI-9
Peacock Gap Golf Country Club—other ... CA-9
Peacock Hammock—island ... FL-3
Peacock Hill—ridge ... WI-6
Peacock Hill—summit ... CT-1
Peacock Hill—summit ... ME-1
Peacock Hill—summit ... NH-1
Peacock Hill—summit ... NM-5
Peacock Hill—summit ... NY-2
Peacock Hill—summit ... WI-6
Peacock Hollow—valley ... AL-4
Peacock Hollow—valley ... OK-5
Peacock Hollow—valley ... TN-4
Peacock House—hist pl ... KY-4
Peacock Island—island ... AK-9
Peacock Island—island ... CT-1
Peacock Island—island ... KY-4
Peacock Lake—lake ... FL-3
Peacock Lake—lake ... GA-3
Peacock Lake—lake ... MI-6
Peacock Lake—lake ... OR-9
Peacock Lake—lake ... WI-6
Peacock Lake—reservoir ... MS-4
Peacock Lake Dam—dam ... MS-4
Peacock Military Acad—school ... TX-5
Peacock Mill Branch—stream ... AL-4
Peacock-Miller House—hist pl ... KY-4
Peacock Mine—mine (2) ... CA-9
Peacock Mine (underground)—mine ... AL-4
Peacock Mountains—range ... AZ-5
Peacock Mtn—summit ... NY-2
Peacock Mtn—summit ... WA-9
Peacock Number 1 Dam—dam ... SD-7
Peacock Park—park ... FL-3
Peacock Peak—summit ... AZ-5
Peacock Point—cape ... AK-9
Peacock Point—cape (2) ... CA-9
Peacock Point—cape ... NY-2
Peacock Point—range ... MP-9
Peacock Pond—lake ... FL-3
Peacock Pond Rsvr—reservoir ... OR-9
Peacock Pool—lake ... CO-8
Peacock Ranch—locale ... NV-8
Peacock Ranch—locale ... NM-5
Peacock Ravine—valley ... CA-9
Peacock Ridge—ridge ... MN-6
Peacock Road Coulee—valley ... WI-6
Peacock Saddle—gap ... CA-9
Peacock Sch—school ... MO-7
Peacocks Crossing ... NC-3
Peacocks Crossing—locale ... GA-3
Peacocks Crossroads—locale ... NC-3
Peacock Slough—gut ... FL-3
Peacock Slough—gut ... IL-6
Peacock Spit—bar ... WA-9
Peacocks Place (historical)—locale ... UT-8
Peacocks Pocket—bay ... FL-3
Peacock Spring ... AZ-5
Peacock Spring—spring ... AZ-5
Peacock Spring—spring ... NV-8
Peacock Springs—spring ... FL-3
Peacock Tank—reservoir ... TX-5
Peacock Tavern—hist pl ... ME-1
**Peacock (Township of)**—pop pl ... MI-6
Peacock Valley—valley ... WI-6
**Peacock Village (subdivision)**—pop pl (2) ... AZ-5
Peacock Wash—arroyo ... AZ-5
Peacock Wildlife Mngmt Area—park ... UT-8
Pea Cove—bay ... ME-1
Pea Cove—locale ... ME-1
Pea Creek ... AL-4
Pea Creek—stream (2) ... AL-4
Pea Creek—stream ... CA-9
Pea Creek—stream ... GA-3
Pea Creek—stream ... ID-8
Pea Creek—stream ... OK-5
Pea Creek—stream ... SC-3
Pea Creek—stream ... TX-5
Pea Creek—stream ... WI-6
Pea Creek Ch—church ... AL-4
Peaden—locale ... FL-3
Peaden Bridge—bridge ... FL-3
Peadenville—locale ... TX-5
Pead Hill—summit ... NH-1
Pea Farm Church ... MS-4
Peaff Town ... NC-3
Pea Field Bayou ... MO-7
Peafield Bayou—stream ... MS-4
Pea Gap—gap ... NC-3
Peagler Store—locale ... MS-4
**Peagreen**—pop pl ... CO-8
Pea Green Cem—cemetery ... CO-8
Pea Green Corner—locale ... CO-8
Pea Green Sch—school ... IL-6
**Peahala Park**—pop pl ... NJ-2
Peahi—civil ... HI-9
Peahi Gulch—valley ... HI-9
Pea Hill—locale ... NC-3
**Pea Hill**—pop pl ... MD-2
Pea Hill Branch—stream ... MD-2
Pea Hill Creek—stream ... NC-3
Pea Hill Creek—stream ... VA-3
Pea Hill Gut—stream ... MD-2
Peahinaia Mountain ... HI-9
Peahi Rsvr—reservoir ... HI-9
**Peaine (Township of)**—pop pl ... MI-6
Peairs Homestead—hist pl ... OH-6
Pea Island ... ME-1
Pea Island—island ... MA-1
Pea Island—island ... NY-2
Pea Island—island ... NC-3
Pea Island—island ... SC-3
Pea Island—rock ... MA-1
Pea Island Bay—bay ... NC-3
Pea Island Creek—stream ... NC-3
Pea Island Natl Wildlife Ref—park ... NC-3
Pea Island Point—cape ... NC-3
Peak—locale ... ND-7
**Peak**—pop pl ... SC-3
**Peak**—pop pl ... TN-4
Peak, George B., House—hist pl ... IA-7
Peak, Henry C., House—hist pl ... KY-4
Peak, Mount—summit ... MA-1
Peak, The—summit ... CA-9
Peak, The—summit ... MT-8
Peak, The—summit (4) ... NC-3
Peak, The—summit ... PA-2
Peak, The—summit ... UT-8
Peak, The—summit (2) ... VA-3
Peak-a-boo Rock—summit ... UT-8
Peakamoose ... NY-2
Peak Branch—stream ... VA-3
Peak Brook—stream ... VT-1
Peak Canyon—valley ... CA-9
Peak Canyon—valley (2) ... NV-8
Peak Canyon—valley (2) ... UT-8
Peak Cem—cemetery ... OH-6
Peak Cem—cemetery (2) ... VA-3
Peak Cemetery ... TN-4
Peak Ch—church ... AR-4
Peak Ch—church ... VA-3
Peak Chapel—church (2) ... TN-4
Peak Cove—valley ... NC-3
Peak Creek—stream (2) ... ID-8
Peak Creek—stream ... NY-2
Peak Creek—stream ... NC-3
Peak Creek—stream ... OR-9
Peak Creek—stream ... VA-3
Peak Creek—stream ... WA-9
Peak Creek Ch—church ... NC-3
Peak Creek (Township of)—fmr MCD ... NC-3
Peake ... VA-3
Peake Brook—stream ... CT-1
Peake Canyon—valley ... NM-5
Peaked Butte—summit ... SD-7
Peaked Cliff—cliff ... MA-1
Peaked Creek—stream ... CA-9
Peakedend ... MS-4
Peaked Hill—summit ... CA-9
Peaked Hill—summit (3) ... ME-1
Peaked Hill—summit (2) ... MA-1
Peaked Hill—summit (7) ... NH-1
Peaked Hill—summit (4) ... NY-2
Peaked Hill Bar—bar ... MA-1
Peaked Hill Pond—lake ... NH-1
Peaked Hill Pond—lake ... NY-2
Peaked Hills—summit ... NY-2
Peaked Hill Trail—trail ... NY-2
Peaked Knob—summit ... NC-3
Peaked Knob—summit ... TN-4
Peaked Mountain Brook—stream ... NY-2
Peaked Mountain Lake—lake ... NY-2
Peaked Mountain Pond—lake (3) ... ME-1
Peaked Mountain Pond—lake ... NY-2
Peaked Mtn—summit (13) ... ME-1
Peaked Mtn—summit ... MA-1
Peaked Mtn—summit (3) ... NH-1
Peaked Mtn—summit (3) ... NY-2
Peaked Mtn—summit ... PA-2
Peaked Mtn—summit (2) ... VT-1
Peaked Prairie—flat ... CA-9
Peaked Rock—pillar ... RI-1
Peaked Rock—summit ... MA-1
Peaked Rock—summit ... NY-2
Peaked Top—summit ... NC-3
Peaked Top—summit ... TN-4
Peak Eight—summit ... CA-9
Peakes Cem—cemetery ... OH-6
Peake Sch—school ... AR-4
Peake Sch—school ... VA-3
Peakes Island ... ME-1
Peak Hill—summit ... OK-5
**Peak (historical)**—pop pl ... OR-9
Peak Hollow—valley ... VA-3
Peak-Hornsby Cem—cemetery ... TN-4
Peak House—hist pl ... KY-4
Peak House—hist pl ... MA-1
Peak Interchange—crossing ... ND-7
Peak Island ... ME-1
Peak Island—island ... AK-9
Peak Island—other ... ME-1
Peak Knob—summit (2) ... NC-3
Peak Knob—summit ... VA-3
Peak Lake ... NV-8
Peak Lake—reservoir ... WY-8
Peakland—locale ... TN-4
**Peakland**—pop pl ... VA-3
Peakland Baptist Church ... TN-4
Peakland Cemetery ... TN-4
Peakland Ch—church ... TN-4
Peakland Post Office (historical)—building ... TN-4
Peakland Sch (historical)—school ... TN-4
Peak Log Pond—reservoir ... OR-9
Peak Mine—mine ... CO-8
Peak Mountain ... VA-3
Peak Mtn—summit (2) ... CA-9
Peak Mtn—summit ... CT-1
Peak Mtn—summit ... KY-4
Peak Mtn—summit ... NY-2
Peak Mtn—summit ... NC-3
Peak o' Moose ... NY-2
Peak One Campground—locale ... CO-8
Peak Post Office (historical)—building ... TN-4
Peak Ridge—ridge (2) ... TN-4
Peak Ridge—ridge ... WV-2
Peak Run—stream ... VA-3
Peaks ... TN-4
**Peaks**—pop pl ... VA-3
Peaks, The—summit ... CA-9
Peaks, The—summit ... OR-9
Peaks, The—summit ... UT-8
Peaks Bald—summit ... NC-3
Peaks Brook—stream ... NY-2
Peaks Cem—cemetery ... NE-7
Peaks Ch—church (2) ... VA-3
Peak Sch—school ... TX-5
Peaks Corner ... AL-4
Peaks Creek—stream ... LA-4
Peaks Hill—summit ... NC-3
Peak's Island ... ME-1
Peaks Island—island ... ME-1
**Peaks Island**—pop pl ... ME-1
Peaks Island Ferry—trail ... ME-1
Peaks Island (Peak Island) ... ME-1
Peaks-kenny State Park—park ... ME-1
Peaks (Magisterial District)—fmr MCD ... VA-3
**Peaks Mill**—pop pl ... KY-4
Peaks Mill (CCD)—cens area ... KY-4
Peaks Mill Creek ... TN-4
Peaks Mill (historical)—locale ... TN-4
Peaks Of Otter Rec Area—park ... VA-3
Peak Spring—spring ... AZ-5
Peak Spring—spring (2) ... NV-8
Peak Spring Canyon ... NV-8
Peaks Ridge—ridge ... CA-9
Peaks Spring—spring ... UT-8
Peaks Tank—reservoir ... NM-5
Peaks Trail—trail ... CO-8
Peaks Turnout ... VA-3
Peaks View Ch—church ... VA-3
Peaksville—locale ... VA-3
**Peaksville**—pop pl ... MO-7
Peaksville Cem—cemetery ... MO-7
Peak Swamp—stream ... NC-3
Peak Tank—reservoir ... NM-5
Peak Trail, The—trail ... VA-3
Peak Valley—valley ... NC-3
Peak Valley Ch—church ... NC-3
Peak View Ch—church ... NC-3
Peak View Golf Course—other ... CO-8
**Peakville**—pop pl ... NY-2
Peak X—summit ... MT-8
Peak Y—summit ... MT-8
Peaky Mtn—summit ... TN-4
Peaky Ridge—ridge ... MO-7
Peaky Top ... TN-4
Peaky Top—summit ... TN-4
Peak 6—summit ... WA-9
Peak 8200 ... WA-9
Peal, Mount—summit ... MT-8
Pea Lake—lake ... MN-6
Pea Lake—lake ... MT-8
Pea Landing ... NC-3
Peal Bend—bend ... MO-7
Peal Bend Bridge (historical)—bridge ... MO-7
Peal Bend Sch (historical)—school ... MO-7
Peal Cem—cemetery ... MO-7
Peal Creek ... ID-8
Peal Creek—stream ... OK-5
Peale—locale ... PA-2
**Peale**—pop pl ... PA-2
Peale, Charles Willson, House—hist pl ... PA-2
Peale, Mount—summit ... UT-8
Pea Ledges—bar ... ME-1
Peale Island—island ... WY-8
Peale Island—island ... MP-9
Peale Passage—channel ... WA-9
Pealer Point—cape ... VA-3
Pealertown—locale ... PA-2
Peale's Baltimore Museum—hist pl ... MD-2
Peales Crossroads—locale ... VA-3
Pealiquor Landing—locale ... MD-2
Pealog Branch—stream ... VA-3
Peal Sch (abandoned)—school ... MO-7
Peals Chapel—church ... KY-4
Pealy Flat—flat ... ID-8
Peamoa Valley—valley ... HI-9
Pea Monk Branch—stream ... TX-5
Peanaskenamset ... MA-1
Peanaz Creek—stream ... KS-7
Peanaz Hill—summit ... KS-7
Pea Neck—cape ... VA-3
Peankishaw Bend—bend ... IL-6
Peankishaw Bend—bend ... IN-6
Peanut—locale ... AR-4
**Peanut**—pop pl ... CA-9
**Peanut**—pop pl (2) ... PA-2
**Peanut**—pop pl ... TN-4
**Peanut**—pop pl ... WV-2
Peanut Belt Research Station—locale ... NC-3
Peanut Creek—stream (2) ... ID-8
Peanut Creek—stream ... WY-8
Peanut Dam—dam ... VT-1
Peanut Hollow—valley ... TN-4
Peanut Hump—summit ... WA-9
Peanut Island—island ... FL-3
Peanut Island—island ... ME-1
Peanut Island—island ... MN-6
Peanut Island Park—park ... FL-3
Peanut Lake—flat ... OR-9
Peanut Lake—lake ... AK-9
Peanut Lake—lake ... CO-8
Peanut Lake—lake (3) ... MI-6
Peanut Lake—lake ... MN-6
Peanut Lake—lake ... WI-6
Peanut Mine—mine ... CO-8
Peanut Mtn—summit ... AR-4
Peanut No 3 Mine—mine ... CO-8
Peanut Post Office (historical)—building ... TN-4
Peanut Ridge—ridge ... AL-4
Peanut Ridge—ridge ... AR-4
Peanuts Park—park ... WI-6
**Peapack**—pop pl ... NJ-2
**Peapack and Gladstone (corporate name for Gladstone)**—pop pl ... NJ-2
Peapack Brook—stream ... NJ-2
Pea Pass—gut ... FL-3
Pea Patch ... DE-2
Peapatch—locale ... VA-3
Peapatch—locale ... WV-2
Peapatch Hollow—valley ... TN-4
Pea Patch Island—island ... DE-2
Pea Patch Island Dike—dam ... DE-2
Pea Patch Lake—lake ... TX-5
Peapatch Ridge—ridge ... MD-2
Pea Patch Shoal—bar ... DE-2
Peapea ... HI-9
Peapea—summit ... HI-9
Peapod Rocks—island ... WA-9
Pea Pond—lake ... NY-2
Pea Porridge Pond ... NH-1
Pea Porridge Pond—lake ... NH-1
Pea Prong Creek—stream ... AR-4
Peaquarter Swamp—swamp ... VA-3
**Pear**—pop pl ... WV-2
Pearall Run—stream ... PA-2
**Pearblossom**—pop pl ... CA-9
Pearblossom Pumping Plant—other ... CA-9
Pear Branch—stream ... TX-5
Pear Butte—summit ... WA-9
Pear Butte Trail—trail ... WA-9
Pear Canal—canal ... CA-9
Pear Canyon—valley ... TX-5
Pearce ... ND-7
**Pearce**—pop pl ... AL-4
**Pearce**—pop pl ... AZ-5
Pearce, George A., House—hist pl ... GA-3
Pearce, John, House—hist pl ... NM-5
Pearce, Nathaniel, House—hist pl ... RI-1
Pearce Branch—stream ... TN-4
Pearce Branch Quarry—mine ... TN-4
Pearce Bridge—bridge ... FL-3
Pearce Brook—stream ... ME-1
Pearce Canal—canal ... FL-3
Pearce Canyon—valley ... AZ-5
Pearce Cem—cemetery ... AZ-5
Pearce Cem—cemetery ... GA-3
Pearce Cem—cemetery ... IL-6
Pearce Cem—cemetery ... PA-2
Pearce Ch—church ... MS-4
Pearce Creek—stream ... MD-2
Pearce Creek—stream ... WY-8
Pearce Crossroads ... NC-3
**Pearce Crossroads**—pop pl ... NC-3
Pearce Ditch—canal ... IN-6
Pearce Draw—valley ... WY-8
Pearce Elem Sch—school ... AZ-5
Pearce Ferry—locale ... AZ-5
Pearce General Store—hist pl ... AZ-5
Pearce Gulch—valley (2) ... OR-9
Pearce Hill—summit ... AZ-5
**Pearce (historical)**—pop pl ... MS-4
Pearce Island—island ... MA-1
Pearce Lake—lake ... MN-6
Pearce Lake—lake ... TX-5
Pearce Lake—lake ... WI-6
Pearce Lake Dam—dam ... MS-4
Pearce Landing—locale ... NC-3
Pearce Lateral—canal ... WY-8
Pear Cem—cemetery ... SC-3
Pearce-McAllister Cottage—hist pl ... CO-8
Pearce Mtn ... AZ-5
Pearce Neck—cape ... MD-2
Pearce Number Seven Mine (underground)—mine ... AL-4
Pearce Peak—summit ... CA-9
Pearce Point—summit ... OR-9
Pearce Pond—reservoir ... RI-1
Pearce Pond Dam—dam ... NC-3
Pearce Post Office—building ... AZ-5
Pearce Ranch—locale ... AZ-5
Pearce Ranch—locale ... NE-7
**Pearces**—pop pl ... NC-3
Pearce Sch—school ... NV-8
Pearce Sch—school ... TX-5
Pearces Creek ... MD-2
Pearces Creek—stream ... MS-4
Pearces Island ... MA-1
Pearces Mill ... AL-4
Pearce's Mill—hist pl ... AL-4
Pearces Mill Cem—cemetery ... AL-4
Pearces Mill Creek—stream ... AL-4
Pearces Mill Creek—stream ... MS-4
Pearces Mills—locale ... AL-4
Pearces Mill (Township of)—fmr MCD ... NC-3
Pearces Neck ... MD-2
Pearces Pond—lake ... GA-3
Pearces Pond—reservoir ... NC-3
Pearce Tank—reservoir ... AZ-5
Pearce Well—well ... AZ-5
Pearce Well—well ... WY-8
Pearcey Creek—stream ... NC-3
Pearch—locale ... VA-3
Pearch Creek—stream ... CA-9
Pearch Creek Campground—locale ... CA-9
Pearch Creek Mine—mine ... CA-9
**Pearcot**—pop pl ... WA-9
Pear Creek—stream ... ID-8
Pear Creek—stream ... MT-8
**Pearcy**—pop pl ... AR-4
Pearcy, J. H., House—hist pl ... TX-5
Pearcy Branch—stream ... TN-4
Pearcy Camp—locale ... IL-6
Pearcy Island—island ... OR-9
Pearcy Mountain—ridge ... AR-4
Pearcy Run—stream ... WV-2
**Peardale**—pop pl ... CA-9
Peard Bay—bay ... AK-9
Peardon Hill—summit ... CA-9
Pear Drain—canal ... CA-9
Pear Drain Waste—canal ... CA-9
Peare Cem—cemetery ... ME-1
Pear Hollow—valley ... TX-5
Pea Ridge ... AL-4
Pea Ridge ... MS-4
Pea Ridge ... TN-4
Pea Ridge ... VA-3
Pea Ridge—locale ... KY-4
Pea Ridge—locale ... ME-1
Pea Ridge—locale ... MO-7
Pea Ridge—locale ... NC-3
**Pea Ridge**—pop pl (4) ... AL-4
**Pea Ridge**—pop pl (2) ... AR-4
**Pea Ridge**—pop pl (2) ... NC-3
**Pea Ridge**—pop pl (2) ... TN-4
Pea Ridge—ridge (7) ... AL-4
Pea Ridge—ridge (4) ... AR-4
Pea Ridge—ridge ... FL-3
Pea Ridge—ridge ... GA-3
Pea Ridge—ridge (2) ... IL-6
Pea Ridge—ridge (2) ... IN-6
Pea Ridge—ridge (10) ... KY-4
Pea Ridge—ridge ... MD-2
Pea Ridge—ridge ... MN-6
Pea Ridge—ridge (3) ... MS-4
Pea Ridge—ridge (6) ... MO-7
Pea Ridge—ridge ... MT-8
Pea Ridge—ridge (2) ... NC-3
Pea Ridge—ridge ... OH-6
Pea Ridge—ridge ... OR-9
Pea Ridge—ridge (13) ... TN-4
Pea Ridge—ridge ... TX-5
Pea Ridge—ridge (2) ... VA-3
Pea Ridge—ridge (3) ... WV-2
Pea Ridge Acad (historical)—school ... MS-4
Pea Ridge Battlefield—locale ... AR-4
Pea Ridge Cem—cemetery ... AL-4
Pea Ridge Cem—cemetery ... GA-3
Pea Ridge Cem—cemetery ... MS-4
Pea Ridge Cem—cemetery (3) ... MO-7
Pea Ridge Cem—cemetery ... TN-4
Pea Ridge Cem—cemetery ... WV-2
Pea Ridge Ch ... AL-4
Pea Ridge Ch—church (4) ... AL-4
Pea Ridge Ch—church ... AR-4
Pea Ridge Ch—church ... FL-3
Pea Ridge Ch—church ... KY-4
Pea Ridge Ch—church (3) ... MO-7
Pea Ridge Ch of Christ—church ... AL-4
Pea Ridge Ch of Christ—church ... TN-4
Pea Ridge Creek ... MO-7
Pea Ridge Creek—stream ... MO-7
**Pea Ridge Crossroads**—pop pl ... AL-4
Pea Ridge Elem Sch—school ... FL-3
Pea Ridge Hall (abandoned)—building ... MO-7
Pea Ridge Hollow—valley ... AR-4
Pea Ridge Hollow—valley ... KY-4
Pea Ridge Hollow—valley (3) ... MO-7
Pea Ridge House of Prayer ... AL-4
Pea Ridge Mine—mine ... MO-7
**Pea Ridge (Mount Moriah)**—pop pl ... TN-4
Pea Ridge Natl Military Park—hist pl ... AR-4
Pea Ridge Number 1 Mine (surface)—mine ... AL-4
Pea Ridge Post Office (historical)—building ... MS-4
Pea Ridge Post Office (historical)—building ... TN-4
**Pea Ridge (Sand Lick)**—pop pl ... KY-4
Pea Ridge Sch—school ... AL-4
Pea Ridge Sch—school ... IL-6
Pea Ridge Sch—school ... KY-4
Pea Ridge Sch—school (3) ... MO-7
Pea Ridge Sch—school ... OK-5
Pea Ridge Sch—school ... TN-4
Pea Ridge Sch—school ... WV-2
Pea Ridge Sch—school ... WI-6
Pea Ridge Sch (historical)—school ... AL-4
Pea Ridge Sch (historical)—school ... MS-4
Pea Ridge Sch (historical)—school ... MO-7
Pea Ridge Sch (historical)—school ... TN-4
Pea Ridge School (historical)—locale ... MO-7
Pea Ridge Store ... TN-4
**Pea Ridge (subdivision)**—pop pl ... AL-4
**Pea Ridge (Township of)**—pop pl ... IL-6
**Pearisburg**—pop pl ... VA-3
**Pearisburg (sta.) (Bluff City)**—pop pl ... VA-3
Pearis Mtn ... VA-3

Pearis Mtn—*summit* ... VA-3
Pearis Thompson Branch—*stream* ... VA-3
Pea River—*stream* ... AL-4
Pea River—*stream* ... FL-3
Pea River Battleground (historical)—*locale* ... AL-4
Pea River Bridge—*bridge* ... AL-4
Pea River Cem—*cemetery* (2) ... AL-4
Pea River Ch—*church* (2) ... AL-4
Pea River P. O. (historical)—*locale* ... AL-4
Pea River Power Company Hydroelectric Facility—*hist pl* ... AL-4
*Pea River Presbyterian Church* ... AL-4
Pea River Sch—*school* ... AL-4
*Pearl* ... MP-9
Pearl—*locale* ... CO-8
Pearl—*locale* ... GA-3
Pearl—*locale* ... ID-8
Pearl—*locale* ... KS-7
Pearl—*locale* ... KY-4
Pearl—*locale* ... LA-4
Pearl—*locale* ... MS-4
Pearl—*locale* ... TX-5
Pearl—*locale* ... WA-9
Pearl—*locale* ... VI-3
**Pearl**—*pop pl* ... IL-6
**Pearl**—*pop pl* ... MD-2
**Pearl**—*pop pl* ... MI-6
**Pearl**—*pop pl* ... MS-4
**Pearl**—*pop pl* ... MO-7
**Pearl**—*pop pl* ... PA-2
**Pearl**—*pop pl* ... UT-8
**Pearl**—*pop pl* ... VT-1
Pearl, Lake—*lake* (5) ... FL-3
Pearl, Lake—*reservoir* ... AL-4
Pearl, Lake—*reservoir* ... MA-1
*Pearl Acad* ... TN-4
*Pear Lake* ... MN-6
Pear Lake—*lake* ... AK-9
Pear Lake—*lake* (2) ... CA-9
Pear Lake—*lake* (3) ... CO-8
Pear Lake—*lake* ... MI-6
Pear Lake—*lake* (3) ... MN-6
Pear Lake—*lake* (3) ... MT-8
Pear Lake—*lake* ... NE-7
Pear Lake—*lake* ... OR-9
Pear Lake—*lake* ... UT-8
Pear Lake—*lake* (3) ... WA-9
Pear Lake—*lake* ... WI-6
Pear Lake Camp—*locale* ... OR-9
Pear Lake Ski Hut—*hist pl* ... CA-9
**Pearland**—*pop pl* ... CA-9
**Pearland**—*pop pl* ... TX-5
Pearl and Hermes Atoll—*island* ... HI-9
*Pearl and Hermes Reef* ... HI-9
Pearl and Hermes Reef—*bar* ... HI-9
Pearl and Hermes Reef—*island* ... MP-9
Pearland Park—*park* ... CA-9
Pear Lateral—*canal* ... ID-8
Pear Lateral One—*canal* ... CA-9
Pearl Bank—*bar* ... FL-3
Pearl Basin—*basin* ... MT-8
Pearl Basin—*bay* ... FL-3
Pearl Bay—*bay* ... FL-3
Pearl Bay—*bay* ... VT-1
Pearl Bayou—*bay* ... FL-3
Pearl Bayou—*gut* ... LA-4
Pearl Bayou—*stream* ... LA-4
Pearl Bayou—*stream* ... MS-4
**Pearl Beach**—*pop pl* (2) ... MI-6
*Pearl Branch* ... MD-2
Pearl Branch—*stream* ... AR-4
Pearl Branch—*stream* ... KY-4
Pearl Branch—*stream* (2) ... MO-7
*Pearlbrook* ... OH-6
Pearl Brook—*stream* ... MA-1
Pearl Brook—*stream* ... NJ-2
Pearl Brook Park—*park* ... NJ-2
Pearl Butte—*summit* (2) ... ND-7
Pearl Camp—*locale* ... IL-6
Pearl Camp—*locale* ... NV-8
Pearl Canyon—*valley* ... NV-8
Pearl Canyon—*valley* ... UT-8
Pearl Cave—*cave* ... AL-4
Pearl (CCD)—*cens area* ... KY-4
Pearl Cem—*cemetery* ... MI-6
Pearl Cem—*cemetery* ... OH-6
Pearl Ch—*church* ... NC-3
Pearl Ch—*church* ... OK-5
Pearl Ch—*church* ... SD-7
Pearl Chapel—*church* ... IL-6
**Pearl (Chili Station)**—*pop pl* ... OH-6
Pearl Ch of God—*church* ... MS-4
Pearl City—*locale* ... TX-5
**Pearl City**—*pop pl* ... HI-9
**Pearl City**—*pop pl* ... IL-6
**Pearl City**—*pop pl* ... TN-4
Pearl City—*uninc pl* ... MS-4
**Pearl City Heights**—*pop pl* ... HI-9
Pearl City Highlands Sch—*school* ... HI-9
Pearl City (historical)—*locale* ... KS-7
Pearl City Kai Intermediate Sch—*school* ... HI-9
Pearl City Peninsula—*cape* ... HI-9
Pearl City Pond—*reservoir* ... MA-1
**Pearl Court**—*pop pl* ... FL-3
*Pearl Creek* ... CO-8
*Pearl Creek* ... WI-6
**Pearl Creek**—*pop pl* ... NY-2
Pearl Creek—*stream* (4) ... AK-9
Pearl Creek—*stream* (3) ... CO-8
Pearl Creek—*stream* ... FL-3
Pearl Creek—*stream* (5) ... ID-8
Pearl Creek—*stream* ... LA-4
Pearl Creek—*stream* ... MD-2
Pearl Creek—*stream* ... MN-6
Pearl Creek—*stream* ... MT-8
Pearl Creek—*stream* ... NE-7
Pearl Creek—*stream* (2) ... NV-8
Pearl Creek—*stream* ... NY-2
Pearl Creek—*stream* (2) ... OR-9
Pearl Creek—*stream* (3) ... SD-7
Pearl Creek—*stream* (2) ... WA-9
Pearl Creek—*stream* ... WI-6
Pearl Creek Camp—*locale* ... NV-8
**Pearl Creek Colony**—*pop pl* ... SD-7
Pearl Creek Guard Station—*locale* ... OR-9
**Pearl Creek Township**—*pop pl* ... SD-7
Pearl Ditch—*canal* ... CO-8
Pearl Elem Sch—*school* ... MS-4
Pearl English Crain Number 1 Dam—*dam* ... SD-7
Pearlette (historical)—*locale* ... KS-7
Pearl Falls—*falls* ... WA-9
Pearl Flat—*flat* ... UT-8
Pearl Gap—*gap* ... CA-9
**Pearl Grange**—*pop pl* ... MI-6
Pearl Hall Sch—*school* ... TX-5
Pearl Handle Pit—*basin* ... AZ-5
Pearl Harbor—*bay* ... AK-9
Pearl Harbor—*bay* ... HI-9
Pearl Harbor—*bay* ... TN-4
Pearl Harbor, U.S. Naval Base—*hist pl* ... HI-9
Pearl Harbor Entrance—*channel* ... HI-9
Pearl Harbor Kai Sch—*school* ... HI-9
**Pearl Harbor Naval Cantonment**—*pop pl* ... HI-9
Pearl Harbor Naval Public Works Center—*military* ... HI-9
Pearl Harbor Naval Shipyard—*military* ... HI-9
Pearl Harbor Naval Station—*military* ... HI-9
Pearl Harbor Naval Submarine Base—*military* ... HI-9
Pearl Harbor Naval Supply Center—*military* ... HI-9
Pearl Harbor Park—*park* ... HI-9
Pearl Harbor Sch—*school* ... HI-9
Pearl Harbor Storage Tank (historical)—*reservoir* ... AZ-5
Pearl Harbor Tank—*reservoir* ... AZ-5
Pearl Harrison Lake Dam—*dam* ... MS-4
Pearlhaven Baptist Ch—*church* ... MS-4
**Pearlhaven (subdivision)**—*pop pl* ... MS-4
*Pearl Hermes Reef* ... HI-9
Pearl Hickory Ch—*church* ... LA-4
**Pearl Hill**—*pop pl* ... MS-4
Pearl Hill—*summit* ... MA-1
Pearl Hill—*summit* ... WA-9
*Pearl Hill Baptist Church* ... MS-4
Pearl Hill Brook—*stream* ... MA-1
Pearl Hill Brook Pond—*lake* ... MA-1
Pearl Hill Ch—*church* ... MS-4
Pearl Hill Sch—*school* ... MO-7
Pearl Hill Sch (historical)—*school* ... MS-4
Pearl (historical)—*locale* ... AL-4
Pearl Hollow—*valley* ... KY-4
Pearl Hot Springs—*spring* ... NV-8
Pearl Howlett School—*locale* ... CO-8
Pearl HS—*school* ... MS-4
Pearl HS—*school* ... TN-4
Pearlie Ch—*church* ... GA-3
Pearlie Grove Ch—*church* (2) ... MS-4
Pearlie Grove Missionary Baptist Ch—*church* ... MS-4
**Pearline**—*pop pl* ... MI-6
**Pearlington**—*pop pl* ... MS-4
*Pearlington Bayou* ... LA-4
Pearl Island—*island* (2) ... AK-9
Pearl Island—*island* ... ID-8
Pearl Island—*island* ... IL-6
Pearl Island—*island* ... IN-6
Pearl Island—*island* ... KY-4
Pearl Island—*island* ... WA-9
Pearl JHS—*school* ... GA-3
Pearl JHS—*school* ... MS-4
*Pearl Lake* ... CO-8
*Pearl Lake* ... CT-1
Pearl Lake—*lake* (2) ... CA-9
Pearl Lake—*lake* (6) ... FL-3
Pearl Lake—*lake* ... ID-8
Pearl Lake—*lake* ... IL-6
Pearl Lake—*lake* (4) ... MI-6
Pearl Lake—*lake* (5) ... MN-6
Pearl Lake—*lake* (2) ... MT-8
Pearl Lake—*lake* ... NV-8
Pearl Lake—*lake* ... NH-1
Pearl Lake—*lake* ... ND-7
Pearl Lake—*lake* ... OR-9
Pearl Lake—*lake* (2) ... UT-8
Pearl Lake—*lake* ... WI-6
Pearl Lake—*reservoir* ... CO-8
Pearl Lake—*reservoir* ... GA-3
Pearl Lake—*reservoir* ... NY-2
Pearl Lake—*reservoir* ... PA-2
Pearl Lake—*reservoir* ... SD-7
Pearl Lake—*reservoir* ... TX-5
Pearl Lake Brook—*stream* ... NH-1
Pearl Lake Dam—*dam* ... SD-7
**Pearl Lake (Marty)**—*pop pl* ... MN-6
Pearl Lake Park—*park* ... MN-6
*Pearl Lakes* ... NV-8
Pearl Lakes—*reservoir* ... CO-8
Pearl Lake Town Hall—*building* ... ND-7
**Pearl Lake Township**—*pop pl* ... ND-7
**Pearll City**—*pop pl* ... MI-6
*Pearl Loch* ... HI-9
Pearlls Resort—*locale* ... MI-6
**Pearl Mill**—*pop pl* ... MO-7
Pearl Mill Village Hist Dist—*hist pl* ... NC-3
Pearl Mine—*mine* ... AZ-5
Pearl Mine—*mine* ... MT-8
Pearl Mtn—*summit* ... CO-8
Pearl Mtn—*summit* ... OK-5
Pearl Municipal Library—*building* ... MS-4
Pearl Oil Field—*other* ... NM-5
Pearl Park—*flat* ... CO-8
Pearl Pass—*gap* ... CO-8
Pearl Peak—*summit* ... CO-8
Pearl Peak—*summit* ... NV-8
*Pearl Peak Lake* ... NV-8
Pearl Plaza (Shop Ctr)—*locale* ... FL-3
Pearl Point—*cape* ... NY-2
Pearl Pond—*lake* ... KY-4
Pearl Pond—*lake* (2) ... ME-1
Pearl Ponds—*lake* ... ME-1
Pearl Post Office—*building* ... MS-4
Pearl Presbyterian Ch—*church* ... MS-4
Pearl Ridge—*post sta* ... HI-9
**Pearl River**—*pop pl* ... LA-4
**Pearl River**—*pop pl* ... MS-4
**Pearl River**—*pop pl* ... NY-2
Pearl River—*stream* ... LA-4
Pearl River—*stream* ... MS-4
*Pearl River Agricultural High School* ... MS-4
Pearl River Bend—*bend* ... TX-5
Pearl River Canal—*canal* ... LA-4
Pearl River Cem—*cemetery* ... MS-4
Pearl River Central Sch—*school* ... MS-4
Pearl River Ch—*church* (2) ... MS-4
**Pearl River County**—*pop pl* ... MS-4
Pearl River County Game Ref—*park* ... MS-4
Pearl River County Hosp—*hospital* ... MS-4
Pearl River Fairgrounds—*locale* ... MS-4
*Pearl River Game Mngmt Area* ... MS-4
Pearl River Island—*island* ... LA-4
Pearl River Junior Coll—*school* (2) ... MS-4
Pearl River Light—*locale* ... LA-4
Pearl River State Waterfowl Ref—*park* ... MS-4
Pearl River State Wildlife Mngmt Area—*park* ... MS-4
Pearl River United Methodist Ch—*church* ... MS-4
*Pearl River Valley Baptist Ch* ... MS-4
Pearl River Valley Ch—*church* ... MS-4
*Pearl River Valley Reservoir* ... MS-4
Pearl Rock—*locale* ... IA-7
Pearl Ross Dam—*dam* ... SD-7
Pearl Rsvr—*reservoir* ... MT-8
Pearl Rsvr—*reservoir* (2) ... WY-8
Pearl Saylor Branch—*stream* ... KY-4
Pearl S Buck Birthplace—*building* ... WV-2
Pearl Sch—*school* ... MI-6
Pearl Sch—*school* ... MT-8
Pearl Sch—*school* ... OH-6
Pearl Sch—*school* (2) ... SD-7
Pearl Sch—*school* ... TN-4
**Pearls Corner**—*pop pl* ... NH-1
Pearl Spring—*spring* ... CO-8
Pearl Spring—*spring* ... PA-2
Pearl Spring—*spring* ... TN-4
Pearl Steam Laundry—*hist pl* ... IN-6
Pearl Street AME Ch—*church* ... MS-4
Pearl Street Cem—*cemetery* ... MA-1
Pearl Street Hist Dist—*hist pl* ... VT-1
Pearl Street Sch—*school* ... CT-1
Pearl Street Sch—*school* ... MA-1
Pearl Street Sch—*school* ... NH-1
Pearl Street Schoolhouse—*hist pl* ... NY-2
Pearl Swamp—*swamp* ... VT-1
Pearl Township—*civil* ... SD-7
**Pearl Township**—*pop pl* ... ND-7
**Pearl Township**—*pop pl* (2) ... SD-7
**Pearl (Township of)**—*pop pl* ... IL-6
Pearl United Methodist Ch—*church* ... MS-4
Pearl Valley—*valley* ... NM-5
*Pearl Valley Baptist Ch* ... MS-4
Pearl Valley Baptist Ch—*church* ... FL-3
Pearl Valley Cem—*cemetery* ... MS-4
Pearl Valley Ch—*church* (2) ... MS-4
Pearl Valley Ch—*church* ... TN-4
Pearl Valley (historical)—*locale* ... MS-4
Pearlville Post Office (historical)—*building* ... TN-4
Pearl Wash—*valley* ... AZ-5
*Pearl Water Creek* ... AL-4
Pearl Wise Canyon—*valley* ... OR-9
Pearl Wise Springs—*spring* ... OR-9
Pearly—*locale* ... VA-3
**Pearly**—*pop pl* ... GA-3
*Pearly Creek* ... AZ-5
Pearly Gate Ch—*church* ... MS-4
Pearly Gates Ch—*church* ... MS-4
Pearly Gates Ranch Airp—*airport* ... WA-9
*Pearly Grove Baptist Ch* ... MS-4
Pearly Grove Cem—*cemetery* ... MS-4
Pearly Island Creek—*stream* ... FL-3
Pearly Lake—*lake* ... NH-1
Pearman—*CDP* ... SC-3
Pearman—*locale* ... KY-4
Pearman Lake—*lake* ... TX-5
Pearman Ranch—*locale* ... SD-7
Pear Mtn—*summit* ... TX-5
Pearogue Branch—*stream* ... AR-4
Pearogue Cem—*cemetery* ... AR-4
Pear Orchard Plantation (historical)—*locale* ... MS-4
Pear Orchard Presbyterian Ch—*church* ... MS-4
Pear Park—*flat* ... UT-8
**Pear Park**—*pop pl* ... CO-8
Pear Park Ch—*church* ... CO-8
Pear Park Gas Field—*oilfield* ... UT-8
Pear Point—*cape* ... WA-9
Pear Pond—*lake* ... NY-2
Pearre—*locale* ... MD-2
Pearre-Metcalfe House—*hist pl* ... MD-2
**Pear Ridge**—*pop pl* ... TX-5
Pear Ridge—*ridge* (2) ... IN-6
Pear Rsvr—*reservoir* ... CO-8
Pearrygin Creek—*stream* ... WA-9
Pearrygin Lake—*lake* ... WA-9
Pearrygin Lake State Park—*park* ... WA-9
Pearrygin Peak—*summit* ... WA-9
Pearrygin Trail—*trail* ... WA-9
**Pearsall**—*pop pl* ... TX-5
Pearsall, Clifford R., House—*hist pl* ... UT-8
Pearsall (CCD)—*cens area* ... TX-5
Pearsall Cem—*cemetery* ... AL-4
Pearsall Cem—*cemetery* ... NY-2
Pearsall Cem—*cemetery* ... TX-5
Pearsall Chapel—*church* ... NC-3
Pearsall Creek—*stream* ... WA-9
**Pearsall Gardens (subdivision)**—*pop pl* ... AL-4
Pearsall Oil Field—*oilfield* ... TX-5
Pearsall Park—*park* ... TX-5
Pearsall Sch—*school* ... MI-6
Pearsall Sch (historical)—*school* ... MS-4
Pearsalls Hassock—*island* ... NY-2
Pearsall Shop Ctr—*locale* ... AL-4
Pearse Canal—*channel* ... AK-9
Pearse Creek—*stream* ... OR-9
Pearse Peak—*locale* ... OR-9
Pear Side Main—*canal* ... CA-9
Pear Slough—*gut* ... CA-9
Pearsol Cem—*cemetery* ... OH-6
Pearsol Creek—*stream* ... ID-8
Pearsol Drain—*canal* ... CA-9
Pearsoll Creek—*stream* ... OR-9
Pearsoll Mine—*mine* ... OR-9
Pearsoll Peak—*summit* ... OR-9
*Pearson* ... DE-2
Pearson—*locale* ... AR-4
Pearson—*locale* (2) ... CA-9
Pearson—*locale* ... ID-8
Pearson—*locale* ... TX-5
Pearson—*locale* ... WA-9
Pearson—*locale* ... WY-8
**Pearson**—*pop pl* ... AL-4
**Pearson**—*pop pl* ... AR-4
**Pearson**—*pop pl* ... GA-3
**Pearson**—*pop pl* ... MS-4
**Pearson**—*pop pl* ... OK-5
**Pearson**—*pop pl* ... WV-2
**Pearson**—*pop pl* ... WI-6
Pearson, Abiel, House—*hist pl* ... MA-1
Pearson, D. O., House—*hist pl* ... WA-9
Pearson, Franklin, House—*hist pl* ... IA-7
Pearson, John, Soda Works—*hist pl* ... CA-9
Pearson, Lake—*lake* ... WY-8
Pearson Airpark Airp—*airport* ... WA-9
Pearson Baptist Ch—*church* ... MS-4
*Pearson Branch* ... GA-3
Pearson Branch—*stream* ... AL-4
Pearson Branch—*stream* ... GA-3
Pearson Branch—*stream* ... KY-4
Pearson Branch—*stream* ... MO-7
Pearson Branch—*stream* ... TN-4
Pearson Branch—*stream* ... WV-2
Pearson Branch Ch—*church* ... MO-7
Pearson Branch Ridge—*ridge* ... MO-7
Pearson Brick House—*hist pl* ... TN-4
Pearson Brook—*stream* ... CT-1
Pearson Butte—*summit* ... OR-9
Pearson Cabin—*locale* ... OR-9
Pearson Cabin—*locale* ... WY-8
Pearson Canyon—*valley* ... OR-9
Pearson Canyon—*valley* ... UT-8
Pearson Cave—*cave* ... TN-4
Pearson (CCD)—*cens area* ... GA-3
Pearson Cem—*cemetery* (3) ... AL-4
Pearson Cem—*cemetery* (2) ... AR-4
Pearson Cem—*cemetery* ... GA-3
Pearson Cem—*cemetery* ... KY-4
Pearson Cem—*cemetery* ... LA-4
Pearson Cem—*cemetery* (4) ... MS-4
Pearson Cem—*cemetery* ... OH-6
Pearson Cem—*cemetery* ... SC-3
Pearson Cem—*cemetery* (9) ... TN-4
Pearson Cem—*cemetery* ... TX-5
Pearson Cem—*cemetery* ... VA-3
Pearson Cem—*cemetery* ... WA-9
Pearson Cem—*cemetery* ... WI-6
Pearson Cemetary—*cemetery* ... AR-4
Pearson Ch—*church* ... OK-5
Pearson Ch—*church* ... VA-3
*Pearson Chapel* ... TX-5
Pearson Chapel—*church* ... AL-4
Pearson Chapel—*church* (2) ... GA-3
Pearson Chapel—*church* ... MS-4
Pearson Chapel—*church* ... NC-3
*Pearson Chapel Ch* ... AL-4
*Pearson Chapel Ch of the Nazarene* ... MS-4
Pearson Chapel Sch—*school* ... TX-5
Pearson Corners—*locale* ... CT-1
Pearson Coulee—*valley* (2) ... MT-8
*Pearson Creek* ... WI-6
Pearson Creek—*bay* ... MD-2
Pearson Creek—*stream* ... AR-4
Pearson Creek—*stream* (2) ... GA-3
Pearson Creek—*stream* ... ID-8
Pearson Creek—*stream* ... MI-6
Pearson Creek—*stream* (2) ... MT-8
Pearson Creek—*stream* (2) ... OR-9
Pearson Creek—*stream* ... SD-7
Pearson Creek—*stream* (2) ... WA-9
Pearson Creek—*stream* ... WI-6
Pearson Creek—*stream* ... WY-8
Pearson Creek Archeol District—*hist pl* ... MO-7
Pearson Dam—*dam* ... OR-9
Pearson Dam—*other* ... WY-8
Pearson Ditch—*canal* ... OR-9
*Pearson Draw* ... WY-8
Pearson Draw—*valley* (3) ... WY-8
Pearson Eddy—*locale* ... WA-9
*Pearson Falls Wash* ... AZ-5
Pearson Falls Wash—*stream* ... AZ-5
Pearson Gap—*gap* ... AL-4
**Pearson Gardens**—*pop pl* ... VI-3
Pearson Grove—*locale* ... DE-2
Pearson Grove Ch—*church* ... GA-3
Pearson Guard Station—*locale* ... OR-9
Pearson Hill—*summit* ... WI-6
**Pearson (historical)**—*pop pl* ... TN-4
Pearson Hollow—*valley* ... TN-4
Pearson House—*hist pl* ... WA-9
Pearson-How, Cooper, and Lawrence Houses—*hist pl* ... NJ-2
Pearsonia—*locale* ... OK-5
Pearson Island—*cape* ... VA-3
Pearson Island—*island* ... FL-3
Pearson JHS—*school* ... MI-6
Pearson Kaolin Mines—*mine* ... IN-6
Pearson Knob—*summit* ... NC-3
*Pearson Lake* ... AL-4
Pearson Lake—*lake* ... MI-6
Pearson Lake—*lake* (2) ... MN-6
Pearson Lake—*lake* ... WI-6
Pearson Lake Dam—*dam* ... AL-4
Pearson Massacre—*locale* ... CA-9
Pearson Mesa—*summit* ... NM-5
Pearson Mill State Rec Area—*park* ... IN-6
Pearson Mine—*mine* ... AK-9
Pearson Mtn—*summit* ... NC-3
Pearson Park—*park* ... CA-9
Pearson Park—*park* ... OH-6
Pearson Park—*park* ... TX-5
Pearson Point—*cape* ... NY-2
Pearson Point—*ridge* ... UT-8
Pearson Point—*summit* ... CO-8
Pearson Pond—*lake* ... CT-1
Pearson Pond—*reservoir* ... NC-3
Pearson Pond Dam—*dam* ... NC-3
Pearson Post Office (historical)—*building* ... MS-4
Pearson Post Office (historical)—*building* ... TN-4
Pearson Ranch—*locale* ... MT-8
Pearson Ranch—*locale* ... NE-7
Pearson Ranch—*locale* ... NV-8
Pearson Ranch—*locale* ... NM-5
Pearson Ranch—*locale* (2) ... WY-8
Pearson Ravine—*valley* ... CA-9
Pearson Ridge—*ridge* ... OR-9
Pearson-Robinson House—*hist pl* ... AR-4
Pearson Rsvr—*reservoir* (2) ... MT-8
Pearson Rsvr—*reservoir* ... OR-9
Pearsons Acad—*school* ... AL-4
*Pearsons Brook* ... CT-1
*Pearsons Canyon* ... UT-8
Pearsons Canyon—*valley* ... UT-8
Pearsons Catfish Pond Dam—*dam* ... MS-4
Pearson Sch—*school* ... AL-4
Pearson Sch—*school* (2) ... IL-6
Pearson Sch—*school* ... NC-3
Pearson Sch—*school* ... SD-7
Pearson Sch—*school* ... TX-5
Pearson Sch—*school* ... WA-9
Pearsons Chapel—*church* ... MS-4
Pearsons Chapel—*locale* ... TX-5
Pearsons Chapel Cem—*cemetery* ... MS-4
*Pearson School* ... IN-6
Pearsons Corner—*locale* ... DE-2
Pearsons Corner—*locale* ... SD-7
Pearsons Corner—*locale* ... VA-3
Pearsons Corner Sch—*school* ... VA-3
Pearsons Coulee—*valley* ... MT-8
Pearsons Creek—*stream* ... TN-4
*Pearsons Cross Roads* ... DE-2
Pearsons Falls—*falls* ... NC-3
*Pearsons Ferry* ... PA-2
Pearson Shaft (Active)—*mine* ... NM-5
Pearsons Hall of Science—*hist pl* ... WI-6
*Pearsons Lake* ... TX-5
Pearson Slough—*lake* ... SD-7
*Pearsons Mill* ... TN-4
Pearsons Mill (historical)—*locale* ... MS-4
*Pearsons Mills* ... AL-4
*Pearsons Mills Post Office* ... AL-4
*Pearsons Point* ... UT-8
Pearsons Pond—*reservoir* ... AL-4
Pearsons Pond—*reservoir* ... SC-3
*Pearsons Ponds* ... LA-4
Pearson Spring—*spring* ... AZ-5
Pearson Spring—*spring* ... CA-9
Pearson Spring—*spring* (2) ... TN-4
Pearson Spring—*spring* ... TX-5
Pearson Spring—*spring* ... WA-9
Pearson Spring—*spring* ... WY-8
Pearson Springs—*spring* ... NM-5
Pearsons Shoal—*bar* ... AL-4
*Pearsons Shoals* ... AL-4
Pearsons Spring—*spring* ... AZ-5
Pearsons Store Post Office (historical)—*building* ... AL-4
**Pearson Subdivision**—*pop pl* ... UT-8
**Pearson Subdivision (subdivision)**—*pop pl* ... AL-4
Pearson Terrace—*hist pl* ... IN-6
**Pearsontown**—*pop pl* ... IN-6
Pearsontown Sch—*school* ... NC-3
Pearson Trail (pack)—*trail* ... OR-9
*Pearsonville* ... IN-6
**Pearsonville**—*pop pl* ... CA-9
Pearson Wash—*valley* ... UT-8
Pear Spring—*spring* ... AZ-5
Pear Spring—*spring* ... CA-9
Pear Tank—*reservoir* ... AZ-5
Peart Cem—*cemetery* ... LA-4
Peart Drain—*canal* ... MI-6
Peart Lateral—*canal* ... CA-9
Peart Lower Ditch—*canal* ... CO-8
*Pear Tree* ... DE-2
Peartree Bay—*bay* ... WA-9
Pear Tree Cove—*bay* ... MA-1
Pear Tree Gulch—*valley* ... CA-9
Pear Tree Park—*park* ... AL-4
Peartree Point—*cape* ... NC-3
Peartree Spring—*spring* ... CA-9
Pear Tree Spring—*spring* ... CA-9
Pear Tree Spring—*spring* ... TX-5
**Peartree (subdivision)**—*pop pl* ... TN-4
Pear Tree Windmill—*locale* ... TX-5
Peart Upper Ditch—*canal* ... CO-8
Pear Valley—*hist pl* ... VA-3
Pear Valley—*locale* ... TX-5
*Pearville* ... TX-5
**Pearwood Park Subdivision**—*pop pl* ... UT-8
Peary—*locale* ... MN-6
Peary—*locale* ... VA-3
*Peary Creek* ... AL-4
Peary Creek—*stream* ... AK-9
Peary HS—*school* ... MD-2
Peary JHS—*school* ... CA-9
Peary Lake—*lake* ... MN-6
Peary Mtn—*summit* ... ME-1
**Peary Place**—*pop pl* ... TX-5
Peary Sch—*school* ... ME-1
Peary Sch—*school* ... OK-5
Peas—*bar* ... FM-9
Peas Cem—*cemetery* ... LA-4
Peas Creek—*stream* ... IA-7
Peas Creek—*stream* ... MT-8
Peas Creek—*stream* ... PA-2
Pease—*locale* ... MO-7
**Pease**—*pop pl* ... MN-6
Pease, George, House—*hist pl* ... OH-6
Pease, Robert L., House—*hist pl* ... KS-7
Pease AFB—*military* ... NH-1
Pease Auditorium—*hist pl* ... MI-6
Pease Bottom—*bend* ... MT-8
Pease Brook—*stream* (2) ... CT-1
Pease Brook—*stream* (3) ... ME-1
Pease Brook—*stream* ... NH-1
Pease Brook—*stream* ... NY-2
Pease Brook—*stream* ... VT-1
Pease Cabin—*locale* ... CA-9
Pease Cem—*cemetery* ... OH-6
Pease Chapel—*church* ... LA-4
Pease Corner—*locale* ... ME-1
Pease Cove—*cove* ... MA-1
Pease Creek—*stream* ... MI-6
Pease Creek—*stream* ... SD-7
Pease Creek Rec Area—*park* ... SD-7
**Peas Eddy**—*pop pl* ... NY-2
Peas Eddy Brook—*stream* ... NY-2
Peas Eddy Island—*island* ... NY-2
Pease Ditch—*canal* ... CO-8
Pease Drain—*canal* ... MI-6
Pease Draw—*valley* ... MT-8
Pease Draw—*valley* ... WY-8
Pease Flat—*flat* ... CA-9
Pease Hill—*summit* ... NY-2
Pease Hill—*summit* ... WA-9
Pease Hill—*summit* ... WI-6
Pease Hollow—*basin* ... OH-6
Pease Homestead—*hist pl* ... OH-6
Pease Island (historical)—*island* ... SD-7
Pease Lake Dam—*dam* ... IN-6
Peasel Branch—*stream* ... MO-7
Pease Ledge—*bar* ... MA-1
Pease MS—*school* ... TX-5
Pease Mtn—*summit* ... ME-1
Pease Mtn—*summit* ... MO-7
Pease Mtn—*summit* ... VT-1
Pease Park—*park* ... TX-5
Pease Peak—*summit* ... AK-9
*Pease Point* ... MA-1
Pease Point—*cape* ... GA-3
Pease Point—*cliff* ... CO-8
Pease Pond—*lake* ... ME-1
Pease Pond—*lake* ... MA-1
Peaser Branch—*stream* ... WV-2
Pease Ridge—*ridge* ... MA-1
*Pease River* ... FL-3
*Pease River* ... TX-5
Pease River—*stream* ... OK-5
Pease River—*stream* ... TX-5
**Peaser Junction**—*pop pl* ... WV-2
Peaser Knob—*summit* ... WV-2
Peaser Ridge—*ridge* ... WV-2
*Peases* ... CT-1
Pease's, George, Second Store—*hist pl* ... MT-8
*Peases Brook* ... MA-1
Pease Sch—*school* ... ME-1
Pease Sch—*school* (5) ... TX-5
Peases Point—*cape* (2) ... MA-1
Pease Spring—*spring* ... CO-8
Pease Spring—*spring* ... OR-9
Pease Spring—*spring* ... SD-7
**Pease (Township of)**—*pop pl* ... OH-6
*Peaseville* ... VT-1
**Peaseville**—*pop pl* ... VT-1
Peas Hill—*summit* ... PA-2
Peas Hollow—*valley* ... MO-7
Peas Lake—*reservoir* ... MI-6
Peaslee Canyon—*valley* ... NV-8
Peaslee Creek—*stream* ... CA-9
Peaslee Creek—*stream* ... OR-9
Peaslee Fish and Wildlife Mngmt Area—*park* ... NJ-2
Peaslee-Gaulbert Warehouse—*hist pl* ... KY-4
Peaslee Hollow—*valley* ... NY-2
Peaslee Lake—*lake* ... WI-6
Peaslee Meadow Brook—*stream* ... NH-1
Peaslees Airstrip—*airport* ... NJ-2
Peasleeville—*locale* ... NY-2
Peasleeville Cem—*cemetery* ... NY-2
*Peasley Brook* ... ME-1
*Peasley Canyon* ... NV-8
Peasley Canyon—*valley* ... WA-9
Peasley Cem—*cemetery* ... IL-6
Peasley Creek—*stream* ... AK-9
Peasley Creek—*stream* ... ID-8
Peasley Drain—*canal* ... MI-6
Peasley Gulch—*valley* ... CA-9
Peasley Hill—*summit* ... ME-1
Peasley Lake—*lake* ... OR-9
Peasley Sch—*school* ... NY-2
Peason—*locale* ... LA-4
Peason Ch—*church* ... LA-4
Peason Fire Tower—*locale* ... LA-4
Pea Soup Bar—*bar* ... CA-9
Peasoup Creek—*stream* ... AZ-5
Pea Soup Lake—*lake* ... MI-6
Pea Soup Lake—*lake* ... MN-6
Peaster—*locale* ... TX-5
Peaster Catfish Ponds Dam—*dam* ... MS-4
Peaster Cem—*cemetery* ... MS-4
Peaster Creek—*stream* ... TX-5
Peasticks—*locale* ... KY-4
Peasys Pond—*lake* ... NY-2
**Peat Corners**—*pop pl* ... NY-2
Peat Creek—*stream* ... OR-9
Peate Hill—*summit* ... CO-8
Peat Hole—*lake* ... MA-1
Peat Lake—*lake* ... MN-6
Peat Lake—*lake* ... WI-6
Peat Lake—*lake* ... WY-8
Peat Marsh—*swamp* ... FL-3
Peat Meadow—*swamp* (2) ... MA-1
*Peatown* ... PA-2
Peatown Branch—*stream* ... TX-5
Peatown Ch—*church* ... TX-5
Peat Pasture Gulch—*valley* ... CA-9
Peat Pond—*lake* ... ME-1
Peatross—*locale* ... VA-3
Peatross Ranch—*locale* ... UT-8
Peats Creek—*stream* ... KS-7
Peats Creek Cem—*cemetery* ... KS-7
Peats Island—*island* ... TN-4
Peats Lake—*bay* ... WI-6
Peat Swamp—*swamp* ... CT-1
Peat Swamp—*swamp* (2) ... NY-2
Peat Swamp Rsvr—*reservoir* ... CT-1
Peatville—*locale* ... MI-6
Peaux, Pointe aux—*cape* ... MI-6
Peaveler Branch—*stream* ... TN-4
Peavey—*locale* ... ID-8
Peavey Bay—*bay* ... NY-2
Peavey Bay—*swamp* ... FL-3
Peavey Branch—*stream* ... LA-4
Peavey Brook—*stream* ... ME-1
Peavey Brook—*stream* ... NH-1
Peavey Creek—*stream* ... AK-9
Peavey Creek—*stream* ... FL-3
Peavey Creek—*stream* ... GA-3
Peavey Falls—*falls* ... WI-6
Peavey Field—*park* ... MN-6
Peavey-Haglin Experimental Concrete Grain Elevator—*hist pl* ... MN-6
**Peavey (historical)**—*pop pl* ... OR-9
Peavey Lake—*lake* (2) ... MN-6
Peavey Mtn—*summit* ... TN-4
Peavey Rsvr—*reservoir* ... OR-9
*Peavey Run* ... VA-3
*Peaveys Bar* ... AL-4
Peaveys Landing Boat Ramp—*locale* ... AL-4
Peavey Well—*well* ... ID-8
Peavier Cem—*cemetery* ... KY-4
*Peavine* ... NV-8
Peavine—*locale* ... CA-9
Peavine—*locale* ... TN-4
Peavine, Mount—*summit* ... OR-9
Peavine Bar—*bar* ... AK-9
Peavine Branch—*stream* ... AL-4
Pea Vine Branch—*stream* (2) ... KY-4
Peavine Branch—*stream* ... MO-7
Peavine Branch—*stream* ... NC-3
Peavine Camp—*locale* ... OR-9
Peavine Campground—*locale* ... CA-9
Peavine Canyon—*valley* ... CA-9
Peavine Canyon—*valley* ... NV-8
Peavine Canyon—*valley* ... NM-5
Peavine Canyon—*valley* ... UT-8
Peavine Canyon—*valley* ... WA-9

Peavine Cem—*cemetery* TN-4
Peavine Ch—*church* GA-3
Peavine Ch—*church* OK-5
*Peavine Creek* NV-8
*Peavine Creek* OK-5
*Peavine Creek* OR-9
Peavine Creek—*stream* AL-4
Peavine Creek—*stream* (3) AR-4
Peavine Creek—*stream* (6) CA-9
Peavine Creek—*stream* (2) GA-3
Pea Vine Creek—*stream* LA-4
Peavine Creek—*stream* MI-6
Peavine Creek—*stream* (2) MO-7
Peavine Creek—*stream* (3) NV-8
Peavine Creek—*stream* NY-2
Pea Vine Creek—*stream* OH-6
Peavine Creek—*stream* (3) OK-5
Peavine Creek—*stream* (4) OR-9
Peavine Creek—*stream* TX-5
Peavine Creek—*stream* WA-9
Peavine Falls—*falls* AL-4
Peavine Flat—*flat* UT-8
Peavine Gap—*gap* VA-3
Peavine Gulch—*valley* CA-9
Pea Vine Hill—*summit* PA-2
Pea Vine Hollow—*valley* AR-4
Pea Vine Hollow—*valley* MO-7
Peavine Hollow—*valley* MO-7
Peavine Hollow—*valley* OK-5
Peavine Hollow—*valley* UT-8
Peavine Hollow—*valley* VA-3
Peavine Hollow Public Access Area—*park* OK-5
Peavine Island—*island* PA-2
Peavine Island—*island* VA-3
Peavine Island—*island* WA-9
Peavine Lake—*reservoir* NC-3
Peavine Lake Dam—*dam* NC-3
Peavine Lookout—*locale* OR-9
Peavine Mtn—*summit* NV-8
Peavine Mtn—*summit* OR-9
Peavine Mtn—*summit* (2) TN-4
Peavine Mtn—*summit* (3) VA-3
Peavine Pass—*channel* WA-9
Peavine Peak—*summit* NV-8
Peavine Point—*ridge* CA-9
Peavine Post Office (historical)—*building* TN-4
Peavine Ranch—*locale* NV-8
*Peavine Ridge* WV-2
Pea Vine Ridge—*ridge* AL-4
Peavine Ridge—*ridge* (4) CA-9
Peavine Ridge—*ridge* GA-3
Peavine Ridge—*ridge* (2) OR-9
Peavine Ridge—*ridge* TN-4
Peavine Ridge—*ridge* WA-9
Pea Viner Lake—*lake* WI-6
Peavine Rsvr—*reservoir* OR-9
Pea Vine Run—*stream* MD-2
Pea Vine Run—*stream* PA-2
Peavine Sch—*school* MI-6
Peavine Sch—*school* MO-7
Peavine Sch—*school* NV-8
Peavine Sch (abandoned)—*school* MO-7
Peavine Spring—*spring* OR-9
*Peavine Springs* OR-9
Peavine Tank—*reservoir* AZ-5
Peavine Trail—*trail* FL-3
Peavine Valley—*valley* GA-3
Peavine Wash—*valley* UT-8
*Peavine Waterfalls* AL-4
Peavler Cem—*cemetery* MO-7
Peavy—*locale* AL-4
Peavy—*locale* TX-5
Peavy Branch—*stream* GA-3
Peavy Cabin—*bar* OR-9
Peavy Cem—*cemetery* GA-3
Peavy Creek—*stream* AL-4
Peavy Creek—*stream* OR-9
Peavy Falls Dam—*dam* MI-6
Peavy Hill—*summit* NH-1
Peavyhouse Hollow—*valley* TN-4
Peavy Lake—*lake* MN-6
Peavy Pond—*reservoir* MI-6
Peavy Pond Dam—*dam* MS-4
Peavys Bar—*bar* AL-4
*Peavys Landing* AL-4
P'eawaar—*locale* FM-9
Peawood Hollow—*valley* TN-4
*Peay* TN-4
P'eayabach—*summit* FM-9
Peay Park—*park* TN-4
*Peay Post Office* TN-4
*Pe-Bam-Ma Lake* MI-6
*Pe-Baumee Lake* MI-6
Pebawma Lake—*lake* MI-6
Pebble—*locale* ID-8
Pebble—*locale* KY-4
**Pebble**—*pop pl* AL-4
**Pebble Acres**—*pop pl* MO-7
**Pebble Acres**—*pop pl* PA-2
Pebble Bay—*bay* OR-9
Pebble Bay Forest Camp—*locale* OR-9
*Pebble Beach* MA-1
Pebble Beach—*beach* (3) CA-9
Pebble Beach—*beach* ME-1
Pebble Beach—*locale* CA-9
**Pebble Beach**—*pop pl* IL-6
**Pebble Beach**—*pop pl* NJ-2
**Pebble Beach**—*pop pl* NY-2
**Pebble Beach**—*pop pl* TX-5
**Pebble Beach**—*pop pl* WA-9
Pebble Beach Golf Course—*other* CA-9
Pebble Beach Park—*park* TX-5
Pebble Beach Riding Stables—*other* CA-9
**Pebble Beach (subdivision)**—*pop pl* NC-3
**Pebble Beach Sunset Acres**—*pop pl* TX-5
*Pebble Brook* MA-1
Pebble Brook—*stream* OH-6
Pebble Brook—*stream* WI-6
Pebblebrook Country Club—*locale* OH-6
Pebblebrook Estates—*locale* GA-3
Pebblebrook Golf Course—*other* AZ-5
**Pebblebrook (subdivision)**—*pop pl* NC-3
Pebble City—*locale* GA-3
Pebble Cow Camp—*locale* ID-8
*Pebble CreeK* ND-7
*Pebble Creek* WY-8
Pebble Creek—*stream* CO-8
Pebble Creek—*stream* ID-8
Pebble Creek—*stream* KS-7
Pebble Creek—*stream* MI-6
Pebble Creek—*stream* (2) MT-8
Pebble Creek—*stream* (3) NE-7
Pebble Creek—*stream* (2) OR-9
Pebble Creek—*stream* (2) WA-9
Pebble Creek—*stream* WI-6
Pebble Creek—*stream* WY-8
Pebble Creek Campground—*locale* WY-8
Pebble Creek Country Club—*locale* FL-3
**Pebble Creek Estates (subdivision)**—*pop pl* NC-3
**Pebble Creek (subdivision)**—*pop pl* NC-3
Pebbledale—*locale* FL-3
Pebble Falls—*falls* OK-5
Pebble Ford Campground—*park* OR-9
**Pebble Glen Subdivision**—*pop pl* UT-8
Pebble Grove Cem—*cemetery* TX-5
Pebble Guard Station—*locale* ID-8
Pebble Hill—*locale* AL-4
**Pebble Hill**—*pop pl* GA-3
**Pebble Hill**—*pop pl* PA-2
**Pebble Hill**—*pop pl* TN-4
Pebble Hill—*summit* MA-1
Pebble Hill—*summit* OR-9
Pebble Hill—*summit* PA-2
Pebble Hill Cem—*cemetery* TN-4
Pebble Hill Ch—*church* FL-3
Pebble Hill Ch—*church* TN-4
Pebble Hill Sch—*school* NY-2
Pebble Hill Sch (historical)—*school* (2) TN-4
**Pebble Hills Subdivision**—*pop pl* UT-8
**Pebble (historical)**—*pop pl* OR-9
Pebble Lake—*lake* MN-6
Pebble Lake—*reservoir* AR-4
Pebble Lake Park—*park* MN-6
Pebble Lake Park—*park* PA-2
Pebble Mound Cem—*cemetery* TX-5
Pebble Mtn—*summit* CA-9
Pebble Ridge Sch (historical)—*school* MO-7
Pebble Run—*stream* IN-6
Pebble Run—*stream* PA-2
Pebble Spring—*spring* CA-9
Pebble Springs Camp—*locale* OR-9
**Pebble Springs Estates Subdivision**—*pop pl* UT-8
Pebblestone Shut-in—*summit* CA-9
*Pebbletown* PA-2
**Pebble Township**—*pop pl* NE-7
**Pebble (Township of)**—*pop pl* OH-6
Pebbly Beach—*beach* MA-1
Pebbly Beach—*locale* CA-9
*Pe-Be-Ma Lake* MI-6
Pebley Mtn—*summit* ME-1
Pebly Sch—*school* PA-2
Peboamauk Fall—*falls* NH-1
Peboan Creek—*stream* MI-6
Pebworth—*locale* KY-4
Peca—*locale* GU-9
Pecadito Tank—*reservoir* TX-5
Pecal, Canal—*gut* LA-4
Pecan—*locale* GA-3
Pecan—*locale* PA-2
**Pecan**—*pop pl* FL-3
**Pecan**—*pop pl* MS-4
Pecan—*post sta* TX-5
Pecan Acres—*CDP* TX-5
**Pecan Acres (subdivision)**—*pop pl* MS-4
**Pecan Acres (subdivision)**—*pop pl* NC-3
*Pecan Bayou* MS-4
*Pecan Bayou* TX-5
Pecan Bayou—*stream* AR-4
Pecan Bayou—*stream* LA-4
Pecan Bayou—*stream* (4) MS-4
Pecan Bayou—*stream* (2) TX-5
Pecan Bayou Cutoff—*gut* MS-4
Pecan Bluff—*cliff* TX-5
Pecan Brake—*swamp* LA-4
*Pecan Branch* TX-5
Pecan Branch—*stream* OK-5
Pecan Branch—*stream* (15) TX-5
Pecan Branch Cem—*cemetery* TX-5
Pecan Cem—*cemetery* OK-5
Pecan Cem—*cemetery* (2) TX-5
Pecan Ch—*church* OK-5
Pecan Ch—*church* TX-5
Pecan Chute—*gut* MO-7
**Pecan City**—*pop pl* GA-3
*Pecan Creek* TX-5
Pecan Creek—*stream* IL-6
Pecan Creek—*stream* KS-7
Pecan Creek—*stream* (2) MO-7
Pecan Creek—*stream* (9) OK-5
Pecan Creek—*stream* OR-9
Pecan Creek—*stream* (33) TX-5
**Pecan Creek (subdivision)**—*pop pl* MS-4
Pecan Crossing—*locale* TX-5
Pecan Draw—*valley* TX-5
**Pecan Gap**—*pop pl* TX-5
Pecan Gap (CCD)—*cens area* TX-5
**Pecan Gardens**—*pop pl* VA-3
Pecan Grove—*hist pl* MS-4
Pecan Grove—*locale* MS-4
**Pecan Grove**—*pop pl* AR-4
**Pecan Grove**—*pop pl* LA-4
**Pecan Grove**—*pop pl* NC-3
**Pecangrove**—*pop pl* TX-5
*Pecan Grove Baptist Church* MS-4
Pecan Grove Cem—*cemetery* LA-4
Pecan Grove Ch—*church* MS-4
Pecan Grove Ch—*church* (4) TX-5
Pecan Grove Community Clubhouse—*building* TX-5
**Pecan Grove Estates (subdivision)**—*pop pl* AL-4
Pecan Grove Sch—*school* AZ-5
Pecan Grove Sch—*school* LA-4
Pecan Grove Sch—*school* MO-7
Pecan Grove Sch—*school* (2) OK-5
Pecan Grove Trailer Park—*locale* AZ-5
**Pecan Heights**—*pop pl* TX-5
**Pecan Hill**—*pop pl* TX-5
Pecan Hollow—*valley* MO-7
Pecan Hollow—*valley* (3) TX-5
Pecan Hollow Creek—*stream* TX-5
Pecaniere—*locale* LA-4
Pecan Island—*island* IL-6
Pecan Island—*island* LA-4
Pecan Island—*island* TX-5
**Pecan Island**—*pop pl* LA-4
Pecan Island Gas Field—*oilfield* LA-4
Pecan Lake—*lake* FL-3
Pecan Lake—*lake* IL-6
Pecan Lake—*lake* (2) MS-4
Pecan Lake—*lake* (2) TX-5
Pecan Lake—*reservoir* AR-4
Pecan Lake Gas Field—*oilfield* LA-4
Pecan Lake (historical)—*lake* MS-4
Pecan Landing—*locale* LA-4
Pecan Lateral—*canal* AR-4
Pecan Park—*park* OK-5
Pecan Park—*park* TX-5
**Pecan Park**—*pop pl* FL-3
**Pecan Park**—*pop pl* TX-5
Pecan Park Elem Sch—*school* MS-4
Pecan Park Rec Area—*park* OK-5
**Pecan Place**—*pop pl* LA-4
Pecan Point—*cape* MS-4
Pecan Point—*locale* AR-4
Pecan Point Cut-Off—*bend* MS-4
Pecan Point Landing—*locale* AR-4
Pecan Point Landing—*locale* MS-4
Pecan Point (Township of)—*fmr MCD* AR-4
Pecan Pool Spring—*spring* TX-5
Pecan Post Office (historical)—*building* MS-4
Pecan Ranch—*locale* TX-5
Pecan Recreation Center—*park* CA-9
Pecan Sch—*school* TX-5
Pecan Slough—*stream* MO-7
Pecan Slough—*stream* OK-5
Pecan Slough—*stream* (2) TX-5
Pecan Spring—*spring* CA-9
Pecan Spring—*spring* (6) TX-5
*Pecan Spring Branch* TX-5
Pecan Spring Branch—*stream* (2) TX-5
Pecan Spring Creek—*stream* (2) TX-5
Pecan Springs—*locale* TX-5
Pecan Springs—*spring* (3) TX-5
*Pecan Springs Branch* TX-5
Pecan Springs Branch—*stream* TX-5
Pecan Springs Draw—*valley* TX-5
Pecan Springs Hollow—*valley* TX-5
Pecan Springs Sch—*school* TX-5
**Pecan Spur**—*pop pl* LA-4
Pecan Station—*locale* TX-5
Pecan Station Oil Field—*oilfield* TX-5
Pecan Tank—*reservoir* NM-5
**Pecan Terrace**—*pop pl* SC-3
Pecan Tree Canal—*canal* LA-4
Pecan Tree Picnic and Camp Ground—*locale* TN-4
**Pecan Valley**—*pop pl* TX-5
Pecan Valley—*valley* LA-4
Pecan Valley Country Club—*other* TX-5
Pecan Valley Golf Course—*other* TX-5
Pecan Way Terrace—*uninc pl* SC-3
Pecan Wells—*locale* TX-5
Pecan Wells Cem—*cemetery* TX-5
Pecan Windmill—*locale* TX-5
**Pecatonica**—*pop pl* IL-6
Pecatonica Cem—*cemetery* IL-6
Pecatonica River—*stream* IL-6
Pecatonica River—*stream* WI-6
**Pecatonica (Township of)**—*pop pl* IL-6
Pecausett Meadows—*forest* CT-1
Pecausett Pond—*lake* CT-1
Pecaut Hollow—*valley* MO-7
Pecaut Ridge—*ridge* MO-7
Pecenka Cem—*cemetery* KS-7
*Pechaca Spring* CA-9
Pechaco Creek—*stream* CA-9
Pechahalee Creek—*stream* MS-4
Pechan, Frantisek, Log House—*hist pl* SD-7
Pechan, Mount—*summit* AZ-5
Pechan Camp—*locale* AZ-5
Pechanga Creek—*stream* CA-9
**Pechanga Ind Res**—*pop pl* CA-9
*Pechapa Spring* CA-9
Peche Coulee—*stream* LA-4
Pechek, Lake—*reservoir* ND-7
**Pechin**—*pop pl* PA-2
*Pechintorama-To* FM-9
*Pechintorma* FM-9
Pechman Creek—*stream* IA-7
Pechner Canyon—*valley* CA-9
Pechochen Swamp—*swamp* MS-4
Pecho Creek—*stream* CA-9
Pecho de la Doncella—*summit* NM-5
Pecho Rock—*island* CA-9
Pechous Lake—*lake* SD-7
Pechstein Lake—*lake* WI-6
Pechstein Rsvr—*reservoir* CA-9
Pechuck Lookout—*locale* OR-9
Peck—*locale* FL-3
Peck—*locale* ID-8
Peck—*locale* OH-6
Peck—*locale* OR-9
**Peck**—*pop pl* ID-8
**Peck**—*pop pl* (2) KS-7
**Peck**—*pop pl* LA-4
**Peck**—*pop pl* MI-6
Peck, Bill, House—*hist pl* ID-8
Peck, Capt. Barton, House—*hist pl* TX-5
Peck, Clarence, Residence—*hist pl* WI-6
Peck, George B., Dry Goods Company Bldg—*hist pl* MO-7
Peck, Judge William V., House—*hist pl* OH-6
Peck, L. W., House—*hist pl* OH-6
Peck, Mount—*summit* CO-8
Peck, Stow & Wilcox Factory—*hist pl* CT-1
Peck, Walter L., House—*hist pl* WI-6
**Peck Addition**—*pop pl* KS-7
Peck and Beede Wash—*stream* CO-8
Peck And Rye Lake—*lake* MI-6
Peck Basin—*basin* AZ-5
Peck Bay—*bay* MI-6
Peck Bay—*bay* NJ-2
Peck Beach—*beach* NJ-2
Peck-Bowen House—*hist pl* MA-1
Peck Branch—*stream* (2) KY-4
Peck Branch—*stream* TN-4
Peck Branch—*stream* TX-5
*Peck Brook* CT-1
*Peck Brook* MA-1
Peck Brook—*stream* CT-1
Peck Cabin—*locale* CA-9
Peck Cabin—*locale* OR-9
*Peck Canyon* UT-8
Peck Canyon—*valley* (3) AZ-5
Peck Canyon—*valley* NM-5
Peck Canyon—*valley* UT-8
Peck Canyon Interchange—*crossing* AZ-5
Peck Cem—*cemetery* (3) AL-4
Peck Cem—*cemetery* ID-8
Peck Cem—*cemetery* (2) IL-6
Peck Cem—*cemetery* KY-4
Peck Cem—*cemetery* MO-7
Peck Cem—*cemetery* (3) NY-2
Peck Cem—*cemetery* PA-2
Peck Cem—*cemetery* TX-5
Peck Cem—*cemetery* VA-3
Peck Cem—*cemetery* WV-2
Peck Cem—*cemetery* WI-6
Peck Corner—*locale* RI-1
Peck Corners—*locale* (2) NY-2
Peck Creek—*stream* CO-8
Peck Creek—*stream* ID-8
Peck Creek—*stream* IA-7
Peck Creek—*stream* (2) NY-2
Peck Creek—*stream* OR-9
Peck-Crim-Chesser House—*hist pl* WV-2
Peck Dam—*dam* SD-7
Peck Ditch—*canal* (2) CO-8
Peckenpaugh Lake—*lake* TX-5
Pecker Branch—*stream* VA-3
Peckermans Pond—*lake* NY-2
Pecker Pond—*lake* NH-1
Peckerwood Branch—*stream* NC-3
Peckerwood Branch—*stream* TN-4
Peckerwood Branch—*stream* (2) VA-3
Peckerwood Creek—*stream* AL-4
Peckerwood Creek—*stream* NC-3
Peckerwood Hill—*summit* OK-5
Peckerwood Hill—*summit* TX-5
Peckerwood (historical P.O.)—*locale* AL-4
Peckerwood Hollow—*valley* MO-7
Peckerwood Hollow—*valley* OH-6
Peckerwood Hollow—*valley* TN-4
Peckerwood Lake—*reservoir* AR-4
Peckerwood Lake—*reservoir* IL-6
Peckerwood Point—*locale* TN-4
Peckerwood Ridge—*ridge* NC-3
Peckerwood Ridge—*ridge* TN-4
Peckerwood Shoals (historical)—*bar* AL-4
Peck Farm Cem—*cemetery* OH-6
Peck Ford—*locale* KY-4
Peck Glacier—*glacier* CO-8
Peck Gulch—*valley* CA-9
Peck Gulch—*valley* (2) CO-8
Peck Gulch—*valley* (2) MT-8
Peck Gulch—*valley* OR-9
Peckham—*fmr MCD* NE-7
Peckham—*locale* CO-8
**Peckham**—*pop pl* OK-5
Peckham Barn—*hist pl* ID-8
Peckham Brook—*stream* CT-1
Peckham Brook—*stream* NY-2
Peckham Brook—*stream* RI-1
Peckham Cem—*cemetery* NE-7
Peckham Lake—*lake* MI-6
Peckham Pond—*lake* NY-2
Peckham Pond—*lake* (2) RI-1
Peckham Ranch—*locale* CA-9
Peckham Ridge—*ridge* CA-9
*Peckhams Pond* RI-1
Peckham West Cem—*cemetery* MA-1
Peckhart Ditch—*canal* IN-6
Peck Hill—*locale* NY-2
Peck Hill—*summit* AL-4
Peck Hill—*summit* CT-1
Peck Hill—*summit* MA-1
Peck Hill—*summit* NY-2
Peck Hill—*summit* OH-6
Peck Hill—*summit* RI-1
Peck (historical)—*locale* MS-4
Peck Hollow—*valley* (2) AL-4
Peck Hollow—*valley* KY-4
Peck Hollow—*valley* MO-7
Peck Hollow—*valley* NY-2
Peck Hollow—*valley* TN-4
Peck Hollow—*valley* WI-6
Peck Hollow Cave—*cave* AL-4
Peck Homestead Gulch—*valley* CO-8
Peck HS—*school* FL-3
Pecking Patch Hollow—*valley* PA-2
Peckinpah Creek—*stream* CA-9
Peckinpah Meadow—*flat* CA-9
Peckinpaugh Ditch—*canal* IN-6
Peckins Airp—*airport* PA-2
Peck Island—*island* MI-6
Peck Lake—*lake* FL-3
Peck Lake—*lake* IL-6
Peck Lake—*lake* (4) MI-6
Peck Lake—*lake* MT-8
Peck Lake—*reservoir* NY-2
Peck Ledge—*bar* CT-1
*Peckman Brook* NJ-2
Peckman River—*stream* NJ-2
*Peckmans Brook* NJ-2
Peck Memorial Ch—*church* TN-4
Peck Mesa—*summit* CO-8
Peck Mill (historical)—*locale* MS-4
Peck Mine—*mine* AZ-5
Peck Mine—*mine* CA-9
Peck Mine—*mine* OR-9
*Peck Mountain* SC-3
Peck Mountain Spring—*spring* AL-4
Peck Mtn—*summit* AL-4
Peck Mtn—*summit* (2) CT-1
Peck Mtn—*summit* ID-8
Peckney Bay—*bay* FL-3
Peck Oil Field—*oilfield* KS-7
Peckout Hollow—*valley* MO-7
Peck Park—*park* CA-9
Peck Park—*park* IL-6
Peck Park—*park* MI-6
Peck Place Plantation (historical)—*locale* AL-4
Peck Point—*cape* CT-1
Peck Pond—*lake* (2) CT-1
Peck Pond—*lake* MA-1
Peck Pond—*reservoir* CT-1
Peck Pond—*reservoir* RI-1
Peck Prospect—*mine* TN-4
Peck Ranch—*locale* NV-8
Peck Ranch—*locale* TX-5
Peck Ranch State Wildlife Mngmt Area—*park* MO-7
Peck Recreation Center—*park* MI-6
Peck Ridge—*ridge* MO-7
Peck Rsvr—*reservoir* CO-8
Peck Rsvr—*reservoir* OR-9
Peck Run—*stream* IN-6
Peck Run—*stream* PA-2
Peck Run—*stream* VA-3
*Pecks Bay* NJ-2
*Pecks Beach* NJ-2
Pecks Branch—*stream* FL-3
Pecks Branch—*stream* KY-4
Pecks Branch—*stream* MO-7
Pecks Brook—*stream* CT-1
Pecks Brook—*stream* MA-1
*Pecks Bun* WV-2
**Pecksburg**—*pop pl* IN-6
Pecks Cabin—*locale* CA-9
Pecks Camp—*locale* CO-8
Pecks Canyon—*valley* CA-9
Pecks Canyon—*valley* ID-8
Pecks Canyon—*valley* UT-8
Pecks Canyon—*valley* WA-9
Pecks Canyon Spring—*spring* ID-8
Pecks Cave—*cave* PA-2
Pecks Cem—*cemetery* CT-1
Pecks Ch—*church* VA-3
Peck Sch—*school* CA-9
Peck Sch—*school* CO-8
Peck Sch—*school* (2) CT-1
Peck Sch—*school* IL-6
Peck Sch—*school* MI-6
Peck Sch—*school* NC-3
Peck Sch—*school* SD-7
Peck Sch—*school* TX-5
Pecks Chapel—*church* GA-3
Pecks Chapel Cem—*cemetery* TN-4
*Pecks Chapel Methodist Church* TN-4
Peck Sch (historical)—*school* PA-2
Peck Sch (historical)—*school* TN-4
**Pecks Corner**—*pop pl* NJ-2
Pecks Corner—*summit* NC-3
Pecks Corner—*summit* TN-4
Pecks Corner Branch—*stream* NC-3
Pecks Corners—*locale* WI-6
**Pecks Corners**—*pop pl* OH-6
*Pecks Creek* CO-8
Pecks Creek—*stream* AK-9
Pecks Creek—*stream* KY-4
Pecks Creek—*stream* NY-2
Pecks Creek—*stream* OH-6
Pecks Creek—*stream* VA-3
Pecks Flat—*flat* CO-8
*Pecks Grove* NE-7
Pecks Gulch—*valley* CO-8
Pecks Gulch—*valley* SD-7
*Pecks Hill Church* AL-4
Pecks (histoical)—*locale* AZ-5
**Peck Siding**—*pop pl* VA-3
*Pecks Lake* FL-3
Pecks Lake—*lake* MI-6
Pecks Lake—*lake* TX-5
Pecks Lake—*reservoir* AZ-5
*Peck's Ledge* CT-1
Peck Slip—*uninc pl* NY-2
Pecks Meadow Pond—*lake* CT-1
**Pecks Mill**—*pop pl* WV-2
Pecks Mill Creek—*stream* GA-3
Pecks Mill (historical)—*locale* TN-4
Pecks Mill Pond—*lake* CT-1
Pecks Mill Sch (historical)—*school* TN-4
Pecks Mill Spring—*spring* TN-4
Pecks No. 1, The—*reservoir* CO-8
Pecks No. 2, The—*reservoir* CO-8
Pecks Point—*cape* MD-2
Pecks Point Tank Number One—*reservoir* AZ-5
Pecks Point Tank Number Three—*reservoir* AZ-5
Pecks Point Tank Number Two—*reservoir* AZ-5
Pecks Pond—*lake* CT-1
Pecks Pond—*lake* MA-1
Pecks Pond—*lake* VT-1
**Pecks Pond**—*pop pl* PA-2
Pecks Pond—*reservoir* OR-9
Pecks Pond—*reservoir* PA-2
Pecks Pond Dam—*dam* PA-2
Pecks Pond Picnic Area—*area* PA-2
**Pecksport**—*pop pl* NY-2
Peck Spring—*spring* AL-4
Peck Spring—*spring* (2) AZ-5
Peck Spring—*spring* CO-8
Peck Spring—*spring* OR-9
Peck Spring—*spring* TN-4
Pecks Puddle—*lake* MN-6
**Pecksridge**—*pop pl* KY-4
Pecks Ridge—*ridge* CA-9
Pecks Ridge—*ridge* KY-4
Pecks Rock—*island* CT-1
Pecks Run—*locale* WV-2
Pecks Run—*stream* WV-2
Pecks Shop (historical)—*locale* MS-4
**Pecks Station**—*pop pl* WI-6
Pecks Store (historical)—*school* AL-4
Pecks Swamp—*swamp* CT-1
Pecks Valley—*basin* CA-9
Pecks Valley Creek—*stream* CA-9
**Pecksville**—*pop pl* NY-2
Pecks Water Mill Cave—*cave* AL-4
Peck Tank—*reservoir* TX-5
Peck Tavern—*hist pl* CT-1
**Pecktonville**—*pop pl* MD-2
**Pecktown**—*pop pl* NY-2
Pecktown Cem—*cemetery* MI-6
**Peck (Town of)**—*pop pl* WI-6
*Peckville* PA-2
**Peckville**—*pop pl* PA-2
Peckville Sch—*school* PA-2
Peckville Station—*building* PA-2
Peck Wash—*stream* AZ-5
Peck Well—*well* AZ-5
Peck Well—*well* CO-8
Pecky Brook—*stream* ME-1
Peco Berwyn Airp—*airport* PA-2
Pecolet Creek—*stream* MT-8
*Peconi Bayou* LA-4
Peconic—*locale* CO-8
**Peconic**—*pop pl* NY-2
*Peconic Bay* NY-2
Peconic Lake—*reservoir* NY-2
Peconic River—*stream* NY-2
Peconic Sch—*school* NY-2
Pecor Cem—*cemetery* NY-2
Pecore Creek—*stream* MN-6
Pecore Creek—*stream* WI-6
Pecor Lake—*lake* WI-6
**Pecos**—*pop pl* NM-5
**Pecos**—*pop pl* TX-5
Pecos Baldy—*summit* NM-5
Pecos Canyon—*valley* TX-5
Pecos Canyon Ranch—*locale* TX-5
Pecos (CCD)—*cens area* NM-5
Pecos (CCD)—*cens area* TX-5
**Pecos (County)**—*pop pl* TX-5
*Pecos Creek* TX-5
Pecos Falls—*falls* NM-5
Pecos High Bridge—*bridge* TX-5
**Pecos Junction**—*pop pl* NM-5
Pecos Natl Monmt—*park* NM-5
Pecos Pasture—*other* NM-5
Pecos Pueblo—*civil* NM-5
Pecos River—*stream* NM-5
Pecos River—*stream* TX-5
Pecos River (Kaiser Channel)—*canal* NM-5
Pecos River (Old Channel)—*stream* NM-5
Pecos River (West Channel)—*canal* NM-5
Pecos Sch—*school* NM-5
Pecos Sch—*school* TX-5
Pecos Shearer Oil Field—*oilfield* TX-5
Pecos Spring—*spring* TX-5
Pecos State Monmt—*park* NM-5
Pecos Tank—*reservoir* TX-5
Pecos Valley Oil Field—*oilfield* TX-5
Pecos Wilderness—*park* NM-5
Pecousic Brook—*stream* MA-1
*Pecowsic Brook* MA-1
Pecoy Notch—*gap* NY-2
Pectil Drain—*canal* MI-6
Pectols Pyramid—*summit* UT-8
**Pectonville**—*pop pl* MD-2
*Pecto Point* MN-6
Pectoria (historical)—*locale* SD-7
*Pectos Point* MN-6
*Pecuanticiot River* MA-1
**Peculiar**—*pop pl* MO-7
Peculiar Cem—*cemetery* MO-7
Peculiar Township—*civil* MO-7
Pecumsaugan Creek—*stream* IL-6
*Pecumsaugum Creek* IL-6
Pecunit Brook—*stream* MA-1
**Pecwan**—*pop pl* CA-9
Pecwan Creek—*stream* CA-9
Pecwan Ridge—*ridge* CA-9
Pecwan Union Sch—*school* CA-9
Pedarosa Camp—*locale* TX-5
Pedarosa Creek—*stream* TX-5
Pedarosa Pens Windmill—*locale* TX-5
Pedarosa Spring—*spring* TX-5
Pedarosa Vats Windmill—*locale* TX-5
**Pedden Acres**—*pop pl* VT-1
*Pedder Island* MP-9
*Pedder Islands* MP-9
Peddicord—*uninc pl* MD-2
Peddicord Point—*ridge* OR-9
Peddicord Sch—*school* MO-7
Peddie Country Club—*other* NJ-2
Peddie Lake—*reservoir* NJ-2
Peddie Lake Dam—*dam* NJ-2
Peddie Prep Sch—*school* NJ-2
Peddlars Grave—*cemetery* PA-2
Peddler Bluff—*cliff* TN-4
Peddler Branch—*stream* SC-3
*Peddler Creek* VA-3
Peddler Creek—*stream* CA-9
Peddler Creek—*stream* MO-7
Peddler Fork—*stream* KY-4
Peddler Gap Sch—*school* KY-4
Peddler Hill—*summit* CA-9
Peddler Lake—*lake* MI-6
Peddler Lake Drain—*canal* MI-6
Peddler Run—*stream* MD-2
Peddler Run—*stream* WV-2
Peddlers Branch—*stream* NC-3
Peddlers Branch—*stream* SC-3
Peddler Sch (abandoned)—*school* MO-7
Peddlers Creek—*stream* OR-9
Peddlers Hill—*summit* TN-4
Peddlers Lake—*lake* FL-3
Peddlers Pond—*lake* RI-1
Peddlers Ridge—*ridge* OR-9
Peddlers Ridge—*ridge* TN-4
Peddlers Village Mall—*locale* FL-3
*Peddock Island* MA-1
Peddocks Island—*island* MA-1
Peddocks Island Channel Light—*locale* MA-1
Peddy Draw—*valley* WY-8
Peddy Draw 1—*reservoir* WY-8
Peddy Draw 2—*reservoir* WY-8
**Peddys Mill**—*pop pl* FL-3
**Pedeco**—*pop pl* TX-5
Pedee—*locale* ID-8
Pedee—*locale* IA-7
**Pedee**—*pop pl* OR-9
Pedee Branch—*stream* MO-7
Pedee Cem—*cemetery* OR-9
*Pedee Creek* TN-4
*Pedee Creek* VA-3
Pedee Creek—*stream* CO-8
Pedee Creek—*stream* ID-8
Pedee Creek—*stream* KS-7
Pedee Creek*—*stream* NE-7
Pedee Creek—*stream* OR-9
Pedee Fork—*stream* WV-2
*Pedee River* NC-3
*Pedee River* SC-3
Pedee Sch—*school* OR-9
*Pedego* TX-5
Pedelo Creek—*stream* MO-7
Pedelo Ridge—*ridge* MO-7
Pedemont Cem—*cemetery* GA-3
Peden—*locale* NC-3
Peden—*locale* TX-5
Peden Cem—*cemetery* AL-4
Peden Cem—*cemetery* (2) KY-4
Peden Cem—*cemetery* SC-3
Peden Chapel—*church* MO-7
Peden Coulee—*valley* MT-8
Peden Ditch—*canal* IN-6
**Peden (historical)**—*pop pl* MS-4
Peden Mill—*locale* KY-4
Peden P.O. (historical)—*building* MS-4
Peden Point—*cape* NC-3
Pedenville—*locale* GA-3
Pedernal—*locale* (2) NM-5
Pedernal Cem—*cemetery* NM-5
Pedernal Creek—*stream* NM-5
Pedernales (Barrio)—*fmr MCD* PR-3

Pedernales Falls—*falls* TX-5
Pedernales River—*stream* TX-5
Pedernal Mtn—*summit* NM-5
Pedersen Glacier—*glacier* AK-9
Pedersen Point—*cape* AK-9
Pedersen Sch—*school* WI-6
**Pedersen Subdivision**—*pop pl* (2) UT-8
Pederson, John, Farm—*hist pl* TX-5
Pederson Cem—*cemetery* ND-7
Pederson Creek—*stream* (2) WA-9
*Pederson Glacier* AK-9
Pederson Hill—*summit* AK-9
Pederson Point—*cape* AK-9
Pederson Ranch—*locale* NE-7
Pederson Slough—*lake* SD-7
Pedestal Peak—*summit* WY-8
Pedestal Rock—*pillar* IN-6
Pedge Branch—*stream* WV-2
Pedia Tank—*reservoir* AZ-5
Pedigo—*locale* TN-4
Pedigo—*locale* WA-9
**Pedigo**—*pop pl* TX-5
Pedigo Cem—*cemetery* OH-6
Pedigo Cem—*cemetery* TN-4
Pedigo Cem—*cemetery* TX-5
Pedigo Cem—*cemetery* VA-3
Pedigo Gulch—*valley* CO-8
Pedigo Hill—*summit* TX-5
Pedigo Post Office (historical)—*building* TN-4
Pedigo Ridge—*ridge* TN-4
Pedigo Sch—*school* KS-7
Pediment Creek—*stream* AK-9
Pediment Wash—*arroyo* NV-8
Pediment Wash—*stream* NV-8
**Pedlar**—*pop pl* WV-2
*Pedlar Creek* VA-3
Pedlar Creek—*stream* MO-7
Pedlar Creek—*stream* NV-8
Pedlar Gap—*gap* VA-3
Pedlar Gap Run—*stream* VA-3
Pedlar Hills—*range* VA-3
Pedlar Hollow—*valley* VA-3
Pedlar (Magisterial District)—*fmr MCD* VA-3
**Pedlar Mills**—*pop pl* VA-3
Pedlar Mtn—*summit* VA-3
Pedlar River—*stream* VA-3
Pedlar Run—*stream* WV-2
*Pedlars Creek* VA-3
Pedler Creek—*stream* WI-6
Pedler Run—*stream* PA-2
**Pedley**—*pop pl* CA-9
Pedley Hills—*range* CA-9
Pedley Lake—*lake* SD-7
Pedley Sch—*school* CA-9
Pedley Valley—*valley* CA-9
Pedlo Branch—*stream* AR-4
Pedlow Drain—*canal* MI-6
Pedmar, Mount—*summit* AK-9
Pednor State Wildlife Mngmt Area—*park* MN-6
*Pedocks Island* MA-1
*Pedo Mountain* OR-9
Pedonlisong—*area* GU-9
Pedora Sch—*school* IN-6
*Pedouriasu* PW-9
*Pedra* CO-8
Pedregal Sch—*school* CA-9
Pedregosa Mountains—*range* AZ-5
*Pedregoso Creek* CA-9
Pedretti Ill—*hist pl* WI-6
Pedrick, Marcellus, House—*hist pl* WI-6
Pedrick Cem—*cemetery* PA-2
Pedrick Pond—*reservoir* PA-2
**Pedricktown**—*pop pl* NJ-2
Pedricktown Station—*locale* NJ-2
*Pedrictown* NJ-2
Pedrioli Creek—*stream* NV-8
*Pedriza Creek* TX-5
*Pedro* OH-6
*Pedro* VA-3
Pedro—*locale* AK-9
Pedro—*locale* AR-4
Pedro—*locale* FL-3
Pedro—*locale* SD-7
Pedro—*locale* WV-2
Pedro—*locale* WY-8
**Pedro**—*pop pl* OH-6
**Pedro**—*pop pl* VA-3
Pedro, Bayou—*stream* LA-4
Pedro Armendaris No 33—*civil* NM-5
Pedro Armendaris No 34—*civil* NM-5
Pedro Avila (Barrio)—*fmr MCD* PR-3
Pedro Bay—*bay* AK-9
Pedro Bay ANV893—*reserve* AK-9
Pedro Cabin—*locale* CA-9
Pedro Camp—*locale* AK-9
Pedro Canyon—*valley* NM-5
Pedro Canyon—*valley* OR-9
Pedro Ch—*church* FL-3
Pedro Cocifacio Grant—*civil* FL-3
Pedro Corrals—*locale* CA-9
*Pedro Creek* WI-6
Pedro Creek—*stream* (2) AK-9
Pedro Creek—*stream* ID-8
Pedro Creek—*stream* MT-8
Pedro Creek—*stream* OR-9
Pedro Creek—*stream* WI-6
**Pedro Dome**—*pop pl* AK-9
Pedro Dome—*summit* AK-9
Pedro Draw—*valley* NM-5
Pedro Flat—*flat* CA-9
Pedro Garcia (Barrio)—*fmr MCD* PR-3
Pedro Garza Zamora Cem—*cemetery* TX-5
Pedro Glacier—*glacier* AK-9
*Pedrogrosa Mountains* AZ-5
Pedro (historical)—*locale* SD-7
**Pedro (historical)**—*pop pl* OR-9
Pedro Hollow—*valley* MO-7
Pedro Jaramillo Cem—*cemetery* TX-5
Pedro Miguel Peak—*summit* NM-5
Pedro Mtn—*summit* AK-9
Pedro Mtn—*summit* OR-9
Pedro Mtns—*range* WY-8
Pedron Lake—*lake* AR-4
Pedro Oil Field—*oilfield* WY-8
Pedro Opening—*gap* CA-9
Pedro Paloo Grant—*civil* FL-3
*Pedro Point* CA-9
Pedro Point—*cape* MT-8
Pedro Ranch—*locale* CA-9
Pedro Ridge—*ridge* CA-9
Pedro Ridge—*ridge* OR-9
Pedro Rsvr—*reservoir* CO-8
*Pedrosa Creek* TX-5
Pedrosa Creek—*stream* TX-5
Pedro Sch—*school* OH-6
Pedroso Creek—*stream* NM-5
Pedro Spring—*spring* ID-8
Pedro Spring—*spring* OR-9
Pedro Tank—*reservoir* TX-5
Pedro Trail—*trail* MT-8
Pedro Trope Grant—*civil* FL-3
*Pedro Valley* CA-9
**Pedro Valley**—*pop pl* CA-9
Pedro Well—*well* NV-8
Pedry Mine—*mine* CA-9
*Pedul* PW-9
*Peduliaes* PW-9
*Peduliaes Point* PW-9
*Peebes Neck* RI-1
*Peeble Point* ME-1
Peebler Sch—*school* KS-7
**Peebles**—*pop pl* OH-6
**Peebles**—*pop pl* WI-6
Peebles Bridge—*bridge* FL-3
Peebles Brook—*stream* MA-1
Peebles Cave—*cave* TN-4
Peebles Cem—*cemetery* AL-4
Peebles Cem—*cemetery* MI-6
Peebles Cem—*cemetery* (2) TN-4
Peebles Cem—*cemetery* TX-5
Peeble's Corner Hist Dist—*hist pl* OH-6
Peebles Coulee—*stream* LA-4
Peebles Ditch—*canal* IN-6
Peebles Elem Sch—*school* PA-2
Peebles Hollow—*valley* MA-1
Peebles House—*hist pl* NC-3
Peebles Landing—*locale* MS-4
Peebles Mill Creek—*stream* AL-4
Peebles Mtn—*summit* VA-3
Peebles (Peobles) Island—*hist pl* NY-2
*Peeble's Point* ME-1
Peebles Ranch—*locale* MT-8
Peebles Run—*stream* PA-2
Peebles Run—*stream* WV-2
Peebles Sch—*school* LA-4
Peebles Sch—*school* MA-1
Peebles Sch—*school* WI-6
*Peebles School* PA-2
*Peebles Tavern* NC-3
Peecher Cem—*cemetery* OH-6
Peedee—*locale* KY-4
**Pee Dee**—*pop pl* (2) NC-3
**Peedee**—*pop pl* SC-3
Pee Dee Acad—*school* SC-3
Peedee Agricultural Experiment Station—*other* SC-3
Pee Dee Bay—*swamp* GA-3
Peedee Branch—*stream* KY-4
Pee Dee Branch—*stream* TN-4
Pee Dee Cem—*cemetery* AR-4
Pee Dee Cem—*cemetery* IA-7
Pee Dee Cem—*cemetery* MS-4
Pee Dee Cem—*cemetery* MO-7
Pee Dee Ch—*church* AR-4
Pee Dee Ch—*church* NC-3
Pee Dee Ch—*church* (3) SC-3
Pee Dee Chapel—*church* SC-3
*Pee Dee Creek* IN-6
*Peedee Creek* OR-9
Pee Dee Creek—*stream* (2) AR-4
Pee Dee Creek—*stream* IN-6
Pee Dee Creek—*stream* (2) IA-7
Pee Dee Creek—*stream* KY-4
Pee Dee Creek—*stream* MS-4
Pee Dee Creek—*stream* MO-7
Pee Dee Creek—*stream* TN-4
Peedee Creek—*stream* VA-3
Pee Dee Crossroads—*locale* SC-3
Peedee Cumberland Presbyterian Ch (historical)—*church* TN-4
Pee Dee Ditch—*canal* IN-6
Peedee Gulch—*valley* SD-7
Pee Dee Gun Club—*other* SC-3
**Pee Dee (historical)**—*pop pl* NC-3
Peedee Hollow—*valley* TN-4
*Pee Dee Island* SC-3
Pee Dee Island—*island* SC-3
Pee Dee Islands—*island* SC-3
Peedee Lake—*lake* SC-3
Pee Dee Natl Wildlife Ref—*park* NC-3
*Pee Dee (Peedee)* SC-3
**Peedee (Pee Dee)**—*pop pl* SC-3
Peedee Plantation Lake—*dam* MS-4
Pee Dee Ridge—*ridge* (2) TN-4
*Peedee River* NC-3
*Peedee River* SC-3
Pee Dee River—*stream* NC-3
Pee Dee River—*stream* SC-3
Pee Dee River Rice Planters Hist Dist—*hist pl* SC-3
Pee Dee River Swamp—*swamp* SC-3
Pee Dee Sch—*school* MO-7
Pee Dee Sch—*school* NC-3
Pee Dee Sch—*school* SC-3
Pee Dee Sch—*school* TX-5
Pee Dee Swamp—*swamp* SC-3
Peedee (Township of)—*fmr MCD* NC-3
Peede's Mill—*other* TX-5
Peedin Sch—*school* NC-3
Peeds—*locale* VA-3
Peeds Lakes—*reservoir* GA-3
*P'eefeereel* FM-9
P'eefreel—*cape* FM-9
*Peek-a-boo* UT-8
**Peekaboo**—*pop pl* MS-4
Peek-a-boo Canyon—*valley* NV-8
Peekaboo Canyon—*valley* UT-8
Peek-a-boo Canyon—*valley* UT-8
Peek-A-Boo Creek—*stream* WA-9
Peekaboo Gulch—*valley* CO-8
Peek-A-Boo Hill—*summit* MI-6
Peek-A-Boo Lake—*lake* WA-9
Peek-A-Boo Lake—*reservoir* IN-6
Peek-A-Boo Lake Dam—*dam* IN-6
Peekaboo Loop Trail—*trail* UT-8
Peekaboo Mtn—*summit* ME-1
Peekaboo Ridge—*ridge* CO-8
Peekaboo Spring—*spring* UT-8
Peekamoose—*locale* NY-2
Peekamoose Lake—*lake* NY-2
Peekamoose Mtn—*summit* NY-2
Peekauai Ditch—*canal* HI-9
Peek Cem—*cemetery* KY-4
Peek Cem—*cemetery* MI-6
Peek Cem—*cemetery* NC-3
Peek Chapel—*church* NC-3
Peek Cut—*gap* IN-6
Peek Forest Park—*park* GA-3
Peekham JHS—*school* WI-6
Peeking Mtn—*summit* AK-9
Peekins Ranch Cove—*bay* FL-3
*Peek o' Moose* NY-2
Peek Run—*stream* IN-6
Peeks Branch Shool Creek—*stream* GA-3
Peeks Chapel—*church* (2) GA-3
*Peeks Chapel Church* AL-4
**Peeks Corner**—*pop pl* AL-4
Peeks Creek—*bay* MD-2
Peeks Creek—*stream* NC-3
Peeks Crossing—*locale* GA-3
*Peeks Crossroads* AL-4
Peeks Hill—*summit* ME-1
Peeks Hill Ch—*church* AL-4
Peeks Hill (historical)—*locale* AL-4
*Peeks Hill United Methodist Church* AL-4
**Peekskill**—*pop pl* NY-2
Peekskill, Lake—*lake* NY-2
Peekskill Bay—*bay* NY-2
*Peekskill Creek* NY-2
*Peekskill Hollow Brook* NY-2
Peekskill Hollow Creek—*stream* NY-2
Peekskill Military Acad—*school* NY-2
Peeks Landing—*locale* FL-3
Peeksville—*locale* WI-6
Peeksville Creek—*stream* GA-3
**Peeksville (Town of)**—*pop pl* WI-6
**Peekville (historical)**—*pop pl* TN-4
Peel—*locale* OR-9
**Peel**—*pop pl* AR-4
Peelaek—*gut* FM-9
Peeloeng—*cape* FM-9
*Peelbark River* WI-6
Peel Cabin—*locale* TX-5
Peel Cem—*cemetery* CO-8
Peel Cem—*cemetery* MS-4
Peel Cem—*cemetery* TN-4
Peel Chapel—*church* NC-3
*Peel Creek* CA-9
Peel Creek—*stream* AL-4
Peel Creek—*stream* MT-8
Peel Creek—*stream* WA-9
Peel Ditch—*canal* IN-6
**Peele Acres (subdivision)**—*pop pl* NC-3
Peele Branch—*stream* NC-3
Peele Cem—*cemetery* SC-3
Peeled Chestnut—*locale* TN-4
Peeled Chestnut Cem—*cemetery* TN-4
Peeled Chestnut Gap—*gap* VA-3
Peeled Chestnut Gap—*gap* WV-2
Peeled Chestnut Methodist Ch—*church* TN-4
Peeled Chestnut Post Office (historical)—*building* TN-4
Peeled Chestnut Sch—*school* TN-4
Peeled Oak—*locale* KY-4
Peeled Oak Branch—*stream* SC-3
Peeled Oak Creek—*stream* KY-4
*Peeled Pine Canyon* CO-8
Peeled Pine Canyon—*valley* CO-8
Peeled Pine Rsvr—*reservoir* CO-8
Peeled Pine Spring—*spring* CO-8
Peeled Poplar Fork—*stream* VA-3
**Peeler**—*pop pl* TX-5
Peeler Basin—*basin* CO-8
Peeler Branch—*stream* MS-4
Peeler Branch—*stream* SC-3
Peeler Cem—*cemetery* (2) TN-4
Peeler Chapel—*church* GA-3
Peeler Creek—*stream* NC-3
Peeler Elem Sch—*school* NC-3
Peeler Gap—*gap* AR-4
Peeler Hollow—*valley* TN-4
Peeler Lake—*lake* (2) AR-4
Peeler Landing—*locale* MS-4
Peeler Park—*park* TN-4
Peeler Peak—*summit* CO-8
Peeler Pond lake FL-3
Peeler Ranch—*locale* TX-5
**Peelers**—*pop pl* MS-4
Peeler Sch—*school* TX-5
Peeler Sch (historical)—*school* MS-4
Peelers Mill Post Office (historical)—*building* MS-4
Peelers Pond—*lake* TN-4
Peeler Spring—*spring* WY-8
Peelers Sch—*school* NC-3
Peeley, Mount—*summit* AZ-5
Peel Island—*island* IA-7
Peel Junction—*locale* OR-9
**Pe Ell**—*pop pl* WA-9
Peel Lake—*reservoir* TX-5
Peel Lake Dam—*dam* MS-4
Pe Ell Prairie—*flat* WA-9
Peelman Pond—*lake* IL-6
Peel Mill Creek—*stream* CA-9
Peel Peak—*summit* CA-9
Peel Point—*summit* CO-8
Peel Pond—*reservoir* GA-3
Peelpoplar Branch—*stream* KY-4
*Peel Private Cemetery* MS-4
Peel Ridge—*ridge* (2) CA-9
Peels Branch—*stream* TN-4
Peels Gap—*gap* NC-3
Peels Gap—*gap* TN-4
Peels High Top—*summit* NC-3
Peels High Top—*summit* TN-4
Peel Spring—*spring* CO-8
Peels Slough—*stream* WA-9
Peels Top—*summit* TN-4
Peeltown—*locale* TX-5
**Peeltown (Liberty)**—*pop pl* TX-5
Peel Tree—*other* WV-2
**Peeltree**—*pop pl* WV-2
Peeltree Ch—*church* WV-2
*Peel Tree Creek* ID-8
Peel Tree Creek—*stream* ID-8
**Peeltree (Peel Tree)**—*pop pl* WV-2
Peeltree Run—*stream* WV-2
*Peely* PA-2
Peely—*other* PA-2
P'eemeqruur—*summit* FM-9
Peemgoy—*summit* FM-9
*Pee-Munky Run* SD-7
Peenie Petroglyph Archeol Site—*hist pl* MO-7
Peenington (historical)—*locale* NC-3
Peeno Cem—*cemetery* KY-4
Peenpack Trail—*trail* NY-2
Peep—*locale* PA-2
Peep a Day Ridge—*ridge* ID-8
Peep Creek—*stream* OR-9
Peep Creek Camp—*locale* OR-9
Peep Creek Trail—*trail* OR-9
*Peepee Creek* OH-6
Pee Pee Creek—*stream* OH-6
Peepee Falls—*falls* HI-9
**Pee Pee (Township of)**—*pop pl* OH-6
Peeper Run—*stream* OH-6
Peepeye Cove—*valley* NC-3
Peeping Tom Spring—*spring* CA-9
Peep Lake—*lake* ME-1
Peeples—*locale* CO-8
Peeples, Robert and John McKee, Houses—*hist pl* IL-6
Peeples Cem—*cemetery* AR-4
Peeples Cem—*cemetery* TN-4
*Peeples Creek* NC-3
Peeples Creek—*stream* AZ-5
Peeples JHS—*school* MS-4
Peeples Pond—*reservoir* SC-3
Peeples Street Sch—*school* GA-3
**Peeples Valley**—*pop pl* AZ-5
Peeples Valley—*valley* AZ-5
Peeples Valley—*valley* GA-3
Peeples Valley Ch—*church* GA-3
Peeples Valley Pioneer Cem—*cemetery* AZ-5
Peeples Valley Sch—*school* AZ-5
Peep Rock—*other* AK-9
Peepsight Creek—*stream* WA-9
Peepsight Lake—*lake* WA-9
Peepsight Mtn—*summit* WA-9
Peep Sight Peak—*summit* CA-9
Peepstem Canyon—*valley* AZ-5
Peepstone Canyon—*valley* UT-8
Peeptoad Brook—*stream* RI-1
Peeptoad Pond—*reservoir* RI-1
*Peer Beaver Creek* CO-8
Peer Field—*flat* ID-8
Peer Island—*island* AK-9
*Peer Lakes* CO-8
Peerless—*locale* TX-5
Peerless—*locale* UT-8
**Peerless**—*pop pl* IL-6
**Peerless**—*pop pl* IN-6
**Peerless**—*pop pl* KY-4
**Peerless**—*pop pl* MT-8
Peerless Coulee—*valley* WY-8
Peerless Lake—*lake* MN-6
Peerless Mine—*mine* AZ-5
Peerless Mine—*mine* CA-9
Peerless Mine—*mine* (2) CO-8
Peerless Mine—*mine* (2) MT-8
Peerless Mine—*mine* SD-7
Peerless Mine—*mine* UT-8
**Peerless Mine**—*pop pl* ND-7
Peerless Motor Company Plant No. 1—*hist pl* OH-6
Peerless Mtn—*summit* CO-8
**Peerless Park**—*pop pl* MO-7
Peerless Saloon—*hist pl* AL-4
Peerless Sch—*school* MN-6
Peerless Spring—*spring* OR-9
Peerless Valley—*valley* CA-9
Peermont—*uninc pl* NJ-2
**Peers**—*pop pl* MO-7
Peers Cem—*cemetery* KY-4
Peers Landing—*locale* NV-8
Peerson Post Office (historical)—*building* AL-4
Peers Park—*park* CA-9
Peers Slough—*stream* MO-7
Peer Trail—*trail* WV-2
P'eeruwol—*summit* FM-9
Peery Apartments—*hist pl* UT-8
Peery Cem—*cemetery* MO-7
Peery Cem—*cemetery* OK-5
Peery Cem—*cemetery* (2) VA-3
Peery Hollow—*valley* TN-4
Peery Hotel—*hist pl* UT-8
Peery Lake—*lake* WA-9
Peery Mill Spring—*spring* UT-8
*Peery Run* VA-3
Peery Sch (abandoned)—*school* MO-7
Peery's Egyptian Theatre—*hist pl* UT-8
Peery Spring—*spring* TN-4
*Pease Creek* IA-7
Pease Ranch—*locale* TX-5
Pees Hollow—*valley* MO-7
Peeso Creek—*stream* WI-6
Peet, David N., Farmstead—*hist pl* MN-6
Peet Brook—*stream* PA-2
Peet Cem—*cemetery* CT-1
Peet Cem—*cemetery* MS-4
*Peet Creek* KS-7
Peet Creek—*stream* MI-6
Peet Creek—*stream* MT-8
Peet Creek—*stream* OR-9
Peete Cem—*cemetery* AL-4
Peetes Pond—*reservoir* NC-3
Peetes Pond Dam—*dam* NC-3
Peethill—*locale* CA-9
Peet Hill—*summit* CT-1
P'eethm'uuth—*cape* FM-9
Peet JHS—*school* IA-7
*Peet Pond* PA-2
Peets Cem—*cemetery* MS-4
Peets Corner—*locale* AL-4
*Peets Creek* KS-7
*Peets Creek* MI-6
*Peets Creek* WY-8
Peet Spring—*spring* AZ-5
*Peetsville* MS-4
**Peetsville**—*pop pl* MS-4
Peetsville Post Office (historical)—*building* MS-4
*P'eetunguun* FM-9
Peetunguun—*cape* FM-9
**Peetz**—*pop pl* CO-8
Peetz Cem—*cemetery* CO-8
Peetz Table—*area* CO-8
Peeve Creek—*stream* WA-9
Pee Vee—*locale* KY-4
*Peeve Pass* WA-9
Peeve Pass—*gap* WA-9
**Peever**—*pop pl* SD-7
Peever Cem—*cemetery* SD-7
**Peever Flats (subdivision)**—*pop pl* SD-7
Peever Slough—*gut* SD-7
Peever Slough State Wildlife Mngmt Area—*park* SD-7
Peevey Creek—*stream* AL-4
Peevyhouse Cem—*cemetery* AR-4
P'eewaar—*cape* FM-9
Peewee—*locale* TN-4
Peewee—*locale* WV-2
Peewee, Lake—*reservoir* KY-4
Peewee Branch—*stream* NC-3
Peewee Cem—*cemetery* IN-6
Peewee Cove—*valley* NC-3
*Peewee Creek* WA-9
Peewee Creek—*stream* ID-8
Pee Wee Creek—*stream* IN-6
Pee Wee Dam—*dam* NM-5
*Peewee Falls* WA-9
Pee Wee Gulch—*valley* ID-8
Pee Wee Hill—*summit* MD-2
Pee Wee Island—*island* PA-2
Peewee Lake—*lake* OR-9
Pee Wee Point—*cape* WV-2
Peewee Sch—*school* WV-2
Pee Wees Nursery and Day Care—*school* FL-3
Peewee Tank—*reservoir* AZ-5
Pee Wee Windmill—*locale* (2) TX-5
Peewink Mtn—*summit* CO-8
Peey—*summit* FM-9
*Peferel* FM-9
Peffer Trail—*trail* PA-2
Peffley Cem—*cemetery* IN-6
Peffley Creek—*stream* OR-9
Pefina Windmill—*locale* TX-5
Pefonio Windmill—*locale* NM-5
Peg, Mount—*summit* VT-1
Pegaham Branch—*stream* GA-3
*Pegamore Creek* GA-3
Pegamore Creek—*stream* GA-3
Pegamore Lake—*reservoir* GA-3
*Pegan* MH-9
Pegan Hill—*summit* MA-1
**Pegasus**—*pop pl* TX-5
Pegasus Airp—*airport* PA-2
Pegasus Gasoline Plant—*oilfield* TX-5
Pegasus Oil Field—*oilfield* TX-5
Pegasus Park—*park* FL-3
Pegati Lake—*lake* AK-9
Peg Branch—*stream* KY-4
Peg Brown Branch—*stream* KY-4
*Pegee Creek* AL-4
Pegeeluk Creek—*stream* AK-9
*Pegees Creek* AL-4
*Pegel Island* FM-9
*Pegerain-to* MP-9
Pegerian—*island* MP-9
*Pegerian Islet* MP-9
*Pegeru-to* FM-9
Peges Creek—*stream* SC-3
Peg Fork—*stream* KY-4
Peg Fork—*stream* WV-2
Pegg Canyon—*valley* WA-9
*Peggatossee* CT-1
Peggies Branch—*stream* VA-3
Pegg Lake—*lake* MN-6
Peggler Butte—*summit* OR-9
Peggley Lake—*lake* MI-6
Peggotty Beach—*beach* MA-1
**Peggs**—*pop pl* OK-5
Peggs Cem—*cemetery* OK-5
Peggs Fork—*stream* KY-4
Peggs Fork—*stream* OH-6
Peggs Point—*cape* NY-2
Peggs Run—*stream* PA-2
Peg Gulch—*valley* OR-9
Peggy—*locale* TX-5
Peggy Ann Bldg—*hist pl* OH-6
Peggy Ann Spring—*spring* KY-4
Peggy Baileys Bluff Lime Works—*mine* AL-4
Peggy Boston Swamp—*swamp* MD-2
Peggy Bottom—*bend* AL-4
Peggy Branch—*stream* GA-3
Peggy Branch—*stream* MD-2
Peggy Branch—*stream* MO-7
Peggy Branch—*stream* WV-2
Peggy Brook—*stream* MN-6
Peggy Butte—*summit* OR-9
*Peggy Creek* MS-4
Peggy Creek—*stream* MS-4
Peggy Creek—*stream* MT-8
Peggy Gap—*gap* NC-3
Peggy Hollow—*valley* UT-8
Peggy Hollow Spring—*spring* UT-8
Peggy Jo Park—*park* NC-3
Peggy Knob—*summit* NC-3
Peggy Lake—*lake* AK-9
Peggy Lake—*lake* CO-8
Peggy Lake—*lake* TX-5
Peggy Lake—*lake* WY-8
Peggy Mesa—*summit* NM-5
Peggy Molton Branch—*stream* AL-4
Peggy Mountain Branch—*stream* NC-3
Peggy Park—*park* TX-5
Peggy Peak—*summit* ID-8
Peggy Peak—*summit* NC-3
Peggy Pond—*lake* TN-4
Peggy Rock—*summit* WY-8
Peggy Row Branch—*stream* MS-4
Peggy Run—*stream* PA-2
Peggys Branch—*stream* KY-4
Peggys Gut—*stream* MD-2
Peggys Island—*island* LA-4
Peggys Island—*island* ME-1
Peggys Pond—*lake* WA-9
Peggy Spring—*spring* MT-8
Peggys Run—*stream* MD-2
Peggys Run—*stream* PA-2
Peggy Steep Trail—*trail* AR-4
Peggy Stewart House—*hist pl* MD-2
Peg Horn Slough—*swamp* FL-3
Pegies Creek—*stream* MS-4
Peg Knob—*summit* MO-7
Pegleg Camp (Site)—*locale* CA-9
Pegleg Canyon—*valley* NV-8
Pegleg Creek—*stream* (3) CA-9
Peg Leg Ditch—*canal* ID-8
Pegleg Falls—*falls* OR-9
Pegleg Falls Camp—*locale* OR-9
Pegleg Gulch—*valley* UT-8
*Pegleg Lake* MI-6
Pegleg Lookout—*locale* CA-9
Peg Leg Mine—*mine* CA-9
Pegleg Mine—*mine* (2) CA-9
Peg Leg Mine—*mine* UT-8
Pegleg Mtn—*summit* CA-9
Pegleg Mtn—*summit* ID-8
*Pegleg Point* MA-1
Pegleg Ridge—*ridge* CA-9
Pegleg Rsvr—*reservoir* NV-8
Pegleg Smith Historical Marker—*park* CA-9
Peg Leg Well—*well* AZ-5
Pegleg Well—*well* CA-9
Pegler, John Carlton, House—*hist pl* CA-9
Pegmatite Creek—*stream* AK-9
Pegmatite Glacier—*glacier* AK-9
Pegmatite Mtn—*summit* AK-9
Pegmatite Points—*ridge* CO-8
Peg Mill Brook—*stream* CT-1
*Peg Mill Pond* MA-1
Peg Millpond—*lake* MA-1
Peg Mtn—*summit* TN-4
Peg Munky Run—*stream* SD-7
Pegnee Landing (historical)—*locale* AL-4
*Pegon* MH-9
*Pegotty Beach* MA-1
Pegram—*locale* ID-8
Pegram—*locale* IL-6
**Pegram**—*pop pl* TN-4
Pegram Creek—*stream* ID-8
Pegram Elem Sch—*school* TN-4
*Pegram Flat* ID-8
Pegram (historical)—*locale* AL-4
Pegram House—*hist pl* NC-3
Pegram Lake—*lake* FL-3
Pegram Lake—*reservoir* (2) NC-3
Pegram Lake Dam—*dam* (2) NC-3
Pegram Post Office—*building* TN-4
*Pegrams* TN-4
Pegram Sch—*school* IL-6
Pegram Sch (historical)—*school* TN-4
*Pegrams Station* TN-4
*Pegrams Station Post Office* TN-4
*Pegram Station* AL-4
Pegrin Well—*well* AZ-5
Peg (RR name for Pinsonfork)—*other* KY-4
Peg Run—*stream* PA-2
Pegs Branch—*stream* NC-3
Pegs Point—*cape* NY-2
Pegs Run—*stream* PA-2
Peg Station—*locale* KY-4
Peg Swamp—*swamp* MA-1
Pegues Branch—*stream* AL-4
Pegues Cem—*cemetery* MS-4
*Pegues Church* MS-4
Pegues Ferry (historical)—*locale* AL-4
Pegues House—*hist pl* TX-5
Pegues Place—*hist pl* SC-3
Pegues Sch—*school* MS-4
Pegun—*island* FM-9
Pegville—*locale* CT-1
*Pehea* HI-9
Pehehoni Point—*cape* HI-9
Pehlam Cem—*cemetery* IA-7
Pehle Brook—*stream* NJ-2
Pehleng, Pillapen—*stream* FM-9
Pehlings Bay—*swamp* MN-6
Pehrson—*locale* UT-8
Pehs—*civil* FM-9
Pehsarep—*summit* FM-9
Peiai—*locale* FM-9
Peiak—*locale* FM-9
Peiakahk—*island* FM-9
Peidie—*locale* FM-9
Peidiker—*summit* FM-9
Peifer Elem Sch—*school* IN-6
Peifers Ch—*church* PA-2
Peifer Sch—*school* MN-6
Peigneur, Lake—*lake* LA-4
Peigneux Ranch—*locale* MT-8
Peiken—*tunnel* FM-9
**Peikin Park (subdivision)**—*pop pl* DE-2
Peil—*unknown* FM-9
*Peilas* FM-9
Peilepwil Island—*island* FM-9
**Peilong**—*pop pl* FM-9
Peimai—*tunnel* FM-9
Peina Island—*island* FM-9
Peina Islands—*island* FM-9
*Peinantomara Islands* FM-9
Peiniot—*island* FM-9
Peinkihr—*island* FM-9
Peinpwe—*cape* FM-9
Pein Semwei—*locale* FM-9
Peinsong—*locale* FM-9
Pein Uh—*swamp* FM-9
*Peipalap* FM-9
*Peipalap-Berg* FM-9
*Peipalap Peak* FM-9
Peipeinap—*bar* FM-9
Peiper Cave—*cave* PA-2
Peirce, John, House—*hist pl* IA-7
Peirce, William S., Sch—*hist pl* PA-2
*Peirce City* MO-7
**Peirce City (corporate name for Pierce City)**—*pop pl* MO-7
Peirce Creek—*stream* VA-3
Peirce Hill—*summit* MA-1
Peirce-Nichols House—*hist pl* MA-1
Peirce Sch—*hist pl* MA-1
Peirce Sch—*school* PA-2
*Peirces Creek* VA-3
Peirunap—*bar* FM-9
Peirusich—*bar* FM-9
Peisar Island—*island* AK-9
Peiser Park—*park* TX-5
**Peiser Spur**—*pop pl* AR-4
*Peisich* FM-9
Peisou—*locale* FM-9
*Peitik* FM-9
*Peitu* FM-9
**Pejepscot**—*pop pl* ME-1
*Pejepscot Mills* ME-1
Pejepscot Mills (RR name for Pejepscot)—*other* ME-1
Pejepscot Paper Company—*hist pl* ME-1
*Pejepscots* ME-1

Pejepscot Site—*hist pl* ... ME-1
Pejuan Cove—*bay* ... FL-3
Pejuan Point—*cape* ... FL-3
Pejuhutazizi Ch—*church* ... MN-6
Pejunkwa Site (FS-571, LA-130)—*hist pl* ... NM-5
*Pekal* ... FM-9
Pekan Lake—*lake* ... MN-6
Pekay Peak—*summit* ... MT-8
*Pekel* ... FM-9
Peken—*civil* ... FM-9
Pekenuht—*summit* ... FM-9
*Pekeru To* ... FM-9
*Pekeshie* ... MP-9
Pekeshie—*island* ... MP-9
*Pekeshire-To* ... MP-9
*Pekin* ... IN-6
*Pekin (2)* ... MD-2
Pekin—*locale* ... KY-4
Pekin—*locale* ... NY-2
**Pekin**—*pop pl* ... IL-6
**Pekin**—*pop pl* ... IN-6
**Pekin**—*pop pl* ... IA-7
**Pekin**—*pop pl* ... NY-2
**Pekin**—*pop pl* ... NC-3
**Pekin**—*pop pl* ... ND-7
**Pekin**—*pop pl (3)* ... OH-6
**Pekin**—*pop pl* ... VT-1
Pekin Brook—*stream* ... NY-2
Pekin Brook—*stream* ... VT-1
Pekin Community Sch—*school* ... IA-7
*Pekin (corporate name New Pekin)* ... IN-6
Pekin Country Club—*other* ... IL-6
Pekin Creek—*stream* ... WA-9
Pekin Federal Bldg—*hist pl* ... IL-6
*Peking* ... MS-4
**Pekin Heights**—*pop pl* ... IL-6
**Pekin (historical)**—*pop pl* ... TN-4
**Pekin Junction**—*pop pl* ... IL-6
Pekin Lake—*lake* ... IL-6
Pekin Post Office (historical)—*building* ... TN-4
Pekin Run—*stream* ... PA-2
Pekin Sch—*school* ... VT-1
*Pekin Station* ... IN-6
Pekin Street Hist Dist—*hist pl* ... RI-1
**Pekin (Township of)**—*pop pl* ... IL-6
Pekkala Creek—*stream* ... MI-6
Pekngasu—*slope* ... MH-9
Pekoa Stream—*stream* ... HI-9
Peko Peak—*summit* ... NV-8
Pektor Hill—*summit* ... PA-2
Pektotolik Slough—*gut* ... AK-9
Pela—*island* ... PR-3
Pelaez Lake—*lake* ... TX-5
Pelagi Islets—*island* ... GU-9
Pelahan Hollow—*valley* ... AR-4
*Pelahatchee* ... MS-4
*Pelahatches* ... MS-4
**Pelahatchie**—*pop pl* ... MS-4
Pelahatchie Attendance Center—*school* ... MS-4
Pelahatchie Baptist Ch—*church* ... MS-4
Pelahatchie Bay—*bay* ... MS-4
Pelahatchie Cem—*cemetery (2)* ... MS-4
Pelahatchie Creek—*stream* ... MS-4
Pelahatchie Depot (historical)—*locale* ... MS-4
Pelahatchie Depot Post Office (historical)—*building* ... MS-4
Pelahatchie Elem Sch—*school* ... MS-4
*Pelahatchie Lake* ... MS-4
Pelahatchie Lake Dam—*dam* ... MS-4
Pelahatchie Methodist Ch—*church* ... MS-4
Pelahatchie MS—*school* ... MS-4
Pelahatchie Oil Field—*oilfield* ... MS-4
Pelahatchie Rec Area—*park* ... MS-4
*Pelahatchie Shore Park* ... MS-4
**Pelahatchie Woods (subdivision)**—*pop pl* ... MS-4
Pela House—*hist pl* ... TX-5
Pelait—*island* ... PR-3
*Pelak* ... FM-9
*Pelak Entrance* ... FM-9
Pelan—*locale* ... MN-6
Pelanconi Park—*park* ... CA-9
*Pelang* ... FM-9
**Pelan (Township of)**—*pop pl* ... MN-6
Pela Seca Spring—*spring* ... AZ-5
*Pelasia Crook* ... MS-4
*Pelau* ... FM-9
Pelau, Cayo—*island* ... FL-3
Pelau Island—*island* ... FM-9
Pelazuk (Site)—*locale* ... AK-9
Pelba—*locale* ... LA-4
Pelcher Pond—*lake* ... NY-2
Pelcher Ranch—*locale* ... WY-8
Pelc Ranch—*locale* ... NE-7
Peleau—*civil* ... HI-9
Peleau Stream—*stream* ... HI-9
Pelee Sch (reduced usage)—*school* ... TX-5
Pelegs Island—*island* ... MA-1
Pelegs Point—*cape* ... MA-1
*Pele Hills* ... HI-9
*Pelekuna Bay* ... HI-9
Pelekunu—*civil* ... HI-9
Pelekunu—*locale* ... HI-9
Pelekunu Bay—*bay* ... HI-9
Pelekunu Gulch—*valley* ... HI-9
Pelekunu Stream—*stream* ... HI-9
*Pelelew* ... PW-9
Pelelilii Gulch—*valley* ... HI-9
*Pelelio* ... PW-9
*Peleliou* ... PW-9
*Peleliu* ... PW-9
*Peleliu Air Field* ... PW-9
Peleliu Battlefield—*hist pl* ... PW-9
Peleliu (County-equivalent)—*civil* ... PW-9
*Peleliu Harbor* ... PW-9
*Peleliu Insel* ... PW-9
Peleliu Sch—*school* ... PW-9
Pelenga Bay—*bay* ... AK-9
Pelen Iak—*swamp* ... FM-9
Peler Creek—*channel* ... FL-3
*Peles Hill* ... HI-9
*Pelesier Lake* ... MI-6
Peletier—*locale* ... NC-3
Peletier Creek—*stream* ... NC-3
Peletier Fire Tower—*locale* ... NC-3
Peleuli Point—*cape* ... HI-9
Pelewski Lake—*lake* ... MN-6
Pelfery Cem—*cemetery* ... KY-4
Pelfrey Branch—*stream* ... KY-4
Pelham—*locale* ... TX-5
**Pelham**—*pop pl (2)* ... AL-4
**Pelham**—*pop pl* ... GA-3
**Pelham**—*pop pl* ... MA-1
**Pelham**—*pop pl* ... NH-1
**Pelham**—*pop pl* ... NY-2
**Pelham**—*pop pl* ... NC-3
**Pelham**—*pop pl* ... SC-3
**Pelham**—*pop pl* ... TN-4
**Pelham**—*pop pl* ... TX-5
Pelham, Charles, House—*hist pl* ... KY-4
Pelham, Lake—*reservoir* ... VA-3
Pelham Baptist Ch—*church* ... AL-4
Pelham Bay—*bay* ... NY-2
Pelham Bay Park—*park* ... NY-2
Pelham Branch—*stream* ... AL-4
Pelham Branch—*stream (2)* ... KY-4
Pelham Bridge—*bridge* ... NY-2
Pelham Brook—*stream* ... MA-1
Pelham (CCD)—*cens area* ... GA-3
Pelham (CCD)—*cens area* ... TN-4
Pelham Cem—*cemetery* ... AL-4
Pelham Cem—*cemetery (2)* ... IN-6
Pelham Cem—*cemetery* ... NY-2
Pelham Cem—*cemetery* ... TN-4
Pelham Cem—*cemetery* ... TX-5
Pelham Ch of Christ—*church* ... TN-4
Pelham Colored Sch (historical)—*school* ... TN-4
Pelham Commercial Hist Dist—*hist pl* ... GA-3
Pelham Country Club—*locale* ... MA-1
Pelham Country Club—*other* ... NY-2
Pelham Creek—*stream* ... AR-4
Pelham Creek—*stream* ... GA-3
Pelham Creek—*stream* ... MT-8
Pelhamdale—*hist pl* ... NY-2
Pelham Division—*civil* ... TN-4
Pelham Elem Sch—*school* ... NC-3
Pelham Elem Sch—*school* ... TN-4
Pelham Flat—*flat* ... CA-9
*Pelham Fort* ... MA-1
*Pelham Heights* ... MA-1
**Pelham Heights**—*pop pl* ... AL-4
Pelham Hollow—*valley (2)* ... MO-7
Pelham Hollow—*valley* ... UT-8
Pelham Hollow Rsvr—*reservoir* ... UT-8
Pelham Industrial Park—*locale* ... AL-4
Pelham Island—*cape* ... MA-1
Pelham JHS—*school* ... MI-6
Pelham Knoll—*summit* ... UT-8
Pelham Lake—*lake* ... UT-8
Pelham Lake—*lake* ... WY-8
Pelham Lake—*reservoir* ... MA-1
Pelham Lake—*reservoir* ... NY-2
Pelham Lake Creek—*stream* ... WY-8
Pelham Lake Dam—*dam* ... MA-1
Pelham Lake Park—*park* ... MA-1
Pelham Lake Trail—*trail* ... WY-8
Pelham Landing (historical)—*locale* ... AL-4
**Pelham Manor**—*pop pl* ... NY-2
Pelham Memorial Garden—*cemetery* ... GA-3
Pelham Memorial Sch—*school* ... NH-1
Pelham Mills Site (38GR165)—*hist pl* ... SC-3
*Pelham Mountain* ... WY-8
Pelham Park—*park* ... AL-4
Pelham Park—*park (2)* ... TX-5
Pelham Parkway—*uninc pl* ... NY-2
Pelham Plaza Shop Ctr—*locale (2)* ... AL-4
Pelham Post Office—*building* ... TN-4
Pelham Range Dam—*dam* ... AL-4
Pelham Ridge—*ridge* ... MO-7
Pelhams Ch—*church* ... VA-3
*Pelhams Landing* ... AL-4
Pelham Swamp—*stream* ... VA-3
Pelham Town Hall Hist Dist—*hist pl* ... MA-1
**Pelham (Town of)**—*pop pl* ... MA-1
**Pelham (Town of)**—*pop pl* ... NH-1
**Pelham (Town of)**—*pop pl* ... NY-2
Pelham (Township of)—*fmr MCD* ... NC-3
Pelham United Methodist Ch—*church* ... AL-4
Pelham United Methodist Ch—*church* ... TN-4
Pelham Valley—*valley* ... TN-4
Pelham Valley Ch—*church* ... TN-4
*Pelia* ... FM-9
P Elia Ranch—*locale* ... NV-8
*Pelican* ... CA-9
*Pelican* ... MI-6
*Pelican* ... OR-9
*Pelican* ... FM-9
**Pelican**—*pop pl* ... AK-9
**Pelican**—*pop pl* ... LA-4
**Pelican**—*pop pl* ... TX-5
Pelican Bank—*bar* ... FL-3
Pelican Bank—*bar* ... SC-3
Pelican Bay—*bay* ... AL-4
Pelican Bay—*bay (2)* ... CA-9
Pelican Bay—*bay (4)* ... FL-3
Pelican Bay—*bay* ... MN-6
Pelican Bay—*bay* ... OR-9
Pelican Bay—*bay* ... UT-8
Pelican Bay—*bay* ... WY-8
**Pelican Bay**—*pop pl* ... FL-3
**Pelican Bay**—*pop pl* ... TX-5
Pelican Bay Camp (historical)—*locale* ... OR-9
Pelican Bayou—*gut* ... LA-4
Pelican Bayou—*stream* ... FL-3
Pelican Bend—*bend* ... MS-4
*Pelican Branch River* ... MN-6
Pelican Brook—*stream* ... MN-6
*Pelican Brook RiA VAR Norway Brook* ... MN-6
*Pelican Brook River* ... MN-6
Pelican Butte—*summit* ... OR-9
Pelican Butte Trail—*trail* ... OR-9
Pelican Canyon—*valley* ... UT-8
Pelican Cay—*island* ... VI-3
*Pelican Channel* ... AL-4
Pelican Channel—*channel* ... AL-4
**Pelican City**—*pop pl* ... OR-9
Pelican Cone—*summit* ... WY-8
Pelican Cone Trail—*trail* ... WY-8
Pelican Cove—*bay (2)* ... FL-3
*Pelican Creek* ... NC-3
Pelican Creek—*stream* ... AK-9
Pelican Creek—*stream* ... MI-6
Pelican Creek—*stream* ... MN-6
Pelican Creek—*stream* ... OR-9
Pelican Creek—*stream* ... WA-9
Pelican Creek—*stream* ... WY-8
Pelican Creek Trail—*trail* ... WY-8
Pelican Drive Ch—*church* ... LA-4
Pelican Elem Sch—*school* ... FL-3
Pelican Group Mines—*mine* ... NM-5
Pelican Guard Station—*locale* ... OR-9
Pelican Harbor Park—*park* ... FL-3
Pelican Hill—*summit* ... CA-9
Pelican Horn—*bay* ... WA-9
*Pelican Island* ... CA-9
*Pelican Island* ... FL-3
*Pelican Island* ... NC-3
Pelican Island—*area* ... MO-7
Pelican Island—*island* ... CA-9
Pelican Island—*island* ... CT-1
Pelican Island—*island (3)* ... FL-3
Pelican Island—*island (3)* ... LA-4
Pelican Island—*island* ... MN-6
Pelican Island—*island* ... NV-8
Pelican Island—*island* ... NJ-2
Pelican Island—*island* ... NY-2
Pelican Island—*island* ... OR-9
Pelican Island—*island (4)* ... TX-5
**Pelican Island**—*pop pl* ... NJ-2
Pelican Island (Bird Sanctuary)—*island* ... FL-3
Pelican Island Elem Sch—*school* ... FL-3
Pelican Island (HISTORICAL)—*island* ... AL-4
Pelican Island Natl Wildlife Refuge—*hist pl* ... FL-3
Pelican Islands—*island* ... LA-4
*Pelican Key* ... FL-3
Pelican Key—*island (2)* ... FL-3
Pelican Key—*island* ... MS-4
Pelican Keys—*island* ... FL-3
Pelican Lake—*lake* ... AR-4
Pelican Lake—*lake* ... CA-9
Pelican Lake—*lake* ... FL-3
Pelican Lake—*lake* ... LA-4
Pelican Lake—*lake* ... MI-6
Pelican Lake—*lake (7)* ... MN-6
Pelican Lake—*lake (2)* ... NE-7
Pelican Lake—*lake (5)* ... ND-7
Pelican Lake—*lake* ... OR-9
Pelican Lake—*lake (2)* ... SD-7
Pelican Lake—*lake* ... TX-5
Pelican Lake—*lake* ... UT-8
Pelican Lake—*lake (3)* ... WI-6
**Pelican Lake**—*pop pl* ... FL-3
**Pelican Lake**—*pop pl* ... WI-6
Pelican Lake—*reservoir* ... UT-8
Pelican Lake Bed—*flat* ... MN-6
Pelican Lake Campground—*park* ... UT-8
Pelican Lake Cem—*cemetery (2)* ... MN-6
Pelican Lake Ch—*church* ... MN-6
Pelican Lake Dam—*dam* ... UT-8
Pelican Lake RR Station—*locale* ... FL-3
*Pelican Lakes* ... MN-6
Pelican Lakes—*other* ... MN-6
Pelican Lake Sch—*school* ... MN-6
Pelican Lake (Township of)—*civ div* ... MN-6
Pelican Mine—*mine (2)* ... CO-8
Pelican Mtn—*summit* ... MO-7
Pelican Oil Field—*oilfield* ... TX-5
Pelican Overlook—*locale* ... UT-8
Pelican Pass—*channel* ... FL-3
Pelican Pass—*channel (2)* ... LA-4
Pelican Pass—*gap* ... WA-9
Pelican Passage—*channel* ... AL-4
Pelican Peak—*summit* ... MI-6
Pelican Plaza Shop Ctr—*locale* ... FL-3
*Pelican Point* ... FL-3
Pelican Point—*cape* ... AL-4
Pelican Point—*cape (4)* ... CA-9
Pelican Point—*cape (2)* ... FL-3
Pelican Point—*cape* ... GA-3
Pelican Point—*cape (3)* ... LA-4
Pelican Point—*cape* ... MN-6
Pelican Point—*cape* ... NV-8
Pelican Point—*cape* ... OR-9
Pelican Point—*cape* ... TX-5
Pelican Point—*cape (2)* ... UT-8
Pelican Point—*cliff* ... OR-9
Pelican Point Campground—*park* ... UT-8
Pelican Pond—*lake* ... CT-1
Pelican Pond—*lake* ... FL-3
Pelican Pond—*lake* ... UT-8
Pelican Pool—*lake* ... MO-7
Pelican Pouch—*ridge* ... IL-6
**Pelican Rapids**—*pop pl* ... MN-6
Pelican Reef—*bar* ... FL-3
Pelican Reef—*bar* ... TX-5
Pelican Ridge—*ridge* ... ID-8
Pelican River—*stream (2)* ... MN-6
Pelican River—*stream* ... WI-6
Pelican Rock—*bar* ... VI-3
Pelican Rock—*island (2)* ... CA-9
Pelican Roost—*island* ... WY-8
Pelican Rsvr—*reservoir* ... OR-9
Pelican Sch—*school* ... FL-3
Pelican Sch—*school* ... LA-4
Pelican Sch—*school* ... WI-6
Pelican Shoal—*bar* ... NC-3
Pelican Shoal Light 26—*locale* ... FL-3
*Pelican Slough* ... ID-8
Pelican Slough—*stream* ... TX-5
*Pelican Spit* ... TX-5
Pelican Spit—*bar (2)* ... GA-3
Pelican Spit Milit Reservation—*military* ... TX-5
Pelican Spring—*spring* ... NM-5
Pelican Spring—*spring* ... TX-5
Pelican Springs—*spring* ... WY-8
Pelican Springs Cabin—*locale* ... WY-8
Pelican State Beach—*park* ... CA-9
**Pelican (Town of)**—*pop pl* ... WI-6
**Pelican Township**—*pop pl* ... ND-7
**Pelican Township**—*pop pl* ... SD-7
**Pelican (Township of)**—*pop pl (2)* ... MN-6
Pelican Valley—*valley* ... WY-8
Pelican Valley Cem—*cemetery* ... MN-6
Pelican Valley Sch—*school* ... MN-6
Pelieniak—*swamp* ... FM-9
*Peliesele* ... FM-9
*Peliesole* ... FM-9
Peligreen Gulch—*valley* ... CA-9
Peligreen Place—*locale* ... CA-9
*Pelik*—*locale* ... FM-9
*Peliklakaha* ... FL-3
*Peliliou* ... PW-9
*Peliliu* ... PW-9
*Peliliu Island* ... PW-9
Pelillos Arroyo—*valley* ... TX-5
*Pelilu* ... PW-9
**Pelion**—*pop pl* ... SC-3
Pelion (CCD)—*cens area* ... SC-3
*Pelior* ... FM-9
Pelishek Corners—*locale* ... WI-6
*Pelisipi River* ... TN-4
Pelissier Lake—*lake* ... MI-6
*Peliysale* ... FM-9
Pelke Divide—*ridge* ... ID-8
Pelke Divide—*ridge* ... WA-9
Pelkey Basin—*basin* ... NY-2
Pelkey Brook—*stream* ... NY-2
Pelkey Lake—*lake* ... MN-6
Pelkey Lake—*lake* ... OR-9
Pelkey Lake Site—*hist pl* ... MN-6
Pelkey Mountan—*summit* ... NY-2
**Pelkie**—*pop pl* ... MI-6
Pelkie Cem—*cemetery* ... MI-6
*Pelkie Creek* ... MI-6
Pelkie Creek—*stream* ... MI-6
Pelkie Reef—*bar* ... MI-6
Pelky Bay—*bay* ... NY-2
Pelky Creek—*stream* ... MI-6
Pelky Creek—*stream* ... WA-9
Pelkys Falls—*falls* ... NY-2
Pelkys Lake—*lake* ... MI-6
Pell, Joe, Bldg—*hist pl* ... KY-4
Pella—*locale* ... ID-8
**Pella**—*pop pl* ... IA-7
**Pella**—*pop pl* ... WI-6
Pella Cem—*cemetery* ... NE-7
Pella Cem—*cemetery* ... TX-5
Pella Community HS—*school* ... IA-7
Pella Community Sch—*school* ... IA-7
Pella Game Mngmt Area—*park* ... IA-7
Pella HS—*school* ... IA-7
**Pelland**—*pop pl* ... MN-6
Pelland Creek—*stream* ... OR-9
Pelland Spring—*spring* ... OR-9
Pellaphalia Creek—*stream (2)* ... MS-4
Pella Pond—*reservoir* ... WI-6
Pella Reformed Ch—*church* ... NE-7
Pella Swamp—*swamp* ... WA-9
**Pella (Town of)**—*pop pl* ... WI-6
**Pella (Township of)**—*pop pl* ... IL-6
Pellatz Ranch—*locale* ... WY-8
Pella Ward Cem—*cemetery* ... ID-8
Pell Branch—*stream* ... KY-4
Pell Branch—*stream* ... TN-4
Pell Brook—*stream* ... IN-6
Pell Cabin—*locale* ... ID-8
Pell Cem—*cemetery* ... AL-4
Pell Cem—*cemetery* ... IN-6
**Pell City**—*pop pl* ... AL-4
Pell City (CCD)—*cens area* ... AL-4
Pell City Ch of God—*church* ... AL-4
Pell City City Hall—*building* ... AL-4
Pell City Civic Center—*building* ... AL-4
Pell City Country Club—*locale* ... AL-4
Pell City Division—*civil* ... AL-4
*Pell City Hospital* ... AL-4
Pell City HS—*school* ... AL-4
*Pell City Intermediate Sch* ... AL-4
Pell City Plaza Shop Ctr—*locale* ... AL-4
Pell Creek—*stream (2)* ... ID-8
Pell Creek—*stream* ... MN-6
Pell Creek—*stream* ... WA-9
*Pelleada Penieta* ... FM-9
Pelled Chestnut Acad (historical)—*school* ... TN-4
Pellegrino Park—*park* ... MO-7
**Pellejas**—*pop pl* ... PR-3
Pellejas (Barrio)—*fmr MCD (2)* ... PR-3
Pellerin-Chauffe House—*hist pl* ... LA-4
*Pelletier* ... NC-3
**Pelletier**—*pop pl* ... ME-1
Pelletier Brook—*stream (2)* ... ME-1
Pelletier Brook Lakes—*lake* ... ME-1
Pelletier Cave—*cave* ... AL-4
Pelletier Hollow—*valley* ... AL-4
*Pelletier Island* ... ME-1
Pelletier Siding—*locale* ... ME-1
Pellet Island—*island* ... MN-6
Pellet Lake—*lake* ... MN-6
Pelletreau Creek—*stream (2)* ... CA-9
Pelletreau Ridge—*ridge* ... CA-9
Pellets Island—*locale* ... NY-2
*Pellett Creek* ... NJ-2
Pellettown—*locale* ... NJ-2
*Pellettown Creek* ... NJ-2
Pellew Creek—*stream* ... MT-8
Pelley Cem—*cemetery* ... IN-6
**Pellez**—*pop pl* ... MS-4
Pell Hill—*summit* ... NY-2
Pell Hollow—*valley* ... KY-4
*Pellia* ... FM-9
Pellicer Creek—*stream* ... FL-3
Pellicer Creek Aquatic Preserve—*park* ... FL-3
Pellicer Creek Cem—*cemetery* ... FL-3
Pellicer Flats—*flat* ... FL-3
*Pellick Ridge* ... MT-8
Pellisier Creek—*stream* ... CA-9
Pellisier Flats—*flat* ... CA-9
Pell Island—*island* ... ME-1
Pellissier Bldg—*hist pl* ... CA-9
Pellissier Ranch—*locale* ... ND-7
Pellissier Spur—*locale* ... CA-9
Pellissippi Boat Dock—*locale* ... TN-4
Pellissippi Point—*cape* ... TN-4
Pellissippi Point Cabin Area—*locale* ... TN-4
Pellitory Point—*cape* ... VA-3
Pell Lake—*lake* ... NY-2
Pell Lake—*lake* ... WI-6
**Pell Lake**—*pop pl* ... WI-6
Pell Lake—*reservoir* ... NC-3
Pell Lake Dam—*dam* ... NC-3
*Pell Mell Creek* ... CA-9
Pell Mell Pocosin—*swamp* ... NC-3
Pellow Place—*locale* ... CA-9
Pell Placer Mine—*mine* ... ID-8
Pell Rsvr—*reservoir* ... CO-8
Pell Run—*stream* ... PA-2
**Pells**—*pop pl* ... NY-2
Pells Cem—*cemetery* ... SC-3
Pell Sch—*school* ... IL-6
Pell Sch—*school* ... WV-2
Pells Island—*island* ... MI-6
*Pells Lsough* ... WA-9
Pells Park—*cemetery* ... IL-6
Pells Pond—*lake* ... NY-2
**Pellston**—*pop pl* ... MI-6
Pellston Lookout Tower—*locale* ... MI-6
Pellucid Bayou—*stream* ... MS-4
Pellucid Bayou Oil Field—*oilfield* ... MS-4
**Pellville**—*pop pl* ... KY-4
Pellville Cem—*cemetery* ... IL-6
**Pellyn Wood (subdivision)**—*pop pl* ... NC-3
Pellyton—*locale* ... KY-4
Pelman Well—*well* ... NM-5
Pelnor Hollow—*valley* ... NY-2
Pelon—*summit* ... NM-5
Pelon, Cerro—*summit* ... AZ-5
Pelona, Loma—*summit* ... TX-5
Pelona, Sierra—*ridge* ... CA-9
Pelona Lookout—*locale* ... CA-9
Pelona Mtn—*summit* ... NM-5
Pelon Canyon—*valley* ... NM-5
*Peloncilla Range* ... NM-5
Peloncillo Mountains—*range* ... AZ-5
Peloncillo Mountains—*range* ... NM-5
Peloncillo Peak—*summit* ... NM-5
Peloncillo Peak—*summit* ... TX-5
*Peloncillo Range* ... AZ-5
*Peloncillo Range* ... NM-5
Peloncillo Tank—*reservoir* ... NM-5
Pelon Ciz Creek—*stream* ... TX-5
Pelon Ciz Ranch—*locale* ... TX-5
Pelone Island—*island* ... TX-5
Pelon Spring—*spring* ... AZ-5
Pelon Tank—*reservoir* ... TX-5
Pelon Windmill—*locale* ... NM-5
*Pelota Creek* ... FL-3
Pelota Fronton—*hist pl* ... OR-9
*Pelot Bay* ... VT-1
Pelot Cem—*cemetery* ... SC-3
Pelote Cem—*cemetery* ... SC-3
Pelotes Island—*island* ... FL-3
*Pelot Point* ... VT-1
*Pelot's Bay* ... VT-1
Pelots Bay—*bay* ... VT-1
Pelots Point—*cape* ... VT-1
*Peloucillo Range* ... NM-5
Pelser Cem—*cemetery* ... IN-6
Pelsey Ditch—*canal* ... IN-6
*Pelsor* ... AR-4
**Pelsor**—*pop pl* ... AR-4
Pelster, Wilhelm, House-Barn—*hist pl* ... MO-7
Pelster Lateral—*canal* ... CO-8
Pelt Cem—*cemetery (2)* ... FL-3
Pelt Creek—*stream* ... FL-3
Pelt Creek—*stream* ... OR-9
*Pelter Drain* ... MI-6
Peltier—*locale* ... CA-9
Peltier Basin—*basin* ... CO-8
*Peltier Creek* ... NC-3
Peltier Creek—*stream* ... CO-8
Peltier Drain—*stream (2)* ... MI-6
Peltier House—*hist pl* ... LA-4
Peltier Lake—*lake* ... CO-8
Peltier Lake—*lake* ... MN-6
Peltier Lakes—*lake* ... TX-5
*Peltier Park*—*park* ... LA-4
Peltier Post Office (historical)—*building* ... TN-4
Peltier Slough—*stream* ... CA-9
Peltis Fork—*stream* ... KY-4
Pelt Lake—*lake* ... MN-6
**Pelto**—*pop pl* ... ND-7
Pelto, Lake—*lake* ... LA-4
*Pelto Bay* ... LA-4
Peltoma Bridge—*bridge* ... ME-1
Pelton—*locale* ... NE-7
Pelton, Bayou—*gut* ... LA-4
Pelton, Ora, House—*hist pl* ... IL-6
Pelton Brook—*stream* ... ME-1
Pelton Cem—*cemetery* ... NY-2
*Pelton Creek* ... WA-9
Pelton Creek—*stream (2)* ... WA-9
Pelton Creek—*stream (2)* ... WY-8
Pelton Creek Campground—*locale* ... WY-8
Pelton Creek Shelter—*locale* ... WA-9
Pelton Dam—*dam* ... MA-1
Pelton Dam*—*dam* ... ND-7
Pelton Dam—*dam* ... OR-9
Pelton Drain—*stream* ... MI-6
*Pelton Hill* ... ME-1
**Pelton Hill**—*pop pl* ... ME-1
Pelton Hill—*summit* ... MA-1
Pelton Hill—*summit* ... NY-2
Pelton Lake—*lake* ... MN-6
Pelton Lake—*lake* ... TX-5
Pelton Mill—*hist pl* ... NY-2
Pelton Oval—*park* ... NY-2
Pelton Park—*park* ... OH-6
Pelton Park—*park* ... OR-9
Pelton Peak—*summit* ... WA-9
Pelton Point—*cape* ... MI-6
Pelton Pond—*lake* ... MI-6
Pelton Pond—*lake* ... NY-2
Pelton Ranch—*locale* ... ND-7
Pelton Regulating Dam—*dam* ... OR-9
Pelton Regulating Rsvr—*reservoir* ... OR-9
Pelton River—*stream* ... MI-6
*Pelton Rsvr* ... OR-9
Pelton Rsvr—*reservoir* ... MA-1
Peltons Posture State Board of Fisheries—*locale* ... CT-1
Pelt Prairie—*flat* ... TX-5
Pelucia Bayou—*gut* ... MS-4
Pelucia Bayou—*stream* ... MS-4
Pelucia Creek—*stream* ... MS-4
Pelucia Creek Structure Y-33A-20 Dam—*dam* ... MS-4
Pelucia Creek Structure Y-33A-23 Dam—*dam* ... MS-4
Pelucia Creek Structure Y-33a-26 Dam—*dam* ... MS-4
Pelucia Creek Structure Y-33a-28 Dam—*dam* ... MS-4
Pelucia Creek Structure Y-33a-39 Dam—*dam* ... MS-4
Pelucia Creek Watershed Y-33A-22 Dam—*dam* ... MS-4
Pelucia Watershed Y-33a-1 Dam—*dam* ... MS-4
Pelucia Watershed Y-33a-10 Dam—*dam* ... MS-4
Pelucia Watershed Y-33a-11 Dam—*dam* ... MS-4
Pelucia Watershed Y-33a-12 Dam—*dam* ... MS-4
Pelucia Watershed Y-33a-13 Dam—*dam* ... MS-4
Pelucia Watershed Y-33a-14 Dam—*dam* ... MS-4
Pelucia Watershed Y-33a-2 Dam—*dam* ... MS-4
Pelucia Watershed Y-33a-25a Dam—*dam* ... MS-4
Pelucia Watershed Y-33a-3 Dam—*dam* ... MS-4
Pelucia Watershed Y-33a-4 Dam—*dam* ... MS-4
Pelucia Watershed Y-33a-5 Dam—*dam* ... MS-4
Pelucia Watershed Y-33a-6 Dam—*dam* ... MS-4
Pelucia Watershed Y-33a-7 Dam—*dam* ... MS-4
Pelucia Watershed Y-33a-8 Dam—*dam* ... MS-4
Pelucia Watershed Y-33a-9 Dam—*dam* ... MS-4
*Pelugaua* ... PW-9
*Pelugauar Island* ... PW-9
*Pelugauer* ... PW-9
*Peluguaur* ... PW-9
Peluk Creek—*stream (2)* ... AK-9
**Pelusrik**—*pop pl* ... FM-9
*Pelveler Chimney Spring* ... AZ-5
Pelvy Creek—*stream* ... WA-9
**Pelzer**—*pop pl* ... IN-6
**Pelzer**—*pop pl* ... SC-3
Pelzer Mills Dam—*dam* ... SC-3
**Pelzer North**—*pop pl* ... SC-3
**Pelzer South**—*pop pl* ... SC-3
**Pelzer (unincorporated)**—*pop pl* ... SC-3
Pemadumcook Lake—*lake* ... ME-1
*Pemagoy* ... FM-9
*Pemaquan Lake* ... ME-1
*Pemaquan River* ... ME-1
**Pemaquid**—*pop pl* ... ME-1
**Pemaquid Beach**—*pop pl* ... ME-1
*Pemaquid Falls* ... ME-1
Pemaquid Harbor—*bay* ... ME-1
**Pemaquid Harbor**—*pop pl* ... ME-1
Pemaquid Ledge—*bar* ... ME-1
Pemaquid Lighthouse—*locale* ... ME-1
Pemaquid Neck—*cape* ... ME-1
Pemaquid Point—*cape* ... ME-1
**Pemaquid Point**—*pop pl* ... ME-1
Pemaquid Point Light—*hist pl* ... ME-1
Pemaquid Pond—*lake* ... ME-1
Pemaquid Restoration and Museum—*hist pl* ... ME-1
Pemaquid River—*stream* ... ME-1
**Pember Corners**—*pop pl* ... NY-2
Pemberthy Crossing—*locale* ... MI-6
Pemberton—*airport* ... NJ-2
Pemberton—*locale* ... VA-3
**Pemberton**—*pop pl* ... MN-6
**Pemberton**—*pop pl* ... NJ-2
**Pemberton**—*pop pl* ... OH-6
**Pemberton**—*pop pl* ... PA-2
**Pemberton**—*pop pl* ... TN-4
**Pemberton**—*pop pl* ... WV-2
Pemberton, Phineas, House—*hist pl* ... PA-2
Pemberton and Hibble Number One Mine (underground)—*mine* ... TN-4
Pemberton Branch—*stream* ... DE-2
Pemberton Branch—*stream (4)* ... TN-4
*Pemberton Canyon* ... OR-9
Pemberton Canyon—*valley* ... OR-9
Pemberton Cem—*cemetery* ... AR-4
Pemberton Cem—*cemetery* ... MS-4
Pemberton Cem—*cemetery (2)* ... MO-7
Pemberton Cem—*cemetery (3)* ... TN-4
*Pemberton Church* ... MS-4
Pemberton Creek—*stream* ... FL-3
Pemberton Creek—*stream* ... NC-3
Pemberton Draw—*valley* ... TX-5
Pemberton Farm—*hist pl* ... KY-4
Pemberton Hall—*hist pl* ... MD-2
Pemberton Hall and Gymnasium—*hist pl* ... IL-6
**Pemberton Heights**—*pop pl* ... NJ-2
Pemberton Hollow—*valley* ... AR-4
Pemberton House—*hist pl* ... GA-3
Pemberton HS—*school* ... TX-5
Pemberton Mansion and Oak—*hist pl* ... TN-4
Pemberton Mine—*mine* ... TN-4
Pemberton Ranch—*locale* ... AZ-5
Pemberton Ridge—*ridge* ... MO-7
Pemberton Sch—*school* ... MI-6
Pemberton Sch—*school* ... MO-7
Pemberton's HQ—*hist pl* ... MS-4
Pemberton Siding—*locale* ... TN-4
Pembertons Point—*cape* ... NY-2
Pemberton Station (historical)—*locale (2)* ... MA-1
**Pemberton (subdivision)**—*pop pl* ... MA-1
Pemberton Tank—*reservoir (2)* ... AZ-5
**Pemberton (Township of)**—*pop pl* ... NJ-2
Pemberty Spring—*spring* ... MO-7
**Pemberville**—*pop pl* ... OH-6
Pemberville Cem—*cemetery* ... OH-6
**Pemberwick**—*pop pl* ... CT-1
**Pembina**—*pop pl* ... ND-7
Pembina Cem—*cemetery* ... MO-7
Pembina Cem—*cemetery* ... ND-7
Pembina City Dam—*dam* ... ND-7
Pembina County—*civil* ... ND-7
Pembina County Courthouse—*hist pl* ... ND-7
Pembina Hills—*range* ... ND-7
Pembina Hills State Game Mngmt Area—*park* ... ND-7
Pembina Interchange—*crossing* ... ND-7
*Pembina Mountain* ... ND-7
*Pembina Mountains* ... ND-7
Pembina Municipal Airp—*airport* ... ND-7
Pembina Prairie Natl Wildlife Mngmt Area—*park* ... ND-7
Pembina River—*stream* ... ND-7
Pembina State Park—*park* ... ND-7
**Pembina Township**—*pop pl* ... ND-7
**Pembina (Township of)**—*pop pl* ... MN-6
*Pembinbemon River* ... WI-6
**Pembine**—*pop pl* ... WI-6
*Pembinebemon River* ... WI-6
Pembine Cem—*cemetery* ... WI-6
*Pembine River* ... WI-6
**Pembine (Town of)**—*pop pl* ... WI-6
Pemble Cem—*cemetery* ... LA-4
**Pembrey**—*pop pl* ... DE-2
*Pembroke* ... IL-6
Pembroke—*locale* ... FL-3
Pembroke—*locale* ... WV-2
Pembroke—*other* ... FL-3
**Pembroke**—*pop pl* ... GA-3
**Pembroke**—*pop pl* ... IN-6
**Pembroke**—*pop pl* ... KY-4
**Pembroke**—*pop pl* ... ME-1
**Pembroke**—*pop pl* ... MA-1
**Pembroke**—*pop pl* ... NH-1
**Pembroke**—*pop pl* ... NY-2
**Pembroke**—*pop pl* ... NC-3
**Pembroke**—*pop pl* ... PA-2
**Pembroke**—*pop pl* ... VA-3
Pembroke, Lake—*lake* ... FL-3
Pembroke Acad—*school* ... NH-1
Pembroke (CCD)—*cens area* ... GA-3
Pembroke (CCD)—*cens area* ... KY-4

Pembroke Cem—*cemetery* CT-1
Pembroke Cem—*cemetery* SD-7
*Pembroke Center* MA-1
Pembroke Center—*other* MA-1
**Pembroke Center**—*pop pl* NY-2
Pembroke Center Sch—*school* MA-1
Pembroke Ch—*church* IL-6
Pembroke Ch—*church* NC-3
Pembroke Christian Acad—*school* FL-3
Pembroke Creek—*stream* NC-3
Pembroke Elem Sch—*school* NC-3
Pembroke Hall—*building* NC-3
Pembroke Hall—*hist pl* NC-3
**Pembroke Heights**—*pop pl* MA-1
Pembroke Hill—*summit* NH-1
Pembroke Hill Sch—*school* NH-1
Pembroke (historical)—*locale* SD-7
Pembroke (historical P.O.)—*locale* MA-1
Pembroke JHS—*school* NC-3
Pembroke Lakes Acad—*school* FL-3
Pembroke Lakes Elem Sch—*school* FL-3
Pembroke Manor—*hist pl* VA-3
**Pembroke Manor**—*pop pl* VA-3
Pembroke Mill—*hist pl* NH-1
Pembroke MS—*school* NC-3
Pembroke Park—*park* MI-6
**Pembroke Park**—*pop pl* FL-3
**Pembroke (Pembroke Center)**—*pop pl* MA-1
**Pembroke Pines**—*pop pl* FL-3
**Pembroke Pines**—*pop pl* MA-1
Pembroke Pines Elem Sch—*school* FL-3
Pembroke Pines General Hosp—*hospital* FL-3
Pembroke Pines Plaza West (Shop Ctr)—*locale* FL-3
Pembroke Pines (Shop Ctr)—*locale* FL-3
Pembroke Road Baptist Ch—*church* FL-3
Pembroke Road Ch—*church* FL-3
Pembroke Road Sch—*school* FL-3
Pembroke Sch—*school* FL-3
Pembroke Sch—*school* IL-6
Pembroke Sch—*school* MI-6
Pembroke Sch—*school* MO-7
Pembroke Sch—*school* NH-1
Pembroke Sch—*school* TN-4
Pembroke Sch—*school* VA-3
Pembroke Shop Ctr—*locale* MA-1
Pembroke Springs—*spring* VA-3
Pembroke State Univ—*school* NC-3
Pembroke Station—*locale* NY-2
Pembroke Stream—*stream* ME-1
Pembroke Town For—*forest* MA-1
Pembroke Town Hall—*building* NC-3
**Pembroke (Town of)**—*pop pl* ME-1
**Pembroke (Town of)**—*pop pl* MA-1
**Pembroke (Town of)**—*pop pl* NH-1
**Pembroke (Town of)**—*pop pl* NY-2
Pembroke (Township of)—*fmr MCD* NC-3
**Pembroke (Township of)**—*pop pl* IL-6
Pembroke Village Hist Dist—*hist pl* PA-2
Pembroke Village (Shop Ctr)—*locale* FL-3
Pembrook Cem—*cemetery* SD-7
Pembrook Chapel—*church* OH-6
Pembrook Colony—*locale* SD-7
**Pembrook Place**—*pop pl* TN-4
Pembrook Rsvr—*reservoir* OR-9
**Pembrook Township**—*pop pl* SD-7
Pemebonwon Dam—*dam* WI-6
Pemebonwon Islands—*island* WI-6
*Peme Bon Won River* WI-6
Pemebonwon River—*stream* WI-6
*Pemedumcook Lake* ME-1
Pemel Ch—*church* SC-3
Pemel Sch—*school* SC-3
Pemene Creek—*stream* MI-6
Pemene Falls—*falls* MI-6
Pemene Falls—*falls* WI-6
*Pemertan* MN-6
Pemeta—*locale* OK-5
Pemetic Mtn—*summit* ME-1
*Pemgoy* FM-9
Pemigewasset, Mount—*summit* NH-1
*Pemigewasset Pond* NH-1
Pemigewasset River—*stream* NH-1
Pemigewassett Camp—*locale* NH-1
Pemilton Sch—*school* LA-4
Pemingewasset Lake—*lake* NH-1
Pemiscot Bayou—*gut* MO-7
Pemiscot Bayou—*stream* AR-4
**Pemiscot County**—*pop pl* MO-7
*Pemiscot County Farm Cemetery* MO-7
Pemiscot County Special Sch—*school* MO-7
Pemiscot County Vocational Sch—*school* MO-7
Pemiscot Lake—*flat* AR-4
Pemiscot Memorial Gardens—*cemetery* MO-7
Pemiscot Township—*civil* MO-7
Pemma Creek—*stream* WI-6
*Pemmaquan River* ME-1
Pemmican Lake—*lake* CA-9
Pemmican Lake—*lake* MN-6
Pemmican Lake—*lake* WA-9
Pemm Windmill—*locale* TX-5
P E Moore Pond Dam—*dam* MS-4
Pemperton Cem—*cemetery* TN-4
Pen, The—*lake* LA-4
Pena Adobe—*hist pl* CA-9
*Penaar* VA-3
*Pena Blanca* CA-9
*Pena Blanca* TX-5
**Pena Blanca**—*pop pl* NM-5
Pena Blanca—*summit* NM-5
*Pena Blanca Arroyo* AZ-5
Pena Blanca Arroyo—*stream* NM-5
*Pena Blanca Canyon* AZ-5
Pena Blanca Canyon —*valley* AZ-5
*Pena Blanca Creek* AZ-5
*Pena Blanca Creek* TX-5
Pena Blanca Creek —*stream* TX-5
*Pena Blanca Hills* TX-5
Pena Blanca Lake —*reservoir* AZ-5
*Pena Blanca Mountains* TX-5
Pena Blanca Mountains —*summit* TX-5
*Pena Blanca Range* TX-5
*Pena Blancas* TX-5
Pena Blanca Spring —*spring* AZ-5
Pena Blanca Spring —*spring* TX-5
Pena Blanca Trail Number Forty-one —*trail* AZ-5
*Pena Blanka Creek* AZ-5
Pena Canyon—*valley* CA-9
Pena Cem—*cemetery* (2) TX-5
*Pena Colorado Creek* TX-5
*Pena Colorado Creek* TX-5
Pena Colorado Creek—*stream* TX-5
*Penacook* (2) NH-1
**Penacook**—*pop pl* NH-1
Penacook Lake—*lake* NH-1
**Pena Cortada**—*pop pl* (2) PR-3
Pena Creek—*stream* CA-9
Pena Creek —*stream* TX-5
Pena Domingo—*summit* PR-3
Pena Flora Banco Number 106—*levee* TX-5
Penaflor Ruins—*locale* NM-5
Pena House (Historic Site) —*locale* CA-9
*Penakese Island* MA-1
Pena La Francia—*summit* PR-3
Penal Farm Dam Number Four—*dam* TN-4
Penal Farm Dam Number One—*dam* TN-4
Penal Farm Dam Number Three—*dam* TN-4
Penal Farm Dam Number Two—*dam* TN-4
Penal Farm Lake Number Four—*reservoir* TN-4
Penal Farm Lake Number One—*reservoir* TN-4
Penal Farm Lake Number Three—*reservoir* TN-4
Penal Farm Lake Number Two—*reservoir* TN-4
**Penalosa**—*pop pl* KS-7
Penalua Gulch—*valley* SD-7
Pena Mountain—*summit* TX-5
**Penantly**—*pop pl* MS-4
Penantly Creek—*stream* MS-4
Penantly Post Office (historical)—*building* MS-4
**Pena Pobre**—*pop pl* (2) PR-3
Pena Pobre (Barrio)—*fmr MCD* PR-3
*Penargil* PA-2
**Pen Argyl**—*pop pl* PA-2
Pen Argyl Borough—*civil* PA-2
Pen Argyl Junior-Senior HS—*school* PA-2
*Pen Argyl Wind Gap* PA-2
**Penarth**—*pop pl* DE-2
**Penarth**—*pop pl* PA-2
Penas, Arroyo—*valley* TX-5
Penasa Lake—*lake* MI-6
*Penasal Lake* MI-6
*Penasca Canyon* AZ-5
*Penascal* TX-5
Penascal, Point—*cape* TX-5
*Penascal Rincon* TX-5
Penascal Rincon—*cape* TX-5
Penascito—*summit* CO-8
**Penasco**—*pop pl* NM-5
Penasco Amarillo—*summit* NM-5
**Penasco Blanco**—*pop pl* NM-5
Penasco Blanco—*summit* NM-5
Penasco Blanco Ruins—*locale* NM-5
Penasco Bluff—*cliff* NM-5
Penasco Canyon —*valley* AZ-5
Penasco Canyon—*valley* (3) NM-5
Penasco (CCD)—*cens area* NM-5
Penasco Dam —*dam* AZ-5
Penasco Flat—*flat* NM-5
Penasco Fosil—*other* PR-3
Penasco Lakes—*lake* NM-5
Penasco Peak—*summit* NM-5
Penasco Ridge—*cliff* NM-5
Penasco River Ranch—*locale* NM-5
Penasco Rock—*summit* CA-9
Penasco Sch—*school* NM-5
Penascoso Mtn—*summit* NM-5
Penasco Spring—*spring* CA-9
Penasco Spring—*spring* NM-5
Penasco Tank —*reservoir* AZ-5
Penasco Tank—*reservoir* NM-5
Penasco Well—*locale* NM-5
Penasco Windmill—*locale* NM-5
Penas Negras Cabin—*locale* NM-5
Penas Negras Cem—*cemetery* NM-5
Penas Negras Trail—*trail* NM-5
Pena Spring—*spring* CA-9
Pena Spring —*spring* TX-5
Pena Springs—*spring* NM-5
Penasquito Canyon—*valley* NM-5
*Penasquitos* CA-9
Penasquitos Ranch—*locale* CA-9
**Penasse**—*pop pl* MN-6
Penasse Island—*island* MN-6
*Penasu* MH-9
Penasula Creek—*stream* FL-3
Pena tank—*reservoir* NM-5
**Penataquit**—*pop pl* NY-2
Penataquit Creek—*stream* NY-2
Penataquit Point—*cape* NY-2
*Penatchie Creek* AL-4
Penateka—*hist pl* OK-5
Pena Wash—*stream* NM-5
**Penawawa**—*pop pl* WA-9
Penawawa Bar—*bar* WA-9
Penawawa Canyon—*valley* WA-9
*Penawawa Creek* WA-9
Penawawa Creek—*stream* WA-9
Pena Windmill—*locale* (2) TX-5
Pena Windmill —*locale* TX-5
Pen Basin—*basin* ID-8
Pen Basin Campground—*locale* ID-8
Pen Basin Driveway (historical)—*trail* ID-8
Pen Bayou—*stream* LA-4
Penber Mine—*mine* CO-8
Pen Bonc Hill—*summit* NY-2
Pen Branch—*stream* MS-4
Pen Branch—*stream* (3) SC-3
Pen Branch—*stream* TX-5
Pen Branch Tank—*reservoir* TX-5
Penbrock Cem—*cemetery* WA-9
Penbroke Sch—*school* IL-6
*Pen Brook* MA-1
**Penbrook**—*pop pl* PA-2
Penbrook Borough—*civil* PA-2
Penbrook JHS—*school* PA-2
*Penbrook MS* PA-2
Penbrook Park—*park* PA-2
Penbrook Run—*stream* MD-2
Penbrook Sch—*school* PA-2
Penbrook Station—*locale* PA-2
Penbryn—*locale* NJ-2
Penbryn—*locale* PA-2
Penbryn Park—*park* PA-2
Pencader—*locale* DE-2
*Pencader Church* DE-2
**Pencader Farms (subdivision)**—*pop pl* DE-2
Pencader Hundred—*civil* DE-2
Pencader Presbyterian Ch—*church* DE-2
**Pencader Village**—*pop pl* DE-2
Pence—*locale* (2) KY-4
**Pence**—*pop pl* AL-4
**Pence**—*pop pl* IN-6
**Pence**—*pop pl* KS-7
**Pence**—*pop pl* TN-4
**Pence**—*pop pl* WI-6
Pence, Adam, House—*hist pl* KY-4
Pence, Mount—*summit* CO-8
Pence Branch—*stream* (2) KY-4
Pence Branch—*stream* TN-4
Pence Butte—*summit* ID-8
Pence Cem—*cemetery* IA-7
Pence Cem—*cemetery* (2) KS-7
Pence Cem—*cemetery* KY-4
Pence Cem—*cemetery* MO-7
Pence Hill—*summit* TN-4
Pence Hill—*summit* VA-3
Pence Hollow—*valley* IN-6
Pence Hot Spring—*spring* ID-8
Pence Lake—*lake* WI-6
Pence Lake Lookout Tower—*locale* WI-6
Pence Mtn—*summit* CA-9
Pence Park—*park* CO-8
**Pencer**—*pop pl* MN-6
Pence Sch—*school* KY-4
Pence Sch (historical)—*school* MO-7
Pence Spring Rsvr—*reservoir* OR-9
**Pence Springs**—*pop pl* WV-2
Pence Springs Hotel Hist Dist—*hist pl* WV-2
**Pence (Town of)**—*pop pl* WI-6
*Penceville* IN-6
Penchant, Bayou—*stream* LA-4
Penchant, Lake—*lake* LA-4
**Penchem (Pinchem)**—*pop pl* KY-4
**Pencil Bluff**—*pop pl* AR-4
Pencil Bluff (Township of)—*fmr MCD* AR-4
Pencil Brook—*stream* NY-2
Pencil Lake—*lake* MI-6
Pencil Lake—*lake* MN-6
Pencil Point—*summit* WY-8
Pencilwood—*uninc pl* CA-9
**Pencoyd**—*pop pl* PA-2
Pencoyo Station—*locale* PA-2
Pen Creek—*stream* ID-8
Pen Creek—*stream* OR-9
Pen Creek—*stream* TX-5
Pendair—*locale* OR-9
**Pendair Heights**—*pop pl* OR-9
Pendant Creek—*stream* MT-8
Pendant Guard Station—*locale* MT-8
Pendant Lake—*lake* CA-9
Pendant Lake—*lake* MN-6
Pendant Point—*cape* AK-9
*Pendar* VA-3
**Pendaries**—*pop pl* NM-5
Pendaries Grist Mill—*hist pl* NM-5
Pendaries Ranch—*locale* NM-5
Pendarvis—*hist pl* WI-6
Pendarvis—*lake* FL-3
Pendarvis—*locale* GA-3
Pendarvis Cem—*cemetery* LA-4
Pendarvis Cove—*bay* FL-3
Pendarvis Point—*cape* FL-3
**Pen Daw**—*pop pl* VA-3
*Pend D'Oreille Lake* MT-8
*Pend D'oreille R* WA-9
Pendegrass Park—*park* TN-4
Pendejo Wash—*stream* NM-5
*Pendeldon Mountain* VA-3
*Pendeldon Mountain* WV-2
Pendell—*locale* TX-5
Pendell Draw—*valley* TX-5
Pendell Pumping Station—*other* TX-5
Pendell Ridge—*ridge* MT-8
**Pendelton**—*pop pl* TX-5
Pendencia Creek—*stream* TX-5
*Pen Dennis* KS-7
Pendennis—*locale* KS-7
**Pen Dennis**—*pop pl* KS-7
**Pendennis Mount**—*pop pl* MD-2
Pendent Lake—*lake* MT-8
Pender—*locale* NC-3
Pender—*locale* VA-3
**Pender**—*pop pl* NE-7
Pender, Joseph John, House—*hist pl* NC-3
Pender Acad—*school* NC-3
Penderborough Sch—*school* SC-3
**Penderbrook**—*pop pl* VA-3
Pender Ch—*church* VA-3
Pender Chapel—*church* MO-7
**Pender County**—*pop pl* NC-3
Pender County Courthouse—*hist pl* NC-3
**Pender Crossroad**—*pop pl* NC-3
Penderdam Bay—*swamp* NC-3
Pendergast Ditch—*canal* MT-8
Pendergast Lake—*lake* MN-6
Pendergast Pup—*stream* AK-9
Pendergast Sch—*school* AZ-5
Pendergests Mill (historical)—*locale* TN-4
Pendergraff Hollow—*valley* MO-7
Pendergraft Peak—*summit* WY-8
**Pendergrass**—*pop pl* AL-4
**Pendergrass**—*pop pl* GA-3
Pendergrass Bluff—*cliff* TN-4
Pendergrass Branch—*stream* NC-3
Pendergrass Canyon—*valley* NM-5
Pendergrass Cem—*cemetery* KY-4
Pendergrass Cem—*cemetery* (2) TN-4
Pendergrass Cem—*cemetery* TX-5
Pendergrass Creek—*stream* CO-8
Pendergrass Creek—*stream* TN-4
Pendergrass Flats—*flat* CO-8
Pendergrass Mine (underground)—*mine* TN-4
Pendergrass Mtn—*summit* NC-3
Pendergrass Tank—*reservoir* NM-5
Pendergrass Well—*locale* NM-5
*Pendergrast* AL-4
*Pendergrast* GA-3
Pender Hollow—*valley* (2) MO-7
Pender HS—*school* NC-3
Penderlan—*locale* VA-3
**Penderlea**—*pop pl* NC-3
Penderlea Ch—*church* NC-3
Penderlea Homesteads—*locale* NC-3
Penderlea Lake—*reservoir* NC-3
Penderlea MS—*school* NC-3
Penders Canyon—*valley* WA-9
Penders Chapel—*church* NC-3
Pender Sch (historical)—*school* PA-2
Penders Creek—*stream* MS-4
**Penders Crossroads**—*pop pl* NC-3
Penders Mill Run—*stream* NC-3
Pender's Store—*hist pl* FL-3
Pender Switch—*locale* MO-7
**Pender Township**—*pop pl* NE-7
Penderville Cem—*cemetery* MS-4
Penderville Ch—*church* MS-4
Penderwood—*locale* VA-3
Pendexter Brook—*stream* ME-1
Pendexter Cem—*cemetery* ME-1
Pendills Bay—*bay* MI-6
Pendills Creek—*stream* MI-6
Pendills Lake—*lake* MI-6
Pendle Hill—*hist pl* ME-1
**Pendle Hill**—*pop pl* PA-2
Pendleton—*locale* AR-4
Pendleton—*locale* KY-4
**Pendleton**—*pop pl* IN-6
**Pendleton**—*pop pl* MO-7
**Pendleton**—*pop pl* NY-2
**Pendleton**—*pop pl* NC-3
**Pendleton**—*pop pl* OR-9
**Pendleton**—*pop pl* (2) SC-3
**Pendleton**—*pop pl* TX-5
**Pendleton**—*pop pl* VA-3
Pendleton, Col. Edmund, House—*hist pl* KY-4
Pendleton, George Hunt, House—*hist pl* OH-6
Pendleton, Mount—*summit* AK-9
Pendleton, William Kimbrough, House—*hist pl* FL-3
*Pendleton Beach* NH-1
**Pendleton Beach**—*pop pl* NH-1
Pendleton Bluff—*cliff* TN-4
Pendleton Branch—*stream* KY-4
Pendleton Branch—*stream* (2) VA-3
Pendleton Canyon—*valley* NM-5
Pendleton Canyon—*valley* (2) WA-9
Pendleton (CCD)—*cens area* CA-9
Pendleton (CCD)—*cens area* OR-9
Pendleton (CCD)—*cens area* SC-3
Pendleton Cem—*cemetery* KY-4
Pendleton Cem—*cemetery* MO-7
Pendleton Cem—*cemetery* TN-4
Pendleton Cem—*cemetery* TX-5
Pendleton Cem—*cemetery* (2) VA-3
**Pendleton Center**—*pop pl* NY-2
Pendleton Ch—*church* GA-3
Pendleton Ch—*church* LA-4
Pendleton Ch—*church* MO-7
Pendleton Ch—*church* VA-3
Pendleton Community Hospital Helipad—*airport* OR-9
Pendleton Country Club—*other* OR-9
**Pendleton (County)**—*pop pl* KY-4
**Pendleton (County)**—*pop pl* WV-2
Pendleton County Poor Farm—*hist pl* WV-2
*Pendleton Cove* ME-1
*Pendleton Creek* AL-4
*Pendleton Creek* MI-6
Pendleton Creek—*stream* GA-3
Pendleton Creek—*stream* MI-6
Pendleton Creek—*stream* NC-3
Pendleton Creek—*stream* PA-2
Pendleton Creek—*stream* WV-2
Pendleton Ferry—*locale* AR-4
Pendleton Gore Ridge—*ridge* MO-7
Pendleton Heights—*hist pl* WV-2
Pendleton Hill—*summit* CT-1
Pendleton Hill—*summit* KY-4
Pendleton Hill—*summit* ME-1
Pendleton Hill—*summit* MA-1
Pendleton Hill Brook—*stream* CT-1
Pendleton Hist Dist—*hist pl* SC-3
Pendleton (historical)—*locale* KS-7
Pendleton Hollow—*valley* KY-4
Pendleton Hollow—*valley* TN-4
Pendleton House—*hist pl* (2) KY-4
Pendleton Island—*island* VA-3
Pendleton Junction—*uninc pl* OR-9
Pendleton Mesa—*summit* AZ-5
Pendleton Mtn—*summit* CO-8
Pendleton Municipal Airp—*airport* OR-9
*Pendleton North* CA-9
Pendleton Park—*park* GA-3
Pendleton Park—*park* OR-9
Pendleton Park—*park* TX-5
Pendleton Point—*cape* ME-1
Pendleton Rec Area—*park* AR-4
Pendleton Ridge—*ridge* VA-3
Pendleton (RR name for Pendletons)—*other* VA-3
Pendleton Run—*stream* IN-6
Pendleton Run—*stream* PA-2
Pendleton Sch—*school* (2) CA-9
Pendletons Mill (historical)—*locale* TN-4
*Pendleton South* CA-9
Pendleton Southwest (CCD)—*cens area* KY-4
Pendleton Spring—*spring* OR-9
Pendleton Spring—*spring* UT-8
Pendleton Springs Ch—*church* GA-3
**Pendletons (RR name (Pendletons)**—*pop pl* VA-3
Pendleton Street Sch—*school* ME-1
**Pendleton (Town of)**—*pop pl* NY-2
Pendleton Township—*civil* MO-7
**Pendleton (Township of)**—*pop pl* IL-6
Pendleton Windmill—*locale* NM-5
Pendley—*locale* AL-4
Pendley Cem—*cemetery* AL-4
Pendley Cem—*cemetery* NC-3
Pendley Chapel—*church* AL-4
Pendley Creek—*stream* AL-4
**Pendley Hills**—*pop pl* GA-3
Pendock Brook—*stream* RI-1
Pendock Hill—*summit* VT-1
*Pendock Pond* MI-6
Pendock Pond—*lake* MI-6
Pendola Campground—*locale* CA-9
Pendola Gardens—*locale* CA-9
Pendola Guard Station—*locale* CA-9
Pendola Point—*Cape* FL-3
Pendola Ranch—*locale* CA-9
Pendora Park—*park* PA-2
Pend Oreille, Lake—*lake* ID-8
Pend Oreille, Mount—*summit* ID-8
**Pend Oreille County**—*pop pl* WA-9
*Pend oreille Creek* WA-9
Pend Oreille Mine—*mine* WA-9
Pend Oreille River—*stream* WA-9
Pend Oreille State Park—*park* WA-9
Pend Oreille State Wildlife Mngmt Area—*park* ID-8
**Pend Oreille Village**—*pop pl* WA-9
*Pendorf Creek* MT-8
**Pendorff**—*pop pl* MS-4
Pendorff Sch—*school* MS-4
*Pendorf Sch* MS-4
*Pend Orielle River* WA-9
Pendorvos Creek—*stream* MS-4
**Pendrew Manor**—*pop pl* DE-2
Pendrey, Arthur, Cottage—*hist pl* ID-8
Pendrey, Joe and Zina, Bungalow—*hist pl* ID-8
Pendrey Drug Store Bldg—*hist pl* ID-8
**Pendroy**—*pop pl* MT-8
Penegor Lake—*lake* MI-6
*Penekese Island* MA-1
*Penekessey Island* MA-1
Penelas Mine—*mine* NV-8
Penelec Retention Dam—*dam* PA-2
Penelo—*locale* NC-3
Penelope—*locale* NY-2
**Penelope**—*pop pl* NC-3
**Penelope**—*pop pl* TX-5
Penelope Creek—*stream* AK-9
Penelope Pond—*lake* NY-2
*Penemakeeset Island* MA-1
Penenuk—*bar* FM-9
Penequa (historical)—*locale* ND-7
*Penequese Island* MA-1
**Penermon**—*pop pl* MO-7
*Penesal Lake* MI-6
*Penescal* TX-5
*Penescal Rincon* TX-5
Penetiw—*spring* FM-9
*Penfield* KS-7
*Penfield* MI-6
Penfield—*locale* KS-7
**Penfield**—*pop pl* GA-3
**Penfield**—*pop pl* IL-6
**Penfield**—*pop pl* NY-2
**Penfield**—*pop pl* OH-6
**Penfield**—*pop pl* (2) PA-2
Penfield Branch—*stream* WV-2
Penfield Cem—*cemetery* KS-7
Penfield Cem—*cemetery* OH-6
**Penfield Center**—*pop pl* NY-2
Penfield Ch—*church* NY-2
Penfield Country Club—*other* NY-2
**Penfield Downs**—*pop pl* PA-2
**Penfield Heights**—*pop pl* AL-4
Penfield Hill—*summit* CT-1
Penfield Hist Dist—*hist pl* GA-3
**Penfield Junction**—*pop pl* OH-6
Penfield Pond—*lake* NY-2
Penfield Reef—*bar* CT-1
Penfield Rsvr—*reservoir* PA-2
Penfield Sch—*school* SD-7
**Penfield (Town of)**—*pop pl* NY-2
**Penfield (Township of)**—*pop pl* OH-6
Penfold Bay—*bay* NY-2
*Penford* MI-6
Pengar Lake—*lake* MN-6
**Pengilly**—*pop pl* MN-6
Penglase Lake—*lake* (2) MI-6
Pengra Bridge—*hist pl* OR-9
*Pengra Pass* OR-9
Pengra Pass—*gap* OR-9
Penguin Creek—*stream* AK-9
Penguins Islands—*island* NC-3
Penhale Sch—*school* OH-6
*Pen Hatch A Pet Mountains* AZ-5
*Penholloway Bay* GA-3
*Pen Holloway Creek* GA-3
*Penholloway Swamp* GA-3
Penholoway Bay—*swamp* GA-3
Penholoway Creek—*stream* GA-3
Penholoway Swamp—*swamp* GA-3
Penhook—*locale* VA-3
Penhook Branch—*stream* KY-4
Penhook Hollow—*valley* AR-4
*Penhorn Creek* NJ-2
Penhorn Creek—*stream* NJ-2
Penia—*locale* GA-3
**Penia**—*pop pl* FM-9
Penia Ch—*church* GA-3
*Penial* FL-3
*Peniamwan* FM-9
Peniamwan—*civil* FM-9
**Peniata**—*pop pl* FM-9
Peni-Bilt Lake—*reservoir* TX-5
Penick—*locale* KY-4
Penick Ch—*church* KY-4
Penick Coulee—*valley* MT-8
Penick Hollow—*valley* KY-4
Penick House—*hist pl* OK-5
Penick Pond—*reservoir* GA-3
Penicks Mill—*locale* VA-3
Penieis—*civil* FM-9
Peniel—*locale* OH-6
Peniel—*locale* WV-2
**Peniel**—*pop pl* FL-3
**Peniel**—*pop pl* NC-3
**Peniel**—*pop pl* TX-5
Peniel Baptist Ch of Orlando—*church* FL-3
Peniel Cem—*cemetery* (2) AL-4
Peniel Ch—*church* AL-4
Peniel Ch—*church* FL-3
Peniel Ch—*church* IL-6
Peniel Ch—*church* IN-6
Peniel Ch—*church* KY-4
Peniel Ch—*church* (2) LA-4
Peniel Ch—*church* (3) NC-3
Peniel Ch—*church* (2) SC-3
Peniel Ch—*church* VA-3
Peniel Ch—*church* WV-2
Peniel Ch—*church* (2) WI-6
Peniel Crossroads—*locale* SC-3
Peniel Run—*stream* IN-6
Peniel Run—*stream* WV-2
Peniel Sch—*school* WV-2
Peniel Sch—*school* WI-6
*Peniel School* TN-4
Peniemuan—*locale* FM-9
**Peniemwan**—*pop pl* FM-9
**Penienuk**—*pop pl* FM-9
Penienuk, Ununen—*cape* FM-9
*Peniesele* FM-9
*Peniesence* FM-9
**Peniesene**—*pop pl* FM-9
*Penieta* FM-9
Penietiw—*civil* FM-9
Penieu—*island* FM-9
*Penigar Cemetery* TN-4
Penikese Island—*island* MA-1
Penile—*locale* KY-4
Penile Ch—*church* (2) AL-4
Penile Ch—*church* NC-3
Penile Ch—*church* WV-2
**Penile Hill**—*pop pl* TN-4
Penile Hill—*summit* TN-4
Penile Sch (historical)—*school* TN-4
Penin Canyon—*valley* CA-9
Peningo Neck—*cape* NY-2
*Penington* NJ-2
**Peninsula**—*pop pl* OH-6
Peninsula—*uninc pl* (2) FL-3
Peninsula, Point—*cape* NY-2
Peninsula, The—*cape* AK-9
Peninsula, The—*cape* (2) CA-9
Peninsula, The—*cape* CO-8
Peninsula, The—*cape* MN-6
Peninsula, The—*cape* (2) OR-9
Peninsula, The—*summit* AK-9
Peninsula Bay—*other* CA-9
Peninsula Boat Ramp—*other* KY-4
*Peninsula Camp* PA-2
Peninsula Campground—*locale* PA-2
Peninsula (CCD)—*cens area* WA-9
Peninsula Center—*locale* WI-6
Peninsula Center—*post sta* CA-9
Peninsula Ch—*church* MO-7
Peninsula Country Club—*other* CA-9
Peninsula County Park—*park* OR-9
Peninsula Drainage Canal—*canal* OR-9
*Peninsula Fee A VAR Peninsula Camp* PA-2
*Peninsula Fee Campground* PA-2
Peninsula Flamenco—*cape* PR-3
Peninsula General Hospital—*post sta* MD-2
Peninsula Hosp—*hospital* CA-9
Peninsula HS—*school* WA-9
Peninsula Island—*island* AK-9
*Peninsula Junction* MD-2
Peninsula Junction—*locale* OR-9
*Peninsula Key* FL-3
Peninsula Lake—*lake* AK-9
Peninsula Lake—*lake* CA-9
Peninsula Lake—*lake* MI-6
Peninsula Lake—*lake* MN-6
Peninsula-McCabe United Methodist Ch—*church* DE-2
Peninsula Med Ctr—*hospital* FL-3
Peninsula Memorial Park Cem—*cemetery* VA-3
Peninsula Park—*park* CA-9
Peninsula Park—*park* OR-9
**Peninsula Park**—*pop pl* SD-7
Peninsula Point—*cape* AK-9
Peninsula Point—*cape* CA-9
Peninsula Point—*cape* FL-3
Peninsula Point—*cape* MI-6
Peninsula Point—*uninc pl* AK-9
Peninsula Point Lighthouse—*hist pl* MI-6
Peninsula Point Shoal—*bar* MI-6
Peninsular Ave Sch—*school* CA-9
Peninsular Cem—*cemetery* WV-2
Peninsula Rec Area—*locale* CO-8
**Peninsular Estates**—*pop pl* TN-4
Peninsular Highway—*channel* MI-6
Peninsula Ridge—*ridge* AK-9
*Peninsular Point* MI-6
Peninsular Point—*cape* AK-9
Peninsular Psychiatric Hosp—*hospital* TN-4
Peninsula Sch—*school* CA-9
Peninsula Sch—*school* OR-9
Peninsula Sch—*school* WA-9
Peninsula State Park—*park* WI-6
**Peninsula (Township of)**—*pop pl* MI-6
Peninsula Village—*locale* PA-2
**Peninsula Village**—*pop pl* CA-9
Peninsula Village Hist Dist—*hist pl* OH-6
Peninsula Windmill—*well* AZ-5
**Penior**—*pop pl* FM-9
Penior, Oror En—*locale* FM-9
*Penis Creek* KS-7
Pen Island—*island* AK-9
Pen Island—*island* LA-4
Penistaja—*locale* NM-5
Penistaja Arroyo—*stream* NM-5
Penistaja Spring—*spring* NM-5
Penistaja Well—*well* NM-5
Peniston Lake—*reservoir* GA-3
**Penitas**—*pop pl* TX-5
Penitas Creek —*stream* TX-5
Penitas Creek—*stream* TX-5
Penitas Gas Field—*oilfield* TX-5
*Penitas Hill* AZ-5
Penitas Hills —*summit* AZ-5
Penitas Ranch—*locale* TX-5
Penitas Wash —*stream* AZ-5
Peniten Bridges—*bridge* NC-3
Peniten Canal—*canal* NC-3
*Penitencia Creek* CA-9
Penitencia Creek—*stream* CA-9
Penitenitiary Hollow—*valley* VA-3
Penitenta Canyon—*valley* CO-8
Penitenta Ch—*church* CO-8
Penitente Canyon—*valley* CO-8
Penitente Canyon—*valley* (2) NM-5
Penitente Peak—*summit* NM-5
Penitente Windmill—*locale* (2) NM-5
Penitentiary—*building* CO-8
Penitentiary, The—*valley* AL-4
Penitentiary, The—*valley* TN-4
Penitentiary Annex Cem—*cemetery* OR-9
Penitentiary Bend—*bend* (2) KY-4
Penitentiary Bottoms—*flat* AL-4
Penitentiary Branch—*stream* AL-4
Penitentiary Branch—*stream* GA-3
Penitentiary Branch—*stream* KY-4
Penitentiary Branch—*stream* MO-7
Penitentiary Branch—*stream* (2) TN-4
Penitentiary Canal—*canal* ID-8
Penitentiary Canyon—*valley* UT-8
Penitentiary Cave—*cave* AR-4
Penitentiary Cove—*bay* GA-3
Penitentiary Creek—*stream* IA-7
Penitentiary Farms—*locale* SD-7
Penitentiary Flat—*flat* CA-9

Penitentiary Gap—gap ... AL-4
Penitentiary Gulf—valley ... TN-4
Penitentiary Hill—summit ... VA-3
Penitentiary Hole—other ... AL-4
Penitentiary Hollow—valley ... AL-4
Penitentiary Hollow—valley ... AR-4
Penitentiary Hollow—valley ... IN-6
Penitentiary Mtn—summit (2) ... AL-4
Penitentiary Mtn—summit ... AZ-5
Penitentiary Mtn—summit ... AR-4
Penitentiary Point—cliff ... UT-8
Penitentiary Spring—spring ... AZ-5
**Penitentiary Spur**—pop pl ... ID-8
Penitentiary Tanks—reservoir ... AZ-5
Penitentiary Valley ... AL-4
Penix Canyon—valley ... WA-9
Penix Cem—cemetery ... AR-4
Peniya ... FM-9
Peniyemwaan ... FM-9
Peniyenuk ... FM-9
Peniyesene ... FM-9
Peniyoor ... FM-9
Penjajawoc Stream—stream ... ME-1
**Penjur**—pop pl ... AR-4
Penknife Brook—stream ... ME-1
Penknife Lakes—lake ... ME-1
Penknife Point—cape ... MD-2
Pen Lake ... MN-6
Penlan—locale ... OH-6
Penlan—locale ... VA-3
Penland—locale ... TX-5
**Penland**—pop pl ... NC-3
Penland, Lake—reservoir ... OR-9
Penland Branch—stream ... NC-3
Penland Cem—cemetery (2) ... NC-3
Penland Cemetery ... OR-9
Penland Cove—valley (2) ... NC-3
Penland Creek ... NC-3
Penland Gap—gap ... NC-3
Penland Island—island ... NC-3
Penland Meadow—flat ... OR-9
Penland Prairie—flat ... OR-9
Penland Ranch—locale ... OR-9
Penland Sch—school ... NC-3
Penlands Creek ... NC-3
Penley Branch ... NC-3
Penley Branch—stream ... KY-4
Penley Branch—stream ... NC-3
Penley Chapel—church ... NC-3
Penley Corner—locale ... ME-1
Penley Corners (2) ... ME-1
Penley Cove—valley ... NC-3
Penley Lake—lake ... WA-9
Penleys Corner ... ME-1
**Penllyn**—pop pl ... PA-2
Penman Airp—airport ... MO-7
Penman Mine—mine ... ID-8
Penman Peak—summit ... CA-9
Penman Rips—rapids ... ME-1
Penman Saddle—gap ... CA-9
Penman Sch—school ... MS-4
Penman Sch—school ... ND-7
**Pen Mar**—pop pl ... MD-2
**Pen Mar**—pop pl ... PA-2
Penmarch Place—hist pl ... SD-7
Penmar Golf Course—other ... CA-9
Pen Mar Park ... MD-2
Penmar Recreation Center—park ... CA-9
Penn ... KS-7
Penn ... MS-4
Penn ... PA-2
Penn—locale ... IA-7
Penn—locale ... OR-9
**Penn**—pop pl ... AL-4
**Penn**—pop pl ... MI-6
**Penn**—pop pl ... NE-7
**Penn**—pop pl ... ND-7
**Penn**—pop pl ... PA-2
Penn, Mount—summit ... PA-2
Penn, William, HS—hist pl ... NC-3
Penn, William, HS for Girls—hist pl ... PA-2
Penn, William, Landing Site—hist pl ... PA-2
Penna Canyon—valley ... NM-5
**Penn Acres**—pop pl ... DE-2
**Penn Acres**—pop pl ... VA-3
**Penn Acres South (subdivision)**—pop pl ... DE-2
Pennahatchee Creek—stream ... GA-3
Pennal Gulch—valley ... ID-8
Penn Allen—locale ... PA-2
Penn Allen Heights ... PA-2
Pennaman Brook—stream ... ME-1
Pennamaquan Lake—lake ... ME-1
Pennamaquan River—stream ... ME-1
Penn and Dauphin Park—park ... PA-2
Penn and Sayford Park—park ... PA-2
Pennan Plaza (Shop Ctr)—locale ... FL-3
Pennant Creek—stream ... AK-9
Pennant Hill—summit ... GA-3
Penn Aqua Cave—cave ... PA-2
Penn Ave Cem—cemetery ... IA-7
Penn Ave Ch—church ... IA-7
Penn Ave Ch—church ... NC-3
Penn Avon—other ... PA-2
Penn Bay—bay ... AR-4
Penn Beach ... NJ-2
Penn Borough—civil ... PA-2
Penn Branch ... SC-3
Penn Branch—stream ... AL-4
Penn Branch—stream ... KY-4
Penn Branch—stream ... MS-4
Penn Branch—stream (2) ... SC-3
Penn Branch—stream (2) ... VA-3
Penn Branch Ch—church ... SC-3
Penn Brook—stream ... MA-1
Pennbrook—uninc pl ... PA-2
Pennbrook Run—stream ... PA-2
Penn Camp—locale ... NC-3
Penn Cave ... PA-2
Penn Cave—cave ... AL-4
Penn Cave—locale ... PA-2
Penn Cem—cemetery (2) ... AL-4
Penn Cem—cemetery ... AR-4
Penn Cem—cemetery ... MO-7
Penn Cem—cemetery ... SC-3
Penn Center—uninc pl ... PA-2
Penn Center Church—locale ... IA-7
Penn Center Hist Dist—hist pl ... SC-3
Penn Central Railway Station—hist pl ... MI-6
Penn Central Station—building ... DE-2
Penn Central Station—hist pl ... MI-6
Penn Central Yard—locale ... NY-2
Penn Channel—channel ... NJ-2
Penn Channel—channel ... PA-2
Penn Chapel ... AL-4
Penn Coal Company Shop—building ... PA-2
Penn Common—park ... PA-2
Penn Community Services—building ... SC-3
Penn Consolidated Sch—school ... IL-6
Penn Cove—bay ... WA-9
**Penn Cove Park**—pop pl ... WA-9
**Penncraft**—pop pl ... PA-2
Penn Creek ... PA-2
Penn Creek—stream ... AK-9
Penn Creek—stream ... CA-9
Penn Creek—stream ... IA-7
Penn Creek—stream ... OK-5
Penn Creek—stream ... OR-9
Penn Creek—stream ... SC-3
Penn Creek Ch—church ... SC-3
Penn Creek Mountain ... PA-2
Penn Creek Oil Field—oilfield ... OK-5
Penn Crest HS—school ... PA-2
**Penn Daw**—pop pl ... VA-3
**Penn Daw Terrace (Trailer Court)**—pop pl ... VA-3
**Penn Daw Village**—pop pl ... VA-3
**Penndel**—pop pl ... PA-2
Penndel Borough—civil ... PA-2
Penn Ditch—canal ... OH-6
Penn Dixie Mine—mine ... ID-8
Penn-Dixie Pond—reservoir ... PA-2
**Penndrew Manor**—pop pl ... DE-2
Penne, Henri, House—hist pl ... LA-4
Pennebackher ... PA-2
Pennebaker Ditch—canal ... CA-9
Pennekamp Sch—school ... CA-9
Pennel Branch—stream ... MO-7
Pennel Creek—stream ... MT-8
Pennel Creek—stream ... OK-5
Penn Elem Sch—school ... PA-2
Pennell ... NJ-2
Pennell, Joseph, Sch—hist pl ... PA-2
Pennell, Mount—summit ... UT-8
Pennell Creek—stream ... KS-7
Pennell Creek—stream ... UT-8
Pennell Creek Bench—bench ... UT-8
Pennell Creek Roughs—summit ... UT-8
Pennell Drain—canal ... MI-6
Pennell Elem Sch—school ... PA-2
Pennellen Pass—gap ... UT-8
Pennell Institute—hist pl ... ME-1
Pennell Lake Dam—dam ... MS-4
Pennell Park—park ... MN-6
Pennell Pond—lake ... ME-1
Pennellville—locale ... ME-1
**Pennellville**—pop pl ... NY-2
Pennellville Cem—cemetery ... NY-2
Pennellville Hist Dist—hist pl ... ME-1
**Pennellwood**—pop pl ... MI-6
Pennel Run—stream ... PA-2
Pennel Run Natural Area—area ... PA-2
Pennel Sch—school ... PA-2
Pennelton Station—building ... PA-2
Penner Cem—cemetery ... MO-7
Penner Lake ... WA-9
Penner Lake—lake ... CA-9
Penner Ponds—lake ... FL-3
Penners Creek ... TN-4
Penners Lake—reservoir ... NJ-2
**Pennersville**—pop pl ... PA-2
Penners Windmill—locale ... TX-5
Pennesseewassee Lake—lake ... ME-1
Penneville ... PA-2
Pennewell Cem—cemetery ... MO-7
Penney—locale ... CA-9
Penney, J. C., Hist Dist—hist pl ... WY-8
Penney, J. C., House—hist pl ... WY-8
Penney Cem—cemetery ... TN-4
Penney Creek ... MI-6
Penney Creek ... WA-9
**Penney Farms**—pop pl ... FL-3
Penney Farms (CCD)—cens area ... FL-3
Penney Farms Sch—school ... FL-3
Penney Glades—flat ... CA-9
Penney Gulch—valley ... WY-8
Penney Hill—summit ... OR-9
Penney Hollow—valley ... UT-8
Penney Hollow Pond—lake ... UT-8
Penney HS—school ... CT-1
Penney-McMillian Cem—cemetery ... SC-3
Penney Peak—summit ... MT-8
Penney Point Lodge Camp—locale ... AL-4
Penney Pond—lake ... ME-1
Penney Ridge—ridge ... CA-9
Penneys Crossroad—locale ... VA-3
Penneywater Pond—lake ... NY-2
Pennfield—locale ... MI-6
**Pennfield**—pop pl ... PA-2
Pennfield Farm Airp—airport ... PA-2
**Pennfield (historical)**—pop pl ... NC-3
Pennfield Sch—school (2) ... MI-6
**Pennfield (Township of)**—pop pl ... MI-6
Penn Five—locale ... PA-2
Penn Forest Airp—airport ... PA-2
Penn Forest Dam—dam ... PA-2
Penn Forest Rsvr—reservoir ... PA-2
**Penn Forest (Township of)**—pop pl ... PA-2
**Penn Glyn**—pop pl ... PA-2
Penn Grange—locale ... PA-2
Penngrove ... NJ-2
Penn Grove ... WA-9
**Penngrove**—pop pl ... CA-9
**Penn Grove**—pop pl ... PA-2
Penn Grove Bible Center—locale ... PA-2
Penn Grove (Penngrove) ... CA-9
**Penngrove (Penn Grove)**—pop pl ... CA-9
Penn Grove Sch—school ... PA-2
Pennhall ... PA-2
**Penn Hall**—pop pl ... PA-2
**Pennhall**—pop pl ... PA-2
Penn Haven Junction—locale ... PA-2
Penn Haven Junction Station ... PA-2
Penn Haven Mtn—summit ... PA-2
Penn Heights—uninc pl ... PA-2
Penn Hill—locale ... PA-2
Penn Hill—summit ... PA-2
**Penn Hill Homes**—pop pl ... PA-2
Penn Hills Ch—church ... PA-2
Penn Hills Junior High School ... PA-2
Penn Hills Senior HS—school ... PA-2
**Penn Hills (subdivision)**—pop pl ... PA-2
**Penn Hills (Township of)**—pop pl ... PA-2
Penn Hollow—valley ... GA-3
Penn Hollow—valley ... WI-6
Penn House—hist pl ... NC-3
Penn HS—school ... IN-6
Penn HS—school ... PA-2
Pennhurst—locale ... PA-2
Pennhurst Center ... PA-2
**Pennhurst (Pennhurst State School and Hospital)**—pop pl ... PA-2
Pennhurst State Sch—school ... PA-2
Pennhurst Station—locale ... PA-2
Penni—bar ... FM-9
Pennichaw—locale ... FL-3
Pennichuck Brook—stream ... NH-1
Pennichuck Pond—lake ... NH-1
Pennick—locale ... GA-3
Pennick Coulee—valley ... MT-8
Pennick-Price Cem—cemetery ... KY-4
Pennie, Daniel, House—hist pl ... MN-6
Penniel Cem—cemetery ... WI-6
Pennike Run—stream ... WV-2
Penniman, Edward, House and Barn—hist pl ... MA-1
Penniman Brook—stream ... MA-1
Penniman Brook—stream ... NH-1
Penniman Cem—cemetery ... NH-1
Penniman Cove—bay ... NY-2
Penniman Creek—bay ... NY-2
Penniman Glaciers—glacier ... AK-9
Penniman Hill—ridge ... NH-1
Penniman Hill—summit ... MA-1
Penniman Lake—reservoir ... VA-3
Penniman Sch—school ... MA-1
Penniman Spit—bar ... VA-3
**Pennine**—pop pl ... TN-4
Pennine Baptist Ch—church ... TN-4
Pennine Post Office (historical)—building ... TN-4
Pennine Station ... TN-4
Penninger Drain—canal ... ID-8
Penninger Lateral—canal ... ID-8
Pennings HS—school ... WI-6
Pennington ... NY-2
Pennington ... NC-3
Pennington—locale (2) ... GA-3
Pennington—locale ... NM-5
Pennington—locale ... WI-6
**Pennington**—pop pl ... AL-4
**Pennington**—pop pl ... AR-4
**Pennington**—pop pl ... CA-9
**Pennington**—pop pl ... GA-3
**Pennington**—pop pl ... MN-6
**Pennington**—pop pl ... NJ-2
**Pennington**—pop pl ... PA-2
**Pennington**—pop pl ... TX-5
Pennington, Governor John L., House—hist pl ... SD-7
Pennington, John-Ford, Henry, House—hist pl ... MI-6
Pennington, Lake—reservoir ... TX-5
Pennington, Sarah, House—hist pl ... MI-6
Pennington Bayou—stream ... AR-4
Pennington Bend—bend ... TN-4
Pennington Bend—uninc pl ... TN-4
Pennington Bend Ch—church ... TN-4
Pennington Branch—stream ... AL-4
Pennington Branch—stream (2) ... TX-5
Pennington Branch—stream ... VA-3
Pennington Bridge—bridge ... VA-3
Pennington Brook—stream ... ME-1
Pennington Butte—summit ... OR-9
Pennington Cave—cave (2) ... TN-4
Pennington Cem—cemetery ... AL-4
Pennington Cem—cemetery ... IL-6
Pennington Cem—cemetery ... IA-7
Pennington Cem—cemetery (4) ... KY-4
Pennington Cem—cemetery ... LA-4
Pennington Cem—cemetery (2) ... NC-3
Pennington Cem—cemetery ... OH-6
Pennington Cem—cemetery (3) ... TN-4
Pennington Cem—cemetery (2) ... TX-5
Pennington Cem—cemetery ... VA-3
Pennington Ch—church ... OK-5
Pennington Ch—church ... TN-4
Pennington Chapel—church ... IN-6
Pennington Chapel—church ... TN-4
Pennington Chapel—church ... TX-5
**Pennington Chapel**—pop pl ... TN-4
Pennington Chapel Ridge—ridge ... IN-6
Pennington Cottage—hist pl ... MD-2
Pennington County—civil ... SD-7
**Pennington (County)**—pop pl ... MN-6
Pennington County Courthouse—hist pl ... SD-7
Pennington Creek—stream ... AK-9
Pennington Creek—stream ... CA-9
Pennington Creek—stream ... IL-6
Pennington Creek—stream ... OK-5
Pennington Creek—stream ... OR-9
Pennington Creek—stream ... TX-5
Pennington Creek Cem—cemetery ... TX-5
Pennington Ford—locale ... MO-7
Pennington Fork—stream ... KY-4
Pennington Gap—gap ... VA-3
**Pennington Gap**—pop pl ... VA-3
**Pennington Gap (RR name Pennington)**—pop pl ... VA-3
Pennington (historical)—locale ... SD-7
Pennington Hollow—valley (2) ... TN-4
Pennington Infirmary—hist pl ... KY-4
Pennington Island—island ... PA-2
Pennington Lake—lake ... IN-6
Pennington Lake—lake ... MN-6
Pennington Lake—reservoir ... MS-4
Pennington Lake—reservoir ... TX-5
Pennington Lake Dam—dam (2) ... MS-4
Pennington Lakes—reservoir ... MS-4
Pennington Mine—mine ... MN-6
Pennington Mtn—summit ... ME-1
Pennington Mtn—summit ... NJ-2
Pennington Mtn—summit ... OR-9
Pennington Park—park ... NJ-2
Pennington P.O. (historical)—locale ... AL-4
Pennington Point—locale ... IL-6
Pennington Pond—lake ... ME-1
Pennington Pond—reservoir ... IN-6
Pennington Post Camp—locale ... FL-3
Pennington Ridge—ridge ... KY-4
Pennington (RR name for Pennington Gap)—other ... VA-3
Pennington RR Station—hist pl ... NJ-2
Pennington Sch—school ... CO-8
Pennington Sch—school ... KY-4
Pennington Sch—school ... NY-2
Pennington Sch—school ... TN-4
**Penningtons Lake Subdivision**—pop pl ... MS-4
Pennington Spring—spring ... WA-9
Pennington Square Sch—school ... SD-7
**Pennington (subdivision)**—pop pl ... DE-2
Pennington (Township of)—fmr MCD ... AR-4
Pennington Well—locale ... NM-5
Penninsula, The ... PA-2
Pennisoaken Creek ... NJ-2
Pennisten Chapel—church ... OH-6
Penniston Cem—cemetery ... MO-7
Penniston House—hist pl ... KY-4
Penniwell Cem—cemetery ... NE-7
Penniwinkle Branch ... AL-4
Penniwinkle Branch ... TN-4
Penniwinkle Creek ... AL-4
Penniwinkle Hollow ... TN-4
Pennix Cove—valley ... NC-3
Penn JHS—school ... MN-6
Penn John Sch—school ... PA-2
Penn Johns Elem Sch ... PA-2
**Penn Junction**—pop pl ... MI-6
**Penn Laird**—pop pl ... VA-3
Penn Lake—lake ... IN-6
Penn Lake—lake ... MN-6
Penn Lake—lake ... OR-9
Penn Lake—reservoir ... PA-2
Penn Lake Dam—dam ... PA-2
Penn Lake Park ... PA-2
**Penn Lake Park**—pop pl ... PA-2
Penn Lake Park Borough—civil ... PA-2
**Penn Lee**—pop pl ... VA-3
Penn-Liberty Hist Dist—hist pl ... PA-2
Penn Lincoln Elem Sch ... PA-2
Penn Lincoln Sch—school ... PA-2
Penn Line ... PA-2
**Pennline**—pop pl ... PA-2
Pennline Ch—church ... OH-6
Penn Line Service Airp—airport ... PA-2
Penn Manor ... PA-2
Penn Manor Junior-Senior High School ... PA-2
Penn-Marshall Stone House—hist pl ... KY-4
Penn Mary Junction—uninc pl ... MD-2
Penn Memorial Hosp—hospital ... NC-3
Penn Mine—mine (2) ... CA-9
Penn Mine—mine ... WY-8
Penn Mountain Cem—cemetery ... NY-2
Penn Mtn—summit ... NY-2
Penn Natl Golf Course—locale ... PA-2
Penn Natl Race Course—park ... PA-2
Penn Nursery—locale ... PA-2
Penn Nursery Dam—dam ... PA-2
**Penn Oaks**—pop pl ... PA-2
**Pennock**—pop pl ... DE-2
**Pennock**—pop pl ... MN-6
Pennock, Martha, House—hist pl ... PA-2
Pennock Brook—stream ... NY-2
Pennock Creek—stream ... CO-8
Pennock Creek—stream ... MT-8
Pennock Creek—stream ... OR-9
Pennock Ditch—canal ... NY-2
Pennock Island—CDP ... AK-9
Pennock Island—island ... AK-9
Pennock Mtn—summit ... WY-8
Pennock Park—park ... MN-6
Pennock Pass—gap ... CO-8
Pennock Reef—bar ... AK-9
Pennow Sch—school ... MI-6
Pennoyer Creek—stream ... OR-9
Pennoyer Park—park ... WI-6
Pennoyer Sch—school ... IL-6
Penn Park—park ... CA-9
Penn Park—park ... WI-6
**Penn Park**—pop pl ... IN-6
Penn Park Station—building ... PA-2
**Penn Pines**—pop pl ... PA-2
Penn Pit—cave ... AL-4
**Penn Pitt**—pop pl ... PA-2
Penn Pitt Elem Sch—school ... PA-2
Penn Place—hist pl ... GA-3
Penn Place—locale ... NJ-2
Penn Point—cape ... NC-3
Penn Post Office (historical)—building ... MS-4
Penn Post Office (historical)—building ... PA-2
Penn Prairie—swamp ... OR-9
**Penn Ridge**—pop pl ... PA-2
Penn Ridge—ridge ... OH-6
Pennridge Airp—airport ... PA-2
Pennridge Central JHS—school ... PA-2
Penn Ridge Ch—church ... IL-6
Pennridge District Education Center—school ... PA-2
Pennridge Industrial Park—locale ... PA-2
Pennridge JHS—school ... PA-2
Pennridge South JHS ... PA-2
**Pennrington**—pop pl ... NC-3
**Pennrock**—pop pl ... DE-2
Penn Roosevelt State Park—park ... PA-2
**Penn Rose**—pop pl ... DE-2
**Penn Rose**—pop pl ... PA-2
**Penn Rose Park**—pop pl ... PA-2
**Penn Run**—pop pl ... PA-2
Penn Run—stream (2) ... PA-2
**Penn Run No. 1**—pop pl ... KY-4
Penn Ryn Private School ... PA-2
**Penns**—pop pl ... MS-4
Penn Salt Fluorite Mill—locale ... KY-4
Pennsalt Hist Dist—hist pl ... PA-2
**Pennsand**—pop pl ... VA-3
**Pennsauken**—pop pl ... NJ-2
Pennsauken Creek ... NJ-2
Pennsauken Creek—stream ... NJ-2
Pennsauken HS—school ... NJ-2
Pennsauken Industrial Park—locale ... NJ-2
Pennsauken JHS—school ... NJ-2
Pennsauken (Pensauken)—CDP ... NJ-2
Pennsauken Shop Ctr—locale ... NJ-2
**Pennsauken (Township of)**—pop pl ... NJ-2
Pennsawken Creek ... NJ-2
**Penns Beach**—pop pl ... NJ-2
**Pennsboro**—pop pl ... MO-7
**Pennsboro**—pop pl ... WV-2
Penns Brook—stream ... NJ-2
**Pennsburg**—pop pl ... PA-2
Pennsburg Borough—civil ... PA-2
Pennsburg-East Greenville (RR name for Pennburg)—other ... PA-2
Pennsburg Golf Course—locale ... PA-2
Pennsburg HS—school ... PA-2
Pennsburg Manor ... PA-2
**Pennsburg (RR name Pennsburg-East Greenville)**—pop pl ... PA-2
Pennsburg Shopping Center ... PA-2
Pennsburg Square—locale ... PA-2
**Pennsbury Heights**—pop pl ... PA-2
Pennsbury HS—school ... PA-2
Pennsbury Inn—hist pl ... PA-2
Pennsbury Manor—hist pl ... PA-2
Pennsbury Manor State Park—park ... PA-2
**Pennsbury (Township of)**—pop pl ... PA-2
**Pennsbury Village**—pop pl ... PA-2
Pennsbury Village Borough—civil ... PA-2
Penns Cave—cave ... PA-2
Penns Cave Airp—airport ... PA-2
Penn's Cave and Hotel—hist pl ... PA-2
Penns Cave Spring—spring ... PA-2
Penn Sch—school ... IL-6
Penn Sch—school ... IA-7
Penn Sch—school ... MN-6
Penn Sch—school ... NE-7
Penn Sch—school ... NH-1
Penn Sch—school ... NJ-2
Penn Sch—school ... OK-5
Penn Sch—school (3) ... PA-2
Penn Sch (abandoned)—school ... PA-2
Penns Chapel—church ... KY-4
Penns Chapel—church ... LA-4
Penn Sch (historical)—school ... AL-4
Penn School Number 49 ... IN-6
**Penns Creek**—pop pl ... PA-2
Penns Creek—stream ... PA-2
Penns Creek Mtn—summit ... PA-2
**Pennsdale**—pop pl ... PA-2
Pennsdale Cem—cemetery ... PA-2
Penns Drive Cave—cave ... PA-2
Penn's Grand Canyon ... PA-2
Pennsgrove ... NJ-2
**Penns Grove**—pop pl ... NJ-2
Penns Grove Ch—church ... PA-2
Penns Grove Sch—school ... PA-2
Penn's Hill ... MA-1
Penns Hill—summit ... MA-1
**Pennside**—pop pl (2) ... PA-2
Penns Lake—reservoir ... GA-3
Penns Landing Pier 36 Heliport—airport ... PA-2
Penn Slough—gut ... OR-9
Penns Manor Ch—church ... PA-2
Penns Manor HS—school ... PA-2
Penns Neck ... NJ-2
**Penns Neck**—pop pl ... NJ-2
Penns Neck Bridge—bridge ... NJ-2
Penns Neck Sch—school ... NJ-2
Pennsoakin Creek ... NJ-2
Penns Park—locale ... PA-2
Penn's Park General Store Complex—hist pl ... PA-2
Penns Park Hist Dist—hist pl ... PA-2
Penns Pocket ... AZ-5
Penn Spring Rsvr—reservoir ... PA-2
Penn Springs—spring ... PA-2
**Penn Square**—pop pl ... PA-2
Penn Square Ch—church ... PA-2
Penn Square Mall—locale ... PA-2
**Penn Square Village**—pop pl ... PA-2
Penns Run—stream (2) ... IN-6
Penns Station ... MS-4
Penns Store—locale ... VA-3
**Penn (sta.)**—pop pl ... IN-6
Penn State College—other ... PA-2
Penn State For—forest ... NJ-2
Penn State Univ (Altoona Campus)—school ... PA-2
Penn State Univ Uniontown Campus ... PA-2
Penn State Wilkes-Barre Campus ... PA-2
**Pennstown**—pop pl ... VA-3
Penn Street Sch—school ... PA-2
**Pennsuco**—pop pl ... FL-3
Pennsuco Canal—canal ... FL-3
Penns Valley—valley ... PA-2
Penns Valley Area HS—school ... PA-2
Penns View—locale ... PA-2
Pennsville ... PA-2
**Pennsville**—pop pl ... NJ-2
**Pennsville**—pop pl ... OH-6
**Pennsville**—pop pl (2) ... PA-2
Pennsville (census name for Pennsville Center)—CDP ... NJ-2
Pennsville Center (census name Pennsville) ... NJ-2
Pennsville Ch—church ... PA-2
Pennsville Shop Ctr—locale ... NJ-2
**Pennsville (Township of)**—pop pl ... NJ-2
Penn Swamp—swamp ... NJ-2
Penn Swamp Branch—stream ... NJ-2
Penn Swamp Pond—lake ... NJ-2
**Penns Woods**—pop pl ... PA-2
Pennsylvania—hist pl ... IN-6
**Pennsylvania**—pop pl ... AL-4
Pennsylvania Acad of the Fine Arts—hist pl ... PA-2
Pennsylvania Ave Hist Dist—hist pl ... IL-6
Pennsylvania Ave Natl Historic Site—hist pl ... DC-2
Pennsylvania Ave Rock Creek Bridge—hist pl ... KS-7
Pennsylvania Ave RR Yard—locale ... DC-2
Pennsylvania Ave Sch—school ... GA-3
Pennsylvania Ave Sch—school ... NY-2
Pennsylvania Ave Sch—school ... NC-3
Pennsylvaniaburg ... IN-6
Pennsylvania Canal—canal (3) ... PA-2
Pennsylvania Canal (Abandoned)—canal ... PA-2
Pennsylvania Canal and Limestone Run Aqueduct—hist pl ... PA-2
Pennsylvania Canyon—valley ... NV-8
Pennsylvania Canyon—valley (2) ... NM-5
Pennsylvania Cem—cemetery ... NE-7
Pennsylvania Charter Sch—school ... PA-2
Pennsylvania Coll of Optometry—school ... PA-2
Pennsylvania Corners—locale ... IL-6
Pennsylvania Creek ... PA-2
Pennsylvania Creek—stream ... AK-9
Pennsylvania Creek—stream ... CA-9
Pennsylvania Creek—stream (2) ... CO-8
Pennsylvania Drift Mine (underground)—mine ... AL-4
Pennsylvania Farm Museum—building ... PA-2
Pennsylvania Fish Commission Access Area—area ... PA-2
Pennsylvania Fish Commission Launch—locale ... PA-2
Pennsylvania Fish Commission Spring—spring ... PA-2
Pennsylvania Fork Dunkard Creek—stream ... PA-2
Pennsylvania Fork Dunkard Creek—stream ... WV-2
Pennsylvania Fork Fish Creek—stream ... PA-2
Pennsylvania Fork Fish Creek—stream ... WV-2
**Pennsylvania Furnace**—pop pl ... PA-2
Pennsylvania Furnace Cem—cemetery ... PA-2
Pennsylvania Game Commission Division Office—building ... PA-2
Pennsylvania Glass Sand Company Station—locale ... PA-2
Pennsylvania Grand Canyon ... PA-2
Pennsylvania Gulch—valley ... CA-9
Pennsylvania Gulch—valley ... CO-8
Pennsylvania Hall, Gettysburg College—hist pl ... PA-2
Pennsylvania Harbor—bay ... NJ-2
Pennsylvania Hill—summit ... CO-8
Pennsylvania Hill—summit ... NV-8
Pennsylvania Hill—summit (2) ... NY-2
Pennsylvania Hollow—valley ... PA-2
Pennsylvania Hosp—hist pl ... PA-2
Pennsylvania Hosp—hospital ... PA-2
Pennsylvania House—hist pl ... OH-6
Pennsylvania HS—school ... PA-2
Pennsylvania Institute for the Deaf and Dumb—hist pl ... PA-2
Pennsylvania Institute of Technology—school ... PA-2
Pennsylvania Lane Ch—church ... IL-6
Pennsylvania Lane Sch—school ... IL-6
Pennsylvania Lincoln Memorial Park Cem—cemetery ... PA-2
Pennsylvania Lumber Museum—building ... PA-2
Pennsylvania Mennonite Ch—church ... KS-7
Pennsylvania Mil Coll—school ... PA-2
Pennsylvania Military College—other ... PA-2
Pennsylvania Mine ... AL-4
Pennsylvania Mine—mine (3) ... CA-9
Pennsylvania Mine—mine (2) ... CO-8
Pennsylvania Mine—mine ... SD-7
Pennsylvania Mtn—summit ... CO-8
Pennsylvania Natl Guard—other ... PA-2
Pennsylvania Natl Guard Camp—locale ... PA-2
Pennsylvania Park—park ... WA-9
Pennsylvania Point—summit ... CA-9
Pennsylvania Ponds—lake ... NJ-2
Pennsylvania Railway Station—hist pl ... OH-6
Pennsylvania Rock—bar ... AK-9
Pennsylvania RR Bridge—hist pl ... NJ-2
Pennsylvania RR Bridge—hist pl ... PA-2
Pennsylvania RR Depot And Baggage Room—hist pl ... OH-6
Pennsylvania RR Passenger Station—hist pl ... PA-2
Pennsylvania RR Passenger Station—locale ... PA-2
Pennsylvania RR Station—hist pl ... IN-6
Pennsylvania RR Station—hist pl ... PA-2
Pennsylvania RR Station-Latrobe—hist pl ... PA-2
Pennsylvania RR Station-Wilkinsburg—hist pl ... PA-2
Pennsylvania Run—stream ... KY-4
Pennsylvania Run—stream ... WV-2
Pennsylvania Run Ch—church ... KY-4
Pennsylvania Run Presbyterian Church—hist pl ... KY-4
Pennsylvania Sch—school ... MI-6
Pennsylvania Sch—school ... TX-5
Pennsylvania Sch for the Deaf ... PA-2
Pennsylvania Soldiers and Sailors Home—building ... PA-2
Pennsylvania State Capitol—building ... PA-2
Pennsylvania State College ... PA-2
Pennsylvania State Correctional Institution—building ... PA-2
Pennsylvania State Fish Hatchery-Corry Number 1 ... PA-2
Pennsylvania State Fish Hatchery-Corry Number 2 ... PA-2
Pennsylvania State Hosp—hospital ... PA-2
Pennsylvania State Hospital And Sch—school ... PA-2
Pennsylvania State Lunatic Asylum ... PA-2
Pennsylvania State Lunatic Hosp—hist pl ... PA-2
Pennsylvania State Police Station—locale ... PA-2
Pennsylvania State Training Sch—school ... PA-2
Pennsylvania State Univ—school ... PA-2
Pennsylvania State Univ Agronomy Research Farm—school ... PA-2
Pennsylvania State Univ Berks Campus—school ... PA-2
Pennsylvania State Univ Capital Campus—school ... PA-2
Pennsylvania State Univ Center—school ... PA-2
Pennsylvania State Univ Delaware Campus—school ... PA-2
Pennsylvania State Univ Dubois Campus—school ... PA-2
Pennsylvania State University, Allentown Campus—school ... PA-2
Pennsylvania State University, Beaver Campus—school ... PA-2
Pennsylvania State University, Hazleton Campus—school ... PA-2
Pennsylvania State University, Wilkes-Barre Campus—school ... PA-2
Pennsylvania State University C E Camp—locale ... PA-2
Pennsylvania State University Experimental For—forest ... PA-2
Pennsylvania State University Experimental Forest Design, The—area ... PA-2
Pennsylvania State University Forestry Camp—locale ... PA-2
Pennsylvania State University Golf Course—locale ... PA-2
Pennsylvania State University Recreation Area—park ... PA-2

Pennsylvania State Univ Experimental Forest—school ... PA-2
Pennsylvania State Univ Fayette Campus—school ... PA-2
Pennsylvania State Univ - Mount Alto Campus—school ... PA-2
Pennsylvania State Univ Ogontz Campus—school ... PA-2
Pennsylvania State Univ Worthington Scranton Campus—school ... PA-2
Pennsylvania State Univ - York Campus—school ... PA-2
Pennsylvania Station—hist pl ... MD-2
Pennsylvania Station—hist pl ... NJ-2
Pennsylvania Street Sch—school ... WI-6
Pennsylvania (Township of)—civ div ... IL-6
Pennsylvania Treaty JHS—school ... PA-2
Pennsylvania Treaty Park—park ... PA-2
Pennsylvania Tunnel—mine ... CO-8
Pennsylvania Tunnnels—tunnel ... NY-2
Pennsylvania Turnpike Interchange 1—crossing ... PA-2
Pennsylvania Turnpike Interchange 10—crossing ... PA-2
Pennsylvania Turnpike Interchange 11—crossing ... PA-2
Pennsylvania Turnpike Interchange 12—crossing ... PA-2
Pennsylvania Turnpike Interchange 13—crossing ... PA-2
Pennsylvania Turnpike Interchange 14—crossing ... PA-2
Pennsylvania Turnpike Interchange 15—crossing ... PA-2
Pennsylvania Turnpike Interchange 16—crossing ... PA-2
Pennsylvania Turnpike Interchange 17—crossing ... PA-2
Pennsylvania Turnpike Interchange 18—crossing ... PA-2
Pennsylvania Turnpike Interchange 19—crossing ... PA-2
Pennsylvania Turnpike Interchange 2—crossing ... PA-2
Pennsylvania Turnpike Interchange 20—crossing ... PA-2
Pennsylvania Turnpike Interchange 21—crossing ... PA-2
Pennsylvania Turnpike Interchange 22—crossing ... PA-2
Pennsylvania Turnpike Interchange 23—crossing ... PA-2
Pennsylvania Turnpike Interchange 24—crossing ... PA-2
Pennsylvania Turnpike Interchange 25—crossing ... PA-2
Pennsylvania Turnpike Interchange 26—crossing ... PA-2
Pennsylvania Turnpike Interchange 27—crossing ... PA-2
Pennsylvania Turnpike Interchange 28—crossing ... PA-2
Pennsylvania Turnpike Interchange 29—crossing ... PA-2
Pennsylvania Turnpike Interchange 3—crossing ... PA-2
Pennsylvania Turnpike Interchange 30—crossing ... PA-2
Pennsylvania Turnpike Interchange 31—crossing ... PA-2
Pennsylvania Turnpike Interchange 32—crossing ... PA-2
Pennsylvania Turnpike Interchange 33—crossing ... PA-2
Pennsylvania Turnpike Interchange 34—crossing ... PA-2
Pennsylvania Turnpike Interchange 35—crossing ... PA-2
Pennsylvania Turnpike Interchange 36—crossing ... PA-2
Pennsylvania Turnpike Interchange 37—crossing ... PA-2
Pennsylvania Turnpike Interchange 38—crossing ... PA-2
Pennsylvania Turnpike Interchange 4—crossing ... PA-2
Pennsylvania Turnpike Interchange 5—crossing ... PA-2
Pennsylvania Turnpike Interchange 6—crossing ... PA-2
Pennsylvania Turnpike Interchange 7—crossing ... PA-2
Pennsylvania Turnpike Interchange 8—crossing ... PA-2
Pennsylvania Turnpike Interchange 9—crossing ... PA-2
Pennsytown—uninc pl ... VA-3
Penn Tank—reservoir (2) ... NM-5
Pennterra—hist pl ... MD-2
Penn Tillery Gas Field—oilfield ... TX-5
**Penntown**—pop pl ... IN-6
Penn Townhall—building ... IA-7
Penn Township—civil ... PA-2
Penn Township—fmr MCD (4) ... IA-7
**Penn Township**—pop pl ... KS-7
**Penn Township**—pop pl ... MO-7
Penn Township Consilidated Sch—school ... PA-2
Penn Township Consolidated Sch—school ... PA-2
Penn Township HS ... PA-2
Penn Township HS—school ... PA-2
**Penn (Township of)**—pop pl (2) ... IL-6
**Penn (Township of)**—pop pl (3) ... IN-6
**Penn (Township of)**—pop pl ... MI-6
**Penn (Township of)**—pop pl ... MN-6
**Penn (Township of)**—pop pl (2) ... OH-6
**Penn (Township of)**—pop pl (13) ... PA-2
Penn Trafford MS—school ... PA-2
Penn Treaty JHS—hist pl ... PA-2
Penn Tunnel—mine ... CO-8
Pennus Hollow—valley ... VA-3
Pennvale ... PA-2
**Pennvale**—pop pl ... PA-2
**Penn Vale (subdivision)**—pop pl ... PA-2
Penn Valley ... PA-2
Penn Valley—basin ... CA-9
Penn Valley—CDP ... CA-9
**Penn Valley**—pop pl (2) ... PA-2
Penn Valley—valley ... AZ-5
Penn Valley Airp—airport ... PA-2
Penn Valley Dam—dam ... AZ-5
Penn Valley Elementary School ... PA-2
Penn Valley Junior Coll—school ... MO-7
Penn Valley Park—park ... MO-7
Penn Valley Sch—school (2) ... PA-2
**Penn Valley Terrace**—pop pl ... PA-2
Penn Valley (Trailer Park)—other ... PA-2
**Penn View**—pop pl ... OH-6
**Penn View**—pop pl ... PA-2
Penn View Lookout Tower—tower ... PA-2
Penn View Mtn—summit ... PA-2
Penn Village—uninc pl ... PA-2
Pennville ... PA-2
Pennville—locale ... MO-7
**Pennville**—pop pl ... GA-3
**Pennville**—pop pl (2) ... IN-6
**Pennville**—pop pl ... PA-2
**Pennville (historical)**—pop pl ... TN-4
Pennwell ... NJ-2
Penn Well—well ... TX-5
Penn Windmill—locale ... TX-5
Pennwood ... PA-2
**Pennwood**—pop pl ... DE-2
**Penn Wood**—pop pl ... PA-2
Pennwood Channel ... MD-2
Penn Wood East JHS—school ... PA-2
Pennwood Farm Airp—airport ... PA-2
Penn Wood HS—school ... PA-2
Pennwood MS ... PA-2
**Pennwood (subdivision)**—pop pl ... PA-2
Penn Wood West JHS—school ... PA-2
Penn-Wyatt House—hist pl ... VA-3
**Pennwyn**—pop pl ... PA-2
**Penn Wynne**—pop pl ... PA-2
Penn Wynne Elem Sch—school ... PA-2
Penny—locale ... KY-4
**Penny**—pop pl ... KY-4
**Penny Acres (subdivision)**—pop pl ... DE-2
**Penn Yan**—pop pl ... NY-2
Pennyan Cem—cemetery ... MI-6
Penn Yan Hist Dist—hist pl ... NY-2
Penny Ante Mine—mine ... OR-9
Pennybaker Island—island ... PA-2
Penny Branch—stream ... KY-4
Penny Branch—stream ... TN-4
Penny Bridge—locale ... NY-2
Penny Brook—stream ... CT-1
Penny Brook—stream ... ME-1
Penny Brook—stream (3) ... MA-1
Penny Brook—stream ... VT-1
Penn-Y-Caerau Cem—cemetery ... NY-2
Penny Cem ... TN-4
Penny Cem—cemetery (2) ... AL-4
Penny Cem—cemetery ... ME-1
Penny Cem—cemetery ... NC-3
Penny Cem—cemetery ... TN-4
Penny Claim—mine ... AZ-5
Penny Cliffs—cliff ... ID-8
Penny Come Quick Area—area ... MD-2
Pennycook Cem—cemetery ... NY-2
Penny Corner—locale ... VA-3
Pennycost Creek—stream ... TN-4
Penny Cove—slope ... GA-3
Pennycove Lump—summit ... NC-3
Penny Creek—stream ... AK-9
Penny Creek—stream ... CA-9
Penny Creek—stream ... FL-3
Penny Creek—stream ... MI-6
Penny Creek—stream ... MS-4
Penny Creek—stream ... NE-7
Penny Creek—stream ... OR-9
Penny Creek—stream (2) ... SC-3
Penny Creek—stream ... VA-3
Penny Creek—stream (3) ... WA-9
**Pennydale (subdivision)**—pop pl ... NC-3
Penny Glades ... CA-9
Penn-Y-Grige Ch—church ... NY-2
Penny-Hester Bridge—bridge ... NC-3
Penny Hill ... DE-2
Penny Hill ... OR-9
**Pennyhill**—pop pl ... DE-2
**Penny Hill**—pop pl ... NC-3
Penny Hill—summit ... NC-3
Penny Hill—summit ... PA-2
Penny Hill—summit ... RI-1
Penny Hill C G Station 167—locale ... NC-3
Penny Hill Lake—reservoir ... NC-3
Penny Hill Lake Dam—dam ... NC-3
**Pennyhill Terrace**—pop pl ... DE-2
Penny Hollow ... MO-7
Penny Hollow—valley (2) ... TN-4
Penny Hollow—valley ... VA-3
Penny Hot Springs—spring ... CO-8
Penny Island ... CT-1
Penny Island—island ... CA-9
Penny Island—island ... MI-6
Penny Island—island ... NH-1
Penny Island—island ... NY-2
Pennykin Branch—stream ... TN-4
Penny Lake ... WI-6
Penny Lake—lake ... ID-8
Penny Lake—lake (6) ... MI-6
Penny Lake—lake ... MN-6
Penny Lake—lake ... WA-9
Penny Lake—lake (2) ... WI-6
Penny Lake—lake ... WY-8
Pennymotley Creek—stream ... AL-4
Penny Mtn—summit ... AL-4
Penny Mtn—summit ... ID-8
Penny Oaks ... IL-6
Pennypack Circle—locale ... PA-2
Pennypack Creek—stream ... PA-2
Pennypack Elem Sch—school ... PA-2
Pennypacker, Benjamin, House—hist pl ... PA-2
Pennypacker, Matthias, Farm—hist pl ... PA-2
Pennypacker, Samuel W., Sch—hist pl ... PA-2
Pennypacker Mansion—hist pl ... PA-2
**Pennypacker Park**—pop pl ... NJ-2
Pennypacker Park Sch—school ... NJ-2
Pennypacker Sch—school ... PA-2
Pennypack Park—park ... PA-2
**Pennypack Woods**—pop pl ... PA-2
Penny Pond—bay ... NY-2
Penny Pond—lake (2) ... NY-2
Penny Pond—reservoir ... NC-3
Penny Pond Dam—dam ... NC-3
Penny Pot—locale ... NJ-2
Penny Pot Mills ... NJ-2
Penny Pot Stream—stream ... NJ-2
Penny Ridge ... CA-9
Pennyrile Lake—reservoir ... KY-4
Pennyrile State For—forest ... KY-4
Penny River—stream ... AK-9
Pennyrock Sch—school ... CA-9
Penny Row ... TN-4
**Pennyroyal**—pop pl ... SC-3
Pennyroyal Bridge—bridge ... SC-3
Pennyroyal Ch—church ... SC-3
Pennyroyal Creek—stream ... SC-3
Pennyroyal Hill—summit ... NH-1
**Pennyroyal Junction**—pop pl ... SC-3
Pennyroyal Sch—school ... SC-3
Pennyroyal Shoals—rapids ... TN-4
Pennyroyal Swamp—stream ... SC-3
**Pennys**—pop pl ... AR-4
Pennys Chapel—church ... KY-4
Penny Sch (historical)—school ... AL-4
Pennys Creek—stream ... SC-3
Pennys Crossroads—locale ... AL-4
Pennys Ford (historical)—crossing ... TN-4
Penny Slough—stream ... TN-4
Penny Slough Landing—locale ... TN-4
Pennysoa ... NJ-2
Pennysoaking Creek ... NJ-2
Penny Spring—spring ... AL-4
Penny Spring—spring (2) ... OR-9
Penny Spring Campground—locale ... ID-8
Penny Springs—stream ... IA-7
Penny Spring Station—locale ... OR-9
Penny Street Sch—school ... VT-1
Penny Town ... NJ-2
**Pennyville**—pop pl ... IN-6
**Pennyville**—pop pl ... VA-3
Pennywash Creek—stream ... FL-3
Pennywinkle Bay—swamp ... FL-3
Pennywinkle Branch—stream ... GA-3
Pennywinkle Branch—stream ... SC-3
Pennywinkle Branch—stream (2) ... TN-4
Pennywinkle Creek—stream ... AL-4
Pennywinkle Creek—stream ... MS-4
Pennywinkle Hollow—valley ... AR-4
Pennywinkle Hollow—valley (2) ... TN-4
Pennywinkle Spring—spring ... AL-4
Pennyworth Island—island ... GA-3
Pennyworth Island—island ... SC-3
Penobscot ... MI-6
**Penobscot**—pop pl ... ME-1
**Penobscot**—pop pl ... PA-2
Penobscot Bald Mtn—summit ... ME-1
Penobscot Bay—bay ... ME-1
Penobscot Brook—stream ... ME-1
Penobscot Ch—church ... ME-1
**Penobscot (County)**—pop pl ... ME-1
Penobscot Creek ... PA-2
Penobscot Creek—stream ... CA-9
Penobscot Expedition Site—hist pl ... ME-1
Penobscot Experimantal For—forest ... ME-1
Penobscot Farm—locale ... CA-9
Penobscot Farm—locale ... ME-1
Penobscot Indian Island Ind Res—348 (1980) ... ME-1
Penobscot Island—island ... ME-1
Penobscot Knob ... PA-2
Penobscot Lake—lake ... ME-1
Penobscot Marine Museum—hist pl ... ME-1
Penobscot Mine—mine ... MT-8
Penobscot Mtn—summit ... PA-2
Penobscot Pond—lake ... ME-1
Penobscot River—stream ... ME-1
Penobscot Salmon Club and Pool—hist pl ... ME-1
Penobscot Sch—school ... KY-4
Penobscott Mine—mine ... SD-7
**Penobscot (Town of)**—pop pl ... ME-1
Penobscot-Valley Country Club—other ... ME-1
Peno Ch (abandoned)—church ... MO-7
Peno Corner—locale ... OK-5
Peno Creek ... MO-7
Peno Creek—stream ... MO-7
Peno Creek—stream ... WY-8
Penoger Lake—lake ... MI-6
Peno Grazing Association Dam—dam ... SD-7
Peno Hill (historical)—summit ... SD-7
Peno (historical)—locale ... SD-7
Penoke—locale ... PA-2
**Penokee**—pop pl ... KS-7
Penokee Cem—cemetery ... KS-7
Penokee Stone Figure—hist pl ... KS-7
Penoke Run—stream ... PA-2
Penola—locale ... VA-3
Penola Brake ... LA-4
Penola (historical)—locale ... AL-4
Peno Lake Dam—dam ... SD-7
Penole ... CA-9
Penole Peak—summit ... CA-9
Penole Point ... CA-9
**Penonales**—pop pl ... PR-3
Penon Blanco ... CA-9
Penon Blanco Peak—summit ... CA-9
Penon Blanco Point—summit ... CA-9
Penon Blanco Ridge—ridge ... CA-9
Penon Brusi—island ... PR-3
Penon de Afuera—island ... PR-3
Penon de los Soldados—summit ... PR-3
Penon de Ponce—summit ... PR-3
Penon de San Jorge—island ... PR-3
Penones de Melones—summit ... PR-3
Peno No. 9 Township—civ div ... SD-7
Penoria Lake ... MI-6
Peno Sch—school ... SD-7
Peno Sch (abandoned)—school ... MO-7
Peno Township—civil ... MO-7
Peno Township—civil (2) ... SD-7
Penovar Lake ... MI-6
**Penowa**—pop pl ... PA-2
Penoyar—locale ... CA-9
Penoyar Creek ... MI-6
Penoyar Lake ... MI-6
Penoyer Creek—stream (2) ... MI-6
Penoyer Drain—canal ... MI-6
Penoyer Farms—locale ... NV-8
Penoyer Lake—lake ... MI-6
Penoyer Lake—lake ... WA-9
Penoyer Springs—spring ... NV-8
Penoyer Valley ... NV-8
Pen Place Windmill—locale ... NM-5
Pen Pocket—reservoir ... AZ-5
Pen Point—cape ... VI-3
Pen Point—summit ... OR-9
Penquite Creek—stream ... MS-4
Penrhos Sch—school ... WI-6
Pen Ridge Cemetery ... MS-4
Penridge HS—school ... PA-2
Penrith—locale ... WA-9
**Penrock**—pop pl ... DE-2
Pen Rock Cave—cave ... AL-4
Penrod ... AZ-5
**Penrod**—pop pl ... KY-4
Penrod Burn—area ... AZ-5
Penrod Cabin—locale ... AZ-5
Penrod Canyon—valley ... CA-9
Penrod Canyon—valley ... NV-8
Penrod (CCD)—cens area ... KY-4
Penrod Cem—cemetery ... PA-2
Penrod Creek—stream ... ID-8
Penrod Creek—stream ... NV-8
Penrod Creek—stream ... UT-8
Penrod Drain—stream ... MI-6
Penrod Flat—flat ... AZ-5
Penrod Hill—summit ... PA-2
Penrod Hollow—valley (2) ... OH-6
Penrod Mtn—summit ... AZ-5
Penrod Sch—school ... NV-8
Penrod Tank—reservoir (3) ... AZ-5
Penrose—locale ... AR-4
Penrose—locale ... PA-2
Penrose—locale ... UT-8
**Penrose**—pop pl ... CO-8
**Penrose**—pop pl ... IL-6
**Penrose**—pop pl ... NC-3
Penrose, Mount—summit ... MT-8
Penrose Branch—stream ... DE-2
Penrose Canal—canal ... NJ-2
Penrose Cem—cemetery ... CO-8
Penrose Cem—cemetery ... UT-8
Penrose Cem—cemetery ... WY-8
Penrose Creek—stream ... WY-8
Penrose Ditch—canal ... WY-8
Penrose Draw—valley ... CO-8
Penrose Guard Station—locale ... WY-8
Penrose Park—flat ... WY-8
Penrose Park—park ... MO-7
Penrose Peak—summit ... MT-8
Penrose Peak—summit ... WY-8
Penrose Point—cape ... WA-9
Penrose Point State Park—park ... WA-9
Penrose-Portland—cens area ... CO-8
Penrose-Rosemont Rsvr—reservoir ... CO-8
Penrose Sch—school ... NC-3
Penrose Trail—trail ... CO-8
Pen Run—stream ... WV-2
**Penryn**—pop pl ... CA-9
**Penryn**—pop pl ... PA-2
Penryn Canal—canal ... CA-9
Penryn Park YMCA Camp—locale ... PA-2
Pen Ryn Sch—school ... PA-2
Penryn Station ... PA-2
Penryth Spring—spring ... PA-2
Pensaco Canyon ... AZ-5
Pensacola ... MS-4
**Pensacola**—pop pl ... FL-3
**Pensacola**—pop pl ... NC-3
**Pensacola**—pop pl ... OK-5
Pensacola Athletic Club—hist pl ... FL-3
Pensacola Baptist Ch—church ... FL-3
Pensacola Bay ... FL-3
Pensacola Bay—bay ... FL-3
Pensacola Bay Bridge—bridge ... FL-3
**Pensacola Beach**—pop pl ... FL-3
Pensacola Beach Community United Ch—church ... FL-3
Pensacola Boys Base—school ... FL-3
Pensacola Branch—stream ... AL-4
Pensacola Catholic HS—school ... FL-3
Pensacola (CCD)—cens area ... FL-3
Pensacola Cem—cemetery ... MS-4
Pensacola Christian Sch—school ... FL-3
Pensacola Dam—dam ... OK-5
Pensacola Hist Dist—hist pl ... FL-3
Pensacola (historical)—locale ... MS-4
Pensacola Hosp—hist pl ... FL-3
Pensacola HS—school ... FL-3
Pensacola Junior Coll—school ... FL-3
Pensacola Junior College, Learning Resource Center—building ... FL-3
Pensacola Junior Coll (Milton Center)—school ... FL-3
Pensacola Lighthouse and Keeper's Quarters—hist pl ... FL-3
Pensacola Memorial Gardens—cemetery (2) ... FL-3
Pensacola Naval Aerospace and Regional Medical Ctr.—military ... FL-3
Pensacola Naval Air Station—locale ... FL-3
Pensacola Naval Air Station Hist Dist—hist pl ... FL-3
Pensacola Naval Public Works Center—military ... FL-3
Pensacola Outlet Mall—locale ... FL-3
Pensacola Plaza (Shop Ctr)—locale ... FL-3
Pensacola Port Authority—locale ... FL-3
Pensacola Private Sch of Liberal Arts—school ... FL-3
Pensacola Regional Airp—airport ... FL-3
Pensacola River ... FL-3
Pensacola Shores ... FL-3
Pensacola Shores—uninc pl ... FL-3
Pensacola (Township of)—fmr MCD ... NC-3
Pensacola Village (Shop Ctr)—locale ... FL-3
**Pensaukee**—pop pl ... WI-6
Pensaukee Lakes—lake ... WI-6
Pensaukee River—stream ... WI-6
Pensaukee Shoal—bar ... WI-6
Pensaukee State Public Hunting Grounds—park ... WI-6
**Pensaukee (Town of)**—pop pl ... WI-6
Pensauken ... NJ-2
Pensauken Creek ... NJ-2
Pensawquin Cr ... NJ-2
Pense Cem—cemetery ... AR-4
Pense Hollow—valley ... AR-4
**Pensfield Place (subdivision)**—pop pl (2) ... AZ-5
Pensinger Canyon ... CA-9
Pension Bldg ... DC-2
Pension Branch—stream ... IN-6
Pension Bureau Bldg—building ... DC-2
Pensioner Pond—lake ... VT-1
Pension Mountain Cem—cemetery ... AR-4
Pension Mountain Sch—school ... AR-4
Pension Mtn—summit ... AR-4
Pension School (historical)—locale ... MO-7
Pensire Pup—stream ... AK-9
Penske—airport ... NJ-2
Penske Airp—airport ... PA-2
Penske Two—airport ... NJ-2
Pens Neck ... NJ-2
Penson Creek—stream ... NC-3
Penson Creek—stream ... TX-5
Penson Knob—summit ... GA-3
Penson Knob—summit ... NC-3
Penson Mtn—summit ... NC-3
Penson Ranch—locale ... NV-8
Penson Spring Branch—stream ... TX-5
Pensons School ... TN-4
Pensoukee Lake ... WI-6
Pen Spring—spring ... CO-8
Penspring Hollow—valley ... TN-4
Penstock—locale ... MO-7
Penstock Bridge—hist pl ... WA-9
Penstock Olsen Ditch—canal ... OR-9
Penstock Ridge—ridge ... CA-9
Penstock Siphon—locale ... NV-8
Pens Windmill—locale ... NM-5
Pens Windmill—locale (2) ... TX-5
Pensyl Creek Dam ... PA-2
Pensyls Mill—locale ... PA-2
Pentacola Field—area ... CA-9
Pentacola Gulch—valley ... CA-9
Pentacostal Ch (historical)—church ... MS-4
Pentacostal Ch of God—church ... MS-4
Pentacostal Workers Assembly Ch—church ... IN-6
Pentacost Church ... AL-4
Pentacre—locale ... WV-2
Pentacrest—hist pl ... IA-7
Pentad Lake—lake ... MT-8
Pentagon—building ... VA-3
Pentagon Barracks—hist pl ... LA-4
Pentagon Clack Creek Trail—trail ... MT-8
Pentagon Creek—stream ... MT-8
Pentagon Guard Station—locale ... MT-8
Pentagon Mtn—summit ... MT-8
Pentagon (U.S. Department of Defense Building)—military ... VA-3
Pen Tank—reservoir (2) ... AZ-5
Penta Sch—school ... OH-6
Pentecost—locale ... MS-4
Pentecostal Bible Institute—school ... MS-4
Pentecostal Campground—locale ... OK-5
Pentecostal Cem—cemetery ... KY-4
Pentecostal Ch ... MO-7
Pentecostal Ch—church (3) ... AL-4
Pentecostal Ch—church (3) ... AR-4
Pentecostal Ch—church ... GA-3
Pentecostal Ch—church (6) ... LA-4
Pentecostal Ch—church (3) ... MI-6
Pentecostal Ch—church (6) ... MO-7
Pentecostal Ch—church ... MT-8
Pentecostal Ch—church ... PA-2
Pentecostal Ch—church ... TN-4
Pentecostal Ch—church (3) ... TX-5
Pentecostal Ch—church ... VA-3
Pentecostal Ch of God—church (2) ... AL-4
Pentecostal Ch of God—church ... FL-3
Pentecostal Ch of God—church (3) ... MS-4
Pentecostal Ch of God—church ... TN-4
Pentecostal Ch of God in Christ—church ... KS-7
Pentecostal Ch of God in Christ—church ... MS-4
Pentecostal Ch of God (Ogden)—church ... UT-8
Pentecostal Ch of God Temple—church ... AL-4
Pentecostal Ch of God (West Valley City)—church ... UT-8
Pentecostal Ch of Promises—church ... IN-6
Pentecostal Faith Ch—church ... AL-4
Pentecostal Grace Ch—church ... KS-7
Pentecostal Holiness Ch—church (3) ... AL-4
Pentecostal Holiness Ch—church ... FL-3
Pentecostal Holiness Ch—church ... MS-4
Pentecostal Holiness Ch—church ... OK-5
Pentecostal Holiness Ch Conference of Florida—church ... FL-3
Pentecostal House of Prayer—church ... FL-3
Pentecostal Miracle Deliverance House of Prayer—church ... FL-3
Pentecostal Mission ... PA-2
Pentecostal Orphanage (historical)—building ... TN-4
Pentecostal Temple Ch of Our Lord Jesus Christ—church ... MS-4
Pentecostal True Holiness Ch—church ... AL-4
Pentecost Cem—cemetery ... AL-4
Pentecost Cem—cemetery ... GA-3
Pentecost Cem—cemetery ... IL-6
Pentecost Cem—cemetery ... IN-6
Pentecost Ch—church (2) ... AL-4
Pentecost Ch—church (2) ... GA-3
Pentecost Ch—church (2) ... LA-4
Pentecost Ch—church ... MI-6
Pentecost Ch—church ... MN-6
Pentecost Ch—church ... MO-7
Pentecost Ch—church (3) ... TN-4
Pentecost Ch—church ... VA-3
Pentecost Ch—church ... WI-6
Pentecost Ch (historical)—church ... MO-7
Pentecost Ch (historical)—church ... TN-4
Pentecost Hollow—valley ... AR-4
Pentecost Methodist Ch ... AL-4
Pentecost Post Office (historical)—building ... MS-4
Pentecost Sch—school ... AL-4
Pentecost Sch—school ... MI-6
Pentenwell Flowage ... WI-6
Penters Bluff ... AR-4
Penthole State Wildlife Mngmt Area—park ... MN-6
Penticutt Pond ... MA-1
Pentitente Canyon—valley ... CO-8
Pentland—locale ... CA-9
Pentland—locale ... PA-2
**Pentland**—pop pl ... DE-2
Pentland Sch—school ... MI-6
**Pentland (Township of)**—pop pl ... MI-6
**Pentoga**—pop pl ... MI-6
**Penton**—pop pl ... AL-4
**Penton**—pop pl ... MS-4
**Penton**—pop pl ... NJ-2
Penton Ch—church ... AL-4
Penton Post Office (historical)—building ... MS-4
Penton Sch—school ... MS-4
Pentonville—locale ... AL-4
Pentrees ... WV-2
**Pentress**—pop pl ... WV-2
Pentress Cem—cemetery ... TX-5
Penttila Butte—summit ... SD-7
Pentucket ... MA-1
Pentucket, Lake—lake ... MA-1
Pentucket Pond Outlet Dam—dam ... MA-1
Pentucket Pond Outlet Rsvr—reservoir ... MA-1
Pentucket Regional HS—school ... MA-1
Pentucket Regional JHS—school ... MA-1
Pentuckett ... MA-1
**Pentwater**—pop pl ... MI-6
Pentwater Lake—lake ... MI-6
Pentwater Oil Field—other ... MI-6
Pentwater River—stream ... MI-6
**Pentwater (Township of)**—pop pl ... MI-6
Pentz—locale ... CA-9
Pentzer Park—park ... NE-7
Pentz Run—stream ... PA-2
Penuasset Island ... MA-1
Penuelas—CDP ... PR-3
Penuelas—locale ... PR-3
**Penuelas**—pop pl ... PR-3
Penuelas (Municipio)—civil ... PR-3
Penuelas (Pueblo)—fmr MCD ... PR-3
Penuel Ch—church (2) ... VA-3
Penville ... NJ-2
Penvir—locale ... CA-9
Penvir—locale ... VA-3
Pen Way Trail—trail ... OR-9
Penwell—locale ... NJ-2
**Penwell**—pop pl ... MT-8
**Penwell**—pop pl ... TX-5
Penwell Ch—church ... TX-5
Penwell House—hist pl ... ID-8
Pen Windmill—locale (3) ... TX-5
Penwood Branch—stream ... NC-3
Penwood Channel—channel ... MD-2
Penwood State Park—park ... CT-1
Penyemwaan ... FM-9
Penzance—cape ... MA-1
Penzance—locale ... AZ-5
Penzance Peninsula ... MA-1
Penzance Point—cape ... MA-1
Penzer Sch—school ... MT-8
Peo, Unai—beach ... MH-9
**Peoa**—pop pl ... UT-8
Peoa Cem—cemetery ... UT-8
Peo Beach ... MH-9
Peobles Island—island ... NY-2
**Peoga**—pop pl ... IN-6
Peoga Lake—reservoir ... IN-6
Peoga Lake Dam (lower)—dam ... IN-6
Peogh Camp—locale ... WY-8
Peoh Point—summit ... WA-9
Peola—locale ... WA-9
Peola Branch—stream ... MO-7
Peola Mills—locale ... VA-3
**Peoli**—pop pl ... OH-6
Peolia Ch—church ... KY-4
Peone—locale ... WA-9
Peone Cem—cemetery ... WA-9
Peone Creek—stream ... WA-9
Peone Creek Park—park ... WA-9
Peone Prairie—flat ... WA-9
Peon Gulch—valley ... CA-9
**Peonia**—pop pl ... KY-4
Peonic ... NY-2
Peon Pit—cave ... AL-4
Peony ... MP-9
Peony Creek—stream ... WA-9
**Peony Gardens Subdivision**—pop pl ... UT-8
Peony Park—park ... NE-7
Peoples ... CO-8
Peoples—locale ... KY-4
Peoples—locale ... MS-4
**Peoples**—pop pl ... CO-8
Peoples A B Ch—church ... DE-2
Peoples Acad—school ... FL-3
Peoples Bank and Trust Company—hist pl ... MS-4
Peoples Bank of Biloxi—hist pl ... MS-4
Peoples Baptist Ch—church ... AL-4
Peoples Baptist Temple ... NC-3
Peoples Bible Sch—school ... NC-3
Peoples Bldg & Loan Building—hist pl ... AR-4
Peoples Branch—stream ... GA-3
Peoples Burial Park—park ... TX-5
Peoples Canal—canal ... ID-8
Peoples Canal—canal ... LA-4
Peoples Canal—canal ... UT-8
Peoples Canal—canal ... WY-8
Peoples Canyon—valley ... AZ-5
Peoples Cem—cemetery (2) ... IA-7
Peoples Cem—cemetery ... KY-4
Peoples Cem—cemetery ... MA-1
Peoples Cem—cemetery ... MS-4
Peoples Cem—cemetery ... MO-7
Peoples Cem—cemetery ... NY-2
Peoples Cem—cemetery (4) ... TN-4
Peoples Cem—cemetery ... TX-5
Peoples Cem—cemetery ... VA-3
Peoples Ch—church (2) ... AL-4
Peoples Ch—church ... AR-4
Peoples Ch—church (2) ... GA-3
Peoples Ch—church ... ME-1
Peoples Ch—church ... MO-7
Peoples Ch—church (6) ... NC-3
Peoples Ch—church ... OH-6
Peoples Ch—church (3) ... PA-2
Peoples Ch—church ... TN-4
Peoples Ch—church ... VA-3
Peoples Chapel—church ... FL-3
Peoples Chapel—church ... IN-6
Peoples Chapel—church ... KY-4
Peoples Chapel—church ... NC-3
Peoples Chapel (historical)—church ... AL-4
Peoples Church, The—church ... NC-3
**Peoples City**—pop pl ... FL-3
Peoples' Congregational Church—hist pl ... MT-8
Peoples Creek—stream (2) ... MT-8
Peoples Creek—stream ... NC-3
Peoples Creek—stream ... SC-3
Peoples Creek—stream ... WA-9
Peoples Creek Rec Area—locale ... MO-7
Peoples Creek Sch—school ... MT-8
Peoples Ditch—canal ... CA-9
People's Federal Savings and Loan Association—hist pl ... OH-6
Peoples Ferry (historical)—locale ... MS-4

People's First Natl Bank and Trust Company Bldg—hist pl ... KY-4
Peoples Forest Museum—hist pl ... CT-1
People's Free Library of South Carolina—hist pl ... SC-3
Peoples Gas Bldg—hist pl ... IL-6
Peoples Gospel Park—park ... MD-2
Peoples High School ... MS-4
Peoples Hollow—valley ... MO-7
Peoples Hosp—hospital ... AL-4
Peoples Hosp—hospital ... IL-6
Peoples Hosp—hospital ... TX-5
Peoples Irrigation Company Ditch—canal ... OR-9
Peoples Lake—lake ... AR-4
Peoples Lake Dam—dam ... AL-4
Peoples Lake Number 2—reservoir ... AL-4
Peoples Lake Number 2 Dam—dam ... AL-4
Peoples Lakes—lake ... GA-3
Peoples Landing—locale ... TN-4
Peoples Landing Post Office (historical)—building ... TN-4
Peoples Memorial Park—cemetery ... DE-2
Peoples Mill (historical)—locale ... TN-4
Peoples Mission—church ... NC-3
Peoples Park—park ... MO-7
Peoples Presbyterian Ch (historical)—church ... MS-4
Peoples Ranch ... AZ-5
People's Savings Bank—hist pl ... IA-7
Peoples Sch—school ... SC-3
Peoples Sch—school ... WI-6
Peoples Sch (historical)—school ... MS-4
Peoples Sch (historical)—school ... PA-2
People's State Bank—hist pl ... NE-7
Peoples State For—forest ... CT-1
Peoples Station ... CO-8
Peoples Still—locale ... GA-3
Peoples Tabernacle—church ... NC-3
Peoples Township—fmr MCD ... IA-7
People's Unitarian Church—hist pl ... NE-7
People Union Ch—church ... VA-3
**Peora**—pop pl ... WV-2
Peoria—locale ... CO-8
Peoria—locale ... MS-4
Peoria—locale ... NC-3
**Peoria**—pop pl ... AZ-5
**Peoria**—pop pl ... IL-6
**Peoria**—pop pl (2) ... IN-6
**Peoria**—pop pl (2) ... IA-7
**Peoria**—pop pl ... KS-7
**Peoria**—pop pl ... MO-7
**Peoria**—pop pl ... NY-2
**Peoria**—pop pl (2) ... OH-6
**Peoria**—pop pl ... OK-5
**Peoria**—pop pl ... OR-9
**Peoria**—pop pl ... TX-5
Peoria Basin—basin ... CA-9
Peoria Bottoms ... SD-7
Peoria Bottoms (historical)—locale ... SD-7
Peoria Cem—cemetery ... CA-9
Peoria Cem—cemetery ... IA-7
Peoria Cem—cemetery ... KS-7
Peoria Cem—cemetery ... OK-5
Peoria Ch—church ... FL-3
Peoria Ch—church ... IA-7
Peoria City—locale ... IA-7
Peoria City Hall—hist pl ... IL-6
**Peoria City (Township of)**—pop pl ... IL-6
Peoria Cordage Company—hist pl ... IL-6
Peoria Country Club—other ... IL-6
**Peoria (County)**—pop pl ... IL-6
Peoria County Park—park ... OR-9
Peoria Creek—stream (2) ... CA-9
Peoria Dam ... AZ-5
Peoria Elem Sch—school ... AZ-5
Peoria Estates (trailer park)—locale ... AZ-5
**Peoria Estates (trailer park)**—pop pl ... AZ-5
Peoria Flat—flat ... CA-9
Peoria Flats—flat ... SD-7
Peoria Flats Rec Area ... SD-7
**Peoria Heights**—pop pl ... IL-6
Peoria Heights Rsvr—reservoir ... IL-6
Peoria (historical)—locale ... KS-7
Peoria HS—school ... AZ-5
Peoria Indian Sch—hist pl ... OK-5
Peoria Kachina Sch—school ... AZ-5
Peoria Lake—lake ... IL-6
Peoria Lock and Dam—dam ... IL-6
Peoria Mineral Springs—hist pl ... IL-6
Peoria Mtn—summit ... CA-9
Peoria Municipal Airp—airport ... IL-6
Peoria Pass—gap ... CA-9
Peoria Polynesian Village (trailer park)—locale ... AZ-5
**Peoria Polynesian Village (trailer park)**—pop pl ... AZ-5
Peoria Post Office—building ... AZ-5
Peoria Sch—school ... CA-9
Peoria Sch—school ... CO-8
Peoria Stadium—other ... IL-6
Peoria State Hosp—hist pl ... IL-6
Peoria State Hosp—hospital ... IL-6
Peoria Substation—locale ... AZ-5
Peoria Tank—reservoir ... NM-5
Peoria Town Hall—building ... AZ-5
Peoria Township—civil ... SD-7
**Peoria Township**—pop pl ... KS-7
**Peoria Township**—pop pl ... NE-7
Peoria Tribal Cemetery—hist pl ... OK-5
Peoria Underpass—crossing ... AZ-5
Peoria Waterworks—hist pl ... IL-6
Peos Bay—bay ... NY-2
**Peosta**—pop pl ... IA-7
Peot Airp—airport ... WA-9
Peotone ... KS-7
**Peotone**—pop pl ... IL-6
Peotone Cem—cemetery ... KS-7
**Peotone (Township of)**—pop pl ... IL-6
Pep—locale ... NM-5
Pep—locale ... TX-5
Pe P'a ... KS-7
Pepacating ... PA-2
Pepack ... NJ-2
Pepacton Rsvr—reservoir ... NY-2
**Pepeekeo**—pop pl ... HI-9
**Pepeekeo Mill**—pop pl ... HI-9
**Pepeekeo Mill Camp**—pop pl ... HI-9
Pepeekeo Point—cape ... HI-9
Pepeekeo Sch—school ... HI-9
Pepeiaohuhu Hill—summit ... HI-9
Pepeiaolepo Bay—bay ... HI-9
Pepeiau Shelter—locale ... HI-9
Pepeopae—summit ... HI-9
Pepercotton Creek ... NJ-2
Pepermint Springs—spring ... MO-7
Pepers Sch (abandoned)—school ... MO-7
Pepertown ... IN-6
Pepe Tank—reservoir ... AZ-5
Pepe Tank—reservoir ... TX-5
Pepetick Creek ... VA-3
**Pepin**—pop pl ... WI-6
Pepin, Lake—lake (3) ... MN-6
Pepin, Lake—lake ... WI-6
**Pepin (County)**—pop pl ... WI-6
Pepin County Courthouse and Jail—hist pl ... WI-6
Pepin Creek—stream ... WA-9
Pepin Hill Ch—church ... WI-6
Pepin Prairie—flat ... WI-6
**Pepin (Town of)**—pop pl ... WI-6
**Pepin (Township of)**—pop pl ... MN-6
**Peplin**—pop pl ... WI-6
Peplin Creek—stream ... WI-6
Peplin Flats—flat ... UT-8
Peplin Mountain ... UT-8
Peplin Mountains ... UT-8
Peplin Mtn—summit ... UT-8
Peplin Pond—reservoir ... UT-8
Peplin Siding—locale ... UT-8
Peplote Windmill—locale ... AZ-5
Pep Marquette Park—park ... TN-4
Pepo ... MH-9
Pepoon Canyon—valley ... WA-9
Pepoon Hollow—valley ... AR-4
Pepoon Lake—lake ... WA-9
Peppard, Joseph Grear, House—hist pl ... MO-7
Peppard Flat—flat ... CA-9
Peppard Gulch—valley ... MT-8
Peppard Sch—school ... IL-6
Pepper—locale ... DE-2
Pepper—locale ... VA-3
Pepper—locale ... WV-2
Pepper, Carlton, David, Farm—hist pl ... DE-2
Pepper Beach State Rec Area—park ... FL-3
Pepperbox—locale ... DE-2
Pepperbox Creek—stream ... NY-2
Pepperbox Hill—summit ... CT-1
Pepperbox Hill—summit ... ID-8
Pepperbox Pond—lake ... NY-2
Pepper Box Ridge—ridge ... AR-4
Pepper Branch ... DE-2
Pepper Branch—stream ... DE-2
Pepper Branch—stream ... LA-4
Pepper Branch—stream ... TX-5
Pepper Brook—stream ... VT-1
Pepper Camp—locale ... OR-9
Peppercamp Creek—stream ... TX-5
Pepper Canyon—valley ... AZ-5
Pepper Canyon—valley ... NM-5
Pepper Canyon—valley ... OR-9
Pepper Cem—cemetery ... KY-4
Pepper Cem—cemetery ... MS-4
Peppercorn Creek—spring ... NV-8
**Pepper Corner**—pop pl ... CA-9
Pepper Corn Hill ... MA-1
Peppercorn Hill—summit ... MA-1
Pepper Cove—bay ... FL-3
Pepper Creek—stream ... AR-4
Pepper Creek—stream ... DE-2
Pepper Creek—stream ... GA-3
Pepper Creek—stream (3) ... ID-8
Pepper Creek—stream ... IN-6
Pepper Creek—stream ... IA-7
Pepper Creek—stream ... KY-4
Pepper Creek—stream (2) ... MS-4
Pepper Creek—stream ... MO-7
Pepper Creek—stream ... NE-7
Pepper Creek—stream ... NC-3
Pepper Creek—stream (2) ... OK-5
Pepper Creek—stream (2) ... OR-9
Pepper Creek—stream ... SD-7
Pepper Creek—stream ... TX-5
Pepper Creek—stream ... VA-3
Pepper Creek—stream ... WA-9
Pepper Creek Ch—church ... NC-3
Pepper Creek Ridge—ridge ... ID-8
Pepperdine Camp—locale ... CA-9
Pepperdine Coll—school ... CA-9
Pepperdine Sch—school ... MO-7
Pepper Drain—canal ... CA-9
Pepper Drive Sch—school ... CA-9
**Pepperdyne (subdivision)**—pop pl ... NC-3
**Pepperell**—pop pl ... AL-4
**Pepperell**—pop pl ... MA-1
**Pepperell Center**—pop pl ... MA-1
Pepperell Centre ... MA-1
Pepperell Cove ... ME-1
Pepperell HS—school ... GA-3
Pepperell Paper Company Dam—dam ... MA-1
Pepperell Park—park ... GA-3
Pepperell Park—park ... ME-1
Pepperell Sch—school ... AL-4
Pepperell(sta.) (RR name for East Pepperell)—other ... MA-1
**Pepperell (Town of)**—pop pl ... MA-1
Pepperfish Keys—island ... FL-3
Pepper Flats—flat ... FL-3
Pepper Fork—stream ... WV-2
Pepper Gap—gap ... CA-9
Peppergrass Flat—flat ... CA-9
Pepper Grass Valley—valley ... CA-9
Pepper Grove Cove—bay ... TX-5
Pepper Gully—stream ... SC-3
Pepper Hammock—basin ... FL-3
Pepper Hammock—island ... FL-3
Pepper Hammock—island ... GA-3
**Pepper Heights Subdivision**—pop pl ... UT-8
**Pepperhill**—pop pl ... SC-3
Pepper Hill—summit ... MO-7
Pepper Hill—summit ... TX-5
Pepper Hill Ch—church ... MS-4
Pepperhill Run—stream ... PA-2
Pepper Hill Trail—trail ... PA-2
Pepper Hollow—valley ... TN-4
Pepper Hollow Branch—stream ... TN-4
**Pepperidge Subdivision**—pop pl ... UT-8
Pepper Island—island ... NY-2
Pepper Lake—lake ... AK-9
Pepper Lake—lake ... AZ-5
Pepper Lake Dam—dam (2) ... MS-4
Pepper Lateral—canal ... CA-9
Pepperleaf Road ... MH-9
Pepperman House—hist pl ... AL-4
Pepper Mill Creek—stream ... VA-3
Peppermill Creek—stream ... WI-6
Peppermill Ditch—canal ... IL-6
**Peppermill Farms**—pop pl ... NJ-2
Peppermill Gulf—valley ... NY-2
Peppermill Lake—reservoir ... WI-6
Pepper Mill Village—uninc pl ... MD-2
Peppermint Branch—stream ... TN-4
Peppermint Brook—stream ... ME-1
Peppermint Brook—stream ... MA-1
Peppermint Brook—stream ... NY-2
**Peppermint Corner**—pop pl ... NH-1
Peppermint Creek—stream (3) ... CA-9
Peppermint Creek—stream ... MN-6
Peppermint Creek—stream ... MO-7
Peppermint Creek—stream ... TX-5
Peppermint Creek—stream ... WV-2
**Peppermint Hills**—pop pl ... TN-4
Peppermint Hollow—valley ... MD-2
Peppermint Meadows—flat ... CA-9
Peppermint Meadows—flat ... WA-9
Peppermint Park—park ... NC-3
**Peppermint Park Subdivision**—pop pl ... UT-8
Peppermint Spring—spring ... ID-8
Pepper Mound Creek—gut ... FL-3
Pepper Mtn—summit ... OR-9
Pepper Park—park ... CA-9
Pepper Park—park ... FL-3
**Pepper Pike**—pop pl ... OH-6
Pepper Pike Country Club—other ... OH-6
Pepper Point—cape ... AK-9
Pepper Point—cape ... FL-3
Pepper Pond—lake ... DE-2
Pepperpot Pond—lake ... ME-1
Pepper Ranch—locale ... WY-8
Pepperrell, William, House—hist pl ... ME-1
Pepperrell Cove—bay ... ME-1
**Pepper Ridge**—pop pl ... DE-2
Pepper Ridge—ridge ... AZ-5
**Pepper Ridge (subdivision)**—pop pl (2) ... AZ-5
**Pepper Ridge (trailer park)**—pop pl ... DE-2
Pepper Run—stream (2) ... PA-2
Pepper Run—stream ... VA-3
Pepper Run—stream ... WV-2
**Peppers**—pop pl ... NC-3
Peppersauce Campground—park ... AZ-5
Peppersauce Cave—cave ... AZ-5
Peppersauce Family Campground ... AZ-5
Peppersauce Wash—stream ... AZ-5
Peppers Cem—cemetery ... GA-3
Peppers Cem—cemetery ... MO-7
Pepper Sch—school ... MI-6
Pepper Sch—school ... TN-4
Peppers Creek—stream ... TN-4
Peppers Lake—lake ... AR-4
Peppers Lake Ch—church ... AR-4
Peppers Landing—locale ... DE-2
Pepper Slough—lake ... SD-7
Peppers Mill Pond—reservoir ... MA-1
Peppers Mill Pond Dam—dam ... MA-1
Pepper Spring—spring ... CA-9
Pepper Spring—spring ... NV-8
Pepper Spring—spring ... NM-5
Pepper Tank—reservoir ... NM-5
**Pepperton**—pop pl ... GA-3
Pepperton Ch—church ... MN-6
**Pepperton (Township of)**—pop pl ... MN-6
Peppertown—locale ... TN-4
**Peppertown**—pop pl ... IN-6
Peppertown Cem—cemetery ... TN-4
Peppertown Ch—church ... TN-4
Peppertown Sch (historical)—school ... TN-4
Pepper Tract—area ... DE-2
Pepper Tree—other ... TX-5
**Pepper Tree**—pop pl ... IL-6
**Peppertree Bay**—pop pl ... FL-3
Peppertree Canyon—valley ... CA-9
Pepper Tree Mobile Home Park—locale ... AZ-5
Peppertree Pointe—cape ... FL-3
Pepper Tree Spring—spring ... CA-9
Pepper Tunnel—tunnel ... VA-3
Pepperville ... MO-7
Pepper Well—well ... TX-5
Pepperwood—locale ... CA-9
**Pepperwood Canyon Subdivision**—pop pl ... UT-8
**Pepperwood Condominium**—pop pl ... UT-8
Pepperwood Corrals—locale ... CA-9
Pepperwood Creek—stream (2) ... CA-9
Pepperwood Falls—falls ... CA-9
Pepperwood Grove—locale ... CA-9
Pepperwood Gulch—valley (2) ... CA-9
Pepperwood Spring—spring (3) ... CA-9
Pepperwood Springs—spring ... CA-9
**Pepperwood (subdivision)**—pop pl (2) ... AZ-5
**Pepperwood Subdivision**—pop pl ... UT-8
**Pepperwood Terrace**—pop pl ... UT-8
Pepperwood Trail—trail ... CA-9
Peppin Canyon—valley ... NM-5
Pepplemeyer Branch—stream ... MO-7
Pepptick Creek ... VA-3
Pepridge Swamp—swamp ... PA-2
Pep Rsvr—reservoir ... MT-8
Pepsi-International Airp—airport ... NC-3
**Pepsin**—pop pl ... MO-7
Pequabuck—locale ... CT-1
Pequabuck Bridge—hist pl ... CT-1
Pequabuck River—stream ... CT-1
Pequag ... MA-1
Pequaket ... NH-1
Pequaket Lake ... ME-1
Pequaket Mountain ... NH-1
**Pequaming**—pop pl ... MI-6
Pequaming Bay—bay ... MI-6
Pequaming Point—cape ... MI-6
Pequamsoggin Creek ... IL-6
Pequanac ... NJ-2
Pequanac River ... NJ-2
Pequannac ... NJ-2
Pequannac River ... NJ-2
Pequannoc ... NJ-2
Pequannock ... CT-1
**Pequannock**—pop pl ... NJ-2
Pequannock HS—school ... NJ-2
Pequannock Lake ... CT-1
Pequannock River ... CT-1
Pequannock River—stream ... NJ-2
Pequannock Sch—school ... NJ-2
Pequannock Station—locale ... NJ-2
Pequannock Township—CDP ... NJ-2
**Pequannock (Township of)**—pop pl ... NJ-2
Pequannock Valley Sch—school ... NJ-2
Pequannoc River ... CT-1
Pequannoc River ... NJ-2
Pequanock River ... CT-1
Pequansoggin creek ... IL-6
**Pequawket**—pop pl ... NH-1
Pequawket Brook—stream ... NH-1
Pequawket ountain ... NH-1
Pequawket Pond—lake ... ME-1
Pequawket Pond—lake ... NH-1
Pequaywan Lake—lake ... MN-6
**Pequaywan Lake**—pop pl ... MN-6
Pequaywan Lookout Tower—locale ... MN-6
**Pequaywan (Township of)**—pop pl ... MN-6
Pequea ... PA-2
**Pequea**—pop pl ... PA-2
Pequea Ch—church (3) ... PA-2
Pequea Creek—stream ... PA-2
Pequea Post Office (historical)—building ... PA-2
Pequea Sch—school ... PA-2
**Pequea (Township of)**—pop pl ... PA-2
Pequea Valley HS—school ... PA-2
Pequeno, Arroyo —stream ... CA-9
Peques Creek—stream ... AL-4
Pequest—locale ... NJ-2
Pequest Fish and Wildlife Mngmt Area—park ... NJ-2
Pequest River—stream ... NJ-2
Pequest Union Cem—cemetery ... NJ-2
Pequest Valley—valley ... NJ-2
Pequet Lake ... MN-6
Pequet Lake—lake ... MI-6
Pequid Brook—stream ... MA-1
Pequimmit ... MA-1
Pequiog ... MA-1
Pequir Brook ... MA-1
Pequit Brook ... MA-1
Pequnock River ... CT-1
**Pequoig**—pop pl ... MA-1
Pequoig Hotel—hist pl ... MA-1
Pequonnock ... CT-1
Pequonnock Lake ... CT-1
Pequonnock River ... CT-1
Pequonnock River—stream ... CT-1
Pequonnock River RR Bridge—hist pl ... CT-1
Pequonnoc River ... CT-1
Pequonnuc River ... CT-1
pequonock Lake ... CT-1
Pequonoc Lake ... CT-1
Pequonuck River ... CT-1
Pequop—locale ... NV-8
Pequop Interchange—crossing ... NV-8
Pequop Maintenance Station—locale ... NV-8
Pequop Mtns—range ... NV-8
Pequop Spring—spring ... NV-8
Pequop Spruce Mountain Pass—gap ... NV-8
Pequop Summit—summit ... NV-8
Pequop Well ... NV-8
Pequop Well—well ... NV-8
**Pequot**—pop pl ... IL-6
Pequot Hill—summit ... CT-1
Pequot Ind Res—locale ... CT-1
Pequot Ind Res Eastern Tribe—reserve ... CT-1
**Pequot Lakes**—pop pl ... MN-6
Pequot Ledge—bench ... CT-1
Pequot Lookout Tower—locale ... MN-6
Pequot Pond—lake ... MA-1
Pequotsepos Brook—stream ... CT-1
Pequotsepos Manor—hist pl ... CT-1
Pequot Swamp ... CT-1
Pequot Swamp Pond—lake ... CT-1
Pera—locale ... AL-4
Pera—locale ... VA-3
Peraku Ko ... FM-9
Peraku Kuchi ... FM-9
Peral—locale ... CA-9
Peral's Run ... VA-3
**Peralta**—pop pl ... NM-5
Peralta, Antonio Maria, House—hist pl ... CA-9
Peralta, Luis Maria, Adobe—hist pl ... CA-9
Peralta and Valencia Cem—cemetery ... NM-5
Peralta Canyon—valley ... AZ-5
Peralta Canyon—valley ... NM-5
Peralta Canyon Camp—locale ... AZ-5
Peralta Canyon Campground—park ... AZ-5
Peralta Cem—cemetery ... NM-5
Peralta Creek—stream ... CA-9
Peralta Ditch—canal ... NM-5
Peralta Ditch—canal (2) ... WY-8
**Peralta Estates**—pop pl ... AZ-5
**Peralta Hills**—pop pl ... CA-9
Peralta Hills—range ... CA-9
Peralta House—hist pl ... CA-9
Peralta JHS—school ... CA-9
Peralta Main Canal—canal ... NM-5
Peralta Park—park ... CA-9
Peralta Ranch—locale ... NM-5
Peralta Ridge—ridge ... NM-5
Peralta Sch—school ... AZ-5
Peralta Sch—school ... CA-9
Peralta Sch—school ... NM-5
Peralta Spring—spring ... AZ-5
Peralta Spring—spring ... WY-8
Peralta Trail—trail ... AZ-5
Peratis Duck Club—other ... CA-9
Peratrovich Island—island ... AK-9
Perau ... FM-9
Perault—locale ... MN-6
Perault, Bayou—stream ... LA-4
Perault Number 1 Dam—dam ... SD-7
Perault Number 2 Dam—dam ... SD-7
Perault Number 3 Dam—dam ... SD-7
Perault Number 4 Dam—dam ... SD-7
Perault Number 5 Dam—dam ... SD-7
Perault Number 6 Dam—dam ... SD-7
Perault Number 7 Dam—dam ... SD-7
Perault Ranch—locale ... SD-7
Perault Sch—school ... MN-6
Perau-To ... FM-9
Perazza Canyon ... CA-9
Perazza Meadows ... CA-9
Perazzo Canyon—valley ... CA-9
Perazzo Meadows—flat ... CA-9
Perazzo Slough—stream ... NV-8
**Percale**—pop pl ... GA-3
Percee, The ... MO-7
Percella Ranch—locale ... NM-5
Percella Tank—reservoir ... NM-5
Perception Park Campground—park ... UT-8
Perch ... TX-5
**Perch**—pop pl ... NC-3
Percha Creek—stream ... NM-5
Percha Dam—dam ... NM-5
Perchade Cem—cemetery ... MA-1
Percha Diversion Dam—hist pl ... NM-5
Percha Lateral—canal ... NM-5
Perchal Drain—canal ... WY-8
**Perchas**—pop pl ... PR-3
Perchas (Barrio)—fmr MCD ... PR-3
Perchas 1 (Barrio)—fmr MCD ... PR-3
Perchas 2 (Barrio)—fmr MCD ... PR-3
Perch Bay—bay ... MT-8
Perch Bay—bay ... NY-2
Perch Bayou—stream ... LA-4
Perch Brook—stream ... NY-2
Perch Cove—bay ... NJ-2
Perch Cove—bay ... RI-1
Perch Cove Run—stream ... NJ-2
Perch Creek ... CA-9
Perch Creek ... TX-5
Perch Creek—stream ... AL-4
Perch Creek—stream ... DE-2
Perch Creek—stream (2) ... GA-3
Perch Creek—stream ... MD-2
Perch Creek—stream ... MN-6
Perch Creek—stream ... MS-4
Perch Creek—stream ... VA-3
Perch Creek State Wildlife Mngmt Area—park ... MN-6
Perche ... MO-7
Perche Ch—church ... MO-7
Perche Creek—stream ... MO-7
Perche (historical)—locale ... MO-7
**Perche (historical)**—pop pl ... MO-7
Perche Post Office (historical)—building ... MO-7
Percheron ... AZ-5
Percheron Creek—stream ... MT-8
Perchetown ... MO-7
Perche Township—civil ... MO-7
Perch Gap—gut ... TX-5
**Perch Hill**—pop pl ... TX-5
Perch Island—island ... CT-1
Perch Island—island (2) ... ME-1
Perch Island—island (2) ... NH-1
Perch Island—island ... NY-2
Perch Lake ... MI-6
Perch Lake ... MN-6
Perch Lake ... WI-6
Perch Lake—lake (5) ... FL-3
Perch Lake—lake ... IN-6
Perch Lake—lake ... LA-4
Perch Lake—lake (33) ... MI-6
Perch Lake—lake (23) ... MN-6
Perch Lake—lake ... MS-4
Perch Lake—lake ... NM-5
Perch Lake—lake ... NY-2
Perch Lake—lake ... SC-3
Perch Lake—lake (2) ... WA-9
Perch Lake—lake (29) ... WI-6
Perch Lake—reservoir ... NY-2
Perch Lake—reservoir ... WI-6
Perch Lake Bayou—stream ... LA-4
Perch Lake Cem—cemetery ... NY-2
Perch Lake Ch—church ... MI-6
Perch Lake Lookout Tower—locale ... MI-6
Perch Lake Mtn—summit ... NY-2
Perch Lakes—lake ... MI-6
**Perch Lake (Township of)**—pop pl ... MN-6
Perchog Brook ... MA-1
Perchog Brook ... NH-1
**Perch Point**—pop pl ... MI-6
Perch Pond ... FL-3
Perch Pond ... ME-1
Perch Pond ... NY-2
Perch Pond—cove ... MA-1
Perch Pond—lake ... ME-1
Perch Pond—lake (3) ... MA-1
Perch Pond—lake (2) ... NH-1
Perch Pond—lake (2) ... NY-2
Perch Pond—lake ... NC-3
Perch Pond—lake ... PA-2
Perch Pond—lake (2) ... VT-1
Perch Pond—reservoir ... NH-1
Perch Pond Ch—church ... FL-3
Perch Pond Dam—dam ... PA-2
Perch Pond Hill Cem—cemetery ... NY-2
Perch River—locale ... NY-2
Perch River—stream ... MI-6
Perch River—stream ... NY-2
Perch River State Game Mngmt Area—park ... NY-2
Perch Rock—island ... AK-9
Perch Run—stream ... PA-2
Perch Slough—gut ... CA-9
Perch Tank—reservoir ... TX-5
**Percilla**—pop pl ... TX-5
Percilla (historical)—locale ... SD-7
Percipany ... NJ-2
Percipeny ... NJ-2
**Percival**—pop pl ... IA-7
Percival, Mount—summit ... ME-1
Percival, Mount—summit ... NH-1
Percival Cem—cemetery ... MA-1
Percival Creek—stream ... OR-9
Percival Creek—stream ... WA-9
Percival Creek—stream ... WI-6
**Percival Crossroads**—pop pl ... SC-3
Percivalli Canyon—valley ... NV-8
Percival Memorial Cem—cemetery ... MO-7
Percival Ponds ... MA-1
Percival Sch—school ... CT-1
Percivals Ponds ... MA-1
Percle—locale ... LA-4
Perco Lakes—reservoir ... MO-7
Percosin Creek—stream ... GA-3
Percussion Rock—pillar ... WI-6
Percy ... WY-8
Percy ... MP-9
Percy—locale ... MS-4
**Percy**—pop pl ... IL-6
**Percy**—pop pl ... NH-1
**Percy**—pop pl ... PA-2
**Percy**—pop pl ... WY-8
Percy, Dr. Edward-Abney House—hist pl ... TX-5
Percy, Lake—lake ... CO-8
Percy and Small Shipyard—hist pl ... ME-1
Percy Campground—locale ... NY-2
Percy Creek—stream ... MS-4
Percy Creek—stream ... WY-8
Percy Creek Sch—school ... MS-4
Percy Dam—dam ... SD-7
Percy (Election Precinct)—fmr MCD ... IL-6
Percy Godwin Park—park ... ND-7
**Percy (historical)**—pop pl ... IA-7
Percy Hollow—valley ... TN-4
Percy Islands—area ... AK-9
**Percy Junction**—pop pl ... IN-6
Percy Lake Trail—trail ... CO-8
Percy-Lobdell Bldg—hist pl ... LA-4
Percy Mines—mine ... TN-4
Percy Peaks—summit ... NH-1
Percy Post Office (historical)—building ... AL-4
Percy Quin Lake ... MS-4
Percy Quin State Park—park ... MS-4
Percy Rsvr—reservoir ... WY-8
Percys Creek ... MS-4
Percys Peak—summit ... NC-3
Percy Spring—spring ... UT-8
Percy Spring—spring ... WY-8
**Percy (Township of)**—pop pl ... MN-6
Percy Vines Camp—locale ... AL-4
Percy Warner Park—park ... TN-4
Percy West Cabin—locale ... OR-9
Percy White Creek ... MS-4
Perdee Creek—stream ... MT-8
**Perdido**—pop pl ... AL-4
Perdido Bay—bay ... AL-4
Perdido Bay—bay ... FL-3
**Perdido Bay**—pop pl ... FL-3
Perdido Bayou—gut ... LA-4
**Perdido Beach**—pop pl ... AL-4
Perdido Canyon—valley ... CA-9
Perdido Cem—cemetery ... AL-4
Perdido Ch—church (3) ... AL-4
Perdido Creek—stream ... AL-4
Perdido Creek—stream (2) ... TX-5
**Perdido Heights**—pop pl ... FL-3
Perdido Hill Sch (historical)—school ... AL-4
Perdido JHS—school ... AL-4
Perdido Key—island ... AL-4
Perdido Key—island ... FL-3
Perdido Key Hist Dist—hist pl ... FL-3
Perdido Lake—reservoir ... IN-6
Perdido Pass—channel ... AL-4
Perdido Pass—channel ... FL-3
Perdido Pass Marina—locale ... AL-4
Perdido Place ... MH-9
Perdido River—stream ... AL-4
Perdido River—stream ... FL-3
Perdido Station ... AL-4
Perdido Tank—reservoir ... NM-5
Perdido Windmill—locale ... TX-5
Perdin Creek—stream ... OR-9
Perdis Tank—reservoir ... TX-5
**Perdix**—pop pl ... PA-2
**Perdiz**—pop pl ... TX-5
Perdiz Canyon—valley ... NM-5
Perdiz Creek—stream ... TX-5
Perdolaria—area ... GU-9
Perdue ... TN-4
Perdue—locale ... MS-4
Perdue, C. A., House—hist pl ... KS-7
Perdue Branch—stream ... TX-5
Perdue Cem—cemetery (2) ... AL-4
Perdue Cem—cemetery ... MO-7
Perdue Cem—cemetery ... TN-4
Perdue Cem—cemetery ... VA-3
Perdue Cem—cemetery (2) ... WV-2
Perdue Ch—church ... AL-4
Perdue Creek—stream ... MD-2
Perdue Creek—stream (2) ... OR-9
Perdue Creek—stream ... UT-8
**Perdue Hill**—pop pl ... AL-4
Perdue Hollow—valley ... OH-6
Perdue Hollow—valley ... WV-2
Perdue Post Office (historical)—building ... TN-4
Perdue University ... IN-6
Perdue University Airp—airport ... IN-6
**Perdueville**—pop pl ... IL-6
Perdu Lake—lake ... MN-6
Perdus Cem—cemetery ... VA-3
Perea—locale (2) ... NM-5
Perea Canyon—valley ... AZ-5
Perea Canyon—valley ... CO-8
**Perea (Iyanbito)**—pop pl ... NM-5
Pere Cheney—locale ... MI-6
Peregoy Cem—cemetery ... TN-4
Peregoy Meadow—flat ... CA-9
Peregrebni Point—cape ... AK-9
Peregrine Creek—stream ... AK-9
Peregrine Ditch—canal ... IN-6
Peregrine Pass—gap ... AK-9
Peregrine Peak—summit ... TN-4
Peregrine Point—cape ... AK-9
Perella—locale ... ND-7
Perelman Antique Toy Museum—building ... PA-2
Perely Pond ... ME-1
Pere Marquette Hotel—hist pl ... IL-6
Pere Marquette Lake—lake ... MI-6
Pere Marquette Park—park ... MO-7
Pere Marquette River—stream ... MI-6
Pere Marquette RR Depot, Bay City Station—hist pl ... MI-6
Pere Marquette Sch—school ... MI-6
Pere Marquette State For—forest ... MI-6
Pere Marquette State Park—park ... IL-6
Pere Marquette State Park Lodge and Cabins—hist pl ... IL-6
Pere Marquette (Township of)—civ div ... MI-6
Perem Insel ... FM-9
Perennial—locale ... GA-3
Perennial Springs—spring ... GA-3
Perenosa Bay—bay ... AK-9
Perenosa Point—cape ... AK-9
Perent Lake—lake ... MN-6
Perent River—stream ... MN-6
Pere-O-Geese Lake ... AR-4
Pereogeethe Lake—lake ... AR-4
Pere Pearson Dam—dam ... SD-7
Pere Pearson 1 Dam—dam ... SD-7
Peresheek Point—cape ... AK-9
Peres Sch—school ... CA-9
Peretti Canyon—valley ... NM-5
Perevalnie Islands—island ... AK-9
Perevalnie Passage—channel ... AK-9

Perez—locale ... CA-9
Perez Artesian Well—well ... TX-5
Perez Baseball Field—park ... TN-4
Perez Beach—beach ... GU-9
Perez Canal—canal ... LA-4
Perez Cem—cemetery (6) ... TX-5
Perez Cove—bay ... CA-9
Perez Drain—canal ... TX-5
**Perez Morris**—pop pl (2) ... PR-3
Perez Ranch—locale (2) ... NM-5
Perez Ranch—locale ... TX-5
Perez Sch—school ... TX-5
**Perezville**—pop pl ... TX-5
Perez Windmill—locale ... TX-5
Perfect Creek—stream ... OH-6
Perfection—locale ... NC-3
**Perfection**—pop pl ... NC-3
**Perfection**—pop pl ... SC-3
Perfection Lake—lake ... WA-9
Perfect Lake—lake ... IN-6
Perfecto Creek ... CO-8
Perfecto Creek—stream ... CO-8
Perfecto Mata Draw—valley ... TX-5
Perfect Pass—gap ... WA-9
Perforate Canyon ... NV-8
Perfumo Canyon ... CA-9
Pergamus Ch—church ... SC-3
Pergram Branch—stream ... KY-4
**Perham**—pop pl ... ME-1
**Perham**—pop pl ... MN-6
Perham Cem—cemetery ... MN-6
**Perham Corner**—pop pl ... NH-1
Perham Creek—stream ... CO-8
Perham Creek—stream ... OR-9
Perham Creek Spring—spring ... OR-9
Perham Hill—summit (2) ... ME-1
Perham Junction—locale ... ME-1
Perhams Four Corners—locale ... NH-1
Perham State Wildlife Mngmt Area—park ... MN-6
Perham Stream—stream ... ME-1
**Perham (Town of)**—pop pl ... ME-1
**Perham (Township of)**—pop pl ... MN-6
Perham Village Hall and Fire Station—hist pl ... MN-6
Perhaps Creek—stream ... AK-9
Periadik ... FM-9
Peria Mountains ... AZ-5
Periander Park—park ... OR-9
Perice, Cape—cape ... AK-9
Pericles Acad (historical)—school ... TN-4
Perico—locale ... TX-5
Perico Bayou—bay ... FL-3
Perico Creek—stream ... NM-5
Perico Island—island ... FL-3
Perico Windmill—locale (2) ... TX-5
**Perida**—pop pl ... WI-6
Perida Cem—cemetery ... WI-6
Perida Sch—school ... WI-6
**Peridiz**—pop pl ... TX-5
**Peridot**—pop pl ... AZ-5
Peridot Flat Tanks—reservoir ... AZ-5
Peridot Hill—summit ... AZ-5
Peridotite Canyon—valley ... CA-9
Peridot Mesa—flat ... AZ-5
Peridot Park—park ... LA-4
Peridot Post Office—building ... AZ-5
Peridot Ridge—ridge ... AZ-5
Peridot Well—well ... AZ-5
Perifer School ... IN-6
Perifukumazo—island ... FM-9
Perigal Creek—stream ... MS-4
Perigen Creek—stream ... OH-6
Perigo—locale ... CO-8
Perigo Cem—cemetery (2) ... IN-6
Perigo Hill—summit ... NY-2
Perigo Mine—mine ... TN-4
Periguα ... AZ-5
Perigua Valley ... AZ-5
Periiruu—bay ... MH-9
Perikomen Bridge Hotel—hist pl ... PA-2
Peril Cape—cape ... AK-9
Peril Cem—cemetery ... TX-5
Peril Creek—stream ... MT-8
**Perilla (historical)**—pop pl ... TN-4
Perilla Mountains—ridge ... AZ-5
Perilla Post Office (historical)—building ... TN-4
Peril Peak—summit ... MT-8
Peril Strait—channel ... AK-9
Perimen Creek ... PA-2
Perimeter—post sta ... GA-3
Perimeter Place Shop Ctr—locale ... TN-4
Perin Canyon—valley ... OR-9
Perington Creek—stream ... CA-9
Perini Creek—stream ... CA-9
Perini Hill—summit ... CA-9
Perino Rsvr—reservoir ... CO-8
Perins Peak—summit ... CO-8
Perinton Park—park ... NY-2
**Perinton (Town of)**—pop pl ... NY-2
**Perintown**—pop pl ... OH-6
Perin Village Site—hist pl ... OH-6
Period Revival House—hist pl ... AZ-5
Perion du Chat, Lake—lake ... LA-4
Perio Point—cape ... ME-1
Perior ... FM-9
Periqua ... AZ-5
Periryu ... PW-9
Periryu To ... PW-9
Periscope Ridge—ridge ... OH-6
Perish ... MS-4
Perisho Sch—school ... IL-6
Perismmon Branch—stream ... TN-4
Peritot You ... TX-5
Peritsa Creek—stream ... MT-8
Periwig Mtn—summit ... NH-1
Periwinkle Bay—bay ... FL-3
Periwinkle Branch ... GA-3
Periwinkle Branch—stream ... AL-4
Periwinkle Branch—stream ... TN-4
Periwinkle Branch—stream ... VA-3
Periwinkle Creek ... ID-8
Periwinkle Creek—stream ... ID-8
Periwinkle Creek—stream ... OR-9
Peri-Winkle Mobile Home Park—locale ... AZ-5
Periwinkle Mtn—summit ... VA-3
Periwinkle Place (Shop Ctr)—locale ... FL-3
Periwinkle Run—stream ... OH-6
Periwinkle Spring—spring ... TN-4
Periz Peak—summit ... AZ-5
Perjue Canyon—valley ... ID-8
Perjury Creek—stream ... MI-6
Perkasey ... PA-2
**Perkasie**—pop pl ... PA-2
Perkasie Borough—civil ... PA-2
Perkasie Cem—cemetery ... PA-2
Perkasie Elem Sch—school ... PA-2
Perk Canyon—valley (2) ... NM-5
Perkens Creek ... ID-8
Perkens Lake ... ID-8
Perkerson Park—park ... GA-3
Perkerson Sch—school ... GA-3
Perkett Mtn—summit (2) ... NY-2
Perkett Sch—school ... ND-7
Perkey Sch—school ... MI-6
**Perkin**—pop pl ... NY-2
Perkingston Lake Dam—dam ... MS-4
Perkins ... NC-3
Perkins—locale ... AR-4
Perkins—locale ... CA-9
Perkins—locale ... FL-3
Perkins—locale ... ID-8
Perkins—locale ... KY-4
Perkins—locale ... ME-1
Perkins—locale ... MN-6
Perkins—locale ... WV-2
**Perkins**—pop pl ... GA-3
**Perkins**—pop pl ... IN-6
**Perkins**—pop pl ... IA-7
**Perkins**—pop pl ... LA-4
**Perkins**—pop pl ... MI-6
**Perkins**—pop pl ... MO-7
**Perkins**—pop pl ... OK-5
**Perkins**—pop pl ... SD-7
**Perkins**—pop pl ... WV-2
**Perkins**—pop pl ... WY-8
Perkins, Arthur, House—hist pl ... VT-1
Perkins, Charles, House—hist pl ... ME-1
Perkins, Col. Simon, Mansion—hist pl ... OH-6
Perkins, Dr. John Milton, House—hist pl ... KY-4
Perkins, Dwight, House—hist pl ... IL-6
Perkins, James A., House—hist pl ... WA-9
Perkins, John, House—hist pl ... ME-1
Perkins, Joseph, House—hist pl ... MA-1
Perkins, Mount—summit ... AZ-5
Perkins, Mount—summit ... CA-9
Perkins, Nicholas Tate, House—hist pl ... TN-4
Perkins, William, House—hist pl ... AL-4
Perkins Beach—beach ... OH-6
Perkins Bend—bend ... AR-4
Perkins Bluff—cliff ... MO-7
Perkins Bluff Landing—locale ... TN-4
Perkins Bottom—bend ... WY-8
Perkins Branch ... AR-4
Perkins Branch—stream ... AR-4
Perkins Branch—stream ... GA-3
Perkins Branch—stream (7) ... KY-4
Perkins Branch—stream ... LA-4
Perkins Branch—stream ... MO-7
Perkins Branch—stream ... OH-6
Perkins Branch—stream (2) ... TN-4
Perkins Branch—stream ... VA-3
Perkins Branch—stream ... WV-2
Perkins Brook ... ME-1
Perkins Brook ... MA-1
Perkins Brook—stream (3) ... ME-1
Perkins Brook—stream (3) ... NH-1
Perkins Brook—stream (4) ... VT-1
Perkins Cabin—locale ... NV-8
Perkins Canyon—valley (2) ... CA-9
Perkins Canyon—valley ... NV-8
Perkins Cay—island ... VI-3
Perkins Cem—cemetery (3) ... AL-4
Perkins Cem—cemetery ... IN-6
Perkins Cem—cemetery (7) ... KY-4
Perkins Cem—cemetery (3) ... LA-4
Perkins Cem—cemetery ... ME-1
Perkins Cem—cemetery (2) ... MI-6
Perkins Cem—cemetery (2) ... MS-4
Perkins Cem—cemetery ... MO-7
Perkins Cem—cemetery ... NY-2
Perkins Cem—cemetery (2) ... OH-6
Perkins Cem—cemetery ... OK-5
Perkins Cem—cemetery (5) ... TN-4
Perkins Cem—cemetery (2) ... TX-5
Perkins Cem—cemetery ... VA-3
Perkins Cem—cemetery ... WA-9
Perkins Ch—church ... TN-4
Perkins Ch—church ... VA-3
Perkins Chapel ... AL-4
Perkins Chapel—church ... MD-2
Perkins Chapel Ch—church ... AL-4
Perkins-Clark House—hist pl ... CT-1
Perkins Clearing—locale ... NY-2
Perkins Consolidated Sch (historical)—school ... MS-4
Perkins Corner ... ME-1
Perkins Corner ... OH-6
Perkins Corner—locale ... CT-1
**Perkins Corner**—pop pl ... CT-1
**Perkins Corner**—pop pl ... NY-2
Perkins Corners—locale ... NY-2
**Perkins Corners**—pop pl ... OH-6
Perkins County—civil ... SD-7
Perkins Cove—bay ... ME-1
Perkins Creek ... MS-4
Perkins Creek ... TN-4
Perkins Creek ... TX-5
Perkins Creek—stream ... AL-4
Perkins Creek—stream ... AK-9
Perkins Creek—stream ... CA-9
Perkins Creek—stream ... ID-8
Perkins Creek—stream ... IA-7
Perkins Creek—stream ... KS-7
Perkins Creek—stream (3) ... KY-4
Perkins Creek—stream ... LA-4
Perkins Creek—stream ... MD-2
Perkins Creek—stream (3) ... MS-4
Perkins Creek—stream (2) ... MO-7
Perkins Creek—stream (2) ... MT-8
Perkins Creek—stream ... NY-2
Perkins Creek—stream (6) ... OR-9
Perkins Creek—stream ... SC-3
Perkins Creek—stream ... TX-5
Perkins Creek—stream (2) ... VA-3
Perkins Creek—stream ... WI-6
Perkins Creek—stream ... WY-8
Perkins Creek Ridge—ridge ... CA-9
Perkins Crossing—locale ... NY-2
**Perkins Crossroads**—pop pl ... SC-3
Perkins Dam—dam ... MT-8
Perkins-Daniel House—hist pl ... KY-4
Perkins Ditch—canal ... MT-8
Perkins Ditch—canal ... OR-9
Perkins Ditch—canal (2) ... WY-8
Perkins Drain—stream ... ID-8
Perkins Draw—valley ... TX-5
Perkins Elem Sch—school ... FL-3
Perkins Engines, Incorporated—facility ... MI-6
Perkins Estate—hist pl ... MA-1
Perkins-Evans Cem—cemetery ... AL-4
Perkins Ferry—locale ... AL-4
Perkins Ferry—locale ... LA-4
Perkins Ferry (historical)—locale ... AL-4
Perkins Flat—flat ... OR-9
Perkins Fork—stream ... KY-4
Perkins Fork—stream ... WA-9
Perkins Fork—stream ... WV-2
Perkins Grove Ch—church ... IL-6
Perkins Gulch—valley ... CA-9
Perkins Gulch—valley ... ID-8
Perkins Gulch—valley ... MT-8
Perkins Gulch—valley ... WA-9
Perkins Hall of Administration—hist pl ... TX-5
Perkins Hill ... MA-1
**Perkins Hill**—pop pl ... NH-1
**Perkins Hill**—pop pl ... TN-4
Perkins Hill—summit ... ME-1
Perkins Hill—summit ... NH-1
Perkins Hill—summit ... NY-2
Perkins Hill—summit ... TN-4
Perkins Hill Park—park ... MN-6
Perkins (historical)—locale ... MS-4
Perkins Hollow—valley ... AL-4
Perkins Hollow—valley (2) ... KY-4
Perkins Hollow—valley (2) ... MO-7
Perkins Hollow—valley ... NY-2
Perkins Hollow—valley (2) ... TN-4
Perkins Hollow—valley ... TX-5
Perkins Hollow—valley ... UT-8
Perkins Hollow—valley ... VT-1
Perkins Hollow—valley ... VA-3
Perkins House—hist pl ... NJ-2
Perkins House—hist pl ... NC-3
Perkins Island ... NY-2
Perkins Island—island ... ME-1
Perkins Island Ledge—bar ... ME-1
Perkins Island Light Station—hist pl ... ME-1
Perkins JHS—school ... OH-6
Perkins Knob—summit ... VA-3
Perkins Knoll—summit ... AZ-5
Perkins Lake—lake ... CA-9
Perkins Lake—lake (2) ... ID-8
Perkins Lake—lake ... IL-6
Perkins Lake—lake ... MT-8
Perkins Lake—lake ... OR-9
Perkins Lake—lake ... TX-5
Perkins Lake—lake ... WA-9
Perkins Lake—reservoir ... MS-4
Perkins Lakes—reservoir ... GA-3
Perkins Landing ... TN-4
Perkins Landing—locale ... AL-4
Perkins Landing (historical)—locale ... MS-4
Perkins Log Pond—reservoir ... OR-9
Perkins Log Pond Dam—dam ... OR-9
Perkins Lookout Tower—locale ... GA-3
Perkins Marsh—swamp ... IA-7
Perkins Marsh Brook—stream ... ME-1
Perkins Marsh State Game Mngmt Area—park ... IA-7
Perkins Meadow Brook—stream ... VT-1
Perkins Memorial Cem—cemetery ... NM-5
Perkins Memorial Ch—church ... MD-2
Perkins Memorial Observatory—building ... NY-2
Perkins Mill (historical)—locale ... MS-4
Perkins Mine (underground)—mine ... TN-4
Perkins Mtn—summit ... CT-1
Perkins Mtn—summit ... ME-1
Perkins Mtn—summit ... NH-1
Perkins Mtn—summit ... TX-5
Perkins Mtn—summit ... VA-3
Perkins Notch—gap ... NH-1
Perkins Nuclear Power Plant—facility ... NC-3
Perkins Observatory—building ... OH-6
Perkins Oil and Gas Field—oilfield ... LA-4
Perkins Oil Field—oilfield ... KS-7
Perkins Old Mill Branch—stream ... NC-3
Perkinson Cem—cemetery ... VA-3
Perkinson Lake—reservoir ... IN-6
Perkinson Lake Dam—dam ... IN-6
Perkinson Spring—spring ... TN-4
Perkins Opera House—hist pl ... FL-3
Perkins Park—park ... IA-7
Perkins Park—park ... MO-7
Perkins Park—park (2) ... OH-6
Perkins Park—park ... WI-6
**Perkins Park**—pop pl ... VA-3
Perkins Peninsula State Park—park ... OR-9
Perkins Place—locale ... GA-3
Perkins Plant—other ... TX-5
Perkins Plantation Pond—lake ... FL-3
**Perkins (P.O.)**—pop pl ... CA-9
Perkins Point—cape (2) ... ME-1
Perkins Point—cape ... MO-7
Perkins Point—cape ... TN-4
Perkins Point—cape ... WI-6
Perkins Point—locale ... VA-3
Perkins Pond ... CT-1
Perkins Pond—lake ... MA-1
Perkins Pond—lake ... MT-8
Perkins Pond—lake (2) ... NH-1
Perkins Pond—lake ... NY-2
Perkins Pond—reservoir ... NY-2
Perkins Pond—reservoir ... PA-2
Perkins Pond—reservoir ... VA-3
Perkins Pond—swamp ... TX-5
Perkins Pond Marsh—swamp ... NH-1
Perkins Prairie—flat ... OR-9
Perkins Ranch—locale ... ID-8
Perkins Ranch—locale (4) ... MT-8
Perkins Ranch—locale (2) ... UT-8
Perkins Reef—bar ... WA-9
Perkins Reservation—park ... TX-5
Perkins Reservoir ... UT-8
Perkins Ridge ... KY-4
Perkins Ridge—ridge ... CA-9
Perkins Ridge—ridge ... ME-1
Perkins Ridge—ridge ... MO-7
Perkins Ridge—ridge ... VA-3
Perkins Road Sch—school ... LA-4
Perkins-Rockwell House—hist pl ... CT-1
Perkins Rsvr—reservoir ... CO-8
Perkins Run—stream ... OH-6
Perkins Run—stream ... WV-2
Perkins Sch—school ... IL-6
Perkins Sch—school (2) ... IA-7
Perkins Sch—school (4) ... MA-1
Perkins Sch—school ... MI-6
Perkins Sch—school ... OH-6
Perkins Sch—school ... SD-7
Perkins Sch—school ... TN-4
Perkins Sch (abandoned)—school ... MO-7
Perkins Slough—gut ... AR-4
Perkins Spring—spring ... AL-4
Perkins Spring—spring ... AZ-5
Perkins Spring—spring ... CA-9
Perkins Spring—spring ... IL-6
Perkins Spring—spring (3) ... NV-8
Perkins Spring—spring ... OR-9
Perkins Spring Draw—valley ... AZ-5
Perkins Square—locale ... OH-6
Perkins Square Gazebo—hist pl ... MD-2
Perkins Store (historical)—locale ... MS-4
Perkins Swamp—swamp ... CT-1
Perkins Swamp—swamp ... NY-2
Perkins Tank—reservoir (2) ... AZ-5
Perkins Tanks—reservoir ... AZ-5
Perkins Telescope—building ... AZ-5
Perkins Tide Mill—hist pl ... ME-1
**Perkinston**—pop pl ... MS-4
Perkinston Attendance Center ... MS-4
Perkinston Elem Sch—school ... MS-4
Perkinston Junior College Dam—dam ... MS-4
Perkinston Junior College Lake Dam—dam ... MS-4
Perkins Town—locale ... ME-1
**Perkinstown**—pop pl ... WI-6
Perkinstown Cem—cemetery ... WI-6
Perkinstown Lookout Tower—locale ... WI-6
**Perkins (Township of)**—pop pl ... OH-6
Perkins (Township of)—unorg (2) ... ME-1
Perkinstown Winter Sports Area—area ... WI-6
Perkins Tunnel—tunnel ... VA-3
Perkins Tunnel Spring—spring ... AZ-5
Perkins United Ch—church ... NC-3
Perkins (Unorganized Territory of)—unorg ... ME-1
Perkinsville—locale ... AZ-5
Perkinsville—locale ... NC-3
**Perkinsville**—pop pl ... AK-9
**Perkinsville**—pop pl ... IN-6
**Perkinsville**—pop pl ... NY-2
**Perkinsville**—pop pl ... NC-3
**Perkinsville**—pop pl ... VT-1
**Perkinsville**—pop pl ... VA-3
Perkinsville Baptist Ch (historical)—church ... MS-4
Perkinsville Cem—cemetery ... IN-6
Perkinsville Cem—cemetery ... MS-4
Perkinsville Ch—church ... NC-3
**Perkinsville (historical)**—pop pl ... MS-4
Perkinsville Post Office (historical)—building ... MS-4
Perkinsville RR Station—building ... AZ-5
Perkins-Wiener House—hist pl ... NE-7
Perkins Windmill—locale (2) ... TX-5
Perkins Woods—park ... IL-6
Perkintown—locale ... NJ-2
Perkintown Cem—cemetery ... NJ-2
Perkintown Station—locale ... NJ-2
**Perkiomen**—pop pl ... PA-2
Perkiomen Ave Sch—school ... PA-2
Perkiomen Bridge—bridge ... PA-2
Perkiomen Bridge—hist pl ... PA-2
Perkiomen Creek—stream ... PA-2
**Perkiomen Heights**—pop pl ... PA-2
Perkiomen Junction—locale ... PA-2
Perkiomen Preparatory Sch—school ... PA-2
**Perkiomen (Township of)**—pop pl ... PA-2
Perkiomen Valley Airp—airport ... PA-2
Perkiomen Valley Cem—cemetery ... PA-2
Perkiomen Valley Convalescent Home—hospital ... PA-2
Perkiomen Valley Elementary North Sch—school ... PA-2
Perkiomen Valley Elementary South Sch ... PA-2
Perkiomen Valley HS ... PA-2
Perkiomen Valley HS—school ... PA-2
**Perkiomen Village**—pop pl ... PA-2
**Perkiomenville**—pop pl ... PA-2
Perk Lake—lake ... WA-9
Perkle Cemetery ... TN-4
Perkons Creek—stream ... ID-8
Perkons Lake—lake ... ID-8
Perk Pond—lake ... ME-1
**Perks**—pop pl ... IL-6
Perks Corner—locale ... CA-9
Perks (Election Precinct)—fmr MCD ... IL-6
Perk Slough—stream ... NV-8
Perks Pasture—flat ... CA-9
Perky—locale ... FL-3
Perky, The ... AZ-5
Perky Rsvr—reservoir ... CO-8
Perkziak Lake ... WI-6
**Perla**—pop pl ... AR-4
Perla Gate Cem—cemetery ... AR-4
Perlantown ... NJ-2
Perlas Point—cape ... AK-9
Perlee—locale ... IA-7
Perles, Lac aux—swamp ... LA-4
**Perley**—pop pl ... MN-6
Perley, Sam, Farm—hist pl ... ME-1
Perley Brook—stream ... ME-1
Perley Brook—stream ... MA-1
Perley Brook Reservoir Dam—dam ... MA-1
Perley Brook Rsvr—reservoir ... MA-1
Perley Ch—church ... WI-6
Perley Creek ... AZ-5
Perley Creek—stream ... AZ-5
Perley Elem Sch—school ... IN-6
Perley Pond—lake (2) ... ME-1
Perley Pond—lake ... NH-1
Perley Sch—school ... MA-1
Perline Sch (historical)—school ... MS-4
Perl Island—island ... AK-9
Perlite Canyon—valley ... NV-8
Perlite Mine—mine ... AZ-5
Perlite Spring—spring ... AZ-5
**Perl-Mack**—pop pl ... CO-8
Perl Mack Manor—locale ... CO-8
Perl Rock—island ... AK-9
Perly, Fred A., House—hist pl ... WV-2
Perly Canyon—valley ... CO-8
**Perma**—pop pl ... MT-8
P'ermach ... FM-9
Perman Dam—dam ... AL-4
Permaneer Log Pond—reservoir ... OR-9
Permanente—locale ... CA-9
**Permanente (Cement Plant)**—pop pl ... CA-9
Permanente Creek—stream ... CA-9
Permanente Foundation Hosp—hospital ... CA-9
Permans Lake—reservoir ... AL-4
Permars Run—stream ... OH-6
Permasse Ranch—locale ... CA-9
Permastone Lake—reservoir ... NC-3
Permastone Lake Dam—dam ... NC-3
**Permco**—pop pl ... NM-5
**Permele**—pop pl ... KY-4
Permele Station—locale ... KY-4
Permelia Creek ... OR-9
Permelia Lake ... OR-9
Permeter Creek—stream ... AL-4
Permian Basin Encampment—locale ... TX-5
Permian General Hosp—hospital ... TX-5
Permian HS—school ... TX-5
Permian Park—park ... TX-5
Permidia Branch—stream ... LA-4
Permielia Post Office (historical)—building ... TN-4
Permita Creek ... AL-4
Permit Mine—mine ... CA-9
Permon—locale ... KY-4
Permuda Island—island ... NC-3
Pernel Branch—stream ... WV-2
Pernell—locale ... OK-5
**Pernell**—pop pl ... AL-4
Pernell Cem ... AL-4
Pernell Cem—cemetery ... AL-4
Pernell Ch—church ... AL-4
Pernell Sch—school ... OK-5
Pernell Sch (historical)—school ... AL-4
Perner Ranch—locale ... TX-5
**Pernitas Point**—pop pl ... TX-5
Pern Lakes—lake ... AK-9
Pern Lock ... PA-2
Pernot, Dr. Henry S., House—hist pl ... OR-9
Pernot Creek—stream ... OR-9
Pernot Meadow—flat ... OR-9
Pernot Mtn—summit ... OR-9
Pernot Trail (historical)—trail ... OR-9
Pero, Mount—summit ... NH-1
Pero Bonito Mine—mine ... AZ-5
Pero Creek—stream ... OK-5
Pero Creek—stream ... SD-7
Pero Grande Windmill—locale ... TX-5
Perogue Ford—locale ... TN-4
Perogue Hollow—valley ... TN-4
Pero Lake—lake ... MI-6
Peromp ... CA-9
Peromp Valley ... NV-8
Perona Lake—reservoir ... NJ-2
Peron Branch—stream ... TX-5
Peron Ch—church ... TX-5
Perone Branch—stream ... AL-4
Perone Ranch (San Samuel)—locale ... TX-5
Peron Lake—lake ... MN-6
Perot, Bayou—gut ... LA-4
**Perota (historical)**—pop pl ... MS-4
**Perote**—pop pl ... AL-4
Perote Cem—cemetery ... AL-4
Perote Ch—church ... AL-4
Perote Creek—stream ... AL-4
Perote Lake—lake ... WI-6
Perote Sch—school ... AL-4
Peroxide Well—well ... AZ-5
Perozzi, Domingo, House—hist pl ... OR-9
Perpendicular Bluff—cliff ... CA-9
Perpertocks Creek ... VA-3
Perpetua, Cape—cape ... OR-9
Perpetual Care Cem—cemetery ... AL-4
Perpetuo Socorro Cem—cemetery ... TX-5
Perphery Gate—dam ... AZ-5
Perquimans Central Sch—school ... NC-3
**Perquimans County**—pop pl ... NC-3
Perquimans County Courthouse—building ... NC-3
Perquimans County Courthouse—hist pl ... NC-3
Perquimans County HS—school ... NC-3
Perquimans River—stream ... NC-3
Perquimons River ... NC-3
Perra Artesian Well—well ... TX-5
Perra Draw—valley ... NM-5
Perrault ... MN-6
Perrault, George O., House—hist pl ... NM-5
Perrault, Lake—lake ... MI-6
Perrault Canyon—valley ... OR-9
Perreau Creek—stream ... ID-8
Perreau Island—island ... LA-4
Perrens Pond ... PA-2
Perret Cem—cemetery ... MO-7
Perret Ridge—ridge ... AK-9
Perrey Ch—church ... MD-2
Perrigo, George, House—hist pl ... MI-6
Perrigo Creek—stream ... NY-2
Perrilla Mountains ... AZ-5
Perrill-Goodman Farm House—hist pl ... OH-6
Perriman Creek—stream ... TX-5
Perrin—locale ... NE-7
Perrin—locale ... VA-3
**Perrin**—pop pl ... AZ-5
**Perrin**—pop pl ... MO-7
**Perrin**—pop pl (2) ... TX-5
Perrin, Lake—reservoir ... GA-3
Perrin, William, House—hist pl ... MA-1
Perrin, Winfield, House—hist pl ... WA-9
Perrin Branch—stream ... MD-2
Perrin Brothers Farm—locale ... TX-5
Perrin (CCD)—cens area ... TX-5
Perrin Church Branch ... AL-4
Perrin Country Club—other ... GA-3
Perrin Cove—bay ... GA-3
Perrin Creek—stream ... CA-9
Perrin Creek—stream ... NE-7
Perrin Creek—stream ... VA-3
Perrin Dam—dam (2) ... AZ-5
Perrin Drain—canal ... MI-6
Perrin Drain—stream ... MI-6
Perrin Draw—valley ... AZ-5
Perrine—locale ... ID-8
**Perrine**—pop pl ... FL-3
Perrine, Lake—reservoir ... IN-6
Perrine Baptist Acad—school ... FL-3
**Perrine Corners**—pop pl ... PA-2
Perrine Coulee—stream ... ID-8
Perrine Coulee Falls—falls ... ID-8
Perrine Elem Sch—school ... FL-3
Perrine Lake Dam—dam ... IN-6
Perrine Memorial Bridge—bridge ... ID-8
Perrine Plaza (Shop Ctr)—locale ... FL-3
Perrine Recreational Center—building ... FL-3
Perrine's Bridge—hist pl ... NY-2
Perrine Sch—school ... IL-6
**Perrineville**—pop pl ... NJ-2
Perrineville Lake—reservoir ... NJ-2
Perrineville Lake Dam—dam ... NJ-2
Perrine Wayside Park—park ... FL-3
Perring Lake—lake ... TX-5
Perrington Creek—stream ... CA-9
Perrin Hist Dist—hist pl ... IN-6
**Perrin Hollow**—pop pl ... TN-4
Perrin Hollow—valley ... TN-4
Perrin Hollow Cem—cemetery ... TN-4
Perrin Hollow Sch (historical)—school ... TN-4
Perrini Mine—mine ... CA-9
Perrin Island—island ... OR-9
Perrin JHS—school ... LA-4
Perrin Lake—lake (2) ... MI-6
Perrin Lateral—canal ... OR-9
Perrin Mine (underground)—mine ... AL-4
Perrin Mtn—summit ... SD-7
Perrino Cem—cemetery ... TX-5
Perrin River—stream ... VA-3
Perrin Run—stream ... OH-6
Perrin Sch ... TN-4
Perrin Sch—school ... AR-4
Perrin Sch—school ... GA-3
Perrin Sch—school ... MA-1
Perrin Sch—school ... MI-6
Perrin Sch—school ... NY-2
**Perrins Crossing**—pop pl ... MA-1
Perrins Island—island ... LA-4
Perrins Ledge—cliff ... IL-6
Perrins Marsh—reservoir ... PA-2
Perrins Marsh Dam—dam ... PA-2
Perrins Pond ... PA-2
Perrins Pond—lake ... MA-1
Perrin Spring—spring ... OR-9
Perrins Sch—school ... MT-8
Perrinsville ... MI-6
Perrin Tank—reservoir (2) ... AZ-5
Perrin-Thomas Sch—school ... SC-3
**Perrinton**—pop pl (2) ... MI-6
**Perrinville**—pop pl ... WA-9
Perrinville Sch—school ... MI-6
Perrin Woods—woods ... OH-6
Perrin Woods Sch—school ... OH-6
**Perris**—pop pl ... CA-9
Perris Hill—summit ... CA-9
Perris Hill Park—park ... CA-9
Perrishoes Creek—gut ... NC-3
Perris Rsvr—reservoir ... CA-9
Perris Union HS—school ... CA-9
Perris Valley—basin ... CA-9
Perris Valley (CCD)—cens area ... CA-9
Perris Valley Cem—cemetery ... CA-9
Perris Valley JHS—school ... CA-9
Perris Valley Storm Drain—canal ... CA-9
Perrito Windmill—locale ... TX-5
**Perritt**—pop pl ... KY-4
Perriwig Channel—channel ... NJ-2
Perriwig Channel—channel ... PA-2
Perriwinkle Branch ... VA-3
Perron Creek—stream ... OR-9
**Perronville**—pop pl ... MI-6
Perrot—locale ... SC-3
Perrot Ridge—ridge ... WI-6
Perrot State Park—park ... WI-6
**Perrott Creek**—pop pl ... CA-9
Perrott Creek—stream ... CA-9
Perrott Grove—woods ... CA-9
Perrow Cem—cemetery ... VA-3
Perrow Point—cape ... ME-1
Perrows—locale ... VA-3
Perrows Chapel—church ... VA-3
Perrowville—locale ... VA-3
Perry ... AL-4
Perry ... ID-8
Perry ... KS-7
Perry ... PA-2
Perry ... SD-7
Perry—locale ... CA-9
Perry—locale ... ME-1
Perry—locale ... NE-7
Perry—locale ... WA-9
Perry—locale ... WV-2
**Perry**—pop pl ... AR-4
**Perry**—pop pl ... CA-9
**Perry**—pop pl ... FL-3
**Perry**—pop pl ... GA-3
**Perry**—pop pl ... IL-6
**Perry**—pop pl ... IA-7
**Perry**—pop pl ... KS-7
**Perry**—pop pl ... LA-4
**Perry**—pop pl ... MI-6
**Perry**—pop pl ... MS-4
**Perry**—pop pl ... MO-7
**Perry**—pop pl ... NY-2
**Perry**—pop pl ... NC-3
**Perry**—pop pl ... OH-6
**Perry**—pop pl ... OK-5
**Perry**—pop pl ... OR-9
**Perry**—pop pl ... SC-3
**Perry**—pop pl ... TN-4
**Perry**—pop pl ... TX-5
**Perry**—pop pl (2) ... UT-8
**Perry**—pop pl ... VT-1
Perry, A. F. and Myrtle-Pitmann House—hist pl ... TX-5
Perry, Bayou—stream ... LA-4
Perry, Capt. William, House—hist pl ... TX-5
Perry, Clark, House—hist pl ... ME-1
Perry, Commodore Oliver, Farm—hist pl ... RI-1
Perry, C. W. Archie-Hallmark House—hist pl ... TX-5
Perry, David, House—hist pl ... CT-1
Perry, Dr. Samuel, House—hist pl ... NC-3
Perry, Ivory, Homestead—hist pl ... NH-1
Perry, James, House—hist pl ... MA-1
Perry, John, Homestead—hist pl ... NH-1
Perry, Lake—reservoir ... IN-6
Perry, Lake—reservoir ... MS-4
Perry, Lake—reservoir ... OK-5

Perry, Mount—summit ... CA-9
Perry, Mount—summit ... MA-1
Perry, Peter D., House—hist pl ... NJ-2
Perry, T. B., House—hist pl ... IA-7
Perry, Warren, House—hist pl ... MI-6
Perry, William F., House—hist pl ... ME-1
Perry Addition—pop pl ... OH-6
Perry Aiken Creek—stream ... CA-9
Perry Aiken Creek—stream ... NV-8
Perry Aiken Flat—flat ... CA-9
Perry Airp—airport ... AL-4
Perry Akin Creek ... CA-9
Perry Akin Creek ... NV-8
Perry And Partridge Ditch—canal ... WY-8
Perry Armory—hist pl ... OK-5
Perry Basin—stream ... UT-8
Perry Bass Camp—locale ... TX-5
Perry Bayou—stream ... TX-5
Perry Bluff—cliff (2) ... AR-4
Perry Bluff Ore Storage Area—other ... PA-2
Perry Bolton Cemetery ... AL-4
Perry Branch ... TN-4
Perry Branch ... VT-1
Perry Branch—bay ... MD-2
Perry Branch—stream (4) ... AL-4
Perry Branch—stream ... AR-4
Perry Branch—stream (3) ... KY-4
Perry Branch—stream ... MS-4
Perry Branch—stream (3) ... MO-7
Perry Branch—stream (2) ... TN-4
Perry Branch—stream ... TX-5
Perry Branch—stream ... VA-3
Perry Branch—stream (3) ... WV-2
Perry Branch—valley ... TN-4
Perry Bridge—bridge (2) ... NC-3
Perry Bridge—other ... IL-6
Perry Brook ... NH-1
Perry Brook ... VT-1
Perry Brook—stream ... CT-1
Perry Brook—stream ... IN-6
Perry Brook—stream (7) ... NH-1
Perry Brook—stream ... NY-2
Perry Brook—stream (2) ... VT-1
Perryburg Cem—cemetery ... NY-2
Perry Butte—summit ... OR-9
Perry Butte Way—trail ... OR-9
Perry Cabin—locale ... WY-8
Perrycamp Branch ... WV-2
Perry Camp Branch—stream ... WV-2
Perry Canal—canal ... CA-9
Perry Canal—canal ... UT-8
Perry Canyon—valley ... MT-8
Perry Canyon—valley ... NV-8
Perry Canyon—valley (3) ... NM-5
Perry Canyon—valley ... UT-8
Perry Canyon Spring—spring ... NM-5
Perry Cary Hollow—valley ... KY-4
Perry (CCD)—cens area ... GA-3
Perry (CCD)—cens area ... OK-5
Perry (CCD)—cens area ... TX-5
Perry Cem—cemetery ... AL-4
Perry Cem—cemetery (2) ... AR-4
Perry Cem—cemetery ... GA-3
Perry Cem—cemetery (2) ... IL-6
Perry Cem—cemetery ... KS-7
Perry Cem—cemetery (6) ... KY-4
Perry Cem—cemetery (2) ... ME-1
Perry Cem—cemetery ... MA-1
Perry Cem—cemetery ... MI-6
Perry Cem—cemetery (4) ... MS-4
Perry Cem—cemetery (3) ... MO-7
Perry Cem—cemetery ... NC-3
Perry Cem—cemetery (2) ... OH-6
Perry Cem—cemetery ... PA-2
Perry Cem—cemetery ... SC-3
Perry Cem—cemetery (11) ... TN-4
Perry Cem—cemetery (3) ... TX-5
Perry Cem—cemetery ... UT-8
Perry Cem—cemetery (2) ... VA-3
Perry Cem—cemetery (6) ... WV-2
Perry Center—pop pl ... NY-2
Perry Center—pop pl ... OH-6
Perry Center School ... IN-6
Perry Central Elem Sch Number 1—school ... IN-6
Perry Central Elem Sch Number 2—school ... IN-6
Perry Central High School ... MS-4
Perry Central JHS—school ... IN-6
Perry Central Junior-Senior HS—school ... IN-6
Perry Ch—church ... IL-6
Perry Ch—church ... ND-7
Perry Ch—church (2) ... OH-6
Perry Ch—church ... PA-2
Perry Ch—church ... TX-5
Perry Chapel—church ... AL-4
Perry Chapel—church (3) ... MS-4
Perry Chapel—church ... OH-6
Perry Chapel Cem—cemetery ... OH-6
Perry Chapel Cem—cemetery (2) ... PA-2
Perry-Cherry House—hist pl ... NC-3
Perry City—pop pl ... NY-2
Perry-Clay Cem—cemetery ... TX-5
Perry-Clay Chapel—church ... TX-5
Perry-Cooper House—hist pl ... MD-2
Perry Corners—locale ... NY-2
Perry Country Club Golf Course—other ... TX-5
Perry County—pop pl ... AL-4
Perry (County)—pop pl ... AR-4
Perry (County)—pop pl ... IL-6
Perry County—pop pl ... IN-6
Perry (County)—pop pl ... KY-4
Perry County—pop pl ... MS-4
Perry County—pop pl ... MO-7
Perry (County)—pop pl ... OH-6
Perry County—pop pl ... PA-2
Perry County—pop pl ... TN-4
Perry County Airp—airport ... AL-4
Perry County Airp—airport ... TN-4
Perry County Courthouse—building ... AL-4
Perry County Courthouse—hist pl ... AR-4
Perry County Courthouse—hist pl ... PA-2
Perry County Courthouse and Jail—hist pl ... OH-6
Perry County General Hosp—hospital ... MS-4
Perry County Hosp—hospital ... AL-4
Perry County HS—school ... TN-4
Perry County HS (historical)—school ... AL-4
Perry County Memorial Hospital Heliport—airport ... WA-9
Perry County Municipal Airp—airport ... IN-6
Perry County Sch—school ... MS-4
Perry County Training Sch (historical)—school ... AL-4
Perry Cove—bay ... MA-1
Perry Cove—pop pl ... ME-1
Perry Cove—valley ... NC-3
Perry Cove Branch—stream ... GA-3
Perry Creek ... MI-6
Perry Creek—gut ... SC-3
Perry Creek—stream (2) ... AK-9
Perry Creek—stream ... AZ-5
Perry Creek—stream (2) ... AR-4
Perry Creek—stream (2) ... CA-9
Perry Creek—stream (2) ... CO-8
Perry Creek—stream (3) ... GA-3
Perry Creek—stream ... ID-8
Perry Creek—stream (2) ... IA-7
Perry Creek—stream ... KS-7
Perry Creek—stream (2) ... KY-4
Perry Creek—stream ... ME-1
Perry Creek—stream (4) ... MI-6
Perry Creek—stream ... MN-6
Perry Creek—stream (2) ... MS-4
Perry Creek—stream ... MT-8
Perry Creek—stream ... NY-2
Perry Creek—stream (4) ... NC-3
Perry Creek—stream ... OK-5
Perry Creek—stream (4) ... OR-9
Perry Creek—stream ... SC-3
Perry Creek—stream ... SD-7
Perry Creek—stream (3) ... TN-4
Perry Creek—stream (3) ... TX-5
Perry Creek—stream ... VA-3
Perry Creek—stream (4) ... WA-9
Perry Creek—stream ... WV-2
Perry Creek—stream ... WI-6
Perry Creek—stream ... WY-8
Perry Creek Rec Area—park ... WI-6
Perry Creek Shelter—locale ... WA-9
Perry Crossing—pop pl ... IN-6
Perry Crossroads—locale ... NC-3
Perrydale—pop pl ... OR-9
Perry Dam—dam ... KS-7
Perry Ditch—canal ... CO-8
Perry Ditch—canal ... IN-6
Perry Drain—canal ... MI-6
Perry Drain—canal ... NE-7
Perry Draw—valley ... CO-8
Perry Draw—valley ... WY-8
Perry East JHS—school ... IN-6
Perry Elem Sch—school ... FL-3
Perry Elem Sch—school (2) ... IN-6
Perry Elem Sch—school (2) ... PA-2
Perry Farm—locale ... MS-4
Perry Field—airport ... NC-3
Perry Ford (historical)—locale ... AL-4
Perry Fork ... WV-2
Perry Fork—stream (2) ... KY-4
Perry Fork—stream ... WV-2
Perry Foundation—locale ... TX-5
Perry Fraser Mill (historical)—locale ... MS-4
Perry Furnace Run—stream ... PA-2
Perry Gap—gap (2) ... NC-3
Perry Golf Course—locale ... PA-2
Perry Go Place (census name Beloit North)—other ... WI-6
Perry Grove Ch—church ... GA-3
Perry Grove Ch—church ... NC-3
Perry Gulch—valley (2) ... CA-9
Perry Gulch—valley ... ID-8
Perry Hall—hist pl ... MD-2
Perry Hall—pop pl ... MD-2
Perry Hall Estates—pop pl ... MD-2
Perry Hall (Fullerton)—CDP ... MD-2
Perry Hall Manor—pop pl ... MD-2
Perry Hall Sch—school ... MD-2
Perryhawkin Ch—church ... MD-2
Perry Hayse House, The—building ... MA-1
Perry Healy Brook—stream ... RI-1
Perry Heights—pop pl ... OH-6
Perry Heights Cem—cemetery ... PA-2
Perry Heights Elementary and JHS—school ... IN-6
Perry Heights Sch ... IN-6
Perry High Top—summit ... KY-4
Perry Highway Ch—church ... PA-2
Perry Highway Interchange ... PA-2
Perry Highway Interchange—locale ... PA-2
Perry Hill ... RI-1
Perry Hill—hist pl ... VA-3
Perry Hill—summit ... AL-4
Perry Hill—summit ... CT-1
Perry Hill—summit (2) ... ME-1
Perry Hill—summit (2) ... MA-1
Perry Hill—summit ... NH-1
Perry Hill—summit ... TN-4
Perry Hill—summit ... VT-1
Perry Hill Ch—church ... MA-1
Perry Hill Ch—church ... TN-4
Perry Hill Methodist Ch—church ... AL-4
Perry Hill Road Baptist Ch—church ... AL-4
Perry Hill Shop Ctr—locale ... AL-4
Perry Hills (subdivision)—pop pl ... AL-4
Perry Hills (subdivision)—pop pl ... NC-3
Perry (historical)—locale ... ND-7
Perry Hollow—valley (4) ... TN-4
Perry Hollow—valley ... TX-5
Perry Homes—pop pl ... GA-3
Perry Hosp—hospital ... IL-6
Perry House—hist pl ... LA-4
Perry HS ... PA-2
Perry HS—hist pl ... MS-4
Perry HS—school (2) ... OH-6
Perry HS—school ... TX-5
Perry Institute—school ... WA-9
Perry Island ... RI-1
Perry Island—island ... AK-9
Perry Island—island ... MD-2
Perry Island—island ... MO-7
Perry Jarvis Branch—stream ... KY-4
Perry JHS—school ... SC-3
Perry Knob—summit ... AR-4
Perry Knob—summit ... KY-4
Perry Knob—summit ... NC-3
Perry Lake ... MI-6
Perry Lake ... WI-6
Perry Lake—lake ... AL-4
Perry Lake—lake ... AZ-5
Perry Lake—lake ... IN-6
Perry Lake—lake ... KS-7
Perry Lake—lake (2) ... MI-6
Perry Lake—lake (3) ... MN-6
Perry Lake—lake (2) ... MS-4
Perry Lake—lake ... NM-5
Perry Lake—lake ... OR-9
Perry Lake—lake ... PA-2
Perry Lake—lake ... TX-5
Perry Lake—lake (3) ... WI-6
Perry Lake—lake ... WY-8
Perry Lake—reservoir ... KS-7
Perry Lake—reservoir ... MI-6
Perry Lake—reservoir ... NC-3
Perry Lake—reservoir ... OK-5
Perry Lake Creek—stream ... MN-6
Perry Lake Dam—dam ... MS-4
Perry Lake Dam—dam ... NC-3
Perry Lake Heights—pop pl ... MI-6
Perry Lake Park—park ... OK-5
Perry Lake Rec Area—park ... AL-4
Perry Lake (Township of)—pop pl ... MN-6
Perryland Farm—locale ... AR-4
Perry Landing—locale ... NC-3
Perry Landing—pop pl ... TX-5
Perry Landing (historical)—locale ... AL-4
Perry Lateral—canal ... SD-7
Perry Lawson Canyon—valley ... NM-5
Perry-Lecompton HS—school ... KS-7
Perry Ledge—bar ... ME-1
Perry Lumber Company Trail—trail ... PA-2
Perry Magee Run—stream ... PA-2
Perryman ... TX-5
Perryman—pop pl ... MD-2
Perryman Branch—stream ... NC-3
Perryman Elem Sch—school ... MS-4
Perry Manor ... IN-6
Perry Manor—pop pl ... IN-6
Perry Manor (subdivision)—pop pl ... MA-1
Perryman Sch—school ... MD-2
Perry Meadows—flat ... OR-9
Perry Memorial Ch—church (2) ... WV-2
Perry Memorial Gardens (Cemetery)—cemetery ... GA-3
Perry Memorial Hosp—hospital ... TN-4
Perry Memorial House—building ... PA-2
Perry Mesa—bench ... NM-5
Perry Mesa—summit ... AZ-5
Perry Mesa Archeol District—hist pl ... AZ-5
Perry Mesa Tank—reservoir ... AZ-5
Perry Mesa Tank—reservoir ... NM-5
Perry Mill—hist pl ... RI-1
Perry Mill Creek ... MS-4
Perry Mill Run—stream ... PA-2
Perry Mills—pop pl ... NY-2
Perry Mill Spring ... UT-8
Perry Mine ... TN-4
Perry Mine—mine ... MN-6
Perry Mine—mine ... WA-9
Perry Monmt—park ... PA-2
Perrymont—uninc pl ... PA-2
Perrymont Ave Sch—school ... VA-3
Perry Moshannon Mine—mine ... PA-2
Perry Mound Cem—cemetery ... NE-7
Perry Mountain ... CO-8
Perry Mountain Creek—stream ... CA-9
Perry Mountain Fire Tower—locale ... AL-4
Perry Mount Park—cemetery ... MI-6
Perry Mount Park—park ... MI-6
Perry MS—school ... FL-3
Perry Mtn—summit ... AL-4
Perry Mtn—summit ... AR-4
Perry Mtn—summit ... CA-9
Perry Mtn—summit ... GA-3
Perry Mtn—summit ... ME-1
Perry Mtn—summit ... NH-1
Perry Mtn—summit ... NY-2
Perry N Boday Creek—stream ... WY-8
Perry N Boday Lake—lake ... WY-8
Perry North (CCD)—cens area ... FL-3
Perry No 1 Sch—school ... IA-7
Perry Number Two Drain—canal ... MI-6
Perryopolis—pop pl ... PA-2
Perryopolis Borough—civil ... PA-2
Perry Park—flat ... CO-8
Perry Park—park ... AZ-5
Perry Park—park ... CA-9
Perry Park—park ... MI-6
Perry Park—park (2) ... MN-6
Perry Park—park ... TX-5
Perry Park—pop pl ... DE-2
Perry Park—pop pl ... KY-4
Perry Park—pop pl ... TN-4
Perry Park (Balls Landing)—pop pl ... KY-4
Perry Park Ranch—locale ... CO-8
Perry Park South Ranch—locale ... CO-8
Perry Parks Placer Mine—mine ... MT-8
Perry Park (subdivision)—pop pl ... NC-3
Perry Passage—channel ... AK-9
Perry-Payne Bldg—hist pl ... OH-6
Perry Peak ... CO-8
Perry Peak—summit ... MA-1
Perry Peak—summit ... WI-6
Perry Plaza—locale ... PA-2
Perry Plaza (Shop Ctr)—locale ... FL-3
Perry Plaza Shop Ctr—locale ... MO-7
Perry Point ... MD-2
Perry Point—cape ... MN-6
Perry Point—cape ... NY-2
Perry Point—cape ... TN-4
Perry Point—pop pl ... MD-2
Perry Point—summit ... OR-9
Perry Point Mansion House and Mill—hist pl ... MD-2
Perry Pond—lake ... AL-4
Perry Pond—lake (2) ... CT-1
Perry Pond—lake ... FL-3
Perry Pond—lake ... GA-3
Perry Pond—lake (2) ... ME-1
Perry Pond—lake ... MA-1
Perry Pond—lake ... MO-7
Perry Pond—lake ... NY-2
Perry Pond—lake ... RI-1
Perry Pond—reservoir ... CO-8
Perry Pond—reservoir ... CT-1
Perry Pond—reservoir ... MA-1
Perry Pond—reservoir (3) ... NC-3
Perry Pond Brook—stream ... NY-2
Perry Pond Dam—dam (2) ... NC-3
Perry Ponds—lake ... NH-1
Perry Primary Sch—school ... FL-3
Perry Public Use Area—locale ... KS-7
Perry Public Use Area—park ... KS-7
Perry Raceway—other ... NY-2
Perry Ranch—locale ... MT-8
Perry Ranch—locale ... OR-9
Perry Ranch—locale (2) ... TX-5
Perry Ranch—locale ... WY-8
Perry Range ... UT-8
Perry Reeves Pond—lake ... FL-3
Perry Reservoir ... KS-7
Perry Ridge—ridge (2) ... CA-9
Perry Ridge—ridge ... LA-4
Perry Ridge—ridge ... NC-3
Perry Ridge—ridge ... OH-6
Perry Ridge—ridge (2) ... WV-2
Perry Ridge Cem—cemetery ... WV-2
Perry Ridge Lake—lake ... CA-9
Perry Ridge Sch (historical)—school ... AL-4
Perry Ridge Trail—trail ... WV-2
Perry Rsvr—reservoir ... UT-8
Perry Run—stream (2) ... OH-6
Perry Run—stream ... PA-2
Perry Run—stream ... WV-2
Perry Salt Log—flat ... CA-9
Perrys Branch—stream ... TN-4
Perrys Branch—stream ... WV-2
Perrysburg ... SC-3
Perrysburg—pop pl ... IN-6
Perrysburg—pop pl ... NY-2
Perrysburg—pop pl ... OH-6
Perrysburg Heights—pop pl ... OH-6
Perrysburg Hist Dist—hist pl ... OH-6
Perrysburg (Town of)—pop pl ... NY-2
Perrysburg (Township of)—pop pl ... OH-6
Perrys Cem—cemetery ... WV-2
Perry Sch ... PA-2
Perry Sch—school ... AL-4
Perry Sch—school (3) ... CA-9
Perry Sch—school ... CO-8
Perry Sch—school ... FL-3
Perry Sch—school ... GA-3
Perry Sch—school (3) ... IL-6
Perry Sch—school ... IA-7
Perry Sch—school (2) ... KY-4
Perry Sch—school ... MA-1
Perry Sch—school (3) ... MI-6
Perry Sch—school ... MN-6
Perry Sch—school ... NH-1
Perry Sch—school (2) ... NY-2
Perry Sch—school ... NC-3
Perry Sch—school (4) ... OH-6
Perry Sch—school ... OK-5
Perry Sch—school ... OR-9
Perry Sch—school ... PA-2
Perry Sch—school ... SC-3
Perry Sch—school ... TN-4
Perry Sch—school ... UT-8
Perry Sch—school ... WI-6
Perry Sch (abandoned)—school ... PA-2
Perrys Chapel—church ... NC-3
Perrys Chapel Church ... AL-4
Perry Sch (historical)—school (2) ... TN-4
Perry School (abandoned)—locale ... OR-9
Perrys Clearing—flat ... NY-2
Perrys Corner—locale ... CA-9
Perrys Corner—other ... PA-2
Perrys Corner—pop pl ... ME-1
Perrys Corner—pop pl ... MD-2
Perrys Corner—pop pl ... MA-1
Perrys Corners—pop pl ... PA-2
Perrys Creek ... MI-6
Perrys Creek—stream ... MI-6
Perrys Ford (historical)—locale ... AL-4
Perrys Glade Run—stream ... MD-2
Perry-Shockley House—hist pl ... DE-2
Perrys Hollow—valley ... UT-8
Perrys Hollow Subdivision—pop pl ... UT-8
Perry Siding—locale ... UT-8
Perrys Knob—summit ... CA-9
Perrys Lake—lake ... AL-4
Perrys Landing (historical)—locale (2) ... AL-4
Perry Slough—gut ... IL-6
Perry Slough—gut ... MN-6
Perry Slough—stream ... CA-9
Perrys Mill—locale ... AL-4
Perrys Mill Cem—cemetery ... AL-4
Perrys Mill (Myrtle)—pop pl ... AL-4
Perrys Millpond—lake ... CT-1
Perrys Mills ... AL-4
Perrys Mills—pop pl ... NY-2
Perrys Natl Monmt—park ... OH-6
Perry South (CCD)—cens area ... FL-3
Perrys Park Spring—spring ... TN-4
Perrys Peak ... MA-1
Perrys Pond—lake ... CT-1
Perrys Pond—reservoir ... GA-3
Perrys Pond—reservoir (2) ... NC-3
Perry Spring—spring ... AZ-5
Perry Spring—spring ... FL-3
Perry Spring—spring ... KY-4
Perry Spring—spring ... MO-7
Perry Spring—spring ... MT-8
Perry Spring—spring (2) ... NV-8
Perry Spring—spring ... NM-5
Perry Spring—spring (2) ... OR-9
Perry Spring—spring ... WA-9
Perry Spring—spring ... WI-6
Perry Spring Canyon—valley ... NM-5
Perry Spring Hollow—valley ... MO-7
Perry Springs Sch—school ... IL-6
Perry Springs Station—locale ... IL-6
Perry-Spruill House—hist pl ... NC-3
Perry Square—locale ... PA-2
Perry Square (Shop Ctr)—locale ... FL-3
Perrys Steam Mill (historical)—locale ... AL-4
Perrys Stove (historical)—locale ... AL-4
Perry Starr Cem (reduced usage)—cemetery ... TX-5
Perry State Game Mngmt Area ... KS-7
Perry State Park—park ... KS-7
Perry State Wildlife Area—park ... MO-7
Perrys Tavern ... DE-2
Perry Store—pop pl ... AL-4
Perry Store (historical)—locale ... AL-4
Perry Stream—stream ... NH-1
Perry Street Hist Dist—hist pl ... AL-4
Perry Street Hist Dist—hist pl ... AR-4
Perry Street Methodist Church ... AL-4
Perry Subdivision—pop pl ... UT-8
Perry's Victory and International Peace Memorial—hist pl ... OH-6
Perry's Victory and International Peace Memorial—park ... OH-6
Perrys Victory and International Peace Memorial—park ... OH-6
Perrys Victory and International Peace Memorial—park ... OH-6
Perrysville ... PA-2
Perrysville—pop pl ... IN-6
Perrysville—pop pl (2) ... OH-6
Perrysville—pop pl (2) ... PA-2
Perrysville Elem Sch—school ... PA-2
Perrysville Sch ... PA-2
Perrys Well (historical)—locale ... AL-4
Perry-Swilley House—hist pl ... TX-5
Perry Switch Ch—church ... TN-4
Perry Tank—reservoir ... NM-5
Perry Tank—reservoir ... TX-5
Perry Tank Canyon—valley ... AZ-5
Perryton—pop pl ... OH-6
Perryton—pop pl ... TX-5
Perryton Ch—church ... IL-6
Perryton Country Club—other ... TX-5
Perryton East (CCD)—cens area ... TX-5
Perryton Sch—school ... IL-6
Perryton (Township of)—pop pl ... IL-6
Perryton West (CCD)—cens area ... TX-5
Perry Top—summit ... NC-3
Perry Towhead ... MO-7
Perrytown—locale ... NC-3
Perrytown—pop pl ... AR-4
Perrytown—pop pl ... KY-4
Perrytown—pop pl (2) ... MS-4
Perrytown Ch—church ... MS-4
Perry (Town of)—pop pl ... NY-2
Perry (Town of)—pop pl ... WI-6
Perrytown Post Office (historical)—building ... MS-4
Perry Township—civil ... MO-7
Perry Township—civil ... PA-2
Perry Township—fmr MCD (5) ... IA-7
Perry Township—pop pl ... IN-6
Perry Township—pop pl ... KS-7
Perry Township—pop pl ... NE-7
Perry Township—pop pl ... ND-7
Perry Township—pop pl (2) ... SD-7
Perry Township Elem Sch—school ... PA-2
Perry (Township of)—fmr MCD (2) ... AR-4
Perry (Township of)—pop pl ... IL-6
Perry (Township of)—pop pl (13) ... IN-6
Perry (Township of)—pop pl ... MI-6
Perry (Township of)—pop pl ... MN-6
Perry (Township of)—pop pl (26) ... OH-6
Perry (Township of)—pop pl (9) ... PA-2
Perry (Town Of)—civ div ... ME-1
Perry Traditional Acad—school ... PA-2
Perry Trail—trail ... PA-2
Perry Valley—valley ... PA-2
Perry Valley Sch—school ... WI-6
Perryville ... MS-4
Perryville ... OH-6
Perryville ... PA-2
Perryville—hist pl ... OK-5
Perryville—locale ... AK-9
Perryville—locale ... IL-6
Perryville—locale (2) ... KY-4
Perryville—locale ... NJ-2
Perryville—locale ... TX-5
Perryville—other ... PA-2
Perryville—pop pl (2) ... AL-4
Perryville—pop pl ... AZ-5
Perryville—pop pl ... AR-4
Perryville—pop pl ... IN-6
Perryville—pop pl ... KY-4
Perryville—pop pl (2) ... LA-4
Perryville—pop pl ... MD-2
Perryville—pop pl (2) ... MA-1
Perryville—pop pl ... MO-7
Perryville—pop pl ... NY-2
Perryville—pop pl (3) ... PA-2
Perryville—pop pl ... RI-1
Perryville—pop pl ... TN-4
Perryville—uninc pl ... VA-3
Perryville Acad (historical)—school ... TN-4
Perryville ANV895—reserve ... AK-9
Perryville Baptist Church ... AL-4
Perryville Battlefield—hist pl ... KY-4
Perryville Battlefield State Park—park ... KY-4
Perryville Bottom—flat ... TN-4
Perryville (CCD)—cens area ... KY-4
Perryville Cem—cemetery ... AR-4
Perryville Ch—church ... AL-4
Perryville Ch—church ... WV-2
Perryville Country Club—locale ... MO-7
Perryville Creek ... OK-5
Perryville Dewatering Area—basin ... TN-4
Perryville Falls—falls ... NY-2
Perryville Ferry (historical)—locale ... TN-4
Perryville First Baptist Ch—church ... TN-4
Perryville Hist Dist—hist pl ... KY-4
Perryville Hollow—valley ... TN-4
Perryville HS—school ... MD-2
Perryville Marina—locale ... TN-4
Perryville Municipal Airp—airport ... MO-7
Perryville Pond—lake ... MA-1
Perryville Pond Dam—dam ... MA-1
Perryville Post Office (historical)—building ... AL-4
Perryville Post Office (historical)—building ... TN-4
Perryville Reservoir ... MA-1
Perryville Run—stream ... PA-2
Perryville Sch (historical)—school ... AL-4
Perryville Sch (historical)—school ... TN-4
Perryville Substation—locale ... AZ-5
Perryville Tavern—hist pl ... NJ-2
Perry Well—locale ... NM-5
Perry Well—well ... MT-8
Perry Well—well (3) ... NM-5
Perry-West Perry Sch—school ... PA-2
Perry Wildlife Area—park ... KS-7
Perry Wilson Canyon—valley ... OR-9
Perry Windmill—locale ... AZ-5
Perry Windmill—locale (2) ... NM-5
Perry Windmill—locale (2) ... TX-5
Perrywinkle Creek ... MS-4
Perrywood Estates—pop pl ... MD-2
Perry Wright—pop pl ... MD-2
Perry Yard—pop pl ... IA-7
Persanti Island—island ... SC-3
Persche Ranch—locale ... SD-7
Persego Wash ... CO-8
Persell Sch—school ... NY-2
Perserverance Ch—church ... VA-3
Perseverance, Lake—lake ... AK-9
Perseverance Bay—bay ... VI-3
Perseverance Cem—cemetery (2) ... IN-6
Perseverance Chapel—church ... IN-6
Perseverance Creek—stream ... AK-9
Perseverance Hall—hist pl ... LA-4
Perseverance Mine—mine ... ID-8
Perseverance Sch—school ... MO-7
Pershall Lakes—reservoir ... MO-7
Pershal Spring—spring ... WY-8
Pershing ... IN-6
Pershing ... PA-2
Pershing—pop pl ... IL-6
Pershing—pop pl ... IN-6
Pershing—pop pl ... IA-7
Pershing—pop pl ... MO-7
Pershing—pop pl ... OK-5
Pershing—pop pl ... TX-5
Pershing—unorg reg ... ND-7
Pershing, Gen. John J., Boyhood Home—hist pl ... MO-7
Pershing, Mount—summit ... WA-9
Pershing Auditorium—other ... NE-7
Pershing (corp ... IN-6
Pershing County—civil ... NV-8
Pershing County Courthouse—hist pl ... NV-8
Pershing Cove—bay ... DE-2
Pershing Creek—stream ... TX-5
Pershing Elem Sch—school ... FL-3
Pershing Elem Sch—school ... IN-6
Pershing Elem Sch—school ... KS-7
Pershing Field—park ... MN-6
Pershing Field—park ... NJ-2
Pershing Hill—summit (2) ... MT-8
Pershing Hill Sch—school ... MD-2
Pershing House—hist pl ... TX-5
Pershing HS—school ... MI-6
Pershing JHS—school ... CA-9
Pershing JHS—school ... TX-5
Pershing Memorial Cem—cemetery ... CO-8
Pershing Mine—mine ... CO-8
Pershing Mine—mine ... NV-8
Pershing Oil and Gas Field—oilfield ... ND-7
Pershing Oil Field—oilfield ... OK-5
Pershing Park—park ... DC-2
Pershing Park—park ... MI-6
Pershing Park—park ... TN-4
Pershing Park—park ... WI-6
Pershing Quicksilver Mine—mine ... NV-8
Pershing Sch—school (3) ... CA-9
Pershing Sch—school ... ID-8
Pershing Sch—school (2) ... IL-6
Pershing Sch—school ... IA-7
Pershing Sch—school ... ME-1
Pershing Sch—school (2) ... MI-6
Pershing Sch—school (6) ... MO-7
Pershing Sch—school (3) ... NE-7
Pershing Sch—school ... NJ-2
Pershing Sch—school (2) ... OK-5
Pershing Sch—school (2) ... SD-7
Pershing Sch—school (2) ... TX-5
Pershing Sch—school (2) ... WI-6
Pershing Sch—school ... WY-8
Pershing School—locale ... IA-7
Pershing Siding—locale ... CA-9
Pershing Square—park ... CA-9
Pershing State Park—park ... MO-7
Pershing State Wildlife Area—park ... WI-6
Pershing Tower—pillar ... LA-4
Pershing (Town of)—pop pl ... WI-6
Pershing Township—pop pl ... NE-7
Pershing Township (historical)—civil ... SD-7
Pershing (Township of)—pop pl ... IN-6
Persia—locale ... NY-2
Persia—pop pl ... IA-7
Persia—pop pl ... TN-4
Persia (historical)—pop pl ... MO-7
Persia M. Robinson Natural Area—area ... OR-9
Persian Creek—stream ... CA-9
Persian Ditch—canal ... CA-9
Persian Sch—school ... MN-6
Persia Post Office (historical)—building ... TN-4
Persia Sch (historical)—school ... TN-4
Persia (Town of)—pop pl ... NY-2
Persico—locale ... GA-3
Persido Bar—bar ... CA-9
Persifer (Township of)—pop pl ... IL-6
Persigo Wash—stream ... CO-8
Persiliano Canyon—valley ... NM-5
Persiliano Windmill—locale ... NM-5
Persimmon—locale ... GA-3
Persimmon—locale ... KY-4
Persimmon Bayou—gut ... TX-5
Persimmon Bayou—stream (2) ... LA-4
Persimmon Bayou—swamp ... LA-4
Persimmon (Blalock)—pop pl ... GA-3
Persimmon Branch—stream (3) ... AL-4
Persimmon Branch—stream ... AR-4
Persimmon Branch—stream (2) ... KY-4
Persimmon Branch—stream ... MS-4
Persimmon Branch—stream ... MO-7
Persimmon Branch—stream ... NC-3
Persimmon Branch—stream (5) ... SC-3
Persimmon Branch—stream (2) ... TN-4
Persimmon Branch—stream (3) ... TX-5
Persimmon Branch—stream ... VA-3
Persimmon-Burntcorn Structure 1 Dam—dam ... MS-4
Persimmon-Burnt Corn Watershed Five Dam—dam ... MS-4
Persimmon Cave—cave ... AL-4
Persimmon Cem—cemetery ... OK-5
Persimmon Chapel—church ... MS-4
Persimmon Creek ... AL-4
Persimmon Creek ... LA-4
Persimmon Creek—pop pl ... NC-3
Persimmon Creek—stream (4) ... AL-4
Persimmon Creek—stream (3) ... GA-3
Persimmon Creek—stream ... KY-4
Persimmon Creek—stream ... MD-2
Persimmon Creek—stream (2) ... MS-4
Persimmon Creek—stream (4) ... NC-3
Persimmon Creek—stream (2) ... OK-5
Persimmon Creek—stream ... SC-3
Persimmon Creek—stream ... TN-4
Persimmon Creek—stream (5) ... TX-5
Persimmon Creek—stream ... VA-3
Persimmon Creek Cem—cemetery ... NC-3

Persimmon Creek Structure Y-21-10 Dam—dam MS-4
Persimmon Creek Structure Y-21-2 Dam—dam MS-4
Persimmon Creek Structure Y-21-3 Dam—dam MS-4
Persimmon Creek Structure Y-21-30 Dam—dam MS-4
Persimmon Creek Structure Y-21-32 Dam—dam MS-4
Persimmon Creek Structure Y-21-4 Dam—dam MS-4
Persimmon Creek Structure Y-21-5 Dam—dam MS-4
Persimmon Creek Structure Y-21-50 Dam—dam MS-4
Persimmon Creek Structure Y-21-51 Dam—dam MS-4
Persimmon Creek Structure Y-21-7 Dam—dam MS-4
Persimmon Creek Structure Y-21-8 Dam—dam MS-4
Persimmon Creek Structure Y-21-9 Dam—dam MS-4
Persimmon Dam—dam NC-3
Persimmon Fork—stream KY-4
Persimmon Fork—stream SC-3
Persimmon Fork Sch—school KY-4
Persimmon Gap—gap (3) GA-3
Persimmon Gap—gap TX-5
Persimmon Gap Ranger Station—locale TX-5
Persimmon Glade Branch—stream NC-3
Persimmon Grove—locale (2) AL-4
**Persimmon Grove**—pop pl KY-4
Persimmon Grove Ch—church AL-4
Persimmon Grove Ch—church (2) MS-4
Persimmon Grove Ch—church NC-3
Persimmon Grove Chapel (historical)—church AL-4
Persimmon Grove Ch (historical)—church TN-4
Persimmon Grove Ch of Christ AL-4
Persimmon Grove Sch—school TN-4
Persimmon Grove Sch (historical)—school TN-4
Persimmon Grove School (historical)—locale MO-7
Persimmon Gully—stream LA-4
Persimmon Hill—summit GA-3
Persimmon Hill—summit MS-4
Persimmon Hill—summit SC-3
Persimmon Hill Ch—church MS-4
Persimmon Hill Country Club—other SC-3
Persimmon Hill Rec Area—park MS-4
Persimmon Hill Sch—school MS-4
Persimmon Hollow—valley FL-3
Persimmon Hollow—valley IL-6
Persimmon Hollow—valley KY-4
Persimmon Hollow—valley (6) MO-7
Persimmon Hollow Tank—reservoir TX-5
Persimmon Hummock—summit DE-2
Persimmon Island—island TN-4
Persimmon Island Bridge—bridge TN-4
Persimmon Knob—summit AL-4
Persimmon Knob—summit KY-4
Persimmon Knob—summit TN-4
Persimmon Knob Spring—spring AL-4
Persimmon Lake—lake FL-3
Persimmon Lake—lake TX-5
Persimmon Lake—reservoir NC-3
Persimmon Lick Drift Mine (underground)—mine AL-4
Persimmon Marsh—stream (2) LA-4
Persimmon Mill Ch—church MS-4
Persimmon Mtn—summit SC-3
Persimmon Mtn—summit VA-3
Persimmon Nursery Branch—stream NC-3
Persimmon Pass—channel LA-4
Persimmon Pit—cave AL-4
Persimmon Point MD-2
Persimmon Point NC-3
Persimmon Point—cape GA-3
Persimmon Point—cape (4) MD-2
Persimmon Point—cape NC-3
Persimmon Point—cape (2) VA-3
Persimmon Point—locale VA-3
Persimmon Point Cem—cemetery KY-4
Persimmon Pond—lake AR-4
Persimmon Pond—lake FL-3
Persimmon Pond—lake LA-4
Persimmon Pond—lake MO-7
Persimmon Pond—reservoir TX-5
Persimmon Pond Branch—stream TN-4
Persimmon Pond Ditch—canal IN-6
Persimmon Pond Hollow—valley MO-7
Persimmon Pond Hollow—valley VA-3
Persimmon Pond Mtn—summit AR-4
Persimmon Pond Sch—school MO-7
Persimmon Pond Slough—swamp TX-5
Persimmon Ridge—ridge (3) IN-6
Persimmon Ridge—ridge (2) KY-4
Persimmon Ridge—ridge NC-3
Persimmon Ridge—ridge SC-3
Persimmon Ridge—ridge (3) TN-4
Persimmon Ridge—ridge VA-3
Persimmon Ridge Ch—church MS-4
Persimmon Run DE-2
Persimmon Run—stream DE-2
Persimmon Run—stream IN-6
Persimmon Run—stream MD-2
Persimmon Run—stream VA-3
Persimmons Branch—stream TX-5
Persimmon Slash—gut AR-4
Persimmon Slough—gut AR-4
Persimmon Slough—gut LA-4
Persimmon Slough Creek—stream KY-4
Persimmon Spring—spring TX-5
Persimmon Swamp—stream (2) NC-3
Persimmon Swamp—stream SC-3
Persimmon Tree Branch—stream NC-3
Persimmon Tree Branch—stream VA-3
Persimmon Tree Landing Gut—gut NC-3
Persimmon Tree Point—cape (3) NC-3
**Persimmon Tree Subdivision**—pop pl UT-8
**Persimon**—pop pl KY-4
**Persinger**—pop pl WV-2
Persinger (abandoned)—building MO-7
Persinger Canyon—valley CA-9
Persinger Cem—cemetery KS-7
Persinger Cemetery TN-4
Persinger Creek—stream WV-2
Persinger Ditch—canal OH-6
Persinger House—hist pl VA-3
Persinger Memorial Chapel—church VA-3
Persis, Mount—summit WA-9
Persist—locale OR-9
PERSISTENCE (log canoe)—hist pl MD-2
Persist Ranch Rsvrs—reservoir OR-9
Persley House TX-5
Personal 500 Sales Co. Heliport—airport WA-9
Person Branch—stream TX-5
Person Cem—cemetery GA-3
Person Cem—cemetery MS-4
Person Cem—cemetery TN-4
**Person County**—pop pl NC-3
Person County Courthouse—hist pl NC-3
Person County Sr HS—school NC-3
Person Creek—stream IL-6
Person Creek—stream NV-8
Person Creek—stream WA-9
Personeni Ranch—locale CA-9
Personett Cem—cemetery IN-6
Person Lake—lake WI-6
Person-McGhee Farm—hist pl NC-3
Person Memorial Cem—cemetery NC-3
Person Memorial Hosp—hospital NC-3
Person Oil Field—oilfield TX-5
Person Ordinary NC-3
Person Place—hist pl NC-3
Person Ranch—locale WA-9
Persons—locale AL-4
Persons Bridge—locale AR-4
Persons Cem—cemetery NY-2
Persons Ch—church VA-3
Persons Chapel—church AR-4
**Persons Corners**—pop pl NY-2
Persons Creek—stream GA-3
Person's Ordinary—hist pl NC-3
Persons Pond—lake PA-2
Persons Post Office (historical)—building AL-4
Persons Spring—spring NV-8
Person Technical Institute—school NC-3
Personville—locale TX-5
Personville (CCD)—cens area TX-5
Perspiration Point—cape CA-9
Persson Draw—valley WY-8
Persun Cem—cemetery PA-2
Pert—locale TX-5
Pert Creek—stream KY-4
Pert Creek Sch—school KY-4
Perteli Windmill—locale NM-5
Perth NJ-2
Perth—locale MN-6
Perth—locale MS-4
Perth—locale NV-8
Perth—locale VA-3
**Perth**—pop pl DE-2
**Perth**—pop pl IN-6
**Perth**—pop pl KS-7
**Perth**—pop pl NV-8
**Perth**—pop pl NY-2
**Perth**—pop pl ND-7
**Perth Amboy**—pop pl NJ-2
Perth Amboy City Hall and Surveyor General's Office—hist pl NJ-2
Perth Amboy Ferry Slip—hist pl NJ-2
Perth Amboy HS—school NJ-2
Perth Amboy Junction—locale NJ-2
Perth Amboy Station—hist pl NJ-2
Perth Amboy Station—locale NJ-2
Perth Cem—cemetery IN-6
Perth Cem—cemetery ND-7
Perth Ch—church NC-3
Perth Oil Field—oilfield KS-7
Perth Post Office (historical)—building MS-4
**Perthshire**—pop pl MS-4
Perthshire Post Office (historical)—building MS-4
Perth Town NJ-2
Perth Town Hall—building ND-7
**Perth (Town of)**—pop pl NY-2
**Perth Township**—pop pl ND-7
Pertie Canyon—valley NM-5
Pertle Creek TN-4
Pertle Creek—stream TX-5
Pertle Springs—spring MO-7
**Pertuits Store**—pop pl LA-4
Peru IA-7
Peru KS-7
Peru VA-3
Peru—locale WV-2
Peru—locale WY-8
**Peru**—pop pl IL-6
**Peru**—pop pl IN-6
**Peru**—pop pl KS-7
**Peru**—pop pl ME-1
**Peru**—pop pl MA-1
**Peru**—pop pl MO-7
**Peru**—pop pl NE-7
**Peru**—pop pl (2) NY-2
**Peru**—pop pl NC-3
**Peru**—pop pl OH-6
**Peru**—pop pl PA-2
**Peru**—pop pl VT-1
**Peru**—pop pl WI-6
Peru Bottoms—flat IA-7
Peru Canyon—valley NV-8
Peru Cem—cemetery KS-7
Peru Cem—cemetery WI-6
Peru Creek—stream CO-8
Perue Peak—summit AK-9
Perue Ranch—locale WY-8
**Peruhill**—pop pl NM-5
Peru Hill—summit MA-1
Peru (historical P.O.)—locale AL-4
Peru HS—school IN-6
Perulack—locale PA-2
Peru Mills—locale PA-2
**Peru Mills**—pop pl PA-2
Peru Municipal Airp—airport IN-6
Perung Sprint—cape FM-9
Peru Peak—summit VT-1
**Peruque**—pop pl MO-7
Peruque Creek—stream MO-7
Peruque Island—island MO-7
Peru Sch—school MO-7
Peru State Coll—school NE-7
Peru State For—forest MA-1
Peru State Hunting Grounds MA-1
Peruton NY-2
Peruton—locale NY-2
**Peru (Town of)**—pop pl MA-1
**Peru (Town of)**—pop pl NY-2
**Peru (Town of)**—pop pl VT-1
**Peru (Town of)**—pop pl WI-6
Peru Township—fmr MCD IA-7
**Peru (Township of)**—pop pl IL-6
**Peru (Township of)**—pop pl IN-6
**Peru (Township of)**—pop pl (2) OH-6
Peru (Town 990f)—civ div ME-1
Peru Tunnel—mine CO-8
Peruvian Branch—stream NC-3
Peruvian Embassy Bldg—building DC-2
Peruvian Gulch—valley CA-9
Peruvian Gulch—valley UT-8
Peruvian Mine—mine CO-8
**Peruvian Park**—pop pl UT-8
Peruvian Park Sch—school UT-8
**Peruvian Park Subdivision**—pop pl UT-8
**Peruville**—pop pl NY-2
Peru Wildlife Mngmt Area—park MA-1
Pervere Ridge—ridge ME-1
Pervis Grove Ch—church GA-3
Perviski Drain—canal MI-6
Pervis Lake—lake MS-4
Perwal FM-9
Peryam Ranch—locale WY-8
Peryear TN-4
Peryear Cem—cemetery TX-5
Peryear Post Office TN-4
Pesabic Lake—lake WI-6
Pesante Canyon—valley CA-9
Pesas (Barrio)—fmr MCD PR-3
Pescadero—civil CA-9
**Pescadero**—pop pl CA-9
**Pescadero**—pop pl ID-8
Pescadero, Arroyo—stream CA-9
Pescadero Beach—beach CA-9
Pescadero Canyon—valley CA-9
Pescadero Creek—stream (3) CA-9
Pescadero High Power Homing Station—other CA-9
Pescadero HS—school CA-9
Pescadero Mtn—summit AZ-5
Pescadero Point—cape (2) CA-9
Pescadero Rocks—island CA-9
Pescadero Wash—stream AZ-5
Pescadito—locale TX-5
Pescadito Tank—reservoir TX-5
Pescado—locale NM-5
Pescado, Canada Del —valley CA-9
Pescado Canyon—valley NM-5
Pescado Creek—stream CA-9
Pescado Creek—stream TX-5
Pescado Draw—valley NM-5
Pescadora MP-9
Pescadore Islands MP-9
Pescadores MP-9
Pescado Reservior—reservoir NM-5
Pescado Spring—spring NM-5
Pescado Tank—reservoir (2) TX-5
Pescara Creek—gut VA-3
Pescar Springs—spring CO-8
Peschani Point—cape AK-9
Pesch Canal—canal AZ-5
Peschi Draw—valley MT-8
Pescio Ranch—locale (2) NV-8
Pesco—uninc pl CA-9
**Peshastin**—pop pl WA-9
Peshastin Cem—cemetery WA-9
Peshastin Creek—stream WA-9
Peshastin Elem Sch—school WA-9
Peshastin Pinnacles—pillar WA-9
**Peshawbestown**—pop pl MI-6
Peshekee River—stream MI-6
Peshette Swamp—swamp NY-2
Peshine Ave Sch—school NJ-2
Peshlakai Point—summit AZ-5
Peshlaki Spring—spring AZ-5
Peshliki Fork—stream UT-8
Peshliki Fork Ticaboo Creek—stream UT-8
**Peshtigo**—pop pl WI-6
Peshtigo Brook—stream WI-6
Peshtigo Brook State Wildlife Area—park WI-6
Peshtigo Fire Cemetery—hist pl WI-6
Peshtigo Harbor—bay WI-6
Peshtigo Harbor State Wildlife Area—park WI-6
Peshtigo Lake—lake WI-6
Peshtigo Lookout Tower—locale WI-6
Peshtigo Point—cape WI-6
Peshtigo River—stream WI-6
**Peshtigo (Town of)**—pop pl WI-6
Pesief Island—island FM-9
Peskeompskut MA-1
Pesketennes Island MA-1
Pesketineasset Island MA-1
Peski Park—park CT-1
Pesk Island MA-1
Pesley Fork—stream KY-4
Pesoadero Creek CA-9
Peso Canyon—valley NM-5
Peson FM-9
Peson—bar FM-9
Peson Reef FM-9
Peso Spring—spring NM-5
**Pesotum**—pop pl IL-6
**Pesotum (Township of)**—pop pl IL-6
Pesquamscot Pond RI-1
Pesqueira Canyon—valley AZ-5
Pesqueira Wash—stream AZ-5
Pesquera Island—island AK-9
Pesqueria Wash AZ-5
Pesquiera Canyon AZ-5
Pesquiera Tank—reservoir AZ-5
Pesquiera Wash AZ-5
Pessell Creek—stream GA-3
**Pesson**—pop pl LA-4
Pesson Sch—school LA-4
Pessou House—hist pl LA-4
Pestchani Point—cape AK-9
Pester Creek—stream KS-7
Pesth KS-7
Pest Hollow—valley PA-2
Pest House—hist pl MA-1
Pest House—hist pl MN-6
Pest House Pond—lake MA-1
Pest House Shore—beach MA-1
Pesthouse Tank—reservoir AZ-5
Pestiga Lake—lake WI-6
Pest Island RI-1
Pest Island—island NH-1
Pestle, The MH-9
Pestle Ravine, The MH-9
Pestletown—locale NJ-2
Pesto Trail—trail PA-2
Pestriak Point—cape AK-9
Pesumpsca River ME-1
Pesumpscatowitt River ME-1
Pesuwan FM-9
Petaca—civil NM-5
Petaca—locale NM-5
Petaca Mesa—summit NM-5
Petaca Peak—summit NM-5
Petaca Pinta—ridge NM-5
Petaca Pinta Dam—dam NM-5
Petaga Point—hist pl MN-6
Petain Lagoon—lake LA-4
Petain Spring—spring NV-8
**Petal**—pop pl MS-4
Petal Cem—cemetery MS-4
Petal Ch of God—church MS-4
Petal Elem Sch—school MS-4
Petal-Harvey Baptist Ch—church MS-4
Petal-Harvey Sch—school MS-4
Petal Hills—summit AZ-5
Petal HS MS-4
Petal JHS—school MS-4
Petal Lookout Tower—locale MS-4
Petal Plaza Shop Ctr—locale MS-4
Petal Presbyterian Ch—church MS-4
Petaluma—civil CA-9
**Petaluma**—pop pl CA-9
Petaluma Adobe—hist pl CA-9
Petaluma Adobe State Historical Monmt—park CA-9
Petaluma Boy Scout Camp—locale CA-9
Petaluma (CCD)—cens area CA-9
Petaluma Creek CA-9
Petaluma Point—cape CA-9
Petaluma River—stream CA-9
Petaluma Rsvr—reservoir CA-9
Petaluma Silk Mill—hist pl CA-9
**Petaluma (subdivision)**—pop pl AL-4
Petal United Methodist Ch—church MS-4
Petal Windmill—locale TX-5
Petan Ranch Airp—airport NV-8
Petarsy Indian Mission—church OK-5
Pet Brook—stream WI-6
Pet Canyon—valley TX-5
Pet Cem—cemetery GA-3
Pet Cem—cemetery IN-6
Pet Cem—cemetery ME-1
Pet Cem—cemetery MD-2
Pet Cem—cemetery NH-1
Pet Cem—cemetery (2) NY-2
Pet Cem—cemetery OH-6
Pet Cem—cemetery PA-2
Petch Creek—stream OR-9
**Petche Gap**—pop pl NC-3
**Pet Crossroads**—pop pl NC-3
Petcuson Lake—lake MI-6
Petdida, As—slope MH-9
**Pete**—pop pl TX-5
Pete, Bayou—stream AR-4
Pete, Bayou—stream LA-4
Pete, The—locale ID-8
Pete and Bill Creek—stream CO-8
Pete and Charlie Creek—stream ID-8
Pete and Joe Mine—mine MT-8
Pete Andrews Creek—stream AK-9
Pete Artesian Well—well TX-5
Pete Basin—basin NV-8
Pete Black Cut—canal UT-8
Pete Branch—stream GA-3
Pete Branch—stream (2) KY-4
Pete Branch—stream MS-4
Pete Buck Hollow—valley PA-2
Pete Canyon—valley CO-8
Pete Canyon—valley NV-8
Pete Canyon—valley (2) UT-8
Pete Cem—cemetery GA-3
Pete Cobb Spring—spring AZ-5
Pete Coll Creek—stream ID-8
Pete Coulee—valley WI-6
Pete Creek CO-8
Pete Creek ID-8
Pete Creek—stream CO-8
Pete Creek—stream (7) ID-8
Pete Creek—stream MT-8
Pete Creek—stream TN-4
Pete Creek—stream TX-5
Pete Creek—stream (2) WA-9
Pete Creek—stream WY-8
Pete Creek Camp—locale MT-8
Pete Creek Campground—locale MT-8
Pete Creek Divide—gap MT-8
Pete Creek Divide—ridge ID-8
Pete Creek Meadows—swamp MT-8
Pete Dahl Slough—gut AK-9
Pete Drain—canal MI-6
Pete Draw—valley ID-8
Pete Enyart Canyon—valley OR-9
**Peteet**—pop pl MS-4
Peteet Creek—stream MO-7
Peteetneet Creek—stream UT-8
Peteetneet Sch—school UT-8
Pete Fann Dam—dam NC-3
Pete Gaines Canyon—valley NM-5
Pete Gaines Tank—reservoir NM-5
Pete Gaines Well—well NM-5
Pete Gay Mtn—summit NY-2
Pete Gibson Bridge—bridge FL-3
Petegrow Cove—bay ME-1
Pete Gulch—valley CO-8
Pete Gulch—valley WA-9
Pete Hanson Creek—stream NV-8
Pete Hills—range CO-8
Pete Hollow—valley KY-4
Pete Hollow—valley TX-5
Pete Holm Spring—spring NV-8
Peteil—locale FM-9
Pete Indian Canyon OR-9
Pete Inyard Canyon OR-9
Pete Inyart Canyon OR-9
Pete Island—island MI-6
Pete Island—island MN-6
Pete King Creek—stream ID-8
Pete Kitchens Museum—building AZ-5
Pete Kitchens Ranch—locale AZ-5
Pete Lagus Brook—stream NY-2
Pete Lake—lake MI-6
Pete Lake—lake (3) MN-6
Pete Lake—lake MS-4
Pete Lake—lake (2) WA-9
Pete Lake—lake WI-6
Pete Lake—reservoir OR-9
Pete Light Spring—spring KY-4
Pete Lish Canyon—valley ID-8
Pete Mathews Coliseum—building AL-4
Pete Mathews State Fire College AL-4
Pete McCombs Hill—summit UT-8
Pete Merrill Canyon—valley CA-9
Pete Miller Creek—stream WA-9
Pete Miller Park—flat WY-8
Pete Moore Island—island WA-9
Pete Moore Spring—spring AZ-5
Pete Mtn—summit AZ-5
Pete Neece Canyon—valley NV-8
Peteneet Creek UT-8
Pete Nelson Hollow—valley UT-8
Pete Number One Tank—reservoir AZ-5
Petenwell County Park—park WI-6
Petenwell Dam—dam WI-6
Petenwell Flowage WI-6
Petenwell Lake—reservoir WI-6
Petenwell Rock—summit WI-6
Petenwell Rsvr WI-6
Petenwell Wilderness Park—park WI-6
Pete Osceola Seminole Village—locale FL-3
Pete Osceolas Farm—locale FL-3
Pete Ott Creek—stream ID-8
Pete Ott Lake—lake ID-8
Pete Parent Peak—summit VT-1
Petepawag Plantation MA-1
Pete Peterson Bridge—bridge AL-4
Peter—locale IA-7
Peter, Mount—summit NY-2
Peter, Mount—summit TN-4
Peter, Point—cape AL-4
Peter and Paul Cem—cemetery IN-6
Peter and Paul Cem—cemetery NJ-2
Peter and Paul Lake MI-6
Peter and Paul Lakes—lake MI-6
Peterball Spring—spring MO-7
Peterbaugh Mountains PA-2
Peter Bay—bay MO-7
Peter Bay—bay VI-3
Peter Beach—beach NJ-2
Peter Blow Bend—bend TN-4
Peterboro (2) NH-1
**Peterboro**—pop pl NY-2
Peterboro Creek—stream AK-9
Peterboro Land Office—hist pl NY-2
Peterboro Street Elem Sch—hist pl NY-2
Peterboro Swamp—swamp NY-2
**Peterborough**—pop pl NH-1
**Peterborough Compact**—pop pl NH-1
**Peterborough (Town of)**—pop pl NH-1
Peterborough Unitarian Church—hist pl NH-1
Peter Branch TX-5
Peter Branch—stream (9) KY-4
Peter Branch—stream MO-7
Peter Branch—stream TN-4
Peter Branch—stream TX-5
Peter Brown Sch—school CO-8
Peter Buck Trail—trail PA-2
Peter Cable Place—locale TN-4
Peter Camp Branch—stream TN-4
Peter Cave—cave IL-6
Peter Cave—cave (2) KY-4
Peter Cave—cave MO-7
Peter Cave—cave (3) TN-4
Peter Cave—locale AR-4
Peter Cave Bluff—cliff KY-4
Petercave Branch—stream KY-4
Peter Cave Branch—stream (3) KY-4
Petercave Branch—stream KY-4
Peter Cave Branch—stream KY-4
Peter Cave Branch—stream TN-4
Peter Cave Branch—stream WV-2
Petercave Branch—stream WV-2
Peter Cave Cove—valley TN-4
Peter Cave Creek TN-4
Peter Cave Creek—stream KY-4
Peter Cave Creek—stream OH-6
Peter Cave Creek—stream TN-4
Petercave Fork—stream KY-4
Peter Cave Fork—stream WV-2
Peter Cave Hill—summit KY-4
Peter Cave Hollow—valley IN-6
Peter Cave Hollow—valley KY-4
Peter Cave Hollow—valley (3) MO-7
Peter Cave Hollow—valley OH-6
Peter Cave Hollow—valley TN-4
Peter Cave No 1—cave MO-7
Peter Cave No 2—cave MO-7
Peter Cave Ridge—ridge TN-4
Peter Cave Run—stream KY-4
Peter Chapel—church NC-3
Peter Cleaver Lake—lake AK-9
Peter Cove ME-1
Peter Cove—bay ME-1
Peter Cove—valley GA-3
Peter Cove—valley NC-3
Peter Cove Branch TN-4
Peter Cove Branch—stream NC-3
Peter Cove Creek—stream NC-3
Peter Cove Creek—stream TN-4
Peter Cove Mtn—summit NC-3
Peter Creek AL-4
Peter Creek KS-7
Peter Creek MI-6
Peter Creek MS-4
Peter Creek OR-9
Peter Creek TX-5
Peter Creek—locale KY-4
Peter Creek—stream AL-4
Peter Creek—stream AK-9
Peter Creek—stream AR-4
Peter Creek—stream CO-8
Peter Creek—stream IN-6
Peter Creek—stream KS-7
Peter Creek—stream (2) KY-4
Peter Creek—stream LA-4
Peter Creek—stream MO-7
Peter Creek—stream NJ-2
Peter Creek—stream NC-3
Peter Creek—stream VA-3
Peter Creek Cem—cemetery MO-7
Peter Creek (Township of)—fmr MCD AR-4
**Peter Dana Point**—pop pl ME-1
Peter Dan Creek—stream WA-9
Peter Deswood Well—well AZ-5
Peter Dick Gap—gap NC-3
Peter Dinsdale Dam—dam OR-9
Peter Ditch—canal IN-6
Peter Dotson Hollow—valley KY-4
Peter Dozier Pond—lake NC-3
Peter Everett Branch—stream KY-4
Peterfish Gap—gap VA-3
Peterfish Run—stream VA-3
Peter Fork—stream (2) KY-4
Peter Fork—stream WV-2
Peter Fouchard Grant—civil FL-3
Peter Gap—gap KY-4
Peter George Lake—lake AR-4
Peter Gibson Pond—lake FL-3
Peter Gold Point—cape AL-4
Peter Green Hollow—valley AR-4
Peter Grove Ch—church FL-3
Peter Grubb Hut—building CA-9
Peter Grube Ditch—canal IN-6
Peter Grube Ditch—canal OH-6
Peter Gulch—valley CA-9
Peter Hall Branch—stream TN-4
Peter Hawks Creek—stream SC-3
Peter Hayes Hill—summit TX-5
Peter Hill MA-1
Peter Hill—summit CA-9
Peter Hill—summit MA-1
Peter Hill—summit TX-5
Peter Hill Cem—cemetery AL-4
Peter Hollow—valley AR-4
Peter Hollow—valley ID-8
Peter House—hist pl AZ-5
Peterhouse Creek—stream TN-4
Peter Hoy Sch—school IL-6
Pete Ridge—ridge MT-8
Peter Island—island AK-9
Pete Ritts Hollow—valley UT-8
Peter Joe Hamilton Elem Sch—school AL-4
Peter John Mtn—summit AK-9
Peter Johnson Run—stream WV-2
Peter Kane Mountain—other CA-9
Peter Kane Water Hole—spring CA-9
Peter Kill Knolls UT-8
Peter King—locale NC-3
Peterkin Pond—lake WI-6
Peterkins Branch—stream DE-2
Peter Knob—summit (2) GA-3
Peter Lake MI-6
Peter Lake—lake CA-9
Peter Lake—lake MI-6
Peter Lake—lake (2) MN-6
Peter Lassen Grave—locale CA-9
Peter Lassen Marker—locale CA-9
Peter Lee Island—island LA-4
Peter Lockett Canyon—valley AZ-5
Peter Lockett Tank—reservoir AZ-5
Peter Long Lake—lake NE-7
Peter L Windmill—locale TX-5
Peterman—locale AL-4
**Peterman**—pop pl AL-4
Peterman Airp—airport MO-7
Peterman Bend—bend TN-4
Peterman Brook—stream WI-6
Peterman (CCD)—cens area AL-4
Peterman Cem—cemetery MO-7
Peterman Creek—stream AL-4
Peterman Creek—stream NV-8
Peterman Division—civil AL-4
Peterman Gulch—valley CO-8
Peterman Hill—summit CA-9
Peterman Island OR-9
Peterman Lake—lake MI-6
Peterman Lookout Tower—locale AR-4
**Peterman Ridge**—pop pl OK-5
Peterman Run—stream PA-2
**Peter Mans Corner**—pop pl PA-2
Peterman Spring Branch—stream TN-4
Petermans Station (historical)—locale AZ-5
Peter Martin Hill—summit AR-4
Peter Mashoes Creek—stream NC-3
Peter May Ditch—canal OH-6
Peter McIntyre County Park—park CA-9
Peter McQueens Village FL-3
Peter Miller Cem—cemetery TN-4
Peter Miranda Grant—civil FL-3
Peter Mooney Mtn—summit MO-7
Peter Mount—summit OR-9
Peter Mtn—summit KY-4
Peter Mtn—summit (2) ME-1
Peter Ogden Sch—school WA-9
Peter Pande Lake—lake CA-9
Peter Pan Park—park KS-7
Peter Pan Park—park NE-7
Peter Pan Sch—school CA-9
Peter Pan Sch—school DC-2
Peter Pan Sch—school MI-6
Peter Paul Prairie—area OR-9
Peter Peak—summit CA-9
Peter Peak—summit VI-3
**Peterpender**—pop pl AR-4
Peter Phalia Creek MS-4
Peter Piper Sch—school CT-1
Peter Point—cape WA-9
Peter Pond MA-1
Peter Pond—lake GA-3
Peter Pond—reservoir MA-1
Peter Pond Dam—dam MA-1
Peter Post Canyon—valley UT-8
Peterptor Creek—stream CA-9
Peter Quarter NC-3
Peter Quin Senior Cemetery MS-4
Peter Ready Creek—stream ID-8
Peter Ready Spring—spring ID-8
Peter Renfro Cave—cave MO-7
Peter River MA-1
Peter Rock Cave—cave TN-4
Peter Rock Point—cape AR-4
Peters IL-6
Peters KS-7
Peters—airport NJ-2
Peters—locale AR-4
Peters—locale CA-9
Peters—locale TX-5
**Peters**—pop pl FL-3
**Peters**—pop pl MI-6
**Peters**—pop pl ND-7
Peters, Charles, Sr., House—hist pl MI-6
Peters, Edward C., House—hist pl GA-3

Peters Spring—spring AZ-5
Peters Spring—spring OR-9
Peters Spring—spring UT-8
Peters Spring Dam PA-2
Peters Spring Run Dam—dam PA-2
Peters Springs—spring CA-9
Peters State Wildlife Mngmt Area—park MN-6
Peters Store—pop pl PA-2
Peters Swale—stream TX-5
Peters Swamp—swamp NC-3
Peters Swamp—swamp SC-3
Peters Switch—pop pl IN-6
Peters Tabernacle—church NC-3
Peters Tank—reservoir (2) AZ-5
Peter Stevens Hill—summit KY-4
Peterstown—locale IL-6
Peterstown—pop pl WV-2
Peterstown House—hist pl IL-6
Peters Township—pop pl KS-7
Peters Township HS—school PA-2
Peters (Township of)—pop pl (2) PA-2
Peters Township Sch—school PA-2
Peters Trail—trail AZ-5
Peters Trail—trail PA-2
Peters Tump—island VA-3
Peter Stuyvesant—uninc pl NY-2
Peters Valley NJ-2
Peters Valley Hist Dist—hist pl NJ-2
Petersville KS-7
Petersville PA-2
Petersville—locale AK-9
Petersville—locale IL-6
Petersville—locale IA-7
Petersville—locale KY-4
Petersville—locale MO-7
Petersville—locale TX-5
Petersville—pop pl AL-4
Petersville—pop pl IN-6
Petersville—pop pl MD-2
Petersville—pop pl NC-3
Petersville—pop pl (2) PA-2
Petersville Cem—cemetery GA-3
Petersville Cem—cemetery ND-7
Petersville Cem—cemetery VA-3
Petersville Ch—church VA-3
Petersville Missionary Baptist Ch—church AL-4
Petersville Post Office (historical)—building PA-2
Petersville Sch—school TX-5
Petersville Township—pop pl ND-7
Peter Swamp—stream NC-3
Peters Wash UT-8
Peters Wash—stream AZ-5
Peters Waterhole—reservoir OR-9
Peters Well—well AZ-5
Peters Well—well NM-5
Peters Windmill—locale NM-5
Peters Windmill—locale TX-5
Peters 1 Dam—dam SD-7
Peterton—locale KS-7
Petertown—pop pl MS-4
Peter Trace—stream KY-4
Peter Weaver Creek—stream NC-3
Peter Wentz Homestead—locale PA-2
Peter White Lake MI-6
Peter White Lake—lake MI-6
Peter Woods Farm (historical)—locale TX-5
Petery, Mount—summit MT-8
Peter Young Mtn—summit GA-3
Pete's Airp—airport WA-9
Petes Branch—stream KY-4
Petes Branch—stream TN-4
Petes Branch Trail—trail TN-4
Petes Cabin—locale NV-8
Petes Cabin Mesa—summit AZ-5
Petes Camp Creek—stream OR-9
Petes Camp (site)—locale OR-9
Petes Canyon—basin NM-5
Petes Canyon—valley MT-8
Petes Canyon—valley NV-8
Petes Canyon—valley (4) UT-8
Petes Canyon—valley WA-9
Petes Canyon—valley WY-8
Pete Sch—school TX-5
Petes Corner—locale OK-5
Petes Coulee—valley MT-8
Petes Cove—bay CO-8
Petes Cove—bay UT-8
Petes Creek KS-7
Pete's Creek WY-8
Petes Creek—stream AK-9
Petes Creek—stream CA-9
Petes Creek—stream ID-8
Petes Creek—stream MI-6
Petes Creek—stream MN-6
Petes Creek—stream NY-2
Petes Creek—stream ND-7
Petes Creek—stream (2) SD-7
Petes Creek—stream UT-8
Petes Creek—stream (3) WA-9
Petes Crossroads—pop pl AL-4
Petes Draw—valley WY-8
Petes Fork—stream UT-8
Petes Fork—stream WV-2
Petes Gap—gap WY-8
Petes Gulch—valley ID-8
Pete Shanty Hollow—valley MO-7
Petes Hill—summit NY-2
Petes Hole—basin WY-8
Petes Hole—lake UT-8
Petes Hole—valley UT-8
Petes Hole Dam—dam UT-8
Petes Hole Rsvr—reservoir (2) UT-8
Petes Hollow—valley UT-8
Pete's Island IL-6
Petes Island—island FL-3
Petes Island—island ME-1
Petes Knoll—summit NV-8
Petes Knoll—summit UT-8
Petes Lagoon—lake LA-4
Petes Lake MS-4
Petes Lake—lake ID-8
Petes Lake—lake MI-6
Petes Lake—lake (2) MS-4
Petes Lake—lake NE-7
Petes Lake—lake OR-9
Petes Lake—lake WY-8
Petes Lake—reservoir CO-8
Petes Lakes—lake MN-6
Petes Lake Trail—trail WY-8
Petes Landing—locale WI-6
Pete Slough—stream MS-4
Petes Mesa—summit UT-8
Pete Smith Hill—summit NE-7
Pete Smith Peak AZ-5
Petes Mountain—ridge OR-9
Petes Mtn AZ-5
Petes Mtn—summit OR-9
Petes Mtn—summit TN-4
Petes Pass—channel AK-9
Petes Pasture—plain CA-9
Petes Peak OR-9
Petes Place—locale CO-8
Petes Place—locale WY-8
Petes Point—summit OR-9
Petes Pond—lake IA-7
Petes Pond—lake ME-1
Petes Pond—reservoir CA-9
Petes Pond—reservoir UT-8
Petes Post—summit CO-8
Pete Spring—spring AZ-5
Pete Spring—spring CA-9
Pete Spring—spring CO-8
Pete Spring—spring MT-8
Pete Spring—spring (2) NV-8
Pete Spring—spring NM-5
Pete Spring—spring WY-8
Pete Spring Gulch—valley CO-8
Petes Puddle—lake OR-9
Petes Rest Cem—cemetery LA-4
Petes Retreat Pond—lake AZ-5
Petes Rsvr—reservoir UT-8
Petes Rsvr—reservoir WY-8
Petes Run—stream IN-6
Petes Run—stream WV-2
Petes Run Cem—cemetery IN-6
Petes Slough Rsvr—reservoir OR-9
Petes Spring—spring CA-9
Petes Spring—spring MT-8
Petes Spring—spring (3) NV-8
Petes Spring—spring (2) UT-8
Petes Summit—gap NV-8
Petes Tank—reservoir (4) AZ-5
Pete Steele Bench—bench UT-8
Pete Stones Creek—gut FL-3
Petes Tractor Salvage Airp—airport ND-7
Petes Valley—valley CA-9
Petes Wash—stream AZ-5
Petes Wash—valley UT-8
Petes Well—well AZ-5
Petes Well—well NV-8
Petes Well—well NM-5
Pete Tank—reservoir (3) AZ-5
Petet Cem—cemetery MO-7
Petetin—pop pl LA-4
Pete Trap Windmill—locale TX-5
Pete Turner Ridge—ridge AR-4
Pete Windmill—locale NM-5
Pete Winward Dam—dam UT-8
Pete Winward Rsvr—reservoir UT-8
Pete W Slough—lake SD-7
Pet Ex Sch—school KY-4
Petey—pop pl AL-4
Peth—locale KY-4
Peth—pop pl NY-2
Peth—pop pl VT-1
Pet Hanson Creek NV-8
Pet Haven Cem—cemetery IL-6
Pet Haven Cem—cemetery IA-7
Pethicks Island MA-1
Pet Hill Ditch—canal CA-9
Pe'thmuth FM-9
Pet Hollow—valley MO-7
Pet Hollow—valley (2) UT-8
Petickfaw MS-4
Petikilos—island FM-9
Petillo Hill Cem—cemetery AR-4
Petit NJ-2
Petit, Bayou—gut LA-4
Petit Amite River LA-4
Petit Bay Chene Fleur—lake LA-4
Petit Bayou Bourbeux—gut LA-4
Petit Bois Bayou—gut LA-4
Petitbois Island MS-4
Petit Bois Island—island MS-4
Petit Bois Pass—channel AL-4
Petit Caillou, Bayou—stream LA-4
Petit Cem—cemetery OH-6
Petit Chackbay, Bayou—stream LA-4
Petit Chaouvanons AL-4
Petit Chou Island GA-3
Petit Creek—stream IL-6
Petite Amite River—stream LA-4
Petite Anse LA-4
Petite Anse, Bayou—stream LA-4
Petite Anse Canal—canal LA-4
Petite Baie—bay LA-4
Petite Baie—gut LA-4
Petite Bay LA-4
Petite Bayou LA-4
Petite Bayou Chene Blanc LA-4
Petite Branch—stream AR-4
Petite Brook—stream ME-1
Petite Gulf MS-4
Petite Lac au Grand Prerion LA-4
Petite Lac Du Grand LA-4
Petite Lac du Grande Prerion LA-4
Petite Lake—lake IL-6
Petite Lake—lake MI-6
Petite Lake—pop pl IL-6
Petite Passe, Bayou—stream LA-4
Petite Pointe au Sable MI-6
Petite Prairie, Bayou—stream LA-4
Petite Riviere—stream LA-4
Petite Riviere de Cansez KS-7
Petite Saline KS-7
Petite Saline Creek—stream MO-7
Petites Gap—gap VA-3
Petite Subdivision—pop pl TN-4
Petit Felix Pond—bay LA-4
Petit Gap AL-4
Petit Gap VA-3
Petit Gouke Hammock Island—island GA-3
Petit Gulf MS-4
Petit Gulf Hills—summit MS-4
Petit Hollow—valley TN-4
Petit Hollow Branch—stream TN-4
Petition Rsvr—reservoir ID-8
Petition Well—well TX-5
Petit Jean—locale AR-4
Petit Jean Creek AR-4
Petit Jean Mountain—ridge AR-4
Petit Jean Mtn—summit AR-4
Petit Jean No. 10—hist pl AR-4
Petit Jean No. 11—hist pl AR-4
Petit Jean No. 4—hist pl AR-4
Petit Jean No. 5—hist pl AR-4
Petit Jean No. 6—hist pl AR-4
Petit Jean No. 7—hist pl AR-4
Petit Jean No. 9—hist pl AR-4
Petit Jean River—stream AR-4
Petit Jean River State Wildlife Mngmt Area—park AR-4
Petit Jean State Park—park AR-4
Petit Jean (Township of)—fmr MCD (3) AR-4
Petit Lac—lake (2) LA-4
Petit Lac Des Allemands—lake LA-4
Petit Lac du Grand Bryon—lake LA-4
Petit Lac L'Huit—lake LA-4
Petit Lake—lake LA-4
Petit Lake—lake (2) MN-6
Petit Lake—lake UT-8
Petit Lake—lake WA-9
Petit Lateral—canal CO-8
Petit Liard, Bayou—gut LA-4
Petit Manan Bar—bar ME-1
Petit Manan Island—island ME-1
Petit Manan Light Station—hist pl ME-1
Petit Manan Point—cape ME-1
Petit Manan Reef—bar ME-1
Petit Pass des Ilettes—gut LA-4
Petit Peak—summit ID-8
Petitpierre-Kleinpeter, Joseph, House—hist pl LA-4
Petitte Rautox MS-4
Petitt Lake ID-8
Petitt Sch—school TX-5
Petitt Spring—spring OK-5
Petiw—locale FM-9
Pet Lake—lake AK-9
Pet Lake—lake MN-6
Petlier (historical)—pop pl TN-4
Petmaker Canyon—valley NM-5
Petmaker Tank—reservoir NM-5
Pet Memorial Cem—cemetery TN-4
Pet Memorial Park—park TX-5
Petobego Pond—lake MI-6
Petoch Butte—summit NM-5
Petoch Wash—stream NM-5
Petogansett Lake CT-1
Petonia, Lake—lake NY-2
Petoskey—pop pl MI-6
Petoskey Downtown Hist Dist—hist pl MI-6
Petoskey Grocery Company Bldg—hist pl MI-6
Petoskey Hunting Club—other MI-6
Petoskey Public Works Utility Bldg—hist pl MI-6
Petosukara MH-9
Petra—locale KY-4
Petra Mills—locale NC-3
Petran—pop pl MN-6
Petranek Number 1 Dam—dam SD-7
Petras Branch—stream VA-3
Petras Ravine—valley WI-6
Petre, Bayou—gut LA-4
Petrea—pop pl OH-6
Petrea Cem—cemetery IL-6
Petree Cem—cemetery MS-4
Petree Cem—cemetery TX-5
Petree Lake—reservoir NC-3
Petree Lake Dam—dam NC-3
Petree Mtn—summit OK-5
Petree Sch—school FL-3
Petre Island—island NY-2
Petrel—locale ND-7
Petrel Bank—other AK-9
Petrel Cem—cemetery ND-7
Petrel Creek—stream MN-6
Petrel-Insel MP-9
Petrel Island MP-9
Petrel Island—island (2) AK-9
Petrelli-DelPizzo House—hist pl CO-8
Petrel Point—cape (2) AK-9
Petrel Point—cape FL-3
Petre Meadows—flat OR-9
Petreo, Arroyo—stream CA-9
Pet Rest Memorial Park (Cemetery)—cemetery NC-3
Petrey—pop pl AL-4
Petrey Cem—cemetery AL-4
Petrey-Highland Home (CCD)—cens area AL-4
Petrey-Highland Home Division—civil AL-4
Petrey Pond—reservoir AL-4
Petri—locale KY-4
Petri Cem—cemetery MN-6
Petric Park—park OR-9
Petrie KY-4
Petrie—locale WY-8
Petrie—pop pl KY-4
Petrie—uninc pl AZ-5
Petrie Cave Hollow—valley AR-4
Petrie Cem—cemetery OH-6
Petrie Cem—cemetery PA-2
Petrie Creek WI-6
Petrie House—hist pl KY-4
Petrie Mesa—summit CO-8
Petrie Playground—park HI-9
Petrie RR Station—building AZ-5
Petries Corners—pop pl NY-2
Petrieville—locale MI-6
Petrified Canyon—valley CA-9
Petrified Canyon—valley NV-8
Petrified Canyon—valley WA-9
Petrified Creek CO-8
Petrified Creek—stream AZ-5
Petrified For—area AZ-5
Petrified For—area UT-8
Petrified Forest MT-8
Petrified Forest—locale CA-9
Petrified Forest Bridge—hist pl AZ-5
Petrified Forest Natl Monmt AZ-5
Petrified Forest Natl Park—park AZ-5
Petrified Forest Overpass—crossing AZ-5
Petrified Forest Tank—reservoir AZ-5
Petrified Forest Trail—trail UT-8
Petrified Hollow—valley UT-8
Petrified Hollow Wash—valley UT-8
Petrified Lake—lake ND-7
Petrified Ridge—ridge WY-8
Petrified Rsvr—reservoir OR-9
Petrified Sand Dunes—area UT-8
Petrified Tank—reservoir AZ-5
Petrified Wash—stream NV-8
Petrified Wood Rsvr—reservoir WY-8
Petrifying Springs Park—park WI-6
Petrillo Lake—reservoir NY-2
Petri Ranch—locale ND-7
Petri Sch—school IL-6
Petri Station KY-4
Petrodie Cem—cemetery SD-7
Petrof Bay—bay AK-9
Petrof Glacier—glacier AK-9
Petrof Point—cape AK-9
Petroglyph Butte—summit NV-8
Petroglyph Canyon—hist pl MT-8
Petroglyph Canyon—valley CA-9
Petroglyph Lake—lake OR-9
Petroglyph Point Archeol Site—hist pl CA-9
Petroglyph Site—hist pl VI-3
Petroglyphs Tank—reservoir AZ-5
Petroglyph Wash—valley AZ-5
Petro Hollow—valley IN-6
Petrokov Lake—lake AK-9
Petrolea CA-9
Petroleum—pop pl IN-6
Petroleum—pop pl KY-4
Petroleum—pop pl OH-6
Petroleum—pop pl WV-2
Petroleum Bldg—hist pl OK-5
Petroleum Center—locale PA-2
Petroleum Centre PA-2
Petroleum City PA-2
Petroleum Club—other CA-9
Petroleum Creek—stream CA-9
Petroleum Creek—stream WA-9
Petroleum Lake—lake CO-8
Petroleum Peak WY-8
Petroleum Peak—summit WY-8
Petroleum Sch—school IN-6
Petrolia—pop pl CA-9
Petrolia—pop pl IL-6
Petrolia—pop pl KS-7
Petrolia—pop pl MT-8
Petrolia—pop pl PA-2
Petrolia—pop pl TX-5
Petrolia Borough—civil PA-2
Petrolia Lake—reservoir MT-8
Petrolia Oil Field—oilfield TX-5
Petrolia Reservoirs—reservoir TX-5
Petrolla—pop pl NY-2
Petrolla Lake MT-8
Petrol Point FL-3
Petronella—locale VI-3
Petronia—pop pl AL-4
Petronia Sch—school AL-4
Petronila—pop pl TX-5
Petronila Creek TX-5
Petronila Creek—stream TX-5
Petronilla TX-5
Petronilla Creek TX-5
Petro Park—park IN-6
Petros TN-4
Petros—locale KY-4
Petros—pop pl OK-5
Petros—pop pl TN-4
Petros First Baptist Ch—church TN-4
Petros HS—school TN-4
Petros Joyner Elem Sch TN-4
Petros Post Office—building TN-4
Petross—locale GA-3
Petross Creek—stream WA-9
Petross Sidehill—summit WA-9
Petroteros Windmill—locale TX-5
Petrow Lake—lake MI-6
Pet Run—stream OH-6
Petruska Park—park NJ-2
Petry Branch—stream MI-6
Petry Bridge—bridge LA-4
Petry Cem—cemetery LA-4
Petry Cem—cemetery MO-7
Petryk Lake—lake WI-6
Petsch Ditch No 1—canal WY-8
Petsch Ranch—locale TX-5
Petsch Ranch—locale WY-8
Petsch Rsvr—reservoir WY-8
Pets Spring—spring UT-8
Petsworth Ch—church VA-3
Petsworth (Magisterial District)—fmr MCD VA-3
Pett MN-6
Pet Tank—reservoir AZ-5
Pet Tank—reservoir TX-5
Pettapiece Badland—area MT-8
Pettaquamscutt Pond RI-1
Pettaquamscutt Cove—bay RI-1
Pettaquamscutt Lake Shores—pop pl RI-1
Pettaquamscutt River—stream RI-1
Pettaquamscutt Rock—pillar RI-1
Pettas Hollow—valley TN-4
Pettee Brook—stream CT-1
Pettee Pond—lake MA-1
Pettees ME-1
Pettees Point—cape ME-1
Pettefer, Harry, House—hist pl AR-4
Pettegrave Point ME-1
Pettegrew Lateral—canal OR-9
Pettegrew Mtn—summit ME-1
Pettegrove Point—cape ME-1
Petteiquaggamack ME-1
Petteiquaggamas ME-1
Pettengill House and Farm—hist pl ME-1
Pettengill Sch—school ME-1
Pettengill Stream—stream ME-1
Petterson Canyon—valley ID-8
Petterson Ranch—locale ID-8
Petterson Tank—reservoir AZ-5
Pettet Pond—reservoir NJ-2
Pettets Pond NJ-2
Petteway—locale TX-5
Petteway Ch—church TX-5
Pettey Cem MS-4
Pettey Post Office (historical)—building AL-4
Petteys Cem—cemetery OR-9
Pettibone—locale TX-5
Pettibone—pop pl ND-7
Pettibone Brook—stream MA-1
Pettibone Cem—cemetery ND-7
Pettibone Creek—stream ID-8
Pettibone Creek—stream MI-6
Pettibone Lake—lake MI-6
Pettibone Park—park WI-6
Pettibone Post Office (historical)—building TN-4
Pettibone Ridge—ridge ID-8
Pettibone Sch—school MO-7
Pettibone Township—pop pl ND-7
Petticamp Swamp—swamp FL-3
Petticks Island MA-1
Petticoat Bayou—stream LA-4
Petticoat Bridge—bridge NJ-2
Petticoat Creek—stream MI-6
Petticoat Creek—stream OR-9
Petticoat Hill—summit MA-1
Petticoat Hill—summit OK-5
Petticoat Lake—lake MI-6
Petticoat Mtn—summit CA-9
Petticoat Peak—summit ID-8
Petties Branch—stream NJ-2
Pettiet Branch—stream GA-3
Pettifer Island—island IL-6
Pettiford Ch—church NC-3
Pettiford Creek—stream NC-3
Pettiford Creek Bay—bay NC-3
Pettifor Lake—lake MI-6
Pettigrew—locale TX-5
Pettigrew—pop pl AR-4
Pettigrew, R. F., and Tate, S. L., Bldg—hist pl SD-7
Pettigrew Bend—bend VA-3
Pettigrew Branch—stream TX-5
Pettigrew Brook—stream NY-2
Pettigrew Cem—cemetery MO-7
Pettigrew Cem—cemetery NC-3
Pettigrew Creek—stream MS-4
Pettigrew Dam—dam SD-7
Pettigrew Family Cem NC-3
Pettigrew Gulch—valley SD-7
Pettigrew House—hist pl CA-9
Pettigrew-Ivy Family Cem—cemetery MS-4
Pettigrew Pond Number 1 Dam—dam SD-7
Pettigrew Pond Number 2 Dam—dam SD-7
Pettigrew Ranch—locale NM-5
Pettigrew Sch (historical)—school MS-4
Pettigrew State Park—park NC-3
Pettigrew Trail—trail SD-7
Pettigrove Point ME-1
Pettigrow State Park Information Center—building NC-3
Pettigrew State Park Office—building NC-3
Pettigru Street Hist Dist—hist pl SC-3
Pettijohn Basin—basin CA-9
Pettijohn Branch—stream TN-4
Pettijohn Creek—stream OR-9
Pettijohn Creek—stream TN-4
Pettijohn Creek—stream WA-9
Pettijohn Hollow—valley MO-7
Pettijohn Lake—lake AR-4
Pettijohn Mtn—summit CA-9
Pettijohn Ranch—locale SD-7
Pettijohns Creek WA-9
Pettingell Lake—lake CO-8
Pettingell Peak—summit CO-8
Pettinger AR-4
Pettinger Canyon—valley CA-9
Pettinghill Pond ME-1
Pettingill Brook—stream ME-1
Pettingill Brook—stream NH-1
Pettingill Island—island ME-1
Pettingill-Morron House—hist pl IL-6
Pettingill Park—park ME-1
Pettingill Pond—lake ME-1
Pettingill Ridge—ridge ME-1
Pettingill Stream ME-1
Pettipoole Hill—summit AL-4
Pettiquah Creek—stream OK-5
Pettis PA-2
Pettis—pop pl IA-7
Pettis—pop pl PA-2
Pettis—pop pl VA-3
Pettis Brook NY-2
Pettis Cem—cemetery TN-4
Pettis Chapel—church MS-4
Pettis Corners—locale PA-2
Pettis County—pop pl MO-7
Pettis Creek GA-3
Pettis Creek—stream MI-6
Pettis Creek—stream MO-7
Pettis Creek—stream PA-2
Pettis Peak—summit ID-8
Pettis Point ID-8
Pettis Pond—lake (2) FL-3
Pettis Ranch—locale AZ-5
Pettis Rocks—island ME-1
Pettis Township—civil (2) MO-7
Pettisville—pop pl OH-6
Pettit—locale OK-5
Pettit—other MS-4
Pettit—pop pl IN-6
Pettit—pop pl KY-4
Pettit—pop pl MN-6
Pettit—pop pl (2) TX-5
Pettit and Pfanders Claim Mine—mine SD-7
Pettit Bay—pop pl OK-5
Pettit Bay Public Use Area—park OK-5
Pettit Branch—stream NY-2
Pettit Branch—stream TX-5
Pettit Branch—stream VA-3
Pettit Campground—locale ID-8
Pettit Cem—cemetery KY-4
Pettit Cem—cemetery MO-7
Pettit Cem—cemetery NY-2
Pettit Cem—cemetery TN-4
Pettit Ch—church AR-4
Pettit Chapel—church OK-5
Pettit Cove—valley GA-3
Pettit Creek—stream AR-4
Pettit Creek—stream (3) GA-3
Pettit Creek—stream OK-5
Pettit Dam—dam OR-9
Pettit Ditch—canal IN-6
Pettit Heights—pop pl WV-2
Pettit Island—island NJ-2
Pettit Island—island VA-3
Pettit Lake—lake ID-8
Pettit Lake—lake MI-6
Pettit Lake—reservoir GA-3
Pettit Marsh—swamp NY-2
Pettit Memorial Chapel—hist pl IL-6
Pettit Mtn—summit NY-2
Pettit Mtn—summit OK-5
Pettit Oil Field—oilfield TX-5
Pettit Park—park IN-6
Pettit Park Elem Sch—school IN-6
Pettit Park School—school IN-6
Pettit Peak—summit CA-9
Pettit Place (Site)—locale CA-9
Pettit Pocosin—swamp VA-3
Pettit Prairie Flats—flat TX-5
Pettit Ranch—locale TX-5
Pettit Ridge—ridge GA-3
Pettit Rsvr—reservoir OR-9
Pettit Run—stream PA-2
Pettits PA-2
Pettits—locale TX-5
Pettit's, James, Mill—hist pl KY-4
Pettit San Andreas Oil Field—oilfield TX-5
Pettits Fishponds—reservoir AL-4
Pettit's Ford—hist pl PA-2
Pettits Peak—summit CA-9
Pettit Spring—spring ID-8
Pettitt Cem—cemetery NC-3
Pettitts Branch—stream IA-7
Pettit Tunnel—tunnel VA-3
Pettry—locale WV-2
Pettry Bottom—pop pl WV-2
Pettry Cem—cemetery (3) WV-2
Petts Draw—valley WY-8
Petts Lake—lake MI-6
Petts Tank—reservoir NM-5
Pettucks Island MA-1
Pettus—locale AR-4
Pettus—pop pl TX-5
Pettus—pop pl WV-2
Pettus Branch—stream TN-4
Pettus Cem—cemetery (2) AL-4
Pettus Cem—cemetery AR-4
Pettus Cem—cemetery MO-7
Pettus Cem—cemetery TN-4
Pettus Cem—cemetery TX-5
Pettus North Oil Field—oilfield TX-5
Pettus Oil Field—oilfield TX-5
Pettus Park—park TN-4
Pettus-Pawnee (CCD)—cens area TX-5
Pettus (Township of)—fmr MCD AR-4
Pettusville—pop pl AL-4
Pettusville Ch—church AL-4
Pettusville Church Cem—cemetery AL-4
Pettusville Methodist Church AL-4
Pettway Cem—cemetery AL-4
Petty—locale TX-5
Petty—pop pl TX-5
Petty, Point—cape UT-8
Petty Bluff—cliff TN-4
Pettyboro—locale NH-1
Pettyboro Brook—stream NH-1
Petty Branch—gut FL-3
Petty Branch—stream AL-4
Petty Branch—stream IL-6
Petty Branch—stream KY-4
Petty Branch—stream (6) TN-4
Petty Brook—stream NH-1
Petty Butte—summit CA-9
Petty Cave—cave (2) TN-4
Petty Cem—cemetery AL-4
Petty Cem—cemetery GA-3
Petty Cem—cemetery (3) KY-4
Petty Cem—cemetery MS-4
Petty Cem—cemetery MO-7
Petty Cem—cemetery (4) TN-4
Petty Chapel—church MS-4
Petty Corner—locale NY-2
Petty Creek ME-1
Petty Creek MT-8
Petty Creek—gut FL-3
Petty Creek—stream CO-8
Petty Creek—stream (3) MT-8
Petty Creek—stream TX-5
Petty Creek—stream UT-8
Petty Crown Creek Trail—trail MT-8
Petty Flat—flat CA-9
Petty Ford Creek Trail—trail MT-8
Petty Gap TN-4
Petty Gap—gap NC-3
Pettygrove, Benjamin S., House—hist pl WA-9
Petty Gulch—valley WA-9
Petty Gulf—bay NC-3
Petty Gulf Lake—lake FL-3
Petty Hill Elem Sch (historical)—school AL-4
Petty Hollow—valley MO-7
Petty Hollow—valley (4) TN-4
Petty Hollow—valley TX-5
Petty Island—island NJ-2
Pettyjohn Cem—cemetery VA-3
Pettyjohn Island—island VA-3
Pettyjohn Mill—locale TN-4
Pettyjohn Place—locale CA-9
Petty Knob—summit KY-4
Petty Knoll—summit AZ-5
Petty Lake MI-6
Petty Lake—lake IN-6
Petty Lake—lake WI-6
Petty Mtn—summit MT-8
Petty Point ME-1
Petty Point—cape NC-3
Petty Point—cape TN-4
Petty Pond FL-3
Petty Post Office AL-4
Petty Ranch—locale WY-8
Petty Ridge—ridge WA-9
Petty-Roberts-Beatty House—hist pl AL-4
Pettys Bayou—bay MI-6
Pettys Bight—bay NY-2
Pettys Bluff—cliff AL-4
Petty Sch—school IL-6
Petty Sch—school NY-2
Pettys Chapel—church AR-4
Pettys Chapel—church TX-5
Pettys Chapel—pop pl TX-5
Pettys Chapel AME Zion Ch—church AL-4
Petty Sch (historical)—school (2) MS-4
Pettys Corner—locale VA-3
Petty's Creek GA-3
Pettys Creek—stream TX-5
Pettys Fork—stream (2) KY-4
Pettys Gap—gap TN-4
Pettys Hill—pop pl MO-7
Pettys Island NJ-2
Pettys Island—pop pl NJ-2
Pettys Lake—lake MI-6
Pettys Lake—reservoir NC-3
Pettys Lake Dam—dam NC-3

Pettys Point ... ME-1
Pettys Pond—lake ... NC-3
Petty Spring—spring ... MO-7
Petty Spring—spring ... TN-4
Petty Spring—spring ... WA-9
**Pettys Shore**—pop pl ... NC-3
Pettys Spring—spring ... MO-7
**Pettysville**—pop pl ... IN-6
**Pettysville**—pop pl ... MI-6
Pettytown—locale ... TX-5
**Petty (Township of)**—pop pl ... IL-6
**Pettyview**—pop pl ... AR-4
Pettyville ... UT-8
**Pettyville**—pop pl ... AR-4
**Pettyville**—pop pl ... WV-2
Petty Well—well ... NM-5
Petty Windmill—locale ... NM-5
Petty Windmill—locale ... TX-5
Pe'tungun ... FM-9
Petunia ... MP-9
**Petunia**—pop pl ... VA-3
Petunia Spring—spring ... NV-8
Petunk Point ... NY-2
**Petuxent Palisades**—pop pl ... MD-2
Petway—locale ... TN-4
Petway Post Office (historical)—building ... TN-4
**Petworth**—pop pl ... DC-2
Petworth Sch—school ... DC-2
Petyt Creek—stream ... KS-7
Petz Lake—lake ... MI-6
Petzold, Richard, House—hist pl ... OR-9
Petzold Ranch (abandoned)—locale ... MT-8
Peufald Lake—lake ... WI-6
Peugh Cem—cemetery ... IL-6
Peugh Cem—cemetery ... IN-6
Peugnet, Captain Louis, House—hist pl ... NY-2
Peumansend Creek—stream ... VA-3
Peus Pond—reservoir ... NC-3
Peutz Valley—valley ... CA-9
Pevah Creek—stream ... WY-8
Pevahouse Hollow—valley ... TN-4
Pevear Hill—summit ... NH-1
Pevehouse Cem—cemetery ... TX-5
Pevehouse Lake—lake ... TX-5
Peveler Cem—cemetery ... TX-5
Peveler Chimney Spring—spring ... AZ-5
Peveler Creek—stream (2) ... TX-5
Peveler Place—locale ... NM-5
Peveler Valley—bend (2) ... TX-5
**Pevely**—pop pl ... MO-7
Pevely Lake—reservoir ... MO-7
Peverly Brook—stream ... NH-1
Peverly Hill—summit ... NH-1
Peveto—locale ... TX-5
Peveto Beach—locale ... LA-4
Pevetot Bayou ... TX-5
Peveyhouse Creek—stream ... OK-5
Peveys Landing ... AL-4
Pevine Creek—stream ... MS-4
Pevitot Gully—stream ... TX-5
Pevitot Gully—valley ... TX-5
**Pevler**—pop pl ... KY-4
Pevley, Isle—island ... LA-4
Pevo Ditch—canal ... ID-8
Pevo Spring—spring ... ID-8
Pevoto Cem—cemetery ... LA-4
Pevov Canyon—valley ... NM-5
Pevy Cem—cemetery ... KY-4
**Pew**—pop pl ... PA-2
Pewabeck Falls—falls ... MI-6
**Pewabic**—pop pl ... MI-6
Pewabic Mine—mine ... MI-6
Pewabic Mtn—summit ... CO-8
Pewabic Pottery—hist pl ... MI-6
Pewabic Shaft (Active)—mine ... NM-5
**Pewamo**—pop pl ... MI-6
Pewamo Cem—cemetery ... MI-6
Pewamo-Westphalia Community Sch—school ... MI-6
Pewangoing Quarry—hist pl ... MI-6
Pewar ... FM-9
Pewaukee—fmr MCD ... NE-7
**Pewaukee**—pop pl ... WI-6
Pewaukee Lake—reservoir ... WI-6
Pewaukee River—stream ... WI-6
**Pewaukee (Town of)**—pop pl ... WI-6
**Pewaukee West**—pop pl ... WI-6
Pewawai Creek—stream ... WA-9
Pew Branch—stream ... SC-3
Pew Branch—stream ... TX-5
Pew Brook ... MA-1
Pew Canyon—valley ... NM-5
Pew Creek—stream ... GA-3
Pewee Creek—stream ... KS-7
Pewee Creek—stream ... OR-9
Pewee Creek—stream ... WA-9
Pewee Creek Rsvr—reservoir ... OR-9
Pewee Falls—falls ... WA-9
Pewee Knob—summit ... WV-2
Pewee Lake—lake ... MI-6
Pewee Lake—lake ... MN-6
Pewee Mines—mine ... TN-4
Pewee Run ... VA-3
Pewee Run ... WV-2
**Pewee Valley**—pop pl ... KY-4
Pewee Valley (CCD)—cens area ... KY-4
Pewee Valley Cem—cemetery ... KY-4
Pewee Valley Sanitarium—hospital ... KY-4
Pewee Valley Temple—church ... KY-4
Pewetole Island—island ... CA-9
Pewett Center (Shop Ctr)—locale ... FL-3
Pew Gulch—valley ... MT-8
Pew Hill—locale ... WV-2
Pew Hollow—valley ... KY-4
Pew Island—island ... OH-6
Pewit ... AL-4
Pewitt Cem—cemetery ... TN-4
Pewitt Chapel—church ... TN-4
Pewitt Hollow—valley (2) ... TN-4
Pewitt Ranch Oil Field—oilfield ... TX-5
Pewitt Sch—school ... TX-5
Pew Landing—locale ... GA-3
Pew Pond—swamp ... TX-5
Pews Creek—stream ... NJ-2
Pew Spring—spring ... NM-5
Pewsville ... NE-7
Pewter Creek—stream ... AL-4
Pewterfork Creek—stream ... AL-4
Pewterpot Brook—stream ... CT-1
Pey ... FM-9
Pe'Yabach ... FM-9
Peyenski Lake ... MN-6
Peyensky Lake ... MN-6
Peyguage ... MA-1
Peyitiw ... FM-9
Peyla—locale ... MN-6
Peyote Cem—cemetery ... SD-7
Peyote Point—summit ... MT-8
Peyrone Camp—locale ... CA-9
Peyrone Grove—woods ... CA-9
Peyron Ranch—locale ... AZ-5
Peyron Tank—reservoir ... AZ-5
Peysenske Lake—lake ... MN-6
Peysenskey Lake ... MN-6
Peysenski Lake ... MN-6
Peyser and Morrison Shirt Company Bldg—hist pl ... NY-2
Peyser Dam—dam ... MA-1
Peytiu ... FM-9
Peyton—locale ... MS-4
Peyton—locale ... WA-9
Peyton—locale ... WI-6
**Peyton**—pop pl ... CO-8
**Peyton**—pop pl ... VA-3
Peytona—locale ... TN-4
**Peytona**—pop pl ... KY-4
**Peytona**—pop pl ... WV-2
Peytona (Magisterial District)—fmr MCD ... WV-2
**Peytona Points**—pop pl ... AL-4
Peyton Branch—stream (2) ... KY-4
Peyton Branch—stream ... TN-4
Peyton Branch—stream ... WV-2
Peyton Cem—cemetery ... GA-3
Peyton Cem—cemetery (2) ... KY-4
Peyton Cem—cemetery ... TN-4
Peyton Cem—cemetery ... TX-5
Peyton Cem—cemetery ... WV-2
**Peyton Creek**—pop pl ... KY-4
Peyton Creek—stream ... AR-4
Peyton Creek—stream (2) ... CA-9
Peyton Creek—stream ... IL-6
Peyton Creek—stream ... KS-7
Peyton Creek—stream ... KY-4
Peyton Creek—stream ... TN-4
Peyton Creek—stream ... TX-5
Peyton Creek—stream ... VA-3
Peyton Creek Ch—church ... TN-4
Peyton-Ellington Bldg—hist pl ... VA-3
Peyton Hill—summit ... PA-2
Peyton (historical)—locale ... MS-4
Peyton House—hist pl ... MS-4
Peytonia ... TN-4
Peytonia Furnace (historical)—locale ... TN-4
**Peytonia Points**—pop pl ... AL-4
Peytonia Slough—gut ... CA-9
Peyton Lake—lake ... IN-6
Peyton Lookout Tower—locale ... MS-4
Peyton Post Office (historical)—building ... MS-4
Peyton Public Use Area—park ... AR-4
Peyton Randolph Sch—school ... VA-3
Peyton Ridge—ridge ... KY-4
Peyton Rock—pillar ... MT-8
Peyton Run ... PA-2
Peyton Run—stream ... VA-3
Peytonsburg—locale ... KY-4
Peytonsburg—locale ... VA-3
Peyton Sch—school ... MD-2
Peyton Sch—school ... WV-2
Peytons Creek ... TN-4
Peytons Creek Baptist Church ... TN-4
Peytons Lick Branch—stream ... KY-4
Peytons Lick Ch—church ... KY-4
**Peytons Store**—pop pl ... KY-4
**Peytonsville**—pop pl ... TN-4
**Peytonsville (Little Texas)**—pop pl ... TN-4
Peytonsville Post Office (historical)—building ... TN-4
Peytontown—locale ... KY-4
Peytonville—locale ... AR-4
Peytonville Branch—stream ... AR-4
Pezhekee Golf Course—other ... MN-6
Pezuela (Barrio)—fmr MCD ... PR-3
Pezuna del Caballo—locale ... TX-5
Pfaff Elem Sch—school ... PA-2
Pfaff Hollow—valley ... NY-2
Pfafflin Lake—lake ... IN-6
Pfaff Peak—summit ... AK-9
Pfafftown ... NC-3
**Pfafftown**—pop pl ... NC-3
**Pfaftown**—pop pl ... NC-3
Pfalzgraf Ridge—ridge ... OH-6
Pfannes Lake—lake ... MI-6
Pfarr Log House—hist pl ... OH-6
Pfau-Creighton Cottage—hist pl ... AL-4
Pfau Lake—reservoir ... IN-6
Pfau Lake Dam—dam ... IN-6
Pfau Private Landing Strip—airport ... ND-7
Pfau Spring—spring ... AZ-5
Pfeffer Cem—cemetery ... TX-5
Pfefferkorn Canyon—valley ... OR-9
Pfefferkorn Ridge—ridge ... OR-9
Pfeffer-Redwood Creek—stream ... CA-9
Pfeffer Valley—valley ... MN-6
**Pfeifer**—pop pl ... KS-7
Pfeifer Airstrip—airport ... ND-7
Pfeifer Camp—locale ... AR-4
Pfeifer Sch—school ... AR-4
Pfeiffer—locale ... AR-4
Pfeiffer Beach—beach ... CA-9
Pfeiffer Big Sur State Park—park ... CA-9
Pfeiffer Canyon—valley ... UT-8
Pfeiffer Coll—school ... NC-3
**Pfeiffer Corners**—pop pl ... MD-2
Pfeiffer Creek ... TX-5
Pfeiffer Creek—stream ... AR-4
Pfeiffer Falls—falls ... CA-9
Pfeiffer Flat—flat ... CA-9
Pfeiffer Gulch—valley ... CA-9
Pfeiffer Hill—summit ... WY-8
Pfeiffer House and Carriage House—hist pl ... AR-4
Pfeiffer Lake—lake ... MN-6
Pfeiffer Park—park ... IA-7
Pfeiffer Point—cape ... CA-9
Pfeiffer Pond—lake ... CT-1
Pfeiffer Ranch—locale ... CA-9
Pfeiffer Ranch—locale ... NE-7
Pfeiffer Ridge—ridge ... CA-9
Pfeiffer Rock—island ... CA-9
Pfeiffer Sch—school ... AR-4
Pfeiffer Sch—school ... CA-9
Pfeiffer Sch—school ... PA-2
Pfeiffers Landing—locale ... GA-3
Pfeiffer Spur—locale ... AR-4
**Pfeiffer Station**—pop pl ... OH-6
Pfeiffle State Public Shooting Area—park ... SD-7
Pfeiler Ranch Airp—airport ... UT-8
Pfennighausen Ridge—ridge ... AR-4
Pferdsteller Park—park ... CO-8
PFE Yard (railroad)—locale ... AZ-5
P-F Hill—summit ... WY-8
Pfiefer Ditch—canal ... IN-6
Pfiefer Keys—island ... LA-4
Pfieffer Branch—stream ... WV-2
Pfiel Cem—cemetery ... AL-4
Pfifer's Cross Roads ... OH-6
Pfingsten—locale ... MN-6
Pfister Draw—valley ... CO-8
Pfister Helistop—airport ... NJ-2
Pfister Park—park ... KS-7
Pfister Pond—lake ... IN-6
Pfister Pond Number 1 Dam—dam ... SD-7
Pfister Pond Number 2 Dam—dam ... SD-7
Pfister Pond Number 3 Dam—dam ... SD-7
Pfister Ranch—locale ... WY-8
Pfisters Pond—lake ... NJ-2
Pfizer, Incorporated—facility ... IN-6
Pfizer, Incorporated (Plant)—facility ... NC-3
Pflamm Sch Number 2 (historical)—school ... SD-7
P-Flat Site (47AS47)—hist pl ... WI-6
Pflaum Gulf—valley ... NY-2
Pfleger Family Houses—hist pl ... OH-6
Pfleiderer Center for Religion and the Humanities—hist pl ... OH-6
Pfletcher Lake—lake ... TX-5
Pflibsen Sch—school ... IL-6
Pflueger General Merchandise Store and Annex Saloon—hist pl ... NM-5
Pflueger Lake—lake ... MN-6
Pfluger Cem—cemetery ... TX-5
Pfluger Park—park ... TX-5
**Pflugerville**—pop pl ... TX-5
Pflug Sch—school ... NE-7
Pflum Hill—summit ... CO-8
Pflum Mine—mine ... NV-8
Pfmester School (historical)—locale ... MO-7
Pforzheimer Memorial Bridge—building ... NY-2
Pfost Gulch—valley ... CA-9
Pfoutz Run—stream ... PA-2
**Pfoutz Valley**—pop pl ... PA-2
Pfoutz Valley—valley ... PA-2
Pfoutz Valley Ch—church ... PA-2
Pfoutz Valley Trail—trail ... PA-2
Pfrimmer Ch—church ... IN-6
PGA Blvd Plaza (Shop Ctr)—locale ... FL-3
P Garr Dam—dam ... SD-7
P Gay Mtn—summit ... NY-2
PGE Service Center Airstrip—airport ... OR-9
P Goicoechea Ranch—locale ... NV-8
PG Tank—reservoir ... AZ-5
Phaelens Butte—summit ... ND-7
Phagan Cem—cemetery ... TN-4
Phair ... ME-1
Phair—locale ... ME-1
Phair Sch—school ... MD-2
Phalan Creek ... NV-8
Phalan Creek Ranch ... NV-8
Phalan Keegan Mine—mine ... NV-8
Phalan Lake ... WA-9
Phalanx—locale ... OH-6
**Phalanx**—pop pl ... NJ-2
Phalanx Lake—lake ... MN-6
Phalanx Station—locale ... OH-6
Phalarope Lake—lake (2) ... AK-9
Phalba—locale ... TX-5
Phalba Sch—school ... TX-5
Phalen, Lake—lake ... MN-6
Phalen Creek—stream ... NV-8
Phalen Creek Ranch—locale ... NV-8
Phalen Gulch—valley ... WA-9
Phalen Mine ... NV-8
Phalen Park—park ... MN-6
Phalen Park Sch—school ... MN-6
Phalen Ranch—locale ... NV-8
Phalen Run—stream ... PA-2
Phalens Creek ... NV-8
Phalen Well—well ... NV-8
Phalia ... MS-4
Phalia, Bogue—stream ... MS-4
Phaline Lake ... MN-6
Phalin (historical)—locale ... AL-4
Phallus, The—pillar ... UT-8
Phalon Lake—lake ... WA-9
Phalti Ch—church (2) ... MS-4
Phaltie Ch—church ... MS-4
Phalti Lakes—reservoir ... MS-4
Phaniels Ch—church ... NC-3
Phantom Banks—area ... NM-5
Phantom Bay—bay ... UT-8
Phantom Bend ... UT-8
Phantom Bluff—cliff ... OR-9
Phantom Canyon—valley ... AZ-5
Phantom Canyon—valley ... CO-8
Phantom Creek—stream ... AZ-5
Phantom Creek—stream (3) ... CO-8
Phantom Creek—stream (3) ... ID-8
Phantom Creek—stream ... MN-6
Phantom Creek—stream ... MT-8
Phantom Creek—stream ... WA-9
Phantom Creek Trail—trail ... CO-8
Phantom Flowage ... WI-6
Phantom Glacier—glacier ... MT-8
Phantom Hill—summit ... ID-8
Phantom Hill Reservoir ... TX-5
Phantom Island—island ... NY-2
Phantom Lake—building ... SD-7
Phantom Lake—lake (2) ... MN-6
Phantom Lake—lake ... MT-8
Phantom Lake—lake ... OR-9
Phantom Lake—lake (2) ... WA-9
Phantom Lake—lake ... WI-6
Phantom Lake—lake (2) ... WY-8
**Phantom Lake**—pop pl ... WI-6
Phantom Lake—reservoir ... MO-7
Phantom Lake—reservoir (2) ... WI-6
Phantom Lake Canal—canal ... TX-5
Phantom Lake Spring—spring ... TX-5
Phantom Meadow—flat ... ID-8
Phantom Meadows—flat ... CA-9
Phantom Mtn—summit ... OK-5
Phantom Natural Bridge—arch ... OR-9
Phantom Pass—gap ... WA-9
Phantom Peak—summit ... WA-9
Phantom Ranch—locale ... AZ-5
Phantom Ranch Boys Camp—locale ... WI-6
Phantom Ranger Station—locale ... AZ-5
Phantom Ridge—ridge ... ID-8
Phantom Ship—island ... OR-9
Phantom Terrace—cliff ... CO-8
Phantom Valley—valley ... UT-8
Phantom Valley Creek ... CO-8
Phantom Valley Ranch—locale ... CO-8
Phantom Valley Trading Post—locale ... CO-8
Phanton Coulee ... MT-8
Phanton Coulee Reservoir ... MT-8
Phantum Campsite—locale ... WY-8
Phantum Fumarole—geyser ... WY-8
Phanuel Ch—church ... IN-6
Pharao Creek ... UT-8
Pharaoh Mtn—summit ... NY-2
Pharaoh Run—stream ... WV-2
Pharaoh Run Sch—school ... WV-2
Pharaohs Country Club—other ... TX-5
Pharaohs Glen—valley ... UT-8
Phard Canyon ... UT-8
Phare Lake—lake ... MN-6
Phares Cem—cemetery ... AL-4
Phares Cem—cemetery ... MS-4
Phares Ditch—canal ... WY-8
**Pharisburg**—pop pl ... OH-6
Pharisee Creek—stream ... NC-3
Pharis Knob—summit ... WV-2
Pharis Sch—school ... IA-7
Pharlin ... AL-4
Pharmacy Coll—school (2) ... NY-2
Pharmacy Hill—summit ... OR-9
Pharm Spring ... GA-3
**Pharoah**—pop pl ... OK-5
**Pharoah**—pop pl ... WV-2
Pharoah Lake—lake ... NY-2
Pharoah Lake Brook—stream ... NY-2
Pharoah Mountain Trail—trail ... NY-2
Pharoah Mtn—summit ... NY-2
**Pharoah's Gardens**—pop pl ... IL-6
Pharo Canyon ... UT-8
Pharo Canyon—valley ... UT-8
Pharo Creek—stream ... UT-8
Pharo House—hist pl ... DE-2
Pharo Ridge—ridge ... UT-8
Pharos Mill ... NJ-2
Pharos Post Office (historical)—building ... AL-4
Pharo Village—hist pl ... UT-8
**Pharr**—pop pl ... TX-5
Pharr Cabin—hist pl ... AR-4
Pharr-Callaway-Sethness House—hist pl ... GA-3
Pharr Canal—canal ... LA-4
Pharr Cem—cemetery ... GA-3
Pharr Flats—flat ... MS-4
Pharr Gas Field—oilfield ... TX-5
Pharris Cem—cemetery ... TN-4
Pharris Chapel (historical)—church ... TN-4
Pharris Hill Ch—church ... KY-4
Pharris Lakes—lake ... TX-5
Pharris Mine (underground)—mine ... AL-4
Pharris Ridge Sch—school ... MO-7
Pharr Memorial Cem—cemetery ... TX-5
Pharr Mounds—hist pl ... MS-4
Pharr Mounds—summit ... MS-4
Pharr-San Juan-Alamo HS—school ... TX-5
Pharr San Juan Main Canal—canal ... TX-5
Pharr San Juan Pumping Station—other ... TX-5
Pharr Sch—school ... FL-3
Pharr Sch (historical)—school ... MS-4
Pharrs Island—island ... MO-7
Pharrs Lake—reservoir ... NC-3
Pharrs Lake Dam—dam ... NC-3
Pharrs Mill—locale ... NC-3
Pharsaha ... MS-4
**Pharsalia**—pop pl ... NY-2
Pharsalia Center Cem—cemetery ... NY-2
Pharsalia Ch (historical)—church ... MS-4
Pharsalia Game Ref—park ... NY-2
Pharsalia (historical)—locale ... MS-4
**Pharsalia (Town of)**—pop pl ... NY-2
P H D Oil Field—oilfield ... TX-5
Pheasant—locale ... TX-5
Pheasant, Mount—summit ... CA-9
**Pheasant Branch**—pop pl ... WI-6
Pheasant Branch—stream (2) ... GA-3
Pheasant Branch—stream (2) ... TN-4
Pheasant Branch—stream ... WI-6
Pheasant Branch—uninc pl ... WI-6
Pheasant Branch Gap—gap ... GA-3
**Pheasantbrook Subdivision**—pop pl ... UT-8
Pheasant Creek ... IL-6
Pheasant Creek—stream ... CA-9
Pheasant Creek—stream ... MT-8
Pheasant Creek—stream (2) ... NC-3
Pheasant Creek—stream ... OK-5
Pheasant Creek—stream (5) ... OR-9
Pheasant Creek—stream ... WA-9
Pheasant Creek—stream ... WY-8
Pheasant Draw—valley ... WY-8
Pheasant Field Rearing Pools—locale ... TN-4
Pheasant Field Trout Rearing Station ... TN-4
Pheasant Fork—stream ... WV-2
Pheasant Gap—gap ... TN-4
**Pheasant Hill**—pop pl ... PA-2
Pheasant Hill—summit (2) ... MA-1
Pheasant Hill—summit ... NJ-2
Pheasant Hill—summit ... OK-5
Pheasant Hill—summit ... VT-1
Pheasant Hill Cem—cemetery ... OK-5
**Pheasant (historical)**—pop pl ... OR-9
Pheasant Hollow—valley ... PA-2
Pheasant Hollow—valley ... WV-2
**Pheasant Hollow Subdivision**—pop pl ... UT-8
Pheasant Lake—lake ... WA-9
Pheasant Lake—reservoir ... ND-7
Pheasant Lake Dam ... ND-7
Pheasant Lick Hollow—valley ... KY-4
**Pheasant Meadows (Trailer Park)**—pop pl ... IL-6
Pheasant Park—park ... MN-6
Pheasant Peak ... PA-2
Pheasant Point—cape ... NE-7
Pheasant Point—summit ... MT-8
Pheasant Ridge ... IL-6
**Pheasant Ridge**—pop pl ... IL-6
Pheasant Ridge—ridge ... MD-2
**Pheasantridge Estates (subdivision)**—pop pl ... UT-8
Pheasant Ridge Resort—locale ... SD-7
**Pheasant Run**—pop pl ... CO-8
**Pheasant Run**—pop pl ... IN-6
**Pheasant Run**—pop pl ... NJ-2
Pheasant Run—stream (2) ... WV-2
**Pheasant Run Estates**—pop pl ... UT-8
Pheasant Spring—spring ... OR-9
Pheasant Springs—spring ... WA-9
Pheasant Terrace State Wildlife Mngmt Area—park ... MN-6
Pheasant Valley ... PA-2
Pheasanty Run—stream ... VA-3
**Pheba**—pop pl ... MS-4
**Phebe (historical)**—pop pl ... TN-4
Phebe Island—island ... ME-1
Phebe Lake—lake ... WA-9
Phebe Post Office (historical)—building ... TN-4
Phebes Neck ... RI-1
Phebus Cem—cemetery ... TN-4
Pheeny Creek—stream ... WA-9
Pheffercorn Lake—lake ... WI-6
Phegley Ridge—ridge ... CA-9
Pheiffer Landing—locale ... AL-4
Pheiffer Sch—school ... TX-5
Phelan—locale ... TX-5
Phelan—other ... TN-4
**Phelan**—pop pl ... AL-4
**Phelan**—pop pl ... CA-9
Phelan Creek—stream ... AK-9
Phelan Creek—stream ... ID-8
Phelan Creek—stream ... MI-6
Phelan Creek—stream ... WA-9
Phelan Creek—stream ... WI-6
Phelan (historical)—locale ... SD-7
Phelan Island—island ... CA-9
Phelan Lake ... WA-9
Phelan Mtn—summit ... ID-8
Phelan Park—park ... AL-4
Phelan Post Office (historical)—building ... TN-4
Phelan Ridge—ridge ... ID-8
Phelan Sch—school ... CA-9
Phelan Sch (historical)—school ... TN-4
Phelans Lake ... MN-6
Phelan State Wildlife Mngmt Area—park ... MN-6
Phelan Tunnel—tunnel ... UT-8
Phelar Memorial Center—building ... MA-1
Phelix Sch—school ... AR-4
Phellis Cem—cemetery ... OH-6
Phelns Brook ... MA-1
Phelon Brook—stream ... MA-1
Phelon Creek ... ID-8
Phelon Dam ... MA-1
Phelon Lake—lake ... MN-6
Phelon Pond—reservoir ... MA-1
Phelon Pond Dam—dam ... MA-1
Phelphs, Kenneth G., Barn—hist pl ... ID-8
Phelphs Cem—cemetery ... KY-4
Phelpps Dam ... AL-4
Phelps ... MD-2
Phelps ... MO-7
Phelps ... SD-7
Phelps—locale ... GA-3
Phelps—locale ... IL-6
Phelps—locale ... KY-4
Phelps—locale (2) ... MI-6
Phelps—locale ... MN-6
Phelps—locale ... TX-5
**Phelps**—pop pl ... IL-6
**Phelps**—pop pl ... KY-4
**Phelps**—pop pl ... MD-2
**Phelps**—pop pl ... MO-7
**Phelps**—pop pl ... NY-2
**Phelps**—pop pl ... WI-6
Phelps, Abner, House—hist pl ... CA-9
Phelps, Alexis, House—hist pl ... IL-6
Phelps, Arah, Inn—hist pl ... CT-1
Phelps, Capt. Elisha, House—hist pl ... CT-1
Phelps, Eli, House—hist pl ... CT-1
Phelps, Ezekiel, House—hist pl ... CT-1
Phelps, Mount—summit ... WA-9
Phelps, Seth S., Farmhouse—hist pl ... MN-6
Phelps Bay—bay ... MN-6
Phelps Bay—bay ... ND-7
Phelps Bay—bay ... VT-1
Phelps Bayou—gut ... LA-4
Phelps Bluff—cliff ... GA-3
Phelps Branch—stream ... AL-4
Phelps Branch—stream ... KY-4
Phelps Branch—stream ... TN-4
Phelps Branch—stream ... VA-3
Phelps Bridge—bridge ... NC-3
Phelps Brook ... MA-1
Phelps Brook—stream (3) ... CT-1
Phelps Brook—stream ... ME-1
Phelps Brook—stream (2) ... MA-1
Phelps Brook—stream (5) ... NY-2
Phelps Cabin Creek—stream ... CO-8
Phelps Canyon—valley ... CO-8
Phelps Canyon—valley ... UT-8
Phelps (CCD)—cens area ... KY-4
Phelps Cem—cemetery ... IN-6
Phelps Cem—cemetery (5) ... KY-4
Phelps Cem—cemetery ... MS-4
Phelps Cem—cemetery ... MO-7
Phelps Cem—cemetery ... NY-2
Phelps Cem—cemetery (2) ... TN-4
Phelps Cem—cemetery ... VA-3
Phelps Cem—cemetery ... WV-2
Phelps Cem—cemetery ... WI-6
Phelps Ch—church ... NC-3
Phelps Chapel—church ... NC-3
Phelps Chapel—church ... PA-2
**Phelps City**—pop pl ... MO-7
Phelps Collins Airp—airport ... MI-6
Phelps Corner—locale ... CA-9
**Phelps Corner**—pop pl ... MD-2
Phelps Corners—locale ... NY-2
Phelps Corners—locale ... PA-2
Phelps Country Estate—hist pl ... MO-7
**Phelps County**—pop pl ... MO-7
Phelps County Canal—canal ... NE-7
Phelps County Hosp—hospital ... MO-7
Phelps Cove ... ME-1
Phelps Creek—gut ... FL-3
Phelps Creek—stream ... AL-4
Phelps Creek—stream ... IA-7
Phelps Creek—stream (2) ... KY-4
Phelps Creek—stream ... MT-8
Phelps Creek—stream ... NY-2
Phelps Creek—stream (2) ... OH-6
Phelps Creek—stream ... OR-9
Phelps Creek—stream (2) ... TX-5
Phelps Creek—stream (3) ... WA-9
Phelps Dam—dam ... CT-1
Phelps Ditch—canal ... MT-8
Phelps Dodge General Office Bldg—hist pl ... AZ-5
Phelps Falls—falls ... NY-2
Phelps Farms Hist Dist—hist pl ... CT-1
Phelps Field—park ... MN-6
Phelps Fire Station—locale ... AZ-5
Phelps Grove Park—park ... MO-7
Phelps (historical)—locale ... KS-7
Phelps Hollow—valley ... AR-4
Phelps Hollow—valley ... KY-4
Phelps Hollow—valley ... TN-4
Phelps Hotel—hist pl ... NE-7
Phelps House—hist pl ... SC-3
Phelps Island—island ... MN-6
Phelps Island—island ... NY-2
Phelps Island (historical)—island ... SD-7
Phelps-Jones House—hist pl ... AL-4
Phelps Junction—locale ... NY-2
Phelps Knob—summit ... KY-4
Phelps Knoll—summit ... MA-1
Phelps Lake ... MN-6
Phelps Lake—lake (2) ... MI-6
Phelps Lake—lake ... MN-6
Phelps Lake—lake ... NC-3
Phelps Lake—lake ... ND-7
Phelps Lake—lake ... TX-5
Phelps Lake—lake ... WY-8
Phelps Lake—reservoir ... GA-3
Phelps Lake—reservoir ... TX-5
Phelps Lake Drain—stream ... MI-6
Phelps Lane Memorial Park—park ... NY-2
Phelps Lane Sch—school ... NY-2
Phelps Library, Shattuck School—hist pl ... MN-6
Phelps Lode Mine—mine ... SD-7
Phelps Mansion—hist pl ... NY-2
Phelps Memorial Hosp—hospital ... NY-2
Phelps Mill—hist pl ... MN-6
Phelps Mill Hist Dist—hist pl ... MN-6
Phelps Mills—uninc pl ... MA-1
Phelps Mtn—summit ... AR-4
Phelps Mtn—summit ... NY-2
Phelps Mtn—summit ... WY-8
Phelps Park—park ... NJ-2
Phelps Pass—gap ... WY-8
Phelps Point ... NC-3
Phelps Point—cape ... VT-1
Phelps Pond—lake ... NY-2
Phelps Pond—lake ... RI-1
Phelps Pond—reservoir ... CT-1
Phelps Ranch—locale ... AZ-5
Phelps Ranch—locale ... CA-9
Phelps Ridge—ridge ... CA-9
Phelps Ridge—ridge ... WA-9
Phelps Rocks—summit ... NY-2
Phelps Rsvr No 1—reservoir ... WY-8
Phelps Rsvr No 2—reservoir ... WY-8
Phelps Run—stream ... PA-2
Phelps Run—stream ... WV-2
Phelps Sch—school ... IL-6
Phelps Sch—school ... MA-1
Phelps Sch—school (2) ... MO-7
Phelps Sch—school ... PA-2
Phelps Sch—school ... UT-8
Phelps Sch—school ... WV-2
Phelps Slough—gut ... IL-6
Phelps Slough—stream ... CA-9
Phelps Spring—spring ... OR-9
Phelps Swamp—swamp ... MA-1
Phelps Swamp—swamp ... PA-2
**Phelps (Town of)**—pop pl ... NY-2
**Phelps (Town of)**—pop pl ... WI-6
Phelps Trail—trail ... NY-2
Phelps Velvet Lake ... MN-6
Phelps Vocational Sch—school ... DC-2
Pheneger Creek—stream ... CA-9
Pheney Lateral—canal ... CO-8
Phenis Creek—stream ... KS-7
Phenita Island—island ... NY-2
Phenix ... AZ-5
Phenix—locale ... AR-4
Phenix—locale ... MO-7
Phenix—locale ... RI-1
**Phenix**—pop pl ... IN-6
**Phenix**—pop pl ... VA-3
**Phenix City**—pop pl ... AL-4
Phenix City (CCD)—cens area ... AL-4
Phenix City Division—civil ... AL-4
Phenix City Elem Sch—school ... AL-4
Phenix Creek ... PA-2
Phenix Drag Strip—locale ... AL-4
Phenix HS—school ... VA-3
Phenix Island ... DE-2
Phenix Lookout Tower—locale ... VA-3
Phenix Municipal Stadium ... AL-4
Phenix Sch—school ... IL-6
**Phenix (Township of)**—pop pl ... IL-6
Phenixville ... PA-2
Phennia Chapel—church ... NC-3
Pherigo Airp—airport ... IN-6
Pherigo Cem—cemetery ... MO-7
Phernetton Lake—lake ... WI-6
Pherrins River—stream ... VT-1
**Pherrin Township**—pop pl ... ND-7
Pherson—locale ... OH-6
P H Hoeft State Park—park ... MI-6
Phibbs Cem—cemetery ... NC-3
Phibbs Cem—cemetery ... TN-4
**Phico**—pop pl ... WV-2
Phi Delta Theta Chapter House—hist pl ... CA-9
Phi Delta Theta Fraternity House—hist pl ... NE-7
Phieffer House—hist pl ... TX-5
Phiel Creek—stream ... KS-7
Phifer—locale ... FL-3
Phifer Cem—cemetery (2) ... TN-4
Phifer Cem—cemetery ... TX-5
Phifer Creek—stream ... ID-8
Phifer Creek—stream ... TX-5
Phifer Ditch—canal ... OH-6
Phiferes—locale ... TN-4
Phifer Hollow—valley ... TN-4
Phifer Landing (historical)—locale ... TN-4
Phifer Mountain Ch—church ... TN-4

Phifer Mtn—summit TN-4
Phifer Plac (historical)—locale TN-4
Phifer Post Office (historical)—building TN-4
Phifer Ranch—locale WY-8
Phigely Creek IN-6
Phi Kappa Campground—locale ID-8
Phi Kappa Creek—stream ID-8
Phi Kappa Mines—mine ID-8
Phi Kappa Mtn—summit ID-8
Phiket Lapali Creek MS-4
Phil—locale KY-4
Phil—locale NV-8
**Phil**—pop pl NC-3
Phil, Lake—lake AK-9
Philadelphia—locale AR-4
Philadelphia—locale (2) TN-4
**Philadelphia**—pop pl (2) AL-4
**Philadelphia**—pop pl AR-4
**Philadelphia**—pop pl IL-6
**Philadelphia**—pop pl IN-6
**Philadelphia**—pop pl MS-4
**Philadelphia**—pop pl MO-7
**Philadelphia**—pop pl NM-5
**Philadelphia**—pop pl NY-2
**Philadelphia**—pop pl (2) NC-3
**Philadelphia**—pop pl PA-2
**Philadelphia**—pop pl (2) TN-4
Philadelphia—uninc pl VA-3
Philadelphia Airp—airport (2) PA-2
Philadelphia and Reading RR Freight Station—hist pl NJ-2
Philadelphia Baptist Ch TN-4
Philadelphia Baptist Ch—church TN-4
Philadelphia Baptist Ch (historical)—church MS-4
Philadelphia Baptist Church AL-4
Philadelphia Baptist Church MS-4
Philadelphia Bar—bar CA-9
Philadelphia Brigade Monmt—park MD-2
Philadelphia Canyon—valley AZ-5
Philadelphia Canyon—valley NV-8
Philadelphia Canyon—valley NM-5
Philadelphia (CCD)—cens area TN-4
Philadelphia Cem—cemetery (4) AL-4
Philadelphia Cem—cemetery (3) AR-4
Philadelphia Cem—cemetery GA-3
Philadelphia Cem—cemetery IN-6
Philadelphia Cem—cemetery IA-7
Philadelphia Cem—cemetery (4) MS-4
Philadelphia Cem—cemetery ND-7
Philadelphia Cem—cemetery OK-5
Philadelphia Cem—cemetery (3) TN-4
Philadelphia Ch MS-4
Philadelphia Ch—church (11) AL-4
Philadelphia Ch—church (5) AR-4
Philadelphia Ch—church (5) FL-3
Philadelphia Ch—church (19) GA-3
Philadelphia Ch—church IL-6
Philadelphia Ch—church IN-6
Philadelphia Ch—church (4) KY-4
Philadelphia Ch—church (2) LA-4
Philadelphia Ch—church (7) MS-4
Philadelphia Ch—church (2) MO-7
Philadelphia Ch—church NY-2
Philadelphia Ch—church (12) NC-3
Philadelphia Ch—church (2) OH-6
Philadelphia Ch—church (4) SC-3
Philadelphia Ch—church (6) TN-4
Philadelphia Ch—church (3) TX-5
Philadelphia Ch—church VA-3
Philadelphia Ch Cemetery AL-4
Philadelphia Ch of Christ—church MS-4
Philadelphia Ch of God—church MS-4
Philadelphia Church Cove—bay NC-3
Philadelphia Church of Christ TN-4
Philadelphia Church of Christ—hist pl TN-4
Philadelphia City Hall—building MS-4
Philadelphia City Hall—hist pl PA-2
Philadelphia College of Art—hist pl PA-2
Philadelphia College of Art (Boundary Increase)—hist pl PA-2
Philadelphia Coll of Pharmacy—school PA-2
Philadelphia Coll Of Textiles And Science—school PA-2
Philadelphia Contributionship—building PA-2
Philadelphia Contributorship—hist pl PA-2
Philadelphia Country Club—other PA-2
Philadelphia (County) PA-2
Philadelphia County—civil PA-2
Philadelphia Creek OK-5
Philadelphia Creek—stream AK-9
Philadelphia Creek—stream AR-4
Philadelphia Creek—stream CO-8
Philadelphia Creek—stream OK-5
Philadelphia Creek—stream WA-9
Philadelphia Cricket Club—other (2) PA-2
Philadelphia Cumberland Presbyterian Ch—church TN-4
Philadelphia Ditch—canal CA-9
Philadelphia Division—civil TN-4
Philadelphia Electric Country Club—other PA-2
Philadelphia Electric Dam—dam PA-2
Philadelphia Elem Sch—school MS-4
Philadelphia Elem Sch—school TN-4
Philadelphia Fire Department Airp—airport PA-2
Philadelphia Flat—flat UT-8
PHILADELPHIA (gundelow)—hist pl DC-2
Philadelphia Hist Dist—hist pl MS-4
Philadelphia (historical)—locale AL-4
Philadelphia HS—school MS-4
Philadelphia HS for Girls—hist pl PA-2
Philadelphia Independent Apostolic Ch—church IN-6
Philadelphia Interchange TN-4
Philadelphia International Airp—airport PA-2
Philadelphia Lake—reservoir NC-3
Philadelphia Lookout Tower—locale SC-3
Philadelphia Market Street Airp—airport PA-2
Philadelphia Memorial Park—park PA-2
Philadelphia Methodist Church MS-4
Philadelphia Methodist Church—hist pl AR-4
Philadelphia Mine—mine (2) AZ-5
Philadelphia Missionary Baptist Ch—church FL-3
Philadelphia Missionary Baptist Church MS-4
Philadelphia Mtn—summit WA-9
Philadelphia Municipal Airp—airport MS-4
Philadelphia Museum Sch of Art—school PA-2
Philadelphia Naval Base Helipad—airport PA-2
Philadelphia Naval Regional Med Ctr—military PA-2
Philadelphia Naval Shipyard—military PA-2
Philadelphia Naval Support Activity—military PA-2
Philadelphia-Neshoba County Industrial Park—locale MS-4
Philadelphia-Neshoba County Public Library—building MS-4
Philadelphia-Neshoba County Vocational Technical Sch—school MS-4
Philadelphia Park—park TN-4
Philadelphia Peak—summit VT-1
**Philadelphia Point**—pop pl LA-4
Philadelphia Post Office—building MS-4
Philadelphia Post Office—building TN-4
Philadelphia Presbyterian Ch (historical)—church AL-4
Philadelphia Presbyterian Church MS-4
Philadelphia Primitive Baptist Ch—church (2) FL-3
Philadelphia Protectory for Boys—school PA-2
Philadelphia Racquet Club—hist pl PA-2
Philadelphia Savings Fund Society Bldg—hist pl PA-2
Philadelphia Sch—school CA-9
Philadelphia Sch—school GA-3
Philadelphia Sch—school IL-6
Philadelphia Sch—school (2) MS-4
Philadelphia Sch—school NC-3
Philadelphia Sch—school TN-4
Philadelphia Sch (historical)—school AL-4
Philadelphia Sch (historical)—school MS-4
Philadelphia Sch (historical)—school TN-4
Philadelphia Seaplane Base PA-2
Philadelphia Sewage Lagoon Dam—dam MS-4
Philadelphia Shaft—mine NM-5
Philadelphia State Hosp—hospital PA-2
Philadelphia Stock Exchange—hist pl PA-2
Philadelphia Suburban Dam—dam PA-2
**Philadelphia (Town of)**—pop pl NY-2
Philadelphia (Township of)—civ div IL-6
Philadelphia United Methodist Ch—church TN-4
Philadelphia United Methodist Church AL-4
Philadelphia Veterans Stadium PA-2
Philadelphia Watch Case Company Bldg—hist pl NJ-2
Philadelphia Wesley Ch—church NC-3
Philadelphia YMCA Camp—locale PA-2
Philadelphia Zoological Garden—park PA-2
**Philadelphus**—pop pl NC-3
Philadelphus Cem—cemetery MS-4
Philadelphus Ch—church MS-4
Philadelphus Ch—church NC-3
Philadelphus Presbyterian Church—hist pl NC-3
Philadelphus (Township of)—fmr MCD NC-3
Philadelpia Missionary Ch—church MS-4
Philander Lee Sch—school OR-9
Philander Smith Coll—school AR-4
Philans Shoal—bar AL-4
Philanthropic Hall, Davidson College—hist pl NC-3
Philatro Ranch (historical)—locale CA-9
Philbates Creek—stream VA-3
Philbeck Crossroads—locale VA-3
Philbin—locale MN-6
Philbrick And Johnson Ditch—canal WY-8
Philbrick Brook—stream ME-1
Philbrick Cem—cemetery ME-1
Philbrick Creek—stream ND-7
Philbrick Hill—summit ME-1
Philbrick Hill—summit (3) NH-1
Philbrick Hills—other MO-7
Philbrick Lake—lake NE-7
Philbrick Mill—locale CA-9
Philbrick Mtn—summit ME-1
Philbrick Pond—lake (2) NH-1
Phil Bright Dam—dam IN-6
**Philbrook**—pop pl MN-6
Philbrook Cem—cemetery MT-8
Philbrook Cove—bay (2) ME-1
Philbrook Creek—stream CA-9
Philbrook Farm Inn—hist pl NH-1
Philbrook Head—summit ME-1
Philbrook Island—island ME-1
Philbrook Rsvr—reservoir CA-9
Philbruek Pond—lake NH-1
Philby—locale IA-7
Philcade Bldg—hist pl OK-5
**Phil Campbell**—pop pl AL-4
Phil Campbell (CCD)—cens area AL-4
Phil Campbell Cem—cemetery AL-4
Phil Campbell Ch—church AL-4
Phil Campbell Ch of Christ—church AL-4
Phil Campbell Ch of God—church AL-4
Phil Campbell Ch of God of Prophecy—church AL-4
Phil Campbell Ch of God - Seventh Day—church AL-4
Phil Campbell Division—civil AL-4
Phil Campbell Elem Sch—school AL-4
Phil Campbell HS—school AL-4
Phil Campbell Medical Clinic—hospital AL-4
Phil Campbell United Methodist Ch—church AL-4
Philcher Creek—stream GA-3
**Philco**—pop pl SC-3
Phil Creek OR-9
Phil Creek—stream MT-8
Phil Creek—stream OR-9
Philedelphia Interchange PA-2
Philema—locale GA-3
Philema, Lake—reservoir GA-3
Philema Branch—stream GA-3
Philema (CCD)—cens area GA-3
Philema Creek—stream GA-3
Phileman Creek NY-2
Philemma Creek MS-4
Philemon Ch—church NJ-2
Philemon Creek NY-2
Phil Harden Park—park MS-4
Philhaven Hosp—hospital PA-2
Philibert Bluff—cliff MO-7
Philibert Cem—cemetery MO-7
Philibert Cem (historical)—cemetery MO-7
Philimena Mine—mine AZ-5
**Philip**—pop pl SC-3
**Philip**—pop pl SD-7
Philip, Bayou—stream MS-4
Philip, Mount—summit ME-1
Philip Bayou—stream LA-4
Philip Billard Municipal Airp—airport KS-7
Philip Brook MA-1
Philip Cary Company (Div. of Panacom Corporation)—facility KY-4
Philip Chapel—church NC-3
Philip County Park—park MI-6
Philip Creek AL-4
Philip Creek TN-4
Philip Creek—stream AL-4
Philip Creek—stream MD-2
Philip Drain—canal MI-6
Philip F. Lauer MS—school PA-2
Philip Head—cape MA-1
Philip H Hamburger Dam—dam SD-7
Philip Junction—locale SD-7
Philip Mtn—summit ME-1
Philip Municipal Airp—airport SD-7
Philip Murray Elem Sch—school PA-2
**Philipp**—pop pl MS-4
Philippa, Lake—lake WA-9
Philippa Creek—stream WA-9
Philippe Park—park FL-3
Philippe Point—cape FL-3
Philippe Prieto Grant—civil FL-3
Philippi WV-2
Philippi—locale TN-4
**Philippi**—pop pl WV-2
Philippian Cem—cemetery LA-4
Philippi B & O RR Station—hist pl WV-2
Philippi Canyon—valley OR-9
Philippi Ch—church AR-4
Philippi Ch—church FL-3
Philippi Ch—church (2) GA-3
Philippi Ch—church (2) KY-4
Philippi Ch—church (3) NC-3
Philippi Ch—church (3) SC-3
Philippi Ch—church (2) TN-4
Philippi Ch—church VA-3
Philippi Ch of Christ NC-3
Philippi Ch of Christ TN-4
Philippi Covered Bridge—hist pl WV-2
Philippi Creek FL-3
Philippi Creek—stream AR-4
Philippine Islands—ridge WI-6
Philippine Sea—sea FM-9
Philippine Sea—sea GU-9
Philipps Cem—cemetery OK-5
Philipps Lake—reservoir GA-3
Philippsville CA-9
Philip Quabes Run MA-1
Philip Quaker Run MA-1
Philip Ranch Airp—airport KS-7
Philip Rock—bar ME-1
Philip Run—stream WV-2
Philip Run Ch—church WV-2
**Philips**—pop pl FL-3
Philips, Hardman, House—hist pl PA-2
Philips Branch—stream FL-3
Philips Brook MA-1
Philips Brook—stream NY-2
Philips Brook Rsvr—reservoir MA-1
Philipsburg NJ-2
**Philipsburg**—pop pl MT-8
**Philipsburg**—pop pl (2) PA-2
Philipsburg Bay—bay MT-8
Philipsburg Borough—civil PA-2
Philipsburg Cem—cemetery PA-2
Philipsburg Elem Sch—school PA-2
Philipsburg Grade Sch—hist pl MT-8
Philipsburgh PA-2
Philipsburg Hist Dist—hist pl MT-8
Philipsburg JHS—school PA-2
Philipsburg Manor—hist pl NY-2
Philipsburg Osceola Area Senior HS PA-2
Philipsburg-Osceola HS—school PA-2
Philipsburg Radio Range Station—locale PA-2
Philipsburg Rsvr—reservoir PA-2
Philipsburg Valley—valley MT-8
Philips Cem—cemetery AR-4
Philips Cem—cemetery MS-4
Philips Cem—cemetery NC-3
Philips Cem—cemetery (2) TX-5
Philips Cemetery TN-4
Philip Sch—school ME-1
Philips Chapel MS-4
Philips Chapel—church NC-3
Philips Chapel—church OH-6
Philips Chapel—church VA-3
Philips Creek AL-4
Philip's Creek MD-2
Philips Creek MS-4
Philips Creek MT-8
Philips Creek PA-2
Philips Creek—stream OK-5
Philips Delight Sch—school MD-2
**Philipse Manor**—pop pl NY-2
Philipse Manor Hall—hist pl NY-2
Philips Fork—stream WV-2
Philips Inlet—bay FL-3
Philips Lake—reservoir AL-4
Philips Lake—reservoir NE-7
Philips Landing—locale NC-3
Philips Lick—stream VA-3
Philips Mill Branch—stream AR-4
Philips Mills PA-2
**Philips Mills**—pop pl NJ-2
Philip Smith Mountains—range AK-9
Philips Point FL-3
Philips Pond RI-1
Philips Sch—school IN-6
Philips Sch—school MT-8
Philips Sch Number 63—school IN-6
Philips Spring—spring ID-8
**Philip Station**—pop pl IN-6
Philips-Thompson Buildings—hist pl DE-2
**Philipston**—pop pl PA-2
**Philipstown (Town of)**—pop pl NY-2
Philipsville PA-2
Philipsville Sch—school SC-3
Philis Hollow—valley MO-7
Phill UT-8
P Hill—locale UT-8
**Phill**—pop pl UT-8
P Hill—ridge OR-9
Philladelphia Mine—mine CA-9
Phillaman Run—stream PA-2
Phillebaum Cem—cemetery MO-7
Phillema Creek GA-3
Philleo Lake—lake WA-9
Philler Cottage—hist pl ME-1
Phil Lewis Sch—school OR-9
Philley Tank—reservoir NM-5
Phillip ME-1
Phillip—locale VA-3
Phillip Adkins Hollow—valley TN-4
Phillip Beach MA-1
Phillip Bengston Dam Number One—dam NC-3
Phillip Bengston Dam Number Two—dam NC-3
Phillip Benston Dam Number Four—dam NC-3
Phillip Bradshaw Lake—reservoir TN-4
Phillip Bradshaw Lake Dam—dam TN-4
Phillip Branch—stream KY-4
Phillip Branch—stream TN-4
Phillip Brook MA-1
Phillip Canyon—valley AZ-5
Phillip Cem—cemetery TN-4
Phillip County Park—locale MI-6
Phillip Cove Ch—church KY-4
Phillip Creek MA-1
Phillip C. Showell Elem Sch—school DE-2
Phillip Ditch—canal IN-6
Phillip Draw—valley ND-7
Phillipe Creek FL-3
Phillipe Hollow—valley IN-6
Phillip George Branch—stream TX-5
Phillip Grove Ch—church AL-4
Phillip Grove Ch—church AR-4
Phillip Grove Ch—church GA-3
Phillip Grove Sch—school GA-3
Phillip Hammond Well—well NV-8
Phillip Hardware Store—hist pl KS-7
Phillipi Ch—church (2) GA-3
Phillipi Ch—church VA-3
Phillipi Ch of Christ—church TN-4
Phillipi Creek FL-3
Phillipi Creek—stream MT-8
Phillipi House—hist pl AL-4
Phillipin Kill—stream NY-2
Phillipi Point FL-3
Phillipis Point FL-3
Phillip Joe Well—well AZ-5
Phillip Jung Number 1 Dam—dam SD-7
Phillip Jung Number 2 Dam—dam SD-7
Phillip Knob—summit NC-3
Phillip Lake WA-9
Phillip Lake WI-6
Phillip Lake—lake MI-6
Phillip Martin Pond—reservoir AL-4
Phillip Martin Pond Dam—dam AL-4
Phillip Morris, Incorporated (Plant)—facility NC-3
**Phillippe**—pop pl IL-6
Phillippe Cem—cemetery IL-6
Phillippe Creek—stream FL-3
Phillippe Creek—stream IL-6
Phillippe Hammock FL-3
Phillippi Baptist Ch TN-4
Phillippi Branch—stream VA-3
Phillippi Ch TN-4
Phillippi Ch—church NC-3
Phillippi Ch—church (5) TN-4
Phillippi Creek FL-3
Phillippi Gardens—CDP FL-3
Phillippi Plantation (historical)—locale MS-4
Phillippi Point FL-3
Phillippi Ranch—locale WY-8
Phillippi Sch (historical)—school PA-2
Phillippi Shores Sch—school FL-3
Phillip Pond—lake MI-6
Phillipps Creek MT-8
**Phillippy**—pop pl TN-4
Phillippy Baptist Ch—church TN-4
Phillippy Post Office (historical)—building TN-4
Phillippy Sch (historical)—school TN-4
Phillip Ridge—ridge (2) TN-4
Phillip R Yonge Grant (landgrant)—civil FL-3
Phillips—locale AK-9
Phillips—locale AR-4
Phillips—locale MT-8
Phillips—locale PA-2
Phillips—locale TX-5
Phillips—other WV-2
**Phillips**—pop pl CA-9
**Phillips**—pop pl IA-7
**Phillips**—pop pl LA-4
**Phillips**—pop pl ME-1
**Phillips**—pop pl NE-7
**Phillips**—pop pl OK-5
**Phillips**—pop pl PA-2
**Phillips**—pop pl (2) TN-4
**Phillips**—pop pl TX-5
**Phillips**—pop pl WV-2
**Phillips**—pop pl WI-6
Phillips, Dr. P., House—hist pl FL-3
Phillips, Duncan, House—hist pl DC-2
Phillips, E. F., House—hist pl TX-5
Phillips, Ernie, House—hist pl MO-7
Phillips, Frank, House—hist pl OK-5
Phillips, George, House—hist pl GA-3
Phillips, Homer G., Hosp—hist pl MO-7
Phillips, John, House—hist pl OR-9
Phillips, Joseph, Farm—hist pl NJ-2
Phillips, Josiah, House—hist pl KY-4
Phillips, Judge Alexander H., House—hist pl TX-5
Phillips, Lake—lake FL-3
Phillips, Lake—lake MI-6
Phillips, Mount—summit MT-8
Phillips, R. O., House—hist pl NE-7
Phillips, Thomas, Mill Complex—hist pl DE-2
Phillips, Waite, Mansion—hist pl OK-5
Phillips, William D., Log Cabin—hist pl GA-3
Phillips Acad—school MA-1
Phillips Airp—airport MO-7
Phillips Airp—airport NC-3
Phillips And Reel Ditch—canal WY-8
Phillips and Trosper Buildings—hist pl TX-5
Phillips Ave Sch—school MA-1
Phillips Banco Number 6—levee TX-5
Phillips Baptist Church AL-4
Phillips Bar—bar AL-4
Phillips-Barnett Cem—cemetery AL-4
Phillips Bay—bay MO-7
Phillips Bay Mill (23CT235)—hist pl MO-7
Phillips Bayou—gut MS-4
**Phillips Bayou**—pop pl AR-4
Phillips Bayou—stream LA-4
Phillips Beach—beach MA-1
Phillips Bend TN-4
Phillips Block—hist pl SD-7
Phillips Bluff—cliff LA-4
Phillips Branch AR-4
Phillips Branch TN-4
Phillips Branch—stream (4) AL-4
Phillips Branch—stream DE-2
Phillips Branch—stream FL-3
Phillips Branch—stream GA-3
Phillips Branch—stream IL-6
Phillips Branch—stream (4) KY-4
Phillips Branch—stream (2) MO-7
Phillips Branch—stream (5) NC-3
Phillips Branch—stream (6) TN-4
Phillips Bridge—bridge LA-4
Phillips Bridge—hist pl IN-6
Phillips Brook—stream CT-1
Phillips Brook—stream ME-1
Phillips Brook—stream (2) MA-1
Phillips Brook—stream (2) NH-1
Phillips Brook—stream NY-2
Phillips Brook—stream RI-1
Phillips Brothers—locale AK-9
Phillipsburg—locale CO-8
Phillipsburg—locale NY-2
**Phillipsburg**—pop pl GA-3
**Phillipsburg**—pop pl KS-7
**Phillipsburg**—pop pl KY-4
**Phillipsburg**—pop pl MO-7
**Phillipsburg**—pop pl NJ-2
**Phillipsburg**—pop pl OH-6
**Phillipsburg**—pop pl PA-2
**Phillipsburg**—pop pl TX-5
Phillipsburg Cem—cemetery OH-6
Phillipsburg Cem—cemetery TX-5
Phillipsburg Ch—church MO-7
Phillipsburg Elem Sch—school KS-7
Phillipsburgh KS-7
Phillipsburg HS—school KS-7
Phillipsburg Mine—mine NV-8
Phillipsburg Municipal Airp—airport KS-7
Phillipsburg Sch—school NE-7
Phillipsburg Township—civil MO-7
**Phillipsburg Township**—pop pl KS-7
Phillipsburg Valley MT-8
Phillips Butte—summit MT-8
Phillips Buttes—summit MT-8
Phillips Camp—locale CO-8
Phillips Camp—locale NE-7
**Phillips Camp**—pop pl TX-5
Phillips Camp Run—stream WV-2
Phillips Canal—canal FL-3
Phillips Canal—canal (2) LA-4
Phillips Canal—canal NC-3
Phillips Canyon—valley AZ-5
Phillips Canyon—valley (2) CO-8
Phillips Canyon—valley NM-5
Phillips Canyon—valley OR-9
Phillips Canyon—valley (2) TX-5
Phillips Canyon—valley WY-8
Phillips Canyon Trail—trail WY-8
Phillips Cave—cave AL-4
Phillips Cave—cave AR-4
Phillips Cave—cave TN-4
Phillips Cem AL-4
Phillips Cem MO-7
Phillips Cem—cemetery (4) AL-4
Phillips Cem—cemetery (8) AR-4
Phillips Cem—cemetery (7) GA-3
Phillips Cem—cemetery (6) IL-6
Phillips Cem—cemetery (4) IN-6
Phillips Cem—cemetery (2) IA-7
Phillips Cem—cemetery (2) KS-7
Phillips Cem—cemetery (6) KY-4
Phillips Cem—cemetery (2) LA-4
Phillips Cem—cemetery MI-6
Phillips Cem—cemetery (5) MS-4
Phillips Cem—cemetery (4) MO-7
Phillips Cem—cemetery NE-7
Phillips Cem—cemetery (2) NY-2
Phillips Cem—cemetery (6) NC-3
Phillips Cem—cemetery OH-6
Phillips Cem—cemetery (2) OK-5
Phillips Cem—cemetery OR-9
Phillips Cem—cemetery (2) PA-2
Phillips Cem—cemetery SC-3
Phillips Cem—cemetery (22) TN-4
Phillips Cem—cemetery (4) TX-5
Phillips Cem—cemetery (5) VA-3
Phillips Cem—cemetery (2) WV-2
Phillips Ch—church AL-4
Phillips Ch—church (2) GA-3
Phillips Ch—church KY-4
Phillips Ch—church MS-4
Phillips Ch—church OH-6
Phillips Ch—church PA-2
Phillips Ch—church TN-4
Phillips Ch—church WV-2
Phillip Sch—school MA-1
Phillip Sch—school TN-4
Phillip Sch—school WI-6
Phillips Ch (abandoned)—church MO-7
Phillip Sch (abandoned)—school MO-7
Phillips Chapel—church (3) AL-4
Phillips Chapel—church KY-4
Phillips Chapel—church MS-4
Phillips Chapel—church OK-5
Phillips Chapel—church TN-4
Phillips Chapel Cem—cemetery AL-4
Phillips Chapel Cemetery TN-4
Phillips Chapel Church AL-4
Phillips Chapel (historical)—church AL-4
Phillips Chapel (historical)—church TN-4
Phillips Ch (historical)—church TN-4
Phillips Christian Methodist Episcopal Temple—church IN-6
Phillips Corner—locale ME-1
Phillips Coulee—valley MT-8
Phillips County—civil KS-7
**Phillips (County)**—pop pl AR-4
Phillips County Carnegie Library—hist pl MT-8
Phillips County Courthouse—hist pl AR-4
Phillip's Court District—hist pl KY-4
Phillips Cove—basin GA-3
Phillips Cove—bay ME-1
Phillips Cove—valley (2) GA-3
Phillips Creek AL-4
Phillips Creek—bay NY-2
**Phillips Creek**—pop pl NY-2
Phillips Creek—stream (3) AL-4
Phillips Creek—stream (2) AR-4
Phillips Creek—stream CO-8
Phillips Creek—stream (3) ID-8
Phillips Creek—stream IN-6
Phillips Creek—stream IA-7
Phillips Creek—stream KS-7
Phillips Creek—stream (3) KY-4
Phillips Creek—stream (2) LA-4
Phillips Creek—stream MD-2
Phillips Creek—stream MA-1
Phillips Creek—stream MI-6
Phillips Creek—stream (3) MS-4
Phillips Creek—stream MO-7
Phillips Creek—stream (3) MT-8
Phillips Creek—stream NJ-2
Phillips Creek—stream NY-2
Phillips Creek—stream (5) NC-3
Phillips Creek—stream OH-6
Phillips Creek—stream (6) OR-9
Phillips Creek—stream (2) PA-2
Phillips Creek—stream (5) TN-4
Phillips Creek—stream TX-5
Phillips Creek—stream (2) VA-3
Phillips Creek—stream (2) WA-9
Phillips Creek—stream WI-6
Phillips Creek—stream (3) WY-8
Phillips Crossing Hollow—valley TN-4
Phillips Crossroads (2) AL-4
Phillips Crossroads—locale AL-4
Phillips Crossroads—locale NC-3
**Phillips Crossroads**—pop pl NC-3
**Phillips Cross Roads**—pop pl NC-3
Phillipsdale RI-1
**Phillipsdale**—pop pl RI-1
Phillips Dam AL-4
Phillips Dam—dam AL-4
Phillips Ditch—canal (4) IN-6
Phillips Ditch—canal (2) MT-8
Phillips Ditch—canal (3) OR-9
Phillips Ditch—stream DE-2
Phillips Drain—canal (3) MI-6
Phillips Draw—valley ID-8
Phillips Draw—valley (2) TX-5
Phillips Elem Sch—school PA-2
**Phillips Estates**—pop pl AL-4
Phillips Exeter Acad—school NH-1
Phillips Family Cem—cemetery AL-4
Phillips Family Cemetery MS-4
Phillips Ferry (historical)—locale AL-4
Phillips Field Airp—airport MO-7
Phillips Flat CA-9
Phillips Flats—flat NE-7
Phillips' Folly—hist pl KY-4
Phillips Ford—locale TN-4
Phillips Ford (historical)—locale MO-7
Phillips Fork—stream KY-4
Phillips Fork—stream OH-6
Phillips Fork—stream WY-8
Phillips Gallery—building DC-2
Phillips Gap—gap (2) AL-4
Phillips Gap—gap GA-3
Phillips Gap—gap KY-4
Phillips Gap—gap NC-3
Phillips Grammer School MA-1
Phillips Grave—cemetery GA-3
Phillips Grove Ch—church GA-3
Phillips Gulch—valley AK-9
Phillips Gulch—valley (3) CA-9
Phillips Gulch—valley CO-8
**Phillips Heights**—pop pl DE-2
Phillip Shields Islands—island NJ-2
Phillips Hill—locale DE-2
Phillips Hill—summit AR-4
Phillips Hill—summit (2) MA-1
Phillips Hill—summit TN-4
Phillips Hill—summit VT-1
Phillips Hill—summit VA-3
Phillips Hills—other NM-5
Phillips (historical)—locale AL-4
Phillips Hole—basin NM-5
Phillips Hollow—valley AR-4
Phillips Hollow—valley (3) KY-4
Phillips Hollow—valley (4) MO-7
Phillips Hollow—valley OH-6
Phillips Hollow—valley OK-5
Phillips Hollow—valley (7) TN-4
Phillips Hollow—valley WV-2
Phillips Hollow Trail—trail TN-4
Phillips House—hist pl CA-9
Phillips House—hist pl NY-2
Phillips HS AL-4
Phillips HS—school (2) AL-4
Phillips HS—school IL-6
Phillipshurst-Riverwood—hist pl CA-9
Phillips International Airp—airport MS-4
Phillips Island SC-3
Phillips Island—island GA-3
Phillips Island—island ME-1
Phillips Island—island NC-3
Phillips Island—island RI-1
Phillips JHS—school MN-6
Phillips JHS—school NC-3
Phillips Knob—summit AR-4
Phillips Knob—summit NC-3
Phillips Lake FL-3
Phillips Lake WA-9
Phillips Lake WI-6
Phillips Lake—lake IN-6
Phillips Lake—lake (2) LA-4
Phillips Lake—lake ME-1
Phillips Lake—lake SC-3
Phillips Lake—lake (2) TX-5
Phillips Lake—lake (4) WA-9
Phillips Lake—lake (3) WI-6
Phillips Lake—lake (2) WY-8
Phillips Lake—reservoir AL-4
Phillips Lake—reservoir AR-4
Phillips Lake—reservoir GA-3
Phillips Lake—reservoir (2) MS-4
Phillips Lake—reservoir (2) OK-5
Phillips Lake—reservoir OR-9
Phillips Lake—reservoir SC-3
Phillips Lake—reservoir TX-5
Phillips Lake Dam—dam MS-4
Phillips Landing—locale (2) MS-4
Phillips Landing Rec Area—park DE-2
Phillips Lateral IN-6
Phillips Mansion—hist pl CA-9
Phillips Marsh—swamp WI-6
Phillips Memorial—cemetery PA-2
Phillips Memorial Gallery Bldg—building DC-2

Phillips Mili—locale TN-4
Phillips Mill—pop pl NY-2
Phillips Mill Branch—stream AL-4
Phillips Mill Ch—church GA-3
Phillips Mill Hist Dist—hist pl PA-2
Phillips Millpond—lake NY-2
Phillips Mills—pop pl NY-2
Phillips Mine AL-4
Phillips Mine—mine AZ-5
Phillips Mine—mine CA-9
Phillips Mine—mine OK-5
Phillips Mine (underground)—mine AL-4
Phillips Mtn SC-3
Phillips Mtn—summit AL-4
Phillips Mtn—summit (2) AR-4
Phillips Mtn—summit ME-1
Phillips Mtn—summit OK-5
Phillips Mtn—summit SC-3
Phillips New Cem—cemetery PA-2
Phillipson Portal—tunnel CO-8
Phillips Park—park FL-3
Phillips Park—park IL-6
Phillips Park—park MA-1
Phillips Park—park NC-3
Phillips Park—park OH-6
Phillips Park—park PA-2
Phillips Park—park (2) TX-5
Phillips Park Dam—dam AZ-5
Phillips Park Lake AZ-5
Phillips Park Tank—reservoir AZ-5
Phillips Pass—gap WY-8
Phillips Peak WY-8
Phillips Petroleum Ambrosia Mill—locale NM-5
Phillips Point FL-3
Phillips Point MA-1
Phillips Point—cape MA-1
Phillips Point—cape (2) NY-2
Phillips Point (subdivision)—pop pl MA-1
Phillips Pond ME-1
Phillips Pond—lake ME-1
Phillips Pond—lake NH-1
Phillips Pond—lake NJ-2
Phillips Pond—lake NY-2
Phillips Pond—lake RI-1
Phillips Pond—reservoir GA-3
Phillips Pond—reservoir MA-1
Phillips Pond—reservoir NC-3
Phillips Pond—reservoir PA-2
Phillips Pond—reservoir VT-1
Phillips Pond—reservoir VA-3
Phillips Pond Dam—dam NC-3
Phillipsport—locale NY-2
Phillips Post Office (historical)—building AL-4
Phillips Post Office (historical)—building TN-4
Phillips Spring—spring ND-7
Phillips Products Company—facility MI-6
Phillips Prospect—mine TN-4
Phillips Ranch—locale (2) AZ-5
Phillips Ranch—locale MT-8
Phillips Ranch—locale NE-7
Phillips Ranch—locale (3) NM-5
Phillips Ranch—locale SD-7
Phillips Ranch—locale (4) TX-5
Phillips Ranch—locale WY-8
Phillips Red Ash Mine (surface)—mine TN-4
Phillips (reduced usage)—locale LA-4
Phillips Ridge—ridge ID-8
Phillips Ridge—ridge NC-3
Phillips Ridge—ridge (2) TN-4
Phillips Ridge—ridge WY-8
Phillips Rock—bar ME-1
Phillips Rock—island AK-9
Phillips Rock—summit TX-5
Phillips Rsvr—reservoir (2) MT-8
Phillips Rsvr—reservoir OR-9
Phillips Rsvr—reservoir WY-8
Phillips Run—stream IN-6
Phillips Run—stream MA-1
Phillips Run—stream PA-2
Phillips Run—stream WV-2
Phillips Sch MA-1
Phillips Sch MO-7
Phillips Sch PA-2
Phillips Sch TN-4
Phillips Sch—school (3) AL-4
Phillips Sch—school (2) CA-9
Phillips Sch—school CO-8
Phillips Sch—school IL-6
Phillips Sch—school IA-7
Phillips Sch—school LA-4
Phillips Sch—school MA-1
Phillips Sch—school (2) MI-6
Phillips Sch—school MN-6
Phillips Sch—school (2) MO-7
Phillips Sch—school NE-7
Phillips Sch—school NJ-2
Phillips Sch—school NY-2
Phillips Sch—school (2) NC-3
Phillips Sch—school OH-6
Phillips Sch—school OK-5
Phillips Sch—school PA-2
Phillips Sch—school (2) TN-4
Phillips Sch—school TX-5
Phillips Sch—school VT-1
Phillips Sch—school VA-3
Phillips Sch—school WV-2
Phillips Sch (historical)—school AL-4
Phillips Sch (historical)—school MS-4
Phillips Sch (historical)—school TN-4
Phillips School IN-6
Phillips School, The MA-1
Phillips-Sims House—hist pl GA-3
Phillips Slough—gut TX-5
Phillips-Smith Cem—cemetery AL-4
Phillips South—cens area MT-8
Phillips-Sprague Mine—hist pl WV-2
Phillips Spring AL-4
Phillips Spring—spring GA-3
Phillips Spring—spring ME-1
Phillips Spring—spring OR-9
Phillips Spring—spring (2) TN-4
Phillips Spring—spring (2) VA-3
Phillips Spring—spring WY-8
Phillips Spring Cove—cave AL-4
Phillips Springs—spring NM-5
Phillips Square—park MA-1
Phillips Store (historical)—locale AL-4
Phillips Store (historical)—locale MS-4
Phillips Street Sch—school NY-2
Phillips Strip Mine—mine OK-5
Phillips Subdivision—pop pl GA-3
Phillips Subdivision—pop pl TN-4
Phillips Subdivision—pop pl UT-8
Phillips Tabernacle—church AL-4
Phillips Tank—reservoir AZ-5
Phillips Tank—reservoir TX-5
Phillips Temple Ch of God AL-4
Phillips Temple Ch of God—church AL-4
Phillips Temple CME Ch—church AL-4
Phillips Thicket—swamp TX-5
Phillipston PA-2
Phillipston—pop pl MA-1
Phillipston—pop pl PA-2
Phillipston Centre MA-1
Phillipston Four Corners—pop pl MA-1
Phillipston Landing (historical)—locale MS-4
Phillipston Pond MA-1
Phillipston Reservoir Dam—dam MA-1
Phillipston Rsvr—reservoir MA-1
Phillipston (Town of)—pop pl MA-1
Phillipstown OH-6
Phillipstown—pop pl IL-6
Phillipstown—pop pl MS-4
Phillipstown Baptist Ch—church MS-4
Phillips (Town of)—pop pl ME-1
Phillipstown Oil Field—other IL-6
Phillips (Township of)—fmr MCD AR-4
Phillips (Township of)—pop pl IL-6
Phillips Univ—school OK-5
Phillips University Camp—locale CO-8
Phillips Village (historical)—locale KS-7
Phillipsville—CDP NC-3
Phillipsville—pop pl AL-4
Phillipsville—pop pl CA-9
Phillipsville—pop pl MI-6
Phillipsville—pop pl (2) PA-2
Phillipsville Cem—cemetery PA-2
Phillips Wash—stream AZ-5
Phillips Wash—stream NV-8
Phillips Well—well MT-8
Phillips Well—well (2) NM-5
Phillips-White Cem—cemetery OH-6
Phillips Woolen Mill—hist pl MA-1
Phillip Tank—reservoir TX-5
Phillip Thompson Ranch—locale TX-5
Phillip Windmill—locale TX-5
Phillis—locale VA-3
Phillis Cem—cemetery OH-6
Phillis Island—island MA-1
Phillis Island—island PA-2
Phillps Subdivision—pop pl TN-4
Phills Lake—lake MT-8
Phil Mar Estates
(subdivision)—pop pl DE-2
Phil Marsin Lake Dam—dam MS-4
Phil Mass Rsvr—reservoir WY-8
Phil Mays Landing (historical)—locale AL-4
Phil McGill Tank—reservoir AZ-5
Philmont—pop pl NY-2
Philmont—pop pl PA-2
Philmont Country Club—locale PA-2
Philmont Golf Course PA-2
Philmont Industrial Park—locale PA-2
Philmont Manor—pop pl PA-2
Philmont Park—pop pl PA-2
Philmont (Philmont Natl Boy Scout
Ranch)—pop pl NM-5
Philmont Rsvr—reservoir NY-2
Philmont Scout Ranch—area NM-5
Philmont Scout Ranch HQ—locale NM-5
Philmont Station—building PA-2
Philo—pop pl CA-9
Philo—pop pl IL-6
Philo—pop pl OH-6
Philo, Lake—lake UT-8
Philo, Mount—summit VT-1
Philoah—pop pl WV-2
Philo Brice Islands—island LA-4
Philo Brook—stream CT-1
Philo Brook—stream MA-1
Philo Hill—summit CT-1
Philo II Archeol District—hist pl OH-6
Phil Olson Dam—dam OR-9
Phil Olson Rsvr—reservoir OR-9
Philomath—locale GA-3
Philomath—pop pl IN-6
Philomath—pop pl OR-9
Philomath Acad (historical)—school TN-4
Philomath Ch—church IN-6
Philomath College—hist pl OR-9
Philomath Hist Dist—hist pl GA-3
Philomathian Sch—school WA-9
Philomel Creek—stream NY-2
Philomena Spring—spring AZ-5
Philomont—locale VA-3
Philo MS—school NC-3
Philo Sch—school KS-7
Philosophical Hall—building PA-2
Philo T. Farnsworth Sch—school UT-8
Philothea—pop pl OH-6
Philothea Catholic Church and Priest
House—hist pl OH-6
Philo (Township of)—pop pl IL-6
Philp Coulee MT-8
Philp Creek MT-8
Phil-Pe-Co Lake—reservoir TX-5
Phil Pico Mtn—summit UT-8
Philpot—pop pl KY-4
Philpot Cem—cemetery IN-6
Philpot Cem—cemetery (2) KY-4
Philpot Chapel—church KY-4
Philpot Creek—stream CA-9
Philpot Dam AL-4
Philpot Dam—building VA-3
Philpot Hollow—valley KY-4
Philpot House—hist pl KY-4
Philpot Lake—lake CA-9
Philpot Lake—reservoir AL-4
Philpot Mtn—summit ME-1
Philpot River DE-2
Philpots Islands—island MD-2
Philpots Mill (historical)—locale TN-4
Philpott—locale VA-3
Philpott Canyon—valley WY-8
Philpott Cem—cemetery MO-7
Philpott Cem—cemetery TN-4
Philpott Cem—cemetery TX-5
Philpott Dam—dam VA-3
Philpott Lake—lake NE-7
Philpott Lake—reservoir VA-3
Philpot Tower (fire tower)—tower FL-3
Philpott Rsvr VA-3
Philpott Site (35 CS 1)—hist pl OR-9
Philpott Valley—valley AR-4
Philp Ranch—locale WY-8
Philrich—pop pl TX-5
Phils Arm Run—stream VA-3
Phils Branch—stream KY-4
Phils Cave—cave PA-2
Phils Creek—stream IL-6
Phils Creek—stream NC-3
Phils Creek—stream SC-3
Phils Creek—stream VA-3
Phil Shop Hollow—valley UT-8
Phils Island—island WI-6
Phils Knob—summit WV-2
Philsmith Peak—summit WY-8
Philson—pop pl PA-2
Philson Crossroads—locale SC-3
Philson Sch (abandoned)—school PA-2
Philson Station PA-2
Phils Tank—reservoir AZ-5
Phils View—summit TN-4
Philton Crossroads SC-3
Philtower—hist pl OK-5
Philview Camp—pop pl TX-5
Philwold—locale NY-2
Phinazee Creek—stream GA-3
Phiney Flat—flat SD-7
Phinholloway Creek GA-3
Phin Holloway Swamp GA-3
Phinizy—locale GA-3
Phinizy Ditch—canal GA-3
Phinizy Sch—school GA-3
Phinizy Swamp—swamp GA-3
Phinney—locale SC-3
Phinney—pop pl IL-6
Phinney—pop pl WA-9
Phinney, William and Jane,
House—hist pl MA-1
Phinney Bay—bay WA-9
Phinney Branch IL-6
Phinney Branch—stream IL-6
Phinney Canyon—valley NV-8
Phinney Creek—stream NY-2
Phinney Draw—valley WY-8
Phinney Harbor MA-1
Phinney Hill—summit NY-2
Phinney Hill—summit OK-5
Phinney (historical)—locale SD-7
Phinney Island ME-1
Phinney Lake—lake UT-8
Phinney Mine—mine NV-8
Phinney Rock—rock MA-1
Phinneys Bay—lake MA-1
Phinney School KS-7
Phinneys Harbor—cove MA-1
Phinneys Harbor Channel Light—locale MA-1
Phinneys Point—cape MA-1
Phinny Hill—summit WA-9
Phipps—locale AL-4
Phipps—locale VA-3
Phipps—pop pl WI-6
Phipps, William H., House—hist pl WI-6
Phipps Arch—arch UT-8
Phipps Bend TN-4
Phipps Bend—bend TN-4
Phipps Bend—locale TN-4
Phipps Branch—stream (2) AR-4
Phipps Branch—stream NC-3
Phipps Brook—stream NY-2
Phippsburg—pop pl CO-8
Phippsburg—pop pl ME-1
Phippsburg (Town of)—pop pl ME-1
Phipps Canyon—valley CA-9
Phipps Cem—cemetery KY-4
Phipps Cem—cemetery LA-4
Phipps Cem—cemetery PA-2
Phipps Cem—cemetery TN-4
Phipps Cem—cemetery (2) VA-3
Phipps Chapel—church NC-3
Phipps Condominium—pop pl UT-8
Phipps Conservatory—hist pl PA-2
Phipps Conservatory—park PA-2
Phipps Corners—locale NY-2
Phipps Cove—bay NC-3
Phipps Cove—valley NC-3
Phipps Creek—stream (2) CA-9
Phipps Creek—stream MS-4
Phipps Creek—stream NC-3
Phipps Creek—stream (3) OR-9
Phipps-Death Hollow Outstanding Natural
Area—area UT-8
Phipps Flowage—channel WI-6
Phipps Fork—stream KY-4
Phipps Gap—gap NC-3
Phipps Gulch—valley OR-9
Phipps Homestead—locale WA-9
Phipps Island—island TN-4
Phipps Lake—lake CA-9
Phipps Lake—lake MI-6
Phipps Lake—lake WI-6
Phipps Lake—reservoir CT-1
Phipps Lateral—canal ID-8
Phipps Meadow—flat OR-9
Phipps Number 1 Dam—dam SD-7
Phipps Pass—gap CA-9
Phipps Peak—summit CA-9
Phipps Peninsula—cape AK-9
Phipps Point—cape AK-9
Phipps Point—cape ME-1
Phipps Ranch—locale CO-8
Phipps Ranch—locale NE-7
Phipps Sch—school IL-6
Phipps Sch—school KY-4
Phipps Site—hist pl IA-7
Phipps Spring—spring WI-6
Phipps Store—locale VA-3
Phipps Street Burying Ground—hist pl MA-1
Phipps Street Cem—cemetery MA-1
Phipps Township—pop pl SD-7
Phipps Wash—valley UT-8
Phipsburg ME-1
Phister Creek—stream SD-7
Phister Tank—reservoir NM-5
Phlegar—locale VA-3
Phlox—pop pl IN-6
Phlox—pop pl WI-6
Phlox Creek—stream WY-8
Phlox Lake—lake MT-8
Phlox Lake—reservoir WI-6
Phlox Point Campground—park OR-9
Phlueger Mine—mine NV-8
Phoca Rock—bar OR-9
Phocena Bay—bay AK-9
Phocena Rocks—other AK-9
Phoeba Bay—swamp GA-3
Phoebe, Lake—lake WA-9
Phoebe, Mount—summit WA-9
Phoebe, Mount—summit WV-2
Phoebe Branch—stream KY-4
Phoebe Branch—stream (2) TN-4
Phoebe Branch—stream VA-3
Phoebe Butt—summit VA-3
Phoebe Creek—stream AK-9
Phoebe Creek—stream ID-8
Phoebe Fork—stream KY-4
Phoebe Forts Corner IN-6
Phoebe Hearst Sch—school (2) CA-9
Phoebe Island—island ME-1
Phoebe Lake—lake MN-6
Phoebe Lake—reservoir GA-3
Phoebe Lake—reservoir VA-3
Phoebe Meadow—flat ID-8
Phoebe Mtn—summit NY-2
Phoebe River—stream MN-6
Phoebe Run—stream PA-2
Phoebes Creek—stream NC-3
Phoebes Knob—summit NY-2
Phoebes Noble Mtn—summit NH-1
Phoebes Sch (historical)—school TN-4
Phoebes Tank—reservoir AZ-5
Phoebe Tip—summit ID-8
Phoebe Trace—stream KY-4
Phoebus—pop pl VA-3
Phoebus Sch—school VA-3
Phoenicia—pop pl NY-2
Phoenician Gardens
Subdivision—pop pl UT-8
Phoenician Woods
(subdivision)—pop pl NC-3
Phoenicia Trail—trail NY-2
Phoenix FL-3
Phoenix—locale CO-8
Phoenix—locale GA-3
Phoenix—locale SC-3
Phoenix—locale TX-5
Phoenix—mine UT-8
Phoenix—other PA-2
Phoenix—pop pl AZ-5
Phoenix—pop pl IL-6
Phoenix—pop pl LA-4
Phoenix—pop pl MD-2
Phoenix—pop pl MI-6
Phoenix—pop pl MS-4
Phoenix—pop pl (2) NJ-2
Phoenix—pop pl NY-2
Phoenix—pop pl NC-3
Phoenix—pop pl OR-9
Phoenix (Aban'd)—locale AK-9
Phoenix Acres Trailer Park—locale AZ-5
Phoenix Baptist Hosp—hospital AZ-5
Phoenix Baptist Hospital
Heliport—airport AZ-5
Phoenix Bay—bay AK-9
Phoenix Bldg—hist pl NY-2
Phoenix Block—hist pl OH-6
Phoenix Bridge—hist pl VA-3
Phoenix Building/Cincinnati Club—hist pl OH-6
Phoenix Canal—canal OR-9
Phoenix Carnegie Library And Library
Park—hist pl AZ-5
Phoenix (CCD)—cens area AZ-5
Phoenix (CCD)—cens area GA-3
Phoenix Cem—cemetery AL-4
Phoenix Cem—cemetery AR-4
Phoenix Cem—cemetery MS-4
Phoenix Cem—cemetery NE-7
Phoenix Cem—cemetery PA-2
Phoenix Ch—church AL-4
Phoenix Ch—church AR-4
Phoenix Ch—church MD-2
Phoenix Ch—church MS-4
Phoenix Ch—church NC-3
Phoenix Chapel—church TN-4
Phoenix Chapel Cem—cemetery TN-4
Phoenix Christian Grade Sch—school AZ-5
Phoenix Christian HS—school AZ-5
Phoenix Club—hist pl IN-6
Phoenix Club—hist pl OH-6
Phoenix Coll AZ-5
Phoenix Community Coll—school AZ-5
Phoenix Community Hosp—hospital AZ-5
Phoenix Community Service
Center—building AZ-5
Phoenix Country Club—other AZ-5
Phoenix Country Club—other IN-6
Phoenix Creek—stream AK-9
Phoenix Creek—stream (2) CA-9
Phoenix Deer Valley Municipal
Airp—airport AZ-5
Phoenix District Airp—airport AZ-5
Phoenix Ditch—canal CA-9
Phoenix Filter Plant—locale AZ-5
Phoenix Furnace (historical)—locale TN-4
Phoenix General Hosp—hospital AZ-5
Phoenix Giants Baseball Park AZ-5
Phoenix Group—mine CA-9
Phoenix Gulch—valley CA-9
Phoenix Gun Club—locale AZ-5
Phoenix Hall-Johnson-Harper
House—hist pl MS-4
Phoenix Hall-Wisconsin Institute for the
Education of the Deaf and
Dumb—hist pl WI-6
Phoenix Hill—summit CA-9
Phoenix Hill—summit MD-2
Phoenix Hill Hist Dist—hist pl KY-4
Phoenix (historical)—pop pl MS-4
Phoenix Hollow—valley PA-2
Phoenix Hollow—valley WV-2
Phoenix Homesteads Hist Dist—hist pl AZ-5
Phoenix Hotel—hist pl GA-3
Phoenix International Raceway—locale AZ-5
Phoenix Junior Coll—school AZ-5
Phoenix Junior Coll (Camelback
Extension)—school AZ-5
Phoenix Junior Coll (Glendale
Extension)—school AZ-5
Phoenix Lake—lake CA-9
Phoenix Lake—lake LA-4
Phoenix Lake—lake NM-5
Phoenix Lake—reservoir CA-9
Phoenix Lake—reservoir MI-6
Phoenix Lake Oil Field—oilfield LA-4
Phoenix Lake Park—park CA-9
Phoenix Landing (historical)—locale MS-4
Phoenix LDS Second Ward
Church—hist pl AZ-5
Phoenix Litchfield Municipal Airp—airport AZ-5
Phoenix Masonic Lodge No. 8—hist pl NC-3
Phoenix Med Ctr—hospital AZ-5
Phoenix Memorial Hosp—hospital AZ-5
Phoenix Memorial Park—cemetery AZ-5
Phoenix Milit Reservation—military AZ-5
Phoenix Mill Farm—hist pl MD-2
Phoenix Mills—hist pl OH-6
Phoenix Mills—pop pl NY-2
Phoenix Mills (historical)—locale MS-4
Phoenix Mills Landing (historical)—locale MS-4
Phoenix Mills Post Office
(historical)—building MS-4
Phoenix Mine—mine AZ-5
Phoenix Mine—mine (2) CA-9
Phoenix Mine—mine (2) CO-8
Phoenix Mine—mine OR-9
Phoenix Mine (Abandoned)—mine CA-9
Phoenix Mobile Home Park—locale AZ-5
Phoenix Mountain AZ-5
Phoenix Mountains AZ-5
Phoenix Mountains—summit AZ-5
Phoenix Mountains Preserve—park AZ-5
Phoenix Mtn—summit NC-3
Phoenix Municipal Stadium—locale AZ-5
Phoenix Opera House Block—hist pl IL-6
Phoenix Park—flat CO-8
Phoenix Park—park AZ-5
Phoenix Park—park MI-6
Phoenix Park—pop pl PA-2
Phoenix Park Canyon—valley AZ-5
Phoenix Park (subdivision)—pop pl FL-3
Phoenix Park Wash—stream AZ-5
Phoenix Peak—summit AK-9
Phoenix Police Acad—school AZ-5
Phoenix Police Compound—other AZ-5
Phoenix Pond—reservoir MA-1
Phoenix Pond Dam—dam MA-1
Phoenix Post Office (historical)—building MS-4
Phoenix Post Office (historical)—building TN-4
Phoenix Powerhouse—other CA-9
Phoenix Proving Grounds—locale AZ-5
Phoenix Proving Grounds—military AZ-5
Phoenix Public Library—building AZ-5
Phoenix Rsvr—reservoir CA-9
Phoenix Run—stream (2) PA-2
Phoenix Sch—school IL-6
Phoenix Sch—school NY-2
Phoenix Sch (abandoned)—school MO-7
Phoenix-Scottsdale Mobile Home Park,
The—locale AZ-5
Phoenix Seed & Feed Company—hist pl AZ-5
Phoenix Service Center—building AZ-5
Phoenix Sewage Treatment Plant—locale AZ-5
Phoenix Shaft (historical)—mine PA-2
Phoenix Sky Harbor International
Airp—airport AZ-5
Phoenix South Mountain Park—park AZ-5
Phoenix South Mountain Park
HQ—building AZ-5
Phoenix South Mountain Water
Storage—reservoir AZ-5
Phoenix Spit—bar MS-4
Phoenix Steam Plant—locale AZ-5
Phoenix Technical Sch—school AZ-5
Phoenix (Township of)—fmr MCD AR-4
Phoenix (Township of)—other IL-6
Phoenix Townsite—hist pl AZ-5
Phoenix Trail—trail (2) PA-2
Phoenix Trap and Skeet Club—other AZ-5
Phoenix Trotting Park—locale AZ-5
Phoenix Union HS Hist Dist—hist pl AZ-5
Phoenixville—pop pl AL-4
Phoenixville—pop pl CT-1
Phoenixville—pop pl PA-2
Phoenixville Area JHS—school PA-2
Phoenixville Area Senior HS—school PA-2
Phoenixville Borough—civil PA-2
Phoenixville Country Club—other PA-2
Phoenixville Dam—dam PA-2
Phoenixville Hist Dist—hist pl PA-2
Phoenixville Park Ponds—lake CT-1
Phoenixville Station—locale PA-2
Phoenix West Mobile Home Park—locale AZ-5
Phoenix Yard RR Station—building AZ-5
Phoenix YMCA Camp—locale AZ-5
Phoenix Zoo—park AZ-5
Phon D Sutton Rec Area—park AZ-5
Phone Booth Tank—reservoir AZ-5
Phone Creek—stream MT-8
Phone Line Canyon—valley TX-5
Phone Line Gap—gap NC-3
Phone Line Tank—reservoir AZ-5
Phone Line Tank—reservoir (2) TX-5
Phone Line Windmill—locale TX-5
Phones Pond—reservoir NM-5
Phoneton—pop pl OH-6
Phonograph Creek—stream AK-9
Phonograph Mine—mine CO-8
Phonolite Hill—summit UT-8
Phonolite Mine—mine NV-8
Phonolite (Site)—locale NV-8
Phorphy Peak WA-9
Phosmico RR Station (historical)—locale FL-3
Phosphate—pop pl MT-8
Phosphate Creek MT-8
Phosphate Creek—stream WY-8
Phosphate Hill—summit UT-8
Phosphate (historical)—pop pl TN-4
Phosphate Junction—pop pl NC-3
Phosphate Spring—spring UT-8
Phosphoria—pop pl FL-3
Phosphoria Gulch—valley ID-8
Phosphorite Creek—stream AK-9
Phospor Lake—lake MN-6
Photographer Gap UT-8
Photographers Point—summit WY-8
Photograph Gap—locale UT-8
Photo Lake—lake OR-9
Photo Pass—gap WY-8
Photovoltaic Array—other UT-8
Phragmites Pond—lake SD-7
Phramtons Run PA-2
Phranton Run—stream PA-2
Phrommer Park—park IN-6
Phroney Spring—spring AZ-5
Phronies Flat—flat CA-9
Phroso—locale OK-5
Phy Cem—cemetery TN-4
Phyfer Creek—stream MS-4
Phylaw Cem—cemetery AR-4
Phylden Subdivision—pop pl UT-8
Phyllip Mine SD-7
Phyllis—pop pl KY-4
Phyllis, Lake—reservoir NV-8
Phyllis Branch—stream FL-3
Phyllis Canal—canal ID-8
Phyllis Cem—cemetery OK-5
Phyllis Lake—lake FL-3
Phyllis Lake—lake ID-8
Phyllis Lake—lake MT-8
Phyllis Lodes Mine SD-7
Phyllis Run—stream PA-2
Phyllis Slough—stream ID-8
Phyllis Spur—ridge GA-3
Phyllis Subdivision—pop pl UT-8
Phyllis Wheatley Middle School AL-4
Phyllis Wheatly Sch—school TX-5
Physa Lake—lake WI-6
Physical Education Building/La Crosse State
Normal Sch—hist pl WI-6
Physic Creek—stream MT-8
Physic Creek Rsvr—reservoir MT-8
Physicians and Dentists Bldg—hist pl PA-2
Physicians and Surgeons Clinic—hospital MS-4
Physicians and Surgeons Hosp—hospital OR-9
Physicians Bldg—hist pl CA-9
Physicians Hosp—hospital NY-2
Physicians Hospital AZ-5
Phys Point—cape OR-9
Phys Slough—stream OR-9
Piaanu FM-9
Piaanu Pass FM-9
Piacenza—pop pl WI-6
Piachee AL-4
Piafa FM-9
Pia Gulch—valley HI-9
Piah Creek—stream (2) ID-8
Pial—island FM-9
Pialoa Fishpond—lake HI-9
Pialu FM-9
Pialu Durchfahrt FM-9
Pia Mill Rsvr—reservoir HI-9
Pianemane—island FM-9
Piankatank (Magisterial
District)—fmr MCD VA-3
Piankatank River VA-3
Piankatank River—stream VA-3
Piankatank Shores—pop pl VA-3
Piank Chapel—church NC-3
Piano—locale IA-7
Piano Box Canyon—valley OR-9
Pianobox Prospect, The—mine CA-9
Piano Hill—summit MT-8
Piano Leg Arch—arch UT-8
Piano Mtn—summit NY-2
Piano Row District—hist pl MA-1
Pianu—island FM-9
Pianu, Mochun—channel FM-9
Pi'ao, Chalan—pop pl MH-9
Pia Oik—pop pl AZ-5
Pia Oik Pass—gap AZ-5
Pia Oik Valley—valley AZ-5
Pia Oik Wash—stream AZ-5
Piapi Canyon—valley NV-8
Piarama—cape MH-9
Piaru FM-9
Piasa—pop pl IL-6
Piasa Creek—stream IL-6
Piasa Hills—pop pl IL-6
Piasa Island—island IL-6
Piasa Island—island FM-9
Piasano Creek TX-5
Piasano Oil Field—oilfield TX-5
Piasa (Township of)—pop pl IL-6
Piasuk River—stream AK-9
Piatka Cem—cemetery TX-5
Piato Vaya—locale AZ-5
Piato Vaya Pass—gap AZ-5
Piatt—locale PA-2
Piatt—pop pl IL-6
Piatt—pop pl WV-2
Piatt, Abram S., House and Piatt, Donn S.,
House—hist pl OH-6
Piatt Cem—cemetery IL-6
Piatt Cem—cemetery KY-4
Piatt (County)—pop pl IL-6
Piatt Creek—stream IL-6
Piatt Lake—lake MI-6
Piatts Lake Dam—dam NC-3
Piatt's Landing—hist pl KY-4
Piatt Spring MO-7
Piattsville—pop pl IN-6
Piatt (Township of)—pop pl PA-2
Pia Valley—valley HI-9
Piave—locale MS-4
Piaya—post sta PR-3
Piaya Lake—lake WY-8
Piazza Lake—lake MS-4
Piazzo Lake Dam—dam MS-4
Pibel Cem—cemetery NE-7
Pibel Lake—lake NE-7
Pibel Lake Rec Area—park NE-7
Pibel Sch—school NE-7
Piber Hollow—valley MO-7
Pi Beta Phi Sorority House—hist pl OR-9
Piburn Sch (historical)—school MO-7
Pica—locale PR-3
Pica—pop pl AZ-5
Pica (Barrio)—fmr MCD PR-3
Picabo—pop pl (2) ID-8
Picabo Hills—range ID-8
Pica Camp—locale AZ-5
Picacheo Peak AZ-5
Picacho—locale AZ-5
Picacho—locale NM-5
Picacho—pop pl AZ-5
Picacho—pop pl CA-9
Picacho—pop pl NM-5
Picacho—summit CA-9
Picacho Bridge—other NM-5

Picacho Butte—summit (2) ... AZ-5
Picacho Canal—canal ... NM-5
Picacho Colorado—summit ... AZ-5
Picacho Creek—stream ... CA-9
Picacho d ... AZ-5
Picacho de la Tea—summit ... PR-3
Picacho del Sentinela ... AZ-5
Picacho del Tucson ... AZ-5
Picacho Drain—canal ... NM-5
Picacho Elem Sch—school ... AZ-5
Picacho Hills—range ... AZ-5
Picacho Interchange ... AZ-5
Picacho Lake ... AZ-5
Picacho Lateral—canal ... NM-5
Picacho Mill Ruins—locale ... CA-9
Picacho Mine—mine ... AZ-5
Picacho Mine—mine (2) ... CA-9
Picacho Mountains—range ... AZ-5
Picacho Mtn—summit ... NM-5
Picacho Nuevo Artesian Well—well ... TX-5
Picacho Overpass—crossing ... AZ-5
Picacho Pass—locale ... AZ-5
Picacho Peak—summit (2) ... AZ-5
Picacho Peak—summit (2) ... CA-9
Picacho Peak—summit ... NM-5
Picacho Peak—summit ... UT-8
Picacho Peak Interchange—crossing ... AZ-5
Picacho Peak State Park—park ... AZ-5
Picacho Prieto ... CA-9
Picacho Reservoir Dam—dam ... AZ-5
Picacho Rock—summit ... CA-9
Picacho RR Overpass ... AZ-5
Picacho RR Station—building ... AZ-5
Picacho Rsvr—reservoir ... AZ-5
Picachos ... CA-9
Picachos, The—ridge ... CA-9
Picacho State Rec Area—park ... CA-9
Picacho Station ... AZ-5
Picacho View Mine—mine ... AZ-5
Picacho Wash—stream ... AZ-5
Picacho Wash—stream ... CA-9
Picaclo Peak Nature Trail—park ... AZ-5
Picada, Pass—channel ... AL-4
Picadilla Creek—stream ... AZ-5
Picadilli Sch—school ... PA-2
Picadilly Bay (carolina bay)—swamp ... NC-3
Picadilly Pond (Carolina Bay)—swamp ... NC-3
Picadilly Ridge—ridge ... CA-9
**Picadilly Terrace**—pop pl ... IL-6
Picadome—uninc pl ... KY-4
Picadome Sch—school ... KY-4
Picara Point—cape ... VI-3
**Picard**—pop pl ... WV-2
Picard, Israel, House—hist pl ... MA-1
Picard Branch—stream ... AL-4
Picard Brook—stream ... ME-1
Picard Cem—cemetery ... CA-9
Picard Cem—cemetery ... LA-4
Picard Hill—summit ... ME-1
Picard Lakes—lake ... MN-6
Picard Point ... MA-1
Picard Point—cape ... ID-8
Picard Ranch—locale ... WY-8
Pica RR Station—building ... AZ-5
Picaso Creek ... TX-5
Picasso Park—park ... SD-7
Picatee Creek—stream ... WI-6
Picatinny Air Park—airport ... NJ-2
Picatinny Arsenal—military ... NJ-2
Picatinny Arsenal (U.S. Army)—military ... NJ-2
Picatinny Lake—reservoir ... NJ-2
Picatinny Lake Dam—dam ... NJ-2
Picawaxen Creek ... MD-2
Picay Creek ... CA-9
Picay Creek—stream ... CA-9
Picayne Gulch—valley ... CO-8
**Picayune**—pop pl ... MS-4
Picayune Branch ... MS-4
Picayune Canyon—valley ... UT-8
Picayune Cem—cemetery ... CA-9
Picayune Chute—stream ... IL-6
Picayune Chute—stream ... IA-7
Picayune City Hall—building ... MS-4
Picayune Creek ... MS-4
Picayune Creek—stream (2) ... CA-9
Picayune Creek—stream (2) ... IA-7
Picayune Creek—stream (2) ... MS-4
Picayune Gulch—valley ... CA-9
Picayune Hollow—valley ... AR-4
Picayune HS—school ... MS-4
Picayune Island—island ... IL-6
Picayune JHS—school ... MS-4
Picayune Lake—lake (2) ... CA-9
Picayune Pearl River County
Airp—airport ... MS-4
Picayune Post Office—building ... MS-4
Picayune Radio Range Station—other ... MS-4
Picayune Sch—school ... IL-6
Picayune Shop Ctr—locale ... MS-4
Picayune Strand—swamp ... FL-3
Picayune Valley—basin ... CA-9
Piccadilly Brook—stream ... MA-1
Piccadily ... DE-2
Piccadune Gulch ... CO-8
Piccard Island—island ... MN-6
Picchetti Brothers Winery—hist pl ... CA-9
Picciola Island—island ... FL-3
Piccolo Creek—stream ... ID-8
Piccolo Creek—stream ... NV-8
Piccowaxen Creek ... MD-2
Piccowaxen Creek—stream ... MD-2
Piccowaxton Creek ... MD-2
Piceance Creek—stream ... CO-8
Pi Chapter House of Psi Upsilon
Fraternity—hist pl ... NY-2
Pichard Slough ... ND-7
Piche—locale ... MT-8
Pichens Cem—cemetery ... AR-4
**Picher**—pop pl ... OK-5
Picher-Peoria (CCD)—cens area ... OK-5
Pichette Rsvr—reservoir ... OR-9
Pichires—bar ... FM-9
Picho Hill—summit ... NM-5
Pichot Ridge—ridge ... LA-4
Pick, George, House—hist pl ... IL-6
**Pickadat Corner**—pop pl ... VA-3
Pickamick River ... IL-6
Pickamick River ... IN-6
Pickamink Ditch ... IN-6
Pickamink Lateral ... IL-6
Pickamink Lateral ... IN-6
Pickamink River ... IL-6
Pickamink River ... IN-6
Pick and Drill Mine—mine ... AZ-5
Pick Anderson Bypass—canal ... CA-9
Pick Anderson Drain—canal ... CA-9
Pick and Pan Creek—stream ... ID-8
Pickands, Jay M., House—hist pl ... OH-6
Pick and Shovel Mine—mine (2) ... CA-9
Pick and Shovel Spring—spring ... NV-8
Pick and Shovel Spring Number
Two—spring ... NV-8
Pick and Shovel Springs Number
One—spring ... NV-8
Pickaninny Buttes—summit ... CA-9
Pickard—locale ... GA-3
Pickard—locale ... WA-9
**Pickard**—pop pl ... IN-6
Pickard, Lake—lake ... ND-7
Pickard Bluff—cliff ... TN-4
Pickard Branch—stream ... TN-4
Pickard Brook—stream ... NH-1
Pickard Cem—cemetery ... AR-4
Pickard Cem—cemetery (2) ... TN-4
Pickard Cem—cemetery ... TX-5
Pickard Creek—stream ... TX-5
Pickard Ditch—canal ... IN-6
Pickard Drain—canal ... MI-6
Pickard Draw—valley ... WY-8
Pickard Falls ... TN-4
Pickard Field—park ... ME-1
Pickard Hill—summit ... ME-1
Pickard Hollow—valley ... TN-4
Pickard HS—school ... TX-5
Pickard Mtn ... ME-1
Pickard Point ... MA-1
Pickard Rec Area—park ... IA-7
Pickard Sch—school ... IL-6
Pickards Mill (historical)—locale ... TN-4
Pickards Mtn—summit ... NC-3
Pickards Point ... MA-1
**Pickard Township**—pop pl ... ND-7
**Pickardville**—pop pl ... ND-7
Pickawaxen Creek ... MD-2
Pickaway—locale ... VA-3
**Pickaway**—pop pl ... WV-2
Pickaway Country Club—other ... OH-6
**Pickaway (County)**—pop pl ... OH-6
Pickaway Settlements Battlesite—hist pl ... OH-6
**Pickaway (Township of)**—pop pl ... IL-6
**Pickaway (Township of)**—pop pl ... OH-6
Pick-aw-Ish Campground—locale ... CA-9
Pickayune ... MS-4
Pick Breeches Ridge—ridge ... VA-3
Pick Bridge—bridge ... WY-8
Pick Cem—cemetery ... IL-6
**Pick City**—pop pl ... ND-7
Pick Creek—stream ... CA-9
Pick Creek—stream ... OR-9
Pick Creek—stream ... WA-9
Pick Ditch—canal ... WY-8
Picked Chicken Hill—summit ... ME-1
Picked Cove—bay ... ME-1
Picked Hill—summit ... NH-1
Pickel, Dr. E. B., Rental House—hist pl ... OR-9
Pickel Cem—cemetery ... MO-7
Pickel Cem—cemetery ... TN-4
Pickel Ditch ... IN-6
Pickel Ditch—canal ... IN-6
Pickel Island—island ... TN-4
Pickel Island (historical)—island ... TN-4
Pickel Lake—lake ... MI-6
Pickel Lake—lake ... WI-6
Pickell Branch—stream ... SC-3
Pickell Hill—summit ... MD-2
Pickell Lake Dam—dam (3) ... MS-4
Pickell Slough—gut ... ND-7
Pickel Meadow—flat ... CA-9
Pickels Island ... TN-4
**Pickelville**—pop pl ... UT-8
Pickem Mtn—summit ... VA-3
Pickenpaw Run—stream ... WV-2
Pickens ... AL-4
Pickens—locale (2) ... AR-4
Pickens—locale ... TX-5
**Pickens**—pop pl ... MS-4
**Pickens**—pop pl ... OK-5
**Pickens**—pop pl ... SC-3
**Pickens**—pop pl ... WV-2
Pickens Acad—school ... AL-4
**Pickens Acres**—pop pl ... TN-4
Pickens Artesian Mill (historical)—locale ... AL-4
Pickens Attendance Center—school ... MS-4
Pickens Bar (historical)—bar ... AL-4
Pickens Bend—bend ... TN-4
Pickens Bend—summit ... SC-3
Pickens Branch—stream ... KY-4
Pickens Branch—stream ... MS-4
Pickens Branch—stream ... TN-4
Pickens Branch—stream ... TX-5
Pickens Bridge—bridge ... TN-4
Pickens Brook—stream ... NY-2
Pickens Canyon—valley ... CA-9
Pickens Canyon Channel—canal ... CA-9
Pickens (CCD)—cens area ... SC-3
Pickens Cem—cemetery (3) ... AL-4
Pickens Cem—cemetery ... KY-4
Pickens Cem—cemetery (3) ... MS-4
Pickens Cem—cemetery (4) ... TN-4
Pickens Cem—cemetery (2) ... WV-2
Pickens Ch—church ... OK-5
Picken Sch—school ... NY-2
Pickens Chapel—church ... SC-3
Pickens Chapel (historical)—church ... TN-4
**Pickens County**—pop pl ... AL-4
**Pickens (County)**—pop pl ... GA-3
**Pickens (County)**—pop pl ... SC-3
Pickens County Country Club—other ... SC-3
Pickens County Courthouse—building ... AL-4
Pickens County Jail—hist pl ... GA-3
Pickens County Training School ... AL-4
Pickens Creek—stream ... GA-3
Pickens Creek—stream ... MS-4
Pickens Creek—stream ... OK-5
Pickens Creek—stream (2) ... SC-3
Pickens Creek Cutoff—trail ... OK-5
Pickens Creek Trail—trail ... OK-5
Pickens Ferry—locale ... AL-4
Pickens Gap—gap ... NC-3
Pickens Gap—gap ... TN-4
Pickens Hill—summit ... KY-4
Pickens Hill—summit ... MA-1
Pickens (historical)—locale ... AL-4
Pickens Hollow—valley ... TN-4
Pickens House—hist pl ... SC-3
Pickens Landing—locale ... AL-4
Pickens Landing (historical)—locale ... MS-4
**Pickens Mill**—pop pl ... SC-3
Pickens Mill (historical)—locale ... AL-4
Pickens Mountian—summit ... WA-9
Pickens Mtn—summit ... NC-3
Pickens Nose—summit ... NC-3
Pickens Oil Field—oilfield ... MS-4
Pickens Pond—lake ... NY-2
Pickens Pone—lake ... AL-4
Pickens Pool—locale ... TX-5
Pickens Run—stream ... WV-2
Pickens Sch—school ... FL-3
Pickens Sch—school ... KS-7
Pickens Sch (historical)—school ... TN-4
Pickens Sewage Lagoon Dam—dam ... MS-4
Pickens Spring—spring ... AL-4
Pickens Spring—spring ... KY-4
Pickens Station ... MS-4
Pickens (Township of)—fmr MCD ... AR-4
Pickens View Ch—church ... SC-3
**Pickensville**—pop pl ... AL-4
**Pickensville**—pop pl ... SC-3
Pickensville Cut Off—channel ... AL-4
Pickensville Ferry (historical)—locale ... AL-4
Pickensville Landing (historical)—locale ... AL-4
Pickensville Lower Landing
(historical)—locale ... AL-4
Pickensville Rec Area—park ... AL-4
Pickens Water Works—other ... SC-3
Pickenville Mtn—summit ... PA-2
Pickeral Creek ... MO-7
Pickeral Creek—stream ... MN-6
Pickeral Lake ... MI-6
Pickeral Lake ... WI-6
Pickeral Lake Creek ... ND-7
Pickerall Ranch—locale ... WY-8
Pickerall Sch—school ... WY-8
Pickeral Pond ... ME-1
Pickeral Pond ... NH-1
Pickeral Pond Dam—dam ... PA-2
Pickerel ... MI-6
Pickerel—locale ... VA-3
**Pickerel**—pop pl ... SD-7
**Pickerel**—pop pl ... WI-6
Pickerel Bay—bay ... MN-6
Pickerel Brook—stream ... ME-1
Pickerel Cem—cemetery ... MN-6
Pickerel Cem—cemetery ... MO-7
Pickerel Ch—church ... MN-6
Pickerel Cove—bay ... CT-1
Pickerel Cove—bay ... ME-1
Pickerel Cove—bay ... MI-6
Pickerel Cove—bay ... NH-1
Pickerel Cove—cove (2) ... MA-1
Pickerel Creek ... KS-7
Pickerel Creek ... MI-6
Pickerel Creek ... SD-7
Pickerel Creek—stream (3) ... MI-6
Pickerel Creek—stream ... MN-6
Pickerel Creek—stream ... MO-7
Pickerel Creek—stream ... NH-1
Pickerel Creek—stream ... OH-6
Pickerel Creek—stream (5) ... WI-6
Pickerel Lake ... MI-6
Pickerel Lake ... MN-6
Pickerel Lake ... WI-6
Pickerel Lake—lake ... CT-1
Pickerel Lake—lake ... IA-7
Pickerel Lake—lake ... ME-1
Pickerel Lake—lake (30) ... MI-6
Pickerel Lake—lake (28) ... MN-6
Pickerel Lake—lake ... ND-7
Pickerel Lake—lake ... SD-7
Pickerel Lake—lake (21) ... WI-6
Pickerel Lake—locale ... SD-7
Pickerel Lake—reservoir ... PA-2
Pickerel Lake Brook—stream ... CT-1
Pickerel Lake Ch—church (2) ... MN-6
Pickerel Lake Creek—stream ... MI-6
Pickerel Lake Creek—stream ... ND-7
Pickerel Lake Creek—stream ... WI-6
Pickerel Lake Lookout Tower—locale ... MI-6
Pickerel Lakes—area ... AK-9
Pickerel Lakes—lake ... AK-9
Pickerel Lakes—lake ... WI-6
Pickerel Lake State Park—park ... SD-7
Pickerel Lake State Wildlife Mngmt
Area—park ... IA-7
Pickerel Lake (Township of)—civ div ... MN-6
Pickerel Lookout Tower—locale ... WI-6
Pickerel Point—cape ... IL-6
Pickerel Point—cape ... ME-1
Pickerel Point—cape ... NJ-2
Pickerel Point—cape ... PA-2
Pickerel Pond ... CT-1
Pickerel Pond ... MA-1
Pickerel Pond ... PA-2
Pickerel Pond—lake (10) ... ME-1
Pickerel Pond—lake (2) ... MA-1
Pickerel Pond—lake ... MI-6
Pickerel Pond—lake (3) ... NH-1
Pickerel Pond—lake (3) ... NY-2
Pickerel Pond—lake ... VT-1
Pickerel Pond—reservoir ... PA-2
Pickerel Pond Dam ... PA-2
Pickerel Pong—lake ... MA-1
Pickerel Ridge—ridge ... VA-3
Pickerel Run—stream ... IA-7
Pickerel Slough—gut ... AK-9
Pickerel Slough—gut ... MN-6
Pickerel Slough—stream ... MN-6
Pickerin Branch—stream ... KY-4
Pickering ... NH-1
Pickering—locale ... IA-7
Pickering—locale ... PA-2
**Pickering**—pop pl ... AL-4
**Pickering**—pop pl ... LA-4
**Pickering**—pop pl ... MO-7
**Pickering**—pop pl ... NH-1
Pickering, I. O., House—hist pl ... KS-7
Pickering, Mount—summit ... CA-9
Pickering, Mount—summit ... NH-1
Pickering Arroyo—stream ... NM-5
Pickering Bar—bar ... CA-9
Pickering Basin—basin ... TX-5
Pickering Beach—beach ... DE-2
**Pickering Beach**—pop pl ... DE-2
Pickering Branch—stream ... WV-2
Pickering Brook—stream ... NH-1
Pickering Cem—cemetery (2) ... MS-4
Pickering Cem—cemetery ... NH-1
Pickering Cove—bay ... ME-1
Pickering Creek—bay ... MD-2
Pickering Creek—stream ... OR-9
Pickering Creek—stream ... PA-2
Pickering Creek—stream (2) ... TX-5
Pickering Creek—stream ... UT-8
Pickering Creek Dam—dam ... PA-2
Pickering Creek Rsvr—reservoir ... PA-2
Pickering Ditch—canal ... CO-8
Pickering Ditch—canal ... IN-6
Pickering Ditch—canal ... NM-5
Pickering Drain—stream ... MI-6
Pickering Farm—hist pl ... WA-9
Pickering Field—other ... PA-2
Pickering (historical)—locale ... MS-4
Pickering Hollow—valley ... MO-7
Pickering House—hist pl ... TX-5
Pickering Island—island ... ME-1
Pickering JHS—school ... MA-1
Pickering Knob—summit ... WV-2
Pickering Lake—reservoir ... AL-4
Pickering Lake Dam—dam ... AL-4
Pickering Passage—channel ... WA-9
Pickering Point—cape ... MA-1
Pickering Pond—lake ... PA-2
Pickering Post Office (historical)—building ... PA-2
Pickering Run—stream ... PA-2
Pickering Sch—school ... LA-4
Pickering Sch—school ... MA-1
Pickering Sch (abandoned)—school ... MO-7
Pickering Sch (historical)—school ... MS-4
**Pickerington**—pop pl ... OH-6
**Pickering Township**—pop pl ... ND-7
Pickering Valley Elementary School ... PA-2
Pickering Wharf—locale ... MA-1
Pickernell Creek—stream ... WA-9
Pickert—locale ... ND-7
Pickert (historical)—locale ... ND-7
Pickerton Ch—church ... GA-3
Pickerton Hill—summit ... MO-7
Pickert Point—cape ... AR-4
Picket Brake—gut ... LA-4
Picket Brook ... CT-1
Picket Brook—stream ... NY-2
Picket Canyon ... UT-8
Picket Canyon—valley ... AZ-5
Picket Canyon—valley ... NM-5
Picket Cem—cemetery ... TN-4
Picket Ch—church ... OK-5
Picket Chapel—church ... OK-5
Picket Corral—other ... NM-5
Picket Corral Canyon—valley ... ID-8
Picket Corral Canyon—valley ... NM-5
Picket Corral Creek—stream ... NV-8
Picket Corral Ranch—locale ... CO-8
Picket Corral Ridge—ridge ... UT-8
Picket Corral Tank—reservoir (2) ... AZ-5
Picket Corral Tank—reservoir ... NM-5
Picket Creek—stream ... CA-9
Picket Creek—stream ... MI-6
Picket Creek—stream ... MN-6
Picket Creek—stream ... MT-8
Picket Creek—stream ... WA-9
Picket Creek—stream ... WY-8
Picket Fork—stream ... UT-8
Picket Gate Crags—summit ... AK-9
Picket Guard Peak—summit ... CA-9
Picket Hollow—valley ... TX-5
Picket Island—island ... LA-4
Picket Island—island ... VT-1
Picket Lake—lake ... FL-3
Picket Lake—lake ... IL-6
Picket Lake—lake ... MI-6
Picket Lake—lake (2) ... MN-6
Picket Lake—lake ... MT-8
Picket Lake—lake ... WY-8
Picket Lake—swamp ... MS-4
Picket Lake Sch—school ... FL-3
Picket Mill Well—well ... AZ-5
Picket Mtn—summit ... CO-8
Picket Mtn—summit ... ID-8
Picket Mtn—summit ... ME-1
Picket Park—flat ... AZ-5
Picket Pass—gap ... WA-9
Picket Pens Tank—reservoir ... NM-5
Picket Pen Tank—reservoir ... AZ-5
Picket Pin Creek—stream ... CO-8
Picket Pin Creek—stream ... ID-8
Picket Pin Creek—stream ... MT-8
Picketpin Flat—flat ... OR-9
Picket Pin Mtn—summit ... MT-8
Picket Pin Park—flat ... CO-8
Picketpin Spring—spring ... OR-9
Picket Pit—cave ... TN-4
Picket Point—cape ... NY-2
Picket Post ... AZ-5
**Picket Post**—pop pl ... SC-3
Picket Post Creek ... AZ-5
Picketpost Inn—locale ... AZ-5
Picketpost Mtn—summit ... AZ-5
Picket Prairie—flat ... OK-5
Picket Range—range ... WA-9
Picket Rock—bar ... NY-2
Picket Spring—spring ... OR-9
Picket Spring Branch—stream ... TX-5
Picket Spring Canyon ... NM-5
Picket Springs (historical)—locale ... AL-4
Pickets Store ... MS-4
Pickett—locale ... AL-4
Pickett—locale ... KY-4
Pickett—locale ... TX-5
**Pickett**—pop pl ... LA-4
**Pickett**—pop pl ... OK-5
**Pickett**—pop pl ... WI-6
Pickett, James A., House—hist pl ... KY-4
Pickett, Lake—lake ... FL-3
Pickett, Mount—summit ... WA-9
Pickett Bay—bay ... LA-4
Pickett Bay—bay ... MI-6
Pickett Bay—swamp ... FL-3
Pickett Branch—stream ... AL-4
Pickett Branch—stream ... GA-3
Pickett Branch—stream ... KY-4
Pickett Brook—stream ... CT-1
Pickett Brook—stream ... NY-2
Pickett Butte Lookout—locale ... OR-9
Pickett Canyon—valley ... NM-5
Pickett Canyon—valley ... UT-8
Pickett Cem—cemetery ... AL-4
Pickett Cem—cemetery ... AR-4
Pickett Cem—cemetery ... FL-3
Pickett Cem—cemetery (2) ... GA-3
Pickett Cem—cemetery ... IN-6
Pickett Cem—cemetery (3) ... MS-4
Pickett Cem—cemetery (3) ... MO-7
Pickett Cem—cemetery (2) ... TN-4
Pickett Cem—cemetery ... TX-5
Pickett Cem—cemetery ... WV-2
Pickett Chapel—church ... VA-3
Pickett Chapel Methodist Church—hist pl ... TN-4
Pickett Corners—locale ... NY-2
Pickett Corral—locale ... AZ-5
Pickett Corral—locale ... CA-9
Pickett Corral Canyon—valley ... UT-8
**Pickett County**—pop pl ... TN-4
Pickett County Court House—building ... TN-4
Pickett County Elem Sch—school ... TN-4
Pickett County HS—school ... TN-4
Pickett Creek ... MI-6
Pickett Creek ... MS-4
Pickett Creek—stream ... AL-4
Pickett Creek—stream ... AR-4
Pickett Creek—stream ... CA-9
Pickett Creek—stream ... GA-3
Pickett Creek—stream ... ID-8
Pickett Creek—stream ... KS-7
Pickett Creek—stream ... MS-4
Pickett Creek—stream ... OR-9
Pickett Creek—stream ... TX-5
Pickett Creek—stream (2) ... WY-8
Pickett Creek Saddle—gap ... ID-8
Pickett Dam—dam ... MI-6
Pickett Drain—canal (2) ... MI-6
Pickett Draw—valley ... NM-5
Pickett Elementary—school ... NC-3
Pickett Gulch—valley ... MT-8
Pickett Gulf—valley ... TN-4
Pickett Henry Mtn—summit ... ME-1
Pickett Hill—summit (2) ... ME-1
Pickett Hill—summit ... NH-1
Pickett Hill—summit ... NM-5
Pickett Hill—summit ... PA-2
Pickett Hollow—valley ... ID-8
Pickett Hollow—valley ... TN-4
Pickett Hollow—valley ... WV-2
Pickett House—hist pl ... WA-9
Pickett Island ... AR-4
Pickett Island—island ... SC-3
Pickett JHS—school ... AZ-5
Pickett Lake ... WY-8
Pickett Lake—lake ... AZ-5
Pickett Lake—lake ... AR-4
Pickett Lake—lake ... MI-6
Pickett Lake—lake ... MS-4
Pickett Lake—lake ... OR-9
Pickett Lake—lake ... TN-4
Pickett Lake Dam—dam ... MS-4
Pickett Ledge—bar ... MA-1
Pickett Mine (surface)—mine ... TN-4
Pickett Mine (underground)—mine ... TN-4
Pickett Mountain Pond—lake ... ME-1
Pickett Mtn—summit ... ME-1
Pickett Mtn—summit ... OR-9
Pickett Park—park ... NV-8
Pickett Park—park ... TN-4
Pickett Peak—summit (2) ... CA-9
Pickett Peak Campground—locale ... CA-9
Pickett Pens—locale ... TX-5
Pickett Playground—park ... MO-7
Pickett Pond—lake ... AL-4
Pickett Pond—lake ... VT-1
Pickett Pond Dam—dam ... MS-4
Pickett Post ... SC-3
**Pickett Post**—pop pl ... SC-3
Pickett Prairie—flat ... OR-9
Picket Trail Dugout—reservoir ... AZ-5
Pickett Ranch—locale ... WY-8
Pickett Ranch Creek—stream ... TX-5
Pickett Revetment—levee ... MS-4
Pickett Run—stream ... OH-6
Pickett Run—stream ... PA-2
Picketts Bay—swamp ... FL-3
Picketts Bayou—gut ... TX-5
Picketts Cem—cemetery ... KY-4
Pickett Sch—school ... FL-3
Pickett Sch—school ... MO-7
Pickett Sch—school ... OH-6
Picketts Corner—locale ... MD-2
Picketts Corners—locale ... NY-2
Picketts Gin (historical)—locale ... AL-4
Picketts Harbor—locale ... VA-3
Picketts Knob—summit ... GA-3
Picketts Lake—lake ... MN-6
Picketts Landing (historical)—locale ... TN-4
Picketts Landing Post Office
(historical)—building ... TN-4
Pickett Slough—gut ... AR-4
Picketts Lower Trough Spring—spring ... ID-8
Pickett's Mill Battlefield Site—hist pl ... GA-3
Picketts Mill Creek—stream ... GA-3
Pickett's Monmt—park ... WA-9
Picketts Pasture—flat ... MT-8
Pickett Spring Canyon—valley ... NM-5
Pickett Spring Creek—stream ... ID-8
Pickett Spring Rsvr—reservoir ... OR-9
Picketts Ranch Creek—stream ... TX-5
Picketts Store (historical)—locale ... MS-4
Pickett State Park And Forest—park ... TN-4
Pickett State Rustic Park ... TN-4
Pickett State Rustic Park Hist
Dist—hist pl ... TN-4
Picketts Upper Trough Spring—spring ... ID-8
**Pickettsville**—pop pl ... NY-2
Picketts Wharf—locale ... VA-3
Pickett Tanks—reservoir ... NM-5
Pickettville ... TN-4
Pickettville—locale ... NY-2
**Pickettville**—pop pl ... FL-3
Pickettville Post Office ... TN-4
Pickett Well—well ... NV-8
Pickett Windmill—locale (2) ... NM-5
Picketville Cem—cemetery ... TX-5
Picketwire ... CO-8
Picketwire Ditch—canal ... CO-8
Picketwire Valley—valley (2) ... CO-8
Pickfoot Creek—stream ... MT-8
**Pickford**—pop pl ... MI-6
Pickford Community Park—park ... MI-6
Pickford Drain—stream ... MI-6
Pickfords Lake Dam—dam ... MS-4
**Pickford (Township of)**—pop pl ... MI-6
Pickhandle Basin—basin ... WA-9
Pickhandle Gap—gap ... WA-9
Pickhandle Gulch—valley ... NV-8
Pickhandle Hills—range ... AZ-5
Pickhandle Mine—mine ... NV-8
Pickhandle Pass—gap ... CA-9
Pickhandle Pass—gap ... NV-8
Pickhandle Point—summit ... WA-9
Picking, D., And Company—hist pl ... OH-6
Pickings Run—stream ... PA-2
Pickings Run - in part ... PA-2
Pickings Sch (historical)—school ... PA-2
Pickinpaugh Homestead—locale ... WY-8
Pickins Creek—stream ... MS-4
Pick Lake—lake ... MN-6
Pickle, Simon, Stone House—hist pl ... PA-2
Pickle Branch—stream ... TX-5
Pickle Butte—summit ... ID-8
Pickle Camp—locale ... CA-9
Pickle Canyon—valley (2) ... CA-9
Pickle Canyon—valley ... ID-8
Pickle Cem—cemetery ... IN-6
Pickle Cem—cemetery (2) ... MS-4
Pickle Cem—cemetery ... TN-4
Pickle Chapel—church ... TX-5
Pickle Creek—stream ... AK-9
Pickle Creek—stream ... IL-6
Pickle Creek—stream ... KS-7
Pickle Creek—stream ... MN-6
Pickle Creek—stream ... MO-7
Pickle Creek—stream ... OK-5
Pickle Creek—stream ... OR-9
Pickle Creek—stream ... TX-5
Pickle Factory Pond—reservoir ... NJ-2
Pickle Fork—stream ... KY-4
Pickle Gap—gap ... AR-4
Pickle Gap Ch—church ... AR-4
Pickle Gap Creek—stream ... AR-4
Pickle Gulch Campground—locale ... CO-8
Pickle Hill—summit ... ME-1
Pickle Hill—summit ... PA-2
Pickle Hollow—valley ... AR-4
Pickle Hollow—valley ... VA-3
Pickle House Slough—gut ... MO-7
Picklekeg Creek—stream ... UT-8
Pickle Lake—lake (3) ... MN-6
Pickle Lake—lake ... WI-6
Pickle Meadow ... CA-9
Pickle Mtn—summit ... WV-2
Pickle Pass—gap ... WY-8
Pickle Pear Knob—summit ... IN-6
Pickle Point ... VT-1
Pickle Pond ... MA-1
Pickle Pond—lake ... FL-3
Pickle Pond—lake ... MI-6
Pickle Prairie Meadows—flat ... WA-9
Pickler, Maj. John A.,
Homestead—hist pl ... SD-7
Pickles Branch—stream ... VA-3
Pickles Butte—summit ... ID-8
Pickles Fork—stream ... WV-2
Picklesimen Mountain ... GA-3
Picklesimer Fields—ridge ... NC-3
Picklesimer Mtn—summit ... GA-3
Pickles Island ... TN-4
Pickles Pond—lake ... VT-1
Pickle Spring—spring ... CA-9
Pickle Spring—spring ... OR-9
Pickles Reef—bar ... FL-3
Pickles Shoals—bar ... TN-4
Pickless Lake ... MI-6
Pickle Street—locale ... WV-2
**Pickle Street (Midway)**—pop pl ... WV-2
Pickle Street Sch—school ... MI-6
Pickletown ... MS-4
Pickletub Branch—stream ... WV-2
Pickleville ... UT-8
Pickliss Lake—lake ... MI-6
Pick Lode Mine—mine ... SD-7
Picklum, Frank, House—hist pl ... IA-7
Pickney ... AR-4
Pickneyville Sch—school ... MS-4
Picknick Cave ... AL-4
Picknitt Creek ... TX-5
Pickowaxon Creek ... MD-2
Pick Peak—summit ... WA-9
Pick Pocket—basin ... WA-9
**Pickpocket Woods**—pop pl ... NH-1
Pick Point—cape ... NH-1
Pick Ranch—locale ... WY-8
**Pickrell**—pop pl ... NE-7
Pickrell Cem—cemetery ... IL-6
Pickrell Cem—cemetery ... OH-6
**Pickrell Corner**—pop pl ... KS-7
Pickrell Creek—stream ... CA-9
Pickrell Mesa—summit ... UT-8
Pickrell Park—park ... TX-5
**Pickrelltown**—pop pl ... OH-6
Pickrelltown Cem—cemetery ... OH-6
Pickrel Ranch—locale ... WY-8
Pickrel Ranch Oil Field—oilfield ... WY-8
Pickren Cem—cemetery ... AR-4
Pickren Hill—summit ... KY-4
Pick River—stream ... AK-9
Picks ... NC-3
**Picks**—pop pl ... NC-3
Picks Creek—stream ... AL-4
Pickseed Swamp—swamp ... SC-3
**Pickshin**—pop pl ... WV-2
Pickshin Nature Center—building ... NC-3
Pick Spring—spring ... OR-9
Pick State Wildlife Mngmt Area—park ... MN-6
**Pickstown**—pop pl ... SD-7
**Pickton**—pop pl ... TX-5
Pickton Oil Field—oilfield ... TX-5
Pickton-Pine Forest (CCD)—cens area ... TX-5
Pickup Drain—canal ... ID-8
Pickup Hill—summit ... NY-2
Pickup Lake—lake ... NY-2
Pickup Wash Lateral—canal ... UT-8
Pickwacket Pond—lake ... NY-2
**Pickwatina Place**—pop pl ... TN-4

Pickwell Park—park TX-5
*Pickwick* TN-4
Pickwick—hist pl PA-2
Pickwick—locale MS-4
Pickwick—locale OK-5
**Pickwick**—pop pl IA-7
**Pickwick**—pop pl MN-6
**Pickwick**—pop pl TX-5
**Pickwick**—pop pl VA-3
Pickwick Cave—cave AL-4
Pickwick (CCD)—cens area TN-4
Pickwick Ch—church TN-4
Pickwick Dam—locale TN-4
**Pickwick Dam (Pickwick)**—pop pl TN-4
Pickwick Division—civil TN-4
Pickwick Hotel—hist pl CA-9
Pickwick Lake—reservoir AL-4
Pickwick Lake—reservoir MS-4
Pickwick Lake—reservoir (2) TN-4
Pickwick Landing Dam—dam (2) TN-4
*Pickwick Landing Rsvr* AL-4
*Pickwick Landing Rsvr* MS-4
Pickwick Landing State Park—park TN-4
Pickwick Mill—hist pl MN-6
Pickwick Mine—mine WY-8
**Pickwick Park**—pop pl IN-6
Pickwick Theater Bldg—hist pl IL-6
*Pickwick Village* TN-4
**Pickwick Village (subdivision)**—pop pl NC-3
*Pickwocket Pond* NY-2
**Pickwood Hills (subdivision)**—pop pl NC-3
**Pickwood (subdivision)**—pop pl AL-4
Pickworth Point—cape MA-1
Picky Pear Canyon—valley TX-5
*Piclaclekeha* FL-3
Piclalene Bayou—stream FL-3
Picle Gulch—valley CO-8
Piclic Run—stream MD-2
Picnic—locale FL-3
Picnic—locale KY-4
Picnic Area Site 4—locale KY-4
Picnic Area Site 5—locale KY-4
Picnic Bayou—gut LA-4
Picnic Beds Picnic Area—locale NC-3
Picnic Bend—bend TX-5
Picnic Boulder Creek—stream OR-9
Picnic Branch—stream MO-7
*Picnic Canyon* MT-8
Picnic Canyon—valley CA-9
Picnic Canyon—valley (2) MT-8
Picnic Canyon—valley (3) NM-5
Picnic Canyon—valley UT-8
Picnic Cave—cave AL-4
Picnic Cave—cave NV-8
Picnic Cove—bay WA-9
Picnic Creek—stream AK-9
Picnic Creek—stream AZ-5
Picnic Creek—stream (2) CA-9
Picnic Creek—stream ID-8
Picnic Creek—stream MN-6
Picnic Creek—stream NV-8
Picnic Creek—stream OR-9
Picnic Creek—stream UT-8
Picnic Flat—flat CO-8
Picnic Flat Sch—school CO-8
*Picnic Four Area* AZ-5
Picnic Grove Rsvr—reservoir CA-9
Picnic Gulch—valley CO-8
Picnic Gulch—valley ID-8
Picnic Harbor—bay AK-9
Picnic Hill—summit AZ-5
Picnic Hill—summit KY-4
Picnic Hill Park—park WI-6
Picnic Hole—lake MS-4
Picnic Hollow—valley AR-4
Picnic Hollow—valley ID-8
Picnic Hollow—valley KY-4
Picnic Hollow—valley MO-7
Picnic Hollow—valley WY-8
Picnic Island—island (3) FL-3
Picnic Island—island (2) MI-6
Picnic Island—island (2) MN-6
Picnic Island—island NH-1
Picnic Island—island (2) NY-2
Picnic Island—island WA-9
Picnic Island—island WI-6
Picnic Island Creek—gut FL-3
Picnic Koy—island FL-3
Picnic Lake—lake AK-9
Picnic Lake—lake (3) FL-3
Picnic Lake—lake GA-3
Picnic Lake—lake (3) MI-6
Picnic Lake—lake WI-6
Picnic Lake—reservoir FL-3
Picnic Lake Park—park CA-9
Picnic Lakes—lake MT-8
Picnic Mine—mine UT-8
Picnic Point—cape AK-9
Picnic Point—cape AR-4
Picnic Point—cape ID-8
Picnic Point—cape ME-1
Picnic Point—cape (3) NY-2
Picnic Point—cape WA-9
Picnic Point—cape (3) WI-6
Picnic Point—locale WA-9
Picnic Pond—reservoir FL-3
Picnic Rocks—island MI-6
Picnic Spring—spring (2) AZ-5
Picnic Spring—spring ID-8
Picnic Spring—spring NV-8
Picnic Spring—spring (3) OR-9
Picnic Spring—spring SD-7
Picnic Spring—spring TX-5
Picnic Spring Campground—park SD-7
Picnic Springs—spring CO-8
Picnic Tank—reservoir (3) AZ-5
Picnic Tank—reservoir TX-5
Pico—locale CA-9
**Pico**—pop pl VA-3
**Pico**—pop pl PR-3
Pico, Pio, Casa—hist pl CA-9
Pico, Romulo, Adobe—hist pl CA-9
Pico Aislado—summit CO-8
Pico Atalaya—summit PR-3
Pico Blanco Boy Scout Camp—locale CA-9
Pico Butte—summit NM-5
Pico Canyon—valley CA-9
Pico Creek—gut GA-3
Pico Creek—stream CA-9
Pico Creek—stream NY-2
Pico Cut—bend GA-3
Pico del Este—summit PR-3
Pico del Oeste—summit PR-3
Pico Derecho Mtn—summit AZ-5
*Picodica Creek* AZ-5
Pico El Yunque—summit PR-3
Pico Fraile—summit PR-3
Pico Heights—uninc pl CA-9
Pico Huton—summit PR-3
Pico Island—island GA-3
Pico Lake—lake NY-2
**Picolata**—pop pl FL-3
Picolata Sch—school FL-3
Pico Lebron—summit PR-3
Pico Montoso—summit PR-3
Pico Mtn—summit NY-2
Pico Park—park CA-9
Pico Peak—summit VT-1
Pico Pinto—summit PR-3
Pico Pond—lake VT-1
Pico Reach—channel GA-3
**Pico Rivera**—pop pl CA-9
Pico Rock—bar CA-9
Pico Rodadero—summit PR-3
Picosa Creek—stream (2) TX-5
Pico San Bernardo—summit PR-3
*Picoso Creek* TX-5
*Picosora Creek* TX-5
Picotte, Dr. Susan, Memorial Hosp—hist pl NE-7
Picou, Bayou—stream LA-4
*Pico Y Cerro De Reyes* CA-9
PIC Ranch—locale WY-8
Picron Hill—summit AR-4
PIC Sch—school WY-8
Pic Swale—valley OR-9
Pictograph Cave—hist pl AR-4
Pictograph Cave—hist pl MT-8
Pictograph Cave—hist pl TX-5
Pictograph Point—cliff CO-8
Picton Island—island NY-2
**Picton Township**—pop pl ND-7
**Pictou**—pop pl CO-8
Pictou Arroyo—stream CO-8
Pictou Mine—mine CO-8
Picture Branch—stream VA-3
Picture Canyon—valley CO-8
Picture Canyon—valley NV-8
Picture Canyon—valley OK-5
Picture Creek—stream MT-8
Picture Creek—stream NC-3
Pictured Pine Knob—summit TN-4
Pictured Rock Lake—lake WI-6
Pictured Rocks—cliff MI-6
Pictured Rocks—OTHER MN-6
Pictured Rocks—other NM-5
Pictured Rocks Natl Lakeshore—park MI-6
Pictured Rocks State Park—park IA-7
Picture Flat—flat OR-9
Picture Gallery Gulch—valley CA-9
Picture Gallery Ranch—locale UT-8
Picture Gorge—valley OR-9
Picture Lake—lake CO-8
Picture Lake—lake MI-6
Picture Lake—lake (2) MT-8
Picture Lake—lake UT-8
Picture Lake—lake WA-9
Picture Lake—lake WI-6
Picture Mtn—summit AZ-5
Picture Point—cliff OR-9
Picture Pond—lake ME-1
Picture Ridge—ridge MT-8
Picture Rock—basin AZ-5
Picture Rock—summit NM-5
Picture Rock Hills—summit UT-8
Picture Rock Island—island OR-9
Picture Rock Mine—mine NV-8
Picture Rock Pass Petroglyphs Site—hist pl OR-9
Picture Rock Prairie—flat OR-9
Picture Rock Rsvr—reservoir UT-8
*Picture Rocks* AZ-5
Picture Rocks—cliff PA-2
**Picture Rocks**—pop pl PA-2
Picture Rocks—summit (2) AZ-5
Picture Rocks Borough—civil PA-2
Picture Rock Wash—valley UT-8
Picture Rock Wash Rsvr—reservoir UT-8
Picturesque Cove—bay AK-9
Picturesque Lake—lake UT-8
Picturesque Windows—arch UT-8
Picture Tree Springs—spring OR-9
Picuda Peak—summit NM-5
**Picuris**—pop pl NM-5
Picuris Canyon—valley NM-5
Picuris (CCD)—cens area NM-5
Picuris Mountains—ridge NM-5
Picuris Peak—summit NM-5
Picuris Pueblo—civil NM-5
Picuris Pueblo—hist pl NM-5
**Picuris Pueblo**—pop pl NM-5
Picuris Pueblo (Indian Reservation)—reserve NM-5
*Pid Branch* GA-3
Pidcock—locale GA-3
Pidcock Creek—stream PA-2
**Pidcoke**—pop pl TX-5
Pidcoke Cem—cemetery TX-5
Pid Creek—stream ID-8
Piddington Cem—cemetery WI-6
Piddler Island—island FL-3
Piddleville—locale GA-3
Piddlins Lake—swamp FL-3
Pidd Sch—school MI-6
Pide Branch—stream TN-4
Pidek Keren—locale FM-9
Pidgeon, Lake—lake OR-9
Pidgeon Creek—stream ID-8
Pidgeon Falls—falls OR-9
Pidgeon Flat—flat CA-9
Pidgeon Flat—flat ID-8
*Pidgeon Hill* MA-1
Pidgeon Hill—summit NY-2
Pidgeon Hill Sch—school NY-2
**Pidgeon Key**—pop pl FL-3
*Pidgeon Mountain* GA-3
Pidgeon Park—park OR-9
Pidgeon Point—summit CA-9
Pidgeon Roost Creek—stream CA-9
Pidgeon Spring—spring AZ-5
Pidgeon Spring—spring NV-8
Pidgeon Springs Cem—cemetery GA-3
Pidgeon Tank—reservoir AZ-5
Pidgeon Tank—reservoir NM-5
*Pidgeon Water Creek* UT-8
*Pidos Kalahe* MH-9
Pidos Kalaho—summit MH-9
**Pie**—pop pl WV-2
Pie, The—locale CO-8
Piebald Gulch—valley AZ-5
Piebald Well—well AZ-5
Pieburn Branch—stream AL-4
Pieburn Creek—stream KY-4
Pie Canyon—valley CA-9
Pie Canyon Trail (Jeep)—trail CA-9
Pie Canyon Trail (Pack)—trail CA-9
Pie Creek—stream (2) ID-8
Pie Creek—stream NV-8
Pie Creek—stream OR-9
Pie Creek—stream VA-3
Pied Branch—stream KY-4
Pied Creek—stream AL-4
Pie de Gallo—cape (2) TX-5
*Piedgeon Creek* AR-4
*Piedmont* FL-3
*Piedmont* VA-3
Piedmont—locale AZ-5
Piedmont—locale GA-3
Piedmont—locale TN-4
Piedmont—locale TX-5
Piedmont—locale (2) VA-3
**Piedmont**—pop pl (2) AL-4
**Piedmont**—pop pl CA-9
**Piedmont**—pop pl (2) CO-8
**Piedmont**—pop pl FL-3
**Piedmont**—pop pl KS-7
**Piedmont**—pop pl KY-4
**Piedmont**—pop pl MO-7
**Piedmont**—pop pl MT-8
**Piedmont**—pop pl OH-6
**Piedmont**—pop pl OK-5
**Piedmont**—pop pl OR-9
**Piedmont**—pop pl SC-3
**Piedmont**—pop pl SD-7
**Piedmont**—pop pl TN-4
**Piedmont**—pop pl VA-3
**Piedmont**—pop pl WA-9
**Piedmont**—pop pl (2) WV-2
**Piedmont**—pop pl WY-8
Piedmont Acad—school GA-3
Piedmont Acad—school NC-3
Piedmont Airp—airport AL-4
Piedmont Ave Sch—school CA-9
Piedmont Baptist Ch—church TN-4
*Piedmont Baptist Church* AL-4
Piedmont Branch—stream TN-4
Piedmont Branch Cave—cave TN-4
Piedmont Butte—summit SD-7
Piedmont (CCD)—cens area AL-4
Piedmont (CCD)—cens area DE-2
Piedmont (CCD)—cens area SC-3
Piedmont Cem—cemetery (2) SC-3
Piedmont Cem—cemetery TN-4
Piedmont Ch—church AL-4
Piedmont Ch—church GA-3
Piedmont Ch—church KY-4
Piedmont Ch—church MS-4
Piedmont Ch—church (3) NC-3
Piedmont Ch—church (2) SC-3
Piedmont Ch—church (5) VA-3
Piedmont Charcoal Kilns—hist pl WY-8
**Piedmont (city)**—pop pl CA-9
Piedmont City Hall—building AL-4
Piedmont Congregational Holiness Ch—church AL-4
Piedmont Creek—stream CA-9
Piedmont Creek—stream OR-9
Piedmont Creek—stream WY-8
Piedmont Crescent Golf Course Lak—reservoir NC-3
Piedmont Dam—dam OH-6
Piedmont Division—civil AL-4
*Piedmont Elementary School* TN-4
*Piedmont Heights* MN-6
Piedmont Heights—locale AL-4
Piedmont Heights—locale GA-3
**Piedmont Heights**—pop pl NC-3
**Piedmont Heights (subdivision)**—pop pl NC-3
Piedmont Hills HS—school CA-9
Piedmont Hollow—valley MO-7
Piedmont Hosp—hospital AL-4
Piedmont Hosp—hospital GA-3
Piedmont HS—school AL-4
Piedmont HS—school CA-9
Piedmont HS—school (2) NC-3
Piedmont Interstate Warehouse System—facility SC-3
Piedmont JHS—school NC-3
Piedmont Lake—lake OH-6
Piedmont Lake—reservoir GA-3
Piedmont Lake—reservoir NC-3
Piedmont Landing—locale TN-4
Piedmont (Magisterial District)—fmr MCD VA-3
Piedmont (Magisterial District)—fmr MCD WV-2
Piedmont Memorial Cem—cemetery NC-3
*Piedmont Memorial Garden Cemetery* AL-4
Piedmont Memorial Gardens—cemetery NC-3
*Piedmont Middle School* NC-3
Piedmont Mill—locale VA-3
Piedmont Mine—mine CO-8
Piedmont Mine—mine NV-8
Piedmont Minerals Dam—dam NC-3
Piedmont Minerals Lake—reservoir NC-3
Piedmont Mine (underground)—mine AL-4
Piedmont Municipal Airp—airport MO-7
Piedmont Natl Wildlife Ref—park GA-3
Piedmont Overlook—locale VA-3
Piedmont Park—hist pl GA-3
Piedmont Park—park CA-9
Piedmont Park—park GA-3
Piedmont Park—park NE-7
Piedmont Park—park NC-3
**Piedmont Park**—pop pl SC-3
Piedmont Park Alliance Ch—church FL-3
Piedmont Park Public Use Area—locale MO-7
Piedmont Picnic Area—locale VA-3
*Piedmont Plateau* AL-4
Piedmont Plaza Shop Ctr—locale NC-3
Piedmont Pond—lake VT-1
Piedmont (P.O. sta.)—uninc pl CA-9
Piedmont Post Office—building AL-4
Piedmont Quarry—basin NC-3
Piedmont Rec Area—park AL-4
*Piedmont Reservoir* OH-6
Piedmont Rsvr—reservoir WY-8
Piedmont Sch—school CA-9
Piedmont Sch—school TN-4
Piedmont Sch—school TX-5
Piedmont Shop Ctr—locale AL-4
**Piedmont Springs**—pop pl AL-4
Piedmont Springs Archeol Site—hist pl TX-5
Piedmont Springs Church Camp—locale AL-4
*Piedmont Springs Mountain* AL-4
Piedmont State Hosp—hospital VA-3
*Piedmont Station* AL-4
*Piedmont Station* VA-3
Piedmont Swamp—swamp MT-8
Piedmont Technical Coll—school SC-3
Piedmont Technical Institute—school NC-3
*Piedmont Triad International Airport* NC-3
Piedmont Upland—area AL-4
Piedmont Vocational Sch—school VA-3
Piedmont Wagon Company—hist pl NC-3
Piedmont Well—well AZ-5
Piedomont RR Station—building AZ-5
Pied Piper Dam Lower—dam NC-3
Pied Piper Dam Upper—dam NC-3
Pied Piper Lake Lower—reservoir NC-3
Pied Piper Lake Upper—reservoir NC-3
Pied Piper Sch—school MI-6
Piedra—locale AZ-5
Piedra—locale CA-9
**Piedra**—pop pl CO-8
Piedra, Tanque—reservoir AZ-5
Piedra Agujero—summit NM-5
**Piedra Aguzada**—pop pl PR-3
Piedra Azul Canyon—valley CA-9
Piedra Azul Creek—stream CA-9
Piedra Azul Spring—spring CA-9
Piedra Blanca—civil CA-9
Piedra Blanca—summit PR-3
Piedra Blanca Camp—locale CA-9
Piedra Blanca Canyon—valley NM-5
Piedra Blanca Creek—stream CA-9
Piedra Blanca Spring—spring NM-5
Piedra Camello—pillar NM-5
Piedra Cook Drain—canal TX-5
Piedra Creek—stream TX-5
Piedra de Degetau—summit PR-3
Piedra de la Aguila—locale NM-5
Piedra de la Mula—summit PR-3
Piedra del Norte—island PR-3
Piedra de Lumbre Canyon—valley CA-9
Piedra Falls—falls CO-8
Piedra Falls Ditch—canal CO-8
Piedra Gorda—CDP PR-3
**Piedra Gorda**—pop pl PR-3
Piedra Gorda (Barrio)—fmr MCD PR-3
Piedra Gorda Canyon—valley CA-9
Piedragosa Tanks—reservoir AZ-5
Piedra Guard Station—locale CO-8
Piedra Lisa Canyon—valley NM-5
Piedra Lumbre—locale NM-5
**Piedra Lumbre**—pop pl NM-5
Piedra Lumbre Canyon—valley (2) NM-5
Piedra Lumbre Ch—church NM-5
Piedra Lumbre Chiquita Canyon—valley NM-5
Piedra Lumbre Grant—civil NM-5
Piedra Lumbre Spring (Polluted)—spring NM-5
Piedra Lumbre Windmill—locale NM-5
Piedra Parada Creek—stream TX-5
Piedra Parada Ranch—locale TX-5
Piedra Parada Tank—reservoir TX-5
Piedra Pass—gap CO-8
Piedra Peak—summit (2) CO-8
Piedra Peak No 2—summit CO-8
**Piedra PO**—pop pl CA-9
Piedra Reinada—summit PR-3
Piedra River—stream CO-8
Piedras Altas—ridge CA-9
Piedras (Barrio)—fmr MCD PR-3
**Piedras Blancas**—pop pl PR-3
Piedras Blancas—ridge NM-5
Piedras Blancas—summit CA-9
Piedras Blancas (Barrio)—fmr MCD (2) PR-3
Piedras China Windmill—locale TX-5
Piedras Grandes—summit CA-9
Piedras Grandes Picnic Ground—park AZ-5
Piedras Island—island AK-9
Piedras Negras Canyon—valley NM-5
Piedras Pintas Creek—stream TX-5
Piedra Stevens—island PR-3
Piedra Stock Trail—trail CO-8
Piedra Substation—other CA-9
Piedra Tank—reservoir (2) NM-5
Piedra Tank—reservoir (2) TX-5
Piedra Trap Windmill—locale TX-5
Piedra Well—well TX-5
Piedra Wells—well NM-5
Piedra Windmill—locale (2) TX-5
Piedres Lumbres (Site)—locale NM-5
Piedritos Hill—summit TX-5
Piedrosa Canyon—valley CO-8
Piedrosa Creek—stream CO-8
Piedroso Windmill—locale NM-5
Pie Flat—flat OK-5
Pie Flat Cem—cemetery OK-5
Piegan—locale (2) MT-8
Piegan Canal—canal MT-8
Piegan Creek—stream MT-8
Piegan Falls—falls MT-8
Piegan Glacier—glacier MT-8
Piegan Mtn—summit MT-8
Piegan Pass—gap MT-8
Piegan Pass Trail—trail MT-8
Pie Hammock—gut VA-3
Pie Hill—summit (2) CT-1
Pie Hill—summit MA-1
Piehle Passage—channel AK-9
Piehl Lookout Tower—locale WI-6
**Piehl (Town of)**—pop pl WI-6
*Pie Hollow* UT-8
*Piei Hill* HI-9
**Pieis**—pop pl FM-9
Pie Island—island MN-6
Pieiss Hollow—valley IN-6
Pieissin—island FM-9
Pie Lake—lake AK-9
Pie Lake—lake MN-6
Pie Lake—lake WY-8
Pielaure Island—island FM-9
Piel Brook—stream ME-1
Piel Creek—stream WI-6
Piele Draw—valley CO-8
Piele Lone Cone Camp—locale CO-8
Pielimal Island—island FM-9
Pie Meadow—flat OR-9
Pie Mesa—bench NM-5
Pien—island FM-9
Pieneluk Island—island AK-9
Pieneluk Slough—gut AK-9
Pienemon—island FM-9
Pienisin—bar FM-9
Pieniwin—island FM-9
Pienkesse—island FM-9
*Pieper Canyon* OR-9
Pieper Hatchery Spring—spring AZ-5
Piepers Lake—lake ND-7
Pieper Tank—reservoir (3) AZ-5
Pieplant Cow Camp—locale CO-8
Pieplant Creek—stream CO-8
Pieplant Mill—locale CO-8
Pieplant Mine—mine CO-8
Pier, Jan, House—hist pl NY-2
Pier A—locale GU-9
**Piera**—pop pl MS-4
Pie Ranch—locale NM-5
Pierano Quarry—mine CA-9
Piera Post Office (historical)—building MS-4
Piera Sch (historical)—school MS-4
Pier Ave Sch—school CA-9
Pier B—locale TX-5
Pier B—locale GU-9
Pier Branch—stream TX-5
Pier Bridge—hist pl NH-1
Pier C—locale GU-9
*Pierce* TN-4
Pierce—locale (2) CA-9
Pierce—locale FL-3
Pierce—locale NM-5
Pierce—locale (2) ND-7
Pierce—locale OK-5
Pierce—locale TN-4
Pierce—locale WA-9
**Pierce**—pop pl AL-4
**Pierce**—pop pl CO-8
**Pierce**—pop pl ID-8
**Pierce**—pop pl KY-4
**Pierce**—pop pl NE-7
**Pierce**—pop pl PA-2
**Pierce**—pop pl TX-5
**Pierce**—pop pl WV-2
Pierce, Bayou—gut LA-4
Pierce, Capt, Mial, Farm—hist pl MA-1
Pierce, Carrie, House—hist pl WI-6
Pierce, Elijah, Properties—hist pl OH-6
Pierce, Franklin, Homestead—hist pl NH-1
Pierce, Franklin, House—hist pl NH-1
Pierce, Harry E., House—hist pl AZ-5
Pierce, James, Jr., House—hist pl IN-6
Pierce, John M., House—hist pl NC-3
Pierce, Joseph, Farm—hist pl RI-1
Pierce, Lake—lake FL-3
Pierce, Lukens, House—hist pl PA-2
Pierce, Mount—summit NH-1
Pierce, Mount (Monument Peak)—summit CA-9
Pierce, Peter, Store—hist pl MA-1
Pierce, William F., House—hist pl AL-4
**Pierce Acres**—pop pl KY-4
Pierce Airp—airport AZ-5
Pierce Arrow Factory Complex—hist pl NY-2
Pierce Ave Dam—dam MA-1
Pierce Ave Missionary Baptist Ch—church TN-4
Pierce Ave Pond—reservoir MA-1
Pierce Beach—beach MA-1
Pierce Bend—bend TN-4
Pierce Block—hist pl OK-5
Pierce-Borah House—hist pl ID-8
Pierce-Bradford Cem—cemetery IL-6
Pierce Branch—stream (2) AL-4
Pierce Branch—stream AR-4
Pierce Branch—stream FL-3
Pierce Branch—stream KY-4
Pierce Branch—stream (2) MS-4
Pierce Branch—stream (3) TN-4
Pierce Branch—stream VA-3
Pierce Breaker—building PA-2
**Pierce Bridge**—pop pl NH-1
Pierce Brook—stream CT-1
Pierce Brook—stream (2) MA-1
Pierce Brook—stream (2) NH-1
Pierce Brook—stream NY-2
Pierce Brook—stream PA-2
Pierce Brook—stream RI-1
**Pierceburg**—pop pl IL-6
Pierce Camp—locale GA-3
Pierce Camp Bay—swamp GA-3
Pierce Canal—canal TX-5
*Pierce Canyon* AZ-5
Pierce Canyon—basin UT-8
Pierce Canyon—valley (2) CA-9
Pierce Canyon—valley ID-8
Pierce Canyon—valley MT-8
Pierce Canyon—valley (6) NM-5
Pierce Canyon—valley TX-5
Pierce Canyon Crossing—locale NM-5
Pierce Canyon Pass—locale NM-5
Pierce Cem—cemetery (2) AL-4
Pierce Cem—cemetery AR-4
Pierce Cem—cemetery (2) IL-6
Pierce Cem—cemetery IN-6
Pierce Cem—cemetery IA-7
Pierce Cem—cemetery (2) KY-4
Pierce Cem—cemetery (6) LA-4
Pierce Cem—cemetery (4) ME-1
Pierce Cem—cemetery MA-1
Pierce Cem—cemetery MN-6
Pierce Cem—cemetery (2) MO-7
Pierce Cem—cemetery NE-7
Pierce Cem—cemetery (2) NC-3
Pierce Cem—cemetery ND-7
Pierce Cem—cemetery OH-6
Pierce Cem—cemetery (2) OK-5
Pierce Cem—cemetery (10) TN-4
Pierce Cem—cemetery TX-5
Pierce Cem—cemetery VA-3
Pierce Cem—cemetery WV-2
*Pierce Cemetery* MS-4
Pierce Ch—church NC-3
Pierce Ch—church OK-5
Pierce Ch—church TX-5
*Pierce Chapel* TX-5
Pierce Chapel—church (2) AL-4
Pierce Chapel—church FL-3
Pierce Chapel—church (3) GA-3
Pierce Chapel—church KY-4
Pierce Chapel—church MS-4
Pierce Chapel—church NE-7
Pierce Chapel—church TN-4
Pierce Chapel—church VA-3
Pierce Chapel—locale GA-3
Pierce Chapel Cem—cemetery AL-4
Pierce Chapel Cem—cemetery (2) GA-3
Pierce Chapel Ch—church GA-3
Pierce Chapel (historical)—church MS-4
*Pierce Chapel Methodist Ch* MS-4
Pierce Chapel Sch (historical)—school AL-4
*Pierce Chapel United Methodist Church* AL-4
**Pierce City**—pop pl MO-7
Pierce Coll—school CA-9
Pierce Community Ch—church IL-6
Pierce Consolidated Sch—school IN-6
Pierce Corners—locale NY-2
Pierce Coulee—valley MT-8
Pierce County—civil ND-7
**Pierce (County)**—pop pl GA-3
**Pierce County**—pop pl WA-9
**Pierce (County)**—pop pl WI-6
Pierce County Courthouse—hist pl GA-3
Pierce County Courthouse—hist pl ND-7
Pierce County Courthouse—hist pl WI-6
Pierce County Islands State Public Hunting Grounds—park WI-6
Pierce County Jail—hist pl GA-3
Pierce County Sch—school WA-9
Pierce County - Thun Field Airp—airport WA-9
Pierce Courthouse—hist pl ID-8
Pierce Cove—bay ME-1
*Pierce Creek* AZ-5
*Pierce Creek* MS-4
*Pierce Creek* OR-9
*Pierce Creek* UT-8
*Pierce Creek* VA-3
Pierce Creek—stream (2) AL-4
Pierce Creek—stream AK-9
Pierce Creek—stream (2) AR-4
Pierce Creek—stream (2) CA-9
Pierce Creek—stream CO-8
Pierce Creek—stream GA-3
Pierce Creek—stream (5) ID-8
Pierce Creek—stream IL-6
Pierce Creek—stream KS-7
Pierce Creek—stream KY-4
Pierce Creek—stream (2) MS-4
Pierce Creek—stream MO-7
Pierce Creek—stream (2) MT-8
Pierce Creek—stream NE-7
Pierce Creek—stream NY-2
Pierce Creek—stream (2) NC-3
Pierce Creek—stream (3) OR-9
Pierce Creek—stream (2) TX-5
Pierce Creek—stream VA-3
Pierce Creek—stream WA-9
*Pierce Creek Cemetery* AL-4
Pierce Crossing—locale MT-8
**Pierce Crossroads**—pop pl MS-4
Pierce Dam—dam OR-9
Pierce Dam—dam SD-7
Pierce Ditch—canal ID-8
Pierce Ditch—canal MT-8
Pierce Ditch—church IN-6
Pierce Divide—gap ID-8
Pierce Draw—valley SD-7
Pierce Draw—valley UT-8
Pierce Draw—valley WY-8
Pierce Farm Hist Dist—hist pl MA-1
*Pierce Ferry* AZ-5
Pierce Ferry Boat Anchorage—harbor AZ-5
**Piercefield**—pop pl NY-2
Piercefield Flow—bay NY-2
**Piercefield (Town of)**—pop pl NY-2
Pierce-Fuller House—hist pl NM-5
Pierce Grove Cem—cemetery GA-3
Pierce Grove Ch—church (2) GA-3
Pierce Grove Park—park WI-6
Pierce Gulch—valley CA-9
Pierce Gulch—valley CO-8
Pierce Gulch—valley ID-8
Pierce-Haley House—hist pl CO-8
Pierce Head—cliff ME-1
Pierce-Headquarters—cens area ID-8
**Pierce Heights**—pop pl NJ-2
Pierce-Hichborn House—building MA-1
Pierce-Hichborn House—hist pl MA-1
Pierce Hill—summit (2) ME-1
Pierce Hill—summit (2) MA-1
Pierce Hill—summit (2) NY-2
Pierce Hill—summit VT-1
Pierce Hill—summit WA-9
Pierce Hill Cem—cemetery ME-1
Pierce Hollow—valley AR-4
Pierce Hollow—valley MO-7
Pierce Hollow—valley OH-6
Pierce Hollow—valley (2) TN-4
Pierce Hollow Cem—cemetery CT-1
Pierce House—hist pl (2) MA-1
Pierce House—hist pl MN-6
Pierce HS—school OK-5
Pierce HS—school WA-9
Pierce Island—island ME-1
Pierce Island—island NH-1
Pierce Island—island WA-9
Pierce JHS—school FL-3
Pierce JHS—school IN-6
Pierce JHS—school (3) MI-6
Pierce Junction—locale TX-5
Pierce-Klingle Mansion—hist pl DC-2
Pierce Lake—lake FL-3
Pierce Lake—lake ME-1
Pierce Lake—lake (3) MI-6
Pierce Lake—lake (2) MN-6
Pierce Lake—lake MS-4
Pierce Lake—lake MT-8
Pierce Lake—lake WA-9
Pierce Lake—reservoir IL-6
Pierce Lake—reservoir NC-3
Pierce Lake—reservoir SD-7

Pierce Lake—*swamp* MN-6
*Pierce Lake Dam* SD-7
Pierce Landing—*locale* AL-4
Pierce Landing (historical)—*locale* TN-4
Pierce Lateral—*canal* CO-8
Pierce Lateral—*canal* ID-8
Pierce Lookout Tower—*tower* FL-3
Pierce Meadow—*flat* CA-9
Pierce Mill—*hist pl* DC-2
Pierce Mill—*locale* KY-4
Pierce Mill—*locale* VA-3
Pierce Mine—*mine* MN-6
Pierce Mine (underground)—*mine* (2) AL-4
Pierce Mountain Way—*trail* WA-9
Pierce Mtn—*summit* AZ-5
Pierce Mtn—*summit* KY-4
Pierce Mtn—*summit* VA-3
Pierce Mtn—*summit* WA-9
**Pierce (New Salem)**—*pop pl* PA-2
Pierce Oil Field—*oilfield* CO-8
Pierce Oil Field—*oilfield* KS-7
Pierce Organ Pipe Factory—*hist pl* MA-1
Pierce Park—*park* AZ-5
Pierce Park—*park* IL-6
Pierce Park—*park* IA-7
Pierce Park—*park* MA-1
Pierce Park—*park* MI-6
Pierce Park—*park* (2) WI-6
Pierce Park Golf Course—*other* MI-6
Pierce Park Sch—*hist pl* ID-8
Pierce Park Sch—*school* ID-8
Pierce Peak—*summit* AK-9
Pierce Peak—*summit* NM-5
Pierce Pennant Motor Hotel—*hist pl* MO-7
**Pierce (Pierce Station)**—*pop pl* TN-4
*Pierce Point* NJ-2
Pierce Point—*cape* NH-1
Pierce Point—*cape* OR-9
Pierce Point (historical)—*locale* IA-7
Pierce Pond—*lake* (2) ME-1
Pierce Pond—*lake* NH-1
Pierce Pond—*lake* NY-2
Pierce Pond—*lake* TN-4
Pierce Pond—*reservoir* MA-1
Pierce Pond Camps—*locale* ME-1
Pierce Pond Dam—*dam* (2) MA-1
Pierce Pond Dam—*dam* MS-4
Pierce Pond Mtn—*summit* ME-1
Pierce Pond Stream—*stream* ME-1
Pierce Pond (Township of)—*unorg* ME-1
Pierce Pool—*lake* IA-7
Pierce Post Office (historical)—*building* TN-4
Pierce Pumping Station—*other* TX-5
Pierce Ranch—*hist pl* CA-9
Pierce Ranch—*locale* CA-9
Pierce Ranch—*locale* (2) MT-8
Pierce Ranch—*locale* NV-8
Pierce Ranch—*locale* (2) NM-5
Pierce Ranch—*locale* (3) TX-5
Pierce Ranch—*locale* WY-8
Pierce Ridge—*ridge* NC-3
Pierce Ridge—*ridge* WI-6
Pierce Rsvr—*reservoir* CO-8
Pierce Rsvr—*reservoir* MT-8
Pierce Rsvr—*reservoir* (2) OR-9
Pierce Rsvr—*reservoir* WY-8
Pierce Run—*stream* NY-2
Pierce Run—*stream* OH-6
Pierce Run—*stream* WV-2
**Pierces**—*pop pl* NJ-2
Pierces Bridge—*bridge* MA-1
**Pierces Bridge**—*pop pl* MA-1
Pierces Campground Ch—*church* NC-3
Pierce Sch—*school* CA-9
Pierce Sch—*school* DC-2
Pierce Sch—*school* (2) IL-6
Pierce Sch—*school* IA-7
Pierce Sch—*school* KY-4
Pierce Sch—*school* ME-1
Pierce Sch—*school* (3) MA-1
Pierce Sch—*school* (6) MI-6
Pierce Sch—*school* NH-1
Pierce Sch—*school* (2) NY-2
Pierce Sch—*school* NC-3
Pierce Sch—*school* ND-7
Pierce Sch—*school* OH-6
Pierce Sch—*school* SD-7
Pierce Sch—*school* TX-5
Pierce Sch—*school* WI-6
Pierces Chapel—*church* GA-3
Pierces Chapel—*church* (3) NC-3
Pierces Chapel—*church* TX-5
**Pierces Chapel**—*pop pl* MS-4
**Pierces Chapel**—*pop pl* TX-5
Pierces Chapel Cem—*cemetery* MS-4
Pierces Chapel Ch—*church* GA-3
Pierces Chapel Sch (historical)—*school* MS-4
Pierce Sch (historical)—*school* MO-7
Pierce Sch (historical)—*school* PA-2
Pierce Sch (historical)—*school* TN-4
Pierce Sch No. 13—*hist pl* IA-7
Pierces Corner—*locale* VT-1
**Pierces Corner**—*pop pl* NY-2
**Pierces Corner**—*pop pl* VA-3
Pierces Corners—*locale* NY-2
*Pierce's Creek* MD-2
*Pierces Creek* MS-4
Pierces Creek—*stream* NV-8
**Pierces Crossroads**—*pop pl* NC-3
Pierces Draw—*valley* CA-9
Pierce Seep—*spring* AZ-5
Pierce's Ferry—*locale* NC-3
Pierces Hill—*summit* AL-4
Pierce Shoal—*bar* FL-3
Pierce Site—*hist pl* FL-3
Pierces Lake—*lake* WI-6
*Pierces Landing* AL-4
Pierces Landing (historical)—*locale* AL-4
Pierce Slough—*stream* OR-9
*Pierces Mill* AL-4
*Pierce's Neck* MD-2
Pierceson Cem—*cemetery* MI-6
Pierces Point—*cape* MA-1
**Pierces Point**—*pop pl* NJ-2
*Pierces Point Landing* NJ-2
Pierces Point Pond—*lake* NJ-2
Pierces Pond—*lake* MA-1
Pierce Spring—*spring* AZ-5
Pierce Spring—*spring* CO-8
Pierce Spring—*spring* (2) MT-8
Pierce Spring—*spring* TN-4
Pierce Spring Branch—*stream* TX-5
Pierce Springhouse and Barn—*hist pl* DC-2
*Pierce Springs* MS-4
Pierces Push Mine (underground)—*mine* AL-4
Pierces Shop—*locale* VA-3
Pierces Springs Ch—*church* MS-4
**Pierces Springs (historical)**—*pop pl* MS-4
**Pierce Station**—*pop pl* TN-4
Pierce Station Post Office (historical)—*building* TN-4
Pierce Store (historical)—*locale* MS-4
Pierce Street Ch—*church* TX-5
Pierce Street Elem Sch—*school* MS-4
Pierce Street Sch—*school* MA-1
Pierce Tank—*reservoir* (2) AZ-5
Pierce Tank—*reservoir* NM-5
**Pierceton**—*pop pl* IN-6
Pierceton Ch—*church* AL-4
Pierceton Elem Sch—*school* IN-6
Pierceton (historical)—*locale* AL-4
*Pierceton Junction* IN-6
Pierceton Lake—*lake* IN-6
Pierceton MS—*school* IN-6
Pierceton Sch (historical)—*school* AL-4
Pierce Tote Road—*trail* ME-1
*Piercetown* TN-4
**Piercetown**—*pop pl* AR-4
**Piercetown**—*pop pl* SC-3
Pierce Town Hall—*building* ND-7
**Pierce (Town of)**—*pop pl* WI-6
Pierce Township—*civil* (2) MO-7
Pierce Township—*fmr MCD* IA-7
**Pierce Township**—*pop pl* MO-7
**Pierce Township**—*pop pl* ND-7
**Pierce (Township of)**—*pop pl* IL-6
**Pierce (Township of)**—*pop pl* IN-6
**Pierce (Township of)**—*pop pl* OH-6
Pierce Tunnel—*mine* ID-8
Pierce Union HS—*school* CA-9
Pierce Valley—*flat* CA-9
*Pierceville* PA-2
Pierceville—*locale* PA-2
**Pierceville**—*pop pl* GA-3
**Pierceville**—*pop pl* IN-6
**Pierceville**—*pop pl* KS-7
**Pierceville**—*pop pl* MA-1
**Pierceville**—*pop pl* NY-2
**Pierceville**—*pop pl* NC-3
**Pierceville**—*pop pl* WI-6
Pierceville Cem—*cemetery* KS-7
Pierceville Cem—*cemetery* WI-6
Pierceville Run—*stream* PA-2
**Pierceville Township**—*pop pl* KS-7
*Piercewans Ferry* NC-3
*Pierce Wash* AZ-5
*Pierce Wash* UT-8
Pierce Wash—*stream* AZ-5
Pierce Wash—*valley* AZ-5
Pierce Wash Tank—*reservoir* (2) AZ-5
Pierce Waterhole—*reservoir* OR-9
Pierce Well—*well* NM-5
Pier Cove—*locale* MI-6
Piercy—*locale* CA-9
Piercy Bald—*summit* NC-3
Piercy Cem—*cemetery* (2) KY-4
Piercy Creek—*stream* CA-9
Piercy Creek—*stream* NC-3
Piercy Farmstead—*hist pl* AR-4
Piercy Hollow—*valley* KY-4
Piercy Quarry—*mine* CA-9
Piercy Ranch—*locale* NE-7
Piercys Mill—*locale* WV-2
Pier Dog—*locale* GU-9
Pier Eighteen—*locale* TX-5
Pier Eleven—*locale* TX-5
Piereus Store—*hist pl* VA-3
Pier Fifteen—*locale* TX-5
Pier Fiftynine Marina—*locale* AL-4
Pier Forty—*locale* TX-5
Pier Fortyone—*locale* TX-5
Pier Fourteen—*locale* TX-5
*Pier Head* MA-1
Pier Head—*cape* MA-1
Pierhead Channel—*channel* NJ-2
Pieri-Elliot House—*hist pl* AZ-5
*Pierimaru To* FM-9
Pier Lake—*lake* MI-6
Pier Lake—*lake* NE-7
Pier Lake—*lake* (3) WI-6
Pierle Bay—*bay* LA-4
Piermont—*other* VT-1
**Piermont**—*pop pl* LA-4
**Piermont**—*pop pl* NH-1
**Piermont**—*pop pl* NY-2
Piermont Creek—*stream* NV-8
Piermont (historical)—*locale* NV-8
Piermont Mtn—*summit* NH-1
**Piermont (Town of)**—*pop pl* NH-1
**Piermont Woods**—*pop pl* DE-2
Pier Number Four—*locale* MA-1
Pier Number Two—*locale* MA-1
Piero—*locale* IA-7
Pierotto Ditch—*canal* WY-8
Pierotto Ranch—*locale* WY-8
Pier Park—*park* NE-7
Pier Park—*park* OR-9
Pier Park (historical)—*park* FL-3
Pier Point Creek—*stream* NJ-2
Pierpoint Meadow Pond—*reservoir* MA-1
Pier Point Neck—*cape* NJ-2
Pier Point Spring—*spring* OR-9
**Pierpont**—*pop pl* MO-7
**Pierpont**—*pop pl* OH-6
**Pierpont**—*pop pl* SC-3
**Pierpont**—*pop pl* SD-7
**Pierpont**—*pop pl* VA-3
**Pierpont**—*pop pl* (2) WV-2
Pierpont Bay—*bay* CA-9
**Pierpont Bay**—*pop pl* CA-9
Pierpont Cem—*cemetery* ME-1
Pierpont Cem—*cemetery* WV-2
Pierpont Dam—*dam* SD-7
Pierpont Lake—*reservoir* SD-7
Pierpont Lake Rec Area—*park* SD-7
*Pierpont Meadow Pond* MA-1
Pierpont Pass—*gap* WY-8
*Pierpont Pond* MA-1
Pierpont Spring—*spring* OR-9
**Pierpont (Township of)**—*pop pl* OH-6
**Pierport**—*pop pl* MI-6
Pierre—*locale* ME-1
**Pierre**—*pop pl* SD-7
Pierre, Bayou—*gut* LA-4
Pierre, Bayou—*stream* (4) LA-4
Pierre, Bayou—*stream* MS-4
Pierre, Lake—*bay* LA-4
Pierre Bay—*bay* (2) LA-4
Pierre Bayou—*stream* LA-4
Pierre Bridge (historical)—*bridge* SD-7
Pierre Cem—*cemetery* LA-4
*Pierre Creek* AR-4
*Pierre Creek* LA-4
*Pierre Creek* MT-8
*Pierre Creek* ND-7
Pierre Creek—*stream* SD-7
Pierre Creek—*stream* WA-9
Pier Reef—*bar* TX-5
Pierre Et Lee, Bayou—*gut* LA-4
Pierre Fleche Creek—*stream* MO-7
Pierre Hill—*summit* MT-8
Pierre (historical)—*locale* IA-7
Pierre Indian Sch—*school* SD-7
*Pierre Island* SD-7
Pierre Lake—*lake* WA-9
Pierre Lake, Bayou—*swamp* LA-4
Pierre Lakes—*lake* CO-8
Pierre Mall—*locale* SD-7
Pierre Marina Rec Area—*park* SD-7
Pierre Moran—*post sta* IN-6
Pierre Moran JHS—*school* IN-6
Pierre Municipal Airp—*airport* SD-7
Pierre Navarre MS—*school* IN-6
*Pierre Navarre Sch* IN-6
Pierre Park—*park* CA-9
**Pierre Part**—*pop pl* LA-4
Pierre Part, Bayou—*stream* LA-4
Pierre Part (Pierre Pass)—*CDP* LA-4
*Pierre Part Settlement* LA-4
*Pierre Pass* LA-4
Pierre Pass—*channel* LA-4
Pierre Pass—*other* LA-4
Pierre Pass Gas Field—*oilfield* LA-4
Pierre Paul Brook—*stream* ME-1
Pierre Point—*cape* LA-4
**Pierrepont**—*pop pl* NY-2
Pierrepont Hill Cem—*cemetery* NY-2
*Pierrepont Lake* CT-1
**Pierrepont Manor**—*pop pl* NY-2
Pierrepont Manor Complex—*hist pl* NY-2
*Pierrepont Pond* CT-1
Pierrepont Sch—*school* NJ-2
Pierrepont Town Buildings—*hist pl* NY-2
**Pierrepont (Town of)**—*pop pl* NY-2
*Pierre Port* LA-4
*Pierre River* ID-8
*Pierre River* WY-8
Pierre Sch—*school* OK-5
Pierre S. Dupont Elem Sch—*school* DE-2
*Pierre S. Dupont HS* DE-2
*Pierre's Hole* ID-8
*Pierres Hole Mountains* ID-8
Pierre's Hole 1832 Battle Area Site—*hist pl* ID-8
*Pierre's River* ID-8
*Pierre's River* WY-8
Pierre Tank—*reservoir* AZ-5
**Pierron**—*pop pl* (2) IL-6
**Pierron (Baden Baden)**—*pop pl* IL-6
*Piers, The* DE-2
Pier Sch—*school* MI-6
Pier Sch—*school* WI-6
Piersol Cem—*cemetery* IA-7
Piersol Hills—*summit* WA-9
Piersol Lake—*lake* TN-4
Piersol Lake—*reservoir* TN-4
Piersol Lake Dam—*dam* TN-4
**Pierson**—*pop pl* FL-3
**Pierson**—*pop pl* IL-6
**Pierson**—*pop pl* IA-7
**Pierson**—*pop pl* MI-6
**Pierson**—*pop pl* WA-9
Pierson, Adrian, House—*hist pl* AZ-5
Pierson, Lake—*lake* FL-3
Pierson, Mount—*summit* UT-8
Pierson, Ole and Ann, Farm—*hist pl* TX-5
Pierson, T., Farm—*hist pl* DE-2
Pierson Basin—*basin* CO-8
Pierson Branch—*stream* MI-6
Pierson Branch—*stream* TX-5
Piers Canyon—*valley* NV-8
Pierson Cem—*cemetery* GA-3
Pierson Cem—*cemetery* MI-6
Pierson Cem—*cemetery* (2) VA-3
Pierson Ch—*church* MO-7
Pierson Chapel—*church* WV-2
Pierson Corners—*locale* (2) NY-2
Pierson County Park—*park* KS-7
Pierson Cove—*bay* DE-2
Pierson Cove—*valley* UT-8
*Pierson Creek* WA-9
Pierson Creek—*stream* (3) ID-8
Pierson Creek—*stream* IA-7
Pierson Creek—*stream* MI-6
Pierson Creek—*stream* MO-7
Pierson Creek—*stream* MT-8
Pierson Creek—*stream* OH-6
Pierson Dam—*dam* OR-9
Pierson Ditch—*canal* WY-8
Pierson Drain—*canal* MI-6
Pierson Elem Sch—*school* FL-3
Pierson Farm—*hist pl* ND-7
**Pierson Farms (subdivision)**—*pop pl* DE-2
Pierson Gap—*gap* NV-8
Pierson-Griffiths House—*hist pl* IN-6
Pierson Hill—*summit* NY-2
Pierson Hill—*summit* VT-1
Pierson JHS—*school* KS-7
*Pierson Lake* MN-6
Pierson Lake—*lake* LA-4
Pierson Lake—*swamp* LA-4
Pierson Ledge—*island* ME-1
Pierson Mtn—*summit* CO-8
Pierson Park—*flat* CO-8
Pierson Park Dam—*dam* KS-7
Pierson Peak—*summit* ID-8
Pierson Peak—*summit* VT-1
Pierson Point—*cape* NC-3
Pierson Ranch—*locale* NE-7
Pierson Ranch (historical)—*locale* UT-8
Pierson Ranch Rec Area—*park* SD-7
Pierson Ridge—*ridge* NJ-2
Pierson Rsvr—*reservoir* OR-9
*Piersons* DE-2
Pierson Sch—*school* CT-1
Pierson Sch—*school* KS-7
Pierson Sch—*school* (2) MI-6
Pierson Sch—*school* NY-2
Pierson Sch—*school* PA-2
Pierson Sch—*school* WA-9
Pierson Sch (historical)—*school* SD-7
*Piersons Cove* DE-2
Pierson-Seville (CCD)—*cens area* FL-3
Piersons Lake—*lake* MN-6
Piersons Point—*cliff* NE-7
Pierson's Ranch—*locale* MT-8
Piersons Run—*stream* PA-2
**Pierson Station**—*pop pl* IN-6
Pierson Summit—*gap* NV-8
**Pierson (Township of)**—*pop pl* IN-6
**Pierson (Township of)**—*pop pl* MI-6
**Piersonville**—*pop pl* NJ-2
Pier Spring—*spring* WI-6
Pierstown—*locale* NY-2
Pier Ten—*locale* TX-5
Pier Thietynine—*locale* TX-5
Pier Thirtyeight—*locale* TX-5
Pier Thirtyfive—*other* TX-5
Pier Thirtyseven—*locale* TX-5
Pier Thirtysix—*locale* TX-5
Pier Thirtythree—*locale* TX-5
Pier Twelve—*locale* TX-5
Pier Twentynine—*locale* TX-5
Pier Twentyone—*locale* TX-5
Pier Twentyseven—*locale* TX-5
Pier Twentysix—*locale* TX-5
Pier Twentythree—*locale* TX-5
Pier Twentytwo—*locale* TX-5
Pierucci Ridge—*ridge* AK-9
**Pierz**—*pop pl* MN-6
Pierz Lake—*lake* MN-6
Pierz Lake—*reservoir* MN-6
**Pierz (Township of)**—*pop pl* MN-6
Pier 90—*locale* WA-9
Pier 91—*locale* WA-9
*Piesich* FM-9
Piesich, Ununen—*cape* FM-9
Piester Lake—*lake* NE-7
**Pieta**—*pop pl* CA-9
Pieta Creek—*stream* CA-9
*Pietala Creek* MI-6
Pietenpol, Bernard H., Workshop and Garage—*hist pl* MN-6
Pietetlot Gulch—*valley* CO-8
Pietila Creek—*stream* MI-6
Pietist Ch—*church* OH-6
*Pieto Creek* CA-9
**Pie Town**—*pop pl* NM-5
*Pietra Lake* MN-6
**Pietri**—*pop pl* (2) PR-3
Pietrock Cem—*cemetery* OR-9
Pietro Lake—*lake* MN-6
Pietrzycki, Dr. Marcel, House—*hist pl* WA-9
Pietrzycki HS—*school* WA-9
*Piets Pond* NY-2
*Piettn Eyland* DE-2
**Piety Corner**—*pop pl* MA-1
**Piety Hill**—*pop pl* IL-6
Piety Hill—*summit* AZ-5
Piety Hill—*summit* IL-6
Piety Hill Hist Dist—*hist pl* MI-6
Piety Island—*island* OR-9
Piety Island Camp—*locale* OR-9
Piety Knob—*summit* OR-9
Pietz Cem—*cemetery* SD-7
Pietz Ranch—*locale* ND-7
Pietzsch Sch—*school* TX-5
Pifer—*locale* WA-9
Pifer Ditch—*canal* IN-6
Pifer Mountain Ch—*church* WV-2
Pifer Mtn—*summit* WV-2
Pifer Run—*stream* VA-3
Pifer Sch—*school* WV-2
Pifer Sch (abandoned)—*school* PA-2
Pifer Sch (historical)—*school* PA-2
**Piffard**—*pop pl* NY-2
Pig—*island* FM-9
Pig—*locale* KY-4
**Piga**—*pop pl* GU-9
Piga Beach—*beach* GU-9
Pig-a-be-ikiti—*lake* NM-5
*Pigamman-to* MP-9
*Piganaarin* MP-9
*Piganigaroyaro Island* MP-9
Piganiyaroyaro Island—*island* MP-9
*Piganiyaroyaro-To* MP-9
Piganman Island—*island* MP-9
Pigaras—*island* FM-9
Piga Spring—*spring* GU-9
Pig-a-ti-ana—*summit* NM-5
Pigback Mtn—*summit* NY-2
Pig Basket Creek—*stream* NC-3
Pig Bayou—*bay* FL-3
Pig Branch—*stream* AL-4
Pig Branch—*stream* KY-4
Pig Branch—*stream* LA-4
Pig Branch—*stream* MS-4
Pig Branch—*stream* TN-4
Pig Branch—*stream* TX-5
*Pig Canyon* KS-7
Pig Canyon—*valley* CA-9
Pig Canyon—*valley* NM-5
Pig Cove—*bay* ME-1
*Pig Creek* ID-8
Pig Creek—*stream* CA-9
Pig Creek—*stream* (3) ID-8
Pig Creek—*stream* IL-6
Pig Creek—*stream* IA-7
Pig Creek—*stream* KS-7
Pig Creek—*stream* MT-8
Pig Creek—*stream* UT-8
Pig Creek—*stream* VA-3
*Pigeeyatto* MP-9
Pigeeyatto Island—*island* MP-9
*Pigeeyatto-To* MP-9
*Pigeji-suido* MP-9
*Pigeji-to* MP-9
Pigelelel—*island* FM-9
*Pigenaarin* MP-9
*Pigenaarin-to* MP-9
*Pigenikarage Island* MP-9
Pigenikarage Island—*island* MP-9
*Pigen Island* MP-9
*Pigenneru* MP-9
*Pigen Pass* MP-9
*Pigen-to* MP-9
*Pigeo* MP-9
Pigeon—*locale* PA-2
Pigeon—*locale* UT-8
Pigeon—*locale* WV-2
**Pigeon**—*pop pl* IN-6
**Pigeon**—*pop pl* IA-7
**Pigeon**—*pop pl* KY-4
**Pigeon**—*pop pl* LA-4
**Pigeon**—*pop pl* MI-6
Pigeon, Bayou—*stream* LA-4
Pigeon Basin—*basin* UT-8
Pigeon Bay—*bay* GA-3
Pigeon Bay—*bay* LA-4
Pigeon Bay—*bay* MN-6
Pigeon Bay—*gut* LA-4
Pigeon Bay—*swamp* NC-3
Pigeon Bay—*swamp* (3) SC-3
Pigeon Bayou—*stream* LA-4
Pigeon Bluff—*cliff* WA-9
*Pigeon Branch* IN-6
*Pigeon Branch* KY-4
*Pigeon Branch* TN-4
Pigeon Branch—*stream* AL-4
Pigeon Branch—*stream* (4) KY-4
Pigeon Branch—*stream* NC-3
Pigeon Branch—*stream* (4) TN-4
Pigeon Branch—*stream* (2) VA-3
Pigeon Branch—*stream* WV-2
Pigeon Branch—*swamp* GA-3
Pigeon Brook—*stream* CT-1
Pigeon Brook—*stream* ME-1
Pigeon Brook—*stream* (2) NY-2
Pigeon Brook Sch—*school* ME-1
Pigeon Butte—*summit* OR-9
Pigeon Cabin—*locale* NM-5
Pigeon Canyon—*valley* (2) AZ-5
Pigeon Canyon—*valley* UT-8
Pigeon Canyon—*valley* WY-8
Pigeon Cave—*cave* PA-2
Pigeon Cove—*bay* MI-6
Pigeon Cove—*bay* WI-6
Pigeon Cove—*cove* MA-1
**Pigeon Cove**—*pop pl* MA-1
Pigeon Cove—*valley* PA-2
Pigeon Cove Creek—*stream* MI-6
Pigeon Cove Sch—*school* MA-1
*Pigeon Creek* AL-4
*Pigeon Creek* AR-4
*Pigeon Creek* CA-9
*Pigeon Creek* GA-3
*Pigeon Creek* IN-6
*Pigeon Creek* MD-2
*Pigeon Creek* MI-6
*Pigeon Creek* PA-2
*Pigeon Creek* TX-5
*Pigeon Creek* WI-6
Pigeon Creek—*locale* AL-4
Pigeon Creek—*stream* (3) AL-4
Pigeon Creek—*stream* (3) AZ-5
Pigeon Creek—*stream* (6) AR-4
Pigeon Creek—*stream* (5) CA-9
Pigeon Creek—*stream* CO-8
Pigeon Creek—*stream* (2) FL-3
Pigeon Creek—*stream* (3) GA-3
Pigeon Creek—*stream* (5) IL-6
Pigeon Creek—*stream* (2) IN-6
Pigeon Creek—*stream* (3) IA-7
Pigeon Creek—*stream* (4) KY-4
Pigeon Creek—*stream* LA-4
Pigeon Creek—*stream* (2) MI-6
Pigeon Creek—*stream* (4) MO-7
Pigeon Creek—*stream* MT-8
Pigeon Creek—*stream* (2) NE-7
Pigeon Creek—*stream* NY-2
Pigeon Creek—*stream* (2) NC-3
Pigeon Creek—*stream* (4) OH-6
Pigeon Creek—*stream* (2) OK-5
Pigeon Creek—*stream* (2) OR-9
Pigeon Creek—*stream* (4) PA-2
Pigeon Creek—*stream* (2) TN-4
Pigeon Creek—*stream* TX-5
Pigeon Creek—*stream* (2) UT-8
Pigeon Creek—*stream* (2) VA-3
Pigeon Creek—*stream* WA-9
Pigeon Creek—*stream* (3) WV-2
Pigeon Creek—*stream* (5) WI-6
Pigeon Creek Bar—*bar* AL-4
Pigeon Creek Cem—*cemetery* IL-6
Pigeon Creek Cem—*cemetery* PA-2
Pigeon Creek Cem—*cemetery* WI-6
Pigeon Creek Ch—*church* AL-4
Pigeon Creek Ch—*church* FL-3
Pigeon Creek Ch—*church* IN-6
Pigeon Creek Ch—*church* PA-2
Pigeon Creek Ditch—*canal* NE-7
Pigeon Creek Flowage—*reservoir* WI-6
Pigeon Creek Lookout Tower—*locale* AL-4
Pigeon Creek No 2—*stream* WA-9
Pigeon Creek Park—*park* MI-6
Pigeon Creek Ridge—*ridge* MT-8
Pigeon Creek Sch—*school* CA-9
Pigeon Creek Sch—*school* MO-7
Pigeon Creek Settling Basin—*basin* IL-6
Pigeon Creek Swamp—*swamp* AL-4
Pigeon Dam Lake—*lake* MN-6
Pigeon Falls—*falls* MN-6
**Pigeon Falls**—*pop pl* WI-6
Pigeonfield Cem—*cemetery* AL-4
Pigeon Flat—*flat* (2) CA-9
**Pigeon Forge**—*pop pl* TN-4
Pigeon Forge Mill—*hist pl* TN-4
Pigeon Fork—*stream* (2) KY-4
Pigeon Fork Ch—*church* KY-4
Pigeon Gap—*gap* (2) NC-3
Pigeon Ground—*bar* ME-1
Pigeon Grove (Township of)—*civ div* IL-6
Pigeon Gulch—*valley* (2) CA-9
Pigeon Gulch—*valley* OR-9
Pigeon Hill—*locale* VA-3
**Pigeon Hill**—*pop pl* ME-1
Pigeon Hill—*summit* CA-9
Pigeon Hill—*summit* CT-1
Pigeon Hill—*summit* GA-3
Pigeon Hill—*summit* (3) ME-1
Pigeon Hill—*summit* (7) MA-1
Pigeon Hill—*summit* MI-6
Pigeon Hill—*summit* (2) NH-1
Pigeon Hill—*summit* NM-5
Pigeon Hill—*summit* (6) NY-2
Pigeon Hill—*summit* (2) PA-2
Pigeon Hill Bay—*bay* ME-1
Pigeon Hill Cem—*cemetery* MA-1
Pigeon Hill Church (historical)—*school* PA-2
Pigeon Hill Cove—*bay* ME-1
Pigeon Hill Playground—*park* IL-6
Pigeon Hills—*range* PA-2
Pigeon Hills—*summit* AR-4
Pigeon Hills—*summit* PA-2
Pigeon Hill Sch—*school* AR-4
Pigeon Hill Sch (historical)—*school* PA-2
Pigeon Hills Sch—*school* PA-2
Pigeon Hill State Wildlife Area—*park* MO-7
Pigeon Hollow—*valley* IL-6
Pigeon Hollow—*valley* KY-4
Pigeon Hollow—*valley* (4) PA-2
Pigeon Hollow—*valley* UT-8
Pigeon Hollow—*valley* WV-2
Pigeon Hollow Junction—*locale* UT-8
Pigeon House Branch—*stream* NC-3
Pigeon House Corner—*locale* MD-2
*Pigeon House Creek* MD-2
Pigeonhouse Creek—*stream* MD-2
Pigeon Island—*island* AK-9
Pigeon Island—*island* GA-3
Pigeon Island—*island* WI-6
Pigeon Key—*island* (3) FL-3
Pigeon Key Banks—*bar* FL-3
Pigeon Knob—*summit* OH-6
Pigeon Knob—*summit* WV-2
*Pigeon Lake* MI-6
Pigeon Lake—*lake* (2) IN-6
Pigeon Lake—*lake* (3) MI-6
Pigeon Lake—*lake* (3) MN-6
Pigeon Lake—*lake* NY-2
Pigeon Lake—*lake* WI-6
Pigeon Lake—*reservoir* (2) WI-6
Pigeon Lake—*swamp* MI-6
Pigeon Milk Spring—*spring* UT-8
Pigeon Mine—*mine* AZ-5
Pigeon Mtn—*summit* (3) GA-3
Pigeon Mtn—*summit* NY-2
Pigeon Mtn—*summit* NC-3
Pigeon Mtn—*summit* OK-5
Pigeon Mtn—*summit* UT-8
Pigeon Number Two Ditch—*canal* IN-6
Pigeon Pass—*gap* CA-9
Pigeon Pass Valley—*valley* CA-9
Pigeon Peak—*summit* CO-8
Pigeon Peak—*summit* WA-9
Pigeon Plains Sch—*school* ME-1
Pigeon Pockets—*basin* AZ-5
Pigeon Point—*cape* (3) CA-9
Pigeon Point—*cape* DE-2
Pigeon Point—*cape* ME-1
Pigeon Point—*cape* MI-6
Pigeon Point—*cape* MN-6
Pigeon Point—*cape* OR-9
Pigeon Point—*cape* SC-3
Pigeon Point—*cape* TN-4
Pigeon Point—*cape* WA-9
Pigeon Point—*cliff* AZ-5
Pigeon Point—*cliff* ND-7
Pigeon Point—*summit* CA-9
Pigeon Point Creek—*stream* SC-3
Pigeon Point Lighthouse—*hist pl* CA-9
Pigeon Point Light Station—*other* CA-9
Pigeon Pond—*lake* AL-4
Pigeon Pond—*lake* VT-1
Pigeon Prairie—*swamp* OR-9
Pigeon Ridge—*ridge* CA-9
Pigeon Ridge—*ridge* IN-6
Pigeon Ridge—*ridge* MO-7
Pigeon Ridge—*ridge* OH-6
*Pigeon River* IN-6
*Pigeon River* NC-3
**Pigeon River**—*pop pl* MN-6
Pigeon River—*stream* IN-6
Pigeon River—*stream* (4) MI-6
Pigeon River—*stream* (2) MN-6
Pigeon River—*stream* NC-3
Pigeon River—*stream* TN-4
Pigeon River—*stream* (3) WI-6
Pigeon River Bay—*bay* MI-6
Pigeon River Ch—*church* MI-6
**Pigeon River Estates**—*pop pl* TN-4
*Pigeon River Fish and Wildlife Area* IN-6
Pigeon River Lookout Tower—*locale* MI-6
Pigeon River Sch—*school* (2) WI-6
Pigeon River State Fish and Wildlife Area—*park* IN-6
Pigeon River State For—*forest* MI-6
*Pigeon River State Game Preserve* IN-6
Pigeon Rock—*pillar* CA-9
Pigeon Rock—*rock* MA-1
Pigeonroost—*locale* KY-4
**Pigeon Roost**—*pop pl* NC-3
**Pigeonroost**—*pop pl* NC-3
**Pigeon Roost**—*pop pl* TN-4
Pigeon Roost—*summit* (2) CA-9
Pigeon Roost—*summit* GA-3
Pigeon Roost—*summit* ID-8
Pigeon Roost—*summit* IN-6
Pigeon Roost—*summit* NY-2
Pigeonroost—*summit* WV-2
Pigeon Roost Bayou—*stream* LA-4
*Pigeon Roost Branch* TN-4
Pigeon Roost Branch—*stream* AL-4
Pigeon Roost Branch—*stream* AR-4
Pigeon Roost Branch—*stream* KY-4
Pigeonroost Branch—*stream* (2) KY-4
Pigeon Roost Branch—*stream* KY-4
Pigeonroost Branch—*stream* (2) KY-4
Pigeon Roost Branch—*stream* KY-4
Pigeonroost Branch—*stream* KY-4
Pigeon Roost Branch—*stream* KY-4
Pigeonroost Branch—*stream* KY-4
Pigeon Roost Branch—*stream* KY-4
Pigeonroost Branch—*stream* (2) KY-4
Pigeon Roost Branch—*stream* KY-4
Pigeon Roost Branch—*stream* LA-4
Pigeon Roost Branch—*stream* (2) MS-4
Pigeon Roost Branch—*stream* SC-3
Pigeonroost Branch—*stream* TN-4
Pigeon Roost Branch—*stream* TN-4

Pigeonroost Branch—stream (2) TN-4
Pigeon Roost Branch—stream TX-5
Pigeon Roost Branch—stream VA-3
Pigeonroost Branch—stream (4) WV-2
Pigeon Roost Canyon—valley CA-9
Pigeon Roost Cave—cave MO-7
Pigeon Roost Cem—cemetery MS-4
Pigeon Roost Ch—church (2) OK-5
Pigeon Roost Creek NC-3
Pigeon Roost Creek—stream (2) AL-4
Pigeonroost Creek—stream (2) AL-4
Pigeon Roost Creek—stream (4) AR-4
Pigeon Roost Creek—stream GA-3
Pigeonroost Creek—stream GA-3
Pigeon Roost Creek—stream IL-6
Pigeon Roost Creek—stream IN-6
Pigeon Roost Creek—stream KY-4
Pigeonroost Creek—stream KY-4
Pigeon Roost Creek—stream KY-4
Pigeon Roost Creek—stream LA-4
Pigeon Roost Creek—stream (2) MS-4
Pigeon Roost Creek—stream MO-7
Pigeonroost Creek—stream (3) NC-3
Pigeon Roost Creek—stream (2) TN-4
Pigeon Roost Creek—stream (4) TX-5
Pigeonroost Creek—stream VA-3
Pigeonroost Creek—stream (2) WV-2
Pigeon Roost Creek Canal—canal MS-4
Pigeon Roost Creek Cave—cave TN-4
Pigeon Roost Fork WV-2
Pigeonroost Fork—stream (2) KY-4
Pigeonroost Fork—stream (6) WV-2
Pigeonroost Gap—gap PA-2
Pigeonroost Gap—gap TN-4
Pigeon Roost Hill—summit IN-6
Pigeon Roost (historical)—locale MS-4
Pigeon Roost Hollow TN-4
Pigeon Roost Hollow—valley AR-4
Pigeonroost Hollow—valley KY-4
Pigeon Roost Hollow—valley (2) KY-4
Pigeonroost Hollow—valley KY-4
Pigeon Roost Hollow—valley (2) KY-4
Pigeon Roost Hollow—valley (4) MO-7
Pigeonroost Hollow—valley OH-6
Pigeonroost Hollow—valley TN-4
Pigeon Roost Hollow—valley TN-4
Pigeonroost Hollow—valley TX-5
Pigeonroost Hollow—valley (2) WV-2
Pigeon Roost Memorial—park IN-6
Pigeon Roost Mine TN-4
Pigeon Roost Mine—mine AR-4
Pigeon Roost Mine (Inactive)—mine CA-9
Pigeon Roost Mountain—ridge AR-4
Pigeon Roost Mtn—summit (2) AR-4
Pigeonroost Ridge—ridge WV-2
Pigeonroost Run—stream OH-6
Pigeonroost Run—stream PA-2
Pigeonroost Run—stream (4) WV-2
Pigeon Roost Run—stream WV-2
Pigeonroost Sch—school KY-4
Pigeon Roost Sch—school (3) KY-4
Pigeon Roost Spring—spring CA-9
Pigeon Roost Stand (historical)—locale MS-4
**Pigeon Roost Station**—pop pl IN-6
Pigeonroost Swamp—stream VA-3
Pigeon Roost Trail—trail CA-9
Pigeon Roost Watershed Y-5-122 Dam—dam MS-4
Pigeon Roost Watershed Y-5-124 Dam—dam MS-4
**Pigeon Run**—pop pl OH-6
Pigeon Run—stream DE-2
Pigeon Run—stream (2) OH-6
Pigeon Run—stream (8) PA-2
Pigeon Run—stream VA-3
Pigeon Run—stream (4) WV-2
Pigeon Run—stream WI-6
Pigeon Run Reservoir PA-2
**Pigeon Run (subdivision)**—pop pl DE-2
Pigeon Sch—school KY-4
Pigeon Sch—school ND-7
Pigeon Spring—spring (7) AZ-5
Pigeon Spring—spring (2) CA-9
Pigeon Spring—spring NV-8
Pigeon Spring—spring OR-9
Pigeon Spring—spring UT-8
Pigeon Spring Number Two—spring AZ-5
Pigeon Springs—locale WA-9
Pigeon Spring Well—well AZ-5
Pigeon Swamp—stream VA-3
Pigeon Swamp—swamp CT-1
Pigeon Swamp—swamp NJ-2
Pigeon Swamp Brook—stream CT-1
Pigeon Tank—mine AZ-5
Pigeon Tank—reservoir (4) AZ-5
Pigeon Top Mtn—summit VA-3
**Pigeon (Town of)**—pop pl WI-6
Pigeon (Township of)—fmr MCD AR-4
Pigeon (Township of)—fmr MCD NC-3
**Pigeon (Township of)**—pop pl (2) IN-6
Pigeon Valley Baptist Church TN-4
Pigeon Valley Cem—cemetery NY-2
Pigeon Valley Ch—church TN-4
Pigeon Wash—valley AZ-5
Pigeon Water UT-8
Pigeon Water Creek—stream UT-8
Pigeon Water Spring UT-8
Pigeon Well—well NV-8
Pigero—island MP-9
Pigero-To MP-9
Piges Creek AL-4
Pigessharukku Island—island MP-9
Pigessharukku-To MP-9
Pigessnarukku Island MP-9
Pigeye—locale AL-4
Pigeye—locale OH-6
Pigeye Creek—stream OH-6
Pig Eye Island Number One MN-6
Pig Eye Island Number Two MN-6
Pig Eye Lake MN-6
Pig Field Airp—airport MO-7
Pigfoot Hollow—valley TX-5
Pig Foot Spring—spring ID-8
Pigford Bldg—hist pl MS-4
Pigford Cem—cemetery MS-4
Pigford House—hist pl NC-3
Pigford Lake—reservoir MS-4
Pigford Lake Dam—dam MS-4
Pigford Sch—school NC-3
Pigg Branch—stream (2) TN-4
Pigg Canyon—valley KS-7
Pigg Cem—cemetery (2) MO-7
Pigg Cem—cemetery (4) TN-4
Piggen—locale VA-3
Pigge Site—hist pl CO-8
Pigg Hollow—valley (2) TN-4
Piggie Tank—reservoir AZ-5
Piggin Run—stream WV-2
Piggly Wiggly Windmill—locale TX-5
Piggot Pond FL-3
**Piggott**—pop pl AR-4
Piggott, Charles, House—hist pl OR-9
Piggott Drain—canal MI-6
Piggott Ranch—locale NM-5
Piggotts Bridge—bridge NC-3
Pigg River—stream VA-3
Pigg River Ch—church (2) VA-3
Pigg Spring AZ-5
**Piggtown**—pop pl MS-4
Piggy Springs—spring CA-9
Pigham Creek—stream TN-4
Pig Hill—summit PA-2
Pig Hill—summit VA-3
Pig Hill Trail—trail PA-2
Pig Hole—valley UT-8
Pig Hole Spring—spring UT-8
Pig Hollow—valley KY-4
Pig In Bay (Carolina Bay)—swamp NC-3
Pigiott Field Cem—cemetery SC-3
Pig Iron Lookout—locale OR-9
Pig Iron Mtn—summit OR-9
Pig Iron Trail—trail OR-9
Pig Island—island AR-4
Pig Island—island (2) FL-3
Pig Island—island ME-1
Pig Island—island MN-6
Pig Island—island NH-1
Pig Island Gut—gut ME-1
Pig Island Ledge—bar ME-1
Pig Key—island FL-3
Pig Knoll—summit ME-1
Pig Lake—lake (2) MN-6
Piglets, The—island MA-1
Pigman Branch—stream KY-4
Pigman Hollow—valley TN-4
Pigman Mound Archeol Site—hist pl MO-7
Pigman Tank—reservoir AZ-5
Pigman Windmill—locale TX-5
Pig Mountain GA-3
Pigmy Mines (Inactive)—mine KY-4
Pignut Gully—valley (3) TX-5
Pignut Hollow—valley MO-7
Pignut Island—island TX-5
Pignut Mtn—summit (2) VA-3
**Pigo**—pop pl GU-9
Pigors Dam—dam SD-7
Pigors Lake—reservoir SD-7
Pigot Bay—bay AK-9
Pigot Glacier—glacier AK-9
Pigott Branch—stream KY-4
Pigott Branch Ch—church GA-3
Pigott Cem—cemetery (2) MS-4
Pigott Ch—church WV-2
Pigott Pond—lake FL-3
Pigotts Run—stream WV-2
Pigowak Island—island MP-9
Pig Pen—gap TN-4
Pigpen Bayou—gut MS-4
Pigpen Bayou—stream LA-4
Pig Pen Bluff—summit NC-3
Pigpen Branch—stream GA-3
Pigpen Branch—stream (3) KY-4
Pig Pen Branch—stream KY-4
Pigpen Branch—stream (2) NC-3
Pigpen Branch—stream SC-3
Pigpen Branch—stream (2) TN-4
Pigpen Branch—stream (2) TX-5
Pigpen Branch—stream WV-2
Pig Pen Canyon—valley TX-5
Pig Pen Cove—cave AL-4
Pig Pen Creek—stream AL-4
Pigpen Creek—stream AL-4
Pigpen Creek—stream CA-9
Pigpen Creek—stream NM-5
Pigpen Creek—stream NC-3
Pigpen Creek—stream OR-9
Pigpen Creek—stream PA-2
Pigpen Creek—stream TX-5
Pigpen Draw—valley CO-8
Pigpen Draw—valley TX-5
Pigpen Flats—summit NC-3
Pig Pen Fork—stream KY-4
Pigpen Fork—stream KY-4
Pigpen Gap—gap GA-3
Pig Pen Gap—gap MO-7
Pigpen Gap—gap NC-3
Pigpen Gulch—valley CA-9
Pigpen Hill—summit CO-8
Pigpen Hollow TN-4
Pig Pen Hollow—valley AR-4
Pigpen Hollow—valley GA-3
Pigpen Hollow—valley (2) KY-4
Pig Pen Hollow—valley MO-7
Pigpen Hollow—valley MO-7
Pigpen Hollow—valley (3) TN-4
Pigpen Hollow—valley TX-5
Pig Pen Hollow—valley TX-5
Pigpen Hollow—valley WV-2
Pigpen Knob—summit (3) NC-3
Pigpen Knoll—summit TX-5
Pigpen Lake MI-6
Pigpen Lakes—lake SC-3
Pigpen Mtn—summit NC-3
Pig Pen Point—cape KY-4
Pigpen Ridge—ridge (2) GA-3
Pigpen Ridge—ridge NC-3
Pigpen Slough—gut MN-6
Pigpen Slough—stream AR-4
Pigpen Slough—stream IA-7
Pig Pen Spring—spring AZ-5
Pigpen Spring—spring CA-9
Pig Pen Tank—reservoir AZ-5
Pig Pig FM-9
Pigpiig—bay FM-9
Pig Plum Creek—stream TX-5
Pig Point—cape NC-3
Pig Point—cape VA-3
Pig Pond—lake MD-2
Pigram Creek TN-4
Pig Ridge—ridge AR-4
Pig Ridge—ridge IL-6
Pigrock MA-1
Pig Rock—rock MA-1
Pig Rock Light—locale MA-1
Pigrum Branch—stream AL-4
Pig Run—stream VA-3
Pig Run—stream WV-2
Pigs Ankle—bay MO-7
Pigs Bath Tub—spring CA-9
Pigs Ear—locale PA-2
Pigs Ear, The—locale WV-2
Pigs Ear Branch—stream PA-2
Pigs Eye NJ-2
Pigs Eye Island Number One—island MN-6
Pigs Eye Island Number Two—island MN-6
Pigs Eye Lake—lake MN-6
Pigsguesset MA-1
Pigshin Ridge—ridge WV-2
Pigskin Ridge—ridge WV-2
Pig Spring—spring (2) AZ-5
Pig Squeal Spring—spring TX-5
Pig Swamp—stream VA-3
Pigtail Alley Hist Dist—hist pl GA-3
Pigtail Branch—stream WV-2
Pigtail Bridge—bridge SD-7
Pigtail Butte—summit ID-8
Pigtail Coulee—valley MT-8
Pigtail Creek—stream CA-9
Pigtail Creek—stream ID-8
Pigtail Gulch—valley CO-8
Pigtail Peak—summit WA-9
Pigtail Ravine—valley CA-9
Pigtail Ridge—ridge MN-6
Pigtail Rsvr—reservoir OR-9
Pigtail Run—stream WV-2
Pig Toe—ridge CA-9
**Pigtown**—pop pl OH-6
Pig Tract AL-4
Pig Trot Sch (historical)—school TN-4
Pig Trough Tank—reservoir AZ-5
Pigua KS-7
**Pigua**—pop pl GU-9
Pigua Pumping Station—other GU-9
Pigua River—stream GU-9
Pigue Island—island FM-9
Pigues Creek AL-4
Pigeut Corners—locale NY-2
Pigwacket Mountain NH-1
Pigwaket Pond NY-2
Piha—civil HI-9
Piha Homesteads—civil HI-9
Pihakapu HI-9
Pihakekua—crater HI-9
**Pihana**—pop pl HI-9
Pihana Heiau—locale HI-9
Pihapono—crater HI-9
Pihea—summit HI-9
Piherar FM-9
Piheraru To FM-9
Piho Stream—stream HI-9
Piiholo—summit HI-9
Piiholo Hill HI-9
Piihonua—civil HI-9
**Piihonua**—pop pl HI-9
Piikea Gulch—valley HI-9
Piilanihale Heiau—hist pl HI-9
Piilani Papa—cape HI-9
Piiloi Stream—stream HI-9
Piinaau Stream—stream HI-9
Piiraai MP-9
Piirai—island MP-9
Piirai-to MP-9
Piiriperiperi Channel—channel FM-9
Piis FM-9
Piis Moen—island FM-9
Piji Island—island MP-9
Pikaareji MP-9
Pikaareji—island MP-9
Pikaarji MP-9
Pikaaru To MP-9
Pika Cirque—basin UT-8
Pika Lake—lake CA-9
Pika Lake—lake OR-9
Pika Mountain MT-8
Pikanoru Island MP-9
Pikanoru Island—island MP-9
Pikanoru-to MP-9
Piku Point—summit MT-8
Pikareji-to MP-9
Pikarezi MP-9
Pikaru-to MP-9
Pik Dunes—area AK-9
Pike AR-4
Pike OH-6
Pike—island FM-9
Pike—locale OK-5
Pike—locale OR-9
Pike—locale TX-5
**Pike**—pop pl CA-9
**Pike**—pop pl IL-6
**Pike**—pop pl IN-6
**Pike**—pop pl NH-1
**Pike**—pop pl NY-2
**Pike**—pop pl WV-2
Pike—stream VA-3
Pike—uninc pl MD-2
Pike, Abram W., House—hist pl MI-6
Pike, Albert, Hotel—hist pl AR-4
Pike Ave Ch—church AL-4
Pike Bay—bay (2) MI-6
Pike Bay—bay (2) MN-6
Pike Bay—swamp FL-3
**Pike Bay (Township of)**—pop pl MN-6
Pike Branch—stream AL-4
Pike Branch—stream GA-3
Pike Branch—stream SC-3
Pike Branch—stream VA-3
Pike Brook—stream (4) NH-1
Pike Brook—stream NY-2
Pike Brook Sch—school NY-2
Pikecamp Run—stream WV-2
Pike Cem—cemetery AL-4
Pike Cem—cemetery ME-1
Pike Cem—cemetery NY-2
Pike Cem—cemetery OH-6
Pike Cem—cemetery OR-9
Pike Cem—cemetery PA-2
Pike Cem—cemetery (2) TN-4
Pike Cem—cemetery (2) VT-1
Pike Central Sch—school IN-6
Pike Ch—church MN-6
Pike Ch—church OH-6
Pike Ch—church PA-2
Pike Ch—church VA-3
Pike City—locale VA-3
**Pike City**—pop pl AR-4
Pike City (Township of)—fmr MCD AR-4
**Pike Corner**—pop pl ME-1
Pike Corners NY-2
Pike Country Public Lake—reservoir AL-4
**Pike County**—pop pl AL-4
**Pike (County)**—pop pl AR-4
**Pike (County)**—pop pl GA-3
**Pike (County)**—pop pl IL-6
**Pike County**—pop pl IN-6
**Pike (County)**—pop pl KY-4
**Pike County**—pop pl MS-4
**Pike County**—pop pl MO-7
**Pike (County)**—pop pl OH-6
**Pike County**—pop pl PA-2
Pike County Courthouse—hist pl AR-4
Pike County Courthouse—hist pl GA-3
Pike County Courthouse—hist pl PA-2
Pike County Fairground—locale AL-4
Pike County Farm—locale MO-7
Pike County Gulch—valley CA-9
Pike County HS—school AL-4
Pike County Lake—dam AL-4
Pike County Lake—lake AL-4
Pike County Lake—reservoir AL-4
Pike County Peak—summit CA-9
Pike County State Forest IN-6
Pike Cove—bay ME-1
Pike Creek IL-6
Pike Creek IN-6
Pike Creek KS-7
Pike Creek NC-3
Pike Creek OR-9
Pike Creek PA-2
Pike Creek—stream AK-9
Pike Creek—stream DE-2
Pike Creek—stream (5) IL-6
Pike Creek—stream (3) IN-6
Pike Creek—stream IA-7
Pike Creek—stream MI-6
Pike Creek—stream (2) MN-6
Pike Creek—stream (2) MO-7
Pike Creek—stream (4) MT-8
Pike Creek—stream (2) NY-2
Pike Creek—stream (2) NC-3
Pike Creek—stream (2) OR-9
Pike Creek—stream SC-3
Pike Creek—stream (3) WI-6
Pike Creek Baptist Ch—church DE-2
Pike Creek-Central Kirkwood (CCD)—cens area DE-2
Pike Creek Ch—church IN-6
Pike Creek Ch—church NC-3
Pike Creek Reservoir PA-2
**Pike Creek (Township of)**—pop pl MN-6
**Pike Creek Valley**—pop pl DE-2
Pike Crossroads—locale NC-3
Pike Cut WA-9
Pike Drain—canal MI-6
Pike Draw—valley WY-8
Pike Five Corners—locale NY-2
Pike-Fletcher-Terry House—hist pl AR-4
Pike-Floyd Hollow—valley KY-4
Pike-Floyd Sch—school KY-4
Pike Fork—stream WV-2
Pike Gap Run—stream WV-2
Pike Hill—locale WV-2
Pike Hill—summit AL-4
Pike Hill—summit IN-6
Pike Hill—summit (2) ME-1
Pike Hill—summit (2) NH-1
Pike Hill—summit TX-5
Pike Hill—summit VT-1
Pike Hill Brook—stream VT-1
Pike (historical)—locale KS-7
Pikehole Bay—swamp FL-3
Pikehole Creek OH-6
Pikehole Creek—stream OH-6
Pike Hollow—valley MO-7
Pike Hollow—valley VT-1
Pike House—hist pl NH-1
Pike HS—school IN-6
Pike Island—island (2) MN-6
Pike Island—island NY-2
Pike Island Lock And Dam—dam OH-6
Pike Island Lock and Dam—dam WV-2
Pike Junction—locale AR-4
Pike Knob—summit VA-3
Pike Knob—summit WV-2
Pike Lake MI-6
Pike Lake MN-6
Pike Lake OR-9
Pike Lake WI-6
Pike Lake—CDP MN-6
Pike Lake—lake (2) AK-9
Pike Lake—lake FL-3
Pike Lake—lake IN-6
Pike Lake—lake (8) MI-6
Pike Lake—lake (10) MN-6
Pike Lake—lake MT-8
Pike Lake—lake OH-6
Pike Lake—lake (9) WI-6
**Pike Lake**—pop pl MI-6
**Pike Lake**—pop pl WI-6
Pike Lake—swamp FL-3
Pike Lake Cem—cemetery MN-6
Pike Lake Creek—stream WI-6
Pike Lake (reduced usage)—lake IL-6
Pike Lakes—lake AK-9
Pike Lakes—lake MI-6
Pike Lake Sch—school (2) MN-6
Pike Lake State Park—park WI-6
Pike Lake Station—locale MI-6
Pikeland—locale PA-2
Pikeleang MP-9
Pike Liberal Arts Sch—school AL-4
Pikelot—island FM-9
Pike Memorial Gardens MS-4
Pike Mills PA-2
Pike Mine—mine PA-2
Pike Mine—uninc pl PA-2
Pike Mountain Spring—spring ID-8
Pike Mtn—summit ID-8
Pike Mtn—summit MN-6
Pikenaarin To MP-9
Pike Natl For—forest CO-8
Pikenekitto To FM-9
Pikengaren FM-9
Pikenkid—beach FM-9
Pikenkid Island FM-9
Pikenkorejo FM-9
Pikenmategan Island—island FM-9
Pikenmenmemchaien MP-9
Pikenmenmenchaien—island MP-9
Pikenuo MP-9
Pike Park—park CA-9
Pike-Pawnee Village Site—hist pl NE-7
Pike Peak TX-5
Pike Peak—summit NV-8
**Pike (Pike City)**—pop pl AR-4
Pike Place Public Market Hist Dist—hist pl WA-9
Pike Point—cape MN-6
Pike Point—cape VA-3
Pike Pond AL-4
Pike Pond—lake GA-3
Pike Pond—lake NH-1
Pike Pond—lake VA-3
Pike Post Office (historical)—building PA-2
Pike Ridge—ridge CO-8
Pike Ridge—ridge KY-4
pike River WI-6
Pike River—locale WI-6
Pike River—stream MI-6
Pike River—stream MN-6
Pike River—stream VT-1
Pike River—stream (2) WI-6
Pike River Cem—cemetery WI-6
Pike River Ch—church MN-6
Pike River Flowage—reservoir MN-6
Pike River Sch—school WI-6
**Pike Road**—pop pl AL-4
**Pike Road**—pop pl NC-3
Pike Road (CCD)—cens area AL-4
Pike Road Ch—church AL-4
Pike Road Division—civil AL-4
Piker Spring—spring WY-8
Pike Run—stream IL-6
Pike Run—stream (2) IA-7
Pike Run—stream NJ-2
Pike Run—stream (4) OH-6
Pike Run—stream (3) PA-2
Pike Run Cem—cemetery OH-6
Pike Run Ch—church OH-6
Pike Run Ch—church PA-2
Pike Run Country Club—other PA-2
Pike's, Zebulon, 1805-1806 Wintering Quarters—hist pl MN-6
Pike-San Isabel Village—locale CO-8
Pikes Bay—bay MN-6
Pikes Bay—bay WI-6
Pikes Beach NY-2
Pikes Bluff—cliff GA-3
Pikes Camp—locale OR-9
Pikes Camp State Wildlife Area—park MO-7
Pike Sch—school AR-4
Pike Sch—school IL-6
Pike Sch—school MA-1
Pike Sch—school (2) OH-6
Pike Sch—school SD-7
Pike Sch (abandoned)—school (5) PA-2
Pike Sch (historical)—school AL-4
Pike Sch (historical)—school TN-4
Pikes Corner—locale NY-2
Pikes Creek NC-3
Pikes Creek—locale PA-2
Pikes Creek—stream GA-3
Pikes Creek—stream MD-2
Pikes Creek—stream PA-2
Pikes Creek—stream WI-6
Pikes Creek Ch—church NC-3
Pikes Creek Dam—dam PA-2
Pikes Creek Marsh—swamp MD-2
Pikes Creek Rsvr—reservoir PA-2
Pikes Crossing—locale OR-9
**Pikes Falls**—pop pl VT-1
Pikes Fork—stream ID-8
Pike's Gap CO-8
Pikes Gulch—valley MT-8
Pikes Hill—summit NH-1
Pikes Hill—summit NY-2
Pikes Hill—summit WA-9
**Pikeslde**—pop pl WV-2
Pike's Island MN-6
Pikes Lake—lake MI-6
Pike Slough—gut WI-6
Pike Slough—stream AK-9
Pike Slough—stream MO-7
Pikes Mtn—summit VA-3
Pikes Neck—cape DE-2
Pikes Peak CA-9
Pikes Peak MT-8
Pikes Peak OR-9
Pikes Peak—cens area CO-8
Pikes Peak—cliff ND-7
Pikes Peak—hist pl CO-8
**Pikes Peak**—pop pl GA-3
**Pikes Peak**—pop pl IN-6
**Pikes Peak**—pop pl LA-4
**Pikes Peak**—pop pl PA-2
Pikes Peak—summit AZ-5
Pikes Peak—summit CA-9
Pikes Peak—summit CO-8
Pikes Peak—summit IN-6
Pikes Peak—summit (2) MI-6
Pikes Peak—summit MO-7
Pikes Peak—summit (2) MT-8
Pikes Peak—summit NY-2
Pikes Peak—summit OK-5
Pikes Peak—summit OR-9
Pikes Peak—summit PA-2
Pikes Peak—summit (4) TX-5
Pikes Peak—summit VT-1
Pikes Peak—summit (4) WI-6
Pikes Peak Airp—airport CO-8
Pikes Peak Bluff—cliff MO-7
Pikes Peak Branch—stream TN-4
Pikes Peak Cave—cave MO-7
Pikes Peak Cem—cemetery LA-4
Pikes Peak Ch—church IN-6
Pikes Peak Creek—stream MT-8
Pikes Peak Draw—valley TX-5
Pikes Peak Gas Field—oilfield TX-5
Pikes Peak Grange—locale CO-8
Pikes Peak Junior Acad—school CO-8
Pikes Peak Lake—swamp LA-4
Pikes Peak Park—uninc pl CO-8
Pikes Peak Ridge—ridge MT-8
Pikes Peak Sch—school IL-6
Pikes Peak Sch (abandoned)—school MO-7
Pikes Peak Sch (abandoned)—school PA-2
Pikes Peak Speedway—other CO-8
Pikes Peak Spring—spring TN-4
Pikes Peak Springs TN-4
Pikes Peak State Park—park IA-7
Pikes Peak Trail—trail PA-2
Pikes Peak Windmill—locale TX-5
Pikes Point—cape CA-9
Pikes Point—cape IA-7
Pikes Point—cape NH-1
Pikes Point—cape WI-6
Pikes Point State Park—park IA-7
Pikes Pond—lake MI-6
Pikes Pond—lake NY-2
Pikes Pond—reservoir AL-4
Pikes Pond—reservoir MA-1
Pikes Pond Dam—dam MA-1
Pike Spring—spring KY-4
Pikes Rocks—pillar PA-2
Pike's Stockade—hist pl CO-8
Pikes Stockade—locale CO-8
Pikestaff Creek—stream TN-4
Pike State For—forest IN-6
Pike Station—other IL-6
Pike Station Public Access Area—locale IL-6
Pike Statue—park DC-2
Pikes Timber Park—park IA-7
Pikesville PA-2
**Pikesville**—pop pl MD-2
Pikesville Armory—hist pl MD-2
Pikesville Rsvr—reservoir MD-2
Pike Swale—stream MI-6
Pike Swamp—swamp GA-3
Pikes Well—well AZ-5
Piketon MS-4
Piketon TN-4
**Piketon**—pop pl OH-6
Piketon Hist Dist—hist pl OH-6
Piketon Mounds—hist pl OH-6
Piketon Post Office TN-4
Piketon Sch—school OH-6
**Piketown**—pop pl MS-4
**Piketown**—pop pl PA-2
**Pike (Town of)**—pop pl NY-2
Pike Township—civil MO-7
Pike Township—fmr MCD IA-7
**Pike Township**—pop pl KS-7
**Pike Township**—pop pl MO-7
**Pike (Township of)**—pop pl IL-6
**Pike (Township of)**—pop pl (4) IN-6
**Pike (Township of)**—pop pl MN-6
**Pike (Township of)**—pop pl (8) OH-6
**Pike (Township of)**—pop pl (4) PA-2
Pike Trap Creek—stream AK-9
Pike Trap Lake—lake AK-9
Pike Valley Elem Sch—school KS-7
Pike Valley HS—school KS-7
Pike Valley JHS—school KS-7
**Pikeview**—pop pl CO-8
**Pike View**—pop pl KY-4
Pikeville MS-4
Pikeville—locale (2) AL-4
Pikeville—locale NY-2
**Pikeville**—pop pl IN-6
**Pikeville**—pop pl KY-4
**Pikeville**—pop pl NC-3
**Pikeville**—pop pl OH-6
**Pikeville**—pop pl PA-2
**Pikeville**—pop pl TN-4
**Pikeville**—pop pl WI-6
Pikeville Branch—stream KY-4
Pikeville (CCD)—cens area KY-4
Pikeville Cem—cemetery AL-4
Pikeville Ch—church AL-4
Pikeville Ch—church KY-4
Pikeville College Acad Bldg—hist pl KY-4
Pikeville Country Club—other AL-4
Pikeville Elem Sch—school NC-3
Pikeville Elem Sch—school TN-4
**Pikeville (historical)**—pop pl MS-4
Pikeville Post Office—building TN-4
Pikeville Public Use Area—park AR-4
Pikeville Sch—school WI-6
Pikeville Sch (historical)—school AL-4
Pikeville School TN-4
Pikeville (Township of)—fmr MCD NC-3
Pike-Whitman Trail—trail PA-2
Pikijin Island MP-9
Pikijin Island—island MP-9
Pikijin-To MP-9
Pikinekit FM-9
Pikinni MP-9
Pikinni-to MP-9
Pikmiktalik—locale AK-9
Pikmiktalik River—stream (2) AK-9
Pikoakea Spring—spring HI-9
Pikoaukea Spring HI-9
Pikonik Mound—summit AK-9
Pikoto MP-9
Pikoto Island MP-9
Pikoto Island—island MP-9
Pikotorikku MP-9
Pikotorikku Island MP-9
Pikotorikku Island—island MP-9
Pikroka Creek—stream AK-9
Piksiksak Creek—stream AK-9
Pikulapnei PW-9
Pikwatina TN-4
Pil PW-9
Pil, Dauen—gut FM-9
Pila, Canada De La —valley CA-9
Pilaa—civil HI-9
Pila Blanca—locale TX-5
Pila Blanca Windmill—locale TX-5
Pila Blance Windmill—locale TX-5
Pila Cerro Well—well AZ-5
Pila Grande Windmill—locale TX-5
Pilakapw FM-9
**Pilaklakha (historical)**—pop pl FL-3
Pilale HI-9
Pilale Bay—bay HI-9
**Pilands Crossroads**—pop pl NC-3
Pilani Ditch—canal HI-9
Pilant Cem—cemetery MO-7
Pilant Lake—reservoir TX-5

*Pilap-en-Lataw River* FM-9
*Pilapen Latwa* FM-9
*Pilap En Lohd* FM-9
**Pilar**—*pop pl* NM-5
Pilarcitos Canyon—*valley* CA-9
Pilarcitos Creek—*stream* CA-9
Pilarcitos Lake—*reservoir* CA-9
Pilarcitos Ridge—*ridge* CA-9
Pilarcitos Tunnel—*tunnel* CA-9
Pilares—*locale* TX-5
Pilares Windmill—*locale* NM-5
*Pilar River* AZ-5
Pilar Tank, El—*reservoir* AZ-5
Pilas Well, Los—*well* AZ-5
*Pilatka* FL-3
Pilchard Creek—*stream* MD-2
Pilcher Branch—*stream* MO-7
Pilcher Cem—*cemetery* GA-3
Pilcher Cem—*cemetery* IL-6
Pilcher Cem—*cemetery* NE-7
Pilcher Chapel—*church* IN-6
Pilcher Creek—*stream* GA-3
Pilcher Creek—*stream* IL-6
Pilcher Creek—*stream* MT-8
Pilcher Creek—*stream* OR-9
Pilcher Hill—*summit* AZ-5
Pilcher Hill—*summit* GA-3
Pilcher Landing—*locale* KY-4
Pilcher Mountain Creek—*stream* AK-9
Pilcher Mtn—*summit* AK-9
Pilcher Park—*park* IL-6
Pilcher Pond—*lake* GA-3
Pilcher Pond—*swamp* FL-3
Pilchs Number 3 Dam—*dam* MA-1
Pilchuck, Mount—*school* WA-9
Pilchuck, Mount—*summit* WA-9
Pilchuck Creek—*stream* (2) WA-9
*Pilchuck Mountain* WA-9
Pilchuck River—*stream* WA-9
Pilchuck State Park, Mount—*park* WA-9
Pile Bay—*bay* AK-9
Pile Bay Village—*locale* AK-9
Pile Cem—*cemetery* KY-4
Pile Creek—*stream* NC-3
Piledriver Cove—*bay* AK-9
Piledriver Creek—*stream* OR-9
Pile Driver Creek—*stream* TX-5
Piledriver Creek—*stream* WI-6
Pile Driver Hollow—*valley* MO-7
Piledriver Lake—*lake* WI-6
Piledriver Rock—*island* AK-9
Piledriver Slough—*stream* AK-9
Pile Hill—*summit* CO-8
*Pilenikiepw* FM-9
*Pilen Keiew* FM-9
*Pilen Keriau* FM-9
*Pilen Leldau* FM-9
*Pilen Senipehn* FM-9
*Pilenuana River* FM-9
Pile of Sticks—*summit* AZ-5
Pile Point—*cape* WA-9
Pilerack Point—*cape* AK-9
*Pilereat* MP-9
Pile River—*stream* AK-9
Pileriver Cove—*bay* AK-9
Piles Branch—*stream* TN-4
Piles Cem—*cemetery* WV-2
Piles Creek—*stream* NJ-2
Piles Creek—*stream* OK-5
Piles Fork—*stream* IL-6
**Pilesgrove (Township of)**—*pop pl* NJ-2
Piletas (Barrio)—*fmr MCD* PR-3
*Piletas Canyon* CA-9
**Pilette**—*pop pl* LA-4
Pileup Canyon—*valley* MT-8
Pileup Canyon—*valley* OR-9
Pileup Creek—*stream* ID-8
Pileup Creek—*stream* OR-9
Pileup Creek—*stream* WA-9
Pile Up Creek—*stream* WA-9
Pileup Saddle—*gap* OR-9
Pilfer Creek—*stream* KY-4
**Pilger**—*pop pl* NE-7
Pilgeram Ditch—*canal* MT-8
Pilger Cem—*cemetery* NE-7
Pilgerheim Cem—*cemetery* ND-7
Pilger Lake—*lake* WY-8
Pilger Lateral—*canal* CA-9
Pilger Mtn—*summit* SD-7
Pilger Ruhe Cem—*cemetery* OH-6
Pilgerts—*locale* PA-2
*Pilgram Church* AL-4
*Pilgram Creek* MT-8
Pilgram Rest Ch—*church* FL-3
Pilgrams Home Ch—*church* NC-3
**Pilgrams Knob (Pilgram Knob)**—*pop pl* VA-3
Pilgreen Pond—*swamp* TX-5
*Pilgrim* RI-1
Pilgrim—*locale* KY-4
Pilgrim—*locale* MI-6
Pilgrim—*locale* MO-7
**Pilgrim**—*pop pl* MI-6
**Pilgrim**—*pop pl* TX-5
Pilgrim—*uninc pl* NY-2
Pilgrim, Mount—*summit* MT-8
Pilgrimage Theater—*building* CA-9
Pilgrim Baptist Ch—*church* (2) AL-4
Pilgrim Baptist Ch—*church* DE-2
Pilgrim Baptist Ch—*church* IN-6
*Pilgrim Baptist Church* MS-4
Pilgrim Beach—*island* MA-1
Pilgrim Bound Baptist Ch—*church* MS-4
Pilgrim Branch—*stream* LA-4
Pilgrim Branch Ch—*church* MS-4
*Pilgrim Branch Missionary Baptist Ch* MS-4
Pilgrim Branch Sch—*school* MS-4
Pilgrim Campground—*park* IN-6
Pilgrim Cem—*cemetery* CO-8
Pilgrim Cem—*cemetery* LA-4
Pilgrim Cem—*cemetery* (2) MS-4
Pilgrim Cem—*cemetery* OK-5
Pilgrim Cem—*cemetery* (2) TX-5
*Pilgrim Ch* AL-4
*Pilgrim Ch* IN-6
*Pilgrim Ch* MS-4
*Pilgrim Ch* TN-4
Pilgrim Ch—*church* (5) AL-4
Pilgrim Ch—*church* (3) AR-4
Pilgrim Ch—*church* CT-1
Pilgrim Ch—*church* DE-2
Pilgrim Ch—*church* (2) GA-3
Pilgrim Ch—*church* IN-6
Pilgrim Ch—*church* (6) KY-4
Pilgrim Ch—*church* (8) LA-4
Pilgrim Ch—*church* (3) MI-6
Pilgrim Ch—*church* (4) MS-4
Pilgrim Ch—*church* (3) NC-3
Pilgrim Ch—*church* (3) OH-6
Pilgrim Ch—*church* (3) OK-5
Pilgrim Ch—*church* (6) PA-2
Pilgrim Ch—*church* (7) SC-3
Pilgrim Ch—*church* (2) TN-4
Pilgrim Ch—*church* (4) TX-5
Pilgrim Ch—*church* (7) VA-3
Pilgrim Ch—*church* (2) WV-2
Pilgrim Chapel—*church* AL-4
Pilgrim Chapel—*church* MA-1
Pilgrim Chapel—*church* (2) NC-3
Pilgrim Ch (historical)—*church* (3) AL-4
Pilgrim Ch (historical)—*church* MS-4
Pilgrim Ch (historical)—*church* TN-4
Pilgrim Christian Fellowship—*church* UT-8
Pilgrim Congregational Church—*hist pl* (2) MA-1
Pilgrim Congregational Church—*hist pl* OH-6
Pilgrim Congregational Church—*hist pl* OK-5
Pilgrim Congregational United Ch of Christ—*church* TN-4
**Pilgrim Corners**—*pop pl* NY-2
Pilgrim Cove—*bay* ID-8
Pilgrim Creek—*stream* (2) CA-9
Pilgrim Creek—*stream* (3) MT-8
Pilgrim Creek—*stream* TX-5
Pilgrim Creek—*stream* WY-8
Pilgrim Creek Experimental Station—*other* CA-9
Pilgrim Creek (historical)—*locale* IA-7
Pilgrim Creek Trail—*trail* WY-8
Pilgrim Evangelical Lutheran Ch—*church* IN-6
Pilgrim Family Farmstead—*hist pl* WI-6
Pilgrim Free Will Ch—*church* AL-4
**Pilgrim Gardens**—*pop pl* DE-2
**Pilgrim Gardens**—*pop pl* PA-2
Pilgrim Green Ch—*church* (2) MS-4
Pilgrim Green Ch (historical)—*church* MS-4
**Pilgrim Grove**—*pop pl* MS-4
Pilgrim Grove Ch—*church* LA-4
Pilgrim Grove Ch—*church* (3) MS-4
Pilgrim Grove Ch—*church* NC-3
*Pilgrim Grove Missionary Baptist Ch* MS-4
Pilgrim Guide Ch—*church* AR-4
Pilgrim Hall—*hist pl* MA-1
Pilgrim Hall Museum—*building* MA-1
**Pilgrimham**—*pop pl* PA-2
**Pilgrimham (Wilson)**—*pop pl* PA-2
**Pilgrim Heights**—*pop pl* MA-1
Pilgrim Heights Camp—*locale* IA-7
Pilgrim Hill Ch—*church* NC-3
Pilgrim Hill Ch—*church* TX-5
Pilgrim Hills Camp—*locale* OH-6
Pilgrim Holiness Ch—*church* NY-2
Pilgrim Holiness Church—*hist pl* NE-7
Pilgrim Holiness Tabernacle—*church* DE-2
Pilgrim Hollow—*valley* AR-4
Pilgrim Home Baptist Ch—*church* (2) MS-4
Pilgrim Home Cem—*cemetery* (2) MI-6
Pilgrim Home Ch—*church* (2) AL-4
Pilgrim Home Ch—*church* GA-3
Pilgrim Home Ch—*church* LA-4
Pilgrim Hot Springs—*hist pl* AK-9
Pilgrim Indian Mission Sch—*school* NM-5
Pilgrim Journey Ch—*church* TX-5
*Pilgrim Knob* VA-3
Pilgrim Knob—*other* VA-3
Pilgrim Lake—*lake* (2) MA-1
Pilgrim Lake—*lake* NV-8
Pilgrim Lake—*lake* PA-2
Pilgrim Lake—*lake* TX-5
Pilgrim Lake—*reservoir* PA-2
Pilgrim Lake Dam—*dam* MS-4
Pilgrim Lakes—*lake* MT-8
Pilgrim Lane Sch—*school* MN-6
Pilgrim Ledge—*bar* MA-1
Pilgrim Lutheran Ch—*church* AL-4
Pilgrim Lutheran Ch—*church* PA-2
Pilgrim Mills—*hist pl* MA-1
Pilgrim Mine—*mine* NV-8
Pilgrim Mine (Inactive)—*mine* CA-9
Pilgrim Missionary Baptist Ch—*church* KS-7
Pilgrim Missionary Baptist Ch—*church* MS-4
Pilgrim Monmt—*park* MA-1
Pilgrim Monument—*cemetery* MA-1
Pilgrim Mtn—*summit* ID-8
Pilgrim Mtn—*summit* NY-2
Pilgrim Mtn—*summit* WY-8
Pilgrim Park Sch—*school* WI-6
**Pilgrim Pines Estates**—*pop pl* MA-1
Pilgrim Playground—*locale* AZ-5
Pilgrim Point—*cape* MI-6
Pilgrim Point—*cape* MN-6
Pilgrim Point Ch—*church* TX-5
Pilgrim Pond—*lake* NY-2
Pilgrim Pond—*reservoir* GA-3
**Pilgrimport**—*pop pl* NY-2
Pilgrim Presbyterian Church—*hist pl* OH-6
*Pilgrim Primitive Baptist Ch* MS-4
Pilgrim Progress Baptist Ch—*church* MS-4
Pilgrim Reformed Ch—*church* NC-3
Pilgrim Reformed Church Cemetery—*hist pl* NC-3
**Pilgrim Rest**—*pop pl* MS-4
*Pilgrim Rest Baptist Ch* AL-4
*Pilgrim Rest Baptist Ch* MS-4
Pilgrim Rest Baptist Ch—*church* (3) AL-4
Pilgrim Rest Baptist Ch—*church* FL-3
Pilgrim Rest Baptist Ch—*church* (2) MS-4
Pilgrimrest Baptist Ch—*church* TN-4
*Pilgrim Rest Cem* MS-4
Pilgrim Rest Cem—*cemetery* (3) AL-4
Pilgrim Rest Cem—*cemetery* (2) AR-4
Pilgrim Rest Cem—*cemetery* (3) LA-4
Pilgrim Rest Cem—*cemetery* (12) MS-4
Pilgrim Rest Cem—*cemetery* WV-2
Pilgrim Rest Cem—*cemetery* WI-6
*Pilgrim Rest Ch* AL-4
*Pilgrim Rest Ch* MS-4
Pilgrim Rest Ch—*church* (12) AL-4
Pilgrim Rest Ch—*church* (8) AR-4
Pilgrim Rest Ch—*church* (2) FL-3
Pilgrim Rest Ch—*church* (3) KY-4
Pilgrim Rest Ch—*church* (8) LA-4
Pilgrim Rest Ch—*church* (26) MS-4
Pilgrim Rest Ch—*church* (3) MO-7
Pilgrim Rest Ch—*church* (2) NC-3
Pilgrim Rest Ch—*church* (4) OK-5
Pilgrim Rest Ch—*church* (2) SC-3
Pilgrim Rest Ch—*church* (2) TN-4
Pilgrim Rest Ch—*church* (6) TX-5
Pilgrim Rest Ch—*church* VA-3
Pilgrim Rest Ch—*church* (3) WV-2
Pilgrim Rest Ch (historical)—*church* (2) MS-4
Pilgrim Rest (historical)—*locale* AL-4
*Pilgrim Rest Primitive Baptist Ch* MS-4
Pilgrim Rest Sch—*school* AR-4
Pilgrim Rest Sch—*school* MS-4
Pilgrim Rest Sch—*school* TN-4
Pilgrim Rest Sch (historical)—*school* MS-4
Pilgrim Rest United American Freewill Ch—*church* FL-3
Pilgrim Ridge—*ridge* AR-4
Pilgrim Ridge Ch—*church* TX-5
Pilgrim River—*stream* AK-9
Pilgrim River—*stream* MI-6
Pilgrim Rock Baptist Ch—*church* TN-4
Pilgrims Ch—*church* AL-4
Pilgrims Ch—*church* TN-4
Pilgrim Sch—*school* IL-6
Pilgrim Sch—*school* OH-6
Pilgrim Sch—*school* SC-3
Pilgrim Sch—*school* TX-5
Pilgrim Sch—*school* VA-3
Pilgrim Sch—*school* WI-6
Pilgrims Chapel—*church* AL-4
Pilgrims Chapel Ch—*church* AL-4
Pilgrims Ch (historical)—*church* AL-4
*Pilgrim School* AL-4
Pilgrims Gospel Tabernacle—*church* VA-3
Pilgrims Home Cem—*cemetery* KS-7
Pilgrims Home Ch—*church* (2) AL-4
Pilgrims Home Ch—*church* GA-3
Pilgrims Home Ch—*church* VA-3
Pilgrims House Ch—*church* KY-4
Pilgrims Knob—*locale* VA-3
Pilgrim Spring—*spring* ID-8
Pilgrim Spring—*spring* MA-1
**Pilgrim Springs**—*pop pl* AK-9
Pilgrim's Progress Road Bridge—*hist pl* NY-2
Pilgrims Refuge Ch—*church* MS-4
*Pilgrims Rest* NC-3
Pilgrim's Rest—*hist pl* MS-4
**Pilgrims Rest**—*pop pl* (2) AR-4
**Pilgrims Rest**—*pop pl* TX-5
*Pilgrims Rest Baptist Ch* AL-4
*Pilgrims Rest Baptist Church* MS-4
*Pilgrims Rest Cem* MS-4
Pilgrims Rest Cem—*cemetery* (5) AL-4
Pilgrims Rest Cem—*cemetery* (3) AR-4
Pilgrims Rest Cem—*cemetery* IN-6
Pilgrims Rest Cem—*cemetery* KY-4
Pilgrims Rest Cem—*cemetery* MI-6
Pilgrims Rest Cem—*cemetery* (4) MN-6
Pilgrims Rest Cem—*cemetery* (4) MS-4
Pilgrims Rest Cem—*cemetery* MO-7
Pilgrims Rest Cem—*cemetery* ND-7
Pilgrims Rest Cem—*cemetery* (2) OK-5
Pilgrims Rest Cem—*cemetery* TN-4
Pilgrims Rest Cem—*cemetery* (3) TX-5
Pilgrims Rest Cem—*cemetery* (3) WI-6
*Pilgrims Rest Ch* AL-4
*Pilgrims Rest Ch* MS-4
Pilgrims Rest Ch—*church* (17) AL-4
Pilgrims Rest Ch—*church* (9) AR-4
Pilgrims Rest Ch—*church* (2) FL-3
Pilgrims Rest Ch—*church* (6) GA-3
Pilgrims Rest Ch—*church* (3) KY-4
Pilgrims Rest Ch—*church* (3) LA-4
Pilgrims Rest Ch—*church* (17) MS-4
Pilgrims Rest Ch—*church* (2) MO-7
Pilgrims Rest Ch—*church* (2) NC-3
Pilgrims Rest Ch—*church* OH-6
Pilgrims Rest Ch—*church* OK-5
Pilgrims Rest Ch—*church* (3) TN-4
Pilgrims Rest Ch—*church* (3) TX-5
Pilgrims Rest Ch—*church* (2) VA-3
Pilgrims Rest Ch (historical)—*church* (4) AL-4
Pilgrims Rest Ch (historical)—*church* (3) MS-4
*Pilgrims Rest Freewill Baptist Ch* AL-4
Pilgrims Rest (historical)—*locale* AL-4
**Pilgrims Rest (historical)**—*pop pl* MS-4
*Pilgrims Rest Missionary Baptist Ch* AL-4
Pilgrims Rest Missionary Baptist Ch—*church* AL-4
Pilgrims Rest Missionary Baptist Ch—*church* MS-4
Pilgrims Rest Number 2 Ch—*church* TX-5
Pilgrims Rest P. O. (historical)—*locale* AL-4
*Pilgrims Rest Primitive Baptist Ch* AL-4
Pilgrims Rest Primitive Baptist Ch—*church* AL-4
Pilgrims Rest Sch—*school* AL-4
Pilgrims Rest Sch—*school* AR-4
Pilgrims Rest Sch (historical)—*school* (3) MS-4
*Pilgrims Rest School* TN-4
**Pilgrims Rest (subdivision)**—*pop pl* AL-4
**Pilgrim Stage Station Historic Site**—*pop pl* ID-8
Pilgrim State Hosp—*hospital* NY-2
Pilgrim Tabernacle—*church* DE-2
Pilgrim Temple—*church* TN-4
**Pilgrim Township**—*pop pl* MO-7
**Pilgrim Village**—*pop pl* MA-1
Pilgrim Wash—*stream* AZ-5
Pilgrim Wash Well—*well* AZ-5
Pilgrim Way Congregational Ch—*church* FL-3
Pilgrim Wesleyan Ch—*church* DE-2
**Pilgrim (Wolfcreek)**—*pop pl* KY-4
Pilgrim 100B Aircraft—*hist pl* AK-9
*Pili* HI-9
Piliamoe Gulch—*valley* HI-9
**Pilibos Ranch**—*pop pl* CA-9
*Pili Hill* HI-9
*Pililau* PW-9
Piling Brake—*swamp* AR-4
Piling Creek—*stream* WA-9
Piling Gulch—*valley* CO-8
Piling Point—*cape* AK-9
Piling Pond—*lake* LA-4
Piliokahe Beach Park—*park* HI-9
Pili o Kahe Gulch—*valley* HI-9
*Pili o Koe Gulch* HI-9
Pilipililau Stream—*stream* HI-9
Pilitas Creek—*stream* CA-9
Pilitas Mtn—*summit* CA-9
Pilkens Rsvr—*reservoir* OR-9
Pilkey Cem—*cemetery* NC-3
Pilkey Creek—*stream* NC-3
Pilkinson Cem—*cemetery* LA-4
Pilkinton—*locale* VA-3
Pilkinton Branch—*stream* MO-7
Pilla, Charles, House—*hist pl* KS-7
**Pillager**—*pop pl* MN-6
Pillager Cem—*cemetery* MN-6
Pillager Creek—*stream* MN-6
Pillager Dam—*dam* MN-6
Pillager Lake—*lake* MN-6
*Pillakapw* FM-9
Pillans Prairie—*flat* FL-3
*Pillap En Kiti* FM-9
*Pillapen Nan Meir Lap* FM-9
Pillar—*locale* AR-4
Pillar, The—*pillar* NM-5
*Pillar Arch* UT-8
Pillar Bay Cannery—*other* AK-9
Pillar Bluff—*cliff* TX-5
Pillar Bluff Creek—*stream* TX-5
Pillar Butte—*summit* ID-8
Pillar Cape—*cape* AK-9
*Pillarcitos Creek* CA-9
*Pillarcitos Lake* CA-9
*Pillar Creek* MT-8
Pillar Creek—*stream* AK-9
Pillar Creek—*stream* ID-8
Pillar Creek Rsvr—*reservoir* AK-9
Pillar Falls—*falls* ID-8
Pillar Lake—*lake* NE-7
Pillar Lake—*lake* (2) WA-9
Pillar Mtn—*summit* AK-9
Pillar of Fire Ch—*church* PA-2
Pillar Of Fire Sch—*school* PA-2
Pillar of Hercules—*pillar* CO-8
Pillar Peak—*summit* OR-9
Pillar Peak—*summit* SD-7
Pillar Point—*cape* AK-9
Pillar Point—*cape* CA-9
Pillar Point—*cape* NY-2
Pillar Point—*cape* WA-9
**Pillar Point**—*pop pl* NY-2
Pillar Point Harbor—*harbor* CA-9
Pillar Point State Rec Area—*park* WA-9
*Pillar Rock* CA-9
Pillar Rock—*island* AK-9
Pillar Rock—*island* OR-9
Pillar Rock—*pillar* TX-5
Pillar Rock—*pillar* WA-9
Pillar Rock—*pillar* WI-6
**Pillar Rock**—*pop pl* WA-9
Pillar Rock Cannery—*building* WA-9
Pillar Rock Island—*island* OR-9
Pillar Rock Lower Range—*channel* OR-9
Pillar Rock Lower Range—*channel* WA-9
Pillar Rock Upper Range—*channel* OR-9
Pillar Rock Upper Range—*channel* WA-9
Pillars, The—*pillar* AK-9
Pillars, The—*ridge* UT-8
Pillars Creek—*stream* LA-4
Pillars of God (open Air Theater)—*basin* CA-9
Pillars of Hercules—*pillar* AZ-5
Pill Berry Creek—*stream* AL-4
Pillbox Cave—*cave* PA-2
Pill Branch—*stream* AR-4
Pill Creek—*stream* WY-8
*Piller Rock* WA-9
Pill Hill—*locale* NJ-2
Pill Hill Hist Dist—*hist pl* MA-1
Pillick Ridge—*ridge* MT-8
Pilliken—*locale* CA-9
Pilling Lake—*lake* NJ-2
*Pilling Pond* MA-1
Pilling Pond—*lake* UT-8
Pilling Ranch—*locale* UT-8
Pillings Cascade—*falls* UT-8
Pillings Cem—*cemetery* WI-6
*Pilling'S Pond* MA-1
Pillings Pond—*lake* MA-1
Pillings Pond Dam—*dam* MA-1
Pillion Cem—*cemetery* VA-3
Pillman Cave—*cave* MO-7
Pillman Cem—*cemetery* MO-7
Pillman Creek—*stream* MO-7
**Pillot**—*pop pl* TX-5
Pillot Bldg—*hist pl* TX-5
Pillot Cem—*cemetery* TX-5
Pillot Gully—*valley* (2) TX-5
**Pillow**—*pop pl* PA-2
Pillow, Jerome Bonaparte, House—*hist pl* AR-4
Pillow, The—*cape* AZ-5
Pillow Acad—*school* MS-4
Pillow-Bethel House—*hist pl* TN-4
Pillow Borough—*civil* PA-2
Pillow Cem—*cemetery* KY-4
Pillow Cem—*cemetery* TN-4
Pillow Cem—*cemetery* TX-5
Pillow Chapel—*church* MS-4
Pillow Lake—*reservoir* TN-4
Pillow Lake Dam—*dam* TN-4
Pillow Mtn—*summit* (2) AZ-5
Pillow Place—*hist pl* TN-4
Pillow Point—*cape* AK-9
Pillow Ridge—*ridge* AZ-5
**Pillows**—*pop pl* MS-4
Pillows Point—*cape* MI-6
Pillow Spring—*spring* TN-4
*Pillowsville* TN-4
Pillowsville Post Office (historical)—*building* TN-4
**Pillowville**—*pop pl* TN-4
Pill Pond—*lake* OR-9
Pillsbery Lake—*lake* MN-6
Pillsboro Landing—*locale* NC-3
**Pillsboro Landing (historical)**—*pop pl* NC-3
**Pillsbury**—*pop pl* KY-4
**Pillsbury**—*pop pl* MN-6
**Pillsbury**—*pop pl* ND-7
Pillsbury, Lake—*reservoir* CA-9
Pillsbury, Mount—*summit* AK-9
Pillsbury Acad Campus Hist Dist—*hist pl* MN-6
Pillsbury A Mill—*hist pl* MN-6
Pillsbury Bay—*bay* NY-2
Pillsbury Coll—*school* MN-6
*Pillsbury Creek* MN-6
Pillsbury Crossing—*locale* KS-7
Pillsbury-French House—*hist pl* MA-1
Pillsbury Hill—*summit* NH-1
Pillsbury Island—*island* ME-1
Pillsbury Island Campsite—*locale* ME-1
*Pillsbury Lake* MN-6
Pillsbury Lake—*lake* NY-2
Pillsbury Lake (historical)—*lake* IA-7
Pillsbury Mine—*mine* MN-6
Pillsbury Mtn—*summit* ME-1
Pillsbury Mtn—*summit* NH-1
Pillsbury Mtn—*summit* NY-2
Pillsbury Point—*cape* AK-9
Pillsbury Point—*cape* IA-7
Pillsbury Point State Park—*park* IA-7
Pillsbury Pond—*lake* ME-1
Pillsbury Ridge—*ridge* NH-1
Pillsbury Sch—*school* MN-6
Pillsbury Sound—*channel* VI-3
Pillsbury State For—*forest* MN-6
Pillsbury State Park—*park* NH-1
**Pillsbury (Township of)**—*pop pl* MN-6
Pills Ponds—*reservoir* GA-3
Pill Tank Number One—*reservoir* AZ-5
**Pilltown**—*pop pl* PA-2
*Pilltown Creek* IA-7
Pill Two Tank—*reservoir* AZ-5
Pilly Fork—*stream* AK-9
**Pilly Green Subdivision**—*pop pl* UT-8
*Pilman Canyon* CA-9
*Pilocklakha* FL-3
*Piloleno Mountain* AZ-5
Pilon Ranch—*locale* MT-8
Pilontary Islands—*island* NC-3
*Pilot* IL-6
Pilot—*locale* KY-4
Pilot—*locale* NV-8
**Pilot**—*pop pl* MD-2
**Pilot**—*pop pl* (2) NC-3
**Pilot**—*pop pl* VA-3
Pilot, The—*summit* KY-4
Pilot, The—*summit* VA-3
Pilot Bluff—*cliff* AK-9
*Pilot Branch* NC-3
Pilot Branch—*stream* AR-4
Pilot Branch—*stream* KY-4
Pilot Branch—*stream* MO-7
Pilot Branch—*stream* NC-3
Pilot Branch—*stream* TX-5
*Pilot Butte* OR-9
Pilot Butte—*summit* CA-9
Pilot Butte—*summit* OR-9
Pilot Butte—*summit* (2) WY-8
Pilot Butte Canal—*canal* OR-9
Pilot Butte Cem—*cemetery* OR-9
Pilot Butte Elem Sch—*school* OR-9
Pilot Butte JHS—*school* OR-9
Pilot Butte North Canal—*canal* OR-9
Pilot Butte Oil Field—*oilfield* WY-8
Pilot Butte Power Plant—*other* WY-8
Pilot Butte Rsvr—*reservoir* WY-8
Pilot Butte South Canal—*canal* OR-9
Pilot Butte State Park—*park* OR-9
Pilot Canal—*canal* WY-8
Pilot Center Cem—*cemetery* IL-6
Pilot Ch—*church* (2) AR-4
Pilot Ch—*church* KY-4
Pilot Channel—*canal* TX-5
Pilot Cone—*summit* NV-8
Pilot Cone Well—*well* NV-8
Pilot Cove—*bay* FL-3
Pilot Cove—*bay* MI-6
Pilot Cove—*valley* NC-3
*Pilot Creek* TX-5
Pilot Creek—*stream* AL-4
Pilot Creek—*stream* (2) AK-9
Pilot Creek—*stream* (3) CA-9
Pilot Creek—*stream* CO-8
Pilot Creek—*stream* (2) ID-8
Pilot Creek—*stream* IA-7
Pilot Creek—*stream* KY-4
Pilot Creek—*stream* NV-8
Pilot Creek—*stream* NC-3
Pilot Creek—*stream* (2) UT-8
Pilot Creek—*stream* WY-8
Pilot Creek Ranches Airp—*airport* NV-8
Pilot Creek Trail—*trail* WY-8
Pilot Creek Valley—*valley* NV-8
Pilot Drain—*canal* WY-8
Pilot Elem Sch—*school* (2) NC-3
Pilotes Ranch—*locale* TX-5
Pilot Falls—*falls* TN-4
Pilot Gap—*gap* NC-3
Pilot Grove—*hist pl* IA-7
**Pilot Grove**—*pop pl* IA-7
**Pilot Grove**—*pop pl* MN-6
**Pilot Grove**—*pop pl* MO-7
**Pilot Grove**—*pop pl* TX-5
Pilot Grove—*woods* CA-9
Pilot Grove Branch—*stream* TX-5
Pilot Grove Cem—*cemetery* AR-4
Pilot Grove Cem—*cemetery* (2) IL-6
Pilot Grove Cem—*cemetery* (2) IA-7
Pilot Grove Cem—*cemetery* MN-6
Pilot Grove Cem—*cemetery* TX-5
Pilot Grove Ch—*church* MO-7
Pilot Grove Ch (abandoned)—*church* MO-7
Pilot Grove Church (historical)—*locale* MO-7
Pilot Grove County Park—*park* IA-7
Pilot Grove Creek—*stream* MO-7
Pilot Grove Creek—*stream* (2) TX-5
Pilot Grove Hill—*summit* MA-1
Pilot Grove Lakebed—*flat* MN-6
Pilot Grove No 1 Ch—*church* MO-7
Pilot Grove Number Two Ch (abandoned)—*church* MO-7
Pilot Grove Sch—*school* (2) IL-6
Pilot Grove Sch—*school* MA-1
Pilot Grove Sch (historical)—*school* MO-7
Pilot Grove Township—*civil* (2) MO-7
Pilot Grove Township—*fmr MCD* IA-7
**Pilot Grove (Township of)**—*pop pl* IL-6
**Pilot Grove (Township of)**—*pop pl* MN-6
Pilot Grove Union Cem—*cemetery* IA-7
*Pilot Gully* TX-5
*Pilot Harbor* MI-6
Pilot Harbor—*bay* AK-9
Pilot Harbor—*bay* FL-3
**Pilot Hill**—*pop pl* CA-9
Pilot Hill—*summit* AL-4
Pilot Hill—*summit* CA-9
Pilot Hill—*summit* IL-6
Pilot Hill—*summit* MA-1
Pilot Hill—*summit* RI-1
Pilot Hill—*summit* TN-4
Pilot Hill—*summit* WY-8
Pilot Hill Cem—*cemetery* AL-4
Pilot Hill Cem—*cemetery* CA-9
Pilot Hill Ch—*church* AL-4
Pilot Hill Grange—*locale* CA-9
Pilot Hill Post Office (historical)—*building* TN-4
Pilot (historical)—*locale* ND-7
Pilot Institute for the Deaf—*school* TX-5
Pilot Island—*island* MI-6
Pilot Island—*island* SC-3
Pilot Island—*island* TN-4
Pilot Island—*island* WI-6
Pilot Island Light—*hist pl* WI-6
*Pilot Knob* OR-9
*Pilot Knob* PA-2
*Pilot Knob* TN-4
Pilot Knob—*cape* MI-6
Pilot Knob—*locale* TN-4
**Pilot Knob**—*pop pl* IN-6
**Pilot Knob**—*pop pl* MO-7
**Pilot Knob**—*pop pl* NY-2
**Pilot Knob**—*pop pl* TN-4
**Pilot Knob**—*pop pl* TX-5
Pilot Knob—*summit* (2) AL-4
Pilot Knob—*summit* AK-9
Pilot Knob—*summit* (2) AZ-5
Pilot Knob—*summit* (9) AR-4
Pilot Knob—*summit* (7) CA-9
Pilot Knob—*summit* (3) CO-8
Pilot Knob—*summit* (2) ID-8
Pilot Knob—*summit* (3) IL-6
Pilot Knob—*summit* (2) IN-6
Pilot Knob—*summit* (2) IA-7
Pilot Knob—*summit* (3) KS-7
Pilot Knob—*summit* (9) KY-4
Pilot Knob—*summit* MI-6
Pilot Knob—*summit* MN-6
Pilot Knob—*summit* (5) MO-7
Pilot Knob—*summit* (2) MT-8
Pilot Knob—*summit* NE-7
Pilot Knob—*summit* NV-8
Pilot Knob—*summit* NM-5
Pilot Knob—*summit* NY-2
Pilot Knob—*summit* (3) NC-3
Pilot Knob—*summit* ND-7
Pilot Knob—*summit* OK-5
Pilot Knob—*summit* SD-7
Pilot Knob—*summit* (15) TN-4
Pilot Knob—*summit* (6) TX-5
Pilot Knob—*summit* (2) VA-3
Pilot Knob—*summit* WA-9
Pilot Knob—*summit* (5) WV-2
Pilot Knob—*summit* (2) WY-8
Pilot Knob Basin—*basin* AZ-5
Pilot Knob Bluff—*cliff* WI-6
Pilot Knob Cem—*cemetery* IL-6
Pilot Knob Cem—*cemetery* KY-4
Pilot Knob Cem—*cemetery* (2) MO-7
Pilot Knob Ch—*church* IN-6
Pilot Knob Ch—*church* IA-7
Pilot Knob Ch—*church* (2) KY-4
Pilot Knob Ch—*church* (2) MO-7
Pilot Knob Ch—*church* TX-5
Pilot Knob Check and Wasteway—*other* CA-9
Pilot Knob Ch (historical)—*church* TN-4
Pilot Knob Golf Club—*locale* NC-3
Pilot Knob Hydro-electric Plant—*other* CA-9
Pilot Knob Lake—*lake* IA-7
Pilot Knob Lake Dam—*dam* IA-7
Pilot Knob Lookout Tower—*locale* OH-6
Pilot Knob Lookout Tower—*locale* WV-2
Pilot Knob Mesa—*summit* CA-9
Pilot Knob Mtn—*summit* TN-4
Pilot Knob Post Office (historical)—*building* TN-4
Pilot Knob Ridge—*ridge* AR-4
Pilot Knob Ridge—*ridge* KS-7
Pilot Knob Ridge—*ridge* NV-8
Pilot Knob Ridge—*ridge* TN-4
*Pilot Knobs* KY-4
Pilot Knobs—*other* MO-7
Pilot Knobs—*ridge* TN-4
Pilot Knob Sch—*school* VA-3
Pilot Knob Sch (historical)—*school* MO-7
Pilot Knob Sch (historical)—*school* (2) TN-4
Pilot Knob Spring—*spring* AZ-5
Pilot Knob State Park—*park* IA-7
Pilot Knob Substation—*other* CA-9
Pilot Knob Tank—*reservoir* AZ-5
*Pilot Knob Township* KS-7
**Pilot Knob (Township of)**—*pop pl* IL-6
Pilot Knob Trail—*trail* ID-8
Pilot Knob Valley—*valley* CA-9
Pilot Knoll—*summit* UT-8
Pilot Knolls Park—*park* TX-5
*Pilot Lake* MI-6
Pilot Lake—*lake* MI-6
Pilot Lake—*lake* WA-9
Pilot Lake (historical)—*lake* IA-7
Pilot Lake Rsvr—*reservoir* OR-9
Pilot Life Dam—*dam* NC-3
Pilot Mine—*mine* CA-9
Pilot Mine—*mine* MN-6
Pilot Mound—*locale* MN-6
**Pilot Mound**—*pop pl* IA-7
**Pilotmound**—*pop pl* MN-6
Pilot Mound Cem—*cemetery* IA-7
Pilot Mound Cem—*cemetery* MN-6
Pilot Mound Township—*fmr MCD* IA-7
**Pilot Mound Township**—*pop pl* ND-7
**Pilot Mound (Township of)**—*pop pl* MN-6
**Pilot Mountain**—*pop pl* NC-3
**Pilot Mountain**—*pop pl* TN-4
Pilot Mountain Ch—*church* AR-4
Pilot Mountain Ch—*church* NC-3
Pilot Mountain Ch—*church* VA-3
Pilot Mountain Filtration Plant—*locale* NC-3
Pilot Mountain Oil Field—*oilfield* TN-4
Pilot Mountain Overlook—*locale* VA-3
Pilot Mountain Post Office (historical)—*building* TN-4
Pilot Mountain Ranch—*locale* NV-8
Pilot Mountain Recreation Facility—*park* NC-3
Pilot Mountain Sch—*school* NC-3

Pine River Lookout Tower—locale ... WI-6
Pine River Park—park ... MI-6
Pine River Park—park ... WA-9
Pine River Point—cape ... MI-6
Pine River Pond—lake ... NH-1
Pine River Reservoir ... CT-1
Pine River Sch—school ... MI-6
Pine River Sch—school (2) ... WI-6
Pine River Site—hist pl ... MI-6
Pine River Southwest Ditch—canal ... CO-8
**Pine River (Town of)**—pop pl ... WI-6
**Pine River (Township of)**—pop pl ... MI-6
**Pine River (Township of)**—pop pl ... MN-6
Pinero—locale ... VA-3
Pine Road Sch—school (2) ... PA-2
Pine Rock—summit ... CA-9
Pine Rock—summit ... MD-2
Pine Rock Hill ... MA-1
Pine Rock Park ... CT-1
**Pine Rock Park**—pop pl ... CT-1
**Pine Rock (Township of)**—pop pl ... IL-6
Pineroot Branch—stream ... NC-3
Pine Root Spring—spring ... CA-9
Pine Root Spring Campground—locale ... CA-9
Pine Rose Ch—church ... FL-3
Piner Point—cape ... WA-9
Piner Sch—school ... CA-9
Pine Rsvr—reservoir ... AZ-5
Pine Rsvr—reservoir ... CO-8
Pine Run ... IN-6
Pine Run ... PA-2
Pine Run ... WV-2
Pine Run—locale ... PA-2
**Pine Run**—pop pl ... MI-6
**Pine Run**—pop pl ... PA-2
Pine Run—stream ... AR-4
Pine Run—stream (2) ... IN-6
Pine Run—stream ... MI-6
Pine Run—stream ... MO-7
Pine Run—stream ... NC-3
Pine Run—stream (6) ... OH-6
Pine Run—stream (44) ... PA-2
Pine Run—stream (3) ... VA-3
Pine Run—stream (7) ... WV-2
Pine Run Camp—locale ... PA-2
Pine Run Cem—cemetery (2) ... OH-6
Pine Run Ch—church (2) ... PA-2
Pine Run Ch—church ... VA-3
Pine Run Creek ... MI-6
Pine Run Dam—dam (2) ... PA-2
Pine Run Dam Number One—dam ... PA-2
Pine Run Dam Sediment Pond—reservoir ... PA-2
Pine Run Rsvr—reservoir ... PA-2
Pine Run Sch—school ... PA-2
**Pine Run (subdivision)**—pop pl ... AL-4
Pine Run Trail—trail (2) ... PA-2
Piner-Visalia (CCD)—cens area ... KY-4
**Pinery, The, The**—pop pl ... CO-8
Pinery Canyon—valley ... AZ-5
Pinery Canyon Campground—park ... AZ-5
Pinery Creek—stream ... AZ-5
Pinery Creek—stream (2) ... MO-7
Pinery Lakes—lake ... MI-6
Pinery Park—park ... MI-6
Pinery Park Sch—school ... MI-6
Pinery Sch (historical)—school ... MO-7
Pinery Station—hist pl ... TX-5
Pines—locale ... NM-5
Pines—locale ... UT-8
**Pines**—pop pl ... WA-9
Pines, Isle Of—island ... MN-6
Pines, Isle Of—island ... NY-2
Pines, Lake—lake ... MT-8
Pines, Lake—reservoir ... GA-3
Pines, Lake O'—lake ... WI-6
Pines, Lake of the—lake ... MI-6
Pines, Lake of the—lake ... SD-7
Pines, Lake of the—lake ... WA-9
Pines, Lake Of the—lake ... WI-6
Pines, Lake O'the—reservoir ... TX-5
Pines, Point of—cape ... FL-3
Pines, Point of—cape ... MT-8
Pines, The ... PA-2
Pines, The—area ... CO-8
Pines, The—area ... UT-8
Pines, The—hist pl ... NY-2
Pines, The—locale ... CA-9
Pines, The—locale ... CO-8
Pines, The—locale (2) ... ME-1
Pines, The—locale ... MN-6
Pines, The—locale ... WA-9
Pines, The—locale ... WY-8
**Pines, The**—pop pl ... AR-4
**Pines, The**—pop pl ... CA-9
**Pines, The**—pop pl ... FL-3
**Pines, The**—pop pl ... MD-2
**Pines, The**—pop pl ... MA-1
**Pines, The**—pop pl ... NC-3
**Pines, The**—pop pl ... OH-6
**Pines, The**—pop pl (2) ... PA-2
Pines, The—summit ... CO-8
Pines, The—summit ... UT-8
Pines, The—woods ... IL-6
Pines, The—woods ... NY-2
Pines, The—woods (3) ... UT-8
Pines, The, The—locale ... MT-8
Pine Saint Cem—cemetery ... PA-2
Pine Savannah Branch—stream ... SC-3
Pine Savannah Sch—school ... SC-3
Pines Bank Plaza (Shop Ctr)—locale ... FL-3
Pines Bridge—bridge ... NY-2
Pines Bridge Hist Dist—hist pl ... CT-1
Pines Brook—stream ... NY-2
Pines Brook Ch—church ... NY-2
Pines Brook Ridge—ridge ... NY-2
**Pinesburg**—pop pl ... MD-2
Pinesburg Station—locale ... MD-2
Pines Campground—locale ... CO-8
Pines Campground—park ... UT-8
Pines Camp Ground, The—locale ... CA-9
Pines Campground, The—locale ... CA-9
Pines Campground, The—locale ... VA-3
Pines Canal, The—canal ... FL-3
Pines Canyon—valley ... NM-5
Pines Cem—cemetery ... AL-4
Pines Cem—cemetery ... ME-1
Pines Cemetery, The—cemetery ... CO-8
Pines Cemetery, The—cemetery ... VA-3
Pines Cemetery, The—cemetery ... WA-9
Pine Sch ... PA-2
Pines Ch—church ... AL-4
Pines Ch—church ... MD-2
Pine Sch—school ... AZ-5
Pine Sch—school ... AR-4
Pine Sch—school ... CA-9
Pine Sch—school ... CT-1
Pine Sch—school (2) ... MI-6
Pine Sch—school (2) ... MO-7
Pine Sch—school ... OK-5
Pine Sch—school (4) ... PA-2
Pines Chapel—church ... VA-3
Pines Ch (historical)—church ... PA-2
Pine Sch (historical)—school (2) ... AL-4
Pine Sch (historical)—school ... MO-7
Pine Sch (historical)—school (3) ... PA-2
Pines Community Ch—church ... MO-7
Pine Scope Hill—summit ... CO-8
Pines Creek—stream ... CA-9
Pines Creek—stream ... TN-4
Pines Creek—stream ... WV-2
**Pinesdale**—pop pl ... MT-8
Pines Draw—valley ... WY-8
Pine Seep—spring ... AZ-5
Pine Set Sch (historical)—school ... TN-4
Pines Ferry (historical)—locale ... MS-4
Pines Golf Course, The—other ... MI-6
Pine Shadow Spring—spring ... NM-5
Pine Shadows Sch—school ... TX-5
Pine Shaft—mine ... NV-8
**Pines (historical)**—pop pl ... TN-4
Pine Shore Golf Course—other ... MI-6
Pine Shore Lakes—reservoir ... NC-3
**Pine Shore Lakes**
**(subdivision)**—pop pl ... NC-3
Pine Shore Park—park ... FL-3
Pine Shores—CDP ... FL-3
**Pine Shores (subdivision)**—pop pl ... AL-4
Pines Island ... PA-2
**Pines Lake**—pop pl ... NJ-2
Pines Lake—reservoir ... NJ-2
Pines Lake Dam—dam ... NJ-2
Pines Lake Sch—school ... NJ-2
Pines Lakes Elem Sch—school ... FL-3
Pine Slash—hist pl ... VA-3
Pine Slooh Chapel ... AL-4
Pines Lookout Tower—locale ... NY-2
Pine Slope Campground—locale ... CA-9
Pine Slope Cem—cemetery ... SD-7
Pine Slough—gut ... MN-6
Pines MS—school ... FL-3
**Pines of Brookhaven**
**(subdivision)**—pop pl ... NC-3
**Pines of Pike Creek, The**—pop pl ... DE-2
**Pines-on-Severn**—pop pl ... MD-2
**Pines on Severn**—pop pl ... MD-2
Pines Park—park ... AL-4
Pines Park—park ... FL-3
Pines Point ... MA-1
Pines Point—cape ... MA-1
Pines Point of—cape ... MA-1
Pines Post Office (historical)—building ... AL-4
Pines Post Office (historical)—building ... TN-4
Pine Spring ... AZ-5
Pine Spring ... ID-8
Pine Spring ... OR-9
Pine Spring ... TX-5
**Pine Spring**—pop pl ... TN-4
**Pine Spring**—pop pl ... VA-3
Pine Spring—reservoir ... AZ-5
Pine Spring—spring ... AL-4
Pine Spring—spring (17) ... AZ-5
Pine Spring—spring (9) ... CA-9
Pine Spring—spring (4) ... ID-8
Pine Spring—spring (8) ... NV-8
Pine Spring—spring (8) ... NM-5
Pine Spring—spring (4) ... OR-9
Pine Spring—spring ... SD-7
Pine Spring—spring ... TN-4
Pine Spring—spring (3) ... TX-5
Pine Spring—spring (17) ... UT-8
Pine Spring—spring (2) ... WA-9
Pine Spring—spring (3) ... WY-8
Pine Spring Basin—basin ... OR-9
Pine Spring Camp ... TX-5
Pine Spring Camp—locale ... PA-2
Pine Spring Campground—locale ... TX-5
Pine Spring Canyon—valley ... AZ-5
Pine Spring Canyon—valley ... CA-9
Pine Spring Canyon—valley (2) ... NM-5
Pine Spring Canyon—valley ... TX-5
Pine Spring Canyon—valley ... UT-8
Pine Spring Cem—cemetery ... MS-4
Pine Spring Ch—church ... TN-4
Pine Spring Ch—church (2) ... TX-5
Pine Spring Creek—stream ... ID-8
Pine Spring Creek—stream ... SD-7
Pine Spring Creek—stream ... TX-5
Pine Spring Draw—valley ... UT-8
Pine Spring Draw Tank—reservoir ... AZ-5
Pine Spring (Dry)—spring ... CA-9
Pine Spring Gulch—valley ... CO-8
Pine Spring Hollow—valley ... OR-9
Pine Spring Knoll—summit ... UT-8
Pine Spring Mtn—summit ... NM-5
Pine Spring Number One And Two ... CA-9
Pine Spring Ridge—ridge ... ID-8
Pine Springs ... AZ-5
Pine Springs—lake ... WI-6
Pine Springs—locale ... AL-4
Pine Springs—locale ... KY-4
Pine Springs—locale ... NM-5
Pine Springs—locale (2) ... TX-5
**Pine Springs**—pop pl ... AZ-5
**Pine Springs**—pop pl ... MN-6
**Pine Springs**—pop pl ... MS-4
**Pine Springs**—pop pl ... OK-5
**Pine Springs**—pop pl ... TN-4
**Pine Springs**—pop pl ... TX-5
**Pine Springs**—pop pl ... VA-3
Pine Springs—spring (2) ... AZ-5
Pine Springs—spring ... CA-9
Pine Springs—spring ... ID-8
Pine Springs—spring (2) ... NV-8
Pine Springs—spring ... WY-8
Pine Springs Airp—airport ... AZ-5
Pine Springs Branch ... AL-4
Pine Springs Camp—locale ... NM-5
Pine Springs Camp—locale ... PA-2
Pine Springs Campground
(historical)—locale ... TX-5
Pine Springs Canyon—valley ... NM-5
Pine Springs Cem—cemetery ... AL-4
Pine Springs Cem—cemetery (2) ... MS-4
Pine Springs Cem—cemetery ... TX-5
Pine Springs Ch—church ... AL-4
Pine Springs Ch—church ... KY-4
Pine Springs Ch—church ... MS-4
Pine Springs Ch—church ... TX-5
Pine Spring Sch—school ... VA-3
Pine Springs Creek—stream ... AL-4
Pine Springs Creek—stream ... SD-7
Pine Springs Hill—summit ... CA-9
Pine Springs Interchange ... AZ-5
Pine Springs Lake—reservoir ... IN-6
Pine Springs Lake Dam—dam ... IN-6
Pine Springs Methodist Ch—church ... MS-4
Pine Springs Methodist Church ... AL-4
Pine Springs Park—park ... MS-4
Pine Springs Post Office
(historical)—building ... AL-4
Pine Springs Presbyterian Ch
(historical)—church ... MS-4
Pine Springs Ranch—locale ... AZ-5
Pine Springs Rsvr—reservoir ... OR-9
Pine Springs Sch—school ... AR-4
Pine Springs Sch—school ... OK-5
Pine Springs Sch—school ... TX-5
Pine Springs Sch (historical)—school ... TN-4
Pine Springs Trail—trail ... PA-2
Pine Springs Wash—stream ... AZ-5
Pine Springs Wash—valley ... AZ-5
Pine Springs Well—well (2) ... AZ-5
Pine Spring Tank—reservoir (2) ... AZ-5
Pine Spring Wash ... UT-8
Pine Spring Wash—valley ... NM-5
Pine Spur—ridge ... KY-4
Pine Spur—ridge (4) ... VA-3
Pine Spur Overlook—locale ... VA-3
Pine Spur Ridge—ridge ... VA-3
Pine Squirrel Rsvr—reservoir ... CO-8
Pines Recreation Area, The—park ... MT-8
Pines Ridge—ridge ... LA-4
Pines River—stream ... MA-1
Pines River Marshes—swamp ... MA-1
Pines Rsvr—reservoir ... MT-8
Pines Run—stream ... NJ-2
Pines Sanatorium, The—hospital ... LA-4
Pines Sch (historical)—school ... AL-4
Pines School, The—school ... NY-2
Pines Shop Ctr, The—locale ... FL-3
Pines Speedway—locale ... MA-1
Pines Station ... NY-2
Pines Subdivision ... UT-8
**Pines (subdivision), The**—pop pl (2) ... NC-3
**Pines Subdivision, The**—pop pl ... UT-8
Pinestand Knob—summit ... TN-4
Pinestand Mtn—summit ... VA-3
Pine Stand Ridge—ridge ... NC-3
Pinestand Ridge—ridge ... TN-4
Pines Tank, The—reservoir ... AZ-5
Pine Station ... PA-2
**Pine Station**—pop pl ... IN-6
Pine Station (historical)—locale ... PA-2
Pine Stem Creek ... ND-7
Pines Theatre—hist pl ... TX-5
Pinestone Creek ... WY-8
Pine Stream—stream ... ME-1
Pine Stream Flowage—lake ... ME-1
Pine Street Baptist Ch—church ... PA-2
Pine Street Cem—cemetery ... ME-1
Pine Street Cem—cemetery ... OH-6
Pine Street Elementary School ... PA-2
Pine Street Hist Dist—hist pl ... RI-1
Pine Street HS—school ... AR-4
Pine Street Park—park ... MS-4
Pine Street Park—park ... TX-5
Pine Street Sch—hist pl ... CA-9
Pine Street Sch—hist pl ... MA-1
Pine Street Sch—school ... CO-8
Pine Street Sch—school ... GA-3
Pine Street Sch—school (2) ... MA-1
Pine Street Sch—school ... MI-6
Pine Street Sch—school ... OH-6
Pine Street Sch—school ... PA-2
Pine Street Sch—school ... SC-3
Pine Street Sch (abandoned)—school ... PA-2
Pine Stub Creek—stream ... OR-9
Pine Stump Hollow—valley ... PA-2
**Pine Stump Junction**—pop pl ... MI-6
Pine Stump Sch (abandoned)—school ... PA-2
**Pine Summit**—pop pl ... PA-2
Pine Summit—summit ... ID-8
Pine Summit Baptist Ch—church ... FL-3
Pine Summit Ch—church ... PA-2
Pinesville—locale ... FL-3
Pinesville—locale ... GA-3
**Pinesville**—pop pl ... NY-2
Pine Swamp ... PA-2
Pine Swamp—locale ... PA-2
Pine Swamp—stream ... VA-3
Pine Swamp—swamp ... AL-4
Pine Swamp—swamp (4) ... CT-1
Pine Swamp—swamp (2) ... MD-2
Pine Swamp—swamp (3) ... MA-1
Pine Swamp—swamp (2) ... NJ-2
Pine Swamp—swamp (6) ... NY-2
Pine Swamp—swamp (5) ... PA-2
Pine Swamp—swamp (3) ... RI-1
Pine Swamp—swamp ... VA-3
Pine Swamp—swamp ... WV-2
Pine Swamp Branch—stream ... NC-3
Pine Swamp Branch—stream ... VA-3
Pine Swamp Brook ... CT-1
Pine Swamp Brook ... MA-1
Pine Swamp Brook—stream (2) ... CT-1
Pine Swamp Brook—stream ... MA-1
Pine Swamp Brook—stream ... NY-2
Pine Swamp Brook—stream ... RI-1
Pine Swamp Ch—church (2) ... NC-3
**Pine Swamp Corner**—pop pl ... DE-2
Pine Swamp Creek—stream (2) ... NC-3
Pine Swamp Knob—summit ... WV-2
Pine Swamp Mtn—summit ... NY-2
Pine Swamp Pond—lake ... PA-2
Pine Swamp Ridge—ridge ... VA-3
Pine Swamp Run ... WV-2
Pine Swamp Run—stream ... MD-2
Pine Swamp Run—stream (2) ... PA-2
Pine Swamp (Township of)—fmr MCD ... NC-3
Pine Tank—reservoir (14) ... AZ-5
Pine Tank—reservoir (9) ... NM-5
Pine Tank Canyon—valley ... AZ-5
Pine Tar Knob—summit ... GA-3
Pine Tavern—locale ... NJ-2
Pine Tavern—locale ... NY-2
Pine Terrace—hist pl ... NY-2
**Pine Terrace**—pop pl ... NJ-2
Pine Thicket Branch ... TN-4
Pine Thicket Branch—stream ... TN-4
Pinethicket Branch—stream ... TN-4
Pine Thicket Cem—cemetery ... KY-4
Pine Thicket Tank—reservoir ... AZ-5
Pinetia—uninc pl ... VA-3
Pine Timber Gulch—valley ... CA-9
**Pine Timbers (subdivision)**—pop pl ... TN-4
Pine Tit—summit ... ID-8
Pinet Lake—lake ... OR-9
**Pineton**—pop pl ... PA-2
Pine Top ... CA-9
Pine Top ... PA-2
Pinetop ... TN-4
Pine Top—locale ... AR-4
Pine Top—locale ... KY-4
Pinetop—locale ... MN-6
Pine Top—locale ... OK-5
Pine Top—locale ... TN-4
Pine Top—locale ... VA-3
**Pinetop**—pop pl ... AZ-5
**Pine Top**—pop pl ... FL-3
**Pine Top**—pop pl ... PA-2
**Pine Top**—pop pl ... TN-4
Pinetop—summit ... PA-2
Pine Top—summit ... TN-4
Pine Top—summit ... VT-1
Pine Top—summit ... WY-8
Pine Top Cem—cemetery ... AL-4
Pinetop Cem—cemetery ... AL-4
Pine Top Cem—cemetery ... MO-7
Pine Top Cem—cemetery ... OK-5
Pine Top Cemetery ... TX-5
Pinetop Ch ... AL-4
Pine Top Ch—church (3) ... AL-4
Pine Top Ch—church ... GA-3
Pine Top Ch—church ... KY-4
Pinetop Ch—church ... KY-4
Pine Top Ch—church ... TN-4
Pine Top Ch—church (3) ... TX-5
Pinetop Chapel—church ... OH-6
Pinetop Country Club—other ... AZ-5
Pinetop Hill—summit ... MT-8
Pinetop Lakes Country Club—other ... AZ-5
**Pinetop-Lakeside**—pop pl ... AZ-5
Pine Top (Magisterial District)—fmr MCD ... VA-3
Pine Top Mountain ... TX-5
Pinetop Mountain Tank—reservoir ... AZ-5
Pinetop Mtn—summit (2) ... AZ-5
Pine Top Mtn—summit (2) ... CA-9
Pine Top Post Office ... TN-4
Pinetop Post Office—building ... AZ-5
Pinetop Post Office (historical)—building ... TN-4
**Pinetops**—pop pl ... NC-3
Pine Top Sch—school ... AL-4
Pine Top Sch (abandoned)—school ... MO-7
Pinetop Sch (abandoned)—school ... PA-2
Pinetop Springs—spring ... AZ-5
Pinetop Tank—reservoir ... AZ-5
Pine Top Tower ... FL-3
Pine Torch Ch—church ... AL-4
Pine Torch Sch (historical)—school ... AL-4
Pinetown ... PA-2
Pinetown—locale ... DE-2
Pinetown—locale (2) ... PA-2
**Pinetown**—pop pl ... NC-3
Pinetown Covered Bridge—hist pl ... PA-2
Pinetown Elem Sch—school ... NC-3
Pinetown Hill—summit ... PA-2
Pine Township—civil ... MO-7
Pine Township—civil ... PA-2
Pine Township (historical)—civil ... SD-7
Pine (Township of)—fmr MCD ... AR-4
**Pine (Township of)**—pop pl (3) ... IN-6
**Pine (Township of)**—pop pl ... MI-6
**Pine (Township of)**—pop pl (8) ... PA-2
Pine Trail—trail ... PA-2
Pine Trail Elem Sch—school ... FL-3
**Pine Trail Estates**—pop pl ... TX-5
Pine Trail Rsvr—reservoir ... CO-8
Pine Trail Shop Ctr—locale ... FL-3
Pinetreat Church Camp—locale ... AL-4
Pine Tree—locale (2) ... VA-3
Pine Tree—locale ... WY-8
**Pinetree**—pop pl ... AR-4
**Pine Tree**—pop pl ... NC-3
**Pinetree**—pop pl ... PA-2
**Pine Tree**—pop pl ... VA-3
Pine Tree Arch—arch ... UT-8
Pinetree Branch—stream ... TN-4
Pine Tree Branch—stream ... TX-5
Pinetree Branch—stream ... VA-3
Pine Tree Brook—stream ... MA-1
Pine Tree Brook Dam—dam ... MA-1
Pine Tree Brook Reservoir Dam—dam ... MA-1
Pine Tree Brook Rsvr—reservoir ... MA-1
Pine Tree Camp—locale ... ME-1
Pine Tree Campground—park ... OR-9
Pine Tree Camp Point—cape ... SC-3
Pine Tree Canyon—valley ... AZ-5
Pine Tree Canyon—valley (2) ... CA-9
Pine Tree Canyon—valley ... CO-8
Pine Tree Canyon—valley (3) ... NM-5
Pinetree Canyon—valley ... NM-5
Pine Tree Canyon—valley ... NM-5
Pine Tree Canyon—valley (2) ... OR-9
Pine Tree Canyon—valley (2) ... WA-9
Pine Tree Cave—cave ... MN-6
Pine Tree Cem—cemetery (3) ... ME-1
Pine Tree Cem—cemetery (2) ... MI-6
Pine Tree Cem—cemetery ... MN-6
Pine Tree Ch—church ... AL-4
Pine Tree Ch (historical)—church ... AL-4
Pine Tree Corner—locale ... OR-9
**Pine Tree Corner**—pop pl ... MA-1
**Pine Tree Corners**—pop pl ... DE-2
Pine Tree Country Club—locale ... AL-4
Pine Tree Country Club—locale ... TN-4
Pine Tree Country Club Dam—dam ... AL-4
Pine Tree Country Club Lake—reservoir ... AL-4
Pine Tree County Sch—school ... MA-1
Pine Tree Cove—valley ... NC-3
Pine Tree Cove Creek—stream ... NC-3
Pine Tree Creek ... SC-3
Pinetree Creek—stream ... NC-3
Pine Tree Creek—stream ... OR-9
Pine Tree Creek—stream ... SC-3
Pine Tree Creek—stream ... WY-8
Pine Tree Crossroads ... DE-2
Pine Tree Draw—valley (3) ... WY-8
Pine Tree Estates ... TN-4
**Pine Tree Estates**—pop pl ... TN-4
**Pinetree Estates**—pop pl ... TN-4
Pine Tree Extension Ditch—canal ... WY-8
Pine Tree Gap—gap ... NC-3
Pine Tree Golf Club—locale ... NC-3
Pine Tree Golf Course—locale ... AL-4
Pinetree Ground—bar ... MA-1
Pine Tree Gulch ... WY-8
Pine Tree Gulch—valley ... CA-9
Pine Tree Gulch—valley ... CO-8
Pine Tree Gulch—valley ... ID-8
Pine Tree Gulch—valley ... MT-8
Pine Tree Gulch—valley ... OR-9
Pine Tree Hill ... SC-3
Pine Tree Holiness Church ... AL-4
Pine Tree Hollow—valley ... CA-9
Pine Tree Hollow—valley ... PA-2
Pine Tree Island—island ... LA-4
Pine Tree Island—island ... NY-2
Pine Tree Knob—summit ... WV-2
Pinetree Lake ... CA-9
Pine Tree Lake—lake ... MN-6
Pine Tree Lake—reservoir ... PA-2
Pinetree Lake Dam—dam ... PA-2
Pine Tree Lake Number One—reservoir ... NC-3
Pine Tree Lake Number One Dam—dam ... NC-3
Pine Tree Landing ... AL-4
Pine Tree Ledge—bar ... ME-1
Pine Tree Lodge—locale ... SC-3
Pine Tree Lumber Company Office
Bldg—hist pl ... MN-6
Pine Tree Mesa—summit ... NM-5
Pine Tree Mine—mine ... CA-9
Pine Tree Mine—mine ... NV-8
Pine Tree Mission—church ... NM-5
Pine Tree Overlook—locale ... VA-3
Pine Tree Park—park ... FL-3
Pine Tree Park—park ... IA-7
Pine Tree Peak—summit ... WY-8
Pine Tree Plaza (Shop Ctr)—locale ... FL-3
Pine Tree Plaza Shop Ctr—locale ... MS-4
Pine Tree Pockets—basin ... AZ-5
Pine Tree Point—cape ... NJ-2
Pine Tree Point—cape ... NC-3
Pine Tree Pond—lake ... WA-9
Pine Tree Ranch—locale ... CA-9
Pine Tree Ranch—locale ... WY-8
Pine Tree Rapids—rapids ... WI-6
Pine Tree Ridge—ridge ... OR-9
Pine Tree Ridge—ridge ... WY-8
Pine Tree Ridge Creek—stream ... OR-9
Pine Tree Rsvr—reservoir ... AZ-5
Pine Tree Rsvr—reservoir ... CO-8
Pine Tree Rsvr—reservoir ... WY-8
Pine Tree Run—stream ... NJ-2
Pine Tree Sch—school ... IL-6
Pine Tree Sch—school ... TX-5
Pine Tree Spring—spring ... CA-9
Pine Tree Spring—spring (4) ... OR-9
Pine Tree Spring—spring ... SD-7
Pine Tree Spring—spring ... WY-8
Pine Tree State Park—park ... MN-6
**Pine Tree Subdivision**—pop pl ... UT-8
Pine Tree Swamp—stream ... NC-3
Pine Tree Tank—reservoir ... AZ-5
Pine Tree Trail—trail ... ME-1
Pine Tree Trail—trail ... VA-3
Pine Tree Trail Natural Area—area ... PA-2
Pine Tree Valley—valley ... AZ-5
Pine Tree Village Shop Ctr—locale ... MS-4
Pine Tree Wash—stream ... NM-5
Pine Tree Wash—valley ... AZ-5
Pine Tree Well—well ... NM-5
Pinetta—locale ... GA-3
Pinetta—locale (2) ... VA-3
**Pinetta**—pop pl ... FL-3
Pinetta Ch—church ... GA-3
Pinetta JHS—school ... FL-3
Pinette Brook—stream (2) ... ME-1
Pinette Draw ... WY-8
Pinette Draw—valley ... WY-8
Pinette Hill—summit ... ME-1
Pine Tuckey ... AL-4
Pine Tuckey—locale ... AL-4
Pine Tuckey Ch—church ... AL-4
Pine Tucky ... AL-4
**Pinetucky**—pop pl ... AL-4
Pine Tucky Branch—stream ... GA-3
Pinetucky Campground—locale ... GA-3
Pinetucky Cemetery ... MS-4
Pinetucky Ch—church ... AL-4
Pinetucky Ch—church ... GA-3
Pine Tucky Ch—church ... GA-3
Pinetucky Ch (historical)—church ... AL-4
Pinetucky Post Office
(historical)—building ... AL-4
Pine Tumbly Creek—stream ... LA-4
Pine Turkey Cem—cemetery ... MS-4
Pine Twist Cem—cemetery ... WV-2
Pine Twist Sch—school ... WV-2
Pineu, Ochen—bar ... FM-9
Pine Union Ch—church ... MO-7
Pine Union Sch—school ... CA-9
Pine Union Sch (abandoned)—school ... MO-7
Pine Union Sch (historical)—school ... AL-4
Pine Vale Ch—church ... LA-4
Pinevale Ch—church ... PA-2
Pinevale HS—school ... GA-3
Pine Valley—basin ... CA-9
Pine Valley—CDP ... NC-3
Pine Valley—locale ... GA-3
Pine Valley—locale ... PA-2
Pine Valley—locale (2) ... TX-5
**Pine Valley**—pop pl ... AR-4
**Pine Valley**—pop pl ... CA-9
**Pine Valley**—pop pl (2) ... GA-3
**Pine Valley**—pop pl ... IN-6
**Pine Valley**—pop pl ... KY-4
**Pine Valley**—pop pl ... MD-2
**Pine Valley**—pop pl ... MS-4
**Pine Valley**—pop pl ... NH-1
**Pine Valley**—pop pl ... NJ-2
**Pine Valley**—pop pl (2) ... NY-2
**Pine Valley**—pop pl ... OH-6
**Pine Valley**—pop pl ... TX-5
**Pine Valley**—pop pl ... UT-8
Pine Valley—post sta ... IN-6
Pine Valley—valley ... AZ-5
Pine Valley—valley (4) ... CA-9
Pine Valley—valley ... NV-8
Pine Valley—valley ... NY-2
Pine Valley—valley ... OR-9
Pine Valley—valley (4) ... UT-8
Pine Valley—valley ... WI-6
Pine Valley Airp—airport ... CO-8
Pine Valley Baptist Ch—church ... MS-4
Pine Valley Camp ... UT-8
Pine Valley Camp—locale ... GA-3
Pine Valley Campsite—locale ... NY-2
Pine Valley Cem—cemetery ... UT-8
Pine Valley Central Sch—school ... NY-2
Pine Valley Ch—church ... GA-3
Pine Valley Ch—church ... KY-4
Pine Valley Ch—church ... MS-4
Pine Valley Ch—church ... MO-7
Pine Valley Ch—church ... NC-3
Pine Valley Ch—church ... PA-2
Pine Valley Ch—church (2) ... TX-5
Pine Valley Chapel and Tithing
Office—hist pl ... UT-8
Pine Valley Christian Ch—church ... KS-7
Pine Valley Church Historical Site—locale ... UT-8
Pine Valley Country Club—locale ... NC-3
Pine Valley Covered Bridge—hist pl ... PA-2
Pine Valley Creek—stream ... CA-9
Pine Valley Creek—stream ... MO-7
Pine Valley Creek—stream ... PA-2
**Pine Valley Estates**
**(subdivision)**—pop pl ... NC-3
**Pine Valley Farms**—pop pl ... DE-2
Pine Valley Golf Club—locale ... MA-1
Pine Valley Golf Club—other ... NH-1
Pine Valley Group Campground—locale ... UT-8
Pine Valley Hardpan—flat ... UT-8
Pine Valley Mtns—range ... UT-8
Pine Valley Peak—summit ... UT-8
Pine Valley Post Office
(historical)—building ... MS-4
Pine Valley Rec Area—park (2) ... UT-8
Pine Valley Reservoir Dam—dam ... UT-8
Pine Valley Rsvr—reservoir ... UT-8
Pine Valley Sch—school ... CO-8
Pine Valley Sch—school ... LA-4
Pine Valley Sch—school ... MS-4
Pine Valley Sch—school ... NC-3
Pine Valley Sch (historical)—school (2) ... MO-7
Pine Valley Shop Ctr—locale ... TN-4
**Pine Valley (Town of)**—pop pl ... WI-6
**Pine Valley (trailer park)**—pop pl ... DE-2
Pine Valley Wash—valley ... UT-8
Pine Valley Work Center—other ... UT-8
Pineveta Interchange ... AZ-5
Pineveta Tank—reservoir ... AZ-5
Pineveta Wash—stream ... AZ-5
Pineview ... TN-4
Pineview—hist pl ... NC-3
Pineview—locale ... ID-8
Pineview—locale ... MS-4
Pineview—locale ... TX-5
Pineview—locale ... UT-8
Pine View—locale ... VA-3
**Pineview**—pop pl (2) ... AL-4
**Pineview**—pop pl ... GA-3
**Pineview**—pop pl ... MS-4
**Pine View**—pop pl ... NM-5
**Pine View**—pop pl ... NC-3
**Pineview**—pop pl ... NC-3
**Pine View**—pop pl ... PA-2
**Pine View**—pop pl ... TN-4
**Pineview Acres (subdivision)**—pop pl ... NC-3
Pineview Baptist Ch ... AL-4
Pineview Baptist Ch—church ... AL-4
Pine View Beach ... AL-4
Pineview (CCD)—cens area ... GA-3
Pineview Cem—cemetery (2) ... AL-4
Pine View Cem—cemetery ... FL-3
Pineview Cem—cemetery ... GA-3
Pine View Cem—cemetery (2) ... GA-3
Pineview Cem—cemetery ... IL-6
Pine View Cem—cemetery ... IA-7
Pineview Cem—cemetery ... ME-1
Pine View Cem—cemetery ... MS-4
Pineview Cem—cemetery ... NY-2
Pine View Cem—cemetery ... NC-3
Pineview Cem—cemetery ... NC-3
Pine View Cem—cemetery ... NC-3
Pineview Cem—cemetery ... WV-2
Pineview Ch ... AL-4
Pineview Ch—church ... AL-4
Pine View Ch—church ... AL-4
Pineview Ch—church (2) ... AL-4
Pine View Ch—church ... AR-4
Pine View Ch—church ... FL-3
Pineview Ch—church (2) ... GA-3
Pine View Ch—church ... GA-3
Pineview Ch—church (4) ... GA-3
Pine View Ch—church ... GA-3
Pineview Ch—church ... GA-3
Pine View Ch—church ... GA-3
Pineview Ch—church (2) ... GA-3
Pineview Ch—church ... LA-4
Pineview Ch—church (2) ... MS-4
Pine View Ch—church (3) ... MS-4
Pineview Ch—church ... MO-7
Pine View Ch—church ... NJ-2
Pine View Ch—church (3) ... NC-3
Pineview Ch—church (2) ... SC-3
Pine View Ch—church ... SC-3
Pineview Ch—church ... TN-4
Pine View Ch—church (2) ... VA-3
Pineview Church Cem—cemetery ... AL-4
Pineview Congregational Methodist Ch ... MS-4
Pineview Drive—other ... PA-2
Pine View Elementary School ... TN-4
Pine View Elem Sch—school ... IN-6
**Pineview Estates**—pop pl ... PA-2
**Pineview Estates**
**(subdivision)**—pop pl ... MS-4
**Pineview Estates**
**(subdivision)**—pop pl ... NC-3
Pineview-Finleyson Ch—church ... GA-3
Pine View Golf Course—other ... MI-6

**Pineview Heights**—*pop pl* ... TN-4
**Pineview Hills (subdivision)**—*pop pl* ... NC-3
Pineview (historical)—*locale* ... AL-4
Pineview Hosp—*hospital* ... GA-3
Pineview HS—*school* ... LA-4
Pineview HS—*school* ... UT-8
*Pineview Lake* ... AL-4
Pineview Lake—*reservoir* ... AL-4
Pine View Lake—*reservoir* ... AL-4
Pineview Lake—*reservoir* ... MS-4
Pineview Lake—*reservoir* ... NC-3
Pineview Lake Dam—*dam* ... MS-4
Pineview Lookout Tower—*locale* ... MO-7
Pineview Manor Sch—*school* ... AL-4
Pineview Memorial Cem—*cemetery* ... AL-4
Pine View Memorial Gardens—*cemetery* ... AL-4
Pineview Memorial Gardens—*cemetery* ... FL-3
Pineview Memorial Gardens—*cemetery* ... GA-3
Pineview Memorial Gardens—*cemetery* ... SC-3
Pineview Memorial Park (Cemetery)—*cemetery* ... OH-6
*Pine View Missionary Baptist Church* ... MS-4
Pine View MS—*school* ... FL-3
Pine View MS—*school* ... UT-8
Pine View Park—*park* ... CO-8
Pineview Park—*park* ... MS-4
Pine View Park—*park* ... WI-6
**Pine View Park**—*pop pl* ... UT-8
*Pineview P.O.* ... AL-4
Pineview Ranch—*locale* ... CO-8
Pine View Ranch—*locale* ... CO-8
*Pine View Reservoir* ... UT-8
**Pine View Resort**—*pop pl* ... UT-8
Pineview Rsvr—*reservoir* ... UT-8
Pineview Sch—*school* (2) ... AL-4
Pine View Sch—*school* ... AR-4
Pineview Sch—*school* (2) ... FL-3
Pineview Sch—*school* ... MI-6
Pine View Sch—*school* ... NC-3
Pineview Sch—*school* ... SC-3
Pineview Sch—*school* ... TN-4
Pineview Sch—*school* ... WI-6
Pineview Sch—*school* ... WY-8
Pineview Sch (historical)—*school* ... TN-4
Pineview School (historical)—*locale* ... MO-7
**Pineview (subdivision)**—*pop pl* ... NC-3
**Pine View (subdivision)**—*pop pl* ... NC-3
**Pine View West Subdivision**—*pop pl* ... UT-8
Pine Villa Elem Sch—*school* ... FL-3
**Pine Village**—*pop pl* ... IN-6
Pine Village Elem Sch—*school* ... IN-6
*Pineville* ... AL-4
Pineville—*locale* ... AL-4
Pineville—*locale* ... CT-1
Pineville—*locale* ... FL-3
Pineville—*locale* ... NY-2
Pineville—*locale* (2) ... PA-2
Pineville—*locale* ... TN-4
Pineville—*other* ... MS-4
**Pineville**—*pop pl* ... AR-4
**Pineville**—*pop pl* ... KY-4
**Pineville**—*pop pl* ... LA-4
**Pineville**—*pop pl* ... MN-6
**Pineville**—*pop pl* ... MS-4
**Pineville**—*pop pl* ... MO-7
**Pineville**—*pop pl* ... NY-2
**Pineville**—*pop pl* ... NC-3
**Pineville**—*pop pl* ... SC-3
**Pineville**—*pop pl* (2) ... TN-4
**Pineville**—*pop pl* ... VA-3
**Pineville**—*pop pl* ... WV-2
Pineville Attendance Center—*school* ... MS-4
Pineville (CCD)—*cens area* ... KY-4
Pineville Cem—*cemetery* ... AL-4
Pineville Ch—*church* ... FL-3
Pineville Ch—*church* ... GA-3
Pineville Ch—*church* (2) ... MS-4
Pineville Ch—*church* (2) ... NC-3
Pineville Ch—*church* ... TX-5
*Pineville Elementary School* ... MS-4
Pineville Elem Sch—*school* ... NC-3
**Pineville Junction**—*pop pl* ... LA-4
Pineville Lanagan Township—*civil* ... MO-7
Pineville Lookout Tower—*locale* ... SC-3
*Pineville Missionary Baptist Ch* ... MS-4
Pineville North Township—*civil* ... MO-7
Pineville P.O. (historical)—*locale* ... AL-4
Pineville Presbyterian Ch—*church* ... MS-4
Pineville Sch—*school* ... LA-4
Pineville Sch—*school* ... MS-4
Pineville Sch—*school* (3) ... SC-3
Pineville Sch—*school* ... TN-4
Pineville Sch (historical)—*school* ... MS-4
Pineville South Township—*civil* ... MO-7
Pineville Town Center Shop Ctr—*locale* ... NC-3
*Pinevita* ... AZ-5
**Pinewald**—*pop pl* ... NJ-2
Pinewan Lake—*lake* ... OR-9
Pine Wash—*stream* ... AZ-5
Pine Wash—*stream* ... NV-8
Pine Wash Well—*well* ... NV-8
**Pinewater Farm (subdivision)**—*pop pl* ... DE-2
Pine Water Landing—*locale* ... DE-2
Pine Water Neck—*cape* ... DE-2
*Pinewater Range* ... NV-8
Pine Waters—*locale* ... PA-2
Pine Water Spring—*spring* ... AZ-5
**Pineway**—*pop pl* ... FL-3
Pine Well—*locale* ... AZ-5
**Pinewell**—*pop pl* ... VA-3
Pine Well—*well* ... NM-5
Pine Wells—*well* ... AZ-5
**Pine Whiff Beach**—*pop pl* ... MD-2
Pine Windmill—*locale* ... NM-5
Pinewold Point—*cape* ... ME-1
*Pine Wood* ... TN-4
Pinewood—*CDP* ... FL-3
Pinewood—*hist pl* ... MS-4
Pine Wood—*locale* ... CA-9
Pinewood—*locale* ... TN-4
**Pinewood**—*pop pl* ... MN-6
**Pinewood**—*pop pl* ... PA-2
**Pinewood**—*pop pl* (2) ... SC-3
Pinewood—*post sta* ... SC-3
Pinewood—*post sta* ... VT-1
Pinewood—*uninc pl* ... TX-5
Pinewood, Lake—*reservoir* ... VA-3
Pinewood Acres Sch—*school* ... FL-3
**Pinewood Acres (subdivision)**—*pop pl* (2) ... NC-3
Pinewood Ave Sch—*school* ... CA-9
Pinewood Branch—*stream* ... TN-4
Pinewood Camp—*locale* ... MI-6
Pine Wood Camp—*locale* ... NY-2
**Pinewood Camp**—*pop pl* ... CA-9
Pine Wood Campground—*locale* ... NY-2
Pinewood Cem—*cemetery* ... FL-3
Pinewood Cem—*cemetery* ... GA-3
Pinewood Cem—*cemetery* (2) ... MN-6
Pinewood Cem—*cemetery* ... NY-2
Pinewood Cem—*cemetery* ... NC-3
Pinewood Chapel—*church* ... MN-6
*Pinewood Church* ... AL-4
Pinewood Country Club—*other* ... WI-6
**Pinewood Downs (subdivision)**—*pop pl* ... NC-3
Pinewood Elem Sch—*school* ... FL-3
**Pinewood Estates**—*pop pl* ... TX-5
**Pinewood Estates (subdivision)**—*pop pl* ... NC-3
Pinewood First Baptist Ch—*church* ... TN-4
**Pinewood Forest**—*pop pl* ... NC-3
**Pinewood Forest (subdivision)**—*pop pl* ... NC-3
**Pinewood Gardens**—*pop pl* ... VA-3
Pinewood Heights Sch—*school* ... TN-4
**Pinewood Hill**—*pop pl* ... MD-2
*Pinewood Lake* ... MA-1
Pinewood Lake—*lake* ... CT-1
Pinewood Lake—*reservoir* ... CO-8
Pinewood Lake—*reservoir* ... SC-3
**Pinewood Lakers (subdivision)**—*pop pl* ... NC-3
Pinewood Landing—*locale* ... MS-4
**Pinewood Lawns**—*pop pl* ... VA-3
Pinewood Lookout Tower—*locale* ... TN-4
Pinewood Memorial Park—*cemetery* ... AR-4
Pine Wood Park—*park* ... FL-3
**Pinewood Park**—*pop pl* ... FL-3
**Pine Wood Park**—*pop pl* ... MI-6
Pinewood Park—*uninc pl* ... VA-3
Pinewood Peak—*summit* ... MT-8
Pinewood Pond—*lake* ... MA-1
*Pine Wood Post Office* ... TN-4
Pinewood Post Office (historical)—*building* ... TN-4
Pinewood Private Sch—*school* ... FL-3
Pinewood Ranch—*locale* (2) ... CO-8
*Pine Woods* ... TN-4
Pinewoods—*hist pl* ... VA-3
**Pine Woods**—*pop pl* ... NY-2
**Pinewoods**—*pop pl* ... PA-2
Pine Woods—*woods* ... TX-5
Pinewood Sanitarium—*hospital* ... NY-2
Pinewoods Camp—*locale* ... MI-6
Pine Woods Cem—*cemetery* ... NY-2
Pine Woods Ch—*church* ... NY-2
Pine Woods Ch—*church* ... NC-3
Pinewood Sch—*school* ... AR-4
Pinewood Sch—*school* ... CO-8
Pinewood Sch—*school* (2) ... MN-6
Pinewood Sch—*school* (2) ... NC-3
Pinewood Sch—*school* ... TN-4
*Pinewoods Creek* ... AL-4
Pinewoods Lake—*lake* ... MO-7
Pinewoods Lake—*locale* ... MO-7
**Pinewood South**—*pop pl* ... VA-3
Pine Woods Pond—*lake* ... VA-3
*Pine Woods Post Office* ... TN-4
Pinewood Springs—*locale* ... CO-8
Pine Woods Ridge—*ridge* ... GA-3
Pine Woods Sch—*school* ... NY-2
**Pine Wood (subdivision)**—*pop pl* ... AL-4
**Pinewood Terrace**—*pop pl* ... AL-4
*Piney* ... TN-4
Piney—*locale* (2) ... AR-4
Piney—*locale* ... KY-4
Piney—*locale* ... NC-3
Piney—*locale* ... OK-5
Piney—*locale* ... TN-4
Piney—*locale* ... TX-5
**Piney**—*pop pl* ... AL-4
**Piney**—*pop pl* (2) ... AR-4
**Piney**—*pop pl* (2) ... TN-4
**Piney**—*pop pl* ... WV-2
**Piney Acres**—*pop pl* ... TN-4
Piney Bald—*summit* ... NC-3
Piney Ball—*summit* ... NC-3
Piney Ball—*summit* ... TN-4
*Piney Baptist Church* ... TN-4
Piney Bay—*bay* ... TN-4
Piney Bay—*stream* ... GA-3
Piney Bay—*swamp* ... FL-3
Piney Bay—*swamp* (4) ... GA-3
Piney Bay—*swamp* (3) ... SC-3
Piney Bayou—*stream* ... LA-4
*Piney Bear Gulch* ... WY-8
Piney Bend—*locale* ... AL-4
Piney Bend Airp—*airport* ... MO-7
Piney Bluff—*cliff* ... KY-4
**Piney Bluff**—*pop pl* ... GA-3
Piney Bluff Landing—*locale* ... FL-3
Piney Bottom Creek—*stream* ... NC-3
*Piney Brake* ... AR-4
Piney Brake—*swamp* ... AR-4
*Piney Branch* ... VA-3
Piney Branch—*stream* ... AL-4
Piney Branch—*stream* ... AR-4
Piney Branch—*stream* ... DE-2
Piney Branch—*stream* ... DC-2
Piney Branch—*stream* ... FL-3
Piney Branch—*stream* ... GA-3
Piney Branch—*stream* ... IL-6
Piney Branch—*stream* ... KY-4
Piney Branch—*stream* (5) ... MD-2
Piney Branch—*stream* ... MS-4
Piney Branch—*stream* ... MO-7
Piney Branch—*stream* (5) ... NC-3
Piney Branch—*stream* ... OK-5
Piney Branch—*stream* (7) ... TN-4
Piney Branch—*stream* ... TX-5
Piney Branch—*stream* (10) ... VA-3
Piney Branch—*stream* (3) ... WV-2
Piney Branch Ch—*church* ... VA-3
Piney Branch Falls—*falls* ... AL-4
Piney Branch Trail—*trail* ... VA-3
Piney Butt—*summit* ... TN-4
Piney Butte—*summit* ... KY-4
Piney Butte—*summit* ... MT-8
Piney Campground—*locale* ... MT-8
Piney Campground—*locale* ... TN-4
Piney Canyon—*valley* ... WY-8
Piney Cem—*cemetery* (4) ... AR-4
Piney Cem—*cemetery* ... OK-5
Piney Cem—*cemetery* (2) ... TN-4
Piney Cem—*cemetery* ... TX-5
Piney Cemeteries—*cemetery* ... WV-2
Piney Ch—*church* (2) ... AR-4
Piney Ch—*church* (2) ... MD-2
Piney Ch—*church* ... MO-7
Piney Ch—*church* ... OK-5
Piney Ch—*church* (2) ... TN-4
Piney Ch—*church* ... TX-5
Piney Chapel—*church* (2) ... AL-4
**Piney Chapel**—*pop pl* ... AL-4
Piney Chapel Cem—*cemetery* ... AL-4
*Piney Chapel Church* ... AL-4
Piney Chapel JHS—*school* ... AL-4
Piney Ch (historical)—*church* ... TN-4
Piney Ch of Christ—*church* ... TN-4
Piney Cliff—*summit* ... NC-3
Piney Court—*locale* ... VA-3
Piney Cove—*bay* ... MD-2
Piney Cove—*bay* ... NC-3
*Piney Creek* ... AL-4
*Piney Creek* ... AR-4
*Piney Creek* ... CA-9
*Piney Creek* ... CO-8
*Piney Creek* ... MO-7
*Piney Creek* ... OH-6
*Piney Creek* ... TN-4
*Piney Creek* ... TX-5
*Piney Creek* ... WY-8
Piney Creek—*bay* ... MD-2
**Piney Creek**—*pop pl* ... NC-3
Piney Creek—*stream* (3) ... AL-4
Piney Creek—*stream* (9) ... AR-4
Piney Creek—*stream* (2) ... CA-9
Piney Creek—*stream* (3) ... CO-8
Piney Creek—*stream* ... FL-3
Piney Creek—*stream* ... GA-3
Piney Creek—*stream* ... ID-8
Piney Creek—*stream* (3) ... KY-4
Piney Creek—*stream* ... LA-4
Piney Creek—*stream* (4) ... MD-2
Piney Creek—*stream* (4) ... MS-4
Piney Creek—*stream* (5) ... MO-7
Piney Creek—*stream* ... MT-8
Piney Creek—*stream* ... NV-8
Piney Creek—*stream* (4) ... NC-3
Piney Creek—*stream* ... OH-6
Piney Creek—*stream* (3) ... OK-5
Piney Creek—*stream* (6) ... PA-2
Piney Creek—*stream* ... SD-7
Piney Creek—*stream* (9) ... TN-4
Piney Creek—*stream* (6) ... TX-5
Piney Creek—*stream* (6) ... VA-3
Piney Creek—*stream* (2) ... WV-2
Piney Creek—*stream* (6) ... WY-8
Piney Creek Campground—*locale* ... CA-9
Piney Creek Cave—*cave* ... MO-7
Piney Creek Ch—*church* ... KY-4
Piney Creek Ch—*church* ... MD-2
Piney Creek Ch—*church* ... TX-5
Piney Creek Cove—*bay* ... MD-2
Piney Creek Falls—*falls* ... TN-4
Piney Creek HS—*school* ... NC-3
Piney Creek (locale)—*locale* ... PA-2
*Piney Creek Missionary Baptist Church* ... TN-4
Piney Creek (Township of)—*fmr MCD* (2) ... NC-3
Piney Creek Trail—*trail* ... MT-8
Piney Creek Trail—*trail* ... WY-8
Piney Creek Watershed Structure 23 Dam—*dam* ... MS-4
Piney Creek Watershed Y-38-21 Dam—*dam* ... MS-4
Piney Creek Watershed Y-38-26 Dam—*dam* ... MS-4
Piney Creek Watershed Y-38-3 Dam—*dam* ... MS-4
Piney Creek Watershed Y-38-35 Dam—*dam* ... MS-4
Piney Crossing Campground—*locale* ... CO-8
*Piney Crossroads* ... NC-3
Piney Cutoff Rsvr—*reservoir* ... WY-8
Piney Dam—*dam* ... PA-2
Piney Dell—*locale* ... MT-8
Piney Draw—*valley* ... WY-8
Piney Field Top—*summit* ... NC-3
Piney Flat—*flat* (2) ... WV-2
*Pineyflats* ... TN-4
**Piney Flats**—*pop pl* ... TN-4
Piney Flats Branch—*stream* ... TN-4
Piney Flats Ch—*church* ... TN-4
*Pineyflats Post Office* ... TN-4
Piney Flats Post Office—*building* ... TN-4
*Piney Flats School* ... TN-4
Piney Flats Siding—*locale* ... TN-4
Piney Forest Ch—*church* ... NC-3
Piney Forest Cross Roads—*locale* ... NC-3
Piney Forest Sch—*school* ... SC-3
*Piney Fork* ... AL-4
Piney Fork—*locale* ... KY-4
**Piney Fork**—*pop pl* ... OH-6
**Piney Fork**—*pop pl* ... PA-2
Piney Fork—*stream* ... AR-4
Piney Fork—*stream* ... KY-4
Piney Fork—*stream* ... NC-3
Piney Fork—*stream* (2) ... OH-6
Piney Fork—*stream* ... PA-2
Piney Fork—*stream* (2) ... TN-4
Piney Fork—*stream* (2) ... VA-3
Piney Fork—*stream* (2) ... WV-2
*Piney Fork Branch* ... DE-2
Piney Fork Branch—*stream* ... TN-4
Piney Fork Ch—*church* ... AR-4
Piney Fork Ch—*church* (2) ... NC-3
Piney Fork Ch—*church* (2) ... VA-3
*Piney Fork Ditch* ... AR-4
Piney Fork Lake—*lake* ... AR-4
*Piney Fork of Strawberry River* ... AR-4
Piney Fork Prospects—*mine* ... TN-4
*Piney Forks* ... PA-2
Piney Fork Sch—*school* ... WV-2
Piney Fork (Township of)—*fmr MCD* ... AR-4
Piney Gap—*gap* ... GA-3
Piney Gap—*gap* ... NC-3
**Piney Glade (subdivision)**—*pop pl* ... DE-2
**Piney Glen Farms**—*pop pl* ... MD-2
*Piney Grace Church* ... AL-4
**Piney Green**—*pop pl* (2) ... NC-3
Piney Green Ch—*church* ... GA-3
Piney Green Ch—*church* ... NC-3
Piney Green-White Oak—*CDP* ... NC-3
*Piney Grove* ... MD-2
Piney Grove—*hist pl* ... VA-3
Piney Grove—*locale* (2) ... AL-4
Piney Grove—*locale* (2) ... AR-4
Piney Grove—*locale* ... DE-2
Piney Grove—*locale* ... FL-3
Piney Grove—*locale* ... GA-3
Piney Grove—*locale* ... KY-4
Piney Grove—*locale* (2) ... MD-2
Piney Grove—*locale* (4) ... TN-4
Piney Grove—*locale* ... TX-5
Piney Grove—*locale* (2) ... VA-3
**Piney Grove**—*pop pl* ... AL-4
**Piney Grove**—*pop pl* ... GA-3
**Piney Grove**—*pop pl* ... MD-2
**Piney Grove**—*pop pl* (4) ... NC-3
**Pineygrove**—*pop pl* ... NC-3
**Piney Grove**—*pop pl* ... NC-3
**Piney Grove**—*pop pl* ... SC-3
**Piney Grove**—*pop pl* (2) ... TN-4
**Piney Grove**—*pop pl* ... TX-5
**Piney Grove**—*pop pl* ... VA-3
*Piney Grove Baptist Ch* ... TN-4
Piney Grove Baptist Ch—*church* (2) ... TN-4
*Piney Grove Baptist Church* ... AL-4
*Piney Grove Baptist Church* ... MS-4
*Piney Grove Baptist Church* ... NC-3
Pineygrove Branch—*stream* ... NC-3
Piney Grove Cem—*cemetery* (6) ... AL-4
Piney Grove Cem—*cemetery* (2) ... AR-4
Piney Grove Cem—*cemetery* (2) ... GA-3
Piney Grove Cem—*cemetery* (2) ... KY-4
Piney Grove Cem—*cemetery* ... LA-4
Piney Grove Cem—*cemetery* ... MD-2
Piney Grove Cem—*cemetery* (4) ... MS-4
Piney Grove Cem—*cemetery* (2) ... NC-3
Piney Grove Cem—*cemetery* (3) ... SC-3
Piney Grove Cem—*cemetery* ... TN-4
Piney Grove Cem—*cemetery* (3) ... TX-5
Piney Grove Cem—*cemetery* ... VA-3
Piney Grove Cemetary—*cemetery* ... AR-4
*Piney Grove Ch* ... AL-4
*Piney Grove Ch* ... MS-4
Piney Grove Ch—*church* (25) ... AL-4
Piney Grove Ch—*church* (5) ... AR-4
Piney Grove Ch—*church* (3) ... FL-3
Piney Grove Ch—*church* (35) ... GA-3
Piney Grove Ch—*church* (4) ... KY-4
Piney Grove Ch—*church* ... LA-4
Piney Grove Ch—*church* ... MD-2
Piney Grove Ch—*church* (11) ... MS-4
Piney Grove Ch—*church* (46) ... NC-3
Piney Grove Ch—*church* (16) ... SC-3
Piney Grove Ch—*church* (11) ... TN-4
Piney Grove Ch—*church* (5) ... TX-5
Piney Grove Ch—*church* (13) ... VA-3
Piney Grove Chapel—*church* ... KY-4
Piney Grove Ch (historical)—*church* ... AL-4
*Piney Grove Ch Number 2* ... AL-4
*Piney Grove Ch of Christ* ... AL-4
Piney Grove Ch of Christ (historical)—*church* ... AL-4
*Piney Grove Christian Church* ... AL-4
Piney Grove Church And Sch—*school* ... GA-3
Piney Grove Crosroad (historical)—*locale* ... TN-4
*Piney Grove Crossroads* ... TN-4
Piney Grove Elem Sch—*school* ... NC-3
Piney Grove Freewill Baptist Ch—*church* ... TN-4
Piney Grove (historical)—*locale* ... MS-4
Piney Grove Hollow—*valley* ... MS-4
Piney Grove Indian Ch—*church* ... NC-3
Piney Grove Landing—*locale* ... NC-3
**Piney Grove Manor**—*pop pl* ... DE-2
*Piney Grove Methodist Ch* ... AL-4
*Piney Grove Methodist Church* ... MS-4
Piney Grove Mine (surface)—*mine* ... AL-4
Piney Grove Missionary Baptist Ch—*church* ... AL-4
*Piney Grove Primitive Baptist Ch* ... AL-4
Piney Grove Rec Area—*park* ... MS-4
Piney Grove Ridge—*ridge* ... KY-4
Piney Grove Ridge—*ridge* ... TN-4
Piney Grove Run—*stream* ... NC-3
Piney Grove Sch—*school* ... AL-4
Piney Grove Sch—*school* ... KY-4
Piney Grove Sch—*school* (2) ... MS-4
Piney Grove Sch—*school* (2) ... NC-3
Piney Grove Sch—*school* (3) ... SC-3
Piney Grove Sch—*school* ... TN-4
Piney Grove Sch (historical)—*school* (2) ... AL-4
Piney Grove Sch (historical)—*school* ... MS-4
Piney Grove Sch (historical)—*school* (3) ... TN-4
**Piney Grove (subdivision)**—*pop pl* ... MS-4
Piney Grove (Township of)—*fmr MCD* ... NC-3
Piney Guard Station—*locale* ... CO-8
Piney Gulch—*valley* ... CO-8
Piney Gut—*gut* ... MD-2
Piney Heights Ch—*church* ... SC-3
*Piney Hill* ... PA-2
**Piney Hill**—*pop pl* ... MD-2
Piney Hill—*summit* ... AZ-5
Piney Hill—*summit* ... VA-3
Piney Hill—*summit* ... WV-2
Piney Hill Cem—*cemetery* ... NY-2
Piney Hill Ch—*church* ... VA-3
Piney Hill Creek—*stream* ... AZ-5
*Piney Hill Wash* ... AZ-5
Piney Hill Wash—*valley* ... AZ-5
**Piney (historical)**—*pop pl* ... OR-9
Piney Hollow—*locale* ... NJ-2
Piney Hollow—*valley* ... MO-7
Piney Hollow—*valley* ... TN-4
Piney Hollow Airfield—*airport* ... NJ-2
*Piney Island* ... DE-2
*Piney Island* ... TN-4
Piney Island—*island* (2) ... FL-3
Piney Island—*island* (2) ... GA-3
Piney Island—*island* (3) ... MD-2
Piney Island—*island* (4) ... NC-3
Piney Island—*island* ... PA-2
Piney Island—*island* ... VA-3
Piney Island Bay—*bay* (2) ... NC-3
Piney Island Canal—*canal* ... NC-3
Piney Island Cove—*bay* ... MD-2
Piney Island Creek—*stream* ... GA-3
Piney Island (historical)—*island* ... TN-4
Piney Island Landing—*locale* ... FL-3
Piney Island Landing—*locale* ... NC-3
Piney Island Point—*cape* ... MD-2
*Piney Jordan United Methodist Church* ... MS-4
*Piney Knob* ... PA-2
Piney Knob—*summit* (4) ... NC-3
Piney Knob—*summit* ... SC-3
Piney Knob—*summit* ... TN-4
Piney Knob—*summit* ... WV-2
Piney Knob Ch—*church* ... NC-3
Piney Knob Creek—*stream* ... NC-3
Piney Knob Fork—*stream* ... NC-3
Piney Knob Ridge—*ridge* ... TN-4
Piney Lake—*lake* ... CO-8
Piney Lake—*lake* ... FL-3
Piney Lake Trail—*trail* ... CO-8
*Piney Level Baptist Church* ... TN-4
Piney Level Cem—*cemetery* ... TN-4
Piney Lick Sch (abandoned)—*school* ... PA-2
Piney Log Creek—*stream* ... AR-4
Piney Lookout Tower—*locale* ... MO-7
Piney Marsh—*locale* ... NC-3
Piney Mountain—*ridge* (2) ... TN-4
Piney Mountain Branch—*stream* ... VA-3
Piney Mountain Ch—*church* (3) ... NC-3
Piney Mountain Creek—*stream* ... NC-3
**Piney Mountain Estates (subdivision)**—*pop pl* ... NC-3
Piney Mountain Mission Union Ch—*church* ... TN-4
Piney Mountain Trail—*trail* ... VA-3
Piney Mount Ch—*church* (2) ... GA-3
*Piney Mtn* ... NC-3
*Piney Mtn* ... VA-3
Piney Mtn—*summit* (2) ... AR-4
Piney Mtn—*summit* ... CO-8
Piney Mtn—*summit* (3) ... GA-3
Piney Mtn—*summit* (3) ... MD-2
Piney Mtn—*summit* (23) ... NC-3
Piney Mtn—*summit* ... OK-5
Piney Mtn—*summit* ... PA-2
Piney Mtn—*summit* (5) ... SC-3
Piney Mtn—*summit* (3) ... TN-4
Piney Mtn—*summit* (13) ... VA-3
Piney Mtn—*summit* ... WV-2
*Piney Neck* ... MD-2
Piney Neck—*cape* ... DE-2
Piney Neck—*cape* (3) ... MD-2
Piney Neck Ch—*church* ... MD-2
Piney Neck Cove—*bay* ... MD-2
Piney Neck Marsh—*swamp* ... MD-2
Piney Neck Point—*cape* ... MD-2
Piney Oaks Sch—*school* ... WV-2
Pineyon (historical)—*locale* ... AZ-5
Piney Park—*flat* (2) ... NM-5
**Piney Park**—*pop pl* ... MO-7
Piney Park Canyon—*valley* (2) ... NM-5
Piney Park Tank—*reservoir* ... NM-5
Piney Park Tank No 1—*reservoir* ... NM-5
Piney Pass—*gap* ... ID-8
Piney Pass—*gap* ... WY-8
Piney Peak—*summit* ... CO-8
Piney Peak—*summit* ... ID-8
Piney Plain Ch—*church* (2) ... SC-3
**Piney Plains**—*pop pl* ... NC-3
Piney Plains Ch—*church* ... MD-2
Piney Plains Sch—*school* ... MD-2
Piney Pocosin—*swamp* ... NC-3
Piney Point—*cape* (10) ... FL-3
Piney Point—*cape* ... LA-4
Piney Point—*cape* (7) ... MD-2
Piney Point—*cape* ... MA-1
Piney Point—*cape* ... MS-4
Piney Point—*cape* ... MT-8
Piney Point—*cape* ... NJ-2
Piney Point—*cape* (5) ... NC-3
Piney Point—*cape* (2) ... TN-4
Piney Point—*cape* ... TX-5
Piney Point—*cape* ... WV-2
Piney Point—*cliff* ... AL-4
Piney Point—*cliff* ... VA-3
**Piney Point**—*pop pl* ... FL-3
**Piney Point**—*pop pl* ... MD-2
Piney Point Beach—*beach* ... MD-2
**Piney Point Beach**—*pop pl* ... MA-1
Piney Point Coast Guard Light Station—*hist pl* ... MD-2
*Piney Point (corporate name Piney Point Village)* ... TX-5
Piney Point Creek—*bay* ... MD-2
Piney Point Creek—*stream* ... FL-3
Piney Point Creek—*stream* (2) ... NC-3
Piney Point Dock—*locale* ... TN-4
**Piney Point Estates**—*pop pl* ... VA-3
Piney Point Gully—*valley* ... TX-5
Piney Point Hollow—*valley* ... MO-7
**Piney Point (Port Manatee)**—*pop pl* ... FL-3
Piney Point Rec Area—*park* ... AL-4
Piney Point Resort—*locale* ... TN-4
Piney Point Sch—*school* ... MD-2
Piney Point Sch—*school* ... WV-2
**Piney Point (subdivision)**—*pop pl* ... AL-4
**Piney Point Village**—*pop pl* ... TX-5
**Piney Point Village (corporate name for Piney Point)**—*pop pl* ... TX-5
*Piney Pond* ... FL-3
Piney Pond Canal—*canal* ... NC-3
Piney Post Office (historical)—*building* ... TN-4
Piney Prairie—*flat* ... FL-3
Piney Prospect—*hist pl* ... NC-3
Piney Reach Slough—*gut* ... FL-3
**Piney Ridge**—*pop pl* ... MI-6
**Piney Ridge**—*pop pl* ... NC-3
Piney Ridge—*ridge* (2) ... CA-9
Piney Ridge—*ridge* (2) ... CO-8
Piney Ridge—*ridge* (2) ... GA-3
Piney Ridge—*ridge* ... MD-2
Piney Ridge—*ridge* ... MT-8
Piney Ridge—*ridge* ... NY-2
Piney Ridge—*ridge* (2) ... NC-3
Piney Ridge—*ridge* (3) ... PA-2
Piney Ridge—*ridge* (12) ... VA-3
Piney Ridge—*ridge* (3) ... WV-2
Piney Ridge—*ridge* ... WY-8
Piney Ridge Branch—*stream* ... AL-4
Piney Ridge Ch—*church* ... AL-4
Piney Ridge Ch—*church* ... AR-4
Piney Ridge Ch—*church* (3) ... NC-3
Piney Ridge Knob—*summit* ... NC-3
Piney Ridge Mine (surface)—*mine* ... AL-4
Piney Ridge Trail—*trail* (2) ... VA-3
**Piney River**—*pop pl* ... VA-3
Piney River—*stream* ... CO-8
Piney River—*stream* (2) ... TN-4
Piney River—*stream* (2) ... VA-3
Piney River Ch—*church* ... TN-4
Piney River Ch—*church* (2) ... VA-3
*Piney River Island* ... TN-4
Piney River Narrows State Natural Area—*park* ... MO-7
Piney River Shoals—*bar* ... TN-4
Piney Rsvr—*reservoir* ... PA-2
*Piney Run* ... PA-2
*Piney Run* ... VA-3
**Piney Run**—*pop pl* ... VA-3
Piney Run—*stream* ... DC-2
Piney Run—*stream* (5) ... MD-2
Piney Run—*stream* (5) ... PA-2
Piney Run—*stream* (3) ... VA-3
Piney Run—*stream* (2) ... WV-2
Piney Run Golf Course—*locale* ... PA-2
Piney Sch—*school* ... IL-6
Piney Sch—*school* (3) ... TN-4
Piney Sch—*school* ... TX-5
Piney Sch (abandoned)—*school* (2) ... MO-7
Piney Sch (historical)—*school* ... AL-4
Piney Sch (historical)—*school* (2) ... TN-4
Piney Shores Estates—*locale* ... TN-4
*Pineys Island* ... TN-4
Piney Spring—*spring* ... CO-8
Piney Spring—*spring* ... MO-7
*Piney Spring Branch* ... AL-4
*Piney Springs* ... AL-4
Piney Springs Ch—*church* ... MS-4
*Piney Springs Creek Church* ... TX-5
Piney Spur—*ridge* ... KY-4
Piney Spur—*ridge* ... SC-3
Piney Spur—*summit* ... TN-4
Piney Swamp—*swamp* ... MD-2
Piney Swamp—*swamp* ... WV-2
Piney Swamp Run—*stream* ... WV-2
Piney Top—*summit* ... GA-3
Piney Top—*summit* ... NC-3
Piney Township—*civil* (2) ... MO-7
**Piney Township**—*pop pl* ... MO-7
Piney (Township of)—*fmr MCD* (3) ... AR-4
**Piney (Township of)**—*pop pl* ... PA-2
**Piney View**—*pop pl* ... WV-2
Piney Watershed Y-38-33 Dam—*dam* ... MS-4
Piney Wood—*locale* (2) ... NC-3
Piney Wood Branch—*stream* ... LA-4
Pineywood Ch—*church* ... AL-4
Piney Wood Ch—*church* ... AL-4
Piney Wood Ch—*church* ... MS-4
Piney Wood Ch—*church* ... NC-3
Piney Wood Chapel—*church* (2) ... NC-3
*Piney Wood Creek* ... GA-3
Pineywood Creek—*stream* ... AL-4
Piney Wood Creek—*stream* ... NC-3
*Piney Woods* ... AL-4
Piney Woods—*locale* ... AL-4
**Piney Woods**—*pop pl* ... MI-6
**Piney Woods**—*pop pl* ... MS-4
**Piney Woods**—*pop pl* ... TN-4
Piney Woods—*woods* ... MS-4
*Piney Woods Baptist Church* ... MS-4
Piney Woods Bay—*swamp* ... FL-3
Piney Woods Branch—*stream* (2) ... GA-3
Piney Woods Branch—*stream* ... LA-4
Pineywoods Camp—*locale* ... AL-4
Piney Woods Camp—*locale* ... TX-5
Piney Woods Cem—*cemetery* ... AL-4
Piney Woods Cem—*cemetery* (2) ... MS-4
Piney Woods Ch—*church* (3) ... AL-4
Pineywoods Ch—*church* ... AL-4
Piney Woods Ch—*church* ... GA-3
Pineywood Sch (historical)—*school* ... AL-4
Piney Woods Community Ch—*church* ... AL-4
Piney Woods Country Life Sch—*school* ... MS-4
**Piney Woods (Country Life School)**—*pop pl* ... MS-4
Piney Woods Creek—*stream* (8) ... AL-4
Piney Woods Creek—*stream* ... FL-3
Piney Woods Creek—*stream* (2) ... GA-3
Piney Woods Creek—*stream* (2) ... LA-4
Piney Woods Creek—*stream* ... MS-4
*Piney Woods Elementary School* ... TN-4
**Pineywoods Estates**—*pop pl* ... NM-5
Piney Woods Fork—*stream* ... LA-4
Piney Woods Lake—*lake* (3) ... GA-3
Piney Woods Lake—*reservoir* ... GA-3
Piney Woods Lake Dam—*dam* ... MS-4
Piney Woods Lookout Tower—*locale* ... MS-4
Piney Woods Lookout Tower—*locale* (2) ... TX-5
Piney Woods Marina—*locale* ... AL-4
Piney Woods Public Use Area—*park* ... MS-4
*Piney Woods Ridge* ... GA-3
Piney Woods Sch—*school* ... TN-4
Piney Woods Sch (historical)—*school* (2) ... AL-4
**Piney Woods (subdivision)**—*pop pl* (2) ... NC-3
Piney Woods Tank—*locale* ... AL-4
Piney Z Lake—*reservoir* ... FL-3
Pinezanita—*locale* ... CA-9
Pinfeather Ridge—*ridge* ... OH-6
Ping—*locale* ... WA-9
Pingally Point—*cape* ... DE-2
Pingaluk River—*stream* ... AK-9
Pingaluligit Mtn—*summit* ... AK-9
Pingaluruk Creek—*stream* ... AK-9
Pin Gap—*gap* ... NC-3
Pingasagruk (abandoned)—*locale* ... AK-9
*Pingaso* ... MH-9
Ping Creek—*stream* ... ID-8
Pingelap—*island* ... FM-9
Pingelap Atoll—*island* ... FM-9
Pingelap (Municipality)—*civ div* ... FM-9
Pingel Cem—*cemetery* ... WI-6
Ping Gulch—*valley* ... OR-9
Ping Gulch—*valley* ... WA-9
Ping Hollow—*valley* ... KY-4
*Pinglag* ... MP-9
*Ping Lake* ... WA-9
*Pinglap Island* ... MP-9
Pinglap Island—*island* ... MP-9
Pingle Drain—*stream* ... MI-6
Pingleton Point—*cape* ... NC-3
Pingok Island—*island* ... AK-9
Pingokraluk Lagoon—*lake* ... AK-9
Pingokraluk Point—*cape* ... AK-9

Pino Draw—valley WY-8
Pino Grande—locale CA-9
Pino Island Lake MN-6
**Pinola**—pop pl IN-6
**Pinola**—pop pl MS-4
**Pinola**—pop pl PA-2
Pinola Attendance Center (historical)—school MS-4
Pinola Cem—cemetery MS-4
Pinola Lake TX-5
Pinole—civil CA-9
**Pinole**—pop pl CA-9
Pinole Creek—stream CA-9
Pinole HS—school CA-9
Pinole Lake—lake TX-5
Pino-Leno Mou AZ-5
Pinole Point—cape CA-9
Pinole Ranch—locale CA-9
Pinole Ridge—ridge CA-9
Pinole Shoal—bar CA-9
Pinole Spring—spring CA-9
Pinole Trap—summit TX-5
Pinoli Peak—summit CA-9
Pinoli Ridge—ridge CA-9
**Pinoliville Rancheria**—pop pl CA-9
Pinon AZ-5
Pinon CA-9
Pinon—locale CO-8
**Pinon**—pop pl AZ-5
**Pinon**—pop pl CO-8
**Pinon**—pop pl CO-8
**Pinon**—pop pl NM-5
**Pinon Acres**—pop pl CO-8
**Pinon Acres**—pop pl CO-8
Pinon Boarding Sch—school AZ-5
Pinon Camp —locale AZ-5
**Pinon Canyon**—pop pl CO-8
Pinon Canyon—valley CO-8
Pinon Canyon—valley (2) NM-5
Pinon Canyon—valley TX-5
Pinon Canyon —valley TX-5
Pinon Canyon—valley UT-8
Pinon (CCD)—cens area AZ-5
Pinon Cem—cemetery NM-5
Pinon Creek AZ-5
Pinon Creek—stream NM-5
Pinon Draw—valley NM-5
Pinon Draw —valley TX-5
**Pinones**—pop pl (2) PR-3
Pinon Flat CA-9
Pinon Grove—area CO-8
Pinon Hill—cliff CO-8
Pinon Hills—other (2) NM-5
**Pinon Hills**—pop pl CA-9
Pinon Hills—range CO-8
Pinon Hills—summit TX-5
Pinon (historical)—locale KS-7
Pinon Hollow—valley AR-4
Pinon Lake—lake CO-8
Pinon Landing Strip—airport AZ-5
Pinon Mesa —summit CA-9
Pinon Mesa—summit CO-8
Pinon Mesa—summit NM-5
Pinon Mountain Tank —reservoir AZ-5
Pinon Mtn—summit CO-8
Pinon Mtn—summit (3) NM-5
Pinon Park—flat CO-8
Pinon Park Hill—summit CO-8
Pinon Park Wash—valley UT-8
Pinon Peak —summit NV-8
Pinon Pines CA-9
Pinon Point —cape UT-8
Pinon Point—cliff UT-8
Pinon Point—ridge NM-5
Pinon Point —summit CA-9
Pinon Post Office—building AZ-5
Pinon Ranch—locale NM-5
Pinon Ranch—locale TX-5
Pinon Range NV-8
Pinon Range —range NV-8
Pinon Ridge—ridge CO-8
Pinon Ridge—ridge NM-5
Pinon Ridge—ridge WY-8
Pinon Rodeo Grounds—park AZ-5
Pinons Hill GA-3
Pinon Spring—spring AZ-5
Pinon Spring —spring AZ-5
Pinon Spring —spring CA-9
Pinon Spring—spring (2) NM-5
Pinon Springs Draw—valley CO-8
Pinon Tank —reservoir AZ-5
Pinon Tank—reservoir AZ-5
Pinon Tank—reservoir (3) NM-5
Pinon Tank —reservoir (2) TX-5
Pinon Tank Number One —reservoir AZ-5
Pinon Tank Number Two —reservoir AZ-5
Pinon Trading Post—locale AZ-5
Pinon Valley Ranch—locale CO-8
Pinon Wash—stream NM-5
Pinon Well—well (2) NM-5
Pinon Windmill—locale NM-5
Pino Place—locale NM-5
**Pinopolis**—pop pl SC-3
Pinopolis Dam—dam SC-3
Pinopolis Hist Dist North—hist pl SC-3
Pinopolis Hist Dist South—hist pl SC-3
**Pinopolis Junction**—pop pl SC-3
Pinopolis Peninsula—cape SC-3
Pinopolis Reservoir SC-3
Pinora Cem—cemetery MI-6
Pinora Lookout Tower—locale MI-6
Pino Ranch—locale NM-5
**Pinora (Township of)**—pop pl MI-6
Pinorealosa Mtn—summit CO-8
Pinoreal Peak—summit NM-5
Pino Real Spring—spring NM-5
Pino Real Tank—reservoir AZ-5
Pinor Point UT-8
Pinos, Mount—summit CA-9
Pinos, Playas de los—flat AZ-5
Pinos, Rio—stream CO-8
Pinosa Canyon—valley NM-5
Pinos Altos—area NM-5
Pinos Altos—locale NM-5
**Pinos Altos**—pop pl NM-5
Pinos Altos (CCD)—cens area NM-5
Pinos Altos Creek—stream NM-5
Pinos Altos Hist Dist—hist pl NM-5
Pinos Altos Mtn—summit NM-5
Pinos Altos Range—range NM-5
Pinos Creek CO-8
Pinos Creek—stream CO-8
Pinoso, Arroyo—stream CA-9
Pino Spring—spring (2) NM-5
Pinos Well—locale NM-5
**Pinoswells**—pop pl NM-5
Pino Tank—reservoir NM-5
Pino Well—well (2) NM-5
Pin Peak—summit (2) AK-9
Pin Peaks—summit AK-9
Pin Point—cape AK-9
Pin Point—cape MD-2
Pin Point—locale GA-3
Pinquickset Cove—cove MA-1
Pin Rock—island AK-9
Pin Rock—island CA-9
Pinrod Hollow—valley AR-4
Pins, Point aux—cape AL-4
Pinschower, Simon, House—hist pl CA-9
Pins Creek—stream NY-2
Pins Creek—stream WA-9
Pinseclair Cem—cemetery LA-4
Pin Shop Pond—reservoir CT-1
Pinski Park—park MT-8
Pinson KY-4
Pinson—locale GA-3
Pinson—locale NC-3
**Pinson**—pop pl TN-4
Pinson, Mount—summit TN-4
Pinson Baptist Ch—church TN-4
Pinson Branch—stream AL-4
Pinson Branch—stream KY-4
Pinson Canyon—valley NV-8
Pinson Cave—cave AL-4
Pinson (CCD)—cens area TN-4
Pinson Cem—cemetery (2) KY-4
Pinson Cem—cemetery MO-7
Pinson Cem—cemetery TN-4
Pinson Ch—church AL-4
Pinson Community Sch—school AL-4
Pinson Division—civil TN-4
Pinson Elem Sch—school AL-4
Pinson Elem Sch—school TN-4
**Pinsonfork**—pop pl KY-4
Pinson Fork—stream KY-4
**Pinsonfork (RR name Peg)**—pop pl KY-4
Pinson Indian Mounds—summit TN-4
Pinson Mine—mine NV-8
Pinson Mine (underground)—mine AL-4
Pinson Mounds—hist pl TN-4
Pinson Mounds State Archaeol Area—park TN-4
Pinson Mounds State Archaeol Park TN-4
**Pinson (Mount Pinson)**—pop pl AL-4
**Pinson (Mt Pinson Station)**—pop pl AL-4
Pinson Post Office—building TN-4
Pinson (RR name for McAndrews)—other KY-4
Pinson Sch (historical)—school TN-4
Pinsons Ferry (historical)—locale AL-4
**Pinson Valley**—pop pl AL-4
Pinson Valley HS—school AL-4
Pins Way Lake—reservoir IN-6
Pins Way Lake Dam—dam IN-6
Pinta—locale AZ-5
Pinta, Loma—summit TX-5
Pinta, Mount—summit (2) AK-9
Pinta, Sierra—range AZ-5
Pinta Bay—bay AK-9
Pinta Cove—bay AK-9
Pintada—locale NM-5
Pintada Arroyo—stream NM-5
Pintada Creek—stream CO-8
Pintada Draw—valley NM-5
Pintada Mine—mine NM-5
Pintada Mtn—summit CO-8
Pintada Peak CO-8
**Pintado**—pop pl PR-3
Pintado Mountain CO-8
Pintado Park—park FL-3
Pintado Point—cliff AZ-5
Pinta Head—cape AK-9
Pintail Creek—gut FL-3
Pintail Duck Club—other CA-9
Pintail Flat—lake LA-4
Pintail Gun Club—other UT-8
Pintail Island—island SC-3
Pintail Lake—lake AK-9
Pintail Lake—reservoir UT-8
Pintail Lane Sch—school NY-2
Pintail Marsh—swamp UT-8
Pintail Neck—cape UT-8
Pintail Point—cape LA-4
Pintail Pond—lake MA-1
Pintail Pond—lake MI-6
Pintail Pond—reservoir OH-6
Pintail Pool—lake MO-7
Pintail Pool—reservoir UT-8
Pintail Rsvr—reservoir ID-8
Pinta Lake—lake AK-9
Pintalla Elem Sch—school AL-4
Pintall Bay—reservoir NV-8
Pinta Playa—flat AZ-5
Pinta Point—cape AK-9
Pintar Canyon—valley ID-8
Pintar Mine—mine ID-8
Pinta Road Interchange—crossing AZ-5
Pinta Rock—other AK-9
Pinta Rocks—area AK-9
Pinta Rocks Light—locale AK-9
Pintas, Point of the—summit AZ-5
Pinta Sands—area AZ-5
Pintas Creek—stream TX-5
Pintchbeck Sch—school VA-3
Pint Cove—bay ME-1
Pint Creek OR-9
Pint Creek—stream IL-6
Pint Creek—stream OR-9
Pinter Creek—stream MS-4
Pinththlocko Creek AL-4
Pint Lake MI-6
Pint Lala AL-4
**Pintlala**—pop pl AL-4
Pintlala Creek—stream AL-4
Pintlalla AL-4
Pintlalla Ch—church AL-4
Pintlar Creek MT-8
Pintlar Falls MT-8
Pintlar Lake MT-8
Pintlar Meadows MT-8
Pintlar Pass MT-8
Pintler Cem—cemetery NY-2
Pintler Creek—stream MT-8
Pintler Creek—stream WA-9
Pintler Falls—falls MT-8
Pintler Lake—lake MT-8
Pintler Meadows—flat MT-8
Pintler Pass—gap MT-8
Pintler Peak—summit MT-8
Pintler Wilderness Area MT-8
Pint Lick Branch—stream KY-4
Pinto NV-8
Pinto—locale TX-5
Pinto—locale (2) UT-8
**Pinto**—pop pl MD-2
Pinto, Lake—lake FL-3
Pinto, Lake—reservoir TX-5
Pinto, William, House—hist pl CT-1
**Pinto Acres Subdivision**—pop pl UT-8
Pinto Arch—arch UT-8
Pinto Ballo Tank—reservoir TX-5
Pinto Basin—basin CA-9
Pinto Basin—basin CO-8
Pinto Basin—basin NV-8
Pinto Bean Tank—reservoir TX-5
Pinto Canyon—valley CA-9
Pinto Canyon—valley NV-8
Pinto Canyon—valley NM-5
Pinto Canyon—valley (2) TX-5
Pinto Canyon—valley UT-8
Pinto Cave—cave MO-7
Pinto Cem—cemetery MO-7
Pinto Cem—cemetery UT-8
Pinto Cow Canyon—valley AZ-5
Pinto Creek AZ-5
Pinto Creek TX-5
Pinto Creek—stream AK-9
Pinto Creek—stream AZ-5
Pinto Creek—stream (2) CA-9
Pinto Creek—stream CO-8
Pinto Creek—stream (3) ID-8
Pinto Creek—stream (3) MT-8
Pinto Creek—stream NV-8
Pinto Creek—stream OR-9
Pinto Creek—stream (4) TX-5
Pinto Creek—stream (3) UT-8
Pinto Creek—stream WA-9
Pinto Creek—stream WY-8
Pinto Creek Ranch—locale NV-8
Pinto Creek Reservoir UT-8
Pinto Creek Springs—spring NV-8
Pinto Creek Well—well AZ-5
Pinto Cutoff—bend LA-4
Pinto Dam—dam WA-9
Pinto Gulch—valley (2) CO-8
Pinto Hill—summit NV-8
Pinto (historical)—locale MS-4
Pinto Horse Rsvr—reservoir OR-9
Pinto Hot Springs—spring NV-8
Pinto Island—island AL-4
**Pinto Island**—pop pl AL-4
Pintojo Ridge—ridge CA-9
Pinto Knoll—summit UT-8
Pinto Lake—lake AZ-5
Pinto Lake—lake CA-9
Pinto Lake—lake OR-9
Pinto Lake—lake UT-8
Pinto Lake—lake WY-8
Pinto Lake—reservoir CA-9
Pinto Lakes—lake CA-9
Pinto Mare—valley UT-8
Pinto Mesa—ridge AZ-5
Pinto Mesa—summit CO-8
Pinto Mesa Spring—spring AZ-5
Pinto Mesa Tank—reservoir (2) AZ-5
Pinto Mesa Windmill—locale CO-8
Pinto Mine—mine CA-9
Pinto Mountains—range CA-9
Pinto Mountain Way—trail OR-9
Pinto Mtn—summit (2) CA-9
Pinto Mtn—summit NV-8
Pinto Mtn—summit OR-9
Pinto Mtn—summit TX-5
Pin Top—summit WY-8
Pinto Park—flat WY-8
Pinto Park Trail—trail WY-8
Pinto Pass—channel AL-4
Pinto Peak MT-8
Pinto Peak—summit AZ-5
Pinto Peak—summit CA-9
Pinto Peak—summit NV-8
Pinto Peak—summit UT-8
Pinto Point—cape ID-8
Pinto Point—summit MT-8
**Pinto (Potomac)**—pop pl MD-2
Pinto Reach—canal AL-4
Pinto Ridge—ridge CA-9
Pinto Ridge—ridge NV-8
Pinto Ridge—ridge WA-9
Pinto Rock UT-8
Pinto Rock—summit WA-9
Pinto Rocks—summit WY-8
Pintosa Canyon NM-5
Pintosa Tank NM-5
Pinto Shaft—mine AZ-5
Pintos Lake—reservoir NM-5
Pintos Pass AL-4
Pinto Spring—spring (3) AZ-5
Pinto Spring—spring NV-8
Pinto Spring—spring OR-9
Pinto Spring—spring (3) UT-8
Pinto Spring—spring WY-8
Pinto Springs—spring NV-8
Pinto Springs—spring OR-9
Pinto Springs—spring TX-5
Pinto Springs—spring UT-8
Pinto Spring Trough—reservoir AZ-5
Pinto Summit—gap NV-8
Pinto Tank AZ-5
Pinto Tank—reservoir (2) AZ-5
Pinto Tank—reservoir (3) NM-5
Pinto Valle Creek—stream TX-5
Pinto Valle Tank—reservoir TX-5
Pinto Valley—basin NV-8
Pinto Valley—valley CA-9
Pinto Valley Tailings Dam Number One—dam AZ-5
Pinto Valley Tailings Dam Number Three—dam AZ-5
Pinto Valley Tailings Dam Number Two—dam AZ-5
Pinto Wash—stream (2) CA-9
Pinto Wash—valley UT-8
Pinto Well—well TX-5
Pinto Wells—well CA-9
Pinto Windmill—locale (2) TX-5
Pinto Wye—locale CA-9
Pint Run—stream IN-6
Pintura—locale UT-8
Pintura Cem—cemetery UT-8
Pintwater Cave—cave NV-8
Pintwater Range—range NV-8
Pinus Creek—stream OR-9
Pinus Creek—stream WA-9
Pinus Lake—lake WA-9
Pinusuk Island—island AK-9
Pinwan Lake OR-9
Pinwood Sch (abandoned)—school MO-7
Piny Branch OK-5
Piny Creek KY-4
Piny Creek TN-4
Piny Grove Cem—cemetery NC-3
Piny Grove Ch—church MS-4
Piny Grove Ch—church NC-3
Piny Knob—summit VA-3
Pinyon CO-8
Pinyon Alta Flat—flat CA-9
Pinyon Butte—summit NV-8
Pinyon Canyon TX-5
Pinyon Canyon—valley CA-9
Pinyon Canyon—valley UT-8
Pinyon Creek AZ-5
Pinyon Creek CO-8
Pinyon Creek—stream (2) CA-9
Pinyon Creek—stream ID-8
Pinyon Creek—stream UT-8
Pinyon Creek Canyon—valley UT-8
Pinyon Crest—locale CA-9
Pinyon Flat—flat CA-9
Pinyon Flat—flat UT-8
Pinyon Flat Camp—locale CA-9
Pinyon Flats—flat CA-9
Pinyon Flats Campground—locale CO-8
Pinyon Gulch—valley ID-8
Pinyon Hill—summit NV-8
Pinyon Hills TX-5
Pinyon Juniper Study Area—area UT-8
Pinyon Knob—summit AZ-5
Pinyon Lake—lake (2) ID-8
Pinyon Mountain ID-8
Pinyon Mountains CA-9
Pinyon Mountains—range CA-9
Pinyon Mountain Valley—valley CA-9
Pinyon Mtn—summit AZ-5
Pinyon Mtn—summit (2) CA-9
Pinyon Pack Trail—trail CO-8
Pinyon Pass—gap NV-8
Pinyon Peak—summit (3) CA-9
Pinyon Peak—summit ID-8
Pinyon Peak—summit UT-8
Pinyon Peak—summit WY-8
**Pinyon Pines**—pop pl CA-9
Pinyon Queen—mine UT-8
Pinyon Ridge—ridge (2) CA-9
Pinyon Ridge—ridge CO-8
Pinyon Spring—spring CA-9
Pinyon Tank TX-5
Pinyon Tank—reservoir AZ-5
Pinyon Terrace—bench WY-8
Pinyon Trail—trail CA-9
Pinyon Wash—stream CA-9
Pinyon Well—well CA-9
Pinyon Well (Site)—locale CA-9
Piny Point—cape NC-3
Piny Run—stream MD-2
Piny Run—stream OH-6
Piny Swamp—stream VA-3
**Pioche**—pop pl NV-8
Pioche Airp—airport NV-8
Pioche-Bristol Mine—mine NV-8
Pioche Creek—stream UT-8
Pioche Hills—summit NV-8
Pioche King Mine—mine NV-8
Pioche Mines Mill—locale NV-8
Pioche Peak NV-8
Pioche Spring—spring UT-8
Pioche Township—inact MCD NV-8
Pio Hill—summit CO-8
Pio Island—island MP-9
Piojo Spring—spring CA-9
Piolett—locale PA-2
Piomingo, Lake—reservoir MS-4
Pio Moses Ranch—locale WY-8
Pioneer MN-6
Pioneer MT-8
Pioneer—fmr MCD NE-7
Pioneer—locale AL-4
Pioneer—locale CA-9
Pioneer—locale IL-6
Pioneer—locale MI-6
Pioneer—locale MT-8
Pioneer—locale OR-9
Pioneer—locale PA-2
Pioneer—locale TX-5
Pioneer—locale WA-9
Pioneer—other KY-4
**Pioneer**—pop pl AZ-5
**Pioneer**—pop pl CA-9
**Pioneer**—pop pl IN-6
**Pioneer**—pop pl IA-7
**Pioneer**—pop pl LA-4
**Pioneer**—pop pl MO-7
**Pioneer**—pop pl NY-2
**Pioneer**—pop pl OH-6
**Pioneer**—pop pl SC-3
**Pioneer**—pop pl TN-4
**Pioneer**—pop pl UT-8
Pioneer—uninc pl MT-8
Pioneer—uninc pl OR-9
Pioneer, The—hist pl CA-9
Pioneer Acad—school MS-4
**Pioneer Acres (subdivision)**—pop pl (2) AZ-5
**Pioneer Addition**—pop pl UT-8
Pioneer Administrative Site—locale UT-8
Pioneer Adobe House—hist pl KS-7
Pioneer and Endicott Buildings—hist pl MN-6
Pioneer Auditorium—building NV-8
Pioneer Aztalan Site—hist pl WI-6
Pioneer Ball Park—park WA-9
Pioneer Baptist Ch—church FL-3
Pioneer Basin—basin AZ-5
Pioneer Basin—basin CA-9
Pioneer Basin Lakes—lake CA-9
Pioneer Bldg—hist pl NY-2
Pioneer Bldg—hist pl OK-5
Pioneer Block—hist pl WI-6
Pioneer Boat Club—other NY-2
Pioneer Bridge—bridge CA-9
Pioneer Bridle Trail—trail OR-9
Pioneer Building, Pergola, and Totem Pole—hist pl WA-9
Pioneer Burying Ground—cemetery NY-2
Pioneer Butte—summit OR-9
Pioneer Cabin—hist pl CO-8
Pioneer Cabin—locale ID-8
Pioneer Camp—locale CA-9
Pioneer Camp—park IN-6
Pioneer Campground—locale UT-8
Pioneer Canal—canal CA-9
Pioneer Canal—canal ID-8
Pioneer Canal—canal (2) UT-8
Pioneer Canal—canal WY-8
Pioneer Canyon—valley UT-8
Pioneer Cem—cemetery AL-4
Pioneer Cem—cemetery AZ-5
Pioneer Cem—cemetery (3) CA-9
Pioneer Cem—cemetery (6) ID-8
Pioneer Cem—cemetery (3) IL-6
Pioneer Cem—cemetery (7) IA-7
Pioneer Cem—cemetery (3) KS-7
Pioneer Cem—cemetery ME-1
Pioneer Cem—cemetery (9) MI-6
Pioneer Cem—cemetery (3) MN-6
Pioneer Cem—cemetery MS-4
Pioneer Cem—cemetery (4) MT-8
Pioneer Cem—cemetery (3) NE-7
Pioneer Cem—cemetery NV-8
Pioneer Cem—cemetery (8) NY-2
Pioneer Cem—cemetery (3) ND-7
Pioneer Cem—cemetery (10) OH-6
Pioneer Cem—cemetery (2) OK-5
Pioneer Cem—cemetery (8) OR-9
Pioneer Cem—cemetery (2) PA-2
Pioneer Cem—cemetery (7) SD-7
Pioneer Cem—cemetery (2) TN-4
Pioneer Cem—cemetery (4) TX-5
Pioneer Cem—cemetery (2) UT-8
Pioneer Cem—cemetery (4) WA-9
Pioneer Cem—cemetery WV-2
Pioneer Cem—cemetery (6) WI-6
Pioneer Cem—cemetery WY-8
Pioneer Ch—church AL-4
Pioneer Ch—church GA-3
Pioneer Ch—church KY-4
Pioneer Ch—church MI-6
Pioneer Ch—church MS-4
Pioneer Ch—church MO-7
Pioneer Ch—church ND-7
Pioneer Ch—church OH-6
Pioneer Ch—church SD-7
Pioneer Ch—church TX-5
Pioneer Ch—church VA-3
Pioneer Ch—church WA-9
Pioneer Chapel—church NE-7
Pioneer Church—hist pl WA-9
Pioneer City ID-8
Pioneer City KS-7
**Pioneer City**—pop pl MD-2
Pioneer Club—hist pl OK-5
Pioneer Community Hall—building KS-7
Pioneer Community Hall—locale OR-9
Pioneer Co-op Spur—locale KS-7
Pioneer Courthouse—hist pl OR-9
Pioneer Cove—bay TX-5
Pioneer Creek MN-6
Pioneer Creek OR-9
Pioneer Creek SC-3
Pioneer Creek—stream (2) AK-9
Pioneer Creek—stream AZ-5
Pioneer Creek—stream CA-9
Pioneer Creek—stream (3) CO-8
Pioneer Creek—stream (2) ID-8
Pioneer Creek—stream IA-7
Pioneer Creek—stream MN-6
Pioneer Creek—stream (2) MT-8
Pioneer Creek—stream NM-5
Pioneer Creek—stream UT-8
Pioneer Creek—stream (4) WA-9
Pioneer Creek—stream WI-6
Pioneer Deep Space Station—hist pl CA-9
Pioneer Ditch—canal CA-9
Pioneer Ditch—canal (3) CO-8
Pioneer Ditch—canal ID-8
Pioneer Ditch—canal (2) MT-8
Pioneer Ditch—canal NV-8
Pioneer Ditch—canal NM-5
Pioneer Ditch—canal UT-8
Pioneer Education Center—school PA-2
Pioneer Elem Sch—school AZ-5
Pioneer Estates IL-6
**Pioneer Estates (subdivision)**—pop pl (2) AZ-5
**Pioneer Estates Subdivision**—pop pl UT-8
Pioneer Express Trail—trail CA-9
Pioneer Falls—falls MT-8
Pioneer Farm—hist pl NY-2
Pioneer Farm—locale MT-8
Pioneer Field—park PA-2
Pioneer First Baptist Ch—church TN-4
Pioneer Ford Campground—park OR-9
Pioneer Forest Camp—locale ID-8
Pioneer Fork—stream UT-8
Pioneer Gap—gap UT-8
Pioneer Gothic Church—hist pl IL-6
Pioneer Grove—cemetery CA-9
Pioneer Gulch—valley (2) AK-9
Pioneer Gulch—valley CO-8
Pioneer Gulch—valley (3) ID-8
Pioneer Gulch—valley MT-8
Pioneer Gulch—valley OR-9
Pioneer Gulch—valley UT-8
Pioneer Hall—hist pl TN-4
Pioneer Hall—hist pl WA-9
Pioneer Hall, Linfield College—hist pl OR-9
Pioneer (historical)—locale KS-7
Pioneer Historic Marker—park CA-9
Pioneer Home—locale WY-8
Pioneer Hosp—hospital OR-9
Pioneer HS—school (4) CA-9
Pioneer Interchange—crossing AZ-5
Pioneer JHS—school (2) CA-9
Pioneer JHS—school (2) WA-9
**Pioneer Junction**—pop pl MT-8
Pioneer Lake—lake CO-8
Pioneer Lake—lake (2) FL-3
Pioneer Lake—lake (3) MN-6
Pioneer Lake—lake MT-8
Pioneer Lake—lake NM-5
Pioneer Lake—lake WI-6
Pioneer Lake—reservoir PA-2
Pioneer Lake Dam—dam PA-2
Pioneer Lake Dam Number Five—dam TN-4
Pioneer Lake Dam Number Four—dam TN-4
Pioneer Lake Dam Number One—dam TN-4
Pioneer Lake Dam Number Three—dam TN-4
Pioneer Lake Dam Number Two—dam TN-4
Pioneer Lake Number Five—reservoir TN-4
Pioneer Lake Number Four—reservoir TN-4
Pioneer Lake Number One—reservoir TN-4
Pioneer Lake Number Three—reservoir TN-4
Pioneer Lake Number Two—reservoir TN-4
Pioneer Lakes—lake MT-8
Pioneer Landing TN-4
Pioneer Lateral—canal WY-8
Pioneer Lodge—locale CA-9
Pioneer Lookout Point—cliff CO-8
Pioneer Lookout Tower—locale MT-8
Pioneer Lutheran Church SD-7
Pioneer Market—hist pl AZ-5
Pioneer Memorial Bridge—bridge CA-9
Pioneer Memorial Cem—cemetery (2) CA-9
Pioneer Memorial Cem—cemetery NE-7
Pioneer Memorial Cem—cemetery OK-5
Pioneer Memorial Cem—cemetery UT-8
Pioneer Memorial Ch—church TX-5
Pioneer Memorial County Park—park WI-6
Pioneer Memorial Hosp—hospital CA-9
Pioneer Memorial Hosp—hospital CO-8
Pioneer Memorial Hosp—hospital OR-9
Pioneer Memorial Park—cemetery UT-8
Pioneer Memorial Park—cemetery WA-9
Pioneer Memorial Park—park OR-9
Pioneer Mesa—summit UT-8
Pioneer Mills—locale NC-3
Pioneer Mine—mine (2) AZ-5
Pioneer Mine—mine (3) CA-9
Pioneer Mine—mine ID-8
Pioneer Mine—mine MN-6
Pioneer Mine—mine NV-8
Pioneer Mine—mine WY-8
Pioneer Mine Buildings and A Headframe—hist pl MN-6
Pioneer Mine Placer Diggings—mine CA-9
Pioneer Monmt—park MA-1
Pioneer Monmt—park WY-8
Pioneer Monmt State Park—park UT-8
Pioneer Monument—other OR-9
Pioneer Mothers Memorial For—forest IN-6
Pioneer MS—school FL-3
Pioneer Mtn—summit AZ-5
Pioneer Mtn—summit MT-8
Pioneer Mtn—summit OR-9
Pioneer Mtns—range ID-8
Pioneer Mtns—range MT-8
Pioneer Mtns—summit ID-8
Pioneer Number Two Canal (historical)—canal UT-8
Pioneer Park—cemetery TX-5
Pioneer Park—flat WY-8
Pioneer Park—park AZ-5
Pioneer Park—park (5) CA-9
Pioneer Park—park CO-8
Pioneer Park—park (2) FL-3
Pioneer Park—park (4) IL-6
Pioneer Park—park (2) IA-7
Pioneer Park—park KY-4
Pioneer Park—park (2) MI-6
Pioneer Park—park MN-6
Pioneer Park—park (2) MT-8
Pioneer Park—park (6) NE-7
Pioneer Park—park NM-5
Pioneer Park—park (2) ND-7
Pioneer Park—park OH-6
Pioneer Park—park (8) OR-9
Pioneer Park—park SD-7
Pioneer Park—park (3) TX-5
Pioneer Park—park (6) WA-9
Pioneer Park—park (2) WI-6
Pioneer Park—park WY-8
Pioneer Park—uninc pl OK-5
Pioneer Park Ground—locale SD-7
Pioneer Park Sch—school WY-8
Pioneer Pass—channel FM-9
Pioneer Pass—gap AZ-5
Pioneer Pass—gap CA-9
Pioneer Pass Campground—park AZ-5
Pioneer Peak OR-9
Pioneer Peak—summit AK-9
Pioneer Peak—summit (2) UT-8
Pioneer Playhouse—building KY-4
Pioneer Point MD-2
Pioneer Point SC-3
Pioneer Point—cape CA-9
**Pioneer Point**—pop pl CA-9
Pioneer Point Campground—locale CA-9
Pioneer Post Office (historical)—building SD-7
Pioneer Post Office (historical)—building TN-4
Pioneer Power Plant—other UT-8
Pioneer Ranch—locale CA-9
Pioneer Register—locale UT-8
Pioneer Rest Cem—cemetery TX-5
Pioneer Rest Cem—cemetery WI-6
Pioneer Ridge—ridge AK-9
Pioneer Ridge—ridge (2) MT-8
Pioneer Ridge—ridge UT-8
Pioneer Ridge—ridge WA-9
Pioneer Ridge Trail—trail MT-8
Pioneer Rock—pillar NV-8
**Pioneer Rocks**—pop pl WV-2
Pioneer Rsvr—reservoir ID-8
Pioneer Saints Cem—cemetery IL-6
Pioneer Salt Well—locale NY-2
Pioneers and Soldiers Cem—cemetery MN-6
Pioneers Cem—cemetery IL-6
Pioneers Cem—cemetery NY-2
Pioneers Cem—cemetery OR-9
Pioneer Sch—school AZ-5
Pioneer Sch—school (4) CA-9
Pioneer Sch—school GA-3
Pioneer Sch—school IL-6

Pisgah Crater—crater ... CA-9
Pisgah Creek—stream ... KY-4
Pisgah Creek—stream ... MO-7
Pisgah Creek—stream ... NC-3
Pisgah Creek—stream ... PA-2
Pisgah Dam—dam ... MN-6
Pisgah Division—civil ... AL-4
Pisgah (Election Precinct)—fmr MCD ... IL-6
Pisgah First Methodist Church ... AL-4
**Pisgah Forest**—pop pl ... NC-3
Pisgah Forest Ch—church (2) ... NC-3
Pisgah Forest Community Building—locale ... NC-3
**Pisgah Forest Farms (subdivision)**—pop pl ... NC-3
Pisgah Freewill Baptist Ch ... TN-4
Pisgah Game Lands—park ... NC-3
Pisgah Gap—gap ... VA-3
Pisgah Gardens—cemetery ... NC-3
Pisgah Heights—locale ... MI-6
Pisgah Heights—uninc pl ... TN-4
Pisgah Hill ... PA-2
Pisgah Hill—summit ... CT-1
Pisgah Hill—summit ... FL-3
Pisgah Hill—summit ... ME-1
Pisgah Hill—summit ... NC-3
Pisgah Hill—summit ... TN-4
Pisgah Hill—summit ... VA-3
Pisgah (historical)—locale ... AL-4
Pisgah Hollow—valley ... TN-4
Pisgah Home Cem—cemetery ... OR-9
Pisgah HS—school ... AL-4
Pisgah HS—school ... MS-4
Pisgah HS—school ... NC-3
Pisgah Knob—summit ... WV-2
Pisgah Lake—lake ... CO-8
Pisgah Lake—lake ... IN-6
Pisgah Lake—reservoir ... IN-6
Pisgah Ledge ... NC-3
Pisgah Methodist Ch—church ... TN-4
Pisgah Methodist Ch (historical)—church ... MS-4
Pisgah Methodist Church ... MS-4
Pisgah Mtn ... ME-1
Pisgah Mtn ... NC-3
Pisgah Mtn—summit ... AL-4
Pisgah Mtn—summit (2) ... AR-4
Pisgah Mtn—summit ... CO-8
Pisgah Mtn—summit ... GA-3
Pisgah Mtn—summit ... ME-1
Pisgah Mtn—summit ... MA-1
Pisgah Mtn—summit ... PA-2
Pisgah Mtn Range—summit ... NH-1
Pisgah Natl For—forest ... NC-3
Pisgah Oil Field ... MS-4
Pisgah Peak—summit ... CA-9
Pisgah (PO)—locale ... GA-3
Pisgah Point Rec Area—park ... KY-4
Pisgah Post Office (historical)—building ... MS-4
Pisgah Post Office (historical)—building ... TN-4
Pisgah Ridge—ridge ... KY-4
Pisgah Ridge—ridge ... NC-3
Pisgah Ridge—ridge ... OH-6
Pisgah Ridge—ridge ... PA-2
Pisgah Ridge—ridge (3) ... TN-4
Pisgah Ridge—ridge ... TX-5
Pisgah Ridge—ridge ... WV-2
Pisgah Rsvr—reservoir ... NH-1
Pisgah Run—stream ... IN-6
Pisgah Run—stream ... PA-2
Pisgah Run—stream ... WV-2
Pisgah Sch ... MS-4
Pisgah Sch—school ... AL-4
Pisgah Sch—school (2) ... KY-4
Pisgah Sch—school ... MS-4
Pisgah Sch—school ... MO-7
Pisgah Sch—school ... NC-3
Pisgah Sch—school ... SC-3
Pisgah Sch—school (3) ... TN-4
Pisgah Sch (abandoned)—school ... MO-7
Pisgah Sch (historical)—school (3) ... AL-4
Pisgah Sch (historical)—school (2) ... MS-4
Pisgah Sch (historical)—school ... PA-2
Pisgah Sch (historical)—school (2) ... TN-4
**Pisgah Shadows**—pop pl ... NC-3
Pisgah Spring—spring ... OR-9
Pisgah Springs Ch—church ... MS-4
Pisgah State Park, Mount—park ... PA-2
Pisgah United Methodist Ch ... MS-4
Pisgah United Methodist Church ... TN-4
Pisgah United Methodist Church—hist pl ... FL-3
Pisgah United Methodist Church and Cemetery—hist pl ... TN-4
Pisgah View—locale ... CA-9
Pisgah View Ch—church ... NC-3
Pisgah View Memorial Park—cemetery ... NC-3
Pisgah View Sch—school ... TN-4
**Pisgah View (subdivision)**—pop pl ... NC-3
Pisgan Ch—church ... GA-3
Pisgy Cem—cemetery ... OH-6
Pishak Island—island ... AK-9
Pishaqua ... IL-6
Pishel Creek—stream ... NE-7
Pishelville—locale ... NE-7
Pishelville Island—island ... NE-7
Pishewaw Creek ... IN-6
Pishkun Canal—canal ... MT-8
Pishkun Natl Wildlife Ref—park ... MT-8
Pishkun Rsvr—reservoir ... MT-8
**Pishon Ferry**—pop pl ... ME-1
Pish River—stream ... AK-9
Pisht ... WA-9
Pishtaka ... IL-6
Pishtaqua ... IL-6
Pisht River ... WA-9
Pisiinuun ... FM-9
Pisiiras ... FM-9
Pisiiwi ... FM-9
Pisiksagiavik Creek—stream ... AK-9
Pisilemo Island—island ... FM-9
Pisililin Reef ... FM-9
Pisilul ... FM-9
Pisimelikon ... FM-9
Pisimonukun—island ... FM-9
Pisinakich—bar ... FM-9
Pisinemelikomo Island ... FM-9
Pisinemo ... AZ-5
Pisinemo (Pisinimo) ... AZ-5
Pisini ... FM-9
Pisiniache—bar ... FM-9
Pisiniap—island ... FM-9
Pisinifach ... FM-9
**Pisinimo**—pop pl ... AZ-5
Pisinimo Sch—school ... AZ-5
Pisinimo Valley ... AZ-5
Pisinimo Wash—stream ... AZ-5
Pisininil ... FM-9
Pisininin—island ... FM-9
Pisininin, Mochun—channel ... FM-9
Pisinion—bar ... FM-9
Pisiniyap ... FM-9
Pisiniyon ... FM-9
Pisinmelikan ... FM-9
Pisinmelikomo ... FM-9
Pisinmelikon ... FM-9
Pisin Menikomo ... FM-9
Pisin Mo ... AZ-5
Pisinuk—bar ... FM-9
Pisinun—island ... FM-9
Pisira Island—island ... FM-9
Pisiras—island ... FM-9
Pisiron Island ... FM-9
Pisisen—bar ... FM-9
Pis Island ... FM-9
Pis Island—island ... FM-9
Pis Islands—island ... FM-9
Pisitin—island ... FM-9
Pisitul ... FM-9
Pisiula Point—cape ... AS-9
Pisiwi—island ... FM-9
Piskorski Canyon ... AZ-5
Piskover Cem—cemetery ... PA-2
Pis-Losap (Municipality)—civ div ... FM-9
Pismire Camp—locale ... OR-9
Pismire Island ... MA-1
Pismire Island—island ... MI-6
Pismire Knolls—summit ... UT-8
Pismire Mtn—summit ... ME-1
Pismire Ridge—ridge ... CA-9
Pismire Ridge—ridge ... PA-2
Pismire Wash—valley ... UT-8
Pismo—civil ... CA-9
**Pismo Beach**—pop pl ... CA-9
**Pismo Beach (Pismo)**—pop pl ... CA-9
Pismo Bench—bench ... CA-9
Pismo Creek—stream ... CA-9
Pismo Lake—swamp ... CA-9
Pismo (Pismo Beach) ... CA-9
Pismo State Beach—park ... CA-9
Pisnel Tank—reservoir ... NM-5
Piso—locale ... KY-4
Pisor Landing Area—airport ... PA-2
Pisor Sch (historical)—school ... PA-2
Piso Sch—school ... KY-4
Pisos Point Rec Area—locale ... MO-7
Pisoun—locale ... FM-9
Pispis Pass—channel ... FM-9
Pispogutt ... MA-1
Pissamwe Island—island ... FM-9
Pissant Knoll—summit ... UT-8
Pissawack River ... NJ-2
Piss Creek ... OR-9
Pissisin Island—island ... FM-9
Pistakee ... IL-6
**Pistakee**—pop pl ... IL-6
Pistakee Bay—bay ... IL-6
**Pistakee Bay**—pop pl ... IL-6
**Pistakee Heights**—pop pl ... IL-6
**Pistakee Highlands**—pop pl ... IL-6
**Pistakee Hills**—pop pl ... IL-6
Pistakee Lake—lake ... IL-6
Pistapaug Mtn—summit ... CT-1
Pistapaug Pond—reservoir ... CT-1
Pistaqua ... IL-6
**Pistaqua Heights**—pop pl ... IL-6
Pistareen Mtn—summit ... NH-1
Pistner Hill—summit ... PA-2
Pisto Hill—summit ... AZ-5
Pistola Peak ... AZ-5
Pistola Windmill—locale ... TX-5
Pistol Bank—bar ... LA-4
Pistol Barrel Hollow—valley ... MO-7
Pistol Brake (historical)—swamp ... LA-4
Pistol Branch—stream ... NC-3
Pistol Branch—stream ... TN-4
Pistol Branch—stream ... VA-3
Pistol Butte—summit ... AZ-5
Pistol Butte—summit ... NM-5
Pistol Butte—summit ... OR-9
Pistol Canyon—valley ... NM-5
Pistol Creek—stream (2) ... AZ-5
Pistol Creek—stream ... CA-9
Pistol Creek—stream ... GA-3
Pistol Creek—stream (2) ... ID-8
Pistol Creek—stream (4) ... MT-8
Pistol Creek—stream ... TN-4
Pistol Creek—stream ... UT-8
Pistol Creek—stream ... WA-9
Pistol Creek Baptist Ch (historical)—church ... TN-4
Pistol Creek Presbyterian Ch (historical)—church ... TN-4
Pistol Creek Ridge—ridge ... ID-8
Pistol Draw—valley (2) ... WY-8
Pistole Ch—church ... TN-4
Pistole Hollow—valley ... TN-4
Pistole Missionary Baptist Church ... TN-4
Pistoles Ferry (historical)—locale ... AL-4
Pistol Gap—gap ... VA-3
Pistol Green—flat ... ME-1
Pistol Grip Mine—mine ... ID-8
Pistol Island—island ... NH-1
Pistol Lake—lake ... ID-8
Pistol Lake—lake (2) ... MN-6
Pistol Lake—lake ... OR-9
Pistol Park—flat ... CO-8
Pistol Park—park ... AL-4
Pistol Pass—gap ... WA-9
Pistol Peaks—summit ... WA-9
Pistol Point—summit ... WY-8
Pistol Pond—reservoir ... MA-1
**Pistol Ridge**—pop pl ... MS-4
Pistol Ridge—ridge ... MS-4
Pistol Ridge—ridge ... UT-8
Pistol Ridge Oil And Gas Field—oilfield ... MS-4
Pistol River—locale ... OR-9
Pistol River—stream ... OR-9
Pistol River Cem—cemetery ... OR-9
Pistol River State Park—park ... OR-9
Pistol Rock—summit ... ID-8
Pistol Rock Picnic Area—locale ... UT-8
Pistol Run—stream ... IN-6
Pistol Run—stream ... WV-2
Pistol Saddle Tank—reservoir ... AZ-5
Pistol Slough—stream ... MS-4
Pistol Spring—spring ... CA-9
Pistol Spring—spring ... WA-9
Pistol Stream—stream ... ME-1
Pistor Draw ... CO-8
Pistor JHS—school ... AZ-5
Pistuk Peak—summit ... AK-9
Pit, The—bay ... CA-9
Pita, Loma de la—summit ... TX-5
Pita Camp—locale ... TX-5
**Pitahaya**—pop pl (3) ... PR-3
Pitahaya (Barrio)—fmr MCD (2) ... PR-3
Pitahaya Canyon—valley ... AZ-5
Pita Island—island ... TX-5
Pitala Creek ... MI-6
Pitalla Windmill—locale ... TX-5
Pitamakan Lake—lake ... MT-8
Pitamakan Pass ... MT-8
Pitamakan Pass—gap ... MT-8
Pitamakan Pass Trail—trail ... MT-8
Pita Oil Field—oilfield ... TX-5
Pita Pasture—flat ... TX-5
Pita Pens—locale ... TX-5
Pitas Point—cape ... CA-9
Pita West Oil Field—oilfield ... TX-5
Pita Windmill—locale (6) ... TX-5
Pit Branch—stream ... NC-3
Pit Branch—stream ... WV-2
Pitcairn—locale ... ND-7
**Pitcairn**—pop pl ... NY-2
**Pitcairn**—pop pl ... PA-2
Pitcairn Bldg—hist pl ... PA-2
Pitcairn Borough—civil ... PA-2
Pitcairn Building Plus Three Elem Sch—school ... PA-2
Pitcairn Creek—stream ... ND-7
Pitcairn Rsvr—reservoir ... CO-8
**Pitcairn (Town of)**—pop pl ... NY-2
Pitcarin Station—building ... PA-2
Pit Cave—cave ... TN-4
Pitchahala ... MS-4
Pitcha Lake—lake ... MN-6
Pitch and Tar Swamp—swamp ... VA-3
Pitchawam Swamp—swamp ... MA-1
Pitchawawache Swamp ... MA-1
Pitch Branch—stream (2) ... KY-4
Pitch Brook—stream ... CT-1
Pitch Creek ... MT-8
Pitch Creek ... SD-7
Pitch Creek—stream ... ID-8
Pitch Creek—stream ... MI-6
Pitch Creek—stream ... OR-9
Pitch Draw—valley ... WY-8
Pitcher—locale ... MO-7
**Pitcher**—pop pl ... NY-2
Pitcher Branch—stream ... KY-4
Pitcher Brook—stream ... ME-1
Pitcher Brook—stream ... MA-1
Pitcher Canyon—valley ... WA-9
Pitcher Cem—cemetery (2) ... ME-1
Pitcher Cem—cemetery ... MO-7
Pitcher Creek ... MT-8
Pitcher Creek—stream ... CA-9
Pitcher Creek—stream ... IN-6
Pitcher Creek—stream ... IA-7
Pitcher Creek—stream ... MT-8
Pitcher Creek—stream (2) ... OR-9
Pitcher Creek—stream ... TX-5
Pitcher Dam Creek—stream ... MD-2
Pitcher Drain—canal ... MI-6
Pitcher-Goff House—hist pl ... RI-1
**Pitcher Hill**—pop pl ... NY-2
Pitcher Hill—summit ... NH-1
Pitcher Hill—summit ... WY-8
Pitcher Hill Sch—school ... NY-2
Pitcher Hollow—valley ... AR-4
Pitcher Hollow—valley ... IN-6
Pitcher House (Fullinwider House)—hist pl ... IN-6
Pitcher Lake ... MI-6
Pitcher Lake ... WI-6
Pitcher Lake—lake ... IN-6
Pitcher Lake—lake (2) ... MI-6
Pitcher Lake—lake ... MN-6
Pitcher Mtn—summit ... CT-1
Pitcher Mtn—summit ... NH-1
Pitcher Mtn—summit ... WA-9
Pitcher Point—cape ... MS-4
Pitcher Point—cape ... OR-9
Pitcher Pond—lake ... NY-2
Pitcher Pond—reservoir ... ME-1
Pitcher Ranch—locale ... OR-9
Pitcher Ridge—ridge ... TN-4
Pitcher Sch—school ... CA-9
Pitcher Sch—school ... MI-6
Pitcher Sch—school ... MO-7
Pitcher Sch—school ... WA-9
Pitchers Cove—bay ... ME-1
Pitchers Point—cape ... ME-1
Pitchers Point—cape ... NY-2
Pitchers Pond—lake ... CT-1
Pitcher Spring—spring ... WY-8
Pitcher Springs—locale ... NY-2
Pitchers Reef—island ... MI-6
Pitchers Shoal—bar ... MA-1
**Pitcher (Town of)**—pop pl ... NY-2
Pitcher Township—fmr MCD ... IA-7
**Pitcherville**—pop pl ... MA-1
Pitchfork Canyon—valley ... AZ-5
Pitchfork Canyon—valley ... NM-5
Pitchfork Canyon—valley ... TX-5
Pitchfork Canyon Wash—stream ... AZ-5
Pitchfork Cave—cave ... TN-4
Pitchfork Creek—stream (2) ... ID-8
Pitchfork Creek—stream ... MT-8
Pitchfork Ditch—canal ... WY-8
Pitchfork Falls—falls ... AK-9
Pitchfork Flats—flat ... TX-5
Pitchfork Flats Windmill—locale ... TX-5
Pitchfork Lake Swamp—swamp ... MI-6
Pitchfork Mines—mine ... CO-8
Pitchfork Oil Field—oilfield ... WY-8
Pitchfork Pond—lake ... NY-2
Pitchfork Ranch—locale ... CA-9
Pitchfork Ranch—locale ... NM-5
Pitchfork Ranch—locale ... TX-5
Pitchfork Ranch—locale ... WY-8
Pitchfork Ridge—ridge ... OR-9
Pitch Fork Rsvr—reservoir ... OR-9
Pitchfork Sch—school ... NM-5
Pitchfork Spring ... UT-8
Pitchfork Tank—reservoir (2) ... AZ-5
Pitchfork Tank—reservoir ... NM-5
Pitchforth Spring—spring ... UT-8
Pitch Haven Lake—lake ... MI-6
Pitch Hole Gut—stream ... NC-3
Pitch HS—school ... CT-1
Pitchin—locale ... IL-6
**Pitchin**—pop pl ... OH-6
Pitchkettle Ch—church ... NC-3
Pitch Kettle Creek ... VA-3
Pitchkettle Creek—stream ... VA-3
Pitchkettle Landing—locale ... NC-3
Pitch Lake—lake ... OR-9
Pitch Lake—lake ... SC-3
Pitch Landing ... NC-3
Pitch Landing—locale ... NC-3
Pitch Landing—locale (4) ... SC-3
Pitch Landing (historical)—locale ... NC-3
Pitch Lick Branch—stream ... KY-4
Pitch Lodge Lake—lake ... SC-3
Pitch Log Creek—stream ... OR-9
Pitchlynn Cem—cemetery ... MS-4
Pitchlynns Ford (historical)—locale ... MS-4
Pitchoff Mtn—summit (2) ... NY-2
Pitch Pine ... PA-2
Pitchpine Creek—stream ... WY-8
Pitchpine Hill—summit ... ME-1
Pitch Pine Hollow—valley ... PA-2
Pitchpine Ledges—bar ... ME-1
Pitchpine Mtn—summit ... CO-8
Pitchpine Ridge—ridge ... PA-2
Pitch Pine Run ... PA-2
Pitchpine Run—stream ... PA-2
Pitch Pine Trail—trail ... PA-2
Pitch Pot Swamp—swamp ... SC-3
Pitch Rapids—bar ... KY-4
Pitch Rsvr—reservoir ... CT-1
Pitch Spring—spring ... NM-5
Pitchstone Plateau—area ... WY-8
Pitchstone Plateau Trail—trail ... WY-8
Pitch Swamp—swamp ... NY-2
Pitchuk Lake—lake ... AK-9
Pitchwam Swamp ... MA-1
Pitch Windmill—locale ... NM-5
Pitchwood Island—island (2) ... NH-1
Pitco—locale ... CA-9
Pitco—other ... PA-2
Pitcock Branch—stream ... KY-4
Pitcock Cem—cemetery ... TN-4
Pitcock Sch—school ... KY-4
Pitfall Lake—lake ... MN-6
**Pitford Acres Subdivision**—pop pl ... UT-8
Pit Fork—stream ... WV-2
Pit Four Powerhouse—other ... CA-9
Pit Four Rsvr—reservoir ... CA-9
Pit Gap—gap ... TN-4
Pit Glacier—glacier ... WA-9
Pithlachascootie River ... FL-3
Pithlachascotee River—stream ... FL-3
Pit Hole ... PA-2
Pithole City—locale ... PA-2
Pithole City, Site of—hist pl ... PA-2
Pithole City Historical Site—park ... PA-2
Pithole Creek—stream ... PA-2
Pithole Stone Arch—hist pl ... PA-2
Pit Hole Tank—reservoir ... AZ-5
**Piti**—pop pl ... GU-9
Piti Bay—bay ... GU-9
Piti Canal—canal ... GU-9
Piti Channel—channel ... GU-9
Piti Coastal Defense Guns—hist pl ... GU-9
Piti (Election District)—fmr MCD ... GU-9
Piti Powerplant—other ... GU-9
Pitis ... FL-3
Pitka Fork Hodzana River—stream ... AK-9
Pitka Fork Middle Fork Kuskokwim River—stream ... AK-9
Pitka Lake—lake ... AK-9
Pitka River—stream ... AK-9
Pitkas Bar—bar ... AK-9
Pitkas Point—cape ... AK-9
**Pitkas Point**—pop pl ... AK-9
Pitka's Point—post sta ... AK-9
Pitkas Point(P.O. Name Pitkas's Point) ANV899—8reserve ... AK-9
Pitkik Creek—stream ... AK-9
Pitkik Lake—lake ... AK-9
**Pitkin**—pop pl ... CO-8
**Pitkin**—pop pl ... LA-4
Pitkin, Elisha, House—hist pl ... CT-1
Pitkin Campground—locale ... CO-8
Pitkin Cem—cemetery ... OH-6
Pitkin Corner—locale ... AR-4
Pitkin County Courthouse—hist pl ... CO-8
Pitkin Creek—stream ... CO-8
Pitkin Glassworks Ruin—hist pl ... CT-1
Pitkin Lake—lake ... CO-8
Pitkin Mesa—summit ... CO-8
Pitkin Place Hist Dist—hist pl ... CO-8
Pitkin Stock Driveway—trail ... CO-8
Pit Lake ... OR-9
Pit Lake—lake ... MI-6
Pit Lake—lake (2) ... MN-6
Pit Lake—lake ... WI-6
Pit Lakes—lake ... WA-9
Pitman—airport ... NJ-2
Pitman—locale ... AR-4
Pitman—locale ... KY-4
**Pitman**—pop pl ... NJ-2
**Pitman**—pop pl ... PA-2
Pitman, Benn, House—hist pl ... OH-6
Pitman-Barnes Cem—cemetery ... NC-3
Pitman Bay—bay ... FL-3
Pitman Branch—stream (2) ... AL-4
Pitman Branch—stream ... FL-3
Pitman Branch—stream ... GA-3
Pitman Branch—stream ... KY-4
Pitman Branch—stream ... SC-3
Pitman Branch—stream ... TX-5
Pitman Canyon—valley (2) ... CA-9
Pitman Cem—cemetery ... IN-6
Pitman Cem—cemetery ... IA-7
Pitman Cem—cemetery ... MO-7
Pitman Cem—cemetery ... TX-5
Pitman Cem—cemetery ... WV-2
Pitman Chapel Cem—cemetery ... IA-7
Pitman Country Club—other ... NJ-2
Pitman Cove—bay ... VA-3
Pitman Creek ... KY-4
Pitman Creek—bay ... NC-3
Pitman Creek—stream ... AR-4
Pitman Creek—stream ... CA-9
Pitman Creek—stream ... IA-7
Pitman Creek—stream (4) ... KY-4
Pitman Creek—stream ... MS-4
Pitman Creek—stream ... VA-3
Pitman Creek Ch—church ... KY-4
Pitman Creek Sch (historical)—school ... MS-4
Pitman Field—park ... AL-4
Pitman Grove ... NJ-2
Pitman Grove—hist pl ... NJ-2
Pitman Hill ... MA-1
Pitman Hill—summit ... MA-1
Pitman Hollow—valley ... AR-4
Pitman Hollow—valley ... TX-5
Pitman Lake—lake ... WA-9
Pitman Mill Branch—stream ... NC-3
Pitman Park—park ... GA-3
Pitman P.O. (historical)—building ... PA-2
Pitman Pond—lake ... ME-1
Pitman Road Mission—church ... NC-3
Pitman Rock—rock ... MA-1
Pitmans Cave—cave ... IN-6
Pitman Sch—school ... KY-4
Pitman Sch—school ... MO-7
Pitman Sch (historical)—school ... MS-4
Pitmans Corner—locale ... ME-1
**Pitmans Corner**—pop pl ... VA-3
Pitmans Creek—stream ... KY-4
Pitmans Grove Ch—church ... NC-3
Pitmans Mill (historical)—locale ... MS-4
Pitmans Point—cape ... WI-6
Pitmans Store ... NC-3
**Pitman (Township of)**—pop pl ... IL-6
Pitman Valley—valley ... AZ-5
Pitman Valley Sch—school ... KY-4
Pitmegea River—stream ... AK-9
Pitmik River—stream ... AK-9
Pitmon Crossroad—locale ... SC-3
Pitner Branch—stream ... GA-3
Pitner Creek—stream ... TN-4
Pitner Ditch—canal ... IN-6
Pitner Field—park ... TN-4
Pitner Hill—summit ... GA-3
Pitner Junction—locale ... TX-5
Pitner Sch—school ... TN-4
Pitney Butte—summit ... WA-9
Pitney Canyon—valley ... CA-9
Pitney Creek—stream ... WA-9
Pitney Ridge—ridge (2) ... CA-9
Pit Number Five Dam—dam ... CA-9
Pit Number Five Powerhouse—other ... CA-9
Pit Number Four Dam—dam ... CA-9
Pit Number Three Dam—dam ... CA-9
Pit Number Two Tank—reservoir ... AZ-5
Pit of Hades ... UT-8
Pitoi Kam ... AZ-5
Pitoikam—locale ... AZ-5
Pitoikam Ranch ... AZ-5
Pitoso Artesian Well—well ... TX-5
Pitot, I—slope ... MH-9
Pitot, Kannat I—stream ... MH-9
Pitot House—hist pl ... LA-4
Pit Place Prairie ... CA-9
Pit Place Prairie—area ... CA-9
Pit Pond—reservoir ... MA-1
Pit Pond Dam—dam ... MA-1
Pitre, Isle au—island ... LA-4
Pitre Cem—cemetery (2) ... LA-4
Pitre Lening Canal—canal ... LA-4
Pitre Sch—school ... LA-4
**Pitreville**—pop pl ... LA-4
Pit River—locale ... CA-9
Pit River—stream ... CA-9
Pit River Arm—bay ... CA-9
Pit River Falls—falls ... CA-9
Pit River Station ... CA-9
Pit Rock—island ... AK-9
**Pitrodie (historical)**—pop pl ... SD-7
Pit Run—stream (2) ... IN-6
**Pitsburg**—pop pl ... OH-6
Pitsch Rsvr—reservoir ... WY-8
Pitsch Sch—school ... WI-6
Pitsebytso ... AZ-5
Pitsehytso ... AZ-5
Pitship Point—cape ... WA-9
Pit Spring—spring ... AZ-5
Pitsua Butte—summit ... OR-9
Pitt ... AL-4
Pitt—locale ... MN-6
**Pitt**—pop pl ... SC-3
**Pitt**—pop pl ... WA-9
Pitt—uninc pl ... NY-2
Pitt, Arthur, House and Distillery—hist pl ... TN-4
Pitt, Newton M., House—hist pl ... NY-2
Pittalukruak Lake—lake ... AK-9
Pitt and Page Hill—summit ... UT-8
Pittang ... PW-9
Pit Tank—reservoir (6) ... AZ-5
Pit Tank—reservoir (5) ... NM-5
Pit Tank—reservoir ... TX-5
Pit Tank Number One—reservoir ... AZ-5
Pit Tank Number Two—reservoir ... AZ-5
Pittard Cave—cave ... TN-4
Pittard Cem—cemetery ... TN-4
Pittard Vocational Sch—school ... AL-4
Pitt Bayou ... FL-3
Pitt Branch—stream ... GA-3
Pitt Branch—stream ... MS-4
Pitt Branch—stream ... SC-3
Pitt Bridge—bridge ... NE-7
Pitt-Bursby Cem—cemetery ... TN-4
Pitt Cem—cemetery ... MO-7
Pitt Cem—cemetery (4) ... TN-4
**Pittco**—pop pl ... VA-3
**Pitt County**—pop pl ... NC-3
Pitt County Administrative Office and Board of Education—building ... NC-3
Pitt County Courthouse—hist pl ... NC-3
Pitt County Memorial Hosp—hospital ... NC-3
Pitt County Memorial Hospital Airp—airport ... NC-3
Pitt County Poor Farm—locale ... NC-3
Pitt County Poor Farms—locale ... NC-3
Pitt Creek—stream ... FL-3
Pitt Creek—stream ... ND-7
Pitt Creek—stream ... TX-5
Pitt Creek Cem—cemetery ... TX-5
Pitt Crossroads—locale ... NC-3
Pitt Dam—dam ... NV-8
Pitt Ditch—canal ... UT-8
Pitt Draw—valley ... CO-8
Pitt Draw—valley ... UT-8
Pitted Plain ... WY-8
Pittenger Cem—cemetery ... OH-6
Pittenger Creek—stream ... OR-9
Pittewomuck Neck ... RI-1
Pitt Gap ... TN-4
**Pitt Gas**—pop pl ... PA-2
**Pitt Gas (Clyde No. 2)**—pop pl ... PA-2
Pitt Grade Trail—trail ... MN-6
Pitt-Greenville Airp—airport ... NC-3
Pitt Hill—summit ... MA-1
Pitt Hill—summit ... TN-4
Pitt (historical)—locale ... KS-7
Pitticfaw ... MS-4
Pittiefaw ... MS-4
Pittillo Lanning Cem—cemetery ... NC-3
**Pittinger**—pop pl ... AR-4
Pitt Island—island ... AK-9
Pitt Island—island ... WA-9
Pitt Lake—lake ... CA-9
Pitt Lake—lake ... OR-9
Pitt Lake Dam—dam ... OR-9
Pitt Land Slide Pond—lake ... FL-3
Pittman ... AL-4
Pittman ... NV-8
Pittman ... PA-2
Pittman—locale ... AK-9
Pittman—locale ... MS-4
**Pittman**—pop pl (2) ... FL-3
**Pittman**—pop pl ... GA-3
**Pittman**—pop pl ... MS-4
**Pittman**—pop pl ... WV-2
Pittman, Lake—reservoir ... AL-4
Pittman Bay—swamp ... AL-4
Pittman Bay—swamp ... FL-3
Pittman Bay—swamp (2) ... GA-3
Pittman Branch—stream (2) ... GA-3
Pittman Branch—stream (2) ... KY-4
Pittman Branch—stream (2) ... MS-4
Pittman Branch—stream ... SC-3
Pittman Branch—stream ... TN-4
Pittman Brothers Lake—reservoir ... AL-4
Pittman Brothers Lake Dam—dam ... AL-4
Pittman Cem ... AL-4
Pittman Cem—cemetery ... AL-4
Pittman Cem—cemetery ... AR-4
Pittman Cem—cemetery (3) ... GA-3
Pittman Cem—cemetery ... IN-6
Pittman Cem—cemetery (2) ... KY-4
Pittman Cem—cemetery (6) ... MS-4
Pittman Cem—cemetery (3) ... NC-3
Pittman Cem—cemetery ... TN-4
**Pittman Center**—pop pl ... TN-4
Pittman Chapel—church ... GA-3
**Pittman Corner**—pop pl ... SC-3
Pittman Creek—stream (2) ... FL-3
Pittman Creek—stream ... GA-3
Pittman Creek—stream ... NC-3
Pittman Creek—stream ... TX-5
Pittman Creek Ch—church ... FL-3
Pittman Ditch—canal ... IN-6
Pittman Draw—valley ... MT-8
Pittman Draw Spring—spring ... MT-8
Pittman Elem Sch—school ... AZ-5
Pittman Gordon Ditch—canal ... IN-6
Pittman Grove Ch—church ... NC-3
Pittman Hill ... MA-1
Pittman Hill—summit ... KY-4
Pittman Hill Ch—church ... FL-3
Pittman Hills JHS—school ... MO-7
Pittman Hollow—valley ... IN-6
Pittman HS—school ... AL-4
Pittman Interchange—crossing ... AZ-5
Pittman Island—area ... MS-4
Pittman Island—island ... LA-4
Pittman Island Landing—locale ... MS-4
Pittman JHS—school ... AL-4
Pittman Lake—lake ... WA-9
Pittman Lake—reservoir ... GA-3
Pittman Lakes Dam Number 2—dam ... AL-4
Pittman Park Ch—church ... GA-3
Pittman Plaza—locale ... VA-3
Pittman Point—cape ... TN-4
Pittman Rsvr—reservoir ... MT-8
Pittman Sch—school ... MO-7
Pittman Sch—school ... NV-8
Pittman Sch—school ... NC-3
Pittman Sch (historical)—school ... AL-4
Pittman Sch (historical)—school ... TN-4
Pittman School—locale ... AR-4
Pittmans Ferry (historical)—locale ... MS-4
Pittmans Lake ... AL-4
Pittmans Mill Branch—stream ... GA-3
Pittmans Pond—lake ... GA-3
Pittman Square Elem Sch—school ... IN-6
Pittman Square Park—park ... IN-6
**Pittmans Store (Hickory Cross Roads)**—pop pl ... NC-3
Pittman-Sullivan Park—park ... TX-5
Pittman Swamp—swamp ... FL-3
Pittmantown—locale ... VA-3
Pittman Trail—trail ... PA-2
Pittman Well—well ... WY-8
Pittman Work Center—locale ... FL-3
Pitt Memorial Hospital ... NC-3
**Pittock**—pop pl ... PA-2
Pittock Bird Sanctuary—park ... OR-9
Pittock Block—hist pl ... OR-9
Pittock Brook—stream ... NY-2
Pittock House—hist pl ... WA-9
Pittock Mansion—hist pl ... OR-9
Pittock Pass—gap ... AK-9
Pitt Passage—channel ... WA-9
Pitt Place Prairie—area ... CA-9
Pitt Place Prairie—flat ... CA-9
Pitt Plaza Shopping Center ... NC-3
Pitt Point—cape ... AK-9
Pitt Post Office (historical)—building ... AL-4
Pitt River ... CA-9
Pitts ... NC-3
Pitts ... TX-5
Pitts—locale ... KY-4
Pitts—locale ... PA-2
**Pitts**—pop pl ... AR-4
**Pitts**—pop pl ... GA-3

**Pitts**—pop pl ... MS-4
**Pitts**—pop pl ... OH-6
Pitts, Thomas H., House and Dairy—hist pl ... GA-3
Pitts Bayou—stream ... FL-3
Pitts Bend—bend ... OK-5
Pitts Bend—bend (3) ... TN-4
*Pittsboro* ... AL-4
**Pittsboro**—pop pl ... IN-6
**Pittsboro**—pop pl ... MS-4
**Pittsboro**—pop pl ... NC-3
Pittsboro Acad (historical)—school ... MS-4
Pittsboro Baptist Ch—church ... MS-4
Pittsboro Cem—cemetery ... MS-4
Pittsboro Elem Sch—school ... NC-3
Pittsboro HS—school ... NC-3
Pittsboro Male and Female Coll (historical)—school ... MS-4
Pittsboro Masonic Lodge—hist pl ... NC-3
Pittsboro Presbyterian Church—hist pl ... NC-3
Pittsboro Sch—school ... IN-6
*Pittsborough* ... AL-4
*Pittsborough* ... IN-6
Pittsboro United Methodist Ch—church ... MS-4
Pitts Branch—stream ... KY-4
Pitts Branch—stream ... LA-4
Pitts Branch—stream ... MS-4
Pitts Branch—stream ... SC-3
Pitts Branch—stream (2) ... TN-4
*Pittsburg* ... IN-6
*Pittsburg* ... MS-4
*Pittsburg* ... PA-2
Pittsburg—locale ... CO-8
Pittsburg—locale ... FL-3
Pittsburg—locale ... PA-2
Pittsburg—locale ... SC-3
Pittsburg—locale ... UT-8
**Pittsburg**—pop pl ... AL-4
**Pittsburg**—pop pl ... CA-9
**Pittsburg**—pop pl ... GA-3
**Pittsburg**—pop pl (2) ... IL-6
**Pittsburg**—pop pl ... IN-6
**Pittsburg**—pop pl ... IA-7
**Pittsburg**—pop pl ... KS-7
**Pittsburg**—pop pl ... KY-4
**Pittsburg**—pop pl ... MI-6
**Pittsburg**—pop pl ... MO-7
**Pittsburg**—pop pl ... NH-1
**Pittsburg**—pop pl ... NC-3
**Pittsburg**—pop pl ... ND-7
**Pittsburg**—pop pl ... OK-5
**Pittsburg**—pop pl ... OR-9
**Pittsburg**—pop pl ... TX-5
Pittsburg, Cincinnati, and St. Louis Depot—hist pl ... OH-6
Pittsburg, Mount—summit ... CO-8
Pittsburg Bar—bar ... ID-8
Pittsburg Bar—bar ... OR-9
Pittsburg (CCD)—cens area ... TX-5
Pittsburg Cem—cemetery ... MS-4
Pittsburg Cem—cemetery ... OK-5
Pittsburg Ch—church ... AR-4
Pittsburg Ch—church ... MO-7
**Pittsburg (County)**—pop pl ... OK-5
Pittsburg County Courthouse—hist pl ... OK-5
Pittsburg Creek—gut ... MI-6
Pittsburg Creek—stream ... OR-9
**Pittsburg East Census Area**—pop pl ... CA-9
Pittsburg Ford—locale ... MS-4
Pittsburg Guard Station—locale ... OR-9
*Pittsburg Gulch* ... OR-9
Pittsburg Gulch—valley ... OR-9
*Pittsburgh* ... IN-6
*PittsbuRgh* ... KS-7
Pittsburgh—locale ... ND-7
**Pittsburgh**—pop pl ... PA-2
Pittsburgh and Lake Erie RR Complex—hist pl ... PA-2
Pittsburgh And Lake Erie Station—locale ... PA-2
Pittsburgh Athletic Association Bldg—hist pl ... PA-2
Pittsburgh Ave Sch—school ... OH-6
Pittsburgh Aviary Conservatory—park ... PA-2
Pittsburgh Boquet Airpark—airport ... PA-2
Pittsburgh Brewing Company—building ... PA-2
Pittsburgh Central Downtown Hist Dist—hist pl ... PA-2
Pittsburgh Childrens Museum—building ... PA-2
Pittsburgh City—civil ... PA-2
Pittsburgh Creek—stream ... AK-9
Pittsburgh Field Club—other ... PA-2
Pittsburgh Hill—summit ... CA-9
Pittsburgh (historical)—locale ... MS-4
Pittsburgh (historical)—locale ... ND-7
Pittsburgh HS for Creative and Performing Arts—school ... PA-2
*Pittsburgh Interchange* ... PA-2
**Pittsburgh Junction**—pop pl ... OH-6
Pittsburgh Junction Stock Yard Station—building ... PA-2
Pittsburgh & Lake Erie RR Station—hist pl ... PA-2
*Pittsburgh Landing* ... TN-4
Pittsburgh-Monroeville Airp—airport ... PA-2
Pittsburgh North Golf Course—locale ... PA-2
Pittsburgh Plate Glass Bldg—building ... PA-2
Pittsburgh Plate Glass Company Bldg—hist pl ... MN-6
**Pittsburgh Plate Plan**—pop pl ... PA-2
Pittsburgh Playhouse—building ... PA-2
Pittsburgh Sch (historical)—school ... MS-4
Pittsburgh Theological Seminary—school ... PA-2
Pittsburgh Tuberculosis Sanitarium—hospital ... PA-2
**Pittsburgh Valley**—pop pl ... PA-2
**Pittsburgh West End**—pop pl ... PA-2
*Pittsburgh YMCA Camp* ... PA-2
*Pittsburgh YMCA Lake* ... PA-2
*Pittsburg Lake* ... MN-6
Pittsburg Lake—lake ... UT-8
Pittsburg Lake—reservoir ... OK-5
Pittsburg Landing—locale ... TN-4
Pittsburg Landing Public Use Area—park ... MO-7
**Pittsburg & Lehigh Junction**—pop pl ... NY-2
Pittsburg Liberty Mine—mine ... CA-9
Pittsburg Mine—mine ... AZ-5
Pittsburg Mine—mine (2) ... CO-8
Pittsburg Mine—mine (2) ... NV-8
Pittsburg MS—school ... KS-7
Pittsburg Oil Field—oilfield ... TX-5
Pittsburg Point—cape ... CA-9
Pittsburg Point—island ... AZ-5
Pittsburg Public Library—hist pl ... KS-7
Pittsburg Saddle—gap ... ID-8
Pittsburg Sch and Gymnasium—hist pl ... OK-5
Pittsburg State Univ—school ... KS-7
Pittsburg Tonto Mine—mine ... AZ-5
**Pittsburg (Town of)**—pop pl ... NH-1
**Pittsburg Township**—pop pl ... KS-7
Pittsburg (Township of)—fmr MCD ... AR-4
*Pittsburg West (census name West Pittsburg)* ... CA-9
Pitts Camp—locale ... FL-3
Pitts (CCD)—cens area ... GA-3
*Pitts Cem* ... TN-4
Pitts Cem—cemetery (2) ... GA-3
Pitts Cem—cemetery ... IA-7
Pitts Cem—cemetery ... KY-4
Pitts Cem—cemetery ... MS-4
Pitts Cem—cemetery ... NC-3
Pitts Cem—cemetery ... SC-3
Pitts Cem—cemetery (4) ... TN-4
Pitts Cem—cemetery ... TX-5
Pitts Cem—cemetery ... WA-9
Pitts Cem (historical)—cemetery ... MO-7
Pitts Chapel—church ... AL-4
Pitts Chapel—church (3) ... GA-3
Pitts Chapel—church ... MS-4
Pitts Chapel—church ... NC-3
Pitts Chapel Cem—cemetery ... AL-4
Pitts Chapel Cem—cemetery ... MO-7
*Pitts Chapel Church* ... AL-4
Pitts Cove—bay ... NC-3
*Pitts Creek* ... MD-2
*Pitts Creek* ... VA-3
Pitts Creek—stream (2) ... FL-3
Pitts Creek—stream (2) ... GA-3
Pitts Creek—stream ... MD-2
Pitts Creek—stream ... MI-6
Pitts Creek—stream ... OK-5
Pitts Creek—stream ... VA-3
Pitts Creek Ch—church ... MD-2
Pitts Cross Roads Post Office (historical)—building ... TN-4
Pitts Drain—stream ... MI-6
Pittsfield—locale ... WI-6
**Pittsfield**—pop pl ... IL-6
**Pittsfield**—pop pl ... ME-1
**Pittsfield**—pop pl ... MA-1
**Pittsfield**—pop pl ... MI-6
**Pittsfield**—pop pl ... NH-1
**Pittsfield**—pop pl ... NY-2
**Pittsfield**—pop pl ... OH-6
**Pittsfield**—pop pl ... PA-2
**Pittsfield**—pop pl ... VT-1
Pittsfield Cem—cemetery ... MA-1
Pittsfield Center (census name Pittsfield)—other ... ME-1
Pittsfield Center Hist Dist—hist pl ... NH-1
**Pittsfield Compact (census name Pittsfield)**—pop pl ... NH-1
Pittsfield Country Club—locale ... MA-1
Pittsfield East Sch—hist pl ... IL-6
Pittsfield Hist Dist—hist pl ... IL-6
Pittsfield HS—school ... MA-1
Pittsfield Mall—locale ... MA-1
Pittsfield Municipal Airp—airport ... MA-1
Pittsfield & North Adams Passenger Station, Baggage & Express House—hist pl ... MA-1
Pittsfield Number Five Drain—stream ... MI-6
**Pittsfield (Pecktown)**—pop pl ... NY-2
Pittsfield Plantation—locale ... LA-4
Pittsfield Plaza, The—locale ... MA-1
Pittsfield Public Library—hist pl ... ME-1
Pittsfield RR Station—hist pl ... ME-1
Pittsfield Sch—school ... MI-6
Pittsfield State For—forest ... MA-1
Pittsfield State Watershed Area—park ... MA-1
Pittsfield (Town of)—civil ... MA-1
**Pittsfield (Town of)**—pop pl ... ME-1
**Pittsfield (Town of)**—pop pl ... NH-1
**Pittsfield (Town of)**—pop pl ... NY-2
**Pittsfield (Town of)**—pop pl ... VT-1
**Pittsfield (Town of)**—pop pl ... WI-6
**Pittsfield (Township of)**—pop pl ... IL-6
**Pittsfield (Township of)**—pop pl ... MI-6
**Pittsfield (Township of)**—pop pl ... OH-6
**Pittsfield (Township of)**—pop pl ... PA-2
Pittsfield Universalist Church—hist pl ... ME-1
*Pittsfield Village* ... MI-6
Pitts Folly—building ... AL-4
Pitts' Folly—hist pl ... AL-4
**Pittsford**—pop pl ... MI-6
**Pittsford**—pop pl ... NY-2
**Pittsford**—pop pl ... VT-1
Pittsford Ditch—canal ... IN-6
Pittsford Green Hist Dist—hist pl ... VT-1
Pittsford HS—school ... NY-2
Pittsford JHS—school ... NY-2
Pittsford Millpond—reservoir ... MI-6
Pittsford State Game Area—park ... MI-6
**Pittsford (Town of)**—pop pl ... NY-2
**Pittsford (Town of)**—pop pl ... VT-1
Pittsford Township—fmr MCD ... IA-7
**Pittsford (Township of)**—pop pl ... MI-6
Pittsford Village Hist Dist—hist pl ... NY-2
Pitts Fork—stream ... KY-4
Pitts Fork Sch—school ... KY-4
Pitts Gap—gap ... TN-4
Pitts Gas Field—oilfield ... TX-5
Pitts Gin (historical)—locale ... AL-4
**Pittsgrove (Pole Tavern)**—pop pl ... NJ-2
Pittsgrove Presbyterian Church—hist pl ... NJ-2
Pitts Grove Sch (historical)—school ... MO-7
**Pittsgrove (Township of)**—pop pl ... NJ-2
*Pitts Hbll* ... MA-1
*Pitts Hollow* ... MO-7
Pitts Hollow—valley ... AL-4
Pitts Hollow—valley (2) ... KY-4
Pitts Hollow—valley (4) ... TN-4
Pitts Homestead Tank—reservoir ... AZ-5
Pitts-Inge—hist pl ... VA-3
Pittsinger Brook—stream ... MA-1
Pitt Sinkhole Cave—cave ... AL-4
Pitts Island—island ... FL-3
Pitts Island—island ... VA-3
Pitts JHS—school ... CO-8
Pitts Lake—lake ... MN-6
Pitts Lake—reservoir ... SC-3
Pitts Meadow—flat ... CO-8
Pitts Memorial Ch—church ... GA-3
Pitts Mill Creek—stream ... FL-3
Pitts Mill Pond—lake ... FL-3
Pitts Mission Ch—church ... KY-4
Pitts Mission Ch—church ... NC-3
Pitts Mtn—summit ... TX-5
Pitts Neck—cape ... VA-3
Pitts Neck—hist pl ... VA-3
Pitts Park—park ... NY-2
Pitts Pasture Tank—reservoir ... NM-5
**Pitts (Pittsville)**—pop pl ... TX-5
Pitts Point—basin ... FL-3
Pitts Point—cape ... VA-3
Pitts Point—locale ... KY-4
Pitts Pond—swamp ... TX-5
Pitt Spring—spring ... VA-3
Pitt Spring Run—stream ... VA-3
Pitts Ranch—locale ... SD-7
*Pitts River* ... CA-9
Pitts River—stream ... FL-3
Pitts Run—stream ... WV-2
Pitts Savanna—basin ... SC-3
Pitts Sch—school ... CO-8
Pitts Sch—school ... IL-6
Pitts Sch—school (2) ... KY-4
Pitts Spring—spring ... TN-4
**Pitts Subdivision**—pop pl ... UT-8
Pitt Stadium—other ... PA-2
Pitts Tank—reservoir ... AZ-5
**Pittston**—pop pl ... ME-1
**Pittston**—pop pl ... PA-2
**Pittston**—pop pl ... VA-3
Pittston Academy Grant—unorg ... ME-1
Pittston City—civil ... PA-2
Pittston Congregational Church—hist pl ... ME-1
Pittston Farm—locale ... ME-1
Pittston Junction—locale ... AR-4
Pittston Junction—locale ... PA-2
Pittston Station—locale ... PA-2
**Pittston (Town of)**—pop pl ... ME-1
**Pittston (Township of)**—pop pl ... PA-2
Pittston Yards—locale ... PA-2
*Pitts Town* ... NJ-2
**Pittstown**—pop pl ... NJ-2
**Pittstown**—pop pl ... NY-2
**Pittstown (Town of)**—pop pl ... NY-2
**Pittsview**—pop pl ... AL-4
Pittsview Cem—cemetery ... AL-4
*Pittsville* ... AL-4
*Pittsville* ... PA-2
Pittsville—locale ... TX-5
Pittsville—locale ... VA-3
**Pittsville**—pop pl ... MD-2
**Pittsville**—pop pl ... MO-7
**Pittsville**—pop pl ... PA-2
**Pittsville**—pop pl ... WI-6
Pittsville Ch—church ... VA-3
**Pittsville (Freedom)**—pop pl ... PA-2
Pittsville Post Office (historical)—building ... PA-2
Pittsylvania Church Camp—locale ... VA-3
**Pittsylvania (County)**—pop pl ... VA-3
Pittsylvania County Courthouse—hist pl ... VA-3
Pittsylvania Wayside Park—park ... VA-3
Pitt Tank—reservoir (2) ... AZ-5
Pitt-Taylor Dam—dam ... NV-8
Pitt-Taylor Diversion Canal—canal ... NV-8
Pitt Technological Institute—school ... NC-3
**Pitt (Township of)**—pop pl ... OH-6
**Pittville**—pop pl ... CA-9
**Pittville**—pop pl ... PA-2
Pit Twentyfive Mine (surface)—mine ... AL-4
Pit Twenty Mine (surface)—mine ... AL-4
Pit Twentytwo Mine (surface)—mine ... AL-4
Pitt Wildwood Club—other ... PA-2
**Pittwood**—pop pl ... IL-6
Pittwood Creek—stream ... ID-8
Pit Windmill—locale ... NM-5
*Pitwood Creek* ... ID-8
Pitzer—locale ... IA-7
Pitzer, Anthony, Jr., House—hist pl ... OH-6
Pitzer Cem—cemetery ... IN-6
Pitzer Coll—school ... CA-9
Pitzer House—hist pl ... CA-9
Pitzer Oil Field—oilfield ... TX-5
Pitzer Run—stream ... IN-6
Pitzer Sch—school ... MT-8
Pitzer Sch—school ... PA-2
Pitzers Chapel Cem—cemetery ... WV-2
Pitzman Sch—school ... IL-6
Pitz Mtn—summit ... ID-8
Pitzner Site (47 Je 676)—hist pl ... WI-6
Piuge Brothers Lake—reservoir ... TN-4
Piuge Brothers Lake Dam—dam ... TN-4
Piumafua Mtn—summit ... AS-9
Pius Aberle Dam—dam ... SD-7
Pius Draw—valley ... AZ-5
Pius Farm Draw—valley ... AZ-5
Pius Heights—uninc pl ... KY-4
Piuss Butte—summit ... ND-7
Pius Spring—spring ... AZ-5
Pius Tank—reservoir ... AZ-5
Pius X Central HS—school ... NY-2
Pius X HS—school ... CA-9
Pius X HS—school ... NE-7
Pius X HS—school ... NM-5
Pius X HS—school ... TX-5
Pius X HS (Pius 10)—school ... PA-2
Piuta Camp—locale ... UT-8
*Piuta MIA Camp* ... UT-8
Piute—locale ... NV-8
Piute Basin—basin ... ID-8
Piute Basin Camp—locale ... ID-8
Piute Basin Rsvr—reservoir ... ID-8
Piute Butte—summit ... CA-9
Piute Butte—summit (2) ... ID-8
Piute Cabin—locale ... CA-9
Piute Campground—park (2) ... UT-8
*Piute Campground and Parking Area* ... UT-8
Piute Canal—canal ... UT-8
Piute Canyon—valley ... AZ-5
Piute Canyon—valley (2) ... CA-9
Piute Canyon—valley (2) ... NV-8
Piute Canyon—valley (3) ... UT-8
*Piute Canyon Creek* ... AZ-5
Piute County—civil ... UT-8
Piute County Courthouse—hist pl ... UT-8
*Piute Creek* ... CO-8
*Piute Creek* ... NV-8
*Piute Creek* ... OR-9
*Piute Creek* ... UT-8
Piute Creek—stream ... AZ-5
Piute Creek—stream (5) ... CA-9
Piute Creek—stream ... CO-8
Piute Creek—stream ... ID-8
Piute Creek—stream ... MT-8
Piute Creek—stream (2) ... NV-8
Piute Creek—stream (2) ... OR-9
Piute Creek—stream ... UT-8
Piute Creek Rsvr—reservoir ... ID-8
Piute Dam—dam ... OR-9
Piute Dam—dam ... UT-8
Piute Farms—locale ... UT-8
Piute Farms Wash—valley ... UT-8
Piute HS—school ... UT-8
Piute Indian Reservation-Cedar City—reserve ... UT-8
*Piute Indian Tribal Lands* ... UT-8
*Piute Ind Res* ... AZ-5
Piute Lake—lake (2) ... CA-9
Piute Lake Bed—flat ... OR-9
*Piute Lake State Beach* ... UT-8
Piute Lake State Park—park ... UT-8
Piute Lateral—canal ... WA-9
Piute Meadow—flat ... CA-9
Piute Mesa—summit ... AZ-5
Piute Mesa—summit ... UT-8
Piute Mine—mine ... CA-9
Piute Mine—mine ... NV-8
Piute Mountains—range ... CA-9
Piute Mtn—summit (2) ... CA-9
*Piute Parking* ... UT-8
Piute Pass—gap (2) ... CA-9
Piute Pass—gap ... UT-8
Piute Pass Archeol District—hist pl ... CA-9
Piute Peak—summit ... CA-9
Piute Point—cliff ... AZ-5
Piute Point—summit ... NV-8
Piute Ponds—reservoir ... CA-9
Piute Ranch—locale ... CA-9
Piute Range—range ... CA-9
Piute Range—range ... NV-8
Piute Rock—pillar ... OR-9
Piute Rsvr—reservoir ... CO-8
Piute Rsvr—reservoir ... OR-9
Piute Rsvr—reservoir ... UT-8
Piute Spring—spring (2) ... CA-9
Piute Spring—spring ... NV-8
Piute Spring—spring ... OR-9
Piute Spring—spring ... UT-8
*Piute Springs* ... CA-9
*Piute State Park* ... UT-8
Piute Valley—valley (3) ... CA-9
Piute Valley—valley ... NV-8
*Piute Wash* ... UT-8
Piute Wash—stream ... CA-9
Piute Wash—stream ... NV-8
Pivahn-hon-kya-pi—locale ... AZ-5
*Pi Va Hon Kia Pi* ... AZ-5
**Pi Va Hon Kia Pi**—pop pl ... AZ-5
Pivash Creek—stream ... ID-8
Piver Bays—swamp ... NC-3
Pivers Island—island ... NC-3
*Pivetot Gully* ... TX-5
*Pivitot Bayou* ... TX-5
Pivot Mtn—summit ... MT-8
Pivoto Cem—cemetery ... TX-5
Pivot Point—cape ... AK-9
Pivot Rock—pillar ... AR-4
Pivot Rock—summit ... PA-2
Pivot Rock Canyon—valley ... AZ-5
Pivot Rock Hollow—valley ... AR-4
*Pivot Rock Spring* ... AZ-5
Pivotrock Spring—spring ... AZ-5
Piwai Rsvr—reservoir ... HI-9
Pi-wan-go-ning Prehistoric District—hist pl ... MI-6
Pix Bldg—hist pl ... TX-5
Pixie Mtn—summit ... NC-3
Pixie Private Sch Dillman Acad—school ... FL-3
Pixley—locale ... KS-7
Pixley—locale ... WY-8
**Pixley**—pop pl ... CA-9
Pixley Basin—basin ... ID-8
Pixley Brook—stream ... MA-1
Pixley Canyon—valley ... CA-9
Pixley (CCD)—cens area ... CA-9
Pixley Creek—stream ... ID-8
Pixley Creek—stream ... NV-8
Pixley Creek—stream ... WI-6
Pixley Creek—stream (2) ... WY-8
Pixley Dam—dam ... WI-6
Pixley Dam—dam ... WY-8
Pixley Ditch—canal ... WY-8
Pixley Falls—falls ... NY-2
Pixley Flowage—reservoir ... WI-6
Pixley Lake—lake ... MN-6
Pixley Natl Wildlife Ref—park ... CA-9
Pixley Park—park ... NY-2
Pixley Rsvr—reservoir ... WY-8
*Pixleys Brook* ... MA-1
Pixley Sch—school ... NE-7
Pixley Slough—stream ... CA-9
**Pixley (Township of)**—pop pl ... IL-6
Pixley Union Sch—school ... CA-9
Pix Mine—mine ... OR-9
*Piyaanu* ... FM-9
Piyas Lake—lake ... SD-7
*Piyesics Piesit* ... FM-9
*Piyokon-to* ... MP-9
*Piyoto Island* ... MP-9
*Piyoto-to* ... MP-9
Piyukenuk River—stream ... AK-9
Pizarro—locale ... VA-3
Pizarro—locale ... WA-9
Pizer Creek—stream ... OR-9
Pizer Meadow—flat ... OR-9
Pizion Pass—channel ... FM-9
Pizitz MS—school ... AL-4
Pizona—locale ... CA-9
Pizona Creek—stream ... CA-9
Pizona Creek—stream ... NV-8
*Pizza Pan Arch* ... UT-8
Pizzle Knob—summit ... NC-3
PI-19 Airp—airport ... NC-3
P J Hoffmaster State Park—park ... MI-6
PJ Lake—lake ... WA-9
P-Kaw-Shun Creek—stream ... LA-4
P K Cow Camp—locale ... WY-8
P K Creek—stream ... MT-8
PK Creek—stream ... OR-9
P K Ditch—canal ... WY-8
P K Draw—valley ... WY-8
Pkin—locale ... VA-3
P K Pass—gap ... ID-8
P K Ranch—locale ... CA-9
P K Ranch—locale ... WY-8
P K Spring—spring ... MT-8
*Pkuiamieg* ... PW-9
*Pkula Belu* ... PW-9
*Pkulagabad* ... PW-9
*Pkulagalid* ... PW-9
*Pkulagalid Point* ... PW-9
*Pkulagasemieg* ... PW-9
*Pkulagolid* ... PW-9
*Pkulaibelau* ... PW-9
*Pkulaklim* ... PW-9
*Pkulamieg* ... PW-9
*Pkulamieg Point* ... PW-9
*Pkul A Mlagalp* ... PW-9
*Pkulangelel* ... PW-9
*Pkulangelul* ... PW-9
*Pkul a Ngesang* ... PW-9
*Pkulapelu* ... PW-9
*Pkulapnei* ... PW-9
*Pkulapngei* ... PW-9
*Pkulatap Erivall* ... PW-9
*Pkulataprangaregolong* ... PW-9
*Pkulataprival* ... PW-9
*Pkul a Tmolial* ... PW-9
*Pkulengril* ... PW-9
*Pkul Medorum* ... PW-9
*Pkulmeig* ... PW-9
*Pkul N* ... PW-9
*Pkul Ngaramudel* ... PW-9
*Pkul Ngariois* ... PW-9
*Pkul Ngerdesiuur* ... PW-9
*Pkulngril* ... PW-9
*Pkulngril Point* ... PW-9
*Pkulopelu* ... PW-9
*Pkulrengereiolong Head* ... PW-9
*Pkulrengereiong Head* ... PW-9
*Pkulrengerelong* ... PW-9
Pkulrengerelong Point—cape ... PW-9
*Pkulrival* ... PW-9
*Pkuludedes* ... PW-9
*Pkurengel* ... PW-9
**Plaat Clove**—pop pl ... NY-2
Plaat Clove Ch—church ... NY-2
*Plaaterkill Clove* ... NY-2
*Plaaterkill Creek* ... NY-2
*Place* ... KY-4
Place—other ... KY-4
**Place**—pop pl ... NH-1
Place Brook—stream ... NY-2
Place Corners—locale ... NY-2
Place Creek—stream ... MT-8
*Place Ditch* ... IN-6
Place Ditch Arm—canal ... IN-6
**Placedo**—pop pl ... TX-5
Placedo Creek—stream ... TX-5
Placedo Oil Field—oilfield ... TX-5
Placedor Gulch—valley ... OR-9
Placedo Windmill—locale ... TX-5
Place for the Gospel Baptist Ch—church ... TN-4
Place JHS—school ... CO-8
Place Mesa—summit ... CO-8
*Placenta Island* ... ME-1
**Placentia**—pop pl ... CA-9
Placentia, Lake—reservoir ... OH-6
Placentia Canal—canal ... GA-3
Placentia Island—island ... ME-1
*Place of Rest* ... MA-1
Place of the Oaks—locale ... CA-9
Place Pond—reservoir ... PA-2
*Place Prairie* ... CA-9
**Placer**—pop pl ... MT-8
**Placer**—pop pl ... OR-9
Placer Basin—basin ... ID-8
Placer Basin—basin ... MT-8
Placer Basin Creek—stream ... MT-8
Placer Canyon—valley ... CA-9
Placer Ch—church ... CA-9
**Placer (County)**—pop pl ... CA-9
Placer County Grove Sierra Redwoods—park ... CA-9
*Placer Creek* ... WY-8
Placer Creek—stream (5) ... AK-9
Placer Creek—stream ... CA-9
Placer Creek—stream (3) ... CO-8
Placer Creek—stream (15) ... ID-8
Placer Creek—stream (6) ... MT-8
Placer Creek—stream (2) ... NM-5
Placer Creek—stream ... UT-8
Placer Creek—stream ... WY-8
Placer Diggings—locale ... CA-9
Placer Ditch—canal ... OR-9
Placer Draw—valley ... CO-8
*Place Reservoir* ... RI-1
Placer Flat—flat ... ID-8
Placer Fork—stream ... NM-5
Placer Gulch—valley ... AZ-5
Placer Gulch—valley ... CO-8
Placer Gulch—valley ... ID-8
Placer Gulch—valley (2) ... MT-8
Placer Gulch—valley ... OR-9
Placer Gulch Spring—spring ... NV-8
Placer Hills Union Sch—school ... CA-9
Placerita—locale ... AZ-5
Placerita Canyon—valley ... CA-9
Placerita Canyon State Park—park ... CA-9
Placerita Creek—stream ... CA-9
Placerita Gulch—valley ... AZ-5
Placerita Gulch—valley ... WY-8
Placeritas Creek—stream ... AZ-5
Placeritas Creek—stream ... CA-9
Placeritas Spring—spring ... CA-9
Placerites—locale ... NV-8
Placerito Canyon—valley ... AZ-5
*Placeritos Canyon* ... CA-9
Placeritos Ranch—locale ... CA-9
Placeritos Wash—stream ... AZ-5
Placer Lake—lake ... OR-9
Placer Lake—lake ... WA-9
Placer Lakes—lake ... AK-9
Placer Mine—mine ... CA-9
Placer Mine—mine ... ID-8
Placer Mine—mine ... OR-9
Placer Mines—mine ... MT-8
Placer Mtn—summit ... NM-5
Placer Peak—summit ... AZ-5
Placer Peak—summit ... ID-8
Placer Queen Mine—mine ... CA-9
Placer River—stream ... AK-9
Placer River Valley—valley ... AK-9
Placer Sch—school ... CA-9
Placer Tank—reservoir ... AZ-5
*Placerville* ... SD-7
**Placerville**—pop pl ... CA-9
**Placerville**—pop pl ... CO-8
**Placerville**—pop pl ... ID-8
Placerville (Aban'd)—locale ... AK-9
Placerville-Camino Junior Acad—school ... CA-9
Placerville Camp—locale ... SD-7
Placerville (CCD)—cens area ... CA-9
Placerville Hist Dist—hist pl ... ID-8
Places Corner—locale ... RI-1
Places Lake—lake ... WI-6
*Places Pond* ... NH-1
Places Pond—lake ... PA-2
Placeway Cem—cemetery ... MI-6
Place Windmill—locale ... NM-5
Placid—locale ... TX-5
Placid, Lake—harbor ... FL-3
Placid, Lake—lake (2) ... FL-3
Placid, Lake—lake ... MI-6
Placid, Lake—lake ... MO-7
Placid, Lake—lake ... OK-5
Placid, Lake—lake ... TX-5
Placid, Lake—lake ... WI-6
Placid, Lake—reservoir ... GA-3
Placid, Lake—reservoir ... IN-6
Placid, Lake—reservoir ... MD-2
Placid, Lake—reservoir ... NY-2
Placid, Lake—reservoir ... TN-4
Placid, Lake—reservoir (2) ... TX-5
**Placida**—pop pl ... FL-3
*Placida Bayou* ... FL-3
Placida Ch—church ... FL-3
Placida Harbor—bay ... FL-3
**Placid Cove Subdivision**—pop pl ... UT-8
Placid Creek—stream ... MT-8
Placid Et Al State No 1—other ... AK-9
*Placidia Lake* ... MA-1
Placid Lake—lake ... CO-8
Placid Lake—lake ... MN-6
Placid Lake—lake ... MT-8
Placid Lake—lake ... WA-9
Placid Lake—reservoir ... PA-2
Placid Lake—reservoir ... VA-3
Placid Lake Dam—dam ... PA-2
Placid Lake Sch—school ... MT-8
**Placid Meadows**—pop pl ... OH-6
Placid Memorial Hosp—hospital ... NY-2
Placido Bayou—bay ... FL-3
*Placido Creek* ... TX-5
*Placido River* ... TX-5
Placid Park—park ... FL-3
Placid Pond—lake ... NY-2
Placid Twin Lakes—lake ... WI-6
*Placita* ... NM-5
Placita—locale ... CO-8
Placita Canyon—valley ... NM-5
**Placita (Rio Pueblo)**—pop pl ... NM-5
Placitas—locale ... NM-5
**Placitas**—pop pl (3) ... NM-5
Placitas Arroyo—stream ... NM-5
Placitas Canyon—valley ... NM-5
**Placitas (Placita)**—pop pl ... NM-5
**Plad**—pop pl ... MO-7
**Plada Heights**—pop pl ... TN-4
Plad Sch (abandoned)—school ... MO-7
Plaggemeyer Homestead—locale ... MT-8
Plagmann Round Barn—hist pl ... IA-7
Plague Mine Creek—stream ... IA-7
**Plaice Cove**—pop pl ... NH-1
*Plain* ... MS-4
*Plain* ... PA-2
Plain—locale ... WA-9
**Plain**—pop pl ... MA-1
**Plain**—pop pl ... MS-4
**Plain**—pop pl ... WI-6
Plain, The—flat ... NH-1
*Plain Brook* ... MA-1
Plain Cem—cemetery ... MA-1
Plain Cem—cemetery (2) ... VT-1
*Plain Cemetery* ... MS-4
*Plain Center Heights* ... OH-6
Plain Center Sch—school ... OH-6
**Plain Center Township**—pop pl ... SD-7
Plain Ch—church (2) ... OH-6
Plain Ch—church ... TX-5
Plain Ch—church ... VA-3
**Plain City**—pop pl ... OH-6
**Plain City**—pop pl ... UT-8
Plain City Canal—canal ... UT-8
Plain City Cem—cemetery ... UT-8
Plain City Sch—school ... UT-8
*Plain (corporate name Richland)* ... MS-4
**Plaincourtville**—pop pl ... LA-4
Plain Dealing—hist pl ... VA-3
**Plain Dealing**—pop pl ... LA-4
Plain Dealing Cem—cemetery ... LA-4
Plaindealing Creek—bay ... MD-2
Plain Dealing Lookout Tower—locale ... LA-4
Plain Dealing Oil Field—oilfield ... LA-4
Plain Drain—stream (2) ... IN-6
**Plainedge**—pop pl ... NY-2
Plainedge HS—school ... NY-2
**Plaines**—pop pl ... IL-6
Plaines Cem—cemetery ... OH-6
Plain Farm House—hist pl ... RI-1
*Plainfield* ... WI-6
Plainfield—locale ... AR-4
Plainfield—locale ... CA-9
Plainfield—locale ... PA-2
**Plainfield**—pop pl ... CT-1
**Plainfield**—pop pl ... GA-3
**Plainfield**—pop pl ... IL-6
**Plainfield**—pop pl (2) ... IN-6
**Plainfield**—pop pl ... IA-7
**Plainfield**—pop pl ... MD-2
**Plainfield**—pop pl (2) ... MA-1
**Plainfield**—pop pl ... MI-6
**Plainfield**—pop pl ... NH-1
**Plainfield**—pop pl ... NJ-2
**Plainfield**—pop pl ... OH-6
**Plainfield**—pop pl ... PA-2
**Plainfield**—pop pl ... TN-4
**Plainfield**—pop pl ... VT-1
**Plainfield**—pop pl ... WV-2

**Plainfield**—*pop pl* WI-6
Plainfield, Lake—*lake* IL-6
**Plainfield Acres**—*pop pl* IL-6
**Plainfield addition (subdivision)**—*pop pl* TN-4
Plainfield Cem—*cemetery* CT-1
Plainfield Cem—*cemetery* KS-7
Plainfield Cem—*cemetery* MI-6
Plainfield Cem—*cemetery* NE-7
Plainfield Cem—*cemetery* NH-1
Plainfield Cem—*cemetery* (2) OH-6
Plainfield Cem—*cemetery* WI-6
**Plainfield Center**—*pop pl* NY-2
Plainfield Center Cem—*cemetery* VT-1
**Plainfield Center (census name Plainfield)**—*pop pl* CT-1
Plainfield Ch—*church* NC-3
Plainfield Ch of God—*church* PA-2
*Plainfield Church* PA-2
Plainfield Country Club—*other* NJ-2
Plainfield Ementary Sch—*school* PA-2
Plainfield Halfway House—*hist pl* IL-6
**Plainfield Heights**—*pop pl* MI-6
Plainfield (historical)—*civil* MA-1
Plainfield (historical)—*locale* SD-7
Plainfield Junior and Senior HS—*school* IN-6
Plainfield Lake—*lake* WI-6
Plainfield Park—*park* MI-6
Plainfield Pond—*lake* MA-1
Plainfield Sch—*school* IL-6
Plainfield Sch—*school* MI-6
Plainfield Sch—*school* PA-2
Plainfields Sch—*school* OH-6
Plainfield Station—*hist pl* NJ-2
Plainfield Station—*locale* NJ-2
**Plainfield Subdivision**—*pop pl* TN-4
Plainfield Town Hall—*hist pl* NH-1
**Plainfield (Town of)**—*pop pl* CT-1
**Plainfield (Town of)**—*pop pl* MA-1
**Plainfield (Town of)**—*pop pl* NH-1
**Plainfield (Town of)**—*pop pl* NY-2
**Plainfield (Town of)**—*pop pl* VT-1
**Plainfield (Town of)**—*pop pl* WI-6
**Plainfield Township**—*pop pl* SD-7
Plainfield Township Elem Sch—*school* PA-2
**Plainfield (Township of)**—*pop pl* IL-6
**Plainfield (Township of)**—*pop pl* (2) MI-6
**Plainfield (Township of)**—*pop pl* PA-2
Plainfield Village Hist Dist—*hist pl* VT-1
Plainfield Woolen Company Mill—*hist pl* CT-1
Plain Grove—*locale* PA-2
**Plain Grove**—*pop pl* TN-4
Plain Grove Sch (historical)—*school* TN-4
**Plain Grove (Township of)**—*pop pl* PA-2
Plain Hill—*locale* CT-1
Plain Landmark Missionary Baptist Ch—*church* MS-4
Plainlawn Cem—*cemetery* NY-2
*Plain Meadow* MA-1
Plainmont Cem—*cemetery* VT-1
Plain Mountain Well—*well* NM-5
Plain Mtn—*summit* AK-9
Plain Nine Dam—*dam* PA-2
Plain Nine Rsvr—*reservoir* PA-2
Plain Pond—*lake* ME-1
Plain Pond—*lake* RI-1
Plain Post Office (historical)—*building* TX-5
Plain Run Branch—*stream* VA-3
*Plains* NH-1
Plains—*locale* FL-3
Plains—*locale* MI-6
Plains—*locale* NJ-2
Plains—*locale* TX-5
**Plains**—*pop pl* GA-3
**Plains**—*pop pl* KS-7
**Plains**—*pop pl* LA-4
**Plains**—*pop pl* MT-8
**Plains**—*pop pl* PA-2
**Plains**—*pop pl* SC-3
**Plains**—*pop pl* TX-5
Plains, Lake of The—*lake* MI-6
*Plains, The* MA-1
*Plains, The* NH-1
Plains, The—*area* RI-1
Plains, The—*flat* (2) ME-1
Plains, The—*flat* (2) MA-1
Plains, The—*flat* NH-1
Plains, The—*flat* (4) NY-2
Plains, The—*flat* (2) OH-6
Plains, The—*plain* ME-1
Plains, The—*plain* NC-3
Plains, The—*plain* UT-8
**Plains, The**—*pop pl* NH-1
**Plains, The**—*pop pl* NY-2
**Plains, The**—*pop pl* OH-6
**Plains, The**—*pop pl* VA-3
**Plains Assembly**—*pop pl* TX-5
**Plainsboro**—*pop pl* NJ-2
Plainsboro Pond—*reservoir* NJ-2
Plainsboro Pond Dam—*dam* NJ-2
**Plainsboro (Township of)**—*pop pl* NJ-2
*Plainsborough* NJ-2
Plains Branch—*stream* NJ-2
**Plainsburg**—*pop pl* CA-9
Plains (CCD)—*cens area* GA-3
Plains (CCD)—*cens area* TX-5
Plains Cem—*cemetery* CT-1
Plains Cem—*cemetery* ME-1
Plains Cem—*cemetery* MI-6
Plains Cem—*cemetery* NH-1
Plains Cem—*cemetery* NY-2
Plains Cem—*cemetery* VT-1
Plains Cem, The—*cemetery* NY-2
Plains Ch—*church* MI-6
Plains Ch—*church* (2) NC-3
Plains Ch—*church* PA-2
Plain Sch—*school* (2) VT-1
Plain Sch (historical)—*school* TX-5
Plains Community—*locale* CO-8
Plains Corral—*locale* TX-5
Plains Creek—*stream* MI-6
Plains Creek—*stream* SD-7
*Plains Crossing* MI-6
*Plains Cross Roads* TN-4
Plains Gas Plant—*oilfield* TX-5
Plains Hist Dist—*hist pl* GA-3
Plains (historical), The—*civil* MA-1
Plains JHS—*school* PA-2
Plains Junction—*locale* TX-5
Plains Junction—*uninc pl* PA-2
*Plains Lake* MI-6
Plains Lake—*lake* (2) MI-6
Plains (Magisterial District)—*fmr MCD* VA-3
Plainsman Club Dam—*dam* AL-4
Plainsman Lake—*reservoir* AL-4
Plains Mill—*locale* VA-3
Plains Municipal Airp—*airport* KS-7
Plains Of San Agustin—*area* NM-5
Plains Oil Field—*oilfield* TX-5
Plains Sch—*school* (2) MA-1
Plains Sch—*school* MI-6
Plains Sch—*school* NH-1
Plains School, The—*school* OH-6
Plains Substation—*other* NM-5
Plains Tank—*reservoir* NM-5
**Plains (Township of)**—*pop pl* PA-2
Plains Valley—*valley* SD-7
**Plainsville**—*pop pl* PA-2
Plainsville Ch—*church* MS-4
Plains Windmill—*locale* (3) TX-5
Plain Tank—*reservoir* AZ-5
Plain Tank Flat—*flat* AZ-5
Plain Township—*civil* SD-7
**Plain Township**—*pop pl* ND-7
**Plain (Township of)**—*pop pl* IN-6
**Plain (Township of)**—*pop pl* (4) OH-6
Plain Tree Sch—*school* IL-6
Plain Truth Apostolic Ch—*church* AL-4
Plain Valley Sch—*school* NE-7
*Plain View* IA-7
*Plainview* MS-4
*Plainview* TX-5
Plainview—*locale* AL-4
Plainview—*locale* AR-4
Plainview—*locale* (3) GA-3
Plainview—*locale* LA-4
Plainview—*locale* MO-7
Plainview—*locale* OH-6
Plainview—*locale* (3) OK-5
Plainview—*locale* OR-9
Plainview—*locale* PA-2
Plainview—*locale* (6) TX-5
Plain View—*locale* VA-3
**Plainview**—*pop pl* AL-4
**Plain View**—*pop pl* AL-4
**Plainview**—*pop pl* AL-4
**Plainview**—*pop pl* (2) AR-4
**Plainview**—*pop pl* CA-9
**Plainview**—*pop pl* CO-8
**Plainview**—*pop pl* IL-6
**Plainview**—*pop pl* IA-7
**Plainview**—*pop pl* LA-4
**Plainview**—*pop pl* MN-6
**Plainview**—*pop pl* MS-4
**Plainview**—*pop pl* MO-7
**Plainview**—*pop pl* NE-7
**Plainview**—*pop pl* NY-2
**Plain View**—*pop pl* NC-3
**Plainview**—*pop pl* NC-3
**Plain View**—*pop pl* OH-6
**Plainview**—*pop pl* (2) OR-9
**Plainview**—*pop pl* SD-7
**Plainview**—*pop pl* TN-4
**Plainview**—*pop pl* (2) TX-5
**Plain View**—*pop pl* VA-3
Plainview—*post sta* KY-4
Plainview Ave Sch—*school* CA-9
Plainview Baptist Ch—*church* AL-4
Plainview Baptist Ch—*church* KS-7
Plainview Baptist Ch—*church* TN-4
Plainview (CCD)—*cens area* TX-5
Plainview Cem—*cemetery* CO-8
Plainview Cem—*cemetery* IN-6
Plainview Cem—*cemetery* IA-7
Plainview Cem—*cemetery* KS-7
Plainview Cem—*cemetery* MA-1
Plainview Cem—*cemetery* (2) MO-7
Plainview Cem—*cemetery* (5) NE-7
Plain View Cem—*cemetery* ND-7
Plainview Cem—*cemetery* OH-6
Plainview Cem—*cemetery* (4) OK-5
Plainview Cem—*cemetery* SD-7
Plainview Cem—*cemetery* TN-4
Plain View Cem—*cemetery* TX-5
Plainview Cem—*cemetery* (2) TX-5
Plainview Cem—*cemetery* (2) WY-8
*Plain View Cemetery* MS-4
*Plainview Ch* AL-4
*Plainview Ch* MO-7
Plainview Ch—*church* (2) AL-4
Plain View Ch—*church* AL-4
Plainview Ch—*church* AL-4
Plainview Ch—*church* (3) AR-4
Plainview Ch—*church* CO-8
Plainview Ch—*church* FL-3
Plainview Ch—*church* GA-3
Plain View Ch—*church* GA-3
Plainview Ch—*church* (2) GA-3
Plainview Ch—*church* IL-6
Plainview Ch—*church* IN-6
Plainview Ch—*church* (2) KS-7
Plainview Ch—*church* KY-4
Plainview Ch—*church* (2) LA-4
Plainview Ch—*church* (3) MS-4
Plainview Ch—*church* (5) MO-7
Plain View Ch—*church* (2) NC-3
Plainview Ch—*church* (4) NC-3
Plainview Ch—*church* OH-6
Plainview Ch—*church* (3) OK-5
Plainview Ch—*church* SD-7
Plainview Ch—*church* (3) TN-4
Plainview Ch—*church* (3) TX-5
Plain View Ch—*church* VA-3
Plainview Ch—*church* WV-2
Plainview Ch of Christ—*church* KS-7
Plainview Ch of God in Christ—*church* KS-7
Plainview Christian Day Sch—*school* OH-6
Plainview Church—*cemetery* IN-6
**Plainview Colony**—*pop pl* SD-7
Plainview Colony Number Two—*locale* SD-7
Plainview Commercial Hist Dist—*hist pl* TX-5
Plainview Community Hall—*building* TX-5
**Plainview (Condon)**—*pop pl* TN-4
*Plainview Congregational Holiness Ch* AL-4
Plainview Country Club—*other* NE-7
Plainview Country Club—*other* TX-5
Plainview Creek—*stream* OR-9
Plainview Creek—*stream* WA-9
Plainview Dam—*dam* TN-4
Plainview Ditch—*canal* OR-9
Plainview Farm—*hist pl* OH-6
Plainview Gate—*locale* AR-4
Plainview Group Mine—*mine* NV-8
**Plainview Heights**—*pop pl* TN-4
Plainview (historical)—*locale* SD-7
Plain View (historical P.O.)—*locale* IA-7
Plainview Lake—*reservoir* TN-4
Plainview Lookout Tower—*locale* LA-4
Plainview Lookout Tower—*locale* MI-6
Plainview Memorial Cem—*cemetery* IN-6
Plainview Memorial Park (Cemetery)—*cemetery* TX-5
Plainview-Old Bethpage HS—*school* NY-2
Plainview-Old Bethpage JHS—*school* NY-2
Plainview Outflow Ditch—*canal* TX-5
Plainview Park—*park* KS-7
Plainview Park (historical)—*park* PA-2
Plain View Peak—*summit* AZ-5
*Plainview Point* AZ-5
Plainview R-8 Sch—*school* MO-7
*Plainview Sch* AL-4
Plainview Sch—*school* (2) AL-4
Plainview Sch—*school* AR-4
Plainview Sch—*school* CO-8
Plainview Sch—*school* (3) IL-6
Plainview Sch—*school* IA-7
Plainview Sch—*school* (3) KS-7
Plainview Sch—*school* LA-4
Plainview Sch—*school* MI-6
Plainview Sch—*school* (2) MO-7
Plainview Sch—*school* MT-8
Plainview Sch—*school* (5) NE-7
Plain View Sch—*school* NE-7
Plainview Sch—*school* NE-7
Plainview Sch—*school* NM-5
Plain View Sch—*school* (2) NC-3
Plainview Sch—*school* ND-7
Plainview Sch—*school* (3) OK-5
Plainview Sch—*school* (2) OR-9
Plainview Sch—*school* SC-3
Plainview Sch—*school* (5) SD-7
Plain View Sch—*school* SD-7
Plainview Sch—*school* (2) SD-7
Plain View Sch—*school* TN-4
Plainview Sch—*school* TX-5
Plainview Sch—*school* (2) WI-6
Plain View Sch—*school* WI-6
Plainview Sch—*school* (3) WI-6
Plainview Sch (historical)—*school* (2) SD-7
Plainview Sch (historical)—*school* (2) TN-4
Plain View Sch (historical)—*school* TN-4
Plainview Sch Number 1—*school* (2) ND-7
Plainview Sch Number 2—*school* (2) ND-7
Plainview School—*locale* CO-8
Plain View School—*locale* CO-8
Plainview School (Abandoned)—*locale* NE-7
Plainview School No 62 (Abandoned)—*locale* NE-7
Plainview Site—*hist pl* TX-5
**Plainview Township**—*pop pl* KS-7
**Plainview Township**—*pop pl* ND-7
**Plainview Township**—*pop pl* SD-7
Plain View (Township of)—*fmr MCD* NC-3
**Plainview (Township of)**—*pop pl* MN-6
*Plainville* (2) RI-1
Plainville—*locale* NJ-2
Plainville—*locale* PA-2
Plainville—*locale* WI-6
**Plainville**—*pop pl* CT-1
**Plainville**—*pop pl* GA-3
**Plainville**—*pop pl* IL-6
**Plainville**—*pop pl* IN-6
**Plainville**—*pop pl* KS-7
**Plainville**—*pop pl* (3) MA-1
**Plainville**—*pop pl* NJ-2
**Plainville**—*pop pl* NY-2
**Plainville**—*pop pl* OH-6
Plainville Airpark—*airport* KS-7
Plainville Cem—*cemetery* IN-6
Plainville Cem—*cemetery* KS-7
Plainville Cem—*cemetery* MA-1
Plainville Ch—*church* NJ-2
Plainville Creek—*stream* WI-6
Plainville Elem Sch—*school* KS-7
**Plainville (historical)**—*pop pl* MA-1
Plainville HS—*school* KS-7
*Plainville Lake* KS-7
Plainville Pond—*lake* MA-1
Plainville Rsvr—*reservoir* CT-1
Plainville Sch—*school* MA-1
Plainville Stadium—*other* CT-1
**Plainville (Town of)**—*pop pl* CT-1
**Plainville (Town of)**—*pop pl* MA-1
*Plainville Township* KS-7
Plainville Township Lake—*reservoir* KS-7
Plainway Baptist Ch—*church* MS-4
**Plainwell**—*pop pl* MI-6
Plain Well—*well* NM-5
Plainwell Dam—*dam* MI-6
Plainwell Ditch—*canal* CO-8
Plair Ch—*church* MS-4
**Plairs**—*pop pl* MS-4
*Plair United Methodist Church* MS-4
**Plaisance**—*pop pl* LA-4
Plaisance Sch—*school* LA-4
**Plaisted**—*pop pl* ME-1
Plaisted Creek—*stream* CA-9
**Plaistow**—*pop pl* NH-1
Plaistow Carhouse—*hist pl* NH-1
**Plaistow (Town of)**—*pop pl* NH-1
Plaman Lake—*lake* MN-6
Plambeck, Joachim, House—*hist pl* IA-7
Plana—*locale* SD-7
**Planada**—*pop pl* CA-9
Planada Canal—*canal* CA-9
Planada-Le Grand (CCD)—*cens area* CA-9
*Planarbis Lake* WI-6
Planas (Barrio)—*fmr MCD* PR-3
**Plan Bonito**—*pop pl* PR-3
Plancha Mtn—*summit* AZ-5
Plan de Barajas, Arroyo—*valley* TX-5
Plan de Monterrey—*flat* TX-5
**Plandome**—*pop pl* NY-2
**Plandome Heights**—*pop pl* NY-2
**Plandome Manor**—*pop pl* NY-2
Plandome Road Sch—*school* NY-2
**Plane Bank**—*pop pl* PA-2
Planebrook—*locale* PA-2
Plane Brook—*stream* CT-1
Planebrook Post Office (historical)—*building* PA-2
**Planehaven**—*pop pl* CA-9
**Plane Number Four**—*pop pl* MD-2
**Planeport**—*pop pl* TX-5
Planer Branch—*stream* MO-7
Planeria Lake—*lake* AK-9
*Planer Mills* LA-4
Plane Rock—*summit* AZ-5
Planet—*locale* AZ-5
Planetarium—*uninc pl* NY-2
Planet Creek—*stream* MT-8
Planet Lake—*lake* WI-6
Planet Mine—*mine* AZ-5
Planet Peak—*summit* AZ-5
Planet Ranch—*locale* AZ-5
Planet Rock—*island* CT-1
Planet Saturn Mine—*mine* AZ-5
Plane View Airfield—*airport* CO-8
Planing Mill Hollow—*valley* PA-2
*Plank* IN-6
Plank—*locale* KY-4
**Plank**—*pop pl* PA-2
Plank Bank—*mine* MO-7
Plank Branch—*stream* KY-4
*Plank Bridge* NC-3
Plank Bridge Bayou—*gut* TX-5
Plank Bridge Creek—*stream* PA-2
Plank Bridge Hill—*summit* NY-2
Plank Bridge Lake—*lake* FL-3
Plank Cabin Spring—*spring* CA-9
Plank Camp Creek—*stream* VA-3
Plank Cem—*cemetery* (2) MO-7
Plank Cem—*cemetery* NY-2
Plank Cem—*cemetery* PA-2
Plank Cem—*cemetery* TN-4
Plank Ch—*church* KY-4
Plank Creek—*stream* GA-3
Plank Creek—*stream* ID-8
Plank Creek—*stream* OR-9
Plank Creek—*stream* PA-2
Plank Hill—*summit* OR-9
Plank Hill—*summit* PA-2
Plank Hollow—*valley* MO-7
Plank Hollow—*valley* PA-2
Plank House—*locale* TX-5
**Plankinton**—*pop pl* SD-7
Plankinton Cem—*cemetery* SD-7
**Plankinton Township**—*pop pl* SD-7
Plankinton-Wells-Water Street Hist Dist—*hist pl* WI-6
Plank Landing—*locale* GA-3
Plank Landing—*locale* NC-3
Plank Pond—*lake* NY-2
Plankroad Branch—*stream* NC-3
Plank Road Cem—*cemetery* OH-6
Plank Road Ch—*church* LA-4
Plank Road Ch—*church* VA-3
Plank Road Gap—*gap* AL-4
Plankroad Gap—*gap* NC-3
Plank Road Hollow—*valley* PA-2
Plank Road Meadow—*flat* IL-6
Plank Road Sch—*school* (3) PA-2
Plank Road Sch (historical)—*school* (2) PA-2
Plank Road Schools—*school* NY-2
Plank Road Shop Ctr—*locale* NC-3
Plank Run—*stream* KY-4
Plank Run—*stream* NJ-2
Plank Run—*stream* WV-2
Plank Sch (abandoned)—*school* PA-2
Plank Shoals (historical)—*bar* AL-4
Plank Spring—*spring* NV-8
Plank Spring—*spring* TN-4
**Plankton**—*pop pl* OH-6
**Planktown**—*pop pl* OH-6
Plank Township—*fmr MCD* IA-7
Plank Trail—*trail* PA-2
Plank Well—*well* NM-5
Planner Cove—*bay* VA-3
Planning Lake—*lake* WI-6
Plano—*locale* MO-7
Plano—*locale* OH-6
**Plano**—*pop pl* AL-4
**Plano**—*pop pl* CA-9
**Plano**—*pop pl* ID-8
**Plano**—*pop pl* IL-6
**Plano**—*pop pl* IN-6
**Plano**—*pop pl* IA-7
**Plano**—*pop pl* KY-4
**Plano**—*pop pl* SD-7
**Plano**—*pop pl* TX-5
Plano, Lake—*lake* IL-6
Plano (CCD)—*cens area* TX-5
Plano Cem—*cemetery* ID-8
Plano Cem—*cemetery* IL-6
Plano Ch—*church* KY-4
Plano de Choche—*area* TX-5
Plano (historical)—*locale* SD-7
Plano Post Office (historical)—*building* AL-4
Planorbis Lake—*lake* WI-6
Plano Sch—*school* MO-7
Plano Sch—*school* SD-7
Plano Sch (historical)—*school* OR-9
**Plano Township**—*pop pl* SD-7
Plano Trabuco—*bench* CA-9
Plans, The—*flat* CT-1
Plans, The—*island* CT-1
**Plant**—*pop pl* AR-4
**Plant**—*pop pl* TN-4
Plant, Morton Freeman, Hunting Lodge—*hist pl* CT-1
Plant, Samuel, House—*hist pl* MO-7
*Plantaganette* MN-6
Plantagenet, Lake—*lake* MN-6
*Plantagenette* MN-6
*Plantagenian Fork* MN-6
Planta Hidroelectrica Comerio Numero 1—*building* PR-3
Planta Hidroelectrica Comerio Numero 2—*building* PR-3
Planta Hidroelectrica de Rio Blanco—*building* PR-3
Plantain, Mount—*summit* MA-1
Plantain Pond—*reservoir* MA-1
Plantain Pond Dam—*dam* MA-1
**Plantaje**—*pop pl* (2) PR-3
Plantatation Trail—*trail* PA-2
Planta Termoelectrica De Palo Seco—*other* PR-3
*Plantation* CT-1
Plantation—*locale* CA-9
Plantation—*locale* VA-3
**Plantation**—*pop pl* (2) FL-3
**Plantation**—*pop pl* KY-4
**Plantation**—*pop pl* MS-4
**Plantation**—*pop pl* TX-5
Plantation, The—*locale* CA-9
**Plantation, The**—*pop pl* NH-1
**Plantation Acres**—*pop pl* LA-4
**Plantation Acres**—*pop pl* NC-3
**Plantation Acres**—*pop pl* OH-6
**Plantation Acres (subdivision)**—*pop pl* FL-3
Plantation (CCD)—*cens area* FL-3
Plantation Center Shopping Plaza—*locale* FL-3
Plantation Ch—*church* MS-4
Plantation Christian Acad—*school* FL-3
Plantation Country Club—*other* LA-4
*Plantation Creek* ID-8
Plantation Creek—*channel* GA-3
Plantation Creek—*stream* ID-8
Plantation Creek—*stream* WV-2
Plantation Early Childhood Sch—*school* FL-3
Plantation Elem Sch—*school* FL-3
**Plantation Estates (subdivision)**—*pop pl* NC-3
Plantation Fork—*stream* (2) WV-2
**Plantation Gardens**—*pop pl* FL-3
Plantation General Hosp—*hospital* FL-3
Plantation Gulch—*valley* CA-9
**Plantation Heights**—*pop pl* VA-3
**Plantation Hills**—*pop pl* TN-4
**Plantation Homes (subdivision)**—*pop pl* MS-4
Plantation HS—*school* FL-3
Plantation Inn Golf Course—*locale* PA-2
Plantation Island—*island* FL-3
Plantation Island—*locale* FL-3
**Plantation Isles**—*pop pl* FL-3
Plantation Key—*island* FL-3
**Plantation Key**—*pop pl* FL-3
**Plantation Key Colony (subdivision)**—*pop pl* FL-3
Plantation Key Elem Sch—*school* FL-3
Plantation Lake—*lake* LA-4
Plantation Lake—*lake* MN-6
Plantation Lake—*lake* (2) WI-6
Plantation Lake—*reservoir* NC-3
Plantation Lake Dam—*dam* NC-3
Plantation Lakes—*lake* MI-6
Plantation Landing—*locale* MS-4
Plantation Library—*building* FL-3
Plantation Methodist Sch—*school* FL-3
Plantation MS—*school* FL-3
Plantation No. 14—*civ div* ME-1
*Plantation No. 21* ME-1
Plantation No. 33—*other* ME-1
*Plantation of East Hoosac* MA-1
**Plantation Park**—*pop pl* FL-3
Plantation Park—*uninc pl* LA-4
Plantation Park Elem Sch—*school* FL-3
**Plantation Park II (trailer park)**—*pop pl* DE-2
Plantation Park Sch—*school* LA-4
Plantation Point—*cape* FL-3
Plantation Point—*cape* MD-2
Plantation Point Public Use Area—*park* MS-4
Plantation Pond—*lake* FL-3
Plantation Post Office (historical)—*building* MS-4
Plantation Sch—*school* CA-9
Plantation Slough—*gut* LA-4
Plantation State Wildlife Mngmt Area—*park* MN-6
Plantation Tank—*reservoir* AZ-5
Plantation Trail—*trail* PA-2
Plantation Trail—*trail* WV-2
Plantation Village Shop Ctr—*locale* FL-3
**Plantation Walk (subdivision)**—*pop pl* NC-3
Plant Branch—*stream* MS-4
Plant Canyon—*valley* OR-9
Plant Cem—*cemetery* AR-4
Plant Cem—*cemetery* TN-4
Plant Cem—*cemetery* WV-2
Plant Ch—*church* AR-4
**Plant City**—*pop pl* AL-4
**Plant City**—*pop pl* FL-3
Plant City (CCD)—*cens area* FL-3
Plant City HS—*hist pl* FL-3
Plant City Plaza (Shop Ctr)—*locale* FL-3
Plant City Public Library—*building* FL-3
Plant City Senior HS—*school* FL-3
Plant City Shop Ctr—*locale* FL-3
Plant City Union Depot—*hist pl* FL-3
Plant Cooling Lake—*reservoir* NC-3
Plant Creek—*stream* (3) ID-8
Plant Creek—*stream* MT-8
Planted Lake—*lake* MN-6
Planter—*locale* GA-3
Planter—*locale* MI-6
*Planter Brook* NY-2
Planter Creek—*stream* MI-6
*Planter Hill* MA-1
*Planters Academy* MS-4
Planters Bank Bldg—*hist pl* AR-4
Planters Bank Bldg—*hist pl* TX-5
Planters Bldg—*hist pl* NC-3
Planter's Cabin—*hist pl* LA-4
Planters Canal—*canal* LA-4
Planters Hall—*hist pl* MS-4
Planters Hall (Boundary Increase)—*hist pl* MS-4
Planters Hill—*summit* MA-1
Planter's Hotel—*hist pl* LA-4
Planters Institute (historical)—*school* AL-4
Planters Natl Bank—*hist pl* VA-3
**Planters Ridge (subdivision)**—*pop pl* (2) NC-3
Planters Row (historical)—*locale* AL-4
Planter's Tobacco Warehouse—*hist pl* KY-4
Planters (Township of)—*fmr MCD* AR-4
Plantersville—*locale* AR-4
Plantersville—*locale* VA-3
**Plantersville**—*pop pl* (2) AL-4
**Plantersville**—*pop pl* MS-4
**Plantersville**—*pop pl* SC-3
**Plantersville**—*pop pl* TX-5
Plantersville Baptist Ch—*church* MS-4
Plantersville (CCD)—*cens area* SC-3
Plantersville Cem—*cemetery* MS-4
Plantersville Grove Ch—*church* AL-4
**Plantersville (historical)**—*pop pl* MS-4
Plantersville Sch—*school* MS-4
Plantersville United Methodist Ch—*church* MS-4
**Planters Walk (subdivision)**—*pop pl* NC-3
Planters Wharf Creek—*stream* MD-2
Plant Hollow—*valley* TN-4
Plant HS—*school* FL-3
*Plantin* MA-1
Planting Camp—*locale* NE-7
Planting Creek—*stream* WA-9
Plantingfield Brook—*stream* MA-1
Planting Fields Arboretum—*hist pl* NY-2
Planting Ground Lake—*lake* WI-6
Planting Island—*cape* MA-1
Planting Island Cove—*cove* MA-1
Planting Spring—*spring* WY-8
*Plantin Pond* MA-1
Plant Island (historical)—*island* TN-4
Plant JHS—*school* CT-1
Plant Pond—*lake* FL-3
Plant Post Office (historical)—*building* TN-4
**Plants**—*pop pl* OH-6
Plants Branch—*stream* MS-4
Plants Chapel—*locale* AR-4
Plants Corner—*locale* NY-2
Plant's Covered Bridge—*hist pl* PA-2
Plants Creek—*stream* TX-5
Plants Dam—*dam* CT-1
**Plantsite**—*pop pl* AZ-5
*Plantsite School* AZ-5
Plants Ridge—*ridge* WV-2
*Plants River* OR-9
Plants Run—*stream* WV-2
Plantsville—*locale* OH-6
**Plantsville**—*pop pl* CT-1
Plantsville Hist Dist—*hist pl* CT-1
Plant System Hosp Number Three (historical)—*hospital* AL-4
Plant Windmill—*locale* TX-5
**Plantz Corners**—*pop pl* NY-2
Plant 2 Heliport—*airport* WA-9
Planz Park—*park* CA-9
Planz Sch—*school* CA-9
**Plaquemine**—*pop pl* LA-4
Plaquemine, Bayou—*stream* LA-4
Plaquemine Bayou—*gut* MS-4
Plaquemine Brule, Bayou—*stream* LA-4
Plaquemine Lock—*dam* LA-4
Plaquemine Point—*cape* LA-4
Plaquemines, Bayou—*gut* LA-4
Plaquemine Southwest (census name Dupont)—*uninc pl* LA-4
**Plaquemines Parish**—*pop pl* LA-4
Plarmigan Creek—*stream* AK-9
Plashes, The—*lake* MA-1
Plashes Brook—*stream* MA-1
Plashes Pond—*lake* MA-1
*Plashes Ponds* MA-1
Plasi Ch—*church* NE-7
**Plaska**—*pop pl* TX-5
Plaskett—*locale* CA-9
Plaskett Creek—*stream* (2) CA-9
Plaskett Meadows—*flat* CA-9
Plaskett Ridge—*ridge* CA-9
Plaskett Rock—*island* CA-9
Plaskett Station—*locale* CA-9
Plass Canyon—*valley* OR-9
Plass Ditch—*stream* IN-6
**Plasse**—*pop pl* CA-9
Plasse Trading Post (Site)—*locale* CA-9
Plass Gap—*gap* NC-3
Plaster Bluff—*cliff* AR-4
Plaster Cem—*cemetery* VA-3
**Plaster City**—*pop pl* CA-9
**Plasterco**—*pop pl* VA-3
Plasterco Lake—*reservoir* TX-5
Plaster Creek—*stream* IN-6
Plaster Creek—*stream* MI-6
Plaster Grove Ch—*church* IL-6
Plaster Mill—*hist pl* NJ-2
Plaster Pit—*cave* AL-4
Plasterville—*locale* NY-2
Plastic—*locale* CO-8
Plastic Park Pond—*reservoir* MA-1
Plastics Park Airp—*airport* IN-6
**Plat**—*pop pl* WI-6
Plat, Bayou—*gut* (2) LA-4
Plat, Bayou—*stream* (2) LA-4
Plata—*locale* AR-4
Plata—*locale* TX-5
**Plata**—*pop pl* AZ-5
Plata, Lake—*lake* OH-6
Plata, Loma—*summit* TX-5
Plata (Barrio)—*fmr MCD* (3) PR-3
*Plata Creek* CA-9
Plata Mine, La—*mine* AZ-5
*Plata River* CO-8
Plata RR Station—*building* AZ-5
Plata Verde Mines—*mine* TX-5
Plat C Park—*park* UT-8
*Plat Creek* AL-4
**Platea**—*pop pl* PA-2
Platea Borough—*civil* PA-2
Plateau—*locale* MT-8
Plateau—*locale* TX-5
**Plateau**—*pop pl* AL-4
**Plateau**—*pop pl* NC-3
**Plateau**—*pop pl* TN-4
Plateau, The—*plain* WA-9
Plateau Baptist Ch—*church* TN-4
Plateau Branch—*stream* NC-3
**Plateau City**—*pop pl* CO-8
*Plateau Creek* WY-8
Plateau Creek—*stream* (2) CO-8
Plateau Creek—*stream* MT-8
Plateau Creek—*stream* OR-9
Plateau Creek—*stream* (2) WY-8
Plateau De Mount Ski Area—*locale* PA-2
Plateau Draw—*valley* TX-5
Plateau Falls—*falls* WY-8
Plateau Glacier—*glacier* AK-9
**Plateau Heights**—*pop pl* PA-2
Plateau Lake—*lake* AK-9
Plateau Lake—*lake* ID-8
Plateau Lake—*lake* WY-8
Plateau (Magisterial District)—*fmr MCD* WV-2
Plateau Mental Health Center—*hospital* TN-4
Plateau Methodist Ch—*church* AL-4
Plateau Mine—*mine* UT-8

P-L Ranch—locale CO-8
Pluck—locale TX-5
Pluckamin NJ-2
Pluck Branch TX-5
Pluckemin—locale NJ-2
Pluckemin Village Hist Dist—hist pl NJ-2
Pluck Sch—school MO-7
Pluenneke Creek—stream TX-5
Plug, The UT-8
Plug, The—pillar UT-8
Plug Hat—summit CO-8
Plug Hat Picnic Area—locale CO-8
Plug Hat Point—cape MN-6
Plug Hat Ranch—locale CO-8
Plug Hat Rock—summit CO-8
Plug Island—island FL-3
Plug Lake—lake MN-6
Plug Peak—summit UT-8
Plug Point—summit CA-9
Plug Pond MA-1
Plug Run—stream IA-7
Plug Run—stream OH-6
Plug Tank—reservoir AZ-5
Plugtown—locale WI-6
Plugtown Branch—stream KY-4
Plugtown Hollow—valley MO-7
Pluhar Sch—school MT-8
Plum PA-2
Plum WV-2
Plum—locale KY-4
**Plum**—pop pl TX-5
**Pluma**—pop pl SD-7
Plumadore Brook—stream NY-2
Plumadore Creek—stream WI-6
Plumadore Outlet—stream NY-2
Plumadore Pond—lake NY-2
Plumadore Range—ridge NY-2
Plum Airp—airport PA-2
Pluma Island—island AK-9
Plumasano Basin—basin NM-5
Plumasano Wash—stream NM-5
**Plumas (County)**—pop pl CA-9
Plumas Eureka Mill—locale CA-9
Plumas-Eureka Mill, Jamison Mines District—hist pl CA-9
Plumas Eureka State Park—park CA-9
Plumas Mine—mine NV-8
Plumas Sch—school (2) CA-9
**Plumb**—pop pl WA-9
Plumb, Mrs. Preston B., House—hist pl KS-7
Plumbago—locale CA-9
Plumbago Canyon—valley NM-5
Plumbago Canyon—valley WY-8
Plumbago Creek WA-9
Plumbago Creek—stream MI-6
Plumbago Creek—stream WA-9
Plumbago Creek—stream WY-8
Plumbago Mine—mine CA-9
Plumbago Mtn—summit ME-1
Plum Bank CT-1
Plum Bank Beach—beach CT-1
Plum Bank Creek—stream CT-1
Plumbar Creek—stream CA-9
**Plum Bayou**—pop pl AR-4
Plum Bayou—stream AR-4
Plum Bayou Homesteads—hist pl AR-4
Plum Bayou (Township of)—fmr MCD AR-4
Plumb Bayou—stream LA-4
Plumb Beach—beach NY-2
Plumb Beach Channel NY-2
Plumb Beach Channel—channel NY-2
Plumbbeach Point RI-1
Plumb Bob Lake—lake MT-8
Plumb Bob Oil and Gas Field—oilfield LA-4
Plumb Boy Lake—lake AK-9
Plumb Branch—stream MO-7
Plumb Brook—stream NY-2
Plumb Bush Creek Oil Field—oilfield CO-8
Plumb Creek IA-7
Plumb Creek KS-7
Plumb Creek MS-4
Plumb Creek OH-6
Plumb Creek SD-7
Plumb Creek—stream KS-7
Plumb Creek—stream OH-6
Plumb Creek—stream OK-5
Plumb Creek—stream SD-7
Plumb Creek stream TN-4
Plumb Ditch—canal CO-8
Plumb Draw—valley ND-7
**Plum Beach**—pop pl RI-1
Plum Beach Lighthouse—hist pl RI-1
Plum Beach Lighthouse—locale RI-1
Plum Beach Point—cape RI-1
Plumber Spring—spring OR-9
Plumbers Slough—gut TX-5
Plumbers Well—well TX-5
Plumb Gulch—valley CA-9
Plumb Hill—summit (2) CT-1
Plumb (historical)—locale KS-7
Plumb Hollow—valley MO-7
Plumb Hollow School (historical)—locale MO-7
Plumb House—hist pl CT-1
Plumb Island MA-1
Plumb Island Point—cape LA-4
Plumb Lake OR-9
Plumb Lake—lake LA-4
Plumb Lake—lake OR-9
Plum Bluff Cutoff—bend MS-4
Plumb Memorial Library—hist pl CT-1
Plumbob Lake—lake MI-6
Plum Bottom Brook NY-2
Plum Bottom Creek—stream (2) NY-2
Plumb Point DE-2
Plumb Point MD-2
Plumb Point NY-2
Plumb Point—cape VA-3
Plumb Point (historical)—cape DE-2
Plumb Point Post Office TN-4
Plum Branch VA-3
**Plum Branch**—pop pl SC-3
Plum Branch—stream AR-4
Plum Branch—stream IL-6
Plum Branch—stream IN-6
Plum Branch—stream (4) KY-4
Plum Branch—stream (6) MO-7
Plum Branch—stream (2) NC-3
Plum Branch—stream SC-3
Plum Branch—stream (4) TN-4
Plum Branch—stream (4) TX-5
Plum Branch—stream VA-3
Plum Branch—stream WV-2
Plum Branch Cem—cemetery TX-5
Plum Branch Ch—church NC-3
Plum Branch Fall River—stream KS-7
**Plumbridge**—pop pl PA-2
**Plumbrook**—pop pl NY-2
Plum Brook—stream CT-1
Plum Brook—stream (2) MA-1
Plum Brook—stream MI-6
Plum Brook—stream NJ-2
Plum Brook—stream (5) NY-2
Plum Brook—stream OH-6
Plum Brook Country Club—other OH-6
Plum Brook Drain—stream MI-6
Plumbrook Estates MI-6
Plumbrook Farms MI-6
Plum Brook Golf Course—other MI-6
**Plum Brook (Nasa)**—pop pl OH-6
**Plumbrook Village**—pop pl MI-6
Plumb Run—stream OH-6
Plumbs—locale CO-8
Plumb Sch—school FL-3
Plumbsock—locale NJ-2
**Plumbsock**—pop pl PA-2
**Plumb Township**—pop pl KS-7
**Plumbush**—pop pl MA-1
Plum Bush Creek—stream CO-8
Plumbush Creek—stream MA-1
Plum Bush Point—cape MA-1
Plum Butte—summit ND-7
Plum Canyon—valley (2) CA-9
Plum Canyon—valley (2) CO-8
Plum Canyon—valley NE-7
Plum Canyon—valley SD-7
Plum Canyon—valley TX-5
Plum Cem—cemetery OH-6
Plum Center Sch—school NE-7
Plum Center Sch—school PA-2
**Plum (Chapmanville)**—pop pl PA-2
**Plum City**—pop pl WI-6
Plum City Union Cem—cemetery WI-6
Plum Corner—locale PA-2
Plum Corners PA-2
Plum Coulee—valley (4) MT-8
Plum Cove—cove (2) MA-1
Plum Cove Sch—school MA-1
Plum creek IA-7
Plum Creek KS-7
Plum Creek MT-8
Plum Creek NE-7
Plum Creek TX-5
Plum Creek—bay NC-3
Plum Creek—fmr MCD (3) NE-7
Plum Creek—locale TX-5
Plum Creek—locale VA-3
**Plum Creek**—pop pl MT-8
**Plum Creek**—pop pl TN-4
Plum Creek—stream (2) AR-4
Plum Creek—stream (4) CA-9
Plum Creek—stream (4) CO-8
Plum Creek—stream (5) IL-6
Plum Creek—stream (6) IN-6
Plum Creek—stream (8) IA-7
Plum Creek—stream (25) KS-7
Plum Creek—stream (3) KY-4
Plum Creek—stream (3) MD-2
Plum Creek—stream (2) MI-6
Plum Creek—stream (4) MN-6
Plum Creek—stream MS-4
Plum Creek—stream (3) MO-7
Plum Creek—stream (8) MT-8
Plum Creek—stream (8) NE-7
Plum Creek—stream NY-2
Plum Creek—stream (4) ND-7
Plum Creek—stream (9) OH-6
Plum Creek—stream OK-5
Plum Creek—stream (9) PA-2
Plum Creek—stream (12) SD-7
Plum Creek—stream (3) TN-4
Plum Creek—stream (22) TX-5
Plum Creek—stream (4) VA-3
Plum Creek—stream (7) WI-6
Plum Creek—stream (2) WY-8
Plum Creek—uninc pl PA-2
Plum Creek Baptist Church SD-7
Plum Creek Canyon—valley NE-7
Plum Creek Cem—cemetery IA-7
Plum Creek Cem—cemetery KS-7
Plum Creek Cem—cemetery NE-7
Plum Creek Cem—cemetery PA-2
Plum Creek Cem—cemetery TN-4
Plum Creek Cem—cemetery (2) TX-5
Plum Creek Ch—church (2) IN-6
Plum Creek Ch—church (2) KS-7
Plum Creek Ch—church (2) KY-4
Plum Creek Ch—church PA-2
Plum Creek Ch—church SD-7
Plum Creek Ch (historical)—church PA-2
Plum Creek Corral Spring—spring MT-8
Plum Creek Country Club—other IA-7
Plum Creek County Park—park IA-7
Plum Creek Cove—bay TX-5
Plum Creek Dam—dam PA-2
Plum Creek Ditch IA-7
Plum Creek Ditch—canal IA-7
Plum Creek Drain—canal MI-6
Plum Creek Draw—valley WY-8
Plum Creek Grazing Association Number 1 Dam—dam SD-7
Plum Creek Grazing Association Number 2 Dam—dam SD-7
Plum Creek (historical)—locale SD-7
Plum Creek Lookout Tower—locale MN-6
Plum Creek Mill Site—locale CA-9
Plum Creek Mine—mine PA-2
Plum Creek Ramp—locale TX-5
Plum Creek Reservoir PA-2
Plum Creek Ridge—ridge (2) CA-9
Plum Creek Rsvr—reservoir MT-8
Plum Creek Sch—school CO-8
Plum Creek Sch—school IA-7
Plum Creek Sch—school KS-7
Plum Creek Sch—school MO-7
Plum Creek Township—civil SD-7
Plum Creek Township—fmr MCD IA-7
**Plum Creek Township**—pop pl KS-7
**Plum Creek Township**—pop pl NE-7
**Plumcreek (Township of)**—pop pl PA-2
Plum Drain—canal CA-9
Plum Draw—valley SD-7
Plum Draw—valley TX-5
Plum Draw Cem—cemetery SD-7
Plume Bayou—stream LA-4
Plume Creek ID-8
Plume Creek—stream MT-8
Plume Lake—lake MN-6
Plumely Canyon—valley CO-8
**Plumer**—pop pl PA-2
Plumer Cem—cemetery IA-7
Plumer Cem—cemetery ME-1
Plumer Creek KS-7
Plumer Creek TX-5
Plumer Fire Tower—tower PA-2
Plumer Grove Christian Methodist Episcopal Church TN-4
Plumer Grove Church TN-4
Plumer Grove Sch (historical)—school TN-4
Plumer Hill—summit NH-1
Plumer House—hist pl PA-2
Plumer-Jones Farm—hist pl NH-1
**Plumer Township**—pop pl ND-7
**Plumerville**—pop pl AR-4
Plumerville Cem—cemetery AR-4
Plumfield—locale IL-6
Plumfield Landing—locale SC-3
Plum Field Sch—school CT-1
Plum Flat—flat (2) CA-9
Plum Ford—locale MO-7
Plumford Branch—stream KY-4
Plum Fork OH-6
Plum Fork—stream KY-4
Plum Garden—area CA-9
Plum Grove KS-7
Plum Grove—fmr MCD NE-7
Plum Grove—hist pl IA-7
Plum Grove—locale TX-5
**Plum Grove**—pop pl MS-4
**Plum Grove**—pop pl TX-5
Plum Grove Archaeol Site—hist pl TN-4
Plum Grove Baptist Church AL-4
Plum Grove Cem—cemetery IN-6
Plum Grove Cem—cemetery KS-7
Plum Grove Cem—cemetery (2) TX-5
Plum Grove Ch—church AL-4
Plum Grove Ch—church IN-6
Plum Grove Ch—church KY-4
Plum Grove Ch—church LA-4
Plum Grove Ch—church MO-7
Plum Grove Ch—church TN-4
Plum Grove Ch—church TX-5
Plum Grove Countryside IL-6
Plum Grove Elementary School MS-4
**Plum Grove Estates**—pop pl IL-6
Plum Grove Gap—gap TN-4
Plum Grove Hills IL-6
Plum Grove Lake—lake MN-6
Plum Grove Post Office (historical)—building TN-4
Plum Grove Sch—school (2) IL-6
Plum Grove Sch—school MS-4
Plum Grove Sch—school (3) MO-7
Plum Grove Sch—school WI-6
Plum Grove Sch (abandoned)—school MO-7
Plum Grove Sch (historical)—school MO-7
Plum Grove Sch (historical)—school PA-2
**Plum Grove Township**—pop pl KS-7
Plum Grove Village IL-6
Plum Grove Ville PA-2
**Plum Grove Woods**—pop pl IL-6
Plum Gulley Brook—stream CT-1
Plum Gut—channel NY-2
Plum Gut Harbor—bay NY-2
Plumhaw Sch—school SC-3
**Plum Hill**—pop pl IL-6
Plum Hill—summit VT-1
Plum Hills—summit MA-1
Plum Hills—summit OR-9
Plum Hill Sch—school LA-4
**Plum Hill (Township of)**—pop pl IL-6
Plumhoff House—hist pl TX-5
Plum Hollow—valley AR-4
Plum Hollow—valley KY-4
Plum Hollow—valley PA-2
Plum Hollow—valley (5) TX-5
Plum Hollow—valley WV-2
Plum Hollow—valley WI-6
Plum Hollow Golf Club—other MI-6
Plum Hollow Golf Course—other IL-6
Plum Hook Creek (historical)—stream PA-2
Plumies Point—cape VT-1
Plum Island SD-7
Plum Island—island IL-6
Plum Island—island MA-1
Plum Island—island NJ-2
Plum Island—island NY-2
Plum Island—island SC-3
Plum Island—island SD-7
Plum Island—island WI-6
**Plum Island**—pop pl MA-1
**Plum Island**—pop pl NY-2
Plum Island (historical)—island SD-7
Plum Island Lighthouse—locale NY-2
Plum Island Point—cape MA-1
Plum Island Range Rear Light—hist pl WI-6
Plum Island River MA-1
Plum Island River—gut MA-1
Plum Island River Marshes—swamp MA-1
Plum Island Rock—bar NY-2
Plum Island Sound—bay MA-1
Plum Island State Park—park MA-1
Plum Lake MN-6
Plum Lake—lake FL-3
Plum Lake—lake MI-6
Plum Lake—lake (2) MN-6
Plum Lake—lake ND-7
Plum Lake—lake SD-7
Plum Lake—lake TX-5
Plum Lake—lake (2) WI-6
Plum Lake—swamp MN-6
**Plum Lake (Town of)**—pop pl WI-6
Plum Lateral—canal CA-9
Plum Lateral—canal ID-8
Plumlee Bottom—bend TN-4
Plumlee Cem—cemetery (2) TN-4
Plumlee Ch—church AR-4
Plumlees Ford—crossing TN-4
Plumlee Spring—spring TN-4
Plumlees Sch (historical)—school TN-4
Plumlee (Township of)—fmr MCD AR-4
Plumley Bay—bay NY-2
Plumley Cem—cemetery WV-2
Plumley Knob—summit WV-2
Plumley Mtn—summit SC-3
Plumley Mtn—summit WV-2
Plumley Point—cape NY-2
Plumley Pond—lake NY-2
Plum Lick Creek—stream KY-4
Plumline Ch—church NC-3
Plumly Sch—school AR-4
Plumly School (Abandoned)—locale MN-6
Plummer KS-7
Plummer PA-2
Plummer—locale FL-3
Plummer—locale MO-7
**Plummer**—pop pl ID-8
**Plummer**—pop pl IN-6
**Plummer**—pop pl MN-6
**Plummer**—pop pl PA-2
Plummer, Henry S., House—hist pl MN-6
Plummer, Mount—summit AK-9
Plummer Airp—airport IN-6
Plummer Branch—stream (2) KY-4
Plummer Branch—stream MS-4
Plummer Brook—stream IN-6
Plummer Brook—stream ME-1
Plummer Butte—summit ID-8
Plummer Canyon—valley WY-8
Plummer Cem—cemetery (2) GA-3
Plummer Cem—cemetery IN-6
Plummer Cem—cemetery NH-1
Plummer Cem—cemetery WI-6
Plummer Ch—church IN-6
Plummer Ch—church KY-4
Plummer Ch—church TN-4
Plummer Cheatham Memorial Park—cemetery NC-3
Plummer Corner—locale ME-1
**Plummer Corner**—pop pl MA-1
Plummer Coulee—valley MT-8
Plummer Creek CA-9
Plummer Creek—stream (3) CA-9
Plummer Creek—stream FL-3
Plummer Creek—stream (2) ID-8
Plummer Creek—stream IN-6
Plummer Creek—stream KS-7
Plummer Creek—stream NC-3
Plummer Creek—stream TX-5
Plummer Crossing—locale TX-5
Plummer Field—park WV-2
Plummer Fork—stream OH-6
Plummer Gulch—valley CA-9
Plummer Gulch—valley OR-9
Plummer Hill—summit CA-9
Plummer Hill—summit IL-6
Plummer Hill—summit ME-1
Plummer Hollow—valley PA-2
Plummer Island ME-1
Plummer Island MD-2
Plummer Island—island (2) ME-1
Plummer Island—island NH-1
**Plummer Island**—pop pl ME-1
Plummer Islands ME-1
Plummer Junction—locale ID-8
Plummer Knob—summit WV-2
Plummer Lake—lake ID-8
Plummer Lake—lake MS-4
Plummer Lake—lake (2) WI-6
Plummer Lake—reservoir AL-4
Plummer Lake Dam AL-4
Plummer Landing—locale ME-1
Plummer Lateral—canal MT-8
Plummer Ledge—bar ME-1
Plummer Meadows—flat CA-9
Plummer Memorial Bridge—bridge MA-1
Plummer Mill—locale ME-1
Plummer Mtn—summit ME-1
Plummer Mtn—summit WA-9
Plummer Oil Field—oilfield TX-5
Plummer Park—park CA-9
Plummer Peak—summit CA-9
Plummer Peak—summit ID-8
Plummer Peak—summit WA-9
Plummer Peninsula—cape ID-8
Plummer Point—cape (2) ME-1
Plummer Point—cape MS-4
Plummer Point—cape NH-1
Plummer Point—cliff ID-8
**Plummer Point**—pop pl WI-6
Plummer Pond NH-1
Plummer Ranch—locale NV-8
Plummer Ridge—ridge CA-9
Plummer Ridge—ridge VA-3
Plummer Run—stream WV-2
Plummers FL-3
Plummers MO-7
**Plummers**—pop pl FL-3
Plummers Branch—stream NE-7
Plummers Branch Cem—cemetery NE-7
Plummers Branch Sch—school NE-7
Plummers Cem—cemetery FL-3
Plummers Cem—cemetery (2) TX-5
Plummer Sch—school CA-9
Plummer Sch—school CO-8
Plummer Sch—school DC-2
Plummer Sch—school MT-8
Plummers Chapel Ch TN-4
Plummers Cove—bay FL-3
Plummers Creek IN-6
Plummers Creek NC-3
Plummers Creek—stream TX-5
Plummers Grove Ch—church TN-4
Plummers Grove School TN-4
Plummers Hill—summit MA-1
Plummers Island ME-1
Plummers Island—island MD-2
Plummers Lake—lake MT-8
Plummers Landing—locale KY-4
Plummer Slough MS-4
Plummer Slough—stream OR-9
Plummer Slu—stream MS-4
Plummers Mill—locale KY-4
Plummers Point—cape FL-3
Plummers Point—cape MN-6
Plummer Spring—spring TN-4
Plummers Run—stream NC-3
Plummers Run Bay—swamp NC-3
Plummers Slough—gut MT-8
Plummer's Station—hist pl AR-4
Plummer Swamp—swamp FL-3
**Plummer Township**—pop pl SD-7
Plummet Brook MA-1
Plummeting Springs—spring TN-4
Plummeting Springs Pot—cave TN-4
Plum Nursery Hollow—valley TN-4
Plumora Sch—school FL-3
Plum Orchard—locale FL-3
Plum Orchard—locale WV-2
Plum Orchard Branch MS-4
Plum Orchard Branch—stream AL-4
Plumorchard Branch—stream MS-4
Plum Orchard Cem—cemetery GA-3
Plumorchard Ch (historical)—church GA-3
Plum Orchard Creek MI-6
Plumorchard Creek WV-2
Plumorchard Creek—stream GA-3
Plum Orchard Creek—stream WV-2
Plumorchard Gap—gap GA-3
Plum Orchard Hist Dist—hist pl GA-3
Plum Orchard Hollow—valley TN-4
Plum Orchard Hunting And Fishing Area—park WV-2
Plum Orchard Island—island LA-4
Plum Orchard Lake—reservoir WV-2
Plum Orchard Landing—locale LA-4
Plum Orchard Run—stream WV-2
Plum Orchard Sch—school WV-2
Plum Orchard Wharf—locale GA-3
Plum Patch Coulee—valley MT-8
Plum Point DE-2
Plumpoint MD-2
Plum Point—cape (2) LA-4
Plum Point—cape (3) MD-2
Plum Point—cape MS-4
Plum Point—cape NJ-2
Plum Point—cape (5) NY-2
Plum Point—cape NC-3
Plum Point—cape RI-1
Plum Point—cape TN-4
Plum Point—cape WA-9
**Plum Point**—pop pl MD-2
**Plum Point**—pop pl MS-4
**Plum Point**—pop pl RI-1
**Plum Point**—pop pl VA-3
Plum Point Bar—bar TN-4
Plum Point Bend—bend TN-4
**Plum Point (Carpenter Beach)**—pop pl MD-2
Plum Point Ch—church KY-4
Plum Point Ch—church MD-2
Plum Point Creek—stream MD-2
Plum Point Creek—stream NY-2
Plum Point Dikes—levee TN-4
**Plum Point Estates (subdivision)**—pop pl NC-3
**Plum Point (Forshee)**—pop pl VA-3
Plum Point Gut—stream NC-3
Plum Point Landing—locale TN-4
Plumpoint Post Office TN-4
Plumpoint Post Office (historical)—building MS-4
Plum Point Post Office (historical)—building TN-4
Plum Point Reach—channel TN-4
Plum Point Rec Area—park MS-4
Plum Point Sch—school MD-2
Plum Point Slough—gut IL-6
Plum Post Office (historical)—building PA-2
Plum Pudding Butte (historical)—summit ND-7
Plum Ridge—ridge CA-9
Plum Ridge—ridge NC-3
Plum Ridge Ch—church TX-5
Plum Rincon Canyon—valley NM-5
Plum River—other IL-6
Plum River—stream IL-6
Plum River Cem—cemetery IL-6
Plum Rsvr—reservoir MT-8
Plum Run PA-2
Plum Run—locale WV-2
**Plum Run**—pop pl DE-2
**Plum Run**—pop pl OH-6
**Plum Run**—pop pl PA-2
Plum Run—stream IN-6
Plum Run—stream KY-4
Plum Run—stream NE-7
Plum Run—stream (17) OH-6
Plum Run—stream (7) PA-2
Plum Run—stream (9) WV-2
Plum Run—stream (2) WI-6
Plum Run Cem—cemetery OH-6
Plum Run Ch—church OH-6
Plum Sch—school TX-5
Plum Senior HS—school PA-2
Plumsock—locale PA-2
Plum Spring AL-4
Plum Spring—spring AL-4
Plum Spring—spring (3) CA-9
**Plum Springs**—pop pl AL-4
**Plum Springs**—pop pl KY-4
Plum Springs Acad (historical)—school AL-4
Plum Springs Branch—stream AL-4
Plum Springs Ch—church AL-4
Plum Springs Ch—church KY-4
Plum Springs (historical)—school AL-4
Plumstead PA-2
Plumstead Airfield—airport PA-2
Plumstead Cem—cemetery PA-2
Plumstead Christian Day Sch—school PA-2
Plumstead Hill—summit PA-2
**Plumstead (Township of)**—pop pl PA-2
**Plumsteadville**—pop pl PA-2
Plumsteadville Industrial Park—locale PA-2
Plumsteadville Sch—school PA-2
Plumsteadville Shop Ctr—locale PA-2
**Plumsted (Township of)**—pop pl NJ-2
Plum Street Temple—hist pl OH-6
**Plum (subdivision)**—pop pl PA-2
Plumtaw Creek—stream CO-8
Plum Thicket Draw—valley MT-8
Plum Thicket Lake—lake LA-4
Plum Thicket Windmill—locale (2) TX-5
**Plum Township**—pop pl KS-7
**Plum (Township of)**—pop pl PA-2
Plum Tree—locale VA-3
**Plum Tree**—pop pl IN-6
**Plumtree**—pop pl NC-3
Plum Tree Branch—stream KY-4
Plumtree Branch—stream (2) MD-2
Plum Tree Branch—stream VA-3
**Plum Tree Condominium**—pop pl UT-8
Plum Tree Country Club—other IL-6
Plumtree Creek—stream NC-3
Plumtree Crossing—locale CA-9
Plum Tree Hollow—valley MO-7
Plumtree Island—island VA-3
Plum Tree Marsh NY-2
Plumtree Marsh—swamp NY-2
Plumtree Point—cape VA-3
Plumtree Run—stream MD-2
Plum Trees—locale OR-9
Plumtrees Sch—school CT-1
Plum Valley—basin CA-9
Plum Valley—locale MO-7
Plum Valley—valley CA-9
Plum Valley—valley CO-8
Plum Valley—valley OR-9
Plum Valley—valley (2) WI-6
Plum Valley Campground—locale CA-9
Plum Valley Cem—cemetery CO-8
Plum Valley Sch (historical)—school MO-7
**Plumville**—pop pl KY-4
**Plumville**—pop pl PA-2
Plumville Borough—civil PA-2
Plumville Ch—church IL-6
**Plumville (historical)**—pop pl MS-4
Plum Windmill—locale CO-8
**Plumwood**—pop pl OH-6
Pluncket Point—cape NY-2
Plunder Branch—stream FL-3
Plunders Creek—stream TN-4
Plunders Creek Sch (historical)—school TN-4
Plunge, The—lake MT-8
Plunge Creek—stream AK-9
Plunge Creek—stream CA-9
Plunge Creek—stream IN-6
Plunge Creek Truck Trail—trail CA-9
Plunger Creek—stream IA-7
Plunge Spring—spring UT-8
Plunk Cem—cemetery MO-7
Plunk Cem—cemetery TN-4
Plunkeet Cemetery AL-4
Plunket Branch—stream AL-4
Plunket Cem—cemetery AL-4
Plunket Creek—stream MT-8
Plunket Draw—valley NM-5
Plunket Hollow—valley TN-4
Plunket Lake—reservoir MT-8
Plunket Oil Wells—well WY-8
Plunket Post Office (historical)—building AL-4
Plunket Reservoir MA-1
Plunket Run—stream PA-2
Plunket Run Sch (historical)—school PA-2
**Plunkets Creek**—pop pl TN-4
**Plunkett**—pop pl PA-2
Plunkett Brook—stream ME-1
Plunkett Cem—cemetery AR-4
Plunkett Cem—cemetery GA-3
Plunkett Cem—cemetery OK-5
Plunkett Cem—cemetery (2) SC-3
Plunkett Cem—cemetery TN-4
Plunkett Cem—cemetery VA-3
Plunkett Creek—stream CA-9
Plunkett Creek—stream GA-3
Plunkett Creek—stream OR-9
Plunkett Creek—stream TN-4
Plunkett Lake—lake WI-6
Plunkett Lake Dam—dam MS-4
Plunkett Mtn—summit AL-4
Plunkett Neck—bay GA-3
Plunkett Park—park MO-7
Plunkett Pond—lake ME-1
Plunkett Rsvr—reservoir MA-1
**Plunketts**—pop pl AR-4
Plunkett Sch—school MA-1
Plunketts Creek TN-4
Plunketts Creek—stream PA-2
Plunketts Creek Baptist Church TN-4
Plunketts Creek Ch—church TN-4
**Plunketts Creek (Township of)**—pop pl PA-2
**Plunkettsville**—pop pl VA-3
**Plunkettville**—pop pl OK-5
Plunketville—locale OK-5
Plunk Sch (abandoned)—school MO-7
Plus WV-2
Plusfour Creek—stream OR-9
**Plush**—pop pl OR-9
Plush Ranch—locale CA-9
Pluss Drain—canal MI-6
Plutarch—locale KY-4
**Plutarch**—pop pl NY-2
Plutarco Tank—reservoir TX-5
Plute Knoll—summit UT-8
Plute Spring—spring OR-9
Pluto—locale WV-2
**Pluto**—pop pl MS-4
Pluto, Mount—summit CA-9
Pluto Canyon—valley NV-8
Pluto Cave—cave CA-9
Pluto Cem—cemetery MS-4
Pluto Ch—church WV-2
Pluto Creek MI-6
Pluto Landing MS-4
Pluto Mine—mine CA-9
Pluto Mine—mine CO-8
Pluto Mtn—summit TX-5
Pluton Cove—bay AK-9
Plutonium Valley—valley NV-8
Pluto Post Office (historical)—building MS-4
Pluto Spring—spring OR-9
Pluto Valley—basin NV-8
Pluvius—locale WA-9
Pluvius Hill—summit WA-9
**Plyers Mill Estates**—pop pl MD-2
**Plyler**—pop pl NC-3
Plyler Lake—reservoir NC-3
Plyler Lake Dam—dam NC-3
Plyler Pond—lake SC-3
Plyler Pond—reservoir GA-3
Plylers Lake—reservoir NC-3
Plyley Ridge—ridge OH-6
Plylies Ferry TN-4
Plymal Cem—cemetery WV-2
Plymale Branch—stream KY-4
Plymale Cem—cemetery AR-4
Plymale Creek—stream GA-3
Plymate Branch—stream WV-2
Plymate Homestead—locale MT-8
**Plymell**—pop pl KS-7
Plymoor Memorial Ch—church NC-3

Plymounth Sch—*school* ... MO-7
Plymount Sch—*school* ... PA-2
*Plymouth* ... AR-4
*Plymouth* ... MI-6
*Plymouth* ... OH-6
*Plymouth* ... PA-2
Plymouth—*hist pl* ... MS-4
Plymouth—*locale* ... OH-6
Plymouth—*locale* ... VA-3
Plymouth—*other* ... OH-6
**Plymouth**—*pop pl* ... CA-9
**Plymouth**—*pop pl* ... CT-1
**Plymouth**—*pop pl* ... DE-2
**Plymouth**—*pop pl* ... FL-3
**Plymouth**—*pop pl* ... IL-6
**Plymouth**—*pop pl* ... IN-6
**Plymouth**—*pop pl* (2) ... IA-7
**Plymouth**—*pop pl* ... KS-7
**Plymouth**—*pop pl* ... ME-1
**Plymouth**—*pop pl* ... MA-1
**Plymouth**—*pop pl* (2) ... MI-6
**Plymouth**—*pop pl* ... MN-6
**Plymouth**—*pop pl* ... MO-7
**Plymouth**—*pop pl* ... NE-7
**Plymouth**—*pop pl* ... NH-1
**Plymouth**—*pop pl* ... NY-2
**Plymouth**—*pop pl* ... NC-3
**Plymouth**—*pop pl* ... OH-6
**Plymouth**—*pop pl* ... PA-2
**Plymouth**—*pop pl* ... UT-8
**Plymouth**—*pop pl* ... VT-1
**Plymouth**—*pop pl* ... WA-9
**Plymouth**—*pop pl* ... WV-2
**Plymouth**—*pop pl* ... WI-6
Plymouth, Lake—*reservoir* ... NJ-2
Plymouth, The—*hist pl* ... DC-2
Plymouth Antiquarian House—*hist pl* ... MA-1
Plymouth Baptist Ch—*church* ... FL-3
Plymouth Baptist Ch—*church* ... MS-4
Plymouth Bay—*bay* ... MA-1
Plymouth Beach—*beach* ... MA-1
Plymouth Bluff—*cliff* ... MS-4
Plymouth Bluff Nature and Cultural Study Center—*building* ... MS-4
Plymouth Bog—*swamp* ... ME-1
Plymouth Borough—*civil* ... PA-2
Plymouth Canal—*canal* ... NV-8
Plymouth-Carver HS—*school* ... MA-1
Plymouth-Carver JHS—*school* ... MA-1
Plymouth Cem—*cemetery* ... FL-3
Plymouth Cem—*cemetery* (2) ... IL-6
Plymouth Cem—*cemetery* ... MS-4
Plymouth Cem—*cemetery* ... MO-7
Plymouth Cem—*cemetery* ... NY-2
Plymouth Cem—*cemetery* ... OK-5
Plymouth Cem—*cemetery* ... TX-5
Plymouth Cem—*cemetery* ... UT-8
Plymouth Cem—*cemetery* ... WI-6
Plymouth (census name for Plymouth Center)—*CDP* ... MA-1
Plymouth Center—*locale* ... OH-6
**Plymouth Center**—*pop pl* ... PA-2
Plymouth Center (census name Plymouth)—*other* ... MA-1
Plymouth Ch—*church* ... FL-3
Plymouth Ch—*church* (2) ... MI-6
Plymouth Ch—*church* ... MN-6
Plymouth Ch—*church* ... MS-4
Plymouth Ch—*church* ... NC-3
Plymouth Ch—*church* ... WI-6
Plymouth Church of the Pilgrims—*hist pl* ... NY-2
*Plymouth Compact* ... NH-1
**Plymouth Compact (census name Plymouth)**—*pop pl* ... NH-1
Plymouth Congregational Ch—*church* ... KS-7
Plymouth Congregational Church—*hist pl* ... CT-1
Plymouth Congregational Church—*hist pl* ... FL-3
Plymouth Country Club—*locale* ... MA-1
Plymouth Country Club—*other* ... PA-2
Plymouth County Courthouse—*hist pl* ... IA-7
Plymouth County Farm—*locale* ... MA-1
Plymouth County Home—*locale* ... IA-7
Plymouth County Hosp—*hospital* ... MA-1
**Plymouth County (in (P)MSA 1120,1200, 5400)**—*pop pl* ... MA-1
*Plymouth Creek* ... IA-7
Plymouth Creek—*stream* ... CO-8
Plymouth Creek—*stream* ... IA-7
Plymouth Creek—*stream* ... PA-2
Plymouth Dam—*dam* ... PA-2
Plymouth Ditch—*canal* ... CA-9
*Plymouth Elementary School* ... PA-2
*Plymouth Farms* ... IL-6
*Plymouth Ferry* ... PA-2
*Plymouth Field* ... MA-1
Plymouth Fire Station—*hist pl* ... IN-6
Plymouth-Five Corners Cem—*cemetery* ... VT-1
Plymouth Friends Meetinghouse—*hist pl* ... PA-2
Plymouth Gas And Oil Field—*oilfield* ... TX-5
Plymouth Harbor—*bay* ... MA-1
Plymouth Harbor Channel—*channel* ... MA-1
Plymouth Haven Ch—*church* ... VA-3
Plymouth Heights Ch—*church* ... OH-6
Plymouth Hist Dist—*hist pl* ... NH-1
Plymouth Hist Dist—*hist pl* ... VT-1
Plymouth (historical)—*locale* ... MS-4
**Plymouth (historical)**—*pop pl* ... MS-4
Plymouth HS—*school* ... IN-6
Plymouth HS—*school* ... MA-1
Plymouth HS—*school* ... NC-3
Plymouth Industrial Center—*locale* ... PA-2
Plymouth Island—*island* ... NY-2
Plymouth JHS West—*school* ... MI-6
*Plymouth Junction* ... MO-7
Plymouth Junction—*locale* ... PA-2
**Plymouth Junction**—*pop pl* ... IA-7
Plymouth Kingdom—*locale* ... VT-1
Plymouth Lake—*lake* ... MI-6
Plymouth Lake—*lake* ... WI-6
Plymouth Lake—*reservoir* ... CT-1
Plymouth Light—*locale* ... MA-1
Plymouth Lighthouse—*locale* ... MA-1
Plymouth Light Station—*hist pl* ... MA-1
Plymouth Lookout Tower—*tower* ... FL-3
Plymouth (Magisterial District)—*fmr MCD* ... VA-3
Plymouth Male and Female Acad (historical)—*school* ... MS-4
**Plymouth Meeting**—*pop pl* ... PA-2
Plymouth Meeting Hist Dist—*hist pl* ... PA-2
Plymouth Meeting Mall—*locale* ... PA-2
Plymouth Methodist Ch—*church* ... NC-3
Plymouth Mine—*mine* ... CA-9
Plymouth Mtn—*summit* ... CO-8
Plymouth Mtn—*summit* ... NH-1
Plymouth Municipal Airp—*airport* ... IN-6
Plymouth Municipal Airp—*airport* ... MA-1
Plymouth Municipal Airp—*airport* ... NC-3
Plymouth Normal Sch (historical)—*school* ... MS-4
Plymouth Notch—*gap* ... VT-1
Plymouth Notch Cem—*cemetery* ... VT-1
Plymouth Oil Camp—*locale* ... TX-5
Plymouth Oil Field—*oilfield* ... TX-5
Plymouth Park—*park* ... MI-6
Plymouth Park—*park* ... TX-5
**Plymouth Park**—*pop pl* (2) ... VA-3
Plymouth Park Ch—*church* ... TX-5
Plymouth Park Sch—*school* ... TX-5
**Plymouth Park (subdivision)**—*pop pl* ... TN-4
Plymouth Playground—*park* ... FL-3
Plymouth Pond—*lake* ... ME-1
Plymouth Pond—*lake* ... NJ-2
Plymouth Post Office Bldg—*hist pl* ... MA-1
Plymouth Post Office (historical)—*building* ... MS-4
Plymouth Preschool of Plymouth Congregational Church—*school* ... FL-3
Plymouth Rd Pond—*reservoir* ... MA-1
Plymouth Refinery—*other* ... TX-5
Plymouth River—*stream* ... MA-1
Plymouth River Sch—*school* ... MA-1
Plymouth Riverside Park—*park* ... MI-6
Plymouth Road Dam—*dam* ... MA-1
Plymouth Rock—*cliff* ... AL-4
Plymouth Rock—*hist pl* ... MA-1
Plymouth Rock—*locale* ... IA-7
Plymouth Rock—*rock* ... MA-1
Plymouth Rock—*summit* ... NY-2
Plymouth Rock Landing (historical)—*locale* ... AL-4
Plymouth Rock Mine—*mine* ... CA-9
Plymouth Rsvr—*reservoir* ... CT-1
Plymouth Rsvr—*reservoir* ... NY-2
Plymouth Rsvr—*reservoir* ... PA-2
Plymouth Sch—*hist pl* ... UT-8
Plymouth Sch—*school* ... CA-9
Plymouth Sch—*school* (2) ... MI-6
Plymouth Sch—*school* ... MN-6
Plymouth Sch—*school* ... MO-7
Plymouth Sch—*school* ... UT-8
Plymouth Sch—*school* ... VT-1
Plymouth Speedway—*other* ... IN-6
Plymouth State Home and Training Sch—*school* ... MI-6
*Plymouth Station* ... PA-2
*Plymouth Street Reservoir* ... MA-1
Plymouth Street Sch—*school* ... MA-1
Plymouth Swamp—*stream* ... VA-3
Plymouth Town Hall—*building* ... MA-1
**Plymouth (Town of)**—*pop pl* ... CT-1
**Plymouth (Town of)**—*pop pl* ... ME-1
**Plymouth (Town of)**—*pop pl* ... MA-1
**Plymouth (Town of)**—*pop pl* ... NH-1
**Plymouth (Town of)**—*pop pl* ... NY-2
**Plymouth (Town of)**—*pop pl* ... VT-1
**Plymouth (Town of)**—*pop pl* (3) ... WI-6
Plymouth Township—*CDP* ... PA-2
Plymouth Township—*fmr MCD* ... IA-7
**Plymouth Township**—*pop pl* ... KS-7
**Plymouth Township**—*pop pl* ... ND-7
Plymouth (Township of)—*fmr MCD* ... NC-3
**Plymouth (Township of)**—*pop pl* ... MI-6
**Plymouth (Township of)**—*pop pl* (2) ... OH-6
**Plymouth (Township of)**—*pop pl* (2) ... PA-2
Plymouth (Township of)—*unorg* ... ME-1
**Plymouth Union**—*pop pl* ... VT-1
**Plymouth Valley**—*pop pl* ... PA-2
Plymouth Valley Ch—*church* ... PA-2
**Plymouth View Subdivision**—*pop pl* ... UT-8
**Plymouth Village**—*pop pl* ... KY-4
Plymouth Village Hist Dist—*hist pl* ... MA-1
Plymouth Whitemarsh HS—*school* ... PA-2
*Plymouth Whitemarsh Senior HS* ... PA-2
Plym Park Golf Course—*other* ... MI-6
**Plympton**—*pop pl* ... MA-1
Plympton Bog North Rsvr—*reservoir* ... MA-1
Plympton Bog West Rsvr—*reservoir* ... MA-1
Plympton Brook—*stream* ... MA-1
Plympton Brook Rsvr—*reservoir* ... MA-1
Plympton Creek—*stream* ... OR-9
Plympton (historical P.O.)—*locale* ... MA-1
Plympton Ridge—*ridge* ... UT-8
Plympton Sch—*school* ... MA-1
**Plympton (Town of)**—*pop pl* ... MA-1
Plymptonville—*CDP* ... PA-2
Plymptonville Elem Sch—*school* ... PA-2
Plymton Sch—*school* ... IA-7
**Plymtonville**—*pop pl* ... PA-2
Plynn Cem—*cemetery* ... AL-4
*Ply Walk* ... IN-6
P. & M. Coal Company—*facility* ... KY-4
P.M. Delaubenfelds Dam—*dam* ... OR-9
P. M. Delaubenfelds Rsvr—*reservoir* ... OR-9
P Measells Lake Dam—*dam* ... MS-4
P Meike Ranch—*locale* ... WY-8
P M Johnston Dam Number One—*dam* ... AL-4
P M Johnston Dam Number Two—*dam* ... AL-4
P M Johnston Lake Number One—*reservoir* ... AL-4
P M Johnston Lake Number Two—*reservoir* ... AL-4
P M Lateral—*canal* ... TX-5
P M Norwood Dam—*dam* ... AL-4
P M Ranch—*locale* ... AZ-5
P Munson Ranch—*locale* ... NE-7
PNB Morton Airp—*airport* ... PA-2
P Neff—*locale* ... TX-5
P Nelson Ranch—*locale* ... ND-7
PN Island—*island* ... MT-8
PN Ranch—*locale* ... MT-8
P Nygard Ranch—*locale* ... ND-7
Po, Dauen—*gut* ... FM-9
Poacher Creek—*stream* ... ID-8
Poacher Gulch—*valley* ... MT-8
Poacher Lake—*lake* ... WY-8
Poacher Spring—*spring* ... ID-8
Poacher Trail—*trail* ... MT-8
Poacher Trail—*trail* ... WY-8
*Poaches Creek* ... TN-4
Poachie Range—*range* ... AZ-5
Poachie Spring—*spring* ... AZ-5
*Poadpis Harbor* ... MA-1
**Poag**—*pop pl* ... IL-6
Poag Branch—*stream* ... TN-4
Poage Cem—*cemetery* ... MO-7
Poage Cem—*cemetery* ... OK-5
Poage Creek—*stream* ... MO-7
Poage Island—*island* ... MO-7
Poage Lake—*lake* ... CO-8
Poage Sch—*school* ... KY-4
Poages Mill—*locale* ... VA-3
Poages Mill Overlook—*locale* ... VA-3
Poags Hole—*valley* ... NY-2
Poague Hollow—*valley* ... MO-7
Poague House—*hist pl* ... KY-4
Poague Run—*stream* (2) ... VA-3
Poague State Wildlife Area—*park* ... MO-7
**Poagville**—*pop pl* ... MS-4
*Poaipoai* ... FM-9
Poa Island—*island* ... AK-9
Poaiwa—*cape* ... HI-9
Poakana Falls—*falls* ... HI-9
Poakod—*unknown* ... FM-9
Poala—*summit* ... HI-9
*Poall Creek* ... OR-9
Poamoho Camp—*locale* ... HI-9
Poamoho Ditch Tunnel—*tunnel* ... HI-9
*Poamoho Gulch* ... HI-9
Poamoho Stream—*stream* ... HI-9
Poamoho Trail—*trail* ... HI-9
Poamoho Tunnel—*tunnel* ... HI-9
Poarch—*locale* ... AL-4
Poarch Cem—*cemetery* ... OK-5
Poarch Community Ch—*church* ... AL-4
Poarch Hollow—*valley* ... TN-4
Poarch Mission Cem—*cemetery* ... AL-4
Poarch Mission Ch—*church* ... AL-4
Poa Ridge Cem—*cemetery* ... MS-4
Poasoile—*island* ... FM-9
*Poasttown* ... OH-6
**Poast Town**—*pop pl* ... OH-6
**Poast Town Heights**—*pop pl* ... OH-6
Poatoapoat—*civil* ... FM-9
Poatoik—*locale* ... FM-9
*Poatopoat* ... FM-9
Po Biddy Crossroads—*locale* ... GA-3
Poblacion de Dolores—*locale* ... TX-5
**Poblado Sitios**—*pop pl* ... PR-3
Poblanos, Canada De Los —*valley* ... CA-9
Po-Boy—*locale* ... TX-5
Pobst Canyon—*valley* ... WA-9
**Poca**—*pop pl* ... WV-2
Poca Cem—*cemetery* ... MO-7
Poca Fiesta Shop Ctr—*locale* ... AZ-5
Poca Fork—*stream* ... WV-2
Poca Hollow—*valley* ... MO-7
Pocahontas—*locale* ... OR-9
Pocahontas—*locale* ... TN-4
**Pocahontas**—*pop pl* ... AL-4
**Pocahontas**—*pop pl* ... AR-4
**Pocahontas**—*pop pl* ... IL-6
**Pocahontas**—*pop pl* ... IA-7
**Pocahontas**—*pop pl* ... MS-4
**Pocahontas**—*pop pl* ... MO-7
**Pocahontas**—*pop pl* ... PA-2
**Pocahontas**—*pop pl* ... TN-4
**Pocahontas**—*pop pl* (2) ... VA-3
Pocahontas, Lake—*reservoir* ... NJ-2
*Pocahontas Baptist Church* ... MS-4
**Pocahontas Bay**—*pop pl* ... WA-9
Pocahontas Branch—*stream* ... TN-4
Pocahontas Cem—*cemetery* ... MS-4
Pocahontas Cem—*cemetery* ... VA-3
Pocahontas Ch—*church* ... AL-4
Pocahontas Ch—*church* ... MS-4
Pocahontas Club Lake Dam—*dam* ... MS-4
**Pocahontas (County)**—*pop pl* ... WV-2
Pocahontas County Courthouse—*hist pl* ... IA-7
Pocahontas Creek—*bay* ... MD-2
Pocahontas Creek—*stream* ... AK-9
Pocahontas Creek—*stream* ... WA-9
Pocahontas Dam—*dam* ... NJ-2
Pocahontas Dam—*dam* ... PA-2
Pocahontas Dam—*dam* ... TN-4
Pocahontas Hill—*summit* ... CO-8
Pocahontas Hist Dist—*hist pl* ... VA-3
Pocahontas Hot Springs—*spring* ... AK-9
Pocahontas HS—*school* ... VA-3
Pocahontas Lake—*reservoir* ... TN-4
Pocahontas Methodist Ch—*church* ... MS-4
Pocahontas Mine—*mine* ... CA-9
Pocahontas Mine—*mine* ... VA-3
Pocahontas Mine (underground)—*mine* ... AL-4
Pocahontas Mound—*summit* ... MS-4
Pocahontas Mound A—*hist pl* ... MS-4
Pocahontas Mound B—*hist pl* ... MS-4
Pocahontas Mounds Roadside Park—*park* ... MS-4
Pocahontas Mtn—*summit* ... OK-5
Pocahontas Picnic And Campground—*locale* ... WV-2
Pocahontas Point—*cape* ... IA-7
Pocahontas Post Office—*building* ... MS-4
Pocahontas Post Office—*building* ... TN-4
Pocahontas Post Office (historical)—*building* ... AL-4
Pocahontas Post Office (historical)—*building* ... TN-4
Pocahontas Sch (historical)—*school* ... TN-4
Pocahontas Schoolhouse—*hist pl* ... SD-7
Pocahontas Spring—*spring* ... NV-8
Pocahontas State For—*forest* ... VA-3
Pocahontas State Park—*park* ... VA-3
Pocahontas Times Print Shop—*hist pl* ... WV-2
Pocahontas Trail—*trail* ... WV-2
**Pocahontas Village**—*pop pl* ... VA-3
Pocalla Creek—*stream* ... SC-3
**Pocalla Springs**—*pop pl* ... SC-3
Pocalla Springs Golf Course—*other* ... SC-3
*Pocame* ... MA-1
*Pocamoonshine Lake* ... ME-1
Pocans Creek—*stream* ... MI-6
**Pocantico Hills**—*pop pl* ... NY-2
Pocantico Hills—*range* ... NY-2
Pocantico Hills Sch—*school* ... NY-2
Pocantico Lake—*reservoir* ... NY-2
Pocantico River—*stream* ... NY-2
Poca Ridge—*ridge* ... WV-2
*Poca River* ... WV-2
Poca Run—*stream* ... WV-2
Poca Sch—*school* ... WV-2
Pocasse, Lake—*reservoir* ... SD-7
*Pocasse Creek* ... SD-7
*Pocassee Creek* ... SD-7
*Pocasset* ... MA-1
**Pocasset**—*pop pl* ... MA-1
**Pocasset**—*pop pl* ... OK-5
**Pocasset**—*pop pl* ... RI-1
Pocasset Cedar Swamp—*swamp* ... MA-1
Pocasset Cedar Swamp—*swamp* ... RI-1
Pocasset Cem—*cemetery* ... OK-5
Pocasset Firehouse No. 7—*hist pl* ... MA-1
Pocasset Firehouse Number Seven—*building* ... MA-1
Pocasset Golf Club—*locale* ... MA-1
Pocasset Harbor—*gut* ... MA-1
*Pocasset Hill* ... MA-1
Pocasset Hill—*summit* ... RI-1
Pocasset Iron Works—*building* ... MA-1
Pocasset Lake—*reservoir* ... ME-1
*Pocasset Pond* ... RI-1
Pocasset Pond—*lake* ... RI-1
Pocasset River—*stream* ... MA-1
Pocasset River—*stream* ... RI-1
**Pocasset Station**—*pop pl* ... MA-1
Pocasset Station (historical)—*building* ... MA-1
*Pocassett Harbor* ... MA-1
*Pocassett Lake* ... ME-1
*Pocasset Village* ... MA-1
*Pocatalago* ... GA-3
Pocatalago (alternate name Pocataligo)—*other* ... GA-3
**Pocatalico**—*pop pl* ... WV-2
Pocatalico Creek—*stream* ... WV-2
Pocatalico (Magisterial District)—*fmr MCD* ... WV-2
Pocatalico River—*stream* ... WV-2
*Pocataligo* ... SC-3
**Pocataligo**—*pop pl* ... GA-3
**Pocataligo**—*pop pl* ... SC-3
**Pocataligo (alternate name for Pocatalago)**—*pop pl* ... GA-3
*Pocataligo River* ... SC-3
*Pocateligo* ... GA-3
**Pocatello**—*pop pl* ... ID-8
Pocatello, Lake—*lake* ... NY-2
Pocatello Bench—*bench* ... ID-8
Pocatello Carnegie Library—*hist pl* ... ID-8
Pocatello Creek—*stream* ... ID-8
Pocatello Federal Bldg—*hist pl* ... ID-8
Pocatello Gulch—*valley* ... UT-8
Pocatello Hist Dist—*hist pl* ... ID-8
Pocatello Municipal Airport—*airport* ... ID-8
Pocatello Range—*range* ... ID-8
Pocatello Valley—*basin* ... ID-8
Pocatello Valley—*valley* ... UT-8
*Pocathunsing* ... DE-2
*Pocatoes Creek* ... PA-2
Pocaty River—*stream* ... VA-3
P O Cave—*cave* ... AL-4
**Poccasett Heights**—*pop pl* ... RI-1
Poccosin Swamp—*stream* ... SC-3
Poccosin Swamp—*swamp* ... SC-3
Pochack Creek—*stream* ... NJ-2
Pochanee Branch—*stream* ... FL-3
Pocha Pond—*lake* ... MA-1
*Pochassic Hill* ... MA-1
Pochassic Hills—*summit* ... MA-1
Pochassic (historical)—*locale* ... MA-1
*Pochassic Mountain* ... MA-1
*Pochasuck Hill* ... MA-1
Poch Creek—*stream* ... WA-9
Poche', Judge Felix, Plantation House—*hist pl* ... LA-4
Poche de Noche—*bend* ... WI-6
Poche Island—*island* ... LA-4
Pocher Creek—*stream* ... OR-9
Pochet Island—*summit* ... MA-1
Pochet Island Marshes—*swamp* ... MA-1
Pochet Neck—*cape* ... MA-1
*Pochisco Creek* ... AL-4
*Pochkapochko* ... PA-2
Pochnoi Point—*cape* ... AK-9
Po Cho Ta—*bar* ... FM-9
Poch Peak—*summit* ... WA-9
Pochuck Creek—*stream* ... NJ-2
Pochuck Creek—*stream* ... NY-2
Pochuck Mtn—*summit* ... NJ-2
Pochuck Mtn—*summit* ... NY-2
Pochuck Neck—*ridge* ... NY-2
Pochung, Lake—*lake* ... NJ-2
*Pochunk Mountains* ... NJ-2
*Po-chuse-hat-che Creek* ... AL-4
Pock, The—*basin* ... WY-8
*Pocker Bill Spring* ... OR-9
**Pocket**—*pop pl* ... VA-3
Pocket, The—*bar* ... CA-9
Pocket, The—*basin* (2) ... AZ-5
Pocket, The—*basin* (2) ... GA-3
Pocket, The—*basin* ... TN-4
Pocket, The—*basin* (2) ... UT-8
Pocket, The—*bay* ... ME-1
Pocket, The—*flat* (2) ... CA-9
Pocket, The—*flat* ... GA-3
Pocket, The—*island* ... FL-3
Pocket, The—*locale* ... FL-3
Pocket, The—*locale* ... UT-8
Pocket, The—*swamp* ... FL-3
*Pocketapaces Neck* ... MA-1
Pocket Bayou—*gut* ... TX-5
Pocket Branch—*stream* ... GA-3
Pocket Canyon—*valley* (2) ... CA-9
Pocket Canyon—*valley* ... NV-8
Pocket Cem—*cemetery* ... GA-3
Pocket Ch—*church* ... NC-3
Pocket Creek—*stream* ... AK-9
Pocket Creek—*stream* ... AZ-5
Pocket Creek—*stream* ... GA-3
Pocket Creek—*stream* ... MN-6
Pocket Creek—*stream* (3) ... MT-8
Pocket Creek—*stream* ... NC-3
Pocket Creek—*stream* ... OR-9
Pocket Creek—*stream* ... TN-4
Pocket Creek—*stream* ... VA-3
Pocket Creek—*stream* ... WY-8
Pocket Creek Lake—*lake* ... WY-8
Pocket Eddy—*basin* ... MO-7
Pocket Gap—*gap* ... GA-3
Pocket Gulch—*valley* ... CA-9
Pocket Hill—*summit* ... AZ-5
Pocket Hollow—*valley* ... IN-6
Pocket Hollow—*valley* ... MO-7
Pocket Hollow—*valley* ... VA-3
Pocket Hollow Canyon—*valley* ... UT-8
Pocket Hollow Spring—*spring* ... UT-8
Pocket Island—*island* ... AK-9
Pocket Island—*island* ... LA-4
Pocket Lake—*lake* ... AZ-5
Pocket Lake—*lake* ... CA-9
Pocket Lake—*lake* ... FL-3
Pocket Lake—*lake* ... GA-3
Pocket Lake—*lake* (2) ... MN-6
Pocket Lake—*lake* ... MT-8
Pocket Lake—*lake* (2) ... OR-9
Pocket Lake—*lake* (3) ... WA-9
Pocket Lake—*lake* ... WY-8
Pocket Lake—*reservoir* ... MN-6
Pocket Meadow—*flat* ... CA-9
Pocket Mesa—*summit* ... UT-8
Pocket Mtn—*summit* ... NH-1
Pocket Opening—*gap* ... CA-9
Pocket Peak—*summit* ... CA-9
Pocket Point—*cliff* ... AZ-5
Pocket Point Tank—*reservoir* ... AZ-5
Pocket Ponds—*lake* ... NY-2
Pocket Rec Area—*locale* ... GA-3
Pocket Ridge—*ridge* ... VA-3
Pocket Rsvr—*reservoir* (2) ... WY-8
Pockets, The—*basin* ... UT-8
Pockets Fork—*stream* ... UT-8
Pocket Slough—*stream* ... TX-5
Pocket Spring—*spring* ... AZ-5
Pocket Spring—*spring* ... ID-8
Pocket Spring—*spring* ... UT-8
Pocket Tank—*reservoir* (3) ... AZ-5
Pockett Knoll—*summit* ... OR-9
*Pocketville* ... UT-8
Pocket Way—*trail* ... OR-9
Pocket Windmill—*locale* ... TX-5
*Pockford School* ... TN-4
Pocknett Neck—*cape* ... MA-1
Pockoy Island—*island* ... SC-3
Pocksha Pond—*lake* ... MA-1
Pockwockamus Deadwater—*channel* ... ME-1
Pockwockamus Falls—*falls* ... ME-1
Pockwockamus Pond—*lake* ... ME-1
Pockwockamus Stream—*stream* ... ME-1
Poco—*other* ... VA-3
Poco, Arroyo—*stream* ... CA-9
Poco, Lake—*reservoir* ... PA-2
Poco Canyon—*valley* ... NV-8
Poco Cem—*cemetery* ... IL-6
*Pocochedie Creek* ... MT-8
Pocochichee Butte—*summit* ... MT-8
Pocochichee Creek—*stream* ... MT-8
*Pocochock* ... VA-3
*Pocock* ... VT-1
Pocock Creek—*stream* ... CA-9
Poco Golf Course—*other* ... TX-5
*Poco Hollow* ... MO-7
Pocohontas Crossing—*locale* ... MO-7
*Pocokannd* ... PA-2
**Pocola**—*pop pl* ... OK-5
Pocola (CCD)—*cens area* ... OK-5
Pocola HS—*school* ... OK-5
Pocola JHS—*school* ... OK-5
*Poco Lake* ... PA-2
Poco Lake—*reservoir* ... TX-5
Pocola Sch—*school* ... OK-5
*Pocolechetto Creek* ... AL-4
*Pocolechetto Creek* ... MS-4
Pocomate Springs—*spring* ... AZ-5
**Pocomo**—*pop pl* ... MA-1
*Pocomocke* ... MD-2
*Pocomocke City* ... MD-2
Pocomo Head—*cape* ... MA-1
**Pocomoke**—*pop pl* ... NC-3
Pocomoke Ch—*church* ... VA-3
**Pocomoke City**—*pop pl* ... MD-2
**Pocomoke City (Pocomoke)**—*pop pl* ... MD-2
*Pocomoke (Pocomoke City)* ... MD-2
Pocomoke River—*stream* ... DE-2
Pocomoke River—*stream* ... MD-2
Pocomoke River—*stream* ... VA-3
Pocomoke Sound—*bay* ... MD-2
Pocomoke Sound—*bay* ... VA-3
Pocomoke State For—*forest* ... MD-2
*Pocomo Marshes* ... MA-1
Pocomo Meadow—*swamp* ... MA-1
Pocomoonshine Branch—*stream* ... ME-1
Pocomoonshine Lake—*lake* ... ME-1
Pocomoonshine Mtn—*summit* ... ME-1
**Pocono**—*pop pl* ... ID-8
**Pocono Country Place**—*pop pl* ... PA-2
Pocono Creek—*stream* ... ID-8
Pocono Creek—*stream* ... PA-2
Pocono Downs—*locale* ... PA-2
Pocono Elementary Center—*school* ... PA-2
Pocono Environmental Education Center—*school* ... PA-2
**Pocono Farms East**—*pop pl* ... PA-2
**Pocono Heights**—*pop pl* ... PA-2
Pocono Hershey Resort Golf Course—*locale* ... PA-2
Pocono Highland Dam—*dam* ... PA-2
Pocono Highlands Lake—*lake* ... PA-2
Pocono Highlands Lake—*reservoir* ... PA-2
Pocono Hill—*summit* ... ID-8
*Pocono Interchange* ... PA-2
Pocono International Raceway—*other* ... PA-2
*Pocono Knob* ... PA-2
**Pocono Lake**—*pop pl* ... PA-2
Pocono Lake—*reservoir* ... PA-2
Pocono Lake Dam—*dam* ... PA-2
Pocono Lake Preserve—*park* ... PA-2
**Pocono Lake Preserve (Preserve)**—*pop pl* ... PA-2
**Pocono Laurel Lake**—*pop pl* ... PA-2
**Pocono Manor**—*pop pl* ... PA-2
Pocono Manor Golf Course—*locale* ... PA-2
Pocono Manor (ski area)—*locale* ... PA-2
Pocono Mission Sch—*school* ... PA-2
Pocono Mountain Junior-Senior HS—*school* ... PA-2
Pocono Mountain Lake—*reservoir* ... PA-2
Pocono Mountain Lake Dam—*dam* ... PA-2
**Pocono Mountain Lake Estates**—*pop pl* (2) ... PA-2
Pocono Mountain Lake Resort—*locale* ... PA-2
Pocono Mountains—*summit* (2) ... PA-2
Pocono Mountains Municipal Airp—*airport* ... PA-2
Pocono Mountain Water Forest—*locale* ... PA-2
**Pocono Mountain Woodland Lakes**—*pop pl* ... PA-2
Pocono Mtn—*summit* ... PA-2
**Pocono Park**—*pop pl* ... PA-2
Pocono Peak Lake—*reservoir* ... PA-2
**Pocono Pines**—*pop pl* ... PA-2
**Pocono Pines (Naomi Pines)**—*pop pl* ... PA-2
Pocono Plateau Lake—*reservoir* ... PA-2
**Pocono Playhouse**—*pop pl* ... PA-2
Pocono Plaza—*locale* ... PA-2
Pocono Point—*cape* ... CT-1
*Pocono Pond* ... PA-2
Pocono Post Office (historical)—*building* ... PA-2
Pocono Raceway Airp—*airport* ... PA-2
Pocono Spring—*spring* ... PA-2
**Pocono Springs**—*pop pl* ... PA-2
**Pocono Summit**—*pop pl* ... PA-2
**Pocono Summit Estates**—*pop pl* ... PA-2
Pocono Summit Lake—*lake* ... PA-2
**Pocono (Township of)**—*pop pl* ... PA-2
Pocono Union Ch—*church* ... PA-2
Pocono Woodland Lake—*reservoir* ... PA-2
Pocono Woodland Lake Dam—*dam* ... PA-2
Pocopson—*locale* ... PA-2
Pocopson Creek—*stream* ... PA-2
Pocopson Home—*building* ... PA-2
**Pocopson (Township of)**—*pop pl* ... PA-2
Pocoshock—*uninc pl* ... VA-3
Pocoshock Creek—*stream* ... VA-3
Pocosin, The—*swamp* (2) ... NC-3
Pocosin, The (historical)—*swamp* ... AL-4
Pocosin Bay—*swamp* ... NC-3
Pocosin Cabin—*locale* ... VA-3
Pocosin Creek—*stream* ... LA-4
Pocosin Fork—*stream* ... WV-2
Pocosin Hollow—*valley* ... VA-3
Pocosin Hollow Trail—*trail* ... VA-3
Pocosinlake, The—*reservoir* ... AL-4
*Pocosin Pond* ... AL-4
Pocosin Pond—*lake* ... FL-3
Pocosin Pond—*lake* ... GA-3
Pocosin Pond Dam—*dam* ... AL-4
*Pocosin River* ... VA-3
Pocosin Trail—*trail* ... VA-3
Pocosin Wilderness—*park* ... NC-3
*Pocoson, The* ... AL-4
Pocoson Branch—*stream* (2) ... NC-3
*Pocoson River* ... VA-3
Pocoson Swamp—*swamp* ... FL-3
Pocosset River—*stream* ... MA-1
**Pocotalaco (historical)**—*pop pl* ... FL-3
*Pocotalago* ... GA-3
*Pocotalca* ... FL-3
*Pocotalico River* ... WV-2
*Pocotaligo* ... WV-2
**Pocotaligo**—*pop pl* ... SC-3
*Pocotaligo River* ... WV-2
Pocotaligo River—*stream* (2) ... SC-3
*Pocotaligo Swamp* ... SC-3
Pocotillo Mine—*mine* ... NV-8
Pocotopaug Creek—*stream* ... CT-1
**Pocotopaug Lake**—*pop pl* ... CT-1
Pocotopaug Lake—*reservoir* ... CT-1
Poco Well—*well* ... NV-8
Pocquette Lake—*lake* ... MN-6
Pocum Cove—*valley* ... AZ-5
Pocumcus Lake—*lake* ... ME-1
Pocumcus Narrows—*channel* ... ME-1
*Pocumpus Lake* ... ME-1
Pocum Tank—*reservoir* ... AZ-5
*Pocumtuck* ... MA-1
Pocumtuck Mtn—*summit* ... MA-1
Pocumtuck Range—*ridge* ... MA-1
Pocumtuck Rock—*summit* ... MA-1
Pocum Wash—*valley* ... AZ-5
*Pocwock Brook* ... ME-1
Pocwock Stream—*stream* ... ME-1
Poda Branch—*stream* ... AR-4
Poddle Mountain Canyon—*valley* ... NV-8
Poddle Mtn—*summit* ... NV-8
Poddong—*slope* ... MH-9
Poddy Creek—*stream* ... WY-8
Poddy Hollow—*valley* ... AR-4
Poddyville Post Office (historical)—*building* ... TN-4
Pode Creek—*stream* ... OR-9
Podell Airp—*airport* ... IN-6
Podell Ditch—*canal* ... IN-6
Podesta Camp—*locale* ... CA-9
Podesva Cem—*cemetery* ... MO-7
Podgys Mtn—*summit* ... NC-3
Pod Meadow—*swamp* ... MA-1
Podmore, Joseph W., Bldg—*hist pl* ... HI-9
Podo—*locale* ... TX-5
Podo Creek—*stream* ... AR-4
Podonque Cem—*cemetery* ... NY-2
Podopholine Post Office (historical)—*building* ... TN-4
*Podoriasu* ... PW-9
*Podpis* ... MA-1
*Podpis Harbor* ... MA-1
Pods Branch—*stream* ... KY-4
Podsopochni Bay—*bay* ... AK-9
Podsopochni Point—*cape* ... AK-9
Podunk—*locale* ... CT-1
Podunk—*locale* (2) ... MI-6
Podunk—*locale* ... NY-2
**Podunk**—*pop pl* ... MA-1
**Podunk**—*pop pl* ... MI-6
**Podunk**—*pop pl* ... VT-1
Podunk Brook—*stream* ... NY-2
Podunk Brook—*stream* ... VT-1
Podunk Cem—*cemetery* ... MA-1
*Podunk Creek* ... UT-8
Podunk Creek—*stream* ... MI-6
Podunk Creek—*stream* ... UT-8
*Podunk Forest Service Station* ... UT-8
Podunk Great Plain—*flat* ... CT-1
Podunk Guard Station—*locale* ... UT-8
*Podunk Lake* ... NY-2
Podunk Lake—*lake* (2) ... MI-6
*Podunk Pass* ... UT-8
*Podunk Pond* ... CT-1
*Podunk Pond* ... MA-1
Podunk Pond—*lake* ... ME-1
*Podunk Pond Quabaug Pond* ... MA-1
Podunk River—*stream* ... CT-1

Podus WI-6
Poe KS-7
Poe—locale CA-9
Poe—locale TX-5
**Poe**—pop pl IL-6
**Poe**—pop pl IN-6
**Poe**—pop pl NM-5
**Poe**—pop pl OH-6
**Poe**—pop pl SC-3
**Poe**—pop pl VA-3
**Poe**—pop pl WV-2
Poe, Bessie, Hall—hist pl OK-5
Poe, Edgar Allan, House—hist pl MD-2
Poe, Edgar Allan, House—hist pl NC-3
Poe, Edgar Allan, House—hist pl PA-2
Poe, Edgar Allen, Sch—hist pl PA-2
Poe Bay—bay AK-9
Poe Branch—stream (2) AL-4
Poe Branch—stream KY-4
Poe Branch—stream (4) TN-4
Poe Bridge Cem—cemetery AL-4
Poe Bridge Mtn—summit AL-4
Poe Cem—cemetery AR-4
Poe Cem—cemetery IL-6
Poe Cem—cemetery (2) MO-7
Poe Cem—cemetery (3) TN-4
Poe Cem—cemetery WV-2
Poeckan Creek VA-3
Poe Cottage—hist pl NY-2
Poe Creek MS-4
Poe Creek PA-2
Poe Creek—stream AR-4
Poe Creek—stream ID-8
Poe Creek—stream KY-4
Poe Creek—stream NC-3
Poe Creek—stream SC-3
Poe Creek—stream WI-6
Poe Dam—dam CA-9
Poe Dam—dam PA-2
Poe Ditch—canal OH-6
Poee Creek—stream ID-8
Poe Field—flat MS-4
Poe Field—locale GA-3
Poe Fish Weir—hist pl NC-3
Poe Gulch WA-9
Poe Hill—summit (2) KY-4
Poe (historical)—locale AL-4
Poehler, August F., House—hist pl MN-6
Poehler Airp—airport OR-9
Poehler Gas Field—oilfield TX-5
Poehnart Pond CT-1
Poehnarts Pond CT-1
Poehnerts Pond—reservoir CT-1
Poe Hollow—valley TX-5
Poe House—building PA-2
Poe Intermediate Sch—school VA-3
Poe Island—island AK-9
Poe Knob—summit GA-3
Poe Lake—lake MN-6
Poe Lake—reservoir IN-6
Poe Lake—reservoir PA-2
Poe Lake Dam—dam IN-6
Poe Lakes—reservoir AL-4
Poe Landing—locale AL-4
Poeleele Stream—stream HI-9
Poeling Lake—lake MO-7
Poelke SD-7
Poellnitz Dam AL-4
Poelua Bay—bay HI-9
Poelua Gulch—valley HI-9
Poelua Stream HI-9
Poe Mine—mine NM-5
Poe Mountain PA-2
Poe Mtn—summit CA-9
Poe Mtn—summit WA-9
Poe Mtn—summit WY-8
Poenarts Pond CT-1
Poenerts Pond CT-1
Poeno Creek—stream SD-7
Poentic Kill—stream NY-2
Poe Paddy State Park—park PA-2
Poe Park—flat MT-8
Poe Park—park NY-2
Poe Park—park WA-9
Poe Peak WA-9
Poe Place—locale OR-9
Poe Point—cape MI-6
Poe Powerhouse—other CA-9
**Poe Prairie**—pop pl TX-5
Poe Prairie Cem—cemetery TX-5
Poer—other TX-5
Poer Dam—dam OR-9
Poe Reef—bar MI-6
Poe Ridge TN-4
Poer Rsvr—reservoir OR-9
Poer Spring—spring AZ-5
Poe Run—other WV-2
Poe Run—stream OH-6
Poe Run—stream PA-2
Poe Run—stream WV-2
**Poes Acres (subdivision)**—pop pl AL-4
Poe Saddle—gap ID-8
Poes Bend—bend AL-4
Poes Branch TN-4
Poe Sch—school (2) IL-6
Poe Sch—school (2) MI-6
Poe Sch—school PA-2
Poe Sch—school TX-5
Poe Sch (abandoned)—school MO-7
Poeschel Cem—cemetery MO-7
Poe Sch (historical)—school AL-4
Poes Ferry AL-4
Poes Ferry (historical)—locale MS-4
Poe Shrine—park VA-3
Poes Mtn—summit VA-3
Poe Spring—spring FL-3
Poe Spring—spring MO-7
Poe Spring—spring OR-9
Poe Spring—spring TN-4
Poesta Creek—stream TX-5
**Poestenkill**—pop pl NY-2
Poesten Kill—stream NY-2
Poesten Kill Gorge Hist Dist—hist pl NY-2
**Poestenkill (Town of)**—pop pl NY-2
**Poesville**—pop pl TX-5
Poet Creek—stream ID-8
Poet Creek Campground—locale ID-8
Poet Drain—stream MI-6
Poetkner Cem—cemetery OH-6
Poet Lake—lake MN-6
**Poetown**—pop pl VA-3
**Poetown (Maple)**—pop pl OH-6
Poe Township—fmr MCD IA-7
**Poe Township**—pop pl ND-7
**Poetry**—pop pl TX-5
Poetry Baptist Ch—church TX-5
Poets Cove ME-1
Poets Seat—rock MA-1
Poe Tunnel—tunnel CA-9
Poe Valley—valley OR-9
Poe Valley (CCD)—cens area OR-9
Poe Valley Fire Tower—tower PA-2
Poe Valley State Park—park PA-2
Poeville (Site)—locale NV-8
Pofahl Lake—lake NE-7
Pofala Hill—summit AS-9
Poff—locale VA-3
Poff Brake—swamp AR-4
Poff Brook—stream IN-6
Poff Cem—cemetery (2) IN-6
Poff Cem—cemetery VA-3
Poff Elem Sch—school PA-2
Poffenberger Caves—cave PA-2
Poffenberger Road Bridge—hist pl MD-2
Poffenbergers Landing—locale CA-9
Pofferman Spring—spring ID-8
Poff Hollow—valley VA-3
Poff Mtn—summit AR-4
Poff School PA-2
Poff (Township of)—fmr MCD AR-4
Poff Trail—trail PA-2
**Poga**—pop pl TN-4
Poga Creek—stream NC-3
Pogami Lake MN-6
Poga Mtn—summit NC-3
Poga Sch (historical)—school TN-4
Poge, Cape—cape MA-1
Poge Branch—stream VA-3
Poge Creek—stream CA-9
Pogel—island FM-9
Pogenaarin MP-9
Pogenaga-to MP-9
Poges Hole—valley PA-2
Poges Mill VA-3
Poges Peak—summit CA-9
Poggi Canyon—valley CA-9
Poggie Strand—swamp FL-3
Poggio Branch—stream VA-3
Pogibshi Point—cape AK-9
Pogie Point Campground—locale CA-9
Pogik Bay—bay AK-9
Pogik Point—cape AK-9
Pogliano Ranch—locale MT-8
Pogo—locale AL-4
Pogo Community Center—building AL-4
Pogo Lake—lake MN-6
Pogond Brook—stream CT-1
Pogones State Wildlife Mngmt Area—park MN-6
Pogonip Ridge—ridge NV-8
Pogopuk Creek—stream AK-9
Pogromni River—stream AK-9
Pogromni Volcano—summit AK-9
Pogue AZ-5
**Pogue**—pop pl PA-2
Pogue, The—lake VT-1
Pogue Branch—stream TN-4
Pogue Branch—stream TX-5
Pogue Canyon—valley CA-9
Pogue Cem—cemetery IN-6
Pogue Cemetery MS-4
Pogue Corners—locale OH-6
Pogue Creek—stream KY-4
Pogue Creek—stream MO-7
Pogue Creek—stream TN-4
Pogue Creek Cave—cave TN-4
Pogue Flat—flat WA-9
Pogue Gulch—valley OR-9
Pogue Hill—summit TN-4
Pogue Hollow—valley KY-4
Pogue Hollow—valley (3) MO-7
Pogue Hollow—valley TN-4
Pogue Hollow Cove—bay (2) MO-7
Pogue Lake—lake IL-6
Pogue Lake—lake TX-5
Pogue Lake—reservoir MO-7
Pogue Mtn—summit NC-3
Pogue Mtn—summit WA-9
Pogue Pit—cave AL-4
Pogue Point—summit OR-9
Pogue Run—stream OH-6
Pogue Run—stream WV-2
Pogue Sch—school IL-6
Pogue Sch—school TN-4
Pogue Spring—spring OR-9
Pogues Run—stream IN-6
Pogues Station—locale NV-8
Pogues Tunnel—tunnel HI-9
Pogue Tank—reservoir NM-5
Poguoy Brook MA-1
Pogy TN-4
Pogy—locale MI-6
Pogy Brook—stream ME-1
Pogy Creek—stream MI-6
Pogy Lake—lake MI-6
Pogy Notch—gap ME-1
Pogy Pond—lake ME-1
Pohachqueunk PA-2
Pohaida Lake—lake WI-6
Pohakaa—valley HI-9
Pohakanele—civil HI-9
Pohakapu HI-9
Pohakaunoho Ridge—ridge HI-9
Pohakea HI-9
Pohakea—cliff HI-9
Pohakea—summit (4) HI-9
Pohakea Gulch—valley HI-9
Pohakea Homesteads—civil HI-9
**Pohakea Homesteads (Lewiston)**—pop pl HI-9
Pohakea Pass—gap HI-9
Pohakea Peak HI-9
Pohakea Sch—school HI-9
Pohakiikii—summit HI-9
Pohakuahalulu—bay HI-9
Pohakuau HI-9
Pohaku Eaea HI-9
Pohaku Eaea Point HI-9
Pohakueaea Point—cape HI-9
Pohakuhaku—civil HI-9
Pohakuhaku Gulch—valley HI-9
Pohaku Hanalei HI-9
Pohaku Hanalei—summit HI-9
Pohakuhonu Gulch—valley HI-9
Pohakuhonu Stream—stream HI-9
Pohakukaanapali—beach HI-9
Pohaku ka luahine—hist pl HI-9
Pohaku Kamalii—cliff HI-9
Pohakukane—cliff HI-9
Pohakulaie—cliff HI-9
Pohakuloa HI-9
Pohakuloa—cape (2) HI-9
Pohakuloa—summit (9) HI-9
Pohakuloa Camp—locale HI-9
Pohakuloa Gulch—valley (3) HI-9
Pohakuloa Harbor—harbor HI-9
Pohakuloa Point—cape (2) HI-9
Pohakuloa Ranger Station—locale HI-9
Pohakuloa Rock HI-9
Pohakuloa Training Area—military HI-9
Pohakulua—civil HI-9
Pohakulua—island HI-9
Pohaku Malumalu—bar HI-9
Pohaku Manamana—island HI-9
Pohakumanu—summit HI-9
Pohakumanu HI-9
Pohakumanu Bay—bay HI-9
Pohakumauliuli—summit HI-9
Pohakumauliuli Gulch—valley HI-9
Pohakunui—summit HI-9
Pohaku o Hanalei—summit HI-9
Pohakuohau—cape HI-9
Pohakuokala Gulch—valley HI-9
Pohaku o Kane HI-9
Pohakuokane—summit HI-9
Pohakuokeaho—bar HI-9
Pohakuopio—bar HI-9
Pohakupaa Stream—stream HI-9
Pohaku Paea—island HI-9
Pohakupala—summit HI-9
Pohaku Palaha—summit HI-9
Pohakupele—summit HI-9
Pohakupili HI-9
Pohaku Pili HI-9
Pohakupili—civil HI-9
Pohakupili—summit HI-9
Pohakupili Gulch—valley HI-9
Pohakupili Peak HI-9
**Pohakupu**—pop pl HI-9
Pohakupuka—civil HI-9
Pohakupuka Stream—stream HI-9
Pohakupule—summit HI-9
Pohakupule Gulch—valley HI-9
Pohakuulaula—summit HI-9
Pohakuwaakauhi—bay HI-9
Poham Rocks Light House—locale RI-1
Pohatcong Creek—stream NJ-2
Pohatcong Lake—reservoir NJ-2
Pohatcong Mtn—summit NJ-2
**Pohatcong (Township of)**—pop pl NJ-2
Pohatcong Valley—valley NJ-2
Pohchishatchee Creek AL-4
Pohclashatchee Creek AL-4
Pohegnut Ledge—bench CT-1
Pohegnut Rsvr—reservoir CT-1
Poheick Bay VA-3
Poheick Creek VA-3
Poheta Cem—cemetery KS-7
Poheta (historical)—locale KS-7
Pohick—locale WV-2
**Pohick**—pop pl VA-3
Pohick Bay—bay VA-3
Pohick Ch—church VA-3
Pohick Church—hist pl VA-3
Pohick Creek—stream VA-3
**Pohick Estates**—pop pl VA-3
**Pohick Hills**—pop pl VA-3
Pohick Hollow—valley WV-2
**Pohick River Pines**—pop pl VA-3
Pohigamet Pond CT-1
Pohina, Pali—cliff HI-9
Pohiokeawe HI-9
Pohl Creek—stream MN-6
**Pohlitz (Township of)**—pop pl MN-6
Pohl Lake—lake MN-6
Pohlmann, Elizabeth, House—hist pl IA-7
Pohlmann, Henry, House—hist pl IA-7
Pohlmann's Hall—hist pl NJ-2
Pohlod Creek—stream MT-8
Pohls Hill—summit WA-9
Pohly Drain—canal MI-6
Pohnahdo, Pilen—stream FM-9
Pohn Ahtik—bar FM-9
Pohnahtik, Kepidau En—channel FM-9
Pohnahtik, Pilen—stream FM-9
Pohnahu—summit FM-9
Pohnallap—locale FM-9
Pohnauleng—civil FM-9
Pohnauleng—locale FM-9
Pohnauleng, Dolen—summit FM-9
Pohn Auwas—locale FM-9
Pohndau—locale FM-9
Pohndauauk—bar FM-9
Pohn Dekehn Awak—bar FM-9
Pohn Diadi—cape FM-9
Pohndimwur—locale FM-9
Pohn Diwi—unknown FM-9
Pohndolap—summit FM-9
Pohn Dolekirou—locale FM-9
Pohn Dollap—summit FM-9
Pohndollap Peak FM-9
Pohn Dollen Net—summit FM-9
Pohn Dolomwar Peiei—locale FM-9
Pohneir En Na—bar FM-9
Pohneken Are—swamp FM-9
Pohnered—locale FM-9
Pohn Iak—locale FM-9
Pohn Imwinsapw—locale FM-9
Pohniot—bar FM-9
Pohn Isamah—summit FM-9
Pohn Isilap—bar FM-9
Pohniso—summit FM-9
**Pohnkalangi**—pop pl FM-9
Pohn Kali—locale FM-9
Pohn Keimw—locale FM-9
Pohn Koi—locale FM-9
Pohn Kotoro—unknown FM-9
Pohn Lahpar—swamp FM-9
**Pohnlangas**—pop pl FM-9
Pohn Lehpwel—swamp FM-9
Pohnlehr—summit FM-9
Pohn Limw, Pilen—stream FM-9
Pohnloang—locale FM-9
Pohn Maka—locale FM-9
Pohnmall—locale FM-9
Pohnmed—locale FM-9
Pohn Mwahu—unknown FM-9
Pohn Mwasowel—locale FM-9
Pohn Mwekioar, Dolen—summit FM-9
Pohn Mwudok—bar FM-9
Pohn Nemwen Parem—bar FM-9
Pohn Ngihn Eni—unknown FM-9
Pohn Pahini—unknown FM-9
Pohn Paip—locale FM-9
Pohnpaip—unknown FM-9
Pohnpe—cape FM-9
Pohn Pehnmen—flat FM-9
Pohnpeil—cliff FM-9
Pohnpeimei—summit FM-9
Pohnpelik—bar FM-9
**Pohn Pw**—pop pl FM-9
Pohn Pwel FM-9
Pohn Pwel Inta—ridge FM-9
Pohn Pwet—locale FM-9
**Pohnrakied**—pop pl FM-9
Pohn Saleng—locale FM-9
Pohnseiuh—locale FM-9
Pohnsekir—summit FM-9
Pohn Semahk—unknown FM-9
**Pohn Semwet**—pop pl FM-9
Pohn Sok—locale FM-9
Pohnsou—locale FM-9
Pohntakai Pwetepwet—summit FM-9
Pohntakaitohr—locale FM-9
Pohn Tehnmei—summit FM-9
Pohntemoar—summit FM-9
Pohn Uh—locale FM-9
Pohn Uhs—locale FM-9
Pohnwet—summit FM-9
Pohocco Cem—cemetery NE-7
Pohocco Ch—church NE-7
**Pohocco Township**—pop pl NE-7
Pohoiki—civil HI-9
Pohoiki—locale HI-9
Pohokea HI-9
Pohokinikini—area HI-9
Pohono CA-9
Pohono Trail—trail CA-9
Pohopoco Creek—stream PA-2
Pohopoco Creek Dam—dam PA-2
Pohopoco Mtn—summit PA-2
Pohopoco Tower—tower PA-2
Pohopoko Creek PA-2
Pohopoko Mountain PA-2
Poho Ridge—ridge CA-9
Pohoula—summit HI-9
Pohrasapw—civil FM-9
Pohsain—unknown FM-9
Pohtakied FM-9
Pohue—civil HI-9
Pohue, Lae—cape HI-9
Pohue Bay—bay HI-9
Pohueloa Valley—valley HI-9
Pohukaina Sch—school HI-9
Pohuku o Kane HI-9
Poio, Mount—summit MT-8
Poia Lake—lake MT-8
Poi Gamliangel PW-9
Poignard, Bayou—gut LA-4
Poikahi—summit HI-9
Poile Zeda Cem—cemetery NJ-2
Poillon-Seguine-Britton House—hist pl NY-2
**Poinciana**—pop pl FL-3
Poinciana Elem Sch—school (2) FL-3
Poinciana Gardens (subdivision)—locale FL-3
Poinciana Hammock—island FL-3
Poinciana Park—park CA-9
Poinciana Park—park FL-3
Poinciana Park Sch—school FL-3
**Poinciana Park (subdivision)**—pop pl FL-3
Poinciana Plaza (Shop Ctr)—locale FL-3
Poinciana Sch—school FL-3
Poincianna Island—island FL-3
**Poincianna Place (subdivision)**—pop pl FL-3
Poindexter—locale KY-4
Poindexter—locale VA-3
**Poindexter**—pop pl TX-5
Poindexter, H. D., Houses—hist pl NC-3
Poindexter, William, House—hist pl KY-4
Poindexter Branch—stream KY-4
Poindexter Branch—stream NC-3
Poindexter Branch—stream TX-5
Poindexter Branch—stream WV-2
Poindexter Cem—cemetery VA-3
Poindexter Ch—church NC-3
Poindexter Elementary School MS-4
**Poindexter Heights (subdivision)**—pop pl TN-4
Poindexter Island—island MS-4
Poindexter Knob—summit GA-3
Poindexter Park—park MS-4
Poindexter Place—locale OR-9
Poindexter Rsvr—reservoir CA-9
**Poindexters**—pop pl VA-3
Poindexter Sch—school MS-4
Poindexter Slough—stream MT-8
Poindexter-Vick Cem—cemetery AL-4
Poineer Square—post sta WA-9
Poinell Point WA-9
Poinrw Au Tourtre MN-6
Poinsett SD-7
Poinsett, Lake—lake FL-3
Poinsett, Lake—lake SD-7
Poinsetta Apartments—hist pl IL-6
Poinsetta Colony—locale SD-7
Poinsett Bridge—hist pl SC-3
Poinsett Cem—cemetery SD-7
Poinsett Community Club—hist pl AR-4
**Poinsett (County)**—pop pl AR-4
Poinsette SD-7
Poinsett (historical)—locale SD-7
Poinsett Hotel—hist pl SC-3
Poinsett House—hist pl DE-2
Poinsettia MP-9
**Poinsettia Park**—pop pl FL-3
**Poinsettia Subdivision**—pop pl TN-4
**Poinsettia Tract**—pop pl CA-9
Poinsett Lodge—locale FL-3
Poinsett MS—school FL-3
Poinsett Park—park CA-9
Poinsett Park Lake—reservoir SC-3
Poinsett Post Office (historical)—building SD-7
Poinsett Rsvr SC-3
Poinsett State For—forest SC-3
Poinsett State Park—park SC-3
Point MS-4
Point OH-6
Point—locale MS-4
**Point**—pop pl LA-4
**Point**—pop pl PA-2
**Point**—pop pl TX-5
Point—post sta PA-2
Point, Bay—cape (3) MI-6
Point, Lake—lake AK-9
Point, Point of—cape VA-3
Point, The PA-2
Point, The—cape (2) AZ-5
Point, The—cape FL-3
Point, The—cape GA-3
Point, The—cape KY-4
Point, The—cape MT-8
Point, The—cape OR-9
Point, The—cape VA-3
Point, The—cliff MT-8
Point, The—cliff UT-8
Point, The—cliff WY-8
**Point, The**—pop pl OH-6
Point, The—summit (3) NV-8
Point, The—summit (2) UT-8
Point, The, Hist Dist—hist pl NY-2
Point Abbaye—cape MI-6
Point Abbaye Reef—bar MI-6
Point a Coquilles LA-4
Point Adam—cape AK-9
Point A Dam—dam AL-4
Point Adams Coast Guard Station—military OR-9
Point Adolphus—cape AK-9
Point Agassiz—cape AK-9
Point Agassiz Peninsula—cape AK-9
Point Aguirre—cape AK-9
Point Agusta—cape AK-9
Point Airy—locale NJ-2
Point Alderton MA-1
Point Aliaksin—cape AK-9
**Point Allerton**—pop pl MA-1
Point Allerton Lifesaving Station—hist pl MA-1
Point Allerton Station (historical)—locale MA-1
Point Alones—cape CA-9
Point Alonzo—cape AK-9
Point Amargura—cape AK-9
Point Amelia—cape AK-9
Point Amelius—cape AK-9
Point Ancon—cape AK-9
Point Animas—cape AK-9
Point Anmer—cape AK-9
Point Anno Nueva CA-9
Point Ano Nuevo—cape CA-9
Point Aquarius AL-4
Point Arboleda—cape AK-9
Point Arena—cape CA-9
**Point Arena**—pop pl CA-9
Point Arena Air Force Station—military CA-9
Point Arena (CCD)—cens area CA-9
Point Arena Creek—stream CA-9
Point Arguello CA-9
Point Arguello—cape CA-9
Point Aries—cape AK-9
Point Aru FM-9
Point Arucenas—cape AK-9
Point Aruncenas AK-9
Point au Chien LA-4
**Point Au Chien**—pop pl LA-4
Point au Fer Channel—channel NY-2
Point Au Fer Island—island (2) LA-4
Point Au Fer Oil Field—oilfield LA-4
Point au Fer Reef—bar NY-2
Point Au Fer Shell Reef—bar LA-4
Point au Frene MI-6
**Point Au Gres**—pop pl MI-6
Point Aulon CA-9
**Point Au Rouche**—pop pl NY-2
Point au Sable MI-6
Point au Sable WI-6
Point Au View—hist pl KY-4
Point Aux Chenes MI-6
Point Aux Chenes Bay—bay MS-4
Point aux Herbes LA-4
Point aux Peaux MI-6
Point aux Pines AL-4
Point Avisadero CA-9
Point Avisadero—cape CA-9
Point B—locale NV-8
**Point Baker**—pop pl AK-9
**Point Baker**—pop pl FL-3
Point Banks—cape AK-9
Point Baptist Ch Innerarity Point Road—church FL-3
Point Barber—cape AK-9
Point Bar Cutoff—bend AR-4
Point Barnes—cape AK-9
**Point Barre**—pop pl LA-4
Point Barringon—cape AK-9
Point Barrow—cape AK-9
Point Barrow Refuge Station—hist pl AK-9
Point Barrow Station—military AK-9
Point Bar Thorofare—channel NJ-2
Point Bartlett—cape CA-9
Point Basse LA-4
Point Bazon—cape AK-9
Point Bazil—cape AK-9
Point Beach CT-1
Point Beach—beach CT-1
Point Beach—cape NC-3
Point Beach—cliff VA-3
Point Beach Nuclear Powerplant—other WI-6
Point Beach State For—forest WI-6
Point Beals—cape WA-9
Point Bede—cape AK-9
Point Beenar—cape CA-9
Point Belcher—cape AK-9
Point Benham—cape AK-9
Point Bennett—cape CA-9
Point Bentinck—cape AK-9
Point Betsie Light Station—hist pl MI-6
Point Blanc MS-4
Point Blanco FL-3
Point Blanco Island FL-3
Point Blank TX-5
Pointblank—locale TX-5
Point Blank (CCD)—cens area TX-5
**Point Blank (corporate name for Pointblank)**—pop pl TX-5
Pointblank (corporate name Point Blank) TX-5
Pointblank Sch—school TX-5
**Point Blue**—pop pl LA-4
Point Bluff WI-6
Point Bluff—cliff WI-6
Point Bluff Cave—cave MO-7
Point Bluff Sch (abandoned)—school MO-7
Point Blunt Rock—island CA-9
Point Bolin—cape WA-9
Point Bolitas CA-9
Point Bolivar TX-5
Point Bolivar Lighthouse—hist pl TX-5
Point Boneta CA-9
Point Bonita—cape CA-9
Point Borlase—cape AK-9
Point Bottom—bend UT-8
Point Branch—stream DE-2
Point Breese—uninc pl MD-2
Point Breeze—cape CT-1
Point Breeze—cape MD-2
Point Breeze—cape PA-2
Point Breeze—hist pl NJ-2
Point Breeze—locale LA-4
Point Breeze—locale NJ-2
Point Breeze—locale (2) PA-2
**Point Breeze**—pop pl DE-2
**Point Breeze**—pop pl NY-2
**Point Breeze**—pop pl (2) PA-2
Point Breeze—uninc pl (2) PA-2
Point Breeze Beach—beach NY-2
Point Breeze Park—park PA-2
Point Breeze Rsvr—reservoir PA-2
Point Bridge—bridge PA-2
Point Bridge—cape AK-9
Point Bridget—cape AK-9
Point Brightman—cape AK-9
**Point Brittany**—pop pl FL-3
Point Brower—cape AK-9
Point Brown WA-9
Point Brown—cape AK-9
Point Brown—cape WA-9
Point Buchon—cape CA-9
Point Buckler—cape CA-9
Point Cabrillo—cape (2) CA-9
Point Cabrillo Light Station—other CA-9
Point Cabrillo Site—hist pl CA-9
Point Caddie MS-4
Point Cadet Plaza Shop Ctr—locale MS-4
Point Cahill—cape LA-4
Point Camden—cape AK-9
Point Campbell—cape AK-9
Point Campbell—locale AK-9
Point Campbell Military Reservation—other AK-9
Point Campground—locale ID-8
Point Campground—locale PA-2
Point Campground—park OR-9
Point Camp Trail—trail CO-8
Point Cangrejo—cape AK-9
Point Canyon—valley ID-8
Point Canyon—valley TX-5
Point Capones—cape AK-9
Point Caracol—cape AK-9
Point Carquinez—locale CA-9
Point Carrew—cape AK-9
Point Castillo—cape CA-9
**Point Caswell**—pop pl NC-3
Point Caution—cape AK-9
Point (CCD)—cens area TX-5
**Point Cedar**—pop pl AR-4
Point Cedar Creek—stream AR-4
Point Cedar Mountains—ridge AR-4
Point Celeste—locale LA-4
Point Cem—cemetery OH-6
Point Cem—cemetery WV-2
Point Cemetery, The—cemetery MS-4
Point Chauncey—cape CA-9
**Point Chautauqua**—pop pl NY-2
Point Cheniere Ronquille—cape LA-4
Point Chester TN-4
Point Chevrette—cape LA-4
Point Chico LA-4
Point Chicot—cape LA-4
Point Chicot Light—locale LA-4
Point Clair—cape LA-4
**Point Clair (U.S. Public Health Service)**—pop pl LA-4
**Point Clear**—pop pl AL-4
Point Clear Bayou MS-4
Point Clear Ch—church AL-4
Point Clear Creek—stream AL-4
Point Clear Hist Dist—hist pl AL-4
Point Clear Island—island MS-4
Point Clear Lake MS-4
Point Clear Sch—school AL-4
Point Cochrane—cape AK-9
Point Cocos—cape AK-9
Point Coke Pit—cape AK-9
Point Collie—cape AK-9
Point Colpoys—cape AK-9
Point Comfort TX-5
Point Comfort VA-3
Point Comfort—cape GA-3
Point Comfort—cape IL-6
Point Comfort—cape IN-6
Point Comfort—cape MD-2
Point Comfort—cape NY-2
Point Comfort—cape SC-3
Point Comfort—cape SD-7
Point Comfort—cape WI-6
Point Comfort—hist pl NH-1
**Point Comfort**—pop pl TX-5
**Point Comfort**—pop pl WI-6
Point Comfort (CCD)—cens area TX-5
Point Comfort Creek—stream SC-3
Point Comfort Landing—locale NC-3
Point Comfort Lodge—hist pl OR-9
Point Comfort Park—park WI-6
Point Comfort State Campsite—locale NY-2
**Point Commerce**—pop pl IN-6
Point Conception—cape CA-9
Point Conception Light Station—hist pl CA-9
Point Conclusion—cape AK-9
Point Coquille LA-4
Point Cornwallis—cape AK-9
Point Cosinas—cape AK-9

Point Cosmos—cape AK-9
Point Countess—cape AK-9
Point Couverden—cape AK-9
Point Craven—cape AK-9
Point Crawford—summit WY-8
Point Creek CO-8
Point Creek—gut NJ-2
Point Creek—stream AK-9
Point Creek—stream CO-8
Point Creek—stream MN-6
Point Creek—stream MT-8
Point Creek—stream SC-3
Point Creek—stream TX-5
Point Creek—stream VA-3
Point Creek—stream WA-9
Point Creek—stream WI-6
Point Crowley—cape AK-9
Point Cruz—cape AK-9
Point Culross—cape AK-9
Point Cypre Mort LA-4
Point Cypress CA-9
Point Davison—cape AK-9
Point Defiance—cape CA-9
Point Defiance—summit WA-9
Point Defiance Park—park WA-9
Point Defiance Sch—school WA-9
Point Delgada—cape AK-9
Point Delgada—cape CA-9
Point Deluce Bayou—stream AR-4
Point Deluce (Township of)—fmr MCD AR-4
Point Demock WA-9
Point Desconocida—cape AK-9
Point Des Ilettes—cape LA-4
Point Dexter—cape AK-9
Point Diablo—cape CA-9
Point Disappointment—cape TN-4
Point Ditch—canal UT-8
Point Divide—cape AK-9
Point Doran—cape AK-9
Point Dougherty—cape AK-9
**Point Douglas**—pop pl MN-6
Point Douglas-St. Louis River Road Bridge—hist pl MN-6
Point Draw—valley TX-5
Point Dume—CDP CA-9
Point Dume—summit CA-9
Point Dumo CA-9
Point Dundas—cape AK-9
Point Dyer—cape AK-9
Pointe, Lake la—lake LA-4
**Pointe A La Hache**—pop pl LA-4
Pointe A La Hache Boat Harbor—bay LA-4
Pointe A La Hache Oil and Gas Field—oilfield LA-4
Pointe A La Hache Relief Outlet—island LA-4
Point Eastern—locale VA-3
Pointeast Shop Ctr—locale FL-3
Point Eaton CA-9
**Pointe at South Mountain (subdivision), The**—pop pl (2) AZ-5
Pointe Au Chien, Bayou—stream LA-4
Pointe au Chien Sch—school LA-4
Pointe au Sable MI-6
**Pointe aux Barques**—pop pl MI-6
Pointe Aux Barques Golf Club—other MI-6
Pointe Aux Barques Lighthouse—hist pl MI-6
Pointe Aux Barques (Township of)—civ div MI-6
Pointe aux Chenes MI-6
Pointe Aux Chenes MI-6
**Pointe aux Chenes**—pop pl MI-6
Pointe aux Chenes Bay—bay MI-6
Pointe aux Chenes Marshes—swamp MI-6
Pointe aux Chenes River—stream MI-6
Pointe aux Frenes MI-6
Pointe aux Herbes—cape LA-4
Pointe Aux Loups, Bayou—stream LA-4
Pointe aux Peaux MI-6
**Pointe aux Peaux Farms**—pop pl MI-6
**Pointe Aux Pins**—pop pl MI-6
**Pointe aux Tremble**—pop pl MI-6
Pointe Basse Plaza—locale MO-7
**Pointe Claire**—pop pl LA-4
Pointe Claire Coulee—stream LA-4
Pointe Coupee—cape LA-4
**Pointe Coupee**—pop pl LA-4
**Pointe Coupee Parish**—pop pl LA-4
Pointe Coupee Parish Courthouse—hist pl LA-4
Pointe Coupee Parish Museum—hist pl LA-4
Pointe Coupee Schexnayder LA-4
Pointe Cypress—locale LA-4
Pointed Branch VA-3
Pointed Butte—summit SD-7
Pointed Butte Ruin (LA 10733)—hist pl NM-5
Pointed Hill—summit ND-7
Pointed Hill—summit TX-5
Point Edith—cape CA-9
Point Edith Crossing Range—channel CA-9
Pointed Mountain MH-9
Pointed Mtn—summit TX-5
Pointed Pond PA-2
Pointed Rock PW-9
Pointed Rocks—pillar CA-9
Point Edward PA-2
Point Edward—cape AK-9
Point Edwards FL-3
Pointe-en-Pointe, Bayou—gut LA-4
Pointe Fienne Bay—lake LA-4
Pointe Lavin Canal—canal LA-4
Point Eleanor—cape AK-9
Point (Election Precinct)—fmr MCD IL-6
Point Elisha MI-6
Point Eliza—cape AK-9
Point Eliza—cape LA-4
Point Elizabeth—cape AK-9
**Point Ellice**—pop pl WA-9
Point Ellis WA-9
Point Ellis—cape AK-9
Point Elrington—cape AK-9
**Point Emerald Villas (subdivision)**—pop pl NC-3
Point Emmet—cape CA-9
Pointe Mouillee State Game Area—park MI-6
**Point Enterprise**—pop pl TX-5
Pointer—locale KY-4
Pointer, Henry, House—hist pl TN-4
Pointer Branch—stream MO-7
Pointer Cem—cemetery AL-4
Pointer Cem—cemetery (3) TN-4
Pointer Club Brook—stream NH-1
Pointer Creek ND-7
Pointer Creek—stream KY-4
Pointer Creek—stream OK-5
**Pointer (Hickorynut)**—pop pl KY-4
Pointer Hollow—valley TN-4
Pointer Island—island WA-9
Pointer Lake—lake CO-8
Pointer Lake—lake MN-6
Pointer Landing VA-3
Pointer Quarters—locale AL-4
Pointer Ridge—ridge TN-4
Pointer Ridge—uninc pl MD-2
Pointer Ridge Rec Area—park MD-2
**Pointers**—pop pl NJ-2
Pointers Airfield—airport OR-9
Pointers Creek—stream MO-7
Pointers Creek Cem—cemetery MO-7
Pointers Creek Public Access—locale MO-7
Pointers Creek Sch (historical)—school MO-7
Pointers Gulch—valley CA-9
Pointers Hill—summit MI-6
Pointers Landing—locale VA-3
Pointers Point OR-9
Pointer Spring—spring AZ-5
Pointe Sowell VA-3
Point Espada—cape AK-9
Point Estero—cape CA-9
Point Esther—cape AK-9
**Pointe (subdivision), The**—pop pl (2) AZ-5
Pointe Tournant—cape LA-4
Pointe Verdra Village Square (Shop Ctr)—locale FL-3
Point Falfan—cape AK-9
Point Farewell—cape AK-9
Point Farm—hist pl DE-2
Point Farm—locale SC-3
Point Fermin—cape CA-9
Point Fermin Lighthouse—hist pl CA-9
Point Fermin Park—park CA-9
Point Fermin Sch—school CA-9
Point Ferry—locale AR-4
Point Fing—cape LA-4
**Point Firmin**—pop pl CA-9
Point Fitzgibbon—cape AK-9
Point Flat MS-4
Point Folly—cape CT-1
Point Fortaleza—cape AK-9
Point Frances WA-9
Point Francis WA-9
Point Francis—cape AK-9
Point Franklin—cape AK-9
Point Freemantle—cape AK-9
Point Fula—cape AK-9
Point Gabert FM-9
Point Gambier—cape AK-9
Point Garcia—cape AK-9
Point Gardner—cape AK-9
Point Gardner—cape LA-4
Point Garnet—cape AK-9
Point George OR-9
Point Glass—cape AK-9
Point Glorious—summit AK-9
Point Gorda CA-9
Point Gorda—cape AK-9
Point Gordon—cape AK-9
Point Grace—cape AK-9
Point Gratiot Beach—beach NY-2
Point Gratiot Lighthouse Complex—hist pl NY-2
Point Gratiot Park—park NY-2
Point Grosbec—cliff LA-4
Point Gustavus—cape AK-9
Point Halliday—cape AK-9
Point Hamilton—cape AK-9
Point Hanus—cape AK-9
Point Happy—summit CA-9
Point Harbor ME-1
Point Harbor—harbor NC-3
**Point Harbor**—pop pl MS-4
**Point Harbor**—pop pl NC-3
**Point Harbor**—pop pl TN-4
Point Hardscrabble—cape AK-9
Point Harmony Sch—school (2) WV-2
Point Harrington—cape AK-9
Point Harris WA-9
Point Harris—cape AK-9
Point Hayes—cape AK-9
Point Hedden—cape CT-1
Point Helen—cape AK-9
Point Hepburn—cape AK-9
Point Hey—cape AK-9
Point Higgins (Port Higgins)—other AK-9
Point Highfield—cape AK-9
Point Highland—cape AK-9
Point Hilda—cape AK-9
Point Hill—locale PA-2
Point Hill—summit WA-9
Point Hill Creek—stream WA-9
Point Hobart—cape AK-9
Point Hogan—cape AK-9
Point Hollenbeck AZ-5
Point Hollow—valley IA-7
Point Hope VA-3
Point Hope—cape (3) AK-9
Point Hope—cape LA-4
**Point Hope**—pop pl AK-9
Point Hope Island—island SC-3
Point Hopson—cape AK-9
Point Horn—cape AK-9
Point Houmas—cape LA-4
Point Howard—cape AK-9
Point Howe—cape AK-9
Point Hueneme—cape CA-9
Point Huerone CA-9
Point Hunt—cape LA-4
**Point Idalawn**—pop pl IN-6
Point Idlefonso—cape AK-9
Point Incarnation—cape AK-9
Point Independence NY-2
**Point Independence**—pop pl MA-1
Point Iroquois Light Station—hist pl MI-6
Point Isabel—cape CA-9
**Point Isabel**—pop pl IN-6
**Point Isabel**—pop pl OH-6
Point Isabel Cem—cemetery IA-7
Point Isabella OH-6
Point Isabel Lighthouse—hist pl TX-5
Point Isleta—cape AK-9
Point Jackson—cape AK-9
Point Jansen—cape AK-9
Point Jefferson—cape LA-4
Point Joe—cape CA-9
Point Joseph—summit OR-9
Point Judith MD-2
Point Judith—cape RI-1
**Point Judith**—pop pl RI-1
Point Judith Harbor of Refuge—bay RI-1
Point Judith Lighthouse—hist pl RI-1
Point Judith Neck—cape RI-1
Point Judith Pond—lake (2) RI-1
Point Judith Pond Breachway RI-1
Point Kadin—cape AK-9
Point Kennedy—cape AK-9
Point Kneeshaw—summit ND-7
Point Knox Shoal—bar CA-9
Point La Fortuna LA-4
Point La Jolla—cape CA-9
Point Lake—lake AK-9
Point Lake—lake (2) FL-3
Point Lake—lake ID-8
Point Lake—lake MN-6
Point Lake—lake NM-5
Point Lake—lake UT-8
Point Lake—lake WI-6
Point Lakeview—cape CA-9
**Point Lakeview**—pop pl MI-6
Point Landing—locale MD-2
Point Las Petes CA-9
Point Las Pitas CA-9
Point Lateral—canal ID-8
Point Latouche—cape AK-9
Point Laurel Lookout Tower—locale MS-4
Point Lavinia—cape AK-9
**Point Lay**—pop pl AK-9
Point Lay ANV903—reserve AK-9
Point League—cape AK-9
Point Leavell—locale KY-4
Point Leflore (historical)—locale MS-4
Point Leflore Landing (historical)—locale MS-4
Point Leleiwi HI-9
Point Lena—cape AK-9
Point Level Ch—church NC-3
Point Lick—other WV-2
Point Lick Branch—stream WV-2
Pointlick Ch—church WV-2
Pointlick Creek WV-2
Pointlick Fork—stream (2) WV-2
**Point Lick Junction (Point Lick)**—pop pl WV-2
Pointlick Sch—school WV-2
Point Lobos—cape (2) CA-9
Point Lobos Archeol Sites—hist pl CA-9
Point Lobos State Res—park CA-9
Point Loma—cape CA-9
**Point Loma**—pop pl TX-5
Point Loma—uninc pl CA-9
Point Loma HS—school CA-9
Point Loma Park—park CA-9
Point Lone—cape CA-9
Point Lonesom—cape FL-3
Point Lookout TN-4
Point Lookout—cape (2) AK-9
Point Lookout—cape CA-9
Point Lookout—cape LA-4
Point Lookout—cape NC-3
Point Lookout—cliff NC-3
Point Lookout—cliff TN-4
Point Lookout—cliff UT-8
Point Lookout—locale CO-8
Point Lookout—locale MD-2
Point Lookout—locale MO-7
**Point Lookout**—pop pl NY-2
**Point Lookout**—pop pl PA-2
Point Lookout—summit CO-8
Point Lookout—summit ID-8
Point Lookout—summit NH-1
Point Lookout—summit NC-3
Point Lookout—summit (2) UT-8
Point Lookout—summit VA-3
Point Lookout Cem—cemetery LA-4
Point Lookout Ch—church (2) WV-2
Point Lookout Creek—bay MD-2
Point Lookout Creek—stream FL-3
Point Lookout-Horace Rockwell-Pony Express Station UT-8
Point Lookout Mountains UT-8
Point Lookout Mtn—summit NC-3
Point Lookout Mtn—summit VA-3
Point Lookout Mtns—summit UT-8
Point Lookout Run—stream WV-2
Point Lookout Station—locale MO-7
Point Los Pitas CA-9
Point Louisa—cape AK-9
Point Lowe—cape AK-9
Point Lull—cape AK-9
Point Lydia—cape LA-4
Point Macartney—cape AK-9
Point Madan—cape AK-9
Point Magu CA-9
Point Malibu AL-4
Point Mallard Park—park AL-4
Point Mallard Parkway Ch—church AL-4
Point Manby—cape AK-9
Point Mansfield—cape AK-9
Point Marabilla—cape AK-9
Point Maria—cape AK-9
Point Marie—cape AK-9
**Point Marion**—pop pl PA-2
Point Marion Borough—civil PA-2
Point Marion Cem—cemetery PA-2
Point Marsden—cape AK-9
Point Marsh—cape AK-9
Point Marsh—swamp AK-9
Point Martin—cape AK-9
Point Mary—cape AK-9
Point Mason Landing (historical)—locale TN-4
Point Mason Post Office (historical)—building TN-4
Point Masons Landing TN-4
Point Mast—cape LA-4
Point McCartey—area AK-9
Point McCloud—locale CA-9
Point McIntyre—cape AK-9
**Point McIntyre**—pop pl AK-9
Point McKenzie—cape AK-9
Point Medanos—cape CA-9
Point Menoir—cape LA-4
Point Meshe—cape LA-4
Point Midgley WA-9
Point Mill Brook—stream MA-1
**Point Mills**—pop pl MI-6
**Point Mills**—pop pl WV-2
Point Mills—uninc pl WV-2
Point Misery—summit NC-3
Point Molate—cape CA-9
Point Montara—cape CA-9
Point Montara Light Station—locale CA-9
Point Moore Landing—locale MS-4
Point Moses—cape AK-9
Point Mouille—cape MI-6
Point Mountain—ridge WV-2
Point Mountain Ch—church WV-2
Point Mountain Run—stream WV-2
Point Mtn—summit NJ-2
Point Mtn—summit NY-2
Point Mtn—summit OR-9
Point Mtn—summit (2) WV-2
Point Mugu—cape CA-9
Point Mugu—post sta CA-9
Point Mugu Naval Air Station—military CA-9
Point Mugu Pacific Missile Test Center—military CA-9
Point Munoz—cape AK-9
Point Muspa FL-3
Point Nankapenparam FM-9
Point Napean—cape AK-9
Point Nardueis PW-9
Point Nashowhak—cape AK-9
Point Nelson—cape AK-9
Point Neptune—cape LA-4
Point Nesbitt—cape AK-9
Point News WA-9
Point Ngateguil PW-9
Point Nip-I-Gon MI-6
**Point Nipigon**—pop pl MI-6
Point No Pass—cliff CA-9
Point No Point PA-2
Point No-Point—cape AK-9
Point No Point—cape CT-1
Point No Point—cape LA-4
Point-no-Point—cape MN-6
Point No Point Creek—stream WA-9
Point No Point Light Station—hist pl WA-9
Point No Point Reach—channel NJ-2
Point Nowell—cape AK-9
Point Nunez—cape AK-9
Point of Beach—cape NC-3
Point of Caddi MS-4
Point of Cedar Mountain—cliff UT-8
Point of Cedars Island—island DE-2
Point of Fork Arsenal—hist pl VA-3
Point of Fork Plantation—hist pl VA-3
Point of Grass—cape (2) NC-3
Point of Grass Creek—bay NC-3
Point of Honor—hist pl VA-3
Point of Island—swamp NC-3
Point of Island Bay—bay NC-3
Point of Marsh—cape NC-3
Point of Marsh Light—tower NC-3
Point of Mountain Spring—spring AZ-5
Point of Narrows NC-3
Point of Narrows—cape NC-3
Point of Pines—cape SC-3
Point of Pines—hist pl AZ-5
**Point of Pines**—pop pl AZ-5
**Point of Pines**—pop pl MA-1
**Point of Pines**—pop pl VT-1
Point of Pines Canyon—valley UT-8
Point of Pines Charco—reservoir AZ-5
Point of Pines Creek—stream AZ-5
Point of Pines Dam—dam AZ-5
Point of Pines (historical)—locale AZ-5
Point of Pines Lake—reservoir AZ-5
Point of Pines Plantation Slave Cabin—hist pl SC-3
Point of Pines Recreation Site—park UT-8
Point of Pines Station (historical)—locale MA-1
**Point of Pines Subdivision (subdivision)**—pop pl AL-4
Point of Ridge—cape DE-2
Point of Rock—peak ID-8
Point of Rock Channel—channel VA-3
Point Of Rock Drain—stream VA-3
Point of Rock Rsvr—reservoir NV-8
Point Of Rock Rsvr—reservoir WY-8
Point of Rocks CA-9
Point Of Rocks CO-8
Point of Rocks ID-8
Point Of Rock's MD-2
Point of Rocks WY-8
Point of Rocks—bar AK-9
Point of Rocks—cape CA-9
Point of Rocks—cape MA-1
Point of Rocks—cape UT-8
Point of Rocks—cliff KS-7
Point of Rocks—cliff VA-3
Point of Rocks—locale AZ-5
Point of Rocks—locale NE-7
Point of Rocks—locale NV-8
Point of Rocks—locale WY-8
Point Of Rocks—locale (2) WY-8
Point of Rocks—pillar NV-8
**Point of Rocks**—pop pl MD-2
Point of Rocks—range CA-9
Point of Rocks—summit CA-9
Point of Rocks—summit (2) CO-8
Point of Rocks—summit (2) NM-5
Point Of Rocks—summit VA-3
Point Of Rocks—summit (2) WY-8
Point of Rocks Canyon—valley NV-8
Point of Rocks Canyon—valley NM-5
Point of Rocks Cem—cemetery MT-8
Point Of Rocks Creek—stream NE-7
Point Of Rocks Creek—stream WY-8
**Point of Rocks Estates**—pop pl MD-2
Point of Rocks Mesa—summit NM-5
Point of Rock Spring—spring AZ-5
Point of Rock Spring—spring NV-8
Point of Rocks Roadside Park—locale TX-5
Point of Rocks RR Station—hist pl MD-2
Point of Rocks Rsvr—reservoir MT-8
Point Of Rocks Rsvr—reservoir WY-8
Point-of-Rocks Spring NV-8
Point of Rocks Spring—spring ID-8
Point of Rocks Springs—spring NV-8
Point Of Rocks Stagecoach Station—locale WY-8
Point of Rocks Stage Station—hist pl WY-8
Point of Rocks Tank—reservoir (2) NM-5
Point of Rocks Windmill—locale NM-5
Point of Rocks Windmill—locale TX-5
Point Of Sand VA-3
Point of Sands—locale NM-5
Point of The Mountain—cape UT-8
Point of the Mountain Tank—reservoir UT-8
Point of the Mountain Well—well NV-8
Point of the Narros—cape NC-3
Point of the Pines AL-4
Point of the Pines—cliff OK-5
Point of the Tongue—cape VT-1
Point of Trees—cape RI-1
**Point of View**—pop pl VA-3
Point Of Woods NY-2
**Point of Woods**—pop pl NJ-2
**Point of Woods**—pop pl VA-3
Point Ohop—cape WA-9
Pointons Store—locale VA-3
Point-O-Pines Ch—church MN-6
Point Option Ranch—locale NE-7
Point Orient—cape CA-9
Point O' Rocks—CDP FL-3
Point O'Rocks—cliff NY-2
**Point O'Rocks**—pop pl FL-3
Point Overlook, The—locale VA-3
**Point O'View (subdivision)**—pop pl TN-4
**Point O'Woods**—pop pl CT-1
**Point o'Woods**—pop pl NY-2
**Point O'Woods**—pop pl VA-3
Point O'Woods Country Club—other MI-6
Point Pakenham—cape AK-9
Point Palo Alto—cape CA-9
Point Park—park AL-4
Point Park—park MN-6
Point Park—park OH-6
Point Park—park TN-4
Point Park Coll—school PA-2
Point Partennoi—cape AK-9
Point Pasture—flat KS-7
Point Patterson Creek—stream MI-6
Point Paulina—cape LA-4
Point Peak—summit TX-5
Point Pedernales—cape CA-9
Point Peiro—cape LA-4
Point Pellew—cape AK-9
Point Pellow—cape AK-9
Point Peninsula—cliff CO-8
**Point Peninsula**—pop pl NY-2
Point Peninsula Cem—cemetery NY-2
Point Percy—cape AK-9
Point Perfection UT-8
Point Perry—cape AK-9
Point Peter WA-9
Point Peter—cape GA-3
Point Peter—cape PA-2
Point Peter—cliff AR-4
Point Peter—locale GA-3
**Point Peter**—pop pl AR-4
Point Peter—summit NY-2
Point Peter Brook—stream NY-2
Point Peter Creek—stream GA-3
Point Peter Mtn—summit AR-4
Point Peters—cape AK-9
Point Petrof—cape AK-9
Point Philips FL-3
Point Phillip—locale PA-2
Point Phillips PA-2
Point Picket CA-9
Point Picnic Area, The—locale UT-8
Point Piedras Blancos—cape CA-9
Point Pigot—cape AK-9
Point Pigot Light—other AK-9
Point Pine MA-1
Point Pinellas—cape FL-3
Point Pines CA-9
Point Pinos—cape CA-9
Point Pinos Lighthouse—hist pl CA-9
Point Pit—cave AL-4
Point Place OH-6
**Point Place**—pop pl OH-6
Point Platte—cape LA-4
Point Plaza (Shop Ctr)—locale FL-3
Point Plaza Shop Ctr—locale MS-4
Point Pleasant NJ-2
Point Pleasant—cape FL-3
Point Pleasant—cape (3) LA-4
Point Pleasant—cliff PA-2
Point Pleasant—locale IA-7
Point Pleasant—locale KY-4
Point Pleasant—locale LA-4
Point Pleasant—locale PA-2
Point Pleasant—locale TN-4
Point Pleasant—locale VA-3
**Point Pleasant**—pop pl CA-9
**Point Pleasant**—pop pl FL-3
**Point Pleasant**—pop pl LA-4
**Point Pleasant**—pop pl MD-2
**Point Pleasant**—pop pl MA-1
**Point Pleasant**—pop pl MO-7
**Point Pleasant**—pop pl (2) NJ-2
**Point Pleasant**—pop pl (2) NY-2
**Point Pleasant**—pop pl OH-6
**Point Pleasant**—pop pl TN-4
**Point Pleasant**—pop pl WV-2
Point Pleasant Baptist Ch—church PA-2
Point Pleasant Baptist Church TN-4
Point Pleasant Battleground—hist pl WV-2
**Point Pleasant Beach**—pop pl NJ-2
Point Pleasant Campground—locale MT-8
Point Pleasant Canal—canal NJ-2
Point Pleasant Cem—cemetery (2) IL-6
Point Pleasant Cem—cemetery IA-7
Point Pleasant Cem—cemetery (2) KY-4
Point Pleasant Cem—cemetery (2) LA-4
Point Pleasant Cem—cemetery MS-4
Point Pleasant Cem—cemetery MO-7
Point Pleasant Cem—cemetery NJ-2
Point Pleasant Cem—cemetery OH-6
Point Pleasant Cemeteries—cemetery LA-4
Point Pleasant Ch TN-4
Point Pleasant Ch—church AR-4
Point Pleasant Ch—church IL-6
Point Pleasant Ch—church (3) KY-4
Point Pleasant Ch—church MS-4
Point Pleasant Ch—church MO-7
Point Pleasant Ch—church OH-6
Point Pleasant Ch—church TN-4
Point Pleasant Ch—church (6) WV-2
Point Pleasant Ch (historical)—church MO-7
Point Pleasant Chute—lake MO-7
Point Pleasant Creek—stream WV-2
Point Pleasant Hist Dist—hist pl WV-2
Point Pleasant Landing—locale TN-4
Point Pleasant Landing (historical)—locale MS-4
**Point Pleasant Manor**—pop pl NJ-2
Point Pleasant Post Office (historical)—building TN-4
Point Pleasant Rec Area—park MS-4
Point Pleasant Sch—school (4) IL-6
Point Pleasant Sch—school KS-7
Point Pleasant Sch—school MD-2
Point Pleasant Sch (abandoned)—school PA-2
Point Pleasant Sch (historical)—school AL-4
Point Pleasant Sch (historical)—school (2) MS-4
Point Pleasant Sch (historical)—school TN-4
Point Pleasant (Township of)—civ div IL-6
Point Pleasent Post Office (historical)—building PA-2
Point Pogibshi—cape AK-9
Point Poleakoon—cape AK-9
Point Polnell WA-9
Point Polocano—cape AK-9
Point Possession—cape AK-9
Point Potrero—cape CA-9
Point Prairie Sch (abandoned)—school MO-7
Point Prominence—summit OR-9
Point Pulley WA-9
Point Pully WA-9
Point Pun—summit CO-8
Point Pybus—cape AK-9
Point Pyke—cape AK-9
Point Quemada—cape AK-9
Point Ranch—locale (2) CA-9
Point Ranch—locale ID-8
Point Razbitie—cape AK-9
Point Recreation Site, The—park AZ-5
Point Remedios—cape AK-9
Point Remove Canal—canal AR-4
Point Remove Creek—stream AR-4
Point Remove Creek Old Channel—stream AR-4
Point Resistance—cape CA-9
Point Rest—locale MO-7
Point Retreat—cape AK-9
**Point Retreat**—pop pl AK-9
Point Return Public Use Area—park AR-4
Point Reyes—cape CA-9
Point Reyes Beach—beach CA-9
Point Reyes Hill—summit CA-9
Point Reyes Lifeboat Rescue Station, 1927—hist pl CA-9
Point Reyes Natl Seashore—park CA-9
**Point Reyes Station**—pop pl CA-9
Point Richards MA-1
Point Richmond CA-9
Point Richmond—cape CA-9
**Point Richmond**—pop pl CA-9
Point Richmond Hist Dist—hist pl CA-9
Point Ridge—ridge MD-2
Point Ridge—ridge TN-4
Point Ringold MD-2
Point Riou—cape AK-9
Point Riou Spit—cape AK-9
Point Rip—bar MA-1
Point River Sch—school WI-6
**Point Roberts**—pop pl WA-9
Point Roberts (CCD)—cens area WA-9
Point Roberts Lighthouse—locale WA-9
Point Roberts-Young Field Airp—airport WA-9
**Point Rochester**—pop pl NY-2
Point Rock MD-2
Point Rock—locale OH-6
Point Rock—pillar AL-4
Point Rock—pillar AR-4
**Point Rock**—pop pl NY-2
Pointrock Branch—stream KY-4
Point Rock Ch—church OH-6
Point Rock Creek—stream NY-2
Point Rok Beach—beach MA-1
Point Romanof—cape AK-9
Point Rosary—cape AK-9
Point Rothsay—cape AK-9
Point Rsvr—reservoir CO-8
Point Run—stream IN-6
Point Run—stream WV-2
**Points**—pop pl CA-9
**Points**—pop pl WV-2
Point Sable MI-6
Point Sacramento—cape CA-9
Point Saint Albans—cape AK-9
Point Saint Boniface—cape AK-9
Point Saint George—cape CA-9
Point Saint Isidor—cape AK-9
Point Saint John—cape AK-9
Point Saint Mary—cape AK-9
Point Saint Sebastian—cape AK-9
Point Saint Thomas—cape AK-9
Point Sal—cape CA-9
Point Sal Beach State Park—park CA-9
Point Salisbury WA-9
Point Salisbury—cape AK-9
Point Sal Ridge—ridge CA-9
Point Salubrious Cem—cemetery NY-2
Point San Bruno—summit CA-9
Point San Francisco—cape AK-9
Point San Joaquin—cape CA-9
Point San Jose—cape AK-9
Point San Leonardo—cape AK-9
Point San Luis—cape CA-9
Point San Mateo CA-9
Point San Matheo CA-9
Point San Pablo—cape CA-9
Point San Pablo Yacht Harbor—bay CA-9
Point San Pasqual—cape AK-9
Point San Pedro—cape (2) CA-9
Point San Quentin—cape CA-9
Point San Rafael—cape AK-9
Point San Roque—cape AK-9
Point Santa Anna—cape AK-9
Point Santa Cruz—cape CA-9
Point Santa Gertrudis—cape AK-9
Point Santa Lucia—cape AK-9
Point Santa Rosa—cape AK-9
Point Santa Rosalia—cape AK-9
Point Santa Theresa—cape AK-9
Point Sares WA-9
Point Satchrun—cape AK-9
Point Sauk WI-6
Point Sch—school IL-6

Poorman Spring—*spring* (2) NV-8
Poor Mans Spring—*spring* AZ-5
Poor Mans Valley—*basin* CA-9
Poormans Wash—*stream* AZ-5
Poorman Valley—*valley* CA-9
*Poor-meadow Brook* MA-1
Poor Meadow Brook—*stream* MA-1
Poor Mountain Overlook—*locale* VA-3
*Poor Mtn* SC-3
Poor Mtn—*summit* GA-3
Poor Mtn—*summit* SC-3
Poor Mtn—*summit* (2) TN-4
Poor Mtn—*summit* (3) VA-3
Poor Ranch—*locale* CA-9
Poor Ridge—*ridge* TN-4
Poor Ridge Landing—*locale* NC-3
Poor Robin Landing—*locale* GA-3
Poor Robin Lower Cut Point—*cape* SC-3
Poor Robin Spring—*spring* GA-3
Poor Robin Upper Cut Point—*cape* SC-3
Poors Ford Ch—*church* NC-3
Poors Hill—*summit* ME-1
Poors Hill—*summit* NH-1
Poor Shoal—*bar* ME-1
Poors Island—*island* NY-2
*Poors Knob* NC-3
**Poors Mill**—*pop pl* ME-1
*Poors Mills* ME-1
Poorspot Cem—*cemetery* FL-3
Poor Tank—*reservoir* AZ-5
Poor Thunder Cem—*cemetery* SD-7
*Poortith* NC-3
Poor Tom Branch—*stream* MO-7
**Poortown**—*pop pl* KY-4
**Poor Town**—*pop pl* NC-3
Poortown Mtn—*summit* VA-3
*Poor Valley* VA-3
Poor Valley—*basin* VA-3
Poor Valley—*valley* (2) TN-4
Poor Valley—*valley* (2) VA-3
Poor Valley Branch—*stream* TN-4
Poor Valley Branch—*stream* VA-3
Poor Valley Ch—*church* VA-3
Poor Valley Creek—*stream* TN-4
Poor Valley Creek—*stream* VA-3
Poor Valley Knobs—*ridge* TN-4
Poor Valley Ridge—*ridge* TN-4
Poor Valley Ridge—*ridge* VA-3
Poor Valley Shoals—*bar* TN-4
*Pooscoos Panha Creek* AL-4
Poose Creek—*stream* CO-8
Poose Run—*stream* PA-2
Poosey Cem—*cemetery* KY-4
Poosey Ridge—*ridge* KY-4
Poosey State For—*forest* MO-7
Poospatuck Creek—*stream* NY-2
Poospatuck Ind Res—*94 (1980)* NY-2
**Pootatuck Park**—*pop pl* CT-1
Pootatuck River—*stream* CT-1
Pootatuck State For—*forest* CT-1
Pooter Branch—*stream* KY-4
*Poot Pond* MA-1
Poovey Chapel—*church* NC-3
**Poovey Estate**—*pop pl* SC-3
Pooveys Grove Ch—*church* NC-3
Poovookpuk Mtn—*summit* AK-9
Poovoot Range—*other* AK-9
Popalito Windmill—*locale* NM-5
*Popano Creek* TX-5
Popash Creek—*stream* FL-3
Popash Slough—*stream* FL-3
Popasquash Island—*island* VT-1
Popasquash Neck—*cape* RI-1
Popasquash Point—*cape* RI-1
**Popasquash Point**—*pop pl* RI-1
Pop Branch—*stream* TN-4
Popcastle—*locale* VA-3
Popcastle Creek—*stream* VA-3
*Popcastle Run* VA-3
**Popcorn**—*pop pl* IN-6
Popcorn Bayou—*gut* LA-4
Popcorn Canyon—*valley* AZ-5
Popcorn Cave—*cave* AR-4
Popcorn Cave—*cave* CA-9
Popcorn Corners—*locale* WI-6
Popcorn Creek—*stream* GA-3
Popcorn Creek—*stream* IN-6
Popcorn Creek—*stream* KS-7
Pop Corn (historical)—*locale* KS-7
Popcorn Ridge—*ridge* IN-6
Popcorn Sch—*school* OR-9
Popcorn Spring—*spring* AZ-5
Popcorn Tank—*reservoir* AZ-5
Pop Creek—*stream* OR-9
*Pope* AL-4
*Pope* KS-7
Pope—*locale* (3) AL-4
Pope—*locale* (2) CA-9
Pope—*locale* KY-4
Pope—*locale* VA-3
**Pope**—*pop pl* MS-4
**Pope**—*pop pl* NM-5
**Pope**—*pop pl* NY-2
**Pope**—*pop pl* TN-4
Pope, John, House—*hist pl* KY-4
Pope, John, House—*hist pl* TN-4
Pope, Lonnie A., House—*hist pl* GA-3
Pope, The—*pillar* UT-8
Pope AFB—*military* NC-3
Pope Air Force Base—*other* NC-3
Pope Arroyo—*stream* CO-8
Pope Ave Sch—*school* CA-9
Pope Baptist Ch—*church* MS-4
*Pope Bay* MD-2
Pope Bay—*bay* MD-2
Pope Bay—*bay* NY-2
Pope Beach—*locale* CA-9
**Pope Beach**—*pop pl* MA-1
Pope Bend—*bend* MO-7
Pope Bend—*bend* TX-5
Pope Branch—*stream* AL-4
Pope Branch—*stream* NJ-2
Pope Branch—*stream* TN-4
Pope Branch Park—*park* DC-2
Pope Brook—*stream* CT-1
Pope Brook—*stream* VT-1
Pope Canyon—*valley* NM-5
Pope Canyon—*valley* UT-8
Pope Canyon Spring—*spring* UT-8
Pope Cave—*cave* (2) AL-4
Pope (CCD)—*cens area* TN-4
Pope Cem—*cemetery* AL-4
Pope Cem—*cemetery* AR-4
Pope Cem—*cemetery* FL-3
Pope Cem—*cemetery* (2) GA-3
Pope Cem—*cemetery* (2) IL-6
Pope Cem—*cemetery* (3) KY-4
Pope Cem—*cemetery* (3) MS-4
Pope Cem—*cemetery* MO-7
Pope Cem—*cemetery* NY-2
Pope Cem—*cemetery* (2) NC-3
Pope Cem—*cemetery* OH-6
Pope Cem—*cemetery* SC-3
Pope Cem—*cemetery* (5) TN-4
Pope Cem—*cemetery* (2) TX-5
Pope Cem—*cemetery* VT-1
Pope Cem—*cemetery* VA-3
Pope Ch—*church* AL-4
Pope Channel—*channel* FL-3
Pope Chapel—*church* MS-4
Pope Chapel—*church* TN-4
Pope Chapel Cem—*cemetery* MO-7
Pope Chapel (historical)—*church* MO-7
Pope Chapel Sch—*school* MS-4
Pope City—*locale* TX-5
**Pope City**—*pop pl* GA-3
Pope City Ch—*church* GA-3
Pope Corner—*locale* OR-9
Pope Country Club—*other* GA-3
**Pope (County)**—*pop pl* AR-4
**Pope (County)**—*pop pl* IL-6
**Pope (County)**—*pop pl* MN-6
Pope County Courthouse—*hist pl* MN-6
*Pope Creek* TX-5
*Pope Creek* VA-3
Pope Creek—*stream* AL-4
Pope Creek—*stream* AK-9
Pope Creek—*stream* AR-4
Pope Creek—*stream* CA-9
Pope Creek—*stream* CO-8
Pope Creek—*stream* GA-3
Pope Creek—*stream* IL-6
Pope Creek—*stream* KY-4
Pope Creek—*stream* LA-4
Pope Creek—*stream* ME-1
Pope Creek—*stream* OK-5
Pope Creek—*stream* OR-9
Pope Creek—*stream* TX-5
Pope Creek—*stream* WA-9
Pope Creek Ch—*church* VA-3
Pope Creek Dome—*summit* AK-9
**Pope Crossing**—*pop pl* NC-3
**Pope Crossroads**—*pop pl* SC-3
Pope Dam—*dam* AL-4
Pope Dam—*dam* NC-3
Pope Division—*civil* TN-4
Pope Drain—*stream* MI-6
*Pope Elementary School* TN-4
Pope Estate—*hist pl* CA-9
Pope Family Cem—*cemetery* AL-4
Pope Field Airp—*airport* IN-6
Pope Head—*island* MA-1
*Pope Head Channel* MA-1
Pope Head Shoal—*bar* MA-1
*Pope Hill* MA-1
Pope Hill—*summit* NY-2
Pope Hill Cem—*cemetery* NY-2
Pope Hollow—*valley* KY-4
Pope Hollow—*valley* TN-4
Pope House—*hist pl* NC-3
Pope Island—*island* GA-3
Pope Island—*island* MD-2
Pope Island—*island* VA-3
Pope Island Ditch—*canal* MD-2
Pope Island (historical)—*island* FL-3
**Popejoy**—*pop pl* IA-7
Popejoy Ditch—*canal* IN-6
Popejoy Sch—*school* IL-6
Pope Knob—*summit* VA-3
Pope Lake—*lake* WA-9
Pope Lake—*lake* WI-6
Pope Lake—*reservoir* AL-4
Pope Lake—*reservoir* GA-3
Pope Lake—*reservoir* NC-3
Pope Lake Number One—*reservoir* AL-4
Pope Lake Number Two—*reservoir* AL-4
Pope-Leighey House—*hist pl* VA-3
Pope Lick—*stream* KY-4
Popelka Ranch—*locale* MT-8
Pope Millpond—*lake* GA-3
**Pope Mills**—*pop pl* NY-2
Pope Mine—*mine* AZ-5
Pope Mine—*mine* NV-8
*Pope Mountain* AL-4
Pope Mtn—*summit* ME-1
Popendick Lake—*lake* MI-6
Pope Neck—*bay* GA-3
Pope Park—*park* CT-1
Pope Park—*park* NC-3
Pope Park—*park* TN-4
Pope Park—*park* TX-5
Pope Pius XII HS—*school* NJ-2
Pope Point—*cape* MN-6
*Pope Pond* NC-3
Pope Pond—*reservoir* GA-3
Pope Pond—*swamp* FL-3
Pope Post Office (historical)—*building* AL-4
Pope Post Office (historical)—*building* TN-4
Pope Ranch—*locale* NM-5
Pope Ranch—*locale* ND-7
Pope Ranch—*locale* TX-5
Poperechnoi Island—*island* AK-9
Pope Ridge—*ridge* OR-9
Pope Ridge—*ridge* WA-9
Pope Rock—*rock* MA-1
Pope Rsvr—*reservoir* OR-9
*Popes* MS-4
*Pope's Bay* MD-2
Popes Beat Sch (historical)—*school* AL-4
Popes Bluffs—*ridge* CO-8
*Popes Branch* TN-4
Popes Branch—*stream* GA-3
Pope Sch—*school* (2) FL-3
Pope Sch—*school* HI-9
Pope Sch—*school* (3) IL-6
Pope Sch—*school* (2) MS-4
Pope Sch—*school* NC-3
Pope Sch—*school* (2) TN-4
*Popes Chapel* TN-4
Popes Chapel—*church* AL-4
Popes Chapel—*church* GA-3
Popes Chapel—*church* MS-4
Popes Chapel—*church* NC-3
Popes Chapel—*church* OK-5
Popes Chapel Cem—*cemetery* OK-5
Popes Chapel Cem—*cemetery* TN-4
*Popes Chapel Ch* AL-4
*Popes Chapel Methodist Church* TN-4
Popes Chapel Sch—*school* OK-5
Pope Sch (historical)—*school* (2) AL-4
Pope Sch (historical)—*school* (2) TN-4
**Popes Creek**—*pop pl* MD-2
Popes Creek—*stream* MD-2
Popes Creek—*stream* MS-4
Popes Creek—*stream* (2) VA-3
Popes Creek Bridge—*bridge* MD-2
Popes Creek Landing—*locale* VA-3
Popes Creek Swamp—*swamp* VA-3
*Popes Depot* MS-4
Popes Ferry—*locale* GA-3
Popes Folly—*island* ME-1
Popes Ford—*locale* AL-4
*Popes Head* MA-1
Popes Head Creek—*stream* VA-3
Pope Shenon Mine—*mine* ID-8
Popes Hill—*summit* CO-8
Popes Hill—*summit* MA-1
Popes Hill Station—*locale* MA-1
Pope Siding—*locale* NM-5
*Popes Island* MD-2
*Popes Island* MO-7
Popes Island—*island* CT-1
Popes Island—*island* MA-1
Popes Lake—*lake* NC-3
Popes Lake—*reservoir* NC-3
Popes Lake Dam—*dam* NC-3
Popes Landing—*locale* NC-3
*Pope's Point* ID-8
Popes Point—*cape* TX-5
Popes Point—*cape* VA-3
Popes Pond—*lake* MA-1
Popes Pond—*swamp* MA-1
Pope Spring—*spring* AZ-5
Pope Spring—*spring* GA-3
Pope Spring—*spring* OR-9
Pope Springs—*spring* WY-8
**Popes Ravine**—*pop pl* NY-2
Popes River Ch—*church* IL-6
Popes Tavern Museum—*building* AL-4
Pope Still—*locale* FL-3
Pope Still Lookout Tower—*tower* FL-3
Pope Street Bridge—*hist pl* CA-9
Pope Swamp—*stream* VA-3
**Popetown**—*pop pl* MS-4
**Pope (Township of)**—*pop pl* IL-6
**Pope Valley**—*pop pl* CA-9
Pope Valley—*valley* CA-9
**Popeville**—*pop pl* KY-4
**Popeville**—*pop pl* ME-1
Pope Well Ridge—*ridge* UT-8
Pope Windmill—*locale* TX-5
Popgun Creek—*stream* ID-8
Popham Beach—*beach* ME-1
**Popham Beach**—*pop pl* ME-1
Popham Branch—*stream* GA-3
Popham Colony Site—*hist pl* ME-1
Popham Creek—*bay* MD-2
Popham Creek Marsh—*swamp* MD-2
Popham Run—*stream* VA-3
Popham Sch—*school* TX-5
*Pophams Creek* MD-2
Pophandusing Brook—*stream* NJ-2
Pop Harvey Park—*park* AZ-5
Pophers Creek—*stream* TX-5
Pophins Hollow—*valley* KY-4
Pop Hollow—*valley* TN-4
Pop Hollow Spring—*spring* TN-4
Popiel Sch—*school* FL-3
Popilleau Bay—*bay* VI-3
Poping—*locale* AR-4
Pop Island—*island* ME-1
Pop Island Ledge—*bar* ME-1
Popitz Ditch—*canal* IN-6
Pop Jackson Tank—*reservoir* NM-5
Popko Lake—*lake* WI-6
Pop Lake—*lake* ND-7
Pop Lake—*lake* OR-9
Poplar—*locale* ID-8
Poplar—*locale* IA-7
Poplar—*locale* KY-4
Poplar—*locale* MN-6
Poplar—*locale* NC-3
Poplar—*locale* TN-4
Poplar—*locale* VA-3
**Poplar**—*pop pl* CA-9
**Poplar**—*pop pl* MD-2
**Poplar**—*pop pl* MT-8
**Poplar**—*pop pl* WI-6
Poplar—*unorg reg* ND-7
Poplar Arbor Ch—*church* GA-3
Poplar Ave Ch of Christ—*church* KS-7
Poplar Ave Sch—*school* CA-9
**Poplar Beach**—*pop pl* MI-6
**Poplar Beach**—*pop pl* NY-2
Poplar Beetree Hollow—*valley* KY-4
**Poplar Bluff**—*pop pl* MO-7
Poplar Bluff Country Club—*other* MO-7
Poplar Bluff Township—*civil* MO-7
Poplar Bottom—*bend* SC-3
**Poplar Branch**—*pop pl* NC-3
Poplar Branch—*stream* (2) AL-4
Poplar Branch—*stream* (4) FL-3
Poplar Branch—*stream* GA-3
Poplar Branch—*stream* IL-6
Poplar Branch—*stream* (3) KY-4
Poplar Branch—*stream* LA-4
Poplar Branch—*stream* MS-4
Poplar Branch—*stream* MO-7
Poplar Branch—*stream* (7) NC-3
Poplar Branch—*stream* (9) SC-3
Poplar Branch—*stream* (5) TN-4
Poplar Branch—*stream* (4) VA-3
Poplar Branch Bay—*bay* NC-3
Poplar Branch Ch—*church* SC-3
Poplar Branch Landing—*locale* (2) NC-3
Poplar Branch (Township of)—*fmr MCD* NC-3
**Poplar Bridge**—*pop pl* PA-2
Poplar Bridge Sch—*school* MN-6
Poplar Bridge Sch (abandoned)—*school* PA-2
*Poplar Brook* MA-1
Poplar Brook—*stream* (3) ME-1
Poplar Brook—*stream* NJ-2
Poplar Camp—*locale* FL-3
Poplar Camp—*locale* VA-3
Poplar Camp Creek—*stream* GA-3
Poplar Camp Creek—*stream* (2) VA-3
Poplar Campground—*locale* CA-9
Poplar Camp Mtn—*summit* VA-3
Poplar Canyon—*valley* NV-8
Poplar Cave—*cave* AL-4
Poplar Cave—*cave* TN-4
Poplar Cem—*cemetery* (3) IN-6
Poplar Cem—*cemetery* MN-6
Poplar Cem—*cemetery* TN-4
Poplar Ch—*church* IL-6
Poplar Ch—*church* LA-4
Poplar Ch—*church* (2) MS-4
Poplar Ch—*church* VA-3
Poplar Ch—*church* WV-2
Poplar Chapel—*church* NC-3
Poplar City—*locale* IL-6
Poplar College—*locale* NC-3
Poplar Community Ch—*church* MN-6
*Poplar Corner* MS-4
Poplar Corner—*hist pl* GA-3
Poplar Corner—*locale* AR-4
Poplar Corner—*locale* KY-4
Poplar Corner—*locale* TN-4
**Poplar Corner**—*pop pl* TN-4
*Poplar Corner Baptist Church* TN-4
Poplar Corner Ch—*church* (2) TN-4
Poplar Corners—*locale* MS-4
Poplar Corners—*locale* NY-2
Poplar-Cotton Center—*CDP* CA-9
Poplar Coulee—*valley* MT-8
Poplar Coulee—*valley* WI-6
Poplar Cove—*basin* GA-3
Poplar Cove—*bay* NY-2
Poplar Cove—*bay* VA-3
Poplar Cove—*locale* VA-3
Poplar Cove—*valley* (2) GA-3
Poplar Cove—*valley* (12) NC-3
Poplar Cove—*valley* TN-4
Poplar Cove Branch—*stream* NC-3
Poplar Cove Ch—*church* NC-3
*Poplar Cove Creek* NC-3
Poplar Cove Creek—*stream* NC-3
Poplar Cove Creek—*stream* TN-4
Poplar Cove Creek Ch—*church* TN-4
Poplar Cove Gap—*gap* GA-3
Poplar Cove Gap—*gap* NC-3
Poplar Cove Knob—*summit* NC-3
Poplar Cove Run—*stream* VA-3
Poplar Cove Trail—*trail* TN-4
*Poplar Cove Wharf* VA-3
*Poplar Creek* AL-4
*Poplar Creek* IL-6
*Poplar Creek* MN-6
*Poplar Creek* NC-3
Poplar Creek—*locale* TN-4
**Poplar Creek**—*pop pl* (2) AL-4
**Poplar Creek**—*pop pl* MS-4
Poplar Creek—*stream* (6) AL-4
Poplar Creek—*stream* AK-9
Poplar Creek—*stream* (4) AR-4
Poplar Creek—*stream* (2) CA-9
Poplar Creek—*stream* (2) FL-3
Poplar Creek—*stream* (2) IL-6
Poplar Creek—*stream* IN-6
Poplar Creek—*stream* (4) KY-4
Poplar Creek—*stream* (3) MI-6
Poplar Creek—*stream* (3) MN-6
Poplar Creek—*stream* (5) MS-4
Poplar Creek—*stream* MT-8
Poplar Creek—*stream* (6) NC-3
Poplar Creek—*stream* (3) OH-6
Poplar Creek—*stream* (2) PA-2
Poplar Creek—*stream* (8) TN-4
Poplar Creek—*stream* TX-5
Poplar Creek—*stream* (5) VA-3
Poplar Creek—*stream* WV-2
Poplar Creek—*stream* WI-6
*Poplar Creek Baptist Church* AL-4
*Poplar Creek Baptist Church* TN-4
Poplar Creek Cabin Site Area—*locale* AL-4
Poplar Creek Cem—*cemetery* (2) AL-4
Poplar Creek Cem—*cemetery* KY-4
Poplar Creek Ch—*church* (3) AL-4
Poplar Creek Ch—*church* AR-4
Poplar Creek Ch—*church* IL-6
Poplar Creek Ch—*church* KY-4
Poplar Creek Ch—*church* NC-3
Poplar Creek Ch—*church* SC-3
Poplar Creek Ch—*church* TN-4
Poplar Creek Ch—*church* VA-3
Poplar Creek (historical)—*locale* AL-4
Poplar Creek Island (historical)—*island* TN-4
Poplar Creek Lake—*lake* AR-4
Poplar Creek Lateral District No 16—*canal* MO-7
Poplar Creek Mine (surface)—*mine* TN-4
Poplar Creek Post Office (historical)—*building* AL-4
Poplar Creek Sch—*school* KY-4
Poplar Creek Sch—*school* VA-3
Poplar Creek Sch (historical)—*school* (2) AL-4
Poplar Creek Slough (inundated)—*stream* AL-4
Poplar Creek Valley—*valley* TN-4
*Poplar Crossroad* GA-3
Poplar Crossroads—*locale* GA-3
Poplar Dam—*dam* SC-3
Poplar Dell Ch—*church* FL-3
Poplar Ditch—*canal* CA-9
Poplar Ditch—*canal* OH-6
**Poplar (Donovan)**—*pop pl* TN-4
**Poplar Estates**—*pop pl* TN-4
Poplar Flat—*locale* KY-4
Poplar Flat—*summit* KY-4
*Poplar Flat Baptist Church* MS-4
Poplar Flat Branch—*stream* TN-4
Poplar Flat Campground—*locale* WA-9
Poplar Flat Ch—*church* MS-4
Poplar Flat Creek—*stream* TN-4
Poplar Flats—*flat* KY-4
Poplar Flats—*flat* NC-3
Poplar Flats—*flat* (2) OH-6
Poplar Flats—*locale* VA-3
Poplar Flats Cem—*cemetery* KY-4
Poplar Forest—*hist pl* VA-3
Poplar Forest—*locale* VA-3
Poplar Forest Ch—*church* TN-4
Poplar Forest Sch—*school* TN-4
Poplar Fork—*stream* (2) KY-4
Poplar Fork—*stream* (3) WV-2
Poplar Fork Cem—*cemetery* OH-6
Poplar Fork Ch—*church* VA-3
Poplar Fork Pine Creek—*stream* OH-6
Poplar Forks—*locale* SC-3
Poplar Gap—*gap* (3) KY-4
Poplar Gap—*gap* NC-3
Poplar Gap—*gap* PA-2
Poplar Gap—*gap* (2) VA-3
Poplar Gap Ch—*church* KY-4
Poplar Gap Sch—*school* KY-4
Poplar Gap Sch—*school* NC-3
**Poplar Gardens (subdivision)**—*pop pl* PA-2
*Poplar Grove* MS-4
*Poplar Grove* NC-3
*Poplar Grove* PA-2
Poplar Grove—*forest* ND-7
Poplar Grove—*hist pl* KY-4
Poplar Grove—*hist pl* NC-3
Poplar Grove—*locale* GA-3
Poplar Grove—*locale* IL-6
Poplar Grove—*locale* (2) KY-4
Poplar Grove—*locale* LA-4
Poplar Grove—*locale* (2) NC-3
Poplar Grove—*locale* OH-6
Poplar Grove—*locale* (3) TN-4
Poplar Grove—*locale* UT-8
Poplar Grove—*locale* VA-3
Poplar Grove—*other* TN-4
**Poplar Grove**—*pop pl* AR-4
**Poplar Grove**—*pop pl* IL-6
**Poplar Grove**—*pop pl* (2) IN-6
**Poplar Grove**—*pop pl* KY-4
**Poplar Grove**—*pop pl* LA-4
**Poplar Grove**—*pop pl* MD-2
**Poplar Grove**—*pop pl* NC-3
**Poplargrove**—*pop pl* OH-6
**Poplar Grove**—*pop pl* (2) PA-2
**Poplar Grove**—*pop pl* (4) TN-4
**Poplar Grove Addition (subdivision)**—*pop pl* UT-8
*Poplar Grove Assembly of God Church* TN-4
*Poplar Grove Baptist Church* TN-4
Poplar Grove Branch—*stream* KY-4
*Poplar Grove Cem* TN-4
Poplar Grove Cem—*cemetery* (2) IN-6
Poplar Grove Cem—*cemetery* KS-7
Poplar Grove Cem—*cemetery* MS-4
Poplar Grove Cem—*cemetery* NY-2
Poplar Grove Cem—*cemetery* NC-3
Poplar Grove Cem—*cemetery* OK-5
Poplar Grove Cem—*cemetery* PA-2
Poplar Grove Cem—*cemetery* (4) TN-4
Poplar Grove Ch—*church* AL-4
Poplar Grove Ch—*church* AR-4
Poplar Grove Ch—*church* GA-3
Poplar Grove Ch—*church* (4) IN-6
Poplar Grove Ch—*church* (8) KY-4
Poplar Grove Ch—*church* (2) MD-2
Poplar Grove Ch—*church* MN-6
Poplar Grove Ch—*church* (3) MS-4
Poplar Grove Ch—*church* (2) NC-3
Poplar Grove Ch—*church* OH-6
Poplar Grove Ch—*church* (7) TN-4
Poplar Grove Ch—*church* WV-2
Poplar Grove Chapel—*church* SC-3
Poplar Grove Ch (historical)—*church* TN-4
*Poplar Grove Ch of God* TN-4
Poplar Grove Dam Number One—*dam* TN-4
**Poplar Grove (Faith)**—*pop pl* KY-4
Poplar Grove (historical)—*locale* MS-4
Poplar Grove (historical P.O.)—*locale* IA-7
Poplar Grove Lake—*reservoir* IN-6
Poplar Grove Lake—*reservoir* TN-4
Poplar Grove Lake Dam—*dam* IN-6
*Poplar Grove Methodist Church* TN-4
Poplar Grove Mill and House—*hist pl* VA-3
*Poplar Grove Missionary Baptist Ch* TN-4
Poplar Grove Missionary Baptist Ch—*church* TN-4
Poplar Grove Natl Cem—*cemetery* VA-3
Poplar Grove Oil Field—*oilfield* MS-4
*Poplar Grove Pentecost Ch* TN-4
*Poplar Grove Plantation* TN-4
**Poplar Grove Plantation**—*pop pl* LA-4
Poplar Grove Plantation House—*hist pl* LA-4
Poplar Grove Post Office (historical)—*building* TN-4
Poplar Grove Ranch—*locale* CA-9
Poplar Grove Sch—*school* IL-6
Poplar Grove Sch—*school* KY-4
Poplar Grove Sch—*school* MS-4
Poplar Grove Sch—*school* NC-3
Poplar Grove Sch—*school* (2) WI-6
Poplar Grove Sch (historical)—*school* (2) AL-4
Poplar Grove Sch (historical)—*school* (4) TN-4
Poplar Grove Sch Number 1—*school* ND-7
Poplar Grove Township—*civil* SD-7
Poplar Grove (Township of)—*civ div* IL-6
Poplar Grove (Township of)—*civ div* MN-6
Poplar Gulch—*valley* CO-8
Poplar Hall—*hist pl* DE-2
**Poplar Halls**—*pop pl* VA-3
Poplar Harbor—*harbor* MD-2
*Poplar Head* AL-4
Poplar Head—*locale* (2) FL-3
Poplar Head—*stream* FL-3
Poplar Head Branch—*stream* FL-3
Poplar Head Branch—*stream* GA-3
Poplar Head Cem—*cemetery* GA-3
Poplar Head Ch—*church* (2) FL-3
Poplar Head Ch—*church* GA-3
Poplarhead Ch—*church* LA-4
Poplar Head Ch—*church* MS-4
Poplar Head Ch and School—*church* GA-3
Poplar Head Hill—*summit* FL-3
**Poplar Heights**—*pop pl* VA-3
*Poplar Heights Baptist Church* TN-4
Poplar Heights Ch—*church* TN-4
**Poplar Highlands**—*pop pl* KY-4
Poplar Hill—*hist pl* KY-4
Poplar Hill—*hist pl* MD-2
Poplar Hill—*hist pl* TN-4
Poplar Hill—*locale* GA-3
Poplar Hill—*locale* MD-2
Poplar Hill—*locale* SC-3
Poplar Hill—*locale* TN-4
Poplar Hill—*locale* VA-3
**Poplar Hill**—*pop pl* SC-3
**Poplar Hill**—*pop pl* TN-4
**Poplar Hill**—*pop pl* VA-3
Poplar Hill—*summit* CT-1
Poplar Hill—*summit* (2) ME-1
Poplar Hill—*summit* (4) MA-1
Poplar Hill—*summit* NH-1
Poplar Hill—*summit* (5) NY-2
Poplar Hill—*summit* PA-2
Poplar Hill—*summit* TN-4
Poplar Hill—*summit* (2) VA-3
Poplar Hill Baptist Ch (historical)—*church* TN-4
Poplar Hill Brook—*stream* MA-1
Poplar Hill Cem—*cemetery* MI-6
Poplar Hill Cem—*cemetery* OH-6
Poplar Hill Cem—*cemetery* WI-6
Poplar Hill Ch—*church* NC-3
Poplar Hill Ch—*church* (2) SC-3
Poplar Hill Ch—*church* (2) TN-4
Poplar Hill Ch—*church* (2) VA-3
Poplar Hill Creek—*stream* MD-2
**Poplar Hill Estates**—*pop pl* MD-2
Poplar Hill Falls—*falls* ME-1
Poplar Hill (historical)—*locale* KS-7
**Poplar Hill (historical)**—*pop pl* NC-3
Poplar Hill Mansion—*hist pl* MD-2
Poplar Hill Post Office (historical)—*building* TN-4
**Poplar Hills**—*pop pl* KY-4
**Poplar Hills**—*pop pl* TN-4
Poplar Hills Ch—*church* SC-3
Poplar Hill Sch—*school* ID-8
Poplar Hill Sch—*school* KY-4
Poplar Hill Sch—*school* MS-4
Poplar Hill Sch—*school* SC-3
Poplar Hill Sch—*school* TN-4
Poplar Hill Sch (historical)—*school* AL-4
Poplar Hill Sch (historical)—*school* MO-7
Poplar Hill Sch (historical)—*school* (2) TN-4
**Poplar (historical)**—*pop pl* OR-9
Poplar Hollow—*valley* (2) AL-4
Poplar Hollow—*valley* IL-6
Poplar Hollow—*valley* (3) KY-4
Poplar Hollow—*valley* MO-7
Poplar Hollow—*valley* OH-6
Poplar Hollow—*valley* (2) PA-2
Poplar Hollow—*valley* SC-3
Poplar Hollow—*valley* (5) TN-4
Poplar Hollow—*valley* (6) VA-3
Poplar Hollow—*valley* (3) WV-2
Poplar Hollow Branch—*stream* NC-3
**Poplar Inn**—*pop pl* VA-3
Poplar Island—*island* (2) MD-2
Poplar Island—*island* NH-1
Poplar Island—*island* NY-2
Poplar Island—*island* PA-2
Poplar Island—*island* WV-2
Poplar Island Brook—*stream* ME-1
*Poplar Island Pot* MD-2
Poplar Island Rapids—*rapids* ME-1
**Poplar Knob**—*pop pl* MD-2
Poplar Knob—*summit* GA-3
Poplar Knob—*summit* OH-6
Poplar Knob—*summit* VA-3
Poplar Knoll—*summit* NY-2
Poplar Lake—*lake* (3) MI-6
Poplar Lake—*lake* (4) MN-6
Poplar Lake—*lake* (2) WI-6
Poplar Lake—*reservoir* (2) SC-3
Poplar Lake—*reservoir* TN-4
Poplar Lake Ch—*church* MN-6
Poplar Landing—*locale* VA-3
Poplar Lane—*hist pl* PA-2
Poplar Lateral—*canal* ID-8
Poplar Lawn Cem—*cemetery* VA-3
Poplar Lawn Ch—*church* (2) VA-3
Poplar Lawn Hist Dist—*hist pl* VA-3
Poplar Level—*locale* KY-4
Poplar Level Ch—*church* KY-4
Poplar Lick Branch—*stream* (2) KY-4
Poplarlick Fork—*stream* KY-4
Poplar Lick Gap—*gap* NC-3
Poplar Lick Run—*stream* MD-2
Poplarlick Run—*stream* WV-2
Poplar Lick Run—*stream* WV-2
Poplarlick Run—*stream* (2) WV-2
Poplar Log Bridge—*bridge* KY-4
Poplar Log Cem—*cemetery* AL-4
Poplar Log Ch—*church* AL-4
Poplar Log Ch—*church* (2) KY-4
Poplar Log Cove—*valley* AL-4
Poplar Log Fork—*stream* KY-4
*Poplar Log Freewill Baptist Church* AL-4
Poplar Log Hollow—*valley* KY-4
Poplar Log Hollow—*valley* WV-2
Poplar Log Sch—*school* KY-4
Poplar Mount (historical)—*locale* NC-3
Poplar Mtn—*summit* ME-1
Poplar Mtn—*summit* MA-1
Poplar Mtn—*summit* NY-2
Poplar Mtn—*summit* (2) NC-3
*Poplar Neck* NJ-2
Poplar Neck—*cape* MD-2
Poplar Neck—*cape* VA-3
Poplar Neck—*flat* PA-2
Poplar Neck—*locale* MD-2
Poplar Neck Creek—*stream* VA-3
**Poplar Place Subdivision**—*pop pl* UT-8
**Poplar Plains**—*pop pl* KY-4
Poplar Plains Brook—*stream* CT-1
Poplar Playground—*park* CA-9
Poplar Plaza Shop Ctr—*locale* TN-4
*Poplar Point* MD-2
Poplar Point—*cape* DE-2
Poplar Point—*cape* ME-1
Poplar Point—*cape* (3) MD-2
Poplar Point—*cape* (2) MI-6
Poplar Point—*cape* (2) NY-2
Poplar Point—*cape* NC-3
Poplar Point—*cape* OH-6
Poplar Point—*cape* RI-1
**Poplar Point**—*pop pl* AL-4
**Poplar Point**—*pop pl* RI-1
Poplar Point—*summit* MT-8
Poplar Point Landing—*locale* NC-3
Poplar Point Lighthouse—*hist pl* RI-1
Poplar Point State Campsite—*locale* NY-2
Poplar Point (Township of)—*fmr MCD* NC-3
Poplar Pole Branch—*stream* (2) NC-3

Poplar Pond—*lake* FL-3
Poplar Pond—*lake* NY-2
Poplar Pond (historical)—*lake* AL-4
Poplar Recreation Center—*park* CA-9
*Poplar Ridge* IL-6
Poplar Ridge—*locale* AL-4
Poplar Ridge—*locale* IL-6
Poplar Ridge—*locale* TN-4
**Poplarridge**—*pop pl* AL-4
**Poplar Ridge**—*pop pl* AR-4
**Poplar Ridge**—*pop pl* NY-2
**Poplar Ridge**—*pop pl* OH-6
Poplar Ridge—*ridge* AL-4
Poplar Ridge—*ridge* AR-4
Poplar Ridge—*ridge* IL-6
Poplar Ridge—*ridge* (2) IN-6
Poplar Ridge—*ridge* KY-4
Poplar Ridge—*ridge* (2) ME-1
Poplar Ridge—*ridge* (2) NC-3
Poplar Ridge—*ridge* (3) OH-6
Poplar Ridge—*ridge* (5) TN-4
Poplar Ridge—*ridge* VA-3
Poplar Ridge—*ridge* WV-2
Poplar Ridge—*summit* ME-1
*Poplar Ridge Baptist Church* TN-4
Poplar Ridge Cem—*cemetery* IN-6
Poplar Ridge Ch—*church* KY-4
Poplar Ridge Ch—*church* NC-3
Poplar Ridge Ch—*church* OH-6
Poplar Ridge Ch—*church* TN-4
Poplar Ridge Ch—*church* VA-3
Poplar Ridge Chapel—*church* AR-4
Poplar Ridge Lake—*lake* MI-6
Poplar Ridge Point—*cape* NC-3
Poplar Ridge Post Office (historical)—*building* AL-4
Poplar Ridge Sch—*school* KS-7
Poplar Ridge Sch (abandoned)—*school* MO-7
Poplar Ridge Sch (historical)—*school* AL-4
Poplar Ridge Sch (historical)—*school* (2) TN-4
**Poplar Ridge (subdivision)**—*pop pl* NC-3
Poplar Ripps—*locale* ME-1
*Poplar River* WI-6
Poplar River—*stream* (2) MN-6
Poplar River—*stream* MT-8
Poplar River—*stream* WI-6
Poplar River Cem—*cemetery* MN-6
Poplar River Diversion Ditch—*canal* MN-6
*Poplar River Lake* MN-6
Poplar River (Township of)—*civ div* MN-6
Poplar Root Branch—*stream* GA-3
Poplar Root Creek—*stream* IN-6
*Poplar Run* PA-2
Poplar Run—*stream* IN-6
Poplar Run—*stream* MD-2
Poplar Run—*stream* (2) OH-6
Poplar Run—*stream* (5) PA-2
Poplar Run—*stream* (3) VA-3
Poplar Run Cem—*cemetery* IN-6
Poplar Run Ch—*church* IN-6
Poplar Run Ch—*church* PA-2
Poplar Run Ch—*church* VA-3
Poplars—*locale* MD-2
**Poplars**—*pop pl* PA-2
Poplar Sch—*school* CA-9
Poplar Sch—*school* KS-7
Poplar Sch—*school* MO-7
Poplar Sch—*school* SC-3
Poplar Sch—*school* WA-9
Poplar Sch (historical)—*school* MS-4
Poplar School Hollow—*valley* WV-2
Poplars Creek—*stream* GA-3
*Poplar Shore* NY-2
Poplars Picnic Area—*locale* WA-9
*Poplar Spring* AL-4
*Poplar Spring* MD-2
*Poplar Spring* TN-4
Poplar Spring—*spring* (5) AL-4
Poplar Spring—*spring* AZ-5
Poplar Spring—*spring* (2) GA-3
Poplar Spring—*spring* KY-4
Poplar Spring—*spring* MS-4
Poplar Spring—*spring* OR-9
Poplar Spring—*spring* PA-2
Poplar Spring—*spring* SD-7
Poplar Spring—*spring* (6) TN-4
Poplar Spring—*valley* AL-4
Poplar Spring Branch—*stream* (2) AL-4
Poplar Spring Branch—*stream* (2) NC-3
Poplar Spring Branch—*stream* (5) TN-4
Poplar Spring Branch—*stream* VA-3
Poplar Spring Cem—*cemetery* (3) AL-4
Poplar Spring Cem—*cemetery* FL-3
Poplar Spring Cem—*cemetery* MS-4
Poplar Spring Cem—*cemetery* SC-3
*Poplar Spring Ch* AL-4
Poplar Spring Ch—*church* AL-4
Poplar Spring Ch—*church* (5) GA-3
Poplar Spring Ch—*church* (2) KY-4
Poplar Spring Ch—*church* MS-4
Poplar Spring Ch—*church* NC-3
Poplar Spring Ch—*church* (2) SC-3
Poplar Spring Creek—*stream* AL-4
Poplar Spring Creek—*stream* GA-3
Poplar Spring Creek—*stream* PA-2
Poplar Spring Furnace (historical)—*locale* TN-4
Poplar Spring Furnace (40MT376)—*hist pl* TN-4
Poplar Spring Hollow—*valley* AL-4
Poplar Spring Hollow—*valley* KY-4
Poplar Spring Hollow—*valley* (3) TN-4
*Poplar Spring Iron Works* TN-4
Poplar Spring Iron Works Post Office (historical)—*building* TN-4
*Poplar Spring Post Office* TN-4
Poplarspring Post Office (historical)—*building* TN-4
*Poplar Spring Run* PA-2
*Poplar Spring Run* VA-3
Poplar Springs—*locale* GA-3
Poplar Springs—*locale* (3) TN-4
Poplar Springs—*locale* VA-3
**Poplar Springs**—*pop pl* (2) AL-4
**Poplar Springs**—*pop pl* MD-2
**Poplar Springs**—*pop pl* (6) MS-4
**Poplar Springs**—*pop pl* NC-3
**Poplar Springs**—*pop pl* (2) SC-3
**Poplar Springs**—*pop pl* (3) TN-4
Poplar Springs—*spring* AL-4
*Poplar Springs Baptist Ch* TN-4
Poplar Springs Baptist Ch—*church* TN-4
*Poplar Springs Baptist Church* MS-4
**Poplar Springs Branch**—*pop pl* AL-4
Poplar Springs Branch—*stream* GA-3
Poplar Springs Branch—*stream* MS-4
Poplar Springs Branch—*stream* TN-4
Poplar Springs Branch—*stream* VA-3
Poplar Springs Branch Cabin Site Area—*locale* AL-4
Poplar Springs Campgrounds—*locale* GA-3
*Poplar Springs Cem* AL-4
Poplar Springs Cem—*cemetery* (5) AL-4
Poplar Springs Cem—*cemetery* GA-3
Poplar Springs Cem—*cemetery* (5) MS-4
Poplar Springs Cem—*cemetery* (3) TN-4
Poplar Springs Cem—*cemetery* VA-3
*Poplar Springs Ch* AL-4
*Poplar Springs Ch* MS-4
Poplar Springs Ch—*church* (18) AL-4
Poplar Springs Ch—*church* FL-3
Poplar Springs Ch—*church* (19) GA-3
Poplar Springs Ch—*church* (3) KY-4
Poplar Springs Ch—*church* LA-4
Poplar Springs Ch—*church* (8) MS-4
Poplar Springs Ch—*church* (12) NC-3
Poplar Springs Ch—*church* (2) SC-3
Poplar Springs Ch—*church* (2) TN-4
Poplar Springs Ch—*church* (2) VA-3
Poplar Spring Sch—*school* (2) FL-3
Poplar Springs Ch (historical)—*church* MS-4
Poplar Spring Sch (historical)—*school* (2) AL-4
Poplar Springs Creek—*stream* AL-4
Poplar Springs Creek—*stream* TN-4
*Poplar Springs Crossroads* AL-4
Poplar Springs Dam—*dam* OR-9
Poplar Springs Drive Baptist Ch—*church* MS-4
Poplar Springs Drive United Methodist Ch—*church* MS-4
*Poplar Springs Elementary School* MS-4
Poplar Springs Gap—*gap* (2) GA-3
Poplar Springs (historical)—*locale* AL-4
Poplar Springs (historical)—*locale* MS-4
Poplar Springs Hollow—*valley* PA-2
Poplar Springs Methodist Ch—*church* MS-4
Poplar Springs Methodist Ch—*church* TN-4
Poplar Springs Mine (surface)—*mine* AL-4
Poplar Springs Normal Coll (historical)—*school* MS-4
Poplar Springs North Ch—*church* GA-3
Poplar Springs Pond—*lake* FL-3
*Poplar Springs Primitive Baptist Church* AL-4
Poplar Springs Rec Area—*park* TN-4
Poplar Springs Ridge—*ridge* (2) TN-4
Poplar Springs Road Hist Dist—*hist pl* MS-4
Poplar Springs Rsvr—*reservoir* OR-9
Poplar Springs Sch—*school* AL-4
Poplar Springs Sch—*school* FL-3
Poplar Springs Sch—*school* KY-4
Poplar Springs Sch—*school* MS-4
Poplar Springs Sch—*school* SC-3
Poplar Springs Sch—*school* TN-4
Poplar Springs Sch (historical)—*school* (6) AL-4
Poplar Springs Sch (historical)—*school* (5) MS-4
Poplar Springs Sch (historical)—*school* (7) TN-4
**Poplar Springs (subdivision)**—*pop pl* NC-3
Poplar Springs Union Ch—*church* MS-4
Poplar Springs Valley—*valley* TN-4
Poplar Spring Top—*summit* NC-3
*Poplar Stand Church* TN-4
Poplar Stand Sch (historical)—*school* TN-4
Poplar Stomp Gap—*gap* GA-3
Poplar Stream—*stream* ME-1
*Poplar Street Church of Christ* AL-4
Poplar Street JHS—*school* AR-4
Poplar Stump Landing (historical)—*locale* TN-4
Poplar Swamp—*stream* SC-3
Poplar Swamp—*stream* VA-3
Poplar Swamp—*swamp* CT-1
Poplar Swamp—*swamp* GA-3
Poplar Swamp Brook—*stream* CT-1
Poplar Tavern Camp—*locale* ME-1
**Poplar Tent**—*pop pl* NC-3
Poplar Tent Ch—*church* NC-3
Poplar Thicket—*hist pl* DE-2
Poplar Thicket Branch—*stream* KY-4
Poplar Top—*locale* TN-4
Poplar Top (CCD)—*cens area* TN-4
Poplar Top Division—*civil* TN-4
Poplartown Branch—*stream* MD-2
Poplar (Township of)—*fmr MCD* NC-3
**Poplar (Township of)**—*pop pl* MN-6
Poplar Training Sch—*school* SC-3
Poplar Tree Bay—*bay* NY-2
Poplar Tree Corners—*locale* NY-2
Poplar Tree Hollow—*valley* OH-6
Poplartree Hollow—*valley* VA-3
Poplar Tree Lake—*reservoir* TN-4
Poplar Tree Lake Dam—*dam* TN-4
Poplar Tree Sch—*school* NY-2
Poplar Union Sch—*school* TN-4
Poplar Valley—*valley* PA-2
Poplar Valley Ch—*church* AR-4
Poplar Valley Ch—*church* PA-2
Poplar Valley Sch (abandoned)—*school* PA-2
Poplarville—*locale* KY-4
**Poplarville**—*pop pl* MS-4
Poplarville City Hall—*building* MS-4
Poplarville Coll (historical)—*school* MS-4
Poplarville Elem Sch—*school* MS-4
Poplarville HS—*school* MS-4
Poplarville JHS—*school* MS-4
Poplarville-Pearl River County Airp—*airport* MS-4
Poplarville Post Office—*building* MS-4
Poplar Wash—*stream* AZ-5
Poplar Well—*cave* TN-4
Poplar Woods Pond—*lake* DE-2
Poplecat Hollow—*valley* WV-2
Pople Hill—*summit* NY-2
Pople Point—*cape* FL-3
*Popler Island Harbor* MD-2
*Poplin* NH-1
Poplin Branch—*stream* NC-3
Poplin Cem—*cemetery* MO-7
Poplin Cem—*cemetery* TN-4
Poplin Creek—*stream* CA-9
Poplin Creek—*stream* NC-3
Poplin Hollow—*valley* (2) TN-4
Poplin Hollow Cem—*cemetery* TN-4
Poplin Lake—*reservoir* OK-5
Poplin School (abandoned)—*locale* MO-7
Poplins Crossroads—*locale* TN-4
Poplins Crossroads Post Office (historical)—*building* TN-4
Poplins Grove Ch—*church* NC-3
Poplus Cem—*cemetery* LA-4
Pop Mtn—*summit* AK-9
Pop Mtn—*summit* CT-1
Popo Agie, Mount—*summit* WY-8
Popo Agie Falls—*falls* WY-8
*Popo Agie River* WY-8
Popo Agie River—*stream* WY-8
*Popo Angie River* WY-8
Popocatepetl, Mount—*summit* OR-9
*Popoff Slough* AR-4
Popof Glacier—*glacier* AK-9
Popof Head—*cliff* AK-9
Popof Island—*island* (2) AK-9
Popof Reef—*bar* AK-9
Popof Strait—*channel* AK-9
Popoiwi Heiau—*locale* HI-9
Popokamiut—*locale* AK-9
Popokanaloa Point—*cape* HI-9
*Popolatic Pond* MA-1
Popoloa—*civil* HI-9
Popoloau Point—*cape* HI-9
Popolopen Bridge—*bridge* NY-2
*Popolopen Brook* NY-2
Popolopen Creek—*stream* NY-2
Popolopen Lake—*lake* NY-2
*Popoloup Island* MA-1
*Popolo Vakamakatuk* AZ-5
*Poponaugh Creek* TX-5
*Poponesset* MA-1
*Poponesset Bay* MA-1
*Poponesset Beach* MA-1
*Poponesset Creek* MA-1
*Poponesset Island* MA-1
*Poponesset Neck* MA-1
*Poponia* MH-9
*Poponoming Lake* PA-2
Poponui—*civil* HI-9
Popoo Gulch—*valley* HI-9
Popo Point—*cape* FL-3
Poposki State Wildlife Mngmt Area—*park* MN-6
Popovich Hill—*summit* NV-8
Popovitch Creek—*stream* AK-9
Poppasguash Swamp—*swamp* MA-1
Poppasquash Farms Hist Dist—*hist pl* RI-1
Poppaw Creek—*stream* NC-3
Popp Drain—*canal* MI-6
*Poppe Creek* MT-8
Poppenesset Bird Sanctuary—*park* MA-1
Poppenheim Crossing—*locale* SC-3
Poppenhusen Institute—*hist pl* NY-2
Popperdam Creek—*stream* SC-3
**Popperton Place Subdivision**—*pop pl* UT-8
Poppet Creek—*stream* CA-9
Poppet Flat—*flat* CA-9
Poppet Flat Divide Truck Trail—*trail* CA-9
Poppet Hollow—*valley* IL-6
Popping Rock—*summit* NM-5
Poppin Rock Tunnel—*tunnel* KY-4
Popple—*locale* MI-6
Popple Branch—*stream* GA-3
*Popple Brook* MA-1
Popple Camp Brook—*stream* MA-1
Popple Cem—*cemetery* MN-6
Popple Creek—*locale* MN-6
Popple Creek—*stream* MI-6
Popple Creek—*stream* (2) WI-6
Popple Creek Cem—*cemetery* WI-6
Popple Dungeon—*valley* VT-1
Popple Dungeon Cem—*cemetery* VT-1
Popple Grove (Township of)—*civ div* MN-6
*Popple Hill* MA-1
Popple Hill—*summit* ME-1
Popple Hill—*summit* NY-2
*Popple Hill Brook* MA-1
Popple Hill Brook—*stream* ME-1
Popple Island—*island* GA-3
Popple Island—*island* MN-6
Popple Island—*island* (2) WI-6
*Popple Lake* MN-6
*Popple Lake* WI-6
Popple Lake—*lake* (5) MN-6
Popple Lake—*lake* (2) WI-6
**Popple Lake**—*pop pl* WI-6
Popple Lake State Wildlife Mngmt Area—*park* MN-6
Popple Mtn—*summit* NH-1
Popple Point—*cape* NY-2
Popple Point Lake—*lake* WI-6
Popple Rapids—*rapids* WI-6
Popple Ridge—*ridge* PA-2
Popple Ridge Snowmobile Trail—*trail* WI-6
**Popple River**—*pop pl* WI-6
Popple River—*stream* MN-6
Popple River—*stream* (2) WI-6
**Popple River (Town of)**—*pop pl* WI-6
Popples Cem—*cemetery* GA-3
Popplestone Beach—*beach* ME-1
Popplestone Beach—*beach* MA-1
Popplestone Cove—*bay* (2) ME-1
Popplestone Ledge—*bar* ME-1
Popplestone Ledge—*rock* MA-1
Popplestone Point—*cape* ME-1
Popple Swamp—*swamp* CT-1
Poppleton Block—*hist pl* NE-7
Poppleton Fire Station—*hist pl* MD-2
Poppleton Landing—*locale* IL-6
Poppleton Park—*park* MI-6
Poppleton Sch—*school* MI-6
**Poppleton (Township of)**—*pop pl* MN-6
**Popple (Township of)**—*pop pl* MN-6
Popplewell Cem—*cemetery* MO-7
Popplewell Drain—*canal* MI-6
Popp Memorial—*locale* LA-4
Pop Point—*cape* AK-9
Poppolton Creek—*stream* FL-3
*Popponeeste Bay* MA-1
Popponesset Bay—*bay* MA-1
Popponesset Beach—*bar* MA-1
**Popponesset Beach**—*pop pl* MA-1
Popponesset Creek—*channel* MA-1
Popponesset Island—*island* MA-1
*Popponessett Bay* MA-1
*Popponessett Beach* MA-1
*Popponessett Island* MA-1
*Popponessit Bay* MA-1
Popp Ridge—*ridge* IN-6
Popp Rsvr—*reservoir* OR-9
Popps Cem—*cemetery* TX-5
Popps Creek—*stream* MI-6
Poppy Canyon—*valley* AZ-5
Poppy Creek—*stream* OR-9
Poppy Drain—*canal* MI-6
Poppy Lode Mine—*mine* SD-7
Poppy Peak—*summit* CA-9
Poppy Well—*well* AZ-5
Pops Branch—*stream* MO-7
Pops Ferry Bridge—*bridge* MS-4
Pops Ferry Elem Sch—*school* MS-4
Pops Ferry (historical)—*locale* MS-4
Pops Ferry Park—*park* MS-4
Pops Ferry Shop Ctr—*locale* MS-4
Pops Gulch—*valley* CA-9
**Pops Hammock Seminole Village**—*pop pl* FL-3
Popshego Creek—*stream* OK-5
Pops Hobby Lake—*reservoir* PA-2
*Popsicle* UT-8
Pops Lake—*lake* OH-6
Pops Landing Campground—*locale* TX-5
**Popsons (historical)**—*pop pl* MS-4
Pop Springs—*spring* WY-8
Popsquatchet Hills—*summit* MA-1
Pops Rocks—*bar* NY-2
Popular Bay (Carolina Bay)—*swamp* NC-3
Popular Bluff—*cliff* KY-4
Popular Bluff Sch (historical)—*school* TN-4
*Popular Branch* FL-3
*Popular Camp Creek* GA-3
*Popular Canyon* NV-8
*Popular Creek* IN-6
Popular Department Store—*hist pl* TX-5
Popular Grove Cem—*cemetery* IL-6
*Popular Grove Church* TN-4
Popular Grove Sch—*school* IN-6
*Popular Gulch* CO-8
*Popular Hill* MA-1
Popularis Cem—*cemetery* MT-8
Popular Mount Ch—*church* VA-3
Popular Mtn—*summit* KY-4
Popular Point—*cape* NJ-2
Popular Price Store—*hist pl* MS-4
Popular Ridge Lake—*lake* MS-4
*Popular River* WI-6
Popular Spring Ch—*church* AL-4
Popular Spring Ch—*church* FL-3
Popular Spring Ch—*church* GA-3
*Popular Springs Baptist Church* MS-4
Popular Springs Cem—*cemetery* MS-4
Popular Springs Cem—*cemetery* NC-3
*Popular Springs Ch* AL-4
*Popular Spring Sch* TN-4
Popular Springs Ch—*church* (4) MS-4
Popular Springs Ch—*church* NC-3
Popular Springs Creek—*stream* MS-4
Popular Springs (historical)—*locale* MS-4
Popular Springs Sch (historical)—*school* MS-4
Popular Springs Sch (historical)—*school* TN-4
Popular State Wildlife Mngmt Area—*park* MN-6
Populatic Pond—*lake* MA-1
*Population Corners* PA-2
Populi Creek—*stream* AR-4
Populis Hollow—*valley* MO-7
Popwell Cem—*cemetery* GA-3
**Popwellville**—*pop pl* GA-3
*Poquaig* MA-1
*Poquannoc* CT-1
*Poquannoc Lake* CT-1
*Poquannoc River* CT-1
Poquanticut Brook—*stream* MA-1
*Poquay Brook* MA-1
*Poque Run* OH-6
Poquessing Creek—*stream* PA-2
Poquessing Sch—*school* PA-2
*Poquetanock* CT-1
*Poquetanock Cove* CT-1
Poquetanuck—*locale* CT-1
Poquetanuck Brook—*stream* CT-1
Poquetanuck Cove—*bay* CT-1
Poquetanuck Sch—*school* CT-1
*Poquet Lake* MN-6
Poquette Ditch—*canal* CO-8
Poquettes Lake—*lake* WI-6
Poquiant Brook—*stream* RI-1
*Poquinunk Brook* RI-1
*Poquita Creek* TX-5
Poquita Mesa—*summit* NM-5
Poquito Bayou—*bay* FL-3
Poquito Mesa—*summit* NM-5
Poquito Oil Field—*oilfield* TX-5
*Poquonoc* CT-1
**Poquonock**—*pop pl* CT-1
**Poquonock Bridge**—*pop pl* CT-1
*Poquonock Lake* CT-1
*Poquonock Pond* CT-1
*Poquonock River* CT-1
Poquonock River—*stream* CT-1
*Poquonoc Lake* CT-1
*Poquonoc river* CT-1
*Poquonrock Bridge* CT-1
*Poquosin River* VA-3
Poquoson Flats—*flat* VA-3
**Poquoson (ind. city)**—*pop pl* VA-3
Poquoson Point—*cape* NC-3
Poquoson River—*stream* VA-3
**Poquoson Shores**—*pop pl* VA-3
**Poquott**—*pop pl* NY-2
Poquoy Brook—*stream* MA-1
*Poquoy Trout Brook* MA-1
P O Ranch—*locale* WY-8
*Poraro* MH-9
Porath Gulch—*valley* CA-9
Porcaville—*locale* NY-2
Porcellian Club—*hist pl* MA-1
Porch Branch—*stream* NJ-2
Porch Cem—*cemetery* PA-2
**Porcher Bluff**—*pop pl* SC-3
Porcher Canal—*canal* TX-5
Porcher House—*hist pl* FL-3
Porcher Ranch—*locale* TX-5
Porcher Windmill—*locale* NM-5
Porches, The—*hist pl* FL-3
Porches Mill—*locale* NJ-2
Porches Mill Dam—*dam* NJ-2
Porches Mill Pond—*reservoir* NJ-2
Porches Spring Cave—*cave* AL-4
Porch Mine—*mine* PA-2
**Porchtown**—*pop pl* NJ-2
Porcupina Island—*island* ME-1
**Porcupine**—*pop pl* ND-7
**Porcupine**—*pop pl* SD-7
**Porcupine**—*pop pl* WI-6
Porcupine, The—*summit* ME-1
Porcupine (Aban'd)—*locale* AK-9
Porcupine Basin—*basin* MT-8
Porcupine Bay—*bay* AK-9
Porcupine Bay—*bay* WA-9
*Porcupine Brook* ME-1
Porcupine Brook—*stream* NH-1
Porcupine Butte—*summit* AK-9
Porcupine Butte—*summit* CA-9
Porcupine Butte—*summit* MT-8
Porcupine Butte—*summit* OK-5
Porcupine Butte—*summit* OR-9
Porcupine Butte—*summit* SD-7
Porcupine Camp—*locale* NM-5
Porcupine Camp—*locale* OR-9
Porcupine Camp—*locale* WA-9
Porcupine Campground—*locale* ID-8
Porcupine Campground—*locale* MT-8
Porcupine Campground—*locale* WY-8
Porcupine Canyon—*valley* AZ-5
Porcupine Canyon—*valley* (2) ID-8
Porcupine Canyon—*valley* MT-8
Porcupine Canyon—*valley* NV-8
Porcupine Canyon—*valley* (4) NM-5
Porcupine Canyon—*valley* (2) OR-9
Porcupine Canyon—*valley* (2) UT-8
Porcupine Cem—*cemetery* WI-6
Porcupine Cone—*summit* CO-8
Porcupine Coulee—*valley* MT-8
Porcupine Cove—*bay* AK-9
*Porcupine Creek* ID-8
*Porcupine Creek* PA-2
Porcupine Creek—*stream* (9) AK-9
Porcupine Creek—*stream* AZ-5
Porcupine Creek—*stream* CA-9
Porcupine Creek—*stream* (6) CO-8
Porcupine Creek—*stream* (15) ID-8
Porcupine Creek—*stream* (2) KS-7
Porcupine Creek—*stream* MN-6
Porcupine Creek—*stream* (16) MT-8
Porcupine Creek—*stream* (2) NV-8
Porcupine Creek—*stream* NM-5
Porcupine Creek—*stream* (2) ND-7
Porcupine Creek—*stream* OH-6
Porcupine Creek—*stream* (3) OR-9
Porcupine Creek—*stream* PA-2
Porcupine Creek—*stream* (4) SD-7
Porcupine Creek—*stream* (4) UT-8
Porcupine Creek—*stream* (2) WA-9
Porcupine Creek—*stream* (3) WI-6
Porcupine Creek—*stream* (15) WY-8
Porcupine Creek Falls—*falls* WY-8
Porcupine Creek Overflow—*stream* MT-8
Porcupine Dam—*dam* UT-8
Porcupine District—*hist pl* AK-9
Porcupine Dome—*summit* AK-9
Porcupine Draft—*valley* PA-2
Porcupine Draw—*valley* NM-5
Porcupine Draw—*valley* SD-7
Porcupine Draw—*valley* (2) UT-8
Porcupine Dry Ledge—*island* ME-1
Porcupine Falls—*falls* WY-8
Porcupine Flat—*flat* CA-9
Porcupine Flat—*flat* ID-8
Porcupine Glacier—*glacier* AK-9
Porcupine Grass Lake—*lake* AK-9
Porcupine Guard Station—*locale* MT-8
Porcupine Guard Station—*locale* OR-9
Porcupine Gulch—*valley* (7) CO-8
Porcupine Gulch—*valley* ID-8
Porcupine Gulch—*valley* (3) MT-8
Porcupine Gulch—*valley* UT-8
*Porcupine Hill* ME-1
Porcupine Hill—*summit* AK-9
Porcupine Hill—*summit* CO-8
Porcupine Hill—*summit* (3) ME-1
Porcupine Hill—*summit* NH-1
Porcupine Hill—*summit* NY-2
Porcupine Hill—*summit* ND-7
Porcupine Hills—*ridge* ND-7
Porcupine Hills—*summit* WY-8
Porcupine Hollow—*valley* (2) ID-8
Porcupine Hollow—*valley* (3) PA-2
Porcupine Inn—*locale* MI-6
Porcupine Island—*island* (2) AK-9
Porcupine Island—*island* ME-1
Porcupine Island—*island* MN-6
Porcupine Islands—*area* AK-9
Porcupine Knoll—*summit* UT-8
*Porcupine Lake* WI-6
Porcupine Lake—*lake* (2) AK-9
Porcupine Lake—*lake* (2) CA-9
Porcupine Lake—*lake* CO-8
Porcupine Lake—*lake* ID-8
Porcupine Lake—*lake* (3) MI-6
Porcupine Lake—*lake* MN-6
Porcupine Lake—*lake* (2) MT-8
Porcupine Lake—*lake* NM-5
Porcupine Lake—*lake* (6) WI-6
Porcupine Lake—*reservoir* ID-8
Porcupine Lakes—*lake* MI-6
Porcupine Ledge—*bench* ME-1
Porcupine Ledges—*bar* ME-1
Porcupine Lookout—*locale* (2) MT-8
Porcupine Lookout Tower—*locale* WI-6
Porcupine Meadow—*flat* ID-8
Porcupine Mine—*mine* MT-8
*Porcupine Mountain* MI-6
Porcupine Mountains—*range* MI-6
Porcupine Mountains State Park—*park* MI-6
*Porcupine Mtn* ME-1
Porcupine Mtn—*summit* (9) ME-1
Porcupine Mtn—*summit* NV-8
Porcupine Mtn—*summit* OR-9
Porcupine Mtn—*summit* UT-8
Porcupine Mtn—*summit* WI-6
Porcupine Park—*flat* CO-8
Porcupine Pass—*gap* (2) ID-8
Porcupine Pass—*gap* MT-8
Porcupine Pass—*gap* NV-8
Porcupine Pass—*gap* UT-8
Porcupine Pass—*gap* WA-9
Porcupine Pass—*gap* WY-8
*Porcupine Peak* SD-7
Porcupine Peak—*summit* AK-9
Porcupine Peak—*summit* CO-8
Porcupine Peak—*summit* MI-6
Porcupine Peak—*summit* OR-9
Porcupine Peak—*summit* UT-8
Porcupine Peak Site—*hist pl* CO-8
Porcupine Pinnacle—*summit* ME-1
Porcupine Point—*cape* AK-9
Porcupine Point—*cape* ME-1
Porcupine Point—*cape* MI-6
Porcupine Ranch—*locale* MT-8
Porcupine Ranch—*locale* UT-8
Porcupine Ranger Station—*locale* ID-8
Porcupine Rapids—*rapids* ID-8
*Porcupine Ridge* WY-8
Porcupine Ridge—*ridge* AK-9
Porcupine Ridge—*ridge* AZ-5
Porcupine Ridge—*ridge* (2) CO-8
Porcupine Ridge—*ridge* ME-1
Porcupine Ridge—*ridge* MT-8
Porcupine Ridge—*ridge* (2) OR-9
Porcupine Ridge—*ridge* (3) UT-8
Porcupine Ridge—*ridge* VT-1
Porcupine Ridge—*ridge* WA-9
Porcupine Ridge—*ridge* WY-8
Porcupine Rim—*cliff* CA-9
Porcupine Rim—*cliff* UT-8
Porcupine River—*stream* (2) AK-9
Porcupine Rock—*other* AK-9
Porcupine Rsvr—*reservoir* CA-9
Porcupine Rsvr—*reservoir* ID-8
Porcupine Rsvr—*reservoir* OR-9
Porcupine Rsvr—*reservoir* (2) UT-8
Porcupine Rsvr—*reservoir* WY-8
Porcupine Run—*stream* (2) PA-2
Porcupines, The—*island* ME-1
Porcupine Saddle—*gap* MT-8
Porcupine Spring—*spring* AZ-5
Porcupine Spring—*spring* CO-8
Porcupine Spring—*spring* (4) ID-8
Porcupine Spring—*spring* MT-8
Porcupine Spring—*spring* NV-8
Porcupine Spring—*spring* (4) OR-9
Porcupine Spring—*spring* (2) UT-8
Porcupine Spring Creek—*stream* MT-8
Porcupine Spring Picnic Area—*locale* ID-8
*Porcupines Tail* SD-7
*Porcupines Tail Butte* SD-7
Porcupine Tank—*reservoir* (3) AZ-5
Porcupine Tank—*reservoir* CA-9
Porcupine Tank—*reservoir* NM-5
Porcupine Tanks—*reservoir* NM-5
Porcupine Trail—*trail* WY-8
Porcupine Valley—*stream* CA-9
Porcupine Valley—*valley* MT-8
Porcupine Wash—*valley* AZ-5
Porcupine Wash—*valley* CA-9
Pordonia Point—*summit* CO-8
*Pores* FM-9
Pores Ford Bridge—*bridge* NC-3
**Pores Knob**—*pop pl* NC-3
Pores Knob—*summit* NC-3
Porfirio—*locale* TX-5
Porfirio Well—*well* TX-5
Porgo Creek—*stream* AK-9
Porgy Key—*island* FL-3
Porgy Shoal—*bar* NY-2
Pori—*locale* MI-6
Pori Creek—*stream* MI-6
Poricy Brook—*stream* NJ-2
Poricy Dam—*dam* NJ-2
Poricy Pond—*reservoir* NJ-2
Porier Canyon—*valley* MT-8
*Po River* VA-3
Po River—*stream* VA-3
Porjoe Key—*island* FL-3
*Pork Barrel* MI-6
Pork Barrel, The—*cove* MA-1
Pork Barrel Island—*island* WI-6
*Pork Barrel Lake* MI-6
Pork Barrel Lake—*lake* ME-1
Pork Barrel Lake—*lake* (2) MI-6
Pork Barrel Pond—*lake* (2) MA-1
Porkbarrel Pond—*lake* NY-2
Pork Bay—*bay* MN-6
Pork Bay—*bay* NY-2
Pork Brook—*stream* ME-1
Pork Chop Pass Site (LA 5661)—*hist pl* NM-5
Porkchop Pond—*lake* MD-2
Pork City Hill—*summit* MN-6
*Pork Creek* MT-8
*Pork Creek* OR-9
Pork Creek—*stream* ID-8
Pork Creek—*stream* NY-2
Porkey—*locale* PA-2
Porkey Lake—*lake* WI-6
*Pork Gulch* MT-8
Pork Hill—*summit* CT-1
Pork Hill—*summit* RI-1
Porkies Pasture—*flat* UT-8
Pork Island—*island* MA-1
Pork Island—*island* NJ-2
Pork Island Hollow—*valley* NY-2
Pork Point—*cape* ME-1
Pork Point—*cape* NC-3
Pork Rips—*rapids* ME-1
Pork Rocks—*island* CT-1
*Porksha Pond* MA-1
*Porky Creek* WI-6
Porky Creek—*stream* OR-9
Porky Creek—*stream* (2) WI-6
Porky Island—*island* SC-3
Porky Lake—*lake* OR-9
Porky Lakes—*lake* MI-6
Porky Run—*stream* PA-2
Porland Bridge—*bridge* ME-1
Porlier Sch—*school* WI-6
Poro, Finol—*summit* FM-9
Poronto Creek—*stream* MT-8
Poroporone Ch—*church* VA-3
Poropotank Bay—*bay* VA-3
Poropotank River—*stream* VA-3
*Porphery Mountain* CO-8
*Porphry Creek* ID-8
*Porphry Peak* MT-8

Porphyry—*locale* CA-9
Porphyry Basin—*basin* (2) CO-8
Porphyry Bench—*bench* UT-8
Porphyry Bridge—*bridge* ID-8
Porphyry Canyon—*valley* NV-8
Porphyry Creek—*stream* AK-9
Porphyry Creek—*stream* (2) CO-8
Porphyry Creek—*stream* (3) ID-8
Porphyry Dike Mine—*mine* MT-8
Porphyry Flat—*flat* UT-8
Porphyry Gulch—*valley* AZ-5
Porphyry Gulch—*valley* (4) CO-8
Porphyry Gulch—*valley* MT-8
Porphyry Hill—*summit* UT-8
Porphyry Knob—*summit* UT-8
Porphyry Lake—*lake* CA-9
Porphyry Lake—*lake* CO-8
Porphyry Lake—*lake* ID-8
*Porphyry Mountain* CO-8
Porphyry Mtn—*summit* AK-9
Porphyry Mtn—*summit* AZ-5
Porphyry Mtn—*summit* (3) CO-8
Porphyry Mtn—*summit* MT-8
Porphyry Park—*flat* CO-8
Porphyry Peak—*summit* CO-8
Porphyry Peak—*summit* (2) ID-8
Porphyry Peak—*summit* (2) MT-8
Porphyry Peak—*summit* NV-8
Porphyry Peak—*summit* WA-9
Porphyry Peaks—*summit* CO-8
Porphyry Reef—*ridge* MT-8
Porphyry Ridge—*ridge* ID-8
Porphyry Spring—*spring* NV-8
Porphyry Spring—*spring* OR-9
Porphyry Wash—*stream* NV-8
Porpoise, Cape—*cape* ME-1
Porpoise Bay—*bay* (2) FL-3
Porpoise Bay—*bay* LA-4
Porpoise Bayou—*gut* LA-4
*Porpoise Bight* FL-3
Porpoise Channel—*channel* NY-2
Porpoise Creek—*stream* (3) FL-3
Porpoise Creek—*stream* MD-2
Porpoise Creek—*stream* NC-3
Porpoise Harbor—*bay* AK-9
Porpoise Islands—*area* AK-9
Porpoise Key—*island* FL-3
Porpoise Point—*cape* AK-9
Porpoise Point—*cape* (4) FL-3
Porpoise Point—*cape* LA-4
Porpoise Point—*cape* VA-3
Porpoise Point Islnnd—*island* FL-3
Porpoise Pond—*lake* MD-2
Porpoise Pond—*lake* NC-3
Porpoise Rocks—*bar* AK-9
Porpoise Rocks—*island* AK-9
Porpoise Rocks—*island* VI-3
Porpoise Shoal—*bar* LA-4
Porpoise Shoal—*bar* MS-4
Porpoise Slough—*gut* VA-3
Porpoise Slough—*stream* NC-3
Porque Tank—*reservoir* AZ-5
Porras Dikes—*summit* AZ-5
Porrell Cem—*cemetery* VT-1
Porrett Lake—*lake* ID-8
Porridge Lake—*lake* MN-6
Porridge Pot—*lake* VA-3
**Port**—*pop pl* OK-5
Port, Dr. Luke A., House—*hist pl* OR-9
Port, Lake—*lake* AR-4
Port, Lake—*lake* TX-5
Porta Bello—*locale* VA-3
Portable Run—*stream* PA-2
**Port Acres**—*pop pl* TX-5
Portaferry Lake—*lake* NY-2
*Portage* MI-6
Portage—*locale* AK-9
Portage—*locale* IL-6
Portage—*locale* LA-4
Portage—*locale* NY-2
Portage—*locale* WA-9
**Portage**—*pop pl* IN-6
**Portage**—*pop pl* LA-4
**Portage**—*pop pl* ME-1
**Portage**—*pop pl* MI-6
**Portage**—*pop pl* MT-8
**Portage**—*pop pl* OH-6
**Portage**—*pop pl* PA-2
**Portage**—*pop pl* UT-8
**Portage**—*pop pl* WI-6
Portage, Bayou—*gut* LA-4
Portage, Bayou—*stream* (5) LA-4
Portage, Bayou—*stream* MS-4
Portage, The—*channel* WA-9
Portage, The—*locale* OR-9
Portage Arm—*bay* AK-9
Portage Arm—*channel* AK-9
Portage Bay—*bay* (5) AK-9
Portage Bay—*bay* LA-4
Portage Bay—*bay* (2) MI-6
Portage Bay—*bay* (2) MN-6
Portage Bay—*bay* (2) WA-9
Portage Bayou—*canal* MO-7
Portage Bight—*bay* AK-9
Portage Borough—*civil* PA-2
Portage Branch—*stream* MN-6
Portage Brook—*stream* ME-1
Portage Brook—*stream* MN-6
Portage-Burns Waterway—*canal* IN-6
Portage Canal—*canal* (2) LA-4
Portage Canal—*canal* WA-9
Portage Canal—*hist pl* WI-6
Portage Canal Number Two—*canal* LA-4
Portage Canyon—*valley* ID-8
Portage Canyon—*valley* UT-8
Portage Cem—*cemetery* OH-6
Portage Cem—*cemetery* UT-8
Portage Channel—*channel* WA-9
Portage Chapel—*church* IN-6
Portage Chapel—*church* OH-6
Portage Coulee—*valley* MT-8
Portage Country Club—*other* OH-6
**Portage (County)**—*pop pl* OH-6
**Portage (County)**—*pop pl* WI-6
Portage Cove—*bay* (2) AK-9
Portage Cove Campground—*locale* AK-9
*Portage Creek* PA-2
Portage Creek—*gut* AL-4
Portage Creek—*stream* (12) AK-9
Portage Creek—*stream* (6) MI-6
Portage Creek—*stream* (2) MN-6
Portage Creek—*stream* WA-9
Portage Creek—*stream* WI-6
Portage Creek ANV905—*reserve* AK-9
Portage Creek (locale)—*locale* PA-2
*Portage Cut* WA-9
**Portage Des Sioux**—*pop pl* MO-7
Portage Detroit Ditch—*canal* SD-7
**Portage Entry**—*pop pl* MI-6
Portage Falls—*falls* MN-6
Portage Glacier—*glacier* AK-9
Portage Head—*cape* WA-9
Portage (historical)—*locale* KS-7
Portage Hotel—*hist pl* OH-6
Portage HS—*school* IN-6
Portage Island—*island* MO-7
Portage Island—*island* NY-2
Portage Island—*island* WA-9
Portage Islands—*area* AK-9
Portage JHS—*school* OH-6
Portage Junction—*uninc pl* WI-6
Portage Junction (Portage)—*other* AK-9
Portage Lagoon—*bay* AK-9
*Portage Lake* MN-6
*Portage Lake* NJ-2
*Portage Lake* NY-2
Portage Lake—*flat* MN-6
Portage Lake—*lake* (5) AK-9
Portage Lake—*lake* LA-4
Portage Lake—*lake* ME-1
Portage Lake—*lake* (6) MI-6
Portage Lake—*lake* (12) MN-6
**Portage Lake**—*pop pl* MI-6
**Portage Lake**—*pop pl* MN-6
Portage Lake—*reservoir* MN-6
Portage Lake Lookout Tower—*locale* MI-6
Portage Lake Park—*park* MI-6
Portage Lakes—*lake* (2) OH-6
**Portage Lakes**—*pop pl* OH-6
Portage Lake Ship Canal—*canal* MI-6
Portage Lakes State Park—*park* OH-6
Portage Lake Swamp—*swamp* MI-6
**Portage Lake (Town of)**—*pop pl* ME-1
Portage Mine—*mine* AK-9
Portage Mountains—*ridge* AK-9
Portage MS—*school* IN-6
Portage Mtn—*summit* AK-9
Portage Open Bay—*stream* MO-7
*Portage Park* IL-6
Portage Park—*park* IL-6
Portage Park—*park* WI-6
Portage Park Sch—*school* IL-6
Portage Pass—*gap* (4) AK-9
Portage Path Sch—*school* OH-6
Portage Point—*cape* AK-9
Portage Point—*cape* (2) MI-6
Portage Point—*cape* WA-9
Portage Point—*cape* WI-6
**Portage Point**—*pop pl* MI-6
Portage Point Inn Complex—*hist pl* MI-6
Portage Prairie—*flat* MI-6
Portage Prairie Cem—*cemetery* WI-6
Portage Prairie Ch—*church* MI-6
Portage River—*channel* MI-6
Portage River—*stream* (3) MI-6
Portage River—*stream* (3) MN-6
Portage River—*stream* OH-6
Portage Roadhouse—*locale* AK-9
Portage Rsvr—*reservoir* PA-2
Portage Run—*stream* VA-3
Portage Sch—*school* (2) OH-6
Portage (Site)—*locale* AK-9
*Portage Slough* WA-9
Portage Slough—*gut* AK-9
Portage South Cem—*cemetery* MI-6
Portage Spring—*spring* WI-6
Portage Street Fire Station—*hist pl* MI-6
**Portage (Town of)**—*pop pl* NY-2
Portage Township—*civil* (2) MO-7
Portage Township—*civil* PA-2
**Portage Township**—*pop pl* SD-7
Portage Township (historical)—*civil* SD-7
*Portage (Township of)* MI-6
Portage (Township of)—*other* OH-6
**Portage (Township of)**—*pop pl* (2) IN-6
**Portage (Township of)**—*pop pl* (2) MI-6
**Portage (Township of)**—*pop pl* MN-6
**Portage (Township of)**—*pop pl* (3) OH-6
**Portage (Township of)**—*pop pl* (3) PA-2
Portage Trail—*trail* OR-9
Portage Valley—*valley* AK-9
**Portageville**—*pop pl* MO-7
**Portageville**—*pop pl* NY-2
Portageville Cem—*cemetery* MO-7
Portageville Cem—*cemetery* NY-2
**Portair**—*pop pl* NM-5
Portairs—*uninc pl* TX-5
Portal—*locale* MT-8
Portal—*locale* NE-7
**Portal**—*pop pl* AZ-5
**Portal**—*pop pl* GA-3
**Portal**—*pop pl* ND-7
Portal, The—*summit* UT-8
Port Albion Airp—*airport* PA-2
Portal Camp—*locale* AK-9
Portal Campground—*locale* CO-8
Portal (CCD)—*cens area* GA-3
Portal Cem—*cemetery* GA-3
Portal Cem—*cemetery* NE-7
Portal Creek—*stream* (2) MT-8
Portal Elem Sch—*school* AZ-5
**Portales**—*pop pl* NM-5
Portales (CCD)—*cens area* NM-5
Portales Creek—*stream* NM-5
Portales Tank—*reservoir* NM-5
Portales Valley—*valley* NM-5
Portales Verde Well—*well* TX-5
Portales Windmill—*locale* TX-5
Port Alexander—*bay* AK-9
**Port Alexander**—*pop pl* (2) AK-9
Port Alice—*bay* AK-9
*Portaligo* MH-9
**Portal Inn**—*pop pl* CA-9
Portal Lake—*lake* CA-9
**Port Allegany**—*pop pl* PA-2
Port Allegany Borough—*civil* PA-2
*Port Allegheny* PA-2
Port Allen—*locale* IA-7
**Port Allen**—*pop pl* HI-9
**Port Allen**—*pop pl* LA-4
Port Allen Canal—*canal* LA-4
**Port Allen (Eleele Landing)**—*pop pl* HI-9
**Port Allen (historical)**—*pop pl* IA-7
Port Allen Landing—*locale* LA-4
Port Allen Lock—*dam* LA-4
Port Allen Oil Field—*oilfield* LA-4
Portal Municipal Airp—*airport* ND-7
Portal Number 1—*mine* PA-2
Portal Number 15—*mine* PA-2
Portal Peak—*summit* AZ-5
Portal Peak—*summit* WA-9
Portal Ranger Station—*locale* AZ-5
Portal Ridge—*ridge* CA-9
Portals, The—*summit* WA-9
Portal Sch—*school* CA-9
Portal Sch—*school* NE-7
*Portal School* AZ-5
**Port Alsworth**—*pop pl* AK-9
**Port Alsworth (Tanalian Point)**—*pop pl* AK-9
Portal Tank—*reservoir* AZ-5
Port Althorp—*bay* AK-9
Port Althorp (abandoned)—*locale* AK-9
**Port Alto**—*pop pl* TX-5
**Portal Township**—*pop pl* ND-7
Portalus Valley—*valley* AK-9
**Port Amherst**—*pop pl* WV-2
**Port Amherst (local name Reed)**—*pop pl* WV-2
**Port Anderson (historical)**—*pop pl* MS-4
**Port Andrew**—*pop pl* WI-6
*Port Andrews* WI-6
**Port Angeles**—*pop pl* WA-9
Port Angeles (CCD)—*cens area* WA-9
Port Angeles Cgas Heliport—*airport* WA-9
Port Angeles Coast Guard Air Station—*military* WA-9
Port Angeles Dam—*dam* WA-9
Port Angeles East—*CDP* WA-9
Port Angeles Harbor—*bay* WA-9
Port Angeles HS—*school* WA-9
Port Angeles Rsvr—*reservoir* WA-9
Portanimicutt—*locale* MA-1
**Port Ann**—*pop pl* PA-2
Port Ann Ch—*church* PA-2
**Port Aransas**—*pop pl* TX-5
Port Aransas (CCD)—*cens area* TX-5
Port Aransas Park—*park* TX-5
Port Arbour Seaplane Base—*airport* OR-9
Port Armstrong—*bay* AK-9
Port Armstrong—*locale* AK-9
Port Arroyo Windmill—*locale* CO-8
**Port Arthur**—*pop pl* TX-5
**Port Arthur**—*pop pl* WI-6
Port Arthur Canal—*canal* TX-5
Port Arthur Coll—*school* TX-5
Port Arthur Country Club—*other* TX-5
Port Arthur Federated Women's Clubhouse—*hist pl* TX-5
Port Arthur Pleasure Pier—*locale* TX-5
Port Arthur Sch (historical)—*school* MO-7
**Port Ashton**—*pop pl* AK-9
Port Asumcion—*bay* AK-9
Port Audrey—*bay* AK-9
**Port-au-Peck**—*pop pl* NJ-2
**Port Austin**—*pop pl* MI-6
Port Austin Air Force Station—*military* MI-6
Port Austin Cem—*cemetery* MI-6
**Port Austin (Township of)**—*pop pl* MI-6
Port Authority—*uninc pl* NY-2
*Port aux Huitres* MA-1
Portavant Indian Mound—*summit* FL-3
Port Bagial—*bay* AK-9
**Port Bailey**—*pop pl* AK-9
Port Bailey Cannery—*locale* AK-9
Port Bainbridge—*bay* AK-9
Port Banks—*bay* AK-9
*Port Barnet* PA-2
**Port Barnett**—*pop pl* PA-2
**Port Barre**—*pop pl* LA-4
**Port Barre Junction**—*pop pl* LA-4
Port Barre Oil and Gas Field—*oilfield* LA-4
Port Barre Oil Field—*oilfield* LA-4
Port Barrow—*uninc pl* AK-9
Port Bay—*bay* NY-2
Port Bay—*bay* TX-5
Port Bazan—*bay* AK-9
Port Beauclerc—*bay* AK-9
Port Benney (Aban'd)—*locale* AK-9
Port Berard—*harbor* FM-9
**Port Bienville**—*pop pl* MS-4
**Port Birmingham**—*pop pl* AL-4
**Port Birmingham (Birminghamport)**—*pop pl* AL-4
Port Blakely—*locale* WA-9
**Port Blakely (community)**—*pop pl* WA-9
**Port Blakely (P.O.)**—*pop pl* WA-9
**Port Blanchard**—*pop pl* PA-2
Port Boca Grande—*locale* FL-3
Port Boca Grande Light—*locale* FL-3
**Port Bolivar**—*pop pl* TX-5
Port Bolivar Cem—*cemetery* TX-5
**Port Boliver**—*pop pl* LA-4
**Port Bowkley**—*pop pl* PA-2
Port Bowkley Station—*locale* PA-2
**Port Byron**—*pop pl* IL-6
**Port Byron**—*pop pl* NY-2
**Port Byron (Township of)**—*pop pl* IL-6
Port Caddo Ch—*church* TX-5
Port Caldera—*bay* AK-9
Port Camden—*bay* AK-9
*Port Canavera* FL-3
*Port Canaveral* FL-3
Port Canaveral—*harbor* FL-3
Port Canaveral—*other* FL-3
**Port Carbon**—*pop pl* PA-2
Port Carbon Borough—*civil* PA-2
*Port Cargil* MN-6
*Port Cargill* MN-6
Port Cargill—*locale* MN-6
Port Chalmers—*bay* AK-9
**Port Chalmette**—*pop pl* LA-4
**Port Charlotte**—*pop pl* FL-3
Port Charlotte Beach State Park—*park* FL-3
Port Charlotte (CCD)—*cens area* FL-3
Port Charlotte Christian Sch—*school* FL-3
Port Charlotte HS—*school* FL-3
Port Charlotte JHS—*school* FL-3
Port Charlotte Public Library—*building* FL-3
Port Charlotte Seventh Day Adventist Sch—*school* FL-3
Port Charlotte Station RR Station—*locale* FL-3
Port Chatham—*bay* AK-9
Port Chester—*bay* AK-9
**Port Chester**—*pop pl* IN-6
**Port Chester**—*pop pl* NY-2
Port Chester Harbor—*bay* CT-1
Port Chester Harbor—*bay* NY-2
**Port Chicago**—*pop pl* CA-9
Port Chicago Reach—*channel* CA-9
**Port Chilkoot**—*pop pl* AK-9
Port Clarence—*harbor* AK-9
**Port Clarence**—*pop pl* AK-9
Port Clarion (historical)—*locale* AL-4
**Port Clinton**—*pop pl* OH-6
**Port Clinton**—*pop pl* PA-2
Port Clinton Borough—*civil* PA-2
**Port Clyde**—*pop pl* ME-1
Port Clyde Harbor—*bay* ME-1
**Port Colden**—*pop pl* NJ-2
Port Columbus Int. Airp—*airport* OH-6
Port Conclusion—*bay* AK-9
**Port Conway**—*pop pl* VA-3
**Port Costa**—*pop pl* CA-9
Port Costa Sch—*hist pl* CA-9
Port Covington—*uninc pl* MD-2
Port Covington Yard—*locale* MD-2
**Port Crane**—*pop pl* NY-2
Port Crawford—*locale* AK-9
Port Creek—*stream* IN-6
Port Creek—*stream* MI-6
Port Creek—*stream* SC-3
Port Creek Sch—*school* MI-6
Port Crescent—*locale* MI-6
Port Crescent Cem—*cemetery* MI-6
Port Crescent State Park—*park* MI-6
Port de Luce Creek—*stream* LA-4
Port Deposit—*hist pl* MD-2
**Port Deposit**—*pop pl* MD-2
Port Deposit Sch—*school* MD-2
Port Dick—*bay* AK-9
Port Dick Creek—*stream* AK-9
**Port Dickinson**—*pop pl* NY-2
*Port Discovery* WA-9
Port Discovery—*locale* WA-9
*Port Discovery Bay* WA-9
Port Divide—*ridge* WY-8
Port Dolomite—*locale* MI-6
Port Dolores—*bay* AK-9
*Port Douglas* NY-2
Port Douglas—*other* NY-2
**Port Douglass**—*pop pl* NY-2
Port Douglass Cem—*cemetery* NY-2
*Port du Mauvais Accueil* FM-9
Port Eads—*locale* LA-4
Porteaux, Bayou—*stream* MS-4
Porter Crayon, Mount—*summit* WV-2
*Porte Des Mortes Passage* WI-6
*Porte des Morts Island* WI-6
Porte Des Morts Passage—*channel* WI-6
Portera des Morts Site—*hist pl* WI-6
**Port Edwards**—*pop pl* WI-6
**Port Edwards (Town of)**—*pop pl* WI-6
Portee Cem—*cemetery* IL-6
**Port Elizabeth**—*pop pl* NJ-2
Port Elsner Airp—*airport* WA-9
**Port Emma (historical)**—*pop pl* ND-7
**Port Emma Township**—*pop pl* ND-7
Port Engel Airp—*airport* PA-2
*Porter* MA-1
*Porter* VA-3
Porter—*fmr MCD* NE-7
Porter—*locale* CA-9
Porter—*locale* DE-2
Porter—*locale* GA-3
Porter—*locale* KY-4
Porter—*locale* MI-6
Porter—*locale* (2) NM-5
Porter—*locale* NY-2
Porter—*locale* PA-2
Porter—*locale* WV-2
**Porter**—*pop pl* AL-4
**Porter**—*pop pl* IN-6
**Porter**—*pop pl* ME-1
**Porter**—*pop pl* MN-6
**Porter**—*pop pl* (2) NC-3
**Porter**—*pop pl* OH-6
**Porter**—*pop pl* OK-5
**Porter**—*pop pl* TN-4
**Porter**—*pop pl* TX-5
**Porter**—*pop pl* VA-3
**Porter**—*pop pl* WA-9
Porter, Bradford, House—*hist pl* KY-4
Porter, Dr. D. T., Bldg—*hist pl* TN-4
Porter, Dr. Joseph Y., House—*hist pl* FL-3
Porter, General, House—*hist pl* NH-1
Porter, Gene Stratton, Cabin—*hist pl* (2) IN-6
Porter, J. K., Farmstead—*hist pl* WI-6
Porter, Lake—*lake* FL-3
Porter, Thomas V., House—*hist pl* FL-3
Porter, Walter C., Farm—*hist pl* TX-5
Porter, William Sidney, House—*hist pl* TX-5
*Porter Acad* TN-4
Porter Acad—*school* SC-3
Portera Lake Dam—*dam* MS-4
Porter and Blankenships Store (historical)—*locale* MS-4
Porter Arroyo—*stream* NM-5
Porter Bay—*bay* VT-1
Porter Bay—*swamp* FL-3
Porter Bayou—*stream* AR-4
Porter Bayou—*stream* MS-4
Porter-Bell-Brackley Estate—*hist pl* ME-1
Porter Bench—*bench* MT-8
Porter Bench Sch—*school* MT-8
Porter Bend Dam—*dam* NC-3
Porter Bldg—*hist pl* CA-9
Porter Bluff—*cliff* AL-4
Porter Bluff Park (historical)—*park* TN-4
Porterboro Sch—*school* VT-1
*Porter Branch* GA-3
Porter Branch—*stream* (2) AL-4
Porter Branch—*stream* (3) KY-4
Porter Branch—*stream* NE-7
Porter Branch—*stream* NC-3
Porter Branch—*stream* PA-2
Porter Branch—*stream* SC-3
Porter Branch—*stream* (3) TN-4
Porter Branch—*stream* (3) TX-5
Porter Branch—*stream* VA-3
Porter Branch Lake Dam—*dam* AL-4
Porter-Brasfield House—*hist pl* OR-9
Porter Bridge—*other* IL-6
Porter Brook—*stream* (2) CT-1
Porter Brook—*stream* (2) ME-1
Porter Brook—*stream* (2) NY-2
Porter Brook—*stream* (2) VT-1
Porter Butte—*summit* OR-9
Porter Cabin Cow Camp—*locale* WY-8
Porter Camp Branch—*stream* KY-4
Portercamp Branch—*stream* WV-2
Porter Canal—*canal* ID-8
Porter Canal—*canal* WY-8
*Porter Canyon* NV-8
Porter Canyon—*valley* AZ-5
Porter Canyon—*valley* CA-9
Porter Canyon—*valley* CO-8
Porter Canyon—*valley* NE-7
Porter Canyon—*valley* (3) NV-8
Porter Canyon—*valley* NM-5
Porter Canyon—*valley* OR-9
Porter Canyon—*valley* UT-8
Porter Cave—*cave* IN-6
Porter Cem—*cemetery* (4) AL-4
Porter Cem—*cemetery* AZ-5
Porter Cem—*cemetery* (2) AR-4
Porter Cem—*cemetery* (2) FL-3
Porter Cem—*cemetery* (2) GA-3
Porter Cem—*cemetery* (3) IL-6
Porter Cem—*cemetery* (4) IN-6
Porter Cem—*cemetery* IA-7
Porter Cem—*cemetery* KS-7
Porter Cem—*cemetery* (4) KY-4
Porter Cem—*cemetery* LA-4
Porter Cem—*cemetery* (2) MI-6
Porter Cem—*cemetery* MN-6
Porter Cem—*cemetery* (2) MS-4
Porter Cem—*cemetery* (2) MO-7
Porter Cem—*cemetery* NM-5
Porter Cem—*cemetery* NY-2
Porter Cem—*cemetery* (2) PA-2
Porter Cem—*cemetery* (2) SC-3
Porter Cem—*cemetery* (13) TN-4
Porter Cem—*cemetery* TX-5
Porter Cem—*cemetery* VT-1
Porter Cem—*cemetery* (4) VA-3
Porter Cem—*cemetery* (4) WV-2
**Porter Center**—*pop pl* NY-2
Porter Center Sch—*school* MI-6
Porter Ch—*church* (2) MI-6
Porter Chapel—*church* AR-4
Porter Chapel—*church* MO-7
Porter Chapel—*church* (2) SC-3
Porter Chapel—*church* TN-4
Porter Chapel Cem—*cemetery* MO-7
Porter Chapel Sch (historical)—*school* TN-4
Porter Clinic—*hospital* TN-4
Porter Corner—*locale* NY-2
**Porter Corners**—*pop pl* NY-2
Porter-Cortner Cem—*cemetery* TN-4
Porter Cottonwood Dam—*dam* SD-7
Porter Coulee—*stream* MT-8
**Porter County**—*pop pl* IN-6
Porter County Jail and Sheriff's House—*hist pl* IN-6
Porter County Memorial Hall—*hist pl* IN-6
Porter County Municipal Airp—*airport* IN-6
**Porter Court**—*pop pl* TN-4
Porter Cove—*bay* AK-9
Porter Cove—*bay* ME-1
Porter Cove—*valley* CO-8
Porter Cove—*valley* (2) NC-3
Porter-Crawford House—*hist pl* MS-4
*Porter Creek* CO-8
*Porter Creek* MT-8
*Porter Creek* OR-9
*Porter Creek* WA-9
*Porter Creek* WY-8
Porter Creek—*bay* MD-2
Porter Creek—*stream* AZ-5
Porter Creek—*stream* AR-4
Porter Creek—*stream* (3) CA-9
Porter Creek—*stream* (4) CO-8
Porter Creek—*stream* (3) GA-3
Porter Creek—*stream* (3) ID-8
Porter Creek—*stream* IN-6
Porter Creek—*stream* IA-7
Porter Creek—*stream* KY-4
Porter Creek—*stream* MD-2
Porter Creek—*stream* (5) MI-6
Porter Creek—*stream* (2) MN-6
Porter Creek—*stream* (3) MS-4
Porter Creek—*stream* MO-7
Porter Creek—*stream* (2) MT-8
Porter Creek—*stream* (2) NY-2
Porter Creek—*stream* (2) NC-3
Porter Creek—*stream* OH-6
Porter Creek—*stream* (8) OR-9
Porter Creek—*stream* PA-2
Porter Creek—*stream* SD-7
Porter Creek—*stream* (3) TX-5
Porter Creek—*stream* UT-8
Porter Creek—*stream* (3) WA-9
Porter Creek—*stream* (2) WV-2
Porter Creek—*stream* (3) WY-8
Porter Creek Dam Number Seventeen—*dam* TN-4
Porter Creek (historical)—*stream* NV-8
Porter Creek Trail—*trail* ID-8
Porter Creek Truck Trail—*trail* WA-9
*Porter Crossroads* VA-3
**Porter Crossroads**—*pop pl* IN-6
**Porterdale**—*pop pl* GA-3
Porterdale Cem—*cemetery* GA-3
Porter Ditch—*canal* CO-8
Porter Ditch—*canal* (2) IN-6
Porter Drain—*canal* MI-6
Porter Drain—*stream* (2) MI-6
*Porter Draw* AZ-5
Porter Draw—*valley* NM-5
Porter Draw—*valley* (2) WY-8
Porter Elem Sch—*school* TN-4
Porter Elem Sch (historical)—*school* AL-4
Porter Family Homestead—*hist pl* MS-4
Porter Field—*flat* OR-9
Porterfield—*locale* IL-6
Porterfield—*locale* ME-1
Porterfield—*locale* TN-4
Porter Field—*park* GA-3
Porter Field—*park* MN-6
**Porterfield**—*pop pl* WI-6
*Porterfield Branch* VA-3
Porterfield Branch—*stream* VA-3
Porterfield Canyon—*valley* CO-8
Porterfield Cem—*cemetery* GA-3
**Porterfield (Center Belpre)**—*pop pl* OH-6
Porterfield Ch—*church* WI-6
Porterfield Creek—*stream* AK-9
Porterfield Creek—*stream* CA-9
Porterfield Creek—*stream* IL-6
Porterfield Creek—*stream* (2) MI-6
Porterfield Gap—*gap* NC-3
Porterfield Gap—*gap* TN-4
Porterfield Hollow—*valley* TN-4
Porterfield HS (historical)—*school* TN-4
Porterfield Lake—*lake* MI-6
Porterfield Ledge—*bar* ME-1
Porterfield Post Office (historical)—*building* TN-4
Porterfield Ranch—*locale* CA-9
Porterfield Run—*stream* OH-6
Porterfield Run—*stream* VA-3
Porterfield Sch—*school* WI-6
**Porterfield (Town of)**—*pop pl* WI-6
Porterfield Well—*well* AZ-5
Porterfield Windmill—*locale* CO-8
Porter Flat—*flat* CO-8
Porter Ford—*locale* TN-4
Porter Fork—*stream* KY-4
Porter Fork—*stream* UT-8
Porter Fork—*stream* WV-2
Porter Fork Ch—*church* WV-2
Porter Gap—*gap* AL-4
Porter Gap—*gap* TX-5
**Porter Gap**—*pop pl* TN-4
Porter Grove Cem—*cemetery* IA-7
*Porter Gulch* OR-9
Porter Gulch—*valley* CA-9
Porter Gulch—*valley* CO-8
Porter Gulch—*valley* MT-8
Porter Gulch—*valley* OR-9
Porter Gulch—*valley* WY-8
Porter Hall—*hist pl* IA-7
Porter-Hays Sch—*school* OH-6
Porter Heights—*CDP* TX-5
**Porter Hill**—*pop pl* OK-5
Porter Hill—*summit* ME-1
Porter Hill—*summit* MA-1
Porter Hill—*summit* (2) NH-1
Porter Hill—*summit* NY-2
Porter Hill—*summit* OR-9
Porter Hill—*summit* TN-4
Porter Hill—*summit* TX-5
Porter Hills—*range* WA-9
**Porter (historical)**—*pop pl* (2) OR-9
*Porter Hollow* VA-3
Porter Hollow—*valley* (2) AL-4
Porter Hollow—*valley* (2) AR-4
Porter Hollow—*valley* IN-6
Porter Hollow—*valley* KY-4
Porter Hollow—*valley* MI-6
Porter Hollow—*valley* (2) MO-7
Porter Hollow—*valley* NY-2
Porter Hollow—*valley* (2) OH-6
Porter Hollow—*valley* PA-2
Porter Hollow—*valley* (3) TN-4
Porter Hollow—*valley* UT-8
Porter Hollow—*valley* (2) VA-3
Porter Hollow—*valley* WY-8
Porter Hosp—*hospital* TX-5
Porter Hosp—*hospital* VT-1
Porter House—*hist pl* TN-4
Porter HS (historical)—*school* TN-4
*Porter Island* FL-3
*Porter Island* MA-1
Porter Island—*island* FL-3
Porter Island—*island* MI-6
Porter JHS—*school* CA-9
Porter JHS—*school* TX-5
Porter Junction—*locale* NC-3
**Porter Junction**—*pop pl* KY-4
*Porter Knob* TX-5
Porter Knob—*summit* KY-4
Porter Knob—*summit* (2) WV-2
*Porter Lake* OR-9
Porter Lake—*lake* AZ-5
Porter Lake—*lake* (2) AR-4
Porter Lake—*lake* (3) FL-3
Porter Lake—*lake* IN-6
Porter Lake—*lake* LA-4
Porter Lake—*lake* ME-1
Porter Lake—*lake* MI-6
Porter Lake—*lake* (2) MN-6
Porter Lake—*lake* MS-4
Porter Lake—*lake* OR-9
Porter Lake—*lake* WY-8
Porter Lake—*reservoir* MA-1
Porter Lake—*reservoir* TN-4
Porter Lake—*reservoir* TX-5
*Porter Lake Dam* MA-1
Porter Lake Dam—*dam* MS-4
Porter Lake Dam—*dam* TN-4
Porter Lakes—*lake* WI-6
**Porter Landing**—*pop pl* ME-1
Porter Landing (historical)—*locale* SD-7
*Porter Lunsford Pond* AL-4
*Porter Lunsford Pond Dam* AL-4
Porter Memorial Hosp—*hospital* CO-8
Porter Memorial Library—*hist pl* ME-1
Porter Mill Bend—*bend* MO-7
*Porter Mill Branch* GA-3
Porter Mill Branch—*stream* TN-4
Porter Mill Creek—*stream* MD-2
Porter Mill Hollow—*valley* MO-7
Porter Mine—*mine* AZ-5
Porter Mine—*mine* CA-9
Porter Mine—*mine* MI-6
Porter Mine—*mine* MO-7
Porter Mine—*mine* (2) NV-8
Porter Moss Agate Dam—*dam* SD-7
Porter Mountain—*ridge* AR-4
Porter Mtn—*summit* (2) AZ-5
Porter Mtn—*summit* CO-8
Porter Mtn—*summit* GA-3
Porter Mtn—*summit* (2) NY-2
Porter Mtn—*summit* (3) VA-3
Porter Neck—*cape* MD-2
Porter Number 2 Mine (underground)—*mine* AL-4

Porter Oil Field—*oilfield* TX-5
Porter Oil Field—*other* (2) MI-6
Porter Old Meetinghouse—*hist pl* ME-1
Porter Park—*park* AZ-5
Porter Park—*park* CA-9
Porter Park—*park* NJ-2
Porter-Parsonfield Bridge—*hist pl* ME-1
Porter Pass—*gap* WA-9
*Porter Peak* UT-8
Porter Peak—*summit* AK-9
Porter Peak—*summit* (2) CA-9
Porter Peak—*summit* NV-8
Porter-Phelps-Huntington House—*hist pl* MA-1
Porter Point—*cape* (2) MD-2
Porter Point—*cape* OR-9
Porter Point—*cape* VT-1
Porter Point—*cape* WA-9
Porter Pond—*lake* CT-1
Porter Pond—*lake* FL-3
Porter Pond—*lake* GA-3
Porter Pond—*lake* (2) ME-1
Porter Poole Mill (historical)—*locale* TN-4
*Porter Ranch* NV-8
Porter Ranch—*locale* (3) CA-9
Porter Ranch—*locale* MT-8
Porter Ranch—*locale* NE-7
Porter Ranch—*locale* NV-8
Porter Ranch—*locale* (2) NM-5
Porter Ranch—*locale* ND-7
Porter Ranch—*locale* (2) OR-9
Porter Ranch—*locale* (3) TX-5
Porter Ranch—*locale* (2) WY-8
Porter Ravine—*valley* CA-9
Porter Reach—*channel* FL-3
Porter Ridge—*ridge* MT-8
Porter Ridge—*ridge* OH-6
Porter Ridge—*ridge* OR-9
Porter Ridge—*ridge* TN-4
Porter Ridge—*ridge* VA-3
Porter River—*bay* MA-1
Porter Rock—*rock* MA-1
Porter Rock—*summit* WY-8
Porter Rsvr—*reservoir* (3) CA-9
Porter Rsvr—*reservoir* (2) CO-8
Porter Rsvr—*reservoir* CT-1
Porter Rsvr—*reservoir* DE-2
Porter Rsvr—*reservoir* KY-4
Porter Rsvr No 1—*reservoir* CO-8
Porter Rsvr No 4—*reservoir* CO-8
Porter Run—*stream* MD-2
Porter Run—*stream* OH-6
Porter Run—*stream* (5) PA-2
*Porters* DE-2
*Porters* MA-1
*Porters* NC-3
Porters—*locale* VA-3
Porters—*locale* WI-6
**Porters**—*pop pl* TN-4
**Porters**—*pop pl* VA-3
*Porter's Bar* MD-2
Porters Bar Cem—*cemetery* FL-3
Porters Bar Creek—*stream* FL-3
Porter's Bar Site—*hist pl* FL-3
*Porters Bayou* MS-4
*Porters Bend Dam* NC-3
Porters Bluff—*cliff* TX-5
Porters Branch—*stream* GA-3
Porters Branch—*stream* TN-4
Porters Bridge—*bridge* PA-2
Portersburg—*locale* KY-4
Porters Camp—*locale* CA-9
Porters Camp—*locale* CO-8
Porters Cave—*cave* AL-4
Porters Cave—*cave* PA-2
Porters Cem—*cemetery* KY-4
Porters Cem—*cemetery* LA-4
Porters Cem—*cemetery* NC-3
Porters Cem—*cemetery* PA-2
Porter Sch—*school* CA-9
Porter Sch—*school* CO-8
Porter Sch—*school* CT-1
Porter Sch—*school* GA-3
Porter Sch—*school* IN-6
Porter Sch—*school* IA-7
Porter Sch—*school* KS-7
Porter Sch—*school* (2) KY-4
Porter Sch—*school* MI-6
Porter Sch—*school* MN-6
Porter Sch—*school* MO-7
Porter Sch—*school* (2) NY-2
Porter Sch—*school* OK-5
Porter Sch—*school* OR-9
Porter Sch—*school* PA-2
Porter Sch—*school* (2) TN-4
Porter Sch—*school* WI-6
Porters Chapel—*church* MS-4
Porters Chapel—*church* NC-3
Porters Chapel—*church* TN-4
Porters Chapel—*church* TX-5
**Porters Chapel**—*pop pl* MS-4
*Porters Chapel Baptist Church* MS-4
*Porters Chapel United Methodist Ch* TN-4
*Porters Chapel United Methodist Church* MS-4
Porter Sch (historical)—*school* MO-7
Porter Sch (historical)—*school* PA-2
Porter Sch (historical)—*school* TN-4
*Porter School* AL-4
**Porters Corner**—*pop pl* MT-8
Porters Corners—*locale* NY-2
**Porters Corners**—*pop pl* PA-2
Porters Cow Camp—*locale* CO-8
*Porter's Creek* MT-8
**Porters Creek**—*pop pl* TN-4
Porters Creek—*stream* GA-3
Porters Creek—*stream* MS-4
Porters Creek—*stream* PA-2
Porters Creek—*stream* (2) TN-4
Porters Creek—*stream* TX-5
Porters Creek—*stream* WI-6
*Porters Creek Baptist Church* TN-4
Porters Creek Ch—*church* TN-4
Porters Creek Dam Number Five—*dam* TN-4
Porters Creek Dam Number Nine—*dam* TN-4
Porters Creek Lake Dam Number Eight—*dam* TN-4
Porters Creek Lake Dam Number Fifteen—*dam* TN-4
Porters Creek Lake Dam Number Four—*dam* TN-4
Porters Creek Lake Dam Number Seven—*dam* TN-4
Porters Creek Lake Dam Number Six—*dam* TN-4
Porters Creek Lake Dam Number Three—*dam* TN-4
Porters Creek Lake Number Eight—*reservoir* TN-4
Porters Creek Lake Number Fifteen—*reservoir* TN-4
Porters Creek Lake Number Five—*reservoir* TN-4
Porters Creek Lake Number Four—*reservoir* TN-4
Porters Creek Lake Number Nine—*reservoir* TN-4
Porters Creek Lake Number Seven—*reservoir* TN-4
Porters Creek Lake Number Seventeen—*reservoir* TN-4
Porters Creek Lake Number Six—*reservoir* TN-4
Porters Creek Lake Number Three—*reservoir* TN-4
Porters Creek Number Sixteen Dam—*dam* TN-4
Porters Creek Slough—*stream* TN-4
Porters Creek Watershed Number Sixteen Lake—*reservoir* TN-4
Porter Screen Company—*hist pl* VT-1
Porters Crossing—*locale* MD-2
*Porters Cross Roads* VA-3
Porters Crossroads—*locale* AL-4
Porters Crossroads—*locale* VA-3
**Porters Cross Roads**—*pop pl* VA-3
Porters Crossroads Sch (historical)—*school* AL-4
**Porters Curve**—*pop pl* LA-4
Porter Settlement—*locale* ME-1
**Porters Falls**—*pop pl* WV-2
Porters Ferry—*locale* ID-8
Porters Ferry Sch (historical)—*school* MS-4
Porters Flat—*flat* OR-9
Porters Flat—*flat* TN-4
Porters Gap—*gap* NC-3
Porters Gap—*gap* TN-4
**Porters Grove**—*pop pl* TN-4
Porters Grove Ch—*church* MD-2
Porters Grove Ch—*church* TN-4
Porters Grove Sch (historical)—*school* TN-4
**Porters (historical)**—*pop pl* TN-4
Porters Hollow—*valley* WV-2
*Porters Inlet* NC-3
*Porters Island* MA-1
Porters Island—*island* (2) LA-4
Porters Island—*island* MI-6
Porters Island—*island* NC-3
Porters Island—*island* OR-9
*Porters Lake* TN-4
Porters Lake—*lake* AL-4
Porters Lake—*lake* LA-4
Porters Lake—*lake* WI-6
Porters Lake—*reservoir* AL-4
Porters Lake—*reservoir* PA-2
Porters Lake Club—*other* PA-2
Porters Lake Dam—*dam* PA-2
Porter Slough—*stream* CA-9
Porter Slough—*stream* FL-3
Porter Slough—*stream* MO-7
Porter Slough—*stream* OR-9
Porter Slough Ditch—*canal* (2) CA-9
Porters Marsh—*swamp* NY-2
Porters Meadow—*stream* PA-2
Porters Mill—*locale* PA-2
Porters Mill Branch—*stream* GA-3
Porters Mill Creek—*stream* AL-4
Porters Mill Creek—*stream* VA-3
Porter Smith Bridge—*bridge* FL-3
Porters Mountain Overlook—*locale* VA-3
Porters Mtn—*summit* ID-8
Porters Mtn—*summit* (2) TN-4
Porters Neck—*cape* NC-3
**Porters Neck Plantation (subdivision)**—*pop pl* NC-3
**Porters Park**—*pop pl* MD-2
Porters Pond—*lake* RI-1
Porters Spring—*spring* (4) AZ-5
Porter Spring—*spring* CA-9
Porter Spring—*spring* CO-8
Porter Spring—*spring* (2) NV-8
Porter Spring—*spring* (3) OR-9
Porter Spring—*spring* WI-6
Porter Spring Rec Area—*park* AZ-5
Porter Springs—*locale* GA-3
**Porter Springs**—*pop pl* TX-5
Porter Springs (CCD)—*cens area* TX-5
Porter Springs Cedar Mtn—*summit* GA-3
Porter Springs Cem—*cemetery* TX-5
Porter Spring Tank—*reservoir* AZ-5
Porter Square Mall Shop Ctr—*locale* AL-4
**Porter Square (subdivision)**—*pop pl* DE-2
Porters Ridge—*ridge* VA-3
*Porters River* MA-1
Porters River—*stream* LA-4
Porters River Landing—*locale* LA-4
Porters (RR name for Porters Sideling)—*other* PA-2
Porters Run—*stream* OH-6
Porters Run—*stream* PA-2
Porters Saint Paul CME Ch—*church* AL-4
Porters Sch (abandoned)—*school* PA-2
*Porters School House* AL-4
**Porters Sideling**—*pop pl* PA-2
**Porters Sideling (RR name Porters)**—*pop pl* PA-2
Porters Station—*locale* PA-2
*Porters Swamp* MA-1
*Porters Tank Wash* AZ-5
Porter Station (Site)—*locale* NV-8
Porterstown—*locale* MD-2
Porterstown Bridge—*bridge* MD-2
*Portersville* AL-4
*Portersville* NC-3
*Portersville* UT-8
Portersville—*locale* WV-2
Portersville—*other* NC-3
**Portersville**—*pop pl* AL-4
**Portersville**—*pop pl* IL-6
**Portersville**—*pop pl* IN-6
**Portersville**—*pop pl* OH-6
**Portersville**—*pop pl* PA-2
**Portersville**—*pop pl* UT-8
Portersville Bat Cave—*cave* AL-4
Portersville Bay—*bay* AL-4
Portersville Borough—*civil* PA-2
Portersville Cave—*cave* PA-2
Portersville Ch—*church* MD-2
Portersville Drain—*stream* IN-6
Portersville Gap—*gap* AL-4
Portersville (historical)—*locale* MS-4
**Portersville (Porterville)**—*pop pl* AL-4
*Portersville Station* PA-2
Porter Swamp—*stream* NC-3
Porter Swamp—*swamp* MA-1
Porter Swamp—*swamp* NC-3
Porter Swamp Ch—*church* NC-3
Porter Tabernacle—*church* OH-6
Porter Tank—*reservoir* (2) AZ-5
Porter Tank Draw—*valley* AZ-5
Porter-Thomsen House—*hist pl* NE-7
Porter-Todd House—*hist pl* KY-4
**Porterton**—*pop pl* MS-4
*Porter Town* AL-4
**Portertown**—*pop pl* NJ-2
Portertown Cem—*cemetery* AL-4
Porter Town Hall—*building* ND-7
Porter Town Hall—*locale* MI-6
**Porter (Town of)**—*pop pl* ME-1
**Porter (Town of)**—*pop pl* NY-2
**Porter (Town of)**—*pop pl* WI-6
Portertown Sch (historical)—*school* AL-4
*Porter Township* KS-7
Porter Township—*civil* MO-7
Porter Township—*civil* PA-2
**Porter Township**—*pop pl* ND-7
Porter (Township of)—*fmr MCD* AR-4
**Porter (Township of)**—*pop pl* IN-6
**Porter (Township of)**—*pop pl* (3) MI-6
**Porter (Township of)**—*pop pl* (2) OH-6
**Porter (Township of)**—*pop pl* (7) PA-2
Porter Valley—*basin* NE-7
Porter Valley—*valley* VA-3
Porter Valley Country Club—*other* CA-9
Porter Valley School (Abandoned)—*locale* NE-7
*Porterville* AL-4
*Porterville* IL-6
*Porterville* NC-3
Porterville—*locale* KS-7
Porterville—*locale* OR-9
**Porterville**—*pop pl* CA-9
**Porterville**—*pop pl* LA-4
**Porterville**—*pop pl* MS-4
**Porterville**—*pop pl* NY-2
**Porterville**—*pop pl* UT-8
Porterville Bridge—*bridge* ID-8
Porterville (CCD)—*cens area* CA-9
Porterville Cem—*cemetery* MS-4
Porterville Cem—*cemetery* UT-8
Porterville Ch—*church* AL-4
Porterville Ch—*church* GA-3
Porterville Coll—*school* CA-9
**Porterville (Eaton Post Office)**—*pop pl* IL-6
*Porterville Gap* AL-4
Porterville Grammar Sch (historical)—*school* MS-4
**Porterville (historical)**—*pop pl* OR-9
Porterville HS (historical)—*school* MS-4
**Porterville Junction**—*pop pl* CA-9
Porterville Lookout Tower—*locale* MS-4
Porterville Methodist Ch—*church* MS-4
**Porterville Northwest**—*pop pl* CA-9
*Porterville (Portersville)* AL-4
Porterville Post Office—*building* MS-4
Porterville Pumping Station—*other* TX-5
Porterville Sch—*school* NC-3
Porterville State Hosp—*hospital* CA-9
**Porterville West (Burton)**—*pop pl* CA-9
Porter-Ward Cem—*cemetery* TN-4
Porter Wash—*stream* AZ-5
Porter Wash—*stream* NV-8
Porter Well—*well* AZ-5
Porter Well—*well* UT-8
**Porterwood**—*pop pl* WV-2
Porter Woods—*woods* WA-9
Porter-York House—*hist pl* GA-3
Port Estrella—*bay* AK-9
Port Etches—*bay* AK-9
Port Everglades—*locale* FL-3
Port Everglades Approach Light—*locale* FL-3
Port Everglades Junction—*locale* FL-3
**Port Ewen**—*pop pl* NY-2
Port Ewen Sch—*school* NY-2
Portezuelo—*gap* CA-9
Port Ferinando (historical)—*bay* NC-3
Port Fidalgo—*bay* AK-9
Port Florence Airp—*airport* PA-2
*Port Fortune* MA-1
Port Fourchon—*locale* LA-4
Port Frederick—*bay* AK-9
**Port Frederick**—*pop pl* AK-9
*Port Fulton* IN-6
**Port Fulton**—*pop pl* IN-6
**Port Gamble**—*pop pl* WA-9
Port Gamble Hist Dist—*hist pl* WA-9
**Port Gamble Ind Res**—*pop pl* WA-9
*Port Gardner* WA-9
**Port Gardner**—*pop pl* LA-4
**Port Gibson**—*pop pl* MS-4
**Port Gibson**—*pop pl* NY-2
*Port Gibson Academy* MS-4
Port Gibson Baptist Ch—*church* MS-4
Port Gibson Battlefield—*hist pl* MS-4
Port Gibson Catholic Cem—*cemetery* MS-4
Port Gibson Ch of Christ—*church* MS-4
Port Gibson Ch of God—*church* MS-4
Port Gibson City Hall—*building* MS-4
Port Gibson Female Acad (historical)—*school* MS-4
Port Gibson HS—*school* MS-4
Port Gibson Methodist Ch—*church* MS-4
Port Gibson Oil Works Mill Bldg—*hist pl* MS-4
Port Gibson Seventh Day Adventist Ch—*church* MS-4
Port Gibson Sewage Lagoon Dam—*dam* MS-4
Port Graham—*bay* AK-9
**Port Graham**—*pop pl* AK-9
Port Graham ANV907—*reserve* AK-9
Port Gravina—*bay* AK-9
**Port Griffith**—*pop pl* PA-2
Port Griffith Sch—*school* PA-2
*Port Gypsum* MI-6
*Port Harbor* ME-1
*Port Hardford* CA-9
Port Harlingen—*locale* TX-5
*Port Hartford* CA-9
**Port Haven (subdivision)**—*pop pl* TN-4
**Port Haywood**—*pop pl* VA-3
Port Heiden—*bay* AK-9
**Port Heiden**—*pop pl* AK-9
Port Heiden Airp—*airport* AK-9
**Port Henry**—*pop pl* NY-2
Port Herbert—*bay* AK-9
Port Herbert—*locale* AK-9
**Port Herman**—*pop pl* MD-2
*Port Herman Beach* MD-2
**Port Herman (Port Herman Beach)**—*pop pl* MD-2
Port Hickey—*locale* LA-4
Port Hickey Landing—*locale* LA-4
Port Higgins—*uninc pl* AK-9
*Port Hill* ID-8
Port Hill—*locale* SC-3
**Porthill**—*pop pl* ID-8
Port Hill Landing—*locale* SC-3
Porth Lake—*lake* MO-7
Port Hobron—*bay* AK-9
Port Hobron—*locale* AK-9
**Port Homer**—*pop pl* OH-6
**Port Hope**—*pop pl* MI-6
**Port Hope (Township of)**—*pop pl* MN-6
Port Houghton—*bay* AK-9
Port Houston—*uninc pl* TX-5
Port Houston Sch—*school* TX-5
Port Hudson—*hist pl* LA-4
Port Hudson—*locale* MO-7
**Port Hudson**—*pop pl* LA-4
Port Hudson Cem—*cemetery* LA-4
Port Hudson Ch—*church* MO-7
Port Hudson Natl Cem—*cemetery* LA-4
Port Hudson Sch—*school* LA-4
**Port Hueneme**—*pop pl* CA-9
Port Hueneme Naval Construction Battalion Center—*military* CA-9
**Port Huron**—*pop pl* MI-6
Port Huron Camp—*locale* MI-6
Port Huron State Game Area—*park* MI-6
**Port Huron (Township of)**—*pop pl* MI-6
Portia—*locale* MO-7
**Portia**—*pop pl* AR-4
Portia Bay—*lake* AR-4
Portia Cem—*cemetery* AR-4
Portia Sch—*hist pl* AR-4
*Portico Bayou* MS-4
Portico Elem Sch—*school* PA-2
*Portico Landing* MS-4
Portico Row—*hist pl* PA-2
Portico Sch—*school* PA-2
Portie Bayou—*stream* LA-4
Portie Lakes—*lake* LA-4
Portier, Bishop, House—*hist pl* AL-4
*Portigo Bayou* MS-4
*Portigo Landing* MS-4
*Portilla* CA-9
**Portilla**—*pop pl* TX-5
Portillo, Mauricio, House—*hist pl* NM-5
Portillo (Barrio)—*fmr MCD* PR-3
Portillo Channel—*channel* AK-9
Port Indian—*locale* PA-2
*Port-industrial Waterway* WA-9
Port Ingleside—*locale* TX-5
Port Inglis—*locale* FL-3
Port Inland—*locale* MI-6
**Portis**—*pop pl* KS-7
*Port Isabel* OH-6
**Port Isabel**—*pop pl* TX-5
Port Isabel Channel—*channel* TX-5
Port Isabel Rsvr (Aban'd)—*reservoir* TX-5
Port Isabel Side Channel—*channel* TX-5
Port Isabel Turning Basin—*harbor* TX-5
Portis Draw—*valley* TX-5
Port Island—*island* AK-9
Portis Pond—*lake* CO-8
Portis Ranch—*locale* CO-8
Port Ivory—*locale* NY-2
Port Jackson—*locale* IL-6
Port Jackson Cem—*cemetery* IL-6
*Port Jefferson* NY-2
**Port Jefferson**—*pop pl* NY-2
**Port Jefferson**—*pop pl* OH-6
Port Jefferson Harbor—*bay* NY-2
Port Jefferson Sch—*hist pl* OH-6
**Port Jefferson Station**—*pop pl* NY-2
**Port Jenkins**—*pop pl* PA-2
Port Jersey—*uninc pl* NJ-2
**Port Jervis**—*pop pl* NY-2
Port Jervis Central Sch—*school* NY-2
Port Johnson—*bay* AK-9
Port Johnson—*locale* NJ-2
Port Junction—*uninc pl* WI-6
Port Kelley—*locale* WA-9
**Port Kennedy**—*pop pl* PA-2
Port Kennedy Cave—*cave* PA-2
Port Kennedy Quarry—*mine* PA-2
**Port Kent**—*pop pl* NY-2
Port Kent Burlington Ferry—*trail* NY-2
**Port Kenyon**—*pop pl* CA-9
Port Krestof—*bay* AK-9
*Portland* IN-6
*Portland* PA-2
*Portland* SD-7
Portland—*CDP* CT-1
Portland—*locale* AL-4
Portland—*locale* GA-3
Portland—*locale* (2) KY-4
Portland—*locale* NY-2
**Portland**—*pop pl* AR-4
**Portland**—*pop pl* (2) CO-8
**Portland**—*pop pl* CT-1
**Portland**—*pop pl* FL-3
**Portland**—*pop pl* IL-6
**Portland**—*pop pl* IN-6
**Portland**—*pop pl* IA-7
**Portland**—*pop pl* KS-7
**Portland**—*pop pl* KY-4
**Portland**—*pop pl* ME-1
**Portland**—*pop pl* MI-6
**Portland**—*pop pl* MO-7
**Portland**—*pop pl* NY-2
**Portland**—*pop pl* ND-7
**Portland**—*pop pl* OH-6
**Portland**—*pop pl* OR-9
**Portland**—*pop pl* PA-2
**Portland**—*pop pl* TN-4
**Portland**—*pop pl* TX-5
**Portland**—*pop pl* WV-2
**Portland**—*pop pl* (3) WI-6
*Portland Access Area Park* AL-4
Portland Adventist Elem Sch—*school* OR-9
Portland AFB—*military* OR-9
Portland and Southwestern RR Tunnel—*hist pl* OR-9
Portland and Westmoreland Places—*hist pl* MO-7
*Portland Arch* IN-6
Portland Arch—*bend* IN-6
Portland Art Museum—*hist pl* OR-9
Portland Auto Port Airstrip—*airport* OR-9
Portland Aventist Med Ctr Heliport—*airport* OR-9
Portland Ave Park—*park* WA-9
Portland Ave Rsvr—*reservoir* WA-9
Portland Borough—*civil* PA-2
Portland Bottoms—*bend* AR-4
Portland Breakwater Light—*hist pl* ME-1
Portland Bridge—*hist pl* CO-8
Portland Burying Ground—*cemetery* CT-1
Portland Canal—*channel* AK-9
Portland (CCD)—*cens area* OR-9
Portland (CCD)—*cens area* TN-4
Portland Cem—*cemetery* AR-4
Portland Cem—*cemetery* IA-7
Portland Cem—*cemetery* KY-4
Portland Cem—*cemetery* WI-6
Portland Ch—*church* MI-6
Portland Ch—*church* TX-5
Portland Christian HS—*school* OR-9
Portland Christian Sch—*school* OR-9
Portland City Hall—*building* TN-4
Portland City Hall—*hist pl* ME-1
Portland City Hall—*hist pl* OR-9
Portland City Hosp—*hist pl* ME-1
Portland City Lake—*reservoir* TN-4
Portland City Lake Dam—*dam* TN-4
Portland City Park—*park* TN-4
Portland Club—*hist pl* ME-1
Portland Community Coll—*school* (2) OR-9
*Portland Corners* (2) IL-6
**Portland Corners**—*pop pl* IL-6
Portland Country Club—*other* ME-1
Portland Country Club—*other* MI-6
Portland Creek—*stream* (2) AK-9
Portland Creek—*stream* CO-8
Portland Creek—*stream* IL-6
Portland Creek—*stream* OR-9
Portland Dam—*dam* ND-7
Portland Division—*civil* TN-4
Portland Fire Station No. 17—*hist pl* OR-9
Portland First Baptist Ch—*church* TN-4
Portland First Congregational Church—*hist pl* MI-6
Portland General Electric Company Station "L" Group—*hist pl* OR-9
Portland Golf Club—*other* OR-9
Portland Gulch—*valley* ID-8
Portland Gulch Spring—*spring* ID-8
Portland Gun Club—*other* OR-9
Portland Harbor—*harbor* ME-1
Portland Headlight—*hist pl* ME-1
Portland Head Lighthouse—*locale* ME-1
**Portland Heights**—*pop pl* OR-9
Portland Heights—*uninc pl* CO-8
Portland-Hillsboro Airp—*airport* OR-9
Portland Hist Dist—*hist pl* KY-4
Portland HS—*hist pl* ME-1
Portland HS—*school* CT-1
Portland HS—*school* TN-4
Portland Hunt Club—*other* OR-9
Portland International Airp—*airport* ME-1
Portland International Airp—*airport* OR-9
*Portland Landis* KS-7
Portland Island—*island* AK-9
*Portland JHS* TN-4
Portland JHS—*school* MN-6
Portland Junction—*locale* ND-7
Portland Junction (historical)—*locale* SD-7
Portland Lake—*lake* ME-1
Portland (Magisterial District)—*fmr MCD* WV-2
Portland Meadows—*flat* OR-9
**Portland Mills**—*pop pl* IN-6
**Portland Mills**—*pop pl* PA-2
Portland Mills Bridge—*hist pl* IN-6
Portland Mills Ch—*church* IN-6
Portland Mine—*mine* AZ-5
Portland Mine—*mine* (2) CO-8
Portland Mine—*mine* (2) ID-8
Portland Mine—*mine* NV-8
Portland Mine—*mine* OR-9
Portland Mine—*mine* SD-7
Portland MS—*school* TN-4
Portland Mtn—*summit* ID-8
Portland Municipal Airp—*airport* TN-4
Portland Municipal Dam—*dam* MI-6
Portland Observatory—*hist pl* ME-1
Portland Oil Field—*oilfield* KS-7
Portland Park—*park* KY-4
Portland Point—*cape* ME-1
Portland Point—*cape* NY-2
**Portland Point**—*pop pl* NY-2
Portland Police Block—*hist pl* OR-9
Portland Post Office—*building* TN-4
Portland Prairie—*flat* MN-6
Portland Prairie Ch—*church* MN-6
Portland Prairie Methodist Episcopal Church—*hist pl* MN-6
Portland Public Use Area—*park* AL-4
Portland Ridge—*ridge* AZ-5
Portland Rsvr—*reservoir* CT-1
Portland Sanatorium—*hospital* OR-9
Portland Sch—*school* IL-6
Portland Sch—*school* (2) KY-4
Portland Sch—*school* MN-6
Portland Sch—*school* MO-7
Portland Skidmore/Old Town Hist Dist—*hist pl* OR-9
Portland South Oil Field—*oilfield* KS-7
Portland Square—*park* MN-6
Portland Stadium—*other* ME-1
Portland State Coll—*school* OR-9
Portland State Game Area—*park* MI-6
Portland Station—*locale* WV-2
Portland Station Cem—*cemetery* ME-1
Portland Stove Foundry—*hist pl* ME-1
Portland Street Hist Dist—*hist pl* AZ-5
Portland Thirteenth Ave Hist Dist—*hist pl* OR-9
Portland Townhall—*building* IA-7
**Portland (Town of)**—*pop pl* NY-2
**Portland (Town of)**—*pop pl* (2) WI-6
Portland Township—*fmr MCD* (3) IA-7
**Portland Township**—*pop pl* SD-7
Portland (Township of)—*fmr MCD* AR-4
Portland (Township of)—*other* OH-6
**Portland (Township of)**—*pop pl* IL-6
**Portland (Township of)**—*pop pl* MI-6
Portland-Troutdale Airp—*airport* OR-9
Portland Union Acad—*school* OR-9
**Portlandville**—*pop pl* NY-2
Portland Wash—*stream* AZ-5
Portland Waterfront—*hist pl* ME-1
Portland Waterfront Hist Dist (Boundary Increase)—*hist pl* ME-1
Portland Yamhill Hist Dist—*hist pl* OR-9
Portland Zoological Gardens—*park* OR-9
Port Largo Plaza (Shop Ctr)—*locale* FL-3
**Port Laudania**—*pop pl* FL-3
**Port Lavaca**—*pop pl* TX-5
Port Lavaca (CCD)—*cens area* TX-5
Port Lawrence—*bay* AK-9
Portledge Sch—*school* NY-2
Port Leon—*locale* FL-3
Port Leon Creek—*stream* FL-3
Port Leon Hammock—*island* FL-3
Port Leon Lake—*reservoir* FL-3
Port Levashef—*locale* AK-9
**Port Leyden**—*pop pl* NY-2
**Port Lions**—*pop pl* AK-9
Portlock—*locale* AK-9
**Portlock**—*pop pl* HI-9
**Portlock**—*pop pl* VA-3
Portlock Glacier—*glacier* AK-9
Portlock Harbor—*bay* AK-9
Portlock Ranch—*locale* ID-8
Port Lock Run—*stream* VA-3
Portlock Sch—*school* VA-3
Portlock Yard—*locale* VA-3
Port Lonesome—*locale* FL-3
**Port Louisa**—*pop pl* IA-7
Port Louisa Cem—*cemetery* IA-7
Port Louisa Township—*fmr MCD* IA-7
Port Lucy—*bay* AK-9
**Port Ludlow**—*pop pl* WA-9
*Port Ludlow Post Office* WA-9
**Port Madison**—*pop pl* WA-9
**Port Madison Ind Res**—*pop pl* WA-9
**Port Mahon**—*pop pl* DE-2
Port Mahon Lighthouse—*hist pl* DE-2
*Port Mahons* DE-2
Port Malabar—*uninc pl* FL-3
Port Malabar Elem Sch—*School* FL-3
Port Malabar Plaza (Shop Ctr)—*locale* FL-3
Port Malabar Shop Ctr—*locale* FL-3
Port Malmesbury—*cape* AK-9
Port Manatee—*harbor* FL-3
Port Manatee—*other* FL-3
Port Manchac—*locale* LA-4
Portman Dam—*dam* SC-3
Portman Hollow—*valley* KY-4
Portman Lagoon—*lake* LA-4
Port-Manning House—*hist pl* OR-9
**Port Mansfield**—*pop pl* TX-5
Port Mansfield Channel—*channel* TX-5
Portman Square—*park* MN-6
*Port Mant* FM-9
Port Marion Elem Sch—*school* PA-2
Port Mary—*bay* AK-9
**Port Matilda**—*pop pl* PA-2
Port Matilda Borough—*civil* PA-2
**Port Mayaca**—*pop pl* FL-3
Port Mayoral—*bay* AK-9
Port McArthur—*harbor* AK-9
Port Meadville Airp—*airport* PA-2
**Port Mercer**—*pop pl* NJ-2
*Port Mich* IN-6
**Port Mitchell**—*pop pl* IN-6
Port Mitchell Lake—*lake* IN-6
Port Moller—*bay* AK-9
Port Moller—*locale* AK-9
Port Moller Hot Springs Village Site—*hist pl* AK-9
**Port Monmouth**—*pop pl* NJ-2
Port Moore—*bay* AK-9
**Port Morris**—*pop pl* NJ-2
**Port Morris**—*pop pl* NY-2
**Port Morris Junction**—*pop pl* NJ-2
Port Mulgrave—*bay* AK-9
**Port Murray**—*pop pl* NJ-2
*Port Murry* NJ-2
**Port Neches**—*pop pl* TX-5
Port Neches Groves HS—*school* TX-5
Port Neches Sch—*school* TX-5
*Port Neck* NY-2
Port Nellie Juan—*bay* AK-9
**Port Nellie Juan**—*pop pl* AK-9
Port Nellie Juan Cannery—*other* AK-9
Portner Pond—*reservoir* NY-2
Portner Rsvr—*reservoir* CO-8
**Portneuf**—*pop pl* ID-8
Portneuf Marsh Valley Canal—*canal* ID-8
Portneuf Marsh Valley Irr Co. Feeder Canal—*canal* ID-8
Portneuf Presto Trail—*trail* ID-8
Portneuf Range—*range* ID-8
*Portneuf Reservoir* ID-8
Portneuf River—*stream* ID-8
Portneuf River Slough—*gut* ID-8
*Portneuf Springs* ID-8
Port Newark—*bay* NJ-2
Port Newark Channel—*channel* NJ-2
Port Newark Elizabeth-Port Authority Marine Terminal—*uninc pl* NJ-2
Port Newark Helistop—*airport* NJ-2
**Port Nickel**—*pop pl* LA-4
**Port Nikiski**—*pop pl* AK-9
*Port Norfolk* MA-1
**Port Norfolk**—*pop pl* VA-3
Port Norfolk Hist Dist—*hist pl* VA-3
Port Norfolk Reach—*channel* VA-3
Port Norfolk Sch—*school* VA-3
**Port Norris**—*pop pl* NJ-2
Portobago Bay—*bay* VA-3
Portobago Creek—*stream* VA-3
Portobago Run—*stream* VA-3

Porto Bello—hist pl MD-2
Porto Bello—hist pl VA-3
Portobello Point—cape MD-2
Port O'Brien—locale AK-9
**Port O'Conner**—pop pl TX-5
**Port O'Connor**—pop pl TX-5
Porto de la Bodega y Cuadra WA-9
Porto de Quadra WA-9
Port of Albany—locale NY-2
Port of Bay City—locale TX-5
Port of Beacon Island, The NC-3
Port of Belau PW-9
Port of Benicia—locale CA-9
Port of Camas-Washougal—locale WA-9
Port of Chickasaw—harbor AL-4
Port of Del Bonita MT-8
Port of Dunkin—locale OK-5
Port of Gulfport—harbor MS-4
Port of History Museum—building PA-2
Port of Iberia—locale LA-4
Port Of Ilwaco Airp—airport WA-9
Port of Indiana IN-6
Port Of Kennewick—locale WA-9
Port of Lake Charles—locale LA-4
Port of Longview—locale WA-9
**Port of Miami**—pop pl FL-3
Port Of Morrow—harbor OR-9
Port of Muskogee—locale OK-5
Port of New Iberia LA-4
**Port of New Iberia**—pop pl LA-4
Port of Palau—harbor PW-9
Port of Palm Beach—harbor FL-3
Port of Palm Beach Junction (railroad junction)—locale FL-3
Port Of Pasco—locale WA-9
Port Of Pasco Industrial Park—locale WA-9
Port of Portland—locale OR-9
Port Of Poulsbo Marina Moorage Seaplane Base—airport WA-9
Port Of Redwood City CA-9
Port of Redwood City—harbor CA-9
Port of Sacramento—locale CA-9
Port of Saint Petersburg—harbor FL-3
Port of Stockton—harbor CA-9
Port of The Dalles—locale OR-9
Port Of Vancouver—locale WA-9
Port Of Vancouver Terminal—other WA-9
Port of Vermilion—locale LA-4
Port of Victoria TX-5
Port of West Saint Mary—locale LA-4
Port of West Saint Mary Parish LA-4
Portohonk Creek—stream NC-3
Portola CA-9
**Portola**—pop pl CA-9
Portola Ave Sch—school CA-9
Portola (CCD)—cens area CA-9
Portola Expedition Historical Marker—park CA-9
Portola JHS—school (2) CA-9
Portola Sch—school (2) CA-9
Portola State Park—park CA-9
Portola Terrace—uninc pl CA-9
**Portola Valley**—pop pl CA-9
Portola Valley—valley CA-9
Portola Valley Sch—hist pl CA-9
Port Oliver Ford—locale KY-4
Portolo Valley CA-9
Port Oneida—locale MI-6
**Port Ontario**—pop pl NY-2
Port Oram NJ-2
Port Orange—locale FL-3
Port Orange—locale NY-2
**Port Orange**—pop pl (2) FL-3
Port Orange (CCD)—cens area FL-3
Port Orange Elem Sch—school FL-3
Port Orange Plaza (Shop Ctr)—locale FL-3
Port Orange Presbyterian Ch—church FL-3
**Port Orchard**—pop pl WA-9
Port Orchard Airp—airport WA-9
Port Orchard (CCD)—cens area WA-9
**Port Orford**—pop pl OR-9
Port Orford (CCD)—cens area OR-9
Port Orford Cedar Experimental For—forest OR-9
Port Orford Cedar State Park—park OR-9
Port Orford Cedar Wayside OR-9
Porto Rico—locale WV-2
**Porto Rico**—pop pl MO-7
Porto Rico Canyon—valley AZ-5
Portoritas Tank—reservoir AZ-5
Portor Sch—school IL-6
Port Pena DE-2
**Port Penn**—pop pl DE-2
Port Penn Hist Dist—hist pl DE-2
Port Perry—locale PA-2
Port Perry Bridge—bridge PA-2
Port Plaza (Shop Ctr)—locale MA-1
Port Protection—bay AK-9
Port Protection—locale AK-9
**Port Providence**—pop pl PA-2
Port Quendall WA-9
Portrait Rock—pillar WA-9
**Port Rayon**—pop pl TN-4
**Port Reading**—pop pl NJ-2
Port Reading Junction—uninc pl NJ-2
Port Reading Reach—channel NJ-2
Port Reading Station—locale NJ-2
Port Real Marina—bay AK-9
Port Refugio—bay AK-9
**Port Republic**—pop pl MD-2
**Port Republic**—pop pl NJ-2
**Port Republic**—pop pl VA-3
Port Republic Battle Monmt—park VA-3
Port Republic Cem—cemetery VA-3
Port Republic Fish and Wildlife Mngmt Area—park NJ-2
Port Republic Hist Dist—hist pl VA-3
**Port Richey**—pop pl FL-3
Port Richey (CCD)—cens area FL-3
Port Richey Shopping Village—locale FL-3
Port Richmond—locale IA-7
Port Richmond—locale PA-2
**Port Richmond**—pop pl NY-2
**Port Richmond**—pop pl VA-3
Port Ridge IL-6
Port Royal—locale GA-3
Port Royal—locale TN-4
**Port Royal**—pop pl AL-4
**Port Royal**—pop pl FL-3
**Port Royal**—pop pl KY-4
**Port Royal**—pop pl (2) PA-2
**Port Royal**—pop pl SC-3
**Port Royal**—pop pl VA-3
Port Royal Borough—civil PA-2
Port Royal Cem—cemetery SC-3
Port Royal Ch—church (2) TN-4
Port Royal Cross Roads—locale VA-3
Port Royal Crossroads—other VA-3
Port Royal Hist Dist—hist pl VA-3
Port Royal (historical)—civil DC-2
Port Royal House—hist pl MA-1
Port Royal Island—island SC-3
Port Royal (Magisterial District)—fmr MCD VA-3
Port Royal Plantation—uninc pl SC-3
Port Royal Post Office (historical)—building TN-4
Port Royal Sound—bay SC-3
Port Royal State Historic Area TN-4
Port Royal State Park—park TN-4
Port Roydel Airp—airport PA-2
Port Rsvr—reservoir NY-2
Port Run—stream (2) IN-6
**Port Safety**—pop pl AK-9
Port Safety Roadhouse—locale AK-9
**Port Saint Joe**—pop pl FL-3
Port Saint Joe (CCD)—cens area FL-3
Port Saint Joe Elem Sch—school FL-3
Port Saint Joe Junior-Senior HS—school FL-3
Port Saint Joe North Channel Range Front Light—locale FL-3
Port Saint John—CDP FL-3
**Port Saint Lucie**—pop pl FL-3
Port Saint Lucie (CCD)—cens area FL-3
Port Saint Lucie Ch of Christ—church FL-3
Port Saint Lucie Elem Sch—school FL-3
Port Saint Lucie Hosp—hospital FL-3
Port Saint Lucie Methodist Ch—church FL-3
Port Saint Nicholas—bay AK-9
**Port Salerno**—pop pl FL-3
Port Salerno Elem Sch—school FL-3
Port Salerno-Hobe Sound (CCD)—cens area FL-3
Port Salerno (RR name Salerno)—CDP FL-3
Port San Antonio—bay AK-9
**Port Sanilac**—pop pl MI-6
Port Sanilac Light Station—hist pl MI-6
Port San Luis—locale CA-9
Port San Luis Site—hist pl CA-9
Port Santa Cruz—bay AK-9
Port Sch—school OK-5
Port Scipio—locale MO-7
Ports Cove ME-1
Ports Creek—stream SC-3
Port Sember Airp—airport PA-2
**Port Serena**—pop pl TN-4
**Port Sewall**—pop pl FL-3
Port Sewell Station RR Station—locale FL-3
Ports Harbor—bay ME-1
**Port Sheldon**—pop pl MI-6
Port Sheldon (Township of)—civ div MI-6
Port Sherman MI-6
Portside—post sta VA-3
Port Smith AL-4
Port Smith P.O. AL-4
Portsmouth—locale KY-4
**Portsmouth**—pop pl IA-7
**Portsmouth**—pop pl NH-1
**Portsmouth**—pop pl NC-3
**Portsmouth**—pop pl OH-6
**Portsmouth**—pop pl RI-1
Portsmouth Athenaeum—hist pl NH-1
Portsmouth Bank NC-3
Portsmouth Banks NC-3
Portsmouth City—civil VA-3
Portsmouth Company Cotton Mills: Counting House—hist pl ME-1
Portsmouth Courthouse—hist pl VA-3
Portsmouth Ditch—canal VA-3
Portsmouth Earthworks, Group A—hist pl KY-4
Portsmouth Fire Department No. 1—hist pl OH-6
Portsmouth Foundry and Machine Works—hist pl OH-6
Portsmouth Friends Meetinghouse Parsonage and Cemetery—hist pl RI-1
Portsmouth Harbor—bay ME-1
**Portsmouth Heights**—pop pl VA-3
Portsmouth Hist Dist (Boundary Increase)—hist pl VA-3
**Portsmouth (ind. city)**—pop pl VA-3
Portsmouth Island—island (2) NC-3
Portsmouth Marine Teminal—locale VA-3
Portsmouth Mine—mine MN-6
Portsmouth Naval Hosp—hist pl VA-3
Portsmouth Naval Regional Med Ctr—military VA-3
Portsmouth Naval Shipyard—military ME-1
Portsmouth Olde Town Hist Dist—hist pl VA-3
Portsmouth Park—park OR-9
**Portsmouth Park**—pop pl RI-1
Portsmouth Plains NH-1
**Portsmouth Plains**—pop pl NH-1
Portsmouth Plaza and Commerce Center (Shop Ctr)—locale VA-3
Portsmouth Public Library—hist pl NH-1
Portsmouth Sch—school OR-9
Portsmouth Square—park CA-9
**Portsmouth (Town of)**—pop pl RI-1
Portsmouth (Township of)—fmr MCD NC-3
**Portsmouth (Township of)**—pop pl MI-6
Portsmouth Village—hist pl NC-3
**Portsmouth Village**—pop pl NC-3
Portsmouth Village Ranger Station—locale NC-3
Port Snettisham—bay AK-9
Port Socony Reach—channel NJ-2
**Port South (subdivision)**—pop pl AL-4
Port Spring—spring ID-8
Port Spring—spring OR-9
Port Stanley—locale WA-9
Port Stewart—bay AK-9
Port Stewart Hollow—valley PA-2
Port Sullivan—locale TX-5
Port Sullivan Ch—church TX-5
**Port Sulphur**—pop pl LA-4
**Port Sutton**—pop pl FL-3
Portsville TN-4
Portsville—locale DE-2
Portsville Ch—church DE-2
Portsville Lighthouse—hist pl DE-2
Portsville Millpond—reservoir DE-2
Portsville Pond DE-2
Port Tabago Creek VA-3
Port Tampa FL-3
**Port Tampa**—pop pl FL-3
Port Tampa Channel—channel FL-3
Port Tampa City FL-3
Port Tampa City (Port Tampa)—uninc pl FL-3
Port Tampa Dock—harbor FL-3
Port Tampa RR Station—locale FL-3
Port Terminal—locale NC-3
Port Tobacco—locale MD-2
Port Tobacco Bay VA-3
Port Tobacco Creek VA-3
Port Tobacco Creek—stream MD-2
Port Tobacco Marina—locale MD-2
Port Tobacco River—stream MD-2
**Port Tobacco Riviera**—pop pl MD-2
Port Tobacco Run VA-3
Port Tobacco Sch—school MD-2
Port Tobacco Station MD-2
**Port Tobacco Village**—pop pl MD-2
Port Tobago Bay VA-3
Port Toledo OH-6
Port Tongass—bar AK-9
**Port Townsend**—pop pl WA-9
Port Townsend Bay WA-9
Port Townsend Canal WA-9
Port Townsend Carnegie Library—hist pl WA-9
Port Townsend Hist Dist—hist pl WA-9
Port Townsend-Oak Bay Canal WA-9
Port Townshend WA-9
**Port Trevorton**—pop pl PA-2
**Port Trinitie (subdivision)**—pop pl NC-3
Portugee Canyon—valley CA-9
Portugese Beach—beach CA-9
Portugese Ch—church MA-1
Portugese Cove MA-1
Portugese Gulch—valley CA-9
Portugese Pasture—flat WY-8
Portugese Springs—spring HI-9
Portugues (Barrio)—fmr MCD (2) PR-3
Portuguese Bench—bench CA-9
Portuguese Bend—bay CA-9
Portuguese Bend—bend CA-9
**Portuguese Bend**—pop pl CA-9
Portuguese Bend Riding Club—other CA-9
Portuguese Canyon—valley (6) CA-9
Portuguese Canyon—valley OR-9
Portuguese Cove—bay MA-1
Portuguese Creek CA-9
Portuguese Creek—stream (4) CA-9
Portuguese Creek—stream ID-8
Portuguese Flat—flat CA-9
Portuguese Flat—flat OR-9
Portuguese Gulch—valley (2) CA-9
**Portuguese Hill**—pop pl IL-6
Portuguese Meadow—flat CA-9
Portuguese Mountain—ridge NV-8
Portuguese Mtn—summit NV-8
Portuguese Pass—gap CA-9
Portuguese Peak—summit (2) CA-9
Portuguese Point—cape CA-9
Portuguese Point—cape MO-7
Portuguese Point—cape WA-9
Portuguese Point—ridge CA-9
Portuguese Ridge—ridge (3) CA-9
Portuguese Rsvr—reservoir ID-8
Portuguese Sheep Camp—locale CA-9
Portuguese Spring—spring CA-9
Portuguese Spring—spring (2) NV-8
Portuguese Spring—spring (2) OR-9
Portugues Urbano (Barrio)—fmr MCD PR-3
**Port Union**—pop pl OH-6
Port Union Cem—cemetery LA-4
Port Valdez—bay AK-9
Port View Elem Sch—school PA-2
Portview Sch—school MN-6
**Portville**—pop pl NY-2
Portville Cem—cemetery NY-2
Portville Ridge—ridge NY-2
**Portville (Town of)**—pop pl NY-2
**Port Vincent**—pop pl LA-4
Port Vita—locale AK-9
Portvue PA-2
**Port Vue**—pop pl PA-2
Port Vue Borough—civil PA-2
Port Wakefield—harbor AK-9
Port Wakefield—locale AK-9
Port Walter—bay AK-9
Port Walthall Channel—channel VA-3
Port Warren—locale NJ-2
**Port Washington**—pop pl NY-2
**Port Washington**—pop pl OH-6
**Port Washington**—pop pl WI-6
Port Washington Bay WA-9
Port Washington Narrows—channel WA-9
**Port Washington North**—pop pl NY-2
Port Washington Town Hall—hist pl OH-6
**Port Washington (Town of)**—pop pl WI-6
Port Wawawai WA-9
**Portway Acres**—pop pl TX-5
Port Wells—bay AK-9
**Port Wentworth**—pop pl GA-3
Port Wentworth (CCD)—cens area GA-3
Port Wentworth Junction—locale GA-3
Port William KS-7
Port William—locale AK-9
**Port William**—pop pl OH-6
Port Williams OH-6
Port Williams—locale KS-7
Port Williams—locale WA-9
**Port Williams**—pop pl AK-9
Port Wine—locale CA-9
Port Wine Lake—lake MI-6
Port Wine Ravine—valley CA-9
Port Wine Ridge—ridge CA-9
**Port Wing**—pop pl WI-6
**Port Wing (Town of)**—pop pl WI-6
Portwood Cem—cemetery KY-4
Portwood Ch—church MS-4
Portwood Hollow—valley MO-7
Portwood Landing (historical)—locale MS-4
Portwood Village and Mound—hist pl MO-7
Port Wrangell—bay AK-9
**Port-980-Dumfries**—pop pl VA-3
Porukunong—spring FM-9
**Porum**—pop pl OK-5
Porum (CCD)—cens area OK-5
Porum Gap—gap OK-5
Porus Islands—island ME-1
Porvenil Well—well TX-5
**Porvenir**—pop pl TX-5
**Porvenir**—pop pl PR-3
Porvenir Canyon—valley NM-5
Porvenir Tank—reservoir AZ-5
Posa, Canada —valley CA-9
Posa Anchorage—bay CA-9
Posa De Los Ositos—civil CA-9
Posa Plain, La—plain AZ-5
Posas AZ-5
Posas, Arroyo Las—stream CA-9
Posas, Cerro De Las—summit CA-9
Posas Plain AZ-5
Posas Valley AZ-5
Posch Site—hist pl MN-6
Posegate Cem—cemetery CO-8
Posehill Springs—spring AL-4
Pose Lake—lake MN-6
Posen NE-7
Posen—fmr MCD NE-7
Posen—locale IL-6
**Posen**—pop pl IL-6
**Posen**—pop pl MI-6
Posen Junction IL-6
Posen Sch—school IL-6
Posen State Wildlife Mngmt Area—park MN-6
**Posen (Township of)**—pop pl MI-6
**Posen (Township of)**—pop pl MN-6
Poser Mtn—summit CA-9
Posey—island WA-9
Posey—locale AR-4
Posey—locale TX-5
Posey—locale WV-2
**Posey**—pop pl CA-9
**Posey**—pop pl IL-6
**Posey**—pop pl TX-5
Posey Bend—bend TN-4
Posey Branch—stream (2) AL-4
Posey Branch—stream GA-3
Posey Branch—stream (2) LA-4
Posey Branch—stream MS-4
Posey Canyon—valley CA-9
Posey Canyon—valley UT-8
Posey Canyon—valley WA-9
Posey Cave—cave AL-4
Posey Cave—cave TN-4
Posey Cem—cemetery AL-4
Posey Cem—cemetery (2) IL-6
Posey Cem—cemetery IN-6
Posey Cem—cemetery MS-4
Posey Cem—cemetery NC-3
Posey Cem—cemetery TN-4
Posey Cem—cemetery WI-6
Posey Chapel—church (2) IN-6
Posey Church AL-4
**Posey County**—pop pl IN-6
Posey Creek—stream (2) AL-4
Posey Creek—stream AR-4
Posey Creek—stream CO-8
Posey Creek—stream ID-8
Posey Creek—stream KS-7
Posey Creek—stream MD-2
Posey Creek—stream MI-6
Posey Creek—stream OK-5
Posey Creek—stream SC-3
Posey Creek—stream WI-6
Posey Creek—stream WY-8
Posey East Oil Field—other IL-6
Posey Field—locale TN-4
Posey Field (airport)—airport AL-4
Posey Field Cem—cemetery TN-4
Posey Flats—hist pl KY-4
Posey Gap—gap AL-4
Posey Gulch—valley CA-9
Posey Hill—summit TN-4
Posey (historical)—locale AL-4
Posey Hollow—valley AL-4
Posey Hollow—valley AR-4
Posey Hollow—valley TN-4
Posey Hollow—valley VA-3
Posey Hollow—valley WV-2
Posey Lake—lake CA-9
Posey Lake—lake TX-5
Posey Lake—lake WI-6
Posey Lake—reservoir MI-6
Posey Lake Drain—stream MI-6
Posey Landing (historical)—locale AL-4
**Posey Mill**—pop pl AL-4
Posey Mill Cem—cemetery AL-4
Posey Mill (historical)—locale AL-4
Posey Mound—locale MS-4
Posey Mound Cem—cemetery MS-4
Posey Mound Plantation MS-4
Posey Mtn—summit GA-3
Posey Mtn—summit SC-3
Posey Oil Field—oilfield KS-7
Posey Oil Field—other IL-6
Posey Pit—cave AL-4
Posey Point—cape TN-4
Posey Pond—reservoir AL-4
Posey Post Office (historical)—building AL-4
Posey Ranch—locale WY-8
Posey Rapids—rapids WI-6
Posey Ridge Lakes—reservoir IL-6
Posey Run—stream WV-2
Poseys Bluff—cliff MD-2
Posey Sch—school AL-4
Posey Sch—school KY-4
Posey Sch—school TN-4
Posey Sch—school TX-5
Poseys Crossroads—locale AL-4
**Poseys Crossroads**—pop pl AL-4
Poseys Draw—valley CO-8
Posey Sink—basin IN-6
Posey Site (22QU500)—hist pl MS-4
Poseys Landing AL-4
Poseys Mill AL-4
Posey Spring—spring MT-8
Posey Spring—spring UT-8
Posey Springs—spring NM-5
**Posey (Township of)**—pop pl (7) IN-6
Posey Tube—tunnel CA-9
Posey Valley OR-9
Posey Valley Ditch OR-9
**Poseyville**—pop pl IN-6
**Poseyville**—pop pl MI-6
Poseyville Cem—cemetery MI-6
Poseyville Ch—church GA-3
Posey Well—well TX-5
Posey Wharf—locale MD-2
Posey Windmill—locale TX-5
Posh Airp—airport PA-2
Posie Tank—reservoir NM-5
Posin Gulch—valley CO-8
Positas, Arroyo Las—stream CA-9
Posita Windmill—locale (3) TX-5
Positeus Creek—stream TX-5
Posito Cerca Windmill—locale TX-5
Posito Creek—stream CO-8
Poskers Settlement IN-6
Poskey Cem—cemetery TX-5
**Poskin**—pop pl WI-6
Poskin Cem—cemetery WI-6
Poskin Lake—lake WI-6
Posky Hollow—valley IN-6
Posley Cem—cemetery IA-7
Posliedni Point—cape AK-9
**Posm**—pop pl VA-3
Posneganset Lake Pond RI-1
Posneganset Pond—lake RI-1
Poso, Mount—summit CA-9
Poso, The—basin CO-8
Poso Blanco AZ-5
Poso Campground—locale CO-8
Poso Canal—canal (3) CA-9
Poso Canal Company HQ—other CA-9
Poso Cow Camp—locale NM-5
Poso Creek—stream CA-9
Poso Creek—stream (2) CO-8
Poso Creek—stream NM-5
Poso Creek Canyon—valley CO-8
Posodera Tank—reservoir NM-5
Poso Drain CA-9
Poso Drain—canal CA-9
Poso Drain One CA-9
Poso Drain 1—canal CA-9
Poso Drain 2—canal CA-9
Poso Farm—locale CA-9
Poso Flat—flat CA-9
Poso Mine—mine CA-9
Poson Gulch CO-8
Poso Ortega—lake CA-9
Poso Ortega Lake CA-9
Poso Park—park NM-5
**Poso Park**—pop pl CA-9
Poso Ranch—locale CA-9
Posos Gulch, Los—valley AZ-5
Posos Lake—lake NM-5
Poso Slough—gut CA-9
Poso Slough Drain CA-9
Poso Spring—spring NM-5
Posos Tank, Los—reservoir AZ-5
Posos Trail—trail CO-8
Poso Tank—reservoir NM-5
Poso Tank—reservoir TX-5
Poso Windmill—locale NM-5
Poso Windmill—locale TX-5
Pospect Hill Lookout Tower—tower PA-2
Pospect Park—uninc pl IA-7
Pospeshil Theatre—hist pl NE-7
Posque Landing—locale NC-3
Poss Branch—stream IN-6
Poss Creek—stream IN-6
Posse Creek—stream MI-6
Posse Lake—lake MN-6
Posser Tabernacle—church SC-3
Possession—locale AK-9
**Possession**—pop pl WA-9
Possession Camp Run—stream WV-2
Possession Hollow—valley NY-2
Possession Point—cape WA-9
Possession Point—other WA-9
Possession Sound—bay WA-9
Possey Branch AL-4
Possey School AL-4
Possible Post Office (historical)—building TN-4
Poss Mtn—summit AK-9
Possum Bayou—gut MS-4
Possum Bayou—stream (3) LA-4
Possum Bend AL-4
Possum Bluff—cliff FL-3
Possum Branch—stream (3) AL-4
Possum Branch—stream (2) GA-3
Possum Branch—stream MS-4
Possum Branch—stream MO-7
Possum Branch—stream (2) NC-3
Possum Branch—stream OK-5
Possum Branch—stream (3) TN-4
Possum Branch—stream TX-5
Possum Branch—stream VA-3
Possum Bridge—other IL-6
Possum Coll (historical)—school TN-4
Possum Community Hall—locale IL-6
Possum Corner AL-4
Possum Corner—locale MS-4
**Possum Corner**—pop pl SC-3
Possum Corner Bridge—bridge SC-3
Possum Creek AL-4
Possum Creek AR-4
Possum Creek OK-5
Possum Creek VA-3
Possum Creek—stream (3) AL-4
Possum Creek—stream AK-9
Possum Creek—stream (4) AR-4
Possum Creek—stream CO-8
Possum Creek—stream (2) GA-3
Possum Creek—stream (2) IL-6
Possum Creek—stream KS-7
Possum Creek—stream (4) MS-4
Possum Creek—stream MO-7
Possum Creek—stream NE-7
Possum Creek—stream (4) OK-5
Possum Creek—stream (8) TN-4
Possum Creek—stream (4) TX-5
Possum Creek—stream (2) VA-3
Possum Creek Rec Area—park TN-4
Possum Ditch—canal IA-7
Possum Eddy—lake GA-3
Possum Eddy—rapids SC-3
Possum Ford Bend—bend OK-5
**Possum Fork**—pop pl AR-4
Possum Gap—gap GA-3
Possum Gap Creek TN-4
Possum Gap Island—island FL-3
Possum Glory PA-2
**Possum Grape**—pop pl AR-4
Possum Head Swamp—swamp FL-3
Possum Head Windmill—locale TX-5
Possum Hollow AL-4
Possum Hollow TN-4
**Possum Hollow**—pop pl PA-2
Possum Hollow—valley AL-4
Possum Hollow—valley AR-4
Possum Hollow—valley IL-6
Possum Hollow—valley (6) IN-6
Possum Hollow—valley IA-7
Possum Hollow—valley (3) KY-4
Possum Hollow—valley MD-2
Possum Hollow—valley (13) MO-7
Possum Hollow—valley NM-5
Possum Hollow—valley (2) NC-3
Possum Hollow—valley (4) OH-6
Possum Hollow—valley OK-5
Possum Hollow—valley (3) PA-2
Possum Hollow—valley (10) TN-4
Possum Hollow—valley TX-5
Possum Hollow—valley (11) VA-3
Possum Hollow—valley (3) WV-2
Possum Hollow Branch—stream TN-4
Possum Hollow Cove—bay MO-7
Possum Hollow Creek—stream OK-5
Possum Hollow Run—stream PA-2
Possum Hollow Sch (historical)—school TN-4
Possum Hollow Woods—woods IL-6
Possum Island MD-2
Possum Kingdom Lake—reservoir TX-5
Possum Kingdom Rsvr TX-5
Possum Kingdom State Park—park TX-5
Possum Knob—summit KY-4
Possum Knobs—range VA-3
Possum Knobs—ridge TN-4
Possum Lake—lake ME-1
Possum Lake—lake TX-5
**Possumneck**—pop pl MS-4
Possumneck Post Office (historical)—building MS-4
Possumneck Public Sch (historical)—school MS-4
Possumneck Sch (historical)—school MS-4
Possum Nose—cliff VA-3
Possumpaw Branch—stream TN-4
Possumpaw Hollow—valley TN-4
Possum Pocket—swamp AL-4
Possum Point—cape DE-2
Possum Point—cape GA-3
Possum Point—cape LA-4
Possum Point—cape (2) MD-2
Possum Point—cape VA-3
**Possum Point**—pop pl VA-3
Possum Point—ridge AZ-5
Possum Point Bayou—gut LA-4
Possum Point Power Station—other VA-3
Possum Poke—hist pl GA-3
Possum Pond—lake TN-4
Possumquarter Creek—stream NC-3
Possum Quarter Landing—locale NC-3
Possum Ridge—ridge IN-6
Possum Ridge—ridge KY-4
Possum Ridge Sch—school IL-6
Possum Run IN-6
Possum Run—stream KY-4
Possum Run—stream OH-6
Possum Run—stream PA-2
Possum Run—stream (2) VA-3
Possum Run—stream WV-2
Possum Run Creek—stream MT-8
Possum Sch—school MO-7
Possum Sch—school OH-6
Possum Spring—spring TX-5
Possum Swamp—stream NC-3
Possum Tank—reservoir AZ-5
Possum Town MS-4
**Possumtown**—pop pl NJ-2
Possumtown Sch (abandoned)—school MO-7
Possum Track Ch—church MS-4
Possum Trail Mine—mine TN-4
Possum Trot (2) AR-4
Possum Trot—locale MO-7
Possum Trot—locale VA-3
**Possum Trot**—pop pl AL-4
**Possum Trot**—pop pl KY-4
**Possum Trot**—pop pl MS-4
**Possumtrot**—pop pl NC-3
Possumtrot Branch—stream GA-3
Possum Trot Branch—stream KY-4
Possumtrot Branch—stream KY-4
Possum Trot Branch—stream KY-4
Possumtrot Branch—stream (3) TN-4
Possumtrot Branch—stream WV-2
Possum Trot Cave—cave TN-4
Possum Trot Cem—cemetery AL-4
Possum Trot Cem—cemetery AR-4
Possum Trot Cem—cemetery GA-3
Possum Trot Cemetery MS-4
Possum Trot Ch—church AR-4
Possum Trot Ch (historical)—church MS-4
Possum Trot Ch (historical)—church (2) TN-4
Possumtrot Church TN-4
Possumtrot Creek TN-4
Possum Trot Creek—stream (2) AR-4
Possum Trot Creek—stream (2) KS-7
Possum Trot Creek—stream MO-7
Possumtrot Creek—stream NC-3
Possum Trot Creek—stream (2) OK-5
Possum Trot Creek—stream TX-5
Possum Trot Ditch—canal IL-6
Possum Trot Hollow—valley AR-4
Possum Trot Hollow—valley (5) MO-7
Possumtrot Hollow—valley TN-4
Possum Trot Hollow—valley (2) TN-4
Possum Trot Hollow—valley VA-3
Possum Trot Lookout (historical)—locale MO-7
Possum Trot Ridge—ridge IN-6
Possum Trot Ridge—ridge KY-4
Possumtrot Ridge—ridge (2) TN-4
Possum Trot Sch—school GA-3
Possum Trot Sch—school IL-6
Possum Trot School MS-4
Possum Valley—valley TN-4
Possum Valley Ridge—ridge TN-4
Possum Walk MS-4
Possum Walk—locale MO-7
**Possumwalk**—pop pl MO-7
Possum Walk Cem—cemetery AR-4
Possum Walk Cem—cemetery TX-5
Possum Walk Creek TX-5
Possum Walk Creek—stream (2) AR-4
Possum Walk Creek—stream (2) MO-7

Possum Walk Hotel—*hist pl* MO-7
**Possum Woods**—*pop pl* OH-6
Possun Park Peninsula—*cape* TX-5
*Possun Point* GA-3
Post—*locale* CA-9
Post—*locale* KY-4
Post—*locale* MS-4
Post—*locale* MT-8
**Post**—*pop pl* OR-9
**Post**—*pop pl* TX-5
Post, Augustus, House—*hist pl* CT-1
Post, Henry, Air Field—*hist pl* OK-5
Post, Joseph W., House—*hist pl* CA-9
Post, Peter P., House—*hist pl* NJ-2
Post, The—*locale* UT-8
*Posta* CO-8
Posta, Canada De La —*valley* CA-9
Post A Canal—*canal* MT-8
Posta de Roque—*gap* TX-5
Post Adjutant's Office—*hist pl* OK-5
Postage Island—*island* MN-6
Postage Stamp Butte—*summit* OR-9
Post-Aire Airp—*airport* IN-6
Postal—*locale* MO-7
Postal Bldg—*hist pl* OR-9
**Postal Concentration Center**—*pop pl* NY-2
Postal Landing—*locale* AR-4
Postal Sch—*school* MO-7
Postalweight Hollow—*valley* PA-2
Postam Gulch—*valley* ID-8
Post and King Saloon—*hist pl* OR-9
*Postaok Creek* MO-7
Posta Quemada Canyon—*valley* AZ-5
Posta Water Hole—*reservoir* TX-5
Posta Windmill—*locale* TX-5
Post Bayou—*gut* LA-4
Post B Canal—*canal* MT-8
Post Blacksmith Shop—*hist pl* OK-5
Postboy—*locale* OH-6
Postboy Creek—*stream* OH-6
*Post Brook* NJ-2
Post Brook—*stream* ME-1
Post Brook Dam—*dam* NJ-2
Post Camp—*locale* (2) CA-9
Post Camp—*locale* ID-8
Post Camp Rsvr—*reservoir* OR-9
Post Camp Spring—*spring* NV-8
Post Canal—*canal* MT-8
*Post Canyon* AZ-5
Post Canyon—*valley* AZ-5
Post Canyon—*valley* (6) CA-9
Post Canyon—*valley* (2) CO-8
Post Canyon—*valley* ID-8
Post Canyon—*valley* NV-8
Post Canyon—*valley* NM-5
Post Canyon—*valley* OR-9
Post Canyon—*valley* TX-5
Post Canyon—*valley* UT-8
Post Canyon—*valley* WY-8
Post Canyon Point—*summit* UT-8
Post Canyon Ridge—*ridge* UT-8
Post Canyon Spring—*spring* NV-8
Post Canyon Spring—*spring* UT-8
Post C Canal—*canal* MT-8
Post Cem—*cemetery* GA-3
Post Cem—*cemetery* MI-6
Post Cem—*cemetery* MT-8
Post Cem—*cemetery* (2) NY-2
Post Cem—*cemetery* OK-5
Post Cem—*cemetery* WV-2
Post Chapel—*church* AL-4
Post Chapel—*church* VA-3
Post Chapel, Fort Sam Houston—*hist pl* TX-5
Post Chapel Cem—*cemetery* WV-2
Post Corner—*locale* NJ-2
Post Corners—*locale* NY-2
Post Corral—*locale* CA-9
Post Corral Canyon—*valley* CA-9
Post Corral Creek—*stream* CA-9
Post Corral Meadow—*flat* CA-9
Post Corral Meadows—*flat* CA-9
Post Cove—*bay* CT-1
*Post Creek* CA-9
*Post Creek* NV-8
*Post Creek* OR-9
Post Creek—*channel* NJ-2
Post Creek—*locale* MT-8
**Post Creek**—*pop pl* NY-2
Post Creek—*stream* AK-9
Post Creek—*stream* AZ-5
Post Creek—*stream* (5) CA-9
Post Creek—*stream* (2) ID-8
Post Creek—*stream* KS-7
Post Creek—*stream* (2) MI-6
Post Creek—*stream* (4) MT-8
Post Creek—*stream* NY-2
Post Creek—*stream* (2) OR-9
Post Creek—*stream* TX-5
Post Creek—*stream* (2) WY-8
Post Creek Basin—*basin* NJ-2
Post Creek Cutoff—*stream* IL-6
Post Creek Guard Station—*locale* CA-9
Post Creek (historical)—*locale* KS-7
Post Creek Picnic Area—*locale* WY-8
Post Ditch—*canal* IN-6
Post Ditch—*canal* OH-6
Post Draft—*valley* PA-2
Post Drain—*canal* MI-6
Post Drain—*stream* MI-6
Post Draw—*valley* SD-7
Post Draw—*valley* TX-5
Post Draw—*valley* (4) WY-8
Post E Canal—*canal* MT-8
Posted Creek—*stream* MI-6
Poste Haste Shop Ctr—*locale* FL-3
Poste Lake—*reservoir* OH-6
Postell—*locale* GA-3
**Postell**—*pop pl* NC-3
Postel Lake—*lake* ND-7
Postell Creek—*stream* GA-3
**Postelle**—*pop pl* AR-4
**Postelle**—*pop pl* TN-4
Postelle Cem—*cemetery* AR-4
Postelle Creek—*stream* GA-3
Postelle Post Office—*building* TN-4
**Postelle (RR name Ducktown (sta.))**—*pop pl* TN-4
Posten Bayou—*bay* FL-3
Posten Bayou—*stream* AR-4
Posten Bayou—*stream* LA-4
Posten Bayou Canal—*canal* LA-4
*Posten Butte* AZ-5
Posten Pond—*reservoir* PA-2
*Posten RR Station* AZ-5
*Poste Ouabache* IN-6
Poster—*cape* NC-3
Poster Creek—*bay* NC-3
Poster Gut—*gut* NC-3
**Post Estates (subdivision)**—*pop pl* MS-4
Postethwait Mtn—*summit* PA-2
**Post Falls**—*pop pl* ID-8
Post Falls Community United Presbyterian Church—*hist pl* ID-8
Post Falls-Rathdrum—*cens area* ID-8
Post F Canal—*canal* MT-8
Post Flat—*flat* CA-9
Post Foot—*locale* SC-3
Post Foot Branch—*stream* SC-3
Post Foot Landing—*locale* SC-3
Post Forest Camp—*locale* OR-9
Post G Canal—*canal* (2) MT-8
Post Golf Course—*other* OK-5
*Post Gulch* MT-8
Post Gulch—*valley* CA-9
Post Gulch—*valley* CO-8
Post Gulch—*valley* MT-8
Post Gulch—*valley* (4) OR-9
Post Gulch Spring—*spring* CO-8
Posthal Township—*civil* SD-7
Post Henderson Trail—*trail* NY-2
Post Hill—*summit* (2) CT-1
Post Hill—*summit* ME-1
Post Hill—*summit* NH-1
Post Hill—*summit* PA-2
Post Hill Cem—*cemetery* PA-2
Posthole Canyon—*valley* ID-8
Posthole Creek—*stream* OR-9
Posthole Tank—*reservoir* NM-5
Post Hollow—*valley* (2) ID-8
Post Hollow—*valley* OR-9
Post Hollow—*valley* (3) PA-2
Post Hollow—*valley* (5) UT-8
Post Hollow Spring—*spring* ID-8
Post Homestead—*locale* CO-8
Post House—*hist pl* IL-6
Postil—*locale* FL-3
Postill Creek—*stream* MT-8
Postillion, Bayou—*stream* LA-4
Post Island—*island* AK-9
Post Island—*summit* NJ-2
**Post Island (subdivision)**—*pop pl* MA-1
Post Junior Coll—*school* CT-1
Post-Kellogg Ditch—*canal* MT-8
*Post Lake* WA-9
*Post Lake* WI-6
Post Lake—*lake* AK-9
Post Lake—*lake* AZ-5
Post Lake—*lake* MI-6
Post Lake—*lake* NM-5
**Post Lake**—*pop pl* WI-6
Post Lake—*reservoir* SD-7
Post Lake—*reservoir* WY-8
*Post Lake Dam* SD-7
Post Lakes—*lake* CA-9
Post Lead—*channel* NY-2
Postle Cem—*cemetery* OH-6
*Postle Ranch* AZ-5
Postles Corner—*locale* DE-2
Postles House—*hist pl* DE-2
Postlethwaite Ridge—*ridge* WV-2
Postlewaite Creek—*stream* MT-8
Post Marsh—*island* NY-2
Postmaster Spring—*spring* AZ-5
Post Meadow—*flat* NV-8
Post Meadows—*flat* OR-9
*Post Mill* VT-1
**Post Mill**—*pop pl* WV-2
**Post Mills**—*pop pl* VT-1
Post Mine, The—*mine* ID-8
Post Montgomery Ranch—*locale* TX-5
Post-Montgomery Site 41 GR 188—*hist pl* TX-5
Post Mountain—*ridge* OR-9
Post Mountain Cem—*cemetery* TX-5
Post Mtn—*summit* OK-5
Post Mtn—*summit* OR-9
Post Mtn—*summit* (2) TX-5
Post Northwest (CCD)—*cens area* TX-5
*Post Oak* TN-4
Postoak—*locale* AL-4
Post Oak—*locale* OK-5
Post Oak—*locale* TN-4
Post Oak—*locale* (2) TX-5
Post Oak—*locale* VA-3
**Post Oak**—*pop pl* AL-4
**Post Oak**—*pop pl* IL-6
**Post Oak**—*pop pl* MO-7
**Post Oak**—*pop pl* TN-4
**Postoak**—*pop pl* TN-4
**Post Oak**—*pop pl* TN-4
**Postoak**—*pop pl* (2) TX-5
**Post Oak**—*pop pl* TX-5
Post Oak Bend—*bend* (2) TX-5
Post Oak Bend—*locale* TX-5
Post Oak Bend Cem—*cemetery* (2) TX-5
**Post Oak Bend City**—*pop pl* TX-5
*Post Oak Branch* TX-5
Post Oak Branch—*stream* (4) TX-5
Post Oak Cem—*cemetery* AR-4
Post Oak Cem—*cemetery* MO-7
Post Oak Cem—*cemetery* OK-5
Post Oak Cem—*cemetery* TN-4
Post Oak Cem—*cemetery* (8) TX-5
Postoak Cem—*cemetery* TX-5
Post Oak Cem—*cemetery* (7) TX-5
*Post Oak Ch* AL-4
*Post Oak Ch* TN-4
Post Oak Ch—*church* AL-4
Post Oak Ch—*church* (2) AR-4
Post Oak Ch—*church* FL-3
Post Oak Ch—*church* (2) GA-3
Post Oak Ch—*church* KY-4
Post Oak Ch—*church* MO-7
Postoak Ch—*church* TN-4
Post Oak Ch—*church* TN-4
Post Oak Ch—*church* (4) TX-5
*Post Oak Chapel* TX-5
Postoak Ch (historical)—*church* MS-4
Postoak Ch (historical)—*church* MO-7
*Post Oak Creek* TN-4
*Postoak Creek* TX-5
Post Oak Creek—*stream* AR-4
Post Oak Creek—*stream* MO-7
Post Oak Creek—*stream* (5) OK-5
Post Oak Creek—*stream* TN-4
Postoak Creek—*stream* TN-4
Post Oak Creek—*stream* (10) TX-5
Postoak Creek—*stream* TX-5
Post Oak Creek—*stream* (9) TX-5
Post Oak Ditch—*canal* AR-4
Post Oak Draw—*valley* CO-8
Post Oak Draw—*valley* (2) TX-5
**Post Oak Estates**—*pop pl* TN-4
Post Oak Falls—*falls* TX-5
**Post Oak Farms**—*pop pl* TN-4
Post Oak Flat—*flat* AL-4
Post Oak Flat—*flat* AR-4
Post Oak Flats—*flat* MO-7
Post Oak Fork—*locale* AL-4
**Postoak (Gantt)**—*pop pl* TX-5
Post Oak Grove Ch—*church* TX-5
Post Oak (historical)—*locale* MS-4
Postoak Hollow—*valley* TX-5
Post Oak Hollow—*valley* TX-5
Post Oak Hunting Lodge—*building* AL-4
Post Oak Island (historical)—*island* TN-4
Post Oak Lake—*lake* OK-5
Post Oak Lake—*lake* TX-5
Post Oak Methodist Ch—*church* TN-4
Post Oak Mission Sch—*school* OK-5
Post Oak Mtn—*summit* TX-5
Post Oak Oil Field—*oilfield* TX-5
**Post Oak Point**—*pop pl* TX-5
Post Oak Point Creek—*stream* TX-5
*Postoak Ridge* TX-5
Post Oak Ridge—*ridge* KY-4
Post Oak Ridge—*ridge* (2) TX-5
Post Oak Sch—*school* AL-4
Post Oak Sch—*school* MI-6
Postoak Sch—*school* TN-4
Post Oak Sch—*school* (3) TX-5
Postoak Sch (abandoned)—*school* MO-7
Postoak Sch (historical)—*school* MO-7
Post Oak Sch (historical)—*school* (3) TN-4
Post Oak Sch (historical)—*school* TX-5
Postoak School (abandoned)—*locale* MO-7
Post Oak Shade Ch—*church* TN-4
Post Oak Slough—*stream* IL-6
Post Oak Spring—*spring* CO-8
Post Oak Spring—*spring* (2) TX-5
*Post Oak Springs* AL-4
*Post Oak Springs* TN-4
Post Oak Springs Ch—*church* AL-4
Post Oak Springs Ch—*church* TN-4
*Post Oak Springs Missionary Baptist Ch* AL-4
Post Oak Springs Post Office (historical)—*building* TN-4
Post Oak Tank—*reservoir* TX-5
Post Oak Township—*civil* MO-7
Post-Oak Valley—*valley* TN-4
Post Oak Waterhole—*lake* TX-5
Post Oak Waterhole Draw—*valley* TX-5
*Post of Arkansas* AR-4
Post Office—*hist pl* ND-7
Post Office, Courthouse, and Federal Office Bldg—*hist pl* OK-5
Post Office Annex—*post sta* CA-9
Post Office Bay—*bay* WA-9
Post Office Bay—*swamp* FL-3
Post Office Bldg—*hist pl* TX-5
Post Office Building, Upper Montclair—*hist pl* NJ-2
Post Office Butte—*summit* ND-7
*Post Office Buttes* ND-7
Post Office Canyon—*valley* AZ-5
Post Office Canyon—*valley* NM-5
Post Office Creek—*gut* GA-3
Postoffice Creek—*stream* ID-8
Post Office Creek—*stream* OR-9
Post Office Department Bldg—*building* DC-2
Post Office Farms—*bend* AZ-5
Post Office Flat—*flat* NM-5
Post Office Hist Dist—*hist pl* AL-4
Post Office Lake—*lake* WA-9
Post Office Saddle—*gap* OR-9
Post Office Spring—*spring* AZ-5
Post Office Spring—*spring* CA-9
Post Office Square Shop Ctr—*locale* MA-1
Post Office Tank—*reservoir* (3) AZ-5
Post Office Terminal—*locale* CA-9
Post Office Windmill—*locale* TX-5
*Poston* IN-6
*Poston* OH-6
Poston—*locale* AZ-5
**Poston**—*pop pl* (2) AZ-5
**Poston**—*pop pl* SC-3
Poston Block—*hist pl* TN-4
Poston Branch—*stream* VA-3
Poston Butte—*summit* (2) AZ-5
Poston Cem—*cemetery* AL-4
Poston Cem—*cemetery* TN-4
Poston Ch—*church* NC-3
Poston Ch—*church* OH-6
Poston Chapel—*church* TN-4
**Poston Crossroads**—*pop pl* SC-3
Poston House—*hist pl* KY-4
Poston JHS—*school* AZ-5
Poston Lake—*lake* WY-8
Poston Meadows—*swamp* WY-8
*Poston Pond* FL-3
Poston Ranch—*locale* WY-8
Poston Ridge—*ridge* TN-4
Poston Road Elem Sch—*school* IN-6
Poston RR Station—*building* AZ-5
Poston Rsvr—*reservoir* WY-8
*Postons Butte* AZ-5
Poston Sch—*school* AZ-5
Poston Sch—*school* KY-4
Poston Sch—*school* OH-6
*Postons Folly* AZ-5
Poston Two—*locale* AZ-5
Post Park—*park* MI-6
Post Park—*park* NY-2
Post Peak—*summit* CA-9
Post Peak Pass—*gap* CA-9
Postpile Camp—*locale* CA-9
Post Pile Rock—*pillar* OR-9
Post Pile Saddle—*locale* ID-8
Post Point—*cape* NY-2
Post Point—*cape* WA-9
Post Point—*summit* OR-9
Post Point—*summit* WY-8
Post Polo Ranch—*other* SC-3
Post Pond—*bay* LA-4
Post Pond—*lake* NH-1
Post Pond—*reservoir* CT-1
Post Pond—*reservoir* PA-2
Post Pond Dam—*dam* PA-2
Post Post Office (historical)—*building* MS-4
Post Post Office (historical)—*building* TN-4
Post Ranch—*locale* AZ-5
Post Ranch—*locale* NM-5
Post Ridge—*ridge* CO-8
Post River—*stream* AK-9
Post Road Sch—*school* NY-2
Post Road Shop Ctr—*locale* MA-1
**Posts**—*pop pl* CA-9
*Post Saint Ange* IN-6
Posts Brook—*stream* NJ-2
Post Sch—*school* AZ-5
Post Sch—*school* AR-4
Post Sch—*school* CA-9
Post Sch—*school* (3) MI-6
Post Sch—*school* NE-7
Post Sch—*school* NY-2
Post Sch—*school* OR-9
Post Sch—*school* TX-5
Post Southeast (CCD)—*cens area* TX-5
Post Spring—*spring* NV-8
Post Spring—*spring* OR-9
*Posts Summit* CA-9
Post Street Tot Lot Park—*park* UT-8
Post Summit—*summit* CA-9
Post Sunny View Cem—*cemetery* ME-1
Post Tank—*reservoir* NM-5
Post Town—*locale* MN-6
**Post Town**—*pop pl* (2) OH-6
Post Township—*fmr MCD* IA-7
Post Township Cem—*cemetery* IA-7
Post Trader's Store and Riallito House—*hist pl* AZ-5
Post Trader's Storehouse—*hist pl* AZ-5
**Post Trailer Park**—*pop pl* LA-4
Postun Bayou—*gut* FL-3
*Postville* ND-7
Postville—*locale* NJ-2
**Postville**—*pop pl* IA-7
**Postville**—*pop pl* WI-6
Postville Cem—*cemetery* WI-6
Postville Ch—*church* NE-7
Postville Sch—*school* NE-7
*Post Vincennes* IN-6
Post Well—*well* AZ-5
Post West Dugout—*hist pl* TX-5
Post-Williams House—*hist pl* NY-2
Postwood Park—*park* NY-2
Post 22-C Lateral—*canal* MT-8
Post 7-D Ditch—*canal* MT-8
Posuk, Unun En—*bar* FM-9
Posvar Ranch—*locale* WY-8
*Posy* MP-9
*Posy Creek* MI-6
*Posy Creek* WY-8
Posy Creek—*stream* MT-8
Posy Lake—*lake* UT-8
Posy Lake Campground—*park* UT-8
Posy Mtn—*summit* AR-4
Posy Spring—*spring* MO-7
Posy Spring—*spring* UT-8
Posy Valley—*valley* OR-9
Posy Valley Ditch—*canal* OR-9
*Pot, The* ME-1
Pot, The—*area* TN-4
Pot, The—*basin* OR-9
Potacocawa Creek Structure Y-3la-17 Dam—*dam* MS-4
Potacocawa Structure Y-31a-34 Dam—*dam* MS-4
Potacocawa Watershed Y-3la-1 Dam—*dam* MS-4
Potacocawa Watershed Y-3la-2 Dam—*dam* MS-4
Potacocawa Watershed Y-31a-13 Dam—*dam* MS-4
Potacocawa Creek—*stream* MS-4
Potacocawa Creek Watershed Y-31a-26 Dam—*dam* MS-4
*Potacocawah Creek* MS-4
Potacocawa Structure Y-31a-5 Dam—*dam* MS-4
Potacocawa Watershed Y-3la-18 Dam—*dam* MS-4
Potacocawa Watershed Y-3la-28 Dam—*dam* MS-4
Potacocawa Watershed Y-31a-10 Dam—*dam* MS-4
Potacocawa Watershed Y-31a-11 Dam—*dam* MS-4
Potacocawa Watershed Y-31a-12 Dam—*dam* MS-4
Potacocawa Watershed Y-31a-15 Dam—*dam* MS-4
Potacocawa Watershed Y-31a-19 Dam—*dam* MS-4
Potacocawa Watershed Y-31a-20 Dam—*dam* MS-4
Potacocawa Watershed Y-31a-3 Dam—*dam* MS-4
Potacocawa Watershed Y-31a-4 Dam—*dam* MS-4
Potacocawa Watershed Y-31a-5 Dam—*dam* MS-4
Potacocawa Watershed Y-31a-6 Dam—*dam* MS-4
Potacocawa Watershed Y-31a-7 Dam—*dam* MS-4
Potacocawa Watershed Y-31a-9 Dam—*dam* MS-4
Potagannissing Bay—*bay* MI-6
Potagannissing River—*stream* MI-6
Potaka Grove Ch—*church* IN-6
*Potake Lake* NJ-2
*Potake Lake* NY-2
Potake Pond—*lake* NJ-2
Potake Pond—*reservoir* NY-2
**Potala**—*pop pl* PR-3
Potala Pastillo—*CDP* PR-3
*Potalca* FL-3
Potaman Creek—*stream* ID-8
Potaman Peak—*summit* ID-8
Potamogeton Park—*flat* MT-8
Potamo-Parke Cem—*cemetery* MN-6
Potamus Creek—*stream* OR-9
Potamus Point—*cliff* OR-9
Potamus Ridge—*ridge* OR-9
Potangeras—*island* FM-9
Potanipo Hill—*summit* NH-1
Potanipo Pond—*lake* NH-1
*Potanjaburo* MH-9
*Potanota Pond* NH-1
*Potanumaquit* MA-1
*Potanumaquut* MA-1
*Potaot Rock* UT-8
**Potapo**—*pop pl* OK-5
Potapo Creek—*stream* OK-5
Potash—*locale* AL-4
Potash—*locale* UT-8
**Potash**—*pop pl* LA-4
Potash Bay—*bay* VT-1
**Potash Bay**—*pop pl* VT-1
*Potash Brook* MA-1
Potash Brook—*stream* (2) CT-1
Potash Brook—*stream* (2) ME-1
Potash Brook—*stream* (11) MA-1
Potash Brook—*stream* NH-1
Potash Brook—*stream* (3) VT-1
Potash Cem—*cemetery* ME-1
Potash Ch—*church* AL-4
Potash Co of America Mine—*mine* NM-5
Potash Corner—*locale* NH-1
Potash Cove—*bay* ME-1
*Potash Creek* VA-3
Potash Creek—*stream* (2) NY-2
Potash Hill—*summit* (2) MA-1
Potash Hollow—*valley* (2) PA-2
Potash Hollow Run—*stream* PA-2
Potash Knob—*summit* NH-1
Potash Lake—*lake* NE-7
Potash Mtn—*summit* NH-1
Potash Mtn—*summit* (3) NY-2
Potash Mtn—*summit* PA-2
Potash Mtn—*summit* VT-1
Potash Oil and Gas Field—*oilfield* LA-4
*Potash Plant* UT-8
Potash Point—*cape* VT-1
**Potash Point**—*pop pl* VT-1
Potash Run—*stream* PA-2
Potash Trail—*trail* PA-2
Potash Wash—*valley* WY-8
Potash Well—*well* NM-5
*Potato Bay* CA-9
Potato Bill Creek—*stream* CO-8
Potato Bottom—*bend* UT-8
Potato Bottom Basin—*basin* UT-8
Potato Branch—*stream* KY-4
Potato Branch—*stream* MS-4
Potato Branch—*stream* NC-3
Potato Branch—*stream* WV-2
Potato Branch Hollow—*valley* TN-4
Potato Bug Hill—*summit* IN-6
Potato Butte—*summit* AZ-5
Potato Butte—*summit* CA-9
Potato Butte—*summit* CO-8
Potato Butte—*summit* OR-9
Potato Butte—*summit* SD-7
Potato Butte—*summit* WA-9
Potato Butte—*summit* WY-8
Potato Butte Draw—*valley* WY-8
Potato Butte Spring—*spring* WY-8
Potato Canyon—*valley* AZ-5
Potato Canyon—*valley* CA-9
Potato Canyon—*valley* CO-8
Potato Canyon—*valley* NV-8
Potato Canyon—*valley* (3) NM-5
Potato Canyon Spring—*spring* NV-8
Potato Cave—*cave* KY-4
Potato Cave—*cave* MO-7
Potato Cave Hollow—*valley* MO-7
Potato City Airp—*airport* PA-2
*Potato Creek* AL-4
*Potato Creek* IN-6
*Potato Creek* TN-4
*Potato Creek* UT-8
**Potato Creek**—*pop pl* SD-7
Potato Creek—*stream* (3) AK-9
Potato Creek—*stream* CA-9
Potato Creek—*stream* CO-8
Potato Creek—*stream* (3) GA-3
Potato Creek—*stream* (2) ID-8
Potato Creek—*stream* IN-6
Potato Creek—*stream* IA-7
Potato Creek—*stream* KS-7
Potato Creek—*stream* KY-4
Potato Creek—*stream* MI-6
Potato Creek—*stream* MN-6
Potato Creek—*stream* MS-4
Potato Creek—*stream* (2) NY-2
Potato Creek—*stream* NC-3
Potato Creek—*stream* OK-5
Potato Creek—*stream* PA-2
Potato Creek—*stream* SC-3
Potato Creek—*stream* (2) SD-7
Potato Creek—*stream* UT-8
Potato Creek—*stream* VA-3
Potato Creek—*stream* WA-9
Potato Creek—*stream* (3) WI-6
Potato Creek—*stream* (2) WY-8
Potato Creek Ch—*church* IN-6
Potato Creek Ch—*church* VA-3
Potato Creek Flowage—*lake* WI-6
**Potato Creek (Lasca)**—*pop pl* VA-3
Potato Creek Reservoir Dam—*dam* IN-6
Potato Creek State Park—*park* IN-6
*Potato Creek State Rec Area* IN-6
Potato Creek State Wildlife Mngmt Area—*park* WI-6
*Potato Draw* WY-8
Potato Draw—*valley* WY-8
**Potatoe**—*pop pl* TN-4
*Potatoe Creek* IN-6
Potatoe Creek—*stream* AL-4
Potatoe Creek—*stream* IA-7
Potatoe Hill—*summit* IL-6
*Potatoe Island* RI-1
*Potatoe Knob* NC-3
Potatoe Knob—*summit* KY-4
*Potatoe Lake* AZ-5
*Potatoe Lake* WI-6
Potatoe Lake—*lake* OR-9
*Potatoe Lakes* MT-8
*Potatoe Point* RI-1
Potato Field Draw—*valley* AZ-5
Potato Field Gap—*gap* NC-3
Potato Flats—*flat* TX-5
Potato Fork—*stream* WV-2
Potato Gap—*gap* (2) NC-3
Potato Garden Run—*stream* PA-2
Potato Garden Valley—*valley* AZ-5
Potato Gulch—*valley* (2) CO-8
Potato Gulch—*valley* (2) MT-8
Potato Gulch—*valley* SD-7
Potato Harbor—*bay* CA-9
*Potato Hill* AR-4
*Potato Hill* OR-9
*Potato Hill* VT-1
*Potato Hill* WV-2
Potato Hill—*summit* (3) AL-4
Potato Hill—*summit* AZ-5
Potato Hill—*summit* (5) AR-4
Potato Hill—*summit* (6) CA-9
Potato Hill—*summit* (2) CO-8
Potato Hill—*summit* (3) GA-3
Potato Hill—*summit* HI-9
Potato Hill—*summit* (3) ID-8
Potato Hill—*summit* (2) IL-6
Potato Hill—*summit* (2) KS-7
Potato Hill—*summit* (4) KY-4
Potato Hill—*summit* LA-4
Potato Hill—*summit* (2) ME-1
Potato Hill—*summit* MS-4
Potato Hill—*summit* (3) NH-1
Potato Hill—*summit* NY-2
Potato Hill—*summit* (3) NC-3
Potato Hill—*summit* ND-7
Potato Hill—*summit* (3) OK-5
Potato Hill—*summit* (3) OR-9
Potato Hill—*summit* PA-2
Potato Hill—*summit* SC-3
Potato Hill—*summit* (10) TN-4
Potato Hill—*summit* (4) TX-5
Potato Hill—*summit* (2) UT-8
Potato Hill—*summit* (2) VA-3
Potato Hill—*summit* WA-9
Potato Hill—*summit* WV-2
Potato Hill—*summit* WI-6
Potato Hill Bald—*summit* NC-3
Potato Hill Bayou—*gut* MS-4
Potato Hill Branch—*stream* AR-4
Potato Hill Branch—*stream* GA-3
Potato Hill Cem—*cemetery* AL-4
*Potato Hill Church* AL-4
Potato Hill Guard Station—*locale* WA-9
Potato Hill Knob—*summit* KY-4
Potato Hill Knob—*summit* VA-3
Potato Hill Knobs—*range* VA-3
Potato Hill Lake—*reservoir* NC-3
Potato Hill Landing—*locale* MS-4
Potato Hill Mtn—*summit* AL-4
Potato Hill Mtn—*summit* AR-4
Potato Hill Mtn—*summit* TN-4
Potato Hill Ridge—*ridge* KY-4
Potato Hill Rsvr—*reservoir* OR-9
Potato Hills—*bar* MS-4
Potato Hills—*range* OK-5
Potato Hill Sch—*school* NH-1
Potato Hill State For—*forest* NY-2
Potato Hole—*bay* ME-1
Potato Hole—*spring* UT-8
Potatohole Fork—*stream* WV-2
Potato Hole Knob—*summit* WV-2
Potato Hollow—*valley* (2) UT-8
Potato Illahe Mtn—*summit* OR-9
Potato Island—*island* CT-1
Potato Island—*island* (2) ME-1
Potato Island—*island* (2) MN-6
Potato Island—*island* NH-1
Potato Island—*island* RI-1
Potato Island—*island* SC-3
Potato Island—*locale* NJ-2
Potato Island—*summit* NJ-2
Potato Islands—*island* MN-6
Potato Knob—*summit* AL-4
Potato Knob—*summit* AR-4
Potato Knob—*summit* IN-6
Potato Knob—*summit* (7) KY-4
Potato Knob—*summit* (5) NC-3
Potato Knob—*summit* OH-6
Potato Knob—*summit* OK-5
Potato Knob—*summit* (5) TN-4
Potato Knob—*summit* (3) WV-2
Potato Knob Mtn—*summit* AR-4
Potato Knob Run—*stream* WV-2
Potato Knoll—*summit* KY-4
*Potato Lake* MN-6
*Potato Lake* OR-9
Potato Lake—*lake* (2) AZ-5
Potato Lake—*lake* CO-8
Potato Lake—*lake* (4) MN-6
Potato Lake—*lake* OR-9
Potato Lake—*lake* (2) WI-6
Potato Lake Draw—*valley* AZ-5
Potato Lakes—*lake* MT-8
Potato Lake Tank—*reservoir* AZ-5
Potato Ledge—*bar* ME-1
**Potato Mound**—*pop pl* IN-6
*Potato Mountain* OR-9
Potato Mountian—*summit* ID-8
Potato Mtn—*summit* AK-9
Potato Mtn—*summit* (2) CA-9
Potato Mtn—*summit* (2) CO-8
Potato Mtn—*summit* NM-5
Potato Neck—*cape* VA-3
Potato Nubble—*summit* ME-1
Potato Park—*flat* CO-8
Potato Patch—*area* (4) AZ-5
Potato Patch—*area* CA-9
Potato Patch—*flat* (2) AZ-5
Potato Patch—*flat* (2) CA-9
Potato Patch—*flat* NM-5
Potato Patch—*gap* NC-3
Potato Patch—*locale* (2) AZ-5
**Potato Patch**—*pop pl* NM-5
Potato Patch, The—*flat* CA-9
Potato Patch, The—*flat* NV-8
Potato Patch Bay—*swamp* FL-3
Potato Patch Branch—*stream* LA-4
Potato Patch Campground—*locale* CA-9
Potato Patch Campground—*locale* CO-8
Potato Patch Canyon—*valley* (2) NM-5
Potato Patch Creek—*stream* AL-4

Potato Patch Creek—*stream* ... CA-9
Potatopatch Creek—*stream* ... GA-3
Potato Patch Creek—*stream* ... OR-9
Potato Patch Draw—*valley* (2) ... AZ-5
Potatopatch Hollow—*valley* ... TN-4
Potatopatch Hollow Mine—*mine* ... TN-4
Potato Patch Lake—*lake* ... TX-5
Potato Patch Mine—*mine* ... OR-9
Potatopatch Mtn—*summit* ... GA-3
Potatopatch Mtn—*summit* ... VA-3
Potato Patch Rec Area—*park* ... AZ-5
Potato Patch Ridge—*ridge* ... LA-4
Potatopatch Shoal—*bar* ... CA-9
Potatopatch Spring—*spring* ... GA-3
Potato Patch Spring—*spring* (5) ... NV-8
Potato Patch Tank—*reservoir* (2) ... AZ-5
Potato Peak—*summit* ... CA-9
Potato Peaks—*summit* ... OK-5
*Potato Point* ... RI-1
Potato Point—*cape* ... AK-9
Potato Point—*cape* ... CA-9
Potato Point—*cape* ... ME-1
Potato Point—*cape* ... RI-1
Potato Pond—*bay* ... LA-4
Potato Pond Slough—*swamp* ... TX-5
Potato Rapids Dam—*dam* ... WI-6
Potato Ridge—*ridge* (2) ... AL-4
Potato Ridge—*ridge* ... TN-4
Potato Ridge—*ridge* ... WY-8
Potato River—*stream* ... MI-6
Potato River—*stream* ... MN-6
Potato River—*stream* ... WI-6
Potato River Falls—*falls* ... WI-6
Potato Rock—*pillar* ... UT-8
Potato Row—*ridge* ... WV-2
Potato Run—*stream* ... IN-6
Potato Run—*stream* ... OH-6
Potato Run—*stream* ... PA-2
Potato Run—*stream* (2) ... VA-3
Potato Run—*stream* ... WV-2
Potato Run Ch—*church* ... IN-6
Potato Slough—*gut* ... CA-9
Potato Spring—*spring* (2) ... NV-8
Potato Spring—*spring* ... SD-7
Potato Spring—*spring* ... TX-5
Potato Spring—*spring* ... UT-8
Potato Tank—*reservoir* (3) ... AZ-5
*Potato Top* ... SC-3
Potato Top—*summit* ... TN-4
*Potato Valley* ... UT-8
Potato Valley—*basin* ... AZ-5
Potato Valley—*basin* ... UT-8
Potato Valley—*valley* ... PA-2
Potato Valley—*valley* ... TN-4
**Potatoville**—*pop pl* ... FL-3
Potatoville RR Station (historical)—*locale* ... FL-3
Potato Wash—*stream* ... AZ-5
*Potawatamie Creek* ... KS-7
*Potawatami Falls* ... MI-6
*Potawatami Lake* ... IN-6
*Potawatami Park* ... IN-6
Potawatomi, Lake—*lake* ... IL-6
*Potawatomi Creek* ... KS-7
*Potawatomie Falls* ... MI-6
*Potawatomie Reservation* ... KS-7
*Potawatomies Creek* ... KS-7
Potawatomi Falls—*falls* ... MI-6
*Potawatomi Ind Res* ... KS-7
**Potawatomi Ind Res**—*pop pl* ... WI-6
**Potawatomi Inn**—*pop pl* ... IN-6
*Potawatomi Lake* ... IN-6
*Potawatomi Park* ... IN-6
**Potawatomi Park**—*pop pl* ... IN-6
**Potawatomi Point**—*pop pl* ... IN-6
*Potawatomi Reservation* ... KS-7
Potawatomi State Park—*park* ... WI-6
**Potawatomi Subdivision**—*pop pl* ... UT-8
Potawatomi Woods—*woods* ... IL-6
Potawatom Park—*park* ... IN-6
*Potawattomie Lake* ... IN-6
*Potawattomie Park* ... IN-6
*Potawotami Lake* ... IN-6
*Potawotami Park* ... IN-6
Potaywadjo Ridge—*ridge* ... ME-1
Pot Branch—*stream* ... NC-3
Pot Branch—*stream* ... TX-5
Pot Branch—*stream* ... WV-2
Potcamp Fork—*stream* ... VA-3
Pot Cem—*cemetery* ... TN-4
Pot Cove—*bay* ... NY-2
**Pot Cove**—*pop pl* ... LA-4
Pot Cove—*valley* ... NC-3
Pot Cove Gap—*gap* ... NC-3
*Pot Creek* ... UT-8
**Pot Creek**—*pop pl* ... NM-5
Pot Creek—*stream* ... AK-9
Pot Creek—*stream* ... CO-8
Pot Creek—*stream* (3) ... ID-8
Pot Creek—*stream* (3) ... OR-9
Pot Creek—*stream* (2) ... TX-5
Pot Creek—*stream* ... UT-8
Pot Creek—*stream* ... WY-8
Pot Creek Cabin—*locale* ... OR-9
Pot Creek Park—*flat* ... WY-8
Pot Creek Recreation Site—*park* ... UT-8
Pot Creek Trail—*trail* ... OR-9
Pot Dam—*dam* ... UT-8
Pote, Capt. Greenfield, House—*hist pl* ... ME-1
Poteat House—*hist pl* ... NC-3
**Poteau**—*pop pl* ... OK-5
Poteau (CCD)—*cens area* ... OK-5
Poteau Community Bldg—*hist pl* ... OK-5
Poteau Community Coll—*school* ... OK-5
*Poteau Creek* ... AR-4
Poteau Lookout Tower—*locale* ... AR-4
Poteau Mtn—*summit* ... AR-4
Poteau Mtn—*summit* ... OK-5
Poteau River—*stream* (2) ... AR-4
Poteau River—*stream* ... OK-5
Poteau Sch
Gymnasium-Auditorium—*hist pl* ... OK-5
*Potecase Bridge* ... NC-3
**Potecasi**—*pop pl* ... NC-3
Potecasi Creek—*stream* ... NC-3
**Poteet**—*pop pl* ... TX-5
Poteet Canyon—*valley* ... TX-5
Poteet (CCD)—*cens area* ... TX-5
Poteet Cem—*cemetery* ... TX-5
Poteete Branch—*stream* ... GA-3
Poteete Cem—*cemetery* ... TN-4
Poteet Ferry Bridge—*bridge* ... VA-3
Poteet Ford—*locale* ... VA-3
Poteet Gap—*gap* ... TN-4
**Poteet (historical)**—*pop pl* ... TN-4
Poteet Hollow—*valley* ... KY-4
Poteet Post Office (historical)—*building* ... TN-4
Poteet Well—*well* ... NM-5
Potem Creek—*stream* ... CA-9
Potem Falls—*falls* ... CA-9
Potential Mine—*mine* ... NV-8
Potent Run—*stream* ... IN-6
*Poterf Creek* ... OR-9
*Poterfield Creek* ... MI-6
Poterfield Creek—*stream* ... MI-6
*Poters Canyon* ... UT-8
**Poteskeet Village**
**(subdivision)**—*pop pl* ... NC-3
**Potetown**—*pop pl* ... PA-2
*Potevin Ditch* ... ID-8
Potfish Lake—*lake* ... WI-6
Pot Flat—*flat* ... OR-9
Pot Fork—*stream* ... WV-2
Pot Gap Ridge—*ridge* ... GA-3
Pot Gut—*stream* ... NC-3
Pot Gut—*valley* ... UT-8
**Poth**—*pop pl* ... TX-5
Poth, Frederick A., Houses,—*hist pl* ... PA-2
Pot Hammock—*island* ... FL-3
Poth and Schmidt Development
Houses—*hist pl* ... PA-2
Poth Brook—*stream* ... NY-2
Poth (CCD)—*cens area* ... TX-5
Pot Head—*summit* ... ME-1
Pothier House—*hist pl* ... RI-1
Pot Hill—*summit* ... AK-9
Pot Hills—*range* ... WA-9
*Pothlochitto Creek* ... AL-4
Pothole—*basin* ... AZ-5
Pot Hole—*basin* ... CO-8
Pothole—*basin* ... OR-9
Pothole—*lake* ... AZ-5
Pothole, The—*basin* (3) ... CA-9
Pothole, The—*basin* ... NV-8
Pothole, The—*basin* ... OR-9
Pothole, The—*basin* ... WA-9
Pot Hole, The—*bend* ... TX-5
Pothole, The—*crater* ... ID-8
Pot Hole, The—*lake* ... MT-8
Pothole Arch—*arch* ... UT-8
Pot Hole Basin—*basin* ... ID-8
Pot Hole Butte—*summit* ... ID-8
Pothole Butte—*summit* ... OR-9
Pothole Camp—*locale* ... OR-9
Pothole Canyon—*valley* (2) ... AZ-5
Pothole Canyon—*valley* ... CA-9
Pothole Canyon—*valley* ... CO-8
Pot Hole Canyon—*valley* ... ID-8
Pothole Canyon—*valley* (2) ... NM-5
Pothole Canyon—*valley* ... UT-8
Pothole Canyon—*valley* ... WA-9
Pot Hole City Canyon—*valley* ... TX-5
Pothole Creek—*stream* (2) ... CA-9
Pot Hole Creek—*stream* ... ID-8
Pothole Creek—*stream* (3) ... OR-9
Pothole Creek—*stream* ... UT-8
Pothole Crossing—*locale* ... CA-9
Pothole Duck Club—*other* ... UT-8
Pothole Glacier—*glacier* ... AK-9
Pothole Gulch—*valley* ... CA-9
Pothole Hollow—*valley* ... MO-7
Pothole Lake—*lake* ... AK-9
Pothole Lake—*lake* ... AR-4
Pothole Lake—*lake* ... ID-8
Pothole Lake—*lake* ... MI-6
Pot Hole Lake—*lake* ... MN-6
Pothole Lake—*lake* ... MN-6
Pothole Lake—*lake* ... NM-5
Pothole Lake—*lake* (3) ... WA-9
Pothole Lake—*lake* ... WI-6
Pothole Meadow—*flat* (2) ... OR-9
Pothole Meadows—*flat* ... CA-9
Pot Hole Peak—*summit* ... AZ-5
Pothole Point—*cliff* ... AZ-5
Pothole Point—*locale* ... UT-8
*Pothole Pond* ... OR-9
*Pot Hole Rsvr* ... AZ-5
Pothole Rsvr—*reservoir* ... AZ-5
Pot Hole Rsvr—*reservoir* ... CO-8
Pothole Rsvr—*reservoir* ... ID-8
Pot Hole Rsvr—*reservoir* ... ID-8
Pothole Rsvr—*reservoir* (2) ... OR-9
Pothole Rsvr No 1—*reservoir* ... CO-8
Pothole Rsvr No 2—*reservoir* ... CO-8
*Pot Holes* ... AZ-5
Pot Holes—*area* ... WA-9
Pot Holes—*lake* ... ID-8
Pot Holes—*lake* ... UT-8
Potholes—*reservoir* ... AZ-5
*Potholes, The* ... WA-9
Potholes, The—*area* ... WA-9
Potholes, The—*area* ... WY-8
Potholes, The—*basin* ... CA-9
Potholes, The—*basin* (2) ... OR-9
Potholes, The—*lake* ... NV-8
Potholes, The—*lake* ... OR-9
Potholes, The—*lake* ... UT-8
Potholes, The—*lava* ... OR-9
Potholes, The—*other* ... ID-8
Potholes, The—*range* ... UT-8
Potholes, The—*spring* ... ID-8
*Potholes Cataract* ... WA-9
Potholes Cem—*cemetery* ... CA-9
Potholes Coulee—*valley* ... WA-9
Potholes Country—*area* ... NM-5
Potholes Creek Rsvr—*reservoir* ... OR-9
Potholes East Canal—*canal* ... WA-9
*Pot Hole Spring* ... OR-9
Pothole Spring—*spring* (2) ... AZ-5
Pothole Spring—*spring* (2) ... CA-9
Pot Hole Spring—*spring* ... CA-9
Pothole Spring—*spring* ... CA-9
Pothole Spring—*spring* (2) ... NV-8
Pothole Spring—*spring* (5) ... OR-9
Pothole Spring—*spring* ... WA-9
Pothole Spring, The—*spring* ... UT-8
Pot Hole Spring No 2—*spring* ... ID-8
Pothole Springs—*spring* ... OR-9
Pothole Springs—*spring* ... UT-8
Potholes Rsvr—*reservoir* ... WA-9
Potholes (Site)—*locale* ... CA-9
Potholes State Park—*park* ... WA-9
Potholes Substation—*other* ... WA-9
Pot Hole Tank—*reservoir* (2) ... AZ-5
Pothole Tank—*reservoir* ... AZ-5
Pot Hole Tank—*reservoir* ... AZ-5
Pothole Tank—*reservoir* ... AZ-5
Pot Hole Tank—*reservoir* ... AZ-5
Pothole Tank—*reservoir* ... AZ-5
Pot Hole Tank—*reservoir* ... AZ-5
Pot Hole Tank—*reservoir* ... NM-5
Pothole Tank—*reservoir* (4) ... NM-5
Pot Hole Tank—*reservoir* ... NM-5
Pothole Tank Number Four—*reservoir* ... AZ-5
Pothole Tank Number One—*reservoir* ... AZ-5
Pothole Tank Number Three—*reservoir* ... AZ-5
Pothole Trail—*trail* ... CA-9
Pothole Valley—*valley* ... CA-9
Pothole Well Guard Station—*locale* ... OR-9
Pot Hole Windmill—*locale* ... NM-5
Pot Hollow—*valley* (2) ... KY-4
Pot Hollow—*valley* ... OK-5
Pot Hollow—*valley* ... UT-8
Pothook—*locale* ... NM-5
Pot Hook Creek—*stream* ... DE-2
Poticaw Bayou—*stream* ... MS-4
Poticaw Landing—*locale* ... MS-4
Potic Creek—*stream* ... NY-2
Potic Mtn—*summit* ... NY-2
Potiller Cem—*cemetery* ... TN-4
Pot Island—*island* ... CT-1
Pot Island—*island* ... MD-2
Pot Island—*island* ... NH-1
Pot Island Creek—*stream* ... MD-2
*Pot Lake* ... UT-8
Pot Lake—*lake* ... ID-8
Pot Lake—*lake* ... MI-6
Pot Lake—*lake* ... MN-6
Pot Lake—*lake* ... MT-8
Pot Lake—*lake* (3) ... WI-6
**Potlatch**—*pop pl* ... ID-8
**Potlatch**—*pop pl* ... WA-9
Potlatch Canyon—*valley* ... OR-9
*Potlatch Creek* ... ID-8
Potlatch Creek—*stream* ... AK-9
Potlatch Grange—*locale* ... WA-9
**Potlatch Junction**—*pop pl* ... ID-8
Potlatch Ridge—*ridge* (2) ... ID-8
Potlatch River—*stream* ... ID-8
Potlicker Flats—*flat* ... PA-2
Pot Lick Hollow—*valley* ... PA-2
Potlick Point—*cliff* ... KY-4
Pot Lick Run—*stream* ... WV-2
Potlid Creek—*stream* ... OR-9
Potlikker Hill—*summit* ... GA-3
*Potlio Creek* ... OR-9
**Potlockney**—*pop pl* ... MS-4
Potlockney Creek—*stream* ... MS-4
Pot Log Branch—*stream* ... NC-3
*Potman Creek* ... OR-9
*Potman Lake* ... MI-6
Pot Mesa—*bench* ... NM-5
Potmesser Knob—*summit* ... KY-4
Pot Mountain Ridge—*ridge* ... ID-8
Pot Mtn—*summit* ... AR-4
Pot Mtn—*summit* ... ID-8
Pot Mtn—*summit* ... MT-8
Pot Mtn—*summit* ... UT-8
**Pot Neck**—*pop pl* ... NC-3
Potnero Well—*well* ... AZ-5
*Potnets* ... DE-2
Pot Nets Cove—*bay* ... DE-2
Pot Nets Point—*cape* ... DE-2
*Poto Chitto Creek* ... MS-4
Pot of Gold Tank—*reservoir* ... TX-5
*Potogannissing* ... MI-6
*Potomac* ... MD-2
Potomac—*locale* ... MD-2
**Potomac**—*pop pl* ... IL-6
**Potomac**—*pop pl* ... MD-2
**Potomac**—*pop pl* ... MT-8
**Potomac**—*pop pl* ... WV-2
Potomac—*uninc pl* ... VA-3
**Potomac Beach**—*pop pl* ... VA-3
Potomac Canal Hist Dist—*hist pl* ... MD-2
Potomac Canal Hist Dist—*hist pl* ... VA-3
Potomac Ch—*church* ... MD-2
Potomac Ch—*church* (3) ... VA-3
Potomac Creek—*stream* ... VA-3
Potomac Creek Site—*hist pl* ... VA-3
**Potomac Falls**—*pop pl* ... MD-2
**Potomac Green**—*pop pl* ... MD-2
**Potomac Heights**—*pop pl* ... DC-2
**Potomac Heights**—*pop pl* ... MD-2
Potomac Heights—*uninc pl* ... MD-2
Potomac Hill—*summit* ... MD-2
**Potomac Hills**—*pop pl* ... VA-3
Potomac HS—*school* ... MD-2
**Potomac Hunt Acres**—*pop pl* ... MD-2
Potomack Canal—*canal* ... WV-2
Potomac (Magisterial District)—*fmr MCD* ... VA-3
Potomac Manor—*locale* ... WV-2
**Potomac Manors**—*pop pl* ... MD-2
Potomac Mills—*locale* ... VA-3
Potomac Mills Pond—*reservoir* ... VA-3
Potomac Mills Shop Ctr—*locale* ... VA-3
Potomac Palisades Parkway—*park* ... DC-2
Potomac Palisades Site—*hist pl* ... DC-2
Potomac Park—*park* ... WV-2
**Potomac Park**—*pop pl* ... MD-2
Potomac Park-Bowling Green—*CDP* ... MD-2
*Potomac (Pinto)* ... MD-2
Potomac Post Office—*locale* ... MT-8
**Potomac Ranch**—*pop pl* ... MD-2
Potomac River—*stream* ... DC-2
Potomac River—*stream* ... MD-2
Potomac River—*stream* ... VA-3
Potomac River—*stream* ... WV-2
*Potomac Run* ... VA-3
**Potomac Run**—*pop pl* ... VA-3
Potomac Run—*stream* ... VA-3
Potomac Sch—*school* ... CA-9
Potomac Sch—*school* ... MD-2
Potomac Sch—*school* (2) ... VA-3
Potomac Shoreline Regional Park—*park* ... VA-3
**Potomac Shores**—*pop pl* (2) ... MD-2
Potomac State Coll—*school* ... WV-2
Potomac State For—*forest* ... MD-2
Potomac Valley—*locale* ... VA-3
**Potomac Valley**—*pop pl* ... MD-2
**Potomac Valley Junction (P.V.**
**Junction)**—*pop pl* ... MD-2
Potomac Valley Nursing Home—*hospital* ... MD-2
*Potomac View* ... MD-2
Potomac View—*locale* ... MD-2
Potomac View Sch—*school* ... VA-3
Potomac Wayside—*locale* ... VA-3
**Potomac Woods**—*pop pl* ... MD-2
Potomac Yard—*uninc pl* ... VA-3
Potomac Yards—*locale* ... VA-3
Potomska Point—*cape* ... MA-1
*Potomus Ridge* ... OR-9
Potoniek Lake—*lake* ... AK-9
*Potopot* ... FM-9
*Potosi* ... CO-8
*Potosi* ... KS-7
*Potosi* ... MS-4
Potosi—*hist pl* ... NV-8
Potosi—*locale* ... PA-2
**Potosi**—*pop pl* ... MO-7
**Potosi**—*pop pl* ... TX-5
**Potosi**—*pop pl* ... WI-6
**Potosia**—*pop pl* ... IA-7
Potosi Brewery—*hist pl* ... WI-6
Potosi Campground—*locale* ... MT-8
Potosi Cem—*cemetery* ... TX-5
Potosi Creek—*stream* ... CA-9
Potosi Creek—*stream* ... MT-8
Potosi Gulch—*valley* ... ID-8
Potosi (historical)—*locale* ... NV-8
Potosi Hot Springs—*spring* ... MT-8
Potosi Island—*island* ... GA-3
Potosi Lake—*reservoir* ... MO-7
Potosi Lookout Tower—*locale* ... MO-7
Potosi Mine—*mine* ... CA-9
Potosi Mine—*mine* (2) ... NV-8
Potosi Mtn—*summit* ... NV-8
Potosi Pass—*gap* ... NV-8
Potosi Peak—*summit* ... CO-8
Potosi Peak—*summit* ... MT-8
Potosi Ranger Station—*locale* ... MT-8
Potosi School (Abandoned)—*locale* ... TX-5
Potosi (Site)—*locale* (2) ... CA-9
Potosi Spring—*spring* ... NV-8
Potosi (Station)—*locale* ... WI-6
**Potosi (Town of)**—*pop pl* ... WI-6
**Potosi Township**—*pop pl* ... KS-7
Potosi Wash—*stream* ... NV-8
*Pototot* ... FM-9
*Potowanek* ... IA-7
*Potowatomie Falls* ... MI-6
*Potowomut* ... RI-1
**Potowomut**—*pop pl* ... RI-1
Potowomut Neck—*cape* ... RI-1
*Potowomut Point* ... RI-1
Potowomut Pond—*lake* ... RI-1
Potowomut Pond—*reservoir* ... RI-1
Potowomut Pond Dam—*dam* ... RI-1
Potowomut River—*stream* ... RI-1
Potowomut Rocks—*pillar* ... RI-1
*Potowoome Neck* ... RI-1
Pot Peak—*summit* ... WA-9
Pot Pie Hollow—*valley* ... PA-2
Potpie Run—*stream* ... OH-6
Potpie Spring—*spring* ... PA-2
Pot Point—*cape* ... NM-5
Pot Point—*cape* ... TN-4
Pot Pond—*reservoir* ... GA-3
Potpourri Shop Ctr—*locale* ... MA-1
*Potquient Brook* ... RI-1
Pot Rack Creek—*stream* ... TX-5
Potranca Creek—*stream* ... TX-5
Potrancas, Loma de las—*summit* ... TX-5
**Potrero**—*pop pl* ... CA-9
Potrero—*uninc pl* ... CA-9
Potrero, The—*flat* ... CA-9
Potrero Arriba Tank—*reservoir* ... TX-5
Potrero Canyon—*valley* ... AZ-5
Potrero Canyon—*valley* (3) ... CA-9
Potrero Canyon Trail—*trail* ... CA-9
Potrero Cercado, Loma del—*summit* ... TX-5
Potrero Chico—*civil* ... CA-9
Potrero Cortado—*summit* ... TX-5
*Potrero Cortados* ... TX-5
Potrero Creek—*stream* ... AZ-5
Potrero Creek—*stream* (6) ... CA-9
Potrero De Felipe Lugo—*civil* ... CA-9
*Potrero de la Canela* ... TX-5
*Potrero de las Cabuyas* ... TX-5
*Potrero de las Canales* ... TX-5
Potrero de las Canelas—*summit* ... TX-5
Potrero De Las Cienega—*civil* ... CA-9
*Potrero de los Caballos* ... TX-5
Potrero de los Caballos—*summit* ... TX-5
*Potrero de los Cabritos* ... TX-5
Potrero De Los Cerritos—*civil* ... CA-9
Potrero De San Luis Obispo—*civil* ... CA-9
**Potrero District**—*pop pl* ... CA-9
Potrero El Cariso—*civil* ... CA-9
Potrero Farias—*summit* ... TX-5
*Potrero Favias* ... TX-5
Potrero Grande—*civil* ... CA-9
Potrero Grande—*summit* ... TX-5
Potrero Heights Sch—*school* ... CA-9
Potrero Hill—*summit* ... CA-9
Potrero Hills—*range* ... CA-9
Potrero John Creek—*stream* ... CA-9
*Potrero Largo* ... TX-5
*Potrero las Canelas* ... TX-5
*Potrero Lopena* ... TX-5
*Potrero Lopeno* ... TX-5
Potrero Lopeno—*summit* ... TX-5
*Potrero los Caballo* ... TX-5
*Potrero los Caballos* ... TX-5
Potrero Los Pinos—*civil* ... CA-9
Potrero Meadows—*flat* ... CA-9
Potrero Number One Well—*well* ... TX-5
Potrero Number Two Windmill—*locale* ... TX-5
Potrero Peak—*summit* (2) ... CA-9
*Potrero Point* ... CA-9
Potrero Point—*cape* ... CA-9
Potrero Sch—*school* ... CA-9
Potrero Seco—*flat* ... CA-9
Potrero Spring—*spring* ... CA-9
Potrero Spring—*spring* ... NM-5
Potrero Valley—*valley* ... CA-9
Potrero Valley Creek—*stream* ... CA-9
Potrero Windmill—*locale* ... TX-5
Potrero Y Rincon De San Padro De
Reglado—*civil* ... CA-9
Pot Ridge—*ridge* ... PA-2
Potrillo—*locale* ... NM-5
Potrillo Canyon—*valley* ... NM-5
Potrillo Creek—*stream* ... NM-5
Potrillo Draw—*valley* ... NM-5
Potrillo Hill—*summit* ... NM-5
Potrillo Tank—*reservoir* ... NM-5
Potrios Windmill—*locale* ... TX-5
Pot Ripple Creek—*stream* ... KY-4
*Pot Rock* ... ME-1
Pot Rock—*island* ... ME-1
Potrock Bald—*summit* ... NC-3
Potrock Branch—*stream* ... NC-3
Pot Rock Hollow—*valley* ... IN-6
Potrock Run—*stream* ... WV-2
Potrock Well—*well* ... TX-5
Pot Rsvr—*reservoir* ... UT-8
Pots, The—*bay* ... RI-1
Pots Branch—*stream* ... NC-3
**Potsdam**—*pop pl* ... MN-6
**Potsdam**—*pop pl* ... NY-2
**Potsdam**—*pop pl* ... OH-6
Potsdam Country Club—*other* ... NY-2
**Potsdam (Town of)**—*pop pl* ... NY-2
**Potsdam Township**—*pop pl* ... ND-7
*Potsh Creek* ... SC-3
Pot Shoals Creek—*stream* ... AR-4
Potshot Creek—*stream* ... MT-8
Potshot Lake—*lake* (2) ... MN-6
Potshot Lake (Unorganized Territory
of)—*unorg* ... MN-6
Pots Lake—*lake* ... MI-6
*Pot Slough* ... AR-4
**Pots Nets North (trailer**
**park)**—*pop pl* ... DE-2
**Pot Spring**—*pop pl* ... MD-2
Pot Spring—*spring* ... NV-8
*Pot Springs* ... NV-8
Pots Sum Pa Spring—*spring* ... UT-8
Pot Tank—*reservoir* ... AZ-5
Pottapaug Hill—*summit* ... MA-1
Pottapaug Pond—*bay* ... MA-1
*Pottaquattuck Hill* ... MA-1
Pottawatomie, Lake—*reservoir* ... MO-7
Pottawatomie Baptist Mission Bldg and Site
(Boundary Increase)—*hist pl* ... KS-7
Pottawatomie Ch—*church* ... TX-5
Pottawatomie County—*civil* ... KS-7
**Pottawatomie (County)**—*pop pl* ... OK-5
Pottawatomie County
Courthouse—*hist pl* ... OK-5
*Pottawatomie County State Fishing Lake* ... KS-7
Pottawatomie County State Park Number
One—*park* ... KS-7
Pottawatomie Creek—*stream* ... KS-7
Pottawatomie Creek—*stream* ... OH-6
Pottawatomie Creek—*stream* ... TX-5
Pottawatomie Creek Bridge—*hist pl* ... KS-7
Pottawatomie (historical)—*locale* (2) ... KS-7
Pottawatomie Indian Pay Station—*hist pl* ... KS-7
**Pottawatomie Ind Res**—*pop pl* ... KS-7
*Pottawatomie Lake* ... IN-6
Pottawatomie Light—*locale* ... WI-6
Pottawatomie Lighthouse—*hist pl* ... WI-6
Pottawatomie Mission Ch—*church* ... KS-7
Pottawatomie Number One State Fishing Lake
and Wildlife Area—*park* ... KS-7
*Pottawatomie Park* ... IN-6
Pottawatomie Park—*park* ... IL-6
Pottawatomie Sch—*school* ... IL-6
Pottawatomie State Fishing Lake Number
Two—*park* ... KS-7
**Pottawatomie Township**—*pop pl* (3) ... KS-7
Pottawatomi Ind Res—*reserve* ... KS-7
Pottawattami County Home—*building* ... IA-7
*Pottawattamie* ... KS-7
Pottawattamie Country Club—*other* ... IN-6
Pottawattamie County Jail—*hist pl* ... IA-7
Pottawattamie County Sub
Courthouse—*hist pl* ... IA-7
*Pottawattamie Creek* ... KS-7
*Pottawattamie Hills* ... IL-6
Pottawattamie Lake—*lake* ... IN-6
Pottawattamie Park—*park* ... IN-6
*Pottawattamie Point* ... IN-6
Pottawattomie Bayou—*bay* ... MI-6
Pottawattomie Gun Club—*other* ... MI-6
*Pottawattomie Lake* ... IN-6
*Pottawattomie Park* ... IN-6
Pottawattomie Park—*park* ... IL-6
**Pottawattomie Park**—*pop pl* ... IN-6
*Pottawattomi Falls* ... MI-6
*Pottawottamie* ... KS-7
*Pottawottomie Lake* ... IN-6
*Pottawottomie Park* ... IN-6
Pott Bluff—*cliff* ... SC-3
Pott Creek—*stream* ... NC-3
Pottebaum Tank—*reservoir* ... AZ-5
Pottenger Run—*stream* ... OH-6
Pottens Brook—*stream* ... CT-1
Potte Point—*cape* ... AL-4
*Potter* ... RI-1
Potter—*locale* ... AK-9
Potter—*locale* ... GA-3
Potter—*locale* ... OK-5
Potter—*locale* ... OR-9
**Potter**—*pop pl* ... AL-4
**Potter**—*pop pl* ... AR-4
**Potter**—*pop pl* ... IA-7
**Potter**—*pop pl* ... KS-7
**Potter**—*pop pl* ... NE-7
**Potter**—*pop pl* ... NJ-2
**Potter**—*pop pl* ... NY-2
**Potter**—*pop pl* ... WI-6
Potter, Carl, Mound—*hist pl* ... OH-6
Potter, Dell, Ranch House—*hist pl* ... AZ-5
Potter, Ephraim B., House—*hist pl* ... NY-2
Potter, H. W., House—*hist pl* ... WA-9
Potter, Judge Joseph, House—*hist pl* ... NY-2
Potter, Lake—*lake* ... IL-6
Potter, William, House—*hist pl* ... IN-6
Potter Acad—*school* ... ME-1
*Potter Airfield* ... AZ-5
Potter-Allison Farm—*hist pl* ... PA-2
Potter Arroyo—*stream* ... NM-5
*Potter Bank* ... PA-2
Potter Basin—*basin* ... CO-8
Potter Bay—*bay* ... NY-2
Potter Bog—*swamp* ... ME-1
Potter Branch—*stream* (3) ... AR-4
Potter Branch—*stream* ... FL-3
Potter Branch—*stream* ... KY-4
Potter Branch—*stream* (3) ... MO-7
Potter Branch—*stream* (2) ... NC-3
Potter Branch—*stream* (2) ... TN-4
Potter Branch—*stream* ... VA-3
Potter Bridge—*bridge* ... IN-6
Potter Bridge—*other* ... MI-6
*Potter Brook* ... CT-1
**Potter Brook**—*pop pl* ... PA-2
Potter Brook—*stream* (2) ... ME-1
Potter Brook—*stream* ... MA-1
Potter Brook—*stream* ... NH-1
Potter Brook—*stream* (2) ... NY-2
Potter Brook—*stream* ... PA-2
Potter Brook—*stream* ... VT-1
Potter Butte—*summit* ... ID-8
Potter Butte—*summit* ... WY-8
Potter Canyon—*valley* ... AZ-5
Potter Canyon—*valley* ... CO-8
Potter Canyon—*valley* ... NM-5
Potter Canyon—*valley* (2) ... OR-9
Potter Canyon—*valley* ... UT-8
Potter/Casey Company Bldg—*hist pl* ... MN-6
Potter Cem—*cemetery* ... FL-3
Potter Cem—*cemetery* ... IL-6
Potter Cem—*cemetery* ... IN-6
Potter Cem—*cemetery* (3) ... KY-4
Potter Cem—*cemetery* ... ME-1
Potter Cem—*cemetery* ... MI-6
Potter Cem—*cemetery* (3) ... MO-7
Potter Cem—*cemetery* ... NH-1
Potter Cem—*cemetery* ... NY-2
Potter Cem—*cemetery* ... NC-3
Potter Cem—*cemetery* ... PA-2
Potter Cem—*cemetery* (6) ... TN-4
Potter Cem—*cemetery* ... TX-5
Potter Cem—*cemetery* ... WI-6
Potter Ch—*church* ... IL-6
Potter Ch—*church* ... MO-7
Potter Ch—*church* ... OK-5
Potter Chapel—*church* ... TN-4
Potter Chapel Sch—*school* ... TN-4
Potterchitto Creek—*stream* ... MS-4
Potter-Collyer House—*hist pl* ... RI-1
Potter Community Cem—*cemetery* ... NE-7
Potter Community Center—*building* ... GA-3
Potter Corners—*locale* ... NY-2
Potter County—*civil* ... SD-7
**Potter County**—*pop pl* ... PA-2
**Potter (County)**—*pop pl* ... TX-5
Potter County Courthouse—*hist pl* ... PA-2
Potter Cove—*bay* (3) ... RI-1
*Potter Creek* ... MT-8
*Potter Creek* ... PA-2
*Potter Creek* ... WA-9
Potter Creek—*bay* ... MD-2
Potter Creek—*stream* ... AK-9
Potter Creek—*stream* ... AR-4
Potter Creek—*stream* (2) ... CA-9
Potter Creek—*stream* (2) ... CO-8
Potter Creek—*stream* ... FL-3
Potter Creek—*stream* (2) ... ID-8
Potter Creek—*stream* ... LA-4
Potter Creek—*stream* ... MI-6
Potter Creek—*stream* (2) ... MS-4
Potter Creek—*stream* ... MO-7
Potter Creek—*stream* (5) ... MT-8
Potter Creek—*stream* ... NJ-2
Potter Creek—*stream* (2) ... NY-2
Potter Creek—*stream* ... NC-3
Potter Creek—*stream* ... OH-6
Potter Creek—*stream* (5) ... OR-9
Potter Creek—*stream* (2) ... PA-2
Potter Creek—*stream* (2) ... TN-4
Potter Creek—*stream* (2) ... TX-5
Potter Creek—*stream* ... VA-3
Potter Creek—*stream* ... WV-2
Potter Creek—*stream* ... WI-6
Potter Creek Cem—*cemetery* ... PA-2
Potter Creek Park—*park* ... TX-5
Potter Dam—*dam* ... MT-8
Potter Ditch—*canal* ... IN-6
Potter Ditch—*canal* ... OH-6
Potter Ditch No 2—*canal* ... CO-8
Potter Elem Sch—*school* ... FL-3
Potter Estate—*hist pl* ... MA-1
Potterf Creek—*stream* ... OR-9
Potter Field Cem—*cemetery* ... KY-4
Potter Flats—*flat* ... KY-4
Potter Flats—*flat* ... TX-5
Potter Flowage—*reservoir* ... WI-6
Potter Ford—*locale* (2) ... TN-4
*Potter Fork* ... KY-4
Potter Fork—*stream* ... KY-4
*Potter Fort* ... PA-2
Potter Gap—*gap* ... KY-4
Potter-Gray Sch—*school* ... KY-4
Potter Gulch—*valley* ... OR-9
Potter Hall—*hist pl* ... MD-2
Potter Highlands Hist Dist—*hist pl* ... CO-8
**Potter Hill**—*pop pl* ... NY-2
**Potter Hill**—*pop pl* ... RI-1
Potter Hill—*summit* ... AR-4
Potter Hill—*summit* (3) ... ME-1
Potter Hill—*summit* (2) ... MA-1
Potter Hill—*summit* (3) ... NY-2
Potter Hill—*summit* ... WA-9
Potter Hill Cem—*cemetery* ... NY-2
Potter Hill Dam—*dam* ... RI-1
**Potter (historical)**—*pop pl* ... OR-9
**Potter Hollow**—*pop pl* ... NY-2
Potter Hollow—*valley* (4) ... TN-4
Potter Hollow—*valley* ... VT-1
Potter House—*hist pl* ... FL-3
Potter Island—*island* ... IN-6
Potter Island—*island* ... NY-2
Potter JHS—*school* ... CA-9
**Potter Junction**—*pop pl* ... AR-4
Potter Knob—*summit* (2) ... TN-4
Potter Lake—*CDP* ... WI-6
Potter Lake—*lake* ... ID-8
Potter Lake—*lake* ... KS-7
Potter Lake—*lake* (4) ... MI-6
Potter Lake—*lake* ... NE-7
Potter Lake—*lake* ... PA-2
Potter Lake—*lake* ... UT-8
Potter Lake—*lake* ... WA-9
Potter Lake—*lake* (2) ... WI-6
Potter Lateral—*canal* ... AZ-5

Pratt, A. W., House—*hist pl* ... IA-7
Pratt, Capt. Josiah, House—*hist pl* ... MA-1
Pratt, Dexter, House—*hist pl* ... MA-1
Pratt, Dr. Ambrose, House—*hist pl* ... CT-1
Pratt, Hannah, House—*hist pl* ... WI-6
Pratt, Humphrey, Tavern—*hist pl* ... CT-1
Pratt, John A., House—*hist pl* ... WI-6
Pratt, John Fenton, Ranch—*hist pl* ... KS-7
Pratt, Miles, House—*hist pl* ... MA-1
Pratt, Mount—*summit* ... AK-9
Pratt, Orson, House—*hist pl* ... UT-8
Pratt, Read and Company Factory Complex—*hist pl* ... CT-1
Pratt, Stillman, House—*hist pl* ... MA-1
Pratt, Wallace, Lodge—*hist pl* ... TX-5
Pratt, Zadock, House—*hist pl* ... NY-2
*Pratt Airport* ... KS-7
Pratt And Ferris Ditch No 1—*canal* ... WY-8
Pratt And Ferris Ditch No 2—*canal* ... WY-8
Pratt And Ferris Ditch No 3—*canal* ... WY-8
Pratt Archeol Site—*hist pl* ... KS-7
Pratt Bayou—*bay* ... FL-3
Pratt Brake—*canal* ... LA-4
Pratt Branch—*stream* ... DE-2
Pratt Branch—*stream* (3) ... TN-4
Pratt Branch—*stream* (2) ... WV-2
Pratt Bridge—*bridge* ... MS-4
*Pratt Brook* ... MA-1
Pratt Brook—*stream* (2) ... ME-1
Pratt Brook—*stream* (2) ... MA-1
Pratt Butte—*summit* ... ID-8
Pratt Canal—*canal* ... WY-8
Pratt Canyon—*valley* ... AZ-5
Pratt Canyon—*valley* ... CA-9
Pratt Canyon—*valley* ... CO-8
Pratt Canyon—*valley* ... MT-8
Pratt Cave—*cave* ... TN-4
Pratt Cem—*cemetery* ... AL-4
Pratt Cem—*cemetery* (3) ... AR-4
Pratt Cem—*cemetery* ... CT-1
Pratt Cem—*cemetery* (2) ... IL-6
Pratt Cem—*cemetery* ... IN-6
Pratt Cem—*cemetery* ... KS-7
Pratt Cem—*cemetery* ... ME-1
Pratt Cem—*cemetery* (2) ... MO-7
Pratt Cem—*cemetery* (2) ... NH-1
Pratt Cem—*cemetery* (3) ... NY-2
Pratt Cem—*cemetery* ... OH-6
Pratt Cem—*cemetery* ... SC-3
Pratt Cem—*cemetery* (6) ... TN-4
Pratt Cem—*cemetery* ... TX-5
Pratt Cem—*cemetery* (2) ... WV-2
*Pratt Center* ... KS-7
Pratt Ch—*church* ... TN-4
Pratt Chapel—*church* ... TN-4
**Pratt City**—*pop pl* ... AL-4
Pratt City Sch—*school* ... AL-4
Pratt Cliff—*cliff* ... WA-9
**Prattco**—*pop pl* ... CA-9
*Pratt Community College* ... KS-7
Pratt Community Junior College—*Pratt Com* ... KS-7
Pratt Consolidated Mines (underground)—*mine* ... AL-4
Pratt Corner—*locale* ... ME-1
**Pratt Corners**—*pop pl* ... NY-2
Pratt Corner Sch—*school* ... ME-1
Pratt County—*civil* ... KS-7
Pratt County Fairgrounds—*locale* ... KS-7
Pratt County (historical)—*civil* ... SD-7
Pratt County Lake—*reservoir* ... KS-7
Pratt Court Baptist Ch—*church* ... AL-4
Pratt Cove—*bay* ... AK-9
Pratt Cove—*bay* ... CT-1
Pratt Cove—*bay* ... ME-1
*Pratt Creek* ... WI-6
Pratt Creek—*stream* ... AL-4
Pratt Creek—*stream* ... CO-8
Pratt Creek—*stream* ... ID-8
Pratt Creek—*stream* ... IA-7
Pratt Creek—*stream* ... KY-4
Pratt Creek—*stream* ... NV-8
Pratt Creek—*stream* ... NY-2
Pratt Creek—*stream* (3) ... WI-6
Pratt Creek Ch—*church* ... IA-7
Pratt Dam—*dam* ... RI-1
Pratt Ditch—*canal* ... IA-7
Pratt Drain—*canal* ... MI-6
Pratter Hollow—*valley* ... VA-3
Pratter Hollow—*valley* ... WV-2
Pratt Ferry Bridge—*bridge* ... AL-4
Pratt Ferry Cave—*cave* ... AL-4
Pratt Ferry (historical)—*locale* ... AL-4
Pratt Fork—*stream* ... KY-4
Pratt Free Sch—*school* ... MA-1
Prattham—*locale* ... NY-2
Pratt Hill—*summit* ... ME-1
Pratt Hill—*summit* (3) ... MA-1
Pratt Hill—*summit* ... OK-5
Pratt Hill Ch—*church* ... LA-4
Pratt Hist Dist—*hist pl* ... WV-2
Pratt Hollow—*valley* ... MD-2
Pratt Hollow—*valley* ... MA-1
Pratt Hollow—*valley* ... MO-7
Pratt Hollow—*valley* (2) ... PA-2
Pratt House—*hist pl* ... CT-1
Pratt House—*hist pl* ... MA-1
Pratt HS—*school* ... KS-7
Prattie Top—*bench* ... NM-5
*Pratti Island* ... OR-9
Pratt Institute—*school* ... NY-2
*Pratt Island* ... CT-1
Pratt Island—*island* ... ME-1
Pratt Island One—*island* ... CT-1
Pratt Island Two—*island* ... CT-1
Pratt Junction—*locale* ... WI-6
**Pratt Junction**—*pop pl* ... MA-1
*Pratt Lake* ... AZ-5
Pratt Lake—*lake* ... AZ-5
Pratt Lake—*lake* ... ID-8
Pratt Lake—*lake* ... IL-6
Pratt Lake—*lake* (2) ... ME-1
Pratt Lake—*lake* (4) ... MI-6
Pratt Lake—*lake* ... MT-8
Pratt Lake—*lake* ... WA-9
Pratt Lake—*lake* ... WI-6
Pratt Lake Creek—*stream* ... MI-6
Pratt Lake (historical)—*lake* ... IA-7
Pratt Lakes—*lake* ... WY-8
Pratt Lake Stream—*stream* ... ME-1
Pratt Lake Trail—*trail* ... WA-9
*Prattles Island* ... RI-1
Pratt Library—*building* ... MD-2
Pratt Lodge—*locale* ... TX-5
Pratt Memorial United Methodist Ch—*church* ... MS-4
*Pratt Mines* ... AL-4
Pratt Mines (underground)—*mine* ... AL-4
Pratt Mine (underground)—*mine* ... AL-4
Prattmont Baptist Ch—*church* ... AL-4
**Prattmont (subdivision)**—*pop pl* ... AL-4
Pratt Mtn—*summit* ... CA-9
Pratt Mtn—*summit* ... ME-1
Pratt Mtn—*summit* ... NH-1
Pratt Mtn—*summit* ... WA-9
Pratt Municipal Airp—*airport* ... KS-7
Pratt Number 1 Mine (underground)—*mine* ... AL-4
*Pratt Number 2 Mine* ... AL-4
*Pratt Number 4 Mine* ... AL-4
Pratton—*locale* ... CA-9
Pratt Park—*flat* ... AZ-5
**Pratt (Petersburg)**—*pop pl* ... KY-4
Pratt Place—*locale* ... CA-9
Pratt Point—*cape* ... AK-9
Pratt Point—*cape* ... ME-1
Pratt Pond—*lake* (2) ... MA-1
Pratt Pond—*lake* (2) ... NH-1
Pratt Pond—*reservoir* ... CT-1
Pratt Pond—*reservoir* ... RI-1
Pratt Pond Brook—*stream* ... NH-1
Pratt Pond Upper Dam—*dam* ... MA-1
Pratt Read Rsvr—*reservoir* ... CT-1
*Pratt Reed Rsvr* ... CT-1
Pratt River—*stream* ... WA-9
Pratt Rocks—*cliff* ... NY-2
Pratt Rsvr—*reservoir* ... AZ-5
Pratt Run—*stream* ... WV-2
Pratts—*locale* ... AL-4
Pratts—*locale* ... NY-2
Pratts—*locale* ... OH-6
Pratts—*locale* ... VA-3
**Pratts**—*pop pl* ... MS-4
Pratt Sandhills State Wildlife Mngmt Area—*park* ... KS-7
Pratt Sandhills Wildlife Area—*park* ... KS-7
Pratts Bluff—*cliff* ... WA-9
Pratts Branch—*stream* ... KY-4
Pratts Branch—*stream* ... NE-7
Pratts Bridge—*bridge* ... LA-4
Pratts Bridge—*bridge* ... MA-1
*Pratts Brook* ... ME-1
Pratts Brook—*stream* ... ME-1
Prattsburg—*locale* ... GA-3
**Prattsburg**—*pop pl* ... IN-6
**Prattsburg**—*pop pl* ... NY-2
Prattsburg Cem—*cemetery* ... KS-7
*Prattsburgh* ... KS-7
Prattsburg (historical)—*locale* ... KS-7
**Prattsburg (Town of)**—*pop pl* ... NY-2
*Pratts Canyon* ... CO-8
Pratts Cem—*cemetery* ... MS-4
Pratts Cem—*cemetery* ... NY-2
Pratts Ch—*church* ... MS-4
Pratt Sch—*school* ... AR-4
Pratt Sch—*school* (2) ... MA-1
Pratt Sch—*school* (2) ... MI-6
Pratt Sch—*school* ... MN-6
Pratt Sch—*school* ... OR-9
Pratt Sch—*school* ... SD-7
Pratt Sch—*school* ... VT-1
Pratt Sch—*school* ... WA-9
Pratt Sch (historical)—*school* ... MS-4
**Pratts Corner**—*pop pl* ... CT-1
**Pratts Corner**—*pop pl* (2) ... MA-1
Pratts Corners—*locale* ... NH-1
Pratts Creek—*stream* ... GA-3
Pratts Falls—*falls* ... NY-2
Pratts Falls County Park—*park* ... NY-2
**Pratts Fork**—*pop pl* ... OH-6
Pratts Fork—*stream* ... OH-6
*Pratts Hill* ... MA-1
**Pratts Hollow**—*pop pl* ... NY-2
Pratts Island—*island* ... ME-1
*Pratts Junction* ... MA-1
**Pratts Junction**—*pop pl* ... MA-1
Pratts Kindergarten—*school* ... FL-3
Pratts Mill Swamp—*swamp* ... VA-3
**Pratts (O'Neal)**—*pop pl* ... VA-3
*Pratts Point* ... VA-3
*Pratts Pond* ... MA-1
Pratts Pond—*lake* ... MA-1
Pratts Pond—*reservoir* ... MA-1
Pratts Pond Dam—*dam* ... MA-1
Pratt Spring—*spring* ... MO-7
Pratt Springs—*spring* ... NV-8
Pratts Rock—*summit* ... NH-1
Pratts Run—*stream* ... OH-6
*Pratts School* ... MS-4
Pratts Soda Lakes—*lake* ... WY-8
*Pratts Station* ... AL-4
**Pratts Subdivision**—*pop pl* (2) ... UT-8
Pratt Stream—*stream* ... ME-1
Pratt Street Hist Dist—*hist pl* ... CT-1
Pratt Street Power Plant—*hist pl* ... MD-2
Prattsville—*locale* ... UT-8
**Prattsville**—*pop pl* ... AR-4
**Prattsville**—*pop pl* ... NY-2
**Prattsville**—*pop pl* ... OH-6
Prattsville Canal—*canal* ... UT-8
**Prattsville (Town of)**—*pop pl* ... NY-2
Pratts Wayne Woods For Preserve—*forest* ... IL-6
Pratt-Tabor House—*hist pl* ... MN-6
*Pratt Tank* ... AZ-5
Pratt Tank—*lake* ... AZ-5
Pratt Tank—*reservoir* ... AZ-5
Pratt (Town of)—*other* ... WI-6
Pratt Township—*civil* ... SD-7
**Pratt Township**—*pop pl* ... ND-7
**Pratt Township**—*pop pl* ... SD-7
Pratt Township No. 10—*civ div* ... KS-7
Pratt Township No. 11—*civ div* ... KS-7
Pratt Township No. 12—*civ div* ... KS-7
Pratt Township No. 6—*civ div* ... KS-7
Pratt Township No. 7—*civ div* ... KS-7
Pratt Township No. 8—*civ div* ... KS-7
Pratt Township No. 9—*civ div* ... KS-7
Pratt Trail—*trail* ... CA-9
Pratt Turner Dam—*dam* ... AL-4
Pratt Valley—*basin* ... NE-7
Pratt Valley—*valley* ... CA-9
Prattville—*locale* ... PA-2
Prattville—*locale* ... TX-5
**Prattville**—*pop pl* ... AL-4
**Prattville**—*pop pl* ... CA-9
**Prattville**—*pop pl* ... MA-1
**Prattville**—*pop pl* ... MI-6
**Prattville**—*pop pl* ... OK-5
Prattville Alliance Ch—*church* ... AL-4
Prattville (CCD)—*cens area* ... AL-4
Prattville Cem—*cemetery* ... MI-6
Prattville Ch—*church* ... AL-4
Prattville Ch of Christ—*church* ... AL-4
Prattville Ch of God—*church* ... AL-4
Prattville City Hall—*building* ... AL-4
Prattville Community Ch—*church* ... AL-4
Prattville Country Club—*locale* ... AL-4
Prattville Division—*civil* ... AL-4
Prattville Drain—*stream* ... MI-6
Prattville East Shop Ctr—*locale* ... AL-4
Prattville Elem Sch—*school* ... AL-4
Prattville HS—*school* ... AL-4
Prattville Industrial Board Waste Pond—*reservoir* ... AL-4
Prattville Intermediate Sch—*school* ... AL-4
Prattville Junction—*locale* ... AL-4
Prattville Lake Dam—*dam* ... AL-4
Prattville Landfill—*locale* ... AL-4
Prattville Missionary Baptist Ch—*church* ... AL-4
Prattville Park—*park* ... AL-4
Prattville Plaza Shop Ctr—*locale* ... AL-4
Prattville Primary Sch—*school* ... AL-4
*Prattville Public Sch* ... AL-4
Prattville Sch—*school* ... MA-1
Prattville Sch—*school* ... MI-6
Prattville Sch (historical)—*school* ... AL-4
Prattville Square Shop Ctr—*locale* ... AL-4
Pratt Well—*well* ... WY-8
Pratt Windmill—*locale* ... TX-5
**Pratum**—*pop pl* (2) ... OR-9
Pratum Cem—*cemetery* ... OR-9
*Pratville* ... CA-9
Praul Ditch—*canal* ... IN-6
*Praul Island* ... PA-2
*Prause Lake* ... MI-6
Prava Peak—*summit* ... OR-9
Prava Peak Rsvr Number Four—*reservoir* ... OR-9
Prava Peak Rsvr Number One—*reservoir* ... OR-9
Prava Peak Rsvr Number Three—*reservoir* ... OR-9
Prava Peak Rsvr Number Two—*reservoir* ... OR-9
Pravo—*locale* ... OH-6
Pray—*locale* ... MT-8
**Pray**—*pop pl* ... WI-6
Pray Cem—*cemetery* ... MI-6
*Pray Cemetery* ... MS-4
Prayer and Faith Ch—*church* ... WV-2
Prayer Ch—*church* ... MI-6
*Prayer Creek* ... TX-5
Prayer Creek—*stream* ... MT-8
Prayer Lake—*lake* ... MN-6
*Prayer Mount Ch* ... MS-4
Prayer Rock—*summit* ... PA-2
*Prayer Rocks* ... PA-2
Pray Hill—*summit* ... ME-1
Pray Hill—*summit* ... NH-1
Pray Hill—*summit* ... NY-2
Pray Hill—*summit* ... RI-1
Praying Monk, The—*summit* ... AZ-5
Pray Lake—*lake* ... MT-8
Pray Pond—*reservoir* ... NY-2
Pray Run—*stream* ... PA-2
Prays Brook—*stream* (2) ... ME-1
Pray Siding—*locale* ... MT-8
Prays Mill Ch—*church* ... GA-3
Prays Pond—*lake* ... FL-3
Pray-Starkweather House—*hist pl* ... OH-6
*Pray Station* ... MT-8
*Praythor Creek* ... OR-9
Praytor Mtn—*summit* ... AL-4
*P R Canyon* ... UT-8
PR Canyon—*valley* ... UT-8
Preacher Berry Creek—*stream* ... AR-4
Preacher Brook—*stream* ... PA-2
Preacher Bryant Pond—*lake* ... FL-3
Preacher Canyon—*valley* (2) ... AZ-5
Preacher Canyon—*valley* ... SD-7
Preacher Canyon—*valley* ... UT-8
Preacher Creek—*stream* ... AK-9
Preacher Creek—*stream* (2) ... ID-8
Preacher Creek—*stream* ... KY-4
Preacher Creek—*stream* ... MT-8
Preacher Creek—*stream* (2) ... OK-5
Preacher Creek—*stream* ... OR-9
Preacher Creek—*stream* ... VA-3
Preacher Creek—*stream* ... WA-9
Preacher Creek—*stream* ... WY-8
Preacher Draw—*valley* ... MT-8
Preacher Draw—*valley* ... WY-8
Preacher Estes Mtn—*summit* ... KY-4
Preacher Flat—*flat* ... OR-9
Preacher Gulch—*valley* ... CA-9
Preacher Gulch—*valley* ... CO-8
Preacher Hill—*summit* ... PA-2
Preacher Hole—*bay* ... FL-3
Preacher Hollow—*valley* ... WY-8
Preacher Lake—*lake* (2) ... MI-6
Preacher Meadow—*flat* ... CA-9
Preacher Meadow Camp Ground—*locale* ... CA-9
Preacher Mtn—*summit* ... ID-8
Preacher Mtn—*summit* ... MT-8
Preacher Mtn—*summit* ... NM-5
Preacher Mtn—*summit* ... WA-9
Preacher Park—*flat* ... WY-8
Preacher Rapids—*rapids* ... WA-9
Preacher Rock ( Campground)—*locale* ... WY-8
Preachers Bay—*bay* ... FL-3
Preachers Cabin—*locale* ... CO-8
Preachers Camp Area—*locale* ... PA-2
Preachers Cove—*valley* ... ID-8
Preachers Creek—*stream* ... TX-5
Preachers Hill—*summit* ... MI-6
Preachers Hole—*basin* ... CO-8
Preachers Hole—*gut* ... FL-3
Preachers Island—*island* (2) ... FL-3
Preachers Mine—*mine* ... NV-8
Preacher Smith Monument—*locale* ... SD-7
Preachers Peak—*summit* ... CA-9
Preachers Peak—*summit* ... OR-9
Preachers Point—*cape* ... WA-9
Preachers Point—*summit* ... NM-5
Preacher Spring—*spring* ... AZ-5
Preacher Spring—*spring* ... SD-7
Preachers Run—*stream* ... SD-7
Preachers Slough—*locale* ... WA-9
Preachers Slough—*stream* ... WA-9
Preachersville—*locale* ... KY-4
Preacher Tank—*reservoir* (2) ... NM-5
Preacher Tank—*reservoir* ... TX-5
Preacher Well—*well* ... NM-5
Preakness—*post sta* ... NJ-2
Preakness Brook—*stream* ... NJ-2
Preakness Ch—*church* ... NJ-2
Preakness Hills Country Club—*other* ... NJ-2
Preakness Mtn—*summit* ... NJ-2
Preakness Sch—*school* ... NJ-2
Preakness Valley—*valley* ... NJ-2
Preakness Valley Park—*park* ... NJ-2
Preasley Branch—*stream* ... TN-4
Prebble Cem—*cemetery* ... VA-3
*Prebble Point* ... ME-1
Prebble Rsvr—*reservoir* ... CO-8
Prebbles Point—*cape* ... ME-1
Preble—*locale* ... NV-8
Preble—*locale* ... TX-5
**Preble**—*pop pl* ... IN-6
**Preble**—*pop pl* ... NY-2
**Preble**—*pop pl* ... WI-6
Preble—*uninc pl* ... WI-6
Preble Ave Station—*building* ... PA-2
Preble Cem—*cemetery* ... ME-1
Preble Corner—*locale* ... ME-1
**Preble (County)**—*pop pl* ... OH-6
Preble Cove—*bay* (2) ... ME-1
Preble Hill—*summit* ... ME-1
Preble Hill—*summit* ... NY-2
Preble Island—*island* ... ME-1
Preble Mtn—*summit* ... NV-8
Preble Park—*park* ... WI-6
Preble Peak—*summit* ... AK-9
Preble Point—*cape* ... ME-1
*Prebles Cove* ... ME-1
**Preble (Town of)**—*pop pl* ... NY-2
**Preble (Township of)**—*pop pl* ... IN-6
**Preble (Township of)**—*pop pl* ... MN-6
Prebyterian Cem—*cemetery* ... PA-2
Precept—*locale* ... NE-7
Preceptor Point—*cape* ... ID-8
Precept Sch—*school* ... NE-7
Prechtle Gulch—*valley* ... CO-8
*Preciena Canyon* ... AZ-5
Precifa Well—*well* ... TX-5
**Precinct**—*pop pl* ... MA-1
Precinct B—*fmr MCD* ... NE-7
Precinct C—*fmr MCD* ... NE-7
Precinct D—*fmr MCD* ... NE-7
Precinct E—*fmr MCD* ... NE-7
Precinct F—*fmr MCD* ... NE-7
Precinct G—*fmr MCD* ... NE-7
Precinct H—*fmr MCD* ... NE-7
Precinct I—*fmr MCD* ... NE-7
Precinct J—*fmr MCD* ... NE-7
Precinct K—*fmr MCD* ... NE-7
Precinct M, Beaver Crossing—*fmr MCD* ... NE-7
Precinct M, Cordova—*fmr MCD* ... NE-7
Precinct N—*fmr MCD* ... NE-7
Precinct O—*fmr MCD* ... NE-7
*Precinct of Cape Cod* ... MA-1
Precinct P—*fmr MCD* ... NE-7
Precinct Sch—*school* ... LA-4
Precinct 1—*fmr MCD* ... NE-7
Precinct 1, Pawnee No. 1—*fmr MCD* ... NE-7
Precinct 1 (Election Precinct)—*fmr MCD* ... IL-6
Precinct 10—*fmr MCD* ... NE-7
Precinct 10 (Election Precinct)—*fmr MCD* ... IL-6
Precinct 11—*fmr MCD* ... NE-7
Precinct 11 (Election Precinct)—*fmr MCD* ... IL-6
Precinct 12—*fmr MCD* ... NE-7
Precinct 12 (Election Precinct)—*fmr MCD* ... IL-6
Precinct 13—*fmr MCD* ... NE-7
Precinct 13 (Election Precinct)—*fmr MCD* ... IL-6
Precinct 14—*fmr MCD* ... NE-7
Precinct 14 (Election Precinct)—*fmr MCD* ... IL-6
Precinct 15—*fmr MCD* ... NE-7
Precinct 15 (Election Precinct)—*fmr MCD* ... IL-6
Precinct 16—*fmr MCD* ... NE-7
Precinct 16 (Election Precinct)—*fmr MCD* ... IL-6
Precinct 17—*fmr MCD* ... NE-7
Precinct 17 (Election Precinct)—*fmr MCD* ... IL-6
Precinct 18—*fmr MCD* ... NE-7
Precinct 18 (Election Precinct)—*fmr MCD* ... IL-6
Precinct 19—*fmr MCD* ... NE-7
Precinct 19 (Election Precinct)—*fmr MCD* ... IL-6
Precinct 2—*fmr MCD* ... NE-7
Precinct 2, Pawnee No. 2—*fmr MCD* ... NE-7
Precinct 2 (Election Precinct)—*fmr MCD* ... IL-6
Precinct 20—*fmr MCD* ... NE-7
Precinct 20 (Election Precinct)—*fmr MCD* ... IL-6
Precinct 21—*fmr MCD* ... NE-7
Precinct 21 (Election Precinct)—*fmr MCD* ... IL-6
Precinct 22 (Election Precinct)—*fmr MCD* ... IL-6
Precinct 23 (Election Precinct)—*fmr MCD* ... IL-6
Precinct 3—*fmr MCD* ... NE-7
Precinct 3, Table Rock—*fmr MCD* ... NE-7
Precinct 3 (Election Precinct)—*fmr MCD* ... IL-6
Precinct 4—*fmr MCD* ... NE-7
Precinct 4, Steinauer—*fmr MCD* ... NE-7
Precinct 4 (Election Precinct)—*fmr MCD* ... IL-6
Precinct 5—*fmr MCD* ... NE-7
Precinct 5, Burchard—*fmr MCD* ... NE-7
Precinct 5 (Election Precinct)—*fmr MCD* ... IL-6
Precinct 6—*fmr MCD* ... NE-7
Precinct 6, South Fork—*fmr MCD* ... NE-7
Precinct 6 (Election Precinct)—*fmr MCD* ... IL-6
Precinct 7—*fmr MCD* ... NE-7
Precinct 7, Turkey Creek—*fmr MCD* ... NE-7
Precinct 7 (Election Precinct)—*fmr MCD* ... IL-6
Precinct 8—*fmr MCD* ... NE-7
Precinct 8 (Election Precinct)—*fmr MCD* ... IL-6
Precinct 9—*fmr MCD* ... NE-7
Precinct 9a—*fmr MCD* ... NE-7
Precinct 9 (Election Precinct)—*fmr MCD* ... IL-6
Precint Ridge—*ridge* ... IN-6
Precious Blood Cem—*cemetery* ... MA-1
Precious Blood Cem—*cemetery* ... OH-6
Precious Blood Convent—*church* ... OH-6
Precious Blood Sch—*school* ... CA-9
Precious Blood Sch—*school* ... IN-6
Precious Blood Sch—*school* ... KY-4
Precious Blood Sch—*school* ... OH-6
Precious Chapel—*church* ... AR-4
Precious Honor Mine No 1—*mine* ... WY-8
Precious Honor Mine No 2—*mine* ... WY-8
Precious Materials Heliport—*airport* ... NV-8
Precipice Bend—*bend* ... AZ-5
*Precipice Canyon* ... CA-9
Precipice Canyon—*valley* ... UT-8
Precipice Creek—*stream* ... ID-8
Precipice Lake—*lake* ... CA-9
Precipice Peak—*summit* ... CO-8
*Precipicio Canyon* ... CA-9
*Precipicio Peak* ... CA-9
Precipitous Canyon—*valley* ... UT-8
Precopia Spring—*spring* ... AZ-5
Precore Creek—*stream* ... MI-6
Precourt Park—*park* ... NH-1
Preddy Creek—*stream* ... VA-3
Preddy Creek Ch—*church* ... VA-3
**Predmore**—*pop pl* ... MN-6
**Predonia (historical)**—*pop pl* ... IA-7
Pred Park—*park* ... LA-4
Preece—*locale* ... KY-4
Preece Cem—*cemetery* ... KY-4
Preece Cem—*cemetery* ... TX-5
Preece Spring—*spring* ... UT-8
Preechey Hollow—*valley* ... NY-2
Pree Creek—*stream* ... MS-4
Pree Eddy—*bay* ... MS-4
Preeminent Sch—*school* ... IL-6
**Preemption**—*pop pl* ... IL-6
**Pre-emption**—*pop pl* ... NY-2
Preemption Cem—*cemetery* ... IL-6
Pre-emption Creek—*stream* ... WI-6
Preemption Creek—*stream* ... WY-8
Pre-emption Creek Pond—*lake* ... WI-6
Preemption Draw—*valley* ... TX-5
Pre-emption Gulch—*valley* ... CO-8
**Preemption (Township of)**—*pop pl* ... IL-6
Preen Cem—*cemetery* ... IA-7
Preers Pond—*reservoir* ... AL-4
Pree Swamp Brook—*stream* ... NJ-2
Pre-exemption Spring—*spring* ... OR-9
Prefedio Creek—*stream* ... CA-9
Prefedio Spring—*spring* ... CA-9
Preference Cem—*cemetery* ... SC-3
Preffitt Run—*stream* ... VA-3
Prefontaine Mesa—*summit* ... CO-8
Prefumo Canyon—*valley* ... CA-9
Prefumo Creek—*stream* ... CA-9
Pregnall—*locale* ... SC-3
Pregnant Spring—*spring* ... CA-9
*Prehan Lake* ... LA-4
Prehistoric Cave Spring Number Two (historical)—*spring* ... UT-8
Prehistoric Indian Village—*hist pl* ... SC-3
Prehistoric Rim—*cliff* ... WY-8
Preis Hot Spring—*spring* ... ID-8
**Preisser**—*pop pl* ... PA-2
Preisser Crossing—*locale* ... PA-2
Preisser Station—*locale* ... PA-2
**Preiss Heights**—*pop pl* ... TX-5
*Preist Hollow* ... UT-8
Preistly Point Campsite—*locale* ... ME-1
Prejean Canal—*canal* ... LA-4
Prellwitz Cem—*cemetery* ... WI-6
Premier—*locale* ... KY-4
**Premier**—*pop pl* ... VA-3
**Premier**—*pop pl* ... WV-2
Premier Creek—*stream* ... AK-9
Premier Mine—*mine* ... AK-9
Premier Mine—*mine* (2) ... NV-8
Premier Mine—*mine* ... WY-8
*Premier Oil Field* ... CA-9
Premier Oil Field—*other* ... NM-5
*Premiscot Bayou* ... AR-4
Premisy Hill—*summit* ... RI-1
**Premium (Hotspot)**—*pop pl* ... KY-4
Premium Millpond—*lake* ... NY-2
Premium Point—*cape* ... NY-2
Premium River—*stream* ... NY-2
Premium Sch—*school* ... IL-6
Premm Sch—*school* ... NY-2
Premo Cem—*cemetery* ... NV-8
Premo Creek—*stream* ... MI-6
Premo Dam—*dam* ... MI-6
Premo Lake—*lake* ... MI-6
**Premont**—*pop pl* ... TX-5
Premont (CCD)—*cens area* ... TX-5
Premont Oil Field—*oilfield* ... TX-5
Premontre HS—*school* ... WI-6
Pren Branch—*stream* ... LA-4
**Prenda**—*pop pl* ... CA-9
Prendergast Cem—*cemetery* ... NY-2
Prendergast Creek—*stream* ... NY-2
**Prendergast Point**—*pop pl* ... NY-2
Prendergast Post Office (historical)—*building* ... TN-4
Prendergast Sch—*school* ... CT-1
Prendergat Ridge—*ridge* ... AK-9
**Prenter**—*pop pl* ... WV-2
Prentice—*locale* ... PA-2
**Prentice**—*pop pl* ... IL-6
**Prentice**—*pop pl* ... WI-6
Prentice, Alonzo T., House—*hist pl* ... MI-6
Prentice Brook—*stream* ... CT-1
Prentice Canyon—*valley* ... NV-8
Prentice Cem—*cemetery* ... WI-6
*Prentice Church* ... IN-6
Prentice Co-operative Creamery Company—*hist pl* ... WI-6
Prentice Cooper State For—*forest* ... TN-4
Prentice-Cooper State Forest and Wildlife Mngmt Area—*park* ... TN-4
**Prentice Corner**—*pop pl* ... MA-1
Prentice Creek—*stream* ... VA-3
Prentice Creek—*stream* ... WI-6
Prentice (Election Precinct)—*fmr MCD* ... IL-6
**Prentice Gardens**—*pop pl* ... MA-1
Prentice Hill—*summit* ... NV-8
Prentice Hill—*summit* ... NH-1
Prentice Mtn—*summit* ... CT-1
Prentice Oil And Gas Field—*oilfield* ... TX-5
Prentice Park—*park* ... CA-9
Prentice Park—*park* ... OH-6
Prentice Park—*park* ... WI-6
Prentice Pond—*lake* ... MN-6
Prentice Presbyterian Ch—*church* ... IN-6
Prentice Ranch—*locale* ... NE-7
Prentice Sch—*school* ... IL-6
Prentice Sch—*school* ... NE-7
**Prentice (Town of)**—*pop pl* ... WI-6
*Prenticeville* ... PA-2
Prentis Branch—*stream* ... GA-3
Prentis Ditch—*canal* ... IL-6
Prentis Draw—*valley* ... OR-9
Prentis Lake—*flat* ... OR-9
Prentis Park—*park* ... SD-7
Prentiss—*locale* ... GA-3
Prentiss—*locale* ... KY-4
Prentiss—*locale* ... ME-1
Prentiss—*locale* ... OK-5
**Prentiss**—*pop pl* ... MS-4
**Prentiss**—*pop pl* ... NC-3
**Prentiss**—*pop pl* ... OH-6
Prentiss, Addison, House—*hist pl* ... MA-1
Prentiss, Frederick, House—*hist pl* ... OH-6
Prentiss, William, House—*hist pl* ... MA-1
Prentiss Baptist Ch—*church* ... MS-4
Prentiss Bar—*bar* ... MS-4
Prentiss Bay—*bay* ... MI-6
Prentiss Bayou—*stream* ... LA-4
Prentiss Bridge—*hist pl* ... NH-1
Prentiss Brook—*stream* ... ME-1
Prentiss Brook—*stream* ... VT-1
Prentiss Cem—*cemetery* ... NY-2
Prentiss Ch—*church* ... MS-4
Prentiss Ch—*church* ... NC-3
Prentis Sch—*school* ... KS-7
Prentiss Christian Sch—*school* ... MS-4
Prentiss City Hall—*building* ... MS-4
Prentiss Club—*hist pl* ... MS-4
Prentiss Country Club—*other* ... MS-4
**Prentiss County**—*pop pl* ... MS-4
Prentiss County Courthouse—*building* ... MS-4
Prentiss County Home (historical)—*building* ... MS-4
Prentiss County Memorial Gardens—*cemetery* ... MS-4
Prentiss County Vocational Sch—*school* ... MS-4
Prentiss Creek—*stream* ... IL-6
Prentiss Creek—*stream* ... MI-6
Prentiss Elem Sch—*school* ... MS-4
Prentiss Hill—*summit* ... MA-1
**Prentiss (historical)**—*pop pl* ... MS-4
Prentiss Hollow—*valley* ... MO-7
Prentiss HS—*school* ... MS-4
Prentiss Institute—*school* ... MS-4
Prentiss Island—*island* ... ME-1
Prentiss-Jefferson Davis County Airp—*airport* ... MS-4
Prentiss Lagoon Dam—*dam* (2) ... MS-4
Prentiss Landing—*locale* ... MS-4
Prentiss Lookout Tower—*locale* ... MS-4
*Prentiss Middle School* ... MS-4
Prentiss Mine—*mine* ... NV-8
Prentiss Mound—*summit* ... MS-4
Prentiss Park—*park* ... OH-6
**Prentiss Park**—*pop pl* ... VA-3
Prentiss-Payson House—*hist pl* ... MA-1
Prentiss Place—*uninc pl* ... VA-3
Prentiss (Plantation of)—*civ div* ... ME-1
Prentiss Pond—*lake* (2) ... ME-1
Prentiss Pond—*lake* ... VT-1
Prentiss Sch—*school* ... MS-4
Prentiss Sch (historical)—*school* ... MS-4
Prentiss Sewage Lagoon Dam—*dam* ... MS-4
Prentiss (Township of)—*unorg* ... ME-1
Prentiss-Tulford House—*hist pl* ... OH-6
*Prentiss Vale* ... PA-2
**Prentisvale**—*pop pl* ... PA-2
Preparation—*locale* ... IA-7
Preparation Canyon Cem—*cemetery* ... IA-7
Preparation Canyon State Park—*park* ... IA-7
Preparatory Institute of Notre Dame—*school* ... CA-9
Presa Antonio Lucchetti—*dam* ... PR-3
Presa Chino—*reservoir* ... TX-5
Presa de Loco—*dam* ... PR-3
Presa de Loco—*reservoir* ... PR-3
Presa de Rayo Windmill—*locale* ... TX-5
*Presa Falcon* ... TX-5
Pres Allen Branch—*stream* ... AR-4
Presa Llorona—*reservoir* ... TX-5
Presa Rincon—*reservoir* ... TX-5
Presa Seca Tank—*reservoir* ... TX-5
Presa Spring—*spring* ... NM-5
Presa Tank—*reservoir* ... TX-5
Presa Viruelas—*reservoir* ... TX-5
Presa Windmill—*locale* ... TX-5
Presbury Cem—*cemetery* ... NH-1
Presbury Meetinghouse—*hist pl* ... MD-2
Presby Creek—*stream* ... ID-8
Presbyerian Ch—*church* ... IL-6
*Presby Ford Branch* ... AL-4
Presby Memorial Iris Gardens Horticultural Center—*hist pl* ... NJ-2
Presbytere, The—*hist pl* ... LA-4
*Presbyterial Female Collegiate Institution of Pontotoc* ... MS-4
Presbyterian Acad (historical)—*school* ... MS-4
Presbyterian Branch—*stream* ... DE-2
Presbyterian Cem—*cemetery* ... IL-6
Presbyterian Cem—*cemetery* ... KS-7
Presbyterian Cem—*cemetery* ... NE-7
Presbyterian Cem—*cemetery* ... NM-5
Presbyterian Cem—*cemetery* ... ND-7
Presbyterian Ch—*church* ... NE-7
Presbyterian Ch—*church* ... OK-5
Presbyterian Childrens Village—*building* ... PA-2
Presbyterian Ch in America—*church* ... FL-3
Presbyterian Ch Number One (historical)—*church* ... AL-4
Presbyterian Ch Number Two (historical)—*church* ... AL-4
Presbyterian Ch of Palm Harbor—*church* ... FL-3
Presbyterian Ch of Sardis—*church* ... MS-4
Presbyterian Ch of the Lakes—*church* ... FL-3
*Presbyterian Church* ... SD-7
Presbyterian Church—*hist pl* ... NE-7
Presbyterian Church—*hist pl* ... OK-5
Presbyterian Church Bldg—*hist pl* ... IN-6
Presbyterian Church Camp—*park* ... SD-7
Presbyterian Church Dam—*dam* ... AL-4
Presbyterian Church in Basking Ridge—*hist pl* ... NJ-2
Presbyterian Church Lakes Dam—*dam* ... MS-4
Presbyterian Church of Fredericksburg—*hist pl* ... VA-3
Presbyterian Church of McGraw—*hist pl* ... NY-2
Presbyterian Church Parsonage—*hist pl* ... AZ-5

Presbyterian Coll—school ... SC-3
Presbyterian Cooperative Parish—church ... DE-2
Presbyterian Falls—falls ... OK-5
Presbyterian Hill Cem—cemetery ... NY-2
Presbyterian Historical Society—building ... PA-2
Presbyterian Hosp—hospital ... PA-2
Presbyterian HS (historical)—school ... AL-4
Presbyterian Lake Dam—dam ... MS-4
Presbyterian Lecture Room—park ... NC-3
Presbyterian Manse—hist pl ... KY-4
Presbyterian Manse—hist pl ... SC-3
Presbyterian Manse—hist pl ... TX-5
Presbyterian Med Ctr—hospital ... CO-8
Presbyterian Mission Church—hist pl ... NM-5
Presbyterian Natl Missions Lake—reservoir ... IN-6
Presbyterian Natl Missions Lake Dam—dam ... IN-6
Presbyterian Orphanage Dam—dam ... NC-3
Presbyterian Parsonage—hist pl ... OH-6
Presbyterian Seminary of Learning (historical)—school ... MS-4
Presbyterian Synod of Florida—church ... FL-3
Presbyterian USA Synod of Florida—church ... FL-3
Presbyterian Well—well ... AZ-5
**Presbytery Camp**—pop pl ... TN-4
Presbytery Point—cape ... MI-6
Presciendo Canon ... AZ-5
Prescimida Pass ... AZ-5
Prescimide Pass ... AZ-5
Prescimido Pass ... AZ-5
Prescot Sch (historical)—school ... MS-4
Prescott ... SC-3
Prescott—locale ... AL-4
Prescott—locale ... MO-7
**Prescott**—pop pl ... AZ-5
**Prescott**—pop pl ... AR-4
**Prescott**—pop pl ... IN-6
**Prescott**—pop pl ... IA-7
**Prescott**—pop pl ... KS-7
**Prescott**—pop pl ... MI-6
**Prescott**—pop pl ... NC-3
**Prescott**—pop pl ... OR-9
**Prescott**—pop pl ... PA-2
**Prescott**—pop pl ... WA-9
**Prescott**—pop pl ... WI-6
Prescott, Benjamin Franklin, House—hist pl ... NH-1
Prescott, Clarence R., House—hist pl ... MT-8
Prescott, J. L., House—hist pl ... ME-1
Prescott, John H., House—hist pl ... KS-7
Prescott Branch—stream ... AL-4
Prescott Brook—stream (2) ... ME-1
Prescott Brook—stream ... MA-1
Prescott Brook—stream ... NH-1
Prescott Brook—stream ... NJ-2
Prescott Cabin—locale ... CA-9
Prescott Canyon ... CA-9
Prescott (CCD)—cens area ... AZ-5
Prescott Cem—cemetery (2) ... AL-4
Prescott Cem—cemetery (2) ... FL-3
Prescott Cem—cemetery (2) ... MS-4
Prescott Cem—cemetery ... OR-9
Prescott Cem—cemetery ... SC-3
Prescott Cem—cemetery ... TX-5
Prescott Ch—church ... AL-4
Prescott Ch—church ... MI-6
Prescott Ch—church ... MO-7
Prescott City Dam—dam ... KS-7
Prescott City Lake—reservoir ... KS-7
Prescott Coll—school ... AZ-5
Prescott Commons—hist pl ... MT-8
**Prescott Corner**—pop pl ... NH-1
Prescott Country Club—other ... AZ-5
Prescott Country Club—other ... AR-4
Prescott Cove—cove ... MA-1
Prescott Creek—stream ... AL-4
Prescott Creek—stream ... OR-9
Prescott Creek—stream ... TX-5
Prescott Creek—stream ... WA-9
Prescott Ditch—canal ... OR-9
Prescott Elem Sch—school ... KS-7
Prescott Elem Sch—school ... PA-2
Prescott Estate—hist pl ... MA-1
Prescott Fork—stream ... CA-9
Prescott Fork Smith River ... CA-9
Prescott Grove Cem—cemetery ... IN-6
Prescott Gulch—valley ... OR-9
Prescott Hill ... MA-1
Prescott Hill—summit (2) ... ME-1
Prescott Hill—summit ... MA-1
Prescott Hill—summit (2) ... NH-1
Prescott Hill Cem—cemetery ... NH-1
**Prescott (historical)**—pop pl ... MA-1
Prescott Hollow—valley ... AL-4
Prescott HS—school ... AZ-5
Prescott Island—island ... MN-6
Prescott JHS—school ... AZ-5
Prescott JHS—school ... LA-4
Prescott Lake—lake ... MI-6
Prescott Lake—lake (2) ... MN-6
Prescott Lake Dam—dam ... MS-4
Prescott Lakes—reservoir ... GA-3
Prescott Memorial Sch—school ... ME-1
Prescott Mtn—summit ... CA-9
Prescott Municipal Airport ... AZ-5
Prescott Natl Bank—hist pl ... AZ-5
Prescott Natl For—forest ... AZ-5
Prescott Old JHS—school ... AZ-5
Prescott Peninsula—cape ... MA-1
Prescott Pond—lake (3) ... ME-1
Prescott Pond—reservoir ... GA-3
Prescott Post Office—building ... AZ-5
Prescott Public Library—hist pl ... AZ-5
Prescott Ranch—locale ... MT-8
Prescott Ranger Station—locale ... AZ-5
Prescott Ridge—ridge ... MA-1
Prescott RR Station—building ... AZ-5
Prescott Rsvr—reservoir ... AZ-5
Prescott Sch—hist pl ... KS-7
Prescott Sch—school ... CA-9
Prescott Sch—school ... IL-6
Prescott Sch—school ... IA-7
Prescott Sch—school ... KS-7
Prescott Sch—school ... ME-1
Prescott Sch—school (2) ... MA-1
Prescott Sch—school ... MN-6
Prescott Sch—school ... MO-7
Prescott Sch—school ... MT-8
Prescott Sch—school ... NE-7
Prescott Sch—school ... NY-2
Prescott Sch—school ... OR-9
Prescott Sch—school ... TX-5
Prescotts Creek—stream ... IA-7
Prescott Shop Ctr—locale ... AZ-5
Prescott Substation—locale ... AZ-5
Prescott Township—fmr MCD ... IA-7
**Prescott Township**—pop pl ... ND-7
**Prescott (Township of)**—pop pl ... MN-6
**Prescott Valley**—pop pl ... AZ-5
**Prescott Valley (Agua Fria)**—pop pl ... AZ-5
Prescott Valley Airp—airport ... AZ-5
Prescott Valley Community Center Park—park ... AZ-5
Prescott Valley Plaza Shop Ctr—locale ... AZ-5
Prescott Valley Rec Area—park ... AZ-5
Prescott Valley Town Park ... AZ-5
**Prescottville**—pop pl ... PA-2
Presely Lake—lake ... TN-4
Presentation Acad—hist pl ... KY-4
Presentation Heights Coll—school ... SD-7
Presentation HS—school ... CA-9
Presentation of Mary Acad—school ... NH-1
Presentation of Our Lord Chapel—hist pl ... AK-9
Presentation Sch—school (2) ... CA-9
Presentation Sch—school ... CO-8
Presentation Sch—school ... IL-6
Presentation Sch—school ... MI-6
Presentation Sch—school ... MN-6
Presentation Sch—school ... PA-2
**Preserve**—pop pl ... PA-2
**Preserve (subdivision), The**—pop pl (2) ... AZ-5
Presgrove Cem—cemetery ... TN-4
Presher Springs—spring ... WA-9
**Presho**—pop pl ... NY-2
**Presho**—pop pl ... SD-7
Presho County (historical)—civil ... SD-7
Presho Municipal Airp—airport ... SD-7
**Presho Township**—pop pl ... SD-7
**President**—pop pl ... PA-2
Presidentail Hills Park—park ... MS-4
President Bay—bay ... AK-9
President Canyon—valley ... AZ-5
President Cem—cemetery ... TX-5
President Channel—channel ... WA-9
President Creek—stream ... ID-8
President Harding Rapids—rapids ... AZ-5
President Hill ... MA-1
President Hotel—hist pl ... MO-7
**Presidential**—pop pl ... CT-1
**Presidential Estates**—pop pl ... AZ-5
**Presidential Heights**—pop pl ... PA-2
**Presidential Hills (subdivision)**—pop pl ... MS-4
**Presidential Lake Estates**—pop pl ... NJ-2
**Presidential Lakes**—pop pl ... NJ-2
Presidential Lakes—reservoir ... NJ-2
Presidential Lakes Estates—CDP ... NJ-2
Presidential Plaza (Shop Ctr)—locale ... FL-3
Presidential Range—ridge ... NH-1
**Presidential Village**—pop pl ... IN-6
President Mine—mine ... AZ-5
President Point—cape ... WA-9
President Polk Water Hole ... TX-5
President Post Office (historical)—building ... PA-2
President Ridge—ridge ... OR-9
President Roads—channel ... MA-1
Presidents Chair—other ... AK-9
Presidents Channel ... WA-9
President's Guest House, The ... DC-2
Presidents Hill—summit ... MA-1
President's Home—hist pl ... KY-4
President's Home, Northwestern State Univ—hist pl ... LA-4
President's House—hist pl ... AZ-5
President's House—hist pl ... AR-4
President's House—hist pl ... GA-3
President's House—hist pl ... NJ-2
President's House—hist pl ... NM-5
President's House—hist pl ... OH-6
President's House, Gallaudet College—hist pl ... DC-2
President's House, Marion Institute—hist pl ... AL-4
President's House, Univ Of Michigan—hist pl ... MI-6
President's House, Univ of Oklahoma—hist pl ... OK-5
President's House, Worthington Female Seminary—hist pl ... OH-6
Presidents Island ... TN-4
Presidents Island Number Forty-five—flat ... TN-4
President's Mansion—hist pl ... AL-4
President's Park South—hist pl ... DC-2
Presidents Roads ... MA-1
**President (Township of)**—pop pl ... PA-2
Presidio—hist pl ... CA-9
Presidio—military ... CA-9
**Presidio**—pop pl ... TX-5
Presidio, The ... CA-9
Presidio (CCD)—cens area ... TX-5
Presidio Cem—cemetery ... TX-5
Presidio Chapel of San Elizario—hist pl ... TX-5
**Presidio (County)**—pop pl ... TX-5
Presidio County Courthouse—hist pl ... TX-5
Presidio JHS—school ... CA-9
Presidio La Bahia—locale ... TX-5
Presidio Nuestra Senora de Loreto de la Bahia—hist pl ... TX-5
Presidio of Monterey—military ... CA-9
Presidio of Monterey (U.S. Army)—military ... CA-9
Presidio of San Francisco ... CA-9
Presidio of San Francisco (U.S. Army)—military ... CA-9
Presidio Park—park ... CA-9
Presidio Park—park ... TX-5
Presidio (Presidio of San Francisco, U.S. Army)—post sta ... CA-9
Presidio Sch—school ... CA-9
Presidio Shoal—bar ... CA-9
Presita Tank—reservoir ... TX-5
Presleano Creek—stream ... TX-5
Presler Cem—cemetery ... TN-4
Presler Lake—lake ... NM-5
Presley ... AL-4
Presley—locale ... ID-8
**Presley**—pop pl ... AR-4
**Presley**—pop pl ... GA-3
Presley Branch ... GA-3
Presley Branch—stream ... AL-4
Presley Branch—stream (2) ... AR-4
Presley Branch—stream ... MO-7
Presley Branch—stream (3) ... VA-3
Presley Cem—cemetery ... IL-6
Presley Cem—cemetery ... MS-4
Presley Cem—cemetery (3) ... TN-4
Presley Cem—cemetery (2) ... VA-3
Presley Cem—cemetery ... WV-2
Presley Chapel—church ... AL-4
**Presley Circle (subdivision)**—pop pl ... MS-4
Presley Creek—stream ... VA-3
Presley Dam—dam ... TN-4
Presley Ford Branch—stream ... AL-4
Presley Hill—summit ... TN-4
Presley House Branch—stream ... KY-4
Presley Junction—locale ... AR-4
Presley Lake—lake ... ME-1
Presley Lake—lake ... OR-9
Presley Lake—reservoir ... TN-4
Presley Memorial Church ... AL-4
Presley Pond—lake ... MS-4
**Presley Ridge**—pop pl ... TN-4
Presley Ridge—ridge ... TN-4
Presleys Airp—airport ... MS-4
Presley Sch—school ... TN-4
Presley Sch—school ... VA-3
Presley Store—hist pl ... AL-4
Presley Tank—reservoir ... AZ-5
Presley Watts Cem—cemetery ... MS-4
Presnall Landing—locale ... AL-4
Presnall Windmill—locale ... TX-5
Presnell Cem—cemetery ... TN-4
Presnell Tailings Pond—reservoir ... TN-4
Presnell Tailings Pond Dam—dam ... TN-4
Presnel Well—well ... NV-8
Presqisle Swamp ... VA-3
Presque Island PO—building ... PA-2
Presque Isle ... LA-4
Presque Isle—cape ... MI-6
Presque Isle—cape ... PA-2
Presque Isle—island ... MI-6
Presque Isle—island ... OH-6
Presque Isle—locale ... VA-3
**Presque Isle**—pop pl ... LA-4
**Presque Isle**—pop pl ... ME-1
**Presque Isle**—pop pl ... MI-6
**Presque Isle**—pop pl ... WI-6
Presque Isle—uninc pl ... PA-2
Presque Isle AFB—military ... ME-1
Presque Isle Bay ... MI-6
Presque Isle Bay—bay ... PA-2
Presque Isle Bay—bay ... WI-6
Presque Isle Cem—cemetery ... MI-6
**Presque Isle (County)**—pop pl ... MI-6
Presque Isle County Courthouse—hist pl ... MI-6
Presque Isle Harbor—bay ... MI-6
Presque Isle Harbor—harbor ... MI-6
Presque Isle Junction—locale ... ME-1
Presque Isle Lake—lake ... ME-1
Presque Isle Lake—lake ... WI-6
Presque Isle Light—hist pl ... PA-2
Presque Isle Lighthouse—locale ... PA-2
Presque Isle Light Station—hist pl ... MI-6
Presque Isle Natl Bank—hist pl ... ME-1
Presque Isle North Lookout Tower—locale ... MI-6
Presque Isle Of The Saint ... ME-1
Presque Isle Park—park (2) ... MI-6
Presque Isle Peninsula ... PA-2
Presque Isle Point—cape ... MI-6
Presque Isle Point—cape ... WI-6
Presque Isle Point Rocks—island ... MI-6
Presque Isle River ... ME-1
Presque Isle River ... MI-6
Presque Isle River ... WI-6
Presque Isle River—stream ... MI-6
Presque Isle River Of The Aroostook ... ME-1
Presque Isle School—locale ... WI-6
Presque Isle South Lookout Tower—locale ... MI-6
Presque Isle State For—forest ... MI-6
Presque Isle State Park—park ... PA-2
Presque Isle Stream ... ME-1
Presque Isle Stream—stream ... ME-1
Presque Isle Swamp—swamp ... VA-3
**Presque Isle (Town of)**—pop pl ... WI-6
Presque Isle (Township of)—civ div ... MI-6
Presque Isle Yacht Club—locale ... PA-2
Presque River ... ME-1
Presque Springs—spring ... WI-6
Presqui'ile—hist pl ... SC-3
Presquile ... LA-4
Presqu'ile ... ME-1
Presqu'Ile ... PA-2
Presqu'Ile Bay ... PA-2
Presquile Natl Wildlife Ref—park ... VA-3
Presquile Swamp ... VA-3
Presquille—locale ... LA-4
Press—locale ... KY-4
Press Cove—valley ... NC-3
Press Creek—stream ... CA-9
Pressee Branch—stream ... KS-7
Pressentin Creek—stream ... WA-9
Presser Cem—cemetery ... MO-7
Presser Creek ... NE-7
Presser Lake ... ND-7
Pressey Brook—stream ... NH-1
Pressey Cove—bay ... ME-1
Pressey House—hist pl ... ME-1
Press Hollow—valley ... MO-7
Press Howard Fork—stream ... KY-4
Press Howard Fork Sch—school ... KY-4
Press Kincaid Branch ... WV-2
Pressler Cemetery ... TN-4
Pressler School ... TN-4
Pressley, Rev. John E., House—hist pl ... NC-3
Pressley Branch—stream ... KY-4
Pressley Branch—stream ... MS-4
Pressley Cem—cemetery ... AL-4
Pressley Cem—cemetery ... SC-3
Pressley Cove—valley ... NC-3
Pressley Cove—valley ... TN-4
Pressley Creek—stream (2) ... NC-3
Pressley Gap—gap (2) ... NC-3
Pressley Hollow—valley ... VA-3
Pressley Mtn—summit ... NC-3
Pressly Ch—church ... NC-3
Pressly Mountain ... NC-3
**Pressly Place (subdivision)**—pop pl ... MS-4
Pressly Sch—school ... NC-3
Pressmens Flume—canal ... TN-4
Pressmens Home ... TN-4
Pressmens Home Cem—cemetery ... TN-4
Pressmens Home Dam—dam ... TN-4
Pressmen's Home Hist Dist—hist pl ... TN-4
Pressmens Home Lake—reservoir ... TN-4
Pressmens Home Post Office (historical)—building ... TN-4
Pressmens Home Power Plant—building ... TN-4
Pressmens Union Power Plant ... TN-4
Presson Cem—cemetery ... NC-3
Presson Point—cape ... MA-1
Press Prong—stream ... NC-3
Press Tank—reservoir ... AZ-5
**Presston**—pop pl ... PA-2
Press Valley—basin ... CA-9
Press Valley—flat ... WA-9
Press Wireless Radio Station—other ... CA-9
Presswood—locale ... CA-9
**Presswood**—pop pl ... PA-2
Presswood Branch—stream ... AL-4
Presswood Branch—stream ... TN-4
Presswood Gap—gap ... TN-4
Presswood Mtn—summit ... TN-4
Presswood Pond—swamp ... TX-5
Pressy State Recreation Grounds—park ... NE-7
Prestages Pot Hole—cave ... AL-4
Pre-Statehood Commercial District—hist pl ... OK-5
**Prestbury**—pop pl ... IL-6
Prestidge Lake ... MN-6
**Prestige**—pop pl ... TN-4
**Prestige Estates Subdivision**—pop pl ... UT-8
Prestige Post Office (historical)—building ... TN-4
Prestile Brook—stream ... ME-1
Prestile Hill—summit ... ME-1
Prestile Stream—stream ... ME-1
Prestle Creek—stream ... MI-6
Prestliens Bluff—cliff ... WA-9
Presto—obs name ... UT-8
**Presto**—pop pl ... PA-2
Preston ... IN-6
Preston ... MS-4
Preston ... PA-2
Preston ... SD-7
Preston ... WV-2
Preston—locale ... AL-4
Preston—locale ... AR-4
Preston—locale ... CA-9
Preston—locale ... LA-4
Preston—locale ... ND-7
Preston—locale ... PA-2
Preston—locale ... SD-7
Preston—locale ... TX-5
Preston—locale ... VA-3
**Preston**—pop pl ... GA-3
**Preston**—pop pl ... ID-8
**Preston**—pop pl ... IL-6
**Preston**—pop pl ... IN-6
**Preston**—pop pl ... IA-7
**Preston**—pop pl ... KS-7
**Preston**—pop pl (2) ... KY-4
**Preston**—pop pl ... MD-2
**Preston**—pop pl ... MN-6
**Preston**—pop pl ... MS-4
**Preston**—pop pl (2) ... MO-7
**Preston**—pop pl ... NE-7
**Preston**—pop pl ... NV-8
**Preston**—pop pl ... NY-2
**Preston**—pop pl ... OK-5
**Preston**—pop pl ... PA-2
**Preston**—pop pl ... WA-9
**Preston**—pop pl ... WV-2
**Preston**—pop pl ... WI-6
Preston—uninc pl ... TX-5
Preston, Lake—lake ... FL-3
Preston, Maj. Walter, House—hist pl ... KY-4
Preston, Thaddeus and Josepha, House—hist pl ... TX-5
**Preston Addition**—pop pl ... OH-6
Preston Bay—bay ... NC-3
Preston B Bird-Mary Heinlein Fruit and Spice Park—park ... FL-3
Preston Beach—beach ... ID-8
Preston Beck—civil ... NM-5
Preston Big Spring—spring ... NV-8
Preston Bluff ... AR-4
Preston Bottoms—bend ... IL-6
Preston Branch ... AL-4
Preston Branch ... IA-7
Preston Branch—stream (2) ... KY-4
Preston Branch—stream ... VA-3
Preston Brewery—hist pl ... MN-6
Preston Brook—stream ... CT-1
Preston Brook—stream ... ME-1
Preston Brook—stream ... NH-1
Preston Brook—stream ... VT-1
Preston Bungalow—hist pl ... ID-8
Prestonburg ... KY-4
Preston Buttes—summit ... MT-8
Preston Cabin Site Area—locale ... AL-4
Preston Canal ... ID-8
Preston Canyon—valley ... CA-9
Preston Canyon—valley ... UT-8
Preston Castle—hist pl ... CA-9
Preston (CCD)—cens area ... GA-3
Preston Cem—cemetery ... AL-4
Preston Cem—cemetery ... GA-3
Preston Cem—cemetery ... ID-8
Preston Cem—cemetery (2) ... IL-6
Preston Cem—cemetery (2) ... KY-4
Preston Cem—cemetery (3) ... MO-7
Preston Cem—cemetery ... NH-1
Preston Cem—cemetery ... OH-6
Preston Cem—cemetery (3) ... TN-4
Preston Cem—cemetery ... WV-2
Preston Center—locale ... NY-2
Preston Center—locale ... PA-2
Preston Ch—church ... MS-4
Preston Ch—church ... ND-7
Preston Ch—church ... SD-7
Preston City—other ... CT-1
Preston City Hist Dist—hist pl ... CT-1
Preston Cliffs—cliff ... WI-6
Preston Corner—locale ... PA-2
Preston Corners—locale ... PA-2
**Preston Corners**—pop pl ... MI-6
**Preston (County)**—pop pl ... WV-2
Preston Creek ... MD-2
Preston Creek—stream (2) ... AK-9
Preston Creek—stream ... CA-9
Preston Creek—stream ... ID-8
Preston Creek—stream ... IL-6
Preston Creek—stream ... IA-7
Preston Creek—stream (2) ... MI-6
Preston Creek—stream ... NC-3
Preston Creek—stream (2) ... OR-9
Preston Creek—stream (2) ... WA-9
Preston Drain—stream ... MI-6
Preston Draw—valley ... WY-8
Preston Falls—falls ... WA-9
Preston Farm—hist pl ... TN-4
**Preston Ferry**—pop pl ... AR-4
Preston Flat Ridge—ridge ... MO-7
**Preston Forest (subdivision)**—pop pl ... TN-4
Preston Fork—stream ... KY-4
Preston Gospel Chapel—church ... NC-3
Preston Guthrie Hollow—valley ... AL-4
**Preston Heights**—pop pl ... IL-6
Preston Heights—uninc pl ... CA-9
Preston Highway Ch—church ... KY-4
Preston Hill—locale ... CT-1
Preston Hill—locale ... PA-2
Preston Hill—summit ... CT-1
Preston Hill—summit (3) ... NY-2
Preston Hill—summit ... VT-1
Preston Hill Cem—cemetery ... OK-5
**Preston Hills**—pop pl ... VA-3
**Preston Hills (subdivision)**—pop pl (2) ... AZ-5
Preston (historical)—locale ... AL-4
Preston (historical)—locale ... MS-4
**Preston (historical)**—pop pl ... OR-9
**Preston (historical)**—pop pl ... TN-4
**Preston Hollow**—pop pl ... NY-2
Preston Hollow—uninc pl ... TX-5
Preston Hollow—valley ... KY-4
Preston Hollow—valley ... OH-6
Preston Hollow—valley ... TN-4
Preston Hollow—valley ... VA-3
Preston Hollow Country Club—other ... TX-5
Preston Hollow Sch—school ... TX-5
Preston House—hist pl ... KY-4
Preston House—hist pl ... MT-8
Preston House—hist pl ... VA-3
Preston HS—school ... NY-2
Prestonia—locale ... WV-2
**Prestonia**—pop pl ... KY-4
**Prestonia**—pop pl ... WV-2
Prestonia Sch—school ... KY-4
**Preston (Industrial Park)**—pop pl ... TN-4
Preston Island ... TN-4
Preston Island—island ... CA-9
Preston Isle—island ... NY-2
**Preston King**—pop pl ... VA-3
Preston Knob—summit ... ID-8
Preston Lake ... PA-2
Preston Lake—lake ... AR-4
Preston Lake—lake ... CA-9
Preston Lake—lake (2) ... MN-6
Preston Lake—lake ... NE-7
Preston Lake (Township of)—civ div ... MN-6
Preston Landing—locale ... TN-4
**Preston Manor**—pop pl ... MD-2
Preston Mesa—summit ... AZ-5
Preston Miles Ditch—canal ... IN-6
Preston Millpond—reservoir ... VA-3
Preston Mine—mine ... CA-9
Preston Mine—mine ... TN-4
Preston Notch—gap ... CT-1
Preston-on-the-Patuxent—hist pl ... MD-2
Preston Park—park ... OH-6
**Preston Park**—pop pl ... PA-2
Preston Park Dam—dam ... PA-2
Preston Park Pond—reservoir ... PA-2
Preston Park Sch—school ... VA-3
Preston Park Sch (historical)—school ... PA-2
Preston Peak—summit ... CA-9
Preston Pilgrim Ch—church ... VA-3
**Preston Place**—pop pl ... AR-4
Preston Point—cape (2) ... CA-9
Preston Point—cape ... TX-5
Preston Point—cape ... WA-9
Preston Point Reach—channel ... CA-9
Preston Pond—lake ... NH-1
Preston Pond—lake ... VT-1
Preston Ponds—lake ... NY-2
Preston Post Office—building ... MS-4
Preston Post Office (historical)—building ... TN-4
Preston Prairie Sch—school ... IL-6
**Preston (Preston City)**—pop pl ... CT-1
Preston Ranch—locale ... TX-5
Preston Ridge—ridge ... WA-9
Preston Riverdale Canal—canal ... ID-8
**Preston Road Highlands**—pop pl ... TX-5
Preston Rsvr ... CA-9
Preston Rsvr—reservoir ... CA-9
Preston Rsvr—reservoir ... NV-8
Preston Run—stream ... MD-2
Preston Run—stream ... OH-6
Preston Run—stream ... PA-2
Prestons ... TN-4
Prestons Bridge—bridge ... AL-4
**Prestonsburg**—pop pl ... KY-4
Prestonsburg (CCD)—cens area ... KY-4
Preston Sch—school ... CA-9
Preston Sch—school ... CT-1
Preston Sch—school ... IL-6
Preston Sch—school ... ME-1
Preston Sch—school ... MI-6
Preston Sch—school (2) ... MS-4
Preston Sch—school ... OH-6
Preston Sch of Industry—school ... CA-9
Preston Seeding Windmill—locale ... NV-8
Prestons Fork ... IN-6
**Preston Shores**—pop pl ... TX-5
**Preston Sights Subdivision (subdivision)**—pop pl ... AL-4
Prestons Island ... TN-4
Prestons Mill Branch—stream ... AL-4
Prestons Mill (historical)—locale ... AL-4
Prestons Point—cliff ... NM-5
Prestons Pond—lake ... NY-2
Preston Spring—spring ... CA-9
Preston Spring—spring ... VA-3
Preston-St. Catherine Street Hist Dist—hist pl ... KY-4
Preston Street Sch—school ... WV-2
**Preston (subdivision)**—pop pl ... NC-3
**Preston Subdivision (subdivision)**—pop pl ... AL-4
Preston Tank—reservoir ... NM-5
Preston Tank—reservoir ... TX-5
Preston Town Hall—building ... ND-7
**Preston (Town of)**—pop pl ... CT-1
**Preston (Town of)**—pop pl ... NY-2
**Preston (Town of)**—pop pl (2) ... WI-6
Preston Township—civil (2) ... MO-7
Preston Township—fmr MCD ... IA-7
**Preston Township**—pop pl ... ND-7
**Preston Township**—pop pl ... SD-7
Preston Township Hall—building ... SD-7
**Preston (Township of)**—pop pl ... IL-6
**Preston (Township of)**—pop pl ... MN-6
**Preston (Township of)**—pop pl ... PA-2
Preston Valley—valley ... MN-6
Preston Valley Campground—locale ... UT-8
Prestonville ... PA-2
Prestonville ... TN-4
**Prestonville**—pop pl ... KY-4
**Prestonville**—pop pl ... NC-3
Prestonville (CCD)—cens area ... KY-4
Prestonville Cem—cemetery ... MI-6
Prestonville Post Office ... TN-4
Preston Well—well (2) ... AZ-5
Prestonwood—post sta ... TX-5
**Preston Woods**—pop pl ... TN-4
Presto Trail ... PA-2
Prestridge Hill—summit ... NM-5
Prestrude Lake—lake ... MN-6
**Prestwick**—pop pl ... AL-4
**Prestwick**—pop pl ... IL-6
Prestwick HS (historical)—school ... AL-4
Prestwood Bridge—bridge ... AL-4
Prestwood Church ... AL-4
Prestwood Country Club—other ... SC-3
Prestwood Creek—stream ... AL-4
Prestwood Dam—dam ... AL-4
Prestwood Lake—reservoir ... AL-4
Prestwood Lake—reservoir ... SC-3
Prestwood Millpond—lake ... AL-4
Prestwood Millpond Dam ... AL-4
Prestwood Sch—school ... CA-9
Prestwould—hist pl ... VA-3
Presumido Canyon—valley ... AZ-5
Presumido Pass—gap ... AZ-5
Presumido Peak—summit ... AZ-5
Presumido Ranch—locale ... AZ-5
Presumido Store—locale ... AZ-5
Presumpscot Falls—falls ... ME-1
Presumpscot Park—park ... ME-1
Presumpscot River—stream ... ME-1
Presums ... ME-1
Presumsca River ... ME-1
Presumskeag River ... ME-1
Preton Hall Sch—school ... PA-2
Pretoria—locale ... GA-3
**Pretoria**—pop pl ... GA-3
**Pretoria**—pop pl ... PA-2
Pre-Trial Detention Center—building ... FL-3
Pretty Bayou—bay ... FL-3
Pretty Bayou—CDP ... FL-3
Pretty Bird Canyon—valley ... NM-5
Pretty Bird Hills—range ... NM-5
Pretty Bird Trail—trail ... WA-9
Pretty Bird Windmill—locale ... NM-5
Pretty Bob Creek—stream ... MO-7
Pretty Bob Sch—school ... MO-7
**Prettyboy**—pop pl ... MD-2
Prettyboy Branch—stream ... MD-2
Prettyboy Cove—bay ... MD-2
Prettyboy Dam—dam ... MD-2
Prettyboy Rsvr—reservoir ... MD-2
Pretty Branch—stream (3) ... AL-4
Pretty Branch—stream ... FL-3
Pretty Branch—stream ... GA-3
Pretty Branch—stream (3) ... KY-4
Pretty Branch—stream ... MS-4
Pretty Branch—stream (2) ... WV-2
**Pretty Branch Estates (subdivision)**—pop pl ... AL-4
Pretty Brook—stream ... ME-1
Pretty Butte—summit ... ND-7
Pretty Canyon—valley ... NM-5
Pretty Cave—cave ... AL-4
Pretty Creek ... CO-8
Pretty Creek ... MO-7
Pretty Creek ... ND-7
Pretty Creek ... WV-2
Pretty Creek—stream ... AL-4
Pretty Creek—stream ... AK-9
Pretty Creek—stream (2) ... CO-8
Pretty Creek—stream ... ID-8
Pretty Creek—stream ... KS-7
Pretty Creek—stream ... LA-4
Pretty Creek—stream (2) ... MS-4
Pretty Creek—stream ... NV-8
Pretty Creek—stream ... NC-3
Pretty Creek—stream ... SC-3
Pretty Creek—stream ... SD-7
Pretty Creek—stream ... TN-4
Pretty Creek—stream ... VA-3
Pretty Creek Archeol Site—hist pl ... MT-8
Pretty Creek Oil Field—oilfield ... MS-4
Pretty Creek Sch—school ... SD-7
Pretty Creek Sch (historical)—school ... TN-4
Pretty Farm Run—stream ... WV-2
Pretty Flat—flat ... CA-9
Pretty Glen Lake ... OH-6
Pretty Gulch—valley ... ID-8
Pretty Gulch Trail—trail ... ID-8
Prettyhair Creek—stream ... OK-5
Pretty Hill—summit ... AR-4
Pretty Hollow Creek—stream ... NC-3
Pretty Hollow Gap—gap ... NC-3
Pretty Island—island ... FL-3
Pretty Joe Rock—island ... FL-3
Prettyklip Point—cape ... VI-3
Pretty Lake ... MI-6
Pretty Lake—lake (3) ... FL-3
Pretty Lake—lake (2) ... IN-6
Pretty Lake—lake (3) ... MI-6
Pretty Lake—lake ... OR-9
Pretty Lake—lake (2) ... WI-6
**Pretty Lake**—pop pl ... IN-6
Pretty Lake Ch—church ... IN-6
Pretty Lake Sch—school ... VA-3
Pretty Lake Trail—trail ... OR-9
Prettyland Mtn—summit ... NC-3

Pretty Little Hole—*cave* ... AL-4
Prettyman—*locale* ... MO-7
Prettyman Ditch—*canal* ... IN-6
Prettyman Landing—*locale* ... NC-3
Prettyman's Meat Market and Grocery/Brigg's Jeweler—*hist pl* ... AZ-5
**Prettyman's Mill**—*pop pl* ... SC-3
*Prettymanville* ... DE-2
**Pretty Marsh**—*pop pl* ... ME-1
Pretty Marsh Harbor—*bay* ... ME-1
Pretty Pine Branch—*stream* ... NC-3
*Pretty Point Creek* ... VA-3
Pretty Point (historical)—*cape* ... ND-7
Pretty Pond—*lake* (2) ... FL-3
Pretty Pond—*lake* (2) ... ME-1
Pretty Pond—*lake* ... NC-3
Pretty Pond—*reservoir* ... FL-3
Pretty Prairie—*flat* ... MT-8
**Pretty Prairie**—*pop pl* ... KS-7
Pretty Prairie Cem—*cemetery* ... IN-6
Pretty Prairie Ch—*church* ... IN-6
Pretty Prairie Creek Road Dam—*dam* ... IN-6
Pretty Prairie Guard Station—*locale* ... MT-8
Pretty Prairie HS—*school* ... KS-7
Pretty Prairie Sch—*school* ... IL-6
Pretty Ridge—*ridge* ... TN-4
Pretty Ridge—*ridge* (3) ... WV-2
Pretty Rock—*pillar* ... NM-5
Pretty Rock—*summit* ... NM-5
Pretty Rock Butte—*summit* ... ND-7
*Pretty Rock Buttes* ... ND-7
Pretty Rock Cem—*cemetery* ... ND-7
Pretty Rock Dam—*dam* ... ND-7
Pretty Rock Lake—*reservoir* ... ND-7
Pretty Rock Natl Wildlife Ref—*park* ... ND-7
Pretty Rock Sch—*school* ... ND-7
**Pretty Rock Township**—*pop pl* ... ND-7
Pretty Run—*stream* (2) ... KY-4
Pretty Run—*stream* ... OH-6
Pretty Run—*stream* ... WV-2
Pretty Soon Tank—*reservoir* ... TX-5
*Prettys Pond* ... NC-3
Pretty Spring—*spring* ... TX-5
Pretty Tank—*reservoir* ... TX-5
Pretty Tree Bench—*bench* ... UT-8
Pretty Tree Rsvr—*reservoir* ... CA-9
Pretty Valley Ridge—*ridge* ... UT-8
Pretty Water Ch—*church* ... OK-5
Pretty Water Creek—*stream* ... WY-8
Pretty Water Lake—*reservoir* ... OK-5
Pretty Water Sch—*school* ... OK-5
Pretzinger, Rudolph, House—*hist pl* ... OH-6
Preuit Cem—*cemetery* (2) ... AL-4
Preuit Oaks—*hist pl* ... AL-4
Preuss—*uninc pl* ... CA-9
Preuss Creek—*stream* ... ID-8
Preusse Lake—*swamp* ... MN-6
*Preuss Peak* ... ID-8
Preuss Range—*range* ... ID-8
Prevatt Cem—*cemetery* ... FL-3
Prevatte Cem—*cemetery* ... NC-3
Prevatt Lake—*lake* ... FL-3
Prevatts Chapel—*church* ... SC-3
*Prevatts Landing* ... TN-4
Prevent Knoll—*summit* ... SC-3
Prevette Ridge—*ridge* ... NC-3
Previs Lake—*lake* ... MN-6
Previt Branch—*stream* ... TN-4
Previtt Canyon—*valley* ... CA-9
Prevo Coulee—*valley* ... MT-8
*Prevo Ditch* ... IN-6
Prevost—*locale* ... WA-9
**Prevost**—*pop pl* ... LA-4
Prevost, Nick, House—*hist pl* ... SC-3
Prevost Catfish Ponds Dam—*dam* ... MS-4
Prevost Cem—*cemetery* ... PA-2
Prevost Harbor—*bay* ... WA-9
Prevost Homestead (abandoned)—*locale* ... MT-8
Prevost Island—*island* ... LA-4
Prevost Manor House—*hist pl* ... NY-2
*Prevosts Ferry* ... PA-2
Prevost Windmill—*locale* ... NM-5
*Prew Creek* ... OR-9
Prewett Cem—*cemetery* ... IN-6
Prewett Creek—*stream* ... MT-8
Prewett Hollow—*valley* ... MO-7
Prewett Sch (abandoned)—*school* ... MO-7
Prewett Spring—*spring* ... MO-7
Prewett Spring—*spring* ... MI-8
Prewit Ranch—*locale* ... TX-5
Prewitt—*locale* ... KY-4
Prewitt—*locale* ... NM-5
Prewitt, Levi, House—*hist pl* ... KY-4
**Prewitt (Baca)**—*pop pl* ... NM-5
Prewitt Bend—*bend* ... KY-4
Prewitt Cem—*cemetery* ... AL-4
Prewitt Cem—*cemetery* (3) ... KY-4
Prewitt Cem—*cemetery* ... LA-4
*Prewitt Creek* ... TX-5
Prewitt Creek—*stream* ... CA-9
Prewitt Gap—*gap* ... KY-4
Prewitt Hollow—*valley* ... AR-4
Prewitt Inlet Canal—*canal* ... CO-8
Prewitt Lake—*reservoir* ... NM-5
Prewitt Outlet Canal—*canal* ... CO-8
Prewitt Post Office—*building* ... NM-5
Prewitt Rsvr—*reservoir* ... CO-8
Prewitt Sch (historical)—*school* ... MS-4
Prewitts Knob—*summit* ... KY-4
Prewitts Lake—*lake* ... KY-4
*Prewitt Slave Cem* ... AL-4
Prey Creek—*stream* ... MI-6
Preza Windmill—*locale* (2) ... TX-5
*Priam* (2) ... IN-6
Priam—*locale* ... MN-6
Priam Run—*stream* ... IN-6
Pribble—*locale* ... VA-3
Pribilof Islands—*island* ... AK-9
Pricco Mine—*mine* ... CO-8
*Price* ... AL-4
Price—*locale* ... AZ-5
Price—*locale* ... GA-3
Price—*locale* ... IA-7
Price—*locale* ... MI-6
Price—*locale* ... OK-5
Price—*locale* ... TX-5
Price—*locale* (2) ... WV-2
**Price**—*pop pl* (2) ... AR-4
**Price**—*pop pl* ... KY-4
**Price**—*pop pl* ... LA-4
**Price**—*pop pl* ... MD-2
**Price**—*pop pl* ... MS-4
**Price**—*pop pl* ... NC-3
**Price**—*pop pl* ... ND-7
**Price**—*pop pl* (2) ... TN-4
**Price**—*pop pl* (2) ... TX-5
**Price**—*pop pl* ... UT-8
**Price**—*pop pl* ... WI-6
Price, Dan, House—*hist pl* ... ID-8
Price, Fred, Bungalow—*hist pl* ... ID-8
Price, Gov. Samuel, House—*hist pl* ... WV-2
Price, Herber, Bungalow—*hist pl* ... ID-8
Price, Hiram/Henry Vollmer House—*hist pl* ... IA-7
Price, Joe, House—*hist pl* ... ID-8
Price, John, House—*hist pl* ... CA-9
Price, Joseph, House—*hist pl* ... PA-2
Price, Lake—*lake* ... FL-3
Price, Mount—*summit* ... CA-9
Price, Mount—*summit* ... WA-9
Price, O. L., House—*hist pl* ... OR-9
Price, Pugh, House—*hist pl* ... KY-4
Price, R. H. and Martha, House—*hist pl* ... TX-5
Price, Rialto, House—*hist pl* ... IA-7
Price, Robert, House—*hist pl* ... ID-8
Price, William, House—*hist pl* ... GA-3
Price, Williamson, House—*hist pl* ... KY-4
Price, W. Y., House—*hist pl* ... AZ-5
Price Acad (historical)—*school* ... MS-4
Price Airp Heliport—*airport* ... UT-8
Price and Davis Mine—*mine* ... NV-8
Price Ave Sch—*school* ... TX-5
Price Bench—*bench* ... UT-8
Price Bench Ditch—*canal* ... UT-8
Price Bend—*bay* ... NY-2
**Priceboro (historical)**—*pop pl* ... OR-9
Price Branch—*stream* (3) ... AL-4
Price Branch—*stream* (2) ... AR-4
Price Branch—*stream* ... GA-3
Price Branch—*stream* ... IA-7
Price Branch—*stream* ... KY-4
Price Branch—*stream* (2) ... MO-7
Price Branch—*stream* ... NJ-2
Price Branch—*stream* (5) ... TN-4
Price Branch—*stream* (2) ... TX-5
Price Branch—*stream* ... VA-3
Price Branch—*stream* (3) ... WV-2
Price Bridge—*bridge* ... MS-4
Price Bridge—*bridge* (2) ... SC-3
Price Bridge—*bridge* ... VA-3
Price Bridge—*other* ... IL-6
Price Bridge—*other* ... MO-7
Price Brook—*stream* ... MI-6
*Priceburg* ... PA-2
Priceburg—*uninc pl* ... PA-2
Price Canal—*canal* ... UT-8
Price Canyon—*valley* (2) ... AZ-5
Price Canyon—*valley* (2) ... CA-9
Price Canyon—*valley* (2) ... CO-8
Price Canyon—*valley* (2) ... ID-8
Price Canyon—*valley* ... MT-8
Price Canyon—*valley* ... OR-9
Price Canyon—*valley* ... TX-5
Price Canyon—*valley* ... UT-8
Price Canyon Campgrounds—*park* ... UT-8
Price Canyon Rec Area—*park* ... UT-8
Price Canyon Trail Two Hundred Twentyfour—*trail* ... AZ-5
**Price (Carlisle)**—*pop pl* ... TX-5
Price Cave—*cave* ... AL-4
*Price Cem* ... TN-4
Price Cem—*cemetery* (5) ... AL-4
Price Cem—*cemetery* (5) ... AR-4
Price Cem—*cemetery* ... GA-3
Price Cem—*cemetery* (5) ... IL-6
Price Cem—*cemetery* (4) ... IN-6
Price Cem—*cemetery* ... IA-7
Price Cem—*cemetery* (2) ... KS-7
Price Cem—*cemetery* (5) ... KY-4
Price Cem—*cemetery* ... LA-4
Price Cem—*cemetery* (3) ... MS-4
Price Cem—*cemetery* (5) ... MO-7
Price Cem—*cemetery* (7) ... NC-3
Price Cem—*cemetery* (3) ... OH-6
Price Cem—*cemetery* (2) ... OK-5
Price Cem—*cemetery* (2) ... PA-2
Price Cem—*cemetery* ... SC-3
Price Cem—*cemetery* (17) ... TN-4
Price Cem—*cemetery* (5) ... TX-5
Price Cem—*cemetery* (5) ... VA-3
Price Cem—*cemetery* (6) ... WV-2
Price Ch—*church* ... AR-4
Price Chapel—*church* ... GA-3
Price Chapel—*church* ... NC-3
Price Chapel—*church* ... UT-8
*Price Chapel Cem* ... TN-4
Price Chapel Cem—*cemetery* ... TX-5
Price City Cem—*cemetery* ... UT-8
Price City Hills—*summit* ... UT-8
Price City (historical)—*locale* ... UT-8
Price Coll—*school* ... TX-5
Price Corners—*locale* ... NY-2
Price Coulee—*valley* ... MT-8
Price-council-Carr Cem—*cemetery* ... GA-3
**Price (County)**—*pop pl* ... WI-6
Price Cove—*bay* ... MD-2
*Price Creek* ... MD-2
*Price Creek* ... NC-3
Price Creek—*locale* ... CO-8
Price Creek—*locale* ... NC-3
Price Creek—*stream* (2) ... AL-4
Price Creek—*stream* (2) ... AK-9
Price Creek—*stream* (3) ... AR-4
Price Creek—*stream* (2) ... CA-9
Price Creek—*stream* (3) ... CO-8
Price Creek—*stream* (3) ... FL-3
Price Creek—*stream* ... GA-3
Price Creek—*stream* (2) ... ID-8
Price Creek—*stream* ... IN-6
Price Creek—*stream* ... IA-7
Price Creek—*stream* (2) ... KY-4
Price Creek—*stream* (3) ... MS-4
Price Creek—*stream* ... MO-7
Price Creek—*stream* (3) ... MT-8
Price Creek—*stream* (2) ... NC-3
Price Creek—*stream* ... OH-6
Price Creek—*stream* (3) ... OR-9
Price Creek—*stream* ... PA-2
Price Creek—*stream* ... SC-3
Price Creek—*stream* ... TN-4
Price Creek—*stream* (4) ... TX-5
Price Creek—*stream* ... VA-3
Price Creek—*stream* ... WA-9
Price Creek—*stream* ... WV-2
Price Creek—*stream* ... WI-6
Price Creek Cem—*cemetery* ... FL-3
Price Creek Ch—*church* ... GA-3
Price Creek Sch—*school* ... CA-9
Price Creek Spring—*spring* ... WI-6
Price Creek (Township of)—*fmr MCD* ... NC-3
Price Crossing—*locale* ... LA-4
Price Cross Road—*locale* ... AL-4
**Price Crossroads**—*pop pl* ... SC-3
**Pricedale**—*pop pl* ... MS-4
**Pricedale**—*pop pl* ... PA-2
Pricedale (RR name Somers)—*uninc pl* ... PA-2
Price Dam—*dam* ... UT-8
Price Ditch—*canal* ... CO-8
Price Ditch—*canal* ... IN-6
Price Division—*civil* ... UT-8
Price Drain—*canal* (3) ... MI-6
Price Drive Sch—*school* ... MI-6
*Price Elementary School* ... MS-4
Price Elem Sch—*school* ... KS-7
Price Elem Sch—*school* ... PA-2
Price Essmann Cem—*cemetery* ... TN-4
Price Falls—*falls* ... OK-5
Price Field—*park* ... OH-6
Price Field—*park* ... TX-5
Price Ford—*locale* ... AR-4
*Price Fork* ... AL-4
Price Fork—*stream* (2) ... WV-2
*Price Forks* ... VA-3
Price Game Farm—*locale* ... UT-8
Price Gap—*gap* ... PA-2
Price Gap—*gap* (2) ... VA-3
Price Glacier—*glacier* ... WA-9
Price Glade Run—*stream* ... WV-2
Price Grove Ch—*church* ... AR-4
Price Grove Ch—*church* ... GA-3
Price Grove Ch—*church* ... TN-4
Price Gulch—*valley* ... ID-8
Price Gulch—*valley* ... MT-8
*Price Hill* ... OH-6
Price Hill—*locale* ... VA-3
**Price Hill**—*pop pl* ... OH-6
**Price Hill**—*pop pl* (3) ... WV-2
Price Hill—*summit* ... WV-2
Price Hill Cemeteries—*cemetery* ... OH-6
Price Hill Ch—*church* ... OH-6
Price Hill Junction—*uninc pl* ... WV-2
Price Hole—*lake* ... KY-4
Price Hollow—*valley* ... AR-4
Price Hollow—*valley* ... CA-9
Price Hollow—*valley* (2) ... MO-7
Price Hollow—*valley* (5) ... TN-4
Price Hollow—*valley* ... VA-3
Price Home—*locale* ... NY-2
Price HS—*school* ... GA-3
Price HS—*school* ... NC-3
Price Inlet—*bay* ... SC-3
Price Island—*island* ... AL-4
Price Island—*island* ... AK-9
Price Island—*island* ... WA-9
Price Kettle—*slope* ... PA-2
Price Knob—*summit* ... PA-2
Price Lake—*lake* ... IN-6
Price Lake—*lake* ... LA-4
Price Lake—*lake* (2) ... MI-6
Price Lake—*lake* (3) ... WA-9
Price Lake—*lake* (4) ... WI-6
Price Lake—*reservoir* ... NC-3
Price Lake—*reservoir* ... TN-4
*Price Lake Dam* ... NC-3
Price Lakes—*lake* ... CO-8
Price Lakes—*lake* ... OH-6
Price Landing—*locale* ... MO-7
Price Landing—*locale* ... SC-3
Priceless Mine—*mine* ... AZ-5
Price Library—*building* ... GA-3
Price Memorial Cem—*cemetery* ... MS-4
Price Memorial Ch—*church* ... TN-4
Price Memorial Hall—*hist pl* ... GA-3
Price Mill—*locale* ... VA-3
Price Mill Creek—*stream* ... NC-3
Price-Miller House—*hist pl* ... MD-2
Price Mill Lake—*reservoir* ... NC-3
Price Mill Lake Dam—*dam* ... NC-3
Price Mine (underground)—*mine* ... AL-4
Price Mtn—*summit* ... AR-4
Price Mtn—*summit* ... GA-3
Price Mtn—*summit* ... NC-3
Price Mtn—*summit* ... TN-4
Price Mtn—*summit* (2) ... VA-3
Price Municipal Bldg—*hist pl* ... UT-8
Price Neck—*bay* ... GA-3
Price Neck—*cape* ... RI-1
Price Northwest Oil Field—*oilfield* ... TX-5
Price Oil Field—*oilfield* ... TX-5
Price Park—*flat* ... CO-8
Price Park—*park* ... OH-6
Price-Patton-Pettis House—*hist pl* ... MS-4
Price Peak—*summit* ... CA-9
Price-Peet Divide—*gap* ... MT-8
Price Place—*locale* ... WY-8
Price Plank Ditch—*stream* ... IN-6
Price Playground—*park* ... CA-9
Price Pocket—*spring* ... AZ-5
Price Point—*cape* ... TN-4
Price Point—*summit* ... AZ-5
Price Pond—*lake* ... PA-2
Price-Portales Ranch—*locale* ... NM-5
Price Post Office—*building* ... UT-8
Price Post Office (historical)—*building* ... TN-4
Price Prong—*stream* ... DE-2
Price Public Elem Sch—*hist pl* ... TN-4
Price Quarry—*mine* ... TN-4
Price Ranch—*locale* (2) ... CO-8
Price Ranch—*locale* (4) ... NM-5
Price Ravine—*valley* ... KS-7
Price Reeves Sch—*school* ... UT-8
Price Ridge—*ridge* ... ID-8
Price Ridge—*ridge* ... PA-2
Price Ridge—*ridge* ... TN-4
Price Ridge—*ridge* (2) ... WV-2
*Price River* ... FL-3
Price River—*stream* ... AK-9
Price River—*stream* ... UT-8
*Price River - in part* ... UT-8
Price Road Baptist Ch—*church* ... AL-4
Pricer Ridge—*ridge* ... OH-6
Price RR Station—*building* ... AZ-5
Price Rsvr—*reservoir* ... CO-8
Price Rsvr—*reservoir* ... MT-8
Price Rsvr—*reservoir* ... OR-9
Price Run—*stream* (5) ... WV-2
Price Run Park—*park* ... DE-2
*Prices* ... MD-2
Prices—*locale* ... TX-5
**Prices**—*pop pl* ... AL-4
Prices Bayou—*gut* ... AR-4
Prices Bluff—*cliff* ... WI-6
**Prices Branch**—*pop pl* ... MO-7
Prices Branch—*stream* ... AR-4
Prices Branch—*stream* ... MO-7
Prices Bridge—*bridge* (2) ... AL-4
Prices Cem—*cemetery* ... SC-3
Prices Cem—*cemetery* ... VA-3
*Price Sch* ... AL-4
Price Sch—*hist pl* ... MO-7
Price Sch—*school* ... AL-4
Price Sch—*school* ... AR-4
Price Sch—*school* (4) ... CA-9
Price Sch—*school* ... IL-6
Price Sch—*school* ... KY-4
Price Sch—*school* (2) ... LA-4
Price Sch—*school* ... MI-6
Price Sch—*school* ... MO-7
Price Sch—*school* ... NC-3
Price Sch—*school* ... ND-7
Price Sch—*school* ... OH-6
Price Sch—*school* ... OR-9
Price Sch—*school* ... TX-5
Price Sch—*school* ... GU-9
Price Sch (abandoned)—*school* ... MO-7
Prices Chapel—*church* ... KY-4
Prices Chapel—*church* ... MD-2
Prices Chapel—*church* ... MS-4
Prices Chapel—*church* ... OK-5
Prices Chapel—*church* ... TN-4
Prices Chapel—*church* ... TX-5
Price Sch (historical)—*school* (2) ... MS-4
*Price School* ... IN-6
**Prices Corner**—*pop pl* ... DE-2
Prices Corner Center (Shop Ctr)—*locale* ... DE-2
Prices Corners—*locale* ... DE-2
*Price's Creek* ... MD-2
*Prices Creek* ... MS-4
*Prices Creek* ... NC-3
*Price's Creek* ... OH-6
Prices Creek—*stream* ... AL-4
Prices Creek—*stream* ... IA-7
Prices Creek—*stream* ... KY-4
Prices Creek Ch—*church* ... KY-4
Prices Creek Ch—*church* ... OH-6
Prices Ferry (historical)—*locale* (2) ... TN-4
**Prices Fork**—*pop pl* ... VA-3
Prices Fork (Magisterial District)—*fmr MCD* ... VA-3
*Prices Grove Baptist Church* ... TN-4
Prices Gulch—*valley* ... MT-8
Price Shake Pine Gulch Trail 235-236—*trail* ... AZ-5
Prices HQ—*building* ... MO-7
*Price's Island* ... WA-9
Prices Island (historical)—*island* ... TN-4
Price Site—*hist pl* ... MO-7
Prices Key—*island* ... FL-3
*Prices Lake* ... AL-4
Prices Lake—*lake* (2) ... AR-4
Prices Landing—*locale* ... SC-3
Price's Mill—*hist pl* ... SC-3
**Prices Mill**—*pop pl* ... KY-4
*Prices Neck* ... RI-1
Prices Peak—*summit* ... WA-9
Prices Ponds—*reservoir* ... AL-4
Price's Post Office—*hist pl* ... SC-3
Price Spring—*spring* ... AL-4
Price Spring—*spring* ... AZ-5
Price Spring—*spring* ... MO-7
Price Spring—*spring* ... TN-4
Price Spring—*spring* ... UT-8
Price's Ranch—*locale* ... MT-8
Prices Shop—*locale* ... VA-3
Prices Spring—*spring* ... PA-2
*Price's Station* ... MD-2
**Prices Store**—*pop pl* ... VA-3
Prices Store (historical)—*locale* ... AL-4
Prices Swamp—*swamp* (2) ... SC-3
Prices Swamp Run—*gut* ... SC-3
Prices Switch—*locale* ... NJ-2
*Prices Tavern* ... PA-2
Price-Stephens House—*hist pl* ... MS-4
Price Store (historical)—*locale* (2) ... TN-4
Price Tank—*reservoir* ... AZ-5
Price Tank—*reservoir* (2) ... NM-5
Price Tank—*reservoir* ... TX-5
Price Tavern/Braffet Block—*hist pl* ... UT-8
Price Tower—*hist pl* ... OK-5
Pricetown—*locale* ... KY-4
**Pricetown**—*pop pl* ... KY-4
**Pricetown**—*pop pl* ... LA-4
**Pricetown**—*pop pl* ... NC-3
**Pricetown**—*pop pl* (2) ... OH-6
**Pricetown**—*pop pl* ... PA-2
**Pricetown**—*pop pl* (2) ... WV-2
**Price (Town of)**—*pop pl* ... WI-6
Price (Township of)—*fmr MCD* ... AR-4
Price (Township of)—*fmr MCD* ... NC-3
**Price (Township of)**—*pop pl* ... PA-2
Price Tunnel—*mine* ... UT-8
Price Valley—*valley* ... ID-8
Price Valley—*valley* ... KY-4
Price Valley Guard Station—*locale* ... ID-8
Price Valley Sch—*school* ... KY-4
Price Villa—*hist pl* ... KS-7
*Priceville* ... IN-6
*Priceville* ... PA-2
Priceville—*locale* ... PA-2
Priceville—*locale* ... SC-3
**Priceville**—*pop pl* ... AL-4
**Priceville**—*pop pl* ... KY-4
**Priceville**—*pop pl* ... MD-2
**Priceville**—*pop pl* ... MS-4
*Priceville Baptist Church* ... MS-4
Priceville Cem—*cemetery* ... MS-4
Priceville Ch—*church* ... MS-4
Priceville JHS—*school* ... AL-4
Priceville Mountain—*ridge* ... AL-4
Priceville Post Office (historical)—*building* ... AL-4
Priceville Sch (abandoned)—*school* ... PA-2
Price Walters Canyon—*valley* ... CO-8
*Price Wash* ... UT-8
Price West Camp—*locale* ... NM-5
Price/Wheeler House—*hist pl* ... IL-6
Prichard—*locale* ... MS-4
Prichard—*locale* ... PA-2
**Prichard**—*pop pl* ... AL-4
**Prichard**—*pop pl* ... ID-8
**Prichard**—*pop pl* ... WV-2
Prichard Airstrip—*airport* ... KS-7
Prichard Athletic Field—*park* ... TX-5
Prichard Branch—*stream* (2) ... KY-4
Prichard Cem—*cemetery* ... KY-4
Prichard Cem—*cemetery* ... MS-4
Prichard Ch—*church* ... KY-4
Prichard Chapel—*church* ... KY-4
*Prichard Creek* ... ID-8
Prichard Creek—*stream* ... ID-8
Prichard Creek—*stream* ... MT-8
Prichard Fork—*stream* ... KY-4
Prichard Hollow—*valley* ... KY-4
Prichard Homes Sch—*school* ... AL-4
*Prichard JHS* ... AL-4
Prichard Lake—*lake* ... MN-6
Prichard Lake—*lake* ... NM-5
Prichard Lake Pumping Station—*other* ... CA-9
Prichard Lakes—*lake* ... NM-5
Prichard Library—*building* ... AL-4
Prichard Methodist Ch—*church* ... AL-4
Prichard Mine—*mine* ... ID-8
Prichard Municipal Park—*park* ... AL-4
Prichard Municipal Stadium—*park* ... AL-4
Prichard Peak—*summit* ... ID-8
**Prichard Place**—*pop pl* ... KY-4
Prichards Branch—*stream* ... SC-3
Prichard Sch—*school* ... IL-6
Prichard Sch (historical)—*school* ... PA-2
Prichard Sewage Treatment Plant—*building* ... AL-4
*Prichards Inlet* ... SC-3
*Prichards Pond* ... MA-1
*Prichard Station* ... AL-4
Prichard Water Treatment Plant—*building* ... AL-4
Prichard Well—*locale* ... NM-5
*Prichard Y* ... ID-8
**Prichard Y**—*pop pl* ... ID-8
**Prichett**—*pop pl* ... CO-8
Prichett Cem—*cemetery* ... IL-6
Prichette (historical)—*locale* ... AL-4
Prichett Hollow—*valley* ... TN-4
Prichett Peaks—*summit* ... CA-9
PRICILLA DAILEY—*hist pl* ... CT-1
*Prickett* ... IL-6
Prickett, Jacob, Jr., Log House—*hist pl* ... WV-2
Prickett Bayou—*gut* ... LA-4
Prickett Branch—*stream* ... TN-4
Prickett Cem—*cemetery* ... WV-2
Prickett Creek—*stream* ... OR-9
Prickett Creek—*stream* ... WV-2
**Prickett Creek Junction**—*pop pl* ... WV-2
*Prickett Dam Backwater* ... MI-6
Prickett Lake—*lake* ... WA-9
Prickett Lake—*reservoir* ... MI-6
Prickett Ranch—*locale* ... SD-7
Prickett Sch—*school* ... ID-8
Prickett Sch (historical)—*school* ... AL-4
Pricketts Pond—*lake* ... CT-1
**Prickettville**—*pop pl* ... AL-4
*Prickley Pear Branch* ... TX-5
Prickley Pear Island—*island* ... DE-2
*Prickly* ... MT-8
Prickly Ash Creek—*stream* ... KY-4
Prickly Ash Mtn—*summit* ... NY-2
Prickly Ash Mtn—*summit* ... NC-3
Prickly Gulch—*valley* ... MT-8
Prickly Pear Bend—*bend* ... UT-8
Prickly Pear Branch—*stream* ... TX-5
Prickly Pear Canyon—*valley* (2) ... UT-8
*Prickly Pear Creek* ... MT-8
*Prickly Pear Creek* ... TX-5
Prickly Pear Creek—*stream* ... MT-8
Pricklypear Creek—*stream* ... TX-5
Prickly Pear Creek—*stream* ... WY-8
Prickly Pear Flat—*flat* ... UT-8
Prickly Pear Hill—*summit* ... NY-2
Prickly Pear Hill—*summit* ... TX-5
Prickly Pear Mtn—*summit* ... NC-3
Prickly Pear Mtn—*summit* ... VA-3
Prickly Pear Point—*cape* ... FL-3
Prickly Pear Point—*cape* ... UT-8
Prickly Point—*cape* ... MD-2
Prick Pond—*lake* ... ME-1
Pricnard Cem—*cemetery* ... TN-4
Pricy Creek—*stream* ... KY-4
Priday Agate Beds—*mine* ... OR-9
Priday Dam—*dam* ... OR-9
Priday Ditch—*canal* ... OR-9
Priday Lake—*lake* ... OR-9
Priday Rsvr—*reservoir* ... OR-9
Priday Spring—*spring* ... OR-9
Priddle Camp—*locale* ... NY-2
*Priddy* ... MS-4
**Priddy**—*pop pl* ... TX-5
Priddy Airp—*airport* ... MS-4
Priddy Cem—*cemetery* ... TN-4
*Priddy Creek* ... VA-3
Priddy Hollow—*valley* ... KY-4
*Priddys Creek* ... VA-3
*Pride* ... WV-2
Pride—*locale* ... AL-4
Pride—*locale* ... ME-1
Pride—*locale* ... TX-5
**Pride**—*pop pl* ... KY-4
**Pride**—*pop pl* ... LA-4
**Pride**—*pop pl* ... OH-6
Prideaux Oil Field—*oilfield* ... TX-5
Pride Basin—*basin* ... WA-9
Pride Bluff—*cliff* ... AL-4
Pride Branch—*stream* ... AR-4
*Pride Cave* ... AL-4
Pride Cem—*cemetery* (2) ... AL-4
Pride Cem—*cemetery* ... TN-4
Pride Cem—*cemetery* ... TX-5
Pride Cem—*cemetery* ... WV-2
Pride Ch—*church* ... AL-4
Pride Chapel—*church* ... LA-4
*Pride Creek* ... ND-7
*Pride Crossing* ... MA-1
Pride Draw—*valley* ... NM-5
Pride Hill—*summit* ... ME-1
Pride Landing—*locale* ... AL-4
Pride Mine—*mine* (2) ... AZ-5
Pride Mine—*mine* ... CA-9
Pridemore Cem—*cemetery* ... TN-4
Pridemore Cem—*cemetery* ... WV-2
Pride of America Mine—*mine* ... CO-8
Pride of Bonita Mine—*mine* ... CO-8
Pride of Green Sch—*school* ... WV-2
Pride of the Valley Ditch—*canal* ... WY-8
Pride of the West Mill—*locale* ... CO-8
Pride of the West Mine—*mine* ... CA-9
Pride of the West Mine—*mine* (2) ... CO-8
Pride of the West Sch—*school* ... MO-7
Pride Peak—*summit* ... OR-9
Pride Ranch—*locale* ... AZ-5
Pride Rock—*rock* ... MA-1
*Prides* ... AL-4
*Prides* ... MA-1
Pride Sch (historical)—*school* ... AL-4
*Prides Corner* ... ME-1
**Prides Corner**—*pop pl* ... ME-1
Prides Creek—*stream* ... IN-6
Prides Creek Lake—*reservoir* ... IN-6
Prides Creek Lake Dam Number 4—*dam* ... IN-6
**Prides Crossing**—*pop pl* ... MA-1
Prides Crossing (RR name Prides)—*uninc pl* ... MA-1
*Prides Ferry* ... NC-3
Prides Ferry (historical)—*locale* ... AL-4
*Prides Point* ... MS-4
Pride Springs—*spring* ... MT-8
Pride Springs Creek—*stream* ... MT-8
Prides (RR name for Prides Crossing)—*other* ... MA-1
*Pride's Station* ... AL-4
Pride Valley Ch—*church* ... AR-4
Pride Well—*well* ... AZ-5
**Pridgen**—*pop pl* ... GA-3
Pridgen Branch—*stream* (2) ... AL-4
Pridgen Cem—*cemetery* ... NC-3
Pridgen Ch—*church* ... NC-3
Pridgen Flats—*flat* ... NC-3
Pridgens Landing—*locale* ... NC-3
Pridgeon Branch—*stream* ... AL-4
Pridgeon Creek—*stream* ... TX-5
Pridgeons Landing—*locale* ... NC-3
Pridham Canyon—*valley* ... AZ-5
Pridham Creek—*stream* ... AZ-5
Pridham Lake—*lake* ... TX-5
Pridham Lake Oil Field—*oilfield* ... TX-5
Priebe Creek—*stream* ... AZ-5
Priebe Creek Tank—*reservoir* ... AZ-5
Priebe Gulch—*valley* ... MT-8
*Priebs Mill* ... AL-4
Priece Ranch—*locale* ... TX-5
Priem Cem—*cemetery* ... IA-7
**Prien**—*pop pl* ... LA-4
Prien, Bayou—*stream* ... LA-4
Prien Bldg—*hist pl* ... IA-7
Prien Lake—*lake* ... LA-4
Prien Memorial Park Cem—*cemetery* ... LA-4
*Priens Lake* ... WI-6
Prier Pond—*lake* ... NY-2
Prieskon Ridge—*ridge* ... MO-7
Priess Hollow—*valley* ... TX-5
Priess Pasture Windmill—*locale* ... TX-5
Priess Pond—*lake* ... CT-1
Priess Sch—*school* ... NY-2
*Priest* ... TN-4
Priest—*locale* ... CA-9
Priest, The—*summit* ... VA-3
Priest and Nuns—*pillar* ... UT-8
Priest Bay—*bay* ... MN-6
Priest Bayou—*stream* ... MS-4
Priest Beavers Oil Field—*oilfield* ... TX-5
Priest Branch—*stream* ... FL-3
Priest Bridge—*bridge* ... MD-2
Priest Brook—*stream* ... MA-1
Priest Butte—*summit* ... MT-8
Priest Butte Lake—*lake* ... MT-8
*Priest Butte Lakes* ... MT-8
Priest Canyon—*valley* ... CA-9
Priest Canyon—*valley* (2) ... NM-5
Priest Canyon—*valley* ... SD-7
Priest Cem—*cemetery* ... FL-3
Priest Cem—*cemetery* ... OH-6
Priest Creek—*stream* ... CO-8
Priest Creek—*stream* ... OR-9
Priest Creek—*stream* ... WI-6
Priest Creek Missionary Baptist Ch—*church* ... MS-4
Priest Ditch—*canal* ... IN-6
Priest Drain—*stream* ... MI-6
Priest Draw—*valley* ... AZ-5
Priest Draw—*valley* ... CO-8
Priester Lake—*lake* ... KY-4
Priester Millpond—*reservoir* ... SC-3
Priester Pond—*reservoir* ... MA-1
Priest Field—*park* ... WI-6
Priest Fork—*stream* ... KY-4
Priest Fork—*stream* ... VA-3
Priest Grade—*slope* ... CA-9
Priest Gulch—*valley* ... CO-8
Priest Gulch—*valley* ... MT-8
Priest Gulch Campground—*locale* ... CO-8
Priest Hill—*summit* (2) ... ME-1
Priest Hill—*summit* ... NH-1
Priest Hill Cem—*cemetery* ... ME-1
Priest Hill Ch—*church* ... NC-3
Priest Hollow—*valley* ... PA-2
Priest Hollow—*valley* ... UT-8
Priest Hollow Sch (historical)—*school* ... PA-2
Priest Lake—*lake* ... MI-6
Priest Lake—*lake* (2) ... WI-6
Priest Lake—*reservoir* ... ID-8
Priest Lake Marina—*other* ... ID-8
Priest Lake Ranger Station—*locale* ... ID-8
Priest Lake Rapids—*rapids* ... WI-6
Priest Lakes—*lake* ... CO-8
Priest Lake Sch—*school* ... ID-8
Priestland Branch—*stream* ... MD-2
Priest Landing—*locale* ... GA-3
Priestland Valley—*valley* ... MD-2
**Priestley**—*pop pl* ... WV-2
Priestley, Dr. Joseph, House—*hist pl* ... PA-2
Priestley, Joseph, House—*hist pl* ... PA-2
Priestley JHS—*school* ... LA-4
Priest Logan—*swamp* ... ME-1
**Priestly**—*pop pl* ... WV-2

Priestly Acad (historical)—*school* TN-4
*Priestly Bayou* MS-4
Priestly Brook—*stream* (2) ME-1
Priestly Cem—*cemetery* MO-7
Priestly Elem Sch—*school* PA-2
Priestly House—*hist pl* KS-7
Priestly House State Historic Site—*locale* PA-2
Priestly Lake—*lake* ME-1
*Priestly Mountains* ME-1
Priestly Mtn—*summit* ME-1
Priestly Rapids—*rapids* (2) ME-1
*Priestly School* PA-2
Priestly's Hydraulic Ram—*hist pl* ID-8
Priestly Tank—*reservoir* NM-5
Priest Mine—*mine* (2) NM-5
Priest Mtn—*summit* CO-8
Priest Overlook, The—*locale* VA-3
Priest Pass—*gap* MT-8
Priest Point—*cape* (2) WA-9
Priest Point Grange—*locale* WA-9
Priest Point Park—*park* WA-9
Priest Pond—*lake* AL-4
Priest Pond—*lake* FL-3
Priest Post Office (historical)—*building* TN-4
Priest Prairie—*flat* FL-3
Priest Ranch—*locale* ID-8
Priest Rapids—*locale* WA-9
Priest Rapids Dam—*dam* WA-9
*Priest Rapids Dam Reservoir* WA-9
Priest Rapids Lake—*reservoir* WA-9
*Priest Rapids Rsvr* WA-9
*Priest River* ID-8
**Priest River**—*pop pl* ID-8
Priest River—*stream* AK-9
Priest River—*stream* ID-8
Priest River Experimental For—*forest* ID-8
Priest River Golf Course—*other* ID-8
Priest River Park—*park* ID-8
Priest Rock—*bar* AK-9
Priest Rock—*island* AK-9
Priest Rock—*other* AK-9
Priest Rock—*pillar* CA-9
Priest Rsvr—*reservoir* CA-9
Priest Run—*stream* OH-6
*Priest'S Brook* MA-1
Priest Sch—*school* MI-6
Priest Sch—*school* TN-4
Priests Creek—*stream* MS-4
Priest Ski Area—*locale* MA-1
Priests Lake—*lake* MI-6
*Priests Pass* MT-8
Priests Point—*cape* MD-2
Priest Spring—*spring* CA-9
Priests Spur—*locale* TN-4
Priest Station—*locale* ID-8
Priest Street Sch—*school* MA-1
Priests Vly—*swamp* NY-2
Priests Vly Mtn—*summit* NY-2
Priests Well—*well* CA-9
*Priest's Well Mountain* MH-9
Priest Tank—*reservoir* AZ-5
Priest Tank—*reservoir* NM-5
Priest Valley—*basin* CA-9
**Priest Valley**—*pop pl* CA-9
Priest Valley Sch—*school* CA-9
Prieta, Loma—*summit* TX-5
Prieta, Sierra—*range* AZ-5
Prieta, Sierra—*ridge* AZ-5
Prieta, Sierra—*summit* AZ-5
Prietal—*summit* AZ-5
Prieta Mesa Site (LA 11251)—*hist pl* NM-5
Prieta Peak—*summit* AZ-5
Prieta Tank—*reservoir* TX-5
Prieta Windmill—*locale* TX-5
Prieto, Cerro—*summit* (2) AZ-5
*Prieto Canyon* CA-9
*Prieto Creek* AZ-5
Prieto Creek—*stream* TX-5
*Prietoe Creek* TX-5
*Prieto Peak* AZ-5
Prieto Plateau—*plain* AZ-5
Prietos Bar—*locale* TX-5
Prieto Windmill—*locale* TX-5
Priet Rsvr—*reservoir* WY-8
Priewe Well—*locale* NM-5
Prigden, O. F. and Mary, House—*hist pl* TX-5
*Priget Hollow* TN-4
Priggooris Park—*park* MI-6
**Prigmore**—*pop pl* TN-4
Prigmore House—*hist pl* AR-4
Prigmore Post Office (historical)—*building* TN-4
*Prigmores Store* TN-4
*Prillamans* VA-3
Prill Draw—*valley* WY-8
Prilliman—*locale* VA-3
*Prill Lake* OR-9
Prill Lake—*lake* OR-9
Prillman Ridge—*ridge* AR-4
Prill Sch—*hist pl* IN-6
Prim—*locale* VA-3
**Prim**—*pop pl* AR-4
Prima Deshecha Canada—*valley* CA-9
**Prima Estates**—*pop pl* TN-4
Primary Childrens Med Ctr—*hospital* UT-8
Primary Childrens Med Ctr Heliport—*airport* UT-8
Primary Day Sch—*school* MD-2
Primative Ch—*church* TX-5
Primavera Sch—*school* AZ-5
**Prima Vista**—*pop pl* CA-9
Prim Bridge—*bridge* AR-4
Prim Cem—*cemetery* MO-7
Primeaux—*locale* NV-8
Primeaux Canyon—*valley* NV-8
Prime Canyon—*valley* AZ-5
Prime Creek—*stream* MO-7
Prime Gully—*stream* LA-4
Primehook Beach—*beach* DE-2
**Primehook Beach**—*pop pl* DE-2
*Prime Hook Creek* DE-2
Primehook Creek—*stream* DE-2
Prime Hook Natl Wildlife Ref—*park* DE-2
*Prime Hook Neck* DE-2
Primehook Neck—*cape* DE-2
Prime House—*hist pl* NY-2
Prime Lake—*lake* AZ-5
Prime-Octagon House—*hist pl* NY-2
**Primera**—*pop pl* TX-5
Primera Agua Canyon—*valley* NM-5
Primera Ch—*church* TX-5
Primera Iglesia Bautista—*church* FL-3
Primera Iglesia Bautista Hispana de Westwood Lake—*church* FL-3
Primera Iglesia Hispana—*church* FL-3
Primera Mine—*mine* CA-9
Primeria Well—*well* AZ-5
*Primer Mine* SD-7
Primero—*locale* CO-8
Primero, Arroyo—*valley* TX-5
Primero (Barrio)—*fmr MCD* PR-3
Primero Branch, Canal (historical)—*canal* AZ-5
Primero HS—*school* CO-8
Primero Island—*island* TX-5
Primero Mine North—*mine* CO-8
Primero Mine South—*mine* CO-8
Primero Mine West—*mine* CO-8
Primero Rsvr—*reservoir* CO-8
Prime Sch—*school* IL-6
**Primghar**—*pop pl* IA-7
*Primisy Hill* RI-1
Primitive Baptist Cem—*cemetery* IL-6
Primitive Baptist Cem—*cemetery* TN-4
Primitive Baptist Ch—*church* AR-4
Primitive Baptist Ch—*church* IA-7
Primitive Baptist Ch (historical)—*church* TX-5
Primitive Baptist Ch of Bethel (historical)—*church* MS-4
Primitive Baptist Church—*hist pl* TN-4
Primitive Baptist Church of Brookfield—*hist pl* NY-2
Primitive Baptist Church of Sweeten's Cove—*hist pl* TN-4
Primitive Camp—*locale* CA-9
*Primitive Cem* MS-4
Primitive Cem—*cemetery* AR-4
Primitive Cem—*cemetery* MS-4
*Primitive Ch* AL-4
*Primitive Ch* MS-4
Primitive Ch—*church* AL-4
Primitive Ch—*church* AR-4
Primitive Ch—*church* IL-6
Primitive Ch—*church* IA-7
Primitive Ch—*church* KY-4
Primitive Ch—*church* MS-4
Primitive Ch—*church* MO-7
Primitive Ch—*church* (3) NC-3
Primitive Ch—*church* (2) TX-5
Primitive Ch (historical)—*church* TN-4
*Primitive Church* TN-4
Primitive Grove Ch—*church* GA-3
Primitive Hall—*hist pl* PA-2
Primitive Methodist Ch—*church* PA-2
**Primitive Ridge**—*pop pl* AL-4
Primitive Stone Ch—*church* TX-5
Primity Ch—*church* KY-4
*Primm* TN-4
Primm Branch—*stream* TN-4
Primm Cem—*cemetery* AR-4
Primm Cem—*cemetery* TN-4
Primmer Lake—*lake* MN-6
Primm Hollow—*valley* TN-4
Primm Post Office (historical)—*building* TN-4
Primm Sch—*school* IL-6
**Primm Springs**—*pop pl* TN-4
Primm Springs—*spring* TN-4
Primm Springs Hist Dist—*hist pl* TN-4
Primmton (historical)—*locale* MS-4
Primo Bay—*bay* FL-3
Primo Island—*island* FL-3
Primo Point—*cape* FL-3
**Primos**—*pop pl* PA-2
Primos Mine—*mine* CO-8
**Primos-Secane**—*pop pl* PA-2
Primo Stables—*locale* TX-5
Primo Tank—*reservoir* NM-5
*Primrose* AL-4
*Primrose* MP-9
Primrose—*locale* AK-9
Primrose—*locale* KY-4
Primrose—*locale* MT-8
Primrose—*locale* OH-6
Primrose—*locale* RI-1
Primrose—*locale* TX-5
Primrose—*mine* UT-8
**Primrose**—*pop pl* GA-3
**Primrose**—*pop pl* IA-7
**Primrose**—*pop pl* NE-7
**Primrose**—*pop pl* (2) PA-2
**Primrose**—*pop pl* TX-5
**Primrose**—*pop pl* WI-6
Primrose, Lake—*reservoir* IN-6
**Primrose Acres**—*pop pl* MD-2
Primrose Branch—*stream* WI-6
Primrose Bridge—*bridge* GA-3
Primrose Brook—*stream* NJ-2
Primrose Brook—*stream* NY-2
Primrose Cem—*cemetery* IA-7
Primrose Ch—*church* AR-4
Primrose Ch—*church* WI-6
Primrose Ch Number Two (historical)—*church* AL-4
*Primrose Ch Number 1* AL-4
Primrose Cirque—*basin* UT-8
Primrose Creek—*stream* MO-7
Primrose Creek—*stream* WY-8
Primrose Creek Campground—*locale* AK-9
Primrose Drain—*canal* ND-7
Primrose Draw—*valley* NV-8
*Primrose Hill* AZ-5
Primrose Hill—*summit* RI-1
Primrose Hill Hist Dist—*hist pl* ME-1
Primrose (historical)—*locale* MS-4
Primrose Hollow—*valley* MO-7
Primrose Lake—*lake* CA-9
Primrose Mill—*hist pl* IA-7
Primrose Mine—*mine* AK-9
Primrose Mine—*mine* CA-9
*Primrose Park* FL-3
Primrose Point—*cape* MD-2
Primrose Pond—*reservoir* RI-1
Primrose Pond Dam—*dam* RI-1
Primrose Ridge—*ridge* AK-9
Primrose Sch—*school* IL-6
Primrose Sch—*school* IA-7
Primrose Sch—*school* MO-7
Primrose Sch—*school* NY-2
Primrose Sch—*school* TX-5
Primrose Sch for the Retarded—*school* FL-3
Primrose Sch (historical)—*school* MS-4
Primrose Shop Ctr—*locale* MA-1
Primrose Slough—*stream* TX-5
Primrose Spring—*spring* AZ-5
Primrose Street Schoolhouse—*hist pl* MA-1
Primrose Town Hall—*building* ND-7
**Primrose Township**—*pop pl* ND-7
Primroy Ch—*church* TN-4
Primroy Creek—*stream* TN-4
**Primroy (historical)**—*pop pl* TN-4
**Primus**—*pop pl* SC-3
Primus Creek—*stream* AK-9
Primus Peak—*summit* WA-9
*Prince* MS-4
Prince—*locale* VA-3
**Prince**—*pop pl* NV-8
**Prince**—*pop pl* WV-2
Prince—*uninc pl* NY-2
Prince, Lake—*reservoir* VA-3
Prince, Thomas, House—*hist pl* OR-9
Prince Albert—*summit* OR-9
*Prince Albert Canyon* TX-5
Prince Albert Creek—*stream* CA-9
Prince Albert Draw—*valley* TX-5
Prince Albert Mine—*mine* AZ-5
Prince Albert Rsvr—*reservoir* OR-9
Prince Albert Spring (historical)—*spring* ID-8
Prince Albert Tank—*reservoir* TX-5
Prince Albert Windmill—*locale* TX-5
Prince and Sons Number 1 Dam—*dam* SD-7
Prince and Sons Number 2 Dam—*dam* SD-7
Prince Barranca—*valley* CA-9
*Prince Bay* NY-2
Prince Branch—*stream* (2) KY-4
Prince Branch—*stream* (3) TN-4
Prince Branch—*stream* WV-2
Prince Brook—*stream* NY-2
Prince Brothers General Store-Berry Store—*hist pl* WV-2
Prince Cem—*cemetery* (3) AL-4
Prince Cem—*cemetery* (2) AR-4
Prince Cem—*cemetery* CO-8
Prince Cem—*cemetery* IL-6
Prince Cem—*cemetery* (2) KY-4
Prince Cem—*cemetery* ME-1
Prince Cem—*cemetery* MO-7
Prince Cem—*cemetery* (2) NC-3
Prince Cem—*cemetery* OH-6
Prince Chapel—*church* FL-3
Prince Chapel—*church* NC-3
Prince Chapel—*church* TX-5
**Prince Chapel**—*pop pl* MS-4
Prince Chapel Sch (historical)—*school* MS-4
Prince Charles Hotel—*hist pl* NC-3
Prince Charming Spring—*spring* AZ-5
Prince Cove—*bay* ME-1
Prince Cove—*cove* MA-1
Prince Creek—*stream* (2) AK-9
Prince Creek—*stream* CO-8
Prince Creek—*stream* ID-8
Prince Creek—*stream* IN-6
Prince Creek—*stream* (2) SC-3
Prince Creek—*stream* WA-9
Prince Creek Campground—*locale* WA-9
Prince Crossing—*locale* IL-6
Prince Crossroads—*locale* AL-4
**Princedale**—*pop pl* AR-4
Prince Ditch—*canal* CO-8
Princedom Cabin—*hist pl* AR-4
Prince Edward Acad—*school* VA-3
Prince Edward And Goodwin Lake State Park—*park* VA-3
**Prince Edward (County)**—*pop pl* VA-3
Prince Edward Lake—*reservoir* VA-3
Prince Edward State For—*forest* VA-3
Prince Ferry (historical)—*locale* TN-4
Prince Field—*park* FL-3
Prince Fork—*stream* KY-4
**Prince Frederick**—*pop pl* MD-2
Prince Frederick Ch—*church* SC-3
Prince Frederick's Chapel Ruins—*hist pl* SC-3
*Prince Fredericktown* MD-2
Prince Fred Knob—*summit* AR-4
*Prince Gallitzin Spring* PA-2
Prince Gallitzin State Park—*park* PA-2
Prince Gap—*gap* TN-4
**Prince George**—*pop pl* VA-3
**Prince George Acres (subdivision)**—*pop pl* DE-2
Prince George Ch—*church* VA-3
**Prince George (County)**—*pop pl* VA-3
Prince George Creek—*stream* NC-3
Prince George Mine—*mine* AZ-5
**Prince Georges**—*pop pl* VA-3
Prince Georges Chapel—*church* DE-2
Prince George's Chapel—*hist pl* DE-2
Prince Georges Country Club—*other* MD-2
**Prince George's (County)**—*pop pl* MD-2
Prince George's Facility—*post sta* MD-2
Prince Georges Hosp—*hospital* MD-2
Prince Georges HS—*school* VA-3
Prince Georges JHS—*school* VA-3
Prince Georges Plaza—*locale* MD-2
Prince Georges Yacht Club—*other* MD-2
Prince George Winyah Church (Episcopal) and Cemetery—*hist pl* SC-3
Prince Gulch—*valley* OR-9
Prince Gurnet—*channel* ME-1
Prince Hall Masonic Temple—*hist pl* DC-2
**Prince Hall Plaza**—*pop pl* IN-6
Prince Head—*isthmus* MA-1
*Prince Hendricks River* DE-2
Prince Henry Sch—*school* NE-7
Prince Hill—*summit* AR-4
Prince Hill—*summit* RI-1
Prince Hollow—*valley* (2) TN-4
Prince Hollow Run—*stream* PA-2
Prince Island—*island* AL-4
Prince Island—*island* AK-9
Prince Island—*island* (2) CA-9
Prince Island—*island* NY-2
Prince Knob—*summit* TN-4
Prince Kuhio Beach Park—*park* HI-9
Prince Lake—*lake* LA-4
Prince Lake—*lake* OR-9
Prince Lake No. 1—*reservoir* CO-8
Prince Lake No. 2—*reservoir* CO-8
*Prince Lakeuikomkenney Creek* MI-6
Prince Mall—*locale* AZ-5
*Prince Maurice River* NJ-2
Prince Mill Swamp—*swamp* SC-3
Prince Mine—*mine* AZ-5
Prince Mine and Camp—*locale* NV-8
Prince Mtn—*summit* GA-3
Prince Mtn—*summit* UT-8
Prince of Peace Catholic Ch—*church* (2) FL-3
Prince of Peace Ch—*church* AR-4
Prince of Peace Ch—*church* (2) IL-6
Prince of Peace Ch—*church* MI-6
Prince of Peace Ch—*church* (2) NC-3
Prince of Peace Ch—*church* PA-2
Prince of Peace Ch—*church* TX-5
*Prince of Peace Church* IN-6
Prince of Peace Lutheran Ch—*church* AL-4
Prince of Peace Lutheran Ch—*church* (2) FL-3
Prince of Peace Lutheran Ch—*church* IN-6
Prince of Peace Lutheran Ch—*church* (3) MS-4
Prince of Peace Lutheran Ch—*church* UT-8
Prince of Peace Lutheran Ch (LCMS)—*church* FL-3
Prince of Peace Lutheran Church-ALC—*church* FL-3
Prince of Peace Lutheran Kindergarten—*school* FL-3
Prince of Peace Lutheran Sch—*school* FL-3
Prince of Peace Sch—*school* CA-9
Prince of Peace Sch—*school* IL-6
Prince Of Wales (Census Subarea)—*cens area* AK-9
Prince of Wales Creek—*stream* AK-9
Prince Of Wales Island—*island* AK-9
Prince of Wales Mine—*mine* NV-8
**Prince of Wales-Outer Ketchikan (Census Area)**—*pop pl* AK-9
Prince Of Wales Passage—*channel* AK-9
Prince of Wales Shaft—*mine* UT-8
Prince of Wales Shoal—*bar* AK-9
Prince Park—*park* IL-6
Prince Peak—*summit* ID-8
Prince Peak Trail—*trail* ID-8
Prince P.O. (historical)—*building* MS-4
Prince Point—*cape* AL-4
Prince Point—*cape* (3) ME-1
Prince Point Ledge—*bar* ME-1
Prince Pond—*lake* RI-1
Prince Ranch—*locale* NM-5
Prince Ridge—*ridge* AR-4
Prince River—*stream* MA-1
Prince Royal Canyon—*valley* NV-8
Prince Rsvr—*reservoir* CO-8
Prince Run—*stream* IL-6
Princesa Island—*island* AK-9
*Prince's Bay* NY-2
Princes Bay—*bay* NY-2
**Princes Bay**—*pop pl* NY-2
Princes Bay Ch—*church* NY-2
Princes Camp—*locale* CA-9
Prince Sch—*school* AZ-5
Prince Sch—*school* CT-1
*Princes Creek* PA-2
*Princes Creek* SC-3
Princes East Lake—*reservoir* IN-6
Princes Hants Lake Dam—*dam* IN-6
*Princes Head* MA-1
*Princes Hill* RI-1
Prince Shoal—*bar* AK-9
*Princes Lake* IN-6
**Princes Lakes**—*pop pl* IN-6
Princes Landing (historical)—*locale* AL-4
Princes Lower Landing (historical)—*locale* AL-4
Princes Northeast Lake—*reservoir* IN-6
Princes North Lake—*reservoir* IN-6
*Princes Point* ME-1
*Princes Pond* RI-1
Princes Pond—*lake* CT-1
Prince Spring—*spring* AL-4
Prince Spring—*spring* TN-4
**Princess**—*pop pl* KY-4
*Princessa Island* MP-9
*Princess Anne* VA-3
**Princess Anne**—*pop pl* MD-2
**Princess Anne**—*pop pl* VA-3
Princess Anne Ch—*church* VA-3
Princess Anne Country Club—*other* VA-3
**Princess Anne Hills**—*pop pl* VA-3
Princess Anne Hist Dist—*hist pl* MD-2
Princess Anne HS—*school* VA-3
**Princess Anne Park**—*pop pl* VA-3
**Princess Anne Plaza**—*pop pl* VA-3
Princess Ann Memorial Park—*cemetery* VA-3
**Princess Ann Plaza**—*pop pl* VA-3
Princess Arch—*arch* KY-4
*Princess Bay* NY-2
Princess Bay—*bay* AK-9
Princess Bay—*bay* VI-3
*Princess Bay Station* NY-2
Princess Blue Ribbon Mine—*mine* ID-8
*Princess Cave* AL-4
*Princess Creek* PA-2
*Princess Creek* SC-3
Princess Creek—*stream* OR-9
Princess Creek—*stream* WA-9
Princess Creek Forest Camp—*locale* OR-9
*Princesse* MP-9
Princess Head—*cliff* AK-9
Princess Ice Cream Co.—*hist pl* TX-5
Princess Jeanne Park and Swimming Pool—*school* NM-5
Princess Lake—*lake* FL-3
Princess Lake—*lake* PA-2
Princess Mine—*mine* AZ-5
Princess Pat Mine—*mine* AZ-5
Princess Pat Mine—*mine* CA-9
Princess Peak—*summit* AK-9
Princess Pine Camp—*locale* WA-9
**Princess Place (subdivision)**—*pop pl* NC-3
Princess Point Bridge—*bridge* WI-6
Princess Point Sch—*school* MI-6
Princess Ridge—*ridge* OR-9
Princess Rock—*island* AK-9
Princess Rock—*pillar* CA-9
Princess Run—*stream* PA-2
Princess Shaft (Active)—*mine* NM-5
Princess Theatre—*hist pl* IN-6
Princes Still—*locale* GA-3
Princes Store (historical)—*locale* TN-4
Princess Trail—*trail* OR-9
Princessville—*locale* NJ-2
*Princes Town* NJ-2
Prince Street Sch—*school* MS-4
Prince Street Sch—*school* VA-3
*Princes Upper Landing* AL-4
Princes White Lake—*reservoir* IN-6
Princes White Lake Dam—*dam* IN-6
Prince Tank—*reservoir* AZ-5
Princeton—*airport* NJ-2
Princeton—*locale* CO-8
Princeton—*locale* MT-8
Princeton—*locale* NC-3
Princeton—*locale* OH-6
**Princeton**—*pop pl* AL-4
**Princeton**—*pop pl* AR-4
**Princeton**—*pop pl* (2) CA-9
**Princeton**—*pop pl* FL-3
**Princeton**—*pop pl* ID-8
**Princeton**—*pop pl* IL-6
**Princeton**—*pop pl* IN-6
**Princeton**—*pop pl* IA-7
**Princeton**—*pop pl* KS-7
**Princeton**—*pop pl* KY-4
**Princeton**—*pop pl* LA-4
**Princeton**—*pop pl* ME-1
**Princeton**—*pop pl* MD-2
**Princeton**—*pop pl* MA-1
**Princeton**—*pop pl* MI-6
**Princeton**—*pop pl* MN-6
**Princeton**—*pop pl* MO-7
**Princeton**—*pop pl* NE-7
**Princeton**—*pop pl* NJ-2
**Princeton**—*pop pl* NC-3
**Princeton**—*pop pl* OR-9
**Princeton**—*pop pl* PA-2
**Princeton**—*pop pl* SC-3
**Princeton**—*pop pl* TN-4
**Princeton**—*pop pl* TX-5
**Princeton**—*pop pl* WV-2
**Princeton**—*pop pl* WI-6
Princeton—*uninc pl* GA-3
Princeton, Mount—*summit* CO-8
Princeton, Mount—*summit* MT-8
Princeton Battlefield—*hist pl* NJ-2
Princeton Battlefield State Park—*park* NJ-2
**Princeton-by-the-Sea**—*pop pl* CA-9
Princeton Canal Number C-102—*canal* (2) FL-3
Princeton Cave—*cave* AL-4
Princeton (CCD)—*cens area* AL-4
Princeton (CCD)—*cens area* KY-4
Princeton (CCD)—*cens area* SC-3
Princeton (CCD)—*cens area* TX-5
Princeton Cem—*cemetery* AR-4
Princeton Cem—*cemetery* ME-1
Princeton Cem—*cemetery* NE-7
Princeton Cem—*cemetery* NJ-2
Princeton Cem—*cemetery* TX-5
Princeton Cemetery—*hist pl* AR-4
*Princeton Centre* MA-1
Princeton Ch—*church* AL-4
Princeton Ch—*church* GA-3
Princeton Ch—*church* PA-2
Princeton Chapter House—*hist pl* IL-6
Princeton Ch of the Nazarene—*church* FL-3
Princeton Club—*hist pl* PA-2
**Princeton Colonial Park**—*pop pl* NJ-2
Princeton Community HS—*school* IN-6
Princeton Country Club—*other* IN-6
Princeton Country Club—*other* KY-4
Princeton Division—*civil* AL-4
Princeton Downtown Commercial District—*hist pl* KY-4
**Princeton Estates**—*pop pl* NJ-2
**Princeton Estates (subdivision)**—*pop pl* DE-2
Princeton Ferry—*locale* CA-9
Princeton Glacier—*glacier* AK-9
Princeton-Goulds (CCD)—*cens area* FL-3
Princeton Gulch—*valley* MT-8
*Princeton Harbor* CA-9
Princeton Harbor—*bay* NJ-2
**Princeton Heights (subdivision)**—*pop pl* AL-4
*Princeton High School* NC-3
**Princeton Hills (subdivision)**—*pop pl* TN-4
Princeton Hist Dist—*hist pl* NJ-2
Princeton (historical)—*locale* KS-7
**Princeton (historical)**—*pop pl* MS-4
Princeton Hotel—*hist pl* CA-9
Princeton HS—*school* OH-6
Princeton Island—*island* ME-1
**Princeton Ivy East**—*pop pl* NJ-2
Princeton JHS—*school* OH-6
**Princeton Junction**—*pop pl* NJ-2
Princeton-Kauffman Memorial Airp—*airport* MO-7
*Princeton Lake* NJ-2
Princeton Landing—*locale* AR-4
Princeton Landing—*locale* MS-4
Princeton Methodist Church—*hist pl* AR-4
Princeton Mine (underground)—*mine* AL-4
Princeton North—*CDP* NJ-2
Princeton Number One Mine—*mine* MI-6
Princeton Number Three Mine—*mine* MI-6
Princeton Number Two Mine—*mine* MI-6
Princeton Park—*park* OH-6
**Princeton Place (subdivision)**—*pop pl* AL-4
**Princeton (P.O.)**—*pop pl* LA-4
Princeton Post Office—*locale* MI-6
Princeton Presbyterian Ch—*church* TN-4
Princeton Public Hunting Area—*area* IA-7
Princeton Public Sch—*school* NJ-2
Princeton Sch—*school* AL-4
Princeton Sch—*school* FL-3
Princeton Sch—*school* MD-2
Princeton Sch—*school* MA-1
Princeton Sch—*school* MI-6
Princeton Sch—*school* OH-6
Princeton Sch (historical)—*school* TN-4
Princeton Siding—*locale* CA-9
Princeton Site—*hist pl* NC-3
**Princeton (sta.)**—*pop pl* LA-4
Princeton Station—*locale* PA-2
**Princeton Station**—*pop pl* MA-1
Princeton Summer Camp—*locale* NJ-2
*Princeton Tower* FL-3
**Princeton (Town of)**—*pop pl* ME-1
**Princeton (Town of)**—*pop pl* MA-1
**Princeton (Town of)**—*pop pl* WI-6
Princeton Township—*fmr MCD* IA-7
**Princeton Township**—*pop pl* NJ-2
Princeton (Township of)—*fmr MCD* AR-4
**Princeton (Township of)**—*pop pl* IL-6
**Princeton (Township of)**—*pop pl* IN-6
**Princeton (Township of)**—*pop pl* MN-6
**Princeton (Township of)**—*pop pl* NJ-2
*Princeton Township (Township of)* NJ-2
Princeton Union Sch—*school* NC-3
Princeton Univ—*school* NJ-2
Princeton Univ Medical Research Center—*school* NJ-2
Princeton Waterworks—*other* IN-6
**Princeton Wood II (subdivision)**—*pop pl* DE-2
**Princeton Woods (subdivision)**—*pop pl* AL-4
Princeton Youth Park—*park* WV-2
*Princetown* KY-4
*Princetown* NJ-2
**Princetown**—*pop pl* NY-2
Princetown Ch—*church* NY-2
**Princetown (Town of)**—*pop pl* NY-2
Prince Valley—*basin* UT-8
Princeville—*CDP* HI-9
Princeville—*locale* SC-3
**Princeville**—*pop pl* (2) IL-6
**Princeville**—*pop pl* NC-3
Princeville Cem—*cemetery* KS-7
Princeville Cem—*cemetery* TX-5
Princeville Ch—*church* SC-3
Princeville Ch—*church* TX-5
Princeville Elem Sch—*school* NC-3
Princeville Ranch—*locale* HI-9
Princeville Town Hall—*building* NC-3
**Princeville (Township of)**—*pop pl* IL-6
**Princewick**—*pop pl* WV-2
**Prince William**—*pop pl* IN-6
Prince William Ch—*church* SC-3
**Prince William (County)**—*pop pl* VA-3
Prince William Forest Park—*park* VA-3
Prince William Hosp—*hospital* VA-3
Prince William Sch—*school* SC-3
Prince William Sound—*bay* AK-9
Prince William Sound (Census Subarea)—*cens area* AK-9
*Principal Meridian* MT-8
**Principia**—*pop pl* MO-7
Principia Coll—*school* IL-6
Principia Coll—*school* (2) MO-7
Principia Page-Park YMCA Gymnasium—*hist pl* MO-7
*Principio* MD-2
*Principio Creek* MD-2
Principio Creek—*stream* MD-2
Principio Furnace—*hist pl* MD-2
Principio Furnace—*locale* MD-2
**Principio Furnace (Principio)**—*pop pl* MD-2
Principio Station—*locale* MD-2
Princton Creek—*stream* OR-9
**Prindle**—*pop pl* WA-9
Prindle, Mount—*summit* AK-9
Prindle, William, Livery Stable—*hist pl* MI-6
**Prindle Corner**—*pop pl* VT-1
**Prindle Corners**—*pop pl* VT-1
Prindle Hill—*summit* MA-1
Prindle Lake—*reservoir* MA-1
Prindle Lake Dam—*dam* MA-1
Prindle Mine—*mine* MN-6
Prindle Peak—*summit* OR-9
*Prindle Pond* MA-1
Prindle Ranch—*locale* NE-7
Prindle Sch—*school* VT-1
Prindle Trail—*trail* PA-2
Prindle Volcano—*summit* AK-9
Prin Drain—*canal* MI-6
*Prine* MS-4
**Prine**—*pop pl* FL-3
Prine Cabin—*locale* CA-9
Prine Cem—*cemetery* IA-7
Prine Ditch—*canal* IN-6
*Prinee Valley* UT-8
*Prinel Lake* WI-6
Prine RR Station—*locale* FL-3
Prine Sch—*school* FL-3
Prines Ditch—*canal* MT-8
**Prineville**—*pop pl* OR-9
Prineville Airp—*airport* OR-9
Prineville Camp—*park* OR-9
*Prineville Dam* OR-9
Prineville Golf and Country Club—*other* OR-9
Prineville Gulch—*valley* OR-9
Prineville Junction—*locale* OR-9
Prineville Rsvr—*reservoir* OR-9
Prineville Rsvr State Park—*park* OR-9
Prineville Southeast—*uninc pl* OR-9
Prineville Valley—*valley* OR-9
Pring—*locale* CO-8
Pringle—*locale* TX-5
**Pringle**—*pop pl* GA-3
**Pringle**—*pop pl* OR-9
**Pringle**—*pop pl* PA-2
**Pringle**—*pop pl* SD-7
Pringle Bend—*locale* SC-3
Pringle Borough—*civil* PA-2
Pringle Branch—*stream* (3) FL-3
Pringle Branch—*stream* MS-4
Pringle Brook—*stream* VT-1
Pringle Butte—*summit* OR-9
Pringle Canyon—*valley* CA-9
Pringle Cem—*cemetery* FL-3
Pringle Cem—*cemetery* SD-7
Pringle community Center—*building* MS-4
Pringle Creek—*stream* NY-2
Pringle Creek—*stream* (2) OR-9
Pringle Creek—*stream* SC-3
Pringle Creek—*stream* TX-5
Pringle Drain—*canal* MI-6
Pringle Falls—*falls* OR-9
Pringle Falls Campground—*park* OR-9
Pringle Falls Experimental For—*forest* OR-9
Pringle Falls Experimental Station—*other* OR-9
Pringle Falt Dam—*dam* OR-9
Pringle Flat Rsvr—*reservoir* OR-9
Pringle Fork—*stream* WV-2
Pringle Hill—*summit* CO-8
Pringle Hill—*summit* PA-2
Pringle Hill Cem—*cemetery* PA-2
Pringle Hollow—*valley* WV-2
Pringle Lake—*lake* TX-5
Pringle Park—*park* OR-9
Pringle Park Plaza—*post sta* OR-9
Pringle Pump—*locale* AZ-5
Pringle Ranch Landing Field—*airport* KS-7
Pringle Ridge—*ridge* CA-9

Pringle Run—*stream* WV-2
Pringle Sch—*school* MA-1
Pringle Sch—*school* NY-2
Pringle Sch—*school* OR-9
Pringle Spring—*spring* OR-9
Pringle Swamp—*swamp* FL-3
**Pringletown**—*pop pl* SC-3
Pringle Wash—*stream* AZ-5
Pringle Well—*well* AZ-5
Prink Rsvr—*reservoir* CO-8
**Prinsburg**—*pop pl* MN-6
Prinsep, Mount—*summit* AK-9
**Prinston Park**—*pop pl* AZ-5
Printer—*locale* KY-4
Printer Boy Hill—*summit* CO-8
Printer Gulch—*valley* CA-9
**Printer (RR name Salisbury)**—*pop pl* KY-4
Printer Run—*stream* PA 2
Printers Alley Hist Dist—*hist pl* TN-4
Printers Knob—*summit* NC-3
Printup, Peter W., Plantation—*hist pl* GA-3
Printup Cem—*cemetery* GA-3
*Print Works* RI-1
Print Works Pond—*lake* RI-1
Printz Basin—*basin* WA-9
Printz Creek—*stream* WI-6
Printz Creek Sch—*school* WI-6
Printz Gulch—*valley* MT-8
Printzhof, The—*hist pl* PA-2
Printz Ridge—*ridge* MT-8
**Prioleau**—*pop pl* SC-3
Prioleau Creek—*stream* SC-3
*Prior* SD-7
Prior—*locale* GA-3
*Prior Bay* TN-4
Prior Branch—*stream* KY-4
Prior Cabin—*locale* NM-5
Prior Cem—*cemetery* MO-7
Prior Ch—*church* MO-7
*Prior Creek* CT-1
*Prior Creek* KY-4
*Prior Creek* TN-4
Prior Creek—*stream* KS-7
Prior Creek—*stream* MI-6
Prior Creek—*stream* NM-5
Priord Lake—*lake* UT-8
Prior Draw—*valley* WY-8
Prior Flat—*flat* WY-8
Prior Grove Ch—*church* IL-6
*Prior Island* KY-4
Prior Lake—*lake* (2) MI-6
Prior Lake—*lake* TX-5
**Prior Lake**—*pop pl* MN-6
Prior Lake Ind Res—*other* MN-6
Prior Lake Ind Res—*reserve* MN-6
Prior Point—*cape* AK-9
Prior Ranch—*locale* WA-9
*Priors* GA-3
Priors Branch—*stream* KY-4
Prior Sch—*school* IL-6
*Priors Creek* CT-1
*Prior Spring* AL-4
**Prior (Township of)**—*pop pl* MN-6
Priory of Saint Mary—*church* MO-7
Pripet—*locale* ME-1
**Priscilla**—*pop pl* IL-6
**Priscilla**—*pop pl* MS-4
Priscilla—*uninc pl* NC-3
Priscilla, Mtn—*summit* NV-8
**Priscilla Beach**—*pop pl* MA-1
Priscilla Brook—*stream* NH-1
Priscilla Ch—*church* FL-3
Priscilla Gulch—*valley* MT-8
Priscilla Mine—*mine* MT-8
Priscilla Peak—*summit* MT-8
Prisehouse Mtn—*summit* VA-3
Priser Mine—*mine* NM-5
Prisk Sch—*school* CA-9
*Prism* MS-4
Prismatic—*locale* MS-4
Prismatic Post Office (historical)—*building* MS-4
Prism Creek—*stream* ID-8
*Prism Post Office* MS-4
Prison Branch—*stream* GA-3
Prison Brickyard Hist Dist—*hist pl* MT-8
Prison Camp No 24—*locale* VA-3
Prison Camp No 31—*locale* VA-3
Prison Camp 116—*locale* NC-3
Prison Canyon—*valley* TX-5
Prison Cem—*cemetery* FL-3
Prison Cem—*cemetery* NY-2
Prison Cem—*cemetery* OK-5
Prison Cem—*cemetery* TX-5
Prison Cem—*cemetery* WV-2
Prisoner Creek—*stream* CA-9
Prisoner Lake—*lake* MT-8
Prisoner of War Camp—*locale* NM-5
Prisoner of War Cem—*cemetery* AL-4
Prisoner Rock—*island* CA-9
Prisoners Harbor—*bay* CA-9
Prisoners Point—*cape* CA-9
Prisoners Rock—*pillar* CA-9
Prison Farm Draw—*valley* WY-8
Prison Hill—*ridge* NV-8
Prison Hill—*summit* AZ-5
*Prison Island* KS-7
Prison Island—*island* NY-2
Prison Lake—*reservoir* OK-5
Prison Lateral—*canal* NM-5
Prison No 601—*locale* NC-3
Prison Point—*cape* MD-2
Prison Spring—*spring* CA-9
Prison Unit No 068—*locale* NC-3
Prison Unit 4043—*locale* NC-3
Prisor Well—*well* NM-5
Prissel Valley—*valley* WI-6
Prissy Wicks Shoal—*bar* NJ-2
Pristine Lake—*lake* CO-8
*Pritchard* PA-2
Pritchard—*locale* OH-6
Pritchard—*locale* OK-5
Pritchard—*locale* PA-2
**Pritchard**—*pop pl* CA-9
**Pritchard**—*pop pl* SC-3
Pritchard, Mount—*summit* VT-1
Pritchard, Paul, Shipyard—*hist pl* SC-3
Pritchard Branch—*stream* TN-4
*Pritchard Brook* CT-1
Pritchard Brook—*stream* NY-2
Pritchard Camp—*locale* LA-4
Pritchard Cave—*cave* TN-4
Pritchard Cem—*cemetery* AL-4
Pritchard Cem—*cemetery* (2) LA-4
Pritchard Cem—*cemetery* MI-6
Pritchard Cem—*cemetery* MS-4
Pritchard Cem—*cemetery* NC-3
Pritchard Cem—*cemetery* SC-3
Pritchard Ch—*church* LA-4
Pritchard Ch—*church* WV-2
Pritchard Creek—*stream* CA-9
Pritchard Creek—*stream* ID-8
Pritchard Creek—*stream* NC-3
Pritchard Creek—*stream* OR-9
Pritchard Creek—*stream* WY-8
Pritchard Field—*park* CA-9
Pritchard Flat—*flat* OR-9
Pritchard Hill *locale* CA-9
**Pritchard (historical)**—*pop pl* PA-2
Pritchard Hollow—*valley* MO-7
Pritchard Hollow—*valley* (2) PA-2
*Pritchard Inlet* SC-3
*Pritchard Island* SC-3
Pritchard Island—*island* FL-3
Pritchard Lake Dam—*dam* MS-4
Pritchard Landing—*locale* MO-7
Pritchard Mill Creek—*stream* NC-3
Pritchard-Moore-Goodrich House—*hist pl* GA-3
Pritchard Park—*park* WI-6
Pritchard Pass—*gap* WY-8
*Pritchard Pond* CT-1
Pritchard Pond—*lake* GA-3
Pritchard Ranch—*locale* TX-5
Pritchard Revetment—*levee* MO-7
Pritchard Rsvr—*reservoir* OR-9
Pritchard Run—*stream* PA-2
Pritchard Run—*stream* WV-2
Pritchards Canyon—*valley* NV-8
Pritchard Sch—*school* IL-6
Pritchard Sch—*school* MS-4
Pritchard Sch—*school* NE-7
Pritchard Sch—*school* TN-4
Pritchard Sch—*school* WV-2
**Pritchards Corner**—*pop pl* PA-2
Pritchards Grove Picnic Area—*locale* WY-8
Pritchards Inlet—*gut* SC-3
Pritchards Island—*island* SC-3
*Pritchards Landing* AL-4
Pritchard's Outlook Hist Dist—*hist pl* MI-6
*Pritchards Pond* MA-1
Pritchards Pond—*lake* CT-1
Pritchard Spring—*spring* CO-8
Pritchards Station—*locale* NV-8
**Pritchardsville**—*pop pl* KY-4
**Pritchardville**—*pop pl* SC-3
Pritchard Wash—*stream* CO-8
Pritchell Mill Branch—*stream* FL-3
Pritcherds Spring—*spring* NV-8
Pritchert Spring—*spring* ID-8
Pritchett—*locale* TX-5
**Pritchett**—*pop pl* CO-8
*Pritchett Arch* UT-8
*Pritchett Branch* TN-4
Pritchett Branch—*stream* TN-4
Pritchett Canyon—*valley* UT-8
Pritchett Cem—*cemetery* AL-4
Pritchett Cem—*cemetery* CO-8
Pritchett Cem—*cemetery* (3) MO-7
Pritchett Cem—*cemetery* (3) TN-4
*Pritchett Creek* CA-9
Pritchett Flat—*flat* UT-8
Pritchett Fork—*stream* KY-4
Pritchett Island Beach—*beach* WA-9
Pritchett Lake—*reservoir* NC-3
Pritchett Lake Dam—*dam* NC-3
Pritchett Mill Creek—*stream* AL-4
Pritchett Mtn—*summit* AL-4
Pritchett Natural Bridge—*arch* UT-8
Pritchett Number 1 Drift Mine (underground)—*mine* AL-4
Pritchett Peaks—*summit* CA-9
Pritchetts—*locale* GA-3
Pritchetts Chapel—*church* KY-4
Pritchett Sch (historical)—*school* AL-4
Pritchett School (historical)—*locale* MO-7
*Pritchetts Cross Roads* MS-4
Pritchetts Landing (historical)—*locale* AL-4
Pritchetts Store (historical)—*locale* AL-4
Pritchett Swamp—*swamp* GA-3
Pritch Lake—*lake* WI-6
*Pritle Creek* IL-6
Prit Mtn—*summit* WV-2
Pritt Hollow—*valley* VA-3
Pritt Hollow—*valley* WV-2
Prittie Swamp—*swamp* NY-2
Pritts Sch (abandoned)—*school* PA-2
**Prittstown**—*pop pl* PA-2
Privateer—*locale* SC-3
Privateer Bay—*bay* VI-3
Privateer Brigantine DEFENCE Shipwreck Site—*hist pl* ME-1
Privateer (CCD)—*cens area* SC-3
Privateer Creek—*stream* SC-3
Privateer Mine—*mine* UT-8
Privateer Point—*cape* SC-3
Privateer Point—*cape* VI-3
Privateer Yacht Club—*locale* TN-4
Private Rsvr—*reservoir* MT-8
Private Sch of Progressive Education—*school* FL-3
*Priveledge Creek* TX-5
Priver Branch—*stream* SC-3
Privet Branch—*stream* AL-4
Privet Branch—*stream* TN-4
Privet Hollow—*valley* MO-7
Privet Mtn—*summit* TN-4
**Privett**—*pop pl* KY-4
**Privette Heights**—*pop pl* GA-3
Privette Lake Number One—*reservoir* NC-3
Privette Lake Number One Dam—*dam* NC-3
Privette Pond Number Two—*reservoir* NC-3
Privette Pond Number Two Dam—*dam* NC-3
Privett Knob—*summit* VA-3
Privetts—*locale* SC-3
*Privilege* MP-9
Privilege Creek—*stream* TX-5
Privilege Sch—*school* TX-5
Privott House—*building* NC-3
Privy Ledge—*bar* MA-1
Privy Pit—*cave* AL-4
Privy Spring—*spring* OR-9
Prize Hill Ch—*church* VA-3
Prize Mine—*mine* WA-9
Prizer Draw—*valley* (2) TX-5
Prizer Point Public Use Area—*locale* KY-4
Prizer's Mill Complex—*hist pl* PA-2
Probable Donner Trail—*trail* CA-9
Probable Route of Donner Party—*trail* (2) CA-9
Probable Route of Donner Party 1847—*trail* CA-9
Probandt Ranch—*locale* TX-5
Probar Creek—*stream* NM-5
Probasco, Henry, House—*hist pl* OH-6
Probasco Fountain—*hist pl* OH-6
**Proberta**—*pop pl* CA-9
**Probe Subdivision**—*pop pl* UT-8
Problem Creek—*stream* AK-9
Probst—*locale* TN-4
Probst Corral—*locale* UT-8
**Probstei**—*pop pl* IA-7
Probstei Sch—*school* IA-7
Probstfield, Randolph M., House—*hist pl* MN-6
Probst Pond—*reservoir* UT-8
Probst Sch (historical)—*school* MO-7
*Probsts Store* NC-3
**Probst Trailer Park**—*pop pl* DE-2
Pro-Cathedral Ch of Jesus of Nazareth—*church* FL-3
Procella Cem—*cemetery* TX-5
Procella Creek—*stream* TX-5
**Process City**—*pop pl* AR-4
Procession Rocks—*bar* AK-9
Pro Ch—*church* IN-6
Prochaska Ditch—*canal* IN-6
Prochnow House—*hist pl* AZ-5
**Procious**—*pop pl* WV-2
**Procious (Camp)**—*pop pl* WV-2
Prock Branch—*stream* TN-4
Prock Hollow—*valley* (2) TN-4
Procks Branch—*stream* TN-4
Procks Ledge—*summit* ME-1
Procks Point—*cape* NC-3
Procopio Spring—*spring* AZ-5
Procopius Cem—*cemetery* TX-5
Procrastination Creek—*stream* AK-9
Procter and Collier-Beau Brummell Bldg—*hist pl* OH-6
Procter Branch—*stream* MO-7
Procter Cem—*cemetery* MI-6
Procter Creek—*stream* CA-9
Procter Creek—*stream* TN-4
Procter Hollow—*valley* OK-5
Procter Hollow—*valley* TN-4
Procter Mtn—*summit* AR-4
Procter Tank—*reservoir* NM-5
Proctor—*locale* AL-4
Proctor—*locale* IL-6
Proctor—*locale* MT-8
Proctor—*locale* NV-8
Proctor—*locale* NC-3
Proctor—*locale* OK-5
Proctor—*locale* PA-2
**Proctor**—*pop pl* AR-4
**Proctor**—*pop pl* CO-8
**Proctor**—*pop pl* FL-3
**Proctor**—*pop pl* KY-4
**Proctor**—*pop pl* MA-1
**Proctor**—*pop pl* MN-6
**Proctor**—*pop pl* MO-7
**Proctor**—*pop pl* OH-6
**Proctor**—*pop pl* TX-5
**Proctor**—*pop pl* (2) VT-1
**Proctor**—*pop pl* WV-2
Proctor—*uninc pl* WA-9
Proctor, F. F., Theatre and Arcade—*hist pl* NY-2
Proctor, John C., Recreation Center—*hist pl* IL-6
Proctor, Lake—*lake* FL-3
Proctor, William, House—*hist pl* MA-1
Proctor Branch—*stream* AL-4
Proctor Branch—*stream* KY-4
Proctor Branch—*stream* (2) NC-3
Proctor Brook—*stream* MA-1
Proctor Canyon—*valley* UT-8
Proctor Cave—*cave* KY-4
Proctor Cem—*cemetery* (2) AL-4
Proctor Cem—*cemetery* IN-6
Proctor Cem—*cemetery* KS-7
Proctor Cem—*cemetery* KY-4
Proctor Cem—*cemetery* MO-7
Proctor Cem—*cemetery* NC-3
Proctor Cem—*cemetery* (2) TX-5
Proctor Ch—*church* OK-5
**Proctor City**—*pop pl* TN-4
Proctor-Clement House—*hist pl* VT-1
Proctor Cove—*bay* MA-1
*Proctor Creek* MI-6
*Proctor Creek* VA-3
Proctor Creek—*gut* AL-4
Proctor Creek—*stream* (2) AL-4
Proctor Creek—*stream* (3) GA-3
Proctor Creek—*stream* ID-8
Proctor Creek—*stream* MO-7
Proctor Creek—*stream* MT-8
Proctor Creek—*stream* NC-3
Proctor Creek—*stream* OR-9
Proctor Creek—*stream* TN-4
Proctor Creek—*stream* WA-9
Proctor Creek—*stream* WV-2
Proctor Creek Ch—*church* AL-4
Proctor Draft—*valley* VA-3
Proctor Drain—*canal* MI-6
Proctor Field Gap—*gap* NC-3
Proctor Hill—*summit* AZ-5
Proctor Hill—*summit* MA-1
Proctor Hill—*summit* (3) NH-1
Proctor Hill—*summit* VT-1
Proctor Hollow—*valley* KY-4
Proctor Hollow—*valley* MO-7
Proctor Hollow—*valley* OK-5
Proctor Hollow—*valley* PA-2
Proctor Hollow—*valley* WV-2
Proctor Hosp—*hospital* IL-6
Proctor House—*hist pl* KY-4
Proctor House—*hist pl* TX-5
Proctor HS—*school* NY-2
*Proctor Island* NY-2
*Proctorknott* MN-6
Proctor Lake—*flat* CA-9
Proctor Lake—*lake* MI-6
Proctor Lake—*lake* NE-7
Proctor Lake—*lake* WA-9
Proctor Lake—*reservoir* MS-4
Proctor Lake—*reservoir* TX-5
Proctor Lake Dam—*dam* MS-4
Proctor Landing—*locale* AL-4
Proctor Lookout—*locale* VT-1
Proctor Lookout Tower—*locale* MO-7
Proctor (Magisterial District)—*fmr MCD* WV-2
Proctor Mountain Ski Lift—*hist pl* ID-8
Proctor Mtn—*summit* ID-8
Proctor Mtn—*summit* OK-5
Proctor Mtn—*summit* PA-2
Proctor Park—*park* NY-2
Proctor Pen I(41HT13)—*hist pl* TX-5
Proctor-Piper State For—*forest* VT-1
Proctor Pit—*cave* AL-4
Proctor Plantation (historical)—*locale* MS-4
Proctor Plaza—*locale* TX-5
Proctor Point—*cape* LA-4
Proctor Point—*cape* MA-1
Proctor Pond—*lake* ME-1
Proctor Pond—*lake* NY-2
Proctor Ranch—*locale* AZ-5
Proctor Ranch—*locale* TX-5
*Proctor Reservoir* TX-5
Proctor Ridge—*ridge* NC-3
Proctor Ridge—*ridge* WV-2
Proctor Run—*stream* OH-6
*Proctors* WV-2
Proctor Sang Branch—*stream* NC-3
Proctors Bridge—*bridge* VA-3
*Proctors Brook* MA-1
Proctors Ch—*church* NC-3
Proctor Sch—*school* CA-9
Proctor Sch—*school* MA-1
Proctor Sch—*school* NC-3
*Proctors City* TN-4
Proctors Corner—*locale* ME-1
**Proctors corner**—*pop pl* MA-1
**Proctors Corner**—*pop pl* NC-3
*Proctors Creek* TN-4
Proctors Creek—*stream* VA-3
*Proctors Landing* LA-4
Proctors Landing—*locale* FL-3
Proctor Spring—*spring* AZ-5
Proctors Station—*locale* MA-1
Proctor's Theater—*hist pl* NY-2
*Proctorsville* LA-4
**Proctorsville**—*pop pl* VT-1
Proctorsville Gulf—*valley* VT-1
Proctors Wharf—*locale* MD-2
Proctor Terrace Sch—*school* CA-9
Proctor Towersite State Wildlife Area—*park* MO-7
Proctor (Township of)—*fmr MCD* AR-4
Proctor Valley—*valley* CA-9
Proctor-Vandenberge House—*hist pl* TX-5
*Proctorville* LA-4
*Proctorville* PA-2
**Proctorville**—*pop pl* MO-7
**Proctorville**—*pop pl* NC-3
**Proctorville**—*pop pl* OH-6
Proctorville Cem—*cemetery* NC-3
Proctorville Elem Sch—*school* NC-3
Proctorville Lookout Tower—*locale* NC-3
Proctorville Sch (abandoned)—*school* MO-7
Proctor Wash—*stream* AZ-5
Proctor Windmill—*locale* TX-5
Procunter Spring—*spring* SD-7
**Prodco**—*pop pl* KS-7
Prodie Creek—*stream* FL-3
Prodigal Ch—*church* SC-3
Produce—*uninc pl* FL-3
Produce Exchange Bldg—*hist pl* MA-1
**Produce Place**—*pop pl* KY-4
Produce Terminal Market—*locale* TX-5
Prody Spring—*spring* NV-8
**Proebstel**—*pop pl* WA-9
Profane Gulch—*valley* OR-9
Profanity Peak—*summit* WA-9
Profanity Ridge—*ridge* AZ-5
Profanity Tank—*reservoir* AZ-5
Professional Bldg—*hist pl* ME-1
Professional Bldg—*hist pl* MO-7
Professional Bldg—*hist pl* NC-3
Professional Bldg Mngmt South Condominium—*locale* UT-8
Professional Center Hosp—*hospital* AL-4
Professional Plaza—*locale* NC-3
Professor Creek—*stream* AZ-5
Professor Creek—*stream* UT-8
Professor Creek Rapids—*rapids* UT-8
Professor Gulch—*valley* CA-9
Professor Spring—*spring* OR-9
Professor Valley—*valley* UT-8
Professorville Hist Dist—*hist pl* CA-9
Proffer Cem—*cemetery* (2) MO-7
*Proffit* TX-5
Proffit—*locale* VA-3
**Proffit**—*pop pl* TX-5
Proffit Grove Ch—*church* NC-3
Proffit Gulch—*valley* CO-8
Proffit Hollow—*valley* TN-4
Proffit Mtn—*summit* MO-7
Proffit Spring—*spring* CO-8
Proffit Spring—*spring* TN-4
**Proffits Store**—*pop pl* VA-3
Proffitt—*locale* TX-5
Proffitt Cem—*cemetery* (2) TN-4
Proffitt Cem—*cemetery* (2) TX-5
*Proffitt Community* TX-5
Proffitt Crossing—*locale* TX-5
Proffitt Lake—*lake* KS-7
Proffitt Spring—*spring* TN-4
Proffitt Spring—*spring* TX-5
Proffitt View—*locale* TN-4
Profile Baptist Ch—*church* AL-4
Profile Butte—*summit* SD-7
Profile Cliff—*cliff* CA-9
Profile Creek—*stream* ID-8
Profile Gap—*gap* ID-8
Profile Golf Club—*other* NH-1
Profile Lake—*lake* (2) ID-8
Profile Lake—*lake* NH-1
Profile Lake Drain—*stream* MI-6
*Profile Mountain* NH-1
*Profile Notch* NH-1
Profile Peak—*summit* ID-8
Profile Point—*cape* AK-9
Profile Point—*cape* CA-9
*Profile Rock* UT-8
Profile Rock—*cliff* CO-8
Profile Rock—*pillar* CO-8
Profile Rock—*summit* MA-1
Profile Rocks—*summit* NY-2
Profile View—*cape* CA-9
Profit—*locale* VI-3
**Profit**—*pop pl* OK-5
Profit Island—*island* AK-9
Profit Island—*island* LA-4
Profit Island Chute—*stream* LA-4
Profit Lake—*lake* MN-6
Profit Post Office (historical)—*building* TN-4
Profits Creek—*stream* MO-7
Profitt Branch—*stream* NC-3
Profitt Prospect—*mine* TN-4
Profitts Pond—*lake* WA-9
Progreso—*CDP* TX-5
**Progreso**—*pop pl* TX-5
Progreso Bend—*bend* TX-5
Progreso District Settling Basin—*reservoir* TX-5
**Progreso Lakes**—*pop pl* TX-5
Progreso Pump—*other* TX-5
Progreso Toll Bridge—*bridge* TX-5
*Progress* MO-7
*Progress* NJ-2
Progress—*locale* CA-9
Progress—*locale* MS-4
Progress—*locale* VA-3
**Progress**—*pop pl* IN-6
**Progress**—*pop pl* (2) MS-4
**Progress**—*pop pl* NY-2
**Progress**—*pop pl* NC-3
**Progress**—*pop pl* OR-9
**Progress**—*pop pl* PA-2
**Progress**—*pop pl* (2) TX-5
**Progress Acres**—*pop pl* IN-6
*Progress Assembly of God Church* MS-4
Progress Baptist Ch—*church* MS-4
Progress Cem—*cemetery* MS-4
Progress Ch—*church* (2) LA-4
Progress Ch—*church* (2) MS-4
Progress Draw—*valley* TX-5
Progressive Baptist Ch—*church* MS-4
Progressive Canal—*canal* ID-8
Progressive Ch—*church* LA-4
Progressive Ch—*church* (2) SC-3
Progressive Ch—*church* TN-4
Progressive Ch—*church* TX-5
Progressive Chapels of Truth—*church* FL-3
Progressive Ch of Our Lord Jesus Christ—*church* FL-3
Progressive Creek—*stream* AK-9
Progressive Day Care—*school* FL-3
Progressive Learning Center—*school* (2) FL-3
Progressive Levee—*levee* CA-9
Progressive Mine—*mine* UT-8
Progressive Missionary Baptist Ch—*church* KS-7
Progressive Park—*park* TX-5
Progressive Sch—*school* MO-7
Progressive Sch—*school* MT-8
Progressive Sch—*school* OK-5
Progressive Sch—*school* WI-6
**Progressive Township**—*pop pl* SD-7
Progressive Union Baptist Ch—*church* AL-4
Progressive Valley—*valley* OH-6
Progress Northwest Oil Field—*oilfield* KS-7
**Progresso**—*pop pl* NM-5
Progress Oil Field—*oilfield* KS-7
Progress Park—*park* CO-8
Progress Park—*park* IL-6
Progress Park—*park* LA-4
Progress Plastics, Incorporated—*facility* OH-6
Progress Plaza Shop Ctr—*locale* AZ-5
Progress Post Office (historical)—*building* AL-4
Progress Ridge Sch—*school* WV-2
Progress Sch—*school* IL-6
Progress Sch—*school* LA-4
Progress Sch—*school* MS-4
Progress Sch—*school* NE-7
Progress Sch—*school* (3) SD-7
Progress Sch—*school* TN-4
Progress Sch—*school* TX 5
Progress Sch—*school* WA-9
Progress Sch (historical)—*school* (7) MS-4
Progress School (Abandoned)—*locale* IL-6
**Progress Subdivision**—*pop pl* UT-8
**Progress Township**—*pop pl* ND-7
Progress Village Elem Sch—*school* FL-3
**Progress Village (subdivision)**—*pop pl* FL-3
Progue Hollow—*valley* KY-4
Progue House—*hist pl* NY-2
Prohibition Creek—*stream* ID-8
Prohibition Flat—*flat* NV-8
*Prohibition Lake* MN-6
Prohibition Mtn—*summit* CO-8
Prohibition Spring—*spring* NV-8
Prohibition Spring—*spring* UT-8
Prohosky Ditch—*canal* MT-8
**Project City**—*pop pl* CA-9
Project Point Rec Area—*park* AR-4
Project Sch—*school* FL-3
Project Sch—*school* MN-6
Project Sch—*school* NJ-2
Project Shoal Monument—*other* NV-8
Prokhoda Point—*cape* AK-9
Prokoda Island—*island* AK-9
Prokor Creek—*stream* WI-6
Proksch Coulee—*valley* WI-6
**Prole**—*pop pl* IA-7
Prolewy Point—*cape* AK-9
Prolewy Rocks—*other* AK-9
P R Olgiati Bridge—*bridge* TN-4
Promenade—*uninc pl* TX-5
Promenade, The—*summit* CA-9
Promenade at Bay Colony (Shop Ctr)—*locale* FL-3
Promenade Plaza (Shop Ctr)—*locale* FL-3
Promenade Shop Ctr—*locale* FL-3
Promenades (Shop Ctr)—*locale* FL-3
Promet Airp—*airport* RI-1
Prometheus, Mount—*summit* NV-8
Prominent Point—*cliff* AZ-5
Prominent Rock—*island* AK-9
Promise—*locale* OR-9
**Promise**—*pop pl* SD-7
**Promise**—*pop pl* TN-4
**Promise City**—*pop pl* IA-7
Promise City Cem—*cemetery* IA-7
Promise Creek—*stream* WA-9
Promised Land—*flat* AR-4
Promised Land—*locale* NY-2
**Promised Land**—*pop pl* (2) AR-4
**Promised Land**—*pop pl* LA-4
**Promised Land**—*pop pl* ME-1
**Promised Land**—*pop pl* PA-2
**Promised Land**—*pop pl* SC-3
**Promised Land**—*pop pl* TN-4
Promised Land Camp—*locale* CA-9
Promised Land Canal—*canal* LA-4
Promised Land Ch—*church* (3) AR-4
Promised Land Ch—*church* MS-4
Promised Land Ch—*church* (2) SC-3
Promised Land Ch—*church* (2) VA-3
Promised Land Coulee—*valley* MT-8
*Promised Land Dam* PA-2
Promised Land Dam—*dam* PA-2
**Promised Land (historical)**—*pop pl* MS-4
Promised Land Hollow—*valley* TN-4
Promised Land Lake—*reservoir* PA-2
*Promised Land Landing* AL-4
*Promised Land Plantation* MS-4
Promised Land P.O. (historical)—*building* MS-4
Promised Land Rec Area—*park* WA-9
*Promised Land Ridge* AR-4
Promised Land Sch—*school* MT-8
Promised Land Sch—*school* (3) SC-3
Promised Land Sch Number 2—*school* MT-8
Promised Land State Park—*park* PA-2
Promised Land State Park-Bear Wallow Cabins—*hist pl* PA-2
Promised Land State Park Whittaker Lodge District—*hist pl* PA-2
Promised Land (Township of)—*fmr MCD* (2) AR-4
Promise Gulch—*valley* WY-8
Promise Lake—*lake* MN-6
Promise Land Ch—*church* AR-4
Promise Land Ch—*church* NC-3
Promiseland Ch—*church* TN-4
Promise Land Ch—*church* VA-3
Promise Land Ch—*church* WV-2
Promise Land Landing—*locale* AL-4
*Promise Land Pond* PA-2
Promise Land Ridge—*ridge* AR-4
Promisla Bay—*bay* AK-9
Promont—*hist pl* OH-6
Promontory—*locale* UT-8
Promontory—*summit* CA-9
Promontory, The—*cliff* UT-8
Promontory, The—*ridge* WY-8
Promontory Butte—*cliff* AZ-5
Promontory Butte Lookout Complex—*hist pl* AZ-5
Promontory Divide—*ridge* CO-8
Promontory Hill—*summit* AK-9
Promontory Hollow—*valley* UT-8
Promontory Lookout Tower—*tower* AZ-5
*Promontory Mountain* UT-8
Promontory Mtns—*range* UT-8
Promontory Point—*cape* UT-8
Promontory Point—*locale* UT-8
Promontory Point—*summit* CA-9
Promontory Point—*summit* NV-8
Promontory Ridge—*ridge* CO-8
**Prompton**—*pop pl* PA-2
Prompton Borough—*civil* PA-2
Prompton Dam—*dam* PA-2
Prompton Lake—*reservoir* PA-2
*Prompton Rsvr* PA-2
Prompton State Park—*park* PA-2
Promrose Creek—*stream* AK-9
Prong, The—*bay* MD-2
*Prong Branch* TN-4
*Prong Creek* OR-9
Prong Creek—*stream* CO-8
Prong Creek—*stream* KS-7
Prong Creek—*stream* (2) OR-9
Prong Creek—*stream* TX-5
Prong Horn Camp—*locale* WY-8
Pronghorn Peak—*summit* WY-8
Pronghorn Ranch—*locale* AZ-5
Pronghorn Rsvr *reservoir* ID-8
Pronghorn Rsvr—*reservoir* WY-8
Pronghorn Run—*stream* IN-6
Pronghorn Tank—*reservoir* AZ-5
Prong Lake—*lake* AZ-5
Prong Lake—*lake* WI-6
Prong Number Two—*stream* DE-2
Prong Pond—*lake* ME-1
*Prong Pond Mtn* ME-1
Prong Pond Mtn—*summit* ME-1
Prong Puss Cuss Creek—*stream* AL-4
*Prongs* MO-7
Pronto—*locale* NM-5
**Pronto**—*pop pl* AL-4
**Pronto**—*pop pl* NV-8
Pronton—*locale* AR-4
Pronto Plata Mine—*mine* NV-8
Propane—*uninc pl* KY-4
Prop Canyon—*valley* NM-5
Prop Cave—*cave* KY-4
Prop Cave Branch—*stream* (2) KY-4
*Propell* AL-4
Propeller Island—*island* MI-6
Propeller Run—*stream* IN-6
Proper Creek—*stream* MI-6
*Properity Cemetery* AL-4
Proper Pond—*lake* VT-1
Proper Sch—*school* (2) MI-6
Propers Corners—*locale* PA-2
**Property Consultants Condominium**—*pop pl* UT-8
*Propest Creek* NC-3
Prophecy Ch—*church* NC-3
Prophecy Ch—*church* SC-3
Prophecy Creek—*stream* PA-2
Prophet, Mount—*summit* WA-9
Prophet Branch—*stream* KY-4
Prophet Branch—*stream* NC-3
*Prophet Bridge* MS-4
Prophet Bridge Crossing—*bridge* MS-4
Prophet Bridge Rec Area—*park* MS-4
Prophet Cem—*cemetery* MS-4
Prophet Elias Greek Orthodox Ch—*church* UT-8
Prophet Elias Monastery—*church* MA-1

Prophetic Ch of the Living God—*church* AL-4
Prophet Knob—*summit* NC-3
Prophet Lake—*lake* AR-4
Prophet Ridge—*ridge* TN-4
Prophet Rock—*pillar* IN-6
Prophets Mountains—*ridge* ND-7
Prophets Sch Number 1—*school* ND-7
Prophets Sch Number 3—*school* ND-7
*Prophets Town* IN-6
**Prophetstown**—*pop pl* IL-6
Prophetstown (Township of)—*civ div* IL-6
*Prophylactic Brush Company Dam* MA-1
Propinquity—*hist pl* LA-4
Prop Lake—*lake* MN-6
Proposal Hill—*summit* ND-7
Proposal Rock—*island* OR-9
Proposal Rock—*pillar* MT-8
Proposition Creek—*stream* WY-8
Proprietary House—*hist pl* NJ-2
*Props Knob* WV-2
Props Lake—*lake* MI-6
*Props Run* WV-2
Props Run—*stream* WV-2
Propst Airfield—*airport* OR-9
Propst Airp—*airport* NC-3
Propstburg—*locale* WV-2
Propst Cem—*cemetery* MS-4
Propst Creek—*stream* AL-4
Propst Crossroads—*locale* NC-3
Propst Gap Ch—*church* WV-2
**Propst Highlands (subdivision)**—*pop pl* MS-4
Propst House—*hist pl* NC-3
Propst Knob—*summit* WV-2
Propst Mountain Mine (surface)—*mine* AL-4
Propst Mtn—*summit* AL-4
Propst Mtn—*summit* NC-3
Propst Park—*park* MS-4
Propst Run—*stream* WV-2
*Propsts Knob* NC-3
Propst Store—*locale* NC-3
Prop Trail—*trail* PA-2
Propulsion and Structural Test Facility—*hist pl* AL-4
Propylaeum, The (John W. Schmidt House)—*hist pl* IN-6
Prosinski Park—*park* WY-8
Prosise Post Office (historical)—*building* TN-4
Prosit—*locale* MN-6
*Prospect* KS-7
*Prospect* MS-4
*Prospect* MO-7
*Prospect* PA-2
Prospect—*hist pl* NJ-2
Prospect—*locale* (2) CA-9
Prospect—*locale* IL-6
Prospect—*locale* IA-7
Prospect—*locale* KS-7
Prospect—*locale* MD-2
Prospect—*locale* MS-4
Prospect—*locale* NJ-2
Prospect—*locale* NC-3
Prospect—*locale* (2) TN-4
Prospect—*locale* (2) TX-5
**Prospect**—*pop pl* AL-4
**Prospect**—*pop pl* CO-8
**Prospect**—*pop pl* (2) CT-1
**Prospect**—*pop pl* IL-6
**Prospect**—*pop pl* IN-6
**Prospect**—*pop pl* KS-7
**Prospect**—*pop pl* KY-4
**Prospect**—*pop pl* LA-4
**Prospect**—*pop pl* ME-1
**Prospect**—*pop pl* NY-2
**Prospect**—*pop pl* OH-6
**Prospect**—*pop pl* OR-9
**Prospect**—*pop pl* (2) PA-2
**Prospect**—*pop pl* (6) TN-4
**Prospect**—*pop pl* VA-3
**Prospect**—*pop pl* WI-6
Prospect—*post sta* FL-3
Prospect—*uninc pl* WI-6
Prospect, Mount—*summit* (3) CT-1
Prospect, Mount—*summit* ME-1
Prospect, Mount—*summit* (2) MA-1
Prospect, Mount—*summit* NH-1
Prospect, Mount—*summit* (2) NY-2
Prospect Ave Hist Dist—*hist pl* CT-1
Prospect Ave Row House Group—*hist pl* OH-6
Prospect Ave Sch—*school* CA-9
Prospect Ave Sch—*school* NY-2
*Prospect Baptist Ch* TN-4
Prospect Baptist Ch—*church* (4) TN-4
*Prospect Baptist Church* AL-4
*Prospect Baptist Church* MS-4
Prospect Basin—*basin* CO-8
Prospect Bay—*bay* MD-2
*Prospect Beach* CT-1
Prospect Beach—*beach* CT-1
*Prospect Bluff* FL-3
Prospect Bog Resevoir—*reservoir* MA-1
Prospect Borough—*civil* PA-2
Prospect Borough Elem Sch—*school* PA-2
Prospect Branch—*stream* DE-2
Prospect Branch—*stream* GA-3
Prospect Branch—*stream* IN-6
Prospect Branch—*stream* NC-3
Prospect Branch—*stream* (2) TN-4
Prospect Branch—*stream* TX-5
Prospect Canyon—*valley* (2) AZ-5
Prospect Canyon—*valley* CA-9
Prospect Canyon—*valley* (2) CO-8
Prospect Canyon—*valley* WA-9
Prospect Canyon—*valley* WY-8
Prospect (CCD)—*cens area* TN-4
*Prospect Cem* MS-4
Prospect Cem—*cemetery* (5) AL-4
Prospect Cem—*cemetery* (2) AR-4
Prospect Cem—*cemetery* FL-3
Prospect Cem—*cemetery* (4) IL-6
Prospect Cem—*cemetery* (7) MS-4
Prospect Cem—*cemetery* (2) MO-7
Prospect Cem—*cemetery* NY-2
Prospect Cem—*cemetery* (2) NC-3
Prospect Cem—*cemetery* ND-7
Prospect Cem—*cemetery* (2) OH-6
Prospect Cem—*cemetery* OK-5
Prospect Cem—*cemetery* (4) PA-2
Prospect Cem—*cemetery* SC-3
Prospect Cem—*cemetery* SD-7
Prospect Cem—*cemetery* (7) TN-4
Prospect Cem—*cemetery* (5) TX-5
Prospect Cem—*cemetery* (2) VT-1
*Prospect Ch* AL-4
*Prospect Ch* GA-3
*Prospect Ch* MS-4
*Prospect Ch* TN-4
Prospect Ch—*church* (17) AL-4
Prospect Ch—*church* (2) AR-4
Prospect Ch—*church* DE-2
Prospect Ch—*church* (3) FL-3
Prospect Ch—*church* (22) GA-3
Prospect Ch—*church* IN-6
Prospect Ch—*church* (2) KY-4
Prospect Ch—*church* (4) LA-4
Prospect Ch—*church* (12) MS-4
Prospect Ch—*church* (5) MO-7
Prospect Ch—*church* NE-7
Prospect Ch—*church* (11) NC-3
Prospect Ch—*church* (3) OH-6
Prospect Ch—*church* PA-2
Prospect Ch—*church* (6) SC-3
Prospect Ch—*church* (8) TN-4
Prospect Ch—*church* (4) TX-5
Prospect Ch—*church* (4) VA-3
Prospect Ch (historical)—*church* AL-4
Prospect Ch (historical)—*church* (2) TN-4
Prospect Congregational Church—*hist pl* MA-1
Prospect Corners—*locale* NY-2
*Prospect Creek* AZ-5
*Prospect Creek* ID-8
Prospect Creek—*stream* (5) AK-9
Prospect Creek—*stream* (4) CA-9
Prospect Creek—*stream* (2) CO-8
Prospect Creek—*stream* (9) ID-8
Prospect Creek—*stream* (4) MT-8
Prospect Creek—*stream* (2) OR-9
Prospect Creek—*stream* UT-8
Prospect Creek—*stream* (2) WA-9
Prospect Creek—*stream* WI-6
Prospect Creek—*stream* (3) WY-8
Prospect Creek Camp—*locale* AK-9
Prospect Creek Trail—*trail* ID-8
**Prospect Crossroads**—*pop pl* SC-3
Prospectdale—*locale* VA-3
Prospect Division—*civil* TN-4
Prospect Draw—*valley* AZ-5
Prospect Draw—*valley* CO-8
*Prospect Elementary School* TN-4
*Prospect Elem Sch* NC-3
Prospect Elem Sch—*school* NC-3
**Prospect Ferry**—*pop pl* ME-1
Prospect Gap—*gap* TN-4
**Prospect Gardens**—*pop pl* PA-2
Prospect Glacier—*glacier* AK-9
Prospect Grove—*locale* MO-7
Prospect Grove Cem—*cemetery* MO-7
Prospect Guard Station—*locale* OR-9
Prospect Gulch—*valley* (2) CO-8
Prospect Gulch—*valley* (2) ID-8
Prospect Gulch—*valley* MT-8
Prospect Gulch—*valley* SD-7
Prospect Gulch—*valley* WY-8
Prospect Hall—*hist pl* MD-2
Prospect Hall Coll—*school* FL-3
Prospect Hall Landing—*locale* NC-3
Prospect Harbor—*bay* ME-1
**Prospect Harbor**—*pop pl* ME-1
Prospect Harbor Light Station—*hist pl* ME-1
Prospect Harbor Point—*cape* ME-1
**Prospect Heights**—*pop pl* CO-8
**Prospect Heights**—*pop pl* IL-6
**Prospect Heights**—*pop pl* NJ-2
**Prospect Heights**—*pop pl* NY-2
**Prospect Heights**—*pop pl* PA-2
Prospect Heights Hist Dist—*hist pl* NY-2
Prospect Heights Sch—*school* CA-9
Prospect Heights Sch—*school* MT-8
Prospect Heights Sch—*school* VA-3
**Prospect Heights (subdivision)**—*pop pl* UT-8
**Prospect Highlands**—*pop pl* NJ-2
*Prospect Hill* CT-1
*Prospect Hill* IA-7
*Prospect Hill* MA-1
*Prospect Hill* MI-6
*Prospect Hill* MS-4
*Prospect Hill* MO-7
*Prospect Hill* WY-8
Prospect Hill—*hist pl* MD-2
Prospect Hill—*hist pl* SC-3
Prospect Hill—*hist pl* (3) VA-3
Prospect Hill—*locale* NY-2
**Prospect Hill**—*pop pl* CT-1
**Prospect Hill**—*pop pl* MA-1
**Prospect Hill**—*pop pl* MO-7
**Prospect Hill**—*pop pl* NY-2
**Prospect Hill**—*pop pl* NC-3
**Prospect Hill**—*pop pl* PA-2
**Prospect Hill**—*pop pl* VT-1
**Prospect Hill**—*pop pl* VA-3
Prospect Hill—*ridge* CA-9
Prospect Hill—*summit* (2) CA-9
Prospect Hill—*summit* CO-8
Prospect Hill—*summit* (9) CT-1
Prospect Hill—*summit* KS-7
Prospect Hill—*summit* (2) ME-1
Prospect Hill—*summit* (28) MA-1
Prospect Hill—*summit* (6) MI-6
Prospect Hill—*summit* MT-8
Prospect Hill—*summit* (9) NH-1
Prospect Hill—*summit* (17) NY-2
Prospect Hill—*summit* OH-6
Prospect Hill—*summit* OR-9
Prospect Hill—*summit* (5) PA-2
Prospect Hill—*summit* TN-4
Prospect Hill—*summit* (6) VT-1
Prospect Hill—*summit* (2) VA-3
Prospect Hill—*summit* WV-2
Prospect Hill—*summit* VI-3
Prospect Hill Bridge—*bridge* VA-3
Prospect Hill Cave—*cave* TN-4
Prospect Hill Cem—*cemetery* DC-2
Prospect Hill Cem—*cemetery* IL-6
Prospect Hill Cem—*cemetery* KS-7
Prospect Hill Cem—*cemetery* ME-1
Prospect Hill Cem—*cemetery* (4) MA-1
Prospect Hill Cem—*cemetery* (2) MI-6
Prospect Hill Cem—*cemetery* (3) NE-7
Prospect Hill Cem—*cemetery* (2) NH-1
Prospect Hill Cem—*cemetery* (2) NJ-2
Prospect Hill Cem—*cemetery* (4) NY-2
Prospect Hill Cem—*cemetery* (3) PA-2
Prospect Hill Cem—*cemetery* SD-7
Prospect Hill Cem—*cemetery* VA-3
Prospect Hill Cemetery Bldg—*hist pl* NY-2
Prospect Hill Ch—*church* NC-3
Prospect Hill Ch—*church* PA-2
Prospect Hill Ch (historical)—*church* PA-2
Prospect Hill Hist Dist—*hist pl* CT-1
Prospect Hill Hist Dist—*hist pl* OH-6
**Prospect Hill (historical)**—*pop pl* TN-4
Prospect Hill Island—*island* SC-3
Prospect Hill Methodist Ch (historical)—*church* TN-4
Prospect Hill Missionary Baptist Church—*hist pl* TX-5
Prospect Hill Park—*park* MA-1
Prospect Hill Park Cem—*cemetery* MD-2
Prospect Hill Pond—*lake* MA-1
Prospect Hill Reservoir Dam—*dam* MA-1
Prospect Hill Rsvr—*reservoir* MA-1
Prospect Hills—*summit* VA-3
Prospect Hill Sch—*school* (2) IA-7
Prospect Hill Sch—*school* KY-4
Prospect Hill Sch—*school* MA-1
Prospect Hill Sch—*school* MI-6
Prospect Hill Sch—*school* NY-2
Prospect Hill Sch—*school* WI-6
Prospect Hill Sch (abandoned)—*school* PA-2
Prospect Hill Station (historical)—*locale* MA-1
Prospect Hist Dist—*hist pl* CA-9
Prospect (historical)—*locale* AL-4
Prospect (historical)—*locale* KS-7
Prospect (historical)—*locale* MS-4
Prospect (historical)—*locale* SD-7
**Prospect (historical)**—*pop pl* MS-4
Prospect Hollow—*valley* AL-4
Prospect Hotel—*hist pl* OR-9
Prospect House—*hist pl* DC-2
Prospect HS—*school* IL-6
Prospect HS (historical)—*school* TN-4
Prospect Island—*island* CA-9
**Prospective**—*pop pl* PA-2
Prospect JHS (historical)—*school* TN-4
Prospect Junior High and Elem Sch—*hist pl* PA-2
Prospect Knob—*summit* TN-4
Prospect Knob—*summit* VA-3
**Prospect Knolls**—*pop pl* MD-2
Prospect Lake—*lake* OR-9
Prospect Lake—*reservoir* CO-8
Prospect Lake—*reservoir* MA-1
Prospect Lake—*reservoir* NY-2
Prospect Lake Dam—*dam* MA-1
Prospect Landing—*locale* FL-3
Prospect Lateral Ditch—*canal* CO-8
Prospect Lateral Sub No. 2 Ditch—*canal* CO-8
Prospect Lawn Cem—*cemetery* NY-2
Prospect (Magisterial District)—*fmr MCD* VA-3
**Prospect Meadows**—*pop pl* IL-6
*Prospect Methodist Church* AL-4
Prospect Mine—*mine* MT-8
Prospect Mines (underground)—*mine* AL-4
*Prospect Mountain* MA-1
*Prospect Mountain* OR-9
*Prospect Mountain* WY-8
Prospect Mountain—*ridge* NV-8
Prospect Mountain Tunnel—*tunnel* CO-8
Prospect MS—*school* PA-2
*Prospect Mtn* NY-2
Prospect Mtn—*summit* AL-4
Prospect Mtn—*summit* (3) CO-8
Prospect Mtn—*summit* (2) ID-8
Prospect Mtn—*summit* (5) NH-1
Prospect Mtn—*summit* (3) NY-2
Prospect Mtn—*summit* VT-1
Prospect Mtn—*summit* WY-8
Prospect Mtn Number One—*summit* MT-8
Prospect Mtn Number Two—*summit* MT-8
Prospect Mtns—*range* WY-8
*Prospect Neck* VA-3
*Prospect Number Two Church* AL-4
Prospector Campground—*locale* CO-8
Prospector Creek—*stream* (2) ID-8
Prospector Creek—*stream* (2) WA-9
Prospector Gulch—*valley* CO-8
**Prospector Hills Subdivision**—*pop pl* UT-8
Prospector Lake—*lake* WY-8
*Prospector Lakes* WY-8
Prospector Mine—*mine* UT-8
Prospector Mtn—*summit* MT-8
Prospector Pass—*gap* NV-8
Prospector-Rawhide Village—*CDP* WY-8
Prospector Ridge—*ridge* ID-8
Prospectors Creek—*stream* MI-6
Prospectors Delight Mine—*mine* NM-5
Prospectors Flat—*flat* UT-8
Prospectors Gap—*gap* CA-9
Prospectors Mtn—*summit* WY-8
Prospector Spring—*spring* CO-8
Prospector Spring—*spring* UT-8
Prospectors Ridge—*ridge* WA-9
Prospectors Trail—*trail* CO-8
Prospector Tank—*reservoir* NM-5
Prospector Well—*well* CO-8
*Prospect Park* IL-6
Prospect Park—*hist pl* NY-2
Prospect Park—*park* CA-9
Prospect Park—*park* (2) CO-8
Prospect Park—*park* (2) IL-6
Prospect Park—*park* (2) IA-7
Prospect Park—*park* KS-7
Prospect Park—*park* MA-1
Prospect Park—*park* (2) MI-6
Prospect Park—*park* MN-6
Prospect Park—*park* NE-7
Prospect Park—*park* NJ-2
Prospect Park—*park* NM-5
Prospect Park—*park* (4) NY-2
Prospect Park—*park* (2) PA-2
Prospect Park—*park* SD-7
Prospect Park—*park* TX-5
Prospect Park—*park* WI-6
**Prospect Park**—*pop pl* IL-6
**Prospect Park**—*pop pl* KS-7
**Prospect Park**—*pop pl* (2) NJ-2
**Prospect Park**—*pop pl* (3) PA-2
Prospect Park Borough—*civil* PA-2
Prospect Park Elem Sch—*school* PA-2
Prospect Park Farm—*hist pl* KS-7
Prospect Park Hist Dist—*hist pl* IA-7
Prospect Park Lake—*lake* NY-2
**Prospect Park (RR name Moore)**—*pop pl* PA-2
Prospect Park Sch—*school* MT-8
Prospect Park South Hist Dist—*hist pl* NY-2
**Prospect Park Subdivision**—*pop pl* UT-8
Prospect Park West—*uninc pl* NY-2
*Prospect Peak* CO-8
Prospect Peak—*summit* CA-9
Prospect Peak—*summit* (4) ID-8
Prospect Peak—*summit* MT-8
Prospect Peak—*summit* (2) NV-8
Prospect Peak—*summit* WA-9
Prospect Peak—*summit* (2) WY-8
Prospect Peak Fire Lookout—*hist pl* CA-9
Prospect Place—*hist pl* OH-6
**Prospect Plains**—*pop pl* NJ-2
Prospect PO—*locale* KY-4
Prospect Point—*cape* (2) AK-9
Prospect Point—*cape* ID-8
Prospect Point—*cape* ME-1
Prospect Point—*cape* MI-6
Prospect Point—*cape* (2) NY-2
Prospect Point—*cape* VT-1
Prospect Point—*cliff* CO-8
**Prospect Point**—*pop pl* NJ-2
Prospect Point—*summit* AZ-5
Prospect Point—*summit* CO-8
Prospect Point—*summit* ID-8
Prospect Point Camp—*hist pl* NY-2
Prospect Point Sch—*school* WA-9
*Prospect Pond* MA-1
Prospect Post Office—*building* TN-4
Prospect Post Office (historical)—*building* AL-4
Prospect Post Office (historical)—*building* MS-4
Prospect Ranch—*locale* CO-8
*Prospect Ridge* AL-4
*Prospect Ridge* NV-8
Prospect Ridge—*ridge* AZ-5
Prospect Ridge—*ridge* ID-8
Prospect Ridge—*ridge* MT-8
Prospect Ridge—*ridge* (2) NC-3
Prospect Ridge—*ridge* PA-2
Prospect Ridge—*ridge* WA-9
Prospect Road—*uninc pl* FL-3
Prospect Road RR Station—*locale* FL-3
*Prospect Rock* PA-2
Prospect Rock—*cape* WV-2
Prospect Rock—*other* PA-2
Prospect Rock—*pillar* CA-9
Prospect Rock—*pillar* NY-2
Prospect Rock—*pillar* PA-2
Prospect Rock—*summit* PA-2
Prospect Rock—*summit* (3) VT-1
Prospect Rsvr—*reservoir* CO-8
Prospect Rsvr—*reservoir* OR-9
Prospect Rsvr—*reservoir* WY-8
*Prospects Cemetery* AL-4
*Prospect Sch* PA-2
Prospect Sch—*school* AR-4
Prospect Sch—*school* FL-3
Prospect Sch—*school* GA-3
Prospect Sch—*school* (3) IL-6
Prospect Sch—*school* IA-7
Prospect Sch—*school* MA-1
Prospect Sch—*school* (2) MS-4
Prospect Sch—*school* (3) MO-7
Prospect Sch—*school* NY-2
Prospect Sch—*school* NC-3
Prospect Sch—*school* (4) OH-6
Prospect Sch—*school* (4) PA-2
Prospect Sch—*school* SD-7
Prospect Sch—*school* (5) TN-4
Prospect Sch (abandoned)—*school* MO-7
Prospect Sch (historical)—*school* (3) AL-4
Prospect Sch (historical)—*school* (4) MS-4
Prospect Sch (historical)—*school* PA-2
Prospect Sch (historical)—*school* (6) TN-4
*Prospect School* AL-4
Prospect Slough—*stream* CA-9
Prospect Spring—*spring* AZ-5
Prospect Spring—*spring* (2) OR-9
Prospect Springs—*spring* NV-8
Prospect State Airp—*airport* OR-9
*Prospect Station* AL-4
Prospect Station (Post Office)—*building* TN-4
Prospect Street Hist Dist—*hist pl* CT-1
Prospect Street Sch—*school* CT-1
Prospect Street Sch—*school* MA-1
**Prospect (Susanna)**—*pop pl* MO-7
Prospect Tank—*reservoir* (3) AZ-5
Prospect Terrace Park—*park* MN-6
**Prospect (Town of)**—*pop pl* ME-1
**Prospect Township**—*pop pl* KS-7
**Prospect Township**—*pop pl* ND-7
**Prospect Township**—*pop pl* SD-7
**Prospect (Township of)**—*pop pl* OH-6
Prospect United Methodist Ch—*church* TN-4
*Prospect United Methodist Church* MS-4
*Prospect Valley* CO-8
Prospect Valley—*basin* CO-8
**Prospect Valley**—*pop pl* CO-8
**Prospect Valley**—*pop pl* WV-2
Prospect Valley—*valley* AZ-5
Prospect Valley—*valley* NY-2
Prospect Valley Sch—*school* (2) CO-8
Prospect View Cem—*cemetery* NE-7
Prospect View Cem—*cemetery* NY-2
**Prospectville**—*pop pl* MA-1
**Prospectville**—*pop pl* (2) PA-2
**Prospect Walk**—*pop pl* MD-2
*Prosper* VT-1
Prosper—*locale* MI-6
Prosper—*locale* NC-3
**Prosper**—*pop pl* MN-6
**Prosper**—*pop pl* ND-7
**Prosper**—*pop pl* OR-9
**Prosper**—*pop pl* TX-5
**Prosper**—*pop pl* VT-1
Prosper Cem—*cemetery* MN-6
Prosper Cem—*cemetery* VT-1
Prosper Center Sch—*school* SD-7
Prosper Ch—*church* MI-6
Prosper East Oil Field—*oilfield* KS-7
Prospere Bayou—*stream* LA-4
**Prosperine**—*pop pl* MO-7
Prosperine Access Point—*locale* MO-7
*Prosperity* TN-4
Prosperity—*locale* (2) AR-4
Prosperity—*locale* FL-3
Prosperity—*locale* GA-3
Prosperity—*locale* KY-4
Prosperity—*locale* VI-3
**Prosperity**—*pop pl* IN-6
**Prosperity**—*pop pl* MO-7
**Prosperity**—*pop pl* PA-2
**Prosperity**—*pop pl* SC-3
**Prosperity**—*pop pl* (2) TN-4
**Prosperity**—*pop pl* WV-2
**Prosperity**—*pop pl* VI-3
Prosperity Archeol Site—*hist pl* VI-3
Prosperity Baptist Ch—*church* AL-4
Prosperity (CCD)—*cens area* SC-3
Prosperity Cem—*cemetery* AL-4
Prosperity Cem—*cemetery* AR-4
Prosperity Cem—*cemetery* GA-3
Prosperity Cem—*cemetery* PA-2
Prosperity Cem—*cemetery* TN-4
Prosperity Cem—*cemetery* WV-2
Prosperity Ch—*church* (2) AR-4
Prosperity Ch—*church* (2) GA-3
Prosperity Ch—*church* (2) LA-4
Prosperity Ch—*church* (4) NC-3
Prosperity Ch—*church* ND-7
Prosperity Ch—*church* PA-2
Prosperity Ch—*church* (4) TN-4
Prosperity Ch—*church* VA-3
Prosperity Ch—*church* (3) WV-2
Prosperity Elem Sch—*school* FL-3
Prosperity Elem Sch—*school* KS-7
Prosperity Flats Sch—*school* SD-7
Prosperity Garden—*locale* VI-3
Prosperity Grange Hall—*locale* OH-6
Prosperity-Granite Ditch—*canal* MT-8
Prosperity Heights Sch—*school* MN-6
Prosperity Hill—*locale* PA-2
Prosperity Mine—*mine* AZ-5
Prosperity Mine No 2—*mine* CO-8
*Prosperity Missionary Baptist Ch* TN-4
Prosperity Playground—*park* MN-6
Prosperity Sch—*school* IL-6
Prosperity Sch—*school* WV-2
Prosperity Sch (abandoned)—*school* MO-7
Prosperity Sch (historical)—*school* TN-4
Prosperity Sch Number 1—*school* ND-7
Prosperity Sch Number 2—*school* ND-7
Prosperity Tank—*reservoir* (2) AZ-5
**Prosperity Township**—*pop pl* ND-7
Prosper Lookout Tower—*locale* MN-6
Prospero—*locale* CA-9
Prospero Tract—*civil* CA-9
Prosperous Bayou—*gut* AR-4
Prosperous Pond—*lake* NV-8
Prosper Post Office (historical)—*building* AL-4
Prosper Ridge—*ridge* CA-9
Prosper Sch—*school* MI-6
*Prosperton* NJ-2
**Prospertown**—*pop pl* NJ-2
Prospertown Dam—*dam* NJ-2
Prospertown Lake—*reservoir* NJ-2
Prospertown Lake Fish and Wildlife Mngmt Area—*park* NJ-2
**Prosper Township**—*pop pl* SD-7
**Prosser**—*pop pl* NE-7
**Prosser**—*pop pl* TX-5
**Prosser**—*pop pl* WA-9
Prosser Airp—*airport* WA-9
Prosser Cem—*cemetery* OH-6
Prosser Cem—*cemetery* TN-4
Prosser Corral—*locale* WY-8
Prosser Creek—*stream* CA-9
Prosser Creek—*stream* CO-8
Prosser Creek—*stream* IA-7
Prosser Creek—*stream* KS-7
Prosser Creek—*stream* NE-7
Prosser Creek—*stream* PA-2
Prosser Creek—*stream* TN-4
Prosser Creek Rsvr—*reservoir* CA-9
Prosser East Lateral—*canal* WA-9
Prosser Gulch—*valley* CO-8
Prosser Heights Sch—*school* WA-9
Prosser Hill—*summit* CA-9
Prosser Hill—*summit* WA-9
Prosser Hollow—*valley* (2) NY-2
Prosser Hollow—*valley* PA-2
Prosser Hollow Sch—*school* NY-2
Prosser Hospital Heliport—*airport* WA-9
Prosser House—*hist pl* IN-6
Prosser HS—*school* IL-6
**Prosser Lakeview Estates**—*pop pl* CA-9
Prosser Rock—*summit* CO-8
*Prosser Run* PA-2
Prosser Sch—*school* MI-6
Prossers Island—*island* GA-3
Prosser Slough—*gut* OR-9
Prossers Mills—*locale* NJ-2
Prosser Steel Bridge—*hist pl* WA-9
Prosser West Lateral—*canal* WA-9
Protar, Feodar, Cabin—*hist pl* MI-6
Protection—*locale* GA-3
**Protection**—*pop pl* KS-7
**Protection**—*pop pl* NY-2
Protection Bay—*bay* AK-9
Protection Cem—*cemetery* KS-7
Protection Cem—*cemetery* NY-2
Protection Elem Sch—*school* KS-7
Protection Head—*summit* AK-9
Protection (historical)—*locale* SD-7
Protection Island—*island* WA-9
Protection Municipal Airp—*airport* KS-7
Protection of the Theotokos Chapel—*hist pl* AK-9
Protection Point—*cape* AK-9
**Protection Township**—*pop pl* KS-7
Protector Mine—*mine* CO-8
Protector Mine—*mine* NM-5
Protectworth Tavern—*hist pl* NH-1
**Protem**—*pop pl* MO-7
Protemus—*locale* KY-4
**Protemus**—*pop pl* TN-4
Protemus Post Office (historical)—*building* TN-4
Protestant Cay—*island* VI-3
Protestant Cem—*cemetery* SD-7
Protestant Cem—*cemetery* TX-5
Protestant Children's Home—*hist pl* AL-4
Protestant Episcopal Church of the Saviour—*hist pl* PA-2
Protestant Episcopal Theological Seminary—*hist pl* VA-3
Protestant Foster Home—*hist pl* NJ-2
*Protestant Grove Church* AL-4
*Protestant Methodist Church* MS-4
Protestant Point—*cape* MD-2
Protestant Reformed Sch—*school* MI-6
Protestant Union Cem—*cemetery* IA-7
Prothero Sch (historical)—*school* MO-7
**Protho Junction**—*pop pl* AR-4
*Prothos Mills* AL-4
Prothro, Nathaniel, Plantation—*hist pl* GA-3
Prothro Creek—*stream* CA-9
Prothro Mill Creek—*stream* LA-4
**Protivin**—*pop pl* IA-7
Proto Canyon—*valley* AZ-5
Protsman Elem Sch—*school* IN-6
Protsmans Knob—*summit* WY-8
*Prot Townsend Harbor* WA-9
Protts Hill—*summit* NY-2
Protzman Canyon—*valley* CA-9
**Protzman Subdivision**—*pop pl* UT-8
Proud Lake—*lake* MI-6
Proud Lake State Rec Area—*park* MI-6
Proud Run—*stream* OH-6
Prough Cem—*cemetery* MO-7
Prough Sch (abandoned)—*school* MO-7
Prouse Canyon—*valley* UT-8
Prouse Cem—*cemetery* WV-2
*Prouse Lake* MI-6
Prous Spring—*spring* UT-8
**Prout**—*pop pl* OH-6
Prout Brook—*stream* CT-1
**Prout Junction**—*pop pl* OH-6
Prout Lake—*lake* MN-6
Prout Lick Trail—*trail* PA-2
*Prout Neck* ME-1
Prout Park—*park* NH-1
Prouts Lake—*lake* AL-4
*Prout's Neck* ME-1
Prouts Neck—*cape* ME-1
**Prouts Neck**—*pop pl* ME-1
Prouts Neck Golf Course—*other* ME-1
Prout Spring—*spring* UT-8
Prout Wash—*valley* UT-8
Prouty—*locale* IL-6
Prouty, Jed, Tavern and Inn—*hist pl* ME-1
*Prouty Branch* PA-2
Prouty Brook—*stream* (2) ME-1
Prouty Corners—*locale* WA-9
Prouty Creek—*stream* OR-9
Prouty Creek—*stream* WA-9
Prouty Ditch—*canal* IN-6
Prouty Drain—*stream* MI-6
Prouty Glacier—*glacier* OR-9
Prouty HS—*school* MA-1
Prouty Memorial Plaque—*other* OR-9
Prouty Peak—*summit* WA-9
Prouty Place Camp—*locale* PA-2
Prouty Place State Park—*park* PA-2
Prouty Run—*stream* PA-2
Prouty Sch—*school* KS-7
Prouty Sch—*school* MI-6
Proux Mtn—*summit* ID-8
Provant Creek—*stream* WY-8
Provault Cem—*cemetery* IN-6
Proveausal Bay—*gut* LA-4
*Provedencia Canyon* AZ-5
Provemont Pond—*lake* MI-6
**Provencal**—*pop pl* LA-4
Provencal, Bayou—*stream* LA-4
Provencal Lake—*swamp* LA-4
Provence—*locale* OK-5
Provence Cem—*cemetery* OK-5
Provence Ch—*church* OK-5
Provence Ranch—*locale* WY-8
Provenger Rincon—*valley* NM-5
Provens Cem—*cemetery* OK-5
Proverbial Creek—*stream* WA-9
Provewell Ch—*church* AL-4
Provewell Sch—*school* AL-4
*Providence* AL-4
*Providence* MS-4
*Providence* NC-3
*Providence* MP-9
Providence—*locale* AL-4
Providence—*locale* KY-4
Providence—*locale* MD-2
Providence—*locale* (2) MO-7
Providence—*locale* NC-3
Providence—*locale* SC-3
Providence—*locale* TN-4
Providence—*locale* TX-5
Providence—*locale* VA-3
Providence—*locale* WA-9
Providence—*locale* WV-2
**Providence**—*pop pl* (6) AL-4
**Providence**—*pop pl* AR-4
**Providence**—*pop pl* (2) FL-3
**Providence**—*pop pl* IL-6
**Providence**—*pop pl* IN-6
**Providence**—*pop pl* (3) KY-4
**Providence**—*pop pl* LA-4
**Providence**—*pop pl* (2) MD-2
**Providence**—*pop pl* MN-6
**Providence**—*pop pl* (3) MS-4
**Providence**—*pop pl* (4) NC-3
**Providence**—*pop pl* OH-6
**Providence**—*pop pl* (2) PA-2
**Providence**—*pop pl* RI-1
**Providence**—*pop pl* (6) TN-4
**Providence**—*pop pl* (3) TX-5
**Providence**—*pop pl* UT-8
**Providence**—*pop pl* VA-3
Providence—*uninc pl* VA-3
Providence, Bayou—*gut* LA-4
Providence, Lake—*lake* LA-4
Providence, Lake—*reservoir* NC-3
Providence, Point—*cape* AK-9
Providence Acad—*school* WA-9
Providence African Methodist Episcopal Ch—*church* IN-6
Providence Airp—*airport* KS-7
*Providence Baptist Ch* AL-4
*Providence Baptist Ch* MS-4
Providence Baptist Ch—*church* (2) AL-4
Providence Baptist Ch—*church* (3) MS-4
*Providence Baptist Church* TN-4
Providence Baptist Church—*hist pl* KY-4
Providence Bar—*bar* AL-4

Providence Bay ... MA-1
Providence Bay ... RI-1
Providence-Biltmore Hotel—hist pl ... RI-1
Providence Branch—stream ... AL-4
Providence Branch—stream ... IN-6
Providence Branch—stream ... MS-4
Providence Branch—stream ... SC-3
**Providence (Brannon)**—pop pl ... KY-4
Providence Camp Ground Cemetery ... MS-4
Providence Camp Ground Church ... MS-4
Providence Canal—canal ... LA-4
Providence Canyon—valley ... UT-8
Providence (CCD)—cens area ... KY-4
Providence Cem—cemetery (12) ... AL-4
Providence Cem—cemetery (3) ... AR-4
Providence Cem—cemetery (4) ... GA-3
Providence Cem—cemetery ... IL-6
Providence Cem—cemetery (3) ... IN-6
Providence Cem—cemetery (2) ... KS-7
Providence Cem—cemetery ... KY-4
Providence Cem—cemetery (2) ... LA-4
Providence Cem—cemetery (15) ... MS-4
Providence Cem—cemetery (6) ... MO-7
Providence Cem—cemetery ... OR-9
Providence Cem—cemetery ... PA-2
Providence Cem—cemetery ... SC-3
Providence Cem—cemetery (6) ... TN-4
Providence Cem—cemetery (9) ... TX-5
Providence Cem—cemetery ... VA-3
Providence Cem—cemetery ... WI-6
Providence Ch ... AL-4
Providence Ch ... MS-4
Providence Ch ... TN-4
Providence Ch—church (47) ... AL-4
Providence Ch—church (15) ... AR-4
Providence Ch—church ... DE-2
Providence Ch—church (6) ... FL-3
Providence Ch—church (26) ... GA-3
Providence Ch—church (10) ... IL-6
Providence Ch—church (5) ... IN-6
Providence Ch—church (12) ... KY-4
Providence Ch—church (5) ... LA-4
Providence Ch—church (3) ... MD-2
Providence Ch—church (35) ... MS-4
Providence Ch—church (14) ... MO-7
Providence Ch—church ... NY-2
Providence Ch—church (31) ... NC-3
Providence Ch—church (6) ... OH-6
Providence Ch—church ... PA-2
Providence Ch—church (16) ... SC-3
Providence Ch—church (12) ... TN-4
Providence Ch—church (14) ... TX-5
Providence Ch—church (26) ... VA-3
Providence Ch—church (7) ... WV-2
Providence Ch (abandoned)—church ... MO-7
Providence Chapel—church ... IL-6
Providence Chapel—church ... NC-3
Providence Chapel—church ... OH-6
Providence Chapel—church ... VA-3
Providence Ch (historical)—church (3) ... MS-4
Providence Ch (historical)—church (3) ... TN-4
Providence Ch of Christ ... AL-4
Providence Christian Sch—school ... FL-3
Providence Church—hist pl ... KY-4
**Providence Church**—pop pl ... VA-3
Providence Church and Cem—cemetery ... GA-3
Providence City Cem—cemetery ... UT-8
Providence City Hall—hist pl ... RI-1
Providence City Lake—reservoir ... KY-4
Providence Club—locale ... TN-4
Providence Coll (historical)—school ... MS-4
Providence Cone—pillar ... NM-5
Providence Coulee—valley ... WA-9
**Providence County (in PMSA 6060, 6480)**—pop pl ... RI-1
Providence Court—hist pl ... MA-1
Providence Creek—stream (2) ... AL-4
Providence Creek—stream ... CA-9
Providence Creek—stream ... DE-2
Providence Creek—stream (2) ... MS-4
Providence Creek—stream ... OR-9
**Providence Downe**—pop pl ... PA-2
Providence Elem Sch—school ... PA-2
**Providence Forge**—pop pl ... VA-3
Providence Gin—locale ... TX-5
Providence Gum Point Ch—church ... AR-4
Providence Harbor bay ... RI-1
Providence Heights Alpha Sch—school ... PA-2
Providence Heights Sch ... PA-2
Providence Hill—summit ... MA-1
Providence Hill—summit ... NH-1
Providence Hill Brook—stream ... NH-1
Providence Hill Mine—mine ... CA-9
Providence Hist Dist—hist pl ... OH-6
Providence (historical)—locale ... AL-4
Providence (historical)—locale ... KS-7
Providence (historical)—locale (2) ... MS-4
Providence (historical)—locale ... SD-7
**Providence (historical)**—pop pl ... NC-3
Providence Hosp—hospital ... AL-4
Providence Hosp—hospital ... DC-2
Providence Hosp—hospital ... KS-7
Providence Hosp—hospital ... NE-7
Providence Hosp—hospital ... OH-6
Providence Hosp—hospital ... OR-9
Providence Hosp—hospital ... SC-3
Providence Hosp—hospital ... TX-5
Providence Hosp—hospital ... WA-9
Providence Hospital Heliport—airport ... OR-9
Providence Hospital Heliport—airport ... WA-9
Providence HS—school ... CA-9
Providence HS—school (2) ... IL-6
Providence HS—school ... TX-5
Providence Infirmary (historical)—hospital ... AL-4
Providence Island ... MP-9
Providence Island—island ... VT-1
Providence Jewelry Manufacturing Hist Dist—hist pl ... RI-1
Providence Junction—locale ... VA-3
Providence Knob Ch—church ... KY-4
Providence Lake—lake ... ID-8
Providence Lake—lake ... UT-8
Providence Landing—locale ... AL-4
Providence Landing—locale ... MD-2
Providence LDS Chapel and Meetinghouse—hist pl ... UT-8
Providence Lookout Tower—locale ... AL-4
Providence Lying-In Hosp—hist pl ... RI-1
Providence (Magisterial District)—fmr MCD (2) ... VA-3
Providence Memorial Cem—cemetery ... NC-3
Providence Memorial Hosp—hospital ... TX-5
Providence Memorial Park—cemetery (2) ... LA-4
Providence Mennonite Ch—church ... PA-2
Providence Methodist Church ... AL-4
Providence Methodist Church ... MS-4
**Providence Mill**—pop pl ... NC-3
Providence Mine—mine (2) ... CA-9
Providence Mission—church ... NC-3
Providence Missionary Baptist Church ... AL-4
Providence Missionary Baptist Church ... MS-4
Providence Missionary Ch—church ... NC-3
Providence Missionary Ch—church ... TX-5
Providence Mound (22HO609)—hist pl ... MS-4
Providence Mountains—range ... CA-9
**Providence Park**—pop pl ... VA-3
**Providence Park (subdivision)**—pop pl ... NC-3
Providence Peak—summit ... UT-8
Providence Plantation (historical)—locale ... MS-4
**Providence Plantation (subdivision)**—pop pl ... NC-3
Providence Plaza (Shop Ctr)—locale ... FL-3
Providence Point—cape ... RI-1
Providence Point—cape ... VI-3
Providence Post Office—building ... UT-8
Providence Post Office (historical)—building ... MS-4
Providence Post Office (historical)—building ... TN-4
Providence Presbyterian Ch—church ... AL-4
Providence Presbyterian Church ... TN-4
Providence Presbyterian Church—hist pl ... VA-3
Providence Presbyterian Church and Cemetery—hist pl ... NC-3
Providence Presbyterian Church of Bustleton—hist pl ... NJ-2
Providence Primitive Baptist Ch—church ... TN-4
Providence Primitive Baptist Church ... MS-4
Providence Reservoir ... RI-1
Providence River—stream ... RI-1
Providence Road Ch—church ... NC-3
Providence Run—stream ... IN-6
Providence Sch—school (2) ... AL-4
Providence Sch—school ... GA-3
Providence Sch—school (3) ... IL-6
Providence Sch—school (2) ... KY-4
Providence Sch—school (2) ... LA-4
Providence Sch—school (3) ... MS-4
Providence Sch—school ... MO-7
Providence Sch—school (4) ... SC-3
Providence Sch—school (3) ... TX-5
Providence Sch—school ... UT-8
Providence Sch—school ... VA-3
Providence Sch (abandoned)—school ... MO-7
Providence Sch (historical)—school (2) ... AL-4
Providence Sch (historical)—school (4) ... MS-4
Providence Sch (historical)—school (2) ... MO-7
Providence Sch (historical)—school (9) ... TN-4
Providence Spring—spring ... KY-4
Providence Square—locale ... PA-2
Providence Square—post sta ... NC-3
Providence State Wildlife Mngmt Area—park ... MN-6
Providence Station—locale ... PA-2
Providence Street Firehouse—hist pl ... MA-1
**Providence (subdivision)**—pop pl ... NC-3
Providence Swamp—stream ... SC-3
Providence Swamp (historical)—swamp ... NC-3
Providence Telephone Company—hist pl ... RI-1
Providence Terrace—uninc pl ... VA-3
Providence Tower (fire tower)—tower ... FL-3
**Providence (Town of)**—pop pl ... NY-2
Providence Township—fmr MCD (2) ... IA-7
Providence Township (historical)—civil ... SD-7
Providence (Township of)—fmr MCD (3) ... NC-3
**Providence (Township of)**—pop pl ... MN-6
**Providence (Township of)**—pop pl ... OH-6
**Providence (Township of)**—pop pl ... PA-2
Providence Union Ch—church ... PA-2
Providence United Methodist Ch—church ... TN-4
Providence Valley Ch—church ... MN-6
**Providence Village**—pop pl ... PA-2
Providence West—locale ... NC-3
**Providence Woods (subdivision)**—pop pl (2) ... NC-3
Providencia—civil ... CA-9
**Providencia**—pop pl ... PR-3
Providencia Canyon—valley ... AZ-5
Providencia Hill—summit ... AZ-5
Providencia Mine—mine ... CA-9
Providencia Sch—school ... CA-9
Providencia Well—well ... AZ-5
**Provident**—pop pl ... OH-6
Provident Central Canal—canal ... CA-9
Provident Ch—church ... AL-4
Provident Ch—church ... TX-5
Provident City—locale ... TX-5
Provident City Gas Field—oilfield ... TX-5
Provident City Refinery—other ... TX-5
Provident Eastern Canal—canal ... CA-9
Provident Heights Sch—school ... TX-5
Provident Hosp—hospital ... FL-3
Provident Hosp—hospital ... IL-6
Provident Main Canal—canal ... CA-9
Provident Sch (historical)—school ... AL-4
Provident Western Canal—canal ... CA-9
Province Branch—stream ... MO-7
Province Brook—stream ... ME-1
Province Brook—stream ... NH-1
Province Brook Trail—trail ... NH-1
Province Hollow—valley ... KY-4
Province Island—island ... PA-2
Province Island—island ... VT-1
Province Lake—lake ... ME-1
Province Lake—lake ... NH-1
Province Lake—locale ... NH-1
Province Lands Visitor Center—building ... MA-1
Province Mtn—summit ... ME-1
Province Mtn—summit ... NH-1
Province of Tusayan ... AZ-5
Province Park—park ... IN-6
Province Point—cape ... VT-1
Province Pond—lake ... NH-1
Province Road State For—forest ... NH-1
Provincetown ... IL-6
**Provincetown**—pop pl ... MA-1
Provincetown Airport Aero Light—locale ... MA-1
Provincetown Beach ... MA-1
**Provincetown Center**—pop pl ... MA-1
Provincetown Harbor—bay ... MA-1
Provincetown Public Library—hist pl ... MA-1
Provincetown Town Hall Spire—locale ... MA-1
**Provincetown (Town of)**—pop pl ... MA-1
**Provincetown Wharf**—pop pl ... MA-1
Province Tusayan ... AZ-5
Province Village—uninc pl ... KS-7
Provincial House Sisters of Saint Joseph—church ... LA-4
**Provincial Point**—pop pl ... OH-6
Provine Cem—cemetery ... TN-4
Provine House—hist pl ... MS-4
Provine HS—school ... MS-4
Provinger Canyon—valley ... NM-5
Provinger Draw—valley (3) ... NM-5
Proving Ground—other ... IL-6
Provin Mountain Reservoir Dam—dam ... MA-1
Provin Mountain Rsvr—reservoir ... MA-1
Provin Mtn—summit ... MA-1
Provins Mountain ... MA-1
**Provins Works**—pop pl ... PA-2
Proviso East HS—school ... IL-6
Proviso (sta.) ... IL-6
**Proviso (Township of)**—pop pl ... IL-6
Proviso West HS—school ... IL-6
Provo—locale ... KY-4
Provo—mine ... UT-8
**Provo**—pop pl ... AR-4
**Provo**—pop pl ... SD-7
**Provo**—pop pl ... UT-8
Provo, Mount—summit ... CA-9
Provo Bay—bay ... UT-8
Provo Bench—bench ... UT-8
Provo Canyon—valley ... NV-8
Provo Canyon—valley ... UT-8
Provo Canyon Guard Quarters—hist pl ... UT-8
Provo Cem—cemetery ... AL-4
Provo Cem—cemetery ... IL-6
Provo Cem—cemetery ... TN-4
Provo City ... UT-8
Provo City Cem—cemetery ... UT-8
Provo Deer Creek—stream ... UT-8
Provo Downtown Hist Dist—hist pl ... UT-8
Provo Hollow—valley ... MO-7
Provo HS—school ... UT-8
Provo Junction—locale ... UT-8
Provo Lake ... WA-9
Provolt—locale ... OR-9
Provo Municipal Airp—airport ... UT-8
Provo Municipal Airp Heliport—airport ... UT-8
Provo-Orem—cens area ... UT-8
Provo-Orem Division—civil ... UT-8
Provo Peak—summit ... UT-8
Provo Post Office—building ... UT-8
Provo Reservoir Canal—canal (2) ... UT-8
Provo River—stream ... UT-8
Provo River Fall Overlook ... UT-8
Provo River Falls—falls ... UT-8
Provo River Falls Overlook—locale ... UT-8
Provo River Overlook—locale ... UT-8
Provo Sch (historical)—school ... AL-4
Provost—locale ... VA-3
Provost, Bayou—gut ... LA-4
Provost Bay—reservoir ... IA-7
Provost Cem—cemetery ... LA-4
Provost Dam—dam ... MA-1
Provost Island—island ... ME-1
Provost Lake—lake ... MI-6
**Provost (Mohemenco)**—pop pl ... VA-3
Provost Point—cape ... ME-1
Provost Sch—school ... PA-2
Provost Sch—school ... UT-8
Provo Tabernacle—hist pl ... UT-8
Provo Third Ward Chapel and Amusement Hall—hist pl ... UT-8
**Provo Township**—pop pl ... SD-7
Provo Town Square—locale ... UT-8
Provo United Pentacostal Ch—church ... UT-8
Provo West Co-op—hist pl ... UT-8
Prow, The—summit ... NV-8
Prow Creek ... ID-8
Prowect Lake—lake ... MN-6
Prowell Cave—cave ... TN-4
Prowell Lake—reservoir ... TN-4
Prowers—locale ... CO-8
Prowers Arroyo—stream ... CO-8
Prowers Bridge—hist pl ... CO-8
Prowers County Bldg—hist pl ... CO-8
Prow Hollow—valley ... IN-6
Prow Pass—gap ... NV-8
Prowse Cem—cemetery ... KY-4
Prowse Spring—spring ... UT-8
Prows Spring ... UT-8
**Prowsville**—pop pl ... IN-6
**Prowswood Plaza Condominium**—pop pl ... UT-8
**Proximity**—pop pl ... NC-3
Proximity Sch ... NC-3
Proximity Sch—school ... NC-3
Proxy Creek—stream ... OR-9
Proxy Falls—falls ... OR-9
Proxy Point—cape ... OR-9
**Proyecto Barracon**—pop pl (2) ... PR-3
P R Prunty Ranch—locale ... NV-8
P R Rankin Dam—dam ... NC-3
P R Spring—spring ... UT-8
P Rsvr—reservoir ... OR-9
Prudden Island ... CT-1
Pruddy Brook—stream ... VT-1
Prude Cem—cemetery ... LA-4
Prude Creek ... AL-4
Prude House—hist pl ... LA-4
Prude Hyde Cem—cemetery ... TX-5
Prude Lake (historical)—lake ... AL-4
Prude Lower Mine (underground)—mine ... AL-4
**Pruden**—pop pl ... KY-4
**Pruden**—pop pl ... TN-4
Prudence ... RI-1
**Prudence**—pop pl ... AL-4
**Prudence**—pop pl ... WV-2
Prudence Chapel—church ... WV-2
Prudence Island ... CT-1
Prudence Island—island ... RI-1
**Prudence Island**—pop pl ... RI-1
Prudence Island Lighthouse—hist pl ... RI-1
Pruden Cem—cemetery ... OH-6
Prudence Park ... AZ-5
**Prudence Park**—pop pl ... RI-1
Prudence Point ... RI-1
Prudencio Tank—reservoir ... NM-5
Prudencio Canyon—valley ... NM-5
Pruden Creek—stream ... CO-8
Pruden Creek—stream ... LA-4
Pruden Creek—stream ... MT-8
Pruden-Fonde ... KY-4
Pruden-Fonde (CCD)—cens area ... KY-4
Pruden Number Six Mile (underground)—mine ... TN-4
Pruden Post Office—building ... TN-4
Pruden Sch—school ... TN-4
Prudential Bldg—hist pl ... NY-2
Prudential Business Campus—school ... PA-2
Prudential Business Campus Airp—airport ... PA-2
Prudential Center—post sta ... MA-1
Prudential Center Shopping Plaza—locale ... MA-1
Prudential Center Skywalk—building ... MA-1
Prudential Ditch—canal ... IN-6
Prudential Florham Park—airport ... NJ-2
Prudential Hollow—valley ... TN-4
Prudential Plaza ... IL-6
Prudential Shopping Plaza ... MA-1
**Prudenville**—pop pl ... MI-6
Prude Ranch—locale ... AZ-5
Prude Ranch—locale ... NM-5
Prudes Creek—stream (2) ... AL-4
Prudes Creek Cem—cemetery ... AL-4
Prudes Creek Ch—church ... AL-4
Prudes Creek Missionary Baptist Ch ... AL-4
Prudes Creek Sch (historical)—school ... AL-4
Prudes Mill (historical)—locale ... AL-4
Prudes Mill Pond—reservoir ... AL-4
Prude Tank—reservoir ... TX-5
Prude Upper Mine (underground)—mine ... AL-4
Prudeville ... MS-4
Prudhoe Bay—bay ... AK-9
Prudhoe Bay—locale ... AK-9
Prudhoe Bay-Kaktovik (Census Subarea)—cens area ... AK-9
Prudhoe Dock—locale ... AK-9
Prudhoe Mound—summit ... AK-9
**Prudhomme**—pop pl ... LA-4
Prud'homme, Jean Pierre Emmanuel, Plantation—hist pl ... LA-4
Prudhomme, Michel, House—hist pl ... LA-4
Prudhon Ranch—locale ... CA-9
Prudue University Limberlost Camp—park ... IN-6
**Prue**—pop pl ... OK-5
Prue, Lake—lake ... WY-8
Prue Ditch ... IN-6
Prue Hollow—valley ... PA-2
Prueitt Ranch—locale ... NM-5
Prue Oil Field—oilfield ... OK-5
Prue Run—stream ... PA-2
Prues Island—island ... MN-6
Pruess Lake—reservoir ... UT-8
Pruess Lake Dam—dam ... UT-8
Pruess Well—well ... NM-5
Pruett—locale ... IL-6
**Pruett**—pop pl ... AL-4
**Pruett**—pop pl ... TX-5
Pruett, Lake—reservoir ... TX-5
Pruett, W., House—hist pl ... KY-4
Pruett Bayou—stream ... TX-5
Pruett Branch—stream ... IL-6
Pruett Branch—stream ... WV-2
Pruett Bridge—bridge ... AL-4
Pruett Cave—cave ... TN-4
Pruett Cem—cemetery ... CO-8
Pruett Cem—cemetery ... IL-6
Pruett Cem—cemetery (3) ... TN-4
Pruett Cem—cemetery ... VA-3
Pruett Chapel—church ... TN-4
Pruett Chapel Sch (historical)—school ... TN-4
Pruett Creek—stream ... MO-7
Pruette Branch—stream ... TN-4
Pruette Cem—cemetery ... TN-4
Pruette Spring—spring ... TN-4
Pruett Hollow—valley ... IN-6
Pruett Hollow—valley ... TN-4
Pruett Mtn—summit ... SC-3
Pruett Pit—cave ... TN-4
Pruetts Branch ... TN-4
Pruett Sch—school ... MS-4
Pruetts Fork—stream ... KY-4
Pruetts Island—island ... AL-4
Pruetts Mtn—summit ... VA-3
Pruetts Spring ... TN-4
Pruett Well—well ... NM-5
Pruetz Municipal Airp—airport ... ND-7
Pru Field Airp—airport ... WA-9
Prugh Branch—stream ... MD-2
Prugh Ditch—canal ... OH-6
Pruill Creek ... MS-4
Pruit Branch ... KY-4
Pruit Canyon—valley ... NM-5
Pruit Lake—lake ... MS-4
Pruiton ... AL-4
Pruitt ... OK-5
Pruitt—locale (2) ... TX-5
**Pruitt**—pop pl ... AR-4
**Pruitt**—pop pl ... OK-5
Pruitt, Lake—reservoir ... AL-4
Pruitt, Pinky, Barn—hist pl ... AR-4
Pruitt Bluff—cliff ... AL-4
Pruitt Branch—stream ... AL-4
Pruitt Branch—stream ... IN-6
Pruitt Branch—stream (4) ... KY-4
Pruitt Branch—stream ... MO-7
Pruitt Branch Sch—school ... KY-4
Pruitt Cem—cemetery ... AL-4
Pruitt Cem—cemetery ... AR-4
Pruitt Cem—cemetery ... IL-6
Pruitt Cem—cemetery ... KY-4
Pruitt Cem—cemetery ... LA-4
Pruitt Cem—cemetery ... MS-4
Pruitt Cem—cemetery ... OK-5
Pruitt Cem—cemetery (2) ... TN-4
Pruitt Cem—cemetery ... TX-5
Pruitt Ch—church ... AR-4
**Pruitt City**—pop pl ... OK-5
Pruitt Creek ... AL-4
Pruitt Creek—stream ... AR-4
Pruitt Creek—stream (3) ... GA-3
Pruitt Draw—valley ... ID-8
Pruitt Fork—stream ... KY-4
Pruitt Hill Sch—school ... TN-4
Pruitt Hollow—valley (2) ... AR-4
Pruitt Hollow—valley (2) ... TN-4
Pruitt Island—island ... AR-4
Pruitt Lake—lake ... CA-9
Pruitt Lake—lake ... LA-4
Pruitt Lake—lake ... TX-5
Pruitt Lake—locale ... TX-5
Pruitt Lake—reservoir ... GA-3
Pruitt Lake Ch—church ... TX-5
Pruitt Memorial Ch—church ... KY-4
Pruitt Mine—mine ... NM-5
Pruitt Mine—mine ... TN-4
Pruitt Mtn—summit ... MO-7
Pruitton—locale ... AL-4
Pruitton Sch (historical)—school ... AL-4
Pruitton Spring—spring ... AL-4
Pruitton Station ... AL-4
Pruitt Park—park ... MT-8
Pruitt Point—summit ... AR-4
Pruitt Ridge—ridge ... AL-4
Pruitt Ridge—ridge ... KY-4
Pruitts Chapel—church ... AR-4
Pruitts Chapel—church ... LA-4
Pruitts Lake—lake ... LA-4
Pruitt Spring—spring ... AL-4
Pruitts Spring—spring ... AL-4
Pruit Valley—valley ... OK-5
Prune Bay—bay ... VI-3
Prune Creek—stream ... WY-8
Prune Creek Campground—locale ... WY-8
Prunedale—locale ... OR-9
**Prunedale**—pop pl ... CA-9
Prune Hill—summit ... OR-9
Prune Hill—summit ... WA-9
Prune Hook Creek ... DE-2
Prune Island—island ... ME-1
Prune Lake ... MN-6
Prune Lake—lake ... MN-6
Prune Lake—lake ... WI-6
Prune Spring—spring ... MT-8
Prune Springs—spring ... NV-8
Pruneville Well—well ... AZ-5
Prunty—locale ... WV-2
Prunty Creek—stream ... ID-8
Prunty Mine—mine ... NV-8
Prunty Run—stream ... WV-2
Prunty-Shively Reservoir ... NV-8
Prunty Spring—spring ... NV-8
**Pruntytown**—pop pl ... WV-2
Prusak Draw—valley ... WY-8
Prusik Pass—gap ... WA-9
Prusik Peak—summit ... WA-9
Pruss Airp—airport ... IN-6
Pruss Hill Dam—dam ... PA-2
**Prussia**—pop pl ... IA-7
Prussia Cem—cemetery ... IA-7
Prussia Centre—locale ... IA-7
Prussian Settlement—locale ... NY-2
Prussia Ridge—ridge ... OH-6
Prussia Run—stream ... OH-6
Prussia Township—fmr MCD ... IA-7
Prussing Sch—school ... IL-6
Pruvan Creek—stream ... ID-8
Pruyn, Casparus F., House—hist pl ... NY-2
Pruyns Island—island ... NY-2
Pryce Canyon—valley ... AZ-5
Pryce Lake—lake ... AZ-5
Pry Chapel (historical)—church ... MO-7
Pry Cove—bay ... MD-2
Pryde Ditch—canal ... MT-8
Pryett Creek ... MT-8
Pry Island—island ... MD-2
Pryor—locale ... AR-4
Pryor—locale ... CO-8
Pryor—locale ... OR-9
**Pryor**—pop pl ... AL-4
**Pryor**—pop pl ... MT-8
**Pryor**—pop pl ... OH-6
**Pryor**—pop pl ... OK-5
**Pryor**—pop pl ... TX-5
Pryor, Frank, House—hist pl ... CO-8
Pryor Bay—bay ... KY-4
Pryor Bay—bay ... TN-4
Pryor Bend—bend ... TN-4
Pryor Branch—stream ... AL-4
Pryor Branch—stream (2) ... KY-4
Pryor Branch—stream ... MD-2
Pryor Branch—stream ... MO-7
Pryor Branch—stream ... TN-4
Pryor Canyon—valley ... CO-8
Pryor Cave—cave ... TN-4
Pryor Cave Spring—spring ... TN-4
Pryor (CCD)—cens area ... OK-5
Pryor Cem—cemetery ... AL-4
Pryor Cem—cemetery (2) ... AR-4
Pryor Cem—cemetery ... IL-6
Pryor Cem—cemetery (2) ... IN-6
Pryor Cem—cemetery (2) ... MS-4
Pryor Cem—cemetery ... MO-7
Pryor Cem—cemetery ... MT-8
Pryor Cem—cemetery (3) ... TN-4
Pryor Cem—cemetery ... TX-5
Pryor Ch ... AL-4
Pryor Chapel—church ... AL-4
Pryor Chapel—church ... KY-4
Pryor Chapel Baptist Ch ... AL-4
Pryor (corporate name Pryor Creek) ... OK-5
Pryor Cove—valley ... TN-4
Pryor Cove Branch—stream ... TN-4
Pryor Creek ... KY-4
Pryor Creek—stream ... AR-4
Pryor Creek—stream ... CO-8
Pryor Creek—stream (2) ... KY-4
Pryor Creek—stream ... MS-4
Pryor Creek—stream ... MO-7
Pryor Creek—stream ... MT-8
Pryor Creek—stream ... OK-5
Pryor Creek—stream ... TN-4
Pryor Creek—stream ... VA-3
Pryor Creek Cave—cave ... MT-8
Pryor Creek Cem—cemetery ... MO-7
**Pryor Creek (corporate name for Pryor)**—pop pl ... OK-5
Pryor Ditch Number One—canal ... MT-8
Pryor Ditch Number Three—canal ... MT-8
Pryor Ditch Number Two—canal ... MT-8
Pryor Field (airport)—airport ... AL-4
Pryor Fork—stream ... KY-4
Pryor Gap—gap ... MT-8
Pryor Grave—cemetery ... CA-9
Pryor Hollow—valley ... KY-4
Pryor Island—island ... KY-4
Pryor Island—island ... TN-4
Pryor JHS—school ... FL-3
Pryor JHS—school ... OK-5
Pryor Knoll—summit ... UT-8
Pryor Lake—lake ... AR-4
Pryor Lake—reservoir ... TX-5
Pryor Meredith Branch—stream ... TN-4
Pryor Mtn—summit (2) ... AR-4
Pryor Mtn—summit ... TX-5
Pryor Mtns—range ... MT-8
Pryor Peak ... UT-8
Pryor Pond Dam—dam ... MS-4
Pryor Ranch—locale ... MT-8
**Pryor Ridge**—pop pl ... TN-4
Pryor Ridge—ridge ... TN-4
Pryor Ridge Sch (historical)—school ... TN-4
Pryor Run—stream ... PA-2
Pryors ... KY-4
Pryors Branch—stream ... MO-7
**Pryorsburg**—pop pl ... KY-4
**Pryorsburg (Pryors)**—pop pl ... KY-4
Pryor Sch—school ... IL-6
**Pryors Chapel**—pop pl ... KY-4
Pryors Chapel Cem—cemetery ... KY-4
Pryors Fork—stream ... KY-4
Pryors Island ... KY-4
Pryors Island ... TN-4
Pryors Mill ... TN-4
Pryors Mill Creek ... AL-4
Pryor Spring—spring ... AL-4
Pryor Spring Hollow—valley ... MO-7
Pryor Street Sch—school ... GA-3
**Pryortown**—pop pl ... IL-6
Pryor Water Intake—other ... OK-5
Pryott Creek ... MT-8
Pryse—locale ... KY-4
Prysock Cem—cemetery ... AR-4
Prys Temple—church ... MS-4
PR-19, Lake—reservoir ... MT-8
P'saganagum ... ME-1
Psalm Lake—lake ... AK-9
Psalms Church, The—church ... FL-3
P S Connell—locale ... TX-5
Psencik Cem—cemetery ... TX-5
Pseudolava Cave—cave ... AL-4
Pshoor ... MP-9
PshorA DESIG channel ... MP-9
Pshorr Durchfahrt ... MP-9
Pshorr Pass ... MP-9
Psimer Hollow—valley ... KY-4
P Simmons Place—locale ... NM-5
Psi Ote Park—park ... IN-6
P Six Ranch—locale ... AZ-5
P S Jones JHS—school ... NC-3
P S Knoll—summit ... AZ-5
P S Knoll Forest Camp—locale ... AZ-5
PS Knoll Lookout Complex—hist pl ... AZ-5
P S Knoll Lookout Tower—tower ... AZ-5
Psotas Lake—lake ... NE-7
P S Ranch—locale ... AZ-5
P S Spring Tank—reservoir ... AZ-5
P Stradinger Number 2 Dam—dam ... SD-7
Psuc-see-que Creek ... OR-9
Psyche Butte—summit ... OR-9
Ptaks Natl Cem—cemetery ... SD-7
Ptarmigan—locale ... AK-9
Ptarmigan Creek—stream (8) ... AK-9
Ptarmigan Creek—stream (3) ... CO-8
Ptarmigan Creek—stream ... MT-8
Ptarmigan Creek—stream ... WA-9
Ptarmigan Creek Trail—trail ... AK-9
Ptarmigan Drop—gap ... AK-9
Ptarmigan Falls—falls ... MT-8
Ptarmigan Glacier—glacier ... AK-9
Ptarmigan Glacier—glacier ... WA-9
Ptarmigan Gulch—valley (2) ... AK-9
Ptarmigan Head—summit ... AK-9
Ptarmigan Hill—summit ... CO-8
Ptarmigan Lake—lake (3) ... AK-9
Ptarmigan Lake—lake (4) ... CO-8
Ptarmigan Lake—lake ... MN-6
Ptarmigan Lake—lake ... MT-8
Ptarmigan Lake—lake ... WA-9
Ptarmigan Lakes—lake ... WA-9
Ptarmigan Mtn—summit ... CO-8
Ptarmigan Mtn—summit ... MT-8
Ptarmigan Mtn—summit ... WY-8
Ptarmigan Pass—gap (3) ... CO-8
Ptarmigan Peak—summit (2) ... AK-9
Ptarmigan Peak—summit (3) ... CO-8
Ptarmigan Peak—summit ... WA-9
Ptarmigan Point—cape ... AK-9
Ptarmigan Point—summit (2) ... CO-8
Ptarmigan Ridge—ridge (3) ... WA-9
Ptarmigan Trail—trail ... CO-8
Ptarmigan Trail—trail ... MT-8
Ptarmigan Tunnel—hist pl ... MT-8
Ptarmigan Tunnel—tunnel ... MT-8
Ptarmigan Valley—valley ... AK-9
Ptarmigan Wall—ridge ... MT-8
PT BOAT 796 (torpedo boat)—hist pl ... MA-1
P T Cox Sch—school ... AZ-5
Pte aux Marchettes—cape ... LA-4
P-To-Ba-Go Pond ... MI-6
Ptomaine Springs—spring ... NV-8
Pt. Shirley ... MA-1
Puaa ... HI-9
Puaahala—civil ... HI-9
**Pua Akala**—pop pl ... HI-9
Puaalaulau Gulch—valley ... HI-9
Puaaluu—civil ... HI-9
Puaaluu Gulch—valley ... HI-9
Puaanaiea ... HI-9
Puaao, Pali—area ... HI-9
Puaa One—civil ... HI-9
Puaa Two-Three—civil ... HI-9
Pua'a-2 Agricultural Fields Archeol District (50HA10229)—hist pl ... HI-9
Puaena ... HI-9
Puaena Point—cape ... HI-9
Puafusi Point—cape ... AS-9
Puahaunui ... HI-9
Puahaunui Point—cape ... HI-9
Puaialua Crater—crater ... HI-9
Puaiki—civil ... HI-9
Puainako Rsvr—reservoir ... HI-9
Puakaa Park—park ... HI-9
Puakaa Stream—stream ... HI-9
Pua Ka Huahua—summit ... HI-9
Puakala ... HI-9
Puakane Gulch—valley ... HI-9
Puakea—civil (2) ... HI-9

Puakea Gulch—*valley* HI-9
Puakea Point—*cape* HI-9
Puakea Ranch—*locale* HI-9
Puakea Rsvr—*reservoir* HI-9
**Puako**—*pop pl* HI-9
Puako Bay—*bay* HI-9
Puako Keamuku Trail—*trail* HI-9
**Puako (Lalamilo)**—*pop pl* HI-9
Puako Petroglyph Archeol District—*hist pl* HI-9
Puako Point—*cape* HI-9
Puako-Waimea Trail—*trail* HI-9
Puakukui Stream—*stream* HI-9
Pualaa—*civil* HI-9
Pualaa—*locale* HI-9
Pualaea—*civil* HI-9
**Pualaea Homestead**—*pop pl* HI-9
Pualanalana—*cape* HI-9
Puale Bay—*bay* AK-9
Puali Gulch—*valley* HI-9
Puali Stream—*stream* HI-9
**Pua Loke**—*pop pl* HI-9
Puama—*cape* HI-9
*Puanaaiea* HI-9
*Puanaaiea Point* HI-9
*Puanaiea* HI-9
Puanaiea Point—*cape* HI-9
Puana Rsvr—*reservoir* HI-9
Puaneva Point—*cape* AS-9
Puanui—*civil* HI-9
Puapua—*locale* AS-9
Puapuaa One—*civil* HI-9
Puapuaa Point—*cape* HI-9
Puapuaa Two—*civil* HI-9
Puasuk—*bar* (2) FM-9
Puatauapa Point—*cape* AS-9
Puawnap—*bar* FM-9
Puawsich—*bar* FM-9
Publ Corral—*locale* NM-5
Public—*locale* KY-4
Public Bath House No. 2—*hist pl* NY-2
Public Bath House No. 3—*hist pl* NY-2
Public Bath House No. 4—*hist pl* NY-2
Public Bath No. 7—*hist pl* NY-2
Public Baths—*hist pl* NY-2
*Public Camp* PA-2
Public Creek—*stream* NC-3
Public Fork—*locale* VA-3
**Public Fork**—*pop pl* VA-3
*Public Grove Hollow* UT-8
Public Grove Hollow—*valley* UT-8
Public Health Administration Bldg—*building* DC-2
Public Health Agency Hosp—*hospital* AZ-5
Public Hollow—*valley* TX-5
Public Hunting Ground and Upland Game Bird Preserve—*park* HI-9
Public Landing—*locale* VA-3
**Public Landing**—*pop pl* MD-2
Public Library of Des Moines—*hist pl* IA-7
Public Lot Brook—*stream* ME-1
Public Lot Ridge—*ridge* ME-1
Public Market—*hist pl* NH-1
*Publico* IN-6
Public Regina HS—*school* NY-2
Public Safety Bldg—*hist pl* MD-2
Public Sch No. 109—*hist pl* MD-2
Public Sch No. 111—*hist pl* MD-2
Public Sch No. 111-C—*hist pl* DE-2
Public Sch No. 19—*hist pl* DE-2
Public Sch No. 25—*hist pl* MD-2
Public Sch No. 27—*hist pl* WI-6
Public Sch No. 29—*hist pl* DE-2
Public Sch No. 37—*hist pl* MD-2
Public Sch No. 99—*hist pl* MD-2
Public Sch Number Two—*hist pl* NJ-2
Public Sch Number 1 (historical)—*school* AL-4
Public Sch Number 2—*school* NJ-2
*Public School Number One* MS-4
Public School Stadium—*other* MO-7
Public Sch 1—*school* NJ-2
Public Sch 1—*school* (4) NY-2
Public Sch 10—*school* NJ-2
Public Sch 10—*school* (4) NY-2
Public Sch 100—*school* (2) NY-2
Public Sch 101—*school* (2) NY-2
Public Sch 102—*school* (4) NY-2
Public Sch 103—*school* (3) NY-2
Public Sch 104—*school* (3) NY-2
Public Sch 105—*school* (3) NY-2
Public Sch 106—*school* (3) NY-2
Public Sch 107—*school* (4) NY-2
Public Sch 108—*hist pl* NY-2
Public Sch 108—*school* (4) NY-2
Public Sch 109—*school* NY-2
Public Sch 11—*hist pl* NY-2
Public Sch 11—*school* NJ-2
Public Sch 11—*school* (7) NY-2
Public Sch 110—*school* (4) NY-2
Public Sch 111—*school* (4) NY-2
Public Sch 111 and Public School 9 Annex—*hist pl* NY-2
Public Sch 112—*school* (2) NY-2
Public Sch 113—*school* (3) NY-2
Public Sch 114—*school* (3) NY-2
Public Sch 115—*school* NY-2
Public Sch 116—*school* (3) NY-2
Public Sch 117—*school* (3) NY-2
Public Sch 118—*school* (2) NY-2
Public Sch 119—*school* (4) NY-2
Public Sch 12—*school* (2) NJ-2
Public Sch 12—*school* (5) NY-2
Public Sch 120—*school* (2) NY-2
Public Sch 121—*school* (4) NY-2
Public Sch 122—*school* (2) NY-2
Public Sch 123—*school* (3) NY-2
Public Sch 124—*school* (3) NY-2
Public Sch 125—*school* (2) NY-2
Public Sch 127—*school* (2) NY-2
Public Sch 128—*school* (2) NY-2
Public Sch 129—*school* (2) NY-2
Public Sch 13—*school* NJ-2
Public Sch 13—*school* (4) NY-2
Public Sch 13 Annex—*school* NY-2
Public Sch 130—*school* (2) NY-2
Public Sch 131—*school* (2) NY-2
Public Sch 132—*school* (4) NY-2
Public Sch 133—*school* (4) NY-2
Public Sch 134—*school* (2) NY-2
Public Sch 135—*school* (2) NY-2
Public Sch 136—*school* NY-2
Public Sch 137—*school* NY-2
Public Sch 138—*school* (3) NY-2
Public Sch 139—*school* (2) NY-2
Public Sch 14—*school* NJ-2
Public Sch 14—*school* (5) NY-2
Public Sch 140—*school* (3) NY-2
Public Sch 141—*school* NY-2
Public Sch 143—*school* NY-2
Public Sch 144—*school* (3) NY-2
Public Sch 145—*school* (2) NY-2
Public Sch 146—*school* (3) NY-2
Public Sch 147—*school* (2) NY-2
Public Sch 148—*school* (3) NY-2
Public Sch 149—*school* NY-2
Public Sch 15—*hist pl* NY-2
Public Sch 15—*school* NJ-2
Public Sch 15—*school* (6) NY-2
Public Sch 150—*school* MD-2
Public Sch 150—*school* (3) NY-2
Public Sch 151—*school* NY-2
Public Sch 152—*school* (3) NY-2
Public Sch 153—*school* (2) NY-2
Public Sch 154—*school* (4) NY-2
Public Sch 155—*school* (3) NY-2
Public Sch 156—*school* (2) NY-2
Public Sch 157—*hist pl* NY-2
Public Sch 157—*school* (3) NY-2
Public Sch 158—*school* (2) NY-2
Public Sch 159—*school* (2) NY-2
Public Sch 16—*school* NJ-2
Public Sch 16—*school* (5) NY-2
Public Sch 160—*school* (2) NY-2
Public Sch 161—*school* NY-2
Public Sch 162—*school* NY-2
Public Sch 163—*school* MD-2
Public Sch 163—*school* (3) NY-2
Public Sch 164—*school* (2) NY-2
Public Sch 165—*school* (3) NY-2
Public Sch 166—*school* (2) NY-2
Public Sch 167—*school* (2) NY-2
Public Sch 168—*school* (2) NY-2
Public Sch 169—*school* (2) NY-2
Public Sch 17—*hist pl* NY-2
Public Sch 17—*school* FL-3
Public Sch 17—*school* NJ-2
Public Sch 17—*school* (6) NY-2
Public Sch 170—*school* (2) NY-2
Public Sch 171—*school* NY-2
Public Sch 172—*school* NY-2
Public Sch 173—*school* (2) NY-2
Public Sch 174—*school* (2) NY-2
Public Sch 175—*school* (3) NY-2
Public Sch 176—*school* (2) NY-2
Public Sch 177—*school* (3) NY-2
Public Sch 178—*school* NY-2
Public Sch 179—*school* (3) NY-2
Public Sch 18—*school* (7) NY-2
Public Sch 180—*school* (2) NY-2
Public Sch 181—*school* (2) NY-2
Public Sch 182—*school* NY-2
Public Sch 184—*school* (2) NY-2
Public Sch 185—*school* (2) NY-2
Public Sch 186—*school* (2) NY-2
Public Sch 187—*school* NY-2
Public Sch 188—*school* (2) NY-2
Public Sch 189—*school* (2) NY-2
Public Sch 19—*school* NJ-2
Public Sch 19—*school* (6) NY-2
Public Sch 190—*school* NY-2
Public Sch 191—*school* (3) NY-2
Public Sch 192—*school* NY-2
Public Sch 193—*school* NY-2
Public Sch 194—*school* (2) NY-2
Public Sch 195—*school* NY-2
Public Sch 196—*school* (2) NY-2
Public Sch 197—*school* (3) NY-2
Public Sch 198—*school* (2) NY-2
Public Sch 199—*school* (3) NY-2
Public Sch 2—*school* (5) NY-2
Public Sch 20—*school* NJ-2
Public Sch 20—*school* (4) NY-2
Public Sch 200—*school* (2) NY-2
Public Sch 201—*school* (3) NY-2
Public Sch 202—*school* NY-2
Public Sch 203—*school* MD-2
Public Sch 203—*school* NY-2
Public Sch 204—*school* (2) NY-2
Public Sch 205—*school* (2) NY-2
Public Sch 206—*school* (2) NY-2
Public Sch 207—*school* NY-2
Public Sch 208—*school* NY-2
Public Sch 209—*school* (2) NY-2
Public Sch 21—*school* NJ-2
Public Sch 21—*school* (7) NY-2
Public Sch 212—*school* NY-2
Public Sch 213—*school* NY-2
Public Sch 214—*school* (2) NY-2
Public Sch 215—*school* NY-2
Public Sch 216—*school* (2) NY-2
Public Sch 217—*school* NY-2
Public Sch 219—*school* (2) NY-2
Public Sch 22—*school* NJ-2
Public Sch 22—*school* (5) NY-2
Public Sch 221—*school* NY-2
Public Sch 222—*school* NY-2
Public Sch 224—*school* NY-2
Public Sch 225—*school* (2) NY-2
Public Sch 226—*school* NY-2
Public Sch 229—*school* NY-2
Public Sch 23—*school* NJ-2
Public Sch 23—*school* (7) NY-2
Public Sch 230—*school* NY-2
Public Sch 232—*school* NY-2
Public Sch 233—*school* NY-2
Public Sch 235—*school* NY-2
Public Sch 236—*school* NY-2
Public Sch 238—*school* NY-2
Public Sch 239—*school* MD-2
Public Sch 24—*school* NJ-2
Public Sch 24—*school* (6) NY-2
Public Sch 241—*school* NY-2
Public Sch 242—*school* NY-2
Public Sch 243—*school* NY-2
Public Sch 244—*school* NY-2
Public Sch 246—*school* NY-2
Public Sch 247—*school* NY-2
Public Sch 248—*school* NY-2
Public Sch 249—*school* NY-2
Public Sch 25—*school* NJ-2
Public Sch 25—*school* (5) NY-2
Public Sch 250—*school* NY-2
Public Sch 251—*school* NY-2
Public Sch 252—*school* NY-2
Public Sch 253—*school* NY-2
Public Sch 254—*school* NY-2
Public Sch 255—*school* NY-2
Public Sch 26—*school* NJ-2
Public Sch 26—*school* (6) NY-2
Public Sch 260—*school* NY-2
Public Sch 262—*school* NY-2
Public Sch 268—*school* NY-2
Public Sch 269—*school* NY-2
Public Sch 27—*school* (4) NY-2
Public Sch 271—*school* NY-2
Public Sch 272—*school* NY-2
Public Sch 273—*school* NY-2
Public Sch 274—*school* NY-2
Public Sch 276—*school* NY-2
Public Sch 277—*school* NY-2
Public Sch 279—*school* NY-2
Public Sch 28—*school* (6) NY-2
Public Sch 286—*school* NY-2
Public Sch 287—*school* NY-2
Public Sch 289—*school* NY-2
Public Sch 29—*school* (4) NY-2
Public Sch 297—*school* NY-2
Public Sch 298—*school* NY-2
Public Sch 299—*school* NY-2
Public Sch 3—*school* (2) NJ-2
Public Sch 3—*school* (7) NY-2
Public Sch 30—*school* (5) NY-2
Public Sch 303—*school* NY-2
Public Sch 304—*school* NY-2
Public Sch 305—*school* NY-2
Public Sch 306—*school* NY-2
Public Sch 307—*school* NY-2
Public Sch 309—*school* NY-2
Public Sch 31—*school* (7) NY-2
Public Sch 312—*school* NY-2
Public Sch 32—*school* (4) NY-2
Public Sch 327—*school* NY-2
Public Sch 328—*school* NY-2
Public Sch 33—*school* (3) NY-2
Public Sch 34—*school* (4) NY-2
Public Sch 35—*hist pl* NY-2
Public Sch 35—*school* (3) NY-2
Public Sch 36—*school* (4) NY-2
Public Sch 37—*school* (3) NY-2
Public Sch 370—*school* NY-2
Public Sch 38—*school* (3) NY-2
Public Sch 39—*hist pl* NY-2
Public Sch 39—*school* (5) NY-2
Public Sch 4—*school* NJ-2
Public Sch 4—*school* (10) NY-2
Public Sch 40—*school* (4) NY-2
Public Sch 41—*school* (5) NY-2
Public Sch 42—*school* (6) NY-2
Public Sch 43—*school* (2) NY-2
Public Sch 44—*school* (4) NY-2
Public Sch 45—*school* (4) NY-2
Public Sch 46—*school* (3) NY-2
Public Sch 47—*school* (4) NY-2
Public Sch 48—*school* (6) NY-2
Public Sch 49—*school* (3) NY-2
Public Sch 5—*school* (2) NJ-2
Public Sch 5—*school* (7) NY-2
Public Sch 50—*school* (4) NY-2
Public Sch 51—*school* (3) NY-2
Public Sch 52—*school* (3) NY-2
Public Sch 53—*school* (3) NY-2
Public Sch 54—*school* (4) NY-2
Public Sch 55—*school* (2) NY-2
Public Sch 56—*school* (3) NY-2
Public Sch 57—*school* (5) NY-2
Public Sch 58—*school* (3) NY-2
Public Sch 59—*school* (4) NY-2
Public Sch 6—*school* (2) NJ-2
Public Sch 6—*school* (5) NY-2
Public Sch 60—*school* NY-2
Public Sch 61—*school* (3) NY-2
Public Sch 615—*school* (2) NY-2
Public Sch 62—*school* (4) NY-2
Public Sch 621—*school* NY-2
Public Sch 63—*school* (5) NY-2
Public Sch 64—*school* (4) NY-2
Public Sch 65—*school* (4) NY-2
Public Sch 65K—*hist pl* NY-2
Public Sch 66—*school* (3) NY-2
Public Sch 67—*school* (3) NY-2
Public Sch 68—*school* (4) NY-2
Public Sch 69—*school* (4) NY-2
Public Sch 7—*hist pl* NY-2
Public Sch 7—*school* NJ-2
Public Sch 7—*school* (6) NY-2
Public Sch 70—*school* (4) NY-2
Public Sch 71—*school* (3) NY-2
Public Sch 71K—*hist pl* NY-2
Public Sch 72—*school* (4) NY-2
Public Sch 73—*school* (3) NY-2
Public Sch 74—*school* (2) NY-2
Public Sch 75—*school* (5) NY-2
Public Sch 76—*school* (4) NY-2
Public Sch 77—*school* (4) NY-2
Public Sch 78—*school* (5) NY-2
Public Sch 79—*school* (5) NY-2
Public Sch 8—*school* NJ-2
Public Sch 8—*school* (4) NY-2
Public Sch 80—*school* (5) NY-2
Public Sch 81—*school* (4) NY-2
Public Sch 82—*school* (3) NY-2
Public Sch 83—*school* (4) NY-2
Public Sch 84—*school* (3) NY-2
Public Sch 85—*school* (2) NY-2
Public Sch 86—*school* (5) NY-2
Public Sch 87—*school* (4) NY-2
Public Sch 88—*school* (4) NY-2
Public Sch 89—*school* (3) NY-2
Public Sch 9—*hist pl* NY-2
Public Sch 9—*school* (3) NY-2
Public Sch 90—*school* (4) NY-2
Public Sch 91—*school* (3) NY-2
Public Sch 92—*school* (3) NY-2
Public Sch 93—*school* (5) NY-2
Public Sch 94—*school* (2) NY-2
Public Sch 95—*school* (3) NY-2
Public Sch 96—*school* (2) NY-2
Public Sch 97—*school* (4) NY-2
Public Sch 98—*school* (3) NY-2
Public Sch 99—*school* (3) NY-2
Public Service Bldg—*hist pl* CO-8
Public Service Bldg—*hist pl* IL-6
Public Service Indiana (Gibson Generating Station)—*facility* IN-6
Public Service of Oklahoma Bldg—*hist pl* OK-5
Public Service Rsvr No 3—*reservoir* OK-5
Public Shooting Grounds Waterfowl Mngmt Area—*park* UT-8
*Public Square* OH-6
Public Square—*park* IL-6
Public Square Hist Dist—*hist pl* AL-4
Public Square Hist Dist—*hist pl* NY-2
Public Waterhole—*spring* OR-9
*Public Well Baptist Church* TN-4
Public Wells Cem—*cemetery* TN-4
Public Wells Ch—*church* TN-4
Publituk Creek—*stream* AK-9
Pucasset River Marshes—*swamp* MA-1
Puch Hollow—*valley* MO-7
*Puchshennubee* MS-4
*Puchshenubbie* MS-4
*Puchshenubee* MS-4
*Puchshenubie* MS-4
*Puchshinnubie* MS-4
Puchshinnubie Creek—*stream* MS-4
*Puchshinubbie* MS-4
*Puchshinubee* MS-4
*Puchshinubie* MS-4
*Puchshunerbie Creek* MS-4
Puchyan River—*stream* WI-6
*Puckanaw* AL-4
*Puckantala* AL-4
*Puckatunna* MS-4
Puckaway Lake—*lake* WI-6
Puck Bldg—*hist pl* NY-2
*Puckell Creek* WA-9
Puckerbrush Lake—*lake* PA-2
Pucker Creek—*stream* OR-9
Puckeroo Spring—*spring* SD-7
Puckerpod Swamp—*swamp* NH-1
*Puckershire* NH-1
**Puckershire**—*pop pl* NH-1
Pucker Spring—*spring* OR-9
Pucker Springs Branch—*stream* TX-5
Pucker Springs Creek—*stream* TX-5
Pucker Street Sch—*school* MI-6
**Puckerville**—*pop pl* NY-2
Puckerville Corners—*locale* NY-2
Pucketa Creek—*stream* PA-2
Pucket Branch—*stream* MO-7
Pucket Creek—*stream* OR-9
Pucket Gap—*gap* AL-4
*Pucket Glade* OR-9
*Puckett* TN-4
**Puckett**—*pop pl* IN-6
**Puckett**—*pop pl* LA-4
**Puckett**—*pop pl* MS-4
**Puckett**—*pop pl* TN-4
Puckett Airp—*airport* TN-4
Puckett Attendance Center—*school* MS-4
*Puckett Branch* SC-3
Puckett Branch—*stream* AL-4
Puckett Branch—*stream* (2) KY-4
Puckett Branch—*stream* NC-3
Puckett Branch—*stream* SC-3
Puckett Branch—*stream* (4) TN-4
Puckett Cem—*cemetery* AL-4
Puckett Cem—*cemetery* IL-6
Puckett Cem—*cemetery* (3) KY-4
Puckett Cem—*cemetery* MS-4
Puckett Cem—*cemetery* TN-4
Puckett Cem—*cemetery* TX-5
Puckett Cem—*cemetery* (3) VA-3
Puckett Cem—*cemetery* WV-2
Puckett Ch—*church* VA-3
*Puckett Creek* TX-5
Puckett Creek—*bay* FL-3
Puckett Creek—*stream* FL-3
Puckett Creek—*stream* GA-3
Puckett Creek—*stream* KS-7
Puckett Creek—*stream* KY-4
Puckett Creek—*stream* OK-5
Puckett Creek—*stream* OR-9
Puckett Creek—*stream* TN-4
Puckett Creek—*stream* VA-3
Puckett Creek—*stream* WA-9
Puckett Draw—*valley* TX-5
*Puckette Branch* SC-3
Puckett Family Farm—*hist pl* NC-3
Puckett Fork—*stream* KY-4
Puckett Gap—*gap* VA-3
Puckett Gas Plant—*oilfield* TX-5
Puckett Glade—*flat* OR-9
Puckett Gulch—*valley* CO-8
Puckett Hollow—*valley* AL-4
Puckett Hollow—*valley* TN-4
Puckett Hollow—*valley* VA-3
Puckett Hollow—*valley* WV-2
Puckett Island—*island* MO-7
Puckett Knob—*summit* KY-4
Puckett Knob—*summit* VA-3
Puckett Lake—*reservoir* KY-4
Puckett Lake—*reservoir* TX-5
Puckett Lake Dam—*dam* MS-4
Puckett Oil And Gas Field—*oilfield* MS-4
Puckett Pond—*lake* TN-4
Puckett Ranch—*locale* (2) TX-5
Puckett Ranch—*locale* WY-8
Puckett Ridge—*ridge* KY-4
Puckett Ridge—*ridge* WV-2
Pucketts Branch—*stream* (2) VA-3
Puckett Sch (abandoned)—*school* MO-7
*Pucketts Creek* TN-4
Pucketts Hole—*bend* VA-3
Pucketts Lake—*lake* LA-4
Puckett Spring—*spring* KY-4
Puckett Spring—*spring* UT-8
Puckett Spring Creek—*stream* KY-4
Puckett Springs—*spring* TX-5
Puckett Store—*locale* TN-4
Puckett Windmill—*locale* TX-5
Pucketty—*locale* PA-2
**Pucketville**—*pop pl* WI-6
Puck Lakes—*lake* OR-9
*Puckshennubie* MS-4
Puckshunnubbe (historical)—*locale* MS-4
Puckshunubbee-Haley Site—*hist pl* MS-4
Puckum Branch—*stream* MD-2
*Puco Point* HI-9
Puddephatt House—*hist pl* AR-4
*Puddin Creek* OR-9
Puddin Creek—*stream* OR-9
Puddin Creek—*stream* VA-3
Pudding Branch—*stream* TN-4
Pudding Brook—*stream* CT-1
Pudding Brook—*stream* ME-1
Pudding Brook—*stream* MA-1
*Pudding Creek* VA-3
Pudding Creek—*gut* VA-3
**Pudding Creek**—*pop pl* CA-9
Pudding Creek—*stream* CA-9
Pudding Creek—*stream* GA-3
Pudding Creek—*stream* OR-9
Pudding Creek—*stream* TN-4
Pudding Creek—*stream* VA-3
Pudding Hill—*summit* CT-1
Pudding Hill—*summit* (2) MA-1
Pudding Hill—*summit* NH-1
Pudding Hill—*summit* (3) VT-1
Pudding Hill Sch—*school* VT-1
Pudding Hollow—*locale* NY-2
Pudding Island—*island* ME-1
Pudding Island—*island* NY-2
*Pudding Point* MA-1
Pudding Pond—*lake* ME-1
Pudding Pond—*lake* NH-1
Pudding Ridge—*ridge* AL-4
Pudding Ridge—*ridge* GA-3
Pudding River—*stream* OR-9
Pudding Rock—*pillar* ME-1
Puddingshear Brook—*stream* MA-1
Puddingstone Diversion Dam—*dam* CA-9
Puddingstone Hill—*summit* AK-9
Puddingstone Reservoir State Rec Area—*park* CA-9
Puddingstone Rsvr—*reservoir* CA-9
Pudding Swamp—*stream* SC-3
Pudding Swamp—*swamp* AL-4
Pudding Valley—*flat* TX-5
Puddin Head Lake—*reservoir* FL-3
Puddin Hill—*summit* AR-4
Puddin Hill—*summit* MA-1
Puddin Lake—*lake* AK-9
Puddin Mtn—*summit* ID-8
Puddin Ridge—*ridge* CO-8
Puddin Rock—*pillar* OR-9
Puddin Rock Creek—*stream* OR-9
*Puddle Creek* TN-4
Puddle Creek—*stream* TX-5
Puddledock Bridge—*bridge* ME-1
Puddledock Hall—*building* ME-1
Puddledock Hollow—*valley* WI-6
Puddle Duck Creek—*stream* PA-2
Puddleford Bridge—*other* MI-6
Puddle Hole—*lake* NY-2
Puddle Lake—*lake* MN-6
Puddle Peak—*summit* NV-8
Puddles, The—*spring* MT-8
Puddle Spring—*spring* OR-9
*Puddle Spring Guard Station* OR-9
Puddle Springs—*spring* WY-8
Puddle Springs Draw—*valley* WY-8
Puddle Springs Ranch—*locale* WY-8
Puddle Spring Work Center—*locale* OR-9
Puddles Tank—*reservoir* NM-5
Puddle Tank—*reservoir* NM-5
Puddle Town—*locale* CT-1
Puddle Valley—*valley* UT-8
Puddle Valley Knolls—*summit* UT-8
*Puddock Brook* MA-1
*Puddy Cemetery* AL-4
Puddy Gulch—*valley* OR-9
Puddy Lake—*reservoir* CA-9
Puddy Run—*stream* WV-2
Puder—*locale* IL-6
Puderbaugh Ridge—*ridge* OR-9
*Pudget Sound Gulch* OR-9
*Pudouriasu* PW-9
Puds Pond—*lake* MA-1
Pudwell Dam—*dam* SD-7
*Pue* FM-9
Puea—*cape* HI-9
Pueblano Trail Camp—*locale* NM-5
*Puebla Viejo* AZ-5
Pueblita Canyon—*valley* NM-5
Pueblito—*locale* (2) NM-5
Pueblito Canyon Ruin (LA 1684)—*hist pl* NM-5
**Pueblito de Ponce**—*pop pl* PR-3
Pueblito East Ruin (LA 55834)—*hist pl* NM-5
Pueblito Point—*cape* NM-5
Pueblito Ranch—*locale* NM-5
**Pueblitos**—*pop pl* NM-5
Pueblitos Canyon—*valley* CA-9
Pueblito Tank—*reservoir* NM-5
Pueblito Well—*locale* NM-5
Pueblo—*locale* KY-4
**Pueblo**—*pop pl* CO-8
**Pueblo**—*pop pl* IN-6
Pueblo—*post sta* PR-3
Pueblo Alto—*uninc pl* AZ-5
Pueblo Alto Ruins—*locale* NM-5
Pueblo Alto Trading Post—*locale* NM-5
Pueblo Army Depot—*military* CO-8
Pueblo Arroyo—*stream* NM-5
Pueblo (Barrio)—*fmr MCD* (5) PR-3
Pueblo Belle Mine—*mine* CO-8
Pueblo Blanco Ruins—*other* NM-5
Pueblo Bonito Ranger Station—*locale* NM-5
Pueblo Bonito Ruins—*locale* NM-5
Pueblo Canon—*valley* NM-5
Pueblo Canyon—*valley* AZ-5
Pueblo Canyon—*valley* NM-5
Pueblo Cem—*cemetery* NM-5
Pueblo Chey Ruins—*locale* NM-5
Pueblo Chey Ruins—*other* NM-5
*Pueblo Colorado* AZ-5
*Pueblo Colorado River* AZ-5
Pueblo Colorado Valley—*valley* AZ-5
*Pueblo Colorado Wash* AZ-5
Pueblo Colorado Wash—*arroyo* AZ-5
Pueblo County Courthouse—*hist pl* CO-8
Pueblo County JHS—*school* CO-8
Pueblo Creek—*stream* NM-5
Pueblo Dam—*dam* CO-8
Pueblo Dam—*dam* NM-5
Pueblo De Cochiti Grant—*civil* NM-5
*Pueblo de la Concepcion* AZ-5
Pueblo del Arroyo Ruins—*locale* NM-5
**Pueblo Del Montana Subdivision**—*pop pl* UT-8
Pueblo Ditch—*canal* NM-5
Pueblo Elem Sch—*school* AZ-5
Pueblo Federal Bldg—*hist pl* CO-8
*Pueblo Ganado* AZ-5
**Pueblo Gardens**—*pop pl* AZ-5
Pueblo Gardens Sch—*school* AZ-5
Pueblo Grande de Nevada—*hist pl* NV-8
Pueblo Grande Museum—*building* AZ-5
Pueblo Grande Park—*park* AZ-5
Pueblo Grande Ruin—*hist pl* AZ-5
Pueblo Grande (ruin)—*locale* AZ-5
Pueblo HS—*school* AZ-5
Pueblo HS—*school* CO-8
Pueblo Intake—*canal* CO-8
Pueblo JHS—*school* NM-5
**Pueblo Junction**—*pop pl* CO-8
Pueblo Junior Coll—*school* CO-8
Pueblo Lands of San Diego—*civil* (2) CA-9
Pueblo Lands of San Jose—*civil* CA-9
Pueblo Lands of Santa Barbara—*civil* CA-9
Pueblo Lands of Sonoma—*civil* CA-9
Pueblo Lateral—*canal* NM-5
Pueblo Lat Number Six—*civil* CA-9
Pueblo los Tanos Ruins—*locale* NM-5
Pueblo Memorial Airport—*airport* CO-8
Pueblo Mesa—*summit* NM-5
Pueblo Mine—*mine* AZ-5
Pueblo Mountain Park—*park* CO-8
*Pueblo Mountains* NV-8
Pueblo Mountains—*range* OR-9
Pueblo Mtn—*summit* OR-9
Pueblo Mtns—*summit* NV-8
**Pueblo Norte**—*pop pl* PR-3
*Pueblo Nueva* FL-3
Pueblo Nuevo—*locale* TX-5
**Pueblo Nuevo**—*pop pl* (4) PR-3
Pueblo Of Acoma—*post sta* NM-5
Pueblo of Nambe—*hist pl* NM-5
Pueblo of Santo Domingo (Kiua)—*hist pl* NM-5
Pueblo of Tesuque—*hist pl* NM-5
Pueblo of The Stone Lions—*summit* NM-5
Pueblo Ordnance Depot—*military* CO-8
Pueblo Park—*park* (2) NM-5
Pueblo Park Corral—*locale* NM-5
*Pueblo Peak* OR-9
Pueblo Peak—*summit* NM-5
Pueblo Pintado—*locale* NM-5
Pueblo Pintado Canyon—*valley* NM-5
**Pueblo Pintado (Indian School)**—*pop pl* NM-5
Pueblo Pintado Sch—*school* NM-5
Pueblo Plaza Shop Ctr—*locale* (2) AZ-5
*pueblo Ruins* KS-7
Pueblo San Cristoval (Ruins)—*locale* NM-5
**Pueblo Seco**—*pop pl* PR-3
Pueblo Sereno Mobile Home Park—*locale* AZ-5
Pueblo Slough—*stream* NV-8
Pueblo Slough—*stream* OR-9
Pueblo Summit—*gap* ID-8
**Pueblo Sur**—*pop pl* PR-3
Pueblo Trick Tank—*reservoir* AZ-5
Pueblo Tuerto—*hist pl* NM-5
Pueblo Valley—*valley* NV-8
Pueblo Valley (depression)—*valley* OR-9
Pueblo Viejo (Barrio)—*fmr MCD* PR-3
Pueblo Viejo (historical)—*locale* AZ-5
Pueblo Viejo Mesa—*summit* NM-5
Pueblo Vista Sch—*school* CA-9
Pueblo Vitoria—*locale* TX-5
Pueblo Well—*locale* NM-5
Pueblo Well—*well* NM-5
**Pueblo West**—*pop pl* CO-8
Pueblo Windmill—*locale* (2) NM-5
Puechenan—*swamp* FM-9
Puehu—*summit* HI-9
Puehuehu—*civil* HI-9
Puehuehuiki—*civil* HI-9
Puehuehunui—*civil* HI-9
Puehu Ridge—*ridge* HI-9
Puehu Stream—*stream* HI-9
*Pueilap Reef* FM-9
*Pueilap-Riff* FM-9
Pueke—*civil* HI-9
Puelelu—*civil* HI-9
Puelz Mine—*mine* NV-8
*Puena Point* HI-9
Puenta Suelas Creek—*stream* TX-5
*Puente* CA-9
Puente—*locale* TX-5
Puente, Arroyo del—*valley* AZ-5
Puente, Canada De La —*valley* CA-9
Puente (Barrio)—*fmr MCD* PR-3
Puente Blanco—*hist pl* PR-3
**Puente Blanco**—*pop pl* PR-3
Puente Constitución—*bridge* PR-3
Puente Creek—*stream* CA-9
Puente Hills—*range* CA-9
Puente Junction—*locale* CA-9
Puente Well—*well* NM-5
Pueo—*cape* HI-9
Pueoao—*cliff* HI-9
Pueo Bay—*bay* HI-9
*Pueo Hill* HI-9
*Pueo Pali* HI-9
Pueo Point—*cape* HI-9
Puerco Beach—*beach* CA-9
Puerco Canyon—*valley* CA-9
Puerco (CCD)—*cens area* AZ-5
Puerco Dam (ruins)—*dam* NM-5
Puerco Elem Sch—*school* AZ-5
Puerco Ridge—*ridge* AZ-5
Puerco River—*stream* AZ-5
Puerco River—*stream* NM-5
Puerco Ruin and Petroglyphs—*hist pl* AZ-5
Puerco Tank—*reservoir* AZ-5
Puerner Block-Breunig's Brewery—*hist pl* WI-6
Puerta Bajita Artesian Well—*well* TX-5
Puertacitas Mountains—*summit* TX-5
Puertacito de los Salado—*gap* NM-5
Puerta Colorada Well—*well* TX-5
Puerta de la Primera Agua—*valley* NM-5
Puerta del Diablo—*summit* CA-9
*Puerta del las Mulas* AZ-5
**Puerta De Tierra**—*pop pl* PR-3
Puerta de Trancas—*gap* TX-5
Puerta de Trasquilar—*gap* (2) NM-5
Puerta La Cruz—*locale* CA-9
Puerta La Cruz Conservation Camp—*locale* CA-9
Puertas Verdes Banco Number 36—*levee* TX-5

Puu Naio—*summit* HI-9
Puu Nana—*summit* (2) HI-9
Puu Nanaha—*summit* HI-9
*Puu-Nana-Hawaii* HI-9
Puu Nanaia—*summit* HI-9
Puu Nananana—*summit* HI-9
Puu Nau—*summit* HI-9
Puu Naue—*summit* HI-9
*Puu Nene* HI-9
**Puunene**—*pop pl* HI-9
Puu Nene—*summit* (3) HI-9
Puunene—*summit* HI-9
Puu Neneakolu—*crater* HI-9
Puunene (CCD)—*cens area* HI-9
Puunene Filtration Plant—*locale* HI-9
Puunene Hosp—*hospital* HI-9
Puu Nianiau—*summit* HI-9
**Puunoa**—*pop pl* HI-9
Puunoa Point—*cape* HI-9
Puu Nole—*summit* HI-9
Puu Nopili—*summit* HI-9
**Puunui**—*pop pl* HI-9
Puu Nukohe—*summit* HI-9
Puu Oahu—*summit* HI-9
*Puu o Ehu* HI-9
Puu o Ehu—*summit* HI-9
Puu Ohai—*civil* HI-9
**Puuohala**—*pop pl* HI-9
**Puuohala Village**—*pop pl* HI-9
Puu o Hanalei—*summit* HI-9
Puu Ohau—*summit* HI-9
Puu o Haupu—*summit* HI-9
Puu Ohelo—*summit* HI-9
Puu o Hewa—*summit* HI-9
Puu o Hewa Rsvr—*reservoir* HI-9
*Puu Ohia* HI-9
Puu Ohia—*summit* HI-9
*Puu Ohio* HI-9
Puu Ohohia—*summit* HI-9
Puu o Hoku Ranch—*locale* HI-9
Puu Ohu—*summit* HI-9
Puuohua—*civil* HI-9
Puu Ohulehule—*summit* HI-9
Puuohulu Beach Park—*park* HI-9
Puu o Hulu Kai—*summit* HI-9
Puu o Hulu Uka—*summit* HI-9
Puu o Ili—*summit* HI-9
Puu o Kaau—*summit* HI-9
Puu o Kaeha—*summit* HI-9
Puu o Kahanui—*summit* HI-9
Puu o Kahaula—*summit* HI-9
Puu o Kahua—*summit* HI-9
Puu o Kahuku—*summit* HI-9
Puu o Kaia—*summit* HI-9
Puu o Kaiaka—*summit* HI-9
Puu o Kakae—*summit* HI-9
Puu o Kalaukani—*summit* HI-9
Puuokalauliko—*summit* HI-9
Puu o Kale—*summit* HI-9
Puuokalepa Stream—*stream* HI-9
*Puu o Kali* HI-9
Puu o Kali—*summit* HI-9
Puu o Kamaoa—*summit* HI-9
Puu o Kanaloa—*summit* HI-9
Puu o Kaopuu—*summit* HI-9
*Puuoka Pele* HI-9
*Puu o Kapolei* HI-9
Puu o Kau—*summit* HI-9
Puu o Kauha—*summit* HI-9
Puu o Kaupo—*summit* HI-9
Puu o Keokeo—*summit* HI-9
Puu o Kihe—*summit* HI-9
Puu o Kila—*summit* (2) HI-9
Puu o Kipahulu—*summit* HI-9
*Puuokoae* HI-9
Puu o Koeke—*summit* HI-9
Puu o Koha—*summit* HI-9
Puu o Kohola—*summit* HI-9
Puu o Kona—*summit* HI-9
Puuokumau—*civil* HI-9
Puuokumau Rsvr—*reservoir* HI-9
Puu Olai—*summit* (2) HI-9
Puu o Lani—*summit* HI-9
Puu Olelo—*summit* (2) HI-9
Puu Oli—*summit* HI-9
Puu o Lokuana—*summit* HI-9
*Puu Olomana* HI-9
Puu o Mahana—*summit* HI-9
*Puu o Mahie* HI-9
Puu o Mahuka Heiau—*hist pl* HI-9
Puu o Mahuka Heiau—*locale* HI-9
*Puu o Mahuku Heiau* HI-9
Puuomaile—*civil* HI-9
Puu o Malei—*summit* HI-9
Puu o Maui—*summit* HI-9
Puu o Mawae—*summit* HI-9
Puu o Miki—*summit* HI-9
Puu o Nale—*summit* HI-9
Puu One—*summit* HI-9
Puu One Pohue—*summit* HI-9
Puu Oo—*summit* (3) HI-9
Puu Oo Ranch—*locale* HI-9
Puu Oo Trail—*trail* HI-9
Puu Oo Volcano Trail—*trail* HI-9
Puu Opae—*summit* (2) HI-9
Puu Opae Rsvr—*reservoir* HI-9
Puu o Papai—*summit* HI-9
Puu o Pele—*summit* HI-9
Puu o Pipika—*summit* HI-9
Puuo Point—*cape* HI-9
Puu Ouli—*summit* HI-9
Puu o Umi—*summit* (2) HI-9
Puu o Uo—*summit* HI-9
Puu o Wahaula—*summit* HI-9
Puu o Wailau—*summit* HI-9
Puu Owaowaka—*summit* HI-9
Puu o Weli—*summit* HI-9
Puu Pa—*summit* HI-9
Puu Paha—*summit* HI-9
Puu Paheehee—*summit* HI-9
Puu Pahoehoe—*summit* HI-9
Puu Pahu—*summit* (2) HI-9
Puu Paipaia—*cape* HI-9
*Puu Paka* HI-9
Puu Pala—*summit* HI-9
Puu Palai—*summit* HI-9
Puu Palailai—*summit* (2) HI-9
Puu Palaolelo—*summit* HI-9
Puu Pane—*summit* (4) HI-9
Puu Papa—*summit* HI-9
Puu Papaa—*summit* HI-9
Puu Papai—*summit* HI-9
Puu Papapa—*summit* (2) HI-9
Puu Pauao—*summit* HI-9
Puu Peahinala—*summit* HI-9
Puupehe—*island* HI-9
Pu'upehe Platform (50La19)—*hist pl* HI-9
*Puupehe Rock* HI-9
*Puu Pehu* HI-9
Puu Pehu—*summit* HI-9
Puu Pelu—*ridge* HI-9
Puu Pia—*summit* HI-9
Puu Piei—*summit* HI-9
Puupiha Cem—*cemetery* HI-9
Puu Pihakapu—*summit* HI-9
*Puu Pihea* HI-9
Puu Pilau—*summit* HI-9
*Puupili* HI-9
Puu Pili—*summit* (4) HI-9
Puu Pilo—*summit* HI-9
*Puu Poa* HI-9
*Puupoa Point* HI-9
Puu Poa Point—*cape* HI-9
Puu Pohaku—*summit* (2) HI-9
Puu Pohakuloa—*summit* (2) HI-9
Puu Pohoulaula—*summit* HI-9
Puu Poliahu—*summit* HI-9
Puu Poopaa—*summit* HI-9
Puu Poo Pueo—*summit* HI-9
Puu Poulihale—*summit* HI-9
Puu Puai—*summit* HI-9
Puu Pueo—*summit* (3) HI-9
Puu Puou—*summit* HI-9
Puutik Mtn—*summit* AK-9
Puutio Creek—*stream* MN-6
Puu Uahia—*summit* HI-9
Puu Uala—*summit* HI-9
Puu Uao—*summit* HI-9
Puu Uau—*summit* (2) HI-9
Puu Ula—*summit* (3) HI-9
Puu Ulaula—*summit* (7) HI-9
Puu Ulaula (Red Hill)—*summit* HI-9
Puu Ulaulua—*summit* HI-9
*Puuwaawaa* HI-9
Puuwaawaa—*civil* HI-9
Puu Waawaa—*summit* (2) HI-9
Puu Waawaa Ranch—*locale* HI-9
**Puuwai**—*pop pl* HI-9
Puu Waiahilahila—*summit* HI-9
Puu Waiau—*summit* HI-9
Puu Waihuena—*summit* HI-9
Puu Waiko Loa—*summit* HI-9
Puu Waimanalo—*summit* HI-9
Puu Wanawana—*summit* HI-9
Puu Wekiu—*summit* HI-9
Puvakrat Mtn—*summit* AK-9
Puvunga Indian Village Sites—*hist pl* CA-9
Puvunga Indian Village Sites (Boundary Increase)—*hist pl* CA-9
Puwainui Falls—*falls* HI-9
Puwaiole Gulch—*valley* HI-9
Puwe—*island* FM-9
PU Well—*well* NV-8
**Puxico**—*pop pl* MO-7
*Puyallop River* WA-9
**Puyallup**—*pop pl* WA-9
Puyallup (CCD)—*cens area* WA-9
Puyallup Cleaver—*ridge* WA-9
Puyallup Glacier—*glacier* WA-9
**Puyallup Ind Res**—*pop pl* WA-9
Puyallup Mine—*mine* AK-9
*Puyallup Peak* WA-9
Puyallup Point—*summit* WA-9
Puyallup River—*stream* WA-9
Puyallup River Fish Hatchery—*other* WA-9
Puyallup River Junction—*locale* WA-9
Puyallup Waterway—*bay* WA-9
Puye—*locale* NM-5
Puyear Chapel—*church* AL-4
Puyear Chapel Cem—*cemetery* AL-4
Puye Ruins—*hist pl* NM-5
Puyuk Lake—*lake* AK-9
Puyulik Creek—*stream* AK-9
Puyulik Mtn—*summit* AK-9
Puzzle Bayou—*stream* MS-4
Puzzle Branch—*stream* WV-2
Puzzle Brook—*stream* ME-1
Puzzle Canyon—*valley* CA-9
Puzzle Creek—*stream* (2) AK-9
Puzzle Creek—*stream* (2) ID-8
Puzzle Creek—*stream* (2) MO-7
Puzzle Creek—*stream* MT-8
Puzzle Creek—*stream* NC-3
Puzzle Creek—*stream* (2) OR-9
Puzzle Draw—*valley* UT-8
Puzzle Gulch—*valley* AK-9
Puzzle Gulch—*valley* MT-8
Puzzle Hills—*spring* MT-8
Puzzle Lake—*lake* (2) FL-3
Puzzle Mine—*mine* CO-8
Puzzle Mtn—*summit* ME-1
Puzzle Pass—*gap* CO-8
Puzzle Point—*cliff* ID-8
Puzzler Gulch—*valley* ID-8
*Puzzle Run* PA-2
*Puzzles Mountains* AZ-5
Puzzle Spring—*spring* WY-8
**Puzzletown**—*pop pl* PA-2
Puzzley Run—*stream* MD-2
Puzzley Run—*stream* PA-2
P.V. Junction—*other* MD-2
*Pvkins Hill* MA-1
Pwadapwad, Pilen—*stream* FM-9
Pwaipwai—*bar* FM-9
Pwairehtik—*locale* FM-9
Pwairehtik, Dolen—*summit* FM-9
Pwakai, Dauen—*gut* FM-9
Pwakorokot, Dolen—*summit* FM-9
Pwapwan Tomu—*bar* FM-9
Pwarapwar, Pilen—*stream* FM-9
Pwasil—*unknown* FM-9
Pwasuk—*bar* FM-9
PW Coulee—*valley* MT-8
*Pwedipwed* FM-9
Pweikamw—*locale* FM-9
Pweikamw, Pilen—*stream* FM-9
Pweilak—*bar* FM-9
*Pwele* FM-9
Pweliko—*island* FM-9
Pwelitik—*unknown* FM-9
Pwellap—*flat* FM-9
Pwelpwel En Soueir—*bar* FM-9
Pwel Weita—*locale* FM-9
*Pwene* FM-9
Pwene—*locale* FM-9
*Pwenees* FM-9
*Pwene Island* FM-9
Pwetenkid—*unknown* FM-9
Pwetik, Dauen—*gut* FM-9
*Pweyinal* FM-9
*Pweyinap* FM-9
Pweynap—*bar* FM-9
Pweynap, Mochun—*channel* FM-9
P W Flats—*flat* MT-8
Pwikieiso—*bar* FM-9
Pwil, Dolen—*summit* FM-9
Pwoaipwoai—*civil* FM-9
*Pwoipwoi* FM-9
Pwok—*civil* FM-9
Pwok, Dauen—*gut* FM-9
Pwokolos—*island* FM-9
Pwong, Pilen—*stream* FM-9
**P & W Patch**—*pop pl* PA-2
P W Ridge—*ridge* MT-8
P Wright Ranch—*locale* ND-7
PWR Spring—*spring* NV-8
P W & S Junction Station—*locale* PA-2
PW Tank—*reservoir* AZ-5
Pwudoi—*civil* FM-9
Pwudoi—*locale* FM-9
Pwudoi, Dauen—*gut* FM-9
Pwuere—*locale* FM-9
Pwulopwul—*unknown* FM-9
*Pwuwe* FM-9
P X Flat—*flat* TX-5
P-X Ranch—*locale* NV-8
P X Ranch—*locale* UT-8
Pyaramid Corners—*locale* OK-5
**Pyatt**—*pop pl* AR-4
Pyatt Cem—*cemetery* MO-7
Pyatt County (historical)—*civil* SD-7
Pyatt Creek—*stream* NC-3
**Pyatte**—*pop pl* NC-3
Pyatt Gulch—*valley* MT-8
Pyatt Hollow—*valley* MO-7
Pyatt Hollow Church (historical)—*locale* MO-7
Pyatts—*locale* IL-6
Pyatts Chapel—*church* NC-3
Pyatt Well—*well* NM-5
*Pyborn Branch* TN-4
Pyborn Creek—*stream* TN-4
Pyborn Ridge—*ridge* TN-4
*Pyborn School* TN-4
**Pyburn**—*pop pl* TN-4
Pyburn Bluff—*cliff* TN-4
Pyburn Creek—*stream* OR-9
Pyburn Gulf—*valley* AL-4
Pyburn Gulf—*valley* GA-3
Pyburn Hollow—*valley* OR-9
Pyburn Place—*locale* TN-4
*Pyburns* TN-4
**Pyburns**—*pop pl* TN-4
Pyburn Sch—*school* TX-5
Pyburn Sch (historical)—*school* TN-4
Pybus Bay—*bay* AK-9
Pybus Lake—*lake* AK-9
Pye Alley—*gut* VA-3
Pyeatt Cave—*cave* AZ-5
Pyeatt Draw—*valley* AZ-5
Pyeatte, Henry, House—*hist pl* AR-4
Pyeatte Mill Site—*hist pl* AR-4
Pyeatt Gulch—*valley* CO-8
Pyeatt Ranch—*locale* AZ-5
Pyeatt's, J. J., General Store—*hist pl* OK-5
Pyeatt Tank—*reservoir* (2) AZ-5
**Pyeattville**—*pop pl* IN-6
Pye Brook—*stream* MA-1
Pye Cem—*cemetery* GA-3
Pye Hill—*summit* KY-4
Pye Islands—*island* AK-9
Pye Key—*island* FL-3
Pye Pond—*lake* GA-3
Pye Reef—*bar* AK-9
Pyerian Ch—*church* SC-3
Pye Slough—*stream* OR-9
Pyette Drain—*canal* MI-6
Pygmy Grove—*woods* CA-9
*Pygmy Lake* MI-6
Pygmy Lake—*lake* OR-9
Pyke—*locale* ID-8
**Pyland**—*pop pl* MS-4
Pyland Cem—*cemetery* TX-5
Pyland Post Office (historical)—*building* MS-4
Pyland Sch (historical)—*school* MS-4
Pylant Cem—*cemetery* TN-4
Pylant Springs—*spring* TN-4
Pyle, Howard, Studios—*hist pl* DE-2
Pyle, Lake—*reservoir* PA-2
Pyle Branch—*stream* MO-7
Pyle Cem—*cemetery* AL-4
Pyle Cem—*cemetery* IL-6
Pyle Cem—*cemetery* LA-4
Pyle Cem—*cemetery* (2) OH-6
Pyle Cem—*cemetery* TN-4
*Pyle Creek* GA-3
Pyle Creek—*stream* ID-8
Pyle Creek—*stream* OR-9
Pyle Creek Point—*summit* ID-8
Pyle Dam—*dam* NC-3
Pyle Ditch—*canal* IN-6
Pyle Ditch—*canal* MT-8
Pyle Draw—*valley* TX-5
Pyle Hollow—*valley* OH-6
Pyle House—*hist pl* SD-7
Pyle HS—*school* TX-5
*Pyle Island* PA-2
Pyle JHS—*school* MD-2
*Pylel* PA-2
Pyle Lake—*reservoir* NC-3
Pyle Mtn—*summit* ME-1
Pyle Mtn—*summit* OK-5
Pyle Mtn—*summit* WV-2
Pyle Ranch—*locale* AZ-5
Pyle Ranch—*locale* (2) NM-5
Pyle Run—*stream* WV-2
Pyles Camp—*locale* CA-9
Pyles Canyon—*valley* OR-9
Pyles Canyon Dam Number Two—*dam* OR-9
Pyles Canyon Rsvr Number Two—*reservoir* OR-9
Pyles Cem—*cemetery* IL-6
Pyles Cem—*cemetery* MO-7
Pyles Cem—*cemetery* (2) TN-4
Pyles Cem—*cemetery* TX-5
*Pyle Sch* DE-2
Pyle Sch—*school* CA-9
*Pyle School* IN-6
*Pyle School Number 90* IN-6
Pyles Creek—*stream* OR-9
Pyles Ferry (historical)—*locale* AL-4
Pyles Fork—*stream* WV-2
Pyles Hollow—*valley* MO-7
Pyles Marsh—*locale* GA-3
Pyles Memorial Ch—*church* VA-3
Pyles Mills—*locale* PA-2
*Pyles Run* WV-2
Pyles Sch—*school* CA-9
Pyles Sch (abandoned)—*school* PA-2
Pyles Site (15MS28)—*hist pl* KY-4
Pyles Swamp—*swamp* GA-3
Pylesville—*locale* MD-2
Pyletown—*locale* VA-3
**Pyletown**—*pop pl* MO-7
Pyle Windmill—*locale* NM-5
Pylon Peak—*summit* WY-8
Pyma-Love Airp—*airport* PA-2
Pymatuning—*locale* PA-2
Pymatuning Creek—*stream* OH-6
Pymatuning Creek—*stream* PA-2
*Pymatuning Lake* OH-6
**Pymatuning Park**—*pop pl* OH-6
Pymatuning Reservoir Dam—*dam* PA-2
Pymatuning Rsvr—*reservoir* OH-6
Pymatuning Rsvr—*reservoir* PA-2
**Pymatuning (sta.)**—*pop pl* PA-2
Pymatuning State Park—*park* OH-6
Pymatuning State Park—*park* PA-2
*Pymatuning Station* PA-2
*Pymatuning Swamp* OH-6
*Pymatuning Swamp* PA-2
Pymatuning Swamp—*swamp* PA-2
**Pymatuning (Township of)**—*pop pl* PA-2
Pymn Canyon—*valley* AZ-5
Pymn Canyon Pond—*lake* AZ-5
Pymosa Township—*fmr MCD* IA-7
Pym Pond—*lake* ME-1
Pynchin Lake—*lake* WY-8
Pynchon Meadows—*flat* MA-1
Pynchon Park—*park* MA-1
*Pynchons Island* CT-1
*Pynchons Little Falls* CT-1
**Pyne**—*pop pl* GA-3
*Pyne Point* NJ-2
Pyne Poynt JHS—*school* NJ-2
Pyne Poynt Park—*park* NJ-2
Pyne Sch—*school* MA-1
Pyne Shaft—*mine* PA-2
Pyneville—*locale* PA-2
Pynor Siding—*locale* SC-3
Pyoca, Lake—*reservoir* IN-6
Pyokon—*island* MP-9
*Pyokon Island* MP-9
**Pyote**—*pop pl* TX-5
Pyote Flats—*flat* TX-5
*Pyoto Island* MP-9
Pyott Branch—*gut* TN-4
Pyott Cem—*cemetery* (2) TN-4
Pyping Point—*cape* VA-3
Pyramid—*locale* IL-6
Pyramid—*locale* KY-4
**Pyramid**—*pop pl* NV-8
*Pyramid, The* WA-9
Pyramid, The—*pillar* NM-5
Pyramid, The—*summit* (3) MT-8
Pyramid, The—*summit* ND-7
Pyramid Block Cave—*cave* TN-4
Pyramid Brook—*stream* (2) NY-2
Pyramid Butte—*summit* AZ-5
Pyramid Butte—*summit* CA-9
Pyramid Butte—*summit* MT-8
Pyramid Butte—*summit* OR-9
Pyramid Butte—*summit* UT-8
Pyramid Buttes—*summit* MT-8
Pyramid Campground—*locale* CA-9
*Pyramid Canyon* NV-8
Pyramid Canyon—*valley* (2) AZ-5
Pyramid Canyon—*valley* NV-8
**Pyramid Corners**—*pop pl* OK-5
Pyramid Cove—*bay* AK-9
Pyramid Cove—*bay* CA-9
Pyramid Creek—*stream* AK-9
Pyramid Creek—*stream* CA-9
Pyramid Creek—*stream* ID-8
Pyramid Creek—*stream* (3) MT-8
Pyramid Creek—*stream* OR-9
Pyramid Creek—*stream* TX-5
Pyramid Creek—*stream* (4) WA-9
Pyramid Creek—*stream* WY-8
Pyramid Glaciers—*glacier* WA-9
Pyramid Guard Station—*locale* CA-9
Pyramid Guard Station—*locale* CO-8
Pyramid Harbor—*bay* AK-9
Pyramid Head—*summit* CA-9
Pyramid Hill—*ridge* CA-9
Pyramid Hill—*summit* MT-8
Pyramid Hills—*other* CA-9
Pyramid Hills Microwave Relay Station—*other* CA-9
Pyramid Island—*island* (2) AK-9
Pyramid Island—*island* (2) NV-8
Pyramid Knoll—*summit* UT-8
Pyramid Lake—*lake* CA-9
Pyramid Lake—*lake* ID-8
Pyramid Lake—*lake* MT-8
Pyramid Lake—*lake* NV-8
Pyramid Lake—*lake* NY-2
Pyramid Lake—*lake* (2) OR-9
Pyramid Lake—*lake* UT-8
Pyramid Lake—*lake* WA-9
Pyramid Lake—*lake* WY-8
Pyramid Lake—*reservoir* CA-9
**Pyramid Lake Ind Res**—*pop pl* NV-8
Pyramid Lake Trail—*trail* WA-9
Pyramid Mine—*mine* (2) CA-9
Pyramid Mine—*mine* NV-8
Pyramid Mine—*mine* UT-8
Pyramid Mine—*mine* WY-8
Pyramid Mound (12k14)—*hist pl* IN-6
*Pyramid Mountain* AZ-5
Pyramid Mountains—*other* NM-5
Pyramid Mountain Trail—*trail* WA-9
*Pyramid Mtn* WA-9
Pyramid Mtn—*summit* (4) AK-9
Pyramid Mtn—*summit* ID-8
Pyramid Mtn—*summit* MT-8
Pyramid Mtn—*summit* NM-5
Pyramid Mtn—*summit* OR-9
Pyramid Mtn—*summit* (2) WA-9
Pyramid Park—*flat* WA-9
Pyramid Pass—*gap* ID-8
Pyramid Pass—*gap* MT-8
Pyramid Pass—*gap* WA 9
Pyramid Pass Trail (pack)—*trail* MT-8
*Pyramid Peak* CO-8
*Pyramid Peak* WA-9
Pyramid Peak—*summit* (5) AK-9
Pyramid Peak—*summit* (3) AZ-5
Pyramid Peak—*summit* (6) CA-9
Pyramid Peak—*summit* (3) CO-8
Pyramid Peak—*summit* (5) ID-8
Pyramid Peak—*summit* (6) MT-8
Pyramid Peak—*summit* (2) NV-8
Pyramid Peak—*summit* (3) NM-5
Pyramid Peak—*summit* (2) UT-8
Pyramid Peak—*summit* (3) WA-9
Pyramid Peak—*summit* (5) WY-8
Pyramid Peak Trail—*trail* WA-9
*Pyramid Point* CA-9
Pyramid Point—*cape* AK-9
Pyramid Point—*cape* CA-9
Pyramid Point—*cape* MI-6
Pyramid Point—*cape* MT-8
Pyramid Point—*cliff* CO-8
Pyramid Point—*summit* (2) ID-8
Pyramid Point Shoal—*bar* MI-6
*Pyramid Range* NV-8
Pyramid Ridge—*ridge* CA-9
Pyramid Rock—*island* AZ-5
Pyramid Rock—*island* CA-9
Pyramid Rock—*island* (3) OR-9
Pyramid Rock—*pillar* HI-9
Pyramid Rock—*pillar* NM-5
Pyramid Rock—*pillar* (2) OR-9
Pyramid Rock—*summit* (2) CA-9
Pyramid Rock—*summit* CO-8
Pyramid Rock—*summit* TX-5
Pyramid Rock—*summit* WA-9
*Pyramids, The* CA-9
Pyramids, The—*summit* AK-9
Pyramids, The—*summit* AZ-5
Pyramids, The—*summit* UT-8
Pyramid Spring—*spring* NV-8
Pyramid State Park—*park* IL-6
Pyramid Tank—*reservoir* TX-5
Pyramid Trail—*trail* MT-8
Pyramid Trail—*trail* (2) OR-9
Pyramid Unicom Airp—*airport* MS-4
Pyramid View Cem—*cemetery* KS-7
Pyramid Well—*well* NV-8
Pyramid Well—*well* NM-5
*Pyramus* NJ-2
Pyre Peak—*summit* AK-9
Pyrite Canyon—*valley* NM-5
Pyrite Channel—*canal* CA-9
Pyrite Creek—*stream* ID-8
Pyrite Mtn—*summit* NM-5
Pyrite Point—*cape* AK-9
Pyrites—*locale* NY-2
**Pyrites**—*pop pl* NY-2
Pyrites Creek—*stream* WA-9
Pyriton—*locale* AL-4
*Pyrmaid Head* CA-9
Pyrmont—*locale* MO-7
**Pyrmont**—*pop pl* IN-6
**Pyrmont**—*pop pl* OH-6
Pyro—*locale* OH-6
**Pyro**—*pop pl* KY-4
*Pyro Creek* AL-4
**Pyron**—*pop pl* AL-4
**Pyron**—*pop pl* TX-5
Pyron Cem—*cemetery* TX-5
Pyron Siding—*locale* TX-5
Pyron Spring Branch—*stream* FL-3
Pyron Spring Chapel—*church* FL-3
Pyrophyllite Mine Lake—*reservoir* NC-3
Pyrophyllite Mine Lake Dam—*dam* NC-3
Pyror Pond—*lake* AL-4
Pyror Ridge Methodist Ch—*church* TN-4
Pyror Slough—*lake* SD-7
*Pyroxene Butte* MT-8
Pyrra—*locale* PA-2
Pyrtle Hollow—*valley* (2) MO-7
Pyrtle Sch—*school* NE-7
Pyrtle Spring—*spring* MO-7
**Pyrus**—*pop pl* KY-4
*Pysche* WA-9
*Pysche River* WA-9
*Pyscht* WA-9
*Pyscht River* WA-9
Pyserts Hole—*basin* UT-8
Pysht—*locale* WA-9
Pysht River—*stream* WA-9
P-Y Tank—*reservoir* AZ-5
Pythagoras Lodge No. 41, Free and Accepted Masons—*hist pl* GA-3
Pythian Castle—*hist pl* CA-9
Pythian Castle—*hist pl* OH-6
Pythian Castle—*hist pl* VA-3
Pythian Castle Lodge—*hist pl* WI-6
Pythian Cave—*cave* CA-9
Pythian Cem—*cemetery* IN-6
Pythian Cem—*cemetery* LA-4
Pythian Grove Cem—*cemetery* KY-4
Pythian Home—*building* OH-6
Pythian Home—*locale* NC-3
Pythian Ridge Cem—*cemetery* KY-4
Pythian Sisters Home—*building* OH-6
Pythian Temple—*hist pl* WA-9
Pythian Temple and James Pythian Theater—*hist pl* OH-6
Pythias, Lake—*lake* FL-3
Pythias Lodge Bldg—*hist pl* CA-9
Pytlovany, Simon, House—*hist pl* TX-5
Pywaosit Lake—*lake* WI-6
Pywiack Cascade—*falls* CA-9
Pywiack Dome—*summit* CA-9
P Y X Mine—*mine* OR-9
PZ Ranch—*locale* AZ-5
P1 Canal—*canal* CA-9
P-38 Crossing—*locale* CA-9
P51 Tank—*reservoir* AZ-5
P-6 Canal—*canal* MT-8

# Q

**Qaaf**—*pop pl* FM-9
Qabaay *summit* FM-9
Qabluul—*cape* FM-9
Qabyaang—*locale* FM-9
Qachangal—*bar* FM-9
**Qadibweg**—*pop pl* FM-9
*Qadibweq* FM-9
Qadigiyelugoch—*bar* FM-9
Qadirgel—*summit* FM-9
*Qadirqel* FM-9
*Qadmaamaang* FM-9
Qaldug—*summit* FM-9
*Qalgath* FM-9
Qaliiyir—*summit* FM-9
Qaloog—*locale* FM-9
Qalqath—*bay* FM-9
Qamin—*locale* FM-9
Qamraaw—*summit* FM-9
Qamun—*locale* FM-9
Qanbalaach—*summit* FM-9
Q and C Ferry (historical)—*locale* MS-4
Qanif—*bay* FM-9
Qanooth—*locale* FM-9
Qapirgog—*summit* FM-9
Qaraq—*bay* FM-9
**Qaringeel**—*pop pl* FM-9
Qarmiilog—*cape* FM-9
Qarngach—*summit* FM-9
Qaruwol—*summit* FM-9
Qatliirow—*channel* FM-9
Qatliw—*locale* FM-9
Qawoch—*summit* FM-9
Qawol—*summit* FM-9
*Qayaan* FM-9
Qayean—*cape* FM-9
Qayeng—*summit* FM-9
**Qayirech**—*pop pl* FM-9
Qayong—*bay* FM-9
Qayong—*channel* FM-9
Q Copeland Lake Dam—*dam* MS-4
Q Creek—*stream* TN-4
Q Ditch—*canal* IL-6
Q Drain—*canal* CA-9
Qeang—*locale* FM-9
Qeedugor—*locale* FM-9
Qeedup Spring—*spring* ID-8
Qeelik'—*island* FM-9
Qeeluul'—*bay* FM-9
Qeetuun—*channel* FM-9
Qeetuun—*gut* FM-9
Qhandlery Corner—*hist pl* PA-2
Qheguechan Club—*hist pl* MA-1
Qichigiyoeg—*locale* FM-9
Qikutulig Bay—*bay* AK-9
Q Lateral—*canal* CA-9
Q Lateral—*canal* MT-8
Q Mart Shop Ctr—*locale* PA-2
Qoer—*bay* FM-9
Qokaaw—*locale* FM-9
Qoon—*locale* FM-9
Q Ranch—*locale* AZ-5
Q Ranch, The—*locale* WY-8
Q Rsvr—*reservoir* OR-9
Qsl Fish Hatchery Dam—*dam* AL-4
Qsl Fish Hatchery Lake—*reservoir* AL-4
Q Street Canal—*canal* OR-9
QT Spring—*spring* OR-9
*Quabaug* MA-1
*Quabaug River* MA-1
Quabbin Aqueduct—*canal* (2) MA-1
*Quabbin Dike* MA-1
Quabbin Goodnough Dike—*dam* MA-1
Quabbin Hill—*summit* MA-1
*Quabbin Lake* MA-1
*Quabbin Mtn* MA-1
Quabbinnight Brook—*stream* NH-1
Quabbin Park Cem—*cemetery* MA-1
Quabbin Regional HS—*school* MA-1
Quabbin Rsvr—*reservoir* MA-1
Quabbin Spillway Dam—*dam* MA-1
Quabbin Winsor Dam—*dam* MA-1
*Quabin Hill* MA-1
*Quabin Lake* MA-1
Quaboag Pond—*lake* MA-1
Quaboag Regional HS—*school* MA-1
Quaboag River—*stream* MA-1
*Quachita City* LA-4
**Quachita City**—*pop pl* LA-4
Quachita Hosp—*hospital* AR-4
*Quackake* PA-2
Quack Branch—*stream* IN-6
Quack Creek—*stream* IN-6
Quackenbush Cem—*cemetery* NY-2
Quackenbush Hardware Store—*hist pl* OR-9
**Quackenbush Hill**—*pop pl* NY-2
Quackenbush Hill—*summit* (2) NY-2
Quackenbush House—*hist pl* NY-2
Quackenbush Lake—*flat* CA-9
Quackenbush Mine—*mine* CA-9
Quackenbush Mtn—*summit* CA-9
Quackenbush Pond—*lake* NY-2
Quackenbush Pumping Station, Albany Water Works—*hist pl* NY-2
Quackenbush Rsvr—*reservoir* OR-9
*Quacken Kill* NY-2
**Quackenkill**—*pop pl* NY-2
Quacken Kill—*stream* NY-2
Quacker Creek—*stream* CO-8
*Quacket River* RI-1
*Quacket Run* MA-1
Quack Hill—*summit* NY-2
Quack Island—*island* NY-2
*Quack Lake* MI-6
Quack Lake—*lake* MI-6
Quack Run—*stream* IN-6
*Quacompawg Pond* RI-1
Quaco Windmill—*locale* TX-5
*Quacumouasit Pond* MA-1
*Quacumquaset Lake* MA-1
Quacumquasit Pond—*lake* MA-1
*Quacut River* RI-1
*Quad Cities* AL-4
*Quad Cities* IL-6
*Quad Cities* IA-7
Quad Cities—*other* IL-6
Quad-City Airp—*airport* IL-6
Quad Creek—*stream* MT-8
Quaddick—*locale* CT-1
Quaddick Mtn—*summit* CT-1
Quaddick Rsvr—*reservoir* CT-1
Quaddick State For—*forest* CT-1
Quaddick State Park—*park* CT-1
Quaderer Creek—*stream* WI-6
Quadga Lake—*lake* MN-6
Quad Hill—*hist pl* OH-6
Quad Lake—*lake* ID-8
**Quadlok**—*pop pl* WA-9
Quadna Mtn—*summit* MN-6
*Quadock Brook* CT-1
*Quadock Brook* RI-1
Quadra Lakes—*area* AK-9
Quadranaou Park—*park* OH-6
Quadrangle, The—*hist pl* TX-5
Quadrangle, The—*locale* CA-9
Quadrangle-Mattoon Street Hist Dist—*hist pl* MA-1
Quadrant Gulch—*valley* ID-8
Quadrant Mtn—*summit* WY-8
Quadra Point—*cape* AK-9
*Quadrate Peak* CO-8
Quadrat Hollow—*valley* UT-8
Quad State Helicopter Heliport—*airport* MO-7
**Quad Subdivision**—*pop pl* UT-8
*Quaduck Brook* CT-1
*Quaduck Brook* RI-1
Quafaloma Landing (historical)—*locale* MS-4
*Quafcacanquen* MA-1
Quag, The—*lake* MA-1
Quagana Hill—*summit* MA-1
Quaggy Joe—*summit* ME-1
Quagle Creek—*stream* MT-8
Quagmire Cave—*cave* AL-4
Quagmire Creek—*stream* CO-8
Quagmire Group—*spring* WY-8
Quagmire Swamp—*swamp* NY-2
*Quag Pond* MA-1
Quag Pond—*lake* MA-1
Quahada Ridge—*ridge* NM-5
*Quahaug Bar* MA-1
*Quahaug Bay* ME-1
Quahaug Point—*cape* RI-1
Quahog Bar—*bar* MA-1
Quahog Bay—*bay* ME-1
*Quahog Point* RI-1
Quahog Pond—*lake* MA-1
**Quaid**—*pop pl* LA-4
*Quaijotoa Mountains* AZ-5
Quail—*locale* CA-9
Quail—*locale* KY-4
Quail—*locale* MO-7
Quail—*locale* VA-3
**Quuil**—*pop pl* TX-5
Quail—*uninc pl* NY-2
Quail Bay—*bay* AK-9
Quail Bay—*bay* NV-8
Quail Brook—*stream* NJ-2
**Quailbrook East Condominium**—*pop pl* UT-8
**Quailbrook Subdivision**—*pop pl* UT-8
Quail Canal—*canal* CA-9
Quail Canyon—*valley* (2) AZ-5
Quail Canyon—*valley* (5) CA-9
Quail Canyon—*valley* (2) NM-5
Quail Canyon—*valley* UT-8
Quail Canyon Ranch—*locale* NV-8
Quail Cem—*cemetery* TX-5
Quail Corners Shop Ctr—*locale* NC-3
**Quail Country Place (subdivision)**—*pop pl* (2) AZ-5
**Quail Cove PUD Subdivision**—*pop pl* UT-8
*Quail Creek* CA-9
*Quail Creek* CO-8
**Quail Creek**—*pop pl* TN-4
Quail Creek—*post sta* OK-5
Quail Creek—*stream* AK-9
Quail Creek—*stream* CA-9
Quail Creek—*stream* NJ-2
Quail Creek—*stream* (2) OR-9
Quail Creek—*stream* UT-8
Quail Creek Country Club—*other* OK-5
Quail Creek Rsvr—*reservoir* OR-9
Quail Creek State Park—*park* UT-8
**Quail Creek (subdivision)**—*pop pl* TN-4
**Quail Creek Subdivision**—*pop pl* UT-8
Quail Draw—*valley* AZ-5
Quail Draw Rsvr—*reservoir* AZ-5
Quail Flat—*flat* AZ-5
Quail Flat—*flat* (4) CA-9
Quail Gulch—*valley* (3) CA-9
Quail Gulch—*valley* MT-8
Quail Gulch—*valley* (2) OR-9
Quail Heights—*post sta* FL-3
Quail Hill—*summit* AZ-5
Quail Hill—*summit* (2) CA-9
Quail Hill—*summit* MT-8
Quail Hill—*summit* NY-2
Quail Hill Mine—*mine* CA-9
**Quail Hollow**—*pop pl* TN-4
Quail Hollow—*valley* NY-2
Quail Hollow Country Club—*locale* FL-3
Quail Hollow Country Club—*locale* NC-3
Quail Hollow Country Club Lake—*reservoir* NC-3
Quail Hollow Country Club Lake Dam—*dam* NC-3
Quail Hollow Elem Sch—*school* FL-3
**Quail Hollow Estates (subdivision)**—*pop pl* NC-3
Quail Hollow HS—*school* NC-3
Quail Hollow Sch—*school* CA-9
Quail Hollow Sch—*school* UT-8
**Quail Hollow (subdivision)**—*pop pl* (7) NC-3
**Quail Hollow (subdivision)**—*pop pl* TN-4
**Quail Hollow Subdivision**—*pop pl* (2) UT-8
Quail Island—*island* AK-9
Quail Lake—*lake* CA-9
Quail Lake—*lake* MT-8
Quail Lake—*reservoir* CA-9
Quail Lake Fire Station—*locale* CA-9
Quail Lake RV Park—*park* UT-8
**Quail Lane (subdivision)**—*pop pl* (2) AZ-5
Quail Meadows—*flat* CA-9
*Quail Meadows Estates* IN-6
**Quail Meadow (subdivision)**—*pop pl* NC-3
Quail Mesa Airp—*airport* AZ-5
Quail Mesa Dam—*dam* AZ-5
Quail Mesa Tank—*reservoir* AZ-5
Quail Mine—*mine* CA-9
Quail Mine—*mine* CO-8
Quail Mountains—*other* CA-9
Quail Mtn—*summit* CA-9
Quail Mtn—*summit* CO-8
Quail Mtn—*summit* TX-5
**Quail Oaks**—*pop pl* VA-3
Quail Park Botanical Garden—*park* CA-9
**Quail Place (subdivision)**—*pop pl* (2) AZ-5
Quail Point—*summit* NV-8
Quail Point Flowage—*reservoir* WI-6
**Quail Point Subdivision**—*pop pl* (3) UT-8
Quail Pond—*lake* FL-3
Quail Post Office (historical)—*building* AL-4
Quail Prairie Creek—*stream* OR-9
Quail Prairie Mtn—*summit* OR-9
**Quail Ridge**—*pop pl* DE-2
**Quail Ridge**—*pop pl* NC-3
Quail Ridge—*ridge* TX-5
**Quail Ridge (subdivision)**—*pop pl* (6) NC-3
**Quail Ridge Subdivision**—*pop pl* UT-8
Quail Roost—*locale* NC-3
Quail Roost Lake Dam Number Three—*dam* NC-3
Quail Roost Lake Number One—*reservoir* NC-3
Quail Roost Lake Number One Dam—*dam* NC-3
Quail Roost Lake Number Three—*reservoir* NC-3
Quail Roost Lake Number Two—*reservoir* NC-3
Quail Roost Lake Number Two Dam—*dam* NC-3
Quail Roost Plaza (Shop Ctr)—*locale* FL-3
Quail Rsvr—*reservoir* UT-8
**Quail Run**—*pop pl* MD-2
**Quail Run** *pop pl* NJ 2
Quail Run—*stream* OH-6
Quail Run—*stream* VA-3
Quail Run Golf Course—*other* AZ-5
**Quail Run (subdivision)**—*pop pl* (3) AL-4
**Quail Run (subdivision)**—*pop pl* NC-3
**Quail Run Subdivision**—*pop pl* (2) UT-8
Quails Cem—*cemetery* TN-4
Quail Sch—*school* PA-2
Quail Site—*hist pl* CA-9
*Quail Slough* CA-9
Quails Pond—*reservoir* NC-3
Quails Pond Dam—*dam* NC-3
Quail Spring—*spring* (14) AZ-5
Quail Spring—*spring* (11) CA-9
Quail Spring—*spring* (2) NV-8
Quail Spring—*spring* TX-5
Quail Spring—*spring* UT-8
Quail Spring—*spring* WY-8
Quail Spring Basin—*basin* CA-9
Quail Spring Canyon—*valley* AZ-5
Quail Spring Rsvr—*reservoir* CA-9
Quail Springs—*spring* AZ-5
Quail Springs (Dry)—*spring* CA-9
Quail Springs Wash—*stream* AZ-5
Quail Springs Wash—*stream* NV-8
Quail Spring Wash—*stream* AZ-5
Quail Spring Wash—*stream* CA-9
Quail Spring Wash—*valley* AZ-5
**Quailstone Subdivision**—*pop pl* UT-8
Quail Tank—*reservoir* (8) AZ-5
Quail Tank—*reservoir* (2) NM-5
Quail Tank—*reservoir* TX-5
Quail Top—*summit* CA-9
Quail Trap Canyon—*valley* CA-9
Quail Trap Cem—*cemetery* MO-7
Quail Trap Cem—*cemetery* OH-6
Quail Trap Ravine—*valley* CA-9
Quail Trap Sch—*school* (2) MI-6
Quail Trap Sch—*school* MN-6
Quail Trick Tank—*reservoir* AZ-5
*Quail Valley* CA-9
**Quail Valley**—*pop pl* CA-9
*Quail Valley Country Club* CA-9
Quail Valley Country Club—*other* CA-9
**Quail Valley (subdivision)**—*pop pl* (2) AZ-5
**Quail Valley (subdivision)**—*pop pl* MS-4
**Quail Valley Subdivision**—*pop pl* UT-8
**Quail Valley Subdivision #3**—*pop pl* UT-8
Quail Walk Golf Course—*locale* AL-4
Quail Wash—*stream* AZ-5
Quail Wash—*stream* CA-9
Quail Water Creek—*stream* CA-9
*Quailwood Farms Lake Number Two* AL-4
Quailwood Farms Lakes—*reservoir* AL-4
**Quaint Acres**—*pop pl* MD-2
Quaintance Park—*flat* MT-8
Quaintance Ranch—*locale* MT-8
**Quaise**—*pop pl* MA-1
Quaise Point—*cape* MA-1
Quaitie Spring—*spring* CO-8
*Quajata Creek* AZ-5
*Quajato* AZ-5
*Quajote* AZ-5
*Quajote Wash* AZ-5
*Quajoto Wash* AZ-5
**Quakake**—*pop pl* PA-2
*Quakake Creek* PA-2
Quakake Creek—*stream* PA-2
Quakake Junction—*locale* PA-2
Quakake Lake—*dam* PA-2
Quakale Lake—*reservoir* PA-2
Quake Lake—*lake* AK-9
Quakenasp Canyon—*valley* WY-8
Quaken Asp Glade—*flat* CA-9
*Quakenbush Creek* CO-8
Quakenbush Drain—*stream* MI-6
Quakenstead Gulch—*valley* WY-8
Quaker—*locale* KS-7
Quaker—*locale* MO-7
Quaker—*locale* PA-2
Quaker—*locale* WV-2
**Quaker**—*pop pl* IL-6
**Quaker**—*pop pl* IN-6
**Quaker Acres (subdivision)**—*pop pl* NC-3
**Quaker Basin**—*pop pl* NY-2
Quaker Branch—*stream* KY-4
Quaker Branch—*stream* SC-3
Quaker Branch—*stream* (2) VA-3
Quaker Bridge—*bridge* (2) NJ-2
Quaker Bridge—*bridge* NY-2
Quaker Bridge—*bridge* NC-3
Quaker Bridge—*bridge* VA-3
Quaker Bridge—*hist pl* PA-2
Quaker Bridge—*locale* NY-2
Quaker Brook—*stream* CT-1
Quaker Brook—*stream* (2) ME-1
Quaker Brook—*stream* MA-1
Quaker Brook—*stream* MI-6
Quaker Brook—*stream* NY-2
Quaker Cem—*cemetery* CT-1
Quaker Cem—*cemetery* (3) IN-6
Quaker Cem—*cemetery* (2) KS-7
Quaker Cem—*cemetery* ME-1
Quaker Cem—*cemetery* MA-1
Quaker Cem—*cemetery* MI-6
Quaker Cem—*cemetery* MO-7
Quaker Cem—*cemetery* NH-1
Quaker Cem—*cemetery* NJ-2
Quaker Cem—*cemetery* (10) NY-2
Quaker Cem—*cemetery* (5) OH-6
Quaker Cem—*cemetery* SD-7
Quaker Cem—*cemetery* VT-1
Quaker Cem—*cemetery* VA-3
Quaker Cemtery—*cemetery* MA-1
Quaker Ch—*church* OH-6
Quaker Ch—*church* VA-3
Quaker Ch (historical)—*church* PA-2
Quaker Ch (historical)—*church* TN-4
*Quaker Church* KS-7
*Qua Church* SD-7
Quaker Church—*locale* NJ-2
Quaker Church Cem—*cemetery* OH-6
**Quaker City**—*pop pl* NH-1
**Quaker City**—*pop pl* OH-6
**Quaker City**—*pop pl* PA-2
Quaker City Mine—*mine* NV-8
Quaker Corral—*locale* CO-8
Quaker Cove—*valley* NY-2
Quaker Creek—*stream* NY-2
Quaker Creek—*stream* NC-3
Quaker Creek—*stream* SC-3
Quaker Creek—*stream* WY-8
Quaker Creek Rsvr—*reservoir* NC-3
Quaker Ditch—*canal* NJ-2
Quakerdom Cem—*cemetery* IN-6
**Quaker Farms**—*pop pl* CT-1
Quaker Field Branch—*stream* VA-3
Quaker Flat—*flat* ID-8
Quaker Flour Mill—*hist pl* CO-8
Quaker Fork—*stream* WV-2
**Quaker Gap**—*pop pl* NC-3
Quaker Gap (Township of)—*fmr MCD* NC-3
**Quaker Gardens**—*pop pl* NJ-2
Quaker Gulch—*valley* CO-8
**Quaker Haven Park**—*pop pl* IN-6
*Quaker Head* ME-1
Quaker Head—*cape* ME-1
Quaker Heights—*uninc pl* NM-5
*Quaker Hill* PA-2
Quaker Hill—*locale* NY-2
**Quaker Hill**—*pop pl* CT-1
**Quaker Hill**—*pop pl* DE-2
**Quaker Hill**—*pop pl* OH-6
**Quaker Hill**—*pop pl* RI-1
Quaker Hill—*summit* CA-9
Quaker Hill—*summit* (4) ME-1
Quaker Hill—*summit* (3) NY-2
Quaker Hill—*summit* (2) PA-2
Quaker Hill—*summit* RI-1
Quaker Hill Cave—*cave* PA-2
Quaker Hill Cem—*cemetery* ME-1
Quaker Hill Cem—*cemetery* NY-2
Quaker Hill Cem—*cemetery* (2) OH-6
Quaker Hill Cem—*cemetery* PA-2
Quaker Hill Ch—*church* ME-1
Quaker Hill Hist Dist—*hist pl* DE-2
Quaker Hill Hist Dist (Boundary Increase)—*hist pl* DE-2
**Quaker Hills**—*pop pl* PA-2
Quaker House Ch—*church* NC-3
Quaker Knobs—*ridge* TN-4
Quaker Knobs Ch—*church* TN-4
Quaker Lake—*lake* MI-6
Quaker Lake—*lake* NY-2
**Quaker Lake**—*pop pl* PA-2
Quaker Lake—*reservoir* NC-3
Quaker Lake—*reservoir* PA-2
Quaker Lake Cem—*cemetery* PA-2
Quaker Lynn Cem—*cemetery* IN-6
Quaker Manor House—*hist pl* PA-2
Quaker Meadow—*locale* CA-9
Quaker Meadow Ch—*church* NC-3
Quaker Meadows—*hist pl* NC-3
Quaker Meadows Cemetery—*hist pl* NC-3
Quaker Meadows Golf Club—*locale* NC-3
Quaker Meadow (Township of)—*fmr MCD* NC-3
Quaker Meeting House—*building* MA-1
Quaker Meetinghouse—*hist pl* MA-1
Quaker Meetinghouse—*locale* NY-2
Quaker Meetinghouse (abandoned)—*church* PA-2
Quaker Mesa—*summit* CO-8
Quaker Mill Pond—*reservoir* IA-7
Quaker Mills Sch—*school* MI-6
Quaker Mine—*mine* CO-8
Quaker Mtn—*summit* CO-8
Quaker Mtn—*summit* NY-2
Quaker Neck—*cape* MD-2
Quaker Neck—*cape* VA-3
Quaker Neck Creek—*stream* VA-3
**Quaker Neck Estates (subdivision)**—*pop pl* NC-3
Quaker Neck Lake—*lake* NC-3
Quaker Neck Lake—*reservoir* NC-3
Quaker Neck Lake Dam—*dam* NC-3
Quaker Neck Landing—*locale* MD-2
Quaker Oats Cereal Factory—*hist pl* OH-6
Quaker Pike Airp—*airport* PA-2
Quaker Plain Sch (abandoned)—*school* PA-2
*Quaker Point* IL-6
*Quaker Point* IN-6
*Quaker Point* KS-7
Quaker Pond—*lake* NY-2
**Quaker Ridge**—*pop pl* MD-2
**Quaker Ridge**—*pop pl* NY-2
Quaker Ridge—*ridge* CT-1
Quaker Ridge—*ridge* OH-6
Quaker Ridge—*ridge* PA-2
Quaker Ridge Cem—*cemetery* CT-1
Quaker Ridge Golf Club—*other* NY-2
Quaker Ridge Sch—*school* NY-2
Quaker Road Ch—*church* NY-2
Quaker Run—*stream* (2) IN-6
Quaker Run—*stream* MA-1
Quaker Run—*stream* NY-2
Quaker Run—*stream* OH-6
Quaker Run—*stream* (3) PA-2
Quaker Run—*stream* VA-3
Quaker Run Area—*area* NY-2
Quaker Run Chapel—*church* NY-2
Quaker Sch—*hist pl* NJ-2
Quaker Sch—*school* IL-6
Quaker Sch—*school* MI-6
Quaker Sch (abandoned)—*school* MO-7
**Quaker Settlement**—*pop pl* NY-2
Quaker Settlement Cem—*cemetery* NY-2
Quaker Settlement Ch—*church* NY-2
**Quakers Heights (subdivision)**—*pop pl* DE-2
Quakers Knob—*summit* PA-2
Quaker Smith Point—*cape* VT-1
Quaker Smith Reef—*bar* VT-1
Quaker Spring—*spring* (2) NV-8
Quaker Spring—*spring* OR-9
**Quaker Springs**—*pop pl* NY-2
Quaker Springs Run—*stream* OH-6
*Quakers Run* MA-1
Quakers Swamp—*stream* MD-2
*Quakers Town, The* PA-2
**Quaker Street**—*pop pl* NY-2
Quaker Street Hist Dist—*hist pl* NY-2
Quaker Swamp—*swamp* VA-3
*Quaker Swamp Brook* PA-2
*Quakertown* MI-6
*Quakertown* NJ-2
Quakertown—*locale* CT-1
**Quakertown**—*pop pl* DE-2
**Quakertown**—*pop pl* IN-6
**Quakertown**—*pop pl* MI-6
**Quakertown**—*pop pl* NJ-2
**Quakertown**—*pop pl* PA-2
Quakertown Airp—*airport* PA-2
Quakertown Borough—*civil* PA-2
Quakertown Elem Sch—*school* PA-2
Quakertown Falls—*falls* PA-2
Quakertown HS—*school* PA-2
*Quakertown Interchange* PA-2
Quakertown Memorial Park—*park* PA-2
Quakertown North—*other* MI-6
Quakertown Shopping Plaza—*locale* PA-2
Quakertown Station—*locale* PA-2
*Quaker Vale* KS-7
Quaker Valley—*basin* PA-2
**Quaker Valley**—*pop pl* PA-2
Quaker Valley—*valley* (2) PA-2
Quaker Valley—*valley* WI-6
Quaker Valley Cem—*cemetery* KS-7
Quaker Valley HS—*school* PA-2
Quaker Valley JHS—*school* PA-2
Quaker Valley Sch—*school* KS-7
Quaker Village Cem—*cemetery* VT-1
Quaker Village Shop Ctr—*locale* PA-2
**Quaker Village (subdivision)**—*pop pl* PA-2
Quakerville Cem—*cemetery* NE-7
Quake Spring—*spring* NV-8
Quaket Creek—*stream* RI-1
Quaket River—*stream* RI-1
Quakey Mountain Trail—*trail* CO-8
Quakey Mtn—*summit* CO-8
Quakie Canyon—*valley* CO-8
Quakie Hollow—*valley* ID-8
Quakie Patch Spring—*spring* AZ-5
Quakie Spring—*spring* CO-8
Quakies Sheep Camp—*locale* NV-8
Quakie Tank—*reservoir* AZ-5
Quaking Asp Canyon—*valley* CA-9
Quaking Asp Canyon—*valley* NV-8
Quaking Asp Canyon—*valley* NM-5
Quaking Asp Canyon—*valley* UT-8
*Quaking Asp Creek* UT-8
Quaking Asp Creek—*stream* CO-8
Quaking Asp Creek—*stream* (2) ID-8
Quaking Asp Creek—*stream* UT-8
Quaking Aspen—*locale* AZ-5
**Quaking Aspen**—*pop pl* CA-9
Quaking Aspen Butte—*summit* ID-8
Quaking Aspen Campground—*locale* CA-9
Quaking Aspen Campground—*locale* NM-5
Quaking Aspen Canyon—*valley* (2) AZ-5
Quaking Aspen Canyon—*valley* (3) NV-8
Quaking Aspen Canyon—*valley* NM-5
Quaking Aspen Canyon—*valley* UT-8
Quaking Aspen Coulee—*valley* MT-8
Quaking Aspen Creek—*stream* (2) MT-8
Quaking Aspen Creek—*stream* NM-5
Quaking Aspen Creek—*stream* (3) UT-8
Quaking Aspen Creek—*stream* WY-8
Quaking Aspen Flat—*flat* OR-9
Quaking Aspen Grove—*woods* CA-9
Quaking Aspen Hollow—*valley* (2) UT-8
Quaking Aspen Hollow—*valley* WY-8
Quaking Aspen Meadow—*flat* CA-9
Quaking Aspen Rsvr—*reservoir* ID-8
Quaking Aspen Spring—*spring* AZ-5
Quaking Aspen Spring—*spring* (2) CA-9
Quaking Aspen Spring—*spring* ID-8
Quaking Aspen Spring—*spring* (3) NV-8
Quaking Aspen Spring—*spring* (3) OR-9
Quaking Aspen Spring—*spring* (2) UT-8
Quaking Aspen Springs—*spring* ID-8
Quaking Aspen Springs—*spring* NV-8
Quaking Aspen Swamp—*swamp* OR-9
Quaking Aspen Tank—*reservoir* AZ-5
Quaking Asp Gap—*gap* WY-8
Quaking Asphalt Spring—*spring* ID-8
Quaking Asp Hollow—*valley* (2) UT-8
Quaking Asp Mtn—*summit* ID-8
Quaking Asp Mtn—*summit* WY-8
Quaking Asp Spring—*spring* AZ-5
Quaking Asp Spring—*spring* CA-9
Quaking Asp Spring—*spring* NV-8
Quakingasp Spring—*spring* UT-8
*Quaking Asp Swamp* OR-9
Quaking Creek—*stream* CA-9
Quaking Hollow Creek—*stream* UT-8
Quakish Bog—*swamp* ME-1
Quakish Brook—*stream* ME-1
Quakish Dam—*dam* ME-1
Quakish Lake—*reservoir* ME-1
Quakish Siding—*locale* ME-1
Quaky Spring—*spring* NV-8
Qualatchee, Lake—*lake* GA-3
Quale Ch—*church* ND-7
Qualey—*locale* OH-6
Quality—*locale* CA-9
Quality—*locale* GA-3
Quality—*locale* KY-4
**Quality**—*pop pl* TX-5
**Quality**—*pop pl* WY-8
Quality Creek—*stream* TN-4
**Quality Estates**—*pop pl* TN-4
Quality Hill—*hist pl* DC-2
Quality Hill—*hist pl* MO-7
**Quality Hill**—*pop pl* NY-2
Quality Hill—*summit* AZ-5
Quality Hill Hist Dist—*hist pl* RI-1
Quality Hill Hist Dist—*hist pl* WV-2
Quality Outlet Center—*locale* FL-3
Quality Ridge Cem—*cemetery* AR-4
Quality Ridge Ch—*church* AR-4
Qualkenbush Hollow—*valley* IN-6
Qualkenbush Spring—*spring* IN-6
Qualla—*locale* NC-3

Qualla Housing Project—locale ... NC-3
Qualla (Township of)—fmr MCD ... NC-3
Quall Coulee—valley ... WI-6
Quallen Lake—lake ... MN-6
Qualley Ranch—locale ... NE-7
Qualliamish River ... WA-9
Qualls—locale ... OK-5
Qualls Bend—bend ... TN-4
Qualls Branch—stream ... AR-4
Qualls Camp—locale ... CA-9
Qualls Cem—cemetery (2) ... TN-4
Qualls Cem—cemetery ... VA-3
Qualls Creek ... NC-3
Qualls Creek—stream ... AR-4
Qualls-Hart Airp—airport ... KS-7
**Qualls (historical)**—pop pl ... TN-4
Qualls Hollow—valley (2) ... TN-4
Qualls Mountain—ridge ... AR-4
Qualls Mtn—summit ... AR-4
Qualls Post Office (historical)—building ... TN-4
Qualls Spring Branch—stream ... TN-4
Qually Creek—stream ... NC-3
**Quamba**—pop pl ... MN-6
Quambaug Ch—church ... CT-1
Quambaug Cove ... CT-1
Quambogue Cove ... CT-1
Quam Lake—lake ... MN-6
Quampache Bottom—valley ... MA-1
Quamphegan Brook—stream ... ME-1
Quamquisset Harbor ... MA-1
Quamquissett Harbor ... MA-1
Quam Slough—gut ... SD-7
Quanacontaug Pond ... RI-1
Quanaduck Cove—bay ... CT-1
**Quanah**—pop pl ... TX-5
Quanah, Acme and Pacific Depot—hist pl ... TX-5
Quanah (CCD)—cens area ... TX-5
Quanah Country Club—other ... TX-5
Quanah Creek—stream ... OK-5
Quanah Mtn—summit ... OK-5
Quanah Municipal Water Wells—well ... TX-5
Quanah Parker Lake—reservoir ... OK-5
Quanai Canyon—valley ... CA-9
Quanapowitt Lake ... MA-1
Quanapowitt Pond ... MA-1
Quanaymes ... MA-1
**Quandahl**—pop pl ... IA-7
Quandary Creek—stream ... AK-9
Quandary Peak—summit ... CO-8
Quandary Tunnel—tunnel ... CO-8
Quandoca Brook ... CT-1
Quandoc Brook ... CT-1
Quandoc Brook ... RI-1
Quandock Brook ... RI-1
Quandock Brook—stream ... CT-1
Quandock River ... CT-1
Quandock River ... RI-1
Quandt Park—park ... MI-6
Quandt Sch—school ... MI-6
Quanduck Brook—stream ... CT-1
Quanduck Brook—stream ... RI-1
Quanduck River ... CT-1
Quanduck River ... RI-1
**Quanicassee**—pop pl ... MI-6
Quanicassee Marsh—swamp ... MI-6
Quanicassee River—stream ... MI-6
Quanicassee Wildlife Area—park ... MI-6
Quanimset ... MA-1
Quankey Ch—church ... NC-3
Quankey Creek—stream ... NC-3
Quannaamuk ... MA-1
Quannacut YMCA Camp—locale ... NY-2
Quannaimes ... MA-1
Quannapowitt, Lake—reservoir ... MA-1
Quannapowitt Lake ... MA-1
Quannessee Rive ... TN-4
Quannissoowauge ... MA-1
Qua-nom-i-ca ... MA-1
Quanset Pond—cove ... MA-1
Quanset Rocks ... MA-1
Quansigamog Pond ... MA-1
Quansigamond Plantation ... MA-1
Quansigomog ... MA-1
Quanso ... MA-1
**Quansoo**—pop pl ... MA-1
Quansue ... MA-1
Quantabacook Lake—lake ... ME-1
**Quantico**—pop pl ... MD-2
**Quantico**—pop pl ... VA-3
Quantico Creek—stream ... MD-2
Quantico Creek—stream ... VA-3
Quantico HS—school ... VA-3
Quantico Marine Corps Dev. and Education Command—military ... VA-3
Quantico Marine Corps Schools—school ... VA-3
Quantico Naval Hospital—military ... VA-3
Quantico Wharf—locale ... MD-2
Quantrell Mine—mine ... AZ-5
Quantrell Sch—school ... MI-6
Quant Slough—gut ... ND-7
Quantuck Bay—bay ... NY-2
Quantuck Canal—canal ... NY-2
Quantuck Creek—stream ... NY-2
**Quapaw**—pop pl ... OK-5
Quapaw Bayou ... LA-4
Quapaw Bayou ... TX-5
Quapaw Creek ... LA-4
Quapaw Creek ... TX-5
Quapaw Creek—stream (3) ... OK-5
Quapaw Creek—stream ... TX-5
Quapaw Mineral Springs—spring ... AR-4
Quapaw Oil Field—oilfield ... OK-5
Quaqua Creek—stream ... NC-3
Quaquechan River ... MA-1
Quarai—hist pl ... NM-5
Quarai Ruins State Monument—other ... NM-5
Quarantine—locale ... SC-3
Quarantine Bay—bay ... LA-4
Quarantine Bay Oil and Gas Field—oilfield ... LA-4
Quarantine Island ... FL-3
Quarantine Island ... HI-9
Quarantine Rocks—bar ... FL-3
Quarantine Rocks—bar ... MA-1
Quarantine Shore—beach ... TX-5
Quarles—locale ... MO-7
**Quarles**—pop pl ... AR-4
Quarles, Charles, House—hist pl ... WI-6
Quarles, W. J., House and Cottage—hist pl ... MS-4
Quarles Branch—stream ... TN-4
Quarles Cem ... TN-4
Quarles Cem—cemetery ... KY-4
Quarles Cem—cemetery (2) ... TN-4
Quarles Creek—stream ... SC-3
Quarles Elem Sch—school ... MS-4
Quarles Peak—summit ... ID-8
Quarles Sch—school ... VA-3
Quarnberg, Peter, House—hist pl ... UT-8
Quarno Dam ... PA-2
Quarrel Creek—stream ... IL-6
Quarrel Creek—stream ... VA-3
**Quarrier**—pop pl ... WV-2
**Quarris Acres**—pop pl ... NM-5
Quarry—locale ... WI-6
**Quarry**—pop pl (2) ... IA-7
**Quarry**—pop pl ... MI-6
**Quarry**—pop pl ... NC-3
**Quarry**—pop pl ... OR-9
**Quarry**—pop pl ... TX-5
**Quarry**—pop pl (2) ... VA-3
Quarry, The—mine ... UT-8
**Quarry, The**—pop pl ... AR-4
Quarry Bay—bay ... WI-6
Quarry Beach—beach ... CA-9
Quarry Branch—stream ... IL-6
Quarry Branch—stream ... KY-4
Quarry Branch—stream ... NC-3
Quarry Branch—stream ... TN-4
Quarry Brook ... CT-1
Quarry Brook—stream ... ME-1
Quarry Brook—stream ... NH-1
Quarry Butte—summit ... WA-9
Quarry Canyon—valley ... AZ-5
Quarry Canyon—valley (2) ... CA-9
Quarry Canyon—valley ... UT-8
Quarry Cave—cave ... AL-4
Quarry Cave—cave (3) ... TN-4
Quarry Cave—cave ... TX-5
Quarry Cottonwood Canyon—valley ... UT-8
Quarry Cottonwood Creek—stream ... UT-8
Quarry Cove—bay ... CO-8
Quarry Cove—bay ... OK-5
Quarry Cove Rec Area—park ... AR-4
Quarry Creek ... DE-2
Quarry Creek ... MT-8
Quarry Creek—stream ... CA-9
Quarry Creek—stream ... CO-8
Quarry Creek—stream ... FL-3
Quarry Creek—stream ... KS-7
Quarry Creek—stream ... MI-6
Quarry Creek—stream ... OH-6
Quarry Creek—stream (2) ... OR-9
Quarry Creek—stream ... TN-4
Quarry Creek—stream ... TX-5
Quarry Creek—stream ... VA-3
Quarry Creek—stream ... WA-9
Quarry Creek—stream ... WY-8
Quarry Creek Archeol Site—hist pl ... KS-7
Quarry Farm—hist pl ... NY-2
Quarry Field Canal—canal ... UT-8
Quarry Gap Hill—summit ... PA-2
Quarry Glen—locale ... PA-2
Quarry Gulch ... CO-8
Quarry Gulch—valley (2) ... MT-8
Quarry Heights—locale ... AR-4
**Quarry Heights**—pop pl ... NY-2
Quarry Hill ... NY-2
Quarry Hill—summit ... CA-9
Quarry Hill—summit (2) ... CT-1
Quarry Hill—summit ... ME-1
Quarry Hill—summit (2) ... MA-1
Quarry Hill—summit ... NV-8
Quarry Hill—summit ... NH-1
Quarry Hill—summit ... NY-2
Quarry Hill—summit ... OK-5
Quarry Hill—summit (2) ... PA-2
Quarry Hill—summit ... TN-4
Quarry Hill—summit ... VT-1
Quarry Hill—summit ... WI-6
Quarry Hill Ch (historical)—church ... TN-4
Quarry Hill Elem Sch—school ... PA-2
Quarry Hill Park—park ... IL-6
Quarry Hill Park—park ... MN-6
Quarry Hills Country Club & Golf Course—locale ... NC-3
Quarry Hollow—valley (2) ... TN-4
Quarry Hollow—valley (2) ... UT-8
Quarry Hollow—valley ... WV-2
Quarry Island—island ... MI-6
Quarry Isle—island ... OK-5
**Quarry Junction**—pop pl ... IN-6
**Quarry Junction**—pop pl ... OH-6
Quarry Junction (historical)—locale ... PA-2
Quarry Junction Station (historical)—locale ... PA-2
Quarry Knob—summit ... TN-4
Quarry Lake ... NY-2
Quarry Lake—lake ... CA-9
Quarry Lake—lake ... MI-6
Quarry Lake—lake ... OH-6
Quarry Lake—lake ... TN-4
Quarry Lake Cave—cave ... AL-4
Quarry Lakes—lake ... NY-2
Quarry Landing—locale ... AR-4
Quarry Lookout Tower—locale ... WI-6
Quarry Mountain ... CO-8
Quarry Mtn—summit ... AL-4
Quarry Mtn—summit ... CO-8
Quarry Mtn—summit ... GA-3
Quarry Mtn—summit ... OK-5
Quarry Mtn—summit ... UT-8
Quarry Overlook—locale ... VA-3
Quarry Park—park ... OH-6
Quarry Peak—summit ... CA-9
Quarry Point ... ME-1
Quarry Point—cape ... CA-9
Quarry Point—cape ... ME-1
Quarry Point—cape ... MA-1
Quarry Point—cape ... MI-6
Quarry Point—cape (3) ... WI-6
Quarry Point Public Use Area—park ... MO-7
Quarry Pond—lake ... IN-6
Quarry Pond—lake ... MA-1
Quarry Pond—lake ... NY-2
Quarry Pond—lake ... VT-1
Quarry Pond—lake ... WA-9
Quarry Pond—reservoir ... MI-6
Quarry Reservoir Dam—dam ... MA-1
Quarry Rsvr—reservoir ... AZ-5
Quarry Rsvr—reservoir ... OR-9
Quarry Run—stream (2) ... OH-6
Quarry Run—stream ... WV-2
Quarry Sch—school ... VT-1
Quarry Sch—school ... WI-6
Quarry Sch (abandoned)—school ... PA-2
Quarry Side Cave—cave ... AL-4
Quarry Sink—reservoir ... AZ-5
Quarry Spring—spring ... CA-9
Quarry Spring—spring ... UT-8
Quarry Square Shop Ctr—locale ... MA-1
Quarry Street Ch—church ... MA-1
Quarry Tank—reservoir (4) ... AZ-5
**Quarry Town**—pop pl ... MO-7
**Quarry (Township of)**—pop pl ... IL-6
Quarryville—locale ... DE-2
Quarryville—locale ... NJ-2
**Quarryville**—pop pl ... CT-1
**Quarryville**—pop pl ... NY-2
**Quarryville**—pop pl ... PA-2
Quarryville Borough—civil ... PA-2
Quarryville Brook—stream ... NJ-2
Quarryville Cem—cemetery ... CT-1
Quarryville Church ... TN-4
Quarryville Creek ... DE-2
**Quarryville (historical)**—pop pl ... TN-4
Quarryville Pond ... CT-1
Quarryville Post Office (historical)—building ... PA-2
Quarryville Post Office (historical)—building ... TN-4
Quarryville Presbyterian Home—building ... PA-2
Quarry Visitor Center—hist pl ... UT-8
Quarsarty Ch—church ... OK-5
Quart Creek ... CA-9
**Quarteles**—pop pl ... NM-5
Quarteles Ditch—canal ... NM-5
Quarter ... TN-4
Quarter, The—bend ... TN-4
Quarter Branch—stream ... DE-2
Quarter Branch—stream (2) ... VA-3
Quarter Butte—summit ... OR-9
Quarter Canal—canal ... NC-3
Quarter Cem—cemetery ... NY-2
Quarter Circle A Ranch—hist pl ... WY-8
Quarter Circle Bar Tank—reservoir ... AZ-5
Quarter Circle Bridge—bridge ... MT-8
Quarter Circle Hills ... WY-8
Quarter Circle J Ranch Landing Strip—airport ... AZ-5
Quarter Circle MC Ranch—locale ... MT-8
Quarter Circle Prong Bitter Creek—stream ... WY-8
Quarter Circle Ranch—locale ... CO-8
Quarter Circle Ranch—locale ... NM-5
Quarter Circle Ranch—locale ... WY-8
Quarter Circle S Ranch—locale ... NV-8
Quarter Circle U Ditch—canal ... MT-8
Quarter Circle U Ranch—locale ... AZ-5
Quarter Circle U Ranch—locale ... MT-8
Quarter Circle U Trail—trail ... AZ-5
Quarter Circle V Bar Ranch—locale ... AZ-5
Quarter Circle W Ranch—locale ... NM-5
Quarter Circle X X Ranch—locale (2) ... AZ-5
Quarter Circle ZN Ranch—locale ... MT-8
Quarter Circle 5 Ranch—locale ... CA-9
Quarter Corner Lake—lake ... UT-8
Quarter Corner Springs—spring ... NM-5
Quarter Corner Tank—reservoir ... AZ-5
Quarter Cove—bay ... MD-2
Quarter Cove—bay ... VA-3
Quarter Creek—bay ... MD-2
Quarter Creek—stream ... AL-4
Quarter Creek—stream (2) ... SC-3
Quarter Creek—stream ... VA-3
Quarter Creek—stream ... WI-6
Quarter Creek—stream ... WY-8
Quarter Domes—summit ... CA-9
Quarter Gulch—valley ... MT-8
Quarter Gut—gut ... DE-2
Quarter Lake—lake ... LA-4
Quarter Landing—locale ... NC-3
Quarter Ledge—bar ... MA-1
Quarterliah Creek—stream ... MS-4
Quarterlial Creek ... MS-4
Quarter Line Lake—lake ... MN-6
Quarterlot Branch—stream ... MS-4
Quarter Lot Cem—cemetery ... AL-4
Quarterman Branch—stream ... SC-3
Quarterman Cem—cemetery ... GA-3
Quarterman Cove—bay ... FL-3
Quarterman Creek—stream ... GA-3
Quarter March Creek—stream ... VA-3
Quartermaster—locale ... WA-9
Quartermaster Canyon—valley ... AZ-5
Quartermaster Creek ... OK-5
Quartermaster Creek—stream ... OK-5
Quartermaster Harbor—bay ... WA-9
Quartermaster's Corrals—hist pl ... AZ-5
Quartermaster Springs—spring ... AZ-5
Quartermaster Storehouse—hist pl ... AZ-5
Quartermaster View Point—locale ... AZ-5
Quarter Mile Creek—stream ... NY-2
Quarter Mile Pond—lake ... MA-1
Quarter Mtn—summit ... AL-4
Quarter Neck Country Club—locale ... NC-3
Quarter Point—cape ... VA-3
Quarter Pond—lake ... AZ-5
Quarter Post Office (historical)—building ... TN-4
Quarters, The ... MS-4
Quarters A—hist pl ... NY-2
Quarters A, B, and C, Norfolk Naval Shipyard—hist pl ... VA-3
Quarters A, Washington Navy Yard—hist pl ... DC-2
Quarters B, Washington Navy Yard—hist pl ... DC-2
Quarters Branch—stream ... SC-3
Quarters Cem—cemetery ... SC-3
Quarters Cem—cemetery ... TX-5
Quarter Section Run—stream ... IA-7
Quarter Shop Ctr, The—locale ... MS-4
Quarters Number 1—hist pl ... TX-5
Quarter Swamp—stream ... NC-3
Quarters 1, Fort Myer—hist pl ... VA-3
Quarter Tank—reservoir ... AZ-5
Quartet Dome—summit ... NV-8
Quartette Mine—mine ... NV-8
Quartite Peak—summit ... AZ-5
Quarton Sch—school ... MI-6
Quarts Creek ... WA-9
Quartsite ... AZ-5
Quartsite Canyon ... AZ-5
Quartsite Peak ... AZ-5
Quartsite Tank—reservoir ... AZ-5
Quartz—locale ... MT-8
Quartz—locale ... OR-9
**Quartz**—pop pl ... CA-9
Quartz Bay—bay ... AK-9
**Quartzburg**—pop pl ... ID-8
Quartzburg Sch—school ... CA-9
Quartz Butte—summit (2) ... OR-9
Quartz Canyon—valley (2) ... CA-9
Quartz Canyon—valley ... OR-9
Quartz Cem—cemetery ... OK-5
Quartz Creek ... CA-9
Quartz Creek ... ID-8
Quartz Creek ... OR-9
Quartz Creek ... WA-9
Quartz Creek—stream (9) ... AK-9
Quartz Creek—stream (3) ... CA-9
Quartz Creek—stream (3) ... CO-8
Quartz Creek—stream (9) ... ID-8
Quartz Creek—stream (6) ... MT-8
Quartz Creek—stream (13) ... OR-9
Quartz Creek—stream ... UT-8
Quartz Creek—stream (11) ... WA-9
Quartz Creek—stream (2) ... WY-8
Quartz Creek Butte—summit ... WA-9
Quartz Creek Campground—locale ... MT-8
Quartz Creek Cow Camp—locale ... WY-8
Quartz Creek Picnic Area—park ... OR-9
Quartz Creek Ridge—ridge ... WA-9
Quartz Creek Trail—trail ... CO-8
Quartz Creek Trail—trail ... WA-9
Quartz Ditch—canal ... WY-8
Quartz Dome—summit ... CO-8
Quartz Guard Station—locale ... MT-8
Quartz Gulch ... MT-8
Quartz Gulch—valley (2) ... AK-9
Quartz Gulch—valley (5) ... ID-8
Quartz Gulch—valley (2) ... MT-8
Quartz Gulch—valley (11) ... OR-9
Quartz Gulch—valley ... WY-8
**Quartz Hill**—pop pl ... CA-9
Quartz Hill—ridge ... CA-9
Quartz Hill—summit ... AZ-5
Quartz Hill—summit (4) ... CA-9
Quartz Hill—summit ... CO-8
Quartz Hill—summit (2) ... MT-8
Quartz Hill—summit ... NM-5
Quartz Hill Gulch—valley ... MT-8
Quartz Hill Sch—school ... CA-9
Quartz Hill Spring—spring ... AZ-5
Quartz Hill Trail—trail ... MT-8
Quartzite ... AZ-5
Quartzite—locale ... KS-7
Quartzite Butte ... OR-9
Quartzite Butte—summit ... ID-8
Quartzite Butte—summit ... NV-8
Quartzite Canyon ... AZ-5
Quartzite Canyon—valley (2) ... AZ-5
Quartzite Canyon—valley ... ID-8
Quartzite Canyon—valley ... NV-8
Quartzite Canyon—valley ... UT-8
Quartzite Creek—stream ... AK-9
Quartzite Creek—stream ... CO-8
Quartzite Hill ... UT-8
Quartzite Hill—summit ... NV-8
Quartzite Lake—lake (2) ... ID-8
Quartzite Mountain ... NV-8
Quartzite Mtn ... AZ-5
Quartzite Mtn—summit ... AZ-5
Quartzite Mtn—summit ... CA-9
Quartzite Mtn—summit ... ID-8
Quartzite Mtn—summit ... MT-8
Quartzite Mtn—summit (2) ... NV-8
Quartzite Mtn—summit ... NM-5
Quartzite Mtn—summit ... WA-9
Quartzite Peak ... AZ-5
Quartzite Peak ... CO-8
Quartzite Peak—summit (2) ... AZ-5
Quartzite Peak—summit ... CA-9
Quartzite Peak—summit ... NM-5
Quartzite Peak—summit ... WY-8
Quartzite Ridge—ridge ... CO-8
Quartzite Ridge—ridge ... ID-8
Quartzite Ridge—ridge ... MT-8
Quartzite Ridge—ridge ... NV-8
Quartzite Ridge—ridge ... NM-5
Quartzite Ridge—ridge ... UT-8
Quartzite Spring—spring ... AZ-5
Quartzite Spring—spring ... NV-8
Quartzite Wash Rsvr—reservoir ... AZ-5
Quartz Knob—summit ... TX-5
Quartz Lake—lake ... AK-9
Quartz Lake—lake ... CO-8
Quartz Lake—lake ... MN-6
Quartz Lake—lake ... MT-8
Quartz Lake—lake (3) ... WA-9
Quartz Lake—lake ... WI-6
Quartz Lake Patrol Cabin—hist pl ... MT-8
Quartz Lake Trail—trail ... MT-8
Quartz Lead Wash—stream ... AZ-5
Quartz Ledge Canyon—valley ... AZ-5
Quartz Ledge Spring—spring ... AZ-5
Quartz Ledge Tank—reservoir ... AZ-5
Quartz Mill Gulch—valley ... OR-9
Quartzmill Peak—summit ... OR-9
Quartz Mine—mine ... CA-9
Quartz Mountain ... UT-8
**Quartz Mountain**—pop pl ... OR-9
Quartz Mountain Basin—basin ... OR-9
Quartz Mountain Guard Station—locale ... OR-9
Quartz Mountain Pass—gap ... OR-9
Quartz Mountain Rsvr ... OR-9
Quartz Mountain (site)—locale ... NV-8
Quartz Mountain State Park—park ... OK-5
Quartz Mtn—summit ... AZ-5
Quartz Mtn—summit (7) ... CA-9
Quartz Mtn—summit ... ID-8
Quartz Mtn—summit ... MT-8
Quartz Mtn—summit (2) ... NV-8
Quartz Mtn—summit ... OK-5
Quartz Mtn—summit (5) ... OR-9
Quartz Mtn—summit (8) ... WA-9
Quartz Peak—summit ... CA-9
Quartz Peak—summit ... MT-8
Quartz Peak—summit ... NV-8
Quartz Point—cape (2) ... AK-9
Quartz Point—cape ... CA-9
Quartz Point—summit ... CA-9
Quartz Point—summit ... OR-9
Quartz Ridge—ridge ... CO-8
Quartz Ridge—ridge (2) ... ID-8
Quartz Ridge—ridge ... MT-8
Quartz Ridge Trail—trail ... CO-8
Quartz Rock—island ... AK-9
Quartz Rock—pillar ... CA-9
**Quartzsite**—pop pl (2) ... AZ-5
Quartzsite Airp—airport ... AZ-5
Quartzsite Elem Sch—school ... AZ-5
Quartz Spring—spring (2) ... CA-9
Quartz Spring—spring ... ID-8
Quartz Spring—spring ... NV-8
Quartz Spring Creek—stream ... ID-8
Quartz Valley—valley ... CA-9
Quartz Valley—valley ... CO-8
Quartz Valley—valley ... OR-9
Quartz Valley Mtn—summit ... OR-9
**Quartz Valley Rancheria**—pop pl ... CA-9
Quartz Valley Sch—school ... CA-9
Quartz Vein Wash—stream ... CA-9
Quartzville—locale ... CO-8
Quartzville Creek—stream ... CO-8
Quartzville Creek—stream ... OR-9
Quartzville Guard Station—locale ... OR-9
Quartzville (site)—locale ... OR-9
Quartz Well—well ... AZ-5
Quarve Sch—school ... ND-7
Quarzite ... AZ-5
Quashnet River—stream ... MA-1
Quasioto ... AL-4
Quasiotos ... AL-4
Quasiponikin ... MA-1
**Quasqueton**—pop pl ... IA-7
Quassaic Creek—stream ... NY-2
Quassapaug, Lake—lake ... CT-1
Quassapaug Lake ... CT-1
Quassapaug Pond ... CT-1
Quasset Cem—cemetery ... CT-1
Quassponikin Hill ... MA-1
Quassuc ... MA-1
Quast—locale ... MT-8
Quast Ditch—canal ... MT-8
Quasuet Neck ... MA-1
Quasuet Point—cape ... MA-1
Quatal Canyon—valley ... CA-9
**Quatama**—pop pl ... OR-9
Quateata—cape ... WA-9
Quates Canyon—valley ... NM-5
Quates Store (historical)—locale ... MS-4
Quation Brook—stream ... VT-1
Quatre, Bayou—gut ... LA-4
Quatre Bayou Pass—channel ... LA-4
Quatre Bayous Pass ... LA-4
Quatre Bayoux Pass ... LA-4
Quatre Pattes, Bayou—stream ... LA-4
Quatro Creek—stream ... CO-8
Quatro Ditch—canal ... CO-8
Quatro Mine—mine ... CO-8
Quatro Windmill—locale ... TX-5
Quatsap Point—cape ... WA-9
Quattlebaum, C. P., House—hist pl ... SC-3
Quattlebaum, C. P., Office—hist pl ... SC-3
Quattlebaum, Paul, House—hist pl ... SC-3
Quattlebaum Cem—cemetery (2) ... AR-4
Quattlebaum Cem—cemetery ... SC-3
Quave Cem—cemetery ... LA-4
Quaw Creek—stream ... MT-8
Quay ... FL-3
Quay—locale ... NM-5
**Quay**—pop pl ... OK-5
Quay, Greer and Jennie, House—hist pl ... ID-8
Quay, Matthew S., House—hist pl ... PA-2
**Quay (County)**—pop pl ... NM-5
**Quay (historical)**—pop pl ... MS-4
Quayle Creek—stream ... CO-8
Quayle Hill—summit ... AZ-5
Quayle Home Park—park ... UT-8
Quayle Ravine—valley ... CA-9
**Quayles Addition (subdivision)**—pop pl ... UT-8
Quayles Lake—lake ... ID-8
Quayle Well—well ... AZ-5
Quay Mine—mine ... CO-8
Quay Run ... PA-2
Quay Sch (abandoned)—school ... PA-2
Quay Sch (historical)—school ... PA-2
Quayz ... MA-1
Quealy—locale ... WY-8
Quealy Creek—stream ... WY-8
Quealy Dome Oil Field—oilfield ... WY-8
Quealy Gap—gap ... WY-8
Quealy Lake—lake ... WY-8
Quealy Peak—summit ... WY-8
Quealy Rsvr—reservoir ... WY-8
Quealy Sch—school ... WY-8
Quealy Spring—spring ... WY-8
Queant Lake—lake ... UT-8
Queantowcap Valley ... AZ-5
Queatchumpah Creek—stream ... CA-9
Quebac Mine—mine ... OR-9
Quebang River ... MA-1
Quebbeman Spring—spring ... MT-8
Quebec ... TN-4
Quebec—locale ... MT-8
Quebec—locale ... TX-5
Quebec—locale ... VA-3
**Quebec**—pop pl ... CT-1
**Quebec**—pop pl ... LA-4
**Quebec**—pop pl ... NC-3
Quebec Branch—stream ... GA-3
Quebec Branch—stream ... VA-3
Quebec Brook—stream ... NY-2
Quebec Hill—summit ... OR-9
Quebec Junction—locale ... NH-1
**Quebeck**—pop pl ... TN-4
Quebeck Cave—cave ... TN-4
Quebec Knob Lookout Tower—locale ... VA-3
Quebeck Sch—school ... TN-4
Quebec Mtn—summit ... NC-3
Quebec Normal Coll (historical)—school ... TN-4
Quebec Pond—lake ... NY-2
Quebec Post Office—building ... TN-4
Quebec Run ... PA-2
Quebec Run Wild Area—area ... PA-2
Quebec Sch—school ... IL-6
Quebodaux Cem—cemetery ... LA-4
Quebodaux Ferry—locale ... LA-4
**Quebrada**—pop pl ... PR-3
Quebrada Abad—valley ... PR-3
Quebrada Abarca—valley ... PR-3
Quebrada Aceituna—valley ... PR-3
Quebrada Achiote—valley ... PR-3
Quebrada Aguacate—valley ... PR-3
Quebrada Agua Fria—valley ... PR-3
Quebrada Aguas Largas—valley ... PR-3
Quebrada Aguas Verdes—valley ... PR-3
Quebrada Agustina—valley ... PR-3
Quebrada Alejandro—stream ... PR-3
Quebrada Algarrobo—valley ... PR-3
Quebrada Alicia—valley ... PR-3
Quebrada Alto Sano—valley ... PR-3
Quebrada Amargura—valley ... PR-3
Quebrada America—valley ... PR-3
Quebrada Amoros—valley ... PR-3
Quebrada Angela—valley ... PR-3
Quebrada Anjilones—valley ... PR-3
Quebrada Anon—valley ... PR-3
Quebrada Anones—valley ... PR-3
Quebrada Antigua—valley ... PR-3
Quebrada Aquas Buenas—valley ... PR-3
Quebrada Aquas Claras—valley ... PR-3
Quebrada Arena—valley ... PR-3
Quebrada Arenas—stream ... PR-3
Quebrada Arenas—valley ... PR-3
Quebrada Arenas (Barrio)—fmr MCD (6) ... PR-3
Quebrada Arenas Chiquita—valley ... PR-3
Quebrada Arriba—valley ... PR-3
Quebrada Arriba (Barrio)—fmr MCD (2) ... PR-3
Quebrada Ausubo—valley ... PR-3
Quebrada A Zumbadura—valley ... PR-3
Quebrada Bacalao—valley ... PR-3
Quebrada Bambua—valley ... PR-3
Quebrada Barbara—valley ... PR-3
Quebrada Barreal—valley ... PR-3
Quebrada (Barrio)—fmr MCD (2) ... PR-3
Quebrada Barros—valley ... PR-3
Quebrada Beatriz—valley ... PR-3
Quebrada Bejuco—valley ... PR-3
Quebrada Bellaca—valley ... PR-3
Quebrada Bello Gallon—valley ... PR-3
Quebrada Berrenchin—valley ... PR-3
Quebrada Blacho—stream ... PR-3
Quebrada Blanca—valley ... PR-3
Quebrada Blasina—valley ... PR-3
Quebrada Bocaforma—valley ... PR-3
Quebrada Bocana—valley ... PR-3
Quebrada Boqueron—valley ... PR-3
Quebrada Botija—valley ... PR-3
Quebrada Branderl—valley ... PR-3
Quebrada Brujas—valley ... PR-3
Quebrada Buena Vista—valley ... PR-3
Quebrada Burgos—valley ... PR-3
Quebrada Caguabo—valley ... PR-3
Quebrada Caimital—valley ... PR-3
Quebrada Calderon—valley ... PR-3
Quebrada Callores—valley ... PR-3
Quebrada Camarones—valley ... PR-3
Quebrada Cambalache—valley ... PR-3
Quebrada Cambute—valley ... PR-3
Quebrada Campo Libre—valley ... PR-3
Quebrada Cana—valley ... PR-3
Quebrada Cana India—valley ... PR-3
Quebrada Cancel—valley ... PR-3
Quebrada Cangilones—valley ... PR-3
Quebrada Canoas—valley ... PR-3
Quebrada Cantara—valley ... PR-3
Quebrada Cantera—valley ... PR-3
Quebrada Caracoles—valley ... PR-3
Quebrada Caricosa—valley ... PR-3
Quebrada Carmen—valley ... PR-3
Quebrada Carraizo—valley ... PR-3
Quebrada Casanga—valley ... PR-3
Quebrada Casanova—valley ... PR-3
Quebrada Catano—valley ... PR-3
Quebrada Cedrito—valley ... PR-3
Quebrada Ceiba—valley ... PR-3
Quebrada Ceiba (Barrio)—fmr MCD ... PR-3
Quebrada Cejas—valley ... PR-3
Quebrada Cepero—valley ... PR-3
Quebrada Cercada—valley ... PR-3
Quebrada Cerrillos—valley ... PR-3
Quebrada Cerro Gordo—valley ... PR-3
Quebrada Charco del Muerto—valley ... PR-3
Quebrada Chicharrones—valley ... PR-3
Quebrada Chinea—valley ... PR-3
Quebrada Chiquita—valley ... PR-3
Quebrada Chorrera—valley ... PR-3
Quebrada Chorro—valley ... PR-3
Quebrada Cienaga—valley ... PR-3
Quebrada Cimarrona—valley ... PR-3
Quebrada Cinfrona—valley ... PR-3
Quebrada Cofi—valley ... PR-3
Quebrada Cofresi—valley ... PR-3
Quebrada Cojolla—valley ... PR-3
Quebrada Cojo Vales—valley ... PR-3
Quebrada Collao—valley ... PR-3
Quebrada Collazo—valley ... PR-3
Quebrada Collera—valley ... PR-3
Quebrada Collores—valley ... PR-3
Quebrada Colorada—valley ... PR-3
Quebrada Columbiana—valley ... PR-3
Quebrada Colzadera—valley ... PR-3
Quebrada Conchita—valley ... PR-3
Quebrada Consejo—valley ... PR-3
Quebrada Convento—valley ... PR-3
Quebrada Corazon—valley ... PR-3
Quebrada Coroco—valley ... PR-3
Quebrada Cortadera—valley ... PR-3
Quebrada Cruz—valley ... PR-3
Quebrada Cruz (Barrio)—fmr MCD ... PR-3
Quebrada Cuesta Pasto—valley ... PR-3
Quebrada Culebra—valley ... PR-3
Quebrada Cumba—valley ... PR-3
Quebrada Dajaos—valley ... PR-3
Quebrada Damian—valley ... PR-3
Quebrada Damiana—valley ... PR-3
Quebrada de Cacaos—valley ... PR-3
Quebrada de El Rayo—valley ... PR-3
Quebrada de la Boca—valley ... PR-3
Quebrada de la Gana—valley ... PR-3
Quebrada de la Garza—valley ... PR-3
Quebrada del Agua—valley ... PR-3
Quebrada de la Majagua—valley ... PR-3
Quebrada del Anon—valley ... PR-3
Quebrada de la Perra—valley ... PR-3
Quebrada de las Avispas—valley ... PR-3
Quebrada de las Cuevas—valley ... PR-3

Quebrada de las Damas—*valley* PR-3
Quebrada de las Gatas—*valley* PR-3
Quebrada de las Lajas—*valley* PR-3
Quebrada de las Mulas—*valley* PR-3
Quebrada de las Quebradillas—*valley* PR-3
Quebrada Del Ausubo—*valley* PR-3
Quebrada de la Zalla—*valley* PR-3
Quebrada del Banco—*valley* PR-3
Quebrada del Bellaco—*valley* PR-3
Quebrada del Guama—*valley* PR-3
Quebrada del Guano—*valley* PR-3
Quebrada del Horno—*valley* PR-3
Quebrada del Ingles—*valley* PR-3
Quebrada del Juicio—*valley* PR-3
Quebrada del Muerto—*valley* PR-3
Quebrada del Oro—*valley* PR-3
Quebrada de los Barros—*valley* PR-3
Quebrada de los Cedros—*valley* PR-3
Quebrada de los Chinos—*valley* PR-3
Quebrada de los Colones—*valley* PR-3
Quebrada de los Cristales—*valley* PR-3
Quebrada de los Guiros—*valley* PR-3
Quebrada de los Llanos—*valley* PR-3
Quebrada de Los Mendez—*valley* PR-3
Quebrada de los Muertos—*valley* PR-3
Quebrada de Los Panes—*valley* PR-3
Quebrada de los Platanos—*valley* PR-3
Quebrada de los Rabanos—*valley* PR-3
Quebrada del Palo—*valley* PR-3
Quebrada del Platano—*valley* PR-3
Quebrada del Pozo Azul—*valley* PR-3
Quebrada del Pozo de Magala—*valley* PR-3
Quebrada del Pozo Redondo—*valley* PR-3
Quebrada del Riego—*valley* PR-3
Quebrada del Suro—*valley* PR-3
Quebrada del Toro—*valley* PR-3
Quebrada de Muertos—*valley* PR-3
Quebrada de Pena Pobre—*valley* PR-3
Quebrada de Quebradas—*valley* PR-3
Quebrada de Utuado—*valley* PR-3
Quebrada de Viejo—*valley* PR-3
Quebrada de Yeguadilla—*valley* PR-3
Quebrada Diego—*valley* PR-3
Quebrada Dona Elena—*valley* PR-3
Quebrada Dona Juana—*valley* PR-3
Quebrada Don Victor—*valley* PR-3
Quebrada Duende—*valley* PR-3
Quebrada Dulce—*valley* PR-3
Quebrada El Cangle—*valley* PR-3
Quebrada El Cedro—*valley* PR-3
Quebrada El Gallinero—*valley* PR-3
Quebrada El Gato—*valley* PR-3
Quebrada El Marques—*valley* PR-3
Quebrada El Negro—*valley* PR-3
Quebrada Elreves—*valley* PR-3
Quebrada El Salto—*valley* PR-3
Quebrada El Toro—*valley* PR-3
Quebrada Emajagua—*valley* PR-3
Quebrada Escarcha—*valley* PR-3
Quebrada Eugenia—*valley* PR-3
Quebrada Fajardo—*valley* PR-3
Quebrada Fajardo (Barrio)—*fmr MCD* PR-3
Quebrada Farallon—*valley* PR-3
Quebrada Felipa—*valley* PR-3
Quebrada Fermina—*valley* PR-3
Quebrada Florida—*valley* PR-3
Quebrada Frailes—*valley* PR-3
Quebrada Franquez—*valley* PR-3
Quebrada Fria—*valley* PR-3
Quebrada Galindo—*valley* PR-3
Quebrada Gandel—*valley* PR-3
Quebrada Gomez—*valley* PR-3
Quebrada Gonzalez—*valley* PR-3
**Quebrada Grande**—*pop pl* PR-3
Quebrada Grande—*valley* PR-3
Quebrada Grande (Barrio)—*fmr MCD* (3) PR-3
Quebrada Grande de Calvache—*valley* PR-3
Quebrada Grande de Morovis—*valley* PR-3
Quebrada Grande de San Lorenzo—*valley* PR-3
Quebrada Grande de Sierra Baja—*valley* PR-3
Quebrada Guama—*valley* PR-3
Quebrada Guanabana—*valley* PR-3
Quebrada Guaracanal—*valley* PR-3
Quebrada Guayabo—*valley* PR-3
Quebrada Guifen—*valley* PR-3
Quebrada Hayales—*valley* PR-3
Quebrada Helechal—*valley* PR-3
Quebrada Hicatea—*valley* PR-3
Quebrada Higuera—*valley* PR-3
Quebrada Higuillo—*valley* PR-3
Quebrada Honda—*post sta* PR-3
Quebrada Honda—*valley* PR-3
Quebrada Honda (Barrio)—*fmr MCD* (2) PR-3
Quebrada Hormiga—*valley* PR-3
Quebrada Hueca—*valley* PR-3
Quebrada Icaco—*valley* PR-3
Quebrada Icacos—*valley* PR-3
Quebrada Indalecia—*valley* PR-3
Quebrada Infierno—*valley* PR-3
Quebrada Infierno (Barrio)—*fmr MCD* PR-3
Quebrada Irizarry—*valley* PR-3
Quebrada Jacana—*valley* PR-3
Quebrada Jacinta—*valley* PR-3
Quebrada Jaguas—*valley* PR-3
Quebrada Jagueyes—*valley* PR-3
Quebrada Jamiel—*valley* PR-3
Quebrada Janer—*valley* PR-3
Quebrada Jimenez—*valley* PR-3
Quebrada Jobos—*valley* PR-3
Quebrada Josefa—*valley* PR-3
Quebrada Josefina—*valley* PR-3
Quebrada Jua—*valley* PR-3
Quebrada Juan—*valley* PR-3
Quebrada Juan Diego—*valley* PR-3
Quebrada Juan Gonzalez—*valley* PR-3
Quebrada Justo—*valley* PR-3
Quebrada La Balza—*valley* PR-3
Quebrada La Caraima—*valley* PR-3
Quebrada La Casimbra—*valley* PR-3
Quebrada La Catalina—*valley* PR-3
Quebrada La Concha—*valley* PR-3
Quebrada La Costa—*valley* PR-3
Quebrada La Cotorra—*valley* PR-3
Quebrada La Granja—*valley* PR-3
Quebrada Laguna—*basin* PR-3
Quebrada Laja—*valley* PR-3
Quebrada Lajas—*valley* PR-3
Quebrada La Luisa—*valley* PR-3
Quebrada La Maquina—*valley* PR-3
Quebrada La Mina—*valley* PR-3
Quebrada La Mocha—*valley* PR-3
Quebrada La Mona—*valley* PR-3
Quebrada La Mota—*valley* PR-3
Quebrada La Palma—*valley* PR-3
Quebrada La Perla—*valley* PR-3
Quebrada La Piedra—*valley* PR-3
Quebrada La Plata—*valley* PR-3
Quebrada La Regadera—*valley* PR-3
Quebrada La Represa—*valley* PR-3
Quebrada Larga—*valley* PR-3
Quebrada Larga (Barrio)—*fmr MCD* PR-3
Quebrada Lasalle—*valley* PR-3
Quebrada Las Animas—*valley* PR-3
Quebrada Las Canas—*valley* PR-3
Quebrada Las Chorreras—*valley* PR-3
Quebrada Las Curias—*valley* PR-3
Quebrada La Sequia—*valley* PR-3
Quebrada Las Guares—*valley* PR-3
Quebrada Las Lajas—*valley* PR-3
Quebrada Las Lugas—*valley* PR-3
Quebrada Las Marias—*valley* PR-3
Quebrada Las Penas—*valley* PR-3
Quebrada Las Piedras—*valley* PR-3
Quebrada Las Pinas—*valley* PR-3
Quebrada Las Torres—*valley* PR-3
Quebrada Las Tunas—*valley* PR-3
Quebrada Las Varas—*valley* PR-3
Quebrada la Tinajera—*valley* PR-3
Quebrada La Toma—*valley* PR-3
Quebrada La Vaca—*valley* PR-3
Quebrada Laya—*valley* PR-3
Quebrada La Yegua—*valley* PR-3
Quebrada Lazania—*valley* PR-3
Quebrada La Zapera—*valley* PR-3
Quebrada Limon—*valley* PR-3
Quebrada Limon (Barrio)—*fmr MCD* PR-3
Quebrada Limones—*valley* PR-3
Quebrada Linguette—*valley* PR-3
Quebrada Llanada—*valley* PR-3
Quebrada Los Cabros—*valley* PR-3
Quebrada Los Canales—*valley* PR-3
Quebrada Los Chorros—*valley* PR-3
Quebrada Los Guanos—*valley* PR-3
Quebrada Los Morones—*valley* PR-3
Quebrada Los Muertos—*valley* PR-3
Quebrada Los Quinones—*valley* PR-3
Quebrada Los Ramos—*valley* PR-3
Quebrada Los Romanes—*valley* PR-3
Quebrada Los Saltos—*valley* PR-3
Quebrada Los Santos—*valley* PR-3
Quebrada Los Terrores—*valley* PR-3
Quebrada Los Verracos—*valley* PR-3
Quebrada Maga—*valley* PR-3
Quebrada Magueyes—*valley* PR-3
Quebrada Maizales—*valley* PR-3
Quebrada Majagual—*valley* PR-3
Quebrada Majina—*valley* PR-3
Quebrada Mambiche—*valley* PR-3
Quebrada Mamey—*valley* PR-3
Quebrada Mamey Chiquita—*valley* PR-3
Quebrada Manglillo—*valley* PR-3
Quebrada Mango Prieto—*valley* PR-3
Quebrada Manicaboa—*valley* PR-3
Quebrada Maolaya—*valley* PR-3
Quebrada Maquina—*valley* PR-3
Quebrada Maracal—*valley* PR-3
Quebrada Maracuto—*valley* PR-3
Quebrada Maresua—*valley* PR-3
Quebrada Margara—*valley* PR-3
Quebrada Margarita—*valley* PR-3
Quebrada Mariana—*valley* PR-3
Quebrada Martina—*valley* PR-3
Quebrada Marunguey—*valley* PR-3
Quebrada Mata de Platano—*valley* PR-3
Quebrada Matadero—*valley* PR-3
Quebrada Mata Redonda—*valley* PR-3
Quebrada Mayaguecillo—*valley* PR-3
Quebrada Mejico—*valley* PR-3
Quebrada Melania—*valley* PR-3
Quebrada Mendoza—*valley* PR-3
Quebrada Minas—*valley* PR-3
Quebrada Minguillo—*valley* PR-3
Quebrada Mohosa—*valley* PR-3
Quebrada Mondongo—*valley* PR-3
Quebrada Mongil—*valley* PR-3
Quebrada Montana—*valley* PR-3
Quebrada Monte Llano—*valley* PR-3
Quebrada Monteria—*valley* PR-3
Quebrada Montones—*valley* PR-3
Quebrada Moralon—*valley* PR-3
Quebrada Morena—*valley* PR-3
Quebrada Morillo—*valley* PR-3
Quebrada Motete—*valley* PR-3
Quebrada Muda—*valley* PR-3
Quebrada Mueresolo—*valley* PR-3
Quebrada Mula—*valley* PR-3
Quebrada Mulas—*valley* PR-3
Quebrada Muro—*valley* PR-3
Quebrada Naranjito—*valley* PR-3
Quebrada Naranjo—*valley* PR-3
Quebrada Negrito—*valley* PR-3
Quebrada Negrito (Barrio)—*fmr MCD* PR-3
Quebrada Noriega—*valley* PR-3
Quebrada Novillo—*valley* PR-3
Quebrada Obispo—*valley* PR-3
Quebrada Olivar—*valley* PR-3
Quebrada Ortiz—*valley* PR-3
Quebrada Padilla—*valley* PR-3
Quebrada Pajaritos—*valley* PR-3
Quebrada Palenque—*valley* PR-3
Quebrada Palma—*valley* PR-3
Quebrada Palmar—*valley* PR-3
Quebrada Palmas Bajas—*valley* PR-3
Quebrada Pasto—*valley* PR-3
Quebrada Pasto Colon—*valley* PR-3
Quebrada Pasto Viejo—*valley* PR-3
Quebrada Pastrana—*valley* PR-3
Quebrada Patos—*valley* PR-3
Quebrada Peces—*valley* PR-3
Quebrada Pedro Avila—*valley* PR-3
Quebrada Pepe Lugo—*valley* PR-3
Quebrada Pepinera—*valley* PR-3
Quebrada Perchas—*valley* PR-3
Quebrada Piedras—*valley* PR-3
Quebrada Pileta—*valley* PR-3
Quebrada Piletas—*valley* PR-3
Quebrada Pilon—*valley* PR-3
Quebrada Pina—*valley* PR-3
Quebrada Placeres—*valley* PR-3
Quebrada Plantina—*valley* PR-3
Quebrada Pozas—*valley* PR-3
Quebrada Prieta—*valley* PR-3
Quebrada Pueblo Viejo—*valley* PR-3
Quebrada Puente—*valley* PR-3
Quebrada Pugnado—*valley* PR-3
Quebrada Pulida—*valley* PR-3
Quebrada Quilan—*valley* PR-3
Quebrada Quintana—*valley* PR-3
Quebrada Quintero—*valley* PR-3
Quebrada Ratones—*valley* PR-3
Quebrada Riachuelo—*valley* PR-3
Quebrada Rincon—*valley* PR-3
Quebrada Rivera—*valley* PR-3
Quebrada Rodadero—*valley* PR-3
Quebrada Rodeo—*valley* PR-3
Quebrada Roncador—*valley* PR-3
Quebrada Rosales—*valley* PR-3
Quebrada Sabalos—*valley* PR-3
Quebrada Sabana Llana—*valley* PR-3
Quebrada Salada—*valley* PR-3
Quebrada Saliente—*valley* PR-3
Quebrada Salsa—*valley* PR-3
Quebrada Salvatierra—*valley* PR-3
Quebrada San Anton—*valley* PR-3
Quebrada San Francisco—*valley* PR-3
Quebrada Sanjelo—*valley* PR-3
Quebrada San Juan—*valley* PR-3
Quebrada San Pedro—*valley* PR-3
Quebrada Santa—*valley* PR-3
Quebrada Santa Catalina—*valley* PR-3
Quebrada Santa Olaya—*valley* PR-3
Quebrada Santo Domingo—*valley* PR-3
Quebradas (Barrio)—*fmr MCD* (2) PR-3
Quebrada Sebastian—*valley* PR-3
**Quebrada Seca**—*pop pl* PR-3
Quebrada Seca—*valley* PR-3
Quebrada Seca (Barrio)—*fmr MCD* PR-3
Quebrada Solano—*valley* PR-3
Quebrada Sonadora—*valley* PR-3
Quebrada Sumaria—*valley* PR-3
Quebrada Sumidero—*valley* PR-3
Quebrada Suspiro—*valley* PR-3
Quebrada Susua—*valley* PR-3
Quebrada Tabonuco—*valley* PR-3
Quebrada Talante—*valley* PR-3
Quebrada Teresa—*valley* PR-3
Quebrada Tigre—*valley* PR-3
Quebrada Tinaja—*valley* PR-3
Quebrada Torres—*valley* PR-3
Quebrada Toruno—*valley* PR-3
Quebrada Toyo—*valley* PR-3
Quebrada Trina—*valley* PR-3
Quebrada Trinidad—*valley* PR-3
Quebrada Tumbada—*valley* PR-3
Quebrada Unidad—*valley* PR-3
Quebrada Urbano—*valley* PR-3
Quebrada Vaca—*valley* PR-3
Quebrada Velez—*valley* PR-3
Quebrada Ventana—*valley* PR-3
Quebrada Verde—*valley* PR-3
Quebrada Verraco—*valley* PR-3
Quebrada Vicente—*valley* PR-3
Quebrada Vieja—*valley* PR-3
Quebrada Villano—*valley* PR-3
Quebrada Villanueva—*valley* PR-3
Quebrada Vueltas (Barrio)—*fmr MCD* PR-3
Quebrada Yagruma—*valley* PR-3
Quebrada Yaurel—*valley* PR-3
Quebrada Yeguas (Barrio)—*fmr MCD* PR-3
Quebrada Zumbon—*valley* PR-3
**Quebradillas**—*pop pl* PR-3
Quebradillas (Barrio)—*fmr MCD* PR-3
Quebradillas (Municipio)—*civil* PR-3
Quebradillas (Pueblo)—*fmr MCD* PR-3
**Quechee**—*pop pl* VT-1
Quechee Gorge—*stream* VT-1
**Quecreek**—*pop pl* PA-2
**Quecreek (RR name Harrison)**—*pop pl* PA-2
Quedo Creek—*stream* OR-9
Quedow Mtn—*summit* CA-9
**Queechy**—*pop pl* NY-2
Queechy Lake—*lake* NY-2
Queechy Lake Brook—*stream* NY-2
*Queechy River* VT-1
*Queen* AZ-5
*Queen* WV-2
Queen—*locale* MT-8
Queen—*locale* NM-5
**Queen**—*pop pl* AZ-5
**Queen**—*pop pl* NC-3
**Queen**—*pop pl* (2) PA-2
**Queen**—*pop pl* VA-3
Queen, Hogan and Martha A. Runkle, House—*hist pl* IA-7
**Queen Acres**—*pop pl* OH-6
*Queenames Pond* MA-1
Queen Ann Bottom—*bend* UT-8
**Queen Anne**—*pop pl* MD-2
**Queen Anne**—*pop pl* WA-9
Queen Anne Bridge—*bridge* MD-2
Queen Anne Club—*hist pl* WA-9
**Queen Anne Colony**—*pop pl* MD-2
*Queen Anne Corner* MA-1
*Queen Anne Corners* MA-1
Queen Anne Cottage and Coach Barn—*hist pl* CA-9
*Queen Anne Creek* NC-3
Queen Anne Creek—*stream* NC-3
Queen Anne Creek—*stream* PA-2
Queen Anne House—*hist pl* NM-5
Queen Anne HS—*hist pl* WA-9
Queen Anne Place Sch—*school* CA-9
Queen Anne Public Sch—*hist pl* WA-9
Queen Anne Sch—*school* OR-9
*Queen Annes Corners* MA-1
**Queen Anne's (County)**—*pop pl* MD-2
*Queen Annes Creek* NC-3
Queen Ann Mine—*mine* NV-8
*Queen Awashonks Marsh* RI-1
Queen Basin—*basin* CO-8
*Queen Bee Butte* SD-7
Queen Bee Campground—*locale* CA-9
Queen Bee Mill—*hist pl* SD-7
Queen Bee Mine—*mine* CO-8
Queen Bee Mine—*mine* MT-8
Queen Bee Mine—*mine* SD-7
Queen Bee Mine—*mine* WA-9
Queen Bee Sch—*school* IL-6
Queen Bess Creek—*stream* GA-3
Queen Bess Island—*island* GA-3
Queen Bess Island—*island* LA-4
Queen Bess Island Oil and Gas Field—*oilfield* LA-4
Queen Bluff—*cliff* WI-6
*Queen Branch* TX-5
Queen Branch—*stream* AL-4
Queen Branch—*stream* GA-3
Queen Branch—*stream* (3) NC-3
Queen Branch—*stream* WV-2
Queen Brook—*stream* MA-1
Queen Camp Creek—*stream* NC-3
Queen Canyon—*valley* CA-9
Queen Canyon—*valley* NV-8
Queen Canyon—*valley* NM-5
Queen Canyon Mine—*mine* NV-8
Queen Cem—*cemetery* (2) GA-3
Queen Cem—*cemetery* MN-6
Queen Cem—*cemetery* NM-5
Queen Cem—*cemetery* (2) NC-3
Queen Cem—*cemetery* WV-2
Queen Chapel—*church* FL-3
Queen Chapel—*church* MS-4
Queen Chapel—*church* (2) NC-3
Queen Chapel—*church* SC-3
*Queen Chapel Crossroads* SC-3
Queen City—*locale* CA-9
**Queen City**—*pop pl* MO-7
**Queen City**—*pop pl* PA-2
**Queen City**—*pop pl* TX-5
*Queen City Airport* PA-2
Queen City Bridge—*bridge* NH-1
Queen City Dam—*dam* ND-7
**Queen City (historical)**—*pop pl* IA-7
Queen City Lake—*lake* FL-3
Queen City Mine—*mine* CO-8
Queen City Municipal Airp—*airport* MO-7
*Queen City of the Delta* MS-4
*Queen City of the East, The* MS-4
*Queen City Park* VT-1
Queen City Park—*park* AL-4
**Queen City Park**—*pop pl* VT-1
Queen City Point—*cape* FL-3
Queen City Prison—*other* NY-2
Queen City Summit—*summit* NV-8
Queen City Tunnel—*mine* CO-8
Queen Claim Mine—*mine* SD-7
*Queen Cove* AL-4
*Queen Cove* FL-3
Queen Cove—*valley* TN-4
*Queen Creek* AZ-5
**Queen Creek**—*pop pl* AZ-5
Queen Creek—*stream* (3) AK-9
Queen Creek—*stream* AZ-5
Queen Creek—*stream* AR-4
Queen Creek—*stream* (3) ID-8
Queen Creek—*stream* (4) NC-3
Queen Creek—*stream* OR-9
Queen Creek—*stream* PA-2
Queen Creek—*stream* VA-3
Queen Creek—*stream* (2) WA-9
Queen Creek Bridge—*hist pl* AZ-5
Queen Creek Canal—*canal* AZ-5
Queen Creek Canyon—*valley* AZ-5
Queen Creek Meadow—*flat* ID-8
Queen Creek Mine—*mine* AZ-5
Queen Creek Mtn—*summit* NC-3
*Queen Creek Reservoir* AZ-5
**Queen Creek (RittenHouse)**—*pop pl* AZ-5
Queen Creek Sch—*school* AZ-5
Queen Creek Siding—*locale* AZ-5
**Queen Creek (sta.)**—*pop pl* AZ-5
Queen Creek Tank—*reservoir* AZ-5
Queen Creek Tunnel—*tunnel* AZ-5
Queendale—*locale* KY-4
Queen Dicks—*locale* CA-9
Queen Dicks Canyon—*valley* CA-9
Queen Ditch—*canal* CO-8
Queen Emma's Summer Home—*hist pl* HI-9
Queener Basin—*basin* MT-8
Queener Cem—*cemetery* TN-4
Queener Creek—*stream* ID-8
Queener Hill—*summit* TN-4
Queener Hollow—*valley* KY-4
Queener Hollow—*valley* TN-4
Queener Mtn—*summit* MT-8
Queener Spring—*spring* TN-4
Queen Esther Flats—*flat* PA-2
Queen Esther Shaft—*mine* UT-8
Queen Gap—*gap* NC-3
Queen Gulch—*valley* AK-9
Queen Gulch—*valley* MT-8
Queen Gutter Brook—*stream* MA-1
Queen Hill—*cliff* NE-7
Queen Hill—*summit* AZ-5
Queen Hill—*summit* TX-5
Queen Hith Plantation Complex Site—*hist pl* VA-3
Queen Hollow—*valley* WV-2
Queen House—*hist pl* GA-3
*Queen Inlet* NC-3
Queen Inlet—*bay* AK-9
Queen Isabella Causeway—*bridge* TX-5
**Queen Junction**—*pop pl* PA-2
Queen Knob—*summit* GA-3
Queen Lake—*lake* GA-3
Queen Lake—*lake* ID-8
Queen Lake—*lake* MI-6
Queen Lake—*lake* MS-4
Queen Lake—*lake* NM-5
Queen Lake—*reservoir* MA-1
Queen Lake Dam—*dam* MA-1
Queen Lane—*uninc pl* PA-2
Queen Lane Baptist Ch—*church* MS-4
Queen Lane Rsvr—*reservoir* PA-2
Queen Lily Campground—*locale* CA-9
Queen Lucas Lake—*lake* WA-9
Queen Mary—*other* CA-9
*Queen Mary Hammock* GA-3
Queen Mary Island—*island* GA-3
Queen Memorial Ch—*church* SC-3
*Queen Mine* SD-7
Queen Mine—*mine* CA-9
Queen Mine—*mine* (2) ID-8
Queen Mine—*mine* (2) NV-8
Queen Mine—*mine* OR-9
Queen Mine—*mine* UT-8
Queen Mine Gap—*gap* GA-3
Queen Mine Knob—*summit* GA-3
Queen Mountain Trail—*trail* ID-8
*Queen Mtn* GA-3
Queen Mtn—*summit* CA-9
Queen Mtn—*summit* ID-8
Queen Mtn—*summit* NC-3
Queen Nefertiti Rock—*pillar* UT-8
Queen of All Saints Sch—*school* IL-6
Queen of All Saints Sch—*school* IN-6
Queen Of Angels Ch—*church* GA-3
Queen of Angels Church—*hist pl* NJ-2
Queen Of Angels Hosp—*hospital* CA-9
Queen of Angels Mission—*church* AZ-5
Queen of Angels Priory—*hist pl* OR-9
Queen of Angels Sch—*school* IN-6
Queen of Angles Sch—*school* CA-9
Queen of Apostles Coll and Seminary—*school* MA-1
Queen of Apostles Sch—*school* CA-9
Queen of Apostles Sch—*school* IL-6
Queen Of apostles Seminary—*school* NY-2
Queen of Heaven Cem—*cemetery* AZ-5
Queen of Heaven Cem—*cemetery* CA-9
Queen of Heaven Cem—*cemetery* FL-3
Queen of Heaven Cem—*cemetery* IL-6
Queen of Heaven Cem—*cemetery* NY-2
Queen Of Heaven Cem—*cemetery* PA-2
Queen Of Heaven Cemeterys—*cemetery* OH-6
Queen of Heaven Ch—*church* NJ-2
Queen of Heaven Ch—*church* NM-5
Queen of Heaven Ch—*church* NY-2
Queen of Heaven Ch—*church* OH-6
Queen of Heaven M C Memorial Sch—*school* CO-8
Queen of Heaven Sch—*school* NM-5
Queen of Heaven Sch—*school* NY-2
Queen of Martyrs Sch—*school* IL-6
Queen of Martyrs Sch—*school* NY-2
Queen of Peace Catholic Ch—*church* MS-4
Queen of Peace Cem—*cemetery* ND-7
Queen of Peace Cem—*cemetery* TX-5
Queen of Peace Ch—*church* FL-3
Queen of Peace Ch—*church* TX-5
Queen of Peace Ch—*church* WI-6
Queen of Peace HS—*school* IL-6
Queen of Peace Monastery—*church* OH-6
Queen of Peace Monastery—*church* WI-6
Queen of Peace Priory—*church* ND-7
Queen of Peace Sch—*school* IN-6
Queen of Peace Sch—*school* MI-6
Queen of Peace Sch—*school* NJ-2
Queen of Peace Sch—*school* (2) NY-2
Queen Of Peace Sch—*school* OH-6
Queen of Peace Sch—*school* OR-9
Queen Of Peace Sch—*school* PA-2
Queen of Sheba—*summit* WA-9
Queen of Sheba Canyon—*valley* UT-8
Queen of Sheba Creek—*stream* AK-9
Queen of Sheba Mine—*mine* (2) CA-9
Queen of Sheba Mine—*mine* NV-8
Queen of Sheba Mine—*mine* NM-5
Queen of Sheba Mine—*mine* UT-8
Queen of the Apostles Ch—*church* NJ-2
Queen of the Apostles Ch—*church* NC-3
Queen of the Hills Mine—*mine* ID-8
Queen of the Hills Mine—*mine* (2) MT-8
Queen of the Hills Mine—*mine* UT-8
Queen of the Holy Rosary HS—*school* MI-6
Queen of the Holy Rosary Sch—*school* KS-7
Queen of the Holy Rosary Shrine—*church* WI-6
Queen of the Mission Chapel—*church* ME-1
Queen of the Rosary Acad—*school* NY-2
Queen of the Rosary Ch—*church* MT-8
Queen of the Rosary Sch—*school* NJ-2
Queen-of-the-West Mine—*mine* CO-8
Queen of the West Tunnel—*mine* CO-8
Queen of the World Sch—*school* PA-2
Queen Oregon Mines—*mine* OR-9
Queen Palmer Sch—*school* CO-8
Queen Peak—*summit* CA-9
Queen Peak—*summit* NV-8
**Queen Pines (subdivision)**—*pop pl* NC-3
Queen Point—*cape* AR-4
Queen Ranch—*locale* MT-8
Queen Ranch—*locale* NM-5
Queen Ridge—*island* VA-3
Queen Ridge—*ridge* (2) NC-3
*Queen River* NV-8
Queen River—*stream* RI-1
Queens—*locale* KY-4
Queens—*locale* WV-2
Queens Arch—*arch* UT-8
Queens Bath—*lake* HI-9
Queens Bay—*bay* FL-3
Queens Bluff—*cliff* MN-6
**Queensboro**—*pop pl* OH-6
Queensboro Bridge—*bridge* NY-2
Queensboro Bridge—*hist pl* NY-2
Queensboro Brook—*stream* NY-2
Queensboro Home for Blind—*building* NY-2
Queensboro Lake—*reservoir* NY-2
*Queensborough* MA-1
**Queensborough**—*pop pl* WA-9
Queensborough—*uninc pl* LA-4
Queensborough Coll—*school* NY-2
Queensborough Sch—*school* LA-4
Queens Branch—*stream* KY-4
Queens Branch—*stream* MO-7
Queens Branch—*stream* OR-9
Queens Branch—*stream* TN-4
Queens Bridge—*bridge* NH-1
Queensbridge—*uninc pl* NY-2
*Queen's Brook* MA-1
**Queensburg (subdivision)**—*pop pl* MS-4
**Queensbury**—*pop pl* NY-2
Queensbury HS—*school* NY-2
Queensbury Mill—*hist pl* NH-1
Queensbury Playground—*park* MD-2
Queensbury Sch—*school* NY-2
Queensbury Shop Ctr—*locale* AL-4
**Queensbury (Town of)**—*pop pl* NY-2
Queenscamp Branch—*stream* WV-2
Queen's Campus, Rutgers Univ—*hist pl* NJ-2
Queens Canyon—*valley* CO-8
Queens Castle—*pillar* UT-8
Queens Cem—*cemetery* KY-4
Queens Cem—*cemetery* NC-3
Queens Chair—*pillar* CO-8
Queens Chapel—*church* FL-3
Queens Chapel—*church* GA-3
Queens Chapel—*church* KY-4
Queens Chapel—*church* MD-2
**Queens Chapel**—*pop pl* MD-2
Queens Chapel Baptist Ch—*church* MS-4
**Queens Chapel Manor**—*pop pl* MD-2
Queens Coll—*school* NC-3
**Queens (County and Borough of New York City)**—*pop pl* NY-2
**Queens Court (subdivision)**—*pop pl* NC-3
**Queens Cove**—*pop pl* FL-3
**Queens Cove (subdivision)**—*pop pl* FL-3
*Queens Creek* ID-8
*Queens Creek* NC-3
*Queens Creek* OR-9
*Queens Creek* TX-5
*Queen's Creek* VA-3
Queens Creek—*stream* AK-9
Queens Creek—*stream* (3) NC-3
Queens Creek—*stream* OR-9
Queens Creek—*stream* TX-5
Queens Creek—*stream* VA-3
Queens Creek—*stream* WV-2
Queens Creek Dam—*dam* NC-3
Queens Creek Lake—*reservoir* NC-3
Queens Crown—*summit* NM-5
**Queensdale (subdivision)**—*pop pl* NC-3
Queens Draw—*valley* CA-9
Queen Seal Mine—*mine* WA-9
*Queen Sewel Cove* MA-1
Queen Sewell Cove—*cove* MA-1
Queen Sewell Pond—*lake* MA-1
*Queen Sewel Pond* MA-1
Queens Falls—*falls* NC-3
Queens Fork—*stream* (2) WV-2
Queen's Fort—*hist pl* RI-1
Queens Fort Brook—*stream* RI-1
Queens Gap—*gap* GA-3
Queens Garden—*area* UT-8
Queens Garden Trail—*trail* UT-8
**Queensgate**—*pop pl* WA-9
Queensgate Shop Ctr—*locale* NC-3
Queensgate Shop Ctr—*locale* PA-2
Queens General Hosp—*hospital* NY-2
**Queens Grant**—*pop pl* PA-2
**Queens Grant (subdivision)**—*pop pl* NC-3
Queens Gulch—*valley* CO-8
Queens Gulch—*valley* MT-8
Queen Shaft—*mine* NV-8
Queens Head—*summit* NM-5
**Queens Hill**—*pop pl* MS-4
Queens Hill—*summit* MT-8
Queens Hill Club Lake Dam—*dam* MS-4
Queens Hill Lake—*reservoir* MS-4
**Queen Shoals**—*pop pl* WV-2
Queen Shoals Creek—*stream* WV-2
Queens Hosp—*hospital* HI-9
Queens Island—*island* IL-6
Queens Knob—*summit* VA-3
Queens Lake—*lake* IL-6
Queens Lake—*lake* VA-3
**Queens Lake**—*pop pl* VA-3
Queens Lake Branch—*stream* IL-6
**Queensland**—*pop pl* GA-3
**Queens Lane (subdivision)**—*pop pl* MS-4
Queens Laundry—*spring* WY-8
Queens Mall West Shop Ctr—*locale* MS-4
Queens Midtown Tunnel—*tunnel* NY-2
*Queens Mill* WV-2
Queens Mirror—*lake* FL-3
Queens Mtn—*summit* GA-3
Queens Mtn—*summit* NC-3
Queens Mtn—*summit* TN-4
Queens of Angeles Sch—*school* WA-9
Queen Sound Channel—*channel* VA-3
*Queens Own* PA-2
Queens Park Cem—*cemetery* TX-5
**Queens Park (subdivision)**—*pop pl* FL-3
Queens Peak—*summit* CA-9
Queens Peak—*summit* TX-5
*Queens Plaza Shopping Center* PA-2
Queens Point—*cape* MD-2
Queens Point—*locale* MT-8
Queens Point Cem—*cemetery* WV-2
Queens Point (historical)—*locale* IA-7
**Queens Point (subdivision)**—*pop pl* NC-3
Queen Springs—*spring* NV-8
**Queens Quest**—*pop pl* DE-2
Queens Ridge—*ridge* (2) WV-2
Queens Ridge Ch—*church* WV-2
*Queens River* NV-8
*Queens River* RI-1
Queens River—*stream* ID-8
Queens River Campground—*locale* ID-8
Queens Road Sch—*school* TX-5
**Queens Run**—*pop pl* PA-2
Queens Run—*stream* PA-2
Queens Sch—*school* MI-6
Queens Station—*locale* AZ-5
Queens Station Bank Mine—*mine* TN-4
**Queens (subdivision)**—*pop pl* NY-2
Queens Tank—*reservoir* AZ-5
*Queen Station* AZ-5
Queen Station—*locale* PA-2
Queen Station (historical)—*locale* TN-4
*Queenstown* NJ-2
Queenstown—*locale* WI-6
**Queenstown**—*pop pl* AL-4
**Queenstown**—*pop pl* (2) MD-2
**Queenstown**—*pop pl* PA-2
**Queenstown**—*pop pl* VA-3
Queenstown Creek—*stream* MD-2
Queenstown Lake—*reservoir* AL-4
Queenstown Lake Number 1 Dam—*dam* AL-4
Queenstown Lake Number 2 Dam—*dam* AL-4
**Queens Village**—*pop pl* NY-2
**Queensville**—*pop pl* IN-6
Queens Vocational HS—*school* NY-2
**Queens Well**—*pop pl* AZ-5
Queens Well—*well* AZ-5
Queens Well—*well* UT-8
**Queen (Township of)**—*pop pl* MN-6
Queen Tree Landing—*locale* MD-2
Queen Tunnel—*mine* UT-8
Queen Twin Creek—*stream* AK-9
**Queen Valley**—*pop pl* AZ-5
Queen Valley—*valley* CA-9
Queen Valley—*valley* NV-8
Queen Valley Golf Course—*other* AZ-5
Queen Victoria—*pillar* UT-8
Queen Victoria Rock—*pillar* UT-8
Queen Victories Profile—*pillar* HI-9
Queen Well—*well* NM-5

Queen Wilhelmina State Park—*park* AR-4
Queeny Township—*civil* MO-7
Queer Branch—*stream* WV-2
Queer Creek—*stream* AK-9
Queer Creek—*stream* MT-8
Queer Creek—*stream* OH-6
Queer Creek—*stream* WA-9
Queer Island—*island* AK-9
Queer Lake—*lake* NY-2
Queer Ponds—*lake* AK-9
**Queets**—*pop pl* WA-9
Queets, Mount—*summit* WA-9
Queets Basin—*basin* WA-9
Queets Campground—*locale* WA-9
Queets-Clearwater Sch—*school* WA-9
Queets Glacier—*glacier* WA-9
*Queetshee River* WA-9
Queets Ranger Station—*locale* WA-9
Queets River—*stream* WA-9
Queguechan Valley Mills Hist Dist—*hist pl* MA-1
*Quehanna* PA-2
Quehanna Trail—*trail* PA-2
Quehanna Wild Area—*area* PA-2
Quekilok Creek—*stream* AK-9
Quella Bottom Spring—*spring* TX-5
Quelland Ranch—*locale* CO-8
Quell House—*hist pl* AR-4
Quell Spring Canyon—*valley* AZ-5
Quemada, Canada—*valley* NM-5
Quemada, Sierra—*summit* TX-5
Quemada Corral Tank—*reservoir* TX-5
Quemada Lateral—*canal* TX-5
Quemada Tank—*reservoir* TX-5
**Quemado**—*pop pl* NM-5
**Quemado**—*pop pl* TX-5
Quemado, Arroyo—*stream* TX-5
Quemado, Arroyo—*valley* CA-9
Quemado, Cerro—*summit* AZ-5
Quemado (Barrio)—*fmr MCD* PR-3
Quemado Canyon—*valley* NM-5
Quemado (CCD)—*cens area* NM-5
Quemado (CCD)—*cens area* TX-5
Quemado Community Cem—*cemetery* NM-5
Quemado Creek—*stream* CO-8
Quemado Creek—*stream* TX-5
Quemado Hills—*ridge* NM-5
Quemado Ranch—*locale* TX-5
**Quemados**—*pop pl* PR-3
Quemados (Barrio)—*fmr MCD* PR-3
Quemado Spring—*spring* TX-5
Quemado Tank—*reservoir* (2) TX-5
Quemado Windmill—*locale* TX-5
Quemahoning Creek—*stream* PA-2
Quemahoning Dam—*dam* PA-2
**Quemahoning Junction**—*pop pl* PA-2
Quemahoning Junction Station—*locale* PA-2
Quemahoning Rsvr—*reservoir* PA-2
**Quemahoning (Township of)**—*pop pl* PA-2
Quemahoning Tunnel (historical)—*tunnel* PA-2
Quema Tank—*reservoir* AZ-5
Quemazon Canyon—*valley* NM-5
Quemazon Trail—*trail* NM-5
Quenames Cove—*lake* MA-1
*Quenames Pond* MA-1
Quenby Mall—*locale* NC-3
Quendall—*uninc pl* WA-9
*Quenebaugh River* MA-1
Quenelda Graphite Mines (underground)—*mine* AL-4
Quenelda (historical)—*locale* AL-4
**Quenemo**—*pop pl* KS-7
Queneska Island—*island* VT-1
*Queniult* WA-9
*Queniult Lake* WA-9
*Queniult River* WA-9
Quenneville Dam—*dam* MA-1
*Quensett Point* RI-1
*Quen Sewell Pond* MA-1
*Quenshehague Run* PA-2
Quenshukeny Run—*stream* PA-2
Quenten Sch—*school* NJ-2
**Quentin**—*pop pl* MS-4
**Quentin**—*pop pl* PA-2
**Quentin (Bismarck)**—*pop pl* PA-2
Quentin Corners—*locale* IL-6
Quentin Creek—*stream* OR-9
Quentin Knob—*summit* OR-9
Quentin Lookout Tower—*tower* MS-4
Quentin Mtn—*summit* AR-4
Quentin Park—*park* MI-6
Quentin Peak—*summit* OK-5
**Queonemysing (historical)**—*pop pl* PA-2
**Queponco ((sta.) Newark)**—*pop pl* MD-2
*Queponco Station* MD-2
Queponco Station—*locale* MD-2
*Quequatuck River* RI-1
Quequechan River—*stream* MA-1
*Quequeteant, Town of* MA-1
Querbes Park—*park* LA-4
Quercus—*locale* TN-4
**Quercus Grove**—*pop pl* IN-6
Quercus Grove Cem—*cemetery* IL-6
Quercus Grove Sch—*school* IL-6
*Quercus Pass* CA-9
Quercus Point—*cape* CA-9
Quercus Post Office (historical)—*building* TN-4
Querecho Plains—*area* NM-5
Querencia Arroyo—*stream* NM-5
*Quereus Pass* CA-9
**Querida**—*pop pl* CO-8
Querida Gulch—*valley* CO-8
**Querinda Park**—*pop pl* NM-5
**Querino**—*pop pl* AZ-5
Querino Canyon Bridge—*hist pl* AZ-5
Querino Interchange—*crossing* AZ-5
Querino Wash—*valley* AZ-5
*Querquellin River* WA-9
*Querquillin River* WA-9
Querry Gap—*gap* PA-2
Query Creek—*stream* AK-9
**Querys Dixons (historical)**—*pop pl* NC-3
Quesada Spring—*spring* CA-9
*Quescado Creek* CA-9
Quesenberry Cem—*cemetery* VA-3
Quesenburg Lateral—*canal* NM-5
Quesenbury Cem—*cemetery* AR-4
**Quesenbury (subdivision)**—*pop pl* NC-3
Queset Brook—*stream* MA-1
Quest, The—*school* FL-3
**Questa**—*pop pl* NM-5
Questa Blanca Canyon—*valley* NM-5
Questa (CCD)—*cens area* NM-5
Questad, Carl and Sedsel, Farm—*hist pl* TX-5
Questa HS—*school* NM-5
Quest-Alb Glacier—*glacier* WA-9
Questa Molybdenum Mine—*mine* NM-5
Questa Ranger Station—*locale* NM-5
Questa Spring—*spring* AZ-5
Questa Spring—*spring* NM-5
Quest End Golf Course—*other* MN-6
Question Creek—*stream* AK-9
Question Creek—*stream* WY-8
Question Lake—*lake* AK-9
Questionmark Lake—*lake* OR-9
Question Mark Rsvr—*reservoir* WY-8
Question Rsvr—*reservoir* OR-9
Quest Oil Field—*oilfield* WY-8
Quetco Wilderness Research Center—*building* MN-6
*Quetenis Island* RI-1
Quetone Point—*summit* OK-5
Quetzal, Point—*cliff* AZ-5
Queue Creek—*stream* MT-8
Queue De Tortue, Bayou—*stream* LA-4
Queue Jughandle Arch—*arch* UT-8
Queue Valley—*valley* NV-8
Quewhiffle Creek—*stream* (2) NC-3
Quewhiffle (Township of)—*fmr MCD* NC-3
*Quhele* NC-3
Quiambog Cove—*bay* CT-1
*Quibbletown* NJ-2
*Quibby Creek* AL-4
*Quibby Creek* MS-4
Quiburi—*hist pl* AZ-5
Quiburi Mission—*church* AZ-5
Quichapa Creek—*stream* UT-8
Quichapa Lake—*lake* UT-8
*Quichupah Creek* UT-8
Quick—*locale* IA-7
Quick—*locale* LA-4
Quick—*locale* NE-7
**Quick**—*pop pl* NC-3
**Quick**—*pop pl* WV-2
Quick, Ben, Ranch and Fort—*hist pl* CO-8
Quick, John Herbert, House—*hist pl* WV-2
*Quickapa Lake* UT-8
*Quick Bend* PA-2
Quickbum Hollow—*valley* OH-6
Quick Cem—*cemetery* KY-4
Quick Cem—*cemetery* MS-4
Quick Cem—*cemetery* MO-7
Quick Cem—*cemetery* NY-2
Quick Cem—*cemetery* PA-2
Quick Cem—*cemetery* (3) SC-3
**Quick City**—*pop pl* MO-7
Quick Creek—*stream* AR-4
Quick Creek—*stream* IN-6
Quick Creek—*stream* (2) MO-7
Quick Creek—*stream* WA-9
*Quick Creek Reservoir* IN-6
Quick Crossroads—*locale* SC-3
Quick Draw Spring—*spring* OR-9
Quickel, Jacob, House—*hist pl* IA-7
Quickels Ch (abandoned)—*church* PA-2
Quick Fill Rsvr—*reservoir* OR-9
Quick Gulch—*valley* OR-9
Quickhaven Lake—*reservoir* AL-4
Quickhaven Lake Dam—*dam* AL-4
Quick Lake—*lake* (2) MN-6
Quick Lake—*lake* NY-2
Quick Lakes—*lake* MI-6
**Quickle**—*pop pl* WV-2
Quick Point—*cape* FL-3
Quick Point—*cape* WI-6
Quick Pond—*reservoir* NJ-2
Quick Pond Dam—*dam* NJ-2
Quick Ranch—*locale* NE-7
*Quick Run* KY-4
**Quicksand**—*pop pl* KY-4
**Quicksand**—*pop pl* TX-5
Quicksand Ch—*church* KY-4
Quicksand Ch—*church* TX-5
Quicksand Cove—*bay* AK-9
*Quicksand Creek* TX-5
Quicksand Creek—*stream* KY-4
Quicksand Creek—*stream* OR-9
Quicksand Creek—*stream* TX-5
Quicksand Fork—*stream* KY-4
*Quicksand Gully* LA-4
Quicksand Gully—*stream* LA-4
Quicksand Lake—*lake* MI-6
*Quicksand Pond* RI-1
Quicksand Pond—*lake* RI-1
*Quicksand River* OR-9
Quicksand Rsvr—*reservoir* OR-9
Quicksands, The—*bar* FL-3
Quicksand Spring—*spring* (2) OR-9
Quicks Bend—*bend* PA-2
**Quicks Bend**—*pop pl* PA-2
Quicks Bend Cem—*cemetery* PA-2
**Quicksburg**—*pop pl* VA-3
Quick Sch—*school* MI-6
Quick Sch (historical)—*school* TN-4
*Quicks Creek* IN-6
*Quicks Hole* MA-1
Quicks Hole—*channel* MA-1
Quicks Hole Pond—*lake* MA-1
Quicksilver Creek—*stream* AK-9
Quicksilver Flat—*flat* CA-9
Quicksilver Mtn—*summit* ID-8
Quicks Island—*island* NJ-2
*Quicks Mill* AL-4
**Quicks Mill**—*pop pl* VA-3
Quicks Run—*stream* KY-4
Quickstad Farm Implement Company—*hist pl* MN-6
Quickstad Park—*park* MI-6
Quickstep Ch—*church* OH-6
Quick Step Spring—*spring* OR-9
*Quickstream* MA-1
Quick Stream—*stream* ME-1
Quick Stream—*stream* MA-1
Quickswipe Lake—*lake* MS-4
**Quicktown**—*pop pl* PA-2
Quicktown Sch (abandoned)—*school* PA-2
Quick Trigger Windmill—*locale* TX-5
Quickville (historical)—*locale* KS-7
Quickwater Spring—*spring* AZ-5
Quick Windmill—*locale* TX-5
*Quidneck* RI-1
*Quidneck Brook* RI-1
*Quidneset* RI-1
*Quidnesit* RI-1
**Quidnessett**—*pop pl* RI-1
*Quidnessett Harbor* RI-1
**Quidnet**—*pop pl* MA-1
*Quidnic Brook* RI-1
Quidnick—*locale* RI-1
Quidnick Brook—*stream* RI-1
*Quidnick Pond* RI-1
Quidnick Reservoir Dam—*dam* RI-1
*Quidnick River* RI-1
Quidnick Rsvr—*reservoir* RI-1
*Quidnit* MA-1
*Quien Sabe* AZ-5
Quien Sabe Canyon—*valley* NM-5
*Quien Sabe Creek* CA-9
Quien Sabe Creek—*stream* AZ-5
Quien Sabe Creek—*stream* CA-9
Quien Sabe Creek—*stream* CO-8
Quien Sabe Draw—*valley* AZ-5
Quien Sabe Glacier—*glacier* WA-9
Quien Sabe Lake—*lake* CO-8
Quien Sabe Mine—*mine* AZ-5
Quien Sabe Mine—*mine* CA-9
Quien Sabe Mtn—*summit* CO-8
Quien Sabe Oil Field—*oilfield* TX-5
Quien Sabe Peak—*summit* AZ-5
Quien Sabe Point—*cape* (2) CA-9
Quien Sabe Ranch—*locale* CA-9
Quien Sabe Ranch—*locale* TX-5
Quien Sabe Ranch—*locale* WY-8
Quien Sabe Spring—*spring* (2) AZ-5
*Quien Sabe Springs* AZ-5
Quien Sabe Tank—*reservoir* AZ-5
Quien Sabe Valley—*valley* CA-9
Quien Sabe Windmill—*locale* TX-5
Quiery Hill—*summit* NY-2
Quiet, Lake—*lake* MT-8
Quiet Acres Airp—*airport* NC-3
Quiet Acres Mobile Home Park—*locale* PA-2
Quiet Bay—*bay* TX-5
Quiet Cove—*bay* NV-8
Quiet Creek—*stream* AK-9
**Quiet Dell**—*pop pl* PA-2
**Quiet Dell**—*pop pl* WV-2
Quiet Dell Ch—*church* WV-2
Quiet Dell Sch—*school* IA-7
Quiet Dell Sch—*school* WV-2
Quiet Harbor—*bay* AK-9
Quiet Lake—*lake* AK-9
Quiet Lake—*lake* FL-3
Quiet Lake—*lake* ID-8
Quiet Pool, A—*channel* MO-7
Quiet Ridge Cem—*cemetery* MS-4
Quiett Cem—*cemetery* AR-4
Quietus—*locale* MT-8
Quiet Valley Farm—*hist pl* PA-2
Quigg Branch—*stream* GA-3
Quigg Lateral—*canal* ID-8
Quiggle Brook—*stream* ME-1
Quiggle Hollow—*valley* PA-2
Quiggle Lake—*lake* MI-6
**Quiggleville**—*pop pl* PA-2
Quiggly Brook—*stream* ME-1
Quigg Peak—*summit* MT-8
Quigg Peak Trail—*trail* MT-8
Quiggs Mtn—*summit* CA-9
Quig Hollow—*valley* NY-2
*Quigley* IA-7
Quigley—*locale* ID-8
Quigley—*locale* LA-4
Quigley—*locale* MT-8
**Quigley**—*pop pl* CA-9
Quigley, G. F., and Son Grocery—*hist pl* KY-4
Quigley Butte—*summit* WA-9
*Quigley Canyon* UT-8
Quigley Canyon—*valley* CA-9
Quigley Cem—*cemetery* IL-6
Quigley Cem—*cemetery* MI-6
Quigley Coulee—*valley* (2) MT-8
*Quigley Creek* WY-8
Quigley Creek—*stream* CA-9
Quigley Creek—*stream* CO-8
Quigley Creek—*stream* (2) ID-8
Quigley Creek—*stream* MI-6
Quigley Creek—*stream* PA-2
Quigley Crossing—*locale* UT-8
Quigley Lake—*lake* MN-6
Quigley Marsh Ditch—*canal* IN-6
Quigley Mtn—*summit* CO-8
Quigley Park—*park* MA-1
**Quigley Park**—*pop pl* NY-2
Quigley Playground—*park* CA-9
Quigley Pond—*lake* ID-8
Quigley Ranch—*locale* MT-8
Quigley Ridge—*ridge* AK-9
Quigley Rsvr—*reservoir* OR-9
Quigleys Camp—*locale* AK-9
Quigley Sch—*school* IL-6
Quigleys Cove—*valley* CA-9
Quigley Seminary (South Branch)—*school* IL-6
Quigleys Point—*cape* WI-6
Quigmy River—*stream* AK-9
*Quigotoa* AZ-5
Quihi—*locale* TX-5
Quihi Cem—*cemetery* TX-5
Quihi Creek—*stream* TX-5
Quijinump Canyon—*valley* NV-8
Quijinump Spring—*spring* NV-8
*Quijotia* AZ-5
*Quijotoa* AZ-5
Quijotoa—*locale* AZ-5
*Quijotoa Draw* AZ-5
Quijotoa (historical)—*locale* AZ-5
Quijotoa Mine—*mine* AZ-5
Quijotoa Mountains—*summit* AZ-5
Quijotoa Pass—*gap* AZ-5
Quijotoa Trading Post—*locale* AZ-5
Quijotoa Valley—*valley* AZ-5
Quijotoa Wash—*stream* AZ-5
*Quijotoa Well* AZ-5
*QUIK-AM* OR-9
Quiktalik Creek—*stream* AK-9
Quik Tung Mine—*mine* NV-8
Quilby Creek—*stream* AL-4
Quilby Creek—*stream* MS-4
Quilby (historical)—*locale* AL-4
Quilceda Creek—*stream* WA-9
**Quilcene**—*pop pl* WA-9
Quilcene Bay—*bay* WA-9
Quilcene Bay (CCD)—*cens area* WA-9
Quilcene Boat Haven—*harbor* WA-9
Quilcene-Quinault Battleground Site—*hist pl* WA-9
Quilcene Range—*range* WA-9
Quilett Drain—*canal* MI-6
**Quileute Ind Res**—*pop pl* WA-9
**Quilhart (historical)**—*pop pl* IA-7
Quilici Creek—*stream* NV-8
Quilici Spring—*spring* (2) NV-8
Quill—*locale* GA-3
Quillan Branch—*stream* KY-4
Quillan Cem—*cemetery* KY-4
Quillan Creek—*stream* AL-4
Quillan Gulch—*valley* CO-8
Quillaree Branch—*stream* NC-3
*Quillayute Needle* WA-9
Quillayute Needles—*pillar* WA-9
Quillayute Needles Natl Wildlife Ref—*park* WA-9
Quillayute Outlying Field Naval Reservation—*other* WA-9
Quillayute Prairie—*flat* WA-9
Quillayute River—*stream* WA-9
Quillayute State Airp—*airport* WA-9
Quillayute Valley HS—*school* WA-9
Quill Branch—*stream* GA-3
Quill Creek—*stream* (2) IN-6
*Quillehute Prairie* WA-9
*Quillehute River* WA-9
Quillen, Mount—*summit* NY-2
Quillen Branch—*stream* MO-7
Quillen Cem—*cemetery* KY-4
Quillen Cem—*cemetery* TN-4
Quillen Cem—*cemetery* (2) VA-3
Quillen Fork—*stream* KY-4
Quillen Hollow—*valley* (2) TN-4
Quillen Hollow—*valley* VA-3
Quillen Mtn—*summit* NC-3
Quillen Mtn—*summit* SC-3
Quillen Park—*park* WV-2
Quillen Ridge—*ridge* VA-3
Quillen Sch—*school* VA-3
Quillens Point—*cape* DE-2
**Quillens Point (subdivision)**—*pop pl* DE-2
Quillens Store (historical)—*locale* TN-4
Quilley Point—*cape* NC-3
Quill Hill—*summit* ME-1
Quilliam Sch—*school* ND-7
Quilliams Rock Cave—*cave* PA-2
Quillian Bay—*bay* AK-9
*Quillian Hollow* TN-4
Quillian Memorial Center—*building* TX-5
Quillian Well—*well* AZ-5
*Quillibee Creek* AL-4
*Quillibee Creek* MS-4
Quillinan Rsvr—*reservoir* CT-1
Quillin Cem—*cemetery* (2) VA-3
**Quillin Siding**—*pop pl* OH-6
Quillin Site—*hist pl* OK-5
Quillin Spring—*spring* VA-3
Quillisascut Creek—*stream* WA-9
Quill Lake—*lake* AK-9
Quill Lake—*lake* MN-6
Quill Lake—*lake* WI-6
Quill Mine—*mine* CA-9
Quillpig Mtn—*summit* ME-1
Quill Pond—*lake* ME-1
Quill Pond Brook—*stream* ME-1
Quill Run—*stream* IN-6
Quill Slough—*gut* CA-9
Quills Pond—*lake* MA-1
Quill Spring—*spring* CA-9
*Quillyhuyte Prairie* WA-9
*Quillyhuyte River* WA-9
Quil Miller Creek—*stream* TX-5
Quilomene Creek—*stream* WA-9
Quilotosa Wash—*stream* AZ-5
Quilt Run—*stream* WV-2
Quilty Creek—*stream* CA-9
*Quiman Creek* TX-5
Quimby—*locale* CO-8
Quimby—*locale* LA-4
Quimby—*locale* ME-1
**Quimby**—*pop pl* IA-7
Quimby Brook—*stream* ME-1
Quimby Brook—*stream* (2) VT-1
Quimby Cem—*cemetery* PA-2
Quimby Creek—*stream* CA-9
Quimby Creek—*stream* KS-7
Quimby Creek—*stream* SC-3
Quimby Hill—*summit* NH-1
Quimby Island—*island* CA-9
Quimby Mtn—*summit* NH-1
Quimby Mtn—*summit* (2) VT-1
Quimby Park—*flat* WY-8
Quimby Pond—*lake* ME-1
Quimper Peninsula—*cape* WA-9
*Quinabaag River* MA-1
**Quinaby**—*pop pl* OR-9
Quinado Canyon—*valley* CA-9
*Quinaielt* WA-9
*Quinaielt Lake* WA-9
*Quinaielt river* WA-9
*Quinames* MA-1
*Quinapaug River* MA-1
**Quinapoxet**—*pop pl* MA-1
*Quinapoxet Pond* MA-1
Quinapoxet River—*stream* MA-1
Quinapoxet Rsvr—*reservoir* MA-1
**Quinault**—*pop pl* WA-9
Quinault, Lake—*lake* WA-9
**Quinault Ind Res**—*pop pl* WA-9
*Quinault Lake* WA-9
Quinault Lake Sch—*school* WA-9
Quinault Reservation (CCD)—*cens area* WA-9
Quinault Ridge—*ridge* WA-9
*Quinault River* WA-9
Quinault River—*stream* WA-9
Quinault R S—*locale* WA-9
**Quinavista**—*pop pl* FL-3
Quinby—*locale* KS-7
**Quinby**—*pop pl* SC-3
**Quinby**—*pop pl* VA-3
Quinby, Ivory, House—*hist pl* IL-6
Quinby Bridge—*bridge* SC-3
*Quinby Creek* KS-7
Quinby Creek—*stream* (2) CA-9
Quinby Estates—*uninc pl* SC-3
Quinby Forest—*uninc pl* SC-3
Quinby Inlet—*bay* VA-3
Quinby Park—*park* OH-6
Quinby Plantation—*locale* SC-3
Quinby Plantation House-Halidon Hill Plantation—*hist pl* SC-3
Quinby Point—*cape* NH-1
Quinby Sch—*school* SC-3
**Quinby Township**—*pop pl* ND-7
Quin Cem—*cemetery* (4) MS-4
Quince Orchard—*locale* MD-2
Quincetree Landing—*locale* NY-2
*Quincie* TN-4
Quinco Mental Health Center—*hospital* TN-4
Quincosin Swamp—*stream* NC-3
*Quincy* IN-6
Quincy—*locale* IA-7
Quincy—*locale* MS-4
Quincy—*locale* TN-4
**Quincy**—*pop pl* CA-9
**Quincy**—*pop pl* FL-3
**Quincy**—*pop pl* IL-6
**Quincy**—*pop pl* IN-6
**Quincy**—*pop pl* KS-7
**Quincy**—*pop pl* KY-4
**Quincy**—*pop pl* MA-1
**Quincy**—*pop pl* MI-6
**Quincy**—*pop pl* MO-7
**Quincy**—*pop pl* NH-1
**Quincy**—*pop pl* OH-6
**Quincy**—*pop pl* OR-9
**Quincy**—*pop pl* PA-2
**Quincy**—*pop pl* WA-9
Quincy—*post sta* CO-8
Quincy, City of—*civil* MA-1
Quincy, Josiah, House—*hist pl* MA-1
Quincy, Missouri, and Pacific RR Station—*hist pl* MO-7
Quincy Adams, Mount—*summit* AK-9
Quincy Adams, Mount—*summit* NH-1
Quincy Bay—*bay* IL-6
Quincy Bay—*bay* MA-1
Quincy Bldg—*hist pl* ME-1
Quincy Bluff—*cliff* WI-6
Quincy (CCD)—*cens area* CA-9
Quincy (CCD)—*cens area* FL-3
Quincy (CCD)—*cens area* WA-9
Quincy Cem—*cemetery* (2) IA-7
Quincy Cem—*cemetery* KS-7
Quincy Cem—*cemetery* MA-1
Quincy Cem—*cemetery* ND-7
Quincy Cem—*cemetery* OH-6
Quincy Cem—*cemetery* TN-4
Quincy Cem—*cemetery* WI-6
**Quincy Center (subdivision)**—*pop pl* MA-1
Quincy Ch—*church* MS-4
Quincy Coll—*school* IL-6
Quincy Creek—*stream* FL-3
Quincy Creek—*stream* MI-6
Quincy Day Sch—*school* FL-3
Quincy East End Hist Dist—*hist pl* IL-6
Quincy-East Quincy—*CDP* CA-9
Quincy Elem Sch—*school* KS-7
Quincy Fire Station—*building* MA-1
Quincy Flying Service Airp—*airport* WA-9
Quincy Granite Railway—*hist pl* MA-1
Quincy Granite Railway Incline—*hist pl* MA-1
Quincy Great Hill—*cliff* MA-1
Quincy Hist Dist—*hist pl* FL-3
Quincy (historical)—*locale* ND-7
**Quincy Hollow**—*pop pl* PA-2
Quincy Homestead—*hist pl* MA-1
Quincy HS—*school* FL-3
Quincy HS—*school* PA-2
Quincy JHS—*school* MA-1
Quincy Junction—*locale* CA-9
Quincy Junction—*locale* IL-6
Quincy Lake—*lake* WA-9
Quincy Lake—*swamp* FL-3
Quincy Library—*hist pl* FL-3
Quincy Lookout Tower—*tower* FL-3
**Quincy Manor**—*pop pl* MD-2
Quincy Market—*hist pl* MA-1
Quincy Market—*locale* MA-1
*Quincy Meadows* WA-9
Quincy Memorial Bridge—*other* IL-6
Quincy Memorial Bridge—*other* MO-7
Quincy Memorial Cem—*cemetery* IL-6
Quincy Mill—*locale* MI-6
Quincy Mine—*mine* NV-8
Quincy Mine—*mine* UT-8
**Quincy Mine**—*pop pl* MI-6
Quincy Mine No. 2 Shaft Hoist House—*hist pl* MI-6
Quincy Mines—*mine* UT-8
Quincy MS—*school* FL-3
Quincy Mtn—*summit* PA-2
Quincy Muni Airp—*airport* WA-9
Quincy Municipal Airp (Baldwin Field)—*airport* IL-6
**Quincy Neck**—*pop pl* MA-1
Quincy Oil Field—*oilfield* (2) KS-7
Quincy Park—*park* NM-5
Quincy Plaza (Shop Ctr)—*locale* FL-3
Quincy Point JHS—*school* MA-1
**Quincy Point (subdivision)**—*pop pl* MA-1
Quincy Pond—*lake* NH-1
*Quincy Reservoir* MA-1
**Quincy (RR name Dickinson)**—*pop pl* WV-2
Quincy Rural Cem—*cemetery* NY-2
Quincy Sch—*hist pl* MA-1
Quincy Sch—*school* MA-1
Quincy Sch—*school* OR-9
Quincy Sch—*school* UT-8
Quincy School (Site)—*locale* CA-9
**Quincy Southeast**—*pop pl* IL-6
Quincy Station (historical)—*locale* MA-1
Quincy Street Hist Dist—*hist pl* MI-6
Quincy Town Hall—*hist pl* MA-1
**Quincy (Town of)**—*pop pl* WI-6
Quincy Township—*fmr MCD* IA-7
**Quincy Township**—*pop pl* KS-7
**Quincy (Township of)**—*pop pl* IL-6
**Quincy (Township of)**—*pop pl* (2) MI-6
**Quincy (Township of)**—*pop pl* MN-6
**Quincy (Township of)**—*pop pl* PA-2
Quincy Valley Hosp—*hospital* WA-9
Quincy Woman's Club—*hist pl* FL-3
Quincy Yacht Club—*locale* MA-1
Quincy Yacht Club Range Light—*locale* MA-1
Quindaro—*uninc pl* KS-7
Quindaro Bend—*bend* MO-7
Quindaro Cem—*cemetery* KS-7
Quindaro (historical)—*loale* KS-7
Quindaro Mine—*mine* CO-8
Quindaro Park—*park* KS-7
Quindocqua Ch—*church* MD-2
**Quinebaug**—*pop pl* CT-1
Quinebaug Mill-Quebec Square Hist Dist—*hist pl* CT-1
Quinebaug Pond—*lake* CT-1
Quinebaug River—*stream* CT-1
Quinebaug River—*stream* MA-1
Quinebaug River Pond Dam—*dam* MA-1
Quinebaug River Rsvr—*reservoir* (2) MA-1
*Quineboag River* MA-1
*Quinepoxet Pond* MA-1
*Quinepoxet River* MA-1
*Quinepoxet Village* MA-1
Quiner Gulch—*valley* CO-8
**Quinerly**—*pop pl* NC-3
*Quines Creek* OR-9
**Quines Creek**—*pop pl* OR-9
Quines Creek—*stream* OR-9
*Quinesshakony Run* PA-2
Quiney—*locale* TX-5
Quiney Flats—*flat* WA-9
Quiney Spring—*spring* UT-8
Quinf—*locale* TX-5
**Quinhagak**—*pop pl* AK-9
*Quiniault* WA-9
*Quiniault Lake* WA-9
*Quiniault River* WA-9
*Quinibaug River* MA-1
Quinientas Well—*well* TX-5
**Quinif**—*pop pl* TX-5
Quinine Bush Tank—*reservoir* AZ-5
Quinine Hill—*summit* SC-3
Quinine Slough—*stream* TX-5
Quinine Swamp—*swamp* NC-3
**Quinlan**—*pop pl* FL-3
**Quinlan**—*pop pl* OK-5
**Quinlan**—*pop pl* TX-5
Quinlan Art Center—*building* GA-3
Quinlan Castle—*hist pl* AL-4
Quinlan (CCD)—*cens area* TX-5
Quinlan Corners—*locale* NY-2
**Quinlan Corners**—*pop pl* PA-2
Quinlan Creek—*stream* TX-5
Quinland—*locale* NC-3
**Quinland**—*pop pl* WV-2
Quinland Ch—*church* WV-2
Quinland Lake—*lake* TN-4
Quinlan Gulch—*valley* CA-9
Quinlan Gulch—*valley* CO-8
Quinlan Lake—*lake* MI-6
Quinlan Mountains—*summit* AZ-5
Quinlan Public Sch—*school* TX-5
Quinlan Sch—*school* IL-6
Quinlan Sch—*school* MN-6
Quinlan's Covered Bridge—*hist pl* VT-1
Quinlantown—*locale* PA-2
Quinlen Lake—*reservoir* NC-3
Quinlen Lake Dam—*dam* NC-3
*Quinless Creek* NV-8
Quinlin—*locale* AZ-5
*Quinlin Mountain* AZ-5
*Quinlin Mountains* AZ-5
**Quinlivan**—*pop pl* MS-4
Quinliven Gulch—*valley* CA-9
*Quinlivin Gulch* CA-9
*Quin Loven Gulch* CA-9
Quinn—*locale* AR-4
Quinn—*locale* KY-4
Quinn—*locale* MT-8
Quinn—*locale* TX-5
**Quinn**—*pop pl* MS-4
**Quinn**—*pop pl* SD-7
Quinn, A. V., House—*hist pl* WY-8
Quinn, Lake—*lake* PA-2
Quinnam Cem—*cemetery* ME-1
Quinnames (historical)—*locale* MA-1
Quinnamose Creek—*stream* WA-9
Quinn Apartments—*hist pl* ID-8
Quinnatisset Brook—*stream* CT-1
Quinnatisset Country Club—*other* CT-1
Quinn Bayou—*stream* FL-3
Quinn Bayou Oil Field—*oilfield* LA-4
Quinn Brake—*swamp* LA-4
Quinn Branch—*stream* AL-4
Quinn Branch—*stream* SC-3
Quinn Branch—*stream* TN-4
Quinn Branch—*stream* VA-3
Quinn Butte—*summit* SD-7
Quinn Camp—*locale* TX-5
Quinn Canyon—*valley* CA-9
Quinn Canyon—*valley* NE-7
Quinn Canyon—*valley* NV-8
Quinn Canyon Division—*forest* NV-8
Quinn Canyon Range—*range* NV-8
*Quinn Canyon Spring* NV-8
Quinn Canyon Springs—*spring* NV-8
Quinn Cem—*cemetery* (2) AL-4
Quinn Cem—*cemetery* (2) IL-6
Quinn Cem—*cemetery* (2) MS-4
Quinn Cem—*cemetery* NC-3
Quinn Cem—*cemetery* VA-3
Quinn Chapel—*church* (2) AR-4
Quinn Chapel—*church* (2) OH-6
Quinn Chapel African Methodist Episcopal Ch—*church* TN-4
Quinn Chapel AME Ch—*church* AL-4
Quinn Chapel AME Church—*hist pl* MO-7
Quinn Chapel of the A.M.E. Church—*hist pl* IL-6
Quinn Coulee—*valley* MT-8
*Quinn Creek* NV-8
*Quinn Creek* OR-9
Quinn Creek—*stream* AK-9
Quinn Creek—*stream* CO-8
Quinn Creek—*stream* (2) ID-8
Quinn Creek—*stream* IA-7
Quinn Creek—*stream* (3) MI-6
Quinn Creek—*stream* MS-4
Quinn Creek—*stream* (2) MT-8
Quinn Creek—*stream* NC-3
Quinn Creek—*stream* OR-9
Quinn Creek—*stream* TX-5
Quinn Creek—*stream* WA-9

# R

*R* NJ-2
R, Mount—*summit* CA-9
Ra, Tower Of—*pillar* AZ-5
*Raab* OH-6
**Raab**—*pop pl* OH-6
**Raab Corners**—*pop pl* OH-6
**Raab Crossroads**—*pop pl* IN-6
Raabe Cem—*cemetery* OH-6
Raabe Lake—*lake* NE-7
RAAB Forest Camp—*locale* OR-9
Raab Sch—*school* IL-6
Raab Spring—*spring* TX-5
Raaen Creek—*stream* MN-6
*Raajerun* MP-9
Raajerun—*island* MP-9
*Raajerun Island* MP-9
Raa JHS—*school* FL-3
*Raarochi Island* MP-9
Raarochi Island—*island* MP-9
*Raarochi-To* MP-9
*Rabaho* AZ-5
*Rabaikesil* PW-9
Rabanal (Barrio)—*fmr MCD* PR-3
Rabassa, Jean Louis, House—*hist pl* LA-4
Rabat—*locale* VA-3
Rabaut JHS—*school* DC-2
Rabb—*locale* TX-5
**Rabb**—*pop pl* AL-4
*Rabb Bayou* TX-5
Rabb Canyon—*valley* NM-5
Rabb Cem—*cemetery* AL-4
Rabb Creek—*stream* OK-5
Rabb Creek Ch—*church* OK-5
Rabbe Well—*well* NM-5
Rabbia Creek—*stream* MT-8
Rabbi Alexander S Gross Hebrew
Acad—*school* FL-3
Rabbidge Creek—*stream* MT-8
*Rabbit* AZ-5
Rabbit and Porcupine Creek Forest
Camp—*locale* OR-9
Rabbit Arroyo—*stream* NM-5
Rabbit Back Creek—*stream* MI-6
Rabbit Back Peak—*summit* MI-6
Rabbit Back Point—*cape* MI-6
Rabbit Bar Point—*cape* GA-3
Rabbit Basin—*basin* OR-9
Rabbit Bay—*bay* (2) MI-6
**Rabbit Bay**—*pop pl* MI-6
Rabbit Bay—*swamp* SC-3
Rabbit Bayou—*gut* LA-4
Rabbit Bayou—*stream* MS-4
Rabbit Bill Tank—*reservoir* AZ-5
**Rabbit Bluff (historical)**—*pop pl* TN-4
Rabbit Bluff Sch (historical)—*school* TN-4
Rabbit Branch—*stream* (4) AL-4
Rabbit Branch—*stream* GA-3
Rabbit Branch—*stream* LA-4
Rabbit Branch—*stream* OK-5
Rabbit Branch—*stream* (2) TN-4
Rabbit Branch—*stream* TX-5
Rabbit Branch—*stream* VA-3
Rabbit Branch Marina—*locale* AL-4
Rabbit Brush Hollow—*valley* UT-8
Rabbit Brush Spring—*spring* NV-8
Rabbit Brush Spring—*spring* (2) UT-8
Rabbit Brush Well—*well* AZ-5
Rabbit Butte—*summit* MT-8
Rabbit Butte—*summit* NM-5
Rabbit Butte—*summit* OR-9
Rabbit Camp—*locale* WY-8
Rabbit Canyon—*valley* AZ-5
Rabbit Canyon—*valley* CO-8
Rabbit Canyon—*valley* (2) NV-8
Rabbit Canyon, The—*valley* NV-8
Rabbit Cave—*cave* AL-4
*Rabbit Chute* MO-7
Rabbit City Lake—*lake* ND-7
**Rabbit Corner**—*pop pl* NC-3
Rabbit Cove—*bay* TX-5
*Rabbit Creek* CA-9
*Rabbit Creek* ID-8
*Rabbit Creek* MT-8
*Rabbit Creek* WA-9
*Rabbit Creek* WI-6
Rabbit Creek—*stream* (3) AL-4
Rabbit Creek—*stream* (5) AK-9
Rabbit Creek—*stream* AR-4
Rabbit Creek—*stream* (2) CA-9
Rabbit Creek—*stream* (3) CO-8
Rabbit Creek—*stream* (13) ID-8
Rabbit Creek—*stream* IA-7
Rabbit Creek—*stream* (2) KS-7
Rabbit Creek—*stream* MN-6
Rabbit Creek—*stream* (4) MT-8
Rabbit Creek—*stream* NE-7
Rabbit Creek—*stream* (3) NV-8
Rabbit Creek—*stream* NC-3
Rabbit Creek—*stream* (6) OK-5
Rabbit Creek—*stream* (4) OR-9
Rabbit Creek—*stream* SD-7
Rabbit Creek—*stream* (2) TN-4
Rabbit Creek—*stream* (4) TX-5
Rabbit Creek—*stream* UT-8
Rabbit Creek—*stream* VA-3
Rabbit Creek—*stream* (4) WA-9
Rabbit Creek—*stream* (7) WY-8
Rabbit Creek Dam—*dam* SD-7
**Rabbit Creek Estates**
**(subdivision)**—*pop pl* AL-4
Rabbit Creek Rsvr—*reservoir* NV-8
Rabbit Creek Rsvr—*reservoir* SD-7
Rabbit Creek Sch—*school* SD-7
Rabbit Creek Spring—*spring* SD-7
Rabbit Creek Summit—*summit* ID-8
Rabbit Draw—*valley* NV-8
*Rabbit Dry Lake* CA-9
*Rabbit Ear Creek* CO-8
Rabbitear Creek—*stream* OR-9
Rabbit Ear Mesa—*summit* NM-5
Rabbit Ear Mtn—*summit* NM-5
*Rabbit Ears* CO-8
Rabbit Ears—*hist pl* NM-5
Rabbit Ears—*pillar* AK-9
Rabbit Ears—*summit* NM-5
Rabbit Ears—*summit* (2) OR-9
*Rabbit Ears Creek* OR-9
Rabbit Ears Creek—*stream* CO-8
Rabbit Ears Lodge—*locale* CO-8
*Rabbit Ears Mountain* CO-8
Rabbit Ears Pass—*gap* CO-8
Rabbit Ears Peak—*summit* CO-8
Rabbit Ears Range—*range* CO-8
Rabbit Flat—*flat* (2) CA-9
Rabbit Flat—*flat* OR-9
Rabbit Flat Ch—*church* KY-4
Rabbit Foot Lake—*lake* AK-9
Rabbit Foot Lake—*reservoir* PA-2
Rabbit Foot Mine—*mine* ID-8
Rabbit Glade Spring—*spring* CA-9
Rabbit Grove Ch—*church* IL-6
Rabbit Gulch—*valley* CA-9
Rabbit Gulch—*valley* (2) CO-8
Rabbit Gulch—*valley* ID-8
Rabbit Gulch—*valley* (2) MT-8
Rabbit Gulch—*valley* SD-7
Rabbit Gulch—*valley* UT-8
Rabbit Gulch Wildlife Mngmt Area—*park* UT-8
**Rabbit Hash**—*pop pl* KY-4
Rabbit Hash Ridge—*ridge* IN-6
Rabbithead Creek—*stream* MO-7
Rabbithead Sch (abandoned)—*school* MO-7
Rabbit Hill—*locale* GA-3
**Rabbit Hill**—*pop pl* WV-2
Rabbit Hill—*summit* (2) CA-9
Rabbit Hill—*summit* CT-1
Rabbit Hill—*summit* NV-8
Rabbit Hill—*summit* NM-5
Rabbit Hill—*summit* (2) OK-5
Rabbit Hill—*summit* PA-2
Rabbit Hill—*summit* RI-1
Rabbit Hill—*summit* TX-5
Rabbit Hill—*summit* VT-1
Rabbit Hill Hist Dist—*hist pl* MA-1
Rabbit Hill Pond—*reservoir* MA-1
*Rabbit Hills* CO-8
Rabbit Hills—*range* OK-5
Rabbit Hills—*spring* MT-8
Rabbit Hills—*summit* OR-9
Rabbit Hill Sch—*school* TN-4
*Rabbit Hole* TN-4
Rabbit Hole—*cave* AL-4
Rabbithole Creek—*stream* NV-8
Rabbit Hole Mine—*mine* CA-9
Rabbithole (Site)—*locale* NV-8
Rabbithole Springs—*spring* NV-8
Rabbit Holes Spring—*spring* CA-9
Rabbit Hollow—*valley* ID-8
Rabbit Hollow—*valley* IN-6
Rabbit Hollow—*valley* (3) MO-7
Rabbit Hollow—*valley* NM-5
Rabbit Hollow—*valley* NY-2
Rabbit Hollow—*valley* OK-5
Rabbit Hollow—*valley* TN-4
Rabbit Hollow—*valley* (3) TX-5
Rabbit Hollow—*valley* UT-8
Rabbit Hollow—*valley* WA-9
Rabbit Hollow Sch—*school* VT-1
Rabbit Hollow Tank—*reservoir* AZ-5
*Rabbit Island* HI-9
*Rabbit Island* SD-7
Rabbit Island—*island* AL-4
Rabbit Island—*island* (3) AK-9
Rabbit Island—*island* AZ-5
Rabbit Island—*island* CA-9
Rabbit Island—*island* FL-3
Rabbit Island—*island* (2) GA-3
Rabbit Island—*island* ID-8
Rabbit Island—*island* (2) IA-7
Rabbit Island—*island* (9) LA-4
Rabbit Island—*island* MI-6
Rabbit Island—*island* MN-6
Rabbit Island—*island* (2) MS-4
Rabbit Island—*island* MO-7
Rabbit Island—*island* (2) NY-2
Rabbit Island—*island* OK-5
Rabbit Island—*island* RI-1
Rabbit Island—*island* (3) SC-3
Rabbit Island—*island* (2) TN-4
Rabbit Island—*island* VT-1
Rabbit Island—*island* VA-3
Rabbit Island Bayou—*gut* LA-4
Rabbit Island Group—*island* NY-2
Rabbit Island Light Twenty-eight—*locale* SC-3
Rabbit Islands—*area* AK-9
*Rabbit Key* FL-3
Rabbit Key—*island* (2) FL-3
Rabbit Key Basin—*bay* FL-3
Rabbit Key Grasses—*flat* FL-3
Rabbit Key Pass—*channel* FL-3
Rabbit Keys—*island* FL-3
Rabbit Knob—*summit* GA-3
Rabbit Knob—*summit* WV-2
Rabbit Knoll—*summit* CA-9
Rabbit Knoll—*summit* ME-1
Rabbit Knoll—*summit* UT-8
*Rabbit Lake* MN-6
Rabbit Lake—*flat* CA-9
Rabbit Lake—*lake* AK-9
Rabbit Lake—*lake* KY-4
Rabbit Lake—*lake* (5) MN-6
Rabbit Lake—*reservoir* AZ-5
Rabbit Lake Cem—*cemetery* MN-6
Rabbit Lake Rsvr—*reservoir* ID-8
**Rabbit Lake (Township of)**—*pop pl* MN-6
Rabbit Meadow—*flat* CA-9
Rabbit Mine—*mine* OR-9
Rabbit Mine, The—*mine* NV-8
*Rabbit Mountain* AZ-5
Rabbit Mtn—*summit* AK-9
Rabbit Mtn—*summit* (3) CO-8
Rabbit Mtn—*summit* ID-8
Rabbit Mtn—*summit* NM-5
Rabbit Mtn—*summit* (2) NC-3
Rabbit Mtn—*summit* OR-9
Rabbit Mtn—*summit* (2) WA-9
Rabbit Patch Pit—*cave* AL-4
Rabbit Peak—*summit* (2) CA-9
Rabbit Peak—*summit* NM-5
*Rabbit Point* FL-3
Rabbit Point—*cape* AK-9
Rabbit Point—*cape* FL-3
Rabbit Point—*cape* MD-2
Rabbit Point—*summit* ID-8
Rabbit Pond—*lake* (2) ME-1
Rabbit Pond—*lake* (2) MA-1
Rabbit Pond—*lake* NY-2
Rabbit Pond—*swamp* TX-5
Rabbit Ranch—*locale* AZ-5
*Rabbit Ridge* MS-4
Rabbit Ridge—*locale* KY-4
Rabbit Ridge—*ridge* AR-4
Rabbit Ridge—*ridge* NC-3
Rabbit Ridge—*ridge* OH-6
Rabbit Ridge—*ridge* OR-9
Rabbit Ridge—*ridge* WA-9
Rabbit Ridge Ch—*church* AR-4
Rabbit Ridge Plantation—*locale* MS-4
Rabbit Ridge Sch—*school* IA-7
Rabbit River—*stream* AK-9
Rabbit River—*stream* MI-6
Rabbit River—*stream* (2) MN-6
Rabbit Rock—*island* OR-9
Rabbit Rock—*summit* CT-1
Rabbit Rock—*summit* WI-6
Rabbit Run—*stream* (2) IN-6
Rabbit Run—*stream* MT-8
Rabbit Run—*stream* OH-6
Rabbit Run—*stream* (2) PA-2
Rabbit Run—*stream* WV-2
Rabbit Run Creek—*stream* NE-7
Rabbit Sch—*school* WI-6
*Rabbit's Ear Creek* CO-8
Rabbits Ear Island—*island* ME-1
Rabbits Ferry Sch—*school* DE-2
Rabbits Foot—*mine* UT-8
Rabbits Foot Lodge—*hist pl* AR-4
Rabbitskin Branch—*stream* NC-3
Rabbits Lake—*lake* MN-6
Rabbit Slough—*gut* AK-9
Rabbits Point—*cape* SC-3
Rabbit Spring—*sp. g* (2) AZ-5
Rabbit Spring—*spring* ID-8
Rabbit Spring—*spring* (4) NV-8
Rabbit Spring—*spring* (2) NM-5
Rabbit Spring—*spring* (3) UT-8
Rabbit Spring Microwave Station—*tower* NV-8
Rabbit Spring Rsvr—*reservoir* UT-8
Rabbit Springs—*spring* CA-9
Rabbit Springs—*spring* ID-8
Rabbit Tank—*reservoir* (2) AZ-5
Rabbit Tank—*reservoir* TX-5
*Rabbitt Creek* AL-4
Rabbitt Hill Pond Dam—*dam* MA-1
*Rabbitt Island* RI-1
Rabbitt Knob—*summit* TN-4
*Rabbit Town* AL-4
Rabbittown—*locale* (2) AL-4
Rabbit Town—*locale* KY-4
**Rabbit Town**—*pop pl* AL-4
**Rabbit Town**—*pop pl* MD-2
Rabbittown Ch—*church* AL-4
Rabbittown Gap—*gap* AL-4
*Rabbittown Missionary Baptist Church* AL-4
Rabbit Trap Corral—*locale* AZ-5
*Rabbitt's Back Peak* MI-6
Rabbit Valley—*basin* CA-9
Rabbit Valley—*valley* AZ-5
Rabbit Valley—*valley* CA-9
Rabbit Valley—*valley* CO-8
Rabbit Valley—*valley* GA-3
Rabbit Valley—*valley* (2) TN-4
Rabbit Valley—*valley* (2) UT-8
Rabbit Valley Rapids—*rapids* UT-8
**Rabbitville**—*pop pl* IN-6
Rabbit Water—*reservoir* AZ-5
Rabbit Well—*locale* NM-5
Rabbit Windmill—*locale* NM-5
**Rabbityard**—*pop pl* AL-4
Rabbitz Lake—*lake* MI-6
Rabbiy Hill Pond—*lake* MA-1
Rabb Lake—*lake* ND-7
Rabb Lake Natl Wildlife Ref—*park* ND-7
Rabble Run—*stream* MD-2
Rabb Park—*flat* NM-5
**Rabbs**—*pop pl* TX-5
Rabbs Bayou—*stream* TX-5
Rabb Sch—*school* IN-6
Rabbs Creek—*stream* TX-5
Rabbs Prairie—*flat* TX-5
Rabbs Prairie—*locale* TX-5
Rabbs Ridge—*ridge* TX-5
Rabdau Park—*park* NE-7
Rabeck Hollow—*valley* TN-4
*Rabe Creek* WI-6
Rabe Creek—*stream* WI-6
Rabe Drain—*stream* MI-6
Rabe Lake—*lake* WI-6
Rabe Lake State Fishery Area—*park* WI-6
Rabenau Cem—*cemetery* MO-7
Rabenberg Airp—*airport* SD-7
Rabenberg Sch—*school* SD-7
Raben Branch—*stream* IN-6
*Rabenes Point* WA-9
Raben Lake—*lake* MN-6
*Rabens Branch* IN-6
Rabensburg House—*hist pl* TX-5
**Raber**—*pop pl* IN-6
**Raber**—*pop pl* MI-6
Raber Bay—*bay* MI-6
Raber Canyon—*valley* OR-9
Raber Lohr Ditch—*canal* CO-8
Raber Point—*cape* MI-6
Raber Ranch—*locale* (2) WY-8
*Rabersburg* PA-2
Raber Sch—*school* SD-7
*Raber School* IN-6
*Rabers Corners* PA-2
**Raber Township**—*pop pl* SD-7
**Raber (Township of)**—*pop pl* MI-6
**Raberts Corner**—*pop pl* PA-2
Rabes Branch—*stream* AL-4
Rabey Cem—*cemetery* VA-3
Rabideau CCC Camp—*hist pl* MN-6
Rabideau Lake—*lake* MN-6
Rabideux Creek—*stream* AK-9
Rabinowitz Bldg—*hist pl* GA-3
*Rabins Point* WA-9
*Rabit Creek* WA-9
*Rabit Town* AL-4
Rabke Cem—*cemetery* TX-5
Rabke Ch—*church* TX-5
*Rab Lake* ND-7
*Rablens Creek* ID-8
Rablens Fork—*stream* ID-8
*Rablissa* PW-9
**Rabo del Buey**—*pop pl* PR-3
Rabon Branch—*stream* SC-3
Rabon Cartwright Cem—*cemetery* TX-5
Rabon Chapel—*church* TX-5
Rabon Creek—*stream* SC-3
Rabon Creek Ch—*church* SC-3
Rabon Crossroads—*locale* SC-3
**Rabon Crossroads**—*pop pl* SC-3
Rabontown—*locale* NC-3
R A Booth Memorial State Park—*park* OR-9
**Rabornville**—*pop pl* OK-5
Rabouin HS—*school* LA-4
Rabourn Cem—*cemetery* MO-7
Rabourn Slough—*gut* MO-7
Rab Ravine—*valley* CA-9
**Rabun**—*pop pl* AL-4
Rabun, Lake—*reservoir* GA-3
Rabun Bald—*summit* GA-3
Rabun Beach Rec Area—*park* GA-3
**Rabun (County)**—*pop pl* GA-3
Rabun Gap—*locale* GA-3
Rabun Gap Nacoochee Sch—*school* GA-3
Raburn Hollow—*valley* TN-4
Raby Bend—*bend* NC-3
Raby Branch—*stream* LA-4
Raby Cem—*cemetery* (2) TN-4
Raby Hollow—*valley* TN-4
Raby Park—*park* TX-5
Racavitch Pond—*lake* PA-2
Raccacious, Bayou—*stream* LA-4
Raccon Branch—*stream* VA-3
*Raccoon* NJ-2
*Raccoon* OH-6
*Raccoon* PA-2
**Raccoon**—*pop pl* IN-6
**Raccoon**—*pop pl* KY-4
Raccoon Bar (historical)—*bar* AL-4
Raccoon Bay—*bay* NC-3
Raccoon Bayou—*gut* (3) LA-4
Raccoon Bayou—*stream* AR-4
Raccoon Bayou—*stream* LA-4
Raccoon Bend—*bend* TX-5
**Raccoon Bend**—*pop pl* TX-5
Raccoon Bend Oil Field—*oilfield* TX-5
**Raccoon Bluff**—*pop pl* GA-3
*Raccoon Branch* MD-2
Raccoon Branch—*stream* AL-4
Raccoon Branch—*stream* (2) GA-3
Raccoon Branch—*stream* IN-6
Raccoon Branch—*stream* (8) KY-4
Raccoon Branch—*stream* LA-4
Raccoon Branch—*stream* MD-2
Raccoon Branch—*stream* MO-7
Raccoon Branch—*stream* (5) NC-3
Raccoon Branch—*stream* (8) TN-4
Raccoon Branch—*stream* (4) VA-3
Raccoon Branch—*stream* (3) WV-2
Raccoon Bridge—*bridge* KY-4
Raccoon Brook—*stream* RI-1
Raccoon Brook Hill—*summit* NY-2
Raccoon Cave—*cave* PA-2
Raccoon Cave—*cave* TN-4
Raccoon (CCD)—*cens area* KY-4
Raccoon Cem—*cemetery* IN-6
Raccoon Cem—*cemetery* KY-4
Raccoon Ch—*church* KY-4
Raccoon Ch—*church* MO-7
Raccoon Ch—*church* PA-2
*Raccoon Cove* AL-4
Raccoon Cove—*bay* DE-2
Raccoon Cove—*bay* ME-1
Raccoon Cove—*valley* NC-3
*Raccoon Creek* AL-4
*Raccoon Creek* IL-6
*Raccoon Creek* IN-6
Raccoon Creek—*bay* NC-3
Raccoon Creek—*gut* SC-3
Raccoon Creek—*stream* AR-4
Raccoon Creek—*stream* CA-9
Raccoon Creek—*stream* (4) GA-3
Raccoon Creek—*stream* (6) IL-6
Raccoon Creek—*stream* (3) IN-6
Raccoon Creek—*stream* IA-7
Raccoon Creek—*stream* (8) KY-4
Raccoon Creek—*stream* (2) MD-2
Raccoon Creek—*stream* MO-7
Raccoon Creek—*stream* NJ-2
Raccoon Creek—*stream* (9) NC-3
Raccoon Creek—*stream* (3) OH-6
Raccoon Creek—*stream* (6) PA-2
Raccoon Creek—*stream* (5) TN-4
Raccoon Creek—*stream* TX-5
Raccoon Creek—*stream* (3) VA-3
Raccoon Creek—*stream* WA-9
Raccoon Creek—*stream* (5) WV-2
Raccoon Creek—*stream* WI-6
Raccoon Creek—*stream* WY-8
Raccoon Creek Ch—*church* GA-3
Raccoon Creek Marsh—*swamp* MD-2
Raccoon Creek Point—*cape* NC-3
Raccoon Creek Public Hunting Area—*park* AL-4
Raccoon Creek State Park—*park* PA-2
Raccoon Creek State Park Dam—*dam* PA-2
*Raccoon Ditch* IN-6
Raccoon Ditch—*canal* IN-6
Raccoon Ditch—*canal* NJ-2
Raccoon Ditch—*stream* DE-2
Raccoon Flat—*flat* GA-3
Raccoon Ford—*locale* VA-3
Raccoon Fork—*stream* KY-4
Raccoon Gap—*gap* TN-4
Raccoon Grange—*locale* PA-2
Raccoon Grove—*woods* IL-6
*Raccoon Gulf* AL-4
Raccoon Hill—*summit* (2) CT-1
Raccoon Hill—*summit* MA-1
Raccoon Hill—*summit* NH-1
Raccoon Hill—*summit* RI-1
Raccoon Hollow—*valley* GA-3
Raccoon Hollow—*valley* (2) KY-4
Raccoon Hollow—*valley* (2) MO-7
Raccoon Hollow—*valley* PA-2
Raccoon Hollow—*valley* (4) TN-4
Raccoon Hollow—*valley* WV-2
Raccoon Hollow Cove—*bay* MO-7
Raccoon Island—*island* AL-4
Raccoon Island—*island* (2) LA-4
Raccoon Island—*island* MA-1
Raccoon Island—*island* (3) NJ-2
Raccoon Island—*island* (2) NC-3
Raccoon Island—*island* SC-3
Raccoon Island—*island* VA-3
Raccoon Island—*locale* OH-6
Raccoon Islands—*island* SC-3
Raccoon Key—*island* (2) FL-3
Raccoon Key—*island* GA-3
**Raccoon Key (Key Haven)**—*pop pl* FL-3
Raccoon Keys—*island* GA-3
Raccoon Key Spit—*bar* GA-3
*Raccoon Lake* IN-6
Raccoon Lake—*lake* FL-3
Raccoon Lake—*lake* LA-4
Raccoon Lake—*lake* SC-3
Raccoon Lake Oil Field—*other* IL-6
Raccoon Lake Park—*park* IL-6
Raccoon Lake State Rec Area—*park* IN-6
*Raccoon Lower Bridge* NJ-2
*Raccoon Mills* GA-3
*Raccoon Mountain* GA-3
Raccoon Mountain—*ridge* NH-1
Raccoon Mountain Pumped Storage Dam and
Rsvr—*reservoir* TN-4
Raccoon Mountain Rsvr—*reservoir* TN-4
*Raccoon Mountains* TN-4
*Raccoon Mtn* AL-4
Raccoon Mtn—*summit* AL-4
Raccoon Mtn—*summit* KY-4
Raccoon Mtn—*summit* NC-3
Raccoon Mtn—*summit* PA-2
Raccoon Mtn—*summit* TN-4
Raccoon Pass—*channel* LA-4
Raccoon Point—*cape* DE-2
Raccoon Point—*cape* FL-3
Raccoon Point—*cape* LA-4
Raccoon Point—*cape* MD-2
Raccoon Point—*cape* NC-3
Raccoon Point—*summit* WA-9
Raccoon Pond—*lake* DE-2
Raccoon Pond—*lake* MA-1
Raccoon Pond—*lake* SC-3
Raccoon Pond—*swamp* IL-6
Raccoon Prong—*stream* DE-2
**Raccoon Ramp**—*pop pl* IN-6
Raccoon Ridge—*ridge* NC-3
Raccoon Ridge—*ridge* (2) PA-2
*Raccoon River* IA-7
Raccoon River—*stream* IA-7
Raccoon (RR name for Joffre)—*other* PA-2
Raccoon Rsvr—*reservoir* WY-8
*Raccoon Run* PA-2
Raccoon Run—*stream* OH-6
Raccoon Run—*stream* (2) PA-2
Raccoon Run—*stream* VA-3
Raccoon Run—*stream* (5) WV-2
Raccoon Sch—*school* IL-6
Raccoon Sch—*school* (3) KY-4
Raccoon Sch—*school* PA-2
Raccoon Slough—*gut* FL-3
Raccoon Spit—*bar* MS-4
Raccoon Spring—*spring* AR-4
Raccoon Strait—*channel* CA-9
*Raccoon Swamp* NC-3
Raccoon Swamp—*swamp* MA-1
Raccoon Swamp—*swamp* (2) NC-3
Raccoon Swash—*channel* MS-4
**Raccoon (Township of)**—*pop pl* IL-6
**Raccoon (Township of)**—*pop pl* IN-6
**Raccoon (Township of)**—*pop pl* OH-6
**Raccoon (Township of)**—*pop pl* PA-2
Raccoon Valley—*basin* VA-3
**Raccoon Valley**—*pop pl* TN-4
Raccoon Valley—*valley* TN-4
Raccoon Valley Post Office
(historical)—*building* TN-4
Raccoon Valley Sch (historical)—*school* TN-4
Raccourci Bay—*lake* LA-4
Raccourci Bayou—*gut* LA-4
Raccourci Cutoff—*bend* LA-4
Raccourci Island—*island* LA-4
*Raccourci Lake* LA-4
Raccourci Old River—*stream* LA-4
Race, Mount—*summit* AK-9
Race, Mount—*summit* MA-1
*Race, The* NJ-2
Race Branch—*stream* MD-2
Race Branch—*stream* VA-3
Race Bridge—*locale* MD-2
Race Brook—*stream* CT-1
Race Brook—*stream* MA-1
Race Brook Falls—*falls* MA-1
Race Brook Sch—*school* CT-1
Race Channel—*channel* FL-3
Race Cove—*bay* NJ-2
*Race Creek* CO-8
*Race Creek* ID-8
Race Creek—*stream* CO-8
Race Creek—*stream* (3) ID-8
Race Creek—*stream* KY-4
Race Creek—*stream* MS-4
Race Creek—*stream* MO-7
Race Creek Campground—*locale* ID-8
Race Creek Ch—*church* KY-4
Raceground Sch (historical)—*school* PA-2
Race Hill—*summit* CT-1
Race Hog Point—*cape* MD-2
Race Hollow—*valley* TN-4
Race Hollow—*valley* UT-8
Racehorse Canyon—*valley* WA-9
Race Horse Cienega—*swamp* AZ-5
*Racehorse Coulee—valley* MT-8
*Racehorse Creek* TX-5
*Race Horse Creek* WI-6
Racehorse Creek—*stream* WA-9
Racehorse Flat—*flat* UT-8
Racehorse Gulch—*valley* MT-8
Racehorse Park—*flat* WY-8
*Race Island* RI-1
Race Lagoon—*bay* WA-9
Race Lake—*lake* MI-6
**Raceland**—*pop pl* KY-4
**Raceland**—*pop pl* LA-4
Raceland Ch—*church* LA-4
Raceland HS—*school* LA-4
Raceland Junction—*locale* LA-4
**Raceland Junction**—*pop pl* KY-4
Raceland Oil and Gas Field—*oilfield* LA-4
Racepath Branch—*stream* GA-3
Race Path Branch—*stream* MS-4
Race Path Branch—*stream* NC-3
Racepath Branch—*stream* VA-3
Race Path Cave—*cave* AL-4
Race Path Ch—*church* NC-3
Racepath Gap—*gap* GA-3
Race Path Gulch—*valley* CO-8
Racepath Hollow—*valley* AL-4
Racepath Hollow—*valley* TN-4
*Race Point* ME-1
Race Point—*bar* MA-1
Race Point—*cape* (3) AK-9
Race Point—*cape* ME-1
Race Point—*cape* NY-2
Race Point—*locale* MA-1
Race Point Beach—*beach* MA-1
Race Point Coast Guard
Station—*building* MA-1
Race Point Ledge—*bar* NY-2
Race Point Light—*locale* MA-1
Race Point Light—*other* AK-9
Race Point Lighthouse—*locale* MA-1
Race Point Light Station—*hist pl* MA-1

Race Point U. S. Life Saving Station (historical)—*locale* MA-1
Race Pond—*lake* (2) FL-3
**Racepond**—*pop pl* GA-3
Racepond Ch—*church* GA-3
**Race Pond (Racepond)**—*pop pl* GA-3
Racer Camp Hollow—*valley* WV-2
Racer Canyon—*valley* UT-8
Racer Canyon Creek—*stream* UT-8
*Race Rock* NH-1
Racer Run—*stream* VA-3
Race Run—*bay* MA-1
Race Run—*stream* IN-6
Race Saint Ch—*church* NC-3
Race Saint Sch—*school* NC-3
Races Point—*cape* FL-3
*Racetrack* WA-9
Race Track—*locale* MS-4
Racetrack—*locale* MT-8
Race Track—*locale* TN-4
Racetrack—*locale* TX-5
Racetrack—*locale* WA-9
Race Track—*other* CA-9
**Racetrack**—*pop pl* MT-8
Race Track—*valley* ID-8
*Racetrack, The* UT-8
Racetrack, The—*flat* CA-9
Race Track, The—*trail* UT-8
Racetrack Bar—*bar* MS-4
Racetrack Basin—*other* AK-9
Racetrack Bayou—*gut* LA-4
Racetrack Bend—*bend* CA-9
Racetrack Bend—*bend* MS-4
Racetrack Bend—*bend* NC-3
Race Track Bluff—*cliff* TN-4
Racetrack Branch—*stream* AR-4
Racetrack Butte—*summit* SD-7
Racetrack Campground—*locale* MT-8
Racetrack Campground—*park* UT-8
Racetrack Canyon—*valley* NM-5
Race Track Ch—*church* AL-4
*Race Track Creek* MT-8
Racetrack Creek—*stream* MT-8
Racetrack Creek—*stream* TX-5
Racetrack Creek—*stream* UT-8
Racetrack Flat—*flat* CO-8
Racetrack Flats—*flat* CO-8
Racetrack Forest Camp—*locale* WA-9
Race Track Hill—*summit* CA-9
*Race Track Hollow* TN-4
Racetrack Hollow—*valley* AR-4
Racetrack Hollow—*valley* KY-4
Racetrack Hollow—*valley* (4) MO-7
Race Track Hollow—*valley* MO-7
Racetrack Hollow—*valley* MO-7
Racetrack Hollow—*valley* (2) TN-4
Racetrack Hollow—*valley* TX-5
Racetrack Hollow—*valley* UT-8
Racetrack Island—*island* PA-2
Racetrack Knoll—*summit* AZ-5
Racetrack Lake—*lake* AR-4
Racetrack Lake—*lake* MT-8
Racetrack Lake—*lake* OR-9
Race Track Landing—*locale* FL-3
Race Track Landing (historical)—*locale* MS-4
Racetrack Meadow—*flat* ID-8
*Race Track Mesa* AZ-5
Racetrack Mesa—*summit* NM-5
*Racetrack Oil Field* CA-9
Racetrack Pass—*gap* MT-8
Racetrack Peak—*summit* MT-8
*Racetrack Playa* CA-9
Race Track Point—*cape* CA-9
Racetrack Prairie—*flat* LA-4
Racetrack Prairie—*flat* (2) OK-5
Race Track Prairie Branch—*stream* TX-5
Racetrack Ranch—*locale* NV-8
Racetrack Ridge—*ridge* MO-7
Racetrack Ridge—*ridge* MT-8
Racetrack Rsvr—*reservoir* NV-8
Race Track Rsvr—*reservoir* UT-8
Racetrack Run—*stream* OH-6
Racetrack Sch—*school* AL-4
Race Track Sch—*school* WI-6
Racetrack Slough—*gut* AK-9
Racetrack Tank—*reservoir* (2) AZ-5
Race Track Tank—*reservoir* AZ-5
Racetrack Tank—*reservoir* AZ-5
Racetrack Towhead—*area* MS-4
Racetrack Valley—*basin* CA-9
Racetrack Wash—*stream* AZ-5
Racetrack Well—*well* AZ-5
Race Track Well—*well* NM-5
Racetrack Windmill—*locale* AZ-5
**Raceville**—*pop pl* NY-2
Raceway Park—*park* IL-6
Raceway Park—*park* NE-7
Racewood Township—*civil* KS-7
Racey Brothers Spring—*spring* OR-9
Racey Cem—*cemetery* WV-2
*Racey Spring* OR-9
Rachael Carson Natl Estuarine Sanctuary—*park* NC-3
Rachael Ch—*church* NC-3
*Rachael Cove* MA-1
Rachael Creek—*gut* NJ-2
Rachael Creek—*stream* SC-3
Rachael Point—*cape* NJ-2
**Rachal**—*pop pl* TX-5
Rachal Oil Field—*oilfield* TX-5
Rachal Siding—*locale* TX-5
*Rachal Station* TX-5
Racheab—*summit* FM-9
Racheal-Patterson Sch—*school* AL-4
*Racheb* FM-9
Rachek Island—*island* AK-9
**Rachel**—*pop pl* WV-2
Rachel, Lake—*lake* MN-6
Rachel, Mount—*summit* GA-3
Rachel Bank—*bar* FL-3
Rachel Branch—*stream* GA-3
Rachel Carson Natl Wildlife Ref—*park* ME-1
Rachel Ch—*church* NC-3
Rachel Chapel—*church* VA-3
Rachel Chapel Sch—*school* VA-3
Rachel Cove—*cove* MA-1
**Rachel (Downs)**—*pop pl* WV-2
Rachel Drain—*stream* ID-8
**Rachel Estates**—*pop pl* TN-4
Rachel Gut—*gut* NJ-2
Rachel Hill Sch—*school* PA-2
Rachel Key—*island* FL-3
Rachel Lake—*lake* FL-3
Rachel Lake—*lake* WA-9
Rachel Mine—*mine* OR-9
*Rachel Patterson Public Sch* AL-4
Rachel Run—*stream* PA-2
Rachels Cem—*cemetery* GA-3
Rachels Delight Riffle—*rapids* OR-9
**Rachels Place Subdivision**—*pop pl* UT-8
Rachel Windmill—*locale* TX-5
Rachelwood—*locale* PA-2
*Rachi Island* MP-9
Rachor Lake—*lake* WA-9
Racho Sch—*school* MI-6
*Racine* PA-2
Racine—*locale* IA-7
**Racine**—*pop pl* IA-7
**Racine**—*pop pl* MN-6
**Racine**—*pop pl* MO-7
**Racine**—*pop pl* OH-6
**Racine**—*pop pl* WV-2
**Racine**—*pop pl* WI-6
*Racine Avenue* IL-6
Racine Brook—*stream* NY-2
Racine College—*hist pl* WI-6
*Racine(corp name Homewood,RR name Homewood Junction)* PA-2
**Racine (County)**—*pop pl* WI-6
Racine County Courthouse—*hist pl* WI-6
Racine Depot—*hist pl* WI-6
Racine Elks Club, Lodge No. 252—*hist pl* WI-6
Racine Harbor Lighthouse and Life Saving Station—*hist pl* WI-6
Racine Junction—*uninc pl* WI-6
Racine Locks and Dam—*dam* WV-2
Racine Public Library—*hist pl* WI-6
Racine Reef—*bar* WI-6
**Racine Township**—*pop pl* SD-7
**Racine (Township of)**—*pop pl* MN-6
**Racing Beach**—*pop pl* MA-1
Racing Creek—*stream* OR-9
Rackard Hollow—*valley* TN-4
Rack Creek—*stream* CA-9
Rack Creek—*stream* VA-3
Rack Creek—*stream* WA-9
Rackensack Canyon—*valley* AZ-5
*Rackensack Gulch* AZ-5
Rackensack Spring—*spring* AZ-5
Rackerby—*locale* CA-9
Rackerby Gulch—*valley* CA-9
Rackerby Jack Spring—*spring* CA-9
Rackerby Ridge—*ridge* CA-9
Racker Vly—*lake* NY-2
Racket—*locale* MO-7
Racket—*locale* WV-2
Racket Branch—*stream* AL-4
Racket Brook—*stream* PA-2
Racket Brook Breaker—*building* PA-2
Racket Creek—*stream* KS-7
Racket Creek—*stream* NC-3
Racket Creek—*stream* WI-6
Racket Island—*island* NY-2
*Racket Lake* NY-2
*Racket Pond* NY-2
Racket Pond—*lake* NY-2
Racket Ridge—*ridge* IN-6
Racket Ridge Sch (abandoned)—*school* MO-7
*Racket River* NY-2
Racket Sch—*school* MO-7
Racket Shaft—*mine* NM-5
**Rackett**—*pop pl* NE-7
Rackett Ch—*church* NE-7
**Rackettown**—*pop pl* VA-3
Rackham Golf Club—*other* MI-6
*Rack Heap Creek* OR-9
Rackheap Creek—*stream* OR-9
Rack Hollow—*valley* VA-3
*Rack Island* VA-3
Rack Lake—*lake* CA-9
Rackleff Bldg—*hist pl* ME-1
Rackley, J. J., Bldg—*hist pl* TX-5
Rackley Hollow—*valley* TN-4
Rackliff Bay—*bay* ME-1
Rackliff Campground—*locale* ID-8
Rackliff Creek—*stream* ID-8
Rackliff Island—*island* ME-1
Rackout Spring—*spring* CA-9
Rack Pond—*lake* ME-1
*Racks, The* FL-3
Racks Creek—*stream* OR-9
Rack Turn Point—*cape* DE-2
*Rackville* PA-2
Raco—*locale* CA-9
Raco—*locale* MI-6
**Raco Junction**—*pop pl* MI-6
**Racola**—*pop pl* MO-7
Racon Creek—*stream* AK-9
Racon Windmill—*locale* TX-5
*Racoon Bend Oil Field* TX-5
Racoon Bend Oil Field—*oilfield* TX-5
Racoon Branch—*stream* NC-3
*Racoon Creek* IL-6
*Racoon Creek* IN-6
*Racoon Creek* TN-4
*Racoon Creek Dam* PA-2
Racoon Creek RDA—*hist pl* PA-2
*Racoon Hill* NH-1
*Racoon Island* MA-1
Racoon Knob—*summit* CO-8
*Racoon Lake* IN-6
*Racoon Lake* PA-2
Racoon Mountain Dam—*dam* TN-4
Racoon Mtn—*summit* NC-3
*Racoon River* IA-7
*Racoon Strait* CA-9
**Racoon Valley**—*pop pl* TN-4
Racops Siding—*locale* PA-2
Raco Ranger Station—*locale* MI-6
Raco-Theodore Park—*park* NH-1
Racquet and Tennis Club Bldg—*hist pl* NY-2
**Racquet Club Drive Condo**—*pop pl* UT-8
**Racquet Club Row Subdivision**—*pop pl* UT-8
Racquet County Club—*other* CA-9
Racquet Creek—*stream* AK-9
Racquet Lake—*lake* NY-2
Racume—*locale* VA-3
Racy—*locale* MI-6
Racy—*locale* WV-2
Racy Ch—*church* MI-6
Racy Point—*cape* FL-3
**Rada**—*pop pl* WV-2
Radabaugh Lake—*lake* MN-6
Radabaugh Run—*stream* WV-2
*Radac* MP-9
*Radack* MP-9
*Radak Chain* MP-9
*Radak Group* MP-9
Radamaker, Mount—*summit* AK-9
**Radar**—*pop pl* MO-7
Radar Ch—*church* VA-3
Radar Creek—*stream* IN-6
*Radar Dam* PA-2
Radar Gulch—*valley* AK-9
*Radar Hill* MI-6
Radar Hill—*summit* AK-9
Radar Hill—*summit* AZ-5
Radar Hill—*summit* OR-9
Radar Station B-71—*hist pl* CA-9
Radas Roosevelt—*channel* PR-3
Radburn—*hist pl* NJ-2
**Radburn**—*pop pl* NJ-2
Radburn-Fair Lawn Station—*hist pl* NJ-2
Radburn Sch—*school* NJ-2
*Radcliff* PA-2
Radcliff—*locale* WV-2
**Radcliff**—*pop pl* KY-4
**Radcliff**—*pop pl* OH-6
Radcliff—*uninc pl* KY-4
Radcliff, Willam, House—*hist pl* IA-7
Radcliff (CCD)—*cens area* KY-4
*Radcliff Creek* GA-3
*Radcliff Creek* ID-8
*Radcliff Creek* MD-2
Radcliff Creek—*stream* ID-8
Radcliffe—*other* VA-3
**Radcliffe**—*pop pl* IA-7
Radcliffe Canal—*canal* NE-7
Radcliffe Cem—*cemetery* IA-7
Radcliffe Cem—*cemetery* WV-2
Radcliffe Coll—*school* (2) MA-1
Radcliffe Creek—*stream* MD-2
Radcliffe-Duvall Farm—*hist pl* KY-4
Radcliffe Glacier—*glacier* AK-9
Radcliffe Landing Strip—*airport* MO-7
Radcliffe Mine—*mine* CA-9
Radcliffe Sch—*school* OH-6
*Radcliff Gulch* CO-8
Radcliff JHS—*school* MI-6
Radcliff No 3 Canal—*canal* NE-7
Radcliff Park—*park* NC-3
Radcliff Ridge—*ridge* ID-8
Radcliff Sch—*school* CA-9
Radcliff Sch—*school* GA-3
Radcliff Sch—*school* KY-4
Raddatz Rockshelter—*hist pl* WI-6
Radden Park—*park* IL-6
*Radder Creek* OR-9
Radder Creek—*stream* NC-3
Raddick Gulch—*valley* SD-7
Radding Bldg—*hist pl* MA-1
**Raddin Station**—*pop pl* MA-1
Raddison Lake—*lake* MN-6
**Raddle**—*pop pl* IL-6
Raddon, LaPage H., House—*hist pl* UT-8
Raddon, Samuel L., House—*hist pl* UT-8
Raddue Guard Station—*locale* OR-9
Raddy Hollow—*valley* MO-7
**Radebaugh**—*pop pl* PA-2
Radec—*locale* CA-9
Radec Valley—*valley* CA-9
Rade Lake—*lake* WI-6
Rademacher, Frank J., House—*hist pl* NE-7
Rademacher Cem—*cemetery* SD-7
Radenbough Cove—*bay* AK-9
Rader—*locale* PA-2
**Rader**—*pop pl* MO-7
**Rader**—*pop pl* TN-4
Rader Branch—*stream* TN-4
Rader Cem—*cemetery* IA-7
Rader Cem—*cemetery* MO-7
Rader Cem—*cemetery* TX-5
Rader Ch—*church* MO-7
Rader Ch—*church* WV-2
Rader Chapel—*church* WV-2
Rader Creek—*stream* KY-4
Rader Creek—*stream* MS-4
Rader Creek—*stream* MT-8
Rader Creek—*stream* OH-6
Rader Creek—*stream* OR-9
Rader Creek—*stream* WA-9
Rader Fork—*stream* WV-2
Rader Gap—*gap* TN-4
*Rader Glade* OR-9
*Rader Hill* OR-9
Rader Hills—*summit* OR-9
Rader Hill Sch—*school* TN-4
Rader Hollow—*valley* AR-4
Rader Hollow—*valley* KY-4
Rader Kindergarten—*school* FL-3
Rader Knob—*summit* VA-3
Rader Mine—*mine* MT-8
Rader Mountain Trail—*trail* VA-3
Rader Mtn—*summit* VA-3
Rader Ridge—*ridge* TX-5
Rader Run—*stream* VA-3
Rader Run—*stream* (3) WV-2
*Raders* TN-4
Raders Branch—*stream* IL-6
Raders Branch Drain—*canal* IL-6
**Radersburg**—*pop pl* MT-8
Radersburg Pass—*gap* MT-8
Rader Sch—*school* IL-6
Rader Sch—*school* SD-7
Radersdorf Ditch—*canal* IN-6
**Raders Run**—*pop pl* WV-2
Raders Valley—*valley* WV-2
Raderville—*locale* WY-8
Rader Windmill—*locale* TX-5
Radey Pond—*lake* CT-1
Radford—*locale* IL-6
**Radford**—*pop pl* AL-4
**Radford**—*pop pl* NC-3
**Radford**—*pop pl* VA-3
Radford Army Ammunition Plant—*other* VA-3
Radford Army Ammun Plant—*military* VA-3
Radford Branch—*stream* GA-3
Radford Branch—*stream* MO-7
Radford Branch—*stream* NC-3
Radford Canyon—*valley* CA-9
Radford Canyon—*valley* UT-8
Radford Cem—*cemetery* (2) MO-7
Radford Cem—*cemetery* NC-3
Radford Coll—*school* VA-3
Radford Creek—*stream* OR-9
Radford Crossroads—*locale* NC-3
Radford Gap—*gap* NC-3
Radford Hollow—*valley* KY-4
Radford Hollow—*valley* (2) MO-7
Radford HS—*school* HI-9
**Radford (ind. city)**—*pop pl* VA-3
Radford Ponds—*reservoir* AL-4
Radford Post Office (historical)—*building* AL-4
Radford Sch—*school* TX-5
Radford Sch (historical)—*school* AL-4
*Radfordsville* AL-4
Radford Top—*summit* NC-3
Radford University—*uninc pl* VA-3
*Radfordville* AL-4
*Radha River* OR-9
Radial Island—*island* AK-9
Radial Mtn—*summit* CO-8
Radiant—*locale* VA-3
Radiant Camp—*locale* CO-8
Radiant City Ch—*church* AL-4
Radiant Life Assembly of God—*church* FL-3
Radiant Mine—*mine* WY-8
Radiant Mine (underground)—*mine* AL-4
**Radiant Valley**—*pop pl* MD-2
Radiator Hill—*summit* NV-8
Radiator Specialty Company—*facility* NC-3
*Radica Creek* TX-5
Radical—*locale* NC-3
*Radical, The* DE-2
Radical Cem—*cemetery* KS-7
Radical Hill—*summit* CO-8
Radical Ridge Sch (abandoned)—*school* MO-7
Radical Sch (historical)—*school* (2) MO-7
Radicha Creek—*stream* TX-5
Radicha Lake—*lake* TX-5
Radigan Flowage—*swamp* WI-6
Radin Kamp Ditch—*canal* CA-9
Radio Astronomical Observatory—*building* TX-5
*Radio Center* MN-6
**Radio Center**—*pop pl* MN-6
Radio Center Shop Ctr—*locale* TN-4
Radio Central Complex—*hist pl* NY-2
Radio City—*uninc pl* NY-2
Radio City Music Hall—*hist pl* NY-2
Radio Creek—*stream* (2) AK-9
Radio Creek—*stream* MT-8
Radio Crystal Mine—*mine* NV-8
**Radio Heights**—*pop pl* OH-6
*Radio Hill* MH-9
Radio Hill—*summit* AZ-5
Radio Hill—*summit* CA-9
Radio Hill—*summit* IL-6
Radio Hill—*summit* NM-5
Radio Hill—*summit* WA-9
Radio Howe Park Facility—*summit* ID-8
Radio Island—*island* MI-6
Radio Island—*island* NY-2
Radio Island—*island* NC-3
**Radio Junction**—*pop pl* TX-5
*Radio Park Elementary School* PA-2
Radio Park( Private)—*locale* PA-2
Radio Park Sch—*school* PA-2
Radio Point—*cape* NY-2
Radio Ridge—*ridge* AZ-5
Radio Shaft—*mine* WA-9
Radio Springs—*locale* GA-3
Radio Springs Dam—*dam* OR-9
Radio Springs Rsvr—*reservoir* OR-9
**Radioville**—*pop pl* IN-6
**Radioville**—*pop pl* PR-3
*Radison* WI-6
**Radison**—*pop pl* NY-2
**Radisson**—*pop pl* WI-6
Radisson Cem—*cemetery* WI-6
Radisson Flowage—*reservoir* WI-6
Radisson Lake—*lake* MN-6
**Radisson (Town of)**—*pop pl* WI-6
Radium—*locale* AZ-5
Radium—*locale* CO-8
Radium—*locale* TX-5
Radium—*locale* VA-3
**Radium**—*pop pl* KS-7
**Radium**—*pop pl* MN-6
Radium Cycle Mine—*mine* CO-8
Radium Elem Sch—*school* KS-7
Radium Group Mines—*mine* CO-8
Radium Hollow—*valley* MO-7
Radium Hot Springs—*locale* AZ-5
Radium Hot Springs—*spring* OR-9
Radium Mtn—*summit* CO-8
Radium Spring—*spring* MO-7
**Radium Springs**—*pop pl* GA-3
**Radium Springs**—*pop pl* NM-5
Radium Springs—*spring* WY-8
Radium Springs Country Club—*other* GA-3
Radium Springs Swimming Pool—*other* CO-8
Radium Townsite Oil Field—*oilfield* KS-7
Radium Trail—*trail* CO-8
Radke Lake—*lake* MN-6
Radke Sawmill—*locale* MT-8
Radle Cem—*cemetery* MO-7
Radley—*locale* IL-6
**Radley**—*pop pl* IN-6
**Radley**—*pop pl* KS-7
Radley Ch—*church* IN-6
Radley Creek—*stream* WI-6
Radley Run—*stream* PA-2
Radley Sch—*school* IL-6
Radloff Cem—*cemetery* MN-6
Radloff Island—*island* WI-6
Radloff Point—*cape* WI-6
**Radmoor**—*pop pl* TN-4
Radney Chapel—*church* AL-4
Radnor—*locale* CA-9
Radnor—*locale* MT-8
**Radnor**—*pop pl* IN-6
**Radnor**—*pop pl* OH-6
**Radnor**—*pop pl* PA-2
**Radnor**—*pop pl* WV-2
Radnor—*uninc pl* TN-4
Radnor ( CDP name: Radnor Township )—*CDP* PA-2
Radnor Ch—*church* TN-4
Radnor Friends Meetinghouse—*hist pl* PA-2
**Radnor Green**—*pop pl* DE-2
**Radnor Heights**—*pop pl* VA-3
Radnor Heliport—*airport* PA-2
Radnor Lake—*reservoir* TN-4
Radnor Lake Dam—*dam* TN-4
Radnor MS—*school* PA-2
Radnor Post Office (historical)—*building* PA-2
Radnor Sch—*school* MD-2
Radnor Senior HS—*school* PA-2
Radnor Station—*building* PA-2
**Radnor Station**—*pop pl* PA-2
**Radnor (Township of)**—*pop pl* IL-6
**Radnor (Township of)**—*pop pl* OH-6
**Radnor (Township of)**—*pop pl* PA-2
Radnor Valley Country Club—*other* PA-2
**Radnor Woods**—*pop pl* DE-2
Radnor Yards—*locale* TN-4
Rado Cem—*cemetery* OH-6
*Radokala Islands* MP-9
**Radom**—*pop pl* IL-6
Radomer Cem—*cemetery* MI-6
Rado Post Office (historical)—*building* TN-4
*Radoriku* MP-9
Rador Springs—*spring* WY-8
Radosevich Ranch—*locale* NM-5
Radovan Gulch—*valley* AK-9
Radovan Prospect—*mine* AK-9
Rad Plzen cis. 9 Z.C.B.J. (SD10-6)—*hist pl* NE-7
Radrick Golf Course—*other* MI-6
Rad Sladkovsky—*hist pl* NE-7
Radson (historical)—*locale* AL-4
Radspur—*locale* WI-6
Radum—*locale* CA-9
Rad Ware Sch—*school* TX-5
Rad Water—*well* AZ-5
**Radwin**—*pop pl* CA-9
Rae, Mount—*summit* MT-8
Raeber Ranch—*locale* WY-8
Raeburn Windmill—*locale* NM-5
Raeco—*locale* WA-9
Rae Creek—*stream* ID-8
Rae Creek—*stream* NE-7
*Raeda* MH-9
Raeder Creek—*stream* WI-6
*Rae Farm Hill* MA-1
**Raeford**—*pop pl* NC-3
Raeford Municipal Airp—*airport* NC-3
Raeford Rhyne Airpark—*airport* NC-3
Raeford Road Shop Ctr—*locale* NC-3
Raeford (Township of)—*fmr MCD* NC-3
*Raej Island* MP-9
Raek—*bay* FM-9
*Rael* PW-9
*Rae Lake* CA-9
Rae Lake—*lake* CA-9
Rae Lakes—*lake* CA-9
Rael Cem—*cemetery* NM-5
Rael Dil—*cape* PW-9
Rael Edeng—*channel* PW-9
*Rael Eding* PW-9
Rael Kedam—*ridge* PW-9
Raelkelat—*bar* PW-9
Rael Orak—*channel* PW-9
Raemer Creek—*stream* KS-7
**Raemon**—*pop pl* NC-3
Raeng—*locale* FM-9
Rae Number 2 Dam—*dam* SD-7
Rae Number 3 Dam—*dam* SD-7
Raes Creek—*stream* GA-3
Raese Cem—*cemetery* WI-6
*Raether Creek* WI-6
*Rae-to* MP-9
Raetz Cem—*cemetery* IA-7
**Raeville**—*pop pl* NE-7
Rae-Wallace Mine—*mine* AK-9
*Rafael* CA-9
**Rafael Arroyo**—*pop pl* PR-3
Rafael Canyon—*valley* NM-5
**Rafael Capo**—*pop pl* PR-3
Rafael Creek—*stream* CA-9
Rafael Creek—*stream* NM-5
Rafael Creek—*stream* TX-5
Rafael Draw—*valley* AZ-5
Rafael Gonzalez—*CDP* PR-3
Rafael Hernandez—*CDP* PR-3
Rafaelito Creek—*stream* NM-5
*Rafael Knob* UT-8
Rafael M. Labra HS—*hist pl* PR-3
Rafael Spring—*spring* NM-5
Rafael Tank—*reservoir* AZ-5
**Rafael Village**—*pop pl* CA-9
Rafe Bay—*swamp* NC-3
Rafe Lake—*lake* TX-5
Rafe Pond—*lake* MA-1
Rafe Run—*stream* WV-2
Rafes Chasm—*valley* MA-1
Rafes Hill—*summit* AR-4
Rafe Swamp—*stream* VA-3
**Rafetown**—*pop pl* IL-6
Raff Creek—*stream* CA-9
Raff Creek—*stream* NC-3
Raffelson Coulee—*valley* WI-6
Rafferty, The—*basin* OR-9
Rafferty Cem—*cemetery* KY-4
*Rafferty Cemetery* OR-9
Rafferty Corners—*locale* NY-2
Rafferty Cove—*valley* VA-3
Rafferty Creek—*stream* CA-9
Rafferty Creek—*stream* MN-6
Rafferty Creek—*stream* MT-8
Rafferty Field—*park* IA-7
Rafferty Peak—*summit* CA-9
Rafferty Ranch (historical)—*locale* SD-7
Raffetto—*locale* CA-9
Raffety Cem—*cemetery* KY-4
Raffety Cem—*cemetery* OR-9
Raffety Knob—*summit* VA-3
Raffety Ranch—*locale* MT-8
Raffia Shop Ctr—*locale* CT-1
Raffield Peninsula—*cape* FL-3
Raffing Creek—*bay* NC-3
Raff Lake—*lake* MN-6
Rafinesque, Mount—*summit* NY-2
Rafn—*locale* MS-4
Rafsnyder-Welsh House—*hist pl* PA-2
*Raft Bayou* AR-4
Raft Bayou—*stream* AR-4
Raft Bayou—*stream* LA-4
Raft Channel—*channel* MN-6
Raft Cove—*bay* ME-1
Raft Creek—*stream* AK-9
Raft Creek—*stream* AR-4
Raft Creek—*stream* (2) ID-8
Raft Creek—*stream* KY-4
Raft Creek—*stream* WY-8
Rafter—*locale* TN-4
*Rafter Gulch* CA-9
Rafter Hollow—*valley* TX-5
Rafter M Bar Tank—*reservoir* AZ-5
Rafter Post Office (historical)—*building* TN-4
Rafter Ranch—*locale* OR-9
Rafter Run—*stream* WV-2
Rafters—*post sta* FL-3
Rafters, The—*locale* FL-3
Rafter Sch (historical)—*school* TN-4
Rafter Six Ranch—*locale* WY-8
Rafters Park—*park* KS-7
Rafter Tank—*reservoir* AZ-5
Raftery, William, Homestead—*hist pl* MT-8
Raft Hollow—*valley* TN-4
*Rafting Creek* SC-3
Rafting Creek—*stream* SC-3
Rafting Creek Ch—*church* SC-3
Rafting Creek Sch—*school* SC-3
Raft Island—*island* WA-9
*Raft Lake* MI-6
Raft Lake—*lake* FL-3
Raft Lake—*lake* ID-8
Raft Lake—*lake* MN-6
Raft Lake—*lake* OR-9
Raft Lake—*lake* (2) UT-8
Raft Lake—*lake* WY-8
Rafton—*locale* OR-9
**Raft River**—*pop pl* ID-8
Raft River—*stream* AL-4
Raft River—*stream* ID-8
Raft River—*stream* UT-8
Raft River—*stream* WA-9
Raft River HS—*school* ID-8
*Raft River Mountains* UT-8
Raft River Mtns—*range* UT-8
Raft River Valley—*valley* ID-8
Raft River Valley—*valley* UT-8
*Raft Rock* WA-9
Raft Rsvr—*reservoir* ID-8
Raft Slough—*stream* AR-4
Raft Swamp—*stream* NC-3
Raft Swamp—*swamp* SC-3
Raft Swamp Ch—*church* NC-3
Raft Swamp (Township of)—*fmr MCD* NC-3
*Ragaen* MP-9
*Ragalin Slough* MO-7
**Ragan**—*pop pl* AR-4
**Ragan**—*pop pl* NE-7
**Ragan**—*pop pl* NC-3
**Ragan**—*pop pl* WY-8
Ragan Branch—*stream* (2) MO-7
Ragan Cem—*cemetery* (2) TN-4
*Ragan Cemetery* MS-4
Ragan Ch—*church* NC-3
**Ragan Chapel**—*pop pl* AL-4
Ragan Chapel Cem—*cemetery* AL-4
*Ragan Chapel United Methodist Church* AL-4
Ragan Creek—*stream* LA-4
Ragan Creek—*stream* NV-8
Ragan Creek—*stream* TX-5
Ragan Draw—*valley* WY-8
Ragan Hollow—*valley* MO-7
*Ragan Lake* CO-8
*Ragan Meadow Ranger Station* CA-9
*Ragans* AL-4
*Ragans Chapel* AL-4
Ragans Chapel CME Ch (historical)—*church* AL-4
Ragan Sch (historical)—*school* TN-4
*Ragans Junction* AL-4
*Ragans Lake* CO-8
Ragan Spring—*spring* MO-7
*Ragan Spur* AR-4
*Ragantown* AL-4
Ragan Way Trail—*trail* WA-9
Rag Branch—*stream* KY-4
Ragby—*locale* CA-9
Ragby Branch—*stream* VA-3
Rag Canyon—*valley* AZ-5
Rag Canyon—*valley* TX-5
Rag Canyon—*valley* WA-9
Rag Creek—*stream* NC-3
Ragdale—*hist pl* IL-6
Rag Dump—*locale* CA-9
R A Gebracht Dam—*dam* SD-7
Rage Hill—*summit* VT-1
*Ragejiaku-Kaikyo* MP-9
Ragen Cem—*cemetery* KY-4
Rager Creek—*stream* IN-6
Rager Creek—*stream* OR-9
Rager Mtn—*summit* PA-2
Rager Rsvr—*reservoir* CA-9
Rager Summit—*locale* PA-2
*Ragers Unit* CO-8
**Ragersville**—*pop pl* OH-6
*Rageziaku Kaikyo* MP-9
Ragford Sch (historical)—*school* MS-4
*Raggain-to* MP-9
*Ragged Ass* CA-9
Ragged Brook—*stream* (2) ME-1
Ragged Brook—*stream* NY-2
Ragged Butte—*summit* ND-7
Ragged Butte—*summit* OR-9
Ragged Butte—*summit* WA-9
Ragged Butte School (Abandoned)—*locale* WA-9
Ragged Cove—*bay* AK-9
*Ragged Creek* CT-1
Ragged Creek—*stream* OR-9
Ragged Falls—*falls* WY-8
Ragged Gulch—*stream* OR-9
Ragged Gulch—*valley* CA-9
Ragged Hill—*summit* CT-1
Ragged Hill—*summit* (2) MA-1
Ragged Hill—*summit* VT-1
Ragged Hill Brook—*stream* CT-1
Ragged Hills—*summit* MI-6
Ragged Island—*island* AK-9
Ragged Island—*island* DE-2
Ragged Island—*island* FL-3
Ragged Island—*island* (2) ME-1
Ragged Island—*island* MD-2
Ragged Island—*island* MA-1

Rainbow Lake—*reservoir* PA-2
Rainbow Lake Campground—*park* AZ-5
Rainbow Lake Dam—*dam* IN-6
Rainbow Lake Dam—*dam* NJ-2
Rainbow Lake Pass—*gap* MT-8
Rainbow Lakes—*lake* CA-9
Rainbow Lakes—*lake* CO-8
Rainbow Lakes—*lake* ID-8
Rainbow Lakes—*lake* (2) MT-8
Rainbow Lakes—*lake* NJ-2
**Rainbow Lakes**—*pop pl* NJ-2
Rainbow Lakes—*reservoir* OH-6
**Rainbow Lakes Estates (subdivision)**—*pop pl* FL-3
**Rainbow Lakes (Rainbow Lakes Estates)**—*pop pl* FL-3
Rainbow Lake Trail—*trail* CO-8
Rainbow Lake Trail—*trail* WA-9
Rainbow Land Mine—*mine* CA-9
Rainbow Lodge—*locale* AZ-5
Rainbow Lodge—*locale* OR-9
Rainbow Lodge Site Trailhead to Rainbow Bridge—*locale* UT-8
Rainbow Lodge Spring—*spring* AZ-5
Rainbow Marina and Resort—*locale* TN-4
Rainbow Memorial Gardens—*cemetery* AL-4
Rainbow Mine—*mine* (2) AZ-5
Rainbow Mine—*mine* (3) CA-9
Rainbow Mine—*mine* CO-8
Rainbow Mine—*mine* NM-5
Rainbow Mine—*mine* (2) OR-9
Rainbow Mine—*mine* UT-8
Rainbow Mine—*mine* WA-9
Rainbow Mine—*mine* WY-8
Rainbow Mines—*locale* AZ-5
Rainbow Mines—*mine* TN-4
Rainbow Mines—*mine* UT-8
Rainbow Mountain—*ridge* NV-8
**Rainbow Mountain Heights**—*pop pl* AL-4
Rainbow MS—*school* AL-4
Rainbow Mtn—*summit* AL-4
Rainbow Mtn—*summit* AK-9
Rainbow Mtn—*summit* (2) CA-9
Rainbow Mtn—*summit* ME-1
Rainbow Mtn—*summit* MT-8
Rainbow Mtn—*summit* (2) NV-8
Rainbow Mtn—*summit* NC-3
Rainbow Mtn—*summit* TN-4
Rainbow Mtn—*summit* WA-9
Rainbow Narrows—*channel* NY-2
*Rainbow Natural Bridge* UT-8
Rainbow Number Four Mine—*mine* SD-7
Rainbow Park—*flat* UT-8
Rainbow Park—*park* IL-6
Rainbow Park—*park* (2) WI-6
Rainbow Park Campground—*park* UT-8
Rainbow Park Sch—*school* FL-3
Rainbow Peak—*summit* CA-9
Rainbow Peak—*summit* ID-8
Rainbow Peak—*summit* MT-8
Rainbow Plantation—*locale* MS-4
Rainbow Plateau—*plain* (2) AZ-5
Rainbow Plateau—*plateau* UT-8
Rainbow Plaza Shop Ctr—*locale* AL-4
*Rainbow Point* FL-3
Rainbow Point—*cape* (3) CA-9
Rainbow Point—*cape* MI-6
Rainbow Point—*cape* MT-8
Rainbow Point—*cape* OR-9
Rainbow Point—*cape* TX-5
Rainbow Point—*cape* UT-8
Rainbow Point Campground—*locale* WA-9
Rainbow Point Viewing Area—*locale* UT-8
Rainbow Pond—*lake* ME-1
Rainbow Pond—*lake* MA-1
Rainbow Pond—*lake* MO-7
Rainbow Pond—*lake* WV-2
Rainbow Pond—*reservoir* (2) NC-3
Rainbow Pond Dam—*dam* (2) NC-3
Rainbow Post Office (historical)—*building* AL-4
Rainbow Presbyterian Ch—*church* AL-4
Rainbow Quarries—*mine* NV-8
Rainbow Quarry—*mine* (2) OR-9
Rainbow (Rainbow Valley)—*CDP* CA-9
*Rainbow Ranch* NC-3
Rainbow Ranch—*locale* (2) CA-9
Rainbow Ranch—*locale* FL-3
Rainbow Ranch—*locale* MT-8
Rainbow Ranch—*locale* ND-7
Rainbow Ranch—*locale* SD-7
Rainbow Ranch—*locale* TX-5
Rainbow Ranch—*locale* WY-8
Rainbow Rancho Fish Hatchery—*other* CO-8
Rainbow Rapids—*falls* WI-6
*Rainbow Reservoir* WI-6
*Rainbow Ridge* ID-8
*Rainbow Ridge* IN-6
Rainbow Ridge—*ridge* AL-4
Rainbow Ridge—*ridge* AK-9
Rainbow Ridge—*ridge* (3) CA-9
Rainbow Ridge—*ridge* (2) ID-8
Rainbow Ridge—*ridge* OH-6
Rainbow Ridge—*ridge* TN-4
Rainbow Ridge—*ridge* TX-5
Rainbow Ridge—*ridge* WA-9
Rainbow Ridge Mine—*mine* NV-8
Rainbow River—*stream* AK-9
Rainbow Rock—*pillar* CA-9
Rainbow Rock—*summit* OR-9
Rainbow Rock Knob—*summit* KY-4
Rainbow Rock (Natural Arch)—*arch* ID-8
Rainbow Rsvrs—*reservoir* OR-9
Rainbow Run—*stream* OH-6
Rainbow Run—*stream* WV-2
Rainbow Run Trout Farm—*locale* CO-8
Rainbow Saddle—*gap* ID-8
Rainbow Sch—*school* IA-7
Rainbow Sch—*school* PA-2
Rainbow Sch—*school* SD-7
Rainbow Sch (historical)—*school* TN-4
Rainbow Shop Ctr—*locale* MS-4
Rainbow Shores—*locale* NY-2
Rainbow Slough—*gut* CA-9
Rainbow Slough—*lake* MO-7
*Rainbow Spring* NV-8
Rainbow Spring—*locale* CA-9
Rainbow Spring—*spring* (2) AZ-5
Rainbow Spring—*spring* CA-9
Rainbow Spring—*spring* ID-8
Rainbow Spring—*spring* MO-7
Rainbow Spring—*spring* NV-8
Rainbow Spring—*spring* NM-5
Rainbow Spring—*spring* OR-9
Rainbow Spring—*spring* TN-4
Rainbow Spring—*spring* WA-9
Rainbow Spring—*spring* WI-6
Rainbow Springs—*locale* NC-3
Rainbow Springs—*spring* FL-3
Rainbow Springs—*spring* NV-8
Rainbow Springs—*spring* OR-9
Rainbow Springs—*spring* WI-6
Rainbow Springs (hot)—*spring* WY-8
Rainbow Springs Lake—*lake* WI-6
*Rainbow Stream* HI-9
Rainbow Stream—*stream* ME-1
Rainbow Tabernacle—*church* AR-4
Rainbow Tabernacle Pentecostal Holiness Ch—*church* KS-7
Rainbow Tank—*reservoir* (2) AZ-5
Rainbow Terraces—*lake* WY-8
Rainbow Thorofare—*channel* NJ-2
**Rainbow Township**—*pop pl* ND-7
**Rainbow Township**—*pop pl* SD-7
Rainbow (Township of)—*unorg* ME-1
Rainbow Trail—*trail* (3) CO-8
Rainbow Trail—*trail* NH-1
Rainbow Trail—*trail* (2) PA-2
Rainbow Trail Camp—*locale* CO-8
Rainbow Trough Spring—*spring* OR-9
Rainbow Trout Lodge—*locale* CO-8
*Rainbow Valley* AZ-5
*Rainbow Valley* CA-9
*Rainbow Valley* UT-8
**Rainbow Valley**—*pop pl* AZ-5
**Rainbow Valley**—*pop pl* CO-8
Rainbow Valley—*valley* AZ-5
Rainbow Valley—*valley* CA-9
Rainbow Valley—*valley* WI-6
Rainbow Valley Ch—*church* ND-7
*Rainbow Valley Lake* NJ-2
Rainbow Valley Substation—*locale* AZ-5
Rainbow View—*locale* CA-9
Rainbow Village Park—*park* FL-3
Rainbow Wash—*stream* AZ-5
Rainbow Wash—*stream* CA-9
Rainbow Wash—*stream* NM-5
Rainbow Well—*well* AZ-5
Rainbow Well—*well* CA-9
Rainbow Well—*well* NM-5
Rainbow Wells—*locale* CA-9
Rainbow Windmill—*locale* NM-5
Rainbow Windmill—*locale* TX-5
Rain Canyon—*valley* UT-8
Rain Cem—*cemetery* AR-4
Rain Cem—*cemetery* FL-3
Rain Cloud Lake—*reservoir* MS-4
*Rain Creek* MT-8
*Rain Creek* TN-4
Rain Creek—*stream* IN-6
Rain Creek—*stream* MT-8
Rain Creek—*stream* NV-8
Rain Creek—*stream* NM-5
Rain Creek—*stream* OK-5
Rain Creek—*stream* WA-9
Rain Creek Divide Trail (Pack)—*trail* NM-5
Rain Creek Mesa—*bench* NM-5
Raine, John, House—*hist pl* KY-4
**Rainelle**—*pop pl* WV-2
**Rainelle Junction**—*pop pl* WV-2
Raine Ranch—*locale* NV-8
Raine Ranch—*locale* WA-9
Rainer Branch—*stream* MO-7
Rainer Brook—*stream* NY-2
Rainer Pond—*lake* NY-2
Rainer Sch (historical)—*school* AL-4
Rainers Gin (historical)—*locale* AL-4
Rainers Store (historical)—*locale* AL-4
Raines—*locale* GA-3
**Raines**—*pop pl* TN-4
Raines, William G., House—*hist pl* GA-3
Raines Branch—*stream* GA-3
*Rainesburg* PA-2
Raines-Carmichael House—*hist pl* GA-3
Raines Cem—*cemetery* MO-7
Raines Cem—*cemetery* (2) TN-4
Raines Corner—*locale* VA-3
Raines Corner—*locale* WV-2
**Raines Corner**—*pop pl* NJ-2
Raines Creek—*stream* ID-8
Raines Creek—*stream* VA-3
*Raines Crossroads* NC-3
*Raines Elementary School* MS-4
Raines-Finley Park—*park* TN-4
Raines Fork—*stream* WV-2
Raineshaven Sch—*school* TN-4
Raines Hollow—*valley* TN-4
Raines Knob—*summit* TN-4
Raines Lake—*lake* TX-5
Raines Lumber Airp—*airport* AL-4
*Raines Ridge* TN-4
Raines Ridge—*ridge* WV-2
Raines Sch—*school* MS-4
Raines Sch—*school* VA-3
**Raines Tavern**—*pop pl* VA-3
Rainey—*locale* MS-4
Rainey, Henry T., Farm—*hist pl* IL-6
Rainey, Joseph H., House—*hist pl* SC-3
Rainey, Matthew, House—*hist pl* AR-4
Rainey Bend—*bend* AR-4
Rainey Branch—*stream* MS-4
Rainey Branch—*stream* SC-3
Rainey Brook—*stream* (2) ME-1
Rainey Cave—*cave* AL-4
Rainey Cem—*cemetery* AL-4
Rainey Cem—*cemetery* AR-4
Rainey Cem—*cemetery* GA-3
Rainey Cem—*cemetery* KY-4
Rainey Cem—*cemetery* (2) MS-4
Rainey Cem—*cemetery* OK-5
Rainey Cem—*cemetery* (2) TN-4
*Rainey Chapel* MS-4
*Rainey Church* AL-4
Rainey Creek—*stream* (2) ID-8
Rainey Creek—*stream* (2) TX-5
Rainey Creek—*stream* VA-3
Rainey Creek—*stream* (2) WA-9
*Rainey Cut* VA-3
Rainey Field (airport)—*airport* AL-4
Rainey Glades—*flat* CA-9
Rainey Gulch—*valley* CA-9
Rainey Gut—*gut* VA-3
Rainey Hollow—*valley* KY-4
Rainey Hollow—*valley* (3) TN-4
Rainey House—*hist pl* TN-4
**Rainey Junction**—*pop pl* PA-2
*Rainey Lake* WY-8
Rainey Lake—*lake* WY-8
Rainey Lake—*reservoir* GA-3
Rainey Lake—*reservoir* MS-4
Rainey Memorial Gates—*hist pl* NY-2
Rainey Mine (surface)—*mine* TN-4
Rainey Mtn—*summit* GA-3
Rainey Park—*park* ID-8
Rainey Park—*park* IL-6
Rainey Park—*park* NY-2
Rainey Point—*cape* VA-3
Rainey Point—*summit* ID-8
Rainey Pond—*reservoir* NC-3
Rainey Pond—*reservoir* VA-3
Rainey Ridge—*ridge* TN-4
Rainey Rsvr—*reservoir* MT-8
Rainey's Cabin—*hist pl* AK-9
Rainey Sch—*school* MI-6
Rainey Sch—*school* MS-4
Raineys Chapel—*church* TX-5
*Raineys Gut* VA-3
*Raineys Lake* GA-3
Raineys Lake—*lake* MS-4
Raineys Lake—*reservoir* FL-3
Rainey Slough—*stream* FL-3
Rainey Spring—*spring* TN-4
Rainey Spring—*spring* WA-9
Rainey Street Hist Dist—*hist pl* TX-5
**Raineytown**—*pop pl* PA-2
Rainey Valley—*valley* WA-9
Rainey Valley—*valley* WI-6
Rainey Well—*well* CA-9
**Rain Forest (subdivision)**—*pop pl* NC-3
Rain God Mesa—*summit* AZ-5
Rain Gulch—*valley* AK-9
Rain Hill Ch—*church* NC-3
Rainie Falls—*falls* OR-9
**Rainier**—*pop pl* OR-9
**Rainier**—*pop pl* WA-9
Rainier, Mount—*summit* WA-9
Rainier Bar—*bar* WA-9
**Rainier Beach**—*pop pl* WA-9
Rainier Brewing Company Bottling Plant—*hist pl* NV-8
Rainier (CCD)—*cens area* OR-9
Rainier Cem—*cemetery* WA-9
Rainier Club—*hist pl* WA-9
Rainier Creek—*stream* CA-9
Rainier Creek—*stream* ID-8
Rainier Elem Sch—*school* OR-9
Rainier Fork American River—*stream* WA-9
Rainier Golf Club—*other* WA-9
Rainier Island—*island* AK-9
Rainier Mesa—*summit* NV-8
Rainier Mtn—*summit* NV-8
Rainier Rapids—*rapids* ID-8
Rainier Rsvr—*reservoir* OR-9
Rainier Sch—*school* WA-9
Rainier Spring—*spring* OR-9
Rainier State Sch—*school* WA-9
**Rainier Valley**—*pop pl* WA-9
Rainie Willis Cave—*cave* AL-4
*Rain Island* ME-1
Rain Lake—*lake* UT-8
Rain Lakes—*lake* (2) UT-8
Rain Mtn—*summit* AZ-5
Rain Place—*locale* NM-5
Rain Point—*cape* TX-5
Rain Pot Cave—*cave* AL-4
Rain Rock—*locale* OH-6
Rainrock—*locale* OR-9
Rain Rock (Indian Ceremonial Site), The—*other* CA-9
Rain Run—*stream* IN-6
Rains—*locale* UT-8
**Rains**—*pop pl* SC-3
Rains, John, House—*hist pl* CA-9
Rains, John P., Hotel—*hist pl* TN-4
*Rainsares Mountain* PA-2
**Rainsboro**—*pop pl* OH-6
Rains Bottom—*bend* TN-4
Rains Branch—*stream* GA-3
Rains Branch—*stream* TN-4
Rains Branch—*stream* TX-5
**Rainsburg**—*pop pl* PA-2
Rainsburg Borough—*civil* PA-2
Rainsburg Gap—*gap* PA-2
Rains Canyon—*valley* OR-9
Rains Canyon—*valley* UT-8
Rains Cem—*cemetery* KY-4
Rains Cem—*cemetery* (3) TN-4
**Rains (County)**—*pop pl* TX-5
Rains Creek—*stream* AL-4
Rains Creek—*stream* TN-4
Rains-Creely Family Cem—*cemetery* MS-4
**Rains Crossroads**—*pop pl* NC-3
Rainsford Hist Dist—*hist pl* WY-8
Rainsford Island—*island* MA-1
Rainsford Pond—*reservoir* SC-3
Rains Grove Cem—*cemetery* TN-4
Rains Gulf—*valley* TN-4
Rains (historical)—*locale* AL-4
Rains Hollow—*valley* TN-4
Rains HS—*school* TX-5
Rains Island—*island* MI-6
**Rains Landing**—*pop pl* GA-3
Rains Pit—*cave* TN-4
Rain Spring Draw—*valley* NM-5
Rain Spring Ranch—*locale* NM-5
Rains Ridge—*ridge* TN-4
*Rains School* AL-4
Rains School, The—*school* NH-1
Rains Springs—*spring* NV-8
Rains Store (historical)—*locale* TN-4
Rainstorm Canyon—*valley* NM-5
*Rainstorm Station* IN-6
**Rainstown**—*pop pl* IN-6
**Rainsville**—*pop pl* AL-4
**Rainsville**—*pop pl* IN-6
**Rainsville**—*pop pl* NM-5
Rainsville Cem—*cemetery* IN-6
Rainsville Civic Center—*building* AL-4
*Rainsville High School* AL-4
Rainsville-Sylvania (CCD)—*cens area* AL-4
Rainsville-Sylvania Division—*civil* AL-4
Rainswood—*locale* VA-3
Rain Tank—*reservoir* AZ-5
Rain Tank Flat—*flat* AZ-5
Rain Tank Wash—*stream* AZ-5
**Raintown**—*pop pl* IN-6
**Raintown**—*pop pl* WV-2
**Raintree Country (subdivision)**—*pop pl* AL-4
**Raintree East Subdivision**—*pop pl* UT-8
**Raintree Equestrian Community Condo**—*pop pl* UT-8
**Raintree Estates (subdivision)**—*pop pl* NC-3
**Raintree Estates (subdivision)**—*pop pl* TN-4
**Raintree Forest**—*pop pl* TN-4
**Raintree Luxury Homes (subdivision)**—*pop pl* (2) AZ-5
**Raintree Place (subdivision)**—*pop pl* MS-4
**Raintree (subdivision)**—*pop pl* (2) AZ-5
**Raintree (subdivision)**—*pop pl* (2) NC-3
**Raintree Subdivision**—*pop pl* UT-8
**Raintree Village (subdivision)**—*pop pl* DE-2
**Raintree Village Subdivision**—*pop pl* UT-8
Rain Valley—*valley* AZ-5
Rain Valley—*valley* TX-5
Rain Valley Ranch—*locale* AZ-5
Rainville Ranch—*locale* AZ-5
Rainville Wash—*stream* AZ-5
*Rain Water Bar* AL-4
Rainwater Bar—*bar* AL-4
Rainwater Branch—*stream* KY-4
Rainwater Cem—*cemetery* AL-4
Rainwater Cem—*cemetery* TN-4
Rainwater Coulee—*valley* MT-8
Rainwater Creek—*stream* TX-5
Rainwater (historical)—*locale* AL-4
Rainwater Hollow—*valley* MO-7
Rainwater Knob—*summit* KY-4
Rainwater Lake—*reservoir* AR-4
Rainwater Lake—*reservoir* GA-3
Rainwater Sch (historical)—*school* TN-4
Rainwater Spring—*spring* WY-8
Rainwater Tank—*reservoir* NM-5
Rainwater Windmill—*locale* NM-5
**Rainy Beach**—*pop pl* MI-6
*Rainy Butte* ND-7
Rainy Butte—*summit* ND-7
Rainy Butte Cem—*cemetery* ND-7
Rainy Butte Ch—*church* ND-7
**Rainy Butte Township**—*pop pl* ND-7
Rainy Camp—*locale* WA-9
*Rainy Camp Branch* TN-4
*Rainy Creek* ID-8
*Rainy Creek* MI-6
*Rainy Creek* WA-9
Rainy Creek—*stream* (4) AK-9
Rainy Creek—*stream* AR-4
Rainy Creek—*stream* GA-3
Rainy Creek—*stream* ID-8
Rainy Creek—*stream* MO-7
Rainy Creek—*stream* (2) MT-8
Rainy Creek—*stream* (2) OR-9
Rainy Creek—*stream* SD-7
Rainy Creek—*stream* TX-5
Rainy Creek—*stream* (5) WA-9
Rainy Creek Mtn—*summit* AR-4
Rainy Creek No. 19 Township—*civ div* SD-7
Rainy Creek Township—*civil* SD-7
Rainy Day Creek—*stream* ID-8
Rainy Day Mine—*mine* CA-9
Rainy Day Point—*summit* ID-8
Rainy Gap—*gap* GA-3
Rainy Glacier—*glacier* AK-9
Rainy Gulch—*valley* WA-9
Rainy Hill Guard Station—*locale* ID-8
**Rainy (historical)**—*pop pl* TN-4
*Rainy Junction* MN-6
Rainy Junction—*locale* MN-6
Rainy Knob—*summit* TN-4
Rainy Knobs—*summit* NC-3
*Rainy Lake* MN-6
Rainy Lake—*lake* CA-9
Rainy Lake—*lake* (2) MI-6
Rainy Lake—*lake* (3) MN-6
Rainy Lake—*lake* MT-8
Rainy Lake—*lake* NM-5
Rainy Lake—*lake* OR-9
Rainy Lake—*lake* (2) WA-9
Rainy Lake—*lake* WI-6
Rainy Lake—*lake* (2) WY-8
*Rainy Lake Campground* OR-9
Rainy Lake Campground—*locale* MT-8
Rainy Lake Recreation Site—*park* OR-9
Rainy Lake (Unorganized Territory of)—*unorg* MN-6
Rainy Mesa—*summit* NM-5
Rainy Mesa Camp—*locale* NM-5
Rainy Mesa Canyon—*valley* NM-5
*Rainy Mountain* MT-8
Rainy Mountain Camp—*locale* GA-3
Rainy Mountain Ch—*church* OK-5
Rainy Mountain Creek—*stream* OK-5
Rainy Mountain Indian Mission—*church* OK-5
Rainy Mountain Indian School Reservation—*reserve* OK-5
Rainy Mtn—*summit* AK-9
Rainy Mtn—*summit* AR-4
Rainy Mtn—*summit* GA-3
Rainy Pass—*gap* AK-9
Rainy Pass—*gap* WA-9
Rainy Pass Lake—*lake* AK-9
Rainy Pass Lodge—*locale* AK-9
Rainy Peak—*summit* OR-9
Rainy Point—*cape* VA-3
Rainy Post Office (historical)—*building* TN-4
Rainy Ridge—*ridge* GA-3
Rainy Ridge—*ridge* OH-6
Rainy Ridge—*ridge* WA-9
Rainy River—*stream* MI-6
Rainy River—*stream* MN-6
Rainy River Dam—*dam* MI-6
Rainy River State Junior Coll—*school* MN-6
Rainy River (Unorganized Territory of)—*unorg* MN-6
Rainy Spring—*spring* AZ-5
*Rainy Valley* WA-9
Rainy Valley—*valley* CA-9
Rainy Valley Creek—*stream* CA-9
Rairden—*locale* WY-8
Rairden Bridge—*hist pl* WY-8
Rairden Gulch—*valley* CA-9
Rairigh Run—*stream* PA-2
Rairik—*island* MP-9
*Rairikku Island* MP-9
*Rairikku-To* MP-9
*Rairok* MP-9
Raise Branch—*stream* KY-4
Raised Spring—*spring* NV-8
**Raish**—*pop pl* WA-9
Raish Dam—*dam* SD-7
Raisin—*locale* TX-5
Raisin, River—*stream* MI-6
Raisin Center—*locale* MI-6
Raisin Center Ch—*church* MI-6
Raisin City Gun Club—*other* CA-9
*Raisin City Oil Field* CA-9
**Raisin City (Raisin Post Office)**—*pop pl* CA-9
*Raisin Creek* MI-6
**Raisin (Raisin City)**—*pop pl* CA-9
*Raisin River* MI-6
Raisin Rock—*island* NC-3
**Raisin (Township of)**—*pop pl* MI-6
Raisin Valley Friends Meetinghouse—*hist pl* MI-6
**Raisinville (P.O.) (Monroe County Community College)**—*61pop pl* MI-6
Raisinville Sch—*school* MI-6
**Raisinville (Township of)**—*pop pl* MI-6
Raisio Creek—*stream* WA-9
*Raison River* MI-6
**Raitt**—*pop pl* VA-3
Raitt Draw—*valley* WY-8
Raitt Hill—*summit* ME-1
Raitt Tunnel—*tunnel* VA-3
Ra Jadero Canyon—*valley* CO-8
Rajah Mine—*mine* CO-8
Rajah Mine (underground)—*mine* AL-4
Rajek Creek—*stream* WI-6
*Rajik Chain* MP-9
*Rajneesh* (2) OR-9
*Rajneeshpuram* OR-9
**Rajneeshpuram**—*pop pl* OR-9
*Ra Jodero Canyon* CO-8
**R A Junction**—*pop pl* OH-6
Rakaaru—*island* MP-9
*Rakaaru-To* MP-9
*Rakahak* NC-3
*Rakaru* MP-9
*Rakaru-to* MP-9
**Rake**—*pop pl* IA-7
Rake Branch—*stream* VT-1
Rake Cem—*cemetery* OH-6
Rake Creek—*stream* FL-3
Rake Creek—*stream* SD-7
Rake Factory Brook—*stream* RI-1
Rake Factory Brook—*stream* VT-1
Rake Pond—*lake* PA-2
*Raker* PA-2
Raker—*other* PA-2
Raker and Thomas Reservoirs—*reservoir* CA-9
Raker Ch—*church* OH-6
Raker Creek—*stream* NV-8
Raker Peak—*summit* CA-9
Raker Point—*summit* OR-9
*Raker Reservoir And Thomas Reservoir* CA-9
Rakes Branch—*stream* KY-4
Rakes Cem—*cemetery* VA-3
Rakes Cem—*cemetery* WV-2
Rakes Creek—*stream* NE-7
Rakes Dam—*dam* PA-2
Rakeshill Sch—*school* KY-4
Rake Shin Bay—*swamp* NC-3
Rakes Knob—*summit* VA-3
Rakes Meadow—*swamp* OR-9
Rakes Millpond—*reservoir* VA-3
Rakes Ridge—*ridge* VA-3
Rakestraw Cem—*cemetery* GA-3
Rakestraw Cemeterys—*cemetery* GA-3
Rakestraw Creek—*stream* GA-3
Rakestraw Ditch—*canal* OH-6
Rakestraw Hollow—*valley* PA-2
Rakestraw House—*hist pl* IN-6
Rakestraw Mtn—*summit* MS-4
Raketail Brook—*stream* ME-1
Rake Tower—*tower* CA-9
**Raketown**—*pop pl* VA-3
**Rakeville**—*pop pl* MA-1
Rakijedr—*island* MP-9
Rakis, Dauen—*bay* FM-9
Rakksan Chapel—*church* NC-3
*Raknru* MP-9
Rakof Islands—*area* AK-9
Rakovoi Bay—*bay* AK-9
Rakuh—*unknown* FM-9
*Rakwis* NC-3
*Ralap* PW-9
**Ralate**—*pop pl* PR-3
**Ralco**—*pop pl* VA-3
*Raleigh* WV-2
Raleigh—*locale* AL-4
Raleigh—*locale* IA-7
Raleigh—*locale* KY-4
Raleigh—*locale* TX-5
**Raleigh**—*pop pl* FL-3
**Raleigh**—*pop pl* GA-3
**Raleigh**—*pop pl* IL-6
**Raleigh**—*pop pl* IN-6
**Raleigh**—*pop pl* MS-4
**Raleigh**—*pop pl* NC-3
**Raleigh**—*pop pl* ND-7
**Raleigh**—*pop pl* TN-4
**Raleigh**—*pop pl* WV-2
Raleigh, Lake—*lake* FL-3
Raleigh, Lake—*lake* NC-3
Raleigh, Lake—*reservoir* NC-3
Raleigh, Sir Walter, Hotel—*hist pl* NC-3
Raleigh Ave Baptist Ch—*church* AL-4
Raleigh Bay—*bay* NC-3
Raleigh Camp—*locale* TN-4
Raleigh (CCD)—*cens area* AL-4
Raleigh Cem—*cemetery* MS-4
Raleigh Cem—*cemetery* TN-4
Raleigh Ch—*church* GA-3
Raleigh Ch—*church* TN-4
*Raleigh Chapel* TN-4
Raleigh Country Club—*locale* NC-3
**Raleigh (County)**—*pop pl* WV-2
Raleigh County Memorial Airp—*airport* WV-2
Raleigh Court Park—*park* VA-3
Raleigh Court Sch—*school* VA-3
*Raleigh Creek* KY-4
*Raleigh Creek* NV-8
*Raleigh Creek* VA-3
Raleigh Creek—*stream* OR-9
Raleigh Creek Sch—*school* KY-4
Raleigh Crossroads Ch—*church* NC-3
Raleigh Dam—*dam* ND-7
Raleigh Division—*civil* AL-4
Raleigh-Durham Airp—*airport* NC-3
Raleigh Elem Sch—*school* MS-4
Raleigh Fork—*stream* KY-4
**Raleigh Heights**—*pop pl* NV-8
**Raleigh Heights (subdivision)**—*pop pl* VA-3
**Raleigh Hills**—*pop pl* OR-9
Raleigh Hills—*summit* OR-9
Raleigh Hills Sch—*school* OR-9
Raleigh HS—*school* MS-4
Raleigh Islands—*island* FL-3
*Raleigh JHS* MS-4
Raleigh Memorial Park—*cemetery* NC-3
*Raleigh Mound* OH-6
Raleigh Mound—*hist pl* OH-6
Raleigh Mtn—*summit* TN-4
Raleigh Municipal Lake—*reservoir* NC-3
Raleigh Municipal Lake Dam—*dam* NC-3
Raleigh Oil Field—*oilfield* MS-4
Raleigh Park Sch—*school* OR-9
Raleigh Peak—*summit* CO-8
*Raleigh Peaks* CO-8
**Raleigh Place**—*pop pl* VA-3
Raleigh Road Ch—*church* (2) NC-3
Raleigh Road Kindergarten—*school* NC-3
Raleigh Road Park—*park* NC-3
Raleigh Road Shop Ctr—*locale* NC-3
*Raleighs Bay* NC-3
Raleigh Tank—*reservoir* TX-5
**Raleigh Terrace**—*pop pl* VA-3
**Raleigh Township**—*pop pl* ND-7
Raleigh (Township of)—*fmr MCD* NC-3
**Raleigh (Township of)**—*pop pl* IL-6
Raleigh United Methodist Ch—*church* MS-4
Raleigh Water Tower—*hist pl* NC-3
Raleigh Well—*well* AZ-5
Raley Cem—*cemetery* AR-4
Raley Family Cem—*cemetery* AL-4
Raley Ford—*locale* KY-4
**Raley Forest Hill (subdivision)**—*pop pl* AL-4
Raley Millpond—*reservoir* SC-3
Raley Pond—*swamp* FL-3
*Ralic* MP-9
*Ralick Chain* MP-9
*Ralick Gruppe* MP-9
Ralik Chain—*island* MP-9
*Ralik-Kette* MP-9
*Ralik Rat* MP-9
Ralive Pen Windmill—*locale* TX-5
Raljon Lake—*reservoir* CA-9
Raljon Ranch—*locale* CA-9
*Rallap* PW-9
R Allen Ranch—*locale* ID-8
R Allgaier Dam—*dam* SD-7
Rall Gulch—*valley* OR-9
Rall Hollow—*valley* TN-4
Rall Mtn—*summit* GA-3
Rallo Cem—*cemetery* IL-6
**Ralls**—*pop pl* MO-7
**Ralls**—*pop pl* TX-5
Ralls, Joe, House—*hist pl* OK-5
Ralls (CCD)—*cens area* TX-5
Ralls Cem—*cemetery* (3) IL-6
Ralls Cem—*cemetery* (2) TN-4
**Ralls County**—*pop pl* MO-7
Ralls County Courthouse and Jail-Sheriff's House—*hist pl* MO-7
Ralls Creek—*stream* KS-7
Ralls Grove Ch—*church* IL-6
Ralls Junction—*locale* MO-7
Ralls Mines—*mine* MT-8
Ralls Ranch—*locale* TX-5
Rall Top—*summit* NC-3
Rally Hill—*hist pl* TN-4
Rally Hill—*locale* AR-4
**Rally Hill**—*pop pl* TN-4
Rally Lake—*lake* MN-6
**Ralmar Park**—*pop pl* NY-2
*Ralmke Pond* CA-9
R A Long HS—*school* WA-9
R A Long Square—*park* WA-9
*Ralph* DE-2
Ralph—*locale* KY-4
Ralph—*locale* MD-2
Ralph—*locale* OK-5
Ralph—*locale* SD-7
Ralph—*locale* WV-2
**Ralph**—*pop pl* AL-4
**Ralph**—*pop pl* AR-4
**Ralph**—*pop pl* CA-9
**Ralph**—*pop pl* MI-6
**Ralph**—*pop pl* PA-2
Ralph Adcock Bridge—*bridge* TN-4
Ralph and Martha Perry Memorial State Wildlife Area—*park* MO-7
Ralph Ave Ch—*church* KY-4
Ralph Branch—*stream* (2) WV-2
Ralph Bunche Sch—*school* MI-6
Ralph Bunche Sch—*school* TX-5
Ralph Cave—*cave* AL-4
Ralph Cem—*cemetery* MI-6
Ralph Cemeterys—*cemetery* KY-4
Ralph Chapel—*church* KY-4
Ralph Cole Cem—*cemetery* TN-4
*Ralph Creek* NV-8
Ralph Creek—*stream* MT-8
Ralph Creek—*stream* NY-2
Ralph Creek—*stream* OR-9
Ralph Dam—*dam* SD-7
Ralph Draw—*valley* SD-7
Ralph Fears Lake Dam—*dam* MS-4
Ralph Fire Lane—*locale* NV-8
Ralph Flowers Dam—*dam* NC-3
Ralph Flowers Lake—*reservoir* NC-3
Ralph Gulch—*valley* CO-8
Ralph Hamptom Dam—*dam* SD-7
Ralph Harris Pond Dam—*dam* MS-4
Ralph Hedman Dam—*dam* SD-7
Ralphine, Lake—*reservoir* CA-9
Ralph Ketchum Lake—*reservoir* IN-6

Rathbun Lake—reservoir IA-7
Rathbun Pond—lake NY-2
Rathbun Ranch—locale WY-8
Rathbun Reservoir IA-7
Rathbun Sch—school PA-2
Rathbun Sch—school WY-8
Rathbun Station—locale PA-2
Rathbunville Sch—school NY-2
Rathburn IA-7
Rathburn—uninc pl TN-4
Rathburn, Levi, House—hist pl OH-6
Rathburn Bridge—bridge PA-2
Rathburn Brook—stream MA-1
Rathburn Cem—cemetery MO-7
Rathburn Cem—cemetery NY-2
Rathburn Creek—stream IA-7
Rathburn Gulch—valley ID-8
Rathburn Lake—swamp MI-6
Rathburn Mine—mine CA-9
Rathburn Run—stream OH-6
Rathburn Sch—school MI-6
Rathburn Station—locale TN-4
Rath Camp—locale SC-3
Rath Creek—stream OR-9
**Rathdrum**—pop pl ID-8
Rathdrum Bald ID-8
Rathdrum Baldy ID-8
Rathdrum Creek—stream ID-8
Rathdrum Mtn—summit ID-8
Rathdrum Prairie—flat ID-8
Rathdrum State Bank—hist pl ID-8
Rather—locale TN-4
Rather, John Daniel, House—hist pl AL-4
Rather Cem—cemetery AL-4
Rather Cem—cemetery (2) TX-5
Rather Ford Bridge—bridge MS-4
Rather House—hist pl TX-5
Rather Sch—school MI-6
Rathgeber Ranch—locale TX-5
Rat Hill—summit CA-9
Rathje, H. A., Mill—hist pl IL-6
Rathje Park—park IL-6
Rath Lake—lake SD-7
Rathlatulik River—stream AK-9
**Rathmel**—pop pl PA-2
Rat Hole—cave AL-4
Rat Hole Canyon—valley CO-8
Rat Hole Canyon—valley UT-8
Rat Hole Cave—cave PA-2
Rathole Mtn—summit VA-3
Rat Hole Ridge—ridge CO-8
Rat Hole Ridge—ridge UT-8
Rat House Lake—lake MN-6
Rath Park—park NY-2
Ratibor—locale TX-5
Ratibor Branch—stream TX-5
Ratigan Lake—lake MI-6
Ratine Campground—locale MT-8
Ratine Creek—stream MT-8
**Ratio**—pop pl AR-4
Ratio Mtn—summit MT-8
Ration Creek CO-8
Rat Island ME-1
Rat Island FM-9
Rat Island—island (2) AK-9
Rat Island—island CT-1
Rat Island—island FL-3
Rat Island—island ID-8
Rat Island—island NY-2
Rat Island—island RI-1
Rat Island—island SC-3
Rat Island—island TN-4
Rat Island—island WA-9
Rat Island Creek—stream SC-3
Rat Island Pass—channel AK-9
Rat Island Pocket—bay TN-4
Rat Islands—island AK-9
Ratison TX-5
Rat Key—island FL-3
Rat Lake MI-6
Rat Lake MN-6
Rat Lake NE-7
Rat Lake WI-6
Rat Lake—lake (3) AK-9
Rat Lake—lake (2) MI-6
Rat Lake—lake (14) MN-6
Rat Lake—lake MT-8
Rat Lake—lake (5) NE-7
Rat Lake—lake (2) WA-9
Rat Lake—lake (3) WI-6
**Rat Lake Township**—pop pl ND-7
Ratler—locale TX-5
Ratler Cem—cemetery TX-5
Ratlief Cem—cemetery TN-4
Ratliff—locale FL-3
Ratliff—locale KY-4
**Ratliff**—pop pl KY-4
**Ratliff**—pop pl LA-4
**Ratliff**—pop pl (2) MS-4
Ratliff Branch—stream (2) KY-4
Ratliff Branch—stream TX-5
Ratliff Branch—stream VA-3
Ratliff Cem TN-4
Ratliff Cem—cemetery (2) AL-4
Ratliff Cem—cemetery AR-4
Ratliff Cem—cemetery (2) KY-4
Ratliff Cem—cemetery MS-4
Ratliff Cem—cemetery MO-7
Ratliff Cem—cemetery TX-5
Ratliff Cem—cemetery (3) VA-3
Ratliff Chapel—church MS-4
Ratliff Chapel (historical)—church MS-4
**Ratliff City**—pop pl OK-5
Ratliff Creek KY-4
Ratliff Creek—stream FL-3
Ratliff Creek—stream (2) KY-4
Ratliff Creek—stream (2) TX-5
Ratliffe Mine (underground)—mine AL-4
Ratliff Hollow—valley VA-3
Ratliff Island—island TN-4
Ratliff Lake—lake LA-4
Ratliff Lake Dam—dam MS-4
Ratliff Landing—locale MS-4
Ratliff Millpond—reservoir SC-3
Ratliff Oil Field—oilfield TX-5
Ratliff Park—park KY-4
Ratliff Pen Windmill—locale TX-5
Ratliff Post Office (historical)—building MS-4
Ratliff Ranch—locale NM-5
Ratliff Ranch—locale (2) TX-5
Ratliff Ridge—ridge VA-3
Ratliff Sch—school KY-4
Ratliffs Ferry (historical)—locale MS-4
Ratliff Spring—spring AZ-5
Ratliff Windmill—locale TX-5
Ratlift Park—park TX-5
Ratlum Brook—stream CT-1
Ratlum Mtn—summit CT-1
Rat Meadow—flat NE-7
Rat Mtn—summit CO-8
Ratnour Bridge—bridge PA-2
**Raton**—pop pl NM-5
Raton Canyon—valley NM-5
Raton (CCD)—cens area NM-5
Raton Creek—stream (2) CO-8
Raton Creek—stream NM-5
Raton Downtown Hist Dist—hist pl NM-5
Raton Mesa CO-8
Raton Mesa NM-5
Raton Park—flat CO-8
Raton Pass—gap NM-5
Raton Pass—hist pl CO-8
Raton Pass—hist pl NM-5
Raton Ranch—locale NM-5
Raton Ski Basin—basin CO-8
Raton Spring—spring NM-5
Raton Tunnel—tunnel NM-5
Rat Pocket—lake TN-4
Rat Pond—lake ME-1
Rat Pond—lake NY-2
Rat Pond—swamp FL-3
Rat River—stream (2) WI-6
Rat Rock—bar CA-9
Rat Root Lake MN-6
Rat Root Lake—lake MN-6
Rat Root River—stream MN-6
Rat Run—stream IL-6
Rat Run—stream IA-7
Rats Branch—stream TX-5
Rat Seep Hollow—valley UT-8
Rats Nest Gulch—valley ID-8
Rat Spring—spring ID-8
Rat Spring—spring UT-8
Rat Spring Branch—stream NC-3
Rats Valley Creek—stream WY-8
Rats Windmill—locale NM-5
Ratta Creek—stream TX-5
Rattail Branch—stream KY-4
Rattail Branch—stream OH-6
Rat Tail Creek IN-6
Rattail Creek—stream IN-6
Rattail Creek—stream MI-6
Rattail Creek—stream OR-9
Rattail Lakes—lake MI-6
Rattail Lateral—canal WI-6
Rattail Point—cliff MO-7
Rattail Ridge—ridge NY-2
Rattail Windmill—locale NM-5
Rattakadokoru Island PW-9
Rattalee Lake—lake MI-6
Rattan—locale LA-4
Rattan—locale TX-5
**Rattan**—pop pl OK-5
Rattan and Belvedere—locale VI-3
Rattan Bay—bay NC-3
Rattan Branch—stream AR-4
Rattan Branch—stream TN-4
Rattan Bridge—bridge TN-4
Rattan Cem—cemetery OK-5
Rattan Creek—stream LA-4
Rattan Creek—stream TX-5
Rattan Spit—bar NC-3
Rattan Trail—trail OK-5
Ratto Post Office (historical)—building MS-4
Ratteree Cem—cemetery TN-4
Ratterman, Bernard, House—hist pl OH-6
Rattermann, Heinrich A., House—hist pl OH-6
**Rattigan**—pop pl PA-2
Rattle and Snap—hist pl TN-4
Rattlebone Lake—lake MT-8
Rattlebox Branch—stream TN-4
Rattle Branch—stream AL-4
Rattle Branch—stream VA-3
Rattle Brook NH-1
Rattle Cem—cemetery MO-7
Rattle Creek—stream ID-8
Rattle Creek—stream UT-8
Rattle Creek—stream (2) VA-3
Rattle Creek Cabin (historical)—locale ID-8
Rattle Hill—summit NY-2
Rattle Lake—lake MN-6
Rattle Mtn—summit ID-8
Rattler Bayou—stream MS-4
Rattler Branch TX-5
Rattler Branch—stream NC-3
Rattler Branch—stream TN-4
Rattler Branch—stream VA-3
Rattler Butte—summit ID-8
Rattler Coulee—valley MN-6
Rattler Creek TX-5
Rattler Creek—stream MT-8
Rattler Ford—locale NC-3
Rattler Gulch—valley MT-8
Rattle River—stream NH-1
Rattle River Shelter—locale NH-1
Rattle River Trail—trail NH-1
Rattler Mine—mine AZ-5
Rattler Mine—mine CA-9
Rattle Rock Saddle—gap AZ-5
Rattler Rsvr—reservoir ID-8
Rattler Run—stream PA-2
Rattler Run Creek—stream WA-9
Rattlers Creek—stream AL-4
**Rattle Run**—pop pl MI-6
Rattle Run—stream MI-6
Rattler Well—well NM-5
Rattle Shoal Creek—stream NC-3
Rattles Islands, The—island OH-6
Rattle Slough—gut KY-4
Rattle Snake PA-2
Rattlesnake—CDP MT-8
Rattlesnake—locale MT-8
**Rattlesnake**—pop pl (2) FL-3
**Rattlesnake**—pop pl NM-5
Rattlesnake Bar—bar AL-4
Rattlesnake Bar—bar (2) CA-9
Rattlesnake Bar—bar (2) ID-8
Rattlesnake Basin—basin (2) AZ-5
Rattlesnake Basin—basin (3) ID-8
Rattlesnake Bay—bay NC-3
Rattlesnake Bay—stream MS-4
Rattlesnake Bay—swamp (2) FL-3
Rattlesnake Bay—swamp NC-3
Rattlesnake Bayou—gut LA-4
Rattlesnake Bayou—stream AL-4
Rattlesnake Bayou—stream FL-3
Rattlesnake Bayou—stream LA-4
Rattlesnake Bayou—stream MS-4
Rattlesnake Bead—locale TX-5
Rattlesnake Bench—bench (3) UT-8
Rattlesnake Bend AL-4
Rattlesnake Bend—bend AL-4
Rattlesnake Bluff—cliff FL-3
Rattlesnake Bluff—cliff IL-6
Rattlesnake Bluff—cliff MN-6
Rattlesnake Bluff—cliff OK-5
Rattlesnake Bluff—cliff WI-6
Rattlesnake Bluff—summit AZ-5
Rattlesnake Bluff—summit IL-6
Rattlesnake Branch MS-4
Rattlesnake Branch NC-3
Rattlesnake Branch—stream (3) AL-4
Rattlesnake Branch—stream (3) FL-3
Rattlesnake Branch—stream GA-3
Rattlesnake Branch—stream IL-6
Rattlesnake Branch—stream (5) KY-4
Rattlesnake Branch—stream MD-2
Rattlesnake Branch—stream (2) MO-7
Rattlesnake Branch—stream (11) NC-3
Rattlesnake Branch—stream OK-5
Rattlesnake Branch—stream (2) SC-3
Rattlesnake Branch—stream (6) TN-4
Rattlesnake Branch—stream TX-5
Rattlesnake Branch—stream (2) VA-3
Rattlesnake Branch—stream WV-2
Rattlesnake Branch Rec Area—park TN-4
Rattlesnake Brook—stream (3) CT-1
Rattlesnake Brook—stream ME-1
Rattlesnake Brook—stream MA-1
Rattlesnake Brook—stream NY-2
Rattlesnake Burn—area AZ-5
Rattlesnake Butte—summit (4) CA-9
Rattlesnake Butte—summit (3) CO-8
Rattlesnake Butte—summit (4) ID-8
Rattlesnake Butte—summit (16) MT-8
Rattlesnake Butte—summit NE-7
Rattlesnake Butte—summit (4) ND-7
Rattlesnake Butte—summit (4) OR-9
Rattlesnake Butte—summit (5) SD-7
Rattlesnake Butte—summit TX-5
Rattlesnake Butte—summit UT-8
Rattlesnake Butte—summit (2) WY-8
**Rattlesnake Buttes**—pop pl CO-8
Rattlesnake Buttes—ridge ND-7
Rattlesnake Buttes—spring MT-8
Rattlesnake Camp—locale CA-9
Rattlesnake Campground—locale (2) ID-8
Rattlesnake Campground—locale WA-9
Rattlesnake Camp (Site)—locale CA-9
Rattlesnake Canal—canal KS-7
Rattlesnake Canyon CA-9
Rattlesnake Canyon NV-8
Rattlesnake Canyon NM-5
Rattlesnake Canyon—valley (14) AZ-5
Rattlesnake Canyon—valley (19) CA-9
Rattlesnake Canyon—valley (2) CO-8
Rattlesnake Canyon—valley (4) ID-8
Rattlesnake Canyon—valley (12) NV-8
Rattlesnake Canyon—valley (9) NM-5
Rattlesnake Canyon—valley OK-5
Rattlesnake Canyon—valley (3) OR-9
Rattlesnake Canyon—valley TX-5
Rattlesnake Canyon—valley (5) UT-8
Rattlesnake Canyon—valley (4) WA-9
Rattlesnake Canyon—valley (2) WY-8
Rattlesnake Canyon Site—hist pl TX-5
Rattlesnake Canyon Wash—stream CA-9
Rattlesnake Cave—cave AL-4
Rattlesnake Cave—cave MO-7
Rattlesnake Cave—cave NM-5
Rattlesnake Cave—cave (2) OR-9
Rattlesnake Cave—cave PA-2
Rattlesnake Cliffs—cliff NC-3
Rattlesnake Cobble—summit NY-2
Rattlesnake Coulee—valley (6) MT-8
Rattlesnake Cove—bay FL-3
Rattlesnake Cove—bay NH-1
Rattlesnake Crater—crater AZ-5
Rattlesnake Creek AZ-5
Rattlesnake Creek CA-9
Rattlesnake Creek ID-8
Rattle Snake Creek IN-6
Rattlesnake Creek KS-7
Rattlesnake Creek MI-6
Rattlesnake Creek NC-3
Rattlesnake Creek OR-9
Rattlesnake Creek—stream AL-4
Rattlesnake Creek—stream AZ-5
Rattlesnake Creek—stream (2) AR-4
Rattlesnake Creek—stream (39) CA-9
Rattlesnake Creek—stream (3) CO-8
Rattlesnake Creek—stream (2) GA-3
Rattlesnake Creek—stream (25) ID-8
Rattlesnake Creek—stream (4) IL-6
Rattlesnake Creek—stream (4) IN-6
Rattlesnake Creek—stream (4) KS-7
Rattlesnake Creek—stream (2) KY-4
Rattlesnake Creek—stream (2) MI-6
Rattlesnake Creek—stream (2) MS-4
Rattlesnake Creek—stream MO-7
Rattlesnake Creek—stream (11) MT-8
Rattlesnake Creek—stream (4) NE-7
Rattlesnake Creek—stream (6) NV-8
Rattlesnake Creek—stream NM-5
Rattlesnake Creek—stream NY-2
Rattlesnake Creek—stream (4) NC-3
Rattlesnake Creek—stream (4) OH-6
Rattlesnake Creek—stream (2) OK-5
Rattlesnake Creek—stream (19) OR-9
Rattlesnake Creek—stream (5) PA-2
Rattlesnake Creek—stream SD-7
Rattlesnake Creek—stream TN-4
Rattlesnake Creek—stream (7) TX-5
Rattlesnake Creek—stream (3) UT-8
Rattlesnake Creek—stream (3) VA-3
Rattlesnake Creek—stream (10) WA-9
Rattlesnake Creek—stream WI-6
Rattlesnake Creek—stream (5) WY-8
Rattlesnake Creek Campground—locale ID-8
Rattlesnake Creek Site—hist pl WA-9
Rattlesnake Creek Trail—trail CA-9
Rattlesnake Creek Trail—trail UT-8
Rattlesnake Crossing TX-5
Rattlesnake Dam—dam AL-4
Rattlesnake Dam—dam AZ-5
Rattlesnake Dam—dam TX-5
Rattlesnake Den—summit NY-2
Rattlesnake Den Creek—stream IL-6
Rattlesnake Den Hollow—valley IL-6
Rattlesnake Den Spring—spring MO-7
Rattlesnake Ditch—canal (2) CA-9
Rattlesnake Draw—valley AZ-5
Rattlesnake Draw—valley ID-8
Rattlesnake Draw—valley (2) NM-5
Rattlesnake Draw—valley OR-9
Rattlesnake Draw—valley (5) TX-5
Rattlesnake Draw—valley WA-9
Rattlesnake Draw—valley (4) WY-8
Rattlesnake Falls—falls TN-4
Rattlesnake Ferry—locale IL-6
Rattlesnake Fire Trail—trail CA-9
Rattlesnake Flat—flat NV-8
Rattlesnake Flat—flat NM-5
Rattlesnake Flat—flat TX-5
Rattlesnake Flat—flat UT-8
Rattlesnake Flat—flat WA-9
Rattlesnake Flats—flat TX-5
Rattlesnake Fork CA-9
Rattlesnake Fork—stream (2) KY-4
Rattlesnake Gap—gap AL-4
Rattlesnake Gap—gap AZ-5
Rattlesnake Gap—gap CA-9
Rattlesnake Gap—gap NC-3
Rattlesnake Gap—gap TN-4
Rattlesnake Gap—gap (3) TX-5
Rattlesnake Gap Camp—locale AZ-5
Rattlesnake Glade—flat CA-9
Rattlesnake Gulch—valley (11) CA-9
Rattlesnake Gulch—valley (7) CO-8
Rattlesnake Gulch—valley (2) ID-8
Rattle Snake Gulch—valley KS-7
Rattlesnake Gulch—valley (3) MT-8
Rattlesnake Gulch—valley NE-7
Rattlesnake Gulch—valley (3) OR-9
Rattlesnake Gulch—valley (2) UT-8
Rattlesnake Gulch—valley (2) WA-9
Rattlesnake Gulch—valley WY-8
Rattlesnake Gulch Rsvr—reservoir OR-9
Rattlesnake Gulf—valley NY-2
Rattlesnake Gully—swamp FL-3
Rattlesnake Gut—gut NJ-2
Rattlesnake Gutter—valley MA-1
Rattlesnake Hammock—island (2) FL-3
Rattlesnake Head—valley FL-3
Rattle Snake Hill MA-1
Rattlesnake Hill—summit (2) AZ-5
Rattlesnake Hill—summit (3) CA-9
Rattlesnake Hill—summit (3) CO-8
Rattlesnake Hill—summit (5) CT-1
Rattlesnake Hill—summit DE-2
Rattlesnake Hill—summit IL-6
Rattlesnake Hill—summit KY-4
Rattlesnake Hill—summit (10) MA-1
Rattlesnake Hill—summit MN-6
Rattlesnake Hill—summit (2) MO-7
Rattlesnake Hill—summit (2) MT-8
Rattlesnake Hill—summit (2) NE-7
Rattlesnake Hill—summit NV-8
Rattlesnake Hill—summit (7) NH-1
Rattlesnake Hill—summit (3) NM-5
Rattlesnake Hill—summit (2) NY-2
Rattlesnake Hill—summit OR-9
Rattlesnake Hill—summit (3) PA-2
Rattlesnake Hill—summit (2) TX-5
Rattlesnake Hill—summit VT-1
Rattlesnake Hill—summit WA-9
Rattlesnake Hill—summit (3) WY-8
Rattlesnake Hills—range WA-9
Rattlesnake Hills—range WY-8
Rattlesnake Hills—summit MI-6
Rattlesnake Hill State Wildlife Mngmt Area—park NY-2
Rattlesnake (historical)—locale KS-7
Rattlesnake Hollow—valley (6) AR-4
Rattlesnake Hollow—valley IL-6
Rattlesnake Hollow—valley (2) IN-6
Rattlesnake Hollow—valley (3) KY-4
Rattlesnake Hollow—valley (3) MO-7
Rattlesnake Hollow—valley OK-5
Rattlesnake Hollow—valley PA-2
Rattlesnake Hollow—valley (5) TN-4
Rattlesnake Hollow—valley TX-5
Rattlesnake Hollow—valley (2) UT-8
Rattlesnake Hollow—valley (2) VA-3
Rattlesnake Hollow—valley (4) WV-2
Rattlesnake Island CA-9
Rattlesnake Island MI-6
Rattlesnake Island—island CA-9
Rattlesnake Island—island (4) FL-3
Rattlesnake Island—island ME-1
Rattlesnake Island—island MD-2
Rattlesnake Island—island NH-1
Rattlesnake Island—island (2) NM-5
Rattlesnake Island—island NY-2
Rattlesnake Island—island NC-3
Rattlesnake Island—island OH-6
Rattlesnake Island—island OK-5
Rattlesnake Island—island (5) TX-5
Rattle Snake Jack Mine—mine SD-7
Rattlesnake Key FL-3
Rattlesnake Key—island (3) FL-3
Rattlesnake Knob—summit (4) GA-3
Rattlesnake Knob—summit (2) KY-4
Rattlesnake Knob—summit MO-7
Rattlesnake Knob—summit NY-2
Rattlesnake Knob—summit (12) NC-3
Rattlesnake Knob—summit OH-6
Rattlesnake Knob—summit (3) WV-2
Rattlesnake Knob—summit WI-6
Rattlesnake Knoll—summit NV-8
Rattlesnake Lake CO-8
Rattlesnake Lake MI-6
Rattlesnake Lake—lake AZ-5
Rattlesnake Lake—lake (3) CA-9
Rattlesnake Lake—lake (3) FL-3
Rattlesnake Lake—lake ID-8
Rattlesnake Lake—lake MI-6
Rattlesnake Lake—lake MS-4
Rattlesnake Lake—lake NE-7
Rattlesnake Lake—lake TX-5
Rattlesnake Lake—lake (3) WA-9
Rattlesnake Lake—reservoir AL-4
Rattlesnake Lake—reservoir SD-7
Rattlesnake Landing MD-2
Rattlesnake Lead—ridge GA-3
Rattlesnake Ledge—bench WA-9
Rattlesnake Ledges—bench (2) CT-1
**Rattlesnake Lodge**—pop pl NC-3
Rattlesnake Lookout Tower—locale PA-2
Rattlesnake Lumps—island FL-3
Rattlesnake Marsh—swamp WI-6
Rattlesnake Meadow—flat (2) CA-9
Rattlesnake Meadows—flat WA-9
Rattlesnake Mesa—summit (2) AZ-5
Rattlesnake Mine—mine (2) AZ-5
Rattlesnake Mine—mine (2) CA-9
Rattlesnake Mine—mine NV-8
Rattlesnake Mine—mine SD-7
Rattlesnake Mine—mine TN-4
Rattlesnake Mound—summit IL-6
Rattlesnake Mound—summit TX-5
Rattlesnake Mound—summit WI-6
Rattlesnake Mountain NV-8
Rattlesnake Mountains WY-8
Rattlesnake Mountains—range OK-5
Rattlesnake Mountains—summit TX-5
Rattlesnake Mountain Trail—trail NH-1
Rattlesnake Mtn MA-1
Rattlesnake Mtn WA-9
Rattlesnake Mtn—summit AL-4
Rattlesnake Mtn—summit (2) AR-4
Rattlesnake Mtn—summit (5) CA-9
Rattlesnake Mtn—summit CO-8
Rattlesnake Mtn—summit CT-1
Rattlesnake Mtn—summit GA-3
Rattlesnake Mtn—summit ID-8
Rattlesnake Mtn—summit (4) ME-1
Rattlesnake Mtn—summit (2) MA-1
Rattlesnake Mtn—summit MT-8
Rattlesnake Mtn—summit (3) NV-8
Rattlesnake Mtn—summit (5) NH-1
Rattlesnake Mtn—summit (2) NY-2
Rattlesnake Mtn—summit (2) NC-3
Rattlesnake Mtn—summit OK-5
Rattlesnake Mtn—summit OR-9
Rattlesnake Mtn—summit (8) TX-5
Rattlesnake Mtn—summit UT-8
Rattlesnake Mtn—summit VT-1
Rattlesnake Mtn—summit VA-3
Rattlesnake Mtn—summit (5) WA-9
Rattlesnake Mtn—summit WY-8
Rattlesnake Narrows—gap AR-4
Rattlesnake Oil Field—other NM-5
Rattlesnake Park—flat CO-8
Rattlesnake Pass—gap AZ-5
Rattlesnake Pass—gap (2) UT-8
Rattlesnake Pass—gap WY-8
Rattlesnake Pasture Tank—reservoir AZ-5
Rattlesnake Peak—summit (3) AZ-5
Rattlesnake Peak—summit (3) CA-9
Rattlesnake Peak—summit (2) ID-8
Rattlesnake Peak—summit MA-1
Rattlesnake Peak—summit NE-7
Rattlesnake Peak—summit NV-8
Rattlesnake Peak—summit (3) UT-8
Rattlesnake Peaks—summit WA-9
Rattlesnake Point—cape (3) CA-9
Rattlesnake Point—cape ID-8
Rattlesnake Point—cape MN-6
Rattlesnake Point—cape NY-2
Rattlesnake Point—cape OR-9
Rattlesnake Point—cape (3) TX-5
Rattlesnake Point—cliff (2) AZ-5
Rattlesnake Point—cliff (2) ID-8
Rattlesnake Point—cliff NV-8
Rattlesnake Point—cliff UT-8
Rattlesnake Point—cliff VT-1
Rattlesnake Point—cliff VA-3
Rattlesnake Point—locale CA-9
Rattlesnake Point—ridge WY-8
Rattlesnake Point—summit AZ-5
Rattlesnake Point—summit (2) ID-8
Rattlesnake Point—summit TX-5
Rattlesnake Point—summit (2) UT-8
Rattlesnake Pond ME-1
Rattlesnake Pond—lake TX-5
Rattlesnake Pond—swamp FL-3
Rattlesnake Prairie—flat OR-9
Rattlesnake Raceway—other TX-5
Rattlesnake Ranch—locale FL-3
Rattlesnake Ranch—locale TX-5
Rattlesnake Ranch Number One Upper Dam—dam UT-8
Rattlesnake Ranch Number Two Dam—dam UT-8
Rattlesnake Ranch Number Two Rsvr—reservoir UT-8
Rattle Snake Range WY-8
Rattlesnake Ranger Station—locale WA-9
Rattlesnake Ravine—valley CA-9
Rattlesnake Reef—bar TX-5
Rattlesnake Reef—spring MT-8
Rattlesnake Reservoir CO-8
Rattlesnake Ridge MD-2
Rattlesnake Ridge NV-8
Rattlesnake Ridge WA-9
Rattlesnake Ridge—ridge AR-4
Rattlesnake Ridge—ridge (6) CA-9
Rattlesnake Ridge—ridge (2) FL-3
Rattlesnake Ridge—ridge GA-3
Rattlesnake Ridge—ridge ID-8
Rattlesnake Ridge—ridge KY-4
Rattlesnake Ridge—ridge LA-4
Rattlesnake Ridge—ridge MN-6
Rattlesnake Ridge—ridge (3) MT-8
Rattlesnake Ridge—ridge NV-8
Rattlesnake Ridge—ridge (3) NM-5
Rattlesnake Ridge—ridge (6) NC-3
Rattlesnake Ridge—ridge (5) OR-9
Rattlesnake Ridge—ridge (3) PA-2
Rattlesnake Ridge—ridge (2) TN-4
Rattlesnake Ridge—ridge UT-8
Rattlesnake Ridge—ridge VT-1
Rattlesnake Ridge—ridge (2) WA-9
Rattlesnake Ridge—ridge (3) WY-8
Rattlesnake Ridge Trail—trail TN-4
Rattlesnake Rock—pillar CA-9
Rattlesnake Rock—pillar OR-9
Rattlesnake Rock—summit TN-4
Rattlesnake Rsvr—reservoir AZ-5
Rattlesnake Rsvr—reservoir CA-9
Rattlesnake Rsvr—reservoir ID-8
Rattlesnake Rsvr—reservoir MT-8
Rattlesnake Rsvr—reservoir NV-8
Rattlesnake Rsvr—reservoir OR-9
Rattlesnake Rsvr—reservoir UT-8
Rattlesnake Run—stream KY-4
Rattlesnake Run—stream MA-1
Rattlesnake Run—stream (8) PA-2
Rattlesnake Run—stream (3) VA-3
Rattlesnake Run—stream (4) WV-2
Rattlesnake Run Sch—school PA-2
Rattlesnakes, The—ridge NH-1
Rattlesnake Sch—school (3) MT-8
Rattlesnake Sch—school PA-2
Rattlesnake Sch (historical)—school MO-7
Rattlesnake Slough—stream (2) FL-3
Rattlesnake Slough—stream LA-4
Rattlesnake Southeast Oil Field—oilfield KS-7
Rattlesnake Southwest Oil Field—oilfield KS-7
Rattlesnake Spring—spring (13) AZ-5
Rattlesnake Spring—spring (14) CA-9
Rattlesnake Spring—spring (9) ID-8
Rattlesnake Spring—spring (4) MO-7
Rattlesnake Spring—spring NE-7
Rattlesnake Spring—spring (9) NV-8
Rattlesnake Spring—spring (2) NM-5
Rattlesnake Spring—spring NC-3
Rattlesnake Spring—spring (11) OR-9
Rattlesnake Spring—spring (4) TN-4
Rattlesnake Spring—spring UT-8
Rattlesnake Spring—spring (4) WA-9
Rattlesnake Spring Branch—stream FL-3
Rattlesnake Spring Branch—stream TN-4
Rattlesnake Spring No 1—spring WY-8
Rattlesnake Spring No 2—spring WY-8
Rattlesnake Spring No 3—spring WY-8
Rattlesnake Spring Picnic Area—area NM-5
Rattlesnake Springs—hist pl TN-4
Rattlesnake Springs—spring CO-8
Rattlesnake Springs—spring (2) ID-8
Rattlesnake Springs—spring NV-8
Rattlesnake Springs—spring WA-9
Rattlesnake Springs—spring WY-8
Rattlesnake Springs Hist Dist—hist pl NM-5
Rattlesnake Springs Sites—hist pl WA-9
Rattlesnake Springs Wayside Park—park OR-9
Rattlesnake Spur—ridge UT-8
Rattlesnake Summit—summit CA-9
Rattlesnake Summit—summit UT-8
Rattlesnake Swamp—stream VA-3
Rattlesnake Swamp—swamp CT-1
Rattlesnake Swamp—swamp NC-3
Rattlesnake Tank TX-5
Rattlesnake Tank—reservoir (13) AZ-5
Rattlesnake Tank—reservoir (9) NM-5
Rattlesnake Tank—reservoir (4) TX-5
Rattlesnake Tanks—reservoir TX-5
Rattlesnake Terminal Island CA-9
Rattlesnake Trail TN-4
Rattlesnake Trail—trail (4) CA-9
Rattlesnake Trail—trail ID-8
Rattlesnake Trail—trail (2) OR-9
Rattlesnake Trail—trail (2) PA-2
Rattlesnake Trail—trail UT-8
Rattlesnake Trail—trail (2) WA-9
Rattlesnake Trail—trail WV-2
Rattlesnake Tunnel—tunnel CO-8
Rattlesnake Tunnel—tunnel NC-3
Rattlesnake Valley—valley (2) CA-9
Rattlesnake Wash—stream AZ-5
Rattlesnake Wash—stream NV-8
Rattlesnake Wash—stream NM-5
Rattlesnake Water Hole No 1—lake ID-8
Rattlesnake Water Hole No 2—lake ID-8
Rattlesnake Way—trail OR-9
Rattlesnake Well—locale NM-5
Rattlesnake Well—well AZ-5
Rattlesnake Well—well CO-8
Rattlesnake Well—well NV-8
Rattlesnake Well—well (4) NM-5
Rattlesnake Well—well TX-5
Rattlesnake Windmill—locale AZ-5
Rattlesnake Windmill—locale (3) NM-5
Rattlesnake Windmill—locale TX-5
Rattlesname Butte OR-9
Rattletrap Cem—cemetery MS-4
Rattling Brook—stream ME-1
Rattling Brook—stream VT-1
Rattling Camp Run—stream PA-2
Rattling Cave—cave TN-4
Rattling Creek—stream PA-2
Rattling Gulch—valley MT-8
Rattling Run—stream NJ-2
Rattling Run—stream (8) PA-2
Rattling Run Trail—trail PA-2
Rattling Slough—gut IL-6
Rattling Springs—spring MN-6
Rattling Springs—spring OR-9
Rattling Valley Hill—summit CT-1
Rattlsnake Mesa—summit CO-8
Ratto Canyon—valley NV-8
Rattogoru Island—island FM-9
Ratto Landing—locale CA-9
Ratton Creek—stream LA-4
Ratto Ranch—locale NV-8
Ratto Spring—spring NV-8
Rat Trap Pass—gap WA-9
Rat Trap Ridge—ridge CA-9
Ratts Cem—cemetery IN-6
Rattz Lake—lake WI-6
Ratz Creek—stream AK-9
Ratz Harbor—bay AK-9
Ratz Point—cape AK-9
Rau, Charles, House—hist pl WI-6
Rau, Herman, House—hist pl MI-6
**Raub**—pop pl IN-6
**Raub**—pop pl ND-7
Raubenstine—locale PA-2
Rauber Hill—summit NY-2
Raub Hollow—valley PA-2
Raub Junior High School PA-2
Raubold House—hist pl NH-1
Raub Sch—school MO-7
Raub Sch—school OH-6
Raubs Ferry PA-2
Raubs Ferry (historical)—locale PA-2
Raubs Island—island PA-2
**Raubs Mills**—pop pl (2) PA-2
**Raubsville**—pop pl PA-2

Raubsville Cem—*cemetery* PA-2
Raubsville Ch—*church* PA-2
*Raubville* PA-2
Rauch—*locale* MN-6
Rauch, Charlton, House—*hist pl* SC-3
Rauch Cem—*cemetery* WI-6
*Rauch Creek* PA-2
Rauch Drain—*stream* MI-6
Rauchfuss Houses—*hist pl* KY-4
Rauchman Sch—*school* IL-6
**Rauchtown**—*pop pl* PA-2
Rauchtown Creek—*stream* PA-2
*Rauchtown Fire Tower* PA-2
Rauchtown Lookout Tower—*locale* PA-2
Rauckman Oil Field—*oilfield* KS-7
Rau Field—*airport* (2) ND-7
Raughs Corners—*locale* PA-2
Raught Run—*stream* PA-2
Raught Sch (historical)—*school* PA-2
Rau Gulch—*valley* MT-8
**Raugust**—*pop pl* WA-9
Rauha Cem—*cemetery* MN-6
Raul Canyon—*valley* UT-8
**Raulerson**—*pop pl* GA-3
Raulerson Cem—*cemetery* GA-3
Raulerson Community Center—*locale* GA-3
Raulerson Cove—*bay* FL-3
Raulerson Creek—*stream* FL-3
Raulerson Hammock—*island* FL-3
Raulerson Memorial Ch—*church* GA-3
Raulerson Prairie—*flat* FL-3
Raulerson Swamp—*swamp* GA-3
Raulison Pond—*reservoir* FL-3
Raulson Head—*swamp* FL-3
Raulston Branch—*stream* TN-4
Raulston Cem—*cemetery* TN-4
*Raulston Creek* GA-3
**Raulstontown**—*pop pl* TN-4
Raum—*locale* IL-6
Raumaker Butte—*summit* ID-8
Raum Chapel—*church* MD-2
Raum Lookout Tower—*locale* IL-6
Raundal Coulee—*valley* MT-8
Raunt, The—*flat* NY-2
Raupp Sch—*school* MI-6
Raups Run—*stream* PA-2
Raur—*island* FM-9
Rau Ranch—*locale* NE-7
*Raurau* MH-9
*Raurau Bay* MH-9
*Raurau Laolao* MH-9
*Raurau-wan* MH-9
Raur Channel—*channel* FM-9
**Raus**—*pop pl* TN-4
*Rausch* PA-2
Rau Sch—*school* MT-8
*Rausch Creek* PA-2
Rausch Creek—*locale* PA-2
Rausch Creek—*stream* (2) PA-2
Rauscher House—*hist pl* KY-4
Rauscher Lagoon Natl Wildlife Mgt Area—*park* NE-7
Rauscher Run—*stream* PA-2
Rausch Gap—*gap* PA-2
Rausch Lake—*lake* MN-6
Rausch Ranch—*locale* TX-5
**Rauschs**—*pop pl* PA-2
Rausch Spring—*spring* WA-9
*Rauseville Chapel* MS-4
Rausin Creek—*stream* TN-4
Rausin Spring—*spring* TN-4
Rauslerson Branch—*stream* FL-3
Raus Post Office (historical)—*building* TN-4
Raus Sch (historical)—*school* TN-4
Rau/Strong House—*hist pl* MN-6
Rauth Trail—*trail* WY-8
Rauville—*locale* SD-7
**Rauville Township**—*pop pl* SD-7
Rava Farms Sch—*school* NJ-2
**Ravalli**—*pop pl* MT-8
Ravalli County Courthouse—*hist pl* MT-8
*Ravalli Creek* MT-8
Ravalli Natl Wildlife Ref—*park* MT-8
Ravalli Potholes—*lake* MT-8
*Ravana* AR-4
Ravanna—*locale* KS-7
**Ravanna**—*pop pl* AR-4
**Ravanna**—*pop pl* MO-7
Ravanna Cem—*cemetery* MO-7
**Ravanna Township**—*pop pl* MO-7
Ravel Creek—*stream* OR-9
*Ravema* MI-6
*Raven* NC-3
Raven—*locale* IL-6
Raven—*locale* KY-4
**Raven**—*pop pl* VA-3
**Raven**—*pop pl* WV-2
Raven, Lake—*reservoir* TX-5
*Ravena* MO-7
**Ravena**—*pop pl* NY-2
*Ravena Gardens* MO-7
Raven Basin—*basin* AK-9
Raven Basin Rsvr—*reservoir* CO-8
Raven Bay—*bay* AK-9
Raven Bay—*swamp* NC-3
Raven Bluff—*cliff* AR-4
Raven Bluff—*cliff* TN-4
Raven Bluff—*cliff* TX-5
Raven Bluff Cave—*cave* TN-4
Raven Branch—*locale* TN-4
Raven Branch—*stream* AL-4
Raven Branch—*stream* (2) KY-4
Raven Branch—*stream* SC-3
Raven Branch—*stream* TN-4
Raven Brook—*stream* MA-1
Ravenbrook Widow Baptist Ch—*church* IN-6
Raven Butte—*summit* AZ-5
Raven Butte Tank—*reservoir* AZ-5
Raven Camp Ch—*church* LA-4
Raven Cave—*cave* NV-8
Raven Ch—*church* PA-2
*Raven Chapel* TN-4
Raven Cliff—*cliff* NC-3
Raven Cliff—*cliff* SC-3
Raven Cliff—*cliff* TN-4
Raven Cliff—*cliff* TX-5
Raven Cliff—*cliff* VA-3
**Ravencliff**—*pop pl* WV-2
Raven Cliff Branch—*stream* NC-3
*Ravencliffe* WV-2
Raven Cliff Falls—*falls* SC-3
Raven Cliff Falls—*rapids* GA-3
Raven Cliff Furnace—*locale* VA-3
Ravencliff Knob—*summit* GA-3
Raven Cliff Ridge—*ridge* NC-3
Raven Cliff Ridge—*ridge* TN-4
Raven Cliffs—*cliff* (2) NC-3
Ravencliff Sch—*school* TN-4
Raven Cliffs Wilderness—*park* GA-3
*Raven Creek* NV-8
**Raven Creek**—*pop pl* PA-2
Raven Creek—*stream* (2) AK-9
Raven Creek—*stream* (2) ID-8
Raven Creek—*stream* IA-7
Raven Creek—*stream* KY-4
Raven Creek—*stream* MN-6
Raven Creek—*stream* MT-8
Raven Creek—*stream* NV-8
Raven Creek—*stream* NC-3
Raven Creek—*stream* PA-2
Raven Creek—*stream* (2) TX-5
Raven Creek—*stream* WA-9
Raven Creek—*stream* (2) WY-8
Raven Creek Campground—*locale* ID-8
Raven Creek Cem—*cemetery* KY-4
Raven Creek Ch—*church* PA-2
Raven Creek Hill—*other* AK-9
Raven Creek Oil Field—*oilfield* TX-5
Raven Creek Oil Field—*oilfield* WY-8
Ravencroft Ranch—*locale* NE-7
*Raven Cross Cemetery* TN-4
**Ravendale**—*pop pl* CA-9
*Ravenden* AR-4
**Ravenden**—*pop pl* AR-4
Raven Den—*summit* NC-3
Raven Den—*summit* TN-4
Raven Den Branch—*stream* AL-4
Raven Den Point—*cape* TN-4
**Ravenden Springs**—*pop pl* AR-4
**Ravenel**—*pop pl* SC-3
Ravenel (CCD)—*cens area* SC-3
Ravenel Lake—*reservoir* NC-3
Ravenel Lake Dam—*dam* NC-3
Ravenell Ponds—*lake* CT-1
Ravenel Ranch—*locale* NV-8
*Ravenels* SC-3
*Raven Fork* TN-4
Raven Fork—*stream* (3) NC-3
Raven Fork—*stream* TN-4
Raven Fork Overlook—*locale* NC-3
Raven Gap—*gap* TN-4
Raven Glacier—*glacier* AK-9
Raven Gulch—*valley* CO-8
Ravenhead—*cliff* TX-5
**Raven Hill**—*pop pl* TN-4
Raven Hill—*summit* NY-2
Raven Hill—*summit* SC-3
Ravenhill Acad—*school* PA-2
Raven Hill Ch—*church* TN-4
Raven Hill Historical Monument—*other* TX-5
*Raven Hill Missionary Baptist Ch* TN-4
Raven Hills—*other* AK-9
**Raven Hill (subdivision)**—*pop pl* PA-2
Raven Hollow—*valley* NC-3
Raven Hollow—*valley* TN-4
Raven Island—*island* AK-9
Raven Knob—*summit* GA-3
Raven Knob—*summit* (3) NC-3
Raven Knob Park Lake—*reservoir* NC-3
Raven Knob Park Lake Dam—*dam* NC-3
*Raven Lake* MN-6
Raven Lake—*lake* AK-9
Raven Lake—*lake* MI-6
Raven Lake—*lake* (2) MN-6
Raven Lake—*lake* NY-2
Raven Lake—*lake* WI-6
Raven Mesa—*summit* CO-8
Raven Mine—*mine* MT-8
Raven Mine—*mine* UT-8
Raven Mine, The—*mine* CO-8
Raven Mtn—*summit* NC-3
Raven Mtn—*summit* TN-4
Ravenna—*hist pl* MS-4
Ravenna—*locale* CA-9
Ravenna—*locale* MT-8
**Ravenna**—*pop pl* KY-4
**Ravenna**—*pop pl* MI-6
**Ravenna**—*pop pl* NE-7
**Ravenna**—*pop pl* OH-6
**Ravenna**—*pop pl* TX-5
**Ravenna**—*pop pl* WA-9
Ravenna Army Ammunition Plant—*other* OH-6
Ravenna (CCD)—*cens area* KY-4
Ravenna Cem—*cemetery* MN-6
Ravenna Park—*park* WA-9
**Ravenna Park**—*pop pl* FL-3
Ravenna Park Bridge—*hist pl* WA-9
Ravenna Sch—*school* MI-6
Ravennaside—*hist pl* MS-4
Ravenna-Telephone (CCD)—*cens area* TX-5
**Ravenna Township**—*pop pl* SD-7
**Ravenna (Township of)**—*pop pl* MI-6
**Ravenna (Township of)**—*pop pl* MN-6
**Ravenna (Township of)**—*pop pl* OH-6
Raven Nest Branch—*stream* VA-3
*Raven Park* CO-8
Raven Park—*flat* CO-8
*Raven Park Basin* CO-8
Raven Park Dam—*dam* CO-8
Raven Pass—*gap* CA-9
Raven Point—*cape* AK-9
Raven Point—*cape* TN-4
Raven Quiver Falls—*falls* MT-8
Raven Ranger Station—*locale* MT-8
Raven Ridge—*other* TN-4
Raven Ridge—*ridge* AK-9
Raven Ridge—*ridge* CO-8
Raven Ridge—*ridge* NC-3
Raven Ridge—*ridge* UT-8
Raven Ridge—*ridge* WA-9
Raven Rock—*pillar* GA-3
Raven Rock—*pillar* PA-2
Raven Rock—*pillar* VA-3
**Raven Rock**—*pop pl* NJ-2
**Raven Rock**—*pop pl* WV-2
Raven Rock—*rock* WV-2
Raven Rock—*summit* KY-4
Raven Rock—*summit* MD-2
Raven Rock—*summit* (2) NC-3
Raven Rock—*summit* OR-9
Raven Rock—*summit* TN-4
Raven Rock Ch—*church* NC-3
Raven Rock Ch—*church* VA-3
Raven Rock Fork—*stream* KY-4
Raven Rock Hollow—*valley* MD-2
Raven Rock Knob—*summit* NC-3
Ravenrock Mtn—*summit* NC-3
Raven Rock Mtn—*summit* PA-2
Ravenrock Ridge—*ridge* NC-3
Raven Rock Ridge—*ridge* NC-3
Raven Rocks—*cliff* MA-1
Raven Rocks—*cliff* NY-2
Raven Rocks—*cliff* (2) WV-2
Raven Rocks—*locale* WV-2
Raven Rocks—*summit* (2) NC-3
Raven Rocks—*summit* (2) WV-2
Raven Rocks Hollow—*valley* VA-3
Raven Rock State Park—*park* NC-3
Raven Rocks Trail—*trail* WV-2
Raven Roost Hollow—*valley* TX-5
Raven Roost Lookout—*locale* WA-9
Raven Rsvr—*reservoir* WY-8
**Raven Run**—*pop pl* PA-2
Raven Run—*stream* KY-4
Raven Run—*stream* (2) PA-2
Raven Run Dam Number Three—*dam* PA-2
Raven Run Dam Number Two—*dam* PA-2
Raven Run Reservoirs—*reservoir* PA-2
Raven Run Rsvr—*reservoir* PA-2
*Ravens Branch* TN-4
Ravensburg State Park—*hist pl* PA-2
Ravensburg State Park—*park* PA-2
Raven Sch—*school* NE-7
*Ravens Crag* MA-1
*Ravenscrag Mountain* MA-1
*Ravens Creek* PA-2
Ravens Crest—*summit* MD-2
Ravens Crest Creek—*stream* MD-2
**Ravenscroft**—*pop pl* TN-4
Ravenscroft Cem—*cemetery* TN-4
Ravenscroft Chapel—*church* OH-6
Ravenscroft Chapel—*church* TN-4
Ravenscroft Post Office (historical)—*building* TN-4
Ravenscroft Sch—*hist pl* NC-3
Ravenscroft Sch—*school* NC-3
Ravenscroft Sch (historical)—*school* TN-4
Ravensdale—*locale* WA-9
Ravensdale Lake—*lake* WA-9
Ravens Den—*basin* MD-2
Ravens Den Cave—*cave* TN-4
Ravens Den Pit—*cave* TN-4
Ravensden Rock—*summit* VA-3
Ravenseye—*locale* WV-2
Ravensford—*locale* NC-3
*Ravens Gap* TN-4
Ravenshurst—*hist pl* MD-2
Raven (Site)—*locale* ID-8
Ravens Knob—*summit* PA-2
Ravens Lore Trail—*trail* TN-4
*Ravens Mountain* TN-4
Ravens Nest—*cliff* ME-1
Ravens Nest—*summit* NV-8
Ravens Point—*cape* MN-6
Ravens Point—*cape* SC-3
Ravens Rock—*pillar* KY-4
Ravens Roost—*summit* AZ-5
Ravens Roost Overlook—*locale* VA-3
Ravens Roost Ridge—*ridge* NC-3
*Raven Stream* MN-6
Raven Stream—*stream* CT-1
Raven Stream—*stream* MN-6
Ravens Window—*arch* KY-4
*Ravenswood* IL-6
Ravenswood—*hist pl* CA-9
Ravenswood—*hist pl* MO-7
Ravenswood—*hist pl* TN-4
Ravenswood—*locale* LA-4
**Ravenswood**—*pop pl* CA-9
**Ravenswood**—*pop pl* IN-6
**Ravenswood**—*pop pl* MI-6
**Ravenswood**—*pop pl* NC-3
**Ravenswood**—*pop pl* WV-2
Ravenswood—*summit* NV-8
**Ravenswood Heights**—*pop pl* MI-6
Ravenswood Hosp—*hospital* IL-6
Ravenswood HS—*school* CA-9
Ravenswood (Magisterial District)—*fmr MCD* WV-2
Ravenswood Oil Field—*oilfield* LA-4
Ravenswood Park—*park* IL-6
Ravenswood Park—*park* MA-1
Ravenswood Peak—*summit* NV-8
Ravenswood Point—*cape* CA-9
Ravenswood Sch—*school* CA-9
Ravenswood Sch—*school* IL-6
Ravenswood Slough—*gut* CA-9
Ravenswood Works—*locale* WV-2
**Ravensworth**—*pop pl* VA-3
**Ravensworth Farms**—*pop pl* VA-3
**Ravensworth Grove**—*pop pl* VA-3
**Ravensworth Park**—*pop pl* VA-3
Ravensworth Sch—*school* VA-3
**Ravensworth (sta.)**—*pop pl* VA-3
Raven Tank—*reservoir* AZ-5
Raventhorp—*hist pl* ME-1
*Ravenwood* LA-4
*Ravenwood* NC-3
Ravenwood—*locale* VA-3
**Ravenwood**—*pop pl* GA-3
**Ravenwood**—*pop pl* MI-6
**Ravenwood**—*pop pl* MO-7
**Ravenwood**—*pop pl* SC-3
**Ravenwood**—*pop pl* VA-3
Ravenwood—*uninc pl* NY-2
Ravenwood Mine—*mine* CO-8
**Ravenwood Park**—*pop pl* VA-3
Ravenwood Sch—*school* GA-3
**Ravenwood (subdivision)**—*pop pl* (7) NC-3
Raver and Michaud Mine—*mine* SD-7
Ravers Gap—*gap* PA-2
Ravers Run—*stream* PA-2
Raves Hill—*summit* MA-1
**Ravia**—*pop pl* OK-5
Raville Siding—*locale* TX-5
**Ravina**—*pop pl* IL-6
**Ravinamy**—*pop pl* IN-6
Ravina Park—*park* IL-6
Ravina Park—*park* IN-6
Ravina Sch—*school* IL-6
*Ravina Township* SD-7
**Ravine**—*pop pl* MS-4
**Ravine**—*pop pl* PA-2
Ravine, The—*valley* AL-4
Ravine Canne—*valley* MS-4
Ravine Cem—*cemetery* OH-6
Ravine Creek—*stream* AK-9
Ravine Ditch—*canal* CO-8
Ravine Drain—*canal* MI-6
*Ravine Elementary School* AL-4
Ravine Gardens Park—*park* FL-3
Ravine House—*building* NH-1
Ravine Lake—*lake* AK-9
Ravine Lake—*reservoir* NJ-2
Ravine Lake Dam—*dam* NJ-2
Ravine Lodge—*locale* NH-1
Ravine Omni Tower—*tower* PA-2
Ravine Park—*park* IL-6
Ravine Park—*park* IN-6
Ravine Park—*park* IA-7
Ravine Park—*park* OH-6
Ravine Park—*park* PA-2
Ravine Park Dam—*dam* SD-7
Ravine Park Lake—*reservoir* SD-7
Ravine Path—*trail* NH-1
Ravine Post Office (historical)—*building* MS-4
Ravine River—*stream* MI-6
Ravine Sch—*school* AL-4
Ravine Shaft (historical)—*mine* PA-2
*Ravinia* IL-6
**Ravinia**—*pop pl* SD-7
*Ravinia Park* IL-6
Ravinia Park Hist Dist—*hist pl* IL-6
**Ravinia Township**—*pop pl* SD-7
Ravin Mine—*mine* CO-8
Raviosa Well (Flowing)—*well* TX-5
Ravisloe Country Club—*other* IL-6
Rawah and Lower Supply Ditch—*canal* CO-8
Rawah Bog—*swamp* CO-8
Rawah Creek—*stream* CO-8
Rawah Lake No. 1—*lake* CO-8
Rawah Lake No. 2—*lake* CO-8
Rawah Lake No. 3—*lake* CO-8
Rawah Lake No. 4—*lake* CO-8
Rawah Lakes—*lake* CO-8
Rawah Ranch—*locale* CO-8
Rawah Trail—*trail* CO-8
Rawah Wilderness Area—*park* CO-8
Rawalts—*locale* IL-6
*Rawaway River* NJ-2
*Raway* NJ-2
*Rawcom Tank* AZ-5
Raw Dog Creek—*stream* OR-9
*Rawdon Landing Field* KS-7
Rawe Creek—*stream* OR-9
Rawe Peak—*summit* NV-8
Rawhead Island—*island* LA-4
*Rawhide* AL-4
*Raw Hide* MS-4
Rawhide—*locale* NV-8
**Rawhide**—*pop pl* CA-9
**Rawhide**—*pop pl* MS-4
**Rawhide**—*pop pl* VA-3
Rawhide Boys Camp—*locale* WI-6
Rawhide Branch—*stream* MS-4
*Rawhide Butte* WY-8
Rawhide Butte—*summit* WY-8
Rawhide Buttes—*range* WY-8
Rawhide Canyon—*valley* AZ-5
Rawhide Canyon—*valley* (3) NV-8
Rawhide Canyon—*valley* NM-5
Rawhide Canyon—*valley* OR-9
*Rawhide Creek* TX-5
Rawhide Creek—*cens area* WY-8
Rawhide Creek—*stream* CO-8
Rawhide Creek—*stream* ID-8
Rawhide Creek—*stream* KY-4
Rawhide Creek—*stream* LA-4
Rawhide Creek—*stream* (2) MT-8
Rawhide Creek—*stream* NE-7
Rawhide Creek—*stream* (2) OR-9
Rawhide Creek—*stream* (3) TX-5
Rawhide Creek—*stream* (3) WY-8
Rawhide Creek Old Channel*—*channel* NE-7
Rawhide Creek (Old Channel)—*stream* NE-7
Rawhide Draw—*valley* NM-5
Rawhide Draw—*valley* TX-5
Rawhide Flat—*flat* CA-9
Rawhide Flats—*flat* CO-8
Rawhide Flats—*flat* NV-8
Rawhide Gulch—*valley* CO-8
Rawhide Gulch—*valley* MT-8
**Rawhide (historical)**—*pop pl* MS-4
Rawhide Hot Springs—*spring* NV-8
Rawhide Mine—*mine* AZ-5
Rawhide Mine—*mine* CA-9
*Rawhide Mountain* WY-8
Rawhide Mountains—*range* AZ-5
Rawhide Mountains—*summit* TX-5
Rawhide Mtn—*summit* AZ-5
Rawhide Mtn—*summit* NV-8
Rawhide Park—*locale* WY-8
*Rawhide Peak* NV-8
Rawhide Ranch—*locale* NV-8
Rawhide Rsvr—*reservoir* NV-8
Rawhide Sch—*school* CA-9
Rawhide Sch—*school* WY-8
Rawhide Sog—*swamp* FL-3
Rawhide Spring—*spring* ID-8
Rawhide Spring—*spring* (2) NV-8
Rawhide Spring—*spring* OR-9
Rawhide Spring—*spring* TX-5
Rawhide Wash—*stream* AZ-5
Rawins Cem—*cemetery* GA-3
*Rawl* FM-9
**Rawl**—*pop pl* WV-2
Rawl, David, House—*hist pl* SC-3
Rawl, John Jacob, House—*hist pl* SC-3
Rawl Canyon—*valley* CA-9
Rawl-Couch House—*hist pl* SC-3
Rawleigh Chapel—*church* TN-4
*Rawlerson Swamp* GA-3
Rawles Bay—*swamp* FL-3
Rawles Canyon—*valley* CA-9
Rawles Cem—*cemetery* KY-4
Rawles Cem—*cemetery* MS-4
Rawles Cem—*cemetery* VA-3
Rawles Hill Cem—*cemetery* AR-4
Rawles Landing (historical)—*locale* TN-4
*Rawles Mill Creek* MS-4
Rawles Mill (historical)—*locale* AL-4
Rawles Mill (historical)—*locale* MS-4
*Rawles Springs* MS-4
Rawles Springs—*spring* MS-4
Rawles Township—*fmr MCD* IA-7
Rawley Cem—*cemetery* OH-6
Rawley Gulch—*valley* CO-8
Rawley House—*hist pl* DE-2
Rawley Island—*island* DE-2
Rawley Mine—*mine* AZ-5
Rawley Mine—*mine* CO-8
Rawley Mines—*mine* CO-8
Rawley Point—*cape* WI-6
Rawley Point Light Station—*hist pl* WI-6
*Rawleys Bay* WI-6
**Rawley Springs**—*pop pl* VA-3
Rawlide Ranch—*locale* NV-8
Rawlie Sch (historical)—*school* MO-7
*Rawling Mountain* ME-1
Rawling Park—*park* FL-3
Rawlings—*locale* VA-3
**Rawlings**—*pop pl* MD-2
Rawlings, Marjorie Kinnan, House—*hist pl* FL-3
Rawlings, Stephen, House—*hist pl* KY-4
Rawlings Branch—*stream* GA-3
Rawlings-Brownell House—*hist pl* OH-6
Rawlings Cem—*cemetery* (2) AR-4
Rawlings Cem—*cemetery* IN-6
Rawlings Cem—*cemetery* KY-4
Rawlings Cem—*cemetery* MS-4
Rawlings Cem—*cemetery* OH-6
Rawlings Cem—*cemetery* VA-3
**Rawlings Heights**—*pop pl* MD-2
Rawlings Hollow—*valley* MO-7
Rawlings JHS—*school* OH-6
Rawlings Knob—*summit* KY-4
Rawlings Lakes—*lake* TX-5
Rawlings Landing—*locale* FL-3
Rawlings Oil Field—*oilfield* TX-5
Rawlings Sch—*school* MO-7
Rawlings Spring Cave—*cave* AL-4
Rawlingsville (historical)—*locale* AL-4
Rawlins—*locale* TX-5
**Rawlins**—*pop pl* WY-8
Rawlins, Capt. R. A., House—*hist pl* TX-5
Rawlins Bend—*bend* IL-6
Rawlins Brook—*stream* CT-1
Rawlins Brook—*stream* ME-1
Rawlins Canyon—*valley* NM-5
Rawlins Cem—*cemetery* (2) KY-4
Rawlins Cem—*cemetery* TX-5
Rawlins Cem—*cemetery* WY-8
Rawlins County—*civil* KS-7
Rawlins Creek—*stream* ID-8
Rawlins Draw—*valley* (2) WY-8
Rawlins (historical)—*locale* KS-7
**Rawlinson**—*pop pl* AR-4
Rawlinsons Channel—*channel* NC-3
Rawlins Peak—*summit* WY-8
Rawlins Run—*stream* PA-2
Rawlins Statue—*park* DC-2
**Rawlins (Township of)**—*pop pl* IL-6
**Rawlinsville**—*pop pl* PA-2
Rawlinsville Ch—*church* PA-2
Rawlinsville Post Office (historical)—*building* PA-2
**Rawlison**—*pop pl* AR-4
Raw Liver Creek—*stream* MT-8
Rawls—*locale* AL-4
Rawls—*locale* AR-4
Rawls—*locale* FL-3
**Rawls**—*pop pl* GA-3
**Rawls**—*pop pl* NC-3
Rawls Bay—*swamp* MS-4
Rawls Branch—*stream* KY-4
Rawls Branch—*stream* LA-4
Rawls Cem—*cemetery* (2) GA-3
Rawls Cem—*cemetery* IL-6
Rawls Cem—*cemetery* (3) MS-4
Rawls Cem—*cemetery* TN-4
Rawls Cem—*cemetery* TX-5
Rawls Chapel—*church* MS-4
Rawls Creek—*stream* AL-4
Rawls Creek—*stream* AR-4
Rawls Creek—*stream* MS-4
Rawls Creek—*stream* SC-3
Rawls Creek—*stream* TN-4
Rawls Creek—*stream* (2) TX-5
Rawls Creek Ch—*church* TN-4
Rawls Creek Sch (historical)—*school* TN-4
Rawls Ferry (historical)—*locale* MS-4
Rawls Gulch—*valley* CA-9
Rawls Hotel—*hist pl* AL-4
Rawls Island—*island* NC-3
Rawls Millpond—*reservoir* SC-3
**Rawls Park (subdivision)**—*pop pl* FL-3
Rawls Point—*cape* AL-4
Rawls Point—*cape* NC-3
Rawls Pond—*lake* TN-4
Rawls Ranch (reduced usage)—*locale* TX-5
Rawls Sch (historical)—*school* AL-4
**Rawls Springs**—*pop pl* MS-4
Rawls Springs Attendance Center—*school* MS-4
Rawls Springs Baptist Ch—*church* MS-4
Rawls Springs Post Office (historical)—*building* MS-4
Rawlston Cem—*cemetery* TN-4
Rawmeat Creek—*stream* NM-5
Rawn Ditch—*canal* IN-6
Rawnee Cove Rec Area—*park* OK-5
Raworth—*locale* MS-4
Raworth Post Office (historical)—*building* MS-4
Rawson—*locale* CA-9
Rawson—*locale* CT-1
**Rawson**—*pop pl* ID-8
**Rawson**—*pop pl* NY-2
**Rawson**—*pop pl* ND-7
**Rawson**—*pop pl* OH-6
Rawson—*uninc pl* WI-6
Rawson, Lake—*lake* IL-6
Rawson, Warren, Bldg—*hist pl* MA-1
Rawson, Warren, House—*hist pl* MA-1
**Rawson Bridge**—*pop pl* IL-6
*Rawson Brook* MA-1
Rawson Brook—*stream* MA-1
Rawson Canal—*canal* CA-9
Rawson Canal—*canal* ID-8
Rawson Canyon—*valley* CA-9
Rawson Cem—*cemetery* MS-4
Rawson Cem—*cemetery* ND-7
Rawson Cem—*cemetery* WV-2
Rawson Ch—*church* NY-2
Rawson Creek—*gut* NC-3
Rawson Creek—*stream* CA-9
Rawson Creek—*stream* ID-8
Rawson Creek—*stream* LA-4
Rawson Creek—*stream* NY-2
Rawson Creek Ch—*church* LA-4
Rawson Drain—*canal* MI-6
Rawson Drain—*stream* MI-6
Rawson Estate—*hist pl* MA-1
Rawson Hill—*summit* MA-1
Rawson Hill Brook—*stream* MA-1
Rawson Hill Brook Dam—*dam* MA-1
Rawson Hollow—*valley* NY-2
Rawson House—*hist pl* OH-6
Rawson Island—*island* MA-1
*Rawson Lakes* MI-6
Rawson Lateral—*canal* WI-6
Rawson Mill Brook Dam A-4-A—*dam* MA-1
Rawson Mill Brook Rsvr—*reservoir* MA-1
Rawson Park—*park* OH-6
Rawson Park—*park* WI-6
Rawson Pond—*reservoir* RI-1
Rawson Pond Dam—*dam* RI-1
Rawson Ridge—*ridge* PA-2
Rawson Sch—*school* CT-1
Rawson Sch—*school* WI-6
Rawson Valley—*valley* NY-2
**Rawsonville**—*pop pl* MI-6
**Rawsonville**—*pop pl* VT-1
Rawsonville (historical)—*locale* MS-4
Raw Tank—*reservoir* AZ-5
Rawul—*summit* FM-9
Raw Water Pond Dam—*dam* PA-2
Ray—*locale* KS-7
Ray—*locale* NV-8
Ray—*locale* NY-2
Ray—*locale* VA-3
Ray—*other* KY-4
**Ray**—*pop pl* AL-4
**Ray**—*pop pl* AZ-5
**Ray**—*pop pl* IL-6
**Ray**—*pop pl* (2) IN-6
**Ray**—*pop pl* MI-6
**Ray**—*pop pl* MN-6
**Ray**—*pop pl* ND-7
**Ray**—*pop pl* OH-6
**Ray**—*pop pl* TX-5
Ray, A., Taylor House—*hist pl* MO-7
Ray, Frank G., House & Carriage House—*hist pl* IA-7
Ray, M. B., House—*hist pl* TX-5
Ray, Mount—*summit* OR-9
Ray, William H., House—*hist pl* UT-8
Rayado—*locale* NM-5
Rayado Base Camp—*locale* NM-5
Rayado Creek—*stream* NM-5
Rayado Mesa—*summit* NM-5
Rayado Peak—*summit* NM-5
Ray Anchorage—*bay* AK-9
Ray Ann Chapel Sch—*school* MS-4
**Rayann Subdivision**—*pop pl* UT-8
**Rayard**—*pop pl* PA-2
Ray Ball Homestead—*locale* CO-8
Ray Baptist Ch—*church* AL-4
Ray Bar—*bar* OR-9
Ray Bay—*bay* NY-2
Ray Behrens Rec Area—*park* MO-7
*Rayberry Hill* MA-1
Raybins Beach—*locale* NJ-2
Ray Bluff Knob—*summit* TN-4
Raybon—*locale* GA-3
**Rayborn**—*pop pl* MO-7
*Rayborn Cemetery* MS-4
Rayborn Ch—*church* TX-5
Rayborn-Easley Cem—*cemetery* MS-4
Ray Bottoms—*flat* VA-3
Raybourn Cem—*cemetery* MS-4
Raybourn Cem—*cemetery* TN-4
Raybourn Ditch—*canal* IN-6
Ray Brake—*swamp* AR-4
Ray Branch—*stream* (3) AL-4
Ray Branch—*stream* AR-4
Ray Branch—*stream* GA-3
Ray Branch—*stream* (3) KY-4
Ray Branch—*stream* (2) MS-4
Ray Branch—*stream* MO-7
Ray Branch—*stream* (2) NC-3
Ray Branch—*stream* SC-3
Ray Branch—*stream* (5) TN-4
Ray Branch—*stream* TX-5
Ray Branch—*stream* WV-2
Ray Bridge—*bridge* TN-4
**Ray Brook**—*pop pl* NY-2
Ray Brook—*stream* ME-1
Ray Brook—*stream* (2) NY-2
Rayburn—*locale* AL-4
Rayburn—*locale* WV-2
**Rayburn**—*pop pl* TX-5
Rayburn, Samuel T., House—*hist pl* TX-5
Rayburn Bayou—*gut* MS-4
Rayburn Brake—*swamp* AR-4
*Rayburn Branch* TN-4
Rayburn Branch—*stream* (2) GA-3
Rayburn Branch—*stream* KY-4
Rayburn Branch—*stream* TX-5
Rayburn Cem—*cemetery* IA-7
Rayburn Cem—*cemetery* (2) KY-4
Rayburn Cem—*cemetery* (2) TN-4
Rayburn Cem—*cemetery* TX-5
*Rayburn Cemetery* AL-4
Rayburn Ch—*church* TX-5
Rayburn Chapel—*church* TN-4
Rayburn Creek—*stream* MI-6
Rayburn Creek—*stream* (2) TN-4
Rayburn Creek—*stream* WV-2
Rayburn Draft—*valley* WV-2
*Rayburn Hollow* AL-4
Rayburn Hollow—*valley* IN-6
Rayburn Hollow—*valley* OH-6
Rayburn Hollow—*valley* TN-4
Rayburn House Office Bldg—*building* DC-2
Rayburn Johnson Shell Mound (15BT41)—*hist pl* KY-4
Rayburn Lake—*lake* TX-5
Rayburn Sch—*school* TX-5
Rayburn Sch (historical)—*school* TN-4
Rayburn Substation—*other* TX-5

**Rayburn (Township of)**—pop pl PA-2
Rayburnville (historical)—locale MS-4
Ray Cabin—locale WA-9
Ray Canada Lake Dam—dam MS-4
Ray Canal—canal WY-8
Ray Canyon—valley NM-5
Ray Canyon—valley TX-5
Ray Cave—cave TN-4
Ray Cem—cemetery (4) AL-4
Ray Cem—cemetery (2) AR-4
Ray Cem—cemetery FL-3
Ray Cem—cemetery GA-3
Ray Cem—cemetery (4) KY-4
Ray Cem—cemetery MN-6
Ray Cem—cemetery MS-4
Ray Cem—cemetery (4) MO-7
Ray Cem—cemetery (3) NC-3
Ray Cem—cemetery OH-6
Ray Cem—cemetery SC-3
Ray Cem—cemetery (8) TN-4
Ray Cem—cemetery (4) TX-5
Ray Cem—cemetery VA-3
Ray Cem—cemetery WV-2
Ray Cem—cemetery WI-6
**Ray Center**—pop pl MI-6
Ray Ch—church TX-5
Ray Chapel—church TN-4
Raychem Corporation—facility NC-3
Ray Church Gulch—valley ID-8
**Ray City**—pop pl GA-3
Ray City (CCD)—cens area GA-3
Ray Cole Campground—park OR-9
Ray Community Center—building AL-4
Ray Corner—locale ME-1
Ray Corner Cem—cemetery TN-4
Ray Cornfield—locale MO-7
**Ray County**—pop pl MO-7
Ray County Courthouse—hist pl MO-7
Ray County Lake—reservoir MO-7
Ray County Poor Farm—hist pl MO-7
Ray Cove—valley NC-3
Ray Cove—valley TN-4
Ray Cowden Tank—spring AZ-5
Raycraft, Arthur, House—hist pl NV-8
Raycraft Ranch—hist pl NV-8
Ray Creek MS-4
Ray Creek—stream (2) AL-4
Ray Creek—stream (2) AK-9
Ray Creek—stream AR-4
Ray Creek—stream IN-6
Ray Creek—stream MI-6
Ray Creek—stream MS-4
Ray Creek—stream (4) MT-8
Ray Creek—stream NE-7
Ray Creek—stream NC-3
Ray Creek—stream OK-5
Ray Creek—stream (6) OR-9
Ray Creek—stream SC-3
Ray Creek—stream TN-4
Ray Creek—stream TX-5
Ray Creek—stream (2) WA-9
Ray Creek School—locale MT-8
Ray Dam OR-9
Ray Dam—dam ND-7
Ray Dam—other WY-8
Rayder Creek—stream TN-4
Ray District Elementary School AZ-5
Ray District HS—school AZ-5
Ray Ditch—canal IN-6
Raydon OK-5
Ray Dorman Pond DE-2
Ray Drain—stream MI-6
Ray Draw—valley WY-8
Raydure—locale KY-4
Ray Elem Sch—school FL-3
Rayen HS—school OH-6
Rayen Sch—hist pl OH-6
Rayes Lake—lake OH-6
Ray E Smith Dam—dam SD-7
Ray Falls—falls TN-4
Rayfield Archeol District—hist pl GA-3
Rayfield Cem—cemetery MO-7
Rayfield Ditch—canal MD-2
Rayfield Hollow—valley MO-7
Ray Flat—flat OR-9
Rayflin—locale SC-3
Rayflin Bridge—bridge SC-3
Rayford—locale OK-5
Rayford—locale TX-5
Rayford Chapel Baptist Ch—church MS-4
Rayford Oil Field—oilfield TX-5
Ray Fork—stream VA-3
Ray Fork—stream WV-2
Ray Gap—gap NC-3
Ray Gap—gap TN-4
Ray Gold—locale OR-9
Ray Gold Dam OR-9
Ray Greene Park—park FL-3
Ray Green Farm—locale MS-4
Ray Gulch—valley CA-9
Ray Gun Tank—reservoir NM-5
Ray Haberman Sr Number 1 Dam—dam SD-7
Ray Haberman Sr Number 2 Dam—dam SD-7
Ray Hill—summit CA-9
Ray Hill—summit FL-3
Ray Hill—summit GA-3
Ray Hill—summit MA-1
Ray Hill—summit NY-2
Rayhill Slough—stream IL-6
Ray Hill Tunnel PA-2
**Ray (historical)**—pop pl TN-4
Ray Hollow—valley AR-4
Ray Hollow—valley (2) MO-7
Ray Hollow—valley OK-5
Ray Hollow—valley (4) TN-4
Ray Hollow—valley WI-6
Ray Hollow Windmill—locale TX-5
Ray House—hist pl KY-4
Ray House—locale MO-7
Ray HS—school TX-5
Ray Hubbard, Lake—reservoir TX-5
Ray Hunter Ranch—locale NM-5
Rayir—cape FM-9
Ray Island—island KY-4
Ray Johnson Airp—airport MO-7
Ray Johnson Park—park OR-9
Ray Junction AZ-5
Ray Junction—locale AZ-5
Ray Knob—summit NC-3
Ray Lake LA-4
Ray Lake*—lake IA-7
Ray Lake—lake MN-6
Ray Lake—lake NY-2
Ray Lake—lake TX-5
Ray Lake—reservoir WY-8
**Rayland**—pop pl OH-6
**Rayland**—pop pl TX-5
**Rayle**—pop pl GA-3
Raylean, Lake—reservoir PA-2
Rayle (CCD)—cens area GA-3
Rayle Cem—cemetery MO-7
Rayleigh Branch—stream TX-5
Ray-Lenox Drain—stream MI-6
Rayley Gulch CO-8
Ray Lode Mine—mine ID-8
Raymack Creek IN-6
Rayman Ch—church PA-2
Rayman Creek CO-8
Rayman Ditch—canal IN-6
Ray-Manship Cem—cemetery TX-5
**Raymar**—pop pl IA-7
Ray Memorial Ch—church VA-3
Rayment Wash AZ-5
Raymer—locale CA-9
**Raymer**—pop pl CO-8
Raymer Cem—cemetery CO-8
Raymer Cem—cemetery KS-7
Raymer Hollow—valley KY-4
Raymer Lake—lake KY-4
Raymers Cem—cemetery MO-7
Raymer Sch—school OH-6
Raymers Fork—stream KY-4
Raymers Gulch—valley CO-8
Raymer Spring—spring ID-8
Raymert AZ-5
**Raymertown**—pop pl NY-2
Ray Mesa—summit CO-8
Ray Mesa—summit UT-8
Raymick Cem—cemetery AR-4
**Raymilton**—pop pl PA-2
Ray Mine—mine AZ-5
Ray Mine—mine OR-9
Ray Mission—church OK-5
Raymond MA-1
Raymond—locale ID-8
Raymond—locale KY-4
Raymond—locale PA-2
Raymond—locale TX-5
Raymond—mine UT-8
**Raymond**—pop pl AR-4
**Raymond**—pop pl CA-9
**Raymond**—pop pl CO-8
**Raymond**—pop pl GA-3
**Raymond**—pop pl IL-6
**Raymond**—pop pl IN-6
**Raymond**—pop pl IA-7
**Raymond**—pop pl KS-7
**Raymond**—pop pl LA-4
**Raymond**—pop pl ME-1
**Raymond**—pop pl MN-6
**Raymond**—pop pl MS-4
**Raymond**—pop pl MT-8
**Raymond**—pop pl NE-7
**Raymond**—pop pl NH-1
**Raymond**—pop pl NY-2
**Raymond**—pop pl OH-6
**Raymond**—pop pl SD-7
**Raymond**—pop pl WA-9
**Raymond**—pop pl WI-6
**Raymond**—pop pl WY-8
Raymond—uninc pl CA-9
Raymond, Charles and Joseph, Houses 3—hist pl PA-2
Raymond, Lake—lake MI-6
Raymond, Lake—reservoir GA-3
Raymond, Liberty G., Tavern and Barn—hist pl OH-6
Raymond, Mount—summit AK-9
Raymond, Mount—summit CA-9
Raymond, Mount—summit UT-8
Raymond, P. P., House—hist pl IA-7
Raymond, Tilley, House—hist pl MA-1
Raymond, Wilbur S., House—hist pl CO-8
**Raymondale**—pop pl VA-3
Raymond Ave Sch—school CA-9
Raymond Ave Sch—school NY-2
Raymond Baptist Ch—church MS-4
Raymond Basin—basin WY-8
Raymond Battlefield Site—hist pl MS-4
Raymond Boston and Maine RR Depot—hist pl NH-1
Raymond-Bradford Homestead—hist pl CT-1
Raymond Branch—stream LA-4
Raymond Branch—stream MS-4
Raymond Bridge—bridge MT-8
Raymond Brook—stream CT-1
Raymond Brook—stream (2) NY-2
Raymond Brothers Lake Dam—dam MS-4
Raymond B Winter State Park—park PA-2
Raymond Canal—canal ID-8
Raymond Canyon—valley WY-8
Raymond Canyon Creek—stream CA-9
Raymond Cape—cape ME-1
Raymond (CCD)—cens area WA-9
Raymond Cem—cemetery CA-9
Raymond Cem—cemetery (2) CT-1
Raymond Cem—cemetery ID-8
Raymond Cem—cemetery LA-4
Raymond Cem—cemetery MI-6
Raymond Cem—cemetery (2) OH-6
Raymond Cem—cemetery OK-5
Raymond Cem—cemetery WI-6
Raymond Ch—church WI-6
Raymond Chapel Presbyterian Church MS-4
**Raymond City**—pop pl WV-2
Raymond Cliff—cliff NH-1
Raymond Corners PA-2
Raymond Corners—locale MI-6
Raymond Cove—bay AK-9
Raymond Creek—stream (3) ID-8
Raymond Creek—stream NC-3
Raymond Creek—stream ND-7
Raymond Creek—stream OR-9
Raymond Creek—stream TX-5
Raymond Creek—stream VA-3
Raymond Creek—stream WI-6
Raymond Creek—stream WY-8
Raymond Dam—dam NJ-2
Raymond Dierickx Dam—dam OR-9
Raymond Dierickx Rsvr—reservoir OR-9
Raymond Ditch IN-6
Raymond Drain—canal CA-9
Raymond Drain—canal MI-6
Raymond Drain—stream MI-6
Raymond E Baldwin Bridge (Toll)—bridge CT-1
Raymond Ely Extension Mine—mine NV-8
Raymond F Brandes Elem Sch—school IN-6
Raymond Flat—flat CA-9
Raymond Fuller Ranch—locale NM-5
Raymond Gary, Lake—reservoir OK-5
Raymond Granite Union HS—school CA-9
Raymond Gulch—valley CA-9
Raymond Gulch—valley (2) OR-9
Raymond Gut—gut DE-2
Raymond Hanzlik Dam—dam SD-7
Raymond Harper Pond Dam—dam MS-4
Raymond Harris Pond Dam—dam MS-4
Raymond Hill—locale KY-4
Raymond Hill—summit CA-9
Raymond Hill—summit ME-1
Raymond Hill—summit VT-1
Raymond Hill Cem—cemetery CT-1
Raymond Hill Cem—cemetery NY-2
Raymond Hill Ch—church GA-3
Raymond Hills—summit NY-2
Raymond Hollow—valley KY-4
Raymond HS—school MS-4
Raymond Island—island NC-3
Raymond Kill PA-2
Raymond Lake—lake AZ-5
Raymond Lake—lake AR-4
Raymond Lake—lake CA-9
Raymond Lake—lake MN-6
Raymond Lake—reservoir MS-4
Raymond Lake Dam—dam MS-4
Raymond Landing (historical)—locale SD-7
Raymond Landing Shoal—bar TX-5
Raymond Lookout Tower—locale MS-4
Raymond L Young Elementary School AL-4
Raymond Meadows—flat CA-9
Raymond Meadows Creek—stream CA-9
Raymond Meyer Dam—dam SD-7
Raymond Mine—mine CA-9
Raymond Mine—mine CO-8
Raymond-Morley House—hist pl TX-5
Raymond Mountain CA-9
Raymond Neck DE-2
Raymond Neck—cape DE-2
Raymond Neck—cape ME-1
Raymond Neck Hist Dist—hist pl DE-2
Raymond O'Conner Park—park NY-2
Raymond-Ogden Mansion—hist pl WA-9
Raymond Oil Field TX-5
Raymond Park—park AZ-5
Raymond Park—park ID-8
Raymond Park—park IL-6
Raymond Park—park NE-7
Raymond Path—trail NH-1
Raymond Peak—summit AK-9
Raymond Peak—summit CA-9
Raymond Point—cape NY-2
Raymond Pond—lake ME-1
Raymond Pond—lake MD-2
Raymond Pond—lake NH-1
Raymond Pool—reservoir DE-2
Raymond Pool Dam—dam DE-2
Raymond Post Office—building MS-4
Raymond Presbyterian Ch—church MS-4
Raymond Public Library—building MS-4
Raymond Public Library—hist pl WA-9
Raymond Quarry—mine CA-9
Raymond Retarding Basin—reservoir CA-9
Raymond Rocks—island CT-1
Raymond Sand—gut NC-3
Raymonds Camp (historical)—locale OR-9
Raymonds Cave—cave AL-4
Raymond Sch—school CA-9
Raymond Sch—school DC-2
Raymond Sch—school IL-6
Raymond Sch—school (2) MA-1
Raymond Sch—school OH-6
Raymond Sch—school TX-5
Raymond Sewage Lagoon Dam—dam MS-4
Raymonds Fork—locale VA-3
Raymonds Hollow—valley UT-8
**Raymond Shupe Addition Subdivision**—pop pl UT 8
**Raymond Shupe Park Addition (subdivision)**—pop pl UT-8
**Raymond Shupe Subdivision**—pop pl UT-8
Raymondskill PA-2
Raymondskill Creek—stream PA-2
Raymondskill Falls—falls PA-2
Raymonds Pit—cave AL-4
Raymonds Point—cape RI-1
Raymonds Pond—lake CT-1
Raymonds Pond—reservoir OR-9
Raymond Spring—spring ID-8
Raymonds (RR name for Raymond)—other OH-6
Raymonds S Bowers Elem Sch—school TN-4
Raymond Street Sch—school NY-2
Raymond Tank—reservoir (3) AZ-5
Raymond Town Hall—building ND-7
**Raymond (Town of)**—pop pl ME-1
**Raymond (Town of)**—pop pl NH-1
**Raymond (Town of)**—pop pl WI-6
**Raymond Township**—pop pl KS-7
**Raymond Township**—pop pl NE-7
**Raymond Township**—pop pl ND-7
**Raymond Township**—pop pl SD-7
Raymond (Township of)—fmr MCD AR-4
**Raymond (Township of)**—pop pl (2) IL-6
**Raymond (Township of)**—pop pl MN-6
Raymond United Methodist Ch—church MS-4
**Raymondville**—pop pl MO-7
**Raymondville**—pop pl NY-2
**Raymondville**—pop pl TX-5
Raymondville (CCD)—cens area TX-5
Raymondville Cem—cemetery TX-5
Raymondville Country Club—other TX-5
Raymondville Oil Field—oilfield TX-5
Raymondville Parabolic Bridge—hist pl NY-2
Raymond W Bliss Army Hosp—hospital AZ-5
Raymore—locale WI-6
**Raymore**—pop pl MO-7
Raymore Cem—cemetery MO-7
Raymore International Airp—airport MO-7
Raymore Pass—gap WI-6
Raymore Township—civil MO-7
Raymound Sch—school MI-6
Ray Mountains—other AK-9
Raymouth Ch—church GA-3
Ray Mtn—summit GA-3
Raynagua, Lake—reservoir AL-4
Raynagua Dam—dam AL-4
Raynal Sch—school TX-5
Rayna Post Office (historical)—building AL-4
Rayne—locale PA-2
**Rayne**—pop pl LA-4
Rayne Airp—airport PA-2
Rayne Ch—church PA-2
**Rayneer Subdivision**—pop pl UT-8
Ray Nell Acres Lake—reservoir IN-6
Ray Nell Acres Lake Dam—dam IN-6
Rayner, Eli, House—hist pl TN-4
Rayner Cem—cemetery TN-4
Rayner Cem—cemetery TX-5
Rayner Hollow—valley TX-5
Rayner Junction—locale TX-5
Rayner Pond—lake FL-3
Rayne Run—stream PA-2
Raynes Ch—church OH-6
**Raynesford**—pop pl MT-8
Raynes Neck—cape ME-1
Raynes Run PA-2
**Rayne (Township of)**—pop pl PA-2
Raynham MA-1
Raynham—hist pl CT-1
**Raynham**—pop pl MA-1
**Raynham**—pop pl NC-3
Raynham Cem—cemetery MA-1
**Raynham Center**—pop pl MA-1
Raynham Center Sch—school MA-1
Raynham Centre MA-1
Raynham Ch—church MA-1
Raynham Hall—hist pl NY-2
Raynham Hill—summit CT-1
Raynham (North Raynham)—other MA-1
Raynham Racetrack—locale MA-1
Raynham Shop Ctr—locale MA-1
Raynham Station (historical)—locale MA-1
Raynham Townhall—building MA-1
**Raynham (Town of)**—pop pl MA-1
Raynis-Ford Cem—cemetery NH-1
Raynolds, Sara, Hall—hist pl NM-5
Raynolds Bay—bay MI-6
Raynolds Pass—gap ID-8
Raynolds Pass—gap MT-8
Raynolds Peak—summit WY-8
Raynolds Point—cape MI-6
Raynor—locale VA-3
**Raynor**—pop pl NC-3
Raynor, John, House—hist pl MI-6
**Raynor Acres Subdivision**—pop pl UT-8
Raynor Creek—stream CA-9
Raynor-Edmonson Ditches—canal CO-8
Raynor Grove Ch—church AR-4
**Raynor Heights**—pop pl MD-2
Raynor Park IL-6
**Raynor Park**—pop pl IL-6
Raynor Park—uninc pl CA-9
Raynor Park Sch—school IL-6
Raynor Sch—school CA-9
Raynor Swamp—stream NC-3
Raynor Town—locale NC-3
Rayns Creek—stream IL-6
Rayns Crossroads NC-3
Rayo—locale CA-9
Rayo (Barrio)—fmr MCD PR-3
Rayo Hills—summit NM-5
Ray Oil Field—oilfield TX-5
Rayon TN-4
**Rayon City**—pop pl TN-4
Rayonet Square (Shop Ctr)—locale FL-3
Rayonier, Lake One—lake FL-3
Rayonier, Lake Two—lake FL-3
Rayon Sch—school WV-2
**Rayon Terrace**—pop pl TN-4
**Rayon Terrace**—pop pl VA-3
Ray Opera House—hist pl ND-7
Ray Orchard—locale MO-7
**Rayo (Shady Grove Corner)**—pop pl VA-3
Ray Park—park CA-9
Ray Park—park CT-1
Ray Park—park TX-5
Ray Placo—locale AZ-5
Ray Point—cape ME-1
Ray Point—locale TX-5
Ray Point Cem—cemetery TX-5
Ray Pond VT-1
Ray Pond—lake FL-3
Ray Post Office (historical)—building TN-4
Ray Ranch—locale CO-8
Ray Ranch—locale ND-7
Ray Ranch—locale (2) OR-9
Ray Ranch—locale TX-5
Ray Reese Ranch—locale WY-8
Ray Ridge—ridge WA-9
Ray River—stream AK-9
Ray River Hot Spring—spring AK-9
Ray Roberts Lake—reservoir TX-5
Ray Ronan Park—park ND-7
Ray RR Dam—dam ND-7
Rays—locale TN-4
**Raysal**—pop pl WV-2
Rays Bar—bar TN-4
Rays Beach—locale NC-3
Rays Big Branch—stream NC-3
Rays Bottom—bend UT-8
Rays Branch—stream IN-6
Rays Branch—stream KY-4
Rays Branch—stream (2) WV-2
Rays Branch Ch—church KY-4
Rays Bridge Ch—church GA-3
Rays Bridge (historical)—bridge AL-4
Rays Cabins—locale MI-6
Rays Camp—locale TN-4
Rays Ch—church GA-3
Ray Sch—school AL-4
Ray Sch—school CA-9
Ray Sch—school (2) IL-6
Ray Sch—school KS-7
Ray Sch—school MD-2
Ray Sch—school NE-7
Ray Sch—school PA-2
Ray Sch—school TX-5
Ray Sch (abandoned)—school MO-7
Rays Chapel—church FL-3
Rays Chapel—church GA-3
Rays Chapel—church NC-3
Rays Chapel—church TN-4
**Rays Chapel**—pop pl TN-4
Rays Chapel Baptist Church TN-4
Rays Chapel United Methodist Church TN-4
Ray Sch (historical)—school MO-7
Ray Sch (historical)—school PA-2
Ray Schnepf Ranch Airstrip—airport AZ-5
Ray School—locale IL-6
Rays Church PA-2
Rays Corner OH-6
Rays Corners—locale PA-2
**Rays Corners**—pop pl NY-2
**Rays Corners**—pop pl (2) OH-6
Rays Cove Ch—church PA-2
Rays Creek—stream CA-9
Rays Creek—stream (2) NC-3
Rays Creek—stream TX-5
**Rays Crossing**—pop pl IN-6
Rays Crossroads—locale AL-4
Rays Ditch—gut DE-2
Rayse Creek IL-6
Rayse Creek—stream IL-6
Ray See Park—park OK-5
Rays Fork—stream KY-4
Rays Fork—stream NC-3
Rays Fork Ch—church KY-4
Rays Gulch—valley CA-9
Rayshill AL-4
Rays Hill PA-2
Rays Hill—ridge PA-2
Rays Hill Tunnel—tunnel PA-2
Ray Siding NV-8
Ray Siding—locale WV-2
Rays Lake—lake OR-9
Rays Lake—reservoir (2) GA-3
Rays Lake—reservoir ID-8
Rays Lake—reservoir TN-4
Rays Lake—swamp IL-6
Rays Lake Canal—canal ID-8
Rays Lake Dam—dam TN-4
Rays Lake Pump—other ID-8
Rays Landing—locale MS-4
Rays Mill Pond—lake ME-1
Rays Millpond—reservoir (2) GA-3
Ray Smiths Lake—reservoir AL-4
Ray Smucker Park—park AZ-5
Raysonde Buttes—summit NV-8
Raysor Bridge—bridge SC-3
Raysor Creek—stream FL-3
Rays Peak—summit (2) CA-9
Rays Point—cape MN-6
Rays Pond GA-3
Rays Pond—reservoir AL-4
Rays Pond—reservoir GA-3
Rays Pond—reservoir MA-1
Rays Pond Dam—dam AL-4
Ray Spring—spring AZ-5
Ray Spring—spring CA-9
Ray Spring—spring MO-7
Ray Spring—spring UT-8
Ray Spring Branch—stream MO-7
Ray Spring Ch—church MO-7
Ray Spring Hill—summit AZ-5
Ray Springhouse—building MO-7
Ray Springs TN-4
Ray Spring Wash—stream AZ-5
Rays Roost Airp—airport MO-7
Rays Rsvr—reservoir ID-8
Rays Run—stream PA-2
Rays (Site)—locale NV-8
Rays Swamp—swamp GA-3
Rays Tank—reservoir (2) AZ-5
Rays Tavern IN-6
Raystone Creek—stream NY-2
Raystown Branch Juniata River—stream PA-2
Raystown Ch—church PA-2
Raystown Dam—dam PA-2
Raystown Lake—reservoir PA-2
Raystown Rsvr PA-2
Ray Street Recreation Center—locale NC-3
Rays Valley—basin UT-8
Raysville—locale GA-3
**Raysville**—pop pl IN-6
**Raysville**—pop pl TN-4
Raysville Bridge—bridge GA-3
Raysville Cem—cemetery TN-4
Raysville Ch—church TN-4
Raysville Run—stream IN-6
Raysville Sch (historical)—school TN-4
Rays Well—well NV-8
Rays Wells—well NV-8
Ray Tank—reservoir AZ-5
Ray T Mantz Dam—dam PA-2
Raytown—locale GA-3
Raytown—locale PA-2
**Raytown**—pop pl MS-4
**Raytown**—pop pl MO-7
Raytown Centre Shops—locale MO-7
Raytown Ch—church GA-3
Ray Town Hall—building ND-7
Raytown Plaza—locale MO-7
**Ray Township**—pop pl ND-7
**Ray (Township of)**—pop pl (2) IN-6
**Ray (Township of)**—pop pl MI-6
Raytown South HS—school MO-7
Raytown South JHS—school MO-7
Ray Trail—trail CO-8
Ray Trail—trail WA-9
Ray Trawick Lake Dam—dam MS-4
Ray Unified District Elem Sch—school AZ-5
Rayville—locale IL-6
Rayville—locale WA-9
**Rayville**—pop pl LA-4
**Rayville**—pop pl ME-1
**Rayville**—pop pl MD-2
**Rayville**—pop pl MO-7
**Rayville**—pop pl NY-2
Rayville (historical)—locale KS-7
Ray Warren NC-3
**Raywick**—pop pl KY-4
Raywick (CCD)—cens area KY-4
Ray Willoughby Dam Number 1—dam IN-6
Ray Willoughby Dam Number 2 North—dam IN-6
Ray Willoughby Lake—reservoir IN-6
Ray Windmill—locale NM-5
Ray Windmill—locale TX-5
Raywood—locale WV-2
**Raywood**—pop pl TX-5
Raywood Flat—flat CA-9
Raywood Flat Trail (Pack)—trail CA-9
Razburg (historical)—locale AL-4
Razer Cem—cemetery OH-6
Raz Lewis Flat—flat OR-9
**Razor**—pop pl TX-5
Razorback—ridge AZ-5
Razorback Lake WI-6
Razorback Lake—lake WI-6
Razorback Mtn—summit MT-8
Razorback Mtn—summit OK-5
Razorback Mtn—summit WA-9
Razorback Pond—lake NY-2
Razor Back Ridge OR-9
Razorback Ridge—ridge CO-8
Razorback Ridge—ridge (2) NV-8
Razorback Ridge—ridge NC-3
Razor Back Ridge—ridge OR-9
Razorblade Branch—stream KY-4
Razor Blade Mesa—summit OK-5
Razor Branch—stream GA-3
Razor Branch—stream KY-4
Razor Brook—stream NH-1
Razor Brook Trail—trail NH-1
Razor Canyon—valley NV-8
Razor Creek—stream CO-8
Razor Creek—stream MT-8
Razor Creek Dome—summit CO-8
Razor Creek Park—flat CO-8
Razor Dome CO-8
Razoredge Mtn—summit MT-8
Razor Fork—stream IN-6
Razor Fork—stream KY-4
Razor Hollow—valley (2) MO-7
Razor Hone Creek—stream WA-9
Razor Island—island ME-1
Razor Lake—lake FL-3
Razor Lake—lake MN-6
Razor Lake—lake WA-9
Razor Mtn—summit NC-3
Razor Ridge—ridge CA-9
Razor Ridge—ridge OR-9
Razor Ridge—ridge VA-3
Razor Ridge Ch—church VA-3
Razor Run—stream OH-6
**Razorville**—pop pl ME-1
Razz Lake—lake OR-9
Razzle Creek—stream MT-8
R Baker—locale TX-5
R Bar C Ranch—locale AZ-5
R Bartels Number 1 Dam—dam SD-7
R Baskin Lake Dam—dam MS-4
R Baye Ranch—locale ND-7
R Bergquist Ranch—locale ND-7
R Berndt Dam—dam SD-7
R B Harrison Junior High School NC-3
R B Hoke Lake Dam—dam MS-4
R B Hunt Elem Sch—school FL-3
R Bierman Dam—dam SD-7
R Bierman Number 2 Dam—dam SD-7
R B Lake—lake WA-9
R B Lynch Catfish Ponds Dam—dam MS-4
R B Middleton Lake Dam—dam MS-4
R B Ricketts Falls—falls PA-2
R B Spires Pond—lake FL-3
R B Squirls Pond—lake FL-3
R B Underwood—lake FL-3
R Burns Ranch—locale ND-7
R B Valley Windmill—locale TX-5
R B Windmill—locale (2) TX-5
R B Worthy HS—school VA-3
R.C.A. Chatham Station—building MA-1
RCA Corporation—facility OH-6
RCA-Lancaster Airp—airport PA-2
R C A Landing Strip—airport NJ-2
R Canal—canal ID-8
R Canal—canal MT-8
R Canal—canal OR-9
RCA Pond—lake AZ-5
R C A Princeton—airport NJ-2
R C A Sommerville—airport NJ-2
R C Balfour Lower Dam—dam NC-3
R C Camp Lake Dam—dam MS-4
R C Farm—locale CA-9
R C Hatch High School AL-4
Rchieb, Ollumelra—ridge PW-9
R Childress Ranch—locale TX-5
**R C Hunter Subdivision**—pop pl UT-8
RC Kremmers Lake—lake IL-6
R C Kreusler Park—park FL-3
R Clark Number 1 Dam—dam SD-7
R Clark Number 2 Dam—dam SD-7
R Clark Number 3 Dam—dam SD-7
R Clem Churchwell Elem Sch—school FL-3
R C Malone Pond Dam—dam MS-4
R C Marina—locale TN-4
R Compton Dam—dam SD-7
R Corner—locale WA-9
R-C Ranch—locale AZ-5
R Cullpepper Dam—dam AL-4
R Cullpepper Lake—reservoir AL-4
R C Withers Tanks—reservoir NM-5
R.D. Bailey Dam—dam WV-2
R D Bearden Pond Dam—dam MS-4
R D Beasley Dam—dam AL-4
R D Beasley Fish Pond—reservoir AL-4
R Dempsey Lake Dam—dam MS-4
R D Goin Pond Dam—dam MS-4
R D Lee Ranch—locale NM-5
R Doolittle Pond Dam—dam MS-4
R Drain—canal CA-9
R Drain—canal NV-8
R D Spring—spring OR-9
R D S Ranch—locale WY-8
R E AL-4
Rea—locale PA-2
**Rea**—pop pl IA-7
**Rea**—pop pl MI-6
**Rea**—pop pl MO-7
Rea, William, Store—hist pl NC-3
Rea Block Field—locale PA-2
Rea Branch TN-4
Reaburn, Mount—summit AK-9
R E A Canyon—valley CO-8
Rea Cem—cemetery AL-4
Rea Cem—cemetery IL-6
Rea Cem—cemetery IN-6
Rea Cem—cemetery OH-6
Rea Cemeteries—cemetery NC-3
Reach ME-1

**Rector**—pop pl PA-2
Rector Brake—swamp AR-4
Rector Branch—stream (2) NC-3
Rector Branch—stream (3) TN-4
Rector Butt—summit NC-3
Rector Canyon—valley CA-9
Rector Canyon—valley TX-5
Rector Cem—cemetery IN-6
Rector Cem—cemetery IA-7
Rector Cem—cemetery KY-4
Rector Cem—cemetery MO-7
Rector Cem—cemetery NC-3
Rector Cem—cemetery OH-6
Rector Cem—cemetery SC-3
Rector Cem—cemetery (2) TN-4
Rector Cem—cemetery WV-2
Rector Ch—church IL-6
Rector Chapel—church NC-3
Rector Creek CA-9
Rector Creek—stream (2) CA-9
Rector Creek—stream IL-6
Rector Creek—stream OR-9
Rector Creek—stream TX-5
Rector Hill—summit AR-4
**Rector (historical)**—pop pl OR-9
Rector Hollow—valley MO-7
Rector Knob—summit GA-3
Rector Knob—summit (2) NC-3
Rector Lake—lake WI-6
Rector Lookout—locale OR-9
Rector Mine (underground)—mine TN-4
Rector Mtn—summit NC-3
Rector Peak—summit CA-9
Rector Post Office (historical)—building AL-4
Rector Ranch—locale CA-9
Rector Ridge—ridge OR-9
Rector Ridge—ridge UT-8
Rector Rsvr—reservoir CA-9
Rector Rsvr—reservoir OR-9
**Rectors**—pop pl NY-2
Rectors Flat Ch—church KY-4
Rector (site)—locale OR-9
Rectors Mill—locale PA-2
Rector Spring—spring OR-9
Rector Spring—spring TN-4
Rectortown—locale VA-3
**Rector (Township of)**—pop pl IL-6
**Rectorville**—pop pl KY-4
Rector Well—well (2) NM-5
Rectory—hist pl MH-9
Rectory—locale VA-3
Rectory, Catholic Church of the Assumption—hist pl CA-9
Rectory and Church of the Immaculate Conception—hist pl CT-1
Rectory of St. George's Episcopal Church—hist pl NY-2
Rectory Sch—school CT-1
Recuerdo Windmill—locale TX-5
Reculusa Ranch—locale WY-8
Recupsido Mine (surface)—mine TN-4
**Recurso**—pop pl PR-3
Red NC-3
Red, Neils, Covered Bridge—hist pl PA-2
Redabaugh Cem—cemetery WV-2
Red Acre (historical)—locale MS-4
**Red Acres (subdivision)**—pop pl NC-3
Red Alder Campground—locale CA-9
Red Aleck Canyon—valley TX-5
Redalia NC-3
Redalir NC-3
Red Alkali Lake—lake WA-9
Redallia—locale NC-3
**Redallia**—pop pl NC-3
Red Amphitheater—basin CA-9
Red Amphitheatre—basin CO-8
Redan—locale GA-3
Redan Ch—church AL-4
Red And Black Trail—trail WV-2
Red and Bonita Mine—mine CO-8
Redan Ditch Second Enlargement—canal WY-8
Red and King Gulch—valley MT-8
Red and White Airp—airport OR-9
Red and White Flying Service Airfield—airport OR-9
Red and White Lake—lake CA-9
Red and White Mtn—summit CA-9
Red and White Mtn—summit CO-8
Red And White Sch—school CT-1
Red And White Tank—reservoir NM-5
Redan Point—cape AK-9
Red Ant—locale CA-9
Red Ant Canyon—valley CA-9
Red Ant Gulch—valley CA-9
Red Ant Mine—mine NV-8
Red Apple—locale CA-9
Red Apple Cem—cemetery AL-4
Red Apple Ch—church AL-4
Red Apple (historical)—locale AL-4
Red Apple Missionary Baptist Church AL-4
**Red Apple Orchard**—pop pl VA-3
Red Arch Mtn—summit UT-8
Red Arrow Cave—cave TX-5
Red Arrow Club—other MO-7
Red Arrow Dome—summit CO-8
Red Arrow Hill—summit MI-6
Red Arrow Mine—mine CO-8
Red Arrow Park—park (2) WI-6
Red Arroyo—stream NM-5
Red Arroyo—valley (3) TX-5
Red Arroyo Camp—locale TX-5
Red Arroyo Tank—locale TX-5
Redart—locale VA-3
Red Ash—locale KY-4
Red Ash—locale TN-4
**Red Ash**—pop pl VA-3
Red Ash Mines—mine TN-4
Red Ballon—post sta FL-3
Red Bank OH-6
Redbank PA-2
Redbank SC-3
Red Bank—island NY-2
Red Bank—levee DE-2
Red Bank—locale AR-4
Red Bank—locale CA-9
Red Bank—locale OH-6
Red Bank—locale TN-4
Red Bank—locale VA-3
**Red Bank**—pop pl AL-4
**Red Bank**—pop pl IN-6
**Red Bank**—pop pl MO-7
**Red Bank**—pop pl (2) NJ-2
**Red Bank**—pop pl (2) PA-2
**Red Bank**—pop pl SC-3
**Red Bank**—pop pl TN-4
**Redbank**—pop pl TX-5
**Red Bank**—pop pl VA-3
Red Bank Baptist Ch—church TN-4
Red Bank Battlefield—hist pl NJ-2
Red Bank Battlefield—park NJ-2
Redbank Branch—stream MS-4
Redbank Branch—stream NC-3
Red Bank Branch—stream NC-3
Red Bank Bridge—bridge AL-4
Red Bank Campground—locale CA-9
Red Bank Cem—cemetery AL-4
Redbank Cem—cemetery CA-9
Red Bank Cem—cemetery IL-6
Red Bank Cem—cemetery NJ-2
Redbank Cem—cemetery NC-3
Red Bank Ch—church AL-4
Red Bank Ch—church MO-7
Red Bank Ch—church NJ-2
Red Bank Ch—church NC-3
Red Bank Ch—church SC-3
Red Bank Ch—church TN-4
Red Bank Ch—church VA-3
Red Bank Ch of Christ—church TN-4
Red Bank City Hall—building TN-4
Red Bank Community Hospital TN-4
Redbank Coulee—valley MT-8
Red Bank Creek MS-4
Red Bank Creek PA-2
Red Bank Creek TX-5
Red Bank Creek—stream AL-4
Redbank Creek—stream AR-4
Red Bank Creek—stream CA-9
Red Bank Creek—stream LA-4
Red Bank Creek—stream MS-4
Red Bank Creek—stream MO-7
Red Bank Creek—stream MT-8
Red Bank Creek—stream NC-3
Redbank Creek—stream OK-5
Redbank Creek—stream (2) PA-2
Red Bank Creek—stream (2) SC-3
Red Bank Creek—stream TN-4
Red Bank Creek—stream (8) TX-5
Red Bank Creek—stream VA-3
Redbank Creek—stream WY-8
Red Bank Cumberland Presbyterian Ch—church TN-4
Red Bank Ditch No 2—canal WY-8
Redbank Drain—stream SC-3
Red Bank Elem Sch—school TN-4
Red Bank Ford—locale AL-4
Redbank Furnace—locale PA-2
Redbank Gorge—valley CA-9
Red Bank Gulch—valley CA-9
Redbank Hill—summit TN-4
Redbank Hill Crossroads—locale TN-4
Red Bank Hollow—valley MO-7
Redbank Hollow—valley OK-5
Red Bank HS—school NJ-2
Red Bank HS—school TN-4
Red Bank JHS—school TN-4
Red Bank JHS—school VA-3
Red Bank Lakes—flat OR-9
Red Bank Landing—locale AR-4
Redbank Landing—locale (2) NC-3
Red Bank Landing—locale SC-3
Red Bank Landing—locale VA-3
Red Bank Landing (historical)—locale NC-3
Red Bank Landing (historical)—locale TN-4
Redbank Lodge—locale NC-3
Redbank (Magisterial District)—fmr MCD VA-3
Red Bank Passenger Station—hist pl NJ-2
Red Bank Plantation—hist pl FL-3
Red Bank Post Office—building TN-4
Red Bank Presbyterian Ch—church TN-4
Red Bank Reach—channel NJ-2
Red Bank Reach—channel NY-2
Red Bank Reserve—reservoir SC-3
Red Banks—cliff UT-8
Redbanks—locale CA-9
Red Banks—locale WI-6
**Red Banks**—pop pl MS-4
**Red Banks** pop pl NC-3
**Red Banks**—pop pl WI-6
Red Banks—ridge CA-9
Red Banks—ridge GA-3
Red Banks Campground—locale UT-8
Red Banks Cem—cemetery MS-4
Red Banks Cem—cemetery OH-6
Red Banks Ch—church NC-3
Red Bank Sch—school ME-1
Redbank Sch—school SC-3
Red Bank Sch (abandoned)—school PA-2
Redbank Sch (abandoned)—school PA-2
Red Bank Sch (historical)—school AL-4
Red Bank Sch (historical)—school PA-2
Red Bank Sch (historical)—school TN-4
Red Bank Sch Number 1—school NJ-2
Red Bank Sch Number 11—school NJ-2
Red Banks Creek—stream MS-4
Red Banks Creek Canal—canal MS-4
Red Bank Shoals TN-4
Redbank Slough—gut CA-9
Red Banks Primary Baptist Ch NC-3
Red Bank Spring—spring AZ-5
Red Bank Spring—spring SD-7
Red Bank Spring—spring UT-8
Redbanks Run—stream VA-3
Red Bank Station—locale PA-2
**Redbank (Township of)**—pop pl (2) PA-2
Red Bank Trail—trail (2) PA-2
Red Bank United Methodist Ch—church TN-4
Redbank Village (2) ME-1
Red Bank Well—well AZ-5
Red Bank-white Oak—other TN-4
**Red Barn**—pop pl PA-2
Red Barn Ch—church MS-4
Red Barn Landing—locale NC-3
Red Barn Tank—reservoir TX-5
Red Barn Well—well NM-5
Red Basin—basin AZ-5
Red Basin—basin ID-8
Red Basin—basin OR-9
Red Basin—basin (3) WY-8
Red Basin Creek—stream ID-8
Red Basin Rsvr—reservoir OR-9
Red Basin Spring—spring AZ-5
Red Bass Lake—lake WI-6
Red Bay FL-3
Red Bay—bay AK-9
Red Bay—bay FL-3
Red Bay—cape VI-3
**Red Bay**—pop pl AL-4
**Red Bay**—pop pl FL-3
**Redbay**—pop pl FL-3
Red Bay—swamp FL-3
Red Bay Bank—bar FL-3
Red Bay Base South East—other AL-4
Red Bay Branch—stream FL-3
Red Bay (CCD)—cens area AL-4
Redbay (CCD)—cens area FL-3
Red Bay Cem—cemetery AL-4
Redbay Cem—cemetery FL-3
Red Bay Division—civil AL-4
Red Bay Freewill Baptist Ch—church AL-4
Red Bay HS—school AL-4
Red Bay Memorial Cemetery AL-4
Red Bay Mtn—summit AK-9
Red Bay Municipal Airp—airport AL-4
Red Bayou LA-4
Red Bayou—gut (2) LA-4
Red Bayou—gut TX-5
Red Bayou—stream (5) LA-4
Red Bayou—stream (3) TX-5
Red Bayou Ch—church LA-4
Red Bayou Ch—church TX-5
Red Bay Point—cape FL-3
Red Bay Pumping Station—other AL-4
Redbay Tower—tower FL-3
Red Beach ME-1
Red Beach MH-9
Red Beach—beach AK-9
**Red Beach**—pop pl ME-1
Red Beach Cove—bay ME-1
Red Beach Lake—lake FL-3
Red Beach Landing—locale ME-1
Red Bear Reach—channel TX-5
Red Bedground Spring—spring UT-8
Red Bed Peak—summit AK-9
Redbell—locale OR-9
Red Belly Lake—lake UT-8
Red Benches—bench UT-8
Red Bench Windmill—locale CO-8
Red Bend—bend TX-5
Red Berry Mtn—summit OK-5
Red Bill Hill—summit WY-8
Red Bill Point—pillar WY-8
Red Birch Sch—school IL-6
Redbird—locale KY-4
Redbird—locale NE-7
Redbird—locale NY-2
Redbird—locale WV-2
Redbird—locale WY-8
**Red Bird**—pop pl KY-4
**Red Bird**—pop pl MO-7
**Redbird**—pop pl MO-7
**Redbird**—pop pl OH-6
**Red Bird**—pop pl OK-5
**Redbird**—pop pl PA-2
Red Bird—uninc pl TX-5
**Red Bird Addition**—pop pl TX-5
Red Bird Branch—stream TN-4
Redbird Canyon—valley CA-9
Redbird Canyon—valley SD-7
Red Bird Cem—cemetery OK-5
Red Bird City Hall—hist pl OK-5
**Redbird (corporate name for Red Bird)**—pop pl OK-5
Red Bird (corporate name Redbird) OK-5
Red Bird Cove—bay TX-5
Redbird Creek—stream CA-9
Redbird Creek—stream GA-3
Redbird Creek—stream ID-8
Red Bird Creek—stream KY-4
Redbird Creek—stream NE-7
Redbird Draw—valley SD-7
Redbird Elem Sch—school AZ-5
Redbird Gulch—valley ID-8
Red Bird Hill Mine—mine TN-4
Red Bird Hills—ridge AZ-5
Redbird I Site—hist pl NE-7
Redbird Island—island FL-3
Redbird Lake—lake MS-4
Red Bird Lake—reservoir OK-5
Red Bird Mine—mine (2) AZ-5
Redbird Mine—mine CO-8
Redbird Mine—mine ID-8
Redbird Mine—mine NV-8
Red Bird Mine—mine (3) NV-8
Red Bird Mine—mine OR-9
Red Bird Mission Hosp—hospital KY-4
Redbird Mtn—summit ID-8
Redbird Point—cape TN-4
Redbird Prairie—swamp GA-3
Redbird Ridge—ridge IL-6
Red Bird River—stream KY-4
Red Bird River Ch—church KY-4
Red Bird Sch—school OH-6
Red Bird Settlement Sch—school KY-4
Red Bird Shop Ctr—locale FL-3
Red Bird Smith Creek—stream OK-5
Redbird Stone WY-8
Red Bird Store WY-8
Red Black Hills—summit TX-5
Red Blanket Butte—summit MT-8
Red Blanket Creek—stream OK-5
Red Blanket Creek—stream OR-9
Red Blanket Mtn—summit OR-9
Red Blanket Peak—summit AZ-5
Red Blanket Ranch—locale AZ-5
Red Blanket Rsvr—reservoir OR-9
Red Blanket Trail—trail OR-9
Red Bluff—cliff (3) AL-4
Red Bluff—cliff (3) AK-9
Red Bluff—cliff AZ-5
Red Bluff—cliff (7) AR-4
Red Bluff—cliff CA-9
Red Bluff—cliff FL-3
Red Bluff—cliff (5) GA-3
Red Bluff—cliff LA-4
Red Bluff—cliff (7) MS-4
Red Bluff—cliff (4) MO-7
Red Bluff—cliff NV-8
Red Bluff—cliff OK-5
Red Bluff—cliff (2) SC-3
Red Bluff—cliff (6) TX-5
Red Bluff—cliff UT-8
Red Bluff—cliff (2) WA-9
Red Bluff—locale AR-4
Red Bluff—locale GA-3
Red Bluff—locale MT-8
Red Bluff—locale NM-5
**Red Bluff**—pop pl CA-9
**Red Bluff**—pop pl GA-3
**Red Bluff**—pop pl SC-3
**Red Bluff**—pop pl (2) TX-5
Red Bluff—summit AK-9
Red Bluff—summit CA-9
Red Bluff Bay—bay AK-9
Red Bluff Branch—stream AR-4
Red Bluff Campground—locale MO-7
Red Bluff Campground—park UT-8
Red Bluff Canyon—valley NM-5
Red Bluff Canyon valley WY-8
Red Bluff (CCD)—cens area CA-9
Red Bluff Cem—cemetery AR-4
Red Bluff Cem—cemetery TX-5
Red Bluff Ch—church (3) GA-3
Red Bluff Ch—church LA-4
Red Bluff Ch—church TX-5
Red Bluff Cove—bay TX-5
Red Bluff Creek TX-5
Red Bluff Creek—stream AK-9
Red Bluff Creek—stream (3) GA-3
Red Bluff Creek—stream ID-8
Red Bluff Creek—stream MT-8
Red Bluff Creek—stream OK-5
Red Bluff Creek—stream SC-3
Red Bluff Creek—stream (3) TX-5
Red Bluff Creek—stream WY-8
Red Bluff Crossing—locale (2) TX-5
**Red Bluff Crossroads**—pop pl SC-3
Red Bluff Cutoff Lake—lake OK-5
Red Bluff Dam—dam TX-5
Red Bluff Diversion Dam—dam CA-9
Red Bluff Draw—valley (2) NM-5
Red Bluff Flint Quarries—hist pl SC-3
Red Bluff General Hosp—hospital TX-5
Red Bluff Hollow—valley MO-7
Red Bluff Lake TX-5
Red Bluff Lake—lake LA-4
Red Bluff Lake—reservoir SC-3
Red Bluff Landing—locale (2) GA-3
Red Bluff Landing—locale SC-3
Red Bluff Light—locale AK-9
Red Bluff Mtn—summit AZ-5
Red Bluff Omni Radio Range Station—locale CA-9
Red Bluff Park—park TX-5
Red Bluff Ranch—locale NM-5
Red Bluff Ridge—ridge OR-9
Red Bluff Ridge—ridge WY-8
Red Bluff Rsvr—reservoir NM-5
Red Bluff Rsvr—reservoir TX-5
Red Bluffs AL-4
Red Bluffs UT-8
Red Bluffs—cliff AK-9
Red Bluffs—cliff FL-3
Red Bluffs—cliff NM-5
Red Bluffs—cliff (2) TX-5
Red Bluffs—cliff UT-8
Red Bluffs—cliff WA-9
Red Bluff Sch—school TX-5
Red Bluffs Dam—dam AZ-5
Red Bluff Slough—gut TX-5
Red Bluff Spring—spring AZ-5
Red Bluff Spring—spring ID-8
Red Bluff Spring—spring (2) NV-8
Red Bluff Tank—reservoir AZ-5
Red Bluff Tank—reservoir NM-5
Red Bluff Village Shop Ctr—locale TX-5
Red Bluff Wash—stream NV-8
Red Bluff Windmill—locale TX-5
Red Bluff Windmill—well AZ-5
Redboat Lake—lake MI-6
Red Boiling Spring TN-4
Redboiling Springs TN-4
**Red Boiling Springs**—pop pl TN-4
Red Boiling Springs (CCD)—cens area TN-4
Red Boiling Springs City Hall—building TN-4
Red Boiling Springs Dam Number One—dam TN-4
Red Boiling Springs Division—civil TN-4
Red Boiling Springs First Baptidst Church—church TN-4
Red Boiling Springs Lake Number One—reservoir TN-4
Redboiling Springs Post Office TN-4
Red Boiling Springs Post Office—building TN-4
Red Boiling Springs Sch—school TN-4
Red Boiling Springs Watershed Lake Number Two—reservoir TN-4
Red Boiling Springs Watershed Number Two Dam—dam TN-4
Redbone—locale GA-3
**Redbone**—pop pl MS-4
Red Bone Cem—cemetery MS-4
Redbone Ch—church MS-4
Red Bone Creek—stream GA-3
Redbone Creek—stream MS-4
**Redbone Crossroads**—pop pl GA-3
Red Bone Ridges—ridge GA-3
Red Bottom Tank—reservoir NM-5
Red Box Corral—locale AZ-5
Red Box Gap—gap CA-9
Red Box Spring—spring AZ-5
Red Box Station—locale CA-9
Redboy Mine OR-9
Red Boy Mine—mine NV-8
Red Boy Mine—mine OR-9
Red Boy Peak—summit AZ-5
Red Branch—locale (2) TX-5
Red Branch—stream (2) AL-4
Red Branch—stream (5) AR-4
Red Branch—stream FL-3
Red Branch—stream (2) GA-3
Red Branch—stream (2) LA-4
Red Branch—stream MS-4
Red Branch—stream (7) OK-5
Red Branch—stream SC-3
Red Branch—stream (2) TN-4
Red Branch—stream (16) TX-5
Red Branch Ch—church (2) NC-3
Red Branch Ch—church SC-3
Red Breaks—cliff (2) UT-8
Red Brick Church MS-4
Red Brick Sch—hist pl ME-1
Red Brick Sch—hist pl MA-1
Red Brick Sch—school KS-7
Red Brick Sch—school (2) MI-6
Red Brick Sch—school NE-7
Red Brick Sch—school WI-6
Red Brick Sch (historical)—school IA-7
Red Brick School—locale KS-7
Red Brick Tavern—hist pl OH-6
Red Bridge MO-7
Red Bridge TN-4
Red Bridge—bridge CA-9
Red Bridge—bridge IN-6
Red Bridge—bridge MA-1
Red Bridge—bridge (2) NJ-2
Red Bridge—bridge OH-6
Red Bridge—bridge OR-9
Red Bridge—bridge PA-2
Red Bridge—bridge RI-1
Red Bridge—bridge VT-1
Red Bridge—locale ME-1
Red Bridge—other (3) MI-6
**Red Bridge**—pop pl IN-6
**Red Bridge**—pop pl MA-1
**Red Bridge**—pop pl MO-7
**Red Bridge**—pop pl (2) PA-2
Red Bridge Bayou—stream MS-4
Red Bridge Campground—locale WA-9
Red Bridge Caves—cave PA-2
Red Bridge Dam—dam MA-1
Red Bridge Ferry (historical)—locale TN-4
**Red Bridge (historical)**—pop pl OR-9
Red Bridge Lookout Tower—locale MI-6
Red Bridge Post Office TN-4
Red Bridge Sch—school MO-7
Redbridge Sch—school MT-8
Red Bridge Slough—gut CA-9
Red Bridge State Park—park OR-9
Redbridge State Rec Area IN-6
Red Bridge State Rec Area—park IN-6
Red Brook NY-2
Red Brook—stream (2) CT-1
Red Brook—stream IN-6
Red Brook—stream (5) ME-1
Red Brook—stream (7) MA-1
Red Brook—stream (7) NH-1
Red Brook—stream (5) NY-2
Red Brook—stream OH-6
Red Brook—stream PA-2
Red Brook—stream (2) VT-1
Red Brook Harbor—cove MA-1
Red Brook Pond—reservoir MA-1
Red Brook Pond Dam—dam MA-1
Red Brook Road Dam—dam MA-1
Red Brook Rsvr—reservoir MA-1
**Red Brush**—pop pl NC-3
Red Brush Cem—cemetery IN-6
Red Brush Ch—church IL-6
Red Brush Hill—summit MA-1
Red Brush Ridge—ridge WV-2
Red Brush Sch—school KY-4
Red Brush Sch—school MO-7
Red Brush Sch—school OH-6
Red Brush School (Abandoned)—locale MO-7
Red Brush Valley—valley VA-3
Red Buck Fork—stream WV-2
Red Buck Hollow—valley AR-4
Red Buck Hollow—valley KY-4
Red Buck Ridge—ridge AR-4
Red Bud AL-4
Redbud—locale GA-3
**Redbud**—pop pl AL-4
**Red Bud**—pop pl IL-6
**Redbud**—pop pl KY-4
**Red Bud**—pop pl TN-4
Red Bud—trail TX-5
Redbud Branch—stream (2) NC-3
Red Bud (CCD)—cens area GA-3
Red Bud Cem—cemetery KS-7
Redbud Cem—cemetery TX-5
Redbud Cem—cemetery VA-3
Red Bud Ch—church (2) MS-4
Red Bud Ch—church NC-3
Red Bud Ch—church TX-5
Redbud Ch—church VA-3
Redbud Creek—stream (2) GA-3
Red Bud Creek—stream (3) MS-4
Red Bud Creek—stream (2) NC-3
Redbud Creek—stream TX-5
Redbud Creek—stream UT-8
Redbud Creek—stream VA-3
Redbud Dam—dam TN-4
Red Bud (Election Precinct)—fmr MCD IL-6
Red Bud Hist Dist—hist pl IL-6
Red Bud (historical)—locale KS-7
**Red Bud (historical)**—pop pl MS-4
Redbud Hollow—hist pl WV-2
Redbud Hollow—valley AL-4
Red Bud Hollow—valley MO-7
Red Bud Knob—summit KY-4
Redbud Lake—lake MO-7
Redbud Lake—reservoir KS-7
Redbud Lake—reservoir TN-4
Red Bud Mine—mine NV-8
Red Bud Mine (underground)—mine AL-4
Redbud Missionary Baptist Church MS-4
Redbud Park—park (2) OK-5
Redbud Pass—gap UT-8
Redbud Plantation (historical)—locale MS-4
Redbud Point—cape AL-4
Redbud Post Office (historical)—building AL-4
Red Bud Ridge—ridge WV-2
Redbud Run—stream VA-3
Redbud Sch—school GA-3
Redbud Sch—school IL-6
Red Bud Sch—school KS-7
Redbud Sch (historical)—school MS-4
Red Bud Sch (historical)—school MS-4
Redbuds Island—island PA-2
Red Bud Springs MS-4
Redbud Springs Park—park MS-4
Red Bud Swamp NC-3
Redbud Tank—reservoir TX-5
Redbud Trail Church Camp—locale MI-6
Redbud Valley Nature Center—park PA-2
Red Buffalo Pass—gap CO-8
**Red Bug**—pop pl NC-3
**Redbug**—pop pl NC-3
Red Bug Elem Sch—school FL-3
Red Bug Island—island FL-3
Red Bug Lake—lake (3) FL-3
Redbug Lake—lake GA-3
Red Bug Point—cape NC-3
Red Bug Sch—school AL-4
Red Bull Canyon—valley AZ-5
Red Bull Canyon—valley NM-5
Red Bull Canyon—valley TX-5
Red Bull Creek MS-4
Red Bull Dam—dam SD-7
Red Bull Draw—valley SD-7
Red Bull Hill—summit TX-5
Red Bull Island—island FL-3
Red Bull Spring—spring TX-5
**Red Bunch Corners**—pop pl NY-2
Redburn Cem—cemetery MO-7
Redburn Ch—church MO-7
Redbush—locale KY-4
**Red Bush**—pop pl IN-6
**Redbush**—pop pl OH-6
Redbush Cem—cemetery WV-2
Redbush Run—stream WV-2
Red Butte AZ-5
Red Butte OR-9
Red Butte—ridge NM-5
Red Butte—summit (5) AZ-5
Red Butte—summit (3) CA-9
Red Butte—summit CO-8
Red Butte—summit (2) ID-8
Red Butte—summit (12) MT-8
Red Butte—summit (3) NV-8
Red Butte—summit (2) NM-5
Red Butte—summit ND-7
Red Butte—summit (5) OR-9
Red Butte—summit (5) SD-7
Red Butte—summit (4) UT-8
Red Butte—summit (3) WA-9
Red Butte—summit (6) WY-8
Red Butte Bay—bay ND-7
Red Butte Bay Public Use Area—park ND-7
Red Butte Burn Camp—locale OR-9
Red Butte Canyon—valley NV-8
Red Butte Canyon—valley OR-9
Red Butte Canyon—valley (3) UT-8
Red Butte Cem—cemetery CO-8
Red Butte Cem—cemetery MT-8
Red Butte Cem—cemetery (2) ND-7
Red Butte Creek—stream (4) MT-8
Red Butte Creek—stream (2) SD-7
Red Butte Creek—stream (2) UT-8
Red Butte Dam—dam UT-8
Red Butte Hills—ridge UT-8
Red Butte Lake—lake OR-9
Red Butte Mine—mine NV-8
Red Butte Rsvr—reservoir UT-8
Red Butte Rsvr Number One—reservoir OR-9
Red Butte Rsvr Number Two—reservoir OR-9
Red Buttes AZ-5
Red Buttes UT-8
**Red Buttes**—pop pl WY-8
Red Buttes—spring MT-8
Red Buttes—summit (2) CA-9
Red Buttes—summit MT-8
Red Buttes—summit NV-8
Red Buttes—summit (2) WY-8
Red Butte Sch—school MT-8
**Red Buttes Village**—pop pl WY-8
Red Butte Tank—reservoir AZ-5
Red Butte Trail—trail (2) OR-9
Red Butte Wash—stream CA-9
**Redby**—pop pl MN-6
Red-byrd Arch—arch KY-4
Red Cabin—locale AZ-5
Red Cabin—locale ID-8
Red Cabin—locale NM-5
Red Cabin—locale (2) WY-8
Red Cabin Creek—stream WA-9
Red Camp—locale TX-5
**Red Campbell**—pop pl WV-2
Red Camp River MI-6
Red Camp Spring—spring TX-5
Red Cane Creek—stream MS-4
Red Canyon CO-8
Red Canyon NV-8
Red Canyon OK-5
Red Canyon OR-9
Red Canyon UT-8
Red Canyon WY-8
Red Canyon—valley (7) AZ-5
Red Canyon—valley CA-9
Red Canyon—valley (10) CO-8
Red Canyon—valley (3) ID-8
Red Canyon—valley (2) MT-8
Red Canyon—valley (3) NV-8
Red Canyon—valley (7) NM-5
Red Canyon—valley OR-9
Red Canyon—valley (3) SD-7
Red Canyon—valley (2) TX-5
Red Canyon—valley (16) UT-8
Red Canyon—valley (11) WY-8
Red Canyon Campground—locale UT-8
Red Canyon Creek UT-8
Red Canyon Creek—stream CO-8
Red Canyon Creek—stream (2) MT-8
Red Canyon Creek—stream SD-7
Red Canyon Creek—stream (8) WY-8
Red Canyon Draw—valley NM-5
Red Canyon Lake—lake CA-9
Red Canyon Lodge—locale UT-8
Red Canyon Mine—mine CO-8
Red Canyon Overlook—locale CO-8
Red Canyon Overlook—locale UT-8
Red Canyon Petroglphs—locale CA-9
Red Canyon Picnic Area—locale UT-8
Red Canyon Picnic Grounds—park NM-5
Red Canyon Ranch—locale AZ-5
Red Canyon Ranch—locale NM-5
Red Canyon Ranch—locale WY-8
Red Canyon Rim—cliff WY-8
Red Canyon Rsvr—reservoir CO-8
Red Canyon Rsvr—reservoir OR-9
Red Canyon Spring—spring (2) AZ-5
Red Canyon Spring—spring NM-5
Red Canyon Station (historical)—locale SD-7
Red Canyon Tank—reservoir (3) AZ-5
Red Canyon Tank Number Two—reservoir AZ-5
Red Canyon Trail—trail NM-5
Red Canyon Visitor Center—locale UT-8
Red Canyon Wash—arroyo NV-8
Red Canyon Wash—stream NV-8
Red Cap Canal—canal UT-8

Red Cap Central Mine—mine CA-9
Red Cap Creek—stream CA-9
Red Cap Glade—flat CA-9
Red Cap Gulch—valley CA-9
Red Cap Hill—summit PA-2
Red Cap Hole—flat CA-9
Redcap Hollow—valley MO-7
Red Cap Lake—lake CA-9
Red Cap Mtn—summit CA-9
Red Cap Prairie—area CA-9
Redcap Swamp GA-3
Redcap Swamp—swamp GA-3
Red Carp River MI-6
Red Castle—summit UT-8
Red Castle Creek—stream WY-8
Red Castle Lake—lake UT-8
Red Castle Peak UT-8
Red Castles—area WY-8
Red Cat Lake—lake AR-4
Red Caty Creek—stream AL-4
Red Cave—cave NM-5
Red Cedar—locale WI-6
Red Cedar Canyon—valley NV-8
Red Cedar Canyon—valley UT-8
Red Cedar Creek—stream OR-9
Red Cedar Creek—stream UT-8
**Red Cedar Hill**—pop pl PA-2
Red Cedar Hill—summit UT-8
Red Cedar Lake—lake (2) WI-6
Red Cedar Lake—reservoir CT-1
Red Cedar Point—cape NY-2
Red Cedar River IA-7
Red Cedar River MN-6
Red Cedar River—stream MI-6
Red Cedar River—stream WI-6
Red Cedar Spring UT-8
Red Cedar Spring—spring CO-8
Redcedar Spring—spring UT-8
Red Cedar Spring—spring (3) UT-8
Red Cedar Springs—spring WI-6
**Red Cedar (Town of)**—pop pl WI-6
Red Cem—cemetery NY-2
Red Cem—cemetery TX-5
Red Ch—church AR-4
Red Ch—church NY-2
Red Ch—church SC-3
Redchain Research Farm—other TX-5
Red Chalk Cem—cemetery NY-2
Red Chalk Hill—summit NY-2
Red Cheek Butte—summit AZ-5
Red Cheek Spring—spring AZ-5
Red Chert Creek—stream CA-9
Red Chief Mine—mine (2) AZ-5
Red Chief Mine—mine OR-9
Red Church MS-4
**Red Chute**—pop pl LA-4
Red Chute—stream AR-4
Red Chute Bayou—stream LA-4
Red Cinder—summit CA-9
Red Cinder Butte—summit OR-9
Red Cinder Cone—summit CA-9
Red Cinder Dome—summit AK-9
Red Cinder Hill CA-9
Red Cinder Mtn CA-9
Red Clay—locale GA-3
**Redclay**—pop pl GA-3
Red Clay Council Ground—hist pl TN-4
Red Clay Council Grounds—locale TN-4
Red Clay Creek DE-2
Red Clay Creek—stream DE-2
Red Clay Creek—stream PA-2
Red Clay Creek Church DE-2
Red Clay Creek Presbyterian Ch—church DE-2
Red Clay Creek Presbyterian Church—hist pl DE-2
Red Clay Dam—dam AZ-5
Red Clay Gap—gap GA-3
Red Clay Hills OR-9
Red Clay Mesa—summit (2) AZ-5
Red Clay Ridge—ridge AZ-5
Red Clay Ridge—ridge TN-4
Red Clay Spring—spring (2) AZ-5
Red Clay State Historic Area—park TN-4
Red Clay Trail—trail AZ-5
Red Clay Wash—arroyo AZ-5
Red Cliff CO-8
Red Cliff PA-2
Red Cliff—cliff AZ-5
Red Cliff—cliff CA-9
Red Cliff—cliff MN-6
Red Cliff—cliff NM-5
Red Cliff—cliff TN-4
Red Cliff—cliff (2) UT-8
Red Cliff—cliff WY-8
**Redcliff**—pop pl CO-8
**Red Cliff**—pop pl CO-8
**Red Cliff**—pop pl WI-6
Redcliff—summit CO-8
Red Cliff Bay—bay WI-6
Red Cliff Bridge—hist pl CO-8
Red Cliff Camp—locale MT-8
Red Cliff Creek—stream WI-6
Redcliffe—hist pl SC-3
**Red Cliff Ind Res**—pop pl WI-6
Redcliff Islands—island AK-9
Red Cliff Lake—lake UT-8
Red Cliff Oasis—park UT-8
Red Cliff Point—cape WI-6
Red Cliffs—cliff CA-9
Red Cliffs—cliff NM-5
Red Cliffs—cliff UT-8
Red Cliffs Campground—park UT-8
Red Cliff Spring—spring AZ-5
Red Cliffs Recreation Site UT-8
Red Clifton Branch—stream TX-5
Redcloud NE-7
**Red Cloud**—pop pl NE-7
Red Cloud Agency (historical)—locale SD-7
Red Cloud Buttes—summit NE-7
Red Cloud Campground—locale TN-4
Red Cloud Canyon—valley CA-9
Red Cloud Canyon—valley NM-5
Red Cloud Cem—cemetery WY-8
Redcloud Cliff—cliff OR-9
Red Cloud Creek—stream ID-8
Red Cloud Creek—stream WY-8
Redcloud Gulch—valley CO-8
Red Cloud Mine—mine (2) AZ-5
Red Cloud Mine—mine (4) CA-9
Red Cloud Mine—mine (2) ID-8
Red Cloud Mine—mine NV-8
Red Cloud Mine—mine OR-9
Red Cloud Mine—mine SD-7
Red Cloud Mines—mine CA-9
Red Cloud Park—park WI-6
Redcloud Peak—summit CO-8
Red Cloud Picnic Ground—locale WY-8
Red Cloud Picnic Grounds—locale NM-5
Red Cloud Ranch—locale OR-9
Red Cloud River—stream AK-9
Red Cloud Sch (historical)—school TN-4
Red Cloud Slough—stream WY-8
Red Cloud Wash—stream (2) AZ-5
Red Cloud Wash—stream CA-9
Red Clover KS-7
Red Clover Creek—stream CA-9
Redclover (historical)—locale KS-7
Red Clover Land Company Demonstration Farm—hist pl MN-6
Red Clover Valley—valley CA-9
Redclyffe—locale PA-2
Redclyffe Ch—church PA-2
**Redco**—pop pl ND-7
Red Coach Farm OH-6
Red Coat Creek—stream SD-7
Redcoat Lake—lake MN-6
Red Colony (Township of)—fmr MCD AR-4
Red Colt Canyon—valley NM-5
Red Cone CO-8
Red Cone OR-9
Red Cone—summit CO-8
Red Cone—summit HI-9
Red Cone—summit NV-8
Red Cone—summit (2) OR-9
Red Cones—summit CA-9
Red Cones—summit HI-9
Red Cone Spring—spring (2) OR-9
Red Cone Spring—spring UT-8
Red Conglomerate Peaks—summit ID-8
Red Conglomerate Peaks—summit MT-8
Red Corner Sch—school IN-6
Red Corner Sch (abandoned)—school PA-2
Red Corner Sch (historical)—school TN-4
Red Cornfield Mesa—summit AZ-5
Red Corral—locale AZ-5
Red Corral—locale CA-9
Red Corral Spring—spring CA-9
Red Coulee—valley MT-8
Red Coulee Tunnel Number 6—tunnel MT-8
Red Cove—basin UT-8
Red Cove—bay AK-9
Red Cove—bay ME-1
Red Cove—bay TX-5
Red Cove—valley UT-8
Redcove Lump—summit NC-3
Red Covered Bridge—bridge IN-6
Red Covered Bridge—hist pl IL-6
Red Covered Bridge—hist pl PA-2
Red Covered Bridge—hist pl VT-1
Red Cove Rsvr—reservoir UT-8
Red Cow Creek—stream NV-8
Red Cow Draw—valley TX-5
Red Crater—crater OR-9
Red Creek AZ-5
Red Creek CO-8
Red Creek ID-8
Red Creek KS-7
Red Creek MT-8
Red Creek OK-5
Red Creek OR-9
Red Creek TN-4
Red Creek TX-5
Red Creek UT-8
Red Creek WY-8
Red Creek—locale WV-2
**Red Creek**—pop pl (2) NY-2
Red Creek—stream (4) AL-4
Red Creek—stream (3) AK-9
Red Creek—stream (2) AZ-5
Red Creek—stream AR-4
Red Creek—stream (2) CA-9
Red Creek—stream (8) CO-8
Red Creek—stream GA-3
Red Creek—stream ID-8
Red Creek—stream KS-7
Red Creek—stream KY-4
Red Creek—stream (2) LA-4
Red Creek—stream (6) MI-6
Red Creek—stream (4) MS-4
Red Creek—stream (3) MT-8
Red Creek—stream (5) NY-2
Red Creek—stream ND-7
Red Creek—stream OH-6
Red Creek—stream (2) OK-5
Red Creek—stream (4) OR-9
Red Creek—stream PA-2
Red Creek—stream (6) TX-5
Red Creek—stream (7) UT-8
Red Creek—stream VA-3
Red Creek—stream (5) WA-9
Red Creek—stream (2) WV-2
Red Creek—stream WI-6
Red Creek—stream (21) WY-8
Red Creek Badlands—area WY-8
Red Creek Basin—basin WY-8
Red Creek Boat Camp—locale UT-8
Red Creek Campground—locale CO-8
Red Creek Campground—locale WV-2
Red Creek Campground—park UT-8
Red Creek Canyon—valley CO-8
Red Creek Cem—cemetery TX-5
Red Creek Ch—church (4) MS-4
Red Creek Dam—dam (2) UT-8
Red Creek Flat—flat UT-8
Red Creek Game Mngmt Area MS-4
**Red Creek Heights (subdivision)**—pop pl AL-4
Red Creek (historical)—locale AL-4
Red Creek Hole—basin UT-8
Red Creek Mtn—summit UT-8
Red Creek Oil Field—area MT-8
Red Creek Plains—flat WV-2
Red Creek Pond—lake NY-2
Red Creek Ranch—locale CO-8
Red Creek Ranch—locale WY-8
Red Creek Rim—cliff WY-8
Red Creek Rsvr—reservoir (2) UT-8
Red Creek Rsvr—reservoir WY-8
Red Creek Sch—school TX-5
Red Creek Spring—spring AZ-5
Red Creek State Wildlife Mngmt Area—park MS-4
Red Creek Trail—trail WV-2
Red Creek Well—well WY-8
Red Creek Wildlife Mngmt Area—park UT-8
**Redcrest**—pop pl CA-9
Red Cross—locale KY-4
Red Cross—locale LA-4
**Red Cross**—pop pl NC-3
**Redcross**—pop pl NC-3
**Red Cross**—pop pl NC-3
**Red Cross**—pop pl PA-2
Red Cross Canteen—hist pl OK-5
Red Cross Cem—cemetery IN-6
Redcross Ch—church NC-3
Red Cross Creek—stream ID-8
Red Cross Draw—valley SD-7
Red Cross Hosp—hospital KY-4
Red Crossing AZ-5
Red Cross Landing (historical)—locale MS-4
Red Cross Mine—mine AZ-5
Red Cross Mine—mine CA-9
Red Cross Park—park CA-9
Red Crossroads—locale NC-3
Red Crossroads (historical)—locale AL-4
Red Cross Sch—school KY-4
Red Cross Sch Number 1—school ND-7
Red Cross Sch Number 2—school ND-7
Red Cross Spring—spring SD-7
Red Cross Trail—trail NH-1
Red Crow Mtn—summit MT-8
**Redcuff Corner**—pop pl IN-6
Red Cut—gut TX-5
**Red Cut Heights**—pop pl TX-5
Red Cut Hollow TN-4
Redcut Hollow—valley TN-4
Red Cut Sch—school AR-4
Red Cut Slough—stream AR-4
Redd—locale MO-7
Redd—locale WA-9
**Redd**—pop pl WA-9
Redd, Lemuel H., Jr., House—hist pl UT-8
Red Dale Gulch Dam—dam SD-7
Red Dale Gulch Rsvr—reservoir SD-7
Red Dam—dam MA-1
Red Dam—dam TX-5
**Reddam**—pop pl TX-5
Red Dam Ch—church SC-3
Red Dam Lake—lake MI-6
Red Dam Tank—reservoir TX-5
Redd Branch—stream VA-3
Redd Cem—cemetery IA-7
Redd Cem—cemetery (2) TN-4
Redd Chapel MS-4
Redd Cow Camp—locale CO-8
Redd Creek OR-9
Redd Creek—stream SC-3
Red Deer Creek—stream CO-8
Red Deer Creek—stream FL-3
Red Deer Creek—stream TX-5
Red Deer Lake—lake CO-8
Red Deer Lake—lake NE-7
Red Deer Park—park TX-5
Red Deer Ranch—locale NE-7
**Reddell**—pop pl LA-4
Reddell Oil and Gas Field—oilfield LA-4
**Reddell's Ranch Acres (subdivision)**—pop pl AZ-5
**Reddells Ranch Acres (subdivision)**—pop pl AZ-5
Redden—locale DE-2
Redden—locale OK-5
Redden, Byron, House—hist pl AZ-5
Redden, Lowell, House—hist pl AZ-5
Reddenbacks Ranch—locale MT-8
Redden Branch—stream GA-3
Redden Branch—stream KY-4
Redden Branch—stream MS-4
Redden Branch—stream NC-3
Redden Branch—stream TN-4
Redden Cem—cemetery (3) TN-4
Redden Creek—stream LA-4
Redden Creek—stream MD-2
Redden Crossroads—locale DE-2
Redden Ditch—canal IN-6
Redden Forest Lodge, Forester's House, and Stable—hist pl DE-2
Redden Park—park AZ-5
Redden Prairie Pond—lake FL-3
Redden Ridge WV-2
Redden Ridge—ridge WV-2
Reddens Chapel (historical)—church TN-4
Reddens Chapel Sch (historical)—school TN-4
Reddens Crossroad DE-2
Redden Spring—spring TN-4
Redden Springs—spring UT-8
Reddens Run PA-2
Redden State For—forest DE-2
Redden State For Bailey Tract—forest DE-2
Reddert Rsvr—reservoir CO-8
Red Desert—locale WY-8
Red Desert—plain (2) UT-8
Red Desert Basin—basin WY-8
**Red Devil**—pop pl AK-9
Red Devil ANV916—reserve AK-9
Red Devil Creek—stream AK-9
Red Devil Ditch—canal MO-7
Red Devil Lake—lake CA-9
Red Devil Mine—mine NV-8
Red Devil Mtn—summit ID-8
Redd Hollow—valley KY-4
Redd Hollow—valley TN-4
Red Diamond—locale OH-6
Red Diamond Mine (underground)—mine AL-4
**Reddick**—pop pl FL-3
**Reddick**—pop pl IL-6
Reddick Branch—stream NC-3
Reddick Branch—stream TN-4
Reddick Camp—locale FL-3
Reddick Canyon—valley UT-8
Reddick Cem—cemetery AR-4
Reddick Cem—cemetery GA-3
Reddick Cem—cemetery IN-6
Reddick-Collier Elem Sch—school FL-3
Reddick Ditch—canal IN-6
Reddick Ditch—canal VA-3
Reddick Hollow—valley AL-4
Reddick Hollow—valley IL-6
Reddick-McIntosh (CCD)—cens area FL-3
Reddick Mill Creek—stream FL-3
Reddick Run—stream IL-6
Reddick Sch—school IL-6
Reddicks Creek—stream NC-3
Reddicks Ferry (historical)—locale AL-4
Reddicks Landing (historical)—locale TN-4
Reddicksville NC-3
Reddick Well—well NM-5
Reddie Point—cape FL-3
Reddies Creek—stream VA-3
Reddies Gap—gap VA-3
**Reddies River**—pop pl NC-3
Reddies River—stream NC-3
Reddies River Ch—church NC-3
Reddies River (Township of)—fmr MCD NC-3
Reddig Creek—stream TX-5
Red Diggings—mine CA-9
Red Dike Pond—lake AZ-5
Redding CT-1
Redding—locale AR-4
Redding—locale MS-4
**Redding**—pop pl CA-9
**Redding**—pop pl CT-1
**Redding**—pop pl IN-6
**Redding**—pop pl IA-7
**Redding**—pop pl ME-1
Redding, Lake—reservoir CA-9
Redding, William, House—hist pl NM-5
Redding-Anderson (CCD)—cens area CA-9
Redding Bay—swamp NC-3
Redding Branch—stream GA-3
Redding Branch—stream (2) TN-4
Redding Canyon—valley CA-9
Redding Cem—cemetery FL-3
Redding Cem—cemetery IA-7
Redding Cem—cemetery LA-4
Redding Cem—cemetery MO-7
Redding Cemetery MS-4
Redding Center CT-1
Redding Creek CA-9
Redding Creek—stream MS-4
Redding Ditch—canal IN-6
Redding Gap—gap VA-3
Redding Glen—valley CT-1
Redding Gun Club—other CA-9
Redding Hammock Cem—cemetery FL-3
Redding-Hill House—hist pl MO-7
**Redding Hills (subdivision)**—pop pl NC-3
Redding (historical)—locale AL-4
Redding (historical P.O.)—locale IA-7
Redding House—hist pl MS-4
Redding Lake WI-6
Redding Lake—lake TX-5
Redding Lookout Tower—locale CT-1
Redding Mine—mine MO-7
Redding MS—school DE-2
Redding Mtn—summit NC-3
Redding Municipal Airp—airport CA-9
Redding Post Office (historical)—building MS-4
Redding Ranch—locale MT-8
Redding Rec Area—park AR-4
**Redding Ridge**—pop pl CT-1
Redding Ridge Cem—cemetery CT-1
Redding Sch DE-2
Redding Sch—school CA-9
Redding Sch—school CT-1
Redding Sch—school GA-3
**Reddings Corner**—pop pl MD-2
Reddings Creek CA-9
Redding Springs Ch—church NC-3
Reddings Run—stream PA-2
Redding (sta.) (West Redding) CT-1
Redding Stream CT-1
Redding Switch MS-4
**Reddington**—pop pl IN-6
Reddington Ditch—canal IN-6
Reddington Island ME-1
**Redding (Town of)**—pop pl CT-1
**Redding (Township of)**—pop pl IN-6
**Redding (Township of)**—pop pl MI-6
Red Dirt Branch—stream TN-4
Red Dirt Creek—stream (3) CO-8
Red Dirt Hollow—valley TN-4
Red Dirt Lookout Tower—locale LA-4
Red Dirt Pass—gap CO-8
Red Dirt Reservoir CO-8
Red Dirt Tank—reservoir AZ-5
Reddish Branch—stream MO-7
Reddish Bridge—other IL-6
Reddish-Dunham Cem—cemetery IL-6
Reddish Hollow—valley MO-7
Reddish Knob—summit VA-3
Reddish Knob—summit WV-2
Reddish Millsite—locale FL-3
Reddish Sch—school IA-7
Reddish Sch (abandoned)—school MO-7
Reddish Township—civil MO-7
Reddis River NC-3
Red Ditch—canal OR-9
Red Ditch—canal TX-5
Redd Level AL-4
Reddmans Square Festival Market—locale NC-3
Reddoch MS-4
**Reddoch**—pop pl MS-4
Reddoch Cem—cemetery AL-4
Reddoch Cem—cemetery MS-4
Reddoch Post Office (historical)—building MS-4
**Reddochs**—pop pl MS-4
Reddochs Bridge—bridge MS-4
Reddochs Ferry MS-4
Reddoch Springs AL-4
Red Dock Canal—canal GA-3
**Reddock Springs**—pop pl AL-4
Reddock Store (historical)—locale MS-4
Red Doe—hist pl SC-3
Red Dog—locale CA-9
Red Dog Creek—stream OR-9
Red Dog Gulch—valley SD-7
Red Dog Lake—lake AK-9
Red Dog Ridge—ridge OH-6
Red Dog School MS-4
Red Dog Table—summit SD-7
Red Dog You Bet Diggings—mine CA-9
Red Dome—summit CA-9
Red Dome—summit NM-5
Red Dome—summit UT-8
Red Dome Siding—locale UT-8
Reddon Lake—lake AR-4
Reddon Lake—lake TX-5
Red Doors Cem—cemetery AR-4
Red Doors Ch—church AR-4
Red Dragon WV-2
Red Dragon Hist Dist—hist pl AK-9
Red Drain—canal OR-9
Red Drain—stream MI-6
Redd Ranch—locale CO-8
Redd Ranchs Summer Camp—locale CO-8
Red Draw CO-8
Red Draw—valley CO-8
Red Draw—valley (5) TX-5
Red Draw—valley UT-8
Red Draw—valley (5) WY-8
Red Drum Drain—gut VA-3
Redd Run—stream PA-2
Redds Beach (Private)—beach PA-2
Redds Branch—stream SC-3
Redds Branch Ch—church SC-3
Redd Shop—locale VA-3
Redds Mill—locale PA-2
Redds Pond—lake MA-1
Red Duck Creek—stream KY-4
Reddus Station NE-7
Redd Valley—valley KS-7
Reddy, Dr. John F. and Mary, House—hist pl OR-9
Reddy Branch—stream MD-2
Reddy Creek GA-3
Reddy Creek—stream MN-6
Reddy Hole Branch—stream VA-3
Reddy Mtn—summit TX-5
Reddy Sch—school KS-7
Reddy Sch—school LA-4
Reddy Tank—reservoir TX-5
Red Eagle MT-8
Red Eagle—locale AL-4
Red Eagle Branch—stream OK-5
Red Eagle Brook—stream NH-1
Red Eagle Cem—cemetery OK-5
Red Eagle Creek—stream MT-8
Red Eagle Glacier MT-8
Red Eagle Glacier—glacier MT-8
Red Eagle Honor Farm AL-4
Red Eagle Lake—lake MT-8
Red Eagle Landing—locale AL-4
Red Eagle Mine—mine NV-8
Red Eagle Mtn—summit MT-8
Red Eagle Pass—gap MT-8
Red Eagle Pond—lake NH-1
Red Eagle Trail—trail MT-8
Red Earth Branch IN-6
Red Earth Creek—stream SD-7
Redeem Ch—church NC-3
Redeemer Cem—cemetery MN-6
Redeemer Cem—cemetery (2) ND-7
Redeemer Cem—cemetery SD-7
Redeemer Ch—church KY-4
Redeemer Ch—church LA-4
Redeemer Ch—church MI-6
Redeemer Ch—church (3) MN-6
Redeemer Ch—church MS-4
Redeemer Ch—church (2) MO-7
Redeemer Ch—church NJ-2
Redeemer Ch—church NM-5
Redeemer Ch—church ND-7
Redeemer Ch—church PA-2
Redeemer Ch—church (2) SC-3
Redeemer Ch—church TX-5
Redeemer Ch—church VA-3
Redeemer Ch—church WY-8
Redeemer Chapel—church IA-7
Redeemer Lutheran Ch MS-4
Redeemer Lutheran Ch—church AL-4
Redeemer Lutheran Ch—church FL-3
Redeemer Lutheran Ch—church KS-7
Redeemer Lutheran Ch—church MT-8
Redeemer Lutheran Ch—church UT-8
Redeemer Lutheran Ch (LCA)—church FL-3
Redeemer Lutheran Chruch—church FL-3
Redeemer Lutheran Sch—school (2) FL-3
Redeemer Lutheran Sch—school KS-7
Redeemer Sch—school CA-9
Redeemer Sch—school CO-8
Redeemer Sch—school IN-6
Redeemer Sch—school MI-6
Redeemer Sch—school OH-6
Redeemer Sch—school (2) TX-5
Redeker Lake—reservoir OK-5
**Redel**—pop pl KS-7
Red Elephant Butte—summit NV-8
Red Elephant Gulch—valley ID-8
Red Elephant Hill—summit CO-8
Red Elephant Mine—mine CA-9
Red Elephant Mine—mine ID-8
Red Elephant Mtn—summit CO-8
Red Elephant Point—cliff CO-8
Red Elk Canyon—valley OR-9
Red Elk Cem—cemetery ID-8
Red Elk Cem—cemetery OR-9
Redell Post Office (historical)—building TN-4
**Red Elm**—pop pl SD-7
Red Elm Creek SD-7
Redelm Township—civil SD-7
Redemption AL-4
**Redemption**—pop pl AR-4
Redemption Cem—cemetery WV-2
Redemption Hill—summit MT-8
Redemption Rock—rock MA-1
Redemptorist HS—school LA-4
Redemptorist Sch—school MO-7
Redenbaugh Pass—gap WY-8
Redenbo Cem—cemetery AR-4
Reder Ranger Station—locale SD-7
Redess—locale OR-9
Redeye—locale VA-3
**Red Eye**—pop pl VA-3
Red Eye Basin—basin WY-8
Red Eye Cem—cemetery MN-6
Redeye Creek—stream VA-3
Red Eye Creek—stream WY-8
Redeye Lake—lake AR-4
Redeye Lake—lake MN-6
Red Eye Ridge—ridge TN-4
Redeye River—stream MN-6
Red Eye Spring—spring CA-9
**Red Eye (Township of)**—pop pl MN-6
Redface Lake—lake MN-6
Red Face Mtn—summit WA-9
**Red Falls (Red Falls)**—pop pl NY-2
Redfearin Cem—cemetery TN-4
Red Feather Lake—lake CO-8
**Red Feather Lakes**—pop pl CO-8
Red Feather Ranch—locale CO-8
Red Feather Well—well NM-5
Redfern—locale AR-4
Redfern—locale SD-7
Redfern Cem—cemetery MS-4
Red Fern Creek—stream WY-8
Redfern Mtn—summit SD-7
Redfern Sch—school NE-7
Redfern Spring—spring CO-8
Redfern Table—summit NE-7
Redfield—hist pl VA-3
**Redfield**—pop pl AR-4
**Redfield**—pop pl IA-7
**Redfield**—pop pl KS-7
**Redfield**—pop pl NY-2
**Redfield**—pop pl OH-6
**Redfield**—pop pl SD-7
**Redfield**—pop pl TX-5
Redfield, Lake—lake AK-9
Redfield, Lake—reservoir SD-7
Redfield, Mount—summit NY-2
Redfield Branch—stream LA-4
Redfield Brook VT-1
Redfield Brook—stream VT-1
Red Field Canyon AZ-5
Redfield Canyon—valley AZ-5
Redfield Carnegie Library—hist pl SD-7
Redfield Cem—cemetery AR-4
Red Field Cem—cemetery GA-3
Redfield Cove—bay AK-9
Redfield Creek—stream WA-9
Redfield Hall—locale MI-6
Redfield Hill—summit ME-1
Redfield Hills—summit SD-7
Redfield Lake—lake LA-4
Redfield Lake—lake MT-8
Redfield Lake Dam—dam SD-7
Redfield Light Plant and Fire Station—hist pl SD-7
Redfield Municipal Airp—airport SD-7
Redfield Post Office (historical)—building AL-4
Redfield Sch—school MA-1
Redfield Sch—school MI-6
Redfield Sch—school PA-2
Redfield State Hosp—hospital SD-7
Redfield Station (reduced usage)—locale TX-5
**Redfield (Town of)**—pop pl NY-2
**Redfield Township**—pop pl SD-7
Redfield Township (historical)—civil SD-7
Red Fin Brook—stream NY-2
Redfin Creek—stream MD-2
Redfin Island—island MI-6
Red Fir Creek—stream OR-9
Red Fir Meadow—flat CA-9
Red Fir Ridge—ridge CA-9
Red Fir Spring—spring (3) OR-9
Red Fir Spring—spring (2) WA-9
**Red Fish**—pop pl LA-4
**Redfish**—pop pl TX-5
Redfish Archeol District—hist pl ID-8
Red Fish Bar—bar TX-5
Redfish Bay—bay AK-9
Redfish Bay—bay LA-4
Redfish Bay—bay TX-5
Red Fish Bay—bay TX-5
Redfish Bay—other TX-5
Redfish Bayou—gut (4) LA-4
Redfish Bayou—gut MS-4
Redfish Bayou—gut (2) TX-5
Redfish Bayou—stream TX-5
Redfish Bend—bay LA-4
Redfish Breaker—bar AK-9
Redfish Camp—locale TX-5
Redfish Cape—cape AK-9
Redfish Cove—bay (3) FL-3
Redfish Cove—bay TX-5
**Red Fish Cove**—pop pl TX-5
Redfish Creek ID-8
Redfish Creek—gut (2) FL-3
Red Fish Creek—stream FL-3
Redfish Creek—stream MS-4
Redfish Inlet Transfer Camp—locale ID-8
Red Fish Island—island TX-5
Redfish Islets—island AK-9
Redfish Key—island FL-3
Redfish Lake—lake AK-9
Red Fish Lake—lake FL-3
Redfish Lake—lake ID-8
Redfish Lake—lake (2) TX-5
**Redfish Lake**—pop pl ID-8
Redfish Lake Creek—stream ID-8
Redfish Outlet Campground—locale ID-8
Redfish Pass—channel FL-3
Red Fish Point FL-3
Redfish Point—cape AK-9
Redfish Point—cape (7) FL-3
Redfish Point—cape (2) LA-4
Redfish Point—cape TX-5
Redfish Point Gas Field—oilfield LA-4
Redfish Reef Oil Field—oilfield TX-5
Redfish Rocks—island OR-9
Redfish Slough—gut TX-5
**Red Fish Township**—pop pl SD-7
Red Flat—flat (2) AZ-5
Red Flat—flat (2) CA-9
Red Flat—flat (3) OR-9
Red Flat—flat WY-8
Red Flat Ch—church TX-5
Red Flat Cow Camp—locale WY-8
Red Flat Pond—reservoir AZ-5
Red Flats—flat NM-5
Red Flats Tank—reservoir NM-5
Red Flat Tank—reservoir (2) AZ-5
Red Flat Wash—stream NM-5
Red Fleet Campground—park UT-8
Red Fleet Rsvr—reservoir UT-8
Redford KS-7
Redford MI-6
**Redford**—pop pl MI-6
**Redford**—pop pl MO-7
**Redford**—pop pl NY-2
**Redford**—pop pl TX-5
Redford A—post sta MI-6
Redford Butte—summit OR-9
Redford Canyon—valley WA-9
Redford Cem—cemetery IL-6
Redford Cem—cemetery MI-6
Redford Cem—cemetery TX-5
Redford Creek—stream OR-9

Redlands, The—*range* CO-8
Redlands Aqueduct—*canal* CA-9
Redlands Canyon—*valley* CA-9
Redlands Cem—*cemetery* (2) TX-5
Redland Sch—*school* FL-3
Redland Sch—*school* OK-5
Redland Sch—*school* OR-9
Redland Sch (historical)—*school* MS-4
Redlands Christian Sch—*school* CA-9
Redlands Country Club—*other* CA-9
Redlands Dam—*dam* CO-8
Redlands First Lift Canal—*canal* CO-8
Redlands Heights—*uninc pl* CA-9
Redlands HS—*school* CA-9
Redlands Lake—*stream* AK-9
Redlands Mesa—*summit* CO-8
Redlands Power Canal, The—*canal* CO-8
Redlands Ranch—*locale* AZ-5
Redlands RV Parks—*park* UT-8
Redlands Sch—*school* CO-8
Redlands Second Lift Canal—*canal* CO-8
Redlands Spring—*spring* CA-9
Redland (Township of)—*fmr MCD* (3) AR-4
**Redland Village (subdivision)**—*pop pl* PA-2
*Redlane* NC-3
**Red Lane**—*pop pl* GA-3
**Red Lane**—*pop pl* VA-3
**Red Lane**—*pop pl* WY-8
Red Lane Gulch—*valley* WY-8
*Red Lassic* CA-9
Red Lassic—*summit* CA-9
Red Lassic Creek—*stream* CA-9
Redlawn—*locale* TX-5
Redlawn—*locale* VA-3
**Red Leaf**—*pop pl* AR-4
Red Leaf Campground—*park* SD-7
Red Leaf Cave—*cave* AL-4
Red Leaf Cem—*cemetery* AR-4
Red Leaf Cem—*cemetery* SD-7
Redleaf Creek—*stream* AK-9
Red Leaf Creek—*stream* SD-7
Red Leaf Pond—*lake* NH-1
Red Ledge—*bar* MA-1
Red Ledge—*beach* ID-8
Red Ledge—*bench* ME-1
Red Ledge—*cliff* (2) UT-8
*Red Ledge, The* UT-8
Red Ledge Canyon—*valley* ID-8
Red Ledge Canyon—*valley* NV-8
Red Ledge Hollow—*valley* UT-8
**Red Ledge Manor Estates**—*pop pl* PA-2
Red Ledge Mesa Tank—*reservoir* AZ-5
Red Ledge Mine—*mine* CA-9
Red Ledge Mine—*mine* ID-8
Red Ledge Ridge—*ridge* PA-2
Red Ledges—*bench* (2) UT-8
Red Ledges—*ridge* NV-8
Red Ledges, The—*cliff* UT-8
Red Ledges, The—*ridge* UT-8
Red Ledges Canyon—*valley* UT-8
Red Ledge Spring—*spring* UT-8
Red Ledge Trail—*trail* ID-8
Red Level—*area* AL-4
Red Level—*locale* (2) AL-4
Red Level—*locale* FL-3
Red Level—*locale* TX-5
Red Level—*locale* VA-3
**Red Level**—*pop pl* AL-4
Red Level Cem—*cemetery* FL-3
Red Level Ch—*church* GA-3
Red Level Ch—*church* VA-3
Red Level Christian Acad—*school* FL-3
Red Level HS—*school* AL-4
**Red Level Junction**—*pop pl* FL-3
Red Level Sch (historical)—*school* MS-4
*Redlew* TX-5
Redlich (Site)—*locale* NV-8
Redlick—*locale* TX-5
**Redlick**—*pop pl* (2) KY-4
**Red Lick**—*pop pl* MS-4
Red Lick Branch—*stream* KY-4
Red Lick Branch—*stream* LA-4
Red Lick (CCD)—*cens area* KY-4
Red Lick Cem—*cemetery* KY-4
Red Lick Cem—*cemetery* MS-4
Red Lick Ch—*church* (2) KY-4
*Red Lick Creek* OK-5
Red Lick Creek—*stream* GA-3
Red Lick Creek—*stream* (2) KY-4
Red Lick Creek—*stream* OK-5
Red Lick Ford—*crossing* TX-5
Red Lick Hollow—*valley* AR-4
Red Lick Mtn—*summit* AR-4
Red Lick Mtn—*summit* WV-2
*Red Lick Run* PA-2
Redlick Run—*stream* PA-2
Red Lick Run—*stream* (2) PA-2
Redlick Run—*stream* PA-2
Redlick Run—*stream* WV-2
Red Lick Run—*stream* WV-2
Redlick Run—*stream* WV-2
Red Lick Run—*stream* WV-2
Redlick Run—*stream* WV-2
Red Lick Sch—*school* KY-4
Red Lick Spring—*spring* (2) OR-9
Red Lick (Township of)—*fmr MCD* AR-4
Red Light Draw—*valley* TX-5
Red Light Windmill—*locale* TX-5
*Red Lily Pond* MA-1
Redlin Dam—*dam* ND-7
**Red Line**—*pop pl* AR-4
**Red Line**—*pop pl* IA-7
Redline Cem—*cemetery* KS-7
Redline Ch—*church* KS-7
Red Line Rsvr—*reservoir* OR-9
Red Line Sch—*school* AR-4
*Redlion* NJ-2
Red Lion—*airport* NJ-2
Red Lion—*locale* CO-8
Red Lion—*locale* DE-2
Red Lion—*locale* OH-6
Red Lion—*locale* (2) PA-2
**Red Lion**—*pop pl* (2) NJ-2
**Red Lion**—*pop pl* (2) PA-2
Red Lion Area JHS—*school* PA-2
Red Lion Area Senior HS—*school* PA-2
Red Lion Borough—*civil* PA-2
Red Lion Branch—*stream* MD-2
Red Lion (CCD)—*cens area* DE-2
Red Lion Cem—*cemetery* PA-2
Red Lion Ch—*church* DE-2
Red Lion Christian Acad—*school* DE-2
Red Lion Circle—*locale* NJ-2
Red Lion Country Club—*locale* PA-2
*Red Lion Creek* MD-2
Red Lion Creek—*stream* DE-2
*Red Lion High School* PA-2
Red Lion Hundred—*civil* DE-2
Red Lion Inn—*building* MA-1
Red Lion Methodist Ch—*church* DE-2
Red Lion Mine—*mine* MT-8
Red Lion Mine—*mine* WA-9
Red Lion Mtn—*summit* MT-8
*Red Lion Pond* MD-2
Red Lion Rsvr—*reservoir* PA-2
Red Lion-Sheraton Hotel Heliport—*airport* UT-8
Red Lion Stadium—*park* PA-2
Red Lion State For—*forest* DE-2
Red Littleton Canyon—*valley* CO-8
**Red Lodge**—*pop pl* MT-8
Red Lodge Cem—*cemetery* MT-8
Red Lodge Commercial Hist Dist—*hist pl* MT-8
Red Lodge Commercial Hist Dist (Boundary Increase)—*hist pl* MT-8
Red Lodge Creek—*stream* AK-9
Red Lodge Creek—*stream* MT-8
Red Lodge Creek Guard Station—*locale* MT-8
Red Lodge Creek Plateau—*plain* MT-8
Red Log Gap—*gap* NC-3
Red Log Gap—*gap* TN-4
Redlouse Lake—*lake* NY-2
*Red Lyon* NJ-2
*Red Lyon Branch* MD-2
*Redman* AL-4
Redman—*locale* MI-6
Redman—*locale* MO-7
**Redman**—*pop pl* CA-9
**Redman**—*pop pl* PA-2
Redman Beach—*beach* ME-1
*Redman Branch* TX-5
Redman Branch—*stream* MD-2
Redman Branch—*stream* TN-4
Redman Branch—*stream* VA-3
Redman Brook—*stream* NH-1
Redman Camp—*locale* TX-5
*Redman Campground* UT-8
Redman Canyon—*valley* UT-8
Redman Cave—*locale* AZ-5
*Redman Cem* MS-4
Redman Cem—*cemetery* AR-4
Redman Cem—*cemetery* IN-6
Redman Cem—*cemetery* IA-7
Redman Cem—*cemetery* KS-7
Redman Cem—*cemetery* KY-4
Redman Cem—*cemetery* MD-2
Redman Cem—*cemetery* MI-6
Redman Cem—*cemetery* MO-7
Redman Cem—*cemetery* NY-2
Redman Cem—*cemetery* NC-3
Redman Cem—*cemetery* OH-6
Redman Cem—*cemetery* VA-3
Red Man Cem—*cemetery* WY-8
**Redman Corners**—*pop pl* NY-2
Redman Cove—*bay* MD-2
Redman Cove—*valley* NC-3
Redman Creek—*stream* AK-9
Redman Creek—*stream* CO-8
Redman Creek—*stream* MO-7
Redman Creek—*stream* (2) NC-3
Red Man Creek—*stream* WA-9
Redman Creek—*stream* WA-9
Redman Creek Rec Area—*park* MO-7
Redman Ditch—*canal* WY-8
Redman Draw—*valley* WY-8
Redman Farm House—*hist pl* MA-1
Redman Forest Camp—*locale* UT-8
Redman Gap—*gap* WV-2
**Redman (historical)**—*pop pl* IA-7
Redman Junior Lake—*lake* LA-4
Redman Lake—*lake* AR-4
Redman Lake—*lake* LA-4
Redman Lake—*lake* (2) WI-6
Redman Lakes—*lake* TX-5
Redman Lake Slough—*stream* AR-4
Redman Lateral—*canal* ID-8
Redman Mesa—*summit* AZ-5
Redman Mesa Tank—*reservoir* AZ-5
Redman Point—*locale* AR-4
Redman Point Bar—*bar* AR-4
Redman Ridge—*ridge* MO-7
Redman Ridge—*ridge* NC-3
*Redman Rim* OR-9
Redman Run—*stream* WV-2
Redmans Bluff Public Use Area—*park* MS-4
Redmans Cem—*cemetery* AR-4
Redman Slough—*lake* SD-7
Redman Slough—*stream* WA-9
Redmans Mtn—*summit* VA-3
*Redmans Pond* MA-1
Red Mans Ridge—*ridge* MT-8
Redman State Wildlife Area—*park* MO-7
Redmans Tooth—*summit* OR-9
Redman Tank—*reservoir* NM-5
Redman Trail—*trail* WV-2
Red Maple Swamp—*swamp* NY-2
Red Marble Ch—*church* NC-3
Red Marble Gap—*gap* NC-3
Red Marsh—*swamp* IN-6
Red Meadow—*flat* MT-8
Red Meadow—*flat* OR-9
Red Meadow Creek—*stream* MT-8
Red Meadow Lake—*lake* MT-8
Red Medicine Bow Creek—*stream* MT-8
*Red Medicine Bow Peak* MT-8
Red Men Cem—*cemetery* DE-2
Redmen Cem—*cemetery* IN-6
Red Men Hall—*hist pl* WA-9
Red Mesa—*bench* NM-5
Red Mesa—*cens area* UT-8
Red Mesa—*locale* AZ-5
**Redmesa**—*pop pl* CO-8
Red Mesa—*summit* (5) AZ-5
Red Mesa—*summit* CO-8
Red Mesa—*summit* (3) NM-5
Red Mesa—*summit* TX-5
Red Mesa—*summit* UT-8
Red Mesa Canyon—*valley* AZ-5
Red Mesa Canyon—*valley* NM-5
Red Mesa Chapter House—*building* UT-8
Red Mesa Day Sch—*school* AZ-5
Red Mesa Division—*civil* UT-8
Red Mesa Pumping Station—*other* UT-8
*Red Mesa Reservoir* CO-8
Red Mesa Rsvr—*reservoir* AZ-5
**Red Mesa (Trading Post)**—*pop pl* AZ-5
Red Metal Canyon—*valley* AZ-5
Red Metal Mine—*mine* NV-8
Red Metals Mine—*mine* ID-8
Red Metal Spring—*spring* AZ-5
Red Metal Tank—*reservoir* AZ-5
Red Mike Hill—*summit* ND-7
*Red Mill* MO-7
Red Mill—*locale* MI-6
Red Mill—*locale* NJ-2
Red Mill—*locale* NM-5
Red Mill—*locale* PA-2
**Red Mill**—*pop pl* NY-2
**Red Mill**—*pop pl* (2) PA-2
Red Mill Bridge—*bridge* TN-4
*Red Mill Brook* PA-2
Red Mill Brook—*stream* PA-2
*Red Mill Creek* DE-2
Red Mill Creek—*stream* GA-3
Red Mill Creek—*stream* OR-9
Red Mill Draw—*valley* (2) TX-5
**Red Mill Farms (subdivision)**—*pop pl* DE-2
Red Mill Lake—*lake* NE-7
Red Millpond—*lake* MI-6
Red Mill Pond—*lake* VT-1
Red Mill Pond—*reservoir* CT-1
Red Mill Pond—*reservoir* DE-2
Red Mill Pond—*reservoir* MO-7
Red Mill Pond Brook—*stream* VT-1
Red Mill Pond Dam—*dam* DE-2
Red Mill Ranch—*locale* TX-5
Red Mill Run—*stream* PA-2
Red Mills—*locale* (2) NY-2
Red Mills—*locale* VA-3
**Red Mills**—*pop pl* (2) NY-2
**Red Mills**—*pop pl* VA-3
**Red Mills, The**—*pop pl* IN-6
*Red Mill Sch* AL-4
Red Mills Ch—*church* NY-2
Red Mill Sch—*school* NE-7
Red Mill Sch—*school* NY-2
**Red Mills Farms (subdivision)**—*pop pl* DE-2
Redmills Sch—*school* AL-4
Red Mill Tank—*reservoir* (2) TX-5
Red Mine—*mine* IL-6
Red Mine—*mine* KY-4
Red Mine—*mine* NM-5
Redmon—*locale* NC-3
**Redmon**—*pop pl* IL-6
Redmon Cem—*cemetery* IL-6
Redmon Ch—*church* NC-3
*Redmon Cove* MD-2
Redmond—*locale* CO-8
Redmond—*locale* WV-2
**Redmond**—*pop pl* OR-9
**Redmond**—*pop pl* PA-2
**Redmond**—*pop pl* UT-8
**Redmond**—*pop pl* WA-9
Redmon Dam—*dam* NC-3
Redmond Bayou—*stream* LA-4
Redmond Branch—*stream* KY-4
Redmond Branch—*stream* TX-5
Redmond Canyon—*valley* UT-8
Redmond Cave—*cave* OR-9
Redmond (CCD)—*cens area* OR-9
*Redmond Cem* MS-4
Redmond Cem—*cemetery* MS-4
Redmond Cem—*cemetery* OR-9
Redmond Cem—*cemetery* TX-5
Redmond Cem—*cemetery* UT-8
Redmond Corner—*locale* NY-2
Redmond Cove North Rec Area—*park* KS-7
Redmond Cove South Rec Area—*park* KS-7
Redmond Creek—*stream* AK-9
Redmond Creek—*stream* KY-4
Redmond Creek—*stream* MT-8
Redmond Creek—*stream* NC-3
Redmond Creek—*stream* TN-4
Redmond Creek—*stream* TX-5
Redmond Creek—*stream* WY-8
Redmond Cut—*gap* CA-9
**Redmond Cut**—*pop pl* CA-9
Redmond Dam—*dam* UT-8
Redmond Drain—*canal* MI-6
Redmond Farm—*locale* ND-7
Redmond Flat—*flat* AZ-5
*Redmond Gap* GA-3
Redmond Gap—*gap* GA-3
Redmond Hill—*summit* MO-7
Redmond Hill—*summit* NY-2
Redmond Hotel—*hist pl* UT-8
Redmond House—*hist pl* KY-4
Redmond HS—*school* OR-9
Redmond HS—*school* WA-9
*Redmond Island* ME-1
Redmond JHS—*school* WA-9
Redmond Lake—*reservoir* UT-8
Redmond Mine—*mine* CA-9
Redmond Mtn—*summit* AZ-5
Redmond Mtn—*summit* NC-3
Redmond Park—*park* IA-7
**Redmond Park**—*pop pl* IN-6
Redmond Pond—*lake* ME-1
Redmond Pond—*lake* SC-3
Redmond Pond—*reservoir* (2) SC-3
Redmond Pumping Plant—*other* OR-9
Redmond Ranch—*locale* OR-9
*Redmond Reservoir* KS-7
Redmond Ridge—*ridge* VA-3
Redmond Ridge—*ridge* WV-2
*Redmond School* MS-4
Redmonds Crossing (historical)—*locale* MS-4
Redmond-Shackelford House—*hist pl* NC-3
Redmond Substation—*locale* OR-9
Redmond Tank—*reservoir* AZ-5
Redmond Terrace—*uninc pl* TX-5
Redmond Town Hall—*hist pl* UT-8
**Redmond Township**—*pop pl* ND-7
**Redmondville**—*pop pl* MO-7
Redmond Wash—*stream* AZ-5
Redmond Well—*well* AZ-5
Redmon House—*hist pl* KY-4
Red Monmt—*pillar* WY-8
**Redmon Park**—*pop pl* IN-6
Redmon Quarry—*mine* TN-4
Redmon Sch—*school* IL-6
Redmont Creek—*stream* OR-9
**Redmont Park**—*pop pl* AL-4
**Redmont (subdivision)**—*pop pl* DE-2
Red Monument—*summit* UT-8
Red Morg Branch—*stream* KY-4
*Redmound* WI-6
Red Mound—*locale* WI-6
Red Mound—*summit* OR-9
Red Mound—*summit* TX-5
Red Mound Sch—*school* WI-6
*Red Mountain* CO-8
Red Mountain—*locale* CO-8
**Red Mountain**—*pop pl* CA-9
**Red Mountain**—*pop pl* NC-3
Red Mountain—*ridge* (3) AL-4
Red Mountain—*ridge* CA-9
Red Mountain—*ridge* NV-8
Red Mountain Bar Siphon—*canal* CA-9
Red Mountain Basin—*basin* (2) CA-9
Red Mountain Branch—*stream* TX-5
Red Mountain Camp—*locale* CA-9
Red Mountain Campground—*locale* WA-9
Red Mountain Ch—*church* NC-3
*Red Mountain Creek* MS-4
*Red Mountain Creek* OR-9
Red Mountain Creek—*stream* (3) AK-9
Red Mountain Creek—*stream* (6) CA-9
Red Mountain Creek—*stream* (3) CO-8
Red Mountain Creek—*stream* NV-8
Red Mountain Creek—*stream* (2) OR-9
Red Mountain Ditch—*canal* CO-8
Red Mountain Field—*flat* CA-9
Red Mountain Fire Station—*locale* CA-9
Red Mountain Gap—*gap* AL-4
Red Mountain Gulch—*valley* CO-8
Red Mountain Lake—*lake* CA-9
Red Mountain Lake—*lake* CO-8
Red Mountain Lake—*lake* OR-9
Red Mountain Lakes—*lake* ID-8
Red Mountain Meadow—*flat* CA-9
Red Mountain Meadows—*flat* CA-9
Red Mountain Mine—*mine* AZ-5
Red Mountain Mine—*mine* OR-9
Red Mountain Mine—*mine* (2) WA-9
Red Mountain Oil Field—*other* NM-5
Red Mountain Pass—*gap* (2) CO-8
Red Mountain Pasture—*flat* CA-9
Red Mountain Plaza Shop Ctr—*locale* AL-4
Red Mountain Prairie—*flat* OR-9
Red Mountain Ranch—*locale* AZ-5
Red Mountain Ranch—*locale* CA-9
*Red Mountain Range* WY-8
*Red Mountain Ridge* CA-9
Red Mountain RR Bridge—*hist pl* WA-9
Red Mountain Rsvr—*reservoir* (3) OR-9
*Red Mountains* NV-8
Red Mountain Shelter—*hist pl* CT-1
Red Mountain Spring—*spring* AZ-5
Red Mountain Spring—*spring* CA-9
Red Mountain Spring—*spring* (2) NV-8
Red Mountain Spring Creek—*stream* WY-8
Red Mountain Spring Number Three—*spring* NV-8
Red Mountain Spring Number Two—*spring* NV-8
Red Mountain Suburbs Hist Dist—*hist pl* AL-4
Red Mountain Tank—*reservoir* AZ-5
Red Mountain Tanks—*reservoir* AZ-5
Red Mountain Trail—*trail* CA-9
Red Mountain Trail—*trail* CO-8
Red Mountain Trail—*trail* MT-8
Red Mountain Trail—*trail* (2) OR-9
Red Mountain Trail—*trail* WA-9
Red Mountain-Trona (CCD)—*cens area* CA-9
Red Mountain Tunnel—*tunnel* CA-9
Red Mountain Twenty-five Trail—*trail* AZ-5
Red Mountan—*ridge* OR-9
Red Mount Ch—*church* PA-2
Red Mountian—*summit* WA-9
Red Mouth Creek—*stream* AL-4
*Red Mtn* AZ-5
*Red Mtn* CA-9
*Red Mtn* NM-5
*Red Mtn* OR-9
*Red Mtn* WA-9
Red Mtn—*summit* AL-4
Red Mtn—*summit* (9) AK-9
Red Mtn—*summit* (12) AZ-5
Red Mtn—*summit* (41) CA-9
Red Mtn—*summit* (14) CO-8
Red Mtn—*summit* (3) CT-1
Red Mtn—*summit* GA-3
Red Mtn—*summit* (7) ID-8
Red Mtn—*summit* MO-7
Red Mtn—*summit* (11) MT-8
Red Mtn—*summit* (10) NV-8
Red Mtn—*summit* (5) NM-5
Red Mtn—*summit* NC-3
Red Mtn—*summit* (7) OR-9
Red Mtn—*summit* PA-2
Red Mtn—*summit* (3) TN-4
Red Mtn—*summit* TX-5
Red Mtn—*summit* (6) UT-8
Red Mtn—*summit* VT-1
Red Mtn—*summit* (8) WA-9
Red Mtn—*summit* (5) WY-8
Red Mtn No 1—*summit* CO-8
Red Mtn No 2—*summit* CO-8
Red Mtn No 3—*summit* CO-8
Red Mtns—*range* UT-8
Red Mtns—*range* WY-8
Red Mud—*locale* TX-5
Red Mud Creek—*stream* OR-9
Red Mud Creek—*stream* TX-5
Redmud Creek—*stream* TX-5
Red Mud Creek—*stream* (2) TX-5
Red Mud Ridge—*ridge* KY-4
Red Mud Tank—*reservoir* TX-5
Rednar Hollow—*valley* MO-7
Red Narrows—*valley* (2) UT-8
Red Narrows, The—*gap* UT-8
Red Needle—*pillar* AZ-5
Red Needle—*pillar* NV-8
**Redne (historical)**—*pop pl* OR-9
Redner Gulch—*valley* CO-8
Redner Hill—*summit* MI-6
Redner Sch—*school* MI-6
Red Nichols Dam—*dam* AL-4
Red Nichols Number One Dam—*dam* AL-4
Red Nichols Number 2 Lake—*reservoir* AL-4
Rednor Hollow—*valley* PA-2
Red Nose—*cliff* CO-8
Red Nose Point—*cape* IA-7
Rednose Rsvr—*reservoir* MT-8
Red Nubs—*summit* UT-8
Red Nubs (historical)—*pillar* UT-8
Red Oak—*locale* AR-4
Redoak—*locale* LA-4
Red Oak—*locale* MI-6
Red Oak—*locale* TN-4
Red Oak—*locale* VA-3
Red Oak—*other* KY-4
**Red Oak**—*pop pl* AL-4
**Red Oak**—*pop pl* GA-3
**Red Oak**—*pop pl* IL-6
**Red Oak**—*pop pl* IA-7
**Red Oak**—*pop pl* LA-4
**Red Oak**—*pop pl* MO-7
**Red Oak**—*pop pl* NC-3
**Redoak**—*pop pl* OH-6
**Red Oak**—*pop pl* OK-5
**Red Oak**—*pop pl* PA-2
**Red Oak**—*pop pl* (2) TX-5
**Red Oak Acres (subdivision)**—*pop pl* NC-3
Red Oak Branch—*stream* (2) GA-3
Red Oak Branch—*stream* KY-4
Red Oak Branch—*stream* SC-3
Red Oak Branch—*stream* (3) TX-5
Red Oak Branch—*stream* WV-2
Red Oak Bridge—*bridge* FL-3
Red Oak Brook—*stream* MA-1
Red Oak Camp Creek—*stream* SC-3
Red Oak Canyon—*valley* CA-9
Red Oak (CCD)—*cens area* OK-5
Red Oak Cem—*cemetery* (2) AR-4
Red Oak Cem—*cemetery* GA-3
Red Oak Cem—*cemetery* IL-6
Red Oak Cem—*cemetery* LA-4
Red Oak Cem—*cemetery* NC-3
Red Oak Cem—*cemetery* (4) OK-5
Red Oak Cem—*cemetery* (2) TX-5
Red Oak Cem—*cemetery* WV-2
*Red Oak Ch* AL-4
*Red Oak Ch* NC-3
Red Oak Ch—*church* (2) AL-4
Red Oak Ch—*church* (2) AR-4
Red Oak Ch—*church* (2) FL-3
Red Oak Ch—*church* (5) GA-3
Red Oak Ch—*church* IL-6
Red Oak Ch—*church* IA-7
Red Oak Ch—*church* (2) KY-4
Redoak Ch—*church* LA-4
Red Oak Ch—*church* LA-4
Red Oak Ch—*church* MO-7
Redoak Ch—*church* NC-3
Red Oak Ch—*church* NC-3
Red Oak Ch—*church* OK-5
Red Oak Ch—*church* SC-3
Red Oak Ch—*church* TX-5
Red Oak Ch—*church* (2) VA-3
Red Oak Ch (historical)—*church* AL-4
*Red Oak Christian Church* NC-3
Red Oak Corner—*locale* SC-3
Red Oak Country Club—*other* IA-7
Red Oak Cove—*valley* NC-3
Red Oak Creek—*stream* AL-4
Redoak Creek—*stream* CA-9
Redoak Creek—*stream* GA-3
Red Oak Creek—*stream* GA-3
Red Oak Creek—*stream* IA-7
Red Oak Creek—*stream* KY-4
Red Oak Creek—*stream* MO-7
Redoak Creek—*stream* OH-6
Red Oak Creek—*stream* (3) OK-5
Red Oak Creek—*stream* (6) TX-5
Red Oak Creek—*stream* VA-3
Red Oak Creek—*stream* WV-2
Red Oak Creek Covered Bridge—*hist pl* GA-3
Red Oak Ditch—*canal* (2) IL-6
*Red Oak Drift Mine* AL-4
Red Oak Elem Sch—*school* NC-3
Red Oak Fork—*stream* LA-4
*Red Oak Gap Sch* TN-4
Redoak Gap Sch—*school* TN-4
Red Oak Grove—*locale* AL-4
Red Oak Grove—*locale* NJ-2
Redoak Grove Cem—*cemetery* AL-4
Red Oak Grove Cem—*cemetery* MN-6
Redoak Grove Ch—*church* AL-4
Red Oak Grove Ch—*church* AR-4
Red Oak Grove Ch—*church* MN-6
Red Oak Grove Ch—*church* (4) MS-4
Red Oak Grove Ch—*church* NC-3
Red Oak Grove Ch—*church* SC-3
Red Oak Grove Ch—*church* VA-3
Red Oak Grove Ch—*church* WV-2
*Red Oak Grove Methodist Ch* AL-4
Red Oak Gulch—*valley* ID-8
Red Oak Hammock—*island* GA-3
*Red-oak Hill* MA-1
Red Oak Hill—*summit* (2) MA-1
Redoak Hill—*summit* NH-1
Red Oak Hill—*summit* TX-5
Red Oak (historical P.O.)—*locale* IA-7
Red Oak Hollow—*locale* VA-3
Red Oak Hollow—*valley* (2) TX-5
Red Oak HS—*school* IA-7
Red Oak Island—*island* FL-3
Red Oak Island—*island* GA-3
Red Oak Island—*island* OH-6
Red Oak JHS—*school* IA-7
Red Oak Knob—*summit* NC-3
Red Oak Knob—*summit* VA-3
Red Oak Knob—*summit* WV-2
Redoak Knob—*summit* WV-2
Red Oak Knobs—*summit* TN-4
Red Oak Lake—*lake* LA-4
Red Oak Lake—*lake* TX-5
Red Oak Lake—*reservoir* TX-5
Red Oak (Magisterial District)—*fmr MCD* VA-3
Redoak Mtn—*summit* NC-3
Red Oak Mtn—*summit* OK-5
Redoak Mtn—*summit* TN-4
Red Oak Mtn—*summit* (3) VA-3
Red Oak-Norris Gas Field—*oilfield* OK-5
Red Oak Park—*park* IA-7
Red Oak Peak—*summit* OK-5
Red Oak Plaza (Shop Ctr)—*locale* NC-3
Red Oak Presbyterian Church—*hist pl* OH-6
Red Oak Public Library—*hist pl* IA-7
Red Oak Range—*ridge* AR-4
Red Oak Ridge—*island* WI-6
Red Oak Ridge—*ridge* IL-6
Red Oak Ridge—*ridge* MI-6
Red Oak Ridge—*ridge* OK-5
Redoak Ridge—*ridge* VA-3
Red Oak Ridge—*ridge* VA-3
Redoak Ridge—*ridge* VA-3
Red Oak Ridge—*ridge* WV-2
Red Oak Ridge—*ridge* WI-6
Red Oak Run—*stream* MD-2
Red Oak Run—*stream* (2) WV-2
*Red Oaks* LA-4
*Red Oaks* PA-2
**Red Oaks**—*pop pl* LA-4
Red Oaks Ch—*church* TX-5
Red Oak Sch—*school* (2) AR-4
Red Oak Sch—*school* GA-3
Red Oak Sch—*school* (4) IL-6
Red Oak Sch—*school* IA-7
Red Oak Sch—*school* LA-4
Red Oak Sch—*school* MA-1
Red Oak Sch—*school* MN-6
Red Oak Sch—*school* NC-3
Red Oak Sch—*school* (2) TN-4
Red Oak Sch—*school* TX-5
Red Oak Sch—*school* WI-6
Red Oak Sch (historical)—*school* AL-4
Red Oak Sch (historical)—*school* MS-4
Redoak Sch (historical)—*school* MO-7
Red Oak Sch (historical)—*school* PA-2
Red Oaks Lakes—*reservoir* PA-2
**Red Oaks Mill**—*pop pl* NY-2
Red Oak Spring—*spring* VA-3
Red Oak Swamp—*swamp* MS-4
*Red Oak Terrace* IL-6
Red Oak Township—*civil* MO-7
Red Oak Township—*fmr MCD* (2) IA-7
Red Oak (Township of)—*fmr MCD* NC-3
Red Oat Mountain Lookout—*locale* CA-9
Red Oat Ridge—*ridge* CA-9
*Redock* PA-2
Redonda, Mesa—*summit* AZ-5
Redonda Mesa—*summit* CA-9
Redonda Ridge—*ridge* CA-9
Redonda Trail—*trail* NM-5
**Redondo**—*pop pl* WA-9
*Redondo Beach* WA-9
**Redondo Beach**—*pop pl* CA-9
Redondo Beach HS—*school* CA-9
Redondo Beach Original Townsite Hist Dist—*hist pl* CA-9
Redondo Beach Public Library—*hist pl* CA-9
Redondo Beach State Park—*park* CA-9
Redondo Border—*ridge* NM-5
Redondo Campground—*locale* NM-5
Redondo Canyon—*valley* CA-9
Redondo Creek—*stream* NM-5
Redondo Elem Sch—*school* FL-3
Redondo Flat—*flat* CA-9
Redondo Junction—*locale* CA-9
*Redondo Mesa* AZ-5
Redondo Peak—*summit* NM-5
Redondo Ranch—*locale* AZ-5
Redondo Ruins (Butterfield Stage Station)—*locale* AZ-5
Redondo Spring—*spring* CA-9
Redondo Tank—*reservoir* AZ-5
Redondo Valle—*area* NM-5
Redondo Wash—*stream* AZ-5
*Red One Beach* MH-9
Red Onion—*locale* KS-7
**Red Onion**—*pop pl* AR-4
**Red Onion**—*pop pl* MO-7
Redore—*locale* MN-6
Red Ore Sch—*school* AL-4
**Red Ore (Woodward Red Ore)**—*pop pl* AL-4
Red Ore 1 Mine—*mine* NV-8
Redoubt, Mount—*summit* WA-9
Redoubt Astro—*cape* AK-9
Redoubt Bay—*bay* (2) AK-9
Redoubt Bayou—*bay* FL-3
Redoubt Creek—*stream* AK-9
Redoubt Creek—*stream* KS-7
Redoubt Creek—*stream* OK-5
Redoubt Creek—*stream* WA-9
Redoubt Glacier—*glacier* WA-9
Redoubt Hill—*summit* ME-1
Redoubt Lake—*lake* AK-9
Redoubt Lake Trail—*trail* AK-9
Redoubt Point—*cape* AK-9
Redoubt Trail—*trail* NY-2
Redoubt Volcano—*summit* AK-9
**Redowl**—*pop pl* SD-7
*Red Owl Creek* SD-7
Red Owl Creek—*stream* MT-8
Red Owl Creek—*stream* SD-7
Red Owl Dam—*dam* SD-7
Red Owl Township (historical)—*civil* SD-7
Red Paint Creek—*stream* AK-9
Red Paint Creek—*stream* TX-5
Red Park—*flat* (2) WY-8
Red Park—*park* IA-7
**Red Park**—*pop pl* MI-6
Red Pass—*gap* (3) UT-8
Red Pass—*gap* WA-9
Red Pass—*gap* WY-8
Red Pass—*gut* LA-4
Red Pass Lake—*flat* CA-9
Red Pasture Pens—*locale* TX-5
Redpath Creek—*stream* SD-7
**Redpath (Township of)**—*pop pl* MN-6
Red Pea Hollow—*valley* TN-4
*Red Peak* CA-9
*Red Peak* WY-8
Red Peak—*summit* AK-9
Red Peak—*summit* AZ-5
Red Peak—*summit* (4) CA-9
Red Peak—*summit* CO-8
Red Peak—*summit* (2) ID-8
Red Peak—*summit* NV-8
Red Peak—*summit* OR-9
Red Peak—*summit* UT-8
Red Peak—*summit* (2) WY-8
Red Peak Fork—*stream* CA-9
Red Peak Tank—*reservoir* NM-5
Red Peak Trail—*trail* CA-9
Red Peak Valley—*valley* AZ-5
Red Pen Windmill—*locale* TX-5
Red Pepper Butte—*summit* NV-8

*Redstar* ... MS-4
Red Star—*locale* ... AL-4
Red Star—*locale* ... AR-4
**Redstar**—*pop pl* ... MS-4
**Red Star**—*pop pl* ... SC-3
**Redstar**—*pop pl* ... WV-2
Red Star Camp—*locale* ... NC-3
Red Star Ch—*church* ... OK-5
Red Star Community Building—*locale* ... MI-6
Redstar Creek—*stream* ... AK-9
Red Star Ditch (Abandoned)—*canal* ... CA-9
Red Star Inn—*facility* ... KY-4
Red Star Mine—*mine* ... AZ-5
Red Star Mine—*mine* ... CA-9
Red Star Mine (underground)—*mine* (2) ... AL-4
Red Star Mining Ditch (Abandoned)—*canal* ... CA-9
Redstar Mtn—*summit* ... AK-9
Red Star Point—*summit* ... CA-9
Red Star Post Office (historical)—*building* ... AL-4
Redstar Post Office (historical)—*building* ... MS-4
Red Star Ravine—*valley* ... CA-9
Red Star Ridge—*ridge* ... CA-9
Red Star (RR name for Redstar)—*other* ... WV-2
**Redstar (RR name Red Star)**—*pop pl* ... WV-2
Red Star Sch—*school* ... MN-6
Red Star Sch—*school* ... MO-7
Red Star Sch—*school* ... NE-7
Red Star Sch—*school* ... WI-6
Red Star Sch (abandoned)—*school* ... MO-7
Red Star Sch (historical)—*school* ... MS-4
Red Star Sch (historical)—*school* ... MO-7
Redstart Creek—*stream* ... MI-6
Redstart Lake—*lake* ... MN-6
Red Steer Canyon—*valley* ... NM-5
Red Steer Spring—*spring* ... NM-5
*Redstone* ... KS-7
*Red Stone* ... PA-2
Redstone—*hist pl* ... IA-7
Redstone—*locale* ... MI-6
Redstone—*locale* ... NM-5
**Redstone**—*pop pl* ... CO-8
**Red Stone**—*pop pl* ... GA-3
**Redstone**—*pop pl* ... MT-8
**Redstone**—*pop pl* ... NH-1
**Redstone**—*pop pl* ... PA-2
Redstone, Lake—*reservoir* ... WI-6
Redstone Army Airfield—*airport* ... AL-4
Redstone Arsenal—*military* ... AL-4
Redstone Arsenal Rec Area—*park* ... AL-4
Red Stone Basin—*basin* ... SD-7
Redstone Branch—*stream* ... VA-3
Redstone Campground—*locale* ... CO-8
Red Stone Cem—*cemetery* ... OK-5
Redstone Cem—*cemetery* ... PA-2
Redstone Cem—*cemetery* ... SD-7
Redstone Ch—*church* ... GA-3
Red Stone Ch—*church* ... OK-5
*Red Stone Creek* ... PA-2
Redstone Creek—*stream* ... CO-8
Redstone Creek—*stream* ... GA-3
Redstone Creek—*stream* ... KY-4
Redstone Creek—*stream* ... MT-8
Redstone Creek—*stream* ... PA-2
Red Stone Creek—*stream* ... SD-7
Redstone Creek—*stream* ... SD-7
Redstone Drain—*canal* ... MI-6
*Red Stone Hill* ... MA-1
Redstone Hill—*summit* ... CT-1
Red Stone Hill—*summit* ... KY-4
Redstone Hill—*summit* ... MA-1
Red Stone (historical)—*locale* ... KS-7
Red Stone (historical)—*locale* ... SD-7
Redstone Inn—*hist pl* ... CO-8
**Redstone Junction**—*pop pl* ... PA-2
Red Stone Lake—*lake* ... MA-1
Redstone Ledge—*bench* ... NH-1
Redstone Marina—*locale* ... AL-4
Redstone MS—*school* ... PA-2
Redstone Park—*flat* ... NM-5
**Redstone Park**—*pop pl* ... AL-4
Redstone Peak—*summit* ... WA-9
Redstone Point—*cape* ... NC-3
Redstone Ridge—*ridge* ... NY-2
Redstone Ridge—*ridge* ... PA-2
*Red Stone River* ... MT-8
*Red Stone River* ... WY-8
Redstone River—*stream* ... AK-9
Redstone Sch—*school* ... MA-1
Redstone Shop Ctr—*locale* ... MA-1
*Redstone Siding* ... AL-4
**Redstone (subdivision)**—*pop pl* ... TN-4
Redstone Test Stand—*hist pl* ... AL-4
**Redstone Township**—*pop pl* ... SD-7
Redstone Township (historical)—*civil* ... SD-7
**Redstone (Township of)**—*pop pl* ... PA-2
Red Store Ch—*church* ... LA-4
*Red Store Crossroad* ... GA-3
Red Store Crossroads—*locale* ... GA-3
Redstreak Peak—*summit* ... MT-8
*Red Stripe Church* ... TN-4
Redstripe (Township of)—*fmr MCD* ... AR-4
Red Sucker Bay—*bay* ... MN-6
Red Sucker Island—*island* ... MN-6
Red Sulfur Spring—*spring* ... TN-4
*Red Sulphur* ... TN-4
*Red Sulphur* ... WV-2
Red Sulphur (Magisterial District)—*fmr MCD* ... WV-2
Red Sulphur Spring—*spring* ... TN-4
*Red Sulphursprings* ... TN-4
Red Sulphur Springs—*locale* ... TN-4
Red Sulphur Springs—*locale* ... WV-2
Red Sulphur Springs Branch—*stream* ... TN-4
Red Sulphur Springs Cabin Area—*locale* ... TN-4
Reds Wallowa Horse Ranch Airstrip—*airport* ... OR-9
Red Swamp—*stream* ... VA-3
Red Swan Golf Course—*other* ... NY-2
*Red Table Mountains* ... CO-8
Red Table Mtn—*summit* ... CO-8
Red Tahquitz—*summit* ... CA-9
*Red Tahquitz Peak* ... CA-9
Redtail Dam Tank—*reservoir* ... AZ-5
Red Tail Ranch—*locale* ... AZ-5
Red Tail Substation—*locale* ... AZ-5
Redtail Tank—*reservoir* ... AZ-5
Red Tail Tank—*reservoir* ... AZ-5
Red Tail Windmill—*locale* ... TX-5
*Red Tank* ... TX-5
Red Tank—*locale* ... PA-2
Red Tank—*reservoir* (29) ... AZ-5
Red Tank—*reservoir* ... HI-9
Red Tank—*reservoir* (29) ... NM-5
Red Tank—*reservoir* (26) ... TX-5
*Red Tank Canyon* ... AZ-5
Red Tank Canyon—*valley* ... AZ-5
Red Tank Canyon—*valley* ... TX-5
Red Tank Creek—*stream* (2) ... NM-5
Red Tank Draw—*valley* ... AZ-5
Red Tank Draw—*valley* ... NM-5
Red Tank Draw—*valley* ... TX-5
Red Tank Number One—*reservoir* ... AZ-5
*Red Tanks* ... UT-8
Red Tanks—*reservoir* (3) ... AZ-5
Red Tanks—*reservoir* ... UT-8
Red Tanks Canyon—*valley* ... AZ-5
Red Tanks Canyon—*valley* ... NM-5
Red Tanks Divide—*gap* ... AZ-5
*Red Tanks Pond* ... AZ-5
Red Tank Spring—*spring* ... CA-9
Red Tank Spring—*spring* ... SD-7
Red Tanks Spring—*spring* ... AZ-5
Red Tanks Trail—*trail* ... AZ-5
Red Tanks Well—*well* ... AZ-5
Red Tank Well—*reservoir* ... AZ-5
Red Tank Well—*well* (2) ... AZ-5
Red Tank Well—*well* ... NM-5
Red Tank Windmill—*locale* ... NM-5
Red Tank Windmill—*locale* (2) ... TX-5
*Red Tavern* ... NJ-2
Red Tavern (historical)—*locale* ... MS-4
Red Terrace Spring—*spring* ... WY-8
*Red Three Beach* ... MH-9
Red Tip Well—*well* ... NM-5
Red Tongue Mesa—*summit* ... NM-5
Red Top—*hist pl* ... MA-1
Red Top—*locale* ... CA-9
Red Top—*locale* ... MS-4
Red Top—*locale* ... MT-8
Red Top—*locale* ... TX-5
Red Top—*locale* ... VA-3
**Red Top**—*pop pl* ... CA-9
**Redtop**—*pop pl* ... MN-6
**Redtop**—*pop pl* ... MO-7
**Red Top**—*pop pl* ... MO-7
**Red Top**—*pop pl* ... SC-3
**Red Top**—*pop pl* ... TN-4
Redtop—*summit* ... CA-9
Red Top—*summit* (2) ... CA-9
Red Top—*summit* ... ID-8
Red Top Canyon—*valley* ... NV-8
Red Top Cem—*cemetery* ... IL-6
Red Top Cem—*cemetery* ... KS-7
Red Top Cem—*cemetery* ... MA-1
Redtop Cem—*cemetery* ... MN-6
Red Top Cem—*cemetery* (2) ... OK-5
Red Top Cem—*cemetery* ... TX-5
*Red Top Cemetery* ... TN-4
Redtop Ch—*church* ... MO-7
*Redtop Cree* ... ID-8
*Redtop Creek* ... MT-8
Red Top Creek—*stream* (2) ... ID-8
Red Top Creek—*stream* ... MT-8
Red Top Creek—*stream* ... WY-8
Red Top Creek Campground—*locale* ... MT-8
Red Top Draw—*valley* (2) ... WY-8
Red Top Gulch—*valley* ... NV-8
Red Top Hill—*summit* ... MT-8
Red Top Lake—*lake* ... CA-9
Red Top Lookout—*locale* ... CA-9
*Red Top Meadow* ... ID-8
Red Top Meadow—*flat* ... OR-9
Red Top Meadows—*flat* ... ID-8
Red Top Meadows—*flat* ... WY-8
*Red Top Mine* ... NV-8
Red Top Mine—*mine* ... AK-9
Red Top Mine—*mine* ... AZ-5
Red Top Mine—*mine* (2) ... CA-9
Red Top Mine—*mine* ... NV-8
Red Top Mine—*mine* ... WA-9
*Red Top Mountain* ... ID-8
Red Top Mountain State Park—*park* ... GA-3
Red Top Mtn—*summit* (2) ... AZ-5
Red Top Mtn—*summit* ... GA-3
Red Top Mtn—*summit* ... MT-8
Red Top Mtn—*summit* ... NV-8
Redtop Mtn—*summit* ... OR-9
Red Top Mtn—*summit* (2) ... WA-9
Red Top Mtn—*summit* ... WY-8
Redtop Peak—*summit* ... CO-8
Red Top Ranch—*locale* ... CA-9
Red Top Ranch—*locale* ... CO-8
Red Top Rsvr—*reservoir* ... CO-8
Red Top Rsvr—*reservoir* (2) ... WY-8
Red Tops—*summit* ... UT-8
Red Tops—*summit* ... WY-8
Red Top Sch—*school* ... ID-8
Red Top Sch—*school* ... MI-6
Red Top Sch—*school* (2) ... NE-7
Red Top Sch—*school* ... SD-7
Redtop Sch (historical)—*school* ... TN-4
Red Top Spring—*spring* (2) ... OR-9
Red Top Tanks—*reservoir* ... NM-5
Red Top Valley Ditch—*canal* ... CO-8
Redtop Windmill—*locale* ... TX-5
Redtower Windmill—*locale* ... NM-5
Red Tower Windmill—*locale* ... NM-5
Red Tower Windmill—*locale* (4) ... TX-5
Redtown—*locale* ... OH-6
**Redtown**—*pop pl* ... AL-4
**Red Town**—*pop pl* ... TX-5
Red Town Sch—*school* ... IL-6
Red Town Sch—*school* ... TX-5
Red Town Windmill—*locale* ... TX-5
Red Trail—*trail* ... ID-8
Red Tree Spring—*spring* ... AZ-5
Red Trough Spring—*spring* ... OR-9
Red Tub Tank—*reservoir* ... TX-5
*Red Two Beach* ... MH-9
**Reduction**—*pop pl* ... PA-2
Redundant Windmill—*locale* ... TX-5
Redus—*locale* ... NE-7
Redus Canyon—*valley* ... AZ-5
Redus Cem—*cemetery* ... TX-5
Redus Hollow—*valley* ... AL-4
**Redvale**—*pop pl* ... CO-8
*Red Valley* ... AL-4
*Red Valley* ... AZ-5
*Red Valley* ... UT-8
Red Valley—*basin* ... UT-8
Red Valley—*locale* ... VA-3
**Red Valley**—*pop pl* ... NJ-2
Red Valley—*post sta* ... AZ-5
Red Valley—*valley* ... AZ-5
Red Valley—*valley* ... NM-5
Red Valley—*valley* ... PA-2
Red Valley—*valley* ... SD-7
Red Valley—*valley* (2) ... UT-8
Red Valley Branch—*stream* ... AL-4
Red Valley Ch—*church* ... AL-4
Red Valley Ch—*church* ... VA-3
Red Valley Dam—*dam* ... NJ-2
Red Valley Lake—*reservoir* ... NJ-2
Red Vermillion Crossing—*locale* ... KS-7
**Red Vermillion Township**—*pop pl* ... KS-7
Redview Forest Service Station—*locale* ... UT-8
Redview Guard Station—*locale* ... UT-8
**Red Village**—*pop pl* ... VT-1
Red Village Sch—*school* ... VT-1
**Redville**—*pop pl* ... WI-6
Redville (historical)—*locale* ... AL-4
Red Wall—*cliff* ... WY-8
Redwall Canyon—*valley* ... AZ-5
Red Wall Canyon—*valley* ... CA-9
Redwall Cavern—*cave* ... AZ-5
Red Wall No 1—*cliff* ... WY-8
Red Wall No 2—*cliff* ... WY-8
Red Walnut—*locale* ... TN-4
**Red Warrior**—*pop pl* ... WV-2
Red Warrior Creek—*stream* (2) ... ID-8
**Red Warrior Junction (Red Warrior)**—*pop pl* ... WV-2
Red Warrior Mine—*mine* ... UT-8
*Red Wash* ... UT-8
**Red Wash**—*pop pl* ... UT-8
Red Wash—*stream* ... AZ-5
Red Wash—*stream* (2) ... CO-8
Red Wash—*stream* ... NM-5
Red Wash—*stream* ... WY-8
Red Wash—*valley* (7) ... UT-8
Red Wash—*valley* ... WY-8
Red Wash Branch—*stream* (3) ... FL-3
Red Wash Butte—*summit* ... CO-8
Red Wash Canyon—*valley* ... NM-5
Red Wash Cem—*cemetery* ... AL-4
Red Wash Creek—*stream* ... CA-9
Red Wash Creek—*stream* ... NV-8
Red Wash Draw—*valley* ... WY-8
Red Wash Hill—*summit* ... AL-4
*Red Wash Hill Cemetery* ... AL-4
Red Wash Oil and Gas Field—*oilfield* ... UT-8
Red Wash Rsvr—*reservoir* ... CO-8
Red Wash Rsvr No 1—*reservoir* ... CO-8
Red Wash Rsvr No 2—*reservoir* ... CO-8
Red Wash Rsvr No 3—*reservoir* ... CO-8
**Redwater**—*pop pl* ... MS-4
**Redwater**—*pop pl* ... MT-8
**Redwater**—*pop pl* ... TX-5
Redwater Bay—*swamp* ... NC-3
Redwater Branch—*stream* ... AL-4
Red Water Branch—*stream* ... AR-4
Redwater Brook—*stream* ... ME-1
Redwater Brook—*stream* ... NH-1
Redwater Brook—*stream* ... NY-2
Redwater Canal—*canal* ... SD-7
Red Water Canyon—*valley* ... NM-5
Redwater Cem—*cemetery* ... MS-4
*Red Water Creek* ... AL-4
*Redwater Creek* ... MT-8
*Red Water Creek* ... SD-7
*Redwater Creek* ... WY-8
Redwater Creek—*stream* ... MS-4
Redwater Creek—*stream* ... NY-2
Redwater Creek—*stream* ... PA-2
Redwater Creek—*stream* (3) ... SD-7
Redwater Creek—*stream* ... TN-4
Redwater Creek—*stream* ... VA-3
Redwater Creek—*stream* ... WY-8
Red Waterhole—*lake* ... OR-9
*Redwater Lake* ... MI-6
Red Water Lake—*lake* ... FL-3
Redwater Lake—*lake* (3) ... FL-3
Red Water Lake—*lake* ... MI-6
Redwater Lookout Tower—*locale* ... TX-5
Red Water Pond—*lake* ... NM-5
*Redwater River* ... SD-7
*Redwater River* ... WY-8
Redwater River—*stream* ... MT-8
Redwater River—*stream* ... SD-7
Redwater Tank—*reservoir* ... AZ-5
Redwater Tank—*reservoir* ... NM-5
Red Water Wash—*valley* ... AZ-5
Redwater Well—*well* ... MT-8
Red Water Well—*well* ... MT-8
**Redway**—*pop pl* ... CA-9
Red Well—*locale* ... NM-5
Red Well—*well* (3) ... NM-5
Red Well—*well* (2) ... OR-9
Red Well—*well* (4) ... TX-5
Red Well—*well* ... UT-8
Redwell Basin—*basin* ... CO-8
Red Wells—*spring* ... UT-8
Red Well Windmill—*locale* ... TX-5
Red Whiskers Spring—*spring* ... AZ-5
Red White and Blue Camp Well—*well* ... TX-5
Red White and Blue Sand Hills—*summit* ... TX-5
Red Willow—*locale* ... NE-7
Red Willow Camp—*locale* ... ND-7
Red Willow Canal—*canal* ... NE-7
Red Willow Canyon—*valley* ... AZ-5
Red Willow Community Center—*locale* ... CO-8
Red Willow Creek—*stream* ... CO-8
Red Willow Creek—*stream* (2) ... NE-7
Red Willow Creek—*stream* ... SD-7
Red Willow Creek—*stream* ... WA-9
Red Willow Creek Diversion Dam—*dam* ... NE-7
Red Willow Dam—*dam* ... NE-7
Red Willow Lake—*lake* ... NE-7
Red Willow Lake—*lake* ... ND-7
Red Willow Rec Area—*park* ... NE-7
*Red Willow Reservoir* ... NE-7
Red Willow Spring—*spring* (3) ... AZ-5
Red Willow Spring—*spring* ... NM-5
Red Willow Spring—*spring* ... OR-9
Red Willow Township (historical)—*civil* ... ND-7
Red Willow Wash—*stream* ... NM-5
Red Windmill—*locale* ... CO-8
Red Windmill—*locale* (8) ... NM-5
Red Windmill—*locale* (20) ... TX-5
Red Windmill Draw—*valley* ... TX-5
Red Windmill Lake—*lake* ... TX-5
Red Windmill Tank—*reservoir* ... NM-5
Red Wind Slough—*gut* ... AK-9
Redwine—*locale* ... GA-3
**Red Wine**—*pop pl* ... AL-4
**Redwine**—*pop pl* ... KY-4
**Redwine**—*pop pl* ... TN-4
Redwine Cabin—*locale* ... CA-9
Redwine Canyon—*valley* ... WA-9
Redwine Cem—*cemetery* ... TX-5
Redwine Ch—*church* (2) ... GA-3
Redwine Cove—*basin* ... GA-3
Redwine Cove Cem—*cemetery* ... GA-3
*Redwine Creek* ... KY-4
Redwine Creek—*stream* ... GA-3
Redwine Creek—*stream* ... LA-4
Redwine Creek—*stream* ... TN-4
Redwine Lake—*reservoir* ... GA-3
Redwine Ranch—*locale* ... CA-9
Redwine Spring—*spring* ... CA-9
*Red Wing* ... KS-7
Red Wing—*locale* ... CO-8
Redwing—*locale* ... WV-2
**Red Wing**—*pop pl* ... AR-4
**Redwing**—*pop pl* ... KS-7
**Redwing**—*pop pl* ... LA-4
**Red Wing**—*pop pl* ... MN-6
Redwing Airpark—*airport* ... NJ-2
Red Wing Area Vocational Tech Institute—*school* ... MN-6
Red Wing Bay—*bay* ... MN-6
*Redwing Brook* ... MA-1
Red Wing Camp—*locale* ... OH-6
Redwing Cem—*cemetery* ... NE-7
Red Wing Cem—*cemetery* ... ND-7
Redwing Ch—*church* ... LA-4
Redwing Ch—*church* ... MS-4
Red Wing City Hall—*hist pl* ... MN-6
Red Wing Country Club—*other* ... MN-6
Red Wing Creek—*stream* ... ND-7
Redwing Creek—*stream* ... WI-6
Red Wing Iron Works—*hist pl* ... MN-6
Redwing Lake—*lake* ... CA-9
Redwing Lake—*lake* ... IN-6
Redwing Lake—*lake* ... VA-3
Red Wing Lake—*lake* ... WY-8
Red Wing Mall Hist Dist—*hist pl* ... MN-6
Red Wing Mine—*mine* ... CA-9
Redwing Oil Field—*oilfield* ... CO-8
Redwing Oil Field—*oilfield* ... KS-7
Redwing Oil Field—*oilfield* ... ND-7
Red Wing Residential Hist Dist—*hist pl* ... MN-6
Red Wing Sch—*school* ... NE-7
Redwing Sch—*school* ... NE-7
Red Wing Sch—*school* ... ND-7
**Red Wing Township**—*pop pl* ... ND-7
Red Wing Well—*well* ... AZ-5
Red Wolf Pass—*gap* ... OR-9
Red Woman Creek—*stream* ... SD-7
Redwood—*CDP* ... OR-9
Redwood—*hist pl* ... ME-1
Redwood—*locale* ... NC-3
**Redwood**—*pop pl* ... MS-4
**Redwood**—*pop pl* (2) ... NY-2
**Redwood**—*pop pl* ... TX-5
**Redwood**—*pop pl* ... UT-8
**Redwood**—*pop pl* ... VA-3
Redwood, Lake—*lake* ... MN-6
Redwood (abandoned)—*locale* ... AK-9
Redwood Acres Fairground—*locale* ... CA-9
Redwood Airp—*airport* ... UT-8
Redwood Bay—*bay* ... AK-9
Redwood Brown Ditch Number One—*canal* ... MN-6
Redwood Camp—*locale* (2) ... CA-9
Redwood Canal—*canal* ... CA-9
Redwood Canyon—*valley* (7) ... CA-9
Redwood Cem—*cemetery* ... CA-9
Redwood Cem—*cemetery* ... FL-3
Redwood Cem—*cemetery* ... IN-6
Redwood Cem—*cemetery* ... LA-4
Redwood Cem—*cemetery* ... NY-2
Redwood Cem—*cemetery* ... TX-5
Redwood Cem—*cemetery* ... VA-3
Redwood Ch—*church* (2) ... LA-4
Redwood Ch—*church* ... MO-7
**Redwood City**—*pop pl* ... CA-9
Redwood City Historic Commercial Buildings—*hist pl* ... CA-9
**Redwood Corral**—*pop pl* ... CA-9
Redwood Cottage—*hist pl* ... WI-6
**Redwood (County)**—*pop pl* ... MN-6
**Redwood Creek**—*pop pl* ... CA-9
Redwood Creek—*stream* ... AK-9
Redwood Creek—*stream* (22) ... CA-9
Redwood Creek—*stream* ... IN-6
Redwood Creek—*stream* ... LA-4
Redwood Creek Beach County Park—*park* ... CA-9
Redwood Creek Camp—*locale* ... CA-9
Redwood Creek Ranch—*locale* ... CA-9
Redwood Elem Sch—*school* ... MS-4
Redwood Empire Country Club—*other* ... CA-9
**Redwood Estates**—*pop pl* ... CA-9
**Redwood Falls**—*pop pl* ... MN-6
Redwood Falls Carnegie Library—*hist pl* ... MN-6
Redwood Falls Cem—*cemetery* ... MN-6
Redwood Falls (Township of)—*civ div* ... MN-6
Redwood Five Drain—*canal* ... CA-9
Redwood Four Drain—*canal* ... CA-9
Redwood Gardens Mobile Home Park—*locale* ... AZ-5
**Redwood Gardens Subdivision**—*pop pl* ... UT-8
Redwood Glen Camp—*locale* ... CA-9
**Redwood Grove**—*pop pl* ... CA-9
Redwood Gulch—*valley* ... CA-9
Redwood Gun Club—*other* ... CA-9
Redwood Harbor (Port Of Redwood City)—*uninc pl* ... CA-9
Redwood Heights Sch—*school* ... CA-9
Redwood Highway—*hist pl* ... CA-9
Redwood Hill—*summit* ... CA-9
Redwood Hill—*summit* ... GA-3
Redwood House—*locale* ... CA-9
Redwood HS—*school* (2) ... CA-9
Redwood Intermediate Sch—*school* ... CA-9
Redwood JHS—*school* ... CA-9
**Redwood Junction**—*pop pl* ... CA-9
Redwood Lake—*lake* ... CA-9
Redwood Landing (historical)—*locale* ... MS-4
Redwood Lateral Eight—*canal* ... CA-9
Redwood Lateral Five—*canal* ... CA-9
Redwood Lateral Four—*canal* ... CA-9
Redwood Lateral One—*canal* ... CA-9
Redwood Lateral Seven—*canal* ... CA-9
Redwood Lateral Ten—*canal* ... CA-9
Redwood Lateral Three—*canal* ... CA-9
Redwood Library—*hist pl* ... RI-1
Redwood Lodge—*locale* ... CA-9
**Redwood Lodge**—*pop pl* ... CA-9
Redwood Log Creek—*stream* ... CA-9
Redwood Meadow—*flat* (2) ... CA-9
Redwood Meadow Grove—*woods* ... CA-9
Redwood Meadow Ranger Station—*hist pl* ... CA-9
Redwood Memorial Estates (Cemetery)—*cemetery* ... UT-8
Redwood Memorial Hosp—*hospital* ... CA-9
Redwood Methodist Ch—*church* ... MS-4
Redwood Mountain—*ridge* ... CA-9
Redwood Mountain Grove—*woods* ... CA-9
Redwood Mtn—*summit* ... CA-9
Redwood Natl Park—*park* ... CA-9
Redwood Nine-A Drain—*canal* ... CA-9
Redwood Nine Drain—*canal* ... CA-9
Redwood Park—*park* (2) ... CA-9
Redwood Peak—*summit* ... CA-9
Redwood Point—*cape* ... CA-9
Redwood-Potter (CCD)—*cens area* ... CA-9
Redwood Primary Sch—*school* ... CA-9
Redwood Ranger Station—*locale* ... CA-9
Redwood Regional Park—*park* ... CA-9
Redwood Retreat—*locale* ... CA-9
Redwood River—*stream* ... MN-6
Redwood (RR name for North Redwood)—*other* ... MN-6
Redwoods—*locale* ... CA-9
Redwood Saddle—*gap* ... CA-9
Redwood Sch—*school* ... AR-4
Redwood Sch—*school* (3) ... CA-9
Redwood Sch—*school* ... OH-6
Redwood Sch—*school* ... OR-9
Redwood Sch—*school* ... UT-8
Redwood Sch—*school* ... VA-3
Redwood Shop Ctr—*locale* ... UT-8
Redwoods Hotel—*hist pl* ... OR-9
Red Wood Spring—*spring* ... AZ-5
Redwood Spring—*spring* ... CA-9
Redwood Spring—*spring* ... NV-8
Redwood Springs—*spring* ... CA-9
Redwood State Park—*park* ... OR-9
Redwood Station—*locale* ... MN-6
Redwood Tank—*spring* ... CO-8
**Redwood Terrace**—*pop pl* ... CA-9
Redwood Union Sch—*school* ... CA-9
**Redwood Valley**—*pop pl* ... CA-9
Redwood Valley—*valley* ... CA-9
**Redwood Valley Rancheria**—*pop pl* ... CA-9
Redwood Village—*locale* ... UT-8
**Redwood Village Condominium**—*pop pl* ... UT-8
Redwood Village Shop Ctr—*locale* ... KS-7
**Redwood Village (subdivision)**—*pop pl* (2) ... NC-3
**Redwood Village Subdivision**—*pop pl* ... UT-8
**Redwood Villa Subdivision**—*pop pl* ... UT-8
Redwood 8 Drain—*canal* ... CA-9
Red Worm Hollow—*valley* ... KY-4
Red Yard Cem—*cemetery* ... AR-4
Redy Drain—*canal* ... MI-6
Ree, Lake—*lake* ... WI-6
R E Earp Pond—*reservoir* ... NC-3
Reeb Ave Sch—*school* ... OH-6
Reebereppu—*island* ... MP-9
*Reebereppu Island* ... MP-9
*Reebereppu-To* ... MP-9
Reeb House—*hist pl* ... MO-7
Reebie Moving and Storage Company—*hist pl* ... IL-6
**Reece**—*pop pl* ... KS-7
*Reece Branch* ... MS-4
Reece Branch—*stream* ... KY-4
Reece Branch—*stream* ... SC-3
Reece Branch—*stream* (2) ... TN-4
Reece Branch—*stream* ... TX-5
Reece Bridge—*bridge* ... GA-3
Reece Canyon—*valley* ... NM-5
Reece Canyon—*valley* ... UT-8
Reece Cave—*cave* ... AL-4
Reece Cem—*cemetery* ... GA-3
Reece Cem—*cemetery* ... KS-7
Reece Cem—*cemetery* ... KY-4
Reece Cem—*cemetery* ... MO-7
Reece Cem—*cemetery* (2) ... OK-5
Reece Cem—*cemetery* ... TN-4
Reece Chapel—*church* ... TN-4
**Reece City**—*pop pl* ... AL-4
*Reece City Bridge* ... AL-4
**Reece City (Reeseville)**—*pop pl* ... AL-4
Reece Creek—*stream* ... AR-4
Reece Creek—*stream* ... GA-3
Reece Creek—*stream* ... TX-5
Reece Hollow—*valley* (3) ... TN-4
Reece Homestead—*locale* ... CA-9
Reece Lake—*lake* ... MI-6
*Reecemore* ... PA-2
Reece Mtn—*summit* ... SC-3
Reece Oil Field—*oilfield* ... KS-7
Reecer Canyon—*valley* ... WA-9
Reecer Creek—*stream* ... WA-9
Reecer Creek Sch—*school* ... WA-9
Reece Ridge Ch—*church* ... AR-4
Reeces Mill (historical)—*locale* ... AL-4
Reece Spring—*spring* ... TN-4
Reece State Memorial—*park* ... GA-3
**Reece Terrace (subdivision)**—*pop pl* ... TN-4
Reeceville—*locale* ... IA-7
**Reeceville**—*pop pl* ... PA-2
Reeceville Cem—*cemetery* ... IA-7
Reeck Drain—*stream* ... MI-6
Ree Creek—*stream* ... SD-7
*Reed* (2) ... IN-6
*Reed* ... PA-2
*Reed* ... WV-2
Reed—*locale* ... CA-9
Reed—*locale* ... ME-1
Reed—*locale* ... OR-9
Reed—*locale* ... PA-2
**Reed**—*pop pl* ... AR-4
**Reed**—*pop pl* ... CA-9
**Reed**—*pop pl* ... KY-4
**Reed**—*pop pl* ... MS-4
**Reed**—*pop pl* ... OK-5
**Reed**—*pop pl* ... SC-3
Reed, Alfred, Mound Group (47Cr311)—*hist pl* ... WI-6
Reed, C. A., House—*hist pl* ... OH-6
Reed, Charles Manning, Mansion—*hist pl* ... PA-2
Reed, Frederick, House—*hist pl* ... KY-4
Reed, G. W., Travellers Home—*hist pl* ... ME-1
Reed, Henry, Jr., House—*hist pl* ... OH-6
Reed, Isaac, House—*hist pl* ... NH-1
Reed, James, House—*hist pl* ... OH-6
Reed, Jehu, House—*hist pl* ... DE-2
Reed, Joseph G., Company—*hist pl* ... OH-6
Reed, J. V., and Company—*hist pl* ... KY-4
Reed, Lake—*lake* ... FL-3
Reed, Lake—*reservoir* (2) ... TX-5
Reed, Mount—*summit* ... AK-9
Reed, Philo, House—*hist pl* ... ME-1
Reed, Pleasant, House—*hist pl* ... MS-4
Reed, Robert, House—*hist pl* ... ME-1
Reed, Samuel Harrison, House—*hist pl* ... NC-3
Reed, Thomas Brackett, House—*hist pl* ... ME-1
Reed, Walter, Birthplace—*hist pl* ... VA-3
Reed, Wilber T., House—*hist pl* ... NE-7
Reed, Will, Farm House—*hist pl* ... AR-4
Reed, William, House—*hist pl* ... AL-4
Reed Airp—*airport* ... PA-2
Reed Airstrip—*airport* ... OR-9
Reed and Barton Complex—*hist pl* ... MA-1
Reed and Benson Mine—*mine* ... UT-8
Reed and Benson Ridge—*ridge* ... UT-8
Reed and Green Bridge Campground—*locale* ... MI-6
Reed and Hawley Mtn—*summit* ... OR-9
Reed Arm Branch—*stream* ... AL-4
Reed Arroyo—*stream* ... NM-5
Reed Attendance Center—*school* ... MS-4
Reed Ave Sch—*school* ... LA-4
Reed Bar—*bar* ... ID-8
Reed Bar Trail—*trail* ... ID-8
Reed Basin—*basin* ... AZ-5
*Reed Bay* ... NJ-2
Reed Bend—*bend* ... MO-7
Reed Bend—*bend* ... TX-5
Reed Bend Ford (historical)—*locale* ... MO-7
Reed Bend Sch (abandoned)—*school* ... MO-7
Reed Bingham State Park—*park* ... GA-3
Reed Bird Island—*island* ... MD-2
Reed Bluff—*cliff* ... AL-4
Reed Bog Rsvr—*reservoir* ... MA-1
Reed Bottom—*bend* ... TN-4
Reed Brake—*stream* ... LA-4
*Reed Brake Branch* ... MS-4
Reed Brake Branch—*stream* (2) ... MS-4
Reedbrake (historical)—*locale* ... AL-4
Reed Brake Research Natural Area—*park* ... AL-4
Reed Brake Swamp—*swamp* ... MS-4
Reed Branch—*stream* ... AL-4
Reed Branch—*stream* ... GA-3
Reed Branch—*stream* ... IN-6
Reed Branch—*stream* (2) ... KY-4
Reed Branch—*stream* ... MS-4
Reed Branch—*stream* ... NJ-2
Reed Branch—*stream* (2) ... NC-3
Reed Branch—*stream* (5) ... TN-4
Reed Branch—*stream* (3) ... TX-5
Reed Branch Swamp—*swamp* ... FL-3
*Reed Break Creek* ... MS-4
Reedbreak Creek—*stream* ... AL-4
Reed Bridge—*bridge* ... GA-3
Reed Bridge—*other* ... IL-6
*Reed Brook* ... NY-2
Reed Brook—*stream* (2) ... CT-1
Reed Brook—*stream* (5) ... ME-1
Reed Brook—*stream* (3) ... MA-1
Reed Brook—*stream* ... MI-6
Reed Brook—*stream* ... NH-1
Reed Brook—*stream* ... NY-2
Reed Butte—*summit* ... MT-8
Reed Butte—*summit* ... NV-8
Reed Camp—*locale* ... TX-5
Reed Canal—*canal* ... FL-3
Reed Canal—*canal* ... ID-8
*Reed Canyon* ... MT-8
Reed Canyon—*valley* ... CA-9
Reed Canyon—*valley* ... CO-8
Reed Canyon—*valley* (2) ... ID-8
Reed Canyon—*valley* (2) ... NV-8
Reed Canyon—*valley* (2) ... NM-5
Reed Canyon—*valley* ... UT-8
Reed Canyon—*valley* ... WA-9
Reed Canyon Windmill—*locale* ... CO-8
Reed Cave—*cave* ... TN-4
*Reed Cem* ... AL-4
Reed Cem—*cemetery* (3) ... AL-4
Reed Cem—*cemetery* (2) ... AR-4
Reed Cem—*cemetery* ... GA-3
Reed Cem—*cemetery* (5) ... IL-6
Reed Cem—*cemetery* (7) ... IN-6
Reed Cem—*cemetery* ... IA-7
Reed Cem—*cemetery* (5) ... LA-4
Reed Cem—*cemetery* (2) ... ME-1
Reed Cem—*cemetery* (2) ... MA-1
Reed Cem—*cemetery* ... MI-6
Reed Cem—*cemetery* ... MS-4
Reed Cem—*cemetery* (6) ... MO-7
Reed Cem—*cemetery* ... NY-2
Reed Cem—*cemetery* ... NC-3
Reed Cem—*cemetery* ... ND-7
Reed Cem—*cemetery* ... PA-2
Reed Cem—*cemetery* (11) ... TN-4
Reed Cem—*cemetery* (6) ... TX-5
Reed Cem—*cemetery* (2) ... VA-3
Reed Cem—*cemetery* (5) ... WV-2
Reed Ch—*church* ... OK-5
Reed Ch—*church* ... WV-2
Reed Channel—*channel* ... NY-2
Reed Chapel—*church* ... KY-4
Reed Chapel—*church* ... TN-4
Reed Chapel (historical)—*church* ... TN-4
Reed-Chatfield Ditch—*canal* ... CO-8
**Reed City**—*pop pl* ... IL-6
**Reed City**—*pop pl* ... MI-6
Reed Club Lake—*lake* ... TX-5
Reed Coll—*school* ... OR-9
**Reed Corners**—*pop pl* (3) ... NY-2

Reef Island—area AK-9
Reef Island—island (2) AK-9
Reef Island—island WA-9
Reef Lake—lake AK-9
Reef Lake—lake CA-9
Reef Mine—mine AZ-5
Reef of Rock—ridge AZ-5
Reef of Rocks—ridge UT-8
Reef Pasture Rsvr—reservoir CO-8
Reef Point—cape (3) AK-9
Reef Point—cape CA-9
Reef Point—cape ME-1
Reef Point—cape WA-9
Reef Point—island WA-9
Reef Point Lake—lake AK-9
Reef Ranch—locale WA-9
Reef Rapids—rapids WA-9
Reef Ridge—ridge AZ-5
Reef Ridge—ridge CA-9
Reef Rock—island AK-9
Reef Rock—summit AZ-5
Reef Rsvr—reservoir UT-8
Reefs, The—island FL-3
Reefs, The—pillar WY-8
Reefs, The—spring MT-8
**Reef Station**—pop pl CA-9
Reef Tank—reservoir AZ-5
Reefy, Frederick, House—hist pl OH-6
Reega—locale NJ-2
Reegan Creek—stream ID-8
Reeh Creek—stream TX-5
**Ree Heights**—pop pl SD-7
Ree Heights—range SD-7
**Ree Heights Township**—pop pl SD-7
Reeher Forest Park—park OR-9
Ree Hills SD-7
Ree Hills—summit SD-7
Ree Indian Village (historical)—locale SD-7
Reekes Mill—locale VA-3
Reek Sch—school WI-6
Reek School—locale MI-6
Reel, Jacob, House—hist pl KY-4
Reel Brook—stream NH-1
Reel Brook Trail—trail NH-1
Reel Cem—cemetery IA-7
**Reel Cove**—pop pl TN-4
Reel Cove—valley TN-4
Reel Cove Mine—mine TN-4
Reel Creek—stream (2) IN-6
Reel Creek—stream TN-4
Reelfoot TN-4
Reelfoot Baptist Church TN-4
Reelfoot Ch—church TN-4
Reelfoot Creek—stream TN-4
Reelfoot Girl Scout Council Camp—locale TN-4
Reelfoot Indian Creek Dam Number Fifteen—dam TN-4
Reelfoot Indian Creek Dam Number Fifteen—reservoir TN-4
Reelfoot Indian Creek Dam Number Fourteen—dam TN-4
Reelfoot-Indian Creek Dam Number Fourteen—reservoir TN-4
Reelfoot Indian Creek Dam Number Ten—dam TN-4
Reelfoot Indian Creek Number Ten Lake—reservoir TN-4
Reelfoot Indian Creek Watershed Number Seven Rsvr—reservoir TN-4
Reel Foot Lake TN-4
Reelfoot Lake—lake TN-4
Reelfoot Lake—reservoir TN-4
Reelfoot Lake Airp—airport TN-4
Reelfoot Lake Biological Station—building TN-4
Reelfoot Lake Campgrounds—locale TN-4
Reelfoot Lake Outlet At Spillway—dam TN-4
Reelfoot Lake State Park—park TN-4
Reelfoot Landing—locale TN-4
Reelfoot Manor Nursing Home—building TN-4
Reelfoot Natl Wildlife Ref—park KY-4
Reelfoot Natl Wildlife Ref—park TN-4
Reelfoot Post Office (historical)—building TN-4
Reelfoot Shop Ctr—locale TN-4
Reelfoot State Wildlife Mngmt Area—park TN-4
Reel Gulf TN-4
Reel Lake—lake MS-4
Reel Lake—reservoir OH-6
Reel Oil Field—oilfield WY-8
Reel Point—cape NY-2
Reel Point—cape VA-3
Reel Run—stream IN-6
Reels—locale IA-7
**Reelsboro**—pop pl NC-3
Reels Chapel—church IN-6
Reels Chapel—church NC-3
**Reels Corners**—pop pl PA-2
Reels Cove Mine TN-4
Reels Hollow—valley TN-4
Reels Mill—locale MD-2
Reels Valley—valley WI-6
Reels Valley Sch—school WI-6
**Reelsville**—pop pl IN-6
Reelsville Elem Sch—school IN-6
**Reeltown**—pop pl AL-4
Reeltown Cem—cemetery AL-4
Reeltown Ch—church AL-4
Reeltown HS—school AL-4
**Reeman**—pop pl MI-6
Reeman Cem—cemetery MI-6
Reem Creek NC-3
Reems Branch—stream NC-3
Reems Creek—stream NC-3
Reems Creek Ch—church NC-3
Reems Creek Falls—falls NC-3
Reems Creek (Township of)—fmr MCD NC-3
Reeny Branch—stream NC-3
Reep Lake—lake MN-6
Reeps Grove Ch—church NC-3
Reeps Lake—reservoir AR-4
**Reepsville**—pop pl NC-3
Reepu MP-9
Reepu—island MP-9
Reepu Island MP-9
Reepville NC-3
**Reepville (Reepsville)**—pop pl NC-3
Reer MP-9
Reere FM-9
Reere—island MP-9
Ree River SD-7
**Rees**—pop pl IL-6
Rees, John, David, and Jacob, House—hist pl WV-2
**Reesburg**—pop pl GA-3
Rees Canal—canal UT-8
Rees Canyon AZ-5
Rees Canyon UT-8
Rees Carillon—other IL-6
Rees Cem—cemetery (2) IN-6
Rees Cem—cemetery PA-2
Rees Cem—cemetery TN-4
Rees Cem—cemetery TX-5
Rees Chapel—church WV-2
Rees Corner—locale WA-9
Rees Creek—stream UT-8
Rees Creek—stream WY-8
Rees Ditch—canal IN-6
Reese—locale AR-4
Reese—locale (2) GA-3
Reese—locale MS-4
Reese—locale NC-3
Reese—locale (2) TX-5
Reese—locale WA-9
**Reese**—pop pl MD-2
**Reese**—pop pl MI-6
**Reese**—pop pl OH-6
**Reese**—pop pl PA-2
**Reese**—pop pl WV-2
Reese, Edwin, House—hist pl AL-4
Reese, Sheldon, Site (39HS23)—hist pl SD-7
Reese AFB—military TX-5
Reese Airp—airport IN-6
Reese and Berry Canyon—valley NV-8
Reese and Berry Mine—mine NV-8
Reese Anderson Creek—stream MT-8
Reese Bay—bay AK-9
Reese Bldg—building NC-3
Reese Branch—stream (2) AL-4
Reese Branch—stream MS-4
Reese Branch—stream SC-3
Reese Branch—stream TN-4
Reese Branch—stream TX-5
Reese Brothers Coal Mine—mine CA-9
Reese Brothers Ranch—locale WY-8
Reeseburg—locale GA-3
Reese Canyon—valley AZ-5
Reese Canyon—valley CA-9
Reese Canyon—valley ID-8
Reese Canyon—valley MT-8
Reese Canyon—valley NM-5
Reese Canyon—valley UT-8
Reese Cave—cave TN-4
Reese Cem—cemetery (2) AR-4
Reese Cem—cemetery MI-6
Reese Cem—cemetery MS-4
Reese Ch—church AL-4
Reese Chapel AL-4
Reese Chapel—church AL-4
Reese Chapel—church SC-3
Reese Chapel Ch AL-4
Reese Ch (historical)—church MS-4
Reese Corners—locale OH-6
Reese Creek LA-4
Reese Creek OR-9
Reese Creek TN-4
Reese Creek—stream CA-9
Reese Creek—stream (3) ID-8
Reese Creek—stream IL-6
Reese Creek—stream KY-4
Reese Creek—stream LA-4
Reese Creek—stream MS-4
Reese Creek—stream (3) MT-8
Reese Creek—stream NC-3
Reese Creek—stream (2) OR-9
Reese Creek—stream TX-5
Reese Creek—stream UT-8
Reese Creek—stream WA-9
Reese Creek—stream (2) WY-8
Reese Creek Cem—cemetery OR-9
Reese Creek Sch—hist pl MT-8
Reese Creek Sch—school MT-8
Reese Creek Sch—school OR-9
Reesedale—locale PA-2
Reesedale—locale VA-3
Reese Dam—dam AL-4
Reese Deadening Hollow—valley TN-4
Reese Ditch—canal MT-8
Reese Drain—canal MI-6
Reese Ferry AL-4
Reese Ferry Landing—locale AL-4
Reese Flat—flat CA-9
Reese Fork—stream MO-7
Reese Gap—gap AL-4
Reese Gap—gap CA-9
Reese Gap—gap NC-3
Reese Gulch CO-8
Reese Gulch—valley CO-8
Reese Gulch—valley WY-8
Reese Hill—summit OR-9
Reese Hill—summit PA-2
Reese Hill—summit WA-9
Reese Hollow—valley KY-4
Reese Hollow—valley MO-7
Reese Hollow—valley (7) PA-2
Reese Hollow—valley (2) TN-4
Reese Hollow—valley VA-3
Reese Hollow Run—stream PA-2
Reese Hosp—hospital IL-6
Reese Lake—lake (2) MN-6
Reese Lake—lake SC-3
Reese Lake—lake TX-5
Reese Lake—lake WA-9
Reese Lake—reservoir GA-3
Reese Lake—reservoir OK-5
Reese Landing—locale MS-4
Reese Marsh—swamp TX-5
Reese Mill IN-6
Reese Mine—mine CA-9
Reese Mtn—summit GA-3
Reese Mtn—summit NC-3
Reese Mtn—summit TN-4
Reese Murrays Dam AL-4
Reese Park—park GA-3
Reese Playground—park MI-6
Reese Pond—lake AL-4
Reeser, C. A., House—hist pl OH-6
Reeser, Lake—lake FL-3
Reese Ranch—locale (2) AZ-5
Reese Ranch—locale SD-7
Reese Ravine—valley CA-9
Reeser Creek WA-9
Reeser Hollow—valley TN-4
**Reese River**—pop pl NV-8
Reese River—stream NV-8
Reese River Butte—summit NV-8
Reese River Canyon—valley NV-8
Reese River Range NV-8
Reese River Ranger Station—locale NV-8
Reese River Valley—valley NV-8
Reeser Post Office (historical)—building TN-4
**Reesers Summit**—pop pl PA-2
Reese Rsvr—reservoir CA-9
Reese Run—stream PA-2
Reeses PA-2
Reeses Branch—stream AL-4
Reese Sch—school (2) CA-9
Reese Sch—school IL-6
Reese Sch—school (2) MO-7
Reese Sch—school NJ-2
Reese Sch (historical)—school AL-4
Reese School TN-4
Reeses Creek—stream AL-4
Reeses Creek—stream VA-3
Reeses Ferry AL-4
Reeses Fork—gut AR-4
Reese Shiloh Ch—church TX-5
**Reese Shop**—pop pl VA-3
Reeses Mill—locale WV-2
Reese Spring CO-8
Reese Spring—spring NV-8
Reeses Run—stream PA-2
**Reeses Spur**—pop pl AL-4
Reeses Tannery WV-2
**Reese Station (Reese)**—pop pl OH-6
Reese Street Hist Dist—hist pl GA-3
Reese Tank—reservoir AZ-5
Reese Tank—reservoir NM-5
Reese Tanks—reservoir AZ-5
Reese Tannery WV-2
Reesetown—locale TN-4
Reese Trail—trail PA-2
**Reese Village**—pop pl TX-5
Reeseville AL-4
Reeseville IL-6
**Reeseville**—pop pl WI-6
Reese Williams Dam—dam SD-7
Reese Windmill—locale TX-5
Rees Flat—flat UT-8
Rees Gulch—valley CO-8
Rees Hills—spring MT-8
Rees Lake—lake FL-3
Rees Lake Dam—dam MS-4
Rees Mill—locale PA-2
Rees Park—park IA-7
Rees Park—park UT-8
Rees Peak—summit AZ-5
Rees Ranch—locale WY-8
Rees Sch—school (2) IL-6
Rees Sch—school UT-8
Rees School TN-4
Rees Spring—spring CO-8
Rees Spring—spring UT-8
Rees Station IL-6
Rees Tannery WV-2
Rees Valley—valley UT-8
**Reesville**—pop pl OH-6
Reesville Sch—school PA-2
Rees Well—well UT-8
Reeths-Puffer Sch—school MI-6
**Ree Township**—pop pl ND-7
**Ree Township**—pop pl SD-7
Ree Valley (historical)—locale SD-7
Reeve KS-7
**Reeve**—pop pl IA-7
**Reeve**—pop pl WI-6
Reeve, Jennie A., House—hist pl CA-9
Reeve, Leander, House—hist pl IA-7
Reeve, Tapping, House and Law Sch—hist pl CT-1
Reeve Cem—cemetery IN-6
Reeve Coulee—valley MT-8
Reeve Field—park TX-5
Reeve Hill—summit GA-3
Reeve Ranch—locale KS-7
Reeve Ranch Spring CA-9
Reeves KS-7
Reeves—locale AR-4
Reeves—locale NC-3
Reeves—locale ND-7
**Reeves**—pop pl FL-3
**Reeves**—pop pl GA-3
**Reeves**—pop pl TN-4
Reeves—uninc pl OK-5
Reeves, Jeremiah, House and Carriage House—hist pl OH-6
Reeves, Sylvester H., House—hist pl UT-8
Reeves, W. L., House—hist pl KY-4
**Reeves Addition (subdivision)**—pop pl UT-8
Reeves Bar—bar AL-4
Reeves Bay—bay NY-2
Reeves Bldg—hist pl GA-3
Reeves Bloomary Forge (historical)—locale TN-4
Reeves Branch—stream AL-4
Reeves Branch—stream (2) AR-4
Reeves Branch—stream (3) KY-4
Reeves Branch—stream (2) MS-4
Reeves Branch—stream NC-3
Reeves Branch—stream SC-3
Reeves Branch—stream (4) TN-4
Reeves Canyon—valley CA-9
Reeves Cattle Company Number 1 Dam—dam SD-7
Reeves Cattle Company Number 2 Dam—dam SD-7
Reeves Cave—cave AL-4
Reeves Cem TN-4
Reeves Cem—cemetery AL-4
Reeves Cem—cemetery (3) AR-4
Reeves Cem—cemetery (3) GA-3
Reeves Cem—cemetery (3) IN-6
Reeves Cem—cemetery KY-4
Reeves Cem—cemetery LA-4
Reeves Cem—cemetery MI-6
Reeves Cem—cemetery (3) MS-4
Reeves Cem—cemetery ND-7
Reeves Cem—cemetery OR-9
Reeves Cem—cemetery SC-3
Reeves Cem—cemetery (4) TN-4
Reeves Cem—cemetery (3) TX-5
Reeves Cem—cemetery WV-2
Reeves Ch—church TN-4
Reeves Chapel—church (2) AL-4
Reeves Chapel—church MS-4
Reeves Chapel—church (2) NC-3
Reeves Chapel—church TX-5
Reeves Chapel Sch—school GA-3
Reeves Community Center—building NC-3
Reeves Corner—locale WY-8
**Reeves (County)**—pop pl TX-5
Reeves County Water Improvement Canal—canal TX-5
Reeves Cove—valley NC-3
Reeves Cox Hollow—valley MO-7
Reeves Creek—stream AL-4
Reeves Creek—stream AZ-5
Reeves Creek—stream CA-9
Reeves Creek—stream (4) GA-3
Reeves Creek—stream (2) ID-8
Reeves Creek—stream KY-4
Reeves Creek—stream LA-4
Reeves Creek—stream MT-8
Reeves Creek—stream NY-2
Reeves Creek—stream OH-6
Reeves Creek—stream (2) OR-9
Reeves Creek—stream TX-5
Reeves Creek—stream UT-8
Reeves Crossing—locale DE-2
Reevesdale—locale PA-2
Reeves-Dougherty Cem—cemetery TN-4
Reeves Ditch—canal IN-6
Reeves Draw—valley (2) WY-8
Reeves Ferry TN-4
Reeves Ferry (historical)—locale NC-3
Reeves Field—locale FL-3
Reeves Field—park CA-9
Reeves Ford—locale NC-3
Reeves Fork—stream AR-4
Reeves-Freeman House—park NC-3
Reeves Grove Ch—church AL-4
Reeve's Hill MA-1
Reeves Hill—summit AL-4
Reeves Hill—summit AR-4
Reeves Hill—summit IN-6
Reeves Hill—summit MA-1
Reeves Hill—summit NY-2
Reeves Hills—range AR-4
Reeves Hollow—valley AR-4
Reeves Hollow—valley (2) OH-6
Reeves Hollow—valley (2) TN-4
Reeves Knob AR-4
Reeves Lake—lake FL-3
Reeves Lake—lake MN-6
Reeves Lake—lake MT-8
Reeves Lake—lake WA-9
Reeves Lake—reservoir AL-4
Reeves Lake—reservoir NC-3
Reeves Lake Dam—dam AL-4
Reeves Lake Dam—dam MS-4
Reeves Lake Dam—dam NC-3
Reeves Lodge—locale SC-3
Reeves-Melson House—hist pl AR-4
Reeves Memorial United Methodist Ch—church FL-3
Reeves Mine—mine CA-9
Reeves Mound—hist pl OH-6
Reeves Mtn—summit AR-4
Reeves Mtn—summit KY-4
Reeves Mtn—summit OR-9
Reeves Number Twelve School TN-4
Reeves Oil Field—oilfield TX-5
Reeves Oil Field—other NM-5
Reeves Park—park FL-3
Reeves Park—park PA-2
**Reeves Park**—pop pl NY-2
Reeves Place—locale (2) CA-9
Reeves Plaza (Shop Ctr)—locale FL-3
Reeves Point—cape AR-4
Reeves Point—cape CA-9
Reeves Pond—lake FL-3
Reeves Pond—lake NY-2
Reeves Pond—lake PA-2
Reeves Powerplant—other NM-5
Reeves Ranch—locale AZ-5
Reeves Ranch—locale MT-8
Reeves Ranch—locale NM-5
Reeves Ranch Springs—spring CA-9
Reeves Ravine—valley OK-5
**Reeves (Reaves School)**—pop pl LA-4
**Reeves (RR name Reaves)**—pop pl LA-4
Reeves RR Station—locale FL-3
Reeves Sch—school IL-6
Reeves Sch—school KY-4
Reeves Sch—school LA-4
Reeves Sch—school MA-1
Reeves Sch—school (2) TN-4
Reeves Sch (historical)—school AL-4
Reeves Sch (historical)—school MS-4
Reeves Sch Number Four TN-4
Reeves Spring—spring CA-9
Reeves Spring Branch—stream NC-3
Reeves Station—locale NJ-2
**Reeves (subdivision)**—pop pl AL-4
Reeves Tank—reservoir (2) AZ-5
Reeves Tank—reservoir TX-5
Reevestown Branch—stream SC-3
Reevestown Cem—cemetery NJ-2
Reeves-Truitt Spring—spring AL-4
**Reevesville**—pop pl IL-6
**Reevesville**—pop pl SC-3
Reevesville (CCD)—cens area SC-3
Reeves-Wheeler Cemetery TN-4
Reeves Windmill—locale NM-5
Reeve Tank AZ-5
Reeve Township—fmr MCD IA-7
**Reeve (Township of)**—pop pl IN-6
Reevhorn Run—stream OH-6
Reevis Creek AZ-5
Reevis Gap AZ-5
Reevis Grave—cemetery AZ-5
Reevis Ranch AZ-5
Reevis Saddle Spring AZ-5
Reevis Trail—trail AZ-5
Reevis Trail Canyon AZ-5
Reevy Branch—stream NJ-2
**Reevytown**—pop pl NJ-2
Reeyes Ranch—locale NM-5
Refeld Cem—cemetery AR-4
Reference Point Creek—stream AZ-5
Reference Point Rapids—rapids AZ-5
Reff, William D., House—hist pl MO-7
Reffett Branch—stream KY-4
Reffits Branch—stream KY-4
Reffitt Cem—cemetery KY-4
Reffitt Hollow—valley KY-4
Refinery Point—cape FM-9
Refish Number One Dam—dam TN-4
Refish Number One Lake—reservoir TN-4
Refish Number Two Dam—dam TN-4
Refish Number Two Lake—reservoir TN-4
Reflection, Lake—lake CA-9
Reflection Canyon UT-8
Reflection Lake PA-2
Reflection Lake—lake AK-9
Reflection Lake—lake (2) CA-9
Reflection Lake—lake GA-3
Reflection Lake—lake ID-8
Reflection Lake—lake MN-6
Reflection Lake—lake NJ-2
Reflection Lake—lake OR-9
Reflection Lake—lake WA-9
Reflection Lake—reservoir WA-9
Reflection Lakes—lake WA-9
Reflection Place—uninc pl VA-3
Reflection Pond—lake NH-1
Reflection Pond—lake WA-9
Reflection Riding—locale TN-4
Reflections Canyon—valley UT-8
Reflection Spring—spring UT-8
Reform—locale AR-4
Reform—locale MO-7
**Reform**—pop pl AL-4
**Reform**—pop pl MS-4
**Reform**—pop pl OH-6
Reformation MS-4
Reformation Canyon—valley UT-8
Reformation Cem—cemetery MS-4
Reformation Ch—church MS-4
Reformation Lutheran Ch—church DE-2
Reformation Lutheran Ch—church KS-7
Reformation Lutheran Ch (LCA)—church FL-3
Reformation Sch (historical)—school MS-4
Reformatory—building MN-6
Reformatory Lake—reservoir KY-4
Reforma Windmill—locale TX-5
Reform (CCD)—cens area AL-4
Reform Cem—cemetery (2) ND-7
Reform Cem—cemetery (2) OH-6
Reform Cem—cemetery (2) SD-7
Reform Cem—cemetery WI-6
Reform Ch—church MO-7
Reform Ch—church NM-5
Reform Chapel—church MS-4
Reform Church AL-4
Reform Consolidated Sch (historical)—school MS-4
Reform Country Club—locale AL-4
Reform Division—civil AL-4
Reformed Cem—cemetery KS-7
Reformed Cem—cemetery KY-4
Reformed Cem—cemetery (2) ND-7
Reformed Cem—cemetery (4) PA-2
Reformed Cem—cemetery (2) SD-7
Reformed Cem—cemetery WI-6
Reformed Cemetery SD-7
Reformed Ch—church NJ-2
Reformed Ch—church NM-5
Reformed Ch—church (2) NY-2
Reformed Ch—church (3) ND-7
Reformed Ch—church OK-5
Reformed Ch—church (2) PA-2
Reformed Ch—church SD-7
Reformed Ch—church WI-6
Reformed Church, The—hist pl NY-2
Reformed Church Cem—cemetery SD-7
Reformed Church of Newtown Complex—hist pl NY-2
Reformed Church of Shawangunk Complex—hist pl NY-2
Reformed Dutch Church and Green—hist pl NJ-2
Reformed Dutch Church of Blawenburg—hist pl NJ-2
Reformed Dutch Church of Fishkill Landing—hist pl NY-2
Reformed Dutch Church of New Hurley—hist pl NY-2
Reformed Dutch Church of Rensselaer in Watervliet—hist pl NY-2
Reformed Dutch Church of Second River—hist pl NJ-2
Reformed Dutch Church of Stone Arabia—hist pl NY-2
Reformed Graveyard—cemetery WV-2
Reformed Jewish Cem—cemetery PA-2
Reformed Presbyterian Ch—church AL-4
Reformed Presbyterian Ch—church FL-3
Reformed Presbyterian Ch—church TN-4
Reformed Presbyterian Church Parsonage—hist pl NY-2
Reformed Theological Seminary—school MS-4
Reformed Trinity Ch—church PA-2
Reform Point—summit AR-4
Reform Presbyterian Ch (historical)—church MS-4
Reform Temple Ch—church AL-4
Refreshing Spring Ch of God in Christ—church FL-3
Refreshment Pavillion—hist pl MA-1
Refrigerator Canyon—valley MT-8
Refrigerator Canyon—valley UT-8
Refrigerator Canyon—valley WA-9
Refrigerator Creek—stream OR-9
Refrigerator Gulch—valley CO-8
**Refton**—pop pl PA-2
Refton Cave—cave PA-2
**Refuge**—pop pl AL-4
**Refuge**—pop pl (2) MS-4
**Refuge**—pop pl TX-5
**Refuge**—pop pl VA-3
Refuge Baptist Ch—church IN-6
Refuge Baptist Church AL-4
Refuge Brake—swamp LA-4
Refuge Camp—locale GA-3
Refuge Canyon—valley CA-9
Refuge Cem—cemetery AL-4
Refuge Cem—cemetery MS-4
Refuge Cem—cemetery TN-4
Refuge Cem—cemetery TX-5
Refuge Ch—church (4) AL-4
Refuge Ch—church AR-4
Refuge Ch—church FL-3
Refuge Ch—church (3) GA-3
Refuge Ch—church IN-6
Refuge Ch—church MS-4
Refuge Ch—church NJ-2
Refuge Ch—church SC-3
Refuge Ch—church TN-4
Refuge Ch—church VA-3
Refuge Chapel—church MS-4
Refuge Ch of Our Lord Jesus Christ—church AL-4
Refuge Community Ch—church MO-7
Refuge Cove—bay AK-9
Refuge Cove—uninc pl AK-9
Refugee Cem—cemetery OH-6
Refuge (historical)—locale AL-4
Refuge HQ—locale MO-7
Refuge HQ—locale TX-5
Refuge Island—island AK-9
Refuge Island—island NY-2
Refuge Key—island FL-3
Refuge Methodist Ch MS-4
**Refuge Mission**—pop pl NC-3
Refuge No. 7 Archeol Site (12BR11)—hist pl IN-6
Refuge P.O. AL-4
Refuge Pond—lake MN-6
Refuge Rock—bar AK-9
Refuge Rock—ridge AZ-5
Refuge Rock—summit NM-5
Refuge Spring—spring OR-9
Refuge Trail—trail (6) PA-2
Refuge Valley—basin CA-9
Refuge Valley—valley AK-9
Refugio—civil CA-9
**Refugio**—pop pl TX-5
Refugio, Canada Del —valley CA-9
Refugio Beach State Park—park CA-9
Refugio (CCD)—cens area TX-5
Refugio Colony—civil NM-5
**Refugio (County)**—pop pl TX-5
Refugio Creek CA-9
Refugio Creek—stream CA-9
Refugio de Aves de Bueron—park PR-3
Refugio Oil Field—oilfield TX-5
Refugio Pass—gap CA-9
Refugio Ramirez Tank—reservoir TX-5
Refugio Tank—reservoir NM-5
Refugio Valley—valley CA-9
Refuse Stilling Basin Dam—dam PA-2
**Rega**—pop pl TN-4
**Regadera**—pop pl PR-3
Regal—locale WA-9
**Regal**—pop pl MN-6
**Regal**—pop pl MO-7
**Regal**—pop pl NC-3
Regal Canyon—valley AZ-5
Regal Creek—stream ID-8
**Regal Estates**—pop pl MD-2
Regal Glacier—glacier AK-9
Regal Mine—mine AK-9
Regal Mine—mine AZ-5
Regal Mine—mine ID-8
Regal Mtn—summit AK-9
Regal Park Sch—school MA-1
**Regal Park (subdivision)**—pop pl FL-3
Regal Sch—school WA-9
**Regan**—pop pl NC-3
**Regan**—pop pl ND-7
Regan, D. H., House—hist pl TX-5
Regan, John, American Legion Hall—hist pl ID-8
Regan, Mount—summit ID-8
Regan Bend—bend ID-8
Regan Branch—stream NC-3
Regan Butte—summit ID-8
Regan Cem—cemetery GA-3
Regan Cem—cemetery MO-7
Regan Cem—cemetery SC-3
Regan Cem—cemetery TN-4
Regan Ch—church NC-3
Regan Creek—stream TX-5
Regan Ditch—canal IN-6
Regan Drain—stream MI-6
Regan Hill—summit MI-6
Regan (historical)—locale MS-4
Regan Island—flat MS-4
Regan Junction—locale PA-2
Regan Knob—summit TN-4
Regan Lake—lake CO-8
Regan Lake—lake ID-8
Regan Lake—lake MI-6
Regan Lake—lake MS-4
Regan Meadow—area CA-9
Regan Meadow Campground CA-9
Regan Mine—mine CA-9
Regan Mine—mine NV-8
Regan Mountain AR-4
Regan Oil Field—oilfield TX-5
Regan Sch—school CT-1
Regan Sch—school TX-5
Regans Lake MS-4
Regan Slough—gut CA-9
**Reganton**—pop pl MS-4
Reganton Post Office (historical)—building MS-4
Regan Valley—valley TN-4
Regar Cem—cemetery KS-7
Regar Cem—cemetery NC-3
Regar Memorial Museum of Natural History—building AL-4
Regatta Park—park OR-9
Regatta Point Park—park MA-1
Regehr State Wildlife Mngmt Area—park MN-6
Regenbogen Lake—lake MN-6
Regency—locale TX-5
**Regency**—pop pl NE-7
Regency—post sta AL-4
Regency—post sta FL-3
Regency Assembly of God Ch—church FL-3
Regency Baptist Temple—church FL-3
Regency Cem—cemetery TX-5
**Regency Estates**—pop pl MD-2
**Regency Estates (subdivision)**—pop pl MS-4
**Regency Estates (subdivision)**—pop pl NC-3
**Regency Forest (subdivision)**—pop pl AL-4

Renshaw Bridge—*bridge* AL-4
Renshaw Cem—*cemetery* AL-4
Renshaw Cem—*cemetery* IL-6
Renshaw Cem—*cemetery* (2) MO-7
Renshaw Creek—*stream* ID-8
Renshaw Creek—*stream* MT-8
Renshaw Creek—*stream* NV-8
Renshaw Creek—*stream* WA-9
Renshaw Lake—*lake* MT-8
Renshaw Mine (underground)—*mine* AL-4
Renshaw Mtn—*summit* MT-8
Renshaw Place—*locale* CA-9
Renshaw Point—*cape* AK-9
Renslaer Rsvr—*reservoir* WY-8
Renslow—*locale* WA-9
Renslow Cem—*cemetery* TN-4
Renslow Spring—*spring* TN-4
Renson—*locale* AL-4
**Rensselaer**—*pop pl* IN-6
**Rensselaer**—*pop pl* MO-7
**Rensselaer**—*pop pl* NY-2
Rensselaer and Saratoga Railroad: Green Island Shops—*hist pl* NY-2
Rensselaer Central HS—*school* IN-6
**Rensselaer (County)**—*pop pl* NY-2
**Rensselaer Falls**—*pop pl* NY-2
Rensselaer Lake—*lake* NY-2
**Rensselaer Park**—*pop pl* OH-6
Rensselaer Polytechnic Institute—*school* NY-2
Rensselaer Rural Cem—*cemetery* NY-2
**Rensselaerville**—*pop pl* NY-2
Rensselaerville Falls—*falls* NY-2
Rensselaerville Hist Dist—*hist pl* NY-2
**Rensselaerville (Town of)**—*pop pl* NY-2
Rensselear Polytechnic Institute (Hartford—*school* CT-1
**Renston**—*pop pl* NC-3
**Rentchler**—*pop pl* IL-6
Rentchler Cem—*cemetery* IL-6
Rentenaar Point—*cape* OR-9
Rentfro Cem—*cemetery* (2) IL-6
Rentfro Junior Tank—*reservoir* NM-5
Rentfro Tank No 2—*reservoir* NM-5
Rentfro Well—*well* NM-5
Rentie Grove Ch—*church* OK-5
**Rentiesville**—*pop pl* OK-5
Rentleman Well—*well* TX-5
*Rento* FM-9
**Renton**—*pop pl* PA-2
**Renton**—*pop pl* WA-9
Renton Elem Sch—*school* PA-2
Renton Highlands—*other* WA-9
**Renton Junction**—*pop pl* PA-2
Renton Mine—*mine* CA-9
Renton Muni Airp—*airport* WA-9
Renton Refuse Bank Pond Four Dam—*dam* PA-2
Renton Slurry Pond Three Dam—*dam* PA-2
**Renton Village**—*pop pl* HI-9
*Rentou* FM-9
Rentschler Ditch—*canal* IN-6
Rentschler For Preserve—*forest* OH-6
Rentschler House—*hist pl* OH-6
**Rentz**—*pop pl* GA-3
Rentz Branch—*stream* GA-3
Rentz (CCD)—*cens area* GA-3
Rentz Cem—*cemetery* MN-6
*Rentz Creek* MT-8
Rentz Ferry (historical)—*locale* AL-4
**Renville**—*pop pl* MN-6
**Renville**—*pop pl* ND-7
Renville Cem—*cemetery* ND-7
Renville County—*civil* ND-7
**Renville (County)**—*pop pl* MN-6
Renville County Courthouse—*hist pl* ND-7
Renville County Courthouse and Jail—*hist pl* MN-6
**Renville Township**—*pop pl* ND-7
**Renwick**—*pop pl* IA-7
**Renwick**—*pop pl* NY-2
Renwick, Lake—*lake* IL-6
Renwick Bldg—*hist pl* IA-7
Renwick Brook—*stream* NY-2
Renwick Canyon—*valley* OR-9
Renwick Dam—*dam* ND-7
Renwick Gallery—*building* DC-2
Renwick Grove Ch—*church* SC-3
Renwick House—*hist pl* IA-7
Renwick Museum—*hist pl* DC-2
Renwood Sch—*school* OH-6
Renwyck Creek—*stream* ID-8
Renz Block—*hist pl* OH-6
Renz Creek—*stream* MT-8
**Renz Farm**—*pop pl* MO-7
Renz Gulch—*valley* CA-9
Renz Hollow—*valley* PA-2
Renziehalusen Park—*park* PA-2
Renzienhausen Slough—*gut* SD-7
Renz Lake—*lake* SD-7
Renzol Nichols Lake—*reservoir* AL-4
Renzol Nichols Lake Dam—*dam* AL-4
**Renz Spur**—*pop pl* MO-7
Reo—*locale* GA-3
**Reo**—*pop pl* IN-6
Reo Ditch—*canal* CA-9
Reola Park—*park* MI-6
Reorganized Ch—*church* MI-6
Reorganized Ch of Jesus Christ of Latter Day Saints—*church* (4) FL-3
Reorganized Church of Latter Day Saints—*hist pl* OR-9
Reo Sch—*school* MI-6
**Reou**—*pop pl* FM-9
Reparatrix Convent—*church* NY-2
Repardo Windmill—*locale* TX-5
**Reparto Sevilla**—*pop pl* PR-3
**Reparto Universitario**—*pop pl* PR-3
**Repass**—*pop pl* VA-3
Repast Lake—*lake* MN-6
**Repaupo**—*pop pl* NJ-2
Repaupo Creek—*stream* NJ-2
Repaupo Station—*locale* NJ-2
Repeat Creek—*stream* ID-8
Repeater Hill—*summit* CA-9
Repeater Station—*locale* PA-2
Repecita Tank—*reservoir* AZ-5
Repetition Point—*cape* AK-9
Repetto Sch—*school* CA-9
Rep (historical)—*locale* AL-4
Repine Run—*stream* PA-2
Replacing Cover Spring—*spring* AZ-5
Replete—*locale* WV-2
Replogle Airp—*airport* PA-2
Replogle Cem—*cemetery* PA-2
*Rep Mountain* MT-8
Reponds Pas, Bayou—*stream* LA-4
Reposa Ranch—*locale* TX-5
**Reppert Addition (subdivision)**—*pop pl* SD-7
*Reppeto Cemetery* TN-4
Repp Hollow—*valley* TN-4
Repplier Park—*park* CA-9
Reppond Branch—*stream* TX-5
Reppond Cem—*cemetery* LA-4
Rep Post Office (historical)—*building* AL-4
Repp Run—*stream* OH-6
Reppto Cem—*cemetery* TN-4
*Reppu-To* MP-9
Reppy Ave Bridge—*hist pl* AZ-5
Represa de Comerio—*reservoir* PR-3
Represa de Mayaguez—*reservoir* PR-3
Represa de San German—*reservoir* PR-3
Represa de San Juan—*reservoir* PR-3
Represa De Toa Vaca—*dam* PR-3
Represa (Folsom State Prison)—*building* CA-9
Represar del Empedrado—*reservoir* NM-5
Repres de las Uvas—*reservoir* NM-5
Represo Tank—*reservoir* AZ-5
Represso, El Cerrito de—*summit* AZ-5
Represso de Lamita, El—*reservoir* AZ-5
Repton—*hist pl* KY-4
**Repton**—*pop pl* AL-4
**Repton**—*pop pl* KY-4
Repton (CCD)—*cens area* AL-4
Repton Cem—*cemetery* AL-4
Repton Cem—*cemetery* KY-4
Repton Division—*civil* AL-4
Repton HS—*school* AL-4
Repton Mills—*locale* VA-3
Republic—*locale* KY-4
Republic—*locale* WV-2
**Republic**—*pop pl* AL-4
**Republic**—*pop pl* IA-7
**Republic**—*pop pl* KS-7
**Republic**—*pop pl* MI-6
**Republic**—*pop pl* MO-7
**Republic**—*pop pl* NY-2
**Republic**—*pop pl* ND-7
**Republic**—*pop pl* OH-6
**Republic**—*pop pl* PA-2
**Republic**—*pop pl* WA-9
*Republican* MS-4
Republican—*locale* AR-4
**Republican**—*pop pl* NC-3
Republican—*uninc pl* PA-2
Republican Bayou—*stream* LA-4
Republican Block—*hist pl* MA-1
Republican Cem—*cemetery* AR-4
Republican Cem—*cemetery* MO-7
Republican Ch—*church* KY-4
Republican Ch—*church* LA-4
Republican Ch—*church* (2) SC-3
Republican Ch—*church* VA-3
*Republican Church* AL-4
**Republican City**—*pop pl* NE-7
Republican City Cem—*cemetery* KS-7
Republican City Cem—*cemetery* NE-7
**Republican City Republican Sta**—*pop pl* NE-7
**Republican City Township**—*pop pl* NE-7
Republican Creek—*stream* KS-7
Republican Creek—*stream* WA-9
Republican Ditch—*canal* MT-8
Republican Flats—*flat* ID-8
Republican Flats—*flat* KS-7
*Republican Fork* KS-7
*Republican Fork of Kanzas River* KS-7
Republican Grove—*locale* VA-3
*Republican Grove Baptist Church* TN-4
Republican Grove Ch—*church* SC-3
Republican Grove Ch—*church* (2) TN-4
*Republican Grove Missionary Baptist Ch* TN-4
Republican Grove Post Office (historical)—*building* TN-4
Republican Gulch—*valley* MT-8
Republican Hall Cem—*cemetery* SC-3
Republican (historical)—*locale* SD-7
Republican Mine—*mine* CA-9
Republican Mine—*mine* CO-8
Republican Mine—*mine* NV-8
Republican Mtn—*summit* CO-8
Republican Point—*cliff* KS-7
*Republican River* NE-7
Republican River—*stream* KS-7
Republican River*—*stream* NE-7
Republican Sch—*school* IL-6
Republican Sch—*school* KY-4
Republican Sch—*school* MO-7
Republican Sch—*school* PA-2
**Republican Township**—*pop pl* KS-7
**Republican (Township of)**—*pop pl* IN-6
Republican Valley Sch—*school* NE-7
Republican Valley Wayside Park—*park* NE-7
Republic Bldg—*hist pl* KY-4
Republic (CCD)—*cens area* WA-9
*Republic City* KS-7
Republic County—*civil* KS-7
Republic Creek—*stream* CO-8
Republic Creek—*stream* MT-8
Republic Creek—*stream* WY-8
Republic Iron and Steel Office Bldg—*hist pl* OH-6
**Republic Junction**—*pop pl* MI-6
Republic Lake—*lake* FL-3
Republic Lake—*reservoir* AL-4
Republic-Merrittstown—*CDP* PA-2
Republic Mine—*mine* (2) AZ-5
Republic Mine—*mine* CA-9
Republic Mine—*mine* MI-6
Republic Mine—*mine* NM-5
Republic Mine Number 2—*mine* MT-8
Republic Mtn—*summit* MT-8
Republic Mtn—*summit* WY-8
Republic No 1 Shaft—*mine* NM-5
Republic No 2 Shaft—*mine* NM-5
Republic Pass—*gap* WY-8
*Republic Peak* MT-8
*Republic Peak* WY-8
Republic Peak—*summit* WY-8
Republic Pit Adit—*mine* NM-5
Republic Powdered Metals—*facility* OH-6
Republic Quarry—*mine* TN-4
Republic Quarry Cave—*cave* TN-4
Republic Shaft—*mine* NM-5
Republic Street Sch—*school* MI-6
Republic Theater—*hist pl* SC-3
Republic (Township of)—*fmr MCD* MO-7
**Republic (Township of)**—*pop pl* MI-6
Republic Trail—*trail* MT-8
*Republicville* AL-4
**Requa**—*pop pl* CA-9
**Requa**—*pop pl* WI-6
Requea Cem—*cemetery* NY-2
Reque Ch—*church* MN-6
R E Rankin Lake—*reservoir* NC-3
R E Rankin Lake Dam—*dam* NC-3
Rerdell—*locale* FL-3
*Rere* FM-9
Rere—*island* (2) MP-9
Reredos of Our Lady of Light—*hist pl* NM-5
Reregulation Rsvr—*reservoir* GA-3
*Rere Island* MP-9
*Rere-To* MP-9
R E Roberts Dam—*dam* NC-3
**Resaca**—*pop pl* GA-3
**Resaca**—*pop pl* OH-6
Resaca Ch—*church* GA-3
Resaca Confederate Cem—*cemetery* GA-3
*Resaca Creek* TX-5
Resaca Creek—*stream* TX-5
Resaca de Enmedio—*stream* TX-5
Resaca de la Gringa—*lake* TX-5
Resaca de la Palma—*lake* TX-5
Resaca de la Palma Battlefield—*hist pl* TX-5
Resaca de las Antonias—*lake* TX-5
Resaca de los Flores—*lake* TX-5
Resaca del Jardin—*lake* TX-5
Resaca de los Cuates—*lake* TX-5
Resaca de los Cuates—*stream* TX-5
Resaca de los Fresnos—*lake* TX-5
Resaca del Rancho Viejo—*lake* (2) TX-5
Resaca Reparo—*lake* TX-5
Resaca Sch—*school* TX-5
*Resaco Creek* TX-5
*Resagonia Mountain* NY-2
Resasep—*bar* FM-9
Resch Creek—*stream* WI-6
R E Scruggs Catfish Ponds Dam—*dam* MS-4
R E Scruggs Pond Dam—*dam* MS-4
Rescue—*locale* AL-4
Rescue—*locale* CA-9
Rescue—*locale* MI-6
**Rescue**—*pop pl* MO-7
**Rescue**—*pop pl* VA-3
Rescue, Lake—*lake* VT-1
Rescue Canyon—*valley* AZ-5
Rescue Canyon—*valley* NV-8
Rescue Cem—*cemetery* AL-4
Rescue Ch—*church* IL-6
Rescue Creek—*stream* ID-8
Rescue Creek—*stream* MT-8
Rescue Creek—*stream* WY-8
Rescue Creek Trail—*trail* MT-8
Rescue Creek Trail—*trail* WY-8
*Rescue Lake* VT-1
Rescue Lake—*lake* AK-9
Rescue Landing—*locale* MS-4
Rescue Landing Revetment—*levee* MS-4
Rescue Mine—*mine* ID-8
Rescue Rock Mesa—*summit* AZ-5
Rescue Sch (historical)—*school* AL-4
Rescue Spring—*spring* AZ-5
**Rescueville**—*pop pl* AL-4
Research Belton Hospital Heliport—*airport* MO-7
Research Cave—*hist pl* MO-7
Research Creek—*stream* AK-9
Research Med Ctr Heliport—*airport* MO-7
Research Mine—*mine* CA-9
Research Pond Number One—*reservoir* NC-3
Research Pond Number One Dam—*dam* NC-3
Research Pond Number Two—*reservoir* NC-3
Research Pond Number Two Dam—*dam* NC-3
Research Ranch HQ—*building* AZ-5
*Research Triangle* NC-3
Research Triangle Park—*park* NC-3
**Research Triangle Park (Industrial Area)**—*pop pl* NC-3
Reseau Bay—*bay* VI-3
**Reseburg**—*pop pl* WI-6
Reseburg Ch—*church* WI-6
**Reseburg (Town of)**—*pop pl* WI-6
*Reseda* IL-6
**Reseda**—*pop pl* CA-9
Reseda Park—*park* CA-9
R E Selph Pond Dam—*dam* MS-4
Reser—*locale* WA-9
Reser Cabin—*locale* OR-9
Reser Creek—*stream* MT-8
Reser Creek—*stream* (2) OR-9
Reser Creek—*stream* WA-9
**Reservation**—*pop pl* NV-8
Reservation—*uninc pl* WA-9
Reservation Basin—*basin* ID-8
*Reservation Bay* WA-9
Reservation Canal—*canal* ID-8
Reservation (CCD)—*cens area* AZ-5
Reservation (CCD)—*cens area* NM-5
Reservation (CCD)—*cens area* OR-9
Reservation Country Club—*locale* MA-1
Reservation Creek—*stream* AZ-5
Reservation Creek—*stream* (3) MT-8
Reservation Creek—*stream* WA-9
Reservation Dam—*dam* AZ-5
Reservation Dam—*dam* PA-2
Reservation Dam—*dam* SD-7
Reservation Dam State Wildlife Mngmt Area—*park* MN-6
Reservation Divide—*ridge* MT-8
Reservation Fence Rsvr—*reservoir* NV-8
Reservation Flat—*flat* AZ-5
Reservation Gulch—*valley* ID-8
Reservation Head—*cape* WA-9
Reservation Hill—*summit* (2) NV-8
Reservation Hill—*summit* NY-2
Reservation Island (historical)—*island* PA-2
Reservation Lake—*reservoir* AZ-5
Reservation Lake Campgrounds—*park* AZ-5
Reservation Levee—*dam* CA-9
Reservation Levee—*levee* CA-9
Reservation Line Lake—*lake* WI-6
Reservation Main Canal—*canal* CA-9
Reservation Main Drain—*canal* CA-9
Reservation Memorial Park—*park* WA-9
Reservation Mine—*mine* NM-5
Reservation Mtn—*summit* MT-8
Reservation Mtn—*summit* OR-9
Reservation Peak—*summit* WY-8
Reservation Point—*cape* CA-9
Reservation Ranch—*locale* (2) AZ-5
Reservation Ridge—*ridge* UT-8
Reservation River—*stream* MN-6
Reservation Sch—*school* ND-7
Reservation Spring—*spring* AZ-5
Reservation Spring—*spring* ID-8
Reservation Spring—*spring* OR-9
Reservation Tank—*reservoir* (7) AZ-5
Reservation Tank Number Two—*reservoir* AZ-5
Reservation Trail—*trail* OR-9
Reservation Well—*well* AZ-5
Reservation Well—*well* NM-5
**Reserve**—*pop pl* KS-7
**Reserve**—*pop pl* LA-4
**Reserve**—*pop pl* MT-8
**Reserve**—*pop pl* NM-5
**Reserve**—*pop pl* WI-6
Reserve Bar—*bar* MS-4
Reserve Basin—*bay* PA-2
Reserve Canyon—*valley* UT-8
Reserve (CCD)—*cens area* NM-5
Reserve Cem—*cemetery* NE-7
Reserve Ch—*church* IN-6
Reserve Creek—*stream* ID-8
Reserve Creek—*stream* MT-8
Reserved Channel—*channel* MA-1
Reserve Elem Sch—*school* KS-7
Reserve Elem Sch—*school* PA-2
*Reserve Lake* MN-6
Reserve Meadow—*flat* OR-9
Reserve Mine—*mine* CA-9
Reserve Mtn—*summit* ID-8
Reserve Pond—*swamp* MA-1
Reserve Relief Canal—*canal* LA-4
Reserve Rsvr—*reservoir* ID-8
Reserve Run—*stream* OH-6
Reserve Sch—*school* MI-6
Reserve Station—*locale* LA-4
Reserve Tank—*reservoir* (2) AZ-5
Reserve Township—*CDP* PA-2
**Reserve (Township of)**—*pop pl* IN-6
**Reserve (Township of)**—*pop pl* PA-2
Reserville Community Hall—*building* KS-7
*Reservoir* TX-5
**Reservoir**—*pop pl* PA-2
Reservoir—*post sta* MS-4
Reservoir—*uninc pl* KY-4
Reservoir—*uninc pl* VA-3
Reservoir, Lake—*reservoir* CO-8
*Reservoir, The* MA-1
*Reservoir, The* RI-1
Reservoir, The—*lake* ID-8
Reservoir, The—*reservoir* MA-1
Reservoir, The—*reservoir* MI-6
Reservoir, The—*reservoir* RI-1
Reservoir Basin—*basin* NV-8
Reservoir Basin Spring—*spring* NV-8
Reservoir Branch—*stream* GA-3
Reservoir Branch—*stream* MO-7
Reservoir Branch—*stream* NC-3
Reservoir Branch—*stream* (2) TN-4
*Reservoir Brook* CT-1
*Reservoir Brook* MA-1
*Reservoir Brook* NJ-2
Reservoir Brook—*stream* (2) CT-1
Reservoir Brook—*stream* NH-1
Reservoir Brook—*stream* (2) VT-1
Reservoir Butte—*summit* CA-9
Reservoir Butte—*summit* OR-9
Reservoir C—*reservoir* CA-9
Reservoir Campground—*locale* CO-8
Reservoir Campground—*locale* UT-8
Reservoir Campground—*park* (2) OR-9
*Reservoir Canyon* CO-8
*Reservoir Canyon* UT-8
Reservoir Canyon—*valley* AZ-5
Reservoir Canyon—*valley* (4) CA-9
Reservoir Canyon—*valley* CO-8
Reservoir Canyon—*valley* (2) ID-8
Reservoir Canyon—*valley* NV-8
Reservoir Canyon—*valley* (5) UT-8
Reservoir Coulee—*valley* MT-8
Reservoir Creek—*stream* CO-8
Reservoir Creek—*stream* (4) ID-8
Reservoir Creek—*stream* MI-6
Reservoir Creek—*stream* (4) MT-8
Reservoir Creek—*stream* (2) NY-2
Reservoir Creek—*stream* (4) OR-9
Reservoir Creek—*stream* PA-2
Reservoir Creek—*stream* (2) UT-8
Reservoir Creek—*stream* (7) WY-8
Reservoir Dam, The—*dam* MA-1
Reservoir Dam Number 2—*dam* MA-1
Reservoir Ditch—*canal* (2) CO-8
Reservoir Ditch—*canal* WY-8
Reservoir Draw—*valley* CO-8
Reservoir Enlargement Ditch—*canal* CO-8
Reservoir F—*reservoir* CA-9
Reservoir F—*reservoir* CO-8
Reservoir Flat—*flat* ID-8
Reservoir Fork—*stream* UT-8
Reservoir G—*reservoir* CA-9
Reservoir Gulch—*valley* CA-9
Reservoir Gulch—*valley* (3) CO-8
Reservoir Gulch—*valley* (2) ID-8
Reservoir Gulch—*valley* MT-8
Reservoir Gulch—*valley* WY-8
**Reservoir Heights**—*pop pl* PA-2
Reservoir Heights Sch—*school* IL-6
*Reservoir Hill* MA-1
**Reservoir Hill**—*pop pl* PA-2
Reservoir Hill—*summit* AL-4
Reservoir Hill—*summit* CA-9
Reservoir Hill—*summit* GA-3
Reservoir Hill—*summit* KY-4
Reservoir Hill—*summit* (2) ME-1
Reservoir Hill—*summit* (4) MA-1
Reservoir Hill—*summit* MO-7
Reservoir Hill—*summit* NH-1
Reservoir Hill—*summit* NY-2
Reservoir Hill—*summit* (2) OK-5
Reservoir Hill—*summit* (2) TN-4
Reservoir Hill—*summit* UT-8
Reservoir Hill—*uninc pl* VA-3
**Reservoir Hill (subdivision)**—*pop pl* PA-2
Reservoir Hollow—*valley* (2) NY-2
Reservoir Hollow—*valley* (2) PA-2
Reservoir Hollow—*valley* VT-1
Reservoir Hollow—*valley* (2) VA-3
Reservoir Hollow—*valley* WV-2
Reservoir Knob—*summit* KY-4
Reservoir Lake—*lake* FL-3
Reservoir Lake—*lake* MN-6
Reservoir Lake—*lake* MT-8
Reservoir Lake—*lake* OR-9
Reservoir Lake—*lake* WY-8
Reservoir Lake—*reservoir* MT-8
Reservoir Lake—*reservoir* NE-7
Reservoir Lake—*reservoir* NC-3
Reservoir Lake—*reservoir* OR-9
Reservoir Lake Dam—*dam* NC-3
*Reservoir Lakes* MN-6
Reservoir Line Canal—*canal* MT-8
*Reservoir Marsh Pond* MA-1
Reservoir Mtn—*summit* ID-8
Reservoir Mtn—*summit* NY-2
Reservoir N—*reservoir* CA-9
*Reservoir No 1* CO-8
Reservoir No 1—*reservoir* CT-1
Reservoir No 1—*reservoir* OK-5
Reservoir No 1—*reservoir* PA-2
Reservoir No 1—*reservoir* (3) WY-8
Reservoir No 12—*reservoir* GA-3
Reservoir No 19—*reservoir* GA-3
Reservoir No 2—*reservoir* (2) CT-1
Reservoir No 2—*reservoir* OK-5
Reservoir No 2—*reservoir* WY-8
Reservoir No 21—*reservoir* GA-3
Reservoir No 3—*reservoir* (2) CT-1
Reservoir No 3—*reservoir* OK-5
Reservoir No 3—*reservoir* WY-8
*Reservoir No. 4* MA-1
Reservoir No 4—*reservoir* CT-1
Reservoir No 4—*reservoir* OK-5
Reservoir No 44—*reservoir* GA-3
Reservoir No 46—*reservoir* GA-3
Reservoir Number Five—*reservoir* MA-1
Reservoir Number Four—*reservoir* MA-1
Reservoir Number Four—*reservoir* PA-2
Reservoir Number Four—*reservoir* TX-5
*Reservoir Number One* MA-1
Reservoir Number One—*reservoir* AZ-5
Reservoir Number One—*reservoir* CA-9
Reservoir Number One—*reservoir* HI-9
Reservoir Number One—*reservoir* MA-1
Reservoir Number Seven—*reservoir* PA-2
Reservoir Number Seven Dam—*dam* PA-2
Reservoir Number Six—*reservoir* MA-1
Reservoir Number Six—*reservoir* OR-9
Reservoir Number Three—*reservoir* AZ-5
Reservoir Number Three—*reservoir* MA-1
Reservoir Number Three—*reservoir* OR-9
Reservoir Number Three—*reservoir* PA-2
Reservoir Number Three—*reservoir* TX-5
Reservoir Number Twenty-nine—*reservoir* IN-6
Reservoir Number Twenty-six—*reservoir* IN-6
*Reservoir Number Two* MA-1
Reservoir Number Two—*reservoir* AZ-5
Reservoir Number Two—*reservoir* CA-9
Reservoir Number Two—*reservoir* (2) MA-1
Reservoir Number Two—*reservoir* OR-9
Reservoir Number Two—*reservoir* PA-2
*Reservoir Number 1* IN-6
*Reservoir Number 1* MA-1
Reservoir Number 1 Dam—*dam* MA-1
*Reservoir Number 2* MA-1
*Reservoir Number 2* PA-2
Reservoir Number 2 Dam—*dam* MA-1
*Reservoir Number 3* MA-1
*Reservoir Number 3* PA-2
Reservoir Number 3 Dam—*dam* MA-1
Reservoir Number 4 Dam—*dam* MA-1
*Reservoir Number 5* PA-2
Reservoir Number 5 Dam—*dam* MA-1
*Reservoir Number 6* PA-2
Reservoir Number 6 Dam—*dam* MA-1
Reservoir Outlet Canal—*canal* TX-5
Reservoir Park—*flat* CO-8
Reservoir Park—*hist pl* MA-1
Reservoir Park—*park* AR-4
Reservoir Park—*park* IL-6
Reservoir Park—*park* IN-6
Reservoir Park—*park* NY-2
Reservoir Park—*park* (2) OH-6
Reservoir Park—*park* (2) PA-2
Reservoir Park—*park* TN-4
Reservoir Park Overlook—*locale* PA-2
*Reservoir Pond* MA-1
Reservoir Pond—*lake* MA-1
Reservoir Pond—*lake* NH-1
Reservoir Pond—*lake* VT-1
Reservoir Pond—*reservoir* MA-1
Reservoir Pond—*reservoir* NE-7
Reservoir Pond—*reservoir* WI-6
*Reservoir PondfWallis Pond* MA-1
Reservoir Public Camp—*locale* CA-9
Reservoir Ridge—*ridge* AL-4
**Reservoir Road Area**—*pop pl* TN-4
Reservoir Road Ch—*church* TN-4
Reservoir Run—*stream* WV-2
Reservoir Sch—*school* VA-3
Reservoirs M—*reservoir* CA-9
Reservoir Spring—*spring* CO-8
Reservoir Spring—*spring* MT-8
Reservoir Square Shop Ctr—*locale* MS-4
Reservoir Station—*locale* MA-1
Reservoir Station—*locale* VA-3
**Reservoir (subdivision)**—*pop pl* MA-1
Reservoir Summit—*summit* CA-9
Reservoir Tank—*reservoir* AZ-5
Reservoir Trail—*trail* NH-1
Reservoir Trail—*trail* OR-9
Reservoir Trail—*trail* PA-2
Reservoir Windmill—*locale* NM-5
Reservoir Windmill—*locale* TX-5
*Reservoir 2* OR-9
*Reservoir 4* OR-9
Reservoir 6-2020—*reservoir* MS-4
*Reservoir 9* MA-1
Resettlement Ditch—*canal* CO-8
Resha Lake—*reservoir* TN-4
Resha Lake Dam—*dam* TN-4
Reshanau Lake—*lake* MN-6
Resh Hill—*summit* MD-2
*Resica Falls* PA-2
Residence, The—*hist pl* VA-3
Residence Lopez—*hist pl* PR-3
*Residence Park* OH-6
**Residence Park**—*pop pl* NY-2
**Residence Park**—*pop pl* OH-6
Residencia Gonzalez Vivaldi—*hist pl* PR-3
Residencia Heygler—*hist pl* PR-3
Residencia Ramirez De Arellano en Guanajibo—*hist pl* PR-3
Resident Ch—*church* MS-4
Residential District—*hist pl* MT-8
**Resighini Rancheria (Indian Reservation)**—*pop pl* CA-9
Resinger Hollis Creek—*stream* LA-4
Resin Ridge—*ridge* TN-4
Resison—*bar* FM-9
*Res. Lake* WY-8
Resler—*locale* PA-2
Resler Sch—*school* IL-6
Resler Sch (abandoned)—*school* PA-2
Resley Creek—*stream* TX-5
Resley Tank—*reservoir* NM-5
*Resnal* AZ-5
Resner Canyon—*valley* WA-9
*Resoe Creek* NC-3
Resoe Creek—*stream* NC-3
**Resolis**—*pop pl* CO-8
**Resolucion**—*pop pl* PR-3
Resolute Sch (historical)—*school* AL-4
Resolution—*locale* VI-3
Resolution, Mount—*summit* NH-1
Resolution Branch—*stream* NC-3
Resolution Creek—*stream* CO-8
Resolution Island—*island* ME-1
Resolution Island—*island* PA-2
Resolution Mine (abandoned)—*mine* AZ-5
Resolution Mtn—*summit* CO-8
Resolution Shelter—*locale* NH-1
Resor, William, House—*hist pl* OH-6
*Resort* MI-6
**Resort**—*pop pl* NY-2
Resort Creek—*stream* OR-9
Resort Creek—*stream* WA-9
Resort Creek Pond—*lake* WA-9
Resort Island—*island* NY-2
Resort Lake—*lake* MI-6
Resort Point—*cape* CA-9
**Resort (Township of)**—*pop pl* MI-6
Resota Beach—*locale* FL-3
Resource Pond—*lake* AZ-5
*Respass Creek* TX-5
Respass Creek—*stream* TX-5
*Respe Creek* TX-5
Respess Field—*airport* NC-3
Respess Shore—*beach* NC-3
*Respini Creek* CA-9
Respondek Ranch—*locale* TX-5
*Respress Creek* TX-5
*Ress* IL-6
Ressaca—*locale* PA-2
Resseau Ch—*church* GA-3
Resseaus Crossroads—*locale* GA-3
Resse Mtn—*summit* WY-8
Resser Ditch—*canal* IN-6
Ressigue Sch—*school* MI-6
Ressler Ditch—*canal* IN-6
Ressurection Sch—*school* AL-4
**Rest**—*pop pl* KS-7
**Rest**—*pop pl* VA-3
Res Tank—*reservoir* AZ-5
Rest Area Eighty-four T Two—*other* AZ-5
Rest Area One-hundred Twenty-nine MP—*other* AZ-5
Rest Area One Hundred Twentythree C—*other* AZ-5
**Restaurada**—*pop pl* PR-3
Restaurant Cave—*cave* AL-4
Resta Well—*well* AZ-5
Rest Cem—*cemetery* ND-7
Rest Cem—*cemetery* TX-5
Rester Cem—*cemetery* (2) LA-4
Rester Cem—*cemetery* MS-4
Rest-Ever Memorial Cem—*cemetery* TX-5
Restful Lake—*lake* OH-6
**Rest Haven**—*pop pl* GA-3
**Resthaven**—*pop pl* IL-6
**Rest Haven**—*pop pl* MD-2
**Rest Haven**—*pop pl* NC-3
Rest Haven Baptist Ch—*church* TN-4
Resthaven Cem—*cemetery* (2) AZ-5
Rest Haven Cem—*cemetery* AR-4
Resthaven Cem—*cemetery* GA-3
Rest Haven Cem—*cemetery* GA-3
Resthaven Cem—*cemetery* IL-6
Resthaven Cem—*cemetery* IN-6
Rest Haven Cem—*cemetery* IN-6
Resthaven Cem—*cemetery* (2) IA-7
Resthaven Cem—*cemetery* KS-7
Resthaven Cem—*cemetery* KY-4
Rest Haven Cem—*cemetery* KY-4
Resthaven Cem—*cemetery* KY-4
Resthaven Cem—*cemetery* LA-4
Rest Haven Cem—*cemetery* MD-2
Rest Haven Cem—*cemetery* NY-2
Rest Haven Cem—*cemetery* NC-3
Resthaven Cem—*cemetery* OK-5
Rest Haven Cem—*cemetery* (2) OK-5
Rest Haven Cem—*cemetery* PA-2
Rest Haven Cem—*cemetery* SD-7
Rest Haven Cem—*cemetery* TN-4
Resthaven Cem—*cemetery* TX-5
Rest Haven Cem—*cemetery* TX-5
Resthaven Cem—*cemetery* (2) TX-5
Rest Haven Cem—*cemetery* (2) TX-5
Resthaven Cem—*cemetery* TX-5
Rest Haven Cem—*cemetery* (3) TX-5
Rest Haven Cem—*cemetery* VT-1
Resthaven Cem—*cemetery* WA-9
Resthaven Cem—*cemetery* WV-2
Rest Haven Cem—*cemetery* WI-6
Resthaven Cem—*cemetery* WI-6
Rest Haven Cem—*cemetery* WI-6
Resthaven Cem—*cemetery* WI-6
Rest Haven Cem—*cemetery* (2) WI-6
Resthaven Cem and Memorial Park—*cemetery* FL-3

**Reynolds**—pop pl ... MO-7
**Reynolds**—pop pl (2) ... NE-7
**Reynolds**—pop pl ... NY-2
**Reynolds**—pop pl ... ND-7
**Reynolds**—pop pl ... OH-6
**Reynolds**—pop pl ... PA-2
**Reynolds**—pop pl ... WV-2
Reynolds, Anson O., House—hist pl ... IA-7
Reynolds, Dr. Carl V., House—hist pl ... NC-3
Reynolds, Gen. John F., Sch—hist pl ... PA-2
Reynolds, George, House—hist pl ... NY-2
Reynolds, Isaac N., House—hist pl ... MI-6
Reynolds, James, House—hist pl ... MO-7
Reynolds, James Culbertson, House—hist pl ... IN-6
Reynolds, James E., House—hist pl ... OK-5
Reynolds, John R., House—hist pl ... OH-6
Reynolds, John T. and Henry T., Jr., House—hist pl ... UT-8
Reynolds, Joseph, House—hist pl ... RI-1
Reynolds, Joseph "Diamond Jo," Office Bldg and House—hist pl ... IA-7
Reynolds, Mount—summit ... CA-9
Reynolds, Mount—summit ... MT-8
Reynolds and Sessions Drain—canal ... MI-6
Reynolds Arcade—hist pl ... NY-2
Reynolds Basin—basin ... CA-9
Reynolds Bay—bay ... ME-1
Reynolds Bend—bend ... GA-3
Reynolds Bend—bend ... TN-4
Reynolds Bend—bend ... TX-5
Reynolds Bend Cem—cemetery ... TX-5
Reynolds Box (historical)—locale ... MS-4
Reynolds Branch—stream ... AL-4
Reynolds Branch—stream (3) ... GA-3
Reynolds Branch—stream ... KY-4
Reynolds Branch—stream ... MO-7
Reynolds Branch—stream (6) ... TN-4
Reynolds Branch—stream (2) ... TX-5
Reynolds Branch—stream ... WV-2
Reynolds Bridge—bridge ... TN-4
**Reynolds Bridge**—pop pl ... CT-1
Reynolds Brook—stream ... ME-1
Reynoldsburg—locale ... IL-6
**Reynoldsburg**—pop pl ... OH-6
**Reynoldsburg (historical)**—pop pl ... TN-4
Reynoldsburg Island (historical)—island ... TN-4
Reynoldsburg Landing (historical)—locale ... TN-4
Reynolds Butte—summit ... OR-9
Reynolds Cabin—locale ... CO-8
Reynold's Candy Company Bldg—hist pl ... DE-2
Reynolds Canyon—valley ... AZ-5
Reynolds Canyon—valley ... NM-5
Reynolds (CCD)—cens area ... GA-3
*Reynolds Cem* ... AL-4
Reynolds Cem—cemetery (2) ... AL-4
Reynolds Cem—cemetery (2) ... AR-4
Reynolds Cem—cemetery (4) ... IL-6
Reynolds Cem—cemetery (3) ... KY-4
Reynolds Cem—cemetery (4) ... ME-1
Reynolds Cem—cemetery ... MA-1
Reynolds Cem—cemetery ... MI-6
Reynolds Cem—cemetery ... MN-6
Reynolds Cem—cemetery ... MS-4
Reynolds Cem—cemetery ... MO-7
Reynolds Cem—cemetery (2) ... NY-2
Reynolds Cem—cemetery ... NC-3
Reynolds Cem—cemetery ... OH-6
Reynolds Cem—cemetery ... OK-5
Reynolds Cem—cemetery ... SC-3
Reynolds Cem—cemetery (12) ... TN-4
Reynolds Cem—cemetery (4) ... TX-5
Reynolds Cem—cemetery ... VA-3
Reynolds Cem—cemetery (4) ... WV-2
Reynolds Cem—cemetery ... WY-8
Reynolds Ch—church ... AL-4
Reynolds Ch—church ... AR-4
Reynolds Ch—church ... DE-2
Reynolds Ch—church ... IL-6
Reynolds Ch—church (2) ... MN-6
Reynolds Ch—church ... PA-2
Reynolds Ch—church ... VA-3
Reynold Sch—school ... MS-4
*Reynold's Channel* ... NY-2
Reynolds Channel—channel ... NY-2
Reynolds Chapel—church ... AL-4
Reynolds Chapel—church (2) ... GA-3
Reynolds Chapel—church ... KY-4
Reynolds Chapel—church ... MS-4
Reynolds Chapel—church ... MO-7
Reynolds Chapel—church ... NC-3
Reynolds Chapel—church ... OK-5
*Reynolds Chapel Ch* ... AL-4
*Reynolds Chapel Pentecostal Independent Ch* ... MS-4
Reynolds Chapel Sch (historical)—school ... AL-4
Reynolds Childrens Home—building ... TX-5
Reynolds Circle Lake—reservoir ... KY-4
Reynolds City—locale ... MT-8
Reynolds Coliseum—locale ... NC-3
Reynolds Coll (historical)—school ... TN-4
Reynolds Corner—locale ... NY-2
Reynolds Corner—locale ... VA-3
**Reynolds Corner**—pop pl ... ME-1
*Reynolds Corners* ... OH-6
Reynolds Corners—locale ... DE-2
Reynolds Corners—locale ... NY-2
**Reynolds Corners**—pop pl ... NY-2
Reynolds Corners Cem—cemetery ... MI-6
Reynolds Coulee—valley ... WI-6
Reynolds Coulee Creek—stream ... WI-6
**Reynolds County**—pop pl ... MO-7
Reynolds Cove—valley ... NC-3
*Reynolds Creek* ... SD-7
*Reynolds Creek* ... TN-4
*Reynolds Creek* ... TX-5
Reynolds Creek—gut ... VA-3
Reynolds Creek—stream (3) ... AK-9
Reynolds Creek—stream ... AZ-5
Reynolds Creek—stream (4) ... CA-9
Reynolds Creek—stream ... CO-8
Reynolds Creek—stream ... GA-3
Reynolds Creek—stream (3) ... ID-8
Reynolds Creek—stream ... IN-6
Reynolds Creek—stream ... IA-7
Reynolds Creek—stream ... KY-4
Reynolds Creek—stream ... MO-7
Reynolds Creek—stream (5) ... MT-8
Reynolds Creek—stream ... NV-8
Reynolds Creek—stream (2) ... NY-2
Reynolds Creek—stream (2) ... NC-3
Reynolds Creek—stream (3) ... OR-9
Reynolds Creek—stream ... TN-4
Reynolds Creek—stream (3) ... TX-5
Reynolds Creek—stream ... UT-8
Reynolds Creek—stream (2) ... VA-3
Reynolds Creek—stream (2) ... WA-9
Reynolds Creek—stream ... WY-8
Reynolds Creek Ranger Station—locale ... AZ-5
Reynolds Creek Springs—spring ... CO-8
Reynolds Creek Trail—trail ... OR-9
Reynolds Crossing—locale ... TX-5
**Reynolds Crossroads**—pop pl ... NC-3
**Reynoldsdale**—pop pl ... PA-2
Reynolds Dam—dam ... MA-1
Reynolds Depot Post Office (historical)—building ... TN-4
Reynolds Ditch—canal ... WY-8
Reynolds Drain—canal ... MI-6
Reynolds Duck Pond—lake ... GA-3
Reynolds Elem Sch—school ... IN-6
*Reynolds Estate* ... GA-3
Reynolds Field—park ... NY-2
Reynolds Flat—flat ... UT-8
Reynolds Ford—locale ... MO-7
Reynolds Ford Bridge—other ... MO-7
Reynolds Fork—stream ... KY-4
Reynolds Gap—gap (2) ... NC-3
Reynolds Gap—gap ... WV-2
Reynolds Gulch—valley ... UT-8
Reynolds Gully—valley ... NY-2
Reynolds Head—cape ... AK-9
**Reynolds Heights**—pop pl ... PA-2
Reynolds Hill—summit ... AL-4
Reynolds Hill—summit ... FL-3
Reynolds Hill—summit ... GA-3
Reynolds Hill—summit ... MT-8
Reynolds Hill—summit ... NY-2
Reynolds Hill—summit ... WV-2
Reynolds Hill—summit ... WY-8
Reynolds (historical)—locale ... MS-4
*Reynolds Holiness Church* ... AL-4
Reynolds Hollow—valley ... AR-4
Reynolds Hollow—valley ... KY-4
Reynolds Hollow—valley (2) ... MO-7
Reynolds Hollow—valley (2) ... TN-4
Reynolds Homestead—hist pl ... VA-3
Reynolds House—hist pl ... NY-2
Reynolds House—hist pl ... NC-3
Reynolds HS—school ... NC-3
Reynolds HS—school ... OR-9
Reynolds JHS—school ... PA-2
Reynolds Knob—summit ... WV-2
Reynolds Lake—lake ... CO-8
Reynolds Lake—lake ... ID-8
Reynolds Lake—lake ... LA-4
Reynolds Lake—lake (3) ... MI-6
Reynolds Lake—reservoir ... NJ-2
Reynolds Lake—reservoir (3) ... NC-3
Reynolds Lake—reservoir (2) ... OK-5
Reynolds Lake Dam—dam ... NJ-2
Reynolds Lake Dam—dam (3) ... NC-3
Reynolds Landing (historical)—locale ... TN-4
Reynolds Landing Strip—airport ... IN-6
Reynolds Landing Strip—airport ... MO-7
Reynolds Lane Sch—school ... FL-3
*Reynold's Ledge* ... ME-1
Reynolds Meadow—flat ... OR-9
Reynolds Memorial Hosp—hospital ... NC-3
Reynolds Memorial Sch—school ... NC-3
Reynolds Mill—locale ... AL-4
Reynolds Mill—locale ... DE-2
Reynolds Mill—locale ... PA-2
Reynolds Mill—locale ... VA-3
Reynolds Mine—mine ... TN-4
Reynolds Mine—mine ... WA-9
Reynolds-Morris House—hist pl ... PA-2
*Reynolds Mountain* ... MT-8
Reynolds Mountain—ridge ... AR-4
Reynolds Mtn—summit (3) ... AR-4
Reynolds Mtn—summit ... KY-4
Reynolds Mtn—summit (2) ... MT-8
Reynolds Mtn—summit ... NC-3
Reynolds Mtn—summit (2) ... TN-4
Reynolds Number 1 Dam—dam ... SD-7
Reynolds Number 2 Dam—dam ... SD-7
Reynoldson—locale ... NC-3
Reynoldson (Township of)—fmr MCD ... NC-3
Reynolds Park—flat ... MT-8
Reynolds Park—park ... NC-3
*Reynolds Park and Golf Course* ... NC-3
*Reynolds Pass* ... ID-8
*Reynolds Pass* ... MT-8
Reynolds Peak—summit ... AK-9
Reynolds Peak—summit ... CA-9
Reynolds Peak—summit ... WA-9
Reynolds Plaza (Shop Ctr)—locale ... PA-2
*Reynolds P.O.* ... MS-4
*Reynolds Point* ... ME-1
Reynolds Point—bench ... UT-8
Reynolds Point—cape ... ID-8
Reynolds Point—cape ... ME-1
Reynolds Point—cape (2) ... VT-1
Reynolds Pond—lake ... NH-1
Reynolds Pond—lake ... PA-2
Reynolds Pond—reservoir ... DE-2
Reynolds Pond—reservoir ... GA-3
Reynolds Pond—reservoir ... MA-1
Reynolds Pond—reservoir ... OR-9
Reynolds Pond—reservoir ... RI-1
Reynolds Pond—reservoir ... SC-3
Reynolds Pond Dam—dam ... DE-2
Reynolds Prairie—flat ... SD-7
Reynolds Prairie Sch—school ... SD-7
Reynolds Ranch—locale ... AZ-5
Reynolds Ranch—locale (3) ... NM-5
Reynolds Ranch—locale ... SD-7
Reynolds Ranch—locale (2) ... TX-5
Reynolds Ranch (historical)—locale ... SD-7
Reynolds Ridge—ridge ... CA-9
Reynolds Ridge—ridge ... IN-6
Reynolds Ridge—ridge ... OR-9
Reynolds Ridge—ridge ... TN-4
Reynolds Ridge—ridge ... VA-3
Reynolds Ridge Lookout—locale ... OR-9
Reynolds Rock—island ... CA-9
Reynolds Rsvr—reservoir (2) ... CO-8
Reynolds Rsvr—reservoir ... OR-9
Reynolds Rsvr—reservoir ... VT-1
Reynolds Rsvr—reservoir (3) ... WY-8
Reynolds Run—stream (2) ... OH-6
Reynolds Run—stream (2) ... PA-2
Reynolds Run—stream ... VA-3
Reynolds Run—stream ... WY-8
Reynolds Sch—school ... AL-4
Reynolds Sch—school ... AZ-5
Reynolds Sch—school ... AR-4
Reynolds Sch—school ... CA-9
Reynolds Sch—school ... CT-1
Reynolds Sch—school ... FL-3
Reynolds Sch—school ... GA-3
Reynolds Sch—school ... IL-6
Reynolds Sch—school ... ME-1
Reynolds Sch—school (2) ... MI-6
Reynolds Sch—school (2) ... MO-7
Reynolds Sch—school ... NY-2
Reynolds Sch—school (2) ... OH-6
Reynolds Sch—school (2) ... TX-5
Reynolds Sch (historical)—school (2) ... MS-4
Reynolds Sch (historical)—school (2) ... PA-2
*Reynolds School* ... MS-4
Reynolds-Seaquist House—hist pl ... TX-5
Reynolds Slough—swamp ... SD-7
Reynolds Spring—spring (2) ... TN-4
Reynolds Spring—spring ... WA-9
Reynolds Spring—spring ... WY-8
Reynolds Spring Bog—swamp ... PA-2
Reynolds Spring Rsvr—reservoir ... UT-8
Reynolds Springs—spring ... ID-8
Reynolds Springs—spring ... NV-8
Reynolds Spring Trail—trail ... PA-2
Reynolds State Wayside Campground—park ... CA-9
*Reynolds Station* ... AL-4
*Reynolds Station* ... TN-4
Reynolds Station—locale ... KY-4
**Reynolds Station (RR name Deanfield)**—pop pl ... KY-4
Reynolds Store—locale ... VA-3
Reynolds Store (historical)—locale (2) ... AL-4
Reynolds Store (historical)—locale (2) ... MS-4
Reynolds Street Sch—school ... GA-3
**Reynolds Subdivision**—pop pl ... UT-8
Reynolds Swamp—swamp ... GA-3
Reynolds Tank—reservoir ... TX-5
Reynoldston—locale ... NY-2
Reynoldstown—locale ... PA-2
Reynolds (Township of)—fmr MCD ... AR-4
**Reynolds (Township of)**—pop pl ... IL-6
**Reynolds (Township of)**—pop pl ... MI-6
**Reynolds (Township of)**—pop pl ... MN-6
Reynolds Trailer Court—locale ... AZ-5
Reynolds Tunnel—mine ... NV-8
*Reynoldsville* ... NY-2
Reynoldsville—locale ... IL-6
Reynoldsville—locale ... KY-4
**Reynoldsville**—pop pl ... GA-3
**Reynoldsville**—pop pl ... NY-2
**Reynoldsville**—pop pl ... OR-9
**Reynoldsville**—pop pl ... PA-2
**Reynoldsville**—pop pl ... WV-2
Reynoldsville Borough—civil ... PA-2
Reynoldsville Cem—cemetery ... PA-2
Reynoldsville Ch—church ... KY-4
Reynoldsville Fire Tower—tower ... PA-2
Reynoldsville Rsvr—reservoir ... PA-2
Reynoldsville Sch—school ... IL-6
*Reynoldsville Station* ... NY-2
Reynoldsville Storage Dam—dam ... PA-2
Reynolds-Weed House—hist pl ... WI-6
Reynolds Well—well (2) ... TX-5
Reynolds Windmill—locale ... NM-5
Reynolds Windmill—locale (3) ... TX-5
Reynon Ranch—locale ... CA-9
Reynosa Banco Number 98—levee ... TX-5
Reyno (Township of)—fmr MCD ... AR-4
Reynovia Lake—reservoir ... VA-3
Reyolds Sch—school ... PA-2
Rey Park—park ... FL-3
**Reywin Acres (subdivision)**—pop pl ... NC-3
Rey Windmill—locale ... TX-5
Rezac Lake—lake ... SD-7
**Rezago**—pop pl ... CO-8
Rezanof Lake—lake ... AK-9
Rezek Post Office (historical)—building ... SD-7
R Farm Lake—lake ... OH-6
R F Fiddyment Ranch—locale ... CA-9
R Fields Number 1 Dam—dam ... SD-7
R Fields Number 2 Dam—dam ... SD-7
R Fields Number 4 Dam—dam ... SD-7
R Fields Number 5 Dam—dam ... SD-7
R F K Stadium—other ... DC-2
R-fourteen Ranch—locale ... AZ-5
R F Smith Ranch—locale ... OR-9
R G Bilbo Lake Dam—dam ... MS-4
R G Goddard Dam—dam ... SD-7
R Grissel—locale ... TX-5
RGW Tunnel—mine ... UT-8
R Hall—locale ... TX-5
**Rhame**—pop pl ... ND-7
Rhame Ave Sch—school ... NY-2
*Rhamer Church* ... AL-4
**Rhame Township**—pop pl ... ND-7
**Rhamkatte**—pop pl ... NC-3
R Hampton Number 1 Dam—dam ... SD-7
R Ham Ranch—locale ... SD-7
R Hanson Dam—dam ... SD-7
R Hardgrave Ranch—locale ... TX-5
Rhawnhurst—locale ... PA-2
Rhawnhurst Sch—school ... PA-2
R H Dana JHS—school ... CA-9
Rhea—locale ... KY-4
Rhea—locale ... OK-5
Rhea—locale ... TX-5
**Rhea**—pop pl ... AR-4
**Rhea**—pop pl ... OR-9
Rhea, John C., House—hist pl ... TX-5
Rhea, Lake—lake ... FL-3
Rhea, Lake—reservoir ... AL-4
Rhea Branch—stream ... NC-3
Rhea Branch—stream (4) ... TN-4
Rhea Cem—cemetery ... MO-7
Rhea Cem—cemetery ... OK-5
Rhea Cem—cemetery (3) ... TN-4
Rhea Central Elem Sch—school ... TN-4
Rhea Central HS—school ... TN-4
Rhea Ch—church ... KY-4
Rhea Ch—church ... MO-7
Rhea Ch—church ... WV-2
Rhea Chapel—church ... TN-4
**Rhea County**—pop pl ... TN-4
Rhea County Courthouse—building ... TN-4
Rhea County Courthouse—hist pl ... TN-4
Rhea County Health Clinic—hospital ... TN-4
Rhea County Hosp—hospital ... TN-4
Rhea County HS—school ... TN-4
Rhea County Vocational Training Center—school ... TN-4
Rhea Cove—valley ... NC-3
Rhea Creek—stream ... CO-8
Rhea Creek—stream ... OR-9
Rhea Creek Cem—cemetery ... OR-9
Rhea Ditch—canal ... CO-8
Rhea Emmanuel Ch—church ... TX-5
Rhea Forge (historical)—locale ... TN-4
Rhea Gap—gap ... TN-4
Rhea Harbor—locale ... TN-4
Rhea (historical)—locale ... AL-4
**Rhea (historical)**—pop pl ... OR-9
Rhea Hollow—valley ... TN-4
Rhea House—hist pl ... TN-4
Rhea Lake Dam—dam ... MS-4
Rhea-McEntire House—hist pl ... AL-4
Rhea Mills—locale ... TX-5
Rhea Ranch—locale ... CO-8
Rheas Bridge—bridge ... AL-4
Rhea Sch (abandoned)—school ... MO-7
Rheas Mill (Township of)—fmr MCD ... AR-4
Rhea Springs—spring (2) ... TN-4
Rhea Springs Cem—cemetery ... TN-4
Rhea Springs Fish Hatchery—locale ... TN-4
**Rhea Springs (historical)**—pop pl ... TN-4
Rhea Springs Post Office (historical)—building ... TN-4
Rhea Springs Rec Area—park ... TN-4
*Rheas Valley* ... TN-4
**Rheasville**—pop pl ... NC-3
R Heath Dam—dam ... SD-7
**Rheatown**—pop pl ... TN-4
Rheatown-Chucky (CCD)—cens area ... TN-4
Rheatown-Chucky Division—civil ... TN-4
Rheatown Creek—stream ... TN-4
Rheatown Post Office (historical)—building ... TN-4
*Rhea Valley* ... TN-4
Rhea Valley—basin ... VA-3
Rheber—locale ... KY-4
*Rhecks Run* ... PA-2
Rhee Cem—cemetery ... TN-4
Rheem—locale ... CA-9
**Rheem**—pop pl ... CA-9
**Rheems**—pop pl ... PA-2
Rheems Elem Sch—school ... PA-2
Rheems Quarry—mine ... PA-2
**Rheem Valley**—pop pl ... CA-9
**Rheiderland (Township of)**—pop pl ... MN-6
Rheims—locale ... NY-2
Rhein Cem—cemetery ... ND-7
*Rhein Durchfahrt* ... MP-9
*Rhein Hafen* ... MP-9
*Rhein-Hafen Durchfahrt* ... MP-9
Rheinlander Sch—school ... IN-6
Rheinstrom Hill—summit ... NY-2
Rhem Creek—stream ... OR-9
Rhems—locale ... SC-3
**Rhems**—pop pl (2) ... NC-3
Rhems Ch—church ... SC-3
Rhems Landing—locale ... NC-3
Rhems Plantation—locale ... SC-3
Rhem Tunnel—mine ... AZ-5
Rhem-Waldrop House—hist pl ... NC-3
R Hendrickson—locale ... TX-5
*Rheonel Hollow* ... OH-6
R Hepper Dam—dam ... SD-7
**Rhett**—pop pl ... SC-3
Rhett, Robert Barnwell, House—hist pl ... SC-3
Rhett Ave Ch—church ... SC-3
Rhett Creek—stream (2) ... ID-8
*Rhett Creek Bar* ... ID-8
Rhett Creek Campground—locale ... ID-8
*Rhett Lake* ... CA-9
Rhett Mill Dam—dam ... NC-3
*Rhettown* ... TN-4
Rhett Sch—school ... SC-3
Rhetts Island—island ... GA-3
Rhetts View—summit ... TN-4
Rheuark Landing—locale ... SC-3
Rheumatism Tank—reservoir ... TX-5
Rheumatiz Gulch—valley ... OR-9
R H Fosters Landing—locale ... AL-4
Rhiley Ranch—locale ... SD-7
Rhimey Lake—lake ... MN-6
Rhin, Port—harbor ... MP-9
*Rhinds Run* ... PA-2
**Rhine**—pop pl ... GA-3
**Rhine**—pop pl ... NC-3
**Rhine**—pop pl ... WI-6
*Rhine, The* ... MT-8
**Rhinebeck**—pop pl ... NY-2
Rhinebeck Kill—stream ... NY-2
Rhinebeck Sch—school ... NY-2
**Rhinebeck (Town of)**—pop pl ... NY-2
Rhinebeck Village Hist Dist—hist pl ... NY-2
Rhine Canyon—valley ... AZ-5
Rhine Canyon—valley ... CA-9
Rhine (CCD)—cens area ... GA-3
Rhine Cem—cemetery ... IL-6
*Rhine Center* ... WI-6
Rhine Center—other ... WI-6
**Rhinecliff**—pop pl ... NY-2
Rhinecliff Hotel—hist pl ... NY-2
*Rhineclift* ... NY-2
*Rhine Creek* ... SD-7
Rhine Creek—stream ... AK-9
Rhine Creek—stream ... IA-7
Rhine Creek—stream ... MN-6
Rhine Creek—stream ... WV-2
Rhinegold Sch—school ... TX-5
Rhinehart—locale ... OR-9
**Rhinehart**—pop pl (2) ... LA-4
Rhinehart Branch—stream ... AL-4
Rhinehart Branch—stream ... AR-4
Rhinehart Brook—stream ... NJ-2
Rhinehart Buttes—summit ... OR-9
Rhinehart Cem—cemetery ... IA-7
Rhinehart Cove—valley ... NC-3
*Rhinehart Creek* ... OR-9
Rhinehart Creek—stream ... LA-4
Rhinehart Creek—stream ... NC-3
Rhinehart Creek—stream ... OR-9
Rhinehart Lake—lake ... LA-4
*Rhinehart Lakes* ... WY-8
Rhinehart Ranch—hist pl ... MO-7
*Rhineharts Mill* ... AL-4
**Rhinehart (Township of)**—pop pl ... MN-6
Rhinehart Valley—valley ... TN-4
Rhinehimmer Hollow—valley ... PA-2
Rhinehimmer Trail—trail ... PA-2
Rhine Hollow—valley ... OH-6
Rhine House—hist pl ... CA-9
Rhine Lake—lake ... MN-6
Rhine Lake—reservoir ... TX-5
**Rhineland**—pop pl ... MO-7
**Rhineland**—pop pl ... TX-5
**Rhinelander**—pop pl ... WI-6
Rhinelander Flowage—channel ... WI-6
Rhinelander-Oneida County Airp—airport ... WI-6
Rhine Point—cape ... ME-1
Rhiner Creek—stream ... MS-4
Rhine Ridge—ridge ... AZ-5
Rhine Run—stream ... PA-2
Rhine School (Abandoned)—locale ... CA-9
Rhines Hollow—valley ... PA-2
Rhinestone Branch—stream ... TN-4
**Rhine (Town of)**—pop pl ... WI-6
Rhiney Creek—stream ... PA-2
Rhino Peak—summit ... AK-9
Rhins Hill—summit ... TX-5
Rhinstad Lake—lake ... WI-6
R H Lamb Lake—reservoir ... AL-4
R H Lamb Lake Dam—dam ... AL-4
**Rhoades**—pop pl ... AL-4
Rhoades—unorg reg ... ND-7
Rhoades Branch—stream ... KY-4
Rhoades Canal—canal ... UT-8
*Rhoades Canyon* ... OR-9
Rhoades Canyon—valley ... UT-8
Rhoades Cem—cemetery ... AL-4
Rhoades Cem—cemetery ... VA-3
Rhoades Creek—stream ... OR-9
Rhoades Creek—stream ... PA-2
Rhoades Ditch—canal ... IN-6
Rhoades Elem Sch—school ... IN-6
**Rhoades Hill (historical)**—pop pl ... TN-4
Rhoades House—hist pl ... CO-8
**Rhoades Lane Subdivision**—pop pl ... UT-8
Rhoades Park—park ... NE-7
Rhoades Sch—school ... TX-5
Rhoades Sch (abandoned)—school ... PA-2
Rhoades Sch (historical)—school (2) ... AL-4
Rhoades School—locale ... CA-9
**Rhoades Township**—pop pl ... SD-7
*Rhoades Valley* ... UT-8
**Rhoadesville**—pop pl ... VA-3
**Rhoads**—pop pl ... PA-2
Rhoads, Peter F., House—hist pl ... OH-6
Rhoads Branch—stream ... KY-4
Rhoads Cem—cemetery ... AR-4
Rhoads Cem—cemetery ... MS-4
Rhoads Creek—stream ... AK-9
Rhoads Creek—stream ... PA-2
Rhoads Fork—stream ... SD-7
Rhoads Gulch—valley ... CO-8
Rhoads Lake—lake ... MI-6
Rhoads Lake—lake ... UT-8
Rhoads Lateral—canal ... ID-8
Rhoads Ranch—locale ... SD-7
Rhoads Sch—school ... PA-2
Rhoads Sch (historical)—school ... AL-4
Rhoads Spring—spring ... SD-7
*Rhoadston* ... NJ-2
*Rhoads Valley* ... UT-8
Rhobaugh Draw—valley ... WY-8
Rhoda—locale ... WV-2
**Rhoda**—pop pl ... KY-4
Rhoda, Lake—lake ... CO-8
Rhoda, Lake—reservoir ... AL-4
Rhoda Ann Memorial Ch—church ... WV-2
Rhoda Branch—stream ... NC-3
Rhoda Branch—stream ... SC-3
Rhodabush Creek—stream ... OR-9
Rhoda Creek—stream ... ID-8
Rhoda Creek—stream ... OK-5
Rhoda Creek—stream ... OR-9
Rhoda Creek—stream ... TN-4
Rhodair Gully—valley ... TX-5
Rhoda Lake—lake ... MT-8
*Rhoda Peak* ... ID-8
Rhoda Point—summit ... ID-8
Rhoda Pond—lake ... MA-1
*Rhoda Ponds* ... NY-2
Rhodarmer Cove—valley ... NC-3
Rhodas Branch—stream ... TN-4
Rhoda Street Sch—school ... CA-9
**Rhoda Township**—pop pl ... SD-7
Rhoda Township Hall—building ... SD-7
Rhoddy Creek—stream ... NC-3
Rhode Creek—stream ... WA-9
Rhode Hall—locale ... NJ-2
Rhodehouse, Nelson, House—hist pl ... MA-1
Rhode Island—island ... CA-9
Rhode Island—island ... RI-1
Rhode Island—locale ... TX-5
**Rhode Island**—pop pl ... NY-2
*Rhode Island Bay* ... MA-1
*Rhode Island Bay* ... RI-1
*Rhode Island Bight* ... MA-1
*Rhode Island Bight* ... RI-1
Rhode Island Cem—cemetery ... NY-2
Rhode Island Ch—church ... TX-5
**Rhode Island Corner**—pop pl ... VT-1
Rhode Island Creek—stream ... AK-9
Rhode Island Hosp Trust Bldg—hist pl ... RI-1
Rhode Island Medical Society Bldg—hist pl ... RI-1
Rhode Island Ponds—lake ... CT-1
Rhode Island Ravine—valley ... CA-9
Rhode Island Rock—rock ... MA-1
Rhode Island Rocks—summit ... CT-1
Rhode Island Sound—bay ... MA-1
Rhode Island Sound—bay ... RI-1
Rhode Island State Airport Terminal—hist pl ... RI-1
Rhode Island Statehouse—hist pl ... RI-1
Rhode Lake—lake ... AK-9
Rhode Lake—lake ... WA-9
Rhodelia—locale ... KY-4
**Rhodelia (historical)**—pop pl ... TN-4
Rhodelia Post Office (historical)—building ... TN-4
**Rhodell**—pop pl ... WV-2
*Rhoden Cem* ... AL-4
Rhoden Cem—cemetery ... AL-4
Rhoden Cem—cemetery ... KY-4
Rhoden Creek—stream ... KY-4
Rhoden Creek—stream ... MS-4
Rhoden Hollow—valley ... OH-6
Rhoden Spring—spring ... AL-4
Rhode Ranch—locale ... TX-5
Rhode River—stream ... MD-2
Rhoder Windmill—locale ... WY-8
*Rhodes* ... ND-7
Rhodes—locale ... AL-4
Rhodes—locale ... LA-4
Rhodes—locale ... MS-4
Rhodes—locale ... MT-8
Rhodes—locale ... NC-3
**Rhodes**—pop pl ... CA-9
**Rhodes**—pop pl ... IL-6
**Rhodes**—pop pl ... IN-6
**Rhodes**—pop pl ... IA-7
**Rhodes**—pop pl ... LA-4
**Rhodes**—pop pl ... MI-6
**Rhodes**—pop pl ... NM-5
**Rhodes**—pop pl ... VA-3
Rhodes—uninc pl ... WA-9
Rhodes, Christopher, House—hist pl ... RI-1
Rhodes and Huddle Cem—cemetery ... OH-6
Rhodes Bay—bay ... KY-4
Rhodes Bay—swamp ... NC-3
Rhodes Branch—stream (2) ... GA-3
Rhodes Branch—stream ... MS-4
Rhodes Bridge—bridge ... NC-3
Rhodes Cabin—hist pl ... NV-8
*Rhodes Canal* ... UT-8
*Rhodes Canyon* ... UT-8
Rhodes Canyon—valley (2) ... AZ-5
Rhodes Canyon—valley ... NV-8
Rhodes Canyon—valley ... NM-5
Rhodes Canyon—valley ... OR-9
Rhodes Canyon Dam—dam ... AZ-5
Rhodes Cem—cemetery ... AL-4
Rhodes Cem—cemetery (2) ... AR-4
Rhodes Cem—cemetery ... GA-3
Rhodes Cem—cemetery ... IL-6
Rhodes Cem—cemetery ... IN-6
Rhodes Cem—cemetery (2) ... IA-7
Rhodes Cem—cemetery ... MD-2
Rhodes Cem—cemetery ... MI-6
Rhodes Cem—cemetery (2) ... MS-4
Rhodes Cem—cemetery (3) ... MO-7
Rhodes Cem—cemetery ... NY-2
Rhodes Cem—cemetery (3) ... NC-3
Rhodes Cem—cemetery (3) ... TN-4
Rhodes Cem—cemetery (2) ... TX-5
Rhodes Cem—cemetery (3) ... WV-2
Rhodes Ch—church ... NC-3
Rhodes Ch—church ... WV-2
Rhodes Chapel—church (3) ... AL-4
Rhodes Chapel—church ... KY-4
Rhodes Chapel—church ... MS-4
Rhodes Chapel—church ... MO-7
Rhodes Chapel—church ... WV-2
*Rhodes Chapel United Methodist Ch* ... MS-4
Rhodes Ch (historical)—church ... MS-4
Rhodes Cove—bay ... GA-3
*Rhodes Creek* ... ID-8
*Rhodes Creek* ... KY-4
Rhodes Creek—channel ... GA-3
Rhodes Creek—stream ... CA-9
Rhodes Creek—stream ... ID-8
Rhodes Creek—stream ... IN-6
Rhodes Creek—stream (3) ... KY-4
Rhodes Creek—stream ... MS-4
Rhodes Creek—stream ... NC-3
Rhodes Creek—stream (2) ... OR-9
Rhodes Creek—stream (2) ... TX-5
Rhodes Creek—stream ... WA-9
Rhodes Creek Ch—church ... MS-4
Rhodes Creek Sch (historical)—school ... MS-4
Rhodes Crossroads—locale ... SC-3
**Rhodes Crossroads**—pop pl ... SC-3
Rhodes Cut—channel ... GA-3
**Rhodesdale**—pop pl ... MD-2
**Rhodesdale**—pop pl ... OH-6
Rhodes Ditch—canal ... OH-6
Rhodes Draw—valley ... MT-8
Rhodes Ferry (historical)—locale ... AL-4
*Rhodes Fork Creek* ... TN-4
Rhodes Gap—gap ... GA-3
Rhodes Gulch—valley ... CO-8
Rhodes Gulf—valley ... AL-4
Rhodes-Haverty Bldg—hist pl ... GA-3
Rhodes Hill—summit ... CA-9
Rhodes Hill—summit ... MD-2
Rhodes Hill—summit ... MA-1
Rhodes (historical)—locale ... KS-7
Rhodes House—hist pl ... TN-4
Rhodes HS—school ... OH-6
**Rhodesia Beach**—pop pl ... WA-9
Rhodes JHS—school ... TX-5
*Rhodes Lake* ... MI-6
Rhodes Lake—lake ... CA-9
Rhodes Lake—lake ... GA-3
Rhodes Lake—lake ... IL-6
Rhodes Lake—lake ... IN-6
Rhodes Lake—lake ... TN-4
Rhodes Lake—lake ... WY-8
Rhodes Lake—reservoir ... AL-4
Rhodesleigh—hist pl ... WA-9
Rhodes Meadow—flat ... CA-9
Rhodes Medical Arts Bldg—hist pl ... WA-9
Rhodes Memorial Hall—hist pl ... GA-3
*Rhodes Mill* ... AL-4
Rhodes Mill—hist pl ... IA-7
Rhodes Mill Creek—stream ... NC-3
Rhodes Mound—summit ... GA-3
Rhodes Mountain Gap—gap ... GA-3
Rhodes Mtn—summit ... GA-3
Rhodes Mtn—summit ... MD-2
Rhodes Mtn—summit ... MO-7
Rhodes-on-the Pawtuxet Ballroom and Gazebo—hist pl ... RI-1
Rhodes Park—hist pl ... AL-4
Rhodes Park—park ... AL-4
Rhodes Park—park ... OK-5
Rhodes Peak—summit ... AZ-5
Rhodes Peak—summit ... ID-8
Rhodes Pharmacy—hist pl ... DE-2
Rhodes Point—cape ... MS-4
Rhodes Point—cape ... NC-3

Rhodes Point—*cape* RI-1
Rhodes Point—*cape* TX-5
**Rhodes Point**—*pop pl* MD-2
Rhodes Point Gut—*gut* MD-2
Rhodes Pond—*lake* NC-3
Rhodes Pond—*reservoir* GA-3
Rhodes Pond Dam—*dam* NC-3
*Rhodes Ranch* AZ-5
Rhodes Ranch—*locale* AZ-5
Rhodes Ranch—*locale* TX-5
Rhodes Ranch—*locale* (2) WY-8
**Rhodes-Rhyne**—*pop pl* NC-3
Rhodes Ridge—*ridge* VA-3
*Rhodes River* MD-2
Rhodes Run—*stream* PA-2
Rhodes Salt Marsh—*flat* NV-8
Rhodes Sch—*school* (2) IL-6
Rhodes Sch—*school* MA-1
Rhodes Sch—*school* (2) SD-7
Rhodes Sch—*school* TX-5
Rhodes Sch—*school* VA-3
Rhodes Sch (historical)—*school* AL-4
Rhodes Sch (historical)—*school* MS-4
*Rhodes School* TN-4
Rhodes (site)—*locale* NV-8
Rhodes Site (31BR90)—*hist pl* NC-3
Rhodes Spring—*spring* CA-9
Rhodes Spring—*spring* NM-5
Rhodes Springs—*spring* (2) FL-3
*Rhodes Station* AL-4
Rhodes Store (historical)—*locale* TN-4
Rhodes Street Hist Dist—*hist pl* RI-1
Rhodes Tank—*reservoir* AZ-5
Rhodes' Tavern—*hist pl* DC-2
**Rhodes Town**—*pop pl* TN-4
*Rhodes Valley* UT-8
*Rhodesville* RI-1
Rhodesville—*locale* AL-4
Rhodesville Cave—*cave* AL-4
Rhodesville Ch—*church* AL-4
Rhodesville Sch—*school* AL-4
Rhodes Wash—*stream* CA-9
Rhodes Windmill—*locale* TX-5
**Rhodhiss**—*pop pl* NC-3
Rhodhiss Dam—*dam* (2) NC-3
Rhodhiss Lake—*reservoir* (2) NC-3
**Rhodhiss (Rhodhiss Junction)**—*pop pl* NC-3
Rhodius Park—*park* IN-6
**Rhodo**—*pop pl* NC-3
Rhodod Creek—*stream* OR-9
**Rhododendron**—*pop pl* OR-9
Rhododendron Cone—*summit* AK-9
Rhododendron Creek—*stream* CA-9
Rhododendron Creek—*stream* OR-9
Rhododendron Creek—*stream* TN-4
Rhododendron Island—*island* OR-9
Rhododendron Meadow—*flat* OR-9
Rhododendron Park—*park* NC-3
Rhododendron Park—*park* OR-9
**Rhododendron Park**—*pop pl* WA-9
Rhododendron Pond—*lake* NY-2
Rhododendron Ridge—*ridge* (2) OR-9
Rhododendron Ridge Shelter—*locale* OR-9
Rhododendron Ridge Trail—*trail* OR-9
Rhododendron Sch—*school* OR-9
Rhododendron Swamp—*swamp* NH-1
Rhododendron Trail—*trail* CA-9
Rhodo Dunes Golf Course—*other* OR-9
Rhodo Lake—*reservoir* NJ-2
Rhodoms Point—*cape* NC-3
Rhodonite Creek—*stream* CA-9
Rhodonite Mine—*mine* CA-9
*Rhodus Cem* MS-4
Rhodus Cem—*cemetery* MS-4
*Rhody Creek* VA-3
Rhody Creek—*stream* MI-6
Rhody Creek—*stream* OR-9
Rhody Creek—*stream* VA-3
Rhody Hollow—*valley* MA-1
Rhody Lake—*lake* OR-9
Rhoe Creek—*stream* LA-4
R Hogans Grant—*civil* FL-3
**Rhome**—*pop pl* TX-5
Rhome Cem—*cemetery* OK-5
R Homer Andrews Elem Sch—*school* NC-3
Rhone—*locale* CO-8
Rhone—*uninc pl* PA-2
Rhone, Leonard, House—*hist pl* PA-2
Rhone Cem—*cemetery* AL-4
Rhone Fork—*stream* KY-4
Rhonemus Branch—*stream* OH-6
Rhonesboro—*locale* TX-5
Rhone Sch—*school* LA-4
**Rhoney**—*pop pl* NC-3
Rhoney Chapel Cem—*cemetery* NC-3
Rhorer Cem—*cemetery* KY-4
Rhoton Cave—*cave* KY-4
Rhoton Cem—*cemetery* (2) VA-3
*Rhoton Crater* AZ-5
Rhoton Ditch—*canal* IN-6
Rhoton Mill—*locale* VA-3
*Rhoton Spring* AZ-5
R Hotter Ranch—*locale* ND-7
R Howie Dam—*dam* (2) SD-7
Rhubarb Patch, The—*area* OR-9
Rhubarb Patch Trail—*trail* MT-8
Rhubens Branch—*stream* KY-4
Rhuda Branch—*stream* FL-3
Rhuda Branch Cem—*cemetery* FL-3
Rhude Hollow—*valley* IN-6
Rhudy Branch—*stream* VA-3
Rhue Creek—*stream* MT-8
Rhuland Ditch—*canal* OH-6
Rhule Cem—*cemetery* IN-6
Rhule Creek—*stream* IL-6
Rhulo Hollow—*valley* PA-2
Rhume Run Gap—*gap* PA-2
**Rhump**—*pop pl* AL-4
Rhumrill Cem—*cemetery* ME-1
Rhus Spring—*spring* UT-8
*R H Watkins High School* MS-4
R H Williams Dam—*dam* TN-4
R H Williams Lake—*reservoir* TN-4
Rhyan Springs—*locale* TN-4
Rhymby Cem—*cemetery* OH-6
Rhyme Creek—*stream* TX-5
Rhymer Creek—*stream* MI-6
Rhymes—*locale* LA-4
Rhymes Campground—*locale* CA-9
Rhymes Cem—*cemetery* MS-4
Rhymes Creek—*stream* TX-5
Rhymes Flat—*flat* CA-9
Rhymes HS—*school* LA-4
Rhymes Missionary Baptist Ch—*church* MS-4
Rhymes Sch—*school* LA-4
Rhymes Spring—*spring* CA-9
**Rhymes Store**—*pop pl* LA-4
*Rhyne* NC-3
Rhyne—*locale* AR-4
**Rhyne**—*pop pl* NC-3
Rhyne Crossroad—*locale* NC-3
**Rhyne Crossroads**—*pop pl* NC-3
Rhyne Lake Dam Number Two—*dam* NC-3
Rhyne Lake Number Two—*reservoir* NC-3
Rhyne Memorial Ch—*church* NC-3
Rhynes Airp—*airport* NC-3
Rhynes Cem—*cemetery* MS-4
Rhyne Sch—*school* NC-3
**Rhyolite**—*pop pl* NV-8
Rhyolite Butte—*summit* UT-8
Rhyolite Canyon—*valley* AZ-5
Rhyolite Creek—*stream* AK-9
Rhyolite Hills—*summit* NV-8
Rhyolite Knob—*summit* NV-8
Rhyolite Mtn—*summit* CO-8
Rhyolite Pass—*gap* NV-8
Rhyolite Peak—*summit* AZ-5
Rhyolite Peak—*summit* NV-8
Rhyolite Ridge—*ridge* NV-8
Rhyolite Spring—*spring* AZ-5
**Rhyse**—*pop pl* MO-7
*Ri* FM-9
Ri—*bar* FM-9
Riadon Branch—*stream* TN-4
Rial, York, House—*hist pl* OH-6
Ria Lake—*lake* MN-6
Rials Branch—*stream* TN-4
Rials Cem—*cemetery* TN-4
Rials Creek—*stream* MS-4
**Rial Side (subdivision)**—*pop pl* MA-1
Rialson Cem—*cemetery* MN-6
**Rialto**—*pop pl* CA-9
**Rialto**—*pop pl* OH-6
**Rialto**—*pop pl* TN-4
Rialto Beach—*beach* WA-9
Rialto Bench—*bench* CA-9
Rialto Bldg—*hist pl* TX-5
Rialto Industrial Park—*locale* TN-4
Rialto Landing—*locale* MS-4
Rialto Mine—*mine* OR-9
Rialto Park—*park* CA-9
Rialto Plantation (historical)—*locale* MS-4
Rialto Post Office (historical)—*building* TN-4
Rialto Sch (historical)—*school* TN-4
Rialto Shop Ctr—*locale* FL-3
Rialto Spring—*spring* CA-9
Rialto Theater—*hist pl* CO-8
Rialto Theatre—*hist pl* AR-4
Rialto Theatre—*hist pl* CA-9
Riansares Mtn—*summit* PA-2
Rias Post Office (historical)—*building* AL-4
Rias Run—*stream* OH-6
*Ribaeon* MP-9
*Ribaion Island* MP-9
*Ribaion-to* MP-9
Ribal Spring—*spring* CO-8
R I Bass Ranch—*locale* NM-5
*Ribault Bay* FL-3
Ribault HS—*school* FL-3
Ribault JHS—*school* FL-3
**Ribault Manor**—*pop pl* FL-3
Ribault Monmt—*park* FL-3
**Ribault Park**—*pop pl* SC-3
*Ribault River* FL-3
Ribault River—*stream* FL-3
*Ribaut Bay* FL-3
Ribaut Monmt—*park* SC-3
*Ribaut River* FL-3
Ribble Lake—*lake* MI-6
Ribble Park—*park* TX-5
Ribble Ranch—*locale* NM-5
Ribbon—*locale* KY-4
Ribbon—*locale* VA-3
Ribbon Arch—*arch* UT-8
Ribbon Beach—*beach* CA-9
Ribbon Branch—*stream* TN-4
Ribbon Canyon—*valley* UT-8
Ribbon Canyon—*valley* WY-8
Ribbon Cascade—*falls* WY-8
Ribbon Ch—*church* OK-5
Ribbon Cliff—*cliff* NV-8
Ribbon Cliff—*cliff* WA-9
Ribbon Creek—*stream* CA-9
Ribbon Creek—*stream* SC-3
Ribbon Fall—*falls* CA-9
Ribbon Falls—*falls* AZ-5
Ribbon Falls—*falls* CO-8
Ribbon Gulch—*valley* MT-8
Ribbon Lakes—*lake* WA-9
Ribbon Lake Trail—*trail* WY-8
Ribbon Meadow—*flat* CA-9
Ribbon Mesa—*summit* CO-8
Ribbon Mesa—*summit* WA-9
*Ribbon Oak School* MS-4
Ribbon Reef—*bar* MA-1
Ribbon Ridge—*ridge* AR-4
Ribbon Ridge—*ridge* OR-9
Ribbon Ridge Sch—*school* OR-9
Ribbon Rock—*ridge* CA-9
Ribbons, The—*cliff* NV-8
Ribbon Tank—*reservoir* NM-5
Ribbonwood—*locale* CA-9
Ribdon River—*stream* AK-9
**Ribera**—*pop pl* NM-5
Ribera Dam—*dam* NM-5
Ribera Ditch—*canal* NM-5
Riberan Pond—*swamp* GA-3
Ribewon—*island* MP-9
Ribeyre Island—*island* IN-6
**Rib Falls**—*pop pl* WI-6
Rib Falls Ch—*church* WI-6
**Rib Falls (Town of)**—*pop pl* WI-6
*Rib Hill* WI-6
Rib Hill—*summit* NV-8
Ribia Tank—*reservoir* NM-5
Ribier—*locale* CA-9
Ribinouri Island—*island* MP-9
*Ribinouri-to* MP-9
Ribiyurigan Island—*island* MP-9
Rib Lake—*lake* MN-6
Rib Lake—*lake* (2) WI-6
**Rib Lake**—*pop pl* WI-6
**Rib Lake (Town of)**—*pop pl* WI-6
Rib Lake Trail—*trail* MN-6
Riblet, Royal, House—*hist pl* WA-9
Riblet Cem—*cemetery* OH-6
Riblets Corners—*locale* OH-6
Rib Mountain Sch—*school* WI-6
Rib Mountain State Park—*park* WI-6
**Rib Mountain (Town of)**—*pop pl* WI-6
Rib Mtn—*summit* WI-6
Ribold—*locale* PA-2
**Ribolt**—*pop pl* KY-4
Ribong Island—*island* MP-9
Ribon Island—*island* MP-9
*Ribon-To* MP-9
Ribot—*locale* PA-2
*Rib River* WI-6
Rib River Lookout Tower—*locale* WI-6
Rib Tank—*reservoir* TX-5
Rib View Cem—*cemetery* WI-6
*Ribyurigan-To* MP-9
Ricabear, Lake—*lake* NJ-2
Ricaby Bayou—*stream* LA-4
Rica Canyon—*valley* WA-9
Rica Creek—*stream* TX-5
**Ricard**—*pop pl* NY-2
Ricardo—*locale* CA-9
Ricardo—*locale* NM-5
**Ricardo**—*pop pl* TX-5
Ricardo Cem—*cemetery* NM-5
Ricardo Creek—*stream* CO-8
Ricardo Creek—*stream* NM-5
Ricardo Tank—*reservoir* NM-5
Ricard Sch—*school* LA-4
**Riccas Corner**—*pop pl* CA-9
Ricci Creek—*stream* WA-9
*Rice* RI-1
Rice—*locale* AL-4
Rice—*locale* IL-6
Rice—*locale* OR-9
**Rice**—*pop pl* AL-4
**Rice**—*pop pl* CA-9
**Rice**—*pop pl* IL-6
**Rice**—*pop pl* KS-7
**Rice**—*pop pl* MN-6
**Rice**—*pop pl* OH-6
**Rice**—*pop pl* SC-3
**Rice**—*pop pl* TX-5
**Rice**—*pop pl* VA-3
**Rice**—*pop pl* WA-9
Rice—*uninc pl* TX-5
Rice, Capt. Peter, House—*hist pl* MA-1
Rice, Ezra, House—*hist pl* MA-1
Rice, Green Pryor, House—*hist pl* AL-4
Rice, Isaac L., Mansion—*hist pl* NY-2
Rice, James A., House—*hist pl* AR-4
Rice, John C., House—*hist pl* ID-8
Rice, John W., Summer Cottage—*hist pl* GA-3
Rice, L. N., House—*hist pl* WA-9
Rice, Mount—*summit* AK-9
Rice, Napoleon, House—*hist pl* OR-9
Rice, Ward, House—*hist pl* CO-8
Rice Acres Lake Dam—*dam* MS-4
Rice Air Base—*military* CA-9
Rice Airfarm—*airport* NC-3
Rice and Black Cem—*cemetery* OH-6
*Rice Ave Middle School* PA-2
Rice Ave Union HS—*school* PA-2
Rice Bar—*bar* WA-9
Rice Bay—*bay* MI-6
Rice Bay—*bay* (2) MN-6
Rice Bay—*bay* WI-6
Rice Bayou—*gut* (2) LA-4
Rice Bayou—*stream* (2) LA-4
*Rice Bed* MN-6
Rice Bed Creek—*stream* WI-6
Rice Bed Creek State Wildlife Area—*park* WI-6
Rice Bed Lake—*lake* MN-6
**Rice Bend**—*pop pl* TN-4
Rice Bend Ch—*church* TN-4
**Riceboro**—*pop pl* GA-3
Riceboro (CCD)—*cens area* GA-3
Riceboro Creek—*stream* GA-3
Rice Branch—*stream* AL-4
Rice Branch—*stream* (2) GA-3
Rice Branch—*stream* (4) KY-4
Rice Branch—*stream* (2) NC-3
Rice Branch—*stream* PA-2
Rice Branch—*stream* (3) TN-4
Rice Branch—*stream* (3) TX-5
Rice Bridge—*bridge* GA-3
Rice Brook—*stream* (2) MA-1
Rice Brook—*stream* (2) NH-1
Rice Brook—*stream* (4) NY-2
Rice Brook—*stream* VT-1
Rice Brothers and Adams Bldg—*hist pl* OR-9
Rice Cabin Creek—*stream* GA-3
Rice Camp Branch—*stream* GA-3
*Rice Canyon* TX-5
Rice Canyon—*valley* (6) CA-9
Rice Canyon—*valley* ID-8
Rice Canyon—*valley* NV-8
Rice Canyon—*valley* (2) NM-5
Rice Canyon—*valley* UT-8
Rice Cave—*cave* (2) TN-4
Rice (CCD)—*cens area* TX-5
Rice Cem—*cemetery* (5) AL-4
Rice Cem—*cemetery* (3) AR-4
Rice Cem—*cemetery* (4) IL-6
Rice Cem—*cemetery* (2) IN-6
Rice Cem—*cemetery* IA-7
Rice Cem—*cemetery* KS-7
Rice Cem—*cemetery* (8) KY-4
Rice Cem—*cemetery* LA-4
Rice Cem—*cemetery* MI-6
Rice Cem—*cemetery* (2) MN-6
Rice Cem—*cemetery* (3) MS-4
Rice Cem—*cemetery* (6) MO-7
Rice Cem—*cemetery* (3) NY-2
Rice Cem—*cemetery* (3) NC-3
Rice Cem—*cemetery* (3) OH-6
Rice Cem—*cemetery* OK-5
Rice Cem—*cemetery* OR-9
Rice Cem—*cemetery* (6) TX-5
Rice Cem—*cemetery* WV-2
*Rice Cemetery* TN-4
Rice Ch—*church* AL-4
Rice Ch—*church* TN-4
Rice Ch—*church* TX-5
*Rice Chapel* AL-4
Rice Chapel—*church* AR-4
Rice Chapel—*church* (2) MS-4
Rice Chapel—*locale* TX-5
Rice Chapel Cem—*cemetery* MS-4
*Rice Chapel Methodist Church* MS-4
**Rice City**—*pop pl* RI-1
Rice City Hist Dist—*hist pl* RI-1
Rice City Pond—*reservoir* MA-1
Rice City Pond Dam—*dam* MA-1
Rice Corner—*locale* ME-1
Rice Corral Rsvr—*reservoir* OR-9
Rice Corral Spring—*spring* OR-9
Rice Coulee—*valley* MT-8
Rice County—*civil* KS-7
**Rice (County)**—*pop pl* MN-6
Rice County Courthouse and Jail—*hist pl* MN-6
Rice Cove—*valley* AL-4
Rice Cove—*valley* (2) NC-3
Rice Cove Creek—*stream* NC-3
Rice Covered Bridge—*hist pl* PA-2
Rice Cow Camp—*locale* WY-8
*Rice Creek* CA-9
*Rice Creek* MS-4
*Rice Creek* ND-7
*Rice Creek* TX-5
Rice Creek—*locale* FL-3
Rice Creek—*locale* MI-6
Rice Creek—*stream* (4) AL-4
Rice Creek—*stream* (4) CA-9
Rice Creek—*stream* (4) FL-3
Rice Creek—*stream* (2) GA-3
Rice Creek—*stream* (5) ID-8
Rice Creek—*stream* KY-4
Rice Creek—*stream* MD-2
Rice Creek—*stream* (3) MI-6
Rice Creek—*stream* (8) MN-6
Rice Creek—*stream* MS-4
Rice Creek—*stream* MO-7
Rice Creek—*stream* (4) MT-8
Rice Creek—*stream* NY-2
Rice Creek—*stream* (3) NC-3
Rice Creek—*stream* ND-7
Rice Creek—*stream* (2) OK-5
Rice Creek—*stream* (5) OR-9
Rice Creek—*stream* SC-3
Rice Creek—*stream* (2) TN-4
Rice Creek—*stream* (4) TX-5
Rice Creek—*stream* (3) UT-8
Rice Creek—*stream* VA-3
Rice Creek—*stream* WA-9
Rice Creek—*stream* (9) WI-6
Rice Creek Bay—*bay* FL-3
Rice Creek Bridge—*bridge* ID-8
Rice Creek Bridge—*bridge* NC-3
Rice Creek Campground—*locale* CA-9
Rice Creek Ch—*church* GA-3
*Rice Creek Field Station* UT-8
*Rice Creek Gap* TN-4
*Rice Creek Gas Field* CA-9
Rice Creek Landing—*locale* AL-4
Rice Creek Sch—*school* MN-6
Rice Creek Spring—*spring* ID-8
Rice Creek Spring—*spring* UT-8
Rice Creek Swamp—*swamp* FL-3
*Rice Crossing* MA-1
Rice Crossing—*locale* CA-9
**Rice Crossroads**—*pop pl* SC-3
Ricedale—*locale* KY-4
Rice Dam—*dam* (2) AL-4
*Rice Depot* VA-3
Rice Ditch—*canal* CA-9
Rice Ditch—*canal* (3) IN-6
Rice Ditch No 1—*canal* WY-8
Rice Drain—*canal* (3) CA-9
Rice Drain—*canal* MI-6
Rice Drain—*stream* MI-6
Rice Drain Five—*canal* CA-9
Rice Drain Four—*canal* CA-9
Rice Drain One—*canal* CA-9
Rice Drain Six—*canal* CA-9
Rice Drain Three—*canal* CA-9
Rice Drain Two—*canal* CA-9
Rice Draw—*valley* MT-8
Rice Draw—*valley* WY-8
Rice Draw Trail—*trail* MT-8
Rice Elem Sch—*school* PA-2
Rice Farm—*hist pl* SD-7
Rice Farm—*locale* ME-1
Ricefield—*locale* NC-3
Rice Field—*locale* TN-4
Rice Field—*swamp* TN-4
Ricefield Bay—*swamp* SC-3
Ricefield Branch—*stream* NC-3
Rice Field Cem—*cemetery* TN-4
Rice Field Cove—*bay* SC-3
Ricefield Pond—*reservoir* MO-7
Rice Field Swamp—*swamp* FL-3
Rice Flat—*flat* CA-9
Rice Flat—*flat* OR-9
**Riceford**—*pop pl* MN-6
Riceford Creek—*stream* MN-6
Rice Fork—*stream* CA-9
Rice Gap—*gap* NC-3
Rice Gap—*gap* TN-4
Rice-Gates House—*hist pl* OR-9
Rice Glen—*valley* NY-2
**Rice Grove**—*pop pl* NY-2
Rice Gulch—*valley* AZ-5
Rice Gulch—*valley* CO-8
Rice Gulch Creek—*stream* AK-9
Rice Hall—*hist pl* NY-2
Rice Heath—*swamp* ME-1
Rice Hill—*locale* OR-9
**Rice Hill**—*pop pl* OR-9
Rice Hill—*summit* CA-9
Rice Hill—*summit* ME-1
Rice Hill—*summit* (2) MA-1
Rice Hill—*summit* (2) NY-2
Rice Hill—*summit* OR-9
Rice Hill—*summit* (3) VT-1
Rice Hill—*summit* WA-9
Rice Hill Ch—*church* GA-3
Rice Hill Sch—*school* KY-4
Rice Hill Wayside—*locale* OR-9
Rice (historical)—*locale* AL-4
Rice Hollow—*valley* AZ-5
Rice Hollow—*valley* ID-8
Rice Hollow—*valley* (2) IL-6
Rice Hollow—*valley* (2) KY-4
Rice Hollow—*valley* MO-7
Rice Hollow—*valley* PA-2
Rice Hollow—*valley* TN-4
Rice Hollow Sch—*school* KY-4
Rice Hollow Trick Tank—*reservoir* AZ-5
**Rice Hope**—*pop pl* SC-3
Rice Hope Ch—*church* SC-3
Rice Hope Plantation—*locale* SC-3
Rice Hotel—*hist pl* TX-5
Rice House—*hist pl* AR-4
Rice House—*hist pl* KY-4
Rice House—*hist pl* LA-4
Rice HS—*school* MI-6
Rice Island—*island* LA-4
Rice Island—*island* NC-3
Rice Island—*island* TN-4
Rice Island—*island* WI-6
*Rice Junction* MN-6
Rice Knob—*summit* (2) NC-3
Rice Knob—*summit* TN-4
*Rice Lake* AL-4
*Rice Lake* CA-9
*Rice Lake* IN-6
*Rice Lake* MN-6
*Rice Lake* WI-6
Rice Lake—*lake* CA-9
Rice Lake—*lake* FL-3
Rice Lake—*lake* ID-8
Rice Lake—*lake* (2) IL-6
Rice Lake—*lake* (6) MI-6
Rice Lake—*lake* (74) MN-6
Rice Lake—*lake* MT-8
Rice Lake—*lake* NY-2
Rice Lake—*lake* (2) ND-7
Rice Lake—*lake* SD-7
Rice Lake—*lake* TX-5
Rice Lake—*lake* WA-9
Rice Lake—*lake* (22) WI-6
Rice Lake—*locale* MN-6
**Rice Lake**—*pop pl* MN-6
**Rice Lake**—*pop pl* WI-6
Rice Lake—*reservoir* (2) AL-4
Rice Lake—*reservoir* IL-6
Rice Lake—*reservoir* IN-6
Rice Lake—*reservoir* (2) IA-7
Rice Lake—*reservoir* (5) MN-6
Rice Lake—*reservoir* TX-5
Rice Lake—*swamp* CA-9
Rice Lake—*swamp* ND-7
Rice Lake Bog—*swamp* MN-6
Rice Lake Bottoms—*swamp* MN-6
*Rice Lake Branch Zumbro River* MN-6
Rice Lake Cem—*cemetery* (6) MN-6
Rice Lake Ch—*church* MI-6
Rice Lake Ch—*church* MN-6
Rice Lake Country Club—*other* WI-6
Rice Lake Creek—*stream* (2) WI-6
Rice Lake Dam—*dam* IN-6
Rice Lake Dam—*dam* MS-4
Rice Lake Dam—*dam* ND-7
Rice Lake Drain—*stream* MI-6
Rice Lake (historical)—*lake* MO-7
Rice Lake Hut Rings—*hist pl* MN-6
Rice Lake Mounds (47 BN-90)—*hist pl* WI-6
Rice Lake Natl Wildlife Ref—*park* MN-6
Rice Lake Prehistoric District—*hist pl* MN-6
Rice Lakes—*lake* MI-6
Rice Lake Sch—*school* MN-6
Rice Lake Sch—*school* SD-7
Rice Lake State Game Mngmt Area—*park* IA-7
Rice Lake State Park—*park* IA-7
Rice Lake Swamp—*swamp* MN-6
**Rice Lake (Town of)**—*pop pl* WI-6
**Rice Lake Township**—*pop pl* ND-7
**Rice Lake (Township of)**—*pop pl* MN-6
**Riceland**—*pop pl* FL-3
**Riceland**—*pop pl* OH-6
Riceland Hotel—*hist pl* AR-4
Rice Landing—*locale* GA-3
Rice Landing—*locale* NV-8
**Riceland (Township of)**—*pop pl* MN-6
Rice Machine Branch—*stream* FL-3
Rice Machine Pond—*lake* FL-3
Rice-Marler House—*hist pl* TN-4
Rice Marsh Lake—*lake* MN-6
Rice Meadow—*flat* MA-1
Rice Meadow Pond—*lake* MA-1
Rice Meetinghouse—*hist pl* ID-8
Rice Memorial Ch—*church* SC-3
Rice Memorial Park—*park* TN-4
Rice Mill—*locale* NY-2
Rice Mill—*locale* NC-3
Rice Mill Creek—*stream* MS-4
Rice Mill (historical)—*locale* AL-4
*Rice Mine* AL-4
Rice Mine (underground)—*mine* AL-4
Rice Mountain Overlook—*locale* VA-3
Rice Mtn—*summit* AK-9
Rice Mtn—*summit* CO-8
Rice Mtn—*summit* KY-4
Rice Mtn—*summit* (2) NH-1
Rice Mtn—*summit* (2) NY-2
Rice Mtn—*summit* UT-8
Rice Mtn—*summit* VT-1
Rice Mtn—*summit* VA-3
Ricenbaw Sch—*school* NE-7
Rice No 3 Rsvr—*reservoir* WY-8
Rice Oil Field—*oilfield* TX-5
Rice Orchard Ridge—*ridge* KY-4
Rice-Packard House—*hist pl* ID-8
Rice Pad Lake—*lake* MN-6
Rice Park—*flat* NM-5
Rice Park—*park* IN-6
Rice Park—*park* KS-7
Rice Park—*park* MN-6
Rice Patch Bay—*bay* SC-3
Rice Patch Branch—*stream* MS-4
Rice Patch Branch—*stream* NC-3
Ricepatch Creek—*stream* SC-3
Rice Patch Lake—*lake* LA-4
Ricepatch Sch—*school* SC-3
*Rice Path* NC-3
Rice Peak—*summit* (2) AZ-5
Rice Peak—*summit* ID-8
Rice Peak—*summit* NV-8
Rice Peak Trail—*trail* (2) ID-8
Rice-Pennebecker Farm—*hist pl* PA-2
Rice Pinnacle—*summit* NC-3
**Rice Plat**—*pop pl* RI-1
*Rice Point* MN-6
Rice Point—*cape* (2) ME-1
Rice Point—*cape* MI-6
Rice Point—*cape* NY-2
Rice Pond—*lake* MA-1
Rice Pond—*lake* MI-6
Rice Pond—*lake* MN-6
Rice Pond—*lake* NY-2
Rice Pond—*reservoir* AL-4
Rice Pond—*reservoir* MA-1
Rice Pond—*swamp* (2) GA-3
Rice Pond Bay—*swamp* NC-3
Rice Portage Lake—*lake* (2) MN-6
Rice Public Library—*hist pl* ME-1
Rice Public Sch—*school* AZ-5
Rice Ranch—*locale* CA-9
Rice Ranch—*locale* MT-8
Rice Ranch—*locale* NM-5
Rice Ranch Airp—*airport* WA-9
Rice Rapids—*rapids* MN-6
*Rice Reservoir* WI-6
Rice Ridge—*ridge* WV-2
*rice River* WI-6
Rice River—*stream* (3) MN-6
Rice River Cem—*cemetery* MN-6
Rice River Flowage—*channel* WI-6
**Rice River (Township of)**—*pop pl* MN-6
Rice Rocks—*island* OR-9
Rice Rsvr—*reservoir* MA-1
Rice Rsvr—*reservoir* MT-8
Rice Rsvr—*reservoir* NY-2
Rice Rsvr—*reservoir* TX-5
Rice Rsvr—*reservoir* (2) WY-8
Rice Rsvr No 1—*reservoir* WY-8
Rice Run—*stream* PA-2
Rices—*locale* NY-2
Rices Airpark—*airport* ND-7
Rices Branch—*stream* AL-4
Rices Bridge—*bridge* ME-1
*Rices Canyon* TX-5
Rices Canyon—*valley* CA-9
Rice Sch—*school* AL-4
Rice Sch—*school* CA-9
Rice Sch—*school* CT-1
Rice Sch—*school* IL-6
Rice Sch—*school* IN-6
Rice Sch—*school* IA-7
Rice Sch—*school* KS-7
Rice Sch—*school* (2) MA-1
Rice Sch—*school* MI-6
Rice Sch—*school* MN-6
Rice Sch—*school* NC-3
Rice Sch—*school* OH-6
Rice Sch—*school* OR-9
Rice Sch—*school* (2) TX-5
Rice Sch (abandoned)—*school* PA-2
Rices Chapel—*church* AL-4
Rices Chapel—*church* SC-3
*Rices Chapel Ch* AL-4
Rice Sch (historical)—*school* AL-4
Rice Sch (historical)—*school* TN-4
Rice School—*cape* MA-1
*Rices Church* AL-4
Rices Corner—*locale* MO-7
Rices Corners—*locale* NY-2
*Rices Creek* AL-4
*Rices Creek* OR-9
Rices Creek—*stream* PA-2
Rices Creek—*stream* SC-3
Rices Creek Ch—*church* SC-3
*Rices Crossing* MA-1
**Rices Crossing**—*pop pl* TX-5
Rices Crossing School—*locale* TX-5
*Rice's Depot* VA-3
Rice Seeps—*spring* AZ-5
Rices Ferry (historical)—*locale* MA-1
Rices Ferry (historical)—*locale* TN-4
Rices Fork—*stream* KY-4
*Rices Hill* MA-1
Rices Hill Cem—*cemetery* AL-4
*Riceshire* SC-3
Rice Sink Cave—*cave* AL-4
Rice-Skunk Lake State Wildlife Mngmt Area—*park* MN-6
**Rices Landing**—*pop pl* PA-2
Rices Landing Borough—*civil* PA-2
Rices Mill—*building* TN-4
*Rices Mill Pond* MA-1
Rices Mills—*locale* OH-6
**Rices Mills**—*pop pl* VT-1
*Rice's Mountain* NY-2
Rices Path—*locale* NC-3
Rices Pocosin—*swamp* NC-3
Rices Point—*cape* MN-6
*Rices Pond* MA-1
*Rices Pond* VA-3
Rice Spring—*spring* AZ-5
Rice Spring—*spring* CA-9
Rice Spring—*spring* (2) ID-8
Rice Spring—*spring* TN-4
Rice Spring—*spring* (2) WY-8
Rice Springs—*spring* CA-9
Rice Springs Branch—*stream* TX-5
Rice Springs Lake—*reservoir* GA-3
**Rice Square (subdivision)**—*pop pl* MA-1
*Rices Reservoir* MA-1
Rices Run—*stream* PA-2
Rices Run—*stream* WV-2
*Rices School* AL-4
Rices Store (historical)—*locale* TN-4
Rice Stadium—*other* NY-2
Rice Station—*locale* KY-4
Riceston Hill—*summit* AL-4
Rice Straw Strand—*swamp* FL-3
*Rice Street* MN-6
Rice Substation—*locale* AZ-5
Rices Valley Ch—*church* AL-4
Rices Valley Plantation (historical)—*locale* AL-4
*Rice Swamp* NC-3
Rice Switch—*locale* MS-4
Rice's Woods—*hist pl* NY-2
Rice Tank—*reservoir* AZ-5
Rice Tank—*reservoir* TX-5
Rice Tobacco Factory—*hist pl* KY-4
Riceton—*locale* CA-9
Riceton Number 5 Mine (underground)—*mine* AL-4
**Ricetown**—*pop pl* KY-4
**Ricetown**—*pop pl* SC-3
Ricetown Chapel—*church* AL-4

*Riley Creek* AL-4
*Riley Creek* IL-6
*Riley Creek* OH-6
Riley Creek—*stream* (2) AL-4
Riley Creek—*stream* (4) AK-9
Riley Creek—*stream* (3) AR-4
Riley Creek—*stream* GA-3
Riley Creek—*stream* (4) ID-8
Riley Creek—*stream* (2) IL-6
Riley Creek—*stream* (3) KS-7
Riley Creek—*stream* MD-2
Riley Creek—*stream* (3) MI-6
Riley Creek—*stream* MN-6
Riley Creek—*stream* MS-4
Riley Creek—*stream* OH-6
Riley Creek—*stream* (3) OR-9
Riley Creek—*stream* (2) PA-2
Riley Creek—*stream* (4) TN-4
Riley Creek—*stream* (4) TX-5
Riley Creek—*stream* (2) WA-9
Riley Creek—*stream* (4) WI-6
Riley Creek—*stream* WY-8
Riley Creek Butte—*summit* OR-9
*Riley Creek Cave* TN-4
Riley Creek Cem—*cemetery* AR-4
Riley Creek Ch—*church* (2) OH-6
Riley Creek Ch—*church* TN-4
Riley Creek Glacier—*glacier* AK-9
**Riley Creek (historical)**—*pop pl* TN-4
Riley Creek Meadows—*flat* OR-9
Riley Creek Ranger Cabin No. 20—*hist pl* AK-9
Riley Creek Rec Area—*park* ID-8
Riley Creek Rec Area—*park* TN-4
Riley-Cutler House—*hist pl* OR-9
Riley Dam—*dam* OR-9
Riley Ditch—*canal* ID-8
Riley Ditch—*canal* IN-6
Riley Ditch—*canal* WY-8
Riley Drain—*canal* MI-6
Riley Draw—*valley* WY-8
Riley Elem Sch—*school* (3) IN-6
Riley Elem Sch—*school* (3) KS-7
Riley Eleven Drain—*canal* CA-9
Riley Extension Ditch—*canal* CO-8
Riley Field—*airport* IN-6
Riley Field—*park* SC-3
Riley Flat—*flat* WY-8
Riley Ford—*locale* TN-4
Riley Fork—*stream* (2) KY-4
Riley Gas Plant—*oilfield* TX-5
Riley Grange—*locale* OH-6
Riley Grove Ch—*church* TX-5
Riley Gulch—*valley* CA-9
Riley Gulch—*valley* CO-8
Riley Gulch—*valley* ID-8
Riley-Harper Cem—*cemetery* TN-4
*Riley-Harpeth Cem* TN-4
Riley High - Northern Wake Optional Sch—*school* NC-3
**Riley Hill**—*pop pl* NC-3
Riley Hill—*summit* CO-8
Riley Hill—*summit* FL-3
Riley Hill—*summit* KY-4
Riley Hill—*summit* ME-1
Riley Hill—*summit* MI-6
Riley Hill—*summit* OH-6
Riley Hill Cem—*cemetery* WV-2
Riley Hollow—*valley* MO-7
Riley Hollow—*valley* (3) TN-4
Riley Hollow—*valley* WI-6
Riley Horn Point—*cliff* OR-9
Riley Horn Rsvr—*reservoir* OR-9
Riley House Heliport—*airport* MO-7
Riley Huff Place--*locale* OR-9
Riley JHS—*school* MI-6
Riley JHS—*school* TX-5
Riley-Kemper Community Hosp—*hospital* MS-4
Riley Kerr Branch—*stream* TN-4
Riley Knob—*summit* (2) NC-3
*Riley Lake* WI-6
Riley Lake—*lake* AK-9
Riley Lake—*lake* FL-3
Riley Lake—*lake* IN-6
Riley Lake—*lake* (5) MI-6
Riley Lake—*lake* MO-7
Riley Lake—*lake* OK-5
Riley Lake—*lake* WA-9
Riley Lake—*lake* (5) WI-6
Riley Lake—*reservoir* IN-6
Riley Lake—*swamp* FL-3
Riley Lakes—*reservoir* KS-7
Riley Lamb Cem—*cemetery* MO-7
Riley Landing—*locale* FL-3
Riley Lateral—*canal* WY-8
Riley Lateral Eleven—*canal* CA-9
Riley Lateral Nine—*canal* CA-9
Riley Maze Creek—*stream* AL-4
Riley Memorial Baptist Ch—*church* TN-4
Riley Memorial Park—*park* IN-6
Riley Mill Branch—*stream* SC-3
*Riley Mill Creek* SC-3
Riley Mill Creek—*stream* MS-4
Riley Mine (underground)—*mine* AL-4
Riley Mound—*summit* CO-8
Riley Mountains—*summit* TX-5
Riley Mtn—*summit* CO-8
Riley Mtn—*summit* CT-1
Riley Mtn—*summit* GA-3
Riley Mtn—*summit* NH-1
Riley Mtn—*summit* NC-3
Riley Mtn—*summit* OR-9
Riley Mtn—*summit* TN-4
Riley Oil Field—*oilfield* TX-5
Riley Park—*park* (4) IN-6
Riley Park—*park* KS-7
Riley Pass—*gap* SD-7
Riley Peak—*summit* CO-8
Riley Peak—*summit* OR-9
Riley Peaks—*summit* NM-5
Riley Place—*locale* NM-5
Riley Playground—*park* MA-1
Riley Point—*cape* NH-1
Riley Point—*cliff* WY-8
Riley Pond—*lake* AL-4
Riley Pond—*lake* FL-3
Riley Pond—*lake* MA-1
Riley Pond—*lake* SC-3
Riley Ponds—*lake* NY-2
Riley Post Office (historical)—*building* MS-4
Riley Ranch—*locale* CO-8
Riley Ranch—*locale* TX-5
Riley Reservation—*civil* AL-4
Riley Ridge—*ridge* (5) CA-9
Riley Ridge—*ridge* GA-3
Riley Ridge—*ridge* IN-6
Riley Ridge—*ridge* TN-4
Riley Ridge—*ridge* WY-8
Riley Rsvr—*reservoir* OH-6
Riley Rsvr—*reservoir* OR-9
*Riley Run* VA-3
Riley Run—*stream* IL-6
Riley Run—*stream* (3) OH-6
Riley Run—*stream* PA-2
Riley Run—*stream* WV-2
Riley Run Dam—*dam* PA-2
**Rileys**—*pop pl* ME-1
Riley Saddle—*gap* AZ-5
Riley Saddle—*gap* ID-8
Rileys Bay—*bay* WI-6
*Rileys Brook* MA-1
**Rileysburg**—*pop pl* IN-6
**Rileysburg**—*pop pl* MO-7
Rileys Butte—*summit* SD-7
Rileys Canyon—*valley* UT-8
*Riley Sch* IN-6
Riley Sch—*school* AL-4
Riley Sch—*school* (3) CA-9
Riley Sch—*school* CT-1
Riley Sch—*school* FL-3
Riley Sch—*school* (2) GA-3
Riley Sch—*school* (2) IL-6
Riley Sch—*school* (10) IN-6
Riley Sch—*school* IA-7
Riley Sch—*school* ME-1
Riley Sch—*school* MI-6
Riley Sch—*school* NE-7
Riley Sch—*school* OH-6
Riley Sch—*school* OK-5
Riley Sch—*school* UT-8
Riley Sch—*school* (2) WI-6
Riley Sch (historical)—*school* TN-4
Riley School Branch—*stream* WI-6
*Rileys Creek* AL-4
*Rileys Creek* IL-6
*Rileys Creek* TN-4
Rileys Creek—*stream* NC-3
Rileys Creek Cem—*cemetery* NC-3
Rileys Creek Ch—*church* NC-3
*Rileys Crossing* AL-4
Rileys El Encinar—*locale* AZ-5
*Rileys Harbor* RI-1
Rileys Lake—*lake* MN-6
Rileys Lake—*reservoir* TX-5
Riley Slope Mine (underground)—*mine* AL-4
Riley Slough—*stream* CA-9
Riley Slough—*stream* WA-9
Riley Smith Number Two Dam—*dam* AL-4
**Rileys Park (Trailer Park)**—*pop pl* FL-3
Rileys Point—*cape* WI-6
Rileys Pond—*reservoir* SC-3
Riley Spring—*spring* AZ-5
Riley Spring—*spring* (3) NM-5
Riley Spring—*spring* (2) OR-9
Riley Spring—*spring* SD-7
Riley Spring—*spring* UT-8
Riley Spring Bridge—*bridge* DC-2
*Riley Springs* WI-6
Riley Springs—*spring* UT-8
Riley Springs Well—*well* TX-5
**Rileys (Riley)**—*pop pl* WI-6
Rileys Spring Branch—*stream* MD-2
*Rileys Store* AL-4
Riley Store (historical)—*locale* AL-4
**Riley Subdivision**—*pop pl* UT-8
Riley Swamp—*swamp* MI-6
*Riley Tank* AZ-5
Riley Tank—*reservoir* AZ-5
Riley Township—*fmr MCD* IA-7
Riley (Township of)—*fmr MCD* AR-4
**Riley (Township of)**—*pop pl* IL-6
**Riley (Township of)**—*pop pl* IN-6
**Riley (Township of)**—*pop pl* (2) MI-6
**Riley (Township of)**—*pop pl* (2) OH-6
Riley (Township of)—*unorg* ME-1
Riley Valley—*stream* CA-9
*Riley Village* IN-6
**Riley Village**—*pop pl* IN-6
Rileyville—*locale* IL-6
Rileyville—*locale* KY-4
Rileyville—*locale* NJ-2
Rileyville—*locale* PA-2
Rileyville—*locale* VA-3
Rileyville Ch—*church* PA-2
Riley Well—*well* AZ-5
Riley Well—*well* NM-5
Rilgrims Rest Cem—*cemetery* LA-4
Riling Draw—*valley* WY-8
Rilla—*locale* LA-4
Rillas Overflow—*channel* UT-8
Rill Creek—*stream* UT-8
*Rillie Lake* PA-2
Rilling Canyon—*valley* CO-8
Rilling Creek—*stream* CO-8
**Rillito**—*pop pl* AZ-5
*Rillito Creek* AZ-5
Rillito Park and Racetrack—*park* AZ-5
Rillito Racetrack-Chute—*hist pl* AZ-5
Rillito River—*stream* AZ-5
Rillito RR Station—*building* AZ-5
Rillito Vista Park—*park* AZ-5
*Rillito Wash* AZ-5
Rills Cem—*cemetery* MS-4
Rills Pond—*lake* OR-9
**Rillton**—*pop pl* PA-2
Rilma (historical)—*locale* AL-4
Rilma Mine (underground)—*mine* AL-4
Riloel—*bay* FM-9
*Rilol* FM-9
RIL Spring—*spring* OR-9
*Rilton* PA-2
Rim, Lake—*reservoir* NC-3
*Rim, The* AZ-5
Rim, The—*cliff* CA-9
Rim, The—*cliff* ME-1
Rim, The—*gap* WY-8
Rim, The—*ridge* NM-5
Rima Flat—*flat* WA-9
Rima Ridge—*ridge* FL-3
Rim Basin—*basin* OR-9
Rim Butte—*summit* AK-9
**Rimby**—*pop pl* MO-7
Rim Canal—*canal* (2) FL-3
Rim Canyon—*valley* NV-8
Rim Canyon Mine—*mine* UT-8
*Rim Creek* ID-8
Rim Creek—*stream* ID-8
Rim Creek—*stream* OR-9
**Rimcrest**—*pop pl* CA-9
Rim Ditch—*canal* FL-3
Rim Draw—*valley* WY-8
*Rimdraw Creek* WY-8
Rime Cem—*cemetery* IA-7
Rimel—*locale* WV-2
Rime Peak—*summit* AK-9
**Rimer**—*pop pl* NC-3
**Rimer**—*pop pl* OH-6
**Rimer**—*pop pl* PA-2
**Rimersburg**—*pop pl* PA-2
Rimersburg Borough—*civil* PA-2
Rimersburg Elem Sch—*school* PA-2
Rimersburg Station—*locale* PA-2
Rimer Sch—*school* OH-6
*Rimerton* PA-2
**Rimerton**—*pop pl* PA-2
Rimes Cem—*cemetery* (2) MS-4
Rimes Millpond—*lake* SC-3
Rimes Sch—*school* FL-3
**Rimforest**—*pop pl* CA-9
Rimiit—*locale* FM-9
**Rimini**—*pop pl* MT-8
**Rimini**—*pop pl* SC-3
**Rimini (Remini)**—*pop pl* SC-3
Rim Island—*island* WA-9
*Rimit* FM-9
Rim Junction—*locale* NH-1
Rimkus Park—*park* TX-5
Rim Lake—*lake* CA-9
Rim Lake—*lake* (2) CO-8
Rim Lake—*lake* ID-8
Rim Lake—*lake* MI-6
Rim Lake—*lake* OR-9
Rim Lake—*lake* UT-8
Rim Lake—*lake* (2) WY-8
Rimlon—*locale* CA-9
Rimmell Branch—*stream* IN-6
Rimmelspacher Spring—*spring* WA-9
Rimmer Creek—*stream* TN-4
Rimmer Ridge—*ridge* SD-7
Rimmon Brook—*stream* CT-1
Rimmon Hill—*summit* CT-1
*Rimmon Mountain* NH-1
Rim-Moody Point Trail—*trail* AZ-5
Rimmy Jims—*locale* AZ-5
**Rimmy Jims (Trading Post)**—*pop pl* AZ-5
Rimmy Jim Tank—*reservoir* AZ-5
Rim of Green Valley—*ridge* AZ-5
Rim Of The Crater—*cliff* OR-9
Rim of the World HS—*school* CA-9
*Rim of Tonto Basin* AZ-5
*Rimpanai* MH-9
Rimpau—*uninc pl* CA-9
Rim Peak—*summit* NV-8
Rim Pit Tank—*reservoir* AZ-5
Rim Point—*cape* AK-9
Rim Pond—*lake* CO-8
Rim Pond—*reservoir* AZ-5
Rim Powerhouse—*other* CA-9
**Rimroad**—*pop pl* MT-8
Rimrock—*cliff* TX-5
Rimrock—*locale* AZ-5
Rimrock—*locale* CA-9
Rimrock—*locale* MT-8
Rimrock—*locale* WA-9
Rim Rock—*pillar* OR-9
Rimrock—*ridge* NM-5
Rim Rock—*ridge* NM-5
Rim Rock—*ridge* OR-9
Rim Rock—*summit* (2) AZ-5
Rimrock—*summit* ID-8
Rimrock—*summit* NM-5
Rimrock, The—*ridge* MT-8
Rim Rock, The—*summit* UT-8
Rimrock Airp—*airport* AZ-5
Rimrock Basin—*basin* WY-8
Rimrock Butte—*summit* MT-8
Rimrock Campground—*locale* CO-8
Rim Rock Canyon—*valley* CA-9
Rimrock Canyon—*valley* NV-8
Rimrock Cem—*cemetery* ID-8
**Rim Rock Colony**—*pop pl* MT-8
Rimrock Creek—*stream* AK-9
Rimrock Creek—*stream* CO-8
Rimrock Creek—*stream* OR-9
Rimrock Creek—*stream* WA-9
Rimrock Dam—*dam* KS-7
Rimrock Divide—*ridge* MT-8
Rim Rock Draw—*valley* WY-8
Rimrock Draw—*valley* WY-8
Rimrock Gulch—*valley* CO-8
Rimrock Lake—*lake* CA-9
Rimrock Lake—*lake* MT-8
Rimrock Lake—*lake* NM-5
Rimrock Lake—*lake* OR-9
Rimrock Lake—*lake* WY-8
Rim Rock Lake—*reservoir* CO-8
Rimrock Lake—*reservoir* WA-9
Rimrock Meadows Airp—*airport* WA-9
Rim Rock Mine—*mine* CO-8
Rimrock Mine—*mine* NV-8
Rimrock Mtn—*summit* NM-5
Rim Rock No 3 Mine—*mine* CO-8
Rimrock Overlook—*locale* PA-2
Rim Rock Plateau—*plain* WA-9
Rimrock Point—*cape* OR-9
Rimrock Post Office—*building* AZ-5
Rimrock Ranch—*locale* AZ-5
Rim Rock Ranch—*locale* AZ-5
Rim Rock Ranch—*locale* CA-9
Rimrock Ranch—*locale* (2) MT-8
Rim Rock Ranch—*locale* OR-9
Rimrock Ranch—*locale* (2) WY-8
Rimrock Reefs—*ridge* MT-8
*Rimrock Reservoir* WA-9
Rim Rock Resort Ranch—*locale* UT-8
Rimrock Retreat—*locale* WA-9
Rimrock Ridge—*ridge* MT-8
Rimrock Ridge—*ridge* OR-9
Rimrock Ridge—*ridge* WA-9
Rim Rock Rsvr—*reservoir* ID-8
Rimrock Rsvr—*reservoir* MT-8
Rimrock Rsvr—*reservoir* NV-8
Rim Rock Rsvr—*reservoir* OR-9
Rimrock Rsvr—*reservoir* OR-9
Rimrocks—*cliff* MT-8
Rim Rocks—*ridge* CO-8
Rimrocks, The—*cliff* UT-8
Rim Rocks Blues No 6 Mine—*mine* CO-8
Rimrock Sch—*school* MT-8
Rimrock School—*locale* CO-8
Rimrock Spring—*spring* CA-9
Rim Rock Spring—*spring* ID-8
Rimrock Spring—*spring* ID-8
Rim Rock Spring—*spring* MT-8
Rimrock Spring—*spring* (2) NV-8
Rim Rock Spring—*spring* NV-8
Rimrock Spring—*spring* NV-8
Rimrock Spring—*spring* (8) OR-9
Rim Rock Spring—*spring* OR-9
Rimrock Spring—*spring* OR-9
Rimrock Spring—*spring* SD-7
Rimrock Spring—*spring* UT-8
Rim Rock Springs—*spring* OR-9
Rimrock Tank—*reservoir* AZ-5
Rimrock Tank—*reservoir* TX-5
Rim Rock Trail—*trail* OR-9
Rimrock Trail—*trail* OR-9
Rimrock Trail—*trail* SD-7
Rim Rock Trail—*trail* TX-5
Rimrock Valley—*valley* CA-9
Rimrock Valley Rsvr—*reservoir* CA-9
Rimrock Waterhole—*reservoir* OR-9
Rim Rock Well—*well* NM-5
Rimrock Windmill—*locale* NM-5
Rim Rsvr—*reservoir* (3) OR-9
Rim Rsvr—*reservoir* UT-8
Rim Run—*stream* IN-6
*Rims Creek* NC-3
Rim Seep—*spring* UT-8
*Rimski-Kirsakoff Atool Airinginae-to* MP-9
*Rimski-Korsakoff* MP-9
*Rimski-Korsakoff Island* MP-9
*Rimski-Korsakoff Islands* MP-9
*Rimski Korsakov* MP-9
*Rimsky Korsacoff* MP-9
*Rimsky-Korsakoff-Inseln* MP-9
Rim Spring—*spring* (2) CO-8
Rim Spring—*spring* ID-8
Rim Spring—*spring* (2) OR-9
Rim Tank—*reservoir* (7) AZ-5
Rim Tank—*reservoir* (7) NM-5
Rim Tank Basin—*basin* AZ-5
Rimtop Spring—*spring* OR-9
Rim Trail—*trail* CA-9
Rim Trail—*trail* CO-8
Rim Trail—*trail* UT-8
Rim View—*locale* UT-8
Rinadis Well—*well* CA-9
Rinaker, Lake—*reservoir* IL-6
Rinaman Run—*stream* PA-2
**Rinard**—*pop pl* IL-6
**Rinard**—*pop pl* IA-7
**Rinard**—*pop pl* WV-2
Rinard Covered Bridge—*hist pl* OH-6
Rinard Creek—*stream* TX-5
Rinard House—*hist pl* MT-8
**Rinard Mills**—*pop pl* OH-6
Rinard North Oil Field—*other* IL-6
Rinard Prong—*canal* IN-6
*Rinch's Island* CT-1
Rinckel—*locale* CA-9
Rinckel Mansion—*hist pl* NV-8
Rincker Cem—*cemetery* IL-6
**Rinco**—*pop pl* PR-3
*Rincoln Creek* CO-8
Rincom Creek—*stream* WA-9
Rincon—*basin* CA-9
Rincon—*CDP* PR-3
Rincon—*locale* AZ-5
Rincon—*locale* CA-9
Rincon—*locale* TX-5
**Rincon**—*pop pl* CA-9
**Rincon**—*pop pl* GA-3
**Rincon**—*pop pl* IN-6
**Rincon**—*pop pl* NM-5
**Rincon**—*pop pl* PR-3
Rincon, Canon—*valley* CO-8
Rincon, The—*basin* (3) AZ-5
Rincon, The—*basin* (2) UT-8
Rincon, The—*cliff* AZ-5
Rincon, The—*cliff* CO-8
Rincon, The—*summit* NM-5
*Rinconada* AZ-5
**Rinconada**—*pop pl* NM-5
Rinconada—*valley* NM-5
Rinconada Canyon—*valley* (2) NM-5
*Rinconada Creek* NM-5
Rinconada Creek—*stream* CA-9
Rinconada Creek—*stream* (2) NM-5
Rinconada Del Arroyo De San Francisquito—*civil* CA-9
Rinconada del Cochino—*valley* NM-5
Rinconada De Los Gatos—*civil* CA-9
Rinconada Isla Ditch—*canal* NM-5
Rinconada Mine—*mine* CA-9
Rinconada Park—*park* CA-9
Rinconada Sch—*school* CA-9
Rinconada Spring—*spring* AZ-5
**Rinconado**—*pop pl* NM-5
*Rinconado Creek* CA-9
Rincon Agua Verde—*area* NM-5
Rincon Alpejo—*valley* NM-5
Rincon Amarillo—*area* NM-5
Rincon Annex—*hist pl* CA-9
Rincon Annex—*uninc pl* CA-9
Rincon Anzures—*valley* NM-5
Rincon Apache—*valley* NM-5
Rincon Arroyo—*stream* NM-5
Rincon Artesian Well—*well* TX-5
Rincon Ave Sch—*school* CA-9
Rincon Bajito—*area* NM-5
Rincon (Barrio)—*fmr MCD* (4) PR-3
Rincon Basin—*basin* (2) AZ-5
Rincon Basin—*basin* NM-5
Rincon Bayou—*gut* TX-5
Rincon Beach—*beach* CA-9
Rincon Bend—*bend* (2) TX-5
Rincon Blanco—*area* NM-5
Rincon Bonito—*area* (2) NM-5
Rincon Bonito Canyon—*valley* CO-8
*Rincon Branch* GA-3
Rincon Branch—*stream* GA-3
Rincon Buena Vista—*cape* TX-5
Rincon Camp—*locale* NM-5
Rincon Canal—*canal* NM-5
Rincon Canyon—*valley* AZ-5
Rincon Canyon—*valley* CA-9
Rincon Canyon—*valley* CO-8
Rincon Canyon—*valley* (4) NM-5
Rincon Canyon—*valley* (2) TX-5
Rincon Canyon—*valley* UT-8
Rincon (CCD)—*cens area* GA-3
Rincon Cem—*cemetery* GA-3
Rincon Cem—*cemetery* NM-5
Rincon Channel—*channel* TX-5
Rincon Chavez—*basin* NM-5
Rincon Chiquito, Loma del—*summit* TX-5
Rincon Colorado—*area* NM-5
Rincon Colorado—*other* NM-5
*Rincon Creek* GA-3
Rincon Creek—*stream* AZ-5
Rincon Creek—*stream* (4) CA-9
Rincon Creek—*stream* (2) CO-8
Rincon Creek—*stream* NV-8
Rincon Creek—*stream* (2) NM-5
Rincon Creek—*stream* OR-9
Rincon Dam—*dam* AZ-5
Rincon De Cochino—*area* NM-5
Rincon de Ebaristo—*valley* NM-5
Rincon de Flores Tank—*reservoir* TX-5
*Rincon de Guajardo* TX-5
Rincon de Guajardo—*cape* TX-5
Rincon de Jaques—*basin* NM-5
Rincon De La Brea—*civil* CA-9
Rincon de la Ciruelita—*area* NM-5
Rincon de la Gorda—*valley* NM-5
Rincon del Aguila—*area* NM-5
Rincon de la Manzanita—*valley* NM-5
Rincon De La Puente Del Monte—*civil* CA-9
Rincon de la Soledad—*basin* TX-5
Rincon de las Salinas—*civil* CA-9
Rincon de las Viejas—*summit* TX-5
Rincon del Cuervo—*basin* NM-5
Rincon Del Cuervo—*ridge* NM-5
Rincon del Dado—*valley* NM-5
Rincon Del Diablo—*civil* CA-9
Rincon del Leon—*valley* NM-5
Rincon De Los Bueyes—*civil* CA-9
Rincon De Los Carneros—*civil* CA-9
Rincon De Los Esteros—*civil* CA-9
Rincon del Oso—*cliff* NM-5
Rincon de los Soldados—*summit* (2) NM-5
Rincon de los Viejos—*valley* NM-5
Rincon de Mora—*ridge* NM-5
Rincon De Musalacon—*civil* CA-9
Rincon de Rosendo Padilla—*valley* NM-5
Rincon De San Francisquito—*civil* CA-9
Rincon De Sanjon—*civil* CA-9
*Rincon de San Jose* TX-5
Rincon de San Jose—*summit* TX-5
Rincon de Tio Francisquito—*basin* NM-5
Rincon de Tio Luis Windmill—*locale* TX-5
Rincon de Tio Pandho Windmill—*locale* TX-5
Rincon de Zixto—*area* NM-5
Rincon Dikes—*levee* NM-5
Rincon Ditch—*canal* CO-8
Rincon Drain—*canal* NM-5
Rincon Draw—*valley* NM-5
Rincon Entranosa—*valley* NM-5
Rincon Entranoso—*area* (2) NM-5
Rincon Flats—*flat* NM-5
Rincon Grande—*summit* PR-3
Rincon Grande—*valley* NM-5
Rincon Grande Tank—*reservoir* NM-5
Rincon Hill—*summit* CA-9
Rincon Hondo—*area* NM-5
Rincon Hondo—*valley* (2) NM-5
Rincon Hondo Canyon—*valley* NM-5
Rincon Hondo Windmill—*locale* NM-5
Rincon HS—*school* AZ-5
**Rincon Ind Res**—*pop pl* CA-9
Rincon Lake—*lake* OR-9
Rincon La Osa—*valley* CO-8
Rincon Largo—*summit* TX-5
Rincon Largo—*valley* (3) NM-5
Rincon Largo Ruin (LA 2436 and LA 2435)—*hist pl* NM-5
Rincon Lateral—*canal* NM-5
Rincon La Vaca—*valley* CO-8
Rincon Leandro—*valley* NM-5
Rincon Lobo—*valley* NM-5
Rincon Madera—*valley* NM-5
Rincon Marquez—*valley* NM-5
Rincon Marquez Arroyo—*stream* NM-5
Rincon Mine—*mine* AZ-5
**Rincon Montoso**—*pop pl* NM-5
Rincon Mountain Foothills Archeol District—*hist pl* AZ-5
Rincon Mountains—*other* NM-5
Rincon Mountains—*ridge* AZ-5
Rincon Mtn—*summit* CA-9
Rincon Mtn—*summit* TX-5
Rincon (Municipio)—*civil* PR-3
Rincon Negro—*basin* NM-5
Rincon Negro—*pillar* NM-5
Rincon Oil Field—*oilfield* TX-5
Rincon Pass—*gap* AZ-5
Rincon Peak—*summit* AZ-5
Rincon Peak—*summit* NM-5
Rincon Peak—*summit* TX-5
Rincon Point—*cape* (2) CA-9
Rincon Point—*cape* TX-5
Rincon (Pueblo)—*fmr MCD* PR-3
Rincon Quemado—*valley* CO-8
Rincon Quemado—*valley* NM-5
Rincon Ranch—*locale* (2) AZ-5
Rincon Rayado—*stream* NM-5
*Rincon Refugio* CA-9
Rincon Rockshelter (LA 55835)—*hist pl* NM-5
Rincon Sanitorium—*hospital* AZ-5
Rincon Sch—*school* AZ-5
Rincon Sch—*school* TX-5
Rincon Seco House Windmill—*locale* TX-5
Rincon Siphon—*other* NM-5
Rincon Spring—*spring* (3) AZ-5
Rincon Spring—*spring* NM-5
Rincon Spring—*spring* OR-9
Rincon Springs—*spring* OR-9
Rincon Tank—*reservoir* (10) AZ-5
Rincon Tank—*reservoir* (6) NM-5
Rincon Tank—*reservoir* (9) TX-5
Rincon Trail—*trail* (2) CA-9
Rincon Valley—*basin* CA-9
Rincon Valley—*uninc pl* CA-9
Rincon Valley—*valley* AZ-5
Rincon Valley—*valley* NM-5
Rincon Valley JHS—*school* CA-9
Rincon Valley Sch—*school* CA-9
Rincon Vigil—*area* NM-5
Rincon Well—*well* AZ-5
Rincon Wells—*well* AZ-5
Rincon Windmill—*locale* CO-8
Rincon Windmill—*locale* (5) NM-5
Rincon Windmill—*locale* (8) TX-5
**Rinda**—*pop pl* TN-4
Rindahl Creek—*stream* WI-6
Rindahl Lake—*lake* MN-6
Rindahl State Wildlife Mngmt Area—*park* MN-6
**Rindal**—*pop pl* MN-6
Rindal Cem—*cemetery* MN-6
Rindal Ch—*church* MN-6
Rindal Ranch—*locale* MT-8
Rinderle Sch—*school* OH-6
Rindesbacher Creek—*stream* IL-6
Rindfleisch Bldg—*hist pl* WI-6
**Rindge**—*pop pl* NH-1
Rindge, Frederick Hastings, House—*hist pl* CA-9
Rindge Cem—*cemetery* CT-1
Rindge Memorial Sch—*school* NH-1
Rindge Mine Number One—*mine* CA-9
Rindge Mine Number Three—*mine* CA-9
Rindge Sch—*school* CA-9
Rindge Sch—*school* MA-1
**Rindge (Town of)**—*pop pl* NH-1
Rindge Tract—*civil* CA-9
Rindler Creek—*stream* CA-9
Rindlishbaker Canyon—*valley* ID-8
Rindy Grove Cem—*cemetery* AR-4
Rinearson Point—*ridge* OR-9
Rinearson Slough—*stream* OR-9
*Rinearsons Slough* OR-9
Rine Cem—*cemetery* MD-2
Rine Corners—*locale* OH-6
Rineer Cave—*cave* PA-2
**Rinehart**—*pop pl* MO-7
**Rinehart**—*pop pl* WV-2
Rinehart, Hugh T., House—*hist pl* OH-6
Rinehart and White Dock (Floating moorage)—*locale* NC-3
Rinehart Branch—*stream* KY-4
Rinehart Branch—*stream* MS-4
*Rinehart Brook* NJ-2
Rinehart Canyon—*valley* OR-9
Rinehart Cem—*cemetery* IL-6
Rinehart Cem—*cemetery* KS-7
Rinehart Cem—*cemetery* (2) MO-7
Rinehart Cem—*cemetery* TN-4
Rinehart Cem—*cemetery* WV-2
Rinehart County (historical)—*civil* SD-7
*Rinehart Creek* OR-9
Rinehart Creek—*stream* (2) OR-9
Rinehart Creek Rsvr—*reservoir* OR-9
Rinehart JHS—*school* AL-4
Rinehart Lake—*lake* TX-5
Rinehart Lake—*lake* WI-6
Rinehart Lakes—*lake* WY-8
Rinehart Ranch—*locale* OR-9
*Rinehart Rsvr* OR-9
Rinehart Run—*stream* WV-2
Rinehart Sch—*school* MO-7
Rinehart Spring—*spring* OR-9
Rinehart Tank—*reservoir* (2) AZ-5
**Rinehart Township**—*pop pl* KS-7
Rinehart Tunnel—*tunnel* VA-3
Rinehart Wash Hole—*lake* AL-4
Rine Lake—*lake* IN-6
Rineltown—*locale* KY-4
Rinely—*locale* PA-2
Rineman Ditch—*canal* OR-9
**Riner**—*pop pl* VA-3
**Riner**—*pop pl* WY-8
Riner Cem—*cemetery* (2) VA-3
Riner Houseworth Ditch—*canal* IN-6
Riner Lake—*reservoir* NM-5
Riner (Magisterial District)—*fmr MCD* VA-3
Riner Mesa—*summit* NM-5
Riner Sch—*school* IL-6
Riner Sch—*school* VA-3
Rines Creek—*stream* NC-3
Rines Hill—*summit* NH-1
Rines Ridge—*ridge* WV-2
Riney, Zachariah, House—*hist pl* KY-4
*Riney Branch* AR-4
Riney (RR name for Rineyville)—*other* KY-4
**Rineyville**—*pop pl* KY-4
Rineyville Cem—*cemetery* KY-4
**Rineyville (RR name Riney)**—*pop pl* KY-4
Rinfroe Springs—*spring* OR-9
Ring—*locale* OR-9
Ring—*locale* WI-6
Ring, Lake—*lake* FL-3
Ring, Walter, House and Mill Site—*hist pl* OH-6
Ring Arch—*arch* UT-8
Ringbo Ch—*church* MN-6
Ringbolt Rapids—*rapids* AZ-5
Ringbolt Rapids—*rapids* NV-8
Ringbone Cayuse Mine—*mine* ID-8
Ringbone Lake—*lake* WY-8
Ringbone Ranch—*locale* NM-5
Ring Branch—*stream* MO-7
Ring Brook—*stream* CT-1
Ring Brook—*stream* ME-1
Ring Brook—*stream* NH-1
Ring Butte—*summit* OR-9
Ring Canyon—*valley* NM-5
Ring Canyon Trail (Pack)—*trail* NM-5
Ring Cem—*cemetery* OH-6
Ring Cem—*cemetery* (2) TN-4
Ring Cem—*cemetery* (2) VA-3
Ring Ch—*church* AR-4
Ring Ch—*church* TX-5
Ring Chapel—*church* VA-3
Ring Cone Tank—*reservoir* AZ-5
Ringcone Tank—*reservoir* AZ-5
Ring Corral Creek—*stream* OR-9
Ring Creek—*stream* AK-9
Ring Creek—*stream* ID-8

Rio Rico Calabasas Interchange—crossing AZ-5
Rio River WY-8
Rio Roncador—stream PR-3
Rio Rosario—stream PR-3
Rio Rsvr—reservoir NY-2
Rio Ruidoso—stream NM-5
Rios—locale TX-5
Rio Sabana—stream PR-3
Rio Salado AZ-5
Rio Salado TX-5
Rio Salado—post sta AZ-5
Rio Salado—stream (2) NM-5
Rio Salado Industrial Recreation Park—park AZ-5
Rio Saliente—stream PR-3
Rio Salientito—stream PR-3
Rio Saltillo—stream PR-3
Rio Sana Muerto—stream PR-3
Rio San Antonio—stream NM-5
Rio san Augustin TX-5
Rio San Carlos AZ-5
Rio San Domingo AZ-5
Rio San Francisco AZ-5
Rio San Gabriel Park—park CA-9
Rio San Gabriel Sch—school CA-9
Rio San Jacinto TX-5
Rio San Jose—stream NM-5
Rio San Leonardo—stream NM-5
Rio San Patricio—stream PR-3
Rio San Pedro AZ-5
Rio Santa Barbara—stream NM-5
Rio Santa Cruz AZ-5
Rio Santa Maria AZ-5
Rio Santa Teresa AZ-5
Rio Santiago—stream PR-3
Rio San Ybon TX-5
Rio Sapo—stream PR-3
Rio Sauz AZ-5
Rios (Barrio)—fmr MCD PR-3
Rios Canyon—valley CA-9
Rio Seco—stream PR-3
Rio Sonador—stream PR-3
Rioso Rsvr—reservoir AZ-5
Rio St Jua de Cuacara FL-3
Rio Suez AZ-5
Rio Tallaboa—stream PR-3
Rio Tanama—stream PR-3
Rio Tank—reservoir AZ-5
Rio Tecate CA-9
Rio Tenmile Wash AZ-5
Rio Tesuque—stream NM-5
Rio Tiajuana CA-9
Rio Tierra JHS—school CA-9
Rio Tijuana CA-9
Rio Tinto Mine—mine NV-8
Rio Toa Vaca—stream PR-3
Rio Toro—stream PR-3
Rio Toro Negro—stream PR-3
Rio (Township of)—pop pl IL-6
Rio Tularosa NM-5
Rio Turabo—stream PR-3
Rio Tusas—stream NM-5
Riou Bay—bay AK-9
Rio Unibon—stream PR-3
Rio Usabon—stream PR-3
Riou Spit AK-9
Rio Vacas—stream PR-3
Rio Valdez—stream NM-5
Rio Valenciano—stream PR-3
Rio Vallecitos—stream NM-5
Rio Veguitas—stream PR-3
Rio Verde AZ-5
Rio Verde CO-8
Rio Verde UT-8
Rio Verde—pop pl AZ-5
Rio Verde Country Club Golf Course—other AZ-5
Rio Verde Well—well AZ-5
Rio Vetaderos TX-5
Rio Viejo—stream PR-3
Rioville and Old Bonelli Ferry (historical)—locale NV-8
Rio Virgin UT-8
Rio Vista TN-4
Rio Vista—locale AR-4
Rio Vista—pop pl CA-9
Rio Vista—pop pl GA-3
Rio Vista—pop pl KY-4
Rio Vista—pop pl MD-2
Rio Vista—pop pl MA-1
Riovista—pop pl TN-4
Rio Vista—pop pl TN-4
Rio Vista—pop pl TX-5
Riovista—pop pl WY-8
Rio Vista—uninc pl GA-3
Rio Vista Campsite—locale TX-5
Rio Vista (CCD)—cens area CA-9
Rio Vista Farms—locale TX-5
Rio Vista Gas Field (2) CA-9
Rio Vista Golf Course—locale FL-3
Rio Vista Isles—pop pl FL-3
Rio Vista Junction—locale CA-9
Rio Vista Mine—mine AZ-5
Rio Vista Sch—school AZ-5
Rio Vista Sch—school (4) CA-9
Rio Vista Sch—school FL-3
Rio Vista Sch—school TX-5
Rio Vista Subdivision—pop pl UT-8
Rio Vivi—stream PR-3
Rio West Run—stream IN-6
Rio Yaguez—stream PR-3
Rio Yahuecas—stream PR-3
Rio Yauco—stream PR-3
Rioyo FM-9
Rio Yunes—stream PR-3
Rio Zamas—stream PR-3
Rip, Point—bar MA-1
Ripaco—pop pl NC-3
Riparia—locale WA-9
Riparia State Wildlife Mngmt Area—park MN-6
Riparius—pop pl NY-2
Riparius (RR name Riverside)—pop pl NY-2
Rip Current MH-9
Rip Current Lake MH-9
Rip Current Point MH-9
Ripgut Creek—stream CA-9
Ripgut Creek—stream UT-8
Ripgut Springs—spring UT-8
Rip Hewes Stadium—other AL-4
Ripinski, Mount—summit AK-9
Ripka Trail—trail PA-2
Rip Lake—lake MN-6
Rip Lake—lake NM-5
Ripley IN-6
Ripley—locale MO-7
Ripley—locale (2) MT-8
Ripley—locale NV-8
Ripley—pop pl AL-4
Ripley—pop pl CA-9
Ripley—pop pl GA-3
Ripley—pop pl IL-6
Ripley—pop pl IN-6
Ripley—pop pl (2) ME-1
Ripley—pop pl MD-2
Ripley—pop pl MI-6
Ripley—pop pl MS-4
Ripley—pop pl NY-2
Ripley—pop pl OH-6
Ripley—pop pl OK-5
Ripley—pop pl TN-4
Ripley—pop pl WV-2
Ripley, Lake—lake MN-6
Ripley, Lake—lake WI-6
Ripley Airp—airport MS-4
Ripley Area Vocational Technical Sch—school TN-4
Ripley Beach—beach NY-2
Ripley Branch—stream TN-4
Ripley Brook—stream MA-1
Ripley Butte—summit ID-8
Ripley Canyon—valley NV-8
Ripley (CCD)—cens area TN-4
Ripley Cem—cemetery AL-4
Ripley Cem—cemetery IL-6
Ripley Cem—cemetery MS-4
Ripley Cem—cemetery OH-6
Ripley Cem—cemetery PA-2
Ripley (census name for Ripley Center)—CDP NY-2
Ripley Center (census name Ripley)—other NY-2
Ripley Ch—church AL-4
Ripley Ch—church OH-6
Ripley Ch—church TN-4
Ripley Ch—church TX-5
Ripley Chapel—church MO-7
Ripley Chapel—church WV-2
Ripley Ch of Christ—church MS-4
Ripley City Hall—building TN-4
Ripley Clinic—hospital TN-4
Ripley Colored School MS-4
Ripley County—pop pl IN-6
Ripley County—pop pl MO-7
Ripley County Courthouse—hist pl MO-7
Ripley County Fairground—locale MO-7
Ripley Cove ME-1
Ripley Cove—bay ME-1
Ripley Cove—cove MA-1
Ripley Creek MA-1
Ripley Creek—stream CA-9
Ripley Creek—stream IN-6
Ripley Creek—stream TN-4
Ripley Creek—stream TX-5
Ripley Creek—stream VA-3
Ripley Creek—stream WA-9
Ripley Creek—stream WI-6
Ripley Creek—stream WY-8
Ripley Creek Ch—church TX-5
Ripley Cumberland Presbyterian Ch (historical)—church MS-4
Ripley Division—civil TN-4
Ripley Elem Sch—school MS-4
Ripley Elem Sch—school TN-4
Ripley Falls—falls NH-1
Ripley Female Acad—school MS-4
Ripley First Baptist Ch—church MS-4
Ripley First Baptist Ch—church TN-4
Ripley First Colored Baptist Ch MS-4
Ripley First United Methodist Ch—church MS-4
Ripley Foundation—building TX-5
Ripley Gulch—valley OR-9
Ripley Hill—summit NY-2
Ripley Hist Dist—hist pl OH-6
Ripley Hollow—valley (2) AR-4
Ripley House—hist pl OH-6
Ripley HS—school MS-4
Ripley HS—school TN-4
Ripley Institute (historical)—school MS-4
Ripley Intaglios—hist pl AZ-5
Ripley Island—island TN-4
Ripley Islands—island ME-1
Ripley JHS—school TN-4
Ripley Knob—summit KY-4
Ripley Lake WI-6
Ripley Lake—lake (2) WI-6
Ripley Lake—reservoir MO-7
Ripley Lake Rec Area—park MO-7
Ripley Landing WV-2
Ripley Landing—locale WV-2
Ripley (Magisterial District)—fmr MCD WV-2
Ripley Male and Female Acad (historical)—school MS-4
Ripley MS—school MS-4
Ripley MS—school TN-4
Ripley Neck—cape ME-1
Ripley Park—park (2) KS-7
Ripley Park—park NM-5
Ripley Plaza Shop Ctr—locale TN-4
Ripley Point—cape NY-2
Ripley Point—summit NM-5
Ripley Pond—lake ME-1
Ripley Post Office—building TN-4
Ripley Post Office (historical)—building AL-4
Ripley Presbyterian Ch—church MS-4
Ripley Primitive Baptist Ch—church MS-4
Ripley Public Library—building MS-4
Ripley Ranch—locale WY-8
Ripley Rock—island MI-6
Ripley Run—stream IN-6
Ripley Run—stream OH-6
Ripleys WV-2
Ripley Sch—school MA-1
Ripley Sch—school OH-6
Ripley Second Baptist Ch—church MS-4
Ripley Sewage Lagoon Dam—dam MS-4
Ripley Shoal—bar MI-6
Ripley Spring—spring NV-8
Ripleys Run—stream PA-2
Ripleys Run—stream WV-2
Ripley Stone House—hist pl TN-4
Ripley Stream—stream ME-1
Ripley Swamp—swamp CT-1
Ripley (Town of)—pop pl ME-1
Ripley (Town of)—pop pl NY-2
Ripley Township—fmr MCD IA-7
Ripley (Township of)—pop pl IL-6
Ripley (Township of)—pop pl (2) IN-6
Ripley (Township of)—pop pl (2) MN-6
Ripley (Township of)—pop pl (2) OH-6
Riplinger—pop pl WI-6
Ripling Waters—pop pl WV-2
Riplow Marsh—swamp MI-6
Ripogenous Lake ME-1
Ripogenus Dam—dam ME-1
Ripogenus Gorge—valley ME-1
Ripogenus Lake—reservoir ME-1
Ripogenus Pond—lake ME-1
Ripogenus Stream ME-1
Ripogenus Stream—stream (2) ME-1
Ripoli—pop pl PR-3
Ripon—pop pl CA-9
Ripon—pop pl WI-6
Ripona Sch—school CA-9
Ripon (CCD)—cens area CA-9
Ripon Coll—school WI-6
Ripon Glacier—glacier AK-9
Ripon (historical)—locale ND-7
Ripon Junction—uninc pl WI-6
Ripon Lodge—hist pl WV-2
Ripon (Town of)—pop pl WI-6
Rippee Creek—stream (2) MO-7
Rippee Island—island ID-8
Rippee Ranch—locale NM-5
Rippee State Wildlife Mngmt Area—park MO-7
Rippee Well—well NM-5
Rippel Field—park NJ-2
Rippentuck WV-2
Ripper Creek—stream MT-8
Ripperdan—pop pl CA-9
Ripperdan Ditch—canal CA-9
Ripperdan Sch—school CA-9
Ripper Hollow—valley PA-2
Ripper Spring—spring AZ-5
Ripper Spring Canyon—valley AZ-5
Ripper Tank—reservoir AZ-5
Ripperton Mine—mine CA-9
Rippet Mtn—summit OR-9
Rippetoe Mtn—summit NC-3
Rippey—pop pl IA-7
Rippey House—hist pl OR-9
Rippey Ridge—ridge TN-4
Rippey Ridge Cove—cave TN-4
Rippeys Corners—locale NY-2
Rippey State Access Area—park IA-7
Rippin Run—stream VA-3
Ripple—locale CO-8
Ripple—pop pl PA-2
Ripple, Lake—reservoir MA-1
Ripple, Otto, Agency—hist pl MO-7
Ripplebrook Forest Camp—locale OR-9
Ripple Cem—cemetery OH-6
Ripple Corners—locale NY-2
Ripple Cove—bay (2) AK-9
Ripple Creek MN-6
Ripple Creek—stream CA-9
Ripple Creek—stream CO-8
Ripple Creek—stream OR-9
Ripple Creek—stream WI-6
Ripple Creek Pass—gap CO-8
Ripple (historical)—pop pl OR-9
Ripple (historical)—pop pl PA-2
Ripple Hollow—valley PA-2
Ripple House—hist pl SD-7
Ripple Island—island MN-6
Ripple Island—island WA-9
Ripple Lake MA-1
Ripple Lake OR-9
Ripple Lake—lake MI-6
Ripple Lake—lake MN-6
Ripple Lake—lake MT-8
Ripplemead—pop pl VA-3
Ripple Pond—lake ME-1
Ripple River—stream MN-6
Ripple River State Wildlife Mngmt Area—park MN-6
Ripple Sch—school PA-2
Rippleside Sch—school MN-6
Ripples Rsvr—reservoir ID-8
Rippleton—pop pl NY-2
Rippleton Creek—stream OR-9
Rippletown—pop pl PA-2
Ripple Valley—valley UT-8
Rippley Gulch—valley CA-9
Rippling Brook—stream CO-8
Rippling Estates—pop pl MD-2
Rippling Ridge—pop pl MD-2
Rippling Run—stream PA-2
Rip Point—cape (2) AK-9
Rippon—pop pl WV-2
Rippon Lodge—hist pl VA-3
Rippon Mine—mine CA-9
Rippon Sch—school VA-3
Rippowam, Lake—lake NY-2
Rippowam HS—school CT-1
Rippowam River—stream CT-1
Rippowam River—stream NY-2
Rippowam Sch—school NY-2
Rippowan river CT-1
Rippy Branch—stream TX-5
Rippy Cem—cemetery MO-7
Rippy Run—stream OH-6
Rippy Sch—school MO-7
Rippys Island (historical)—island TN-4
Rip Rap—pop pl VA-3
Riprap Coulee—valley MT-8
Riprap Creek—stream WA-9
Riprap Dam—dam CO-8
Riprap Hollow—valley VA-3
Riprap Island—island IA-7
Rip Rap Landing State Fish And Waterfowl Mngmt Area—park IL-6
Rip-Raps VA-3
Riprap Shelter—locale VA-3
Rip Raps Plantation—hist pl SC-3
Riprap Springs—spring NV-8
Rip Rap Tank—reservoir AZ-5
Riprap Tank—reservoir NM-5
Riprap Trail—trail VA-3
Rip Rock—bar AK-9
Rip Rock—island AK-9
Ripsaw Ridge—ridge WA-9
Rips Dam—dam ME-1
Ripsey Hill—summit AZ-5
Ripsey Ranch—locale AZ-5
Ripsey Spring—spring AZ-5
Ripsey Wash—stream AZ-5
Ripshin—hist pl VA-3
Ripshin—summit GA-3
Ripshin Branch—stream (2) NC-3
Ripshin Creek—stream VA-3
Ripshin Dam—dam TN-4
Ripshin Lake—lake TN-4
Ripshin Lake—reservoir TN-4
Rip Shin Mountain TN-4
Rip Shin Mtn NC-3
Ripshin Mtn—summit (2) NC-3
Rip Shin Post Office (historical)—building TN-4
Ripshin Ridge—ridge AL-4
Ripshin Ridge—ridge KY-4
Ripshin Ridge—ridge NC-3
Ripshin Ridge—ridge TN-4
Rips Lake—reservoir TX-5
Rip Slough—reservoir IL-6
Ripsnorter Creek—stream AK-9
Rip Spring—spring AZ-5
Ripstein Camp—locale CA-9
Ripstein Creek—stream TX-5
Ripstein Gulch—valley CA-9
Ripton CT-1
Ripton—pop pl VT-1
Ripton Community House—hist pl VT-1
Ripton (Town of)—pop pl VT-1
Rip Van Winkle, Lake—reservoir NY-2
Rip Van Winkle Bridge—bridge NY-2
Rip Van Winkle Hollow—valley NY-2
Rip Van Winkle Mine—mine AZ-5
Rip Van Winkle Mine—mine NV-8
Ripville Mill (historical)—locale AL-4
Ripy, T. B., House—hist pl KY-4
Ripyville—pop pl KY-4
Riqiir—cape FM-9
Riquen FM-9
Riqueza Artesian Well—well TX-5
Riri MP-9
Ririe—pop pl ID-8
Ririe Cem—cemetery ID-8
Ririe Lake—lake ID-8
Ri Rii Island MP-9
Riri Island MP-9
Riri Island—island MP-9
Ririi-to MP-9
Rirs Bital—island PW-9
Risbeck—locale WA-9
Risberg Lake—lake WI-6
Risby Cem—cemetery MO-7
Risco—pop pl MO-7
Risco Park—park FL-3
Risden NC-3
Rise Branch—stream MO-7
Rise Mill Hollow—valley TN-4
Rise Mills Post Office (historical)—building TN-4
Risen Cem—cemetery KY-4
Rise of Crab Creek WA-9
Riser Butte—summit OR-9
Riser Cem—cemetery LA-4
Riser Chapel—church AL-4
Riser Creek NV-8
Riser Creek—stream ID-8
Riser Creek—stream MS-4
Riser Creek—stream NV-8
Riser Creek—stream (2) OR-9
Riser Dam—dam AL-4
Riser Ditch—stream NJ-2
Riser Lake—lake OR-9
Riser Lake—reservoir AL-4
Riser Mine—mine AL-4
Riser Mtn AL-4
Riser Mtn—summit AL-4
Risers—pop pl AL-4
Risers Mill AL-4
Risers Store AL-4
Rishaberger Gulch—valley CO-8
Rishaberger Mtn—summit CO-8
Rishaberger Spring—spring CO-8
Rishabh Mountain OR-9
Rish Cem—cemetery TX-5
Rishel—locale KS-7
Rishel Covered Bridge—hist pl PA-2
Rishelieu—pop pl PA-2
Rishel JHS—school CO-8
Rishell Run—stream PA-2
Rishell Peak—summit UT-8
Risher—locale AR-4
Risher Lake Dam—dam MS-4
Risher Mine Siding—uninc pl PA-2
Rish Well—well NM-5
Rising NE-7
Rising—locale IL-6
Rising—locale ND-7
Rising—other MA-1
Rising—pop pl PA-2
Rising Bull Ridge—ridge MT-8
Rising Butte—summit ID-8
Rising Cem—cemetery NC-3
Rising Ch—church ND-7
Rising Chapel—church MS-4
Rising Chapel Cem—cemetery MS-4
Rising City—pop pl NE-7
Rising Corner—pop pl CT-1
Rising Creek—stream ID-8
Rising Creek—stream MO-7
Rising Dale MA-1
Risingdale—pop pl MA-1
Risingdale (Rising)—pop pl MA-1
Risinger Cem—cemetery SC-3
Risinger Creek—stream TX-5
Risinger Hill—summit TX-5
Risinger Run—stream PA-2
Risinger Sch—school PA-2
Risinger Woods—pop pl LA-4
Rising Fawn—pop pl GA-3
Rising Grove Ch—church GA-3
Rising Hail Colony—hist pl SD-7
Rising Mountain Trail—trail PA-2
Rising Mount Zion Ch—church (3) VA-3
Rising Mtn—summit PA-2
Rising Paper Company Dam—dam MA-1
Rising Paper Mill—hist pl MA-1
Rising Park—park OH-6
Rising River—locale ID-8
Rising River—stream CA-9
Rising River Lake—lake CA-9
Rising River Ranch—locale CA-9
Rising Sch—school FL-3
Rising Slough—stream LA-4
Rising Spring—spring PA-2
Rising Spring Ch—church TN-4
Rising Springs (RR name for Spring Mills)—other PA-2
Rising Springs Sch (historical)—school TN-4
Rising Spring Station (historical)—building PA-2
Rising Star—pop pl TX-5
Rising Star Baptist Ch—church (2) AL-4
Rising Star Baptist Ch—church KS-7
Rising Star Baptist Ch—church MS-4
Rising Star (CCD)—cens area TX-5
Rising Star Cem—cemetery AL-4
Rising Star Cem—cemetery LA-4
Rising Star Cem—cemetery MS-4
Rising Star Cem—cemetery MO-7
Rising Star Ch—church (8) AL-4
Rising Star Ch—church (2) GA-3
Rising Star Ch—church (2) LA-4
Rising Star Ch—church (2) MS-4
Rising Star Ch—church NC-3
Rising Star Ch—church (2) TX-5
Rising Star Ch—church (4) VA-3
Rising Star Ch (historical)—church AL-4
Rising Star Ch (historical)—church (2) MS-4
Rising Star Methodist Ch AL-4
Rising Star Methodist Ch—church AL-4
Rising Star Mine—mine ID-8
Rising Star Public Use Area—park AR-4
Rising Star Sch—school AL-4
Rising Star Sch—school LA-4
Rising Star Sch—school MS-4
Rising Star Sch—school TX-5
Rising Star Sch (historical)—school AL-4
Rising States Ledge—rock MA-1
Rising Sun NJ-2
Rising Sun OH-6
Rising Sun—locale IL-6
Rising Sun—locale (2) PA-2
Rising Sun—pop pl DE-2
Rising Sun—pop pl IL-6
Rising Sun—pop pl IN-6
Rising Sun—pop pl IA-7
Risingsun—pop pl IA-7
Rising Sun—pop pl MD-2
Rising Sun—pop pl MS-4
Rising Sun—pop pl MT-8
Risingsun—pop pl OH-6
Rising Sun—pop pl WI-6
Rising Sun Baptist Ch—church MS-4
Rising Sun Cem—cemetery IN-6
Rising Sun Cem—cemetery MS-4
Rising Sun Cem—cemetery NE-7
Rising Sun Cem—cemetery OK-5
Rising Sun Cem—cemetery TX-5
Rising Sun Ch—church (2) AR-4
Rising Sun Ch—church IL-6
Rising Sun Ch—church (2) LA-4
Rising Sun Ch—church (2) MS-4
Rising Sun Ch—church MO-7
Rising Sun Ch—church OK-5
Rising Sun Ch—church TN-4
Rising Sun Ch—church (4) VA-3
Rising Sun Ch (historical)—church MS-4
Rising Sun (corporate name for Risingsun)—pop pl OH-6
Rising Sun Ditch—canal CO-8
Rising Sun Elementary School MS-4
Rising Sun Inn—hist pl MD-2
Rising Sun Landing (historical)—locale MS-4
Rising Sun-Lebanon—CDP DE-2
Rising Sun Mine—mine UT-8
Rising Sun Mine (Inactive)—mine CA-9
Rising Sun Post Office (historical)—building AL-4
Rising Sun Ridge—ridge KY-4
Rising Sun Sch—school CA-9
Rising Sun Sch—school MS-4
Rising Sun Sch—school MO-7
Rising Sun Sch—school PA-2
Rising Sun Sch—school WV-2
Rising Sun Sch—school WI-6
Rising Sun Sch (historical)—school MS-4
Rising Sun Sch (historical)—school TN-4
Rising Sun Square NJ-2
Rising Sun Tavern—hist pl CT-1
Rising Sun Tavern—hist pl VA-3
Rising Sun (trailer park)—pop pl DE-2
Rising Valley Ch—church VA-3
Risingville—pop pl NY-2
Rising Water Creek ND-7
Rising Wolf Mtn—summit MT-8
Rising Zion Ch—church (4) VA-3
Risk—locale IL-6
Risk Brothers Site—hist pl KY-4
Risk Cem—cemetery (2) IN-6
Risk Creek—stream WA-9
Risk Creek—stream WI-6
Risken Lookout Tower—locale TX-5
Risken Well—well TX-5
Risk Hill—summit IN-6
Riskin Drain—canal MI-6
Risky Creek—stream AK-9
Risley KS-7
Risley (2) NJ-2
Risley Branch—stream NJ-2
Risley Canyon—valley CO-8
Risley Cem—cemetery IN-6
Risley Center Sch—school GA-3
Risley Channel—channel NJ-2
Risley Creek—stream OR-9
Risley Hollow—valley AR-4
Risley Hollow—valley MO-7
Risley HS GA-3
Risley JHS—school CO-8
Risley Park—park OR-9
Risley Pond CT-1
Risley Rsvr—reservoir CT-1
Risley Sch—school GA-3
Risley Sch—school NV-8
Risley Sch (historical)—school MO-7
Risley Township—pop pl KS-7
Rismiller—pop pl PA-2
Risner—locale KY-4
Risner Branch—stream (2) KY-4
Risner-Bull Creek (CCD)—cens area KY-4
Risner Cem—cemetery (3) KY-4
Risner Cem—cemetery TN-4
Risner Sch—school OK-5
Rison—locale MD-2
Rison—pop pl AR-4
Risong—bay PW-9
Rison Sch—school AL-4
Rison (Township of)—fmr MCD AR-4
Risse—pop pl IN-6
Rissers Ch—church PA-2
Risser Sch—school MO-7
Risser's Mill Covered Bridge—hist pl PA-2
Riss Lake—reservoir (2) MO-7
Rissler Draw—valley WY-8
Rissler Ranch—locale WY-8
Rissler Rsvr—reservoir WY-8
Risslers Lake—reservoir IN-6
Risslers Lake Dam—dam IN-6
Rista—pop pl ME-1
Rista Siding—locale ME-1
Rist Benson Lake—lake CO-8
Rist Canyon—valley CO-8
Rist Canyon Picnic Area—locale CO-8
Risters Creek—stream SC-3
Ristine—locale MO-7
Rist Mine TN-4
Rist Mtn—summit NY-2
Ristow Branch—stream IN-6
Rist Sch—school IL-6
Risue Canyon—valley NV-8
Risue Canyon Spring—spring NV-8
Risum Round Barn—hist pl WI-6
Riswold Creek—stream ID-8
Rita ND-7
Rita TN-4
Rita—locale TX-5
Rita—pop pl LA-4
Rita—pop pl PA-2
Rita—pop pl WV-2
Rita Blanca Creek TX-5
Rita Blanca Creek—stream TX-5
Rita Blanca Lake—reservoir TX-5
Rita Blanca Spring—spring NM-5
Rita Blanca Tank—reservoir TX-5
Rita Blanca Windmill—locale TX-5
Rita Branch AL-4
Rita Branch—stream AL-4
Rita Branch—stream NC-3
Rita Branch—stream (2) VA-3
Rita Canyon—valley CO-8
Rita Creek AZ-5
Rita Interchange—crossing AZ-5
Rital—locale FL-3
Rita Mine—mine CA-9
Ritas Draw—valley NM-5
Ritas Sch—school OH-6
Rita Windmill—locale TX-5
R Itcaina Ranch NV-8
Ritch—locale GA-3
Ritchal—locale KS-7
Ritchards Cem—cemetery FL-3
Ritch Cem—cemetery NC-3
Ritch Ch—church GA-3
Ritchea Cem—cemetery WV-2
Ritche Brothers—locale TX-5
Ritcher Park—park MO-7
Ritchey IL-6
Ritchey MS-4
Ritchey—pop pl MO-7
Ritchey, Mathew H., House—hist pl MO-7
Ritchey Branch—stream AR-4
Ritchey Bridge—bridge KY-4
Ritchey Bridge—bridge PA-2
Ritchey Cem—cemetery MS-4
Ritchey Cem—cemetery PA-2
Ritchey Creek—stream KS-7
Ritchey Ditch—canal WY-8
Ritchey Knob—summit (2) PA-2
Ritchey Peak—summit AZ-5
Ritchfield Junction—locale NY-2
Ritch Hall—hist pl NM-5
Ritchie—locale AR-4
Ritchie—locale KY-4
Ritchie—locale PA-2
Ritchie—locale TX-5
Ritchie—pop pl IL-6
Ritchie—pop pl IN-6
Ritchie—pop pl MD-2
Ritchie—pop pl TN-4
Ritchie, Z., House—hist pl NY-2
Ritchie Bldg—hist pl MA-1
Ritchie Block—hist pl VT-1
Ritchie Branch—stream MD-2
Ritchie Branch—stream TN-4
Ritchie Cem—cemetery IL-6
Ritchie Cem—cemetery KS-7
Ritchie Cem—cemetery LA-4
Ritchie Cem—cemetery (2) TN-4
Ritchie Ch—church WV-2
Ritchie (County)—pop pl WV-2
Ritchie Creek—stream (2) CA-9
Ritchie Creek—stream GA-3
Ritchie Creek—stream OR-9
Ritchie Creek—stream TX-5
Ritchie Creek—stream WI-6
Ritchie Dam—dam NC-3
Ritchie Gulch—valley ID-8
Ritchie Heights—pop pl MD-2
Ritchie Hill—ridge VA-3
Ritchie Hollow—valley TN-4
Ritchie Ledges—bench OH-6
Ritchie Manor—pop pl MD-2
Ritchie Point—cape VA-3
Ritchie Ridge—ridge WA-9
Ritchie Run—stream OH-6
Ritchie Run—stream PA-2
Ritchie Sch—school GA-3
Ritchie Sch—school IA-7
Ritchie Sch—school TN-4
Ritchie Sch (abandoned)—school MO-7
Ritchies Lake—reservoir NC-3
Ritchies Lake Dam—dam NC-3
Ritchies Pond—lake WV-2
Ritchie Station—locale IL-6
Ritchie Trail—trail VA-3

Ritchie Webster Center (Magisterial District)—fmr MCD WV-2
Ritchland Cem—cemetery KS-7
Ritch Ranch—locale NM-5
Ritch Rim—ridge NM-5
Ritch Sch—school GA-3
Ritchson Hollow—valley MO-7
Ritell—locale WA-9
Ritell Siding WA-9
Ritenour HS—school MO-7
Ritenour Run—stream VA-3
Riter—locale UT-8
Riter Canal—canal UT-8
Riter Creek OR-9
Riter Drain—canal UT-8
Riter Siding—locale UT-8
Riterville—locale PA-2
Riterville Station PA-2
Ritger Wagonmaking and Blacksmith Shop, —hist pl WI-6
Ritidian Beach—beach GU-9
Ritidian Channel—channel GU-9
Ritidian Point—summit GU-9
Ritito Canyon—valley NM-5
Ritmer Creek—stream CA-9
Ritner—locale KY-4
Ritner—locale OR-9
Ritner Creek—stream OR-9
Ritner Creek Bridge—hist pl OR-9
Ritner Lake—lake OK-5
Rito Alta Mine—mine CO-8
Rito Alto Ch—church CO-8
Rito Alto Lake—lake CO-8
Rito Alto Peak—summit CO-8
Rito Alto Trail—trail CO-8
Rito Anastacio—stream NM-5
Rito Anastacio—trail NM-5
Rito Angostura—stream NM-5
Rito Agua Creek CO-8
Rito Arean CO-8
Rito Atascoso—stream NM-5
Rito Axul CO-8
Rito Azul—stream (2) NM-5
Rito Bonito—stream NM-5
Rito Cafe—stream NM-5
Rito Canejo—stream NM-5
Rito Cebolla—stream NM-5
Rito Chaperito—stream NM-5
Rito Chavez—stream NM-5
Rito Cieneguilla—stream NM-5
Rito Claro—stream NM-5
Rito Colorado—stream NM-5
Rito con Agua—stream NM-5
Rito Creek—stream NM-5
Rito de Abiquiu—stream NM-5
Rito de Agua Fria NM-5
Rito de Gascon—stream NM-5
Rito de Juan Manuel—stream NM-5
Rito de la Nutria Ciega NM-5
Rito de la Olla—stream NM-5
Rito de la Osha—stream NM-5
Rito de las Palomas—stream NM-5
Rito de las Perchas—stream NM-5
Rito de las Sillas—locale NM-5
Rito de las Sillas—stream NM-5
Rito del Gato—stream NM-5
Rito del Indio—stream NM-5
Rito del Medio—stream (2) NM-5
Rito del Ojo—stream NM-5
Rito de los Alamitos—stream NM-5
Rito de los Chimayosos—stream NM-5
Rito de los Frijoles—stream NM-5
Rito De Los Indios—stream NM-5
Rito de los Indios—stream NM-5
Rito del Oso—stream (2) NM-5
Rito de los Ojos—stream NM-5
Rito de los Pinos—stream NM-5
Rito de los Utes—stream NM-5
Rito del Padre—stream NM-5
Rito de Tierra Amarilla—stream NM-5
Rito Encino—stream NM-5
Rito Frijoles—stream NM-5
Rito Gallina—stream NM-5
Rito Garcia—stream NM-5
Rito Gulch—valley CO-8
Rito Hondo Rsvr—reservoir CO-8
Rito Jarosa—stream NM-5
Rito Jaroso—stream NM-5
Rito la Cueva—stream NM-5
Rito la Cueva Spring—spring NM-5
Rito la Presa—stream NM-5
Rito Las Trampas—stream NM-5
Rito la Vega—stream NM-5
Rito Leche—stream NM-5
Rito los Esteros—stream NM-5
Rito Maestas—stream NM-5
Rito Manzanares—stream NM-5
Rito Morphy—stream NM-5
Rito Olguin—stream NM-5
Rito Oscuro—stream NM-5
Rito Osha—stream NM-5
Rito Pelon—stream NM-5
Rito Penas Negras—stream NM-5
Rito Perro—stream NM-5
Rito Primero—stream NM-5
Rito Quemado—stream NM-5
Rito Quemazon—stream NM-5
Rito Quien Sabe—stream NM-5
Rito Redondo—stream NM-5
Rito Resumidero—stream NM-5
Rito Rsvr—reservoir NM-5
Rito Ruidoso—stream NM-5
Rito Sandoval—stream NM-5
Rito San Jose—stream NM-5
Rito Sebadilloses—stream NM-5
Rito Seco—stream (2) NM-5
Rito sin Agua—stream NM-5
Rito Spring—spring NM-5
Rito Torito—stream NM-5
Rito Windmill—locale TX-5
Ritschard Ranch—locale CO-8
Ritsenburg Meadow—flat MT-8
Ritt PA-2
Ritta—locale TN-4
**Ritta**—pop pl FL-3
Ritta Elem Sch—school TN-4
Ritta Island—island FL-3
**Ritta (Labor Camp)**—pop pl FL-3
Rittenhouse—locale AZ-5
Rittenhouse—locale PA-2
**Rittenhouse**—pop pl PA-2
Rittenhouse, Lake—lake TX-5
Rittenhouse Air Force Auxillary Field (closed)—military AZ-5
Rittenhouse Branch—stream KS-7
Rittenhouse Cem—cemetery WV-2
Rittenhouse Dam—dam AZ-5
Rittenhouse Ditch—canal IN-6
Rittenhouse Gap—gap PA-2
**Rittenhouse Gap**—pop pl PA-2
Rittenhouse Hist Dist—hist pl PA-2
Rittenhouse JHS—school PA-2
Rittenhouse Park—park DE-2
Rittenhouse (Queen Creek)—other AZ-5
Rittenhouse Slough—gut KY-4
Rittenhouse Square—hist pl PA-2
Rittenhouse Square—park PA-2
Rittenhouse Substation—locale AZ-5
**Rittenhouse Town**—pop pl PA-2
Rittenmeyer, F. X., House—hist pl IA-7
Rittenour Cem—cemetery OH-6
Rittenour Ridge—ridge VA-3
Rittenours—locale OH-6
Ritter—locale IA-7
**Ritter**—pop pl MO-7
**Ritter**—pop pl OR-9
**Ritter**—pop pl SC-3
**Ritter**—pop pl WV-2
Ritter, Andrew, Farm—hist pl KY-4
Ritter, John, House—hist pl KY-4
Ritter, Mount—summit CA-9
Ritter, William, House—hist pl OH-6
Ritter, William M., House—hist pl ID-8
Ritter Airpark—airport NC-3
Ritter Arroyo—stream CO-8
Ritter Ave Free Methodist Ch—church IN-6
Ritter Bay—bay SD-7
Ritter Branch—stream IN-6
Ritter Branch—stream KY-4
Ritter Branch—stream MO-7
Ritter Branch—stream SC-3
Ritter Bridge—other IL-6
Ritterbusch Flat—flat OR-9
Ritterbush Camp—locale VT-1
Ritterbush Pond—lake VT-1
Ritter Butte—summit AZ-5
Ritter Butte—summit OR-9
Ritter Butte Summit—summit OR-9
Ritter Canyon—valley CA-9
Ritter Canyon—valley CO-8
Ritter Cem—cemetery IL-6
Ritter Cem—cemetery MO-7
Ritter Cem—cemetery OH-6
Ritter Cem—cemetery OR-9
Ritter Cem—cemetery (3) TN-4
Ritter Cem—cemetery TX-5
Ritter Creek OK-5
Ritter Creek—stream AZ-5
Ritter Creek—stream AR-4
Ritter Creek—stream IN-6
Ritter Creek—stream MO-7
Ritter Creek—stream OR-9
Ritter Dam SD-7
Ritter Dam—dam AZ-5
Ritter Draw—valley CO-8
Ritter Elem Sch—school PA-2
Ritter Farm Park—park MN-6
Ritter Grange—locale OR-9
Ritter Hammock—island GA-3
Ritter Hills MI-6
Ritter Hollow—valley (2) MO-7
Ritter Hot Springs OR-9
Ritter Hot Springs—spring OR-9
Ritter House—hist pl KY-4
Ritter House—hist pl MA-1
Ritter HS—school IN-6
Ritter Lake—lake TX-5
Ritter Lake—lake WI-6
Ritter-Morton House—hist pl TN-4
Ritter Mountain CA-9
Ritter Mtn—summit AZ-5
Ritter Park—park FL-3
Ritter Park—park WV-2
Ritter Peak—summit AZ-5
Ritter Point—cape AK-9
Ritter Point—cape TX-5
Ritter Ranch—locale CA-9
Ritter Range—range CA-9
Ritter Rsvr—reservoir OR-9
Ritter Run—stream PA-2
Ritters—locale WV-2
Ritter Sch—school AZ-5
Ritter Sch—school CA-9
Ritter Sch—school CO-8
Ritter Sch—school MI-6
Ritter Sch—school MO-7
Ritter Sch—school OR-9
Ritters Corners Sch—school WI-6
Ritters Crossroads—locale PA-2
Ritter Siphon—canal CA-9
Ritters Lake—reservoir NC-3
Ritter Spring—spring AZ-5
Ritter Springs Park—park MO-7
Rittersville PA-2
Ritter Tank—reservoir (2) AZ-5
Rittertown Baptist Church TN-4
Rittertown Ch—church TN-4
**Ritterville (subdivision)**—pop pl PA-2
Ritter Well—well NM-5
Ritte's Corner Hist Dist, Latonia—hist pl KY-4
Rittgers—cemetery IA-7
Rittiman Creek—stream TX-5
Rittle Fork—stream NC-3
Rittle Hollow—valley TN-4
Rittle Knob—summit NC-3
Rittlo Mtn NC-3
**Rittman**—pop pl OH-6
Ritts—locale PA-2
Ritts Area County Park—park IA-7
Ritts Junction—locale OK-5
Ritts Mill (Abandoned)—locale CA-9
Ritts Ridge—ridge TN-4
Ritts Ridge Prospect—mine TN-4
Ritts Station PA-2
Rittswood Golf Course—locale PA-2
Ritual Lake—lake MN-6
Ritz—locale AR-4
Ritz—locale ID-8
Ritz—uninc pl NJ-2
Ritz Apartment, The—hist pl FL-3
Ritz Canton Oil Field—oilfield KS-7
Ritz Center—locale MO-7
Ritz Center (Shop Ctr)—locale MO-7
Ritzer Grove—woods CA-9
Ritz Hill—summit NY-2
**Ritzie Village**—pop pl PA-2
Ritzius Sch—school CO-8
Ritzman Sch—school OH-6
Ritz Sch (abandoned)—school PA-2
**Ritzville**—pop pl WA-9
Ritzville Carnegie Library—hist pl WA-9
Ritzville (CCD)—cens area WA-9
**Riva**—pop pl MD-2
Riva Bridge—bridge MD-2
**Rivajana**—pop pl NM-5
Rival KY-4
Rival—locale ND-7
Riva Lake TN-4
Riva Lake Baptist Church TN-4
Riva Lake Camp—locale TN-4
Riva Lake Ch—church TN-4
Rival Creek—stream MT-8
Rivale Spring—spring CO-8
**Rival (historical)**—pop pl TN-4
Rivalier Canyon—valley CA-9
**Rival Junction**—pop pl ND-7
Rival Post Office (historical)—building AL-4
Rivalry Lake—lake MN-6
**Rivals**—pop pl KY-4
Rivals Park—park IL-6
Rivanna—locale VA-3
Rivanna (Magisterial District)—fmr MCD VA-3
Rivanna River—stream VA-3
**Rivare**—pop pl IN-6
Rivaux Creek—stream MO-7
**Rivco**—pop pl VA-3
Rive Lake WI-6
**Rivelon**—pop pl SC-3
Rivenbark Ponds—reservoir AL-4
Rivendell Childrens and Youth Center UT-8
**Rivendell Condominium**—pop pl UT-8
Rivendell of Utah—hospital UT-8
Riven Oak Sch—school MS-4
Riven Rock Mtn—summit VA-3
Riven Rock Picnic Area—park VA-3
Riven Rocks—summit VA-3
River IN-6
River MA-1
River MS-4
River TX-5
River—locale KY-4
River—locale VI-3
**River**—pop pl IL-6
**River**—pop pl IN-6
**River**—pop pl MD-2
**River**—pop pl TX-5
River—stream (3) AK-9
River—uninc pl NY-2
River, The NJ-2
River, The—bay MA-1
Rivera CA-9
**Rivera**—pop pl PR-3
Rivera—uninc pl CA-9
Rivera, Nazario, Residencia—hist pl PR-3
Rivera Beach MD-2
Rivera Beach (Shop Ctr)—locale FL-3
Rivera Canyon—valley CA-9
Rivera Canyon—valley NM-5
Rivera Cem—cemetery CO-8
Rivera Cem—cemetery NM-5
Rivera Cow Camp—locale NM-5
**River Acres**—pop pl NC-3
Rivera Hotel—hist pl AR-4
**Riverair**—pop pl IL-6
Rivera JHS—school CA-9
Rivera Mesa—summit NM-5
Rivera Park—park CA-9
Rivera Park—park KS-7
River Archeol Site—hist pl VI-3
**Rivera Townhouses (subdivision)**—pop pl UT-8
River au Cabris SD-7
River Aux Chenes LA-4
River Aux Chenes, Bay of—bay LA-4
River aux Ecorces MI-6
**River aux Vases**—pop pl MO-7
River aux Vases—stream MO-7
River Ave Baptist Ch—church IN-6
**Rivera y Lomas**—pop pl PR-3
Riverbank—locale CT-1
Riverbank—locale NY-2
**Riverbank**—pop pl CA-9
**River Bank**—pop pl NJ-2
Riverbank Army Ammun Plant—military CA-9
Riverbank Cem—cemetery VT-1
River Bank Ch—church IN-6
Riverbank Lateral—canal CA-9
River Bank Park—park NJ-2
River Bar Campground—locale WA-9
River Bay—bay AK-9
Riverbay Plaza (Shop Ctr)—locale FL-3
Riverbed Butte—summit OR-9
Riverbed Butte Spring—spring OR-9
Riverbed Pond—reservoir OR-9
Riverbed Pony Express Station—locale UT-8
Riverbed Rsvr OR-9
River Bed Rsvr—reservoir UT-8
River Bed Rsvr No 2—reservoir UT-8
Riverbend—hist pl WI-6
Riverbend—locale CA-9
River Bend—locale CO-8
Riverbend—locale GA-3
River Bend—locale GA-3
River Bend—locale VA-3
**Riverbend**—pop pl AL-4
**River Bend**—pop pl AL-4
**River Bend**—pop pl (2) LA-4
**River Bend**—pop pl MD-2
**Riverbend**—pop pl NC-3
**River Bend**—pop pl NC-3
**Riverbend**—pop pl TN-4
**Riverbend**—pop pl WV-2
River Bend Airp—airport WA-9
River Bend Baptist Church TN-4
River Bend Campground—locale ID-8
Riverbend Campground—locale WA-9
River Bend Campground—locale WA-9
River Bend (CCD)—cens area AL-4
River Bend Cem—cemetery CO-8
River Bend Cem—cemetery (2) MI-6
River Bend Cem—cemetery VA-3
River Bend Center for Mental Health—hospital AL-4
River Bend Ch AL-4
Riverbend Ch—church AL-4
River Bend Ch—church (2) GA-3
Riverbend Ch—church NC-3
River Bend Ch—church NC-3
River Bend Ch—church (2) TN-4
River Bend Ch—church TX-5
Riverbend Ch of Christ AL-4
Riverbend Country Club—other TX-5
River Bend Country Club—other VA-3
River Bend Dam—dam OR-9
River Bend Division—civil AL-4
**River Bend Estates**—pop pl MD-2
**River Bend Estates**—pop pl MO-7
**River Bend Estates**—pop pl TN-4
**Riverbend Estates**—pop pl TN-4
**River Bend Estates**—pop pl VA-3
River Bend Estates Golf And Country Club—locale TN-4
River Bend Farm—hist pl PA-2
River Bend Forge Number One (historical)—locale TN-4
River Bend Forge Number Two (historical)—locale TN-4
River Bend Golf Course—locale NC-3
River Bend (historical)—locale AL-4
River Bend Hollow—valley OK-5
River Bend Hunting and Fishing Club—locale AL-4
River Bend Lodge—building CA-9
Riverbend Marina—locale AL-4
River Bend Nuclear Power Plant—facility LA-4
River Bend Park—park MI-6
River Bend Park—park NC-3
River Bend Post Office (historical)—building TN-4
River Bend Ranch—locale WY-8
River Bend Rec Area—park TN-4
River Bend Rsvr Number Two—reservoir OR-9
River Bend Sch—school CA-9
River Bend Sch—school GA-3
River Bend Sch—school MI-6
River Bend Sch—school WY-8
River Bend Shop Ctr—locale KS-7
**River Bend (subdivision)**—pop pl AL-4
**Riverbend (subdivision)**—pop pl NC-3
**Riverbend Subdivision**—pop pl UT-8
River Bend (Township of)—fmr MCD NC-3
**Riverbend Trailer Park**—pop pl UT-8
River Bethel Ch—church GA-3
River Birch Bottom County Park—park IA-7
River Blanche AR-4
River Bluff—hist pl VA-3
**River Bluff**—pop pl MI-6
**River Bluff Addition**—pop pl SD-7
**River Bluff Farms**—pop pl KY-4
River Bluff Rec Area—park GA-3
River Bluff Small Wild Area—park TN-4
River Bluffs Park—park MO-7
River Bluff Trail—trail TN-4
Riverboat Museum—building IA-7
**Riverbottom**—pop pl TX-5
River Bottom Rsvr—reservoir WY-8
River Bottom Sch Number 50 (historical)—school SD-7
River Botton Rsvr—reservoir CA-9
River Branch—stream AL-4
River Branch—stream KY-4
River Branch—stream TN-4
River Branch—stream WV-2
River Branch Canal—canal CA-9
River Branch Columbia Canal—canal CA-9
River Branch Junction IL-6
River Bridge—locale FL-3
River Bridge—locale VA-3
River Brook—stream NJ-2
Riverby—locale TX-5
River Camp—locale WA-9
River Campground—locale MT-8
River Campground—park OR-9
River Camp Sch—school TX-5
River Canyon—valley (2) NE-7
River Canyon—valley WY-8
River Cave—cave (2) MO-7
River Cave—cave (2) TN-4
Rivercene—hist pl MO-7
River Ch—church KY-4
River Ch—church PA-2
River Chapel AL-4
Riverchase Country Club—locale AL-4
Riverchase Galleria Shop Ctr—locale AL-4
Riverchase Hosp—hospital TN-4
Riverchase MS—school AL-4
Riverchase Stables—locale AL-4
**Riverchase (subdivision)**—pop pl AL-4
**Riverchase (subdivision)**—pop pl TN-4
Rivercliff CT-1
**Rivercliff**—pop pl CT-1
River Cliff Cem—cemetery OH-6
River Cliffs—cliff NC-3
**Rivercliff (subdivision)**—pop pl NC-3
**River Club Estates**—pop pl MD-2
River Club Marsh—swamp MD-2
River Colderan Ranch—locale AZ-5
River Coll—school NH-1
Rivercombs Corner VA-3
River Corner Ch—church PA-2
**River Corners**—pop pl OH-6
River Creek NC-3
River Creek—stream AR-4
**River Creek Acres**—pop pl TX-5
**Rivercrest**—pop pl NH-1
**Rivercrest**—pop pl VA-3
**Rivercrest**—pop pl WA-9
River Crest—uninc pl OR-9
Rivercrest Camp—locale NE-7
River Crest Country Club—other TX-5
River Crest Lake—reservoir TX-5
**Rivercrest Manor**—pop pl NJ-2
Rivercrest Park—park FL-3
Rivercrest Park—park OR-9
River Crest Preventurium—building PA-2
River Crest Sch—school PA-2
**Rivercrest (subdivision)**—pop pl NC-3
**River Crest Subdivision**—pop pl UT-8
River Cusitie AL-4
Riverdahl Sch—school IL-6
Riverdale KS-7
Riverdale OH-6
Riverdale—hist pl AL-4
Riverdale—hist pl DE-2
Riverdale—locale AR-4
Riverdale—locale CO-8
Riverdale—locale CT-1
Riverdale—locale DE-2
Riverdale—locale ID-8
Riverdale—locale IA-7
Riverdale—locale MT-8
Riverdale—locale OH-6
Riverdale—locale SC-3
Riverdale—locale TX-5
Riverdale—locale VA-3
**Riverdale**—pop pl AL-4
**Riverdale**—pop pl (2) CA-9
**Riverdale**—pop pl (3) FL-3
**Riverdale**—pop pl GA-3
**Riverdale**—pop pl ID-8
**Riverdale**—pop pl (2) IL-6
**Riverdale**—pop pl IA-7
**Riverdale**—pop pl KS-7
**Riverdale**—pop pl (2) MD-2
**Riverdale**—pop pl (3) MA-1
**Riverdale**—pop pl MI-6
**Riverdale**—pop pl MS-4
**Riverdale**—pop pl MO-7
**Riverdale**—pop pl NE-7
**Riverdale**—pop pl NH-1
**Riverdale**—pop pl NJ-2
**Riverdale**—pop pl (2) NY-2
**Riverdale**—pop pl NC-3
**Riverdale**—pop pl ND-7
**Riverdale**—pop pl OR-9
**Riverdale**—pop pl SC-3
**Riverdale**—pop pl TN-4
**Riverdale**—pop pl UT-8
**Riverdale**—pop pl (5) VA-3
Riverdale Baptist Ch—church TN-4
Riverdale Bench Canal—canal UT-8
Riverdale (CCD)—cens area CA-9
Riverdale (CCD)—cens area GA-3
Riverdale Cem—cemetery GA-3
Riverdale Cem—cemetery KS-7
Riverdale Cem—cemetery MA-1
Riverdale Cem—cemetery MI-6
Riverdale Cem—cemetery MN-6
Riverdale Cem—cemetery NH-1
Riverdale Cem—cemetery NY-2
Riverdale Cem—cemetery TX-5
Riverdale Center—locale UT-8
Riverdale Ch—church AR-4
Riverdale Ch—church MO-7
Riverdale Ch—church NC-3
Riverdale Ch—church TN-4
Riverdale Ch—church TX-5
Riverdale Community Hall—locale OK-5
Riverdale Country Sch—school NY-2
Riverdale Creek—stream MS-4
Riverdale Dam—dam MA-1
Riverdale Ditch—canal CA-9
Riverdale Elem Sch—school IN-6
**Riverdale Estates (trailer park)**—pop pl DE-2
Riverdale Ferry (historical)—crossing TN-4
Riverdale Flowage—reservoir WI-6
**Riverdale Gardens**—pop pl MD-2
Riverdale Grange Hall—locale CO-8
**Riverdale Heights**—pop pl MD-2
Riverdale Hill—summit OR-9
**Riverdale Hills**—pop pl MD-2
Riverdale Hills Sch—school MD-2
Riverdale HS—school FL-3
Riverdale HS—school IN-6
Riverdale HS—school LA-4
Riverdale Industrial Park—locale UT-8
Riverdale Junction—locale ND-7
Riverdale Landing Camp—locale AL-4
Riverdale Mill—hist pl TN-4
Riverdale Mtn—summit NY-2
Riverdale Oil Field—oilfield CA-9
Riverdale Park—park CA-9
Riverdale Park—park IL-6
Riverdale Park—park MA-1
Riverdale Park—park NY-2
Riverdale Park—park SD-7
Riverdale Park—park WA-9
Riverdale Park Airp—airport DE-2
Riverdale Plantation MS-4
Riverdale Plaza Shop Ctr—locale VA-3
Riverdale-Pompton (Riverdale) NJ-2
Riverdale Pond—reservoir MA-1
Riverdale Post Office (historical)—building TN-4
Riverdale Power Plant—other UT-8
Riverdale Presbyterian Church Complex—hist pl NY-2
Riverdale Recreation Center—park MD-2
**Riverdale (Riverdale-Pompton)**—pop pl NJ-2
Riverdale Sch—school (2) CA-9
Riverdale Sch—school IL-6
Riverdale Sch—school IN-6
Riverdale Sch—school (2) IA-7
Riverdale Sch—school MA-1
Riverdale Sch—school NE-7
Riverdale Sch—school ND-7
Riverdale Sch—school (2) OR-9
Riverdale Sch—school SD-7
Riverdale Sch—school TN-4
Riverdale Sch—school UT-8
Riverdale Sch—school WA-9
Riverdale Sch (Abon'-d)—school ID-8
Riverdale Shop Ctr—locale FL-3
Riverdale Shop Ctr—locale MA-1
Riverdale State Game Mngmt Area—park ND-7
**Riverdale Station**—pop pl MA-1
**Riverdale (subdivision)**—pop pl AL-4
**Riverdale (subdivision)**—pop pl DE-2
**Riverdale (subdivision)**—pop pl MA-1
**Riverdale (subdivision)**—pop pl NC-3
Riverdale Township—fmr MCD IA-7
**Riverdale Township**—pop pl NE-7
**Riverdale Township**—pop pl ND-7
**Riverdale (Township of)**—pop pl MN-6
River de Flag AZ-5
Riverdell Canal—canal UT-8
River Deshee IN-6
River Deshee ditch IN-6
River des Peres—stream MO-7
River des Peres Drainage Channel—canal MO-7
River Des Peres Drainage Channel—channel MO-7
River District Hosp—hospital MI-6
River Ditch—canal NC-3
River Ditch—canal UT-8
River Ditch—canal WY-8
River Downs Racetrack—other OH-6
River Drain—canal TX-5
River Drain—stream IN-6
River Dubois IL-6
River Dubois MO-7
River Echo School—locale MT-8
**River Edge**—pop pl NJ-2
**River Edge**—pop pl OH-6
Riveredge Country Club—other OH-6
River Edge Manor—uninc pl NJ-2
**Riveredge Park (subdivision)**—pop pl DE-2
**River Edge (Riverside)**—pop pl NJ-2
River Edge Sch—school OH-6
**Riveredge (Township of)**—pop pl OH-6
River End (historical)—locale MA-1
**River Falls**—pop pl AL-4
**River Falls**—pop pl MD-2
**River Falls**—pop pl SC-3
**River Falls**—pop pl WI-6
River Falls Baptist Ch—church AL-4
River Falls Cem—cemetery AL-4
**River Falls (Town of)**—pop pl WI-6
**River Falls (Township of)**—pop pl MN-6
River Field Lake—lake SC-3
Riverfield Sch—school CT-1
River Ford—locale UT-8
River Ford Forest Camp—locale OR-9
River Forest—locale FL-3
**River Forest**—pop pl IL-6
**River Forest**—pop pl IN-6
**River Forest**—pop pl MD-2
River Forest Acad—school LA-4
River Forest Elem Sch—school IN-6
River Forest Golf Club—other IL-6
River Forest Golf Course—other LA-4
River Forest Hist Dist—hist pl IL-6
River Forest Junior-Senior HS—school IN-6
River Forest Lake—reservoir OR-9
River Forest Nursing Home—hospital MI-6
**River Forest Shores**—pop pl VA-3
River Forest Shores Shop Ctr—locale VA-3
River Forest (Township of)—civ div IL-6
River Fork—stream KY-4
River Fork—stream WV-2
River Forks—locale NY-2
River Forks County Park—park OR-9
River Forks Park—locale GA-3
**River Front**—pop pl AR-4
**River Front**—pop pl VA-3
Riverfront—uninc pl KY-4
Riverfront Park—park AL-4
River Front Park—park IL-6
Riverfront Park—park IL-6
Riverfront Park—park IN-6
Riverfront Park—park MO-7
Riverfront Park—park PA-2
River Front Park—park PA-2
Riverfront Park—park TN-4
Riverfront Park—park VA-3
River Gap—gap AL-4
River Gardner—area CA-9
River Gate NY-2
Rivergate—civil OR-9
Rivergate—locale NY-2
**Rivergate**—pop pl OR-9
Rivergate—post sta FL-3
Rivergate Plaza (Shop Ctr)—locale FL-3
River Gate Plaza (Shop Ctr)—locale FL-3
Rivergate Shop Ctr—locale NC-3
Rivergate Village (Shop Ctr)—locale FL-3
**River Glen**—pop pl CT-1
**River Glen**—pop pl IL-6
River Glen Sch—school CA-9
River Grange Plantation (historical)—locale TN-4
River Group—spring WY-8
**River Grove**—pop pl IL-6
**Rivergrove**—pop pl OR-9
**River Grove**—pop pl OR-9
River Grove Cem—cemetery ME-1
River Grove Ch of Christ—church FL-3
River Grove Sch—school IL-6
River Grove Sch—school OR-9
River Grove Sch—school WI-6
**River Haven**—pop pl IN-6
**River Haven**—pop pl (2) NC-3
**River Haven Estates Subdivision**—pop pl UT-8
**Riverhaven (River Haven)**—pop pl IN-6
**Riverhead**—pop pl NY-2
Riverhead Beach—beach MA-1
River Head Camp—locale OR-9
Riverhead Cem—cemetery NY-2
Riverhead Raceway—other NY-2
Riverheads HS—school VA-3
Riverheads (Magisterial District)—fmr MCD VA-3
**Riverhead (Town of)**—pop pl NY-2
River Heights IL-6
**River Heights**—pop pl (2) TN-4
**River Heights**—pop pl UT-8
River Heights Park—park MN-6
River Heights Sch—school MN-6
River Heights Sch—school UT-8
River Heights Sch—school WI-6
**River Heights (subdivision)**—pop pl NC-3
River Hill AL-4
River Hill NH-1
Riverhill NH-1
River Hill NC-3
Riverhill TN-4
River Hill—locale TN-4
Riverhill—locale VA-3
**Riverhill**—pop pl NH-1
**River Hill**—pop pl PA-2
**River Hill**—pop pl TN-4
**River Hill**—pop pl TX-5
River Hill—summit (2) AL-4
River Hill—summit CA-9
River Hill—summit CO-8

Robert L Hopkins Dam—*dam* ... TN-4
Robert L Huff Sch—*school* ... TN-4
Robert Livingston, Birthplace Of—*locale* ... NY-2
Robert Lotts (historical)—*locale* ... MS-4
Robert Louis Stevenson Memorial State Park—*park* ... CA-9
Robert Louis Stevenson Sch—*school* ... CA-9
Robert L. Roberts—*uninc pl* ... KS-7
Robert L. Taylor Meml Airpark Airp—*airport* ... WA-9
Robert Lucas Sch—*school* ... IA-7
Robert McCord Oral Sch—*school* ... FL-3
Robert McHardy Grant—*civil* ... FL-3
Robert Miller Ditch—*canal* ... MT-8
Robert Morgan Vocational Technical Institute—*school* ... FL-3
Robert Morris Coll—*school* ... PA-2
Robert Morris Junior Coll—*school* ... IL-6
Robert Morris Sch—*school* ... NJ-2
Robert Morris Sch—*school* ... NY-2
Robert Moses State Park—*park* ... NY-2
Robert Moton Sch—*school* ... MD-2
Robert Mount Pisgan African Methodist Episcopal Ch—*church* ... FL-3
Robert Mueller Municipal Airp—*airport* ... TX-5
Robert M Watkins Regional State Park—*park* ... MD-2
Roberto Clemente Memorial Park—*park* ... PA-2
Roberto Clemente Park—*park* ... FL-3
*Roberto Creek* ... SD-7
Roberto-Sunol Adobe—*hist pl* ... CA-9
Robert Packer Hosp—*hospital* ... PA-2
Robert Pfluger Ranch—*locale* ... TX-5
Robert Pinkston Junior Lake—*reservoir* ... AL-4
Robert Pinkston Junior Lake Dam—*dam* ... AL-4
Robert Reeder Dam—*dam* ... SD-7
Robert Richard Drain—*stream* ... IN-6
Robert Riley Lake Dam—*dam* ... MS-4
Robert Rives Cem—*cemetery* ... AL-4
Robert Rooke, Lake—*reservoir* ... NJ-2
Robert Rsvr—*reservoir* ... CO-8
Robert Run—*stream* ... PA-2
Robert Run—*stream* ... WV-2
Robert R Young Memorial Yard—*other* ... IN-6
*Roberts* ... CA-9
*Roberts* ... ME-1
*Roberts* ... OH-6
Roberts—*locale* ... IA-7
Roberts—*locale* ... ME-1
Roberts—*locale* (2) ... MD-2
Roberts—*locale* ... MS-4
Roberts—*locale* (2) ... OR-9
Roberts—*locale* ... TN-4
Roberts—*locale* ... WV-2
Roberts—*other* ... FL-3
Roberts—*other* ... OH-6
**Roberts**—*pop pl* ... AL-4
**Roberts**—*pop pl* ... CO-8
**Roberts**—*pop pl* ... ID-8
**Roberts**—*pop pl* ... IL-6
**Roberts**—*pop pl* ... IN-6
**Roberts**—*pop pl* ... MT-8
**Roberts**—*pop pl* ... OH-6
**Roberts**—*pop pl* ... OR-9
**Roberts**—*pop pl* ... PA-2
**Roberts**—*pop pl* ... TN-4
**Roberts**—*pop pl* ... WV-2
**Roberts**—*pop pl* ... WI-6
Roberts—*uninc pl* ... MA-1
Roberts, Alfred W., House—*hist pl* ... GA-3
Roberts, Dr. Rufus A., House—*hist pl* ... TX-5
Roberts, Edward C., House—*hist pl* ... IA-7
Roberts, Enoch, House—*hist pl* ... PA-2
Roberts, Gov. Albert H., Law Office—*hist pl* ... TN-4
Roberts, James D., House—*hist pl* ... NV-8
Roberts, John N., House—*hist pl* ... KS-7
Roberts, John Spencer, House—*hist pl* ... GA-3
Roberts, Judge Nathan S., House—*hist pl* ... NY-2
Roberts, Lake—*lake* (2) ... FL-3
Roberts, Lake—*reservoir* ... IL-6
Roberts, Lake—*reservoir* ... NM-5
Roberts, Martin W., House—*hist pl* ... MI-6
Roberts, Morris, Store—*hist pl* ... ID-8
Roberts, Mount—*summit* ... NH-1
Roberts, Point—*cape* ... WA-9
Roberts, Wesley, House—*hist pl* ... KY-4
Roberts, William D., House—*hist pl* ... UT-8
Roberts, William H., House—*hist pl* ... IL-6
Roberts Air Field—*airport* ... KS-7
Roberts Ave Ch—*church* ... TX-5
Roberts Ave Sch—*school* ... CT-1
Robert Sawyer State Park—*park* ... OR-9
Roberts-Banner Bldg—*hist pl* ... TX-5
Roberts Bay—*bay* (3) ... FL-3
Roberts Bay—*bay* ... OR-9
Roberts Bay—*swamp* ... GA-3
Roberts Bayou—*stream* ... AL-4
Roberts Bayou—*stream* ... LA-4
Roberts Bench—*bench* ... MT-8
Roberts Bend—*bend* ... KY-4
Roberts Bend—*bend* ... TN-4
Roberts Bend Branch—*stream* ... TN-4
Roberts Bldg—*hist pl* ... MT-8
Roberts Bluff—*cliff* ... KY-4
Roberts Bluff—*cliff* ... ME-1
Roberts Bluff—*cliff* ... MS-4
Roberts Bluff Bridge—*other* ... MO-7
Roberts Bottom—*bend* ... UT-8
Roberts Branch—*stream* (4) ... AL-4
Roberts Branch—*stream* ... AR-4
Roberts Branch—*stream* ... FL-3
Roberts Branch—*stream* (2) ... GA-3
Roberts Branch—*stream* (7) ... KY-4
Roberts Branch—*stream* ... LA-4
Roberts Branch—*stream* ... MS-4
Roberts Branch—*stream* (3) ... MO-7
Roberts Branch—*stream* ... NJ-2
Roberts Branch—*stream* (3) ... NC-3
Roberts Branch—*stream* ... PA-2
Roberts Branch—*stream* ... SC-3
Roberts Branch—*stream* (6) ... TN-4
Roberts Branch—*stream* ... TX-5
Roberts Branch—*stream* (2) ... VA-3
Roberts Branch Cem—*cemetery* ... KY-4
Roberts Branch Cem—*cemetery* ... TX-5
Roberts Bridge—*bridge* ... GA-3
*Roberts Brook* ... MA-1
Roberts Brook—*stream* ... CT-1
Roberts Brook—*stream* ... IN-6
Roberts Brook—*stream* ... ME-1
Roberts Brook—*stream* ... MA-1
Roberts Brook—*stream* ... VT-1
Roberts Brooks—*stream* ... NH-1
Robertsburg—*locale* ... OH-6
**Robertsburg**—*pop pl* ... WV-2
*Roberts Butte* ... AZ-5
Roberts Butte—*locale* ... OR-9
Roberts Butte—*summit* ... CA-9
Roberts Butte—*summit* ... OR-9
Roberts Camp—*locale* ... AZ-5
Roberts Camp—*locale* ... CA-9
Roberts Camp—*locale* ... FL-3
Roberts Camp—*locale* ... TX-5
Roberts Canal—*canal* ... FL-3
*Roberts Canyon* ... ID-8
Roberts Canyon—*valley* (3) ... CA-9
Roberts Canyon—*valley* (2) ... CO-8
Roberts Canyon—*valley* (2) ... NM-5
Roberts Canyon—*valley* ... OR-9
Roberts-Carter House—*hist pl* ... NC-3
Roberts Cave—*cave* ... TN-4
*Roberts Cem* ... TN-4
Roberts Cem—*cemetery* (4) ... AL-4
Roberts Cem—*cemetery* (2) ... AR-4
Roberts Cem—*cemetery* ... FL-3
Roberts Cem—*cemetery* (2) ... GA-3
Roberts Cem—*cemetery* (4) ... IL-6
Roberts Cem—*cemetery* (3) ... IN-6
Roberts Cem—*cemetery* (2) ... IA-7
Roberts Cem—*cemetery* ... KS-7
Roberts Cem—*cemetery* (7) ... KY-4
Roberts Cem—*cemetery* (5) ... LA-4
Roberts Cem—*cemetery* ... ME-1
Roberts Cem—*cemetery* ... MA-1
Roberts Cem—*cemetery* ... MI-6
Roberts Cem—*cemetery* (10) ... MS-4
Roberts Cem—*cemetery* (8) ... MO-7
Roberts Cem—*cemetery* ... MT-8
Roberts Cem—*cemetery* ... NY-2
Roberts Cem—*cemetery* (3) ... NC-3
Roberts Cem—*cemetery* (5) ... OH-6
Roberts Cem—*cemetery* ... OR-9
Roberts Cem—*cemetery* ... PA-2
Roberts Cem—*cemetery* (25) ... TN-4
Roberts Cem—*cemetery* (10) ... TX-5
Roberts Cem—*cemetery* ... VT-1
Roberts Cem—*cemetery* (3) ... VA-3
Roberts Cem—*cemetery* (4) ... WV-2
Roberts Cem Number 1—*cemetery* ... OH-6
Roberts Cem Number 2—*cemetery* ... OH-6
Roberts Ch—*church* ... AL-4
Roberts Ch—*church* ... KY-4
Roberts Ch—*church* ... SC-3
Roberts Ch—*church* ... TX-5
Roberts Ch—*church* ... VA-3
Robert Sch—*school* ... MA-1
Robert Sch—*school* ... MI-6
*Roberts Chapel* ... AL-4
Roberts Chapel—*church* (2) ... AL-4
Roberts Chapel—*church* ... IN-6
Roberts Chapel—*church* (2) ... KY-4
Roberts Chapel—*church* (2) ... MS-4
Roberts Chapel—*church* (3) ... NC-3
Roberts Chapel—*church* ... OH-6
Roberts Chapel—*church* ... TN-4
Roberts Chapel—*hist pl* ... KY-4
Roberts Chapel Cem—*cemetery* ... IN-6
Roberts Chapel Cem—*cemetery* ... IA-7
Roberts Chapel Cem—*cemetery* ... MS-4
Roberts Chapel Cem—*cemetery* ... SD-7
*Roberts Chapel Ch* ... AL-4
*Roberts Chapel Church* ... MS-4
Roberts Chapel (historical)—*church* ... TN-4
*Robert School* ... IN-6
Robert Schuelke Dam—*dam* ... SD-7
Roberts Community Park—*park* ... MI-6
Roberts Corner—*locale* (2) ... ME-1
**Roberts Corner**—*pop pl* ... MI-6
**Roberts Corner**—*pop pl* ... NY-2
*Roberts Corners* ... MI-6
Roberts Corners—*locale* ... NY-2
**Roberts Corners**—*pop pl* ... MI-6
*Roberts Corners Pond* ... NY-2
Roberts Coulee—*valley* ... WI-6
Roberts County—*civil* ... SD-7
**Roberts (County)**—*pop pl* ... TX-5
Roberts County Courthouse—*hist pl* ... SD-7
Roberts County State Wildlife Mngmt Area—*park* ... SD-7
Roberts Cove—*bay* ... NH-1
Roberts Cove—*valley* ... GA-3
Roberts Cove—*valley* (2) ... NC-3
Roberts Cove—*valley* ... VA-3
Roberts Covered Bridge—*hist pl* ... OH-6
Roberts Creek—*reservoir* ... IA-7
Roberts Creek—*stream* (4) ... AL-4
Roberts Creek—*stream* ... AK-9
Roberts Creek—*stream* ... AR-4
Roberts Creek—*stream* ... CA-9
Roberts Creek—*stream* (2) ... CO-8
Roberts Creek—*stream* ... FL-3
Roberts Creek—*stream* ... ID-8
Roberts Creek—*stream* ... IA-7
Roberts Creek—*stream* ... KS-7
Roberts Creek—*stream* ... MN-6
Roberts Creek—*stream* ... MS-4
Roberts Creek—*stream* (7) ... MT-8
Roberts Creek—*stream* ... NV-8
Roberts Creek—*stream* ... NY-2
Roberts Creek—*stream* ... NC-3
Roberts Creek—*stream* ... OK-5
Roberts Creek—*stream* (6) ... OR-9
Roberts Creek—*stream* (2) ... TN-4
Roberts Creek—*stream* (4) ... TX-5
Roberts Creek—*stream* (3) ... VA-3
Roberts Creek—*stream* (2) ... WI-6
Roberts Creek Mtn—*summit* ... NV-8
Roberts Creek Ranch—*locale* ... NV-8
Roberts Creek Sch—*school* ... OR-9
Roberts Creek Trail (historical)—*trail* ... OR-9
**Roberts Cross Road**—*pop pl* ... GA-3
Roberts Crossroads—*locale* ... AL-4
Roberts Crossroads—*locale* ... GA-3
*Robertsdale* ... IN-6
**Robertsdale**—*pop pl* ... AL-4
**Robertsdale**—*pop pl* ... IN-6
**Robertsdale**—*pop pl* ... PA-2
Robertsdale Baptist Ch—*church* ... AL-4
Robertsdale (CCD)—*cens area* ... AL-4
Robertsdale Ch of Christ—*church* ... AL-4
Robertsdale Division—*civil* ... AL-4
Robertsdale Elem Sch—*school* ... PA-2
Roberts Dam—*dam* ... TX-5
*Roberts Ditch* ... IN-6
Roberts Ditch—*canal* (4) ... IN-6
Roberts Ditch—*canal* ... KY-4
Roberts Ditch—*canal* ... MI-6
Roberts Ditch—*canal* ... NM-5
Roberts Ditch—*canal* (4) ... OH-6
Roberts Drain—*stream* ... MI-6
Roberts Draw—*valley* ... SD-7
Roberts Draw—*valley* ... WY-8
Roberts Draw Tank—*reservoir* ... AZ-5
*Roberts Elem Sch* ... PA-2
Roberts Elem Sch—*school* ... PA-2
Roberts Farm—*locale* ... WA-9
Roberts Farm Site (36LA1)—*hist pl* ... PA-2
Roberts Ferry Cem—*cemetery* ... CA-9
Roberts Ferry Sch—*school* ... CA-9
Roberts Field—*park* ... CA-9
Roberts Field (Airport)—*airport* ... OR-9
Roberts Field (airport)—*airport* ... OR-9
Roberts Field Campsite—*park* ... MO-7
Roberts Field River Access—*locale* ... MO-7
Roberts Folly Cave—*cave* ... AL-4
Roberts Ford—*locale* ... TN-4
Roberts Fork—*stream* ... KY-4
Roberts Fork—*stream* ... WV-2
Roberts Gap—*gap* ... FL-3
Roberts Gap—*gap* ... NC-3
Roberts Gap—*gap* ... TN-4
Roberts Gap Ch—*church* ... AR-4
**Roberts Glen**—*pop pl* ... MD-2
Roberts Grove Ch—*church* ... GA-3
Roberts Grove Ch—*church* ... NC-3
Roberts Gulch—*valley* ... CO-8
Roberts Gulch—*valley* ... ID-8
Roberts Gulch—*valley* (2) ... MT-8
Roberts Gulch Rsvr—*reservoir* ... MT-8
Roberts Hall—*hist pl* ... NY-2
Roberts Harbor—*bay* ... ME-1
Robert Shaw Acres—*locale* ... PA-2
**Roberts (Herrens Chapel)**—*pop pl* ... TN-4
Roberts Hill—*locale* ... NY-2
Roberts Hill—*summit* ... CT-1
Roberts Hill—*summit* ... IN-6
Roberts Hill—*summit* (2) ... ME-1
Roberts Hill—*summit* ... MA-1
Roberts Hill—*summit* ... NY-2
**Roberts (historical)**—*pop pl* ... OR-9
Roberts Hollow—*valley* (4) ... KY-4
Roberts Hollow—*valley* ... MO-7
Roberts Hollow—*valley* ... NY-2
Roberts Hollow—*valley* (8) ... TN-4
Roberts Hollow—*valley* ... TX-5
Roberts Hollow—*valley* ... UT-8
Roberts Hollow—*valley* ... VA-3
Roberts Horn—*summit* ... UT-8
Roberts Hotel—*hist pl* ... IN-6
Roberts House—*hist pl* ... AZ-5
Roberts House—*hist pl* ... MA-1
Roberts House—*hist pl* ... PA-2
Roberts House—*hist pl* ... WI-6
Robert Shrader Dam—*dam* ... AL-4
Robert Shrader Lake—*reservoir* ... AL-4
Roberts HS—*school* ... SC-3
Robert Sibley Airp—*airport* ... TN-4
Robert Simpson Ranch—*locale* ... NE-7
Roberts Island—*island* ... CA-9
Roberts Island—*island* ... FL-3
Roberts Island—*island* ... ME-1
Roberts Island—*island* ... MN-6
Roberts Island Farm Center—*other* ... CA-9
Roberts Island Slough—*gut* ... FL-3
Roberts-Jacobi Restricted Airp—*airport* ... IN-6
Roberts JHS—*school* ... MA-1
Roberts JHS—*school* ... TX-5
Roberts-Justice House—*hist pl* ... NC-3
Robert S Kerr Dam—*dam* (2) ... OK-5
Robert S Kerr Rsvr—*reservoir* ... OK-5
Roberts Lake—*lake* ... FL-3
Roberts Lake—*lake* ... GA-3
Roberts Lake—*lake* ... IN-6
Roberts Lake—*lake* ... MI-6
Roberts Lake—*lake* ... MS-4
Roberts Lake—*lake* ... MO-7
Roberts Lake—*lake* ... ND-7
Roberts Lake—*lake* ... TX-5
Roberts Lake—*lake* ... UT-8
Roberts Lake—*lake* (2) ... WA-9
Roberts Lake—*lake* ... WI-6
Roberts Lake—*lake* ... WY-8
Roberts Lake—*reservoir* ... AL-4
Roberts Lake—*reservoir* ... FL-3
Roberts Lake—*reservoir* ... KS-7
Roberts Lake—*reservoir* ... NC-3
Roberts Lake—*reservoir* ... PA-2
Roberts Lake Dam—*dam* ... KS-7
Roberts Lake Dam—*dam* ... MS-4
Roberts Lakes Strand—*swamp* ... FL-3
Roberts Landing—*locale* ... CA-9
Roberts Landing—*locale* ... FL-3
Roberts Landing—*locale* ... NC-3
**Roberts Landing**—*pop pl* ... MI-6
Roberts Lateral—*canal* ... NM-5
Roberts Lookout Tower—*locale* ... MT-8
Roberts (Magisterial District)—*fmr MCD* ... VA-3
Roberts-McGregor House—*hist pl* ... GA-3
Roberts Meadow—*flat* ... MA-1
Roberts Meadow Brook—*stream* ... MA-1
Roberts Meadow Rsvr—*reservoir* ... MA-1
Roberts Memorial Ch—*church* ... NC-3
Roberts Mesa—*summit* ... AZ-5
Roberts Mesa—*summit* ... TX-5
Roberts Mesa—*summit* ... UT-8
Roberts Mill—*locale* ... VA-3
Roberts Mill Branch—*stream* ... TN-4
Roberts Mill (historical)—*locale* (2) ... AL-4
Roberts Millikin Ditch—*canal* ... OH-6
Roberts Mission—*church* ... WY-8
Robert Smith Cave Number 1—*cave* ... TN-4
Robert Smith Cave Number 2—*cave* ... TN-4
Roberts-Morton House—*hist pl* ... IN-6
Roberts Mound—*hist pl* ... OH-6
Roberts Mount—*summit* ... AK-9
Roberts Mtn—*summit* ... AL-4
Roberts Mtn—*summit* ... AR-4
Roberts Mtn—*summit* ... ID-8
Roberts Mtn—*summit* ... ME-1
Roberts Mtn—*summit* ... MT-8
Roberts Mtn—*summit* (2) ... NC-3
Roberts Mtn—*summit* (2) ... OR-9
Roberts Mtn—*summit* ... VA-3
Roberts Mtn—*summit* ... WY-8
Roberts Mtns—*range* ... NV-8
Roberts Municipal Stadium—*other* ... IN-6
Roberts Octagon Barn—*hist pl* ... IA-7
Roberts Oil Field—*other* ... NM-5
*Robertson* ... TN-4
Robertson—*locale* ... IA-7
Robertson—*locale* (2) ... TX-5
**Robertson**—*pop pl* ... AL-4
**Robertson**—*pop pl* ... GA-3
**Robertson**—*pop pl* ... MO-7
**Robertson**—*pop pl* ... OR-9
**Robertson**—*pop pl* ... TN-4
**Robertson**—*pop pl* ... WY-8
Robertson, Col. Elijah Sterling Clack, Plantation—*hist pl* ... TX-5
Robertson, Dr. and Mrs. Charles G., House and Garden—*hist pl* ... OR-9
Robertson, Eugene P., House—*hist pl* ... MI-6
Robertson, James, Hotel—*hist pl* ... TN-4
Robertson, Samuel, House—*hist pl* ... KY-4
Robertson, Smith, Elem Sch—*hist pl* ... MS-4
Robertson, William, House—*hist pl* ... SC-3
Robertson Acad—*school* ... TN-4
Robertson Bayou—*stream* ... LA-4
*Robertson Bend* ... AL-4
Robertson Boys Camp—*locale* ... TX-5
*Robertson Branch* ... IN-6
*Robertson Branch* ... TN-4
Robertson Branch—*stream* (2) ... AL-4
Robertson Branch—*stream* (2) ... AR-4
Robertson Branch—*stream* ... LA-4
Robertson Branch—*stream* ... MO-7
Robertson Branch—*stream* (2) ... SC-3
Robertson Branch—*stream* (3) ... TN-4
Robertson Branch—*stream* ... TX-5
Robertson Branch—*stream* (2) ... VA-3
Robertson Bridge—*bridge* ... OR-9
Robertson Bridge—*bridge* ... VA-3
Robertson-Buck Cem—*cemetery* ... MO-7
Robertson Canyon—*valley* ... NM-5
*Robertson Cem* ... MS-4
Robertson Cem—*cemetery* (3) ... AL-4
Robertson Cem—*cemetery* ... IL-6
Robertson Cem—*cemetery* (2) ... IN-6
Robertson Cem—*cemetery* ... KS-7
Robertson Cem—*cemetery* (4) ... KY-4
Robertson Cem—*cemetery* (2) ... LA-4
Robertson Cem—*cemetery* (2) ... ME-1
Robertson Cem—*cemetery* (5) ... MS-4
Robertson Cem—*cemetery* (3) ... MO-7
Robertson Cem—*cemetery* ... NC-3
Robertson Cem—*cemetery* (6) ... TN-4
Robertson Cem—*cemetery* (2) ... VA-3
Robertson Cem—*cemetery* (2) ... WV-2
Robertson Cem Number One—*cemetery* ... MS-4
Robertson Cem Number Two—*cemetery* ... MS-4
Robertson Chapel—*church* (2) ... AL-4
Robertson Chapel—*church* ... GA-3
Robertson Chapel—*church* (2) ... LA-4
*Robertson Church* ... TN-4
**Robertson (County)**—*pop pl* ... KY-4
**Robertson County**—*pop pl* ... TN-4
**Robertson (County)**—*pop pl* ... TX-5
Robertson County Courthouse—*hist pl* ... KY-4
Robertson County Courthouse—*hist pl* ... TN-4
Robertson County Courthouse and Jail—*hist pl* ... TX-5
Robertson County Fairgrounds—*locale* ... TN-4
Robertson County Farm (historical)—*locale* ... TN-4
Robertson County Vocational Center—*school* ... TN-4
Robertson Cove—*bay* ... ME-1
Robertson Cove—*valley* ... AL-4
*Robertson Creek* ... AL-4
*Robertson Creek* ... AR-4
*Robertson Creek* ... CA-9
*Robertson Creek* ... TX-5
Robertson Creek—*stream* ... AL-4
Robertson Creek—*stream* (2) ... AR-4
Robertson Creek—*stream* ... CA-9
Robertson Creek—*stream* ... ID-8
Robertson Creek—*stream* ... IN-6
Robertson Creek—*stream* ... KY-4
Robertson Creek—*stream* (4) ... MS-4
Robertson Creek—*stream* (4) ... MT-8
Robertson Creek—*stream* (2) ... NC-3
Robertson Creek—*stream* ... OR-9
Robertson Creek—*stream* (2) ... TN-4
Robertson Creek—*stream* (2) ... TX-5
Robertson Creek—*stream* ... WA-9
*Robertson Creek Baptist Church* ... TN-4
Robertson Creek Ch—*church* ... TN-4
Robertson Creek Sch (historical)—*school* ... TN-4
Robertson Dam—*dam* ... AL-4
Robertson Ditch—*canal* ... ID-8
Robertson Ditch—*canal* ... OR-9
Robertson Drain—*canal* ... MI-6
Robertson Draw—*valley* ... MT-8
Robertson Draw—*valley* ... OR-9
Robertson Draw—*valley* ... WY-8
Robertson-Easterling-McLaurin House—*hist pl* ... SC-3
Robertson Fence Tank—*reservoir* ... NM-5
*Robertson Field* ... ND-7
Robertson Field—*airport* ... NC-3
*Robertson Flat* ... CA-9
Robertson Flat—*flat* ... KY-4
Robertson Flat—*flat* ... TX-5
Robertson Flat—*flat* ... WY-8
Robertson Fork—*locale* ... TN-4
*Robertson Fork Baptist Church* ... TN-4
Robertson Fork Cem—*cemetery* ... TN-4
Robertson Fork Ch—*church* ... TN-4
Robertson Fork Creek—*stream* ... TN-4
Robertson Glacier—*glacier* ... AK-9
Robertson Gulch—*valley* ... ID-8
Robertson Hill—*summit* ... AR-4
Robertson Hill—*summit* ... ME-1
Robertson Hill—*summit* ... NY-2
Robertson Hill—*summit* ... TX-5
Robertson (historical)—*locale* ... AL-4
*Robertson Hollow* ... TN-4
Robertson Hollow—*valley* ... AZ-5
Robertson Hollow—*valley* (2) ... TN-4
Robertson House—*hist pl* ... KY-4
Robertson HS—*school* ... NM-5
Robertson Island—*island* ... FL-3
Robertson Island—*island* ... TN-4
Robertson Island—*island* ... WV-2
Robertson JHS—*school* ... OK-5
*Robertson Lake* ... MS-4
Robertson Lake—*lake* ... MS-4
Robertson Lake—*lake* ... TN-4
Robertson Lake—*lake* ... TX-5
Robertson Lake—*reservoir* (2) ... TN-4
Robertson Lake Dam—*dam* (2) ... TN-4
Robertson Landing—*locale* ... AL-4
Robertson Landing—*locale* ... DE-2
Robertson Lateral—*canal* ... CA-9
Robertson (Magisterial District)—*fmr MCD* ... VA-3
Robertson Mill (historical)—*locale* ... AL-4
Robertson Millpond—*reservoir* ... AL-4
Robertson Mine—*mine* ... OR-9
Robertson Mountain Site—*hist pl* ... VA-3
Robertson Mountain Trail—*trail* ... VA-3
Robertson Mtn—*summit* ... ME-1
Robertson Mtn—*summit* ... NC-3
Robertson Mtn—*summit* (2) ... VA-3
Robertson Number 1 Dam—*dam* ... SD-7
Robertson Park—*park* ... CA-9
Robertson Park—*park* ... CT-1
Robertson Park—*park* ... MS-4
Robertson Park—*park* ... VA-3
Robertson Park Site—*hist pl* ... MN-6
Robertson Pasture—*flat* ... UT-8
Robertson Place—*hist pl* ... KY-4
*Robertson Point* ... FL-3
*Robertson Pond* ... LA-4
Robertson Post Office (historical)—*building* ... TN-4
Robertson Prospect—*mine* ... TN-4
Robertson Ranch—*locale* ... MT-8
Robertson Ranch—*locale* ... OR-9
Robertson Ranch—*locale* (2) ... WY-8
Robertson Recreation Center—*park* ... CA-9
Robertson Reservation—*reserve* ... AL-4
Robertson Ridge—*ridge* ... OR-9
Robertson Ridge—*ridge* ... TN-4
Robertson Ridge—*summit* ... OR-9
*Robertson River* ... VA-3
Robertson River—*stream* ... AK-9
Robertson Road Sch—*school* ... CA-9
*Robertson Run* ... VA-3
Robertson Run—*stream* ... PA-2
Robertson Run—*stream* ... VA-3
**Robertsons**—*pop pl* ... VA-3
Robertson Saltpeter Cave—*cave* ... TN-4
Robertson Sch—*school* ... CA-9
Robertson Sch—*school* ... CT-1
Robertson Sch—*school* ... KY-4
Robertson Sch—*school* ... LA-4
Robertson Sch—*school* ... ME-1
Robertson Sch—*school* (2) ... MS-4
Robertson Sch—*school* ... MT-8
Robertson Sch—*school* ... OK-5
Robertson Sch—*school* ... TN-4
Robertson Sch—*school* ... VA-3
Robertson Sch—*school* ... WA-9
Robertsons Chapel—*church* ... AL-4
Robertson Sch (historical)—*school* ... MS-4
Robertson Sch (historical)—*school* ... MO-7
Robertson Sch (historical)—*school* ... TN-4
*Robertsons Creek* ... OR-9
*Robertsons Cross Roads* ... MS-4
*Robertsons Cross Roads* ... TN-4
Robertsons Cross Roads Post Office (historical)—*building* ... TN-4
*Robertsons Ferry* ... AL-4
*Robertsons Fork Post Office* ... TN-4
Robertsons Island (historical)—*island* ... AL-4
Robertsons Lake—*reservoir* (2) ... AL-4
*Robertsons Landing* ... AL-4
Robertsons Mill (historical)—*locale* ... AL-4
Robertsons Pond—*reservoir* ... NC-3
Robertsons Pond Dam—*dam* ... NC-3
Robertsons Post Office (historical)—*building* ... TN-4
Robertson Spring—*spring* (2) ... AL-4
Robertson Spring—*spring* ... ID-8
Robertson Spring—*spring* ... MT-8
Robertson Spring—*spring* ... OR-9
Robertson Spring—*spring* ... TN-4
Robertson Springs—*spring* ... WA-9
Robertsons Ranch—*locale* ... NM-5
*Robertsons Store* ... MS-4
Robertson State Wildlife Mngmt Area—*park* ... MN-6
Robertson Store—*locale* ... VA-3
Robertson Tank—*reservoir* (3) ... NM-5
Robertson Wash—*stream* ... AZ-5
Robertson Wells—*locale* ... NM-5
Robertson Windmill—*locale* ... TX-5
*Roberts Park* ... IL-6
Roberts Park—*flat* ... NM-5
Roberts Park—*park* ... FL-3
Roberts Park—*park* ... IN-6
Roberts Park—*park* ... IA-7
Roberts Park—*park* ... MO-7
Roberts Park—*park* (2) ... NE-7
Roberts Park—*park* ... NJ-2
Roberts Park—*park* ... NC-3
**Roberts Park**—*pop pl* ... VA-3
Roberts Park Corral—*locale* ... NM-5
Roberts Park Methodist Episcopal Church—*hist pl* ... IN-6
Roberts Park Sch—*school* ... IL-6
Roberts Park Sch—*school* ... VA-3
Roberts Park Tank—*reservoir* ... NM-5
Roberts Park United Methodist Ch—*church* ... IN-6
Roberts Pass—*gap* ... UT-8
Roberts Peak—*summit* ... AK-9
Roberts Place—*locale* ... CA-9
Roberts Place Tank—*reservoir* ... NM-5
*Robert's Point* ... WA-9
Roberts Point—*cape* ... TN-4
*Roberts Pond* ... MA-1
Roberts Pond—*lake* (2) ... ME-1
Roberts Pond—*lake* ... NH-1
Roberts Pond—*lake* ... NY-2
Roberts Pond—*lake* ... PA-2
Roberts Pond—*lake* ... TN-4
Roberts Pond—*reservoir* ... AL-4
Roberts Pond—*reservoir* ... CO-8
Roberts Pond—*reservoir* ... FL-3
Roberts Pond—*reservoir* ... OR-9
Roberts Pond—*swamp* ... FL-3
*Roberts Pond Dam* ... MA-1
Roberts Post Office (historical)—*building* ... MS-4
Roberts Prairie—*flat* ... FL-3
Roberts Prairie Branch—*stream* ... TX-5
Robert Springs Branch—*stream* ... TX-5
Roberts Quarry—*mine* ... CO-8
Roberts-Quay House—*hist pl* ... PA-2
Roberts Ranch—*locale* (2) ... AZ-5
Roberts Ranch—*locale* ... CA-9
Roberts Ranch—*locale* ... MT-8
Roberts Ranch—*locale* ... NV-8
Roberts Ranch—*locale* ... NM-5
Roberts Ranch—*locale* ... OR-9
Roberts Ranch—*locale* (2) ... TX-5
Roberts Ranch—*locale* ... WA-9
Roberts Ranch ( Abandoned)—*locale* ... WY-8
Roberts Recreation Center—*park* ... CA-9
*Roberts Ridge* ... WV-2
Roberts Ridge—*ridge* ... CA-9
Roberts Ridge—*ridge* ... ME-1
Roberts Ridge—*ridge* ... TN-4
Roberts Ridge—*ridge* ... WV-2
Roberts River—*stream* ... FL-3
Roberts Rocky Brook—*stream* ... ME-1
Roberts Roost—*park* ... UT-8
Roberts Roost Creek—*stream* ... KS-7
*Roberts Run* ... MA-1
*Roberts Run* ... PA-2
Roberts Run—*stream* ... OH-6
Roberts Run—*stream* (5) ... PA-2
Roberts Run—*stream* (2) ... WV-2
*Roberts Sch* ... PA-2
Roberts Sch—*school* ... AL-4
Roberts Sch—*school* ... AZ-5
Roberts Sch—*school* ... CA-9
Roberts Sch—*school* ... LA-4
Roberts Sch—*school* ... MI-6
Roberts Sch—*school* (3) ... MO-7
Roberts Sch—*school* ... NJ-2
Roberts Sch—*school* ... NY-2
Roberts Sch—*school* ... PA-2
Roberts Sch—*school* (3) ... TN-4
Roberts Sch—*school* (4) ... TX-5
Roberts Sch (abandoned)—*school* (2) ... MO-7
Roberts Sch (historical)—*school* ... MO-7
Roberts Sch (historical)—*school* ... SD-7
Roberts Sch (historical)—*school* ... TN-4
Roberts School—*locale* ... OR-9
*Roberts School Number 97* ... IN-6
Roberts Sheep Camp—*locale* ... WY-8
**Roberts Siding**—*pop pl* ... SC-3
Roberts Slough—*bay* ... TN-4
Roberts Slough—*gut* ... FL-3
Roberts Slough—*gut* ... ID-8
Roberts Spring—*spring* ... AL-4
Roberts Spring—*spring* ... CA-9
Roberts Spring—*spring* ... ID-8
Roberts Spring—*spring* (2) ... MT-8
Roberts Spring—*spring* ... TN-4
Roberts Spring—*spring* ... UT-8
Roberts Spring No 1—*spring* ... CO-8
Roberts Spring No 2—*spring* ... CO-8
Roberts Spring No 3—*spring* ... CO-8
Roberts Square Park—*park* ... IL-6
**Roberts Subdivision (subdivision)**—*pop pl* ... AL-4
Roberts Swamp—*stream* ... SC-3
Roberts Swamp Brook—*stream* ... NJ-2
Roberts Tabernacle—*church* ... TN-4
Roberts Tank—*reservoir* ... NM-5
Roberts Tanks—*reservoir* (2) ... NM-5
**Robertstown**—*pop pl* ... GA-3
*Roberts Town Elementary School* ... AL-4
Robertstown Sch—*school* ... AL-4
Roberts (Township of)—*fmr MCD* ... AR-4
**Roberts (Township of)**—*pop pl* ... IL-6
**Roberts (Township of)**—*pop pl* ... MN-6
Robert Stuart Jr HS—*school* ... ID-8
Roberts Valley—*basin* ... NE-7
Roberts-Vaughan House—*hist pl* ... NC-3
Robertsville—*locale* ... AR-4
Robertsville—*locale* ... CA-9
Robertsville—*locale* ... CT-1
Robertsville—*locale* ... GA-3
Robertsville—*locale* ... NJ-2
Robertsville—*locale* ... PA-2
**Robertsville**—*pop pl* ... MO-7
**Robertsville**—*pop pl* ... OH-6
**Robertsville**—*pop pl* ... PA-2
**Robertsville**—*pop pl* ... TN-4
Robertsville Cem—*cemetery* ... AR-4
**Robertsville (Furnondaga)**—*pop pl* ... PA-2
**Robertsville (historical)**—*pop pl* ... MS-4
Robertsville HS—*school* ... TN-4
Robertsville Post Office (historical)—*building* ... TN-4
Roberts Vocational Center—*school* ... PA-2
Roberts Wagon Mine (underground)—*mine* ... AL-4
Robert Swamp—*swamp* ... PA-2
Roberts Well—*well* ... AZ-5
Roberts Well—*well* (2) ... NM-5
Roberts Well—*well* ... TX-5
Roberts Wesleyan Coll—*school* ... NY-2
Roberts Windmill—*locale* ... NM-5
Roberts Windmill—*locale* ... TX-5
Robert Taft JHS—*school* ... IN-6
Robert Tank (historical)—*reservoir* ... AZ-5
**Robertville**—*pop pl* ... SC-3
Robertville Baptist Church—*hist pl* ... SC-3
*Robertville Station* ... SC-3
Robert Weir Dam—*dam* ... AL-4
Robert Weir Pond—*reservoir* ... AL-4
Robert Whitmore Grant—*civil* ... FL-3
Robert Williams Dam—*dam* ... TN-4
Robert Williams Lake—*reservoir* ... TN-4
Robert Williams Pond Dam—*dam* ... MS-4
Robert W Matthews Dam—*dam* ... CA-9
**Robeson**—*pop pl* ... PA-2
Robeson, Dr. Donovan, House—*hist pl* ... OH-6
Robeson, Paul, Home—*hist pl* ... NY-2
Robeson Branch—*stream* ... SC-3
Robeson Branch—*stream* ... TN-4
Robeson Branch—*stream* ... TX-5
Robeson Ch—*church* ... PA-2
Robeson County—*civil* ... NC-3
Robeson County Sch—*school* ... NC-3

*Robeson Creek* ... NC-3
Robeson Crossing—*locale* ... PA-2
**Robeson Extension**—*pop pl* ... PA-2
Robeson Hills—*summit* ... IL-6
**Robesonia**—*pop pl* ... PA-2
Robesonia Borough—*civil* ... PA-2
Robeson Memorial Park—*cemetery* ... NC-3
*Robeson Mill* ... AL-4
Robeson Millpond—*reservoir* ... SC-3
Robeson Peak—*summit* ... CO-8
Robeson Pond—*lake* ... IL-6
Robeson Sch—*school* ... IL-6
Robeson Sch—*school* ... MA-1
Robesons Mill (historical)—*locale* ... DE-2
**Robeson (Township of)**—*pop pl* ... PA-2
**Robey**—*pop pl* ... WV-2
Robey Cem—*cemetery* ... KY-4
Robey Elem Sch—*school* ... IN-6
Robey George Park—*park* ... FL-3
Robey Gulch—*valley* ... CO-8
Robey (historical)—*locale* ... SD-7
Robey Hollow—*valley* ... MO-7
Robey Hollow—*valley* ... WV-2
*Robey Sch Number 12* ... IN-6
Robeys Mill—*locale* ... VA-3
Robey Swamp—*swamp* ... KY-4
Rob Fork—*stream* ... KY-4
Rob Hollow—*valley* ... AL-4
Rob Hollow—*valley* ... MO-7
Rob Hollow—*valley* ... TN-4
Rob Horse Trail—*trail* ... PA-2
Robichaud HS—*school* ... MI-6
Robichaux House—*hist pl* ... LA-4
Robideau Landing—*locale* ... OR-9
Robideaux Meadows—*flat* ... ID-8
*Robidoux Airport* ... AZ-5
Robidoux Compressor Station—*other* ... UT-8
Robidoux Creek—*stream* ... KS-7
*Robidoux Fork* ... KS-7
Robidoux Inscription—*hist pl* ... UT-8
Robidoux Inscription—*other* ... UT-8
Robidoux Pass—*hist pl* ... NE-7
Robidoux Row—*hist pl* ... MO-7
Robidoux Sch—*hist pl* ... MO-7
Robie, Frederick C., House—*hist pl* ... IL-6
Robie, Reuben, House—*hist pl* ... NY-2
*Robie Bar* ... ID-8
Robie Creek—*stream* ... ID-8
Robie Lake—*lake* ... WI-6
Robie Point—*summit* ... CA-9
Robie Sch—*school* ... ME-1
Robin—*locale* ... ID-8
Robin—*locale* ... IA-7
Robin, Lake—*reservoir* ... AL-4
Robina Draw—*valley* (2) ... NM-5
Robina (historical)—*locale* ... MS-4
Robina Lake—*lake* ... MN-6
Robin Bay—*bay* ... VI-3
Robin Bay—*swamp* ... GA-3
Robin Bay—*swamp* ... NC-3
*Robin Branch* ... TX-5
Robin Branch—*stream* ... KY-4
Robin Branch—*stream* (2) ... NC-3
Robin Bridge—*bridge* ... LA-4
Robin Cem—*cemetery* ... ID-8
Robin Coal Mines (underground)—*mine* ... AL-4
Robin Cove—*bay* ... MD-2
*Robin Creek* ... MD-2
Robin Creek—*stream* (2) ... AK-9
Robin Creek—*stream* (3) ... ID-8
Robin Creek—*stream* ... MN-6
Robin Creek—*stream* ... MT-8
Robin Creek—*stream* ... OR-9
Robincroft—*hist pl* ... TN-4
**Robindale**—*pop pl* ... MD-2
**Robindale**—*pop pl* ... PA-2
*Robindale Heights* ... PA-2
Robindreau, Alfred E., House—*hist pl* ... MA-1
**Robin Estates**—*pop pl* ... NJ-2
Robinet Drain—*canal* ... MI-6
**Robinet (historical)**—*pop pl* ... NC-3
*Robinett* ... OR-9
Robinett Branch—*stream* ... TX-5
Robinett Cem—*cemetery* ... MO-7
Robinett Cem—*cemetery* ... TX-5
Robinett Cem—*cemetery* ... VA-3
Robinett Cem—*cemetery* ... WV-2
*Robinett Creek* ... TN-4
**Robinette**—*pop pl* ... OR-9
**Robinette**—*pop pl* ... WV-2
Robinette Branch—*stream* (2) ... VA-3
Robinette Branch—*stream* ... WV-2
Robinette Cem—*cemetery* (6) ... VA-3
Robinette Cem—*cemetery* ... WV-2
Robinette Chapel—*church* ... VA-3
*Robinette Creek* ... OR-9
Robinette Creek—*stream* ... IL-6
Robinette Creek—*stream* ... OR-9
Robinette Creek—*stream* ... TN-4
Robinette Gap—*gap* ... VA-3
Robinette Memorial Ch—*church* ... VA-3
Robinette Mine—*mine* ... NV-8
Robinette Mtn—*summit* ... WA-9
Robinette Point—*cape* ... TX-5
Robinette Prospect—*mine* ... TN-4
Robinette Sch (historical)—*school* ... MO-7
Robinette Valley—*basin* ... VA-3
Robinett Hollow—*valley* ... KY-4
Robinett Ridge—*ridge* (2) ... OH-6
Robing Cem—*cemetery* ... GA-3
**Robin Heights**—*pop pl* ... PA-2
*Robin Hill* ... MA-1
**Robin Hill**—*pop pl* ... FL-3
**Robin Hill**—*pop pl* ... IL-6
**Robin Hill**—*pop pl* ... MA-1
Robin Hill—*summit* ... CT-1
Robin Hill Cem—*cemetery* ... MA-1
Robin Hill Ch—*church* ... AL-4
Robin (historical P.O.)—*locale* ... IA-7
Robin Hollow—*valley* ... MA-1
Robin Hollow—*valley* ... PA-2
Robin Hollow—*valley* ... RI-1
Robin Hollow—*valley* ... WV-2
Robin Hollow—*valley* ... WI-6
Robin Hollow Pond—*reservoir* ... MA-1
Robin Hollow Pond—*reservoir* (2) ... RI-1
Robin Hollow Pond Dam—*dam* ... RI-1
**Robinhood**—*pop pl* ... ME-1
Robin Hood, Lake—*lake* ... FL-3
Robin Hood, Lake—*reservoir* ... MO-7
Robinhood, Lake—*reservoir* ... TX-5
*Robinhood Baptist Church* ... MS-4
Robin Hood Bay—*bay* ... VA-3
Robinhood Brook—*stream* ... PA-2
Robinhood Campground—*park* ... OR-9
Robinhood Ch—*church* ... MS-4
Robinhood Country Estates—*locale* ... PA-2
Robinhood Cove—*bay* ... ME-1
Robinhood Creek—*stream* ... OR-9
**Robinhood Forest**—*pop pl* ... VA-3
**Robinhood Forest (subdivision)**—*pop pl* ... NC-3
Robinhood Guard Station—*locale* ... OR-9
**Robin Hood Homes**—*pop pl* ... NJ-2
Robinhood Lake—*reservoir* ... MS-4
Robin Hood Lake—*reservoir* ... NY-2
Robin Hood Lake Dam—*dam* ... MA-1
Robin Hood Lake Number 1 Dam—*dam* ... MS-4
Robin Hood Lake Number 2 Dam—*dam* ... MS-4
Robin Hood Lake Number 3 Dam—*dam* ... MS-4
Robin Hood Lake Number 4 Dam—*dam* ... MS-4
Robin Hood Lake Number 5 Dam—*dam* ... MS-4
**Robin Hood Lakes**—*pop pl* ... PA-2
**Robin Hood Park**—*pop pl* ... NM-5
Robinhood Road Ch—*church* ... NC-3
Robin Hood Road Shop Ctr—*locale* ... NC-3
Robin Hood (RR name Twilight)—*other* ... WV-2
Robin Hood Sch—*school* ... MA-1
**Robin Hood Trace (subdivision)**—*pop pl* ... NC-3
Robin Lake—*lake* ... MN-6
Robin Lake—*lake* ... WY-8
Robin Lake—*reservoir* ... GA-3
**Robin Lake Estates (subdivision)**—*pop pl* ... NC-3
Robin Lakes—*lake* ... WA-9
*Robin Landing* ... GA-3
Robin Landing Field—*airport* ... AZ-5
Robin Lick Creek—*stream* ... KY-4
Robin Park—*park* ... OR-9
Robin Park—*park* ... WI-6
**Robin Park**—*pop pl* ... VA-3
*Robin Point* ... MD-2
Robin Ridge—*ridge* ... TN-4
Robin Rsvr—*reservoir* ... MT-8
Robin Rsvr—*reservoir* ... OR-9
Robin Run—*stream* ... IN-6
Robin Run—*stream* ... KY-4
Robin Run—*stream* ... MT-8
Robin Run—*stream* ... PA-2
Robin Run Dam—*dam* ... PA-2
Robin Run Lake—*reservoir* ... PA-2
**Robins**—*pop pl* ... IA-7
**Robins**—*pop pl* ... OH-6
Robins Air Force Base—*military* ... GA-3
Robins Arroyo—*valley* ... TX-5
Robins Bayou—*stream* ... MS-4
*Robins Branch* ... VT-1
Robins Branch—*stream* ... VA-3
Robins Brook—*stream* ... NY-2
Robins Canal—*canal* ... LA-4
Robins Canyon—*valley* ... CO-8
Robins Cem—*cemetery* ... IA-7
*Robins Cemetery* ... TN-4
Robin Sch—*school* ... LA-4
Robin Sch—*school* ... MS-4
Robin Sch (abandoned)—*school* ... PA-2
*Robin's Creek* ... MD-2
Robins Creek—*stream* ... GA-3
Robins Creek—*stream* (2) ... MD-2
Robins Creek—*stream* ... TX-5
Robins Creek—*stream* ... WA-9
Robins Gap—*stream* ... TX-5
Robins Grove Point—*cape* ... VA-3
*Robins Hill* ... MA-1
Robins Hill—*summit* ... MO-7
*Robin's Island* ... NY-2
Robins Island—*island* ... NY-2
Robins Island—*island* ... OR-9
**Robins Island**—*pop pl* ... NY-2
Robins Lake—*lake* ... UT-8
Robins Landing—*locale* ... NC-3
Robin Slough—*stream* ... AR-4
Robins Marsh—*swamp* ... MD-2
Robins Neck—*cape* ... VA-3
Robins Nest Lake—*reservoir* ... NC-3
Robins Nest Lake Dam—*dam* ... NC-3
**Robins Nest (subdivision)**—*pop pl* ... NC-3
*Robinson* ... AL-4
*Robinson* ... MS-4
*Robinson* ... TN-4
Robinson—*locale* ... GA-3
Robinson—*locale* ... KY-4
Robinson—*locale* ... LA-4
Robinson—*locale* ... MN-6
Robinson—*locale* ... MT-8
Robinson—*locale* ... NY-2
Robinson—*locale* ... OR-9
Robinson—*locale* ... PA-2
Robinson—*locale* (2) ... WA-9
Robinson—*locale* ... WY-8
Robinson—*other* ... MS-4
Robinson—*other* ... TN-4
**Robinson**—*pop pl* ... AR-4
**Robinson**—*pop pl* ... GA-3
**Robinson**—*pop pl* ... IL-6
**Robinson**—*pop pl* ... IA-7
**Robinson**—*pop pl* ... KS-7
**Robinson**—*pop pl* ... ME-1
**Robinson**—*pop pl* ... MD-2
**Robinson**—*pop pl* ... MI-6
**Robinson**—*pop pl* ... ND-7
**Robinson**—*pop pl* (2) ... PA-2
**Robinson**—*pop pl* ... SC-3
**Robinson**—*pop pl* ... TX-5
**Robinson**—*pop pl* ... VT-1
Robinson, A. W., Bldg—*hist pl* ... AZ-5
Robinson, Capt. Joel, House—*hist pl* ... MA-1
Robinson, Charles, House—*hist pl* ... WI-6
Robinson, Col. William H., House—*hist pl* ... ND-7
Robinson, Daniel Webster, House—*hist pl* ... VT-1
Robinson, Edmund, House—*hist pl* ... OH-6
Robinson, Edward Arlington, House—*hist pl* ... ME-1
Robinson, Horney, House—*hist pl* ... IN-6
Robinson, James E., House—*hist pl* ... UT-8
Robinson, J. C., House—*hist pl* ... NE-7
Robinson, Jesse, House—*hist pl* ... DE-2
Robinson, J. L., General Store—*hist pl* ... IL-6
Robinson, John, House—*hist pl* ... AL-4
Robinson, John Roosevelt "Jackie", House—*hist pl* ... NY-2
Robinson, Joseph Taylor, House—*hist pl* ... AR-4
Robinson, Lake—*bay* ... LA-4
Robinson, Lake—*reservoir* ... SC-3
Robinson, Lake (historical)—*lake* ... ND-7
Robinson, Leonard, House—*hist pl* ... MN-6
Robinson, Mount—*summit* ... CO-8
Robinson, Mrs. William, House—*hist pl* ... AL-4
Robinson, P., Fur Cutting Company—*hist pl* ... CT-1
Robinson, Virginia, Estate—*hist pl* ... CA-9
Robinson, William, House—*hist pl* ... UT-8
Robinson Access Point—*locale* ... GA-3
Robinson Airp—*airport* ... IN-6
**Robinson Arms Landing**—*pop pl* ... TX-5
Robinson Arroyo—*stream* ... CO-8
Robinson Baptist Ch—*church* ... MS-4
**Robinson Bar**—*pop pl* ... ID-8
Robinson Bar Peak—*summit* ... ID-8
Robinson Basin—*basin* ... CO-8
Robinson Bay—*bay* ... AR-4
Robinson Bay—*bay* ... CA-9
Robinson Bay—*bay* ... MI-6
Robinson Bay—*bay* ... MN-6
Robinson Bay—*bay* ... NY-2
Robinson Bay—*lake* ... AR-4
Robinson Bay—*swamp* ... FL-3
Robinson Bay Archeol District—*hist pl* ... NY-2
*Robinson Bayou* ... LA-4
Robinson Bayou—*bay* ... FL-3
Robinson Bayou—*gut* ... MS-4
Robinson Bayou—*stream* ... AL-4
Robinson Bayou—*stream* (2) ... MS-4
Robinson Bayou—*stream* ... MO-7
Robinson Bayou—*stream* (2) ... TX-5
Robinson Bayou Revetment—*levee* ... TN-4
*Robinson Bend* ... AL-4
Robinson Bend—*bend* (2) ... AL-4
Robinson Bend—*bend* ... LA-4
Robinson Bldg—*hist pl* ... TX-5
Robinson Blue Springs—*spring* ... TX-5
Robinson Bluff—*cliff* ... MO-7
Robinson Bluff—*cliff* ... TX-5
Robinson Bog—*swamp* ... ME-1
Robinson Bottom—*valley* ... MS-4
Robinson-Bowman Mine—*mine* ... AK-9
Robinson Brake—*swamp* ... LA-4
*Robinson Branch* ... AR-4
*Robinson Branch* ... VA-3
Robinson Branch—*stream* (2) ... AL-4
Robinson Branch—*stream* ... AR-4
Robinson Branch—*stream* ... FL-3
Robinson Branch—*stream* ... GA-3
Robinson Branch—*stream* (2) ... IN-6
Robinson Branch—*stream* ... KS-7
Robinson Branch—*stream* (2) ... KY-4
Robinson Branch—*stream* ... MS-4
Robinson Branch—*stream* ... MO-7
Robinson Branch—*stream* ... NE-7
Robinson Branch—*stream* ... NC-3
Robinson Branch—*stream* (2) ... SC-3
Robinson Branch—*stream* (6) ... TN-4
Robinson Branch—*stream* (7) ... TX-5
Robinson Branch—*stream* ... VA-3
Robinson Branch—*stream* ... WV-2
Robinson Bridge—*bridge* ... AL-4
Robinson Bridge—*bridge* ... GA-3
Robinson Bridge—*bridge* ... MA-1
Robinson Brook—*stream* (2) ... ME-1
Robinson Brook—*stream* (2) ... MA-1
Robinson Brook—*stream* ... MN-6
Robinson Brook—*stream* ... NH-1
Robinson Brook—*stream* ... NY-2
Robinson Brothers Ranch (historical)—*locale* ... SD-7
Robinson Butte—*summit* ... OR-9
Robinson Butte—*summit* ... WY-8
Robinson Canal—*canal* (2) ... LA-4
*Robinson Canyon* ... OR-9
Robinson Canyon—*valley* (2) ... AZ-5
Robinson Canyon—*valley* (4) ... CA-9
Robinson Canyon—*valley* ... MT-8
Robinson Canyon—*valley* (3) ... NV-8
Robinson Canyon—*valley* (4) ... OR-9
Robinson Canyon—*valley* ... UT-8
Robinson Canyon—*valley* (3) ... WA-9
Robinson Canyon—*valley* (2) ... WY-8
Robinson Cave—*cave* ... AL-4
Robinson Cave—*cave* (2) ... TN-4
*Robinson Cem* ... MS-4
*Robinson Cem* ... MO-7
Robinson Cem—*cemetery* (8) ... AL-4
Robinson Cem—*cemetery* (4) ... AR-4
Robinson Cem—*cemetery* ... FL-3
Robinson Cem—*cemetery* (3) ... GA-3
Robinson Cem—*cemetery* (5) ... IL-6
Robinson Cem—*cemetery* (7) ... IN-6
Robinson Cem—*cemetery* (6) ... KY-4
Robinson Cem—*cemetery* (2) ... LA-4
Robinson Cem—*cemetery* (2) ... ME-1
Robinson Cem—*cemetery* ... MI-6
Robinson Cem—*cemetery* (7) ... MS-4
Robinson Cem—*cemetery* (4) ... MO-7
Robinson Cem—*cemetery* ... NH-1
Robinson Cem—*cemetery* (2) ... NY-2
Robinson Cem—*cemetery* (9) ... NC-3
Robinson Cem—*cemetery* (6) ... OH-6
Robinson Cem—*cemetery* (3) ... PA-2
Robinson Cem—*cemetery* ... SC-3
Robinson Cem—*cemetery* (16) ... TN-4
Robinson Cem—*cemetery* (3) ... TX-5
Robinson Cem—*cemetery* ... VT-1
Robinson Cem—*cemetery* (6) ... VA-3
Robinson Cem—*cemetery* (3) ... WV-2
*Robinson Cemetery* ... OR-9
Robinson Cem Number One—*cemetery* ... MS-4
Robinson Ch—*church* ... GA-3
Robinson Ch—*church* ... LA-4
Robinson Ch—*church* ... MD-2
Robinson Ch—*church* ... NC-3
Robinson Ch—*church* ... OK-5
Robinson Chapel—*church* ... IN-6
Robinson Chapel—*church* ... KY-4
Robinson Chapel—*church* (5) ... MS-4
Robinson Chapel—*church* (2) ... NC-3
Robinson Chapel—*church* ... OK-5
Robinson Chapel—*church* (3) ... TN-4
Robinson Chapel Cem—*cemetery* ... TN-4
*Robinson Chapel Methodist Church* ... TN-4
Robinson Chapel Sch (historical)—*school* ... MS-4
Robinson Ch of God in Christ Temple—*church* ... IN-6
**Robinson Church Community (subdivision)**—*pop pl* ... NC-3
Robinson Community Hall—*locale* ... TX-5
Robinson Corner—*locale* ... NH-1
Robinson Corner—*locale* ... OK-5
**Robinson Corner**—*pop pl* ... ME-1
**Robinson Corners**—*pop pl* ... NY-2
Robinson Corner Shop Ctr—*locale* ... TN-4
Robinson Coulee—*valley* ... MT-8
Robinson Coulee—*valley* ... ND-7
Robinson County Park—*park* ... IA-7
*Robinson Cove* ... ME-1
*Robinson Cove* ... MD-2
Robinson Cove—*bay* ... MD-2
Robinson Cove—*bay* ... NY-2
Robinson Cove—*valley* ... NC-3
Robinson Cove—*valley* ... TN-4
Robinson Cow Camp—*locale* ... CA-9
Robinson Crater—*crater* ... AZ-5
*Robinson Creek* ... MT-8
*Robinson Creek* ... NC-3
*Robinson Creek* ... WA-9
**Robinson Creek**—*pop pl* ... KY-4
Robinson Creek—*stream* (8) ... AL-4
Robinson Creek—*stream* (2) ... AK-9
Robinson Creek—*stream* (2) ... AR-4
Robinson Creek—*stream* (9) ... CA-9
Robinson Creek—*stream* (2) ... CO-8
Robinson Creek—*stream* (2) ... FL-3
Robinson Creek—*stream* (3) ... GA-3
Robinson Creek—*stream* (6) ... ID-8
Robinson Creek—*stream* (3) ... IL-6
Robinson Creek—*stream* (3) ... IN-6
Robinson Creek—*stream* (2) ... KS-7
Robinson Creek—*stream* (4) ... KY-4
Robinson Creek—*stream* ... MA-1
Robinson Creek—*stream* (4) ... MI-6
Robinson Creek—*stream* ... MN-6
Robinson Creek—*stream* (4) ... MS-4
Robinson Creek—*stream* ... MO-7
Robinson Creek—*stream* (2) ... MT-8
Robinson Creek—*stream* ... NE-7
Robinson Creek—*stream* (3) ... NV-8
Robinson Creek—*stream* (2) ... NY-2
Robinson Creek—*stream* (2) ... NC-3
Robinson Creek—*stream* (2) ... OK-5
Robinson Creek—*stream* (2) ... OR-9
Robinson Creek—*stream* (7) ... TN-4
Robinson Creek—*stream* (4) ... TX-5
Robinson Creek—*stream* ... UT-8
Robinson Creek—*stream* (3) ... VA-3
Robinson Creek—*stream* (5) ... WA-9
Robinson Creek—*stream* ... WV-2
Robinson Creek—*stream* (2) ... WI-6
Robinson Creek—*stream* (7) ... WY-8
Robinson Creek Campground—*locale* ... CA-9
Robinson Creek (CCD)—*cens area* ... KY-4
Robinson Creek Ch—*church* ... KY-4
Robinson Creek Dam—*dam* ... MI-6
Robinson Creek Flooding—*reservoir* ... MI-6
Robinson Creek Sch—*school* ... IL-6
Robinson Creek Sch—*school* ... KY-4
Robinson Crossroad—*locale* ... SC-3
Robinson Crossroads—*locale* (2) ... AL-4
Robinson Cross Roads—*locale* ... TN-4
Robinson Crossroads—*locale* ... TN-4
Robinson Crusoe Camp—*locale* ... MA-1
**Robinson Crusoe Camp**—*pop pl* ... MA-1
Robinson Crusoe Island—*island* ... TN-4
Robinson Crusoe Island—*island* ... VA-3
Robinson Dam—*dam* (4) ... AL-4
Robinson Dam—*dam* ... OR-9
Robinson Dam—*dam* ... PA-2
Robinson Dam—*locale* ... ME-1
Robinson-Dickson Cem—*cemetery* ... AL-4
Robinson Dike Mine—*mine* ... ID-8
Robinson District Cem—*cemetery* ... NY-2
Robinson Ditch—*canal* ... AZ-5
Robinson Ditch—*canal* (2) ... IN-6
Robinson Ditch—*canal* ... MI-6
Robinson Ditch—*canal* ... MT-8
Robinson Ditch—*canal* ... OH-6
Robinson Drain—*canal* (2) ... MI-6
Robinson Drain—*stream* ... MI-6
*Robinson Draw* ... MT-8
*Robinson Draw* ... WY-8
Robinson Draw—*valley* ... CO-8
Robinson Draw—*valley* ... ID-8
Robinson Draw—*valley* ... MT-8
Robinson Draw—*valley* ... NM-5
Robinson Draw—*valley* ... OR-9
Robinson Draw—*valley* ... TX-5
Robinson Draw—*valley* (3) ... WY-8
*Robinson Elementary School* ... AL-4
Robinson Elem Sch—*school* ... FL-3
Robinson Falls Creek—*stream* ... AK-9
Robinson Ferry (historical)—*locale* ... AL-4
Robinson Ferry (historical)—*locale* ... TN-4
Robinson Ferry Shoals—*bar* ... TN-4
*Robinson Flat* ... CA-9
Robinson Flat—*flat* ... AZ-5
Robinson Flat—*flat* (2) ... CA-9
Robinson Flat—*flat* ... WA-9
Robinson Flats—*flat* ... SD-7
Robinson Ford (historical)—*locale* ... TN-4
Robinson Ford Shoals—*bar* ... TN-4
**Robinson Forest (subdivision)**—*pop pl* ... TN-4
Robinson Fork—*stream* ... KY-4
Robinson Fork—*stream* ... PA-2
Robinson Fork—*stream* (2) ... VA-3
Robinson Fork—*stream* ... WA-9
Robinson Fork—*stream* (3) ... WV-2
Robinson Gap—*gap* ... NC-3
Robinson Gap—*gap* ... TN-4
Robinson Gap—*gap* ... VA-3
Robinson Gap—*gap* ... WV-2
**Robinson Gin**—*pop pl* ... MS-4
Robinson Group—*island* ... NY-2
Robinson Grove—*woods* ... CA-9
*Robinson Gulch* ... WA-9
Robinson Gulch—*valley* (3) ... CA-9
Robinson Gulch—*valley* (3) ... CO-8
Robinson Gulch—*valley* ... MT-8
Robinson Gulch—*valley* (3) ... OR-9
Robinson Gulch—*valley* ... UT-8
Robinson Gulch—*valley* (2) ... WA-9
Robinson Gulch—*valley* ... WY-8
Robinson Gulch Rapids—*rapids* ... ID-8
Robinson Gulch Rapids—*rapids* ... OR-9
Robinson Gully—*valley* ... TX-5
Robinson Hammock—*island* ... GA-3
**Robinson Heights**—*pop pl* ... FL-3
**Robinson Heights (subdivision)**—*pop pl* ... NC-3
Robinson-Herrling Sawmill—*hist pl* ... WI-6
Robinson Hill—*summit* (4) ... ME-1
Robinson Hill—*summit* ... MA-1
Robinson Hill—*summit* (2) ... NH-1
Robinson Hill—*summit* (2) ... NY-2
Robinson Hill—*summit* (2) ... TN-4
Robinson Hill—*summit* (3) ... VT-1
Robinson Hill Ch—*church* ... TX-5
Robinson Hill Sch—*school* ... MA-1
Robinson Hill Sch—*school* ... NY-2
Robinson Hillside—*other* ... WI-6
**Robinson (historical)**—*pop pl* ... IN-6
**Robinson (historical)**—*pop pl* ... TN-4
*Robinson Hole* ... MA-1
Robinson Hole—*bay* ... NV-8
Robinson Hollow—*valley* ... AL-4
Robinson Hollow—*valley* ... AR-4
Robinson Hollow—*valley* ... IN-6
Robinson Hollow—*valley* ... KY-4
Robinson Hollow—*valley* (3) ... MO-7
Robinson Hollow—*valley* ... NY-2
Robinson Hollow—*valley* (8) ... TN-4
Robinson Hollow—*valley* ... VA-3
Robinson Hollow—*valley* ... WY-8
Robinson Hollow Branch—*stream* ... TN-4
Robinson Hollow State For—*forest* ... NY-2
Robinson Hotel—*hist pl* ... CA-9
Robinson House—*building* ... VA-3
Robinson House—*hist pl* ... CO-8
Robinson House—*hist pl* ... DE-2
Robinson House—*hist pl* ... MA-1
Robinson House—*hist pl* ... PA-2
Robinson HS—*school* ... FL-3
*Robinson Hunting Creek* ... NC-3
Robinson Island—*island* (2) ... AL-4
Robinson Island—*island* ... NY-2
Robinson JHS—*school* (2) ... KS-7
Robinson JHS—*school* ... OH-6
*Robinson Junction* ... MS-4
**Robinson Junction**—*pop pl* ... MS-4
Robinson Knob—*summit* ... VA-3
Robinson Laboratory Sch—*school* ... MD-2
*Robinson Lake* ... AL-4
*Robinson Lake* ... LA-4
*Robinson Lake* ... MI-6
*Robinson Lake* ... OR-9
Robinson Lake—*lake* ... AR-4
Robinson Lake—*lake* ... CA-9
Robinson Lake—*lake* ... FL-3
Robinson Lake—*lake* (2) ... ID-8
Robinson Lake—*lake* ... IN-6
Robinson Lake—*lake* (5) ... MI-6
Robinson Lake—*lake* (4) ... MN-6
Robinson Lake—*lake* ... MO-7
Robinson Lake—*lake* (2) ... NE-7
Robinson Lake—*lake* ... NV-8
Robinson Lake—*lake* ... OR-9
Robinson Lake—*lake* ... PA-2
Robinson Lake—*lake* (2) ... TX-5
Robinson Lake—*lake* (3) ... WI-6
Robinson Lake—*reservoir* (3) ... AL-4
Robinson Lake—*reservoir* ... CO-8
Robinson Lake—*reservoir* (2) ... GA-3
Robinson Lake—*reservoir* ... ID-8
Robinson Lake—*reservoir* ... OR-9
Robinson Lake—*reservoir* (2) ... PA-2
Robinson Lake—*reservoir* (2) ... TN-4
Robinson Lake—*swamp* ... LA-4
Robinson Lake Dam—*dam* ... AL-4
Robinson Lake Dam—*dam* ... MS-4
Robinson Lake Dam—*dam* ... TN-4
Robinson Lake Number 2—*reservoir* ... AL-4
Robinson Landing—*locale* ... DE-2
Robinson Landing—*locale* ... TN-4
Robinson Landing (inundated)—*locale* ... AL-4
Robinson Laurel—*valley* ... NC-3
Robinson-Lewis-G. F. Fessenden House—*hist pl* ... MA-1
Robinson-Macken House—*hist pl* ... TX-5
Robinson (Magisterial District)—*fmr MCD* ... VA-3
Robinson (Magisterial District)—*fmr MCD* ... WV-2
Robinson Marsh—*swamp* ... TX-5
Robinson-McElvin Cem—*cemetery* ... MS-4
Robinson Meadow—*swamp* ... ME-1
Robinson Memorial Chapel—*church* ... PA-2
Robinson Memorial Park—*park* ... AL-4
Robinson Memorial Presbyterian Ch—*church* ... AL-4
Robinson Memorial Sch—*school* ... VA-3
Robinson Mesa—*summit* ... AZ-5
Robinson Mesa Twenty-seven Trail—*trail* ... AZ-5
*Robinson Middle School* ... TN-4
Robinson Mill—*hist pl* ... KY-4
Robinson Mill—*hist pl* ... TN-4
Robinson Mill—*locale* ... TN-4
Robinson Mill Branch—*stream* ... NC-3
Robinson Mill Creek—*gut* ... AL-4
Robinson Mill Creek—*stream* ... AL-4
Robinson Mills—*locale* ... CA-9
Robinson Mine—*mine* ... CA-9
Robinson Mine—*mine* ... TN-4
Robinson Mine—*mine* ... UT-8
Robinson Mine (underground)—*mine* ... AL-4
Robinson Missionary Baptist Ch—*church* ... MS-4
Robinson Mountains—*range* ... AK-9
*Robinson Mtn* ... ME-1
Robinson Mtn—*summit* ... AL-4
Robinson Mtn—*summit* ... AZ-5
Robinson Mtn—*summit* ... AR-4
Robinson Mtn—*summit* (2) ... ME-1
Robinson Mtn—*summit* ... MT-8
Robinson Mtn—*summit* ... NV-8
Robinson Mtn—*summit* ... WA-9
Robinson Neck—*cape* ... MD-2
Robinson Number 2 Dam—*dam* ... AL-4
Robinson Oil Field—*oilfield* ... TX-5
Robinson Oil Field—*other* ... IL-6
Robinson Oil Field—*other* ... NM-5
Robinson Park—*park* ... CO-8
Robinson Park—*park* ... IL-6
Robinson Park—*park* (2) ... MI-6
Robinson Park—*park* ... MN-6
Robinson Park—*park* ... MS-4
Robinson Park—*park* ... NM-5
Robinson Park—*park* ... NC-3
Robinson Park—*park* ... PA-2
Robinson Park—*park* ... TX-5
Robinson Park—*park* ... UT-8
Robinson Park—*park* ... WI-6
Robinson-Parsons Farm—*hist pl* ... ME-1
Robinson Pass—*gap* ... WA-9
Robinson-Pavey House—*hist pl* ... OH-6
Robinson Peak—*summit* ... CA-9
Robinson Peak—*summit* ... ME-1
Robinson Peak—*summit* ... NM-5
Robinson Peak—*summit* ... TX-5
Robinson Place—*locale* ... CO-8
Robinson Place—*locale* ... WY-8
Robinson Plateau—*area* ... CO-8
Robinson Plaza—*post sta* ... TX-5
*Robinson Point* ... NC-3
Robinson Point—*cape* (2) ... CA-9
Robinson Point—*cape* ... FL-3
Robinson Point—*cape* ... ME-1
Robinson Point—*cape* (2) ... NC-3
Robinson Point—*cape* (2) ... VT-1
Robinson Point—*cape* ... WA-9
**Robinson Point**—*pop pl* ... FL-3
Robinson Point—*summit* ... TN-4
Robinson Point Ch—*church* ... AR-4
Robinson Point Landing—*locale* ... AR-4
*Robinson Pond* ... LA-4
Robinson Pond—*bay* ... LA-4
Robinson Pond—*lake* ... CT-1
Robinson Pond—*lake* ... GA-3
Robinson Pond—*lake* (3) ... ME-1
Robinson Pond—*lake* ... MO-7
Robinson Pond—*lake* ... NH-1
Robinson Pond—*lake* (2) ... NY-2
Robinson Pond—*lake* ... SC-3
Robinson Pond—*reservoir* (2) ... MA-1
Robinson Pond—*reservoir* ... NY-2
Robinson Pond—*reservoir* ... PA-2
Robinson Pond—*reservoir* ... VA-3
Robinson Pond—*swamp* ... AL-4
Robinson Pond Dam—*dam* ... MA-1
Robinson Pond Outler—*stream* ... ME-1
Robinson Prairie—*flat* ... OR-9
Robinson Primary Sch—*school* ... AL-4
Robinson Private Airp—*airport* ... AL-4
Robinson Ranch—*locale* ... CA-9
Robinson Ranch—*locale* (2) ... CO-8
Robinson Ranch—*locale* ... MT-8
Robinson Ranch—*locale* ... NV-8
Robinson Ranch—*locale* (2) ... NM-5
Robinson Ranch—*locale* ... OR-9
Robinson Ranch—*locale* ... SD-7
Robinson Ranch—*locale* (4) ... TX-5
Robinson Ranch—*locale* ... UT-8
Robinson Ranch—*locale* (4) ... WY-8
**Robinson Rancheria**—*pop pl* ... CA-9
Robinson Ravine—*valley* ... CA-9
Robinson Reef—*bar* ... CA-9
Robinson Ridge—*ridge* ... CA-9
Robinson Ridge—*ridge* ... KY-4
Robinson Ridge—*ridge* ... ME-1
Robinson Ridge—*ridge* ... MO-7
Robinson Ridge—*ridge* (2) ... MT-8
Robinson Ridge—*ridge* ... OK-5
Robinson Ridge—*ridge* (3) ... OR-9
Robinson Ridge—*ridge* (3) ... TN-4
Robinson Ridge—*ridge* ... VA-3
Robinson Ridge—*ridge* (2) ... WV-2
Robinson Ridge Ch—*church* ... WV-2
Robinson Ridge Saltpeter Cave—*cave* ... TN-4
Robinson River—*stream* ... NY-2
Robinson River—*stream* ... VA-3
Robinson River Ch—*church* ... VA-3
Robinson Road Cem—*cemetery* ... KY-4
Robinson Road (190-191-3M)—*hist pl* ... MS-4
**Robinson (Robinson Hillside)**—*pop pl* ... WI-6
**Robinson (Robinsons)**—*pop pl* ... ME-1
Robinson Rock—*island* ... ME-1
Robinson Round—*cape* ... GA-3
Robinson (RR name for North Robinson)—*other* ... OH-6
Robinson Rsvr—*reservoir* ... AZ-5
Robinson Rsvr—*reservoir* (2) ... OR-9
Robinson Rsvr—*reservoir* ... UT-8
Robinson Rsvr—*reservoir* ... WY-8
*Robinson Run* ... PA-2
*Robinson Run* ... VA-3
Robinson Run—*stream* ... NY-2
Robinson Run—*stream* (6) ... OH-6
Robinson Run—*stream* (6) ... PA-2
Robinson Run—*stream* ... VA-3
Robinson Run—*stream* (8) ... WV-2
Robinson Run Cem—*cemetery* ... PA-2
Robinson Run Sch—*school* ... WV-2
**Robinsons**—*pop pl* ... AL-4
**Robinsons**—*pop pl* ... ME-1
*Robinsons Branch* ... VA-3
Robinsons Branch—*stream* ... NJ-2
*Robinsons Brook* ... MA-1
*Robinson Sch* ... TN-4
Robinson Sch—*school* (4) ... AL-4
Robinson Sch—*school* (3) ... AR-4
Robinson Sch—*school* (2) ... CA-9
Robinson Sch—*school* ... GA-3
Robinson Sch—*school* ... IL-6
Robinson Sch—*school* ... KY-4
Robinson Sch—*school* (4) ... MI-6
Robinson Sch—*school* (3) ... MO-7
Robinson Sch—*school* ... MT-8
Robinson Sch—*school* ... NC-3
Robinson Sch—*school* ... OH-6
Robinson Sch—*school* ... OK-5
Robinson Sch—*school* ... SD-7
Robinson Sch—*school* ... TN-4
Robinson Sch—*school* (2) ... VT-1
Robinson Sch—*school* (2) ... WV-2
Robinson Sch—*school* ... WI-6
Robinson Sch—*school* ... WY-8
Robinson Sch—*school* ... PR-3
Robinson Sch (abandoned)—*school* (2) ... MO-7
*Robinsons Chapel Presbyterian Church* ... TN-4
Robinson Sch (historical)—*school* ... MS-4
Robinson Sch (historical)—*school* ... SD-7
Robinson Sch (historical)—*school* ... TN-4
*Robinson School* ... IN-6
Robinson School (historical)—*locale* ... MO-7
Robinsons Corner—*locale* ... CA-9
*Robinsons Cove* ... ME-1

Rockbridge Post Office (historical)—*building* TN-4
Rockbridge Sch—*school* KY-4
Rock Bridge Sch—*school* NC-3
Rock Bridge Shop Ctr—*locale* MO-7
**Rockbridge (Town of)**—*pop pl* WI-6
**Rockbridge (Township of)**—*pop pl* IL-6
Rock Bridge Trail—*trail* KY-4
*Rock Brook* ME-1
*Rockbrook* NE-7
Rock Brook—*stream* CT-1
Rock Brook—*stream* NJ-2
Rock Brook—*stream* VT-1
Rockbrook Camp—*locale* NC-3
Rock Brothers—*island* NY-2
Rock Buffalo Ch—*church* SC-3
Rockburn Branch—*stream* MD-2
*Rock Butte* AZ-5
Rock Butte—*summit* AK-9
Rock Butte—*summit* AZ-5
Rock Butte—*summit* ID-8
Rock Butte—*summit* (2) OR-9
Rock Butte No 2 Rsvr—*reservoir* WY-8
Rock Butte Well—*well* MT-8
Rockby—*hist pl* GA-3
Rockby Dam—*dam* PA-2
Rock Cabin—*locale* WA-9
Rock Cabin Avalanche—*cliff* WA-9
Rock Cabin Camp—*locale* CA-9
*Rock Cabin Creek* PA-2
Rock Cabin Creek—*stream* OR-9
Rock Cabin Creek—*stream* WY-8
Rock Cabin Dugway—*locale* WY-8
Rock Cabin (Freeman)—*locale* NM-5
**Rock Cabin (Freeman)**—*pop pl* NM-5
Rock Cabin Lake—*reservoir* GA-3
Rock Cabin Mine—*mine* NV-8
Rock Cabin Run—*stream* (2) PA-2
Rock Cabin Spring—*spring* ID-8
Rock Cabin Spring—*spring* WY-8
Rock Cabin Spring Number Two—*spring* OR-9
Rock Cabin Spring Number 1—*spring* OR-9
Rock Cabin Well—*well* CA-9
Rock Cabin Well—*well* NV-8
Rock Cairns—*locale* ID-8
Rock Camp—*locale* TX-5
**Rock Camp**—*pop pl* (2) OH-6
**Rock Camp**—*pop pl* WV-2
*Rockcamp Branch* WV-2
Rock Camp Branch—*stream* KY-4
Rock Camp Branch—*stream* NC-3
Rock Camp Branch—*stream* TN-4
Rockcamp Branch—*stream* WV-2
Rock Camp Branch—*stream* WV-2
Rockcamp Branch—*stream* (2) WV-2
Rockcamp Ch—*church* WV-2
Rockcamp Creek—*stream* OH-6
Rock Camp Creek—*stream* WV-2
Rock Camp Draw—*valley* OR-9
Rockcamp Fork—*stream* (3) WV-2
Rock Camp Guard Station—*locale* CA-9
Rockcamp Knob—*summit* WV-2
Rock Camp Lake—*flat* OR-9
Rockcamp Ridge—*ridge* WV-2
Rock Camp Run—*stream* NC-3
Rockcamp Run—*stream* OH-6
Rockcamp Run—*stream* PA-2
Rockcamp Run—*stream* (7) WV-2
Rock Camp Run—*stream* WV-2
Rockcamp Run—*stream* (8) WV-2
Rock Camp Sch—*school* WV-2
Rock Camp Spring—*spring* OR-9
Rock Candy Creek—*stream* AK-9
Rock Candy Mountain Mine—*mine* AZ-5
Rock Candy Mtn—*summit* MT-8
Rock Candy Mtn—*summit* WA-9
*Rock Canon Creek* MT-8
*Rock Canyon* AZ-5
*Rock Canyon* CA-9
*Rock Canyon* NV-8
*Rock Canyon* UT-8
**Rock Canyon**—*pop pl* NM-5
Rock Canyon—*valley* (9) AZ-5
Rock Canyon—*valley* AR-4
Rock Canyon—*valley* (4) CA-9
Rock Canyon—*valley* (4) CO-8
Rock Canyon—*valley* (2) MT-8
Rock Canyon—*valley* (2) NE-7
Rock Canyon—*valley* (3) NV-8
Rock Canyon—*valley* (7) NM-5
Rock Canyon—*valley* (4) OR-9
Rock Canyon—*valley* (4) TX-5
Rock Canyon—*valley* (32) UT-8
Rock Canyon—*valley* (2) WY-8
Rock Canyon Assembly of God Ch—*church* UT-8
Rock Canyon Bridge—*bridge* UT-8
*Rock Canyon Campground* UT-8
*Rock Canyon Creek* OK-5
*Rock Canyon Creek* UT-8
Rock Canyon Creek—*stream* OR-9
Rock Canyon Creek—*stream* UT-8
Rock Canyon Flat—*flat* UT-8
Rock Canyon Picnic Area—*locale* UT-8
Rock Canyon Point—*cliff* AZ-5
Rock Canyon Rsvr—*reservoir* (2) AZ-5
Rock Canyon Rsvr—*reservoir* UT-8
Rock Canyon Sch—*school* UT-8
Rock Canyon Spring—*spring* (2) AZ-5
Rock Canyon Spring—*spring* UT-8
Rock Canyon Tank—*reservoir* AZ-5
Rock Canyon Tank—*reservoir* (2) NM-5
Rock Canyon Trail Two Hundred Fiftynine—*trail* AZ-5
Rock Canyon Trick Tank—*reservoir* AZ-5
Rock Canyon Well—*well* NV-8
Rock Canyon Well—*well* TX-5
*Rock Castle* KS-7
*Rockcastle* WV-2
Rock Castle—*building* TN-4
Rock Castle—*hist pl* TN-4
Rock Castle—*hist pl* VA-3
Rockcastle—*locale* AL-4
Rockcastle—*locale* KY-4
Rock Castle—*locale* VA-3
Rock Castle—*locale* WV-2
**Rock Castle**—*pop pl* AL-4
**Rock Castle**—*pop pl* TN-4
Rock Castle Ch—*church* WV-2
**Rockcastle (County)**—*pop pl* KY-4
Rockcastle Cove—*valley* TN-4
*Rock Castle Creek* AL-4
*Rockcastle Creek* KY-4
*Rock Castle Creek* OR-9
Rockcastle Creek—*stream* AL-4
Rockcastle Creek—*stream* IL-6
Rockcastle Creek—*stream* KY-4
Rockcastle Creek—*stream* TN-4
Rock Castle Creek—*stream* (2) VA-3
Rockcastle Creek—*stream* VA-3
Rockcastle Creek—*stream* (2) WV-2
Rock Castle Gap—*gap* VA-3
Rock Castle Hollow—*valley* AR-4
Rock Castle Mine (underground)—*mine* AL-4
Rock Castle Missionary Baptist Ch (historical)—*church* TN-4
Rockcastle River—*stream* KY-4
Rock Castle Sch—*school* TN-4
Rock Castle Sch—*school* VA-3
Rockcastle Shores—*locale* KY-4
**Rock Cave**—*pop pl* WV-2
Rock Cem—*cemetery* AL-4
Rock Cem—*cemetery* IL-6
Rock Cem—*cemetery* IA-7
Rock Cem—*cemetery* KY-4
Rock Cem—*cemetery* MI-6
Rock Cem—*cemetery* MS-4
Rock Cem—*cemetery* MO-7
Rock Cem—*cemetery* (2) OK-5
Rock Cem—*cemetery* TX-5
Rock Cem—*cemetery* VA-3
Rock Cem—*cemetery* WI-6
*Rock Ch* AL-4
Rock Ch—*church* (2) AL-4
Rock Ch—*church* AR-4
Rock Ch—*church* (4) GA-3
Rock Ch—*church* MD-2
Rock Ch—*church* (3) MO-7
Rock Ch—*church* NC-3
Rock Ch—*church* (2) PA-2
Rock Ch—*church* SC-3
Rock Ch—*church* (2) TN-4
Rock Ch—*church* TX-5
Rock Ch—*church* VA-3
*Rock Chapel* AL-4
Rock Chapel—*church* AL-4
Rock Chapel—*church* AR-4
Rock Chapel—*church* GA-3
Rock Chapel—*church* MO-7
Rock Chapel Cem—*cemetery* PA-2
Rock Chapel Sch—*school* PA-2
Rock Chimney Ranch—*locale* TX-5
Rock Chimney Tank—*reservoir* NM-5
Rock Chuck Pass—*gap* WY-8
Rockchuck Peak—*summit* WY-8
Rock Church—*hist pl* WY-8
Rock Church, The—*church* TX-5
Rock Church Cem—*cemetery* OK-5
Rock Church Cem—*cemetery* TX-5
Rock Church Cem—*cemetery* (2) WI-6
Rock Chute—*canal* TN-4
Rock Chute—*stream* MS-4
Rock Chute Creek—*stream* CA-9
Rock City—*locale* CA-9
Rock City—*locale* NY-2
Rock City—*park* KS-7
Rock City—*pillar* AL-4
**Rock City**—*pop pl* (2) AL-4
**Rock City**—*pop pl* IL-6
**Rock City**—*pop pl* (2) NY-2
**Rock City**—*pop pl* (2) TN-4
Rock City Cabin—*locale* ID-8
Rock City Cem—*cemetery* IL-6
**Rock City Falls**—*pop pl* NY-2
Rock City Gardens—*locale* GA-3
Rock City Park—*park* NY-2
Rock City Park—*park* TN-4
Rock City Pond Peak Trail—*trail* ID-8
Rock City Sch (historical)—*school* TN-4
Rock Cliff—*cliff* CO-8
Rock Cliff—*locale* WV-2
**Rockcliff Addition (subdivision)**—*pop pl* UT-8
Rock Cliff Cave—*cave* AL-4
Rockcliff Ch—*church* TN-4
*Rockcliff Ch of Christ* TN-4
Rockcliffe Mansion—*hist pl* MO-7
Rock Cliff Rsvr—*reservoir* TX-5
Rock Cliff Tank—*reservoir* NM-5
Rock Clift—*hist pl* MD-2
Rock Cobble Hill—*summit* CT-1
Rockcola Ch—*church* GA-3
Rock Coll Sch (historical)—*school* TN-4
Rock Cone—*summit* OR-9
Rock Corner Ch—*church* LA-4
Rock Corral—*locale* CA-9
Rock Corral—*locale* (2) UT-8
Rock Corral Bench—*bench* AZ-5
Rock Corral Butte—*summit* ID-8
Rock Corral Canyon—*valley* AZ-5
Rock Corral Canyon—*valley* OR-9
Rock Corral Draw—*valley* WY-8
Rock Corral on the Barlow Road—*hist pl* OR-9
*Rock Corral Peak* AZ-5
Rock Corral Quarry—*mine* UT-8
Rock Corral Ranch—*locale* AZ-5
Rock Corral Recreation Site—*park* UT-8
Rock Corral Rsvr—*reservoir* UT-8
Rock Corral Spring—*spring* AZ-5
Rock Corral Spring—*spring* CA-9
Rock Corral Spring—*spring* UT-8
*Rock Coulee* MT-8
**Rock (County)**—*pop pl* MN-6
**Rock (County)**—*pop pl* WI-6
Rock County Airp—*airport* WI-6
Rock County Courthouse and Jail—*hist pl* MN-6
*Rock Courthouse* TN-4
Rock Cove—*bay* MD-2
Rock Cowan Number 1 Dam—*dam* SD-7
Rock Cowan Number 2 Dam—*dam* SD-7
Rock Cowan Number 3 Dam—*dam* SD-7
Rock Cowan Number 4 Dam—*dam* SD-7
*Rock Creek* AL-4
*Rock Creek* AZ-5
*Rock Creek* AR-4
*Rock Creek* CA-9
*Rock Creek* FL-3
*Rock Creek* GA-3
*Rock Creek* ID-8
*Rock Creek* IN-6
*Rock Creek* IA-7
*Rock Creek* KS-7
*Rock Creek* (2) MD-2
*Rock Creek* MA-1
*Rock Creek* MS-4
*Rock Creek* MO-7
*Rock Creek* MT-8
*Rock Creek* NE-7
*Rock Creek* NV-8
*Rock Creek* NC-3
*Rock Creek* OH-6
*Rock Creek* OR-9
*Rock Creek* PA-2
*Rock Creek* SC-3
*Rock Creek* TN-4
*Rock Creek* TX-5
*Rock Creek* UT-8
*Rock Creek* WA-9
*Rock Creek* WY-8
Rock Creek—*bay* MD-2
Rock Creek—*fmr MCD* (3) NE-7
Rock Creek—*gut* (2) FL-3
Rock Creek—*gut* (2) MD-2
Rock Creek—*gut* VA-3
Rock Creek—*locale* AL-4
Rock Creek—*locale* CA-9
Rock Creek—*locale* (2) FL-3
Rock Creek—*locale* ID-8
Rock Creek—*locale* (2) IL-6
Rock Creek—*locale* KY-4
Rock Creek—*locale* OK-5
Rock Creek—*locale* (2) OR-9
Rock Creek—*locale* (2) TX-5
Rock Creek—*locale* WV-2
Rock Creek—*locale* WY-8
**Rock Creek**—*pop pl* (2) AL-4
**Rockcreek**—*pop pl* IN-6
**Rock Creek**—*pop pl* IA-7
**Rock Creek**—*pop pl* KS-7
**Rock Creek**—*pop pl* MN-6
**Rock Creek**—*pop pl* (2) MS-4
**Rock Creek**—*pop pl* MO-7
**Rock Creek**—*pop pl* MT-8
**Rock Creek**—*pop pl* NC-3
**Rock Creek**—*pop pl* OH-6
**Rock Creek**—*pop pl* (2) TN-4
**Rock Creek**—*pop pl* WV-2
Rock Creek—*stream* (18) AL-4
Rock Creek—*stream* (8) AK-9
Rock Creek—*stream* (14) AZ-5
Rock Creek—*stream* (26) AR-4
Rock Creek—*stream* (52) CA-9
Rock Creek—*stream* (22) CO-8
Rock Creek—*stream* DC-2
Rock Creek—*stream* (7) FL-3
Rock Creek—*stream* (15) GA-3
Rock Creek—*stream* (46) ID-8
Rock Creek—*stream* (12) IL-6
Rock Creek—*stream* (9) IN-6
Rock Creek*—*stream* IA-7
Rock Creek—*stream* (24) IA-7
Rock Creek—*stream* (35) KS-7
Rock Creek—*stream* (7) KY-4
Rock Creek—*stream* (2) LA-4
Rock Creek—*stream* (5) MD-2
Rock Creek—*stream* (3) MN-6
Rock Creek—*stream* (3) MS-4
Rock Creek—*stream* (17) MO-7
Rock Creek—*stream* (38) MT-8
Rock Creek—*stream* (13) NE-7
Rock Creek—*stream* (10) NV-8
Rock Creek—*stream* NJ-2
Rock Creek—*stream* (6) NM-5
Rock Creek—*stream* NY-2
Rock Creek—*stream* (20) NC-3
Rock Creek—*stream* ND-7
Rock Creek—*stream* (3) OH-6
Rock Creek—*stream* (66) OK-5
Rock Creek—*stream* (85) OR-9
Rock Creek—*stream* (3) PA-2
Rock Creek—*stream* (6) SC-3
Rock Creek—*stream* (3) SD-7
Rock Creek—*stream* (21) TN-4
Rock Creek—*stream* (30) TX-5
Rock Creek—*stream* (12) UT-8
Rock Creek—*stream* (10) VA-3
Rock Creek—*stream* (33) WA-9
Rock Creek—*stream* (4) WV-2
Rock Creek—*stream* (15) WI-6
Rock Creek—*stream* (25) WY-8
Rock Creek and Piney Diversion Ditch—*canal* WY-8
*Rock Creek Apostolic Church* AL-4
Rock Creek Assembly of God Ch—*church* AL-4
*Rock Creek Baptist Ch* AL-4
Rock Creek Baptist Ch—*church* AL-4
Rock Creek Baptist Ch—*church* NC-3
Rock Creek Basin—*basin* ID-8
Rock Creek Bay—*bay* MT-8
Rock Creek Bay—*bay* UT-8
Rock Creek Bench Spring—*spring* UT-8
Rock Creek Bicycle Trail—*trail* TN-4
**Rock Creek (Bone Lick)**—*pop pl* WV-2
Rock Creek Bridge—*bridge* TN-4
Rock Creek Butte—*summit* CA-9
Rock Creek Butte—*summit* (2) OR-9
Rock Creek Butte—*summit* WA-9
Rock Creek Butte Point—*cape* CA-9
*Rock Creek Buttes* WY-8
Rock Creek Buttes—*summit* WY-8
Rock Creek Camp—*locale* CA-9
Rock Creek Camp—*locale* ID-8
**Rock Creek Camp**—*pop pl* CA-9
Rock Creek Campground—*locale* CA-9
Rock Creek Campground—*locale* (2) CO-8
Rock Creek Campground—*locale* ID-8
Rock Creek Campground—*locale* MT-8
Rock Creek Camp Ground—*locale* MT-8
Rock Creek Camp Ground—*locale* TN-4
Rock Creek Campground—*park* (2) OR-9
Rock Creek Canal—*canal* MT-8
*Rock Creek Canyon* OR-9
*Rock Creek Canyon* UT-8
Rock Creek Canyon—*valley* (2) NV-8
Rock Creek Canyon—*valley* NM-5
Rock Creek Canyon—*valley* OK-5
*Rock Creek Canyon Spring* OR-9
Rock Creek Cave—*cave* AL-4
Rock Creek Cave—*cave* TN-4
Rock Creek (CCD)—*cens area* GA-3
Rock Creek (CCD)—*cens area* TN-4
*Rock Creek Cem* AL-4
Rock Creek Cem—*cemetery* AL-4
Rock Creek Cem—*cemetery* (2) AR-4
Rock Creek Cem—*cemetery* CO-8
Rock Creek Cem—*cemetery* DC-2
Rock Creek Cem—*cemetery* GA-3
Rock Creek Cem—*cemetery* (2) IL-6
Rock Creek Cem—*cemetery* IN-6
Rock Creek Cem—*cemetery* (2) IA-7
Rock Creek Cem—*cemetery* (5) KS-7
Rock Creek Cem—*cemetery* KY-4
Rock Creek Cem—*cemetery* MO-7
Rock Creek Cem—*cemetery* MT-8
Rock Creek Cem—*cemetery* (3) NE-7
Rock Creek Cem—*cemetery* (2) OH-6
Rock Creek Cem—*cemetery* (3) OK-5
Rock Creek Cem—*cemetery* (2) OR-9
Rock Creek Cem—*cemetery* SD-7
Rock Creek Cem—*cemetery* TX-5
Rock Creek Cem—*cemetery* WI-6
Rock Creek Cemeteries—*cemetery* ID-8
**Rock Creek Center**—*pop pl* IN-6
*Rock Creek Ch* NC-3
Rock Creek Ch—*church* (6) AL-4
Rock Creek Ch—*church* AR-4
Rock Creek Ch—*church* (2) GA-3
Rock Creek Ch—*church* IL-6
Rock Creek Ch—*church* (2) IN-6
Rock Creek Ch—*church* MD-2
Rock Creek Ch—*church* MS-4
Rock Creek Ch—*church* MO-7
Rock Creek Ch—*church* (5) NC-3
Rock Creek Ch—*church* (6) OK-5
Rock Creek Ch—*church* OR-9
Rock Creek Ch—*church* SC-3
Rock Creek Ch—*church* TN-4
Rock Creek Ch—*church* (5) TX-5
Rock Creek Ch—*church* VA-3
Rock Creek Ch—*church* WI-6
Rock Creek Ch (historical)—*church* TN-4
Rock Creek Church And Cem—*cemetery* IA-7
Rock Creek Church Cem—*cemetery* AL-4
*Rock Creek Church of Christ* AL-4
Rock Creek Church Yard and Cemetery—*hist pl* DC-2
Rock Creek Clear Creek Ditch—*canal* MT-8
Rock Creek Community Hall—*building* KS-7
Rock Creek Community Hall—*locale* OR-9
Rock Creek Corner—*locale* OR-9
Rock Creek Corral—*locale* UT-8
Rock Creek Cove—*bay* AL-4
Rock Creek Cow Camp—*locale* (2) CO-8
Rock Creek Crossing—*locale* CA-9
Rock Creek Crossing Campground—*locale* WA-9
Rock Creek Dam—*dam* (2) CA-9
Rock Creek Dam—*dam* (3) OR-9
Rock Creek Ditch—*canal* (2) CA-9
Rock Creek Ditch—*canal* MO-7
Rock Creek Ditch—*canal* MT-8
Rock Creek Ditch—*canal* NV-8
Rock Creek Ditch—*canal* OR-9
Rock Creek Ditch—*canal* WY-8
Rock Creek Division—*civil* TN-4
Rock Creek (Election Precinct)—*fmr MCD* (2) IL-6
*Rock Creek Elem Sch* TN-4
Rock Creek Elem Sch—*school* TN-4
Rock Creek Falls—*falls* MT-8
Rock Creek Falls—*falls* NC-3
Rock Creek Falls—*falls* OK-5
Rock Creek Falls—*falls* PA-2
Rock Creek Falls—*falls* WA-9
Rock Creek Falls Trail—*trail* TN-4
Rock Creek Fish Hatchery—*locale* OR-9
Rock Creek Flat—*flat* OR-9
**Rock Creek Forest**—*pop pl* MD-2
Rock Creek Forest Camp—*locale* OR-9
Rock Creek Forest Sch—*school* MD-2
Rock Creek Forest Service Station—*locale* MT-8
Rock Creek Gap—*gap* NC-3
**Rock Creek Gardens**—*pop pl* MD-2
Rock Creek Gas Field—*oilfield* AR-4
Rock Creek Guard Station—*locale* CA-9
Rock Creek Guard Station—*locale* (2) MT-8
Rock Creek Guard Station—*locale* OR-9
Rock Creek Guard Station—*locale* WA-9
Rock Creek Guard Station (24GN165)—*hist pl* MT-8
Rock Creek Gun Club—*other* WA-9
Rock Creek Hideout—*locale* OR-9
Rock Creek Hill—*summit* CO-8
**Rock Creek Hills**—*pop pl* MD-2
Rock Creek (historical P.O.)—*locale* IA-7
*Rock Creek Junction* MO-7
Rock Creek Junction—*locale* MO-7
Rock Creek Knob—*summit* NC-3
Rock Creek Knoll—*summit* WY-8
**Rock Creek Knolls**—*pop pl* MD-2
Rock Creek Lake—*lake* (2) CA-9
Rock Creek Lake—*lake* MT-8
Rock Creek Lake—*lake* OR-9
Rock Creek Lake—*reservoir* CA-9
Rock Creek Lake—*reservoir* GA-3
Rock Creek Lake—*reservoir* IA-7
Rock Creek Lake—*reservoir* KS-7
Rock Creek Lake—*reservoir* MT-8
Rock Creek Lake—*reservoir* NE-7
Rock Creek Lake—*reservoir* OR-9
Rock Creek Lake Dam—*dam* IA-7
Rock Creek Lake Dam—*dam* KS-7
Rock Creek Lake Dam—*dam* OR-9
*Rock Creek Lakes* KS-7
Rock Creek Lakes—*lake* WY-8
Rock Creek Lake Trail (pack)—*trail* OR-9
Rock Creek-Lima (Township of)—*civ div* IL-6
**Rock Creek Manor**—*pop pl* MD-2
Rock Creek Meadow—*flat* UT-8
Rock Creek Meadows—*flat* MT-8
Rock Creek Mesa—*summit* NM-5
Rock Creek Methodist Ch—*church* NC-3
Rock Creek Methodist Church—*hist pl* OR-9
Rock Creek Mine (underground)—*mine* AL-4
Rock Creek Mtn—*summit* NC-3
Rock Creek Mtn—*summit* TN-4
Rock Creek Mtn—*summit* WY-8
Rock Creek Oil Field—*oilfield* WY-8
Rock Creek Oil Field—*other* WV-2
Rock Creek Pack Trail—*trail* ID-8
**Rock Creek Palisades**—*pop pl* MD-2
Rock Creek Palisades Sch—*school* MD-2
Rock Creek Park—*flat* (3) CO-8
Rock Creek Park—*flat* WY-8
Rock Creek Park—*park* DC-2
Rock Creek Park—*park* MD-2
Rock Creek Park—*park* NC-3
**Rock Creek Park (subdivision)**—*pop pl* AL-4
Rock Creek Patrol Cabin—*locale* CA-9
*Rock Creek Picnic Area* UT-8
Rock Creek Picnic Area—*park* AZ-5
Rock Creek Picnic Ground—*locale* WY-8
Rock Creek Point—*cape* OR-9
Rock Creek Point—*cliff* ID-8
Rock Creek Point—*summit* WY-8
Rock Creek Post Office (historical)—*building* MS-4
Rock Creek Post Office (historical)—*building* TN-4
*Rock Creek Powerhouse* CA-9
Rock Creek Powerhouse—*other* CA-9
Rock Creek Powerplant—*locale* OR-9
**Rock Creek Pprk**—*pop pl* CO-8
Rock Creek Public Use Area—*park* AR-4
Rock Creek Public Use Area—*park* KS-7
Rock Creek Public Use Area—*park* TN-4
Rock Creek Ranch—*locale* AZ-5
Rock Creek Ranch—*locale* ID-8
Rock Creek Ranch—*locale* MT-8
Rock Creek Ranch—*locale* (2) NV-8
Rock Creek Ranch—*locale* (2) OR-9
Rock Creek Ranch—*locale* (2) UT-8
Rock Creek Ranger Station—*locale* ID-8
Rock Creek Ranger Station—*locale* MT-8
Rock Creek Rapids—*rapids* UT-8
Rock Creek Rec Area—*park* NE-7
Rock Creek Recreation Site—*park* OR-9
*Rock Creek Resort* UT-8
Rock Creek Ridge—*ridge* (2) WY-8
*Rock Creek Rsvr* OR-9
Rock Creek Rsvr—*reservoir* CA-9
Rock Creek Rsvr—*reservoir* MT-8
Rock Creek Rsvr—*reservoir* NV-8
Rock Creek Rsvr—*reservoir* (6) OR-9
Rock Creek Rsvr Campground—*park* OR-9
Rock Creek Scenic Area—*park* TN-4
Rock Creek Sch—*school* AL-4
Rock Creek Sch—*school* (2) ID-8
Rock Creek Sch—*school* IL-6
Rock Creek Sch—*school* (2) KS-7
Rock Creek Sch—*school* MO-7
Rock Creek Sch—*school* MT-8
Rock Creek Sch—*school* (2) NE-7
Rock Creek Sch—*school* (2) OR-9
Rock Creek Sch—*school* TN-4
Rock Creek Sch—*school* (2) WV-2
Rock Creek Sch (abandoned)—*school* (2) MO-7
Rock Creek Sch (historical)—*school* AL-4
Rock Creek School (historical)—*locale* MO-7
Rock Creek Schoolhouse—*school* MT-8
Rock Creek Shearing Corral—*locale* NV-8
Rock Creek Shelter—*locale* WA-9
Rock Creek Ski Area—*locale* CO-8
*Rock Creek Spring* OR-9
Rock Creek Spring—*spring* (2) AZ-5
Rock Creek Springs—*spring* OR-9
Rock Creek Stable—*building* DC-2
Rock Creek Stage Station—*hist pl* CO-8
Rock Creek State Bank—*hist pl* MT-8
Rock Creek State Fish Hatchery—*other* NE-7
Rock Creek State Park—*park* IA-7
Rock Creek State Park—*park* MT-8
Rock Creek Station—*locale* AZ-5
**Rock Creek (Town of)**—*pop pl* WI-6
Rock Creek Township—*fmr MCD* IA-7
**Rock Creek Township**—*pop pl* (7) KS-7
**Rock Creek Township**—*pop pl* NE-7
**Rock Creek Township**—*pop pl* SD-7
Rock Creek Township (historical)—*civil* SD-7
Rock Creek (Township of)—*civ div* IN-6
Rock Creek (Township of)—*fmr MCD* AR-4
Rock Creek (Township of)—*fmr MCD* (2) NC-3
Rock Creek (Township of)—*other* MN-6
**Rock Creek (Township of)**—*pop pl* (2) IL-6
**Rock Creek (Township of)**—*pop pl* (3) IN-6
Rock Creek Trail—*trail* (2) CO-8
Rock Creek Trail—*trail* ID-8
Rock Creek Trail—*trail* MT-8
Rock Creek Trail—*trail* OR-9
Rock Creek Trail—*trail* TN-4
Rock Creek Trail—*trail* (2) WA-9
Rock Creek Trail—*trail* WY-8
Rock Creek Truck Trail—*trail* WA-9
Rock Creek Valley—*valley* ID-8
Rock Creek Valley Sch—*school* MD-2
**Rock Creek Village**—*pop pl* MD-2
Rock Creek Vista—*summit* MT-8
*Rock Creek Wash* CA-9
Rock Creek Windmill—*locale* TX-5
**Rock Crest**—*pop pl* CA-9
**Rockcrest**—*pop pl* MD-2
Rockcrest Park—*park* MD-2
Rock Crest-Rock Glen Hist Dist—*hist pl* IA-7
Rock Crossing—*locale* AZ-5
Rock Crossing—*locale* (2) CO-8
Rock Crossing—*locale* MT-8
Rock Crossing—*locale* (2) TX-5
Rock Crossing Campground—*park* AZ-5
Rock Crossing Ch—*church* TX-5
Rock Crossing Rsvr—*reservoir* AZ-5
Rock Crossing Trail—*trail* AZ-5
Rock Crossing Windmill—*well* AZ-5
Rock Crusher Canyon—*valley* OR-9
*Rock Crusher Creek* OR-9
Rock Crusher Creek—*stream* OR-9
Rock Crusher Lake—*lake* TX-5
Rock Curve Ch—*church* AL-4
Rock Cut—*gap* CO-8
Rock Cut—*gut* ID-8
Rock Cut—*locale* OH-6
Rock Cut—*locale* WY-8
**Rock Cut**—*pop pl* MD-2
**Rock Cut**—*pop pl* NY-2
Rock Cut—*uninc pl* GA-3
Rock Cut Bridge—*bridge* WA-9
Rock Cut Brook—*stream* NY-2
*Rock Cut Cave* TN-4
Rock Cut Cem—*cemetery* FL-3
Rock Cut Ch—*church* FL-3
Rock Cut Lookout Tower—*locale* MN-6
Rock Cut Sch—*school* IL-6
Rock Cut State Park—*park* IL-6
**Rockcut (subdivision)**—*pop pl* AL-4
Rock Cutter Gap—*gap* AL-4
*Rockdale* MA-1
Rockdale—*hist pl* KY-4
Rockdale—*hist pl* MD-2
Rockdale—*locale* GA-3
Rockdale—*locale* KY-4
Rockdale—*locale* (2) MD-2
Rockdale—*locale* (5) PA-2
Rockdale—*locale* TX-5
Rockdale—*locale* WA-9
**Rockdale**—*pop pl* (2) AL-4
**Rockdale**—*pop pl* CO-8
**Rockdale**—*pop pl* FL-3
**Rockdale**—*pop pl* IL-6
**Rockdale**—*pop pl* IN-6
**Rockdale**—*pop pl* IA-7
**Rockdale**—*pop pl* KY-4
**Rockdale**—*pop pl* MD-2
**Rockdale**—*pop pl* (2) MA-1
**Rockdale**—*pop pl* NY-2
**Rockdale**—*pop pl* NC-3
**Rockdale**—*pop pl* OH-6
**Rockdale**—*pop pl* (3) PA-2
**Rockdale**—*pop pl* (2) TN-4
**Rockdale**—*pop pl* TX-5
**Rockdale**—*pop pl* WV-2
**Rockdale**—*pop pl* WI-6
**Rockdale Acres**—*pop pl* PA-2
Rockdale Branch—*stream* TX-5
Rockdale (CCD)—*cens area* TX-5
Rockdale Cem—*cemetery* MA-1
Rockdale Cem—*cemetery* MO-7
Rockdale Cem—*cemetery* PA-2
Rockdale Cem—*cemetery* TX-5
Rockdale Cem—*cemetery* WA-9
Rockdale Center HS—*school* PA-2
Rockdale Ch—*church* (2) AL-4
Rockdale Ch—*church* AR-4
Rockdale Ch—*church* GA-3
Rockdale Ch—*church* IA-7
Rockdale Ch—*church* KY-4
Rockdale Ch—*church* LA-4
Rockdale Ch—*church* MO-7
Rockdale Ch—*church* NC-3
Rockdale Ch—*church* (2) TX-5
Rockdale Common Housing District—*hist pl* MA-1
**Rockdale (County)**—*pop pl* GA-3
Rockdale County Jail—*hist pl* GA-3
Rockdale Creek—*stream* PA-2
Rockdale Furnace Hist Dist (40MU487)—*hist pl* TN-4
*Rockdale Junction* IL-6
Rockdale Junction—*locale* IL-6
**Rockdale Keys**—*pop pl* FL-3
Rockdale Lake—*lake* WA-9
Rockdale Lake—*reservoir* GA-3
Rockdale Lake—*reservoir* VA-3
Rockdale Millpond—*reservoir* WI-6
*Rock Dale Mills* MA-1
**Rockdale Mills**—*pop pl* MA-1
Rock Dale Mills (historical P.O.)—*locale* MA-1
Rockdale Park—*park* FL-3
*Rockdale P.O.* AL-4
Rockdale Pond—*reservoir* MA-1
Rockdale Run—*stream* MD-2
Rockdale Sch—*school* CA-9
Rockdale Sch—*school* MO-7
Rockdale Sch—*school* OH-6
Rockdale Sch—*school* OK-5
Rockdale Sch (abandoned)—*school* PA-2
Rockdale Sch (historical)—*school* AL-4
Rockdale Sch (historical)—*school* PA-2
**Rockdale Township**—*pop pl* SD-7
Rockdale Township Hall—*building* SD-7
**Rockdale (Township of)**—*pop pl* PA-2
*Rock Dam* AZ-5
Rock Dam—*dam* AZ-5
Rock Dam—*dam* ME-1
Rock Dam—*dam* OR-9
Rock Dam—*dam* TX-5
Rock Dam Canal—*canal* UT-8
Rock Dam County Park Falls—*falls* WI-6
Rockdam Creek—*stream* NC-3
Rock Dam Creek—*stream* SC-3
Rock Dam Ditch—*canal* NV-8
Rock Dam Heath—*swamp* ME-1
Rock Dam Lake—*lake* WI-6
Rock Dam Rsvr—*reservoir* CO-8
Rock Dam Rsvr—*reservoir* UT-8
Rockdedundy Island—*island* GA-3
Rockdedundy River—*channel* GA-3
Rockdell—*locale* VA-3
**Rock Dell**—*pop pl* MN-6
Rock Dell Ch—*church* MN-6
**Rock Dell (Township of)**—*pop pl* MN-6
Rock Dike Tank—*reservoir* AZ-5
Rock Ditch Hollow—*valley* TN-4
Rock Door Mesa—*summit* UT-8
Rock Draw—*valley* KS-7
Rock Draw—*valley* TX-5
Rock Draw—*valley* (2) WY-8
Rock Draw Rsvr—*reservoir* WY-8
Rock Dundee—*summit* ME-1
Rock Dunder—*bar* VT-1
Rock Dunder Island—*island* NY-2
Rockeagle—*locale* WY-8
Rock Eagle Lake—*reservoir* GA-3
Rock Eagle Monmt—*park* GA-3
Rock Eagle Site—*hist pl* GA-3
Rockedge Creek—*stream* FL-3
Rocked Spring—*spring* KY-4
Rockefeller, John D., Estate—*hist pl* NY-2
Rockefeller Bldg—*hist pl* OH-6
Rockefeller Brook—*stream* NY-2
Rockefeller Center—*building* NY-2
Rockefeller Center—*hist pl* NY-2
Rockefeller Cottage—*hist pl* GA-3
Rockefeller Creek—*stream* WA-9
*Rockefeller Foundation Wildlife Sanctuary* LA-4
Rockefeller Institute—*building* NY-2
Rockefeller Lookout—*locale* NJ-2
Rockefeller Mine—*mine* NV-8
Rockefeller Park—*park* OH-6
Rockefeller Park Bridges—*hist pl* OH-6

Rockhouse Tank—*reservoir* TX-5
Rockhouse Trail—*trail* CA-9
Rockhouse Trough—*spring* AZ-5
Rock House Well—*locale* NM-5
Rockhouse Well—*well* AZ-5
Rock House Well—*well* (3) NM-5
Rock House Wells—*well* NM-5
Rock House West Windmill—*locale* NM-5
Rock House Windmill—*locale* (2) NM-5
Rock House Windmill—*locale* TX-5
**Rockhurst**—*pop pl* NY-2
Rockhurst Coll—*school* MO-7
Rockhurst HS—*school* MO-7
*Rockie Creek* OR-9
Rockie Four Corners—*locale* OR-9
Rockies, The—*summit* WA-9
Rockies Creek—*stream* WA-9
Rocking Bar Spring—*spring* OR-9
*Rockingchair Branch* NC-3
Rocking Chair Branch—*stream* NC-3
Rocking Chair Cow Camp—*locale* WY-8
Rocking Chair Creek—*stream* MT-8
Rockingchair Creek—*stream* OR-9
Rocking Chair Park—*flat* MT-8
Rocking Chair Ranch—*locale* AZ-5
Rocking Chair Ranch—*locale* TX-5
Rocking Chair Ranch—*locale* WY-8
Rocking Chair Tank—*reservoir* TX-5
Rocking D Ranch—*locale* TX-5
*Rockingham* PA-2
*Rockingham* VA-3
Rockingham—*hist pl* NJ-2
Rockingham—*locale* GA-3
Rockingham—*locale* NJ-2
Rockingham—*other* VA-3
**Rockingham**—*pop pl* IA-7
**Rockingham**—*pop pl* MO-7
**Rockingham**—*pop pl* NH-1
**Rockingham**—*pop pl* NC-3
**Rockingham**—*pop pl* PA-2
**Rockingham**—*pop pl* VT-1
Rockingham (CCD)—*cens area* GA-3
Rockingham Cem—*cemetery* GA-3
Rockingham Ch—*church* SC-3
Rockingham Community Coll—*school* NC-3
**Rockingham County**—*pop pl* NC-3
**Rockingham (County)**—*pop pl* VA-3
Rockingham County Airp—*airport* NC-3
Rockingham County Courthouse—*hist pl* NC-3
Rockingham County HS—*school* NC-3
**Rockingham County(in (P)MSA 4160, 4760,6450)**—*pop pl* NH-1
Rockingham Court Ch—*church* VA-3
Rockingham-Hamlet Airp—*airport* NC-3
Rockingham Hist Dist—*hist pl* NC-3
Rockingham Hotel—*hist pl* NH-1
Rockingham JHS—*school* NC-3
*Rockingham Junction* NH-1
Rockingham Lake—*reservoir* NC-3
Rockingham Meetinghouse—*hist pl* VT-1
Rockingham Park—*park* NH-1
Rockingham Square Shop Ctr—*locale* NC-3
**Rockingham (Town of)**—*pop pl* VT-1
Rockingham (Township of)—*fmr MCD* NC-3
Rockinghan County Courthouse—*hist pl* VA-3
**Rocking Horse Ranchos**—*pop pl* CA-9
Rocking Horse Road Sch—*school* MD-2
Rocking H Ranch Lake—*reservoir* AL-4
Rocking K Ranch—*locale* AZ-5
Rocking K Ranch Estates Dam—*dam* AZ-5
Rocking Point—*cape* MD-2
Rocking Point Gut—*gut* MD-2
Rocking R Ranch—*locale* TX-5
Rocking R Sky Ranch—*locale* CO-8
**Rock Inn Estates (subdivision)**—*pop pl* AL-4
Rock Institute (historical)—*school* AL-4
*Rockinstraw Butte* AZ-5
Rockinstraw Mtn—*summit* AZ-5
Rockinstraw Tank—*reservoir* AZ-5
Rockinstraw Tank Number Two—*reservoir* AZ-5
*Rock Island* AL-4
*Rock Island* FL-3
*Rock Island* IN-6
*Rock Island* MA-1
*Rock Island* NY-2
*Rock Island* OR-9
*Rock Island* WA-9
*Rock Island* WY-8
Rock Island—*CDP* FL-3
Rock Island—*flat* OR-9
Rock Island—*island* AK-9
Rock Island—*island* AZ-5
Rock Island—*island* (2) CT-1
Rock Island—*island* (3) FL-3
Rock Island—*island* GA-3
Rock Island—*island* ID-8
Rock Island—*island* (2) IL-6
Rock Island—*island* IN-6
Rock Island—*island* (3) ME-1
Rock Island—*island* MD-2
Rock Island—*island* MA-1
Rock Island—*island* MI-6
Rock Island—*island* (2) MN-6
Rock Island—*island* (2) MT-8
Rock Island—*island* NV-8
Rock Island—*island* NH-1
Rock Island—*island* (2) NY-2
Rock Island—*island* (2) OR-9
Rock Island—*island* (2) RI-1
Rock Island—*island* TN-4
Rock Island—*island* TX-5
Rock Island—*island* UT-8
Rock Island—*island* (2) VT-1
Rock Island—*island* VA-3
Rock Island—*island* (2) WA-9
Rock Island—*island* (4) WI-6
Rock Island—*locale* FL-3
Rock Island—*locale* (4) TX-5
**Rock Island**—*pop pl* ID-8
**Rock Island**—*pop pl* IL-6
**Rock Island**—*pop pl* OK-5
**Rock Island**—*pop pl* TN-4
**Rock Island**—*pop pl* TX-5
**Rock Island**—*pop pl* WA-9
Rock Island Arsenal—*hist pl* IL-6
Rock Island Arsenal—*military* IL-6
Rock Island Baptist Ch—*church* TN-4
Rock Island Bay—*bay* FL-3
Rock Island Bay—*bay* NY-2
Rock Island Branch—*stream* TN-4
Rock Island Bridge—*bridge* NY-2
Rock Island Butte—*summit* MT-8
Rock Island Campground—*locale* WA-9
Rock Island Cem—*cemetery* OK-5
Rock Island Cem—*cemetery* TN-4
Rock Island Cem—*cemetery* TX-5
Rock Island Ch—*church* TX-5
Rock Island Country Club—*other* IL-6
**Rock Island (County)**—*pop pl* IL-6
Rock Island Cove—*cove* MA-1
Rock Island Cove Marshes—*swamp* MA-1
Rock Island Creek—*stream* VA-3
Rock Island Creek—*stream* WA-9
Rock Island Dam—*dam* WA-9
Rock Island Depot—*flat* OK-5
Rock Island Depot—*hist pl* (2) AR-4
Rock Island Depot—*hist pl* KS-7
Rock Island Depot—*hist pl* (2) MN-6
Rock Island Depot—*hist pl* NE-7
Rock Island Depot—*hist pl* (3) OK-5
Rock Island Depot—*hist pl* SD-7
Rock Island Depot and Freight House—*hist pl* IL-6
Rock Island Elem Sch—*school* FL-3
Rock Island Gulch—*valley* CO-8
Rock Island Haul—*island* VA-3
Rock Island Head—*cape* MA-1
Rock Island Hist Dist—*hist pl* WI-6
Rock Island (historical)—*island* AL-4
Rock Island (historical P.O.)—*locale* IN-6
Rock Island HS—*school* IL-6
*Rock Island - in part* NV-8
*Rock Island Junction* IL-6
**Rock Island Junction**—*pop pl* AR-4
**Rock Island Junction**—*pop pl* TX-5
Rock Island Junction—*uninc pl* OK-5
*Rock Island Lake* TN-4
Rock Island Lake—*lake* CA-9
Rock Island Lake—*lake* (2) ID-8
Rock Island Lake—*lake* LA-4
Rock Island Lake—*lake* MN-6
Rock Island Lake—*lake* MT-8
Rock Island Lake—*reservoir* (2) MO-7
Rock Island Lake—*reservoir* NJ-2
Rock Island Lake Dam—*dam* NJ-2
Rock Island Lakes—*lake* MT-8
Rock Island Light Station—*hist pl* NY-2
Rock Island Lines Passenger Station—*hist pl* IL-6
Rock Island Marina—*other* IL-6
Rock Island Mine—*mine* MT-8
Rock Island Mine—*mine* NV-8
Rock Island Park—*park* KS-7
Rock Island Park—*park* OK-5
Rock Island Pass—*gap* CA-9
Rock Island Passage—*channel* WI-6
Rock Island Plow Bldg—*hist pl* OK-5
Rock Island Point—*cape* AK-9
Rock Island Pond—*lake* FL-3
Rock Island Post Office—*building* TN-4
Rock Island Prairie—*flat* FL-3
**Rock Island Quarters**—*pop pl* AR-4
Rock Island Railway Depot—*hist pl* AR-4
Rock Island Ranch—*locale* (2) MT-8
Rock Island Resort—*locale* SD-7
Rock Island Ridge—*ridge* CA-9
Rock Island RR Bridge—*hist pl* WA-9
*Rock Island Run* VA-3
Rock Island Sch—*school* MO-7
Rock Island Sch—*school* WA-9
Rock Island Sch (abandoned)—*school* MO-7
Rock Island State Park—*park* WA-9
Rock Island State Rustic Park—*park* TN-4
Rock Island Station—*locale* TX-5
**Rock Island (subdivision)**—*pop pl* MA-1
Rock Island Table—*summit* NE-7
**Rock Island Township**—*pop pl* ND-7
**Rock Island (Township of)**—*pop pl* IL-6
**Rock Island Village**—*pop pl* FL-3
Rock Island Waterfowl Mngmt Area—*park* UT-8
Rock Jetty—*locale* MD-2
Rock Job Spring—*spring* MT-8
Rock Jolly—*hist pl* TN-4
Rock Junction—*locale* PA-2
*Rock Knob* IN-6
*Rock Knob* NC-3
Rock Knob—*summit* AZ-5
Rock Knob—*summit* IN-6
Rock Knob—*summit* KY-4
Rock Knob—*summit* MO-7
Rock Knob—*summit* (2) NC-3
Rock Knob—*summit* OR-9
Rock Knob Trail—*trail* PA-2
Rock Knoll—*summit* ID-8
Rock Knoll Rsvr—*reservoir* OR-9
*Rock Lake* CO-8
*Rock Lake* IL-6
*Rock Lake* MI-6
*Rock Lake* MN-6
*Rock Lake* MT-8
*Rock Lake* NM-5
*Rock Lake* NY-2
*Rocklake* ND-7
*Rock Lake* WA-9
*Rock Lake* WI-6
Rock Lake—*lake* (4) AK-9
Rock Lake—*lake* (7) CA-9
Rock Lake—*lake* (8) CO-8
Rock Lake—*lake* (6) FL-3
Rock Lake—*lake* GA-3
Rock Lake—*lake* (7) ID-8
Rock Lake—*lake* IL-6
Rock Lake—*lake* IN-6
Rock Lake—*lake* KY-4
Rock Lake—*lake* LA-4
Rock Lake—*lake* (5) MI-6
Rock Lake—*lake* (15) MN-6
Rock Lake—*lake* MS-4
Rock Lake—*lake* (4) MT-8
Rock Lake—*lake* NV-8
Rock Lake—*lake* (7) NM-5
Rock Lake—*lake* (7) NY-2
Rock Lake—*lake* (2) ND-7
Rock Lake—*lake* OK-5
Rock Lake—*lake* (3) OR-9
Rock Lake—*lake* PA-2
Rock Lake—*lake* (2) TX-5
Rock Lake—*lake* (6) UT-8
Rock Lake—*lake* (9) WA-9
Rock Lake—*lake* (10) WI-6
Rock Lake—*lake* (3) WY-8
**Rock Lake**—*pop pl* IN-6
**Rock Lake**—*pop pl* ND-7
**Rock Lake**—*pop pl* PA-2
**Rock Lake**—*pop pl* WV-2
Rock Lake—*reservoir* CA-9
Rock Lake—*reservoir* CO-8
Rock Lake—*reservoir* CT-1
Rock Lake—*reservoir* MT-8
Rock Lake—*reservoir* ND-7
Rock Lake—*reservoir* WV-2
Rock Lake Campground—*locale* MN-6
Rock Lake Campground—*locale* MT-8
Rock Lake (CCD)—*cens area* WA-9
Rock Lake Cem—*cemetery* WI-6
*Rock Lake Church* PA-2
Rock Lake Creek—*stream* ID-8
Rock Lake Creek—*stream* MN-6
Rock Lake Creek—*stream* TX-5
Rock Lake Dam—*dam* ND-7
Rock Lake Dam—*dam* OR-9
Rock Lake Elem Sch—*school* FL-3
Rock Lake Grange—*locale* WY-8
Rock Lake MS—*school* FL-3
Rock Lake Mtn—*summit* NY-2
Rock Lake Peak—*summit* WY-8
Rock Lake Pothole—*lake* AZ-5
Rock Lake Rsvr—*reservoir* NM-5
Rock Lakes—*lake* CO-8
Rock Lakes—*lake* (2) ID-8
Rock Lakes—*lake* OR-9
Rock Lakes—*lake* UT-8
Rock Lakes—*lake* WA-9
Rock Lakes—*reservoir* AL-4
Rock Lake Sch (historical)—*school* PA-2
Rock Lake School (Abandoned)—*locale* WA-9
Rock Lake Tank—*reservoir* NM-5
**Rock Lake Township**—*pop pl* ND-7
**Rock Lake (Township of)**—*pop pl* MN-6
**Rock Lake Village**—*pop pl* WV-2
Rock Lake Windmill—*locale* TX-5
*Rockland* AL-4
*Rockland* OH-6
Rockland—*hist pl* MD-2
Rockland—*hist pl* VA-3
Rockland—*locale* CO-8
Rockland—*locale* KS-7
Rockland—*locale* KY-4
Rockland—*locale* MD-2
Rockland—*locale* NV-8
Rockland—*locale* SC-3
Rockland—*locale* VA-3
Rockland—*locale* (2) WV-2
**Rockland**—*pop pl* CT-1
**Rockland**—*pop pl* DE-2
**Rockland**—*pop pl* FL-3
**Rockland**—*pop pl* ID-8
**Rockland**—*pop pl* ME-1
**Rockland**—*pop pl* (2) MD-2
**Rockland**—*pop pl* MA-1
**Rockland**—*pop pl* MI-6
**Rockland**—*pop pl* NV-8
**Rockland**—*pop pl* (2) NY-2
**Rockland**—*pop pl* OH-6
**Rockland**—*pop pl* (2) PA-2
**Rockland**—*pop pl* TN-4
**Rockland**—*pop pl* TX-5
**Rockland**—*pop pl* WI-6
Rockland—*summit* NV-8
Rockland Almshouse—*hist pl* MA-1
Rockland Breakwater Lighthouse—*hist pl* ME-1
Rockland Canyon—*valley* NV-8
Rockland Cem—*cemetery* CO-8
Rockland Cem—*cemetery* NY-2
Rockland Cem—*cemetery* OH-6
Rockland Cem—*cemetery* PA-2
Rockland Cem—*cemetery* TX-5
Rockland Cem—*cemetery* VA-3
Rockland Ch—*church* GA-3
Rockland Ch—*church* PA-2
Rockland Channel—*channel* FL-3
Rockland Country Club—*other* NY-2
**Rockland (County)**—*pop pl* NY-2
Rockland Day Sch—*school* NY-2
Rockland Farm—*hist pl* (2) MD-2
Rockland Golf Course—*other* ME-1
Rockland Harbor—*bay* ME-1
Rockland Hist Dist—*hist pl* DE-2
Rockland Hist Dist—*hist pl* MD-2
**Rockland (historical)**—*pop pl* RI-1
Rockland HS—*school* MA-1
*Rock Landing* NC-3
Rock Landing—*locale* CT-1
Rock Landing—*locale* (2) FL-3
Rock Landing—*locale* GA-3
Rock Landing—*locale* VT-1
**Rock Landing**—*pop pl* MA-1
Rock Landing Shoal Channel—*channel* VA-3
Rockland JHS—*school* MA-1
Rockland Junction (railroad junction)—*locale* FL-3
Rockland Key—*island* FL-3
*Rockland Lake* CO-8
Rockland Lake—*lake* NY-2
Rockland Lake—*lake* WI-6
**Rockland Lake**—*pop pl* NY-2
Rockland Lake—*reservoir* CO-8
Rockland Landing (Aban'd)—*locale* CA-9
Rockland Mill Complex—*hist pl* NY-2
Rockland Mines—*mine* NV-8
Rockland Plaza (Shop Ctr)—*locale* MA-1
Rockland Pond—*lake* CT-1
Rockland Ponds—*lake* CT-1
Rockland Post Office (historical)—*building* PA-2
Rockland Public Library—*hist pl* ME-1
Rockland Rec Area—*park* TN-4
Rockland Residential Hist Dist—*hist pl* ME-1
Rockland RR Station—*hist pl* ME-1
Rockland RR Station—*locale* FL-3
Rocklands—*hist pl* VA-3
Rockland Sch—*school* CA-9
Rockland Sch—*school* IL-6
Rockland Sch (historical)—*school* TN-4
Rockland State Hosp—*hospital* NY-2
*Rockland Station* PA-2
Rockland Station (historical)—*locale* MA-1
**Rockland (Town of)**—*pop pl* MA-1
**Rockland (Town of)**—*pop pl* NY-2
**Rockland (Town of)**—*pop pl* (2) WI-6
**Rockland (Township of)**—*pop pl* MI-6
**Rockland (Township of)**—*pop pl* (2) PA-2
Rockland Valley—*valley* ID-8
**Rockland Village**—*pop pl* VA-3
**Rockland Woods (subdivision)**—*pop pl* DE-2
**Rocklane**—*pop pl* IN-6
Rocklane Creek—*stream* IN-6
Rock Lane Lodge Marina—*locale* MO-7
Rock Laurel Branch—*stream* SC-3
Rock Lawn and Carriage House—*hist pl* NY-2
Rocklawn Cem—*cemetery* MA-1
Rock Ledge—*cape* ME-1
Rock Ledge—*hist pl* CT-1
Rockledge—*hist pl* KY-4
Rock Ledge—*hist pl* TN-4
Rockledge—*hist pl* VA-3
Rockledge—*locale* TN-4
Rockledge—*locale* TX-5
**Rockledge**—*pop pl* AL-4
**Rockledge**—*pop pl* AZ-5
**Rockledge**—*pop pl* FL-3
**Rockledge**—*pop pl* GA-3
**Rockledge**—*pop pl* PA-2
Rockledge Baptist Ch—*church* AL-4
**Rock Ledge Beach**—*pop pl* NY-2
Rockledge Borough—*civil* PA-2
Rockledge Branch—*stream* PA-2
Rockledge Country Club—*locale* FL-3
Rockledge Country Club—*other* CT-1
**Rock Ledge Estates**—*pop pl* TN-4
Rockledge HS—*school* FL-3
Rock Ledge Park—*park* WI-6
Rockledge Ranch—*locale* NM-5
Rock Ledge Sch—*school* WI-6
Rock Ledge Spring—*spring* (2) AZ-5
Rockledge Tank—*reservoir* AZ-5
**Rockleigh**—*pop pl* NJ-2
Rockleigh Country Club—*other* NJ-2
Rockleigh Hist Dist—*hist pl* NJ-2
Rock Levee—*locale* MO-7
*Rock Lick* WV-2
Rock Lick—*locale* KY-4
Rocklick—*locale* WV-2
**Rocklick**—*pop pl* (2) WV-2
Rock Lick—*stream* (2) KY-4
Rock Lick—*stream* OH-6
Rock Lick—*stream* (2) VA-3
Rock Lick—*summit* (2) OH-6
*Rock Lick Branch* KY-4
Rock Lick Branch—*stream* IN-6
Rock Lick Branch—*stream* KY-4
Rocklick Branch—*stream* (2) KY-4
Rock Lick Branch—*stream* (3) KY-4
Rocklick Branch—*stream* KY-4
Rock Lick Branch—*stream* KY-4
Rocklick Branch—*stream* KY-4
Rock Lick Branch—*stream* (3) KY-4
Rocklick Branch—*stream* KY-4
Rocklick Branch—*stream* MO-7
Rock Lick Branch—*stream* TX-5
Rocklick Branch—*stream* (2) VA-3
Rock Lick Branch—*stream* VA-3
Rocklick Branch—*stream* (2) WV-2
Rock Lick Branch—*stream* WV-2
Rocklick Branch—*stream* (2) WV-2
Rocklick Ch—*church* KY-4
Rocklick Ch—*church* VA-3
Rocklick Creek—*stream* KY-4
Rock Lick Creek—*stream* KY-4
Rocklick Creek—*stream* KY-4
Rock Lick Creek—*stream* (5) KY-4
Rocklick Creek—*stream* MD-2
Rocklick Creek—*stream* OH-6
Rocklick Creek—*stream* PA-2
Rocklick Creek—*stream* VA-3
Rocklick Creek—*stream* WV-2
Rocklick Fork—*stream* KY-4
Rock Lick Fork—*stream* KY-4
Rocklick Fork—*stream* WV-2
Rock Lick Gap—*gap* TN-4
Rock Lick Gap—*gap* VA-3
Rock Lick Hollow—*valley* KY-4
Rock Lick Hollow—*valley* MD-2
Rock Lick Hollow—*valley* OH-6
Rock Lick Hollow—*valley* TN-4
Rock Lick Hollow—*valley* WV-2
Rocklick Knob—*summit* KY-4
Rock Lick (Magisterial District)—*fmr MCD* VA-3
**Rock Lick (Minersville)**—*pop pl* WV-2
Rock Lick Mission Hall—*church* KY-4
Rocklick Point—*cliff* AR-4
*Rocklick Run* WV-2
Rock Lick Run—*stream* PA-2
Rocklick Run—*stream* PA-2
Rocklick Run—*stream* (2) WV-2
Rock Lick Run—*stream* WV-2
Rocklick Run—*stream* (2) WV-2
Rock Lick Sch—*school* KY-4
Rocklick Sch—*school* MO-7
Rocklick Sch (abandoned)—*school* PA-2
Rock Lick Spring—*spring* VA-3
**Rocklin**—*pop pl* CA-9
Rock Lodge Pond—*lake* NJ-2
Rock Lookout Tower—*locale* MO-7
Rocklyn—*locale* WA-9
**Rocklyn**—*pop pl* PA-2
Rock Manor—*locale* DE-2
Rock Maple Cem—*cemetery* ME-1
**Rockmart**—*pop pl* GA-3
Rockmart (CCD)—*cens area* GA-3
Rockmart Memorial Gardens—*cemetery* GA-3
Rock Mary—*hist pl* OK-5
Rock Mary—*pillar* OK-5
Rock Meadow—*flat* CA-9
Rock Meadow—*flat* OR-9
Rock Meadow Brook—*stream* (2) MA-1
*Rock Meadows* MT-8
Rock Meadow Sch—*school* CT-1
*Rockmeer* PA-2
Rockmere—*locale* PA-2
**Rockmere**—*pop pl* PA-2
Rock Mesa—*summit* AZ-5
Rock Mesa—*summit* NM-5
Rock Mesa—*summit* OR-9
*Rockmill* NJ-2
Rock Mill—*hist pl* WI-6
Rock Mill—*locale* OH-6
**Rock Mill**—*pop pl* NJ-2
Rock Mill Ch—*church* AL-4
Rock Mill Ch—*church* GA-3
Rock Mill Covered Bridge—*hist pl* OH-6
Rock Mill Fish Hatchery—*other* GA-3
*Rock Mills* CA-9
Rock Mills—*locale* VA-3
**Rock Mills**—*pop pl* AL-4
**Rock Mills**—*pop pl* OH-6
Rock Mills Cem—*cemetery* OH-6
Rock Mills Ch—*church* AL-4
*Rock Mills First Baptist Ch* AL-4
Rock Mills JHS—*school* AL-4
Rockmont—*locale* WI-6
Rockmore Creek—*stream* GA-3
Rock Mound Archeol Site—*hist pl* FL-3
*Rock Mountain* NJ-2
Rock Mountain—*ridge* OR-9
Rock Mountain Ch (historical)—*church* AL-4
*Rock Mountain Creek* CO-8
Rock Mountain Creek—*stream* (2) GA-3
*Rock Mountain Lake* AL-4
Rock Mountain Lake Dam—*dam* AL-4
Rock Mountian—*summit* WA-9
*Rock Mtn* AZ-5
Rock Mtn—*summit* AK-9
Rock Mtn—*summit* (4) CA-9
Rock Mtn—*summit* CO-8
Rock Mtn—*summit* (3) GA-3
Rock Mtn—*summit* OR-9
Rock Mtn—*summit* SC-3
Rock Mtn—*summit* VA-3
Rock Mtn—*summit* (2) WA-9
Rock Mtn—*summit* (2) WY-8
Rock Narrows Branch—*stream* WV-2
**Rockne**—*pop pl* TX-5
Rockne Gulch—*valley* OR-9
*Rockoak* WV-2
Rock Oak—*locale* WV-2
Rockoak—*other* WV-2
Rock Oak Park (historical)—*park* PA-2
Rock Oak Ridge—*ridge* PA-2
*Rock Oak Ridge Trail* PA-2
**Rock Oak (Rockoak)**—*pop pl* WV-2
Rock Oak Trail—*trail* (2) PA-2
Rock-O-Dundee Hill—*summit* ME-1
Rock of Ages—*island* AK-9
Rock Of Ages—*pillar* ID-8
Rock Of Ages—*pillar* WY-8
Rock of Ages Baptist Ch—*church* AL-4
Rock of Ages Baptist Ch—*church* DE-2
Rock of Ages Baptist Ch—*church* IN-6
*Rock of Ages Baptist Church* TN-4
Rock of Ages Bluff—*cliff* MO-7
Rock of Ages Cem—*cemetery* AR-4
Rock of Ages Cem—*cemetery* MS-4
Rock of Ages Ch—*church* AR-4
Rock of Ages Ch—*church* (3) MS-4
Rock of Ages Ch—*church* TN-4
Rock Of Ages Ch—*church* VA-3
Rock of Ages Ch (historical)—*church* MS-4
Rock of Ages Lake—*lake* MN-6
Rock of Ages Lighthouse—*locale* MI-6
Rock of Ages Light Station—*hist pl* MI-6
Rock of Ages Mine—*mine* CO-8
Rock of Ages Mine—*mine* NM-5
Rock of Ages Missionary Baptist Ch—*church* MS-4
Rock of Ages Sch (historical)—*school* TN-4
Rock of Faith Missionary Baptist Ch—*church* AL-4
Rock of Mount Zion Ch—*church* LA-4
Rock of Mount Zion Ch—*church* MS-4
Rock of the Ages Mine—*mine* CO-8
*Rock of the Cross* MO-7
Rock of Will Ch—*church* FL-3
Rock of Zion Ch—*church* NC-3
Rocko Hollow—*valley* VA-3
Rock Oil Field—*oilfield* (2) KS-7
Rock on Dam Tank—*reservoir* AZ-5
Rock O' the Range Bridge—*hist pl* OR-9
Rock Park Rsvr—*reservoir* CO-8
Rock Pass—*gap* WA-9
Rock Pasture Spring—*spring* TX-5
*Rock Peak* AZ-5
Rock Peak—*summit* AZ-5
Rock Peak—*summit* MT-8
Rock Peak—*summit* WA-9
Rockpen Branch—*stream* WV-2
Rock Pen Creek—*stream* OK-5
Rock Pen Draw—*valley* TX-5
Rock Pens Windmill—*locale* TX-5
Rock Pen Windmill—*locale* TX-5
Rock Peon Mtn—*summit* NJ-2
Rock Pike Ch—*church* VA-3
Rock Pile—*summit* CA-9
Rockpile, The—*summit* TX-5
Rockpile, The—*summit* WY-8
Rockpile Ch (historical)—*church* TN-4
Rock Pile Creek—*stream* AL-4
Rockpile Creek—*stream* CA-9
Rockpile Creek—*stream* WA-9
Rockpile Hill—*summit* MS-4
Rockpile House Windmill—*locale* TX-5
Rockpile Lake—*lake* (2) OR-9
Rock Pile Mountain Wilderness—*forest* MO-7
Rock Pile Mtn—*summit* AL-4
Rock Pile Mtn—*summit* MO-7
Rockpile Mtn—*summit* OR-9
Rockpile Pass—*gap* AK-9
Rockpile Peak—*summit* CA-9
Rockpile Pond—*lake* WI-6
Rockpile Ranch—*locale* OR-9
Rock Pile Spring—*spring* OR-9
Rock Pile Spring—*spring* SD-7
Rock Pile Tank—*reservoir* AZ-5
Rockpile Tanks—*reservoir* NM-5
Rock Pillar—*summit* ID-8
*Rock Pine Mtn* AL-4
Rock Pinnacles—*area* UT-8
Rock Pisgah Ch—*church* MS-4
Rock Pit—*reservoir* NM-5
Rock Pit Creek—*stream* OR-9
Rock Pit Lake—*lake* FL-3
Rock Pit Number 57—*mine* FL-3
Rock Pit Rsvr—*reservoir* OR-9
*Rock Point* ID-8
*Rock Point* RI-1
Rock Point—*cape* (7) AK-9
Rock Point—*cape* AR-4
Rock Point—*cape* DE-2
Rock Point—*cape* (4) FL-3
Rock Point—*cape* (2) ME-1
Rock Point—*cape* (4) MD-2
Rock Point—*cape* NJ-2
Rock Point—*cape* NY-2
Rock Point—*cape* (2) NC-3
Rock Point—*cape* OR-9
Rock Point—*cape* VA-3
Rock Point—*cliff* AZ-5
Rock Point—*cliff* (2) CO-8
Rock Point—*cliff* UT-8
Rock Point—*cliff* WY-8
Rock Point—*locale* OR-9
Rock Point—*other* AK-9
Rock Point—*pillar* CO-8
**Rock Point**—*pop pl* AZ-5
**Rock Point**—*pop pl* MD-2
**Rock Point**—*pop pl* PA-2
Rock Point—*summit* CA-9
Rock Point—*summit* OR-9
Rock Point—*summit* WA-9
Rock Point Airp—*airport* AZ-5
Rock Point Boarding Sch—*school* AZ-5
Rock Point Canal—*canal* UT-8
Rock Point Cem—*cemetery* MO-7
Rock Point Cem—*cemetery* UT-8
*Rockpoint Cemetery* UT-8
Rock Point Ch—*church* OK-5
Rock Point Creek—*stream* VA-3
Rock Point Hill—*summit* AK-9
Rock Point Hotel—*hist pl* OR-9
Rock Pointing West—*ridge* AZ-5
Rock Point Lodge—*locale* AR-4
Rock Point Overlook—*locale* VA-3
Rock Point Rsvr—*reservoir* ID-8
Rock Point Rsvr—*reservoir* UT-8
Rock Point Sch—*school* TX-5
Rock Point Spring—*spring* AZ-5
Rock Point Trading Post—*locale* AZ-5
Rock Point Valley—*valley* NM-5
*Rock Pond* NY-2
Rock Pond—*lake* (2) AL-4
Rock Pond—*lake* CT-1
Rock Pond—*lake* (6) FL-3
Rock Pond—*lake* (2) GA-3
Rock Pond—*lake* (4) ME-1
Rock Pond—*lake* MD-2
Rock Pond—*lake* (2) NH-1
Rock Pond—*lake* (13) NY-2
Rock Pond—*lake* (2) OR-9
Rock Pond—*reservoir* MA-1
Rock Pond Brook—*stream* NY-2
Rock Pond Courthouse—*building* GA-3
Rock Pond Dam—*dam* MA-1
Rock Pond Mtn—*summit* (2) NY-2
Rock Pond Sch—*school* GA-3
Rock Pond Stream—*stream* ME-1
Rock Pond Trail—*trail* NY-2
Rockpool Gully—*valley* TX-5
*Rock Port* KS-7
*Rockport* MO-7
*Rockport* SD-7
Rockport—*locale* CO-8
Rockport—*locale* MI-6
Rockport—*locale* (2) NJ-2
Rockport—*locale* TN-4
Rockport—*locale* WV-2
**Rockport**—*pop pl* AR-4
**Rockport**—*pop pl* CA-9
**Rockport**—*pop pl* FL-3
**Rockport**—*pop pl* IL-6
**Rockport**—*pop pl* (2) IN-6
**Rockport**—*pop pl* KY-4
**Rockport**—*pop pl* ME-1
**Rockport**—*pop pl* MA-1
**Rockport**—*pop pl* MS-4
**Rock Port**—*pop pl* MO-7
**Rockport**—*pop pl* OH-6
**Rockport**—*pop pl* PA-2
**Rockport**—*pop pl* SD-7
**Rockport**—*pop pl* TX-5
**Rockport**—*pop pl* WA-9
**Rockport**—*pop pl* WV-2
Rockport Art Association—*building* MA-1
Rockport Bay—*bay* CA-9
Rockport Beach—*beach* TX-5
Rockport Breakwater Light—*locale* MA-1
Rockport Bridge—*bridge* IN-6
Rockport Bridge—*bridge* MS-4
Rockport Bridge—*hist pl* MS-4
Rockport Campground—*park* UT-8
Rockport (CCD)—*cens area* TX-5
Rockport Cem—*cemetery* AR-4
Rockport Cem—*cemetery* ME-1
Rockport Cem—*cemetery* TX-5
**Rockport (census name Rockport Center)**—*pop pl* MA-1
Rockport Center (census name Rockport)—*other* MA-1
Rockport Ch—*church* MS-4
Rockport Ch (historical)—*church* MS-4
**Rockport Colony**—*pop pl* SD-7
Rockport Community Sch—*school* MA-1
*Rockport (corporate name Rock Port)* MO-7
*Rockport Creek* CA-9
Rockport Creek—*stream* CA-9
Rock Port Creek—*stream* PA-2
Rockport Downtown Main Street Hist Dist—*hist pl* MA-1
Rockport Fire Station—*locale* CA-9
Rockport Game Farm—*park* NJ-2
Rockport Golf Club—*locale* MA-1
Rockport Harbor—*harbor* ME-1
Rockport Harbor—*harbor* MA-1
Rockport Hist Dist—*hist pl* ME-1
Rockport (historical)—*locale* KS-7
**Rockport (historical)**—*pop pl* MS-4
Rockport Historic Kiln Area—*hist pl* ME-1
Rockport Information Center—*building* MA-1
Rockport Island (historical)—*island* TN-4
**Rockport Junction**—*pop pl* IN-6
Rockport Lake—*reservoir* UT-8
Rockport Landing—*locale* TN-4
*Rockport Mills* IN-6
Rock Port Municipal Airp—*airport* MO-7
Rockport Park—*park* WI-6
Rockport Pond—*lake* NY-2
Rockport Post Office (historical)—*building* (2) MS-4
Rockport Post Office (historical)—*building* TN-4
*Rockport Reservoir* UT-8
Rockport RR Station—*locale* FL-3

Rockport Sch—school MS-4
Rockport Sch—school WV-2
Rockport State Park—park UT-8
Rockport State Park—park WA-9
Rockport Station—locale MA-1
Rockport Station—locale PA-2
**Rockport (Town of)**—pop pl ME-1
**Rockport (Town of)**—pop pl MA-1
Rockport Tunnel—tunnel PA-2
Rock Port United Methodist Church MS-4
Rockport Village. MA-1
Rock Prairie—area CA-9
Rock Prairie—flat WA-9
Rock Prairie—locale MO-7
Rock Prairie—swamp FL-3
Rock Prairie Cem—cemetery IA-7
Rock Prairie Cem—cemetery MO-7
Rock Prairie Ch—church IN-6
Rock Prairie Ch—church MO-7
Rock Prairie Ch—church (2) TX-5
Rock Prairie County Park—park OR-9
Rock Prairie School (historical)—locale MO-7
Rock Prairie Township—civil MO-7
Rock Primitive Baptist Church AL-4
Rock Quarry Bar—bar TN-4
Rock Quarry Branch—stream AL-4
Rock Quarry Branch—stream AR-4
Rock Quarry Branch—stream KY-4
Rock Quarry Branch—stream MS-4
Rock Quarry Branch—stream TX-5
Rock Quarry Canyon—valley OR-9
Rock Quarry Canyon Dam—dam OR-9
Rock Quarry Cave—cave AL-4
Rock Quarry Cem—cemetery KY-4
Rock Quarry Ch—church GA-3
Rock Quarry County Park—park AL-4
Rock Quarry Creek—stream TX-5
Rock Quarry Draw—valley TX-5
Rock Quarry Gulch MT-8
Rock Quarry Gulch—valley ID-8
Rock Quarry Hill TX-5
Rock Quarry Hill—summit AR-4
**Rockquarry (historical)**—pop pl TN-4
Rock Quarry Hollow—valley (2) TN-4
Rock Quarry Hollow Mine—mine TN-4
Rock Quarry Landing Public Use
Area—park AL-4
Rock Quarry Mtn—summit AL-4
Rock Quarry Mtn—summit GA-3
Rock Quarry Pond—reservoir SC-3
Rock Quarry Prison—other GA-3
Rock Quarry Rsvr—reservoir OR-9
Rock Quarry Spring—spring UT-8
Rock Quarry Tank—reservoir NM-5
Rock Rabbit Lakes—lake WA-9
Rock Ramond—summit NH-1
Rock Ranch—locale AZ-5
Rock Ranch—locale CA-9
Rock Ranch—locale NM-5
Rock Ranch—locale (2) SD-7
Rock Ranch Canal—canal WY-8
Rock Ranch ( Historical)—locale WY-8
Rock Ranch Sch—school SD-7
**Rock Rapids**—pop pl IA-7
Rock Rapids—rapids MI-6
Rock Raven Mine—mine CO-8
**Rock Raymond**—pop pl CT-1
Rock Reef Pass—ridge FL-3
Rock Reservoir AZ-5
**Rock Rest**—pop pl NC-3
Rock Rest Ch—church AL-4
**Rock Rest (subdivision)**—pop pl NC-3
Rock Ridge—hist pl MA-1
Rock Ridge—locale FL-3
**Rock Ridge**—pop pl CT-1
**Rockridge**—pop pl GA-3
**Rock Ridge**—pop pl NC-3
**Rockridge**—pop pl WV-2
Rock Ridge—ridge AL-4
Rock Ridge—ridge AR-4
Rock Ridge—ridge GA-3
Rock Ridge—ridge KY-4
Rock Ridge—ridge MD-2
Rock Ridge—ridge NM-5
Rock Ridge—ridge PA-2
Rock Ridge—ridge WY-8
Rockridge—uninc pl CA-9
Rock Ridge Cem—cemetery IL-6
Rock Ridge Cem—cemetery MA-1
Rock Ridge Cem—cemetery NY-2
Rock Ridge Ch—church VA-3
Rock Ridge Chapel—church PA-2
Rock Ridge Country Club—other CT-1
Rock Ridge Elem Sch—school NC-3
**Rock Ridge Lake**—pop pl NJ-2
Rock Ridge Lake—reservoir NJ-2
Rock Ridge Lake Dam—dam NJ-2
Rock Ridge Park—park CT-1
Rockridge Pond—lake MA-1
Rock Ridge Rsvr—reservoir WY-8
Rockridge Sch—school CA-9
Rock Ridge Sch—school OH-6
Rock Ridge Sch (abandoned)—school PA-2
Rock Ridge Slough—gut MO-7
Rock Ridge Trail—trail PA-2
Rock Riffle—rapids IN-6
Rockriffle Run—stream WV-2
Rock Rift—locale NY-2
Rock Rift Mtn—summit NY-2
Rock Rim Lake—lake OR-9
**Rockrimmin Ridge**—pop pl PA-2
**Rockrimmon**—pop pl CO-8
Rock Rimmon—summit CT-1
Rock Rimmon—summit MA-1
Rockrimmon Country Club—other NY-2
Rock Rimmon Hill—summit NH-1
Rock Rimmon Park—park NH-1
Rock Rimmon State For—forest NH-1
Rock River IN-6
Rock River MN-6
**Rock River**—pop pl MI-6
**Rock River**—pop pl WY-8
Rock River—stream IL-6
Rock River—stream IA-7
Rock River—stream (3) MI-6
Rock River—stream MN-6
Rock River—stream NY-2
Rock River—stream (2) VT-1
Rock River—stream WI-6
Rock River Bay—bay VT-1

Rock River Cem—cemetery (3) WI-6
Rock River Country Club—other WI-6
Rock River Falls—falls MI-6
Rock River Mine—mine CA-9
Rock River Park—park WI-6
Rock River Sch—school (2) IL-6
Rock River Sch—school (2) WI-6
**Rock River (Township of)**—pop pl MI-6
Rock River View Cem—cemetery IL-6
Rock Road Cem—cemetery VA-3
Rock Robinson Creek—stream OR-9
**Rock (Rock Quarry)**—pop pl (2) LA-4
Rock Roe Bayou AR-4
Rock Roe Lake AR-4
Rock Roll Canyon—valley ID-8
Rock Rovers' Land UT-8
Rock Row—ridge AR-4
Rock Row Cem—cemetery LA-4
Rock Rsvr—reservoir (3) OR-9
Rock Rsvr—reservoir UT-8
Rock Rsvr—reservoir WY-8
Rock Run IN-6
Rock Run OH-6
Rock Run PA-2
Rock Run WV-2
Rock Run WI-6
Rock Run—locale MD-2
Rock Run—locale PA-2
**Rock Run**—pop pl AL-4
**Rock Run**—pop pl WV-2
Rock Run—stream AL-4
Rock Run—stream (2) IL-6
Rock Run—stream (3) IN-6
Rock Run—stream (3) KY-4
Rock Run—stream (3) MD-2
Rock Run—stream NY-2
Rock Run—stream (4) OH-6
Rock Run—stream (34) PA-2
Rock Run—stream (2) VA-3
Rock Run—stream (12) WV-2
Rock Run Cem—cemetery IL-6
Rock Run Cem—cemetery OH-6
Rock Run Ch—church AL-4
Rock Run Ch—church IN-6
Rock Run Ch—church MD-2
Rock Run Ch—church PA-2
Rock Run Ch—church VA-3
Rock Run Ch—church WV-2
Rock Run Creek IL-6
Rock Run Creek—stream IN-6
Rock Run Creek—stream IA-7
Rock Run Creek—stream OH-6
Rock Run Dam—dam (3) PA-2
Rock Run (historical P.O.)—locale IA-7
Rock Run Post Office
(historical)—building AL-4
Rock Run Sch (historical)—school (2) PA-2
**Rock Run Station**—pop pl AL-4
Rock Run Station Post Office
(historical)—building AL-4
**Rock Run (Township of)**—pop pl IL-6
Rock Run Trail—trail (3) PA-2
Rock Run Vista—summit PA-2
Rocks—locale MD-2
**Rocks**—pop pl WV-2
Rocks, Lake of the—lake MT-8
Rocks, Point of—cape MT-8
Rocks, Point of—cape TX-5
Rocks, Point of—cape (2) VA-3
Rocks, Point of—cliff MT-8
Rocks, Point of—pillar MT-8
Rocks, Point of—summit (2) MT-8
Rocks, The AZ-5
Rocks, The—cape NH-1
Rocks, The—dam NC-3
Rocks, The—island DE-2
Rocks, The—island GA-3
Rocks, The—locale AL-4
Rocks, The—locale DE-2
Rocks, The—locale FL-3
Rocks, The—pillar NY-2
**Rocks, The**—pop pl KY-4
Rocks, The—ridge CA-9
Rocks, The—rock UT-8
Rocks, The—summit AZ-5
Rocks, The—summit CO-8
Rocks, The—summit MA-1
Rocks, The—summit UT-8
Rocks, The—summit VA-3
Rocks, The—summit (2) WY-8
Rock Salt River KS-7
Rocks at Laurel Creek Reservoir—cliff PA-2
Rocks Bar, The—bar AL-4
Rocks Bayou—gut LA-4
Rocks Bridge—bridge MA-1
Rocksburg PA-2
**Rocksbury (Township of)**—pop pl MN-6
Rocks Cem—cemetery (2) SC-3
Rocks Ch—church VA-3
Rock Sch—school CO-8
Rock Sch—school IL-6
Rock Sch—school (2) KS-7
Rock Sch—school MN-6
Rock Sch—school MO-7
Rock Sch—school OK-5
Rock Sch—school PA-2
Rock Sch—school SC-3
Rock Sch—school (3) WI-6
Rock Sch (abandoned)—school PA-2
Rocks Chapel—church AL-4
Rocks Chapel Cem—cemetery AL-4
Rock Sch (historical)—school (2) AL-4
Rocks Creek—stream LA-4
Rocksdale—locale WV-2
Rock Seep—spring AZ-5
Rocks Estate—hist pl NH-1
Rock Settee—pillar UT-8
Rock Shale Rsvr—reservoir CO-8
Rockshire—uninc pl MD-2
Rockshire Square—uninc pl MD-2
Rockshire Village—uninc pl MD-2
Rock Shoals Cumberland Ch—church TX-5
Rockside Sch—school OH-6
Rock Sink—basin FL-3
Rock Sink Ch—church FL-3
Rock sjprings—spring TN-4
Rock Skree Trail—trail PA-2
Rock Slide—cliff OR-9
Rock Slide, The—locale WY-8
Rockslide Canyon—valley ID-8

Rock Slide Canyon—valley UT-8
Rockslide Lake—lake CA-9
Rock Slide Lake—lake ID-8
Rockslides—cliff CA-9
Rock Slope—flat WY-8
Rock Slope Mine (underground)—mine
(2) AL-4
Rock Slope Number 4 Mine
(underground)—mine AL-4
Rock Slough—gut TX-5
Rock Slough—lake ND-7
Rock Slough—stream AK-9
Rock Slough—stream CA-9
Rock Slough—stream (2) TN-4
Rocks Mountain Trail—trail VA-3
Rocks Mtn—summit VA-3
Rocks Nose—island ME-1
Rock Southwest Oil Field—oilfield KS-7
Rocks Park, The—flat IL-6
Rocks Plantation—hist pl SC-3
Rock Spring AZ-5
Rock Spring MO-7
Rock Spring PA-2
Rock Spring—locale GA-3
Rock Spring—locale KY-4
**Rock Spring**—pop pl AL-4
**Rock Spring**—pop pl AR-4
**Rock Spring**—pop pl NC-3
**Rockspring**—pop pl PA-2
Rock Spring—spring (8) AL-4
Rock Spring—spring (21) AZ-5
Rock Spring—spring AR-4
Rock Spring—spring (17) CA-9
Rock Spring—spring (10) CO-8
Rock Spring—spring FL-3
Rock Spring—spring (9) ID-8
Rock Spring—spring IL-6
Rock Spring—spring (3) MO-7
Rock Spring—spring (5) MT-8
Rock Spring—spring (28) NV-8
Rock Spring—spring (11) NM-5
Rock Spring—spring (31) OR-9
Rock Spring—spring PA-2
Rock Spring—spring (6) TN-4
Rock Spring—spring (2) TX-5
Rock Spring—spring (28) UT-8
Rock Spring—spring (2) VA-3
Rock Spring—spring (4) WA-9
Rock Spring—spring WY-8
Rock Spring Arroyo—stream CO-8
Rock Spring Baptist Church TN-4
Rock Spring Branch—stream (2) GA-3
Rock Spring Branch—stream IL-6
Rockspring Branch—stream KY-4
Rock Spring Branch—stream TN-4
Rockspring Branch—stream TN-4
Rock Spring Branch—stream (2) TN-4
Rock Spring Branch—stream TX-5
Rock Spring Branch—stream VA-3
Rock Spring Camp—locale OR-9
Rock Spring Canyon UT-8
Rock Spring Canyon—valley AZ-5
Rock Spring Canyon—valley ID-8
Rock Spring Canyon—valley (2) NV-8
Rock Spring Canyon—valley OR-9
Rock Spring Canyon—valley UT-8
Rock Spring (CCD)—cens area GA-3
Rock Spring Cem—cemetery GA-3
Rock Spring Cem—cemetery IA-7
Rock Spring Cem—cemetery MO-7
Rock Spring Cem—cemetery OK-5
Rock Spring Cem—cemetery TX-5
Rock Spring Cem—cemetery WV-2
Rock Spring Ch TN-4
Rock Spring Ch—church AL-4
Rock Spring Ch—church (2) GA-3
Rock Spring Ch—church (2) KY-4
Rock Spring Ch—church LA-4
Rock Spring Ch—church MD-2
Rock Spring Ch—church MO-7
Rock Spring Ch—church (7) NC-3
Rock Spring Ch—church (3) SC-3
Rock Spring Ch—church (2) TN-4
Rock Spring Ch—church (3) VA-3
Rock Spring Ch—church WV-2
Rock Spring Creek TN-4
Rock Spring Creek—stream CO-8
Rock Spring Creek—stream GA-3
Rock Spring Creek—stream MI-6
Rock Spring Creek—stream NV-8
Rock Spring Creek—stream OR-9
Rock Spring Creek—stream WY-8
Rock Spring Draw—valley AZ-5
Rock Spring Draw—valley (3) CO-8
Rock Spring Draw—valley (2) UT-8
Rock Spring Draw Tank—reservoir AZ-5
Rock Spring Gap—gap AL-4
Rock Spring Gap—gap TN-4
Rock Spring Gulch—valley CO-8
Rock Spring Gulch—valley (2) WA-9
Rock Spring Hollow—valley AR-4
Rock Spring Hollow—valley MO-7
Rock Spring Island—island FL-3
Rock Spring Junction—locale AL-4
Rock Spring Mesa—summit UT-8
Rock Spring Mtn—summit VA-3
Rock Spring Navajo Mission—church NM-5
Rock Spring Peak—summit CA-9
Rock Spring P.O. (historical)—locale AL-4
Rock Spring Pond—lake SC-3
Rock Spring Quarry—uninc pl AL-4
Rock Spring Ranch—locale MT-8
Rock Spring Ranch—locale NM-5
Rock Spring Ridge—ridge TN-4
Rock Spring Ridge—ridge UT-8
Rock Spring Rsvr—reservoir OR-9
Rock Spring Rsvr—reservoir WY-8
Rock Spring Run—stream (3) PA-2
Rock Springs AL-4
Rock Springs FL-3
Rock Springs GA-3
Rock Springs NV-8
Rock Springs OR-9
Rock Springs PA-2
Rock Springs UT-8
Rock Springs—locale (2) AL-4
Rock Springs—locale AZ-5
Rock Springs—locale (2) AR-4
Rocksprings—locale FL-3
Rock Springs—locale GA-3

Rock Springs—locale KY-4
Rock Springs—locale MT-8
Rock Springs—locale OH-6
Rock Springs—locale (3) TN-4
Rock Springs—locale (3) TX-5
**Rock Springs**—pop pl (2) AL-4
**Rock Springs**—pop pl FL-3
**Rock Springs**—pop pl KY-4
**Rock Springs**—pop pl MD-2
**Rock Springs**—pop pl MO-7
**Rock Springs**—pop pl NM-5
**Rock Springs**—pop pl NC-3
**Rocksprings**—pop pl PA-2
**Rock Springs**—pop pl (2) TN-4
**Rocksprings**—pop pl TX-5
**Rock Springs**—pop pl (2) VA-3
**Rock Springs**—pop pl WI-6
**Rock Springs**—pop pl WY-8
Rock Springs—spring AL-4
Rock Springs—spring AR-4
Rock Springs—spring (3) CA-9
Rock Springs—spring CO-8
Rock Springs—spring FL-3
Rock Springs—spring (2) ID-8
Rock Springs—spring IN-6
Rock Springs—spring (4) NV-8
Rock Springs—spring NC-3
Rock Springs—spring OR-9
Rock Springs—spring TN-4
Rock Springs—spring (3) TX-5
Rock Springs—spring (3) UT-8
Rock Springs—spring WA-9
Rock Springs—spring (2) WY-8
Rock Springs—valley NV-8
Rock Springs Baptist Church AL-4
Rock Springs Baptist Church TN-4
Rock Springs Bench—bench (2) UT-8
Rock Springs Bible Ch—church MO-7
Rock Springs Branch—stream (2) AL-4
Rock Springs Branch—stream AR-4
Rock Springs Branch—stream GA-3
Rock Springs Branch—stream KY-4
Rock Springs Branch—stream TN-4
Rocksprings Branch—stream TN-4
Rock Springs Branch—stream TX-5
Rock Springs Butte—summit AZ-5
Rock Springs Camp—locale OR-9
Rock Springs Campground—locale CO-8
Rock Springs Campground—locale NC-3
Rock Springs Camp Meeting
Ground—hist pl NC-3
Rock Springs Canyon UT-8
Rock Springs Canyon—valley CA-9
Rock Springs Canyon—valley KS-7
Rock Springs Canyon—valley (2) NV-8
Rock Springs Canyon—valley (5) NM-5
Rock Springs Canyon—valley WY-8
Rock Springs Cem—cemetery AL-4
Rock Springs Cem—cemetery (2) AR-4
Rock Springs Cem—cemetery PA-2
Rock Springs Cem—cemetery (4) TN-4
Rock Springs Ch AL-4
Rock Springs Ch NC-3
Rock Springs Ch—church (13) AL-4
Rock Springs Ch—church (5) AR-4
Rock Springs Ch—church FL-3
Rock Springs Ch—church (10) GA-3
Rock Springs Ch—church (3) IL-6
Rock Springs Ch—church (2) IN-6
Rock Springs Ch—church (3) KY-4
Rock Springs Ch—church (2) MO-7
Rock Springs Ch—church (5) NC-3
Rock Springs Ch—church (2) OK-5
Rock Springs Ch—church PA-2
Rock Springs Ch—church (2) SC-3
Rock Springs Ch—church (4) TN-4
Rock Springs Ch—church (3) TX-5
Rock Springs Ch—church (2) VA-3
Rock Spring Sch—school GA-3
Rock Spring Sch—school IA-7
Rock Spring Sch—school KY-4
Rock Spring Sch—school TX-5
Rock Spring Sch (abandoned)—school PA-2
Rock Spring Sch (historical)—school TN-4
Rock Springs Ch of Christ TN-4
Rock Springs Cow Camp—locale NV-8
Rock Springs Creek NV-8
Rock Springs Creek UT-8
Rock Springs Creek—stream CA-9
Rock Springs Creek—stream (3) MT-8
Rock Springs Creek—stream SC-3
Rock Springs Creek—stream (3) TX-5
Rock Springs Creek—stream UT-8
Rock Springs Draw—valley WY-8
Rock Springs Elementary School NC-3
Rock Springs Elem Sch—school TN-4
Rock Springs Hollow—valley IL-6
Rock Springs Hollow—valley TX-5
Rock Springs Interchange—crossing AZ-5
Rock Spring Siphon—other OR-9
Rock Springs Landing—locale GA-3
Rock Springs Methodist Ch—church TN-4
Rock Springs Mission AL-4
Rock Springs North—cens area WY-8
Rocksprings North (CCD)—cens area TX-5
Rock Springs Park—park (2) IL-6
Rock Springs Park—park TN-4
Rock Springs Pass—gap NV-8
Rock Springs Peak UT-8
Rock Springs Peak—summit CA-9
Rock Springs Peak—summit NM-5
Rock Springs Pit—cave TN-4
Rock Springs Ranch—locale KS-7
Rock Springs Ridge—ridge UT-8
Rock Springs (RR name
Rockspring)—other GA-3
Rock Springs Run—stream FL-3
Rock Springs Sch—school GA-3
Rock Springs Sch—school (2) KY-4
Rock Springs Sch—school MT-8
Rock Springs Sch—school NC-3
Rock Springs Sch—school PA-2
Rock Springs Sch—school TN-4
Rock Springs Sch—school TX-5
Rock Springs Sch—school WV-2
Rock Springs Sch (abandoned)—school MO-7
Rock Springs Sch (historical)—school AL-4
Rock Springs Sch (historical)—school (2) TN-4
Rock Springs School (historical)—locale MO-7
Rock Springs South—cens area WY-8

Rocksprings South (CCD)—cens area TX-5
**Rock Springs (subdivision)**—pop pl NC-3
**Rock Springs Subdivision**—pop pl UT-8
Rock Springs Substation—locale AZ-5
Rock Springs-Sweetwater County
Airport—airport WY-8
Rock Springs Tank—reservoir TX-5
Rock Springs Trail—trail CO-8
Rock Springs Trail—trail OR-9
Rock Springs Valley—valley TN-4
Rock Springs Wash—valley UT-8
Rock Springs Windmill—locale TX-5
Rock Springs 4 H Camp KS-7
Rock Spring Table—flat NV-8
Rock Spring Table Rsvr—reservoir NV-8
Rock Spring Tank—reservoir AZ-5
Rock Spring Tank—reservoir NM 5
Rock Spring Top—summit (2) GA-3
Rock Spring Trail—trail SD-7
Rock Spring Trail (pack)—trail OR-9
Rock Spring Warehouse—hist pl KY-4
Rock Spring Wash UT-8
Rock Spring Well—well AZ-5
Rock Spur Drain—canal ID-8
Rocks Rsvr—reservoir ID-8
Rocks Sch (historical)—school MS-4
Rocks (Stage station site), The—locale ID-8
Rockstack—summit NC-3
Rockstack—summit TN-4
Rockstad Lake—reservoir MN-6
Rockstand AL-4
Rock Stand—locale AL-4
Rock Stand Ch—church AL-4
Rock Star Baptist Ch—church MS-4
Rock Station MA-1
Rock Station—locale AZ-5
Rock Station—locale TN-4
Rock Station (historical)—locale KS-7
Rock Station (historical)—locale MA-1
Rockstep Run—stream WV-2
Rock Stile Ch—church KY-4
**Rock Stream**—pop pl NY-2
Rock Stream—stream NY-2
Rock Stream Cem—cemetery NY-2
Rock Stream Point—cape NY-2
**Rocks Village**—pop pl MA-1
Rocks Village Hist Dist—hist pl MA-1
Rocksville MA-1
Rocksville PA-2
Rock Switch—locale VA-3
**Rocks Works**—pop pl (2) PA-2
Rock Tank AZ-5
Rock Tank NM-5
Rock Tank—lake NM-5
Rock Tank—reservoir (34) AZ-5
Rock Tank—reservoir (23) NM-5
Rock Tank—reservoir (15) TX-5
Rock Tank—spring UT-8
Rock Tank Canyon AZ-5
Rock Tank Canyon—valley (4) AZ-5
Rock Tank Canyon—valley (4) NM-5
Rock Tank Creek AZ-5
Rock Tank Creek—stream TX-5
Rock Tank Dam—dam AZ-5
Rock Tank Draw—valley NM-5
Rock Tanks—reservoir (3) AZ-5
Rock Tanks—reservoir NM-5
Rock Tanks Spring—spring AZ-5
Rock Tank Well—well (2) NM-5
Rock Tank West—reservoir AZ-5
Rock Tank Windmill—locale (2) NM-5
Rock Tank Windmill—locale (3) TX-5
Rock Tavern—locale NY-2
Rock Terrace HS—school MD-2
Rockton—locale WV-2
**Rockton**—pop pl IL-6
**Rockton**—pop pl IA-7
**Rockton**—pop pl NY-2
**Rockton**—pop pl NC-3
**Rockton**—pop pl PA-2
**Rockton**—pop pl SC-3
**Rockton**—pop pl WI-6
Rockton and Rion RR Hist Dist—hist pl SC-3
Rockton Archeol District—hist pl WI-6
Rockton Cem—cemetery NE-7
Rockton Ch—church SC-3
Rockton Fire Tower—tower PA-2
Rockton Hist Dist—hist pl IL-6
Rockton (historical)—locale KS-7
Rockton Station—locale PA-2
**Rockton (Township of)**—pop pl IL-6
Rock Top—summit AZ-5
Rock Top—summit PA-2
Rocktop Airp—airport PA-2
Rock Top Butte OR-9
Rocktop Butte—summit OR-9
Rock Top Spring—spring AZ-5
Rock Top Wash—valley AZ-5
Rock Tower Well—well KS-7
Rocktown—locale VA-3
**Rocktown**—pop pl NJ-2
**Rocktown**—pop pl PA-2
**Rock Town**—pop pl TN-4
Rock Town—ridge OK-5
Rocktown Branch—stream GA-3
Rocktown Ch (historical)—church TN-4
**Rock (Town of)**—pop pl (2) WI-6
Rock Township—civil MO-7
Rock Township—fmr MCD (4) IA-7
**Rock Township**—pop pl KS-7
**Rock Township**—pop pl (2) ND-7
**Rock (Township of)**—pop pl MN-6
Rock Trail (Jeep), The—trail CA-9
Rock Trail Tank—reservoir TX-5
Rocktram—locale CA-9
Rocktree Creek—stream CA-9
Rocktree Valley—basin CA-9
Rock Trick Tank—reservoir AZ-5
Rock Turn Point DE-2
Rock United Methodist Ch—church FL-3
Rock United Presbyterian Church—hist pl MD-2
Rockvale—locale KY-4
Rockvale—locale MT-8
**Rockvale**—pop pl CO-8
**Rockvale**—pop pl TN-4
Rockvale Cem—cemetery MT-8
Rockvale Cem—cemetery TX-5
Rockvale Ch—church TN-4
Rockvale Elementary School TN-4
Rockvale Heights Sch—school IL-6

Rockvale Sch—school (2) CO-8
Rockvale Sch—school MT-8
Rockvale Sch—school TN-4
**Rockvale (Township of)**—pop pl IL-6
**Rock Valley**—pop pl IA-7
**Rock Valley**—pop pl MA-1
**Rock Valley**—pop pl NY-2
Rock Valley—valley NV-8
Rock Valley Cem—cemetery (2) IA-7
Rock Valley Cem—cemetery MI-6
Rock Valley Cem—cemetery WI-6
Rock Valley Ch—church MN-6
Rock Valley Ch—church NY-2
Rock Valley Coll—school IL-6
Rock Valley HS—school IA-7
Rock Valley Sch (abandoned)—school
(2) MO-7
Rock Valley Wash—stream NV-8
Rockview PA-2
Rockview WV-2
Rockview—locale MI-6
Rockview—locale NC-3
**Rockview**—pop pl MO-7
**Rock View**—pop pl WV-2
Rockview Baptist Church TN-4
Rock View Beach MD-2
**Rockview Beach**—pop pl MD-2
Rockview Cem—cemetery MI-6
Rockview Cem—cemetery MO-7
Rockview Ch—church NC-3
Rockview Ch—church TN-4
Rockview Lake—reservoir AL-4
Rockview Lookout Tower—locale MI-6
Rockview Penitentiary PA-2
Rockview Reservoir Dam—dam PA-2
Rockview Rsvr—reservoir PA-2
Rockview Sch—school WI-6
Rockview (State Correctional
Institution)—building PA-2
Rockview State Penitentary PA-2
Rock Village MA-1
Rockville NC-3
Rockville ND-7
Rockville PA-2
Rockville—locale AL-4
Rockville—locale GA-3
Rockville—locale IA-7
Rockville—locale OH-6
Rockville—locale OR-9
Rockville—locale (2) PA-2
Rockville—locale WV-2
**Rockville**—pop pl CA-9
**Rockville**—pop pl CT-1
**Rockville**—pop pl IN-6
**Rockville**—pop pl ME-1
**Rockville**—pop pl MD-2
**Rockville**—pop pl MA-1
**Rockville**—pop pl MN-6
**Rockville**—pop pl MO-7
**Rockville**—pop pl NE-7
**Rockville**—pop pl (2) NY-2
**Rockville**—pop pl OH-6
**Rockville**—pop pl (10) PA-2
**Rockville**—pop pl (2) RI-1
**Rockville**—pop pl SC-3
**Rockville**—pop pl TN-4
**Rockville**—pop pl UT-8
**Rockville**—pop pl VT-1
**Rockville**—pop pl (2) VA-3
**Rockville**—pop pl WV-2
**Rockville**—pop pl (2) WI-6
Rockville Acad (historical)—school AL-4
Rockville Baptist Church AL-4
Rockville Bench—bench UT-8
Rockville Bridge—bridge PA-2
Rockville Bridge—hist pl PA-2
Rockville Butte UT-8
Rockville Cem—cemetery (2) KS-7
Rockville Cem—cemetery MO-7
Rockville Cem—cemetery NY-2
Rockville Cem—cemetery OR-9
Rockville Cem—cemetery UT-8
**Rockville Centre**—pop pl NY-2
Rockville Ch—church AL-4
Rockville Ch—church SC-3
Rockville Country Club—other NY-2
Rockville Elem Sch—school IN-6
Rockville Estates—uninc pl MD-2
Rockville Gap—gap PA-2
Rockville Hist Dist—hist pl CT-1
Rockville Hist Dist—hist pl SC-3
Rockville (historical)—locale KS-7
**Rockville (historical)**—pop pl (2) OR-9
Rockville HS—school CT-1
Rockville Junior-Senior HS—school IN-6
Rockville Lake—lake MN-6
Rockville Lake—lake NY-2
**Rockville Lake**—pop pl NY-2
Rockville Lookout Tower—locale GA-3
Rockville RR Station—hist pl MD-2
Rockville Sch—school KS-7
Rockville Sch—school OH-6
Rockville Sch—school OR-9
Rockville Sch—school SC-3
Rockville Sch—school VA-3
Rockville Sch (abandoned)—school PA-2
Rockville Square—locale PA-2
Rockville Township—civ div NE-7
**Rockville Township**—pop pl KS-7
**Rockville Township**—pop pl MO-7
**Rockville (Township of)**—pop pl IL-6
**Rockville (Township of)**—pop pl MN-6
Rockville Trail—trail PA-2
Rockville Training Center—school IN-6
Rock Wall—cliff AK-9
Rock Wall—cliff MT-8
Rockwall—cliff OR-9
Rock Wall—locale NM-5
**Rockwall**—pop pl TX-5
Rock Wall, The—ridge NM-5
Rockwall Branch—stream GA-3
Rockwall Branch—stream NC-3
Rockwall Cem—cemetery TX-5
Rockwall Ch—church TX-5
Rock Wall Corral—locale HI-9
**Rockwall (County)**—pop pl TX-5
Rockwall Creek TX-5
Rockwall Creek—stream NV-8
Rockwall Creek—stream TX-5
Rock Wall Draw—valley CO-8

Rockwall-Forney Reservoir TX-5
Rockwall Gap—gap GA-3
Rockwall Gulch—valley AZ-5
Rockwall Hollow—valley KY-4
Rockwall Lake—reservoir TX-5
Rockwall Post Office (historical)—building MS-4
Rockwall Sch (abandoned)—school PA-2
Rockwall Spring—spring AZ-5
Rockwall Spring—spring OR-9
Rockwall Windmill—locale TX-5
Rock Wash CA-9
Rock Wash—stream NM-5
Rock Waterfall Cave—cave AL-4
Rock Water Hole—bay TX-5
Rockwater Hole—lake TX-5
Rock Waterhole—lake TX-5
Rock Waterhole—spring CO-8
Rock Waterhole Canyon—valley (3) NM-5
Rock Waterhole Creek—stream WY-8
Rock Water Spring—spring AZ-5
Rockwater Spring—spring UT-8
Rock Water Spring Branch—stream SC-3
**Rock Way**—pop pl OH-6
Rockway Elem Sch—school FL-3
Rockway JHS—school FL-3
Rockway Point—cape NY-2
Rockwell IL-6
Rockwell—CDP AR-4
Rockwell—locale KS-7
Rockwell—locale WA-9
**Rockwell**—pop pl CA-9
**Rockwell**—pop pl FL-3
**Rockwell**—pop pl IA-7
**Rockwell**—pop pl KY-4
**Rockwell**—pop pl MD-2
**Rockwell**—pop pl NC-3
**Rockwell**—pop pl TX-5
Rock Well—well AZ-5
Rock Well—well NM-5
Rockwell, Bertrand, House—hist pl MO-7
Rockwell, Lake—reservoir OH-6
Rockwell, Mount—summit MT-8
Rockwell, Samuel, House—hist pl GA-3
Rockwell, Solomon, House—hist pl CT-1
Rockwell, Stoddard, House—hist pl GA-3
Rockwell Bay—bay VT-1
Rockwell Cave—cave TN-4
Rockwell Cem—cemetery FL-3
Rockwell Cem—cemetery IL-6
Rockwell Cem—cemetery (2) MO-7
Rockwell Cem—cemetery NC-3
Rockwell Cem—cemetery (2) OH-6
Rockwell Cem—cemetery TN-4
Rockwell Ch—church AL-4
Rockwell Ch—church (3) GA-3
Rockwell Ch—church (2) NC-3
Rockwell City KS-7
**Rockwell City**—pop pl IA-7
Rockwell City Park—park IA-7
Rockwell Corners—locale NY-2
Rockwell Creek—stream CO-8
Rockwell Creek—stream NY-2
Rockwell Creek—stream PA-2
Rockwell Dam—dam MA-1
Rockwell Ditch IN-6
Rockwell Ditch—canal CO-8
Rockwell Ditch—canal IN-6
Rockwell Drain—canal MI-6
Rockwell Elem Sch—school NC-3
Rockwell Falls—falls MT-8
Rockwell Flat—flat (2) UT-8
Rockwell-Forney Dam—dam TX-5
Rockwell Gap—gap CA-9
Rockwell Hill—summit CT-1
Rockwell Hill—summit GA-3
Rockwell Hill—summit NY-2
Rockwell (historical)—locale MS-4
Rockwell Hollow—valley TN-4
Rockwell House—hist pl CT-1
Rockwell House—hist pl NY-2
Rockwell International Airp—airport PA-2
Rockwell International Corporation—facility KY-4
Rockwell International Corporation—facility OH-6
Rockwell Lake—lake MI-6
Rockwell Lake—lake MN-6
Rockwell Lake—lake NM-5
Rockwell Lake—lake TX-5
**Rockwell Mills**—pop pl NY-2
Rockwell Mills Sch—school WI-6
Rockwell Mound—hist pl IL-6
Rockwell Park—hist pl CT-1
Rockwell Park—park CT-1
Rockwell Park—park IL-6
**Rockwell Park (subdivision)**—pop pl NC-3
Rockwell Playground—park MI-6
Rockwell Point—cape AK-9
Rockwell Pond—basin CA-9
Rockwell Pond—lake PA-2
Rockwell Pond—reservoir MA-1
Rockwell Pond Dam—dam MA-1
Rockwell Ranch—locale CO-8
Rockwell Ranch—locale UT-8
Rockwell Ridge—ridge CA-9
Rockwell Rsvr—reservoir UT-8
**Rockwell Run**—pop pl WV-2
Rockwell Run—stream WV-2
Rockwell Sch—school ME-1
Rockwell Sch—school MI-6
Rockwell Sch—school NH-1
Rockwell Sch—school NY-2
Rockwell Sch—school WI-6
Rockwell Sch (historical)—school NC-3
Rockwell School AL-4
**Rockwells Mills**—pop pl NY-2
Rockwell Spring—spring UT-8
Rockwell Springs—reservoir NY-2
Rockwell Standard Plant—facility IN-6
Rockwell Township KS-7
**Rockwell (Township of)**—pop pl MN-6
Rockwell Universalist Church—hist pl GA-3
Rockwell Windmill—locale NM-5
Rock West—island NY-2
Rockwest—locale AL-4
Rockwest Ch AL-4
Rock West Ch—church (3) AL-4
Rock West Creek AL-4
Rockwest Creek—stream AL-4
Rock West Island NY-2
Rock Windmill—locale NM-5
Rock Windmill—locale TX-5
Rock Window—arch AZ-5
Rock Woman Cave—cave TN-4
Rockwood OH-6
Rockwood—hist pl DE-2
Rockwood—locale CA-9
Rockwood—locale CO-8
Rockwood—locale NH-1
Rockwood—locale NJ-2
**Rockwood**—pop pl AL-4
**Rockwood**—pop pl IL-6
**Rockwood**—pop pl KY-4
**Rockwood**—pop pl ME-1
**Rockwood**—pop pl MI-6
**Rockwood**—pop pl NY-2
**Rockwood**—pop pl OH-6
**Rockwood**—pop pl OR-9
**Rockwood**—pop pl (2) PA-2
**Rockwood**—pop pl TN-4
**Rockwood**—pop pl TX-5
**Rockwood**—pop pl WI-6
Rockwood—uninc pl NC-3
Rockwood Acad—school MA-1
**Rockwood Acres (subdivision)**—pop pl NC-3
Rockwood Borough—civil PA-2
Rockwood Brook—stream ME-1
Rockwood Camp—locale PA-2
Rockwood Canal—canal CA-9
Rockwood Canyon—valley CA-9
Rockwood (CCD)—cens area TN-4
Rockwood Cem—cemetery OH-6
Rockwood Ch—church AL-4
Rockwood Ch—church AR-4
Rockwood Ch—church NC-3
Rockwood Chocolate Factory Hist Dist—hist pl NY-2
Rockwood Ch of Christ—church TN-4
Rockwood Community Park—park TN-4
Rockwood Country Club—other MO-7
Rockwood Creek—stream OR-9
Rockwood Division—civil TN-4
Rockwood Dock—locale TN-4
Rockwood Drain—canal CA-9
Rockwood Drain—canal MI-6
Rockwood (Election Precinct)—fmr MCD IL-6
**Rockwood Estates Subdivision**—pop pl UT-8
Rockwood Ferry (historical)—locale TN-4
Rockwood Filtration Plant—building TN-4
Rockwood First Baptist Ch—church TN-4
**Rockwood Gardens (subdivision)**—pop pl UT-8
Rockwood Golf and Country Club—locale TN-4
Rockwood Heading—other CA-9
Rock Wood Hill TN-4
**Rockwood Hill**—pop pl TN-4
Rockwood Hill—summit GA-3
Rockwood Hills TN-4
**Rockwood Hills (subdivision)**—pop pl DE-2
Rockwood HS—school TN-4
Rockwood Island—island IL-6
Rockwood JHS—school TN-4
Rockwood Junction Station—locale PA-2
Rockwood Lake—lake AL-4
Rockwood Lake—lake NY-2
Rockwood Lake—reservoir CT-1
Rockwood Lake Brook—stream CT-1
Rockwood Landing (historical)—locale TN-4
Rockwood Lateral B—canal CA-9
Rockwood Lateral Four—canal CA-9
Rockwood Lateral Seven—canal CA-9
Rockwood Mine (underground)—mine TN-4
Rockwood Municipal Airp—airport TN-4
Rockwood Municipal Park TN-4
Rockwood Park—park DE-2
Rockwood Park—park TX-5
Rockwood Peak UT-8
Rockwood Point—cape MO-7
Rockwood Point Rec Area—park MO-7
Rockwood Pond—lake NH-1
Rockwood Post Office—building TN-4
Rockwood Ranger Station—locale UT-8
Rockwood Rsvr—reservoir PA-2
Rockwood Sch—school AL-4
Rockwood Sch—school CA-9
Rockwood Sch—school OK-5
Rockwood Sch—school TN-4
Rockwood Spring—spring AL-4
**Rockwood Spur**—pop pl MT-8
Rockwoods Range—park MO-7
Rockwoods Reservation—area MO-7
Rockwood State Wildlife Mngmt Areas—park MN-6
**Rockwood Station**—pop pl PA-2
Rockwood Strip T1R1—unorg ME-1
Rockwood Strip T2R1—unorg ME-1
**Rockwood (subdivision)**—pop pl NC-3
Rockwood Town Hall—building SD-7
**Rockwood (Township of)**—pop pl (2) MN-6
Rockwood United Methodist Ch—church TN-4
**Rockwood Woods (subdivision)**—pop pl DE-2
**Rock Works**—pop pl PA-2
Rocky NC-3
Rocky TN-4
Rocky—locale CO-8
**Rocky**—pop pl (2) AR-4
**Rocky**—pop pl OK-5
**Rocky Acres**—pop pl MD-2
Rocky Acres Bible Camp—locale GA-3
Rocky Arbor State Park—park WI-6
Rock Yard Creek—gut FL-3
Rocky Arroyo—stream (4) NM-5
Rocky Arroyo—valley AZ-5
Rocky Arroyo—valley NM-5
Rocky Arroyo Cem—cemetery NM-5
Rocky Arroyo Sch—school NM-5
Rock-Yatesville (CCD), The—cens area GA-3
Rocky Bald—summit (2) NC-3
Rocky Bald Branch—stream NC-3
Rocky Bald Mtn—summit SC-3
Rocky Bald Ridge—ridge NC-3
Rocky Bar—bar (2) ID-8
Rocky Bar—cliff TN-4
**Rocky Bar**—pop pl ID-8
**Rocky Bar**—pop pl VA-3
Rocky Bar Campground—locale CA-9
Rocky Bar Creek—stream OR-9
Rocky Bar Guard Station—locale ID-8
Rocky Bar Gulch—valley OR-9
Rockybar Hollow—valley VA-3
Rocky Basin—basin CA-9
Rocky Basin—basin (2) NV-8
Rocky Basin—basin OR-9
Rocky Basin—basin UT-8
Rocky Basin—lake CO-8
Rocky Basin Creek—stream (2) CA-9
Rocky Basin Lakes—lake CA-9
Rocky Basin Ridge—ridge CA-9
Rocky Basin Tank Number One—reservoir AZ-5
Rocky Basin Tank Number Two—reservoir AZ-5
Rocky Bay—bay (5) AK-9
Rocky Bay—bay FL-3
Rocky Bay—bay MN-6
Rocky Bay—bay (2) WA-9
Rocky Bayou LA-4
Rocky Bayou—bay FL-3
Rocky Bayou—stream (2) AR-4
Rocky Bayou—stream (2) LA-4
Rocky Bayou—stream MS-4
Rocky Bayou State Park—park FL-3
Rocky Bayou State Park Aquatic Preserve—park FL-3
Rocky Beach RI-1
Rocky Beach—beach CT-1
Rocky Bedground—summit OR-9
Rocky Bench Spring—spring ID-8
Rocky Bend Campground—park OR-9
Rocky Bluff—cliff FL-3
Rocky Bluff—summit NV-8
Rocky Bluff Branch—stream MS-4
Rocky Bluff Campground—locale ID-8
Rocky Bluff Ch (historical)—church MS-4
Rocky Bluff Creek—stream TX-5
Rocky Bluff Crossroads—locale SC-3
Rocky Bluff Recreation Site—locale NC-3
Rocky Bluff Swamp—stream SC-3
Rocky Bog—lake ME-1
**Rocky Bottom**—pop pl SC-3
Rocky Bottom, The—basin MT-8
Rocky Bottom Branch—stream GA-3
Rocky Bottom Ch—church GA-3
Rockybottom Creek—stream AK-9
Rocky Bottom Creek—stream MS-4
Rocky Bottom Creek—stream SC-3
Rocky Bottom Lake—lake CA-9
Rocky Bottom Rsvr—reservoir OR-9
Rocky Bottom Tank—reservoir AZ-5
Rockybound Pond—lake NH-1
**Rocky Boy**—pop pl MT-8
Rocky Boy Gravel—cemetery MT-8
Rocky Boy Mine—mine MT-8
Rocky Boy Peak—summit AZ-5
**Rocky Boy's Ind Res**—pop pl MT-8
Rocky Boys Ind Res—reserve MT-8
Rocky Branch AL-4
Rocky Branch GA-3
Rocky Branch TX-5
Rocky Branch—locale TX-5
**Rocky Branch**—pop pl AL-4
**Rockybranch**—pop pl KY-4
**Rocky Branch**—pop pl LA-4
**Rocky Branch**—pop pl MS-4
**Rocky Branch**—pop pl TN-4
Rocky Branch—stream (50) AL-4
Rocky Branch—stream (17) AR-4
Rocky Branch—stream (3) FL-3
Rocky Branch—stream (20) GA-3
Rocky Branch—stream (13) IL-6
Rocky Branch—stream IN-6
Rocky Branch—stream (2) IA-7
Rocky Branch—stream KS-7
Rocky Branch—stream (26) KY-4
Rocky Branch—stream (5) LA-4
Rocky Branch—stream MD-2
Rocky Branch—stream (7) MS-4
Rocky Branch—stream (14) MO-7
Rocky Branch—stream NH-1
Rocky Branch—stream (2) NY-2
Rocky Branch—stream (28) NC-3
Rocky Branch—stream (2) OH-6
Rocky Branch—stream (3) OK-5
Rocky Branch—stream (15) SC-3
Rocky Branch—stream (37) TN-4
Rocky Branch—stream (25) TX-5
Rocky Branch—stream (33) VA-3
Rocky Branch—stream (8) WV-2
Rocky Branch—stream WI-6
Rocky Branch—valley KY-4
Rocky Branch Baptist Ch—church MS-4
Rocky Branch Cem—cemetery GA-3
Rocky Branch Cem—cemetery MO-7
Rocky Branch Cem—cemetery WV-2
Rocky Branch Cemeteries—cemetery MS-4
Rocky Branch Ch—church (2) AL-4
Rocky Branch Ch—church (4) GA-3
Rocky Branch Ch—church KY-4
Rocky Branch Ch—church (2) MS-4
Rocky Branch Ch—church NC-3
Rocky Branch Ch—church SC-3
Rocky Branch Ch—church TN-4
Rocky Branch Ch—church TX-5
Rocky Branch Ch—church (3) VA-3
Rocky Branch Ch—church WV-2
Rocky Branch Coulee—valley WA-9
Rocky Branch Hollow—valley (2) AL-4
Rocky Branch Hollow—valley IL-6
Rocky Branch Mine (underground)—mine TN-4
Rocky Branch Post Office (historical)—building TN-4
Rocky Branch Public Use Area—park AL-4
Rocky Branch Public Use Area—park AR-4
Rocky Branch Ridge—ridge NH-1
Rocky Branch Ridge—ridge NC-3
Rocky Branch Sch—hist pl AR-4
Rocky Branch Sch—school AL-4
Rocky Branch Sch—school (2) IL-6
Rocky Branch Sch—school (2) KY-4
Rocky Branch Sch—school TN-4
Rocky Branch Sch—school WI-6
Rocky Branch Sch (abandoned)—school MO-7
Rocky Branch Sch (historical)—school MS-4
Rocky Branch Trail—trail NH-1
Rocky Bridge Sch—school MO-7
Rocky Brook ME-1
Rocky Brook MA-1
Rocky Brook VT-1
**Rocky Brook**—pop pl RI-1
Rocky Brook—stream AL-4
Rocky Brook—stream CO-8
Rocky Brook—stream CT-1
Rocky Brook—stream (15) ME-1
Rocky Brook—stream (3) MA-1
Rocky Brook—stream (3) NH-1
Rocky Brook—stream NJ-2
Rocky Brook—stream (2) NY-2
Rocky Brook—stream WA-9
Rocky Brook Mountains—summit ME-1
**Rocky Brook Park**—pop pl MD-2
Rocky Brook Rsvr—reservoir RI-1
**Rocky Brook (subdivision)**—pop pl AL-4
**Rocky Brook (subdivision)**—pop pl NC-3
Rocky Brook Swamp—swamp ME-1
Rocky Brook Village RI-1
Rocky Butte WY-8
**Rocky Butte**—pop pl WA-9
Rocky Butte—summit CA-9
Rocky Butte—summit ID-8
Rocky Butte—summit (5) MT-8
Rocky Butte—summit ND-7
Rocky Butte—summit (5) OR-9
Rocky Butte—summit SD-7
Rocky Butte—summit WA-9
Rocky Butte—summit (3) WY-8
Rocky Butte Gulch—valley WY-8
Rocky Butte Lookout—locale CA-9
Rocky Buttes—summit CA-9
Rocky Buttes—summit MT-8
Rocky Butte Spring—spring OR-9
Rocky Buttes Sch—school CO-8
Rocky Butte Waterhole—lake OR-9
Rocky Butte Way Trail—trail OR-9
Rocky Cabin Spring—spring CA-9
Rocky Camp—locale CA-9
Rocky Campground—locale CA-9
Rocky Canal—canal LA-4
Rocky Canyon CA-9
Rocky Canyon ID-8
Rocky Canyon UT-8
Rocky Canyon—valley AZ-5
Rocky Canyon—valley (3) CA-9
Rocky Canyon—valley CO-8
Rocky Canyon—valley (14) ID-8
Rocky Canyon—valley (3) MT-8
Rocky Canyon—valley (11) NV-8
Rocky Canyon—valley NM-5
Rocky Canyon—valley (2) OR-9
Rocky Canyon—valley (9) UT-8
Rocky Canyon—valley WY-8
Rocky Canyon Campgroud—locale NM-5
Rocky Canyon Creek—stream MT-8
Rocky Canyon Creek—stream OK-5
Rocky Canyon Creek—stream OR-9
Rocky Canyon Spring—spring CA-9
Rocky Canyon Spring—spring NV-8
Rocky Canyon Spring—spring UT-8
Rocky Canyon Trail (Pack)—trail NM-5
Rocky Carry Park—park WI-6
Rocky Carry Rapids—rapids WI-6
Rocky Cave—cave AL-4
Rocky Cedar Creek—stream TX-5
Rocky Cem—cemetery AR-4
Rocky Cem—cemetery FL-3
Rocky Ch—church AR-4
Rocky Ch—church TX-5
Rocky Channel—channel (3) FL-3
Rocky Chapel—church NC-3
Rocky Chapel—church (2) TX-5
Rocky Cliff—cliff TN-4
Rocky Cliff Canyon—valley NM-5
Rocky Clifty Creek—stream KY-4
**Rocky Comfort**—pop pl MO-7
Rocky Comfort Ch—church AR-4
Rocky Comfort Creek—stream FL-3
Rocky Comfort Creek—stream GA-3
Rocky Comfort Flat—flat ID-8
Rocky Community Ch—church TX-5
**Rocky Corners**—pop pl WI-6
Rocky Corner Trail—trail PA-2
Rocky Coulee MT-8
Rocky Coulee—valley (4) MT-8
Rocky Coulee—valley (2) WA-9
Rocky Coulee Wasteway—canal WA-9
Rocky Cove—bay (3) AK-9
Rocky Cove—bay FL-3
Rocky Cove—bay GA-3
Rocky Cove—bay ME-1
Rocky Cove—valley (5) NC-3
Rocky Cove Branch—stream NC-3
Rocky Cove Knob—summit NC-3
Rocky Creek AL-4
Rocky Creek AZ-5
Rocky Creek FL-3
Rocky Creek GA-3
Rocky Creek ID-8
Rocky Creek MO-7
Rocky Creek MT-8
Rocky Creek NC-3
Rocky Creek OK-5
Rocky Creek SC-3
Rocky Creek TN-4
Rocky Creek TX-5
Rocky Creek UT-8
Rocky Creek—gut (2) FL-3
Rocky Creek—locale TX-5
**Rocky Creek**—pop pl FL-3
**Rocky Creek**—pop pl GA-3
Rocky Creek—stream (8) AL-4
Rocky Creek—stream (4) AK-9
Rocky Creek—stream AZ-5
Rocky Creek—stream (5) AR-4
Rocky Creek—stream (9) CA-9
Rocky Creek—stream (16) FL-3
Rocky Creek—stream (28) GA-3
Rocky Creek—stream (2) ID-8
Rocky Creek—stream (2) KY-4
Rocky Creek—stream (5) LA-4
Rocky Creek—stream MI-6
Rocky Creek—stream (11) MS-4
Rocky Creek—stream (2) MO-7
Rocky Creek—stream (3) MT-8
Rocky Creek—stream (12) NC-3
Rocky Creek—stream (3) OK-5
Rocky Creek—stream (5) OR-9
Rocky Creek—stream (15) SC-3
Rocky Creek—stream (4) TN-4
Rocky Creek—stream (76) TX-5
Rocky Creek—stream UT-8
Rocky Creek—stream (6) VA-3
Rocky Creek—stream (8) WA-9
Rocky Creek—stream WI-6
Rocky Creek—stream WY-8
Rocky Creek Bay—bay FL-3
Rocky Creek Camp—locale CA-9
Rocky Creek Cave—cave AL-4
Rocky Creek Cem—cemetery (2) MS-4
Rocky Creek Ch—church (2) AL-4
Rocky Creek Ch—church (10) GA-3
Rocky Creek Ch—church (2) MS-4
Rocky Creek Ch—church (2) NC-3
Rocky Creek Ch—church (5) SC-3
Rocky Creek Ch—church TX-5
Rocky Creek Farms—locale AL-4
Rocky Creek High School MS-4
Rocky Creek Mine—mine WA-9
Rocky Creek Mtn—summit AR-4
Rocky Creek Number Six Mine (underground)—mine TN-4
Rocky Creek Park—park TX-5
Rocky Creek Ranch—locale TX-5
Rocky Creek Sch—school AL-4
Rocky Creek Sch—school GA-3
Rocky Creek Sch—school MS-4
Rocky Creek Sch (historical)—school MS-4
Rocky Creek State For—forest MO-7
Rocky Creek State Park—park OR-9
**Rocky Creek Subdivision**—pop pl TN-4
Rocky Creek Swamp—swamp FL-3
Rocky Creek Wayside OR-9
Rocky Crest HS—school TX-5
Rocky Crest Sch—school TX-5
**Rocky Cross**—pop pl NC-3
Rocky Cross Ch—church NC-3
Rocky Crossing—locale AR-4
Rocky Crossing—locale MT-8
Rocky Crossing—locale (2) WY-8
Rocky Crossing Rsvr—reservoir MT-8
Rocky Cypress Creek—stream AR-4
**Rocky Dale**—pop pl VT-1
Rockydale Cem—cemetery TN-4
Rocky Dale Ch TN-4
Rockydale Ch—church TN-4
Rocky Dale Ch—church WV-2
Rocky Dell—hist pl TX-5
Rocky Dell Hollow—valley AR-4
Rocky Doblin Spring AZ-5
Rocky Draft—valley PA-2
Rocky Draw—valley AZ-5
Rocky Draw—valley CO-8
Rocky Draw—valley ID-8
Rocky Draw—valley KS-7
Rocky Draw—valley MT-8
Rocky Draw—valley (2) NM-5
Rocky Draw—valley (4) WY-8
Rocky Draw Creek—stream WY-8
Rocky Draw Rsvr—reservoir MT-8
Rocky Draw Rsvr—reservoir WY-8
Rocky Dublin Spring—spring AZ-5
**Rocky Face**—pop pl GA-3
Rocky Face—summit GA-3
Rocky Face—summit KY-4
Rocky Face—summit (5) NC-3
Rocky Face Branch—stream (2) NC-3
Rocky Face Cem—cemetery GA-3
Rockyface Ch—church NC-3
Rocky Face Knob—summit NC-3
Rockyface Lead—ridge GA-3
Rocky Face Mine—mine NC-3
Rocky Face Mtn GA-3
Rocky Face Mtn KY-4
Rocky Face Mtn—summit GA-3
Rocky Face Mtn—summit NC-3
Rockyface Mtn—summit (3) NC-3
Rocky Face Mtn—summit NC-3
Rocky Face Mtn—summit TN-4
Rocky Face Ridge—ridge NC-3
Rocky Face Trail—trail PA-2
Rocky Falls—falls MS-4
Rocky Falls—falls MO-7
Rocky Falls—falls NY-2
Rocky Falls Picnic Area—locale MO-7
Rocky Fence Ridge—ridge NC-3
Rocky Flat WA-9
Rocky Flat—flat AZ-5
Rocky Flat—flat (3) OR-9
Rocky Flat—flat WA-9
Rocky Flats—flat CO-8
Rocky Flats A.e.c. Plant CO-8
Rocky Flats Branch—stream TN-4
Rocky Flats Plant CO-8
Rocky Flat Spring—spring OR-9
Rocky Flats Trail—trail TN-4
Rocky Flat Tank—reservoir CA-9
Rocky Ford ND-7
Rocky Ford TN-4
Rocky Ford—crossing WY-8
Rocky Ford—locale (3) AL-4
Rocky Ford—locale AR-4
Rocky Ford—locale CO-8
Rocky Ford—locale IL-6
Rocky Ford—locale KS-7
Rocky Ford—locale MO-7
Rocky Ford—locale OK-5
Rocky Ford—locale (2) OR-9
Rockyford—locale SD-7
Rocky Ford—locale SD-7
Rocky Ford—locale TN-4
Rocky Ford—locale (2) VA-3
Rocky Ford—locale WV-2
Rocky Ford—locale WY-8
**Rocky Ford**—pop pl CO-8
**Rocky Ford**—pop pl GA-3
**Rocky Ford**—pop pl IN-6
**Rocky Ford**—pop pl KS-7
**Rocky Ford**—pop pl MS-4
**Rocky Ford**—pop pl NC-3
Rocky Ford—stream OH-6
Rocky Ford Branch—stream (2) AL-4
Rocky Ford Branch—stream (2) GA-3
Rocky Ford Branch—stream MO-7
Rocky Ford Branch—stream (2) NC-3
Rocky Ford Branch—stream SC-3
Rocky Ford Branch—stream VA-3
Rocky Ford Bridge—bridge GA-3
Rocky Ford Bridge—bridge WA-9
Rocky Ford Bridge—other IL-6
Rocky Ford Campground—park OR-9
Rocky Ford Canal—canal CO-8
Rocky Ford Canal—canal UT-8
Rocky Ford Canyon—valley CA-9
Rocky Ford (CCD)—cens area GA-3
Rocky Ford Cem—cemetery FL-3
Rocky Ford Cem—cemetery GA-3
Rocky Ford Cem—cemetery KS-7
Rockyford Cem—cemetery TX-5
Rocky Ford Ch—church KY-4
Rocky Ford Ch—church NC-3
Rockyford Ch—church OK-5
Rockyford Ch—church SD-7
Rocky Ford Ch—church (2) TX-5
Rocky Ford Ch—church VA-3
Rocky Ford Creek OH-6
Rocky Ford Creek—stream (2) AL-4
Rocky Ford Creek—stream MO-7
Rocky Ford Creek—stream NC-3
Rocky Ford Creek—stream (2) SC-3
Rocky Ford Creek—stream (2) TN-4
Rocky Ford Creek—stream TX-5
Rocky Ford Creek—stream UT-8
Rocky Ford Creek—stream VA-3
Rocky Ford Creek—stream WA-9
Rocky Ford Creek—stream (2) WY-8
Rocky Ford Dam—dam (2) UT-8
Rockyford Ditch—canal CA-9
Rocky Ford Ditch—canal CO-8
Rocky Ford Diversion Dam—dam CO-8
Rocky Ford Draw—valley CO-8
Rocky Ford Highline Canal—canal CO-8
Rocky Ford (historical)—locale (2) MS-4
Rocky Ford Hollow—valley UT-8
Rocky Ford Irrigation Company Canal UT-8
Rocky Ford Lakes—reservoir IL-6
Rocky Ford Lateral—canal CO-8
Rocky Ford Lateral—canal WA-9
Rocky Ford Mill (historical)—locale MS-4
Rocky Ford Mine—mine AZ-5
Rocky Ford Ranch—locale TX-5
Rockyford Reservoir UT-8
Rocky Ford Rsvr—reservoir (4) UT-8
Rocky Ford Sch—school KY-4
Rocky Ford Sch—school NC-3
Rockyford Sch—school OK-5
Rocky Ford Sch—school OK-5
Rocky Ford Sch—school TX-5
Rocky Ford Sch (historical)—school AL-4
Rocky Ford Sch (historical)—school MS-4
Rocky Ford Swamp—stream SC-3
**Rocky Ford Township**—pop pl SD-7
Rocky Ford Trail—trail UT-8
**Rocky Forest**—pop pl PA-2
Rocky Forest Creek—stream PA-2
Rocky Forge—locale MD-2
Rocky Fork CO-8
Rocky Fork MO-7
Rocky Fork OH-6
Rocky Fork—locale SC-3
**Rocky Fork**—pop pl OH-6
**Rocky Fork**—pop pl (2) TN-4
**Rocky Fork**—pop pl WV-2
Rocky Fork—stream AR-4
Rocky Fork—stream (2) IL-6
Rocky Fork—stream IN-6
Rocky Fork—stream (4) KY-4
Rocky Fork—stream (2) MO-7
Rocky Fork—stream (2) NC-3
Rocky Fork—stream (15) OH-6
Rocky Fork—stream PA-2
Rocky Fork—stream SC-3
Rocky Fork—stream TN-4
Rocky Fork—stream (2) VA-3
Rocky Fork—stream WA-9
Rocky Fork—stream (7) WV-2
Rocky Fork Branch—stream TN-4
Rocky Fork Campground—locale CO-8
Rocky Fork Cem—cemetery WV-2
Rocky Fork Ch—church IL-6
Rocky Fork Ch—church NC-3
Rocky Fork Ch—church OH-6
Rocky Fork Ch—church SC-3
Rocky Fork Ch—church TN-4
Rocky Fork Ch—church WV-2
Rocky Fork Covered Bridge—bridge IN-6
Rocky Fork Creek OH-6
Rockyfork Creek TN-4
Rocky Fork Creek WA-9
Rocky Fork Creek—stream CO-8
Rocky Fork Creek—stream IN-6
Rocky Fork Creek—stream MO-7
Rocky Fork Creek—stream NC-3
Rocky Fork Creek—stream TN-4
**Rocky Fork Lake**—pop pl IN-6
Rocky Fork Lake—reservoir IN-6
Rocky Fork Lake—reservoir OH-6
Rocky Fork Lake Dam—dam IN-6
Rocky Fork Park Group—hist pl OH-6
Rocky Fork Park Site—hist pl OH-6
Rocky Fork Ridge—ridge NC-3
Rocky Fork Sch—school VA-3
Rocky Fork Sch (historical)—school TN-4
Rocky Fork State Park—park OH-6
Rocky Fork Township—civil MO-7
Rocky Fountain Run—stream MD-2
Rocky Four Corners OR-9
Rocky Gap—gap AL-4
Rocky Gap—gap (2) GA-3
Rocky Gap—gap KY-4
Rocky Gap—gap MD-2
Rocky Gap—gap MT-8
Rocky Gap—gap SC-3
Rocky Gap—gap (2) TN-4
Rocky Gap—gap (2) VA-3
Rocky Gap—gap WV-2
Rocky Gap—gap (3) WY-8
**Rocky Gap**—pop pl VA-3
Rocky Gap Creek MT-8
Rocky Gap Creek—stream MT-8
Rocky Gap (Magisterial District)—fmr MCD VA-3
Rocky Gap Park—park MI-6
Rocky Gap Run—stream MD-2
Rocky Gap Run—stream PA-2
Rocky Gap School TN-4
Rocky Gap Spring—spring NV-8
Rocky Glade Ch—church TN-4
**Rocky Glen**—pop pl CT-1
**Rocky Glen**—pop pl PA-2
Rocky Glen—valley CA-9
Rocky Glen Cem—cemetery PA-2

Rocky Run—*stream* (15) ... VA-3
Rocky Run—*stream* (2) ... WA-9
Rocky Run—*stream* (9) ... WV-2
Rocky Run—*stream* (13) ... WI-6
*Rocky Run Brook* ... MA-1
Rocky Run Cem—*cemetery* ... WI-6
Rocky Run Ch—*church* ... NC-3
Rocky Run Ch—*church* (2) ... VA-3
*Rocky Run Creek* ... WI-6
Rocky Run Creek—*stream* ... ID-8
Rocky Run Creek—*stream* ... NC-3
Rocky Run Creek—*stream* ... VA-3
Rocky Run Flowage—*channel* ... WI-6
Rocky Run Guard Station—*locale* ... WA-9
Rocky Run Point—*summit* ... ID-8
Rocky Run Sch—*school* ... NC-3
Rocky Run Sch—*school* ... WI-6
Rocky Run Springs—*spring* ... WI-6
**Rocky Run (Township of)**—*pop pl* ... IL-6
Rocky Run Trail—*trail* ... PA-2
Rocky Saddle—*gap* ... WA-9
Rocky Sch—*school* ... TX-5
Rocky Sch (historical)—*school* ... TN-4
Rocky Sea Pass—*gap* ... UT-8
Rocky Shoal Creek—*stream* ... WV-2
Rocky Shoals Creek—*stream* ... GA-3
Rocky Siding—*locale* ... NC-3
Rocky Sink Ch—*church* ... FL-3
Rockys Lakes—*lake* ... AK-9
Rocky Slough—*gut* ... TX-5
Rocky Slough—*stream* ... NV-8
Rocky Slough—*stream* ... WA-9
Rockys Park—*park* ... SD-7
Rockys Plaza—*locale* ... MA-1
*Rocky Spring* ... WA-9
Rocky Spring—*locale* ... PA-2
Rocky Spring—*locale* ... TN-4
Rocky Spring—*spring* (2) ... AZ-5
Rocky Spring—*spring* ... GA-3
Rocky Spring—*spring* ... OR-9
Rocky Spring—*spring* (2) ... PA-2
Rocky Spring—*spring* ... TN-4
Rocky Spring—*spring* ... UT-8
Rocky Spring—*spring* ... VA-3
Rocky Spring Branch—*stream* (2) ... NC-3
Rocky Spring Branch—*stream* ... PA-2
Rocky Spring Branch—*stream* ... TN-4
Rocky Spring Camp—*locale* ... PA-2
Rocky Spring Cem—*cemetery* ... KY-4
Rocky Spring Cem—*cemetery* ... OH-6
Rocky Spring Cem—*cemetery* ... PA-2
Rocky Spring Cem—*cemetery* ... TN-4
Rocky Spring Ch—*church* (3) ... MS-4
Rocky Spring Ch—*church* ... SC-3
Rocky Spring Ch—*church* ... VA-3
Rocky Spring Ch (historical)—*church* ... MS-4
*Rocky Spring Coulee* ... MT-8
*Rocky Spring Creek* ... MS-4
*Rocky Spring Creek* ... SC-3
Rocky Spring Dam—*dam* ... PA-2
Rocky Spring Golf Club—*other* ... NJ-2
Rocky Spring Lake—*reservoir* ... PA-2
Rocky Spring Mine—*mine* ... AZ-5
*Rocky Spring Park* ... PA-2
*Rocky Springs* ... TN-4
Rocky Springs—*locale* ... AL-4
Rocky Springs—*locale* ... MS-4
Rocky Springs—*locale* ... TN-4
**Rocky Springs**—*pop pl* ... MD-2
**Rocky Springs**—*pop pl* ... NC-3
Rocky Springs—*spring* ... WY-8
Rocky Springs Acad (historical)—*school* ... MS-4
*Rocky Springs Baptist Ch* ... TN-4
Rocky Springs Baptist Ch—*church* ... TN-4
*Rocky Springs Canyon* ... UT-8
*Rocky Springs Cem* ... TN-4
Rocky Springs Cem—*cemetery* ... AR-4
Rocky Springs Cem—*cemetery* ... MD-2
Rocky Springs Cem—*cemetery* (2) ... MS-4
Rocky Springs Cem—*cemetery* ... PA-2
Rocky Springs Cem—*cemetery* (2) ... TN-4
Rocky Springs Cem—*cemetery* ... TX-5
Rocky Springs Ch—*church* ... FL-3
Rocky Springs Ch—*church* ... GA-3
Rocky Springs Ch—*church* ... LA-4
Rocky Springs Ch—*church* (2) ... MS-4
Rocky Springs Ch—*church* ... PA-2
Rocky Springs Ch—*church* (2) ... SC-3
Rocky Springs Ch—*church* (4) ... TN-4
Rocky Springs Ch—*church* (2) ... TX-5
Rocky Springs Ch (historical)—*church* ... MS-4
Rocky Spring Sch (historical)—*school* ... TN-4
Rocky Springs Coulee—*valley* ... MT-8
Rocky Springs Creek—*stream* ... SC-3
Rocky Springs Hollow—*valley* ... TN-4
Rocky Springs Methodist Ch—*church* ... MS-4
*Rocky Springs Methodist Church* ... TN-4
Rocky Springs Park—*park* ... PA-2
*Rocky Springs Peak* ... UT-8
Rocky Springs Post Office (historical)—*building* ... TN-4
Rocky Springs Sch—*school* ... KY-4
Rocky Springs Sch—*school* ... TN-4
Rocky Springs Sch (historical)—*school* ... MS-4
Rocky Springs Sch (historical)—*school* ... TN-4
Rocky Springs Station—*locale* ... MD-2
Rocky Springs (Township of)—*fmr MCD* ... NC-3
Rocky Spring Top—*summit* ... NC-3
Rocky Sprur Hollow—*valley* ... VA-3
Rocky Spur—*ridge* ... SC-3
Rocky Spur—*ridge* ... TN-4
Rocky Spur Branch—*stream* ... TN-4
Rocky Station (Magisterial District)—*fmr MCD* ... VA-3
Rocky Store Sch—*school* ... NY-2
Rocky Stream—*stream* ... MT-8
*Rocky Summit Baptist Church* ... TN-4
Rocky Summit Cem—*cemetery* ... TN-4
Rocky Summit Ch—*church* ... TN-4
**Rocky Summit (historical)**—*pop pl* ... TN-4
Rocky Swamp—*stream* ... NC-3
Rocky Swamp Ch—*church* ... NC-3
Rocky Swamp Ch—*church* ... SC-3
Rocky Swamp Creek—*stream* ... SC-3
Rocky Tank—*reservoir* (7) ... AZ-5
Rocky Tank—*reservoir* (3) ... NM-5
Rocky Tank—*reservoir* ... TX-5
*Rocky Top* ... VA-3
Rocky Top—*summit* (2) ... AZ-5
Rocky Top—*summit* ... GA-3
Rocky Top—*summit* (3) ... NC-3
Rocky Top—*summit* (4) ... OR-9
Rocky Top—*summit* (3) ... TN-4
Rocky Top—*summit* ... UT-8
Rockytop—*summit* ... VA-3
Rocky Top—*summit* ... WY-8
Rocky Top Ch—*church* ... AL-4
**Rocky Top Estates (subdivision)**—*pop pl* ... AL-4
Rocky Top Gap—*gap* ... TN-4
Rockytop Overlook—*locale* ... VA-3
Rocky Top Shelter—*locale* ... OR-9
Rocky Top Trail—*trail* ... OR-9
Rockytop Trail—*trail* ... VA-3
Rocky Trail—*trail* ... UT-8
Rocky Twins—*summit* ... OK-5
**Rocky Valley**—*pop pl* ... PA-2
**Rocky Valley**—*pop pl* ... TN-4
Rocky Valley—*valley* ... PA-2
Rocky Valley—*valley* ... TN-4
*Rocky Valley Baptist Church* ... TN-4
Rocky Valley Cem—*cemetery* ... AR-4
Rocky Valley Cem—*cemetery* ... TN-4
Rocky Valley Ch—*church* ... MS-4
Rocky Valley Ch—*church* (2) ... TN-4
Rocky Valley Sch (historical)—*school* (2) ... MS-4
Rocky Valley Sch (historical)—*school* ... TN-4
Rockyview Lake—*reservoir* ... AL-4
*Rocky Wash* ... UT-8
Rocky Wash—*stream* ... CA-9
Rocky Wash Rsvr—*reservoir* ... CO-8
Rocky Waterhole—*lake* ... OR-9
Rocky Waterhole—*reservoir* ... OR-9
**Rocky Waters**—*pop pl* ... TN-4
Rocky Well—*locale* ... NM-5
Rocky Well—*well* ... TX-5
Rocky Windmill—*locale* ... MT-8
Rocky Windmill—*locale* ... NM-5
Rocky Windmill—*locale* ... TX-5
**Rockywold**—*pop pl* ... NH-1
Rocky Woods—*woods* ... MA-1
*Rocky Woods Hills* ... MA-1
Rocky Woods Range—*summit* ... MA-1
Rocky Zion Ch—*church* ... AL-4
*Rocky Zion Missionary Baptist Ch* ... AL-4
Rock Zion Ch—*church* ... GA-3
Rock 1 And Rock 2 Township—*fmr MCD* ... IA-7
Roc Mar Ton Lake—*reservoir* ... IN-6
Roc Mar Ton Lake Dam—*dam* ... IN-6
*Rocoon Creek Park Dam* ... PA-2
Roco Roja, Rancho—*locale* ... AZ-5
*Rocquist* ... NC-3
Roc Roe Bayou—*stream* ... AR-4
Roc Roe Cem—*cemetery* ... AR-4
Roc Roe Lake—*lake* ... AR-4
Roc Roe (Township of)—*fmr MCD* (2) ... AR-4
Roda—*locale* ... VA-3
Rodabaugh Run—*stream* ... WV-2
Roda Ditch—*canal* (2) ... IN-6
Rodakowski Ranch—*locale* ... ND-7
Rodamaker Canyon—*valley* ... NM-5
*Rodamer* ... WV-2
Rod and Gun Campground—*park* ... SD-7
Rod and Gun Club—*locale* ... MA-1
Rod and Gun Club Dam—*dam* ... IN-6
Rod and Gun Club Lake—*reservoir* ... IN-6
Rod and Reel Dam—*dam* ... AL-4
Rod And Reel Lake—*reservoir* ... AL-4
**Rodanthe**—*pop pl* ... NC-3
**Rodarte**—*pop pl* ... NM-5
Rod Bay—*bay* ... VI-3
Rodburn—*locale* ... KY-4
Rodburn Hollow—*valley* ... KY-4
Rodburn Hollow Campsite—*locale* ... KY-4
Rod Creek—*stream* ... OR-9
Rodden—*locale* ... IL-6
Rodden—*locale* ... VA-3
Roddenberry—*locale* ... GA-3
Rodden Ch—*church* ... MO-7
Rodden Creek—*stream* ... CA-9
Rodden Lake—*reservoir* ... CA-9
Rodden Lateral—*canal* ... CA-9
*Rodder Creek* ... OR-9
**Roddey**—*pop pl* ... SC-3
Rodd Fork—*stream* ... WV-2
Roddick Creek—*stream* ... AL-4
Roddy—*locale* ... TN-4
Roddy—*locale* ... TX-5
**Roddy**—*pop pl* ... GA-3
**Roddy**—*pop pl* ... OR-9
**Roddy**—*pop pl* ... SC-3
Roddy Bayou—*stream* ... LA-4
Roddy Branch—*stream* ... NC-3
Roddy Branch—*stream* ... TN-4
Roddy Branch—*stream* ... TX-5
Roddy Branch—*stream* ... VA-3
Roddy Cem—*cemetery* ... NC-3
Roddy Cem—*cemetery* ... TN-4
Roddy Gap—*gap* ... TN-4
Roddy (historical)—*locale* ... PA-2
Roddy Hollow—*valley* ... TN-4
Roddy Island—*island* ... TX-5
Roddy Mtn—*summit* ... NC-3
Roddy Post Office (historical)—*building* ... TN-4
Roddy Road Covered Bridge—*hist pl* ... MD-2
**Roddys**—*pop pl* ... PA-2
Roddy Spring—*spring* ... TN-4
Roddy Springs—*spring* ... TN-4
Roddys Station—*locale* ... PA-2
*Roddy Station* ... TN-4
Roddy Storage Bins—*locale* ... OR-9
Roddy-Yarnell Cem—*cemetery* ... TN-4
Rodear Flat—*flat* ... NV-8
Rode Artesian Well—*well* ... TX-5
Rodebaugh Dam—*reservoir* ... PA-2
Rode Cem—*cemetery* ... TN-4
Rode Cem—*cemetery* (2) ... TX-5
Rode Centre Shop Ctr—*locale* ... MS-4
Rodecker Flat—*flat* ... CA-9
Rodee Ford (historical)—*locale* ... SD-7
Rodee Grove—*woods* ... SD-7
R O Dees Pond Dam—*dam* ... MS-4
Rodefer Hollow—*valley* ... TN-4
Rodef Shalom Congregation—*church* ... PA-2
Rodef Shalom Temple—*hist pl* ... PA-2
Rode Hasvold Road Dam—*dam* ... SD-7
Rodeheaven Boys Ranch—*locale* ... FL-3
Rodeheaver Ch—*church* ... TN-4
**Rodell**—*pop pl* ... WI-6
*Rodelm* ... TN-4
**Rodemacher**—*pop pl* ... LA-4
Rodemacher, Lake—*reservoir* ... LA-4
Rodemer—*locale* ... KY-4
Rodemer—*locale* ... TN-4
Rodemer—*locale* ... WV-2
**Rodemich**—*pop pl* ... IL-6
**Rodena Beach**—*pop pl* ... WA-9
*Roden Baptist Church* ... AL-4
Roden Branch—*stream* ... AL-4
Roden Cem—*cemetery* (4) ... AL-4
Roden Ch—*church* ... AL-4
Roden Crater—*crater* ... AZ-5
Roden Creek—*stream* ... TX-5
Roden Gap—*gap* ... AL-4
Roden Hollow—*valley* ... TX-5
Rodenhouse Wash—*valley* ... UT-8
Roden Mill Gap—*gap* ... AR-4
*Roden Point* ... NC-3
Roden Ridge—*ridge* ... AL-4
Roden Sch (historical)—*school* ... AL-4
Rodens Creek—*stream* ... SC-3
Roden Spring—*spring* ... AZ-5
Rodent Creek—*stream* ... WY-8
Rodent Creek Trail—*trail* ... WY-8
Rodent Island—*island* ... SC-3
**Rodentown**—*pop pl* ... AL-4
Roden Valley—*valley* ... AL-4
**Rodeo**—*pop pl* ... CA-9
**Rodeo**—*pop pl* ... NM-5
Rodeo, Arroyo Del—*civil* ... CA-9
Rodeo, Canada Del —*valley* ... CA-9
Rodeo Arena—*building* ... MO-7
Rodeo Artesian Well—*well* ... TX-5
Rodeo Butte—*summit* ... OR-9
*Rodeo Canyon* ... CA-9
Rodeo Canyon—*valley* ... CA-9
Rodeo Cove—*bay* ... CA-9
Rodeo Creek—*stream* (3) ... CA-9
Rodeo Creek—*stream* ... ID-8
Rodeo Creek—*stream* (3) ... NV-8
Rodeo Creek Gulch—*valley* ... CA-9
Rodeo Flat—*flat* ... AZ-5
Rodeo Flat—*flat* (4) ... CA-9
Rodeo Flat—*flat* ... NV-8
Rodeo Flat Spring—*spring* ... AZ-5
Rodeo Flat Tank—*reservoir* ... AZ-5
Rodeo Ground Corral—*locale* ... AZ-5
Rodeo Grounds—*area* ... CA-9
Rodeo Gulch—*valley* ... ID-8
Rodeo Lagoon—*lake* ... CA-9
Rodeo Lake—*lake* ... NM-5
Rodeo Lake Rsvr—*reservoir* ... ID-8
Rodeo Park—*park* ... AZ-5
Rodeo Park—*park* ... IA-7
Rodeo Park—*park* ... WY-8
Rodeo Ridge—*ridge* ... CA-9
Rodeo Spring—*spring* (2) ... CA-9
Rodeo Spring—*spring* (2) ... ID-8
Rodeo Spring—*spring* ... NV-8
Rodeo Spring—*spring* (2) ... OR-9
Rodeo Tank—*reservoir* (2) ... AZ-5
Rodeo Valley—*basin* ... CA-9
Rodeo Windmill—*locale* (7) ... TX-5
Rodeph Shalom Center—*building* ... PA-2
Rodere Canal—*canal* ... LA-4
**Roderfield**—*pop pl* ... WV-2
*Roder Hill* ... MA-1
Roderick, Mount—*summit* ... NY-2
Roderick Butte—*summit* ... MT-8
Roderick Cem—*cemetery* ... MO-7
Roderick Cem—*cemetery* ... TN-4
Roderick Creek—*stream* ... LA-4
Roderick Creek—*stream* ... OR-9
Roderick Ditch—*canal* ... CO-8
Roderick Head—*cape* ... ME-1
*Roderick Hill* ... CO-8
Roderick Hollow—*valley* ... MO-7
Roderick Hollow—*valley* ... TN-4
Roderick Hollow Mine—*mine* ... TN-4
Roderick Lake—*lake* ... MI-6
Roderick Mtn—*summit* ... MT-8
Roderick Mtn—*summit* ... TN-4
Roderick Oil Field—*oilfield* ... CO-8
Roderick Plantation (historical)—*locale* ... TN-4
Roderique Pond—*lake* ... ME-1
Rodero Creek—*stream* ... NV-8
Rodero Flat—*flat* ... NV-8
Rodero Springs—*spring* ... NV-8
**Rodes**—*pop pl* ... WV-2
Rodes Cem—*cemetery* ... MO-7
Rodes Ch—*church* ... VA-3
Rode School—*locale* ... MT-8
*Rodes Creek* ... MS-4
Rodes Creek—*stream* ... VA-3
Rodes Post Office (historical)—*building* ... TN-4
**Rodessa**—*pop pl* ... LA-4
Rodessa Oil and Gas Field—*oilfield* ... LA-4
Rodessa Oil Field—*oilfield* ... TX-5
Rodessa Oil Pool—*oilfield* ... MS-4
Rodet—*locale* ... TX-5
*Rodewald Ditch* ... IN-6
Rodewald Ranch—*locale* ... NM-5
Rodewald Sch—*school* ... NE-7
Rodewald Well—*locale* ... NM-5
**Rodey**—*pop pl* ... NM-5
Rodey Canyon—*valley* ... NM-5
Rodey Cem—*cemetery* ... NM-5
Rodey Dam—*dam* ... NM-5
Rodey Lateral—*canal* ... NM-5
Rodford Bridge—*bridge* ... IA-7
Rodger Bluff—*cliff* ... WA-9
*Rodger Canyon* ... CA-9
**Rodger Corner**—*pop pl* ... NY-2
Rodger Creek—*stream* ... AZ-5
Rodger Ford (historical)—*locale* ... MO-7
Rodger Gulch—*valley* ... CO-8
Rodger Hill—*summit* ... WA-9
*Rodger Island* ... ME-1
Rodger Iverson Dam—*dam* ... OR-9
Rodger Iverson Rsvr—*reservoir* ... OR-9
*Rodger Peak* ... CA-9
Rodger Ranch—*locale* ... OR-9
Rodger Rsvr—*reservoir* ... OR-9
*Rodgers* ... AL-4
Rodgers—*locale* ... SC-3
**Rodgers**—*pop pl* ... AL-4
**Rodgers**—*pop pl* ... GA-3
Rodgers, Moses, House—*hist pl* ... CA-9
Rodgers, Thomas, House—*hist pl* ... KY-4
*Rodgers Branch* ... GA-3
Rodgers Branch—*stream* ... AL-4
Rodgers Branch—*stream* (2) ... KS-7
Rodgers Branch—*stream* ... TN-4
Rodgers Break—*bar* ... CA-9
Rodgers Brook—*stream* ... ME-1
Rodgers Canyon—*valley* (2) ... CA-9
Rodgers Canyon—*valley* ... NE-7
Rodgers Cave—*cave* ... TN-4
Rodgers Cem—*cemetery* ... AL-4
Rodgers Cem—*cemetery* (2) ... AR-4
Rodgers Cem—*cemetery* ... KY-4
Rodgers Cem—*cemetery* ... NC-3
Rodgers Cem—*cemetery* (2) ... TN-4
Rodgers Cem—*cemetery* ... TX-5
Rodgers Ch—*church* ... GA-3
Rodgers Chapel—*church* ... AR-4
Rodgers Coulee—*valley* ... MT-8
*Rodgers Creek* ... TN-4
Rodgers Creek—*stream* (2) ... CA-9
Rodgers Creek—*stream* ... FL-3
Rodgers Creek—*stream* ... GA-3
Rodgers Creek—*stream* ... MO-7
Rodgers Creek—*stream* (2) ... OR-9
Rodgers Creek—*stream* ... TX-5
Rodgers Crossing—*locale* ... CA-9
Rodgers Dam—*dam* ... NV-8
*Rodgers Ditch* ... IN-6
Rodgers Ditch—*canal* ... IN-6
Rodgers Draw—*valley* ... AZ-5
Rodgers Farm—*locale* ... AR-4
**Rodgers Forge**—*pop pl* ... MD-2
Rodgers Gulch—*valley* (2) ... CA-9
Rodgers Gulch—*valley* ... MT-8
Rodgers Gulch—*valley* ... OR-9
Rodgers Gulch—*valley* ... WA-9
Rodgers Herr JHS—*school* ... NC-3
Rodgers Highway—*channel* ... MI-6
Rodgers Hill—*locale* ... MT-8
Rodgers Hill—*summit* ... NY-2
Rodgers (historical)—*locale* ... KS-7
**Rodgers (historical)**—*pop pl* ... MS-4
Rodgers Hollow—*valley* ... KY-4
Rodgers Hollow—*valley* (2) ... TN-4
Rodgers House—*hist pl* ... KY-4
*Rodgers Island* ... ME-1
*Rodgers Island* ... NY-2
Rodgers Island—*island* ... ME-1
Rodgers JHS—*school* ... MI-6
Rodgers JHS—*school* ... TX-5
*Rodgers Knob* ... GA-3
Rodgers Lake—*lake* ... CA-9
Rodgers Lake—*lake* ... MI-6
Rodgers Lake—*lake* ... MN-6
Rodgers Lake—*lake* ... OH-6
Rodgers Lake—*lake* ... TX-5
Rodgers Lakes—*lake* ... CA-9
Rodgers Meadow—*flat* ... CA-9
*Rodgers Mountain* ... CA-9
Rodgers Mountain—*ridge* ... WV-2
Rodgers Park—*park* ... TX-5
Rodgers Peak—*summit* ... AK-9
Rodgers Peak—*summit* (2) ... CA-9
*Rodgers Point* ... ME-1
Rodgers Point—*cape* ... AK-9
Rodgers Prairie Cem—*cemetery* ... TX-5
Rodger Spring—*spring* ... ID-8
Rodgers Ridge—*ridge* ... CA-9
Rodgers Ridge—*ridge* ... KY-4
Rodgers Ridge—*ridge* ... OR-9
Rodgers Ridge—*ridge* ... TN-4
**Rodgers Ridge Subdivision**—*pop pl* ... TN-4
Rodgers River—*stream* ... FL-3
Rodgers River Bay—*bay* ... FL-3
Rodgers Rsvr—*reservoir* ... AR-4
Rodgers Sch—*school* ... KS-7
Rodgers Sch—*school* ... NJ-2
Rodgers Sch—*school* ... NC-3
Rodgers Sch (historical)—*school* ... MS-4
Rodgers Sch (historical)—*school* ... TN-4
Rodgers School (historical)—*locale* ... MO-7
Rodgers Shelter Archeol Site—*hist pl* ... MO-7
Rodgers Shoal—*bar* ... MA-1
Rodgers Shoals—*bar* ... TN-4
*Rodgers Spring* ... TN-4
Rodgers Spring—*spring* ... GA-3
Rodgers Spring—*spring* ... TN-4
*Rodgers Tank* ... AZ-5
Rodgers Tank—*reservoir* (2) ... AZ-5
Rodgers Tavern—*hist pl* ... MD-2
Rodgers Trap Windmill—*locale* ... TX-5
*Rodgersville* ... AL-4
*Rodgersville* ... MO-7
*Rodgersville* ... TN-4
Rodgers-Wade Furniture Company—*hist pl* ... TX-5
Rodgers-Wilson Cem—*cemetery* ... TN-4
Rodger Tank—*reservoir* ... AZ-5
Rodger Well—*well* ... NM-5
Rodges Chapel—*church* ... VA-3
Rodges Run—*stream* ... PA-2
Rod Hollow—*valley* ... VA-3
**Rodi**—*pop pl* ... PA-2
*Rodin Crater* ... AZ-5
Rodine Creek—*stream* ... OR-9
Rodin Museum—*building* ... PA-2
Rodkey—*locale* ... KS-7
*Rodky River* ... IN-6
Rod Lake—*reservoir* ... OH-6
*Rodlers Creek* ... DE-2
Rodley Butte—*summit* ... OR-9
Rodley Butte Trail—*trail* ... OR-9
Rodley Cem—*cemetery* ... CO-8
Rodman—*locale* ... FL-3
**Rodman**—*pop pl* ... IA-7
**Rodman**—*pop pl* ... NY-2
**Rodman**—*pop pl* ... PA-2
**Rodman**—*pop pl* ... SC-3
Rodman—*uninc pl* ... AK-9
Rodman Bay—*bay* ... AK-9
Rodman Branch—*stream* ... AR-4
Rodman Brook—*stream* ... VT-1
Rodman Creek—*stream* ... AK-9
Rodman Creek—*stream* ... NC-3
**Rodman Crossing (historical)**—*pop pl* ... RI-1
Rodman Dam—*dam* ... FL-3
Rodman Glacier—*glacier* ... AK-9
*Rodman Heights* ... VA-3
Rodman Hill—*summit* ... AR-4
Rodman Hollow—*valley* ... RI-1
Rodman Island—*island* ... AK-9
Rodman Mountains—*range* ... CA-9
Rodman Mountains Petroglyphs Archeol District—*hist pl* ... CA-9
Rodman Neck—*cape* ... NY-2
Rodman Octagonal Barn—*hist pl* ... ND-7
Rodman Peak—*summit* ... AK-9
Rodman Point—*cape* ... NC-3
Rodman Pond—*lake* ... MA-1
Rodman Pond—*lake* ... RI-1
Rodman Ranch—*locale* ... TX-5
Rodman Reach—*channel* ... AK-9
Rodman Rim—*cliff* (2) ... OR-9
Rodman Rock—*bar* ... AK-9
Rodman Rock—*summit* ... OR-9
*Rodman Rsvr* ... FL-3
Rodman Rsvr—*reservoir* ... FL-3
Rodman Sch—*school* ... MA-1
Rodman Sch—*school* ... MO-7
Rodman Sch—*school* ... OK-5
Rodman Slough—*stream* ... CA-9
Rodman Spring—*spring* ... OR-9
Rodmans Quarter—*locale* ... NC-3
Rodmans Quarter Sch—*school* ... NC-3
**Rodman (Town of)**—*pop pl* ... NY-2
Rodna—*locale* ... WA-9
Rodnes Ch—*church* ... MN-6
Rodney—*locale* ... AR-4
Rodney—*locale* ... PA-2
Rodney—*locale* ... TX-5
**Rodney**—*pop pl* ... IA-7
**Rodney**—*pop pl* ... MI-6
**Rodney**—*pop pl* ... MS-4
**Rodney**—*pop pl* ... OH-6
Rodney Baptist Ch—*church* ... MS-4
Rodney Bend—*bend* ... MS-4
Rodney Branch—*stream* ... AL-4
Rodney Branch—*stream* ... IN-6
Rodney Cem—*cemetery* ... IN-6
Rodney Cem—*cemetery* ... MS-4
Rodney Center Hist Dist—*hist pl* ... MS-4
Rodney Ch—*church* ... IN-6
Rodney Court—*hist pl* ... DE-2
Rodney Creek—*stream* ... AK-9
Rodney Crump Slope Mine (underground)—*mine* ... AL-4
Rodney Cutoff—*bend* ... LA-4
Rodney Draw—*valley* ... ID-8
Rodney Hill—*summit* ... KS-7
Rodney Island—*island* ... LA-4
Rodney Island Bar—*bar* ... MS-4
Rodney Lake—*lake* ... LA-4
Rodney Lake—*lake* ... MS-4
Rodney Lake (historical)—*lake* ... MS-4
Rodney Landing—*locale* ... MS-4
Rodney Mortimer Lake Dam—*dam* ... MS-4
Rodney Mtn—*summit* ... OK-5
Rodney Point—*cape* ... MD-2
Rodney Pond—*lake* ... MD-2
Rodney Post Office (historical)—*building* ... MS-4
Rodney Presbyterian Church—*hist pl* ... MS-4
Rodney Run—*stream* ... OH-6
Rodney Sacred Heart Catholic Ch—*church* ... MS-4
*Rodney Sch* ... DE-2
Rodney Sch (historical)—*school* ... MS-4
Rodney Square—*post sta* ... DE-2
*Rodney Station* ... DE-2
**Rodney Village**—*pop pl* ... DE-2
Rodney Village Shop Ctr—*locale* ... DE-2
Rodney Winkler Dam Number 1—*dam* ... SD-7
*Rodo* ... MP-9
Rodokakat—*locale* ... AK-9
Rodolfo Wash—*arroyo* ... AZ-5
Rodonnel (RR name for Bluehole)—*other* ... KY-4
Rodophil—*locale* ... VA-3
Rodo River—*stream* ... AK-9
*Rodo-to* ... MP-9
Rodrick Bridge—*hist pl* ... OH-6
**Rodric Village**—*pop pl* ... DE-2
Rod Ridge—*ridge* ... NC-3
Rodrigues, Canada De —*valley* ... CA-9
Rodriguez Arroyo—*valley* ... TX-5
Rodriguez-Avero-Sanchez House—*hist pl* ... FL-3
Rodriguez Canyon—*valley* ... CA-9
Rodriguez Canyon—*valley* ... NM-5
Rodriguez Cem—*cemetery* (2) ... TX-5
Rodriguez Flat—*flat* ... CA-9
**Rodriguez Hevia**—*pop pl* (2) ... PR-3
Rodriguez Key—*island* ... FL-3
Rodriguez Mtn—*summit* ... CA-9
Rodriguez Oil Field—*oilfield* ... TX-5
Rodriguez Park—*park* ... TX-5
Rodriguez Spur Truck Trail—*trail* ... CA-9
Rodriguez Tank—*reservoir* ... TX-5
Rodriquena Lateral—*canal* ... TX-5
Rodriques Canyon—*valley* ... CO-8
**Rodriquez**—*pop pl* ... LA-4
Rodriquez Ch—*church* ... TX-5
*Rod Rocks* ... PA-2
*Rodsch* ... FM-9
Rods Gap—*gap* ... WA-9
Rods Spring—*spring* ... UT-8
Rods Valley—*valley* ... UT-8
Rods Winter Camp Tank—*reservoir* ... AZ-5
Rod Tank—*reservoir* ... AZ-5
*Rodthy Creek* ... OK-5
Rodtky Creek—*stream* ... OK-5
**Roduco**—*pop pl* ... NC-3
R O Duncan Lake Dam—*dam* ... MS-4
Rody Creek—*stream* ... CA-9
Rody Mtn—*summit* ... AR-4
*Roe* ... MP-9
Roe—*locale* ... CO-8
**Roe**—*pop pl* ... AR-4
**Roe**—*pop pl* ... NC-3
**Roe**—*pop pl* ... TN-4
Roe, L.I., House—*hist pl* ... WI-6
Roe, Ole K., House—*hist pl* ... WI-6
Roe and Cooper Creek—*stream* ... MT-8
Roebecker Homestead (abandoned)—*locale* ... MT-8
Roebell Mtn—*summit* ... MO-7
Roeber Rsvr—*reservoir* ... CO-8
Roebert and Warren Ditch—*canal* ... MT-8
**Roebling**—*pop pl* ... NJ-2
Roebling, Donald, Estate—*hist pl* ... FL-3
Roebling, John, House—*hist pl* ... PA-2
Roebling Hist Dist—*hist pl* ... NJ-2
Roebling Range—*channel* ... NJ-2
Roebling Range—*channel* ... PA-2
Roe Branch—*stream* ... AL-4
Roe Branch—*stream* ... KY-4
Roe Bridge—*bridge* ... AL-4
Roebuck—*locale* ... AL-4
Roebuck—*locale* ... VA-3
**Roebuck**—*pop pl* ... AL-4
**Roebuck**—*pop pl* ... MS-4
**Roebuck**—*pop pl* ... SC-3
Roebuck Branch—*stream* ... MS-4
Roebuck Cem—*cemetery* ... OH-6
Roebuck Cem—*cemetery* ... PA-2
Roebuck Creek—*stream* ... FL-3
**Roebuck Crest Estates**—*pop pl* ... AL-4
**Roebuck Forest**—*pop pl* ... AL-4
**Roebuck Gardens**—*pop pl* ... AL-4
Roebuck Lake—*lake* ... MS-4
Roebuck Lake—*lake* ... OK-5
Roebuck Landing (historical)—*locale* ... MS-4
Roebuck Mine (underground)—*mine* ... AL-4
Roebuck Municipal Golf Course—*other* ... AL-4
**Roebuck Park**—*pop pl* ... AL-4
**Roebuck Plaza**—*pop pl* ... AL-4
Roebuck Plaza Sch—*school* ... AL-4
Roebuck Plaza Shop Ctr—*locale* ... AL-4
Roebuck Recreation Center—*park* ... AL-4
Roebuck Sch—*school* ... PA-2
Roebuck Sch (historical)—*school* ... MS-4
Roebuck Shopping City Shop Ctr—*locale* ... AL-4
**Roebuck Springs**—*pop pl* ... AL-4
Roebuck Tank—*reservoir* ... NM-5
Roebuck Tavern—*hist pl* ... MA-1
**Roebuck Terrace**—*pop pl* ... AL-4
Roe Cem—*cemetery* ... AR-4
Roe Cem—*cemetery* ... IL-6
Roe Cem—*cemetery* (4) ... NY-2
Roe Cem—*cemetery* ... SD-7
Roe Cem—*cemetery* (2) ... TN-4
Roe Cem—*cemetery* ... VA-3
Roe Cem—*cemetery* ... WV-2
Roe Creek—*stream* ... KY-4
Roe Creek—*stream* ... PA-2
Roedecker Lake—*lake* ... WI-6
Roe Deer Spring—*spring* ... NV-8
Roedel Ditch—*canal* ... ID-8
Roeder, Victor A., House—*hist pl* ... WA-9
Roeder Cem—*cemetery* ... TX-5
*Roeder Creek* ... CO-8
Roeder Oil Field—*oilfield* ... TX-5
Roeders—*locale* ... PA-2
Roeder Sch—*school* ... WA-9
Roeder Spring—*spring* ... TN-4
Roedersville—*locale* ... PA-2
Roeding Park—*park* ... CA-9
Roeding Sch—*school* ... CA-9
Roe Drain—*stream* ... MI-6
*Roe Gulch* ... MT-8
Roe Gulch—*valley* (2) ... MT-8
Roe-Harper House—*hist pl* ... GA-3
Roehl-Lenzmeier House—*hist pl* ... MN-6
Roehm JHS—*school* ... OH-6
Roehm Park—*park* ... LA-4
Roehm Ranch—*locale* ... WY-8
Roe Hollow—*valley* ... PA-2
Roe Hollow—*valley* (2) ... TN-4
Roe Hollow—*valley* ... WV-2
Roe Island—*island* ... CA-9
Roe Island Channel—*channel* ... CA-9
**Roe Junction**—*pop pl* ... TN-4
Roe Junction Baptist Ch—*church* ... TN-4
Roe Junction Sch (historical)—*school* ... TN-4
Roe Lake—*lake* ... MN-6
Roe Lake—*lake* ... WI-6
Roe Landing—*locale* ... AL-4
**Roeland Park**—*pop pl* ... KS-7
Roeland Park Elem Sch—*school* ... KS-7
Roeland Park Shop Ctr—*locale* ... KS-7
Roeliff Jansen Kill—*stream* ... NY-2
Roeliff Jansen Sch—*school* ... NY-2
Roelker, John H., House—*hist pl* ... IN-6
Roell Creek—*stream* ... CO-8
**RoEllen**—*pop pl* ... TN-4
Roellen Baptist Ch—*church* ... TN-4
Ro Ellen (CCD)—*cens area* ... TN-4
*Roellen Cem* ... TN-4
RoEllen Cem—*cemetery* ... TN-4
RoEllen Creek—*stream* ... TN-4
Ro Ellen Division—*civil* ... TN-4
Roelofs—*locale* ... PA-2
Roelofs Gully—*valley* ... MI-6
**Roelyn**—*pop pl* ... IA-7
Roemer Park—*park* ... IL-6
**Roemersville**—*pop pl* ... PA-2
Roemerville Sch—*school* ... TX-5
Roemhildts Lake—*lake* ... MN-6
Roemich Dam—*dam* ... ND-7
*Roen* ... MP-9
Roena Gulch—*valley* ... WY-8
*Roen-to* ... MP-9
**Roe Park**—*pop pl* ... NY-2
Roe-Parker House—*hist pl* ... OR-9
Roepcke Pond—*lake* ... MI-6
Roe Peak—*summit* ... NV-8
Roeper Sch—*school* ... MI-6
Roepke Landing Strip—*airport* ... KS-7
Roe Point—*cape* ... AK-9
Roe Point—*cape* ... WI-6
*Roe Pond* ... NJ-2
Roe Pond—*lake* ... CT-1
Roe Pond—*lake* ... SC-3
Roe Pond—*reservoir* ... NY-2
Roe River—*stream* ... MT-8
*Roers Island* ... OH-6
*Roes Basin* ... MT-8
Roe Sch—*school* ... MO-7
Roe Sch—*school* (2) ... NC-3
Roeschel-Toennes-Oswald Property—*hist pl* ... MO-7
Roesch Well—*well* ... WY-8
*Roes Creek* ... MT-8
Roeser, Oscar, House—*hist pl* ... NE-7
Roeser Park—*park* ... MI-6
Roesiger, Lake—*lake* ... WA-9
Roesiger Creek—*stream* ... WA-9
Roesland Elem Sch—*school* ... KS-7
Roesler Coulee—*valley* ... WI-6
Roesler House—*hist pl* ... TX-5
Roesler Oil Field—*oilfield* ... KS-7
Roesler Timber Company Heliport—*airport* ... WA-9
Roesley Park—*park* ... AZ-5

Rohrs—*locale* NE-7
**Rohrsburg**—*pop pl* PA-2
Rohrsburg Cem—*cemetery* PA-2
Rohr Sch—*school* CA-9
Rohrs Hill—*summit* ME-1
Rohrville—*locale* ND-7
Rohunta, Lake—*reservoir* MA-1
*Rohunta Lake* MA-1
**Rohwer**—*pop pl* AR-4
Rohwer Relocation Center Site—*hist pl* AR-4
*Roi* FM-9
Roi—*island* MP-9
Roi Anchorage—*harbor* MP-9
Roida Mesa—*summit* CA-9
**Roi-Dell Subdivision**—*pop pl* UT-8
**Roi Dell Subdivision**—*pop pl* UT-8
**Roie**—*pop pl* FM-9
**Roig**—*pop pl* PR-3
*Roi-Ganofmine* FM-9
*Roi Gen* FM-9
*Roi Hill* FM-9
*Roi-iwa* FM-9
Roi-Kwajalein Highway Channel—*channel* MP-9
Roiles Harbor—*bay* RI-1
Roiley Creek—*stream* AL-4
Roiley Pond—*lake* NY-2
*Roi-mine* FM-9
Roi-Namur—*island* MP-9
Roi-Namur Battlefield—*hist pl* MP-9
Roi (not verified)—*harbor* MP-9
*Roi Peak* FM-9
**Rois**—*pop pl* PW-9
*Rois Aias* PW-9
*Roisbong* PW-9
*Rois Buiel* PW-9
*Rois-Buiel Peak* PW-9
Rois Buked—*island* PW-9
Roischemiangel—*summit* PW-9
*Rois Eaur* PW-9
Roiseaur—*summit* PW-9
Roisebong—*summit* PW-9
Roisemelachel—*summit* PW-9
Rois-Emiangel—*summit* PW-9
Roisersuul—*summit* PW-9
*Roishibuiru Mtn* PW-9
*Roishibuiru San* PW-9
Roiskebesang—*summit* PW-9
*Rois Ketun* PW-9
*Rois Kobasang* PW-9
*Rois Malkiabesek* PW-9
*Rois-Malk-Ra-B* PW-9
*Rois Mlungui* PW-9
*Rois Ngchemiangel* PW-9
*Rois Omleblochel* PW-9
*Rois Sias* PW-9
*Roi-to* MP-9
Roix Springs—*spring* WI-6
Rojas Cem—*cemetery* TX-5
*Roji* MP-9
*Roj Island* FM-9
*Roji To* FM-9
*Roji-To* MP-9
*Rojoa* MP-9
Rojoa—*island* MP-9
*Rojoa Island* MP-9
*Rojoa-To* MP-9
Rojo Spring—*spring* NV-8
*Rok* AZ-5
*Rokar Island* MP-9
Rokeby—*hist pl* NY-2
Rokeby—*hist pl* VT-1
Rokeby—*hist pl* VA-3
**Rokeby**—*pop pl* NE-7
Rokeby (historical)—*locale* MS-4
**Rokeby Lock**—*pop pl* OH-6
Roke Ranch—*locale* MT-8
**Rokey**—*pop pl* AR-4
Rokow Lake—*lake* NE-7
Rok Siding—*locale* AZ-5
Rokumw—*unknown* FM-9
Rolan—*locale* KY-4
Roland—*locale* GA-3
Roland—*locale* ID-8
Roland—*locale* IL-6
Roland—*locale* KS-7
Roland—*locale* MN-6
Roland—*locale* TX-5
**Roland**—*pop pl* AL-4
**Roland**—*pop pl* AR-4
**Roland**—*pop pl* IN-6
**Roland**—*pop pl* IA-7
**Roland**—*pop pl* OK-5
Roland—*summit* ID-8
Roland, Lake—*lake* MI-6
Roland, Lake—*reservoir* MD-2
Roland Bar Rapids—*rapids* ID-8
Roland Bar Rapids—*rapids* OR-9
Roland Branch—*stream* NC-3
Roland Branch—*stream* VA-3
Roland Canyon—*valley* OR-9
Roland (CCD)—*cens area* OK-5
Roland Cem—*cemetery* AR-4
Roland Cem—*cemetery* IL-6
Roland Cem—*cemetery* NC-3
Roland Cem—*cemetery* OK-5
Roland Ch—*church* MO-7
Roland Chimney Hollow—*valley* VA-3
Roland Cooper State Park—*park* AL-4
Roland Creek—*stream* NC-3
Roland Creek—*stream* (2) OR-9
Roland Creek—*stream* TN-4
Roland Creek—*stream* WA-9
Roland Creek Canal—*canal* NC-3
Roland Day Pond—*reservoir* AL-4
Roland Day Pond Dam—*dam* AL-4
Roland Divide—*gap* AR-4
Roland-Grise JHS—*school* NC-3
Roland Gulch—*valley* CO-8
Roland Hall Plantation—*locale* SC-3
Roland Hill Ch (historical)—*church* TN-4
Roland (historical P.O.)—*locale* IA-7
Roland Hollow—*valley* NC-3
Roland Industrial Sch (historical)—*school* AL-4
*Roland Island* ME-1
Roland Kimbrell Lake Dam—*dam* MS-4
Roland Knob—*summit* NC-3
Roland Lake—*lake* MI-6
Roland Lake—*lake* (2) MN-6
Roland Lake—*lake* NE-7
Roland Lake—*lake* SC-3
Roland Lake—*lake* WI-6
Roland Lake Dam—*dam* MS-4
Roland Landing—*locale* KY-4
Roland Memorial Ch—*church* KY-4
Roland Oil Field—*other* IL-6
Rolando Park—*park* CA-9
Rolando Park Sch—*school* CA-9
Rolando Sch—*school* CA-9
*Roland Park* KS-7
**Roland Park**—*pop pl* MD-2
**Roland Park**—*pop pl* NH-1
**Roland Park**—*pop pl* VA-3
Roland Park Ch—*church* MD-2
Roland Park Elem Sch—*school* FL-3
Roland Park Hist Dist—*hist pl* MD-2
Roland Park Shop Ctr—*locale* VA-3
**Roland Park (subdivision)**—*pop pl* NC-3
Roland Point—*summit* WA-9
Roland Pond—*lake* AZ-5
Roland Pond—*lake* ME-1
Roland Pond—*lake* NC-3
Roland Ridge—*ridge* GA-3
Roland Ridge—*ridge* NC-3
Roland Run—*stream* MD-2
Roland Run—*stream* PA-2
**Rolands**—*pop pl* CA-9
Rolands Canyon—*valley* NV-8
Rolands Cem—*cemetery* AL-4
Roland Sch—*school* NC-3
Roland Sch (abandoned)—*school* PA-2
Rolands Chapel—*church* NC-3
Rolands Fork—*stream* AR-4
Roland Site—*hist pl* AR-4
Rolands Mill—*locale* VA-3
Rolands Pond—*reservoir* GA-3
Roland Spring—*spring* KY-4
Rolands Run Branch—*stream* VA-3
Roland Summit—*summit* ID-8
Roland Township—*fmr MCD* IA-7
**Roland Township**—*pop pl* ND-7
Rolandus—*locale* OH-6
**Roland Valley**—*pop pl* CO-8
*Rolapp* UT-8
Rolapp Mine—*mine* UT-8
Rolator Park Hist Dist—*hist pl* GA-3
**Ro-Len Lake Gardens**—*pop pl* FL-3
*Roler* PA-2
**Roler**—*pop pl* PA-2
Roles Inn of America (trailer park)—*other* AZ-5
**Roles Inn of America (trailer park)**—*pop pl* AZ-5
**Rolesville**—*pop pl* NC-3
Rolesville Cem—*cemetery* NC-3
Rolesville Elem Sch—*school* NC-3
Roleta Post Office (historical)—*building* TN-4
**Rolette**—*pop pl* ND-7
Rolette Airp—*airport* ND-7
Rolette Cem—*cemetery* ND-7
Rolette County—*civil* ND-7
Rolette House—*hist pl* WI-6
Roley Cem—*cemetery* KY-4
Roley Ch—*church* KY-4
**Rolfe**—*pop pl* IA-7
**Rolfe**—*pop pl* PA-2
**Rolfe**—*pop pl* WV-2
Rolfe Brook—*stream* (2) ME-1
Rolfe Brook Pond—*lake* ME-1
Rolfe Cape—*cape* WA-9
Rolfe Cem—*cemetery* (2) MI-6
Rolfe Cem—*cemetery* NY-2
Rolfe Ch—*church* AR-4
Rolfe Chapel—*church* AR-4
Rolfe Cove—*bay* ME-1
Rolfe Gulch—*valley* MT-8
Rolfe Hill—*summit* NH-1
**Rolfe (historical)**—*pop pl* IA-7
Rolfe Junction—*locale* AR-4
Rolfe Park—*park* NH-1
Rolfe Sch—*school* AR-4
Rolff Lake—*lake* WY-8
Rolf Lake—*lake* MN-6
Rolford Brook—*stream* ME-1
Rolford Dam—*locale* ME-1
Rolf Pond—*lake* NH-1
Rolf Sch—*school* PA-2
Rolfs Hall—*hist pl* FL-3
Rolfson Canyon—*valley* UT-8
Rolfson House—*hist pl* MT-8
Rolfson Reservoir Dam—*dam* UT-8
Rolfson Rsvr—*reservoir* UT-8
Rolf Survey Assembly of God Ch—*church* AL-4
Rolhausen Ditch—*canal* IN-6
**Rolinda**—*pop pl* CA-9
Roling Cem—*cemetery* WV-2
Rolin Hollow—*valley* AL-4
Rolin Hollow—*valley* TN-4
Rolins Store (historical)—*locale* TN-4
*Roll* PW-9
**Roll**—*pop pl* AZ-5
**Roll**—*pop pl* IN-6
**Roll**—*pop pl* OK-5
*Rolla* VA-3
Rolla—*locale* CO-8
Rolla—*locale* TX-5
**Rolla**—*pop pl* AR-4
**Rolla**—*pop pl* KS-7
**Rolla**—*pop pl* MO-7
**Rolla**—*pop pl* ND-7
Rolla, Lake—*reservoir* OK-5
Rolla Cem—*cemetery* KS-7
Rolla Cem—*cemetery* MO-7
Rolla Downtown Airp—*airport* MO-7
Rolla Elem Sch—*school* KS-7
**Rollag**—*pop pl* MN-6
Rolla HS—*school* KS-7
Rolla Municipal Airp—*airport* ND-7
Rolla Natl Airp—*airport* MO-7
Rollan Creek—*stream* OR-9
Rolland Branch—*stream* FL-3
Rolland Cem—*cemetery* GA-3
Rolland Center—*locale* MI-6
Rolland Hollow—*valley* TN-4
*Rolland Island* ME-1
Rolland Lagoon N W M A—*park* NE-7
**Rolland (Township of)**—*pop pl* MI-6
Rollang Field (airport)—*airport* MS-4
Rolla Township—*civil* KS-7
Rolla Township—*civil* MO-7
Rolla Vocational-Technical Sch—*school* MO-7
Rollaway—*cliff* NY-2
Roll Cem—*cemetery* KS-7
Roll Creek—*stream* ID-8
Roll Dam Brook—*stream* ME-1
*Rollefson Lake* WI-6
*Rollekl* PW-9
Rollem Fork—*stream* WV-2
Rollen Spring—*spring* TN-4
*Roller* TN-4
Roller—*locale* MD-2
Roller Bay—*bay* AK-9
Roller Canal—*canal* LA-4
Roller Canyon—*valley* ID-8
*Roller Cem* MO-7
Roller Cem—*cemetery* KY-4
Roller Cem—*cemetery* (2) MO-7
Roller Cem—*cemetery* VA-3
Roller Chapel—*church* VA-3
Roller Coaster Knob—*summit* NV-8
Roller Creek—*stream* OH-6
Roller Gulch—*valley* CA-9
Roller Hollow—*valley* MO-7
Roller Hollow Sch (abandoned)—*school* MO-7
Roller Memorial Chapel—*church* TN-4
Roller Mill Hill—*summit* UT-8
Roller Office Supply—*hist pl* ND-7
Roller-Pettyjohn Mill—*hist pl* TN-4
Roller Ridge (Township of)—*fmr MCD* AR-4
Roller Sch—*school* SD-7
Roller Sch (abandoned)—*school* MO-7
Rollers Lake—*lake* CO-8
Rollers Lake—*lake* WI-6
Roller Stone Well—*well* CO-8
**Rollersville**—*pop pl* OH-6
Rollertown Cem—*cemetery* KY-4
Rolle Sch—*school* AZ-5
**Rollestown (historical)**—*pop pl* FL-3
Rolley Canyon—*valley* UT-8
Rolleys Point—*cape* CA-9
Rollick Bay—*bay* MN-6
Rollick Creek—*stream* MN-6
Rollin—*locale* KS-7
**Rollin**—*pop pl* MI-6
Rollin Canyon—*valley* OR-9
Rollin Cem—*cemetery* TX-5
Rollin Center Cem—*cemetery* MI-6
Rollin Center Ch—*church* MI-6
Rollin Ch—*church* MI-6
*Rolling Acres* (2) IL-6
**Rolling Acres**—*pop pl* FL-3
**Rolling Acres**—*pop pl* IN-6
**Rolling Acres**—*pop pl* KY-4
**Rolling Acres**—*pop pl* (4) MD-2
**Rolling Acres**—*pop pl* NY-2
**Rolling Acres**—*pop pl* NC-3
**Rolling Acres**—*pop pl* (3) TN-4
**Rolling Acres**—*pop pl* TX-5
**Rolling Acres Estates**—*pop pl* MA-1
Rolling Acres Farm Airp—*airport* PA-2
Rolling Acres Golf Club—*other* KS-7
Rolling Acres Golf Course—*locale* PA-2
Rolling Acres Lake Dam—*dam* TN-4
Rolling Acres Memory Gardens—*cemetery* GA-3
Rolling Acres Pitch and Putt Golf Course—*locale* PA-2
Rolling Acres Rsvr—*reservoir* TN-4
Rolling Acres Sch—*school* IL-6
Rolling Acres Sch—*school* WI-6
**Rolling Acres (subdivision)**—*pop pl* (2) AL-4
**Rolling Acres (subdivision)**—*pop pl* (2) NC-3
**Rolling Acres (subdivision)**—*pop pl* (3) TN-4
*Rolling Bay* WA-9
Rolling Bay—*bay* AK-9
Rolling Bay—*bay* WA-9
**Rollingbay**—*pop pl* WA-9
Rolling Bayou—*stream* MS-4
**Rolling Brook**—*pop pl* TN-4
**Rolling Brook**—*pop pl* VA-3
Rolling Brook—*stream* CA-9
**Rollingburg**—*pop pl* KY-4
Rolling Camp Gap—*gap* NC-3
Rolling Cem—*cemetery* WI-6
Rolling Chapel—*church* NC-3
Rolling Creek—*stream* AR-4
Rolling Creek—*stream* CO-8
Rolling Creek—*stream* MS-4
*Rolling Creek Baptist Church* MS-4
Rolling Creek Ch—*church* MS-4
Rollingcrest JHS—*school* MD-2
Rolling Dam Brook—*stream* ME-1
Rolling Drain—*canal* MI-6
Rolling Draw—*valley* CA-9
Rollinger Creek—*stream* WA-9
Rolling Fields—*area* AL-4
**Rolling Fields**—*pop pl* KY-4
**Rolling Fields**—*pop pl* TN-4
Rolling Fields Ch—*church* IN-6
Rolling Field Sch—*school* OH-6
Rolling Fields Golf Course—*locale* PA-2
*Rolling Fork* KY-4
*Rolling Fork* LA-4
**Rolling Fork**—*pop pl* MS-4
Rolling Fork—*stream* AR-4
Rolling Fork—*stream* (2) KY-4
Rolling Fork—*stream* TX-5
Rolling Fork Ch—*church* (3) KY-4
*Rolling Fork Creek* AR-4
Rolling Fork Creek—*stream* MS-4
Rolling Fork Elem Sch—*school* MS-4
**Rolling Fork Estates (subdivision)**—*pop pl* MS-4
Rolling Fork HS—*school* MS-4
Rolling Fork Landing—*locale* MS-4
Rolling Fork Methodist Ch—*church* MS-4
Rolling Fork Mounds—*hist pl* MS-4
*Rolling Fork Of Salt River* KY-4
Rolling Fork Presbyterian Ch—*church* MS-4
*Rolling Fork River* AR-4
*Rolling Fork River* KY-4
Rolling Fork Slough—*stream* KY-4
Rolling Forks (Township of)—*civ div* MN-6
Rolling G Dam—*dam* TN-4
Rolling G Lake—*reservoir* TN-4
**Rolling Glen**—*pop pl* PA-2
*Rolling Green* KS-7
Rolling Green—*locale* PA-2
Rolling Green Amusement Park—*park* PA-2
Rolling Green Cem—*cemetery* MN-6
Rolling Green Country Club—*other* IL-6
Rolling Green Elem Sch—*school* FL-3
Rolling Green Golf Club—*other* PA-2
Rolling Green Memorial Cem—*cemetery* OH-6
Rolling Green Memorial Gardens (cemetery)—*cemetery* PA-2
Rolling Green Memorial Park—*park* PA-2
*Rolling Green Park* PA-2
Rolling Green Run—*stream* PA-2
Rolling Green Sch—*school* IL-6
Rolling Green Sch—*school* KS-7
Rolling Green Sch—*school* SD-7
Rolling Greens Country Club—*locale* FL-3
**Rolling Greens Subdivision**—*pop pl* UT-8
**Rolling Green (subdivision)**—*pop pl* NC-3
Rolling Green Township—*civil* SD-7
**Rolling Green Township**—*pop pl* ND-7
**Rolling Green Township**—*pop pl* SD-7
Rolling Green (Township of)—*civ div* MN-6
**Rolling Ground**—*pop pl* WI-6
Rolling Grounds—*area* OR-9
Rolling Grounds Camp—*park* OR-9
Rolling Hill—*locale* VA-3
Rolling Hill—*summit* TN-4
**Rolling Hill Acres**—*pop pl* PA-2
Rolling Hill Cem—*cemetery* WV-2
**Rolling Hill Estates**—*pop pl* IN-6
Rolling Hill Hosp—*hospital* PA-2
*Rolling Hills* AL-4
*Rolling Hills* CO-8
Rolling Hills—*locale* AL-4
**Rolling Hills**—*pop pl* (2) CA-9
**Rolling Hills**—*pop pl* DE-2
**Rolling Hills**—*pop pl* FL-3
**Rolling Hills**—*pop pl* (3) IN-6
**Rolling Hills**—*pop pl* KS-7
**Rolling Hills**—*pop pl* KY-4
**Rolling Hills**—*pop pl* NY-2
**Rolling Hills**—*pop pl* (2) PA-2
**Rolling Hills**—*pop pl* (3) TN-4
**Rolling Hills**—*pop pl* TX-5
**Rolling Hills**—*pop pl* VA-3
**Rolling Hills**—*pop pl* WY-8
**Rolling Hills**—*pop pl* PR-3
Rolling Hills—*summit* AK-9
Rolling Hills—*summit* NV-8
Rolling Hills—*uninc pl* FL-3
Rolling Hills—*uninc pl* KS-7
Rolling Hills—*uninc pl* WV-2
**Rolling Hills Additions 2-7 (subdivision)**—*pop pl* UT-8
Rolling Hills Camp—*locale* AL-4
Rolling Hills Cem—*cemetery* AZ-5
Rolling Hills Cem—*cemetery* (2) KY-4
Rolling Hills Ch—*church* KS-7
Rolling Hills Ch—*church* NC-3
Rolling Hill Sch (historical)—*school* TN-4
Rolling Hills Ch of God—*church* KS-7
Rolling Hills Christian Ch—*church* KS-7
*Rolling Hills Church Camp* AL-4
Rolling Hills Community Ch—*church* FL-3
Rolling Hills Convalescent Center Airp—*airport* IN-6
Rolling Hills Country Club—*locale* NC-3
Rolling Hills Country Club—*locale* TN-4
Rolling Hills Country Club—*other* CO-8
Rolling Hills Country Club—*other* KS-7
Rolling Hills Country Club—*other* KY-4
Rolling Hills Country Club—*other* MO-7
Rolling Hills Country Club—*other* NE-7
Rolling Hills Country Club—*other* OH-6
Rolling Hills Country Club—*other* TX-5
*Rolling Hills Country Club and Golf Course* NC-3
**Rolling Hills Country Club Estates**—*pop pl* AZ-5
Rolling Hills Country Day Sch—*school* CA-9
*Rolling Hills Elementary School* AL-4
Rolling Hills Elem Sch—*school* FL-3
Rolling Hills Elem Sch—*school* PA-2
**Rolling Hills Estates**—*pop pl* (2) CA-9
**Rolling Hills Estates Subdivision**—*pop pl* UT-8
Rolling Hills Girl Scout Camp—*locale* OH-6
Rolling Hills Golf and Racquet Club—*locale* AL-4
Rolling Hills Golf Club—*locale* TN-4
Rolling Hills Golf Course—*locale* NC-3
Rolling Hills Golf Course—*other* AZ-5
Rolling Hills Golf Course—*other* IN-6
Rolling Hills HS—*school* CA-9
Rolling Hills JHS—*school* CA-9
**Rolling Hills Meadows Subdivision**—*pop pl* UT-8
Rolling Hills Moravian Ch—*church* FL-3
Rolling Hills Plaza Shop Ctr—*locale* CA-9
Rolling Hills (P.O.)—*uninc pl* CA-9
Rolling Hills Ranch Lake—*reservoir* MS-4
**Rolling Hills Riviera**—*pop pl* CA-9
Rolling Hills Rsvr—*reservoir* NV-8
Rolling Hills Sch—*school* CA-9
Rolling Hills Sch—*school* PA-2
Rolling Hills Shop Ctr—*locale* AZ-5
**Rolling Hills (subdivision)**—*pop pl* (2) AL-4
**Rolling Hills (subdivision)**—*pop pl* FL-3
**Rolling Hills (subdivision)**—*pop pl* MS-4
**Rolling Hills (subdivision)**—*pop pl* (3) NC-3
**Rolling Hills (subdivision)**—*pop pl* (3) TN-4
Rolling Hills Youth Camp—*locale* AL-4
Rolling Island—*island* ME-1
**Rolling Knolls Estate**—*pop pl* OH-6
Rolling Knolls Golf Club—*other* IL-6
**Rolling Knolls Subdivision**—*pop pl* UT-8
Rolling Lake—*lake* MN-6
Rolling Lake—*reservoir* AL-4
Rolling Lake Bayou—*gut* LA-4
Rolling Lakes Dam—*dam* AL-4
**Rolling Lakes (subdivision)**—*pop pl* AL-4
Rolling Meadow Bridge—*bridge* DC-2
*Rolling Meadows* IL-6
**Rolling Meadows**—*pop pl* IL-6
**Rolling Meadows**—*pop pl* NY-2
**Rolling Meadows**—*pop pl* TN-4
**Rolling Meadows**—*pop pl* TX-5
Rolling Meadows Golf Course—*locale* PA-2
Rolling Meadows Sch—*school* IL-6
Rolling Meadows Sch—*school* UT-8
**Rolling Meadows (subdivision)**—*pop pl* AL-4
**Rolling Meadows (subdivision)**—*pop pl* DE-2
**Rolling Meadows (subdivision)**—*pop pl* MS-4
**Rolling Meadows (subdivision)**—*pop pl* NC-3
**Rolling Meadows (subdivision)**—*pop pl* TN-4
**Rolling Meadows Subdivision**—*pop pl* UT-8
*Rolling Mill Mine* AL-4
**Rolling Mill Park**—*pop pl* OH-6
Rolling Mill Shoals—*bar* TN-4
Rolling Mounds—*other* NM-5
Rolling M Ranch—*locale* CA-9
Rolling Mtn—*summit* CO-8
**Rolling Oak Acres**—*pop pl* FL-3
**Rolling Oaks**—*pop pl* TX-5
Rolling Oaks Park—*park* FL-3
**Rolling Oaks Subdivision**—*pop pl* UT-8
**Rolling Park**—*pop pl* DE-2
Rolling Park—*uninc pl* PA-2
**Rolling Park (subdivision)**—*pop pl* NC-3
Rolling Pin Creek—*stream* AK-9
**Rolling Pine Acres (subdivision)**—*pop pl* NC-3
**Rolling Pines (subdivision)**—*pop pl* NC-3
Rolling Pin Ranch—*locale* WY-8
Rolling Plains Research Station—*other* TX-5
Rolling Point—*cape* AK-9
**Rolling Prairie**—*pop pl* IN-6
**Rolling Prairie**—*pop pl* WI-6
Rolling Prairie Elem Sch—*school* IN-6
Rolling Prairie Sch—*school* CO-8
Rolling Prairie Sch—*school* NE-7
Rolling Prairie Sch—*school* WI-6
**Rolling Prairie Township**—*pop pl* ND-7
**Rolling Ranches (subdivision)**—*pop pl* FL-3
**Rollingreen (subdivision)**—*pop pl* NC-3
*Rolling Ridge* IN-6
**Rolling Ridge**—*pop pl* DE-2
**Rolling Ridge**—*pop pl* IN-6
**Rolling Ridge**—*pop pl* MD-2
Rolling Ridge Farm—*hist pl* NY-2
Rolling Ridge Shop Ctr—*locale* KS-7
**Rolling Ridge (subdivision)**—*pop pl* AL-4
Rolling Riffle Campground—*park* OR-9
Rolling Riffle Creek—*stream* OR-9
Rolling Road Golf Course—*other* MD-2
**Rolling Roads (subdivision)**—*pop pl* NC-3
Rolling Rock—*pillar* MA-1
Rolling Rock Creek—*stream* PA-2
Rolling Rock Lookout Tower—*locale* PA-2
*Rolling Sage Plains* OR-9
*Rollings Creek* TN-4
Rolling Shoals Farm Airp—*airport* MO-7
Rollingson Oil Field—*oilfield* KS-7
*Rolling Spring Branch* TN-4
Rolling Spring Ch—*church* KY-4
Rolling Springs—*spring* WY-8
Rolling Stone—*locale* PA-2
**Rollingstone**—*pop pl* MN-6
Rolling Stone Bridge—*bridge* IN-6
Rollingstone Creek—*stream* MN-6
Rolling Stone Lake—*lake* WI-6
Rolling Stone Ranch—*locale* NE-7
Rolling Stone Run—*stream* PA-2
Rollingstone (Township of)—*civ div* MN-6
**Rollings Woods (subdivision)**—*pop pl* MS-4
**Rolling Terrace**—*pop pl* MD-2
Rolling Terrace Sch—*school* MD-2
Rolling Thunder Mtn—*summit* WY-8
**Rollington**—*pop pl* KY-4
**Rolling (Town of)**—*pop pl* WI-6
Rolling Turf Golf Club—*locale* PA-2
Rolling Turf Golf Course—*locale* PA-2
**Rolling Valley**—*pop pl* VA-3
**Rolling View**—*pop pl* MD-2
Rollingwall Sch—*school* AR-4
Rolling Water Cem—*cemetery* AR-4
Rolling Waters Sch (historical)—*school* MS-4
**Rollingwood**—*pop pl* CA-9
**Rollingwood**—*pop pl* MD-2
**Rollingwood**—*pop pl* TN-4
**Rollingwood**—*pop pl* TX-5
**Rollingwood**—*pop pl* VA-3
**Rollingwood Estates (subdivision)**—*pop pl* NC-3
*Rollingwood Hills* TN-4
Rollingwood Sch—*school* CA-9
Rollingwood Sch—*school* MD-2
**Rolling Woods (subdivision)**—*pop pl* AL-4
**Rolling Woods (subdivision)**—*pop pl* MS-4
**Rollingwood (subdivision)**—*pop pl* AL-4
**Rollingwood (subdivision)**—*pop pl* (4) NC-3
**Rollingwoood Acres (subdivision)**—*pop pl* NC-3
Roll Inn Spring—*spring* ID-8
Rollin Ridge Ranch—*locale* CO-8
Rollin Run—*stream* PA-2
*Rollins* (2) CO-8
*Rollins* IN-6
Rollins—*locale* IL-6
Rollins—*locale* MN-6
Rollins—*locale* WV-2
**Rollins**—*pop pl* (2) AL-4
**Rollins**—*pop pl* IN-6
**Rollins**—*pop pl* MT-8
**Rollins**—*pop pl* NC-3
**Rollins**—*pop pl* WA-9
Rollins, Gov. Frank West, House—*hist pl* NH-1
Rollins, Ralph, House—*hist pl* IA-7
Rollins Bay—*swamp* NC-3
Rollins Bluff Hollow—*valley* MO-7
Rollins Bottom—*bend* WY-8
**Rollins Branch**—*pop pl* WV-2
Rollins Branch—*stream* AL-4
Rollins Branch—*stream* NC-3
Rollins Branch—*stream* TN-4
Rollins Branch—*stream* WV-2
Rollins Brook—*stream* ME-1
Rollins Brook—*stream* NH-1
Rollins Building Airp—*airport* DE-2
Rollins Cem—*cemetery* MS-4
Rollins Cem—*cemetery* MO-7
Rollins Cem—*cemetery* OK-5
Rollins Cem—*cemetery* (3) TN-4
Rollins Chapel Ch (historical)—*church* TN-4
Rollins Chapel Sch—*school* TN-4
Rollins Coll—*school* FL-3
Rollins Corner—*locale* FL-3
Rollins Cove—*bay* MD-2
Rollins Creek—*stream* AL-4
Rollins Creek—*stream* MN-6
Rollins Creek—*stream* MS-4
Rollins Creek—*stream* (3) MO-7
Rollins Creek—*stream* WA-9
Rollins Farm—*locale* NH-1
Rollins Ferry Public Access Area—*locale* MO-7
**Rollinsford**—*pop pl* NH-1
Rollinsford (Salmon Falls)—*CDP* NH-1
**Rollinsford Station**—*pop pl* NH-1
**Rollinsford (Town of)**—*pop pl* NH-1
Rollins Fork—*locale* (2) VA-3
Rollins Hill—*summit* (2) NH-1
Rollins (historical)—*locale* AL-4
Rollins (historical)—*locale* SD-7
Rollins Hollow—*valley* TN-4
Rollin (Site)—*locale* CA-9
Rollins Jersey City Helistop—*airport* NJ-2
Rollins Lake—*lake* (2) WI-6
Rollins Lake—*reservoir* WV-2
Rollins Mill—*locale* ME-1
Rollins Mill Branch—*stream* AL-4
Rollins Mills—*locale* ME-1
Rollins Mine—*mine* CO-8
*Rollins Mountain* AR-4
Rollins Mtn—*summit* ME-1
Rollinson Channel Beacon—*tower* NC-3
Rollinson Channel Light (C)—*tower* (2) NC-3
*Rollinson Creek* MS-4
*Rollinson Prairie* MS-4
Rollinson Run—*stream* PA-2
Rollins Park—*park* NH-1
**Rollins Park**—*pop pl* MD-2
Rollins Pass—*gap* CO-8
Rollins Point—*cape* FL-3
Rollins Point—*summit* AR-4
Rollins Pond—*lake* (2) NH-1
Rollins Pond—*lake* NY-2
Rollins Ridge—*ridge* (2) TN-4
Rollins Rsvr—*reservoir* CA-9
Rollins Sch—*school* GA-3
Rollins Sch—*school* MA-1
Rollins Sch—*school* MI-6
Rollins Sch—*school* MO-7
Rollins Sch—*school* NC-3
Rollins Sch—*school* TX-5
Rollins Sch (historical)—*school* AL-4
Rollins Spring—*spring* MO-7
Rollins Spring Branch—*stream* AL-4
**Rollins Subdivision**—*pop pl* TN-4
Rollins Trail—*trail* NH-1
**Rollinsville**—*pop pl* CO-8
Rollins Well—*well* UT-8
**Rollin (Township of)**—*pop pl* MI-6
Rollinwall Sch (historical)—*school* MS-4
Rollin W Mobile Home Ranch—*locale* AZ-5
Rollison Branch—*stream* MS-4
Rollison Creek—*stream* MS-4
Rollison Prairie—*flat* MS-4
**Rollis (Township of)**—*pop pl* MN-6
*Rollito Creek* AZ-5
Rollman Ditch—*canal* WY-8
Rollman Rsvr—*reservoir* WY-8
Roll-N-Ridge Airp—*airport* IN-6
**Rollo**—*pop pl* IL-6
Rolloff Bluff—*cliff* AR-4
Rolloff Mtn—*summit* AR-4
Rollofson Lake—*lake* WI-6
Rollo Mine (underground)—*mine* AL-4
Rollo Pasture—*flat* KS-7
**Rollo Sand Pit**—*pop pl* GA-3
Rollover—*locale* TX-5
Rollover Bay—*bay* TX-5
Rollover Bayou—*stream* LA-4
Rollover Creek—*stream* NC-3
Rollover Lake—*lake* LA-4
Rollover Pass—*channel* TX-5
Rollow Airp—*airport* KS-7
Roll Pone Branch—*stream* VA-3
Roll Ranch—*locale* AZ-5
Rolls, The—*area* AZ-5
Rolls Hollow—*valley* VA-3
*Rolls Mill* MS-4
Rollstone Hill—*summit* MA-1
Rollstone Machinery Company—*hist pl* AL-4
Rollstone Mtn—*summit* NH-1
*Rollston Hill* MA-1
*Rollwar School* MS-4
Rollway Bay—*bay* NY-2
Rollway Lake—*lake* (3) MI-6
Rollways Lookout Tower—*locale* MI-6
Rolly Creek—*stream* KY-4
Rolly Lake—*lake* WA-9
Rollyson—*locale* WV-2
Rollyson Hollow—*valley* WV-2
*Rollyston* WV-2
*Rolmore Creek* MS-4
Rolo, Mount—*summit* WA-9
Roloff Cem—*cemetery* ND-7
**Roloff Township**—*pop pl* ND-7
**Rolon**—*pop pl* PR-3
Roloson, Robert, Houses—*hist pl* IL-6
*Rolph* CA-9
Rolph Canyon—*valley* ID-8
Rolph Grove—*woods* CA-9
Rolph Landing—*locale* MD-2
Rolphs—*locale* MD-2
Rolph Sch—*school* CA-9
Rolphs Creek—*stream* NJ-2
Rolph Slough—*gut* AK-9
R Olson Ranch—*locale* ND-7
Rolston—*locale* GA-3
Rolston Cem—*cemetery* OK-5
Rolston Creek—*stream* GA-3
Rolston Creek—*stream* MI-6
Rolston Draw—*valley* TX-5
Rolston Gap—*gap* GA-3
Rolston Rsvr—*reservoir* WY-8
Rolston Sch (historical)—*school* GA-3
Rolston Spring—*spring* TX-5
Roluf Spring—*spring* MO-7
Rolvaag, O. E., House—*hist pl* MN-6
*Roma* TX-5
Roma, Arroyo—*valley* TX-5
Romaas Sch Number 1—*school* ND-7
Romaas Sch Number 2—*school* ND-7
Romaas Sch Number 3—*school* ND-7
Roma Bakery—*hist pl* CA-9
Romac—*uninc pl* CA-9
*Roma (corporate name Roma-Los Saenz)* TX-5
Romaggi Adobe—*building* CA-9

Rosenwall Sch—*school* AL-4
Rosenwall Sch—*school* AR-4
Rosenwall Sch—*school* MS-4
Rosenwall Sch—*school* TX-5
Rosenward Sch—*school* MS-4
Rosenworth Drain—*stream* MI-6
Rose O'Connell Mine—*mine* NV-8
Rose of Lima Sch—*school* NJ-2
Rose of Peru Mine—*mine* CA-9
Rose of Sharon Baptist Ch—*church* TN-4
Rose Of Sharon Campground—*locale* TN-4
Rose of Sharon Campground Ch—*church* TN-4
Rose of Sharon Ch—*church* AR-4
Rose Of Sharon Ch—*church* GA-3
Rose of Sharon Ch—*church* KY-4
Rose of Sharon Ch—*church* LA-4
Rose of Sharon Ch—*church* MD-2
Rose of Sharon Ch—*church* MI-6
Rose of Sharon Ch—*church* (2) NC-3
Rose Of Sharon Ch—*church* OH-6
Rose of Sharon Ch—*church* SC-3
Rose Of Sharon Ch—*church* VA-3
Rose of Sharon Ch of God in Christ—*church* MS-4
Rose Oil Field—*oilfield* KS-7
Rose Outlet—*canal* CA-9
Rose Park—*park* CA-9
Rose Park—*park* (2) IN-6
Rose Park—*park* MT-8
Rose Park—*park* TN-4
**Rose Park**—*pop pl* AL-4
**Rose Park**—*pop pl* UT-8
Rose Park Ch—*church* VA-3
Rose Park Christian Sch—*school* MI-6
**Rose Park Circle Subdivision**—*pop pl* UT-8
Rose Park Golf Course—*other* UT-8
Rose Park JHS—*school* TN-4
Rose Park Sch—*school* UT-8
Rose Park Shop Ctr—*locale* UT-8
**Rose Park Subdivision**—*pop pl* UT-8
Rose Park Tot Lot Park—*park* UT-8
Rose Peak—*summit* (2) AZ-5
Rose Peak—*summit* CA-9
Rose Peak—*summit* NV-8
Rose Peak—*summit* NM-5
**Rosepine**—*pop pl* LA-4
Rose Pine (RR name for Rosepine)—*other* LA-4
**Rosepine (RR name Rose Pine)**—*pop pl* LA-4
Rose Place—*locale* AR-4
Rose Place—*locale* CA-9
Rose Place—*locale* NM-5
Rose Place Hist Dist—*hist pl* MI-6
*Rose Point* PA-2
*Rose Point* RI-1
Rose Point—*cape* (2) AK-9
Rose Point—*cape* MA-1
Rose Point—*cape* NJ-2
Rose Point—*cliff* AZ-5
**Rose Point**—*pop pl* PA-2
Rose Point Cave—*cave* PA-2
Rose Polytechnic Institute—*school* IN-6
Rose Pond—*lake* NY-2
Rose Pond—*lake* PA-2
Rose Pond—*reservoir* NC-3
Rose Pond—*reservoir* PA-2
Rose Pond Branch—*stream* PA-2
Rose Pond Dam—*dam* NC-3
Rose Pond Ditch—*canal* IN-6
Rose Pond Lateral—*canal* AR-4
*Roseport* KS-7
*Roseport* MN-6
Roseport—*locale* MN-6
Rose Port Airp—*airport* KS-7
Rose Post Office (historical)—*building* TN-4
Rose Quartz Mine—*mine* CA-9
Rose Quartz Mine—*mine* SD-7
Rose Rabenberg Number 1 Dam—*dam* SD-7
Rose Rabenberg Number 2 Dam—*dam* SD-7
Rose Ranch—*locale* (3) CA-9
Rose Ranch—*locale* CO-8
Rose Ranch—*locale* NV-8
Rose Ranch—*locale* (3) TX-5
Rose Ranch—*locale* UT-8
Rose Ranch—*locale* (2) WA-9
Rose Ranch Rsvr—*reservoir* UT-8
*Roserdale* IA-7
*Rose Ridge* OH-6
Rose Ridge—*ridge* AR-4
Rose Ridge—*ridge* ID-8
Rose Ridge—*ridge* KY-4
Rose Ridge—*ridge* NC-3
Rose Ridge Cem—*cemetery* NY-2
Rose Ridge Golf Course—*locale* PA-2
Rose River—*stream* VA-3
Rose River Ch—*church* VA-3
Rose River Falls—*falls* VA-3
Rose River Trail—*trail* VA-3
Rose Rock—*other* (3) AK-9
Rose Rock—*summit* CA-9
Roser Park Sch—*school* FL-3
Rosers Pond—*lake* CT-1
Rose Rsvr—*reservoir* CA-9
*Rose Run* WV-2
Rose Run—*stream* (2) KY-4
Rose Run—*stream* (2) OH-6
Rose Run—*stream* (2) PA-2
Rose Run—*stream* (4) WV-2
**Roses**—*pop pl* PA-2
Roses Bluff—*cliff* AL-4
Roses Bluff—*cliff* FL-3
**Roses Bluff (subdivision)**—*pop pl* MS-4
Roses Branch—*stream* NC-3
Roses Brook—*stream* CT-1
Roses Cem—*cemetery* PA-2
Rose Sch—*hist pl* TN-4
Rose Sch—*school* AZ-5
Rose Sch—*school* (3) CA-9
Rose Sch—*school* LA-4
Rose Sch—*school* MI-6
Rose Sch—*school* NV-8
Rose Sch—*school* PA-2
Rose Sch—*school* TN-4
Rose Sch (abandoned)—*school* (2) MO-7
Rose Sch (historical)—*school* TN-4
Rose School (historical)—*locale* MO-7
*Roses Creek* TN-4
Roses Creek—*stream* GA-3
Roses Creek—*stream* (2) NC-3
Roses Creek—*stream* VA-3
Rose Seven Drain—*canal* CA-9
Roses Fork—*stream* KY-4
Roses Gap—*gap* NC-3
Rose Shoal (historical)—*bar* AL-4
Rose Shoals—*rapids* TN-4
Rose Siding—*locale* WV-2
Roses Lake—*lake* WA-9
Roses Lake—*reservoir* NC-3
Roses Mill—*locale* VA-3
Roses Point—*cape* NC-3
Roses Point—*locale* NY-2
Roses Pond—*reservoir* NC-3
Rosespout—*locale* VA-3
Rose Spring—*spring* (2) AZ-5
Rose Spring—*spring* (2) CA-9
Rose Spring—*spring* ID-8
Rose Spring—*spring* (4) NV-8
Rose Spring—*spring* TN-4
Rose Spring—*spring* (3) UT-8
Rose Spring—*spring* WA-9
Rose Spring Canyon—*valley* UT-8
Rose Spring Ditch—*canal* CA-9
Rose Spring Hollow—*valley* MO-7
**Rose Springs**—*pop pl* WA-9
Roses Run—*stream* OH-6
Roses Run—*stream* VA-3
Roses Run—*stream* WV-2
Roses Shop Ctr—*locale* AL-4
Roses Spring—*spring* NV-8
**Rose (sta.)**—*pop pl* PA-2
Rose Stadium—*other* TX-5
Rose Stage Station Historical Marker—*park* CA-9
Rose Station (Site)—*locale* CA-9
Rose Street—*locale* CA-9
Roses Well—*well* NV-8
Rose Tank—*reservoir* (3) AZ-5
Rose Tead, Lake—*lake* AK-9
Rose Terrace—*hist pl* IN-6
Rose Terrace—*hist pl* VA-3
**Rose Terrace**—*pop pl* KY-4
Rose Terrace Trailer Park—*locale* AZ-5
Roseth Dam—*dam* SD-7
Rose Theatre—*hist pl* LA-4
Rosethorn Park—*park* LA-4
Rosethorn Sch—*school* LA-4
**Roseto**—*pop pl* PA-2
*Rose to Bangor Branch* PA-2
Roseto Borough—*civil* PA-2
Roseton—*locale* NY-2
Roseton Sch—*school* NY-2
Rose Top—*summit* NC-3
Rose Tourist Camp—*hist pl* AZ-5
Rosetown Creek—*stream* PA-2
**Rose (Town of)**—*pop pl* NY-2
**Rose (Town of)**—*pop pl* WI-6
**Rose Township**—*pop pl* ND-7
**Rose Township**—*pop pl* SD-7
**Rose (Township of)**—*pop pl* IL-6
**Rose (Township of)**—*pop pl* (2) MI-6
**Rose (Township of)**—*pop pl* OH-6
**Rose (Township of)**—*pop pl* PA-2
Rosetrail Hunting Club—*locale* AL-4
Rosetrail Park—*park* AL-4
*Rosetree* PA-2
**Rose Tree**—*pop pl* PA-2
Rose Tree Elem Sch—*school* PA-2
Rose Tree Park—*park* PA-2
Rose Tree Ranch—*locale* AZ-5
**Rosetree Woods**—*pop pl* PA-2
Rosetta—*locale* AR-4
Rosetta—*locale* KY-4
**Rosetta**—*pop pl* MS-4
Rosetta Creek—*stream* ID-8
Rosetta Creek—*stream* MT-8
**Rosetta (historical)**—*pop pl* IA-7
Rosetta Landing—*locale* MS-4
Rosetta Mine—*mine* MT-8
Rosetta Mine—*mine* NV-8
Rosette—*locale* MS-4
**Rosette**—*pop pl* UT-8
Rosette Cem—*cemetery* KS-7
Rosette Dam—*dam* SD-7
Rosette Hall—*locale* KS-7
Rosette (historical)—*locale* KS-7
Rosette Lake—*reservoir* SD-7
Rosette Park Congregational Ch (historical)—*church* SD-7
**Rosette Township**—*pop pl* SD-7
Rose Union Ch—*church* VA-3
*Rose Vale* KS-7
*Rosevale* PA-2
**Rosevale**—*pop pl* CO-8
Rose Valley—*locale* NV-8
Rose Valley—*locale* (2) PA-2
**Rose Valley**—*pop pl* PA-2
**Rose Valley**—*pop pl* TN-4
**Rose Valley**—*pop pl* WA-9
Rose Valley—*school* MT-8
Rose Valley—*stream* NV-8
Rose Valley—*valley* CA-9
Rose Valley—*valley* MN-6
Rose Valley—*valley* NE-7
Rose Valley—*valley* NY-2
Rose Valley—*valley* OH-6
Rose Valley—*valley* PA-2
Rose Valley—*valley* WA-9
Rose Valley—*valley* WI-6
**Rose Valley Acres**—*pop pl* PA-2
Rose Valley Borough—*civil* PA-2
Rose Valley (CCD)—*cens area* WA-9
Rose Valley Cem—*cemetery* (4) KS-7
Rose Valley Cem—*cemetery* MO-7
Rose Valley Cem—*cemetery* ND-7
Rose Valley Cem—*cemetery* PA-2
Rose Valley Cem—*cemetery* WA-9
Rose Valley Ch—*church* KS-7
Rose Valley Ch—*church* PA-2
Rose Valley Ch—*church* TN-4
Rose Valley Creek—*stream* CA-9
Rose Valley Creek—*stream* OH-6
**Rose Valley Estates**—*pop pl* MD-2
Rose Valley Falls—*falls* CA-9
*Rose Valley Lake* PA-2
Rose Valley Lake Dam—*dam* PA-2
Rosevalley Mills—*locale* PA-2
Rose Valley Pond—*lake* MI-6
Rose Valley Rsvr—*reservoir* UT-8
*Rose Valley Run* OH-6
Rose Valley Sch—*school* DE-2
Rose Valley Sch—*school* KS-7
Rose Valley Sch—*school* (2) NE-7
Rose Valley Sch—*school* OK-5
Rose Valley Sch—*school* (2) PA-2
Rose Valley Sch—*school* WA-9
Rose Valley Sch (abandoned)—*school* MO-7
**Rose Valley Township**—*pop pl* KS-7
**Rosevear**—*pop pl* MI-6
Rosevear Gulch—*valley* ID-8
Rosevear Park—*park* MI-6
Rosevere Canyon—*valley* UT-8
Rosevere Fork—*stream* UT-8
Rosevere Point—*cliff* UT-8
Rose View Cem—*cemetery* LA-4
*Roseville* IN-6
Roseville—*locale* AR-4
Roseville—*locale* KY-4
Roseville—*locale* NJ-2
Roseville—*locale* ND-7
Roseville—*locale* VA-3
**Roseville**—*pop pl* (2) CA-9
**Roseville**—*pop pl* IL-6
**Roseville**—*pop pl* IA-7
**Roseville**—*pop pl* KY-4
**Roseville**—*pop pl* MI-6
**Roseville**—*pop pl* MN-6
**Roseville**—*pop pl* NJ-2
**Roseville**—*pop pl* NC-3
**Roseville**—*pop pl* OH-6
**Roseville**—*pop pl* (4) PA-2
**Roseville**—*pop pl* TN-4
**Roseville Addition**—*pop pl* WV-2
Roseville Ave. (Roseville)—*other* NJ-2
Roseville Ave Station—*locale* NJ-2
Roseville Borough—*civil* PA-2
Roseville Bridge—*hist pl* IN-6
Roseville Cave—*cave* TN-4
Roseville (CCD)—*cens area* CA-9
Roseville Cem—*cemetery* CA-9
Roseville Cem—*cemetery* KY-4
Roseville Cem—*cemetery* (2) MN-6
Roseville Ch—*church* NC-3
Roseville Ch—*church* (2) WV-2
Roseville Ch—*church* WI-6
Roseville Covered Bridge—*bridge* IN-6
Roseville Drain Number 19—*canal* ND-7
Roseville HS—*hist pl* OH-6
Roseville HS—*school* MI-6
**Roseville (Lyonia)**—*pop pl* KY-4
Roseville Number 1 Sch—*school* ND-7
Roseville Number 2 Sch—*school* ND-7
**Roseville Park**—*pop pl* DE-2
Roseville (Roseville Ave.)—*uninc pl* NJ-2
Roseville Rsvr—*reservoir* CA-9
Roseville Run—*stream* VA-3
**Roseville (Rutland)**—*pop pl* PA-2
Roseville Sch—*school* ND-7
Roseville Sch—*school* TN-4
Roseville School—*locale* MI-6
Roseville State Wildlife Mngmt Area—*park* MN-6
Roseville Town Hall—*building* ND-7
**Roseville Township**—*pop pl* ND-7
Roseville Township (historical)—*civil* ND-7
Roseville (Township of)—*fmr MCD* AR-4
**Roseville (Township of)**—*pop pl* IL-6
**Roseville (Township of)**—*pop pl* (2) MN-6
**Rosevine**—*pop pl* TX-5
Rosewald Consolidated Sch—*school* SC-3
Rosewald Sch—*school* AL-4
Rosewald Sch—*school* AR-4
Rosewall Sch—*school* MS-4
Rosewall Sch (historical)—*school* MS-4
Rosewarne Sch—*school* MI-6
Rosewater Sch—*hist pl* NE-7
Rosewater Sch—*school* NE-7
Rosewell—*hist pl* VA-3
Rose Well—*locale* NM-5
**Rose Well**—*pop pl* AZ-5
Rose Well—*well* NV-8
Rose Well Camp—*locale* AZ-5
*Rosewells Canyon* UT-8
Rosewood—*locale* CA-9
Rosewood—*locale* FL-3
Rosewood—*locale* LA-4
Rosewood—*locale* MO-7
Rosewood—*locale* TX-5
**Rosewood**—*pop pl* CA-9
**Rosewood**—*pop pl* IL-6
**Rosewood**—*pop pl* IN-6
**Rosewood**—*pop pl* KY-4
**Rosewood**—*pop pl* MN-6
**Rosewood**—*pop pl* NC-3
**Rosewood**—*pop pl* OH-6
**Rosewood**—*pop pl* OR-9
**Rosewood**—*pop pl* WA-9
**Rosewood**—*pop pl* WI-6
Rosewood—*uninc pl* KS-7
Rosewood—*uninc pl* SC-3
Rosewood Ave Sch—*school* CA-9
Rosewood (CCD)—*cens area* KY-4
Rosewood Cem—*cemetery* DC-2
Rosewood Cem—*cemetery* NE-7
Rosewood Cem—*cemetery* NY-2
Rosewood Cem—*cemetery* NC-3
Rosewood Cem—*cemetery* TX-5
Rosewood Cem—*cemetery* WA-9
Rosewood Ch—*church* MN-6
Rosewood Ch—*church* VA-3
Rosewood Convalescent Center—*hospital* AR-4
Rosewood Elem Sch—*school* FL-3
Rosewood Elem Sch—*school* NC-3
**Rosewood Estates (subdivision)**—*pop pl* UT-8
**Rosewood Gardens**—*pop pl* PA-2
Rosewood General Hosp—*hospital* TX-5
Rosewood Gulch—*valley* OR-9
**Rosewood Heights**—*pop pl* IL-6
Rosewood (historical)—*locale* AL-4
Rosewood (historical P.O.)—*locale* IN-6
Rosewood Lake—*lake* TX-5
Rosewood Lane Nazarene Chapel—*church* UT-8
Rosewood Lodge—*locale* TX-5
Rosewood Manor—*building* MS-4
**Rosewood Manor Condominium**—*pop pl* UT-8
Rosewood Manor Nursing Home—*hospital* IA-7
Rosewood Memorial Park—*cemetery* VA-3
Rosewood Park—*hist pl* IL-6
Rosewood Park—*park* CA-9
Rosewood Park—*park* SC-3
Rosewood Park—*park* (2) TX-5
Rosewood Park—*park* UT-8
**Rosewood Park**—*pop pl* PA-2
Rosewood Park Cem—*cemetery* TX-5
Rosewood Park Schoool—*school* CA-9
Rosewood Plantation (historical)—*locale* MS-4
Rosewood Point—*cliff* AZ-5
Rosewood Sch—*school* OH-6
Rosewood Sch—*school* SC-3
Rosewood Sch—*school* TX-5
Rosewood Sch—*school* WI-6
Rosewood State Training Sch—*school* MD-2
**Rosewood (subdivision)**—*pop pl* AL-4
**Rosewood (subdivision)**—*pop pl* (2) NC-3
**Rosewood (subdivision)**—*pop pl* TN-4
**Rosewood Subdivision**—*pop pl* UT-8
**Rosewood (Township of)**—*pop pl* MN-6
Roseworth—*locale* ID-8
Rosey Cem—*cemetery* KS-7
Rosey Creek—*stream* AZ-5
Rosey Creek—*stream* OR-9
Rosey Creek—*stream* WI-6
Rosey Creek Campground—*park* AZ-5
Rosey Lake—*lake* WI-6
Rosey Windmill—*locale* NM-5
**Rosharon**—*pop pl* TX-5
Rosharon Lateral—*canal* TX-5
Rosharon Sch—*school* TX-5
*Rosholf* SD-7
**Rosholt**—*pop pl* SD-7
**Rosholt**—*pop pl* WI-6
Rosholt Creek—*stream* MN-6
Rosholt Lake—*lake* MN-6
Rosias, Canada —*valley* TX-5
**Rosiclare**—*pop pl* IL-6
Rosiclare Mine—*mine* IL-6
Rosicrucian Museum And Planetarium—*building* CA-9
**Rosie**—*pop pl* AR-4
Rosie, Lake—*lake* MN-6
Rosie Creek—*stream* (2) AK-9
Rosie Creek Pass—*gap* AK-9
Rosie Draw—*valley* WY-8
Rosie Hollow—*valley* UT-8
Rosie Point—*cape* MI-6
**Rosier**—*pop pl* GA-3
Rosier, Cape—*cape* ME-1
Rosier Bluff—*cliff* MD-2
Rosier Cem—*cemetery* GA-3
Rosier Creek—*stream* VA-3
**Rosiere**—*pop pl* NY-2
**Rosiere**—*pop pl* (2) WI-6
Rosier Grove Ch—*church* GA-3
*Rosie Rsvr* OR-9
Rosies Ridge—*ridge* WY-8
Rosie (Township of)—*fmr MCD* AR-4
Rosignal Brook—*stream* ME-1
Rosilda Spring—*spring* AZ-5
Rosilda Spring Canyon—*valley* AZ-5
Rosilla Peak—*summit* NM-5
*Rosillas Mountains* TX-5
Rosillo Creek—*stream* TX-5
*Rosillo Mountain* TX-5
Rosillo Peak—*summit* TX-5
Rosillos Mountain Ranch—*locale* TX-5
Rosillos Mountains—*summit* TX-5
*Rosin* NC-3
Rosin Branch—*stream* AR-4
Rosin Camp Fork—*stream* VA-3
Rosin Cem—*cemetery* WA-9
Rosin Creek—*stream* MD-2
Rosindale—*locale* NC-3
Rosin Dam Branch—*stream* GA-3
Rosindhall Ch—*church* MN-6
Rosine—*locale* MS-4
**Rosine**—*pop pl* KY-4
Rosin Ford—*locale* GA-3
**Rosing (Township of)**—*pop pl* MN-6
**Rosin Hill**—*pop pl* NC-3
Rosin Hill—*summit* AR-4
*Rosin Hill Church* AL-4
Rosin Mine—*mine* WY-8
Rosin Ridge—*ridge* TX-5
Rosin Ridge Cem—*cemetery* AL-4
Rosin Ridge Ch—*church* TX-5
**Rosinton**—*pop pl* AL-4
*Rosinton Ch* AL-4
Rosinton Ch—*church* (2) AL-4
*Rosinton Methodist Ch* AL-4
Rosinton Road Ch—*church* AL-4
Rosinton Sch—*school* AL-4
Rosinvick Ch—*church* GA-3
**Rosinville**—*pop pl* SC-3
Rosinweed Sch—*school* NE-7
Rosio Rsvr—*reservoir* OR-9
*Ros Island* FM-9
**Rosita**—*pop pl* CO-8
**Rosita**—*pop pl* (2) TX-5
Rosita Artesian Well—*well* TX-5
Rosita Banco Number 73—*levee* TX-5
Rosita Cem—*cemetery* CO-8
Rosita Cem—*cemetery* TX-5
Rosita Creek—*stream* (4) TX-5
Rosita Gulch—*valley* CO-8
Rosita Hills—*range* CO-8
Rosita Lake—*lake* TX-5
Rosita Lake—*reservoir* TX-5
Rosita Post Office (historical)—*building* TN-4
*Rosita Ranch* TX-5
Rosita Ranch—*locale* TX-5
Rosita San Juan Creek—*stream* TX-5
Rositas Canal—*canal* CA-9
Rosita Sch—*school* CA-9
Rositas Dam—*dam* CA-9
Rositas Waste—*canal* CA-9
Rosita Tank—*reservoir* TX-5
Rosita Windmill—*locale* (2) TX-5
Roske Gulch—*valley* ID-8
**Roskelley Subdivision**—*pop pl* UT-8
Roskey Drain—*canal* MI-6
Roskos Valley—*valley* WI-6
Roskruge JHS—*school* AZ-5
*Roskruge Mountains* AZ-5
Roskruge Mountains—*range* AZ-5
*Rosland* OR-9
Roslin—*locale* NC-3
Roslin—*locale* TN-4
Roslin Creek—*stream* MD-2
Roslindale Station (historical)—*locale* MA-1
**Roslindale (subdivision)**—*pop pl* MA-1
Roslin Post Office (historical)—*building* TN-4
Roslin Sch—*school* TN-4
Roslund Elem Sch—*school* PA-2
*Roslyn* OH-6
Roslyn—*building* TN-4
Roslyn—*locale* IL-6
**Roslyn**—*pop pl* NY-2
**Roslyn**—*pop pl* (2) PA-2
**Roslyn**—*pop pl* SD-7
**Roslyn**—*pop pl* WA-9
Roslyn Air Natl Guard Station—*building* NY-2
Roslyn Cascade Mine 4—*mine* WA-9
Roslyn Cem—*cemetery* NY-2
Roslyn Cem—*cemetery* SD-7
Roslyn Creek—*stream* AK-9
*Roslyn Elementary School* PA-2
**Roslyn Estates**—*pop pl* NY-2
Roslyn Flats—*hist pl* IA-7
Roslyn Flower Hill Sch—*school* NY-2
Roslyn Grist Mill—*hist pl* NY-2
**Roslyn Harbor**—*pop pl* NY-2
**Roslyn Heights**—*pop pl* NY-2
**Roslyn Heights**—*pop pl* PA-2
Roslyn Heights (RR name Rosalyn (sta.))—*CDP* NY-2
Roslyn Highlands Sch—*school* NY-2
**Roslyn Hills**—*pop pl* VA-3
Roslyn Hist Dist—*hist pl* WA-9
Roslyn (historical)—*locale* SD-7
Roslyn Lake—*reservoir* OR-9
Roslyn Natl Bank and Trust Company Bldg—*hist pl* NY-2
Roslyn Pond—*lake* NY-2
Roslyn Ranch—*locale* CO-8
Roslyn Road Park—*park* NY-2
Roslyn Savings Bank Bldg—*hist pl* NY-2
Roslyn Sch—*school* PA-2
Roslyn (sta.) (RR name for Roslyn Heights)—*other* NY-2
Roslyn Village Hist Dist—*hist pl* NY-2
**Rosmait Park Subdivision**—*pop pl* UT-8
**Rosman**—*pop pl* NC-3
Rosman Elem Sch—*school* NC-3
Rosman HS—*school* NC-3
Rosner Pond—*reservoir* PA-2
Rosner Pond Dam—*dam* PA-2
Rosney—*locale* VA-3
Rosney Creek—*stream* VA-3
*Rosney Siding* NV-8
Rosnick Branch—*stream* KY-4
Rosny—*locale* NV-8
Rosom Hill—*summit* SC-3
Rosom Hill Cem—*cemetery* SC-3
*Ross* PA-2
*Ross* TN-4
Ross—*locale* AR-4
Ross—*locale* CA-9
Ross—*locale* DE-2
Ross—*locale* GA-3
Ross—*locale* MI-6
Ross—*locale* MN-6
Ross—*locale* OR-9
Ross—*locale* TX-5
Ross—*locale* WV-2
Ross—*locale* WI-6
Ross—*locale* WY-8
**Ross**—*pop pl* CA-9
**Ross**—*pop pl* (2) GA-3
**Ross**—*pop pl* IN-6
**Ross**—*pop pl* IA-7
**Ross**—*pop pl* KY-4
**Ross**—*pop pl* MN-6
**Ross**—*pop pl* ND-7
**Ross**—*pop pl* OH-6
**Ross**—*pop pl* TX-5
**Ross**—*pop pl* VA-3
Ross, David M., House—*hist pl* MI-6
Ross, Dr. Robert M., House—*hist pl* NM-5
Ross, Edith, Mound—*hist pl* OH-6
Ross, Gov. William H., House—*hist pl* DE-2
Ross, John, House—*hist pl* GA-3
Ross, John, House—*hist pl* MO-7
Ross, Moses, House—*hist pl* PA-2
Ross, Mount—*summit* WA-9
Ross, Seymour, Round Barn—*hist pl* IA-7
Ross Airp—*airport* AZ-5
Rossakatum Branch—*stream* DE-2
Ross Allen Lake—*lake* WI-6
Ross and Branch Drain—*canal* MI-6
Ross and Dilly Sch—*school* LA-4
Ross Barnett, Lake—*reservoir* MS-4
Ross Barnett Reservoir Dam—*dam* MS-4
Ross Barnett Reservoir Lower Dam—*dam* MS-4
Ross Basin—*basin* CO-8
Ross Bay—*bay* AK-9
Ross Bayou—*stream* LA-4
Ross Bayou Oil Field—*oilfield* LA-4
Rossberg Cem—*cemetery* TX-5
**Rossboro**—*pop pl* TN-4
Ross Brake—*swamp* LA-4
Ross Branch—*stream* (4) AL-4
Ross Branch—*stream* KS-7
Ross Branch—*stream* (5) KY-4
Ross Branch—*stream* MD-2
Ross Branch—*stream* MI-6
Ross Branch—*stream* MS-4
Ross Branch—*stream* (3) OK-5
Ross Branch—*stream* SC-3
Ross Branch—*stream* (5) TN-4
Ross Branch—*stream* (2) TX-5
Ross Branch—*stream* VA-3
Ross Branch—*stream* WV-2
Ross Branch Cave—*cave* AL-4
Ross Branch Richland Creek—*stream* KY-4
Ross Branch Rsvr—*reservoir* MS-4
*Ross Bridge* MS-4
Ross Bridge—*bridge* AL-4
Ross Bridge—*bridge* OR-9
**Ross Bridge**—*pop pl* MO-7
Ross Brook—*stream* MA-1
Ross Brook—*stream* MN-6
Ross Brook—*stream* NJ-2
Ross Brook—*stream* VT-1
*Rossburg* IN-6
Rossburg—*locale* MN-6
**Rossburg**—*pop pl* IN-6
**Rossburg**—*pop pl* NY-2
**Rossburg**—*pop pl* OH-6
Rossburg Cem—*cemetery* IN-6
*Rossburgh* IN-6
Ross Butte—*summit* OR-9
Ross Butte—*summit* WY-8
Ross Camp—*park* IN-6
Ross Campground—*locale* TN-4
**Ross Camp Ground**—*pop pl* TN-4
Ross Camp Ground United Methodist Ch—*church* TN-4
Ross Camp Hollow—*valley* VA-3
Ross Camp Sch (historical)—*school* TN-4
Ross Camp Trail—*trail* VA-3
Ross Canal—*canal* LA-4
*Ross Canyon* UT-8
Ross Canyon—*valley* (2) CA-9
Ross Canyon—*valley* MT-8
Ross Canyon—*valley* NM-5
Ross Canyon—*valley* OR-9
Ross Canyon—*valley* TX-5
Ross Canyon—*valley* WA-9
Ross Cem—*cemetery* (3) AL-4
Ross Cem—*cemetery* (4) AR-4
Ross Cem—*cemetery* (3) IL-6
Ross Cem—*cemetery* (2) IN-6
Ross Cem—*cemetery* IA-7
Ross Cem—*cemetery* KS-7
Ross Cem—*cemetery* (2) KY-4
Ross Cem—*cemetery* (4) MS-4
Ross Cem—*cemetery* (5) MO-7
Ross Cem—*cemetery* (3) OH-6
Ross Cem—*cemetery* (2) OK-5
Ross Cem—*cemetery* SC-3
Ross Cem—*cemetery* (10) TN-4
Ross Cem—*cemetery* (6) TX-5
Ross Cem—*cemetery* (4) VA-3
Ross Cem—*cemetery* (3) WV-2
Ross Center Sch—*school* PA-2
Ross Ch—*church* (2) NC-3
Ross Ch—*church* OH-6
Ross Ch—*church* PA-2
Ross Ch—*church* WV-2
Ross Chapel—*church* AL-4
Ross Chapel—*church* (2) GA-3
Ross Chapel—*church* (2) KY-4
Ross Chapel Cem—*cemetery* MS-4
Ross Chapel Creek—*stream* KY-4
Ross Chapel (historical)—*church* AL-4
Ross Chapel Sch (historical)—*school* TN-4
Ross Ch (historical)—*church* MS-4
Ross Chimneys—*pillar* CA-9
*Ross Church* TN-4
**Ross City**—*pop pl* TX-5
Ross Collins Vocational Center—*school* MS-4
Ross Common—*locale* PA-2
Ross Common Creek—*stream* PA-2
Ross Common Manor—*hist pl* PA-2
Ross Complex Heliport—*airport* WA-9
Ross Corner—*locale* CA-9
Ross Corner—*locale* ME-1
Ross Corner—*locale* NJ-2
Ross Corners—*locale* (2) NY-2
Ross Corners—*locale* PA-2
**Ross Corners**—*pop pl* NY-2
**Rosscott Manor**—*pop pl* DE-2
**Ross (County)**—*pop pl* OH-6
Ross Cove—*bay* AK-9
Ross Cove—*bay* ME-1
*Ross Creek* KY-4
*Ross Creek* TX-5
Ross Creek—*bay* FL-3
Ross Creek—*stream* AK-9
Ross Creek—*stream* (3) AR-4
Ross Creek—*stream* (7) CA-9
Ross Creek—*stream* GA-3
Ross Creek—*stream* ID-8
Ross Creek—*stream* (2) KY-4
Ross Creek—*stream* LA-4
Ross Creek—*stream* MD-2
Ross Creek—*stream* (2) MI-6
Ross Creek—*stream* MO-7
Ross Creek—*stream* (3) MT-8
Ross Creek—*stream* NV-8
Ross Creek—*stream* NM-5
Ross Creek—*stream* (3) NC-3
Ross Creek—*stream* (3) OR-9
Ross Creek—*stream* PA-2
Ross Creek—*stream* SC-3
Ross Creek—*stream* (2) TN-4
Ross Creek—*stream* (2) TX-5
Ross Creek—*stream* UT-8
Ross Creek—*stream* (3) WA-9
Ross Creek Cave—*cave* TN-4
Ross Creek Picnic Area—*park* MT-8
Ross Creek Sch—*school* KY-4
Ross Crossing—*locale* CA-9
Ross Crossing—*locale* KY-4
Ross Crossing—*locale* MS-4
Ross Crossing—*locale* WI-6
Ross Crossing Creek—*stream* WI-6
Ross Cutoff—*bend* FL-3
Ross Dam—*dam* (2) PA-2
Ross Dam—*dam* (2) WA-9
*Ross Ditch* IN-6
Ross Ditch—*canal* CO-8
Ross Ditch—*canal* (5) IN-6
Ross Ditch Extension—*canal* CO-8
Ross Drain—*canal* ID-8
Ross Drain—*stream* MI-6
Ross Draw—*valley* AZ-5
Ross Draw—*valley* WY-8
Ross East End Drain—*canal* ID-8
*Rosseau* MI-6
Rosseau—*locale* OH-6
Ross E Jeffries Elem Sch—*school* FL-3
Rosse Key—*island* FL-3
Rosseland Ch—*church* ND-7
*Ross Elem Sch* PA-2
Ross Elem Sch—*school* PA-2
Rossella Cem—*cemetery* OH-6
Rossel Lake—*lake* MI-6
*Rosselle* IA-7
Rosser—*locale* AL-4
Rosser—*locale* NC-3
**Rosser**—*pop pl* GA-3
**Rosser**—*pop pl* TN-4
**Rosser**—*pop pl* TX-5
Rosser Cem—*cemetery* (2) TN-4
Rosser Cem—*cemetery* TX-5
Rosser Cem—*cemetery* VA-3
Rosser Creek—*stream* AL-4

Rosserdale—*locale* IA-7
Rosser Mtn—*summit* VA-3
Rosser Pond—*lake* TN-4
Rosser Run—*stream* WV-2
Rossers Bluff Landing (historical)—*locale* AL-4
Rossers Bridge—*bridge* NC-3
Rossers Mill (historical)—*locale* AL-4
Rosses—*locale* NY-2
Rosses Cem—*cemetery* TX-5
*Rosses Island* TN-4
*Rosses Run* PA-2
*Rosset Gulch* CO-8
Ross-Etheridge Cem—*cemetery* TX-5
Rosse Tunnel—*mine* CO-8
Ross Farm—*locale* WA-9
Ross Farm Sch—*school* IL-6
*Ross Ferry* TN-4
Ross Ferry—*locale* PA-2
Ross Ferry (historical)—*crossing* TN-4
Ross Ferry (historical)—*locale* MS-4
Ross F Gray Memorial Park—*cemetery* AL-4
Ross Field (Airport)—*airport* MI-6
Ross Field Branch—*stream* GA-3
Ross Finch Lake—*lake* CA-9
*Ross First Island* TN-4
Ross First Shoals—*bar* TN-4
Ross-Flannigan Ditch—*canal* MT-8
Ross Flat—*flat* OR-9
Ross Flat—*flat* WY-8
Ross Ford—*locale* AL-4
**Rossford**—*pop pl* OH-6
**Rossford**—*pop pl* PA-2
Rossford (Township of)—*other* OH-6
*Ross Fork* ID-8
*Rossfork* MT-8
Ross Fork—*locale* MT-8
Ross Fork—*stream* (4) ID-8
Ross Fork—*stream* MT-8
Ross Fork—*stream* WV-2
Ross Fork Basin—*basin* ID-8
Ross Fork Cem—*cemetery* ID-8
*Ross Fork Creek* ID-8
Ross Fork Creek—*stream* MT-8
Ross Fork Episcopal Church—*hist pl* ID-8
Ross Fork Indian Sch—*school* ID-8
*Ross Fork Judith River* MT-8
Ross Fork Lakes—*lake* ID-8
Ross Fork Oregon Short Lines RR Depot—*hist pl* ID-8
Ross Fork Wasteway—*canal* ID-8
Ross Fort Park—*flat* CO-8
Ross Franks Pond Dam—*dam* MS-4
Ross Gap—*gap* GA-3
Ross Gap—*gap* TN-4
Ross Gates Spring—*spring* CA-9
Ross General Hosp—*hospital* CA-9
Ross-Gowdy House—*hist pl* OH-6
Ross Green Lake—*lake* AK-9
Ross Grove Ch—*church* KY-4
Ross Grove Ch—*church* NC-3
Ross Grove Sch—*school* MO-7
Ross Grove Sch (abandoned)—*school* PA-2
Ross Gulch—*valley* (2) CA-9
Ross Gulch—*valley* (2) ID-8
Ross Gulch—*valley* (2) MT-8
Ross Gulch—*valley* NV-8
Ross Gulch—*valley* OR-9
Ross Hall—*locale* MT-8
Ross Hammock Site—*hist pl* FL-3
Ross-Hand Mansion—*hist pl* NY-2
Ross Hannibal Mine—*mine* SD-7
Ross-Harbour Ch—*church* VA-3
Ross Hardware—*hist pl* OH-6
**Ross Heights (subdivision)**—*pop pl* AL-4
Ross Hill—*summit* CA-9
Ross Hill—*summit* CT-1
Ross Hill—*summit* GA-3
Ross Hill—*summit* ME-1
Ross Hill—*summit* MA-1
Ross Hill—*summit* MS-4
Ross Hill—*summit* NY-2
Ross Hill—*summit* VT-1
Ross Hill—*summit* WA-9
Ross Hill Cem—*cemetery* MS-4
Ross Hill Ch—*church* MS-4
Ross Hill Corners—*locale* PA-2
*Ross Hill Missionary Baptist Ch* MS-4
Ross Hill Sch—*school* PA-2
Ross Hole—*bend* MT-8
Ross Hollow—*valley* (2) AR-4
Ross Hollow—*valley* GA-3
Ross Hollow—*valley* KY-4
Ross Hollow—*valley* (2) OH-6
Ross Hollow—*valley* OK-5
Ross Hollow—*valley* (3) PA-2
Ross Hollow—*valley* TN-4
Ross Hollow—*valley* WV-2
Ross Homestead—*locale* MT-8
Ross House—*hist pl* CA-9
Ross House—*hist pl* MO-7
Ross HS—*school* LA-4
Ross HS—*school* OH-6
Rossi—*locale* CA-9
Rossi, Mrs. A. F., House—*hist pl* ID-8
**Rossie**—*pop pl* IA-7
**Rossie**—*pop pl* NY-2
Rossie, Lake—*reservoir* GA-3
Rossie Purcell Library—*building* AL-4
Rossier Lake—*lake* MN-6
**Rossie (Town of)**—*pop pl* NY-2
*Rossignal Station* LA-4
Rossignol—*locale* LA-4
**Rossignol Hill**—*pop pl* GA-3
Rossi Highline Ditch—*canal* CO-8
Rossi Hill—*summit* UT-8
Rossi Mine—*mine* NV-8
Rossin Bayou—*stream* MS-4
**Rossington**—*pop pl* KY-4
Ross Inlet—*stream* ME-1
Rossin Sch (historical)—*school* IA-7
Rossi Playground—*park* CA-9
Rossi Sch—*school* MN-6
*Ross' Island* ME-1
*Ross Island* TN-4
Ross Island—*island* FL-3
Ross Island—*island* ID-8
Ross Island—*island* ME-1
Ross Island—*island* MI-6
Ross Island—*island* OR-9
Ross Island—*island* PA-2
Ross Island—*island* WA-9
Ross Island Bridge—*bridge* OR-9
**Rossiter**—*pop pl* PA-2
Rossiter, William, House—*hist pl* NH-1
Rossiter Cem—*cemetery* IA-7
Rossiter Creek—*stream* MT-8
Rossiter Dam—*dam* PA-2
Rossiter Island—*island* FL-3
Rossiter Lake—*lake* MT-8
Rossiter Station—*locale* PA-2
Rossi Tungsten Mine—*mine* CA-9
Ross JHS—*school* TX-5
Ross Knob—*summit* NC-3
Ross Knob—*summit* TN-4
Ross Knob—*summit* VA-3
*Ross Lake* MI-6
*Ross Lake* MN-6
*Ross Lake* NY-2
Ross Lake—*lake* (2) FL-3
Ross Lake—*lake* GA-3
Ross Lake—*lake* (2) ID-8
Ross Lake—*lake* ME-1
Ross Lake—*lake* (4) MI-6
Ross Lake—*lake* (2) MN-6
Ross Lake—*lake* MS-4
Ross Lake—*lake* MO-7
Ross Lake—*lake* NE-7
Ross Lake—*lake* NV-8
Ross Lake—*lake* NY-2
Ross Lake—*lake* ND-7
Ross Lake—*lake* OK-5
Ross Lake—*lake* WA-9
Ross Lake—*lake* (3) WI-6
Ross Lake—*lake* WY-8
Ross Lake—*reservoir* CA-9
Ross Lake—*reservoir* MI-6
Ross Lake—*reservoir* (2) OH-6
Ross Lake—*reservoir* PA-2
Ross Lake—*reservoir* WA-9
Ross Lake—*swamp* LA-4
Ross Lake Guards Station—*locale* WA-9
Ross Lake Natl Rec Area—*park* WA-9
**Ross Lake (Township of)**—*pop pl* MN-6
Ross Lake Trail—*trail* WY-8
Rossland—*locale* KY-4
Rossland—*locale* PA-2
**Rossland City**—*pop pl* AL-4
**Rossland City (Sipsey)**—*pop pl* AL-4
Ross Landing—*locale* AL-4
Ross Landing City Park—*park* TN-4
Ross Landing (historical)—*locale* MS-4
Ross Lateral—*canal* ID-8
**Rosslyn**—*pop pl* KY-4
**Rosslyn**—*pop pl* TX-5
**Rosslyn**—*pop pl* VA-3
**Rosslyn Farms**—*pop pl* PA-2
Rosslyn Farms Borough—*civil* PA-2
**Rosslyn Farms (RR name Rosslyn)**—*pop pl* PA-2
*Rosslyn Gap* CA-9
Rosslyn Heights Sch—*school* UT-8
Rosslyn (RR name for Rosslyn Farms)—*other* PA-2
**Rossman**—*pop pl* NY-2
Rossman Cem—*cemetery* NY-2
Rossman Creek—*stream* WI-6
Rossman Falls—*falls* NY-2
*Rossman Fly* NY-2
Rossman Gap—*gap* PA-2
Rossman Hill—*summit* NY-2
Rossman Lake—*lake* MI-6
Rossman Pond—*lake* NY-2
Rossman-Prospect Ave Hist Dist—*hist pl* NY-2
Rossman Sch—*school* MN-6
Rossman Sch—*school* NY-2
Rossman Sch—*school* PA-2
Rossman Sch—*school* WY-8
Ross Mayes Cem—*cemetery* OK-5
Ross Meadow—*flat* CA-9
Ross Memorial Park—*cemetery* MA-1
**Rossmere**—*pop pl* PA-2
Rossmere Ch—*church* AR-4
*Ross Mill* MS-4
**Ross Mill**—*pop pl* NY-2
Ross Mill (historical)—*locale* MS-4
Ross Mills Cem—*cemetery* NY-2
Ross Mine—*mine* (2) MT-8
Ross Mine—*mine* SD-7
Ross Mine—*mine* TX-5
**Rossmoor**—*pop pl* CA-9
**Rossmoor**—*pop pl* MD-2
**Rossmoor Highlands**—*pop pl* CA-9
**Rossmoor Leisure World**—*pop pl* CA-9
Rossmoor Sch—*school* CA-9
Rossmoor Storm Channel—*canal* CA-9
**Rossmore**—*pop pl* WV-2
Rossmore Apartment House—*hist pl* KY-4
*Ross Mountain* VA-3
Ross Mountain—*park* PA-2
Rossmoyne—*locale* PA-2
**Rossmoyne**—*pop pl* OH-6
**Rossmoyne**—*pop pl* PA-2
**Rossmoyne Manor**—*pop pl* PA-2
Rossmoyne Sch—*school* PA-2
Ross Mtn—*summit* AL-4
Ross Mtn—*summit* (2) AR-4
Ross Mtn—*summit* CA-9
Ross Mtn—*summit* ME-1
Ross Mtn—*summit* NY-2
Ross Mtn—*summit* OR-9
Ross Mtn—*summit* SC-3
Ross Mtn—*summit* (2) TN-4
Ross Mtn—*summit* TX-5
Rossnecker Draw—*valley* WY-8
Rossner Rsvr—*reservoir* OR-9
Ross N Robinson JHS—*school* TN-4
Ross Oil Field—*oilfield* TX-5
Rosson, Dr. Roland Lee, House—*hist pl* AZ-5
Rosson Branch—*stream* MS-4
Rosson Cem—*cemetery* AL-4
Rosson Cem—*cemetery* MO-7
Rosson Cem—*cemetery* (2) TN-4
Rosson Hollow—*valley* AR-4
Rosson Hollow—*valley* TN-4
Rosson Hollow Run—*stream* VA-3
Rosson Sch (historical)—*school* MO-7
Ross Park—*park* CA-9
Ross Park—*park* ID-8
Ross Park—*park* NM-5
Ross Park—*park* NY-2
*Ross Pass* VA-3
Ross Pass—*gap* (2) MT-8
Ross Pass—*gap* WA-9
Ross Pass—*summit* MT-8
Ross Peak—*summit* (2) ID-8
Ross-Pike County Tabernacle—*church* OH-6
Ross Pocosin—*swamp* VA-3
Ross Point—*cape* AL-4
Ross Point—*cape* (2) AK-9
Ross Point—*cape* NY-2
Ross Point—*cape* VA-3
Ross Point—*cliff* ID-8
Ross Point—*cliff* MT-8
Rosspoint—*locale* KY-4
Ross Point Sch—*school* DE-2
Rosspoint Sch—*school* KY-4
Ross Pond—*dam* PA-2
Ross Pond—*lake* CT-1
Ross Pond—*lake* FL-3
Ross Pond—*lake* (2) ME-1
Ross Pond—*lake* NY-2
Ross Pond—*lake* NC-3
Ross Pond—*reservoir* PA-2
Ross Pond—*reservoir* RI-1
Ross Prairie—*flat* FL-3
Ross Prong—*stream* DE-2
Ross Ranch—*locale* CA-9
Ross Ranch—*locale* NM-5
Ross Ranch—*locale* OR-9
Ross Ranch—*locale* TX-5
Ross Ranch—*locale* WY-8
Ross Ranch Meadow—*flat* CA-9
Ross Rapids—*rapids* UT-8
Ross R Barnett Lake Dam—*dam* MS-4
Ross R Barnett Rsvr—*reservoir* MS-4
Ross Ridge—*ridge* CO-8
Ross Ridge—*ridge* GA-3
Ross Ridge—*ridge* TN-4
Ross Ridge—*ridge* TX-5
Ross Ridge—*ridge* WY-8
Ross Road Sch—*school* CA-9
Ross Rogers Golf Course—*other* TX-5
Ross Rsvr—*reservoir* CA-9
Ross Rsvr—*reservoir* CO-8
Ross Rsvr—*reservoir* NV-8
Ross Rsvr—*reservoir* OR-9
*Ross Rsvr 2* OR-9
*Ross Run* VA-3
Ross Run—*stream* IN-6
Ross Run—*stream* (5) OH-6
Ross Run—*stream* (4) PA-2
Ross Run—*stream* VA-3
Ross Run—*stream* WV-2
Ross Run Junction—*locale* PA-2
Ross Sanatorium—*hospital* NY-2
Ross Sch—*school* AR-4
Ross Sch—*school* (5) CA-9
Ross Sch—*school* HI-9
Ross Sch—*school* (2) IL-6
Ross Sch—*school* LA-4
Ross Sch—*school* ME-1
Ross Sch—*school* MA-1
Ross Sch—*school* MI-6
Ross Sch—*school* (2) MO-7
Ross Sch—*school* MT-8
Ross Sch—*school* NE-7
Ross Sch—*school* (2) OK-5
Ross Sch—*school* (2) PA-2
Ross Sch—*school* SD-7
Ross Sch—*school* TN-4
Ross Sch—*school* (3) TX-5
Ross Sch (abandoned)—*school* MO-7
Ross Sch (abandoned)—*school* PA-2
Ross Sch (historical)—*school* (2) MS-4
*Ross's Corner* NY-2
**Ross's Corners (Algona)**—*pop pl* NY-2
*Rosss Creek* TN-4
Ross Second Island (historical)—*island* TN-4
Ross Second Island Shoals—*bar* TN-4
Ross-Sewell House—*hist pl* TN-4
*Ross's Ferry* TN-4
Ross Siding—*locale* PA-2
Ross Site (3CL401)—*hist pl* AR-4
Ross's Landing—*hist pl* TN-4
Ross Slough—*stream* ID-8
Ross Slough—*stream* OR-9
Ross Slough—*swamp* ND-7
*Ross Spring* VA-3
Ross Spring—*spring* AL-4
Ross Spring—*spring* (2) AZ-5
Ross Spring—*spring* ID-8
Ross Spring—*spring* MT-8
Ross Spring—*spring* NM-5
Ross Spring—*spring* (2) OR-9
Ross Spring—*spring* PA-2
Ross Spring—*spring* TN-4
Ross Spring—*spring* (2) UT-8
**Ross Store**—*pop pl* NC-3
Ross Street Christian Ch—*church* AL-4
Ross Swamp—*stream* NC-3
Ross Tank—*reservoir* AZ-5
Ross Tank—*reservoir* TX-5
**Rosston**—*pop pl* AR-4
**Rosston**—*pop pl* IN-6
**Rosston**—*pop pl* OK-5
**Rosston**—*pop pl* PA-2
**Rosston**—*pop pl* TX-5
Rosston Creek—*stream* GA-3
Rosston Lake—*reservoir* AR-4
Ross Towhead—*bar* TN-4
Rosstown—*locale* NY-2
**Rosstown**—*pop pl* IN-6
**Ross (Town of)**—*pop pl* WI-6
Ross Township—*CDP* PA-2
Ross Township—*fmr MCD* (2) IA-7
**Ross Township**—*pop pl* (2) KS-7
**Ross Township**—*pop pl* ND-7
Ross Township Cem—*cemetery* IA-7
Ross (Township of)—*other* OH-6
**Ross (Township of)**—*pop pl* (3) IL-6
**Ross (Township of)**—*pop pl* (2) IN-6
**Ross (Township of)**—*pop pl* MI-6
**Ross (Township of)**—*pop pl* MN-6
**Ross (Township of)**—*pop pl* (3) OH-6
**Ross (Township of)**—*pop pl* (3) PA-2
Ross Trail—*trail* PA-2
Ross Trails Adena Circle—*hist pl* OH-6
Ross Tyrell Ditch—*canal* IL-6
Ross Valley—*valley* CA-9
Ross Valley—*valley* TX-5
Ross Valley (CCD)—*cens area* CA-9
Ross Van Ness Sch—*school* AR-4
*Ross View* TN-4
Rossview—*locale* TN-4
Rossview Post Office (historical)—*building* TN-4
Rossview Sch (historical)—*school* TN-4
**Rossview (subdivision)**—*pop pl* TN-4
*Rossville* IN-6
*Rossville* OH-6
Rossville—*locale* MD-2
Rossville—*locale* TX-5
**Rossville**—*pop pl* GA-3
**Rossville**—*pop pl* IL-6
**Rossville**—*pop pl* IN-6
**Rossville**—*pop pl* IA-7
**Rossville**—*pop pl* KS-7
**Rossville**—*pop pl* MO-7
**Rossville**—*pop pl* (2) NY-2
**Rossville**—*pop pl* OH-6
**Rossville**—*pop pl* OK-5
**Rossville**—*pop pl* PA-2
**Rossville**—*pop pl* SC-3
**Rossville**—*pop pl* TN-4
Rossville Baptist Ch—*church* TN-4
Rossville-Beverly Hills (CCD)—*cens area* GA-3
Rossville (CCD)—*cens area* TN-4
Rossville Cem—*cemetery* IA-7
Rossville Cem—*cemetery* OK-5
Rossville Cem—*cemetery* TX-5
Rossville Ch—*church* NY-2
Rossville Christian Ch—*church* KS-7
Rossville City Hall—*building* TN-4
Rossville Division—*civil* TN-4
Rossville Gap—*gap* GA-3
Rossville Hist Dist—*hist pl* OH-6
Rossville (historical)—*locale* SD-7
Rossville HS—*school* GA-3
Rossville Junction—*locale* IL-6
**Rossville Junction**—*pop pl* TN-4
Rossville Post Office—*building* TN-4
Rossville Sch (historical)—*school* TN-4
**Rossville Township**—*pop pl* KS-7
Ross Well—*well* NM-5
*Rosswell Station* SD-7
Ross-Wise Lake—*reservoir* IN-6
Rosswood—*hist pl* MS-4
Rossylyn Station—*building* PA-2
Rost—*locale* MN-6
Rostad Ranch—*locale* MT-8
Rost Cem—*cemetery* TX-5
Rost Creek—*stream* AK-9
Rosteet Sch—*school* LA-4
Rosten Slough—*lake* ND-7
Rostislaf Lakes—*area* AK-9
*Rost Lake* ND-7
Rost Lake—*lake* WI-6
**Rostok**—*pop pl* WI-6
Rost Plaza (Shop Ctr)—*locale* FL-3
**Rostraver**—*pop pl* (2) PA-2
Rostraver Airp—*airport* PA-2
Rostraver Grange—*locale* PA-2
*Rostraver High School* PA-2
Rostraver JHS—*school* PA-2
**Rostraver (Township of)**—*pop pl* PA-2
Rost Run—*stream* IN-6
**Rost (Township of)**—*pop pl* MN-6
Rosvold Lake—*lake* MN-6
Roswell—*locale* MO-7
**Roswell**—*pop pl* AL-4
**Roswell**—*pop pl* CO-8
**Roswell**—*pop pl* GA-3
**Roswell**—*pop pl* ID-8
**Roswell**—*pop pl* NM-5
**Roswell**—*pop pl* OH-6
**Roswell**—*pop pl* SD-7
**Roswell**—*pop pl* TX-5
Roswell-Alpharetta (CCD)—*cens area* GA-3
Roswell (CCD)—*cens area* NM-5
Roswell Cem—*cemetery* ID-8
Roswell Cem—*cemetery* SD-7
Roswell Chapel—*church* GA-3
Roswell Country Club—*other* NM-5
Roswell Creek—*stream* AL-4
Roswell Creek Cem—*cemetery* AL-4
Roswell Creek Ch—*church* AL-4
Roswell Grade Sch—*hist pl* ID-8
Roswell Hist Dist—*hist pl* GA-3
Roswell Industrial Air Center—*other* NM-5
*Roswell Lake* MI-6
Roswell Park Hosp—*hospital* NY-2
Roswell Post Office (historical)—*building* AL-4
Roswells Canyon—*valley* UT-8
Roswell Sch (historical)—*school* TN-4
**Roswell Township**—*pop pl* SD-7
Rosy—*locale* MN-6
Rosy Bayou—*stream* TX-5
Rosy Branch—*stream* NC-3
Rosy Canyon—*valley* AZ-5
Rosy Canyon—*valley* (2) UT-8
Rosy Cem—*cemetery* MN-6
Rosy Creek—*stream* KY-4
Rosy Draw—*valley* NM-5
Rosy Lake—*lake* MN-6
Rosy Lane Campground—*locale* CO-8
**Rosy Mound**—*pop pl* MI-6
Rosy Mound Sch—*school* MI-6
Rosy Run—*stream* MI-6
Rosy Tank—*reservoir* NM-5
*Rota* MH-9
Rota—*island* MH-9
Rota Airp—*airport* MH-9
*Rota Bay* MH-9
*Rota Insel* MH-9
*Rota Island* MH-9
Rota Lake—*lake* MN-6
Rotalata—*locale* SC-3
Rota Latte Stone Quarry—*hist pl* MH-9
**Rota (Municipality)**—*pop pl* MH-9
**Rotan**—*pop pl* AR-4
**Rotan**—*pop pl* TX-5
Rotan (CCD)—*cens area* TX-5
Rotan Cem—*cemetery* TX-5
Rotan-Dossett House—*hist pl* TX-5
Rotary, Lake—*reservoir* SC-3
Rotary Camp—*locale* MO-7
Rotary Club Dam—*dam* TN-4
Rotary Cove—*bay* NV-8
*Rotary Creek* WA-9
Rotary Creek—*stream* WA-9
Rotary Field—*park* TN-4
Rotary Grove Park—*park* CA-9
Rotary Hill—*summit* MT-8
**Rotary Hills (subdivision)**—*pop pl* TN-4
Rotary Island—*island* NJ-2
Rotary Park—*park* (2) AZ-5
Rotary Park—*park* CA-9
Rotary Park—*park* CO-8
Rotary Park—*park* (2) FL-3
Rotary Park—*park* (2) MI-6
Rotary Park—*park* OH-6
Rotary Park—*park* (4) OK-5
Rotary Park—*park* (3) TN-4
Rotary Park—*park* TX-5
Rotary Park—*park* (2) UT-8
Rotary Park—*park* WY-8
Rotary Park Picnic Area—*park* UT-8
Rotary Playground—*park* MI-6
Rotary Springs Camp—*park* IN-6
Rotate (historical)—*locale* KS-7
*Rotate Township* KS-7
Rotavele—*locale* CA-9
*Rota Village* MH-9
Rotch and Cassidy Dam—*dam* AL-4
Rotch And Cassidy Lake—*reservoir* AL-4
**Rote**—*pop pl* PA-2
Rotella Park—*park* CO-8
**Roten**—*pop pl* NC-3
Rotenberg Sch—*school* MI-6
Rotenberry Cem—*cemetery* WV-2
Roten Cabin—*locale* AZ-5
Roten Creek—*stream* NC-3
Rotenhouse Well—*well* AZ-5
Rotenis—*spring* FM-9
Roten Valley—*valley* NE-7
*Roth* ND-7
Roth—*locale* IL-6
Roth—*locale* VA-3
**Roth**—*pop pl* ND-7
Roth, Lottie, Block—*hist pl* WA-9
**Rothbury**—*pop pl* MI-6
Roth Cem—*cemetery* (2) IN-6
Roth Cem—*cemetery* IA-7
Roth Cem—*cemetery* (2) MO-7
Roth Cem—*cemetery* OH-6
Roth Ch—*church* PA-2
Roth-Childs Acad and Day Save—*school* FL-3
Rothchild Sch—*school* IL-6
Roth Cigar Factory—*hist pl* FL-3
Roth Creek—*stream* MO-7
Roth Creek—*stream* OR-9
Roth Ditch—*canal* (2) IN-6
**Rothe**—*pop pl* OR-9
Rothe Cem—*cemetery* TX-5
Rothe Ditch—*canal* IN-6
Rothenbeger Lake—*lake* IN-6
Rothenberg Sch—*school* OH-6
Rotheram Mill House—*hist pl* DE-2
Rother Sch—*school* CA-9
*Rotherwood* TN-4
Rotherwood—*locale* TX-5
**Rotherwood**—*pop pl* TN-4
Rotherwood Bridge—*bridge* TN-4
*Rotherwood Cemetery* TN-4
Rotherwood Ch—*church* GA-3
Rotherwood Estates—*uninc pl* SC-3
Rotherwood Heights—*locale* TN-4
**Rotherwood Hills**—*pop pl* TN-4
Rotherwood Oil Field—*oilfield* TX-5
Rotherwood Post Office (historical)—*building* TN-4
**Rotherwood (Rotherwood Heights)**—*pop pl* TN-4
Roth Farm—*hist pl* KY-4
Roth Farms Airp—*airport* MO-7
Rothgeb Park—*park* NC-3
Rothgeb Pond—*reservoir* NC-3
Rothgeb Pond Dam—*dam* NC-3
Roth Hall—*locale* MT-8
**Rothiemay**—*pop pl* MT-8
Roth Island—*area* MO-7
Rothlisberger Mine—*mine* WA-9
Rothlisberger Ranch—*locale* NM-5
Rothlisburg Sch—*school* WA-9
Rothman—*locale* MN-6
Rothmann Cem—*cemetery* WI-6
**Rothmoor Estates Subdivision**—*pop pl* UT-8
Roth Park—*park* IN-6
**Roth Park**—*pop pl* IN-6
Roth Point—*cape* TN-4
Roth Private Airstrip—*airport* PA-2
Roth Ranch—*locale* NE-7
Rothrick Lake—*lake* MI-6
Roth Rock—*summit* MD-2
Rothrock, Joseph, House—*hist pl* PA-2
Rothrock Campground—*locale* PA-2
Rothrock Cem—*cemetery* PA-2
Rothrock Ridge—*ridge* WA-9
*Rothrock State For* PA-2
Rothrock State For—*forest* PA-2
*Rothrocksville* PA-2
*Rothrockville* PA-2
Roth-Rosenzweig House—*hist pl* AR-4
**Rothruck**—*pop pl* PA-2
**Roths**—*pop pl* WI-6
**Rothsay**—*pop pl* MN-6
Roth Sch—*school* NE-7
Roth Sch—*school* NY-2
**Rothschild**—*pop pl* WI-6
Rothschild, David, House—*hist pl* GA-3
Rothschild House—*hist pl* WA-9
Rothschild's, David, Wholesale Dry Goods—*hist pl* GA-3
Roths Swamp—*swamp* WA-9
**Rothsville**—*pop pl* PA-2
Rothsville Post Office (historical)—*building* PA-2
**Rothville**—*pop pl* MO-7
Rothwell—*locale* KY-4
Rothwell Cem—*cemetery* MO-7
Rothwell Creek—*stream* GA-3
Rothwell Hollow—*valley* KY-4
Rothwell Lake—*lake* NE-7
Rothwell Park—*park* MO-7
Rothwell Ranch—*locale* (2) NE-7
Rothwell Valley—*basin* NE-7
**Rothwood**—*pop pl* TN-4
Rothy Creek—*stream* AR-4
Rotofly Inc Heliport—*airport* WA-9
*Rotoin* MP-9
*Roto Island* MP-9
**Rotonda**—*pop pl* FL-3
**Rotonda West**—*pop pl* FL-3
Roton Point—*cape* CT-1
*Roto-To* MH-9
Roto Wing Inc Airp—*airport* AL-4
**Rottaken**—*pop pl* AR-4
Rott Brothers Airstrip—*airport* ND-7
Rotten Bananas Butte—*summit* AZ-5
Rotten Bayou—*stream* MS-4
Rotten Bluff Hollow—*valley* AR-4
Rotten Bottom—*bend* ID-8
Rotten Coulee—*valley* MT-8
Rotten Creek—*stream* NC-3
Rotten Egg Slough—*gut* FL-3
Rotten Egg Spring—*spring* NV-8
Rotten Fish Slough—*lake* AK-9
Rotten Fork Sch—*school* TN-4
Rotten Fork Wolf River—*stream* TN-4
Rotten Grass Canyon—*valley* MT-8
Rotten Grass Creek—*stream* MT-8
Rotten Hill—*summit* TX-5
Rotten Lake—*lake* OR-9
Rotten Point—*summit* KY-4
*Rotten Pond* NJ-2
Rotten Pumpkin Pond—*lake* MA-1
*Rottens Fork* TN-4
*Rottens Fork School* TN-4
Rotten Spring—*spring* (2) AZ-5
Rotten Springs—*spring* WY-8
Rottenwood Creek—*stream* GA-3
Rottenwood Island—*island* MN-6
**Rotterdam**—*pop pl* NY-2
**Rotterdam Junction**—*pop pl* NY-2
Rotterdam Lateral—*canal* CA-9
Rotterdam Pumping Station—*other* NY-2
Rotterdam (South Schenectady)—*CDP* NY-2
**Rotterdam (Town of)**—*pop pl* NY-2
Rotto Cay—*island* VI-3
*Rotto-ko* FM-9
Rotton Creek—*stream* AL-4
*Rottopaa* FM-9
*Rottopoue* FM-9
*Rottopour* FM-9
Rott Sch—*school* MO-7
*Rotts Lakes* IL-6
*Rotunda* FL-3
Rotunda, Univ of Virginia—*hist pl* VA-3
Rotunda Cirque—*basin* MT-8
Rotunda of the Pennsylvania RR Station—*hist pl* PA-2
**Rotunda-West**—*pop pl* FL-3
Rouark Ditch—*canal* IN-6
Roubadeau—*fmr MCD* NE-7
Roubadeau Pass—*gap* NE-7
Roubadeau Ranch—*locale* NE-7
Roubadeau Trading Post—*locale* NE-7
Roubaix—*locale* SD-7
Roubaix Lake—*reservoir* SD-7
Roubaix Lake Dam—*dam* SD-7
*Roubedeau Pass* NE-7
Roubideau—*locale* CO-8
Roubideau Bench—*bench* CO-8
Roubideau Bridge—*hist pl* CO-8
Roubideau Conservation Training Camp—*locale* CO-8
Roubideau Creek—*stream* CO-8
*Roubideau Pass* NE-7
Roubidoux—*locale* MO-7
Roubidoux Creek—*stream* MO-7
*Roubidoux Pass* NE-7
Roubidoux Spring—*spring* MO-7
Roubidoux Township—*civil* MO-7
**Roubidoux Township**—*pop pl* MO-7
Roubillard Creek—*stream* MI-6
Roub's Ranch—*locale* MT-8
Rouch Cem—*cemetery* IA-7
Rouch Ditch—*canal* (2) IN-6
Rouch Gulch—*valley* CO-8
Rouchleau Mine—*mine* MN-6
Rouch Well—*well* AZ-5
Roucker Cem—*cemetery* TX-5
Roudebush Ditch—*canal* IN-6
Roudebush Farm—*hist pl* OH-6
Roudoth Spring—*spring* OR-9
Roudy Lake—*lake* IN-6
**Roueche Hills Subdivision**—*pop pl* UT-8
Roueche House—*hist pl* PA-2
Rouen Gulch—*valley* OR-9
*Roug* FM-9
Rouge, Bayou—*stream* (3) LA-4
Rouge, River—*stream* MI-6
Rougeau Cem—*cemetery* (2) LA-4
Rouge Creek—*stream* MT-8
Rouge Golf Course—*other* MI-6
*Rougemere* MI-6
**Rougemont**—*pop pl* NC-3
*Rouge River* MI-6
*Rouge Riviere* TX-5
*Rouges Fork Creek* TN-4
Rouggly Cem—*cemetery* MO-7
Rouggly Ch—*church* MO-7
*Rough* NC-3
Rough Acres Dam—*dam* NJ-2
Rough Acres Pond—*reservoir* NJ-2
Rough And Muddy Tank—*reservoir* NM-5
Rough and Ready—*locale* NY-2
Rough and Ready—*locale* PA-2
**Rough and Ready**—*pop pl* CA-9
Rough and Ready Cem—*cemetery* AR-4
Rough and Ready Creek—*stream* (2) CA-9
Rough and Ready Creek—*stream* OR-9
Rough And Ready Creek Forest Way Side State Park—*park* OR-9
Rough And Ready Ditch—*canal* CA-9
Rough and Ready Ditch—*canal* CO-8
Rough and Ready Furnace (40SW215)—*hist pl* TN-4
Rough And Ready Hills—*other* NM-5
Rough and Ready (historical)—*locale* AL-4
Rough and Ready Island—*island* CA-9
Rough and Ready Lakes—*lake* OR-9
Rough and Ready Landing—*locale* MS-4
Rough and Ready Landing (historical)—*locale* TN-4
Rough and Ready Log Pond—*reservoir* OR-9
Rough and Ready Mill Pond Dam—*dam* OR-9
Rough and Ready Mine—*mine* SD-7
Rough and Ready Mtn—*summit* CA-9

Rough and Ready Post Office (historical)—building TN-4
Rough and Ready Rsvr—reservoir CA-9
Rough and Ready Trail—trail CA-9
Rough and Tough Branch—stream KY-4
Rough And Tough Creek—stream KY-4
Rough and Tough Sch—school KY-4
Rough and Tumbling Creek—stream CO-8
Roughan Hall—hist pl MA-1
Rough Arm—ridge NC-3
Rough Arm Branch—stream NC-3
Rough Bay—bay AK-9
Rough Bayou—stream TX-5
Rough Branch AR-4
Rough Branch—stream (2) AR-4
Rough Branch—stream GA-3
Rough Branch—stream (6) KY-4
Rough Branch—stream (4) NC-3
Rough Branch—stream (2) OK-5
Rough Branch—stream (3) TN-4
Rough Branch—stream (3) TX-5
Rough Branch—stream VA-3
Rough Branch—stream WV-2
Rough Butt Bald—summit NC-3
Rough Butt Creek—stream NC-3
Rough Canyon TX-5
Rough Canyon—valley (3) AZ-5
Rough Canyon—valley (4) CO-8
Rough Canyon—valley (5) ID-8
Rough Canyon—valley (2) NV-8
Rough Canyon—valley (4) NM-5
Rough Canyon—valley OK-5
Rough Canyon—valley (2) OR-9
Rough Canyon—valley (7) TX-5
Rough Canyon—valley (6) UT-8
Rough Canyon Creek OR-9
Rough Canyon Creek—stream UT-8
Rough Canyon Marina—other TX-5
Rough Canyon Rsvr—reservoir (2) OR-9
Rough Canyon Tank—reservoir AZ-5
Rough Channel—channel AK-9
Roughcorn Cem—cemetery IA-7
Rough Coulee—valley (3) MT-8
Rough Coulee—valley ND-7
Rough Cove—valley NC-3
Rough Creek CO-8
Rough Creek KY-4
Rough Creek TN-4
Rough Creek TX-5
Rough Creek WY-8
Rough Creek—locale VA-3
Rough Creek—stream (3) AR-4
Rough Creek—stream (5) CA-9
Rough Creek—stream (3) CO-8
Rough Creek—stream (4) GA-3
Rough Creek—stream (9) ID-8
Rough Creek—stream IN-6
Rough Creek—stream (2) KY-4
Rough Creek—stream MO-7
Rough Creek—stream (10) MT-8
Rough Creek—stream NV-8
Rough Creek—stream (2) NM-5
Rough Creek—stream NC-3
Rough Creek—stream ND-7
Rough Creek—stream (2) OK-5
Rough Creek—stream (4) OR-9
Rough Creek—stream (2) TN-4
Rough Creek—stream (20) TX-5
Rough Creek—stream (3) VA-3
Rough Creek—stream (4) WY-8
Rough Creek Canyon—valley NV-8
Rough Creek Cem—cemetery (2) TX-5
Rough Creek Ch—church (2) KY-4
Rough Creek Ch—church TX-5
Rough Creek Crossing—locale TX-5
Rough Creek Sch—school KY-4
Rough Creek Trail—trail CO-8
Rough Creek Trail—trail OR-9
Rough Creek Trail—trail TN-4
Rough Draw—valley CO-8
Rough Draw—valley (4) MT-8
Rough Draw—valley NV-8
Rough Draw—valley NM-5
Rough Draw—valley UT-8
Rough Draw—valley (2) WY-8
Rough Draw North Oil Field—oilfield TX-5
Rough Draw Oil Field—oilfield TX-5
**Rough Edge**—pop pl MS-4
**Roughedge**—pop pl NC-3
Roughedge Ford—locale AR-4
Roughedge Hollow—valley AR-4
Rough Edge Sch (historical)—school TX-5
Rough Fork—stream KY-4
Rough Fork—stream (3) NC-3
Rough Fork—stream WV-2
Rough Gap Run—stream WV-2
Rough Gulch—valley (4) CA-9
Rough Gulch—valley CO-8
Rough Gulch—valley ID-8
Rough Gulch—valley MT-8
Rough Gulch—valley WY-8
Rough Gulch Trail—trail CA-9
Rough-hew Ridge—ridge NC-3
Rough Hill—summit PA-2
Rough Hill Ch—church KY-4
Rough Hill Ch—church TN-4
Rough Hills—summit NV-8
Rough Hollow—valley (6) AR-4
Rough Hollow—valley (4) KY-4
Rough Hollow—valley (6) MO-7
Rough Hollow—valley (2) OK-5
Rough Hollow—valley PA-2
Rough Hollow—valley TN-4
Rough Hollow—valley (10) TX-5
Rough Hollow—valley (3) UT-8
Rough Horn Bay—swamp NC-3
Rough Horn Branch—stream NC-3
Roughhouse Gulch ID-8
Rough House Tank—reservoir AZ-5
Rough Island—island (2) FL-3
Rough Island—island (3) GA-3
Rough Island—island SC-3
Rough Knob—summit KY-4
Rough Knob—summit (2) NC-3
Rough Knob—summit WV-2
Rough Lake—lake (2) ID-8
Rough Lake—lake MT-8
Rough Lake—reservoir ID-8
Rough Leg Hollow—valley AL-4
Roughlock Falls—falls SD-7
Roughlock Hill—ridge MT-8
Roughlock Hill—summit WY-8
Rough Log AL-4
Rough Log Church AL-4
Roughlook Hill WY-8
Rough Mountain Branch—stream TN-4
Rough Mountain Creek—stream AK-9
Rough Mountain State For—forest NJ-2
Rough Mtn—summit (2) AZ-5
Rough Mtn—summit CO-8
Rough Mtn—summit GA-3
Rough Mtn—summit (3) ID-8
Rough Mtn—summit NV-8
Rough Mtn—summit NM-5
Rough Mtn—summit (2) NC-3
Rough Mtn—summit OK-5
Rough Mtn—summit TX-5
Rough Mtn—summit VA-3
Rough Posture Draw—valley TX-5
Rough Posture Windmill—locale TX-5
Roughpoint TN-4
Rough Point—cape RI-1
Rough Point—cape VI-3
Rough Point—locale TN-4
**Roughpoint**—pop pl TN-4
Rough Point Post Office TN-4
Roughpoint Post Office (historical)—building TN-4
Rough Point Wells—well AZ-5
Rough Prong—stream TN-4
Rough Prong McGuire Creek—stream MT-8
Rough Prong Spring—spring MT-8
Roughrider Dam—dam ND-7
Rough Rider Mine—mine SD-7
Rough Rider Oilfield—oilfield ND-7
Rough Ridge—ridge AR-4
Rough Ridge—ridge (2) GA-3
Rough Ridge—ridge KY-4
Rough Ridge—ridge (4) NC-3
Rough Ridge—ridge OR-9
Rough Ridge—ridge (5) TN-4
Rough Ridge—ridge TX-5
Rough Ridge—ridge VA-3
Rough Ridge Creek—stream TN-4
Rough Ridge Tank—reservoir AZ-5
Rough River KY-4
Rough River—stream KY-4
Rough River Dam—dam KY-4
Rough River Dam State Park—park KY-4
Rough River Lake—reservoir KY-4
Rough River Rsvr KY-4
Rough River Rsvr—reservoir KY-4
Rough Rock—pillar AZ-5
**Rough Rock**—pop pl AZ-5
Rough Rock Airstrip—airport AZ-5
Rough Rock Demonstration Sch—school AZ-5
Rough Rock Point—cliff AZ-5
**Rough Rock (Rough Rock Demonstration School)**—pop pl AZ-5
Rough Rock Spring—spring (2) AZ-5
Rough Rock Spring—spring NM-5
Rough Rock Trail Canyon—valley AZ-5
Rough Rock Well—well AZ-5
Rough Run—locale WV-2
Rough Run—stream KY-4
Rough Run—stream NC-3
Rough Run—stream OH-6
Rough Run—stream (2) PA-2
Rough Run—stream TX-5
Rough Run—stream (5) WV-2
Rough Run Ch—church WV-2
Roughs, The—ridge (2) CA-9
Rough Shack Creek—stream AR-4
Rough Sheep Creek—stream MT-8
Rough Shoals Branch—stream TN-4
Rough Shoals Creek—stream KY-4
Rough Spring—spring TX-5
Rough Spring Canyon—valley TX-5
Rough Springs Coulee—valley MT-8
Rough Spur—ridge CA-9
Roughs Rsvr—reservoir WY-8
Rough Sycamore Creek—stream TX-5
Roughtons Store (historical)—locale AL-4
Roughtop Mtn—summit AK-9
Rough Trail—trail ID-8
Rough Trail—trail KY-4
Rough Trap—cliff TX-5
Rough Run PA-2
Roughts Chapel—church TX-5
Roughwood—hist pl MA-1
Roughwood—hist pl PA-2
Rough Wood Branch—stream MS-4
Rough Woods Cem—cemetery IA-7
Rough Woods Hill—locale IA-7
Rougin Creek—stream ID-8
**Rougon**—pop pl LA-4
Rougon Chenal LA-4
**Rougon (Chenal)**—pop pl LA-4
**Rougue Elk**—pop pl OR-9
Roulac Pond—lake FL-3
Roulard Lake—reservoir CO-8
Roulard Lateral—canal CO-8
Roulbac MS—school FL-3
Roulet PA-2
Roulet Pond—lake OR-9
**Roulette**—pop pl PA-2
Roulette Creek—stream OK-5
Roulette Mine—mine CA-9
**Roulette (Township of)**—pop pl PA-2
Roulhac Cem—cemetery FL-3
Roulhac Pond—swamp FL-3
**Roulo**—pop pl MI-6
Roulo Sch—school MI-6
Roulston-Rogers Site—hist pl OK-5
Roumain Bldg—hist pl LA-4
Round SC-3
Round, Bay—bay LA-4
Roundabout Bay—bay NC-3
Roundabout Branch—stream NC-3
Roundabout Ch—church NC-3
Roundabout Creek—stream AL-4
Roundabout Creek—stream NJ-2
Roundabout Creek—stream NC-3
Roundabout Creek—stream (3) VA-3
Roundabout Hill—summit MO-7
Roundabout Island—island FL-3
Roundabout Lake—lake FL-3
Roundabout Lake—lake SC-3
Roundabout Mountains—other AK-9
Roundabout Mtn—summit (2) AK-9
Roundabout Ridge—ridge TN-4
Roundabout Swamp—swamp FL-3
Roundabout Swamp—swamp (2) GA-3
Roundabout Swamp—swamp KY-4
Roundabout Swamp—swamp SC-3
Roundabout Thorofare—channel NJ-2
Rounda Lake Dam—dam NC-3
Rounda Lake Dam—reservoir NC-3
**Roundaway**—pop pl (2) MS-4
Roundaway Baptist Church MS-4
Roundaway Bayou—gut LA-4
Roundaway Bayou—stream MS-4
Roundaway-Bayou Vidal Cutoff—bend LA-4
Roundaway Ch—church MS-4
Roundaway Elementary School MS-4
Roundaway Lake—lake (2) MS-4
Roundaway Post Office (historical)—building MS-4
Roundaway Sch (historical)—school MS-4
Round Bald—summit NC-3
Round Bald—summit TN-4
Round Ball Mtn—summit NY-2
Round Bar—bar CA-9
Round Barn—hist pl (5) OH-6
Round Barn—locale VT-1
Round Barn—post sta IL-6
Round Barn, Bruce Township Section 3—hist pl IA-7
Round Barn, Bruce Township Section 6—hist pl IA-7
Round Barn, Buckingham Township—hist pl IA-7
Round Barn, Cooper Township—hist pl IA-7
Round Barn, Dubuque Township—hist pl IA-7
Round Barn, Millville Township—hist pl IA-7
Round Barn, Norway Township—hist pl IA-7
Round Barn, Pilot Grove Township—hist pl IA-7
Round Barn, The—locale CA-9
Round Barn, Washington Township—hist pl (2) IA-7
Round Barn Rsvr OR-9
Round Basin—lake AR-4
Round Basin Sch—school OR-9
Round Bay FL-3
Round Bay MD-2
Round Bay NH-1
Round Bay—basin SC-3
Round Bay—bay MD-2
Round Bay—bay MO-7
Round Bay—bay VI-3
**Round Bay**—pop pl MD-2
Round Bay Cem—cemetery NH-1
Round Bayou—gut (2) LA-4
**Round Beach**—pop pl CT-1
Round Bear Island—island MN-6
Round Birch Creek—stream UT-8
Round Bluff—cliff IL-6
Round Bluff—cliff WI-6
Round Bluff—summit WI-6
Round Bluff Landing—locale GA-3
Round Bog—lake ME-1
Round Bottom—bend AL-4
Round Bottom—bend AR-4
Round Bottom—bend CA-9
Round Bottom—bend CO-8
Round Bottom—bend (2) KY-4
Roundbottom—bend PA-2
Round Bottom—bend WV-2
Round Bottom—locale VA-3
**Round Bottom**—pop pl OH-6
**Round Bottom**—pop pl WV-2
Round Bottom Branch—stream KY-4
Roundbottom Branch—stream WV-2
Round Bottom Campground—locale NC-3
Round Bottom Cem—cemetery OH-6
Round Bottom Ch—church WV-2
Round Bottom Creek—stream NC-3
Roundbottom Creek—stream (2) WV-2
Round Bottom Ford (historical)—locale MO-7
Round Bottom Hollow—valley AR-4
Round Bottom Hollow—valley WV-2
Round Bottom Meadows—flat ID-8
Round Bottom Ridge—ridge WV-2
Round Bottom Run—stream WV-2
Roundbottom Run—stream WV-2
Round Bottom Sch—school (2) IL-6
Round Brake—lake LA-4
Round Brake—swamp AR-4
Round Brake (historical)—swamp LA-4
Round Branch Ch—church NC-3
Round Brook—stream CT-1
Round Brown Pond—reservoir FL-3
Round Butte AZ-5
Round Butte—locale MT-8
Round Butte—summit (3) AZ-5
Round Butte—summit CO-8
Round Butte—summit (7) MT-8
Round Butte—summit NM-5
Round Butte—summit (8) OR-9
Round Butte Dam—dam OR-9
Round Butte Lake—flat OR-9
Round Butte Rsvr—reservoir CO-8
Round Butte Rsvr—reservoir MT-8
Round Butte Spring—spring AZ-5
Round Canyon—valley CA-9
Round Canyon—valley UT-8
Round Canyon Hollow—valley OK-5
Round Church—hist pl VT-1
Round Cienaga Creek—stream CA-9
Round Cienega—flat AZ-5
Round Cliff—cliff KY-4
Round Corner House—building MA-1
Round Corner Tank—reservoir TX-5
Round Corral—locale (2) AZ-5
Round Corral—locale (2) CA-9
Round Corral Canyon—valley CA-9
Round Corral Creek—stream CO-8
Round Corral Creek—stream NV-8
Round Corral Meadow—flat CA-9
Round Corral Rsvr—reservoir WY-8
Round Corral Spring—spring CO-8
Round Corral Windmill—locale CO-8
Round Cove—basin TN-4
Round Cove—bay AK-9
Round Cove—bay ME-1
Round Cove—cove (2) MA-1
Round Cove—valley AL-4
Round Cove—valley (2) NC-3
Round Cove—valley TN-4
Round Cove Cave—cave AL-4
Round Cove Cem—cemetery TN-4
Round Cow Rsvr—reservoir MT-8
Round Creek OK-5
Round Creek—stream CO-8
Round Creek—stream (2) OR-9
Round Creek—stream WI-6
Round Cypress Brake—swamp AR-4
Round Eddy—lake MS-4
Rounded Hill—summit AR-4
Rounded Island—island WA-9
Rounded Islet WA-9
Rounded Ridge—ridge NV-8
Round Flat—flat (2) UT-8
Round Flat Ch—church TX-5
Round Gap MA-1
Round Glade Run—stream MD-2
Round Granite Hill summit CA-9
Round Grove KS-7
Round Grove—locale IA-7
**Round Grove**—pop pl IL-6
**Round Grove**—pop pl IN-6
**Round Grove**—pop pl MO-7
Round Grove—swamp OR-9
Round Grove—woods UT-8
Round Grove Cem—cemetery (2) IL-6
Round Grove Cem—cemetery OK-5
Round Grove Ch—church (2) TX-5
Round Grove Creek—stream MO-7
Round Grove Creek—stream NE-7
Round Grove (historical P.O.)—locale IA-7
Round Grove Lake—lake MN-6
Round Grove Ranch—locale MT-8
Round Grove Ranch—locale OR-9
Round Grove Sch—school IL-6
Round Grove Sch—school (3) IA-7
Round Grove Sch—school MO-7
Round Grove Sch—school NE-7
Round Grove Sch—school WI-6
Round Grove Sch (abandoned)—school MO-7
Round Grove Township—civil (2) MO-7
**Round Grove (Township of)**—pop pl IL-6
**Round Grove (Township of)**—pop pl IN-6
**Round Grove (Township of)**—pop pl MN-6
Round Gulch—valley CO-8
Round Gut—gut VA-3
Round Hammock Bay—bay (2) NC-3
Round Hammock Point—cape NC-3
Round Head—cliff AK-9
Round Head—locale PA-2
**Roundhead**—pop pl OH-6
Round Head—summit PA-2
Roundhead—summit (2) TX-5
Round Head—summit VA-3
Roundhead Butte—summit MT-8
Round Head Mtn—summit PA-2
Roundhead Mtn—summit VA-3
Roundhead Ridge VA-3
**Roundhead (Township of)**—pop pl OH-6
Roundhill AL-4
Round Hill AZ-5
Round Hill—hist pl OH-6
Roundhill—locale AL-4
Round Hill—locale AR-4
Round Hill—locale CT-1
Roundhill—locale KY-4
Roundhill—locale NC-3
Round Hill—locale PA-2
Round Hill—locale TN-4
Round Hill—locale (2) VA-3
**Round Hill**—pop pl AL-4
**Round Hill**—pop pl KY-4
**Round Hill**—pop pl MD-2
**Round Hill**—pop pl VA-3
Round Hill—summit (2) AK-9
Round Hill—summit (2) AZ-5
Round Hill—summit (2) AR-4
Round Hill—summit (3) CA-9
Round Hill—summit (2) CO-8
Round Hill—summit (9) CT-1
Round Hill—summit IN-6
Round Hill—summit KY-4
Round Hill—summit (7) MA-1
Round Hill—summit MS-4
Round Hill—summit MO-7
Round Hill—summit NV-8
Round Hill—summit (3) NH-1
Round Hill—summit NM-5
Round Hill—summit (7) NY-2
Round Hill—summit (5) PA-2
Round Hill—summit RI-1
Round Hill—summit SD-7
Round Hill—summit (2) TN-4
Round Hill—summit (3) TX-5
Round Hill—summit (3) UT-8
Round Hill—summit (2) VT-1
Round Hill—summit (12) VA-3
Round Hill—summit WI-6
Round Hill—summit (2) WY-8
Round Hill Baptist Ch (historical)—church TN-4
Round Hill Branch—stream NC-3
Round Hill Brook—stream (2) CT-1
Round Hill Cem—cemetery GA-3
Round Hill Cem—cemetery IN-6
Roundhill Cem—cemetery NC-3
Roundhill Cem—cemetery PA-2
Round Hill Cem—cemetery (2) TN-4
Round Hill Cem—cemetery (2) VA-3
Round Hill Cem—cemetery WI-6
Round Hill Ch—church AR-4
Round Hill Ch—church (2) NC-3
Round Hill Ch—church PA-2
Round Hill Ch—church (3) VA-3
Round Hill Ch (historical)—church TN-4
Round Hill Country Club—other CA-9
Round Hill Country Club—other CT-1
Round Hill County Regional Park—park PA-2
Round Hill Gulch—valley CO-8
Round Hill Missionary Baptist Ch—church TN-4
Round Hill Park—park NY-2
Round Hill Point—cape MA-1
Round Hill Pond—lake MA-1
Round Hill Post Office—building PA-2
Roundhill Ranch—locale TX-5
Round Hill Rock MA-1
Round Hill Rsvr—reservoir VA-3
Round Hills—summit CA-9
Round Hills—summit UT-8
Round Hill Sch—school (2) NE-7
Round Hill Sch—school PA-2
Round Hill Sch—school SC-3
Round Hill Sch—school VA-3
Round Hill Sch (historical)—school TN-4
Round Hills Sch—school PA-2
Round Hill Swamp—stream VA-3
Round Hill Tank—reservoir AZ-5
Roundhill Tank—reservoir NM-5
Round Hill Trail—trail CO-8
Round Hole—bay PA-2
Round Hole—lake AR-4
Round Hole—lake MA-1
Round Hole—lake MS-4
Round Hole—lake MO-7
Round Hole—lake WI-6
Roundhole Branch—stream (2) KY-4
Round Hole Branch—stream KY-4
Round Hole Branch—stream TX-5
Round Hole Draw—valley TX-5
Round Hole Lake—lake SC-3
Round Hole Mtn—summit TN-4
Round Holes, The—lake TX-5
Round Hole Spring—spring NV-8
Round Hole Spring—spring TX-5
Round Hollow—valley KY-4
Round Hollow—valley (2) MO-7
Round Hollow Public Access Area—park OK-5
Round House—hist pl MA-1
Roundhouse, The—building MT-8
Roundhouse Branch—stream MS-4
Roundhouse Branch Cutoff—channel MS-4
Round House Canyon—valley NM-5
Roundhouse Creek—stream TX-5
Roundhouse Gulch—valley ID-8
Roundhouse Meadow CA-9
Roundhouse Pool—lake TX-5
Round House Rock—summit KS-7
Roundhouse Rock—summit NE-7
Round Island ME-1
Round Island MA-1
Round Island NY-2
Round Island SD-7
Round Island—gut FL-3
Round Island—island (2) AL-4
Round Island—island (8) AK-9
Round Island—island AR-4
Round Island—island CT-1
Round Island—island (2) FL-3
Round Island—island IN-6
Round Island—island (3) LA-4
Round Island—island (7) ME-1
Round Island—island MD-2
Round Island—island MA-1
Round Island—island (9) MI-6
Round Island—island MN-6
Round Island—island MS-4
Round Island—island NH-1
Round Island—island (4) NY-2
Round Island—island OH-6
Round Island—island PA-2
Round Island—island SC-3
Round Island—island TN-4
Round Island—island WA-9
Round Island—island (2) WI-6
Round Island—summit MA-1
Round Island Baptist Church AL-4
Round Island Branch—stream AL-4
Round Island Cem—cemetery AL-4
Round Island Ch—church AL-4
Round Island Creek—stream AL-4
Round Island Creek Church AL-4
Round Island Creek Public Use Area—park AL-4
Round Island Flats—bar ME-1
Round Island Gut—stream MD-2
Round Island (historical)—island AZ-5
Round Island (historical)—island TN-4
Round Island Lake—lake MN-6
Round Island Lighthouse—hist pl MI-6
Round Island Lighthouse—hist pl MS-4
Round Island Lighthouse—locale MS-4
Round Island Park—park FL-3
Round Island Point—cape MI-6
Round Island Run—stream PA-2
Round Island Run Trail—trail PA-2
Round Islands—area AK-9
Round Islet—island AK-9
Round Key—island (2) FL-3
Round Knob GA-3
**Round Knob**—pop pl IL-6
**Round Knob**—pop pl PA-2
**Round Knob**—pop pl WV-2
Round Knob—summit (3) AL-4
Round Knob—summit CA-9
Round Knob—summit ID-8
Round Knob—summit IL-6
Round Knob—summit IN-6
Round Knob—summit (5) KY-4
Round Knob—summit (2) NC-3
Round Knob—summit OH-6
Round Knob—summit (5) PA-2
Round Knob—summit (4) TN-4
Round Knob—summit (3) VA-3
Round Knob—summit WA-9
Round Knob—summit (4) WV-2
Roundknob—summit WV-2
Round Knob—summit (2) WV-2
Round Knob Branch—stream TN-4
Round Knob Campground—locale TN-4
Round Knob Cem—cemetery IL-6
Round Knob Cem—cemetery WV-2
Round Knob Ch—church NC-3
Round Knob Ch—church (2) VA-3
Round Knob Rec Area TN-4
Round Knob Run—stream WV-2
Roundknob Run—stream WV-2
Round Knob Sch—school WV-2
Round Knob Sch (abandoned)—school PA-2
Round Knoll—summit ID-8
Round Knoll—summit NV-8
Round Knoll—summit (5) UT-8
Round Knoll—summit VT-1
Round Knoll Pond—reservoir UT-8
Round Lake MI-6
Round Lake MN-6
Round Lake NY-2
Round Lake ND-7
Round Lake TN-4
Round Lake UT-8
Round Lake WA-9
Round Lake WI-6
Round Lake—bay LA-4
Round Lake—flat (2) OR-9
Round Lake—lake AL-4
Round Lake—lake (5) AK-9
Round Lake—lake (11) AR-4
Round Lake—lake (3) CA-9
Round Lake—lake (3) CO-8
Round Lake—lake (8) FL-3
Round Lake—lake (5) GA-3
Round Lake—lake (5) ID-8
Round Lake—lake (6) IL-6
Round Lake—lake (10) IN-6
Round Lake—lake (2) IA-7
Round Lake—lake (20) LA-4
Round Lake—lake (2) ME-1
Round Lake—lake (55) MI-6
Round Lake—lake (55) MN-6
Round Lake—lake (16) MS-4
Round Lake—lake (3) MO-7
Round Lake—lake MT-8
Round Lake—lake (5) NE-7
Round Lake—lake (9) NY-2
Round Lake—lake (10) ND-7
Round Lake—lake OH-6
Round Lake—lake OK-5
Round Lake—lake (8) OR-9
Round Lake—lake SC-3
Round Lake—lake (6) SD-7
Round Lake—lake (3) TN-4
Round Lake—lake (15) TX-5
Round Lake—lake (4) UT-8
Round Lake—lake (12) WA-9
Round Lake—lake (41) WI-6
Round Lake—lake (2) WY-8
Round Lake—locale FL-3
**Round Lake**—pop pl IL-6
**Round Lake**—pop pl IN-6
**Round Lake**—pop pl (2) MI-6
**Round Lake**—pop pl MN-6
**Roundlake**—pop pl MS-4
**Round Lake**—pop pl MS-4
**Round Lake**—pop pl NY-2
Round Lake—reservoir CO-8
Round Lake—reservoir FL-3
Round Lake—reservoir (2) ID-8
Round Lake—reservoir IA-7
Round Lake—reservoir MN-6
Round Lake—reservoir TX-5
Round Lake—reservoir UT-8
Round Lake—swamp LA-4
Round Lake—swamp MI-6
Round Lake—swamp MN-6
Round Lake Bayou—gut TX-5
**Round Lake Beach**—pop pl IL-6
Round Lake Campground—locale MI-6
Round Lake Canal—canal LA-4
Round Lake Cem—cemetery MI-6
Round Lake Cem—cemetery MS-4
Round Lake Cem—cemetery OK-5
Round Lake Cem—cemetery WI-6
Round Lake Ch—church IN-6
Round Lake Ch—church MN-6
Round Lake Ch—church OK-5
Round Lake Christian Camp—locale OR-9
Round Lake Country Club—other IL-6
Round Lake Dam IN-6
**Round Lake Heights**—pop pl IL-6
Round Lake Hill—summit OR-9
Round Lake Hills—summit ME-1
Round Lake Hist Dist—hist pl NY-2
Round Lake (historical)—lake IA-7
**Round Lake Junction**—pop pl MI-6
Round Lake Logging Dam—hist pl WI-6
Round Lake Outlet—stream NY-2
Round Lake Outlet Control Dam—dam ND-7
**Round Lake Park**—pop pl IL-6
Round Lake Recreation Site—park OR-9
Round Lake Sch—school MI-6
Round Lake Sch—school WI-6
Round Lake School—locale MI-6
Round Lake Springs—spring UT-8
Round Lake State Game Mngmt Area—park IA-7
Round Lake State Park—park ID-8
Round Lake State Wildlife Mngmt Area—park IA-7
Round Lake State Wildlife Mngmt Area—park SD-7
**Round Lake (Town of)**—pop pl WI-6
**Round Lake Township**—pop pl ND-7
**Round Lake (Township of)**—pop pl (2) MN-6
Round Lake Trail—trail (2) OR-9
Roundland Lake WI-6
Round Lick Acad (historical)—school TN-4
Round Lick Creek—stream TN-4
Round Meadow—flat (5) CA-9
Round Meadow—flat (2) ID-8
Round Meadow—flat (2) MT-8
Round Meadow—flat NV-8
Round Meadow—flat (6) OR-9
Round Meadow—flat UT-8
Round Meadow—flat WA-9
Round Meadow—flat WY-8
Round Meadow—summit CA-9
Round Meadow—swamp CT-1
Round Meadow—swamp (2) OR-9
Round Meadow Branch—stream KY-4
Round Meadow Brook—stream MA-1
Round Meadow Canyon—valley NV-8
Round Meadow Community Club—cliff WI-6
Round Meadow Country Club—other VA-3
Round Meadow Creek—stream CO-8
Round Meadow Creek—stream ID-8
Round Meadow Creek—stream VA-3
Round Meadow Elem Sch PA-2
Round Meadow Overlook—locale VA-3
Round Meadow Pond—reservoir MA-1
Round Meadow Pond Dam—dam MA-1
Round Meadow Run—stream PA-2
Round Meadows—flat CA-9
Round Meadows—flat ID-8
Round Meadows—flat OR-9
Round Meadow Spring—spring OR-9
Round Meadow Trail—trail OR-9
Round Mesa CO-8
Round Mesa—summit NM-5
Round Mott—locale TX-5
Round Mound—pillar (2) KS-7
Round Mound—summit CO-8

Roup Ranch—*locale* NV-8
Roup Run—*stream* PA-2
*Roups Run* PA-2
Roup Station—*locale* PA-2
*Roups Valley* AL-4
Rourke, Eugene, House—*hist pl* CO-8
Rourke Canyon—*valley* CO-8
Rourke Ranch—*locale* CO-8
Rourke Rsvr—*reservoir* CO-8
Rourke Rsvr—*reservoir* WY-8
Rourkes Gap—*gap* VA-3
**Rourkes Gap**—*pop pl* VA-3
Rourks Ch—*church* NC-3
*Rourks Cove* TN-4
Rousa Bridge—*bridge* OR-9
Rousch Ditch—*canal* IN-6
Rousch Drain—*canal* MI-6
Rouschelback Cem—*cemetery* MO 7
Rousch Ranch—*locale* MT-8
**Rousculp**—*pop pl* OH-6
Rousculp Ch—*church* OH-6
Rouse—*locale* CO-8
Rouse—*locale* ID-8
Rouse—*locale* SC-3
Rouse—*locale* WI-6
**Rouse**—*pop pl* MS-4
Rouse—*uninc pl* KY-4
Rouse, Lake—*lake* FL-3
Rouse Branch—*stream* KY-4
Rouse Branch—*stream* TX-5
Rouse Bridge—*bridge* MS-4
Rouse Camp—*locale* NM-5
Rouse Canyon—*valley* (2) NM-5
Rouse Cem—*cemetery* AL-4
Rouse Cem—*cemetery* FL-3
Rouse Cem—*cemetery* IA-7
Rouse Cem—*cemetery* KY-4
Rouse Cem—*cemetery* MS-4
Rouse Cem—*cemetery* MO-7
Rouse Cem—*cemetery* NY-2
Rouse Chapel—*church* NC-3
Rouse Creek—*stream* AR-4
Rouse Creek—*stream* OR-9
Rouse Creek—*stream* WI-6
Rouse Drain—*canal* MI-6
Rouse Field Cem—*cemetery* MS-4
Rouse Flat—*area* CA-9
Rouse Gardens—*flat* CA-9
Rouse Hill—*summit* CA-9
Rouse Hill-Bautista Canyon Trail—*trail* CA-9
*Rouse Hollow* TN-4
Rouse Hollow—*valley* MO-7
Rouse Hollow—*valley* TN-4
Rouse House—*hist pl* MT-8
Rouse Meadow—*flat* CA-9
Rouse Mine—*mine* CO-8
Rousensock Canyon—*valley* AZ-5
*Rousensock Creek* AZ-5
Rousensock Creek—*stream* AZ-5
Rouse Place—*locale* NM-5
*Rouse Point* NY-2
Rouse Pond—*lake* PA-2
Rouse Pond—*reservoir* NC-3
Rouse Prospect—*mine* TN-4
Rouser House—*hist pl* TX-5
Rouse Ridge—*ridge* CA-9
Rouse Rsvr—*reservoir* WY-8
**Rousertown**—*pop pl* MO-7
*Rouses Bridge* MS-4
Rouses Cem—*cemetery* NY-2
Rouse Sch—*school* MI-6
Rouses Chapel—*church* NC-3
**Rouses Point**—*pop pl* NY-2
Rouses Point Bridge—*bridge* NY-2
Rouses Point Bridge—*bridge* VT-1
Rouse Spring—*spring* CO-8
Rouse Spring—*spring* NM-5
**Rouse Township**—*pop pl* SD-7
**Rouseville**—*pop pl* PA-2
Rouseville Borough—*civil* PA-2
Rouse Well—*well* NM-5
Roush Cem—*cemetery* IA-7
Roush Cem—*cemetery* OH-6
Roush Creek—*stream* CA-9
Roush Creek—*stream* ID-8
Roush Creek—*stream* WA-9
Roush Creek—*stream* WY-8
Roush Ditch—*canal* IN-6
Roush Draw—*valley* CO-8
Roush Ranch—*locale* AZ-5
Roush Run—*stream* OH-6
Roush Sch—*school* CO-8
Roush Well No 2—*well* WY-8
Roushy Cem—*cemetery* NY-2
Rousons Gin (historical)—*locale* AL-4
Rousseau—*locale* KY-4
Rousseau—*locale* LA-4
Rousseau—*locale* MI-6
Rousseau—*locale* SD-7
Rousseau, Lake—*reservoir* FL-3
Rousseau Cave—*cave* AL-4
Rousseau (CCD)—*cens area* KY-4
Rousseau Cem—*cemetery* (2) AL-4
Rousseau Cem—*cemetery* SD-7
*Rousseau Creek* SD-7
Rousseau Creek—*stream* GA-3
Rousseau Creek—*stream* SD-7
Rousseau (historical P.O.)—*locale* IA-7
Rousseau Hollow—*valley* AL-4
*Rousseau Hollow Pit* AL-4
Rousseau McClellan Elem Sch—*school* IN-6
Rousseau Pioneer Cem—*cemetery* FL-3
Rousseau Range—*range* AK-9
Rousseau Recreation and Overlook Area—*park* SD-7
Rousseau Sch—*school* NE-7
Rousseau Sch—*school* SD-7
Rousseau Station and Post Office (historical)—*building* SD-7
Rousseau Township—*civil* SD-7
Rousseau Well Cave—*cave* AL-4
Rousseaux Cem—*cemetery* LA-4
Rousse Key—*island* FL-3
Rousselle Sch—*school* MT-8
Roussin Sch—*school* ND-7
Rouss Spring—*spring* VA-3
Roustabout Camp—*locale* TX-5
Roust Cem—*cemetery* TN-4
Routan Creek—*stream* CA-9
Route Creek—*stream* MT-8
Route Creek—*stream* WA-9
Route Creek Pass—*gap* MT-8
Routen Store (historical)—*building* MS-4
Route of Butterfield Stage—*trail* AZ-5
Route Of California Trail—*trail* NV-8
Route of Donner-Reed Party and Mormon Pioneers—*trail* UT-8
Route of Elko-Hamilton Stage Lines—*trail* NV-8
*Route of Pony Express* NV-8
Route of Pony Express—*trail* UT-8
Route Sixtysix Grotto—*cave* AL-4
Route 100 Shoppes—*locale* PA-2
Route 106 At Robbins Reservoir Dam—*dam* MA-1
Route 128-38 Shop Ctr—*locale* MA-1
Route 22 Cave—*cave* PA-2
Route 30 Mall *locale* MA-1
Route 327 Ch—*church* OH-6
Route 6 Plaza—*locale* (2) PA-2
Routh Bayou—*gut* LA-4
Routh Cem—*cemetery* MS-4
Routh Cem—*cemetery* (2) TX-5
Routh Chapel—*church* MO-7
Routh Creek—*stream* LA-4
Routh Ditch—*canal* LA-4
Routherford Branch—*stream* IA-7
Rout Hill—*summit* AR-4
Routhland—*hist pl* MS-4
Rout Hollow—*valley* AR-4
Routh Point—*cape* LA-4
Routhwood Cem—*cemetery* LA-4
**Routier**—*pop pl* CA-9
Routley Creek—*stream* MI-6
**Routon**—*pop pl* LA-4
**Routon**—*pop pl* TN-4
Routon Hollow—*valley* MO-7
Routon Post Office (historical)—*building* TN-4
Routon Sch (abandoned)—*school* MO-7
Routons Crossroads—*locale* GA-3
Routson County Park—*park* OR-9
Routson Creek—*stream* ID-8
Routt—*locale* KY-4
**Routt**—*pop pl* CO-8
Routt, J. R., House—*hist pl* TX-5
Routt Branch—*stream* TN-4
Routt Creek—*stream* MT-8
Routt Gulch—*valley* CO-8
Routt Hill Ch—*church* TX-5
Routt Natl For—*forest* CO-8
Routt Point Cem—*cemetery* TX-5
Routt Point Ch—*church* TX-5
Routt Sch—*school* IL-6
Routt Sch—*school* TX-5
Routzhan Park—*park* CA-9
Rouvideau Trail—*trail* CO-8
*Roux Creek* OR-9
**Roux Quarters**—*pop pl* FL-3
Rouzer—*locale* WV-2
**Rouzerville**—*pop pl* PA-2
Rouzie Chapel—*church* VA-3
Rouzie Swamp—*stream* VA-3
**Rovana**—*pop pl* CA-9
*Rove Lake* MN-6
Rove Lake—*lake* MN-6
Rover—*locale* ID-8
Rover—*locale* MO-7
Rover—*locale* NC-3
Rover—*locale* WV-2
**Rover**—*pop pl* AR-4
**Rover**—*pop pl* GA-3
**Rover**—*pop pl* TN-4
Rover, Hanna, House—*hist pl* WA-9
Rover Airp—*airport* PA-2
Rover Baptist Ch—*church* TN-4
Rover Branch—*stream* MO-7
Rover Branch—*stream* WV-2
Rover Cave—*cave* AL-4
Rover Ch—*church* NC-3
Rover Creek—*stream* AK-9
Rover Creek—*stream* ID-8
Rover Creek—*stream* OR-9
Roveres Lake—*lake* NJ-2
Rover Hill—*summit* UT-8
Rover (historical)—*locale* AL-4
Rover Island—*island* MI-6
ROVER (log canoe)—*hist pl* MD-2
Rover Mine—*mine* MT-8
Rover Oil Field—*oilfield* OK-5
Rover Peak—*summit* AZ-5
Rover Post Office (historical)—*building* TN-4
Rovers Branch—*stream* AL-4
Rover Sch—*school* AZ-5
Rover (Township of)—*fmr MCD* AR-4
Rovey Cem—*cemetery* IL-6
Rovey Park—*park* AZ-5
Roving House—*hist pl* GA-3
Roving Volunteers in Christ Service—*church* FL-3
**Rovohl Township**—*pop pl* KS-7
Row—*locale* OK-5
Rowallan—*hist pl* FL-3
*Rowan* MS-4
*Rowan* NC-3
Rowan—*locale* WA-9
**Rowan**—*pop pl* IA-7
**Rowan**—*pop pl* NC-3
Rowan, Lake—*lake* FL-3
Rowan Ave Sch—*school* CA-9
Rowan Bay—*bay* AK-9
Rowan Branch—*stream* KY-4
Rowan Branch—*stream* (2) NC-3
Rowan Cem—*cemetery* MS-4
Rowan Cem—*cemetery* TX-5
Rowan Ch—*church* NC-3
Rowan Ch—*church* SC-3
**Rowan Corners**—*pop pl* NY-2
Rowan Correction Center—*locale* NC-3
*Rowan County* NC-3
**Rowan (County)**—*pop pl* KY-4
**Rowan County**—*pop pl* NC-3
Rowan County Airp—*airport* NC-3
Rowan County Courthouse—*hist pl* KY-4
Rowan County Wildlife Lake—*reservoir* NC-3
Rowan County Wildlife Lake Dam—*dam* NC-3
Rowan Creek—*stream* KY-4
Rowan Creek—*stream* NC-3
Rowan Creek—*stream* TX-5
Rowan Creek—*stream* WI-6
Rowan Ditch—*canal* IN-6
Rowand Lake—*lake* NJ-2
Rowan Hill—*summit* GA-3
Rowan Hope Oil Field—*oilfield* TX-5
Rowan HS—*school* MS-4
Rowan JHS—*school* MS-4
Rowan Lake—*lake* NJ-2
Rowan Lake Dam—*dam* MS-4
Rowan Mall—*locale* NC-3
Rowan Memorial Home Cem—*cemetery* WV-2
Rowan Memorial Hosp—*hospital* NC-3
Rowan Memorial Park Cem—*cemetery* NC-3
**Rowan Mill**—*pop pl* NC-3
**Rowan Mills**—*pop pl* NC-3
**Rowan Mills (historical)**—*pop pl* NC-3
Rowan Museum—*building* NC-3
Rowan Oil Field—*oilfield* TX-5
Rowan Park—*park* IL-6
*Rowan Run* VA-3
Rowan Run—*stream* VA-3
Rowan Sch—*school* CA-9
Rowans Creek—*stream* TN-4
Rowan Spring—*spring* AL-4
Rowan Spring—*stream* WY-8
Rowan Swamp—*swamp* NC-3
**Rowanta**—*pop pl* VA-3
Rowanta Ch—*church* VA-3
Rowan Technical Coll—*school* NC-3
**Rowan Terrace (subdivision)**—*pop pl* NC-3
Rowanty Creek—*stream* VA-3
Rowanty (Magisterial District)—*fmr MCD* VA-3
Rowardale Sch (historical)—*school* MS-4
*Roward Cove School* TN-4
*Rowark Cove* TN-4
Rowark Ranch (reduced usage)—*locale* TX-5
*Rowarks Cove* TN-4
Rowaruerii Channel—*channel* FM-9
Rowaryu Channel—*channel* FM-9
*Rowayton* CT-1
**Rowayton**—*pop pl* CT-1
Rowayton Station—*locale* CT-1
Rowback Mtn—*summit* MT-8
Row Bench—*bench* UT-8
Row Bend—*bend* KY-4
Rowbotham Dam—*dam* SD-7
Row Branch—*stream* NC-3
Row Branch—*stream* TN-4
*Row Brook* MA-1
Row Cem—*cemetery* OK-5
Rowcroft Ranch—*locale* CA-9
*Rowdells Knob* GA-3
Rowden—*locale* TX-5
**Rowden**—*pop pl* TX-5
Rowden Branch—*stream* TN-4
Rowdon Sch—*school* WI-6
*Rowdy* KY-4
Rowdy Bar Creek—*stream* CA-9
Rowdy Bend Towhead—*area* AR-4
Rowdy Branch—*stream* KY-4
Rowdy Creek—*stream* CA-9
Rowdy Creek—*stream* (2) OR-9
Rowdy Creek—*stream* TN-4
Rowdy Creek—*stream* TX-5
Rowdy Creek—*stream* WY-8
Rowdy Mtn—*summit* AR-4
Rowdy Ridge—*ridge* TN-4
**Rowdy (Stacy)**—*pop pl* KY-4
*Rowe* OR-9
Rowe—*locale* VA-3
**Rowe**—*pop pl* IL-6
**Rowe**—*pop pl* KY-4
**Rowe**—*pop pl* MA-1
**Rowe**—*pop pl* NM-5
**Rowe**—*pop pl* WA-9
Rowe, John, House—*hist pl* MN-6
Rowe, Mount—*summit* MT-8
Rowe, Mount—*summit* NH-1
Rowe, Nicholas, House—*hist pl* UT-8
Rowe,The—*hist pl* VA-3
Rowe and Weed Houses—*hist pl* CT-1
Rowe Bayou—*gut* MT-8
Rowe Bench—*bench* MT-8
Rowe Branch—*stream* KY-4
Rowe Branch—*stream* MO-7
Rowe Branch—*stream* TN-4
Rowe Branch—*stream* TX-5
Rowe Branch Elk River—*stream* KS-7
Rowe Brook—*stream* (?) ME-1
Rowe Brothers Rsvr—*reservoir* CO-8
Rowe Camp—*locale* MA-1
Rowe Cem—*cemetery* (3) AL-4
Rowe Cem—*cemetery* IL-6
Rowe Cem—*cemetery* (3) IN-6
Rowe Cem—*cemetery* ME-1
Rowe Cem—*cemetery* MI-6
Rowe Cem—*cemetery* (3) MO-7
Rowe Cem—*cemetery* NC-3
Rowe Cem—*cemetery* (2) OH-6
Rowe Cem—*cemetery* (3) TN-4
Rowe Cem—*cemetery* (2) TX-5
Rowe Cem—*cemetery* (3) WV-2
Rowe Ch—*church* NY-2
Rowe Ch—*church* PA-2
Rowe Corner—*locale* ME-1
**Rowe Corner**—*pop pl* ME-1
*Rowe Corners* ME-1
Rowe Coulee—*valley* MT-8
Rowe Cove—*bay* ME-1
Rowe Creative Arts Bldg—*building* NC-3
Rowe Creek—*stream* AR-4
Rowe Creek—*stream* ID-8
Rowe Creek—*stream* MT-8
Rowe Creek—*stream* NV-8
Rowe Creek—*stream* OR-9
Rowe Creek—*stream* TN-4
Rowe Creek Dam—*dam* OR-9
Rowe Creek Rsvr—*reservoir* OR-9
Rowe Crossroads—*locale* VA-3
*Rowe Ditch* IN-6
Rowe Ditch—*canal* (2) IN-6
Rowe Ditch—*canal* WY-8
Rowe Drain—*canal* MI-6
Rowe-Eden Ditch—*canal* IN-6
Rowe Fork—*stream* VA-3
Rowe Gap—*gap* TN-4
Rowe Gap Cave—*cave* TN-4
Rowe Gap Ch—*church* TN-4
Rowe Glacier—*glacier* CO-8
*Rowe Gulch* MT-8
Rowe Hill—*summit* (3) ME-1
Rowe Hill—*summit* NM-5
Rowe Hill—*summit* PA-2
Rowe Hill—*summit* VT-1
Rowe Hill Cem—*cemetery* ME-1
**Rowe Hills Condominium**—*pop pl* UT-8
Rowe Hollow—*valley* AR-4
Rowe Hollow—*valley* KY-4
Rowe House—*hist pl* MI-6
Rowe Island—*island* AK-9
Rowe Island—*island* MI-6
Rowe Kamp Sch—*school* MT-8
Rowe Lake—*lake* ME-1
Rowe Lake—*lake* (2) MI-6
Rowe Lake—*reservoir* TN-4
Rowe Lake Dam—*dam* TN-4
Rowel Branch—*stream* NC-3
Rowel Canyon—*valley* WA-9
Rowell—*locale* AR-4
Rowell—*locale* IL-6
Rowell—*locale* SC-3
Rowell, Lake—*lake* FL-3
Rowel Lake—*lake* WA-9
Rowell Bog—*swamp* ME-1
Rowell Branch—*stream* AL-4
Rowell Brook—*stream* ME-1
Rowell Brook—*stream* NH-1
Rowell Brook—*stream* NY-2
Rowell Brook—*stream* VT-1
Rowell Cem—*cemetery* (2) AL-4
Rowell Cem—*cemetery* GA-3
Rowell Cem—*cemetery* OH-6
Rowell Cove—*bay* ME-1
Rowell Creek—*stream* FL-3
Rowell Creek—*stream* (2) OR-9
Rowell Creek—*stream* SC-3
Rowell Gulch—*valley* CO-8
Rowell Hill—*summit* CO-8
Rowell Hill—*summit* (2) ME-1
Rowell Hill—*summit* (2) NH-1
Rowell Hill—*summit* NY-2
Rowell Hill—*summit* VT-1
Rowell House—*hist pl* MA-1
Rowell Lake—*lake* NE-7
Rowell Lake Dam—*dam* MS-4
Rowell Meadow—*flat* CA-9
Rowell Mtn—*summit* ME-1
Rowell Pond—*lake* ME-1
Rowell Ranch—*locale* NM-5
Rowell Run—*stream* OH-6
Rowells Brook—*stream* NH-1
Rowells Cem—*cemetery* AL-4
Rowell Sch—*school* CA-9
Rowell's Covered Bridge—*hist pl* NH-1
*Rowells Cross Road* AL-4
**Rowells Crossroad**—*pop pl* AL-4
*Rowells Cross Roads* AL-4
Rowells Crossroads—*locale* AL-4
Rowells Island—*island* GA-3
Rowell Spring—*spring* AL-4
Rowell (Township of)—*fmr MCD* AR-4
Rowe Lot Hill—*summit* MA-1
Rowe Mine—*mine* MN-6
Rowe Mine (underground)—*mine* AL-4
*Rowe Mountain* AL-4
Rowe Mtn—*summit* CO-8
Rowe Mtn—*summit* VA-3
Rowen—*locale* CA-9
Rowen, William, Sch—*hist pl* PA-2
Rowena—*locale* GA-3
Rowena—*locale* KY-4
Rowena—*locale* MN-6
Rowena—*other* PA-2
**Rowena**—*pop pl* CO-8
**Rowena**—*pop pl* MO-7
**Rowena**—*pop pl* OR-9
**Rowena**—*pop pl* PA-2
**Rowena**—*pop pl* SD-7
**Rowena**—*pop pl* TX-5
Rowena, Lake—*lake* AK-9
Rowena, Lake—*lake* FL-3
Rowena, Lake—*lake* WA-9
Rowena, Lake—*reservoir* PA-2
Rowena (CCD)—*cens area* TX-5
Rowena Creek—*stream* OR-9
Rowena Crest—*ridge* OR-9
Rowena Dell—*valley* OR-9
Rowena Dell Airstrip—*airport* OR-9
Rowena Gap *gap* OR 9
Rowena Gap—*gap* WA-9
Rowena Kyle Elem Sch—*school* IN-6
*Rowena Lake* WA-9
Rowena Lookout Tower—*locale* GA-3
Rowena Oil Field—*oilfield* TX-5
Rowen Bayou—*gut* MS-4
**Rowenna**—*pop pl* PA-2
Rowen Sch—*school* PA-2
Rowen Sch—*school* SD-7
Rowenton—*locale* OH-6
Rowe Peak—*summit* CO-8
Rowe Peak—*summit* NM-5
Rowe Point—*cape* MA-1
Rowe Pond—*lake* (2) ME-1
Rowe Rsvr—*reservoir* CO-8
Rowe Run—*stream* PA-2
*Rowes* AL-4
*Rowes* AZ-5
Rowes Bayou—*stream* LA-4
Rowe Sch—*school* IL-6
Rowe Sch—*school* KS-7
Rowe Sch—*school* MA-1
Rowe Sch—*school* MI-6
Rowe Sch—*school* NV-8
Rowe Sch—*school* OH-6
Rowe Sch—*school* SC-3
Rowe Sch—*school* TN-4
Rowe Sch—*school* WI-6
Rowes Chapel—*church* AR-4
Rowe Sch (historical)—*school* TN-4
Rowe School—*locale* MI-6
*Rowes Corner* ME-1
Rowes Corner—*locale* MI-6
Rowes Corner—*locale* NC-3
**Rowes Corner**—*pop pl* (2) NH-1
Rowes Creek—*stream* CA-9
Rowes Creek—*stream* VA-3
Rowes Ferry (historical)—*locale* AL-4
Rowes Hill—*summit* NH-1
Rowes Hole Channel—*channel* VA-3
Rowes Landing—*locale* LA-4
Rowes Landing—*locale* VA-3
Rowes Mine (underground)—*mine* AL-4
*Rowes Mountain* AL-4
*Rowes Point* AZ-5
Rowes Point—*cape* VA-3
Rowe Spring—*spring* CO-8
Rowe Spring—*spring* TN-4
**Rowes Run**—*pop pl* PA-2
Rowes Run—*stream* PA-2
*Rowes Station* AZ-5
Rowes Tank—*reservoir* AZ-5
**Rowe Street**—*pop pl* NJ-2
Rowe Street Station—*locale* NJ-2
*Rowesville* TN-4
**Rowesville**—*pop pl* SC-3
Rowesville Bridge—*bridge* SC-3
Rowesville United Methodist Ch—*church* TN-4
Rowes Well—*well* AZ-5
Rowes Wharf—*locale* MA-1
Rowetown Cem—*cemetery* KY-4
Rowe Town Ch—*church* GA-3
**Rowe (Town of)**—*pop pl* MA-1
Rowetown Sch—*school* KY-4
**Rowe Township**—*pop pl* SD-7
Rowe Wash—*stream* AZ-5
Rowe Well Picnic Area—*park* AZ-5
Rowe Williams Canyon—*valley* OR-9
Row Gulch—*valley* OR-9
Rowher Canyon—*valley* CA-9
Rowher Gulch—*valley* NV-8
Row Hollow—*valley* UT-8
Row House—*hist pl* ME-1
Row House Buildings (Boundry Increase)—*hist pl* MO-7
Rowhouses at 256-274 Haven Street—*hist pl* MA-1
Rowhouses at 303-327 East North Ave—*hist pl* MD-2
Rowhouses at 322-344 East 69th Street—*hist pl* NY-2
Rowhouses at 702-712 Kirkwood Blvd—*hist pl* IA-7
Rowin Branch—*stream* MS-4
Rowing Bayou—*stream* LA-4
*Rowing Lake* WA-9
Rowing Lake—*lake* AR-4
*Rowing Run* VA-3
*Rowin Lake* AR-4
Row Lake—*lake* MT-8
Row Lakes—*lake* UT-8
*Rowland* GA-3
*Rowland* TX-5
Rowland—*locale* CA-9
Rowland—*locale* GA-3
Rowland—*locale* OR-9
Rowland—*locale* PA-2
Rowland—*locale* TN-4
Rowland—*locale* TX-5
**Rowland**—*pop pl* KY-4
**Rowland**—*pop pl* MN-6
**Rowland**—*pop pl* NV-8
**Rowland**—*pop pl* NC-3
**Rowland**—*pop pl* PA-2
**Rowland**—*pop pl* TN-4
**Rowland**—*pop pl* WV-2
Rowland—*uninc pl* KY-4
Rowland, Henry August, House—*hist pl* MD-2
Rowland, John A., House—*hist pl* CA-9
Rowland, Lake—*lake* WA-9
Rowland Ave Sch—*school* CA-9
Rowland Bend—*bend* TN-4
Rowland Branch—*stream* KY-4
Rowland Branch—*stream* (2) MS-4
Rowland Branch—*stream* NC-3
Rowland Canal—*canal* FL-3
Rowland Cave—*cave* AR-4
*Rowland Cem* MS-4
Rowland Cem—*cemetery* AL-4
Rowland Cem—*cemetery* GA-3
Rowland Cem—*cemetery* IN-6
Rowland Cem—*cemetery* (2) KY-4
Rowland Cem—*cemetery* MS-4
Rowland Cem—*cemetery* MO-7
Rowland Cem—*cemetery* NC-3
Rowland Cem—*cemetery* (2) OH-6
Rowland Cem—*cemetery* (2) TN-4
Rowland Cem—*cemetery* VA-3
Rowland Chapel—*church* GA-3
*Rowland Church* PA-2
Rowland Creek—*stream* CA-9
Rowland Creek—*stream* NC-3
Rowland Creek—*stream* OK-5
Rowland Creek—*stream* (2) OR-9
Rowland Creek—*stream* TN-4
Rowland Creek—*stream* VA-3
Rowland Creek Cem—*cemetery* VA-3
Rowland Creek Ch—*church* VA-3
Rowland Grove Sch—*school* GA-3
Rowland Hall Sch—*school* UT-8
Rowland Hall-St. Mark's Sch—*hist pl* UT-8
**Rowland Heights**—*pop pl* CA-9
Rowland Hollow—*valley* TN-4
Rowland Hollow Creek—*stream* NY-2
Rowland House—*hist pl* PA-2
Rowland HS—*school* CA-9
Rowland Island—*island* (2) MD-2
Rowland Lake—*lake* WA-9
Rowland Lake Dam Number One—*dam* NC-3
Rowland Lake Number One—*reservoir* NC-3
Rowland Mill Ch—*church* MS-4
Rowland Mills—*locale* NJ-2
Rowland Mills Cem—*cemetery* MS-4
Rowland Mills Sch (historical)—*school* MS-4
Rowland MS—*school* NC-3
Rowland Mtn—*summit* NV-8
Rowland Norment Sch—*school* NC-3
**Rowland Park**—*pop pl* PA-2
Rowland Picnic Area—*area* PA-2
Rowland Point—*cape* NC-3
Rowland Pond Dam—*dam* NC-3
*Rowland Post Office* AL-4
Rowland Post Office (historical)—*building* TN-4
Rowland Prairie—*area* OR-9
Rowland Row Camp—*locale* KY-4
Rowlands—*locale* MS-4
Rowland Sch—*school* CA-9
Rowland Sch—*school* IL-6
Rowland Sch—*school* OH-6
Rowland Sch—*school* PA-2
Rowland Sch (abandoned)—*school* MO-7
Rowland Sch for Young Children—*school* PA-2
*Rowlands Island* ME-1
Rowland Site—*hist pl* MS-4
*Rowlands Mills* NJ-2
Rowlands Pond—*reservoir* NC-3
Rowland Spring—*locale* GA-3
Rowland Spring—*spring* NV-8
Rowland Spring—*spring* WA-9
Rowland Spring Creek—*stream* GA-3
*Rowland Station* TN-4
**Rowland Station**—*pop pl* TN-4
Rowlands Towhead—*bar* TN-4
**Rowlandsville**—*pop pl* MD-2
Rowland Swamp—*swamp* PA-2
Rowland Tank—*reservoir* TX-5
Rowland Theater—*hist pl* PA-2
**Rowlandtown**—*pop pl* KY-4
Rowland (Township of)—*fmr MCD* NC-3
*Rowland Wilkinson Cemetery* MS-4
Rowlan Tank—*reservoir* AZ-5
Rowledge Pond—*lake* CT-1
Rowlee Point—*cape* AK-9
Rowlee Sch—*school* MI-6
Rowles—*locale* (2) PA-2
Rowles, Donaldson, House—*hist pl* ID-8
*Rowles Bay* WA-9
**Rowlesburg**—*pop pl* WV-2
Rowles Run—*stream* WV-2
Rowles Run Sch—*school* WV-2
Rowles Station—*locale* PA-2
Rowlesville—*locale* OH-6
**Rowlett**—*pop pl* TX-5
Rowlett Branch—*stream* TN-4
Rowlett Cem—*cemetery* TN-4
Rowlett Cem—*cemetery* TX-5
Rowlett Ch—*church* TX-5
Rowlett Creek—*stream* TX-5
Rowlett Creek Ch—*church* TX-5
*Rowlette* TX-5
Rowlette Branch—*stream* KY-4
Rowlett Hollow—*valley* AR-4
Rowlett House—*hist pl* KY-4
Rowlett Park—*park* FL-3
**Rowletts**—*pop pl* KY-4
Rowletts Creek—*stream* FL-3
Rowlett's Grocery—*hist pl* KY-4
Rowley—*locale* MT-8
Rowley—*locale* UT-8
**Rowley**—*pop pl* IA-7
**Rowley**—*pop pl* MA-1
Rowley Bay—*bay* MD-2
Rowley Bay—*bay* WI-6
Rowley Bridge—*bridge* MA-1
Rowley Burial Ground—*cemetery* MA-1
Rowley Cabin Spring—*spring* OR-9
Rowley Canyon—*valley* CA-9
Rowley Canyon—*valley* (2) ID-8
Rowley Cem—*cemetery* PA-2
Rowley (census name for Rowley Center)—*CDP* MA-1
Rowley Center (census name Rowley)—*other* MA-1
Rowley Ch—*church* MI-6
Rowley Cove—*bay* MD-2
Rowley Creek—*stream* ID-8
Rowley Creek—*stream* MD-2
Rowley Creek—*stream* WI-6
Rowley Flat—*flat* UT-8
Rowley Gulch—*valley* OR-9
Rowley Hill—*summit* MA-1
Rowley Hill—*summit* PA-2
Rowley Hill Cem—*cemetery* IA-7
Rowley (historical P.O.)—*locale* MA-1
*Rowley Junction* UT-8
Rowley Mine—*mine* OR-9
Rowley Mound—*summit* OH-6
Rowley Park—*park* CA-9
Rowley Pond—*lake* CT-1
Rowley Ranch—*locale* ID-8
Rowley River—*stream* MA-1
Rowley Run—*stream* OH-6
*Rowleys Bay* WI-6
**Rowleys Bay**—*pop pl* WI-6
Rowley Sch—*school* LA-4
Rowley Sch (historical)—*school* PA-2
Rowleys Mine—*mine* UT-8
**Rowleys Trailer Park**—*pop pl* UT-8
**Rowley (Town of)**—*pop pl* MA-1
*Rowley Village* MA-1
Rowlin Creek—*stream* NC-3
Rowling Hill—*summit* TN-4
Rowlin Sch—*school* NC-3
Rownd, C. A., Round Barn—*hist pl* IA-7
Row of Pines Bench—*bench* UT-8
Rowood—*locale* AZ-5
*Row River* OR-9
Row River—*stream* OR-9
**Row River (historical)**—*pop pl* OR-9
R O W Rsvr—*reservoir* WY-8
*Row Run* PA-2
*Rows Branch* AL-4
**Rowsburg**—*pop pl* OH-6
Rowser Lake—*lake* SC-3
Rowsey Creek—*stream* MS-4
Rowski Creek—*stream* CA-9
*Rowston Chapel* MS-4
**Rowtown**—*pop pl* PA-2
Row Water Canyon—*valley* AZ-5
Row Water Spring—*spring* AZ-5
**Rox**—*pop pl* NV-8
*Roxabel* OH-6
**Roxabell**—*pop pl* OH-6
Roxalana—*locale* WV-2
**Roxalana**—*pop pl* WV-2
Roxalana Sch—*school* WV-2
Roxalia—*locale* WV-2
*Roxana* GA-3
Roxana—*locale* AL-4
Roxana—*locale* DE-2
Roxana—*locale* OK-5
**Roxana**—*pop pl* (2) AL-4
**Roxana**—*pop pl* IL-6
**Roxana**—*pop pl* KY-4
**Roxana**—*pop pl* LA-4
*Roxana Branch* DE-2
Roxana Cem—*cemetery* AL-4
Roxana Ch—*church* AL-4
*Roxana Crossroads* GA-3
*Roxana Methodist Ch* AL-4
Roxana Methodist Ch—*church* DE-2
Roxana Park Sch—*school* MI-6
Roxana Sch (historical)—*school* (2) AL-4

**Roxana (subdivision)**—*pop pl* ... NC-3
Roxana Wesleyan Ch—*church* ... DE-2
Roxand Center Sch—*school* ... MI-6
**Roxand (Township of)**—*pop pl* ... MI-6
*Roxanna* ... GA-3
Roxanna—*locale* ... OH-6
**Roxanna**—*pop pl* ... GA-3
Roxanna Cem—*cemetery* ... AL-4
Roxanna Cem—*cemetery* ... OH-6
*Roxanna Ch* ... AL-4
Roxanna Ch—*church* (3) ... AL-4
*Roxboro* ... PA-2
Roxboro—*locale* ... WA-9
**Roxboro**—*pop pl* ... NC-3
Roxboro—*uninc pl* ... MD-2
Roxboro City Lake—*reservoir* ... NC-3
Roxboro Commercial Hist Dist—*hist pl* ... NC-3
Roxboro Country Club Lake—*reservoir* ... NC-3
Roxboro Country Club Lake Dam—*dam* ... NC-3
Roxboro JHS—*school* ... OH-6
Roxboro Lake—*reservoir* ... NC-3
Roxboro Male Acad and Methodist Parsonage—*hist pl* ... NC-3
Roxboro Municipal Lake Dam—*dam* ... NC-3
Roxboro Plaza (Shop Ctr)—*locale* ... NC-3
Roxboro Road Sch—*school* ... NY-2
Roxboro (Township of)—*fmr MCD* ... NC-3
**Roxborough**—*pop pl* ... PA-2
**Roxborough**—*pop pl* ... UT-8
Roxborough Cem—*cemetery* ... PA-2
Roxborough Park—*flat* ... CO-8
Roxborough State Park Archaeol District—*hist pl* ... CO-8
*Roxbory* ... PA-2
*Roxburg* ... PA-2
**Roxburg**—*pop pl* ... NJ-2
*Roxburgh* ... NJ-2
Roxburg Station—*locale* ... NJ-2
*Roxbury* ... CT-1
*Roxbury* ... MD-2
Roxbury—*hist pl* ... VA-3
Roxbury—*locale* ... IL-6
Roxbury—*locale* ... MD-2
Roxbury—*locale* ... OH-6
Roxbury—*locale* ... VA-3
**Roxbury**—*pop pl* ... CT-1
**Roxbury**—*pop pl* ... KS-7
**Roxbury**—*pop pl* ... ME-1
**Roxbury**—*pop pl* (2) ... NY-2
**Roxbury**—*pop pl* (4) ... PA-2
**Roxbury**—*pop pl* ... VT-1
**Roxbury**—*pop pl* ... VA-3
**Roxbury**—*pop pl* ... WI-6
Roxbury Brook—*stream* ... CT-1
*Roxbury Canada* ... MA-1
*Roxbury Canada Plantation* ... MA-1
Roxbury Cem—*cemetery* ... WI-6
Roxbury Center—*hist pl* ... CT-1
Roxbury Center—*locale* ... NH-1
Roxbury Ch—*church* ... CT-1
Roxbury Creek—*stream* ... MI-6
Roxbury Creek—*stream* ... WI-6
Roxbury Creek Campgrounds—*locale* ... MI-6
**Roxbury Crossing (subdivision)**—*pop pl* ... MA-1
Roxbury Falls—*locale* ... CT-1
Roxbury Fire Tower—*locale* ... CT-1
Roxbury Flat—*locale* ... VT-1
Roxbury Gap—*gap* ... VT-1
Roxbury High Fort—*hist pl* ... MA-1
Roxbury (historical P.O.)—*locale* ... MA-1
Roxbury Iron Mine and Furnace Complex—*hist pl* ... CT-1
Roxbury Latin Sch—*school* ... MA-1
Roxbury Mills—*locale* ... MD-2
Roxbury Mtn—*summit* ... ME-1
Roxbury Notch—*gap* ... ME-1
Roxbury Oil Field—*oilfield* ... KS-7
Roxbury Park—*park* ... CA-9
Roxbury Park—*park* ... PA-2
Roxbury Sch—*school* ... CT-1
Roxbury Sch—*school* ... NH-1
Roxbury Sch—*school* ... OH-6
Roxbury State For—*forest* ... VT-1
Roxbury (State Reformatory for Males)—*building* ... MD-2
Roxbury Station—*locale* ... MD-2
**Roxbury Station**—*pop pl* ... CT-1
Roxbury Station (historical)—*locale* ... MA-1
**Roxbury (subdivision)**—*pop pl* ... MA-1
**Roxbury (Town of)**—*pop pl* ... CT-1
**Roxbury (Town of)**—*pop pl* ... ME-1
**Roxbury (Town of)**—*pop pl* ... NH-1
**Roxbury (Town of)**—*pop pl* ... NY-2
**Roxbury (Town of)**—*pop pl* ... VT-1
**Roxbury (Town of)**—*pop pl* ... WI-6
**Roxbury (Township of)**—*pop pl* ... NJ-2
**Roxie**—*pop pl* ... IA-7
**Roxie**—*pop pl* ... MS-4
Roxie Attendance Center—*school* ... MS-4
Roxie Cem—*cemetery* ... MS-4
Roxie Post Office (historical)—*building* ... TN-4
*Roxiticus* ... NJ-2
**Roxobel**—*pop pl* ... NC-3
Roxobel-Kelford Cem—*cemetery* ... NC-3
Roxobel-Kelford Sch—*school* ... NC-3
Roxobel (Township of)—*fmr MCD* ... NC-3
Roxton—*locale* ... AR-4
**Roxton**—*pop pl* ... PA-2
**Roxton**—*pop pl* ... TX-5
Roxton (CCD)—*cens area* ... TX-5
Roxton Station—*locale* ... PA-2
Roxy Ann Lake—*lake* ... CO-8
Roxy Ann Peak—*summit* ... OR-9
Roxy Hotel—*hist pl* ... NY-2
Roxy Islands—*island* ... NY-2
Roxy Lake—*lake* ... WI-6
Roxy Pond—*swamp* ... FL-3
*Roy* ... AL-4
*Roy* ... OR-9
Roy—*locale* ... AR-4
Roy—*locale* ... CO-8
Roy—*locale* ... FL-3
Roy—*locale* ... GA-3
Roy—*locale* ... ID-8
Roy—*locale* ... MS-4
Roy—*locale* ... TX-5
**Roy**—*pop pl* ... AR-4
**Roy**—*pop pl* ... GA-3
**Roy**—*pop pl* ... LA-4
**Roy**—*pop pl* ... MO-7
**Roy**—*pop pl* ... MT-8
**Roy**—*pop pl* ... NM-5
**Roy**—*pop pl* ... OR-9
**Roy**—*pop pl* ... TN-4
**Roy**—*pop pl* ... UT-8
**Roy**—*pop pl* ... WA-9
Roy, Dr. E. G., House—*hist pl* ... NJ-2
Roy, Dr. Thomas A., Sr., House—*hist pl* ... LA-4
Roy, J. Arthur, House—*hist pl* ... LA-4
Roy, John, Site—*hist pl* ... IL-6
Roy, Lake—*lake* ... FL-3
Roy, Lake—*lake* ... PA-2
*Royal* ... WA-9
Royal—*locale* ... AR-4
Royal—*locale* ... GA-3
Royal—*locale* ... KY-4
Royal—*locale* ... MO-7
Royal—*locale* ... OR-9
Royal—*locale* ... PA-2
Royal—*locale* ... UT-8
Royal—*locale* ... WV-2
**Royal**—*pop pl* ... AL-4
**Royal**—*pop pl* ... FL-3
**Royal**—*pop pl* ... IL-6
**Royal**—*pop pl* ... IA-7
**Royal**—*pop pl* ... NE-7
**Royal**—*pop pl* (2) ... NC-3
**Royal**—*pop pl* ... OH-6
**Royal**—*pop pl* ... PA-2
**Royal**—*pop pl* ... TN-4
**Royal**—*pop pl* ... TX-5
**Royal**—*pop pl* ... WA-9
Royal, Mount—*summit* ... AL-4
Royal, Mount—*summit* ... MA-1
Royal, Mount—*summit* ... MT-8
Royal, Mount—*summit* ... NM-5
*Royal Advent Church* ... AL-4
Royal Ambassador Camp—*locale* (2) ... VA-3
Royal Arch—*arch* ... AZ-5
Royal Arch Cascade—*falls* ... CA-9
Royal Arch Creek—*stream* ... AZ-5
Royal Arch Creek—*stream* ... CA-9
Royal Arches—*arch* ... AZ-5
Royal Arches—*pillar* ... CA-9
Royal Arch Hill—*summit* ... NH-1
Royal Arch Lake—*lake* ... CA-9
Royal Ave Ch of Christ—*church* ... AL-4
Royal Basin—*basin* ... WA-9
**Royal Beach**—*pop pl* ... MD-2
**Royal Blue**—*pop pl* ... TN-4
Royal Blue Mine—*mine* ... AZ-5
Royal Blue Sch—*school* ... TN-4
Royal Bluff—*cliff* ... FL-3
Royal Branch Canal—*canal* ... WA-9
Royal Branch Canal Wasteway—*canal* ... WA-9
Royal Brewery—*hist pl* ... HI-9
Royal Camp—*locale* ... WA-9
Royal Cem—*cemetery* ... AL-4
Royal Cem—*cemetery* ... NE-7
**Royal Center**—*pop pl* ... IN-6
Royal Center Cem—*cemetery* ... IN-6
Royal Ch—*church* ... AL-4
Royal Ch—*church* ... AR-4
Royal Ch—*church* ... SC-3
Royal Chapel—*church* ... AR-4
Royal Chapel—*church* (2) ... MS-4
Royal Chapel—*church* (2) ... NC-3
Royal Chapel Cem—*cemetery* ... MS-4
**Royal City**—*pop pl* ... AL-4
**Royal City**—*pop pl* ... VA-3
**Royal City**—*pop pl* ... WA-9
**Royal City Junction**—*pop pl* ... WA-9
**Royal Corner**—*pop pl* ... ME-1
**Royal Court**—*pop pl* ... VA-3
*Royal Creek* ... NC-3
Royal Creek—*stream* ... ID-8
Royal Creek—*stream* ... MT-8
Royal Creek—*stream* ... NC-3
Royal Creek—*stream* ... TX-5
Royal Creek—*stream* (2) ... WA-9
Royal Creek Cabin—*locale* ... WA-9
Royal Creek Trail—*trail* ... WA-9
Royal Crown Cola Company—*facility* ... OH-6
Royal-Crumpler-Parker House—*hist pl* ... NC-3
Royal Drift Mine—*mine* ... CA-9
Royal Drift Mine (underground)—*mine* ... AL-4
Royale, Isle—*island* ... MI-6
Royale, Lake—*reservoir* ... NC-3
*Royale Heliport* ... PA-2
**Royal Estates**—*pop pl* ... NJ-2
**Royal Estates West (subdivision)**—*pop pl* (2) ... AZ-5
Roy Alexander Dam—*dam* ... AL-4
Roy Alexander Lake—*reservoir* ... AL-4
**Royal Farms Estates Subdivision**—*pop pl* ... UT-8
Royal Flush Claim Mine—*mine* ... SD-7
Royal Flush Mine—*mine* ... AZ-5
Royal Flush Mine—*mine* ... CO-8
Royal Flush Mine—*mine* ... NM-5
Royal Galdes Canal—*canal* ... FL-3
**Royal Gardens**—*pop pl* ... CA-9
**Royal Gardens**—*pop pl* ... PR-3
**Royal Gardens Estates**—*pop pl* ... FL-3
Royal Gate Park—*park* ... TX-5
Royal Gate Sch—*school* ... TX-5
*Royal Glades Canal* ... FL-3
Royal Glen Mobile Home Park—*locale* ... AZ-5
Royal Gold Creek—*stream* ... MT-8
Royal Gorge—*gap* ... MO-7
**Royal Gorge**—*pop pl* ... CO-8
Royal Gorge—*valley* ... CO-8
Royal Gorge—*valley* (2) ... ID-8
Royal Gorge Bridge—*bridge* ... CO-8
Royal Gorge Bridge and Incline Railway—*hist pl* ... CO-8
Royal Gorge Park—*park* ... CO-8
Royal Gorge River—*stream* ... CA-9
**Royal Grant**—*pop pl* ... DE-2
Royal Green Elem Sch—*school* ... FL-3
Royal Green Park—*park* ... FL-3
Royal Gulch—*valley* ... CO-8
Royal Gulch—*valley* ... UT-8
Royal Gulf Hills Golf Course—*locale* ... MS-4
**Royal Harbor**—*pop pl* ... FL-3
Royal Hawaiian—*post sta* ... HI-9
*Royal Heights* ... MO-7
**Royal Heights**—*pop pl* ... IL-6
Royal Heights Baptist Ch—*church* ... TN-4
Royal Heights Park—*park* ... MO-7
Royal Highlanders Bldg—*hist pl* ... NE-7
Royal Hill—*summit* ... NY-2
Royal Hill Ch—*church* ... AR-4
**Royal Hills (subdivision)**—*pop pl* ... NC-3
Royal (historical)—*locale* ... MS-4
Royal HS—*school* ... CA-9
Royal HS—*school* ... TX-5
Royal HS—*school* ... WA-9
*Royalist* ... FM-9
Royal John Mine—*mine* ... NM-5
Royal Junction—*locale* ... ME-1
Royall, Isaac, House—*hist pl* ... MA-1
Royal Lake—*lake* ... IL-6
Royal Lake—*lake* ... MN-6
Royal Lake—*lake* (2) ... WA-9
**Royal Lake**—*pop pl* ... IL-6
Royal Lake—*reservoir* ... GA-3
Royal Lake Resort—*locale* ... IL-6
**Royal Lake Resort**—*pop pl* ... IL-6
**Royal Lakes**—*pop pl* ... IL-6
Royal Lane—*uninc pl* ... TX-5
Royal Lane Park—*park* ... NC-3
**Royal Lane Subdivision**—*pop pl* ... UT-8
Roy Allen Elem Sch—*school* ... FL-3
Royall Lake—*reservoir* ... NC-3
Royall Lake Dam—*dam* ... NC-3
Royalls Cove—*bay* ... NH-1
*Royalls Side* ... MA-1
Royal Manor Sch—*school* ... OH-6
Royal Mausoleum—*cemetery* ... HI-9
Royal Mausoleum—*hist pl* ... HI-9
Royal McKnight Dam Number 1—*dam* ... SD-7
Royal McKnight Dam Number 2—*dam* ... SD-7
**Royal Meadows Subdivision**—*pop pl* ... UT-8
Royal Memorial Cem—*cemetery* ... FL-3
**Royal Mills**—*pop pl* ... NC-3
Royal Mine—*mine* (2) ... CA-9
Royal Mine—*mine* (2) ... CO-8
Royal Mtn—*summit* ... CO-8
Royal Oak—*locale* ... MD-2
**Royal Oak**—*pop pl* ... AR-4
**Royal Oak**—*pop pl* ... MD-2
**Royal Oak**—*pop pl* ... MI-6
**Royal Oak**—*pop pl* (2) ... TN-4
**Royal Oak Beach**—*pop pl* ... MI-6
Royal Oak Bridge—*bridge* ... NC-3
Royal Oak Cem—*cemetery* ... MI-6
Royal Oak Ch—*church* ... IN-6
Royal Oak Ch—*church* ... LA-4
Royal Oak Ch—*church* ... OK-5
Royal Oak Golf Course—*other* ... MI-6
**Royal Oak Hills**—*pop pl* ... FL-3
Royal Oak HS—*school* ... CA-9
Royal Oak Lake—*lake* ... SC-3
Royal Oak (Magisterial District)—*fmr MCD* ... VA-3
Royal Oak Ranch—*locale* ... CA-9
**Royal Oaks**—*pop pl* ... IN-6
**Royal Oaks**—*pop pl* ... NC-3
**Royal Oaks**—*pop pl* (2) ... TN-4
Royal Oak Sch—*school* ... KY-4
Royal Oak Sch—*school* ... MD-2
Royal Oak Sch—*school* ... MN-6
Royal Oak Sch—*school* ... NC-3
Royal Oak Sch (abandoned)—*school* ... MO-7
Royal Oaks Country Club—*other* ... WA-9
Royal Oaks Sch—*school* ... CA-9
Royal Oaks Sch—*school* ... NC-3
**Royal Oaks (subdivision)**—*pop pl* ... AL-4
**Royal Oaks (subdivision)**—*pop pl* ... NC-3
**Royal Oaks (subdivision)**—*pop pl* ... TN-4
**Royal Oaks Subdivision**—*pop pl* ... UT-8
Royal Oak Swamp—*stream* ... NC-3
**Royal Oak Township**—*pop pl* ... MI-6
**Royal Oak (Township of)**—*pop pl* ... MI-6
*Royal Palm* ... FL-3
**Royal Palm Beach**—*pop pl* ... FL-3
Royal Palm Beach Lake—*lake* ... FL-3
Royal Palm Beach-West Jupiter (CCD)—*cens area* ... FL-3
Royal Palm Bridge—*bridge* ... FL-3
Royal Palm Cem—*cemetery* ... FL-3
Royal Palm Cem—*cemetery* ... TX-5
Royal Palm Christian Ch—*church* ... FL-3
Royal Palm Country Club—*locale* ... FL-3
Royal Palm Elem Sch—*school* (2) ... FL-3
Royal Palm Hammock—*island* ... FL-3
**Royal Palm Hammock**—*pop pl* ... FL-3
Royal Palm Hammock Creek—*gut* ... FL-3
Royal Palm Island—*island* ... FL-3
**Royal Palm Isles**—*pop pl* ... FL-3
Royal Palm Memorial Gardens—*cemetery* (2) ... FL-3
Royal Palm of Saint Petersburg—*cemetery* ... FL-3
Royal Palm Park—*park* ... AZ-5
Royal Palm Plaza (Shop Ctr)—*locale* ... FL-3
Royal Palm Polo Grounds—*locale* ... FL-3
Royal Palm Ranger Station—*locale* ... FL-3
Royal Palms Beach Park—*beach* ... CA-9
Royal Palm Sch—*school* ... AZ-5
Royal Palms of Mesa Shop Ctr—*locale* ... AZ-5
**Royal Palms Park**—*pop pl* ... FL-3
Royal Palm Travel Trailer and Mobile Home Park—*locale* ... AZ-5
Royal Palm Village (trailer park)—*locale* ... AZ-5
**Royal Palm Village (trailer park)**—*pop pl* ... AZ-5
Royal Palm Yacht Club—*locale* ... FL-3
Royal Palo Verde Shop Ctr—*locale* ... AZ-5
**Royal Pal Village (Trailer Park)**—*pop pl* ... FL-3
Royal Park—*flat* ... CO-8
Royal Park—*locale* ... NC-3
Royal Park—*park* ... CO-8
Royal Park—*park* ... MA-1
Royal Park—*park* ... OR-9
Royal Park Plaza (Shop Ctr)—*locale* ... FL-3
**Royal Park (subdivision)**—*pop pl* ... NC-3
**Royal Pines**—*pop pl* ... NC-3
**Royal Pines**—*pop pl* ... TN-4
**Royal Pines (subdivision)**—*pop pl* ... AL-4
Royal Pit Mine (surface)—*mine* ... AL-4
Royal Playground—*park* ... NY-2
Royal Plaza (Shop Ctr)—*locale* ... FL-3
Royal Plaza Shopping and Office Complex—*locale* ... FL-3
Royal Poinciana Chapel—*church* ... FL-3
**Royal Poinciana Park**—*pop pl* ... FL-3
Royal Poinciana Plaza (Shop Ctr)—*locale* ... FL-3
Royal Point—*cape* ... NC-3
Royal Point Bay—*bay* ... NC-3
Royal Pond—*reservoir* ... MA-1
Royal Pond Dam—*dam* ... MA-1
Royal Presidio Chapel—*hist pl* ... CA-9
Royal Princess Mine—*mine* ... IL-6
Royal Purple Creek—*stream* ... OR-9
**Royal Ranch**—*pop pl* ... CO-8
Royal Reservoir Dam—*dam* ... PA-2
Royal Ridge (historical P.O.)—*locale* ... IA-7
Royal Ridge Sch—*school* ... OH-6
Royal River—*stream* ... ME-1
Royal River—*stream* ... MN-6
Royal Run—*stream* ... IN-6
Royals Cem—*cemetery* ... FL-3
Royals Cem—*cemetery* ... MS-4
Royal Sch—*school* ... FL-3
Royal Sch—*school* ... HI-9
Royal Sch—*school* ... KY-4
Royal Sch—*school* (2) ... MO-7
Royal Sch—*school* ... TX-5
Royal Sch—*school* ... WA-9
**Royals Cross Roads**—*pop pl* ... FL-3
Royal Shaft Cave—*cave* ... AL-4
*Royalshire, Town of* ... MA-1
Royal Side Sch—*school* ... MA-1
Royal Slope—*slope* ... WA-9
Royal Spring—*spring* ... CA-9
Royal Spring Park—*hist pl* ... KY-4
Royal Springs—*spring* ... FL-3
Royal Springs—*spring* ... KY-4
Royal Springs Ch—*church* ... GA-3
Royals Shop Ctr—*locale* ... FL-3
**Royalston**—*pop pl* ... MA-1
Royalston Cem—*cemetery* ... TN-4
Royalston Center Cem—*cemetery* ... MA-1
*Royalston Centre* ... MA-1
Royalston Common Hist Dist—*hist pl* ... MA-1
Royalston State For—*forest* ... MA-1
*Royalston Station* ... MA-1
**Royalston (Town of)**—*pop pl* ... MA-1
Royal Substation—*other* ... WA-9
Royal Tank—*reservoir* ... TX-5
**Royal Terrace**—*pop pl* ... FL-3
Royal Terrace Park—*park* ... PA-2
Royal Theater—*hist pl* ... PA-2
Royal Tiger Basin—*basin* ... CO-8
Royal Tiger Creek—*stream* ... CO-8
Royal Tiger Mine—*mine* ... CO-8
*Royalton* ... NY-2
**Royalton**—*pop pl* ... IL-6
**Royalton**—*pop pl* ... IN-6
**Royalton**—*pop pl* ... KY-4
**Royalton**—*pop pl* ... MN-6
**Royalton**—*pop pl* ... OH-6
**Royalton**—*pop pl* ... PA-2
**Royalton**—*pop pl* ... VT-1
**Royalton**—*pop pl* ... WI-6
Royalton Borough—*civil* ... PA-2
Royalton (CCD)—*cens area* ... KY-4
Royalton Cem—*cemetery* ... MN-6
Royalton Cem—*cemetery* ... OH-6
**Royalton Center**—*pop pl* ... NY-2
Royalton Center (local name for Royalton)—*other* ... NY-2
**Royalton Heights**—*pop pl* ... MI-6
Royalton Hill—*summit* ... VT-1
Royalton House—*hist pl* ... OH-6
**Royalton (local name Royalton Center)**—*pop pl* ... NY-2
Royalton Lookout Tower—*locale* ... IL-6
Royalton Mill Complex—*hist pl* ... VT-1
Royalton Mount Ridge Cem—*cemetery* ... NY-2
Royalton Road Sch—*school* ... OH-6
**Royalton (Town of)**—*pop pl* ... NY-2
**Royalton (Town of)**—*pop pl* ... VT-1
**Royalton (Town of)**—*pop pl* ... WI-6
**Royalton (Township of)**—*pop pl* ... MI-6
**Royalton (Township of)**—*pop pl* ... MN-6
**Royalton (Township of)**—*pop pl* ... OH-6
Royalton Waterworks—*other* ... IL-6
**Royal Town**—*pop pl* ... PR-3
**Royal Township**—*pop pl* ... KS-7
**Royal Township**—*pop pl* ... NE-7
**Royal Township**—*pop pl* ... ND-7
Royal Township (historical)—*civil* ... SD-7
Royal (Township of)—*fmr MCD* ... AR-4
**Royal (Township of)**—*pop pl* ... MN-6
**Royalty**—*pop pl* ... TX-5
**Royalty Acres**—*pop pl* ... TN-4
Royalty Cem—*cemetery* (2) ... KY-4
Royalty Park—*park* ... TX-5
Royalty Ridge—*ridge* ... TX-5
Royalty-Smith Farm—*hist pl* ... KY-4
Royal University Plaza (Shop Ctr)—*locale* ... FL-3
Royal Valley Elem Sch—*school* ... KS-7
Royal Valley HS—*school* ... KS-7
**Royal View**—*pop pl* ... IN-6
**Royal View**—*pop pl* ... MD-2
Royalview Sch—*school* ... OH-6
**Royal West Subdivision**—*pop pl* ... UT-8
Royal White Mine—*mine* ... OR-9
Royal Wood Aerodrome Airp—*airport* ... MO-7
*Royan Hollow* ... VA-3
Roy Atchinson Lake Dam—*dam* ... MS-4
Roy Bailey Camp—*locale* ... ME-1
Roybal, Ignacio, House—*hist pl* ... NM-5
Royball Spring—*spring* ... CA-9
Roybals Spring—*spring* ... NM-5
Roybals Tank—*reservoir* ... NM-5
Roy Barrett Lake Dam—*dam* ... MS-4
Roy Bible Ch—*church* ... UT-8
Roy Bogan Pond Dam—*dam* ... MS-4
Roy Branch—*stream* ... KY-4
Roy Branch—*stream* ... TX-5
Roy Brook—*stream* ... VT-1
Roy Brown Dam—*dam* ... SD-7
Roy Canyon—*valley* ... AZ-5
Roy Canyon—*valley* ... OR-9
Roy (CCD)—*cens area* ... WA-9
*Royce* ... NJ-2
Royce—*locale* ... NM-5
**Royce**—*pop pl* ... MS-4
Royce, Deodatus, House—*hist pl* ... NY-2
Royce, J. B., House and Farm Complex—*hist pl* ... NY-2
Royce, Steven, House—*hist pl* ... MI-6
Royce Brook—*stream* ... NJ-2
Royce Brook—*stream* ... VT-1
Royce Cave—*cave* ... MT-8
*Royce Cove* ... TN-4
Royce Creek—*stream* ... OR-9
Royce Darling Memorial Golf Course—*other* ... CO-8
Roycefield Station—*locale* ... NJ-2
*Royce Lake* ... MI-6
Royce Lakes—*lake* ... CA-9
*Roy Cem* ... AL-4
Roy Cem—*cemetery* ... AL-4
Roy Cem—*cemetery* ... AR-4
Roy Cem—*cemetery* ... GA-3
Roy Cem—*cemetery* ... SD-7
Roy Cem—*cemetery* ... TN-4
Roy Cem—*cemetery* ... WV-2
Roycemore Sch—*hist pl* ... IL-6
Royce Mtn—*summit* ... OR-9
Royce Peak—*summit* ... CA-9
Royce Ranch—*locale* ... OR-9
*Royces Branch* ... NJ-2
*Royces Brook* ... NJ-2
Royce Sch—*school* (2) ... WI-6
Royce Trail—*trail* ... ME-1
**Royce Valley**—*pop pl* ... NJ-2
Royce Valley—*valley* ... NJ-2
**Royce (VA Supply Depot)**—*pop pl* ... NJ-2
Roy Chester Park—*park* ... PA-2
Roy Christian Ch—*church* ... UT-8
Roy City Cem—*cemetery* ... UT-8
Roy City Municipal Heliport—*airport* ... UT-8
Roy Cook Ponds—*reservoir* ... AL-4
Roy Cove Branch—*stream* ... TN-4
*Roy Creek* ... MN-6
Roy Creek—*stream* ... AK-9
Roy Creek—*stream* ... CA-9
Roy Creek—*stream* ... DE-2
Roy Creek—*stream* ... MI-6
Roy Creek—*stream* (2) ... OR-9
Roy Creek—*stream* ... TX-5
Roy Creek—*stream* ... WI-6
Roy Creek Park—*park* ... OR-9
Roycroft Campus—*hist pl* ... NY-2
Roycroft Gulch—*valley* ... CA-9
Roycroft Lake—*reservoir* ... NC-3
Roycroft Lake Dam—*dam* ... NC-3
Roycroft Lookout—*locale* ... MA-1
Roydale—*locale* ... CO-8
**Roydale**—*pop pl* ... CO-8
Royder—*locale* ... TX-5
*Roy Draw* ... WY-8
**Royer**—*pop pl* ... PA-2
Royer, Christian, House—*hist pl* ... MD-2
Royer, Daniel, House—*hist pl* ... PA-2
Royer, Lake—*lake* ... MD-2
Roy E Ray Airp—*airport* ... AL-4
Royer Cave—*cave* ... AL-4
Royer Cem—*cemetery* ... KS-7
Royer Cem—*cemetery* ... LA-4
Royer Cem—*cemetery* (2) ... MO-7
Royer Cem—*cemetery* ... PA-2
Royer Cem—*cemetery* ... WI-6
Royer Chapel—*church* ... OH-6
Royer Creek—*stream* ... IA-7
Royer Ditch—*canal* ... OH-6
**Royer Estates**—*pop pl* ... TN-4
Royer Gulch—*valley* ... CO-8
Royer Lake—*lake* ... IN-6
Royer Lake—*lake* ... MI-6
**Royer Lake**—*pop pl* ... IN-6
Royer-Nicodemus House and Farm—*hist pl* ... PA-2
Royers Ch—*church* ... PA-2
*Royer's Ford* ... PA-2
**Royersford**—*pop pl* ... PA-2
Royersford Borough—*civil* ... PA-2
Royersford Ch—*church* ... PA-2
Royersford Elem Sch—*school* ... PA-2
Royersford Station—*locale* ... PA-2
*Royers Meeting House* ... PA-2
**Royersville**—*pop pl* ... OH-6
Royersville Ch—*church* ... OH-6
**Royerton**—*pop pl* ... IN-6
Royer-Williams House—*hist pl* ... NE-7
Royes Brook—*stream* ... MA-1
Roy Everett Hunting Club Pond—*reservoir* ... NC-3
Roy Everett Hunting Club Pond Dam—*dam* ... NC-3
Roy Farnes Spring—*spring* ... ID-8
Roy Ford—*locale* ... AL-4
Roy Forehand Ranch—*locale* ... NM-5
Roy Gap—*gap* ... WV-2
Roy Gulch—*valley* ... CA-9
Roy Gulch—*valley* ... MT-8
Roy Guyton Lake Dam—*dam* ... MS-4
Roy Hollow—*valley* ... KY-4
Roy Hollow—*valley* ... UT-8
Roy HS—*school* ... UT-8
Roy Inks Dam—*dam* ... TX-5
Roy Island—*island* ... AK-9
Roy JHS—*school* ... UT-8
Roy Johnson Ranch—*locale* ... ID-8
Roy Johnston Mine—*mine* ... CO-8
Roy Jones Mtn—*summit* ... AK-9
Roy Jordan Lake Dam—*dam* ... MS-4
**Roy Junction**—*pop pl* ... MT-8
Roy Knob—*summit* ... TN-4
Roy Lake—*lake* ... MI-6
Roy Lake—*lake* (2) ... MN-6
Roy Lake—*lake* ... SD-7
**Roy Lake**—*pop pl* ... MN-6
Roy Lake—*reservoir* ... MN-6
Roy Lake Creek—*stream* ... MN-6
Roy Lake State Park Number 1—*park* ... SD-7
Roy Lake State Park Number 2—*park* ... SD-7
Royland Sch—*school* ... VA-3
Roy Lazenby Dam—*dam* ... AL-4
Royle, Jonathan C. and Eliza K., House—*hist pl* ... UT-8
Roy-LeBlanc House—*hist pl* ... LA-4
**Roylene Acres (subdivision)**—*pop pl* ... NC-3
Royle Sch—*school* ... CT-1
Roy Marketplace Plaza—*locale* ... UT-8
Roy McGinnis Dam—*dam* ... SD-7
Roy Mill Branch—*stream* ... AL-4
Roy Miller—*uninc pl* ... TX-5
Roy Mtn—*summit* ... VT-1
Roynon Sch—*school* ... CA-9
Roy Otten Memorial Airfield Airp—*airport* ... MO-7
**Roy Park Addition Subdivision**—*pop pl* ... UT-8
Roy Parker Lake—*reservoir* ... AL-4
Roy Parker Lake Dam—*dam* ... AL-4
Roy Post Office—*building* ... UT-8
Roy Post Office (historical)—*building* (2) ... MS-4
Roy Post Office (historical)—*building* ... SD-7
Royrader—*locale* ... KY-4
Roy Reese Lake Dam—*dam* ... MS-4
Roy Rinker Homestead—*locale* ... WY-8
Roy Robinson Ranch—*locale* ... WY-8
Roy Royall—*uninc pl* ... TX-5
Roy Rsvr—*reservoir* (2) ... CO-8
Roy Rsvr—*reservoir* ... OR-9
Roy Run—*stream* ... IN-6
Roys—*locale* ... NJ-2
Roys Branch—*stream* ... MO-7
Roy Sch—*school* ... IL-6
Roy Sch—*school* ... UT-8
Roy Schull Number 1 Dam—*dam* ... SD-7
Roy Schull Number 2 Dam—*dam* ... SD-7
*Roys Creek* ... TX-5
Roys Creek—*stream* ... KS-7
Roys Creek—*stream* ... NE-7
**Royse City**—*pop pl* ... TX-5
Royse (historical)—*locale* ... AL-4
*Royse P.O.* ... AL-4
**Royset Park Addition and Annex (subdivision)**—*pop pl* ... UT-8
Roy Shaw Dam—*dam* ... AL-4
Roys Hill—*summit* ... NY-2
Roy Shop Ctr—*locale* ... UT-8
*Roys Island* ... SD-7
Roy Smith Mine—*mine* ... AR-4
Roy's Office Supply Bldg—*hist pl* ... AR-4
Roys Peak—*summit* ... TX-5
Roys Point—*cape* ... ME-1
Roys Point—*cape* ... VA-3
Roys Point—*cape* ... WI-6
Roys Point—*summit* ... NV-8
Roys Pond—*lake* ... AZ-5
*Roy Spring* ... AZ-5
Roy Spring—*spring* ... AL-4
Roy Spring—*spring* ... AZ-5
Roy Spring Hollow—*valley* ... AR-4
Roys Run—*stream* ... VA-3
Roys Spring—*spring* ... OR-9
Roys Tank—*reservoir* ... AZ-5
Roy Starnes Pond Dam—*dam* ... MS-4
Royster—*locale* ... FL-3
Royster—*locale* ... NC-3
Royster, John Henry, Farm—*hist pl* ... NC-3
Royster, Marcus, Plantation—*hist pl* ... NC-3
Royster Cem—*cemetery* ... NC-3
Royster Creek—*stream* ... TN-4
Royster Creek Drainage Canal—*canal* ... TN-4
*Royster Golf Course and City Park* ... NC-3
Royster Hollow—*valley* ... KY-4
Royster JHS—*school* ... KS-7
Royster Lake—*lake* ... LA-4
Royster Memorial Golf Course—*locale* ... NC-3
Royster Memorial Park—*cemetery* ... NC-3
Royster Mine—*mine* ... FL-3
Royster Sch—*school* ... MO-7
Royston—*locale* ... TX-5
**Royston**—*pop pl* ... GA-3
**Royston**—*pop pl* ... MI-6
Royston, Grandison D., House—*hist pl* ... AR-4
Royston Branch—*stream* ... MD-2
Royston (CCD)—*cens area* (2) ... GA-3
Royston Chapel—*church* ... MS-4
Royston Commercial Hist Dist—*hist pl* ... GA-3
Royston Dam—*dam* ... AL-4
Royston Drain—*canal* ... MI-6
**Roystone**—*pop pl* ... PA-2
Roystone Hot Springs—*spring* ... ID-8
Roystone Run—*stream* ... PA-2
Royston Hill—*summit* ... TX-5
Royston Hills—*summit* ... NV-8
**Royston (historical)**—*pop pl* ... OR-9
Royston Island—*island* ... MD-2
Royston Lake—*reservoir* ... AL-4
Royston Spring—*spring* ... OR-9
Roy Stout Number 1 Dam—*dam* ... SD-7
Roy Stout Number 2 Dam—*dam* ... SD-7
Roy Summit—*locale* ... ID-8
Roy Tank—*reservoir* (2) ... AZ-5
Roy Tank—*reservoir* ... TX-5
**Roytown**—*pop pl* ... PA-2
Roytown Ridge—*ridge* ... KY-4
Roy Township—*civil* ... SD-7
Roy Valley Ch—*church* ... MS-4
Roy Veit Number 4 Dam—*dam* ... SD-7
*Royville* ... LA-4
**Royville**—*pop pl* ... IN-6
**Royville**—*pop pl* ... KY-4
**Roy Webb**—*pop pl* ... AL-4
*Roy Webb School* ... AL-4
**Roy West Subdivision**—*pop pl* ... UT-8
Roy White Dam—*dam* ... TN-4
Roy White Lake—*reservoir* ... TN-4
Roy-Winifred Junction—*locale* ... MT-8
Roy Young Dam—*dam* ... MS-4
Roy Zornes Branch—*stream* ... KY-4
Roza—*locale* ... WA-9
Roza Canal—*canal* ... WA-9
Roza Creek—*stream* ... WA-9
Rozas House—*hist pl* ... CA-9
Roza Wasteway No 4—*canal* ... WA-9
Rozel—*locale* ... UT-8
**Rozel**—*pop pl* ... KS-7
Rozel Bay—*bay* ... UT-8
Rozel Cem—*cemetery* ... KS-7
Rozel Flat—*flat* ... UT-8
Rozel Hills—*summit* ... UT-8
Rozelle Creek—*stream* ... OH-6
Rozelle Elem Sch—*hist pl* ... TN-4
Rozelle Sch—*school* ... OH-6
Rozelle Sch—*school* ... TN-4
*Rozell Lake* ... MI-6
**Rozells Mill**—*pop pl* ... TN-4
**Rozellville**—*pop pl* ... WI-6
**Rozel Park**—*pop pl* ... PA-2
Rozel Point—*summit* ... UT-8
Rozel Point Oil Field—*oilfield* ... UT-8
Rozencrantz Sch—*school* ... NE-7
Rozet—*locale* ... WY-8
Rozet Oil Field—*oilfield* ... WY-8
Rozetta—*locale* ... IL-6
**Rozetta (Township of)**—*pop pl* ... IL-6

Rozier Branch—stream GA-3
Rozier Cem—cemetery GA-3
Rozier Ch—church NC-3
Rozier Island—island GA-3
**Roziers**—pop pl NC-3
Roziers Cem—cemetery SC-3
Rozier Siding—locale NC-3
Roznov—locale TX-5
Rozzel Lake MI-6
Rozzell Ch—church KY-4
Rozzelle Bridge—bridge NC-3
R Paine Dam—dam SD-7
R Perez Ranch—locale NM-5
R Pritchards Heirs Grant—civil FL-3
**Rrai**—pop pl PW-9
R.R. Banks Dam AL-4
R R Banks Lake Dam—dam AL-4
R R B Lateral—canal TX-5
R R G Lateral—canal TX-5
R Rivers Pond Dam—dam MS-4
R R Lateral—canal TX-5
R R Moton Elem Sch—school FL-3
RRR Ranch—locale AZ-5
R R Smith Lake Dam—dam MS-4
R R Spring—spring CO-8
R Rsvr—reservoir OR-9
RR Tank—reservoir AZ-5
R R Tank—reservoir NM-5
R R Vance Pond Dam—dam MS-4
R Sanchez or Atkinson Grant—civil FL-3
R & S Bldg—hist pl NY-2
R Schrempp Dam—dam SD-7
R-seven Spring—spring AZ-5
R Seven Tank—reservoir AZ-5
R S Hill—summit AZ-5
R Side Main Canal—canal CA-9
R Skorpil Ranch—locale ND-7
R S Ranch—locale WY-8
RS Spring—spring AZ-5
R S Tank—reservoir AZ-5
R Talley Number 1 Dam—dam SD-7
R Talley Number 2 Dam—dam SD-7
R Taylor Ranch—locale CO-8
R T Spring—spring OR-9
Ru' FM-9
Ruac FM-9
Ruac Island FM-9
Rua Cove—bay AK-9
Rua Island FM-9
Rua Island—island (2) MP-9
**Rual**—pop pl VA-3
Rual Island MP-9
Rua Mine SD-7
Rua Mine—mine AK-9
Ruan, John, House—hist pl PA-2
Ruan Bay—locale VI-3
Ruark—locale VA-3
Ruark Bluff—cliff MO-7
Ruark Sch—school MO-7
Rua-to MP-9
Ruotsale, Matt, Homestead—hist pl ID-8
**Ruback Camp**—pop pl NY-2
Ruba won MP-9
Rubberboot Gap—gap CA-9
Rubber Boot Lake—lake AK-9
Rubber Canal—canal (2) CA-9
Rubber Drain—canal CA-9
Rubber Drain One—canal CA-9
Rubber Drain Three—canal CA-9
Rubber Drain Two—canal CA-9
Rubber Hill—summit NV-8
Rubber Lake—lake NV-8
Rubber Lateral—canal CA-9
Rubber Lateral Six—canal CA-9
Rubber Lateral Two—canal CA-9
Rubber Latera One—canal CA-9
Rubbert Aerial Landing Strip—airport ND-7
Rubber Thread Pond—reservoir MA-1
Rubble Creek—stream OR-9
Rubble Dam—dam AZ-5
Rubble Dam Three—dam AZ-5
Rubble Lake—lake MT-8
Rubble Number One Dam—dam AZ-5
Rubboard Crossing TX-5
Rubboard Crossing—locale TX-5
Rube—locale WI-6
Rube Bayou—stream AR-4
Rube Branch—stream KY-4
Rube Cem—cemetery CO-8
Rube Creek—stream AK-9
Rube Creek—stream (3) CA-9
Rube Creek—stream CO-8
Rube Creek—stream NC-3
Rube Fork—stream KY-4
Rubegeshi MP-9
Rubegeshi—island MP-9
Rubegeshi-To MP-9
Rube Green Top—summit NC-3
Rube Hollow—valley (2) KY-4
Rube Hollow—valley OH-6
Rube Hollow—valley TN-4
Rube Hollow—valley WV-2
Rubekij—island MP-9
Rubel Ave Sch—school KY-4
Rubel Creek—stream MO-7
Rubel Lake—reservoir OH-6
Rubel Ranch AZ-5
Rubel Ranch Landing Strip AZ-5
Rube Meadow—flat CA-9
Rube Mine—mine UT-8
Ruben Blue Spring—spring WA-9
Ruben Canyon—valley NM-5
Ruben Chapel—church MS-4
Ruben Creek—stream SD-7
Rubendall Ranch—locale SD-7
Rubeneau Branch—stream MO-7
Ruben Gulch—valley MT-8
Ruben Hollow—valley ID-8
Rubenhouse Bluff—cliff MS-4
Ruben Larosh Dam—dam SD-7
Ruben Mtn—summit NC-3
Ruben Oil Field—oilfield WY-8
Ruben Point—cape MD-2
Rubens—locale IA-7
Rubens Branch—stream WV-2
Rubens Chapel Cem—cemetery MS-4
Rubenser Ridge—ridge WA-9
Rubens (historical)—locale KS-7
Ruben Springs Hollow—valley VA-3
Rubens Rialto Square Theater—hist pl IL-6
**Rubens Siding**—pop pl IA-7
Ruben Windmill—locale TX-5
Rube Point—cape MP-9
Rube Ranch—locale CA-9
Rubermont—locale VA-3
Rubermount VA-3
Rube Rock Branch—stream NC-3
Rubert Ford—locale KY-4
Rubert Sch—school SD-7
Rube-saki MP-9
Rubes Creek—stream GA-3
Rube-Spitze MP-9
Rube Well—well TX-5
Rubias (Barrio)—fmr MCD PR-3
Rubiatt NC-3
**Rubicam**—pop pl PA-2
Rubicam Station—locale PA-2
Rubicon Keys FL-3
Rubicon—locale ID-8
**Rubicon**—pop pl AR-4
**Rubicon**—pop pl WI-6
**Rubicon**—pop pl TX-5
Rubicon Bay—bay CA-9
Rubicon Beach—beach MI-6
Rubicon Ch—church IL-6
Rubicon Creek CA-9
Rubicon Creek—stream CA-9
Rubicon Creek—stream IL-6
Rubicon Farm—hist pl OH-6
Rubicon Gulch—valley SD-7
Rubicon Keys—island FL-3
Rubicon Lake—lake CA-9
Rubicon Peak—summit CA-9
Rubicon Point—cape CA-9
Rubicon River—stream CA-9
Rubicon River—stream WI-6
Rubicon Rsvr—reservoir CA-9
Rubicon Springs—spring CA-9
**Rubicon (Town of)**—pop pl WI-6
**Rubicon (Township of)**—pop pl IL-6
**Rubicon (Township of)**—pop pl MI-6
Rubicon Trail—trail CA-9
Rubideau Creek—stream MT-8
Rubideau Spring—spring MT-8
**Rubidoux**—pop pl CA-9
Rubidoux, Mount—summit CA-9
Rubidoux HS—school CA-9
Rubidoux (West Riverside)—CDP CA-9
Rubie Creek—stream ID-8
Rubin Cooley Branch—stream KY-4
Rubin Creek—stream WA-9
Rubin Glacier—glacier AK-9
Rubin Lake—lake GA-3
Rubin Lake—lake MS-4
Rubino Ditch—canal CA-9
Rubino Gun Club—other CA-9
Rubins Run—stream NJ-2
Rubin Tank—reservoir UT-8
**Rubin Township**—pop pl ND-7
**Rubio**—pop pl IA-7
Rubio Access Public Hunting Area IA-7
Rubio Canyon—valley CA-9
Rubio Friends Ch—church IA-7
Rubio State Access Area—area IA-7
Rubio Wash—stream CA-9
Rubio Woods—woods IL-6
Rubison Gulch—valley MT-8
Ruble PA-2
Ruble—locale IA-7
Ruble—locale MO-7
**Ruble**—pop pl MS-4
**Ruble**—pop pl PA-2
Ruble Cem—cemetery (2) MO-7
Ruble Cem—cemetery OH-6
Ruble Cem—cemetery VA-3
Ruble Cem—cemetery (2) WV-2
Ruble Church—hist pl WV-2
Ruble Creek—stream ID-8
Ruble Creek—stream WY-8
Ruble Knob—summit WV-2
**Ruble Mill**—pop pl PA-2
Ruble Mtn—summit MO-7
Ruble Post Office (historical)—building MS-4
Ruble Run—stream OH-6
Ruble Run—stream WV-2
Ruble Sch—school MN-6
Rubles Run—stream PA-2
Rubles Run—stream WV-2
Rubles Store (historical)—locale MS-4
Rublin Mine—mine CA-9
Rubochi—island MP-9
Rubochi Island MP-9
**Rubonia**—pop pl FL-3
**Rubottom**—pop pl OK-5
Rubow Sch—school KS-7
Rubs Berg PA-2
Rubush Run—stream VA-3
Ruby MP-9
Ruby—hist pl AZ-5
Ruby—locale (3) CO-8
Ruby—locale ID-8
Ruby—locale MS-4
Ruby—locale NE-7
Ruby—locale NV-8
Ruby—locale VA-3
Ruby—locale (3) WA-9
Ruby—locale WI-6
**Ruby**—pop pl AK-9
**Ruby**—pop pl AZ-5
**Ruby**—pop pl GA-3
**Ruby**—pop pl KY-4
**Ruby**—pop pl LA-4
**Ruby**—pop pl MI-6
**Ruby**—pop pl MS-4
**Ruby**—pop pl MT-8
**Ruby**—pop pl NY-2
**Ruby**—pop pl OR-9
**Ruby**—pop pl SC-3
**Ruby**—pop pl VI-3
Ruby, Lake—lake (2) FL-3
Ruby, Lake—reservoir CO-8
Ruby, Turner, House—hist pl KY-4
**Ruby Acres Subdivision**—pop pl UT-8
Ruby Administrative Site NV-8
Ruby Anthracite Creek—stream CO-8
Ruby Arm—bay WA-9
Rubyatt—locale NC-3
Ruby Beach—beach WA-9
Ruby Belle Mine (historical)—mine SD-7
Ruby Bluff—cliff CA-9
Ruby Brook—stream CT-1
Ruby Canyon—valley AZ-5
Ruby Canyon—valley (8) CA-9
Ruby Canyon—valley CO-8
Ruby Canyon—valley UT-8
Ruby Canyon Creek WA-9
Ruby Canyon Ditch—canal MT-8
Ruby Cem—cemetery KS-7
Ruby Cem—cemetery KY-4
Ruby Cem—cemetery MI-6
Ruby Cem—cemetery PA-2
Ruby Christensen Memorial Youth Forest—pillar UT-8
Ruby City—locale NC-3
Ruby City Creek—stream NV-8
Ruby City (historical)—locale NV-8
Ruby City (Site)—locale ID-8
Ruby Clearwater Truck Trail—trail CA-9
Ruby Corner—locale NY-2
Ruby Creek ID-8
Ruby Creek MT-8
Ruby Creek TX-5
Ruby Creek—stream (6) AK-9
Ruby Creek—stream (2) CA-9
Ruby Creek—stream (3) CO-8
Ruby Creek—stream (11) ID-8
Ruby Creek—stream MI-6
Ruby Creek—stream (9) MT-8
Ruby Creek—stream NV-8
Ruby Creek—stream (3) OR-9
Ruby Creek—stream SD-7
Ruby Creek—stream (6) WA-9
Ruby Creek Campground—locale ID-8
Ruby Creek Ditch MT-8
Ruby Creek Mines—mine OR-9
Ruby Creek Trail—trail WA-9
Ruby Crest Trail—trail NV-8
Ruby Dam—dam MT-8
Ruby Dam—dam OR-9
Ruby Ditch—canal CO-8
Ruby Ditch—canal WY-8
Ruby Dome—summit NV-8
Ruby Drain—canal ID-8
Ruby Drift Mine (underground)—mine AL-4
Ruby Drive Sch—school CA-9
Ruby Falls—locale TN-4
Ruby Falls Cave—cave TN-4
Ruby Flats—flat SD-7
**Ruby (Geren)**—pop pl MS-4
RUBY G. FORD—hist pl MD-2
Ruby Grove Sch—school TN-4
Ruby Gulch—valley (4) AK-9
Ruby Gulch—valley (4) CO-8
Ruby Gulch—valley (2) ID-8
Ruby Gulch—valley (2) MT-8
Ruby Gulch—valley (2) SD-7
Ruby Hill—summit CO-8
Ruby Hill—summit NV-8
Ruby Hill—summit WA-9
Ruby Hill—summit WY-8
Ruby Hill Mine—mine (2) NV-8
Ruby Hill Park—park CO-8
Ruby Hills—summit NV-8
Ruby Hill Spring—spring CA-9
Ruby (historical)—locale AL-4
Ruby (historical)—locale KS-7
**Ruby (historical)**—pop pl OR-9
Ruby Hollow—valley UT-8
Ruby Interchange—crossing AZ-5
Ruby Jewel Lake CO-8
Ruby Junction MN-6
Ruby Junction—locale MN-6
Ruby King Mine—mine CA-9
Ruby Knolls—summit WY-8
Ruby Lake IN-6
Ruby Lake—lake CO-8
Ruby Lake—lake (2) CA-9
Ruby Lake—lake (5) CO-8
Ruby Lake—lake ID-8
Ruby Lake—lake (3) MN-6
Ruby Lake—lake NE-7
Ruby Lake—lake NV-8
Ruby Lake—lake OH-6
Ruby Lake—lake WA-9
Ruby Lake—lake (2) WI-6
Ruby Lake—reservoir CT-1
Ruby Lake—reservoir TX-5
Ruby Lake East Sump—reservoir NV-8
Ruby Lake Migratory Waterfowl Refuge NV-8
Ruby Lake Natl Wildlife HQ NV-8
Ruby Lake Natl Wildlife Ref—park NV-8
Ruby Lake Natl Wildlife Refuge HQ—locale NV-8
Ruby Lake North Sump—reservoir NV-8
Ruby Lakes—lake AZ-5
Ruby Lakes—lake CO-8
Ruby Lake South Sump—reservoir NV-8
Ruby Lake Unit Fourteen—reservoir NV-8
Ruby Lake Unit Ten—reservoir NV-8
Ruby Lake Unit Thirteen—reservoir NV-8
Ruby Lake Unit Twenty—reservoir NV-8
Ruby Lake Unit Twenty-one—reservoir NV-8
Ruby Landing—locale MS-4
Ruby Lee Rsvr—reservoir CO-8
Ruby Lee Well—well CA-9
Ruby Lookout Tower—locale LA-4
Ruby Lookout Tower—locale SC-3
Ruby Meadows—flat ID-8
Ruby Mill Canyon—valley OK-5
Ruby Mine—mine AZ-5
Ruby Mine—mine (3) CA-9
Ruby Mine—mine (4) CO-8
Ruby Mine—mine (4) MT-8
Ruby Mine—mine NM-5
Ruby Mine—mine OR-9
Ruby Mine—mine WA-9
Ruby Mountain CO-8
Ruby Mountain Ranger District—forest NV-8
Ruby Mountains ID-8
Ruby Mountains NV-8
Ruby Mountains OR-9
Ruby Mountain Scenic Area NV-8
Ruby Mountains Scenic Area—park NV-8
Ruby Mtn—summit CA-9
Ruby Mtn—summit (3) CO-8
Ruby Mtn—summit (2) ID-8
Ruby Mtn—summit MT-8
Ruby Mtn—summit NY-2
Ruby Mtn—summit (2) WA-9
Ruby Mtns—range NV-8
Ruby Parks—flat MT-8
Ruby Pass—gap ID-8
Ruby Peak—summit AZ-5
Ruby Peak—summit CO-8
Ruby Peak—summit OR-9
Ruby Point—summit ID-8
Ruby Post Office (historical)—building AL-4
Ruby Post Office (historical)—building MS-4
Ruby Ranch—locale TX-5
Ruby Ranch—locale UT-8
Ruby Ranch—locale WY-8
Ruby Range NV-8
Ruby Range—range CO-8
Ruby Range—range MT-8
Ruby Ranger Station NV-8
Ruby Rapids—rapids ID-8
Ruby Reservoir WA-9
Ruby Ridge—ridge (2) ID-8
Ruby Ridge Trail—trail ID-8
Ruby River—stream MT-8
Ruby River Rsvr—reservoir MT-8
Ruby Roadhouse—hist pl AK-9
Ruby Roadhouse—locale AK-9
Ruby Rsvr—reservoir OR-9
Rubys Bay—bay MI-6
Ruby Sch—school MT-8
**Rubys Corner**—pop pl WI-6
Rubys Grove Sch TN-4
Ruby Shaft—mine UT-8
Rubys Inn—locale UT-8
Rubys Inn RV Campground UT-8
Ruby Slough—stream AK-9
Ruby Spring—spring AR-4
Ruby Spring—spring (2) CA-9
Ruby Spring—spring NV-8
Ruby Springs—spring NV-8
Ruby Springs—spring OR-9
Ruby-Star Ranch—locale AZ-5
Ruby Station MS-4
Ruby Swamps—swamp WI-6
Ruby Tank AZ-5
Ruby Tank—reservoir AZ-5
Ruby Theatre—hist pl MT-8
**Ruby (Town of)**—pop pl WI-6
Ruby Trail Dam—dam AZ-5
**Ruby Valley**—pop pl NV-8
Ruby Valley—valley MT-8
Ruby Valley (depression)—basin NV-8
Ruby Valley Ditch—canal MT-8
Ruby Valley Forest Service Station—locale NV-8
Ruby Valley Ind Res—reserve NV-8
Ruby Valley Pony Express Station—hist pl NV-8
Ruby Valley Rsvr Number One—reservoir NV-8
Ruby Valley Sch—school (2) NV-8
**Rubyville**—pop pl OH-6
Ruby Wash—stream AZ-5
Ruby Wash—stream NV-8
Ruby Wells—well NM-5
Ruby Wells Ranch—locale NM-5
Ruby-Wise JHS—school LA-4
Ruc FM-9
Ruces Creek—stream TX-5
**Ruch**—pop pl OR-9
Rucher Gap—gap WV-2
Ruchert Camp—locale WA-9
Ruchert Spring—spring WA-9
Ruchi MP-9
Ruchi Island MP-9
Ru chi-to MP-9
Ruch Sch—school OR-9
**Ruchsville**—pop pl PA-2
**Rucio**—pop pl PR-3
Rucio (Barrio)—fmr MCD PR-3
Rucio Windmills—locale TX-5
Ruck-A-Chucky Rapids—rapids CA-9
Ruckavina Well Number One—well MT-8
Ruckavina Well Number Three—well MT-8
Ruckavina Well Number Two (flowing)—well MT-8
Ruck Cem—cemetery TX-5
Ruckdashel Cem—cemetery WI-6
Ruckel Creek—stream OR-9
Ruckel Hollow—valley KY-4
Ruckel Junction—locale OR-9
Ruckel Ridge—ridge OR-9
Ruckel Spring—spring OR-9
Rucker—locale CA-9
Rucker—locale (2) MO-7
Rucker—locale TX-5
**Rucker**—pop pl TN-4
Rucker Airp—airport (2) KS-7
Rucker Bend—bend WV-2
Rucker Branch—stream TN-4
Rucker Branch—stream WV-2
Rucker Canyon—valley AZ-5
Rucker Canyon—valley NM-5
Rucker Canyon Dam—dam AZ-5
Rucker Canyon Ranch—locale AZ-5
Rucker Canyon Trail Two Hundred Twentytwo—trail AZ-5
Rucker Cave—cave TN-4
Rucker Cem—cemetery AZ-5
Rucker Cem—cemetery IN-6
Rucker Cem—cemetery MI-6
Rucker Cem—cemetery (3) MS-4
Rucker Cem—cemetery MO-7
Rucker Cem—cemetery OH-6
Rucker Cem—cemetery (4) TN-4
Rucker Cem—cemetery WV-2
Rucker Cemetery TX-5
Rucker Chapel—church IL-6
Rucker Creek MS-4
Rucker Creek—stream CA-9
Rucker Creek—stream MS-4
Rucker Creek—stream TX-5
Rucker Dam—dam TN-4
Ruckerd Knob—summit TN-4
Rucker Draw—valley WY-8
Rucker Forest Camp—locale AZ-5
Rucker Fork—stream WV-2
Rucker Gap—gap VA-3
Rucker Goodloe Cem—cemetery TN-4
Rucker Hill—summit CA-9
Rucker Hill Tank—reservoir CA-9
Rucker Hollow—valley VA-3
Rucker House—hist pl AR-4
Rucker House—hist pl GA-3
Rucker House—hist pl WA-9
Rucker Knob—summit TN-4
Rucker Lake—lake NE-7
Rucker Lake—lake NM-5
Rucker Lake—reservoir AZ-5
Rucker Lake—reservoir CA-9
Rucker Lake—reservoir TN-4
Rucker Lake Campground—park AZ-5
Rucker Mountain TN-4
Rucker Ranger Station—locale AZ-5
Rucker Raspberry Ridge Trail Two Hundred Twentyeight—trail AZ-5
Rucker Run—stream VA-3
Ruckers Branch—stream TN-4
Rucker Sch—school AZ-5
Rucker Sch—school OK-5
Rucker Sch—school TX-5
Ruckers Crossing MS-4
Ruckers Ferry (historical)—locale IN-6
Ruckers Grove Ch—church GA-3
Ruckers Lake—reservoir GA-3
Ruckers Point—cape TN-4
Ruckers Point Landing (historical)—locale TN-4
Ruckers Pond—reservoir SC-3
Rucker Spring—spring CA-9
Rucker Spring—spring NM-5
Ruckersville—locale GA-3
**Ruckersville**—pop pl VA-3
Ruckersville Baptist Church MS-4
Ruckersville Cem—cemetery VA-3
Ruckersville (historical)—locale MS-4
Ruckersville (Magisterial District)—fmr MCD VA-3
Rucker Tank—reservoir (3) AZ-5
**Ruckerville**—pop pl KY-4
Ruckerville Cem—cemetery MS-4
Ruckerville Ch—church MS-4
Ruckerville Sch—school MS-4
Ruck Island IL-6
Ruckles—locale OR-9
Ruckles Creek—stream OR-9
Ruckles Lake—swamp MN-6
Ruckle Spring OR-9
Ruckman, John, House—hist pl TX-5
Ruckman Cem—cemetery IA-7
Ruckman Cem—cemetery MO-7
Ruckman Ch—church WV-2
Ruckman Dam—dam OR-9
Ruckman Draft—valley VA-3
Ruckman Rsvr—reservoir OR-9
Ruckman Run VA-3
Ruckman Run—stream WV-2
Ruckman's Rsvr—reservoir OR-9
Ruckman Windmill—locale NM-5
**Rucks**—pop pl MS-4
Rucks Run—stream PA-2
**Rucks Spur**—pop pl AR-4
Ruction Ditch—canal CO-8
Rucum Hill—summit CT-1
Ruda Canyon—valley CA-9
Rudakof Mtn—summit AK-9
Rudasill Branch—stream VA-3
Rudberg Creek CA-9
Rudco—locale NY-2
Rudd—locale AR-4
**Rudd**—pop pl IA-7
**Rudd**—pop pl NC-3
Rudd Branch—stream SC-3
Rudd Branch—stream (2) TN-4
Rudd Branch—stream VA-3
Rudd Canyon—valley MT-8
Rudd Cem—cemetery AR-4
Rudd Cem—cemetery KY-4
Rudd Cem—cemetery SC-3
Rudd Creek—stream AZ-5
Rudd Creek—stream UT-8
Rudd Creek—stream WI-6
Rudd Creek Public Use Area—park VA-3
Rudd Ditch—canal MT-8
Rudd Draw—valley TX-5
Ruddell Ditch—canal IN-6
**Ruddell Hill**—pop pl AR-4
Ruddell Hill—summit AR-4
Ruddell Hill—summit CA-9
Ruddell Lake—lake AR-4
Ruddells Cem—cemetery AR-4
Ruddell Sch—school AR-4
Ruddell Sch—school IL-6
Ruddell (Township of)—fmr MCD AR-4
**Ruddels Mills**—pop pl KY-4
Rudden—locale GA-3
Rudder Branch—stream KY-4
Rudder Cave—cave PA-2
Rudder Cem—cemetery TN-4
Rudder Creek—stream OR-9
Rudder Hill Hunting Club—locale AL-4
Rudder Mine (underground)—mine AL-4
Rudder Rock—bar ME-1
Rudders Chapel—church AL-4
Rudders Ferry (historical)—locale AL-4
**Rudderville**—pop pl TN-4
Rudderville Post Office (historical)—building TN-4
Rudderville School TN-4
Rudd Hills—summit WI-6
Rudd (historical)—locale AL-4
Rudd Hollow—valley TN-4
Rudd Hollow—valley UT-8
Ruddick Cem—cemetery MO-7
Ruddick Ch—church AR-4
Ruddick Park—park TX-5
Ruddick Pond—lake NY-2
Ruddick Ranch—locale CA-9
Ruddiman Creek—stream MI-6
Ruddiman HS—school MI-6
Ruddiman Lagoon—lake MI-6
Ruddiman Terrace MI-6
Rudd JHS—school AL-4
Rudd Knoll Spring—spring AZ-5
Rudd Lake—lake MI-6
Rudd Lake—lake WA-9
**Ruddle**—pop pl WV-2
Ruddle Ch—church WV-2
**Ruddle Mill**—pop pl AR-4
Rudd-Moore Lakes—lake ID-8
Ruddo LA-4
**Ruddock**—pop pl LA-4
Ruddock Brook—stream MA-1
Ruddock Canal—canal LA-4
Ruddock Sch—school CA-9
Rudd Park—park CO-8
Rudd P.O. AL-4
Rudd Pond—lake NY-2
Rudd Pond—reservoir MA-1
Rudd Pond Brook—stream MA-1
Rudd Pond North Dam—dam MA-1
Rudd Quarry (Abandoned)—mine KY-4
Rudd Ranch—locale NE-7
Rudd Rsvr—reservoir AZ-5
Ruddsboro Sch—school NH-1
Rudd Sch—school IL-6
Rudd School Cem—cemetery MO-7
Rudd School (historical)—locale MO-7
Rudds Creek MD-2
Rudds Mill—locale MI-6
Rudd Spring—spring TN-4
Rudd Spring Branch—stream TN-4
Rudd Spring Creek—stream UT-8
Rudds Tank—reservoir AZ-5
Rudd Tank—reservoir OK-5
Rudd Township—fmr MCD IA-7
Rudd Township Cem—cemetery IA-7
Rudd Well—well TX-5
Ruddy Bay—swamp GA-3
Ruddy Branch FL-3
Ruddy Branch—stream NC-3
Ruddy Gulch—valley ID-8
Ruddy Hill—summit OR-9
Ruddy Mtn—summit AK-9
Ruddy Pool—lake IA-7
Ruddy Sch—school IL-6
Ruddy Slough—lake ND-7
Rudebusch Corner—locale SD-7
Rudebush Island—island WI-6
Rude Cem—cemetery IN-6
Rude Cem—cemetery KY-4
Rudee, Lake—lake VA-3
**Rudee Heights**—pop pl VA-3
Rudee Inlet—gut VA-3
Rudefeha—locale WY-8
Rude Hollow—valley UT-8
Rude Lake MI-6
Rude Lake—lake AK-9
Rudell CA-9
Rudell School (historical)—building AR-4
**Rudement**—pop pl IL-6
**Ruden**—pop pl GA-3
Rudenvale Spring—spring SD-7
Rude Park—park CO-8
Ruder Cove—bay ME-1
Rude River—stream AK-9
Rudes Corner—locale PA-2
Rudes Creek WI-6
Rudes Hill WI-6
Rudes Hill—summit VA-3
Rude Spring—spring CA-9
**Rudeston**—pop pl NY-2
Rudeville—locale NJ-2
Rudeville Sch—school NJ-2
Rudey Creek SD-7
Rudge Memorial Park—park NE-7
Rudge Rizzi Ranch—locale NV-8
Rudi, Lars, House—hist pl MN-6
Rudicell Cem—cemetery AL-4
Rudie Coulee—valley MT-8
Rudie Dam—dam MT-8
Rudie Lake—lake MT-8
Rudifor Lake—lake CO-8
Rudio Creek—stream OR-9
Rudio Meadows—flat OR-9
Rudio Mtn—summit OR-9
Rudisel, Ludwick, Tannery House—hist pl MD-2
Rudisill Cem—cemetery VA-3
Rudisill Mills—other NC-3
Rudisill Sch—school IN-6
Rudisill-Wilson House—hist pl NC-3
Rudkin, Frank, House—hist pl WA-9
Rudledge Bluff—cliff MO-7
Rudner Drain—canal MI-6
Rudnu FM-9
Rudo—locale ID-8
Rudo Creek—stream ID-8
Rudolf Bennitt State Wildlife Area—park MO-7
Rudolf Canyon—valley CA-9
Rudolf Hill—locale AL-4
Rudolf Hotel—hist pl ND-7
Rudolf Run WV-2
Rudolf Run—stream PA-2
Rudolph—locale SD-7
Rudolph—locale TX-5
**Rudolph**—pop pl OH-6
**Rudolph**—pop pl TN-4
**Rudolph**—pop pl WI-6
Rudolph, Mount—summit CA-9
Rudolph and Arthur Covered Bridge—hist pl PA-2
Rudolph Cem—cemetery IL-6
Rudolph Coulee—valley MT-8
Rudolph Creek—stream AK-9
Rudolph Creek—stream OR-9
Rudolph Creek—stream WA-9
Rudolph Gulch—valley CO-8
Rudolph Hill AL-4
Rudolph Hill—summit CO-8
Rudolph Lake—lake ND-7
Rudolph Lake—lake UT-8
Rudolph Lake—lake (2) WI-6
Rudolph Larson Dam—dam SD-7
Rudolph Mountain Trail—trail CO-8
Rudolph Mtn—summit CO-8
Rudolph Post Office (historical)—building TN-4
Rudolph Run PA-2
Rudolph Run—stream WV-2
Rudolphs Canyon—valley NV-8
Rudolph Sch—school DC-2
Rudolph Sch (abandoned)—school PA-2
Rudolph School AL-4
Rudolph Tank—reservoir NM-5
Rudolph Temple—church AL-4
**Rudolphtown**—pop pl TN-4
**Rudolph (Town of)**—pop pl WI-6
Rudolph Valley—basin MT-8
Rudser Ch—church ND-7
Rudy—locale NE-7
**Rudy**—pop pl AR-4
Rudyard—locale MS-4
**Rudyard**—pop pl MI-6
**Rudyard**—pop pl MT-8
Rudyard Cem—cemetery MI-6
Rudyard Gun Club—other MT-8
Rudyard Post Office (historical)—building MS-4
**Rudyard (Township of)**—pop pl MI-6

*Rudy Branch* ... FL-3
Rudy Branch—*stream* ... FL-3
Rudy Branch—*stream* ... MS-4
Rudy Branch Ch—*church* ... TN-4
Rudy Canal—*canal* ... ID-8
*Rudy Canyon* ... WY-8
Rudy Cem—*cemetery* ... IL-6
Rudy Cem—*cemetery* ... MO-7
Rudy Ch—*church* ... AR-4
Rudy Ch (historical)—*church* ... TN-4
*Rudy Creek* ... MS-4
Rudy Creek—*stream* ... AK-9
Rudy Creek—*stream* ... SD-7
Rudy Ditch—*canal* ... OH-6
Rudy Drain—*stream* ... UT-8
Rudy Duck Club—*other* ... UT-8
Rudyerd Bay—*bay* ... AK-9
Rudyerd Island—*island* ... AK-9
Rudy Gas Field—*oilfield* ... AR-4
Rudy Hill Dam—*dam* ... NC-3
Rudy Hollow—*valley* ... TN-4
Rudyk Park—*park* ... NJ-2
Rudy Lake—*lake* ... MN-6
Rudy Lake—*lake* ... WI-6
Rudy Mine—*mine* ... CA-9
Rudy Park—*park* ... TX-5
Rudy Pass—*gap* ... AZ-5
Rudy Rapids—*rapids* ... AZ-5
Rudy Ridge—*ridge* ... PA-2
Rudy Run—*stream* ... WV-2
Rudys—*airport* ... NJ-2
Rudys Flat—*summit* ... UT-8
Rudys Island—*island* ... WI-6
Rudy Slough—*gut* ... FL-3
Rudys Tank—*reservoir* ... AZ-5
**Rudytown**—*pop pl* ... PA-2
Rudy (Township of)—*fmr MCD* ... AR-4
*Rudy Trail* ... PA-2
Rue—*island* ... MP-9
Rue—*locale* ... VA-3
**Rue**—*pop pl* ... KY-4
Rueb Cem—*cemetery* ... SD-7
Rueb Dam—*dam* ... ND-7
Rueben Hollow—*valley* ... KY-4
*Ruebenville* ... AL-4
Rueben Windmill—*locale* ... TX-5
Ruebe Ranch—*locale* ... MT-8
Rue Branch—*stream* ... GA-3
*Ruechayam* ... FM-9
Rue Creek—*stream* ... MT-8
Rue Creek—*stream* ... WA-9
Rueda—*slope* ... MH-9
Rueda, Kannat—*stream* ... MH-9
Rueda, Laderan—*cliff* ... MH-9
*Rueda Cliffs* ... MH-9
*Rueda Valley* ... MH-9
**Ruedi**—*pop pl* ... CO-8
Ruedi Creek—*stream* ... CO-8
Ruediger Cem—*cemetery* ... MO-7
Ruediger Sch—*school* ... FL-3
Ruedi Rsvr—*reservoir* ... CO-8
Ruedloff Draw—*valley* ... CO-8
Ruedloff Draw—*valley* ... WY-8
Ruedloff Ridge—*ridge* ... WY-8
Rueechayaam—*locale* ... FM-9
Rueger Springs—*spring* ... ID-8
Rue Gut—*gut* ... VA-3
Ruehrmond Ditch—*canal* ... OH-6
*Rueisisu* ... FM-9
*Rue Island* ... MP-9
*Rueisu* ... FM-9
Ruel-A-Lou Lake—*lake* ... MS-4
Ruelas Canyon—*valley* ... AZ-5
Ruelas Spring—*spring* ... AZ-5
*Ruelas Spring Number Four* ... AZ-5
Ruelas Spring Number Two and Three—*spring* ... AZ-5
*Ruelas Spring 4* ... AZ-5
*Ruelas 4* ... AZ-5
Ruel Drain—*canal* ... MI-6
Ruella—*locale* ... KS-7
Ruell Snead Dam Number One—*dam* ... AL-4
Ruell Snead Dam Number Two—*dam* ... AL-4
*Ruells Township* ... KS-7
Ruen Creek—*stream* ... ID-8
Rueppele Mine—*mine* ... MO-7
*Ruer-Amehem Airport* ... PA-2
Rue Ranch—*locale* ... ND-7
Rue Sch—*school* ... IA-7
Ruesch Spring—*spring* ... AZ-5
Ruess Island—*island* ... FL-3
Rueter—*locale* ... MO-7
*Rue-to* ... MP-9
**Ruf**—*pop pl* ... NE-7
**Rufe**—*pop pl* ... OK-5
Rufe Cem—*cemetery* ... OK-5
Rufe Evans Hollow—*valley* ... TX-5
Rufelio Spring—*spring* ... NM-5
Rufe Sch—*school* ... OK-5
*Rufes Corner* ... PA-2
Rufe Williams Hollow—*valley* ... TX-5
**Ruff**—*pop pl* ... SC-3
**Ruff**—*pop pl* ... VA-3
**Ruff**—*pop pl* ... WA-9
Ruffans Run—*stream* ... VA-3
Ruffa Ranch—*locale* ... CA-9
Ruffa Ridge—*ridge* ... CA-9
Ruffatte Sch—*school* ... MT-8
*Ruff Branch* ... IA-7
Ruff Canyon—*valley* ... UT-8
Ruff Cem—*cemetery* ... GA-3
Ruff Cem—*cemetery* ... MS-4
Ruff Cem—*cemetery* ... OH-6
**Ruff Creek**—*pop pl* ... PA-2
**Ruffcreek**—*pop pl* ... PA-2
Ruff Creek—*stream* ... GA-3
Ruff Creek—*stream* ... ID-8
Ruff Creek—*stream* ... KY-4
Ruff Creek—*stream* ... PA-2
Ruff Creek Cabin Area—*park* ... KY-4
Ruff Draw—*valley* ... WY-8
Ruffed Grouse Campground—*locale* ... WA-9
Ruffener Sch (abandoned)—*school* ... PA-2
Ruff Estate Dam—*dam* ... MS-4
Ruffey Creek—*stream* ... CA-9
Ruffey Gap—*gap* ... CA-9
Ruffey Ind Res—*reserve* ... CA-9
Ruffey Lakes—*lake* ... CA-9
Ruff Field—*airport* ... PA-2
Ruff Gap—*gap* ... PA-2
Ruff Gap Trail—*trail* ... PA-2
Ruff Hill—*summit* ... CA-9
Ruff Hollow—*valley* ... TN-4
Ruffian Cem—*cemetery* ... TN-4
Ruffie Branch—*stream* ... WV-2
**Ruffin**—*pop pl* ... NC-3
**Ruffin**—*pop pl* ... SC-3
Ruffin, Edmund, Plantation—*hist pl* ... VA-3
Ruffin Cem—*cemetery* ... VA-3
Ruffin Creek—*stream* ... GA-3
Ruffingham Meadow State Game Mngmt Area—*park* ... ME-1
Ruffin Grove Ch—*church* ... MS-4
Ruffin (historical)—*locale* ... MS-4
Ruffin Mine (underground)—*mine* ... AL-4
Ruffin-Roulhac House—*hist pl* ... NC-3
Ruffins Pond—*lake* ... VA-3
Ruffins Pond—*reservoir* ... VA-3
Ruffin Swamp—*swamp* ... AL-4
**Ruffin (Tillmans)**—*pop pl* ... VA-3
Ruffin (Township of)—*fmr MCD* ... NC-3
Ruffle Bar—*island* ... NY-2
*Ruff Log* ... AL-4
Ruffneck Lake—*lake* ... ID-8
Ruffneck Peak—*summit* ... ID-8
**Ruffner**—*pop pl* ... AL-4
Ruffner Branch—*stream* ... WV-2
Ruffner Cem—*cemetery* ... AR-4
Ruffner Cem—*cemetery* ... OH-6
Ruffner Cem—*cemetery* ... WV-2
Ruffner Ch—*church* ... PA-2
Ruffner Creek—*stream* ... IL-6
Ruffner Fork—*stream* ... WV-2
Ruffner Hollow—*valley* (2) ... WV-2
Ruffner JHS—*school* ... VA-3
Ruffner Mines—*mine* ... AL-4
Ruffner Monmt—*park* ... OH-6
Ruffner Mtn—*summit* ... CO-8
**Ruffner Number Two**—*pop pl* ... AL-4
Ruffner Sch—*school* ... IL-6
Ruff Post Office (historical)—*building* ... AL-4
Ruff Sch—*school* ... MI-6
Ruff's Chapel—*hist pl* ... SC-3
Ruff Sch (historical)—*school* ... SD-7
*Ruffs Creek* ... PA-2
*Ruffsdale* ... PA-2
**Ruffs Dale**—*pop pl* ... PA-2
Ruffsdale Arpk Airp—*airport* ... PA-2
Ruffsdale Elem Sch—*school* ... PA-2
Ruffsdale (RR name for Ruffs Dale)—*other* ... PA-2
**Ruffs Dale (RR name Ruffsdale)**—*pop pl* ... PA-2
Ruff's Mill and Concord Covered Bridge—*hist pl* ... GA-3
*Ruffy Branch* ... MN-6
Ruffy Brook—*stream* ... MN-6
*Ruffy Creek* ... CA-9
*Ruffy Lakes* ... CA-9
Ruffys Fork—*stream* ... WV-2
Rufina (Barrio)—*fmr MCD* ... PR-3
Rufino Butte—*summit* ... OR-9
Rufino Butte Rsvr—*reservoir* ... OR-9
Rufino Gulch—*valley* ... OR-9
Rufledt Cem—*cemetery* ... WI-6
**Ruflin Acres Subdivision**—*pop pl* ... UT-8
**Ruflin Circle Subdivision**—*pop pl* ... UT-8
Rufner Camp Spring—*spring* ... CO-8
Ruf Sch—*school* ... ND-7
Rufus—*locale* ... KY-4
Rufus—*locale* ... MS-4
Rufus—*locale* ... NC-3
**Rufus**—*pop pl* ... OR-9
**Rufus**—*pop pl* ... TX-5
**Rufus**—*pop pl* ... WI-6
Rufus Baptist Ch—*church* ... NC-3
Rufus Brook—*stream* ... CT-1
Rufus Cem—*cemetery* ... NC-3
Rufus Cove—*bay* ... NV-8
Rufus Creek—*stream* ... AK-9
Rufus Creek—*stream* ... LA-4
Rufus Elememtary Sch—*school* ... OR-9
Rufus Gray Dam—*dam* ... SD-7
Rufus Meadows—*flat* ... WA-9
Rufus Post Office (historical)—*building* ... MS-4
Rufus Rayburn Arm—*canal* ... IN-6
Rufus Shaw Lake Dam—*dam* ... MS-4
Rufus Woods Lake—*reservoir* ... WA-9
*Rug* ... FM-9
*Rugaji-to* ... MP-9
Rugby—*locale* ... CO-8
Rugby—*locale* ... IL-6
Rugby—*locale* ... TX-5
Rugby—*locale* (2) ... VA-3
**Rugby**—*pop pl* ... IN-6
**Rugby**—*pop pl* ... NC-3
**Rugby**—*pop pl* ... ND-7
**Rugby**—*pop pl* ... TN-4
Rugby—*uninc pl* ... NY-2
Rugby, Lake—*reservoir* ... NC-3
Rugby Canyon—*valley* ... CO-8
Rugby Cem—*cemetery* ... OH-6
Rugby Cem—*cemetery* ... TN-4
Rugby Cem—*cemetery* ... VA-3
Rugby Ch—*church* ... VA-3
Rugby Colony—*hist pl* ... TN-4
Rugby Creek—*stream* ... MT-8
Rugby Grange—*hist pl* ... NC-3
**Rugby Hall**—*pop pl* ... MD-2
Rugby Highlands—*uninc pl* ... AL-4
Rugby Hills—*uninc pl* ... TN-4
Rugby JHS—*school* ... NC-3
Rugby Junction—*locale* ... WI-6
Rugby Municipal Airp—*airport* ... ND-7
Rugby Point—*cape* ... ND-7
*Rugby Road* ... TN-4
Rugby Road (RR name for Elgin)—*other* ... TN-4
Rugby Road Sch (historical)—*school* ... TN-4
Rugby Road Station—*locale* ... TN-4
Rugby Road-University Corner Hist Dist—*hist pl* ... VA-3
Rugby Rock—*summit* ... CO-8
Rugby Sch—*school* ... IL-6
Rugby Sch—*school* ... VA-3
Rugby Sch (historical)—*school* ... TN-4
Rugeley—*locale* ... TX-5
Rugen Park—*park* ... IL-6
Rugen Sch—*school* ... IL-6
Ruger Lake—*lake* ... MT-8
*Rugg* ... MS-4
Rugg Brook—*stream* ... CT-1
Rugg Brook—*stream* ... VT-1
Rugg Brook Rsvr—*reservoir* ... CT-1
Rugg Canyon—*valley* ... OR-9
Rugg Cem—*cemetery* ... OR-9
Rugge, A. S., House—*hist pl* ... NY-2
Rugged Creek—*stream* ... ID-8
Rugged Crest—*ridge* ... OR-9
Rugged Crest Palisades—*cliff* ... OR-9
Rugged Island—*island* ... AK-9
Rugged Mesa—*ridge* ... AZ-5
Rugged Mesa—*summit* ... AZ-5
Rugged Ridge—*ridge* ... WA-9
Rugged Well—*well* ... AZ-5
Rugg Hill—*summit* ... CT-1
Ruggle Cem—*cemetery* ... KY-4
Ruggles—*locale* ... NC-3
Ruggles—*locale* ... PA-2
**Ruggles**—*pop pl* ... OH-6
**Ruggles**—*pop pl* ... PA-2
Ruggles, Charles, House—*hist pl* ... OH-6
Ruggles, Draper, House—*hist pl* ... MA-1
**Ruggles Beach**—*pop pl* ... OH-6
Ruggles Camp—*locale* ... KY-4
Ruggles Cem—*cemetery* ... IN-6
Ruggles Cem—*cemetery* ... MI-6
Ruggles Cem—*cemetery* ... OK-5
Ruggles Cem—*cemetery* ... WI-6
Ruggles Dam—*dam* ... KS-7
Ruggles Draw—*valley* ... KS-7
Ruggles Ferry Bridge (historical)—*bridge* ... TN-4
Ruggles Ferry (historical)—*crossing* ... TN-4
Ruggles Grade—*trail* ... OR-9
Ruggles Gulch—*valley* ... ID-8
Ruggles Hill—*summit* ... MA-1
Ruggles House—*hist pl* ... ME-1
Ruggles Lane Sch—*school* ... MA-1
Ruggles Park—*hist pl* ... MA-1
Ruggles Park—*park* ... MA-1
*Ruggles Point* ... MA-1
Ruggles Pond—*reservoir* ... MA-1
Ruggles Pond Dam—*dam* ... MA-1
Ruggles Sch—*school* ... IL-6
Ruggles Sch—*school* ... KS-7
Ruggles Sch—*school* ... KY-4
Ruggles Sch—*school* ... MA-1
**Ruggles (Township of)**—*pop pl* ... OH-6
Rugg Pond—*lake* ... NH-1
Rugg Pond—*reservoir* ... MI-6
Ruggs—*locale* ... OR-9
Ruggs Bluff Cem—*cemetery* ... LA-4
Rugg Sch—*school* ... LA-4
Ruggs Lake—*lake* ... SC-3
Ruggs Lake—*lake* ... WA-9
*Ruggs Pond* ... NY-2
Ruggs Post Office (historical)—*building* ... MS-4
Rugg Spring—*spring* ... OR-9
Rugh Cem—*cemetery* ... AR-4
Rugh Hill—*summit* ... TX-5
Rugh Lake—*lake* ... ND-7
*Rughsville* ... PA-2
Rughton Sch—*school* ... PA-2
Rugh Town Hall—*building* ... ND-7
**Rugh Township**—*pop pl* ... ND-7
*Rugi* ... MH-9
*Rugii* ... MH-9
Rug Lake—*lake* ... MI-6
Rug Lake—*lake* ... MN-6
Rug le Cem—*cemetery* ... ME-1
Rugless—*locale* ... KY-4
Rugley Sch (abandoned)—*school* ... MO-7
*Rugoddagai* ... MP-9
*Rugoddagai Island* ... MP-9
*Rugoddagai-to* ... MP-9
Rugureru Island—*island* ... FM-9
*Ruhama* ... AL-4
*Ruhama Baptist Ch* ... AL-4
Ruhama Baptist Ch—*church* (2) ... AL-4
*Ruhama Baptist Church* ... MS-4
Ruhama Cem—*cemetery* ... AL-4
Ruhama Cem—*cemetery* ... MS-4
Ruhama Ch—*church* ... AL-4
Ruhamach Ch—*church* ... MS-4
Ruhama Church Branch—*stream* ... AL-4
Ruhamah, Mount—*summit* ... AK-9
Ruhamah Ch—*church* ... GA-3
Ruhamah Ch—*church* ... KS-7
Ruhamah Ch—*church* (2) ... SC-3
Ruhamah Mission—*church* ... GA-3
Ruhama JHS—*school* ... AL-4
Ruh Creek—*stream* ... OR-9
Ruhe Park—*park* ... PA-2
Ruhff—*locale* ... TX-5
Ruhl—*locale* ... MD-2
Ruhl Cem—*cemetery* ... PA-2
Ruhle Road Stone Arch Bridge—*hist pl* ... NY-2
*Ruhlers Run* ... PA-2
Ruhls Ch—*church* ... PA-2
Ruhl Sch—*school* ... MO-7
Ruhm Ditch—*canal* ... OH-6
Ruhrah Sch—*school* ... MD-2
Ruhstaller Bldg—*hist pl* ... CA-9
*Ruida* ... MH-9
*Ruidene* ... TX-5
Ruidosa—*locale* ... TX-5
Ruidosa Hot Springs—*spring* ... TX-5
Ruidosa Sch—*school* ... TX-5
**Ruidoso**—*pop pl* ... NM-5
Ruidoso (CCD)—*cens area* ... NM-5
**Ruidoso Downs**—*pop pl* ... NM-5
Ruidoso Lookout Tower—*hist pl* ... NM-5
Ruidoso Ridge—*ridge* ... NM-5
Ruidoso Rsvr—*reservoir* ... NM-5
Ruihley Park—*park* ... OH-6
Ruiler Cave—*cave* ... AL-4
Ruin—*locale* ... KY-4
Ruin Basin—*basin* ... AZ-5
Ruin Branch—*stream* ... VA-3
*Ruin Canon* ... UT-8
Ruin Canyon—*valley* ... CO-8
Ruin Canyon—*valley* ... UT-8
Ruin Creek—*stream* ... NC-3
Ruin Hill—*summit* ... AZ-5
Ruin Mtn—*summit* ... AZ-5
Ruin Park—*flat* ... UT-8
Ruin Point—*cape* ... UT-8
Ruin Point—*cliff* ... CO-8
Ruin Point Tank—*reservoir* ... AZ-5
Ruin Rock—*pillar* ... UT-8
Ruins, The—*locale* ... SC-3
Ruins Creek—*stream* ... CA-9
Ruins (Fort Frederick)—*locale* ... SC-3
Ruins of Fort Maginnis—*locale* ... MT-8
Ruins of Fort Mason—*locale* ... NM-5
*Ruins of Fort McRae, The* ... FL-3
Ruins of Georgias First Brewery—*locale* ... GA-3
Ruins of Mission Nuestra Senora del Rosario de los Cujanes—*hist pl* ... TX-5
*Ruins of Old Brunswick* ... NC-3
Ruins Point—*cape* ... AK-9
Ruins Point—*cliff* ... AZ-5
Ruin Spring—*spring* ... UT-8
Ruin Spring Point—*cliff* ... UT-8
Ruin Springs—*spring* ... AZ-5
Ruins Ridge—*ridge* ... AZ-5
Ruins Rsvr—*reservoir* ... MT-8
Ruins Spring—*spring* ... AZ-5
Ruins Tank—*reservoir* (3) ... AZ-5
Ruins Tank Number Two—*reservoir* ... AZ-5
Ruinsville—*locale* ... SC-3
Ruinsville Creek—*stream* ... SC-3
Ruins Wash—*stream* ... AZ-5
Ruin Tank—*reservoir* (4) ... AZ-5
Ruin Wash—*stream* ... AZ-5
*Rui River* ... FM-9
*Ruisaka* ... FM-9
*Ruiso-To* ... MP-9
*Ruisu* ... MP-9
*Ruisu Island* ... MP-9
*Ruisu-to* ... MP-9
*Ruisuwa* ... MP-9
*Ruisuwaa Island* ... MP-9
Ruisuwaa Island—*island* ... MP-9
*Ruisuwa-To* ... MP-9
Ruiz, The—*locale* ... AZ-5
Ruiz-Alvarado Ranch Site—*hist pl* ... CA-9
*Ruizappu-to* ... MP-9
Ruiz Canyon—*valley* ... AZ-5
Ruiz Canyon—*valley* (2) ... CA-9
Ruiz Canyon—*valley* ... NM-5
Ruiz Cem—*cemetery* (2) ... TX-5
Ruiz Creek—*stream* ... TX-5
Ruiz Lake—*lake* ... ID-8
Ruiz Peak—*summit* ... NM-5
Ruiz Sch—*school* ... TX-5
Ruiz Windmill—*locale* ... TX-5
Rujada Point—*cape* ... OR-9
*Rujerukku Island* ... MP-9
Rujerukku Island—*island* ... MP-9
*Rujerukku-To* ... MP-9
*Ruji* ... MP-9
*Rujiyoru* ... MP-9
Rujiyoru—*island* ... MP-9
*Rujiyoru-to* ... MP-9
*Rujoro* ... MP-9
*Rujoru Island* ... MP-9
*Ruk* ... FM-9
**Rukavina Subdivision**—*pop pl* ... UT-8
Rukes Cem—*cemetery* ... IN-6
Rukgaber Trail—*trail* ... ID-8
*Rukgruppe* ... FM-9
*Rukochi* ... MP-9
*Rukochi-To* ... MP-9
Rukoey—*bay* ... FM-9
Rukoji—*island* ... MP-9
*Rukoji Island* ... MP-9
Rukoji Pass—*channel* ... MP-9
*Rukoji-suido* ... MP-9
*Rukoji-to* ... MP-9
*Rukoppu* ... FM-9
*Rukoy* ... FM-9
*Ruku* ... FM-9
*Rukunooru* ... MP-9
*Rukunooru Island* ... MP-9
*Rukunooru-Suido* ... MP-9
*Rukunooru To* ... MP-9
*Rukunoru* ... MP-9
*Rukunoru Passage* ... MP-9
*Rukunoru-Suido* ... MP-9
*Rukunoru-to* ... MP-9
*Rukys Valley* ... AL-4
*Rul* ... FM-9
Ruland Spring—*spring* ... WY-8
**Rulane**—*pop pl* ... SC-3
Rulby Creek—*stream* ... AK-9
Rule—*locale* ... AR-4
**Rule**—*pop pl* ... TX-5
Rule, Duncan, House—*hist pl* ... IA-7
Ruleau Creek—*stream* ... MI-6
Rule Canyon—*valley* ... CO-8
Rule (CCD)—*cens area* ... TX-5
Rule Cem—*cemetery* ... MS-4
Rule Cem—*cemetery* ... TX-5
Rule Ch—*church* ... KY-4
**Rule Corners**—*pop pl* ... PA-2
Rule Creek—*stream* (2) ... CO-8
Rule Creek—*stream* ... MO-7
Rule Creek—*stream* ... WA-9
Rule Creek Trail—*trail* ... CO-8
Rule Gap—*gap* ... TN-4
Rule Gulch—*valley* ... CO-8
**Rule (historical)**—*pop pl* ... TN-4
Rule HS—*school* ... TN-4
Ruleman Mtn—*summit* ... WV-2
Rule Post Office (historical)—*building* ... TN-4
Ruler Bench—*bench* ... MT-8
Rulers Bar—*bar* ... NY-2
Rulers Bar Hassock—*island* ... NY-2
Rules Branch—*stream* ... MS-4
Rules Hill—*summit* ... CO-8
**Ruleton**—*pop pl* ... KS-7
**Ruleville**—*pop pl* ... MS-4
Ruleville Baptist Ch—*church* ... MS-4
Ruleville City Hall—*building* ... MS-4
Ruleville-Drew Airp—*airport* ... MS-4
Ruleville Health Care Center—*hospital* ... MS-4
*Ruleville High School* ... MS-4
Ruleville JHS—*school* ... MS-4
Ruleville Lagoon Dam—*dam* ... MS-4
Ruleville Memorial Park—*park* ... MS-4
Ruleville Public Library—*building* ... MS-4
Ruleville United Methodist Ch—*church* ... MS-4
Ruley Ch—*church* ... WV-2
**Ruley (historical)**—*pop pl* ... OR-9
Rulford Branch—*stream* ... AL-4
**Ruliff**—*pop pl* ... TX-5
Ruliffson Cem—*cemetery* ... NY-2
Ruling Creek—*stream* ... CA-9
Rulison—*locale* ... CO-8
Rulison Gulch—*valley* ... CO-8
Rulison Oil Shale Mine—*mine* ... CO-8
*Rull* ... FM-9
Rulland Coulee—*valley* ... WI-6
Rull Men's Meetinghouse—*hist pl* ... FM-9
Rull (Municipality)—*civ div* ... FM-9
Rulman Branch—*stream* ... VA-3
Rulo—*locale* ... WA-9
**Rulo**—*pop pl* ... NE-7
Rulon Road—*locale* ... NJ-2
Rulo Sch—*school* ... KY-4
**Ruma**—*pop pl* ... IL-6
Rumac, Lake—*reservoir* ... AL-4
Rumac Dam—*dam* ... AL-4
Ruma Convent—*church* ... IL-6
Ruma (Election Precinct)—*fmr MCD* ... IL-6
*Rumalum* ... FM-9
*Rumarumum* ... FM-9
Rumbarger Cem—*cemetery* ... PA-2
Rumbaugh—*locale* ... PA-2
Rumbaugh Campground—*locale* ... MT-8
Rumbaugh Cem—*cemetery* ... OH-6
Rumbaugh Corners—*locale* ... PA-2
Rumbaugh Creek—*stream* ... MT-8
Rumbaugh Creek—*stream* ... OR-9
Rumbaugh Sch (abandoned)—*school* ... PA-2
*Rum Bay* ... TX-5
*Rumbel* ... WV-2
**Rumbels**—*pop pl* ... PA-2
**Rumble**—*pop pl* ... IN-6
**Rumble**—*pop pl* ... WV-2
*Rumble Creek* ... MT-8
Rumble Creek—*stream* ... AK-9
Rumble Creek—*stream* ... MT-8
Rumble Creek Lake— *lake* ... MT-8
Rumble Hill—*summit* ... WA-9
Rumble Lake—*lake* ... MI-6
**Rumble (Lick Creek)**—*pop pl* ... WV-2
Rumble Sch—*school* ... GA-3
*Rumble Town* ... IN-6
**Rumbley**—*pop pl* ... MD-2
Rumbley Cem—*cemetery* ... AL-4
Rumbley Cem—*cemetery* ... TN-4
*Rumbling Bald* ... NC-3
Rumbling Bald Mtn—*summit* ... NC-3
Rumbling Mtn—*summit* ... AK-9
Rumbly Point—*cape* ... MD-2
Rumbo Branch—*stream* ... MO-7
Rumbold Park—*park* ... MO-7
Rumbough Hill—*summit* ... OK-5
*Rum Branch* ... TN-4
**Rum Branch**—*pop pl* ... MO-7
Rum Branch—*stream* ... SC-3
Rum Bridge—*bridge* ... DE-2
Rum Bridge Branch—*stream* ... DE-2
Rum Brook—*stream* (2) ... ME-1
Rum Brook—*stream* ... MA-1
Rum Brook—*stream* ... NY-2
Rum Brook Campsite—*locale* ... ME-1
Rumburg Cem—*cemetery* ... MO-7
**Rum Center**—*pop pl* ... LA-4
*Rum Corner* ... PA-2
Rum Cove—*bay* (3) ... ME-1
Rum Creek—*stream* (2) ... AL-4
Rum Creek—*stream* (3) ... GA-3
Rum Creek—*stream* ... MI-6
Rum Creek—*stream* ... NJ-2
Rum Creek—*stream* ... OH-6
Rum Creek—*stream* ... OR-9
Rum Creek—*stream* ... SC-3
Rum Creek—*stream* ... TN-4
Rum Creek—*stream* ... WV-2
Rum Creek Ch—*church* ... GA-3
Rum Creek Ch—*church* ... OH-6
Rumel, Eliza Gray, House—*hist pl* ... UT-8
Rumell Island—*island* ... ME-1
**Rumely**—*pop pl* ... MI-6
**Rumer**—*pop pl* ... WV-2
Rumery Cem—*cemetery* ... WI-6
*Rumford* ... NH-1
Rumford—*locale* ... VA-3
**Rumford**—*pop pl* ... ME-1
**Rumford**—*pop pl* ... RI-1
**Rumford**—*pop pl* ... SD-7
Rumford, Count, Birthplace—*hist pl* ... MA-1
**Rumford Center**—*pop pl* ... ME-1
Rumford Chemical Works and Mill House Hist Dist—*hist pl* ... RI-1
Rumford Compact (census name Rumford)—*other* ... ME-1
**Rumford Corner**—*pop pl* ... ME-1
*Rumford Falls* ... ME-1
Rumford Falls—*falls* ... ME-1
Rumford Falls Power Company Bldg—*hist pl* ... ME-1
Rumford Hist Dist—*hist pl* ... RI-1
Rumford HS—*school* ... ME-1
*Rumford Junction* ... ME-1
Rumford Junction—*locale* ... ME-1
**Rumford Point**—*pop pl* ... ME-1
Rumford Point Congregational Church—*hist pl* ... ME-1
Rumford River—*stream* ... MA-1
Rumford Sch—*school* ... NH-1
**Rumford (Town of)**—*pop pl* ... ME-1
Rum Gully—*stream* ... SC-3
Rum Gully Sch—*school* ... SC-3
Rum Harbor—*bay* ... MD-2
Rum Harbor Cove—*bay* ... MD-2
Rum Harbor Ditch—*channel* ... MD-2
Rum Harbor Marsh—*swamp* ... MD-2
Rum Hill—*summit* ... NH-1
Rum Hill—*summit* ... NY-2
**Rumilla**—*pop pl* ... PA-2
*Rumill Island* ... ME-1
*Rum Island* ... WA-9
Rum Island—*island* ... FL-3
Rum Island—*island* ... ME-1
Rum Junction—*locale* ... WV-2
Rum Key—*island* ... ME-1
Rum Lake—*lake* (2) ... MN-6
*Rumley* ... MI-6
Rumley—*locale* ... AR-4
Rumley—*locale* ... TX-5
**Rumley**—*pop pl* ... AR-4
**Rumley**—*pop pl* ... OH-6
Rumley Bay—*bay* ... NC-3
Rumley Branch—*stream* ... VA-3
*Rumley Brook* ... RI-1
Rumley Creek—*stream* ... OR-9
*Rumley Fire Tower* ... AL-4
Rumley Hammock—*island* ... NC-3
Rumley Hollow—*valley* ... AR-4
Rumley Lookout Tower—*locale* ... AL-4
Rumley Marsh—*stream* ... VA-3
Rumley Marsh—*swamp* ... NC-3
**Rumley (Township of)**—*pop pl* ... OH-6
**Rummel**—*pop pl* ... PA-2
Rummel Creek—*stream* ... TX-5
Rummel Creek Sch—*school* ... TX-5
Rummel HS—*school* ... LA-4
Rummel Lake—*basin* ... WA-9
Rummell Cem—*cemetery* ... WV-2
Rummell Mill—*hist pl* ... OH-6
Rummel Run—*stream* ... PA-2
Rummel Windmill—*locale* ... NM-5
**Rummerfield**—*pop pl* ... PA-2
Rummerfield Creek—*stream* ... PA-2
*Rummerling Creek* ... PA-2
Rum Mtn—*summit* (2) ... ME-1
Rummy Creek—*stream* ... ID-8
**Rumney**—*pop pl* ... NH-1
*Rumney Creek* ... MD-2
**Rumney Depot**—*pop pl* ... NH-1
Rumney Hill—*summit* ... NH-1
*Rumney Marsh* ... MA-1
*Rumney Marsh, Town of* ... MA-1
Rumney Marsh Brook—*stream* ... MA-1
**Rumney (Town of)**—*pop pl* ... NH-1
*Rumo* ... FM-9
Rumph Cem—*cemetery* ... AR-4
Rumph Cem—*cemetery* ... SC-3
Rumph Drain—*canal* ... MI-6
Rumph Sch—*school* ... MT-8
Rumphs Hill Creek—*stream* ... SC-3
Rumph Windmill—*locale* ... NM-5
Rump Mtn—*summit* ... ME-1
Rum Point—*cape* (2) ... MD-2
Rum Point—*cape* ... NH-1
Rum Point—*cape* ... NJ-2
Rum Point—*cape* ... VA-3
Rum Pond—*lake* (2) ... ME-1
Rum Pond—*lake* ... OR-9
Rum Pond—*lake* ... RI-1
Rum Pond—*swamp* ... FL-3
Rumppe Cem—*cemetery* ... WI-6
Rump Pond—*lake* ... ME-1
Rumpus Creek—*stream* ... ID-8
Rumpus Ridge—*locale* ... SD-7
Rumpuss Lake—*lake* ... MN-6
Rum River—*locale* ... MN-6
Rum River—*stream* ... MN-6
Rum River Golf Club—*other* ... MN-6
Rum River State For—*forest* ... MN-6
Rum Rock Lake—*lake* ... MA-1
*Rum Rock Plateau* ... WA-9
*Rumsey* ... KS-7
Rumsey—*locale* ... MT-8
**Rumsey**—*pop pl* ... CA-9
**Rumsey**—*pop pl* ... KY-4
**Rumsey**—*pop pl* ... NE-7
Rumsey Bay—*bay* ... CA-9
Rumsey Canyon—*valley* ... CA-9
Rumsey Creek—*stream* (2) ... TX-5
Rumsey Farm—*hist pl* ... DE-2
Rumsey Hall—*hist pl* ... WV-2
Rumsey Hall Sch—*school* ... CT-1
Rumsey Hill—*summit* ... NY-2
Rumsey Hollow—*valley* ... TN-4
Rumsey Monument—*other* ... WV-2
Rumsey Mtn—*summit* ... MT-8
*Rumsey Park* ... NY-2
Rumsey Park—*park* ... AZ-5
Rumsey Park—*park* ... MI-6
**Rumsey Rancheria (Indian Reservation)**—*pop pl* ... CA-9
**Rumsey Ridge**—*pop pl* ... NY-2
Rumsey Slough—*stream* ... CA-9
Rumsey Town Hall—*hist pl* ... CA-9
*Rumsford River* ... MA-1
Rum Sink—*basin* ... FL-3
**Rumson**—*pop pl* ... NJ-2
Rumson Country Club—*other* ... NJ-2
Rumson HS—*school* ... NJ-2
Rumson Neck—*cape* ... NJ-2
Rum Spring Creek—*stream* ... KY-4
Rumstead Valley—*valley* ... WI-6
*Rumstick Cove* ... RI-1
Rumstick Neck—*cape* ... RI-1
Rumstick Point—*cape* ... RI-1
**Rumstick Point**—*pop pl* ... RI-1
Rum Still Branch—*stream* ... FL-3
*Rumsy Mountain* ... MT-8
*Rumu'* ... FM-9
*Rumun* ... FM-9
Rumung—*island* ... FM-9
Rumung Elem Sch—*school* ... FM-9
*Rumung Island* ... FM-9
*Rumung Islands* ... FM-9
Rumung (Municipality)—*civ div* ... FM-9
*Rumungu* ... FM-9
*Rumungu To* ... FM-9
**Rumuug**—*pop pl* ... FM-9
Rum Village Park—*park* ... IN-6
Run—*locale* ... TX-5
Run, Lake—*stream* ... NC-3
*Run, The* ... MA-1
Run, The—*bay* ... NY-2
Runa—*locale* ... WV-2
Runaround Brook—*stream* ... ME-1
Runaround Butte—*summit* ... SD-7
Runaround Lake—*lake* ... OK-5
Runaround Pond—*lake* ... ME-1
**Runaway Bay**—*pop pl* ... TX-5
*Runaway Branch* ... AL-4
Runaway Branch Area Number 1—*park* ... AL-4
Runaway Branch Area Number 2—*park* ... AL-4
*Runaway Brook Country Club* ... MA-1
Runaway Brook Country Club—*locale* ... MA-1
*Runaway Creek* ... OR-9
Runaway Creek—*stream* ... ID-8
Runaway Creek—*stream* (3) ... MT-8
Runaway Creek—*stream* ... OR-9
Runaway Creek—*stream* ... VA-3
Runaway Farm Lake—*reservoir* ... NC-3
Runaway Farm Lake Dam—*dam* ... NC-3
Runaway Gap—*gap* ... NC-3
Runaway Gulch—*valley* ... CO-8
Runaway Hill—*summit* ... OR-9
Runaway Hollow—*valley* ... OK-5
Runaway Knob—*summit* ... NC-3

Runaway Negro Creek—*stream* GA-3
Runaway Point—*cape* CA-9
Runaway Point—*cape* MD-2
Runaway Point—*summit* ID-8
Runaway Pond—*lake* VT-1
Runaway Pond Heath—*swamp* ME-1
Runaway Ridge—*ridge* ID-8
Runaway Ridge—*ridge* NC-3
Runaway Run—*stream* PA-2
Run Branch—*stream* MS-4
Run Branch—*stream* (2) NC-3
Run Brook—*stream* MA-1
*Run Creek* TN-4
Run Creek—*stream* AL-4
Run Creek—*stream* (2) NJ-2
Run Creek—*stream* WA-9
Rundahl Coulee—*valley* WI-6
Rundale Creek—*stream* TX-5
Rundall Creek—*stream* PA-2
Rundback Ranch—*locale* (3) NE-7
**Rundell**—*pop pl* PA-2
Rundell Cem—*cemetery* PA-2
Rundell Ditch—*canal* MT-8
Rundelltown Creek—*stream* PA-2
Rundel Memorial Library—*hist pl* NY-2
Rundlet-May House—*hist pl* NH-1
Rundlett Hill—*summit* (2) NH-1
Rundlett JHS—*school* NH-1
Rundy Cup Mtn—*summit* NY-2
Runeberg Ch—*church* MN-6
**Runeberg (Township of)**—*pop pl* MN-6
*Rune Lake* WA-9
Runestone Hill—*summit* MN-6
*Runey Canyon* TX-5
Run Gap—*gap* PA-2
Rungay Sch—*school* CT-1
Rungchu—*bar* FM-9
**Runge**—*pop pl* TX-5
Runge (CCD)—*cens area* TX-5
Runge Oil Field—*oilfield* TX-5
Runge Ranch Airstrip—*airport* SD-7
Runge State Wildlife Mngmt Area—*park* SD-7
Rung Sch—*school* PA-2
*Runguch* FM-9
Run Gulch—*valley* OR-9
Rungun Creek—*stream* AK-9
*Runik Island* MP-9
*Runins River* MA-1
*Runins River* RI-1
Runion—*locale* NC-3
Runion Cem—*cemetery* NC-3
Runion Creek—*stream* VA-3
Runion Hollow—*valley* TN-4
Runion Hollow—*valley* VA-3
Runit—*island* (2) MP-9
*Runitto-to* MP-9
**Run Junction**—*pop pl* OH-6
Runk Cem—*cemetery* OH-6
Runkel (historical)—*locale* SD-7
Runkel Sch—*school* ND-7
Runkels Creek—*stream* AK-9
**Runkle**—*pop pl* WV-2
Runkle Canyon—*valley* CA-9
Runkle Cem—*cemetery* WI-6
Runkle Ditch—*canal* IN-6
Runkle Lake—*lake* MI-6
Runkle Mtn—*summit* VA-3
Runkle Rsvr—*reservoir* CA-9
Runkles Cem—*cemetery* IA-7
Runkle Sch—*school* MA-1
Runkles Gap—*gap* VA-3
Runlett Park—*flat* CO-8
Runlett Peak—*summit* CO-8
*Run Mill* PA-2
*Runnamede* KS-7
Runnel Bay—*bay* VI-3
Runnel Drain—*stream* MI-6
*Runnell Creek* TN-4
**Runnells**—*pop pl* IA-7
Runnells, Lake—*lake* LA-4
Runnells Bridge—*bridge* NH-1
Runnells Creek—*stream* TX-5
*Runnells Run* PA-2
Runnells Sch—*school* IA-7
**Runnels**—*pop pl* TX-5
Runnels, B. F., House—*hist pl* IA-7
Runnels Branch—*stream* AR-4
Runnels Branch—*stream* KY-4
Runnels Cem—*cemetery* MS-4
Runnels Cem—*cemetery* (3) TX-5
**Runnels (County)**—*pop pl* TX-5
Runnels Drain—*canal* MI-6
Runnels Fork—*stream* KY-4
Runnels JHS—*school* TX-5
Runnels Mtn—*summit* OK-5
**Runnelstown**—*pop pl* MS-4
Runnelstown Elem Sch—*school* MS-4
**Runnemede**—*pop pl* NJ-2
Runnemede Lake—*lake* NJ-2
Runnemede Lake Park—*park* NJ-2
Runnenede, Lake—*lake* VT-1
*Runner Branch* LA-4
Runner Branch—*stream* TN-4
Runner Cem—*cemetery* FL-3
Runner Gulch—*valley* MT-8
Runner Slough—*lake* ND-7
Runner Tank—*reservoir* AZ-5
*Runnet Bag Creek* VA-3
*Runnett Bag Creek* VA-3
Running Bayou—*stream* MS-4
**Running Bird Township**—*pop pl* SD-7
Running Branch—*stream* AR-4
Running Branch—*stream* KY-4
Running Branch—*stream* NC-3
Running Branch—*stream* SC-3
Running Branch—*stream* (3) TX-5
Running Branch Ch—*church* NC-3
**Running Brook**—*pop pl* MD-2
**Running Brook (subdivision)**—*pop pl* AL-4
Running Channel—*channel* (2) VA-3
Running Crane Lake—*lake* MT-8
Running Crane Mtn—*summit* MT-8
*Running Creek* TN-4
*Running Creek* TX-5
Running Creek—*stream* AR-4
Running Creek—*stream* (2) CO-8
Running Creek—*stream* ID-8
Running Creek—*stream* MS-4
Running Creek—*stream* NC-3
Running Creek—*stream* OK-5
Running Creek—*stream* SC-3
Running Creek—*stream* (2) TX-5
Running Creek Ch—*church* NC-3
Running Creek Ranch—*locale* ID-8
Running Crow Creek—*stream* MT-8
Running Deer Creek—*stream* MT-8
Running Drain—*stream* IN-6
Running Dutchman Ditch—*canal* WY-8
Running Eagle Falls—*falls* MT-8
Running Edge Canyon—*valley* NM-5
Running Enemy Creek—*stream* SD-7
Running Fork—*stream* AR-4
Running Gap—*gap* PA-2
*Running Gutter* MA-1
Running Gutter—*stream* MA-1
*Running Gutter Brook* MA-1
Running Hill—*summit* ME-1
Running Knob Hollow—*valley* TN-4
Running Lake—*lake* FL-3
Running Lake—*lake* ID-8
Running Lake—*stream* AR-4
Running Lake—*stream* SC-3
Running Lake Ditch—*stream* IL-6
Running Lake (Township of)—*fmr MCD* AR-4
Running Owl Mtn—*summit* MT-8
Running Park—*park* MN-6
*Running Pond* FL-3
Running Rabbit Mtn—*summit* MT-8
Running Reelfoot Bayou—*stream* TN-4
Running Reelfoot Ditch—*canal* TN-4
Running Ridge—*ridge* GA-3
*Running Slough* MS-4
Running Slough—*gut* (2) IL-6
Running Slough—*gut* TN-4
Running Slough—*gut* (2) WI-6
Running Slough—*stream* (2) IL-6
Running Slough—*stream* IA-7
Running Slough—*stream* KY-4
Running Slough—*stream* MN-6
Running Slough—*stream* (2) TN-4
Running Slough Ditch—*stream* MS-4
Running Slough Drain—*stream* IA-7
Running Slough Site (15FU67)—*hist pl* KY-4
Running Slu—*stream* MS-4
Running Spring—*spring* SD-7
Running Spring Cem—*cemetery* TX-5
*Running Springs* ID-8
**Running Springs**—*pop pl* CA-9
Running Springs—*spring* FL-3
Running Springs Sch—*school* CA-9
Running Springs Station—*locale* CA-9
Running Tiger Creek—*stream* MS-4
Running Turkey Creek—*stream* KS-7
Running Valley Creek—*stream* WI-6
Runningville (historical)—*locale* SD-7
Running Water—*locale* SD-7
Running Water Bend—*bend* AR-4
Running Water Bridge—*bridge* NE-7
Running Water Canyon—*valley* NM-5
Running Water Creek—*stream* AR-4
Running Water Creek—*stream* CO-8
Running Water Creek—*stream* MS-4
Running Water Creek—*stream* MO-7
Running Water Creek—*stream* TN-4
Running Water Creek—*stream* (2) TX-5
Running Water Creek—*stream* WY-8
Running Water Creek Bridge—*hist pl* MS-4
Running Water Creek Ch—*church* MS-4
Running Water Ditch—*canal* AR-4
*Runningwater Draw* TX-5
Running Water Draw—*valley* NM-5
Running Water Draw—*valley* (3) TX-5
Running Water Post Office (historical)—*building* TN-4
Running Water Public Use Area—*park* TN-4
Running Water Sch—*school* NE-7
Running Water Spring—*spring* NV-8
Running Water Spring—*spring* UT-8
Running Water Stage Station Site—*hist pl* NE-7
Running Water Township—*civil* SD-7
Running Water Township (historical)—*civil* SD-7
Running W Oil Field—*oilfield* TX-5
*Running Wolf Creek* MT-8
Running Wolf Creek—*stream* MT-8
Runnins River—*stream* MA-1
Runnins River—*stream* RI-1
Runnion Cem—*cemetery* NC-3
Runnion Ridge—*ridge* WV-2
Runnoe Park—*park* WI-6
*Runnymeade* KS-7
*Runnymeade* MS-4
*Runnymeade* VA-3
**Runnymeade**—*pop pl* DE-2
*Runnymeade Plantation* SC-3
**Runnymeade (subdivision)**—*pop pl* (2) NC-3
*Runnymede* OH-6
Runnymede—*locale* FL-3
Runnymede—*locale* KS-7
Runnymede—*locale* MS-4
Runnymede—*locale* SC-3
Runnymede—*locale* VA-3
**Runnymede**—*pop pl* IN-6
Runnymede, Lake—*lake* FL-3
*Runo* MP-9
*Run Of Four Mile Creek* VA-3
Run of Swamp—*swamp* NC-3
*Run Plateau* MT-8
Run Pond—*lake* MA-1
*Run River* MN-6
*Runs, The* GA-3
Runs Branch—*stream* GA-3
Runs Ch—*church* SC-3
Runs Close Creek—*stream* SD-7
*Runs Creek* GA-3
*Runstick Neck* RI-1
Run Swamp Canal—*canal* NC-3
Runswick Wash—*valley* UT-8
Runt Brook—*stream* ME-1
Runt Creek—*stream* AK-9
Runt Creek—*stream* MT-8
Runt Mtn—*summit* ID-8
Runt Mtn—*summit* MT-8
Run Trail—*trail* VA-3
Runt Run—*stream* IN-6
Runts Knob—*summit* UT-8
*Runu* FM-9
Rununder Branch—*stream* SC-3
*Run-up, The* WA-9
*Runuw* FM-9
**Runville**—*pop pl* PA-2
Runville Post Office (historical)—*building* PA-2
Runway Branch—*stream* AL-4
*Runway Creek* VA-3
Runway Ranch Airp—*airport* MO-7
Runway Rsvr—*reservoir* WY-8
Runyan Bench—*bench* MT-8
Runyan Bluff—*cliff* OK-5
Runyan Cem—*cemetery* AR-4
Runyan Cem—*cemetery* OH-6
Runyan Cem—*cemetery* VA-3
Runyan Ch—*church* AR-4
Runyan Creek—*stream* MI-6
Runyan Field—*park* CO-8
Runyan Hollow—*valley* KY-4
Runyan Key—*island* FL-3
Runyan Lake—*lake* MI-6
Runyan Line Shack—*locale* NM-5
Runyan Place—*locale* NM-5
Runyan Ranch—*locale* (3) NM-5
Runyan Sch—*school* OH-6
Runyan Spring Branch—*stream* TN-4
**Runyantown**—*pop pl* IN-6
Runyan Trail—*trail* AR-4
Runyon—*locale* NJ-2
**Runyon**—*pop pl* FL-3
Runyon Acad—*school* FL-3
Runyon Branch—*stream* KY-4
Runyon Cem—*cemetery* TN-4
*Runyon Creek* NC-3
Runyon Creek—*stream* MI-6
Runyon Creek—*stream* (2) NC-3
Runyon Creek—*stream* OR-9
Runyon Fork—*stream* KY-4
Runyon Gap—*gap* NC-3
Runyon Hills—*range* TX-5
Runyon Line Shack—*locale* NM-5
*Runyon Pond* NJ-2
Runyon Ridge—*ridge* NC-3
Runyon Sch—*school* KY-4
Runyon Spring—*spring* CA-9
Runyon Springs—*spring* CA-9
*Runzel Lake* WI-6
*Ruo* FM-9
Ruo—*island* FM-9
Ruof Ditch—*canal* MT-8
Ruo Island—*island* FM-9
Ruo (Municipality)—*civ div* FM-9
Ruona Camp—*locale* MI-6
Ruona Ranch—*locale* SD-7
Ruoruchierochieji—*bar* MP-9
Ruoruchierochieraru—*bar* MP-9
*Ruot Islet* MP-9
*Ruotto* MP-9
*Ruotto-to* MP-9
Rupard Cem—*cemetery* KY-4
Rupe Branch—*stream* MO-7
Rupe Hill—*summit* WY-8
Rupe Hinton Branch—*stream* WV-2
**Rupel**—*pop pl* IN-6
Rupel Ditch—*canal* IN-6
Rupel Lake—*lake* IN-6
Rupels—*locale* OH-6
*Rupels Lake* IN-6
Rupe Peak—*summit* ID-8
Rupert—*locale* AR-4
Rupert—*locale* OH-6
Rupert—*locale* PA-2
**Rupert**—*pop pl* CA-9
**Rupert**—*pop pl* GA-3
**Rupert**—*pop pl* ID-8
**Rupert**—*pop pl* VT-1
**Rupert**—*pop pl* WV-2
Rupert, Lake—*reservoir* OH-6
Rupert Bayou—*swamp* MI-6
Rupert Cave—*cave* PA-2
Rupert (CCD)—*cens area* GA-3
Rupert Cem—*cemetery* ID-8
Rupert Cem—*cemetery* OH-6
Rupert Cem—*cemetery* OK-5
Rupert Cem—*cemetery* TX-5
Rupert Ch—*church* AR-4
Rupert Country Club—*other* ID-8
Rupert Covered Bridge No. 56—*hist pl* PA-2
*Rupert Elem Sch* PA-2
Rupert Mtn—*summit* VT-1
Ruperto Tank—*reservoir* TX-5
Rupert Point—*cape* TX-5
Rupert Rock—*island* VI-3
Rupert Sch—*school* PA-2
Rupert Siding—*locale* CA-9
Rupert State For—*forest* VT-1
**Rupert (Town of)**—*pop pl* VT-1
Rupert Valley—*valley* VT-1
Rupes Grove Ch—*church* MO-7
Rupes Grove Sch—*school* MO-7
*Rupes Valley* AL-4
Rupe Tank—*reservoir* AZ-5
*Rupged* FM-9
Rupgeed—*locale* FM-9
**Ruple**—*pop pl* LA-4
Ruple Ch—*church* LA-4
Ruple Ditch—*canal* IN-6
Ruple Point—*summit* UT-8
Ruple Ranch—*locale* UT-8
Ruple Ridge—*ridge* UT-8
Rupley Cabin—*locale* CA-9
Rupley Lake—*lake* TX-5
Rupley Run—*stream* PA-2
Rupley Sch—*school* IL-6
Rupley Wash—*stream* AZ-5
Rupley Well—*well* AZ-5
*Rupoku* MH-9
Rupp Airp—*airport* KS-7
Rupp Cem—*cemetery* (3) OH-6
Ruppee Sch (historical)—*school* TN-4
**Ruppe (historical)**—*pop pl* TN-4
Ruppel Meadow—*flat* MT-8
Ruppel Sch—*school* IL-6
Ruppenthal JHS—*school* KS-7
Ruppert Cem—*cemetery* IN-6
Ruppert Ditch—*canal* IN-6
Ruppert Home—*locale* DC-2
Ruppert Island—*island* MD-2
Ruppert Lake—*lake* MI-6
Ruppert Lake—*reservoir* LA-4
Ruppertown—*locale* TN-4
Ruppertown Post Office (historical)—*building* TN-4
Ruppert Point—*summit* CA-9
Ruppert Ridge—*ridge* CA-9
Rupperts Sch—*school* PA-2
Ruppes Boghole—*spring* NV-8
Ruppes Place—*locale* NV-8
Rupp Gulch—*valley* CO-8
Rupp Hill—*summit* PA-2
Rupp Hollow—*valley* PA-2
Rupple—*locale* WA-9
Rupple Creek—*stream* IA-7
**Ruppletown**—*pop pl* (2) PA-2
Rupp Mtn—*summit* PA-2
Rupp Run—*stream* IL-6
Rupp Run—*stream* PA-2
*Rupps* PA-2
Rupp Sch (abandoned)—*school* PA-2
Rupp State Wildlife Mngmt Area—*park* MN-6
**Ruppsville**—*pop pl* PA-2
Ruprecht Hollow—*valley* AR-4
Ruprecht Hollow—*valley* MO-7
Ruprecht Spring—*spring* AR-4
Ruprecht Spring—*spring* MO-7
Rura Cem—*cemetery* NY-2
*Rural* AL-4
*Rural* KS-7
Rural—*locale* AL-4
Rural—*locale* IA-7
Rural—*locale* KS-7
Rural—*locale* KY-4
**Rural**—*pop pl* IN-6
**Rural**—*pop pl* OH-6
**Rural**—*pop pl* WI-6
Rural Cem—*cemetery* CA-9
Rural Cem—*cemetery* KS-7
Rural Cem—*cemetery* ME-1
Rural Cem—*cemetery* (2) MA-1
Rural Cem—*cemetery* (13) NY-2
Rural Cem—*cemetery* PA-2
Rural Center Ch—*church* KS-7
Rural Ch—*church* IL-6
Rural Chapel—*church* OH-6
Rural Choice Sch (historical)—*school* PA-2
Ruraldale—*locale* WV-2
**Ruraldale**—*pop pl* OH-6
Ruraldale Cem—*cemetery* OH-6
Rural Dale Ch—*church* MO-7
Rural Dale Sch—*school* AR-4
Rural Dale Sch (historical)—*school* MO-7
Rural Dell—*locale* OR-9
Rural Ditch—*canal* CO-8
Rural Glen Cem—*cemetery* (2) MA-1
**Rural Grove**—*pop pl* NY-2
Rural Grove Ch—*church* AL-4
Rural Grove Sch (abandoned)—*school* MO-7
**Rural Hall**—*pop pl* NC-3
Rural Hall Depot—*hist pl* NC-3
Rural Hall Elem Sch—*school* NC-3
Rural Hall Plantation House—*hist pl* SC-3
Rural Heights Sch—*school* WI-6
*Rural Hill* MS-4
*Ruralhill* TN-4
Rural Hill—*locale* IL-6
Rural Hill—*locale* MS-4
Rural Hill—*locale* NY-2
**Rural Hill**—*pop pl* TN-4
Rural Hill Acad (historical)—*school* TN-4
Rural Hill Cem—*cemetery* MI-6
Rural Hill Cem—*cemetery* MS-4
Rural Hill Cem—*cemetery* NC-3
Rural Hill Ch—*church* GA-3
Rural Hill Ch—*church* TN-4
Rural Hill Ch of Christ (historical)—*church* MS-4
**Rural Hill (historical)**—*pop pl* TN-4
Rural Hill Methodist Ch—*church* MS-4
Rural Hill Plantation (historical)—*locale* AL-4
Rural Hill Post Office (historical)—*building* TN-4
Rural Hill Sch—*school* PA-2
Rural Hill Sch (historical)—*school* MS-4
**Rural (historical)**—*pop pl* OR-9
Rural Home—*locale* AL-4
Rural Home Cem—*cemetery* NY-2
Rural Home Cem—*cemetery* WI-6
Rural Home Sch—*school* IA-7
*Rural Home School* AL-4
Ruralia—*building* TN-4
Rural Mount—*hist pl* TN-4
Rural Otter Creek Valley Hist Dist—*hist pl* VT-1
**Rural Park**—*pop pl* LA-4
Rural Plains—*hist pl* VA-3
Rural Point—*hist pl* SC-3
Rural Point—*locale* VA-3
**Rural Retreat**—*pop pl* VA-3
Rural Retreat Lake—*reservoir* VA-3
**Rural Ridge**—*pop pl* PA-2
**Rural Ridge (subdivision)**—*pop pl* TN-4
Rural Sch—*school* AZ-5
Rural Sch—*school* IL-6
Rural Shade—*locale* TX-5
Rural Shade Ch—*church* TX-5
Rural Special Sch—*school* AR-4
**Rural Subdivision**—*pop pl* UT-8
Rural Town Hall Sch—*school* IL-6
**Rural Township**—*pop pl* (2) KS-7
**Rural (Township of)**—*pop pl* (2) IL-6
*Ruralvale* TN-4
Rural Vale—*locale* TN-4
*Rural Vale Baptist Church* TN-4
Rural Vale Cem—*cemetery* TN-4
Rural Vale Ch—*church* TN-4
*Rural Vale Elementary School* TN-4
Ruralvale Post Office (historical)—*building* TN-4
Rural Vale Sch—*school* TN-4
Rural Valley—*locale* PA-2
**Rural Valley**—*pop pl* PA-2
Rural Valley Borough—*civil* PA-2
*Rural Village* PA-2
**Ruralville**—*pop pl* MA-1
*Rurbal'* FM-9
Rurdue Cem—*cemetery* IL-6
Rurick Strait—*channel* MP-9
*Rurick-Strasse* MP-9
*Rurid Island* PW-9
Ruriid—*island* PW-9
Rurik Harbor—*bay* AK-9
*Rurikku-Kaikyo* MP-9
*Rurikstrasse* MP-9
*Ruru* FM-9
Ruru—*gut* FM-9
*Ruruck Strait* MP-9
Rusaias Hole—*lake* TX-5
Rusby Gulch—*valley* CA-9
Rusch Creek—*stream* CA-9
Rusche Cem—*cemetery* TX-5
Rusche Sch—*school* IL-6
Ruschin Sch—*school* CA-9
Rusch Lake—*lake* MN-6
Rusch Park—*park* CA-9
Rusco Cem—*cemetery* KS-7
Rusco Creek—*stream* NE-7
Ruscoe (historical)—*locale* ND-7
Ruscoe Ridge—*ridge* CT-1
**Ruscombmanor (Township of)**—*pop pl* PA-2
Ruscom Pond—*lake* CT-1
**Rusco Township**—*pop pl* NE-7
Rush—*locale* AR-4
Rush—*locale* MD-2
Rush—*locale* OH-6
Rush—*locale* PA-2
**Rush**—*pop pl* CO-8
**Rush**—*pop pl* GA-3
**Rush**—*pop pl* KY-4
**Rush**—*pop pl* NY-2
Rush, Benjamin, House—*hist pl* PA-2
Rush, Lake—*reservoir* OK-5
Rusha Cem—*cemetery* OH-6
Rusha Creek—*stream* OH-6
Rush Airp—*airport* IN-6
Rush Airp—*airport* KS-7
Rush and Brown Mine—*mine* AK-9
Rusha Pond—*swamp* TX-5
Rushart Ditch—*canal* IN-6
*Rushaw Creek* OH-6
Rush Basin—*basin* CO-8
Rush Bayou—*gut* AR-4
Rush Bayou—*gut* MS-4
*Rush Bed Creek* MI-6
*Rush Bed Drain* MI-6
Rush Beds—*area* UT-8
Rushboro—*locale* PA-2
Rush Bottom—*flat* CA-9
Rush Branch—*stream* IN-6
Rush Branch—*stream* (5) KY-4
Rush Branch—*stream* (5) NC-3
Rush Branch—*stream* (3) TN-4
Rush Branch—*stream* (3) TX-5
Rush Branch—*stream* (2) VA-3
Rush Branch—*stream* (2) WV-2
Rush Branch Ch—*church* IN-6
Rush Branch Ch—*church* KY-4
Rush Branch Ch—*church* WV-2
Rush Brook—*stream* ME-1
Rush Brook—*stream* MD-2
Rush Brook—*stream* MN-6
Rush Brook—*stream* PA-2
Rush Brook—*stream* RI-1
Rush Brook Rsvr—*reservoir* PA-2
Rush Canyon—*valley* CA-9
Rush Canyon—*valley* OK-5
Rush Canyon—*valley* UT-8
Rush Canyon—*valley* WA-9
Rush Cem—*cemetery* AL-4
Rush Cem—*cemetery* AR-4
Rush Cem—*cemetery* IL-6
Rush Cem—*cemetery* (2) IN-6
Rush Cem—*cemetery* MS-4
Rush Cem—*cemetery* (2) MO-7
Rush Cem—*cemetery* NC-3
Rush Cem—*cemetery* (2) OH-6
Rush Cem—*cemetery* SC-3
Rush Cem—*cemetery* (2) TN-4
Rush Cem—*cemetery* TX-5
Rush Cem—*cemetery* VA-3
Rush Cem—*cemetery* WV-2
**Rush Center**—*pop pl* KS-7
*Rush Center Cemetery* PA-2
Rush Center Elem Sch—*school* KS-7
Rush Center Memorial Park—*cemetery* PA-2
Rush Center Oil Field—*oilfield* KS-7
*Rush Centre* KS-7
Rush Ch—*church* MD-2
Rush Ch—*church* OH-6
Rush Ch—*church* (2) PA-2
Rush Chapel—*church* GA-3
Rush Chapel—*church* MO-7
Rush Chapel (historical)—*church* MO-7
Rush Chute—*stream* IA-7
**Rush City**—*pop pl* MN-6
Rush Consolidated Elem Sch—*school* PA-2
Rush Corner—*locale* VA-3
Rush Coulee—*valley* (2) WI-6
Rush County—*civil* KS-7
**Rush County**—*pop pl* IN-6
Rush County Airp—*airport* KS-7
Rush County Courthouse—*hist pl* IN-6
Rush County Courthouse—*hist pl* KS-7
Rush County Dam—*dam* KS-7
Rush County Fairgrounds—*locale* KS-7
Rush County Line Bridge—*hist pl* KS-7
Rush Cove—*bay* ME-1
*Rush Creek* AR-4
*Rush Creek* CO-8
*Rush Creek* GA-3
*Rush Creek* NE-7
*Rush Creek* OH-6
*Rush Creek* TX-5
*Rush Creek* VA-3
*Rush Creek* WV-2
*Rush Creek* WI-6
Rush Creek—*locale* CA-9
**Rush Creek**—*pop pl* WV-2
Rush Creek—*stream* (2) AL-4
Rush Creek—*stream* AR-4
Rush Creek—*stream* (15) CA-9
Rush Creek—*stream* (3) CO-8
Rush Creek—*stream* (5) GA-3
Rush Creek—*stream* (5) ID-8
Rush Creek—*stream* (2) IL-6
Rush Creek—*stream* (4) IN-6
Rush Creek—*stream* IA-7
Rush Creek—*stream* (4) KS-7
Rush Creek—*stream* (5) KY-4
Rush Creek—*stream* (3) MI-6
Rush Creek—*stream* (4) MN-6
Rush Creek—*stream* (3) MO-7
Rush Creek—*stream* (4) NE-7
Rush Creek—*stream* NV-8
Rush Creek—*stream* (4) NY-2
Rush Creek—*stream* (3) OH-6
Rush Creek—*stream* (5) OK-5
Rush Creek—*stream* (7) OR-9
Rush Creek—*stream* (2) SD-7
Rush Creek—*stream* (2) TN-4
Rush Creek—*stream* (12) TX-5
Rush Creek—*stream* (2) VA-3
Rush Creek—*stream* WA-9
Rush Creek—*stream* (2) WV-2
Rush Creek—*stream* (5) WI-6
Rush Creek—*stream* (4) WY-8
Rush Creek Bridge—*bridge* NY-2
Rush Creek Bridge—*hist pl* IN-6
Rush Creek Camp—*locale* MO-7
Rush Creek Cem—*cemetery* IN-6
Rush Creek Ch—*church* (2) IN-6
Rush Creek Ch—*church* KY-4
Rush Creek Ch—*church* VA-3
Rush Creek Ch—*church* WV-2
Rush Creek Hill—*summit* CA-9
*Rush Creek Lake* OH-6
Rush Creek Lake—*lake* CA-9
Rushcreek Lake—*reservoir* OH-6
Rush Creek Lakes—*lake* CA-9
Rush Creek Mtn—*summit* CA-9
Rush Creek Point—*summit* ID-8
Rush Creek Public Camp—*locale* CA-9
Rush Creek Ranch—*locale* CO-8
Rush Creek Ranch—*locale* TX-5
Rush Creek Rapids—*rapids* OR-9
Rush Creek Reservoir—*canal* CO-8
Rush Creek Sch—*school* NE-7
Rush Creek Sch (abandoned)—*school* MO-7
Rush Creek Spring—*spring* CA-9
**Rush Creek (Township of)**—*pop pl* OH-6
**Rushcreek (Township of)**—*pop pl* OH-6
**Rush Creek Valley**—*pop pl* IN-6
Rush Crossroads—*locale* PA-2
Rush Cut—*channel* MI-6
Rush Dam—*dam* AL-4
Rush Ditch—*canal* TX-5
Rush Drain—*canal* MI-6
*Rush Elem Sch* PA-2
Rush Elem Sch—*school* PA-2
Rushenville Ch—*church* AL-4
Rusheon JHS—*school* LA-4
Rusher Hotel—*hist pl* AR-4
Rushes Lake—*lake* WI-6
Rush Field—*airport* KS-7
Rush Field—*park* FL-3
Rushfieldt Lake—*lake* MN-6
**Rushford**—*pop pl* MN-6
**Rushford**—*pop pl* NY-2
Rushford City Mill—*hist pl* MN-6
**Rushford Lake**—*pop pl* NY-2
Rushford Lake—*reservoir* NY-2
**Rushford (Town of)**—*pop pl* NY-2
**Rushford (Town of)**—*pop pl* WI-6
**Rushford Township**—*pop pl* ND-7
**Rushford Village**—*pop pl* MN-6
Rushford Wagon and Carriage Company—*hist pl* MN-6
Rush Fork—*stream* AR-4
Rush Fork—*stream* (3) KY-4
Rush Fork—*stream* NC-3
Rush Fork—*stream* TN-4
Rush Fork—*stream* VA-3
Rush Fork—*stream* (4) WV-2
Rush Fork Cem—*cemetery* AR-4
Rush Fork Ch—*church* AR-4
Rush Fork Gap—*gap* NC-3
Rush Foundation Hosp—*hospital* MS-4
Rush Gulch—*valley* CA-9
**Rush Hill**—*pop pl* MO-7
Rush Hill—*summit* AK-9
Rush Hill—*summit* MD-2
Rush Hist Dist—*hist pl* AR-4
Rush Hollow—*valley* AR-4
Rush Hollow—*valley* MD-2
Rush Hollow—*valley* (3) TN-4
Rush Hollow—*valley* VT-1
Rush Hollow—*valley* VA-3
Rush Hollow—*valley* WV-2
Rush Hosp—*hospital* PA-2
Rush House—*hist pl* PA-2
Rush House—*park* DC-2
*Rushian Creek* TN-4
Rushie Branch—*stream* GA-3
Rushing—*locale* AR-4
**Rushing**—*pop pl* MS-4
**Rushing**—*pop pl* TX-5
Rushing Bay—*bay* TN-4
Rushing Bluff—*cliff* TN-4
Rushing Branch—*stream* FL-3
Rushing Branch—*stream* MS-4
Rushing Branch—*stream* NC-3
Rushing Branch—*stream* TN-4
Rushing Cem—*cemetery* AR-4
Rushing Cem—*cemetery* IL-6
Rushing Cem—*cemetery* KY-4
Rushing Cem—*cemetery* (2) MS-4
Rushing Cem—*cemetery* (7) TN-4
Rushing Cem—*cemetery* TX-5
Rushing Ch—*church* KY-4
Rushing Ch—*church* TN-4
*Rushing Chapel* TN-4
Rushing Chapel Cem—*cemetery* TX-5
*Rushing Creek* TN-4
Rushing Creek—*stream* AL-4
Rushing Creek—*stream* (2) TN-4
Rushing Creek Campground—*locale* TN-4
Rushing Creek Cem—*cemetery* TN-4
Rushing Creek Ch—*church* (2) TN-4
Rushing Creek Community Center—*locale* TN-4
Rushing Creek Draingage Ditch—*canal* TN-4
Rushing Creek (historical)—*stream* TN-4
Rushing Cutoff—*stream* FL-3
*Rushing Dam* AL-4
Rushing Grove Ch—*church* TN-4
Rushing Hall—*building* NC-3
*Rushing Hill* CA-9
Rushing Hill—*summit* TN-4
**Rushing (historical)**—*pop pl* TN-4
Rushing Hollow—*valley* TN-4
Rushing Lake—*reservoir* AL-4
Rushing Lake—*reservoir* CA-9
Rushing Meadow—*flat* CA-9

Rushing Mtn—summit ... CA-9
Rushing Pond—bay ... TN-4
Rushing Run—stream ... IN-6
Rushings Chapel—church ... AL-4
Rushing Sch (historical)—school ... TN-4
Rushings Creek ... TN-4
Rushings Creek Baptist Church ... TN-4
Rushings Creek Cem—cemetery ... TN-4
Rushings Grove United Pentecostal Church ... TN-4
Rushings Hill ... CA-9
Rushings Mill (historical)—locale ... TN-4
Rushings Mtn ... CA-9
Rushing Spring—spring ... OR-9
Rushing Spring Ch—church (2) ... AL-4
Rushing Springs (historical)—locale ... AL-4
Rushing Springs Sch—school ... TN-4
Rushing Store (historical)—locale ... MS-4
Rushingville Church ... AL-4
Rushing Water Creek—stream ... OR-9
Rushingwater Creek—stream ... WA-9
Rush Island—island (2) ... AR-4
Rush Island—island ... FL-3
Rush Island—island ... IA-7
Rush Island—island ... KY-4
Rush Island—island (2) ... MO-7
Rush Island—island ... NE-7
Rush Island—island ... NJ-2
Rush Island—island ... NY-2
Rush Island—island ... NC-3
Rush Island Lake—lake ... MN-6
Rush Island Lake—lake ... ND-7
Rush Knob—summit ... WV-2
Rush Lake ... MN-6
Rush Lake ... MS-4
Rush Lake ... NE-7
Rush Lake ... ND-7
Rush Lake ... OH-6
Rush Lake ... SD-7
Rush Lake—lake ... AK-9
Rush Lake—lake ... AR-4
Rush Lake—lake ... FL-3
Rush Lake—lake ... ID-8
Rush Lake—lake (2) ... IA-7
Rush Lake—lake (6) ... MI-6
Rush Lake—lake (16) ... MN-6
Rush Lake—lake (2) ... MT-8
Rush Lake—lake (6) ... NE-7
Rush Lake—lake (6) ... ND-7
Rush Lake—lake (2) ... SD-7
Rush Lake—lake (2) ... TX-5
Rush Lake—lake (2) ... UT-8
Rush Lake—lake (5) ... WI-6
Rush Lake—lake (2) ... WY-8
Rush Lake—pop pl ... WI-6
Rush Lake—swamp (2) ... MN-6
Rush Lake—swamp ... NE-7
Rush Lake—swamp ... ND-7
Rush Lakebed—flat (2) ... MN-6
Rush Lake Dam—dam ... MS-4
Rush Lake Drain—canal ... MI-6
Rush Lake (historical)—lake ... ND-7
Rush Lake Junction ... WI-6
Rush Lake Junction (Rush Lake)—pop pl ... WI-6
Rush Lake Outlet—stream ... IA-7
Rush Lake Sch—school ... MI-6
Rush Lake State Game Mngmt Area—park ... IA-7
Rush Lake State Public Shooting Area—park ... SD-7
Rush Lake State Wildlife Mngmt Area—park ... IA-7
Rush Lake State Wildlife Mngmt Area—park ... MN-6
Rush Lake Township—fmr MCD ... IA-7
Rush Lake Township—pop pl ... ND-7
Rush Lake (Township of)—pop pl ... MN-6
Rushland—locale ... PA-2
Rushland Ditch ... OH-6
Rush Landing—locale ... CA-9
Rushland Post Office (historical)—building ... PA-2
Rush Lick Run—stream ... WV-2
Rush Memorial Hosp—hospital ... IN-6
Rushmer Canyon—valley ... CO-8
Rushmere—pop pl ... VA-3
Rushmere Shores—locale ... VA-3
Rushmeyer Lake—lake ... MN-6
Rush-Miller House—hist pl ... WV-2
Rush Mill Pond ... VA-3
Rushmore—pop pl ... MN-6
Rushmore—pop pl ... OH-6
Rushmore, Mount—summit ... SD-7
Rushmore Airp—airport ... SD-7
Rushmore Cave—cave ... SD-7
Rushmore Mall—locale ... SD-7
Rushmore Sch—school ... OH-6
Rush Mtn—summit (2) ... NC-3
Rusho Bay—bay ... NY-2
Rusho Creek—stream ... WA-9
Rushpatch Branch—stream ... WV-2
Rush Peak—summit ... AK-9
Rush Peak—summit ... ID-8
Rush Pipeline Well—well ... NM-5
Rush Place Windmill—locale ... AZ-5
Rush Point—cape (2) ... AK-9
Rush Point—cape ... NC-3
Rush Point—pop pl ... MN-6
Rush Point Sch—school ... KY-4
Rush Point State Public Hunting Grounds—park ... WI-6
Rush Pond ... MA-1
Rush Pond ... MI-6
Rush Pond—lake ... GA-3
Rush Pond—lake (2) ... ME-1
Rush Pond—lake ... NY-2
Rush Pond—lake ... UT-8
Rush Pond—lake ... VT-1
Rush Pond—swamp ... TX-5
Rush Prairie ... TX-5
Rush Prairie—pop pl ... TX-5
Rush Ridge—ridge ... IN-6
Rush Ridge—ridge ... KY-4
Rush Ridge Ch—church ... MO-7
Rush Ridge Sch (abandoned)—school ... MO-7
Rush River ... MN-6
Rush River—locale ... MN-6
Rush River—stream ... MN-6
Rush River—stream ... ND-7
Rush River—stream ... VA-3
Rush River—stream ... WI-6
Rush River Ch—church ... WI-6
Rush River (Town of)—pop pl ... WI-6
Rush River Township—pop pl ... ND-7
Rush Rock—bar ... AK-9
Rush Rsvr—reservoir ... NY-2
Rush Run ... MI-6
Rush Run ... WV-2
Rush Run—pop pl ... NY-2
Rush Run—pop pl ... OH-6
Rush Run—stream (3) ... KY-4
Rush Run—stream ... MD-2
Rush Run—stream (6) ... OH-6
Rush Run—stream (6) ... PA-2
Rush Run—stream (20) ... WV-2
Rush Run Ch—church ... OH-6
Rush Run Ch—church (2) ... WV-2
Rush Run Chapel—church ... OH-6
Rush Run Sch (abandoned)—school ... PA-2
Rush Run Wildlife Area—park ... OH-6
Rush Sch—school ... CA-9
Rush Sch—school (3) ... IL-6
Rush Sch—school ... OH-6
Rush Sch—school ... TX-5
Rush Sch—school ... WI-6
Rush Sch (historical)—school (2) ... MS-4
Rush Sch (historical)—school (2) ... TN-4
Rushseba (Township of)—pop pl ... MN-6
Rushs Enemy Cem—cemetery ... SD-7
Rushs Lake—reservoir ... AL-4
Rush Slough—gut ... TN-4
Rush Slough—gut ... WY-8
Rush Slough—stream ... TN-4
Rush Slough Sch (historical)—school ... TN-4
Rush Spring—spring ... AZ-5
Rush Spring—spring ... CO-8
Rush Spring—spring (2) ... OR-9
Rush Spring—spring ... TN-4
Rush Springs—pop pl ... OK-5
Rush Springs (CCD)—cens area ... OK-5
Rush Station—locale ... KY-4
Rush Strip Airp—airport ... IN-6
Rush Strong Elementary School ... TN-4
Rush Strong Sch—school (4) ... TN-4
Rush Strong Sch (historical)—school ... TN-4
Rush Swamp—swamp ... ME-1
Rush Swamp—swamp ... MI-6
Rush Swamp Brook—stream ... ME-1
Rushsylvania—pop pl ... OH-6
Rushsylvania Cem—cemetery ... OH-6
Rushton—pop pl ... MI-6
Rushton Acres Subdivision—pop pl ... UT-8
Rushton Addition (subdivision)—pop pl ... UT-8
Rushton Cem—cemetery ... MS-4
Rushton Elem Sch—school ... KS-7
Rushton Hill—summit ... NV-8
Rushton Park—park ... AL-4
Rushton Station—locale ... PA-2
Rushton (subdivision)—pop pl ... TN-4
Rush Tower—locale ... MO-7
Rush Tower Sch (abandoned)—school ... MO-7
Rushtown—pop pl ... OH-6
Rushtown—pop pl ... PA-2
Rush (Town of)—pop pl ... NY-2
Rush Township ... KS-7
Rush Township—civil ... MO-7
Rush (Township of)—pop pl ... IL-6
Rush (Township of)—pop pl ... MI-6
Rush (Township of)—pop pl (3) ... OH-6
Rush (Township of)—pop pl (5) ... PA-2
Rush Valley—pop pl ... UT-8
Rush Valley—valley ... UT-8
Rush Valley Creek ... NV-8
Rushville ... PA-2
Rushville—locale ... MD-2
Rushville—locale ... PA-2
Rushville—locale ... VA-3
Rushville—locale ... WV-2
Rushville—pop pl ... IL-6
Rushville—pop pl ... IN-6
Rushville—pop pl ... IA-7
Rushville—pop pl ... MO-7
Rushville—pop pl ... NE-7
Rushville—pop pl ... NY-2
Rushville—pop pl (2) ... OH-6
Rushville—pop pl ... SC-3
Rushville Cem—cemetery ... IA-7
Rushville Cem—cemetery ... SC-3
Rushville Consolidated HS—school ... IN-6
Rushville Hist Dist—hist pl ... OH-6
Rushville (historical)—locale ... KS-7
Rushville Sch (historical)—school ... MO-7
Rushville Township—pop pl ... KS-7
Rushville Township—pop pl ... ND-7
Rushville (Township of)—pop pl ... IL-6
Rushville (Township of)—pop pl ... IN-6
Rushwater Creek—stream ... MT-8
Rush Windmill—locale ... CO-8
Rush Windmill—locale ... NM-5
Rushy Hollow—valley ... TN-4
Rushy Marsh Pond—lake ... MA-1
Rushy Ponds—cape ... MD-2
Rushy Spring—spring ... TN-4
Rushy Springs—locale ... TN-4
Rusin, Oror En—pop pl ... FM-9
Rusk ... MS-4
Rusk—locale ... WV-2
Rusk—pop pl ... IN-6
Rusk—pop pl ... IA-7
Rusk—pop pl ... MI-6
Rusk—pop pl ... TX-5
Rusk—pop pl ... WI-6
Ruskaup House—hist pl ... MO-7
Rusk Camp—locale ... WI-6
Rusk (CCD)—cens area ... TX-5
Rusk Cem—cemetery ... IL-6
Rusk Cem—cemetery ... OH-6
Rusk Cem—cemetery (2) ... OK-5
Rusk Ch—church ... WI-6
Rusk City Park—park ... TX-5
Rusk (County)—pop pl ... TX-5
Rusk (County)—pop pl ... WI-6
Rusk Creek—stream ... WA-9
Rusk Glacier—glacier ... WA-9
Rusk Hill—summit ... NM-5
Rusk (historical)—locale ... NC-3
Ruskin ... MO-7
Ruskin—locale ... MN-6
Ruskin—locale ... NC-3
Ruskin—pop pl ... FL-3
Ruskin—pop pl ... GA-3
Ruskin—pop pl ... MO-7
Ruskin—pop pl ... NE-7
Ruskin—pop pl ... TN-4
Ruskin, Mount—summit ... CA-9
Ruskin (CCD)—cens area ... FL-3
Ruskin Cem—cemetery ... FL-3
Ruskin Colony Grounds—hist pl ... TN-4
Ruskin Elem Sch—school ... FL-3
Ruskin Heights ... MO-7
Ruskin Heights—pop pl ... MO-7
Ruskin Heights—uninc pl ... GA-3
Ruskin Inlet—gut ... FL-3
Ruskin Memorial Gardens—cemetery ... FL-3
Ruskin Park—pop pl ... SD-7
Ruskin Park (historical)—park ... SD-7
Ruskin Sch—school ... MN-6
Ruskin Sch—school ... OH-6
Rusk JHS—school ... TX-5
Rusk Lake—lake ... WI-6
Rusk Lookout Tower—locale ... TX-5
Rusk Mtn—summit ... NY-2
Rusk Oil Field—oilfield ... KS-7
Rusk Park—park ... TX-5
Rusk Post Office (historical)—building ... MS-4
Rusk Ranch—locale ... TX-5
Rusk Sch—school (5) ... TX-5
Rusk State Hosp—hospital ... TX-5
Rusk (Town of)—pop pl (2) ... WI-6
Rusk Township—pop pl ... SD-7
Rusland Township—pop pl ... ND-7
Ruslin Hill Cem—cemetery ... OH-6
Ruslor ... MS-4
Ruslor Junction—locale ... MS-4
Rusmag Oil Field—oilfield ... TX-5
Rusnak Mine—mine ... PA-2
Rusnaks Private Strip—airport ... NJ-2
Ruso—pop pl ... ND-7
Russ—locale ... CA-9
Russ—pop pl ... MO-7
Russ, Joseph W., Jr., House—hist pl ... FL-3
Russaw (historical)—pop pl ... NC-3
Russ Branch—stream ... TN-4
Russ Canyon—valley ... NM-5
Russ Cem—cemetery ... CT-1
Russ Cem—cemetery ... MO-7
Russcher Sch—school ... MI-6
Russ Coalings—summit ... TN-4
Russ Creek—stream ... CA-9
Russ Creek—stream ... OR-9
Russ Creek—stream ... SC-3
Russel, Lake—lake ... GA-3
Russel, Robert, House—hist pl ... KY-4
Russel Camp—locale ... WY-8
Russel Cem—cemetery ... GA-3
Russel Cem—cemetery ... MS-4
Russel Cemetery ... TN-4
Russel Chapel Cem—cemetery ... TX-5
Russel Church ... TN-4
Russel Creek ... MT-8
Russel Creek—stream ... AK-9
Russel Creek—stream (4) ... OR-9
Russel Creek—stream ... SC-3
Russel Creek—stream ... WY-8
Russel Draw—valley ... MT-8
Russel Draw—valley ... WY-8
Russel Fork—pop pl ... TN-4
Russel Fork Deep Creek ... MT-8
Russel Fork River ... KY-4
Russel Grove HS—school ... VA-3
Russel Gulch ... CO-8
Russel Gulch—valley ... ID-8
Russel Gulch—valley ... NV-8
Russel Hills—other ... NM-5
Russel Hollow ... MO-7
Russel Key—island ... FL-3
Russell ... CA-9
Russell ... NV-8
Russell ... OH-6
Russell—fmr MCD (3) ... NE-7
Russell—locale ... CA-9
Russell—locale ... NH-1
Russell—locale ... OH-6
Russell—locale ... OK-5
Russell—locale ... TX-5
Russell—locale ... VA-3
Russell—locale ... WA-9
Russell—pop pl ... AR-4
Russell—pop pl ... CO-8
Russell—pop pl (2) ... FL-3
Russell—pop pl ... GA-3
Russell—pop pl ... IL-6
Russell—pop pl ... IA-7
Russell—pop pl ... KS-7
Russell—pop pl ... KY-4
Russell—pop pl ... MA-1
Russell—pop pl ... MN-6
Russell—pop pl ... MS-4
Russell—pop pl ... NY-2
Russell—pop pl ... ND-7
Russell—pop pl ... OH-6
Russell—pop pl ... OK-5
Russell—pop pl ... OR-9
Russell—pop pl ... PA-2
Russell—pop pl ... SC-3
Russell—pop pl ... VA-3
Russell—pop pl ... WI-6
Russell—uninc pl ... AL-4
Russell—uninc pl ... CA-9
Russell, Avery, House—hist pl ... TN-4
Russell, Charles B., House—hist pl ... OH-6
Russell, Charles M., House and Studio—hist pl ... MT-8
Russell, Edward Augustus, House—hist pl ... CT-1
Russell, Jason House—hist pl ... MA-1
Russell, John, House—hist pl ... AR-4
Russell, Joseph and William, House—hist pl ... RI-1
Russell, Lake—lake ... FL-3
Russell, Lake—reservoir ... AL-4
Russell, Lake—reservoir ... GA-3
Russell, Lake—reservoir ... PA-2
Russell, Mark, House—hist pl ... OH-6
Russell, Mount—summit ... AK-9
Russell, Mount—summit (2) ... CA-9
Russell, Nathaniel, House—hist pl ... SC-3
Russell, Rensselaer, House—hist pl ... IA-7
Russell, The—hist pl ... MA-1
Russell, William, House—hist pl ... DE-2
Russell, William, House—hist pl ... MI-6
Russell-Arnold House—hist pl ... TX-5
Russell Arnold Ranch—locale ... NM-5
Russel Lateral—canal ... CA-9
Russell Baptist Ch—church ... MS-4
Russell Bar—bar ... ID-8
Russell Bay—bay ... FL-3
Russell Bayou—bay ... FL-3
Russell Bayou—stream ... LA-4
Russell Bend—bend ... IN-6
Russell Bend—bend ... LA-4
Russell Bend—bend ... TN-4
Russell Bird Ranch—locale ... NM-5
Russell Blvd Sch—school ... MO-7
Russell Bog—swamp ... ME-1
Russell Bogs—swamp ... MA-1
Russell Branch—stream (2) ... AL-4
Russell Branch—stream (2) ... AR-4
Russell Branch—stream (2) ... GA-3
Russell Branch—stream (3) ... IN-6
Russell Branch—stream (6) ... KY-4
Russell Branch—stream ... MD-2
Russell Branch—stream ... MS-4
Russell Branch—stream ... NC-3
Russell Branch—stream (5) ... TN-4
Russell Branch—stream (2) ... TX-5
Russell Branch—stream (2) ... VA-3
Russell Branch Sch (historical)—school ... MS-4
Russell Bridge—bridge ... GA-3
Russell Bridge—bridge ... SC-3
Russell Brook ... CT-1
Russell Brook—stream ... CA-9
Russell Brook—stream ... CT-1
Russell Brook—stream (4) ... ME-1
Russell Brook—stream ... NY-2
Russell Brook—stream (2) ... VT-1
Russell Brown Elem Sch—school ... TN-4
Russellburg ... PA-2
Russell Butte—summit ... ND-7
Russell Cabin—locale (2) ... CA-9
Russell Camp—locale ... CA-9
Russell Camp—locale ... CO-8
Russell Camp (historical)—locale ... ME-1
Russell Camp Ridge—ridge ... AR-4
Russell Canyon—valley ... CA-9
Russell Canyon—valley ... OR-9
Russell Cave—cave ... AL-4
Russell Cave—cave ... KY-4
Russell Cave—cave ... TN-4
Russell Cave Natl Monmt—hist pl ... AL-4
Russell Cave Natl Monmt—park ... AL-4
Russell Cave Sch—school ... KY-4
Russell (CCD)—cens area ... AL-4
Russell (CCD)—cens area ... KY-4
Russell Cem ... AL-4
Russell Cem—cemetery (3) ... AL-4
Russell Cem—cemetery (3) ... AR-4
Russell Cem—cemetery ... GA-3
Russell Cem—cemetery ... ID-8
Russell Cem—cemetery (6) ... IL-6
Russell Cem—cemetery ... IN-6
Russell Cem—cemetery (2) ... IA-7
Russell Cem—cemetery (13) ... KY-4
Russell Cem—cemetery ... LA-4
Russell Cem—cemetery ... ME-1
Russell Cem—cemetery ... MN-6
Russell Cem—cemetery (3) ... MS-4
Russell Cem—cemetery (3) ... MO-7
Russell Cem—cemetery ... NY-2
Russell Cem—cemetery ... NC-3
Russell Cem—cemetery (4) ... OH-6
Russell Cem—cemetery (3) ... OK-5
Russell Cem—cemetery ... OR-9
Russell Cem—cemetery ... SC-3
Russell Cem—cemetery (17) ... TN-4
Russell Cem—cemetery (2) ... TX-5
Russell Cem—cemetery (2) ... WV-2
Russell Center—pop pl ... OH-6
Russell Ch ... TN-4
Russell Ch—church ... GA-3
Russell Ch—church ... LA-4
Russell Ch—church ... TX-5
Russell Ch—church ... WV-2
Russell Channel—channel ... WA-9
Russell Chapel—church ... AL-4
Russell Chapel—church ... AR-4
Russell Chapel—church ... IN-6
Russell Chapel—church ... KY-4
Russell Chapel—church ... MO-7
Russell Chapel—church ... MT-8
Russell Chapel—church (2) ... TN-4
Russell Chapel—church (2) ... VA-3
Russell Chapel Baptist Ch ... AL-4
Russell Chapel Cem—cemetery ... IN-6
Russell Chapel (historical)—church ... TN-4
Russell Chapel Sch—school ... TX-5
Russell City—pop pl ... CA-9
Russell City—pop pl ... PA-2
Russell City (RR name for DeYoung)—other ... PA-2
Russell Cliff—cliff ... WA-9
Russell-Colbath House—hist pl ... NH-1
Russell Common—hist pl ... MA-1
Russell Company Upper Mill—hist pl ... CT-1
Russell Corner—locale ... KY-4
Russell Corner—locale ... VA-3
Russell Corners—locale ... PA-2
Russell Cottage Sch—school ... CO-8
Russell County—civil ... KS-7
Russell County—pop pl ... AL-4
Russell (County)—pop pl ... KY-4
Russell (County)—pop pl ... VA-3
Russell County Courthouse at Seale—hist pl ... AL-4
Russell County Vocational Sch—school ... AL-4
Russell Court—hist pl ... KY-4
Russell Cove—bay ... ME-1
Russell Cove—lake ... MA-1
Russell Cove—valley ... AL-4
Russell Crag—cliff ... NH-1
Russell Creek ... SC-3
Russell Creek—pop pl ... OK-5
Russell Creek—pop pl ... VA-3
Russell Creek—stream ... CA-9
Russell Creek—stream ... CO-8
Russell Creek—stream ... GA-3
Russell Creek—stream (2) ... ID-8
Russell Creek—stream (3) ... KY-4
Russell Creek—stream (2) ... MI-6
Russell Creek—stream (2) ... MS-4
Russell Creek—stream (3) ... MT-8
Russell Creek—stream ... NE-7
Russell Creek—stream (3) ... NC-3
Russell Creek—stream ... OH-6
Russell Creek—stream ... OK-5
Russell Creek—stream (7) ... OR-9
Russell Creek—stream ... SC-3
Russell Creek—stream (4) ... TN-4
Russell Creek—stream (5) ... TX-5
Russell Creek—stream (2) ... VA-3
Russell Creek—stream (2) ... WA-9
Russell Creek—stream ... WV-2
Russell Creek—stream ... WY-8
Russell Creek Cem—cemetery ... OK-5
Russell Creek Ch—church ... VA-3
Russell Creek Ch (historical)—church ... TN-4
Russell Creek Sch—school ... KY-4
Russell Crossing—locale ... ME-1
Russell Crossing—locale ... TX-5
Russell Crossroad—locale ... TN-4
Russell Crossroads ... AL-4
Russell Crossroads—locale ... TN-4
Russell C Struble Elem Sch—school ... PA-2
Russell Dairy Spring—spring ... CA-9
Russelldale—locale ... WV-2
Russell Dayton Ranch—locale ... WY-8
Russell Ditch—canal ... IN-6
Russell Division—civil ... AL-4
Russell Drain—canal ... MI-6
Russell Drain—canal ... OR-9
Russell Drain—stream ... MI-6
Russell Draw—valley ... WY-8
Russell Falls—falls ... NY-2
Russell Farm Ch—church ... AL-4
Russell Farms Airp—airport ... PA-2
Russell Ferry Estates (subdivision)—pop pl ... AL-4
Russell Ferry (historical)—locale ... TN-4
Russell Field—flat ... TN-4
Russell Field—park ... MA-1
Russell Field—ridge ... NC-3
Russell Field Branch—stream ... TN-4
Russell Field Lookout Tower—locale ... TN-4
Russell Field Trail—trail ... TN-4
Russell Fiord—bay ... AK-9
Russell Fire Tower—locale ... AL-4
Russell Flat—flat ... KY-4
Russell Flat Cem—cemetery ... KY-4
Russell Ford (historical)—crossing ... TN-4
Russell Fork—pop pl ... TN-4
Russell Fork—stream ... KY-4
Russell Fork—stream ... VA-3
Russell Fork Ch—church ... VA-3
Russell Fork Deep Creek—stream ... MT-8
Russell Fork River ... VA-3
Russell Fork San Gabriel River—stream ... TX-5
Russell Fork Stout Creek—stream ... OH-6
Russell For Preserve—forest ... IL-6
Russell Gap—gap ... NM-5
Russell Gap—gap (2) ... NC-3
Russell Gap—gap ... TN-4
Russell Gap—gap ... TX-5
Russell Gap Ch—church ... NC-3
Russell Gardens—pop pl ... NY-2
Russell Glacier—glacier ... AK-9
Russell Glacier—glacier ... OR-9
Russell Glacier—glacier ... WA-9
Russell-Graves House—hist pl ... CO-8
Russell Grove Ch—church ... TN-4
Russell Grove Sch—school ... TN-4
Russell Gulch—locale ... CO-8
Russell Gulch—valley ... AZ-5
Russell Gulch—valley (2) ... CO-8
Russell Gulch—valley ... MT-8
Russell Gulch—valley ... UT-8
Russell Gulch Cem—cemetery ... CO-8
Russell Gulch Tank—reservoir ... AZ-5
Russell Harrington Mill Pond ... MA-1
Russell Harrington Mill Pond Dam—dam ... MA-1
Russell Hay Camp—locale ... NV-8
Russell Heights—pop pl ... AL-4
Russell Heights—pop pl ... KY-4
Russell Heights—pop pl ... OH-6
Russell Heights Cem—cemetery ... MO-7
Russell Hill ... AL-4
Russell Hill—pop pl ... PA-2
Russell Hill—pop pl ... TN-4
Russell Hill—summit ... AL-4
Russell Hill—summit ... AZ-5
Russell Hill—summit ... KY-4
Russell Hill—summit ... ME-1
Russell Hill—summit (2) ... MA-1
Russell Hill—summit (2) ... NH-1
Russell Hill—summit ... NY-2
Russell Hill—summit (3) ... PA-2
Russell Hill—summit ... TX-5
Russell Hill—summit ... VT-1
Russell Hill Baptist Ch—church ... TN-4
Russell Hill Presbyterian Ch—church ... TN-4
Russell Hill Sch—school ... PA-2
Russell HillSchool (historical)—school ... TN-4
Russell Hills (subdivision)—pop pl ... NC-3
Russell Hill (subdivision)—pop pl ... AL-4
Russell Hist Dist—hist pl ... KY-4
Russell Hollow ... MO-7
Russell Hollow ... TN-4
Russell Hollow—valley ... CA-9
Russell Hollow—valley (2) ... MO-7
Russell Hollow—valley ... PA-2
Russell Hollow—valley (7) ... TN-4
Russell Hollow—valley ... TX-5
Russell Hollow—valley ... UT-8
Russell Hollow—valley ... VA-3
Russell Hollow Run—stream ... PA-2
Russell Homeplace Hist Dist—hist pl ... GA-3
Russell Hosp—hospital ... AL-4
Russell House—hist pl ... AR-4
Russell House—hist pl ... CT-1
Russell House—hist pl ... MA-1
Russell House—hist pl ... PA-2
Russell House—hist pl ... WA-9
Russell HS—school (2) ... AL-4
Russell HS—school ... GA-3
Russell HS—school ... KS-7
Russell HS—school ... KY-4
Russell HS—school ... MT-8
Russell HS—school ... VA-3
Russell Independent District Sch (historical)—school ... IA-7
Russell Island—flat ... AR-4
Russell Island—island ... AL-4
Russell Island—island ... AK-9
Russell Island—island ... KY-4
Russell Island—island ... MI-6
Russell Island—island ... TN-4
Russell Island—island ... VA-3
Russell Island—pop pl ... MI-6
Russell Jennings pond ... CT-1
Russell JHS—school ... CA-9
Russell Key—island (2) ... FL-3
Russell Knob—summit ... VA-3
Russell Lake ... AL-4
Russell Lake ... GA-3
Russell Lake ... MI-6
Russell Lake ... WA-9
Russell Lake—lake ... CA-9
Russell Lake—lake ... CO-8
Russell Lake—lake (2) ... IN-6
Russell Lake—lake (4) ... MI-6
Russell Lake—lake ... MN-6
Russell Lake—lake ... MT-8
Russell Lake—lake (2) ... NY-2
Russell Lake—lake ... ND-7
Russell Lake—lake ... OR-9
Russell Lake—lake ... TX-5
Russell Lake—lake ... WI-6
Russell Lake—lake ... WY-8
Russell Lake—pop pl ... IN-6
Russell Lake—reservoir ... MS-4
Russell Lake—reservoir ... PA-2
Russell Lake—reservoir ... TX-5
Russell Lake Dam—dam (2) ... MS-4
Russell Lake Landing—locale ... SC-3
Russell Lakes—lake ... CO-8
Russell Landing—locale ... FL-3
Russell Landing—locale ... WA-9
Russell Lateral—canal ... CA-9
Russell Lateral—canal ... WI-6
Russell Lee Lake—reservoir ... AL-4
Russell Lee Lake Dam—dam ... AL-4
Russellmann Creek—stream ... CA-9
Russellmann Park—park ... CA-9
Russell Memorial Bridge—bridge ... AL-4
Russell Memorial Cem—cemetery ... VA-3
Russell Memorial Park—park ... MA-1
Russell Memorial Park—park ... WI-6
Russell Mill—locale ... TN-4
Russell Mill—uninc pl ... AL-4
Russell Mill Pond ... MA-1
Russell Millpond—lake ... MA-1
Russell Millpond—lake ... NH-1
Russell Millpond—reservoir (2) ... MA-1
Russell Mill Pond Dam—dam ... MA-1
Russell Millpond Dam—dam ... MA-1
Russell Mills Dam—dam ... AL-4
Russell Mills Lake ... AL-4
Russell Mills Pond ... MA-1
Russell Mine—mine ... CA-9
Russell Mines (underground)—mine ... TN-4
Russell Missionary Ch—church ... FL-3
Russell Mountain ... OR-9
Russell MS—school ... OR-9
Russell Mtn—summit ... AL-4
Russell Mtn—summit ... AR-4
Russell Mtn—summit ... GA-3
Russell Mtn—summit ... ID-8
Russell Mtn—summit (3) ... ME-1
Russell Mtn—summit ... MA-1
Russell Mtn—summit (2) ... MO-7
Russell Mtn—summit ... NH-1
Russell Mtn—summit ... OK-5
Russell Mtn—summit ... SC-3
Russell Mtn—summit ... TN-4
Russell Municipal Airp—airport ... KS-7
Russell No 2 Cem—cemetery ... OH-6
Russell Number 1 Cem—cemetery ... OH-6
Russell Octagon House—hist pl ... IA-7
Russell Oil Field—oilfield ... KS-7
Russell Oil Field—oilfield ... TX-5
Russell Park—park ... IL-6
Russell Park—park ... IA-7
Russell Park—park ... MT-8
Russell Park—park ... NY-2
Russell Park—park ... TX-5
Russell Park Subdivision—pop pl ... UT-8
Russell Pass—channel ... FL-3
Russell Pass—gap ... NV-8
Russell Peak—summit ... CA-9
Russell Peak—summit ... NV-8
Russell Peak—summit ... WY-8
Russell Point—cape ... AL-4
Russell Point—cape ... AR-4
Russell Point—cape ... ME-1
Russell Point—cape (2) ... MD-2
Russell Point—cape ... MT-8
Russell Point—cape ... NH-1
Russell Point—cape ... OR-9
Russell Point—cliff ... AL-4
Russell Point—summit ... AL-4
Russell Point—summit ... AZ-5
Russell Pond ... ME-1
Russell Pond ... MA-1
Russell Pond—lake ... IL-6
Russell Pond—lake (2) ... ME-1
Russell Pond—lake (2) ... NH-1
Russell Pond—reservoir (2) ... AL-4
Russell Pond—reservoir (2) ... MA-1
Russell Pond Brook—stream ... NH-1
Russell Pond Dam—dam (2) ... MA-1
Russell Pond Rec Area—park ... NH-1
Russell Pond (Township of)—unorg ... ME-1
Russell Post Office ... SD-7
Russell Post Office (historical)—building ... MS-4
Russell Prater Ch—church ... VA-3
Russell Prater Creek—stream ... VA-3
Russell Pretty Branch—stream ... OK-5
Russell Quarry—mine ... AZ-5
Russell Ranch—locale ... CO-8
Russell Ranch—locale ... NE-7
Russell Ranch—locale ... TX-5
Russell Ranch—locale ... WY-8
Russell Ranch Oil Field ... CA-9
Russell Reservoir—lake ... NH-1
Russell Ridge—ridge ... AL-4
Russell Ridge—ridge ... AR-4
Russell Ridge—ridge ... CA-9
Russell Ridge—ridge ... CO-8
Russell Ridge—ridge ... ID-8
Russell Ridge—ridge (2) ... KY-4
Russell Ridge—ridge (4) ... TN-4
Russell Ridge—ridge ... VA-3

Ruthland Sch—school ... IL-6
**Ruthland (subdivision)**—pop pl ... FL-3
Ruthledge Ford—locale ... TN-4
Ruthledge Hill—locale ... TN-4
Ruth Lookout Tower—locale ... MS-4
Ruth Mansion House—hist pl ... DE-2
Ruth Memorial Ch—church ... NC-3
Ruth Mine—mine ... AZ-5
Ruth Mine—mine ... CA-9
Ruth Mine—mine ... ID-8
Ruth Mine—mine (2) ... NV-8
Ruth Mine—mine ... NM-5
Ruth Mtn ... WA-9
Ruth Mtn—summit ... CO-8
Ruth Mtn—summit ... OR-9
Ruth Mtn—summit ... WA-9
Ruth Palmer Elem Sch—school ... IN-6
Ruth Park—park ... MO-7
Ruth Park—park ... WA-9
Ruth Peak ... WA-9
Ruth Pierce Mine—mine ... CA-9
Ruth Pit ... NV-8
Ruth Point—cape ... ME-1
Ruth Pond—lake ... MA-1
Ruth Post Office (historical)—building ... MS-4
Ruth Prairie—flat ... WA-9
Ruth Reservoir ... CA-9
Ruth River—stream ... AK-9
Ruthruff Sch—school ... MI-6
**Ruthsburg**—pop pl ... MD-2
Ruth Sch—school ... MI-6
Ruth Sch—school ... MS-4
Ruth Sch—school ... NC-3
Ruths Chapel ... TN-4
Ruths Chapel—church ... NC-3
Ruths Chapel Cem—cemetery ... TN-4
Ruth Sch (historical)—school ... AL-4
Ruths Island—island ... MN-6
Ruths Pond—lake ... UT-8
Ruth Spring—spring ... NV-8
Ruth Spring—spring ... OR-9
Ruth Spring—spring ... WA-9
Ruths Tank—reservoir ... AZ-5
Ruth Tank—reservoir ... AZ-5
Ruthton—locale ... KY-4
Ruthton—locale ... NE-7
**Ruthton**—pop pl ... MN-6
**Ruthton**—pop pl ... TN-4
Ruthton Cem—cemetery ... MN-6
**Ruthton (historical)**—pop pl (2) ... OR-9
Ruthton Post Office (historical)—building ... TN-4
Ruthton State Wildlife Mngmt Area—park ... MN-6
Ruth (Township of)—fmr MCD ... MO-7
Ruth Trace Branch—stream ... WV-2
Ruthven ... AL-4
Ruthven—locale ... CA-9
**Ruthven**—pop pl ... AL-4
**Ruthven**—pop pl ... IA-7
Ruthville—locale ... VA-3
**Ruthville**—pop pl ... ND-7
**Ruthville**—pop pl ... TN-4
Ruthville Baptist Ch—church ... TN-4
Ruticle Sch (historical)—school ... MS-4
Rutland ... MO-7
Rutland—locale ... FL-3
Rutland—locale ... KY-4
Rutland—other ... PA-2
**Rutland**—pop pl ... GA-3
**Rutland**—pop pl ... IL-6
**Rutland**—pop pl ... IN-6
**Rutland**—pop pl ... IA-7
**Rutland**—pop pl ... MA-1
**Rutland**—pop pl ... ND-7
**Rutland**—pop pl ... OH-6
**Rutland**—pop pl ... SD-7
**Rutland**—pop pl ... TX-5
**Rutland**—pop pl ... VT-1
**Rutland**—pop pl ... WI-6
Rutland Branch—stream ... TN-4
Rutland Branch—stream ... WI-6
Rutland Brook—stream ... MA-1
Rutland (CCD)—cens area ... GA-3
Rutland Cem—cemetery ... AL-4
Rutland Cem—cemetery ... FL-3
Rutland Cem—cemetery ... IL-6
Rutland Cem—cemetery ... KS-7
Rutland Cem—cemetery ... MI-6
Rutland Cem—cemetery (2) ... MS-4
Rutland Cem—cemetery ... SC-3
Rutland Cem—cemetery (2) ... TN-4
Rutland Cem—cemetery ... TX-5
Rutland (census name for Rutland Center)—CDP ... MA-1
Rutland Center ... MA-1
**Rutland Center**—pop pl ... NY-2
Rutland Center Cem—cemetery ... WI-6
Rutland Center (census name Rutland)—other ... MA-1
Rutland Centre ... MA-1
Rutland Ch—church ... TN-4
Rutland Chapel—church ... AL-4
Rutland City For—forest ... VT-1
Rutland City Rsvr—reservoir ... VT-1
Rutland CME Chapel ... AL-4
**Rutland County**—pop pl ... VT-1
Rutland Courthouse Hist Dist—hist pl ... VT-1
Rutland Creek—stream ... FL-3
Rutland Downtown Hist Dist—hist pl ... VT-1
Rutland Heights ... MA-1
Rutland Heights Hosp—hospital ... MA-1
Rutland Hollow—valley ... NY-2
Rutland Hollow—valley ... TX-5
Rutland Hollow Cem—cemetery ... NY-2
Rutland Island—island ... MI-6
Rutland Lake—lake ... NY-2
Rutland Lake—reservoir (2) ... AL-4
Rutland Plaza (Shop Ctr)—locale ... FL-3
Rutland Pond ... MA-1
Rutland Pond—reservoir ... AL-4
Rutland Pond Dam—dam ... AL-4
Rutland Post Office (historical)—building ... PA-2
Rutlands Baptist Ch ... TN-4
Rutland Sch—school ... IL-6
Rutland Sch—school ... ND-7
Rutland Sch—school ... TN-4
Rutland Sch Number 2—school ... ND-7
Rutland Sportsmens Club—locale ... MA-1
Rutland Store (historical)—locale ... AL-4
**Rutland (Town of)**—pop pl ... MA-1
**Rutland (Town of)**—pop pl ... NY-2
**Rutland (Town of)**—pop pl ... VT-1
**Rutland (Town of)**—pop pl ... WI-6
Rutland Township—fmr MCD (2) ... IA-7
**Rutland Township**—pop pl ... KS-7
**Rutland Township**—pop pl ... ND-7
**Rutland Township**—pop pl ... SD-7
Rutland Township Cem—cemetery ... IA-7
**Rutland (Township of)**—pop pl (2) ... IL-6
**Rutland (Township of)**—pop pl ... MI-6
**Rutland (Township of)**—pop pl ... MN-6
**Rutland (Township of)**—pop pl ... OH-6
**Rutland (Township of)**—pop pl ... PA-2
Rutledge ... NY-2
Rutledge—locale ... IA-7
Rutledge—locale ... MD-2
Rutledge—locale ... OR-9
Rutledge—locale ... WI-6
**Rutledge**—pop pl ... AL-4
**Rutledge**—pop pl ... FL-3
**Rutledge**—pop pl ... GA-3
**Rutledge**—pop pl ... MN-6
**Rutledge**—pop pl ... MO-7
**Rutledge**—pop pl ... PA-2
**Rutledge**—pop pl ... TN-4
**Rutledge**—pop pl ... WV-2
Rutledge—uninc pl ... AL-4
Rutledge, Edward, House—hist pl ... SC-3
Rutledge, Gov. John, House—hist pl ... SC-3
Rutledge, Lake—reservoir ... GA-3
Rutledge Bay—basin ... SC-3
Rutledge Borough—civil ... PA-2
Rutledge Branch—stream ... MS-4
Rutledge Camp—locale ... AR-4
Rutledge Canyon—valley ... OR-9
Rutledge Cave—cave ... TN-4
Rutledge (CCD)—cens area ... GA-3
Rutledge (CCD)—cens area ... TN-4
Rutledge Cem—cemetery ... AL-4
Rutledge Cem—cemetery ... IL-6
Rutledge Cem—cemetery ... TN-4
Rutledge Ch—church ... AL-4
Rutledge Coll—school ... NC-3
Rutledge Creek—stream (2) ... ID-8
Rutledge Creek—stream ... MO-7
Rutledge Creek—stream ... NC-3
Rutledge Creek—stream (2) ... VA-3
Rutledge Creek Trail—trail ... ID-8
Rutledgedale—locale ... PA-2
Rutledge Division—civil ... TN-4
Rutledge Elem Sch—school ... TN-4
Rutledge Falls—falls ... TN-4
Rutledge Falls—locale ... TN-4
Rutledge Falls Baptist Ch—church ... TN-4
Rutledge Field (airport)—airport ... TN-4
**Rutledge Heights**—pop pl ... AL-4
Rutledge Heights—uninc pl ... AL-4
Rutledge Hill Hist Dist—hist pl ... TN-4
**Rutledge Hills**—pop pl ... TN-4
Rutledge Hill Sch (historical)—school ... TN-4
Rutledge Hollow—valley ... TN-4
Rutledge Hollow—valley ... TX-5
Rutledge House—hist pl ... GA-3
Rutledge HS—school ... TN-4
Rutledge Lake ... WA-9
Rutledge Lake—lake ... SC-3
Rutledge Lake—reservoir ... AL-4
Rutledge Lake—reservoir ... GA-3
Rutledge Lateral—canal ... ID-8
Rutledge Methodist Ch—church ... TN-4
Rutledge MS—school ... TN-4
Rutledge Mtn—summit ... NC-3
Rutledge Point—cape ... AL-4
Rutledge Point—cape ... TN-4
Rutledge Point Mine (underground)—mine ... TN-4
Rutledge Post Office—building ... TN-4
Rutledge Presbyterian Ch—church ... TN-4
Rutledge Ranch—locale ... MT-8
Rutledge Recreational Park—park ... TN-4
Rutledge Run—stream ... MO-7
Rutledge Salem Cemetery ... MS-4
Rutledge Salem Ch—church ... MS-4
Rutledge Salem Sch (historical)—school ... MS-4
Rutledge Sch—school ... AL-4
Rutledge Sch—school ... IA-7
**Rutledge Springs**—pop pl ... AL-4
Rutledge Store (historical)—locale ... TN-4
**Rutledge (Township of)**—pop pl ... IL-6
Rutled Opening—flat ... CA-9
Rutledy Creek—stream ... NC-3
Rutman Creek ... NC-3
Rutman Creek—stream ... NC-3
Rutsen, Mount—summit ... NY-2
**Rutsonville**—pop pl ... NY-2
Rutstrum State Wildlife Mngmt Area—park ... MN-6
Rutt Branch—stream ... IA-7
Rutten Lake—lake ... ND-7
Rutter—locale ... NM-5
Rutter Branch—stream ... TN-4
Rutter Canyon—valley ... OR-9
Rutter Cem—cemetery ... MO-7
Rutter Cem—cemetery ... OH-6
Rutter JHS—school ... CA-9
Rutter Ridge—ridge ... TN-4
Rutters Brook—stream ... MA-1
Rutter Sch (historical)—school ... PA-2
Rutthven—locale ... AL-4
Rutty Creek—stream ... CT-1
Rutz Lake—lake ... MN-6
Rutz Lake Cem—cemetery ... MN-6
Ruu ... FM-9
Ruud Canyon—valley ... WA-9
Ruud Mtn—summit ... ID-8
Ruuisu To ... MP-9
Ruul—civil ... FM-9
Ruul District ... FM-9
Ruunguch—island ... FM-9
Ruunitto ... MP-9
Ruun'uw—locale ... FM-9
Ruuq—locale ... FM-9
Ruurbaal—summit ... FM-9
Ruuru ... FM-9
Ruus Park—park ... CA-9
Ruus Sch—school ... CA-9
Ruuwa To ... MP-9
Ruvi Pit—reservoir ... NM-5
Ruwaamaaw'—locale ... FM-9
Ruwa-to ... MP-9
Ruwau Lake—lake ... CA-9
Ruwbal ... FM-9
Ruwe Ditch—canal ... NE-7
Ruwemaw ... FM-9
Ruwe Park—park ... NE-7
Ruwo ... FM-9
Ruwul ... FM-9
Ruwwe Cem—cemetery ... MO-7
Ruxby—locale ... WA-9
Rux Cem—cemetery ... MN-6
Ruxer Lake—reservoir ... IN-6
Ruxer Lake Dam—dam ... IN-6
Ruxton—locale ... CO-8
**Ruxton**—pop pl ... MD-2
Ruxton Creek—stream ... CO-8
Ruxton Draw—valley ... CO-8
**Ruxton (historical)**—pop pl ... VA-3
Ruxton Park—park ... CO-8
Ruyan Cem—cemetery ... TN-4
Ruybalid Lake—lake ... CO-8
Ruybalid Trail—trail ... CO-8
Ruyle Bridge—bridge ... TX-5
Ruyle Place—locale ... NM-5
**Ruyle (Township of)**—pop pl ... IL-6
Ruy Point—cape ... VI-3
Ruyter Bay—bay ... VI-3
Ruzic Hunting Club—locale ... AL-4
Ruzicka Airp—airport ... IN-6
Ruzicka Drain—stream ... IN-6
RV Acres Campground—park ... UT-8
R Van Bockle Dam—dam ... SD-7
R Vandewart Ranch—locale ... NM-5
R V Daniels Elem Sch—school ... FL-3
R.V. Phinney Elem Sch—school ... KS-7
Rwawak River ... NJ-2
R W Clark Elem Sch—school ... PA-2
R Wightman Grant—civil ... FL-3
R W Lindsey Sch—school ... GA-3
R Wolff Dam—dam ... SD-7
R Wolf Ranch—locale ... ND-7
RWPZ No 25 Windmill—locale ... NM-5
R Wray—locale ... TX-5
RWR Landing Strip—airport ... KS-7
R W Spring—spring ... OR-9
R W Stribling Lake Dam—dam ... MS-4
RW Taylor—locale ... TX-5
Ryal Canyon—valley ... AZ-5
Ryal Corners—locale ... NY-2
Ryal Gap—gap ... GA-3
Ryalis Cem—cemetery ... TX-5
Ryal Island—island ... TN-4
Ryall Branch—stream ... TN-4
Ryall Chapel—church ... MS-4
Ryall Drain—stream ... MI-6
Ryall Side ... MA-1
Ryall Spring—spring ... TN-4
**Ryall Springs**—pop pl ... TN-4
Ryall Springs Branch—stream ... TN-4
Ryals Branch—stream ... AL-4
Ryals Cem—cemetery (2) ... GA-3
Ryals Cem—cemetery ... MS-4
Ryal Side ... MA-1
Ryals Lake—reservoir (2) ... AL-4
Ryals Mill Creek—stream ... AL-4
Ryals Post Office (historical)—building ... AL-4
Ryal Spring—spring ... AZ-5
Ryals Run ... VA-3
Ryals Sch—school ... OK-5
Ryals Swamp—swamp ... FL-3
Ryan ... MS-4
Ryan—locale ... AL-4
Ryan—locale ... AZ-5
Ryan—locale ... IL-6
Ryan—locale ... KY-4
Ryan—locale ... MN-6
Ryan—locale ... VA-3
Ryan—locale ... WA-9
Ryan—locale ... WV-2
Ryan—locale ... VI-3
**Ryan**—pop pl ... AR-4
**Ryan**—pop pl ... CA-9
**Ryan**—pop pl ... IA-7
**Ryan**—pop pl ... MI-6
**Ryan**—pop pl ... OH-6
**Ryan**—pop pl ... OK-5
**Ryan**—pop pl ... TX-5
Ryan, Mount—summit ... AK-9
Ryan Airport—other ... LA-4
Ryan Appleton Ditch—canal ... IN-6
Ryan Baptist Church ... AL-4
Ryan Branch—stream ... IL-6
Ryan Branch—stream ... KY-4
Ryan Branch—stream ... SC-3
Ryan Branch—stream ... TN-4
Ryan Branch—stream ... TX-5
Ryan Bridge—bridge ... AL-4
Ryan Bridge—other ... IL-6
Ryan Brook—stream ... NH-1
Ryan Brook—stream ... NY-2
Ryan Butte—summit ... MT-8
Ryan Cabin—locale ... OR-9
Ryan Cabin—locale (2) ... WA-9
Ryan Campground—locale ... CA-9
Ryan Canyon—valley ... CA-9
Ryan Canyon—valley (2) ... NV-8
Ryan Cem ... AL-4
Ryan Cem—cemetery ... AL-4
Ryan Cem—cemetery (2) ... KY-4
Ryan Cem—cemetery ... MO-7
Ryan Cem—cemetery ... OH-6
Ryan Cem—cemetery ... OK-5
Ryan Cem—cemetery ... TN-4
Ryan Cem—cemetery ... TX-5
Ryan Cem—cemetery (3) ... WV-2
Ryan Ch—church (2) ... AL-4
Ryan Chapel—church ... TX-5
Ryan Chapel—church ... WV-2
Ryan Childs Grave—cemetery ... TN-4
**Ryan Corner**—pop pl ... OR-9
Ryan Coulee—valley ... MN-6
Ryan Coulee—valley (2) ... MT-8
Ryan Cove—valley ... AL-4
Ryan Creek—stream (2) ... AL-4
Ryan Creek—stream (2) ... AK-9
Ryan Creek—stream (2) ... CA-9
Ryan Creek—stream ... CO-8
Ryan Creek—stream (3) ... ID-8
Ryan Creek—stream ... IA-7
Ryan Creek—stream (4) ... MI-6
Ryan Creek—stream (2) ... MN-6
Ryan Creek—stream ... MS-4
Ryan Creek—stream (2) ... MT-8
Ryan Creek—stream ... NC-3
Ryan Creek—stream (6) ... OR-9
Ryan Creek—stream ... TX-5
Ryan Creek—stream ... UT-8
Ryan Creek—stream ... VA-3
Ryan Creek—stream ... WA-9
Ryan Creek—stream (3) ... WI-6
Ryan Creek—stream ... WY-8
Ryan Creek Mine (surface)—mine ... AL-4
Ryan Creek Post Office (historical)—building ... AL-4
Ryan Creek Rsvr—reservoir ... OR-9
**Ryan Crossroads**—pop pl ... AL-4
Ryan Dam—dam ... MT-8
Ryan Detention Dam—dam ... AZ-5
Ryan Ditch ... IN-6
Ryan Ditch—canal (4) ... IN-6
Ryan Ditch—canal ... OH-6
Ryan Drain—canal (2) ... MI-6
Ryan Drain—stream ... MI-6
Ryan Draw—valley ... AZ-5
Ryan Field—airport ... AZ-5
Ryan Foreman And Elk Hollow Ditch—canal ... WY-8
Ryan Gulch—valley ... AK-9
Ryan Gulch—valley (4) ... CO-8
Ryan Gulch—valley ... MT-8
Ryan Gulch—valley ... OR-9
Ryan Gulch Lake—reservoir ... CO-8
Ryan Hall Sch—school ... VA-3
Ryan Hill—ridge ... OH-6
Ryan Hill—summit (2) ... NH-1
Ryan Hill—summit ... WA-9
Ryan Hill—summit ... WY-8
Ryan Hill Canyon—valley ... NM-5
Ryan Hill Spring—spring ... NM-5
Ryan (historical)—locale ... KS-7
Ryan Hollow ... WI-6
Ryan Hollow—valley ... OH-6
Ryan Hollow—valley ... PA-2
Ryan Hollow—valley ... VA-3
Ryan Hollow—valley (2) ... WV-2
Ryan Hollow—valley ... WI-6
Ryan House—building ... IA-7
Ryan House—hist pl ... WA-9
Ryan House and Lost Horse Well—hist pl ... CA-9
Ryan HS—school ... AL-4
Ryan HS—school ... NY-2
Ryan Island ... ME-1
Ryan Island—island ... CA-9
Ryan Island—island ... IA-7
Ryan Island—island ... MI-6
Ryan Island—island ... WA-9
Ryan JHS—school ... TX-5
Ryan Kraisinger Ditch—canal ... IN-6
Ryan Lake ... AK-9
Ryan Lake ... WI-6
Ryan Lake—lake ... AK-9
Ryan Lake—lake ... AR-4
Ryan Lake—lake ... LA-4
Ryan Lake—lake ... ME-1
Ryan Lake—lake (3) ... MI-6
Ryan Lake—lake (4) ... MN-6
Ryan Lake—lake ... MT-8
Ryan Lake—lake ... NE-7
Ryan Lake—lake ... OR-9
Ryan Lake—lake ... TX-5
Ryan Lake—lake (2) ... WA-9
Ryan Lake—reservoir ... TN-4
Ryan Lake (historical)—lake ... IA-7
Ryan Lake State Game Mngmt Area—park ... IA-7
Ryan Lauffler Ditch—canal ... MT-8
Ryan Memorial Gardens—cemetery ... AL-4
Ryan Mine—mine ... MT-8
Ryan Mine (underground)—mine ... AL-4
Ryan Mountain Cave—cave ... AL-4
Ryan Mountain Trail—trail ... CA-9
Ryan Mtn—summit ... CA-9
Ryan Mtn—summit ... NY-2
Ryan Mtn—summit ... VT-1
Ryan Park—flat (2) ... CO-8
Ryan Park—flat ... WY-8
Ryan Park—park ... AL-4
Ryan Park—park ... MN-6
Ryan Park—park ... TX-5
Ryan Park—park ... WY-8
**Ryan Park**—pop pl ... WY-8
Ryan Park Ski Course—locale ... WY-8
Ryan Pasture—flat ... ID-8
Ryan Peak—summit (2) ... ID-8
Ryan Peak—summit ... OK-5
**Ryan Place**—pop pl ... IN-6
Ryan Playground—park ... MA-1
Ryan Point—cape ... WA-9
Ryan Pond—lake ... NY-2
Ryan Pond—lake ... WI-6
Ryan Ponds—lake ... UT-8
Ryan Post Office (historical)—building ... AL-4
Ryan Ranch—hist pl ... WY-8
Ryan Ranch—locale (2) ... AZ-5
Ryan Ranch—locale ... MT-8
Ryan Ranch—locale ... UT-8
Ryan Ranch—locale ... WY-8
Ryan Ranch Meadow—flat ... OR-9
Ryan Ranch (42 BE 618)—hist pl ... UT-8
Ryan Ridge ... ID-8
Ryan Ridge—ridge ... CA-9
Ryan Ridge—ridge ... WI-6
Ryan Round Barn—hist pl ... IL-6
Ryan Rsvr—reservoir ... CO-8
Ryan Run—stream (2) ... OH-6
Ryan's, John, House—hist pl ... MT-8
Ryans Bay—bay ... MN-6
Ryans Branch—stream ... VA-3
Ryans Branch Campsite—locale ... VA-3
Ryans Brook—stream ... NY-2
Ryan Sch—school ... CA-9
Ryan Sch—school ... CT-1
Ryan Sch—school ... IA-7
Ryan Sch—school ... ME-1
Ryan Sch—school ... MI-6
Ryan Sch—school ... OH-6
Ryan Sch—school ... PA-2
Ryan Sch—school ... SD-7
Ryan Sch—school (2) ... TX-5
Ryan Sch—school ... WI-6
Ryan School—locale ... CO-8
Ryans Corner—locale ... PA-2
Ryans Corner—locale ... WI-6
Ryans Creek ... MI-6
Ryans Creek—stream ... KY-4
Ryans Creek Ch—church ... AL-4
Ryans Creek Ch—church ... KY-4
Ryans Creek Mtn—summit ... KY-4
Ryans Creek Sch—school ... KY-4
Ryans Dam—dam ... VA-3
Ryans Fork—stream ... MT-8
Ryans Gulch—valley ... UT-8
Ryans Hill—summit ... GA-3
Ryans Hill—summit ... MA-1
Ryans L'Argent Landing—locale ... MS-4
Ryan Slough—stream ... CA-9
Ryans Lower Cow Camp—locale ... CA-9
Ryan Spring—spring ... AL-4
Ryan Spring—spring ... NV-8
Ryan Spring—spring (2) ... UT-8
Ryan Spring—spring ... WI-6
Ryan Springs—spring ... MT-8
**Ryan Spur**—pop pl ... ID-8
Ryans Ridge ... WV-2
Ryans Slough (census name Myrtletowne)—other ... CA-9
Ryans Trail—trail ... PA-2
Ryans Upper Cow Camp—locale ... CA-9
Ryansville (historical)—locale ... KS-7
Ryans Well (historical)—locale ... MS-4
Ryan Tank—reservoir (2) ... AZ-5
Ryan Tank—reservoir ... NM-5
Ryant Drain—canal ... MI-6
Ryan Town Hall—building ... ND-7
Ryan Township—civil ... SD-7
**Ryan Township**—pop pl ... KS-7
**Ryan Township**—pop pl ... ND-7
**Ryan (Township of)**—pop pl ... PA-2
Ryan Trail (Camp)—locale ... NY-2
Ryan Trick Tanks—reservoir ... AZ-5
Ryan Village—locale ... MN-6
**Ryanville**—pop pl ... WV-2
Ryberg Lake—lake ... WI-6
Ryberg Ranch—locale ... NM-5
Ryberg Tank—reservoir ... AZ-5
Rybery Tank—reservoir ... AZ-5
Ryburn Memorial Ch—church ... NC-3
Rycade—locale ... LA-4
**Rycerville**—pop pl ... MD-2
**Ryceville**—pop pl ... MD-2
Ryckman Creek—stream ... WY-8
Rydal—locale ... GA-3
Rydal—locale ... KS-7
Rydal—locale ... PA-2
Rydalch Canyon—valley (2) ... UT-8
Rydalch Pass—gap ... UT-8
Rydal County Club—locale ... PA-2
**Rydal East**—pop pl ... PA-2
**Rydal Park**—pop pl ... PA-2
Rydal Station—building ... PA-2
Rydberg Creek—stream ... CA-9
Ryde—locale ... CA-9
**Ryde**—pop pl ... PA-2
Rydel ... KS-7
Ryden Cave—cave ... MO-7
Ryden Lakes—lake ... IN-6
Ryder—locale ... MO-7
**Ryder**—pop pl ... ND-7
**Ryder**—pop pl ... OK-5
Ryder—uninc pl ... NY-2
Ryder Brook—stream ... VT-1
Ryder Cem—cemetery ... KY-4
Ryder Cem—cemetery ... WV-2
Ryder Church ... TN-4
Ryder Corner—locale ... NH-1
Ryder Cove—cove ... MA-1
Ryder Creek—stream (2) ... OR-9
Ryder Drain—stream ... MI-6
Ryder Gap—gap ... VA-3
Ryder Gap—gap ... WV-2
Ryder Hill—summit ... NY-2
Ryder Hollow—valley ... VA-3
Ryder Lake—lake ... UT-8
Ryder Lakes—lake ... CO-8
Ryder Mountain ... CO-8
Ryder MS—school ... MA-1
Ryder Municipal Airfield—airport ... ND-7
Ryder Pond—lake ... MA-1
Ryder Pond—lake ... NY-2
Ryder Pond—lake ... VT-1
Ryder Ridge—ridge ... WI-6
Ryder Run—stream ... VA-3
Ryder Run—stream ... WV-2
Ryder Sch—school ... IL-6
Ryder Sch—school ... NY-2
Ryder Sch—school ... OH-6
Ryder Sch—school ... PA-2
Ryders Cove ... MA-1
Ryders Pond—lake ... MA-1
Ryders Pond—reservoir ... NC-3
**Ryder Township**—pop pl ... ND-7
**Ryderwood**—pop pl ... WA-9
Rydners Branch—stream ... KY-4
Rydners Branch Sch—school ... KY-4
Rydolph Cem—cemetery ... TX-5
Rye (2) ... IN-6
Rye—locale ... AZ-5
Rye—locale ... AR-4
Rye—locale ... PA-2
Rye—locale ... TX-5
Rye—locale ... WA-9
**Rye**—pop pl ... CO-8
**Rye**—pop pl ... FL-3
**Rye**—pop pl ... NH-1
**Rye**—pop pl ... NY-2
**Rye**—pop pl (2) ... TX-5
**Rye**—pop pl ... WA-9
Rye, Chris, House—hist pl ... IA-7
Rye Beach ... OH-6
Rye Beach—beach ... NY-2
**Rye Beach**—pop pl ... NH-1
Rye Branch—stream ... FL-3
Rye Branch—stream (2) ... KY-4
Rye Branch—stream ... OR-9
Rye Bread Sch (historical)—school ... PA-2
Rye Bridge—bridge ... NY-2
**Rye Brooke**—pop pl ... NY-2
Rye Cem—cemetery ... WV-2
Rye Coulee ... MT-8
Rye Coulee—valley (2) ... MT-8
Rye Country Club—other ... NY-2
**Rye Cove**—pop pl ... VA-3
Rye Cove Branch—stream (2) ... KY-4
Rye Cove Cem—cemetery ... NC-3
Rye Cove Creek—stream ... VA-3
Rye Cove Memorial Sch—school ... VA-3
Rye Creek ... AZ-5
Rye Creek ... NV-8
Rye Creek—stream ... AK-9
Rye Creek—stream ... AZ-5
Rye Creek—stream ... ID-8
Rye Creek—stream ... MS-4
Rye Creek—stream (3) ... MO-7
Rye Creek—stream (2) ... MT-8
Rye Creek—stream ... NV-8
Rye Creek—stream ... WA-9
Rye Creek Rsvr—reservoir ... NV-8
Rye Creek Sch (abandoned)—school ... MO-7
Rye Creek Sch (historical)—school ... MO-7
Rye Creek Tank—reservoir ... AZ-5
Rye Creek Well—well ... AZ-5
Ryecroft Canyon—valley ... NV-8
Ryecroft Spring—spring ... NV-8
Rye Elem Sch—school ... NH-1
Rye Field—flat ... OR-9
Rye Field (airport)—airport ... MS-4
Ryefield Branch—stream ... KY-4
Ryefield Branch—stream ... NC-3
Ryefield Brook—stream ... NH-1
Ryefield Cem—cemetery ... ME-1
Ryefield Creek—stream ... VA-3
Ryefield Landing—locale ... VA-3
Ryefield Neck ... MA-1
Ryefield Point—cape ... MA-1
Rye Field Ridge—ridge ... KY-4
Rye Field Ridge—ridge ... NY-2
Ryefield Ridge—ridge ... TN-4
Rye Flat—flat ... ID-8
Rye Flat—flat (2) ... OR-9
**Ryegate**—pop pl ... MT-8
**Ryegate Corner**—pop pl ... VT-1
**Ryegate (Ryegate Corner)**—pop pl ... VT-1
**Ryegate (Town of)**—pop pl ... VT-1
Rye Grass—flat ... NV-8
Ryegrass Archeol District—hist pl ... WA-9
Ryegrass Canyon—valley ... NV-8
Rye Grass Canyon—valley (2) ... NV-8
Ryegrass Coulee—valley ... WA-9
Rye Grass Coulee—valley ... WA-9
Ryegrass Creek—stream ... ID-8
Rye Grass Creek—stream (2) ... ID-8
Rye Grass Creek—stream (3) ... MT-8
Ryegrass Creek—stream (2) ... OR-9
Ryegrass Ditch—canal ... OR-9
Rye Grass Draw—valley ... CO-8
Rye Grass Draw—valley ... UT-8
Ryegrass Draw—valley ... WY-8
Ryegrass Flat—flat ... ID-8
Rye Grass Flat—flat ... ID-8
Rye Grass Flat—flat ... WA-9
Rye Grass Gulch—valley ... WY-8
Ryegrass Hollow—valley ... OR-9
Ryegrass Junction—locale ... WY-8
Ryegrass Lake—lake ... OR-9
Ryegrass Mtn—summit ... WA-9
Rye Grass Patch—flat ... NV-8
Rye Grass Pinnacle—pillar ... ID-8
Ryegrass Ranch—locale ... NV-8
Ryegrass Ranch—locale ... OR-9
Rye Grass Rsvr—reservoir ... ID-8
Ryegrass Rsvr—reservoir (2) ... OR-9
Ryegrass Rsvr—reservoir ... WY-8
Rye Grass Spring—spring ... ID-8
Ryegrass Spring—spring (2) ... ID-8
Ryegrass Spring—spring ... NV-8
Rye Grass Spring—spring (2) ... NV-8
Ryegrass Spring—spring ... OR-9
Rye Grass Swale—valley ... CA-9
Ryegrass Table—summit ... OR-9
Ryegrass Trail—trail ... ID-8
Ryegrass Valley—basin ... OR-9
Rye Grass Well—well (2) ... NV-8
Rye Gulch—valley ... WY-8
Rye Harbor—harbor ... NH-1
Rye Harbor State Park—park ... NH-1
Rye Hill—locale ... AR-4
**Rye Hill**—pop pl ... MA-1
Rye Hill—summit ... CT-1
Rye Hill—summit ... ME-1
Rye Hill—summit ... MA-1
Rye Hill—summit ... OR-9
Rye Hill Ch—church ... AR-4
**Rye Hills-Rye Brook**—pop pl ... NY-2
**Rye (historical)**—pop pl ... MS-4
Rye Hole—bay ... DE-2
Rye Hollow—valley ... KY-4
Rye Hollow—valley ... MO-7
Rye Hollow—valley ... TN-4
Rye Hollow—valley ... VA-3
Rye Key—island ... FL-3
Rye Lake—lake ... NY-2
Ryeland—locale ... PA-2
Rye Ledge—bar ... NH-1
Ryemoor Hill—summit ... ME-1
Rye Mtn—summit ... NC-3
Rye Mtn—summit ... OR-9
Rye Neck ... NY-2
Rye-Neck HS—school ... NY-2
Rye North Beach—beach ... NH-1
**Rye North Beach**—pop pl ... NH-1
Ryen Sawmill—locale ... MT-8
Rye Park—park ... CO-8
Rye Pasture Well—well ... TX-5
Rye Patch—flat (2) ... ID-8
Rye Patch—flat (2) ... NV-8
Rye Patch—flat ... UT-8
Rye Patch—gap ... NC-3
**Rye Patch**—pop pl ... NV-8
Rye Patch Archeol Sites—hist pl ... NV-8
Rye Patch Branch—stream ... NC-3
Ryepatch Canyon ... NV-8
**Rye Patch Canyon**—pop pl ... NV-8
Rye Patch Canyon—valley ... CA-9
Rye Patch Canyon—valley (2) ... NV-8
Rye Patch Ch—church ... GA-3
Rye Patch Creek—stream ... ID-8
Rye Patch Dam—dam ... NV-8
Ryepatch Gulch ... NV-8
Rye Patch Hollow—valley ... TN-4
Ryepatch Mine ... NV-8
Rye Patch Mine—mine ... NV-8

# S

S ... MI-6
Saa Betoh—spring ... AZ-5
Saachi Beach ... OR-9
Saafelo Point—cape ... AS-9
Saager Canyon—valley ... MT-8
Saap Cem—cemetery ... MO-7
Saaraners Beach Access Area—park ... SD-7
Saar Creek—stream ... WA-9
Saarela Ditch—canal ... MT-8
Saathoff House—hist pl ... TX-5
Saathoff Mtn—summit ... TX-5
Saathoff Sch—school ... SD-7
Sabac Lake ... ME-1
**Sabael**—pop pl ... NY-2
Saba Island—island ... VI-3
Sabaka, Lake—lake ... AK-9
Sabal Chase Park—park ... FL-3
Sabal Elem Sch—school (2) ... FL-3
Sabal Lake—lake ... FL-3
**Sabalos**—pop pl (2) ... PR-3
Sabalos (Barrio)—fmr MCD ... PR-3
Sabal Palm Baptist Ch—church ... FL-3
Sabal Palm Elem Sch—school ... FL-3
**Sabal Palm Estates**—pop pl ... FL-3
Sabal Palm Sch—school (2) ... FL-3
**Sabal Palms Estates**—pop pl ... FL-3
Sabal Point Elem Sch—school ... FL-3
Sabana ... MH-9
Sabana—CDP ... PR-3
**Sabana**—pop pl (4) ... PR-3
Sabana—summit ... MH-9
**Sabana Abajo**—pop pl ... PR-3
Sabana Abajo (Barrio)—fmr MCD ... PR-3
**Sabana Alta**—pop pl ... PR-3
Sabana (Barrio)—fmr MCD (3) ... PR-3
Sabana Batea—summit ... GU-9
**Sabana Eneas**—pop pl ... PR-3
Sabana Eneas (Barrio)—fmr MCD ... PR-3
**Sabana Gardens**—pop pl ... PR-3
**Sabana Grande**—pop pl ... PR-3
Sabana Grande Abajo (Barrio)—fmr MCD ... PR-3
Sabana Grande (Barrio)—fmr MCD ... PR-3
Sabana Grande (Municipio)—civil ... PR-3
Sabana Grande (Pueblo)—fmr MCD ... PR-3
**Sabana Hoyos**—pop pl (2) ... PR-3
Sabana Hoyos (Barrio)—fmr MCD ... PR-3
**Sabana Llana**—pop pl ... PR-3
**Sabana Llana Abajo**—pop pl ... PR-3
**Sabana Llana Arriba**—pop pl ... PR-3
Sabana Llana (Barrio)—fmr MCD ... PR-3
Sabana Llana Norte (Barrio)—fmr MCD ... PR-3
Sabana Llana Sur (Barrio)—fmr MCD ... PR-3
Sabana Maagas—area ... GU-9
Sabana Maleyuc—summit ... GU-9
Sabanan Achugau ... MH-9
Sabanan Adelup—summit ... GU-9
Sabanan Hagman ... MH-9
Sabanan I Eddot ... MH-9
Sabanan Laulau ... MH-9
Sabanan Pagat—other ... GU-9
Sabanan Rapugau ... MH-9
Sabanan Talofofo ... MH-9
Sabanan Unai Nanasu ... MH-9
Sabana River—stream ... TX-5
**Sabana Seca**—pop pl (2) ... PR-3
Sabana Seca (Barrio)—fmr MCD ... PR-3
Sabana Seca Naval Security Group—military ... PR-3
Sabana Tank—reservoir ... TX-5
Sabana Yeguas (Barrio)—fmr MCD ... PR-3
Sabaneta—slope ... MH-9
Sabaneta, Puntan—cape ... MH-9
Sabanetan Chiguet ... MH-9
Sabanetan Famalauan ... MH-9
Sabanetan Toro Latte Site—hist pl ... MH-9
Sabaneta Point ... MH-9
**Sabanetas**—pop pl ... PR-3
Sabanetas (Barrio)—fmr MCD (2) ... PR-3
Sabanettan Abas ... MH-9
Sabanettan Asiga ... MH-9
Sabanettan Chiget ... MH-9
Sabanettan Famalauan ... MH-9
Sabanettan Mangpang ... MH-9
Sabanettan Tahgong ... MH-9
Sabanettan Unai Babui ... MH-9
Sabanettan Unai Lamlam ... MH-9
**Sabanno**—pop pl ... TX-5
Sabanno Cem—cemetery ... TX-5
Saban Pond—lake ... ME-1
Sabao Dam—dam ... ME-1
Sabao Mtn—summit ... ME-1
Sabarney Gile Swamp—swamp ... NY-2
S A Barrett Dam—dam ... AL-4
**Sabarto East**—pop pl ... DE-2
Sabathany—locale ... TX-5
Sabatia Pond ... MA-1
Sabatka Creek—stream ... WY-8
Sabattis—locale ... NY-2
Sabattis, Mount—summit ... NY-2
Sabattos Mtn ... ME-1
**Sabattus**—pop pl ... ME-1
**Sabattus Heights**—pop pl ... NH-1
Sabattus Mtn—summit (2) ... ME-1
Sabattus Pond—lake ... ME-1
Sabattus River—stream ... ME-1
**Sabattus (Town of)**—pop pl ... ME-1
Sabbaday Brook—stream ... NH-1
Sabbaday Brook Trail—trail ... NH-1
Sabbaday Falls—falls ... NH-1
Sabbat Channel—channel ... VI-3
Sabbath Ch—church ... MD-2
Sabbath Creek—stream ... GA-3
Sabbathday Harbor—bay ... ME-1
Sabbathday House—hist pl ... CT-1
Sabbath Day House—hist pl ... MA-1
Sabbathday Lake ... ME-1
**Sabbathday Lake**—pop pl ... ME-1
**Sabbath Day Point**—pop pl ... NY-2
Sabbathday Pond—lake ... ME-1
Sabbath Day Pond—lake ... ME-1
Sabbath Haven Ch—church ... NC-3
Sabbath Home Cem—cemetery ... NC-3
Sabbath Home Ch—church ... MO-7
Sabbath Home Ch—church ... NC-3
Sabbath Rest Sch (abandoned)—school ... PA-2
Sabbatia, Lake—reservoir ... MA-1
Sabbatia Lake ... MA-1
Sabbat Point—cape ... VI-3
Sabbou ... FM-9
Sabe Branch—stream ... LA-4
Sabe Creek—stream ... ID-8
Sabedra-Huerta House—hist pl ... AZ-5
Sabe Lake—lake ... MN-6
Sabe Mtn—summit ... ID-8
Saben Canyon—valley ... WA-9
Sabers Creek—stream ... MD-2
Sabe Saddle—gap ... ID-8
**Sabetha**—pop pl ... KS-7
Sabetha City Lake—reservoir ... KS-7
Sabetha Elem Sch—school ... KS-7
Sabetha HS—school ... KS-7
Sabetha MS—school ... KS-7
Sabetha Municipal Landing Field—airport ... KS-7
Sabetiu ... FM-9
Sabe Vista Point—cape ... ID-8
Sabie Creek—stream (2) ... UT-8
Sabie Mtn—summit ... UT-8
Sabies Canyon—valley ... CA-9
Sabie Spring—spring ... UT-8
**Sabillasville**—pop pl ... MD-2
Sabille Creek ... WY-8
Sabin ... WI-6
Sabin—locale ... NM-5
**Sabin**—pop pl ... MN-6
**Sabina**—pop pl ... IL-6
**Sabina**—pop pl ... OH-6
Sabina Creek ... TX-5
Sabinal—locale ... NM-5
**Sabinal**—pop pl ... TX-5
Sabinal Canyon—valley ... TX-5
Sabinal (CCD)—cens area ... TX-5
Sabinal Cem—cemetery ... TX-5
Sabinal Ditch—canal ... NM-5
Sabinal Lateral No 1—canal ... NM-5
Sabinal Lateral No 2—canal ... NM-5
Sabinal River—stream ... TX-5
Sabinal Siding—locale ... NM-5
Sabinas Creek—stream ... TX-5
Sabinas Mtn—summit ... TX-5
Sabina Sola Tank—reservoir ... NM-5
Sabinata Flat—flat ... NM-5
Sabinata Flat Arroyo—arroyo ... NM-5
Sabinat Flat Arroyo ... NM-5
Sabinat Flat Arroyo—stream ... NM-5
Sabin Ch—church ... IL-6
Sabine ... RI-1
**Sabine**—pop pl ... TX-5
**Sabine**—pop pl ... WV-2
Sabine Canal—canal ... LA-4
Sabine (CCD)—cens area ... TX-5
Sabine Cem—cemetery ... MS-4
Sabine Ch—church ... AL-4
Sabine Ch—church ... TX-5
Sabine City ... TX-5
**Sabine (County)**—pop pl ... TX-5
Sabine Creek ... TX-5
Sabine Creek—stream ... MT-8
Sabine Creek—stream ... TX-5
Sabine Hall—building ... VA-3
Sabine Hall—hist pl ... VA-3
Sabine Hill—hist pl ... TN-4
Sabine Hill—summit ... TN-4
Sabine (historical P.O.)—locale ... IN-6
Sabine HS—school ... TX-5
Sabine Inlet—gut ... FL-3
Sabine Island—island ... LA-4
Sabine Lake—lake ... LA-4
Sabine Lake—lake ... MI-6
Sabine Lake—lake ... TX-5
Sabine Lookout Tower—locale ... TX-5
Sabine Natl For—forest ... TX-5
Sabine Natl Wildlife Ref—park ... LA-4
Sabine Neches Canal—canal ... TX-5
**Sabine Parish**—pop pl ... LA-4
Sabine Park—park ... TX-5
Sabine Pass—channel ... LA-4
Sabine Pass—channel ... TX-5
**Sabine Pass**—pop pl ... TX-5
Sabine Pass (CCD)—cens area ... TX-5
Sabine Pass Lighthouse—hist pl ... LA-4
Sabine Pass Lighthouse Reservation—locale ... LA-4
Sabine Point ... RI-1
Sabine Point—cape ... FL-3
Sabine River ... TX-5
**Sabine River**—pop pl ... TX-5
Sabine River—stream ... LA-4
Sabine River—stream (2) ... TX-5
Sabine Sand Hills—summit ... FL-3
Sabine Sch—school ... TX-5
Sabinetown—locale ... TX-5
Sabine Valley Ch—church ... TX-5
Sabine Valley Sch—school ... TX-5
Sabin Lake—lake ... CA-9
Sabin Lake—lake ... MN-6
Sabin Lake—lake ... WI-6
Sabino—locale ... NM-5
**Sabino**—pop pl ... AZ-5
**Sabino**—pop pl ... ME-1
**Sabino**—pop pl ... MS-4
Sabino (Abandoned)—locale ... NM-5
Sabino Canyon—valley (2) ... AZ-5
Sabino Canyon—valley ... NM-5
Sabino Canyon Picnic Area ... AZ-5
Sabino Cem—cemetery ... TX-5
Sabino Creek—stream ... AZ-5
Sabino Creek—stream ... NM-5
Sabino Head—cape ... ME-1
Sabino Hill—summit ... ME-1
Sabino HS—school ... AZ-5
Sabino Junior High—school ... AZ-5
Sabino Lake—lake ... NM-5
Sabino Lake—reservoir ... AZ-5
Sabino-Palisade Trail Twenty-Three—trail ... AZ-5
Sabino Ranch (abandoned)—locale ... NM-5
Sabino RR Station—building ... AZ-5
Sabinosa Windmill—locale ... NM-5
Sabino Sch (historical)—school ... MS-4
**Sabinoso**—pop pl ... NM-5
Sabino Springs—spring ... NM-5
Sabino Visitor Center—building ... AZ-5
Sabino Visitor Center Picnic Area—park ... AZ-5
Sabino Wash—stream ... AZ-5
Sabin Point—cape ... RI-1
Sabin Point Lighthouse—locale ... RI-1
Sabin Pond—lake ... MA-1
Sabin Pond—lake ... VT-1
Sabin Pond—lake ... WI-6
Sabin Sch—school ... CO-8
Sabin Sch—school ... IL-6
Sabin Sch—school (2) ... IA-7
Sabin Sch—school ... MI-6
Sabin Sch—school ... OR-9
Sabins Point ... RI-1
**Sabinsville**—pop pl ... PA-2
Sabinsville-Consolidated Airp—airport ... PA-2
Sabin Well—well ... AZ-5
Sabio Lake ... ME-1
Sabiston Crossing—locale ... NC-3
Sabito Wash—valley ... AZ-5
Sablatura Park—park ... TX-5
Sable—locale ... CO-8
Sable—locale ... MS-4
Sable, Cape—cape ... FL-3
Sable, Lake—lake ... FL-3
Sable, Point—cape ... WI-6
Sable Branch—stream ... KY-4
Sable Creek ... UT-8
Sable Creek—stream ... ID-8
Sable Creek—summit ... MI-6
Sable Creek—stream ... WA-9
Sable Falls—falls ... MI-6
Sable Hill—summit ... ID-8
Sable Hill—summit ... ME-1
Sable Island—island ... LA-4
Sable Island—island ... NY-2
Sable Lake—lake ... CO-8
Sable Lake—lake ... MN-6
Sable Mill Brook—stream ... ME-1
Sable Mountain Brooks—stream ... VT-1
Sable Mountains—ridge ... NY-2
Sable Mountain Trail—trail ... NH-1
Sable Mtn—summit ... AK-9
Sable Mtn—summit (3) ... ME-1
Sable Mtn—summit ... NH-1
Sable Mtn—summit (3) ... VT-1
Sable Oil Field—oilfield ... TX-5
Sable Pass—gap ... AK-9
Sable Point ... WI-6
Sable Point—cliff ... CO-8
Sable Post Office (historical)—building ... MS-4
Sable Ridge—ridge ... ME-1
Sable Ridge—ridge ... WA-9
Sable River ... MI-6
Sable Sch—school ... CO-8
Sablon—locale ... CA-9
Sabnettan Gatut ... MH-9
Saboeru ... FM-9
Saboeru Island ... FM-9
Sabo-Johnson-Curry Ditch—canal ... MT-8
Sabola ... MS-4
Sabold Sch—school ... PA-2
Sabo Pond—reservoir ... CT-1
Sabo Ranch—locale ... MT-8
Sabore ... FM-9
Saborelong ... FM-9
Sabot—locale ... VA-3
Sabota ... FM-9
Sabotage Pond—lake ... AZ-5
Sabot Hill—summit ... VA-3
Sabot Island—island ... VA-3
Sabotiu ... FM-9
Sabot Pond—bay ... LA-4
Sabougala ... MS-4
**Sabougla**—pop pl ... MS-4
Sabougla Cem—cemetery ... MS-4
Sabougla Creek—stream ... MS-4
Sabougla Creek Canal—canal ... MS-4
Sabougla Hatchie River ... MS-4
Sabra Ch—church ... WV-2
**Sabraton**—pop pl ... WV-2
Sabraton Ch—church ... WV-2
Sabratus Creek ... UT-8
Sabre Army Airp—airport ... TN-4
**Sabre City**—pop pl ... CA-9
Sabre Creek—stream ... OR-9
Sabre Lake—lake ... MN-6
Sabre Lake Cem—cemetery ... MN-6
Sabrey Branch ... DE-2
Sabrina, Lake—lake ... CA-9
Sabrina Lake—lake ... MA-1
Sabuk ... FM-9
Sabuk, Cape ... FM-9
**Sabula**—pop pl ... IA-7
**Sabula**—pop pl ... MO-7
**Sabula**—pop pl ... PA-2
Sabula, Lake—reservoir ... PA-2
Sabula Creek—stream ... AK-9
Sabula Hatchie ... MS-4
Sabula Hollow—valley ... MO-7
**Sabula Junction**—pop pl ... IA-7
Sabula Lakes—lake ... IA-7
Sabula Slough—stream ... IA-7
Sabylund Cem—cemetery ... WI-6
Sabylund Ch—church ... WI-6
Sabzin Mine—mine ... MT-8
Sac—cemetery ... OK-5
Sac, The ... MI-6
Sacacawea Monument ... SD-7
Sacagawea, Mount—summit ... WY-8
Sacagawea Glacier—glacier ... WY-8
Sacagawea Lagoon—channel ... MT-8
Sacagawea Park—park ... MT-8
Sacagawea Peak—summit ... MT-8
Sacagawea Ridge—ridge ... WY-8
Sacagawea River—stream ... MT-8
Sacahuista Butte—summit ... TX-5
Sacahuista Windmill—locale ... TX-5
Sacahuiste Draw—valley ... NM-5
Sacajawea, Lake—lake ... WA-9
Sacajawea, Lake—reservoir ... WA-9
Sacajawea Campground—locale ... WY-8
Sacajawea Forest Camp—locale ... OR-9
Sacajawea Hotel—hist pl ... MT-8
Sacajawea Island—island ... MT-8
Sacajawea JHS—school ... WA-9
Sacajawea Lake ... WA-9
Sacajawea Memorial Camp—locale ... MT-8
Sacajawea Monmt—park ... ID-8
Sacajawea Mtn—summit ... MT-8
Sacajawea Park—park ... MT-8
Sacajawea Peak ... MT-8
Sacajawea Peak—summit ... MT-8
Sacajawea Peak—summit ... OR-9
Sacajawea Sch—school ... MT-8
Sacajawea Sch—school ... OR-9
Sacajawea Sch—school ... WA-9
Sacajawea Spring—spring (2) ... OR-9
Sacajawea State Park—park ... WA-9
Saca Lake—lake ... MN-6
**Sacanap**—pop pl ... CA-9
**Sacandaga**—pop pl ... NY-2
Sacandaga Camp—locale ... NY-2
Sacandaga Lake—lake ... NY-2
**Sacandaga Park**—pop pl ... NY-2
Sacandaga Park Rsvr—reservoir ... NY-2
Sacandaga Public Campsite—locale ... NY-2
Sacandaga Reservoir ... NY-2
Sacandaga River—stream ... NY-2
Sacandaga Sch—school ... NY-2
Sacandago River ... NY-2
Sac And Fox Day Sch—school ... IA-7
Sac And Fox Indian Trail Park—park ... IA-7
Sac and Fox Ind Res—reserve ... IA-7
Sac And Fox Ind Res—reserve ... KS-7
Sac And Fox Ind Res—reserve ... NE-7
Sac and Fox Reservation ... KS-7
Sa Canyon—valley ... NM-5
Sacapee Pond—lake ... ME-1
Sacaponack Lake ... NY-2
Sacarider Lake—lake ... IN-6
Sacarma Bay ... FL-3
Sacata Creek ... CA-9
Sacatal, Rancho—locale ... AZ-5
Sacatan Wash ... AZ-5
Sacatara Creek—stream ... CA-9
Sacatar Canyon—valley ... CA-9
Sacata Ridge ... CA-9
Sacatar Meadow—flat ... CA-9
Sacate—locale ... AZ-5
Sacate—locale ... CA-9
Sacate, Canada Del —valley ... CA-9
Sacate Creek—stream ... CA-9
Sacate Ridge—ridge ... CA-9
Sacate Tank—reservoir ... TX-5
Sacaton ... AZ-5
**Sacaton**—pop pl ... AZ-5
Sacaton Ball Field Park—park ... AZ-5
Sacaton Butte—summit ... AZ-5
Sacaton Cem—cemetery ... AZ-5
Sacaton Community Ch—church ... AZ-5
Sacaton Creek—stream ... NM-5
Sacaton Dam—dam ... AZ-5
Sacaton Dam Bridge—hist pl ... AZ-5
Sacaton Draw—valley (2) ... NM-5
Sacaton Draw—valley ... TX-5
Sacatones Windmill—locale ... TX-5
Sacatone Wash—stream ... NV-8
Sacaton Fairgrounds—park ... AZ-5
Sacaton Flat—flat ... CA-9
Sacaton Flats—flat ... AZ-5
Sacaton Flats—locale ... AZ-5
Sacaton Flats Community Center—building ... AZ-5
Sacaton Mountain ... AZ-5
Sacaton Mountains—summit ... AZ-5
Sacaton Mountain Trail (Pack)—trail ... NM-5
Sacaton Mtn—summit ... NM-5
Sacaton Peak—summit ... AZ-5
Sacaton (Pima Agency)—CDP ... AZ-5
Sacaton Public Sch—school ... AZ-5
Sacaton Ranch—locale ... AZ-5
Sacaton Section ... AZ-5
Sacaton Spring—spring ... AZ-5
Sacaton Spring—spring ... CA-9
Sacaton Station ... AZ-5
Sacaton Tank—reservoir (2) ... AZ-5
Sacaton Tank—reservoir ... NM-5
Sacaton Wash—stream (2) ... AZ-5
Sacaton Windmill—locale ... NM-5
Sacatosa Creek—stream ... TX-5
Sacatosa Oil Field—oilfield ... TX-5
Sacatosa Tank—reservoir (3) ... TX-5
Sac Bay—bay ... MI-6
SAC Bay—bay ... UT-8
Sac Bay—locale ... MI-6
Sac Branch—stream ... KS-7
Saccamochee River ... MS-4
Saccarappa (historical)—locale ... MA-1
Saccarappa Pond ... MA-1
Saccarappo Sch—school ... ME-1
Sacchi Beach—beach ... OR-9
**Sac City**—pop pl ... IA-7
**Sac City Junction (historical)**—pop pl ... IA-7
Sacconesset ... MA-1
Saco-Pettee Machine Shops—hist pl ... MA-1
Sac County Courthouse—hist pl ... IA-7
Sac Creek—stream ... KS-7
Sachacha ... MA-1
Sachacha Pond ... MA-1
Sacheen Lake—lake ... WA-9
Sachem Brook ... MA-1
Sachem Creek—stream ... MA-1
**Sachem Head**—pop pl ... CT-1
Sachem Head—summit ... MA-1
Sachem Head Harbor—bay ... CT-1
Sachem HS—school ... NY-2
Sachem Island—island ... AK-9
Sachem Lodge Cem—cemetery ... MA-1
Sachem Peak—summit ... NH-1
Sachem Point ... WA-9
Sachem Pond—lake ... RI-1
Sachems Head ... CT-1
Sachem's Head Harbor ... CT-1
Sachem Spring ... MA-1
Sachem Village ... NH-1
**Sachem Village**—pop pl ... NH-1
Sachett Mtn—summit ... CO-8
Sachile ... FL-3
**Sac (historical)**—pop pl ... TN-4
**Sachse**—pop pl ... TX-5
Sachse Monument—summit ... CA-9
Sachueest Point ... RI-1
Sachuest—cape ... RI-1
**Sachuest**—pop pl ... RI-1
Sachuest Bay—bay ... RI-1
Sachuest Beach ... RI-1
Sachuest Neck ... RI-1
Sachuest Point—cape ... RI-1
Sacia Cem—cemetery ... WI-6
Sacier Pond Dam—dam ... MS-4
Sack, Johnny, Cabin—hist pl ... ID-8
Sack Bay ... MI-6
Sack Canyon—valley ... OR-9
Sack Canyon Rsvr—reservoir ... OR-9
Sack Creek—stream ... ID-8
Sack Creek Campground—locale ... ID-8
Sacker Branch—stream ... KY-4
Sacker Brook ... MA-1
Sacker Cem—cemetery ... KY-4
Sacker Creek—stream ... KY-4
Sacker Sch—school ... KY-4
Sackerson Lake—lake ... WI-6
**Sackertown**—pop pl ... MD-2
Sacket, Cornelius, House—hist pl ... NY-2
Sacket, General, House—hist pl ... NY-2
Sacket Brook—stream ... MA-1
Sacket Harbor ... NY-2
Sacket Run—stream ... OH-6
Sackets Brook ... MA-1
Sackets Harbor—bay ... NY-2
**Sackets Harbor**—pop pl ... NY-2
Sackets Harbor Battlefield—hist pl ... NY-2
Sackets Harbor Battlefield State Park—park ... NY-2
Sackets Harbor Village Hist Dist—hist pl ... NY-2
Sackett—locale ... KY-4
**Sackett**—pop pl ... PA-2
Sackett, Russell, House—hist pl ... MI-6
Sackett Tank—reservoir ... AZ-5
Sackett Brook ... MA-1
Sackett Brook—stream ... MA-1
Sackett Canyon—valley ... WY-8
Sackett Cem—cemetery ... OH-6
Sackett Creek—stream ... NY-2
Sackett Creek—stream ... PA-2
Sackett Creek—stream ... WY-8
Sackett Hill ... MA-1
Sackett Hollow—valley ... PA-2
Sackett Hollow—valley ... UT-8
Sackett Lake—lake ... NY-2
Sackett Lake—lake ... WI-6
Sackett Rsvr—reservoir ... CO-8
Sackett Rsvr—reservoir ... MA-1
Sacketts Brook—stream ... VT-1
Sacketts Brook Stone Arch Bridge—hist pl ... VT-1
Sackett Sch—school ... OH-6
Sacketts Gulch—valley ... CA-9
Sacketts Harbor ... NY-2
Sacketts Harbor—locale ... NY-2
**Sacketts Harbor**—pop pl ... NY-2
Sacketts Lake ... WI-6
**Sacketts Lake**—pop pl ... NY-2
Sackit Canyon—valley ... WA-9
Sack Lake—lake ... WI-6
Sackmeister Lake ... MN-6
Sackos Pond—reservoir ... OR-9
Sack Point—cape ... VA-3
Sackrider Cem—cemetery ... NY-2
Sackrider Hill—summit ... MI-6
Sackrider Lake ... IN-6
Sacks Lake—lake ... NE-7
**Sacksonia**—pop pl ... LA-4
Sacktaloosa Bluff ... AL-4
Sack Tongue Tank—reservoir ... AZ-5
Sackukupakupaku ... MH-9
**Sackville**—pop pl ... PA-2
Sackville House—hist pl ... PA-2
Saco—locale ... CA-9
Saco—locale ... MN-6
Saco—locale ... MO-7
Saco—locale ... PA-2
**Saco**—pop pl ... AL-4
**Saco**—pop pl ... ME-1
**Saco**—pop pl ... MT-8
**Saco**—pop pl ... PA-2
Saco (Barrio)—fmr MCD ... PR-3
Saco Bay—bay ... ME-1
Saco City Hall—hist pl ... ME-1
Saco HS (old)—hist pl ... ME-1
Saco Lake—lake ... NH-1
Sacondaga River ... NY-2
Sacondago River ... NY-2
**Saconesset Hills**—pop pl ... MA-1
Saconesset Homestead and Museum—locale ... MA-1
Saconon—locale ... NC-3
Saconon Creek—stream ... NC-3
Sacony Bridge—bridge ... PA-2
Sacony Creek—stream ... PA-2
Sacopatoy Creek ... AL-4
Saco River—stream ... ME-1
Saco River—stream ... NH-1
**Sac-o-Sage Heights**—pop pl ... MO-7
Sacotone Spring—spring ... CA-9
Sacra Farm—locale ... NM-5
Sacramento—locale ... CO-8
Sacramento—locale ... IL-6
Sacramento—locale ... NE-7
**Sacramento**—pop pl ... CA-9
**Sacramento**—pop pl ... KY-4
**Sacramento**—pop pl ... NM-5
**Sacramento**—pop pl ... PA-2
Sacramento Army Depot—military ... CA-9
Sacramento Bank Bldg—hist pl ... CA-9
Sacramento Bar—bar ... CA-9
Sacramento Boy Scout Camp—locale ... CA-9
Sacramento Butte—summit ... OR-9
Sacramento Bypass—other ... CA-9
Sacramento Canyon—valley ... CA-9
Sacramento Canyon—valley ... NV-8
Sacramento Canyon—valley ... NM-5
Sacramento Canyon (CCD)—cens area ... CA-9
Sacramento (CCD)—cens area ... CA-9
Sacramento (CCD)—cens area ... KY-4
Sacramento City (Abandoned)—locale ... NM-5
Sacramento City Coll—school ... CA-9
**Sacramento (County)**—pop pl ... CA-9
Sacramento County Animal Pound—building ... CA-9
Sacramento County Juvenile Center—building ... CA-9
Sacramento Creek—stream ... CO-8
Sacramento Creek—stream ... NE-7
Sacramento Drainage Canal—canal ... CA-9
Sacramento Gulch—valley ... CA-9
Sacramento Gulch—valley ... UT-8
Sacramento Hill—summit ... AZ-5
Sacramento Hill—summit ... CA-9
Sacramento Hill—summit ... OR-9
Sacramento (historical)—locale ... WI-6
Sacramento HS—school ... CA-9
Sacramento Landing—locale ... CA-9
Sacramento Lookout Tower—other ... NM-5
Sacramento Memorial Auditorium—hist pl ... CA-9
Sacramento Memorial Lawn (Cemetery)—cemetery ... CA-9
Sacramento Metropolitan Airp—airport ... CA-9
Sacramento Mine—mine ... CA-9
Sacramento Mine—mine (2) ... UT-8
Sacramento Mountains ... NM-5
Sacramento Mountains ... TX-5
Sacramento Mountains—range ... CA-9
Sacramento Mountains—range ... NM-5
Sacramento Mtn—summit ... CA-9
Sacramento Natl Wildlife Ref—park ... CA-9
Sacramento Pass—gap ... NV-8
Sacramento Peak—summit ... NM-5
Sacramento Range ... AZ-5
Sacramento River ... CA-9
Sacramento River—stream ... AK-9
Sacramento River—stream ... CA-9
Sacramento River—stream ... NM-5
Sacramento River Arm—bay ... CA-9

Sacramento River Deep Water Ship Channel—channel ... CA-9
Sacramento River Sch—school ... CA-9
Sacramento Sch—school ... OR-9
Sacramento Side Camp—locale ... NM-5
Sacramento Slough—gut ... CA-9
Sacramento South—uninc pl ... CA-9
Sacramento Springs—spring ... CA-9
Sacramento Square—park ... IL-6
Sacramento State Coll—school ... CA-9
Sacramento Union Acad—school ... CA-9
Sacramento Valley—valley ... AZ-5
Sacramento Valley—valley ... CA-9
Sacramento Wash—stream ... AZ-5
Sacramento Weir—levee ... CA-9
Sacramento-Wilcox State Wildlife Mgt Are—park ... NE-7
Sacramore Playground—park ... MA-1
Sacra Ranch—locale ... NM-5
Sacrarrappa Pond—reservoir ... MA-1
Sacratone Flat—flat ... CA-9
Sacra Via Park—park ... OH-6
Sacre Coeur Sch—school ... IL-6
Sacre Coeur Sch—school ... MA-1
Sacred Canyon—valley ... NV-8
Sacred Dancing Cascade—falls ... MT-8
Sacred Falls (Kaliuwaa)—falls ... HI-9
Sacred Falls Trail—trail ... HI-9
Sacred Hear Cem—cemetery ... NY-2
Sacred Heart—church ... FL-3
Sacred Heart—locale ... AR-4
Sacred Heart—locale ... OK-5
**Sacred Heart**—pop pl ... MN-6
Sacred Heart Acad—hist pl ... OH-6
Sacred Heart Acad—school ... CA-9
Sacred Heart Acad—school (2) ... CT-1
Sacred Heart Acad—school ... DC-2
Sacred Heart Acad—school ... FL-3
Sacred Heart Acad—school (2) ... IL-6
Sacred Heart Acad—school ... LA-4
Sacred Heart Acad—school (2) ... MA-1
Sacred Heart Acad—school (2) ... MI-6
Sacred Heart Acad—school ... MO-7
Sacred Heart Acad—school ... NM-5
Sacred Heart Acad—school (2) ... NY-2
Sacred Heart Acad—school ... ND-7
Sacred Heart Acad—school ... OH-6
Sacred Heart Acad—school ... OR-9
Sacred Heart Acad—school (2) ... TX-5
Sacred Heart Acad—school ... UT-8
Sacred Heart Camp—locale ... GA-3
Sacred Heart Cathedral—church ... IA-7
Sacred Heart Cathedral—church ... NJ-2
Sacred Heart Cathedral—hist pl ... KS-7
Sacred Heart Cathedral and Cathedral Sch—hist pl ... MN-6
Sacred Heart Catholic Ch—church (4) ... AL-4
Sacred Heart Catholic Ch—church ... DE-2
Sacred Heart Catholic Ch—church ... FL-3
Sacred Heart Catholic Ch—church ... KS-7
Sacred Heart Catholic Ch—church (5) ... MS-4
Sacred Heart Catholic Ch—church (2) ... TN-4
Sacred Heart Catholic Ch—church ... UT-8
Sacred Heart Catholic Church—hist pl ... CA-9
Sacred Heart Catholic Church—hist pl ... GA-3
Sacred Heart Catholic Church and Parsonage—hist pl ... MO-7
Sacred Heart Catholic Church and Rectory—hist pl ... AZ-5
Sacred Heart Catholic Church and Rectory—hist pl ... OK-5
Sacred Heart Catholic Church and Sch—hist pl ... TX-5
Sacred Heart Catholic Church Complex—hist pl ... NE-7
Sacred Heart Catholic Sch—school ... TN-4
Sacred Heart Cem—cemetery ... AZ-5
Sacred Heart Cem—cemetery (2) ... AR-4
Sacred Heart Cem—cemetery ... CO-8
Sacred Heart Cem—cemetery ... CT-1
Sacred Heart Cem—cemetery (9) ... IL-6
Sacred Heart Cem—cemetery (2) ... IN-6
Sacred Heart Cem—cemetery (16) ... IA-7
Sacred Heart Cem—cemetery (8) ... KS-7
Sacred Heart Cem—cemetery (2) ... LA-4
Sacred Heart Cem—cemetery (2) ... MD-2
Sacred Heart Cem—cemetery (5) ... MA-1
Sacred Heart Cem—cemetery (6) ... MI-6
Sacred Heart Cem—cemetery (10) ... MN-6
Sacred Heart Cem—cemetery (6) ... MO-7
Sacred Heart Cem—cemetery (6) ... NE-7
Sacred Heart Cem—cemetery (2) ... NH-1
Sacred Heart Cem—cemetery (3) ... NJ-2
Sacred Heart Cem—cemetery (11) ... NY-2
Sacred Heart Cem—cemetery (6) ... ND-7
Sacred Heart Cem—cemetery (2) ... OH-6
Sacred Heart Cem—cemetery (5) ... OK-5
Sacred Heart Cem—cemetery (2) ... OR-9
Sacred Heart Cem—cemetery (9) ... PA-2
Sacred Heart Cem—cemetery (8) ... SD-7
Sacred Heart Cem—cemetery (8) ... TX-5
Sacred Heart Cem—cemetery ... VA-3
Sacred Heart Cem—cemetery (8) ... WI-6
*Sacred Heart Cemetery* ... TN-4
Sacred Heart Center—church ... WI-6
Sacred Heart Ch—church ... AL-4
Sacred Heart Ch—church (2) ... CO-8
Sacred Heart Ch—church ... CT-1
Sacred Heart Ch—church ... FL-3
Sacred Heart Ch—church (3) ... GA-3
Sacred Heart Ch—church (2) ... IN-6
Sacred Heart Ch—church (2) ... IA-7
Sacred Heart Ch—church ... KS-7
Sacred Heart Ch—church ... KY-4
Sacred Heart Ch—church (5) ... LA-4
Sacred Heart Ch—church (3) ... MD-2
Sacred Heart Ch—church ... MA-1
Sacred Heart Ch—church (6) ... MI-6
Sacred Heart Ch—church ... MT-8
Sacred Heart Ch—church (3) ... NE-7
Sacred Heart Ch—church (3) ... NJ-2
Sacred Heart Ch—church (2) ... NM-5
Sacred Heart Ch—church (4) ... NY-2
Sacred Heart Ch—church (3) ... OH-6
Sacred Heart Ch—church (2) ... SC-3
Sacred Heart Ch—church (3) ... SD-7
Sacred Heart Ch—church (7) ... TX-5
Sacred Heart Ch—church (2) ... VA-3
Sacred Heart Ch—church (3) ... WI-6
Sacred Heart Chapel—church (2) ... LA-4
Sacred Heart Chapel—church ... NM-5
Sacred Heart Church—hist pl ... KY-4
Sacred Heart Church—hist pl ... MT-8
Sacred Heart Church—hist pl ... OH-6
Sacred Heart Church—hist pl ... WI-6
Sacred Heart Church, Rectory, Sch and Convent—hist pl ... MA-1
Sacred Heart Church, Sch and Rectory—hist pl ... MO-7
Sacred Heart Church (abandoned)—locale ... NM-5
Sacred Heart Church and Sch—school ... TN-4
Sacred Heart Coll—school ... KS-7
Sacred Heart Coll—school ... MA-1
Sacred Heart Coll—school ... NC-3
Sacred Heart Coll and Acad—school ... AL-4
Sacred Heart Convent—church ... CT-1
Sacred Heart Convent—church ... IL-6
Sacred Heart Convent—church ... ND-7
Sacred Heart Convent—church ... PA-2
Sacred Heart Convent—school ... FL-3
Sacred Heart Convent—school ... MO-7
Sacred Heart Convent—school ... PA-2
Sacred Heart Country Day Sch—school ... MD-2
Sacred Heart Creek—stream ... MN-6
Sacred Heart Dominican Coll—school ... TX-5
Sacred Heart Elem Sch—school ... IN-6
Sacred Heart Elem Sch—school ... KS-7
Sacred Heart Elem Sch—school ... MS-4
Sacred Heart General Hosp—hospital ... OR-9
Sacred Heart General Hospital Heliport—airport ... OR-9
Sacred Heart Grade Sch—school (3) ... KS-7
Sacred Heart Home—building ... IN-6
Sacred Heart Home—building ... NY-2
Sacred Heart Home—building ... PA-2
Sacred Heart Hosp—hospital ... FL-3
Sacred Heart Hosp—hospital ... ID-8
Sacred Heart Hosp—hospital (2) ... PA-2
Sacred Heart Hosp—hospital ... WI-6
Sacred Heart Hosp of Pensacola—hospital ... FL-3
Sacred Heart HS—school ... CA-9
Sacred Heart HS—school ... CT-1
Sacred Heart HS—school ... IN-6
Sacred Heart HS—school ... MA-1
Sacred Heart HS—school ... MI-6
Sacred Heart HS—school ... MS-4
Sacred Heart HS—school ... NE-7
Sacred Heart Institute—school ... NJ-2
Sacred Heart Juniorate—school ... MA-1
Sacred Heart Med Ctr Helistop Heliport—airport ... WA-9
Sacred Heart Mission—church ... MD-2
Sacred Heart Mission—church ... MN-6
Sacred Heart Mission—church ... MS-4
Sacred Heart Mission (historical)—church ... ND-7
Sacred Heart Mission Site—hist pl ... OK-5
Sacred Heart Monastery—church ... MD-2
Sacred Heart Monastery—church ... VA-3
Sacred Heart Monastery—church ... WI-6
Sacred Heart Novitiate—church ... OH-6
Sacred Heart Novitiate—school ... MD-2
Sacred Heart Novitiate—school ... OH-6
Sacred Heart of Jesus Church—hist pl ... TN-4
Sacred Heart of Jesus Churches—hist pl ... OH-6
Sacred Heart of Jesus HS—school ... LA-4
Sacred Heart of Jesus Rectory—hist pl ... OH-6
Sacred Heart of Jesus Roman Catholic Ch—church ... IN-6
Sacred Heart of Jesus Sch—school ... IN-6
Sacred Heart of Jesus Sch—school ... NY-2
Sacred Heart of Jesus Sch—school ... PA-2
Sacred Heart Of Jesus Sch—school ... PA-2
Sacred Heart of Mary Cem—cemetery ... MD-2
Sacred Heart of Mary HS—school ... CA-9
Sacred Heart Parish Educational Center—school ... AL-4
Sacred Heart Parochial Sch—school ... TN-4
Sacred Heart Primary Sch—school ... IN-6
Sacred Heart Priory—church ... ND-7
Sacred Heart Retreat—church ... CA-9
Sacred Heart Retreat House—locale ... CO-8
Sacred Heart Roman Catholic Cathedral Complex—hist pl ... IA-7
Sacred Heart Roman Catholic Church—hist pl ... MS-4
Sacred Heart Roman Catholic Church, Convent and Rectory—hist pl ... MI-6
Sacred Hearts Acad—school ... HI-9
Sacred Heart Sanitarium—hospital ... WI-6
Sacred Hearts Cem—cemetery ... IA-7
Sacred Hearts Cem—cemetery ... NY-2
Sacred Heart Sch—hist pl ... MA-1
Sacred Heart Sch—school ... AL-4
Sacred Heart Sch—school (2) ... AZ-5
Sacred Heart Sch—school (12) ... CA-9
Sacred Heart Sch—school ... CO-8
Sacred Heart Sch—school (9) ... CT-1
Sacred Heart Sch—school (4) ... FL-3
Sacred Heart Sch—school (3) ... GA-3
Sacred Heart Sch—school ... ID-8
Sacred Heart Sch—school (6) ... IL-6
Sacred Heart Sch—school (7) ... IN-6
Sacred Heart Sch—school (11) ... IA-7
Sacred Heart Sch—school (8) ... KS-7
Sacred Heart Sch—school ... KY-4
Sacred Heart Sch—school (4) ... LA-4
Sacred Heart Sch—school (2) ... ME-1
Sacred Heart Sch—school (12) ... MA-1
Sacred Heart Sch—school (8) ... MI-6
Sacred Heart Sch—school (3) ... MN-6
Sacred Heart Sch—school (3) ... MS-4
Sacred Heart Sch—school (5) ... MO-7
Sacred Heart Sch—school ... MT-8
Sacred Heart Sch—school (4) ... NE-7
Sacred Heart Sch—school ... NH-1
Sacred Heart Sch—school (12) ... NJ-2
Sacred Heart Sch—school (9) ... NY-2
Sacred Heart Sch—school ... NC-3
Sacred Heart Sch—school (11) ... OH-6
Sacred Heart Sch—school (4) ... OK-5
Sacred Heart Sch—school (2) ... OR-9
Sacred Heart Sch—school (15) ... PA-2
Sacred Heart Sch—school (2) ... SD-7
Sacred Heart Sch—school ... TN-4
Sacred Heart Sch—school (8) ... TX-5
Sacred Heart Sch—school ... VA-3
Sacred Heart Sch—school (2) ... WA-9
Sacred Heart Sch—school (2) ... WV-2
Sacred Heart Sch—school (7) ... WI-6
*Sacred Heart School* ... KS-7
Sacred Heart Schools—school ... IN-6
Sacred Heart Schools—school ... NJ-2
Sacred Hearts Convent—school ... HI-9
Sacred Heart Seminary—church ... OH-6
Sacred Heart Seminary—hist pl ... MI-6
Sacred Heart Seminary—school ... DC-2
Sacred Heart Seminary—school ... HI-9
Sacred Heart Seminary—school (2) ... IL-6
Sacred Heart Seminary—school ... MA-1
Sacred Heart Seminary—school ... MI-6
Sacred Heart Seminary—school ... OH-6
Sacred Hearts of Jesus and Mary Church—hist pl ... ID-8
Sacred Hearts Sch—school ... MA-1
Sacred Hearts Sch—school (2) ... NY-2
Sacred Heart (Township of)—civ div ... MN-6
Sacred Heart Univ—school ... CT-1
Sacred Heart University—facility ... PR-3
Sacred Home—hist pl ... KY-4
Sacred Lake—lake ... AK-9
Sacred Mound Mine—mine ... CA-9
Sacred Mountain—hist pl ... AZ-5
Sacred Mountain Trading Post—locale ... AZ-5
**Sacred Mountain (Trading Post)**—pop pl ... AZ-5
Sacred Mtn—summit ... AZ-5
Sacred Point—summit ... NV-8
Sacred Sch—school ... MA-1
Sacred Spring—spring ... NM-5
S A Creek—stream ... NM-5
SA Creek—stream ... WY-8
Sacre Gap—gap ... CA-9
*Sacremento Mountains* ... NM-5
*Sacremento Wash* ... CA-9
Sacrifice Ch (historical)—church ... MS-4
Sacrifice Cliff—cliff ... MT-8
Sacrifice Creek—stream ... ID-8
Sac River—stream ... MO-7
Sactone Spring—spring ... AZ-5
Sac Township—fmr MCD ... IA-7
**Sac Township**—pop pl ... MO-7
**Sacul**—pop pl ... TX-5
Sacville—locale ... MO-7
Sadaquada Golf Club—other ... NY-2
Sadatanak Island—island ... AK-9
Sadawga Lake—lake ... VT-1
Sadberry Creek—stream ... TX-5
Sad Branch—stream ... VA-3
Sadd Creek—stream ... OR-9
*Saddle* ... ME-1
Saddle—locale ... AZ-5
Saddle—locale ... AR-4
Saddle—locale ... UT-8
**Saddle**—pop pl ... NC-3
Saddle, The—gap ... CA-9
Saddle, The—gap (3) ... CO-8
Saddle, The—gap ... ID-8
Saddle, The—gap ... OR-9
Saddle, The—gap ... TN-4
Saddle, The—gap ... UT-8
Saddle, The—gap ... VA-3
*Saddle Back* ... ME-1
*Saddleback* ... PA-2
*Saddleback* ... UT-8
Saddleback—bar ... ME-1
Saddleback—gap (2) ... CA-9
Saddle Back—gap ... NV-8
Saddle Back—ridge ... CA-9
Saddle Back—ridge ... KS-7
Saddleback—summit ... AZ-5
Saddleback, The—summit (2) ... ME-1
Saddleback Brook—stream ... ME-1
Saddleback Butte—summit ... CA-9
Saddleback Butte—summit ... MT-8
Saddleback Butte State Park—park ... CA-9
Saddleback Hill—summit ... MA-1
*Saddleback Hills* ... WY-8
Saddleback Hills—range ... WY-8
Saddleback Hills—ridge ... ME-1
Saddleback Island—island ... ME-1
Saddleback Junior—summit ... ME-1
Saddle Back Knob—summit ... WV-2
Saddleback Lake—lake ... FL-3
Saddleback Lake—lake ... ME-1
Saddleback Lake—lake (2) ... MI-6
Saddleback Ledge—bar (2) ... ME-1
Saddleback Ledge Light Station—hist pl ... ME-1
Saddleback Ledge Shoal—bar ... ME-1
Saddleback Mesa—summit ... NM-5
*Saddleback Mound* ... WI-6
*Saddleback Mountain* ... OR-9
Saddle Back Mountains—summit ... TX-5
Saddleback Mountain Trail—trail ... VA-3
*Saddle Back Mtn* ... AZ-5
*Saddleback Mtn* ... ME-1
Saddleback Mtn—summit ... AZ-5
Saddle Back Mtn—summit ... AR-4
Saddleback Mtn—summit (2) ... CA-9
Saddleback Mtn—summit (2) ... CO-8
Saddleback Mtn—summit (5) ... ME-1
Saddleback Mtn—summit (2) ... MT-8
Saddleback Mtn—summit ... NH-1
Saddleback Mtn—summit ... NM-5
Saddleback Mtn—summit (2) ... NY-2
Saddleback Mtn—summit (2) ... TX-5
Saddleback Mtn—summit ... VT-1
Saddleback Mtn—summit ... VA-3
Saddleback Mtn—summit (2) ... WY-8
Saddleback Opening—flat ... CA-9
Saddleback Pond—lake ... ME-1
Saddleback Ranch—locale ... CO-8
Saddleback Ridge—ridge ... NC-3
Saddle Back Ridge—ridge ... PA-2
Saddleback Stream—stream ... ME-1
Saddleback Swamps—swamp ... MI-6
Saddlebag Campground—locale ... CA-9
Saddlebag Creek—stream ... MS-4
Saddlebag Glacier—glacier ... AK-9
*Saddle Bag Island* ... MI-6
Saddlebag Island—island ... MI-6
Saddlebag Island—island ... WA-9
Saddlebag Island State Park—park ... WA-9
Saddlebag Lake—lake ... CA-9
Saddlebag Lake—lake ... FL-3
Saddle Bag Lake—lake ... FL-3
Saddlebag Lake—lake ... FL-3
Saddlebag Lake—lake (4) ... MI-6
Saddlebag Lake—lake ... NY-2
Saddlebag Lake—lake ... WI-6
*Saddlebag Mtn* ... OR-9
Saddle Bag Mtn—summit ... OR-9
Saddlebags Creek—stream ... MS-4
*Saddlebags Island* ... MI-6
Saddlebags Lake—lake ... FL-3
*Saddle Ball* ... MA-1
Saddle Ball Mtn—summit ... MA-1
Saddle Basin—basin ... OR-9
Saddle Basin Creek—stream ... OR-9
Saddle Blanket Flat—flat ... CA-9
Saddle Blanket Lakes—lake ... FL-3
Saddleblanket Mtn—summit ... OR-9
Saddle Blanket Pond—lake ... TX-5
Saddle Blanket Ridge—ridge ... ID-8
Saddle Blanket Well—well ... TX-5
Saddle Bow Mtn—summit ... WA-9
Saddle Branch—stream ... KY-4
Saddle Branch—stream ... LA-4
Saddle Branch—stream ... MO-7
Saddle Bridge—bridge ... MO-7
**Saddle Brook**—pop pl ... NJ-2
Saddle Brook—stream (2) ... ME-1
Saddle Brook—stream ... NJ-2
**Saddle Brook (Township of)**—pop pl ... NJ-2
Saddlebunch Harbor—bay ... FL-3
*Saddlebunch Key* ... FL-3
Saddlebunch Keys—island ... FL-3
Saddlebunch Number 2 Channel—channel ... FL-3
Saddlebunch Number 3 Channel—channel ... FL-3
Saddlebunch Number 4 Channel—channel ... FL-3
Saddlebunch Number 5 Channel—channel ... FL-3
*Saddle Butte* ... ID-8
*Saddle Butte* ... SD-7
Saddle Butte—ridge ... OR-9
Saddle Butte—summit (2) ... AZ-5
Saddle Butte—summit ... ID-8
Saddle Butte—summit (5) ... MT-8
Saddle Butte—summit (3) ... ND-7
Saddle Butte—summit (9) ... OR-9
Saddle Butte—summit (5) ... SD-7
Saddle Butte—summit ... TX-5
Saddle Butte—summit ... WA-9
Saddle Butte Bay—bay ... ND-7
Saddle Butte Creek—stream ... OR-9
Saddle Butte Lava Field—lava ... OR-9
Saddle Butte Lava Tube—lava ... OR-9
Saddle Butte Public Use Area—park ... ND-7
Saddle Butte Rsvr—reservoir (3) ... OR-9
Saddle Butte Rsvr 2—reservoir ... OR-9
*Saddle Buttes* ... ND-7
Saddle Buttes—range ... ND-7
**Saddle Butte Township**—pop pl ... ND-7
Saddle Camp—locale ... CA-9
Saddle Camp—locale (2) ... ID-8
Saddle Camp—locale (3) ... OR-9
Saddle Camp—locale ... WA-9
Saddle Camp Butte—summit ... OR-9
Saddle Camp Creek—stream ... OR-9
Saddle Campground—locale ... NM-5
Saddle Campground—locale ... WA-9
Saddle Camp Guard Station—locale ... CA-9
Saddle Camp Pass—gap ... CA-9
Saddle Camp Spring—spring (2) ... OR-9
Saddle Canyon—valley (3) ... AZ-5
Saddle Canyon Tank—reservoir ... AZ-5
Saddle Cave—cave ... TN-4
Saddle Corral—locale ... AZ-5
Saddle Crater—crater ... AZ-5
**Saddle Creek**—pop pl ... FL-3
**Saddle Creek**—pop pl ... NE-7
Saddle Creek—stream ... AK-9
Saddle Creek—stream (2) ... CO-8
Saddle Creek—stream ... FL-3
Saddle Creek—stream (6) ... ID-8
Saddle Creek—stream (2) ... IN-6
Saddle Creek—stream (2) ... MT-8
Saddle Creek—stream (3) ... OR-9
Saddle Creek—stream ... SD-7
Saddle Creek—stream (2) ... TX-5
Saddle Creek—stream ... UT-8
Saddle Creek—stream ... VA-3
Saddle Creek—stream (4) ... WA-9
Saddle Creek—stream ... WY-8
Saddle Creek Ch—church ... VA-3
Saddle Creek (historical)—locale ... SD-7
Saddle Creek Park—park ... FL-3
Saddle Creek Spring—spring ... UT-8
Saddle Dam—dam ... OR-9
Saddle Dam—dam (2) ... TN-4
Saddle Dam No 2—dam ... IL-6
Saddle Dam No 3—dam ... IL-6
Saddle Dam 1—dam ... NC-3
Saddle Dam 1—dam ... TN-4
Saddle Dam 10—dam ... TN-4
Saddle Dam 2—dam ... NC-3
Saddle Dam 3—dam ... NC-3
Saddle Dam 3—dam ... TN-4
Saddle Dam 4—dam ... TN-4
Saddle Dam 5—dam ... TN-4
Saddle Dam 6—dam ... TN-4
Saddle Dam 7—dam ... TN-4
Saddle Dam 8—dam ... TN-4
Saddle Dam 9—dam ... TN-4
Saddle Draw—valley ... OR-9
Saddle Flats—flat ... CA-9
*Saddle Fork* ... UT-8
Saddle Fork—stream ... ID-8
Saddle Fork—stream ... KY-4
Saddle Gap—gap ... AL-4
Saddle Gap—gap ... AZ-5
Saddle Gap—gap ... AR-4
Saddle Gap—gap (2) ... GA-3
Saddle Gap—gap ... NE-7
Saddle Gap—gap ... NC-3
Saddle Gap—gap ... TN-4
Saddle Gap—gap ... TX-5
Saddle Gap—gap ... VA-3
Saddle Gap—gap (2) ... WA-9
Saddle Gap Branch—stream ... GA-3
Saddle Gap Cave—cave ... TN-4
*Saddle Gulch* ... ID-8
Saddle Gulch—valley (2) ... CA-9
Saddle Gulch—valley ... ID-8
Saddle Gulch—valley (2) ... OR-9
Saddle Hammock—island (2) ... FL-3
Saddle Hill—summit ... FL-3
Saddle Hill—summit ... ME-1
Saddle Hill—summit ... MA-1
Saddle Hill—summit ... NH-1
Saddle Hill—summit ... NY-2
Saddle Hill—summit ... WA-9
Saddlehill Key—island ... FL-3
Saddle Hollow—valley ... OR-9
Saddle Hollow—valley ... VA-3
Saddlehorn—summit ... CO-8
**Saddlehorn Ranch (subdivision)**—pop pl (2) ... AZ-5
Saddle Horn Rock—pillar ... AZ-5
Saddle Horse Basin—basin ... ID-8
Saddle Horse Bottom—bend ... UT-8
Saddle Horse Butte—summit ... MT-8
Saddle Horse Butte—summit ... WY-8
Saddle Horse Canyon—valley ... AZ-5
Saddle Horse Canyon—valley ... TX-5
Saddle Horse Canyon—valley ... UT-8
Saddlehorse Canyon—valley ... UT-8
Saddlehorse Creek—stream ... OR-9
Saddle Horse Draw—valley ... AZ-5
Saddle Horse Draw—valley ... WY-8
Saddle Horse Flat—flat ... WA-9
*Saddle Horse Lake* ... CA-9
Saddle Horse Lake—lake ... CA-9
Saddle Horse Park—flat ... CO-8
Saddle Horse Point—cliff ... UT-8
Saddle Horse Ridge—ridge ... ID-8
Saddle Horse Spring—spring ... AZ-5
Saddlehorse Spring—spring ... OR-9
Saddle Horse Spring—spring ... UT-8
Saddle Horse Tank—reservoir (3) ... AZ-5
Saddle Indian Creek—stream ... LA-4
*Saddle Island* ... MI-6
Saddle Island—island ... ME-1
Saddle Island—island ... NV-8
Saddle Island—island ... OK-5
Saddle Junction—locale ... CA-9
Saddle Key—island ... FL-3
Saddle Knob—summit ... WV-2
Saddle Knoll—summit ... UT-8
Saddle Lake—lake ... CA-9
Saddle Lake—lake (2) ... ID-8
Saddle Lake—lake ... MI-6
Saddle Lake—lake ... MN-6
Saddle Lake—lake ... NY-2
Saddle Lake—lake ... OR-9
Saddle Lake—lake ... WA-9
Saddle Lake—lake ... WI-6
**Saddle Lake**—pop pl ... IN-6
**Saddle Lake**—pop pl ... MI-6
Saddle Lake—reservoir (2) ... IN-6
Saddle Lake Camp—locale ... NY-2
Saddle Lake Dam—dam ... IN-6
Saddle Lake Dam—dam ... PA-2
Saddle Lake Sch—school ... MI-6
Saddle Mound—summit ... FL-3
Saddle Mound—summit ... WI-6
*Saddle Mount* ... PW-9
*Saddle Mountain* ... NY-2
*Saddle Mountain* ... WY-8
Saddle Mountain—locale ... OK-5
Saddle Mountain, The—summit ... NM-5
Saddle Mountain Ch—church ... NC-3
Saddle Mountain Creek—stream ... NC-3
Saddle Mountain Creek—stream ... OK-5
Saddle Mountain Highline Ditch—valley ... CO-8
Saddle Mountain Indian Mission—church ... OK-5
Saddle Mountain Natl Wildlife Ref—park ... WA-9
Saddle Mountains—range ... WA-9
*Saddle Mountains Gap* ... WA-9
Saddle Mountain Spring—spring ... AZ-5
Saddle Mountain Spring—spring ... OR-9
Saddle Mountain Springs—spring ... OR-9
Saddle Mountain State Park—park ... OR-9
Saddle Mountain Tank—reservoir (2) ... AZ-5
*Saddle Mtn* ... AZ-5
*Saddle Mtn* ... MA-1
*Saddle Mtn* ... OR-9
Saddle Mtn—summit (4) ... AK-9
Saddle Mtn—summit (7) ... AZ-5
Saddle Mtn—summit (5) ... CA-9
Saddle Mtn—summit (4) ... CO-8
Saddle Mtn—summit ... GA-3
Saddle Mtn—summit (3) ... ID-8
Saddle Mtn—summit (6) ... MT-8
Saddle Mtn—summit (2) ... NV-8
Saddle Mtn—summit (2) ... NM-5
Saddle Mtn—summit ... NC-3
Saddle Mtn—summit ... OK-5
Saddle Mtn—summit (6) ... OR-9
Saddle Mtn—summit ... UT-8
Saddle Mtn—summit ... VT-1
Saddle Mtn—summit (3) ... WA-9
Saddle Mtn—summit (2) ... WY-8
Saddle Notch—gap ... CO-8
Saddle Notch Gulch—valley ... CO-8
Saddle Opening—flat ... CA-9
Saddle Park Hills—other ... CA-9
Saddle Pass—gap ... UT-8
Saddle Pass Spring—spring ... UT-8
*Saddle Peak* ... OR-9
Saddle Peak—summit ... AK-9
Saddle Peak—summit (2) ... CA-9
Saddle Peak—summit ... MT-8
Saddle Peak—summit ... WA-9
Saddle Peak Hills—other ... CA-9
Saddle Peaks—summit ... OR-9
Saddle & Pilgrim Graves—cemetery ... MA-1
Saddle Pit—cave ... TN-4
Saddle Point—cape (2) ... AK-9
Saddle Point—cape ... CA-9
Saddle Point—cape ... ID-8
Saddle Point—cape ... SD-7
Saddle Point—summit ... WA-9
Saddle Pond—lake ... ME-1
Saddle Pond—lake ... VT-1
**Saddler**—pop pl ... ID-8
*Saddle Range* ... MA-1
Saddler Bend—bend ... OK-5
Saddler Bend—bend ... TN-4
*Saddler Branch* ... TN-4
Saddler Branch—stream ... KY-4
Saddler Cem—cemetery ... KY-4
Saddler Cem—cemetery ... VA-3
Saddler Creek—stream ... ID-8
Saddler Creek—stream ... MI-6
Saddler Creek—stream ... PA-2
Saddler Creek—stream (2) ... TX-5
Saddler Falls—falls ... AR-4
*Saddle Ridge* ... NV-8
Saddle Ridge—ridge (2) ... AZ-5
Saddle Ridge—ridge ... GA-3
Saddle Ridge—ridge ... ID-8
Saddle Ridge—ridge ... UT-8
Saddle Ridge—ridge ... WA-9
Saddle Ridge—ridge ... WY-8
Saddle Ridge Pasture—flat ... AZ-5
Saddle Ridge Pasture Tank—reservoir ... AZ-5
Saddleridge Point—cape ... AK-9
Saddle Ridge Tank—reservoir ... AZ-5
Saddle Ridge Windmill—locale ... TX-5
*Saddle River* ... NJ-2
**Saddle River**—pop pl ... NJ-2
Saddle River—stream ... NJ-2
Saddle River—stream ... NY-2
Saddle River Center Hist Dist—hist pl ... NJ-2
Saddle River County Park—park ... NJ-2
Saddle River Golf Club—other ... NJ-2
Saddle River Valley—valley ... NJ-2
*Saddler Lake* ... CA-9
Saddler Lake Dam—dam ... MS-4
Saddler Mtn—summit ... AL-4
Saddle Road Junction—locale ... HI-9
Saddle Rock—island ... OR-9
Saddle Rock—pillar ... CA-9
Saddle Rock—pillar ... CO-8
**Saddle Rock**—pop pl ... NY-2
Saddle Rock—rock ... MA-1
Saddle Rock—summit ... AZ-5
Saddle Rock—summit ... CA-9
Saddle Rock—summit ... CO-8
Saddle Rock—summit ... NE-7
Saddle Rock—summit ... NM-5
Saddle Rock—summit ... UT-8
Saddle Rock—summit (2) ... WY-8
Saddlerock Brook—stream ... ME-1
Saddle Rock Canyon—valley ... NM-5
*Saddlerock Creek* ... SD-7
**Saddle Rock Estates**—pop pl ... NY-2
Saddle Rock Grist Mill—hist pl ... NY-2
Saddlerock Lake—lake ... CA-9
Saddlerock Pond—lake ... ME-1
Saddle Rock Ranch Pictograph Site—hist pl ... CA-9
Saddle Rock Sch—school ... NY-2
Saddle Rock Trail—trail ... CO-8
*Saddler Run* ... PA-2
Saddlers Ch—church ... PA-2
*Saddlers Creek* ... GA-3
*Saddlers Creek* ... PA-2
Saddlers Creek—stream ... MS-4
Saddlers Creek—stream ... TX-5
Saddlers Crossroads—locale ... VA-3
Saddlers Hill—summit ... MS-4
Saddlers Mistake—other ... AK-9
Saddlers Neck—cape ... VA-3
Saddlers Run Dam—dam ... PA-2
Saddle Rsvr—reservoir (2) ... CO-8
Saddle Rsvr—reservoir ... ID-8
Saddle Rsvr—reservoir ... OR-9
Saddler Swamp—stream ... SC-3
Saddlers Well—cave ... TN-4
Saddler Windmill—locale ... TX-5
Saddles, The—summit ... NY-2
*Saddles Island* ... MS-4
*Saddle Spring* ... OR-9
Saddle Spring—spring (3) ... CA-9
Saddle Spring—spring (3) ... ID-8
Saddle Spring—spring ... ME-1
Saddle Spring—spring (2) ... NV-8
Saddle Spring—spring (4) ... OR-9
Saddle Spring—spring (2) ... UT-8
Saddle Spring—spring ... WA-9
Saddle Spring Pass—gap ... CA-9
Saddle Springs—spring ... OR-9
Saddle Springs Guard Station—locale ... WA-9
**Saddlestring**—pop pl ... WY-8
Saddle String Ranch—locale ... CO-8
Saddle Swamp—stream ... VA-3
Saddle Tank—reservoir (9) ... AZ-5
Saddle Tank—reservoir (3) ... NM-5
Saddle Tanks—reservoir ... AZ-5
Saddle Trail—trail ... ME-1
Saddle Trail—trail ... OR-9
Saddle Trail—trail ... VA-3
**Saddletree**—pop pl ... NC-3
Saddletree Ch—church ... NC-3
Saddletree Creek—stream ... VA-3
Saddletree Draw—valley ... UT-8
Saddle Tree Gap—gap ... NC-3
Saddletree Lake—lake ... LA-4
Saddletree Swamp—swamp ... NC-3
Saddletree (Township of)—fmr MCD ... NC-3
Saddle Tunnel (Abandoned)—tunnel ... SC-3
Saddle Windmill—locale ... NM-5
Saddok Tasi—beach ... MH-9
Sadds Mill—locale ... CT-1
Sadds Mill Pond—reservoir ... CT-1
*Sadds Mills* ... CT-1
Sadducee Hollow—valley ... ID-8
Sadducee Spring—spring ... ID-8
*Sa del Caballo Muerto* ... TX-5
Saderbalm Creek—stream ... MT-8
Sadie—locale ... OK-5
**Sadie**—pop pl ... LA-4
**Sadie**—pop pl ... TN-4
Sadie Cove—bay ... AK-9
Sadie Creek—stream ... MT-8
Sadie Creek—stream ... WA-9
Sadie D Mine—mine ... CA-9
**Sadie Heights (subdivision)**—pop pl ... NC-3
Sadie Lake—lake ... AK-9
Sadie Morris Creek—stream ... GA-3
*Sadie Saulter Elementary School* ... NC-3
Sadies Dam—dam ... NJ-2
Sadies Flat—flat ... UT-8
Sadies Hollow—valley ... UT-8
Sadies Nipple—pillar ... UT-8
Sadies Peak—summit ... AZ-5
Sadie Spring—spring ... OR-9
Sadie Thomas Park—park ... TX-5
**Sadieville**—pop pl ... KY-4
Sadieville (CCD)—cens area ... KY-4
Sad Lake—lake ... OR-9
Sadler—locale ... KY-4
Sadler—locale ... MO-7
Sadler—locale ... TN-4
**Sadler**—pop pl ... NC-3
**Sadler**—pop pl ... TX-5
Sadler, Gov. Reinhold, House—hist pl ... NV-8
Sadler, Herbert A., House—hist pl ... MA-1
Sadler, Samuel, House—hist pl ... NY-2

Sagokutashii MH-9
**Sagola**—*pop pl* MI-6
Sago Lake—*lake* MI-6
Sago Lake—*lake* MN-6
Sagola Lakes—*lake* MI-6
Sagola Swamp—*swamp* MI-6
**Sagola (Township of)**—*pop pl* MI-6
**Sagon**—*pop pl* PA-2
**Sagon (Hickory Ridge)**—*pop pl* PA-2
**Sagon Junction**—*pop pl* PA-2
Sago School AL-4
Sago Spring—*spring* ID-8
**Sago (Township of)**—*pop pl* MN-6
Sagouspe Dam—*dam* NV-8
Sag Pond—*lake* ME-1
Sagrada—*locale* MO-7
Sagrada Familia de Lemitar Church, Los Dulces Nombres—*hist pl* NM-5
**Sagrado Corazon**—*pop pl* (2) PR-3
Sagrado Corazon Cem—*cemetery* NM-5
Sagtikos Manor—*hist pl* NY-2
Sagtikos Sch—*school* NY-2
Sag Top—*summit* VA-3
**Sagu**—*pop pl* CA-9
Sagua—*area* GU-9
Sagua'—*slope* MH-9
Sagua Beach—*beach* GU-9
**Saguache**—*pop pl* CO-8
Saguache Arroyo CO-8
Saguache Creek CO-8
Saguache Flour Mill—*hist pl* CO-8
Saguache Municipal Airp—*airport* CO-8
Saguache Park—*flat* CO-8
Saguache Peak—*summit* CO-8
Saguache Rsvr—*reservoir* CO-8
Saguache Sch and Jail Buildings—*hist pl* CO-8
Sagua'gahga, Puntan—*cape* MH-9
Sagualao—*area* GU-9
Sagua Pagpag MH-9
Saguapagupagu MH-9
Sagua Pakpak—*slope* MH-9
Saguapugupugu MH-9
Saguapupupagu MH-9
Sagua River—*stream* GU-9
Saguaro Airp—*airport* AZ-5
Saguaro del Norte Rec Area—*park* AZ-5
Saguaro Gap—*gap* AZ-5
Saguaro Gap Well—*well* AZ-5
Saguaro (historical)—*locale* AZ-5
Saguaro HS—*school* AZ-5
Saguaro Lake—*reservoir* AZ-5
Saguaro Mine—*mine* AZ-5
Saguaro Natl Monmt East Unit—*park* AZ-5
Saguaro Natl Monument (Tucson Mountain Section)—*park* AZ-5
Saguaro Power Plant—*locale* AZ-5
Saguaro Sch—*school* AZ-5
Saguaro Slope Ranch—*locale* AZ-5
Saguaro Tank—*reservoir* (3) AZ-5
Saguaro Vista Shop Ctr—*locale* AZ-5
Saguaro Well—*well* AZ-5
Sague House—*hist pl* NY-2
Saguish Head MA-1
Sagulla Airp—*airport* PA-2
Sagunada Ranch—*locale* TX-5
**Sagunay Lake**—*pop pl* IN-6
Sagus Lake—*lake* MN-6
Sagwon—*locale* AK-9
Sagwup Draw—*valley* WY-8
Sagy at Sosi Canyon AZ-5
Sahale Arm—*cape* WA-9
Sahale Creek WA-9
Sahalee Tyee, Lake—*lake* WA-9
Sahale Falls—*falls* OR-9
Sahale Glacier WA-9
Sahale Glacier—*glacier* WA-9
Sahale Mtn—*summit* WA-9
Sahalie Falls OR-9
Sahalie Falls—*falls* OR-9
Sahalie Peak WA-9
**Sahama Village (subdivision)**—*pop pl* AL-4
Sahara Cem—*cemetery* TX-5
Sahara Draw—*valley* WY-8
Sahara Mine No 16—*mine* IL-6
Sahara Mine No 5—*mine* IL-6
Sahara Mobile Home Park—*locale* AZ-5
Sahara Sand Dunes Heliport—*airport* UT-8
**Sahara Sands**—*pop pl* OH-6
**Sahara Village**—*pop pl* UT-8
Sahauro AZ-5
Sahdbush Cove—*bay* NH-1
Sahdy Grove Ch—*church* MS-4
Sahgzie Creek—*stream* UT-8
Sahhawotung PA-2
Sahhonnotung PA-2
S A Hill—*summit* AZ-5
Sahkoo Park—*park* AZ-5
Sahlee Creek—*stream* NC-3
Sahlin Creek—*stream* AK-9
Sahlin Falls—*falls* AK-9
Sahlin Lagoon—*lake* AK-9
Sahlin Lake—*lake* AK-9
Sahm Cem—*cemetery* TX-5
Sahoma, Lake—*reservoir* OK-5
Sahot Lake—*lake* AK-9
Sahotsaidbeazhe Canyon AZ-5
Sa Hot soid be azhe Canyon AZ-5
Sahs Sch—*school* IL-6
Sah Tah Mine—*mine* AZ-5
Sahtlikwu River WA-9
**Sahuarita**—*pop pl* AZ-5
Sahuarita Air Force Range—*military* AZ-5
Sahuarita Bombing and Gunnery Range—*military* AZ-5
Sahuarita Butte AZ-5
Sahuarita Elem Sch—*school* AZ-5
**Sahuarita Heights**—*pop pl* AZ-5
Sahuarita HS—*school* AZ-5
Sahuarita JHS—*school* AZ-5
Sahuarita Post Office—*building* AZ-5
Sahuarita RR Station—*building* AZ-5
Sahuarita Wash—*arroyo* AZ-5
Sahuarito AZ-5
Sahuarito Butte AZ-5
Sahuaro AZ-5
Sahuaro HS—*school* AZ-5
Sahuaro Lake AZ-5
Sahuaro Ranch—*hist pl* AZ-5
Sahuaro Ranch—*locale* AZ-5
Sahuaro Sch—*school* (2) AZ-5
Sahuaro School, The—*school* AZ-5
Sahuaro Tank—*reservoir* AZ-5
S A Hull Elem Sch—*school* FL-3
Sahura AZ-5
Sahurito Peak AZ-5
Sahwa Creek—*stream* MI-6
Sahwaralap—*stream* FM-9
Sahwartik—*stream* FM-9
Sahwave Mtns—*range* NV-8
Sahwick Mountain AZ-5
Sah-wik Mountain AZ-5
Said Cem—*cemetery* IA-7
Saidora—*locale* IL-6
Said Valley—*valley* CA-9
Said Valley Rsvr—*reservoir* CA-9
**Saienni Farms (subdivision)**—*pop pl* DE-2
Saikan River OR-9
Sail Bay—*bay* CA-9
Sail Boat Bridge—*bridge* OK-5
Sailboat Lake—*lake* FL-3
**Sailele**—*pop pl* AS-9
Sailes—*locale* LA-4
Sailes Lookout Tower—*locale* LA-4
Sailes Oil Field—*oilfield* LA-4
Sailiga Hulo MH-9
Sailigai, Puntan—*cape* MH-9
Sailigai Hulo'—*slope* MH-9
Sailigai Papa'—*slope* MH-9
Sailiagi Ridge—*ridge* AS-9
Sailing Branch MO-7
Sailing Sch—*school* ID-8
Sail Island—*island* AK-9
Sail Loft—*hist pl* ME-1
Sailor—*locale* OR-9
Sailor Bar—*bar* CA-9
Sailor Boy Mine—*mine* WA-9
Sailor Canyon—*valley* CA-9
Sailor Canyon Mine—*mine* CA-9
Sailor Cap Butte—*summit* ID-8
Sailor Cem—*cemetery* AL-4
Sailor Cem—*cemetery* KS-7
Sailor Cem—*cemetery* OH-6
Sailor Creek—*stream* ID-8
Sailor Creek—*stream* TX-5
Sailor Creek—*stream* VA-3
Sailor Creek—*stream* (2) WI-6
Sailor Creek Butte ID-8
Sailor Creek Flowage—*reservoir* WI-6
Sailor Flat—*flat* (2) CA-9
Sailor Flat Trail—*trail* CA-9
Sailor Gulch—*valley* AK-9
Sailor Gulch—*valley* CA-9
Sailor Gulch—*valley* (2) ID-8
Sailor Gulch—*valley* (3) OR-9
Sailor Hammock—*island* FL-3
Sailor Hammock Slough—*gut* FL-3
Sailor Harris Ridge—*ridge* AR-4
Sailor Hole—*lake* FL-3
Sailor Island MA-1
Sailor Island TN-4
Sailor Island—*island* TN-4
Sailor Jack Creek—*stream* OR-9
Sailor Lake—*lake* CA-9
Sailor Lake—*lake* MN-6
Sailor Lake—*lake* MT-8
Sailor Lake—*lake* WI-6
Sailor Meadow—*flat* CA-9
Sailor Peak WY-8
Sailor Pioneer-Noti Cem—*cemetery* OR-9
Sailor Point—*cliff* CA-9
Sailor Ravine—*valley* (3) CA-9
Sailor Ridge—*ridge* AR-4
Sailor Run—*stream* WV-2
Sailors Branch—*stream* NC-3
Sailors Cem AL-4
Sailors Creek VA-3
Sailors Creek—*stream* MI-6
Sailors Encampment MI-6
Sailors Gulch—*valley* OR-9
Sailor Shoals—*bar* TN-4
Sailors Isle MA-1
Sailors Pond NJ-2
Sailor Spring—*spring* AR-4
**Sailor Springs**—*pop pl* IL-6
Sailor Springs Oil Field—*other* IL-6
Sailors Ravine—*valley* CA-9
Sailors Rest—*locale* TN-4
Sailors Rest Ch TN-4
Sailors Rest Ch—*church* TN-4
Sailors Rest Ch (historical)—*church* TN-4
Sailors Rest Furnace (historical)—*locale* TN-4
Sailor's Rest Furnace (40MT375)—*hist pl* TN-4
**Sailors Rest (historical)**—*pop pl* TN-4
Sailors Rest Landing (historical)—*locale* TN-4
Sailors Rest Post Office (historical)—*building* TN-4
Sailors Rest Station TN-4
Sailors Rest United Methodist Church TN-4
Sailors Snug Harbor—*building* NY-2
Sailors Snug Harbor—*cove* MA-1
Sailors' Snug Harbor Natl Register District—*hist pl* NY-2
Sail River—*stream* WA-9
Sail Rock—*bar* WA-9
Sail Rock—*island* (2) CA-9
Sail Rock—*island* ME-1
Sail Rock Point—*cape* AS-9
Saima Pond—*lake* MA-1
Sain Cem—*cemetery* TN-4
Sain Creek IN-6
Sain Creek—*stream* OR-9
Saines Creek IN-6
Sain Johns Sch—*school* TX-5
Sainovich Airp—*airport* PA-2
Sain Park—*park* IL-6
Sains Branch—*stream* NC-3
Sains Creek IN-6
Saint Aaron Ch—*church* AL-4
Saint Abalberts Sch—*school* NY-2
Saint Abraham Ch—*church* LA-4
Saint Adalbert Cem—*cemetery* IL-6
Saint Adalbert Cem—*cemetery* OH-6
Saint Adalbert Ch—*church* WI-6
Saint Adalberts Cem—*cemetery* IL-6
Saint Adalberts Cem—*cemetery* MN-6
Saint Adalberts Cem—*cemetery* WI-6
Saint Adalbert Sch—*school* IN-6
Saint Adalbert Sch—*school* MN-6
Saint Adalbert Sch—*school* (2) OH-6
Saint Adalbert Sch—*school* (4) WI-6
Saint Adalberts Sch—*school* MI-6
Saint Adalberts Sch—*school* NY-2
Saint Adalberts Sch—*school* (2) OH-6
Saint Adalherts Sch—*school* IN-6
Saint Adelaide Sch—*school* CA-9
Saint Adelbert Cem—*cemetery* OH-6
Saint Adelbert Cem—*cemetery* PA-2
Saint Adrian Cem—*cemetery* MN-6
Saint Adrian Cem—*cemetery* PA-2
Saint Adrians Ch—*church* FL-3
Saint Adrian Sch—*school* IL-6
Saint Aedans Sch—*school* CT-1
Saint Aedans Sch—*school* NJ-2
Saint Aemillian Home—*building* WI-6
**Saint Agatha**—*pop pl* ME-1
Saint Agatha Campground—*park* AZ-5
Saint Agatha Catholic Ch—*church* AL-4
Saint Agatha Cem—*cemetery* IL-6
Saint Agatha Cem—*cemetery* MI-6
Saint Agatha Cem—*cemetery* NY-2
Saint Agatha Cem—*cemetery* (2) PA-2
Saint Agatha Ch—*church* FL-3
Saint Agatha Home—*building* NY-2
Saint Agatha Mission—*church* AZ-5
Saint Agathas Cem—*cemetery* PA-2
Saint Agatha Sch—*school* CA-9
Saint Agatha Sch—*school* (2) FL-3
Saint Agatha Sch—*school* MI-6
Saint Agatha Sch—*school* (2) OH-6
Saint Agathas Sch—*school* NY-2
Saint Agathas Sch—*school* OR-9
**Saint Agatha (Town of)**—*pop pl* ME-1
Saint Agey Ch—*church* SC-3
Saint Agnes, Lake—*lake* LA-4
Saint Agnes Acad—*school* FL-3
Saint Agnes Acad—*school* IN-6
Saint Agnes Acad—*school* TN-4
Saint Agnes Acad—*school* TX-5
Saint Agnes Catholic Ch—*church* FL-3
Saint Agnes Cem—*cemetery* CT-1
Saint Agnes Cem—*cemetery* IL-6
Saint Agnes Cem—*cemetery* KS-7
Saint Agnes Cem—*cemetery* KY-4
Saint Agnes Cem—*cemetery* (2) MN-6
Saint Agnes Cem—*cemetery* (9) NY-2
Saint Agnes Cem—*cemetery* (4) PA-2
Saint Agnes Cem—*cemetery* SD-7
Saint Agnes Cem—*cemetery* WI-6
Saint Agnes Ch—*church* FL-3
Saint Agnes Ch—*church* IN-6
Saint Agnes Ch—*church* IA-7
Saint Agnes Ch—*church* LA-4
Saint Agnes Ch—*church* (2) MN-6
Saint Agnes Ch—*church* MO-7
Saint Agnes Ch—*church* NJ-2
Saint Agnes Ch—*church* (2) NY-2
Saint Agnes Ch—*church* TX-5
Saint Agnes Ch—*church* WI-6
Saint Agnes Church—*hist pl* NC-3
Saint Agnes Church—*hist pl* SD-7
Saint Agnes Convent—*church* NY-2
Saint Agnes Home—*other* MO-7
Saint Agnes Hosp—*hospital* CA-9
Saint Agnes Hosp—*hospital* MD-2
Saint Agnes Hosp—*hospital* NY-2
Saint Agnes Hosp—*hospital* PA-2
Saint Agnes HS—*school* MO-7
Saint Agnes HS—*school* (2) NY-2
Saint Agnes Sacred Heart Sch—*school* PA-2
Saint Agnes Sch—*school* AZ-5
Saint Agnes Sch—*school* (3) CA-9
Saint Agnes Sch—*school* (3) IL-6
Saint Agnes Sch—*school* (2) IN-6
Saint Agnes Sch—*school* KS-7
Saint Agnes Sch—*school* (2) KY-4
Saint Agnes Sch—*school* LA-4
Saint Agnes Sch—*school* (3) MA-1
Saint Agnes Sch—*school* (2) MI-6
Saint Agnes Sch—*school* (2) MN-6
Saint Agnes Sch—*school* MO-7
Saint Agnes Sch—*school* NE-7
Saint Agnes Sch—*school* (2) NJ-2
Saint Agnes Sch—*school* (5) NY-2
Saint Agnes Sch—*school* (6) OH-6
Saint Agnes Sch—*school* (3) PA-2
Saint Agnes Sch—*school* SD-7
Saint Agnes Sch—*school* TX-5
Saint Agnes Sch—*school* (2) VA-3
Saint Agnes Sch—*school* WV-2
Saint Agnes Sch—*school* (3) WI-6
Saint Agnes Sch For Girls—*school* NY-2
Saint Agustines Cem—*cemetery* KY-4
Saint Aidans Catholie Ch—*church* MA-1
Saint Aidans Ch—*church* MI-6
Saint Aidans Ch—*church* VA-3
Saint Aidan's Church and Rectory—*hist pl* MA-1
Saint Aidans Sch—*school* NY-2
Saint Aidans Sch—*school* VA-3
Saint Aiden Episcopal Ch—*church* PA-2
Saint Aidens Cem—*cemetery* MN-6
Saint Ailbe Sch—*school* IL-6
Saint Aioysius Cem—*cemetery* MO-7
Saint Albans MS-4
Saint Albans WV-2
**Saint Albans**—*pop pl* ME-1
**Saint Albans**—*pop pl* MO-7
**Saint Albans**—*pop pl* NY-2
**Saint Albans**—*pop pl* PA-2
**Saint Albans**—*pop pl* VT-1
**Saint Albans**—*pop pl* WV-2
Saint Albans American Episcopal Ch—*church* FL-3
Saint Albans Bay—*bay* (2) MN-6
Saint Albans Bay—*bay* VT-1
**Saint Albans Bay**—*pop pl* VT-1
Saint Albans Bay Cem—*cemetery* VT-1
Saint Albans Bay State Park—*park* VT-1
Saint Albans Ch—*church* AL-4
Saint Albans Ch—*church* FL-3
Saint Albans Ch—*church* KY-4
Saint Albans Ch—*church* MN-6
Saint Albans Ch—*church* MS-4
Saint Albans Ch—*church* NY-2
Saint Albans Ch—*church* OH-6
Saint Albans Ch—*church* SC-3
Saint Albans Ch—*church* SD-7
Saint Albans Ch—*church* TX-5
Saint Albans Chapel (historical)—*church* TN-4
Saint Albans Church DE-2
Saint Albans Church IN-6
Saint Albans Day Nursery (Main Branch)—*school* FL-3
Saint Albans Day Nursery (2nd Campus)—*school* FL-3
Saint Albans Day Sch—*school* CA-9
Saint Albans Episcoal Ch—*church* FL-3
Saint Albans Episcopal Ch AL-4
Saint Albans Episcopal Ch MS-4
Saint Albans Episcopal Ch—*church* DE-2
Saint Albans Episcopal Ch—*church* IN-6
Saint Alban's Episcopal Church—*hist pl* NY-2
Saint Alban's Hall—*hist pl* VA-3
**Saint Albans Hill**—*pop pl* VT-1
Saint Albans Hill—*summit* VT-1
Saint Albans Hosp—*hospital* VA-3
Saint Albans Island—*island* MO-7
Saint Albans Memorial Park—*park* NY-2
Saint Albans Mtn—*summit* ME-1
Saint Albans Naval Hosp—*hospital* NY-2
Saint Albans Point—*cape* VT-1
Saint Albans Point Cem—*cemetery* VT-1
Saint Albans Road Cem—*cemetery* VT-1
Saint Albans Rsvr—*reservoir* VT-1
Saint Albans Sch—*school* CA-9
Saint Albans Sch—*school* SC-3
Saint Albans Sch—*school* TX-5
Saint Albans Site—*hist pl* WV-2
**Saint Albans Subdivision**—*pop pl* UT-8
Saint Albans-Tacoma Girl Scout Camp—*locale* WA-9
**Saint Albans (Town of)**—*pop pl* ME-1
**Saint Albans (Town of)**—*pop pl* VT-1
Saint Albans (Township of)—*civ div* IL-6
Saint Albans (Township of)—*civ div* OH-6
Saint Albans University Episcopal Parish—*church* KS-7
Saint Albans Warehouse—*facility* WV-2
Saint Alba Subdivision UT-8
Saint Albert Cem—*cemetery* IA-7
Saint Albert Cem—*cemetery* MN-6
Saint Albert Ch—*church* WY-8
Saint Alberts Cem—*cemetery* PA-2
Saint Albert Sch—*school* IL-6
Saint Albert Sch—*school* MN-6
Saint Albert Sch—*school* NV-8
Saint Albert Sch—*school* PA-2
Saint Albert Sch—*school* WI-6
Saint Alberts Coll—*school* NY-2
Saint Alberts Sch—*school* MI-6
Saint Alberts Sch—*school* NY-2
Saint Alberts Sch—*school* (2) PA-2
Saint Albert the Great Sch—*school* CA-9
Saint Albert the Great Sch—*school* (2) OH-6
Saint Albert the Greats Sch—*school* KY-4
Saint Alexander Cem—*cemetery* PA-2
Saint Alexanders Cem—*cemetery* NY-2
Saint Alexander Sch—*school* (2) IL-6
Saint Alexanders Sch—*school* NY-2
Saint Alexanders Sch—*school* WI-6
Saint Alexis Ch—*church* NY-2
Saint Alexis Hosp—*hospital* ND-7
Saint Alexis Hosp—*hospital* OH-6
Saint Alexis Sch—*school* IL-6
Saint Alfreds Ch—*church* FL-3
Saint Alfred Sch—*school* MI-6
Saint Alfreds Chapel—*church* IL-6
Saint Alfreds Episcopal Ch—*church* FL-3
Saint Alice Ch—*church* AL-4
Saint Alice Sch—*school* OR-9
Saint Alice Sch—*school* PA-2
Saint Alma Sch—*school* LA-4
Saint Almond Brook—*stream* ME-1
Saint Almond Pond—*lake* ME-1
Saint Alogsius Cem—*cemetery* IA-7
Saint Alovsius Sch—*school* OH-6
Saint Alovsius Sch—*school* WI-6
Saint Aloysins Sch—*school* WI-6
Saint Aloysius Acad—*school* NJ-2
Saint Aloysius Acad—*school* OH-6
Saint Aloysius Acad—*school* PA-2
Saint Aloysius Catholic Church—*hist pl* DC-2
Saint Aloysius Catholic Sch—*school* IN-6
Saint Aloysius Cem—*cemetery* (2) IL-6
Saint Aloysius Cem—*cemetery* IA-7
Saint Aloysius Cem—*cemetery* KS-7
Saint Aloysius Cem—*cemetery* LA-4
Saint Aloysius Cem—*cemetery* (2) MA-1
Saint Aloysius Cem—*cemetery* MN-6
Saint Aloysius Cem—*cemetery* NE-7
Saint Aloysius Cem—*cemetery* NY-2
Saint Aloysius Cem—*cemetery* (3) PA-2
Saint Aloysius Cem—*cemetery* TX-5
Saint Aloysius Cem—*cemetery* WI-6
Saint Aloysius Ch—*church* IA-7
Saint Aloysius Ch—*church* MD-2
Saint Aloysius Ch—*church* MN-6
Saint Aloysius Ch—*church* OH-6
Saint Aloysius Ch—*church* (2) PA-2
Saint Aloysius Ch—*church* WI-6
Saint Aloysius Convent—*church* AL-4
Saint Aloysius HS—*school* LA-4
Saint Aloysius HS—*school* MS-4
Saint Aloysius Sch IN-6
Saint Aloysius Sch—*school* AL-4
Saint Aloysius Sch—*school* (2) CA-9
Saint Aloysius Sch—*school* (2) IL-6
Saint Aloysius Sch—*school* KY-4
Saint Aloysius Sch—*school* LA-4
Saint Aloysius Sch—*school* (2) MA-1
Saint Aloysius Sch—*school* MO-7
Saint Aloysius Sch—*school* NJ-2
Saint Aloysius Sch—*school* (4) NY-2
Saint Aloysius Sch—*school* (3) OH-6
Saint Aloysius Sch—*school* PA-2
Saint Aloysius Sch—*school* WA-9
Saint Aloysius Sch—*school* WI-6
Saint Alphonse Cem—*cemetery* MI-6
Saint Alphonse Sch—*school* OH-6
Saint Alphonsus Catholic Ch—*church* (2) MS-4
Saint Alphonsus Cem—*cemetery* MD-2
Saint Alphonsus Cem—*cemetery* MO-7
Saint Alphonsus Cem—*cemetery* NY-2
Saint Alphonsus Ch—*church* IA-7
Saint Alphonsus Church—*hist pl* LA-4
Saint Alphonsus' Church, Rectory, Convent and Halle—*hist pl* MD-2
Saint Alphonsus HS—*school* IL-6
Saint Alphonsus Parochial Sch—*school* MS-4
Saint Alphonsus Sch—*school* (2) CA-9
Saint Alphonsus Sch—*school* IL-6
Saint Alphonsus Sch—*school* IA-7
Saint Alphonsus Sch—*school* LA-4
Saint Alphonsus Sch—*school* (2) MI-6
Saint Alphonsus Sch—*school* MN-6
Saint Alphonsus Sch—*school* NY-2
Saint Alphonsus Sch—*school* PA-2
Saint Alvido Creek TX-5
Saint Alvido Creek—*stream* TX-5
Saint Amadeus Cem—*cemetery* VT-1
Saint Amandas Ch—*church* NC-3
Saint Amand Creek—*stream* AK-9
**Saint Amant**—*pop pl* LA-4
Saint Amants Brook—*stream* ME-1
Saint Amant Swamp—*swamp* LA-4
Saint Ambrose Catholic Ch—*church* UT-8
Saint Ambrose Cem—*cemetery* IN-6
Saint Ambrose Cem—*cemetery* IA-7
Saint Ambrose Cem—*cemetery* LA-4
Saint Ambrose Cem—*cemetery* SD-7
Saint Ambrose Cem—*cemetery* WI-6
Saint Ambrose Ch—*church* (2) FL-3
Saint Ambrose Ch—*church* KY-4
Saint Ambrose Ch—*church* LA-4
Saint Ambrose Ch—*church* MI-6
Saint Ambrose Ch—*church* NY-2
Saint Ambrose Ch—*church* OH-6
Saint Ambrose Coll—*school* IA-7
Saint Ambrose Episcopal Ch—*church* FL-3
Saint Ambrose Episcopal Sch—*school* FL-3
Saint Ambroses Ch—*church* NJ-2
Saint Ambrose Sch—*school* AZ-5
Saint Ambrose Sch—*school* CA-9
Saint Ambrose Sch—*school* CT-1
Saint Ambrose Sch—*school* FL-3
Saint Ambrose Sch—*school* IL-6
Saint Ambrose Sch—*school* (2) IN-6
Saint Ambrose Sch—*school* KY-4
Saint Ambrose Sch—*school* (2) MI-6
Saint Ambrose Sch—*school* NY-2
Saint Ambrose Sch—*school* OH-6
Saint Ambrose Sch—*school* PA-2
Saint Ambrose Sch—*school* TX-5
Saint Ambroses Sch—*school* MD-2
Saint Ambrosius Sch—*school* PA-2
Saint Amelias Sch—*school* NY-2
Saint Ames Ch—*church* MD-2
Saint Ames Ch—*church* NC-3
Saint Anastasia Cem—*cemetery* MN-6
Saint Anastasia Sch—*school* IL-6
Saint Anastasia Sch—*school* NY-2
Saint Anastasia Sch—*school* PA-2
Saint Anastasias Sch—*school* NJ-2
Saint Andes Ch—*church* MS-4
Saint Andies Church AL-4
Saint Andreas Cem—*cemetery* SD-7
Saint Andres Catholic Ch—*church* FL-3
Saint Andre Sch—*school* ME-1
Saint Andres Hosp—*hospital* ME-1
**Saint Andrew**—*pop pl* FL-3
**Saint Andrew**—*pop pl* NY-2
Saint Andrew Apostle Ch—*church* MD-2
Saint Andrew Assembly of God Ch—*church* FL-3
Saint Andrew Avellino Sch—*school* NY-2
Saint Andrew Bay—*bay* FL-3
Saint Andrew Bay West Light 14—*locale* FL-3
Saint Andrew Beach—*beach* GA-3
Saint Andrew Catholic Sch—*school* FL-3
Saint Andrew Cem—*cemetery* KS-7
Saint Andrew Cem—*cemetery* MI-6
Saint Andrew Cem—*cemetery* ND-7
Saint Andrew Cem—*cemetery* TX-5
Saint Andrew Ch—*church* AR-4
Saint Andrew Ch—*church* FL-3
Saint Andrew Ch—*church* IL-6
Saint Andrew Ch—*church* KS-7
Saint Andrew Ch—*church* MI-6
Saint Andrew Ch—*church* (2) MS-4
Saint Andrew Ch—*church* NC-3
Saint Andrew Ch—*church* (3) TX-5
Saint Andrew Church AL-4
Saint Andrew Greek Orthodox Ch of Kendall—*church* FL-3
Saint Andrew Lutheran Ch—*church* (2) FL-3
Saint Andrew Memorial Ch—*church* TN-4
Saint Andrew Memorial Methodist Ch TN-4
Saint Andrew Point—*cape* FL-3
Saint Andrew Ridge—*ridge* IL-6
Saint Andrews—*CDP* SC-3
Saint Andrews—*locale* TN-4
**Saint Andrews**—*pop pl* SC-3
**Saint Andrews**—*pop pl* TN-4
**Saint Andrews**—*pop pl* WA-9
Saint Andrews—*uninc pl* FL-3
Saint Andrews, Frank, House—*hist pl* WI-6
Saint Andrews African Methodist Episcopal Ch—*church* FL-3
Saint Andrews Anglican Ch—*church* FL-3
Saint Andrews Baptist Church AL-4
Saint Andrews Bay—*bay* AL-4
Saint Andrews Brook—*stream* NJ-2
Saint Andrews Camp—*locale* PA-2
Saint Andrew's Cathedral—*hist pl* HI-9
Saint Andrews Catholic Cathedral—*hist pl.* AR-4
Saint Andrews Catholic Ch—*church* AL-4
Saint Andrews Catholic Ch—*church* (2) FL-3
Saint Andrews Cem—*cemetery* AL-4
Saint Andrews Cem—*cemetery* (2) GA-3
Saint Andrews Cem—*cemetery* (2) IL-6
Saint Andrews Cem—*cemetery* IN-6
Saint Andrews Cem—*cemetery* IA-7
Saint Andrews Cem—*cemetery* KS-7
Saint Andrews Cem—*cemetery* KY-4
Saint Andrews Cem—*cemetery* (2) LA-4
Saint Andrews Cem—*cemetery* MD-2
Saint Andrews Cem—*cemetery* MI-6
Saint Andrews Cem—*cemetery* (4) MN-6
Saint Andrews Cem—*cemetery* MS-4
Saint Andrews Cem—*cemetery* MO-7
Saint Andrews Cem—*cemetery* NE-7
Saint Andrews Cem—*cemetery* (2) NJ-2
Saint Andrews Cem—*cemetery* NY-2
Saint Andrews Cem—*cemetery* (2) ND-7
Saint Andrews Cem—*cemetery* (2) OH-6
Saint Andrews Cem—*cemetery* OR-9
Saint Andrews Cem—*cemetery* (2) PA-2
Saint Andrews Cem—*cemetery* SC-3
Saint Andrews Cem—*cemetery* TN-4
Saint Andrews Cem—*cemetery* TX-5
Saint Andrews Cem—*cemetery* (2) VA-3
Saint Andrews Cem—*cemetery* WA-9
Saint Andrews Ch IN-6
Saint Andrews Ch—*church* (3) AL-4
Saint Andrews Ch—*church* (2) AR-4
Saint Andrews Ch—*church* (5) CT-1
Saint Andrews Ch—*church* DE-2
Saint Andrews Ch—*church* (5) FL-3
Saint Andrews Ch—*church* GA-3
Saint Andrews Ch—*church* (2) IL-6
Saint Andrews Ch—*church* (2) IN-6
Saint Andrews Ch—*church* IA-7
Saint Andrews Ch—*church* (3) KY-4
Saint Andrews Ch—*church* (3) LA-4
Saint Andrews Ch—*church* (2) ME-1
Saint Andrews Ch—*church* (3) MD-2
Saint Andrews Ch—*church* (2) MI-6
Saint Andrews Ch—*church* (3) MS-4
Saint Andrews Ch—*church* (2) MO-7
Saint Andrews Ch—*church* NE-7
Saint Andrews Ch—*church* NH-1
Saint Andrews Ch—*church* (5) NJ-2
Saint Andrews Ch—*church* (6) NY-2
Saint Andrews Ch—*church* (6) NC-3
Saint Andrews Ch—*church* ND-7
Saint Andrews Ch—*church* (3) OH-6
Saint Andrews Ch—*church* (9) PA-2
Saint Andrews Ch—*church* (5) SC-3
Saint Andrews Ch—*church* (4) TN-4
Saint Andrews Ch—*church* (6) TX-5
Saint Andrews Ch—*church* (9) VA-3
Saint Andrews Ch—*church* WV-2
Saint Andrews Ch—*church* WI-6
Saint Andrew Sch—*school* CA-9
Saint Andrew Sch—*school* FL-3
Saint Andrew Sch—*school* IL-6
Saint Andrew Sch—*school* KS-7
Saint Andrew Sch—*school* LA-4
Saint Andrew Sch—*school* MN-6
Saint Andrew Sch—*school* MO-7
Saint Andrews Chapel—*church* GA-3
Saint Andrews Chapel—*church* VA-3
Saint Andrew's Chapel—*hist pl* MA-1
Saint Andrews Ch of God of Prophecy—*church* FL-3
Saint Andrew's Church—*hist pl* AL-4
Saint Andrew's Church—*hist pl* MD-2
Saint Andrew's Church—*hist pl* VA-3
Saint Andrews Coll—*school* NC-3
Saint Andrews College Lake—*reservoir* NC-3
Saint Andrews College Lake Dam—*dam* NC-3
Saint Andrews Creek—*stream* WA-9
Saint Andrews Dam—*dam* TN-4
Saint Andrews Day Sch—*school* TX-5
Saint Andrew Seminary—*school* CO-8
Saint Andrews Episcopal Ch—*church* (3) AL-4
Saint Andrews Episcopal Ch—*church* FL-3
Saint Andrews Episcopal Ch—*church* MS-4
Saint Andrew's Episcopal Chapel—*hist pl.* MD-2
Saint Andrews Episcopal Church AL-4
Saint Andrews Episcopal Church TN-4
Saint Andrew's Episcopal Church—*hist pl* AL-4
Saint Andrew's Episcopal Church—*hist pl* FL-3
Saint Andrew's Episcopal Church—*hist pl* LA-4
Saint Andrew's Episcopal Church—*hist pl* (2) NY-2
Saint Andrew's Episcopal Church—*hist pl* SD-7
Saint Andrew's Episcopal Church—*hist pl* TX-5
Saint Andrew's Episcopal Church—*hist pl* WA-9
Saint Andrew's Episcopal Church and Cemetery—*hist pl* NC-3
Saint Andrews Episcopal Day Sch—*school* FL-3
Saint Andrews Episcopal Parish—*church* FL-3
**Saint Andrews Estates**—*pop pl* MD-2
Saint Andrew's Evangelical Lutheran Church Complex—*hist pl* NY-2
Saint Andrews Golf Club—*other* NY-2
Saint Andrews Golf Course—*locale* MS-4
Saint Andrew's Gore VT-1
Saint Andrews (historical)—*locale* ND-7
Saint Andrews Lake—*lake* FL-3
Saint Andrews Lake—*lake* WA-9
Saint Andrews Lake—*reservoir* (2) TN-4
Saint Andrews Lutheran Ch—*church* DE-2
Saint Andrews Lutheran Ch—*church* IN-6
Saint Andrews Lutheran Ch—*church* KS-7
Saint Andrews Memorial Chapel—*church* FL-3
Saint Andrew's Memorial Episcopal Church—*hist pl* MI-6
Saint Andrews Missionary Baptist Ch—*church* KS-7
Saint Andrews Mission Cem—*cemetery* OR-9
Saint Andrews on the Hudson—*school* NY-2
Saint Andrew Sound—*bay* FL-3
Saint Andrew Sound—*bay* GA-3
Saint Andrews Park—*flat* WA-9
**Saint Andrews Park Condo**—*pop pl* UT-8
Saint Andrews Plaza (Shop Ctr)—*locale* FL-3
Saint Andrews Point FL-3
Saint Andrews Post Office—*building* TN-4
Saint Andrews Preparatory Sch—*school* FL-3
Saint Andrews Presbyterian Ch—*church* FL-3
Saint Andrews Presbyterian Ch of Dunedin—*church* FL-3
Saint Andrews Presbyterian College NC-3
Saint Andrews Priory—*church* CA-9
Saint Andrews Rock—*summit* WA-9
Saint Andrew's Roman Catholic Church—*hist pl* VA-3
Saint Andrews Sch IN-6
Saint Andrews Sch—*school* AR-4
Saint Andrews Sch—*school* CA-9
Saint Andrews Sch—*school* CT-1
Saint Andrews Sch—*school* DE-2
Saint Andrews Sch—*school* FL-3
Saint Andrews Sch—*school* (5) IL-6
Saint Andrews Sch—*school* (2) IN-6
Saint Andrews Sch—*school* (3) MI-6
Saint Andrews Sch—*school* MN-6
Saint Andrews Sch—*school* MS-4
Saint Andrews Sch—*school* (3) NJ-2
Saint Andrews Sch—*school* (7) NY-2
Saint Andrews Sch—*school* (3) OH-6
Saint Andrews Sch—*school* (2) OR-9
Saint Andrews Sch—*school* (3) PA-2
Saint Andrews Sch—*school* SC-3
Saint Andrews Sch—*school* TN-4
Saint Andrews Sch—*school* (2) TX-5
Saint Andrews Sch—*school* (2) WV-2
Saint Andrews Sch—*school* WI-6

Saint Benedict Ch—church ... ND-7
Saint Benedict Ch—church (2) ... SD-7
Saint Benedict Chapel—church ... LA-4
Saint Benedict Convent—church ... MO-7
Saint Benedict Elem Sch—school ... KS-7
Saint Benedict Home—building ... ND-7
Saint Benedict Hosp—hospital ... UT-8
Saint Benedict HS—school ... IL-6
Saint Benedict JHS—school ... KS-7
Saint Benedict Joseph Labre Sch—school ... NY-2
Saint Benedict Mission (historical)—church ... SD-7
Saint Benedict Monastery—church ... MI-6
Saint Benedict Monastery—other ... CO-8
**Saint Benedict (Religious Institution)**—pop pl ... LA-4
Saint Benedicts Abbey—church ... OR-9
Saint Benedicts Abbey—church ... WI-6
Saint Benedicts Acad—school (2) ... PA-2
Saint Benedict's Catholic Church—hist pl ... HI-9
Saint Benedicts Cem—cemetery ... MA-1
Saint Benedicts Cem—cemetery ... MI-6
Saint Benedicts Cem—cemetery ... MO-7
Saint Benedicts Cem—cemetery ... NE-7
Saint Benedicts Cem—cemetery ... PA-2
Saint Benedicts Ch—church ... KY-4
Saint Benedicts Ch—church ... ND-7
Saint Benedict Sch—school ... CA-9
Saint Benedict Sch—school ... IN-6
Saint Benedict Sch—school ... KS-7
Saint Benedict Sch—school ... LA-4
Saint Benedict Sch—school (2) ... MI-6
Saint Benedict Sch—school ... NY-2
Saint Benedict Sch—school ... OK-5
Saint Benedict Sch—school ... PA-2
Saint Benedict Sch—school ... TX-5
Saint Benedicts College ... KS-7
Saint Benedicts Episcopal Ch—church ... FL-3
Saint Benedicts Hosp—hospital ... UT-8
Saint Benedicts Hospital Heliport—airport ... UT-8
Saint Benedicts Mission—church ... MN-6
Saint Benedicts Novitiate—church ... MI-6
Saint Benedicts Sch ... IN-6
Saint Benedicts Sch—school ... DC-2
Saint Benedicts Sch—school (2) ... IN-6
Saint Benedicts Sch—school ... MI-6
Saint Benedicts Sch—school ... NJ-2
Saint Benedicts Sch—school (2) ... NY-2
Saint Benedicts Sch—school ... OH-6
Saint Benedicts Sch—school ... OR-9
Saint Benedicts Sch—school (3) ... PA-2
Saint Benedicts Sch—school ... VA-3
Saint Benedict (St. Benedict Abbey & Mt Angel Seminary)—facility ... OR-9
Saint Benignus Ch—church ... OH-6
Saint Bernadette Catholic Ch—church (2) ... FL-3
Saint Bernadette Ch—church ... MO-7
Saint Bernadette Ch—church ... PA-2
Saint Bernadette Roman Catholic Ch—church ... IN-6
Saint Bernadettes Catholic Ch—church ... MS-4
Saint Bernadettes Ch—church ... FL-3
Saint Bernadette Sch—school ... CA-9
Saint Bernadette Sch—school ... CO-8
Saint Bernadette Sch—school ... FL-3
Saint Bernadette Sch—school (2) ... IL-6
Saint Bernadette Sch—school ... IN-6
Saint Bernadette Sch—school ... MI-6
Saint Bernadette Sch—school ... WI-6
Saint Bernadettes Sch ... IN-6
Saint Bernadettes Sch—school ... CA-9
Saint Bernadettes Sch—school ... CT-1
Saint Bernadettes Sch—school ... MD-2
Saint Bernadettes Sch—school ... MO-7
Saint Bernadettes Sch—school (2) ... NY-2
Saint Bernadettes Sch—school ... PA-2
Saint Bernadetts Sch—school ... VA-3
Saint Bernadine Ch—church ... NY-2
Saint Bernadines Monastery—church ... PA-2
Saint Bernard ... IN-6
Saint Bernard ... KS-7
**Saint Bernard**—pop pl ... AL-4
**Saint Bernard**—pop pl ... CA-9
**Saint Bernard**—pop pl ... LA-4
**Saint Bernard**—pop pl ... NE-7
**Saint Bernard**—pop pl ... OH-6
Saint Bernard Cem—cemetery ... AR-4
Saint Bernard Cem—cemetery (2) ... IL-6
Saint Bernard Cem—cemetery ... IN-6
Saint Bernard Cem—cemetery ... KS-7
Saint Bernard Cem—cemetery ... LA-4
Saint Bernard Cem—cemetery (2) ... MN-6
Saint Bernard Cem—cemetery ... NE-7
Saint Bernard Cem—cemetery ... NY-2
Saint Bernard Cem—cemetery (3) ... OH-6
Saint Bernard Cem—cemetery ... PA-2
Saint Bernard Cem—cemetery ... SD-7
Saint Bernard Cem—cemetery ... TX-5
Saint Bernard Cem—cemetery (2) ... WI-6
Saint Bernard Ch—church ... IL-6
Saint Bernard Ch—church ... IN-6
Saint Bernard Ch—church ... ND-7
Saint Bernard Ch—church ... TN-4
Saint Bernard Ch—church ... TX-5
Saint Bernard Ch—church ... VA-3
Saint Bernard Church and Cemetery—hist pl ... WV-2
Saint Bernard Coll—school ... AL-4
Saint Bernard College Camp—locale ... AL-4
Saint Bernard Elem Sch—school ... IN-6
Saint Bernard Elem Sch—school ... PA-2
Saint Bernardette Sch—school ... OH-6
Saint Bernardettes Sch—school ... OH-6
Saint Bernard Golf Club—other ... OH-6
Saint Bernard Grade Sch—school ... IA-7
**Saint Bernard Grove**—pop pl ... LA-4
Saint Bernard HS—school ... CA-9
Saint Bernard HS—school ... IA-7
Saint Bernard HS—school ... LA-4
Saint Bernardine Hosp—hospital ... CA-9
Saint Bernardine of Sienna College ... NY-2
Saint Bernardine Sch—school ... IL-6
Saint Bernard Memorial Gardens—cemetery ... LA-4
Saint Bernardo ... AZ-5
**Saint Bernard Parish**—pop pl ... LA-4
Saint Bernard Post Office (historical)—building ... AL-4
Saint Bernards Acad—school ... TN-4
Saint Bernard's Catholic Church—hist pl ... SD-7
Saint Bernards Cem—cemetery (2) ... CT-1
Saint Bernards Cem—cemetery ... IL-6
Saint Bernards Cem—cemetery ... IN-6
Saint Bernards Cem—cemetery (2) ... IA-7
Saint Bernards Cem—cemetery ... KS-7
Saint Bernards Cem—cemetery (2) ... MA-1
Saint Bernards Cem—cemetery ... NJ-2
Saint Bernards Cem—cemetery (3) ... NY-2
Saint Bernards Cem—cemetery ... ND-7
Saint Bernards Cem—cemetery (2) ... PA-2
Saint Bernards Cem—cemetery ... WI-6
Saint Bernards Ch—church ... FL-3
Saint Bernards Ch—church ... IN-6
Saint Bernards Ch—church ... KS-7
Saint Bernards Ch—church ... MA-1
Saint Bernards Ch—church ... MT-8
Saint Bernards Ch—church ... NE-7
Saint Bernards Ch—church ... NJ-2
Saint Bernards Ch—church ... NY-2
Saint Bernards Ch—church ... PA-2
Saint Bernards Ch—church ... WV-2
Saint Bernard Sch—school (2) ... CA-9
Saint Bernard Sch—school (3) ... IL-6
Saint Bernard Sch—school ... MA-1
Saint Bernard Sch—school (2) ... MI-6
Saint Bernard Sch—school (2) ... MN-6
Saint Bernard Sch—school (3) ... WI-6
Saint Bernard Seminary—school ... MI-6
Saint Bernards Episcopal Ch—church ... FL-3
Saint Bernards Episcopal Church ... TN-4
Saint Bernards Parochial Sch—school ... PA-2
Saint Bernards Sch—school ... CT-1
Saint Bernards Sch—school (2) ... KY-4
Saint Bernards Sch—school ... MD-2
Saint Bernards Sch—school ... MA-1
Saint Bernards Sch—school ... NE-7
Saint Bernards Sch—school (2) ... NJ-2
Saint Bernards Sch—school (4) ... NY-2
Saint Bernards Sch—school ... PA-2
Saint Bernards Sch—school ... WI-6
Saint Bernards School ... IN-6
Saint Bernard (Township of)—other ... OH-6
**Saint Bernice**—pop pl ... IN-6
Saint Bertha Cem—cemetery ... PA-2
Saint Bethany Ch—church ... AR-4
Saint Bethany Ch (historical)—church ... AL-4
Saint Bethards Cem—cemetery ... CT-1
Saint Bethel Ch—church ... AL-4
Saint Bethel Ch—church ... GA-3
Saint Bethel Ch—church ... NC-3
**Saint Bethlehem**—pop pl ... TN-4
Saint Bethlehem (CCD)—cens area ... TN-4
Saint Bethlehem Ch—church ... TN-4
Saint Bethlehem Civitan Sports Complex—park ... TN-4
Saint Bethlehem Division—civil ... TN-4
Saint Bethlehem Elem Sch—school ... TN-4
Saint Bethlehem Missionary Baptist Church ... TN-4
Saint Bethlehem Post Office—building ... TN-4
Saint Beulah Ch—church ... TX-5
Saint Beulahs Ch—church ... NC-3
Saint Blaise ... TN-4
Saint Blaise Ch—church ... MA-1
Saintblaise Post Office (historical)—building ... TN-4
Saint Blase Ch—church ... MI-6
Saint Blase Sch—school ... IL-6
Saint Bonaface Sch—school ... WA-9
Saint Bonafice Cem—cemetery ... ND-7
Saint Bonafice Cem—cemetery ... SD-7
Saint Bonaventure—CDP ... NY-2
Saint Bonaventure Cem—cemetery ... MO-7
Saint Bonaventure Cem—cemetery ... NY-2
Saint Bonaventure Cem—cemetery ... PA-2
Saint Bonaventure Cem—cemetery ... SD-7
Saint Bonaventure Ch—church ... PA-2
Saint Bonaventure Sch—school ... IL-6
Saint Bonaventure Sch—school ... MN-6
Saint Bonaventure Sch—school ... MO-7
Saint Bonaventure Sch—school ... OH-6
Saint Bonaventure Sch—school ... PA-2
Saint Bonaventure Sch—school ... WI-6
Saint Bonaventures Sch—school ... NJ-2
Saint Bonaventure Univ—school ... NY-2
**Saint Boniface**—pop pl ... PA-2
Saint Boniface Cem—cemetery (4) ... IL-6
Saint Boniface Cem—cemetery ... IN-6
Saint Boniface Cem—cemetery (5) ... IA-7
Saint Boniface Cem—cemetery (4) ... KS-7
Saint Boniface Cem—cemetery (3) ... MN-6
Saint Boniface Cem—cemetery ... MO-7
Saint Boniface Cem—cemetery (2) ... NE-7
Saint Boniface Cem—cemetery (5) ... ND-7
Saint Boniface Cem—cemetery ... OR-9
Saint Boniface Cem—cemetery ... PA-2
Saint Boniface Cem—cemetery (2) ... SD-7
Saint Boniface Cem—cemetery ... TX-5
Saint Boniface Cem—cemetery (2) ... WI-6
Saint Boniface Ch—church (2) ... IL-6
Saint Boniface Ch—church ... MA-1
Saint Boniface Ch—church ... ND-7
Saint Boniface Ch—church ... TX-5
Saint Boniface Ch—church ... WV-2
Saint Boniface Chapel—church ... PA-2
Saint Boniface JHS—school ... IN-6
Saint Boniface Lookout Tower—tower ... PA-2
Saint Boniface Roman Catholic Church—hist pl ... PA-2
Saint Boniface Sch—school (2) ... CA-9
Saint Boniface Sch—school ... CT-1
Saint Boniface Sch—school ... IL-6
Saint Boniface Sch—school ... IN-6
Saint Boniface Sch—school ... IA-7
Saint Boniface Sch—school ... KY-4
Saint Boniface Sch—school (2) ... MN-6
Saint Boniface Sch—school (4) ... NY-2
Saint Boniface Sch—school (2) ... OH-6
Saint Boniface Sch—school ... PA-2
Saint Bonifaces Sch—school ... OH-6
Saint Bonifacius ... PA-2
**Saint Bonifacius**—pop pl ... MN-6
Saint Bonifacius Ch—church ... IN-6
Saint Bonifacius Kirche Complex—hist pl ... KY-4
Saint Bonitaffee Church and Sch—school ... AR-4
Saint Bookers Chapel ... AL-4
Saint Borgia Cem—cemetery ... MI-6
Saint Bosco Sch—school ... PA-2
Saint Branch—stream ... VA-3
Saint Brendan Ch—church ... FL-3
Saint Brendan HS—school ... FL-3
Saint Brendans Cem—cemetery ... MO-7
Saint Brendans Ch—church ... NY-2
Saint Brendans Ch—church ... PA-2
Saint Brendan Sch—school ... CA-9
Saint Brendan Sch—school ... FL-3
Saint Brendan Sch—school ... NJ-2
Saint Brendan Sch—school ... OH-6
Saint Brendans Sch—school ... CT-1
Saint Brendans Sch—school ... IL-6
Saint Brendans Sch—school ... MI-6
Saint Brendans Sch—school ... MO-7
Saint Brendans Sch—school ... NY-2
Saint Brendans Sch—school ... OH-6
Saint Brendens Cem—cemetery ... WV-2
Saint Brendens Sch—school ... WV-2
**Saint Brides**—pop pl ... VA-3
Saint Brides Ch—church ... VA-3
Saint Brides Sch—school ... IL-6
Saint Bridget—locale ... KS-7
Saint Bridget Catholic Ch—church ... AL-4
Saint Bridget Cem—cemetery ... IN-6
Saint Bridget Cem—cemetery (2) ... KS-7
Saint Bridget Cem—cemetery ... MN-6
Saint Bridget Cem—cemetery ... NY-2
Saint Bridget Cem—cemetery (4) ... WI-6
Saint Bridget Ch—church (2) ... IA-7
Saint Bridget Ch—church ... LA-4
Saint Bridget Ch—church ... MN-6
Saint Bridget Ch—church ... TN-4
Saint Bridget Ch—church (2) ... WI-6
Saint Bridgets Cem—cemetery (2) ... CT-1
Saint Bridgets Cem—cemetery ... MA-1
Saint Bridgets Cem—cemetery (2) ... WI-6
Saint Bridgets Ch—church ... MN-6
Saint Bridgets Ch—church ... NY-2
Saint Bridgets Ch—church ... WV-2
Saint Bridgets Ch—church ... WI-6
Saint Bridget Sch—school ... CA-9
Saint Bridget Sch—school ... IN-6
Saint Bridget Sch—school ... IA-7
Saint Bridget Sch—school ... MN-6
Saint Bridget Sch—school ... NY-2
Saint Bridgets Sch ... IN-6
Saint Bridgets Sch—school ... CT-1
Saint Bridgets Sch—school ... IL-6
Saint Bridgets Sch—school (2) ... IN-6
Saint Bridgets Sch—school (2) ... MA-1
Saint Bridgets Sch—school ... NY-2
Saint Bridgets Sch—school ... PA-2
Saint Bridgett Cem—cemetery ... IA-7
**Saint Bridget Township**—pop pl ... KS-7
Saint Bridgids Cem—cemetery ... PA-2
Saint Brigade Cem—cemetery ... MA-1
Saint Brigid Ch—church ... NY-2
Saint Brigids Cem—cemetery ... KY-4
Saint Brigids Cem—cemetery (2) ... MA-1
Saint Brigids Cem—cemetery ... OH-6
Saint Brigids Cem—cemetery ... PA-2
Saint Brigids Ch—church ... NJ-2
Saint Brigid Sch—school (2) ... CA-9
Saint Brigid Sch—school ... CT-1
Saint Brigid Sch—school ... MI-6
Saint Brigid Sch—school ... NY-2
Saint Brigids Sch—school (2) ... KY-4
Saint Brigids Sch—school ... NJ-2
Saint Brigids Sch—school (2) ... NY-2
Saint Brigids Sch—school ... OH-6
Saint Bronislava Ch—church ... WI-6
Saint Bronislava Sch—school ... IL-6
Saint Bruno Cem—cemetery ... IL-6
Saint Brunos Ch—church ... WI-6
Saint Bruno Sch—school ... CA-9
Saint Bruno Sch—school ... IL-6
Saint Bulah Baptist Ch—church ... AL-4
Saint Cabrini Sch—school ... IL-6
Saint Caecilias Cem—cemetery ... NY-2
Saint Caecilias Sch—school ... NY-2
Saint Cajetan Sch—school ... CO-8
Saint Callistus Cem—cemetery ... PA-2
Saint Callistus Sch—school ... CA-9
Saint Callistus Sch—school ... PA-2
Saint Callistus Sch (abandoned)—school ... PA-2
Saint Camillus Acad—hist pl ... KY-4
Saint Camillus Acad—school ... KY-4
Saint Camillus Hosp—hospital ... MA-1
Saint Camillus Hosp—hospital ... WI-6
Saint Camillus Sch—school ... IL-6
Saint Camillus Sch—school ... MD-2
Saint Camillus Sch—school ... NY-2
Saint Campbell Ch—church ... AL-4
Saint Campbells Baptist Ch ... AL-4
Saint Canice Sch—school ... PA-2
Saint Cares Sch—school ... NY-2
Saint Carmel Cem—cemetery ... CA-9
Saint Carthages Sch—school ... PA-2
Saint Casimer Cem—cemetery ... MN-6
Saint Casimer Cem—cemetery ... PA-2
Saint Casimir Cem—cemetery ... IL-6
Saint Casimir Cem—cemetery ... NY-2
Saint Casimir Ch—church ... PA-2
Saint Casimir Convent—church ... IL-6
Saint Casimir HS—school ... IL-6
Saint Casimirs Cem—cemetery ... CT-1
Saint Casimirs Cem—cemetery ... IL-6
Saint Casimirs Cem—cemetery ... NH-1
Saint Casimirs Cem—cemetery ... OH-6
Saint Casimirs Cem—cemetery ... PA-2
Saint Casimirs Cem—cemetery ... WI-6
Saint Casimir Sch—school ... CA-9
Saint Casimir Sch—school ... IN-6
Saint Casimir Sch—school (4) ... MI-6
Saint Casimir Sch—school ... MN-6
Saint Casimir Sch—school ... OH-6
Saint Casimir Sch—school ... WI-6
Saint Casimirs Sch—school ... IL-6
Saint Casimirs Sch—school ... IN-6
Saint Casimirs Sch—school ... NJ-2
Saint Casimirs Sch—school (3) ... NY-2
Saint Casimirs Sch—school ... OH-6
Saint Casimirs Sch—school ... PA-2
Saint Casmirs Cem—cemetery ... PA-2
Saint Cassian Sch—school ... NJ-2
Saint Catharina Cem—cemetery ... KS-7
Saint Catharine—hist pl ... MD-2
**Saint Catharine**—pop pl ... KY-4
**Saint Catharine**—pop pl ... MO-7
Saint Catharine Bend ... MS-4
Saint Catharine Creek ... MS-4
Saint Catharine Lake ... VT-1
Saint Catharine Mountain ... VT-1
Saint Catharine Post Office—locale ... KY-4
Saint Catharines Cem—cemetery ... NJ-2
Saint Catharines Sch—school ... OH-6
**Saint Catherine**—pop pl (2) ... FL-3
**Saint Catherine**—pop pl ... MS-4
Saint Catherine, Lake—lake ... LA-4
Saint Catherine, Lake—lake ... VT-1
Saint Catherine Acad—school ... KY-4
Saint Catherine Acad—school ... NY-2
Saint Catherine Bend—bend ... MS-4
Saint Catherine Cem—cemetery ... LA-4
Saint Catherine Cem—cemetery ... MI-6
Saint Catherine Cem—cemetery ... MN-6
Saint Catherine Cem—cemetery ... NE-7
Saint Catherine Cem—cemetery ... PA-2
Saint Catherine Cem—cemetery (2) ... WI-6
Saint Catherine Ch—church ... LA-4
Saint Catherine Ch—church ... MI-6
Saint Catherine Ch—church ... MN-6
Saint Catherine Ch—church ... MS-4
Saint Catherine Ch—church ... NH-1
Saint Catherine Ch—church ... SD-7
Saint Catherine Ch—church ... WI-6
Saint Catherine Chapel—church ... CO-8
Saint Catherine Chapel—church ... LA-4
Saint Catherine Convent—church ... NY-2
Saint Catherine Cove—bay ... AK-9
Saint Catherine Creek—stream ... CA-9
Saint Catherine Creek—stream ... MS-4
Saint Catherine Island—island (2) ... MD-2
Saint Catherine Laboure Sch—school ... CA-9
Saint Catherine Laboure Sch—school ... MD-2
Saint catherine lake ... VT-1
Saint Catherine Lake—lake ... MN-6
Saint Catherine Mtn—summit ... VT-1
Saint Catherine of Siena Catholic Ch—church ... AL-4
Saint Catherine of Siena Catholic Ch—church ... FL-3
Saint Catherine of Siena Ch—church (2) ... FL-3
Saint Catherine of Siena Ch—church ... NJ-2
Saint Catherine of Siena Ch—church ... NY-2
Saint Catherine of Siena Ch—church ... PA-2
Saint Catherine of Siena Sch—school ... CA-9
Saint Catherine of Siena Sch—school ... IN-6
Saint Catherine of Siena Sch—school ... NY-2
Saint Catherine of Siena School ... PA-2
Saint Catherine Pass—gut ... LA-4
Saint Catherine Roman Catholic Ch—church ... IN-6
**Saint Catherines Bay**—pop pl (2) ... WI-6
Saint Catherines Bend ... MS-4
Saint Catherines CA VAR Saint Catharine Creek ... MS-4
Saint Catherines Cem—cemetery ... CT-1
Saint Catherines Cem—cemetery ... IN-6
Saint Catherines Cem—cemetery ... MA-1
Saint Catherines Cem—cemetery ... MN-6
Saint Catherines Cem—cemetery ... NY-2
Saint Catherines Cem—cemetery ... ND-7
Saint Catherines Cem—cemetery (5) ... PA-2
Saint Catherines Ch—church ... AZ-5
Saint Catherines Ch—church ... CT-1
Saint Catherines Ch—church ... LA-4
Saint Catherines Ch—church (3) ... NJ-2
Saint Catherines Ch—church ... ND-7
Saint Catherines Ch—church ... OH-6
Saint Catherines Ch—church ... SC-3
Saint Catherines Ch—church ... TX-5
Saint Catherines Ch—church ... FM-9
Saint Catherine Sch—school ... CO-8
Saint Catherine Sch—school (3) ... IL-6
Saint Catherine Sch—school ... KS-7
Saint Catherine Sch—school (2) ... LA-4
Saint Catherine Sch—school ... MO-7
Saint Catherine Sch—school ... NJ-2
Saint Catherine Sch—school ... OH-6
Saint Catherine Sch—school ... OK-5
Saint Catherine Sch—school ... PA-2
Saint Catherine Sch—school ... WI-6
Saint Catherines Creek ... MS-4
Saint Catherines Episcopal Ch—church (2) ... FL-3
Saint Catherines Greek Orthodox Ch—church ... FL-3
Saint Catherines Hosp—hospital ... IN-6
Saint Catherines Hosp—hospital (2) ... NE-7
Saint Catherines Indian Sch—school ... NM-5
Saint Catherine's Island—hist pl ... GA-3
Saint Catherines Island—island ... GA-3
Saint Catherines Lake ... MN-6
Saint Catherines Military Sch—school ... CA-9
Saint Catherine Sound—bay ... MD-2
Saint Catherines Sch—school ... AL-4
Saint Catherines Sch—school (3) ... CA-9
Saint Catherines Sch—school ... CO-8
Saint Catherines Sch—school ... HI-9
Saint Catherines Sch—school ... IN-6
Saint Catherines Sch—school ... KY-4
Saint Catherines Sch—school ... MA-1
Saint Catherines Sch—school ... MN-6
Saint Catherines Sch—school ... NH-1
Saint Catherines Sch—school (2) ... NJ-2
Saint Catherines Sch—school (2) ... NY-2
Saint Catherines Sch—school (2) ... OH-6
Saint Catherines Sch—school (3) ... PA-2
Saint Catherines Sch—school ... VA-3
Saint Catherines Sound—bay ... GA-3
Saint Catherine Towhead—island ... LA-4
Saint Cecelia Cem—cemetery ... WI-6
Saint Cecelia Ch—church ... IL-6
Saint Cecelias Acad—school ... IA-7
Saint Cecelias Cem—cemetery ... IL-6
Saint Cecelias Cem—cemetery ... NJ-2
Saint Cecelias Ch—church ... NY-2
Saint Cecelia Sch—school ... OH-6
Saint Cecelias Sch—school ... FL-3
Saint Cecilia Acad—hist pl ... TN-4
Saint Cecilia Catholic Ch—church ... FL-3
Saint Cecilia Catholic Church ... AL-4
Saint Cecilia Cem—cemetery ... MO-7
Saint Cecilia Cem—cemetery ... PA-2
Saint Cecilia Ch—church ... AL-4
Saint Cecilia Ch—church ... IA-7
Saint Cecilia Ch—church ... PA-2
Saint Cecilia Episcopal Ch—church ... FL-3
Saint Cecilias Acad—school ... TN-4
Saint Cecilias Cem—cemetery ... KY-4
Saint Cecilias Cem—cemetery ... PA-2
Saint Cecilia Sch—hist pl ... LA-4
Saint Cecilia Sch—school ... CA-9
Saint Cecilia Sch—school ... IL-6
Saint Cecilia Sch—school ... IA-7
Saint Cecilia Sch—school ... LA-4
Saint Cecilia Sch—school ... MI-6
Saint Cecilia Sch—school ... NY-2
Saint Cecilia Sch—school ... OH-6
Saint Cecilia Sch—school ... OR-9
Saint Cecilia Sch—school ... PA-2
Saint Cecilia Sch—school (2) ... TX-5
Saint Cecilia Sch—school ... WI-6
Saint Cecilia Sch—school ... FM-9
Saint Cecilia's Church and Convent—hist pl ... NY-2
Saint Cecilias Convent—church ... TN-4
Saint Cecilias HS—school ... DC-2
Saint Cecilias Park—park ... PA-2
Saint Cecilias Sch—school ... CA-9
Saint Cecilias Sch—school ... CT-1
Saint Cecilias Sch—school ... KY-4
Saint Cecilias Sch—school ... NE-7
Saint Cecilias Sch—school (3) ... NJ-2
Saint Cecilias Sch—school (2) ... NY-2
Saint Cecilias Sch—school ... OH-6
Saint Cecilias Sch—school ... OR-9
Saint Cecilias Sch—school ... PA-2
Saint Cecilias Sch—school ... TX-5
Saint Cecilla Cem—cemetery ... IA-7
Saint Celestine Sch ... IN-6
Saint Celestine Sch—school ... IL-6
Saint Celments Bay—bay ... MD-2
Saint Cem—cemetery ... IN-6
Saint Ch—church ... LA-4
Saint Chads Episcopal Ch—church ... FL-3
Saint Charies Cem—cemetery ... WI-6
Saint Charles—locale ... GA-3
Saint Charles—locale ... NE-7
Saint Charles—locale ... PA-2
**Saint Charles**—pop pl (2) ... AR-4
**Saint Charles**—pop pl ... GA-3
**Saint Charles**—pop pl ... ID-8
**Saint Charles**—pop pl (2) ... IL-6
**Saint Charles**—pop pl ... IA-7
**Saint Charles**—pop pl ... KY-4
**Saint Charles**—pop pl ... LA-4
**Saint Charles**—pop pl ... MD-2
**Saint Charles**—pop pl ... MI-6
**Saint Charles**—pop pl ... MN-6
**Saint Charles**—pop pl ... MO-7
**Saint Charles**—pop pl (2) ... OH-6
**Saint Charles**—pop pl ... SC-3
**Saint Charles**—pop pl ... SD-7
**Saint Charles**—pop pl ... VA-3
Saint Charles, Lake—lake ... FL-3
Saint Charles, Point—summit ... MT-8
Saint Charles Acad—school ... LA-4
Saint Charles Airp—airport ... MO-7
Saint Charles Barromeo Ch—church ... FL-3
Saint Charles Battle Site—hist pl ... AR-4
Saint Charles Bay—bay ... TX-5
Saint Charles Boromeo Sch—school ... IN-6
Saint Charles Borremeo Seminary—church ... NY-2
Saint Charles Borromen Sch—school ... NJ-2
Saint Charles Borromeo Catholic Ch—church ... FL-3
Saint Charles Borromeo Sch—school ... CA-9
Saint Charles Borromeo Sch—school ... FL-3
Saint Charles Borromeo Sch—school ... IN-6
Saint Charles Borromeo Sch—school (2) ... NY-2
Saint Charles Borromeo Seminary—school ... PA-2
Saint Charles Borromeos Sch—school ... KY-4
Saint Charles Boys Home—building ... WI-6
Saint Charles Campground—locale ... ID-8
Saint Charles Canal—canal (2) ... LA-4
Saint Charles Canyon—valley ... ID-8
Saint Charles Catholic Ch—church ... AL-4
Saint Charles Catholic Ch—church ... MS-4
Saint Charles (CCD)—cens area ... KY-4
Saint Charles (CCD)—cens area ... SC-3
Saint Charles Cem—cemetery ... IL-6
Saint Charles Cem—cemetery ... IA-7
Saint Charles Cem—cemetery (2) ... KS-7
Saint Charles Cem—cemetery ... LA-4
Saint Charles Cem—cemetery ... MA-1
Saint Charles Cem—cemetery ... MI-6
Saint Charles Cem—cemetery (2) ... MN-6
Saint Charles Cem—cemetery ... MO-7
Saint Charles Cem—cemetery ... NH-1
Saint Charles Cem—cemetery (2) ... NY-2
Saint Charles Cem—cemetery ... ND-7
Saint Charles Cem—cemetery ... OH-6
Saint Charles Cem—cemetery ... SD-7
Saint Charles Cem—cemetery (4) ... WI-6
Saint Charles Ch—church ... FL-3
Saint Charles Ch—church ... IA-7
Saint Charles Ch—church ... KY-4
Saint Charles Ch—church (2) ... LA-4
Saint Charles Ch—church (2) ... MD-2
Saint Charles Ch—church ... MN-6
Saint Charles Ch—church ... MS-4
Saint Charles Ch—church ... NY-2
Saint Charles Ch—church (3) ... PA-2
Saint Charles Ch—church ... TN-4
Saint Charles Ch—church ... TX-5
Saint Charles Chapel—church ... WI-6
Saint Charles College Hist Dist—hist pl ... MD-2
Saint Charles College Hist Dist (Boundary Increase)—hist pl ... MD-2
Saint Charles Country Club—other ... IL-6
**Saint Charles County**—pop pl ... MO-7
Saint Charles County Smart Field Airp—airport ... MO-7
Saint Charles Creek ... FL-3
Saint Charles Creek ... ID-8
Saint Charles Creek—stream ... AK-9
Saint Charles Creek—stream ... ID-8
Saint Charles Elem Sch—school ... FL-3
Saint Charles Flood Ditch—canal ... CO-8
**Saint Charles Furnace**—pop pl ... PA-2
Saint Charles Hill—summit ... CA-9
Saint Charles Hosp—hospital ... NY-2
Saint Charles Hosp—hospital ... OH-6
Saint Charles Hotel—hist pl ... SD-7
Saint Charles HS—school ... KY-4
Saint Charles Lake—lake ... WA-9
Saint Charles Med Ctr—hospital ... OR-9
Saint Charles Med Ctr Heliport—airport ... OR-9
**Saint Charles Mesa**—pop pl ... CO-8
Saint Charles Mission Sch—school ... MT-8
**Saint Charles Parish**—pop pl ... LA-4
Saint Charles Park—park ... MI-6
Saint Charles Peak—summit ... CO-8
Saint Charles Place Park—park ... CO-8
Saint Charles Plaza—locale ... MO-7
Saint Charles Reservoir No 1 ... CO-8
Saint Charles River ... CO-8
Saint Charles River—stream ... CO-8
Saint Charles Rsvr No 2—reservoir ... CO-8
Saint Charles Rsvr No 3—reservoir ... CO-8
Saint Charles Sch ... IN-6
Saint Charles Sch—school (4) ... CA-9
Saint Charles Sch—school ... CT-1
Saint Charles Sch—school ... IL-6
Saint Charles Sch—school ... IN-6
Saint Charles Sch—school ... KY-4
Saint Charles Sch—school ... LA-4
Saint Charles Sch—school ... MD-2
Saint Charles Sch—school (2) ... MA-1
Saint Charles Sch—school (2) ... MI-6
Saint Charles Sch—school ... MO-7
Saint Charles Sch—school ... NJ-2
Saint Charles Sch—school ... NM-5
Saint Charles Sch—school ... NY-2
Saint Charles Sch—school (6) ... OH-6
Saint Charles Sch—school ... OR-9
Saint Charles Sch—school (2) ... PA-2
Saint Charles Sch—school (2) ... TX-5
Saint Charles Sch—school ... WA-9
Saint Charles Sch—school (2) ... WI-6
Saint Charles School Cem—cemetery ... VA-3
Saint Charles Seminary—school (2) ... OH-6
Saint Charles Spring—spring ... ID-8
Saint Charles Streetcar Line—hist pl ... LA-4
Saint Charles Township—civil ... MO-7
**Saint Charles Township**—pop pl ... SD-7
Saint Charles (Township of)—civ div ... IL-6
Saint Charles (Township of)—civ div ... MI-6
**Saint Charles (Township of)**—pop pl ... MN-6
Saint Charles Trail—trail ... CO-8
Saint Charles Windmill—locale ... TX-5
Saint Charlottes Ch—church ... SC-3
Saint Ch (historical)—church ... PA-2
Saint Chretiennes Acad—school ... MA-1
Saint Christina Cem—cemetery ... SD-7
Saint Christines Ch—church ... OH-6
Saint Christine Sch—school ... MI-6
Saint Christines Sch—school (2) ... OH-6
Saint Christoper's Normal and Industrial Parish Sch—hist pl ... GA-3
Saint Christopher ... UT-8
Saint Christopher By The Sea Ch—church ... MD-2
Saint Christopher Ch—church ... AL-4
Saint Christopher Ch—church ... WI-6
Saint Christopher Episcopal Ch ... AL-4
Saint Christopher in the Bighorn—church ... WY-8
Saint Christopher Key—island ... FL-3
Saint Christopher Mine—mine ... AZ-5
Saint Christopher Roman Catholic Ch—church ... IN-6
Saint Christophers By the Sea Ch—church ... FL-3
Saint Christophers by the Sea Montessori Sch—school ... FL-3
Saint Christophers Ch—church ... FL-3
Saint Christophers Ch—church ... IN-6
Saint Christophers Ch—church ... KY-4
Saint Christophers Ch—church (3) ... NY-2
Saint Christophers Ch—church ... NC-3
Saint Christophers Ch—church (2) ... PA-2
Saint Christopher Sch—school (2) ... CA-9
Saint Christopher Sch—school ... IL-6
Saint Christopher Sch—school ... IN-6
Saint Christopher Sch—school ... LA-4
Saint Christopher Sch—school (2) ... MI-6
Saint Christopher Sch—school ... TX-5
Saint Christophers Episcopal Ch—church ... FL-3
Saint Christophers Episcopal Ch—church ... KS-7
Saint Christophers Episcopal Ch—church ... MS-4
Saint Christophers Hosp—hospital ... PA-2
Saint Christophers Mission—church ... UT-8
Saint Christophers Sch—school ... CA-9
Saint Christophers Sch—school ... CT-1
Saint Christophers Sch—school ... NV-8
Saint Christophers Sch—school ... NH-1
Saint Christophers Sch—school ... NJ-2
Saint Christophers Sch—school (4) ... NY-2
Saint Christophers Sch—school (2) ... OH-6
Saint Christophers Sch—school ... TX-5
Saint Christophers Sch—school ... VA-3
Saint Christopher Wayside Shrine—church ... AL-4
Saint Clair ... AL-4
Saint Clair—locale ... IA-7
Saint Clair—locale ... TN-4
Saint Clair—locale ... VA-3
**Saint Clair**—pop pl (2) ... AL-4
**Saint Clair**—pop pl ... GA-3
**Saint Clair**—pop pl ... LA-4
**SAINT Clair**—pop pl ... MI-6
**Saint Clair**—pop pl ... MI-6
**Saint Clair**—pop pl ... MN-6
**Saint Clair**—pop pl ... MO-7
**Saint Clair**—pop pl (4) ... PA-2
**Saint Clair**—pop pl (2) ... TN-4
**Saint Clair**—pop pl ... WA-9
Saint Clair, Alexander, House—hist pl ... VA-3
Saint Clair, Bayou—stream ... LA-4
Saint Clair, Lake—lake ... MI-6
Saint Clair, Lake—lake ... WA-9
Saint Clair, Lake—reservoir ... AZ-5
Saint Clair, Lake—reservoir ... VA-3
**Saint Clair Acres**—pop pl ... PA-2
Saint Clair Baptist Ch—church ... TN-4
Saint Clair Borough—civil ... PA-2
Saint Clair Bottom—locale ... VA-3
Saint Clair Branch—stream ... TN-4
Saint Clair Brooks Memorial Park—cemetery ... VA-3
Saint Claírce Cem—cemetery ... IA-7
Saint Clair Cem—cemetery ... AL-4
Saint Clair Cem—cemetery ... IN-6
Saint Clair Cem—cemetery ... IA-7
Saint Clair Cem—cemetery ... LA-4
Saint Clair Cem—cemetery ... MO-7
Saint Clair Cem—cemetery (2) ... PA-2
Saint Clair Cem—cemetery (2) ... VA-3
Saint Clair Ch—church ... AR-4
Saint Clair Ch—church ... GA-3
Saint Clair Ch—church (2) ... LA-4
Saint Clair Ch—church ... MS-4
Saint Clair Ch—church ... NC-3

*Saint Ferdinand High School* ... IN-6
Saint Ferdinand Sch—*school* ... IL-6
Saint Ferdinand Township—*civil* ... MO-7
Saint Fidelis Catholic Church—*hist pl* ... KS-7
Saint Fidelis Cem—*cemetery* ... KS-7
Saint Fidelis Sch—*school* ... NY-2
Saint Filumena Shrine—*other* ... PA-2
Saint Finbarrs Cem—*cemetery* ... MN-6
Saint Finbars Cem—*cemetery* ... WI-6
Saint Finbar Sch—*school* ... CA-9
Saint Finbar Sch—*school* ... NY-2
Saint Finbars Sch—*school* ... WI-6
Saint Florence Ch—*church* ... MI-6
**Saint Florian**—*pop pl* ... AL-4
Saint Florian Branch—*stream* ... AL-4
Saint Florian Ch—*church* ... WI-6
Saint Florian HS—*school* ... MI-6
Saint Florian Sch—*school* ... PA-2
Saint Florian Sch—*school* ... WI-6
Saint Florians Sch—*school* ... IL-6
Saint Fortunata Sch—*school* ... NY-2
Saint Frances Cabrini Ch—*church* ... MN-6
Saint Frances Cabrini Hosp—*hospital* ... LA-4
Saint Frances Cabrini Sch—*school* (2) ... CA-9
Saint Frances Cabrini Sch—*school* (2) ... LA-4
Saint Frances Cabrini Sch—*school* ... PA-2
Saint Frances Cabrini Sch—*school* ... TX-5
Saint Frances Cem—*cemetery* ... NE-7
Saint Frances Hosp—*hospital* ... CT-1
Saint Frances Methodist Church—*hist pl* ... NC-3
Saint Frances of Assisi Catholic Ch—*church* ... MS-4
Saint Frances of Rome Sch—*hist pl* ... KY-4
Saint Frances of Rome Sch—*school* ... CA-9
Saint Frances of Rome Sch—*school* ... KY-4
Saint Frances Sch—*school* ... OK-5
Saint Frances Sch—*school* ... WI-6
Saint Francie Convent—*church* ... IN-6
*Saint Francis* ... ME-1
Saint Francis—*locale* ... TX-5
**Saint Francis**—*pop pl* (2) ... AR-4
**Saint Francis**—*pop pl* ... FL-3
**Saint Francis**—*pop pl* ... KS-7
**Saint Francis**—*pop pl* ... KY-4
**Saint Francis**—*pop pl* ... ME-1
**Saint Francis**—*pop pl* (2) ... MN-6
**Saint Francis**—*pop pl* ... SD-7
**Saint Francis**—*pop pl* ... WI-6
Saint Francis, Lake—*lake* ... NM-5
Saint Francis, Lake—*reservoir* ... AR-4
Saint Francis Acad—*school* ... IL-6
Saint Francis Acad—*school* ... PA-2
Saint Francis Acad—*school* ... TX-5
Saint Francis Assisi Sch—*school* ... MI-6
Saint Francis Bay—*bay* ... SD-7
Saint Francis Bay—*stream* ... AR-4
Saint Francis Bend—*bend* ... MS-4
Saint Francis Borgia Cem—*cemetery* ... MO-7
Saint Francis Borgia Ch—*church* ... AZ-5
Saint Francis Borgia Sch—*school* ... IL-6
Saint Francis Boys Camp—*locale* ... IL-6
Saint Francis Boys Home—*building* (2) ... KS-7
*Saint Francis Boys Sch* ... PA-2
Saint Francis Brook—*stream* ... ME-1
Saint Francis by the Lake Chapel—*church* ... NC-3
Saint Francis by-the-Sea American Catholic Church—*hist pl* ... CA-9
Saint Francis Cabrini Ch—*church* ... MO-7
Saint Francis Cabrini HS—*school* ... MI-6
Saint Francis Camp—*locale* ... NY-2
Saint Francis Catholic Ch—*church* ... MS-4
Saint Francis Catholic Ch—*church* ... UT-8
Saint Francis Cem—*cemetery* ... AZ-5
Saint Francis Cem—*cemetery* ... AR-4
Saint Francis Cem—*cemetery* ... CA-9
Saint Francis Cem—*cemetery* ... CO-8
Saint Francis Cem—*cemetery* ... IL-6
Saint Francis Cem—*cemetery* (2) ... IN-6
Saint Francis Cem—*cemetery* (4) ... IA-7
Saint Francis Cem—*cemetery* (6) ... KS-7
Saint Francis Cem—*cemetery* (2) ... KY-4
Saint Francis Cem—*cemetery* ... LA-4
Saint Francis Cem—*cemetery* (2) ... MA-1
Saint Francis Cem—*cemetery* ... MI-6
Saint Francis Cem—*cemetery* (2) ... MN-6
Saint Francis Cem—*cemetery* ... MO-7
Saint Francis Cem—*cemetery* (2) ... NE-7
Saint Francis Cem—*cemetery* ... NM-5
Saint Francis Cem—*cemetery* (6) ... NY-2
Saint Francis Cem—*cemetery* ... NC-3
Saint Francis Cem—*cemetery* ... ND-7
Saint Francis Cem—*cemetery* ... OR-9
Saint Francis Cem—*cemetery* (2) ... PA-2
Saint Francis Cem—*cemetery* ... TX-5
Saint Francis Cem—*cemetery* (5) ... WI-6
Saint Francis Centre—*church* ... WV-2
Saint Francis Ch—*church* (3) ... AL-4
Saint Francis Ch—*church* ... AR-4
Saint Francis Ch—*church* ... FL-3
Saint Francis Ch—*church* ... GA-3
Saint Francis Ch—*church* ... IA-7
Saint Francis Ch—*church* ... KS-7
Saint Francis Ch—*church* (2) ... KY-4
Saint Francis Ch—*church* ... MD-2
Saint Francis Ch—*church* ... MA-1
Saint Francis Ch—*church* (4) ... MI-6
Saint Francis Ch—*church* ... MT-8
Saint Francis Ch—*church* (2) ... NE-7
Saint Francis Ch—*church* ... NH-1
Saint Francis Ch—*church* ... NJ-2
Saint Francis Ch—*church* (3) ... NY-2
Saint Francis Ch—*church* (3) ... NC-3
Saint Francis Ch—*church* (3) ... PA-2
Saint Francis Ch—*church* ... SD-7
Saint Francis Ch—*church* (3) ... TX-5
Saint Francis Ch—*church* ... VA-3
Saint Francis Ch—*church* (3) ... WI-6
Saint Francis Ch—*church* ... WY-8
Saint Francis Chapel—*church* ... TX-5
Saint Francis Chapel—*church* ... WI-6
Saint Francis Chapel—*hist pl* ... LA-4
Saint Francis Ch (historical)—*church* ... SD-7
**Saint Francis (Chicago)**—*pop pl* ... KY-4
Saint Francis Childrens Home—*building* ... MI-6
*Saint Francis City* ... KS-7
Saint Francis Coll—*school* ... IN-6
Saint Francis Coll—*school* ... ME-1
Saint Francis Coll—*school* ... NH-1
Saint Francis Coll—*school* ... PA-2
Saint Francis Convent—*church* ... IA-7
Saint Francis Convent—*church* ... MO-7
Saint Francis Convent—*church* ... WI-6
Saint Francis Convent Sch—*school* ... HI-9
Saint Francis Country Home—*building* ... PA-2
**Saint Francis (County)**—*pop pl* ... AR-4
Saint Francis Creek—*stream* ... CO-8
Saint Francis Dead River—*stream* ... FL-3
Saint Francis de Chantal Sch—*school* ... NY-2
*Saint Francis De Sales* ... PA-2
Saint Francis de Sales Cem—*cemetery* ... MN-6
Saint Francis DeSales Cem—*cemetery* ... NY-2
Saint Francis deSales Cem—*cemetery* ... WI-6
Saint Francis de Sales Ch—*church* ... FL-3
Saint Francis De Sales Ch—*church* ... MD-2
Saint Francis de Sales Ch—*church* ... NE-7
Saint Francis De Sales Ch—*church* ... NY-2
Saint Francis de Sales Coll—*school* ... PA-2
Saint Francis De Sales HS—*school* ... CO-8
Saint Francis de Sales HS—*school* ... IL-6
Saint Francis de Sales HS—*school* ... OH-6
Saint Francis DeSales Roman Catholic Church—*hist pl* ... KY-4
Saint Francis de Sales Sch—*school* ... CA-9
Saint Francis de Sales Sch—*school* (2) ... MI-6
Saint Francis DeSales Sch—*school* ... MN-6
Saint Francis De Sales Sch—*school* ... NJ-2
Saint Francis DeSales Sch—*school* ... NY-2
Saint Francis DeSales Sch—*school* ... NC-3
Saint Francis DeSales Sch—*school* ... OH-6
Saint Francis De Sales Sch—*school* (3) ... OH-6
Saint Francis De Sales Sch—*school* ... VA-3
Saint Francis-Desales Sch—*school* ... WV-2
Saint Francis DeSales Seminary—*school* ... OK-5
Saint Francis East Wing Secondary Sch—*school* ... PA-2
Saint Francis Elem Sch—*school* ... KS-7
Saint Francis Episcopal Ch—*church* ... FL-3
Saint Francis Episcopal Ch—*church* ... MS-4
Saint Francis Floodway—*canal* ... AR-4
Saint Francis Floodway—*flat* ... AR-4
Saint Francis Friary—*building* ... PA-2
*Saint Francis Game Mngmt Area* ... KS-7
Saint Francis Heights—*uninc pl* ... CA-9
Saint Francis Heights Sch—*school* ... WI-6
Saint Francis Hosp—*hospital* ... CA-9
Saint Francis Hosp—*hospital* ... CO-8
Saint Francis Hosp—*hospital* ... DE-2
Saint Francis Hosp—*hospital* ... FL-3
Saint Francis Hosp—*hospital* ... GA-3
Saint Francis Hosp—*hospital* (3) ... IL-6
Saint Francis Hosp—*hospital* ... IN-6
Saint Francis Hosp—*hospital* ... IA-7
Saint Francis Hosp—*hospital* ... KS-7
Saint Francis Hosp—*hospital* ... MN-6
Saint Francis Hosp—*hospital* ... NE-7
Saint Francis Hosp—*hospital* (6) ... NY-2
Saint Francis Hosp—*hospital* ... OH-6
Saint Francis Hosp—*hospital* ... PA-2
Saint Francis Hosp—*hospital* ... SC-3
Saint Francis Hosp—*hospital* ... WI-6
Saint Francis Hospital Airp—*airport* ... PA-2
Saint Francis Hospital Heliport—*airport* (2) ... MO-7
Saint Francis HS—*school* (2) ... CA-9
Saint Francis HS—*school* ... IL-6
Saint Francis HS—*school* ... KS-7
Saint Francis HS—*school* ... KY-4
Saint Francis HS—*school* ... MN-6
Saint Francis HS—*school* (2) ... OR-9
Saint Francis HS—*school* ... WV-2
Saint Francis in the Fields Ch—*church* ... PA-2
Saint Francis Island Landing—*locale* ... MS-4
Saint Francis Island Lodge—*locale* ... AR-4
Saint Francis Lake—*lake* ... ME-1
Saint Francis Lake—*swamp* ... AR-4
Saint Francis Levee—*levee* (2) ... AR-4
Saint Francis Levee—*levee* ... TN-4
Saint Francis M C Helistop—*airport* ... NJ-2
Saint Francis Mission—*church* (2) ... AZ-5
Saint Francis Mission—*church* ... KY-4
Saint Francis Mission—*hist pl* ... SD-7
Saint Francis Mission at White Sulphur—*hist pl* ... KY-4
Saint Francis Mission (historical)—*church* ... SD-7
Saint Francis Monastery—*church* ... WI-6
Saint Francis Municipal Airp—*airport* ... KS-7
Saint Francis Natl For—*forest* ... AR-4
Saint Francis of Assisi Catholic Ch—*church* (2) ... FL-3
Saint Francis of Assisi Catholic Ch—*church* (3) ... MS-4
Saint Francis of Assisi Cem—*cemetery* ... NY-2
Saint Francis Of Assisi Ch—*church* ... CT-1
Saint Francis Of Assisi Ch—*church* ... GA-3
Saint Francis of Assisi Ch—*church* ... KS-7
Saint Francis of Assisi Ch—*church* ... NC-3
Saint Francis of Assisi Ch—*church* ... VA-3
Saint Francis of Assisi Ch—*church* ... WI-6
Saint Francis of Assisi Ch—*church* ... FM-9
Saint Francis of Assisi Complex—*hist pl* ... KY-4
Saint Francis of Assisi Episcopal Ch—*church* (2) ... FL-3
*Saint Francis of Assisi Sch* ... PA-2
Saint Francis of Assisi Sch—*school* ... CA-9
Saint Francis Of Assisi Sch—*school* ... CT-1
Saint Francis of Assisi Sch—*school* ... IL-6
Saint Francis of Assisi Sch—*school* ... KS-7
Saint Francis of Assisi Sch—*school* ... KY-4
Saint Francis of Assisi Sch—*school* ... MO-7
Saint Francis of Assisi Sch—*school* (2) ... NY-2
Saint Francis Of Assisi Sch—*school* ... PA-2
Saint Francis of Assisi Sch—*school* ... TX-5
Saint Francis Of Oak Ridge Hosp—*hospital* ... OH-6
Saint Francis of Xavier Cem—*cemetery* ... IN-6
Saint Francis of Xavier Ch—*church* ... SD-7
Saint Francis Point—*cape* ... AL-4
Saint Francis Retreat—*building* ... PA-2
Saint Francis Retreat—*church* ... IL-6
Saint Francis Retreat—*locale* ... CA-9
Saint Francis Retreat—*locale* ... MA-1
Saint Francis Revet—*levee* ... AR-4
Saint Francis River—*stream* ... AR-4
Saint Francis River—*stream* ... ME-1
Saint Francis River—*stream* ... MN-6
Saint Francis River—*stream* ... MO-7
Saint Francis Sch—*school* ... AZ-5
Saint Francis Sch—*school* ... AR-4
Saint Francis Sch—*school* (5) ... CA-9
Saint Francis Sch—*school* ... CT-1
Saint Francis Sch—*school* (7) ... IL-6
Saint Francis Sch—*school* ... IA-7
Saint Francis Sch—*school* ... KY-4
Saint Francis Sch—*school* ... LA-4
Saint Francis Sch—*school* (3) ... MA-1
Saint Francis Sch—*school* (3) ... MI-6
Saint Francis Sch—*school* (2) ... MN-6
Saint Francis Sch—*school* (3) ... MS-4
Saint Francis Sch—*school* ... MO-7
Saint Francis Sch—*school* ... NE-7
Saint Francis Sch—*school* ... NV-8
Saint Francis Sch—*school* ... NM-5
Saint Francis Sch—*school* (5) ... NY-2
Saint Francis Sch—*school* (4) ... OH-6
Saint Francis Sch—*school* (2) ... OK-5
Saint Francis Sch—*school* (3) ... OR-9
Saint Francis Sch—*school* (7) ... PA-2
Saint Francis Sch—*school* ... SD-7
Saint Francis Sch—*school* ... TN-4
Saint Francis Sch—*school* ... WA-9
Saint Francis Sch—*school* ... WV-2
Saint Francis Sch—*school* (2) ... WI-6
Saint Francis Sch—*school* ... GU-9
Saint Francis Seminary—*church* ... NY-2
Saint Francis Seminary—*school* ... CA-9
Saint Francis Seminary—*school* ... OH-6
Saint Francis Seminary—*school* ... PA-2
Saint Francis Seminary—*school* ... WI-6
Saint Francis Solanus Mission—*church* ... WI-6
Saint Francis Street Baptist Ch (historical)—*church* ... AL-4
Saint Francis Street Methodist Ch—*church* ... AL-4
Saint Francis Street Methodist Church—*hist pl* ... AL-4
Saint Francis Sunk Lands—*flat* ... AR-4
Saint Francis Towhead—*island* ... MS-4
**Saint Francis (Town of)**—*pop pl* ... ME-1
Saint Francis (Township of)—*civ div* ... IL-6
Saint Francis (Township of)—*fmr MCD* (4) ... AR-4
**Saint Francis Village**—*pop pl* ... TX-5
**Saint Francisville**—*pop pl* (2) ... IL-6
**Saint Francisville**—*pop pl* ... LA-4
**Saint Francisville**—*pop pl* ... MO-7
Saint Francisville Hist Dist—*hist pl* ... LA-4
Saint Francisville Hist Dist (Boundary Increase)—*hist pl* ... LA-4
Saint Francis Vocational Sch—*school* ... PA-2
Saint Francis Wildlife Area—*park* ... KS-7
Saint Francis Xaviar Sch—*school* ... IL-6
Saint Francis Xavier Cathedral—*hist pl* ... LA-4
Saint Francis Xavier Cathedral Complex (Boundary Increase)—*hist pl* ... LA-4
Saint Francis Xavier Catholic Ch—*church* ... AL-4
Saint Francis Xavier Cem—*cemetery* ... CA-9
Saint Francis Xavier Cem—*cemetery* (2) ... KS-7
Saint Francis Xavier Cem—*cemetery* ... KY-4
Saint Francis Xavier Cem—*cemetery* ... MA-1
Saint Francis Xavier Cem—*cemetery* (3) ... MN-6
Saint Francis Xavier Cem—*cemetery* (2) ... PA-2
Saint Francis Xavier Ch—*church* ... FL-3
Saint Francis Xavier Ch—*church* (2) ... MD-2
Saint Francis Xavier Ch—*church* ... MN-6
Saint Francis Xavier Ch—*church* ... PA-2
Saint Francis Xavier Ch—*church* (2) ... TX-5
Saint Francis Xavier Church—*hist pl* ... MD-2
Saint Francis Xavier Church—*hist pl* ... WV-2
Saint Francis Xavier Church and Newtown Manor House—*hist pl* ... MD-2
Saint Francis Xavier Coll—*school* ... NY-2
Saint Francis Xavier Convent—*hist pl* ... MS-4
Saint Francis Xavier Grade Sch—*school* ... AZ-5
Saint Francis Xavier Mission—*church* ... WA-9
Saint Francis Xavier Novitiate—*school* ... OR-9
Saint Francis Xaviers Cem—*cemetery* ... MA-1
Saint Francis Xavier Sch—*school* ... AL-4
Saint Francis Xavier Sch—*school* ... CA-9
Saint Francis Xavier Sch—*school* ... CT-1
Saint Francis Xavier Sch—*school* ... DC-2
Saint Francis Xavier Sch—*school* (2) ... FL-3
Saint Francis Xavier Sch—*school* (2) ... MA-1
Saint Francis Xavier Sch—*school* ... MI-6
Saint Francis Xavier Sch—*school* ... MO-7
Saint Francis Xavier Sch—*school* ... MT-8
Saint Francis Xavier Sch—*school* ... NM-5
Saint Francis Xavier Sch—*school* ... NY-2
Saint Francis Xavier Sch—*school* (3) ... PA-2
Saint Francis Xaviers Sch—*school* ... WV-2
Saint Francois Cem—*cemetery* ... MO-7
Saint Francois Country Club—*other* ... MO-7
**Saint Francois County**—*pop pl* ... MO-7
Saint Francois Plaza—*locale* ... MO-7
*Saint Francois River* ... AR-4
*Saint Francois River* ... MO-7
Saint Francois Township—*civil* (4) ... MO-7
*Saint Francoisville* ... MO-7
Saint Francois Xavier Academie—*school* ... NH-1
Saint Francois Xavier Cem—*cemetery* ... NH-1
*Saint Francois Xavier du Bac* ... AZ-5
Saint Fredericks Cem—*cemetery* ... MN-6
Saint Frederick Sch—*school* ... MI-6
Saint Frederick Sch—*school* ... WI-6
Saint Fredrick Cem—*cemetery* ... IL-6
Saint Fredrick Cem—*cemetery* ... NE-7
Saint Fridolin Cem—*cemetery* ... MN-6
Saint Fridolin Cem—*cemetery* ... WI-6
Saint Froid Lake—*lake* ... ME-1
**Saint Gabriel**—*pop pl* ... LA-4
Saint Gabriel Acad—*school* ... MI-6
Saint Gabriel Catholic Ch—*church* ... FL-3
Saint Gabriel Cem—*cemetery* ... IL-6
Saint Gabriel Cem—*cemetery* ... MD-2
Saint Gabriel Cem—*cemetery* ... MN-6
Saint Gabriel Cem—*cemetery* ... MT-8
Saint Gabriel Cem—*cemetery* ... ND-7
Saint Gabriel Ch—*church* ... NJ-2
Saint Gabriel Coll—*school* ... NJ-2
*Saint Gabriel Convent* ... NC-3
Saint Gabriel Episcopal Ch—*church* ... FL-3
Saint Gabriel Hall—*building* ... PA-2
Saint Gabriel Hill—*summit* ... PA-2
Saint Gabriel HS—*school* ... IL-6
Saint Gabriel Roman Catholic Ch—*church* ... IN-6
Saint Gabriel Roman Catholic Church—*hist pl* ... LA-4
Saint Gabriels Cem—*cemetery* ... MD-2
Saint Gabriels Cem—*cemetery* ... PA-2
Saint Gabriels Ch—*church* ... NY-2
Saint Gabriels Ch—*church* (2) ... NC-3
Saint Gabriel Sch—*school* ... IN-6
Saint Gabriel Sch—*school* ... NC-3
Saint Gabriel Sch—*school* ... OH-6
Saint Gabriel Sch—*school* (2) ... PA-2
Saint Gabriel's Episcopal Church—*hist pl* ... FL-3
Saint Gabriel's Episcopal Church—*hist pl* ... PA-2
Saint Gabriels Home—*locale* ... MD-2
Saint Gabriels Hosp—*hospital* ... MN-6
Saint Gabriels Monastery (historical)—*church* ... IA-7
Saint Gabriels Park—*park* ... NY-2
Saint Gabriels Sch—*school* ... AR-4
Saint Gabriels Sch—*school* ... DC-2
Saint Gabriels Sch—*school* ... KY-4
Saint Gabriels Sch—*school* ... MA-1
Saint Gabriels Sch—*school* ... MO-7
Saint Gabriels Sch—*school* (4) ... NY-2
Saint Gabriels Sch—*school* ... NC-3
Saint Gabriels Sch—*school* ... OH-6
Saint Gabriels Sch—*school* (3) ... PA-2
Saint Gabriels Sch—*school* ... WI-6
Saint Galilee Ch—*church* ... NC-3
Saint Galilee Ch—*church* ... TX-5
Saint Gall Cem—*cemetery* ... IL-6
Saint Galls Cem—*cemetery* ... MN-6
Saint Gall Sch—*school* ... IL-6
Saint Gaspars Ch—*church* ... IN-6
Saint Gaudens Memorial—*other* ... NH-1
Saint-Gaudens Natl Historic Site—*hist pl* ... NH-1
Saint Gemmas Sch—*school* ... MI-6
**Saint Genevieve**—*pop pl* ... LA-4
Saint Genevieve Cem—*cemetery* ... MN-6
Saint Genevieve Cem—*cemetery* ... VT-1
Saint Genevieve Ch—*church* ... VT-1
Saint Genevieve HS—*school* ... CA-9
Saint Genevieve Sch—*school* ... LA-4
Saint Genevieve Sch—*school* ... MI-6
Saint Genevieves Sch—*school* ... PA-2
Saint Geneview Sch—*school* ... NJ-2
*Saint George* ... DE-2
*Saint George* ... ND-7
*Saint George* ... WV-2
Saint George—*locale* ... DE-2
Saint George—*locale* ... MN-6
**Saint George**—*pop pl* ... AK-9
**Saint George**—*pop pl* ... DE-2
**Saint George**—*pop pl* ... FL-3
**Saint George**—*pop pl* ... GA-3
**Saint George**—*pop pl* (2) ... IL-6
**Saint George**—*pop pl* ... KS-7
**Saint George**—*pop pl* ... ME-1
**Saint George**—*pop pl* (2) ... MO-7
**Saint George**—*pop pl* ... NY-2
**Saint George**—*pop pl* (2) ... PA-2
**Saint George**—*pop pl* ... SC-3
**Saint George**—*pop pl* ... UT-8
**Saint George**—*pop pl* ... WV-2
**Saint George**—*pop pl* ... WI-6
Saint George, Cape—*cape* ... FL-3
Saint George and Washington Canal—*canal* ... UT-8
Saint George Anglican Ch—*church* ... FL-3
Saint George Antiochian Eastern Orthodox—*church* ... IN-6
Saint George Barber Marsh—*swamp* ... MD-2
Saint George Canyon—*valley* ... AZ-5
Saint George (CCD)—*cens area* ... GA-3
Saint George (CCD)—*cens area* ... SC-3
Saint George Cem—*cemetery* ... GA-3
Saint George Cem—*cemetery* (2) ... IL-6
Saint George Cem—*cemetery* (2) ... KS-7
Saint George Cem—*cemetery* (2) ... MI-6
Saint George Cem—*cemetery* ... MO-7
Saint George Cem—*cemetery* (2) ... NY-2
Saint George Cem—*cemetery* (2) ... ND-7
Saint George Cem—*cemetery* (2) ... SC-3
Saint George Cem—*cemetery* ... SD-7
Saint George Cem—*cemetery* ... TX-5
Saint George Cem—*cemetery* (2) ... WI-6
*Saint George Ch* ... IN-6
Saint George Ch—*church* ... FL-3
Saint George Ch—*church* ... GA-3
Saint George Ch—*church* ... MA-1
Saint George Ch—*church* ... NY-2
Saint George Ch—*church* (3) ... SC-3
Saint George Channel—*channel* ... CA-9
Saint George City Cem—*cemetery* ... UT-8
Saint George Creek—*bay* ... MD-2
Saint George Creek—*stream* ... AK-9
Saint George Eastern Orthodox Ch—*church* ... KS-7
Saint George East Sch—*school* ... UT-8
Saint George Elem Sch—*school* ... KS-7
Saint George Fields—*flat* ... UT-8
Saint George Harbor—*harbor* ... MD-2
Saint George Hill—*summit* ... VT-1
Saint George Hill—*summit* ... VI-3
**Saint George (historical)**—*pop pl* ... ND-7
Saint George Hosp—*hospital* ... OH-6
Saint George Hotel—*hist pl* ... CA-9
Saint George HS—*school* ... IL-6
Saint George HS—*school* ... KS-7
*Saint George Island* ... FL-3
Saint George Island—*island* ... AK-9
Saint George Island—*island* ... FL-3
Saint George Island—*island* ... MD-2
**Saint George Island**—*pop pl* ... MD-2
Saint George Island—*post sta* ... AK-9
Saint George Island Beach—*beach* ... MD-2
Saint George Island Bridge—*bridge* ... MD-2
Saint George Island West Jetty Light 1—*locale* ... FL-3
Saint George Lake—*lake* ... FL-3
Saint George Lake—*lake* ... MI-6
Saint George Lake—*reservoir* ... ME-1
Saint George Lake—*reservoir* ... TN-4
Saint George Lake Dam—*dam* ... TN-4
Saint George (Magisterial District)—*fmr MCD* ... WV-2
Saint George Melkite Catholic Church—*hist pl* ... WI-6
Saint George Melkite Greek Catholic Ch—*church* ... AL-4
Saint George Mines—*mine* ... CA-9
Saint George Municipal Airp—*airport* ... UT-8
Saint George Orthodox Ch—*church* ... PA-2
**Saint George Park**—*pop pl* ... MD-2
Saint George Plantation House—*hist pl* ... LA-4
**Saint George (P.O. Name St. George Island)**—*pop pl* ... AK-9
Saint George Post Office—*building* ... UT-8
Saint George River—*stream* ... ME-1
Saint George Rock—*bar* ... AK-9
Saint George Rsvr—*reservoir* ... CO-8
Saint George RV Campground—*park* ... UT-8
**Saint Georges**—*pop pl* (2) ... DE-2
**Saint Georges**—*pop pl* ... MD-2
Saint Georges and Sallys Fancy—*locale* ... VI-3
Saint Georges Archeol Site—*hist pl* ... VI-3
*Saint Georges Bank* ... MA-1
Saint Georges Cem—*cemetery* ... DE-2
Saint Georges Cem—*cemetery* ... KS-7
Saint Georges Cem—*cemetery* (2) ... MA-1
Saint Georges Cem—*cemetery* ... NY-2
Saint Georges Cem—*cemetery* (3) ... PA-2
Saint Georges Cemetery Caretaker's House—*hist pl* ... DE-2
Saint Georges Ch—*church* ... DE-2
Saint Georges Ch—*church* ... IN-6
Saint Georges Ch—*church* (2) ... MD-2
Saint Georges Ch—*church* (2) ... NJ-2
Saint Georges Ch—*church* (4) ... NY-2
Saint Georges Ch—*church* ... OH-6
Saint Georges Ch—*church* (2) ... PA-2
Saint Georges Ch—*church* (3) ... VA-3
Saint Georges Ch—*church* ... WV-2
Saint George Sch—*school* ... CA-9
Saint George Sch—*school* (2) ... IL-6
Saint George Sch—*school* ... KY-4
Saint George Sch—*school* ... LA-4
Saint George Sch—*school* ... ME-1
Saint George Sch—*school* ... MA-1
Saint George Sch—*school* ... NJ-2
Saint George Sch—*school* (2) ... OH-6
Saint George Sch—*school* ... TX-5
Saint George Sch—*school* ... VT-1
Saint George Sch—*school* ... WI-6
*Saint Georges Chapel* ... DE-2
Saint George's Chapel—*hist pl* ... DE-2
Saint George's Church—*hist pl* ... NY-2
Saint George's Church—*hist pl* ... VA-3
Saint Georges Country Club—*other* ... NY-2
Saint Georges Creek—*stream* ... DE-2
Saint Georges Episcopal Ch—*church* ... FL-3
Saint Georges Episcopal Ch—*church* ... MS-4
Saint George's Episcopal Church—*hist pl* ... NY-2
Saint George Shaft—*mine* ... CA-9
**Saint Georges Heights**—*pop pl* (2) ... DE-2
Saint Georges Hundred—*civil* ... DE-2
*Saint George's Island* ... ME-1
*Saint Georges Island* ... MD-2
*Saint Georges Island* ... MA-1
**Saint Georges Island**—*pop pl* ... FL-3
*Saint George's Lake* ... MI-6
Saint George's Methodist Church—*hist pl* ... PA-2
Saint George Sound—*bay* ... FL-3
Saint George's Parish Vestry House—*hist pl* ... MD-2
**Saint Georges Park**—*pop pl* ... MD-2
*Saint Georges Point* ... CA-9
Saint Georges Presbyterian Church—*hist pl* ... DE-2
Saint George's Protestant Episcopal Church—*hist pl* ... MD-2
Saint George's Protestant Episcopal Church—*hist pl* ... NY-2
Saint George's Roman Catholic Church—*hist pl* ... KY-4
Saint Georges Sch—*school* ... CA-9
Saint Georges Sch—*school* ... FL-3
Saint Georges Sch—*school* ... IL-6
Saint Georges Sch—*school* ... MA-1
Saint Georges Sch—*school* ... MS-4
Saint Georges Sch—*school* ... NH-1
Saint Georges Sch—*school* ... PA-2
Saint Georges Sch—*school* ... TN-4
Saint Georges Sch—*school* ... WA-9
*Saint Georges Sound* ... FL-3
*Saint Georges Station* ... DE-2
Saint Georges United Methodist Ch—*church* (2) ... DE-2
Saint Georges United Presbyterian Ch—*church* ... DE-2
*Saint Georges Village* ... DE-2
Saint George Tank—*reservoir* ... AZ-5
Saint George the Great Martyr Orthodox Church—*hist pl* ... AK-9
**Saint George (Town of)**—*pop pl* ... ME-1
**Saint George (Town of)**—*pop pl* ... VT-1
**Saint George Township**—*pop pl* ... KS-7
**Saint George (Township of)**—*pop pl* ... MN-6
Saint George Valley Lateral—*canal* ... UT-8
Saint George Well—*well* ... NM-5
Saint George West Sch—*school* ... UT-8
Saint Gerald Majella Sch—*school* ... CA-9
Saint Gerald Sch—*school* ... IL-6
Saint Gerard HS—*school* ... TX-5
Saint Gerard JHS—*school* ... TX-5
Saint Gerard-Majella Sch—*school* ... IL-6
Saint Gerard Mission House—*locale* ... MN-6
Saint Gerard Sch—*school* ... GA-3
Saint Gerard Sch—*school* ... LA-4
Saint Gerard Sch—*school* (2) ... MI-6
Saint Gerard Sch—*school* ... SC-3
Saint Gerards Coll—*school* ... OH-6
Saint Gerards Sch—*school* ... MT-8
Saint Gerards Sch—*school* (2) ... NY-2
Saint Gerards Sch—*school* ... WI-6
**Saint Germain**—*pop pl* ... WI-6
Saint Germain Cem—*cemetery* ... WI-6
Saint Germaine Brook—*stream* ... NY-2
Saint Germaine Ditch—*canal* ... SD-7
Saint Germaine Sch—*school* ... MI-6
Saint Germaine Sch—*school* ... PA-2
Saint Germain Foundation—*church* ... FL-3
Saint Germain Foundation—*locale* ... CO-8
Saint Germain Pond—*lake* ... NY-2
Saint Germain River—*stream* ... WI-6
**Saint Germain (Town of)**—*pop pl* ... WI-6
**Saint Gertrude**—*pop pl* ... ND-7
Saint Gertrude Acad—*school* ... ID-8
Saint Gertrude Acad—*school* ... MD-2
Saint Gertrude Cem—*cemetery* ... MI-6
Saint Gertrude Cem—*cemetery* ... NM-5
Saint Gertrude Cem—*cemetery* ... PA-2
Saint Gertrude Ch—*church* ... LA-4
Saint Gertrude Convent—*church* ... LA-4
Saint Gertrude HS—*school* ... MI-6
**Saint Gertrude (Religious Institution) (Ramsay)**—*pop pl* ... LA-4
Saint Gertrude Roman Catholic Church—*hist pl* ... PA-2
Saint Gertrudes Cem—*cemetery* ... IL-6
Saint Gertrudes Cem—*cemetery* ... NJ-2
Saint Gertrudes Ch—*church* ... CT-1
Saint Gertrudes Ch—*church* ... NY-2
Saint Gertrudes Ch—*church* ... PA-2
Saint Gertrude Sch—*school* ... IL-6
Saint Gertrude Sch—*school* ... OH-6
Saint Gertrudes Sch—*school* (2) ... CA-9
Saint Gertrudes Sch—*school* ... DC-2
Saint Gertrudes Sch—*school* ... PA-2
Saint Gertrudes Sch—*school* ... TX-5
Saint Gilbert Ch—*church* ... PA-2
Saint Gilberts Sch—*school* ... IL-6
Saint Gilbert Terminal—*locale* ... MI-6
Saint Giles—*hist pl* ... MD-2
Saint Giles Ch—*church* ... ME-1
Saint Giles Ch—*church* ... NC-3
Saint Giles Ch—*church* ... VA-3
Saint Giles Hosp—*hospital* ... NY-2
Saint Giles Sch—*school* ... IL-6
Saint Gobki Cem—*cemetery* ... WI-6
Saint Gregory Barbarigo Sch—*school* ... NY-2
Saint Gregory Catholic Ch—*church* ... FL-3
Saint Gregory Cem—*cemetery* ... MN-6
Saint Gregory Cem—*cemetery* ... PA-2
Saint Gregory Ch—*church* ... FL-3
Saint Gregory Coll—*school* ... OK-5
Saint Gregory HS—*school* ... IL-6
Saint Gregory's Abbey and College—*hist pl* ... OK-5
Saint Gregorys Catholic Ch—*church* ... MS-4
Saint Gregorys Cem—*cemetery* ... KS-7
Saint Gregorys Cem—*cemetery* ... KY-4
Saint Gregorys Ch—*church* ... PA-2
Saint Gregory Sch—*school* ... AZ-5
Saint Gregory Sch—*school* ... CA-9
Saint Gregory Sch—*school* ... FL-3
Saint Gregory Sch—*school* ... MA-1
Saint Gregory Sch—*school* ... MI-6
Saint Gregory Sch—*school* ... NJ-2
Saint Gregory Sch—*school* ... TX-5
Saint Gregory Sch—*school* ... WI-6
Saint Gregory's Church—*hist pl* ... WI-6
Saint Gregorys Priory—*church* ... MI-6
Saint Gregorys Sch—*school* ... CT-1
Saint Gregorys Sch—*school* ... KS-7
Saint Gregorys Sch—*school* ... KY-4
Saint Gregorys Sch—*school* (3) ... NY-2
Saint Gregorys Sch—*school* (2) ... OH-6
Saint Gregorys Sch—*school* (2) ... PA-2
Saint Gregorys Sch—*school* ... TX-5
Saint Gregorys Seminary—*church* ... OH-6
Saint Gregory the Great Sch—*school* ... CA-9
Saint Gualberts Sch—*school* ... NY-2
Saint Hans Ch—*church* ... ND-7
Saint Harmony Ch—*church* ... AR-4
Saint Hawthornes Ch—*church* ... FL-3
Saint Hebron Cem—*cemetery* ... FL-3
Saint Hebron Ch—*church* ... FL-3
Saint Hedricks Sch—*school* ... IN-6
**Saint Hedwig**—*pop pl* ... TX-5
Saint Hedwig Cem—*cemetery* ... MI-6
Saint Hedwig Cem—*cemetery* ... WI-6
Saint Hedwigs Cem—*cemetery* ... NJ-2
Saint Hedwigs Cem—*cemetery* ... NY-2
Saint Hedwigs Ch—*church* ... NJ-2
Saint Hedwigs Ch—*church* ... NY-2
Saint Hedwig Sch—*school* ... CA-9
Saint Hedwig Sch—*school* ... MA-1
Saint Hedwig Sch—*school* (2) ... MI-6
Saint Hedwig Sch—*school* ... MN-6
Saint Hedwig Sch—*school* ... WI-6
Saint Hedwigs Elem Sch—*school* ... DE-2
Saint Hedwig's Roman Catholic Church—*hist pl* ... DE-2
Saint Hedwigs Sch—*school* ... CT-1
Saint Hedwigs Sch—*school* ... NJ-2
Saint Hedwigs Sch—*school* ... NY-2
Saint Hedwigs Sch—*school* (3) ... OH-6
Saint Hedwigs Sch—*school* (2) ... PA-2
Saint Hegwigs Cem—*cemetery* ... MN-6
*Saint Heirelda Creek* ... TX-5
*Saint Heivelda Creek* ... TX-5
Saint Heivelda Creek—*stream* ... TX-5
**Saint Helen**—*pop pl* ... MI-6
Saint Helen, Lake—*lake* ... MI-6
**Saint Helena**—*pop pl* (2) ... CA-9
**Saint Helena**—*pop pl* (2) ... MD-2
**Saint Helena**—*pop pl* ... NE-7
**Saint Helena**—*pop pl* ... NC-3
Saint Helena, Mount—*summit* ... CA-9
**Saint Helena Baltimore**—*pop pl* ... MD-2
Saint Helena Bay—*bay* ... LA-4
Saint Helena Catholic Church—*hist pl* ... CA-9
Saint Helena (CCD)—*cens area* ... CA-9
Saint Helena (CCD)—*cens area* ... SC-3
Saint Helena Cem—*cemetery* ... NE-7
Saint Helena Cem—*cemetery* ... NY-2
Saint Helena Cem—*cemetery* ... ND-7
Saint Helena Ch—*church* ... LA-4
Saint Helena Ch—*church* ... NH-1
Saint Helena Chapel—*church* ... NE-7
Saint Helena Creek—*stream* ... CA-9
Saint Helena HS—*hist pl* ... CA-9
Saint Helena Island—*island* ... CT-1
Saint Helena Island—*island* ... ME-1
Saint Helena Island—*island* ... MD-2
Saint Helena Island—*island* ... MI-6
Saint Helena Island—*island* ... NE-7
Saint Helena Island—*island* ... NY-2
Saint Helena Island—*island* ... SC-3
**Saint Helena Parish**—*pop pl* ... LA-4
Saint Helena Public Library—*hist pl* ... CA-9
*Saint Helena Range* ... CA-9
Saint Helena Sanitarium—*hospital* ... CA-9
Saint Helenas Catholic Ch—*church* ... DE-2
Saint Helenas Ch—*church* ... SC-3
Saint Helena Sch—*school* ... LA-4
Saint Helena Sch—*school* ... MD-2
Saint Helena Sch—*school* ... PA-2
Saint Helena Sch—*school* ... SC-3
Saint Helenas Chapel—*church* ... MA-1
Saint Helena Shoal—*bar* ... MI-6
Saint Helena Sound—*bay* ... SC-3
Saint Helenas Sch—*school* ... DE-2
Saint Helenas Sch—*school* ... PA-2

Saint Joseph Ch—church OK-5
Saint Joseph Ch—church (3) PA-2
Saint Joseph Ch—church (3) SC-3
Saint Joseph Ch—church (3) SD-7
Saint Joseph Ch—church (9) TX-5
Saint Joseph Ch—church VT-1
Saint Joseph Ch—church WA-9
Saint Joseph Ch—church (4) WI-6
Saint Joseph Chapel—church IL-6
Saint Joseph Chapel—church NY-2
Saint Joseph Chapel—church TX-5
Saint Joseph Church KS-7
Saint Joseph Church—hist pl KY-4
Saint Joseph Church—hist pl TN-4
Saint Joseph Church-Convent of the Most Holy Sacrament Complex—hist pl LA-4
Saint Joseph City Hall—building TN-4
Saint Joseph City Park—park TN-4
Saint Joseph Coll—school NM-5
Saint Joseph Coll—school WI-6
Saint Joseph Convent—church (2) MO-7
Saint Joseph Convent—church WI-6
Saint Joseph Convent and Acad—hist pl OK-5
Saint Joseph Coulee—valley WI-6
**Saint Joseph County**—pop pl IN-6
**Saint Joseph (County)**—pop pl MI-6
Saint Joseph Creek—stream FL-3
Saint Joseph Creek—stream IA-7
Saint Joseph Creek—stream MI-6
Saint Joseph Elem Sch—school TN-4
Saint Joseph Elmina Cem—cemetery TX-5
Saint Joseph First Baptist Ch—church TN-4
Saint Joseph Gonzagas Sch—school PA-2
Saint Joseph Grade Sch—school KS-7
Saint Joseph Hall—locale IL-6
Saint Joseph Hall HS—school PA-2
**Saint Joseph Hill**—pop pl IN-6
Saint Joseph Hill—summit IN-6
Saint Joseph Hist Dist—hist pl LA-4
Saint Joseph (historical)—locale SD-7
Saint Joseph Home—building IL-6
Saint Joseph Home—building LA-4
Saint Joseph Home—building UT-8
Saint Joseph Home for Aged—building NY-2
Saint Joseph Home for Girls—building TX-5
Saint Joseph Hosp—hospital AZ-5
Saint Joseph Hosp—hospital AR-4
Saint Joseph Hosp—hospital CA-9
Saint Joseph Hosp—hospital CO-8
Saint Joseph Hosp—hospital FL-3
Saint Joseph Hosp—hospital (3) IL-6
Saint Joseph Hosp—hospital (2) KS-7
Saint Joseph Hosp—hospital LA-4
Saint Joseph Hosp—hospital ME-1
Saint Joseph Hosp—hospital (4) MI-6
Saint Joseph Hosp—hospital (2) MO-7
Saint Joseph Hosp—hospital NE-7
Saint Joseph Hosp—hospital NC-3
Saint Joseph Hosp—hospital ND-7
Saint Joseph Hosp—hospital PA-2
Saint Joseph Hosp—hospital SD-7
Saint Joseph Hosp—hospital (2) TX-5
Saint Joseph Hosp—hospital WA-9
Saint Joseph Hosp—hospital (4) WI-6
Saint Joseph Hosp and Health Care Center PA-2
Saint Joseph Hospital Airp—airport TN-4
Saint Joseph Hospital Campus Heliport—airport WA-9
Saint Joseph Hospital Heliport—airport WA-9
Saint Joseph Hosp of Port Charlotte—hospital FL-3
Saint Joseph HS—school AR-4
Saint Joseph HS—school CO-8
Saint Joseph HS—school (2) IL-6
Saint Joseph HS—school IN-6
Saint Joseph HS—school KS-7
Saint Joseph HS—school MI-6
Saint Joseph HS—school MS-4
Saint Joseph HS—school OH-6
Saint Joseph HS—school (2) TX-5
Saint Joseph HS—school UT-8
Saint Joseph Industrial Sch—school DE-2
Saint Josephinum HS—school IL-6
Saint Joseph Island TX-5
Saint Joseph Island—island AK-9
Saint Joseph Lake ID-8
Saint Joseph Lake—lake WI-6
Saint Joseph Landing (historical)—locale MS-4
Saint Joseph Lead Mines (historical)—mine MO-7
Saint Joseph Life Flight Helipad Heliport—airport MO-7
Saint Joseph Military Acad—school IL-6
Saint Joseph Minor Seminary—school NH-1
Saint Joseph Mission—church ID-8
Saint Joseph Mission—church WA-9
Saint Joseph Missionary Baptist Ch—church AL-4
Saint Joseph Missionary Baptist Ch—church FL-3
Saint Joseph Missionary Baptist Church MS-4
Saint Joseph Mountains ID-8
Saint Joseph Novitiate—church IN-6
Saint Joseph Novitiate—church MI-6
Saint Joseph Novitiate—church VT-1
Saint Joseph of the Maumee IN-6
Saint Joseph of the Valley Ch—church KS-7
Saint Joseph Oil Field—oilfield TX-5
Saint Joseph on-the-Brandywine—church DE-2
Saint Joseph Orphanage—building WI-6
Saint Joseph Orphan Home—building MT-8
Saint Joseph Parish Complex—hist pl NE-7
Saint Joseph Park—park IL-6
Saint Joseph Park—park MI-6
Saint Joseph Peak—summit MT-8
Saint Joseph Peninsula—bar FL-3
Saint Joseph Peninsula State Park—park FL-3
Saint Joseph Plantation—locale LA-4
Saint Joseph Point—cape FL-3
Saint Joseph Point—cape MS-4
Saint Joseph Post Office—building TN-4
Saint Joseph Proto Cathedral—hist pl KY-4
Saint Joseph Ridge—ridge WI-6
Saint Joseph River—stream (2) IN-6
Saint Joseph River—stream (2) MI-6
Saint Joseph River—stream OH-6
Saint Joseph River Dam—dam IN-6
Saint Joseph Roman Catholic Ch—church IN-6
Saint Joseph Roman Catholic Ch—church KS-7
Saint Joseph Roman Catholic Church—hist pl KY-4
Saint Joseph Roman Catholic Church and Rectory—hist pl NY-2
saint Joseph Run OH-6
**Saint Josephs**—pop pl FL-3
**Saint Josephs**—pop pl NY-2
Saint Josephs Abbey—church MA-1
Saint Josephs Acad—school AZ-5
Saint Josephs Acad—school (2) FL-3
Saint Josephs Acad—school GA-3
Saint Josephs Acad—school (2) OH-6
Saint Josephs Acad—school PA-2
Saint Josephs Acad—school (2) TX-5
Saint Josephs Acad—school WI-6
Saint Joseph's African Methodist Episcopal Church—hist pl NC-3
Saint Joseph Salesian Juniorate school CA-9
Saint Josephs and Highland Cem—cemetery KS-7
Saint Josephs Baptist Ch—church AL-4
Saint Joseph's Basilica—hist pl CA-9
Saint Josephs Bay FL-3
Saint Josephs Boys Sch—school MA-1
Saint Josephs Carrollton Manor—church MD-2
Saint Josephs Cathedral—church NY-2
Saint Joseph's Cathedral—hist pl OK-5
Saint Josephs Catholic Cemetery SD-7
Saint Josephs Catholic Ch AL-4
Saint Josephs Catholic Ch—church AL-4
Saint Josephs Catholic Ch—church (2) DE-2
Saint Josephs Catholic Ch—church (4) FL-3
Saint Josephs Catholic Ch—church (4) MS-4
Saint Joseph's Catholic Ch—church MT-8
Saint Josephs Catholic Ch—church PA-2
Saint Josephs Catholic Ch—church UT-8
Saint Joseph's Catholic Church—hist pl FL-3
Saint Joseph's Catholic Church—hist pl GA-3
Saint Joseph's Catholic Church—hist pl KS-7
Saint Joseph's Catholic Church—hist pl NC-3
Saint Joseph's Catholic Church—hist pl OH-6
Saint Joseph's Catholic Church—hist pl OK-5
Saint Joseph's Catholic Church and Cemetery—hist pl KY-4
Saint Joseph's Catholic Church Complex—hist pl WI-6
Saint Josephs Catholic Sch—school AZ-5
Saint Josephs Catholic Sch—school FL-3
Saint Josephs Cem—cemetery (2) AR-4
Saint Josephs Cem—cemetery (2) CA-9
Saint Josephs Cem—cemetery (3) CT-1
Saint Josephs Cem—cemetery (9) IL-6
Saint Josephs Cem—cemetery (12) IN-6
Saint Josephs Cem—cemetery (25) IA-7
Saint Josephs Cem—cemetery (4) KS-7
Saint Josephs Cem—cemetery (4) KY-4
Saint Josephs Cem—cemetery LA-4
Saint Josephs Cem—cemetery (4) ME-1
Saint Josephs Cem—cemetery MD-2
Saint Josephs Cem—cemetery (17) MA-1
Saint Josephs Cem—cemetery (6) MI-6
Saint Josephs Cem—cemetery (5) MN-6
Saint Josephs Cem—cemetery (3) MO-7
Saint Josephs Cem—cemetery (8) NE-7
Saint Josephs Cem—cemetery NH-1
Saint Josephs Cem—cemetery (3) NJ-2
Saint Josephs Cem—cemetery NM-5
Saint Josephs Cem—cemetery (27) NY-2
Saint Josephs Cem—cemetery (2) ND-7
Saint Josephs Cem—cemetery (14) OH-6
Saint Josephs Cem—cemetery (4) OK-5
Saint Josephs Cem—cemetery (23) PA-2
Saint Josephs Cem—cemetery (3) SD-7
Saint Josephs Cem—cemetery (2) TX-5
Saint Josephs Cem—cemetery VT-1
Saint Josephs Cem—cemetery WA-9
Saint Josephs Cem—cemetery (2) WV-2
Saint Josephs Cem—cemetery (9) WI-6
Saint Josephs Ch AL-4
Saint Josephs Ch MS-4
Saint Josephs Ch PA-2
Saint Josephs Ch TX-5
Saint Josephs Ch—church (3) AL-4
Saint Josephs Ch—church CO-8
Saint Josephs Ch—church (2) CT-1
Saint Josephs Ch—church (3) FL-3
Saint Josephs Ch—church (2) GA-3
Saint Josephs Ch—church (6) IN-6
Saint Josephs Ch—church (2) IA-7
Saint Josephs Ch—church KS-7
Saint Josephs Ch—church (3) LA-4
Saint Josephs Ch—church ME-1
Saint Josephs Ch—church (3) MD-2
Saint Josephs Ch—church MA-1
Saint Josephs Ch—church (4) MI-6
Saint Josephs Ch—church (2) MN-6
Saint Josephs Ch—church (2) MS-4
Saint Josephs Ch—church MO-7
Saint Josephs Ch—church MT-8
Saint Josephs Ch—church NE-7
Saint Josephs Ch—church (4) NJ-2
Saint Josephs Ch—church (12) NY-2
Saint Josephs Ch—church (5) NC-3
Saint Josephs Ch—church ND-7
Saint Josephs Ch—church OH-6
Saint Josephs Ch—church (14) PA-2
Saint Josephs Ch—church SC-3
Saint Josephs Ch—church (2) SD-7
Saint Josephs Ch—church TX-5
Saint Josephs Ch—church VT-1
Saint Josephs Ch—church VA-3
Saint Josephs Ch—church WV-2
Saint Josephs Ch—church WI-6
Saint Josephs Ch—church FM-9
Saint Josephs Ch—church VI-3
Saint Josephs Sch—school AL-4
Saint Josephs Sch—school (2) AR-4
Saint Josephs Sch—school (10) CA-9
Saint Josephs Sch—school CO-8
Saint Josephs Sch—school CT-1
Saint Josephs Sch—school (4) FL-3
Saint Josephs Sch—school GA-3
Saint Josephs Sch—school ID-8
Saint Josephs Sch—school (16) IL-6
Saint Josephs Sch—school (5) IN-6
Saint Josephs Sch—school (3) IA-7
Saint Josephs Sch—school (6) KS-7
Saint Josephs Sch—school (4) LA-4
Saint Josephs Sch—school MD-2
Saint Josephs Sch—school (2) MA-1
Saint Joseph Sch—school (14) MI-6
Saint Joseph Sch—school (4) MN-6
Saint Joseph Sch—school MS-4
Saint Joseph Sch—school (4) MO-7
Saint Joseph Sch—school (2) MT-8
Saint Joseph Sch—school (3) NE-7
Saint Joseph Sch—school NV-8
Saint Joseph Sch—school NH-1
Saint Joseph Sch—school (2) NJ-2
Saint Joseph Sch—school NY-2
Saint Joseph Sch—school (3) ND-7
Saint Joseph Sch—school (2) OH-6
Saint Joseph Sch—school (5) OK-5
Saint Joseph Sch—school OR-9
Saint Joseph Sch—school (4) PA-2
Saint Joseph Sch—school (2) SD-7
Saint Joseph Sch—school TN-4
Saint Joseph Sch—school (9) TX-5
Saint Joseph Sch—school WA-9
Saint Joseph Sch—school (10) WI-6
Saint Joseph Sch—school WY-8
Saint Joseph Sch (abandoned)—school PA-2
Saint Josephs Chapel—church AL-4
Saint Josephs Chapel—church OH-6
Saint Joseph's Chapel—hist pl WI-6
Saint Josephs Ch (historical)—church AL-4
Saint Joseph Sch (historical)—school AL-4
Saint Joseph Sch (historical)—school MS-4
Saint Joseph's Church—hist pl DE-2
Saint Joseph's Church—hist pl NY-2
Saint Joseph's Church—hist pl TX-5
Saint Joseph's Church and Complex—hist pl CA-9
Saint Joseph's Church Buildings—hist pl FL-3
Saint Josephs Church Cem—cemetery UT-8
Saint Joseph's Co-Cathedral and Rectory—hist pl LA-4
Saint Josephs Coll—school CT-1
Saint Josephs Coll—school IN-6
Saint Josephs Coll—school ME-1
Saint Josephs Coll—school MD-2
Saint Josephs College PA-2
Saint Joseph's College and Mother Seton Shrine—hist pl MD-2
Saint Josephs Collegiate Institute—school NY-2
Saint Josephs Coll for Women—school NY-2
Saint Josephs Convent—church ME-1
Saint Josephs Convent—church MI-6
Saint Josephs Convent—school PA-2
Saint Josephs Convent of Mercy—church MO-7
Saint Josephs Convent of Mercy—school MO-7
Saint Joseph's District—hist pl KY-4
Saint Joseph Seminary—church IL-6
Saint Joseph Seminary—school CA-9
Saint Joseph Seminary—school (2) IL-6
Saint Josephs Seminary—school MI-6
Saint Josephs Episcopal Ch—church FL-3
Saint Joseph's Episcopal Church—hist pl NC-3
Saint Josephs Hall—building NY-2
Saint Josephs Hall—church NY-2
**Saint Joseph's (Health Resort)**—pop pl IL-6
Saint Josephs Hill—summit CA-9
Saint Josephs Hill Acad—school NY-2
Saint Josephs Hill Infirmary—hospital MO-7
Saint Josephs Home—building PA-2
Saint Joseph's Home—hist pl AR-4
Saint Josephs Home—other DC-2
Saint Josephs Home For Childern—building PA-2
Saint Josephs Hosp NC-3
Saint Joseph's Hosp—hist pl CA-9
Saint Josephs Hosp—hospital AZ-5
Saint Josephs Hosp—hospital (2) CA-9
Saint Josephs Hosp—hospital FL-3
Saint Josephs Hosp—hospital (2) GA-3
Saint Josephs Hosp—hospital (3) IL-6
Saint Josephs Hosp—hospital (4) IN-6
Saint Josephs Hosp—hospital IA-7
Saint Josephs Hosp—hospital KY-4
Saint Josephs Hosp—hospital MD-2
Saint Josephs Hosp—hospital MA-1
Saint Josephs Hosp—hospital (2) MN-6
Saint Josephs Hosp—hospital MO-7
Saint Josephs Hosp—hospital NJ-2
Saint Josephs Hosp—hospital (4) NY-2
Saint Josephs Hosp—hospital NC-3
Saint Josephs Hosp—hospital ND-7
Saint Josephs Hosp—hospital OH-6
Saint Josephs Hosp—hospital (4) PA-2
Saint Josephs Hosp—hospital TX-5
Saint Josephs Hosp—hospital (2) WV-2
Saint Josephs Hosp—hospital WI-6
Saint Josephs Hospital Helistop—airport AZ-5
Saint Josephs HS IN-6
Saint Josephs HS—school CT-1
Saint Josephs HS—school HI-9
Saint Josephs HS—school (2) MA-1
Saint Josephs HS—school MO-7
Saint Josephs HS—school NJ-2
Saint Josephs HS—school NY-2
Saint Josephs HS—school OH-6
Saint Josephs HS—school PA-2
Saint Josephs Indian Sch—school SD-7
Saint Josephs (Infirmary)—church GA-3
Saint Josephs Infirmary—hospital KY-4
Saint Josephs Institute—school NY-2
Saint Josephs Island TX-5
Saint Josephs Island (historical)—island MS-4
Saint Josephs Key FL-3
Saint Josephs Lake—lake IN-6
Saint Josephs Lake—reservoir NY-2
Saint Josephs Lighthouse (historical)—locale MS-4
Saint Josephs Manor—building CT-1
Saint Josephs Mission—church GA-3
Saint Joseph's Mission—hist pl WA-9
Saint Josephs Mission—locale NM-5
Saint Josephs Monastery—church MD-2
Saint Josephs New Catholic Cem—cemetery PA-2
Saint Josephs Novitiate—church MA-1
Saint Josephs Novitiate—school MA-1
Saint Josephs Novitiate—school NY-2
Saint Josephs of the Lake IN-6
Saint Joseph's on the Brandywine—hist pl DE-2
Saint Josephs Orphanage—building AR-4
Saint Josephs Orphanage—building (2) KY-4
Saint Josephs Orphanage—building MN-6
Saint Josephs Orphanage—building OH-6
Saint Josephs Orphanage—locale WY-8
Saint Josephs Orphans Home—building OH-6
Saint Joseph Sound—bay FL-3
Saint Joseph Spit FL-3
**Saint Joseph 53079**—pop pl WI-6
Saint Joseph **54082**—post sta WI-6
Saint Josephs Point FL-3
Saint Josephs Preparatory Sch—school KY-4
Saint Joseph Springs—spring PA-2
Saint Josephs Priory—church OH-6
Saint Josephs Protectorate—other PA-2
Saint Josephs Retreat—church AL-4
Saint Josephs River IN-6
Saint Joseph's Roman Catholic Church—hist pl CA-9
Saint Joseph's Roman Catholic Church—hist pl WI-6
Saint Joseph's Roman Catholic Church Rectory and Sch—hist pl NJ-2
Saint Josephs Rsvr—reservoir AZ-5
Saint Josephs Sanatarium—other NY-2
Saint Josephs Sch IN-6
Saint Joseph's Sch—hist pl LA-4
Saint Josephs Sch—school (3) AL-4
Saint Josephs Sch—school AZ-5
Saint Josephs Sch—school AR-4
Saint Josephs Sch—school (6) CA-9
Saint Josephs Sch—school CO-8
Saint Josephs Sch—school (10) CT-1
Saint Josephs Sch—school DE-2
Saint Josephs Sch—school (5) FL-3
Saint Josephs Sch—school GA-3
Saint Josephs Sch—school HI-9
Saint Josephs Sch—school ID-8
Saint Josephs Sch—school (3) IL-6
Saint Josephs Sch—school (6) IN-6
Saint Josephs Sch—school (2) IA-7
Saint Josephs Sch—school KS-7
Saint Josephs Sch—school (3) KY-4
Saint Josephs Sch—school (2) LA-4
Saint Josephs Sch—school (2) MD-2
Saint Josephs Sch—school (15) MA-1
Saint Josephs Sch—school (2) MI-6
Saint Josephs Sch—school (3) MN-6
Saint Josephs Sch—school (2) MS-4
Saint Josephs Sch—school NE-7
Saint Josephs Sch—school (4) NH-1
Saint Josephs Sch—school (11) NJ-2
Saint Josephs Sch—school (25) NY-2
Saint Josephs Sch—school (16) OH-6
Saint Josephs Sch—school (17) PA-2
Saint Josephs Sch—school (2) TN-4
Saint Josephs Sch—school (5) TX-5
Saint Josephs Sch—school UT-8
Saint Josephs Sch—school (2) VA-3
Saint Josephs Sch—school (3) WA-9
Saint Josephs Sch—school (3) WV-2
Saint Josephs Sch—school (6) WI-6
Saint Josephs Sch for Girls—school PA-2
Saint Josephs Sch (historical)—school (2) AL-4
Saint Josephs Sch (historical)—school MS-4
Saint Josephs Seminary—school AL-4
Saint Josephs Seminary—school DC-2
Saint Josephs Seminary—school IL-6
Saint Josephs Seminary—school (2) NY-2
Saint Josephs Seminary—school WV-2
Saint Josephs Shrine—church CA-9
Saint Josephs Shrine—church NJ-2
**Saint Josephs Shrine**—pop pl IN-6
Saint Josephs Sound FL-3
**Saint Josephs (St. Josephs Sanatarium)**—pop pl NY-2
Saint Joseph State Park FL-3
Saint Josephs the Worker Sch—school NY-2
Saint Josephs Univ—school PA-2
Saint Josephs Ursuline Acad—school NY-2
Saint Josephs Villa—building NY-2
Saint Josephs Villa—church NJ-2
Saint Josephs Villa—church NY-2
**Saint Josephs Villa**—pop pl VA-3
Saint Josephs Village—locale NJ-2
Saint Josephs Wayside Shrine—church NY-2
Saint Joseph the Worker—church MA-1
Saint Joseph The Worker Catholic Ch—church UT-8
Saint Joseph the Worker Sch—school IN-6
Saint Joseph the Worker Sch—school MN-6
Saint Joseph the Worker Sch—school NY-2
**Saint Joseph (Town of)**—pop pl WI-6
Saint Joseph Township—civil ND-7
Saint Joseph Township (historical)—civil ND-7
Saint Joseph (Township of)—civ div IL-6
Saint Joseph (Township of)—civ div MI-6
Saint Joseph (Township of)—civ div OH-6
**Saint Joseph (Township of)**—pop pl IN-6
**Saint Joseph (Township of)**—pop pl (2) MN-6
Saint Joseph United Methodist Ch—church FL-3
Saint Joseph United Methodist Ch—church TN-4
Saint Joseph Ursuline Novitiate—church MO-7
Saint Joseph Valley Memorial Park—park IN-6
Saint Joseph Wash AZ-5
Saint Joseph Youth Camp—locale AZ-5
**Saint Joseph Youth Camp**—pop pl AZ-5
Saint Joseph 1930 Hosp—hist pl NM-5
Saint Joshaphat Sch—school MI-6
Saint Joy—locale VA-3
Saint Joys Ch—church VA-3
Saint Jude, Lake—lake MI-6
Saint Jude Acad—school CA-9
**Saint Jude Acres (subdivision)**—pop pl MO-7
Saint Jude at Assumption Catholic Church-Melkite Rite—church FL-3
Saint Jude Catholic Ch—church AL-4
Saint Jude Catholic Ch—church FL-3
Saint Jude Catholic Ch—church MS-4
Saint Jude Catholic Ch—church TN-4
Saint Jude Catholic School TN-4
Saint Jude Ch—church FL-3
Saint Jude Ch—church LA-4
Saint Jude Ch—church MI-6
Saint Jude Ch—church MO-7
Saint Jude Ch—church NC-3
Saint Jude Ch—church TX-5
Saint Jude Chapel—church MN-6
Saint Jude Deliverance Center—church IN-6
Saint Jude Elem Sch—school (2) IN-6
Saint Jude Golf Course PA-2
Saint Jude Hosp—hospital CA-9
Saint Jude Hosp—hospital TX-5
Saint Jude Hospital AL-4
Saint Jude Institution—school AL-4
Saint Jude Manor Nursing Home—building FL-3
Saint Jude Roman Catholic Ch—church IN-6
Saint Jude Roman Catholic Ch—church KS-7
Saint Judes Catholic Cemetery ND-7
Saint Judes Cem—cemetery IL-6
Saint Judes Cem—cemetery MO-7
Saint Judes Ch—church CT-1
Saint Judes Ch—church MA-1
Saint Judes Ch—church (2) NY-2
Saint Judes Ch—church PA-2
Saint Jude Sch—school FL-3
Saint Jude Sch—school (2) IL-6
Saint Jude Sch—school LA-4
Saint Jude Sch—school (2) MI-6
Saint Jude Sch—school NY-2
Saint Jude Sch—school SC-3
Saint Jude Sch—school TN-4
Saint Jude Sch—school WI-6
Saint Judes Chapel—church MA-1
Saint Judes Chapel—church NY-2
Saint Jude's Episcopal Church—hist pl ME-1
Saint Judes Nursing Home—hospital TX-5
Saint Jude Spring—spring CO-8
Saint Judes Sch IN-6
Saint Judes Sch—school IN-6
Saint Judes Sch—school MD-2
Saint Judes Sch—school MA-1
Saint Judes Sch—school NY-2
Saint Judes Sch—school (4) OH-6
Saint Judes Sch—school TX-5
Saint Judes Sch—school WI-6
Saint Judes Seminary—school IL-6
Saint Jude Thaddeus Ch—church FL-3
Saint Jude the Apostle Sch—school IL-6
Saint Jude Well—well AZ-5
Saint Jules Ch—church LA-4
Saint Jules Ch—church VA-3
Saint Julia Cem—cemetery SD-7
Saint Julian, Bayou—gut LA-4
Saint Juliana Ch—church GA-3
Saint Juliana Ch—church LA-4
Saint Julianas Catholic Ch—church FL-3
Saint Julianas Cem—cemetery PA-2
Saint Julianas Ch—church PA-2
Saint Juliana Sch—school FL-3
Saint Juliana Sch—school IL-6
Saint Julian Creek—stream VA-3
Saint Julian Eymard Sch—school LA-4
Saint Julian Mine—mine MT-8
Saint Julians Creek VA-3
Saint Julians Sch—school KY-4
Saint Julien—hist pl VA-3
Saint Julien Chapel—church LA-4
Saint Julien House—hist pl LA-4
Saint Just—locale VA-3
**Saint Just**—pop pl (2) PR-3
Saint Just—post sta PR-3
Saint Justens Sch—school CA-9
Saint Justin Martyr Catholic Ch—church FL-3
Saint Justin Martyr Sch—school CA-9
Saint Justin Martyr Sch—school IL-6
Saint Justins Sch—school CT-1
Saint Justins Sch—school MI-6
Saint Katharine Sch—school IA-7
Saint Katharines Convent—church MD-2
Saint Katherine Cem—cemetery KS-7
Saint Katherine Ch—church MI-6
Saint Katherine Ch—church WI-6
Saint Katherine Day School PA-2
Saint Katherines Cem—cemetery ND-7
Saint Katherines Ch—church MD-2
Saint Katherines Island MD-2
Saint Katherines Sch—school (2) PA-2
Saint Kathryn Cem—cemetery MN-6
Saint Kets Ch—church NC-3
Saint Kevin Catholic Sch—school FL-3
Saint Kevin Ch—church FL-3
Saint Kevin Gulch—valley CO-8
Saint Kevin Lake—lake CO-8
Saint Kevin Sch—school FL-3
Saint Kevin Sch—school MN-6
Saint Kevin Sch—school PA-2
Saint Kevin Shaft—mine CO-8
Saint Kevins Sch—school IL-6
Saint Kevins Sch—school MI-6
Saint Kevins Sch—school NY-2
Saint Kierahs Cem—cemetery IA-7
Saint Kieran Cem—cemetery NH-1
Saint Kieran Ch—church MI-6
Saint Kierans Ch—church FL-3
Saint Kieran Sch—school IL-6
Saint Kilian—locale MN-6
**Saint Kilian**—pop pl WI-6
Saint Kilian Ch—church (2) WI-6
Saint Kilians Sch—school MA-1
Saint Kilians Sch—school NY-2
Saint Killian MN-6
Saint Killian WI-6
**Saint Killian**—pop pl MN-6
Saint Killian Cem—cemetery WI-6
Saint Killian Ch—church WI-6
Saint Killian Sch—school IL-6
Saint Killian Sch—school WI-6
Saint Killians Creek WI-6
Saint Kolala Ch MS-4
Saint Labre Mission—church MT-8
Saint Ladislaus Ch—church PA-2
Saint Ladislaus HS—school MI-6
Saint Ladislaus Sch—school IL-6
Saint Ladislaus Sch—school NY-2
Saint Ladislaus Sch—school (3) OH-6
Saint Ladislaus Sch—school PA-2
Saint Lake Ch—church AR-4
Saint Lamberts Cem—cemetery NH-1
Saint Lambert Sch—school IL-6
Saint Lambert Sch—school SD-7
**Saint Landry**—pop pl LA-4
Saint Landry Catholic Church—hist pl LA-4
Saint Landry Ch—church LA-4
**Saint Landry Parish**—pop pl LA-4
Saint Lasalle Sch—school CA-9
Saint Laurence HS—school IL-6
Saint Laurence Sch—school TX-5
Saint Laurent Creek—stream MO-7
Saint Laurents Cem—cemetery CT-1
Saint Lawrance Ch—church FL-3
Saint Lawrance Sch—school FL-3
Saint Lawrence MN-6
Saint Lawrence—locale TX-5
**Saint Lawrence**—pop pl NY-2
**Saint Lawrence**—pop pl (2) PA-2
**Saint Lawrence**—pop pl SD-7
**Saint Lawrence**—pop pl WI-6
Saint Lawrence, Lake—reservoir NY-2
Saint Lawrence, Patrick, House—hist pl NC-3
Saint Lawrence African Methodist Episcopal Ch—church FL-3
Saint Lawrence Basin—basin WY-8
Saint Lawrence Bluff—cliff WI-6
Saint Lawrence Borough—civil PA-2
Saint Lawrence Catholic Ch—church FL-3
Saint Lawrence Catholic Ch—church UT-8
Saint Lawrence Cem—cemetery CT-1
Saint Lawrence Cem—cemetery (3) IL-6
Saint Lawrence Cem—cemetery IA-7
Saint Lawrence Cem—cemetery (3) KS-7
Saint Lawrence Cem—cemetery (2) MI-6
Saint Lawrence Cem—cemetery (4) MN-6
Saint Lawrence Cem—cemetery NE-7
Saint Lawrence Cem—cemetery (3) NY-2
Saint Lawrence Cem—cemetery ND-7
Saint Lawrence Cem—cemetery (2) OH-6
Saint Lawrence Cem—cemetery SC-3
Saint Lawrence Cem—cemetery (2) SD-7
Saint Lawrence Cem—cemetery WI-6
Saint Lawrence Central Sch—school NY-2
Saint Lawrence Ch—church IA-7
Saint Lawrence Ch—church LA-4
Saint Lawrence Ch—church MI-6
Saint Lawrence Ch—church MN-6
Saint Lawrence Ch—church MS-4
Saint Lawrence Ch—church OH-6
Saint Lawrence Ch—church PA-2
Saint Lawrence Ch—church (2) WI-6
Saint Lawrence Chapel—church MD-2
Saint Lawrence Convent—church IN-6
**Saint Lawrence (County)**—pop pl NY-2
Saint Lawrence Creek WI-6
Saint Lawrence Creek—stream MT-8
Saint Lawrence Creek—stream WY-8
Saint Lawrence Elem Sch—school IN-6
Saint Lawrence HS—school CA-9
Saint Lawrence Island—island AK-9
Saint Lawrence Lookout Tower—tower PA-2
Saint Lawrence Mine—mine MT-8
Saint Lawrence Mine—mine NV-8
Saint Lawrence Neck—cape MD-2
Saint Lawrence-O'Toole Sch—school IL-6
**Saint Lawrence Park**—pop pl NY-2
Saint Lawrence Ranger Station—locale WY-8
Saint Lawrence Ridge—ridge WY-8
Saint Lawrence River—stream NY-2
Saint Lawrence Roman Catholic Ch—church IN-6
Saint Lawrences Ch—church NY-2
Saint Lawrence Sch—school CA-9
Saint Lawrence Sch—school FL-3
Saint Lawrence Sch—school (3) IL-6
Saint Lawrence Sch—school IN-6
Saint Lawrence Sch—school (2) KY-4
Saint Lawrence Sch—school MA-1
Saint Lawrence Sch—school MI-6
Saint Lawrence Sch—school NJ-2
Saint Lawrence Sch—school (2) NY-2
Saint Lawrence Sch—school (3) OH-6
Saint Lawrence Sch—school OR-9
Saint Lawrence Sch—school (2) PA-2
Saint Lawrence Sch—school SC-3
Saint Lawrence Sch—school SD-7
Saint Lawrence Sch—school TN-4
Saint Lawrence Sch—school TX-5
Saint Lawrence Sch—school WI-6
Saint Lawrence Sch—school WY-8
Saint Lawrence Seaway—channel NY-2
Saint Lawrence Seminary—church NY-2
Saint Lawrence Seminary—school WI-6
Saint Lawrence State For—forest NY-2
Saint Lawrence State For Number 10—forest NY-2
Saint Lawrence State For Number 12—forest NY-2
Saint Lawrence State For Number 15—forest NY-2
Saint Lawrence State For Number 2—forest NY-2
Saint Lawrence State For Number 23—forest NY-2
Saint Lawrence State For Number 28—forest NY-2
Saint Lawrence State For Number 31—forest NY-2
Saint Lawrence State For Number 6—forest NY-2
Saint Lawrence State For Number 8—forest NY-2
Saint Lawrence State Hosp—hospital NY-2
Saint Lawrence State Park—park NY-2
**Saint Lawrence Terrace**—pop pl CA-9
Saint Lawrence the Martyr Sch—school LA-4
**Saint Lawrence (Town of)**—pop pl WI-6
**Saint Lawrence Township**—pop pl SD-7
Saint Lawrence (Township of)—civ div MN-6
Saint Lawrence Univ—school NY-2
Saint Lawrence University-Old Campus Hist Dist—hist pl NY-2
Saint Lazaria Islands—area AK-9
Saint Lazaria Natl Wildlife Ref—park AK-9
Saint Lazarus Nursery/Kindergarten Sch—school FL-3
Saint Lazarus Sch—school MA-1
Saint Ledger Island—island MI-6
Saint Leger—locale MO-7
Saint Lena Ch—church LA-4
Saint Lena Sch—school AR-4
**Saint Leo**—pop pl FL-3
**Saint Leo**—pop pl KS-7
**Saint Leo**—pop pl MN-6
**Saint Leo**—pop pl WV-2
Saint Leo Catholic Ch—church AL-4
Saint Leo Cem—cemetery MA-1
Saint Leo Cem—cemetery (2) MN-6
Saint Leo Cem—cemetery NY-2
Saint Leo Cem—cemetery ND-7
Saint Leo Cem—cemetery OK-5

Saint Leo Cem—cemetery SD-7
Saint Leo Ch—church IL-6
Saint Leo Ch—church (2) LA-4
Saint Leo Ch—church MO-7
Saint Leo Ch—church NY-2
Saint Leo Coll—school FL-3
Saint Leo College Library—building FL-3
**Saint Leon**—pop pl ID-8
**Saint Leon**—pop pl IN-6
Saint Leonard—locale PA-2
**Saint Leonard**—pop pl MD-2
Saint Leonard Creek—stream MD-2
Saint Leonards Cem—cemetery NE-7
Saint Leonards Ch—church MT-8
Saint Leonards Ch—church TX-5
Saint Leonard Sch—school IL-6
Saint Leonard Sch—school WI-6
Saint Leonards Coll—school OH-6
Saint Leonards Sch—school KY-4
Saint Leonards Sch—school MI-6
Saint Leonards Sch—school NY-2
Saint Leonards Sch—school PA-2
Saint Leon Grange—locale ID-8
Saint Leon Sch—school ID-8
Saint Leos Cem—cemetery NE-7
Saint Leos Cem—cemetery PA-2
Saint Leos Cem—cemetery (2) WI-6
Saint Leos Ch—church MI-6
Saint Leos Ch—church NY-2
Saint Leos Ch—church VA-3
Saint Leo Sch—school CA-9
Saint Leo Sch—school IL-6
Saint Leo Sch—school KS-7
Saint Leo Sch—school MI-6
Saint Leo Sch—school MN-6
Saint Leo Sch—school (2) OH-6
Saint Leo Sch—school PA-2
Saint Leo Sch—school TX-5
Saint Leo Sch—school WA-9
Saint Leo Sch—school WI-6
Saint Leo's Church—hist pl MD-2
Saint Leos Hosp—hospital NC-3
Saint Leos Sch—school CA-9
Saint Leos Sch—school MA-1
Saint Leos Sch—school (2) NJ-2
Saint Leos Sch—school (2) NY-2
Saint Leos Sch—school (3) PA-2
Saint Leos Sch—school VA-3
Saint Leo State Wildlife Mngmt Areas—park MN-6
Saint Leo Tower—tower FL-3
Saint Lewis FL-3
**Saint Lewis**—pop pl NC-3
Saint Liberty Ch—church LA-4
Saint Liborives Cemetery SD-7
**Saint Libory**—pop pl (2) IL-6
**Saint Libory**—pop pl NE-7
Saint Liguori Cem—cemetery MN-6
Saint Linus Sch—school CA-9
Saint Linus Sch—school IL-6
Saint Linus Sch—school MI-6
Saint Lonis Univ (School of Medicine)—school MO-7
Saint Lorenz Ch—church MI-6
Saint Lorenzo Ch—church NM-5
Saint Lorenz Sch—school MI-6
Saint Louis IN-6
Saint Louis KS-7
Saint Louis—locale CA-9
Saint Louis—locale VA-3
**Saint Louis**—pop pl CA-9
**Saint Louis**—pop pl GA-3
**Saint Louis**—pop pl (2) LA-4
**Saint Louis**—pop pl MI-6
**Saint Louis**—pop pl MO-7
**Saint Louis**—pop pl OK-5
**Saint Louis**—pop pl (2) OR-9
**Saint Louis**—pop pl TX-5
**Saint Louis**—pop pl VA-3
Saint Louis, Lake—reservoir MO-7
Saint Louis Acad—school NY-2
Saint Louis Academy IN-6
Saint Louis and O'Fallon Mine—mine IL-6
Saint Louis Area Support Center—military IL-6
Saint Louis Ave Ch of Christ—church AL-4
Saint Louis Bay—bay MN-6
Saint Louis Bay—bay MS-4
Saint Louis Bay—bay WI-6
Saint Louis Bayou—stream LA-4
Saint Louis Bertrand Sch—school CA-9
Saint Louis Cabins—locale WY-8
Saint Louis Campground—locale CO-8
Saint Louis Canal—canal (2) LA-4
Saint Louis Canyon—valley ID-8
Saint Louis Cathedral—church LA-4
Saint Louis Catholic Ch—church (2) FL-3
Saint Louis Catholic Ch—church MS-4
Saint Louis Catholic Church—hist pl CA-9
Saint Louis Cem—cemetery CA-9
Saint Louis Cem—cemetery (2) KS-7
Saint Louis Cem—cemetery (2) KY-4
Saint Louis Cem—cemetery ME-1
Saint Louis Cem—cemetery MD-2
Saint Louis Cem—cemetery MN-6
Saint Louis Cem—cemetery MO-7
Saint Louis Cem—cemetery ND-7
Saint Louis Cem—cemetery (2) OH-6
Saint Louis Cem—cemetery (3) TX-5
Saint Louis Cem—cemetery VT-1
Saint Louis Cemetery No. 1—hist pl LA-4
Saint Louis Cemetery No. 2—hist pl LA-4
Saint Louis Cem Number 3—cemetery LA-4
Saint Louis Centre (Shop Ctr)—locale MO-7
Saint Louis Ch—church (4) AL-4
Saint Louis Ch—church FL-3
Saint Louis Ch—church (2) GA-3
Saint Louis Ch—church NC-3
Saint Louis Ch—church PA-2
Saint Louis Ch—church VA-3
Saint Louis Chapel—church LA-4
Saint Louis Childrens Hospital Heliport—airport MO-7
Saint Louis City MO-7
Saint Louis City—civil MO-7
Saint Louis City Waterworks—other MO-7
Saint Louis Coast Guard Base—military MO-7
Saint Louis Country Club—other MO-7
**Saint Louis (County)**—pop pl MN-6
**Saint Louis County**—pop pl MO-7
Saint Louis County Park—park MO-7
Saint Louis Creek—stream AK-9
Saint Louis Creek—stream CO-8
Saint Louis Creek—stream MT-8
Saint Louis Crossing IN-6
**Saint Louis Crossing**—pop pl IN-6
Saint Louis de France Ch—church NY-2
Saint Louis De Gonzagues Cem—cemetery NH-1
Saint Louis De Montfort Seminary—school CT-1
Saint Louis Ditch—canal CO-8
Saint Louis Downtown Heliport—airport MO-7
Saint Louise, Lake—reservoir MO-7
Saint Louis Field—locale MA-1
Saint Louis Field—park ME-1
Saint Louis Galleria—locale MO-7
Saint Louis Gulch—valley ID-8
Saint Louis Gulch—valley (2) MT-8
**Saint Louis Heights**—pop pl HI-9
Saint Louis HS—school HI-9
Saint Louis King of France Sch—school LA-4
Saint Louis Lake—lake CO-8
Saint Louis Mine—mine (2) AZ-5
Saint Louis Mine—mine (3) CA-9
Saint Louis Mine—mine (2) CO-8
Saint Louis Mine—mine (3) ID-8
Saint Louis Mine—mine NV-8
Saint Louis Mine—mine NM-5
Saint Louis Mine—mine SD-7
Saint Louis Mine—mine WA-9
Saint Louis Mines—mine WY-8
Saint Louis No 2 Ditch—canal CO-8
Saint Louis Park—park MO-7
**Saint Louis Park**—pop pl MN-6
Saint Louis Park HS—school MN-6
Saint Louis Pass—gap CO-8
Saint Louis Peak—summit CO-8
Saint Louis Plantation—hist pl LA-4
**Saint Louis Plantation**—pop pl LA-4
Saint Louis Point AL-4
Saint Louis Preparatory Seminary—school MO-7
Saint Louis Reach—channel AL-4
Saint Louis River—stream MN-6
Saint Louis River—stream WI-6
Saint Louis River Hall—locale MN-6
Saint Louis Sch—school AL-4
Saint Louis Sch—school CA-9
Saint Louis Sch—school CO-8
Saint Louis Sch—school CT-1
Saint Louis Sch—school IL-6
Saint Louis Sch—school IN-6
Saint Louis Sch—school KS-7
Saint Louis Sch—school LA-4
Saint Louis Sch—school MD-2
Saint Louis Sch—school (3) MA-1
Saint Louis Sch—school (3) MI-6
Saint Louis Sch—school MO-7
Saint Louis Sch—school (2) OH-6
Saint Louis Sch—school OR-9
Saint Louis Sch—school PA-2
Saint Louis Sch—school TN-4
Saint Louis Sch—school (2) TX-5
Saint Louis Sch—school VA-3
Saint Louis Sch—school (2) WI-6
**Saint Louis Spur**—pop pl LA-4
Saint Louis State Training Sch—school MO-7
Saint Louis Station—locale OR-9
Saint Louis Straight Ditch—canal NV-8
Saint Louis Street Baptist Ch—church AL-4
Saint Louis Street Missionary Baptist Church—hist pl AL-4
Saint Louis the King Sch—school MI-6
Saint Louis Trail—trail CO-8
Saint Louis Tunnel—mine CO-8
Saint Louis Univ—school MO-7
Saint Louis University Hospital Heliport—airport MO-7
Saint Louis Valley—valley AR-4
**Saint Louisville**—pop pl OH-6
**Saint Lucas**—pop pl IA-7
Saint Lucas Cem—cemetery IL-6
Saint Lucas Cem—cemetery MO-7
Saint Lucas Cem—cemetery ND-7
Saint Lucas Ch—church IN-6
Saint Lucas Ch—church (2) MN-6
Saint Lucas Ch—church ND-7
Saint Luce (RR name for Upper Frenchville)—other ME-1
Saint Luce Station—locale ME-1
Saint Lucians Childrens Home—school CT-1
**Saint Lucie**—pop pl FL-3
Saint Lucie Canal—canal FL-3
Saint Lucie Catholic Ch—church FL-3
**Saint Lucie County**—pop pl FL-3
Saint Lucie County Schools—school FL-3
Saint Lucie Cut—channel FL-3
Saint Lucie Elem Sch—school FL-3
Saint Lucie HS—hist pl FL-3
Saint Lucie Inlet—gut FL-3
Saint Lucie Inlet State Park—park FL-3
Saint Lucie Lock and Dam—dam FL-3
Saint Lucie Plaza (Shop Ctr)—locale FL-3
Saint Lucie Primary—school FL-3
Saint Lucie River—stream FL-3
Saint Lucie Shoal—bar FL-3
Saint Lucins Ch—church NC-3
Saint Lucys Cem—cemetery NY-2
Saint Lucys Ch—church NY-2
Saint Lucy Sch—school CA-9
Saint Lucys Priory Sch—school CA-9
Saint Lucys Sch—school CA-9
Saint Lucys Sch—school MI-6
Saint Lucys Sch—school NY-2
Saint Ludger Cem—cemetery MO-7
Saint Ludgers Cem—cemetery MO-7
Saint Ludmilas Sch—school IA-7
Saint Luise Creek—stream WA-9
Saint Luke TN-4
Saint Luke—locale VA-3
Saint Luke and Saint Peters Episcopal Ch—church FL-3
Saint Luke Baptist Ch MS-4
Saint Luke Baptist Ch—church IN-6
Saint Luke Baptist Ch—church MS-4
Saint Luke Baptist Church TN-4
Saint Luke Bldg—hist pl VA-3
Saint Luke Catholic Ch—church (2) FL-3
Saint Luke Catholic Sch—school FL-3
Saint Luke Cem—cemetery AR-4
Saint Luke Cem—cemetery (2) LA-4
Saint Luke Cem—cemetery MN-6
Saint Luke Cem—cemetery MS-4
Saint Luke Cem—cemetery NC-3
Saint Luke Cem—cemetery OK-5
Saint Luke Cem—cemetery SD-7
Saint Luke Cem—cemetery (3) TX-5
Saint Luke Cem—cemetery (2) WI-6
Saint Luke Ch AL-4
Saint Luke Ch—church (9) AL-4
Saint Luke Ch—church (8) AR-4
Saint Luke Ch—church (2) FL-3
Saint Luke Ch—church (5) GA-3
Saint Luke Ch—church IL-6
Saint Luke Ch—church IN-6
Saint Luke Ch—church (8) LA-4
Saint Luke Ch—church (2) MI-6
Saint Luke Ch—church (10) MS-4
Saint Luke Ch—church MO-7
Saint Luke Ch—church (5) NC-3
Saint Luke Ch—church (3) SC-3
Saint Luke Ch—church (3) SD-7
Saint Luke Ch—church (4) TN-4
Saint Luke Ch—church (12) TX-5
Saint Luke Ch—church WI-6
Saint Luke Ch (historical)—church AL-4
Saint Luke Ch (historical)—church MS-4
Saint Luke Ch of God in Christ—church KS-7
Saint Luke Ch of God in Christ—church (2) MS-4
Saint Luke Christian Church MS-4
Saint Luke Episcopal Ch—church MS-4
Saint Luke Episcopal Church—hist pl TN-4
Saint Luke Evangelist Catholic Sch PA-2
Saint Luke Freewill Baptist Ch—church AL-4
Saint Luke Hosp—hospital CO-8
Saint Luke Hosp—hospital MI-6
Saint Luke Kindergarten—school FL-3
Saint Luke Methodist Ch—church (2) AL-4
Saint Luke Missionary Baptist Ch AL-4
Saint Luke Missionary Baptist Ch—church FL-3
Saint Luke Missionary Baptist Ch—church MS-4
Saint Luke Post Office (historical)—building TN-4
Saint Luke Presbyterian Ch—church FL-3
Saint Luke Primitive Baptist Ch—church FL-3
Saint Luke (reduced usage)—locale MO-7
Saint Luke Roman Catholic Ch—church IN-6
Saint Lukes—locale MD-2
Saint Lukes African Methodist Episcopal Ch AL-4
Saint Lukes AME Ch—church AL-4
Saint Lukes Baptist Ch—church AL-4
Saint Lukes Branch—stream LA-4
Saint Lukes Cem—cemetery AL-4
Saint Lukes Cem—cemetery CO-8
Saint Lukes Cem—cemetery GA-3
Saint Lukes Cem—cemetery (4) IL-6
Saint Lukes Cem—cemetery IN-6
Saint Lukes Cem—cemetery KS-7
Saint Lukes Cem—cemetery (3) LA-4
Saint Lukes Cem—cemetery MD-2
Saint Lukes Cem—cemetery (2) MA-1
Saint Lukes Cem—cemetery (4) MN-6
Saint Lukes Cem—cemetery NY-2
Saint Lukes Cem—cemetery NC-3
Saint Lukes Cem—cemetery (2) ND-7
Saint Lukes Cem—cemetery (3) OH-6
Saint Lukes Cem—cemetery OR-9
Saint Lukes Cem—cemetery (5) PA-2
Saint Lukes Cem—cemetery (2) SC-3
Saint Lukes Cem—cemetery SD-7
Saint Lukes Cem—cemetery TX-5
Saint Lukes Cem—cemetery VA-3
Saint Lukes Cem—cemetery (3) WI-6
Saint Lukes Ch AL-4
Saint Lukes Ch IN-6
Saint Luke Sch TN-4
Saint Lukes Ch—church (12) AL-4
Saint Lukes Ch—church (4) AR-4
Saint Lukes Ch—church DE-2
Saint Lukes Ch—church (10) FL-3
Saint Lukes Ch—church (17) GA-3
Saint Lukes Ch—church IL-6
Saint Lukes Ch—church (4) IN-6
Saint Lukes Ch—church (2) KS-7
Saint Lukes Ch—church KY-4
Saint Lukes Ch—church (7) LA-4
Saint Lukes Ch—church (8) MD-2
Saint Lukes Ch—church (2) MA-1
Saint Lukes Ch—church (2) MI-6
Saint Lukes Ch—church MN-6
Saint Lukes Ch—church (5) MS-4
Saint Lukes Ch—church MO-7
Saint Lukes Ch—church (6) NJ-2
Saint Lukes Ch—church (2) NM-5
Saint Lukes Ch—church (5) NY-2
Saint Lukes Ch—church (21) NC-3
Saint Lukes Ch—church ND-7
Saint Lukes Ch—church (4) OH-6
Saint Lukes Ch—church (14) PA-2
Saint Lukes Ch—church (27) SC-3
Saint Lukes Ch—church SD-7
Saint Lukes Ch—church (4) TN-4
Saint Lukes Ch—church (7) TX-5
Saint Lukes Ch—church VT-1
Saint Lukes Ch—church (17) VA-3
Saint Lukes Ch—church (3) WV-2
Saint Lukes Ch—church (5) WI-6
Saint Lukes Ch—church VI-3
Saint Luke Sch—school AR-4
Saint Luke Sch—school GA-3
Saint Luke Sch—school IL-6
Saint Luke Sch—school IN-6
Saint Luke Sch—school LA-4
Saint Luke Sch—school (2) MI-6
Saint Luke Sch—school MN-6
Saint Luke Sch—school PA-2
Saint Luke Sch—school TN-4
Saint Luke Sch—school (2) TX-5
Saint Lukes Chapel—church MD-2
Saint Lukes Ch (historical)—church AL-4
Saint Lukes Ch (historical)—church MS-4
Saint Luke Sch (historical)—school MS-4
Saint Luke Sch Number 2—school MS-4
Saint Lukes Ch of God in Christ—church MS-4
Saint Lukes Church—hist pl KY-4
Saint Luke's Church—hist pl (2) MD-2
Saint Luke's Church—hist pl NJ-2
Saint Luke's Church—hist pl NY-2
Saint Luke's Church—hist pl VA-3
Saint Lukes Church Sch—school AR-4
Saint Lukes CME Ch—church AL-4
Saint Lukes Episcocal Ch—church TN-4
Saint Lukes Episcopal Ch—church (3) AL-4
Saint Lukes Episcopal Ch—church FL-3
Saint Lukes Episcopal Ch—church UT-8
Saint Lukes Episcopal Church—church NC-3
Saint Luke's Episcopal Church—hist pl AL-4
Saint Luke's Episcopal Church—hist pl AR-4
Saint Luke's Episcopal Church—hist pl DC-2
Saint Lukes Episcopal Church—hist pl PA-2
Saint Luke's Episcopal Church—hist pl TN-4
Saint Luke's Episcopal Church, Chapel, Guildhall, and Rectory—hist pl WI-6
Saint Lukes Fork—stream VA-3
Saint Lukes Freewill Baptist Ch—church FL-3
Saint Luke's Home for Destitute and Aged Women—hist pl CT-1
Saint Lukes Hosp—hospital AZ-5
Saint Lukes Hosp—hospital CA-9
Saint Lukes Hosp—hospital CT-1
Saint Lukes Hosp—hospital FL-3
Saint Lukes Hosp—hospital ID-8
Saint Lukes Hosp—hospital IA-7
Saint Lukes Hosp—hospital KY-4
Saint Lukes Hosp—hospital (2) MA-1
Saint Lukes Hosp—hospital MI-6
Saint Lukes Hosp—hospital MN-6
Saint Lukes Hosp—hospital (2) MO-7
Saint Lukes Hosp—hospital (2) NY-2
Saint Lukes Hosp—hospital ND-7
Saint Lukes Hosp—hospital OH-6
Saint Luke Hosp—hospital (2) PA-2
Saint Lukes Hosp—hospital SD-7
Saint Lukes Hosp—hospital TX-5
Saint Lukes Hosp—hospital VA-3
Saint Lukes Hosp (historical)—hospital AL-4
Saint Lukes Hospital Heliport—airport MO-7
Saint Lukes in the Desert Hosp—hospital AZ-5
Saint Lukes Lutheran Ch—church FL-3
Saint Luke's Lutheran Church Cemetery—hist pl NC-3
Saint Lukes Methodist Ch—church IN-6
Saint Lukes Missionary Baptist Ch—church KS-7
Saint Luke's Protestant Episcopal Church—hist pl DE-2
Saint Luke's Protestant Episcopal Church—hist pl NE-7
Saint Luke's Protestant Episcopal Church—hist pl NY-2
Saint Lukes Protestant Episcopal Church—hist pl NY-2
Saint Lukes Sch IN-6
Saint Lukes Sch PA-2
Saint Lukes Sch—school (2) CA-9
Saint Lukes Sch—school CT-1
Saint Lukes Sch—school FL-3
Saint Lukes Sch—school (2) IL-6
Saint Lukes Sch—school IN-6
Saint Lukes Sch—school MD-2
Saint Lukes Sch—school MA-1
Saint Lukes Sch—school MI-6
Saint Lukes Sch—school MN-6
Saint Lukes Sch—school NE-7
Saint Lukes Sch—school (2) NJ-2
Saint Lukes Sch—school (3) NY-2
Saint Lukes Sch—school (3) OH-6
Saint Lukes Sch—school OR-9
Saint Lukes Sch—school (3) PA-2
Saint Lukes Sch—school SC-3
Saint Lukes Sch—school TN-4
Saint Lukes Sch—school TX-5
Saint Lukes Sch—school VA-3
Saint Lukes United Methodist Ch—church MS-4
Saint Lukes United Methodist Ch at Windemere—church FL-3
Saint Luke United Methodist Ch—church (2) MS-4
Saint Luke United Methodist Church TN-4
Saint Luther Baptist Ch—church MS-4
Saint Lytton Sch—school TX-5
Saint Madeleine Sch—school CA-9
Saint Madeleines Sch—school PA-2
Saint Madelene Sophe Ch—church NY-2
Saint Madeline Sch—school PA-2
**Saint Magdalen**—pop pl IN-6
Saint Mahala Chapel—church NC-3
Saint Makarius Point—cape AK-9
Saint Malachi Ch—church PA-2
Saint Malachy Cem—cemetery MN-6
Saint Malachy Cem—cemetery WI-6
Saint Malachy Ch—church WI-6
Saint Malachys Cem—cemetery KS-7
Saint Malachys Ch—church IA-7
Saint Malachy Sch—school FL-3
Saint Malachy Sch—school IN-6
Saint Malachy Sch—school PA-2
Saint Malachys Sch—school (2) CA-9
Saint Malachys Sch—school NY-2
Saint Malachys Sch—school PA-2
Saint Malachy West Cem—cemetery IN-6
Saint Malo, Bayou—gut LA-4
Saint Manes Cem—cemetery CT-1
Saint Marcus Cem—cemetery MN-6
Saint Marcus Cem—cemetery MO-7
Saint Marcus Ch—church IL-6
Saint Marcus Sch—school WI-6
Saint Margaret Cem—cemetery IA-7
Saint Margaret Cem—cemetery MI-6
Saint Margaret Cem—cemetery (3) MN-6
Saint Margaret Ch—church FL-3
Saint Margaret Ch—church MI-6
Saint Margaret Ch—church MO-7
Saint Margaret Field KS-7
Saint Margaret Hosp—hospital AL-4
Saint Margaret Hosp—hospital IL-6
Saint Margaret Island—island MD-2
Saint Margaret Mary Catholic Ch—church FL-3
Saint Margaret-Mary Ch—church NM-5
Saint Margaret Mary Ch—church NY-2
Saint Margaret Mary Ch—church OK-5
Saint Margaret Mary Elem Sch—school FL-3
Saint Margaret Mary Roman Catholic Ch—church KS-7
Saint Margaret Marys Ch—church CT-1
Saint Margaret Mary Sch—school LA-4
Saint Margaret Mary Sch—school (2) NY-2
Saint Margaret Mary Sch—school OH-6
Saint Margaret Mary Sch—school TX-5
Saint Margaret Mary Sch—school WI-6
Saint Margaret Marys Sch—school IN-6
Saint Margaret Marys Sch—school KY-4
Saint Margaret Marys Sch—school PA-2
Saint Margaret Marys Sch—school WV-2
Saint Margaret Mission—church MI-6
**Saint Margarets**—pop pl MD-2
Saint Margarets Acad—school MN-6
Saint Margarets Catholic Ch—church AL-4
Saint Margarets Cem—cemetery OH-6
Saint Margarets Cem—cemetery SD-7
Saint Margarets Cem—cemetery WI-6
Saint Margarets Ch—church FL-3
Saint Margarets Ch—church LA-4
Saint Margarets Ch—church ME-1
Saint Margarets Ch—church NY-2
Saint Margarets Ch—church SD-7
Saint Margarets Ch—church VA-3
Saint Margaret Sch—school IL-6
Saint Margaret Sch—school (2) MI-6
Saint Margaret Sch—school OH-6
Saint Margarets Chapel—church NY-2
Saint Margaret's Episcopal Church—hist pl FL-3
Saint Margarets Hosp—hospital IN-6
Saint Margarets Hospital AL-4
Saint Margarets Sch—school AL-4
Saint Margarets Sch—school CA-9
Saint Margarets Sch—school CT-1
Saint Margarets Sch—school LA-4
Saint Margarets Sch—school (2) MD-2
Saint Margarets Sch—school MA-1
Saint Margarets Sch—school (2) NJ-2
Saint Margarets Sch—school (4) NY-2
Saint Margarets Sch—school VA-3
Saint Margarets Vocational Sch—school PA-2
Saint Margarettes Island—island NY-2
Saint Margaret Villa—building NY-2
Saint Margarita TX-5
Saint Margarite Mary Ch—church MO-7
Saint Marguerites Catholic Ch—church UT-8
Saint Marguerites Sch—school NJ-2
Saint Maria Cem—cemetery MS-4
Saint Maria Church MS-4
Saint Mariaes Sch—school NY-2
Saint Maria Goretti Ch—church LA-4
Saint Maria Goretti Ch—church MI-6
Saint Maria Goretti HS PA-2
Saint Maria Goretti Sch—school CA-9
Saint Maria Goretti Sch—school TX-5
Saint Mariah Ch—church SC-3
Saint Mariahs Ch—church NC-3
Saint Marianne de Paredes Sch—school CA-9
Saint Marians Sch—school OH-6
Saint Marie Cem—cemetery WI-6
Saint Marie Goreffis HS—school PA-2
Saint Marie Goretti Sch—school IL-6
Saint Marie Goretti Sch—school PA-2
**Saint Maries**—pop pl ID-8
Saint Maries Ch—church CA-9
Saint Maries Country Club—other ID-8
Saint Maries Peak CA-9
Saint Maries Peak—summit ID-8
Saint Maries River ID-8
Saint Maries River—stream ID-8
Saint Maries Sch—school NH-1
**Saint Marie (Town of)**—pop pl WI-6
Saint Marietta Sch—school NE-7
Saint Marion Brake—swamp AR-4
Saint Marion Cem—cemetery AR-4
Saint Marion Ch—church AR-4
Saint Mark KS-7
**Saint Mark**—pop pl KS-7
Saint Mark African Methodist Episcopal Ch—church KS-7
Saint Mark American Lutheran Ch—church FL-3
Saint Mark Baptist Ch—church (3) AL-4
Saint Mark Baptist Ch—church MS-4
Saint Mark by the Sea Lutheran Ch—church FL-3
Saint Mark Cem—cemetery AL-4
Saint Mark Cem—cemetery AR-4
Saint Mark Cem—cemetery LA-4
Saint Mark Cem—cemetery MN-6
Saint Mark Cem—cemetery (2) MS-4
Saint Mark Ch AL-4
Saint Mark Ch MS-4
Saint Mark Ch TN-4
Saint Mark Ch—church (9) AL-4
Saint Mark Ch—church (2) AR-4
Saint Mark Ch—church DE-2
Saint Mark Ch—church FL-3
Saint Mark Ch—church GA-3
Saint Mark Ch—church IL-6
Saint Mark Ch—church KY-4
Saint Mark Ch—church (5) LA-4
Saint Mark Ch—church (3) MI-6
Saint Mark Ch—church MN-6
Saint Mark Ch—church (7) MS-4
Saint Mark Ch—church (2) NC-3
Saint Mark Ch—church OH-6
Saint Mark Ch—church (5) SC-3
Saint Mark Ch—church SD-7
Saint Mark Ch—church TN-4
Saint Mark Ch—church (6) TX-5
Saint Mark Ch—church WI-6
Saint Mark Ch of God in Christ MS-4
Saint Mark Christian Ch—church AL-4
Saint Mark Christian Sch—school FL-3
Saint Markellas Park—park WV-2
Saint Mark Episcopal Ch—church MT-8
Saint Mark Freewill Baptist Ch—church AL-4
Saint Mark Lutheran Ch—church FL-3
Saint Mark Lutheran Ch—church MT-8
Saint Mark Methodist Ch—church AL-4
Saint Mark Methodist Church—hist pl GA-3
Saint Mark Missionary Baptist Ch TN-4
Saint Mark Missionary Baptist Ch—church FL-3
Saint Mark Missionary Baptist Ch—church MS-4
Saint Mark Primitive Baptist Ch AL-4
Saint Mark Roman Catholic Ch—church IN-6
Saint Marks FL-3
**Saint Marks**—pop pl FL-3
**Saint Marks**—pop pl GA-3
**Saint Marks**—pop pl (2) IN-6
**Saint Marks**—pop pl KS-7
Saint Marks African Methodist Episcopal Ch—church AL-4
Saint Marks AME Ch—church AL-4
Saint Marks Ave Sch—school NY-2
Saint Marks Baptist Ch—church FL-3
Saint Marks Catholic Ch—church FL-3
Saint Marks Cem—cemetery AL-4
Saint Marks Cem—cemetery (4) AR-4
Saint Marks Cem—cemetery IN-6
Saint Marks Cem—cemetery (2) LA-4
Saint Marks Cem—cemetery MI-6
Saint Marks Cem—cemetery (2) MN-6
Saint Marks Cem—cemetery (2) MS-4
Saint Marks Cem—cemetery (2) NE-7
Saint Marks Cem—cemetery NY-2
Saint Marks Cem—cemetery ND-7
Saint Marks Cem—cemetery (5) PA-2
Saint Marks Cem—cemetery (2) SC-3
Saint Marks Cem—cemetery (2) TN-4
Saint Marks Cem—cemetery (2) VA-3
Saint Marks Cem—cemetery (2) WI-6
Saint Mark's Cemetery—hist pl NY-2
Saint Marks Ch AL-4
Saint Marks Ch PA-2
Saint Marks Ch—church (15) AL-4
Saint Marks Ch—church (7) AR-4
Saint Marks Ch—church DE-2
Saint Marks Ch—church (10) FL-3
Saint Marks Ch—church (16) GA-3
Saint Marks Ch—church IL-6
Saint Marks Ch—church (4) IN-6
Saint Marks Ch—church IA-7
Saint Marks Ch—church (3) KY-4
Saint Marks Ch—church (12) LA-4
Saint Marks Ch—church (15) MD-2
Saint Marks Ch—church MA-1
Saint Marks Ch—church MI-6
Saint Marks Ch—church MN-6
Saint Marks Ch—church (14) MS-4
Saint Marks Ch—church NE-7
Saint Marks Ch—church (2) NJ-2
Saint Marks Ch—church NM-5
Saint Marks Ch—church (6) NY-2
Saint Marks Ch—church (20) NC-3
Saint Marks Ch—church (5) OH-6
Saint Marks Ch—church (21) PA-2
Saint Marks Ch—church (25) SC-3
Saint Marks Ch—church (2) SD-7
Saint Marks Ch—church (4) TN-4
Saint Marks Ch—church (3) TX-5
Saint Marks Ch—church (17) VA-3
Saint Marks Ch—church WI-6
Saint Mark Sch—school FL-3
Saint Mark Sch—school IL-6
Saint Mark Sch—school (2) IN-6
Saint Mark Sch—school MI-6
Saint Mark Sch—school MN-6
Saint Mark Sch—school OK-5
Saint Mark Sch—school (4) SC-3
Saint Mark Sch—school (2) TX-5
Saint Marks Ch (abandoned)—church PA-2
Saint Marks Chapel—church NC-3
Saint Marks Ch (historical)—church (2) AL-4
Saint Marks Ch (historical)—church TN-4
Saint Marks Ch in the Fork of Greene AL-4
Saint Marks Ch of God in Christ—church KS-7
Saint Mark's Church—hist pl DC-2
Saint Marks Early Learning Center—school FL-3
Saint Marks Episcopal Ch AL-4
Saint Marks Episcopal Ch—church (2) AL-4
Saint Marks Episcopal Ch—church FL-3
Saint Marks Episcopal Ch—church KS-7
Saint Marks Episcopal Ch—church MS-4
Saint Mark's Episcopal Church—hist pl AR-4
Saint Marks Episcopal Church—hist pl FL-3
Saint Mark's Episcopal Church—hist pl NJ-2
Saint Mark's Episcopal Church—hist pl (3) NY-2
Saint Mark's Episcopal Church—hist pl NC-3
Saint Mark's Episcopal Church—hist pl (2) PA-2
Saint Mark's Episcopal Church—hist pl WV-2
Saint Mark's Episcopal Church—hist pl WI-6
Saint Mark's Episcopal Church, Guild Hall and Vicarage—hist pl WI-6
Saint Marks Episcopal Day Sch—school (2) FL-3
Saint Marks Episcopal Sch—school FL-3
Saint Mark's Hist Dist—hist pl NY-2
Saint Mark's Hist Dist (Boundary Increase)—hist pl NY-2
Saint Marks Hosp—hospital UT-8
Saint Marks Hosp (abandoned)—hospital UT-8
Saint Marks Hospital Heliport—airport UT-8
Saint-Marks-In-The-Bowery—hist pl NY-2
Saint Marks Island—island FL-3
Saint Marks Light—locale FL-3
Saint Marks Lighthouse—hist pl FL-3
Saint Marks Lutheran Ch AL-4
Saint Marks Lutheran Ch—church UT-8
Saint Mark's Lutheran Church—hist pl AL-4
Saint Mark's Lutheran Church—hist pl NY-2
Saint Marks Methodist Ch—church AL-4
Saint Marks Missionary Baptist Church MS-4
Saint Marks Mission Ch—church LA-4
Saint Marks Natl Wildlife Ref—park FL-3
Saint Marks Park—park MA-1
Saint Marks Park—park NJ-2
Saint Marks Point FL-3
Saint Marks Pond Swamp—swamp FL-3
Saint Marks Precinct—civil FL-3
Saint Marks Presbyterian Ch—church FL-3
Saint Marks Reformed Episcopal Ch—church PA-2
Saint Marks River—stream (2) FL-3
Saint Marks Sch IN-6
Saint Marks Sch—school AZ-5
Saint Marks Sch—school CA-9
Saint Marks Sch—school CT-1
Saint Marks Sch—school FL-3
Saint Marks Sch—school HI-9
Saint Marks Sch—school (2) IL-6
Saint Marks Sch—school (2) IN-6
Saint Marks Sch—school LA-4
Saint Marks Sch—school MD-2
Saint Marks Sch—school (2) MA-1
Saint Marks Sch—school MN-6
Saint Marks Sch—school (3) NY-2
Saint Marks Sch—school (4) OH-6

Saint Patrick Ch—church SD-7
Saint Patrick Ch—church TN-4
Saint Patrick Ch—church (2) WI-6
Saint Patrick Ch (historical)—church AL-4
Saint Patrick Church MO-7
Saint Patrick Community Center—locale NY-2
Saint Patrick Creek—stream (2) AK-9
Saint Patrick Creek—stream MD-2
Saint Patrick Creek—stream MT-8
Saint Patrick Creek—stream NM-5
Saint Patrick HS—school IL-6
Saint Patrick Lake—lake MN-6
Saint Patrick Mine—mine AZ-5
Saint Patrick Mtn—summit OR-9
Saint Patrick Oil Field—oilfield TX-5
Saint Patrick Peak—summit MT-8
Saint Patrick Roman Cathlic Ch—church PA-2
Saint Patrick Roman Catholic Ch—church IN-6
Saint Patrick Roman Catholic Ch—church KS-7
Saint Patricks Acad—school IL-6
Saint Patricks Acad—school NY-2
Saint Patricks Butte SD-7
Saint Patricks Cathedral—church NY-2
Saint Patrick's Cathedral—hist pl NY-2
Saint Patricks Catholic Ch—church DE-2
Saint Patricks Catholic Ch—church FL-3
Saint Patrick's Catholic Ch—church MT-8
Saint Patricks Catholic Ch (historical)—church IA-7
Saint Patrick's Catholic Church—hist pl AL-4
Saint Patricks Catholic Church—school SD-7
Saint Patrick's Catholic Church and Rectory—hist pl TN-4
Saint Patricks Cem—cemetery (5) CT-1
Saint Patricks Cem—cemetery (6) IL-6
Saint Patricks Cem—cemetery (3) IN-6
Saint Patricks Cem—cemetery (18) IA-7
Saint Patricks Cem—cemetery (4) KS-7
Saint Patricks Cem—cemetery KY-4
Saint Patricks Cem—cemetery MD-2
Saint Patricks Cem—cemetery (14) MA-1
Saint Patricks Cem—cemetery (4) MI-6
Saint Patricks Cem—cemetery (3) MN-6
Saint Patricks Cem—cemetery MS-4
Saint Patricks Cem—cemetery (2) MO-7
Saint Patricks Cem—cemetery (6) NE-7
Saint Patricks Cem—cemetery (3) NH-1
Saint Patricks Cem—cemetery (21) NY-2
Saint Patricks Cem—cemetery (2) ND-7
Saint Patricks Cem—cemetery (8) OH-6
Saint Patricks Cem—cemetery (6) PA-2
Saint Patricks Cem—cemetery SC-3
Saint Patricks Cem—cemetery (4) SD-7
Saint Patricks Cem—cemetery WA-9
Saint Patricks Cem—cemetery (10) WI-6
Saint Patricks Ch—church CT-1
Saint Patricks Ch—church (3) FL-3
Saint Patricks Ch—church (5) IL-6
Saint Patricks Ch—church IN-6
Saint Patricks Ch—church (5) IA-7
Saint Patricks Ch—church (2) KS-7
Saint Patricks Ch—church KY-4
Saint Patricks Ch—church ME-1
Saint Patricks Ch—church MD-2
Saint Patricks Ch—church (2) MA-1
Saint Patricks Ch—church MI-6
Saint Patricks Ch—church (3) MN-6
Saint Patricks Ch—church (3) MO-7
Saint Patricks Ch—church (2) NE-7
Saint Patricks Ch—church (7) NY-2
Saint Patricks Ch—church (3) OH-6
Saint Patricks Ch—church OK-5
Saint Patricks Ch—church (4) PA-2
Saint Patricks Ch—church SD-7
Saint Patricks Ch—church TN-4
Saint Patricks Ch—church TX-5
Saint Patricks Ch—church (5) WI-6
Saint Patrick Sch—school AZ-5
Saint Patrick Sch—school (4) CA-9
Saint Patrick Sch—school (5) IL-6
Saint Patrick Sch—school (3) IN-6
Saint Patrick Sch—school (3) IA-7
Saint Patrick Sch—school (4) KS-7
Saint Patrick Sch—school MS-4
Saint Patrick Sch—school MO-7
Saint Patrick Sch—school NJ-2
Saint Patrick Sch—school NY-2
Saint Patrick Sch—school OH-6
Saint Patrick Sch—school TX-5
Saint Patrick Sch—school WA-9
Saint Patrick Sch—school (3) WI-6
Saint Patrick School PA-2
Saint Patrick School—locale PA-2
Saint Patrick's Church—hist pl LA-4
Saint Patrick's Church—hist pl WI-6
Saint Patricks Colliery—building PA-2
Saint Patricks Convent Sch—school NH-1
Saint Patricks Creek—stream AK-9
Saint Patricks Episcopal Ch—church FL-3
Saint Patricks Glencoe Cem—cemetery IN-6
Saint Patricks Hosp—hospital LA-4
Saint Patricks HS—school IL-6
Saint Patricks HS—school (2) NE-7
Saint Patricks HS—school NY-2
Saint Patricks Lake MI-6
Saint Patricks Mission—church TX-5
Saint Patrick's Mission Church and Sch—hist pl KS-7
Saint Patricks Monastery—church DE-2
Saint Patricks Orphanage—building CA-9
Saint Patricks Orphanage—building NH-1
Saint Patrick's Parish and Buildings—hist pl NJ-2
Saint Patrick's Pro Cathedral—hist pl NJ-2
Saint Patrick's Roman Catholic Church—hist pl OR-9
Saint Patrick's Roman Catholic Church—hist pl PA-2
Saint Patrick's Roman Catholic Church—hist pl (4) WI-6
Saint Patrick's Roman Catholic Church, Rectory, and School—hist pl KY-4
Saint Patrick's Roman Catholic Church and Rectory—hist pl OR-9
Saint Patricks Roman Catholic Sch (historical)—school AL-4
Saint Patricks Sch IN-6
Saint Patricks Sch—school AR-4
Saint Patricks Sch—school (5) CA-9
Saint Patricks Sch—school CO-8
Saint Patricks Sch—school (4) FL-3
Saint Patricks Sch—school HI-9
Saint Patricks Sch—school (7) IL-6
Saint Patricks Sch—school (2) IN-6
Saint Patricks Sch—school (4) IA-7
Saint Patricks Sch—school (4) KS-7
Saint Patricks Sch—school (7) MA-1
Saint Patricks Sch—school (4) MI-6
Saint Patricks Sch—school (2) MN-6
Saint Patricks Sch—school (2) MO-7
Saint Patricks Sch—school (3) NE-7
Saint Patricks Sch—school (2) NH-1
Saint Patricks Sch—school (3) NJ-2
Saint Patricks Sch—school NM-5
Saint Patricks Sch—school (14) NY-2
Saint Patricks Sch—school ND-7
Saint Patricks Sch—school (5) OH-6
Saint Patricks Sch—school OK-5
Saint Patricks Sch—school (5) PA-2
Saint Patricks Sch—school SD-7
Saint Patricks Sch—school (2) TX-5
Saint Patricks Sch—school VA-3
Saint Patricks Sch—school (3) WA-9
Saint Patricks Sch—school (6) WI-6
Saint Patricks Sch—school VI-3
Saint Patricks School NC-3
Saint Patricks Sch Station PA-2
Saint Patricks Seminary—school CA-9
Saint Patricks Seminary—school NE-7
Saint Patrick State Wildlife Mngmt Area—park MN-6
Saint Patrick Station—locale IA-7
Saint Patrick Tank—reservoir NM-5
Saint Pats—locale KS-7
Saint Pats Park—park WI-6
Saint Paul SD-7
Saint Paul—locale KS-7
Saint Paul—locale (2) TX-5
**Saint Paul**—pop pl AK-9
**Saint Paul**—pop pl (2) AR-4
**Saint Paul**—pop pl (2) IL-6
**Saint Paul**—pop pl (2) IN-6
**Saint Paul**—pop pl IA-7
**Saint Paul**—pop pl KS-7
**Saint Paul**—pop pl (2) KY-4
**Saint Paul**—pop pl MN-6
**Saint Paul**—pop pl MS-4
**Saint Paul**—pop pl MO-7
**Saint Paul**—pop pl NE-7
**Saint Paul**—pop pl ND-7
**Saint Paul**—pop pl OH-6
**Saint Paul**—pop pl OR-9
**Saint Paul**—pop pl PA-2
**Saint Paul**—pop pl SC-3
**Saint Paul**—pop pl TN-4
**Saint Paul**—pop pl (3) TX-5
**Saint Paul**—pop pl (2) VA-3
Saint Paul, Butte—summit ND-7
Saint Paul Acad—school MN-6
Saint Paul African Methodist Episcopal Ch—church (2) AL-4
Saint Paul African Methodist Episcopal Ch—church (6) FL-3
Saint Paul African Methodist Episcopal Ch—church IN-6
Saint Paul African Methodist Episcopal Ch—church KS-7
Saint Paul AME Ch—church (6) AL-4
Saint Paul A.M.E. Church—hist pl NC-3
Saint Paul AME Zion Ch—church AL-4
Saint Paul Baptist Ch MS-4
Saint Paul Baptist Ch—church (2) AL-4
Saint Paul Baptist Ch—church (2) FL-3
Saint Paul Baptist Ch—church (2) MS-4
Saint Paul Baptist Ch (historical)—church MS-4
Saint Paul Baptist Church TN-4
Saint Paul Baptist Church—hist pl NC-3
Saint Paul Bayou—stream LA-4
Saint Paul Bible Coll—school MN-6
Saint Paul Branch—stream GA-3
Saint Paul Branch—stream MD-2
Saint Paul Branch—stream SC-3
Saint Paul Cathedral—church MN-6
Saint Paul Catholic Cem—cemetery OR-9
Saint Paul Catholic Ch—church AL-4
Saint Paul Catholic Ch—church FL-3
Saint Paul Catholic Sch—school FL-3
Saint Paul (CCD)—cens area OR-9
Saint Paul Cem—cemetery (3) AL-4
Saint Paul Cem—cemetery (6) AR-4
Saint Paul Cem—cemetery GA-3
Saint Paul Cem—cemetery (9) IL-6
Saint Paul Cem—cemetery (2) IN-6
Saint Paul Cem—cemetery (5) IA-7
Saint Paul Cem—cemetery (6) KS-7
Saint Paul Cem—cemetery (3) LA-4
Saint Paul Cem—cemetery (3) MI-6
Saint Paul Cem—cemetery (7) MN-6
Saint Paul Cem—cemetery (11) MS-4
Saint Paul Cem—cemetery (9) MO-7
Saint Paul Cem—cemetery (4) NE-7
Saint Paul Cem—cemetery (4) NY-2
Saint Paul Cem—cemetery (5) ND-7
Saint Paul Cem—cemetery (2) OH-6
Saint Paul Cem—cemetery OK-5
Saint Paul Cem—cemetery OR-9
Saint Paul Cem—cemetery (2) PA-2
Saint Paul Cem—cemetery SC-3
Saint Paul Cem—cemetery (7) SD-7
Saint Paul Cem—cemetery (5) TN-4
Saint Paul Cem—cemetery (6) TX-5
Saint Paul Cem—cemetery VA-3
Saint Paul Cem—cemetery (18) WI-6
Saint Paul Ch AL-4
Saint Paul Ch MS-4
Saint Paul Ch TN-4
Saint Paul Ch—church (19) AL-4
Saint Paul Ch—church (18) AR-4
Saint Paul Ch—church DE-2
Saint Paul Ch—church (4) FL-3
Saint Paul Ch—church (12) GA-3
Saint Paul Ch—church (4) IL-6
Saint Paul Ch—church IN-6
Saint Paul Ch—church (6) IA-7
Saint Paul Ch—church KS-7
Saint Paul Ch—church (18) LA-4
Saint Paul Ch—church (2) MD-2
Saint Paul Ch—church (7) MI-6
Saint Paul Ch—church (5) MN-6
Saint Paul Ch—church (36) MS-4
Saint Paul Ch—church (5) MO-7
Saint Paul Ch—church (5) NE-7
Saint Paul Ch—church NM-5
Saint Paul Ch—church (11) NC-3
Saint Paul Ch—church (7) ND-7
Saint Paul Ch—church (7) OH-6
Saint Paul Ch—church (4) OK-5
Saint Paul Ch—church (6) PA-2
Saint Paul Ch—church (15) SC-3
Saint Paul Ch—church SD-7
Saint Paul Ch—church (10) TN-4
Saint Paul Ch—church (30) TX-5
Saint Paul Ch—church (13) WI-6
Saint Paul Ch (abandoned)—church (2) MO-7
Saint Paul Chapel TN-4
Saint Paul Chapel—church MO-7
Saint Paul Ch (historical)—church AL-4
Saint Paul Ch (historical)—church (2) MS-4
Saint Paul Ch (historical)—church TN-4
Saint Paul Ch Number 2—church (2) LA-4
Saint Paul Christian Day Sch and Kindergarten—school IN-6
Saint Paul Christian Methodist Episcopal Ch—church IN-6
Saint Paul Church—locale IL-6
**Saint Paul Church**—pop pl (2) MN-6
Saint Paul CME Ch—church (2) AL-4
Saint Paul Creek—stream MI-6
Saint Paul Creek—stream TX-5
Saint Paul Elem Sch—school IN-6
Saint Paul Evangelical Lutheran Ch (historical)—church SD-7
Saint Paul Evangelistic Lutheran Ch AL-4
**Saint Paul Forks**—pop pl SC-3
Saint Paul Friedhol Cem—cemetery WI-6
Saint Paul German Lutheran Ch AL-4
Saint Paul Gulch—valley MT-8
Saint Paul Harbor—bay AK-9
Saint Paul Hill—summit FL-3
Saint Paul Hist Dist—hist pl OR-9
Saint Paul (historical)—locale SD-7
Saint Paul Holiness Ch—church AL-4
Saint Paul Hollow—valley KY-4
Saint Paul HS—school MN-6
Saint Paul HS—school NC-3
Saint Paul HS—school TX-5
Saint Pauli Cem—cemetery (2) MN-6
Saint Pauli Ch—church MN-6
Saint Pauli Ch—church SD-7
Saint Paul Indian Sch—school SD-7
Saint Paul Industrial Sch—school TX-5
Saint Pauline Cem—cemetery ND-7
Saint Paulinus Cem—cemetery LA-4
Saint Paulinus Ch—church IL-6
Saint Paulinus Sch—school PA-2
Saint Paul Island—island AK-9
Saint Paul Island—island MN-6
Saint Paul Island—post sta AK-9
Saint Paul Island Airp—airport AK-9
Saint Paul Junction IL-6
Saint Paul Lake—lake MT-8
Saint Paul Lutheran Cem—cemetery OR-9
Saint Paul Lutheran Cemetery SD-7
Saint Paul Lutheran Ch TN-4
Saint Paul Lutheran Ch—church (2) AL-4
Saint Paul Lutheran Ch—church FL-3
Saint Paul Lutheran Ch—church (2) PA-2
Saint Paul Lutheran Church SD-7
Saint Paul Lutheran Preschool—school FL-3
Saint Paul Lutheran Sch—school FL-3
Saint Paul Lutheran Sch—school IN-6
Saint Paul Lutheran Sch—school MI-6
Saint Paul Methodist Ch AL-4
Saint Paul Methodist Ch TN-4
Saint Paul Methodist Ch—church (3) AL-4
Saint Paul Methodist Ch—church (3) MS-4
Saint Paul Methodist Episcopal Ch MS-4
Saint Paul Mine—mine MN-6
Saint Paul Mine—mine MT-8
Saint Paul Mine—mine OR-9
Saint Paul Mission—church TX-5
Saint Paul Missionary Baptist Ch AL-4
Saint Paul Missionary Baptist Ch MS-4
Saint Paul Missionary Baptist Ch—church AL-4
Saint Paul Missionary Baptist Ch—church (2) FL-3
Saint Paul Missionary Baptist Ch—church (3) MS-4
Saint Paul Monastery—church MI-6
Saint Paul Mtn—summit OR-9
Saint Paul-North Water Streets Hist Dist—hist pl NY-2
Saint Paul of the Cross Catholic Ch—church FL-3
Saint Paul of the Cross Sch—school CA-9
Saint Paul Orphange—building MN-6
**Saint Paul Park**—pop pl MN-6
Saint Paul Pass—gap ID-8
Saint Paul Pass—gap (2) MT-8
Saint Paul Pass Tunnel—tunnel ID-8
Saint Paul Pass Tunnel—tunnel MT-8
Saint Paul Peak—summit MT-8
Saint Paul P. O. (historical)—locale AL-4
**Saint Paul (P.O. Name St. Paul Island)**—pop pl AK-9
Saint Paul Presbyterian Church—hist pl TN-4
Saint Paul Roman Catholic Church—hist pl OR-9
Saint Paul (RR name for St. Pauls)—other NC-3
Saint Pauls—locale SC-3
**Saint Pauls**—pop pl NC-3
**Saint Pauls**—pop pl OH-6
**Saint Pauls**—pop pl SC-3
Saint Pauls Abbey—church NJ-2
Saint Pauls African Methodist Episcopal Ch MS-4
Saint Pauls AME Ch—church (2) AL-4
Saint Pauls Baptist Ch—church (2) MS-4
Saint Paul's Baptist Church—hist pl TX-5
Saint Paul's Bottoms—hist pl LA-4
Saint Pauls Branch—stream SC-3
Saint Pauls by the Sea Episcopal Ch—church FL-3
Saint Pauls by the Sea Episcopal Day Sch—school FL-3
Saint Pauls Camp—locale WI-6
Saint Pauls Cathedral—church AL-4
Saint Pauls Cathedral—church CA-9
Saint Pauls Cathedral—church PA-2
Saint Paul's Cathedral—hist pl NY-2
Saint Paul's Cathedral—hist pl OK-5
Saint Paul's Cathedral and Parish House—hist pl NY-2
Saint Pauls Catholic Ch AL-4
Saint Pauls Catholic Ch—church AL-4
Saint Pauls Catholic Ch—church DE-2
Saint Pauls Catholic Ch—church (3) FL-3
Saint Pauls Catholic Ch—church MS-4
Saint Pauls Catholic Ch—church NC-3
Saint Pauls Catholic Ch—church TN-4
Saint Paul's Catholic Church—hist pl AL-4
Saint Pauls Catholic Sch—school TN-4
Saint Pauls Cem—cemetery (3) AL-4
Saint Pauls Cem—cemetery (4) AR-4
Saint Pauls Cem—cemetery CT-1
Saint Pauls Cem—cemetery (2) FL-3
Saint Pauls Cem—cemetery (2) GA-3
Saint Pauls Cem—cemetery (4) IL-6
Saint Pauls Cem—cemetery (6) IN-6
Saint Pauls Cem—cemetery (7) IA-7
Saint Paul's Cem—cemetery IA-7
Saint Pauls Cem—cemetery IA-7
Saint Pauls Cem—cemetery (2) KS-7
Saint Pauls Cem—cemetery KY-4
Saint Pauls Cem—cemetery (5) LA-4
Saint Pauls Cem—cemetery (2) MD-2
Saint Pauls Cem—cemetery (3) MA-1
Saint Pauls Cem—cemetery (2) MI-6
Saint Pauls Cem—cemetery (15) MN-6
Saint Pauls Cem—cemetery (6) MS-4
Saint Pauls Cem—cemetery (7) MO-7
Saint Pauls Cem—cemetery (6) NE-7
Saint Pauls Cem—cemetery (9) NY-2
Saint Pauls Cem—cemetery (5) ND-7
Saint Pauls Cem—cemetery (10) OH-6
Saint Pauls Cem—cemetery OR-9
Saint Pauls Cem—cemetery (12) PA-2
Saint Pauls Cem—cemetery (7) SC-3
Saint Pauls Cem—cemetery (6) SD-7
Saint Pauls Cem—cemetery (4) TN-4
Saint Pauls Cem—cemetery (2) TX-5
Saint Pauls Cem—cemetery VT-1
Saint Pauls Cem—cemetery (6) VA-3
Saint Pauls Cem—cemetery WV-2
Saint Pauls Cem—cemetery (12) WI-6
Saint Paul's Cemetery—hist pl MD-2
Saint Pauls Ch AL-4
Saint Pauls Ch DE-2
Saint Pauls Ch IN-6
Saint Pauls Ch MS-4
Saint Pauls Ch TN-4
Saint Pauls Ch—church (24) AL-4
Saint Pauls Ch—church (11) AR-4
Saint Pauls Ch—church (2) CT-1
Saint Pauls Ch—church (3) DE-2
Saint Pauls Ch—church DC-2
Saint Pauls Ch—church (26) FL-3
Saint Pauls Ch—church (49) GA-3
Saint Pauls Ch—church (12) IL-6
Saint Pauls Ch—church (20) IN-6
Saint Pauls Ch—church (4) IA-7
Saint Paul's Ch—church IA-7
Saint Pauls Ch—church (9) IA-7
Saint Pauls Ch—church (6) KS-7
Saint Pauls Ch—church (3) KY-4
Saint Pauls Ch—church (10) LA-4
Saint Pauls Ch—church (22) MD-2
Saint Pauls Ch—church MA-1
Saint Pauls Ch—church (5) MI-6
Saint Pauls Ch—church (12) MN-6
Saint Pauls Ch—church (18) MS-4
Saint Pauls Ch—church (8) MO-7
Saint Pauls Ch—church (18) NE-7
Saint Pauls Ch—church (10) NJ-2
Saint Pauls Ch—church (22) NY-2
Saint Pauls Ch—church (35) NC-3
Saint Pauls Ch—church (4) ND-7
Saint Pauls Ch—church (27) OH-6
Saint Pauls Ch—church (70) PA-2
Saint Pauls Ch—church (36) SC-3
Saint Pauls Ch—church (4) SD-7
Saint Pauls Ch—church (16) TN-4
Saint Pauls Ch—church (10) TX-5
Saint Pauls Ch—church (41) VA-3
Saint Pauls Ch—church (3) WV-2
Saint Pauls Ch—church (19) WI-6
Saint Paul Sch—school AR-4
Saint Paul Sch—school CA-9
Saint Paul Sch—school (2) FL-3
Saint Paul Sch—school (9) IL-6
Saint Paul Sch—school IN-6
Saint Paul Sch—school (3) IA-7
Saint Paul Sch—school KS-7
Saint Paul Sch—school (2) LA-4
Saint Paul Sch—school (9) MI-6
Saint Paul Sch—school MN-6
Saint Paul Sch—school MS-4
Saint Paul Sch—school MO-7
Saint Paul Sch—school (4) NE-7
Saint Paul Sch—school NY-2
Saint Paul Sch—school OR-9
Saint Paul Sch—school (4) SC-3
Saint Paul Sch—school (8) TX-5
Saint Paul Sch—school (7) WI-6
Saint Paul Sch (abandoned)—school MO-7
Saint Paul Sch (abandoned)—school PA-2
Saint Pauls Chapel MS-4
Saint Pauls Chapel—church GA-3
Saint Pauls Chapel—church ME-1
Saint Pauls Chapel—church TN-4
Saint Pauls Chapel—church (2) VA-3
Saint Paul's Chapel—hist pl MD-2
Saint Paul's Chapel—hist pl NY-2
Saint Pauls Ch (historical)—church (3) AL-4
Saint Pauls Ch (historical)—church PA-2
Saint Paul Sch (historical)—school (5) AL-4
Saint Paul Sch (historical)—school (3) MS-4
Saint Paul Sch (historical)—school MO-7
Saint Paul Sch (historical)—school TN-4
Saint Pauls Childrens Home—building PA-2
Saint Paul's Ch Number 1—church MS-4
Saint Pauls Church PA-2
Saint Paul's Church—hist pl MD-2
Saint Paul's Church—hist pl PA-2
Saint Paul's Church—hist pl (5) VA-3
**Saint Pauls Church**—pop pl (2) PA-2
Saint Paul's Church, Chapel, and Parish House—hist pl MA-1
Saint Paul's Church and Cemetery—hist pl NC-3
Saint Paul's Church Natl Historic Site—hist pl NY-2
Saint Paul's Church Rectory—hist pl MD-2
Saint Pauls CME Ch—church AL-4
Saint Pauls Coll—school DC-2
Saint Pauls Coll—school LA-4
Saint Pauls Coll—school MO-7
Saint Pauls Coll—school VA-3
Saint Paul's College—hist pl VA-3
Saint Pauls Convent—church FL-3
Saint Pauls Day Sch—school FL-3
Saint Pauls Elem Sch—school NC-3
Saint Paul Seminary—school MN-6
Saint Paul's Episcopal Cathedral—hist pl NY-2
Saint Pauls Episcopal Ch TN-4
Saint Pauls Episcopal Ch—church (3) AL-4
Saint Pauls Episcopal Ch—church FL-3
Saint Pauls Episcopal Ch—church IN-6
Saint Pauls Episcopal Ch—church (4) MS-4
Saint Pauls Episcopal Ch—church (2) NC-3
Saint Paul's Episcopal Chapel—hist pl AL-4
Saint Pauls Episcopal Ch (historical)—church AL-4
Saint Paul's Episcopal Church—hist pl (2) AL-4
Saint Paul's Episcopal Church—hist pl (2) AZ-5
Saint Paul's Episcopal Church—hist pl DE-2
Saint Paul's Episcopal Church—hist pl DC-2
Saint Paul's Episcopal Church—hist pl GA-3
Saint Paul's Episcopal Church—hist pl (2) KY-4
Saint Paul's Episcopal Church—hist pl (2) MD-2
Saint Paul's Episcopal Church—hist pl MO-7
Saint Paul's Episcopal Church—hist pl NY-2
Saint Paul's Episcopal Church—hist pl OH-6
Saint Paul's Episcopal Church—hist pl PA-2
Saint Paul's Episcopal Church—hist pl (2) TN-4
Saint Paul's Episcopal Church—hist pl TX-5
Saint Paul's Episcopal Church—hist pl (2) VA-3
Saint Paul's Episcopal Church—hist pl WA-9
Saint Paul's Episcopal Church—hist pl (3) WI-6
Saint Paul's Episcopal Church and Cemetery—hist pl NC-3
Saint Paul's Episcopal Church and Churchyard—hist pl NC-3
Saint Paul's Episcopal Church and Rectory—hist pl NY-2
Saint Paul's Episcopal Church Complex—hist pl NY-2
Saint Pauls Episcopal Ch (Vernal)—church UT-8
Saint Pauls Episcopal Sch—school AL-4
Saint Paul's Evangelical Lutheran Church—hist pl IN-6
Saint Paul's German Evangelical Church and Parish House—hist pl KY-4
Saint Pauls HS—school AR-4
Saint Pauls HS—school CA-9
Saint Pauls HS—school NC-3
Saint Pauls JHS—school VA-3
Saint Paul Slough—channel IA-7
Saint Pauls Lutheran Ch—church (2) AL-4
Saint Pauls Lutheran Ch—church DE-2
Saint Pauls Lutheran Ch—church (2) KS-7
Saint Pauls Lutheran Ch—church PA-2
Saint Pauls Lutheran Ch—church TN-4
Saint Pauls Lutheran Ch (historical)—church AL-4
Saint Pauls Lutheran Ch (Ogden)—church UT-8
Saint Paul's Lutheran Church, Parsonage and Cemetery—hist pl NY-2
Saint Pauls Lutheran Sch—school AL-4
Saint Pauls Memorial Cem—cemetery TX-5
Saint Paul's Memorial Church and Rectory—hist pl NY-2
Saint Paul's Memorial Episcopal Church and Guild Hall—hist pl NM-5
Saint Pauls Memorial Park—park NC-3
Saint Pauls Methodist Ch—church MA-1
Saint Pauls Methodist Ch (historical)—church AL-4
Saint Pauls Methodist Episcopal Ch (historical)—church AL-4
Saint Paul's Methodist Episcopal Church—hist pl AL-4
Saint Pauls Millpond—reservoir MD-2
Saint Pauls Mission—church NC-3
Saint Paul's Mission—hist pl WA-9
Saint Pauls Mission—school MT-8
Saint Pauls Mission Sch—school VA-3
Saint Pauls Mission State Historical Site—park WA-9
Saint Pauls Monastery—church OH-6
Saint Pauls MS—school NC-3
Saint Pauls No 3 Ch—church GA-3
Saint Pauls Number 1 Ch—church SC-3
Saint Pauls Number 2 Ch AL-4
Saint Pauls Orphanage—building PA-2
Saint Paul's Parish Church—hist pl AR-4
Saint Paul's Parish Church—hist pl MD-2
Saint Pauls Parochial Sch—school AL-4
Saint Pauls Polish Natl Catholic Ch—church FL-3
Saint Pauls Presbyterian Ch—church FL-3
Saint Paul's Protestant Episcopal Church—hist pl MD-2
Saint Paul's Rectory—hist pl MA-1
Saint Pauls Reformed Episcopal Ch—church (2) FL-3
Saint Pauls Roman Catholic Church—building IA-7
Saint Paul's Roman Catholic Church—hist pl NC-3
**Saint Pauls (RR name St. Paul)**—pop pl NC-3
Saint Pauls Sch IN-6
Saint Pauls Sch—school AL-4
Saint Pauls Sch—school (8) CA-9
Saint Pauls Sch—school DE-2
Saint Pauls Sch—school (2) FL-3
Saint Pauls Sch—school ID-8
Saint Pauls Sch—school (9) IL-6
Saint Pauls Sch—school (4) IN-6
Saint Pauls Sch—school (2) IA-7
Saint Pauls Sch—school KY-4
Saint Pauls Sch—school (2) LA-4
Saint Pauls Sch—school MD-2
Saint Pauls Sch—school (2) MA-1
Saint Pauls Sch—school (3) MI-6
Saint Pauls Sch—school (2) MN-6
Saint Pauls Sch—school (2) MO-7
Saint Pauls Sch—school (2) NE-7
Saint Pauls Sch—school NH-1
Saint Pauls Sch—school (4) NJ-2
Saint Pauls Sch—school (8) NY-2
Saint Pauls Sch—school NC-3
Saint Pauls Sch—school (10) OH-6
Saint Pauls Sch—school (2) OR-9
Saint Pauls Sch—school (2) PA-2
Saint Pauls Sch—school (3) SC-3
Saint Pauls Sch—school TN-4
Saint Pauls Sch—school (2) TX-5
Saint Pauls Sch—school VA-3
Saint Pauls Sch—school (2) WA-9
Saint Pauls Sch—school (8) WI-6
Saint Pauls School—locale TX-5
Saint Pauls School Camp—locale NH-1
Saint Pauls School Cem—cemetery NH-1
Saint Pauls Seminary—school NY-2
Saint Pauls Spiritual Ch—church AL-4
Saint Pauls (Township of)—fmr MCD NC-3
Saint Pauls Union Ch—church PA-2
Saint Pauls United Methodist Ch—church (3) DE-2
Saint Pauls United Methodist Ch—church FL-3
Saint Pauls United Methodist Ch—church MS-4
Saint Pauls Woods—woods IL-6
Saint Paul the Apostle Catholic Ch—church FL-3
Saint Paul Township—civil ND-7
Saint Paul United Ch of Christ—church IN-6
Saint Paul United Methodist Ch AL-4
Saint Paul United Methodist Ch—church (8) MS-4
Saint Paul United Methodist Church TN-4
Saint Paul United Presbyterian Church TN-4
Saint Paulus Ch—church IN-6
Saint Paulus Lutheran Church—hist pl CA-9
Saint Paul Waterway—bay WA-9
Saint Paul Waterworks—other MN-6
Saint Paus Methodist Ch—church TN-4
Saint Perpetuas Ch—church MI-6
Saint Pete Plaza (Shop Ctr)—locale FL-3
Saint Peter AZ-5
Saint Peter KS-7
Saint Peter—locale MT-8
**Saint Peter**—pop pl FL-3
**Saint Peter**—pop pl (2) IL-6
**Saint Peter**—pop pl IN-6
**Saint Peter**—pop pl KS-7
**Saint Peter**—pop pl MN-6
**Saint Peter**—pop pl OH-6
**Saint Peter**—pop pl WI-6
**Saint Peter**—pop pl VI-3
Saint Peter—school MI-6
Saint Peter—school PA-2
Saint Peter—summit VI-3
Saint Peter African Methodist Church—hist pl TN-4
Saint Peter African Methodist Episcopal Ch—church MS-4
Saint Peter AME Ch—church (2) AL-4
Saint Peter A.M.E. Church—hist pl LA-4
Saint Peter and Paul Catholic Ch—church FL-3
Saint Peter and Paul Catholic Ch—church TN-4
Saint Peter and Paul Cem—cemetery PA-2
Saint Peter And Paul Cem—cemetery TX-5
Saint Peter and Paul Ch—church OH-6
Saint Peter and Paul Ch—church PA-2
Saint Peter and Pauls Ch—church TX-5
Saint Peter and Paul Sch—school IN-6
Saint Peter and Paul Sch—school MT-8
Saint Peter and Paul Sch—school TX-5
Saint Peter and Saint Paul Historic District-Oliver's Second addition—hist pl OH-6
Saint Peter Baptist Ch AL-4
Saint Peter Baptist Ch—church FL-3
Saint Peter Cem—cemetery AR-4
Saint Peter Cem—cemetery IL-6
Saint Peter Cem—cemetery (5) IA-7
Saint Peter Cem—cemetery (3) LA-4
Saint Peter Cem—cemetery MI-6
Saint Peter Cem—cemetery (5) MN-6
Saint Peter Cem—cemetery (4) MS-4
Saint Peter Cem—cemetery MO-7
Saint Peter Cem—cemetery (2) NE-7
Saint Peter Cem—cemetery (2) ND-7
Saint Peter Cem—cemetery (3) SD-7
Saint Peter Cem—cemetery TN-4
Saint Peter Cem—cemetery (3) WI-6
Saint Peter Ch MS-4
Saint Peter Ch PA-2
Saint Peter Ch—church (3) AL-4
Saint Peter Ch—church (3) AR-4
Saint Peter Ch—church FL-3
Saint Peter Ch—church GA-3
Saint Peter Ch—church KS-7
Saint Peter Ch—church KY-4
Saint Peter Ch—church (6) LA-4
Saint Peter Ch—church (2) MN-6
Saint Peter Ch—church (13) MS-4
Saint Peter Ch—church MO-7
Saint Peter Ch—church NJ-2
Saint Peter Ch—church (3) NC-3
Saint Peter Ch—church ND-7
Saint Peter Ch—church (2) PA-2
Saint Peter Ch—church (3) SC-3
Saint Peter Ch—church (4) SD-7
Saint Peter Ch—church TN-4
Saint Peter Ch—church (3) TX-5
Saint Peter Ch—church (6) WI-6
Saint Peter Ch (historical)—church (2) AL-4
Saint Peter Ch (historical)—church MS-4
Saint Peter Claver—school FL-3
Saint Peter Clavers Roman Catholic Ch (historical)—church AL-4
Saint Peter Clavers Sch (historical)—school AL-4
Saint Peter Creek—stream OR-9
Saint Peter Creek—stream WA-9
Saint Peter Flat—flat WA-9
Saint Peter Free Will Baptist Ch—church FL-3
Saint Peter-Greenfield Cemetery SD-7
Saint Peter HS—school CA-9
Saint Peter-Immanuel Lutheran Sch—school IN-6
Saint Peter Lutheran Cemetery SD-7
Saint Peter Lutheran Ch—church FL-3
Saint Peter Lutheran Ch—church IN-6
Saint Peter Lutheran Sch—school (4) IN-6
Saint Peter Methodist Ch MS-4

Saints Cyril and Mehodius Ch—*church* ... SD-7
Saints Cyril and Methodius Sch—*school* ... NY-2
Saints Cyril and Methodius Sch—*school* ... TX-5
Saints Delight Ch—*church* (4) ... NC-3
Saints Delite Ch—*church* ... NC-3
Saint Sebald—*locale* ... IA-7
**Saint Sebastian**—*pop pl* ... OH-6
Saint Sebastian Catholic Ch—*church* ... FL-3
Saint Sebastian Cem—*cemetery* ... CT-1
Saint Sebastian Cem—*cemetery* ... WI-6
Saint Sebastian River—*stream* ... FL-3
Saint Sebastians Cem—*cemetery* ... WV-2
Saint Sebastians Ch—*church* ... IL-6
Saint Sebastian Sch—*school* (2) ... CA-9
Saint Sebastian Sch—*school* ... IL-6
Saint Sebastian Sch—*school* ... KY-4
Saint Sebastian Sch—*school* (2) ... MI-6
Saint Sebastian Sch—*school* ... PA-2
Saint Sebastian Sch—*school* ... WI-6
Saint Sebastians Sch—*school* ... MA-1
Saint Sebastians Sch—*school* ... OH-6
Saints Edward—*church* ... WI-6
Saint Sehastians Sch—*school* ... NY-2
Saint Seraphim Ch—*church* ... NY-2
Saint Seraphim Chapel—*hist pl* ... AK-9
Saint Sergius Chapel—*hist pl* ... AK-9
Saint Severin Cem—*cemetery* ... KS-7
Saint Severin Ch—*church* ... KS-7
Saint Severins Cem—*cemetery* ... PA-2
Saint Severin's Old Log Church—*hist pl* ... PA-2
Saints Flat—*flat* ... WA-9
Saints Francis and Ann Ch—*church* ... LA-4
Saint Silovam Baptist Ch—*church* ... AL-4
Saint Simeons Ch—*church* ... WI-6
Saint Simeon Sch—*school* ... IL-6
Saint Simon and Jude Sch—*school* ... AZ-5
Saint Simona Sch—*school* ... IL-6
*Saint Simon Island* ... GA-3
Saint Simon Roman Catholic Ch—*church* ... IN-6
*Saint Simons* ... GA-3
**Saint Simons**—*pop pl* ... GA-3
Saint Simons (CCD)—*cens area* ... GA-3
Saint Simons (census name St. Simons Island)—*other* ... GA-3
Saint Simons Ch—*church* ... FL-3
Saint Simons Ch—*church* ... LA-4
Saint Simons Ch—*church* ... MD-2
Saint Simons Ch—*church* ... SC-3
*Saint Simon School* ... IN-6
Saint Simons Episcopal Ch—*church* ... FL-3
*Saint Simon's Island* ... GA-3
Saint Simons Island—*island* ... GA-3
**Saint Simons Island**—*pop pl* ... GA-3
Saint Simons Island (census name for St. Simons)—*CDP* ... GA-3
Saint Simons Lighthouse—*locale* ... GA-3
Saint Simons Lighthouse and Lighthouse Keepers' Bldg—*hist pl* ... GA-3
Saint Simons Mill Ch—*church* ... GA-3
Saint Simons Mills—*locale* ... GA-3
Saint Simons Sch—*school* ... NY-2
Saint Simons Sch—*school* ... OH-6
Saint Simons Sch—*school* ... PA-2
Saint Simons Sound—*bay* ... GA-3
*Saint Simons Village* ... GA-3
Saint Simons Yacht Club—*other* ... GA-3
Saint Simon the Apostle Sch—*school* ... IN-6
Saint Sinai Ch—*church* ... SC-3
Saints James and Phillip Cem—*cemetery* ... NJ-2
Saints Joachim and Ann Sch—*school* ... NY-2
Saints John—*locale* ... CO-8
Saints John and Anne Ch—*church* ... MI-6
Saints John and Mary Sch—*school* ... NY-2
Saints John and Paul Sch—*school* ... NY-2
Saints John Creek—*stream* ... CO-8
Saints John Mine—*mine* ... CO-8
Saints Margaret and Marys Sch—*school* ... NY-2
Saint Smyrna Ch—*church* ... GA-3
*Saint Sophia* ... KS-7
Saint Sophia Camp—*locale* ... CA-9
Saint Sophia Greek Orthodox Cathedral—*church* ... FL-3
Saint Sophia Home of the Little Sisters of the Poor—*hist pl* ... VA-3
Saint Sophia Ridge—*ridge* ... CO-8
Saint Sophias Ch—*church* ... FL-3
*Saint Sophias School* ... FL-3
Saint Southwest Park Ch—*church* ... TX-5
Saints Patrick and George Sch—*school* ... NY-2
Saints Patricks Cem—*cemetery* ... KY-4
Saints Peter—*school* ... FL-3
Saints Peter—*school* ... KY-4
Saints Peter—*school* ... WI-6
Saints Peter And Mary Cem—*cemetery* ... NE-7
Saints Peter and Paul Catholic Ch—*church* ... FL-3
Saints Peter and Paul Catholic Ch—*church* ... UT-8
Saints Peter and Paul Catholic Church and Buildings—*hist pl* ... TN-4
Saints Peter and Paul Catholic Church Complex—*hist pl* ... ND-7
Saints Peter and Paul Catholic Sch—*school* ... MO-7
Saints Peter And Paul Cem—*cemetery* ... CT-1
Saints Peter and Paul Cem—*cemetery* (2) ... IL-6
Saints Peter And Paul Cem—*cemetery* ... IL-6
Saints Peter and Paul Cem—*cemetery* ... IL-6
Saints Peter And Paul Cem—*cemetery* ... IL-6
Saints Peter and Paul Cem—*cemetery* ... IL-6
Saints Peter And Paul Cem—*cemetery* ... IA-7
Saints Peter and Paul Cem—*cemetery* (2) ... KS-7
Saints Peter and Paul Cem—*cemetery* (2) ... MA-1
Saints Peter and Paul Cem—*cemetery* (2) ... MI-6
Saints Peter And Paul Cem—*cemetery* ... MN-6
Saints Peter And Paul Cem—*cemetery* ... MO-7
Saints Peter and Paul Cem—*cemetery* (2) ... NE-7
Saints Peter and Paul Cem—*cemetery* (2) ... NJ-2
Saints Peter and Paul Cem—*cemetery* ... NY-2
Saints Peter And Paul Cem—*cemetery* ... NY-2
Saints Peter and Paul Cem—*cemetery* ... NY-2
Saints Peter and Paul Cem—*cemetery* (4) ... ND-7
Saints Peter and Paul Cem—*cemetery* ... OH-6
Saints Peter And Paul Cem—*cemetery* (2) ... OH-6
Saints Peter and Paul Cem—*cemetery* (2) ... OH-6
Saints Peter And Paul Cem—*cemetery* ... OK-5
Saints Peter And Paul Cem—*cemetery* (2) ... PA-2
Saints Peter and Paul Cem—*cemetery* ... PA-2
Saints Peter And Paul Cem—*cemetery* (4) ... PA-2
Saints Peter and Paul Cem—*cemetery* ... PA-2
Saints Peter And Paul Cem—*cemetery* ... PA-2
Saints Peter and Paul Cem—*cemetery* ... PA-2
Saints Peter And Paul Cem—*cemetery* (2) ... WI-6
Saints Peter and Paul Ch—*church* ... FL-3
Saints Peter And Paul Ch—*church* ... IA-7
Saints Peter and Paul Ch—*church* ... IA-7
Saints Peter And Paul Ch—*church* ... IA-7
Saints Peter And Paul Ch—*church* (2) ... KS-7
Saints Peter and Paul Ch—*church* ... MN-6
Saints Peter And Paul Ch—*church* ... MN-6
Saints Peter and Paul Ch—*church* (2) ... NJ-2
Saints Peter and Paul Ch—*church* ... NC-3
Saints Peter and Paul Ch—*church* ... ND-7
Saints Peter And Paul Ch—*church* ... OH-6
Saints Peter and Paul Ch—*church* ... OH-6
Saints Peter And Paul Ch—*church* ... PA-2
Saints Peter and Paul Ch—*church* ... PA-2
Saints Peter And Paul Ch—*church* (2) ... PA-2
Saints Peter and Paul Ch—*church* ... PA-2
Saints Peter And Paul Ch—*church* ... WI-6
Saints Peter and Paul Ch—*church* ... WI-6
Saints Peter and Paul Church—*hist pl* ... AK-9
Saints Peter And Paul Church—*hist pl* ... MI-6
Saints Peter and Paul Church—*hist pl* ... ND-7
Saints Peter and Paul Church-Ukranian Catholic—*hist pl* ... MN-6
Saints Peter And Paul HS—*school* ... IL-6
Saints Peter and Paul HS—*school* ... MI-6
Saints Peter and Paul Roman Catholic Cathedral—*church* ... IN-6
Saints Peter and Paul Roman Catholic Church—*hist pl* ... IA-7
Saints Peter and Paul Sch—*school* ... AZ-5
Saints Peter and Paul Sch—*school* ... CO-8
Saints Peter And Paul Sch—*school* ... CT-1
Saints Peter and Paul Sch—*school* ... FL-3
Saints Peter and Paul Sch—*school* (2) ... IL-6
Saints Peter And Paul Sch—*school* ... IA-7
Saints Peter and Paul Sch—*school* ... KS-7
Saints Peter And Paul Sch—*school* ... KS-7
Saints Peter and Paul Sch—*school* (2) ... MA-1
Saints Peter and Paul Sch—*school* (3) ... MI-6
Saints Peter and Paul Sch—*school* ... MN-6
Saints Peter And Paul Sch—*school* ... MN-6
Saints Peter and Paul Sch—*school* ... NJ-2
Saints Peter And Paul Sch—*school* ... NY-2
Saints Peter and Paul Sch—*school* (3) ... NY-2
Saints Peter and Paul Sch—*school* ... ND-7
Saints Peter And Paul Sch—*school* (3) ... OH-6
Saints Peter and Paul Sch—*school* ... OH-6
Saints Peter And Paul Sch—*school* ... OH-6
Saints Peter and Paul Sch—*school* (2) ... OK-5
Saints Peter and Paul Sch—*school* ... WI-6
Saints Peter And Paul Sch—*school* ... WI-6
Saints Peter And Paul Seminary—*school* ... OH-6
Saints Peter and Paul Ukrainian Orthodox Ch—*church* ... DE-2
Saints Philip And James Sch—*school* ... NY-2
Saints Phillip and James Ch—*church* ... MO-7
Saints Phillips and James Sch—*school* ... NY-2
Saint Spyridon Ch—*church* ... PA-2
**Saints Rest**—*pop pl* ... MS-4
Saints Rest—*summit* ... NY-2
Saint's Rest, Tukey's Pioneer Cabin and Homestead House—*hist pl* ... WA-9
Saints Rest Bar—*bar* ... CA-9
Saints Rest Cem—*cemetery* ... GA-3
Saints Rest Cem—*cemetery* ... MD-2
Saints Rest Cem—*cemetery* ... TX-5
Saints Rest Ch—*church* (3) ... LA-4
Saints Rest Ch—*church* ... MS-4
Saints Rest Ch—*church* ... NC-3
Saints Rest Ch—*church* ... TX-5
Saints Rest Creek—*stream* ... CA-9
Saints Rest Gulch—*valley* ... UT-8
Saints Rest Plantation (historical)—*locale* ... MS-4
Saints Rest P.O. (historical)—*building* ... MS-4
Saints Rest Sch—*school* (2) ... LA-4
Saints Sergius and Herman of Valaam Chapel—*hist pl* ... AK-9
Saints Sergius and Herman of Valaam Church—*hist pl* ... AK-9
Saints Simon and Jude Catholic Sch—*school* ... PA-2
Saints Simon and Jude Ch—*church* ... AL-4
Saints Simon and Jude Sch—*school* ... NY-2
Saint Stanilaus Cem—*cemetery* ... MA-1
Saint Stanisclaus Sch—*school* ... CT-1
Saint Stanislas Sch—*school* ... PA-2
Saint Stanislaus Cem—*cemetery* ... CT-1
Saint Stanislaus Cem—*cemetery* ... IN-6
Saint Stanislaus Cem—*cemetery* ... MD-2
Saint Stanislaus Cem—*cemetery* (3) ... MA-1
Saint Stanislaus Cem—*cemetery* ... MI-6
Saint Stanislaus Cem—*cemetery* ... MN-6
Saint Stanislaus Cem—*cemetery* ... NH-1
Saint Stanislaus Cem—*cemetery* ... NJ-2
Saint Stanislaus Cem—*cemetery* (2) ... NY-2
Saint Stanislaus Cem—*cemetery* ... ND-7
Saint Stanislaus Cem—*cemetery* (4) ... PA-2
Saint Stanislaus Cem—*cemetery* ... TX-5
Saint Stanislaus Cem—*cemetery* (3) ... WI-6
Saint Stanislaus Ch—*church* ... IN-6
Saint Stanislaus Ch—*church* ... IA-7
Saint Stanislaus Ch—*church* ... MD-2
Saint Stanislaus Ch—*church* ... MI-6
Saint Stanislaus Ch—*church* ... NC-3
Saint Stanislaus Ch—*church* (2) ... PA-2
Saint Stanislaus Ch—*church* ... TX-5
Saint Stanislaus Ch—*church* ... WI-6
Saint Stanislaus Coll—*school* ... MS-4
Saint Stanislaus Convent—*church* ... CA-9
Saint Stanislaus Kostka Cem—*cemetery* ... MA-1
Saint Stanislaus Kostka Roman Catholic Church—*hist pl* ... PA-2
Saint Stanislaus Kostka Sch—*school* ... NJ-2
Saint Stanislaus Kostka Sch—*school* ... VT-1
Saint Stanislaus Novitiate—*church* ... OH-6
Saint Stanislaus Polish Ch—*church* ... PA-2
Saint Stanislaus Sch—*school* ... CT-1
Saint Stanislaus Sch—*school* ... ID-8
Saint Stanislaus Sch—*school* (2) ... IL-6
Saint Stanislaus Sch—*school* (2) ... IN-6
Saint Stanislaus Sch—*school* (3) ... MA-1
Saint Stanislaus Sch—*school* (4) ... MI-6
Saint Stanislaus Sch—*school* (2) ... MN-6
Saint Stanislaus Sch—*school* ... NE-7
Saint Stanislaus Sch—*school* ... NJ-2
Saint Stanislaus Sch—*school* (5) ... NY-2
Saint Stanislaus Sch—*school* (2) ... OH-6
Saint Stanislaus Sch—*school* (3) ... PA-2
Saint Stanislaus Sch—*school* ... TX-5
Saint Stanislaus Sch—*school* (2) ... WI-6
Saint Stanislaus Seminary—*school* ... MO-7
Saint Stanislaus Stadium—*park* ... MS-4
Saint Stanislawa Sch—*school* ... IN-6
Saint Stanslaus Sch—*school* ... OH-6
Saint Stephans Ch—*church* ... IN-6
Saint Stephans Ch—*church* ... LA-4
Saint Stephans Ch—*church* ... ND-7
Saint Stephan's Church—*hist pl* ... NJ-2
Saint Stephanus Sch—*school* ... MI-6
*Saint Stephen* ... OH-6
**Saint Stephen**—*pop pl* ... MD-2
**Saint Stephen**—*pop pl* ... MN-6
**Saint Stephen**—*pop pl* ... SC-3
Saint Stephen Catholic Ch—*church* ... TN-4
Saint Stephen (CCD)—*cens area* ... SC-3
Saint Stephen Cem—*cemetery* ... CA-9
Saint Stephen Cem—*cemetery* ... MI-6
Saint Stephen Cem—*cemetery* ... MN-6
Saint Stephen Cem—*cemetery* ... SD-7
Saint Stephen Ch—*church* ... AR-4
Saint Stephen Ch—*church* ... IN-6
Saint Stephen Ch—*church* ... MI-6
Saint Stephen Ch—*church* ... MN-6
Saint Stephen Ch—*church* ... MS-4
Saint Stephen Ch—*church* ... MO-7
Saint Stephen Ch—*church* (4) ... NC-3
Saint Stephen Ch—*church* ... PA-2
Saint Stephen Ch—*church* (2) ... SC-3
Saint Stephen Ch—*church* ... WI-6
Saint Stephen Episcopal Sch—*school* ... FL-3
Saint Stephen HS—*school* ... LA-4
Saint Stephen Lutheran Ch—*church* ... FL-3
Saint Stephen Lutheran Ch (LCA)—*church* ... FL-3
Saint Stephen Lutheren Ch LCA—*church* ... FL-3
Saint Stephen Martyr Sch—*school* ... KY-4
Saint Stephen Presbyterian Ch—*church* ... FL-3
Saint Stephen Run—*stream* ... MD-2
*Saint Stephens* ... AL-4
*Saint Stephens* ... MN-6
*Saint Stephens* ... SC-3
Saint Stephens—*locale* ... NC-3
**Saint Stephens**—*pop pl* ... AL-4
**Saint Stephens**—*pop pl* ... NE-7
**Saint Stephens**—*pop pl* ... OH-6
**Saint Stephens**—*pop pl* ... VA-3
**Saint Stephens**—*pop pl* ... WY-8
Saint Stephens African Methodist Episcopal Ch—*church* ... FL-3
Saint Stephens AME Ch—*church* ... AL-4
Saint Stephens Baptist Ch—*church* ... AL-4
Saint Stephens Bible Ch—*church* ... AL-4
Saint Stephens Catholic Ch—*church* (2) ... FL-3
Saint Stephens Catholic Ch—*church* ... MS-4
Saint Stephens Cem—*cemetery* ... AL-4
Saint Stephens Cem—*cemetery* ... AR-4
Saint Stephens Cem—*cemetery* (2) ... IL-6
Saint Stephens Cem—*cemetery* (2) ... KY-4
Saint Stephens Cem—*cemetery* (2) ... MD-2
Saint Stephens Cem—*cemetery* ... MA-1
Saint Stephens Cem—*cemetery* ... MN-6
Saint Stephens Cem—*cemetery* ... MO-7
Saint Stephens Cem—*cemetery* (2) ... NJ-2
Saint Stephens Cem—*cemetery* (2) ... NY-2
Saint Stephens Cem—*cemetery* ... NC-3
Saint Stephens Cem—*cemetery* (3) ... OH-6
Saint Stephens Cem—*cemetery* (2) ... PA-2
Saint Stephens Cem—*cemetery* ... SD-7
Saint Stephens Cem—*cemetery* (4) ... WI-6
Saint Stephens Ch—*church* (4) ... AL-4
Saint Stephens Ch—*church* ... AR-4
Saint Stephens Ch—*church* (3) ... FL-3
Saint Stephens Ch—*church* (4) ... GA-3
Saint Stephens Ch—*church* ... IN-6
Saint Stephens Ch—*church* (2) ... KY-4
Saint Stephens Ch—*church* ... LA-4
Saint Stephens Ch—*church* (4) ... MD-2
Saint Stephens Ch—*church* (2) ... MA-1
Saint Stephens Ch—*church* (4) ... MI-6
Saint Stephens Ch—*church* ... MO-7
Saint Stephens Ch—*church* (3) ... NJ-2
Saint Stephens Ch—*church* (2) ... NY-2
Saint Stephens Ch—*church* (10) ... NC-3
Saint Stephens Ch—*church* ... ND-7
Saint Stephens Ch—*church* ... OH-6
Saint Stephens Ch—*church* (5) ... PA-2
Saint Stephens Ch—*church* (5) ... SC-3
Saint Stephens Ch—*church* (2) ... SD-7
Saint Stephens Ch—*church* (12) ... VA-3
Saint Stephens Ch—*church* ... WI-6
Saint Stephen Sch—*school* (2) ... MI-6
Saint Stephen Sch—*school* ... PA-2
Saint Stephen Sch—*school* ... VA-3
Saint Stephen Sch—*school* ... WI-6
Saint Stephens Chapel—*church* ... AL-4
Saint Stephens Ch (historical)—*church* ... PA-2
Saint Stephen's Church—*hist pl* ... PA-2
Saint Stephen's Church—*hist pl* ... VA-3
Saint Stephens Church—*locale* ... VA-3
Saint Stephens Convent—*church* ... CT-1
Saint Stephens Episcopal Ch—*church* ... AL-4
Saint Stephens Episcopal Ch—*church* ... KS-7
Saint Stephens Episcopal Ch—*church* (2) ... MS-4
Saint Stephens Episcopal Ch—*church* ... UT-8
Saint Stephen's Episcopal Church—*hist pl* ... LA-4
Saint Stephen's Episcopal Church—*hist pl* ... MD-2
Saint Stephen's Episcopal Church—*hist pl* ... PA-2
Saint Stephen's Episcopal Church—*hist pl* ... VA-3
Saint Stephens HS—*school* ... MI-6
Saint Stephens HS—*school* ... NC-3
Saint Stephens JHS (historical)—*school* ... AL-4
Saint Stephens Landing (historical)—*locale* ... AL-4
Saint Stephens Methodist Ch—*church* ... MA-1
Saint Stephens Mission (historical)—*church* ... SD-7
Saint Stephens Mission (historical)—*church* ... TN-4
Saint Stephens Priory—*church* ... MA-1
Saint Stephens Road Ch of God—*church* ... AL-4
Saint Stephens Sch—*school* ... CA-9
Saint Stephens Sch—*school* (2) ... CT-1
Saint Stephens Sch—*school* (3) ... FL-3
Saint Stephens Sch—*school* ... IL-6
Saint Stephens Sch—*school* ... IN-6
Saint Stephens Sch—*school* (2) ... MA-1
Saint Stephens Sch—*school* (3) ... MI-6
Saint Stephens Sch—*school* (2) ... MN-6
Saint Stephens Sch—*school* ... MO-7
Saint Stephens Sch—*school* (2) ... NJ-2
Saint Stephens Sch—*school* ... NY-2
Saint Stephens Sch—*school* ... NC-3
Saint Stephens Sch—*school* (4) ... OH-6
Saint Stephens Sch—*school* ... OR-9
Saint Stephens Sch—*school* ... PA-2
Saint Stephens Sch—*school* ... TN-4
Saint Stephens Sch—*school* ... TX-5
Saint Stephens Sch—*school* ... VA-3
Saint Stephens Sch—*school* (3) ... WI-6
Saint Stephens Sch (historical)—*school* ... AL-4
Saint Stephens Seminary—*school* ... HI-9
Saint Stephens State For—*forest* ... AL-4
Saint Stephens The Martyr Ch—*church* ... VA-3
Saint Stephens United Methodist Ch—*church* ... AL-4
Saint Stephen Weekday Sch—*school* ... FL-3
Saint Stevens Cem—*cemetery* ... GA-3
Saint Stevens Cem—*cemetery* ... KY-4
Saint Stevens Cem—*cemetery* ... NC-3
Saint Stevens Ch—*church* ... AR-4
Saint Stevens Ch—*church* (2) ... FL-3
Saint Stevens Ch—*church* ... GA-3
Saint Stevens Ch—*church* ... MD-2
Saint Stevens Ch—*church* ... NJ-2
Saint Stevens Ch—*church* ... NC-3
Saint Stevens Ch—*church* ... PA-2
Saint Stevenson Baptist Ch—*church* ... AL-4
Saint Stevens Sch—*school* ... CT-1
Saint Stevens Sch—*school* ... KY-4
Saints Thomas and Peter Sch—*school* ... MI-6
Saint Susanna Sch—*school* ... IL-6
Saint Susanna Sch—*school* ... IN-6
Saint Suzanne Sch—*school* ... MI-6
Saintsville—*locale* ... NY-2
Saint Sylester Sch—*school* ... IL-6
Saint Sylvan Cem—*cemetery* ... ND-7
Saint Sylvan Mission—*church* ... ND-7
Saint Sylvester Catholic Ch—*church* ... FL-3
Saint Sylvester Cem—*cemetery* ... OH-6
Saint Sylvester Ch—*church* ... KY-4
Saint Sylvester Ch—*church* ... MO-7
Saint Sylvester Ch—*church* ... PA-2
Saint Sylvesters Ch—*church* ... NY-2
Saint Sylvester Sch—*school* ... MI-6
Saint Sylvester Sch—*school* ... NY-2
Saint Sylvester Sch—*school* ... PA-2
Saint Sylvesters Sch—*school* ... NY-2
Saint Sylvias Ch—*church* ... NY-2
Saint Symphorosa Sch—*school* ... IL-6
**Saint Tammany**—*pop pl* ... LA-4
Saint Tammany Corner—*locale* ... LA-4
*Saint Tammany Island* ... MI-6
**Saint Tammany Parish**—*pop pl* ... LA-4
Saint Tammany Sch—*school* ... LA-4
Saint Tarcisius Cem—*cemetery* ... MA-1
Saint Tarcisius Sch—*school* ... MA-1
Saint Tarcissus Sch—*school* ... IL-6
**Saint Teresa**—*pop pl* ... FL-3
Saint Teresa Acad—*school* (2) ... IL-6
Saint Teresa Acad—*school* ... TX-5
*Saint Teresa Beach* ... FL-3
**Saint Teresa Beach**—*pop pl* ... FL-3
Saint Teresa Catholic Ch—*church* ... FL-3
Saint Teresa Cem—*cemetery* (2) ... KS-7
Saint Teresa Cem—*cemetery* ... NJ-2
Saint Teresa Cem—*cemetery* ... OH-6
Saint Teresa Cem—*cemetery* ... PA-2
Saint Teresa Ch—*church* ... LA-4
Saint Teresa Ch—*church* ... MA-1
Saint Teresa Ch—*church* ... NM-5
Saint Teresa Ch—*church* ... TX-5
Saint Teresa of Avila Sch—*school* ... CA-9
Saint Teresa of Avila Sch—*school* ... NY-2
Saint Teresas Ch—*church* ... OH-6
Saint Teresa Sch—*school* ... CA-9
Saint Teresa Sch—*school* ... DC-2
Saint Teresa Sch—*school* ... ME-1
Saint Teresa Sch—*school* ... MI-6
Saint Teresa Sch—*school* ... MO-7
Saint Teresa Sch—*school* ... NY-2
Saint Teresa Sch—*school* ... OH-6
Saint Teresa Sch—*school* (2) ... PA-2
Saint Teresa Sch—*school* ... WI-6
Saint Teresas Sch—*school* ... GA-3
Saint Teresas Sch—*school* (2) ... NJ-2
Saint Teresas Sch—*school* (3) ... NY-2
Saint Teresas Sch—*school* ... OH-6
**Saint Terese**—*pop pl* ... AK-9
Saint Thaddaeus Ch—*church* ... TN-4
*Saint Thaddaeus Episcopal Ch* ... TN-4
Saint Thaddeus Ch—*church* ... SC-3
Saint Thecia Sch—*school* ... IL-6
Saint Thecla Sch—*school* ... MI-6
Saint Theodore Ch—*church* ... MI-6
Saint Theodores Cem—*cemetery* (2) ... MN-6
Saint Theodores Ch—*church* ... NY-2
Saint Theodores Sch—*school* ... NY-2
Saint Theodosius Cem—*cemetery* ... OH-6
Saint Therasas Chapel—*church* ... NY-2
Saint Theresa Acad—*school* ... KY-4
Saint Theresa Catholic Ch—*church* (2) ... AL-4
Saint Theresa Catholic Ch—*church* (4) ... MS-4
Saint Theresa Catholic Ch—*church* ... UT-8
Saint Theresa Cem—*cemetery* ... FL-3
Saint Theresa Cem—*cemetery* ... IL-6
Saint Theresa Cem—*cemetery* ... MI-6
Saint Theresa Cem—*cemetery* ... NE-7
Saint Theresa Cem—*cemetery* ... NY-2
Saint Theresa Cem—*cemetery* ... PA-2
Saint Theresa Cem—*cemetery* ... VT-1
Saint Theresa Cem—*cemetery* ... WI-6
Saint Theresa Ch—*church* ... IA-7
Saint Theresa Ch—*church* ... KS-7
Saint Theresa Ch—*church* ... KY-4
Saint Theresa Ch—*church* (2) ... LA-4
Saint Theresa Ch—*church* ... OH-6
Saint Theresa Ch—*church* ... PA-2
Saint Theresa Ch—*church* ... SC-3
Saint Theresa Ch—*church* ... WI-6
Saint Theresa Convent—*church* ... IL-6
Saint Theresa (historical)—*locale* ... KS-7
Saint Theresa Hosp—*hospital* ... IL-6
Saint Theresa Mine—*mine* ... AZ-5
Saint Theresa Mission—*church* ... AZ-5
Saint Theresa Roman Catholic Church—*hist pl* ... KY-4
Saint Theresas Cem—*cemetery* ... VA-3
Saint Theresas Ch—*church* ... FL-3
Saint Theresas Ch—*church* ... MA-1
Saint Theresa Sch—*school* ... AL-4
Saint Theresa Sch—*school* ... AZ-5
Saint Theresa Sch—*school* ... AR-4
Saint Theresa Sch—*school* ... FL-3
Saint Theresa Sch—*school* (2) ... HI-9
Saint Theresa Sch—*school* (4) ... IL-6
Saint Theresa Sch—*school* ... IN-6
Saint Theresa Sch—*school* ... IA-7
Saint Theresa Sch—*school* ... KY-4
Saint Theresa Sch—*school* ... LA-4
Saint Theresa Sch—*school* ... MN-6
Saint Theresa Sch—*school* ... MS-4
Saint Theresa Sch—*school* ... NV-8
Saint Theresa Sch—*school* ... NY-2
Saint Theresa Sch—*school* ... OH-6
Saint Theresa Sch—*school* (4) ... PA-2
Saint Theresa Sch—*school* ... SD-7
Saint Theresa Sch—*school* (5) ... TX-5
Saint Theresas Girls Sch—*school* ... AS-9
Saint Theresas Sch—*school* ... CT-1
Saint Theresas Sch—*school* ... MA-1
Saint Theresas Sch—*school* ... NJ-2
Saint Theresas Sch—*school* (3) ... NY-2
Saint Theresas Shrine—*church* ... OH-6
Saint Therese Acad—*school* ... CA-9
*Saint Theresea Sch* ... IN-6
Saint Therese Cem—*cemetery* ... VT-1
Saint Therese Ch—*church* ... NM-5
Saint Therese Ch—*church* ... TN-4
Saint Therese of Lisieux Monastery—*church* ... PA-2
*Saint Therese of the Infant Jesus Roman Catholic Church* ... IN-6
Saint Therese Roman Catholic Ch—*church* ... IN-6
Saint Therese Roman Catholic Church, School, and Rectory—*hist pl* ... KY-4
Saint Thereses Catholic Church-Byzantine Rite—*church* ... FL-3
*Saint Therese Sch* ... MS-4
Saint Therese Sch—*school* (2) ... CA-9
Saint Therese Sch—*school* (2) ... CO-8
Saint Therese Sch—*school* ... IN-6
Saint Therese Sch—*school* ... MI-6
Saint Therese Sch—*school* ... NE-7
Saint Therese Sch—*school* ... NH-1
Saint Therese Sch—*school* ... NM-5
Saint Therese Sch—*school* ... OR-9
Saint Therese Sch—*school* ... SD-7
Saint Thereses Sch—*school* ... MO-7
Saint Thereses Sch—*school* (2) ... NJ-2
Saint Thereses Sch—*school* ... OH-6
Saint Theresia Cem—*cemetery* ... MN-6
Saint Thomas—*island* ... VI-3
**Saint Thomas**—*pop pl* (2) ... AR-4
**Saint Thomas**—*pop pl* ... CO-8
**Saint Thomas**—*pop pl* (2) ... IL-6
**Saint Thomas**—*pop pl* ... IN-6
**Saint Thomas**—*pop pl* ... LA-4
**Saint Thomas**—*pop pl* ... MN-6
**Saint Thomas**—*pop pl* ... MO-7
**Saint Thomas**—*pop pl* ... ND-7
**Saint Thomas**—*pop pl* ... PA-2
Saint Thomas Acad—*school* ... MN-6
Saint Thomas Aquinas Catholic Ch—*church* ... FL-3
Saint Thomas Aquinas Catholic Ch—*church* ... TN-4
Saint Thomas Aquinas Cem—*cemetery* ... MS-4
Saint Thomas Aquinas Ch—*church* ... MS-4
Saint Thomas Aquinas Coll—*school* ... NY-2
Saint Thomas Aquinas HS—*school* ... CT-1
Saint Thomas Aquinas HS—*school* ... FL-3
Saint Thomas Aquinas Roman Catholic Ch—*church* ... IN-6
Saint Thomas Aquinas Roman Catholic Ch—*church* ... KS-7
Saint Thomas Aquinas Sch—*school* (2) ... CA-9
Saint Thomas Aquinas Sch—*school* (2) ... IN-6
Saint Thomas Aquinas Sch—*school* ... KS-7
Saint Thomas Aquinas Sch—*school* (2) ... MI-6
Saint Thomas Aquinas Sch—*school* ... NH-1
Saint Thomas Aquinas Sch—*school* (4) ... NY-2
Saint Thomas Aquinas Sch—*school* ... OH-6
Saint Thomas Aquinas Sch—*school* (2) ... PA-2
Saint Thomas Aquinas Sch—*school* ... TX-5
Saint Thomas Aquinas Sch—*school* ... WI-6
*Saint Thomas Assembly of God* ... AL-4
Saint Thomas Boys Home—*building* ... GA-3
Saint Thomas by the Sea Episcopal Ch—*church* ... FL-3
Saint Thomas Camp—*locale* ... MT-8
Saint Thomas Catholic Ch—*church* ... MS-4
Saint Thomas Cem—*cemetery* ... AL-4
Saint Thomas Cem—*cemetery* (4) ... CT-1
Saint Thomas Cem—*cemetery* ... IN-6
Saint Thomas Cem—*cemetery* (2) ... KS-7
Saint Thomas Cem—*cemetery* (2) ... KY-4
Saint Thomas Cem—*cemetery* ... MD-2
Saint Thomas Cem—*cemetery* (3) ... MA-1
Saint Thomas Cem—*cemetery* ... MI-6
Saint Thomas Cem—*cemetery* (3) ... MN-6
Saint Thomas Cem—*cemetery* ... MS-4
Saint Thomas Cem—*cemetery* (2) ... MO-7
Saint Thomas Cem—*cemetery* ... NJ-2
Saint Thomas Cem—*cemetery* (2) ... NY-2
Saint Thomas Cem—*cemetery* ... NC-3
Saint Thomas Cem—*cemetery* (3) ... ND-7
Saint Thomas Cem—*cemetery* (2) ... OH-6
Saint Thomas Cem—*cemetery* (2) ... PA-2
Saint Thomas Cem—*cemetery* (4) ... SD-7
Saint Thomas Cem—*cemetery* ... TX-5
Saint Thomas Cem—*cemetery* (2) ... WI-6
Saint Thomas Ch—*church* (5) ... AL-4
Saint Thomas Ch—*church* ... AR-4
Saint Thomas Ch—*church* ... CT-1
Saint Thomas Ch—*church* (2) ... DE-2
Saint Thomas Ch—*church* ... DC-2
Saint Thomas Ch—*church* (4) ... FL-3
Saint Thomas Ch—*church* (2) ... GA-3
Saint Thomas Ch—*church* ... IL-6
Saint Thomas Ch—*church* ... IN-6
Saint Thomas Ch—*church* (2) ... KY-4
Saint Thomas Ch—*church* (4) ... LA-4
Saint Thomas Ch—*church* (2) ... MD-2
Saint Thomas Ch—*church* (3) ... MI-6
Saint Thomas Ch—*church* ... MN-6
Saint Thomas Ch—*church* (2) ... MS-4
Saint Thomas Ch—*church* ... MO-7
Saint Thomas Ch—*church* ... MT-8
Saint Thomas Ch—*church* (3) ... NJ-2
Saint Thomas Ch—*church* (4) ... NY-2
Saint Thomas Ch—*church* ... NC-3
Saint Thomas Ch—*church* ... ND-7
Saint Thomas Ch—*church* (7) ... PA-2
Saint Thomas Ch—*church* (4) ... SC-3
Saint Thomas Ch—*church* ... SD-7
Saint Thomas Ch—*church* (3) ... TX-5
Saint Thomas Ch—*church* ... VT-1
Saint Thomas Ch—*church* (7) ... VA-3
Saint Thomas Ch—*church* (2) ... WI-6
Saint Thomas Chapel—*church* ... MA-1
Saint Thomas Chapel—*church* ... TX-5
Saint Thomas Chapel—*hist pl* ... VA-3
Saint Thomas Ch (historical)—*church* ... AL-4
Saint Thomas Ch (historical)—*church* ... MS-4
Saint Thomas Ch (historical)—*church* ... SD-7
Saint Thomas Church—*hist pl* ... MD-2
Saint Thomas Church—*hist pl* ... VA-3
Saint Thomas Church and Parish House—*hist pl* ... NY-2
Saint Thomas Coll—*school* ... MN-6
Saint Thomas Creek—*stream* ... MD-2
Saint Thomas Elem Sch—*school* ... MS-4
Saint Thomas Elem Sch—*school* ... PA-2
*Saint Thomas Episcopal Ch* ... AL-4
Saint Thomas Episcopal Ch—*church* ... AL-4
Saint Thomas Episcopal Ch—*church* (2) ... FL-3
Saint Thomas Episcopal Ch—*church* ... TN-4
Saint Thomas Episcopal Ch (historical)—*church* ... SD-7
Saint Thomas Episcopal Church—*hist pl* ... DE-2
Saint Thomas Episcopal Church—*hist pl* ... KY-4
Saint Thomas Episcopal Church—*hist pl* (2) ... NJ-2
Saint Thomas Episcopal Church—*hist pl* ... NC-3
Saint Thomas' Episcopal Church—*hist pl* ... OR-9
Saint Thomas Episcopal Church and Rectory—*hist pl* ... RI-1
Saint Thomas Episcopal Parish Sch—*school* ... FL-3
Saint Thomas Gap—*gap* ... NV-8
Saint Thomas Hall (historical)—*school* ... MS-4
Saint Thomas Harbor—*bay* ... VI-3
**Saint Thomas (historical)**—*pop pl* ... NV-8
Saint Thomas Home on the Hill Sch—*school* ... AL-4
Saint Thomas Hosp—*hospital* ... KS-7
Saint Thomas Hosp—*hospital* ... OH-6
Saint Thomas Hosp—*hospital* ... TN-4
Saint Thomas Hospital Airp—*airport* ... TN-4
Saint Thomas HS—*school* ... MI-6
Saint Thomas (Island) (County-equivalent)—*44218 (1980)* ... VI-3
Saint Thomas JHS—*school* ... TX-5
Saint Thomas Manor—*hist pl* ... MD-2
Saint Thomas Mine—*mine* ... CA-9
Saint Thomas Moore Ch—*church* ... FL-3
Saint Thomas Moore Sch—*school* ... IL-6
Saint Thomas More Catholic Ch—*church* ... FL-3
Saint Thomas More Catholic Ch—*church* ... UT-8
Saint Thomas More Chapel—*church* ... FL-3
Saint Thomas More Sch—*school* (2) ... CA-9
Saint Thomas More Sch—*school* ... DC-2
Saint Thomas More Sch—*school* ... FL-3
Saint Thomas More Sch—*school* ... GA-3
Saint Thomas More Sch—*school* ... IL-6
Saint Thomas More Sch—*school* ... IN-6
Saint Thomas More Sch—*school* ... KY-4
Saint Thomas More Sch—*school* ... LA-4
Saint Thomas More Sch—*school* ... NY-2
Saint Thomas More Sch—*school* ... NC-3
Saint Thomas More Sch—*school* ... OH-6
Saint Thomas More Sch—*school* ... PA-2
Saint Thomas More Sch—*school* (2) ... TX-5
Saint Thomas More Sch—*school* ... VA-3
Saint Thomas More Sch—*school* ... WA-9
Saint Thomas More Sch—*school* ... WI-6
*Saint Thomas Mores Sch* ... IN-6
Saint Thomas Mores Sch—*school* ... MA-1
Saint Thomas Municipal Airp—*airport* ... ND-7
Saint Thomas of The Pines Ch—*church* ... MN-6
Saint Thomas Orphange—*building* ... KY-4
Saint Thomas Parish—*church* ... DE-2
Saint Thomas Point—*cape* ... NV-8
Saint Thomas' Protestant Episcopal Church—*hist pl* ... SC-3
Saint Thomas Rec Area—*park* ... SD-7
Saint Thomas Roman Catholic Church and Howard-Flaget House—*hist pl* ... KY-4
Saint Thomas-Saint Peter Sch—*school* ... MI-6
*Saint Thomas Sch* ... IN-6
Saint Thomas Sch—*school* ... AL-4
Saint Thomas Sch—*school* ... AZ-5
Saint Thomas Sch—*school* (3) ... CA-9
Saint Thomas Sch—*school* (3) ... CT-1
Saint Thomas Sch—*school* (5) ... IL-6
Saint Thomas Sch—*school* ... IN-6
Saint Thomas Sch—*school* ... KS-7
Saint Thomas Sch—*school* ... KY-4
Saint Thomas Sch—*school* (2) ... MA-1
Saint Thomas Sch—*school* (4) ... MI-6
Saint Thomas Sch—*school* (3) ... MN-6
Saint Thomas Sch—*school* ... MS-4
Saint Thomas Sch—*school* ... NJ-2
Saint Thomas Sch—*school* (3) ... NY-2
Saint Thomas Sch—*school* (3) ... OH-6
Saint Thomas Sch—*school* ... PA-2
Saint Thomas Sch—*school* (2) ... SD-7
Saint Thomas Sch—*school* ... TN-4
Saint Thomas Sch—*school* ... TX-5
Saint Thomas Sch—*school* ... WI-6
Saint Thomas Sch (historical)—*school* ... MS-4
Saint Thomas Schol—*school* ... OH-6
*Saint Thomas School* ... DE-2
Saint Thomas Seminary—*school* ... CO-8
Saint Thomas Seminary—*school* ... CT-1
Saint Thomas Seminary—*school* ... KY-4

Saint Thomas Seminary—*school* MO-7
Saint Thomas Sink Cave Number Four—*cave* PA-2
Saint Thomas Sink Cave Number One—*cave* PA-2
Saint Thomas Sink Cave Number Three—*cave* PA-2
Saint Thomas Sink Cave Number Two—*cave* PA-2
Saint Thomas State Wildlife Mngmt Area—*park* MN-6
Saint Thomas the Apostle Ch—*church* DE-2
Saint Thomas the Apostle Sch—*school* DE-2
Saint Thomas the Apostle Sch—*school* FL-3
Saint Thomas the Apostle Sch—*school* IN-6
Saint Thomas the Apostle Sch—*school* (2) NY-2
Saint Thomas Township—*civil* ND-7
**Saint Thomas (Township of)**—*pop pl* PA-2
Saint Thomas United Methodist Ch—*church* AL-4
Saint Thomas Univ—*school* FL-3
Saint Thomas Wash—*stream* NV-8
Saint Thomas Yuma Indian Mission—*church* CA-9
*Saint Thompson Sch* MS-4
*Saint Tide Baptist Church* TN-4
Saint Tide Ch—*church* TN-4
Saint Tide Hollow—*valley* TN-4
*Saint Tikhons Theological Seminary* PA-2
Saint Timethys Sch—*school* CT-1
Saint Timothy Catholic Ch—*church* FL-3
Saint Timothy Cem—*cemetery* IA-7
Saint Timothy Cem—*cemetery* MN-6
Saint Timothy Cem—*cemetery* ND-7
Saint Timothy Ch—*church* CO-8
Saint Timothy Ch—*church* FL-3
Saint Timothy Ch—*church* GA-3
Saint Timothy Ch—*church* IA-7
Saint Timothy Ch—*church* LA-4
Saint Timothy Ch—*church* MI-6
Saint Timothy Ch—*church* NE-7
Saint Timothy Ch—*church* NC-3
Saint Timothy Ch—*church* OH-6
Saint Timothy Ch—*church* OK-5
Saint Timothy Ch—*church* PA-2
Saint Timothy Ch—*church* SC-3
Saint Timothy Ch—*church* TX-5
Saint Timothy Episcopal Ch (historical)—*church* AL-4
Saint Timothy Lutheran Ch—*church* AL-4
Saint Timothy Lutheran Church Preschool—*school* FL-3
Saint Timothys Cem—*cemetery* PA-2
Saint Timothys Ch—*church* (2) FL-3
Saint Timothys Ch—*church* IN-6
Saint Timothys Ch—*church* NM-5
Saint Timothys Ch—*church* NY-2
Saint Timothys Ch—*church* NC-3
Saint Timothys Ch—*church* PA-2
Saint Timothys Ch—*church* VA-3
Saint Timothy Sch—*school* (2) CA-9
Saint Timothy Sch—*school* FL-3
Saint Timothy Sch—*school* IL-6
Saint Timothy Sch—*school* MI-6
Saint Timothy Sch—*school* MN-6
Saint Timothy Sch—*school* (2) OH-6
Saint Timothy Sch (historical)—*school* AL-4
Saint Timothys Episcopal Ch—*church* MS-4
Saint Timothys Episcopal Ch—*church* NC-3
Saint Timothys Episcopal Ch—*church* TN-4
Saint Timothys Sch—*school* MD-2
Saint Timothys Sch—*school* NY-2
Saint Titusville Sch—*school* PA-2
Saint Trinity Sch—*school* MI-6
**Saint Truitt**—*pop pl* TN-4
Saint Truitt Cem—*cemetery* TN-4
Saint Truitt Sch (historical)—*school* TN-4
Saint Turibius Sch—*school* CA-9
Saint Turibius Sch—*school* IL-6
Saint Ubaldus Cem—*cemetery* IL-6
*Saint Union Baptist Church* AL-4
Saint Union Ch—*church* AL-4
Saint Union Ch—*church* TX-5
Saint Union Primitive Baptist Ch—*church* MS-4
Saint Urban—*locale* WA-9
**Saint Urbans**—*pop pl* WA-9
Saint Ursalas Acad—*school* OH-6
Saint Ursula Sch—*school* MD-2
Saint Ursula Sch—*school* PA-2
Saint Urusulas Acad—*school* OH-6
Saint Valberts Cem—*cemetery* OH-6
Saint Valentine Ch—*church* IL-6
Saint Valentines Cem—*cemetery* IL-6
Saint Valentine Sch—*school* IL-6
Saint Valentine Sch—*school* MI-6
Saint Valentine Sch—*school* PA-2
Saint Valentines Sch—*school* NY-2
*Saint Valley Sch* TN-4
**Saint Vencent de Paul Camp**—*pop pl* NY-2
Saint Veronica of Lima Sch—*school* PA-2
Saint Veronicas Ch—*church* PA-2
Saint Veronica Sch—*school* MI-6
Saint Veronicas Sch—*school* IL-6
Saint Veronicas Sch—*school* OH-6
Saint Veronicas Sch—*school* PA-2
Saint Viator Sch—*school* (2) IL-6
Saint Viator Sch—*school* NV-8
Saint Vibiana Sch—*school* CA-9
Saint Victors Ch—*church* PA-2
Saint Victor Sch—*school* CA-9
Saint Victors Chapel—*church* TX-5
Saint Victors Sch—*school* IL-6
Saint Victors Sch—*school* WI-6
*Saint Vincent* LA-4
Saint Vincent—*locale* AR-4
Saint Vincent—*locale* KY-4
Saint Vincent—*other* LA-4
**Saint Vincent**—*pop pl* AR-4
**Saint Vincent**—*pop pl* MN-6
Saint Vincent, Bayou—*stream* LA-4
Saint Vincent Acad—*school* KY-4
Saint Vincent Acad—*school* LA-4
Saint Vincent Acad—*school* NM-5
Saint Vincent Archabbey Gristmill—*hist pl* PA-2
Saint Vincent Catholic Ch—*church* FL-3
Saint Vincent Cem—*cemetery* CA-9
Saint Vincent Cem—*cemetery* (2) IL-6
Saint Vincent Cem—*cemetery* IA-7
Saint Vincent Cem—*cemetery* LA-4
Saint Vincent Cem—*cemetery* MN-6
Saint Vincent Cem—*cemetery* NJ-2
Saint Vincent Cem—*cemetery* NY-2
Saint Vincent Cem—*cemetery* ND-7
Saint Vincent Cem—*cemetery* PA-2
Saint Vincent Cem—*cemetery* TX-5
Saint Vincent Ch—*church* ND-7
Saint Vincent Ch—*church* PA-2
Saint Vincent Childrens Home—*building* IL-6
Saint Vincent Coll—*school* PA-2
Saint Vincent DePaul Camp—*locale* MD-2
Saint Vincent De Paul Camp—*locale* PA-2
Saint Vincent de Paul Camp—*park* MA-1
Saint Vincent De Paul Catholic Ch—*church* AL-4
Saint Vincent Depaul Cem—*cemetery* IN-6
Saint Vincent De Paul Cem—*cemetery* KY-4
Saint Vincent de Paul Cem—*cemetery* MI-6
Saint Vincent de Paul Cem—*cemetery* MN-6
Saint Vincent De Paul Cem—*cemetery* MN-6
Saint Vincent de Paul Cem—*cemetery* (2) NY-2
Saint Vincent DePaul Ch—*church* FL-3
Saint Vincent de Paul Ch—*church* (2) FL-3
Saint Vincent de Paul Ch—*church* KS-7
Saint Vincent DePaul Ch—*church* NJ-2
Saint Vincent De Paul Ch—*church* (2) NY-2
Saint Vincent DePaul Ch—*church* PA-2
Saint Vincent DePaul Chapel—*church* NJ-2
Saint Vincent DePaul Church, Rectory, School, Saint Ursula Home and Convent—*hist pl* KY-4
Saint Vincent De Paul Hosp—*hospital* VA-3
Saint Vincent De Paul HS—*school* MI-6
Saint Vincent de Paul Regional Seminary—*school* FL-3
Saint Vincent De Paul Roman Catholic Church—*hist pl* LA-4
Saint Vincent De Paul Roman Catholic Church—*hist pl* MD-2
*Saint Vincent De Paul Sch* IN-6
Saint Vincent de Pauls Ch—*church* PA-2
Saint Vincent de Paul Sch—*school* AZ-5
Saint Vincent de Paul Sch—*school* AR-4
Saint Vincent De Paul Sch—*school* CO-8
Saint Vincent de Paul Sch—*school* IL-6
Saint Vincent Depaul Sch—*school* IN-6
Saint Vincent DePaul Sch—*school* IN-6
Saint Vincent de Paul Sch—*school* IN-6
Saint Vincent de Paul Sch—*school* MI-6
Saint Vincent DePaul Sch—*school* NJ-2
Saint Vincent de Paul Sch—*school* (3) NY-2
Saint Vincent De Paul Sch—*school* OH-6
Saint Vincent de Paul Sch—*school* OR-9
Saint Vincent de Paul Sch—*school* TN-4
*Saint Vincent de Pauls Sch* IN-6
Saint Vincent de Pauls Sch—*school* OH-6
Saint Vincent Ferrer—*school* FL-3
Saint Vincent Ferrer Church and Priory—*hist pl* NY-2
Saint Vincent Ferrer Sch—*school* MI-6
*Saint Vincent Health Center* PA-2
Saint Vincent Health Center Airp—*airport* PA-2
Saint Vincent Hosp—*hospital* AL-4
Saint Vincent Hosp—*hospital* IA-7
Saint Vincent Hosp—*hospital* MA-1
Saint Vincent Hosp—*hospital* MT-8
Saint Vincent Hosp—*hospital* NM-5
Saint Vincent Hosp—*hospital* OR-9
Saint Vincent Hosp—*hospital* WI-6
Saint Vincent Hospital Health Care Center Airp—*airport* IN-6
Saint Vincent Hospital Heliport—*airport* OR-9
Saint Vincent HS—*school* CA-9
Saint Vincent HS—*school* MO-7
Saint Vincent Infirmary—*hospital* AR-4
Saint Vincent Island—*island* FL-3
Saint Vincent Junction—*locale* MN-6
**Saint Vincent Junction**—*pop pl* MN-6
Saint Vincent Lake—*reservoir* PA-2
Saint Vincent of Paul Catholic Church—*hist pl* NY-2
Saint Vincent Orphanage and Sch Bldg—*hist pl* CA-9
Saint Vincent Point—*cape* FL-3
Saint Vincents Acad—*school* AL-4
Saint Vincents Acad—*school* MO-7
Saint Vincent Sanitarium—*hospital* MO-7
Saint Vincents Catholic Ch—*church* AL-4
Saint Vincents Catholic Ch—*church* UT-8
Saint Vincents Cem—*cemetery* AR-4
Saint Vincents Cem—*cemetery* OH-6
Saint Vincents Cem—*cemetery* PA-2
Saint Vincents Cem—*cemetery* SD-7
Saint Vincents Ch—*church* MO-7
Saint Vincents Ch—*church* OH-6
Saint Vincent Sch—*school* CA-9
Saint Vincent Sch—*school* IN-6
Saint Vincent Sch—*school* MO-7
Saint Vincents Childrens Home—*building* PA-2
Saint Vincent Schools—*school* OH-6
Saint Vincents Coll—*school* MO-7
**Saint Vincent Shaft**—*pop pl* PA-2
Saint Vincents Home And Sch—*school* DC-2
Saint Vincents Home for Boys—*other* CO-8
Saint Vincents Hosp—*hospital* CT-1
Saint Vincents Hosp—*hospital* FL-3
Saint Vincents Hosp—*hospital* IL-6
Saint Vincents Hosp—*hospital* IN-6
Saint Vincents Hosp—*hospital* NJ-2
Saint Vincents Hosp—*hospital* (3) NY-2
Saint Vincents Hosp—*hospital* (2) OH-6
Saint Vincents Hosp—*hospital* PA-2
Saint Vincent's Hotel—*hist pl* SD-7
Saint Vincent's Infant Asylum—*hist pl* WI-6
Saint Vincents Infants Home—*locale* MD-2
*Saint Vincents Island* FL-3
Saint Vincents Med Ctr—*hospital* FL-3
Saint Vincents Orphanage—*building* OH-6
Saint Vincents Orphanage—*school* IN-6
Saint Vincents Orphan Home—*school* IN-6
Saint Vincent Sound—*bay* FL-3
Saint Vincents Roman Catholic Select Sch—*school* AL-4
Saint Vincents Sch—*school* (4) CA-9
Saint Vincents Sch—*school* IN-6
Saint Vincents Sch—*school* (2) IA-7
Saint Vincents Sch—*school* KY-4
Saint Vincents Sch—*school* NJ-2
Saint Vincents Sch—*school* (2) NY-2
Saint Vincents Sch—*school* OH-6
Saint Vincents Sch—*school* PA-2
Saint Vincents Sch—*school* TX-5
Saint Vincents Sch—*school* VA-3
Saint Vincents Sch—*school* WV-2
Saint Vincents Sch—*school* WI-6
Saint Vincents Seminary—*school* CA-9
Saint Vincents Seminary—*school* PA-2
**Saint Vincent (St. Vincent Shaft)**—*pop pl* PA-2
Saint Vincent (Township of)—*fmr MCD* AR-4
**Saint Vincent (Township of)**—*pop pl* MN-6
Saint Viola Cem—*cemetery* TX-5
Saint Viola Ch—*church* TX-5
Saint Virgilius Sch—*school* NY-2
Saint Virgils Sch—*school* NJ-2
Saint Vital Bay—*bay* MI-6
Saint Vital Island—*island* MI-6
Saint Vital Point—*cape* (2) MI-6
Saint Vital Shoal—*bar* MI-6
Saint Vitos Sch—*school* NY-2
Saint Vitus Cem—*cemetery* NE-7
Saint Vitus Cem—*cemetery* PA-2
Saint Vitus Sch—*school* OH-6
Saint Vitus Sch—*school* PA-2
Saint Vladimer Cem—*cemetery* PA-2
Saint Vladimir Ch—*church* PA-2
**Saint Vladimirs**—*pop pl* NJ-2
Saint Vladimirs Cem—*cemetery* PA-2
Saint Vladimirs Ch—*church* NJ-2
Saint Vladimirs Ch—*church* PA-2
**Saint Vrain**—*pop pl* NM-5
Saint Vrain Cem—*cemetery* NM-5
Saint Vrain Creek—*stream* CO-8
Saint Vrain Glaciers—*glacier* CO-8
Saint Vrain Glacier Trail—*trail* CO-8
Saint Vrain Mountain Trail—*trail* CO-8
Saint Vrain Mtn—*summit* CO-8
Saint Vrains—*locale* CO-8
Saint Vrain Sch—*school* CO-8
*Saint Vrains Creek* CO-8
Saint Vrain's Mill—*hist pl* NM-5
Saint Vrain Supply Canal—*canal* CO-8
Saint Vrain Supply Tunnel—*tunnel* CO-8
Saint Walburgas Ch—*church* PA-2
*Saint Walden Church* AL-4
Saint Waldons Ch—*church* AL-4
Saint Walley Cem—*cemetery* IN-6
Saint Walter Sch—*school* IL-6
Saint Walters Sch—*school* IL-6
Saint Wenceslas Sch—*school* OH-6
Saint Wenceslaus Catholic Church and Parish House—*hist pl* SD-7
Saint Wenceslaus Cem—*cemetery* IA-7
Saint Wenceslaus Cem—*cemetery* KS-7
Saint Wenceslaus Cem—*cemetery* MT-8
Saint Wenceslaus Cem—*cemetery* (5) NE-7
Saint Wenceslaus Cem—*cemetery* ND-7
Saint Wenceslaus Cem—*cemetery* OK-5
Saint Wenceslaus Cem—*cemetery* OR-9
Saint Wenceslaus Cem—*cemetery* (3) WI-6
Saint Wenceslaus Ch—*church* IA-7
Saint Wenceslaus Ch—*church* MI-6
Saint Wenceslaus Ch—*church* NE-7
Saint Wenceslaus Ch—*church* TX-5
Saint Wenceslaus Ch—*church* (3) WI-6
Saint Wenceslaus Roman Catholic Church—*hist pl* WI-6
Saint Wenceslaus Sch—*school* IL-6
Saint Wenceslaus Sch—*school* ND-7
*Saint Wendel* WI-6
**Saint Wendel**—*pop pl* IN-6
**Saint Wendel**—*pop pl* MN-6
Saint Wendel—*uninc pl* WI-6
**Saint Wendelin**—*pop pl* OH-6
Saint Wendelin Cem—*cemetery* IL-6
Saint Wendelin Cem—*cemetery* OH-6
Saint Wendelin Sch—*school* OH-6
Saint Wendelin Sch—*school* PA-2
*Saint Wendells* IN-6
**Saint Wendells**—*pop pl* IN-6
Saint Wendells Sch—*school* PA-2
**Saint Wendel (Township of)**—*pop pl* MN-6
Saint Wilfrid Cem—*cemetery* SD-7
Saint Wilfrids Cem—*cemetery* AL-4
Saint Wilfrids Episcopal Ch—*church* AL-4
Saint William Catholic Ch—*church* FL-3
Saint William Ch—*church* MO-7
Saint William Of York Ch—*church* VA-3
Saint Williams Cem—*cemetery* MN-6
Saint Williams Cem—*cemetery* SC-3
Saint Williams Cem—*cemetery* SD-7
Saint Williams Cem—*cemetery* (2) TX-5
Saint Williams Cem—*cemetery* WI-6
Saint Williams Ch—*church* (2) GA-3
Saint Williams Ch—*church* (2) KY-4
Saint Williams Ch—*church* MA-1
Saint Williams Ch—*church* MS-4
Saint Williams Ch—*church* NY-2
Saint Williams Ch—*church* SC-3
Saint Williams Ch—*church* TX-5
Saint Williams Ch—*church* WV-2
Saint Williams Chapel—*church* MI-6
Saint Williams Sch—*school* IL-6
Saint Williams Sch—*school* MI-6
Saint Williams Sch—*school* NY-2
Saint Williams Sch—*school* (2) OH-6
Saint Williams Sch—*school* PA-2
Saint Williams Sch—*school* TX-5
Saint William the Abbot Sch—*school* NY-2
Saint Willibrorb Robey Ch—*church* SD-7
Saint Willibrord Cem—*cemetery* MN-6
Saint Winfred Ch—*church* LA-4
Saint Wisdom Ch—*church* (2) AL-4
**Saint Xavier**—*pop pl* MT-8
Saint Xavier Acad—*school* PA-2
Saint Xavier Academy—*hist pl* FM-9
Saint Xavier Cem—*cemetery* PA-2
Saint Xavier Ch—*church* LA-4
Saint Xavier Coll—*school* IL-6
Saint Xavier Coulee—*valley* MT-8
Saint Xavier HS—*school* OH-6
*Saint Xaviers Academy* FM-9
Saint Xaviers Cem—*cemetery* MO-7
Saint Xaviers Cem—*cemetery* WV-2
Saint Xavier Sch—*school* NY-2
Saint Xavier Sch—*school* OH-6
Saint Xavier Sch—*school* WA-9
Saint Xaviers Sch—*school* KY-4
Saint Yues Bog Dam (breeched)—*dam* MA-1
Saint Yues Bog Rsvr—*reservoir* MA-1
Saint Zachary Sch—*school* IL-6
Saint Zephryns Cem—*cemetery* MA-1
Sainville—*locale* TN-4
Sainville Branch—*stream* TN-4
Sainville Post Office (historical)—*building* TN-4
*Saipan* PW-9
Saipan—*island* MH-9
*Saipan Airport* MH-9
Saipan Channel—*channel* MH-9
*Saipan Harbor* MH-9
Saipan Harbor—*harbor* MH-9
*Saipan Harbour* MH-9
*Saipan Insel* MH-9
Saipan International Airp—*airport* MH-9
*Saipan Island* MH-9
*Saipan Kanal* MH-9
*Saipan-Ko* MH-9
**Saipan (Municipality)**—*pop pl* MH-9
*Saipan -Suido* MH-9
*Saipan-To* MH-9
*Saira* VA-3
Sais—*locale* NM-5
**Sais**—*pop pl* NM-5
*Saisaginaga Lake* MN-6
Sais Lateral—*canal* NM-5
Sais Tank—*reservoir* NM-5
Saitchuck, The—*bay* AK-9
Saiz Ditch—*canal* CO-8
Saiz Place—*locale* NM-5
*Sa-jini* AZ-5
*Sajini Butte* AZ-5
Sak—*locale* FM-9
*Sakagawia Peak* MT-8
Sakakawea, Lake—*reservoir* ND-7
Sakakawea Monument—*locale* SD-7
*Sakaki To* FM-9
Sakala Cem—*cemetery* CO-8
*Sakapatayi Creek* AL-4
Sakarakapw—*locale* FM-9
Sakaralap—*locale* FM-9
Sakariso—*locale* FM-9
Sakarkoatoan—*cape* FM-9
Sakartik—*locale* FM-9
Sakartik, Pilen—*stream* FM-9
Sakatah Cem—*cemetery* MN-6
Sakatah Lake—*lake* MN-6
Sakatah State Park—*park* MN-6
Sakawawin Boy Scout Camp—*locale* NJ-2
Sakaya—*slope* MH-9
*Sakesville* PA-2
*Sakhainotung* PA-2
Sakie Bay—*bay* AK-9
Sakie Point—*cape* AK-9
Sakima Country Club—*other* NJ-2
Saki Mana—*locale* HI-9
Saki Mana Shaft—*reservoir* HI-9
Saklolik Mtn—*summit* AK-9
**Sakonnet**—*pop pl* RI-1
*Sakonnet Cove* RI-1
*Sakonnet Harbor* RI-1
Sakonnet Harbor—*bay* RI-1
Sakonnet Light—*locale* RI-1
Sakonnet Light Station—*hist pl* RI-1
Sakonnet Point—*cape* RI-1
Sakonnet River—*stream* RI-1
Sakonowyak River—*stream* AK-9
Sakoonang Channel—*channel* AK-9
*Sakotucket River* RI-1
Sakpik Mtn—*summit* AK-9
Sakrorak Creek—*stream* AK-9
Sakrorak Mtn—*summit* AK-9
**Saks**—*pop pl* AL-4
Saksaia Glacier—*glacier* AK-9
Saks Baptist Ch—*church* AL-4
Saks Ch of God of Prophecy—*church* AL-4
Saks Cove—*bay* AK-9
Saks Creek—*stream* AK-9
Saks Elem Sch—*school* AL-4
Saks HS—*school* AL-4
Saks Lake—*lake* AK-9
Saks MS—*school* AL-4
Saksro, Infal—*stream* FM-9
Saks Shop Ctr—*locale* AL-4
Sakston Heights Assembly of God Ch—*church* AL-4
Saktehke Cem—*cemetery* OK-5
*Sakti Homma* AL-4
Saktuina Point—*cape* AK-9
*Sakunk* PA-2
*Sakura Shima* FM-9
*Sakura To* FM-9
Sakvelak Creek—*stream* AK-9
Sal, Laguna la—*lake* TX-5
Sal, Lake—*lake* MA-1
Sala—*locale* NY-2
Salaam Temple—*hist pl* NJ-2
Salabar Draw—*valley* CO-8
Salacoa—*locale* GA-3
Salacoa Ch—*church* GA-3
Salacoa Creek—*stream* (2) GA-3
Salacoa Valley—*valley* GA-3
Salada, Laguna—*bay* TX-5
Salada, Laguna—*lake* AZ-5
Salada, Laguna—*lake* (2) TX-5
Saladak—*civil* FM-9
Saladak—*locale* FM-9
Saladar Flat—*flat* NM-5
Salada Windmill—*locale* NM-5
Salada Windmill—*locale* (2) TX-5
Saladen Kimai—*ridge* FM-9
Saladenre—*unknown* FM-9
Saladenre, Dolen—*summit* FM-9
Salad Hollow—*valley* KY-4
Saladillo Tank—*reservoir* TX-5
Saladito Creek—*stream* (3) NM-5
Saladito Point Windmill—*locale* NM-5
Saladito Ranch—*locale* NM-5
Saladito Springs—*spring* NM-5
Saladito Trap Windmill—*locale* NM-5
Saladito Windmill—*locale* NM-5
Salado—*locale* NM-5
Salado—*locale* OR-9
**Salado**—*pop pl* AZ-5
**Salado**—*pop pl* AR-4
**Salado**—*pop pl* TX-5
Salado, Arroyo—*stream* (2) CA-9
Salado, Arroyo—*valley* (3) TX-5
Salado Battlefield and Archeol Site—*hist pl* TX-5
Salado Canyon—*valley* (2) NM-5
Salado Cem—*cemetery* TX-5
Salado College Archeol Site—*hist pl* TX-5
*Salado Creek* TX-5
Salado Creek—*stream* AR-4
Salado Creek—*stream* CA-9
Salado Creek—*stream* CO-8
Salado Creek—*stream* (8) NM-5
Salado Creek—*stream* (9) TX-5
Salado Draw—*valley* NM-5
Salado Draw Oil Field—*other* NM-5
**Salado Junction**—*pop pl* TX-5
Salado Mountains—*other* NM-5
Salado Mtn—*summit* AR-4
Saladon Creek—*stream* NM-5
Saladone Tank—*reservoir* NM-5
Saladon Lake—*lake* NM-5
Salado Park—*park* TX-5
Salado Sch—*school* TX-5
Salado Spring—*spring* NM-5
Salado Springs—*spring* AZ-5
Salado Substation—*other* CA-9
Salado Tank—*reservoir* NM-5
Salado Tank—*reservoir* TX-5
Salado (Township of)—*fmr MCD* AR-4
Salado United Methodist Chruch—*hist pl* TX-5
Salado Well—*well* NM-5
Salado Windmill—*locale* (5) TX-5
*Salaggo Road* MH-9
Salaglula—*area* GU-9
Salagna—*area* GU-9
*Salahkai Mesa* AZ-5
*Salahkai Point* AZ-5
Salailago—*area* GU-9
*Salaiseau* OK-5
*Salaiseau Creek* OK-5
Salak—*locale* SC-3
*Sa La kai Mesa* AZ-5
*Salal Creek* OR-9
Salal Creek—*stream* OR-9
Salal Gulch—*valley* CA-9
Salal Point—*summit* OR-9
*Salal Slough* OR-9
Salal Spring—*spring* CA-9
Salal Spring—*spring* OR-9
*Salamalcato* FL-3
*Salamanas* IL-6
**Salamanca**—*pop pl* NY-2
**Salamanca (Town of)**—*pop pl* NY-2
**Salamanca Township**—*pop pl* KS-7
Salamander, Lake—*reservoir* UT-8
Salamander Butte—*summit* ID-8
Salamander Cave—*cave* AL-4
*Salamander Creek* OR-9
Salamander Creek—*stream* CA-9
Salamander Creek—*stream* (2) ID-8
Salamander Falls—*falls* MT-8
Salamander Glacier, The—*glacier* MT-8
Salamander Lake—*lake* AK-9
Salamander Lake—*lake* CO-8
Salamander Lake—*lake* OR-9
Salamander Lake—*lake* (2) UT-8
Salamander Pit—*cave* TN-4
Salamander Point—*cape* NH-1
Salamander Ridge—*ridge* ID-8
Salamander Rock—*summit* MD-2
*Salamanic River* IN-6
*Salamanie River* IN-6
Salamatof—*locale* AK-9
Salamatof ANV926—*reserve* AK-9
Salamatof Beach—*beach* AK-9
Salamatof Creek—*stream* AK-9
Salamatof Lake—*lake* AK-9
Salam Cem—*cemetery* OK-5
Salam Ch—*church* PA-2
**Salamonia**—*pop pl* IN-6
Salamonia Grange—*locale* WA-9
*Salamonia River* IN-6
Salamonie Ch—*church* IN-6
Salamonie Dam—*dam* IN-6
Salamonie Lake—*reservoir* IN-6
Salamonie River—*stream* IN-6
Salamonie River State For—*forest* IN-6
*Salamonie Rsvr* IN-6
Salamonie Sch—*school* IN-6
**Salamonie (Township of)**—*pop pl* IN-6
Salander Creek—*stream* OR-9
Salano Sch—*school* AZ-5
Salapwuk—*civil* FM-9
Sala Ranch—*locale* AZ-5
Saleratus Draw—*valley* AZ-5
Saleratus Pond—*reservoir* AZ-5
Salas Arroyo—*stream* NM-5
Salas Spring—*spring* NV-8
*Salat* FM-9
*Salat Island* FM-9
*Salat Pass* FM-9
Salatral Lateral—*canal* TX-5
*Salatrillo Creek* TX-5
Salavador Canyon—*valley* NM-5
*Salavilla Creek* TX-5
Salaya Creek—*stream* CO-8
Salazar, Vidal and Elisa, House—*hist pl* NM-5
Salazar Arroyo—*stream* CO-8
Salazar Arroyo—*stream* NM-5
Salazar Butte—*summit* WY-8
Salazar-Candal House—*hist pl* PR-3
Salazar Canyon—*valley* CA-9
Salazar Canyon—*valley* (3) NM-5
Salazar Cem—*cemetery* AZ-5
Salazar Cem—*cemetery* TX-5
Salazar Ditch—*canal* NM-5
Salazar Ranch—*locale* NM-5
Salazar Rincon—*other* NM-5
Salazar Rincon—*valley* CO-8
Salazar Rsvr—*reservoir* WY-8
Salazar Sch—*school* NM-5
Salazar Sch—*school* TX-5
*Salazar's Lake* CO-8
Salazar Spring—*spring* CA-9
Salazar Spring—*spring* (3) NM-5
Salazar Tank—*reservoir* (3) NM-5
Salazar Wash—*stream* NM-5
Salaza Windmill—*locale* NM-5
Sal Branch—*stream* AL-4
Sal Branch—*stream* KY-4
Sal Branch—*stream* TN-4
Sal Brown Branch—*stream* AL-4
*Salceda Mountains* AZ-5
**Salcedo**—*pop pl* MO-7
Salcedo Tank—*reservoir* AZ-5
Salcedo Well—*well* AZ-5
Salcha—*CDP* AK-9
Salcha Bluff—*cliff* AK-9
Salchaket—*other* AK-9
Salchaket Slough—*stream* AK-9
Salcha River—*stream* AK-9
Salcha River State Recreation Site—*park* AK-9
Salchow Cem—*cemetery* KS-7
Salcido Canyon—*valley* TX-5
Salcido Windmill—*locale* TX-5
*Salcilla* AZ-5
Salcita Spring—*spring* AZ-5
Sal City—*locale* TN-4
*Sal City Crossing* TN-4
Sal City Spring—*spring* TN-4
Salco—*locale* AL-4
**Salco**—*pop pl* PA-2
Salco Landing—*locale* AL-4
*Salco Mines* PA-2
Salco Mines—*locale* PA-2
Sal Creek—*stream* AK-9
Sal Creek—*stream* NC-3
Saldana—*CDP* PR-3
**Saldana**—*pop pl* PR-3
*Saldee* KY-4
**Saldee (Copland)**—*pop pl* KY-4
Saldeer Gap—*gap* NC-3
Sal del Ray—*lake* TX-5
Sal del Rey Gas Field—*oilfield* TX-5
*Sal del Rey Lake* TX-5
Salduro—*locale* UT-8
Sale, Bayou—*gut* LA-4
Sale, Bayou—*stream* LA-4
Sale, Reuben, House—*hist pl* KY-4
Saleaudo—*hist pl* MD-2
Sale Barn Canyon—*valley* CO-8
*Salec* AZ-5
**Sale City**—*pop pl* GA-3
Sale City (CCD)—*cens area* GA-3
*Sale Creek* TN-4
**Sale Creek**—*pop pl* TN-4
Sale Creek—*stream* TN-4
Sale Creek (CCD)—*cens area* TN-4
Sale Creek Division—*civil* TN-4
Sale Creek Dock—*locale* TN-4
*Sale Creek Marina* TN-4
*Salecreek Post Office* TN-4
Sale Creek Post Office—*building* TN-4
Sale Creek Rec Area—*park* TN-4
Sale Creek Sch—*school* TN-4
Sale Creek Shoals—*bar* TN-4
*Salee Creek* ID-8
Salee Creek—*stream* ID-8
*Sale Elementary School* MS-4
Salefsky Creek—*stream* MT-8
Sale Gulch—*valley* AK-9
Saleh Lake—*lake* TX-5
Sale Lake—*lake* MN-6
Sale Lake—*reservoir* CO-8
*Salem* KS-7
*Salem* MS-4
*Salem* MO-7
*Salem* NJ-2
*Salem* PA-2
*Salem* TN-4
Salem—*locale* AL-4
Salem—*locale* AR-4
Salem—*locale* CT-1
Salem—*locale* FL-3
Salem—*locale* (2) GA-3
Salem—*locale* KS-7
Salem—*locale* KY-4
Salem—*locale* (4) MS-4
Salem—*locale* MT-8
Salem—*locale* NC-3
Salem—*locale* OH-6
Salem—*locale* OK-5
Salem—*locale* (3) TN-4
Salem—*locale* (6) TX-5
Salem—*locale* (2) VA-3
Salem—*other* MO-7
**Salem**—*pop pl* (3) AL-4
**Salem**—*pop pl* (3) AR-4
**Salem**—*pop pl* GA-3
**Salem**—*pop pl* ID-8
**Salem**—*pop pl* IL-6
**Salem**—*pop pl* (4) IN-6
**Salem**—*pop pl* IA-7
**Salem**—*pop pl* KY-4
**Salem**—*pop pl* ME-1
**Salem**—*pop pl* MD-2
**Salem**—*pop pl* MA-1
**Salem**—*pop pl* MI-6
**Salem**—*pop pl* MO-7
**Salem**—*pop pl* NE-7
**Salem**—*pop pl* NH-1
**Salem**—*pop pl* NJ-2
**Salem**—*pop pl* NM-5
**Salem**—*pop pl* NY-2
**Salem**—*pop pl* (6) NC-3
**Salem**—*pop pl* OH-6
**Salem**—*pop pl* OK-5
**Salem**—*pop pl* OR-9
**Salem**—*pop pl* (4) PA-2
**Salem**—*pop pl* (4) SC-3
**Salem**—*pop pl* SD-7
**Salem**—*pop pl* (4) TN-4
**Salem**—*pop pl* TX-5
**Salem**—*pop pl* UT-8
**Salem**—*pop pl* VA-3
**Salem**—*pop pl* (2) WV-2
**Salem**—*pop pl* (2) WI-6
Salem, City of—*civil* MA-1
Salem, Mount—*summit* OR-9
*Salem, Town of* MA-1
Salem Acad—*school* OR-9
*Salem Academy* MS-4
Salem Acres Ch—*church* VA-3
**Salem Acres (subdivision)**—*pop pl* NC-3
Salem Airfield—*airport* NJ-2
Salem and Bristol Sch—*school* WI-6
Salem Apostolic Ch—*church* MO-7
Salem Associated Reformed Presbyterian Ch—*church* TN-4
Salem Attendance Center—*school* MS-4
Salem-Auburn Streets Hist Dist—*hist pl* MA-1
Salem Ave Ch—*church* MO-7
Salem Ave Sch—*school* MD-2
*Salem Baptist Ch* AL-4

*Samples Memorial Baptist Church* ... TN-4
Samples Memorial Cem—*cemetery* ... TN-4
Samples Memorial Ch—*church* ... TN-4
Sample Spur Junction—*uninc pl* ... PA-2
Sample Square—*post sta* ... FL-3
Sample Swamp—*swamp* ... FL-3
Samples Windmill—*locale* ... NM-5
**Sampleville**—*pop pl* ... OH-6
Sample Wash—*stream* ... AZ-5
Samp Meredith Cem—*cemetery* ... TN-4
Samp Meredith Hollow—*valley* ... TN-4
**Samp Mortar**—*pop pl* ... CT-1
Samp Mortar Rsvr—*reservoir* ... CT-1
Sampo—*locale* ... WY-8
Sam Point—*cape* ... WI-6
Sam Pollock Arch—*arch* ... UT-8
Sam Pond—*lake* ... MA-1
*Sam-Po-Wans Brook* ... NY-2
Sam Powell Peak—*summit* ... AZ-5
Sampre Branch—*stream* ... LA-4
**Sampsel**—*pop pl* ... MO-7
*Sampsell* ... MO-7
Sampsel Lake—*lake* ... OK-5
**Sampsel Township**—*pop pl* ... MO-7
*Sampson* ... AL-4
Sampson—*locale* ... FL-3
Sampson—*locale* ... KY-4
Sampson—*locale* ... MO-7
Sampson—*locale* ... NY-2
Sampson—*locale* ... PA-2
Sampson—*locale* ... TN-4
Sampson—*locale* ... VA-3
Sampson—*locale* ... WA-9
**Sampson**—*pop pl* ... FL-3
**Sampson**—*pop pl* ... PA-2
**Sampson**—*pop pl* ... WI-6
Sampson, George W., House—*hist pl* ... TX-5
Sampson, Lake—*lake* ... FL-3
Sampson, Mount—*summit* ... ID-8
Sampson Acres Lake—*reservoir* ... NC-3
Sampson Acres Lake Dam—*dam* ... NC-3
Sampson Bog—*swamp* ... NY-2
Sampson Branch—*stream* ... KY-4
Sampson Branch—*stream* ... MO-7
Sampson Branch—*stream* ... NE-7
Sampson Branch—*stream* ... NC-3
Sampson Branch—*stream* ... VA-3
*Sampson Brook* ... MA-1
Sampson Brook—*stream* (2) ... MA-1
Sampson Butte—*summit* ... OR-9
Sampson Cabin—*locale* ... CO-8
Sampson Cabin—*locale* ... WA-9
Sampson Cem—*cemetery* ... FL-3
Sampson Cem—*cemetery* ... IN-6
Sampson Cem—*cemetery* ... MI-6
Sampson Cem—*cemetery* ... WA-9
Sampson Ch—*church* ... TX-5
Sampson Channel—*channel* ... LA-4
Sampson Chapel—*church* ... AL-4
Sampson Chapel—*church* ... NC-3
*Sampson City* ... FL-3
**Sampson City**—*pop pl* ... FL-3
Sampson Community Club—*locale* ... CO-8
Sampson County—*civil* ... NC-3
Sampson County Airp—*airport* ... NC-3
*Sampson Cove* ... MA-1
Sampson Cove—*bay* (2) ... ME-1
*Sampson Creek* ... TX-5
Sampson Creek—*stream* ... AK-9
Sampson Creek—*stream* (2) ... CA-9
Sampson Creek—*stream* ... FL-3
Sampson Creek—*stream* ... GA-3
Sampson Creek—*stream* ... ID-8
Sampson Creek—*stream* ... MO-7
Sampson Creek—*stream* ... NV-8
Sampson Creek—*stream* ... NY-2
Sampson Creek—*stream* ... NC-3
Sampson Creek—*stream* (2) ... OR-9
Sampson Creek—*stream* ... TX-5
Sampson Creek—*stream* ... VA-3
Sampson Creek—*stream* ... WI-6
Sampson Drain—*canal* ... MI-6
Sampson Drain—*stream* ... MI-6
Sampson Draw—*valley* ... WY-8
Sampson Flat—*flat* ... CA-9
Sampson Gap—*gap* ... NC-3
Sampson Gulch—*valley* ... CO-8
Sampson Gulch—*valley* ... OR-9
Sampson Hill—*summit* ... IN-6
Sampson Hill—*summit* ... ME-1
Sampson Hill—*summit* ... MA-1
Sampson Hill—*summit* ... PA-2
Sampson (historical)—*locale* ... IA-7
**Sampson (historical)**—*pop pl* ... OR-9
Sampson Hollow—*valley* ... IN-6
Sampson House—*hist pl* ... AZ-5
*Sampson Island* ... MA-1
Sampson Island—*island* ... MA-1
Sampson Island—*island* (2) ... SC-3
Sampson Island Creek—*stream* ... SC-3
Sampson Island Marshes—*swamp* ... MA-1
Sampson Lake—*lake* ... FL-3
Sampson Lake—*lake* (2) ... MN-6
Sampson Lake—*lake* ... MT-8
Sampson Lake—*lake* ... NY-2
Sampson Lake—*lake* ... OR-9
Sampson Lakes—*lake* ... SC-3
Sampson Landing—*locale* ... SC-3
Sampson Landing Creek—*stream* ... NC-3
Sampson Memorial Hospital Airp—*airport* ... NC-3
Sampson Mills Ch—*church* ... PA-2
Sampson Mine—*mine* ... CA-9
Sampson Mine—*mine* ... NM-5
Sampson Mine—*mine* ... UT-8
*Sampson Mountain* ... ID-8
Sampson Mountain—*ridge* ... OR-9
Sampson MS—*school* ... NC-3
Sampson Mtn—*summit* ... CO-8
Sampson Mtn—*summit* ... NC-3
Sampson Mtn—*summit* (2) ... TN-4
Sampson Peak—*summit* ... CA-9
Sampson Peak—*summit* ... NC-3
Sampson Pike Hollow—*valley* ... WV-2
Sampson Point—*cape* ... AL-4
Sampson Point—*cape* ... ME-1
Sampson Point—*cape* ... NC-3
Sampson Pond—*lake* ... ME-1
Sampson Pond—*lake* ... MA-1
Sampson Pond—*lake* ... NY-2
Sampson Pond—*lake* ... NC-3
Sampson Pond—*reservoir* ... CT-1
Sampson Pond Outlet—*stream* ... NY-2
Sampson Post Office (historical)—*building* ... TN-4
Sampson Ridge—*ridge* ... IN-6
Sampson Ridge—*ridge* ... TN-4
Sampson River—*stream* ... FL-3
Sampson Rock—*summit* ... MD-2
*Sampsons Brook* ... MA-1
Sampson Sch—*school* ... CO-8
Sampson Sch—*school* ... MI-6
Sampson Sch—*school* ... NC-3
Sampson Sch (historical)—*school* ... TN-4
Sampson Sch Number 1—*school* ... ND-7
Sampson School—*locale* ... IL-6
**Sampsons Corner**—*pop pl* ... MA-1
Sampsons Cove—*bay* ... LA-4
Sampsons Cove—*cove* ... MA-1
Sampson's Folly-Josiah Sampson House—*hist pl* ... MA-1
*Sampsons Hill* ... IN-6
*Sampsons Hill* ... MA-1
Sampsons Island—*cape* ... MA-1
Sampsons Island Sanctuary—*park* ... MA-1
*Sampsons Pond* ... MA-1
Sampson Spring—*spring* ... NV-8
Sampson Spring—*spring* ... OR-9
Sampson-Star Sch—*school* ... PA-2
Sampson State Park—*park* ... NY-2
Sampsons Wharf—*locale* ... VA-3
Sampson Tank—*reservoir* ... AZ-5
**Sampson (Town of)**—*pop pl* ... WI-6
**Sampsonville**—*pop pl* ... NY-2
Sampson Well—*well* (2) ... AZ-5
Sampson Well—*well* ... NM-5
Sampson Well—*well* (2) ... TX-5
Sampson Windmill—*locale* ... AZ-5
Sampson Windmill—*locale* (2) ... TX-5
Sampson-Wood Lake—*reservoir* ... TN-4
Sampson-Wood Lake Dam—*dam* ... TN-4
*Samptown* ... NJ-2
Samptown—*locale* ... NJ-2
Sampusand—*locale* ... LA-4
*Sampusand Hill* ... LA-4
Sampy Ch—*church* ... AL-4
Sam Queen Gap—*gap* ... NC-3
**Sam Rayburn**—*pop pl* ... TX-5
Sam Rayburn HS—*school* ... TX-5
Sam Rayburn JHS—*school* ... TX-5
Sam Rayburn Rsvr—*reservoir* ... TX-5
Sam Rice Brook—*stream* ... MA-1
Sam Rice Ditch—*canal* ... CO-8
Sam Ridge—*ridge* ... WV-2
Sam Ross Coulee—*valley* ... MT-8
Sam Rowe Hill—*summit* ... ME-1
Sam Rowe Ridge—*ridge* ... ME-1
Sams—*locale* ... CO-8
**Sams**—*pop pl* ... TN-4
Sams Bayou—*bay* ... FL-3
Sams Bayou—*gut* ... FL-3
Sams Bayou—*stream* ... LA-4
Sams Big Lake—*lake* ... AK-9
*Sams Branch* ... NC-3
Sams Branch—*stream* ... KY-4
Sams Branch—*stream* ... MS-4
Sams Branch—*stream* ... MO-7
Sams Branch—*stream* (3) ... NC-3
Sams Branch—*stream* ... TN-4
Sams Branch—*stream* (3) ... WV-2
Sams Butte—*summit* ... AZ-5
Sams Butte—*summit* ... TX-5
Sams Butte Tank—*reservoir* ... AZ-5
Sams Cabin—*locale* ... OR-9
Sams Cabin—*locale* ... UT-8
Sams Camp Rsvr—*reservoir* ... NV-8
Sams Camp Wash—*stream* ... NV-8
Sams Camp Well—*well* ... NV-8
Sams Canyon—*valley* ... CA-9
Sams Canyon—*valley* ... NV-8
Sams Canyon—*valley* (3) ... UT-8
Sams Cave—*cave* ... TN-4
Sams Cem—*cemetery* ... IA-7
Sams Cem—*cemetery* ... NC-3
Sams Cem—*cemetery* ... WV-2
Sams Cove—*bay* ... MA-1
Sams Cove—*bay* ... VA-3
Sams Cove—*valley* ... TN-4
*Sams Creek* ... AR-4
Sams Creek—*locale* ... MD-2
Sams Creek—*stream* ... AL-4
Sams Creek—*stream* ... AR-4
Sams Creek—*stream* ... CO-8
Sams Creek—*stream* (2) ... GA-3
Sams Creek—*stream* (2) ... ID-8
Sams Creek—*stream* ... IN-6
Sams Creek—*stream* ... MD-2
Sams Creek—*stream* ... MO-7
Sams Creek—*stream* ... MT-8
Sams Creek—*stream* ... NY-2
Sams Creek—*stream* (2) ... NC-3
Sams Creek—*stream* (2) ... OH-6
Sams Creek—*stream* (2) ... OR-9
Sams Creek—*stream* (3) ... TN-4
Sams Creek—*stream* ... UT-8
Sams Creek—*stream* ... VA-3
Sams Creek—*stream* ... WA-9
Sams Creek—*stream* ... WV-2
Sams Creek—*stream* ... WY-8
Sams Creek Campground—*locale* ... ID-8
Sams Creek Ch—*church* ... GA-3
Sams Creek Ch—*church* ... TN-4
Sams Creek Ch—*church* ... WV-2
Sams Creek Cutoff—*stream* ... FL-3
Sams Creek Sch (historical)—*school* ... TN-4
*Sams Cut Off* ... FL-3
Sams Dam Tank—*reservoir* ... AZ-5
Sams Divide—*ridge* ... CO-8
Sams Dock—*locale* ... TN-4
Samsel Cem—*cemetery* ... TN-4
Samsel Mines—*mine* ... AZ-5
Samsel Spring—*spring* ... AZ-5
Sams Fork—*stream* ... WV-2
Sams Gap—*gap* (2) ... NC-3
Sams Gap—*gap* (2) ... TN-4
Sams Gulch—*valley* (2) ... ID-8
Sams Gulch—*valley* (2) ... MT-8
Sam Shafer Hollow—*valley* ... WV-2
Sams Hill—*summit* ... NH-1
Sams Hill—*summit* ... ND-7
Sams Hole—*lake* ... GA-3
Sams Hollow—*valley* ... ID-8
Sams Hollow Mine (underground)—*mine* ... AL-4
Samsil Cem—*cemetery* ... KY-4
Sam Simon Barrier Structure Dam—*dam* ... AZ-5
*Sam Sing Camp* ... HI-9
Samsing Cove—*bay* ... AK-9
**Sam Sing Village**—*pop pl* ... HI-9
Sams Island (historical)—*island* ... FL-3
SAM Site—*hist pl* ... SC-3
Sams Knob—*summit* ... NC-3
Sams Knob—*summit* ... OH-6
Sams Knob—*summit* ... VA-3
Sams Lake—*lake* ... FL-3
Sams Lake—*lake* ... MS-4
Sams Lake—*lake* ... WI-6
Sams Lake—*reservoir* ... GA-3
Sams Land—*ridge* ... NC-3
Sams Mesa—*summit* ... UT-8
*Sams Mesa Box* ... UT-8
Sams Mesa Box Canyon—*valley* ... UT-8
*Sams Mesa Canyon* ... UT-8
Sams Mesa Spring—*spring* ... UT-8
Sam Smith Cem—*cemetery* ... TN-4
*Sam Smith Creek* ... OK-5
Sam Smith Creek—*stream* ... WA-9
Sam Snead Golf Course—*other* ... CA-9
Sams Neck—*cape* ... CA-9
**Samson**—*pop pl* ... AL-4
**Samson**—*pop pl* ... KY-4
Samson Bayou—*stream* ... TX-5
*Samson Branch* ... KY-4
Samson Branch—*stream* ... AL-4
*Samson Butte* ... OR-9
Samson Canyon—*valley* ... CA-9
Samson (CCD)—*cens area* ... AL-4
*Samson Church* ... AL-4
*Samson Creek* ... CA-9
Samson Creek—*stream* ... KY-4
Samson Creek—*stream* ... OR-9
**Samsondale**—*pop pl* ... NY-2
Samson Division—*civil* ... AL-4
Samson Draw—*valley* ... TX-5
*Samson Flat* ... CA-9
Samson Hollow—*valley* ... MO-7
Samson Hotel—*hist pl* ... WA-9
Samson HS—*school* ... AL-4
Samson Lake—*lake* ... MN-6
Samson Lake—*lake* ... NM-5
Samson Mesa—*summit* ... CO-8
Samson Methodist Ch—*church* ... AL-4
Samson Mtn—*summit* ... NY-2
Samson Ridge—*ridge* ... CA-9
*Samsons Brook* ... MA-1
Samson Slough—*stream* ... CA-9
Samson Station—*locale* ... KY-4
**Samsonville**—*pop pl* ... NY-2
**Samsonville**—*pop pl* ... VT-1
Samson Well—*well* ... NE-7
Samson Windmill—*locale* (3) ... TX-5
Sams Peak—*summit* ... CO-8
Sams Point—*cape* ... SC-3
Sams Point—*cliff* ... NY-2
**Sams Point**—*pop pl* ... OK-5
Sams Pond—*reservoir* ... ID-8
Sams Ponds—*reservoir* ... OR-9
Sams Prairie—*flat* ... TX-5
Sam Spring—*spring* ... AZ-5
Sam Spring—*spring* (2) ... CA-9
Sam Spring—*spring* ... UT-8
*Sam Springs Wash* ... NV-8
Sam Spring Wash—*stream* ... NV-8
Sams Rapids—*rapids* ... WA-9
Sams Ridge—*ridge* ... KY-4
Sams Ridge—*ridge* ... NC-3
Sams Ridge—*ridge* ... TN-4
Sams Ridge—*ridge* ... VA-3
Sams Ridge—*ridge* ... WA-9
Sams Ridge—*ridge* ... WV-2
Sams Ridge Trail—*trail* ... VA-3
Sams River—*stream* ... WA-9
*Sams Rocks* ... PA-2
Sams Run—*stream* ... PA-2
Sams Run—*stream* ... VA-3
Sams Run—*stream* (3) ... WV-2
Sams Spring—*spring* ... AZ-5
Sams Spring—*spring* ... NV-8
Sams Tank—*reservoir* ... TX-5
Sams Throne—*cliff* ... AR-4
Sams Throne—*summit* ... ID-8
*Sam Stover Canyon* ... UT-8
Sam Stowe Canyon—*valley* ... UT-8
Sam Stowe Creek—*stream* ... UT-8
**Samstown**—*pop pl* ... LA-4
Sam Stuart Canyon—*valley* ... UT-8
Sam Suell Hollow—*valley* ... OK-5
**Samsula**—*pop pl* ... FL-3
Samsula Camp—*locale* ... FL-3
Samsula Canal—*canal* ... FL-3
Samsula Elem Sch—*school* ... FL-3
Samsula-Spruce Creek—*CDP* ... FL-3
**Sams Valley**—*pop pl* ... OR-9
Sams Valley—*valley* ... OR-9
Sams Valley (CCD)—*cens area* ... OR-9
Sams Valley Dam—*dam* ... OR-9
Sams Valley Rsvr—*reservoir* ... OR-9
**Samsville**—*pop pl* ... IL-6
Sams Wash—*valley* ... UT-8
Sams Windmill—*locale* ... NM-5
Sam Talen Hollow—*valley* ... AR-4
Sam Tank—*reservoir* ... AZ-5
Sam Tank—*reservoir* (2) ... NM-5
Sam Taylor Lake—*lake* ... MI-6
Samtown—*locale* ... MO-7
**Samtown**—*pop pl* ... LA-4
*Samtown School* ... TN-4
*Samuals Lake* ... UT-8
Samuel, Point—*cape* ... AK-9
*Samuel A Boardman Wayside* ... OR-9
Samuel Artesian Well—*well* ... TX-5
Samuel Ayer HS—*school* ... CA-9
*Samuel Baird Maxwills Run* ... PA-2
Samuel Betts Grant—*civil* ... FL-3
Samuel Blodget Park—*park* ... NH-1
Samuel Cave—*cave* ... KY-4
Samuel Cem—*cemetery* ... GA-3
Samuel Cem—*cemetery* ... MO-7
*Samuel Chapel* ... MS-4
Samuel Chapel—*church* (2) ... NC-3
Samuel Chapel—*church* ... TX-5
Samuel Chapel Cem—*cemetery* ... MS-4
Samuel Dale Cem—*cemetery* ... MS-4
**Samuel Davila**—*pop pl* ... PR-3
Samuel Dysant Sch—*school* ... IL-6
*Samuel Elisha Rushing Cem* ... MS-4
Samuel Fairbanks Grant—*civil* (2) ... FL-3
Samuel-Fisher Cem—*cemetery* ... TN-4
Samuel Gompers JHS—*school* ... CA-9
Samuel Grove Ch—*church* ... GA-3
Samuel Hartwell Farm Site—*locale* ... MA-1
Samuel H Boardman State Park—*park* ... OR-9
Samuel Hill—*summit* ... KY-4
**Samuel (historical)**—*pop pl* ... TN-4
Samuel HS—*school* ... TX-5
Samuel Inman Sch—*school* ... GA-3
*Samuel J. Bargh Reservoir* ... NY-2
*Samuel J. Bargh Rsvr* ... CT-1
Samuel Key Reservation—*park* ... AL-4
Samuel K Faust Sch—*school* ... PA-2
Samuel L Clemens Memorial Airp—*airport* ... MO-7
Samuell-Crawford Memorial Park—*cemetery* ... TX-5
Samuell Mesquite Park—*park* ... TX-5
Samuell New Hope Park Site—*park* ... TX-5
Samuell Park—*park* ... TX-5
*Samuel McGehee Cem* ... MS-4
Samuel Memorial Cem—*cemetery* ... MN-6
Samuel Miller (Magisterial District)—*fmr MCD* ... VA-3
Samuel Mtn—*summit* ... AR-4
Samuel P Kyger Elem Sch—*school* ... IN-6
Samuel P Large Ditch—*canal* ... WY-8
Samuel Post Office (historical)—*building* ... TN-4
Samuel P Taylor (State Park)—*park* ... CA-9
Samuel Rayburn Memorial Bridge—*bridge* ... TN-4
Samuel Ready Sch—*school* ... MD-2
Samuel Run—*stream* ... WV-2
Samuel R Young Sch—*school* ... GA-3
Samuels—*locale* ... ID-8
**Samuels**—*pop pl* ... KY-4
Samuels, T. W., Distillery Hist Dist—*hist pl* ... KY-4
Samuels Cem—*cemetery* ... KS-7
Samuels Cem—*cemetery* ... KY-4
Samuels Cem—*cemetery* ... TN-4
Samuels Cem—*cemetery* ... VA-3
Samuels Ch—*church* (2) ... PA-2
Samuels Chapel—*church* (2) ... MS-4
Samuels Chapel—*locale* ... AL-4
*Samuels Chapel Church* ... AL-4
Samuels Chapel Creek—*stream* ... AL-4
Samuels Chapel United Methodist Ch—*church* ... AL-4
Samuels Corner—*locale* ... VA-3
Samuels Creek—*stream* ... KY-4
Samuels Ditch—*canal* ... IL-6
Samuel S Dixon Elem Sch—*school* ... PA-2
Samuels Grove Ch—*church* ... VA-3
Samuel Slade Cem—*cemetery* ... MS-4
Samuels Lake—*lake* ... UT-8
Samuel S Lewis State Park—*park* ... PA-2
Samuelson Brothers Number 1 Dam—*dam* ... SD-7
Samuelson Brothers Number 2 Dam—*dam* ... SD-7
Samuelson Brothers Number 4 Dam—*dam* ... SD-7
Samuelson Dam—*dam* ... SD-7
Samuelson Ranch—*locale* ... MT-8
Samuelson Ranch—*locale* ... SD-7
Samuelsons Rock—*pillar* ... CA-9
Samuels Point—*cliff* ... NY-2
Samuels Pond Dam—*dam* ... MS-4
Samuel Spring—*spring* ... MS-4
Samuel Springs—*locale* ... CA-9
Samuels Sch—*school* ... CA-9
Samuels Sch—*school* ... MA-1
Samuels Sch (abandoned)—*school* ... PA-2
Samuel Strong Sch—*school* ... IN-6
Samuel W Houston Sch—*school* ... TX-5
Samuel Wilson Grant—*civil* ... FL-3
*Samuel Word Cemetery* ... MS-4
Samuel W Wolfson Senior HS—*school* ... FL-3
Sam Watt Creek—*stream* ... CA-9
Sam Watt Rock—*summit* ... CA-9
Samway, Lake—*lake* ... WI-6
*Samway Lake* ... WI-6
Sam White Lake—*lake* ... AK-9
Sam White Spring—*spring* ... WA-9
Sam Williams Grant—*civil* ... FL-3
Sam Willies Camp—*locale* ... FL-3
Sam Willie Seminole Village—*locale* ... FL-3
Sam Windmill—*locale* (2) ... TX-5
*Sam Windsors Lump* ... NC-3
Sam Winsors Lump—*island* ... NC-3
*Sam Winter Lump* ... NC-3
Sam Winter Lump—*island* ... NC-3
Sam Wolfin Spring—*spring* ... CA-9
Sam Wood Hollow—*valley* ... MO-7
Samyn Creek—*stream* ... MI-6
*San* ... AZ-5
**San Acacia**—*pop pl* ... NM-5
San Acacia Drainage Canal—*canal* ... NM-5
**San Acacio**—*pop pl* ... CO-8
San Acacio Ch—*church* ... NM-5
San Acacio Stock Ditch No 1—*canal* ... CO-8
San Acacio Stock Ditch No 2—*canal* ... CO-8
San Adrian Island—*island* ... AK-9
Sanaguich River—*stream* ... AK-9
San Agustin—*locale* ... AZ-5
**San Agustin**—*pop pl* (3) ... PR-3
San Agustin, Arroyo—*valley* ... CA-9
Sanak—*locale* ... AK-9
Sanak Bank—*bar* ... AK-9
Sanak Harbor—*bay* ... AK-9
Sanak Island—*island* ... AK-9
Sanak Islands—*island* ... AK-9
Sanak Peak—*summit* ... AK-9
Sanak Reefs—*bar* ... AK-9
**San Alberto**—*pop pl* ... PR-3
San Alberto Bay—*bay* ... AK-9
San Albino Cem—*cemetery* ... NM-5
San Alfonso Ranch—*locale* ... TX-5
San Altos Sch—*school* ... CA-9
San Ambrosia Creek—*stream* ... TX-5
**Sana Muerto**—*pop pl* ... PR-3
Sana Muertos—*CDP* ... PR-3
**San Andreas**—*pop pl* ... CA-9
San Andreas (CCD)—*cens area* ... CA-9
San Andreas Creek—*stream* ... CA-9
San Andreas Creek—*stream* ... TX-5
San Andreas Lake—*reservoir* ... CA-9
San Andreas Rift Zone—*area* (2) ... CA-9
San Andreas Sch—*school* ... CA-9
San Andreas Shoal—*bar* ... CA-9
San Andreas Windmill—*locale* ... TX-5
San Andrecito Canyon—*valley* ... NM-5
San Andres—*civil* ... CA-9
San Andres-Alameda Estates—*CDP* ... NM-5
San Andres Canyon—*valley* ... NM-5
San Andres Catholic Ch—*church* ... UT-8
San Andres Cem—*cemetery* ... TX-5
*San Andres Coata* ... AZ-5
*San Andres Creek* ... TX-5
*San Andres Lake* ... CA-9
San Andres Mountains—*range* ... NM-5
San Andres Peak—*summit* ... NM-5
San Andres Sch—*school* ... TX-5
San Andres Trail—*trail* ... NM-5
San Andres Well—*well* ... TX-5
**San Angelo**—*pop pl* ... TX-5
San Angelo (CCD)—*cens area* ... TX-5
San Angelo City Hall—*hist pl* ... TX-5
San Angelo Coll—*school* ... TX-5
*San Angelo College* ... TX-5
San Angelo Country Club—*other* ... TX-5
*San Angelo del Botum* ... AZ-5
San Angelo Gun Club—*other* ... TX-5
San Angelo High School Stadium—*other* ... TX-5
San Angelo Junction—*locale* ... TX-5
San Angelo Natl Bank, Johnson and Taylor, and Schwartz and Raas Bldgs—*hist pl* ... TX-5
San Angelo Natl Bank Bldg—*hist pl* ... TX-5
San Angelo Telephone Company Bldg—*hist pl* ... TX-5
San Angelo Yard—*locale* ... TX-5
San Anita Mine—*mine* ... MT-8
**San Anselmo**—*pop pl* ... CA-9
San Anselmo Creek—*stream* ... CA-9
*San Antinio* ... FL-3
**San Anton**—*pop pl* ... PR-3
San Anton (Barrio)—*fmr MCD* (2) ... PR-3
*San Antone* ... NV-8
San Antone Creek—*stream* ... OR-9
San Antone Lake—*lake* ... NM-5
San Antone Well—*well* (2) ... AZ-5
*San Antonia* ... NV-8
*San Antonia Peak* ... CA-9
San Antonio—*CDP* ... PR-3
San Antonio—*locale* ... NV-8
**San Antonio**—*pop pl* ... CO-8
**San Antonio**—*pop pl* ... FL-3
**San Antonio**—*pop pl* ... MO-7
**San Antonio**—*pop pl* (3) ... NM-5
**San Antonio**—*pop pl* ... TX-5
**San Antonio**—*pop pl* ... GU-9
**San Antonio**—*pop pl* ... MH-9
**San Antonio**—*pop pl* (4) ... PR-3
San Antonio, Estero De—*stream* ... CA-9
San Antonio, Mount—*summit* ... CA-9
San Antonio, Point—*cape* ... AK-9
San Antonio, Rio—*stream* ... CO-8
San Antonio Air Force Station—*military* ... TX-5
San Antonio (A M Peralta)—*civil* ... CA-9
San Antonio Art Institute—*building* ... TX-5
San Antonio (Barrio)—*fmr MCD* (2) ... PR-3
San Antonio Bay—*bay* ... TX-5
San Antonio Cabin—*locale* ... NM-5
San Antonio Camp—*locale* ... CA-9
San Antonio Camp—*locale* ... TX-5
San Antonio Campground—*locale* ... NM-5
San Antonio Canyon—*valley* ... AZ-5
San Antonio Canyon—*valley* ... CA-9
San Antonio Canyon—*valley* ... TX-5
San Antonio Casino Club Bldg—*hist pl* ... TX-5
San Antonio (CCD)—*cens area* ... TX-5
San Antonio Cem—*cemetery* ... CO-8
San Antonio Cem—*cemetery* (3) ... NM-5
San Antonio Cem—*cemetery* (5) ... TX-5
San Antonio Ch—*church* (6) ... NM-5
San Antonio Coll—*school* ... TX-5
San Antonio Country Club—*other* ... TX-5
*San Antonio Creek* ... CA-9
*San Antonio Creek* ... CO-8
San Antonio Creek—*stream* (7) ... CA-9
San Antonio Creek—*stream* ... NM-5
San Antonio Creek Channel—*canal* ... CA-9
San Antonio Dam—*dam* ... CA-9
San Antonio De Las Huertas Grant—*civil* ... NM-5
San Antonio de Padua Church—*hist pl* ... NM-5
San Antonio de Padua del Quemado Chapel—*hist pl* ... NM-5
San Antonio de Padua del Rancho—*locale* ... NM-5
San Antonio de Padua Mission—*hist pl* ... CA-9
San Antonio Ditch—*canal* (2) ... NM-5
San Antonio Elem Sch—*school* ... FL-3
*San Antonio Estuary* ... CA-9
San Antonio Falls—*falls* ... CA-9
**San Antonio Heights**—*pop pl* ... CA-9
San Antonio Hill—*summit* ... NM-5
San Antonio Hosp—*hospital* ... CA-9
San Antonio Hot Spring—*spring* ... NM-5
San Antonio International Airp—*airport* ... TX-5
San Antonio Lake—*lake* ... TX-5
San Antonio Loan and Trust Bldg—*hist pl* ... TX-5
San Antonio (Lugo)—*civil* ... CA-9
San Antonio (Mesa)—*civil* ... CA-9
San Antonio Mine—*mine* ... AZ-5
San Antonio Mine—*mine* ... CA-9
San Antonio Mine—*mine* (2) ... NV-8
San Antonio Mine—*mine* ... TX-5
San Antonio Mission—*church* ... CA-9
San Antonio Mission—*church* ... NM-5
San Antonio Missions Natl Historic Park—*park* ... TX-5
San Antonio Mtn—*summit* (2) ... NM-5
San Antonio Mtn—*summit* ... TX-5
San Antonio Mtns—*range* ... NV-8
San Antonio Or Pescadero—*civil* ... CA-9
San Antonio Or Rodeo De Las Aguas—*civil* ... CA-9
San Antonio Park—*park* ... CA-9
San Antonio Pass—*gap* ... TX-5
*San Antonio Peak* ... CA-9
San Antonio Prairie Cem—*cemetery* ... TX-5
San Antonio Raceway—*other* ... TX-5
San Antonio Ranch—*locale* ... NV-8
San Antonio Ranger Station—*locale* ... CA-9
San Antonio Reef—*bar* ... MI-6
San Antonio Ridge—*ridge* ... CA-9
*San Antonio River* ... CO-8
San Antonio River—*stream* ... CA-9
San Antonio River—*stream* ... TX-5
*San Antonio Rsvr* ... CA-9
San Antonio Rsvr—*reservoir* (2) ... CA-9
San Antonio Sch—*school* (5) ... CA-9
San Antonio Spring—*spring* (2) ... NM-5
*San Antonio Station* ... NV-8
San Antonio Tank—*reservoir* ... NM-5
San Antonio Tank—*reservoir* ... TX-5
San Antonio Terrace—*bench* ... CA-9
San Antonio Union Sch—*school* ... CA-9
San Antonio Valley—*valley* (2) ... CA-9
San Antonio Valley—*valley* ... NM-5
San Antonio (V and D Peralta)—*civil* ... CA-9
**San Antonio Viejo**—*pop pl* ... TX-5
San Antonio Water Works Pump Station No. 2—*hist pl* ... TX-5
San Antonio Well—*locale* ... NM-5
San Antonio Well—*well* ... NV-8
San Antonio Windmill—*locale* (2) ... TX-5
San Antonio (Y Peralta)—*civil* ... CA-9
**San Antonito**—*pop pl* (2) ... NM-5
Sana Post Office (historical)—*building* ... SD-7
*San Aqueda Creek* ... CA-9
**San Ardo**—*pop pl* ... CA-9
San Ardo (CCD)—*cens area* ... CA-9
San Arroyo—*valley* ... UT-8
San Arroyo Camp—*locale* ... UT-8
San Arroyo Canyon—*valley* ... UT-8
*San Arroyo Creek* ... CO-8
San Arroyo Gas Field—*oilfield* ... UT-8
San Arroyo Ridge—*ridge* ... UT-8
*San Arroyo Wash* ... CO-8
*San Arroyo Wash* ... UT-8
San Arroyo Wash—*valley* ... UT-8
*Sanastee Wash* ... AZ-5
Sanat—*island* ... FM-9
Sanatag Creek—*stream* ... OK-5
**Sanatoga**—*pop pl* ... PA-2
Sanatoga Creek—*stream* ... PA-2
Sanatoga Dam—*dam* ... PA-2
**Sanatoga Park**—*pop pl* ... PA-2
Sanatoga Station—*locale* ... PA-2
Sanator—*locale* ... SD-7
*Sanatoricho* ... MH-9
Sanatorio Ruiz Soler—*hospital* ... PR-3
**Sanatorium**—*pop pl* ... MS-4
**Sanatorium (Blue Ridge Sanatorium)**—*pop pl* ... VA-3
Sanatorium (Eastern Oklahoma State TB Sanatorium)—*hospital* ... OK-5
**Sanatorium (McKnight State Tuberculosis Hospital)**—*pop pl* ... TX-5
Sanatorium (RR for McCain)—*other* ... NC-3
*Sanat Pass* ... FM-9
San Augustin—*civil* ... CA-9
San Augustin Canyon—*valley* ... CA-9
San Augustin Dam—*dam* ... NM-5
San Augustin de Laredo Hist Dist—*hist pl* ... TX-5
San Augustine—*locale* ... CA-9
**San Augustine**—*pop pl* ... TX-5
San Augustine (CCD)—*cens area* ... TX-5
**San Augustine (County)**—*pop pl* ... TX-5
San Augustine Draw—*valley* ... TX-5
*San Augustine Inlet* ... FL-3
San Augustine Plaza—*park* ... AZ-5
San Augustines Springs—*spring* ... TX-5
**San Augustin (Lourdes Post Office)**—*pop pl* (2) ... NM-5
San Augustin Mountains—*other* ... NM-5
San Augustin Pass—*gap* ... NM-5
San Augustin Peak—*summit* ... NM-5
San Augustin Spring—*spring* ... NM-5
San Bacino Dam—*dam* ... NM-5
Sanbar Lake—*lake* ... FL-3
*San Barnardo River* ... TX-5
San Bartolo, Arroyo—*valley* ... TX-5
*San Bartolomeo* ... MP-9
San Benancio Gulch—*valley* ... CA-9
San Benancio Sch—*school* ... CA-9
*San Benard River* ... TX-5
San Benito—*civil* ... CA-9
San Benito—*locale* ... CA-9
**San Benito**—*pop pl* ... TX-5
San Benito-Bitterwater (CCD)—*cens area* ... CA-9
**San Benito (County)**—*pop pl* ... CA-9
San Benito County Golf And Country Club—*other* ... CA-9
San Benito County HS and Junior Col—*school* ... CA-9
San Benito Mill (Site)—*locale* ... CA-9
San Benito Mtn—*summit* ... CA-9
San Benito Pumping Station—*other* ... TX-5
San Benito River—*stream* ... CA-9
*San Benito Valley* ... CA-9
San Bernabe—*civil* ... CA-9
*San Bernadino* ... AZ-5
San Bernadino Peak—*summit* ... CA-9
*San Bernardino* ... AZ-5
San Bernardino—*civil* ... CA-9
San Bernardino—*locale* ... AZ-5
**San Bernardino**—*pop pl* ... CA-9
San Bernardino Asistencia—*church* ... CA-9
San Bernardino (CCD)—*cens area* ... CA-9
**San Bernardino (County)**—*pop pl* ... CA-9
San Bernardino East Peak—*summit* ... CA-9
San Bernardino HS—*school* ... CA-9
*San Bernardino Mountains* ... CA-9
San Bernardino Mountains—*range* ... CA-9
San Bernardino Mtn—*summit* ... CA-9
San Bernardino Peak Divide Trail (Pack)—*trail* ... CA-9
San Bernardino Ranch—*hist pl* ... AZ-5
San Bernardino Ranch—*locale* ... AZ-5
San Bernardino Valley—*valley* ... AZ-5
San Bernardino Valley Coll—*school* ... CA-9
San Bernardino Wash—*stream* ... CA-9
San Bernard Natl Wildlife Ref—*park* ... TX-5
*San Bernardo* ... CA-9
San Bernardo—*hist pl* ... OK-5
San Bernardo (Cane)—*civil* ... CA-9
San Bernardo Creek—*stream* ... CA-9
San Bernardo Junior Mine—*mine* ... AZ-5
San Bernardo Mine—*mine* ... CO-8
San Bernardo Mtn—*summit* ... CO-8
*San Bernardo River* ... TX-5
San Bernardo (Snook)—*civil* ... CA-9

San Bernardo (Soberanes)—*civil* CA-9
San Bernardo Valley—*valley* CA-9
San Bernard River—*stream* TX-5
**San Blas**—*pop pl* FL-3
San Blas, Cape—*cape* FL-3
*San Bois Creek* OK-5
*Sanbois Mountains* OK-5
Sanborn—*locale* CA-9
Sanborn—*locale* FL-3
Sanborn—*locale* NE-7
**Sanborn**—*pop pl* GA-3
**Sanborn**—*pop pl* IA-7
**Sanborn**—*pop pl* KY-4
**Sanborn**—*pop pl* MN-6
**Sanborn**—*pop pl* NY-2
**Sanborn**—*pop pl* ND-7
**Sanborn**—*pop pl* WI-6
Sanborn, Lake—*lake* MN-6
Sanborn, Rev. Peter, House—*hist pl* MA-1
Sanborn Bay—*bay* NH-1
Sanborn Brook—*stream* CT-1
Sanborn Brook—*stream* ME-1
Sanborn Brook—*stream* (2) NH-1
Sanborn Cabin—*locale* CA-9
Sanborn Canal—*channel* AK-9
Sanborn Cem—*cemetery* FL-3
Sanborn Cem—*cemetery* (2) ME-1
Sanborn Cem—*cemetery* (2) MI-6
Sanborn Cem—*cemetery* MN-6
Sanborn Cem—*cemetery* (2) NH-1
Sanborn Ch—*church* WI-6
Sanborn Corner—*locale* ME-1
**Sanborn Corners**—*pop pl* NH-1
Sanborn Country Park—*park* MI-6
Sanborn County—*civil* SD-7
Sanborn Cove—*bay* ME-1
Sanborn Creek—*stream* CO-8
Sanborn Creek—*stream* GA-3
Sanborn Creek—*stream* ID-8
Sanborn Creek—*stream* MI-6
Sanborn Cutoff—*bend* FL-3
Sanborn Ditch—*canal* CO-8
Sanborn Drain—*canal* MI-6
Sanborn Draw—*valley* CO-8
Sanborn Field and Soil Erosion Plots—*hist pl* MO-7
Sanborn Hall—*hist pl* OH-6
Sanborn Harbor—*bay* AK-9
Sanborn Hill—*summit* CA-9
Sanborn Hill—*summit* ME-1
Sanborn Hill—*summit* NH-1
Sanborn House—*hist pl* MA-1
Sanborn Lake—*lake* FL-3
Sanborn Lake—*lake* MN-6
Sanborn Lake—*lake* ND-7
Sanborn Lake—*lake* WI-6
Sanborn Lake—*reservoir* OK-5
Sanborn Lookout Tower—*tower* FL-3
Sanborn Marsh—*swamp* ME-1
Sanborn Mine—*locale* CA-9
Sanborn Park—*flat* CO-8
Sanborn Park—*park* CA-9
Sanborn Park—*park* MN-6
*Sanborn Pond* ME-1
Sanborn Pond—*lake* (2) ME-1
Sanborn Pond—*lake* NH-1
Sanborn Ridge—*ridge* VT-1
Sanborn River—*stream* ME-1
Sanborn Rsvr—*reservoir* (2) CO-8
**Sanborns**—*pop pl* ME-1
Sanborn Sch—*school* CA-9
Sanborn Sch—*school* CO-8
Sanborn Sch—*school* FL-3
Sanborn Sch—*school* MA-1
Sanborn Sch—*school* NE-7
Sanborn Sch—*school* NH-1
Sanborn Seminary—*hist pl* NH-1
Sanborns Gut—*bay* NC-3
Sanborn Slough—*stream* CA-9
Sanborn Slough Gun Club—*other* CA-9
**Sanbornton**—*pop pl* NH-1
Sanbornton Mtn—*summit* NH-1
*Sanbornton Square* NH-1
Sanbornton Square Hist Dist—*hist pl* NH-1
**Sanbornton (Town of)**—*pop pl* NH-1
**Sanborn (Town of)**—*pop pl* WI-6
**Sanborn (Township of)**—*pop pl* MI-6
**Sanbornville**—*pop pl* NH-1
**Sanbourn**—*pop pl* PA-2
Sanbourn Run—*stream* PA-2
Sanbourn Sch—*school* IN-6
Sanbout, Bayou—*gut* LA-4
San Branch—*stream* KY-4
**San Bruno**—*pop pl* CA-9
San Bruno Canyon—*valley* CA-9
San Bruno Channel—*channel* CA-9
San Bruno Creek—*stream* CA-9
San Bruno Mtn—*summit* CA-9
San Bruno Shoal—*bar* CA-9
*San Buenaventura* CA-9
*San Buenaventura* CO-8
San Buena Ventura—*civil* CA-9
**San Buenaventura (corporate name for Ventura)**—*pop pl* CA-9
**San Buenaventura (historical)**—*pop pl* FL-3
San Buenaventura Mission Aqueduct—*hist pl* CA-9
*San Buenaventura River* UT-8
*San Buenaventura River* WY-8
San Buenaventura State Beach—*park* CA-9
Sanburg Ditch—*canal* CO-8
**Sanburne Park**—*pop pl* VA-3
Sanburn Hill—*summit* NY-2
*Sanburn Lake* MN-6
Sanburn Rsvr—*reservoir* MT-8
San Caja Hill—*summit* TX-5
San Caja Hollow—*valley* TX-5
San Cajo—*summit* TX-5
San Carlo Cem—*cemetery* IL-6
*San Carlos* MH-9
San Carlos—*locale* TX-5
**San Carlos**—*pop pl* AZ-5
**San Carlos**—*pop pl* CA-9
**San Carlos**—*pop pl* FL-3
**San Carlos**—*pop pl* TX-5
**San Carlos**—*pop pl* PR-3
San Carlos—*uninc pl* CA-9
San Carlos, Arroyo—*valley* TX-5
San Carlos Bay—*bay* FL-3
San Carlos Bay Light 1—*locale* FL-3
San Carlos Beach—*beach* FL-3
San Carlos Bolsa—*basin* CA-9
San Carlos Canyon—*valley* CA-9
San Carlos (CCD)—*cens area* AZ-5
**San Carlos Chacatos (historical)**—*pop pl* FL-3
*San Carlos Creek* TX-5
San Carlos Creek—*stream* CA-9
San Carlos Creek—*stream* FL-3
San Carlos Creek—*stream* TX-5
San Carlos De Jonata—*civil* CA-9
San Carlos Gas Field—*oilfield* TX-5
San Carlos Golf Course—*other* CA-9
San Carlos (historical)—*locale* AZ-5
San Carlos Hosp—*hospital* AZ-5
San Carlos Hotel—*hist pl* (2) AZ-5
San Carlos Hotel—*hist pl* FL-3
San Carlos Indian Agency—*building* AZ-5
**San Carlos Ind Res**—*pop pl* AZ-5
*San Carlos Island* AZ-5
*San Carlos Island* UT-8
San Carlos Island—*island* FL-3
San Carlos Job Corporation Conservation Center—*locale* AZ-5
*San Carlos Lake* AZ-5
San Carlos Landing Strip—*airport* AZ-5
San Carlos Mine—*mine* TX-5
San Carlos Mines—*mine* CA-9
San Carlos Park—*park* AZ-5
San Carlos Park—*park* CA-9
**San Carlos Park**—*pop pl* FL-3
San Carlos Park Elem Sch—*school* FL-3
San Carlos Peak—*summit* CA-9
San Carlos Plaza (Shop Ctr)—*locale* FL-3
San Carlos Police Station—*building* AZ-5
San Carlos Post Office—*building* AZ-5
San Carlos Project Substation—*locale* AZ-5
San Carlos Ranch—*locale* CA-9
*San Carlos Reservation* AZ-5
San Carlos River—*stream* AZ-5
San Carlos Rsvr—*reservoir* AZ-5
San Carlos (San Carlos Agency)—*CDP* AZ-5
**San Carlos (subdivision)**—*pop pl* (2) AZ-5
San Carlos Tank—*reservoir* AZ-5
San Carlos Trail—*trail* CO-8
San Carlos Windmill—*locale* (3) TX-5
*San Caropjoro Creek* CA-9
San Carpoforo Creek—*stream* CA-9
*San Carpoforo Valley* CA-9
*San Carpojo Creek* CA-9
San Casimiro Creek—*stream* TX-5
**Sancassa**—*pop pl* FL-3
San Catanio Creek—*stream* CA-9
San Cayetano de Tumacacori (historical)—*locale* AZ-5
*San Cayetano Mountain* AZ-5
San Cayetano Mountains—*summit* AZ-5
San Cayetano Mtn—*summit* CA-9
San Cayetano Peak—*summit* AZ-5
San Cayetano Ranch—*locale* AZ-5
*Sanchacantacket Pond* MA-1
Sancher Pond—*lake* FL-3
Sanches Cem—*cemetery* CO-8
*Sanches Creek* TX-5
Sanchez—*locale* NM-5
**Sanchez**—*pop pl* AZ-5
Sanchez, Samuel, Barns—*hist pl* NM-5
Sanchez, Samuel, House—*hist pl* NM-5
Sanchez Adobe—*locale* CA-9
Sanchez Adobe Park—*hist pl* CA-9
Sanchez Canal—*canal* CO-8
Sanchez Canyon—*valley* (5) NM-5
Sanchez Cem—*cemetery* NM-5
Sanchez Creek—*stream* CA-9
Sanchez Creek—*stream* TX-5
Sanchez Creek—*stream* WY-8
Sanchez Drain—*canal* NM-5
Sanchez Draw—*valley* CO-8
Sanchez Draw—*valley* TX-5
Sanchez Lake—*lake* FL-3
Sanchez Lakes—*lake* CO-8
Sanchez-March House—*hist pl* NM-5
Sanchez Mine—*mine* CO-8
Sanchez Monmt—*park* AZ-5
Sanchez Place—*locale* (2) NM-5
Sanchez Powder House Site—*hist pl* FL-3
Sanchez Prairie—*swamp* FL-3
Sanchez Ranch—*locale* (3) NM-5
Sanchez Rsvr—*reservoir* CO-8
Sanchez Sch—*school* (2) CA-9
Sanchez Sch—*school* TX-5
Sanchez Sch—*school* GU-9
Sanchez Spring—*spring* CO-8
Sanchez Spring—*spring* (2) TX-5
Sanchez Spring—*spring* WY-8
Sanchez Tank—*reservoir* NM-5
Sanchez Tank—*reservoir* TX-5
Sanchez Well—*well* (2) NM-5
Sanchez Well—*well* TX-5
Sanchez Windmill—*locale* CO-8
Sancho Ch—*church* WV-2
Sancho Creek—*stream* WV-2
*Sancho Fork* WV-2
Sancho Panza Mine—*mine* TX-5
San Christoval Channel—*channel* AK-9
*San Christoval Creek* TX-5
San Christoval Creek—*stream* TX-5
San Christoval Rock—*other* AK-9
San Cirilo Creek—*stream* TX-5
Sancity Ch—*church* GA-3
San Clair Ch—*church* GA-3
**San Clemente**—*pop pl* CA-9
**San Clemente**—*pop pl* PR-3
San Clemente Beach Club—*hist pl* CA-9
San Clemente Canyon—*valley* CA-9
San Clemente Creek—*stream* (3) CA-9
San Clemente Dam—*dam* CA-9
San Clemente Golf Course—*other* CA-9
San Clemente Grant—*civil* NM-5
San Clemente Island—*island* AK-9
San Clemente Island—*island* CA-9
San Clemente Park—*park* CA-9
San Clemente Pier—*locale* CA-9
San Clemente Ridge—*ridge* CA-9
San Clemente Sch—*school* CA-9
San Clemente Shop Ctr—*locale* AZ-5
San Clemente State Beach—*park* CA-9
San Clemente Trail—*trail* CA-9
Sanco—*locale* TX-5
*San Cosme Del Tucson* AZ-5
*San Cosme y San Damian de Escambe* FL-3
*Sancoty Head* MA-1
San Cristobal—*locale* PR-3
**San Cristobal**—*pop pl* NM-5
**San Cristobal**—*pop pl* PR-3
San Cristobal, Lake—*reservoir* CO-8
San Cristobal Arroyo—*valley* NM-5
San Cristobal Canyon—*valley* NM-5
San Cristobal Cem—*cemetery* NM-5
*San Cristobal Creek* TX-5
San Cristobal Creek—*stream* NM-5
*San Cristobal Lake* CO-8
San Cristobal Valley—*valley* AZ-5
San Cristobal Wash—*stream* AZ-5
San Cristobal Windmill—*locale* TX-5
*San Cristobas Wash* AZ-5
*San Cristopal Lake* CO-8
*San Cristovaal Lake* CO-8
San Cristoval—*civil* NM-5
*San Cristoval Creek* TX-5
Sancta Clara Monastery—*church* OH-6
*Sanctified Ch* MS-4
Sanctified Ch—*church* (5) AL-4
Sanctified Ch—*church* AR-4
Sanctified Ch—*church* (2) FL-3
Sanctified Ch—*church* (4) LA-4
Sanctified Ch—*church* (10) MS-4
Sanctified Ch—*church* MO-7
Sanctified Ch—*church* (4) SC-3
Sanctified Ch—*church* TN-4
Sanctified Ch (historical)—*church* (3) AL-4
Sanctified Ch (historical)—*church* (3) MS-4
Sanctified Ch (historical)—*church* (2) TN-4
Sanctified Ch of God—*church* IN-6
Sanctified Hill—*summit* TN-4
Sanctified Saints Ch—*church* LA-4
Sanctified Tabernacle (historical)—*church* AL-4
Sanctify Ch—*church* AR-4
Sanctity Ch—*church* VA-3
**Sanctuario**—*pop pl* NM-5
**Sanctuary**—*pop pl* TX-5
Sanctuary, The—*church* FL-3
Sanctuary Bay—*bay* NJ-2
Sanctuary Cem—*cemetery* OH-6
Sanctuary Pond—*lake* MA-1
Sanctuary Ridge—*summit* AZ-5
Sanctuary River—*stream* AK-9
Sanctuary River Cabin No. 31—*hist pl* AK-9
Sanctuary River Campground—*locale* AK-9
Sanctuary Sound—*bay* FL-3
*Sanctuit* MA-1
Sanctum Ch—*church* GA-3
Sancudo Windmill—*locale* TX-5
Sand—*locale* TX-5
Sand, Lake—*lake* LA-4
Sandabacka Lake—*lake* MN-6
Sandage Buttes—*summit* MT-8
Sandage Coulee—*valley* MT-8
Sandager—*locale* LA-4
Sandager Canal—*canal* LA-4
Sandager Park—*park* ND-7
Sandago (historical)—*locale* KS-7
Sandal Canal—*canal* CA-9
*Sandal Cave* OR-9
**Sandale**—*pop pl* IN-6
Sandalee Glacier—*glacier* WA-9
Sandale Sch Number 1—*school* ND-7
Sandale Sch Number 3—*school* ND-7
Sandalfoot Cove—*CDP* FL-3
Sandal Foot Cove Park—*park* FL-3
Sandal Gulch—*valley* WA-9
Sandal House—*locale* CO-8
Sandals Cem—*cemetery* MO-7
**Sandalwood**—*pop pl* FL-3
**Sandalwood**—*pop pl* GA-3
Sandalwood Country Club—*other* WI-6
Sandalwood Junior-Senior HS—*school* FL-3
Sandalwood Playground—*park* OH-6
**Sandalwood Square Subdivision**—*pop pl* UT-8
**Sandalwood (subdivision)**—*pop pl* (2) AZ-5
**Sandalwood (subdivision)**—*pop pl* MS-4
**Sandalwood Village**—*pop pl* TN-4
San Damiano Retreat—*locale* CA-9
Sand Arroya Creek—*stream* CO-8
Sand Arroyo—*stream* (3) CO-8
Sand Arroyo—*stream* NM-5
Sand Arroyo—*valley* MT-8
Sand Arroyo Badlands—*area* MT-8
Sand Arroyo Bay—*bay* MT-8
Sand Arroyo Cem—*cemetery* CO-8
Sand Arroyo Creek—*stream* KS-7
San Davis Spring—*spring* OR-9
Sandback Lake—*lake* MN-6
Sandback Pond—*lake* MI-6
Sand Ball Hill—*summit* NC-3
*Sand Bank* NY-2
**Sand Bank**—*pop pl* ID-8
*Sandbank, The* PA-2
Sandbank Cem—*cemetery* IN-6
Sand Bank Cove—*bay* RI-1
Sand Bank Creek—*stream* CA-9
Sandbank Creek—*stream* FL-3
Sandbank Creek—*stream* NC-3
*Sand Bank Hill* CT-1
Sand Bank Hill—*summit* IN-6
Sandbank Hollow—*valley* AR-4
Sandbank Hollow—*valley* MO-7
Sandbank Hollow—*valley* VA-3
Sandbank Lake—*lake* LA-4
Sandbank Mtn—*summit* VA-3
Sandbank Ridge—*ridge* NC-3
*Sand Banks* NY-2
*Sand Banks* TN-4
Sand Banks—*bar* NC-3
Sand Banks—*slope* CA-9
Sandbank Sch—*school* IL-6
Sand Bank Sch—*school* IL-6
Sand Bank Sch—*school* KY-4
Sandbank Sch (abandoned)—*school* PA-2
Sandbank Spring—*spring* NV-8
Sand Banks Ridge—*ridge* TN-4
Sandbank Stream—*stream* ME-1
Sand Bank Trail—*trail* ME-1
Sandbank Trail—*trail* ME-1
Sand Bar—*ridge* UT-8
*Sand Bar, The* CT-1
Sand Bar, The—*bar* ME-1
Sandbar, The—*bar* ME-1
Sandbar, The—*bar* MT-8
Sand Bar Bridge—*bridge* VT-1
Sandbar Creek—*stream* MT-8
Sand Bar Flat Dam—*dam* CA-9
Sand Bar Gulch—*valley* OR-9
Sand Bar Island—*island* IL-6
Sand Bar Island—*island* ME-1
Sandbar Island—*island* MN-6
*Sand Bar Lake* MN-6
Sandbar Lake—*lake* FL-3
Sandbar Lake—*lake* LA-4
Sandbar Lake—*lake* MS-4
Sand Bar Lake—*lake* WI-6
Sandbar Lakes—*lake* WI-6
Sand Bar Landing—*locale* NC-3
Sandbar Point—*cape* ME-1
Sand Bar Point—*cape* ME-1
Sand Bar Point—*cape* NJ-2
Sand Bar Point—*cape* NY-2
**Sand Barrens**—*pop pl* IL-6
Sandbar Slough—*gut* IA-7
Sand Bar State Park—*park* VT-1
Sandbar Tract—*unorg* ME-1
Sandbar West Oil Field—*oilfield* WY-8
Sand Basin—*basin* MT-8
Sand Basin—*basin* OR-9
Sand Basin—*basin* WY-8
Sand Basin Creek—*stream* MT-8
Sand Bay—*bay* (2) AK-9
Sand Bay—*bay* FL-3
Sand Bay—*bay* (6) MI-6
Sand Bay—*bay* MN-6
Sand Bay—*bay* NY-2
Sand Bay—*bay* VA-3
Sand Bay—*bay* (2) WI-6
Sand Bay—*lake* IL-6
**Sand Bay**—*pop pl* AK-9
**Sand Bay**—*pop pl* WI-6
Sand Bay Cem—*cemetery* NY-2
Sand Bay Island—*island* MN-6
*Sand Bayou* LA-4
Sand Bayou—*gut* (2) AL-4
Sand Bayou—*gut* LA-4
Sand Bayou—*gut* (2) MS-4
Sand Bayou—*gut* TX-5
Sand Bayou—*stream* LA-4
Sand Bay Park—*park* WI-6
*Sand Beach* LA-4
*Sand Beach* MI-6
Sand Beach—*beach* CA-9
Sand Beach—*beach* FL-3
**Sand Beach**—*pop pl* OH-6
**Sand Beach**—*pop pl* PA-2
**Sandbeach**—*pop pl* PA-2
Sand Beach, The—*locale* AK-9
Sand Beach Bayou—*stream* LA-4
Sand Beach Branch—*stream* FL-3
Sand Beach Brook—*stream* ME-1
Sand Beach Campground—*park* OR-9
Sand Beach Church—*hist pl* NY-2
Sand Beach Creek—*bay* NC-3
Sandbeach Creek—*stream* CO-8
Sand Beach Creek—*stream* NC-3
Sandbeach Lake—*lake* CO-8
Sand Beach Lake—*lake* (2) NE-7
Sandbeach Lake—*lake* NE-7
Sandbeach Lake Trail—*trail* CO-8
Sand Beach Mission—*church* PA-2
Sand Beach Mtn—*summit* NY-2
**Sand Beach (Township of)**—*pop pl* MI-6
**Sand Bed**—*pop pl* GA-3
Sand Bench—*bench* (3) UT-8
Sand Bench Rim—*cliff* UT-8
Sand Bench Rsvr—*reservoir* UT-8
Sand Bench Trail—*trail* UT-8
Sand Bend Draw—*valley* TX-5
Sand Bend Tank—*lake* TX-5
Sandberg—*locale* CA-9
Sandberg Creek—*stream* MI-6
Sandberg Valley—*valley* WI-6
Sandberry Cem—*cemetery* TX-5
Sand Bethel Ch—*church* GA-3
Sand Blow Ridge—*ridge* MO-7
Sand Bluff—*cliff* AL-4
Sand Bluff—*cliff* AK-9
Sand Bluff—*locale* OK-5
**Sandbluff**—*pop pl* OK-5
Sand Bluff Draw—*valley* TX-5
**Sandborn**—*pop pl* IN-6
Sandborn Canal—*channel* AK-9
Sandborn Cem—*cemetery* IN-6
Sandborn Creek—*stream* MT-8
*Sandborn Drain* MI-6
Sandborn Hill—*summit* NH-1
*Sandborn Lake* MI-6
*Sandborn Lake* MN-6
Sandborn Park—*park* TX-5
Sandborn Sch—*school* TX-5
*Sand Bottom Lake* MI-6
Sandbottom Lake—*lake* MI-6
Sand Bottom Lake—*lake* ND-7
Sandbottom Sch—*school* AL-4
*Sand Branch* AL-4
*Sand Branch* IL-6
*Sand Branch* TN-4
Sand Branch—*stream* (10) AL-4
Sand Branch—*stream* (3) FL-3
Sand Branch—*stream* (5) GA-3
Sand Branch—*stream* (4) IL-6
Sand Branch—*stream* (2) IN-6
Sand Branch—*stream* (3) KY-4
Sand Branch—*stream* (4) LA-4
Sand Branch—*stream* MD-2
Sand Branch—*stream* (8) MS-4
Sand Branch—*stream* (7) MO-7
Sand Branch—*stream* (5) NC-3
Sand Branch—*stream* (4) OK-5
Sand Branch—*stream* (3) SC-3
Sand Branch—*stream* (4) TN-4
Sand Branch—*stream* (38) TX-5
Sand Branch—*stream* (2) VA-3
Sand Branch—*stream* (6) WV-2
Sand Branch—*stream* WI-6
Sand Branch—*swamp* SC-3
Sand Branch Cem—*cemetery* TX-5
Sand Branch Ch—*church* (2) TN-4
Sand Branch Ch—*church* (2) TX-5
Sand Branch Number One—*stream* TX-5
Sand Branch Number Two—*stream* TX-5
Sand Branch Rsvr—*reservoir* WY-8
Sand Branch Sch—*school* WI-6
*Sand Branch United Methodist Ch* TN-4
*Sand Bridge* VA-3
*Sand Bridge Beach* VA-3
**Sandbridge Beach**—*pop pl* VA-3
Sand Bridge Beach—*uninc pl* VA-3
Sand Bridge State Park—*park* PA-2
*Sandbrook* NJ-2
**Sand Brook**—*pop pl* NJ-2
Sand Brook—*stream* ME-1
Sand Brook—*stream* MA-1
Sand Brook—*stream* NH-1
Sand Brook—*stream* (2) NY-2
Sandburg Creek—*stream* NY-2
Sandburg House—*hist pl* MI-6
Sandburg JHS—*school* CA-9
Sandburg JHS—*school* IL-6
Sandburg JHS—*school* MN-6
Sandburg JHS—*school* PA-2
Sandburg Sch—*school* CA-9
Sandburg Sch—*school* (2) IL-6
Sandburg Sch—*school* MI-6
Sandburg Sch—*school* WI-6
Sandburn—*locale* IL-6
Sandburn Brook—*stream* NY-2
Sandburn Coulee—*valley* MT-8
**Sandburr Corners**—*pop pl* OH-6
**Sand Burr Hill**—*pop pl* KS-7
Sand Burr Sch—*school* IL-6
*Sandbury Creek* NY-2
Sand Butte—*summit* ID-8
Sand Butte—*summit* OR-9
Sand Butte—*summit* WA-9
Sand Butte—*summit* (3) WY-8
Sand Butte Basin—*basin* WY-8
Sand Butte Coulee—*valley* MT-8
Sand Butte Lateral—*canal* WY-8
Sand Butte Rim—*cliff* WY-8
Sand Buttes—*summit* MT-8
Sand Butte Spring—*spring* WY-8
Sand Camp—*locale* CO-8
Sand Camp—*locale* TX-5
Sand Camp Lake—*lake* OR-9
Sand Camp Well—*well* TX-5
*Sand Canyon* CA-9
*Sand Canyon* CO-8
Sand Canyon—*valley* (2) AZ-5
Sand Canyon—*valley* (12) CA-9
Sand Canyon—*valley* (6) CO-8
Sand Canyon—*valley* ID-8
Sand Canyon—*valley* KS-7
Sand Canyon—*valley* (5) NE-7
Sand Canyon—*valley* (6) NV-8
Sand Canyon—*valley* (7) NM-5
Sand Canyon—*valley* OK-5
Sand Canyon—*valley* (4) OR-9
Sand Canyon—*valley* UT-8
Sand Canyon—*valley* (2) WA-9
Sand Canyon Airp—*airport* WA-9
Sand Canyon Creek—*stream* NE-7
Sand Canyon Rsvr—*reservoir* CA-9
Sand Canyon Tank—*reservoir* NM-5
Sand Canyon Wash—*stream* CA-9
Sand Canyon Wash—*valley* UT-8
Sand Canyon Windmill—*locale* NM-5
*Sand Cape* OR-9
Sandcastle Creek—*stream* AK-9
Sand Castle Kindergarten—*school* FL-3
Sandcastle Park—*park* MN-6
Sand Cave—*cave* AL-4
Sand Cave—*cave* (3) KY-4
Sand Cave Branch—*stream* (2) KY-4
Sand Cave Hollow—*valley* KY-4
Sand Cave Island—*island* KY-4
*Sand Caves* UT-8
S and C Echelon—*airport* NJ-2
Sand Cem—*cemetery* IA-7
Sand Cem—*cemetery* MO-7
**Sand City**—*pop pl* CA-9
Sand City Island—*island* NY-2
Sand Cliff—*cliff* (2) KY-4
Sand Cliff Spring—*spring* UT-8
Sandclift—*locale* KY-4
**Sandco**—*pop pl* VA-3
Sand Column Tank—*reservoir* NM-5
Sand Cone Springs—*spring* AZ-5
Sand Corner—*locale* NM-5
*Sand Coulee* MT-8
*Sand Coulee* WY-8
**Sand Coulee**—*pop pl* MT-8
Sand Coulee—*stream* WY-8
Sand Coulee—*valley* MN-6
Sand Coulee—*valley* (8) MT-8
Sand Coulee—*valley* SD-7
Sand Coulee—*valley* WA-9
Sand Coulee Cem—*cemetery* MT-8
*Sand Coulee Creek* SD-7
Sand Coulee Creek—*stream* MT-8
Sand Cove—*bay* FL-3
Sand Cove—*bay* (13) ME-1
Sand Cove—*bay* NC-3
Sand Cove—*valley* (2) AZ-5
Sand Cove North—*bay* ME-1
*Sand Cove Reservoir* UT-8
Sand Cove Spring—*spring* UT-8
Sand Cove Wash—*valley* UT-8
*Sand Cranch* WV-2
*Sand Creek* AL-4
*Sand Creek* AZ-5
*Sand Creek* CA-9
*Sand Creek* (2) CO-8
*Sand Creek* IN-6
*Sand Creek* KS-7
*Sand Creek* MN-6
*Sand Creek* MS-4
*Sand Creek* MT-8
*Sand Creek* NE-7
*Sand Creek* ND-7
*Sand Creek* OK-5
*Sand Creek* SD-7
*Sand Creek* TX-5
*Sand Creek* WY-8
Sand Creek—*channel* VA-3
Sand Creek—*gut* FL-3
Sand Creek—*locale* KS-7
Sand Creek—*locale* WV-2
Sandcreek—*other* MI-6
**Sand Creek**—*pop pl* MI-6
**Sand Creek**—*pop pl* MT-8
**Sand Creek**—*pop pl* OK-5
**Sand Creek**—*pop pl* OR-9
**Sand Creek**—*pop pl* WI-6
Sand Creek—*stream* (7) AL-4
Sand Creek—*stream* (4) AK-9
Sand Creek—*stream* (4) AZ-5
Sand Creek—*stream* (6) AR-4
Sand Creek—*stream* (13) CA-9
Sand Creek—*stream* (23) CO-8
Sand Creek—*stream* (7) FL-3
Sand Creek—*stream* (5) GA-3
Sand Creek—*stream* (13) ID-8
Sand Creek—*stream* (6) IL-6
Sand Creek—*stream* (7) IN-6
Sand Creek—*stream* (9) IA-7
Sand Creek—*stream* (39) KS-7
Sand Creek—*stream* (2) KY-4
Sand Creek—*stream* (2) LA-4
Sand Creek—*stream* MA-1
Sand Creek—*stream* (11) MI-6
Sand Creek—*stream* (7) MN-6
Sand Creek—*stream* (13) MS-4
Sand Creek—*stream* (7) MO-7
Sand Creek—*stream* (30) MT-8
Sand Creek—*stream* (22) NE-7
Sand Creek*—*stream* NE-7
Sand Creek—*stream* (7) NE-7
Sand Creek—*stream* (4) NV-8
Sand Creek—*stream* (4) NM-5
Sand Creek—*stream* (2) NY-2
Sand Creek—*stream* (2) NC-3
Sand Creek—*stream* (7) ND-7
Sand Creek—*stream* OH-6
Sand Creek—*stream* (43) OK-5
Sand Creek—*stream* (16) OR-9
Sand Creek—*stream* (4) SC-3
Sand Creek—*stream* (12) SD-7
Sand Creek—*stream* (2) TN-4
Sand Creek—*stream* (33) TX-5
Sand Creek—*stream* (3) UT-8
Sand Creek—*stream* (9) WA-9
Sand Creek—*stream* WV-2
Sand Creek—*stream* (8) WI-6
Sand Creek—*stream* (25) WY-8
Sand Creek Agriculture Sch—*school* MI-6
Sand Creek Basin—*basin* SC-3
Sand Creek Canal—*canal* MT-8
Sand Creek Canal—*canal* OR-9
Sand Creek Canyon—*valley* WY-8
Sand Creek Cem—*cemetery* (2) IN-6
Sand Creek Cem—*cemetery* IA-7
Sand Creek Cem—*cemetery* KS-7
Sand Creek Cem—*cemetery* MI-6
Sand Creek Cem—*cemetery* MS-4
Sand Creek Cem—*cemetery* ND-7
Sand Creek Cem—*cemetery* (2) OK-5
*Sand Creek Cemetery* SD-7
*Sand Creek Ch* MS-4
Sand Creek Ch—*church* AL-4
Sand Creek Ch—*church* IL-6
Sand Creek Ch—*church* (3) IN-6
Sand Creek Ch—*church* KS-7
Sand Creek Ch—*church* (2) OK-5
Sand Creek Chapel—*church* MN-6
Sand Creek Chapel Missionary Baptist Ch—*church* MS-4
Sand Creek Crossing—*locale* WY-8
Sand Creek Dam Number One—*dam* AL-4
Sand Creek Ditch—*canal* (2) CO-8
Sand Creek Extension Ditch—*canal* MT-8
Sand Creek Hill—*summit* MT-8
Sand Creek Hills—*range* MS-4
*Sand Creek - in part* MS-4
Sand Creek Junction—*locale* OR-9
Sand Creek Lake—*lake* WY-8
Sand Creek Lake Number One—*reservoir* AL-4
Sand Creek Lateral—*canal* CO-8
Sand Creek Marshes—*swamp* MA-1
Sand Creek Mtn—*summit* WA-9
Sand Creek Pass—*gap* CO-8
Sand Creek Pilot Watershed Dam Number One—*dam* TN-4
Sand Creek Point—*cape* WY-8
Sand Creek Rec Area—*park* SD-7
Sand Creek Rsvr—*reservoir* ID-8
Sand Creek Rsvr—*reservoir* WY-8
Sand Creek Sch—*school* KS-7
Sand Creek Sch—*school* (2) MI-6
Sand Creek Sch—*school* MN-6
Sand Creek Sch—*school* OK-5
Sand Creek Sch—*school* SD-7
Sand Creek Sch—*school* WV-2
Sand Creek Sch—*school* WI-6
Sand Creek Sch—*school* WY-8
Sand Creek School—*locale* CO-8
Sand Creek Spring—*spring* UT-8
**Sand Creek Station**—*pop pl* IN-6
**Sand Creek (Town of)**—*pop pl* WI-6
*Sand Creek Township* KS-7
Sand Creek Township—*fmr MCD* IA-7
**Sand Creek Township**—*pop pl* KS-7
**Sand Creek Township**—*pop pl* NE-7
**Sand Creek Township**—*pop pl* ND-7
**Sand Creek Township**—*pop pl* SD-7
**Sand Creek (Township of)**—*pop pl* (3) IN-6
**Sand Creek (Township of)**—*pop pl* MN-6
Sand Creek Trail Rsvr—*reservoir* WY-8
Sand Creek Watershed Dam Number Two—*dam* TN-4
Sand Creek Well—*well* WY-8
Sand Creek Wildlife Mngmt Area HQ—*locale* ID-8
Sand Creek Windmill—*locale* TX-5
*Sand Cut* FL-3
Sand Cut—*gut* WI-6
**Sand Cut**—*pop pl* AL-4
**Sandcut**—*pop pl* CA-9
**Sand Cut**—*pop pl* (2) FL-3
**Sand Cut**—*pop pl* IL-6
**Sandcut**—*pop pl* IN-6
*Sandcute* IN-6
Sand Cut Shoals—*bar* WI-6
Sand Cut Siding—*locale* FL-3
Sand Cut Slough—*gut* WI-6
*Sand Dam* RI-1
Sand Dam Bridge—*bridge* SC-3
*Sand Dam Reservoir* RI-1
Sand Ditch—*canal* CA-9
Sand Ditch—*canal* NJ-2
Sand Ditch—*gut* DE-2
Sand Ditch—*stream* MN-6

**Sand Dollar Shores (subdivision)**—pop pl NC-3
**Sand Draw**—pop pl WY-8
Sand Draw—valley AZ-5
Sand Draw—valley CA-9
Sand Draw—valley (6) CO-8
Sand Draw—valley KS-7
Sand Draw—valley MT-8
Sand Draw—valley (2) NE-7
Sand Draw*—valley NE-7
Sand Draw—valley (3) NE-7
Sand Draw—valley (4) NM-5
Sand Draw—valley OK-5
Sand Draw—valley (2) SD-7
Sand Draw—valley TX-5
Sand Draw—valley (31) WY-8
Sand Draw Coal Mine—mine WY-8
Sand Draw Mngmt Area—park CO-8
Sand Draw Rsvr No 4—reservoir WY-8
Sand Draw Siphon—canal CA-9
Sand Draw Tank—reservoir AZ-5
Sand Draw Windmill—locale NM-5
**S and D Subdivision**—pop pl UT-8
Sand Dune Arch—arch UT-8
Sand Dunes CA-9
Sand Dunes Lookout Tower—locale MN-6
**Sand Dunes Village (subdivision)**—pop pl DE-2
Sand Dunes Well—well (2) NV-8
Sand Dune Windmill—locale NV-8
Sandee Lake—reservoir VA-3
Sandefer Butte—summit MT-8
**San de Fuca**—pop pl WA-9
Sandefur Crossing—locale KY-4
Sandefur Sch (historical)—school MO-7
S and E Junction—locale FL-3
Sandel—locale LA-4
Sandel Cave OR-9
Sandel Cem—cemetery LA-4
Sandell Creek—stream WY-8
Sandell Farms—locale CA-9
Sanden Landing Strip—airport ND-7
Sanden Sch—school PA-2
Sander Branch—stream MO-7
Sander Cem—cemetery MO-7
Sander Cem—cemetery TX-5
Sander Cem—cemetery VA-3
Sander Cem—cemetery WV-2
Sandercock Spring—spring WY-8
Sanderfur Training Sch—school KY-4
**Sanderling**—pop pl NC-3
Sanderlin Mtn—summit GA-3
Sander Rsvr—reservoir OR-9
Sanders AL-4
Sanders—locale AL-4
Sanders—locale AR-4
Sanders—locale CA-9
Sanders—locale (2) OK-5
**Sanders**—pop pl AZ-5
**Sanders**—pop pl ID-8
**Sanders**—pop pl IN-6
**Sanders**—pop pl KY-4
**Sanders**—pop pl MT-8
**Sanders**—pop pl TN-4
Sanders, Erick Gustave, Mansion—hist pl WA-9
Sanders, G. O., House—hist pl NH-1
Sanders, Robert, House—hist pl KY-4
Sanders Airp—airport AZ-5
Sanders Airp—airport PA-2
Sanders Airp—airport TN-4
Sanders Bay—bay NH-1
Sanders Bay—bay NC-3
Sanders Bay—bay VI-3
Sanders Beach—beach ID-8
Sanders Beach—locale FL-3
Sanders Bluff—cliff TX-5
Sanders Branch—stream AL-4
Sanders Branch—stream AR-4
Sanders Branch—stream (2) FL-3
Sanders Branch—stream KY-4
Sanders Branch—stream (2) MS-4
Sanders Branch—stream (2) MO-7
Sanders Branch—stream SC-3
Sanders Branch—stream (3) TN-4
Sanders Branch—stream (3) TX-5
Sanders Branch—stream WV-2
Sanders Branch Richland Creek—stream KY-4
Sanders Branch Sch—school SC-3
Sanders Bridge—bridge NC-3
Sanders Bridge—hist pl AZ-5
Sanders Brook—stream MA-1
Sanders Brook—stream (2) NH-1
Sanders Brook—stream (2) VT-1
Sanders Canyon NM-5
Sanders Canyon—valley NM-5
Sanders Cape—cape AK-9
Sanders Causeway—bridge TN-4
Sanders Cem—cemetery (8) AL-4
Sanders Cem—cemetery (7) AR-4
Sanders Cem—cemetery (4) GA-3
Sanders Cem—cemetery (3) IL-6
Sanders Cem—cemetery (2) IN-6
Sanders Cem—cemetery (2) KY-4
Sanders Cem—cemetery (4) MS-4
Sanders Cem—cemetery (5) MO-7
Sanders Cem—cemetery NE-7
Sanders Cem—cemetery NH-1
Sanders Cem—cemetery NC-3
Sanders Cem—cemetery (2) OH-6
Sanders Cem—cemetery (3) SC-3
Sanders Cem—cemetery (8) TN-4
Sanders Cem—cemetery (5) TX-5
Sanders Cem—cemetery (3) VA-3
Sanders Cem—cemetery (4) WV-2
Sanders Ch—church MS-4
Sanders Ch—church TN-4
Sanders Chapel MS-4
Sanders Chapel—church FL-3
Sanders Chapel—church LA-4
Sanders Chapel—church (2) MS-4
Sanders Chapel—church OK-5
Sanders Chapel—church (3) TN-4
Sanders Chapel (historical)—church MS-4
**Sanders (Chetco)**—pop pl AZ-5
Sanders Corner DE-2
Sanders Corner—locale SC-3
Sanders Corral—locale SD-7
Sanders County Jail—hist pl MT-8
Sanders Cove—valley VA-3
Sanders Creek IN-6
Sanders Creek NE-7
Sanders Creek OR-9
Sanders Creek SC-3
Sanders Creek TN-4
Sanders Creek TX-5
Sanders Creek—bay NC-3
Sanders Creek—gut NC-3
Sanders Creek—stream (3) AL-4
Sanders Creek—stream (3) AR-4
Sanders Creek—stream FL-3
Sanders Creek—stream GA-3
Sanders Creek—stream IA-7
Sanders Creek—stream KY-4
Sanders Creek—stream LA-4
Sanders Creek—stream MS-4
Sanders Creek—stream (2) MO-7
Sanders Creek—stream MT-8
Sanders Creek—stream NY-2
Sanders Creek—stream NC-3
Sanders Creek—stream PA-2
Sanders Creek—stream SC-3
Sanders Creek—stream (2) TN-4
Sanders Creek—stream (4) TX-5
Sanders Creek—stream VA-3
Sanders Creek—stream WA-9
Sanders Creek—stream WI-6
Sanders Creek Ch—church SC-3
Sanders Crossing—locale TN-4
Sanders Crossing School TN-4
**Sandersdale**—pop pl MA-1
Sanders Dam—dam AL-4
Sanders Dam—dam SD-7
Sanders Draft—valley (2) PA-2
Sanders Draw—valley CO-8
Sanders East Well—well NM-5
Sanders Elem Sch—school (2) IN-6
Sanders Ferry (historical)—locale AL-4
Sanders Ferry Landing (historical)—locale AL-4
Sanders Ferry Park TN-4
Sanders Field—park WA-9
Sanders Ford (historical)—crossing TN-4
Sanders Fork TN-4
Sanders Fork—stream VA-3
Sanders Fork Church TN-4
Sanders Fork Sch (historical)—school TN-4
Sanders Gift Ch—church GA-3
Sanders Grove Ch—church NC-3
Sanders Gulch—valley OR-9
Sanders-Hairr House—hist pl NC-3
Sanders Hammock Pond—lake FL-3
Sanders Hill—hist pl GA-3
**Sanders Hill**—pop pl AL-4
Sanders Hill—summit AR-4
Sanders Hill—summit ME-1
Sanders Hill—summit VA-3
Sanders Hill—summit WA-9
Sanders Hill Brook—stream CT-1
Sanders Hill Sch—school IL-6
Sanders Hollow—valley MS-4
Sanders Hollow—valley MO-7
Sanders Hollow—valley (5) TN-4
Sanders Hollow—valley (2) TX-5
Sanders Hollow Windmill—locale TX-5
Sanders House—hist pl AR-4
Sanders House—hist pl TX-5
Sanders Interchange—crossing AZ-5
Sanders Island—island NC-3
Sanders Island—island TN-4
Sanders Kill—stream NY-2
Sanders Knob—summit (2) NC-3
Sanders Lake AL-4
Sanders Lake MI-6
Sanders Lake—lake AR-4
Sanders Lake—lake (2) MN-6
Sanders Lake—lake MT-8
Sanders Lake—lake TN-4
Sanders Lake—reservoir (2) AL-4
Sanders Lake—reservoir MS-4
Sanders Lake—reservoir SC-3
Sanders Lake—reservoir TX-5
Sanders Lake—swamp AR-4
Sanders Lake Bayou—gut AR-4
Sanders Lake Dam—dam MS-4
Sanders Ledge MA-1
Sanders Ledge—bar ME-1
Sanders Memorial Sch—school FL-3
Sanders Mesa—summit AZ-5
Sanders Mill Branch AL-4
Sanders Mill Creek—stream AL-4
Sanders Mine—mine TN-4
Sanders Mtn—summit MT-8
Sanders Mtn—summit OK-5
**Sanderson**—pop pl FL-3
**Sanderson**—pop pl TX-5
**Sanderson**—pop pl WV-2
Sanderson, James S., House—hist pl TX-5
Sanderson, Julia, Theater—hist pl MA-1
Sanderson Acad—school MA-1
Sanderson Bluff—cliff MO-7
Sanderson Branch—stream MS-4
Sanderson Branch—stream (3) TN-4
Sanderson Bridge—bridge NC-3
Sanderson Bridge—bridge OR-9
Sanderson Bridge—bridge VT-1
Sanderson Brook—stream ME-1
Sanderson Brook—stream MA-1
Sanderson Brook—stream NH-1
Sanderson Brook—stream OR-9
Sanderson Cabin (reduced usage)—locale TX-5
Sanderson Canyon—valley TX-5
Sanderson Canyon Crossing—locale TX-5
Sanderson (CCD)—cens area FL-3
Sanderson Cem—cemetery (2) AL-4
Sanderson Cem—cemetery FL-3
Sanderson Cem—cemetery MS-4
Sanderson Cem—cemetery MO-7
Sanderson Cem—cemetery NC-3
Sanderson Cem—cemetery SC-3
Sanderson Cem—cemetery TX-5
Sanderson Cem—cemetery VT-1
Sanderson Ch—church TN-4
Sanderson Chapel Ch—church AL-4
Sanderson Corner DE-2
**Sanderson Corner**—pop pl VT-1
Sanderson Corners—locale ME-1
Sanderson Cove—valley AL-4
Sanderson Cove—valley NC-3
Sanderson Covered Bridge—hist pl VT-1
Sanderson Creek—stream AK-9
Sanderson Creek—stream MI-6
Sanderson Creek—stream TX-5
Sanderson Creek—stream WA-9
Sanderson Crossing DE-2
Sanderson Crossroad DE-2
Sanderson Crossroads DE-2
Sanderson Ditch—canal CO-8
Sanderson Drain—stream MI-6
Sanderson Farms Pond Dam—dam MS-4
Sanderson Ferry (historical)—locale AL-4
Sanderson Field Airp—airport WA-9
Sanderson Fish Pond—reservoir NC-3
Sanderson Gulch—valley (2) CO-8
Sanderson Gulch—valley OR-9
Sanderson Harbor—locale WA-9
Sanderson Hollow—valley TN-4
Sanderson House—hist pl NC-3
Sanderson House and Munroe Tavern—hist pl MA-1
Sanderson HS—school NC-3
Sanderson Lake—lake MI-6
Sanderson Lake Dam—dam MS-4
Sanderson Number 1 Dam—dam SD-7
Sanderson Number 2 Dam—dam SD-7
Sanderson Number 3 Dam—dam SD-7
Sanderson Park—flat CO-8
Sanderson Pass—gap AZ-5
Sanderson Point—cape MO-7
Sanderson Pond Dam—dam MS-4
Sanderson Sch—school TX-5
Sanderson Sch—school WI-6
Sandersons Chapel AL-4
Sanderson Sch (historical)—school TN-4
Sanderson Spring—spring CO-8
Sanderson Spring—spring OR-9
Sanderson Town AL-4
Sanders Park—park IL-6
Sanders Park—park WI-6
Sanders Park—park WY-8
**Sanders Park**—pop pl FL-3
**Sanders Park**—pop pl MD-2
Sanders Park Elem Sch—school FL-3
Sanders Peak—summit AZ-5
Sanders Point—cape (2) NC-3
Sanders Pond—lake FL-3
Sanders Pond—reservoir AL-4
Sanders Pond—reservoir GA-3
Sanders Pond Dam—dam AL-4
Sanders Post Office—building AZ-5
Sanders Post Office (historical)—building AL-4
Sanders Ranch—locale CO-8
Sanders Ranch—locale NM-5
Sanders Rangeline Cabin—locale AZ-5
Sanders Ridge—ridge CA-9
Sanders Ridge—ridge KY-4
Sanders Ridge—ridge LA-4
Sanders Ridge—ridge VA-3
Sanders Run—stream PA-2
Sanders Sch—school CA-9
Sanders Sch—school CO-8
Sanders Sch—school (3) IL-6
Sanders Sch—school KY-4
Sanders Sch—school MA-1
Sanders Sch—school MI-6
Sanders Sch—school NV-8
Sanders Sch—school SC-3
Sanders Sch—school TN-4
Sanders Sch—school TX-5
Sanders Sch—school WI-6
Sanders Shoals—bar AL-4
Sanders-Sikes Gymnasium—building NC-3
Sanders Site (47WP26 and 47WP70)—hist pl WI-6
Sanders Slough—gut IL-6
Sanders Slough—gut TX-5
Sanders Spring TX-5
Sanders Spring—spring (2) AZ-5
Sanders Spring—spring TN-4
Sanders Spring Rsvr—reservoir KY-4
Sanders Spur—locale AL-4
Sanders Store (historical)—locale AL-4
Sanders Tank—reservoir NM-5
Sanders Theater—building MA-1
Sanderstown RI-1
**Sanders (Township of)**—pop pl MN-6
Sandersville IN-6
Sandersville TN-4
**Sandersville**—pop pl GA-3
**Sandersville**—pop pl MS-4
Sandersville Baptist Ch—church MS-4
Sandersville (CCD)—cens area GA-3
Sandersville Cem—cemetery MS-4
Sandersville Elementary School MS-4
Sandersville Sch—school MS-4
Sanders Wash—stream AZ-5
Sanders Waterhold OR-9
Sanders Well—well NM-5
**Sandertown**—pop pl PA-2
Sanderville—locale KY-4
**Sandestin**—pop pl FL-3
S and E Tank—reservoir AZ-5
Sandeval Draw AZ-5
Sandfall Mtn—summit AL-4
**Sandfield**—pop pl AL-4
Sand Field Cem—cemetery AR-4
Sandfield Cem—cemetery MS-4
Sandfield Ch—church KY-4
Sandfield Ch—church MS-4
Sandfield Ford—locale TN-4
Sandfield Sch—school KY-4
Sandfield Well—well TX-5
Sandflat AL-4
Sand Flat CA-9
Sand Flat—flat AZ-5
Sand Flat—flat (7) CA-9
Sand Flat—flat CO-8
Sand Flat—flat MD-2
Sand Flat—flat OR-9
Sand Flat—flat (3) UT-8
Sand Flat—flat WA-9
Sand Flat—locale (2) TX-5
**Sand Flat**—pop pl TX-5
**Sandflat**—pop pl TX-5
Sand Flat Campground—locale (2) CA-9
Sand Flat Canyon—valley NM-5
Sand Flat Cem—cemetery TX-5
Sand Flat Ch—church TX-5
Sand Flat Community Center—locale TX-5
Sand Flats—flat MS-4
Sand Flats—flat NM-5
Sand Flats—locale TX-5
Sand Flat Sch—school TX-5
Sand Flat School MS-4
Sand Flats JHS—school MS-4
Sand Flat Tabernacle—church MD-2
Sand Flat Tank—reservoir (2) AZ-5
Sand Flat Well—well CA-9
Sandfly GA-3
**Sandfly**—pop pl GA-3
Sandfly Bay—bay AK-9
Sandfly Creek—gut FL-3
Sandfly Creek—stream FL-3
Sandfly Gully—stream FL-3
Sandfly Island—island FL-3
Sandfly Key—island (2) FL-3
Sandfly Pass—channel FL-3
Sandfly Point—cape FL-3
Sand Ford KS-7
**Sandford**—pop pl IN-6
Sandford Blvd—post sta NY-2
Sandford Branch—stream TN-4
Sandford Brook CT-1
Sandford Creek KS-7
Sandford JHS—school MN-6
Sandford Landing—locale NC-3
Sandford P.O. (historical)—locale AL-4
Sandford Point—cape WA-9
Sandford Sch—school MI-6
Sandfords Corners NY-2
**Sandfordville**—pop pl NY-2
Sand Fork WV-2
Sand Fork—locale OH-6
Sand Fork—locale WV-2
**Sand Fork**—pop pl WV-2
Sand Fork—stream (2) OH-6
Sand Fork—stream (9) WV-2
Sandfork Ch—church OH-6
Sand Fork Ch—church WV-2
**Sand Fork (corporate name for Layopolis)**—pop pl WV-2
Sand Fork Crab Creek—stream WV-2
Sand Fork Creek—stream KY-4
Sand Fork Sch—school WV-2
Sandfort—locale AL-4
Sandfort Creek—stream MO-7
Sandfort Fire Tower—locale AL-4
Sand Fort Sch AL-4
Sandfort Sch—school AL-4
Sandgap AR-4
Sand Gap—gap NM-5
Sand Gap—gap OK-5
Sand Gap—gap (2) OR-9
Sand Gap—gap (3) TN-4
Sand Gap—gap (2) WV-2
Sand Gap—gap WY-8
Sand Gap—locale WV-2
**Sand Gap**—pop pl AR-4
**Sandgap**—pop pl KY-4
Sand Gap Arch—arch KY-4
Sand Gap Branch—stream KY-4
Sand Gap (CCD)—cens area KY-4
Sand Gap Ch—church KY-4
Sand Gate—other NM-5
**Sandgate**—pop pl VT-1
Sandgate Brook—stream VT-1
Sand Gate Cem—cemetery TX-5
**Sandgates**—pop pl MD-2
Sandgates On Cat Creek—hist pl MD-2
**Sandgate (Town of)**—pop pl VT-1
S and G Canyon—valley SD-7
S and G Ranch (historical)—locale SD-7
Sand Grove Ch—church GA-3
Sand Grove Ch—church TX-5
S and G Saddle—gap MT-8
Sand Gulch—valley CA-9
Sand Gulch—valley (8) CO-8
Sand Gulch—valley MT-8
Sand Gulch—valley OR-9
Sand Gulch—valley (3) UT-8
Sand Gulch—valley (2) WY-8
Sand Gulch Lateral—canal WY-8
Sand Gulley—stream MS-4
Sand Gully—locale FL-3
Sand Gully—stream (2) FL-3
Sand Hagen Creek—stream IA-7
Sandham SD-7
Sand Hammock Pond—lake FL-3
Sand Harbor—bay NV-8
Sand Harbor Beach State Rec Area—park NV-8
S and H Cave—cave AL-4
Sand Hill AL-4
Sand Hill MA-1
Sandhill MS-4
Sand Hill NC-3
Sand Hill—locale DE-2
Sand Hill—locale (2) GA-3
Sand Hill—locale (2) KY-4
Sand Hill—locale (2) MS-4
Sand Hill—locale MO-7
Sand Hill—locale NY-2
Sandhill—locale NC-3
Sand Hill—locale PA-2
Sandhill—locale TN-4
Sand Hill—locale TX-5
Sandhill—locale TX-5
Sand Hill—locale TX-5
Sandhill—locale WV-2
**Sand Hill**—pop pl (2) AR-4
**Sand Hill**—pop pl CA-9
**Sand Hill**—pop pl FL-3
**Sand Hill**—pop pl (2) GA-3
**Sand Hill**—pop pl (2) KY-4
**Sand Hill**—pop pl MA-1
**Sand Hill**—pop pl MI-6
**Sand Hill**—pop pl (2) MS-4
**Sandhill**—pop pl MS-4
**Sand Hill**—pop pl (2) NY-2
**Sand Hill**—pop pl NC-3
**Sand Hill**—pop pl (3) OH-6
**Sandhill**—pop pl OH-6
**Sand Hill**—pop pl PA-2
**Sandhill**—pop pl PA-2
**Sandhill**—pop pl TN-4
**Sand Hill**—pop pl TX-5
**Sand Hill**—pop pl (2) WV-2
Sand Hill—summit (2) AR-4
Sand Hill—summit (3) CA-9
Sand Hill—summit DE-2
Sand Hill—summit (2) FL-3
Sand Hill—summit HI-9
Sand Hill—summit IL-6
Sand Hill—summit (5) IN-6
Sand Hill—summit IA-7
Sand Hill—summit (2) KY-4
Sand Hill—summit ME-1
Sand Hill—summit MD-2
Sand Hill—summit (2) MS-4
Sand Hill—summit MT-8
Sand Hill—summit (2) NM-5
Sand Hill—summit (3) NY-2
Sand Hill—summit (2) NC-3
Sand Hill—summit (5) OH-6
Sand Hill—summit (2) OR-9
Sand Hill—summit (2) PA-2
Sand Hill—summit (3) TN-4
Sand Hill—summit (5) TX-5
Sand Hill—summit VT-1
Sand Hill—summit (2) WA-9
Sand Hill—summit WY-8
Sand Hill Archeol Site 12J62—hist pl IN-6
Sand Hill Arroyo—stream NM-5
Sand Hill Attendance Center—school MS-4
Sand Hill Baptist Ch MS-4
Sandhill Baptist Ch—church MS-4
Sand Hill Baptist Church TN-4
Sand Hill Bay—basin SC-3
Sand Hill Bay—bay FL-3
Sand Hill Bay—swamp FL-3
Sandhill Bay—swamp GA-3
Sand Hill Bay—swamp GA-3
Sandhill Bay—swamp GA-3
Sand Hill Bay—swamp NC-3
Sand Hill Bay—swamp SC-3
Sandhill Bay—swamp SC-3
Sand Hill Bayou—gut LA-4
Sand Hill Beach RI-1
Sand Hill Bluff—cliff CA-9
Sand Hill Branch—stream (2) GA-3
Sand Hill Branch—stream MO-7
Sandhill Branch—stream SC-3
Sandhill Brook—stream RI-1
Sand Hill Camp—locale MN-6
Sandhill Campground—park OR-9
Sandhill Canal—canal NC-3
Sandhill Cem MS-4
Sandhill Cem—cemetery AL-4
Sand Hill Cem—cemetery (2) AL-4
Sand Hill Cem—cemetery AR-4
Sand Hill Cem—cemetery CT-1
Sandhill Cem—cemetery (2) FL-3
Sand Hill Cem—cemetery (6) GA-3
Sand Hill Cem—cemetery IL-6
Sandhill Cem—cemetery IL-6
Sandhill Cem—cemetery IN-6
Sand Hill Cem—cemetery (5) IN-6
Sand Hill Cem—cemetery IA-7
Sand Hill Cem—cemetery (3) KY-4
Sand Hill Cem—cemetery (2) LA-4
Sand Hill Cem—cemetery (2) MI-6
Sand Hill Cem—cemetery (2) MS-4
Sandhill Cem—cemetery MS-4
Sand Hill Cem—cemetery MS-4
Sandhill Cem—cemetery MS-4
Sand Hill Cem—cemetery (3) MS-4
Sand Hill Cem—cemetery (2) MO-7
Sand Hill Cem—cemetery (5) NY-2
Sand Hill Cem—cemetery (2) NC-3
Sand Hill Cem—cemetery OH-6
Sandhill Cem—cemetery OH-6
Sand Hill Cem—cemetery OK-5
Sand Hill Cem—cemetery SC-3
Sandhill Cem—cemetery TN-4
Sand Hill Cem—cemetery TN-4
Sand Hill Cem—cemetery (3) TX-5
Sand Hill Cem—cemetery WI-6
Sand Hill Ch MS-4
Sand Hill Ch—church (3) AL-4
Sand Hill Ch—church AR-4
Sand Hill Ch—church DE-2
Sand Hill Ch—church (2) GA-3
Sandhill Ch—church GA-3
Sand Hill Ch—church (5) GA-3
Sand Hill Ch—church IL-6
Sand Hill Ch—church IN-6
Sand Hill Ch—church (5) KY-4
Sand Hill Ch—church (2) MN-6
Sand Hill Ch—church (3) MS-4
Sandhill Ch—church (2) MS-4
Sand Hill Ch—church MS-4
Sandhill Ch—church MS-4
Sand Hill Ch—church MS-4
Sand Hill Ch—church MO-7
Sand Hill Ch—church NY-2
Sand Hill Ch—church (3) NC-3
Sandhill Ch—church NC-3
Sand Hill Ch—church (2) PA-2
Sand Hill Ch—church (2) SC-3
Sandhill Ch—church SC-3
Sand Hill Ch—church SC-3
Sand Hill Ch—church (3) TN-4
Sandhill Ch—church TN-4
Sand Hill Ch—church (7) TX-5
Sand Hill Ch—church (2) WV-2
Sand Hill Chapel—church MN-6
Sand Hill Ch (historical)—church (3) MS-4
Sand Hill Ch (historical)—church TN-4
Sandhill Corner—locale ME-1
Sand Hill Cove—bay CA-9
Sand Hill Cove—bay RI-1
Sandhill Crack AZ-5
Sand Hill Crack—gap AZ-5
Sand Hill Creek AL-4
Sand Hill Creek—stream (2) AL-4
Sand Hill Creek—stream (2) FL-3
Sandhill Creek—stream (2) GA-3
Sandhill Creek—stream MI-6
Sand Hill Creek—stream MS-4
Sand Hill Creek—stream NY-2
Sand Hill Creek—stream NC-3
Sandhill Creek—stream OH-6
Sand Hill Creek—stream PA-2
Sand Hill Creek Ch—church MS-4
Sandhill Crossing—locale OR-9
Sand Hill Ditch—canal CO-8
Sand Hill Drain—stream MI-6
Sandhill Forge (historical)—locale TN-4
Sand Hill Gap—gap AK-9
Sand Hill Gardens—cemetery SC-3
Sand Hill Golf Course—other GA-3
Sand Hill High School MS-4
**Sand Hill (historical)**—pop pl MS-4
Sand Hill Hollow—valley MO-7
Sand Hill Hosp—hospital MS-4
Sandhill Lake—lake CA-9
Sand Hill Lake—lake FL-3
Sand Hill Lake—lake (2) GA-3
Sand Hill Lake—lake MI-6
Sand Hill Lake—lake MN-6
Sand Hill Lake—lake NC-3
Sand Hill Lake—lake SC-3
Sandhill Lake—lake WI-6
Sand Hill Lake Ditch—canal IA-7
Sand Hill Landing—locale NC-3
Sand Hill Lookout Tower—locale AL-4
Sand Hill Lookout Tower—locale KY-4
Sand Hill Lookout Tower—tower FL-3
Sand Hill Methodist Church MS-4
Sandhill Missionary Baptist Ch—church MS-4
Sand Hill MS—school NC-3
Sandhill Pass CO-8
Sand Hill Point—cape NC-3
Sand Hill Pond—lake (2) FL-3
Sand Hill Pond—lake GA-3
Sandhill Pond—lake NH-1
Sandhill Pond—lake RI-1
Sand Hill Pond—lake SC-3
Sandhill Post Office (historical)—building TN-4
Sand Hill Primary Sch—school NC-3
Sandhill Ranch Airp—airport AZ-5
Sand Hill Ridge—ridge CA-9
Sandhill Ridge—ridge WV-2
Sandhill Ridge—ridge WI-6
Sandhill River MN-6
Sand Hill River—stream (2) MN-6
Sandhill Rsvr—reservoir NV-8
Sand Hill Rsvr—reservoir WY-8
Sandhills MA-1
Sand Hills MT-8
Sand Hills NJ-2
Sand Hills—area NE-7
Sand Hills—locale (2) NJ-2
Sandhills—other MA-1
**Sand Hills**—pop pl HI-9
**Sand Hills**—pop pl MA-1
**Sand Hills**—pop pl NJ-2
Sand Hills—range AZ-5
Sand Hills—range CA-9
Sand Hills—range ID-8
Sand Hills—range KS-7
Sand Hills—range MS-4
Sand Hills—range NV-8
Sand Hills—range UT-8
Sand Hills—range (2) WA-9
Sand Hills—range (3) WY-8
Sand Hills—ridge MT-8
Sand Hills—ridge SC-3
Sand Hills—summit AZ-5
Sand Hills—summit FL-3
Sand Hills—summit KY-4
Sand Hills—summit OR-9
Sand Hills—summit SC-3
Sand Hills—summit (2) TX-5
Sand Hills—summit UT-8
Sand Hills, The—range WY-8
Sand Hills, The—summit CO-8
Sand Hills, The—summit TX-5
Sand Hills, The—summit (2) UT-8
**Sand Hill (Sandhill)**—pop pl KY-4
Sand Hill Sch—school FL-3
Sand Hill Sch—school IL-6
Sand Hill Sch—school IN-6
Sand Hill Sch—school IA-7
Sand Hill Sch—school (4) KY-4
Sand Hill Sch—school (2) LA-4
Sandhill Sch—school ME-1
Sandhill Sch—school (2) MI-6
Sand Hill Sch—school MS-4
Sand Hill Sch—school OK-5
Sand Hill Sch—school PA-2
Sandhill Sch—school SC-3
Sand Hill Sch—school SC-3
Sandhill Sch—school SC-3
Sand Hill Sch—school WV-2
Sandhill Sch—school WV-2
Sand Hill Sch—school WV-2
Sand Hill Sch (historical)—school (2) AL-4
Sand Hill Sch (historical)—school (8) MS-4
Sand Hill Sch (historical)—school PA-2
Sand Hill Sch (historical)—school (2) TN-4
Sand Hill Sch Number 5—school NY-2
Sand Hills Coulee—valley WA-9
Sand Hills Golf Course—other TX-5
Sand Hills Grange Hall—locale WA-9
Sandhill Shaft—mine NV-8
Sandhills Lateral—canal NM-5
Sand Hills Lighthouse—locale MI-6
Sand Hills Oil Field—oilfield TX-5
Sand Hills Park—park CA-9
Sand Hills Park—park MT-8
Sandhills Pasture—flat KS-7
Sand Hill Spring—spring AZ-5
Sand Hills South Oil Field—oilfield TX-5
Sandhills State For—forest SC-3
Sand Hills State For—forest SC-3
Sand Hills Tanks—reservoir NM-5
**Sand Hill (subdivision)**—pop pl AL-4
**Sandhill (subdivision)**—pop pl PA-2
**Sand Hill Subdivision (subdivision)**—pop pl SD-7
Sand Hills Well—well TX-5
Sandhill Tank—reservoir TX-5
Sand Hill Township—civil MO-7
Sand Hill (Township of)—fmr MCD NC-3
Sand Hill Well—well (2) NM-5
Sandhill Well—well TX-5
Sand Hill Well—well TX-5
Sand Hill Windmill—locale (2) NM-5
Sandhill Windmill—locale (2) TX-5
Sand Hill Windmill—locale TX-5
Sand Hole—lake FL-3
Sand Hole, The—bay NY-2
Sand Hole Creek—stream NC-3
Sandhole Creek—stream SC-3
Sandhole Lake—reservoir ID-8
Sand Hole Ridge—ridge PA-2
Sand Hollow OR-9
Sand Hollow TX-5
Sand Hollow—basin (2) OR-9
Sand Hollow—locale OR-9

Sandrock Post Office (historical)—building..AL-4
Sand Rock Reservoir—spring ....UT-8
Sand Rock Ridge—ridge ....KY-4
Sand Rock Ridge—ridge ....TN-4
Sand Rock Ridge—ridge ....UT-8
Sand Rock Rsvr—reservoir ....CO-8
Sand Rock Rsvr—reservoir ....MT-8
Sand Rock Rsvr—reservoir ....WY-8
Sandrock Run—stream ....PA-2
Sand Rocks—rock ....MT-8
Sandrocks—summit ....CA-9
**Sand Rock (Sandrock)**—pop pl ....AL-4
Sandrock Spring—spring ....AZ-5
Sandrock Spring—spring ....MT-8
Sand Rock Spring—spring ....TX-5
Sandrock Springs—spring ....OR-9
Sandrock Tank—reservoir ....AZ-5
Sandrock Tank—reservoir ....NM-5
Sand Rock Tank—reservoir ....TX-5
Sand Rock Trail—trail ....PA-2
Sand Rsvr—reservoir ....WY-8
Sand Rsvr No. 1—reservoir ....CO-8
Sand Rsvr No. 2—reservoir ....CO-8
Sand Run ....ID-8
Sand Run ....PA-2
Sand Run—channel ....WI-6
Sand Run—locale ....OH-6
**Sandrun**—pop pl ....OH-6
**Sand Run**—pop pl ....WV-2
Sand Run—stream (3) ....IN-6
Sand Run—stream ....KY-4
Sand Run—stream ....MD-2
Sand Run—stream ....MO-7
Sand Run—stream (7) ....OH-6
Sand Run—stream (4) ....PA-2
Sand Run—stream ....VA-3
Sand Run—stream (8) ....WV-2
Sand Run Ch—church ....KY-4
Sand Run Ch—church ....MO-7
Sand Run Ch—church (2) ....WV-2
Sand Run Junction—locale ....OH-6
**Sand Run Junction**—pop pl ....WV-2
Sand Run Metropolitan Park—park ....OH-6
Sand Run Sch—school ....WV-2
Sands ....MI-6
Sands—locale ....CA-9
Sands—locale ....VA-3
**Sands**—pop pl (2) ....MI-6
**Sands**—pop pl ....NM-5
**Sands**—pop pl ....NC-3
Sands, Hiram, House—hist pl ....MA-1
Sands, Ivory, House—hist pl ....MA-1
Sands, Robert, Estate—hist pl ....NY-2
Sands, The—area ....NM-5
Sands, The—bar ....ME-1
Sands, The—beach ....NC-3
Sands, The—beach ....VA-3
Sands, The—flat ....ME-1
Sands, The—summit ....NH-1
Sand Sand Springs Sand Dune ....NV-8
Sands Basin—basin ....ID-8
Sands Branch—stream ....TX-5
Sandsbury Creek ....TN-4
Sands Camp—locale ....ME-1
Sands Canyon—valley ....ID-8
Sands Cem—cemetery ....GA-3
Sands Cem—cemetery ....NY-2
Sands Cem—cemetery ....OH-6
Sands Cem—cemetery ....PA-2
Sands Ch—church ....PA-2
Sand Sch—school ....IL-6
Sand Sch—school ....ND-7
Sands Cove—bay ....MD-2
Sands Creek ....WI-6
Sands Creek—stream (3) ....ID-8
Sands Creek—stream ....LA-4
Sands Creek—stream (2) ....MI-6
Sands Creek—stream ....NY-2
Sands Creek—stream ....WA-9
Sands Cut—channel ....FL-3
Sands Ditch—canal ....ID-8
Sands Ditch—canal ....IN-6
Sands Draw—valley ....AZ-5
Sands Draw Detention Dam—dam ....AZ-5
Sandsea Kill—stream ....NY-2
Sand Seeps—spring ....AZ-5
Sand Shoal Channel—channel ....VA-3
Sand Shoal Inlet—bay ....VA-3
Sands Hollow—valley ....TN-4
Sandshore Lake—lake ....MN-6
Sands House Sanatorium—other ....CO-8
Sandsing Hollow—valley ....AR-4
Sands Island, The—island ....ME-1
Sands Key—island ....FL-3
Sand S Lake—lake ....AL-4
Sands Lake—lake ....MN-6
Sands Lake—lake ....MT-8
Sands Lake—reservoir ....TX-5
Sandslide Point—cliff ....UT-8
Sand Slough—gut ....AR-4
Sand Slough—gut (3) ....CA-9
Sand Slough—gut (2) ....IL-6
Sand Slough—gut ....KY-4
Sand Slough—gut ....TX-5
Sand Slough—lake (2) ....ND-7
Sand Slough—stream (3) ....AR-4
Sand Slough—stream ....CA-9
Sand Slough—stream (2) ....FL-3
Sand Slough—stream ....MN-6
Sand Slough Ditch—canal ....IL-6
Sand Slough Ditch—canal ....MO-7
Sands Meadow—flat ....CA-9
S and S Oil Field—oilfield ....KS-7
Sand Spit, The ....MA-1
Sandspit, The—bar ....MA-1
Sandspit Point—cape ....AK-9
SandS Plaza (Shop Ctr)—locale ....FL-3
Sands Point ....ME-1
Sands Point—cape (2) ....NY-2
**Sands Point**—pop pl ....NJ-2
**Sands Point**—pop pl ....NY-2
Sands Point Country Club—locale ....NY-2
Sands Point Harbor—bay ....NJ-2
Sands Point Sch—school ....NY-2
Sands Pond—lake ....RI-1
Sands Pond—reservoir ....GA-3
S and S Pond Dam—dam ....AL-4
Sand Spring ....IA-7
Sand Spring ....NV-8
Sand Spring ....PA-2
Sand Spring—locale ....MD-2
**Sand Spring**—pop pl ....IA-7
**Sand Spring**—pop pl ....KS-7
**Sand Spring**—pop pl ....PA-2
Sand Spring—spring (2) ....AL-4
Sand Spring—spring (15) ....AZ-5
Sand Spring—spring ....AR-4
Sand Spring—spring ....CA-9
Sand Spring—spring (2) ....CO-8
Sand Spring—spring ....GA-3
Sand Spring—spring (2) ....ID-8
Sand Spring—spring ....KS-7
Sand Spring—spring ....MA-1
Sand Spring—spring (2) ....MO-7
Sand Spring—spring ....MT-8
Sand Spring—spring (8) ....NV-8
Sand Spring—spring (6) ....NM-5
Sand Spring—spring (8) ....OR-9
Sand Spring—spring (5) ....PA-2
Sand Spring—spring ....TN-4
Sand Spring—spring ....TX-5
Sand Spring—spring (7) ....UT-8
Sand Spring—spring ....VA-3
Sand Spring—spring ....WA-9
Sand Spring—spring ....WV-2
Sand Spring—spring (4) ....WY-8
Sandspring Branch—stream ....TN-4
Sand Spring Branch—stream ....TN-4
Sand Spring Branch—stream (2) ....TX-5
Sand Spring Brook—stream ....NY-2
Sand Spring Butte—summit ....OR-9
Sand Spring Camp (abandoned)—locale ....PA-2
Sand Spring Canyon—valley ....CA-9
Sand Spring Canyon—valley ....NV-8
Sand Spring Canyon—valley ....UT-8
Sand Spring Canyon—valley ....WA-9
Sand Spring Cem—cemetery ....KY-4
Sand Spring Cem—cemetery ....MS-4
Sand Spring Cem—cemetery ....OK-5
Sand Spring Ch—church (2) ....KY-4
Sand Spring Ch—church (2) ....MS-4
Sand Spring Ch—church ....TX-5
Sand Spring Church ....AL-4
Sand Spring Creek—stream (2) ....PA-2
Sand Spring Creek—stream ....TX-5
Sand Spring Creek—stream ....WI-6
Sand Spring Creek—stream ....WY-8
Sand Spring Creek (historical)—stream ....PA-2
Sand Spring Draw—valley ....WY-8
Sand Spring Flat—flat ....PA-2
Sand Spring Forge (historical)—locale ....TN-4
Sand Spring Gulch—valley ....CO-8
Sand Spring Hill—summit ....MD-2
Sand Spring (historical)—locale ....AL-4
Sand Spring (historical)—spring ....PA-2
Sand Spring Hollow—valley ....AR-4
Sand Spring Lake—reservoir (2) ....PA-2
Sand Spring Lookout Tower—locale ....WV-2
Sand Spring Mountain Trail—trail ....VA-3
Sand Spring Mtn—summit ....VA-3
Sand Spring Post Office (historical)—building ....AL-4
Sand Spring Run ....PA-2
Sand Spring Run—stream (2) ....MD-2
Sand Spring Run—stream (8) ....PA-2
Sand Spring Run Dam—dam ....PA-2
Sand Springs ....AZ-5
Sand Springs ....KS-7
Sand Springs ....OR-9
Sand Springs ....TN-4
Sand Springs ....TX-5
Sand Springs ....WV-2
Sand Springs—locale ....AZ-5
Sand Springs—locale ....KY-4
Sand Springs—locale ....MT-8
Sand Springs—locale ....TN-4
**Sand Springs**—pop pl ....AZ-5
**Sand Springs**—pop pl ....IA-7
**Sand Springs**—pop pl ....KY-4
**Sand Springs**—pop pl ....NM-5
**Sand Springs**—pop pl ....OK-5
**Sand Springs**—pop pl ....PA-2
**Sand Springs**—pop pl ....TX-5
Sand Springs—spring ....NV-8
Sand Springs—spring (2) ....NM-5
Sand Springs—spring ....PA-2
Sand Springs—spring ....VA-3
Sand Springs—spring (3) ....WY-8
Sand Springs Arroyo—stream ....NM-5
Sand Springs Baptist Ch—church ....TN-4
Sand Springs Baptist Church ....AL-4
Sand Springs Bend—bend ....OK-5
Sand Springs Branch—stream ....MO-7
Sand Springs Branch—stream ....OK-5
Sand Springs Branch—stream (2) ....TX-5
Sand Springs Cem—cemetery (2) ....AL-4
Sand Springs Cem—cemetery ....IA-7
Sand Springs Ch ....TN-4
Sand Springs Ch—church (4) ....AL-4
Sand Springs Ch—church ....AR-4
Sand Springs Ch—church ....GA-3
Sand Springs Ch—church ....MS-4
Sand Springs Ch—church ....OK-5
Sand Springs Ch—church (2) ....TX-5
Sand Spring Sch—school ....KY-4
Sand Spring Sch—school ....VA-3
Sand Spring Sch—school ....WV-2
Sand Spring Sch (abandoned)—school ....MO-7
Sand Springs Creek—stream ....ID-8
Sand Springs Creek—stream ....WY-8
Sand Springs Draw—valley ....SD-7
Sand Springs Draw—valley (2) ....WY-8
Sand Springs Dune ....NV-8
Sand Springs Lake—reservoir ....OK-5
Sand Springs Lake—reservoir ....TX-5
Sand Springs Mesa—summit ....AZ-5
Sand Springs Overnight Campground—park ....UT-8
Sand Springs Park—park ....PA-2
Sand Springs Pass—gap ....NV-8
Sand Springs Pony Express Station Historical Marker—park ....NV-8
Sand Springs Ranch—locale ....NM-5
Sand Springs Range—range ....NV-8
Sand Springs Sch—school ....KY-4
Sand Springs Sch (historical)—school ....MS-4
Sand Springs School ....TN-4
Sand Springs Station—hist pl ....NV-8
Sand Springs Trail—trail ....PA-2
Sand Springs United Methodist Church ....MS-4
Sand Springs Wash—stream ....NV-8
Sand Springs Well No 1—well ....WY-8
Sand Spring Trail—trail ....PA-2
Sand Spring Valley ....NV-8
Sand Spring Valley—basin ....NV-8
Sand Spring Wash—stream ....CO-8
Sand Spring Wash—valley ....UT-8
Sandsprit Park—park ....FL-3
Sandspru Lake—reservoir ....TX-5
Sand Spur—locale ....LA-4
**Sand Spur**—pop pl ....ID-8
Sandspur Island—island ....FL-3
Sands Ranch—locale ....AZ-5
Sands (reduced usage)—locale ....IL-6
Sands Sch—school (2) ....OH-6
Sands Sch—school ....TX-5
Sands Small World Sch—school ....FL-3
Sands Spring—spring ....TN-4
Sands Station—locale ....MI-6
Sand Steps—cliff ....AL-4
**Sandston**—pop pl ....VA-3
**Sandstone**—pop pl ....MI-6
**Sandstone**—pop pl ....MN-6
**Sandstone**—pop pl ....WV-2
Sandstone and Cobblestone Schools—hist pl ....MT-8
Sandstone Basin—basin ....UT-8
Sandstone Blackman Drain—canal ....MI-6
Sandstone Bluff ....KS-7
Sandstone Bluff—cliff ....AK-9
Sandstone Bluff—cliff ....NV-8
**Sandstone Bluff**—pop pl ....WI-6
Sandstone Bluffs—cliff ....NV-8
Sandstone Bluffs (historical)—cliff ....ND-7
Sandstone Branch—stream ....TN-4
Sandstone Butte—summit ....UT-8
Sandstone Butte—summit ....WY-8
Sandstone Camp—locale ....AZ-5
Sandstone Camp—locale ....CA-9
Sandstone Canyon—valley ....AZ-5
Sandstone Canyon—valley ....CA-9
Sandstone Canyon—valley ....CO-8
Sandstone Canyon—valley ....NM-5
Sandstone Cave—cave ....AL-4
Sandstone Cave—cave ....TN-4
Sandstone Cem—cemetery ....MO-7
Sandstone Coulee—valley ....MT-8
Sandstone Creek ....AL-4
Sandstone Creek—stream ....AR-4
Sandstone Creek—stream (2) ....MI-6
Sandstone Creek—stream (2) ....MT-8
Sandstone Creek—stream ....OK-5
Sandstone Creek—stream ....OR-9
Sandstone Creek—stream ....WA-9
Sandstone Dam—dam ....WI-6
Sandstone Ditch—canal (3) ....WY-8
Sandstone Divide Trail—trail ....WY-8
Sandstone Draw—valley ....UT-8
Sandstone Falls—falls ....MI-6
Sandstone Falls—falls ....WV-2
Sandstone Federal Correctional Institution—other ....MN-6
Sandstone Flat—flat ....SD-7
Sandstone Flowage—channel ....WI-6
Sandstone Hill—summit ....AL-4
Sandstone Hill—summit ....NC-3
Sand Stone (historical)—locale ....IA-7
Sandstone HS—school ....WV-2
Sandstone Indian Cave ....PA-2
Sandstone Knob—summit ....TN-4
Sandstone Knolls—summit ....UT-8
Sandstone Mesa—summit ....NM-5
Sandstone Mine—mine ....NM-5
Sandstone Mine (underground)—mine ....AL-4
Sandstone Mountain Windmill—locale ....NM-5
Sandstone Mtn—summit ....AR-4
Sandstone Mtn—summit ....CO-8
Sandstone Mtn—summit ....TX-5
Sandstone Mtn—summit ....UT-8
Sandstone Mtn—summit ....WY-8
Sandstone Natl Wildlife Ref—park ....MN-6
Sandstone Peak—summit ....CA-9
Sandstone Point—cape ....CA-9
Sandstone Point—cape ....OR-9
Sandstone Ranch—hist pl ....CO-8
Sandstone Ranch—hist pl ....NV-8
Sandstone Ranger Station—locale ....WY-8
Sandstone Ridge—ridge ....AL-4
Sandstone Ridge—ridge ....CA-9
Sandstone Ridge—ridge ....MT-8
Sandstone Ridge—ridge ....VA-3
Sandstone Ridge—summit ....PA-2
Sandstone Ridge Trail—trail ....MT-8
Sandstone Rsvr—reservoir (2) ....WY-8
Sandstone Sch—hist pl ....MN-6
Sandstone Sch—school ....MI-6
Sandstone Sch—school ....MO-7
Sandstone Sch—school ....OK-5
Sandstone Sch—school ....PA-2
Sandstone Spring—spring ....AZ-5
Sandstone Spring—spring (2) ....NV-8
Sandstone Spring—spring ....WA-9
Sandstone Spring—spring ....WV-2
Sandstone Springs—spring ....PA-2
Sandstone Springs Picnic Ground—locale ....PA-2
Sandstone Tank—reservoir (4) ....AZ-5
**Sandstone (Township of)**—pop pl ....MI-6
**Sandstone (Township of)**—pop pl ....MN-6
Sandstone Trail—trail ....OR-9
Sandstone Wash—arroyo ....AZ-5
Sandstorm Creek ....OK-5
**Sands (Township of)**—pop pl ....MI-6
Sandstrom Cem—cemetery ....NE-7
Sandstrom Coulee—valley ....MT-8
Sandstrom Lake—lake ....MI-6
Sandstrum Lake ....MI-6
Sandsuck Branch—stream ....TN-4
Sandsuck Creek—stream ....KY-4
Sandsuck Hollow—valley ....OH-6
Sandsville Sch—school ....MN-6
**Sandsville (Township of)**—pop pl ....MN-6
Sands Well—well ....AZ-5
Sands West Camp—locale ....AZ-5
Sands-Willets Homestead—hist pl ....NY-2
**Sand Switch**—pop pl ....TN-4
Sand Tank—reservoir (13) ....AZ-5
Sand Tank—reservoir (6) ....NM-5
Sand Tank—reservoir (9) ....TX-5
Sand Tank Canyon—valley ....AZ-5
Sand Tank Mountains—summit ....AZ-5
Sand Tanks—reservoir ....NM-5
Sand Tank Wash—stream ....AZ-5
Sand Tank Well—well ....AZ-5
Sand Thorofare—channel ....NJ-2
Sandtown ....AL-4
Sand Town ....MS-4
Sandtown ....NJ-2
Sandtown—locale ....AL-4
Sandtown—locale ....DE-2
Sandtown—locale ....GA-3
Sandtown—locale ....MS-4
Sandtown—locale ....NJ-2
**Sandtown**—pop pl (2) ....AR-4
Sandtown Bottom—bend ....OK-5
Sandtown Bottoms—flat ....AR-4
Sandtown Branch—stream ....DE-2
Sandtown Branch—stream ....MD-2
Sandtown Cem—cemetery ....AL-4
Sandtown Cem—cemetery ....IA-7
Sandtown Cem—cemetery ....MI-6
Sandtown Cem—cemetery ....MS-4
Sandtown Cem—cemetery ....OK-5
Sandtown Ch—church ....OK-5
Sandtown Community House—locale ....GA-3
Sandtown Lookout Tower—locale ....MS-4
Sand Town Mine (surface)—mine ....AL-4
Sandtown Sch—school ....GA-3
Sandtown Sch (historical)—school ....AL-4
Sand Town School ....AL-4
Sandtown United Methodist Ch—church ....MS-4
Sand Trace Hollow—valley ....TN-4
Sand Trap Tank—reservoir (2) ....AZ-5
Sand Trap Wash ....AZ-5
**Sandts Eddy**—pop pl ....PA-2
Sandts Eddy Station (historical)—building ....PA-2
Sand Tub Tank—reservoir ....TX-5
Sandtuck ....AL-4
Sandtuck Ch—church ....AL-4
Sand Turn—locale ....WY-8
Sandune—locale ....TX-5
Sanduski Ridge—ridge ....AL-4
Sandusky—locale ....TX-5
Sandusky—locale ....WV-2
Sandusky—locale ....WI-6
**Sandusky**—pop pl ....AL-4
**Sandusky**—pop pl ....IL-6
**Sandusky**—pop pl ....IN-6
**Sandusky**—pop pl ....IA-7
**Sandusky**—pop pl ....MI-6
**Sandusky**—pop pl ....NY-2
**Sandusky**—pop pl ....OH-6
Sandusky Bay—bay ....OH-6
Sandusky Branch—stream ....TN-4
Sandusky Brook—stream ....VT-1
Sandusky Cem—cemetery (2) ....IL-6
Sandusky Cem—cemetery ....IA-7
Sandusky Cem—cemetery ....KY-4
Sandusky Cem—cemetery (2) ....OH-6
Sandusky Chapel—church ....KY-4
**Sandusky (County)**—pop pl ....OH-6
Sandusky Creek—stream ....AK-9
Sandusky Creek—stream ....CA-9
Sandusky Creek—stream ....IL-6
Sandusky Creek—stream ....OH-6
Sandusky Creek North Public Use Area—locale ....IL-6
Sandusky Creek South Public Use Area—locale (2) ....IL-6
Sandusky Creek West Public Use Area—locale ....IL-6
Sandusky (Election Precinct)—fmr MCD ....IL-6
Sandusky Elem Sch—school ....AL-4
Sandusky House—hist pl ....KY-4
Sandusky House—hist pl ....VA-3
Sandusky Mine (underground)—mine ....AL-4
Sandusky Norwalk Interchange 7—other ....OH-6
Sandusky Post Office (historical)—building ....TN-4
Sandusky River—stream ....OH-6
Sandusky Sch—school ....AL-4
Sandusky South—CDP ....OH-6
Sandusky Street Hist Dist—hist pl ....OH-6
**Sandusky (Township of)**—pop pl (3) ....OH-6
Sand Valley—basin (2) ....NE-7
Sand Valley—bend ....TX-5
Sand Valley—valley (2) ....AL-4
Sand Valley—valley ....NE-7
Sand Valley—valley ....TN-4
Sand Valley Assembly of God Church ....AL-4
Sand Valley Baptist Church ....AL-4
Sand Valley Cem—cemetery ....AL-4
Sand Valley Cem—cemetery ....MN-6
Sand Valley Cem—cemetery ....NE-7
Sand Valley Ch—church (2) ....AL-4
Sand Valley Ch—church ....GA-3
Sand Valley Creek—stream (3) ....AL-4
Sand Valley Sch—school ....NE-7
Sand Valley Well—well ....AZ-5
Sandvick Ranch—locale ....ND-7
Sandville Cem—cemetery ....MO-7
Sandville Ch—church ....AL-4
Sand Wash—stream (6) ....AZ-5
Sand Wash—stream ....ID-8
Sand Wash—stream (2) ....NV-8
Sand Wash—stream ....NM-5
Sand Wash—valley (2) ....CO-8
Sand Wash—valley (13) ....UT-8
Sand Wash—valley (2) ....WY-8
Sand Wash Airp—airport ....UT-8
Sand Wash Bench—bench ....UT-8
Sand Wash Creek ....CO-8
Sand Wash Creek ....UT-8
Sandwash Creek—swamp ....GA-3
Sand Wash Ferry—locale ....UT-8
Sandwash Mill—locale ....AZ-5
Sand Wash Ranch—locale ....CO-8
Sand Wash River Ranger Station and Put In Site—locale ....UT-8
Sandwash Rsvr—reservoir ....MA-1
Sandwash Spring ....AZ-5
Sand Wash Spring—spring (2) ....AZ-5
Sand Wash Spring Number Two—spring ....AZ-5
S And W Cafeteria—hist pl ....NC-3
Sand Well—locale (2) ....NM-5
Sand Well—well (2) ....AZ-5
Sand Well—well (6) ....NM-5
Sand Well—well (8) ....TX-5
Sand Well Canyon—valley ....NM-5
Sand Wells—well ....AZ-5
Sand Wells—well ....NM-5
Sand Well Windmill—locale ....TX-5
Sandwich—locale ....NH-1
**Sandwich**—pop pl ....IL-6
**Sandwich**—pop pl ....MA-1
Sandwich, Town of ....MA-1
Sandwich Academy Grant—unorg ....ME-1
Sandwich Bay—bay ....NH-1
Sandwich (census name for Sandwich Center)—CDP ....MA-1
Sandwich Center (census name Sandwich)—other ....MA-1
Sandwich City Hall—hist pl ....IL-6
Sandwich Cove—bay ....FL-3
Sandwich Creek—stream ....WA-9
Sandwich Dome ....NH-1
Sandwich Glass Museum—building ....MA-1
Sandwich Harbor—harbor ....MA-1
Sandwich Harbor Marshes—swamp ....MA-1
Sandwich Lake ....MN-6
Sandwich Landing—locale ....NH-1
Sandwich Mountain Trail—trail ....NH-1
Sandwich Mtn—summit ....NH-1
Sandwich Notch—gap ....NH-1
Sandwich Range—range ....NH-1
Sandwich Town Hall, The—building ....MA-1
**Sandwich (Town of)**—pop pl ....MA-1
**Sandwich (Town of)**—pop pl ....NH-1
**Sandwich (Township of)**—pop pl ....IL-6
Sandwich Village ....MA-1
Sandwick Lake—lake ....MN-6
Sandwick Lakes ....MN-6
Sand Windmill—locale (6) ....NM-5
Sand Windmill—locale (9) ....TX-5
**Sandwood**—pop pl ....SC-3
Sandwood Drain—stream ....AZ-5
Sandy ....AL-4
Sandy ....NV-8
Sandy ....UT-8
Sandy—locale ....FL-3
Sandy—locale ....KY-4
Sandy—locale ....OK-5
Sandy—locale ....TN-4
Sandy—locale ....TX-5
**Sandy**—pop pl ....AR-4
**Sandy**—pop pl ....GA-3
**Sandy**—pop pl ....NV-8
**Sandy**—pop pl ....OR-9
**Sandy**—pop pl ....PA-2
**Sandy**—pop pl ....SC-3
**Sandy**—pop pl ....TN-4
**Sandy**—pop pl ....UT-8
**Sandy**—pop pl (2) ....WV-2
Sandy, Bayou—stream ....LA-4
Sandy, Lake—lake ....TX-5
**Sandy Acres**—pop pl ....MD-2
**Sandy Acres**—pop pl ....TX-5
**Sandy Acres**—pop pl ....UT-8
Sandy Acres Park—park ....IN-6
Sandy Arroyo—stream ....CO-8
Sandy Arroyo Creek ....KS-7
Sandy Baker Pass—gap ....UT-8
**Sandy Bank**—pop pl ....PA-2
Sandy Bank Cem—cemetery ....PA-2
Sandy Baptist Ch—church ....UT-8
Sandy Bar Creek—stream (2) ....CA-9
Sandy Barren Desarts ....NJ-2
Sandy Bay ....MA-1
Sandy Bay ....MI-6
Sandy Bay—bay ....AL-4
Sandy Bay—bay (3) ....AK-9
Sandy Bay—bay ....ME-1
Sandy Bay—bay ....MA-1
Sandy Bay—bay ....NY-2
Sandy Bay—bay (2) ....NC-3
Sandy Bay—bay (2) ....VA-3
Sandy Bay—bay ....VI-3
Sandy Bay—locale ....WI-6
**Sandy Bay**—pop pl ....NY-2
Sandy Bay—stream ....SC-3
Sandy Bay—swamp ....SC-3
Sandy Bay Cem—cemetery ....WI-6
Sandy Bay Ch—church ....SC-3
Sandy Bay Farm—locale ....ME-1
Sandy Bay Historical Society—building ....MA-1
Sandy Bay Ledge—rock ....MA-1
Sandy Bay Mtn—summit ....ME-1
Sandy Bayou ....AL-4
Sandy Bayou ....MS-4
Sandy Bayou—gut (3) ....AR-4
Sandy Bayou—gut (7) ....LA-4
Sandy Bayou—gut (4) ....MS-4
**Sandy Bayou**—pop pl ....MS-4
Sandy Bayou—stream (3) ....AR-4
Sandy Bayou—stream (8) ....LA-4
Sandy Bayou—stream (3) ....MS-4
Sandy Bayou—swamp ....MI-6
Sandy Bayou Bend—bend ....AR-4
Sandy Bayou Cem—cemetery ....MS-4
Sandy Bayou Ch—church ....LA-4
Sandy Bayou Ch—church ....MS-4
Sandy Bayou Oil Field—oilfield ....LA-4
Sandy Bayou Sch (historical)—school ....MS-4
Sandy Bay Point ....NC-3
Sandy Bay Sch—school (2) ....SC-3
Sandy Bay (Township of)—unorg ....ME-1
Sandy Beach ....PA-2
Sandy Beach—beach (2) ....CA-9
Sandy Beach—beach (3) ....MA-1
Sandy Beach—beach ....NY-2
Sandy Beach—beach ....TX-5
Sandy Beach—beach ....WA-9
Sandy Beach—locale ....CT-1
Sandy Beach—locale ....MN-6
Sandy Beach—locale ....NY-2
Sandy Beach—locale ....WA-9
**Sandy Beach**—pop pl ....CT-1
**Sandy Beach**—pop pl ....IN-6
**Sandy Beach**—pop pl ....ME-1
**Sandy Beach**—pop pl (2) ....MA-1
**Sandy Beach**—pop pl (2) ....MI-6
**Sandy Beach**—pop pl ....NY-2
Sandy Beach Bay—bay ....UT-8
Sandy Beach Lake—lake ....GA-3
Sandy Beach Lake—lake ....WI-6
Sandy Beach Lake—reservoir ....NY-2
Sandy Beach Park—park ....AR-4
Sandy Beach Park—park ....HI-9
Sandy Beach Park—park ....TX-5
Sandy Beach Picnic Area—locale ....WY-8
Sandy Beach Public Use Area—park ....IA-7
Sandy Beach Rec Area—park ....AK-9
**Sandy Beach (subdivision)**—pop pl ....DE-2
Sandy Bear Cem—cemetery ....OK-5
Sandy Bear Creek—stream ....OK-5
Sandy Beaver Canal—canal (2) ....OH-6
Sandy-Beaver Canal Tunnel (Abandoned)—locale ....OH-6
Sandybend—locale ....AR-4
**Sandy Bend (Sandybend)**—pop pl ....AR-4
Sandy Bend Sch—school ....WA-9
Sandyberry Creek—stream ....NC-3
Sandy Big Bend Rsvr No 1—reservoir ....WY-8
Sandy Big Bend Rsvr No 2—reservoir ....WY-8
Sandy Bight—bay ....AK-9
Sandy Bluff—hist pl ....KY-4
Sandy Bluff Bridge—bridge ....SC-3
Sandy Bluff Cem—cemetery ....GA-3
Sandy Bluff Landing—locale ....NC-3
Sandy Bob Canyon—valley ....AZ-5
Sandy Bob Springs Windmill—locale ....AZ-5
Sandy Bob Tank—reservoir ....AZ-5
Sandy Bob Windmill—locale ....AZ-5
Sandy Bois d'Arc Creek—stream ....AR-4
Sandy Bottom ....VA-3
Sandy Bottom—bend ....NC-3
Sandy Bottom—flat ....GA-3
Sandy Bottom—locale ....MD-2
Sandy Bottom—locale ....NC-3
Sandy Bottom—locale ....VA-3
**Sandy Bottom**—pop pl ....GA-3
**Sandy Bottom**—pop pl ....NC-3
**Sandybottom**—pop pl ....VA-3
**Sandy Bottom**—pop pl ....VA-3
Sandy Bottom Branch—stream ....VA-3
Sandy Bottom Chapel—church ....VA-3
Sandy Bottom Creek—stream ....OH-6
Sandy Bottom (Daileys Store)—uninc pl ....VA-3
Sandy Bottom Fire District—civil ....NC-3
Sandy Bottom Fire Station—building ....NC-3
Sandy Bottom Island—island ....TN-4
Sandy Bottom Lake ....MI-6
Sandy Bottom Lake—lake ....MI-6
Sandy Bottom Overlook—locale ....VA-3
Sandy Bottom Pond—lake ....LA-4
Sandy Bottom Pond—lake ....ME-1
**Sandy Bottoms**—pop pl ....NC-3
Sandy Bouis d'Arc Creek ....AR-4
**Sandy Brae**—pop pl ....DE-2
Sandy Branch ....AL-4
Sandy Branch ....TX-5
Sandy Branch—stream (4) ....AL-4
Sandy Branch—stream (4) ....AR-4
Sandy Branch—stream (2) ....DE-2
Sandy Branch—stream (2) ....FL-3
Sandy Branch—stream (3) ....GA-3
Sandy Branch—stream (3) ....IL-6
Sandy Branch—stream (5) ....IN-6
Sandy Branch—stream ....IA-7
Sandy Branch—stream (5) ....KY-4
Sandy Branch—stream (3) ....LA-4
Sandy Branch—stream (2) ....MD-2
Sandy Branch—stream (4) ....MS-4
Sandy Branch—stream (3) ....MO-7
Sandy Branch—stream (7) ....NC-3
Sandy Branch—stream ....OK-5
Sandy Branch—stream (4) ....SC-3
Sandy Branch—stream (10) ....TN-4
Sandy Branch—stream (23) ....TX-5
Sandy Branch—stream (4) ....VA-3
Sandy Branch Cem—cemetery ....MS-4
Sandy Branch Cem—cemetery ....TN-4
Sandy Branch Ch—church (2) ....NC-3
Sandy Branch Ch—church ....TN-4
Sandy Branch Public Use Area—park ....GA-3
Sandy Branch Sch—school ....IL-6
Sandy Branch Sch (historical)—school ....TN-4
Sandy Bray—summit ....DE-2
Sandy Bridge Post Office (historical)—building ....TN-4
**Sandy Brook**—pop pl ....ME-1
Sandy Brook—stream (2) ....CT-1
Sandy Brook—stream (4) ....ME-1
Sandy Brook—stream (2) ....MA-1
Sandy Burr Country Club—locale ....MA-1
Sandy Butte—summit ....MT-8
Sandy Butte—summit ....OR-9
Sandy Butte—summit ....WA-9
Sandy Butte Rsvr—reservoir ....WY-8
Sandy Butte Well—well ....ID-8
Sandy Campground—locale ....CA-9
Sandy Canyon—valley (2) ....CA-9
Sandy Canyon—valley ....NM-5
Sandy Canyon—valley ....OR-9
Sandy Canyon—valley ....WA-9
Sandy Canyon Tank—lake ....NM-5
Sandy Canyon Wash ....UT-8
Sandy Canyon Wash—stream ....AZ-5
Sandy Cove—cave ....AL-4
Sandy Cave—cave ....PA-2
Sandy (CCD)—cens area ....OR-9
Sandy Cem—cemetery ....AL-4
Sandy Cem—cemetery ....MN-6
Sandy Cem—cemetery ....OH-6
Sandy Cem—cemetery (2) ....TX-5
Sandy Cem—cemetery ....WV-2
Sandy Ch—church ....MN-6
Sandy Ch—church ....MS-4
Sandy Ch—church (2) ....MO-7
Sandy Ch—church ....OK-5
Sandy Ch—church (2) ....TX-5
Sandy Chapel—church ....AL-4
Sandy Chapel—church ....OH-6
Sandy Chapel—church ....TN-4
Sandy Chapel Access Area—park ....TN-4
Sandy Chapel Cem—cemetery ....AL-4
Sandy Chapel Cem—cemetery ....TX-5
Sandy Chapel United Methodist Church ....AL-4
Sandy Chute—stream ....MO-7
**Sandy City**—pop pl ....UT-8
Sandy City—uninc pl ....KY-4
Sandy City Cem—cemetery ....UT-8
Sandy Clay Sch—school ....MS-4
**Sandy Corner**—pop pl ....TX-5
**Sandy Corners**—pop pl ....OH-6
Sandy Cove ....MA-1
Sandy Cove—bay (3) ....AK-9
Sandy Cove—bay ....CT-1
Sandy Cove—bay (5) ....ME-1
Sandy Cove—bay (2) ....MD-2
Sandy Cove—bay ....NV-8
Sandy Cove—bay ....NC-3

Sandy Valley Post Office (historical)—*building* PA-2
Sandy Valley Sch—*school* KY-4
Sandy View Sch—*school* MI-6
**Sandy Village Subdivision**—*pop pl* UT-8
Sandyville—*locale* OH-6
**Sandyville**—*pop pl* IA-7
**Sandyville**—*pop pl* MD-2
**Sandyville**—*pop pl* PA-2
**Sandyville**—*pop pl* WV-2
Sandyville Cem—*cemetery* IA-7
**Sandyville (Sandymount)**—*pop pl* MD-2
*Sandy Wash* UT-8
Sandy Wash—*stream* CA-9
Sandy Wash—*stream* NM-5
Sandy Wash Bend—*bend* MS-4
Sandy Wash Lake—*reservoir* GA-3
Sandy Well—*well* NM-5
Sandy Well—*well* TX-5
Sandy Windmill—*locale* TX-5
Sandy Woods Lake—*reservoir* NC-3
Sandy Woods Lake Dam—*dam* NC-3
Sandy Woods Settlement Archeol Site—*hist pl* MO-7
Sandywoods Township—*civil* MO-7
San Eduardo Windmills—*locale* TX-5
Sanel—*civil* CA-9
San Eladio—*locale* PR-3
San Elijo Canyon—*valley* CA-9
San Elijo Lagoon—*swamp* CA-9
San Elijo State Beach—*park* CA-9
**San Elizario**—*pop pl* TX-5
San Elizario Island—*island* TX-5
San Elizario Lateral—*canal* TX-5
Sanel Mtn—*summit* CA-9
Sanel Valley—*valley* CA-9
*San Emedio Creek* CA-9
*San Emedio Mountain* CA-9
San Emidio—*civil* CA-9
San Emidio—*locale* CA-9
San Emidio Canyon—*valley* NV-8
*San Emidio Creek* CA-9
San Emidio Desert—*plain* NV-8
*San Emidio Mountain* CA-9
*San Emidion Creek* CA-9
*San Emidion Mountain* CA-9
San Emidio Spring—*spring* NV-8
San Emigdio Creek—*stream* CA-9
San Emigdio Girl Scout Camp—*locale* CA-9
San Emigdio Mesa—*bench* CA-9
San Emigdio Mtn—*summit* CA-9
San Emigdio Ranch—*locale* CA-9
*Sanencheck Rock* AZ-5
*Sanenecheck Rock* AZ-5
*Sa-ne-ne-heck Rock* AZ-5
Saneneheck Rock—*summit* AZ-5
*Sanenehec Rock* AZ-5
Saner Spring—*spring* AZ-5
Sanes Creek—*stream* IN-6
Sanes Creek Ch—*church* IN-6
San Estaban Lake—*reservoir* TX-5
San Estevan del Rey Mission Church—*hist pl* NM-5
San Expedito Ch—*church* LA-4
*San Fancisco Wash* AZ-5
San Felasco Hammock State Preserve—*park* FL-3
*San Felipe* NM-5
San Felipe—*canal* NM-5
San Felipe—*locale* (2) CA-9
**San Felipe**—*pop pl* TX-5
**San Felipe**—*pop pl* PR-3
San Felipe Arroyo—*valley* TX-5
San Felipe Butterfield Stage Station Historical Site—*other* CA-9
San Felipe Cem—*cemetery* TX-5
San Felipe Ch—*church* NM-5
San Felipe Country Club—*other* TX-5
San Felipe Courts Hist Dist—*hist pl* TX-5
San Felipe Creek—*stream* (3) CA-9
San Felipe Creek—*stream* TX-5
San Felipe Creek Archeol District—*hist pl* TX-5
*San Felipe de Jesus Guevavi* AZ-5
San Felipe de Neri Church—*hist pl* NM-5
San Felipe East Side Ditch—*canal* NM-5
San Felipe Hills—*range* (2) CA-9
San Felipe Ind Res—*reserve* (2) NM-5
San Felipe Lake—*lake* CA-9
San Felipe Mesa—*summit* NM-5
San Felipe Oil Field—*oilfield* TX-5
**San Felipe Pueblo**—*pop pl* NM-5
San Felipe Pueblo Grant—*civil* NM-5
**San Felipe Pueblo (Indian Reservation)**—*pop pl* NM-5
San Felipe Pueblo (Place)—*CDP* NM-5
San Felipe Pueblo Ruin—*hist pl* NM-5
San Felipe Ranch—*locale* CA-9
San Felipe Ranch—*locale* TX-5
San Felipe Riverside Drain—*canal* NM-5
San Felipe/Santa Ana Joint Area—*reserve* NM-5
San Felipe/Santo Domingo Joint Area—*reserve* NM-5
San Felipe Sch—*school* NM-5
San Felipe Sch—*school* TX-5
San Felipe Siding—*locale* TX-5
San Felipe Springs—*spring* TX-5
San Felipe Valley—*valley* (2) CA-9
San Felipe Wash—*stream* CA-9
San Felipe Windmill—*locale* (2) TX-5
San Fernandez Drain—*canal* NM-5
San Fernandez Lateral—*canal* NM-5
**San Fernando**—*pop pl* CA-9
**San Fernando**—*pop pl* PR-3
San Fernando Building, The—*hist pl* CA-9
San Fernando Cem Number 1—*cemetery* TX-5
San Fernando Cem Number 2—*cemetery* TX-5
*San Fernando Creek* TX-5
San Fernando Creek—*stream* (2) TX-5
San Fernando Hosp—*hospital* CA-9
San Fernando HS—*school* CA-9
San Fernando Island—*island* AK-9
San Fernando JHS—*school* CA-9
San Fernando Pass—*gap* CA-9
San Fernando Ranger Station—*locale* CA-9
San Fernando Valley—*valley* CA-9
San Fernando Valley Country Club—*other* CA-9
San Fernando Valley Juvenile Hall—*other* CA-9
San Fernando Valley State Coll—*school* CA-9
San Fernando Windmill—*locale* TX-5
**San Fidel**—*pop pl* NM-5
*Sanford* AZ-5
*Sanford* KS-7
Sanford—*locale* (2) GA-3
Sanford—*locale* NY-2
Sanford—*locale* PA-2
Sanford—*locale* TN-4
**Sanford**—*pop pl* AL-4
**Sanford**—*pop pl* CO-8
**Sanford**—*pop pl* FL-3
**Sanford**—*pop pl* KS-7
**Sanford**—*pop pl* ME-1
**Sanford**—*pop pl* MD-2
**Sanford**—*pop pl* MI-6
**Sanford**—*pop pl* MS-4
**Sanford**—*pop pl* NY-2
**Sanford**—*pop pl* NC-3
**Sanford**—*pop pl* TX-5
**Sanford**—*pop pl* VA-3
**Sanford**—*pop pl* WV-2
Sanford—*uninc pl* CA-9
Sanford, Esbon, House—*hist pl* RI-1
Sanford, Mount—*summit* AK-9
Sanford, Mount—*summit* CT-1
Sanford Acad (historical)—*school* MS-4
Sanford Airp—*airport* FL-3
Sanford Alliance Ch—*church* FL-3
Sanford Assembly of God Ch—*church* AL-4
*Sanford Baptist Church* TN-4
Sanford Basin—*basin* CO-8
Sanford Bayou—*gut* MI-6
Sanford Branch—*stream* MO-7
Sanford Brook—*stream* CT-1
Sanford Brook—*stream* ME-1
Sanford Brook—*stream* VT-1
Sanford B Shaffer Elem Sch—*school* PA-2
Sanford Butte—*summit* AZ-5
Sanford Calhoun HS—*school* NY-2
Sanford Canyon—*valley* AZ-5
Sanford Canyon—*valley* (2) NV-8
Sanford Canyon—*valley* OR-9
Sanford Canyon—*valley* WA-9
Sanford (CCD)—*cens area* FL-3
Sanford Cem—*cemetery* CO-8
Sanford Cem—*cemetery* FL-3
Sanford Cem—*cemetery* (2) MI-6
Sanford Cem—*cemetery* NY-2
Sanford Cem—*cemetery* OH-6
Sanford Cem—*cemetery* TN-4
Sanford Cem—*cemetery* TX-5
*Sanford Cemetery* MS-4
Sanford Center (census name Sanford)—*other* ME-1
Sanford Ch—*church* MI-6
Sanford Ch—*church* TN-4
Sanford Commercial District—*hist pl* FL-3
*Sanford Corners* NY-2
*Sanford Corners* PA-2
Sanford Corners—*locale* NY-2
Sanford Corners Cem—*cemetery* NY-2
Sanford Country Club—*other* ME-1
*Sanford County* AL-4
Sanford Cove—*bay* AK-9
Sanford Cove—*bay* ME-1
*Sanford Creek* UT-8
Sanford Creek—*stream* AL-4
Sanford Creek—*stream* AR-4
Sanford Creek—*stream* (2) CA-9
Sanford Creek—*stream* CO-8
Sanford Creek—*stream* KS-7
Sanford Creek—*stream* MI-6
Sanford Creek—*stream* MO-7
Sanford Creek—*stream* NY-2
Sanford Creek—*stream* NC-3
Sanford Creek—*stream* OR-9
Sanford Creek—*stream* UT-8
Sanford Dam—*dam* TX-5
Sanford Ditch—*canal* (2) CO-8
Sanford Ditch—*canal* OH-6
Sanford Drain—*canal* MI-6
Sanford Draw—*valley* WY-8
**Sanford Farms**—*pop pl* FL-3
Sanford Ferry (historical)—*locale* AL-4
Sanford Flat—*island* MA-1
Sanford Glacier—*glacier* AK-9
Sanford Grammar Sch—*hist pl* FL-3
*Sanford Grant* FL-3
Sanford Gray Lake Dam Number One—*dam* TN-4
Sanford Gray Lake Number One—*reservoir* TN-4
Sanford Health Camp—*locale* ME-1
Sanford Heights Ch—*church* NJ-2
Sanford Heights Playground—*park* OR-9
**Sanford Hill**—*pop pl* TN-4
Sanford Hill—*summit* IN-6
Sanford Hill—*summit* ME-1
Sanford Hill—*summit* NY-2
Sanford Hill—*summit* VA-3
Sanford Hill Baptist Ch—*church* TN-4
Sanford Hills—*range* CO-8
Sanford Hollow—*valley* NY-2
Sanford Hotel—*hist pl* NE-7
Sanford-Humphreys House—*hist pl* CT-1
Sanford Island—*island* NY-2
Sanford JHS—*school* FL-3
Sanford Johnson Dam—*dam* AL-4
Sanford Johnson Lake—*reservoir* AL-4
Sanford Knob—*summit* TN-4
*Sanford Lake* IN-6
*Sanford Lake* NC-3
Sanford Lake—*lake* CA-9
Sanford Lake—*lake* IN-6
Sanford Lake—*lake* MI-6
Sanford Lake—*lake* (2) NY-2
Sanford Lake—*lake* WI-6
Sanford Lake—*reservoir* MI-6
Sanford Lake Park—*park* MI-6
Sanford-Lee County Brick Field—*airport* NC-3
Sanford Lookout Tower—*locale* MS-4
Sanford Memorial Hosp—*hospital* MN-6
Sanford Mill Dam—*dam* MA-1
Sanford Mill Pond—*reservoir* MA-1
*Sanford Mines* NY-2
Sanford Mine (underground)—*mine* AL-4
Sanford Missionary Baptist Ch—*church* MS-4
Sanford Naval Acad—*school* FL-3
Sanford Naval Academy—*military* FL-3
Sanford Naval Air Station—*military* FL-3
Sanford Neal Drain—*canal* MI-6
Sanford Oil Field—*other* MI-6
Sanford-Orlando Kennel Club—*locale* FL-3
Sanford Park—*park* IA-7
Sanford Park—*park* MO-7
Sanford Park—*park* MT-8
Sanford Pass—*gap* CA-9
Sanford Pasture—*flat* WA-9
Sanford Plaza (Shop Ctr)—*locale* FL-3
Sanford Post Office (historical)—*building* MS-4
Sanford Post Office (historical)—*building* TN-4
*Sanford Preparatory School* DE-2
*Sanford Ranch* AZ-5
Sanford Ranch—*locale* NM-5
Sanford Ranch—*locale* TX-5
Sanford Ranch—*locale* (2) WY-8
*Sanford Reservoir* TX-5
Sanford Residence Hall—*building* NC-3
*Sanford Ridge* CA-9
Sanford Ridge—*ridge* CA-9
Sanford River—*stream* AK-9
Sanford Sch—*school* DE-2
Sanford Sch—*school* FL-3
Sanford Sch—*school* MI-6
Sanford Sch—*school* MN-6
Sanford Sch—*school* MO-7
Sanford Sch—*school* VA-3
Sanford Sch—*school* WV-2
Sanford Sch (historical)—*school* MS-4
Sanford Sch (historical)—*school* TN-4
*Sanfords Corner* NY-2
Sanfords Corners—*locale* NY-2
Sanfords (historical)—*locale* AZ-5
Sanford Speedway—*other* ME-1
Sanford Spinning Co.—*hist pl* MA-1
*Sanford's Pond* CT-1
Sanfords Pond—*lake* CT-1
Sanford Spring—*spring* AL-4
Sanford Spring—*spring* ID-8
Sanford Spring—*spring* (2) OR-9
Sanford Spring—*stream* UT-8
*Sanford Springs* NV-8
Sanford Springs—*locale* AL-4
Sanfords Ridge Ch—*church* NY-2
Sanford Stream—*stream* ME-1
Sanford Tabernacle of Prayer—*church* FL-3
Sanfordtown—*locale* CT-1
Sanfordtown—*locale* KY-4
**Sanford (Town of)**—*pop pl* ME-1
**Sanford (Town of)**—*pop pl* NY-2
**Sanford (Township of)**—*pop pl* MN-6
Sanford United Methodist Ch—*church* MS-4
*Sanfordville* TN-4
*Sanfordville Post Office* TN-4
Sanford Windmill—*locale* CO-8
Sanford Yake Oil Field—*oilfield* TX-5
*San Franciesquito Canyon* CA-9
San Francis Cem—*cemetery* MN-6
*San Francisco* CO-8
San Francisco—*civil* CA-9
San Francisco—*locale* NM-5
San Francisco—*locale* TX-5
San Francisco—*locale* PR-3
**San Francisco**—*pop pl* CA-9
**San Francisco**—*pop pl* CO-8
**San Francisco**—*pop pl* PR-3
San Francisco, Arroyo—*valley* TX-5
San Francisco, La Cadena—*range* PR-3
San Francisco Artesian Well—*well* TX-5
San Francisco Banco Number 60—*levee* TX-5
San Francisco Bay—*bay* CA-9
San Francisco Bay Discovery Site—*hist pl* CA-9
San Francisco Cable Cars—*hist pl* CA-9
San Francisco Camp—*locale* CA-9
San Francisco Canal North Branch—*canal* AZ-5
San Francisco Canal South Branch—*canal* AZ-5
*San Francisco Canyon* NV-8
San Francisco Canyon—*valley* NV-8
San Francisco Canyon—*valley* NM-5
San Francisco (CCD)—*cens area* CA-9
San Francisco Cemeteries—*cemetery* TX-5
San Francisco Ch—*church* NM-5
San Francisco Ch—*church* TX-5
San Francisco Civic Center Hist Dist—*hist pl* CA-9
San Francisco Coll For Women—*school* CA-9
**San Francisco Condo**—*pop pl* UT-8
San Francisco Conservatory of Music—*school* CA-9
San Francisco Creek—*stream* AK-9
San Francisco Creek—*stream* (3) CO-8
San Francisco Creek—*stream* TX-5
San Francisco Crossing—*locale* TX-5
San Francisco de Assisi Mission Church—*hist pl* NM-5
*San Francisco del Adid* AZ-5
San Francisco De Las Llagas—*civil* CA-9
**San Francisco de Oconi (historical)**—*pop pl* FL-3
San Francisco Golf Club—*other* CA-9
San Francisco Hosp—*hospital* CA-9
San Francisco Hot Springs—*spring* NM-5
San Francisco International Airp—*airport* CA-9
San Francisco Island—*island* AK-9
San Francisco Jail Site—*locale* CA-9
San Francisco Lakes—*lake* CO-8
San Francisco Lateral—*canal* NM-5
San Francisco Log Cabin Boys Sch—*school* CA-9
San Francisco Mine—*mine* AZ-5
San Francisco Mine—*mine* CA-9
*San Francisco Mountains* AZ-5
San Francisco Mountains—*range* NM-5
San Francisco Mountains—*summit* AZ-5
San Francisco Mtn—*summit* AZ-5
*San Francisco Mtn Plateau* AZ-5
San Francisco Mtns—*range* UT-8
San Francisco Natl Guard Armory and Arsenal—*hist pl* CA-9
San Francisco Naval Public Works Center—*military* CA-9
San Francisco-Oakland Bay Bridge—*bridge* CA-9
San Francisco Opera House—*building* CA-9
San Francisco Park—*park* CA-9
San Francisco Pass—*gap* CO-8
*San Francisco Peak* AZ-5
San Francisco Peak—*summit* CA-9
*San Francisco Peaks* AZ-5
San Francisco Peaks Natural Area—*park* AZ-5
San Francisco Perez Creek—*stream* TX-5
San Francisco Plantation—*locale* LA-4
San Francisco Plantation House—*hist pl* LA-4
*San Francisco Plateau* AZ-5
San Francisco Plateau—*plain* AZ-5
**San Francisco Plaza**—*pop pl* NM-5
San Francisco Port of Embarkation, US Army—*hist pl* CA-9
**San Francisco Potano (historical)**—*pop pl* FL-3
San Francisco Ranch—*hist pl* TX-5
San Francisco Ranch—*locale* TX-5
*San Francisco River* AR-4
San Francisco River—*stream* AZ-5
San Francisco River—*stream* NM-5
San Francisco Riverside Drain—*canal* NM-5
San Francisco (Ruins)—*locale* NM-5
San Francisco Shutups—*valley* TX-5
San Francisco Solano (Site)—*locale* CA-9
San Francisco Spring—*spring* NM-5
San Francisco State Coll—*school* CA-9
San Francisco State Fish and Game Refuge—*park* CA-9
San Francisco Theological Seminary—*school* CA-9
San Francisco (Township of)—*civ div* MN-6
San Francisco Volcanic Field (historical)—*lava* AZ-5
*San Francisco Wash* AZ-5
San Francisco Wash—*stream* AZ-5
San Francisco Well—*well* TX-5
San Francisco Windmill—*locale* (2) TX-5
San Francisco Xavier—*church* AZ-5
San Franciso Ch—*church* NM-5
*San Franciso Peak* AZ-5
San Francisquito—*civil* CA-9
San Francisquito Canyon—*valley* CA-9
San Francisquito Creek—*stream* CA-9
San Francisquito (Dalton)—*civil* CA-9
San Francisquito Flat—*flat* CA-9
San Francisquito Powerhouse Number One—*other* CA-9
San Francisquito Powerhouse Number Two—*other* CA-9
San Francisquito Ranger Station—*locale* CA-9
San Francisquito (Rodriguez)—*civil* CA-9
Sang, Rois Ra—*ridge* PW-9
**San Gabriel**—*pop pl* CA-9
**San Gabriel**—*pop pl* TX-5
San Gabriel Ave Sch—*school* CA-9
San Gabriel Canyon—*valley* CA-9
San Gabriel Ch—*church* CA-9
San Gabriel Christian Sch—*school* CA-9
San Gabriel Country Club—*other* CA-9
San Gabriel (Courtney)—*civil* CA-9
San Gabriel Dam—*dam* CA-9
San Gabriel de Yungue-Ouinge—*hist pl* NM-5
San Gabriel HS—*school* CA-9
San Gabriel (Ledesma)—*civil* CA-9
San Gabriel Mission—*hist pl* CA-9
San Gabriel Mountains—*range* CA-9
San Gabriel Peak—*summit* CA-9
San Gabriel River—*stream* CA-9
San Gabriel River—*stream* TX-5
San Gabriel Rsvr—*reservoir* CA-9
**San Gabriel (subdivision)**—*pop pl* (2) AZ-5
San Gabriel Valley Gun Club—*other* CA-9
San Gabriel Valley Hosp—*hospital* CA-9
Sangaina Creek—*stream* AK-9
Sangamaw Ridge—*ridge* IN-6
Sangamon—*locale* IL-6
Sangamon Ave Interchange—*other* IL-6
Sangamon Bay—*bay* IL-6
**Sangamon (County)**—*pop pl* IL-6
*Sangamon Lake* IL-6
Sangamon River—*stream* IL-6
Sangamon School—*locale* IL-6
Sangamon State Univ—*school* IL-6
**Sangamon Township**—*pop pl* SD-7
**Sangamon (Township of)**—*pop pl* IL-6
Sangamon Valley (Township of)—*civ div* IL-6
Sangamore Fork—*stream* WV-2
Sang Branch—*stream* (2) KY-4
Sang Branch—*stream* TN-4
Sang Branch—*stream* WV-2
Sang Cem—*cemetery* TN-4
Sangchris Lake—*lake* IL-6
*Sang Cove* TN-4
*Sang Cove Branch* TN-4
*Sangemon Lake* IL-6
Sanger—*locale* WV-2
**Sanger**—*pop pl* CA-9
**Sanger**—*pop pl* ND-7
**Sanger**—*pop pl* TX-5
Sanger, Asa, House—*hist pl* MA-1
Sanger, Casper M., House—*hist pl* WI-6
Sanger, Richard, III, House—*hist pl* MA-1
**San Gerardo**—*pop pl* PR-3
Sanger Ave Sch—*school* TX-5
Sanger Branch—*stream* TX-5
Sanger Brook—*stream* NH-1
Sanger Brothers Complex—*hist pl* TX-5
Sanger Canyon—*valley* CA-9
Sanger (CCD)—*cens area* CA-9
Sanger (CCD)—*cens area* TX-5
Sanger Cem—*cemetery* CA-9
Sanger Cem—*cemetery* ND-7
Sanger Cem—*cemetery* TX-5
Sanger Creek—*gut* NC-3
Sanger Draw—*valley* WY-8
**Sangerfield**—*pop pl* NY-2
Sangerfield River—*stream* NY-2
**Sangerfield (Town of)**—*pop pl* NY-2
*Sanger Fork* WV-2
Sanger Gulch—*valley* OR-9
Sanger Hill—*summit* NY-2
**Sanger (historical)**—*pop pl* OR-9
Sanger Lake—*lake* CA-9
Sanger Lake—*lake* WA-9
San German—*CDP* PR-3
**San German**—*pop pl* PR-3
San German (Municipio)—*civil* PR-3
San German (Pueblo)—*fmr MCD* PR-3
Sanger Meadow—*flat* CA-9
Sanger Mine—*mine* NV-8
Sanger Mine—*mine* OR-9
Sanger Oil Field—*oilfield* TX-5
**San Geromino**—*pop pl* TX-5
San Geronimo—*civil* (2) CA-9
San Geronimo—*locale* NM-5
**San Geronimo**—*pop pl* CA-9
**San Geronimo**—*pop pl* NM-5
San Geronimo Cabin—*locale* NM-5
San Geronimo Cem—*cemetery* TX-5
San Geronimo Creek—*stream* CA-9
San Geronimo Creek—*stream* TX-5
San Geronimo Hist Dist—*hist pl* NM-5
Sanger Peak—*summit* CA-9
Sanger Ranch—*locale* WY-8
Sanger Sch—*school* NM-5
Sanger Sch—*school* TX-5
Sangers Slough—*swamp* CA-9
Sanger Substation—*other* CA-9
Sangerville—*locale* VA-3
**Sangerville**—*pop pl* ME-1
**Sangerville (Town of)**—*pop pl* ME-1
Sangeta Creek—*stream* MN-6
Sang Fork—*stream* WV-2
*Sang Hollow* KY-4
Sangls Slough—*gut* MN-6
Sangl State Wildlife Mngmt Area—*park* MN-6
**Sango**—*pop pl* TN-4
Sango Creek—*stream* AK-9
*Sango Point* RI-1
Sango Post Office (historical)—*building* TN-4
*San Gorgonio* CA-9
San Gorgonio Campground—*locale* CA-9
San Gorgonio HS—*school* CA-9
*San Gorgonio Mtn* CA-9
San Gorgonio Mtn—*summit* CA-9
San Gorgonio Pass—*gap* CA-9
San Gorgonio Pass (CCD)—*cens area* CA-9
San Gorgonio Pass Memorial Hosp—*hospital* CA-9
San Gorgonio River—*stream* CA-9
Sango Sch (historical)—*school* TN-4
Sang Pour Sang Hill—*summit* LA-4
San Grabiel Cem—*cemetery* TX-5
Sangraco, Lake—*reservoir* CO-8
Sangre De Cristo—*civil* CO-8
Sangre De Cristo—*civil* NM-5
Sangre de Cristo Camp—*locale* NM-5
Sangre de Cristo Creek—*stream* CO-8
Sangre de Cristo Ditch No 3—*canal* CO-8
Sangre De Cristo Mountains—*range* NM-5
Sangre de Cristo Pass—*gap* CO-8
**Sangre De Cristo Ranches**—*pop pl* CO-8
Sangre De Cristo-Trinchera Diversion Canal—*canal* CO-8
**Sangree (subdivision)**—*pop pl* PA-2
*San Gregorio* AZ-5
**San Gregorio**—*pop pl* CA-9
San Gregorio Beach—*beach* CA-9
San Gregorio (Castro)—*civil* CA-9
*San Gregorio Creek* CA-9
San Gregorio Creek—*stream* CA-9
San Gregorio House—*hist pl* CA-9
San Gregorio (Rodriguez)—*civil* CA-9
San Gregorio Rsvr—*reservoir* NM-5
Sangrey Sch—*school* MT-8
Sang Run—*locale* MD-2
Sang Run—*stream* WV-2
Sangster Branch—*stream* VA-3
Sangston Prong—*stream* DE-2
San Guadalupe Windmill—*locale* TX-5
Sanguijuela Arroyo—*stream* NM-5
Sanguijuela Arroyo—*valley* TX-5
*San Guillemo River* KS-7
San Guillermo Ch—*church* TX-5
San Guillermo Creek—*stream* CA-9
San Guillermo Mtn—*summit* CA-9
Sanguinary Mtn—*summit* NH-1
Sanguinet, Marshall R., House—*hist pl* TX-5
Sanguinetti Field—*park* AZ-5
Sanguinetti Memorial Park—*cemetery* AZ-5
**Sangully**—*pop pl* FL-3
*Sanhaaja Bay* MH-9
*Sanhaajiya Wan* MH-9
*Sanhaja Wan* MH-9
*Sanhaji-Wan* MH-9
*Sanhajiya-Wan* MH-9
*Sanhajiyi-Wan* MH-9
**San Haven**—*pop pl* ND-7
*San Haven State Hospital* ND-7
*Sanhazaya Wan* MH-9
*Sanhazya Wan* MH-9
*Sanhedrin, The* CA-9
Sanhedrin Creek—*stream* CA-9
Sanhedrin Mtn—*summit* CA-9
Sanhedrin Ridge—*ridge* CA-9
Sanhill Memorial Park Cem—*cemetery* IL-6
San Houston Sch—*school* TX-5
**Sanibel**—*pop pl* FL-3
Sanibel Bayou—*lake* FL-3
Sanibel Bayous—*cove* FL-3
Sanibel Cem—*cemetery* FL-3
Sanibel Community Ch—*church* FL-3
Sanibel Congregational United Ch of Christ—*church* FL-3
Sanibel Island—*island* FL-3
Sanibel Island Causeway—*bridge* FL-3
Sanibel Island (CCD)—*cens area* FL-3
Sanibel Island Light—*locale* FL-3
Sanibel Island Lighthouse—*locale* FL-3
Sanibel Lighthouse and Keeper's Quarters—*hist pl* FL-3
Sanibel Rocks—*bar* FL-3
Sanibel Sch—*school* FL-3
San Idelfonso Creek—*stream* TX-5
San Idelfonso Tank—*reservoir* TX-5
*San Idlefenso* MP-9
**Sanie**—*pop pl* AL-4
*Sanie Baptist Church* AL-4
Sanie Ch—*church* AL-4
Saniford Cem—*cemetery* TN-4
Sanift Ditch—*canal* OH-6
Sanigaruak Island—*island* AK-9
Sanigaruak Pass—*channel* AK-9
San Ignacio—*locale* CA-9
San Ignacio—*locale* NM-5
**San Ignacio**—*pop pl* NM-5
San Ignacio Artesian Well—*well* TX-5
San Ignacio Cem—*cemetery* (2) NM-5
San Ignacio Church—*hist pl* NM-5
*San Ignacio Creek* TX-5
San Ignacio Creek—*stream* NM-5
San Ignacio de la Canoa—*civil* AZ-5
San Ignacio del Babocomari—*civil* AZ-5
**San Ignacio de Loyola**—*pop pl* TX-5
San Ignacio Ranch—*locale* AZ-5
San Ignacio Sch—*school* CA-9
San Ignacio Sch—*school* NM-5
San Ignacio Spring—*spring* NM-5
San Ignacio Windmill—*locale* TX-5
San Ignacio Windmill Number One—*locale* TX-5
San Ignacio Windmill Number Two—*locale* TX-5
Sanilac and Saint Clair Drain—*canal* MI-6
**Sanilac (County)**—*pop pl* MI-6
Sanilac Huron Creek—*stream* MI-6
Sanilac Petroglyphs—*hist pl* MI-6
**Sanilac (Township of)**—*pop pl* MI-6
San Ildefonso—*post sta* PR-3
San Ildefonso (Barrio)—*fmr MCD* PR-3
*San Ildefonso Mesa* NM-5
San Ildefonso Pueblo—*hist pl* NM-5
**San Ildefonso Pueblo**—*pop pl* NM-5
San Ildefonso Pueblo Grant—*civil* NM-5
**San Ildefonso Pueblo (Indian Reservation)**—*pop pl* NM-5
**San Ildefonso Pueblo (Place)**—*pop pl* NM-5
**San Isabel**—*pop pl* CO-8
*San Isabel Creek* CA-9
*San Isabel Creek* TX-5
San Isabel Creek—*stream* CO-8
San Isabel Lake—*lake* CO-8
*San Isabel Mountain* CA-9
San Isabel Natl For—*forest* CO-8
San Isabel Ranch—*locale* CO-8
*San Isabel Valley* CA-9
**Sanish**—*pop pl* ND-7
Sanish Bay—*bay* ND-7
**San Isidoro**—*pop pl* PR-3
San Isidro—*CDP* PR-3
**San Isidro**—*pop pl* TX-5
**San Isidro**—*pop pl* (2) PR-3
San Isidro Arroyo—*stream* NM-5
San Isidro (Barrio)—*fmr MCD* PR-3
San Isidro Cem—*cemetery* (2) NM-5
San Isidro Cem—*cemetery* (2) TX-5
San Isidro Ch—*church* CO-8
San Isidro Ch—*church* FL-3
San Isidro Ch—*church* (3) NM-5
San Isidro Chapel—*church* GU-9
San Isidro Creek—*stream* CO-8
San Isidro Creek—*stream* NM-5
San Isidro Lake—*lake* NM-5
San Isidro Sch—*school* NM-5
San Isidro Spring—*spring* NM-5
San Isidro Valley—*valley* NM-5
San Isidro Wash—*stream* NM-5
San Island—*island* AK-9
*San Island Recreation Site* UT-8
**Sanita Clarita**—*pop pl* CA-9
Sanita Hills Camp—*locale* NY-2
**Sanitaria Springs**—*pop pl* NY-2
**Sanitarium**—*pop pl* CA-9
Sanitary, Lake—*lake* FL-3
Sanitary Ditch—*canal* IN-6
Sanitary Spring—*spring* ID-8
*Sanit Bonifacius* PA-2
Sanitol Bldg—*hist pl* MO-7
Sanitorium—*post sta* MS-4
San Jacino Park—*park* TX-5
San Jacinto—*locale* TX-5
**San Jacinto**—*pop pl* CA-9
**San Jacinto**—*pop pl* IN-6
**San Jacinto**—*pop pl* NV-8
San Jacinto—*uninc pl* TX-5
San Jacinto Battlefield—*hist pl* TX-5
*San Jacinto Bayou* TX-5
San Jacinto Ch—*church* TX-5
San Jacinto Coll—*school* TX-5
**San Jacinto (County)**—*pop pl* TX-5
San Jacinto County Jail—*hist pl* TX-5
San Jacinto Creek—*stream* CA-9
San Jacinto Dam—*dam* TX-5
San Jacinto HS—*school* TX-5
San Jacinto JHS—*school* (2) TX-5
San Jacinto Lake—*reservoir* NJ-2
San Jacinto Memorial Hosp—*hospital* TX-5
San Jacinto Memorial Park—*cemetery* TX-5
San Jacinto Monument—*other* TX-5
San Jacinto Mountains—*range* CA-9
San Jacinto Mtn—*summit* TX-5
San Jacinto Nuevo Y Potrero—*civil* CA-9
San Jacinto Park—*park* FL-3
San Jacinto Park—*park* TX-5
*San Jacinto Peak* CA-9
San Jacinto Peak—*summit* CA-9
San Jacinto Ranch—*locale* NV-8
San Jacinto Ranch—*locale* TX-5
San Jacinto Ridge Truck Trail—*trail* CA-9
*San Jacinto River* CA-9
*San Jacinto River* TX-5
San Jacinto River—*stream* CA-9
San Jacinto River—*stream* TX-5
San Jacinto River Authority Canal—*canal* TX-5
San Jacinto Rsvr—*reservoir* CA-9
San Jacinto Sch—*school* (8) TX-5
San Jacinto Spring—*spring* TX-5
San Jacinto State Park—*park* TX-5
San Jacinto Valley—*valley* CA-9
San Jacinto Viejo—*civil* CA-9
*San Jacome De La Marca* CA-9
*Sanja Cota Creek* CA-9
San Jasinto Cem—*cemetery* TX-5
*San Jaun Creek* TX-5
San Javier de Ajuera Windmill—*locale* TX-5
San Joachim Cem—*cemetery* CA-9
San Joaquin—*civil* (2) CA-9
**San Joaquin**—*pop pl* CA-9
San Joaquin, Canada De —*valley* CA-9
*San Joaquin And Kings River Canal* CA-9
*San Joaquin And Kings River Irrigation Company Canal* CA-9
**San Joaquin Bridge**—*pop pl* CA-9
San Joaquin Cem—*cemetery* (2) CA-9
San Joaquin Church—*hist pl* NM-5
San Joaquin City (site)—*locale* CA-9
San Joaquin Country Club—*other* CA-9
**San Joaquin (County)**—*pop pl* CA-9
San Joaquin Delta Coll—*school* CA-9
San Joaquin Experimental Range—*forest* CA-9
San Joaquin Gun Club—*other* CA-9
San Joaquin Hills—*range* CA-9
San Joaquin Main Canal—*canal* CA-9
San Joaquin Memorial HS—*school* CA-9
San Joaquin Mine—*mine* CA-9
San Joaquin Mines—*mine* CA-9

Santa Margarita Creek—stream ................ CA-9
Santa Margarita Fire Control Station—locale ................ CA-9
Santa Margarita Lake—reservoir ................ CA-9
Santa Margarita Mine—mine ................ CA-9
Santa Margarita Mountains—range ................ CA-9
Santa Margarita Ranch—locale ................ AZ-5
Santa Margarita Ranchhouse—hist pl ................ CA-9
Santa Margarita River—stream ................ CA-9
Santa Margarita Sch—school (2) ................ CA-9
Santa Margarita Tank—reservoir ................ AZ-5
Santa Margarita Valley—valley ................ CA-9
Santa Margarita Wash—stream ................ AZ-5
Santa Margarita Y Las Flores—civil ................ CA-9
Santa Marguerita ................ TX-5
Santa Maria ................ FL-3
**Santa Maria**—pop pl ................ AZ-5
**Santa Maria**—pop pl ................ CA-9
**Santa Maria**—pop pl ................ CO-8
**Santa Maria**—pop pl ................ FL-3
**Santa Maria**—pop pl ................ TX-5
**Santa Maria**—pop pl (7) ................ PR-3
Santa Maria—valley ................ PR-3
Santa Maria Aida Cem—cemetery ................ TX-5
Santa Maria Bay—bay ................ VI-3
Santa Maria Camp—locale ................ TX-5
Santa Maria Canyon—valley ................ CA-9
Santa Maria Cem—cemetery ................ CA-9
Santa Maria Cem—cemetery ................ TX-5
Santa Maria Country Club—other ................ CA-9
Santa Maria Creek—stream (2) ................ CA-9
Santa Maria del Agua Caliente ................ AZ-5
Santa Maria Del Mar Catholic Ch—church ................ FL-3
Santa Maria Estate—locale ................ VI-3
Santa Maria Gulch—valley ................ CA-9
Santa Maria Main Canal—canal ................ TX-5
Santa Maria Mine—mine ................ AZ-5
Santa Maria Mission—church ................ NM-5
Santa Maria Mountain ................ CA-9
Santa Maria Mountains—range ................ AZ-5
Santa Maria Novitiate—church ................ NY-2
Santa Maria Pass—gap ................ CO-8
Santa Maria Plantation House—hist pl ................ LA-4
Santa Maria Public Airp—airport ................ CA-9
Santa Maria Pumping Station—other ................ TX-5
Santa Maria Ranch—locale ................ AZ-5
Santa Maria Ranch—locale ................ CO-8
Santa Maria River ................ AZ-5
Santa Maria River—stream ................ AZ-5
Santa Maria River—stream ................ CA-9
Santa Maria River North Fork—stream ................ AZ-5
Santa Maria Rsvr—reservoir ................ CO-8
Santa Maria Sch—school (2) ................ CA-9
Santa Maria Sch—school ................ IL-6
Santa Maria Sch—school ................ MI-6
Santa Maria Sch—school ................ TX-5
**Santa Maria South**—pop pl ................ CA-9
Santa Maria Spring—spring ................ AZ-5
**Santa Maria (subdivision)**—pop pl ................ AZ-5
Santa Maria Valley—valley (3) ................ CA-9
Santa Maria Valley (CCD)—cens area ................ CA-9
Santa Maria Valley Oil Field ................ CA-9
Santa Maria Windmill—locale (2) ................ TX-5
Santa Marie Cem—cemetery ................ FL-3
Santa Marie Valley ................ CA-9
**Santa Marta**—pop pl ................ PR-3
Santa Marta Windmill—locale ................ TX-5
Santa Martha Catholic Ch—church ................ FL-3
Santa Mission Ch—church ................ NM-5
**Santa Monica**—pop pl ................ CA-9
**Santa Monica**—pop pl ................ FL-3
**Santa Monica**—pop pl ................ TX-5
**Santa Monica**—pop pl (2) ................ PR-3
Santa Monica—uninc pl ................ FL-3
Santa Monica Bay—bay ................ CA-9
Santa Monica Beach—beach ................ MI-6
Santa Monica Beach State Park—park (2) ................ CA-9
Santa Monica Blvd Sch—school ................ CA-9
Santa Monica Camp—locale ................ AZ-5
Santa Monica Canyon—uninc pl ................ CA-9
Santa Monica Canyon—valley (2) ................ CA-9
Santa Monica (CCD)—cens area ................ CA-9
Santa Monica Cem—cemetery ................ TX-5
Santa Monica City Coll—school ................ CA-9
Santa Monica Creek—stream ................ CA-9
Santa Monica HS—school ................ CA-9
Santa Monica Junior Acad—school ................ CA-9
Santa Monica Looff Hippodrome—hist pl ................ CA-9
Santa Monica Mountains—range ................ CA-9
Santa Monica Mountains Natl Rec Area—park ................ CA-9
Santa Monica Ridge—ridge ................ CA-9
Santa Monica Shop Ctr—locale ................ FL-3
Santa Monica State Beach—beach ................ CA-9
Santa Monica Well (flowing)—well ................ TX-5
Santan—locale ................ AZ-5
**Santana**—pop pl ................ PR-3
San Tana, Lake—reservoir ................ TX-5
Santana (Barrio)—fmr MCD (2) ................ PR-3
Santana Butte—summit ................ CO-8
Santana Canyon—valley ................ CO-8
Santana Canyon—valley ................ TX-5
Santana HS—school ................ CA-9
Santana Mesa—summit ................ TX-5
Santana Place—locale ................ NM-5
Santana Spring—spring ................ CO-8
Santana Tank—reservoir ................ TX-5
Santana Trail—trail ................ CO-8
Santan Canal—canal ................ AZ-5
San Tan Canal Bridge—hist pl ................ AZ-5
Santan Day Sch—school ................ AZ-5
**Santa Nella**—pop pl (2) ................ CA-9
**Santa Nella Village**—pop pl ................ CA-9
Santa Nina Ch—church ................ NM-5
Santa Nino Cem—cemetery (2) ................ NM-5
Santanka Cove ................ CO-8
San Tan Mobile Village—locale ................ AZ-5
Santan Mountains—summit ................ AZ-5
Santan Mtn—summit ................ AZ-5
Santanoni Brook—stream (2) ................ NY-2
Santanoni Mountains—summit ................ NY-2
Santanoni Peak—summit ................ NY-2
Santan RR Station—building ................ AZ-5
Santan Substation—locale ................ AZ-5
Santanta ................ KS-7
Santanta Peak—summit ................ CO-8
Santa Olaya (Barrio)—fmr MCD ................ PR-3
**Santa Paula**—pop pl ................ CA-9
Santa Paula Canyon—valley (2) ................ CA-9
Santa Paula (CCD)—cens area ................ CA-9
Santa Paula Cem—cemetery ................ CA-9
Santa Paula Creek—stream ................ CA-9
Santa Paula Hardware Company Block-Union Oil Company—hist pl ................ CA-9
Santa Paula Peak—summit ................ CA-9
Santa Paula Ridge—ridge ................ CA-9
Santa Paula Y Saticoy—civil ................ CA-9
Santa Peak—summit ................ ID-8
Santa Pentecostes Ch—church ................ TX-5
Santa Petronilla Creek ................ TX-5
Santapogue Creek—stream ................ NY-2
Santapogue Neck—cape ................ NY-2
Santapogue Point—cape ................ NY-2
Santapogue Sch—school ................ NY-2
**Santapoque**—pop pl ................ NY-2
**Santaquin**—pop pl ................ UT-8
Santaquin Canyon—valley ................ UT-8
Santaquin City Cem—cemetery ................ UT-8
Santaquin Creek ................ UT-8
Santaquin Debris Basin Dam—dam ................ UT-8
Santaquin Debris Basin Rsvr—reservoir ................ UT-8
Santaquin Draw—valley ................ UT-8
Santaquin JHS—hist pl ................ UT-8
Santaquin Meadows—flat ................ UT-8
Santaquin Peak—summit ................ UT-8
Santaquin Post Office—building ................ UT-8
Santaquin Reservoir ................ UT-8
Santaquin Sch—school ................ UT-8
Santaquin Spring—spring ................ UT-8
Santa Renia Fields—flat ................ NV-8
Santa Renia Mtns—range ................ NV-8
Santa Rita—civil ................ CA-9
Santa Rita—locale ................ TX-5
**Santa Rita**—pop pl ................ CA-9
**Santa Rita**—pop pl ................ MT-8
**Santa Rita**—pop pl ................ NM-5
**Santa Rita**—pop pl ................ GU-9
**Santa Rita**—pop pl (4) ................ PR-3
Santa Rita Bridge—bridge ................ CA-9
Santa Rita Canyon—valley ................ NM-5
Santa Rita Cem—cemetery (3) ................ TX-5
Santa Rita Ch—church ................ NM-5
Santa Rita Creek—stream ................ CA-9
Santa Rita Creek—stream ................ NM-5
Santa Rita Ditch—canal ................ CA-9
Santa Rita Drain—canal ................ CA-9
Santa Rita (Election District)—fmr MCD ................ GU-9
Santa Rita Experimental Range and Wildlife Area—park ................ AZ-5
Santa Rita Flat—flat ................ CA-9
Santa Rita Hills—ridge ................ CA-9
Santa Rita (historical)—locale ................ AZ-5
Santa Rita HS—school ................ AZ-5
Santa Rita Island—island ................ AK-9
Santa Rita Lodge—locale ................ AZ-5
Santa Rita (Malo)—civil ................ CA-9
Santa Rita Mesa—summit ................ NM-5
Santa Rita Mountains—range ................ AZ-5
Santa Rita Park—locale ................ CA-9
Santa Rita Park—park ................ AZ-5
**Santa Rita Park (Dos Palos Y)**—pop pl ................ CA-9
Santa Rita Peak ................ AZ-5
**Santa Rita Peak**—pop pl ................ CA-9
Santa Rita Ranch—locale ................ AZ-5
Santa Rita Ranch—locale (2) ................ CA-9
Santa Rita Ranch—locale ................ TX-5
Santa Rita Rehabilitation Center (Alameda County)—hospital ................ CA-9
Santa Rita Rehabilitation Center Annex—hospital ................ CA-9
Santa Rita Sch—school (2) ................ CA-9
Santa Rita Sch—school ................ TX-5
Santa Rita Shrine—church ................ AZ-5
Santa Rita Slough—gut ................ CA-9
Santa Rita Spring—spring ................ CA-9
Santa Rita Spring—spring ................ GU-9
Santa Rita State Farm ................ CA-9
Santa Rita Station—locale ................ NM-5
Santa Rita Valley—valley ................ CA-9
Santa Rita Well—well ................ AZ-5
Santa Rita Windmill—locale ................ TX-5
Santa Rosa ................ AZ-5
Santa Rosa ................ CA-9
Santa Rosa ................ FL-3
Santa Rosa—civil ................ CA-9
Santa Rosa—other ................ FL-3
**Santa Rosa**—pop pl ................ AZ-5
**Santa Rosa**—pop pl ................ CA-9
**Santa Rosa**—pop pl ................ MS-4
**Santa Rosa**—pop pl ................ MO-7
**Santa Rosa**—pop pl ................ NM-5
**Santa Rosa**—pop pl ................ TX-5
**Santa Rosa**—pop pl ................ GU-9
**Santa Rosa**—pop pl (5) ................ PR-3
Santa Rosa, Arroyo—stream ................ CA-9
Santa Rosa, Canada De —stream ................ CA-9
Santa Rosa, Mount—summit ................ GU-9
Santa Rosa, Sierra de—range ................ AZ-5
Santa Rosa (Barrio)—fmr MCD (3) ................ PR-3
Santa Rosa Bay ................ FL-3
**Santa Rosa Beach**—pop pl ................ FL-3
Santa Rosa Boarding and Day Sch—school ................ AZ-5
Santa Rosa (CCD)—cens area ................ CA-9
Santa Rosa (CCD)—cens area ................ NM-5
Santa Rosa Cem—cemetery ................ CA-9
Santa Rosa Cem—cemetery ................ FL-3
Santa Rosa Cem—cemetery ................ TX-5
Santa Rosa (Coto)—civil ................ CA-9
**Santa Rosa County**—pop pl ................ FL-3
Santa Rosa County Adult HS—school ................ FL-3
Santa Rosa Creek—stream (3) ................ CA-9
Santa Rosa Creek Rsvr—reservoir ................ CA-9
Santa Rosa Crossing—locale ................ TX-5
Santa Rosa De Cubero Grant—civil ................ NM-5
Santa Rosa de Lima Ch—church ................ TX-5
Santa Rosa de Lima de Abiquiu—hist pl ................ NM-5
Santa Rosa Flat—flat ................ CA-9
Santa Rosa Flood Control Channel—canal ................ CA-9
Santa Rosa Francisco Cem—cemetery ................ AZ-5
Santa Rosa Gas Plant—oilfield ................ TX-5
Santa Rosa Gulch—valley ................ AZ-5
Santa Rosa Hills—other ................ CA-9
Santa Rosa Hills—range ................ CA-9
Santa Rosa Hills—summit ................ CA-9
Santa Rosa Hosp—hospital ................ FL-3
**Santa Rosa Ind Res**—pop pl ................ CA-9
Santa Rosa Infirmary—hospital ................ TX-5
Santa Rosa Island—island ................ CA-9
Santa Rosa Island—island ................ FL-3
Santa Rosa Lake—lake ................ TX-5
Santa Rosa Lake—reservoir ................ NM-5
Santa Rosa Lake—reservoir ................ TX-5
Santa Rosalia Cem—cemetery ................ TX-5
Santa Rosalia Mtn—summit ................ CA-9
Santa Rosalis Mtn ................ CA-9
Santa Rosa Memorial Park—cemetery ................ CA-9
Santa Rosa Mine—locale ................ AZ-5
Santa Rosa Mine—mine ................ CA-9
Santa Rosa Mine—mine ................ NV-8
Santa Rosa Mines—mine ................ CA-9
Santa Rosa (Morino)—civil ................ CA-9
Santa Rosa Mountains ................ AZ-5
Santa Rosa Mountains ................ NV-8
Santa Rosa Mountains—range ................ AZ-5
Santa Rosa Mountains—range ................ CA-9
Santa Rosa Mtn ................ AZ-5
Santa Rosa Mtn—summit ................ AZ-5
Santa Rosa Mtn—summit ................ CA-9
Santa Rosa Mountain ................ AZ-5
Santa Rosa of Lima Catholic Ch—church ................ FL-3
Santa Rosa Park—park ................ AZ-5
Santa Rosa Park—park (2) ................ CA-9
Santa Rosa Peak—summit ................ NV-8
Santa Rosa Peaks—other ................ NM-5
Santa Rosa Pens—locale ................ TX-5
Santa Rosa Ranch ................ AZ-5
Santa Rosa Ranch—locale ................ CA-9
Santa Rosa Ranch—locale ................ TX-5
**Santa Rosa Rancheria (Indian Reservation)**—pop pl ................ CA-9
Santa Rosa Ranch Sch—school ................ AZ-5
Santa Rosa Range—range ................ NV-8
Santa Rosa Reef—bar ................ CA-9
Santa Rosa River ................ AL-4
Santa Rosa Roundup Rodeo Grounds—locale ................ TX-5
Santa Rosa Sch—school ................ AZ-5
Santa Rosa Sch—school (3) ................ CA-9
Santa Rosa Sch—school ................ NM-5
Santa Rosa Shores Baptist Ch—church ................ FL-3
Santa Rosa Sound—bay ................ FL-3
Santa Rosa Spring—spring ................ CA-9
Santa Rosa Spring—spring ................ TX-5
Santa Rosa Summit—gap ................ CA-9
Santa Rosa Trading Post—locale ................ AZ-5
**Santa Rosa Tres**—pop pl ................ PR-3
Santa Rosa Valley—valley ................ AZ-5
Santa Rosa Valley—valley ................ CA-9
Santa Rosa Wash ................ AZ-5
Santa Rosa Wash—stream ................ AZ-5
Santa Rosa Wash—stream ................ CA-9
Santa Rosa Well ................ AZ-5
Santa Rosa Well—well ................ GU-9
Santa Rosa Windmill—locale ................ TX-5
Santa Sinforosa Ridge—ridge ................ CA-9
Santa's Land—park ................ NC-3
Santastevens Spring—spring ................ CO-8
**Santa Susana**—pop pl ................ CA-9
Santa Susana County Park—park ................ CA-9
**Santa Susana Knolls**—pop pl ................ CA-9
Santa Susana Mountains—ridge ................ CA-9
Santa Susana Oil Field ................ CA-9
Santa Susana Pass—gap ................ CA-9
Santa Susana Pass Wash—stream ................ CA-9
Santa Susana Tunnel—tunnel ................ CA-9
Santa Tereso—civil ................ CA-9
Santa Teresa—civil ................ NM-5
**Santa Teresa**—pop pl ................ PR-3
Santa Teresa Ch—church ................ NM-5
Santa Teresa Ch—church ................ TX-5
Santa Teresa Golf Course—other ................ CA-9
Santa Teresa Hills—summit ................ CA-9
Santa Teresa Mine—mine ................ CA-9
Santa Teresa Mountains—range ................ AZ-5
Santa Teresa Spring—spring ................ CA-9
Santa Teresa Valley—valley ................ CA-9
Santa Teresa Well—well ................ AZ-5
Santa Teresa Windmill—locale (2) ................ TX-5
**Santa Teresita**—pop pl ................ PR-3
Santa Teresita Ch—church ................ NM-5
Santa Teresita Ch—church ................ GU-9
Santa Teresita Sch—school ................ CA-9
Santa Theresas Roman Catholic Ch—church ................ FL-3
Santaug Lake ................ MA-1
Santauruf ................ MH-9
**Santa Venetia**—pop pl ................ CA-9
Santa Venetia Sch—school ................ CA-9
Santa Western—uninc pl ................ CA-9
**Santa Ynez**—pop pl ................ CA-9
Santa Ynez Campground—locale ................ CA-9
Santa Ynez Canyon—valley ................ CA-9
**Santa Ynez Ind Res**—pop pl ................ CA-9
Santa Ynez Lake—lake ................ CA-9
Santa Ynez Mountains—range ................ CA-9
Santa Ynez Peak—summit ................ CA-9
Santa Ynez Point—cape ................ CA-9
Santa Ynez River—stream ................ CA-9
Santa Ynez Union HS—school ................ CA-9
Santa Ynez Valley—valley ................ CA-9
Santa Ynez Valley (CCD)—cens area ................ CA-9
Santa Ysabel—civil (2) ................ CA-9
**Santa Ysabel**—pop pl ................ CA-9
Santa Ysabel Creek ................ CA-9
Santa Ysabel Creek—stream ................ CA-9
**Santa Ysabel Ind Res**—pop pl ................ CA-9
Santa Ysabel Mountain ................ CA-9
Santa Ysabel Peak—summit ................ CA-9
Santa Ysabel Ranch—locale ................ CA-9
Santa Ysabel Sch—school ................ CA-9
Santa Ysabel Shaft—mine ................ CA-9
Santa Ysabel Truck Trail—trail ................ CA-9
Santa Ysabel Valley ................ CA-9
Santa Ysabel Valley—valley ................ CA-9
Sant Creek—stream ................ ID-8
Sante, Cap—cape ................ WA-9
Santee ................ SC-3
Santee—hist pl ................ VA-3
**Santee**—pop pl ................ CA-9
**Santee**—pop pl ................ MS-4
**Santee**—pop pl ................ NE-7
**Santee**—pop pl ................ SC-3
Santee, Lake—reservoir ................ IN-6
Santee Branch ................ TN-4
Santee Branch—stream ................ MS-4
Santee Branch—stream ................ SC-3
Santee Canal—canal ................ SC-3
Santee Canal—hist pl ................ SC-3
Santee Cem—cemetery ................ MS-4
Santee Ch—church ................ MS-4
Santee Ch—church (2) ................ SC-3
**Santee Circle**—pop pl ................ SC-3
Santee Cooper Project (Power Plant)—facility ................ SC-3
Santee Cooper Reservation—reserve ................ SC-3
Santee Creek—stream ................ PA-2
Santee Creek—stream ................ TN-4
Santee Creek Hollow—valley ................ TN-4
Santee Dam—dam ................ SC-3
Santee Indian Mound and Fort Watson—hist pl ................ SC-3
**Santee Ind Res**—pop pl ................ NE-7
Santee Lake—lake ................ GA-3
Santee Methodist Ch ................ MS-4
Santee Natl Wildlife Ref—park ................ SC-3
Santee Pass—channel ................ SC-3
Santee Path Creek—gut ................ SC-3
Santee Point—cape ................ SC-3
Santee Rec Area—park ................ NE-7
Santee Recreational Lakes—reservoir ................ CA-9
Santee Reservoir ................ SC-3
Santee Ridge—ridge ................ PA-2
Santee Ridge—ridge ................ WV-2
Santee River—stream ................ SC-3
Santee Run—stream ................ WV-2
Santee Sch—school ................ CA-9
Santee Sch—school ................ MI-6
Santee Sch—school ................ PA-2
Santee Sch—school ................ SC-3
Santee Sch (abandoned)—school ................ MO-7
Santee Sch (historical)—school ................ MS-4
Santees Slope Mine (underground)—mine ................ AL-4
Santee State Park—park ................ SC-3
Santee Swamp—swamp ................ SC-3
Santeetla ................ NC-3
**Santeetlah**—pop pl ................ NC-3
Santeetlah Ch—church ................ NC-3
Santeetlah Creek—stream ................ NC-3
Santeetlah Dam—building ................ NC-3
Santeetlah Dam—dam ................ NC-3
Santeetlah Gap—gap ................ NC-3
Santeetlah Lake—reservoir ................ NC-3
Santeetlah Power House—locale ................ NC-3
**Santee Township**—pop pl ................ NE-7
Sante Fe ................ IN-6
**Sante Fe**—pop pl ................ FL-3
Sante Fe Apartments—hist pl ................ MI-6
Sante Fe Depot and Reading Room—hist pl ................ OK-5
Sante Fe Lake ................ OK-5
Sante Fe Old Fields ................ FL-3
Sante Fe Trail Ruts—hist pl ................ KS-7
Santell Ch—church ................ GA-3
Santer River—stream ................ MI-6
San Texas Mine—mine ................ NM-5
San Tex Mine—mine ................ NM-5
S. Anthony Ponds ................ NY-2
Santhuff Cem—cemetery ................ MO-7
Santiago—locale ................ MI-6
Santiago—locale ................ MO-7
Santiago—locale (2) ................ PR-3
**Santiago**—pop pl ................ IA-7
**Santiago**—pop pl ................ MN-6
**Santiago**—pop pl ................ WV-2
**Santiago**—pop pl ................ PR-3
Santiago Artesian Well—well (2) ................ TX-5
Santiago (Barrio)—fmr MCD ................ PR-3
Santiago Bog—swamp ................ ME-1
Santiago Canyon—valley (2) ................ CA-9
Santiago Canyon—valley ................ NV-8
Santiago Cem—cemetery ................ MN-6
Santiago Coal Mine—mine ................ CA-9
Santiago Creek ................ TX-5
Santiago Creek—stream (2) ................ CA-9
Santiago Creek—stream ................ IA-7
Santiago Creek—stream ................ NM-5
Santiago Dam—dam ................ CA-9
Santiago De Santa Ana—civil ................ CA-9
Santiago Draw ................ TX-5
Santiago Draw—valley ................ TX-5
Santiago Golf Course—other ................ CA-9
Santiago HS—school ................ CA-9
**Santiago Iglesias**—pop pl ................ PR-3
Santiago Lake—lake ................ NM-5
Santiago Mine—mine ................ CO-8
Santiago Mountains ................ TX-5
Santiago Mountains—range ................ TX-5
Santiago Park—park ................ CA-9
Santiago Peak—summit ................ CA-9
Santiago Peak—summit ................ TX-5
Santiago Pond—lake ................ NM-5
Santiago Ramirez Grant—civil ................ NM-5
Santiago Range ................ TX-5
Santiago Rsvr—reservoir ................ CA-9
Santiago Sch—school ................ CA-9
Santiago Sch (abandoned)—school ................ MO-7
Santiago Sierra ................ TX-5
**Santiago (subdivision)**—pop pl (2) ................ AZ-5
Santiago Tank—reservoir ................ TX-5
**Santiago (Township of)**—pop pl ................ MN-6
Santiago Truck Trail—trail ................ CA-9
**Santiago (Tyre Post Office)**—pop pl ................ PA-2
**Santiago y Lima**—pop pl ................ PR-3
Santiago y Lima (Barrio)—fmr MCD ................ PR-3
Santiague—locale ................ LA-4
Santiam ................ OR-9
Santiam City ................ OR-9
Santiam Creek—stream ................ ID-8
Santiam Junction—locale ................ OR-9
Santiam Junction State Airp—airport ................ OR-9
Santiam Lake—lake ................ OR-9
Santiam Memorial Hospital Heliport—airport ................ OR-9
Santiam Pass—gap ................ OR-9
Santiam Peak—summit ................ OR-9
Santiam River ................ OR-9
Santiam River—stream ................ OR-9
Santiam River Safety Rest Area—locale ................ OR-9
Santiam Sch—school ................ OR-9
Santiam State For—forest ................ OR-9
Santiam Terrace—locale ................ OR-9
Santiam Valley Grange—locale ................ OR-9
**Santiam City (historical)**—pop pl ................ OR-9
Santianez Lake—reservoir ................ NM-5
Santiego Coleman Grant—civil ................ FL-3
Santillana Gas Field—oilfield ................ TX-5
Santillana Windmill—locale ................ TX-5
Santillane—hist pl ................ VA-3
Santillanes Creek—stream ................ NM-5
Santilla River ................ GA-3
Santimaw Brook—stream ................ NY-2
San Timoteo Canyon—valley ................ CA-9
San Timoteo Wash—stream ................ CA-9
Santina Bay—bay ................ FL-3
Santini Bight—bay ................ FL-3
Santio Crossing—locale ................ UT-8
Santio Knolls—summit ................ UT-8
Santistevan Canyon—valley ................ CO-8
Santistevan Creek—stream ................ NM-5
Santi Vaya ................ AZ-5
Santle Branch—stream ................ LA-4
Santlin Sch (historical)—school ................ AL-4
Santo ................ MH-9
**Santo**—pop pl ................ TX-5
Santo Arroyo Creek—stream ................ MT-8
Santo Christo Ch—church ................ MA-1
Santo Christo Church—hist pl ................ MA-1
**Santo Domingo**—pop pl ................ MD-2
**Santo Domingo**—pop pl ................ PR-3
Santo Domingo Banco Number 55—levee ................ TX-5
Santo Domingo (Barrio)—fmr MCD ................ PR-3
Santo Domingo (CCD)—cens area ................ NM-5
Santo Domingo Creek—stream ................ PA-2
Santo Domingo De Cundiyo Grant—civil ................ NM-5
Santo Domingo Ditch—canal ................ NM-5
Santo Domingo Drain—canal ................ NM-5
Santo Domingo East Side Riverside Drain—canal ................ NM-5
Santo Domingo Gulch ................ AZ-5
Santo Domingo Mission Ruins—locale ................ GA-3
Santo Domingo Pubelo Grant—civil ................ NM-5
**Santo Domingo Pueblo**—pop pl ................ NM-5
**Santo Domingo Pueblo (Indian Reservation)**—pop pl ................ NM-5
Santo Domingo Pueblo (Place)—CDP ................ NM-5
Santo Domingo Tank—reservoir ................ TX-5
Santo Domingo Wash ................ AZ-5
Santo Domingo West Side Drain—canal ................ NM-5
Santo Domingo Windmill—locale (3) ................ TX-5
Santo East Cem—cemetery ................ TX-5
Santo Gertrudis Memorial Cem—cemetery ................ TX-5
**San Tomas**—pop pl ................ CA-9
San Tomas Aquinas Creek—stream ................ CA-9
San Tomas Artesian Well—well ................ TX-5
San Tomas Camp—locale ................ TX-5
San Tomas Sch—school ................ CA-9
San Tomas Windmill—locale ................ TX-5
San Tomas Well—well ................ AZ-5
**Santo Nino**—pop pl (2) ................ NM-5
Santo Nino Canyon—valley ................ NM-5
Santo Nino Cem—cemetery (3) ................ NM-5
Santo Nino Cemetery—cemetery ................ TX-5
Santo Nino Ch—church (6) ................ NM-5
Santo Nino Chapel—church ................ NM-5
Santonino Creek—stream ................ TX-5
Santo Nino Mine —mine ................ AZ-5
Santonino Sch—school ................ NM-5
Santo Nino Sch—school ................ TX-5
Santora Bldg—hist pl ................ CA-9
Santo Rsvr ................ OR-9
**Santos**—pop pl ................ FL-3
Santos Apostoles San Simon y Judas ................ AZ-5
Santos Banco Number 95—levee ................ TX-5
Santos Bar—bar ................ AL-4
Santosch Slough ................ OR-9
Santos Creek—stream ................ CA-9
Santosh Slough—stream ................ OR-9
Santos Mesa—summit ................ NM-5
Santos Ninos Ch—church ................ NM-5
Santos Peak—summit ................ NM-5
Santos Ranch—locale ................ NE-7
Santo Tomas—locale ................ TX-5
**Santo Tomas**—pop pl ................ NM-5
Santo Tomas Cem—cemetery ................ TX-5
Santo Tomas Creek—stream ................ TX-5
Santo Tomas De Yturbide Colony Tract No 1—civil ................ NM-5
Santo Tomas De Yturbide Colony Tract No 2—civil ................ NM-5
Santo Tomas Drain—canal ................ NM-5
Santo Tomas Lateral—canal ................ NM-5
Santo Tomas HS—summit ................ NM-5
Santo Tomas River Drain—canal ................ NM-5
Santo Tomas River Lateral—canal ................ NM-5
**Santo Tomas (subdivision)**—pop pl (2) ................ AZ-5
Santo Tomas Tank—reservoir ................ TX-5
Santo Toribio Ch—church ................ NM-5
Santown—locale ................ WV-2
**Santoy**—pop pl ................ OH-6
**San Toy**—pop pl ................ OH-6
San Toy Creek—stream ................ OH-6
San Toy Dam—dam ................ OH-6
San Toy Mtn—summit ................ CO-8
Sant Punt ................ NJ-2
Santrock Sch—school ................ OH-6
Sants Branch—stream ................ IA-7
Santuario de la Monserate de Hormigueros and Casa de Peregrinos—hist pl ................ PR-3
**Santuc**—pop pl ................ SC-3
Santuck ................ SC-3
**Santuck**—pop pl ................ AL-4
**Santuck**—pop pl ................ AR-4
Santuet River ................ MA-1
**Santuit**—pop pl ................ MA-1
Santuit Hist Dist—hist pl ................ MA-1
Santuit Pond—lake ................ MA-1
Santuit Post Office—hist pl ................ MA-1
Santuit River—stream ................ MA-1
Santultah ................ NC-3
**Santurce**—pop pl ................ PR-3
Santurce (Barrio)—fmr MCD ................ PR-3
Santway Park—park ................ NY-2
Santwer Lake ................ MN-6
Sant Willow Ch—church ................ TX-5
Santwire Lake—lake ................ MN-6
Santy Rsvr—reservoir ................ OR-9
Sanuk ................ FM-9
**Sanuk**—pop pl ................ FM-9
Sanuk, Oror En—locale ................ FM-9
Sanup Plateau—plain ................ AZ-5
Sanur Plateau ................ AZ-5
Sanusi Creek—stream ................ AL-4
San Valentine Windmill—locale ................ TX-5
Sanvantine Creek ................ PA-2
San Ventura Palica ................ FL-3
San Vicente—CDP ................ MH-9
San Vicente—civil ................ CA-9
San Vicente—locale ................ AZ-5
**San Vicente**—pop pl ................ GU-9
**San Vicente**—pop pl ................ PR-3
San Vicente Arroyo—stream ................ NM-5
San Vicente (Berreyesa)—civil ................ CA-9
San Vicente Cem—cemetery ................ TX-5
San Vicente Creek—stream (3) ................ CA-9
San Vicente Crossing—locale ................ TX-5
San Vicente Drainage Ditch—canal ................ TX-5
San Vicente (Escarrillo)—civil ................ CA-9
San Vicente Mtn—summit (2) ................ CA-9
San Vicente (Munrass)—civil (2) ................ CA-9
San Vicente Rsvr—reservoir ................ CA-9
San Vicente Sch—school ................ CA-9
San Vicente Sch—school ................ TX-5
San Vicente Sch—school ................ GU-9
San Vicente (Site)—locale ................ TX-5
San Vicente Valley—valley ................ CA-9
San Vicente Wash—stream ................ AZ-5
San Vicente Y Santa Monica—civil (2) ................ CA-9
**Sanville**—pop pl ................ VA-3
San Vincent Canyon—valley ................ TX-5
San Vincente—locale ................ NM-5
**San Vincente**—pop pl ................ MH-9
San Vincente, Sierra—summit ................ TX-5
San Vincente Cem—cemetery ................ TX-5
San Vitores Martyrdom Site—hist pl ................ GU-9
**San Xavier**—pop pl ................ AZ-5
San Xavier del Bac ................ AZ-5
San Xavier del Bac—hist pl ................ AZ-5
San Xavier del Bac Mission—church ................ AZ-5
San Xavier Ind Res—reserve ................ AZ-5
San Xavier Interchange—crossing ................ AZ-5
San Xavier Mine—mine ................ AZ-5
San Xavier Mission Complex Archeol District—hist pl ................ TX-5
San Xavier Plaza Shop Ctr—locale ................ AZ-5
San Ysdiro Cem—cemetery ................ NM-5
San Ysidro Ch—church ................ NM-5
Sanybel Island ................ FL-3
Sanybel River ................ FL-3
San Y Ca Spring—spring ................ CA-9
**San Ygnacio**—pop pl ................ TX-5
San Ygnacio (CCD)—cens area ................ TX-5
San Ygnacio Creek—stream ................ TX-5
San Ygnacio Hist Dist—hist pl ................ TX-5
San Ygnacio Ranch—locale ................ TX-5
San Ysabell Creek ................ CA-9
San Ysidro ................ AZ-5
San Ysidro—civil ................ NM-5
**San Ysidro**—pop pl (2) ................ CA-9
**San Ysidro**—pop pl ................ NM-5
San Ysidro Acad—school ................ CA-9
San Ysidro Canyon—valley ................ CA-9
San Ysidro Cem—cemetery ................ TX-5
San Ysidro Ch—church (2) ................ NM-5
San Ysidro Ch and Cemetery—church ................ NM-5
San Ysidro Church—hist pl ................ NM-5
San Ysidro Creek—stream (3) ................ CA-9
San Ysidro (Gilroy)—civil ................ CA-9
San Ysidro Hacienda—hist pl ................ AZ-5
San Ysidro Mountains—range ................ CA-9
San Ysidro Mtn—summit ................ CA-9
San Ysidro Oratorio—hist pl ................ NM-5
San Ysidro (Ortega)—civil ................ CA-9
San Ysidro Sch—school ................ CA-9
San Ysidro Tank—reservoir ................ TX-5
San Ysidro Trail—trail ................ CA-9
Saoksa—locale ................ FM-9
Saoksa, Foko—reef ................ FM-9
Sa'ole (County of)—civ div ................ AS-9
Sa-ol-Sooth, Lake—lake ................ MT-8
Saook Bay—bay ................ AK-9
Saook Point—cape ................ AK-9
**Sapa**—pop pl ................ MS-4
Sapa Baptist Ch—church ................ MS-4
Sapa Cem—cemetery ................ MS-4
Sapa Chitto (historical)—locale ................ MS-4
Sapala River ................ GA-3
Sapaloop Creek ................ WA-9
Sapan ................ MH-9
Sapan Anang, Ochen—bar ................ FM-9
Sapano Vaya—locale ................ AZ-5
Sapa Post Office (historical)—building ................ MS-4
Sapaque Creek—stream ................ CA-9
Sapaque Valley—valley ................ CA-9
Sapa Sch (historical)—school ................ MS-4
Sapata—civil ................ FM-9
Sapata Kumi ................ FM-9
Sapata Lake ................ TX-5
**Sapato, Oror En**—pop pl ................ FM-9
Sap Branch—stream ................ KY-4
Sap Brook—stream ................ PA-2
Sapbush Creek—stream ................ NY-2
Sapello—locale ................ NM-5
Sapello River—stream ................ NM-5
Sapelo ................ GA-3
Sapeloe Island ................ GA-3
Sapelo Island—island ................ GA-3
**Sapelo Island**—pop pl ................ GA-3
Sapelo River—stream ................ GA-3
Sapelo Sound—bay ................ GA-3
Sap Gulch—valley ................ UT-8
Sapho ................ WA-9
Saphom Ruins—locale ................ ID-8
Sapila River ................ GA-3
Sapillo Creek—stream ................ NM-5
Sapillo Trail—trail ................ NM-5
Sapillo Trail (Pack)—trail ................ NM-5
Sapinaro Creek ................ CO-8
Sapinero—locale ................ CO-8
Sapinero Creek ................ CO-8
Sapinero Mesa ................ CO-8
Sapinero Mesa—summit ................ CO-8
Sapinero Ranger Station—locale ................ CO-8
Sapington Chapel ................ OK-5
Sapinimatok Island—island ................ FM-9
Sapino, Unun En—bar ................ FM-9
**Sapitiu**—pop pl ................ FM-9
Sapitiw ................ FM-9
Sap Lake—lake ................ MN-6
Saplin Bay—swamp ................ FL-3
Sapling Branch—stream ................ FL-3
Sapling Creek—stream (2) ................ MS-4
Sapling Gap—gap (2) ................ GA-3
Sapling Hill Cem—cemetery ................ ME-1
Sapling Mine—mine ................ TN-4
Sapling Mtn—summit ................ MS-4
Sapling Mtn—summit ................ NC-3

Sargent Brook—*stream* ... MA-1
Sargent Brook—*stream* ... VT-1
Sargent Butte—*summit* ... OR-9
Sargent Canyon—*valley* ... CA-9
Sargent Canyon—*valley* (2) ... NM-5
Sargent Cem—*cemetery* ... AL-4
Sargent Cem—*cemetery* ... ME-1
Sargent Cem—*cemetery* ... MS-4
Sargent Cem—*cemetery* ... MO-7
Sargent Cem—*cemetery* ... NH-1
Sargent Cem—*cemetery* ... TX-5
**Sargent Corners**—*pop pl* ... NH-1
Sargent County—*civil* ... ND-7
Sargent County Courthouse—*hist pl* ... ND-7
*Sargent Cove* ... ME-1
Sargent Cove—*bay* ... NH-1
Sargent Creek—*stream* (5) ... AK-9
Sargent Creek—*stream* (2) ... CA-9
Sargent Creek—*stream* ... MI-6
Sargent Creek—*stream* ... MN-6
Sargent Creek—*stream* ... MT-8
Sargent Creek—*stream* ... OR-9
*Sargent Dam* ... SD-7
Sargent Dam—*dam* ... AL-4
Sargent Ditch—*canal* ... IN-6
Sargent Ditch—*canal* ... NM-5
Sargent Head—*cape* ... ME-1
Sargent Hill—*summit* ... MA-1
Sargent Hill—*summit* (3) ... NH-1
Sargent Hill—*summit* (3) ... VT-1
Sargent Hills—*area* ... CA-9
Sargent Hollow—*valley* ... VA-3
Sargent House—*hist pl* ... LA-4
Sargent HS—*school* ... CO-8
Sargent Ice Field—*glacier* ... AK-9
Sargent Irrigation Project Dam—*dam* ... SD-7
Sargent Island—*island* ... NY-2
Sargent Lake—*lake* ... LA-4
Sargent Lake—*lake* ... MI-6
Sargent Lake—*lake* ... MN-6
Sargent Lake—*lake* ... NH-1
Sargent Lake—*lake* (2) ... UT-8
Sargent Lakes—*reservoir* ... UT-8
Sargent Millpond—*lake* ... MA-1
Sargent Mine—*mine* ... MN-6
Sargent Mtn—*summit* (2) ... ME-1
Sargent Mtn—*summit* ... UT-8
Sargent-Murray-Gilmon-Hough House—*building* ... MA-1
Sargent Number One Dam—*dam* ... UT-8
Sargent Number One Rsvr—*reservoir* ... UT-8
Sargent Oil Field—*oilfield* ... CA-9
Sargent Park—*park* ... MN-6
Sargent Place—*locale* ... OR-9
Sargent Point—*cape* ... LA-4
Sargent Point—*cape* ... ME-1
Sargent Pond—*lake* ... MA-1
Sargent Pond—*reservoir* ... MA-1
Sargent Pond—*reservoir* ... VT-1
Sargent Pond Dam—*dam* ... MA-1
Sargent Ponds—*lake* ... NY-2
Sargent Ranch—*locale* ... NM-5
*Sargent Reservoir* ... NH-1
Sargent River—*stream* ... CT-1
**Sargents**—*pop pl* ... CO-8
**Sargents**—*pop pl* ... OH-6
Sargents Bay—*bay* ... WY-8
Sargent Sch—*school* ... MA-1
Sargent Sch—*school* ... MO-7
Sargents Chapel—*church* ... MO-7
*Sargent's Cove* ... ME-1
Sargents Creek—*stream* ... MI-6
Sargents Creek—*stream* ... NC-3
*Sargents Island* ... NY-2
Sargents Island—*island* ... ME-1
Sargent Slough—*stream* ... IL-6
Sargents Mesa—*summit* ... CO-8
Sargents Point—*cape* ... ME-1
*Sargents Pond* ... MA-1
Sargent's Pond—*hist pl* ... MA-1
Sargents Pond—*lake* ... NH-1
Sargents Purchase—*civil* ... NH-1
Sargents Ridge—*ridge* ... CA-9
**Sargents School**—*pop pl* ... CO-8
Sargents Spur—*ridge* ... IA-7
Sargents Wharf—*locale* ... MA-1
Sargent Tank—*reservoir* (3) ... NM-5
**Sargent Township**—*pop pl* ... MO-7
**Sargent Township**—*pop pl* ... NE-7
**Sargent Township**—*pop pl* ... ND-7
**Sargent (Township of)**—*pop pl* ... IL-6
Sargent Valley—*valley* ... NE-7
Sargent Valley Sch—*school* ... NE-7
**Sargentville**—*pop pl* ... ME-1
Sargent Well—*well* ... AZ-5
Sargent Yards—*locale* ... TN-4
Sarges Branch—*stream* ... KY-4
Sarghum Belt Tank—*reservoir* ... TX-5
Sargon (historical)—*locale* ... AL-4
Sargs Run—*stream* ... IN-6
Sarheen Cove—*bay* ... AK-9
*Sari* ... MH-9
Sarian, Bayou—*stream* ... LA-4
Sarichef Island—*island* ... AK-9
Sarichef Strait—*channel* ... AK-9
Sarietta Ch—*church* ... WV-2
Sarigan—*island* ... MH-9
*Sarigan Insel* ... MH-9
*Sarigan Island* ... MH-9
*Sarignan* ... MH-9
*Sarigoan* ... MH-9
*Sariguan* ... MH-9
Sarikoski Cem—*cemetery* ... MN-6
*Sarillo Creek* ... TX-5
Sario Canyon—*valley* ... CA-9
Sarion Ch—*church* ... SC-3
Sario Ranch—*locale* ... CA-9
Sario Well—*well* ... NV-8
Sarisfield Mine—*mine* ... CO-8
**Sarita**—*pop pl* ... TX-5
Sarita Airp—*airport* ... AZ-5
Sarita Artesian Well—*well* ... TX-5
Sarita (CCD)—*cens area* ... TX-5
Sarita Cem—*cemetery* ... TX-5
Sarita Windmill—*locale* ... TX-5
Sarkar Cove—*bay* ... AK-9
Sarkar Creek—*stream* ... AK-9
Sarkar Lake—*lake* ... AK-9
Sarker Point—*cape* ... AK-9
*Sarkey* ... MO-7
Sarle Drain—*stream* ... MI-6
*Sarles* ... ND-7
**Sarles**—*pop pl* ... ND-7
Sarles, O. C., House—*hist pl* ... ND-7
Sarles Cem—*cemetery* ... NY-2
**Sarles Corners**—*pop pl* ... NY-2
Sarles Hill—*summit* ... NY-2
Sarles Lake—*reservoir* ... TX-5
Sarles' Tavern—*hist pl* ... NY-2
Sarnia Dam—*dam* ... ND-7
**Sarnia Township**—*pop pl* ... ND-7
Sarno Plaza (Shop Ctr)—*locale* ... FL-3
Sarnosa Hill—*summit* ... TX-5
Sarnosa Oil Field—*oilfield* ... TX-5
Sarnoski Hill—*summit* ... PA-2
**Sarona**—*pop pl* ... WI-6
Sarona Cem—*cemetery* ... WI-6
**Sarona (Town of)**—*pop pl* ... WI-6
Saron Cem—*cemetery* ... KS-7
Saron Cem—*cemetery* (2) ... MN-6
Saron Cem—*cemetery* ... NE-7
Saron Cem—*cemetery* ... ND-7
Saron Cem—*cemetery* ... OK-5
Saron Cem—*cemetery* ... SD-7
Saron Cem—*cemetery* ... TX-5
Saron Ch—*church* ... IL-6
Saron Ch—*church* (3) ... MN-6
Saron Ch—*church* (3) ... NC-3
Saron Ch—*church* ... ND-7
Saron Ch—*church* ... OK-5
Saron Ch—*church* (3) ... SD-7
Saron Ch—*church* ... WI-6
Saroni Canal—*canal* ... NV-8
**Saronville**—*pop pl* ... NE-7
Saronville Cem—*cemetery* ... NE-7
*Saroute Creek* ... OR-9
*Saroutte Creek* ... OR-9
*Sarpan* ... MH-9
*Sarpana O'Rota* ... MH-9
*Sarpanta* ... MH-9
*Sar Passage* ... PW-9
Sar Passage—*channel* ... PW-9
Sarpsborg Ch—*church* ... MN-6
*Sarpy* ... LA-4
Sarpy, Peter A., Trading Post Site—*hist pl* ... NE-7
Sarpy Center Sch—*school* ... NE-7
Sarpy Creek—*stream* ... MT-8
Sarpy Creek Mine—*mine* ... MT-8
**Sarpy Junction**—*pop pl* ... MT-8
Sarpy Mtns—*summit* ... MT-8
Sarpy Sch—*school* ... MT-8
Sarracino Ranch—*locale* ... NM-5
Sarrah Hollow—*valley* ... IL-6
Sarratt Cem—*cemetery* ... AL-4
Sarratt Creek—*stream* ... SC-3
Sarratt House—*hist pl* ... SC-3
Sarrett Branch—*stream* ... NC-3
Sarrett Cem—*cemetery* ... WV-2
Sarrett-Lemon Cem—*cemetery* ... WV-2
Sarsaparilla Windmill—*locale* ... NM-5
Sarsapkin Creek—*stream* ... WA-9
Sarsapkin Creek Trail—*trail* ... WA-9
Sarshalom Hebrew Acad—*school* ... FL-3
*Sarsilla Canyon* ... CO-8
*Sarsillo Canyon* ... CO-8
Sarson Island—*island* ... MA-1
*Sarsons Island* ... MA-1
Sartain Bend—*bend* ... AL-4
Sartain Branch—*stream* ... TN-4
Sartain Branch—*stream* ... VA-3
*Sartain Cem* ... TN-4
Sartain Cem—*cemetery* ... TN-4
Sartain Hollow—*valley* ... TN-4
Sartain Sch—*school* ... PA-2
Sartain Spring—*spring* ... TN-4
**Sartain Springs**—*pop pl* ... TN-4
Sartain Springs Ch—*church* ... TN-4
**Sartains Ridgecrest Subdivision (subdivision)**—*pop pl* ... AL-4
Sartan Lake Dam—*dam* ... MS-4
**Sartell**—*pop pl* ... MN-6
Sartell State Wildlife Mngmt Area—*park* ... MN-6
Sartell Swamp—*swamp* ... MN-6
Sarter Creek—*stream* ... MS-4
*Sartex* ... SC-3
Sartin Bluff—*cliff* ... TX-5
*Sartin Branch* ... TN-4
Sartin Cem—*cemetery* ... MO-7
Sartin Cem—*cemetery* ... TN-4
Sartin Draw—*valley* ... MT-8
Sartin Draw Rsvr—*reservoir* ... MT-8
Sartin Draw Spring—*spring* ... MT-8
Sartin Mill Branch—*stream* ... AL-4
*Sartinsville* ... MS-4
**Sartinsville**—*pop pl* ... MS-4
Sartinville—*locale* ... MS-4
Sartinville Cem—*cemetery* ... MS-4
Sartinville Ch—*church* ... MS-4
Sartinville Post Office (historical)—*building* ... MS-4
Sartin Windmill—*locale* ... NM-5
**Sarton**—*pop pl* ... WV-2
Sarton Branch—*stream* ... WV-2
Sarton Ridge—*ridge* ... VA-3
Sartor Cem—*cemetery* ... MS-4
Sartor Ditch—*canal* ... IN-6
Sartorette Sch—*school* ... CA-9
Sartoria—*locale* ... NE-7
**Sartoria Township**—*pop pl* ... NE-7
Sartori Gulch—*valley* ... CA-9
Sartori Hosp—*hospital* ... IA-7
Sartori Sch—*school* ... WA-9
Sartorius Sch—*school* ... MO-7
**Sartwell**—*pop pl* ... PA-2
Sartwell Creek—*stream* ... PA-2
Sartwell Creek Ch—*church* ... PA-2
Sartwelle Lakes—*lake* ... TX-5
Sartwell Oil Field—*oilfield* (2) ... PA-2
Saruche Canyon—*valley* ... CO-8
Saruche Canyon—*valley* ... NM-5
*Saru Jima* ... FM-9
Sarum—*hist pl* ... MD-2
*Sarupaniya* ... MH-9
*Saru-Shi* ... FM-9
*Sarutoeshi* ... MP-9
*Sarutoeshi-To* ... MP-9
*Sar Valley Creek* ... AL-4
*Sarvant Glacier* ... WA-9
Sarvant Glaciers—*glacier* ... WA-9
*Sarvent Glacier* ... WA-9
**Sarver**—*pop pl* ... PA-2
Sarver Cem—*cemetery* ... VA-3
Sarver Ch—*church* ... PA-2
Sarver Hollow—*valley* ... VA-3
Sarver Run—*stream* (2) ... PA-2
Sarver Sch—*school* ... WV-2
**Sarversville**—*pop pl* ... PA-2
*Sarvice Creek* ... OR-9
*Sarvice Hollow* ... WA-9
Sarvis Branch—*stream* ... KY-4
Sarvis Branch—*stream* ... MO-7
Sarvis Branch—*stream* ... TN-4
*Sarvis Buttes* ... OR-9
*Sarvis Canyon* ... OR-9
Sarvis Ch (historical)—*church* ... AL-4
Sarvis Cove Creek—*stream* ... TN-4
Sarvis Crossroads—*locale* ... SC-3
Sarvis Fork—*stream* ... WV-2
Sarvis Fork Covered Bridge—*hist pl* ... WV-2
Sarvis Fork Sch—*school* ... WV-2
Sarvis Gap—*gap* ... GA-3
Sarvis Gap—*gap* ... NC-3
Sarvis Park—*park* ... MI-6
Sarvis Ridge—*ridge* ... NC-3
Sarvls Cove—*valley* ... TN-4
Sarvorum Mtn—*summit* ... CA-9
Sarzotti Park—*park* ... CA-9
Sasa—*area* ... GU-9
**Sasabe**—*pop pl* ... AZ-5
Sasabe, Arroyo del—*valley* ... AZ-5
*Sasabe Flat* ... AZ-5
*Sasacaeheh Pond* ... MA-1
Sasacat Creek—*stream* ... WI-6
Sasacat Lake—*lake* ... WI-6
*Sasagachah Pond* ... MA-1
Sasajyan—*area* ... GU-9
**Sasakwa**—*pop pl* ... OK-5
Sasalaguan, Mount—*summit* ... GU-9
*Sasanha* ... MH-9
*Sasanhaia* ... MH-9
*Sasanhaia Bucht* ... MH-9
*Sasanhaya*—*bay* ... MH-9
*Sasanhiya* ... MH-9
*Sasan Island* ... MA-1
*Sasanlago* ... MH-9
*Sasanlago Bucht* ... MH-9
Sasanlagu—*harbor* ... MH-9
Sasanoa Point—*cape* ... ME-1
Sasanoa River—*gut* ... ME-1
Sasa River—*stream* ... GU-9
Sasby Island—*island* ... AK-9
*Sasco* ... AZ-5
*Sasco Beach* ... CT-1
Sasco Brook—*stream* ... CT-1
Sasco Cem—*cemetery* ... AZ-5
Sasco Hill—*summit* ... CT-1
Sasco Hill Beach—*beach* ... CT-1
Sasco Ruins—*locale* ... AZ-5
Sasco Tank—*reservoir* ... AZ-5
Sasedni Island—*island* ... AK-9
Sase Nasket—*bench* ... AZ-5
Sash—*locale* ... TX-5
Sashabaw Creek—*stream* ... MI-6
Sashabaw Presbyterian Church—*hist pl* ... MI-6
Sashabaw Sch—*school* ... MI-6
Sash Factory Creek—*stream* ... NY-2
Sashin Creek—*stream* ... AK-9
Sashin Lake—*lake* ... AK-9
Sash Lake—*lake* ... MN-6
Saska Peak—*summit* ... WA-9
Saskatchewan Butte—*summit* ... MT-8
Saskatoon Golf Course—*other* ... MI-6
Sasnett Mill Branch—*stream* ... NC-3
*Sason Island* ... MA-1
*Sasons Island* ... MA-1
**Saspamco**—*pop pl* ... TX-5
*Saspan* ... MH-9
Sasqua Hill—*summit* ... CT-1
Sasquatch Steps—*area* ... WA-9
*Sassacowens Pond* ... MA-1
Sassacus Creek—*stream* ... NE-7
*Sassafras* ... NC-3
Sassafras—*locale* ... VA-3
Sassafras—*locale* ... WV-2
**Sassafras**—*pop pl* ... IN-6
**Sassafras**—*pop pl* ... KY-4
**Sassafras**—*pop pl* ... MD-2
Sassafras Bayou—*gut* ... LA-4
*Sassafras Branch* ... OK-5
Sassafras Branch—*stream* ... GA-3
Sassafras Branch—*stream* ... LA-4
Sassafras Branch—*stream* (6) ... NC-3
Sassafras Branch—*stream* ... TX-5
Sassafras Cem—*cemetery* ... IL-6
*Sassafras Creek* ... OK-5
Sassafras Creek—*stream* ... AR-4
Sassafras Creek—*stream* ... KY-4
Sassafras Creek—*stream* (3) ... NC-3
Sassafras Creek—*stream* (3) ... OK-5
Sassafras Falls—*falls* ... NC-3
*Sassafras Fork* ... NC-3
Sassafras Fork (Township of)—*fmr MCD* ... NC-3
Sassafras Gap—*gap* (3) ... GA-3
Sassafras Gap—*gap* (10) ... NC-3
Sassafras Gap—*gap* ... SC-3
Sassafras Grove Ch—*church* ... KY-4
Sassafras Grove Ch—*church* ... NC-3
Sassafras Grove Ch (historical)—*church* ... TN-4
Sassafras Hill—*summit* ... SC-3
Sassafras Island—*island* (2) ... LA-4
Sassafras Island—*island* ... NJ-2
Sassafras Island—*island* ... PA-2
Sassafras Island—*island* ... RI-1
Sassafras Knob—*summit* ... AR-4
Sassafras Knob—*summit* ... GA-3
Sassafras Knob—*summit* (7) ... NC-3
Sassafras Knob—*summit* ... TN-4
Sassafras Knob—*summit* ... WV-2
Sassafras Lake—*lake* ... MI-6
Sassafras Landing—*locale* ... DE-2
*Sassafras Mtn* ... TN-4
Sassafras Mtn—*summit* (2) ... GA-3
Sassafras Mtn—*summit* (3) ... NC-3
Sassafras Mtn—*summit* ... SC-3
Sassafras Mtn—*summit* ... TN-4
Sassafras Neck—*cape* ... MD-2
Sassafras Point—*cape* ... OH-6
Sassafras Point—*cape* ... RI-1
**Sassafras Ridge**—*pop pl* ... KY-4
Sassafras Ridge—*ridge* ... KY-4
Sassafras Ridge—*ridge* (4) ... NC-3
Sassafras Ridge—*ridge* (2) ... TN-4
Sassafras Ridge—*ridge* ... WV-2
*Sassafras Ridge Cemetery* ... MO-7
Sassafras Ridge Ch—*church* ... KY-4
Sassafras Ridge Ch (abandoned)—*church* ... MO-7
Sassafras Ridge Sch (abandoned)—*school* ... MO-7
Sassafras Ridge (Site 15 FU 3)—*hist pl* ... KY-4
Sassafras River—*stream* ... DE-2
Sassafras River—*stream* ... MD-2
Sassafras Run—*stream* ... WV-2
Sassafras Sch—*school* ... KY-4
Sassafras Site, RI-55—*hist pl* ... RI-1
*Sassafrass Ridge* ... MO-7
Sassafras Stand Ridge—*ridge* ... TN-4
*Sassafras Station* ... DE-2
**Sassafras Switch**—*pop pl* ... WV-2
Sassafras Trail—*trail* ... PA-2
Sassamans Sch—*school* ... PA-2
**Sassamansville**—*pop pl* ... PA-2
*Sassanoa River* ... ME-1
Sassaquin—*uninc pl* ... MA-1
Sassaquin Pond—*lake* ... MA-1
*Sassaquins Pond* ... MA-1
Sassarini Sch—*school* ... CA-9
Sassarixa Creek—*stream* ... NC-3
Sassas Creek—*stream* ... MN-6
*Sassawitch Beach* ... RI-1
Sasse Lake—*lake* ... MN-6
Sasse Mountain Trail—*trail* ... WA-9
Sasse Mtn—*summit* ... WA-9
*Sassenow River* ... ME-1
Sasser—*locale* ... KY-4
**Sasser**—*pop pl* ... GA-3
Sasse Ranch—*locale* ... SD-7
Sasser Branch—*stream* (2) ... AL-4
Sasser Branch—*stream* ... KY-4
Sasser (CCD)—*cens area* ... GA-3
Sasser Cem—*cemetery* (2) ... GA-3
Sasser Cem—*cemetery* ... KY-4
Sasser Cem—*cemetery* ... NC-3
Sasser Cem—*cemetery* ... TN-4
Sasser Ch—*church* ... AL-4
Sasser Commercial Hist Dist—*hist pl* ... GA-3
Sasser Farm—*hist pl* ... GA-3
Sasse Ridge—*ridge* ... WA-9
Sasser Lake—*lake* ... GA-3
Sasser Landing Cem—*cemetery* ... FL-3
Sasser Millpond—*reservoir* ... NC-3
Sasser Playground—*park* ... MI-6
Sasser Pond Dam—*dam* ... MS-4
Sasser Sch (historical)—*school* (2) ... AL-4
**Sassers Mill**—*pop pl* ... NC-3
Sassers Mill Ch—*church* ... AL-4
Sassers Mill Creek—*stream* ... MS-4
Sasser Store (historical)—*locale* ... AL-4
Sasses Branch—*stream* ... NC-3
Sassfrass Branch—*stream* ... NC-3
Sassick Butte—*summit* ... WY-8
Sassie Grove Ch—*church* ... GA-3
Sassin Cem—*cemetery* ... WA-9
Sassin Ch—*church* ... VA-3
Sassman Cem—*cemetery* ... WI-6
Sassman Gulch—*valley* ... MT-8
Sasso Park—*park* ... FL-3
Sasspan Bay—*swamp* ... NC-3
Sasspan Branch—*stream* ... NC-3
Sass Sch—*school* ... IL-6
Sassy Branch—*stream* ... KY-4
*Sastanha Mesa* ... AZ-5
*Sastonho Mesa* ... AZ-5
Satago Lake—*lake* ... MI-6
Satailak Creek—*stream* ... AK-9
**Satala**—*pop pl* ... AS-9
Satan Butte—*summit* ... AZ-5
Satan Canyon—*valley* ... TX-5
Satan Creek Forest Camp—*locale* ... OR-9
Satan Hill—*summit* ... IN-6
**Satank**—*pop pl* ... CO-8
S A Tank—*reservoir* ... AZ-5
SA Tank—*reservoir* ... NM-5
Satanka Cove—*bay* ... CO-8
Satank Bridge—*hist pl* ... CO-8
Satan Lake—*lake* ... ID-8
Satan Pass—*gap* ... NM-5
Satan Pass Canyon—*valley* ... NM-5
Satan Rock—*rock* ... MA-1
Satan Shoal—*bar* ... FL-3
Satans Kingdom—*other* ... CT-1
**Satans Kingdom**—*pop pl* ... MA-1
**Satans Kingdom**—*pop pl* ... VT-1
Satans Kingdom—*ridge* ... MA-1
Satans Toe—*cape* ... NY-2
**Satanta**—*pop pl* ... KS-7
Satanta Canal—*canal* ... CO-8
*Satanta Landing Strip* ... KS-7
Satanta Municipal Airp—*airport* ... KS-7
**Satartia**—*pop pl* ... MS-4
Satartia Landing—*locale* ... MS-4
Satartia Sch—*school* ... MS-4
*Satas* ... WA-9
*Satas River* ... WA-9
Satathite Mtn—*summit* ... AZ-5
Satathite Place—*locale* ... NM-5
Satawal—*island* ... FM-9
Satawal (Municipality)—*civ div* ... FM-9
Satawan—*CDP* ... FM-9
Satawan—*island* ... FM-9
Satawan Anchorage—*harbor* ... FM-9
Satawan Atoll—*island* ... FM-9
Satawan (Municipality)—*civ div* ... FM-9
Sat Brown Branch—*stream* ... GA-3
Satchel Cem—*cemetery* ... OH-6
Satchel Creek—*stream* ... KS-7
Satchel Ford Road Sch—*school* ... SC-3
*Satchel Mountain* ... NC-3
Satchel Pond—*reservoir* ... GA-3
Satcher Branch—*stream* ... SC-3
Satchin Cliff—*cliff* ... AZ-5
**Satellite Beach**—*pop pl* ... FL-3
Satellite Beach Public Library—*building* ... FL-3
Satellite HS—*school* ... FL-3
Satellite Island—*island* ... WA-9
Satellite Lake—*lake* ... CA-9
Satenfield Cem—*cemetery* ... IN-6
Sater Cem—*cemetery* ... OH-6
Sater Meadows—*flat* ... ID-8
Sater Run—*stream* ... IN-6
Sater Run—*stream* ... OH-6
Saters Ch—*church* ... MD-2
Satersdal Cem—*cemetery* ... MN-6
Sates Gamble Cem—*cemetery* ... OH-6
Sather Dam—*dam* ... ND-7
Sather Gate—*uninc pl* ... CA-9
Sather Gate and Bridge—*hist pl* ... CA-9
Sather Lake—*lake* (2) ... MN-6
Sather Lake—*reservoir* ... ND-7
Sather Lake Rec Area—*park* ... ND-7
Sather Park—*park* ... WA-9
Sather Rsvr—*reservoir* ... ND-7
Sather Tower—*hist pl* ... CA-9
**Saticoy**—*pop pl* ... CA-9
Saticoy Country Club—*other* ... CA-9
Saticoy Sch—*school* ... CA-9
Satilla—*locale* ... GA-3
Satilla Bluff—*cliff* ... GA-3
Satilla Cem—*cemetery* ... GA-3
Satilla Ch—*church* (3) ... GA-3
*Satilla Creek* ... GA-3
Satilla Creek—*stream* (2) ... GA-3
Satilla Creek (CCD)—*cens area* ... GA-3
*Satilla River* ... GA-3
Satilla River—*stream* ... GA-3
Satilla Sch—*school* ... GA-3
**Satilla Shores**—*pop pl* ... GA-3
Satilla Swamp—*swamp* ... GA-3
*Satilpa Creek* ... AL-4
**Satin**—*pop pl* ... TX-5
Satinfield Ch—*church* ... IL-6
Satin Peak—*summit* ... CA-9
Satire Mtn—*summit* ... MT-8
Satler Cem—*cemetery* ... TX-5
Satlerfield Cem—*cemetery* ... TN-4
*Satler Run* ... PA-2
Sato—*locale* ... IL-6
Sato—*uninc pl* ... SC-3
Satolah—*locale* ... GA-3
Satopa Park—*park* ... MI-6
*Satres Gulch* ... CO-8
Satser Branch—*stream* ... NC-3
**Satsop**—*pop pl* ... WA-9
Satsop Guard Station—*locale* ... WA-9
Satsop Lakes—*lake* ... WA-9
Satsop River—*stream* ... WA-9
Satsuit Meadow—*swamp* ... MA-1
Satsuma—*locale* ... LA-4
Satsuma—*locale* ... TX-5
**Satsuma**—*pop pl* ... AL-4
**Satsuma**—*pop pl* ... FL-3
Satsuma Assembly of God Ch—*church* ... AL-4
Satsuma Cem—*cemetery* ... AL-4
Satsuma Cem—*cemetery* ... FL-3
Satsuma Ch—*church* ... LA-4
Satsuma Chapel—*church* ... TX-5
**Satsuma Heights**—*pop pl* ... FL-3
Satsuma HS—*school* ... AL-4
Satsuma Lions Park—*park* ... AL-4
Satsuma Methodist Ch—*church* ... AL-4
Satsuma Municipal Park—*park* ... AL-4
Sattazahn Ch—*church* ... PA-2
*Sattellite Island* ... WA-9
Sattell Knoll Substation—*locale* ... AZ-5
Satter Creek—*stream* ... OR-9
Satterfield—*locale* ... PA-2
**Satterfield**—*pop pl* ... PA-2
Satterfield, Emory Edward, House—*hist pl* ... GA-3
Satterfield Branch—*stream* ... GA-3
Satterfield Branch—*stream* ... OK-5
Satterfield Camp—*locale* ... AL-4
Satterfield Cem—*cemetery* ... OH-6
Satterfield Chapel—*church* ... OH-6
*Satterfield Creek* ... NC-3
Satterfield Creek—*stream* ... NC-3
Satterfield Hollow—*valley* ... MO-7
*Satterfield Junction* ... PA-2
**Satterfield Junction**—*pop pl* ... PA-2
Satterfield Sch (historical)—*school* ... MO-7
Satterfield Store—*building* ... GA-3
Satterlee Creek—*stream* ... PA-2
Satterlee Hollow—*valley* ... NY-2
Satterlee Run—*stream* ... PA-2
Satterlee Sch—*school* ... MI-6
*Satterley* ... MD-2
*Satterley Point* ... MD-2
Satterlund Sch Number 2—*school* ... ND-7
Satterly Corners—*locale* ... NY-2
Satterly Creek—*stream* ... NY-2
Satterly Gulch—*valley* ... CO-8
Satterly Hill—*summit* ... NY-2
Satterly Lake—*lake* ... MI-6
Satterthwaite, John, House—*hist pl* ... OH-6
Satterthwaite Creek—*stream* ... NC-3
Satterthwaite Point—*cape* ... NC-3
Satterthwaites Run—*stream* ... OH-6
Satterwhite—*locale* ... OK-5
**Satterwhite**—*pop pl* ... NC-3
Satterwhite Branch—*stream* ... GA-3
Satterwhite Point—*cape* ... NC-3
Satterwhite Rec Area—*park* ... NC-3
**Sattes**—*pop pl* ... WV-2
Sattison Ditch—*canal* ... IN-6
**Sattler**—*pop pl* ... TX-5
Sattler Draw—*valley* ... WY-8
**Sattley**—*pop pl* ... CA-9
Sattre—*locale* ... IA-7
*Satucket* ... MA-1
**Satucket**—*pop pl* ... MA-1
*Satucket, Town of* ... MA-1
*Satucket River* ... MA-1
Satucket River—*stream* ... MA-1
*Satuckett* ... MA-1
*Satuckett, Town of* ... MA-1
*Satuit* ... MA-1
Satuit Brook—*stream* ... MA-1
Satulah Branch—*stream* ... NC-3
Satulah Falls—*falls* ... NC-3
Satulah Mtn—*summit* ... NC-3
*Satula Mtn* ... NC-3
Satulick Mtn—*summit* ... WA-9
Satuma—*locale* ... AR-4
Saturday Bay—*bay* ... MN-6
Saturday Camp—*locale* ... CA-9
Saturday Cave—*cave* ... AL-4
Saturday Cem—*cemetery* ... GA-3
Saturday Club—*hist pl* ... PA-2
Saturday Cove—*bay* ... ME-1
Saturday Cove Cem—*cemetery* ... ME-1
Saturday Creek—*stream* (2) ... AK-9
Saturday Creek—*stream* ... ID-8
*Saturday Island* ... FM-9
Saturday Islands—*island* ... WI-6
Saturday Mtn—*summit* ... ID-8
Saturday Night Hill—*summit* ... MT-8
Saturday Night Ledge—*rock* ... MA-1
Saturday Peak—*summit* ... CA-9
Saturday Pond—*lake* ... ME-1
Saturday Pond (historical)—*lake* ... ME-1
Saturday Ridge—*ridge* ... ID-8
Saturday Rock—*summit* ... WA-9
Saturday Spring—*spring* ... CA-9
Saturday Spring Creek—*stream* ... CA-9
Saturn—*lake* ... AK-9
**Saturn**—*pop pl* ... IN-6
**Saturn**—*pop pl* ... TX-5
Saturn Ch—*church* ... IN-6
Saturn Ch—*church* ... TN-4
Saturn Ch—*church* ... TX-5
Saturn Creek—*stream* ... OR-9
Saturn Elem Sch—*school* ... FL-3
Saturno-Breen Truck Garden—*hist pl* ... WA-9
Saturn V Dynamic Test Stand—*hist pl* ... AL-4
Saturn V Space Vehicle—*hist pl* ... AL-4
Satus—*locale* ... WA-9
Satus Bar—*bar* ... WA-9
Satus Creek—*stream* ... WA-9
Satus Longhouse—*locale* ... WA-9
Satus No 2 Pump Canal—*canal* ... WA-9
Satus No 2 Pumping Station—*other* ... WA-9
Satus No 3 Pump Canal—*canal* ... WA-9
Satus No 3 Pumping Station—*other* ... WA-9
Satus Pass—*gap* ... WA-9
Satus Peak—*summit* ... WA-9
Satus Ranger Station—*locale* ... WA-9
**Satyr Hill**—*pop pl* ... MD-2
*Satzer Creek* ... WA-9
Sau—*island* ... FM-9
Saua—*locale* ... AS-9
Sauaimoe Stream—*stream* ... AS-9
SAU at Dorado—*hist pl* ... AR-4
Saubee Lake—*lake* ... MI-6
Saubel Hill—*summit* ... PA-2
Saubel Sch (abandoned)—*school* ... PA-2
Saubert Creek—*stream* ... OR-9
*Sauble* ... MI-6
Sauble—*locale* ... MI-6
Sauble Circle Dot Ranch—*locale* ... NM-5
*Sauble Lake* ... MI-6
Sauble Lakes—*lake* ... MI-6
*Sauble River* ... MI-6
**Sauble (Township of)**—*pop pl* ... MI-6
Sauce Arroyo—*stream* ... CO-8
*Sauceda* ... AZ-5
Sauceda Cem—*cemetery* ... TX-5
Sauceda Creek—*stream* ... TX-5
Sauceda Mountains—*range* ... AZ-5
Sauceda Ranch—*locale* ... TX-5
Sauceda Wash—*stream* ... AZ-5
*Sauceda Well* ... AZ-5
Sauceda Windmill—*locale* ... TX-5
*Saucedo Mountains* ... AZ-5
*Saucelito* ... CA-9
Saucelito—*civil* ... CA-9
Saucelito Creek—*stream* ... CA-9
Saucelito Ridge—*ridge* ... CA-9
Saucepan Creek—*stream* ... NC-3
Sauce Pan Rsvr—*reservoir* ... ID-8
**Saucer**—*pop pl* ... AL-4
Saucer, The—*basin* ... UT-8
Saucer Basin—*basin* ... CO-8
Saucer Basin—*basin* ... UT-8
Saucer Basin Rsvr—*reservoir* ... UT-8
Saucer Basin Well—*well* ... UT-8
Saucer Branch—*stream* ... GA-3
Saucer Branch—*valley* ... CA-9
Saucer Creek—*stream* ... MS-4
Saucer Creek Cem—*cemetery* ... MS-4
Saucer Creek Ch—*church* ... MS-4
*Saucer Creek Ch of Christ* ... MS-4
Saucer Creek Rec Area—*park* ... MS-4
Saucer Lake—*lake* (2) ... CA-9
Saucer Lake—*lake* ... KS-7
Saucer Lake—*lake* ... MN-6
Saucer Lake—*lake* ... UT-8
Saucer Lake—*lake* ... WA-9
Saucerman Cem—*cemetery* ... WI-6
Saucer Meadow—*flat* ... CA-9
Saucer Mesa—*summit* ... NV-8
Sauces, Canada De Los —*valley* (2) ... CA-9
Sauces Well—*well* ... TX-5
Sauce Tank—*reservoir* ... TX-5
Sauce Verde Tank—*reservoir* ... TX-5
Sauch—*tunnel* ... FM-9
*Saucida* ... AZ-5
Saucie Cem—*cemetery* ... SC-3
**Saucier**—*pop pl* ... MS-4
Saucier Camp—*locale* (2) ... ME-1
Saucier Cem—*cemetery* ... MS-4
Saucier Creek—*stream* ... MS-4
Saucier Elem Sch—*school* ... MS-4
Saucier Ranch—*locale* ... TX-5
*Saucita* ... AZ-5
*Saucita Mountains* ... AZ-5
Saucita Tank—*reservoir* ... AZ-5
*Saucito* ... AZ-5
Saucito—*civil* ... CA-9
Saucito Canyon—*valley* ... AZ-5
Saucito Canyon—*valley* ... CA-9
Saucito Mtn—*summit* (2) ... AZ-5
Saucito Ranch—*locale* ... CA-9
Saucito Spring—*spring* (2) ... AZ-5
*Saucito Tank* ... AZ-5
Saucito Wash—*stream* (2) ... AZ-5
Saucito Well—*well* ... AZ-5
Sauck's Covered Bridge—*hist pl* ... PA-2
**Saucon**—*pop pl* ... PA-2
*Saucona* ... PA-2
**Saucona**—*pop pl* ... PA-2
Saucona Pond—*lake* ... PA-2
Saucon Ch—*church* ... PA-2
Saucon Creek—*stream* ... PA-2
Saucon Creek—*stream* ... WA-9
Saucon Gap—*gap* ... PA-2
Saucon Hill—*summit* ... PA-2
Saucon Park—*park* ... PA-2
**Saucon Valley**—*pop pl* ... PA-2
Saucon Valley Country Club—*other* ... PA-2
Saucon Valley JHS—*school* ... PA-2

Sawtooth City—hist pl ... ID-8
Sawtooth City—locale ... ID-8
Sawtooth Cove—valley ... UT-8
Sawtooth Crater—gap ... OR-9
Sawtooth Creek—stream ... CO-8
Sawtooth Creek—stream ... ID-8
Sawtooth Creek—stream ... MT-8
Sawtooth Creek—stream ... OR-9
Sawtooth Creek—stream ... UT-8
Sawtooth Flow—lava (2) ... ID-8
Sawtooth Knob—summit ... NV-8
Sawtooth Lake ... ID-8
Sawtooth Lake—lake ... ID-8
Sawtooth Lake—lake ... MT-8
Sawtooth Lake—lake ... WY-8
Sawtooth Meadows—flat ... OR-9
Sawtooth Meadows—flat ... WY-8
Sawtooth Mountain ... CO-8
Sawtooth Mountains ... CA-9
Sawtooth Mountains—range ... AZ-5
Sawtooth Mountains—range ... CA-9
Sawtooth Mountains—range ... MN-6
Sawtooth Mountains—ridge ... NM-5
Sawtooth Mountains—summit ... NY-2
Sawtooth Mtn—summit (2) ... AK-9
Sawtooth Mtn—summit (2) ... AZ-5
Sawtooth Mtn—summit (4) ... CA-9
Sawtooth Mtn—summit (4) ... CO-8
Sawtooth Mtn—summit (7) ... MT-8
Sawtooth Mtn—summit (2) ... NV-8
Sawtooth Mtn—summit (2) ... OR-9
Sawtooth Mtn—summit ... TX-5
Sawtooth Mtn—summit ... UT-8
Sawtooth Mtn—summit ... WA-9
Sawtooth Mtn—summit (2) ... WY-8
Sawtooth Natl Forest-Raft River Division—forest ... UT-8
Sawtooth Park—flat ... CO-8
Sawtooth Pass—gap ... CA-9
Sawtooth Peak ... CA-9
Sawtooth Peak ... MT-8
Sawtooth Peak—summit ... AZ-5
Sawtooth Peak—summit (2) ... CA-9
Sawtooth Peak—summit ... CO-8
Sawtooth Peak—summit (2) ... ID-8
Sawtooth Peak—summit ... OR-9
Sawtooth Peak—summit ... UT-8
Sawtooth Range ... MT-8
Sawtooth Range ... WA-9
Sawtooth Range—range (2) ... CA-9
Sawtooth Range—range ... CO-8
Sawtooth Range—range ... ID-8
Sawtooth Range—range ... MT-8
Sawtooth Range—ridge ... AK-9
Sawtooth Ridge ... MT-8
Sawtooth Ridge ... UT-8
Sawtooth Ridge—ridge ... AZ-5
Sawtooth Ridge—ridge (5) ... CA-9
Sawtooth Ridge—ridge ... CO-8
Sawtooth Ridge—ridge (2) ... MT-8
Sawtooth Ridge—ridge (4) ... OR-9
Sawtooth Ridge—ridge ... UT-8
Sawtooth Ridge—ridge (5) ... WA-9
Sawtooth Ridge—ridge ... WY-8
Sawtooth Rock—pillar ... CO-8
Sawtooth Rock—pillar (2) ... OR-9
Sawtoothrock Mountain ... OR-9
Sawtooth Rocks—pillar ... CO-8
Sawtooth Rocks—summit ... CT-1
Sawtooths—summit ... CA-9
Sawtooth Sch—school ... AZ-5
Sawtooth Spring—spring ... NV-8
Sawtooth Spring—spring (2) ... OR-9
Sawtooth Tank—reservoir (2) ... AZ-5
Sawtooth Tank—reservoir (2) ... NM-5
Sawtooth Tank Number Two—reservoir ... AZ-5
Sawtooth Trail—trail ... MT-8
Sawtooth Valley—valley ... ID-8
Sawtooth Valley Ranger Station—locale ... ID-8
Sawtooth Way—trail ... OR-9
Sawtooth Windmill—locale ... TX-5
**Sawtown**—pop pl ... PA-2
Sawtucket River Rsvr—reservoir ... MA-1
Sawyar Creek ... WI-6
Sawyer ... PA-2
Sawyer—fmr MCD ... NE-7
Sawyer—locale ... ID-8
Sawyer—locale ... KY-4
Sawyer—locale ... NM-5
Sawyer—locale ... NY-2
Sawyer—locale ... WA-9
**Sawyer**—pop pl ... IA-7
**Sawyer**—pop pl ... KS-7
**Sawyer**—pop pl ... MI-6
**Sawyer**—pop pl ... MN-6
**Sawyer**—pop pl ... MS-4
**Sawyer**—pop pl ... NM-5
**Sawyer**—pop pl (2) ... NY-2
**Sawyer**—pop pl ... NC-3
**Sawyer**—pop pl ... ND-7
**Sawyer**—pop pl ... OK-5
Sawyer, David, House—hist pl ... KY-4
Sawyer, Lake—lake ... FL-3
Sawyer, Lake—lake ... OH-6
Sawyer, Lake—lake ... WA-9
Sawyer, Louis, House—hist pl ... OH-6
Sawyer, Mount—summit ... WA-9
Sawyer, W. P., House And Orchard—hist pl ... WA-9
Sawyer Bar—bar ... OR-9
Sawyer Bay—bay ... NY-2
Sawyer Bay—bay ... VT-1
Sawyer Bend—bend ... TN-4
Sawyer Bldg—hist pl ... NH-1
Sawyer Bluff—cliff ... MA-1
Sawyer Branch—stream ... AL-4
Sawyer Branch—stream ... AR-4
Sawyer Branch—stream ... NC-3
Sawyer Branch—stream ... SC-3
Sawyer Branch—stream ... TX-5
Sawyer Brook—stream (3) ... ME-1
Sawyer Brook—stream ... MA-1
Sawyer Brook—stream (2) ... NH-1
Sawyer Brook—stream ... OH-6
Sawyer Brook—stream ... VT-1
Sawyer Camp—locale ... FL-3
Sawyer Camp—locale ... WA-9
Sawyer Canal—canal ... NC-3
Sawyer Canyon—valley ... KS-7
Sawyer Canyon—valley ... NM-5
Sawyer Canyon—valley ... UT-8
Sawyer Cem—cemetery (2) ... AL-4
Sawyer Cem—cemetery ... AR-4
Sawyer Cem—cemetery ... IL-6
Sawyer Cem—cemetery ... IA-7
Sawyer Cem—cemetery ... LA-4
Sawyer Cem—cemetery (4) ... ME-1
Sawyer Cem—cemetery ... NY-2
Sawyer Cem—cemetery ... NC-3
Sawyer Cem—cemetery ... ND-7
Sawyer Cem—cemetery ... OH-6
Sawyer Cem—cemetery (2) ... SC-3
Sawyer Cem—cemetery (3) ... TN-4
Sawyer Cem—cemetery ... TX-5
Sawyer Cem—cemetery ... VT-1
Sawyer Cem—cemetery ... VA-3
Sawyer Ch—church ... PA-2
**Sawyer City**—pop pl ... PA-2
Sawyer Corner—locale ... ME-1
**Sawyer (County)**—pop pl ... WI-6
Sawyer Cove—basin ... AL-4
Sawyer Cove—bay ... FL-3
Sawyer Cove—bay ... ME-1
Sawyer Cove—valley (2) ... NC-3
Sawyer Creek—stream ... AL-4
Sawyer Creek—stream ... AK-9
Sawyer Creek—stream ... CA-9
Sawyer Creek—stream ... CO-8
Sawyer Creek—stream ... MA-1
Sawyer Creek—stream ... MI-6
Sawyer Creek—stream ... MO-7
Sawyer Creek—stream ... MT-8
Sawyer Creek—stream (2) ... NM-5
Sawyer Creek—stream (2) ... NY-2
Sawyer Creek—stream (3) ... NC-3
Sawyer Creek—stream (2) ... OR-9
Sawyer Creek—stream (2) ... WA-9
Sawyer Creek—stream (3) ... WI-6
Sawyer Creek Cem—cemetery ... NC-3
Sawyer Creek Ch—church ... NC-3
Sawyer Creek Conduit—canal ... CO-8
Sawyer Creek Springs—spring ... WI-6
Sawyer Creek State Wildlife Area—park ... WI-6
Sawyer-Curtis House—hist pl ... OH-6
Sawyerdale Sch—school ... SC-3
Sawyer Dock (Floating moorage)—locale ... NC-3
Sawyer Draw—valley ... TX-5
Sawyer Elementary School ... TN-4
Sawyer Glacier—glacier ... AK-9
Sawyer Gulch—valley ... CO-8
Sawyer Harbor—bay ... WI-6
Sawyer Hill ... ME-1
Sawyer Hill—ridge ... NH-1
Sawyer Hill—summit ... CT-1
Sawyer Hill—summit ... ME-1
Sawyer Hill—summit ... MA-1
Sawyer Hill—summit ... NH-1
Sawyer Hill Burying Ground—cemetery ... MA-1
Sawyer Hill Ridge—ridge ... ME-1
Sawyer Hollow—valley ... KY-4
Sawyer Hollow—valley ... MO-7
Sawyer Hollow—valley ... NY-2
Sawyer Hollow—valley (3) ... TN-4
Sawyer Hollow—valley ... TX-5
Sawyer Hollow—valley ... WV-2
Sawyer House—hist pl ... MI-6
Sawyer Island—island (3) ... ME-1
Sawyer Island—island ... VT-1
Sawyer Key—island (2) ... FL-3
Sawyer Kill—stream ... NY-2
Sawyer Lake ... IN-6
Sawyer Lake ... ME-1
Sawyer Lake—lake ... CO-8
Sawyer Lake—lake ... FL-3
Sawyer Lake—lake ... GA-3
Sawyer Lake—lake ... MI-6
Sawyer Lake—lake (2) ... MN-6
Sawyer Lake—lake ... NH-1
Sawyer Lake—lake ... NC-3
Sawyer Lake—lake (2) ... WI-6
**Sawyer Lake**—pop pl ... MI-6
Sawyer Lake—reservoir ... AL-4
Sawyer Lake Dam—dam ... AL-4
Sawyer Lake Trail—trail ... CO-8
Sawyer Ledge—bar ... ME-1
Sawyer Memorial Bridge—bridge ... SC-3
Sawyer Memorial Ch—church ... ME-1
Sawyer Mesa—summit ... NM-5
Sawyer Motor Company Bldg—hist pl ... NC-3
Sawyer Mtn—summit ... KY-4
Sawyer Mtn—summit (3) ... ME-1
Sawyer Mtn—summit ... NY-2
Sawyer Mtn—summit ... TN-4
Sawyer Mtn—summit ... VT-1
Sawyer Notch—gap ... ME-1
Sawyer Park—park ... FL-3
Sawyer Park—park ... NY-2
Sawyer Peak—summit ... CA-9
Sawyer Playground—park ... MI-6
Sawyer Point—cape ... MI-6
Sawyer Point—cape ... NY-2
Sawyer Point—cape ... UT-8
Sawyer Pond ... MA-1
Sawyer Pond ... NH-1
Sawyer Pond—lake ... LA-4
Sawyer Pond—lake (2) ... ME-1
Sawyer Pond—lake ... NH-1
Sawyer Pond—reservoir ... MA-1
Sawyer Pond Bayou—gut ... LA-4
Sawyer Pond Dam—dam ... MA-1
Sawyer Ponds—lake ... MA-1
Sawyer Pond Trail—trail ... NH-1
Sawyer Ranch—locale (2) ... TX-5
Sawyer Rapids—rapids ... OR-9
Sawyer Reservoir ... NH-1
Sawyer Ridge—ridge ... CA-9
Sawyer Ridge—ridge ... ID-8
Sawyer Ridge Lookout—locale ... ID-8
Sawyer River—stream ... NH-1
Sawyer River Station ... NH-1
Sawyer Rock—bar ... ME-1
Sawyer Rock—summit ... NH-1
Sawyer Rocks—summit ... VT-1
Sawyer Run—stream (2) ... WV-2
Sawyers ... NH-1
Sawyers ... NY-2
**Sawyers**—pop pl ... NH-1
Sawyers Bar—bar ... CA-9
**Sawyers Bar**—pop pl ... CA-9
Sawyers Bar Camp Ground—locale ... CA-9
Sawyers Bar Catholic Church—hist pl ... CA-9
Sawyers Basin—gut ... FL-3
Sawyers Branch ... MO-7
Sawyers Cave—cave ... AL-4
Sawyers Cave—cave ... OR-9
Sawyers Cem—cemetery ... MO-7
Sawyer Sch—school ... IL-6
Sawyer Sch—school ... IA-7
Sawyer Sch—school ... KY-4
Sawyer Sch—school ... MI-6
Sawyer Sch—school ... NH-1
Sawyer Sch—school ... NC-3
Sawyer Sch—school ... TN-4
**Sawyers Corner**—pop pl ... NY-2
Sawyers Cove—bay ... LA-4
Sawyers Cove—bay ... ME-1
Sawyers Creek—stream ... NC-3
Sawyers Creek Ch—church ... NC-3
Sawyers Crossing Covered Bridge—hist pl ... NH-1
Sawyers Ferry ... NC-3
Sawyers Ferry (historical)—locale ... OR-9
Sawyers Fork—stream ... KY-4
Sawyers Hill ... MA-1
Sawyers Hill—summit ... NH-1
Sawyers (historical)—locale ... NC-3
Sawyers Island—island ... ME-1
Sawyers Island—island ... SC-3
Sawyers Keys ... FL-3
Sawyers Lakes—reservoir ... TX-5
Sawyers Landing—locale ... NC-3
Sawyers Ledge—bench ... VT-1
Sawyers Ledge—locale ... NC-3
Sawyer Slough—lake ... IL-6
Sawyer Slough—stream ... OR-9
Sawyer Slough—swamp ... AR-4
**Sawyers Mill**—pop pl ... TN-4
Sawyer Snell Park—park ... NE-7
Sawyers Peak—summit ... NM-5
Sawyers Point—cape ... NH-1
Sawyers Pond ... MA-1
Sawyers Pond—lake ... KY-4
Sawyer Spring—spring ... CA-9
Sawyer Spring—spring ... UT-8
**Sawyers Rapids (historical)**—pop pl ... OR-9
**Sawyers River**—pop pl ... NH-1
Sawyers Rock—pillar ... IA-7
Sawyers Run—stream ... WV-2
Sawyer-Stand Cem—cemetery ... VT-1
Sawyersville ... IL-6
Sawyersville Ch—church ... NC-3
Sawyer Swamp—swamp ... AL-4
Sawyer Tank—reservoir ... AZ-5
Sawyer Tavern—hist pl ... NH-1
**Sawyer Township**—pop pl ... ND-7
**Sawyerville**—pop pl ... AL-4
**Sawyerville**—pop pl ... IL-6
Sawyerville (CCD)—cens area ... AL-4
Sawyerville Division—civil ... AL-4
Sawyerville Elementary School ... AL-4
Sawyerville Lake ... MI-6
Sawyerville Sch—school ... AL-4
Sawyer-Wayside House—hist pl ... OH-6
**Sawyerwood**—pop pl ... OH-6
Sax—locale ... MN-6
**Saxapahaw**—pop pl ... NC-3
Saxby—locale ... WA-9
Saxe—locale ... OR-9
Saxe—locale ... VA-3
Saxe Brook—stream ... VT-1
Saxe Cem—cemetery ... NY-2
Saxe Corner—locale ... NY-2
Saxe-Gotha Millpond—reservoir ... SC-3
Saxe Pond—reservoir ... PA-2
Saxe Pond Dam—dam ... PA-2
Saxet—locale ... TX-5
Saxet Center—locale ... TX-5
Saxet Lakes—lake ... TX-5
Saxet Oil Field—oilfield ... TX-5
**Saxeville**—pop pl ... WI-6
**Saxeville (Town of)**—pop pl ... WI-6
Saxine Creek—stream ... WI-6
**Saxis**—pop pl ... VA-3
Saxis Island—island ... VA-3
Saxman—locale ... WV-2
**Saxman**—pop pl ... AK-9
**Saxman**—pop pl ... KS-7
Saxman East—CDP ... AK-9
Saxman Run—stream ... PA-2
Saxman Site—hist pl ... KS-7
Saxman Totem Park—hist pl ... AK-9
Saxon ... SC-3
Saxon—locale ... CA-9
Saxon—locale ... GA-3
Saxon—locale ... WA-9
Saxon—locale ... WV-2
**Saxon**—pop pl ... IA-7
**Saxon**—pop pl ... MS-4
**Saxon**—pop pl ... SC-3
**Saxon**—pop pl ... WI-6
Saxon, Harry, House—hist pl ... AZ-5
Saxon Airp—airport ... PA-2
Saxon Bay—bay ... AL-4
Saxon Branch—stream ... TX-5
Saxon Bridge—bridge ... WA-9
**Saxonburg**—pop pl ... PA-2
Saxonburg Borough—civil ... PA-2
Saxonburg Cem—cemetery ... WI-6
Saxonburg Elem Sch—school ... PA-2
**Saxonburg (sta.) (Ivywood)**—pop pl ... PA-2
Saxon Cem—cemetery ... GA-3
Saxon Cem—cemetery ... WI-6
Saxon Creek—stream ... AL-4
Saxon Creek—stream (2) ... CA-9
Saxon Crossroads—locale ... AL-4
Saxon Dairy ... AZ-5
Saxon Dam—dam ... AL-4
Saxon Drain—canal ... MI-6
Saxon Falls—falls ... MI-6
Saxon Falls—falls ... WI-6
Saxon Golf Course—locale ... PA-2
Saxon Harbor—bay ... WI-6
Saxon Harbor County Park—park ... WI-6
Saxon Heights Sch—school ... GA-3
Saxon Hill—summit ... VT-1
Saxonia Lake—lake ... CA-9
Saxonia Park—locale ... CA-9
Saxon Lake—lake ... FL-3
Saxon Lake—reservoir ... AR-4
Saxon Motor Car Store—hist pl ... TX-5
Saxon Mtn—summit ... CO-8
**Saxon Park**—pop pl ... NY-2
Saxon Sch—school ... IL-6
Saxons Dairy Ranch ... AZ-5
Saxons Lake—reservoir ... AL-4
Saxon Tank—reservoir ... NM-5
**Saxon (Town of)**—pop pl ... WI-6
Saxon Union Ch—church ... WI-6
Saxonville ... RI-1
**Saxonville**—pop pl ... MA-1
Saxonville Dam ... MA-1
Saxonville Pond ... MA-1
Saxon Woods Park—park ... NY-2
**Saxony**—pop pl ... IL-6
Saxony Apartment Bldg—hist pl ... OH-6
Saxony Mill—hist pl ... CT-1
**Saxsony (Glenn Mills)**—pop pl ... NC-3
Saxton ... AZ-5
Saxton—locale ... AK-9
Saxton—locale ... CO-8
Saxton—locale ... FL-3
**Saxton**—pop pl ... KY-4
**Saxton**—pop pl ... MO-7
**Saxton**—pop pl ... NY-2
**Saxton**—pop pl ... PA-2
Saxton And Lockwood Drain—canal ... MI-6
Saxton Borough—civil ... PA-2
Saxton Branch—stream ... SC-3
Saxton Brook—stream ... CT-1
Saxton (CCD)—cens area ... KY-4
Saxton Dam—dam ... PA-2
Saxton Drain—canal (2) ... MI-6
**Saxton Falls**—pop pl ... NJ-2
Saxton Falls Dam—dam ... NJ-2
Saxton House—hist pl ... OH-6
Saxton Lake—lake ... NJ-2
Saxton Lake—lake ... WI-6
Saxton Lake—reservoir ... CO-8
Saxton Mtn—summit ... PA-2
Saxton Peak—summit ... NV-8
Saxton Point—cape ... VT-1
Saxton Pond—reservoir ... PA-2
Saxton Reef—bar ... VT-1
Saxton Rock—pillar ... WA-9
Saxton Shaft—mine ... NV-8
Saxtons Knob—summit ... PA-2
**Saxtons River**—pop pl ... VT-1
Saxtons River—stream ... VT-1
Saxtons River Village Hist Dist—hist pl ... VT-1
Saxtown Cem—cemetery ... IL-6
Saxvik Sch—school ... ND-7
Saxville ... WI-6
Sayalik Creek—stream ... AK-9
Sayan Gigane ... MH-9
Sayan Gigani—slope ... MH-9
**Sayard**—pop pl ... TX-5
Saybrook ... CT-1
Say Brook ... IL-6
**Saybrook**—pop pl ... FL-3
**Saybrook**—pop pl ... IL-6
**Saybrook**—pop pl ... OH-6
**Saybrook**—pop pl ... PA-2
Saybrook Beacon—locale ... CT-1
**Saybrook (historical)**—pop pl ... SD-7
Saybrook Jetties—other ... CT-1
Saybrook Lighthouse—locale ... CT-1
**Saybrook Manor**—pop pl ... CT-1
**Saybrook-on-the-lake**—pop pl ... OH-6
Saybrook Point—cape ... CT-1
**Saybrook Point**—pop pl ... CT-1
Saybrook Sch—school ... NJ-2
Saybrook Sch (abandoned)—school ... SD-7
**Saybrook (Township of)**—pop pl ... OH-6
Say Canyon—valley ... NV-8
**Saydel**—pop pl ... IA-7
Saydel HS—school ... IA-7
Saye Draw—valley ... TX-5
Sayees Corners—locale ... PA-2
Sayer Butte—summit ... MT-8
Sayer House—hist pl ... MN-6
Sayer Lake—lake ... MN-6
Sayer Park ... OH-6
**Sayers**—pop pl ... TX-5
Sayers, Gov. Joseph, House—hist pl ... TX-5
Sayers Cem—cemetery (2) ... IA-7
Sayers Cem—cemetery (2) ... KY-4
Sayer Sch—school ... NY-2
Sayers Gulch ... CO-8
Sayers Hill—summit ... NY-2
Sayers Park—park ... IA-7
Sayer Spring—spring ... AZ-5
**Sayers (Sayersville)**—pop pl ... TX-5
**Sayersville**—pop pl ... TX-5
**Sayersville**—pop pl ... VA-3
**Sayerwood South**—pop pl ... NJ-2
Sayesville ... WI-6
Saykes Creek ... AL-4
Sayle—locale ... MT-8
Sayle Cem—cemetery ... TX-5
Sayle Hall—locale ... MT-8
Sayler Airp—airport ... PA-2
Sayler Branch—stream ... VA-3
Sayler Cem—cemetery ... OH-6
Sayler Chapel—church ... VA-3
**Sayler Park**—pop pl ... OH-6
Saylers Creek—stream ... VA-3
Sayler's Creek Battlefield—hist pl ... VA-3
Saylers Creek Battlefield State Park—park ... VA-3
**Sayles**—pop pl ... NC-3
Sayles, Deborah Cook, Public Library—hist pl ... RI-1
Sayles, Henry, House—hist pl ... TX-5
Sayles, Richard, House—hist pl ... MA-1
**Sayles Bleachery**—pop pl ... RI-1
Sayles Canyon—valley ... CA-9
Sayles Canyon—valley ... CO-8
Sayles Cem—cemetery ... MS-4
Sayles Corners—locale (2) ... NY-2
Sayles Creek ... WY-8
Sayles Creek—stream (2) ... SD-7
Sayles Creek—stream ... WY-8
Sayles Flat—flat ... CA-9
Sayles Hill—summit ... RI-1
Sayles Lake—lake ... MI-6
Sayles Pond ... RI-1
Sayless Island ... MA-1
**Sayles Village**—pop pl ... NC-3
Saylesville—locale ... WI-6
**Saylesville**—pop pl ... RI-1
**Saylesville**—pop pl ... WI-6
**Saylesville Highlands**—pop pl ... RI-1
Saylesville Hist Dist—hist pl ... RI-1
Saylesville (historical)—locale ... SD-7
Saylesville Meetinghouse—hist pl ... RI-1
Saylesville Millpond—reservoir ... WI-6
Saylesville Sch—school ... WI-6
Saylings Creek—stream ... IA-7
Saylor—locale ... IA-7
Saylor—locale ... KY-4
Saylor Bottom—bend ... OK-5
Saylor Branch—stream (3) ... KY-4
Saylor Branch Ch—church ... KY-4
Saylor Cap Butte ... ID-8
Saylor Cem—cemetery ... KY-4
Saylor Cem—cemetery ... OH-6
Saylor Cem—cemetery ... TN-4
Saylor Cem—cemetery ... VA-3
Saylor Center Sch—school ... IA-7
Saylor Creek ... ID-8
Saylor Creek—stream ... IA-7
Saylor Creek—stream ... KY-4
Saylor Creek—stream ... TN-4
Saylor Creek—stream ... WY-8
Saylor Flat ... UT-8
Saylor Fork—stream ... KY-4
Saylor Gap—gap ... AL-4
Saylor Gulch—valley ... CA-9
Saylor Hollow—valley ... KY-4
Saylor Island—island ... TN-4
Saylor Lake—reservoir ... NC-3
Saylor Park (2) ... OH-6
Saylor Park—flat ... CO-8
**Saylorsburg**—pop pl ... PA-2
Saylorsburg Junction (historical)—locale ... PA-2
Saylors Cabin—locale ... CA-9
Saylor Sch—school ... KY-4
Saylor Sch (abandoned)—school ... PA-2
Saylor School ... IN-6
Saylors Creek ... TN-4
**Saylors Crossing**—pop pl ... SC-3
**Saylors Crossroads**—pop pl ... SC-3
Saylors Lake—lake ... PA-2
Saylors Lake—lake ... SC-3
Saylors Lake—reservoir ... NC-3
Saylors Lake Dam—dam ... NC-3
Saylors Pond—reservoir ... NJ-2
Saylor Spring ... UT-8
Saylor Springs ... IL-6
Saylor Station—locale ... IA-7
**Saylor Station**—pop pl ... IA-7
Saylorsville—locale ... PA-2
Saylor Township—fmr MCD ... IA-7
**Saylorville**—pop pl ... IA-7
Saylorville Dam—dam ... IA-7
Saylorville Lake—reservoir ... IA-7
Saylorville Reservoir ... IA-7
Saylorville Reservoir—unorg reg ... IA-7
**Sayner**—pop pl ... WI-6
Saypan ... MH-9
Saypo—locale ... MT-8
Sayre—locale ... AR-4
Sayre—locale ... KS-7
**Sayre**—pop pl ... AL-4
**Sayre**—pop pl ... OH-6
**Sayre**—pop pl ... OK-5
**Sayre**—pop pl ... PA-2
Sayre and Fisher Reading Room—hist pl ... NJ-2
Sayre Borough—civil ... PA-2
Sayre (CCD)—cens area ... OK-5
Sayre Cem—cemetery ... OK-5
Sayre Cem—cemetery (4) ... WV-2
Sayre Ch—church ... AL-4
Sayre-Dewey Cem—cemetery ... OK-5
Sayre Female Institute—hist pl ... KY-4
Sayre Hollow—valley ... TN-4
Sayre Hollow—valley ... WV-2
Sayre Homestead—hist pl ... NJ-2
Sayre House—hist pl ... NJ-2
Sayre Impoundment Number 1—reservoir ... AL-4
Sayre Impoundment Number 1 Dam—dam ... AL-4
Sayre JHS—school ... PA-2
Sayre Lake—lake ... LA-4
Sayre-Mann House—hist pl ... OK-5
Sayre Mines ... AL-4
Sayre Mines (Sayre) ... AL-4
Sayre Mine (surface)—mine ... AL-4
Sayre Mine (underground)—mine ... AL-4
Sayre Neck ... NJ-2
Sayre Park Field—park ... PA-2
Sayre Pond—lake ... NY-2
Sayre Rsvr—reservoir ... PA-2
**Sayre (Sayre Mines)**—pop pl ... AL-4
Sayres Branch—stream ... IN-6
Sayre Sch—school ... AL-4
Sayre Sch—school ... IL-6
Sayre Sch—school ... MI-6
Sayre Sch—school ... WV-2
Sayre Sch (historical)—school ... PA-2
Sayres Gulch—valley ... CO-8
Sayre's Lake ... OH-6
Sayres Neck—cape ... NJ-2
**Sayres Neck**—pop pl ... NJ-2
Sayres Point—cape ... NJ-2
Sayres Ponds—lake ... OH-6
Sayre Street Sch ... AL-4
Sayre Street Sch—hist pl ... AL-4
Sayre Tank—reservoir ... AZ-5
**Sayreton**—pop pl ... AL-4
Sayreton Number 2 Mine (underground)—mine ... AL-4
**Sayreville**—pop pl ... NJ-2
Sayreville Junction—locale ... NJ-2
**Sayreville Station**—pop pl ... NJ-2
**Sayre Woods**—pop pl ... NJ-2
**Sayre Woods South**—pop pl ... NJ-2
Says Canyon—valley ... OR-9
**Sayville**—pop pl ... NY-2
Sayville HS—school ... NY-2
**Saywards Corner**—pop pl ... ME-1
Saywood Cem—cemetery ... ME-1
Saywood Hill—summit ... NY-2
Sazarine Creek—stream ... GA-3
Sazini Butte ... AZ-5
S Baker Ranch—locale ... NV-8
S Baker Ranch—locale ... TX-5
Sbarbaro Ranch Airp—airport ... PA-2
Sbarbaro Sch—school ... IL-6
S-Bar Creek—stream ... WY-8
S-Bar Ranch—locale ... TX-5
S Baxter Number 1 Dam—dam ... SD-7
S B Boone Sch—school ... TX-5
S B Canyon ... AZ-5
SBD Trucking Station ... PA-2
S B Elliott State Park—park ... PA-2
S Bend—bend ... TX-5
S Bluff Park—park ... TX-5
S B Mtn—summit ... AZ-5
S B Point—cliff ... AZ-5
S Bridge—hist pl ... PA-2
"S" Bridge—hist pl ... PA-2
S Bridge—mine ... ID-8
S B Ridge—ridge ... UT-8
S Bridge, Natl Road—hist pl ... OH-6
"S" Bridge II—hist pl ... OH-6
S Bryan Jennings Elem Sch—school ... FL-3
S B Thorton Lake Dam—dam ... MS-4
Scaarborough ... TN-4
Scabbard Bay—bay ... AK-9
Scabbard Lake—lake ... MN-6
Scabbler Branch—stream ... SC-3
Scab Branch—stream ... TN-4
Scabby Creek—stream ... SD-7
Scabby Island Ledge—bar ... ME-1
Scabby Islands—island ... ME-1
Scab Creek ... WY-8
Scab Creek—stream ... ND-7
Scab Creek—stream ... WA-9
Scab Creek—stream ... WY-8
Scab Creek Trail—trail ... WY-8
Scab Gulch—valley (2) ... OR-9
**Scab Hill**—pop pl ... PA-2
Scab Hollow—valley ... IL-6
Scab Hollow—valley ... UT-8
Scab Lake—lake ... WY-8
Scab Mill Brook—stream ... NH-1
Scab Rock Mtn—summit ... MT-8
Scab Rsvr—reservoir ... OR-9
Scab Run—stream ... WV-2
Scab Sage Trail—trail ... WY-8
Scab Spring—spring ... OR-9
Scab Windmill—locale ... TX-5
Scace Brook—stream ... MA-1
Scachse Cem—cemetery ... MO-7
Scaddan Mtn—summit ... AZ-5
Scaddan Wash—stream ... AZ-5
Scadden Brook—stream ... MA-1
Scadden Flat—flat ... CA-9
Scaddens Island—island ... MI-6
Scadding Pond ... MA-1
Scad Ridge—ridge ... UT-8
Scad Valley—valley ... UT-8
Scad Valley Creek—stream ... UT-8
Scad Valley Divide—gap ... UT-8
Scaff Branch ... TN-4
Scaffold Branch—stream ... TN-4
Scaffold Camp Creek—stream ... WA-9
Scaffold Cane Branch—stream ... KY-4
Scaffold Cane Ch—church ... KY-4
Scaffold Creek—bay ... MD-2
Scaffold Creek—stream ... KY-4
Scaffold Creek—stream ... OR-9
Scaffold Creek Marsh—swamp ... MD-2
Scaffold Lake—lake ... WI-6
Scaffold Lick ... CO-8
Scaffold Lick—stream (2) ... KY-4
Scaffold Lick—stream ... OH-6
Scaffold Lick Branch—stream ... KY-4
Scaffold Lick Ch—church ... IN-6
Scaffold Lick Creek ... KY-4
Scaffold Lick Creek—stream ... KY-4
Scaffold Lick Run—stream ... PA-2
Scaffold Meadows—flat ... CA-9
Scaffold Mtn—summit ... OK-5
Scaffold Peak—summit ... WA-9
Scaffold Point—cape ... MD-2
Scaffold Point Marsh—swamp ... MD-2
Scaffold Ridge—ridge ... WA-9
Scaffold Run—stream ... VA-3
Scaffold Run—stream ... WV-2
Scaffold Spring ... OR-9
Scafford Lick Canyon—valley ... CO-8
Scafford Prairie Cem—cemetery ... IN-6
Scafold Lick ... CO-8
**Scaggs**—pop pl ... WV-2
Scaggs Bluff—cliff ... TN-4
Scaggs Cem—cemetery ... WV-2
Scaggs Ford—locale ... VA-3
Scaggs Hollow—valley ... MO-7
Scaggs Hollow—valley ... TN-4
Scaggsville—locale ... MD-2
Scahonda—locale ... PA-2
Scahonda Run ... PA-2
Scaife—locale ... TN-4
Scaife Hill—summit ... PA-2
Scairt Woman Draw—valley ... ND-7
Scajaquada Creek—stream ... NY-2
Scajaquady Creek ... NY-2
Scajawea Sch—school ... WA-9
Scalan Mine—mine ... CA-9
Scalawag Ridge—ridge ... WA-9
Scalcucci's Grocery—hist pl ... MI-6
Scald Branch—stream ... NC-3
Scaldhog Hollow ... AR-4
Scald Point—cape ... AK-9
**Scale**—pop pl ... KY-4
Scale Branch—stream ... GA-3
Scale Creek—stream ... TN-4
Scale Hollow—valley (2) ... WV-2
Scale Key—island ... FL-3
Scale Leader Hollow—valley ... KY-4
Scalem Branch—stream ... KY-4
Scale Pen Windmill—locale (2) ... TX-5
Scaler Creek—stream ... ID-8
Scaler Guard Station—locale ... WY-8
Scale Rsvr—reservoir ... OR-9
Scale Run—stream (2) ... WV-2
**Scales**—pop pl ... CA-9
Scales, Absalom, House—hist pl ... TN-4
Scales, Alfred Moore, Law Office—hist pl ... NC-3
Scales, James, House—hist pl ... TN-4
Scales, Joseph, House—hist pl ... TN-4
Scales Brook—stream ... NH-1
Scales Brook—stream ... VT-1
Scales Canyon—valley ... NM-5
Scales Cave—cave ... TN-4
Scales Cem—cemetery ... AL-4
Scales Creek—stream ... MI-6
Scales Creek—stream ... NC-3

Scales Elem Sch—school TN-4
Scalese Ranch—locale MT-8
Scales (historical)—locale AL-4
Scales Hollow—valley KY-4
Scale Siding—locale PA-2
Scales Lake—lake AL-4
Scales Lake County Park—park IN-6
Scales Lake No. 1—reservoir CO-8
Scales Lake No. 2—reservoir CO-8
Scales Mine AL-4
**Scales Mound**—pop pl IL-6
Scales Mound—summit IL-6
Scales Mound (Township of)—civ div IL-6
Scales Mtn—summit TN-4
Scales Point—cape NY-2
Scale Springs—spring AR-4
Scales Sch—school AZ-5
Scales Sch—school IL-6
Scales Station MS-4
**Scalesville**—pop pl IN-6
**Scalesville**—pop pl NC-3
Scales Well—well NM-5
Scalf—locale KY-4
Scalf Branch—stream KY-4
Scalf Cem—cemetery KY-4
Scalf Cem—cemetery TN-4
Scalf Cem—cemetery TX-5
Scaling Oil Field—oilfield TX-5
**Scalley Spur**—pop pl WA-9
Scallop, The—summit VT-1
Scallop Point—cape MD-2
Scallop Point Gut—gut MD-2
Scallop Pond—lake NY-2
Scallop Tank Windmill—locale TX-5
Scallorn—locale TX-5
Scally Lake—lake MI-6
Scallys Golf Course PA-2
Scalous Creek—stream LA-4
Scalp, The—locale PA-2
Scalp Butte (historical)—summit SD-7
Scalp Creek TX-5
Scalp Creek—stream ID-8
Scalp Creek—stream MI-6
Scalp Creek—stream MT-8
Scalp Creek—stream TX-5
Scalp Creek Indian Site (historical)—locale SD-7
Scalp Lake—lake MN-6
Scalp Level PA-2
**Scalp Level**—pop pl PA-2
Scalp Level Borough—civil PA-2
Scalp Level Sch (abandoned)—school PA-2
Scalplock Mountain Fire Lookout—hist pl MT-8
Scalplock Mtn—summit MT-8
Scalp Mtn—summit MT-8
Scalte Knob—summit PA-2
Scaly NC-3
Scaly—other NC-3
Scaly Bark Creek—stream MO-7
Scaly Bark Creek—stream NC-3
Scaly Bark Mtn—summit OK-5
Scaly Knob—summit GA-3
Scaly Mountain—locale NC-3
**Scaly Mountain (Scaly)**—pop pl NC-3
Scaly Mtn—summit NC-3
Scaly Point Sch—school IL-6
Scaly Ridge—ridge NC-3
Scaly Sch—school NC-3
Scambe FL-3
Scambler Cem—cemetery MN-6
**Scambler (Township of)**—pop pl MN-6
Scamen Brook—stream NH-1
Scammel Bridge—bridge NH-1
**Scammells Corner**—pop pl PA-2
**Scammon**—pop pl KS-7
Scammon Bay—bay AK-9
**Scammon Bay**—pop pl AK-9
Scammon Cove—bay (2) MI-6
Scammon Creek—stream WA-9
Scammon Elem Sch—school KS-7
Scammon Landing—locale WA-9
Scammon Point—cape MI-6
Scammon Pond—lake ME-1
Scammon Ridge—ridge ME-1
Scammons Arrowhead Ranch—locale CA-9
Scammon Sch—school IL-6
Scammon's Cove MI-6
Scammonville KS-7
Scamp Creek—stream WA-9
S Canal—canal ID-8
S Canal—canal (3) MT-8
S Canal—canal NV-8
S Canal—canal OR-9
Scanawah Island—island SC-3
Scandard Gulch—valley CO-8
Scandea Sch—school ND-7
**Scandia**—pop pl KS-7
**Scandia**—pop pl MN-6
**Scandia**—pop pl PA-2
**Scandia**—pop pl WA-9
Scandia Air Park—airport PA-2
Scandia-Belleville Airp—airport KS-7
Scandia Bridge (historical)—bridge IA-7
Scandia Cem—cemetery (4) MN-6
Scandia Cem—cemetery MT-8
Scandia Cem—cemetery SD-7
Scandia Ch—church (3) MN-6
Scandia Ch—church (2) ND-7
Scandia Lake—lake MN-6
Scandia Mine—mine CO-8
Scandian Grove Cem—cemetery (2) MN-6
Scandia Sch—school MT-8
Scandia Sch—school ND-7
Scandia Township—civil KS-7
**Scandia Township**—pop pl ND-7
**Scandia (Township of)**—pop pl MN-6
Scandia Tunnel—mine OR-9
Scandia Valley Cem—cemetery MN-6
Scandia Valley Ch—church ND-7
Scandia Valley Town Hall—locale MN-6
Scandia Valley (Township of)—civ div MN-6
**Scandia Village Condominium**—pop pl UT-8
**Scandia Village Subdivision**—pop pl UT-8
**Scandinavia**—pop pl WI-6
Scandinavia Cem—cemetery WI-6
Scandinavia Ch—church ND-7
Scandinavia Ch—church WI-6
Scandinavian Cem—cemetery (2) IL-6
Scandinavian Cem—cemetery IA-7
Scandinavian Cem—cemetery MN-6
Scandinavian Ch—church (2) MN-6
Scandinavian Ch—church (2) WI-6
Scandinavian Creek—stream AK-9
Scandinavian Ditch—canal CO-8
Scandinavian Gulch—valley CO-8
Scandinavian Lake—lake MN-6
Scandinavian Lutheran Ch—church SD-7
Scandinavian Lutheran Ch (historical)—church SD-7
Scandinavian Sch—school CA-9
Scandinavian Slough—stream AK-9
Scandinavia Post Office (historical)—building SD-7
**Scandinavia (Town of)**—pop pl WI-6
Scandinavia Township SD-7
**Scandinavia Township**—pop pl NE-7
**Scandinavia Township**—pop pl SD-7
Scandlyn—locale TN-4
Scandlyn Post Office (historical)—building TN-4
Scanlan, Michael, House—hist pl MN-6
Scanlan Bldg—hist pl TX-5
Scanland Branch—stream KY-4
Scanland Cem—cemetery TX-5
Scanlan Lake—lake MT-8
Scanlan Sch—school IL-6
**Scanlin**—pop pl PA-2
Scanlin Branch—stream AL-4
Scanlon—locale FL-3
**Scanlon**—pop pl MN-6
Scanlon Bay—bay NV-8
Scanlon Brook—stream MA-1
Scanlon Creek—stream OK-5
Scanlon Draw—valley NM-5
Scanlon Dugway—locale NV-8
Scanlon Farm—hist pl WV-2
Scanlon Ferry AZ-5
Scanlon Gulch—valley CA-9
Scanlon Hill—summit NV-8
**Scanlon (historical)**—pop pl MS-4
Scanlon Lake—lake MN-6
Scanlon Lake—lake WA-9
Scanlon Sch—school WI-6
Scanlon Spring—spring AZ-5
Scanlon Tunnel—mine AZ-5
**Scanlonville**—pop pl SC-3
Scanlon Wash—stream (2) AZ-5
Scanlon Wash—stream NV-8
Scanlon Well—well AZ-5
Scant Branch—stream KY-4
**Scant City**—pop pl AL-4
Scantic—locale CT-1
Scantic Brook MA-1
Scantic Cem—cemetery CT-1
Scantic Ch—church CT-1
Scantic (historical)—locale MA-1
Scantick River CT-1
Scanticook River CT-1
Scantic Pond CT-1
Scantic River—stream (2) CT-1
Scantic River—stream MA-1
Scantic Village CT-1
Scantigrease Creek WA-9
Scantik Village CT-1
Scantland Cem—cemetery MO-7
Scantlin Branch TN-4
Scantlin Cem—cemetery AR-4
Scantlin Cem—cemetery MO-7
Scantling Branch—stream TN-4
Scantling Run—stream OH-6
Scantlin Island (historical)—island TN-4
Scanton Wash AZ-5
Scantuck River CT-1
Scanty Branch—stream TN-4
S Canyon—valley (2) AZ-5
Scapborough Water Hole—lake ID-8
Scapecat Branch—stream NC-3
Scapegoat Mtn—summit MT-8
Scape Ore Swamp—stream SC-3
Scaper Rsvr—reservoir WY-8
Scapin ME-1
Scapin Lake ME-1
Scaponia Recreation Site—park OR-9
**Scappoose**—pop pl OR-9
Scappoose Bay—bay OR-9
Scappoose (CCD)—cens area OR-9
Scappoose Creek OR-9
Scappoose Creek—stream OR-9
Scappoose Industrial Airpark—airport OR-9
Scarab Club—hist pl MI-6
Scarabin Island—island LA-4
Scarabin Pass—gut LA-4
Scarabin Pond—bay LA-4
Scarab Lake—lake CA-9
Scarab Rock—island AK-9
Scarber Cem—cemetery MS-4
Scarberry Branch—stream KY-4
Scarberry Branch—stream WV-2
Scarberry Cem—cemetery KY-4
Scarb Hill AZ-5
Scarbo Creek—stream AL-4
Scarboro ME-1
Scarboro—locale MD-2
Scarboro—locale TN-4
Scarboro—other ME-1
**Scarboro**—pop pl GA-3
**Scarboro**—pop pl IL-6
**Scarboro**—pop pl MD-2
**Scarboro**—pop pl WI-6
Scarboro Beach ME-1
Scarboro Branch—stream GA-3
Scarboro Brook—stream MA-1
Scarboro Ch—church (2) GA-3
Scarboro Ch of Christ—church TN-4
Scarboro Creek AL-4
Scarboro Creek—bay NC-3
Scarboro Creek—stream (2) MD-2
Scarboro Creek—stream TN-4
Scarboro Creek—stream WI-6
Scarboro Hill—summit MA-1
Scarboro Hill—summit WA-9
Scarboro Landing—locale MD-2
Scarboro Point—cape NC-3
Scarboro Pond—lake MA-1
Scarboro Post Office (historical)—building TN-4
Scarboro River ME-1
**Scarborough**—pop pl ME-1
**Scarborough**—pop pl NY-2
Scarborough, Lake—reservoir TX-5
Scarborough, Maj. James, House—hist pl NC-3
Scarborough Airstrip—airport SD-7
Scarborough Beach—beach ME-1
Scarborough Bend—bend FL-3
Scarborough Cem—cemetery AL-4
Scarborough Cem—cemetery SC-3
Scarborough Cem—cemetery TN-4
Scarborough Creek—stream MS-4
Scarborough Creek—stream TX-5
Scarborough Downs—other ME-1
Scarborough Gut—gut VA-3
**Scarborough Hills**—pop pl RI-1
Scarborough Hist Dist—hist pl NY-2
Scarborough Hollow—valley (2) TN-4
Scarborough House—hist pl NC-3
Scarborough House Archaeol Site (44AC4)—hist pl VA-3
Scarborough Island—island VA-3
Scarborough Lake LA-4
Scarborough Lake—lake IA-7
Scarborough Lake—lake LA-4
Scarborough Lake Dam—dam MS-4
Scarborough Lake Number One—reservoir NC-3
Scarborough Lake Number One Dam—dam NC-3
Scarborough Neck—cape VA-3
**Scarborough Park (subdivision)**—pop pl DE-2
Scarborough Point—cape VA-3
Scarborough Post Office TN-4
Scarborough River—stream ME-1
Scarborough's MD-2
Scarboroughs Branch—stream TX-5
Scarborough Sch—school TX-5
Scarborough's Creek MD-2
Scarboroughs Creek—stream LA-4
**Scarboroughs Neck**—pop pl VA-3
Scarborough Springs TN-4
**Scarborough (subdivision)**—pop pl NC-3
Scarborough Tank—reservoir TX-5
Scarborough Tank Number One—reservoir AZ-5
Scarborough Tank Number Two—reservoir AZ-5
**Scarborough (Town of)**—pop pl ME-1
Scarbough Cem—cemetery TN-4
Scarbough JHS—school TX-5
Scarbow Lake—reservoir OK-5
Scar Branch—stream MD-2
**Scarbro**—pop pl WV-2
Scarbro Cem—cemetery WV-2
Scarbrough, William, House—hist pl GA-3
Scarbrough Bridge (historical)—bridge MS-4
Scarbrough Cem—cemetery WV-2
Scarbrough Creek—stream AL-4
Scarbrough Cross Roads—locale GA-3
Scarbrough Lake—reservoir MS-4
Scarbrough Lake Dam—dam MS-4
Scarbrough Memorial Ch—church TN-4
Scarburg PA-2
Scarce Creek—stream TN-4
Scarce Grease—locale AL-4
Scarce Grease Branch—stream AL-4
Scarce Grease Branch—stream TN-4
Scarce of Fat Ridge—ridge IN-6
Scar Creek—stream OR-9
Scardino Park—park ID-8
Scardos—airport NJ-2
Scare Canyon—valley UT-8
Scarecorn Creek—stream GA-3
Scare Creek—stream OR-9
Scarecrow Draw—valley WY-8
Scarecrow Gulch—valley MT-8
Scarecrow Island—island MI-6
Scarecrow Peak—summit UT-8
Scared Dog Creek—stream TX-5
Scared Heart Sch—school IN-6
Scaredman Camp—locale OR-9
Scaredman Creek—stream OR-9
Scaredman Creek Recreation Site—park OR-9
Scare Mtn—summit CO-8
Scare Ridge—ridge OR-9
Scare Ridge Lookout—locale OR-9
Scareum Mtn—summit AL-4
Scarey Creek—stream OH-6
Scarface NY-2
Scarface—cape WA-9
Scarface—locale CA-9
Scarface Brook—stream NH-1
Scarface Creek—stream MT-8
Scarface Mtn—summit AZ-5
Scarface Mtn—summit ID-8
Scarface Mtn—summit MT-8
Scarface Mtn—summit NH-1
Scarface Mtn—summit NY-2
Scarface Peak—summit MT-8
Scarface Ridge—ridge CA-9
**Scarff**—pop pl MD-2
Scarff Hill—summit NY-2
Scargo Hill—summit MA-1
Scargo Hill Observation Tower—tower MA-1
Scargo Lake—lake MA-1
Scarhain Creek AL-4
Scarham Creek—stream AL-4
Scar Hill—summit PA-2
Scar Hill—summit WA-9
Scar Hill Bluffs—cliff MA-1
**Scarlan Hill**—pop pl PA-2
Scarlat Lake—lake PA-2
**Scarlet**—pop pl GA-3
**Scarlet**—pop pl IN-6
**Scarlet**—pop pl WV-2
Scarlet and Davis Canyon—valley CA-9
Scarlet Brook—stream MA-1
Scarletelli Pond—lake NJ-2
**Scarlet Glen**—pop pl WV-2
Scarlet Mtn—summit MT-8
Scarlet Number One Beach MH-9
Scarlet Number Two Beach MH-9
Scarlet Oaks—hist pl OH-6
**Scarlet Oaks**—pop pl IN-6
Scarlet Oak Trail—trail TN-4
Scarlet Oak Trail—trail WV-2
Scarlet One Beach MH-9
Scarlet Ridge—ridge NC-3
Scarlet Ridge Creek—stream NC-3
Scarlets Mill (White Bear Station)—locale PA-2
Scarlet Spring—spring AZ-5
Scarlett And Davis Canyon CA-9
Scarlett Hill—summit NC-3
Scarlett JHS—school MI-6
Scarlett Ranch—locale WY-8
Scarletts Brook—stream MA-1
Scarlet Two Beach MH-9
Scar Mountain Trail—trail OR-9
Scar Mtn—summit OR-9
Scar Mtn—summit WA-9
Scarp Canyon—valley NV-8
Scarp Creek—stream AK-9
Scarpet Peak—summit CA-9
Scarp Hill—summit AZ-5
Scarp Ridge—ridge CO-8
Scarred Branch—stream NC-3
Scar Ridge—ridge NH-1
Scarrit Bible and Training School for Women TN-4
Scarritt, Edward Lucky, House—hist pl MO-7
Scarritt, Rev. Nathan, House—hist pl MO-7
Scarritt, William Chick, House—hist pl MO-7
Scarritt Bldg and Arcade—hist pl MO-7
Scarritt Brook—stream NH-1
Scarritt Coll—school TN-4
Scarritt College Hist Dist—hist pl TN-4
Scarritt Hill—summit NH-1
Scarritt Sch—school MO-7
Scar Run—stream PA-2
Scar Run Trail—trail PA-2
Scarsdale IL-6
**Scarsdale**—pop pl LA-4
**Scarsdale**—pop pl NY-2
Scarsdale Canal—canal LA-4
Scarsdale Country Club—other NY-2
**Scarsdale Downs**—pop pl NY-2
**Scarsdale Park**—pop pl NY-2
Scarsdale Pumping Station—locale LA-4
**Scarsdale (subdivision)**—pop pl NC-3
Scarsdale (Town of)—civ div NY-2
Scarse Grease AL-4
Scarsland Lake—reservoir SD-7
Scar Tank—reservoir AZ-5
Scar Top Mtn—summit CO-8
Scarum Creek AL-4
**Scarville**—pop pl IA-7
**Scary**—pop pl WV-2
Scary Ch—church WV-2
Scary Creek—stream (2) WV-2
Scary Hollow—valley TN-4
Scary Sch—school WV-2
Scataway Creek—stream GA-3
Scatchet Head—cliff WA-9
Scat Creek—stream ID-8
Scates Branch—stream VA-3
Scates Cem—cemetery KS-7
Scates Millstream—stream VA-3
Scat Lake—lake LA-4
Scat Lake—lake WI-6
Scatter Branch—locale TX-5
Scatter Branch Cem—cemetery TX-5
Scatterbranch Creek—stream TX-5
Scatter Creek WA-9
Scatter Creek—stream AR-4
Scatter Creek—stream (2) KS-7
Scatter Creek—stream OK-5
Scatter Creek—stream TX-5
Scatter Creek—stream (7) WA-9
Scatter Creek—stream WY-8
Scatter Creek Campground—locale WA-9
Scatter Creek Ch—church AR-4
Scatterday Cem—cemetery OH-6
Scattered Rice Lake—lake WI-6
Scattered Rocks—rock FL-3
Scattered Willow Wash—stream AZ-5
Scattergood Cem—cemetery GA-3
Scattergood Sch—school IA-7
Scattering Branch—stream MO-7
Scattering Fork—stream IL-6
Scattering Fork—stream MO-7
Scattering Point Creek—stream IL-6
Scattering Springs—spring MT-8
Scatterman Lake—lake TX-5
Scatter Peak, The—summit AK-9
Scatter Ridge—ridge (2) OH-6
**Scattersville**—pop pl TN-4
Scattersville Sch (historical)—school TN-4
**Scattertown**—pop pl (2) PA-2
Scatter Wash—stream AZ-5
Scatterwood Ch—church SD-7
Scatterwood Community Bldg—building SD-7
Scatterwood (historical)—locale SD-7
Scatterwood Lake SD-7
Scatterwood Lake—lake SD-7
Scatterwood Lakes SD-7
Scatterwood Township (historical)—civil SD-7
Scaup Lake—lake (2) AK-9
Scaup Lake—lake (2) MI-6
Scaup Lake—lake WY-8
Scaur, The—summit NH-1
Scaur Peak—summit NH-1
Scawley Creek—stream TN-4
S & C Distribution Center Airp—airport PA-2
S. C. DOBSON (log canoe)—hist pl MD-2
Sceantocke River CT-1
Scearce Gammon Cem—cemetery VA-3
Scearce House—hist pl KY-4
Scearces—locale MO-7
Scearcorn Creek GA-3
Scecina High School IN-6
Scecina Memorial HS—school IN-6
Sceggins Creek GA-3
Scelebsprung Islet PW-9
Scelly Creek AZ-5
Sce Mohave Heliport—airport NV-8
Scenery Cove—bay AK-9
Scenery Creek—stream AK-9
Scenery Gulch—valley CO-8
**Scenery Hill**—pop pl PA-2
Scenery Hill—summit PA-2
Scenery Lake—lake AK-9
Scenery Mtn—summit MT-8
Scenia Ridge Creek AL-4
Scenic—locale UT-8
Scenic—locale WA-9
**Scenic**—pop pl SD-7
Scenic Basin—basin SD-7
Scenic Bay—bay ID-8
Scenic Bay Baptist Ch—church FL-3
Scenic Beach—beach WA-9
**Scenic Brook Estates**—pop pl CA-9
Scenic Cem—cemetery SD-7
Scenic Center—uninc pl CA-9
Scenic City Cooperative Oil Company—hist pl MN-6
Scenic Creek—stream ID-8
Scenic Creek—stream WA-9
Scenic Drive Hist Dist—hist pl MS-4
**Scenic Heights**—pop pl AL-4
**Scenic Heights**—pop pl IN-6
**Scenic Heights**—pop pl TN-4
Scenic Heights—ridge CA-9
Scenic Heights—summit WA-9
Scenic Heights Baptist Ch—church FL-3
Scenic Heights Sch—school FL-3
Scenic Heights Sch—school MN-6
**Scenic Hill**—pop pl IN-6
Scenic Hills—locale GA-3
**Scenic Hills**—pop pl PA-2
Scenic Hills Cem—cemetery OR-9
Scenic Hills Ch—church FL-3
Scenic Hill Sch—school TN-4
Scenic Hills Club Lake Dam—dam MS-4
Scenic Hills Country Club—locale FL-3
Scenic Hills Elem Sch—school PA-2
Scenic Hills Lake—reservoir AR-4
Scenic Hills Sch PA-2
**Scenic Hills (subdivision)**—pop pl (2) AL-4
Scenic Hotel—hist pl MN-6
Scenic Lake—lake AK-9
Scenic Lake—lake ID-8
Scenic Lake—reservoir KY-4
Scenic Lake—reservoir TN-4
Scenic Lake Dam—dam TN-4
Scenic Lakes—lake MT-8
Scenic Land Ch—church GA-3
Scenic Lodge—locale ID-8
Scenic Lookout Tower—locale MN-6
Scenic Meadow—flat CA-9
Scenic Mesa—summit CO-8
Scenic Mtn—summit TX-5
Scenic No. 7 Township—civ div SD-7
Scenic Park—park NE-7
**Scenic Park**—pop pl VA-3
Scenic Park Ch—church VA-3
Scenic Pass—gap WY-8
Scenic Point—cape TX-5
Scenic Point—summit MT-8
Scenic Point Estates—locale TN-4
Scenic State Park—park MN-6
**Scenic Terrace (subdivision)**—pop pl TN-4
Scenic Township—civil SD-7
Scenic View Golf Course—locale TN-4
**Scenic View (subdivision)**—pop pl AL-4
Scenic Vista Trail—trail PA-2
**Scenic West Estates (subdivision)**—pop pl AL-4
Scenic Woods—locale TN-4
**Scenic Woods**—pop pl TN-4
**Scenic Woods**—pop pl TX-5
Scenic Woods Park—park TX-5
Scenic Woods Sch—school TX-5
Scepter Creek—stream CA-9
Scepter Lake—lake CA-9
Scepter Pass—gap CA-9
Sceptre Tunnel—mine CO-8
Scera Park Sch—school UT-8
Schaad Creek—stream NE-7
Schaad Rsvr—reservoir OR-9
Schaad Spring—spring TN-4
Schaads Rsvr—reservoir CA-9
Schaaf Creek—stream MO-7
Schaaf Ditch—canal IN-6
Schaaf Ditch—canal OH-6
Schaaf Hollow—valley IL-6
Schaaf Lake—lake MI-6
Schaaf Lake—lake WI-6
Schaak Ranch—locale MT-8
Schaal—locale AR-4
Schaal Branch—stream AR-4
Schaat Creek—stream MI-6
Schaawe Creek MI-6
Schaawe Lake—lake MI-6
Schaback Strip—airport MO-7
Schaben Oil Field—oilfield KS-7
Schaberg—locale AR-4
Schaberg Cem—cemetery AR-4
Schaber Rsvr—reservoir OR-9
Schabert Mine—mine MT-8
Schacht Cem—cemetery NE-7
Schacht Lake Dam—dam IN-6
Schackle Creek—stream WA-9
Schackman Lake—lake MN-6
Schacte Creek—stream WI-6
Schact Lake—reservoir IN-6
Schadel Cem—cemetery OH-6
Schadel Oil Field—oilfield KS-7
Schadels Airp—airport PA-2
Schader, Mount—summit NV-8
**Schades Corner**—pop pl PA-2
Schade Trail—trail PA-2
Schadler Cow Camp—locale OR-9
Schadler Ditch—canal CA-9
Schadts PA-2
Schaede Cem—cemetery KS-7
**Schaefer**—pop pl WA-9
Schaefer Bay—bay MN-6
Schaefer Creek—stream CO-8
Schaefer Creek—stream ID-8
Schaefer Creek—stream PA-2
Schaefer Creek—stream WA-9
Schaefer Creek Campground—locale WA-9
Schaefer Draw—valley CO-8
Schaefer Field—park IA-7
Schaefer-Goodman Mine—mine TN-4
Schaefer Head—summit PA-2
Schaefer JHS—school OH-6
Schaefer Lake—lake WA-9
**Schaefer Lake**—pop pl IN-6
Schaefer Lake—reservoir IN-6
Schaefer Lake Dam—dam IN-6
Schaefer-Marks House—hist pl GA-3
Schaefer Park—park WI-6
Schaefer Ranch—locale NV-8
Schaefer Run—stream PA-2
Schaefers Bldg—hist pl OR-9
Schaefers Run PA-2
**Schaeferville**—pop pl IL-6
**Schaeferville**—pop pl SD-7
Schaeffer, Charles, Sch—hist pl PA-2
Schaeffer, Michael, House—hist pl IN-6
Schaeffer, W. F., House—hist pl TX-5
Schaeffer Cem—cemetery MO-7
Schaeffer Cem—cemetery WV-2
Schaeffer Ch—church PA-2
Schaeffer Creek—stream NY-2
Schaeffer Hill—summit IL-6
Schaeffer Hollow—valley IL-6
Schaeffer Lake—lake MN-6
Schaeffer Meadow—flat (2) CA-9
Schaeffer Mtn—summit CA-9
Schaeffer Point—cape MI-6
Schaeffer Pond—lake IL-6
Schaeffer Ranch—locale ND-7
Schaeffer Run PA-2
Schaeffers Brook—stream NY-2
Schaeffer Sch PA-2
Schaeffer Sch—school MI-6
Schaeffer Sch—school (2) PA-2
Schaeffer Sch—school SD-7
Schaeffer Spur—locale WA-9
**Schaefferstown**—pop pl PA-2
Schaefferstown Elem Sch—school PA-2
Schaefferstown Spring—spring PA-2
Schaeffer Stringer—stream CA-9
Schaer, Theodore B., Mound—hist pl OH-6
Schaer House—hist pl AR-4
**Schafer**—pop pl ND-7
Schafer Airfield—airport KS-7
Schafer Basin—basin CO-8
Schafer Cem—cemetery ND-7
Schafer Creek—stream (2) MT-8
Schafer Creek—stream OR-9
Schafer Creek—stream (3) WA-9
Schafer Gulch—valley CO-8
Schafer Gulch—valley ID-8
Schafer House—hist pl OH-6
Schafer HS—school MI-6
Schafer Lake—lake (2) MN-6
Schafer Meadows—flat MT-8
Schafer Memorial Camp—locale KY-4
Schafer Mine—mine ID-8
Schafer Park—park CO-8
Schafer Park Sch—school CA-9
Schafer Peak—summit ID-8
Schafer Pocket—basin WA-9
Schafer Ranch—locale MT-8
Schafer Ranger Station—locale MT-8
Schafer Rsvr—reservoir CO-8
Schafer Sch—school IL-6
Schafer Spring—spring MO-7
Schafers Tank—reservoir AZ-5
Schafer State Park—park WA-9
**Schafer Township**—pop pl ND-7
Schafer Trail UT-8
Schaffenaker Mtn—summit WV-2
Schaffer—locale KS-7
**Schaffer**—pop pl MI-6
Schaffer Cabin—locale OR-9
Schaffer Cem—cemetery MI-6
Schaffer Cem—cemetery OH-6
Schaffer Creek CO-8
Schaffer Creek—stream GA-3
Schaffer Creek—stream IA-7
Schaffer Creek—stream KS-7
Schaffer Farmstead—hist pl SD-7
Schaffer Island—island IL-6
Schaffer Lake—lake CO-8
Schaffer Lake—lake MI-6
Schaffer Mtn—summit CA-9
Schaffer Sch—school KS-7
Schaffer Sch (abandoned)—school PA-2
Schaffer Sch (historical)—school (2) PA-2
Schaffers Ponds—reservoir NJ-2
Schaffer Spring—spring CA-9
Schaffers Run—stream PA-2
Schaffer Wash AZ-5
Schaffer Well Number One—well NV-8
Schaffhauser Cem—cemetery AR-4
Schaff JHS—school OH-6
Schaffline Creek—stream TX-5
Schaffner Creek—stream ND-7
Schaffner Lake—lake IL-6
Schaffner Sch—school KY-4
Schaff Sch—school ND-7
**Schaghticoke**—pop pl NY-2
**Schaghticoke Hill**—pop pl NY-2
Schaghticoke Ind Res—reserve CT-1
Schaghticoke Mtn—summit NY-2
**Schaghticoke (Town of)**—pop pl NY-2
Schagrin, Charles, Bldg—hist pl DE-2
Schaible ND-7
**Schaidt**—pop pl MD-2
Schalar Creek OK-5
Schales Branch—stream AR-4
Schales Cem—cemetery (2) AR-4
Schalks—locale NJ-2
Schalks Creek—stream MI-6
Schall Cem—cemetery MO-7
Schallcross Sch—school PA-2
Schallenberger Ridge—ridge CA-9
Schallenberger Sch—school CA-9
**Schaller**—pop pl IA-7
Schaller Cem—cemetery IA-7
Schaller Sch—school WI-6
Schallert Sch—school TX-5
Schallow Mountain WA-9
Schall Sch (abandoned)—school PA-2
Schalls Gap—gap PA-2
Schalls Sch—school MO-7
Schalm Sch—school MI-6
Schalow Mtn—summit WA-9
Schambaugh-Cope Cem—cemetery MO-7
Schamberg Bridge—bridge OR-9
Schamber (historical)—locale SD-7
**Schamberville**—pop pl MS-4
Schamp Creek—stream CA-9
Schampinal Lake LA-4
Schampinol Lake LA-4
Schanade Brook—stream CT-1
Schanbacher Hollow—valley PA-2
Schanbacher Trail—trail (2) PA-2
Schanen Estates Sch—school TX-5
Schanen-Zolling House—hist pl OR-9
Schang Ditch—canal IN-6
Schanning Cem—cemetery MO-7
Schannon Cem—cemetery MO-7
Schant Drain—canal MI-6
Schantz, Adam Sr., House—hist pl OH-6
Schantz, George, House and Store—hist pl MI-6
Schantzen Lake—lake MN-6
Schantz Hill—summit PA-2
Schantz-Inseln MP-9
Schantz Spring—spring PA-2
Schantzs Spring PA-2

Schanz Atoll ... MP-9
Schanz Inseln ... MP-9
Schapeler Bend—bend ... MO-7
Schapler, Frank, House—hist pl ... MI-6
Schapps Pond ... PA-2
**Schapville**—pop pl ... IL-6
**Scharbauer City**—pop pl ... TX-5
Scharbauer Oil Field—oilfield ... TX-5
Scharbauer Ranch—locale ... NM-5
Scharbauer Ranch—locale (2) ... TX-5
Scharbrough Well—well ... NM-5
Schardein Cem—cemetery ... KY-4
Scharen Gulch—valley ... WY-8
Scharer Drain—stream ... MI-6
Scharff Cabin Creek—stream ... OR-9
Scharff Sch—school ... IA-7
Scharf Mesa—summit ... UT-8
Scharf Playground—park ... MA-1
Scharf Rsvr—reservoir ... OR-9
Scharman Dam*—dam ... SD-7
Scharnagel Cem—cemetery ... AL-4
Scharnagel-Rauschenberg Cem ... AL-4
Scharnagle Branch—stream ... AL-4
Scharnagle Cem—cemetery ... AL-4
Scharnberg County Park—park ... IA-7
Scharrer Bayou—bay ... FL-3
Scharrer Canal ... FL-3
Scharrer Cut—channel ... FL-3
Scharsch Ranch—locale (2) ... CA-9
Schartner Cem—cemetery ... SD-7
Scharwtz Creek ... OR-9
Schasse Hill—summit ... TX-5
Schasser Lake—lake ... MI-6
Schatley Ditch ... IN-6
Schattel—locale ... TX-5
Schattinger Homestead—locale ... CO-8
Schattinger Ranch—locale ... CO-8
Schatulga—locale ... GA-3
Schatz ... MT-8
Schatz, Jacob, House—hist pl ... SD-7
Schatz Dam—dam ... ND-7
Schatzley Ditch—canal ... IN-6
Schatz Sch—school ... SD-7
Schaub, John Jacob, House—hist pl ... NC-3
Schaub Butte—summit ... WY-8
Schaub Dam—dam ... SD-7
Schaudel Rsvr—reservoir ... MT-8
Schauder Hotel—hist pl ... IA-7
Schauer Filling Station—hist pl ... TX-5
Schauer Lake ... MN-6
Schauer Lake—lake ... MN-6
**Schauers Acres**—pop pl ... OH-6
Schauger Hill ... MI-6
Schaulon ... FM-9
Schaulon Point ... FM-9
Schaumberg ... IL-6
Schaumboch's Tavern—hist pl ... PA-2
**Schaumburg**—pop pl ... IL-6
Schaumburg Center ... IL-6
Schaumburg Center—other ... IL-6
Schaumburg Green ... IL-6
Schaumburg Sch—school ... IL-6
Schaumburg Sch—school ... LA-4
**Schaumburg (sta.)**—pop pl ... IL-6
**Schaumburg (Township of)**—pop pl ... IL-6
Schaunamann School (Abandoned)—locale ... MN-6
Schau Peak—summit ... CA-9
**Schaupps**—pop pl ... NE-7
Schaur Dam—dam ... SD-7
Schaut Creek—stream ... MI-6
Schautz Memorial Stadium—park ... PA-2
Schauweker Lake—lake ... IN-6
Schave Drain—canal ... MI-6
**Schawana**—pop pl ... WA-9
Schawanes Springs Branch—stream ... MO-7
Schawe Cem—cemetery ... TX-5
Schayots Canal—canal ... LA-4
Schcro Gana—summit ... NM-5
Scheaffer Traditional A Elem Sch—school ... PA-2
Schebler, Richard, House—hist pl ... IA-7
Schechs Mill—hist pl ... MN-6
Schechs Mill—locale ... MN-6
Schechtman Branch—stream ... IA-7
Scheckels Dam—dam ... OR-9
Scheckels Rsvr—reservoir ... OR-9
Schecker Gulch—valley ... CO-8
Scheck Skyline Airp—airport ... PA-2
Schedule Brook—stream ... ME-1
Scheeker Spring—spring ... CO-8
Scheel Cem—cemetery ... TX-5
Scheeldre Mine—mine ... CA-9
Scheele Creek—stream ... OR-9
**Scheel Estates Subdivision**—pop pl ... UT-8
**Scheelite**—pop pl ... CA-9
Scheelite Canyon—valley ... AZ-5
Scheelite Lake—lake ... WA-9
Scheelite Pass—gap ... WA-9
Scheelite Ridge—ridge ... AZ-5
Scheer Ranch—locale ... NE-7
Scheffenburg Valley—basin ... NE-7
Scheffer Ditch—canal ... IN-6
Scheffer Mountain ... CA-9
Scheffer Sch—school ... MN-6
Scheffle Drain—stream ... MI-6
Schefflin—locale ... OR-9
Schefflin Sch—school ... OR-9
**Schefield**—pop pl ... ND-7
Scheggs Draw—valley ... WY-8
Scheh Sch—school ... TX-5
Scheiben Insel ... FM-9
Scheiben Island ... FM-9
Scheiben Islet ... FM-9
Scheiben Reef—bar ... MP-9
Scheiben Riff ... MP-9
Scheid Ditch—canal ... OH-6
**Scheideck**—pop pl ... CA-9
Scheideck Camp—locale ... CA-9
Scheider's Opera House—hist pl ... NE-7
Scheidler Run—stream ... WV-2
Scheid Park—park ... MI-6
Scheid Quarry—mine ... AR-4
Scheids Park—park ... MN-6
Scheidy—locale ... PA-2
Scheifferstadt—hist pl ... MD-2
Scheiller Cem—cemetery ... KS-7
Scheiman Bridge—bridge ... IN-6
Scheimersville ... PA-2
Scheiner Creek—stream ... WA-9
Scheiriern Sch—school ... MI-6
Scheisinger ... WI-6
Scheiss Creek ... ID-8
Schekaha (historical)—locale ... MS-4
Schelburne Centre ... MA-1
Schelfhout Point—cape ... MN-6
Schelicher Lake—lake ... MN-6
Schelin Lake—lake ... MN-6
Schelite Pass ... WA-9
Schelke Drain—canal ... MI-6
Schell—locale ... MD-2
Schell—locale ... WV-2
Schell, August, Brewing Company—hist pl ... MN-6
Schell, Otto, House—hist pl ... MN-6
Schellbach Butte—summit ... AZ-5
Schellbourne—locale ... NV-8
Schellbourne Maintenance Station—locale ... NV-8
Schellbourne Pass—gap ... NV-8
Schellbourne Ranch ... NV-8
Schellbourne Station—locale ... NV-8
Schell Bridge—bridge ... MA-1
Schellburg ... PA-2
Schell Canyon—valley ... AZ-5
Schell Cem—cemetery ... OH-6
**Schell City**—pop pl ... MO-7
Schell Creek ... NV-8
Schell Creek—stream ... CA-9
Schell Creek—stream ... KS-7
Schell Creek—stream ... NV-8
Schell Creek Division—forest ... NV-8
Schell Creek Range—range ... NV-8
Schelldorf Draw—valley ... WY-8
Schellenberger Island ... PA-2
Schellenbergers Island—island ... PA-2
Schellenger Creek—stream ... NJ-2
Schellenger Landing—locale ... NJ-2
Schellengers Landing—uninc pl ... NJ-2
**Scheller**—pop pl ... IL-6
Scheller Lakes—lake ... IL-6
Schellers Cem—cemetery ... WI-6
Schelley Knob—summit ... TN-4
Schell Gulch—valley ... AZ-5
Schellinger Creek ... NJ-2
Schellin Park—park ... OH-6
Schell Mtn—summit ... CA-9
Schell Park—park ... KS-7
Schell Run—stream ... PA-2
**Schellsburg**—pop pl ... PA-2
Schellsburg Borough—civil ... PA-2
Schell Slough—stream ... CA-9
Schell Spring—spring ... AZ-5
Schell Spring—spring ... NV-8
**Schellville**—pop pl ... CA-9
Schellys Station ... PA-2
Schemehorn Cem—cemetery ... NY-2
Schemerhorn Ridge—ridge ... KY-4
Schemmel Cem—cemetery ... OH-6
Schemmel Island—island ... IA-7
Schemn Drain—canal ... MI-6
Schenak Job Corps Camp ... NC-3
Schenck Creek—stream ... OH-6
**Schenck Estates**—pop pl ... VA-3
Schenck Job Corps Center—locale ... NC-3
Schenck's ... OH-6
Schencks Cem—cemetery ... PA-2
Schenck Sch—school ... CO-8
Schenck Sch—school ... MI-6
Schenck Sch—school ... OH-6
Schenck Sch—school ... TX-5
Schencks Pond—reservoir ... MA-1
Schencks Pond Dam—dam ... MA-1
Schencks Station ... PA-2
Schenck Sulpher Springs ... AL-4
Schendel Lake—lake ... MN-6
Schendel Sch—school ... CA-9
Schendler Cem—cemetery ... IL-6
**Schenectady**—pop pl ... NY-2
Schenectady Camp—locale ... NY-2
Schenectady City Hall and Post Office—hist pl ... NY-2
**Schenectady (County)**—pop pl ... NY-2
Schenectady General Depot—other ... NY-2
Schenectady Memorial Park—cemetery ... NY-2
Schenectady Mine—mine ... AZ-5
Schenectady Museum and Park—park ... NY-2
Schenectady Pumping Station—other ... NY-2
Schenectady Stadium—other ... NY-2
**Schenevus**—pop pl ... NY-2
Schenevus Creek—stream (2) ... NY-2
Schengen ... KS-7
Schenk Canyon—valley ... SD-7
Schenk Corners—locale ... MD-2
Schenk Creek—stream ... CA-9
Schenkel Ch—church ... PA-2
Schenk Lake—reservoir ... WV-2
Schenk Ranch—locale ... NE-7
Schenks Branch—stream ... VA-3
Schenks Ch—church ... PA-2
Schenk Sch—school ... WI-6
Schenk Seven Drain—canal ... CA-9
Schenk Six Drain—canal ... CA-9
**Schenks (Sulphur Springs)**—pop pl ... AL-4
Schenks White Sulpher Springs—spring ... AL-4
Schenks White Sulphur Springs ... AL-4
Schenk Ten Drain—canal ... CA-9
Schenk Two Drain—canal ... CA-9
Schenley—locale ... PA-2
Schenley Farms Hist Dist—hist pl ... PA-2
**Schenley Heights**—pop pl ... PA-2
Schenley HS—hist pl ... PA-2
Schenley HS—school ... PA-2
Schenley Park—hist pl ... PA-2
Schenley Park—park ... PA-2
Schenley Park Golf Course—locale ... PA-2
Schenley Ranch—locale ... CA-9
Schenley Station ... PA-2
Schenly Park—park ... FL-3
Schenob Brook—stream ... CT-1
Schenob Brook—stream ... MA-1
Schenop Brook ... MA-1
Schep Creek—stream ... TX-5
**Schepps Corner**—pop pl ... WY-8
**Schepps Corners**—pop pl ... NY-2
**Schepps Valley**—pop pl ... NJ-2
Scheraden School ... PA-2
Scherer, Frank C., Wagon Works—hist pl ... PA-2
Scherer Canyon—valley ... AZ-5
Scherer Cem—cemetery ... IN-6
Scherer Cem—cemetery ... NY-2
Scherer Ch—church ... SC-3
Scherer Ditch—canal ... OH-6
Scherer Gulch—valley ... CO-8
Scherer Hollow—valley ... OH-6
Scherer House—hist pl ... MS-4
Scherer Island—island ... IL-6
Scherer Park—park ... CA-9
Scherers Sch (abandoned)—school ... PA-2
**Scherersville**—pop pl ... PA-2
**Schererville**—pop pl ... IN-6
Schererville Ditch—canal ... IN-6
Scherman Ditch—canal ... IN-6
Schermerhorn Corners—locale ... NY-2
Schermerhorn Creek—stream ... WI-6
Schermerhorn Hill—summit ... CT-1
Schermerhorn Lake—lake ... MI-6
Schermerhorn Landing—locale ... NY-2
Schermerhorn Park—park ... MA-1
Schermerhorn Row Block—hist pl ... NY-2
Scherr—locale ... WV-2
**Schertz**—pop pl ... TX-5
Schertz-Cibolo (CCD)—cens area ... TX-5
Schertz-Cibolo HS—school ... TX-5
Schertz Sportmans Club—other ... TX-5
Schervier Hosp—hospital ... NY-2
Scherzberg Bayou—lake ... NE-7
Scherzberg Ranch—locale ... NE-7
Scherz Ditch—canal ... OH-6
Scherz School (Abandoned)—locale ... TX-5
Schesberger Drain—stream ... MI-6
Schess Cem—cemetery ... PA-2
Schesslers Sch—school ... PA-2
Schetter Creek—stream ... MI-6
Scheuer Creek—stream ... WI-6
Scheuer Ditch—canal ... IN-6
Scheuer Sch—school ... IL-6
Scheu Park—park ... NY-2
Scheurer, William Riley, House—hist pl ... OR-9
Scheurman Mtn—summit ... AZ-5
Scheurman Mtn Tank—summit ... AZ-5
Scheuter Spring—spring ... OR-9
Scheve Community Center—locale ... MO-7
Schexneyder ... LA-4
Schiager Sch—school ... SD-7
Schiben Reef ... MP-9
Schick—locale ... IL-6
Schick, Henry, Barn—hist pl ... ID-8
Schick Lake—lake ... NE-7
Schick Ranch—locale ... MT-8
Schicks Crossing ... IL-6
Schick's Express and Transfer Co.—hist pl ... IA-7
Schidler, Mount—summit ... WY-8
Schiebel Sch—school ... IL-6
Schieber Ditch—canal ... IN-6
Schiedler Rsvr—reservoir ... OR-9
Schieffelin Creek—stream ... AK-9
Schieffelin Gulch—valley ... OR-9
Schieffelin Neck ... ME-1
Schieffelin Point—cape ... ME-1
Schiele Museum—building ... NC-3
Schiele Nature Museum ... NC-3
Schiel Sch—school ... OH-6
Schiemann Lake—lake ... MI-6
Schierling Rsvr—reservoir ... OR-9
Schiesher Sch—school ... IL-6
Schiess Creek ... ID-8
Schiess Creek—stream ... ID-8
Schiesser Ranch—locale ... SD-7
Schiestel Drain—stream ... MI-6
Schiestler Peak—summit ... WY-8
Schiete Scout Reservation—locale ... SC-3
Schiever Sch—school ... PA-2
Schifferdecker Park—park ... MO-7
Schiffern Ranch—locale ... NE-7
Schiffman Bldg—hist pl ... AL-4
Schiffman Cove—valley ... AL-4
Schiff Trail—trail ... NY-2
Schildgen Pond—lake ... CT-1
Schildhauer Pond—reservoir ... WI-6
Schildkrote Rock—bar ... MH-9
Schildmeier Cem—cemetery ... IN-6
Schili Creek ... AZ-5
Schiller—locale ... ID-8
Schiller—other ... WI-6
Schiller Canyon—valley ... WY-8
Schiller Cem—cemetery ... TX-5
Schiller Classical Acad—school ... PA-2
Schiller Creek—stream ... ID-8
Schiller Creek—stream ... MT-8
Schiller Elem Sch—hist pl ... PA-2
Schiller Park—park (2) ... NY-2
Schiller Park—park ... OH-6
**Schiller Park**—pop pl ... IL-6
Schiller Pond—lake ... IL-6
Schiller Pond—reservoir ... NJ-2
Schiller Pond Dam—dam ... NJ-2
Schiller Rsvr—reservoir ... MT-8
Schiller Sch—school (2) ... IL-6
Schiller Sch—school ... MN-6
Schiller Sch Number 1—school ... ND-7
Schiller Sch Number 2—school ... ND-7
Schiller Sch Number 3—school ... ND-7
**Schiller Township**—pop pl ... ND-7
Schiller Woods North—woods ... IL-6
Schiller Woods South—woods ... IL-6
Schilling ... CA-9
Schilling—locale ... CA-9
Schilling—locale ... MT-8
Schilling Archeol District—hist pl ... MN-6
Schilling Branch—stream ... TX-5
Schilling Bridge—bridge ... ND-7
Schilling Cem—cemetery (2) ... LA-4
Schilling Creek—stream ... AK-9
Schilling Creek—stream ... WA-9
Schilling Hollow—valley ... OH-6
Schilling Lake—lake ... CA-9
Schilling Lake—lake ... MN-6
Schilling Park—park ... OK-5
Schillings Cem—cemetery ... LA-4
Schilling Sch—school ... CA-9
Schilling Sch—school ... MN-6
Schillings Gap ... VA-3
Schilling Siding—locale ... MT-8
Schillings Lake—lake ... NY-2
Schilling Spring—spring ... OR-9
Schillings Spring ... CO-8
Schilling Windmill—locale ... TX-5
Schillpades Creek ... DE-2
**Schills**—pop pl ... PA-2
Schilpatts Creek ... DE-2
Schilter Creek—stream ... AK-9
Schimanel Bridge—bridge ... OR-9
Schiminoe Creek—stream ... VA-3
Schimke Creek—stream (2) ... MI-6
Schimke Sch—school ... SD-7
Schimmel Cave—cave ... AL-4
Schimmelhorn Creek—stream ... MN-6
Schimmelpfennig, Johann, Farmstead—hist pl ... MN-6
Schimmel Slough—lake ... SD-7
Schimmer, Lake—lake ... ND-7
Schimmerhorn Lake—lake ... FL-3
Schimnel Ditch—canal ... IN-6
Schinasi House—hist pl ... NY-2
**Schindler**—pop pl ... TX-5
Schindler,R.M. House—hist pl ... CA-9
Schindler Cem—cemetery ... MO-7
Schindler Creek—stream ... CA-9
Schindler Creek—stream ... NE-7
Schindler Landing—locale ... OR-9
Schindler Ranch—locale ... MT-8
Schindler Rsvr—reservoir ... OR-9
Schindorff Hill—summit ... MO-7
Schinery Well—well ... TX-5
Schine State Theatre—hist pl ... OH-6
Schinette Hollow—valley ... AR-4
Schinn Lake—lake ... MN-6
Schinzel Flats—flat ... CO-8
Schinzel Meadows ... CO-8
Schipper Campground—locale ... ID-8
Schipple Sch—school ... KS-7
Schirmer Ravine—valley ... CA-9
Schischareff Strait ... MP-9
Schischmareff-Strasse ... MP-9
Schischmarev Strait—channel ... MP-9
Schisel Lake—lake ... WI-6
Schishmarer ... MP-9
Schisler Lake—lake ... MN-6
Schissler Creek—stream ... ID-8
Schist Creek—stream ... AK-9
Schisto Basin—basin ... CO-8
Schivelly Gulch ... MT-8
Schively Gulch—valley ... MT-8
Schladoer Creek—stream ... TX-5
Schladoer Ranch—locale ... TX-5
Schlag Draw—valley ... NV-8
Schlagel Creek—stream ... NE-7
Schlagel Sch—school ... NE-7
Schlager, Ferdinand, House—hist pl ... WA-9
Schlamm Lake ... MN-6
Schlamm Lake—reservoir ... IN-6
Schlamm Lake Dam—dam ... IN-6
Schlamn Lake—lake ... MN-6
Schlamp Lake ... MN-6
Schlanger Park—park ... KS-7
Schlanker Branch—stream ... MO-7
Schlapp, George E., House—hist pl ... IA-7
Schlarman HS—school ... IL-6
**Schlater**—pop pl ... MS-4
Schlater Baptist Ch—church ... MS-4
Schlater Consolidated Sch—school ... MS-4
Schlater Ditch—canal ... IN-6
Schlather Cem—cemetery ... TX-5
**Schlatitz**—pop pl ... MO-7
Schlatoz ... MO-7
Schlatter Cem—cemetery ... IN-6
Schlatter Lake—lake ... MI-6
Schlatterville—locale ... GA-3
Schlaudt Hills—summit ... TX-5
Schlautmann Sch—school ... WY-8
Schlechts Butte—summit ... AZ-5
Schlecht-Thom Dam—dam ... ND-7
Schlecht-Wiexel Dam—dam ... ND-7
Schlect Hollow—valley ... IA-7
Schlee Brewery Hist Dist—hist pl ... OH-6
Schlee-Kemmler Bldg—hist pl ... OH-6
**Schlegal**—pop pl ... OK-5
Schlegel—locale ... OK-5
Schlegel Lake—lake ... CO-8
Schlegel Lake—reservoir ... NJ-2
Schlegel Park—park ... PA-2
Schlegel Road Sch—school ... NY-2
Schlegel Run—stream ... PA-2
Schlegels Grove—locale ... OH-6
Schlehubers Marsh—lake ... MI-6
Schlei Bayou—stream ... LA-4
Schleichart Draw—valley ... SD-7
Schleichart Draw Rsvr—reservoir ... SD-7
**Schleicher (County)**—pop pl ... TX-5
Schleicher Mtn—summit ... TX-5
Schleiders Ditch—canal ... LA-4
Schleier, George, Mansion—hist pl ... CO-8
Schleighsingerville ... WI-6
Schlein Ranger Station—locale ... CA-9
Schlein Trail—trail ... CA-9
Schleisinger ... WI-6
Schleisingerville ... WI-6
Schlem Cem—cemetery ... IL-6
Schlemmer, Otto, Bldg—hist pl ... IN-6
Schlemmer Airp—airport ... MO-7
Schlemmer Swamp—swamp ... MI-6
**Schlemville**—pop pl ... PA-2
Schlender Cem—cemetery ... KS-7
Schlenke Lake ... WI-6
Schlenker Dam—dam ... ND-7
Schlensker Ditch—canal ... IN-6
Schlepp Ranch—locale ... MT-8
Schlesinger Ranch—locale ... MT-8
Schlesinger Sch—school ... IL-6
Schlesser-Burrows House—hist pl ... TX-5
Schlessers Corners—locale ... PA-2
Schlessinger House—hist pl ... CO-8
Schlessman Ditch—canal ... OH-6
**Schleswig**—pop pl ... IA-7
Schleswig Cem—cemetery ... WI-6
**Schleswig (Town of)**—pop pl ... WI-6
Schleur Creek—stream ... OR-9
Schleur Gulch—valley ... OR-9
Schleuter Ranch—locale ... NE-7
Schley—locale ... AL-4
Schley—locale ... MN-6
Schley—locale ... MS-4
Schley—locale ... MT-8
Schley—locale ... OH-6
Schley—locale ... VA-3
**Schley**—pop pl ... GA-3
**Schley**—pop pl ... IN-6
**Schley**—pop pl ... IA-7
**Schley**—pop pl ... KY-4
**Schley**—pop pl ... NC-3
Schley Cem—cemetery ... GA-3
**Schley (County)**—pop pl ... GA-3
Schley County Courthouse—hist pl ... GA-3
Schley Creek ... MT-8
Schley Creek—stream ... AK-9
Schley Creek—stream ... MT-8
Schley Mine—mine ... MN-6
Schley Mtn—summit ... MT-8
Schley Pond—lake ... NY-2
Schley Pond—reservoir ... GA-3
Schley Sch—school ... IL-6
Schley School—locale ... CO-8
Schleys Lake ... WI-6
**Schley (Town of)**—pop pl ... WI-6
Schley Township—civil ... SD-7
Schlicher Covered Bridge—bridge ... PA-2
Schlicher Covered Bridge—hist pl ... PA-2
Schlicht Draw—valley ... WY-8
**Schlichter**—pop pl ... PA-2
Schlichtig House—hist pl ... MO-7
Schlichting Ditch—canal (2) ... WY-8
Schlichting Mountain ... WY-8
Schlichtling Bldg—hist pl ... MI-6
Schlicker Ditch—canal ... OH-6
Schlict Draw ... WY-8
Schlieght Lake—lake ... ID-8
Schlieper Spring—spring ... AR-4
Schlight Cem—cemetery ... MO-7
Schlimmer Point—cape ... MN-6
Schlimmer Sch (abandoned)—school ... PA-2
Schlinke Windmill—locale ... TX-5
Schlinkman Creek—stream ... OR-9
Schlitz, Joseph, Brewing Company Saloon—hist pl ... WI-6
Schlitz, Victor, House—hist pl ... WI-6
Schlitz Creek—stream ... AK-9
Schlitz Hotel—hist pl ... MN-6
Schlomberg Cabin—locale ... CA-9
Schlomer—locale ... WA-9
Schlopata Cem—cemetery ... TX-5
Schlosser, Frank, Complex—hist pl ... IL-6
Schlosser Creek—stream ... MT-8
Schlosser Lake—lake ... WI-6
Schlosser Park—park ... IA-7
Schlosser Sch—school ... SD-7
Schlot Creek—stream ... MI-6
Schlotz Branch—stream ... MO-7
Schluckbier Drain—canal ... MI-6
**Schluersburg**—pop pl ... MO-7
Schluersburg Branch ... MO-7
Schluersburg Creek—stream ... MO-7
Schlupe Spring—spring ... OR-9
Schly Creek ... NV-8
Schmadeke Rsvr—reservoir ... OR-9
Schmadel Ditch—canal ... IN-6
Schmader Airp—airport ... PA-2
Schmaderer Sch—school ... NE-7
Schmale Bros Ranch—locale ... WY-8
Schmale Ranch—locale ... WY-8
Schmall Marsh—swamp ... MN-6
Schmals Stadt ... PA-2
Schmaltz Drain—canal ... MI-6
Schmalzstadt ... PA-2
Schman Gulch ... UT-8
Schmardebeck Ditch—canal ... OH-6
Schmeider Gulch—valley ... CA-9
Schmelzel, H. A., House—hist pl ... ID-8
Schmerschall, John F., House—hist pl ... ID-8
Schmid Airp—airport ... TN-4
Schmidelkoffer Dutton Vogers Ditch—canal ... MT-8
Schmidell, Lake—lake ... CA-9
Schmid Lake ... MI-6
Schmid Lake—lake ... MN-6
Schmid Meadows—flat ... WA-9
Schmid Ridge—ridge ... ID-8
Schmid Rsvr—reservoir ... OR-9
Schmid Sch—school ... IL-6
Schmids Lake—lake ... IL-6
**Schmidt**—pop pl ... ND-7
Schmidt, F. Jacob, House—hist pl ... IA-7
Schmidt, George, House—hist pl ... CO-8
Schmidt Arch—arch ... UT-8
Schmidt Block—hist pl ... IA-7
Schmidt Bottom—bend ... ND-7
Schmidt Branch ... TN-4
Schmidt Branch—stream ... TX-5
Schmidt Camp—locale ... CA-9
Schmidt Cem—cemetery ... IL-6
Schmidt Cem—cemetery (3) ... MO-7
Schmidt Cem—cemetery ... ND-7
Schmidt Cem—cemetery (2) ... TX-5
Schmidt Corner—locale ... WI-6
**Schmidt Corner**—pop pl ... MI-6
Schmidt Coulee—valley ... MN-6
Schmidt Creek—stream ... CA-9
Schmidt Creek—stream ... ID-8
Schmidt Creek—stream ... MI-6
Schmidt Creek—stream ... MN-6
Schmidt Creek—stream ... MT-8
Schmidt Creek—stream ... NV-8
Schmidt Dam—dam ... ND-7
Schmidt Ditch—canal ... CA-9
Schmidt Ditch—canal ... IN-6
Schmidt Drain—canal ... MI-6
Schmidt Hill—summit ... TX-5
Schmidt Hollow—valley ... TN-4
Schmidt House—hist pl ... IA-7
Schmidt House—hist pl ... MO-7
Schmidt Island—island ... WI-6
Schmidt Lake ... MN-6
Schmidt Lake—lake ... MI-6
Schmidt Lake—lake (4) ... MN-6
Schmidt Lake—lake ... ND-7
Schmidt Lake Dam—dam ... MS-4
**Schmidt Landing**—pop pl ... SD-7
Schmidtlein Ranch (historical)—locale ... NV-8
Schmidt Marsh—swamp ... NY-2
Schmidt Number 2 Dam—dam ... SD-7
Schmidt Park—park ... MN-6
Schmidt Ranch—locale (2) ... CA-9
Schmidt Ranch—locale ... NE-7
Schmidt Ranch—locale ... WA-9
Schmidt Road Number 1 Dam—dam ... SD-7
Schmidt Rsvr—reservoir (2) ... MT-8
Schmidt Sch—school ... MN-6
Schmidt Sch—school ... MO-7
Schmidt Sch—school ... WA-9
Schmidt School—locale ... MN-6
Schmidts Island—island ... MN-6
Schmidts Island—island ... MO-7
Schmidt Site—hist pl ... MI-6
Schmidts Lake ... MN-6
Schmidts Mill ... AL-4
Schmidt Spring—spring ... CO-8
Schmidt State Wildlife Mngmt Area—park ... MN-6
Schmidts Woods—woods ... NJ-2
Schmidt Telescope—building ... AZ-5
Schmidtt Lake ... MN-6
Schmidt Valley—valley ... WI-6
Schmieder Landing—locale ... IL-6
Schmit Creek—stream ... CO-8
Schmith Knob—summit ... WA-9
Schmit Ranch—locale ... NE-7
**Schmits Mill**—pop pl ... AL-4
Schmitt, Gottlieb, House—hist pl ... SD-7
Schmitt Cem—cemetery ... ND-7
Schmitt Creek ... NV-8
Schmitt Creek—stream ... MI-6
Schmitt Creek—stream ... TX-5
Schmitt Creek—stream ... WI-6
Schmitt Dam—dam ... AL-4
Schmitt Ford—locale ... MO-7
Schmitthenner Lake—lake ... PA-2
Schmitt-Laemmle House—hist pl ... NM-5
Schmitt Lake—lake ... MI-6
Schmitt Lake—reservoir ... AL-4
Schmittou Cem—cemetery ... TN-4
Schmitts Bayou—gut ... OR-9
Schmitt Sch—school ... CA-9
Schmitt Sch—school ... CO-8
Schmitt School ... IN-6
Schmitz Block—hist pl ... IN-6
Schmitz Creek—stream ... OR-9
Schmitz Ditch—canal ... OH-6
Schmitz Lakes—lake ... MT-8
Schmitz Mtn—summit ... MT-8
Schmitz Park—park ... WA-9
Schmitz Park Bridge—hist pl ... WA-9
Schmitz Park Sch—school ... WA-9
Schmitz Ranch—locale ... NM-5
Schmmuck Mountain—ridge ... AL-4
Schmoke Lake—lake ... WI-6
Schmoker Spring—spring ... OR-9
Schmoker Valley—basin ... NE-7
Schmoker Well—well ... OR-9
Schmoll Cem—cemetery ... IL-6
Schmore Place—locale ... OR-9
Schmoutz Creek—stream ... PA-2
Schmucker Cem—cemetery ... PA-2
Schmucker Creek—stream ... MI-6
Schmucker MS—school ... IN-6
Schmucker Run—stream ... PA-2
Schmucke Sch ... IN-6
Schmuck Park—park ... WA-9
Schmudlack Creek—stream ... WI-6
Schmuhl Lake—lake ... WI-6
Schmuhl Sch—school ... IL-6
Schmuland Flowage—lake ... WI-6
Schmul Playground—park ... NY-2
Schmutz Cem—cemetery ... MO-7
Schmutz Ranch—locale ... AZ-5
Schmutz Spring—spring ... AZ-5
Schnabaum Lake—lake ... AR-4
Schnabel, Charles J. and Elsa, House—hist pl ... OR-9
Schnabel Park—park ... TX-5
Schnable Brook—stream ... MI-6
Schnable Creek—stream ... OR-9
Schnable Diggings—locale ... CA-9
Schnable Lake—lake ... MI-6
Schnabletown ... PA-2
Schnaible Cem—cemetery ... SD-7
Schnake Lake—reservoir ... IN-6
Schnake Lake Dam—dam ... IN-6
Schnapps Creek—stream ... IN-6
**Schnappsville**—pop pl ... WI-6
Schnarr Draft—valley ... PA-2
Schnasse County (historical)—civil ... SD-7
Schnauber, Fred, House—hist pl ... SD-7
Schnauber Hill—summit ... NY-2
Schnaubert Ranch—locale ... TX-5
Schneblin Cem—cemetery ... IL-6
Schnebly Canyon—valley ... WA-9
Schnebly Coulee—valley ... WA-9
Schnebly Creek—stream ... WA-9
Schnebly Hill—summit ... AZ-5
Schnebly Hill Vista—locale ... AZ-5
Schnebly Number Two Tank—reservoir ... AZ-5
Schnebly Tank—reservoir ... AZ-5
Schnebly Well—well ... AZ-5
Schneck Airp—airport ... PA-2
Schneck Brook—stream ... MA-1
Schneck Hosp—hospital ... IN-6
Schneckloth Spring—spring ... WA-9
**Schnecksville**—pop pl ... PA-2
Schnecksville Elem Sch—school ... PA-2
Schneckville ... PA-2
Schneede Ranch—locale ... NE-7
Schneeman Draw ... TX-5
Schneemann, William, House—hist pl ... TX-5
Schneemann Draw—valley ... TX-5
Schneemann Ranch—locale ... NM-5
Schnee Sch—school ... OH-6
**Schneider**—pop pl ... IN-6
Schneider, Charles W., House—hist pl ... MN-6
Schneider, J. P., Store—hist pl ... TX-5
Schneider, R. B., House—hist pl ... NE-7
Schneider Butte—summit ... OR-9
Schneider Campground—locale ... ID-8
Schneider Canyon—valley ... AZ-5
Schneider Cem—cemetery ... IL-6
Schneider Cem—cemetery ... KS-7
Schneider Cem—cemetery ... MO-7
Schneider Cem—cemetery (2) ... TX-5
Schneider China Drain—stream ... MI-6
Schneider Creek—stream (2) ... CA-9
Schneider Creek—stream ... CO-8
Schneider Creek—stream ... ID-8
Schneider Creek—stream ... WA-9
Schneider Crossroads—locale ... VA-3
Schneider Dam—dam ... AL-4
Schneider Ditch—canal ... CO-8
Schneider Ditch—canal ... IN-6
Schneider Drain—canal ... MI-6
Schneider Field Airp—airport ... MO-7
Schneider Gulch—valley ... CA-9
Schneider Hill—summit (2) ... CA-9
Schneider Hill—summit ... TX-5

Schneider Hotel—*hist pl* ... TX-5
Schneider Lake—*lake* ... IN-6
Schneider Lake—*lake* (2) ... MI-6
Schneider Lake—*lake* (2) ... MN-6
Schneider Lake—*reservoir* ... AL-4
Schneider Lake—*reservoir* ... CO-8
Schneider Log Pond—*reservoir* ... OR-9
Schneider Meadows—*flat* ... OR-9
Schneider Memorial Cem—*cemetery* ... TX-5
Schneider Park—*park* ... OH-6
Schneider Prairie—*flat* ... WA-9
Schneider Ranch—*locale* ... NM-5
Schneider Ranch—*locale* ... WY-8
Schneider Ravine—*valley* ... CA-9
Schneider Ridge—*ridge* ... WY-8
Schneider Rsvr—*reservoir* ... OR-9
Schneiders Bar—*bar* ... CA-9
Schneider Sch—*school* (2) ... IL-6
Schneider Sch—*school* ... ND-7
Schneider Sch—*school* ... SC-3
Schneider Sch (abandoned)—*school* ... MO-7
**Schneiders Crossroads**—*pop pl* ... VA-3
Schneiders Field—*airport* ... PA-2
Schneiders Lake—*lake* ... MN-6
**Schneiders Prairie**—*pop pl* ... WA-9
Schneider Springs—*spring* ... WA-9
Schneider Springs Branch—*stream* ... IL-6
**Schneidersville**—*pop pl* ... PA-2
**Schneider Township**—*pop pl* ... NE-7
Schneider Triangle—*hist pl* ... DC-2
Schneider Vocational Sch—*school* ... CA-9
Schneidman Road Ch—*church* ... KY-4
Schneikert, Valentine, House—*hist pl* ... KY-4
**Schneiter Subdivision**—*pop pl* ... UT-8
Schnell—*locale* ... IL-6
Schnellbacher, John and Fredericka Meyer, House—*hist pl* ... IA-7
Schnell East Oil Field—*other* ... IL-6
*Schnell Run* ... PA-2
**Schnellville**—*pop pl* ... IN-6
*Schnellville Conservation Lake* ... IN-6
Schnellville Conservation Lake Dam—*dam* ... IN-6
Schnellville Lake—*reservoir* ... IN-6
Schnelock Brook—*stream* ... MA-1
Schnepf State Wildlife Mngmt Area—*park* ... MN-6
*Schnerbusch* ... MO-7
Schneringer Valley—*basin* ... NE-7
**Schneyville**—*pop pl* ... WI-6
*Schnick Lake* ... NE-7
Schnick Ranch—*locale* ... NE-7
Schnieder Cem—*cemetery* ... MN-6
Schnieder Lake—*lake* ... AK-9
Schnieral Drain—*stream* ... MI-6
*Schnippe Thal* ... PA-2
Schnipps Valley—*valley* ... OR-9
Schnipps Valley Spring—*spring* ... OR-9
Schnitzelbank Creek—*stream* ... MI-6
Schnitzler Ranch—*locale* ... MT-8
*Schnoble Brook* ... MI-6
*Schnoble Lake* ... MI-6
Schnoor Ranch—*locale* ... WY-8
Schnoor Rsvr—*reservoir* ... WY-8
Schnoors—*locale* ... ID-8
Schnoor Windmill—*locale* ... CO-8
Schnose Dam Number 1—*dam* ... SD-7
Schnose Dam Number 2—*dam* ... SD-7
Schnull-Rauch House—*hist pl* ... IN-6
*Schnurbusch* ... MO-7
Schnurbusch—*other* ... MO-7
Schnur Lake—*lake* ... WI-6
*Schoal Creek* ... AL-4
*Schoate Hollow* ... TN-4
Schobe Cem—*cemetery* ... MO-7
Schober Lakes—*lake* ... CA-9
Schober Mine—*mine* ... CA-9
Schocalog Lake—*reservoir* ... OH-6
Schocalog Run—*stream* ... OH-6
Schoch Creek—*stream* ... PA-2
**Schochoh**—*pop pl* ... KY-4
Schoch Sch (abandoned)—*school* ... PA-2
*Schock Bar* ... UT-8
Schock Cem—*cemetery* ... IN-6
*Schock Creek* ... MS-4
Schocken Hill—*summit* ... CA-9
Schockopee Lake—*lake* ... IN-6
Schock Rapids (inundated)—*rapids* ... UT-8
Schock Trail Base (inundated)—*locale* ... UT-8
*Schodack* ... NY-2
Schodack Brook—*stream* ... NY-2
**Schodack Center**—*pop pl* ... NY-2
**Schodack Center (Schodack)**—*pop pl* ... NY-2
Schodack Creek—*stream* ... NY-2
*Schodack Island* ... NY-2
**Schodack Junction**—*pop pl* ... NY-2
**Schodack Landing**—*pop pl* ... NY-2
Schodack Landing Hist Dist—*hist pl* ... NY-2
Schodack Pond—*lake* ... NY-2
**Schodack (Town of)**—*pop pl* ... NY-2
**Schodde**—*pop pl* ... ID-8
Schodde Mine—*mine* ... NV-8
Schodde Well—*well* ... ID-8
Schoeber Draw—*valley* ... WY-8
Schoeberl State Wildlife Mngmt Area—*park* ... MN-6
**Schoeb Switch**—*pop pl* ... OK-5
Schoechler Lake—*lake* ... TX-5
Schoeffel Creek—*stream* ... WA-9
Schoeffel Ditch—*canal* ... OH-6
Schoemann Cutoff—*channel* ... IL-6
**Schoen**—*pop pl* ... GA-3
**Schoenau**—*pop pl* ... TX-5
*Schoenauer Ditch* ... IN-6
Schoenauer Ditch—*canal* ... IN-6
Schoenberger, Anton, Homestead—*hist pl* ... MT-8
Schoenberger, Charlie, Homestead—*hist pl* ... MT-8
Schoenberger Cem—*cemetery* ... OH-6
Schoenberger Creek—*stream* (2) ... IL-6
Schoenberger Hall—*hist pl* ... NC-3
Schoenberg Lake—*lake* ... TX-5
Schoenberg Marsh—*swamp* ... WI-6
*Schoenbrun* ... OH-6
**Schoenbrunn**—*pop pl* ... OH-6
Schoenbrunn Site—*hist pl* ... OH-6
Schoenbrunn State Memorial—*park* ... OH-6
Schoenburger Spring—*spring* ... UT-8
**Schoenchen**—*pop pl* ... KS-7
Schoenchen Elem Sch—*school* ... KS-7
Schoen Creek—*stream* ... IN-6
**Schoeneck**—*pop pl* (2) ... PA-2
*Schoeneck Creek* ... PA-2
Schoeneck Elem Sch—*school* ... PA-2
Schoeneck Post Office (historical)—*building* ... PA-2
Schoenenberger, Nicholas, House and Barn—*hist pl* ... IA-7
Schoener Drain—*canal* ... MI-6
Schoener Island—*island* ... AK-9
**Schoenersville**—*pop pl* ... PA-2
*Schoenerville* ... PA-2
Schoenfeld Cem—*cemetery* ... KS-7
Schoenhals Sch—*school* ... MI-6
Schoenhofen Brewery Hist Dist—*hist pl* ... IL-6
Schoenholzer Canyon—*valley* ... AZ-5
Schoenicke Barn—*hist pl* ... WI-6
Schoenick Lake—*lake* ... WI-6
Schoeniger Valley—*valley* ... MN-6
Schoening Cem—*cemetery* ... IL-6
Schoening Creek—*stream* ... WY-8
Schoen Mtn—*summit* ... TX-5
Schoens Crossing—*locale* ... AZ-5
Schoenstein and Company Pipe Organ Factory—*hist pl* ... CA-9
Schoentown—*uninc pl* ... PA-2
*Schoenvrunn* ... OH-6
Schoepf Divide—*ridge* ... WY-8
**Schoepke (Town of)**—*pop pl* ... WI-6
Schoepp Valley—*valley* ... WI-6
Schoer Creek—*stream* ... NV-8
Schoer Place—*locale* ... NV-8
Schoettgen Pass—*gap* ... CA-9
Schoettlin Mtn—*summit* ... WY-8
Schofer—*locale* ... PA-2
Schoffelman Sch—*school* ... SD-7
Schoffner Corner—*locale* ... PA-2
Schoffs Island—*island* ... ID-8
Schofield—*locale* ... CO-8
Schofield—*locale* ... MO-7
**Schofield**—*pop pl* ... SC-3
**Schofield**—*pop pl* ... WI-6
Schofield, James, House—*hist pl* ... MA-1
Schofield, Robert, House—*hist pl* ... WI-6
Schofield Barracks—*military* ... HI-9
Schofield Barracks For Res—*forest* ... HI-9
Schofield Barracks Milit Reservation—*military* ... HI-9
Schofield Barracks (U.S. Army)—*military* ... HI-9
Schofield Cem—*cemetery* ... WI-6
Schofield Cobble—*summit* ... NY-2
**Schofield Corners**—*pop pl* ... PA-2
*Schofield Cove* ... ME-1
*Schofield Creek* ... OR-9
Schofield Creek—*stream* ... ID-8
Schofield Creek—*stream* ... MI-6
Schofield Creek—*stream* ... WA-9
Schofield Dam—*dam* ... ND-7
Schofield Flat—*flat* ... OR-9
Schofield Gulch—*valley* ... CA-9
Schofield Hall—*hist pl* ... WI-6
Schofield Hill—*summit* ... NY-2
Schofield HS—*school* ... SC-3
*Schofield Island* ... CT-1
*Schofield Lake* ... WI-6
Schofield Mine—*mine* ... CO-8
Schofield Mtn—*summit* ... NH-1
Schofield Opening—*flat* ... CA-9
Schofield Park—*flat* ... CO-8
Schofield Pass—*gap* ... CO-8
Schofield Pass—*gap* ... NV-8
Schofield Pass—*gap* ... WY-8
Schofield Peak—*summit* (2) ... CA-9
*Schofield Pond* ... CT-1
Schofield Pond—*lake* ... NY-2
Schofield Pond—*lake* ... VT-1
Schofield Run—*stream* ... PA-2
Schofield Sch—*school* ... KS-7
Schofield Sch—*school* ... MA-1
Schofield Sch—*school* ... MI-6
Schofield Sch—*school* ... MT-8
Schofield Swamp—*swamp* ... SC-3
Schofield Tower—*locale* ... LA-4
Schofield Waikane Trail—*trail* ... HI-9
Schofiled Mine—*mine* ... NV-8
**Schoharie**—*pop pl* ... NY-2
**Schoharie (County)**—*pop pl* ... NY-2
Schoharie Creek—*stream* ... NY-2
Schoharie Hill—*summit* ... NY-2
Schoharie (historical)—*locale* ... KS-7
Schoharie Junction—*locale* ... NY-2
Schoharie Junction Sch—*school* ... NY-2
*Schoharie Ridge* ... PA-2
Schoharie Rsvr—*reservoir* ... NY-2
**Schoharie (Town of)**—*pop pl* ... NY-2
Schoharie Valley RR Complex—*hist pl* ... NY-2
Schohr Ranch—*locale* ... CA-9
Schoitz Hosp—*hospital* ... IA-7
*Schola* ... MS-4
Scholar Creek—*stream* ... OK-5
Scholars Run—*stream* ... PA-2
Scholder Creek—*stream* ... CA-9
Scholefield Canyon—*valley* ... AZ-5
Scholefield Spring—*spring* ... AZ-5
Scholer Ditch—*canal* ... IN-6
Scholes—*locale* ... NY-2
Scholes Branch—*stream* ... IL-6
Scholes Hall—*hist pl* ... NM-5
Scholes Hollow—*valley* ... TN-4
Scholey Gulch—*valley* ... OR-9
Scholfield—*locale* ... VA-3
Scholfield Creek—*stream* ... OR-9
Scholfield Pond—*lake* ... CT-1
*Scholing Creek* ... WY-8
**Scholl**—*pop pl* ... NC-3
Schollaert Hills—*range* ... ND-7
**Schollard**—*pop pl* ... PA-2
Scholl Canyon—*valley* ... CA-9
Scholl Cem—*cemetery* ... NC-3
Scholle—*locale* ... NM-5
Scholle, Mattias, House—*hist pl* ... IN-6
Scholle Siding—*locale* ... NM-5
Scholle Well—*well* ... NM-5
Schollmeyer Bldg—*hist pl* ... MO-7
Scholl Pond—*lake* ... IN-6
**Scholls**—*pop pl* ... OR-9
Scholls Bridge—*bridge* ... OR-9
Scholls Grange Hall—*locale* ... OR-9
**Schollsville**—*pop pl* ... KY-4
Scholte, Dominie Henry P., House—*hist pl* ... IA-7
**Scholten**—*pop pl* ... MO-7
Scholtie Lateral—*canal* ... ID-8
Scholts, Lake—*lake* ... MI-6
Scholtz Ditch—*canal* ... IN-6
Scholtztown—*locale* ... MT-8
Scholze-Sayles House—*hist pl* ... RI-1
Scholz Garten—*hist pl* ... TX-5
Scholz Lake—*reservoir* ... AZ-5
Schomberg—*locale* ... MI-6
Schomberg—*locale* ... NM-5
Schomberg County Park—*park* ... WI-6
Schombrug Canyon—*valley* ... NM-5
Schomburg Center for Research in Black Culture—*hist pl* ... NY-2
Schonberg—*locale* ... IA-7
Schonberg (historical P.O.)—*locale* ... IA-7
*Schonbrunn* ... OH-6
Schonchin Butte—*summit* ... CA-9
Schonchin Spring—*spring* ... CA-9
Schoneman Ditch Camp—*locale* ... CO-8
Schoner Lake—*lake* ... MI-6
Schonhar Ranch—*locale* ... NE-7
Schonholm (historical)—*locale* ... KS-7
*Schonian Harbor* ... PW-9
Schonna Chapel—*church* ... MS-4
**Schonowe**—*pop pl* ... NY-2
Schonthda Hill—*summit* ... AK-9
Schoodac Brook—*stream* ... NH-1
Schoodic—*locale* ... ME-1
**Schoodic**—*pop pl* ... ME-1
Schoodic Bay—*bay* ... ME-1
Schoodic Bog—*swamp* ... ME-1
Schoodic Brook—*stream* ... ME-1
Schoodic Cem—*cemetery* ... ME-1
Schoodic Deadwater—*lake* ... ME-1
Schoodic Harbor—*bay* ... ME-1
Schoodic Head—*summit* ... ME-1
Schoodic Island—*island* ... ME-1
*Schoodic Lake* ... ME-1
Schoodic Lake—*lake* (2) ... ME-1
*Schoodic Mtn* ... ME-1
Schoodic Mtn—*summit* (2) ... ME-1
Schoodic Nubble—*summit* ... ME-1
Schoodic Peninsula—*cape* ... ME-1
Schoodic Point—*cape* ... ME-1
Schoodic Ridge—*ridge* ... ME-1
Schoodic Stream—*stream* (2) ... ME-1
Schoof Drain—*canal* ... MI-6
*Schooks Creek* ... PA-2
*Schook Toahk* ... AZ-5
**School Acres (subdivision)**—*pop pl* ... NC-3
School Bldg Number 2—*hist pl* ... NM-5
School Board Lake Dam—*dam* ... AL-4
Schoolboy Rapids—*rapids* ... UT-8
*School Branch* ... TN-4
School Branch—*stream* ... AL-4
School Branch—*stream* ... GA-3
School Branch—*stream* ... IN-6
School Branch—*stream* (2) ... KS-7
School Branch—*stream* ... MO-7
School Branch—*stream* ... TN-4
School Branch—*stream* (3) ... TX-5
School Branch Immanuel Ch—*church* ... NE-7
*School Brook* ... MA-1
School Brook—*stream* ... CT-1
School Brook—*stream* ... IN-6
School Brook—*stream* ... ME-1
School Bus Corral—*locale* ... UT-8
School Bus Windmill—*locale* ... TX-5
School Butte—*summit* ... MT-8
School Canyon—*valley* (2) ... AZ-5
School Canyon—*valley* ... CO-8
School Canyon—*valley* ... NM-5
School Canyon—*valley* ... WA-9
School Cave—*cave* ... AL-4
School City Administration—*locale* ... NC-3
Schoolcraft—*fmr MCD* ... NE-7
**Schoolcraft**—*pop pl* ... MI-6
Schoolcraft, John, House—*hist pl* ... NY-2
Schoolcraft Airp—*airport* ... KS-7
Schoolcraft Coll—*school* ... MI-6
**Schoolcraft (County)**—*pop pl* ... MI-6
Schoolcraft Creek—*stream* ... OR-9
Schoolcraft Furnace Site—*hist pl* ... MI-6
Schoolcraft Island—*island* ... MN-6
Schoolcraft Lake—*lake* ... MN-6
Schoolcraft River—*stream* ... MN-6
Schoolcraft Run—*stream* ... WV-2
Schoolcraft Sch—*school* ... MI-6
School Craft State Rec Area—*park* ... MN-6
**Schoolcraft (Township of)**—*pop pl* (2) ... MI-6
**Schoolcraft (Township of)**—*pop pl* ... MN-6
*School Creek* ... IN-6
*School Creek* ... KS-7
School Creek—*stream* ... AR-4
School Creek—*stream* ... CO-8
School Creek—*stream* ... ID-8
School Creek—*stream* ... IN-6
School Creek—*stream* (2) ... IA-7
School Creek—*stream* (10) ... KS-7
School Creek—*stream* ... MI-6
School Creek—*stream* (7) ... NE-7
School Creek—*stream* ... NV-8
School Creek—*stream* ... OH-6
School Creek—*stream* (4) ... OR-9
School Creek—*stream* ... PA-2
School Creek—*stream* (2) ... TX-5
School Creek—*stream* ... WA-9
School Creek—*stream* (2) ... WI-6
School Creek—*stream* (6) ... WY-8
School Creek Ch—*church* ... TX-5
School Creek School (Abandoned)—*locale* ... NE-7
School Creek Spring—*spring* ... NV-8
School Ditch—*canal* ... CA-9
School Ditch—*canal* ... IL-6
School Drain—*canal* ... TX-5
School Draw—*valley* ... WY-8
Schooler Cem—*cemetery* ... MO-7
Schooler Creek—*stream* ... ID-8
Schooler Creek—*stream* ... IN-6
Schooler Lake—*reservoir* ... OK-5
Schooler Point Landing—*locale* ... IN-6
Schooler Ranch—*locale* ... SD-7
Schooler Ranch—*locale* ... TX-5
Schoolerville—*locale* ... TX-5
Schooler Windmill—*locale* ... TX-5
*Schooley* ... FL-3
Schooley—*locale* ... OH-6
**Schooley**—*pop pl* ... FL-3
Schooley, Dr. Lindley, House and Office—*hist pl* ... OH-6
Schooley Airp—*airport* ... MO-7
Schooley Breaker (historical)—*mine* ... PA-2
Schooley Cem—*cemetery* ... KS-7
Schooley Cem—*cemetery* ... OH-6
Schooley Creek—*stream* ... TX-5
Schooley Creek—*stream* ... WA-9
Schooley Mtn—*summit* ... PA-2
Schooley Pond—*reservoir* ... PA-2
**Schooleys**—*pop pl* ... OH-6
**Schooleys Mountain**—*pop pl* ... NJ-2
Schooleys Mountain Park—*park* ... NJ-2
**Schooleys Mountian**—*pop pl* ... NJ-2
Schooleys Mtn—*summit* ... NJ-2
Schooley Station RR Station—*locale* ... FL-3
**Schoolfield**—*pop pl* ... VA-3
Schoolfield Ch—*church* ... PA-2
Schoolfield Ch—*church* ... VA-3
*School Field Creek* ... OR-9
**Schoolfield (historical)**—*pop pl* ... TN-4
Schoolfield Post Office (historical)—*building* ... TN-4
School Flat—*flat* ... OR-9
School for Boys—*school* ... PA-2
School for Cerebral Palsied Children—*school* ... CA-9
School for Deaf—*school* ... NY-2
School Fork—*stream* ... OR-9
School For Mentally Retarded—*school* ... PA-2
School For The Blind—*school* ... PA-2
School Girl Tank—*reservoir* ... NM-5
School Grove Lake—*lake* ... MN-6
*School Gulch* ... MT-8
School Gulch—*valley* ... CO-8
School Gulch Creek—*stream* ... MT-8
**School Hill**—*pop pl* ... WI-6
School Hill—*summit* ... AZ-5
School Hill—*summit* ... CA-9
School Hill—*summit* ... CT-1
School Hill—*summit* ... ND-7
School Hill Cem—*cemetery* ... TX-5
School Hollow—*valley* ... MO-7
School Hollow—*valley* ... OR-9
*School House* ... PA-2
Schoolhouse—*hist pl* ... NJ-2
School House—*hist pl* ... UT-8
School House—*school* ... FL-3
Schoolhouse—*school* ... NC-3
Schoolhouse, Denton—*hist pl* ... MD-2
School House, The—*locale* ... MT-8
School House and Town Hall—*hist pl* ... VT-1
Schoolhouse Bay—*bay* ... MO-7
Schoolhouse Bay—*bay* ... NY-2
Schoolhouse Bay—*swamp* ... FL-3
Schoolhouse Bay—*swamp* (2) ... GA-3
Schoolhouse Bay—*swamp* ... NC-3
School House Bayou—*gut* ... LA-4
School House Bend—*bend* ... AR-4
Schoolhouse Bluff—*cliff* ... TX-5
Schoolhouse Branch—*stream* ... AL-4
School House Branch—*stream* ... AL-4
Schoolhouse Branch—*stream* (4) ... AL-4
School House Branch—*stream* ... AR-4
Schoolhouse Branch—*stream* (3) ... AR-4
Schoolhouse Branch—*stream* (4) ... FL-3
Schoolhouse Branch—*stream* ... IL-6
Schoolhouse Branch—*stream* (12) ... KY-4
School House Branch—*stream* ... KY-4
Schoolhouse Branch—*stream* (8) ... KY-4
Schoolhouse Branch—*stream* (5) ... LA-4
Schoolhouse Branch—*stream* (3) ... MD-2
Schoolhouse Branch—*stream* ... MS-4
Schoolhouse Branch—*stream* ... NJ-2
School House Branch—*stream* ... NC-3
Schoolhouse Branch—*stream* (7) ... NC-3
Schoolhouse Branch—*stream* (3) ... SC-3
Schoolhouse Branch—*stream* (2) ... TN-4
Schoolhouse Branch—*stream* (7) ... TX-5
Schoolhouse Branch—*stream* (3) ... VA-3
Schoolhouse Branch—*stream* (3) ... WV-2
Schoolhouse Branch—*swamp* ... FL-3
Schoolhouse Brook—*stream* (3) ... CT-1
Schoolhouse Brook—*stream* (4) ... ME-1
Schoolhouse Brook—*stream* (2) ... MA-1
Schoolhouse Brook—*stream* (2) ... NH-1
Schoolhouse Brook—*stream* ... NY-2
Schoolhouse Brook—*stream* (2) ... VT-1
Schoolhouse Butte—*summit* ... MT-8
Schoolhouse Butte—*summit* ... NV-8
Schoolhouse Butte—*summit* ... WY-8
*School House Canyon* ... AZ-5
*Schoolhouse Canyon* ... ID-8
Schoolhouse Canyon—*valley* ... AZ-5
School House Canyon—*valley* ... AZ-5
Schoolhouse Canyon—*valley* ... AZ-5
Schoolhouse Canyon—*valley* (6) ... CA-9
Schoolhouse Canyon—*valley* (2) ... CO-8
Schoolhouse Canyon—*valley* (2) ... ID-8
Schoolhouse Canyon—*valley* (3) ... NV-8
Schoolhouse Canyon—*valley* (6) ... NM-5
Schoolhouse Canyon—*valley* (3) ... OR-9
Schoolhouse Canyon—*valley* ... WY-8
Schoolhouse Cem—*cemetery* ... ME-1
Schoolhouse Coulee—*valley* (3) ... MT-8
Schoolhouse Cove—*bay* ... ME-1
Schoolhouse Cove—*bay* ... MD-2
*School House Creek* ... AL-4
*Schoolhouse Creek* ... OK-5
School House Creek—*stream* ... AL-4
Schoolhouse Creek—*stream* ... AR-4
Schoolhouse Creek—*stream* (7) ... CA-9
Schoolhouse Creek—*stream* ... GA-3
Schoolhouse Creek—*stream* ... ID-8
School House Creek—*stream* ... LA-4
Schoolhouse Creek—*stream* ... LA-4
Schoolhouse Creek—*stream* ... MI-6
Schoolhouse Creek—*stream* ... MN-6
Schoolhouse Creek—*stream* (12) ... OR-9
Schoolhouse Creek—*stream* ... PA-2
Schoolhouse Creek—*stream* (2) ... TN-4
Schoolhouse Creek—*stream* ... UT-8
Schoolhouse Creek—*stream* ... WA-9
Schoolhouse Creek—*stream* (2) ... WI-6
Schoolhouse Creek—*stream* (2) ... WY-8
Schoolhouse Debris Basin—*basin* ... CA-9
School House Ditch—*canal* ... CA-9
Schoolhouse Ditch Number One—*canal* ... MT-8
Schoolhouse Divide—*ridge* ... CA-9
School House Drain—*canal* ... MI-6
Schoolhouse Drain—*canal* ... MI-6
Schoolhouse Draw—*valley* (2) ... AZ-5
Schoolhouse Draw—*valley* ... CO-8
School House Draw—*valley* ... CO-8
Schoolhouse Draw—*valley* (2) ... MT-8
Schoolhouse Draw—*valley* ... TX-5
Schoolhouse Draw—*valley* ... WA-9
Schoolhouse Draw—*valley* (2) ... WY-8
Schoolhouse Falls—*falls* ... NC-3
Schoolhouse Flat—*flat* (2) ... CA-9
Schoolhouse Fork—*stream* ... WV-2
*School House Gap* ... TN-4
Schoolhouse Gap—*gap* ... GA-3
Schoolhouse Gap—*gap* ... NC-3
Schoolhouse Gap—*gap* (2) ... TN-4
*School House Gulch* ... CA-9
Schoolhouse Gulch—*valley* ... AZ-5
Schoolhouse Gulch—*valley* (4) ... CA-9
Schoolhouse Gulch—*valley* (6) ... CO-8
Schoolhouse Gulch—*valley* (3) ... ID-8
Schoolhouse Gulch—*valley* (2) ... MT-8
Schoolhouse Gulch—*valley* (5) ... OR-9
Schoolhouse Gulch—*valley* ... SD-7
Schoolhouse Gulch—*valley* (2) ... WY-8
Schoolhouse Gut—*stream* ... NC-3
Schoolhouse Hill—*summit* (2) ... AR-4
Schoolhouse Hill—*summit* (2) ... CA-9
Schoolhouse Hill—*summit* (2) ... CT-1
Schoolhouse Hill—*summit* (2) ... IN-6
Schoolhouse Hill—*summit* ... MD-2
Schoolhouse Hill—*summit* ... MA-1
Schoolhouse Hill—*summit* ... NC-3
Schoolhouse Hill—*summit* ... OR-9
School House Historical Site—*locale* ... UT-8
Schoolhouse Hollow—*valley* (4) ... AR-4
Schoolhouse Hollow—*valley* ... ID-8
Schoolhouse Hollow—*valley* (4) ... KY-4
School House Hollow—*valley* ... KY-4
Schoolhouse Hollow—*valley* (4) ... KY-4
Schoolhouse Hollow—*valley* (2) ... MO-7
School House Hollow—*valley* ... MO-7
Schoolhouse Hollow—*valley* (6) ... MO-7
Schoolhouse Hollow—*valley* ... NY-2
Schoolhouse Hollow—*valley* (9) ... PA-2
Schoolhouse Hollow—*valley* (12) ... TN-4
Schoolhouse Hollow—*valley* (4) ... TX-5
Schoolhouse Hollow—*valley* (4) ... VA-3
Schoolhouse Hollow—*valley* (7) ... WV-2
Schoolhouse Knob—*summit* (2) ... KY-4
*Schoolhouse Lake* ... MI-6
Schoolhouse Lake—*lake* ... FL-3
Schoolhouse Lake—*lake* ... LA-4
Schoolhouse Lake—*lake* (4) ... MI-6
Schoolhouse Lake—*lake* (3) ... MN-6
School House Lake—*lake* ... MN-6
Schoolhouse Lake—*lake* ... MT-8
Schoolhouse Lake—*lake* ... NE-7
Schoolhouse Lake—*lake* ... NY-2
Schoolhouse Lake—*lake* (3) ... WI-6
Schoolhouse Landing—*locale* ... NC-3
Schoolhouse Ledge—*cliff* ... ME-1
Schoolhouse Ledge—*cliff* ... UT-8
Schoolhouse Marsh—*swamp* ... VT-1
Schoolhouse Meadow—*flat* ... OR-9
Schoolhouse Mesa—*summit* ... NM-5
Schoolhouse Mine—*mine* ... CA-9
School House Mine (underground)—*mine* ... AL-4
Schoolhouse Mtn—*summit* ... AL-4
Schoolhouse Mtn—*summit* ... AR-4
Schoolhouse Mtn—*summit* (2) ... NM-5
Schoolhouse Mtn—*summit* ... NY-2
Schoolhouse Mtn—*summit* ... OK-5
Schoolhouse Mtn—*summit* ... TN-4
Schoolhouse Mtn—*summit* (2) ... TX-5
Schoolhouse Mtn—*summit* ... VA-3
Schoolhouse Opening—*area* ... CA-9
Schoolhouse Park—*flat* ... WY-8
Schoolhouse Pasture Rock—*pillar* ... CA-9
Schoolhouse Peak—*summit* ... CA-9
Schoolhouse Point—*cape* ... WA-9
Schoolhouse Point—*cliff* ... CO-8
Schoolhouse Point—*summit* ... AZ-5
Schoolhouse Point—*summit* ... CA-9
Schoolhouse Point Rec Area—*park* ... AZ-5
*School House Pond* ... MA-1
Schoolhouse Pond—*lake* (3) ... FL-3
Schoolhouse Pond—*lake* ... GA-3
Schoolhouse Pond—*lake* ... ME-1
Schoolhouse Pond—*lake* ... MD-2
Schoolhouse Pond—*lake* (3) ... MA-1
School House Pond—*lake* ... RI-1
Schoolhouse Pond—*swamp* ... FL-3
Schoolhouse Prong—*stream* ... WY-8
Schoolhouse Ranch—*locale* ... OR-9
Schoolhouse Rapids—*rapids* ... ME-1
Schoolhouse Ridge—*ridge* (2) ... CA-9
Schoolhouse Ridge—*ridge* ... IN-6
Schoolhouse Ridge—*ridge* ... KY-4
Schoolhouse Ridge—*ridge* (3) ... NC-3
Schoolhouse Ridge—*ridge* (2) ... TN-4
Schoolhouse Ridge—*ridge* ... WV-2
Schoolhouse Ridge—*summit* ... AR-4
Schoolhouse Rsvr—*reservoir* ... CO-8
Schoolhouse Run—*stream* ... MD-2
Schoolhouse Run—*stream* (8) ... PA-2
Schoolhouse Run—*stream* ... VA-3
Schoolhouse Run—*stream* (2) ... WV-2
Schoolhouse Slough—*stream* ... MT-8
Schoolhouse Spring—*spring* ... AZ-5
Schoolhouse Spring—*spring* ... AR-4
Schoolhouse Spring—*spring* (2) ... CA-9
Schoolhouse Spring—*spring* ... MO-7
Schoolhouse Spring—*spring* (2) ... NV-8
School House Spring—*spring* ... NV-8
Schoolhouse Spring—*spring* ... NV-8
Schoolhouse Spring—*spring* ... NM-5
Schoolhouse Spring—*spring* ... SD-7
Schoolhouse Springs—*spring* ... UT-8
Schoolhouse Swamp—*swamp* ... NY-2
Schoolhouse Swamp—*swamp* ... RI-1
Schoolhouse Tank—*reservoir* (5) ... AZ-5
Schoolhouse Tank—*reservoir* (2) ... NM-5
Schoolhouse Trail—*trail* ... PA-2
School House Trail—*trail* ... PA-2
Schoolhouse Wash—*stream* ... AZ-5
Schoolhouse Well—*well* ... CA-9
Schoolhouse Windmill—*locale* ... NM-5
School House Windmill—*locale* ... NM-5
Schoolhouse Windmill—*locale* (2) ... NM-5
Schoolhouse Windmill—*locale* (3) ... TX-5
Schoolhouse #6—*hist pl* ... NY-2
Schoolie Flat—*flat* ... OR-9
Schoolie Pasture—*flat* ... OR-9
Schoolie Pasture Ranger Station—*locale* ... OR-9
Schooling Cem—*cemetery* ... MO-7
School Island—*island* ... NE-7
School Key—*island* ... FL-3
*School Lake* ... MI-6
*School Lake* ... MN-6
*School Lake* ... WI-6
School Lake—*lake* (5) ... MI-6
School Lake—*lake* (13) ... MN-6
School Lake—*lake* ... MS-4
School Lake—*lake* ... ND-7
School Lake—*lake* ... SD-7
School Lake—*lake* ... WI-6
School Lake—*swamp* ... MN-6
School Lake Dam—*dam* ... MS-4
*School Lakes* ... CO-8
**School Land**—*pop pl* ... TX-5
School Land Bay—*bay* ... OR-9
School Land Branch—*stream* ... AL-4
School Land Ch—*church* ... OH-6
School Land Creek—*stream* ... TX-5
School Land Dam—*dam* (3) ... SD-7
School Land Gulch—*valley* ... CA-9
*School Lands Hollow* ... OH-6
**School Lane**—*pop pl* ... PA-2
School Lane Hills—*locale* ... PA-2
School Lateral—*canal* (2) ... ID-8
School Lot Cem—*cemetery* ... OH-6
Schoolma'am Creek—*stream* ... OR-9
*Schoolmaam Mountain* ... CO-8
*School Mam Gulch* ... MT-8
Schoolmam Gulch—*valley* ... ID-8
Schoolmam Spring—*spring* ... OR-9
Schoolman Basin—*basin* ... NV-8
Schoolman Ditch—*canal* ... IN-6
Schoolman Spring—*spring* ... OR-9
Schoolmarm Butte—*summit* ... WY-8
Schoolmarm Buttes—*summit* ... MT-8
Schoolmarm Creek—*stream* ... CA-9
Schoolmarm Creek—*stream* ... OR-9
Schoolmarm Draw—*valley* ... CO-8
Schoolmarm Gulch—*valley* (2) ... MT-8
Schoolmarm Lake—*lake* ... CA-9
Schoolmarm Lake—*reservoir* ... MT-8
Schoolmarm Mtn—*summit* ... CO-8
Schoolmarm Peak—*summit* ... ID-8
Schoolmarm Ridge—*ridge* ... CA-9
*School Marms Pants* ... UT-8
Schoolmarm Spring—*spring* ... MT-8
Schoolmarm Spring—*spring* ... OR-9
School Meadow Brook—*stream* ... MA-1
School Neck Point—*cape* ... VA-3
School No—*school* ... NY-2
School No C-14—*school* ... NE-7
School No R 5—*school* ... MO-7
School No 1—*school* ... IL-6
School No 1—*school* ... KY-4
School No 1—*school* (14) ... NE-7
School No 1—*school* (62) ... NY-2
School No 1 (Abandoned)—*locale* ... MN-6
School No 10—*school* ... IL-6
School No 10—*school* (3) ... NE-7
School No 10*—*school* ... NE-7
School No 10—*school* (16) ... NE-7
School No 10—*school* ... NH-1
School No 10—*school* (38) ... NY-2
School No 100—*school* (4) ... NE-7
School No 100R—*school* ... NE-7
School No 101—*school* (2) ... NE-7
School No 101 East—*school* ... NE-7
School No 101 West—*school* ... NE-7
School No 10 1/2—*school* ... NE-7
School No 102—*school* (4) ... NE-7
School No 103—*school* (3) ... NE-7
School No 104—*school* ... NE-7
School No 105—*school* ... NE-7
School No 106—*school* ... NE-7
School No 106—*school* ... OK-5
School No 107—*school* (2) ... NE-7
School No 108—*school* ... IL-6
School No 108—*school* ... NE-7
School No 109—*school* (3) ... NE-7
School No 11—*school* ... MO-7
School No 11—*school* (12) ... NE-7
School No 11—*school* (42) ... NY-2
School No 11 (Abandoned)—*locale* ... NE-7
School No 110—*school* ... NE-7
School No 110 (Abandoned)—*locale* ... NE-7
School No 112—*school* (3) ... NE-7
School No 113—*school* ... NE-7
School No 114—*school* (2) ... NE-7
School No 115—*school* (2) ... NE-7
School No 116—*school* (3) ... NE-7
School No 117—*school* (2) ... NE-7
School No 118—*school* (2) ... NE-7
School No 119—*school* (2) ... NE-7
School No 12—*school* (12) ... NE-7
School No 12—*school* (39) ... NY-2
School No 12—*school* ... OK-5
School No 12 (Abandoned)—*locale* ... NE-7
School No 120—*school* ... NE-7
School No 121—*school* (2) ... NE-7
School No 122—*school* (2) ... NE-7
School No 123—*school* ... NE-7
School No 124—*school* (2) ... NE-7
School No 127—*school* (3) ... NE-7
School No 128—*school* (2) ... NE-7
School No 129—*school* (2) ... NE-7
School No 13—*school* (15) ... NE-7
School No 13—*school* (30) ... NY-2
School No 130—*school* ... NE-7
School No 131—*school* (3) ... NE-7
School No 133—*school* (2) ... NE-7
School No 134—*school* (2) ... NE-7
School No 136—*school* ... KY-4
School No 136—*school* ... NE-7
School No 137—*school* ... NE-7
School No 138—*school* (2) ... NE-7
School No 14—*school* (13) ... NE-7
School No 14—*school* (25) ... NY-2
School No 14 R—*school* ... NE-7
School No 141—*school* ... NE-7
School No 142—*school* ... NE-7
School No 143—*school* (2) ... NE-7
School No 145—*school* ... NE-7
School No 146—*school* ... NE-7
School No 147—*school* ... NE-7

School Number 42 (historical)—school (2) ... SD-7
School Number 43 ... SD-7
School Number 43—school ... MN-6
School Number 43 (historical)—school ... SD-7
School Number 44 ... SD-7
School Number 44—school (3) ... MN-6
School Number 44 (historical)—school ... SD-7
School Number 45 ... SD-7
School Number 45—locale ... MN-6
School Number 45—school ... FL-3
School Number 45—school (2) ... MN-6
School Number 45 (historical)—school ... SD-7
School Number 46 ... SD-7
School Number 46—locale ... MN-6
School Number 46—school ... FL-3
School Number 46 (historical)—school ... SD-7
School Number 47—school ... MN-6
School Number 47—school ... NE-7
School Number 47—school ... ND-7
School Number 47—school ... SD-7
School Number 47 (historical)—school (2) ... SD-7
School Number 48—school ... IL-6
School Number 48—school ... MN-6
School Number 48 (historical)—school ... SD-7
School Number 49—school (2) ... MN-6
School Number 4-9—school ... SD-7
School Number 49 (historical)—school (2) ... SD-7
School Number 498—school ... MN-6
School Number 5—school ... MN-6
School Number 5—school (7) ... NJ-2
School Number 5—school (16) ... ND-7
School Number 5—school (6) ... SD-7
School Number 5—school (2) ... VT-1
School Number 5 (historical)—school (14) ... SD-7
School Number 50 ... SD-7
School Number 50—locale ... MN-6
School Number 50—school ... MN-6
School Number 50—school (2) ... SD-7
School Number 50 (historical)—school ... SD-7
School Number 508—school ... MN-6
School Number 51—school (3) ... MN-6
School Number 51—school ... NE-7
School Number 51—school ... SD-7
School Number 51 (historical)—school (2) ... SD-7
School Number 5-16—school ... SD-7
School Number 52—school ... IN-6
School Number 52—school (2) ... SD-7
School Number 52 (historical)—school (2) ... SD-7
School Number 525—school ... MN-6
School Number 53—school ... MN-6
School Number 53—school ... SD-7
School Number 53 (Abandoned)—locale ... MN-6
School Number 53 (historical)—school ... SD-7
School Number 54—locale ... MN-6
School Number 54—school ... MN-6
School Number 54 (historical)—school (2) ... SD-7
School Number 55—locale ... MN-6
School Number 55—school ... MN-6
School Number 55 (historical)—school ... SD-7
School Number 55W—locale ... MN-6
School Number 56—school (2) ... MN-6
School Number 56—school ... SD-7
School Number 56 (historical)—school ... SD-7
School Number 57—school ... KS-7
School Number 57—school (3) ... MN-6
School Number 57—school ... ND-7
School Number 57 (historical)—school (2) ... SD-7
School Number 58—school ... MN-6
School Number 59—school (2) ... MN-6
School Number 59—school ... ND-7
School Number 59 (historical)—school (2) ... SD-7
School Number 6 ... SD-7
School Number 6—school ... ME-1
School Number 6—school (3) ... MI-6
School Number 6—school (6) ... NJ-2
School Number 6—school (3) ... ND-7
School Number 6—school (2) ... SD-7
School Number 6—school (4) ... VT-1
School Number 6 (abandoned)—school ... PA-2
School Number 6 (historical)—school (11) ... SD-7
School Number 6 West—locale ... MN-6
School Number 60—school (2) ... MN-6
School Number 60 (historical)—school (3) ... SD-7
School Number 607—school ... MN-6
School Number 61—school (4) ... MN-6
School Number 61—school (2) ... SD-7
School Number 6-16—school ... SD-7
School Number 62—locale (2) ... MN-6
School Number 62—school ... MN-6
School Number 62—school ... SD-7
School Number 62 (historical)—school ... SD-7
School Number 623—school ... MN-6
School Number 63—school ... SD-7
School Number 63 (historical)—school (2) ... SD-7
School Number 633—school ... MN-6
School Number 64—school (4) ... MN-6
School Number 64—school ... SD-7
School Number 65—school (3) ... MN-6
School Number 65 (historical)—school ... SD-7
School Number 66 (historical)—school (2) ... SD-7
School Number 669—school ... MN-6
School Number 67—school (2) ... MN-6
School Number 67 (historical)—school ... SD-7
School Number 671—school ... MN-6
School Number 68 ... SD-7
School Number 68—school ... MN-6
School Number 68—school ... NE-7
School Number 69—school ... NE-7
School Number 6-9—school ... SD-7
School Number 69 (historical)—school (2) ... SD-7
School Number 7 ... SD-7
School Number 7—school ... IA-7
School Number 7—school (2) ... MI-6
School Number 7—school (4) ... MN-6
School Number 7—school (3) ... NJ-2
School Number 7—school ... ND-7
School Number 7—school ... SD-7
School Number 7—school (2) ... VT-1
School Number 7 (historical)—school ... PA-2
School Number 7 (historical)—school (9) ... SD-7
School Number 70—locale ... MN-6
School Number 70—school (2) ... MN-6
School Number 70 (historical)—school ... SD-7
School Number 71 (historical)—school ... SD-7
School Number 72—school ... MN-6
School Number 72 (historical)—school ... SD-7
School Number 73—school (2) ... MN-6
School Number 73—school (2) ... SD-7
School Number 74—school (2) ... MN-6
School Number 75—school ... MN-6
School Number 75 (historical)—school ... SD-7
School Number 76 (historical)—school ... SD-7
School Number 761—school (2) ... MN-6
School Number 761 N—school ... MN-6
School Number 761 S—school ... MN-6
School Number 769—school ... MN-6
School Number 77—school (2) ... MN-6
School Number 77 (historical)—school ... SD-7
School Number 776—school ... MN-6
School Number 78—school ... MN-6
School Number 780—school ... MN-6
School Number 781—school ... MN-6
School Number 783—school ... MN-6
School Number 79—school ... MN-6
School Number 79 (historical)—school ... SD-7
School Number 790—school ... MN-6
School Number 8—school ... MI-6
School Number 8—school (2) ... MN-6
School Number 8—school ... NE-7
School Number 8—school (5) ... NJ-2
School Number 8—school (2) ... ND-7
School Number 8—school (2) ... SD-7
School Number 8—school (2) ... VT-1
School Number 8 (historical)—school (8) ... SD-7
School Number 80—school ... NE-7
School Number 801—school ... MN-6
School Number 809—school ... MN-6
School Number 81—school ... MN-6
School Number 81—school (2) ... SD-7
School Number 812—school ... MN-6
School Number 815—school ... MN-6
School Number 819—school ... MN-6
School Number 82—school ... MN-6
School Number 82—school ... SC-3
School Number 82—school (2) ... SD-7
School Number 820—school ... MN-6
School Number 83—school ... ND-7
School Number 83—school ... SD-7
School Number 836—school ... MN-6
School Number 839—school ... MN-6
School Number 84—school ... SD-7
School Number 841—school ... MN-6
School Number 842—locale ... MN-6
School Number 85—school ... MN-6
School Number 85—school ... SD-7
School Number 86—school ... MN-6
School Number 86—school ... NE-7
School Number 86—school ... SD-7
School Number 866—school ... MN-6
School Number 867—school ... MN-6
School Number 87—school (2) ... MN-6
School Number 87—school ... ND-7
School Number 871—school ... MN-6
School Number 88—school ... MN-6
School Number 88—school ... SD-7
School Number 89—school ... SD-7
School Number 9 ... SD-7
School Number 9—school ... ME-1
School Number 9—school ... NE-7
School Number 9—school (4) ... NJ-2
School Number 9—school (2) ... ND-7
School Number 9—school ... VT-1
School Number 9 (abandoned)—school ... ND-7
School Number 9 (historical)—school (5) ... SD-7
School Number 90—school (2) ... MN-6
School Number 90—school ... SD-7
School Number 91—school ... SD-7
School Number 93 ... IN-6
School Number 93—school ... MN-6
School Number 96—school (2) ... MN-6
School Number 97 (Abandoned)—locale ... MN-6
School Number 985—school ... MN-6
School Number 987—school ... MN-6
School Number 988—school ... MN-6
School Number 99—school ... NJ-2
School Number 99—school ... SD-7
School Number 993—school ... MN-6
School Number 994—school ... MN-6
School Number 996—school ... MN-6
School of Esthetic Experience—school ... FL-3
School of Hope—school ... CA-9
School of Hope—school ... MD-2
School Of Hope—school ... OH-6
School of Hope for Exceptional Children—school ... FL-3
School of Organic Education—hist pl ... AL-4
School of Saints—school ... IL-6
School of Santa Isabel—school ... CA-9
School of the Arts—school ... FL-3
School of the Evangelists ... TN-4
School of the Good Shepherd—school ... TN-4
School Of The Holy Family—school ... GA-3
School of the Little Flower—school ... NY-2
School of the Osage—school ... MO-7
School of the Ozarks ... MO-7
School of the Ozarks, The—school ... MO-7
School of the Redwoods—school ... CA-9
School of the Resurrection—school ... FL-3
School of the Sacred Heart of Jesus ... AL-4
School of Tropical Medicine—hist pl ... PR-3
School of Visitation—school ... MN-6
School Park—park ... WY-8
Schoolpath Branch—stream ... NC-3
School Point ... FL-3
School Point—summit ... MT-8
School Pond—lake ... MD-2
School Pond—lake ... MI-6
School Pond—lake ... NH-1
School Ridge—ridge ... CA-9
Schoolridge Farm—hist pl ... MD-2
School Rock—pillar ... TX-5
Schoolroom Glacier—glacier ... WY-8
School Rsvr—reservoir ... WY-8
School R-14—school ... MO-7
School R-3—school ... MO-7
Schools ... OR-9
School Seat Lake ... WI-6
School Section ... MN-6
School Section—locale ... OR-9
School Section Bay—bay (2) ... MN-6
School Section Brook—stream ... MI-6
School Section Butte—summit ... SD-7
School Section Camp—locale ... WY-8
School Section Canyon—valley (3) ... CO-8
School Section Canyon—valley (2) ... NM-5
School Section Canyon—valley ... UT-8
School Section Canyon—valley ... WY-8
School Section Coulee—valley (2) ... MT-8
School Section Creek—stream ... CA-9
School Section Creek—stream ... CO-8
School Section Creek—stream ... ID-8
School Section Creek—stream ... MT-8
School Section Dam—dam ... SD-7
School Section Ditch—canal ... WY-8
School Section Divide—ridge ... MT-8
School Section Draw—valley ... CO-8
School Section Draw—valley ... NM-5
School Section Draw—valley ... SD-7
School Section Draw—valley (10) ... WY-8
School Section Flat—flat ... NE-7
School Section Hollow—valley ... WI-6
School Section Lake ... MI-6
School Section Lake—lake ... CO-8
School Section Lake—lake ... ID-8
School Section Lake—lake (6) ... MI-6
School Section Lake—lake (4) ... MN-6
School Section Lake—lake (4) ... NE-7
School Section Lake—lake (3) ... ND-7
School Section Lake—lake (2) ... OR-9
School Section Lake—lake (2) ... WI-6
School Section Lake—reservoir ... WI-6
School Section Lake Natl Wildlife Ref—park ... ND-7
School Section Lakes—lake ... NE-7
School Section Lakes—lake ... SD-7
School Section Mine—mine ... CO-8
School Section Mtn—summit ... WY-8
School Section Number 5 Dam—dam ... SD-7
School Section Pond—reservoir ... AZ-5
School Section Ranch—locale ... UT-8
School Section Rsvr—reservoir (3) ... CO-8
School Section Rsvr—reservoir ... WY-8
School Section Spring—spring ... CO-8
School Section Spring—spring (3) ... MT-8
School Section Spring—spring (3) ... WY-8
School Section Springs—spring ... MT-8
School Section Table—summit ... OR-9
School Section Tank—reservoir ... AZ-5
School Section Tank—reservoir (8) ... NM-5
School Section Tanks—reservoir ... NM-5
School Section Well—locale ... NM-5
School Section Well—well ... CO-8
School Section Well—well (6) ... NM-5
School Section Well—well ... WY-8
School Section Windmill—locale ... CO-8
School Section Windmill—locale (3) ... NM-5
School Section Windmills—locale ... NM-5
Schools for the Deaf and Blind—school ... MS-4
School Side Manor—pop pl ... PA-2
School Spring—spring ... CA-9
School Spring—spring ... NV-8
School Station (historical)—pop pl ... OR-9
School Stream ... MA-1
School Street Brook—stream ... MA-1
School Street Cem—cemetery ... MA-1
School Street Elem Sch—school ... NC-3
School Street JHS—school ... PA-2
School Street Sch—hist pl (2) ... MA-1
School Street Sch—school ... ME-1
School Street Sch—school (3) ... MA-1
School Street Sch—school ... NY-2
School Tank—reservoir (3) ... NM-5
Schoolteacher Hill—summit ... CA-9
Schoolton—locale ... OK-5
Schoolton Chapel—church ... OK-5
Schoolview—pop pl ... DE-2
School Village—pop pl ... HI-9
Schoolville—pop pl ... KY-4
School Wash—valley ... UT-8
School Well—well ... NM-5
School 1—locale ... MI-6
School 1—school ... MI-6
School 1 North—school ... MI-6
School 1 South—school ... MI-6
School 2—locale ... MI-6
School 2—school ... MI-6
School 4—school ... MI-6
School 7—school ... MI-6
Schoomaker Lake—lake ... MI-6
Schoo Mine—mine ... UT-8
Schoona ... MS-4
Schoona Chapel Baptist Church ... MS-4
Schoonamaker Lake—lake ... CA-9
Schoonaver Cem—cemetery ... MO-7
Schoonbeck Lake—reservoir ... NC-3
Schoonbeck Lake Dam—dam ... NC-3
Schoon Ditch—canal ... IN-6
Schooner ... MS-4
Schooner Bank—bar ... FL-3
Schooner Bar—bar ... MA-1
Schooner Bay—bay ... AK-9
Schooner Bay—bay ... CA-9
Schooner Bayou ... LA-4
Schooner Bayou—stream (2) ... LA-4
Schooner Bayou Canal—canal ... LA-4
Schooner Bayou Cutoff ... LA-4
Schooner Bayou Cuttoff ... LA-4
Schooner Bend—bend ... AK-9
Schooner Brook—stream ... ME-1
Schooner Brook Cove ... ME-1
Schooner Canal—canal ... LA-4
Schooner Canyon—valley ... WY-8
Schooner Channel—channel ... AK-9
Schooner Channel—channel ... SC-3
Schooner Cove—bay (2) ... ME-1
Schooner Creek ... IN-6
Schooner Creek—stream ... ID-8
Schooner Creek—stream ... MO-7
Schooner Creek—stream ... NJ-2
Schooner Creek—stream (2) ... OR-9
Schooner Creek—stream (3) ... SC-3
Schooner Creek Campground—park ... OR-9
Schooner Gulch—valley ... CA-9
Schooner Head—summit ... ME-1
Schooner Island—island ... LA-4
Schooner Island—island ... MI-6
Schooner Island—island ... NY-2
Schooner Landing (Site)—locale ... CA-9
Schoonermaker Well—well ... NM-5
Schooner Point—cape ... ME-1
Schooner Point—cape ... RI-1
Schooner Point—locale ... OR-9
Schooner Post Office (historical)—building ... MS-4
Schooner Ridge Subdivision)—pop pl ... NC-3
Schooner Rock—island ... AK-9
Schooner Valley Baptist Church ... MS-4
Schooner Valley Ch—church ... MS-4
Schooner Valley Sch (historical)—school ... MS-4
Schoonhorer Creek ... NV-8
Schoonhover Creek ... NV-8
Schoonnorer Creek ... NV-8
Schoonover—locale ... WA-9
Schoonover, Frank E., Studios—hist pl ... DE-2
Schoonover Bridge—bridge ... WY-8
Schoonover Buttes—summit ... CO-8
Schoonover Cem—cemetery ... NE-7
Schoonover Cem—cemetery ... PA-2
Schoonover Creek—stream (2) ... NV-8
Schoonover Flats—flat ... WY-8
Schoonover Gulch—valley ... CO-8
Schoonover Gulch—valley ... ID-8
Schoonover Hollow—valley ... PA-2
Schoonover House—hist pl ... MO-7
Schoonover Knob—summit ... WV-2
Schoonover Lake—lake ... NE-7
Schoonover Mountain House—hist pl ... PA-2
Schoonover Park—park ... OH-6
Schoonover Pasture—flat ... CO-8
Schoonovers Lake ... PA-2
Schoon Sch—school ... IL-6
Schoop Lake ... NE-7
Schoosett—pop pl ... MA-1
Schoosett Cem—cemetery ... MA-1
Schootarza Stream ... ME-1
Schootaza Brook ... ME-1
Schootaza Stream ... ME-1
Schoothouse Lake—lake ... AK-9
Schoper—locale ... IL-6
Schoper Lake—reservoir ... IL-6
Schoppe Bay—bay ... AK-9
Schoppe Brook—stream ... NH-1
Schoppe Cem—cemetery ... TX-5
Schoppe Ridge—ridge ... ME-1
Schoppert, Phillip, House—hist pl ... AL-4
Schoppman Drain—canal ... IN-6
Schoppmann Hollow—valley ... UT-8
Schori Lake—lake ... IN-6
Schori Lake Dam—dam ... IN-6
Schorlig House—hist pl ... CA-9
Schorn Brook Cem—cemetery ... LA-4
Schorns Creek ... TN-4
Schorns Ferry ... TN-4
Schornstein Grocery and Saloon—hist pl ... MN-6
Schorr Lake—reservoir ... AL-4
Schorr Lake Dam—dam ... AL-4
Schorsch Forest View ... IL-6
Schortemeyers Triangle—locale ... FL-3
Schortz Sch (abandoned)—school ... PA-2
Schote Creek—stream ... MO-7
Schote Hollow—valley ... TN-4
Schott Canyon—valley ... CA-9
Schott Canyon—valley ... OR-9
Schott Ditch—canal ... IN-6
Schott Lateral—canal ... ID-8
Schott Mtn—summit ... TX-5
Schottner Drain ... NV-8
Schott Ranch—locale ... TX-5
Schounmaker Ditch—canal ... WY-8
Schoun Sch—school ... SD-7
Schouts Creek—stream ... MI-6
Schoverling, Carl F., Tobacco Warehouse—hist pl ... CT-1
Schow—locale ... ID-8
Schowengerdt, Ernst, House—hist pl ... MO-7
Schraalenburgh ... NJ-2
Schracktown—pop pl ... PA-2
Schrader—locale ... WV-2
Schrader—pop pl ... OH-6
Schrader, Lake—lake ... AK-9
Schrader, Mount—summit ... AK-9
Schrader Archeol Site—hist pl ... NE-7
Schrader Bluff—cliff ... AK-9
Schrader Branch—stream ... KS-7
Schrader Branch Towanda Creek ... PA-2
Schrader Corners—locale ... OH-6
Schrader Creek—stream ... AK-9
Schrader Creek—stream ... CO-8
Schrader Creek—stream ... PA-2
Schrader Crossroads—locale ... PA-2
Schrader Ditch—canal ... IN-6
Schrader Elem Sch—school ... FL-3
Schrader Flats—flat ... WY-8
Schrader Gap—gap ... PA-2
Schrader Gulch—valley ... WY-8
Schrader Hill—summit ... NY-2
Schrader Hollow ... WV-2
Schrader Island—island ... AK-9
Schrader Lake—lake ... AK-9
Schrader Lake—reservoir ... VA-3
Schrader Mill (historical)—locale ... AL-4
Schrader Rsvr—reservoir ... CO-8
Schrader Sch—school ... MO-7
Schrader Sch (historical)—school ... AL-4
Schrader Sch (historical)—school ... TN-4
Schrador Cemetery ... TN-4
Schrag—locale ... WA-9
Schrag Cem—cemetery ... OR-9
Schrage Sch—school ... IL-6
Schrag Station ... WA-9
Schralenburg ... NJ-2
Schram Branch—stream ... MI-6
Schram City—pop pl ... IL-6
Schram Drain—canal ... MI-6
Schram Lake—lake (2) ... MN-6
Schram Lake—lake ... NM-5
Schramling Creek—stream ... IA-7
Schramm—locale ... CO-8
Schramm Cem—cemetery ... IA-7
Schramm Creek—stream ... WI-6
Schramm Dam—dam ... ND-7
Schrammeck Lake—lake ... MT-8
Schramm Lake ... MN-6
Schramm Sch—school ... IL-6
Schramsberg Winery Historical Marker—locale ... CA-9
Schrams Cem—cemetery ... MN-6
Schrams Lake—lake ... MN-6
Schram Well—locale ... NM-5
Schraner Cem—cemetery ... IN-6
Schrauger Sch (historical)—school ... PA-2
Schraum Creek—stream ... WI-6
Schrawders Creek ... PA-2
Schrawn Creek ... MO-7
Schreck—pop pl ... WA-9
Schreckengast Gap—gap ... PA-2
Schrecks Plaza—locale ... KS-7
Schreck Tank—reservoir ... AZ-5
Schreeder Brook—stream ... MI-6
Schreeder Pond—lake ... CT-1
Schreffler Cem—cemetery ... PA-2
Schreiber, Adolph, House—hist pl ... ID-8
Schreiber, Brock, Boathouse and Beach—hist pl ... CA-9
Schreiber Cem—cemetery ... SD-7
Schreiber Creek ... MT-8
Schreiber Ditch—canal ... MI-6
Schreiber Ditch—canal ... OH-6
Schreiber Lake ... MT-8
Schreiber Lake—lake ... IL-6
Schreiber Park—park ... IL-6
Schreiber Promenade—park ... FL-3
Schreiers Lake—lake ... MN-6
Schreiner, Capt. Charles, Mansion—hist pl ... TX-5
Schreiner Cem—cemetery ... KS-7
Schreiner Institute—school ... TX-5
Schreiner Peak—summit ... OR-9
Schreiver Tank—reservoir ... TX-5
Schremmer Hollow—valley ... AR-4
Schremmer Hollow—valley ... MO-7
Schremp Sch—school ... NE-7
Schrewsbury Pond ... VT-1
Schreyer Ranch—locale ... WY-8
Schriber, Hyman, Bldg—hist pl ... OH-6
Schriborough Canyon—valley ... AR-4
Schricker, John, House—hist pl ... IA-7
Schricker, John C., House—hist pl ... IA-7
Schricker Slough—stream ... IA-7
Schrieber ... PA-2
Schrieber Creek—stream ... MT-8
Schrieber HS—school ... NY-2
Schrieber Lake—lake ... MT-8
Schriebers Meadow—flat ... WA-9
Schrier Cem—cemetery ... TX-5
Schrier Park—park ... TX-5
Schriever—pop pl ... LA-4
Schriever Sch—school ... LA-4
Schriever Township—pop pl ... SD-7
Schrike Rsvr—reservoir ... ID-8
Schrimpsher Cem—cemetery ... OK-5
Schrites Coulee—valley ... MT-8
Schriver Cem—cemetery (2) ... OH-6
Schriver Fork—stream ... OH-6
Schriver Sch—school ... PA-2
Schrivnor Lake—lake ... TX-5
Schrob Gulch ... OR-9
Schrock (2) ... IN-6
Schrock, Peter, Jr., Farm—hist pl ... OH-6
Schrock Cem—cemetery ... IN-6
Schrock Cem—cemetery ... IA-7
Schrock Cem—cemetery ... MO-7
Schrock Run—stream ... PA-2
Schrocks Cem—cemetery ... OH-6
Schrode Lake—lake ... CA-9
Schroder Arroyo—valley ... TX-5
Schroder Branch—stream ... MO-7
Schroder Ranch—locale ... MT-8
Schroder Sch—school ... OH-6
Schroder Sch (abandoned)—school ... MO-7
Schroder Subdivision—pop pl ... UT-8
Schrodts Station—pop pl ... IL-6
Schrodt (Sugar Creek)—pop pl ... IL-6
Schroeder—pop pl ... MN-6
Schroeder—pop pl ... TX-5
Schroeder, Mount—summit ... GU-9
Schroeder Branch—stream ... VA-3
Schroeder Bros, Meat Market—hist pl ... IA-7
Schroeder Cem—cemetery ... IL-6
Schroeder Cem—cemetery ... LA-4
Schroeder Cem—cemetery ... MO-7
Schroeder Cem—cemetery ... TX-5
Schroeder Creek—stream ... MI-6
Schroeder Creek—stream ... OR-9
Schroeder Ditch—canal ... CO-8
Schroeder Ditch—canal ... IN-6
Schroeder Ditch—canal ... OH-6
Schroeder Drain—canal (2) ... MI-6
Schroeder Field—airport ... ND-7
Schroeder Gulch—valley ... MT-8
Schroeder House—hist pl ... TX-5
Schroeder JHS—school ... ND-7
Schroeder Junction—locale ... GU-9
Schroeder Lake—lake (2) ... MN-6
Schroeder Lake—reservoir ... NV-8
Schroeder Lumber Company Bunkhouse—hist pl ... MN-6
Schroeder Mine—mine (2) ... CA-9
Schroeder Mtn—summit ... NV-8
Schroeder Park—park ... IL-6
Schroeder Park—park ... MI-6
Schroeder Park—park ... MN-6
Schroeder Park—park ... OR-9
Schroeder Ranch—locale (2) ... NE-7
Schroeder Ranch—locale ... SD-7
Schroeder Rock—pillar ... CA-9
Schroeder Sch—school ... CA-9
Schroeder Sch—school ... NY-2
Schroeder Sch—school ... SD-7
Schroeder Tank—reservoir (4) ... AZ-5
Schroeder (Township of)—pop pl ... MN-6
Schroeder-Yturri House—hist pl ... TX-5
Schroeppel Bridge—bridge ... NY-2
Schroeppel House—hist pl ... NY-2
Schroeppel Island—island ... NY-2
Schroeppel (Town of)—pop pl ... NY-2
Schroff-O'Neil Mine—mine ... AK-9
Schroll Draw—valley ... WY-8
Schrom Cem—cemetery ... IA-7
Schrom Creek—stream ... IN-6
Schrom Hills Recreation Center—park ... MD-2
Schroon Falls—locale ... NY-2
Schroon Lake—lake ... NY-2
Schroon Lake—pop pl ... NY-2
Schroon River ... NY-2
Schroon River—stream ... NY-2
Schroon River Cem—cemetery ... NY-2
Schroon (Town of)—pop pl ... NY-2
Schrop JHS—school ... OH-6
Schroth Sch—school ... IL-6
Schroy Cem—cemetery ... OH-6
Schroyer ... KS-7
Schroyer Gap—gap ... PA-2
Schroyer Trail—trail ... PA-2
Schrum—pop pl ... IL-6
Schrum Creek—stream ... OR-9
Schrum Hollow—valley ... MO-7
Schrum Ranch—locale ... WA-9
Schrum Sch—school ... IL-6
Schrunk Sch Number 1—school ... ND-7
Schrunk Sch Number 2—school ... ND-7
Schrunk Township—pop pl ... ND-7
Schryer Dam—dam ... AL-4
Schubarth Trail—trail ... CO-8
Schubee Glacier—glacier ... AK-9
Schubert—locale ... MO-7
Schubert—pop pl ... PA-2
Schubert Cem—cemetery ... IN-6
Schubert Creek—stream ... KS-7
Schubert Flat—flat ... CO-8
Schubert House—hist pl ... TX-5
Schubert Lake ... MN-6
Schubert Ranch—locale ... CO-8
Schubert Sch—school ... IL-6
Schubert Sch—school ... SD-7
Schuchk—locale ... AZ-5
Schuchk Ka Wuacho Awotam ... AZ-5
Schuchman Cem—cemetery ... MO-7
Schuchuli—pop pl ... AZ-5
Schuck ... FM-9
Schucken Hausen ... PA-2
Schucks Corners—locale ... MD-2
Schuck Waterhole—reservoir ... OR-9
Schudel No. 2 Site—hist pl ... IL-6
Schuebe School ... OR-9
Schuelke Gulch—valley ... WA-9
Schuelke Spring—spring ... WA-9
Schueller, Erwin W., House—hist pl ... OH-6
Schueltheis Canyon ... WA-9
Schuerman Heights ... MO-7
Schuermann Heights—pop pl ... MO-7
Schuessler Dam—dam ... AL-4
Schuessler Hill—summit ... TX-5
Schuessler Tank—reservoir ... TX-5
Schuetz, E.K., House—hist pl ... WI-6
Schuetz Creek—stream ... TX-5
Schuetzen Hill—summit ... TX-5
Schuetzen Park—park ... NJ-2
Schuetz Ranch—locale ... MT-8
Schuffenecker, August Bldg—hist pl ... OH-6
Schuff Hollow—valley ... TN-4
Schufler ... AL-4
Schug—pop pl ... AR-4
Schugart Flat—flat ... WA-9
Schug Dam—dam ... ND-7
Schugg Ditch—canal ... IN-6
Schugh Cem—cemetery ... TX-5
Schugtown ... AR-4
Schuh Bend—bend ... IL-6
Schuh Ditch—canal ... IN-6
Schukar Table—summit ... NE-7
Schuk Cowlik—summit ... AZ-5
Schulderman, Peter, House—hist pl ... WA-9
Schuleen—pop pl ... VA-3
Schulenburg—pop pl ... TX-5
Schulenburg (CCD)—cens area ... TX-5
Schulenburg Cotton Compress—hist pl ... TX-5
Schuler, Hans, Studio and Residence—hist pl ... MD-2
Schuler Branch—stream ... KS-7
Schuler Branch—stream ... KY-4
Schuler Gulch—valley (2) ... CA-9
Schuler (historical)—locale ... AL-4
Schuler Hollow—valley ... OH-6
Schuler Park—flat ... WY-8
Schules Creek ... AL-4
Schuline—pop pl ... IL-6
Schulines (Schuline)—pop pl ... IL-6
Schull Cove—cave ... PA-2
Schullenberger Lake—lake ... WI-6
Schuller Gulch ... CA-9
Schuller Lateral—canal ... CA-9
Schuller Well—well ... NM-5
Schulls Rock—summit ... PA-2
Schulmeier Cem—cemetery ... TX-5
Schulmeyer Gulch—valley ... CA-9
Schult—pop pl ... MO-7
Schulte—pop pl ... KS-7
Schulte Archeol Site—hist pl ... NE-7
Schulte Cem—cemetery ... MI-6
Schulte Creek—stream ... MO-7
Schulteis Airp—airport ... PA-2
Schulte Mine (historical)—mine ... MO-7
Schulter—pop pl ... OK-5
Schulte Sch—school ... IL-6
Schulte Sch—school ... IN-6
Schultheis Canyon—valley ... WA-9
Schultice Mtn—summit ... NY-2
Schultie Crossroad ... DE-2
Schultie Crossroads—locale ... DE-2
Schult Lake—lake ... MN-6
Schultys Landing—locale ... AL-4
Schultz ... WI-6
Schultz—locale ... MI-6
Schultz—locale ... WI-6
Schultz—pop pl ... MD-2
Schultz—pop pl ... WV-2
Schultz, Charles S. House—hist pl ... NJ-2
Schultz, Raymond, Round Barn—hist pl ... IL-6
Schultz, Tobias and Wilhelmine, Farm—hist pl ... TX-5
Schultz Bar—bar ... WA-9
Schultz Branch—stream ... KY-4
Schultz Canyon—valley ... CO-8
Schultz Cem—cemetery ... IN-6
Schultz Cem—cemetery ... IA-7
Schultz Cem—cemetery ... NE-7
Schultz Cem—cemetery ... WV-2
Schultz Coulee ... MT-8
Schultz Coulee—valley (2) ... MT-8
Schultz Creek ... OK-5
Schultz Creek ... OR-9
Schultz Creek ... WA-9
Schultz Creek—stream ... AL-4
Schultz Creek—stream ... AZ-5
Schultz Creek—stream ... CA-9

Scott Knob—*summit* VA-3
Scott Lagoon—*lake* AK-9
*Scott Lake* MI-6
Scott Lake—*CDP* FL-3
Scott Lake—*lake* AL-4
Scott Lake—*lake* (2) AK-9
Scott Lake—*lake* (2) AR-4
Scott Lake—*lake* CA-9
Scott Lake—*lake* CO-8
Scott Lake—*lake* (2) FL-3
Scott Lake—*lake* (5) MI-6
Scott Lake—*lake* (6) MN-6
Scott Lake—*lake* (2) MT-8
Scott Lake—*lake* NY-2
Scott Lake—*lake* OR-9
Scott Lake—*lake* SC-3
Scott Lake—*lake* TX-5
Scott Lake—*lake* WA-9
Scott Lake—*lake* (4) WI-6
Scott Lake—*locale* MI-6
Scott Lake—*reservoir* GA-3
Scott Lake—*reservoir* IN-6
Scott Lake—*reservoir* MS-4
Scott Lake—*reservoir* NC-3
Scott Lake—*reservoir* TN-4
Scott Lake—*reservoir* TX-5
Scott Lake—*reservoir* WV-2
Scott Lake—*reservoir* WY-8
Scott-Lake Baptist Ch—*church* FL-3
Scott Lake Dam—*dam* (2) MS-4
Scott Lake Dam—*dam* NC-3
Scott Lake Elem Sch—*school* FL-3
Scott Lake Golf Course—*other* MI-6
Scott Lakes—*lake* MI-6
Scott Lake Sch—*school* FL-3
*Scott Land* IL-6
Scottland—*locale* AL-4
**Scottland**—*pop pl* IL-6
*Scott Landing* MD-2
Scott Landing—*locale* LA-4
Scott Landing—*locale* NC-3
Scottland Plantation House—*hist pl* LA-4
Scott Lane Sch—*school* CA-9
Scott Lateral—*canal* IN-6
Scott Lewis Sch—*school* VA-3
Scott Libby Elem Sch—*school* AZ-5
Scott Lookout Tower—*locale* NE-7
Scott Lookout Tower—*tower* FL-3
Scott (Magisterial District)—*fmr MCD* VA-3
Scott (Magisterial District)—*fmr MCD* (2) WV-2
Scott-Majors House—*hist pl* TX-5
Scott Marsh—*lake* TX-5
Scott Memorial Ch—*church* VA-3
Scott Memorial Ch of God—*church* TN-4
*Scott Memorial Hospital* TN-4
Scott Memorial Park—*park* TX-5
Scott Memorial Sch—*school* VA-3
Scott Mennonite Cem—*cemetery* KS-7
Scott Mennonite Ch—*church* KS-7
Scott Mesa—*summit* NM-5
Scott Middle Ground—*bar* MI-6
Scott Mill Creek—*stream* GA-3
Scott Mill Pond Public Fishing Area—*park* IN-6
*Scott Millpond State Fishing Area* IN-6
Scott Mills Sch—*school* OR-9
Scott Mine—*mine* AZ-5
Scott Mountain Creek—*stream* CA-9
Scott Mountain Driveway (historical)—*trail* ID-8
**Scott Mountain Summit**—*pop pl* CA-9
Scott Mtn—*summit* AL-4
Scott Mtn—*summit* AZ-5
Scott Mtn—*summit* CA-9
Scott Mtn—*summit* ID-8
Scott Mtn—*summit* KY-4
Scott Mtn—*summit* NH-1
Scott Mtn—*summit* (2) NC-3
Scott Mtn—*summit* (4) OR-9
Scott Mtn—*summit* TN-4
Scott Mtn—*summit* VT-1
Scott Mtn—*summit* (6) VA-3
Scott Mtn—*summit* WA-9
*Scott Mtn Cemetery* AL-4
Scott Municipal Airp—*airport* TN-4
Scott Nicholson Catfish Ponds Dam—*dam* MS-4
Scott No. 2 Mine—*other* WV-2
Scott Oil Field—*oilfield* KS-7
Scott Oil Field—*oilfield* TX-5
**Scotton Corner**—*pop pl* WA-9
*S. Cottonwood Township* ND-7
Scottow Bog—*swamp* ME-1
Scottow Hill—*summit* ME-1
Scottown—*locale* KY-4
**Scottown**—*pop pl* OH-6
Scottown Covered Bridge—*hist pl* OH-6
Scottown Marsh—*swamp* MD-2
Scott Paper Company Dam—*dam* AL-4
Scott Paper Company Lake Dam—*dam* MS-4
Scott Paper Company Pond—*reservoir* AL-4
Scott Park—*locale* CA-9
Scott Park—*park* CA-9
Scott Park—*park* FL-3
Scott Park—*park* IL-6
Scott Park—*park* MI-6
Scott Park—*park* OH-6
**Scott Park**—*pop pl* NC-3
Scott Pass—*gap* NV-8
Scott Pass—*gap* OR-9
Scott Patent Ch—*church* NY-2
Scott Patent Hill—*summit* NY-2
Scott Peak—*summit* (2) AK-9
Scott Peak—*summit* CA-9
Scott Peak—*summit* ID-8
Scott Peak—*summit* NM-5
Scott Peak—*summit* WA-9
Scott Pierce Ditch—*canal* CO-8
Scott Pinnacle—*summit* TN-4
Scott Place—*locale* CA-9
Scott Place—*locale* ID-8
*Scott Point* TN-4
Scott Point—*cape* (2) AK-9
Scott Point—*cape* MD-2
Scott Point—*cape* MI-6
Scott Point—*cape* OH-6
Scott Point—*cape* VT-1
Scott Point—*summit* AZ-5
Scott Point Shoal—*bar* OH-6
Scott Point Site—*hist pl* MI-6
Scott Pond—*lake* IN-6
Scott Pond—*lake* ME-1
Scott Pond—*lake* MO-7
Scott Pond—*lake* NH-1
Scott Pond—*lake* (2) NY-2
Scott Pond—*lake* TN-4
Scott Pond—*lake* VT-1
Scott Pond—*reservoir* AL-4
Scott Pond—*reservoir* FL-3
Scott Pond—*reservoir* RI-1
Scott Post Office (historical)—*building* SD-7
Scott Prospect—*mine* (2) TN-4
Scott Quarry—*mine* MI-6
Scott Ranch—*locale* CA-9
Scott Ranch—*locale* MT-8
Scott Ranch—*locale* NV-8
Scott Ranch—*locale* (2) NM-5
Scott Ranch—*locale* SD-7
Scott Ranch—*locale* TX-5
Scott Ranch—*locale* WY-8
Scott Ravine—*valley* CA-9
Scott Reservoir Dam—*dam* MA-1
Scott Residence Hall—*building* NC-3
Scott Ridge—*ridge* AZ-5
Scott Ridge—*ridge* AR-4
Scott Ridge—*ridge* (2) CA-9
Scott Ridge—*ridge* CT-1
Scott Ridge—*ridge* IN-6
Scott Ridge—*ridge* (2) KY-4
Scott Ridge—*ridge* NC-3
Scott Ridge—*ridge* TX-5
Scott Ridge—*ridge* VA-3
Scott Ridge—*ridge* WV-2
Scott Ridge Ch—*church* TX-5
*Scott River* CA-9
Scott River—*stream* CA-9
Scott Road Mine (surface)—*mine* AL-4
Scott-Robbins Cem—*cemetery* MS-4
Scottrock—*locale* AL-4
Scott Rock—*summit* CA-9
Scott-Roden Mansion—*hist pl* TX-5
Scott (RR name for Scott Depot)—*other* WV-2
*Scott Rsvr* OR-9
Scott Rsvr—*reservoir* AZ-5
Scott Rsvr—*reservoir* MA-1
Scott Rsvr—*reservoir* MT-8
Scott Rsvr—*reservoir* (2) OR-9
Scott Rsvr—*reservoir* WY-8
*Scott Run* WV-2
Scott Run—*locale* WV-2
Scott Run—*stream* CO-8
Scott Run—*stream* DE-2
Scott Run—*stream* (5) OH-6
Scott Run—*stream* (5) PA-2
Scott Run—*stream* VA-3
Scott Run—*stream* (4) WV-2
Scott Run Community Park—*park* VA-3
*Scotts* DE-2
*Scott's* OH-6
Scotts—*locale* CA-9
Scotts—*other* KY-4
**Scotts**—*pop pl* MI-6
**Scotts**—*pop pl* (2) NC-3
**Scotts**—*pop pl* WV-2
**Scotts Acres Subdivision**—*pop pl* UT-8
Scott Saddle—*gap* ID-8
Scotts Barn Cave—*cave* AL-4
Scotts Basin—*basin* AZ-5
Scotts Beach—*beach* NY-2
Scotts Bend—*bend* AR-4
*Scotts Bluff* LA-4
*Scotts Bluff* NE-7
Scotts Bluff—*cliff* ID-8
Scotts Bluff—*cliff* NY-2
**Scottsbluff**—*pop pl* NE-7
Scotts Bluff—*summit* NE-7
Scottsbluff Carnegie Library—*hist pl* NE-7
Scottsbluff Country Club—*other* NE-7
Scotts Bluff County Airp—*airport* NE-7
Scottsbluff Drain—*canal* NE-7
Scotts Bluff Lateral—*canal* NE-7
Scotts Bluff Natl Monmt—*hist pl* NE-7
Scotts Bluff Natl Monmt—*park* NE-7
*Scottsboro* AL-4
**Scottsboro**—*pop pl* AL-4
**Scottsboro**—*pop pl* GA-3
**Scottsboro**—*pop pl* TN-4
Scottsboro (CCD)—*cens area* AL-4
Scottsboro Country Club And Golf Course—*other* AL-4
Scottsboro Crossroads—*locale* AL-4
Scottsboro Division—*civil* AL-4
Scottsboro HS—*school* AL-4
Scottsboro Mission—*church* TN-4
Scottsboro Municipal Airp—*airport* AL-4
Scottsboro Municipal Park—*park* AL-4
Scottsboro Plaza Shop Ctr—*locale* AL-4
Scottsboro Public Sch (historical)—*school* AL-4
Scottsboro Sch (historical)—*school* AL-4
Scottsboro Shop Ctr—*locale* AL-4
Scotts Bottom—*bend* KY-4
*Scott's Branch* NY-2
*Scotts Branch* SC-3
Scotts Branch—*stream* (3) KY-4
Scotts Branch—*stream* MS-4
Scotts Branch—*stream* (2) MO-7
Scotts Branch—*stream* NC-3
Scotts Branch—*stream* VA-3
Scotts Bridge—*bridge* MS-4
Scotts Bridge—*bridge* NY-2
*Scotts Brook* MA-1
*Scotts Brook* RI-1
Scotts Brook—*stream* CT-1
Scotts Brook—*stream* ME-1
Scotts Brook—*stream* MA-1
Scotts Brook—*stream* NY-2
*Scottsburg* PA-2
Scottsburg—*locale* IL-6
Scottsburg—*locale* KY-4
**Scottsburg**—*pop pl* (2) IN-6
**Scottsburg**—*pop pl* NY-2
**Scottsburg**—*pop pl* OR-9
**Scottsburg**—*pop pl* VA-3
Scottsburg Airp—*airport* IN-6
Scottsburg Cem—*cemetery* OR-9
Scottsburg Drain—*stream* IN-6
*Scottsburgh* IN-6
Scottsburg JHS—*school* IN-6
Scottsburg Memorial Hosp—*hospital* IN-6
Scottsburg Park—*park* OR-9
Scottsburg Rsvr—*reservoir* IN-6
Scottsburg Sch—*school* VA-3
Scottsburg Senior HS—*school* IN-6
Scottsburg Water Works Dam—*dam* IN-6
*Scotts Butte* OR-9
*Scotts Butte Creek* OR-9
Scotts Cabin Creek—*stream* OR-9
Scotts Cabin Spring—*spring* OR-9
Scotts Cache Spring—*spring* OR-9
Scotts Camp—*locale* KS-7
Scotts Camp—*locale* MO-7
Scotts Campground—*park* OR-9
Scotts Canyon—*valley* NV-8
Scotts Canyon—*valley* OR-9
Scotts Cem—*cemetery* MS-4
Scotts Cem—*cemetery* OH-6
Scotts Cem—*cemetery* SC-3
Scotts Ch—*church* KY-4
Scott Sch—*school* AL-4
Scott Sch—*school* FL-3
Scott Sch—*school* (2) GA-3
Scott Sch—*school* (4) IL-6
Scott Sch—*school* IA-7
Scott Sch—*school* KS-7
Scott Sch—*school* MD-2
Scott Sch—*school* (4) MI-6
Scott Sch—*school* (3) MO-7
Scott Sch—*school* NJ-2
Scott Sch—*school* NY-2
Scott Sch—*school* NC-3
Scott Sch—*school* OK-5
Scott Sch—*school* OR-9
Scott Sch—*school* SD-7
Scott Sch—*school* (2) TX-5
Scott Sch—*school* VA-3
Scott Sch—*school* (3) WI-6
Scotts Chapel—*church* (2) GA-3
Scotts Chapel—*church* KY-4
Scotts Chapel—*church* MS-4
Scotts Chapel Cem—*cemetery* TN-4
Scotts Chapel Cem—*cemetery* TX-5
Scotts Chapel (historical)—*church* AL-4
Scotts Chapel Sch—*school* KY-4
Scott Sch (historical)—*school* MS-4
Scott Sch (historical)—*school* MO-7
Scott Sch (historical)—*school* TN-4
*Scott School* TN-4
Scott School—*locale* IL-6
Scott School (historical)—*locale* (2) MO-7
Scotts Cliff—*cliff* KY-4
Scotts Cobble—*summit* NY-2
Scotts Corner—*locale* CA-9
Scotts Corner—*locale* DE-2
Scotts Corner—*locale* GA-3
Scotts Corner—*locale* MO-7
Scotts Corner—*locale* TX-5
Scotts Corner—*locale* VA-3
**Scotts Corner**—*pop pl* MN-6
**Scotts Corner**—*pop pl* NY-2
*Scott's Corner Brook* CT-1
*Scotts Corners* DE-2
*Scotts Corners* NY-2
Scotts Corners—*locale* DE-2
Scotts Corners—*locale* ME-1
Scotts Corners—*locale* NJ-2
Scotts Corners—*locale* (2) NY-2
**Scotts Corners**—*pop pl* NY-2
Scotts Cove—*bay* MD-2
*Scotts Creek* MI-6
*Scotts Creek* TN-4
*Scotts Creek* VA-3
Scotts Creek—*stream* AR-4
Scotts Creek—*stream* (2) CA-9
Scotts Creek—*stream* NC-3
Scotts Creek—*stream* PA-2
Scotts Creek—*stream* SC-3
Scotts Creek—*stream* (3) TN-4
Scotts Creek—*stream* TX-5
*Scotts Creek Basin* PA-2
Scotts Creek Ch—*church* NC-3
Scotts Creek Sch—*school* NC-3
Scotts Crossing—*locale* PA-2
Scotts Crossing—*locale* (2) TX-5
**Scotts Crossing**—*pop pl* OH-6
Scotts Crossroad—*locale* VA-3
*Scotts Crossroads* DE-2
**Scotts Crossroads**—*pop pl* NC-3
**Scotts Crossroads**—*pop pl* VA-3
*Scottsdale* UT-8
**Scottsdale**—*pop pl* AZ-5
Scottsdale, Canal (historical)—*canal* AZ-5
*Scottsdale Ballpark* AZ-5
Scottsdale Community Coll—*school* AZ-5
Scottsdale Community Hosp—*hospital* AZ-5
Scottsdale Country Club—*other* AZ-5
Scottsdale Country Club Golf Course—*other* AZ-5
Scottsdale East Shop Ctr—*locale* AZ-5
Scottsdale Fashion Square Shop Ctr—*locale* AZ-5
Scottsdale Horsemens Park—*park* AZ-5
Scottsdale HS—*school* AZ-5
Scottsdale Mall—*locale* AZ-5
Scottsdale Mall—*locale* IN-6
Scottsdale Memorial Hosp—*hospital* AZ-5
Scottsdale Mobile Home Park—*locale* AZ-5
Scottsdale Municipal Airp—*airport* AZ-5
Scottsdale Oak Plaza Shop Ctr—*locale* AZ-5
Scottsdale Park—*park* IL-6
**Scottsdale Park (trailer park)**—*pop pl* DE-2
Scottsdale Plaza—*locale* PA-2
Scottsdale Plaza Shop Ctr—*locale* AZ-5
Scottsdale Post Office—*building* AZ-5
**Scottsdale Ranch**—*pop pl* AZ-5
Scottsdale Regional Shop Ctr—*locale* AZ-5
Scottsdale Shop Ctr—*locale* AZ-5
Scottsdale Stadium—*building* AZ-5
**Scottsdale (subdivision)**—*pop pl* AL-4
**Scottsdale (subdivision)**—*pop pl* NC-3
**Scotts Dale Subdivision**—*pop pl* UT-8
**Scottsdale Subdivision**—*pop pl* UT-8
Scottsdale Trailer Corral—*locale* AZ-5
Scottsdale Village Shop Ctr—*locale* AZ-5
Scott Seed Farm Airp—*airport* WA-9
Scott Settlement Cem—*cemetery* MN-6
Scotts Factory Pond—*reservoir* VA-3
Scotts Ferry—*locale* KY-4
**Scotts Ferry**—*pop pl* FL-3
Scotts Flat Rsvr—*reservoir* CA-9
Scotts Ford—*crossing* TN-4
*Scotts Fork* CA-9
Scotts Fork—*locale* VA-3
Scotts Glade—*flat* CA-9
Scotts Grove Ch—*church* (2) KY-4
Scotts Gulch—*valley* CA-9
Scotts Gulch—*valley* NV-8
*Scotts Hill* MA-1
**Scotts Hill**—*pop pl* (2) NC-3
**Scotts Hill**—*pop pl* TN-4
*Scotts Hill Baptist Church* TN-4
Scotts Hill Cem—*cemetery* TN-4
Scotts Hill Coll (historical)—*school* TN-4
Scotts Hill First Baptist Ch—*church* TN-4
Scotts Hill Post Office—*building* TN-4
*Scotts Hills* TN-4
Scotts Hill Sch—*school* TN-4
*Scotts Hills Post Office* TN-4
Scottshire Girl Scout Camp—*locale* AL-4
Scotts Hole—*basin* AZ-5
Scotts Hollow—*valley* TN-4
Scotts Hollow—*valley* UT-8
Scotts Island—*island* FL-3
Scotts Island—*island* VA-3
Scotts Island—*island* WV-2
Scotts John Creek—*stream* CA-9
Scotts Junction—*locale* WI-6
Scotts Knob—*summit* AZ-5
*Scotts Lake* WA-9
Scotts Lake—*lake* CA-9
Scotts Lake—*lake* CO-8
Scotts Lake—*lake* MI-6
Scotts Lake—*lake* MS-4
Scotts Lake—*lake* NE-7
Scotts Lake—*lake* NM-5
Scotts Lake—*lake* ND-7
Scotts Lake—*reservoir* GA-3
Scotts Lake—*reservoir* NC-3
Scotts Lake Dam—*dam* NC-3
*Scotts Landing* AL-4
Scotts Landing—*locale* MD-2
**Scotts Landing**—*pop pl* OH-6
**Scottslawn**—*pop pl* OH-6
**Scotts Level**—*pop pl* MD-2
Scotts Level Branch—*stream* MD-2
Scotts Meadow—*flat* WY-8
*Scott's Middle Ground* MI-6
*Scotts Mill* AL-4
**Scotts Mill**—*pop pl* TN-4
Scotts Mill Branch—*swamp* NC-3
Scotts Mill (historical)—*locale* AL-4
Scotts Mill (historical)—*locale* MS-4
Scotts Millpond—*reservoir* VA-3
**Scotts Mills**—*pop pl* OR-9
**Scottsmoor**—*pop pl* FL-3
Scotts Mtn—*summit* CA-9
Scotts Mtn—*summit* NJ-2
Scotts Neck—*cape* ME-1
Scotts Neck—*cape* SC-3
Scotts Opening—*gap* CA-9
Scotts Pass—*gap* UT-8
*Scott's Point* OH-6
Scotts Point—*cape* MD-2
Scotts Point—*cape* TX-5
Scotts Point—*cape* WA-9
Scotts Point—*cliff* AZ-5
*Scotts Pond* MA-1
*Scotts Pond* NH-1
*Scotts Pond* RI-1
Scotts Pond—*lake* MA-1
Scotts Pond—*reservoir* VA-3
Scotts Prairie—*area* AL-4
Scotts Prairie Cem—*cemetery* IN-6
Scotts Prairie Ch—*church* IN-6
Scott Spring—*spring* AL-4
Scott Spring—*spring* (2) AZ-5
Scott Spring—*spring* AR-4
Scott Spring—*spring* CO-8
Scott Spring—*spring* ID-8
Scott Spring—*spring* KS-7
Scott Spring—*spring* (2) MO-7
Scott Spring—*spring* NV-8
Scott Spring—*spring* (3) NM-5
Scott Spring—*spring* (2) OR-9
Scott Spring—*spring* TN-4
Scott Spring—*spring* TX-5
Scott Spring—*spring* (2) WY-8
Scott Spring Branch—*stream* MO-7
Scott Springs—*spring* MT-8
Scott Springs—*spring* WI-6
Scotts Quarry—*mine* AL-4
Scotts Ridge—*ridge* CA-9
Scotts Ridge—*ridge* IN-6
Scotts Ridge—*ridge* KY-4
Scotts Ridge Ch—*church* OH-6
*Scotts River* CA-9
Scotts Rsvr—*reservoir* NY-2
*Scotts Run* DE-2
*Scotts Run* PA-2
*Scotts Run* VA-3
*Scotts Run* WV-2
Scotts Run—*stream* OH-6
Scotts Run—*stream* (3) PA-2
Scotts Run—*stream* WV-2
Scott's Run Dam—*dam* PA-2
Scotts Run Lake—*lake* PA-2
Scott's Run Lake—*reservoir* PA-2
Scotts Sch—*school* NC-3
Scotts Slough—*gut* LA-4
Scotts Slough—*lake* SD-7
Scotts Slough—*stream* ID-8
Scotts Slough—*stream* MO-7
Scotts Slough—*stream* ND-7
Scotts Slough Canal—*canal* ID-8
Scotts Spring—*spring* MI-6
Scotts Spring—*spring* NE-7
Scotts Spring—*spring* NV-8
Scotts Spring—*spring* TX-5
*Scotts Station* AL-4
*Scotts Station* MS-4
Scotts Station—*locale* KY-4
Scotts Station Post Office (historical)—*building* AL-4
**Scotts Station (Scotts)**—*pop pl* KY-4
Scott's Store—*hist pl* DE-2
**Scotts Store**—*pop pl* (2) NC-3
Scott Stadium—*other* VA-3
Scotts Tank—*reservoir* AZ-5
Scott State For—*forest* TN-4
Scott State Public Shooting Area—*park* SD-7
Scott Station—*locale* AL-4
Scott Station—*locale* PA-2
Scott Statue—*park* DC-2
Scott Store—*hist pl* OK-5
*Scottstown* KS-7
Scott Street Dam—*dam* IA-7
Scott Street Firehouse—*hist pl* AL-4
Scott Street Pavilion—*hist pl* IN-6
Scott Street Sch—*school* LA-4
**Scotts Valley**—*pop pl* CA-9
Scotts Valley—*valley* (2) CA-9
Scotts Valley—*valley* OR-9
Scotts Valley—*valley* WA-9
Scotts Valley Rancheria—*locale* CA-9
*Scottsville* CA-9
*Scottsville* PA-2
Scottsville—*locale* CA-9
Scottsville—*locale* IL-6
Scottsville—*locale* LA-4
Scottsville—*locale* PA-2
**Scottsville**—*pop pl* AL-4
**Scottsville**—*pop pl* AR-4
**Scottsville**—*pop pl* IL-6
**Scottsville**—*pop pl* IN-6
**Scottsville**—*pop pl* KS-7
**Scottsville**—*pop pl* KY-4
**Scottsville**—*pop pl* NY-2
**Scottsville**—*pop pl* PA-2
**Scottsville**—*pop pl* (2) SC-3
**Scottsville**—*pop pl* TX-5
**Scottsville**—*pop pl* VT-1
**Scottsville**—*pop pl* VA-3
Scottsville (CCD)—*cens area* KY-4
Scottsville Cem—*cemetery* VT-1
Scottsville Cem—*cemetery* VA-3
Scottsville Ch—*church* AL-4
Scottsville Ch—*church* IN-6
Scottsville Ch—*church* SC-3
Scottsville Hist Dist—*hist pl* VA-3
Scottsville Lake—*reservoir* IN-6
Scottsville Lake—*reservoir* TX-5
Scottsville (Magisterial District)—*fmr MCD* VA-3
Scottsville Oil Field—*oilfield* TX-5
Scottsville Recreation Center—*park* VA-3
Scottsville Sch—*school* AL-4
Scottsville Union Ch—*church* AL-4
Scott Swamp—*swamp* CT-1
Scott Swamp Brook—*stream* CT-1
Scotts Well—*well* AZ-5
Scottswood—*locale* IA-7
**Scottswood**—*pop pl* IL-6
**Scottswood**—*pop pl* VA-3
Scotts Woodyard Landing (historical)—*locale* AL-4
*Scotts X Roads* NC-3
Scott Table—*flat* NV-8
Scott Table—*summit* ID-8
Scott Table Rsvr—*reservoir* NV-8
Scott Tank—*reservoir* (5) AZ-5
Scott Tank—*reservoir* (4) NM-5
Scott Tank—*reservoir* TX-5
Scott-Taylor Creek—*stream* WI-6
Scott Teays Sch—*school* WV-2
Scott Tower—*pillar* LA-4
**Scott (Town of)**—*pop pl* NY-2
**Scott (Town of)**—*pop pl* (7) WI-6
Scott Township—*CDP* PA-2
Scott Township—*civ div* NE-7
Scott Township—*civil* KS-7
Scott Township—*civil* MO-7
Scott Township—*fmr MCD* (12) IA-7
**Scott Township**—*pop pl* (3) KS-7
**Scott Township**—*pop pl* (2) NE-7
**Scott Township**—*pop pl* ND-7
**Scott Township**—*pop pl* PA-2
Scott Township Ditch—*canal* IA-7
Scott (Township of)—*fmr MCD* (4) AR-4
**Scott (Township of)**—*pop pl* (2) IL-6
**Scott (Township of)**—*pop pl* (4) IN-6
**Scott (Township of)**—*pop pl* MN-6
**Scott (Township of)**—*pop pl* (4) OH-6
**Scott (Township of)**—*pop pl* (4) PA-2
Scott Trail—*trail* OR-9
Scott Union Cem—*cemetery* NY-2
Scott Union Cem—*cemetery* WI-6
Scott United Methodist Ch—*church* IN-6
*Scott Valley* CA-9
Scott Valley—*basin* ID-8
**Scott Valley**—*pop pl* AR-4
Scott Valley—*valley* CA-9
Scott Valley—*valley* WI-6
Scott Valley Cem—*cemetery* PA-2
Scott Valley Ch—*church* KS-7
Scott Valley Sch—*school* KS-7
*Scottville* KS-7
Scottville—*locale* NC-3
**Scottville**—*pop pl* IL-6
**Scottville**—*pop pl* MI-6
**Scottville**—*pop pl* NC-3
Scottville Cem—*cemetery* NE-7
Scottville Sch—*school* LA-4
**Scottville (Township of)**—*pop pl* IL-6
Scott-Vrooman House—*hist pl* IL-6
Scott Wash—*stream* AZ-5
Scott Water—*lake* AR-4
Scott Well—*well* AZ-5
Scott Well—*well* NM-5
Scott Wildlife Area—*park* KS-7
Scott Wincoop Ditch—*canal* IN-6
Scott Wincorp Ditch—*canal* IN-6
Scott Windmill—*locale* NM-5
Scott Windmill—*locale* TX-5
Scottwood Sch—*school* OH-6
Scott Woods Park—*park* MI-6
Scotty, Mount—*summit* MT-8
Scott-Yarbrough House—*hist pl* AL-4
Scotty Basin—*basin* UT-8
Scotty Bay—*bay* MI-6
Scotty Brook—*stream* ME-1
Scotty Brown Bridge—*bridge* MT-8
Scotty Butte—*summit* MT-8
Scotty Canyon—*valley* NM-5
Scotty Canyon—*valley* WY-8
Scotty Creek—*stream* CA-9
Scotty Creek—*stream* MT-8
Scotty Creek—*stream* (4) OR-9
Scotty Creek—*stream* WA-9
Scotty Creek—*stream* WY-8
Scotty Creek Campground—*locale* WA-9
Scotty Creek Lodge—*locale* AK-9
Scotty Draw—*valley* WY-8
Scotty Gulch—*valley* AK-9
**Scotty Hills (subdivision)**—*pop pl* NC-3
Scotty Hollow—*valley* MA-1
*Scotty Lake* MI-6
Scotty Lake—*lake* (2) AK-9
Scotty Lake—*lake* (2) NE-7
Scotty Lake—*lake* WY-8
Scotty Oil Field—*oilfield* TX-5
Scott-Youngman Ditch—*canal* IN-6
Scotty Peak—*summit* AK-9
Scotty Peak—*summit* MT-8
Scotty Philip Cem—*cemetery* SD-7
Scotty Place—*locale* CA-9
Scotty Point—*cape* CA-9
Scottys Cabin—*locale* NV-8
Scottys Canyon—*valley* CA-9
Scottys Castle—*locale* CA-9
Scottys Island—*island* AK-9
Scottys Junction—*locale* NV-8
Scottys Junction Airp—*airport* NV-8
Scottys Meadow—*flat* NV-8
Scottys Pond—*lake* OR-9
Scotty Spring—*spring* AZ-5
Scotty Spring—*spring* CA-9
Scotty Spring—*spring* NV-8
Scotty Spring—*spring* OR-9
Scotty Spring Mine—*mine* AZ-5
Scottys Ranch—*locale* CA-9
Scottys Springs—*spring* OR-9
Scotty Wash—*stream* NV-8
Scotty Windmill—*locale* NM-5
S Cotulla—*locale* TX-5
Scoubes Creek—*stream* OR-9
*Scout, The* ID-8
Scout, The—*summit* ID-8
Scoutana Ranch—*locale* MT-8
Scout-a- Vista—*locale* WA-9
Scout Branch—*stream* IN-6
Scout Branch—*stream* SC-3
Scout Branch—*stream* VA-3
Scout Canyon—*valley* AK-9
Scout Canyon—*valley* NV-8
Scout Canyon—*valley* WY-8
Scout Carson Lake—*lake* CA-9
Scout Cave—*cave* IL-6
Scout Creek—*stream* AL-4
Scout Creek—*stream* MT-8
Scout Creek—*stream* NE-7
Scout Creek—*stream* OK-5
Scout Creek—*stream* (3) OR-9
Scouten Brook—*stream* PA-2
Scouten Canyon—*valley* WA-9
Scouter Branch—*stream* SC-3
Scouters Pond—*lake* MI-6
Scout Falls—*falls* UT-8
Southaven Camp—*locale* NY-2
Scout Hill—*summit* OR-9
Scout Hollow—*valley* TN-4
Scout Hollow—*valley* UT-8
Scout Island—*island* AR-4
Scout Island—*island* CA-9
Scout Island—*island* CO-8
Scout Island—*island* FL-3
Scout Island—*island* MT-8
Scout Island—*island* NE-7
Scout Island—*island* NY-2
Scout Island—*island* SC-3
Scout Island—*island* SD-7
Scout Island—*island* WV-2
Scout Island—*island* WI-6
*Scout Lake* WA-9
Scout Lake—*lake* (3) AK-9
Scout Lake—*lake* CO-8
Scout Lake—*lake* FL-3
Scout Lake—*lake* IN-6
Scout Lake—*lake* (2) MI-6
Scout Lake—*lake* MT-8
Scout Lake—*lake* (4) OR-9
Scout Lake—*lake* (2) UT-8
Scout Lake—*lake* (2) WA-9
Scout Lake—*lake* (3) WI-6
Scout Lake—*reservoir* GA-3
Scout Lake Forest Camp—*locale* OR-9
Scout Lookout—*locale* UT-8
*Scout Mountain* MT-8
Scout Mountain Campground—*locale* ID-8
Scout Mtn—*summit* ID-8
Scout Mtn—*summit* IN-6
Scout Park—*park* MI-6
Scout Pass—*gap* WA-9
*Scout Peak* CO-8
Scout Peak—*summit* CA-9
Scout Peak—*summit* UT-8
Scout Point—*cape* NY-2
Scout Pond—*lake* MA-1
Scout Pond—*swamp* FL-3
Scouts Bay—*bay* NC-3
Scouts Cove—*valley* CA-9
**Scoutshire Woods (subdivision)**—*pop pl* AL-4
Scout's Rest Ranch—*hist pl* NE-7
Scout Tank—*reservoir* AZ-5
Scout Tank—*reservoir* TX-5
Scout Trail—*trail* KY-4
Scoval Branch—*stream* PA-2
S Cove—*bay* NV-8
Scove Canyon—*valley* CA-9
Scove Hill—*summit* VT-1
Scovel—*locale* IL-6
Scovell Island—*island* PA-2
*Scovells Island* PA-2
Scovern Hot Springs—*spring* CA-9
Scovill—*fmr MCD* NE-7
Scoville—*locale* ID-8
Scoville—*locale* NE-7
**Scoville**—*pop pl* KY-4
Scoville Arm—*canal* IN-6
Scoville Cem—*cemetery* CT-1
Scoville Corners—*locale* NY-2
Scoville Hill—*summit* CT-1
Scoville (historical)—*locale* ND-7
Scoville Memorial Library—*hist pl* CT-1
Scoville Memorial Library-Carlton College—*hist pl* MN-6
Scoville Park—*park* IL-6
Scoville Point—*cape* MI-6
Scoville Powerhouse—*hist pl* CT-1
Scoville Rsvr—*reservoir* CT-1
Scoville Spring—*spring* OR-9
Scoville Town Hall—*building* ND-7

**Scoville Township**—pop pl ND-7
Scovill Gardens—park IL-6
Scovill Rock—summit CT-1
Scovill Rsvr—reservoir CT-1
Scovill's Rock CT-1
Scovils Lake—lake WI-6
**Scovil Township**—pop pl SD-7
Scow Bay—bay AK-9
Scow Bay—bay WA-9
**Scow Bay**—pop pl AK-9
Scow Canyon—valley CA-9
Scow Cove—bay AK-9
Scow Creek—channel NY-2
Scow Creek—stream WA-9
Scowcroft Warehouse—hist pl UT-8
Scowden, Mount—summit CA-9
Scow Harry Creek—stream AK-9
Scow Island—island (2) AK-9
Scow Island—island NY-2
Scow Lake—lake UT-8
**Scow Landing**—pop pl NJ-2
Scow Mtn—summit AK-9
Scow Pass—channel LA-4
Scow Point—cape ME-1
Scoy Pond—lake NY-2
Scrabble—locale VA-3
Scrabble—locale WV-2
Scrabble Branch—stream WI-6
Scrabble Canyon—valley UT-8
Scrabble Creek—stream AR-4
Scrabble Creek—stream KY-4
Scrabble Creek—stream WV-2
Scrabble Creek Ch—church WV-2
Scrabble Hill Sch (historical)—school AL-4
Scrabble Lake—lake WA-9
Scrabble Mtn—summit WA-9
Scrabbler Mtn—summit WA-9
Scrabblers Flat—flat WA-9
**Scrabbletown**—pop pl MD-2
Scrabbletown Brook—stream RI-1
Scrabbletown Creek RI-1
Scrabbletown Historic and Archeol District—hist pl RI-1
Scraboltown NJ-2
Scrag Cedars—summit NC-3
Scraggly Lake—lake (2) ME-1
Scragg Neck MA-1
Scraggy Brook—stream ME-1
Scraggy Creek—stream NJ-2
Scraggy Island—island AK-9
Scraggy Island—island CT-1
Scraggy Island—island ME-1
Scraggy Islands—area AK-9
Scraggy Ledge—island ME-1
Scraggy Mtn—summit CA-9
Scraggy Neck MA-1
Scraggy Neck—cape MA-1
Scraggy Peaks—summit CO-8
Scraggy Point—cape (2) AK-9
Scraggy Ridge—ridge NC-3
Scrag Hill—summit NH-1
Scrag Island—area AK-9
Scrag Island—island (2) ME-1
Scrag Mtn—summit VT-1
Scramble Creek—stream WA-9
Scrambled Eggs Windmills—locale NM-5
Scramble Point—cape WA-9
Scramblers Knob—summit TN-4
Scram Lake—lake MI-6
Scrams Creek—stream MI-6
Scrams Marsh—lake MI-6
Scrange AL-4
**Scrange**—pop pl AL-4
Scranton MS-4
Scranton—locale AL-4
Scranton—locale CA-9
Scranton—locale KY-4
Scranton—locale MN-6
Scranton—locale TX-5
**Scranton**—pop pl AR-4
**Scranton**—pop pl IA-7
**Scranton**—pop pl KS-7
**Scranton**—pop pl NY-2
**Scranton**—pop pl NC-3
**Scranton**—pop pl ND-7
**Scranton**—pop pl PA-2
**Scranton**—pop pl SC-3
Scranton, Lake—reservoir PA-2
Scranton Army Ammunition Plant—military PA-2
Scranton Brook—stream CT-1
Scranton Butte ND-7
Scranton Canyon UT-8
Scranton Cem—cemetery IA-7
Scranton Cem—cemetery KS-7
Scranton Cem—cemetery ND-7
Scranton Cem—cemetery PA-2
Scranton City—civil PA-2
Scranton City Dam—dam KS-7
Scranton City Mine—mine CO-8
**Scranton Corners**—pop pl PA-2
Scranton Country Club—other PA-2
Scranton Creek—stream NC-3
Scranton Elem Sch—school KS-7
Scranton Grove Cem—cemetery TX-5
Scranton (historical)—locale SD-7
Scranton Hollow—valley PA-2
Scranton Hollow Sch (historical)—school PA-2
Scranton House—hist pl NH-1
Scranton Interchange PA-2
Scranton Mine—mine MN-6
Scranton Mine—mine UT-8
Scranton Mtn—summit CT-1
Scranton Municipal Airp—airport PA-2
Scranton Municipal Golf Course—locale PA-2
Scranton Sch—school CT-1
Scranton Sch—school OH-6
Scranton State Hosp—hospital PA-2
Scranton State Sch for the Deaf—school PA-2
Scranton Steel Mill (historical)—building PA-2
Scranton Technical HS—school PA-2
Scranton Township—civil SD-7
Scranton Township—fmr MCD IA-7
**Scranton Township**—pop pl KS-7
**Scranton Township**—pop pl ND-7
Scranton Univ—school PA-2
Scranton Water Company Rsvr—reservoir PA-2
Scranton Well—well UT-8
Scraper—locale OK-5
Scraper Canyon—valley CA-9
Scraper Cem—cemetery (2) OK-5
Scraper Coulee—valley MT-8
Scraper Creek MT-8
Scraper Hill—summit AL-4
Scraper Hill Cave—cave AL-4
Scraper Hollow—valley OK-5
Scraper Knoll—summit AZ-5
**Scraper-Moecherville**—pop pl IL-6
Scraper Mountain AL-4
Scraper Spring—spring CA-9
Scraper Spring—spring NV-8
Scraper Spring—spring (2) UT-8
Scraper Spring Draw—valley UT-8
Scraper Springs—locale NV-8
Scraper Springs Creek—stream NV-8
Scraper Tank—reservoir NM-5
Scrapetown—locale NJ-2
Scrap (historical)—locale AL-4
Scrapper Lake—lake MN-6
Scrapping Ridges—ridge CO-8
Scrapping Valley—locale TX-5
Scrappy Corner—locale NJ-2
Scrappy Mtn—summit AR-4
Scrap Tavern Crossroads—locale DE-2
Scraptown (historical)—locale AL-4
**Scratch Ankle**—pop pl AL-4
Scratch Ankle Hollow—valley TN-4
Scratch Britches—area TN-4
Scratch Canyon—valley AZ-5
Scratch Canyon—valley UT-8
Scratch Creek—stream ID-8
Scratchers Branch—stream MO-7
Scratchers Run—stream WV-2
Scratchgravel Hills—spring MT-8
Scratch Hill—locale AL-4
Scratch Hill—summit CA-9
Scratch Hill—summit OK-5
Scratch Hollow—valley OH-6
Scratchill AL-4
Scratching Post Spring—spring ID-8
Scratch Key FL-3
Scratchnose Creek SC-3
Scratchnose Swamp—stream SC-3
Scratch Post Butte OR-9
Scratch Post Butte—summit OR-9
Scratch Ranch—locale TX-5
Scratch Rapids—rapids WI-6
Scratch Ridge—locale NJ-2
Scratchunder Cem—cemetery TN-4
Scraunchers Rock Bluff—cliff TN-4
Scravel Hill—summit OR-9
Scrawls Branch—stream TN-4
Scrawls Ridge—ridge TN-4
Scray Hill—summit WI-6
Screamer—locale TN-4
**Screamer**—pop pl AL-4
Screamer Lake—lake MN-6
Screamer Mtn—summit GA-3
Screamer Sch—school GA-3
**Screamersville**—pop pl VA-3
Scream Ridge—ridge (2) NC-3
Screamsville AL-4
Screech Cem—cemetery VA-3
Screeches Branch—stream SC-3
Screech Lake—lake MN-6
Screech Owl Beach—beach TX-5
Screech Owl Canyon—valley CA-9
Screech Owl Creek—stream CA-9
Screech Owl Creek—stream WI-6
S Creek—gut NJ-2
Scree Lake—lake ID-8
Screen Islands—area AK-9
Screen Tank—reservoir AZ-5
Screeton—locale AR-4
Screggs Draw WY-8
Screptah Ch—church AL-4
Screvan GA-3
**Screven**—pop pl GA-3
Screven (CCD)—cens area GA-3
Screven Cem—cemetery GA-3
**Screven (County)**—pop pl GA-3
**Screven Fork**—pop pl GA-3
Screven Fork Ch—church GA-3
Screvens Point—cape GA-3
Screwauger Canyon—valley CA-9
Screw Auger Falls—falls (2) ME-1
Screw Bean Arroyo TX-5
Screw Bean Draw—valley TX-5
Screw Bean Hills—summit TX-5
Screw Bean Northeast Oil Field—oilfield TX-5
Screw Bean Oil Field—oilfield TX-5
Screwbean Spring—spring AZ-5
Screw Bean Spring—spring TX-5
Screwbean Windmill—locale TX-5
Screw Creek—stream MT-8
Screwdriver Creek—stream CA-9
Screwgee Creek—stream MN-6
Screw Plate Canyon—valley NM-5
Screw Windmill—locale NM-5
**Scriba**—pop pl NY-2
**Scriba Center (Scriba)**—pop pl NY-2
Scriba Creek—stream NY-2
**Scriba (Town of)**—pop pl NY-2
Scribbner Cem—cemetery MN-6
Scribe Creek—stream ID-8
Scriber Lake—lake WA-9
Scribnar Lake MN-6
Scribner—locale MN-6
Scribner—locale TN-4
Scribner—locale WA-9
**Scribner**—pop pl NE-7
Scribner Air Force Base—locale NE-7
Scribner Bldg—hist pl NY-2
Scribner Bog—swamp (2) ME-1
Scribner Brook—stream MA-1
Scribner Brook—stream NY-2
Scribner Cem—cemetery AR-4
Scribner Cem—cemetery NY-2
**Scribner Corners**—pop pl NY-2
Scribner Covered Bridge—hist pl VT-1
Scribner Creek—stream KS-7
Scribner Drain—canal MI-6
Scribner Fellows State Forest—park NH-1
Scribner Gulch—valley AZ-5
Scribner Hill—summit ME-1
Scribner Hill—summit MA-1
Scribner Hill—summit NY-2
Scribner Hill—summit VT-1
Scribner Hollow—valley TN-4
Scribner House—hist pl IN-6
Scribner JHS—school IN-6
Scribner Lake—lake ID-8
Scribner Lake—lake MN-6
Scribner Lake—reservoir MS-4
Scribner Lake Dam—dam MS-4
Scribner Mtn—summit CA-9
Scribner Municipal Cem—cemetery NE-7
Scribner Pond—reservoir NY-2
Scribner Road Cem—cemetery MI-6
Scribner School SD-7
Scribners Corner—locale NH-1
Scribners Creek KS-7
Scribners Hill MA-1
**Scribners Mill**—pop pl ME-1
Scribners Mill Bridge—bridge TN-4
**Scribners Mills**—pop pl ME-1
Scribner Spring—spring UT-8
Scribners Spring—spring OR-9
Scripps, George H., Memorial Marine Biological Laboratory—hist pl CA-9
Scripps Annex Sch—school MI-6
Scripps Bay—bay AK-9
Scripps Canyon—valley CA-9
Scripps Coll—school CA-9
Scripps College for Women—hist pl CA-9
Scripps Institution Of Oceanography (Univ Of Cal.)—school CA-9
Scripps Memorial Hosp—hospital CA-9
Scripps Park—park CA-9
Scripps Park—park MI-6
Scripps Ranch—locale CA-9
Scripps Sch—school CA-9
Scripps Sch—school MI-6
Script Canyon Number One—valley CA-9
Script Canyon Number Two—valley CA-9
Script Coulee—valley MT-8
Script Spring—spring MT-8
Script Tank—reservoir NM-5
Scripture Cem—cemetery NY-2
Scritchfield Cem—cemetery (2) WV-2
Scriven Dam Number One—dam PA-2
Scriver Creek—stream ID-8
Scriver Creek—stream WA-9
Scrivner—locale MO-7
Scrivner Branch—stream KY-4
Scrivner Butte—summit WY-8
Scrivner Canyon—valley WY-8
Scrivner Cem—cemetery (2) KY-4
Scrivner Cem—cemetery MO-7
Scrivner Road State Wildlife Area—park MO-7
Scrivner Windmill—locale NM-5
Scroggie Canyon—valley WA-9
Scroggin Cem—cemetery AR-4
Scroggin Creek OR-9
Scroggin Creek—stream MT-8
Scrogging Lake—lake SC-3
Scroggin Knob—summit GA-3
Scroggins—locale TX-5
Scroggins Branch—stream GA-3
Scroggins Branch—stream TN-4
Scroggins Cem—cemetery IL-6
Scroggins Cem—cemetery IN-6
Scroggins Cem—cemetery TN-4
Scroggins Creek—stream AR-4
Scroggins Ditch—canal KY-4
Scroggins Draw—valley TX-5
Scroggins Draw—valley WY-8
Scroggins Hollow—valley TN-4
Scroggins Store (historical)—locale AL-4
Scroggs Arroyo—stream CO-8
**Scroggsfield**—pop pl OH-6
Scroggsfield Ch—church OH-6
Scroggs House—hist pl OH-6
Scroggs Wash UT-8
S Crossing—locale CO-8
Scroton Neck MA-1
Scrouge About Cemetery AL-4
Scrougeabout Creek AL-4
Scrouge Branch—stream IN-6
Scrouge Cem—cemetery AL-4
Scrouge Creek—stream AR-4
Scrougeout—locale AL-4
Scrougetown Cem—cemetery GA-3
Scrougetown Ch—church GA-3
Scrougetown Creek GA-3
Scroungeabout Creek AL-4
Scrounge Springs Cave—cave AL-4
Scrub Bull Spring—spring OR-9
Scrubby Bluff—cliff GA-3
Scrubby Neck—cape MA-1
Scrub Creek—stream IL-6
Scrub Creek—stream MS-4
Scrub Creek—stream NC-3
Scrub Creek—stream TX-5
Scrub Creek Ch—church FL-3
Scrub Creek Ch—church TX-5
Scrub Flat—flat UT-8
Scrub Flat Rsvr—reservoir UT-8
Scrub Glade Creek PA-2
Scrub Grass PA-2
Scrubgrass Bayou—stream AR-4
Scrubgrass Bend—bend MS-4
Scrubgrass Branch—stream KY-4
Scrub Grass Branch—stream NC-3
Scrubgrass Campground—locale AR-4
Scrubgrass Ch—church PA-2
Scrubgrass Creek—stream KY-4
Scrubgrass Creek—stream (3) PA-2
Scrubgrass Run—stream PA-2
**Scrubgrass (Township of)**—pop pl PA-2
Scrub Hill—summit FL-3
Scrub Hill—summit VT-1
Scrub Island—island AK-9
Scrub Island—island (2) FL-3
Scrub Island—island (2) GA-3
Scrub Island—island ME-1
Scrub Lake FL-3
Scrub Lake—lake GA-3
Scrub Monday OH-6
Scrub Mtn—summit PA-2
Scrub Oak Cem—cemetery TN-4
Scrub Oak Ranch—locale TX-5
Scrub Point—cape AL-4
Scrub Point—summit AZ-5
Scrub Pond—lake FL-3
Scrub Ridge—locale OH-6
Scrub Ridge—ridge FL-3
Scrub Ridge—ridge MO-7
Scrub Ridge—ridge (2) PA-2
Scrub Ridge Sch (historical)—school PA-2
Scrub Run—stream PA-2
Scrub Slough—stream FL-3
Scrub Tank—reservoir TX-5
Scrugg Gap—gap GA-3
Scrugg Knob—summit GA-3
Scruggs—locale MO-7
Scruggs—locale VA-3
Scruggs Branch—stream (2) MS-4
Scruggs Branch—stream TN-4
Scruggs Bridge Overlook Area—park MS-4
Scruggs Cem—cemetery (3) AL-4
Scruggs Cem—cemetery FL-3
Scruggs Cem—cemetery GA-3
Scruggs Cem—cemetery MS-4
Scruggs Cem—cemetery NC-3
Scruggs Cem—cemetery SC-3
Scruggs Cem—cemetery (2) TN-4
Scruggs Chapel—church AR-4
Scruggs Creek—stream TX-5
Scruggs Hollow—valley TN-4
Scruggs Lake—lake MS-4
Scruggs Lake—reservoir SC-3
Scruggs Landing—locale AL-4
Scruggs Pond—lake TN-4
Scruggs Pond—reservoir GA-3
Scruggs Pond—reservoir VA-3
Scruggs Sch—school MO-7
Scruggs Shoals—bar TN-4
Scruggs Spring—spring TN-4
Scruggs Top—summit GA-3
Scruggs-Vandervoort-Barney Warehouse—hist pl MO-7
Scrugham Peak—summit NV-8
Scrum Branch—stream TN-4
Scrutchin Ranch—locale TX-5
Scrutchins—locale GA-3
Scruton Mtn—summit SD-7
Scruton Pond—reservoir NH-1
Scsally Sch (historical)—school MS-4
SCS Dam Pa-447 PA-2
SCS Pa-103 PA-2
SCS Pa-611 PA-2
SCS Pa-612 PA-2
SCS Pa-617 PA-2
SCS Pa-620 Dam PA-2
SCS Pa-656 PA-2
SCS Tank—reservoir (2) AZ-5
S C S Tank—reservoir NM-5
S C Townhouse Mobile Home Estates—locale AZ-5
Scudday Tank—reservoir TX-5
Scudder—locale OH-6
Scudder, B. H., Rental House—hist pl AZ-5
Scudder Ave Sch—school NY-2
Scudder Bay—lake MA-1
Scudder Brook—stream ME-1
Scudder Brook—stream NY-2
Scudder Camp—locale MO-7
Scudder Cem—cemetery NY-2
Scudder Creek—stream MT-8
Scudder Hill—summit IN-6
Scudder Lake—lake UT-8
Scudder Oaks Sch—school CA-9
Scudders Bay MA-1
Scudder Sch—school IN-6
Scudder Sch—school MO-7
Scudder Sch (historical)—school MO-7
Scudders Falls—falls PA-2
Scudders Falls—locale NJ-2
Scudders Rock—rock MA-1
Scudder Trail—trail NH-1
Scudding Pond MA-1
**Scuddy**—pop pl KY-4
Scuddy Branch—stream KY-4
Scuddy Sch—school KY-4
Scuds Lake—lake IL-6
Scuffeltown Creek—stream VA-3
Scuffe Pasture—flat NV-8
Scuffleburg—locale VA-3
Scuffle Creek—stream GA-3
Scuffle Creek—stream IN-6
Scuffle Creek—stream KY-4
Scuffle Creek—stream TN-4
Scuffle Grit Cem—cemetery AL-4
Scufflehill Methodist Ch (historical)—church AL-4
Scufflehill School AL-4
Scuffle Hollow—valley TX-5
**Scuffleton**—pop pl (2) NC-3
Scuffletown—locale GA-3
Scuffletown—locale (2) KY-4
Scuffletown—locale VA-3
Scuffletown Hollow—valley KY-4
Scull Bay—bay NJ-2
Scullcamps Bridge (historical)—bridge TN-4
Scull Cem—cemetery NC-3
Scull Creek—stream AR-4
Scull Creek—stream KS-7
Scullen Sch—school MO-7
Scull Hill—summit PA-2
Scullin—locale OK-5
Scullion Gulch—valley CO-8
Scull Island—island AK-9
**Scull Landing**—pop pl NJ-2
Scull Lick Creek MO-7
Scull Sch—school PA-2
Sculls Creek—stream GA-3
Sculls Creek Ch—church GA-3
Sculls Creek No 2 Ch—church GA-3
Sculls Crossing—crossing TX-5
Scull Shoal Creek—stream GA-3
Scull Shoals Historic Area—locale GA-3
Sculls Lodge—locale NC-3
**Scullton**—pop pl PA-2
Sculltown NJ-2
**Scullville**—pop pl NJ-2
Scully Canal—canal LA-4
Scully Creek MT-8
Scully Creek—stream ID-8
Scully Hill—summit CA-9
Scully Mtn—summit NM-5
Scully Ranch—hist pl CA-9
Scullys Gap—locale WY-8
**Scullyville**—pop pl OK-5
Scully Yard—locale PA-2
Sculpin Cave—cave TN-4
Sculpin Ledge—rock MA-1
Sculpin Ledge Channel—channel MA-1
Sculpin Point—cape ME-1
Sculptured Rocks—rock NH-1
Sculthorp Cem—cemetery VA-3
Scuma Creek—stream AL-4
Scuna MS-4
Scupernong Creek WI-6
Scupernong River WI-6
**Scuppernong**—pop pl NC-3
Scuppernong Ch—church NC-3
Scuppernong Creek WI-6
Scuppernong Creek—stream WI-6
Scuppernong River—stream NC-3
Scuppernong River—stream WI-6
Scuppernong (Township of)—fmr MCD (2) NC-3
Scuppo Hill—summit CT-1
Scup Rock—pillar RI-1
Scurff Mtn—summit VA-3
Scurlock—locale TX-5
Scurlock Cem—cemetery (2) TN-4
Scurlock Lake—reservoir MS-4
Scurlocks Camp—locale TX-5
Scurlock Sch—school NC-3
Scurlock Sch (historical)—school MS-4
Scurry—locale TX-5
**Scurry (County)**—pop pl TX-5
Scurry Creek—stream ID-8
Scurrycut Pond—lake FL-3
Scurry-Rosser Sch—school TX-5
Scurry-Spring Hill Ch—church SC-3
Scurvy Creek—stream ID-8
Scurvy Lake—lake ID-8
Scusset Beach MA-1
Scusset Beach—beach MA-1
Scusset Creek MA-1
Scusset Harbor—harbor MA-1
Scusset Harbour MA-1
Scusset Mill Creek—stream MA-1
Scusset River (historical)—stream MA-1
Scussett Beach MA-1
Scussett Harbor MA-1
Scutarzy Brook ME-1
Scutaze Stream—stream ME-1
Scutaze Trail—trail ME-1
Scutchalo Creek—stream MS-4
Scutchalo Falls—falls MS-4
Scutcheon Creek—stream TN-4
Scutchillo Hills—ridge MS-4
Scutt Hill—summit NY-2
Scuttle Hole—basin NY-2
Scuttle Hole—lake NY-2
Scuttlehole—locale NY-2
Scuttle Hole Creek—stream NY-2
Scuttlehole Gap—gap KY-4
Scuylkill Rowing Basin—reservoir PA-2
Scylla—summit CA-9
Scylla Butte—summit AZ-5
Scylla Peak CA-9
**Scyoc**—pop pl PA-2
Scyphers Coulee—valley MT-8
Scyrene—locale AL-4
Scythe Branch—stream TN-4
Scythia—locale KY-4
S & C 8th & Market Helistop—airport PA-2
S D A Cem—cemetery CA-9
SDA Ch—church MN-6
SDA Church Sch—school IN-6
S D Bishop State Junior Coll—school AL-4
S D Ingram Pond One—lake FL-3
S D Ingram Pond Two—lake FL-3
S D Lee High School MS-4
Sdoh-doh-hohbsh River WA-9
S Drain—canal CA-9
SDSU Extension Bldg—hist pl SD-7
Sea Acre—locale WA-9
Sea-Aire Park—park CA-9
**Sea Air (trailer park)**—pop pl DE-2
Sea and Land Church—hist pl NY-2
Seaback Ranch—locale CA-9
Seabaugh Cem—cemetery MO-7
Seabaugh Ford—locale MO-7
Seabaugh Hollow—valley MO-7
Seabaugh Sch—school MO-7
Seab Cem—cemetery MS-4
Seabeck—locale WA-9
Seabeck Bay—bay WA-9
Seabeck Creek—stream WA-9
Seabee Creek—stream AK-9
Seabes Creek—stream AL-4
Sea Bird Beach MH-9
**Sea Bluff**—pop pl CT-1
Seaboard—locale VA-3
**Seaboard**—pop pl AL-4
**Seaboard**—pop pl NC-3
Seaboard—uninc pl NJ-2
Seaboard Air Line RR Passenger Station—hist pl NC-3
Seaboard Airline RR Station—hist pl FL-3
Seaboard Bluff—cliff AL-4
Seaboard Church AL-4
Seaboard Coastline Bldg—hist pl VA-3
Seaboard Coastline Depot—hist pl AL-4
Seaboard Coast Line Passenger Depot—hist pl NC-3
Seaboard Coast Line RR Company Office Bldg—hist pl NC-3
Seaboard Coast Line RR Depot—hist pl AL-4
Seaboard Coast Line RR Depot—hist pl FL-3
Seaboard Coastline RR Passenger Station—hist pl FL-3
Seaboard-Coates Elem Sch NC-3
**Seaboard Junction**—pop pl SC-3
Seaboard Landing—locale AL-4
Seaboard Pond—lake FL-3
Seaboard Sch—school VA-3
Seaboard (Township of)—fmr MCD NC-3
Seaboard Windmill—locale TX-5
**Seabold**—pop pl WA-9
Seabold Lake—lake MN-6
Seabolt Branch—stream GA-3
Seabolt Cem—cemetery (2) OK-5
Seabolt Cem—cemetery WV-2
Seabolt Creek AL-4
Seabolt Creek—stream GA-3
Seabolt Mtn—summit GA-3
Seabolt Pond—reservoir GA-3
Seabolt Spring—spring AL-4
Seaborg Bay—bay AK-9
Seaborn Cem—cemetery TN-4
Sea-Born Sch—school FL-3
Seabourne Creek—stream TX-5
Sea Branch—stream TN-4
**Seabreak (subdivision)**—pop pl DE-2
Sea Breeze—locale TX-5
**Seabreeze**—pop pl DE-2
**Seabreeze**—pop pl FL-3
**Sea Breeze**—pop pl NJ-2
**Sea Breeze**—pop pl NY-2
**Seabreeze**—pop pl NC-3
**Sea Breeze**—pop pl NC-3
Seabreeze Bridge—bridge FL-3
Seabreeze Creek—stream FL-3
Seabreeze Island—island FL-3
Sea Breeze Oil Field—oilfield TX-5
Seabreeze Pass—channel LA-4
Sea Breeze Point—cape FL-3
Seabreeze Sch—school CT-1
Seabreeze Sch—school FL-3
Seabreeze Senior HS—school FL-3
Seabreeze Shop Ctr—locale FL-3
Seabright NJ-2
**Sea Bright**—pop pl NJ-2
Seabright—uninc pl CA-9
Seabright Hollow—valley WV-2
Seabrock Spring—spring WA-9
Seabron Shaw Lake Dam—dam MS-4
Seabrook SC-3
Seabrook—airport NJ-2
Seabrook—locale GA-3
Seabrook—locale SC-3
**Seabrook**—pop pl MD-2
**Seabrook**—pop pl NH-1
**Seabrook**—pop pl NJ-2
**Seabrook**—pop pl SC-3
**Seabrook**—pop pl TX-5
Seabrook—uninc pl LA-4
Seabrook, John, Plantation Bridge—hist pl SC-3
Seabrook, William, House—hist pl SC-3
**Seabrook Acres**—pop pl MD-2
Seabrook Beach—beach SC-3
**Seabrook Beach**—pop pl NH-1
Seabrook Cem—cemetery TX-5
Seabrook (census name Seabrook Farms) NJ-2
Seabrook Farms (census name for Seabrook)—CDP NJ-2
**Seabrook Hills (subdivision)**—pop pl NC-3
Seabrook Island—island SC-3
**Seabrook Island**—pop pl SC-3
Seabrook Landing SC-3
Seabrook Landing—locale SC-3
Seabrook Park—park KS-7
Seabrook Park—park MD-2
**Seabrook Park Estates**—pop pl MD-2
Seabrook Point—cape SC-3
Seabrook Pond—lake SC-3
Seabrook Sch—school MD-2
Seabrook Sch—school NC-3
Seabrooks Island SC-3
**Seabrook Station**—pop pl NH-1
**Seabrook (Town of)**—pop pl NH-1
Seabrook United Ch of Christ—church KS-7
Seabrook-Wilson House—hist pl NJ-2
Seaburg—locale ID-8
Seaburg Hammock—island FL-3
Seaburg Lookout ID-8
Seaburg Point ID-8
Seaburgs Well—well CA-9
Seaburn Branch—stream NC-3
Seaburn House Bayou—stream LA-4
Seaburn Rsvr—reservoir OR-9
Seaburn Spring—spring NC-3
Seaburn Well—well OR-9
**Seabury**—pop pl ME-1
**Seabury**—pop pl WA-9
Seabury Brook—stream NY-2
Seabury-Calkins Mine (historical)—mine SD-7
Seabury Creek—stream (2) AL-4
Seabury Creek—stream MS-4
Seaburys Creek AL-4
Seaburys Mill (historical)—locale AL-4
Sea Camp—locale NM-5
Sea Captains House—building DC-2
Seacat Bros Landing Strip—airport KS-7
Seacat Oil Field—oilfield KS-7
Seace Brook—stream MA-1
Sea Cem—cemetery KY-4
Seachi Canyon AZ-5
Seachi Canyon—valley AZ-5
Seach Sch—school MA-1
**Sea City**—pop pl IA-7
Sea Cliff—locale CA-9
**Seacliff**—pop pl AL-4
**Seacliff**—pop pl CA-9
**Sea Cliff**—pop pl NY-2
Sea Cliff County Park—park CA-9
Sea Cliff RR Station—hist pl NY-2
Seacliff State Beach—park CA-9
**Seacoast**—pop pl VA-3
Seacoast Assembly of God Ch—church FL-3
Seacock Corner—locale VA-3
Seacock Creek VA-3
Seacock Swamp—stream VA-3
Seacoll—locale FL-3
**Sea Colony East (subdivision)**—pop pl DE-2
**Sea Colony (subdivision)**—pop pl DE-2
Seaconnet Point RI-1
Seaconnett Mills—hist pl MA-1
Seaconset Island MA-1
Seacord Hill—summit NY-2
Seacorrie Swamp—stream VA-3
Sea Cove—bay ME-1
Sea Creek—stream GA-3
Sea Creek Bay—bay SC-3
Sea Creek Falls—falls GA-3
Seacrest Field—park NE-7
Seacrest HS—school FL-3
Sea Crest Park TX-5
**Sea Crest Park**—pop pl TX-5
Seacrest Sch—school FL-3
Seacrist Junior High—school AZ-5
Seacunck, Town of MA-1
Seacunk MA-1
**Sea Del Estates (subdivision)**—pop pl DE-2
Sea Dog Creek—channel NY-2
Sea Dog Island—island NY-2
**Seadrift**—pop pl TX-5
Seadrift (CCD)—cens area TX-5
Seadrift Cem—cemetery TX-5
Seaduck Point—cape ME-1
Seaduck Rock—island ME-1
**Sea Dunes**—pop pl DE-2
Seafarers Sch—school NY-2

**Seafarers Village (subdivision)**—pop pl ... DE-2
Seafarm Cove—bay ... WA-9
Seafert County Park—park ... OR-9
Seaffold Fork—stream ... KY-4
**Seafield**—pop pl ... IN-6
Seafield Lake—lake ... WA-9
Sea First—uninc pl ... WA-9
Seaflower Reef Light—locale ... CT-1
Seafoam Creek—stream ... ID-8
Seafoam Lake—lake ... ID-8
Seafoam Mine—mine ... ID-8
Seafood Creek—stream ... NY-2
**Seaford**—pop pl ... DE-2
**Seaford**—pop pl ... NY-2
**Seaford**—pop pl ... VA-3
Seaford Armory—military ... DE-2
Seaford Ave Sch—school ... NY-2
Seaford (CCD)—cens area ... DE-2
Seaford Ch—church ... VA-3
Seaford Ch of Christ—church ... DE-2
Seaford Christian Acad—school ... DE-2
Seaford City ... DE-2
Seaford Harbor Sch—school ... NY-2
**Seaford Heights**—pop pl ... DE-2
Seaford HS—school ... NY-2
Seaford Hundred—civil ... DE-2
Seaford JHS—school ... DE-2
Seaford Kindergarten—school ... DE-2
Seaford Manor Sch—school ... NY-2
Seaford Pond—reservoir ... NC-3
Seaford Pond Dam—dam ... NC-3
Seaford Sch—school ... VA-3
Seaford Senior HS—school ... DE-2
**Seaford Shores**—pop pl ... VA-3
Seaford Station Complex—hist pl ... DE-2
**Seaforth**—pop pl ... MN-6
**Seaforth**—pop pl ... NC-3
Seaforth Homestead (abandoned)—locale ... MT-8
Seaforth Lake—lake ... NC-3
Seafuse Marsh—swamp ... MI-6
Seagate—hist pl ... FL-3
**Seagate**—pop pl ... NY-2
**Seagate**—pop pl ... NC-3
Seagate Baptist Ch—church ... FL-3
Sea Gate Elem Sch—school ... FL-3
Seagels Lake—lake ... WI-6
Seager—locale ... NY-2
Seager Hill—summit ... VT-1
Seager Hill Sch—school ... NY-2
**Seagers**—pop pl ... PA-2
Seagersville ... PA-2
Seager West Branch Trail—trail ... NY-2
Seagirt ... NJ-2
**Sea Girt**—pop pl ... NJ-2
**Sea Girt Estates**—pop pl ... NJ-2
Sea Girt Inlet—gut ... NJ-2
**Seaglades**—pop pl ... FL-3
Seagle, Andrew, Farm—hist pl ... NC-3
Seagle Cem—cemetery ... NC-3
Seagle Ch—church ... VA-3
**Seagles Store (historical)**—pop pl ... NC-3
Seago Hollow—valley ... KY-4
**Seagoville**—pop pl ... TX-5
Seagoville Federal Correctional Institution—other ... TX-5
Seagoville Sewage Disposal—other ... TX-5
Seagram, Joseph, Warehouse—facility ... IN-6
Seagrape Hammock—island ... FL-3
Sea Grape Point—cape ... FL-3
**Seagraves**—pop pl ... TX-5
Seagraves, Lake—reservoir ... GA-3
Seagraves (CCD)—cens area ... TX-5
Seagraves Cem—cemetery ... IL-6
Seagraves Creek—stream ... KY-4
Seagrid Creek—stream ... MT-8
**Seagrove**—pop pl ... NC-3
**Seagrove Beach**—pop pl ... FL-3
Sea Grove Cape ... NJ-2
Seagrove Elem Sch—school ... NC-3
Seagrove Lake—lake ... GA-3
SEA GULL—hist pl ... MD-2
Seagull—locale ... NC-3
Seagull Bar—cape ... WI-6
Seagull Bay—bay ... ID-8
Seagull Bay—bay ... UT-8
Sea Gull Beach—beach ... MA-1
Seagull Canyon—valley ... CA-9
Seagull Creek ... MN-6
Seagull Creek—stream (2) ... AK-9
Sea Gull Creek—stream ... MN-6
Sea Gull Flat—flat ... AK-9
Seagull Island ... AK-9
Seagull Island—island ... AK-9
Seagull Lake—lake ... AK-9
Sea Gull Lake—lake ... MN-6
Sea Gull Point—cape ... AK-9
Seagull Point—cape ... MI-6
Sea Gull Point—cape ... UT-8
Seagull Pond—bay ... LA-4
Sea Gull River—stream ... MN-6
Seagull Sch—school ... FL-3
**Seahaven**—pop pl ... CA-9
Sea Hawk Stadium—locale ... CA-9
**Sea Hawk (subdivision)**—pop pl ... NC-3
Sea Hill—summit ... CT-1
Seaholm HS—school ... MI-6
Seahorn Chapel—church ... TN-4
Seahorn Creek ... TN-4
Seahorn Mine—mine ... WY-8
Seahorn Pond (historical)—lake ... TN-4
Seahorn Ranch—locale ... TX-5
Seahorns Chapel United Methodist Church ... TN-4
Seahorse Island ... FL-3
Seahorse Islands—area ... AK-9
Sea-Horse Key ... FL-3
Seahorse Key—island ... FL-3
Seahorse Lake—lake ... MN-6
Seahorse Reef—bar ... FL-3
Seahorse Rock—island ... ME-1
Seahpo Peak—summit ... WA-9
**Seahurst**—pop pl ... WA-9
Seahurst Park—park ... WA-9
Sea Island—island ... GA-3
**Sea Island**—pop pl ... GA-3
Sea Island Beach ... GA-3
Sea Island Beach—beach ... GA-3
Sea Island Cove Head—cape ... ME-1
Sea Island Golf Course—other ... GA-3
Sea Island Yacht Club—other ... GA-3
**Sea Isle**—pop pl ... TX-5
**Sea Isle City**—pop pl ... NJ-2
Sea Isle Park—park ... TN-4
Sea Isle Sch—school ... TN-4
Seajaquada Creek ... NY-2
**S E A Junction (Savannah & Atlantic Junction)**—pop pl ... GA-3
Seakonk ... MA-1
Seakoovook Bay—bay ... AK-9
Seaks Run—stream ... PA-2
Seal—locale ... PA-2
**Seal**—pop pl ... OH-6
Sea Lake—lake (2) ... MN-6
Sealand—locale ... ME-1
Sealander Brook—stream ... ME-1
Sealand of Cape Cod—locale ... MA-1
Sea-Land Service Terminal—locale ... VA-3
Sea Lark Drain—stream ... AZ-5
Seal Bay—bay (4) ... AK-9
Seal Bay—bay ... ME-1
**Seal Beach**—pop pl ... CA-9
Seal Beach City Hall—hist pl ... CA-9
Seal Beach Naval Weapons Station—military ... CA-9
Seal Branch—stream ... TN-4
Seal Cape—cape (2) ... AK-9
Seal Castle—summit ... UT-8
Seal Castle Butte ... UT-8
Seal Cem ... TN-4
Seal Cem—cemetery ... IL-6
Seal Cem—cemetery (3) ... LA-4
Seal Cem—cemetery ... MS-4
Seal Cem—cemetery ... MO-7
Seal Cem—cemetery ... NC-3
Seal Cem—cemetery (3) ... TN-4
Seal Channel—channel ... OR-9
Seal Chapel ... TN-4
Seal Chapel Missionary Baptist Ch—church ... TN-4
Seal Chapel Sch (historical)—school ... TN-4
Seal Cove ... ME-1
Seal Cove—bay ... AK-9
Seal Cove—bay ... CA-9
Seal Cove—bay (12) ... ME-1
Seal Cove—bay ... OR-9
Seal Cove—locale ... ME-1
**Seal Cove**—pop pl ... CA-9
Seal Cove Head ... ME-1
Seal Cove Ledge—bar (2) ... ME-1
Seal Cove Pond—lake ... ME-1
Seal Creek ... CA-9
Seal Creek—stream ... AK-9
Seal Creek—stream ... CA-9
Seal Creek—stream ... VA-3
Seal Creek—stream ... WA-9
Seal Draw—valley ... SD-7
Seale—locale ... LA-4
Seale—locale ... TX-5
**Seale**—pop pl ... AL-4
**Seale**—pop pl ... TX-5
Seale Cem—cemetery (2) ... TX-5
Seale Cemetery ... AL-4
Seale Creek—stream ... TX-5
Sea Ledge—bar ... MA-1
Sealed Passage—channel ... AK-9
Seale (historical)—locale ... AL-4
Seale Road Ch—church ... AL-4
Seale-Round Prairie Cem—cemetery ... TX-5
Sealers Island—island ... AK-9
Seale Sch—school ... AL-4
Seales Lakes—lake ... TX-5
**Sealevel**—pop pl ... NC-3
Sea Level Creek—stream ... AK-9
Sealevel Mine (Aban'd)—mine ... AK-9
Sea Level Slough—gut ... AK-9
Sea Level (Township of)—fmr MCD ... NC-3
Sealey Cem—cemetery ... FL-3
Sealey Cem—cemetery ... NC-3
Sealey Lake—lake ... NM-5
Sealey Sch—school ... FL-3
Seal Harbor—bay (3) ... ME-1
**Seal Harbor**—pop pl ... ME-1
Seal Harbor Congregational Church—hist pl ... ME-1
Seal Head Point—cape ... ME-1
Seal Hollow—valley (2) ... TN-4
Seal Hollow Branch—stream ... TN-4
Sealholtz Run—stream ... PA-2
Sealing Cove—bay ... AK-9
Sealing Reef—bar ... AK-9
Sea Lion Caves—cave ... OR-9
Sealion Cove—bay ... AK-9
Sea Lion Cove—bay (2) ... CA-9
Sea Lion Gulch—valley ... CA-9
Sealion Islands—area ... AK-9
Sea Lion Lake—lake ... UT-8
Sea Lion Lake—lake ... WI-6
Sea Lion Pass—channel ... AK-9
Sealion Point—cape ... AK-9
Sea Lion Point—cape ... OR-9
Sea Lion Rock—bar ... AK-9
Sea Lion Rock—island (2) ... AK-9
Sea Lion Rock—island (2) ... CA-9
Sea Lion Rock—island ... OR-9
Sea Lion Rock—island (2) ... WA-9
Sealion Rocks—area ... AK-9
Sealion Rocks—island (2) ... AK-9
Sea Lion Rocks—island ... AK-9
Sea Lion Rocks—island (2) ... CA-9
Sea Lion View Point—locale ... OR-9
Seal Island ... MA-1
Seal Island—island ... AK-9
Seal Island—island ... DE-2
Seal Island—island (5) ... ME-1
Seal Island—island (2) ... MA-1
Seal Island—island ... OR-9
Seal Island—island ... RI-1
Seal Island Rocks—bar ... MA-1
Seal Islands—island ... AK-9
Seal Islands—island ... CA-9
Seal Lake—lake ... AK-9
Seal Lake—lake ... OR-9
Seal Lake—lake ... WI-6
Seal Ledge—bar (7) ... ME-1
Seal Ledges—bar (2) ... ME-1
Seally Canyon—valley ... NM-5
Seal Mathis Elementary School ... TN-4
Seal Mathis Sch—school ... TN-4
Seal Mountain Trail—trail ... AZ-5
Seal Mtn—summit ... AZ-5
Sealock Lake—reservoir ... KS-7
Seal Oil Creek—stream ... AK-9
**Sealover**—pop pl ... OH-6
Seal Point—cape ... AK-9
Seal Point—cape ... ME-1
Seal Point—cape ... OR-9
Seal River ... WA-9
Seal River—stream (2) ... AK-9
Seal Rock ... CA-9
Seal Rock ... ME-1
Seal Rock ... RI-1
Seal Rock ... WA-9
Seal Rock—bar (2) ... ME-1
Seal Rock—bar ... MA-1
Seal Rock—bar ... WA-9
Seal Rock—island ... AK-9
Seal Rock—island (3) ... CA-9
Seal Rock—island ... CT-1
Seal Rock—island (2) ... ME-1
Seal Rock—island (2) ... OR-9
Seal Rock—other ... AK-9
Seal Rock—pillar (3) ... RI-1
**Seal Rock**—pop pl ... OR-9
**Seal Rock**—pop pl ... WA-9
Seal Rock—rock (3) ... MA-1
Seal Rock Beach ... OR-9
Seal Rock Creek ... OR-9
Seal Rock Creek—stream ... CA-9
Seal Rocks ... CA-9
Seal Rocks—area ... AK-9
Seal Rocks—bar ... AK-9
Seal Rocks—bar (4) ... ME-1
Seal Rocks—bar (2) ... MA-1
Seal Rocks—bar ... NH-1
Seal Rocks—bar ... NY-2
Seal Rocks—island (2) ... AK-9
Seal Rocks—island (3) ... CA-9
Seal Rocks—island ... CT-1
Seal Rocks—island ... OR-9
Seal Rocks, The ... ME-1
Seal Rock Shell Mounds (45JE15)—hist pl ... WA-9
Seal Rock State Park—park ... OR-9
**Seals**—pop pl ... GA-3
Seals Bay—bay ... GA-3
Seals Branch ... TN-4
Seals Branch—stream ... GA-3
Seals Branch—stream ... KY-4
Seals Branch—stream ... MS-4
Seals Cem—cemetery (2) ... MS-4
Seals Cem—cemetery (4) ... TN-4
Seals Creek—stream ... AL-4
Seals Creek—stream ... AR-4
Seals Creek—stream (2) ... GA-3
Seals Creek—stream ... TX-5
Seals Fork—stream ... IN-6
Seals Gully—valley ... TX-5
**Seals (historical)**—pop pl ... TN-4
Seals Knob—summit ... GA-3
Seals Lake—reservoir ... GA-3
Seal Slough—gut ... AK-9
Seal Slough—gut ... CA-9
Seal Slough—stream (2) ... WA-9
Seal Spit—cape ... AK-9
Seals Point—cape ... DE-2
Seals Post Office (historical)—building ... TN-4
Seal Spring—spring ... AL-4
Seals Ridge—ridge ... GA-3
Seals Sch (historical)—school ... TN-4
Seals School ... TN-4
Seals Swamp—swamp ... GA-3
Seal Station ... AL-4
Sealston—locale ... VA-3
**Seal (Township of)**—pop pl ... OH-6
Seal Trap, The—bay ... ME-1
Sealy—locale ... OK-5
**Sealy**—pop pl ... TX-5
Sealy, George, House—hist pl ... TX-5
Sealy, Lake—reservoir ... TX-5
Sealy (CCD)—cens area ... TX-5
Sealy Cem—cemetery ... AL-4
Sealy Cem—cemetery ... OK-5
Sealy Cem—cemetery ... TX-5
Sealy Creek—stream ... OR-9
Sealy Plantation—locale ... GA-3
**Sealy Springs**—pop pl ... AL-4
Sealy Springs Post Office (historical)—building ... AL-4
**Sealy Township**—pop pl ... ND-7
**Seama**—pop pl ... NM-5
Seama Mesa—summit ... NM-5
Seaman—locale ... TX-5
Seaman—locale ... WV-2
**Seaman**—pop pl ... OH-6
Seaman Baptist Ch—church ... KS-7
Seaman Bridge—other ... MO-7
Seaman Canyon—valley ... UT-8
Seaman Cem—cemetery ... IL-6
Seaman Congregational Ch—church ... KS-7
Seaman Creek—stream ... MO-7
Seaman Creek—stream ... OR-9
Seaman Draw—valley ... MT-8
Seaman Farm—hist pl ... NY-2
Seaman Fork—stream ... WV-2
Seaman Gulch—valley ... CA-9
Seaman Gulch—valley ... ID-8
Seaman Hill Rsvr—reservoir ... WY-8
Seaman Hills—range ... WY-8
Seaman (historical)—locale ... KS-7
Seaman HS—school ... KS-7
**Seaman Junction**—pop pl ... OK-5
Seaman Lake—lake (2) ... MI-6
Seaman Lake—lake ... MN-6
Seaman Narrows—gap ... NV-8
Seaman Park—flat ... CO-8
Seaman Point—cape ... UT-8
Seaman Pond—reservoir ... NY-2
Seaman Ranch—locale ... WY-8
Seaman Range—range ... NV-8
Seaman Rsvr—reservoir ... CO-8
Seaman Run—stream ... WV-2
Seamans Cem—cemetery ... MI-6
Seaman Sch—school ... KS-7
Seaman Sch—school ... NY-2
Seaman Sch—school ... WI-6
Seamans Chapel—church ... TX-5
Seamans Ch Institute (historical)—church ... AL-4
Seamans Creek—stream ... ID-8
Seamans Creek—stream ... NY-2
Seamans Ditch—canal ... CO-8
Seamans Field—airport ... PA-2
Seamans Field Airp ... PA-2
Seamans Island—island ... NY-2
Seaman Sisters' House—hist pl ... KY-4
Seamans Neck Park—park ... NY-2
Seamans Neck Sch—school ... NY-2
Seamans Park—park ... FL-3
Seamans Point—cape ... MI-6
Seamans Point—cape ... NH-1
Seaman Spring—spring ... NV-8
Seamans Wash ... NV-8
Seamanville Cem—cemetery ... NY-2
Seaman Wash—arroyo ... UT-8
Seaman Wash—stream ... AZ-5
Seaman Wash—stream ... NV-8
Seama Sch—school ... NM-5
Seamens Bethel Museum—building ... MA-1
Seamens Cem—cemetery ... NY-2
Seamen's Church Institute of Newport—hist pl ... RI-1
**Seamentown**—pop pl ... PA-2
**Seamersville**—pop pl ... OH-6
Seamon Park—park ... NY-2
Seamons Ditch—canal ... IN-6
Seamore Gulch—valley ... SD-7
Seamore Mtn—summit ... AL-4
Seams Brook—stream ... ME-1
Seams Chapel ... MS-4
Seaney Cem—cemetery ... IL-6
Seanlan Marsh—swamp ... MI-6
**Seanor**—pop pl ... PA-2
Seanor Ch—church ... PA-2
Sea Oat Island—island ... FL-3
Sea of Kalohi ... HI-9
Sea Otter Creek—stream ... AK-9
Sea Otter Glacier—glacier ... AK-9
Sea Otter Harbor—bay ... AK-9
Sea Otter Island—island ... AK-9
Sea Otter Pass—channel ... AK-9
Sea Otter Point—cape (2) ... AK-9
Sea Otter Rock—island ... AK-9
Sea Otter Sound—bay ... AK-9
Sea Park Elem Sch—school ... FL-3
Sea Pines—hist pl ... SC-3
Sea Pines—uninc pl ... SC-3
Seapines—uninc pl ... VA-3
Seapit River—stream ... MA-1
Seaplane Basin—bay ... FL-3
Seaplane Dock Of Philadelphia Airp—airport ... PA-2
Seaplane Harbor—harbor ... CA-9
Seapo (historical)—locale ... KS-7
Seapoint—cape ... ME-1
Seapoint Beach—beach ... ME-1
Sea Pond—lake ... FL-3
Sea Pond—lake ... GA-3
Seapowet Cove ... RI-1
Seapowet Creek ... RI-1
Seapowet Point ... RI-1
Seapuit River—gut ... MA-1
Seaquest State Park—park ... WA-9
**Sea Ranch, The**—pop pl ... CA-9
**Sea Ranch Lakes**—pop pl ... FL-3
Sea Ranch Village (Shop Ctr)—locale ... FL-3
Sea Ranger Drain—canal ... AZ-5
Sea Ranger Reef—bar ... AK-9
Search Bay—bay ... MI-6
Search Creek—stream ... ID-8
Search Lake—lake ... ID-8
**Searchlight**—pop pl ... NV-8
Searchlight Airp—airport ... NV-8
Searchlight Creek—stream ... ID-8
Searchlight Junction ... CA-9
Searchlight M and M Mine—mine ... NV-8
Searchlight Sch (historical)—school ... MS-4
Searchlight Township—inact MCD ... NV-8
Searchright Parallel Mine—mine ... NV-8
Search Sch—school ... IL-6
Searchs Island—island ... PA-2
Search Well—hist pl ... MD-2
Searcy—locale ... AL-4
**Searcy**—pop pl ... AR-4
**Searcy**—pop pl ... LA-4
Searcy, Lake—lake ... FL-3
Searcy Branch—stream ... AL-4
Searcy Branch—stream ... KY-4
Searcy Branch—stream ... MS-4
Searcy Branch—stream ... MO-7
Searcy Branch—stream ... TX-5
Searcy Cem—cemetery ... AR-4
Searcy Cem—cemetery ... MS-4
Searcy Cem—cemetery ... MO-7
Searcy Cem—cemetery ... TX-5
Searcy Country Club—other ... AR-4
**Searcy (County)**—pop pl ... AR-4
Searcy County Courthouse—hist pl ... AR-4
Searcy Creek—stream ... FL-3
Searcy Creek—stream ... NC-3
Searcy Creek—stream ... OR-9
Searcy Creek Parkway—park ... MO-7
**Searcy Crossroads**—pop pl ... IN-6
**Searcy Farms (subdivision)**—pop pl ... AL-4
Searcy Flat—flat ... OR-9
Searcy Gulch—valley ... CO-8
Searcy House—hist pl ... AL-4
Searcy Ridge—ridge ... IN-6
Searcy Sch (historical)—school ... MO-7
Searcys Ferry (historical)—crossing ... TN-4
Searcy State Hosp—hospital ... AL-4
Searcy Town—locale ... MS-4
Searcy (Township of)—fmr MCD ... AR-4
Searfoss Pond ... PA-2
Seargeante Bluff ... IA-7
**Sea Ridge (subdivision)**—pop pl ... NC-3
**Searight**—pop pl ... AL-4
**Sea Right**—pop pl ... PA-2
Searight Mtn—summit ... CO-8
Searight Oil Field—oilfield ... OK-5
**Searights**—pop pl ... PA-2
Searights Ch—church ... PA-2
Searight's Fulling Mill—hist pl ... PA-2
Searights Toll House—building ... PA-2
Searights Tollhouse, Natl Road—hist pl ... PA-2
**Searingtown**—pop pl ... NY-2
Searite Well—well ... NM-5
Searl Coulee—valley ... MT-8
Searle Gulch—valley ... CO-8
Searle Hill—summit ... MA-1
Searle Park—park ... IL-6
Searle Pass—gap ... CO-8
Searle Rock—rock ... MA-1
Searles—locale ... CA-9
**Searles**—pop pl ... AL-4
**Searles**—pop pl ... MN-6
Searles Brook—stream ... MA-1
Searles Brook—stream ... NY-2
Searles Castle—building ... MA-1
Searles Castle—hist pl ... MA-1
Searles Cem—cemetery ... MA-1
Searle Sch—school ... CA-9
Searles Creek—stream ... WI-6
Searles Hill ... MA-1
Searles Hill—summit ... ME-1
Searles Hill—summit (2) ... NH-1
Searles Hollow—valley ... WI-6
Searles HS—hist pl ... MA-1
Searles Lake—flat ... CA-9
Searles Number 2 Mine (underground)—mine ... AL-4
Searles Pond—lake ... MA-1
Searles Pond Dam—dam ... MA-1
Searles Prairie Cem—cemetery ... WI-6
Searles Ranch—locale ... NV-8
Searles Rsvr—reservoir ... NV-8
Searles Sch—school ... MA-1
Searles Sch—school ... NH-1
Searles Sch and Chapel—hist pl ... NH-1
Searles Slope Mine (underground)—mine ... AL-4
Searles Valley—CDP ... CA-9
Searles Valley (Depression)—basin ... CA-9
Searl Ranch—locale ... CA-9
Searl Ridge Cem—cemetery ... IL-6
Searls Memorial Park—park ... IL-6
Searls Rock ... MA-1
Sea Rock—other ... AK-9
**Searose Beach**—pop pl ... OR-9
Sear Point ... MA-1
Sear Pond ... MA-1
Searra Casa Rsvr—reservoir ... OR-9
Sears—locale ... FL-3
Sears—locale ... KS-7
Sears—locale ... NE-7
**Sears**—pop pl ... MI-6
Sears—uninc pl ... NC-3
Sears—uninc pl ... PA-2
Sears, A. B., House—hist pl ... OH-6
Sears, Albert H., House—hist pl ... IL-6
Sears, David, House—hist pl ... MA-1
Sears, Joshua, Bldg—hist pl ... WA-9
Sears, Roebuck and Company Complex—hist pl ... IL-6
Sears, Roebuck and Company Store—hist pl ... KY-4
**Sears Addition Subdivision**—pop pl ... UT-8
**Searsboro**—pop pl ... IA-7
Searsboro Sully Lynville Sch—school ... IA-7
**Searsburg**—pop pl ... NY-2
**Searsburg**—pop pl ... VT-1
Searsburg Rsvr—reservoir ... VT-1
**Searsburg (Town of)**—pop pl ... VT-1
Sears Camp—locale ... AL-4
Sears Canyon ... UT-8
Sears Canyon—valley ... UT-8
Sears Canyon Wildlife Mngmt Area—park ... UT-8
Sears Cem—cemetery ... AL-4
Sears Cem—cemetery ... IL-6
Sears Cem—cemetery ... KY-4
Sears Cem—cemetery ... MA-1
Sears Cem—cemetery ... MS-4
Sears Cem—cemetery (2) ... NY-2
Sears Cem—cemetery ... WV-2
Sear Sch—school ... AL-4
Sears Chapel—church ... AL-4
Sears Chapel Cem—cemetery ... AL-4
Sears Chapel Church ... AL-4
Sears Community Lake—reservoir ... MO-7
**Sears Corners**—pop pl ... NY-2
Sears Coulee—valley ... MT-8
Sears Creek—stream ... AK-9
Sears Creek—stream ... ID-8
Sears Creek—stream (2) ... MT-8
Sears Creek—stream ... OR-9
Sears Creek—stream ... UT-8
Sears Creek—stream (2) ... WA-9
Sears' Crescent and Sears' Block—hist pl ... MA-1
Sears Ditch—canal ... WY-8
Sears Draw—valley ... WY-8
Sears Flat—flat ... CA-9
Sears Flat—flat ... OR-9
Sears Flat Spring—spring ... CA-9
Sears Gulch—valley ... MT-8
Sears Highway—channel ... MI-6
Sears Hill Sch (abandoned)—school ... PA-2
Sears Hollow—valley ... PA-2
Sears Home Cem—cemetery ... KY-4
Sears House—hist pl ... VA-3
Sear's Island ... ME-1
Sears Island—island ... ME-1
Sears Island—island ... MA-1
Sears Island Ledge—bar ... ME-1
Sears Islands—island ... NY-2
Sears Kay Ranch—locale ... AZ-5
Sears Lake—lake (2) ... FL-3
Sears Lake—lake ... MI-6
Sears Lake—lake ... MT-8
Sears Lake—lake ... OR-9
Sears Lake—lake ... WA-9
Sears Landing—locale ... NC-3
Sears Marina—locale ... AL-4
Sears Meadow—flat ... MA-1
Sears Meadow Dam—dam ... MA-1
Sears Meadow Rsvr—reservoir ... MA-1
**Searsmont**—pop pl ... ME-1
**Searsmont (Town of)**—pop pl ... ME-1
Sears Park—park ... AZ-5
Sears Park—park ... CA-9
Sears Point ... MA-1
Sears Point—cape ... MA-1
Sears Point—cliff ... AZ-5
Sears Point—locale ... CA-9
Sears Point Archaeol District—hist pl ... AZ-5
Sears Pond ... MA-1
Sears Pond—lake ... ME-1
Sears Pond—lake (3) ... NY-2
**Searsport**—pop pl ... ME-1
Searsport Center (census name Searsport)—other ... ME-1
Searsport Harbor—bay ... ME-1
Searsport Hist Dist—hist pl ... ME-1
**Searsport (Town of)**—pop pl ... ME-1
Sears Ranch—locale ... NE-7
Sears Ranch—locale ... SD-7
Sears Ravine—valley ... CA-9
Sears Ridge—ridge ... VA-3
Sears Rock—bar ... CA-9
Sears Run—stream ... PA-2
Sears Run—stream ... WV-2
Sears Sch—school ... IL-6
Sears Sch—school ... KY-4
Sears Sch—school ... NE-7
Sears Spring—spring ... CO-8
Sears Spring—spring ... UT-8
Sears Tank—reservoir ... AZ-5
Sears Tower-Harvard Observatory—hist pl ... MA-1
Searstown—uninc pl ... FL-3
**Searsville**—pop pl ... MA-1
**Searsville**—pop pl ... NY-2
Searsville Ch—church ... TX-5
Searsville Historical Marker—locale ... CA-9
Searsville Lake—reservoir ... CA-9
Sears Well—well ... NM-5
Sears Wharf (historical)—locale ... NC-3
Sears Youth Center—locale ... MO-7
Sea Run—stream ... WV-2
Searway Brook—stream ... ME-1
Seas Branch—stream ... KY-4
Seas Branch—stream ... WI-6
Seascout Point—cape ... OK-5
Sease Hollow—valley ... PA-2
**Seasha**—pop pl ... AL-4
Seashore Campground Sch—hist pl ... MS-4
Seashore Ledge—bar ... ME-1
Seashore Mtn—summit ... ME-1
Seashore State Park—park ... VA-3
Seaside ... MA-1
Seaside—locale ... NC-3
Seaside—locale ... SC-3
**Seaside**—pop pl ... CA-9
**Seaside**—pop pl ... CT-1
**Seaside**—pop pl ... FL-3
**Seaside**—pop pl ... NY-2
**Seaside**—pop pl ... OR-9
Seaside (CCD)—cens area ... CA-9
Seaside (CCD)—cens area ... OR-9
Seaside Cem—cemetery ... ME-1
Seaside Cem—cemetery (2) ... MA-1
Seaside Cem—cemetery ... NJ-2
Seaside Creek—stream ... CA-9
Seaside Creek—stream ... SC-3
Seaside Dam—dam ... OR-9
Seaside Gardens County Park—park ... CA-9
**Seaside Heights**—pop pl ... NJ-2
**Seaside Heights Harbor**—pop pl ... NJ-2
Seaside Heights Sch—school ... OR-9
Seaside HS—school ... OR-9
Seaside Institute—hist pl ... CT-1
Seaside Memorial Cem—cemetery ... TX-5
Seaside Memorial Hosp—hospital ... CA-9
Seaside-Monterey (CCD)—cens area ... CA-9
Seaside Park—hist pl ... CT-1
Seaside Park—park ... CT-1
Seaside Park—park ... MA-1
Seaside Park—park ... NY-2
**Seaside Park**—pop pl ... NJ-2
Seaside Plantation—hist pl ... SC-3
Seaside Plantation House—hist pl ... SC-3
Seaside Point—cape ... CT-1
Seaside Point—cape ... FL-3
Seaside Rsvr—reservoir ... OR-9
Seaside Sch—school (3) ... CA-9
Seaside State Airp—airport ... OR-9
**Seaside Villas (subdivision)**—pop pl ... DE-2
Seasonal Springs—spring ... AZ-5
Seasongoer Squarė—park ... OH-6
Seasongood Homestead—locale ... MT-8
**Sea Spray Village (subdivision)**—pop pl ... DE-2
Seass Cem—cemetery ... IL-6
S East Bald Peak Drain—stream ... NE-7
Seasted Lake—lake ... MN-6
Seastone Point—cape ... MI-6
Seastrand Creek—stream ... WA-9
Seastrand Ridge—ridge ... WA-9
Sea Street Beach—beach ... MA-1
Seastrunk Cem—cemetery ... TX-5
**Seatack**—pop pl ... VA-3
Seat Cem—cemetery ... MO-7
Seatco Prison Site—hist pl ... WA-9
Seat Creek—stream ... ID-8
Seaths Point ... MD-2
Seat Island Branch—stream ... VA-3
Seat Lake—lake ... MN-6
Seaton—hist pl ... VA-3
Seaton—locale ... MO-7
**Seaton**—pop pl ... AR-4
**Seaton**—pop pl ... IL-6
**Seaton**—pop pl ... TN-4
**Seaton**—pop pl ... TX-5
Seaton Branch—stream ... TN-4
Seaton Canyon—valley ... WA-9
Seaton Cem—cemetery ... MO-7
Seaton Cem—cemetery ... NE-7
Seaton Cem—cemetery ... TN-4
Seaton Cem—cemetery (2) ... TX-5
Seaton Ch—church ... MD-2
Seaton Ch—church ... MO-7
Seaton Creek—stream ... AR-4
Seaton Creek—stream ... FL-3
Seaton Creek—stream ... MI-6
Seaton Creek—stream ... PA-2
Seaton Dump—locale ... AR-4
Seaton Gulch—valley ... CO-8
Seaton-Hackney Farm Park—park ... NJ-2
Seaton (historical)—locale ... AL-4
Seaton (historical P.O.)—locale ... IA-7
Seaton Hollow—valley ... TN-4
Seaton Landing—locale ... FL-3
Seaton Mtn—summit ... CO-8
Seaton P.O. ... AL-4
Seaton Post Office (historical)—building ... TN-4
Seaton Ranch (reduced usage)—locale ... MT-8
Seaton Roadhouse—locale ... AK-9
Seaton Run—stream ... PA-2
Seatons Brook ... CT-1
Seaton Sch—school ... DC-2
Seaton Sch (historical)—school ... PA-2
Seatons Dam ... PA-2

Seatons Grove—*locale* ... WA-9
*Seatons Lake* ... PA-2
Seaton Spring—*locale* ... TN-4
Seaton Spring—*spring* ... AZ-5
Seaton Spring—*spring* (2) ... TN-4
**Seaton Subdivision**—*pop pl* ... TN-4
Seaton Top—*summit* ... TN-4
Seatonville—*locale* ... KY-4
**Seatonville**—*pop pl* ... IL-6
**Seatonville Junction**—*pop pl* ... IL-6
Seatonville Springs Country Club—*other* ... KY-4
**Seatowne (subdivision)**—*pop pl* ... DE-2
**Seat Pleasant**—*pop pl* ... MD-2
Seat Pleasant Ch—*church* ... MD-2
Seat Pleasant Recreation Center—*park* ... MD-2
Seat Pleasant Sch—*school* ... MD-2
Seatra Canal—*canal* ... LA-4
**Sea Trail Plantation**—*pop pl* ... NC-3
Seats Chapel—*church* ... TN-4
Seats Dam—*dam* ... OR-9
Seatter Creek—*stream* ... WA-9
Seatter Lake—*lake* ... WA-9
**Seattle**—*pop pl* ... WA-9
Seattle, Chief of the Suquamish,
Statue—*hist pl* ... WA-9
Seattle, Mount—*summit* ... AK-9
Seattle, Mount—*summit* ... WA-9
Seattle Air Natl Guard Base—*building* ... WA-9
**Seattle Bar (historical)**—*pop pl* ... OR-9
Seattle (CCD)—*cens area* ... WA-9
Seattle Center—*locale* ... WA-9
Seattle Chinatown Hist Dist—*hist pl* ... WA-9
Seattle Coll—*school* ... WA-9
Seattle Country Club—*other* ... WA-9
Seattle Creek—*stream* (6) ... AK-9
Seattle Creek—*stream* ... CA-9
Seattle Creek—*stream* (3) ... WA-9
Seattle Electric Company Georgetown Steam
Plant—*hist pl* ... WA-9
Seattle Flat—*flat* ... OR-9
Seattle Gulch—*valley* ... AK-9
**Seattle Heights**—*pop pl* ... WA-9
Seattle Junior Creek—*stream* ... AK-9
Seattle Naval Support Activity—*military* ... WA-9
Seattle Pacific Coll—*school* ... WA-9
Seattle Park—*flat* ... WA-9
Seattle Private Number One
Heliport—*airport* ... WA-9
Seattle Public Library—*hist pl* ... WA-9
Seattle Quartermaster Depot—*other* ... WA-9
Seattle Spring—*spring* ... WA-9
Seattle-Tacoma International
Airp—*airport* ... WA-9
Seattle Water Supply Intake—*other* ... WA-9
Seatuck Cove—*bay* ... NY-2
Seatuck Creek—*stream* ... NY-2
Seavarda Lake—*reservoir* ... CO-8
Seavarda Springs—*spring* ... CO-8
Seaver Branch—*stream* ... VT-1
Seaver Brook—*stream* ... NH-1
Seaver Brook—*stream* ... VT-1
Seaver Drain—*canal* ... MI-6
Seaver Hill—*summit* ... VT-1
Seaver Mtn—*summit* ... NY-2
Seaverns, George, House—*hist pl* ... ME-1
Seaverns Brook—*stream* ... MA-1
**Seaver Park**—*pop pl* ... MT-8
Seavers Brook—*stream* ... VT-1
Seaverson Ditch—*canal* ... WY-8
Seaverson Rsvr—*reservoir* (2) ... WY-8
Seavey, A. B., House—*hist pl* ... ME-1
Seavey, Dr. John B., House and
Cemetery—*hist pl* ... NC-3
Seavey Brook—*stream* (3) ... ME-1
Seavey Cem—*cemetery* ... NC-3
Seavey Cove—*bay* ... ME-1
Seavey Creek—*stream* ... NH-1
Seavey Drainage Ditch—*canal* ... IL-6
Seavey Hill—*summit* ... NH-1
Seavey House—*hist pl* ... NH-1
Seavey Island—*island* (2) ... ME-1
**Seavey Island**—*pop pl* ... ME-1
Seavey Lake—*lake* (2) ... ME-1
Seavey Ledges—*bar* ... ME-1
Seavey Pass—*gap* ... CA-9
Seavey Point—*cape* ... ME-1
Seavey Pond—*reservoir* ... NH-1
Seavey Ridge—*ridge* ... ME-1
Seavey-Robinson House—*hist pl* ... ME-1
Seaveys Corner—*locale* ... ME-1
Seavey Stream—*stream* ... ME-1
**Seavey (Township of)**—*pop pl* ... MN-6
Seaview—*locale* ... VA-3
**Sea View**—*pop pl* ... MA-1
**Seaview**—*pop pl* ... NY-2
**Seaview**—*pop pl* ... WA-9
**Seaview Beach**—*pop pl* ... CT-1
Seaview Cem—*cemetery* ... CA-9
Seaview Cem—*cemetery* (2) ... ME-1
Seaview Center (Shop Ctr)—*locale* ... FL-3
Seaview Country Club—*other* ... NJ-2
Seaview Heights Sch—*school* ... WA-9
Sea View (historical P.O.)—*locale* ... MA-1
Sea View Hosp—*hospital* ... NY-2
Seaview Park—*park* ... CT-1
**Seaview Park**—*pop pl* ... NJ-2
Seaview School (Abandoned)—*locale* ... CA-9
Sea View Station (historical)—*locale* ... MA-1
**Seaville**—*pop pl* ... KY-4
**Seaville**—*pop pl* ... NJ-2
Seaville Camp—*locale* ... NJ-2
Seaville Ch—*church* ... NJ-2
Seavy-Lull Mine—*mine* ... TN-4
**Seawall**—*pop pl* ... ME-1
*Seawall Point* ... ME-1
Sea Wall Point—*cape* ... ME-1
Seawall Point—*cape* ... ME-1
Seawall Pond—*lake* ... ME-1
Seawane Country Club—*other* ... NY-2
Seawanhaka Corinthian Yacht
Club—*hist pl* ... NY-2
Seaward Mills—*locale* ... ME-1
Sea Warrior Creek—*stream* ... AL-4
Seaway Hosp—*hospital* ... MI-6
Seaway Shop Ctr—*locale* ... NY-2
**Seaweed Beach**—*pop pl* ... RI-1
Seaweed Cove—*bay* ... RI-1
Seaweed Pass—*channel* ... AK-9
Seaweed Point—*cape* ... NJ-2
Seawell Creek—*stream* ... ID-8
Seawell-Ross-Isom House—*hist pl* ... OK-5
Seawell Sch—*school* ... NC-3
*Seawells Ferry* ... AL-4
*Seawells Point* ... VA-3
**Seawillow**—*pop pl* ... TX-5
Sea World Aquatic Park—*park* ... CA-9
Seawre Cave—*cave* ... PA-2
**Seawright Spring**—*pop pl* ... VA-3
Seawright Springs—*spring* ... VA-3
Seay, Jammie, House—*hist pl* ... SC-3
Seay Cem—*cemetery* (2) ... AL-4
Seay Cem—*cemetery* ... AR-4
Seay Cem—*cemetery* ... IA-7
Seay Cem—*cemetery* ... KY-4
Seay Cem—*cemetery* ... SC-3
Seay Chapel—*church* ... VA-3
Seay Chapel Cem—*cemetery* ... AL-4
Seay Chapel (historical)—*church* ... AL-4
Seay Creek—*stream* ... AR-4
Seay Creek—*stream* ... VA-3
Seay Hill—*summit* ... TN-4
Seay Hollow—*valley* ... TN-4
Seay Mansion—*hist pl* ... OK-5
Seay Mtn—*summit* ... NC-3
Seay Sch—*school* ... TN-4
Seays Ch (historical)—*church* ... TN-4
Seay Spring—*spring* ... TN-4
*Seays School* ... TN-4
Seba—*locale* ... AR-4
Seba Dalkai—*locale* ... AZ-5
Seba Dalkai—*school* ... AZ-5
Seba Dalkai Spring—*spring* ... AZ-5
*Seba Dalkai Wash* ... AZ-5
Sebadilla Creek—*stream* ... NM-5
*Sebago* ... ME-1
Sebago, Lake—*lake* ... WA-9
Sebago, Lake—*reservoir* ... NY-2
**Sebago Center**—*pop pl* ... ME-1
Sebago Lake—*lake* ... ME-1
**Sebago Lake**—*pop pl* ... ME-1
Sebago Lake Basin—*lake* ... ME-1
Sebago Lake State Park—*park* ... ME-1
**Sebago (Town of)**—*pop pl* ... ME-1
*Sebaim Lake* ... ME-1
Sebands Branch—*stream* ... TN-4
*Sebasco* ... ME-1
**Sebasco**—*pop pl* ... ME-1
*Sebascodegan* ... ME-1
Sebascodegan Island—*island* ... ME-1
*Sebascodeggin* ... ME-1
*Sebascodiggin* ... ME-1
*Sebasco Estates* ... ME-1
**Sebasco Estates**—*pop pl* ... ME-1
Sebasco Harbor—*bay* ... ME-1
Sebasco Sch—*school* ... ME-1
*Sebaskahegan Island* ... ME-1
*Sebastapol* ... MS-4
**Sebastapol**—*pop pl* ... LA-4
Sebastian—*locale* ... FL-3
Sebastian—*locale* ... KY-4
**Sebastian**—*pop pl* ... FL-3
**Sebastian**—*pop pl* ... OH-6
**Sebastian**—*pop pl* ... TX-5
Sebastian, Cape—*cape* ... OR-9
Sebastian Branch—*stream* (2) ... KY-4
Sebastian Canyon—*valley* ... NM-5
Sebastian (CCD)—*cens area* ... TX-5
Sebastian Cem—*cemetery* ... FL-3
Sebastian Cem—*cemetery* ... KY-4
Sebastian Cem—*cemetery* ... LA-4
Sebastian Cem—*cemetery* ... MO-7
Sebastian Center (Shop Ctr)—*locale* ... FL-3
**Sebastian (County)**—*pop pl* ... AR-4
Sebastian County Park—*park* ... AR-4
*Sebastian Creek* ... FL-3
Sebastian De Vargas—*civil* ... NM-5
Sebastian Elem Sch—*school* ... FL-3
Sebastian Highlands—*uninc pl* ... FL-3
Sebastiani—*uninc pl* ... CA-9
Sebastian Inlet—*channel* ... FL-3
Sebastian Inlet North Jetty Light—*locale* ... FL-3
Sebastian Island—*island* ... IN-6
Sebastian Lake—*lake* ... AR-4
Sebastian Log House—*hist pl* ... KY-4
Sebastian Martin Grant—*civil* ... NM-5
Sebastian Methodist Ch—*church* ... FL-3
Sebastian Point—*cape* ... VA-3
Sebastian Pond—*lake* ... TN-4
*Sebastian River* ... FL-3
Sebastian River Med Ctr—*hospital* ... FL-3
Sebastian River Middle-JHS—*school* ... FL-3
**Sebastians Branch**—*pop pl* ... KY-4
Sebastian Sch (abandoned)—*school* ... MO-7
Sebasticook Lake—*lake* ... ME-1
*Sebasticook River* ... ME-1
Sebasticook River—*stream* ... ME-1
Sebastopol—*hist pl* ... TX-5
Sebastopol—*locale* ... CA-9
Sebastopol—*locale* ... IL-6
Sebastopol—*locale* ... TX-5
**Sebastopol**—*pop pl* ... CA-9
**Sebastopol**—*pop pl* ... LA-4
**Sebastopol**—*pop pl* ... MS-4
**Sebastopol**—*pop pl* ... PA-2
Sebastopol Attendance Center—*school* ... MS-4
Sebastopol Baptist Ch—*church* ... MS-4
Sebastopol Canal—*canal* ... LA-4
Sebastopol (CCD)—*cens area* ... CA-9
Sebastopol Creek—*stream* ... OR-9
Sebastopol Grange—*locale* ... CA-9
Sebastopol Plantation House—*hist pl* ... LA-4
Sebastopol Sch—*school* ... CA-9
*Sebatos Mountain* ... ME-1
*Sebattis* ... ME-1
Sebbas Creek—*stream* ... CA-9
Seb Basin—*basin* ... NC-3
*Sebbathday Point* ... NY-2
Sebbins Brook—*stream* ... NH-1
Sebbins Pond—*lake* ... NH-1
Sebbles Mill (historical)—*locale* ... TN-4
Seb Craft Island—*island* ... GA-3
**Sebec**—*pop pl* ... ME-1
**Sebec Corners**—*pop pl* ... ME-1
Sebec Lake—*lake* ... ME-1
**Sebec Lake**—*pop pl* ... ME-1
Sebec-Piscataquis River Confluence Prehistoric
Archeol District—*hist pl* ... ME-1
Sebec River—*stream* ... ME-1
Sebec Station—*locale* ... ME-1
**Sebec (Town of)**—*pop pl* ... ME-1
**Sebeka**—*pop pl* ... MN-6
Sebeka Cem—*cemetery* ... MN-6
Sebeka Lake—*lake* ... MN-6
Seberger Park—*park* ... MN-6
*Seberson Dam* ... ND-7
Sebert Ditch—*canal* ... IN-6
Sebert Prospect—*mine* ... TN-4
Seberts Point—*cape* ... NY-2
Sebeseb—*bay* ... PW-9
Sebesta Sch—*school* ... NE-7
**Sebewa Center**—*pop pl* ... MI-6
Sebewa Center Ch—*church* ... MI-6
Sebewa Ch—*church* ... MI-6
**Sebewa Corners**—*pop pl* ... MI-6
Sebewa Creek—*stream* ... MI-6
*Sebewaine River* ... MI-6
**Sebewaing**—*pop pl* ... MI-6
Sebewaing River—*stream* ... MI-6
**Sebewaing (Township of)**—*pop pl* ... MI-6
**Sebewa (Township of)**—*pop pl* ... MI-6
Sebie Lake—*lake* ... MN-6
**Sebille Manor**—*pop pl* ... MI-6
Sebille Pond—*lake* ... RI-1
Seblin Bridge—*bridge* ... ND-7
*Sebocis* ... ME-1
*Seboeis* ... ME-1
**Seboeis**—*pop pl* ... ME-1
Seboeis Deadwater—*lake* ... ME-1
Seboeis Farm—*locale* ... ME-1
Seboeis Fish and Game Club
Camps—*locale* ... ME-1
*Seboeis Lake* ... ME-1
Seboeis Lake—*lake* ... ME-1
Seboeis (Plantation of)—*civ div* ... ME-1
Seboeis River—*stream* ... ME-1
*Seboeis Stream* ... ME-1
Seboeis Stream—*stream* ... ME-1
*Sebois Grand Lake* ... ME-1
*Sebois Lakes* ... ME-1
*Sebois River* ... ME-1
Sebonac Creek—*stream* ... NY-2
*Sebonack Neck* ... NY-2
Sebonac Neck—*cape* ... NY-2
Sebonibus Rapids—*rapids* ... ME-1
*Seboois Lake* ... ME-1
*Seboois Lakes* ... ME-1
*Seboois Stream* ... ME-1
Seboomook—*locale* ... ME-1
Seboomook Dam—*dam* ... ME-1
Seboomook Island—*island* ... ME-1
Seboomook Lake—*reservoir* ... ME-1
Seboomook Lake (Unorganized Territory
of)—*unorg* ... ME-1
Seboomook Mtn—*summit* ... ME-1
Seboomook Point—*cape* ... ME-1
Seboomook (Township of)—*unorg* ... ME-1
Seborn, Frederick Augustus,
House—*hist pl* ... OH-6
**Seboruco**—*pop pl* ... PR-3
*Sebos Branch* ... KS-7
Sebosis Brook—*stream* ... NH-1
Sebowisha—*locale* ... TN-4
**Seboyeta**—*pop pl* ... NM-5
Seboyeta Canyon—*valley* ... NM-5
Seboyeta Creek—*stream* ... NM-5
**Seboyetita (Bibo)**—*pop pl* ... NM-5
Seboyetita Creek—*stream* ... NM-5
Sebras Chapel—*church* ... VA-3
Sebra Tank—*reservoir* ... AZ-5
Sebree—*locale* ... ID-8
Sebree—*locale* ... MO-7
**Sebree**—*pop pl* ... KY-4
Sebree Branch—*stream* ... KY-4
Sebree (CCD)—*cens area* ... KY-4
Sebree Cove—*bay* ... AK-9
Sebree Island—*island* ... AK-9
Sebree Springs Park—*park* ... KY-4
*Sebre Lake* ... MN-6
Sebre Lake Site (21-CW-55)—*hist pl* ... MN-6
Sebrell—*locale* ... VA-3
Sebrell-Reese Cem—*cemetery* ... VA-3
*Sebrina Lake* ... CA-9
**Sebring**—*pop pl* ... FL-3
**Sebring**—*pop pl* ... MD-2
**Sebring**—*pop pl* ... OH-6
**Sebring**—*pop pl* ... PA-2
Sebring, Lake—*lake* ... FL-3
Sebring Branch—*stream* ... PA-2
Sebring (CCD)—*cens area* ... FL-3
Sebring Cem—*cemetery* ... MI-6
Sebring Cem—*cemetery* ... NY-2
Sebring Christian Sch—*school* ... FL-3
Sebring Country Club—*other* ... OH-6
Sebring Hill—*ridge* ... NY-2
Sebring HS—*school* ... FL-3
Sebring MS—*school* ... FL-3
Sebring Public Library—*building* ... FL-3
**Sebring Shores (subdivision)**—*pop pl* ... FL-3
Sebring Southgate—*post sta* ... FL-3
Sebron-Kilgore Cem—*cemetery* ... KY-4
Seca, Canada —*valley* ... CA-9
**Secane**—*pop pl* ... PA-2
**Secane Highlands**—*pop pl* ... PA-2
Secar Rock—*island* ... WA-9
*Secata Creek* ... CA-9
*Secata Ridge* ... CA-9
Secatogue Sch—*school* ... NY-2
**Secaucus**—*pop pl* ... NJ-2
*Secaucus Creek* ... NJ-2
Secaucus Station—*locale* ... NJ-2
Secca—*building* ... NC-3
Seccaium Park—*park* ... OH-6
**Secedar Corners**—*pop pl* ... OH-6
Seceder Cem—*cemetery* ... IN-6
Seceder Cem—*cemetery* ... OH-6
Seceders Cem—*cemetery* ... OH-6
Secelid Tank—*reservoir* ... AZ-5
*Secellpot Creek* ... DE-2
Secena Creek—*stream* ... OR-9
Secesakut Hill—*summit* ... RI-1
*Secesh Fork* ... ID-8
Secesh Gulch—*valley* ... OR-9
Secesh Hollow—*valley* ... MO-7
Secesh Meadows—*flat* ... ID-8
*Secesh River* ... ID-8
Secesh River—*stream* ... ID-8
Secesh Summit—*gap* ... ID-8
Secession—*locale* ... NC-3
Secession Bluff—*cliff* ... AL-4
Secession Lake—*reservoir* ... SC-3
**Secessionville**—*pop pl* ... SC-3
Secessionville Creek—*stream* ... SC-3
Secessionville Hist Dist—*hist pl* ... SC-3
*Sechacha Pond* ... MA-1
*Se chil Canyon* ... UT-8
Sechler Run—*stream* ... PA-2
Sechlers Lake—*reservoir* ... PA-2
**Sechlerville**—*pop pl* ... WI-6
Sechlerville Cem—*cemetery* ... WI-6
Sechrest Cem—*cemetery* ... KY-4
Sechrist Ditch—*canal* ... IN-6
Sechrist Lake—*lake* ... IN-6
Sechrist Mill—*locale* ... PA-2
Sechrist Sch—*school* ... AZ-5
Sechrist Sch (abandoned)—*school* ... PA-2
*Seckler's Run* ... PA-2
**Seckman**—*pop pl* ... MO-7
Seck Memorial Park—*park* ... WI-6
*Seclock Run* ... PA-2
Secluded Bay—*bay* ... AK-9
Secluded Lake Rsvr—*reservoir* ... OR-9
Seclusaval—*hist pl* ... KY-4
Seclusaval and Windsor Spring—*hist pl* ... GA-3
Seclusia Rsvr—*reservoir* ... OR-9
Seclusion—*locale* ... TX-5
Seclusion, Lake—*lake* (2) ... AK-9
Seclusion Creek—*stream* ... WY-8
Seclusion Harbor—*bay* ... AK-9
**Seco**—*pop pl* ... AZ-5
**Seco**—*pop pl* ... KY-4
Seco, Arroyo—*stream* ... AZ-5
Seco, Arroyo—*stream* (6) ... CA-9
Seco, Arroyo—*valley* ... TX-5
Seco, Rancho—*locale* ... AZ-5
Seco, Rito—*stream* (2) ... CO-8
**Secoal**—*pop pl* ... WV-2
Seco Canyon—*valley* ... CO-8
Seco Canyon—*valley* (3) ... NM-5
Seco Canyon Windmill—*locale* ... NM-5
*Seco Creek* ... CA-9
Seco Creek—*stream* (2) ... NM-5
Seco Creek—*stream* (2) ... TX-5
Seco Creek, Arroyo—*stream* ... CA-9
Seco Del Diablo, Arroyo—*stream* ... CA-9
Seco Ditch, Arroyo—*canal* ... CA-9
Secody Well—*well* ... AZ-5
Secoma Beach—*locale* ... WA-9
**Seco Mines**—*pop pl* ... TX-5
**Seco Mines (La Gloria)**—*pop pl* ... TX-5
Seco Mtn—*summit* ... TX-5
Second, Bayou—*bay* ... AL-4
Second Alkali Creek—*stream* ... CO-8
Second Alligator Branch—*stream* ... MS-4
Second and Market Streets Hist
Dist—*hist pl* ... KY-4
Second Anvil Creek—*stream* ... CO-8
Second Apache Canyon—*valley* ... NM-5
Second Apache Canyon Tank—*reservoir* ... NM-5
Second Arenac County
Courthouse—*hist pl* ... MI-6
*Secondary Agricultural School* ... AL-4
Secondary Industrial Sch—*hist pl* ... GA-3
Secondary Retenston Rsvr—*reservoir* ... TN-4
Secondary Retention Reservoir
Dam—*dam* ... TN-4
*Secondary Retention Rsvr* ... TN-4
Secondary Rsvr—*reservoir* ... TX-5
Secondary Tank—*reservoir* ... AZ-5
Second Aspen Canyon—*valley* ... AZ-5
Second Ave Baptist Ch—*church* (2) ... AL-4
Second Ave Baptist Ch—*church* ... MS-4
Second Ave Ch—*church* ... GA-3
Second Ave Ch—*church* ... SC-3
Second Ave Ch of Christ—*church* ... TN-4
Second Ave Commercial District—*hist pl* ... TN-4
Second Ave Elem Sch—*school* ... PA-2
Second Ave Sch—*school* ... NE-7
Second Ave Sch—*school* ... OH-6
Second Bank of the United
States—*building* ... PA-2
Second Bank of the United
States—*hist pl* ... PA-2
Second Baptist Cem—*cemetery* ... MS-4
Second Baptist Ch—*church* (9) ... AL-4
Second Baptist Ch—*church* ... IN-6
Second Baptist Ch—*church* ... KS-7
Second Baptist Ch—*church* ... LA-4
Second Baptist Ch—*church* (9) ... MS-4
Second Baptist Ch—*church* ... SC-3
Second Baptist Ch—*church* (5) ... TN-4
Second Baptist Ch (historical)—*church* (2) ... AL-4
Second Baptist Ch of Selma—*church* ... AL-4
Second Baptist Ch (Ogden)—*church* ... UT-8
Second Baptist Church—*hist pl* ... MO-7
Second Baptist Church—*hist pl* ... NY-2
Second Baptist Church—*hist pl* ... OH-6
Second Baptist Church Day Care
Center—*school* ... FL-3
Second Baptist Church Of Detroit—*hist pl* ... MI-6
Second Baptist Church Park—*park* ... TX-5
Second Baptist Sch—*school* ... AR-4
Second Basin—*lake* ... IN-6
Second Bass Lake—*lake* ... MI-6
Second Bay—*bay* ... CT-1
Second Bay—*bay* ... FL-3
Second Bay—*bay* ... LA-4
Second Bay—*lake* ... LA-4
Second Bayou—*stream* ... LA-4
Second Bayou—*stream* ... MS-4
Second Beach—*locale* ... RI-1
Second Belmont Ch—*church* ... GA-3
Second Bench—*bench* ... MT-8
Second Bethel Ch—*church* ... VA-3
Second Bethesda Ch—*church* ... GA-3
*Second Bethlehem Baptist Ch* ... TN-4
Second Bethlehem Ch—*church* ... AL-4
Second Bethlehem Ch—*church* ... TN-4
Second Big Creek Fork—*stream* ... KY-4
Second Big Fork—*stream* ... PA-2
Second Big Run—*stream* (2) ... WV-2
Second Blackburn Canyon—*valley* ... UT-8
Second Black Lake—*lake* ... WI-6
Second Boulder Creek—*stream* ... NV-8
Second Bow Creek—*stream* ... NE-7
Second Box Canyon—*valley* ... CO-8
*Second Branch* ... WV-2
Second Branch—*stream* ... KY-4
Second Branch—*stream* ... NJ-2
Second Branch—*stream* (2) ... TN-4
Second Branch—*stream* ... VA-3
Second Branch—*stream* (2) ... WV-2
Second Branch Columbia Glacier—*glacier* ... AK-9
Second Branch McGraw Creek—*stream* ... TX-5
Second Branch Sch—*school* ... VA-3
Second Branch White River—*stream* ... VT-1
Second Brazer Bldg—*hist pl* ... MA-1
Second Broad River—*stream* ... NC-3
Second Brook—*stream* ... CT-1
Second Brook—*stream* ... ME-1
Second Brook—*stream* (3) ... MA-1
Second Brook—*stream* ... NH-1
Second Brook—*stream* ... NY-2
Second Brook—*stream* ... VT-1
Second Brooklyn Zion Ch—*church* ... AL-4
Second Brother—*summit* ... NY-2
Second Brushy Canyon—*valley* ... CA-9
Second Buffalo Ch—*church* ... VA-3
Second Bull Creek—*stream* ... SD-7
Second Burnt Hill—*summit* ... NY-2
*Second Butte* ... MT-8
Second Butte—*summit* ... CA-9
Second Butte—*summit* ... NV-8
Second Buttermilk Pond—*lake* ... ME-1
Second Callahan Block—*hist pl* ... ME-1
Second Calvary Ch—*church* (2) ... SC-3
Second Cambridge Savings Bank
Bldg—*hist pl* ... MA-1
Second Canaan Ch—*church* ... GA-3
Second Canal—*canal* ... LA-4
*Second Canal System* ... AZ-5
Second Caney Creek—*stream* ... TX-5
Second Canyon—*valley* ... CO-8
Second Canyon—*valley* ... TX-5
Second Canyon—*valley* (2) ... UT-8
Second Cape—*cape* ... AK-9
Second Cave—*cave* ... AL-4
Second Cedar Rapids—*rapids* ... WI-6
Second Cem—*cemetery* ... CT-1
Second Ch—*church* ... NJ-2
Second Ch—*church* ... NC-3
Second Ch—*church* (2) ... SC-3
Second Ch—*church* (2) ... TX-5
Second Chain Lake—*lake* ... ME-1
Second Chain of Islands—*island* ... TX-5
Second Channel—*channel* ... VA-3
Second Ch Christian Science—*church* ... KS-7
Second Christian Ch—*church* ... AL-4
Second Christian Ch—*church* ... IN-6
Second Christian Church—*hist pl* ... MO-7
Second Church of Christ—*hist pl* ... CT-1
Second Church of Christ,
Scientist—*hist pl* ... CA-9
Second Church of Christ Scientist—*hist pl* ... WI-6
Second Cliff—*cliff* ... MA-1
**Second Cliff**—*pop pl* ... MA-1
Second Coffee Hollow—*valley* ... TX-5
Second Cokedale Mine—*mine* ... CO-8
Second College Grant—*civil* ... NH-1
Second Concord Ch—*church* ... MS-4
Second Congregational Church—*hist pl* ... ME-1
Second Congregational Church—*hist pl* ... TN-4
Second Connecticut Lake—*reservoir* ... NH-1
Second Corinth—*locale* ... TX-5
Second Corinth Ch—*church* ... TX-5
Second Cove—*bay* ... MD-2
Second Cow Creek—*stream* ... KS-7
Second Credit Hill Ch—*church* ... GA-3
*Second Creek* ... MI-6
*Second Creek* ... WV-2
Second Creek—*locale* ... TN-4
Secondcreek—*locale* ... WV-2
Second Creek—*stream* (5) ... AL-4
Second Creek—*stream* ... AK-9
Second Creek—*stream* (2) ... AR-4
Second Creek—*stream* (4) ... CA-9
Second Creek—*stream* (8) ... CO-8
Second Creek—*stream* ... FL-3
Second Creek—*stream* (7) ... ID-8
Second Creek—*stream* ... IL-6
Second Creek—*stream* ... IA-7
Second Creek—*stream* (2) ... KS-7
Second Creek—*stream* (3) ... KY-4
Second Creek—*stream* ... MD-2
Second Creek—*stream* ... MI-6
Second Creek—*stream* (2) ... MN-6
Second Creek—*stream* ... MS-4
Second Creek—*stream* (2) ... MO-7
Second Creek—*stream* (14) ... MT-8
Second Creek—*stream* (2) ... NV-8
Second Creek—*stream* (3) ... NY-2
Second Creek—*stream* (5) ... NC-3
Second Creek—*stream* ... ND-7
Second Creek—*stream* (2) ... OH-6
Second Creek—*stream* ... OK-5
Second Creek—*stream* (9) ... OR-9
Second Creek—*stream* (2) ... SC-3
Second Creek—*stream* (2) ... SD-7
Second Creek—*stream* (6) ... TN-4
Second Creek—*stream* (4) ... TX-5
Second Creek—*stream* (2) ... UT-8
Second Creek—*stream* (5) ... WA-9
Second Creek—*stream* (3) ... WV-2
Second Creek—*stream* (4) ... WY-8
Second Creek Baptist Ch—*church* ... TN-4
Second Creek Baptist Ch
(historical)—*church* ... TN-4
Second Creek Cabin Area—*locale* ... AL-4
Second Creek Campground—*locale* ... CO-8
Second Creek Cave—*cave* ... TN-4
Second Creek Cem—*cemetery* ... TN-4
*Second Creek Ch* ... TN-4
Second Creek Ch—*church* ... MO-7
Second Creek Ch—*church* ... NC-3
Second Creek Ch—*church* ... OH-6
Second Creek Ch—*church* ... TN-4
*Second Creek Ch of Christ* ... TN-4
Second Creek Island—*island* ... TN-4
Second Creek (Magisterial
District)—*fmr MCD* ... WV-2
Second Creek Methodist Ch
(historical)—*church* ... TN-4
Second Creek Point—*cape* ... NC-3
Second Creek Rec Area—*park* ... AL-4
Second Creek Ridge—*ridge* ... CO-8
Second Creek Sch—*school* ... MT-8
Second Creek Sch—*school* ... WV-2
Second Creek Sch (abandoned)—*school* ... MO-7
Second Creek Sch (historical)—*school* (2) ... TN-4
Second Creek Spring—*spring* ... OR-9
Second Creek Structure 10b Dam—*dam* ... MS-4
Second Creek Structure 11 Dam—*dam* ... MS-4
Second Creek Structure 12 Dam—*dam* ... MS-4
Second Creek Structure 7 Dam—*dam* ... MS-4
Second Creek Structure 8 Dam—*dam* ... MS-4
Second Creek Structure 9 Dam—*dam* ... MS-4
*Second Creek Subdivision* ... AL-4
Second Creek Tunnel—*tunnel* ... WV-2
Second Creek Watershed Structure One
Dam—*dam* ... MS-4
Second Creek Watershed Structure 6a
Dam—*dam* ... MS-4
Second Creek Watershed Structure 6b
Dam—*dam* ... MS-4
Second Crichton Baptist Ch—*church* ... AL-4
Second Crossing—*locale* ... CA-9
Second Crossing—*locale* (2) ... TX-5
Second Cross Swamp—*stream* ... NC-3
Second Crow Wing Lake—*lake* ... MN-6
Second Cumberland Presbyterian Ch—*church*
(2) ... AL-4
Second Currier Brook—*stream* ... ME-1
Second Currier Pond—*lake* ... ME-1
Second Darien Ch—*church* ... GA-3
Second Davidson Creek—*stream* ... TX-5
Second Davis Pond—*lake* ... ME-1
Second Debsconeag Lake—*lake* ... ME-1
Second Dinkey Lake—*lake* ... CA-9
Second District Elem Sch—*school* ... PA-2
Second Divide—*gap* ... CA-9
Second Division Brook—*stream* ... MA-1
Second Division Hill—*summit* ... TX-5
Second Division Monmt—*park* ... DC-2
Second Dog Lake—*lake* ... MN-6
Second East Branch Magalloway
River—*stream* ... ME-1
Second Ebenezer Ch—*church* ... GA-3
Second Elam Ch—*church* ... VA-3
Second Elizabeth Ch—*church* ... GA-3
Second Euhaw Ch—*church* ... SC-3
Second Evening Star Ch—*church* ... LA-4
Second Fall Creek Ch—*church* ... IN-6
Second Falls—*falls* ... NC-3
Second Flat Mesa—*summit* ... AZ-5
*Second Forest* ... AZ-5
Second Fork—*stream* ... KY-4
Second Fork—*stream* ... PA-2
Second Fork—*stream* (3) ... WV-2
Second Fork Barney Run—*stream* ... PA-2
Second Fork Cedar Creek—*stream* ... MT-8
Second Fork Larrys Creek—*stream* ... PA-2
*Second Fork Mad River* ... WA-9
Second Fork Millers Creek—*stream* ... KY-4
Second Fork Rock Creek—*stream* ... ID-8
Second Fork Sch—*school* ... WV-2
Second Fork Silver Creek—*stream* ... NV-8
Second Fork Squaw Creek—*stream* ... ID-8
Second Fork West Fork Buffalo
Fork—*stream* ... MT-8
Second Gap—*gap* ... PA-2
Second Gap Trail—*trail* ... PA-2
**Second Garrotte**—*pop pl* ... CA-9
Second Garrotte Basin—*basin* ... CA-9
Second Garrotte Ridge—*ridge* ... CA-9
Second Grass—*summit* ... NC-3
Second Green Knob—*summit* ... PA-2
Second Grove Ch—*church* ... TN-4
Second Gulch—*valley* ... CO-8
Second Gulch—*valley* ... ID-8
Second Gulch—*valley* ... MT-8
Second Gulch—*valley* ... WY-8
*Second Hammock Hills* ... NC-3
Second Hamongog—*summit* ... UT-8
Secondhand Spring—*spring* ... NV-8
*Second Hanson Lake* ... MN-6
Second Hay Creek—*stream* ... MT-8
Second Herring Brook—*stream* ... MA-1
Second Hill—*island* ... DE-2
Second Hill—*summit* (2) ... CT-1
Second Hill—*summit* ... ME-1
Second Hill Brook—*stream* ... CT-1
Second Hill Lake—*lake* ... AK-9
Second Hill Lane Sch—*school* ... CT-1
Second Hole—*basin* ... UT-8
Second Hollow—*valley* ... AZ-5
Second Hollow—*valley* (2) ... ID-8
Second Hollow—*valley* ... KY-4
Second Hollow—*valley* ... VA-3
Second Hollow Spring—*spring* ... AZ-5
Second Hollow Tank—*reservoir* ... AZ-5
*Second Holly Grove Church* ... MS-4
Second Home Cem—*cemetery* ... WI-6
Second Hosack House—*hist pl* ... OH-6
Second Hurricane Branch—*stream* ... NC-3
Secondine Cem—*cemetery* ... OK-5
Second Island—*cape* ... MA-1
Second Island—*island* ... LA-4
Second Island—*island* (2) ... MN-6
Second Island—*island* (2) ... NY-2
Second Island—*island* ... PA-2
Second James Creek Ch—*church* ... MS-4
Second Kekur—*island* ... AK-9
Second Kent Ch—*church* ... NY-2
Second Knoll—*summit* ... AZ-5
Second Knolls—*summit* ... AZ-5
Second Knoll Tank—*reservoir* ... AZ-5
*Second Kokadjo Lake* ... ME-1
Second Lafayette—*fmr MCD* ... NE-7
*Second Laguna* ... AZ-5
*Second Lake* ... ME-1
*Second Lake* ... MI-6
*Second Lake* ... MN-6
Second Lake—*lake* (2) ... AK-9
Second Lake—*lake* ... CA-9
Second Lake—*lake* ... KY-4
Second Lake—*lake* (2) ... LA-4
Second Lake—*lake* (6) ... ME-1
Second Lake—*lake* (10) ... MI-6
Second Lake—*lake* (7) ... MN-6
Second Lake—*lake* ... MS-4
Second Lake—*lake* (5) ... NY-2
Second Lake—*lake* ... OR-9
Second Lake—*lake* ... WA-9
Second Lake—*lake* (6) ... WI-6
Second Lake Dam—*dam* ... ME-1
Second Lake Ridge—*ridge* ... ME-1
Second Larson Coulee—*valley* ... ND-7
Second Laurel Branch—*stream* ... TN-4
Second Ledges—*cliff* ... UT-8
Second Left Fork Rock Canyon—*valley* ... UT-8
Second Left Hand Canyon—*valley* ... UT-8

Second Lefthand Fork—*stream* UT-8
Second Level Canal—*canal* MA-1
Second Liberty Ch—*church* (2) VA-3
Second Lift—*canal* CA-9
Second Lift Canal—*canal* CA-9
*Second Little River* NC-3
Second Los Angeles Aqueduct—*canal* CA-9
Second Lower Falls Creek Lake—*lake* MT-8
Second Macedonia Ch—*church* GA-3
Second Mace Trail—*trail* CO-8
Second Machias Lake—*lake* ME-1
Second Mallard Branch—*stream* CA-9
Second Marks Lake—*lake* ME-1
Second Meadows—*flat* CO-8
**Second Mesa**—*pop pl* AZ-5
Second Mesa—*summit* AZ-5
Second Mesa Campground—*park* AZ-5
Second Mesa Day Sch—*school* AZ-5
Second Mesa Post Office—*building* AZ-5
Second Methodist Church—*hist pl* GA-3
*Second Methodist Episcopal Ch* AL-4
Second Midland Sch—*hist pl* CO-8
*Second Mill Lake* SC-3
Second Millpond—*reservoir* SC-3
**Second Milo**—*pop pl* NY-2
Second Mine Branch—*stream* MD-2
Second Mineral Springs Ch—*church* VA-3
Second Missionary Baptist Ch—*church* FL-3
Second Missionary Baptist Ch—*church* (2) MS-4
Second Moose Plain—*bench* MA-1
Second Moravian Ch—*church* IN-6
Second Morningstar Ch—*church* FL-3
Second Mound—*summit* UT-8
*Second Mountain* NJ-2
Second Mountain Trail—*trail* PA-2
Second Mountain Trail—*trail* VA-3
Second Mountan—*summit* VA-3
Second Mount Carmel Ch—*church* GA-3
Second Mount Morris Ch—*church* VA-3
Second Mount Olive Ch—*church* SC-3
Second Mount Olive Ch—*church* VA-3
Second Mount Zion Ch—*church* AL-4
Second Mouth—*channel* FL-3
Second Mtn—*range* PA-2
Second Mtn—*summit* (2) OK-5
Second Mtn—*summit* PA-2
Second Mtn—*summit* VA-3
Second Musquacook Lake—*lake* ME-1
Second Musquash Pond—*lake* ME-1
Second Napa Slough—*gut* CA-9
Second Narrows—*channel* AK-9
Second Narrows—*channel* ME-1
Second Narrows—*gap* PA-2
Second Narrows—*valley* UT-8
Second Neck—*cape* NH-1
Second Neck Creek—*stream* NY-2
*Second Negro Brook Lake* ME-1
Second Neshanic River—*stream* NJ-2
Second New Hope Ch—*church* MS-4
Second New Hope Ch—*church* VA-3
Second Newlight Ch—*church* NC-3
Second Newlin Creek—*stream* CO-8
Second Nicolson Creek—*stream* MO-7
*Second Nigger brook Lake* ME-1
Second Old River—*stream* TX-5
Second Old River Lake—*lake* AR-4
Second Order Creek Ch—*church* KY-4
Second O'Shea Bldg—*hist pl* MA-1
Second Owsley Canal—*canal* ID-8
*Second Parish of Lynn* MA-1
Second Park—*flat* CO-8
Second Peak—*summit* OR-9
Second Peak—*summit* VA-3
Second Pelletier Brook Lake—*lake* ME-1
Second Perch Lake—*lake* MN-6
*Second Periwinkle Creek* OR-9
Second Pilgrim Rest Ch—*church* MS-4
Second Point—*cape* FL-3
Second Point—*cape* ME-1
Second Point—*cape* MA-1
Second Point—*cape* RI-1
Second Point—*cape* UT-8
Second Point—*cape* WI-6
*Second Pond* NY-2
*Second Pond* PA-2
Second Pond—*lake* (2) ME-1
Second Pond—*lake* MA-1
Second Pond—*lake* (5) NY-2
Second Pond—*reservoir* PA-2
Second Pond—*swamp* TX-5
Second Pond Brook—*stream* NY-2
Second Pond Dam—*dam* PA-2
Second Porcupine Rapids—*rapids* WI-6
*Second Potts Creek* NC-3
Second Prairie Mtn—*summit* OR-9
Second Presbyterian Ch—*church* FL-3
Second Presbyterian Ch—*church* KS-7
Second Presbyterian Ch—*church* (2) TN-4
Second Presbyterian Ch (historical)—*church* AL-4
Second Presbyterian Church—*hist pl* AL-4
Second Presbyterian Church—*hist pl* IL-6
Second Presbyterian Church—*hist pl* KY-4
Second Presbyterian Church—*hist pl* MO-7
Second Presbyterian Church—*hist pl* OH-6
Second Presbyterian Church—*hist pl* (2) TN-4
Second Presbyterian Church—*hist pl* VA-3
Second Presbyterian Church Sch—*school* FL-3
Second Price Pond—*lake* OH-6
Second Prong—*stream* TN-4
Second Puncheon Branch—*stream* FL-3
Second Pup—*stream* AK-9
Second Recess—*valley* CA-9
Second Red Knoll—*summit* UT-8
*Second Redtown* IL-6
Second Reformed Dutch Church—*hist pl* NJ-2
Second Ridge—*ridge* ME-1
Second Ridge—*ridge* MT-8
Second Right Fork Rock Canyon—*valley* UT-8
*Second Right Hand Fork* WV-2
Second Rindge Meetinghouse, Horsesheds and Cemetery—*hist pl* NH-1
*Second River* NJ-2
Second River—*stream* MI-6
Second River—*stream* NJ-2
Second Roach Pond—*reservoir* ME-1
Second Robertson Ch—*church* VA-3
Second Rock Lake—*lake* MT-8
Second Rocky Tunnel—*tunnel* NC-3
Second RR Car No. 21—*hist pl* NV-8
Second Rsvr—*reservoir* AZ-5
Second Rsvr—*reservoir* NY-2
Second Run—*stream* WV-2
*Second Sabao Lake* ME-1
Second Saint John Pond—*reservoir* ME-1
Second Saint Paul Baptist Ch—*church* IN-6
Second Saint Pauls Ch—*church* GA-3
Second Salem Ch—*church* GA-3
Second Salt Creek—*stream* IL-6
Second Salt Creek—*stream* UT-8
Second Sand Beach Park—*park* MI-6
Second Sand Creek—*stream* SD-7
Second Sand Creek—*stream* WY-8
Second San Diego Aqueduct—*canal* CA-9
Second Sawmill Spring—*spring* NV-8
Second Set—*valley* UT-8
Second Set Spring—*spring* CO-8
Second Set Spring—*spring* UT-8
Second Shady Grove Ch—*church* AL-4
Second Sheep Camp Spring—*spring* OR-9
*Second Siding* ND-7
Second Silver Lake—*lake* MN-6
Second Silver Run—*stream* NC-3
Second Sister Creek—*stream* SC-3
Second Sister Lake—*lake* MI-6
Second South Branch Oconto River—*stream* WI-6
Second South Branch Russell Pond—*lake* ME-1
Second Southern Baptist Ch—*church* IN-6
Second South Fork East Fork Clear Creek—*stream* CA-9
Second Southwark Church Archeol Site (44SY65)—*hist pl* VA-3
Second Spring—*spring* CO-8
Second Spring—*spring* UT-8
Second Spring Creek—*stream* ID-8
Second Spring Creek—*stream* UT-8
Second Springfield Ch—*church* GA-3
Second Stillwater—*lake* NY-2
Second Stillwater—*reservoir* NY-2
Second St. Joseph Hotel—*hist pl* IN-6
Second Stony Island—*island* WI-6
Second Street Bridge—*hist pl* MI-6
Second Street Bridge—*hist pl* PA-2
Second Street Cem—*cemetery* NY-2
Second Street Ch of Christ—*church* TN-4
Second Street Commercial District—*hist pl* WI-6
Second Street Elem Sch—*school* PA-2
Second Street Hist Dist—*hist pl* NY-2
Second Street Hist Dist—*hist pl* OH-6
Second Street Park—*park* KS-7
Second Street Sch—*school* CA-9
Second Street Sch—*school* MA-1
Second Sugarloaf—*summit* CA-9
Second Swale Creek—*stream* OR-9
Second Swamp—*stream* VA-3
Second Temple Ch of Christ—*church* MS-4
Second Texas Lunette (historical)—*locale* MS-4
Second Tompkins County Courthouse—*hist pl* NY-2
Second Top—*summit* WA-9
Second Trail Canyon—*valley* AZ-5
Second Trap Windmill—*locale* NM-5
Second Trestle Lake—*lake* MN-6
Second Trinity Univ Campus—*hist pl* TX-5
Second Union Ch—*church* GA-3
Second Union Ch—*church* (2) LA-4
Second Union Ch—*church* (2) MS-4
Second Union Ch—*church* (2) VA-3
Second Union Sch—*school* VA-3
Second Union Sch (historical)—*school* MS-4
Second Unitarian Church—*hist pl* MA-1
Second United Methodist Ch—*church* TN-4
Second United Presbyterian Ch—*church* IN-6
Second United Presbyterian Ch—*church* TN-4
Second United Presbyterian Church—*hist pl* NM-5
*Second Upper Saint John Pond* ME-1
Second Valley—*valley* NM-5
Second Valley Creek—*stream* CA-9
Second Wannigan Rapids—*rapids* WI-6
Second Ward Grade Sch (historical)—*school* PA-2
Second Ward HS—*school* NC-3
Second Ward Park—*park* NJ-2
Second Ward Sch—*hist pl* NM-5
Second Ward Sch—*school* (2) LA-4
Second Ward Sch—*school* (5) PA-2
Second Ward Sch—*school* WV-2
Second Washburn Tunnel—*tunnel* NC-3
Second Watchung Mtn—*summit* NJ-2
Second Water—*lake* UT-8
Second Water Canyon—*valley* AZ-5
Second Water Canyon—*valley* TX-5
Second Water Canyon—*valley* UT-8
Secondwater Creek—*stream* ID-8
Second Water Creek—*stream* UT-8
Second Waterfall Creek—*stream* AK-9
Second Waterfall Hollow—*valley* UT-8
Second Water Gulch—*valley* CO-8
Second Water Gulch—*valley* OR-9
Second Waterhouse House—*hist pl* MA-1
Second Water Ridge—*ridge* UT-8
Second Water Spring—*spring* AZ-5
Second Water Spring—*spring* CO-8
Second Water Trail—*trail* AZ-5
Second Water Trough Creek—*stream* CA-9
Second Weches Sch (historical)—*school* TX-5
Second West Branch Pond—*lake* ME-1
*Second West Fork Sanpoil River* WA-9
Second West Prong Windmill—*locale* TX-5
Second Wolverine Creek—*stream* MT-8
Second Woodland Ch—*church* GA-3
Second Yadkin County Jail—*hist pl* NC-3
*Second Yegua Creek* TX-5
Second Yellow Mule Creek—*stream* MT-8
*Second Zion Church* MS-4
*Seconet* MA-1
*Seconnet* MA-1
*Seconod Pond* ME-1
Seconsett Island—*cape* MA-1
*Seconsset Island* MA-1
Seco Pass—*gap* TX-5
**Secor**—*pop pl* IL-6
Secor, Joseph K., House—*hist pl* OH-6
Secor Brook—*stream* NY-2
Secor Cem—*cemetery* IL-6
Secor Corners—*locale* NY-2
Secord—*locale* MI-6
Secord Ch—*church* MI-6
Secord Lake—*lake* (2) MI-6
Secord Lake—*reservoir* MI-6
Secord Lake Campground—*locale* MI-6
*Secord Pond* MI-6
**Secord (Township of)**—*pop pl* MI-6
*Secor Gardens* OH-6
**Secor Gardens**—*pop pl* NY-2
**Secor (historical)**—*pop pl* IA-7
Secor Hotel—*hist pl* OH-6
Secor Lake—*lake* NY-2
Secor Park—*park* OH-6
Seco Rsvr—*reservoir* TX-5
Seco Spring—*spring* NM-5
*Secota* NC-3
Secotan—*locale* FL-3
Secotan (historical)—*area* NC-3
Seco Tank—*lake* NM-5
Seco Tank—*reservoir* AZ-5
Seco Tank—*reservoir* (3) NM-5
Secotan Lookout Tower—*tower* FL-3
*Secoton* NC-3
*SE Cove Point* NJ-2
Seco Windmill—*locale* NM-5
Secrest Cem—*cemetery* TN-4
Secrest Cottage Sch No 1—*school* CO-8
Secrest Cottage Sch No 2—*school* CO-8
Secrest Grove Ch—*church* NC-3
Secrest Octagon Barn—*hist pl* IA-7
Secrest Sch—*school* CO-8
Secret—*locale* CA-9
Secret, Bayou—*stream* LA-4
**Secretary**—*pop pl* MD-2
*Secretary Creek* MD-2
Secret Basin—*basin* NV-8
Secret Bay—*bay* AK-9
Secret Bog—*lake* ME-1
Secret Brook—*stream* ME-1
Secret Cabin—*locale* AZ-5
Secret Cabin Butte—*summit* ID-8
*Secret Canyon* UT-8
Secret Canyon—*valley* AZ-5
Secret Canyon—*valley* (3) CA-9
Secret Canyon—*valley* CO-8
Secret Canyon—*valley* ID-8
Secret Canyon—*valley* (3) NV-8
Secret Canyon—*valley* UT-8
Secret Cave—*cave* TN-4
Secret Caverns—*cave* NY-2
Secret Creek—*stream* AK-9
Secret Creek—*stream* (2) CA-9
Secret Creek—*stream* ID-8
Secret Creek—*stream* (3) NV-8
Secret Creek—*stream* OR-9
Secret Diggings—*mine* CA-9
Secret Flat—*flat* CA-9
Secret Forest Camp—*locale* OR-9
Secret Gulch—*valley* CA-9
Secret Gulch—*valley* MT-8
Secret Harbor—*bay* NV-8
Secret Harbor—*bay* WA-9
Secret Harbor Creek—*stream* NV-8
Secret House—*locale* CA-9
Secret Lake—*lake* (4) CA-9
Secret Lake—*lake* CT-1
Secret Lake—*lake* FL-3
Secret Lake—*lake* RI-1
Secret Lake—*'ake* WI-6
**Secret Lake**—*pop pl* CT-1
Secret Lake—*reservoir* UT-8
Secret Lakes—*lake* MT-8
Secret Mesa—*summit* UT-8
Secret Mtn—*summit* AZ-5
Secret Pass—*gap* AZ-5
Secret Pass—*gap* (2) NV-8
Secret Pass Canyon—*valley* AZ-5
Secret Pass Spring—*spring* AZ-5
Secret Pass Wash—*stream* AZ-5
Secret Pasture—*area* CA-9
Secret Pasture—*flat* AZ-5
Secret Peak—*summit* NV-8
Secret Pit—*cave* AL-4
Secret Pocket—*basin* AZ-5
Secret Pond—*lake* (4) ME-1
Secret Pond—*lake* NY-2
Secret Prayer Hollow—*valley* TN-4
Secret Ravine—*valley* (2) CA-9
Secret Ridge—*ridge* CA-9
Secrets Creek—*stream* NC-3
Secret Spring—*spring* CA-9
Secret Spring—*spring* ID-8
Secret Spring—*spring* (3) NV-8
Secret Spring—*spring* (3) UT-8
Secret Spring Canyon—*valley* NV-8
Secret Spring Mtn—*summit* CA-9
Secret Springs—*spring* (2) UT-8
Secret Spring Summit—*gap* NV-8
Secret Tank—*reservoir* (2) AZ-5
Secret Town—*locale* CA-9
Secret Valley—*valley* (2) CA-9
Secret Valley—*valley* NV-8
Secret Valley—*valley* (2) OR-9
Secret Valley—*valley* WY-8
Secret Valley Creek—*stream* WY-8
Secret Woods Park—*park* FL-3
Secrist Well—*well* NV-8
Sec Tank—*reservoir* NM-5
Sect Ditch—*canal* UT-8
Section—*locale* AL-4
**Section**—*pop pl* AL-4
Section and a Half Windmill—*locale* TX-5
Section Base Channel Range Front Light—*locale* FL-3
Section Bluff Cabin Site Area—*locale* AL-4
*Section Bluff Subdivision* AL-4
Section Brake—*swamp* AR-4
Section Branch—*stream* AL-4
Section Branch—*stream* AR-4
Section Branch—*stream* MS-4
Section Branch—*stream* MO-7
Section (CCD)—*cens area* AL-4
Section Cem—*cemetery* (2) AR-4
Section Cem—*cemetery* IL-6
Section Corner Canyon—*valley* ID-8
Section Corner Creek—*stream* WA-9
Section Corner Lake—*lake* WY-8
Section Corner Lake Trail—*trail* WY-8
Section Corner Rsvr—*reservoir* ID-8
Section Corner Spring—*spring* OR-9
*Section Corner Tank* AZ-5
Section Corner Tank—*reservoir* AZ-5
Section Creek—*stream* AK-9
Section Creek—*stream* IL-6
Section Creek—*stream* MS-4
Section Creek—*stream* (2) OR-9
Section Creek—*stream* TX-5
Section Division—*civil* AL-4
Section Eight Ch—*church* WI-6
Section Eighteen Mine—*mine* MN-6
Section Eighteen Tank—*reservoir* (2) AZ-5
Section Eight Rsvr—*reservoir* ID-8
Section Eight Sch—*school* MN-6
Section Eight Well—*well* AZ-5
*Section Eleven Lake* MN-6
Section Eleven Lake—*lake* MI-6
Section Eleven Lake—*lake* MN-6
Section Eleven Tank—*reservoir* (2) AZ-5
Section Eleven Well—*well* AZ-5
Section Eleven Well—*well* NM-5
Section F Dam—*dam* PA-2
Section Ferry (historical)—*locale* AL-4
Section Fifteen Lake—*lake* MN-6
Section Fifteen Spring—*spring* CA-9
Section Fifteen Tank—*reservoir* AZ-5
Section Fifteen Tank—*reservoir* NM-5
Section Fifteen Windmill—*locale* AZ-5
Section Five Creek—*stream* MN-6
Section Five Lake—*lake* MI-6
Section Five Lake—*swamp* MI-6
Section Five Tank—*reservoir* (5) AZ-5
Section Ford—*locale* AL-4
Section Four Creek—*stream* CA-9
Section Four Lake—*lake* (2) MI-6
Section Four Rsvr—*reservoir* MT-8
Section Four Tank—*reservoir* AZ-5
Section Fourteen Lake—*lake* MN-6
Section Fourteen Well—*well* AZ-5
Section Gap—*gap* AL-4
Section Grove Ch—*church* GA-3
Section (historical)—*locale* KS-7
Section Hollow—*valley* AL-4
Section Hollow—*valley* AR-4
Section Hollow—*valley* MO-7
Section House—*building* AK-9
**Section House**—*pop pl* AK-9
*Section House Creek* LA-4
Sectionhouse Creek—*stream* MT-8
*Sectionhouse Draw* CO-8
Section House Draw—*valley* CO-8
Section House Draw—*valley* MT-8
Section House Hill—*summit* KY-4
Sectionhouse Hollow—*valley* TN-4
Section House Lake—*lake* AK-9
Section House Spring—*spring* AZ-5
Section HS—*school* AL-4
Section Lake—*lake* MN-6
Sectionline Creek—*stream* AL-4
Section Line Gap—*gap* OR-9
Section Line Lake—*lake* CA-9
Section Line Rsvr—*reservoir* ID-8
Section Line Rsvr—*reservoir* OR-9
Section Line Rsvr—*reservoir* WY-8
Sectionline Slough—*lake* ND-7
Section Line Spring—*spring* MT-8
Section Line Spring—*spring* (2) OR-9
Section Line Tank—*reservoir* AZ-5
Section Line Trail—*trail* OR-9
Section Mtn—*summit* AL-4
Section Nine Lake—*lake* MI-6
Section Nine Lake—*lake* MN-6
Section Nine Tank—*reservoir* AZ-5
Section Nineteen Creek—*stream* MI-6
Section Nineteen Well—*well* AZ-5
Section Nine Well—*well* AZ-5
Section One Lake—*lake* MI-6
Section One Lake—*lake* MN-6
Section One Spring—*spring* OR-9
Section One Tank—*reservoir* AZ-5
Section One Well—*reservoir* AZ-5
Section Point—*summit* CO-8
Section Pond—*lake* MN-6
Section Pond—*swamp* TX-5
Section Sch—*school* IL-6
Section Sch (historical)—*school* MO-7
Section Seven Gun Club—*other* CA-9
Section Seven Lake—*lake* MI-6
Section Seven Swamp—*swamp* WI-6
Section Seventeen Lake—*lake* MI-6
Section Seventeen Tank—*reservoir* AZ-5
Section Seven Well—*well* AZ-5
Section Seven Windmill—*locale* TX-5
Section Six Draw—*valley* WY-8
Section Six Mine—*mine* MN-6
Section Six Tank—*reservoir* AZ-5
Section Sixteen Cem—*cemetery* AR-4
Section Sixteen Hill—*summit* AZ-5
Section Sixteen Lake—*lake* FL-3
Section Sixteen Lake—*lake* MN-6
Section Sixteen Tank—*reservoir* (2) AZ-5
Section Sixteen Windmill—*locale* MT-8
Section Six Well—*well* NM-5
Section Spring—*spring* ID-8
Section Spring Hollow—*valley* MO-7
Section Tank—*reservoir* (2) AZ-5
Section Tank—*reservoir* (2) TX-5
Section Ten Lake—*lake* (3) MN-6
Section Ten Lake—*lake* WI-6
Section Ten Sch—*school* WI-6
Section Ten Tank—*reservoir* (3) AZ-5
Section Thirteen Creek—*stream* MI-6
Section Thirteen Sch—*school* AR-4
Section Thirteen Tank—*reservoir* (2) AZ-5
Section Thirteen Well—*well* AZ-5
Section Thirt-six Creek—*stream* MN-6
**Section Thirty**—*pop pl* MN-6
Section Thirty Creek—*stream* MN-6
Section Thirtyfour Creek—*stream* MI-6
Section Thirty-four Tank—*reservoir* (2) AZ-5
Section Thirty Lake—*lake* MN-6
Section Thirty Lake—*lake* WI-6
Section Thirty Sch—*school* MN-6
Section Thirtysix Lake—*lake* MI-6
Section Thirtysix Lake—*lake* MN-6
Section Thirty Spring—*spring* AZ-5
Section Thirty Tank—*reservoir* (3) AZ-5
Section Thirty-three Number One Tank—*reservoir* AZ-5
Section Thirty-three Number Two Tank—*reservoir* AZ-5
Section Thirty-three Spring—*spring* AZ-5
Section Thirty-three Tank—*reservoir* AZ-5
Section Thirtythree Tank—*reservoir* AZ-5
Section Thirty Windmill—*locale* AZ-5
Section Three Draw—*valley* WY-8
Section Three Windmill—*locale* TX-5
Section Twelve Lake—*lake* (3) MN-6
Section Twelve Spring—*spring* AZ-5
Section Twelve Tank—*reservoir* (2) AZ-5
Section Twenty Creek—*stream* WI-6
Section Twenty-eight Lake—*lake* MI-6
Section Twenty-eight Tank—*reservoir* AZ-5
Section Twenty-Five Lake—*lake* MN-6
Section Twentyfive Tank—*reservoir* (2) AZ-5
Section Twenty-four Tank—*reservoir* AZ-5
Section Twentyfour Tank—*reservoir* AZ-5
Section Twenty-four Tank—*reservoir* AZ-5
Section Twenty-nine Lake—*lake* MN-6
Section Twentynine Rsvr—*reservoir* AZ-5
Section Twenty Nine Tank—*reservoir* AZ-5
Section Twentynine Well—*well* AZ-5
Section Twentyone Tank—*reservoir* AZ-5
Section Twenty-one Tank—*reservoir* AZ-5
Section Twentyone Tank—*reservoir* AZ-5
Section Twentyseven Spring—*spring* ID-8
Section Twenty-seven Tank—*reservoir* AZ-5
Section Twentysix Cave—*cave* AL-4
Section Twentysix Pit—*cave* AL-4
Section Twenty-six Tank—*reservoir* AZ-5
Section Twenty Tank—*reservoir* (3) AZ-5
Section Twentythree Tank—*reservoir* AZ-5
Section Twenty-three Tank—*reservoir* AZ-5
Section Twentytwo Tank—*reservoir* AZ-5
Section Two Dam Tank—*reservoir* AZ-5
*Section Two Lake* MN-6
Section Two Tank—*reservoir* (2) AZ-5
Section Two Tank—*reservoir* NM-5
Section Two Windmill—*locale* TX-5
Section United Methodist Ch—*church* AL-4
Section Valley Sch (historical)—*school* AL-4
Section Well—*well* AZ-5
Section Well—*well* (2) NM-5
Section Windmill—*locale* (2) NM-5
Section Windmill—*locale* TX-5
Section 11 Spring—*spring* OR-9
Section 16 Cem—*cemetery* MI-6
Section 16 Cem—*cemetery* MS-4
Section 16 Lake—*lake* AR-4
Section 17 Cabin—*locale* MI-6
Section 18 JHS—*school* MI-6
Section 18 Tank—*reservoir* NM-5
Section 2 Spring—*spring* WY-8
Section 20 Rsvr—*reservoir* WY-8
Section 20 Tank—*reservoir* AZ-5
Section 21 Well—*well* NM-5
*Section 24 Lake* MI-6
Section 25 Lake—*lake* ID-8
Section 26 Tank—*reservoir* NM-5
Section 28 Oil and Gas Field—*oilfield* LA-4
Section 28 Rsvr—*reservoir* ID-8
Section 3 Lake—*lake* WA-9
Section 30 Tank—*reservoir* NM-5
Section 31 Well—*well* NM-5
Section 33 Mine—*mine* NM-5
Section 34 Tank—*reservoir* AZ-5
Section 34 Tank—*reservoir* NM-5
Section 5 Lake—*lake* MI-6
Section 5 Spring—*spring* WA-9
Section 5 Tank—*reservoir* NM-5
*Section 7 Lake* MI-6
Section 7 Rsvr—*reservoir* CO-8
Section 9 Spring—*spring* ID-8
Section 9 Spring—*spring* OR-9
Section 9 Spring—*spring* WA-9
Sector—*locale* WV-2
Secucito Spring—*spring* AZ-5
Secum Brook—*stream* MA-1
Secunda Creek—*stream* ID-8
Secundino—*locale* AZ-5
Secundino Tank—*reservoir* NM-5
Secundino Well—*well* AZ-5
Secundino Windmill—*locale* NM-5
*Secunke* MA-1
Securities and Exchange Commission—*building* DC-2
Security—*CDP* MD-2
Security—*locale* MD-2
Security—*locale* TX-5
**Security**—*pop pl* CO-8
**Security**—*pop pl* LA-4
**Security**—*pop pl* MD-2
**Security Acres (subdivision)**—*pop pl* (2) AZ-5
Security Bank and Trust Company Bldg—*hist pl* CA-9
Security Bank Bldg—*hist pl* AL-4
Security Bank Bldg—*hist pl* SD-7
Security Bay—*bay* AK-9
Security Bldg—*hist pl* AZ-5
Security Bldg—*hist pl* IA-7
Security Cem—*cemetery* TX-5
Security Club Lake—*reservoir* IL-6
Security Copper Mine—*mine* WA-9
Security Cove—*bay* (2) AK-9
**Security Junction**—*pop pl* MD-2
Security Mine—*mine* CO-8
Security Point—*cape* AK-9
Security Savings Bank—*hist pl* WI-6
Security Siding—*locale* TX-5
Security State Bank—*hist pl* KS-7
Security State Bank Bldg—*hist pl* NE-7
Security Trust and Savings—*hist pl* CA-9
Security Trust Bldg—*hist pl* ME-1
Security-Widefield—*CDP* CO-8
*Sec 31* NV-8
*Sec 32* MT-8
*sec 35* AL-4
Sedal Canyon—*valley* AZ-5
*Sedalia* OH-6
*Sedalia* TN-4
Sedalia—*locale* SC-3
Sedalia—*locale* VA-3
**Sedalia**—*pop pl* CO-8
**Sedalia**—*pop pl* IN-6
**Sedalia**—*pop pl* KY-4
**Sedalia**—*pop pl* MO-7
**Sedalia**—*pop pl* NC-3
**Sedalia**—*pop pl* TX-5
**Sedalia**—*pop pl* WV-2
Sedalia (CCD)—*cens area* KY-4
Sedalia Ch—*church* KS-7
Sedalia Ch—*church* TX-5
*Sedalia (corporate name Midway)* OH-6
Sedalia Elem Sch—*school* NC-3
Sedalia Lookout Tower—*locale* SC-3
Sedalia Memorial Airp—*airport* MO-7
Sedalia Post Office (historical)—*building* TN-4
Sedalia Public Library—*hist pl* MO-7
Sedalia Rsvr—*reservoir* MO-7
Sedalia Township—*civil* MO-7
Sedal Pass—*gap* UT-8
Sedal Valley—*basin* UT-8
*Sedamsville* OH-6
**Sedamsville**—*pop pl* OH-6
Sedan—*locale* NE-7
Sedan—*locale* OH-6
Sedan—*locale* OK-5
Sedan—*locale* WV-2
**Sedan**—*pop pl* IN-6
**Sedan**—*pop pl* IA-7
**Sedan**—*pop pl* KS-7
**Sedan**—*pop pl* MN-6
**Sedan**—*pop pl* MT-8
**Sedan**—*pop pl* NM-5
Sedan Brook—*stream* MN-6
Sedan Cem—*cemetery* IN-6
Sedan Cem—*cemetery* MT-8
Sedan Cem—*cemetery* NM-5
Sedan City Airp—*airport* KS-7
Sedan City Dam—*dam* KS-7
Sedan City Lake—*reservoir* KS-7
Sedan Crater—*crater* NV-8
Sedanka Island—*island* AK-9
Sedanka Pass—*channel* AK-9
Sedanka Point—*cape* AK-9
*Sedan Lake* KS-7
*Sedan Lake* MT-8
Sedan Sch—*hist pl* MT-8
Sedan Sch—*school* NE-7
Sedan State Wildlife Mngmt Areas—*park* MN-6
Sedan Township—*civil* KS-7
Sedative Lake—*lake* MN-6
Sedberry Cem—*cemetery* NC-3
Sedberry Cem—*cemetery* TN-4
Sedberry Hollow—*valley* TX-5
Sedberry-Holmes House—*hist pl* NC-3
Sedberry House—*hist pl* TX-5
**Sedco Hills**—*pop pl* CA-9
*Seddon* VA-3
**Seddon**—*pop pl* AL-4
Seddon Cem—*cemetery* AL-4
Seddon Channel—*channel* FL-3
*Seddon Island* FL-3
*Seddon Island Channel* FL-3
Seddon (Magisterial District)—*fmr MCD* VA-3
*Seddon Shores* AL-4
Sederlin Slide—*cliff* WY-8
Sedge Cove—*cove* MA-1
Sedge Creek—*stream* MT-8
Sedge Creek—*stream* (2) NJ-2
Sedge Creek—*stream* WY-8
*Sedgedale* PA-2
Sedgefield—*locale* AL-4
**Sedgefield**—*pop pl* AL-4
**Sedgefield**—*pop pl* NJ-2
**Sedgefield**—*pop pl* NC-3
**Sedgefield**—*pop pl* VA-3
**Sedgefield Acres (subdivision)**—*pop pl* NC-3
Sedgefield Country Club—*locale* NC-3
Sedgefield Elem Sch—*school* NC-3
Sedgefield JHS—*school* NC-3
Sedgefield Lake—*reservoir* AL-4
Sedgefield Lake Dam—*dam* AL-4
**Sedgefield Lakes (subdivision)**—*pop pl* NC-3
Sedgefield Landing (historical)—*locale* MS-4
**Sedgefield Manor**—*pop pl* VA-3
**Sedgefield Park (subdivision)**—*pop pl* NC-3
Sedgefield Plantation—*locale* AL-4
Sedgefield Sch—*school* NC-3
Sedgefield Sch—*school* VA-3
**Sedgefield (subdivision)**—*pop pl* (4) NC-3
Sedge Garden Ch—*church* NC-3
Sodgo Gardon Chapol church NC 3
Sedge Garden Sch—*school* NC-3
Sedge Grass Island (historical)—*island* AL-4
*Sedge Island* NJ-2
Sedge Island—*island* CT-1
Sedge Island—*island* (3) NJ-2
Sedge Island—*island* (3) NY-2
Sedge Island—*island* NC-3
Sedge Island—*island* VA-3
Sedge Island Point—*cape* VA-3
Sedge Islands—*island* NJ-2
Sedge Lake—*lake* CA-9
Sedge Lake—*lake* (2) MT-8
Sedgely Brook—*stream* ME-1
Sedge Marsh—*swamp* SC-3
Sedge Meadow—*flat* MT-8
Sedge Meadows—*swamp* MA-1
*Sedge Point* MD-2
Sedge Ridge—*ridge* WA-9
*Sedger River* VA-3
Sedges Creek—*stream* VA-3
**Sedges Garden (historical)**—*pop pl* NC-3
Sedge Spring—*spring* AZ-5
Sedge Spring—*spring* UT-8
**Sedge-Town**—*pop pl* NC-3
Sedgeunkedunk Stream—*stream* ME-1
Sedgewich (historical)—*locale* IA-7
Sedgewick—*locale* CO-8
*Sedgewick Church* SD-7
Sedgewick (historical P.O.)—*locale* IA-7
Sedgewick Meadows—*flat* WY-8
Sedgewick Sch (abandoned)—*school* PA-2
**Sedgewickville**—*pop pl* MO-7
Sedgewood Club—*locale* NY-2
**Sedgewood (subdivision)**—*pop pl* NC-3
Sedgley, John, Homestead—*hist pl* ME-1
**Sedgley Farms**—*pop pl* DE-2
Sedgwick—*locale* WI-6
**Sedgwick**—*pop pl* AR-4
**Sedgwick**—*pop pl* CO-8
**Sedgwick**—*pop pl* KS-7
**Sedgwick**—*pop pl* ME-1
**Sedgwick**—*pop pl* PA-2
Sedgwick—*uninc pl* PA-2

Sedgwick Bar State Game Preserve—*park* ... CO-8
Sedgwick Cem—*cemetery* ... CO-8
Sedgwick Cem—*cemetery* ... CT-1
Sedgwick Cem—*cemetery* ... WA-9
Sedgwick Ch—*church* ... SD-7
Sedgwick County—*civil* ... KS-7
Sedgwick County Park—*park* ... KS-7
Sedgwick Draw—*valley* ... CO-8
Sedgwick Draw*—*valley* ... NE-7
Sedgwick Elem Sch—*school* ... KS-7
Sedgwick (historical)—*locale* ... SD-7
Sedgwick House—*hist pl* ... NY-2
Sedgwick HS—*school* ... KS-7
Sedgwick Mtn—*summit* ... CT-1
Sedgwick Peak—*summit* ... ID-8
Sedgwick Ridge—*ridge* ... ME-1
Sedgwick Sch—*school* ... CA-9
Sedgwick Sch—*school* ... CT-1
**Sedgwick (Town of)**—*pop pl* ... ME-1
**Sedgwick Township**—*pop pl* ... KS-7
*Sedgy Creek* ... VA-3
Sedgy Point—*cape* ... MD-2
Sedgy Point Cove—*bay* ... MD-2
Sedgy Point Gut—*gut* ... MD-2
Sedil—*locale* ... MN-6
Sedilap—*bar* ... FM-9
**Sedillo**—*pop pl* ... NM-5
Sedillo Canyon—*valley* ... NM-5
**Sedillo Hill**—*pop pl* ... NM-5
Sedillo Hill—*reservoir* ... NM-5
Sedillo Spring—*spring* ... NM-5
Sedillo Well—*well* ... NM-5
Sedimentation Pond Number Three—*reservoir* ... PA-2
*Sedimentation Pond 3* ... PA-2
Sedimentation Rsvr—*reservoir* ... PA-2
Sedimentation Tank—*reservoir* ... AZ-5
Sedivy Lake—*lake* ... MN-6
Sedivy Landing Strip—*airport* ... KS-7
Sedlacek, Jacob, Chalkrock House—*hist pl* ... SD-7
Sedlak Creek—*stream* ... MT-8
Sedlak Park—*flat* ... MT-8
Sedlano Creek—*stream* ... SD-7
**Sedley**—*pop pl* ... IN-6
**Sedley**—*pop pl* ... VA-3
**Sedona**—*pop pl* ... AZ-5
Sedona Airp—*airport* ... AZ-5
Sedona Interchange—*crossing* ... AZ-5
Sedona Memorial Park—*cemetery* ... AZ-5
Sedona-Oak Creek Golf Course—*other* ... AZ-5
Sedona Ranger Station—*locale* ... AZ-5
Sedona Sch—*school* ... AZ-5
*Sedro Woolley* ... WA-9
**Sedro-Woolley**—*pop pl* ... WA-9
Sedro-Woolley (CCD)—*cens area* ... WA-9
**Sedro-Woolley (corporate name for Sedro Woolley)**—*pop pl* ... WA-9
*Sedro Woolley (corporate name Sedro-Woolley)* ... WA-9
*Sedro Wooly* ... WA-9
Seduciton Point—*cape* ... AK-9
Sedum Gulch—*valley* ... ID-8
Sedum Point—*summit* ... WA-9
Sedwick—*locale* ... TX-5
Sedwick Chapel—*church* ... IN-6
*Sedwick Community* ... TX-5
Sedwick Ditch—*canal* ... IN-6
Sedwick Sch—*school* ... IL-6
Sedwicks Mill—*locale* ... PA-2
*See-All* ... WV-2
See All—*summit* ... WV-2
Seeall, Mount—*summit* ... ME-1
Seebaugh Cem—*cemetery* ... WV-2
Seeber Cem—*cemetery* ... TN-4
Seeber Creek—*stream* (2) ... TN-4
Seeber Flats—*locale* ... TN-4
Seeberger-Loring-Kilburn House—*hist pl* ... IA-7
Seeber Lane Sch—*school* ... NY-2
Seebers Branch—*stream* ... MO-7
**Seebert**—*pop pl* ... WV-2
*Seebewaing River* ... MI-6
Seebolt-Wilhoite-Pendergrass House—*hist pl* ... KY-4
Seeboy Ridge—*ridge* ... CA-9
See Branch—*stream* (2) ... KY-4
**Seeburger**—*pop pl* ... MO-7
Seeburn Hazerig Lake—*reservoir* ... AL-4
Seeburn Hezerig Dam—*dam* ... AL-4
See Camp Gap—*gap* ... WV-2
See Canyon—*valley* ... AZ-5
See Canyon—*valley* ... CA-9
See Cem—*cemetery* ... GA-3
See Chapel—*church* ... KY-4
*Seecombe Brook* ... MA-1
*Seeconesset Island* ... MA-1
*Seeconosset Island* ... MA-1
Seed—*locale* ... GA-3
Seed, Miles A., Carriage House—*hist pl* ... MO-7
Seed Branch—*stream* ... SC-3
Seed Cane Creek—*stream* ... NC-3
Seed Chapel—*church* ... IL-6
Seed Creek—*stream* ... IL-6
Seed Hill—*summit* ... AZ-5
Seedhouse Campground—*locale* ... CO-8
Seedhouse Guard Station—*locale* ... CO-8
Seeding Rsvr—*reservoir* ... ID-8
*Seed Lake* ... MN-6
Seed Lake—*lake* ... MN-6
Seed Lake—*lake* ... WI-6
Seed Lake—*reservoir* ... GA-3
Seed Lakes—*lake* ... UT-8
Seedland Cutoff—*channel* ... FL-3
Seedling Mile Sch—*school* ... NE-7
Seed Run—*stream* ... IN-6
Seeds Cem—*cemetery* ... OH-6
Seedshadee Natl Wildlife Ref—*park* ... WY-8
*Seedskeedee-agie River* ... CO-8
*Seedskeedee-agie river* ... UT-8
*Seedskeedee Range* ... WY-8
Seedtick Branch—*stream* ... KY-4
Seed Tick Branch—*stream* ... SC-3
Seed Tick Branch—*stream* ... TN-4
Seedtick Cem—*cemetery* ... IN-6
Seedtick Church (historical)—*locale* ... MO-7
Seed Tick Creek—*stream* ... IN-6
Seedtick Creek—*stream* ... TN-4
Seed Tick Hollow—*valley* ... AR-4
Seed Tick Hollow—*valley* ... MO-7
Seed Tick Hollow—*valley* ... TX-5
Seed Tick Knob—*summit* ... KY-4
Seed Tick Lake—*reservoir* ... IN-6
Seedtick Mine (abandoned)—*mine* ... MO-7
Seed Tick Ridge—*ridge* ... MO-7
*Seedtick School* ... TN-4
Seed Unity Ch—*church* ... GA-3
Seefar Glacier—*glacier* ... AK-9
Seefeldt-Limesand Dam—*dam* ... ND-7
Seefield Ditch—*canal* ... MT-8
Seegar Ditch—*canal* ... IN-6
Seegars Point—*cape* ... VA-3
*Seeger* ... IL-6
Seeger Memorial Junior-Senior HS—*school* ... IN-6
*Seeger Memorial Sch* ... IN-6
Seeger Place—*locale* ... PA-2
Seeglitz JHS—*school* ... MA-1
Seegmiller Canyon—*valley* ... AZ-5
Seegmiller Mtn—*summit* ... AZ-5
Seegmiller Point—*cliff* ... AZ-5
Seegmiller Spring—*spring* ... AZ-5
Seegmiller Trick Tank—*reservoir* ... AZ-5
*Seegmuller Mountain* ... AZ-5
Seego Hollow—*valley* ... MO-7
Seehafer Sch—*school* ... ND-7
See Hollow—*valley* ... WV-2
*Seehoo Mountain* ... NV-8
Seehorn—*locale* ... IL-6
Seehorn Creek—*stream* ... TN-4
See House—*hist pl* ... AK-9
*Seeinsville* ... PA-2
**Seek**—*pop pl* ... PA-2
Seek and Follow Ch—*church* ... AL-4
Seekatz Cove—*bay* ... TX-5
Seekeks Lake—*lake* ... TX-5
Seekens Cem—*cemetery* ... ME-1
**Seekonk**—*pop pl* ... MA-1
*Seekonk Brook* ... MA-1
Seekonk Brook—*stream* ... MA-1
*Seekonk Cove* ... RI-1
Seekonk HS—*school* ... MA-1
Seekonk JHS—*school* ... MA-1
Seekonk River—*stream* ... RI-1
Seekonk Shop Ctr—*locale* ... MA-1
Seekonk Square—*locale* ... MA-1
Seekonk Townhall—*building* ... MA-1
**Seekonk (Town of)**—*pop pl* ... MA-1
*Seek-seek-qua Creek* ... OR-9
*Seekseekwa* ... OR-9
*Seekseekwa creek* ... OR-9
Seekseequa Cem—*cemetery* ... OR-9
Seekseequa Creek—*stream* ... OR-9
Seekseequa Junction—*locale* ... OR-9
Seekseequa Spring—*spring* ... OR-9
Seeks Village Res—*reserve* ... IN-6
Seekwell Ch—*church* ... SC-3
Seel, William, Bldg—*hist pl* ... PA-2
See Lake—*lake* ... MO-7
Seelander Creek—*stream* ... OR-9
Seelbach Branch—*stream* ... TX-5
Seelbach Hotel—*hist pl* ... KY-4
Seele Sch—*school* ... TX-5
Seeley—*locale* ... NJ-2
**Seeley**—*pop pl* ... CA-9
**Seeley**—*pop pl* ... WI-6
Seeley, Edward B., House—*hist pl* ... KY-4
Seeley, Justis Wellington II, House—*hist pl* ... UT-8
Seeley, Samuel W., House—*hist pl* ... NJ-2
Seeley, Uri, House—*hist pl* ... OH-6
Seeley Brook—*stream* ... NY-2
Seeley Brook—*stream* ... PA-2
Seeley Canyon—*valley* ... NM-5
Seeley Canyon—*valley* (2) ... UT-8
Seeley Cem—*cemetery* ... NY-2
Seeley Cem—*cemetery* ... OK-5
**Seeley Creek**—*pop pl* ... NY-2
Seeley Creek—*stream* ... CA-9
Seeley Creek—*stream* (2) ... MT-8
Seeley Creek—*stream* (3) ... NY-2
Seeley Creek—*stream* ... NC-3
Seeley Creek—*stream* (3) ... OR-9
Seeley Creek—*stream* ... PA-2
Seeley Creek—*stream* ... SC-3
Seeley Creek—*stream* ... WI-6
Seeley Drain—*canal* ... CA-9
Seeley Drain—*stream* (2) ... MI-6
Seeley Drain One—*canal* ... CA-9
Seeley Farmhouse—*hist pl* ... NY-2
Seeley Flat—*flat* ... CA-9
Seeley Hill—*summit* ... NY-2
Seeley Hill—*summit* ... VT-1
Seeley Hill Cem—*cemetery* ... PA-2
Seeley Hollow—*valley* (2) ... PA-2
Seeley Lake—*lake* ... AK-9
Seeley Lake—*lake* ... CO-8
Seeley Lake—*lake* ... MI-6
Seeley Lake—*lake* ... MT-8
Seeley Lake—*lake* ... WI-6
**Seeley Lake**—*pop pl* ... MT-8
Seeley Lake-Blackfoot Valley—*cens area* ... MT-8
Seeley Lake Campground—*locale* ... MT-8
Seeley Lake Game Preserve—*park* ... MT-8
Seeley Lake Ranger Station—*locale* ... MT-8
Seeley Lookout Tower—*locale* ... WI-6
Seeley Mtn—*summit* ... UT-8
Seeley Pond—*reservoir* ... NJ-2
Seeley Ranch—*locale* ... NE-7
Seeley Ranch—*locale* ... SD-7
Seeley Ranch—*locale* ... UT-8
Seeley Run—*stream* ... PA-2
*Seeleys* ... WI-6
**Seeleys**—*pop pl* ... WI-6
Seeley Sch—*school* ... CT-1
Seeley Sch—*school* (2) ... MI-6
Seeleys Pond—*lake* ... CT-1
Seeleys Pond—*reservoir* ... NJ-2
Seeleys Pond Dam—*dam* ... NJ-2
Seeley Spring—*spring* ... OR-9
Seeley Spring—*spring* ... UT-8
Seeley Spring—*spring* ... WA-9
*Seeley's Ranch* ... MT-8
Seeley Swan HS—*school* ... MT-8
Seeley Tank—*reservoir* ... AZ-5
*Seeleyville* ... PA-2
Seeley-Wick Oil Field—*oilfield* ... KS-7
Seelig Cem—*cemetery* ... OH-6
Seeliger Ranch—*locale* ... CA-9
Seeligson—*locale* ... TX-5
Seeligson Oil Field—*oilfield* ... TX-5
Seeligson Ranch—*locale* ... TX-5
Seeling Park—*park* ... TX-5
Seelmaer Hill—*summit* ... IN-6
Seelovers Spur—*locale* ... ID-8
Seely—*locale* ... WY-8
**Seely**—*pop pl* ... IL-6
Seely, Dr. John W., House—*hist pl* ... OH-6
Seely, John H., House—*hist pl* ... UT-8
Seely Brook—*stream* ... NY-2
Seely Cabin—*locale* ... UT-8
Seely Chapel—*church* ... OK-5
*Seely Creek* ... NY-2
*Seely Creek* ... PA-2
*Seely Creek* ... WI-6
Seely Creek—*stream* ... CA-9
Seely Creek—*stream* ... IA-7
Seely Creek—*stream* ... MI-6
Seely Creek—*stream* ... UT-8
Seely Creek Campground—*locale* ... UT-8
Seelye, A. B., House—*hist pl* ... KS-7
Seelye, Seth, House—*hist pl* ... CT-1
Seelye Brook—*stream* ... MN-6
Seelye Point—*cape* ... MN-6
Seely Fork—*stream* ... WY-8
Seely Guard Station—*locale* ... UT-8
Seely Hill—*summit* ... NY-2
Seely Hill—*summit* ... PA-2
Seely (historical)—*locale* ... KS-7
Seely Hollow—*valley* ... PA-2
*Seely Mountain* ... UT-8
Seely Ranch—*locale* ... WY-8
Seely School (abandoned)—*locale* ... MO-7
Seely Tank—*reservoir* ... AZ-5
Seelytown Creek—*stream* ... NY-2
Seely Township—*fmr MCD* ... IA-7
**Seely (Township of)**—*pop pl* ... MN-6
**Seelyville**—*pop pl* ... IN-6
**Seelyville**—*pop pl* ... PA-2
Seemalik Butte—*summit* ... AK-9
*Seeman Hills* ... WY-8
Seeman Park—*park* ... ND-7
*Seemans Hills* ... WY-8
Seematter Cem—*cemetery* ... MO-7
Seematter Hollow—*valley* ... MO-7
*S E Emmons Cemetery* ... AL-4
Seemo Creek—*stream* ... MT-8
Seemo Pass—*gap* ... MT-8
*See-Mor Lake* ... IN-6
Seemsville—*locale* ... PA-2
Seeneytown—*locale* ... DE-2
Seenic Hill Cem—*cemetery* ... IL-6
Seeny Lake—*lake* ... TX-5
See Off Mtn—*summit* ... NC-3
Seep, Bayou—*gut* ... LA-4
*Seep, The* ... UT-8
Seep, The—*gut* ... TX-5
Seep, The—*lake* ... NV-8
Seep, The—*spring* ... NM-5
Seep, The—*spring* ... TX-5
Seepage Canyon—*valley* ... AZ-5
Seepage Creek—*stream* ... CO-8
Seepage Creek—*stream* ... WY-8
Seepage Ditch—*canal* ... IL-6
Seepage Draw—*valley* ... WY-8
Seepage Lake—*reservoir* ... CO-8
Seepage Mtn—*summit* ... AZ-5
Seepage Spring—*spring* ... WA-9
Seepage Tank—*reservoir* ... AZ-5
Seepanpak Lagoon—*lake* ... AK-9
Seepay Creek—*stream* ... MT-8
Seep Canyon—*valley* (2) ... NM-5
Seep Canyon—*valley* (2) ... TX-5
Seep Canyon—*valley* (2) ... UT-8
Seep Creek—*stream* (2) ... CO-8
Seep Creek—*stream* ... MT-8
Seep Creek—*stream* ... UT-8
Seep Draw—*valley* ... TX-5
*Seepe Canyon* ... TX-5
Seepela Lake—*lake* ... MT-8
*Seepelo Lake* ... MT-8
Seep Flat—*flat* ... UT-8
Seep Gulch—*valley* ... CO-8
Seep Hole Spring—*spring* ... CA-9
Seep Hollow—*valley* (2) ... UT-8
Seeping Spring Gulch—*valley* ... CO-8
Seeping Springs Lakes—*lake* ... NM-5
Seeping Springs Windmill—*locale* ... TX-5
*Seepit River* ... MA-1
Seep Ridge—*ridge* ... UT-8
Seeps, The—*locale* ... UT-8
Seeps, The—*spring* ... CO-8
Seeps, The—*spring* ... NV-8
Seeps, The—*spring* ... SD-7
Seeps, The—*spring* (3) ... UT-8
Seeps, The—*spring* ... WY-8
Seeps, The—*stream* ... UT-8
Seep Spring—*spring* (8) ... AZ-5
Seep Spring—*spring* ... CA-9
Seep Spring—*spring* (3) ... NV-8
Seep Spring—*spring* ... NM-5
Seep Spring—*spring* (2) ... OR-9
Seep Spring—*spring* (2) ... TX-5
Seep Spring—*spring* (2) ... UT-8
Seep Spring, The—*spring* ... NM-5
Seep Spring Canyon—*valley* (3) ... AZ-5
Seep Spring Canyon—*valley* (2) ... NM-5
*Seep Spring Creek* ... UT-8
Seep Spring Draw—*valley* ... NM-5
Seep Spring Draw—*valley* ... TX-5
Seep Spring Hollow—*valley* ... MO-7
Seep Spring Mtn—*summit* ... AZ-5
Seep Spring Mtn—*summit* ... TX-5
*Seep Springs* ... UT-8
Seep Springs Canyon—*valley* ... NM-5
Seep Springs Draw—*valley* ... CO-8
Seep Springs Gap—*gap* ... NM-5
Seep Springs Hollow—*valley* ... TX-5
Seep Spring Tank—*reservoir* ... TX-5
Seeps Well—*well* ... NM-5
Seep Tank—*reservoir* (3) ... AZ-5
Seep Tank—*reservoir* ... NM-5
Seep Tank—*reservoir* ... TX-5
*Seep Wash* ... UT-8
Seep Wash—*valley* ... UT-8
Seep Well—*well* ... TX-5
Seepwell Ch—*church* ... MS-4
Seepy Tank—*reservoir* ... TX-5
Seer Creek—*bay* ... NC-3
Seering Island—*island* ... WI-6
Seerley Creek—*stream* ... IN-6
Seerley Creek Christian Ch—*church* ... IN-6
See Rocks—*summit* ... KY-4
*Seerum Brook* ... MA-1
Seery Cem—*cemetery* ... OH-6
Seesaw Tank—*reservoir* ... NM-5
Sees Chapel—*church* ... MS-4
*Sees Creek* ... MO-7
Sees Creek—*stream* ... MO-7
*See See Ah Creek* ... WA-9
Seese Run—*stream* ... PA-2
Seese Sch—*school* ... FL-3
See Shanty Run—*stream* ... WV-2
**Seeshore**—*pop pl* ... NC-3
Sees Old Mill—*locale* ... GA-3
See Spring—*spring* ... AZ-5
Seestrom Creek—*stream* ... OR-9
**Seetaga**—*pop pl* ... AS-9
**Se'etaga**—*pop pl* ... AS-9
See Tal Lake—*reservoir* ... MO-7
Seetau Island—*island* ... FM-9
Seevee Island—*island* ... FL-3
Seever Cem—*cemetery* ... OH-6
Seevookhan Mtn—*summit* ... AK-9
Seevoonah Mtn—*summit* ... AK-9
Seevoo Point—*cape* ... AK-9
See-Ward House—*hist pl* ... WV-2
Seewhy—*locale* ... MI-6
*Sefago Lake* ... MI-6
S & E Farms Independence Airstrip—*airport* ... OR-9
**Sefcikville**—*pop pl* ... TX-5
Seferino Canyon—*valley* ... NM-5
Seferino Hill—*summit* ... NM-5
Sefert Hill—*summit* ... IN-6
**Seffner**—*pop pl* ... FL-3
Seffner Elem Sch—*school* ... FL-3
Seffner Hills Acad—*school* ... FL-3
*Seford* ... DE-2
Sefrit, Mount—*summit* ... WA-9
Sefrna Sch—*school* ... SD-7
Sefton—*locale* ... IL-6
**Sefton (Township of)**—*pop pl* ... IL-6
*Segahatosi Canyon* ... AZ-5
Segaita Gun Club—*other* ... CA-9
Segal—*locale* ... KY-4
**Sega Lake**—*pop pl* ... NC-3
Segal Bldg—*hist pl* ... NJ-2
*Segal Creek* ... ID-8
Segal Ditch—*canal* ... IN-6
Segal Park—*park* ... FL-3
*Seganic Island* ... NY-2
Seganus Thatch—*island* ... NY-2
Segar Cem—*cemetery* ... NY-2
Segar Cove—*bay* ... RI-1
Segar Gulch—*valley* ... CO-8
Segar Gully—*valley* ... NY-2
Segar Mtn—*summit* ... CO-8
Segar Mtn—*summit* ... CT-1
Segar Mtn—*summit* ... VA-3
*Segar Pond* ... NY-2
**Segars**—*pop pl* ... SC-3
Segars Airp—*airport* ... MS-4
Segars Cem—*cemetery* ... MS-4
Segar Sch—*school* ... MI-6
*Segars Cove* ... RI-1
Segars Creek—*stream* ... MS-4
Segars Millpond—*reservoir* ... SC-3
Segars Mill Stream—*stream* ... SC-3
Segars Pond—*reservoir* ... GA-3
Segars Road Ch—*church* ... AL-4
Segaser Ranch—*locale* ... CA-9
Segassia Canyon—*valley* ... CA-9
**Segco**—*pop pl* ... AL-4
Segco Mine (underground)—*mine* ... AL-4
Sege Creek—*stream* ... WA-9
Segeke Butte—*summit* ... AZ-5
Segelke, C., Bldg—*hist pl* ... NE-7
Segelke Windmills—*locale* ... CO-8
Segelsen Creek—*stream* ... WA-9
Segelsen Lake—*lake* ... WA-9
Segelsen Ridge—*ridge* ... WA-9
Seger—*locale* ... TX-5
**Seger**—*pop pl* ... PA-2
Seger Recreation Center—*park* ... PA-2
*Seger Road Church* ... AL-4
Segers Hole—*basin* ... UT-8
Segerstrom Creek—*stream* ... CO-8
Segerstrom Creek—*stream* ... NM-5
*Segersville* ... PA-2
*Segetoa Spring* ... AZ-5
*Segeunkedunk Stream* ... ME-1
Seghers—*locale* ... OR-9
Seghis Lakes—*lake* ... PA-2
Segihatsosi Canyon—*valley* ... AZ-5
Segi Ho Cho Mesa—*summit* ... AZ-5
*Se-gi-ke Butte* ... AZ-5
Segi Mesas—*summit* ... AZ-5
Segito Canyon—*valley* ... AZ-5
**Seglar**—*pop pl* ... TX-5
Segloch Run—*stream* ... PA-2
*Seglock Run* ... PA-2
Segnette, Bayou—*stream* ... LA-4
Segnette Waterway, Bayou—*canal* ... LA-4
**Segno**—*pop pl* ... TX-5
Segno Oil Field—*oilfield* ... TX-5
Sego—*locale* ... UT-8
**Sego**—*pop pl* ... OH-6
Sego Canyon—*valley* ... UT-8
Sego Cem—*cemetery* ... KS-7
Sego Dam—*dam* ... NM-5
Sego Flat—*flat* ... UT-8
Sego (historical)—*locale* ... KS-7
Sego Island (historical)—*island* ... SD-7
Sego Lily Sch—*school* ... UT-8
Sego Place—*locale* ... ID-8
*Sego Presbyterian Church* ... AL-4
Sego Ridge—*ridge* ... CA-9
Sego Sch (historical)—*school* ... AL-4
Sego Spring—*spring* ... UT-8
Sego Springs—*spring* ... CO-8
Sego Tank—*reservoir* ... AZ-5
Segovia—*locale* ... TX-5
Seg Post Office (historical)—*building* ... TN-4
Segrado Carazon Windmill—*locale* ... TX-5
Segraves Mtn—*summit* ... NC-3
**Segreganset**—*pop pl* ... MA-1
Segreganset JHS—*school* ... MA-1
Segreganset River—*stream* ... MA-1
Segreganset River Dam—*dam* ... MA-1
Segreganset River Rsvr—*reservoir* ... MA-1
*Segregansett* ... MA-1
Segregated Iron Hill Mine—*mine* ... SD-7
Segrest Cem—*cemetery* ... MS-4
Segrest Draw—*valley* ... NM-5
Segrest-Gibson Cem—*cemetery* ... AL-4
Segrest Waterhole—*reservoir* ... NM-5
Seguam Island—*island* ... AK-9
Seguam Pass—*channel* ... AK-9
**Segui**—*pop pl* ... PR-3
**Seguin**—*pop pl* ... KS-7
**Seguin**—*pop pl* ... TX-5
Seguin Auxiliary Airfield—*military* ... TX-5
Seguin Branch—*stream* ... TX-5
Seguin (CCD)—*cens area* ... TX-5
Seguin Commercial Hist Dist—*hist pl* ... TX-5
Seguin East (CCD)—*cens area* ... TX-5
Seguine House—*hist pl* ... NY-2
Seguine Point—*cape* ... NY-2
Seguine Point Bend—*bend* ... NY-2
Seguin Island—*island* (2) ... ME-1
Seguin Ledge—*bar* ... ME-1
Seguin Ledges—*bar* ... ME-1
Seguin North (CCD)—*cens area* ... TX-5
Seguin Passage—*channel* ... ME-1
Seguin Sch—*school* ... IL-6
Seguin Southwest (CCD)—*cens area* ... TX-5
Segula Island—*island* ... AK-9
Segula Pass—*channel* ... AK-9
Segula Peak—*summit* ... AK-9
Segunda Creek—*stream* ... NV-8
Segunda Deshecha Canada —*valley* ... CA-9
Segunda Tank—*reservoir* ... TX-5
**Segundo**—*pop pl* ... CO-8
Segundo, Arroyo—*valley* ... TX-5
Segundo (Barrio)—*fmr MCD* ... PR-3
Segundo Canyon—*valley* ... UT-8
**Segundo Castillo**—*pop pl* ... PR-3
Segundo Ditch—*canal* ... OR-9
Segundo Spring—*spring* ... OR-9
Segur—*locale* ... AR-4
**Segura**—*pop pl* ... LA-4
Segura Branch Canal—*canal* ... LA-4
Segura Ranch—*locale* ... NV-8
Segura-Saenz Cem—*cemetery* ... TX-5
Segura Spring—*spring* ... NV-8
Seguro—*locale* ... CA-9
Seguro Canyon—*valley* ... CO-8
Seguro Canyon—*valley* ... NM-5
*Seguva River* ... FL-3
**Segwun**—*pop pl* ... MI-6
Seha Sorghum Mill—*hist pl* ... MN-6
*Sehcee Creek* ... WA-9
Seher, William, House—*hist pl* ... OH-6
*Sehesengel* ... PW-9
*Sehili* ... AZ-5
Sehili—*locale* ... AZ-5
Sehkapw—*island* ... FM-9
*Sehler* ... MI-6
Sehm Wahu—*unknown* ... FM-9
Sehome Hill—*summit* ... WA-9
Sehome Hill Park—*park* ... WA-9
Sehome HS—*school* ... WA-9
Sehoo Mtn—*summit* ... NV-8
Sehorn Creek—*stream* ... CA-9
*Sehorns Creek* ... TN-4
Sehoy Airp—*airport* ... AL-4
Sehoy Dam—*dam* ... AL-4
Sehoy Lake—*reservoir* ... AL-4
Sehoy Plantation Lake Dam—*dam* ... AL-4
Sehp—*locale* ... FM-9
*Seh-quu River* ... WA-9
*Sehrader Creek* ... KS-7
Sehrt Creek—*stream* ... MO-7
*Sehuster Creek* ... UT-8
Seiad Creek—*stream* ... CA-9
**Seiad Valley**—*pop pl* ... CA-9
Seiad Valley—*valley* ... CA-9
Seiba Point—*cape* ... AK-9
Seibel Cave—*cave* ... PA-2
*Seiben Creek* ... CO-8
Seiber Cem—*cemetery* ... TN-4
Seiber Chapel (historical)—*church* ... TN-4
Seiberling Mansion—*hist pl* ... IN-6
Seiberling Sch—*school* ... OH-6
*Seiberlingsville* ... PA-2
Seiberlingville—*locale* ... PA-2
Seiber Point—*cliff* ... AZ-5
**Seibert**—*pop pl* (2) ... CO-8
Seibert, Henry J., II, House—*hist pl* ... WV-2
Seibert Ch—*church* ... PA-2
Seibert Creek—*stream* ... KY-4
Seibert Sch—*school* ... CA-9
Seibert Sch (historical)—*school* ... MO-7
Seiberts Creek—*stream* ... MI-6
Sei Betoh—*spring* ... AZ-5
Sei Be Toh—*well* ... AZ-5
Sei Billikoon—*stream* ... UT-8
Seibold Branch—*stream* ... AL-4
Seibold Branch—*stream* ... NC-3
Seibold Ranch—*locale* ... AZ-5
Seidel Creek—*stream* ... PA-2
Seidel Creek—*stream* ... WA-9
Seidel Creek—*stream* ... WI-6
Seidel Hill—*summit* ... PA-2
Seidel Lake—*lake* ... WI-6
Seidel Sch—*school* ... PA-2
Seidels Hill—*summit* ... PA-2
Seideltown Sch—*school* ... PA-2
Seidenberd Canal—*canal* ... ID-8
Seidensticker Ditch—*canal* ... MT-8
Seidensticker Number Two Spring—*spring* ... MT-8
Seider Coulee—*valley* ... MT-8
Seiders Sch (abandoned)—*school* ... PA-2
*Seiders Tavern* ... PA-2
Seidersville—*locale* ... PA-2
Seidihne—*locale* ... FM-9
Seidler Beach—*beach* ... NJ-2
**Seidler Corners**—*pop pl* ... MI-6
Seidlers—*locale* ... MI-6
*Seidl Lake* ... WI-6
Seifarth Cem—*cemetery* ... TN-4
*Seifarths Landing* ... AL-4
Seif Cem—*cemetery* ... WI-6
Seifers Gulch—*valley* ... CO-8
**Seifert Corners**—*pop pl* ... NY-2
Seifert Ranch—*locale* ... MT-8
**Seif (Town of)**—*pop pl* ... WI-6
*Seigal Creek* ... ID-8
Seigal Mtn—*summit* ... CO-8
*Seiganaga Lake* ... MN-6
*Seiganagaw lake* ... MN-6
*Seiganagooh Lake* ... MN-6
Seigars Cem—*cemetery* ... ME-1
**Seigel**—*pop pl* ... IA-7
Seigel Administrative Site—*locale* ... NV-8
*Seigel Creek* ... ID-8
*Seigel Creek* ... NV-8
*Seigel Mines* ... NV-8
Seigel Sch—*school* ... IL-6
*Seigers* ... MS-4
Seigers Post Office (historical)—*building* ... MS-4
*Seigersville* ... PA-2
Seights Creek—*stream* ... IA-7
Seigle Homestead—*hist pl* ... NJ-2
Seigler Canyon—*valley* ... CA-9
Seigler Canyon Creek—*stream* ... CA-9
Seigler Cem—*cemetery* ... SC-3
Seigler Mtn—*summit* ... CA-9
**Seiglers Crossroads**—*pop pl* ... SC-3
*Seigler Spring* ... CA-9
**Seigler Springs**—*pop pl* ... CA-9
Seigler Valley—*valley* ... CA-9
Seigling—*locale* ... SC-3
*Seiglingville* ... SC-3
Seig Ponds—*lake* ... OR-9
Seigrist's Mill Covered Bridge—*hist pl* ... PA-2
Seigs Hill—*summit* ... IN-6
Sei Haasgaii Wash—*stream* ... AZ-5
Seikel Creek—*stream* ... CA-9
**Seilcrest Acres**—*pop pl* ... OH-6
Seiler Bldg—*hist pl* ... ND-7
Seiler Elem Sch—*school* ... PA-2
Seilers Dam—*dam* ... SD-7
**Seiling**—*pop pl* ... OK-5
Seiling (CCD)—*cens area* ... OK-5
Seiling Creek—*stream* ... OK-5
Seiling Milling Company—*hist pl* ... OK-5
*Seilz Creek* ... CO-8
Seim Dam—*dam* ... ND-7
Seim Lake—*lake* ... MN-6
Seim Township—*civil* ... SD-7
*Sein Creek* ... OR-9
Seine Bay—*bay* ... NY-2
*Seine Creek* ... OR-9
Seine Creek—*stream* ... GA-3
Seine Hill—*summit* ... WI-6
Seine Pond—*lake* ... MA-1
Seiners Creek—*stream* ... MI-6
Seiners Point—*cape* ... MI-6
*Seines Creek* ... IN-6
Seines Landing—*locale* ... GA-3
Seinwar—*civil* ... FM-9
*Seipan* ... MH-9
Seip Earthworks and Dill Mounds District—*hist pl* ... OH-6
*Seiper Creek* ... LA-4
Seip House—*hist pl* ... OH-6
Seiple—*locale* ... PA-2
*Seiples Station* ... PA-2
Seip Mound State Memorial—*locale* ... OH-6
Seipon—*tunnel* ... FM-9
Seipp Sch—*school* ... IL-6
*Seips* ... PA-2
Seips Sch (abandoned)—*school* ... PA-2
**Seipstown**—*pop pl* ... PA-2
*Seipsville* ... PA-2
Seipsville—*other* ... PA-2
Seipsville Hotel—*hist pl* ... PA-2
Seisein—*summit* ... FM-9
Seisholtzville—*locale* ... PA-2
Seismo Creek—*stream* ... AK-9
Seismograph Rsvr No 2—*reservoir* ... WY-8
Seismograph Rsvr No 3—*reservoir* ... WY-8
Seis-wilson Detention Dam No 1—*dam* ... NM-5
Seis-wilson Detention Dam No 2—*dam* ... NM-5
Seis-wilson Dike and Pit No 2—*mine* ... NM-5
Seis-Wilson Ranch—*locale* ... NM-5
Seiten—*locale* ... FM-9
Seiter, Joseph, House—*hist pl* ... KY-4
Seiter Park—*park* ... IL-6
Seites Cem—*cemetery* ... WV-2
Seits Ridge—*ridge* ... OR-9
**Seitter Acres (subdivision)**—*pop pl* ... NC-3
Seitz—*locale* ... KY-4
Seitz Canyon—*valley* ... NV-8
Seitz Cem—*cemetery* ... MS-4
Seitz Cem—*cemetery* ... PA-2
Seitz Creek—*stream* ... CO-8
Seitz Drain—*stream* ... MI-6
Seitz Field—*airport* ... PA-2
Seitz (historical)—*locale* ... MS-4
Seitz JHS—*school* ... MI-6
Seitz Lake—*lake* ... NV-8
Seitz Lake—*lake* ... WI-6
Seitz Lake Dam—*dam* ... MS-4
**Seitzland**—*pop pl* ... PA-2
Seitz Sch—*school* ... PA-2
*Seitzville* ... PA-2
Seitzville—*locale* ... PA-2
**Seivern**—*pop pl* ... SC-3
Seivers Brothers Ranchhouse and Barn—*hist pl* ... WA-9
Seivers Cem—*cemetery* ... TN-4
**Seivert Township**—*pop pl* ... ND-7
Sejita—*locale* ... TX-5
Sejita Oil Field—*oilfield* ... TX-5
Sekere—*civil* ... FM-9
Sekeren—*cape* ... FM-9
Sekeren Iap—*locale* ... FM-9
Sekeren Kahle—*locale* ... FM-9
Sekeren Lapahu—*locale* ... FM-9
Sekeren Pei—*locale* ... FM-9
*Sekeren Peilong* ... FM-9
Sekeren Senipohn—*swamp* ... FM-9
Sekere Riau—*unknown* ... FM-9
Sekereriau, Pilap En—*stream* ... FM-9
Sekinak Lagoon—*bay* ... AK-9
*Sekiou Point* ... WA-9
*Sekiou River* ... WA-9
**Sekiu**—*pop pl* ... WA-9
Sekiu Airp—*airport* ... WA-9
Sekiu Mtn—*summit* ... WA-9
Sekiu Point—*cape* ... WA-9
*Sekiu River* ... WA-9
Sekiu River—*stream* ... WA-9
*Seklagaidesa Canyon* ... AZ-5
Seknak River—*stream* ... AK-9
*Sekou Point* ... WA-9

Sekou River WA-9
Sekuiak Bluff—cliff AK-9
Sekwan Peak CA-9
S E Lackey Hospital MS-4
Selado Creek CO-8
**Selah**—pop pl WA-9
Selah Butte—summit WA-9
Selah Ch—church NC-3
Selah Christian Acad—school FL-3
Selah Creek—stream WA-9
Selah Heights—summit WA-9
**Selah (historical)**—pop pl OR-9
Selah Moxee Irrigation Canal—canal WA-9
Selah Springs—spring WA-9
Selah Tabernacle—church FL-3
Selah Valley—valley WA-9
Selah Valley Canal—canal WA-9
Selap, Foko—reef FM-9
Selaris Lake—lake TN-4
Selat, Mount—summit AK-9
SE Lateral—canal TX-5
Selatna Mtn—summit AK-9
Selatna River—stream AK-9
**Selawik**—pop pl AK-9
Selawik Hills—other AK-9
Selawik Lake—lake AK-9
Selawik River—stream AK-9
Selba Dalkai Spring AZ-5
Selbee Branch—stream WV-2
Selbie Bldg—hist pl SD-7
Selbrook Park—park AL-4
**Selbrook (subdivision)**—pop pl AL-4
Selbu Ch—church WA-9
Selby MD-2
Selby—locale CA-9
Selby—locale ID-8
**Selby**—pop pl SD-7
Selby, Lake—lake AK-9
Selby, Orland, House—hist pl OH-6
Selby Bay—bay MD-2
**Selby Beach**—pop pl MD-2
Selby Branch—stream KY-4
Selby Branch—stream MS-4
Selby Caves—cave TN-4
Selby Cem—cemetery (2) TN-4
Selby Creek—stream TN-4
Selby Draw—valley WY-8
Selby Field—hist pl OH-6
Selby Flat—flat CA-9
Selby Grove Sch—school CA-9
Selby Gut MD-2
Selby Hill—summit GA-3
**Selby (historical)**—pop pl TN-4
Selby Hosp—hospital OH-6
Selby Knob—summit OH-6
Selby Lane Sch—school CA-9
Selby Mill Branch—stream VA-3
Selby-on-the-Bay MD-2
Selby-on-the-Bay—CDP MD-2
Selby Opera House—hist pl SD-7
Selby Pond—lake CT-1
Selby Post Office (historical)—building TN-4
Selby Public Library—building FL-3
Selby Ranch—locale CA-9
Selby Ranch Cow Camp—locale CA-9
Selby Resort—locale MT-8
Selby River—stream AK-9
Selby's Bay MD-2
Selby Sch—school (2) MI-6
Selbys Gut—stream MD-2
Selbys Landing—locale MD-2
**Selbysport**—pop pl MD-2
Selby Spring—spring AL-4
**Selby (Township of)**—pop pl IL-6
Selby Union Cem—cemetery SD-7
**Selbyville**—pop pl DE-2
**Selbyville**—pop pl WV-2
Selbyville-Frankford (CCD)—cens area DE-2
Selbyville MS—school DE-2
Selby Windmill—locale NE-7
Selcer Branch—stream VA-3
Selck and Taylor Canal—canal ID-8
Selden OH-6
Selden—fmr MCD NE-7
Selden—locale ME-1
Selden—locale VA-3
**Selden**—pop pl KS-7
**Selden**—pop pl NY-2
**Selden**—pop pl TX-5
Selden Bicycle Path Sch—school NY-2
Selden Cem—cemetery CT-1
Selden Cem—cemetery KS-7
Selden Cem—cemetery ME-1
Selden Cove—bay CT-1
Selden Creek—stream CT-1
Selden Drain—canal NM-5
Selden Island—island MD-2
Selden Island Site—hist pl CT-1
Selden Neck—cape CT-1
Selden Neck State Park—park CT-1
Selden Pass—gap CA-9
Selden's Island MD-2
Selder Creek—stream OR-9
Selders Creek OR-9
Selders Lake—lake MI-6
Selders Ranch—locale CO-8
**Seldersville**—pop pl PA-2
Seldevoe Lagoon—lake AK-9
Seldom Cem—cemetery CT-1
Seldom Creek—stream OR-9
Seldom Point—cape VA-3
Seldom Ridge Draw—valley CO-8
Seldom Rsvr—reservoir OR-9
Seldom Seen Corners—locale PA-2
Seldom Seen Hollow—valley PA-2
Seldom Seen Hollow—valley VA-3
Seldom Seen Hollow—valley WV-2
Seldom Seen Mtn—summit WA-9
Seldom Seen Park MT-8
Seldom Seen Park—flat MT-8
Seldom Seen Point—cape GA-3
Seldom Seen Pond—lake CT-1
Seldom Seen Sch—school WV-2
Seldon Park—park GA-3
Seldon Pass CA-9
Seldon Skidmore Site—hist pl KY-4
Seldons Store—locale VA-3
**Seldovia**—pop pl AK-9
Seldovia Bay—bay AK-9
Seldovia Lagoon—lake AK-9
Seldovia Lake—lake AK-9
Seldovia Point—cape AK-9
Seldovia River—stream AK-9
Seldovia Slough—gut AK-9
Sele FM-9
Selea—locale PA-2
**Selea (Brownsville)**—pop pl PA-2
Select—locale KY-4
**Selection**—pop pl IA-7
Select Private Sch (historical)—school MS-4
Seledonio—canal CO-8
Seleeta Cemetery AL-4
Selema Hall—hist pl KY-4
Selena Baptist Ch—church AL-4
Selene Bayou—stream LA-4
Selenie Lagoon AK-9
Selenie Lagoon Archeol Site—hist pl AK-9
Selenite Peak—summit NV-8
Selenite Range—range NV-8
Selesian Sch—school NY-2
Seles Point—flat LA-4
Seleta Cem—cemetery AL-4
Seley Sch—school NY-2
Selezen Bay—bay AK-9
Selezen Point—cape AK-9
Self FL-3
Self—locale AR-4
Self, James C., House—hist pl SC-3
Self Bayou—stream TX-5
Self Branch MO-7
Self Branch—stream AR-4
Self Cem—cemetery (2) LA-4
Self Cem—cemetery MO-7
Self Cem—cemetery (2) TN-4
Self Chapel Sch—school MO-7
Self Creek—locale AL-4
**Self Creek**—pop pl MS-4
Self Creek—stream (2) AL-4
Self Creek—stream AR-4
Self Creek—stream (2) MS-4
Self Creek—stream TX-5
Self Creek Bible Baptist Church MS-4
Self Creek Cem—cemetery MS-4
Self Creek Ch—church MS-4
Self Creek Christian Acad—school MS-4
Self Creek Consolidated Sch (historical)—school MS-4
Self Creek Mine (underground)—mine AL-4
Self Creek Public Use Area—park AR-4
Self Creek Southern Baptist Church MS-4
Self Creek (Township of)—fmr MCD AR-4
Self Dam—dam AL-4
Self Drift Mine (underground)—mine AL-4
Selfe Cem—cemetery VA-3
Self Farm Slough TN-4
Self Help Hollow—valley ID-8
Self Help Spring—spring ID-8
Self Hollow—valley (2) TN-4
Selfice Swamp—swamp PA-2
Selfield Airp—airport AL-4
Self Island—island IN-6
Self Lake—reservoir GA-3
Self Landing—locale TN-4
Self-locking Carton Company Lower Dam MA-1
Self-locking Carton Company Upper Dam MA-1
Self Memorial Hosp—hospital SC-3
Self Mountain—ridge AL-4
Self Mtn—summit AR-4
Self Mtn—summit GA-3
Self Mtn—summit OK-5
Selfour Ranch—locale WY-8
Self Place—locale NM-5
**Selfridge**—pop pl ND-7
Self Ridge—ridge CA-9
Selfridge AFB—military MI-6
Selfridge Air Natl Guard Base—building MI-6
**Selfridge Aviation Field Siding (RR name)**—pop pl MI-6
Selfridge Base—other MI-6
Selfridge-Capehart (census name Sebille Manor)—other MI-6
Selfridge Cem—cemetery GA-3
Selfridge Knoll—summit WI-6
Selfridge Sch—school MI-6
**Selfs**—pop pl TX-5
Selfs Airp—airport MS-4
Solfs Branch TX-5
Self Settlement AL-4
Selfs Lake—reservoir VA-3
Self Slough—stream TN-4
**Selfville**—pop pl AL-4
Selfville Ch—church AL-4
Selfville Fire House—building AL-4
Selgar Family Cem—cemetery AL-4
**Selgas**—pop pl PR-3
Selgato Canyon—valley CA-9
**Selhaven (subdivision)**—pop pl FL-3
**Selica**—pop pl NC-3
Selic Canyon—valley CA-9
Selief Bay—bay AK-9
Selie (historical P.O.)—locale AL-4
Selig Canal—canal CO-8
**Seligman**—pop pl AZ-5
**Seligman**—pop pl MO-7
Seligman Airp—airport AZ-5
Seligman Canyon—valley AZ-5
Seligman Canyon—valley NV-8
Seligman Cem—cemetery MO-7
Seligman Compressor Station—other AZ-5
Seligman Dam—dam AZ-5
Seligman Elementary and HS—school AZ-5
Seligman Hollow—valley (2) MO-7
Seligman Interchange—crossing AZ-5
Seligman Junction Substation—locale AZ-5
Seligman Mine—mine NV-8
Seligman Post Office—building AZ-5
Seligman RR Station—building AZ-5
Seligman Spring—spring NV-8
Seligman Substation—locale AZ-5
Selig's Dry Goods Company Bldg—hist pl IN-6
Selina SD-7
Selin Creek—stream AK-9
Selins Grove PA-2
**Selinsgrove**—pop pl PA-2
Selinsgrove Area MS—school PA-2
Selinsgrove Borough—civil PA-2
Selinsgrove Creek—stream PA-2
Selinsgrove Elem Sch—school PA-2
Selinsgrove Hall and Seibert Hall—hist pl PA-2
Selinsgrove Junction—locale PA-2
Selinsgrove State Colony PA-2
Selinsgrove State School And Hosp—hospital PA-2
Selinsky Lake—lake MN-6
Selisa MD-2
Selisco Creek TX-5
Selish Lake MT-8
Seljord Ch—church MN-6
Selke Valley—valley MN-6
Selking Ditch—canal IN-6
Selkirk—locale PA-2
**Selkirk**—pop pl KS-7
**Selkirk**—pop pl MI-6
**Selkirk**—pop pl (2) NY-2
**Selkirk Beach**—pop pl NY-2
Selkirk Canyon UT-8
Selkirk Farm—hist pl SC-3
Selkirk Gulch—valley CO-8
**Selkirk (historical)**—pop pl TN-4
Selkirk HS—school WA-9
Selkirk Island—island TX-5
**Selkirk Junction**—pop pl NY-2
Selkirk Lake MI-6
Selkirk Lake—lake MI-6
Selkirk Lakes MI-6
Selkirk Lighthouse—hist pl NY-2
Selkirk Mountains—summit WA-9
Selkirk Post Office (historical)—building TN-4
Selkirk Sch (historical)—school PA-2
Selkirk Shores State Park—park NY-2
Selkirk Yards—locale NY-2
Selk State Wildlife Mngmt Area—park MN-6
Sell—locale WV-2
**Sell**—pop pl PA-2
Sella—area GU-9
**Sella**—pop pl GU-9
Sella Bay—bay GU-9
Sella Bay Site—hist pl GU-9
Sellar Creek—stream CO-8
Sellards Branch—stream WV-2
Sellards Lake—lake MN-6
Sella River—stream GU-9
Sellar Lake—lake CO-8
Sellar Park—flat CO-8
Sellar Peak—summit CO-8
Sellars WV-2
Sellars—locale KY-4
Sellars Cem—cemetery NC-3
Sellars Creek—stream ID-8
Sellars Creek—stream (2) MO-7
Sellars Fork—stream KY-4
Sellars HS—school NC-3
Sellars Indian Mound—hist pl TN-4
Sellars Lake FL-3
Sellars Memorial Park—park NC-3
Sellars Portrero—flat CA-9
Sellars Store—locale GA-3
Sell Branch—stream AL-4
Sell Branch—stream IN-6
Sell Cem—cemetery IL-6
Sell Cem—cemetery OH-6
Selle—locale ID-8
**Selleck**—pop pl WA-9
Selleck Drain—stream MI-6
Selleck-Espeland Ditch—canal MT-8
Sellecks Corners—locale NY-2
**Sellecks Corners**—pop pl CT-1
Selleck-Scott Ditch—canal MT-8
Sellecks Lower Camp—locale NY-2
Selle Gap—gap OR-9
Selle Gap Rsvr—reservoir OR-9
Selle Gap Rsvr Number Two—reservoir OR-9
Selleh Park—park AZ-5
S Ellen Jones Elem Sch—school IN-6
Sellen Lake—lake AK-9
Sellen Lake—lake MI-6
Sellens Creek—stream KS-7
Seller Cem—cemetery PA-2
Seller Cem—cemetery TX-5
Seller Creek KS-7
Sellers WV-2
Sellers—fmr MCD NE-7
Sellers—locale IL-6
Sellers—locale LA-4
Sellers—locale MO-7
**Sellers**—pop pl AL-4
**Sellers**—pop pl (2) MS-4
**Sellers**—pop pl SC-3
Sellers, Salome, House—hist pl ME-1
Sellers Airp—airport MO-7
Sellers Bar—bar AL-4
Sellers Bear Hole—lake FL-3
Sellers Bluff—cliff TN-4
Sellers Branch—stream AL-4
Sellers Branch—stream NC-3
Sellers Branch—stream TN-4
Sellers Bridge—bridge MS-4
**Sellersburg**—pop pl IN-6
Sellers Butte—summit OR-9
Sellers Canal—canal LA-4
Sellers Cem MS-4
Sellers Cem—cemetery AL-4
Sellers Cem—cemetery FL-3
Sellers Cem—cemetery (2) GA-3
Sellers Cem—cemetery (2) MS-4
Sellers Cem—cemetery OK-5
Sellers Cem—cemetery OR-9
Sellers Cem—cemetery TN-4
Sellers Cem—cemetery VA-3
Sellers Cem—cemetery WV-2
Sellers Ch—church MO-7
Sellers Creek—stream AL-4
Sellers Creek—stream AR-4
Sellers Creek—stream MI-6
Sellers Creek—stream (2) MS-4
Sellers Creek—stream OR-9
**Sellers Crossroads**—pop pl AL-4
Sellers - Crowell Rsvr—reservoir CO-8
Sellers Ditch—canal IN-6
Sellers Ditch—canal KY-4
Sellers Farm—hist pl AR-4
Sellers Field—flat NC-3
Sellers Field—park NY-2
Sellers Fishpond—reservoir AL-4
Sellers Gulch—valley CO-8
Sellers Hill—summit TX-5
Sellers Hole—bend CO-8
Sellers Hollow—valley AL-4
Sellers Hollow—valley (2) MO-7
Sellers Hollow—valley TN-4
Sellers House—hist pl PA-2
Sellers Lake—dam NC-3
Sellers Lake—lake FL-3
Sellers Lake—lake IN-6
Sellers Lake—lake TX-5
Sellers Lake—lake WA-9
**Sellers Lake**—pop pl IN-6
Sellers Lake—reservoir AL-4
Sellers Lake—reservoir NC-3
Sellers Lake Dam—dam (2) MS-4
Sellers Lake Number Four—reservoir AL-4
Sellers Lake Number Three—reservoir AL-4
Sellers Lake Number Two—reservoir AL-4
Sellers Landing—locale AL-4
Sellers Landing Strip—airport NC-3
Sellers Lookout Tower—locale MS-4
Sellers Manufacturing Company Lak reservoir NC-3
Sellers Marsh—swamp OR-9
Sellers Memorial Ch—church AL-4
Sellers Mfg Company Dam—dam NC-3
Sellers Mtn—summit OK-5
Sellers Mtn—summit WY-8
Sellers Point—cape OH-6
**Sellers Point**—pop pl OH-6
Sellers Pond—reservoir SC-3
Sellers Ponds—reservoir AL-4
Sellers Potrero CA-9
Sellers Prairie—flat FL-3
Seller Spring—spring AZ-5
Sellers Ridge—ridge AR-4
Sellers Ridge—ridge KY-4
Sellers Run—stream KY-4
Sellers Sch—school CA-9
Sellers Sch (historical)—school MS-4
Sellers School (historical)—locale MO-7
Sellers Shoal (historical)—bar AL-4
**Sellers Store**—pop pl AR-4
Sellers Store (historical)—locale (2) AL-4
Sellers Tank—reservoir AZ-5
Sellers Tavern PA-2
Sellersville—locale FL-3
**Sellersville**—pop pl AL-4
**Sellersville**—pop pl PA-2
Sellersville Borough—civil PA-2
Sellersville Cem—cemetery FL-3
Sellersville Ch—church AL-4
Sellersville Ch—church FL-3
Sellersville Elem Sch—school PA-2
Sellersville Post Office (historical)—building PA-2
Sellery Sch—school CA-9
Selle Sch (abandoned)—school MO-7
Sell Field—park PA-2
Sellick Creek—stream AK-9
Sellie Dam—dam ND-7
Sellier Creek—stream CA-9
Selliez Spring—spring WY-8
Sellin Lake—lake WI-6
Sell Lake—lake CO-8
Sell Lake Ch—church MN-6
Sellman—locale MD-2
**Sellman**—pop pl TX-5
**Sellman (Barnesville (sta.))**—pop pl MD-2
Sellman Berth—rock MA-1
Sellman Creek—bay MD-2
Sellman Creek Marsh—swamp MD-2
Sellman Recreation Center—building MD-2
Sellmans Creek MD-2
Sellpaws Landing TN-4
**Sells**—pop pl AZ-5
**Sells**—pop pl GA-3
Sells, Benjamin, Barn #1—hist pl OH-6
Sells, Benjamin, Barn #2—hist pl OH-6
Sells, Benjamin, House—hist pl OH-6
Sells, Benjamin, Wash House—hist pl OH-6
Sells, David, Barn—hist pl OH-6
Sells, Eliud, House—hist pl OH-6
Sells, William Henry, House—hist pl OH-6
Sells Airp—airport AZ-5
Sells Cave—cave AL-4
Sells Cave—cave TN-4
Sells Cem—cemetery IN-6
Sells Cem—cemetery TN-4
Sells Cemetary—cemetery TN-4
Sells Consolidated Sch—school AZ-5
Sells Hollow—valley KY-4
Sells Knob—summit VA-3
Sells Lake—lake (2) MN-6
Sells Lake—lake (2) WI-6
Sells Lateral—canal CA-9
Sells Mill Creek—stream TN-4
Sells (Papago Agency)—CDP AZ-5
Sells Papago Indian Agency AZ-5
Sells Sch—school MO-7
Sells Station—locale PA-2
Sells Tunnel—mine UT-8
Sells Valley—valley AZ-5
Sells Valley—valley NE-7
Sells Valley Cem—cemetery NE-7
Sells Wash AZ-5
Sells Wash—stream AZ-5
Sells Well—well TX-5
**Sellwood**—pop pl OR-9
Sellwood Bridge—bridge OR-9
Sellwood Creek—stream MI-6
Sellwood-Moreland OR-9
Sellwood Moreland—uninc pl OR-9
Sellwood Park—park OR-9
Sellwood Sch—school OR-9
Selma AL-4
Selma—locale AR-4
Selma—locale CO-8
Selma—locale MI-6
Selma—locale MS-4
**Selma**—pop pl AL-4
**Selma**—pop pl CA-9
**Selma**—pop pl IN-6
**Selma**—pop pl IA-7
**Selma**—pop pl KS-7
**Selma**—pop pl LA-4
**Selma**—pop pl MO-7
**Selma**—pop pl NC-3
**Selma**—pop pl OH-6
**Selma**—pop pl OR-9
**Selma**—pop pl SC-3
**Selma**—pop pl (3) TX-5
**Selma**—pop pl (2) VA-3
Selma Airp—airport IN-6
Selma Airp—airport NC-3
Selma Ave Baptist Ch—church AL-4
Selma Ave Sch—school CA-9
Selma Baptist Ch AL-4
Selma Bar—bar AL-4
Selma Baseball Park AL-4
Selma Branch—canal CA-9
Selma Branch Ditch—canal CA-9
Selmac, Lake—lake OR-9
Selmac, Lake—reservoir OR-9
Selma (CCD)—cens area AL-4
Selma (CCD)—cens area CA-9
Selmac County Park, Lake—park OR-9
Selma Cem—cemetery AL-4
Selma Cem—cemetery FL-3
Selma Cem—cemetery MI-6
Selma Cem—cemetery OR-9
Selma Cem—cemetery TX-5
Selma Center School—locale MI-6
Selma Ch—church (2) AL-4
Selma Ch—church OH-6
Selma Ch—church SC-3
Selma City Hall—building AL-4
Selma City Marina—locale AL-4
Selma Colony Ditch—canal CA-9
**Selma Cotton Mills**—pop pl NC-3
Selma Country Club—other AL-4
Selma Creek—arroyo TX-5
Selma Creek—stream NC-3
Selma Ditch—canal IL-6
Selma Division—civil AL-4
Selma Elem Sch—school IN-6
Selma Elem Sch—school NC-3
Selma Free Will Baptist Ch—church NC-3
Selma High School AL-4
Selma (historical)—locale IA-7
Selma Hollow—valley MO-7
Selma Hunting Club—locale AL-4
Selma Hunting Club Lake—reservoir AL-4
Selma Hunting Club Lake Dam—dam AL-4
Selma Infirmary (historical)—hospital AL-4
Selma JHS—school AR-4
Selma Mall Shop Ctr—locale AL-4
Selma Memorial Cem—cemetery NC-3
Selma Memorial Gardens (Cemetery)—cemetery NC-3
Selma Methodist Church—hist pl AR-4
Selma Mine—mine UT-8
Selma MS—school IN-6
Selman—locale FL-3
Selman—locale TX-5
**Selman**—pop pl OK-5
Selman Canyon—valley TX-5
Selman Cem—cemetery TX-5
**Selman City**—pop pl TX-5
Selman Creek—stream GA-3
Selman Drain—stream MI-6
Selman Draw—valley NM-5
Selman Lake—reservoir GA-3
Selman Lakes—lake GA-3
Selmann Creek GA-3
Selman Rsvr—reservoir UT-8
Selmans Lake—reservoir GA-3
Selman Tank—reservoir AZ-5
Selman Tank—reservoir NM-5
Selman Tank—reservoir TX-5
Selman Windmill—locale NM-5
Selma Plantation MS-4
Selma Post Office—building TN-4
Selma Sch—school MI-6
Selma Sch—school MO-7
Selma Speedway—other CA-9
Selma State Docks AL-4
Selma State Park—park AL-4
Selma (Station)—locale MO-7
Selma Street Elementary School AL-4
Selma Street Sch—school AL-4
**Selma Subdivision**—pop pl UT-8
Selma (Township of)—fmr MCD NC-3
**Selma (Township of)**—pop pl MI-6
**Selma (Township of)**—pop pl MN-6
Selma Union Cem—cemetery ND-7
Selma Univ—school AL-4
**Selmaville**—pop pl IL-6
Selmaville South Sch—school IL-6
Selmek Oil Field—oilfield WY-8
**Selmer**—pop pl TN-4
Selmer (CCD)—cens area TN-4
Selmer Ch—church TN-4
Selmer Ditch—canal IN-6
Selmer Division—civil TN-4
Selmer Elem Sch—school TN-4
Selmer Lake WI-6
Selmer MS—school TN-4
Selmes—locale MT-8
Selmier State For—forest IN-6
Selmo Gulch—valley MT-8
**Selmont**—pop pl AL-4
Selmont Ch—church AL-4
Selmont-West Selmont—CDP AL-4
**Selmore**—pop pl MO-7
**Seloc**—pop pl SC-3
**Seloca**—pop pl AL-4
Selock Sch—school IL-6
Seloga AL-4
Selow Creek—stream MT-8
Selph Bldg—hist pl OK-5
Selph Branch—stream MO-7
Selph Sch (historical)—school TN-4
Selsa—locale MO-7
Selser Canal—canal LA-4
Selser Cut-off—bend AR-4
Selser Sch—school MA-1
Selsers Creek—stream LA-4
Selsertown (historical)—locale MS-4
Selsertown Mounds MS-4
Selso Martinez Tank—reservoir NM-5
Selsor Ford—locale IL-6
Selso Well—well NM-5
Sels Prairie—locale MS-4
Selstrom Sch—school MT-8
Selt Cem—cemetery TX-5
Seltice—locale WA-9
Selting Sch—school SD-7
**Selton**—pop pl VA-3
Selton Sch—school MO-7
**Seltzer**—pop pl PA-2
Seltzer Ch—church KS-7
Seltzer City PA-2
Seltzer Elem Sch—school KS-7
Seltzer Park—park OH-6
Seltzer Spring—spring KS-7
Selvage Hollow—valley MO-7
Selva Marina Country Club—locale FL-3
**Selvern**—pop pl SC-3
Selvester Ranch—locale CA-9
**Selvin**—pop pl IN-6
Selvin Johnson Dam—dam SD-7
Selvo Ranch—locale MT-8
Selway Creek—stream MT-8
Selway Falls—falls ID-8
Selway Falls Campground—locale ID-8
Selway Falls Guard Station—locale ID-8
Selway Gulch—valley MT-8
Selway Lake—lake MT-8
Selway Lodge—locale ID-8
Selway Meadows—flat MT-8
Selway Mtn—summit MT-8
Selway Ranch—locale MT-8
Selway River—stream ID-8
Selway Slough—stream MT-8
Selway Spring—spring MT-8
**Selwin**—pop pl NC-3
Selwood Plantation (historical)—locale AL-4
**Selwyn**—pop pl WV-2
**Selwyn Park (subdivision)**—pop pl NC-3
Selwyn Sch—school NC-3
**Selz**—pop pl ND-7
Selzers Creek LA-4
Sema Creek—stream WA-9
Sema Lake—lake MN-6
Sema Meadows—flat WA-9
**Seman**—pop pl AL-4
Seman Ch—church AL-4
Semans Corner—locale NY-2
Semans Trail—trail PA-2
Semar Block—hist pl WA-9
Semas Mtn—summit CA-9
Semco Sch—school IA-7
Semem Creek—stream MT-8
Semen Cistern—well AZ-5
Semer Park—park MN-6
Semevolos Farm—hist pl ND-7
Semiahmoo WA-9
Semiahmoo—locale WA-9
Semiahmoo Bay—bay WA-9
Semiahmoo Spit—bar WA-9
Semiahmoo Spit—cape WA-9
Semiamo Bay WA-9
Semiamoo Bay WA-9
Semiamu Bay WA-9
Semicek Windmill—locale TX-5
Semi-Centennial Geyser—geyser WY-8
Semichi Islands—island AK-9
Semichi Pass—channel AK-9
Semiconon Run—stream PA-2
Semi Crater—crater CA-9
Semidi Islands—island AK-9
Semidi Natl Wildlife Ref—park AK-9
**Semil**—pop pl PR-3
Semilla Canyon—valley NM-5
**S E Miller Subdivision**—pop pl TN-4
Semi Lonesome Windmill—locale NM-5
Seminacum Lake ID-8
Seminacum Lake WA-9
Seminario Episcopal del Caribe—school PR-3
Seminary—locale IL-6
Seminary—locale KY-4
**Seminary**—pop pl MS-4
**Seminary**—pop pl VA-3
Seminary, Lake—lake FL-3
Seminary, The MS-4
Seminary, The—hist pl GA-3
Seminary at River Cem—cemetery MS-4
Seminary Attendance Center—school MS-4
Seminary Baptist Ch—church MS-4
Seminary Branch—stream KY-4
Seminary Brook—stream ME-1
Seminary Cem—cemetery IL-6
Seminary Cem—cemetery (2) TN-4
Seminary Cem—cemetery VA-3
Seminary Ch—church AR-4
Seminary Ch—church MS-4
Seminary Ch—church TN-4
Seminary Creek—stream (2) IL-6
Seminary Creek—stream MO-7
Seminary Falls—falls MS-4
Seminary Fork—stream IL-6
Seminary Hill—facility TX-5
Seminary Hill—summit KY-4
Seminary Hill—summit WA-9
Seminary Hill Sch (historical)—school TN-4
Seminary Lake—reservoir MO-7
Seminary Methodist Ch—church MS-4
Seminary of Our Lady Queen of the Angels—school CA-9
Seminary Of Pius X—church KY-4
Seminary of Saint Charles Borromed PA-2
Seminary Presbyterian Ch (historical)—church MS-4
Seminary Ridge—facility VA-3
Seminary Ridge—ridge CA-9
Seminary Ridge—ridge PA-2
Seminary Sch TN-4
Seminary Sch—school (2) IL-6
Seminary Sch—school (2) KY-4
Seminary Sch—school MO-7
Seminary Sch—school TN-4
Seminary Spring—spring OK-5
**Seminary Springs**—pop pl WI-6
Seminary Square Hist Dist—hist pl KY-4
Seminary Square Park—hist pl IN-6
**Seminary (Township of)**—pop pl IL-6
**Seminary Valley**—pop pl VA-3
**Seminary Village**—pop pl KY-4
Semino Creek—stream WY-8
Seminoe Canyon—valley WY-8
Seminoe Dam—dam WY-8
**Seminoe Dam**—pop pl WY-8
Seminoe Mine—mine WY-8
Seminoe Mtns—range WY-8
Seminoe Rsvr—reservoir WY-8
Seminole SD-7
Seminole—locale PA-2
Seminole—locale WV-2
**Seminole**—pop pl AL-4
**Seminole**—pop pl (2) FL-3
**Seminole**—pop pl NC-3
**Seminole**—pop pl OK-5
**Seminole**—pop pl PA-2
**Seminole**—pop pl TX-5

**Seminole**—pop pl WV-2
Seminole, Lake—lake (3) FL-3
Seminole, Lake—reservoir FL-3
Seminole, Lake—reservoir GA-3
Seminole Arkeba Ch—church OK-5
Seminole Baptist Ch—church FL-3
Seminole Bayou FL-3
Seminole Beach—beach FL-3
Seminole Blvd Square (Shop Ctr)—locale FL-3
Seminole Bridge—bridge FL-3
Seminole Canyon—valley (2) TX-5
Seminole Canyon Archeol District—hist pl TX-5
Seminole Canyon District (Boundary Increase)—hist pl TX-5
Seminole Canyon State Park—park TX-5
Seminole (CCD)—cens area TX-5
Seminole Cem—cemetery FL-3
Seminole Ch—church (2) AL-4
Seminole Ch—church (2) FL-3
Seminole Ch—church OK-5
Seminole Christian Ch Disciples of Christ—church FL-3
Seminole Community Coll—school FL-3
**Seminole County**—pop pl FL-3
**Seminole (County)**—pop pl GA-3
**Seminole (County)**—pop pl OK-5
Seminole County Courthouse—hist pl GA-3
Seminole County Courthouse—hist pl OK-5
Seminole Creek—stream FL-3
Seminole Creek—stream OK-5
Seminole Draw—valley NM-5
Seminole Draw—valley TX-5
Seminole East Oil Field—oilfield TX-5
Seminole Elem Sch—school FL-3
Seminole First Baptist Ch—church FL-3
Seminole Golf Club—locale FL-3
Seminole Heights—uninc pl FL-3
**Seminole Heights (subdivision)**—pop pl AL-4
**Seminole Hills**—pop pl FL-3
**Seminole Hot Springs**—pop pl CA-9
Seminole HS—school FL-3
Seminole Hunt Club—other VA-3
Seminole Indian Scout Cem—cemetery TX-5
Seminole Island—island OH-6
Seminole JHS—school FL-3
Seminole JHS—school MI-6
Seminole Junior Coll—school OK-5
Seminole Lake—gut FL-3
Seminole Lake—reservoir VA-3
**Seminole Lake Country Club**—pop pl FL-3
Seminole Lookout Tower—tower AL-4
Seminole Lookout Tower—tower FL-3
Seminole Mall—locale FL-3
**Seminole Manor**—pop pl FL-3
Seminole Manor—uninc pl FL-3
Seminole Mountains WY-8
Seminole MS—school FL-3
Seminole Municipal Country Club—other OK-5
Seminole North (CCD)—cens area OK-5
Seminole Northwest Oil Field—oilfield TX-5
Seminole Oil Field—oilfield OK-5
Seminole Oil Field—oilfield TX-5
Seminole Park FL-3
Seminole Park MI-6
Seminole Park—park AZ-5
Seminole Park—park FL-3
Seminole Park Raceway—locale FL-3
Seminole Plaza (Shop Ctr)—locale FL-3
Seminole Point—cape FL-3
Seminole Presbyterian Sch—school FL-3
Seminole Road Sch—school SC-3
Seminole RR Station—locale FL-3
Seminole Sch—school (2) FL-3
Seminole Senior HS—school FL-3
**Seminole Shores**—pop pl FL-3
Seminole South (CCD)—cens area OK-5
Seminole Springs—locale FL-3
**Seminole Subdivision**—pop pl TN-4
Seminole Swamp—swamp FL-3
Seminole Tower FL-3
Seminole Trail—trail TX-5
Seminole Valley Farmstead—hist pl IA-7
Seminole Valley Park—park IA-7
Seminole Vocational Education Center—school FL-3
Seminole Wayside Park—park FL-3
Seminole Whipping Tree—hist pl OK-5
**Seminole Woods (subdivision)**—pop pl TN-4
Semi Point—cape MD-2
Semirah Springs Ch—church AL-4
Semisopochnoi Island—island AK-9
Semitropic—locale CA-9
Semitropic Ridge—ridge CA-9
Semitropic Substation—other CA-9
Semiutak Bend—bend AK-9
Semiway—locale KY-4
**Semmes**—pop pl AL-4
Semmes, Lake—lake FL-3
Semmes, Raphael, House—hist pl AL-4
Semmes (CCD)—cens area AL-4
Semmes Cem—cemetery AL-4
Semmes Cem—cemetery MS-4
Semmes Division—civil AL-4
Semmes Elem Sch—school AL-4
Semmes Lake—reservoir SC-3
Semmes Lookout Tower—tower AL-4
Semmes Sch—school AL-4
Semmes Sch—school FL-3
Semmes Sch—school LA-4
SEMO Camp—locale MO-7
Semoco—other WV-2
Semon Cem—cemetery LA-4
**Semora**—pop pl NC-3
Semore Gulch—valley CA-9
Semorile Bldg—hist pl CA-9
Semper—locale CO-8
Semper Spring—spring CA-9
Sempervirens Creek—stream CA-9
Sempervirens Rsvr—reservoir CA-9
Semple, James, House—hist pl VA-3
Semple Creek—stream OH-6
Semple House—hist pl AL-4
Semple Plateau—bench WA-9
Semple Point—cape CA-9
Semple Run—stream MD-2
Semple Run—stream OH-6
**Semples**—pop pl OH-6
Semples Bluff AL-4
Semple Sch—school KY-4
Semple Sch—school PA-2
**Sempronius**—pop pl NY-2
**Sempronius (Town of)**—pop pl NY-2
Sempter CO-8
Semwei—civil FM-9
Semwei, Dauen—gut FM-9
Semwei, Pilapen—stream FM-9
Semwei, Pilen—stream FM-9
**Sena**—pop pl NM-5
Senac, Lake—lake FL-3
Senac Creek—stream CO-8
Sena Cem—cemetery NM-5
Senachwine Creek—stream (2) IL-6
Senachwine Lake—lake IL-6
Senachwine Sch—school (2) IL-6
**Senachwine (Township of)**—pop pl IL-6
Sena Dam—dam NM-5
Sena Ditch—canal NM-5
Senaham, Lake—reservoir VA-3
Senal Lake—lake MT-8
Senani—summit FM-9
Sena Ranch—locale NM-5
Senate—locale TX-5
Senate Brook—stream CT-1
Senate Creek—stream ID-8
Senate Creek—stream MT-8
**Senate Grove**—pop pl MO-7
Senate Grove Ch—church MO-7
Senate Hotel—hist pl PA-2
Senate House—hist pl NY-2
Senate Island—island IL-6
Senate Mine—mine AZ-5
Senate Mine—mine MT-8
Senate Mtn—summit MT-8
Senate Valley Sch—school NE-7
**Senath**—pop pl MO-7
Senatis Mtn—summit AK-9
**Senatobia**—pop pl MS-4
Senatobia Christian Ch—church MS-4
Senatobia Community Hosp—hospital MS-4
Senatobia Creek—stream MS-4
Senatobia Creek Watershed Y-7-1 Dam—dam MS-4
Senatobia Creek Watershed Y-7-2 Dam—dam MS-4
Senatobia Creek Watershed Y-7-3 Dam—dam MS-4
Senatobia Creek Watershed Y-7-7 Dam—dam MS-4
Senatobia Creek Watershed Y-7-8 Dam—dam MS-4
Senatobia Elem Sch—school MS-4
Senatobia HS—school MS-4
Senatobia JHS—school MS-4
**Senatobia Lakes**—pop pl MS-4
Senatobia Lakes Incorporated Pond Dam—dam MS-4
Senatobia Plaza Shop Ctr—locale MS-4
Senatobia Presbyterian Ch—church MS-4
Senator Beck Mine—mine CO-8
Senator Clarke Field (Airport)—airport NM-5
Senator Creek—stream (2) ID-8
Senator Creek Campground—locale ID-8
Senator Gulch—valley CO-8
Senator Mine—mine (2) AZ-5
Senator Mine—mine CA-9
Senator Mine—mine CO-8
Senator Morgan Mine—mine AZ-5
Senator Mtn—summit AZ-5
Senator Shoal—bar MA-1
Senator Stewart Mine—mine NV-8
Senator Wash—stream CA-9
Senator Young Dam—dam ND-7
Sen Beck Ditch—canal IL-6
Sencchotoconet River MA-1
Senczszyn Christian Acad—school FL-3
**Sendero (subdivision)**—pop pl NC-3
Seneacquoteen—locale ID-8
Seneagouteen ID-8
Seneaguoteen ID-8
Seneaquoteen ID-8
Seneas—bar FM-9
Seneasha MS-4
Seneasha Cem—cemetery MS-4
Seneasha Ch—church MS-4
Seneasha Creek—stream MS-4
Seneasha Sch (historical)—school MS-4
Seneatcha MS-4
Seneca NY-2
Seneca ND-7
Seneca—locale AZ-5
Seneca—locale FL-3
Seneca—locale MI-6
Seneca—locale MS-4
Seneca—locale NM-5
Seneca—locale VA-3
**Seneca**—pop pl CA-9
**Seneca**—pop pl IL-6
**Seneca**—pop pl IA-7
**Seneca**—pop pl KS-7
**Seneca**—pop pl MD-2
**Seneca**—pop pl MI-6
**Seneca**—pop pl MO-7
**Seneca**—pop pl NE-7
**Seneca**—pop pl (2) OR-9
**Seneca**—pop pl PA-2
**Seneca**—pop pl SC-3
**Seneca**—pop pl SD-7
**Seneca**—pop pl WI-6
Seneca, Lake—lake (2) FL-3
Seneca, Mount—summit NY-2
Seneca Access Public Hunting Area—area IA-7
Seneca Airp—airport PA-2
Seneca Airpark—airport PA-2
Seneca Airport KS-7
Seneca Army Depot—military NY-2
Seneca Ave East Hist Dist—hist pl NY-2
Seneca Ave School PA-2
Seneca Breaker (historical)—building PA-2
Seneca Brook—stream ME-1
Seneca Campground—locale WV-2
Seneca Canal NY-2
Seneca Canyon—valley NM-5
**Seneca Castle**—pop pl NY-2
Seneca Caverns—cave OH-6
Seneca Caverns—cave WV-2
Seneca (CCD)—cens area OR-9
Seneca (CCD)—cens area SC-3
Seneca Cem—cemetery FL-3
Seneca Cem—cemetery MS-4
Seneca Cem—cemetery WI-6
Seneca Ch—church NY-2
Seneca Ch—church WV-2
Seneca Common Sch—school SD-7
Seneca Country Club—other NY-2
Seneca Country Club—other TX-5
**Seneca (County)**—pop pl NY-2
**Seneca (County)**—pop pl OH-6
Seneca County Courthouse Complex at Ovid—hist pl NY-2
Seneca Creek NY-2
Seneca Creek OH-6
Seneca Creek—stream AL-4
Seneca Creek—stream CA-9
Seneca Creek—stream (2) MD-2
Seneca Creek—stream MT-8
Seneca Creek—stream NM-5
Seneca Creek—stream OK-5
Seneca Creek—stream SC-3
Seneca Creek—stream VA-3
Seneca Creek—stream WV-2
Seneca Ditch—canal CO-8
Seneca Drain—stream MI-6
Seneca Elem Sch—school KS-7
Seneca Falls SD-7
Seneca Falls—falls PA-2
**Seneca Falls**—pop pl NY-2
Seneca Falls Country Club—other NY-2
**Seneca Falls (Town of)**—pop pl NY-2
Seneca Fork Wills Creek—stream OH-6
Seneca Fouts State Park—park OR-9
**Seneca Gardens**—pop pl KY-4
Seneca Glass Company Bldg—hist pl WV-2
**Seneca Heights**—pop pl NY-2
**Seneca Hill**—pop pl NY-2
Seneca Hist Dist—hist pl MD-2
Seneca Hist Dist—hist pl SC-3
Seneca Hist Dist (Boundary Increase)—hist pl SC-3
Seneca (historical P.O.)—locale IA-7
Seneca Hollow VA-3
Seneca Hollow—valley NY-2
Seneca Hollow—valley VA-3
Seneca Hotel—hist pl OH-6
Seneca HS—school NY-2
Seneca HS—school PA-2
Seneca Hunt Camp—locale PA-2
Seneca Indian Park—park NY-2
Seneca Indian Sch—school OK-5
Seneca Island NY-2
Seneca Island—area MO-7
Seneca JHS (historical)—school PA-2
**Seneca Knolls**—pop pl NY-2
Seneca Lake—lake AZ-5
Seneca Lake—lake MI-6
Seneca Lake—lake NJ-2
Seneca Lake—lake NY-2
Seneca Lake—lake PA-2
Seneca Lake—lake WI-6
Seneca Lake—lake WY-8
Seneca Lake—reservoir WV-2
Seneca Lake Dam—dam AZ-5
Seneca Lake Inlet—stream NY-2
Seneca Lake (RR name for Himrod)—other NY-2
Seneca Lake State Park—park NY-2
Seneca Lake Trail—trail WY-8
Senecal Creek—stream OR-9
**Seneca Location**—pop pl MI-6
Senecal Spring—spring OR-9
Seneca Mills—locale NY-2
Seneca Mtn—summit NY-2
Seneca Mtn—summit VT-1
Seneca Municipal Airp—airport KS-7
Seneca-Onderdonk-Woodward Hist Dist—hist pl NY-2
Seneca Park—park (2) IL-6
Seneca Park—park KS-7
Seneca Park—park KY-4
Seneca Park—park (2) NY-2
**Seneca Park**—pop pl MD-2
Seneca Point—cape MD-2
Seneca Point—cape NY-2
**Seneca Point**—pop pl NY-2
Seneca Point Gully—valley NY-2
Seneca Presbyterian Church—hist pl NY-2
Seneca Pumped Storage Area—reservoir PA-2
Seneca Quarry—hist pl MD-2
Seneca River VA-3
Seneca River—stream NY-2
Seneca River—stream SC-3
Seneca Rock WV-2
Seneca Rocks—cliff WV-2
**Seneca Rocks**—pop pl WV-2
Seneca Rocks Sch—school WV-2
Seneca Rsvr—reservoir CA-9
Seneca Rsvr—reservoir SC-3
Seneca Run—stream (2) PA-2
Senecas, Isle of the—island NY-2
Seneca Sch—school MD-2
Seneca Sch—school VA-3
Seneca Sch—school WV-2
Seneca Sch (historical)—school MO-7
Seneca Shop Ctr—locale NC-3
Seneca Slough—stream MO-7
Seneca Spring—spring CA-9
Seneca Springs—spring AL-4
Seneca Square Mall—locale KS-7
Seneca State For—forest WV-2
Seneca Substation—locale OR-9
Seneca Tanks—reservoir NM-5
**Seneca (Town of)**—pop pl NY-2
**Seneca (Town of)**—pop pl (4) WI-6
Seneca Township—civil (2) MO-7
Seneca Township—civil SD-7
Seneca Township—fmr MCD IA-7
**Seneca (Township of)**—pop pl IL-6
**Seneca (Township of)**—pop pl MI-6
**Seneca (Township of)**—pop pl (3) OH-6
**Seneca Valley**—pop pl PA-2
Seneca Valley Ch—church OH-6
Seneca Valley JHS—school PA-2
Seneca Valley Senior HS—school PA-2
**Senecaville**—pop pl OH-6
Senecaville Dam—dam OH-6
Senecaville Lake—reservoir OH-6
Senecaville Natl Fish Hatchery—other OH-6
Senecaville Reservoir OH-6
Seneca Vista—uninc pl KY-4
Seneca Well—well OR-9
Senechtoconet River RI-1
Senecio Creek—stream WY-8
Senectaconnet Pond RI-1
Senegai MP-9
Senegai Island MP-9
Senegambia Missionary Baptist Ch (historical)—church MS-4
Seneger, Mount—summit CA-9
Sen-eh-say Creek WA-9
Seneker Cem—cemetery TN-4
Senepetuit Pond MA-1
Senepuxent DE-2
Senesha Creek MS-4
Seneson—bar FM-9
Senethem Cem—cemetery MO-7
Seney—locale GA-3
Seney—locale IA-7
**Seney**—pop pl MI-6
Seney, Charles, House—hist pl IA-7
Seney Point—cape WY-8
**Seney (Township of)**—pop pl MI-6
Senff Ditch—canal WY-8
Senff Draw—valley WY-8
Senft Sch Number One (abandoned)—school PA-2
Senft Sch Number Two (abandoned)—school PA-2
Sengall PW-9
Seng Branch—stream (4) KY-4
Seng Branch—stream NC-3
Seng Branch—stream TN-4
Seng Branch—stream (2) WV-2
**Seng Camp**—pop pl VA-3
Seng Camp Branch—stream KY-4
Seng Camp Creek—stream WV-2
Seng Camp Fork—stream VA-3
Seng Camp Hollow—valley WV-2
Seng Camp Run—stream WV-2
Seng Cove—valley KY-4
Seng Cove—valley TN-4
Seng Cove Branch—stream TN-4
**Seng Creek**—pop pl WV-2
Seng Creek—stream WV-2
Sengegontacket Pond MA-1
Sengekontacket Pond—lake MA-1
Sengekontacket Pond Marshes—swamp MA-1
Sengekontakit (historical)—locale MA-1
Senger Creek CA-9
Senger Creek—stream CA-9
Senger Gully—valley TX-5
Senger Lake—lake ND-7
Sengers Mountain Lake—reservoir VA-3
Seng Fork—stream KY-4
Seng Fork—stream WV-2
Seng Gap—gap NC-3
Seng Hollow—valley KY-4
Senging Branch—stream WV-2
Seng Mtn—summit VA-3
Seng Patch Branch—stream TN-4
Seng Ridge—ridge NC-3
Seng Run—stream (4) WV-2
**Sengtown**—pop pl TN-4
Senhanom, Puntan—cape MH-9
**Senia**—pop pl NC-3
Senia Creek—stream (2) MT-8
Seniahdak, Pilapen—stream FM-9
Seniard Creek—stream NC-3
Seniard Mtn—summit (2) NC-3
Seniard Ridge—ridge NC-3
Senico Lake—lake MN-6
Senior—locale OH-6
**Senior**—pop pl TX-5
Senior Canyon—valley CA-9
Senior Creek—stream VA-3
Senior Hall—hist pl CA-9
Senior Hall—hist pl MO-7
Senior Hill—summit NY-2
Senior Lake—lake ND-7
Senior Lakes—lake NJ-2
**Seniors Five-Acre Plat Subdivision**—pop pl UT-8
Senipehn—civil FM-9
Senipehn, Pillap En—stream FM-9
Senipeu—bar FM-9
Senisoco Windmill—locale TX-5
Senita Basin—basin AZ-5
Senita Pass—gap AZ-5
Senita Sch—school AZ-5
Senita Tank—reservoir AZ-5
Senith KS-7
Senix Creek—stream NY-2
Senks Rapids ID-8
Senn, John L., House—hist pl WI-6
Senna Bean Lake—lake TX-5
Sennatoba MS-4
Senn Branch—stream SC-3
Senn Cem—cemetery IN-6
Sennebec Pond—lake ME-1
Sennet Canyon—valley CA-9
**Sennett**—pop pl NY-2
Sennett Canyon—valley MT-8
Sennett Draw—valley WY-8
Sennett Point—cape AK-9
Sennetts Corner—locale ME-1
**Sennett (Town of)**—pop pl NY-2
Senn HS—school IL-6
Sennicant Lake WY-8
Senn Lake—lake WI-6
Senn Marsh—swamp MN-6
Senno Creek KS-7
Sennott Park—park MA-1
Senn Park—park IL-6
Senn Sch—school SD-7
**Senoia**—pop pl GA-3
Senoia (CCD)—cens area GA-3
Senoia State Park—park GA-3
Senoj Lake—lake OR-9
Senoj Trail—trail OR-9
Senora—locale VA-3
Senora Cem—cemetery OK-5
Senora Peak CA-9
Senor Canyon CA-9
Senorita Artesian Well—well TX-5
**Senorito**—pop pl NM-5
Senorito Canyon—valley NM-5
Senpehn, Dauen—gut FM-9
Senrac Lake—reservoir AR-4
Sensabaugh Branch TN-4
Sensabaugh Branch—stream (2) TN-4
Sensabaugh Cave—cave TN-4
Sensabaugh Cem—cemetery TN-4
Sensabaugh Ridge—ridge TN-4
Sensabaugh Saltpeter Cave—cave TN-4
Sensabaugh Tunnel—tunnel TN-4
Sensaboy Spring—spring TN-4
Senseball Creek—stream UT-8
Senseball Lake—lake UT-8
Sensebaugh Canyon—valley WY-8
Sensenbrenner-Seldon Camp—locale MI-6
Sensenig—locale PA-2
Senseny Road Sch—school VA-3
Sensiba State Wildlife Area—park WI-6
Sensing Cem—cemetery TN-4
Sentell—locale LA-4
Sentell Cem—cemetery AL-4
Sentell Cem—cemetery (2) NC-3
Sentell Creek—stream NC-3
Sentell Knob—summit NC-3
Sentell Lake—reservoir TX-5
Sentell Plantation—locale LA-4
Sentenac Canyon—valley CA-9
Sentenac Creek—stream CA-9
Sentenac Mtn—summit CA-9
Sentence Cienaga—swamp CA-9
Senteney Creek—stream CA-9
Senteney Rock—pillar CA-9
Senteney Sch—school IL-6
Senter—locale ID-8
**Senter**—pop pl MI-6
**Senter**—pop pl NC-3
Senter Cem—cemetery NH-1
Senter Ch—church NC-3
Senterfitt—locale TX-5
Senter Hill TN-4
Senter Hill Ch—church TN-4
Senter Lake Dam—dam MS-4
Senter Park—park TX-5
Senter Point—cape MI-6
Senter-Rooks House—hist pl TN-4
Senter's Point ME-1
**Sentertown**—pop pl TN-4
Sentertown Missionary Baptist Ch—church TN-4
**Senterville**—pop pl KY-4
Sentill Hollow—valley AL-4
Sentill Hollow Cave—cave AL-4
Sentinal Butte ND-7
Sentinal Buttes ND-7
Sentinal Mtn—summit CO-8
Sentinal Peak—summit AK-9
Sentinal Point Lookout Tower—locale WI-6
Sentinal Rock—pillar PA-2
Sentinel—locale OH-6
**Sentinel**—pop pl AZ-5
**Sentinel**—pop pl MO-7
**Sentinel**—pop pl OK-5
Sentinel, Lake—lake FL-3
Sentinel, Mount—summit (2) MT-8
Sentinel, The—pillar UT-8
Sentinel, The—summit ID-8
Sentinel, The—summit (2) MT-8
Sentinel, The—summit UT-8
Sentinela Tank—reservoir TX-5
Sentinel Bldg—hist pl IL-6
Sentinel Bluffs—range WA-9
Sentinel Butte UT-8
**Sentinel Butte**—pop pl ND-7
Sentinel Butte—summit AZ-5
Sentinel Butte—summit CA-9
Sentinel Butte—summit NM-5
Sentinel Butte—summit ND-7
Sentinel Butte—summit WA-9
Sentinel Butte Dam—dam ND-7
Sentinel Butte Public Sch—hist pl ND-7
Sentinel Cem—cemetery OK-5
Sentinel Creek—stream CA-9
Sentinel Creek—stream ID-8
Sentinel Creek—stream MT-8
Sentinel Creek—stream NV-8
Sentinel Creek—stream OR-9
Sentinel Creek—stream WA-9
Sentinel Creek—stream WY-8
Sentinel Dome—summit (2) CA-9
Sentinel Elem Sch—school AZ-5
Sentinel Fall—falls CA-9
Sentinel Falls—falls MT-8
Sentinel Gap—gap WA-9
**Sentinel Heights**—pop pl NY-2
**Sentinel Heights**—pop pl TN-4
**Sentinel Hill**—pop pl OR-9
Sentinel Hill—summit AK-9
Sentinel Hill—summit CA-9
Sentinel Hill—summit KS-7
Sentinel Hills—summit OR-9
Sentinel HS—school MT-8
Sentinel Interchange—crossing AZ-5
Sentinel Island—island AK-9
Sentinel Island—island CO-8
Sentinel Island—island NV-8
Sentinel Island—island WA-9
Sentinel Islet—island AK-9
Sentinel Meadow—flat CA-9
Sentinel Meadows CA-9
Sentinel Meadows—flat WY-8
Sentinel Mesa—summit UT-8
Sentinel Mine—mine ID-8
Sentinel Mtn—summit ME-1
Sentinel Mtn—summit (2) MT-8
Sentinel Mtn—summit NV-8
Sentinel Mtn—summit (2) NH-1
Sentinel Mtn—summit NY-2
Sentinel Mtn—summit WA-9
Sentinel Peak—summit AK-9
Sentinel Peak—summit (4) AZ-5
Sentinel Peak—summit CA-9
Sentinel Peak—summit CO-8
Sentinel Peak—summit ID-8
Sentinel Peak—summit MT-8
Sentinel Peak—summit NV-8
Sentinel Peak—summit (3) OR-9
Sentinel Peak—summit (2) WA-9
Sentinel Peak Park—park AZ-5
Sentinel Peak Rsvr—reservoir NV-8
Sentinel Plain AZ-5
Sentinel Plain—plain AZ-5
Sentinel Point AZ-5
Sentinel Point—cape AK-9
Sentinel Point—summit CO-8
Sentinel Point—summit VA-3
Sentinel Ranch—locale MT-8
Sentinel Range—range NY-2
Sentinel Ridge—ridge CA-9
Sentinel Rock—bar WA-9
Sentinel Rock—island CA-9
Sentinel Rock—other AK-9
Sentinel Rock—pillar AZ-5
Sentinel Rock—pillar CA-9
Sentinel Rock—pillar MT-8
Sentinel Rock—pillar NE-7
Sentinel Rock—pillar OR-9
Sentinel Rock—pillar WA-9
Sentinel Rock—summit NV-8
Sentinel Rock—summit WY-8
Sentinel Rocks—ridge WY-8
Sentinels, The—area AK-9
Sentinels, The—island AK-9
Sentinel South Flow—lava ID-8
Sentinel Spire—pillar CO-8
Sentinel Spring AZ-5
Sentinels Sister—summit WA-9
**Sentinel Township**—pop pl ND-7
Sentinel Wash—stream AZ-5
Sentinel West Flow—lava ID-8
**Sentous**—pop pl CA-9
Sentry, The—summit UT-8
Sentry Mount Ch (historical)—church MS-4
Sentry Mtn—summit TX-5
Sentry Peak MA-1
Sentry Ridge—locale MO-7
Sentry Rock—island AK-9
Sentz Lick Branch—stream WV-2
**Senyah**—pop pl FL-3
Senyaquateen ID-8
Seny Sch (historical)—school MO-7
Seoconnet River RI-1
Seogmiller Cem—cemetery IA-7
**Seola Beach**—pop pl WA-9
**Seopus**—pop pl MO-7
Seoria Creek—stream WY-8
Sepaessing Creek PA-2
Sepam MH-9
Separ—locale NM-5
Separate Hill—summit AZ-5
Separate Pond (historical)—lake TN-4
Separation Canyon—valley AZ-5
Separation Corrals Camp—locale OR-9
Separation Creek OR-9
Separation Creek—stream OR-9
Separation Creek—stream WY-8
Separation Creek Cutoff—trail OR-9
Separation Creek Meadow—flat OR-9
Separation Creek Trail—trail OR-9
Separation Flats—flat WY-8
Separation Lake—lake OR-9
Separation Lake—lake WY-8
Separation Peak—summit WY-8
Separation Point—summit WY-8
Separation Point Lake—lake WY-8
Separation Rapids—rapids AZ-5
Separation Rim—ridge WY-8
Separator Brook—stream NY-2
Separ Ranch—locale NM-5
Separ Windmill—locale NM-5
Sepasco Lake—lake NY-2
Sep Creek—stream WA-9
Sepeipei—ridge FM-9
Sepeipei, Pilen—stream FM-9
Sepenter Cem—cemetery TX-5
Seperation Creek WY-8
Sepere—unknown FM-9
Sepo—locale IL-6
Sepo Cem—cemetery IL-6
Sepo Creek—stream IL-6
Seponack Neck NY-2
Sepowet Cove RI-1
Seppings Lagoon—lake AK-9
Seppman Mill—hist pl MN-6
Septa—locale VA-3
September, Lake—lake AK-9
September Creek—stream (2) AK-9
September Morn Lake—lake MT-8
September Morn Mine—mine NV-8
September Morn Spring—spring MT-8
Sepuit River MA-1
Sepulcher Creek—stream VA-3
Sepulcher Loop Trail—trail WY-8
Sepulcher Mtn—summit WY-8
Sepulga Ch—church AL-4
Sepulga Fire Tower AL-4
Sepulgah Creek AL-4
Sepulga Lookout Tower—locale AL-4
Sepulga P.O. (historical)—locale AL-4
Sepulga River—stream AL-4
Sepultura Canyon—valley NM-5
Sepultura Flat—flat NM-5
**Sepulveda**—pop pl (2) CA-9
Sepulveda Canyon—valley (2) CA-9
Sepulveda Cem—cemetery TX-5
Sepulveda Channel—canal CA-9
Sepulveda Creek—stream AZ-5
Sepulveda Dam Rec Area(Flood Control)—other CA-9
Sepulveda Flood Control Basin—basin CA-9
Sepulveda Military Sch—school CA-9
Sepulveda Sch—school (2) CA-9
Sepulveda Wash AZ-5
Sepu Ridge—ridge AS-9
Sequa, Lake—lake WY-8
Sequachee College Post Office TN-4
Sequalichew Creek WA-9
Sequalitchew Archeol Site—hist pl WA-9
Sequalitchew Creek—stream WA-9
Sequalitchew Lake—lake WA-9
Sequallitchew Lake WA-9
Sequan Ind Res CA-9
Sequan Ind Res—reserve CA-9
Sequan Peak—summit CA-9
Sequassett Station (historical)—locale MA-1
**Sequatchie**—pop pl TN-4
Sequatchie-Bledsoe Vocational Center—school TN-4
Sequatchie-Bledsoe Vocational Training Center—school TN-4
Sequatchie Chapel—church TN-4
Sequatchie College Post Office (historical)—building TN-4
**Sequatchie County**—pop pl TN-4
Sequatchie County Courthouse—building TN-4
Sequatchie County Courthouse—hist pl TN-4

Seven Troughs Spring—spring ... NV-8
Seven Troughs Wash—stream ... NV-8
Seven T X Camp—locale ... NM-5
Seventy Acre Canyon—valley ... CA-9
Seventy Buck Lick Run—stream ... VA-3
Seventy Creek—stream ... ID-8
Seventy Creek—stream ... OR-9
Seventy Eight—locale ... IA-7
Seventyeighth Street Sch—school ... WI-6
Seventy-Fifth Street Sch—school ... CA-9
Seventy-first and Rockhill Shops—locale .. MO-7
Seventy-First Elem Sch—school ... NC-3
Seventyfirst HS—school ... NC-3
Seventy-First (Township of)—fmr MCD ... NC-3
Seventy-Five Creek—stream ... ID-8
Seventyfive Mile Creek—stream ... AZ-5
Seventyfive Mile Rapids ... AZ-5
Seventy-Five Mile Rapids—rapids ... AZ-5
Seventyfive Well—well ... TX-5
Seventy Flats—flat ... SD-7
Seventyfour Canyon—valley ... NM-5
Seventyfour Draw—valley ... NM-5
Seventyfour Mine—mine ... CA-9
Seventyfour Mountain Tank—reservoir ... NM-5
Seventyfour Mtn—summit ... NM-5
Seventyfour Plains—plain ... AZ-5
Seventy-Four Ranch—locale ... TX-5
Seventy-Fourth Street Sch—school ... CA-9
Seventy-fourth Street Sch—school ... FL-3
Seventyfour Windmill—locale ... NM-5
Seventy Holes Lake—lake ... CO-8
Seventymile River—stream ... AK-9
Seventy Mtn—summit ... NY-2
Seventy-nine Ch (historical)—church ... TN-4
Seventy Nine Coulee ... MT-8
Seventy Nine Coulee—valley ... MT-8
Seventynine Coulee—valley (2) ... MT-8
Seventynine Hill—summit ... MT-8
Seventynine Mine—mine ... AZ-5
Seventynine Ranch—locale ... MT-8
Seventy-nine Sch (historical)—school ... TN-4
Seventynine Spring—spring (2) ... MT-8
Seventy-Ninth Street Baptist
Kindergarten—school ... FL-3
Seventy-Ninth Street Sch—school ... CA-9
Seventyninth Street Sch—school ... NY-2
Seventy One—stream ... PA-2
Seventyone Camp—locale ... NV-8
Seventy One Gulch—valley ... ID-8
Seventyone Ranch—locale ... MT-8
Seventyone Ranch—locale ... NV-8
Seventy-one Rsvr—reservoir ... WY-8
Seventyone Table—summit ... SD-7
Seventyone Well—well ... TX-5
Seventy Ranch—locale ... CO-8
Seventyseven, Lake—lake ... TX-5
Seventyseven Flat—flat ... UT-8
Seventy-Seven Hills—range ... WY-8
Seventy-seven Ranch—locale ... TX-5
Seventy-seven Ranch—locale ... WY-8
Seventyseven Tank—reservoir ... AZ-5
Seventyseventh Street Ch of
Christ—church ... AL-4
Seventyseven Well—well ... TX-5
Seventyseven Windmill—locale ... NM-5
Seventy Six—locale ... KY-4
**Seventysix**—pop pl ... MO-7
**Seventy-Six**—pop pl ... MO-7
Seventysix Creek—stream ... MT-8
Seventysix Creek—stream (2) ... NV-8
Seventysix Creek—stream (2) ... WY-8
Seventysix Creek Pasture—flat ... NV-8
Seventysix Draw—valley ... NM-5
Seventysix Draw—valley ... SD-7
Seventysix Draw—valley ... WY-8
**Seventy-Six Estates**
**(subdivision)**—pop pl ... TN-4
Seventy Six Falls—falls ... KY-4
Seventysix Gulch—arroyo ... AZ-5
Seventysix Gulch—valley ... WA-9
Seventy Six Hill—summit ... MA-1
Seventysix Mine—mine ... AZ-5
Seventy Six Ranch—locale ... AZ-5
Seventysix Ranch—locale ... AZ-5
Seventysix Shaft—mine ... NV-8
Seventysix Spring—spring ... AZ-5
Seventysixth Street Presbyterian
Ch—church ... AL-4
Seventy-Six Townhall—building ... IA-7
Seventy Six Township—civil ... KS-7
Seventy-Six Township—fmr MCD (2) ... IA-7
Seventysix Well—well ... NM-5
Seventytwo Bench—bench ... MT-8
Seventytwo Hills—spring ... MT-8
Seventytwo Well—well ... TX-5
Seventy Wash—stream ... AZ-5
Seventy Well—well ... TX-5
Seven-Up Creek—stream ... MT-8
Seven-up Creek—stream ... OR-9
Seven-Up Gulch—valley ... MT-8
Seven Up Pasture Tank—reservoir ... AZ-5
Seven Up Peak—summit ... CA-9
Seven-up-Pete Creek—stream ... MT-8
Seven Up Ranch—locale ... AZ-5
Seven-Up Rsvr—reservoir ... MT-8
Seven Up Spring—spring ... AZ-5
Seven Up Spring—spring ... OR-9
Seven Up Tank—reservoir ... AZ-5
Seven Up Tank—reservoir ... TX-5
Seven Utes Mtn—summit ... CO-8
**Seven Valleys**—pop pl ... PA-2
Seven Valleys Borough—civil ... PA-2
Seven Valleys Ch—church ... PA-2
**Seven Valleys (RR name**
**Smyser)**—pop pl ... PA-2
Seven V Ranch—locale ... AZ-5
Seven VT Draw—valley ... AZ-5
Seven Well Canyon—valley ... CA-9
Seven Wells, The—well ... NY-2
Seven Wells Monmt—park ... TX-5
Seven Wells Sch—school ... TX-5
Seven Winds of the Lake—lake ... MT-8
Seven W Ranch—locale ... MT-8
Seven X Ranch—locale ... CO-8
Seven X Tank—reservoir ... AZ-5
Seven-11 Ranch—locale ... MT-8
Seven-11 Ranch—locale ... SD-7
Severance—locale ... NY-2
**Severance**—pop pl ... CO-8
**Severance**—pop pl ... KS-7
**Severance**—pop pl ... NH-1
**Severance**—pop pl ... NY-2
Severance, Cordenio, House—hist pl ... MN-6
Severance Creek—stream ... MI-6
Severance Drain—canal ... MI-6
Severance Hill—summit ... NH-1
Severance Hill—summit ... NY-2
Severance Lake—lake ... MN-6
Severance-Millikin Sch—school ... OH-6
Severance Stadium—other ... OH-6
**Severance (Township of)**—pop pl ... MN-6
Severe Creek—stream ... ID-8
Severence ... KS-7
Severence Creek—stream ... MI-6
Severe Post Office (historical)—building ... AL-4
Severe Spring—spring ... ID-8
Sever Hall, Harvard Univ—hist pl ... MA-1
Severin Canyon—valley ... AZ-5
Severin Openings—flat ... CA-9
Severly ... KS-7
**Severn**—pop pl ... MD-2
**Severn**—pop pl ... NC-3
**Severn**—pop pl ... VA-3
**Severna Forest**—pop pl ... MD-2
**Severna Park**—pop pl ... MD-2
Severn Beach—beach ... MD-2
Severn Ch—church ... VA-3
Severn Creek—stream ... KY-4
Severn Crossroads—locale ... MD-2
Severne Point—cape ... NY-2
Severn Forest—locale ... MD-2
**Severn Grove**—pop pl ... MD-2
Severn Gulch—valley ... MT-8
Severn Gut—gut ... MD-2
**Severn Heights**—pop pl ... MD-2
Severn Island—bend ... TX-5
Severn Manor—locale ... VA-3
Severn Peak—summit ... CO-8
Severn River—stream ... MD-2
Severn River—stream ... VA-3
Severn River Bridge—bridge (2) ... MD-2
Severn Run—stream ... MD-2
Severn Sch—school ... MD-2
Severn Sch—school ... NY-2
**Severnside**—pop pl ... MD-2
Severns Run ... KY-4
Severns Sch—school ... SD-7
**Severn Township**—pop pl ... ND-7
Severn Wharf—locale ... VA-3
**Severs**—pop pl ... IA-7
Severs Creek—stream ... IA-7
**Seversens**—pop pl ... AK-9
Severs Hotel—hist pl ... OK-5
Severson, Nels, Barn—hist pl ... IA-7
Severson Canal—canal ... ID-8
Severson Cem—cemetery ... IA-7
Severson Cem—cemetery ... NE-7
Severson Cem—cemetery ... NY-2
Severson Cem—cemetery ... ND-7
Severson Cem—cemetery ... WI-6
Severson Coulee—valley (2) ... WI-6
Severson Creek—stream ... MN-6
Severson Flats—flat ... WY-8
Severson Lake—lake ... MN-6
Severson Lake—lake ... WI-6
Severson Peninsula—cape ... AK-9
Severson Sch—school ... MN-6
Seversville—uninc pl ... NC-3
Seversville Sch—school ... NC-3
Severt Creek—stream ... OR-9
Severt-Iverson County Park—park ... OR-9
**Severville (subdivision)**—pop pl ... NC-3
**Severy**—pop pl ... KS-7
Severy City Dam—dam ... KS-7
Severy Creek—stream ... CO-8
Severy Elem Sch—school ... KS-7
Severy Hill—summit ... ME-1
Severy Hill Cem—cemetery ... ME-1
Severy Municipal Rsvr—reservoir ... KS-7
Sevevin Cem—cemetery ... TX-5
Sevey—locale ... NY-2
Sevey Corners—locale ... NY-2
Sevey Pond—lake ... NY-2
Seveys Well—well ... UT-8
Sevier—locale ... OR-9
**Sevier**—pop pl ... NC-3
**Sevier**—pop pl ... UT-8
Sevier and Weed Bldg—hist pl ... WA-9
Sevier Branch—stream ... KY-4
Sevier Branch—stream ... TN-4
Sevier Bridge Dam—dam ... UT-8
Sevier Bridge Rsvr—reservoir ... UT-8
Sevier Canal ... UT-8
Sevier Canal—canal ... UT-8
Sevier Canyon ... UT-8
Sevier Canyon—valley (2) ... UT-8
Sevier Cem—cemetery ... TN-4
Sevier Cem—cemetery ... UT-8
Sevier County—civil ... UT-8
**Sevier (County)**—pop pl ... AR-4
**Sevier County**—pop pl ... TN-4
Sevier County Courthouse—hist pl ... TN-4
Sevier County Park—park ... TN-4
Sevier Desert—plain ... UT-8
Sevier Dry lake ... UT-8
Sevier Ferry ... TN-4
Sevier Flat—flat ... AZ-5
Sevier-Gatlinburg Airp—airport ... TN-4
Sevier Heights Baptist Ch—church ... TN-4
**Sevier Heights (subdivision)**—pop pl ... TN-4
**Sevier Home**—pop pl ... TN-4
Sevier Home Sch (historical)—school ... TN-4
Sevier HS—school ... LA-4
Sevier Lake—lake ... UT-8
Sevier Lake—stream ... MS-4
Sevier Lake Rsvr—reservoir ... UT-8
Sevier Lake Rsvr No 1—reservoir ... UT-8
Sevier Lake Rsvr No 4—reservoir ... UT-8
Sevier Lake Rsvr No 5—reservoir ... UT-8
Sevier Lake Rsvr No 6—reservoir ... UT-8
Sevier Mine—mine ... UT-8
Sevier MS ... TN-4
Sevier Park—park ... TN-4
Sevier Plateau—plateau ... UT-8
Sevier Reservoir ... UT-8
Sevier River—stream ... UT-8
Sevier River Bend Recreation Site—park ... UT-8
Seviers Cem—cemetery ... TN-4
Seviers Ferry ... TN-4
Sevier Station—hist pl ... TN-4
Sevier Station—locale ... TN-4
Sevier Tank—reservoir ... AZ-5
**Sevier Terrace (subdivision)**—pop pl ... TN-4
Sevier Valley ... UT-8
Sevier Valley—valley ... UT-8
Sevier Valley Canal—canal ... UT-8
Sevier Valley Hosp—hospital ... UT-8
Sevier Valley Hospital Heliport—airport ... UT-8
**Sevierville**—pop pl ... TN-4
Sevierville (CCD)—cens area ... TN-4
Sevierville Commercial Hist Dist—hist pl ... TN-4
Sevierville Division—civil ... TN-4
Sevierville Masonic Lodge—hist pl ... TN-4
Sevier Ward Church—hist pl ... UT-8
Sevilla Sch—school ... AZ-5
Seville—locale ... IL-6
**Seville**—pop pl ... CA-9
**Seville**—pop pl ... FL-3
**Seville**—pop pl ... GA-3
**Seville**—pop pl ... OH-6
Seville, The—hist pl ... IN-6
Seville Bridge—hist pl ... IL-6
Seville Ch—church ... MI-6
Seville Community Hall—locale ... MT-8
Seville Elem Sch—school ... PA-2
Seville Flat—flat ... MT-8
Seville Lake—lake ... CA-9
Seville Lookout Tower—tower ... FL-3
Seville-Midway Mine—mine ... MN-6
Seville Public Sch—school ... FL-3
Seville Sch ... PA-2
Seville Square—park ... FL-3
Sevilleta Grant—civil ... NM-5
Sevilleta Natl Wildlife Ref—park ... NM-5
**Seville (Township of)**—pop pl ... MI-6
Sevin, Bayou—gut ... LA-4
Sevin Canal—canal ... LA-4
Sevisok Slough—gut ... AK-9
Sevona Cabin—hist pl ... WI-6
Sevuokuk Mtn—summit ... AK-9
Sevy Canyon—valley ... UT-8
Sevy Draw—valley ... AZ-5
Sevy Draw Rsvr Number One—reservoir ... AZ-5
Sevy Draw Rsvr Number Two—reservoir ... AZ-5
Sevy Hollow—valley ... UT-8
Sevy Ranch—locale ... UT-8
Sevy Spring—spring ... UT-8
Sewaft Bridge—bridge ... ME-1
Sewage Disposal Pond Number 1
Dam—dam ... MS-4
Sewage Disposal Pond Number 2
Dam—dam ... MS-4
Sewage Lagoon Dam North—dam ... AL-4
Sewage Lagoon Dam South—dam ... AL-4
Sewage Lagoon North—reservoir ... AL-4
Sewage Lagoon South—reservoir ... AL-4
Sewah Creek—stream ... AK-9
**Sewal**—pop pl ... IA-7
Sewal Brook ... MA-1
Sewall, Cleveland Harding,
House—hist pl ... TX-5
Sewall, Edward, Garrison—hist pl ... NH-1
Sewall, William, House—hist pl ... ME-1
Sewall Anderson Sch—school ... MA-1
Sewall-Belmont House Natl Historic
Site—hist pl ... DC-2
Sewall Brook—stream (3) ... MA-1
Sewall Brook—stream ... VT-1
Sewallcrest Park—park ... OR-9
Sewallcrest Sch—school ... OR-9
Sewall Deadwater Pond—lake ... ME-1
Sewall Hill—summit ... ME-1
Sewall Hill—summit ... MA-1
Sewall House—hist pl ... AZ-5
Sewall Point ... VA-3
Sewall Point—cape ... FL-3
Sewall Pond—lake ... ME-1
Sewall Pond—lake ... MA-1
Sewall Ridge—ridge ... ME-1
Sewall Sch—school ... MA-1
Sewall-Scripture House—hist pl ... MA-1
Sewalls Falls—falls ... NH-1
Sewalls Island—island ... NY-2
Sewalls Point ... VA-3
Sewalls Point—cape ... NH-1
**Sewalls Point**—pop pl ... FL-3
**Sewall's Point**—pop pl ... FL-3
Sewall Station ... ND-7
Sewall-Ware House—hist pl ... MA-1
Sewall Woods Park—park ... MA-1
Sewal Pond ... MA-1
Sewals Pond ... MA-1
Sewammock Neck—cape ... MA-1
Sewanee—CDP ... TN-4
**Sewanee**—pop pl ... TN-4
Sewanee Acad—school ... TN-4
Sewanee (CCD)—cens area ... TN-4
Sewanee Ch—church ... TN-4
Sewanee Creek ... TN-4
Sewanee Creek—stream ... TN-4
Sewanee Cumberland Presbyterian
Ch—church ... TN-4
Sewanee Division—civil ... TN-4
Sewanee Gulf—valley ... TN-4
Sewanee Military Academy ... TN-4
Sewanee Peak—summit ... CO-8
Sewanee Plateau—plain ... TN-4
Sewanee Post Office—building ... TN-4
Sewanee Post Office
(historical)—building ... TN-4
Sewanee Public Sch—school ... TN-4
Sewanhaka HS—school ... NY-2
**Seward**—pop pl ... AK-9
**Seward**—pop pl ... IL-6
**Seward**—pop pl ... KS-7
**Seward**—pop pl ... MD-2
**Seward**—pop pl ... NE-7
**Seward**—pop pl ... NY-2
**Seward**—pop pl ... NC-3
**Seward**—pop pl ... OH-6
**Seward**—pop pl ... OK-5
**Seward**—pop pl ... PA-2
Seward, John, House—hist pl ... TN-4
Seward, William H., House—hist pl ... NY-2
Seward Ave Baptist Ch—church ... KS-7
Seward Borough—civil ... PA-2
Seward Brook—stream ... NH-1
Seward Brook—stream ... NY-2
Seward Cem—cemetery ... KS-7
Seward Cem—cemetery ... NE-7
Seward Cem—cemetery ... NY-2
Seward Cem—cemetery ... OK-5
Seward Cem—cemetery ... TN-4
Seward (Census Subarea)—cens area ... AK-9
Seward County—civil ... KS-7
Seward County Community Coll—school ... KS-7
Seward County Country Club—other ... NE-7
Seward County Courthouse Square Hist
Dist—hist pl ... NE-7
Seward Creek ... CA-9
Seward Creek—stream (2) ... AK-9
Seward Creek—stream ... CA-9
Seward-Curks Cem—cemetery ... OR-9
Seward Depot—hist pl ... AK-9
Seward Ditch—canal ... AK-9
Seward Flat—flat ... OR-9
Seward Glacier—glacier ... AK-9
Seward Hill—summit ... NJ-2
Seward (historical)—locale ... KS-7
**Seward (historical)**—pop pl ... OR-9
Seward Hotel—hist pl ... OR-9
Seward Island ... ME-1
Seward Junction—locale ... TX-5
Seward Lake—lake ... FL-3
Seward Lake—lake ... NM-5
Seward Lake—lake ... NY-2
Seward Mountains—summit ... AK-9
Seward Mountains—summit ... NY-2
Seward Mtn—summit ... MT-8
Seward Mtn—summit ... NY-2
Seward Neck—cape ... ME-1
Seward Park—park ... IL-6
Seward Park—park ... MN-6
Seward Park—park ... NY-2
Seward Park—park ... WA-9
Seward Pass—gap ... WY-8
Seward Passage—channel ... AK-9
Seward Peak—summit ... WA-9
Seward Peninsula—cape ... AK-9
Seward Point—cape ... NY-2
Seward Point—cliff ... GA-3
Seward Pond—lake ... NY-2
Seward Ridge ... ME-1
Sewards ... MD-2
Seward Sch—school ... IL-6
Seward Sch—school ... MN-6
Seward Sch—school ... NY-2
Seward Sch—school ... WI-6
Sewards Cove—bay ... ME-1
Sewards Point—cape ... ME-1
Seward Square—park ... DC-2
Seward Street Hist Dist—hist pl ... NE-7
**Seward (Town of)**—pop pl ... NY-2
**Seward Township**—pop pl ... KS-7
**Seward (Township of)**—pop pl (2) ... IL-6
**Seward (Township of)**—pop pl ... IN-6
**Seward (Township of)**—pop pl ... MN-6
Sewardville ... DE-2
**Sewaren**—pop pl ... NJ-2
Sewaren Station—locale ... NJ-2
Sewarren ... NJ-2
Sewarrior Creek ... AL-4
Sewart AFB—military ... TN-4
Sewart Mtn—summit ... CA-9
Sewayiah Creek—stream ... MS-4
Sewee—locale ... TN-4
Sewee Bay—bay ... SC-3
Sewee Camp—locale ... SC-3
Sewee Ch—church ... SC-3
Sewee Ch—church ... TN-4
Sewee Creek ... SC-3
Sewee Creek—stream ... TN-4
Sewee Fork Sch (historical)—school ... TN-4
Sewee Grove Sch (historical)—school ... TN-4
Sewee Iron Works (historical)—locale ... TN-4
Sewee Landing—locale ... TN-4
Sewee Mill (historical)—locale ... TN-4
Sewee Mound—hist pl ... SC-3
Sewee Post Office (historical)—building ... TN-4
Sewee Sch (historical)—school ... TN-4
Sewel Fire Tower—locale ... MI-6
Sewell ... ME-1
Sewell ... OK-5
Sewell—locale ... AL-4
Sewell—locale ... KY-4
Sewell—locale ... WV-2
**Sewell**—pop pl ... MD-2
**Sewell**—pop pl ... NJ-2
**Sewell**—pop pl ... OR-9
Sewell, William C. B., House—hist pl ... IN-6
Sewell Bay—swamp (2) ... NC-3
Sewell Bend (historical)—bend ... TN-4
Sewell-Bowers Cem—cemetery ... TN-4
Sewell Branch—stream ... DE-2
Sewell Branch—stream (2) ... FL-3
Sewell Branch—stream (2) ... MD-2
Sewell Branch—stream (2) ... TN-4
Sewell Branch—stream ... TX-5
Sewell Branch—stream ... WV-2
Sewell Bridge—bridge ... MO-7
Sewell Bridge—bridge ... VA-3
Sewell Brook ... MA-1
Sewell Cem ... TN-4
Sewell Cem—cemetery (2) ... AL-4
Sewell Cem—cemetery ... AR-4
Sewell Cem—cemetery ... GA-3
Sewell Cem—cemetery ... KY-4
Sewell Cem—cemetery (2) ... MO-7
Sewell Cem—cemetery ... OH-6
Sewell Cem—cemetery ... TN-4
Sewell Ch—church ... GA-3
**Sewell Chief**—pop pl ... WV-2
Sewell Circle Park—park ... GA-3
Sewell Cove—valley ... NC-3
Sewell Creek ... TX-5
Sewell Creek—stream ... AR-4
Sewell Creek—stream ... ME-1
Sewell Creek—stream ... MO-7
Sewell Creek—stream ... TN-4
Sewell Creek—stream ... TX-5
Sewell Creek—stream ... WV-2
Sewell Ferry (historical)—locale ... AL-4
Sewell Ford—locale ... MO-7
Sewell Gulch—valley ... CO-8
Sewell Lake—lake ... FL-3
Sewell Lake—lake ... MN-6
Sewell Memorial School ... AL-4
Sewell Mill Creek—stream ... GA-3
Sewell Millpond—reservoir ... GA-3
Sewell Mills—locale ... MD-2
Sewell Mtn—summit ... KY-4
Sewell Mtn—summit ... WV-2
Sewell Park—park ... FL-3
Sewell Point ... VA-3
Sewell Point—cape ... NJ-2
Sewell Pond ... FL-3
Sewell Pond—lake ... ME-1
Sewell Pond—reservoir ... TX-5
Sewell Ranch—locale (2) ... WY-8
Sewell Rsvr—reservoir ... ID-8
Sewell Run—stream ... NC-3
Sewell Run—stream ... OH-6
Sewell Sch—school ... AL-4
Sewell Sch—school ... AZ-5
Sewell Sch—school ... NV-8
Sewell Sch (historical)—school ... MO-7
Sewells Ferry (historical)—locale ... MS-4
**Sewells Gardens**—pop pl ... VA-3
Sewells Hill ... MA-1
**Sewell Shop**—pop pl ... KY-4
Sewells Lake—reservoir ... GA-3
Sewells Point—cape ... VA-3
Sewells Point Spit—bar ... VA-3
Sewells Pond ... MA-1
Sewells Pond—lake ... MN-6
Sewell Station—locale ... MD-2
**Sewell Subdivision**
**(subdivision)**—pop pl ... AL-4
**Sewellsville**—pop pl ... OH-6
Sewell Tank—reservoir ... NM-5
Sewellton—locale ... KY-4
Sewell Valley ... WV-2
Sewell Vocational Center—school ... GA-3
Sewelson Creek—stream ... GA-3
Sewemup Mesa—summit ... CO-8
Sewemup Stock Trail—trail ... CO-8
Sewer Branch—stream ... MO-7
Sewer Branch—stream ... ND-7
Sewer Branch—stream ... SD-7
Sewer Canyon—valley ... AZ-5
Sewer Cave—cave (2) ... AL-4
Sewer Creek—stream ... AR-4
Sewer Creek—stream ... IL-6
Sewer Creek—stream (2) ... IA-7
Sewer Creek—stream ... MO-7
Sewer Creek—stream ... TX-5
Sewer Lake No 1—lake ... NE-7
Sewer Lake No 2—lake ... NE-7
Sewer Lake No 3—lake ... NE-7
Sewer Number One Tank—reservoir ... AZ-5
Sewer Number Two Tank—reservoir ... AZ-5
Sewer Trail—trail ... OR-9
Sewickey Creek ... PA-2
**Sewickley**—pop pl ... PA-2
Sewickley Acad—school ... PA-2
Sewickley Borough—civil ... PA-2
Sewickley Bridge—bridge ... PA-2
Sewickley Cem—cemetery ... PA-2
Sewickley Ch—church (3) ... PA-2
Sewickley Creek ... PA-2
Sewickley Creek—stream ... PA-2
Sewickley Grange—locale ... PA-2
**Sewickley Heights**—pop pl ... PA-2
Sewickley Heights Borough—civil ... PA-2
Sewickley Heights Sch
(abandoned)—school ... PA-2
Sewickley Heights (Township of)—other ... PA-2
**Sewickley Hills**—pop pl ... PA-2
Sewickley Hills Borough—civil ... PA-2
Sewickley Manor—hist pl ... PA-2
Sewickley Mills ... PA-2
Sewickley Post Office
(historical)—building ... AL-4
Sewickley (Township of)—other ... PA-2
**Sewickley (Township of)**—pop pl ... PA-2
Sewihso—civil ... FM-9
Sewing Machine, The—rock ... UT-8
Sewing Machine Pass—gap ... UT-8
Sewish Creek—stream ... VA-3
Sewll Pond ... MA-1
Sexauer Park—park ... SD-7
Sexauer Sch (historical)—school ... IA-7
Sex Peak—summit ... MT-8
Sexsmith Lake—lake ... NY-2
Sexson—locale ... IL-6
Sexson Branch—stream ... IL-6
**Sexson Corner**—pop pl ... IL-6
Sexson Spring—spring ... IN-6
Sextant Point—cape ... AK-9
Sexto (Barrio)—fmr MCD ... PR-3
Sexto Creek ... CO-8
Sexto Creek ... NM-5
Sexton—locale ... TN-4
Sexton—locale ... TX-5
**Sexton**—pop pl ... IN-6
**Sexton**—pop pl ... IA-7
**Sexton**—pop pl ... NC-3
Sexton And Kilfoil Drain—stream ... MI-6
Sexton Bend—bend ... AL-4
Sexton Branch—stream ... KY-4
Sexton Branch—stream (2) ... TN-4
Sexton Branch—stream ... TX-5
Sexton Branch—stream ... VA-3
Sexton Canyon—valley ... AZ-5
Sexton Canyon—valley ... CA-9
Sexton Cem—cemetery ... AR-4
Sexton Cem—cemetery (2) ... KY-4
Sexton Cem—cemetery ... OH-6
Sexton Cem—cemetery (6) ... TN-4
Sexton Cem—cemetery (2) ... VA-3
Sexton Ch—church ... LA-4
Sexton Ch—church ... NC-3
Sexton Chapel—church ... TX-5
**Sexton City**—pop pl ... TX-5
Sexton Coal Mines—mine ... MT-8
Sexton Cove—bay ... FL-3
Sexton Creek—stream ... AR-4
Sexton Creek—stream ... IL-6
Sexton Creek—stream ... KY-4
Sexton Ditch—canal ... IN-6
Sexton Ditch—canal ... OH-6
Sexton Fork—stream ... KY-4
Sexton Fork Ch—church ... KY-4
Sexton Gap—gap ... TN-4
Sexton Glacier—glacier ... MT-8
Sexton Hill—summit ... CT-1
Sexton Hill—summit ... FL-3
Sexton Hill Branch—stream ... VA-3
Sexton (historical)—locale (2) ... KS-7
Sexton Hollow—valley ... KY-4
Sexton Hollow—valley ... VA-3
Sexton HS—school ... MI-6
Sexton Island—island ... MN-6
Sexton Island—island ... NY-2
Sexton Mtn—summit (2) ... OR-9
Sexton Mtn—summit ... TN-4
Sexton Pond—lake ... TN-4
Sexton Pond—reservoir ... SC-3
Sexton Post Office (historical)—building ... TN-4
Sexton Ridge—ridge ... GA-3
Sexton Rsvr—reservoir (2) ... OR-9
Sextons Bend—bend ... AL-4
Sextons Branch—stream ... AL-4
Sexton Sch—school (2) ... IL-6
Sextons Creek—locale ... KY-4
Sextons Landing (historical)—locale ... TN-4
Sextons Point—cape ... MN-6
Sexton Spring—spring ... OR-9
Sexton Spring—spring ... TN-4
Sexton Spring Branch—stream ... AL-4
Sextons Station ... KS-7
Sexton Summit ... OR-9
**Sextonville**—pop pl ... WI-6
Sexton Well—well ... NM-5
Seybert—locale ... MO-7
Seybert Ch—church ... OH-6
Seybert Chapel—church ... VA-3
Seybert Hills—summit ... VA-3
**Seybertown**—pop pl ... PA-2
**Seyberts**—pop pl ... IN-6
Seybold Canal—canal ... FL-3
Seybold Cem—cemetery ... IN-6
Seybold Spring—spring ... MT-8
Seyfert—locale ... PA-2
Seyferth Playground—park ... MI-6
Seyffer Public Use Area—park ... IA-7
Seyforth Cem—cemetery ... OH-6
Seyler Mountain ... NV-8
Seyler Peak—summit ... NV-8
Seyler Rsvr—reservoir ... NV-8
Seyler Spring—spring ... NV-8
Seyler-Tash Ditch—canal ... MT-8
Seyler Valley—flat ... WA-9
Seyleys Pond ... PA-2
Seylor Valley ... WA-9
Seymanski Ranch—locale ... ND-7
Seymore—locale ... TX-5
Seymore Branch—stream ... AL-4
Seymore Branch—stream ... IL-6
Seymore Cem—cemetery ... AR-4
Seymore Cem—cemetery ... OH-6
Seymore Cem—cemetery ... TX-5
Seymore Cemetery ... TN-4
Seymore Creek ... MI-6
Seymore Mtn—summit ... MT-8
Seymore Peak ... WA-9
Seymore Springs—spring ... OR-9
Seymore Station—locale ... PA-2
Seymour ... MI-6
Seymour ... MS-4
Seymour ... NE-7
Seymour ... ND-7
Seymour—locale ... AL-4
Seymour—locale ... KY-4
Seymour—locale ... TN-4
Seymour—locale ... WV-2
**Seymour**—pop pl (2) ... CT-1
**Seymour**—pop pl ... GA-3
**Seymour**—pop pl ... IL-6
**Seymour**—pop pl ... IN-6
**Seymour**—pop pl ... IA-7
**Seymour**—pop pl ... MO-7
**Seymour**—pop pl ... TX-5
**Seymour**—pop pl ... WI-6
Seymour, Edward B., House—hist pl ... PA-2
Seymour, Elisha, Jr., House—hist pl ... CT-1
Seymour, Lake—lake ... MN-6
Seymour, William H., House—hist pl ... OH-6
Seymour Bay—bay ... MI-6
Seymour Bluff—cliff (2) ... AL-4
Seymour Branch—stream (2) ... AL-4
Seymour Branch Hazel Creek—stream ... MO-7
Seymour Brook—stream ... MA-1
Seymour Brook—stream ... NY-2
Seymour Brook—stream ... VT-1
Seymour Canal—channel ... AK-9
Seymour Canyon—valley ... UT 8
Seymour (CCD)—cens area (2) ... TX-5
Seymour Cem—cemetery ... IL-6
Seymour Cem—cemetery ... MS-4
Seymour Cem—cemetery ... WI-6
Seymour Central Sch—school (2) ... WI-6
Seymour City Rsvr—reservoir ... IA-7
Seymour Country Club—other ... TX-5
Seymour Cove—bay ... ME-1
Seymour Creek ... MI-6
Seymour Creek—stream ... CA-9
Seymour Creek—stream (2) ... MI-6
Seymour Creek—stream ... MT-8
Seymour Creek—stream ... OH-6
Seymour Creek—stream ... TX-5
Seymour Creek—stream ... WA-9
Seymour Creek—stream ... WI-6
Seymour Dam ... UT-8
Seymour Ditch No 2—canal ... CO-8
Seymour Downs Race Track—other ... TX-5
Seymoure Cem—cemetery ... TN-4
Seymour Flat—flat ... CA-9
Seymour Gulch—valley ... CO-8
Seymour Heights—locale ... TN-4
Seymour High School ... IN-6
Seymour Hill—summit ... WA-9
Seymour Hollow—valley ... CT-1
Seymour HS and Annex—hist pl ... CT-1
Seymour-Jackson Elem Sch—school ... IN-6
Seymour JHS—school ... MI-6
Seymour Johnson AFB—military ... NC-3
Seymour Johnson Air Force Base—other ... NC-3
**Seymour Johnson Homes**
**(subdivision)**—pop pl ... NC-3
Seymour Lake ... MT-8
Seymour Lake ... UT-8
Seymour Lake—lake ... MI-6
Seymour Lake—lake ... VT-1
Seymour Lake—lake ... WI-6
**Seymour Lake**—pop pl ... VT-1
Seymour Lake Ch—church ... MI-6
Seymour Library—building ... MS-4
Seymour McKinley Drain—canal ... MI-6
Seymour Meadow Lake Dam—dam ... UT-8

Seymour Mine—*mine* CO-8
Seymour Mtn—*summit* (2) MA-1
Seymour Mtn—*summit* (2) NY-2
Seymour Oil Field—*oilfield* TX-5
Seymour Park—*locale* NE-7
Seymour Park—*park* NY-2
Seymour Park—*park* (2) WI-6
Seymour Peak—*summit* WA-9
Seymour Pickett Grant—*civil* FL-3
Seymour Point—*cape* CT-1
Seymour Point—*cape* FL-3
Seymour Pond—*lake* MA-1
Seymour Pond—*lake* NY-2
Seymour Póst Office—*locale* TN-4
Seymour Ranch—*locale* CO-8
Seymour-Redding Elem Sch—*school* IN-6
Seymour River—*stream* VT-1
Seymour Rock—*summit* CT-1
Seymour Rsvr—*reservoir* (2) MT-8
Seymour Rsvr No 4—*reservoir* CT-1
Seymour Run—*stream* OH-6
Seymour Rural (CCD)—*cens area* TX-5
*Seymours Bluff* AL-4
Seymours Bridge Marina—*locale* TN-4
Seymour Sch—*school* IL-6
Seymour Sch—*school* IA-7
Seymour Sch—*school* (2) MI-6
Seymour Sch—*school* (2) NY-2
Seymour Sch—*school* TN-4
Seymour Senior HS—*school* IN-6
Seymours Lake—*reservoir* GA-3
Seymours Point—*cape* ME-1
*Seymours Pond* MA-1
*Seymour Square* MI-6
Seymour State Wildlife Mngmt Area—*park* MO-7
*Seymoursville* WV-2
**Seymour (Town of)**—*pop pl* (3) WI-6
Seymourville—*locale* WV-2
**Seymourville**—*pop pl* LA-4
Seymourville Sch—*school* LA-4
Seymour Watson Branch—*stream* TX-5
Seynor Creek—*stream* MI-6
Seyoc—*locale* PA-2
Seyour Corners—*locale* WI-6
Seyouyah Creek—*stream* AL-4
*Seyoyah Creek* AL-4
*Seypan Island* MH-9
*Sey Pond* PA-2
**Seyppel**—*pop pl* AR-4
Seyppel Lodge—*locale* AR-4
**Seyton**—*pop pl* MN-6
*Sezhini Butte* AZ-5
Se-1 Canal—*canal* CA-9
S.F.A.(Stephen F. Austin College)—*uninc pl* TX-5
S F Campfire Girls Camp—*locale* CA-9
SF Lateral—*canal* TX-5
S-Fourteen Creek—*stream* MT-8
S-F Scout Ranch—*locale* MO-7
S F State College Camp—*locale* CA-9
S Garrard Ditch—*canal* IN-6
S G Drain—*canal* WY-8
*Sguaw Creek* ND-7
S Gulch—*valley* WY-8
*Sh* AL-4
Shaaf Pond—*reservoir* VA-3
*Shaantoh Spring* AZ-5
Shaarcy Zedek Temple—*church* MI-6
Shaar Hollow—*valley* PA-2
*Shaatkam* AZ-5
Shabakunk Creek—*stream* NJ-2
Shabbit Island—*island* ME-1
Shabbit Island Ledge—*bar* ME-1
**Shabbona**—*pop pl* IL-6
**Shabbona**—*pop pl* MI-6
Shabbona County Park—*park* IL-6
**Shabbona Grove**—*pop pl* IL-6
Shabbona Park—*park* (2) IL-6
Shabbona Sch—*school* IL-6
**Shabbona (Township of)**—*pop pl* IL-6
Shabby Island—*island* ME-1
Shabbyroom Branch—*stream* WV-2
Shabikeshchee Ruins—*locale* NM-5
Shabodock Creek—*stream* WI-6
Shabodock Lake—*lake* WI-6
*Shabunaren* MP-9
Shabunaren—*island* MP-9
*Shabunaren-To* MP-9
Shack, The—*hist pl* OH-6
Shackaford Cem—*cemetery* KY-4
Shack Allen Cem—*cemetery* KY-4
Shackaloa Creek—*stream* MS-4
Shackamaxon—*uninc pl* PA-2
Shackamaxon Dam—*dam* NJ-2
Shackamaxon Golf Course—*other* NJ-2
Shackamaxon Lake—*reservoir* NJ-2
Shackamaxon Sch—*school* NJ-2
Shackatan (Township of)—*other* MN-6
Shack Branch—*stream* AL-4
Shack Branch—*stream* (2) KY-4
Shack Branch—*stream* TN-4
Shack Camp—*locale* HI-9
Shack Creek—*stream* AL-4
Shack Creek—*stream* AK-9
Shack Creek—*stream* (2) AR-4
Shack Creek—*stream* ID-8
Shack Creek—*stream* NV-8
Shack Creek—*stream* TN-4
Shack Creek—*stream* WA-9
*Shack Eddy Lake* MN-6
*Shackelford* LA-4
*Shackelford* MO-7
Shackelford Branch—*stream* MS-4
Shackelford Branch—*stream* MO-7
Shackelford Canyon—*valley* TX-5
Shackelford Cem—*cemetery* (2) AL-4
Shackelford Cem—*cemetery* (2) VA-3
**Shackelford (County)**—*pop pl* TX-5
Shackelford County Courthouse Hist Dist—*hist pl* TX-5
Shackelford Ditch—*canal* IN-6
Shackelford Lake—*lake* MS-4
Shackelford Lake—*reservoir* MS-4
Shackelford Pond Dam—*dam* MS-4
*Shackelfords* VA-3
**Shackelford (Shackleford)**—*pop pl* MO-7
Shackelton Point—*cape* NY-2
Shackford Brook—*stream* ME-1
Shackford Corners—*locale* NH-1
Shackford Head—*summit* ME-1
Shackford Ledge—*bar* ME-1
Shackford Point—*cape* NH-1
Shackham Brook—*stream* NY-2
Shack Hill—*summit* CT-1
Shack Hill—*summit* (2) ME-1
Shack Huddle Sch—*school* MI-6
Shack Lake—*lake* AK-9
Shack Lake—*reservoir* TN-4
Shack Lake Dam—*dam* TN-4
Shacklefoot Channel—*channel* NC-3
Shacklefoot Pond—*lake* FL-3
Shackleford—*locale* MS-4
**Shackleford**—*pop pl* FL-3
**Shackleford**—*pop pl* MO-7
Shackleford Banks—*bar* NC-3
Shackleford Bar—*bar* AL-4
Shackleford Bayou—*stream* LA-4
Shackleford Cem—*cemetery* KY-4
Shackleford Cem—*cemetery* MS-4
Shackleford Cem—*cemetery* MO-7
Shackleford Ch—*church* LA-4
Shackleford Ch—*church* MS-4
Shackleford Creek—*stream* AK-9
Shackleford Creek—*stream* CA-9
Shackleford Creek—*stream* TX-5
Shackleford Crossing—*locale* MO-7
Shackleford Gap—*gap* AL-4
Shackleford Lake—*lake* LA-4
Shackleford Lake—*lake* SC-3
Shackleford Landing—*locale* GA-3
Shackleford Point—*cape* NC-3
Shackleford Ridge—*ridge* VA-3
*Shacklefords* NC-3
*Shackleford's* VA-3
**Shacklefords**—*pop pl* VA-3
**Shacklefords (Centerville)**—*pop pl* VA-3
Shackleford Sch—*school* CA-9
Shacklefords Chapel—*church* VA-3
Shackleford Sch (historical)—*school* AL-4
Shackleford Sch (historical)—*school* MS-4
**Shacklefords Fork**—*pop pl* VA-3
Shackleford Slue—*channel* NC-3
Shacklefords Mill (historical)—*locale* TN-4
Shackleford Well—*locale* VA-3
Shackleford Well—*well* TX-5
Shackleford Windmill—*locale* TX-5
Shackle Hollow—*valley* TN-4
Shackle Island—*locale* TN-4
Shackle Island Ch—*church* TN-4
Shackle Island Hist Dist—*hist pl* TN-4
Shackle Run—*stream* KY-4
**Shacklesville**—*pop pl* AL-4
Shacklesville Cem—*cemetery* AL-4
Shacklesville Ch—*church* AL-4
**Shackleton**—*pop pl* OH-6
Shackleton Pond—*lake* NY-2
**Shacklett**—*pop pl* TN-4
Shacklett Cem—*cemetery* MO-7
Shackletts Mill (historical)—*locale* TN-4
Shackleville Sch (historical)—*school* AL-4
Shackley Hill—*summit* ME-1
Shackley Island—*island* VA-3
Shackley Point—*cape* VA-3
*Shackley Slough* ND-7
*Shackleys Point* VA-3
*Shackly Point* VA-3
Shack Mountain—*hist pl* VA-3
Shackolo Cem—*cemetery* MS-4
Shack Pond—*lake* ME-1
Shackport—*locale* NY-2
Shack Ranch—*locale* TX-5
Shacks Branch—*stream* KY-4
Shacks Branch—*stream* VA-3
**Shacks Corner**—*pop pl* NJ-2
Shacks (historical)—*locale* MS-4
Shack Spring—*spring* AZ-5
Shack Tank—*reservoir* AZ-5
Shack Tank—*reservoir* NM-5
Shacktown—*locale* NC-3
Shacktown Mtn—*summit* NY-2
*Shadack Stream* NY-2
*Shadagee Brook* ME-1
Shadagee Falls—*falls* ME-1
Shadberry Landing—*locale* NC-3
Shadbolt Ranch—*locale* NE-7
*Shadbush Bay* NH-1
Shadbush Cove—*bay* NH-1
Shad Cem—*cemetery* SC-3
Shad Cove—*bay* NC-3
Shad Creek—*gut* (2) FL-3
Shad Creek—*stream* (2) MA-1
Shad Creek—*stream* MI-6
Shadden Cem—*cemetery* IL-6
Shadden Cem—*cemetery* TN-4
*Shadden Creek* OR-9
Shadden Creek—*stream* TN-4
*Shaddens Mill* TN-4
Shaddock Branch—*stream* AR-4
Shaddock Creek—*stream* GA-3
Shaddock Hollow—*valley* TN-4
*Shaddocks Weir* RI-1
Shaddon Mill—*locale* TN-4
Shaddon Mill Cave—*cave* TN-4
Shaddox Branch—*stream* AR-4
Shaddox Creek—*stream* NC-3
Shadd Sch—*school* DC-2
Shaddtown Cem—*cemetery* TN-4
Shadduck Creek—*stream* WI-6
Shadduck Drain—*canal* MI-6
Shadduck Park—*park* KS-7
Shade—*locale* KY-4
**Shade**—*pop pl* MO-7
**Shade**—*pop pl* OH-6
Shade Branch—*stream* (2) KY-4
Shade Branch—*stream* (2) NC-3
Shade Branch—*stream* VA-3
Shade Branch Johns Creek—*stream* KY-4
Shade Ch—*church* PA-2
*Shade Creek* AL-4
*Shade Creek* MT-8
Shade Creek—*stream* AK-9
Shade Creek—*stream* MT-8
Shade Creek—*stream* OH-6
Shade Creek—*stream* OR-9
Shade Creek—*stream* (2) PA-2
Shade Creek—*stream* WV-2
Shaded Spring—*spring* AZ-5
Shade Fork—*stream* PA-2
*Shade Furnace* PA-2
Shade Furnace Post Office (historical)—*building* PA-2
**Shade Gap**—*pop pl* PA-2
Shade Gap Borough—*civil* PA-2
Shade Gap Elem Sch—*school* PA-2
Shade Gap Station (abandoned)—*building* PA-2
**Shadehill**—*pop pl* SD-7
Shade Hill—*summit* MD-2
Shadehill Dam—*dam* SD-7
Shadehill Dike Number 1—*dam* SD-7
Shadehill Rsvr—*reservoir* (2) SD-7
Shade Lake—*lake* TX-5
Shadeland—*hist pl* PA-2
**Shadeland**—*pop pl* (2) IN-6
**Shadeland**—*pop pl* KY-4
**Shadeland**—*pop pl* PA-2
Shadeland Ch—*church* TN-4
Shadeland Elem Sch—*school* IN-6
Shadeland Post Office (historical)—*building* TN-4
Shadeland Sch—*school* IN-6
Shadelands Ranch House—*hist pl* CA-9
Shadeland Station—*locale* PA-2
Shade Loftin Branch—*stream* TN-4
**Shademoore**—*pop pl* OH-6
*Shademore* OH-6
**Shademore**—*pop pl* OH-6
Shade Mountain Fire Tower—*tower* PA-2
Shade Mtn—*range* (2) PA-2
*Shaden Mountain* AR-4
Shadepen Branch—*stream* NC-3
Shadequarter Mtn—*summit* CA-9
Shade River—*locale* OH-6
Shade River—*stream* OH-6
Shade Run—*stream* MD-2
Shades, The—*hist pl* LA-4
**Shades Acres (subdivision)**—*pop pl* AL-4
Shades Beach County Boat Livery (historical)—*locale* PA-2
*Shades Branch* AL-4
*Shades Branch* DE-2
*Shades-Cahaba Elementary School* AL-4
Shades-Cahaba Sch—*school* AL-4
Shade Sch—*school* OH-6
**Shades Cliff**—*pop pl* AL-4
Shades Creek—*stream* AL-4
Shades Creek—*stream* PA-2
**Shades Crest Estates**—*pop pl* AL-4
Shades Death Creek—*stream* WV-2
**Shades Glen**—*pop pl* PA-2
Shades Mountain—*ridge* AL-4
Shades Mountain Bible Ch—*church* AL-4
Shades Mountain Elem Sch—*school* AL-4
Shades Mtn—*range* AL-4
Shades Pond—*reservoir* IN-6
Shades Pond Dam—*dam* IN-6
Shade Springs—*spring* NV-8
*Shade Spur* KY-4
Shades Run—*stream* PA-2
Shades State Park—*park* IN-6
Shades State Park Airp—*airport* IN-6
Shades Valley—*valley* AL-4
*Shades Valley Elementary School* AL-4
Shades Valley HS—*school* AL-4
Shades Valley Sch—*school* AL-4
Shades Valley Sewage Treatment Plant—*building* AL-4
Shade Swamp—*swamp* CT-1
Shade Swamp Shelter—*hist pl* CT-1
**Shade (Township of)**—*pop pl* PA-2
*Shadetree* IL-6
Shade Valley—*basin* PA-2
**Shade Valley**—*pop pl* PA-2
Shade Valley Lake—*reservoir* OH-6
**Shadeville**—*pop pl* FL-3
**Shadeville**—*pop pl* OH-6
Shadeville Elem Sch—*school* FL-3
Shadeville Park Memorial Cem—*cemetery* MS-4
Shad Factory Pond—*reservoir* MA-1
Shad Factory Pond Dam—*dam* MA-1
Shad Gully—*valley* ME-1
Shad Hill—*ridge* NH-1
Shad Hollow—*valley* MO-7
Shad Hollow—*valley* TN-4
Shadick Spring—*spring* WI-6
**Shadigee**—*pop pl* NY-2
Shadigee Creek—*stream* PA-2
Shadigee Sch—*school* ME-1
Shadinger, J. Alvin, House—*hist pl* HI-9
Shad Island—*island* NJ-2
Shad Island—*island* NY-2
Shad Island—*island* PA-2
Shad Island—*island* VT-1
Shad Lake—*lake* LA-4
Shad Lake—*reservoir* IL-6
Shad Landing—*locale* MD-2
Shad Landing—*locale* VA-3
Shad Landing State Park—*park* MD-2
Shadle—*locale* PA-2
Shadle Bridge—*other* WV-2
Shadle Cem—*cemetery* MO-7
Shadle Cem—*cemetery* TX-5
Shadle Drain—*stream* IN-6
Shadle Garland—*post sta* WA-9
Shadle Park—*park* IA-7
Shadle Park—*park* WA-9
Shadle Park HS—*school* WA-9
Shadley Cem—*cemetery* OH-6
Shadley Creek—*stream* AR-4
Shadley Creek—*stream* CA-9
Shadley Creek—*stream* NE-7
Shadley Creek—*stream* SD-7
Shadley Vale Creek—*stream* NE-7
Shadley Valley Creek—*stream* OH-6
*Shadly Creek* NE-7
*Shadly Creek* SD-7
Shadmon Sch (historical)—*school* MS-4
Shadnor Ch—*church* GA-3
Shadoan Sawmill—*locale* MT-8
Sha Donde Tank—*reservoir* AZ-5
Shadow—*locale* VA-3
Shadow—*locale* WA-9
Shadow, Lake—*lake* FL-3
Shadow Bay—*bay* AK-9
Shadow Bay—*bay* WA-9
Shadow Bay Forest Camp—*locale* OR-9
Shadow Bluff—*cliff* IL-6
Shadow Box Arch—*arch* UT-8
Shadow Brook—*stream* MA-1
Shadow Brook—*stream* NY-2
Shadowbrook Dam—*dam* DE-2
Shadow Brook Farm Hist Dist—*hist pl* MA-1
Shadow Brook Golf Course—*locale* PA-2
Shadowbrook Novitiate—*school* MA-1
Shadowbrook Pond—*reservoir* DE-2
**Shadow Canyon**—*pop pl* AZ-5
Shadow Canyon—*valley* CA-9
Shadow Canyon—*valley* CO-8
Shadow Canyon—*valley* NV-8
Shadow Canyon—*valley* OR-9
Shadow Cave—*cave* AZ-5
Shadow Cem—*cemetery* TN-4
Shadow Creek—*stream* (2) CA-9
Shadow Creek—*stream* OR-9
Shadow Creek—*stream* WA-9
Shadow Creek Campground—*locale* CA-9
Shadow Falls—*falls* MN-6
Shadow Falls—*falls* OR-9
Shadow Falls Campground—*park* OR-9
Shadow Farm—*hist pl* RI-1
**Shadow Glen**—*pop pl* TX-5
*Shadow Hall* MD-2
Shadow Hills—*summit* CA-9
Shadow Hills Country Club—*other* OR-9
**Shadow Hills East Subdivision**—*pop pl* UT-8
**Shadow Hills (subdivision)**—*pop pl* (2). AZ-5
Shadow Hill State For—*forest* NH-1
*Shadow Lake* NE-7
*Shadow Lake* WI-6
Shadow Lake—*lake* AR-4
Shadow Lake—*lake* (5) CA-9
Shadow Lake—*lake* CO-8
Shadow Lake—*lake* IL-6
Shadow Lake—*lake* MA-1
Shadow Lake—*lake* (3) MI-6
Shadow Lake—*lake* MN-6
Shadow Lake—*lake* (5) MT-8
Shadow Lake—*lake* NH-1
Shadow Lake—*lake* NY-2
Shadow Lake—*lake* (2) OR-9
Shadow Lake—*lake* TX-5
Shadow Lake—*lake* (3) UT-8
Shadow Lake—*lake* VT-1
Shadow Lake—*lake* (4) WA-9
Shadow Lake—*lake* (3) WI-6
Shadow Lake—*lake* WY-8
**Shadow Lake**—*pop pl* VT-1
Shadow Lake—*reservoir* AL-4
Shadow Lake—*reservoir* CA-9
Shadow Lake—*reservoir* CO-8
Shadow Lake—*reservoir* FL-3
Shadow Lake—*reservoir* IN-6
Shadow Lake—*reservoir* MI-6
Shadow Lake—*reservoir* MS-4
Shadow Lake—*reservoir* MO-7
Shadow Lake—*reservoir* NH-1
Shadow Lake—*reservoir* (2) NJ-2
Shadow Lake—*reservoir* NY-2
Shadow Lake—*reservoir* (2) NC-3
Shadow Lake—*reservoir* OH-6
Shadow Lake Dam—*dam* (2) NJ-2
Shadow Lake Dam—*dam* (2) NC-3
**Shadow Lake Estates (subdivision)**—*pop pl* MS-4
*Shadow Lakes* WY-8
Shadow Lakes—*reservoir* ID-8
Shadowland—*locale* TX-5
Shadowlawn—*building* MS-4
Shadow Lawn—*hist pl* NJ-2
Shadow Lawn—*hist pl* NC-3
Shadow Lawn—*hist pl* VA-3
**Shadow Lawn**—*pop pl* IL-6
**Shadowlawn**—*pop pl* TN-4
Shadowlawn—*uninc pl* FL-3
Shadow Lawn—*uninc pl* WV-2
Shadowlawn Baptist Ch—*church* AL-4
Shadowlawn Cem—*cemetery* GA-3
Shadowlawn Elem Sch—*school* FL-3
**Shadow Lawn Estates**—*pop pl* FL-3
**Shadowlawn Heights**—*pop pl* VA-3
Shadowlawn Memorial Park—*cemetery* AL-4
*Shadow Lawn Sch* FL-3
Shadowlawn Sch—*school* FL-3
Shadowlawn Sch—*school* TN-4
Shadow Lawn Sch—*school* WI-6
**Shadowlawn (subdivision)**—*pop pl* NC-3
Shadowmere Lake—*lake* NY-2
**Shadow Mountain**—*pop pl* CO-8
Shadow Mountain Dam—*dam* CO-8
Shadow Mountain Lake—*reservoir* CO-8
Shadow Mountain Lookout—*hist pl* CO-8
Shadow Mountain Mine—*mine* CA-9
Shadow Mountain Natl Rec Area—*park* CO-8
*Shadow Mountain Reservoir* CO-8
Shadow Mountains—*range* CA-9
Shadow Mountains—*ridge* CA-9
Shadow Mountain Sch—*school* AZ-5
**Shadow Mountain (subdivision)**—*pop pl* (2) AZ-5
**Shadow Mountain Subdivision**—*pop pl* UT-8
Shadow Mountain Trail—*trail* CO-8
**Shadow Mountain Village Scottsdale (trailer pa**—*pop pl* AZ-5
Shadow Mountain Village Scottsdale (trailer park)—*locale* AZ-5
Shadow Mountain Well—*well* AZ-5
*Shadow Mtn* AZ-5
Shadow Mtn—*summit* AZ-5
Shadow Mtn—*summit* (2) CA-9
Shadow Mtn—*summit* (2) CO-8
Shadow Mtn—*summit* MT-8
Shadow Mtn—*summit* WA-9
Shadow Mtn—*summit* WY-8
**Shadowns Subdivision**—*pop pl* UT-8
Shadow Oaks Sch—*school* TX-5
**Shadow Oaks Subdivision**—*pop pl* UT-8
**Shadowood**—*pop pl* OR-9
Shadowood Farm Airp—*airport* PA-2
Shadowood Square (Shop Ctr)—*locale* FL-3
**Shado-Wood Village**—*pop pl* PA-2
Shadow Peak—*summit* WY-8
Shadow Point—*cape* MD-2
*Shadow Pond* CT-1
Shadow Pond—*lake* ME-1
Shadow Pond—*lake* VT-1
Shadow Pond—*reservoir* VA-3
Shadow Pool—*lake* NH-1
**Shadow Ridge II (subdivision)**—*pop pl* (2) AZ-5
**Shadow Ridge Subdivision**—*pop pl* (2) UT-8
Shadow Rim Camp—*locale* AZ-5
Shadow Rock Public Use Area—*locale* MO-7
**Shadow Run Estates Subdivision**—*pop pl* UT-8
Shadows Glacier—*glacier* AK-9
**Shadow Shuttle**—*pop pl* PA-2
Shadows-on-the-Teche—*hist pl* LA-4
Shadow Spring—*spring* CA-9
Shadow Spring—*spring* TN-4
**Shadow Valley**—*pop pl* VA-3
Shadow Valley—*valley* CA-9
Shadow Valley—*valley* WA-9
**Shadow Valley Estates (subdivision)**—*pop pl* UT-8
Shadow Valley Lake—*reservoir* MO-7
**Shadow Wood**—*pop pl* TN-4
**Shadow Wood (subdivision)**—*pop pl* MS-4
Shad Point—*cape* MD-2
Shad Point—*cape* NC-3
**Shad Point**—*pop pl* MD-2
Shad Pond—*lake* ME-1
Shadrach—*reservoir* IL-6
Shadrach Draft—*valley* PA-2
Shadrach Pond—*lake* NH-1
Shadrack Bluff—*cliff* MO-7
*Shadrick Creek* WV-2
Shadrick Creek—*stream* NC-3
Shadrick Fork—*stream* WV-2
Shadrick Hill—*locale* TN-4
Shad River—*channel* GA-3
*Shad Rock* OR-9
Shadrow Ditch—*canal* IN-6
Shadscale Canyon—*valley* UT-8
Shadscale Canyon Trailer Wash—*stream* UT-8
Shadscale Flat—*flat* OR-9
Shadscale Mesa—*summit* UT-8
Shadscale Spring—*spring* OR-9
Shad Spring Gulch—*valley* CA-9
Shad Swamp—*swamp* NY-2
Shadtown—*locale* TN-4
*Shadtown Cemetery* TN-4
Shadura Lake—*lake* AK-9
Shadwell—*locale* VA-3
Shadwell Creek—*stream* MT-8
Shadwell Creek—*stream* ND-7
Shadwell Creek—*stream* VA-3
Shadwell Sch—*school* ND-7
Shadwick Branch—*stream* NC-3
Shadwick Branch—*stream* TN-4
Shadwick Cem—*cemetery* TN-4
*Shady* MS-4
*Shady* TN-4
Shady—*locale* FL-3
**Shady**—*pop pl* AR-4
**Shady**—*pop pl* NY-2
**Shady**—*pop pl* OR-9
**Shady Acres**—*pop pl* AL-4
**Shady Acres**—*pop pl* PA-2
**Shady Acres**—*pop pl* (2) TN-4
Shady Acres Airp—*airport* WA-9
**Shady Acres Estates (subdivision)**—*pop pl* AL-4
Shady Acres Golf Course—*other* MO-7
Shady Acres Sch—*school* FL-3
**Shady Acres (subdivision)**—*pop pl* (2) AL-4
**Shady Acres (subdivision)**—*pop pl* MS-4
**Shady Acres Trailer Park**—*pop pl* DE-2
**Shady Banks**—*pop pl* IN-6
**Shady Banks**—*pop pl* NC-3
Shady Beach—*beach* TN-4
Shady Beach—*locale* WA-9
**Shady Beach**—*pop pl* IL-6
**Shady Beach**—*pop pl* SD-7
Shady Bend—*locale* KS-7
**Shady Bend**—*pop pl* OH-6
Shady Bend Creek—*stream* AL-4
Shady Bend Sch—*school* AR-4
Shady Bend Spring—*spring* NM-5
**Shady Bluff (subdivision)**—*pop pl* TN-4
**Shady Bower**—*pop pl* MD-2
Shady Bowl Speedway—*other* OH-6
Shady Bradley Lake—*lake* LA-4
Shady Branch—*stream* AL-4
Shady Branch—*stream* IA-7
Shady Branch—*stream* NC-3
Shady Branch—*stream* VA-3
*Shady Brodley Lake* LA-4
Shady Brook—*locale* KS-7
**Shady Brook**—*pop pl* AL-4
**Shady Brook**—*pop pl* NM-5
**Shady Brook**—*pop pl* NC-3
**Shady Brook**—*pop pl* WV-2
Shady Brook—*stream* (2) CT-1
Shady Brook—*stream* FL-3
Shady Brook—*stream* WI-6
Shady Brook Camp—*locale* CO-8
Shady Brook Canyon—*valley* NM-5
Shady Brook Ch—*church* NC-3
**Shady Brook Estates Subdivision**—*pop pl* UT-8
Shady Brook Farm—*hist pl* KY-4
Shady Brook Hosp—*hospital* SC-3
Shady Brook Park—*park* PA-2
Shady Brook Run—*stream* PA-2
Shady Brook Sch—*school* NC-3
**Shady Brook Subdivision**—*pop pl* UT-8
Shady Campground—*locale* WA-9
Shady Canyon—*valley* CA-9
Shady Cem—*cemetery* IN-6
Shady Ch—*church* GA-3
Shady Ch—*church* MO-7
Shady Ch—*church* TN-4
Shady Corner Curve—*locale* NY-2
Shady Cove—*bay* AK-9
**Shady Cove**—*pop pl* OR-9
Shady Cove Campground—*park* OR-9
Shady Cove (CCD)—*cens area* OR-9
Shady Cove Public Use Area—*park* MS-4
Shady Cove Resort—*locale* TN-4
*Shady Creek* NE-7
*Shady Creek* SD-7
Shady Creek—*stream* AK-9
Shady Creek—*stream* AR-4
Shady Creek—*stream* CA-9
Shady Creek—*stream* CO-8
Shady Creek—*stream* (3) ID-8
Shady Creek—*stream* KS-7
Shady Creek—*stream* MN-6
Shady Creek—*stream* MO-7
Shady Creek—*stream* NV-8
Shady Creek—*stream* (5) OR-9
Shady Creek Ch—*church* AL-4
Shady Creek Fire Camp—*locale* CA-9
**Shady Dale**—*pop pl* GA-3
Shady Dale (CCD)—*cens area* GA-3
Shadydale Ch—*church* OK-5
Shadydale Ch—*church* WV-2
Shadydale Sch—*school* TX-5
*Shady Del* CA-9
Shady Dell—*basin* AZ-5
Shady Dell—*locale* CA-9
Shady Dell—*locale* MO-7
Shady Dell—*locale* WI-6
**Shady Dell**—*pop pl* MO-7
**Shady Dell**—*pop pl* OR-9
Shady Dell—*valley* CA-9
Shady Dell Camp—*locale* OR-9
Shady Dell Campground—*locale* UT-8
Shady Dell Ch—*church* MO-7
Shady Dell Grange Hall—*locale* MD-2
**Shady Dell (historical)**—*pop pl* MS-4
Shady Dell Park—*park* MS-4
Shady Dell Sch—*school* MO-7
Shady Dell Sch (historical)—*school* MO-7
**Shady Dell (trailer park)**—*pop pl* DE-2
Shady Field Landing—*locale* GA-3
Shady Ford (historical)—*locale* TN-4
**Shady Forest**—*pop pl* NC-3
Shady Forest Camp—*locale* OR-9
Shady Fork—*stream* WV-2
*Shady Gap* PA-2
Shady Gap—*gap* OR-9
Shady Gap—*gap* TN-4
Shady Glade Ch—*church* AR-4
**Shady Glen**—*pop pl* CA-9
**Shady Glen**—*pop pl* OH-6
Shady Glen Ch—*church* OH-6
**Shady Glen (Knockemstiff)**—*pop pl* OH-6
Shady Glenn Ch—*church* VA-3
*Shady Grove* NC-3
*Shady Grove* PA-2
*Shady Grove* TN-4
Shady Grove—*hist pl* KY-4
Shady Grove—*hist pl* VA-3
Shady Grove—*locale* (5) AR-4
Shady Grove—*locale* FL-3
Shady Grove—*locale* GA-3
Shady Grove—*locale* IA-7
Shady Grove—*locale* KY-4
Shady Grove—*locale* LA-4
Shady Grove—*locale* OH-6
Shady Grove—*locale* OK-5
Shady Grove—*locale* (9) TN-4
Shady Grove—*locale* (8) TX-5
Shady Grove—*locale* (3) VA-3
Shady Grove—*locale* WV-2
**Shady Grove**—*pop pl* (7) AL-4
**Shady Grove**—*pop pl* (3) AR-4
**Shady Grove**—*pop pl* FL-3
**Shady Grove**—*pop pl* IL-6
**Shady Grove**—*pop pl* (2) KY-4
**Shady Grove**—*pop pl* (8) MS-4
**Shady Grove**—*pop pl* (2) MO-7
**Shady Grove**—*pop pl* NC-3
**Shady Grove**—*pop pl* OH-6
**Shady Grove**—*pop pl* (2) OK-5
**Shady Grove**—*pop pl* OR-9
**Shady Grove**—*pop pl* PA-2
**Shady Grove**—*pop pl* (6) TN-4
**Shady Grove**—*pop pl* (4) TX-5
**Shady Grove**—*pop pl* VA-3
Shady Grove Access Area—*park* TN-4
*Shady Grove Baptist Ch* MS-4
*Shady Grove Baptist Ch* TN-4
Shady Grove Baptist Ch—*church* (2) MS-4
Shady Grove Baptist Ch—*church* TN-4
Shady Grove Baptist Ch—*church* TX-5
Shady Grove Baptist Ch (historical)—*church* TN-4
*Shady Grove Baptist Church* AL-4
Shady Grove Boat Harbor—*locale* TN-4
Shady Grove Branch—*stream* AL-4
Shady Grove Branch—*stream* LA-4
Shady Grove (CCD)—*cens area* TN-4
*Shady Grove Cem* TN-4
Shady Grove Cem—*cemetery* (13) AL-4
Shady Grove Cem—*cemetery* (16) AR-4
Shady Grove Cem—*cemetery* CA-9
Shady Grove Cem—*cemetery* (2) FL-3
Shady Grove Cem—*cemetery* (2) GA-3
Shady Grove Cem—*cemetery* KY-4
Shady Grove Cem—*cemetery* (5) LA-4
Shady Grove Cem—*cemetery* (24) MS-4
Shady Grove Cem—*cemetery* (4) MO-7
Shady Grove Cem—*cemetery* (2) NC-3
Shady Grove Cem—*cemetery* (5) OK-5
Shady Grove Cem—*cemetery* SC-3
Shady Grove Cem—*cemetery* (9) TN-4
Shady Grove Cem—*cemetery* (10) TX-5
Shady Grove Cem—*cemetery* VA-3
*Shady Grove Ch* AL-4
*Shady Grove Ch* MS-4
Shady Grove Ch—*church* (67) AL-4
Shady Grove Ch—*church* (34) AR-4
Shady Grove Ch—*church* (10) FL-3
Shady Grove Ch—*church* (35) GA-3
Shady Grove Ch—*church* (2) IN-6
Shady Grove Ch—*church* (9) KY-4
Shady Grove Ch—*church* (20) LA-4
Shady Grove Ch—*church* (57) MS-4
Shady Grove Ch—*church* (9) MO-7
Shady Grove Ch—*church* NM-5
Shady Grove Ch—*church* (30) NC-3
Shady Grove Ch—*church* OH-6
Shady Grove Ch—*church* (4) OK-5
Shady Grove Ch—*church* (19) SC-3
Shady Grove Ch—*church* (23) TN-4
Shady Grove Ch—*church* (4) TX-5
Shadygrove Ch—*church* TX-5
Shady Grove Ch—*church* (26) TX-5
Shady Grove Ch—*church* (8) VA-3
Shady Grove Ch—*church* (4) WV-2
Shady Grove Chapel—*church* NC-3
Shady Grove Ch (historical)—*church* (4) AL-4
Shady Grove Ch (historical)—*church* (5) MS-4

Shady Grove Ch (historical)—church MO-7
Shady Grove Ch (historical)—church (4) TN-4
Shady Grove Ch Number 1 AL-4
Shady Grove Ch Number 2 AL-4
Shady Grove Ch of Christ AL-4
Shady Grove Ch of Christ TN-4
Shady Grove Ch (reduced usage)—church TX-5
Shady Grove Christian Church AL-4
Shady Grove CME Ch AL-4
Shady Grove Community Hall—locale AR-4
Shady Grove Community Hall—locale TX-5
Shady Grove Congregational Methodist Ch AL-4
Shady Grove Corner—locale VA-3
Shady Grove Creek—stream MO-7
Shady Grove Creek—stream OK-5
Shady Grove Cumberland Presbyterian Ch TN-4
Shady Grove Dam Number One—dam AL-4
Shady Grove Dam Number Two—dam AL-4
Shady Grove Division—civil TN-4
Shady Grove Dock—locale TN-4
**Shady Grove Duck River**—pop pl TN-4
Shady Grove East Church AL-4
Shady Grove Elementary School NC-3
Shady Grove Elementary School PA-2
Shady Grove Elem Sch—school KS-7
Shady Grove Elem Sch—school MS-4
Shady Grove (historical)—locale (2) AL-4
**Shady Grove (historical)**—pop pl MS-4
**Shady Grove (historical)**—pop pl TN-4
Shady Grove Hollow—valley TN-4
Shady Grove JHS—school PA-2
Shady Grove Lake—lake MN-6
Shady Grove Lake Number One—reservoir AL-4
Shady Grove Lake Number Two—reservoir AL-4
Shady Grove Lakes—reservoir AL-4
Shady Grove Lookout Tower—locale TX-5
Shady Grove Meeting Ground (historical)—locale TN-4
Shady Grove Methodist Ch AL-4
Shady Grove Methodist Ch TN-4
Shady Grove Methodist Ch—church AL-4
Shady Grove Methodist Ch—church TN-4
Shady Grove Methodist Church MS-4
Shady Grove Mission—church MS-4
Shady Grove Missionary Baptist Ch AL-4
Shady Grove Missionary Baptist Ch MS-4
Shady Grove Mobile and Recreational Vehicle Park—locale AZ-5
Shady Grove Music Fair Theater—other MD-2
Shady Grove Nazarene Ch AL-4
Shady Grove Park—park CA-9
Shady Grove Park—park GA-3
Shady Grove Park—park (2) MS-4
Shady Grove Park—park PA-2
Shady Grove Pentecostal Holiness Church MS-4
Shady Grove Pond—reservoir GA-3
Shady Grove Post Office TN-4
Shadygrove Post Office (historical)—building TN-4
Shady Grove Primitive Baptist Ch AL-4
Shady Grove Primitive Baptist Ch—church FL-3
Shady Grove Primitive Baptist Church TN-4
Shady Grove Ridge—ridge KY-4
Shady Grove Ridge—ridge MO-7
Shady Grove Run—stream CA-9
Shady Grove Run—stream VA-3
Shady Grove Sanitorium—hospital KY-4
Shady Grove Sch AL-4
Shady Grove Sch—hist pl AR-4
Shady Grove Sch—school (3) AL-4
Shady Grove Sch—school (4) AR-4
Shady Grove Sch—school FL-3
Shady Grove Sch—school (2) IL-6
Shady Grove Sch—school (2) KY-4
Shady Grove Sch—school (4) LA-4
Shady Grove Sch—school (2) MS-4
Shady Grove Sch—school (5) MO-7
Shady Grove Sch—school (2) NC-3
Shady Grove Sch—school (3) OK-5
Shady Grove Sch—school (3) SC-3
Shady Grove Sch—school (4) TN-4
Shady Grove Sch—school TX-5
Shady Grove Sch—school WI-6
Shady Grove Sch (abandoned)—school (3) MO-7
Shady Grove Sch (abandoned)—school (3) PA-2
Shady Grove Sch (historical)—school (8) AL-4
Shady Grove Sch (historical)—school (14) MS-4
Shady Grove Sch (historical)—school (4) MO-7
Shady Grove Sch (historical)—school (13) TN-4
Shady Grove Sch (historical)—school TX-5
Shady Grove School (Abandoned)—locale IA-7
Shady Grove School (historical)—locale MO-7
**Shady Grove Shores**—pop pl TN-4
Shady Grove Site (22OU525)—hist pl MS-4
**Shady Grove (subdivision)**—pop pl DE-2
**Shady Grove Subdivision**—pop pl UT-8
Shady Grove (Township of)—fmr MCD (2) AR-4
Shady Grove (Township of)—fmr MCD NC-3
Shady Grove United Methodist Church AL-4
Shady Grove United Methodist Church MS-4
Shady Grove Youth Camp—locale FL-3
Shady Gulch—valley (2) CA-9
**Shady Harbor**—pop pl RI-1
Shady Haven Camper Park and Marina—locale IA-7
**Shady Heights (subdivision)**—pop pl AL-4
Shadyhill TN-4
**Shady Hill**—pop pl IL-6
**Shady Hill**—pop pl TN-4
Shady Hill Branch—stream TN-4
Shady Hill Ch—church (2) AL-4
Shady Hill Ch—church NC-3
Shady Hill Ch—church TN-4
Shady Hill Ch—church VA-3
Shady Hill Hist Dist—hist pl MA-1
Shady Hill Post Office TN-4
Shadyhill Post Office (historical)—building TN-4
**Shady Hills**—pop pl IN-6
Shady Hills—post sta FL-3
Shady Hill Sch—school MA-1
Shady Hill Sch—school MO-7
Shady Hill Sch—school TN-4
Shady Hills Elem Sch—school FL-3
**Shady Hills Estates**—pop pl IN-6
Shady Hollow—valley OH-6
Shady Hollow Country Club—other OH-6
Shady Hollow Lake—reservoir IN-6
Shady Hollow Lake Dam—dam IN-6
Shady Hollow Lakes—reservoir MO-7
Shady Hollow Sch—school NE-7
Shady Island—island (2) MN-6
Shady Isle—island MA-1
**Shady Knoll Mobile Estates**—pop pl NC-3
Shady Lake MN-6
Shady Lake—lake AR-4
Shady Lake—lake CT-1
Shady Lake—lake (2) IL-6
Shady Lake—lake IN-6
Shady Lake—lake KY-4
Shady Lake—lake (2) MI-6
Shady Lake—lake MN-6
Shady Lake—reservoir (2) GA-3
Shady Lake—reservoir MO-7
Shady Lake—reservoir NJ-2
Shady Lake—reservoir (2) PA-2
Shady Lake—reservoir TN-4
Shady Lake (Mud Lake)—lake WA-9
Shady Land Ch—church KY-4
Shadyland Point—cape MN-6
**Shady Lane**—pop pl AL-4
**Shady Lane**—pop pl DE-2
**Shady Lane**—pop pl IN-6
**Shady Lane**—pop pl VA-3
Shady Lane Canyon—valley CA-9
Shady Lane Cem—cemetery PA-2
Shady Lane Park—park TX-5
Shady Lane Sch—school IL-6
Shady Lane Sch—school NJ-2
Shady Lane Sch—school OH-6
Shady Lane Stock Farm—hist pl MN-6
**Shady Lawn**—pop pl IN-6
**Shady Lawn Manor**—pop pl NJ-2
Shady Lea—summit RI-1
Shady Lea Hist Dist—hist pl RI-1
Shady Mine TN-4
Shady Mountain Creek—stream VA-3
Shady Mtn—summit (2) VA-3
Shady Nook—locale ME-1
**Shady Nook**—pop pl IN-6
Shady Nook Basin—basin WA-9
Shady Nook Ch—church MO-7
Shady Nook Chapel—church IN-6
Shady Nook Lake—lake FL-3
Shady Nook Sch—school MO-7
Shady Nook Sch—school NE-7
Shady Nook Sch—school WI-6
**Shadynook (Shady Nook)**—pop pl KY-4
Shady Oak—locale IA-7
Shady Oak—locale VA-3
**Shady Oak**—pop pl MS-4
Shady Oak Brook—stream RI-1
Shady Oak Ch—church MS-4
Shady Oak Ch—church NC-3
Shady Oak Ch—church SC-3
Shady Oak Lake—lake MN-6
Shady Oak Lake Cem—cemetery MN-6
Shady Oak Mission—church TX-5
Shady Oak Park—park IL-6
Shady Oak Park—park LA-4
Shady Oaks—hist pl NC-3
**Shady Oaks**—pop pl LA-4
**Shady Oaks**—pop pl MD-2
Shady Oaks—uninc pl TX-5
Shady Oaks Airstrip—airport OR-9
Shady Oaks Camp—locale CA-9
Shady Oaks Camp—locale IL-6
Shady Oaks Ch—church (2) TX-5
Shady Oak Sch—school FL-3
Shady Oak Sch (historical)—school MS-4
Shady Oaks Country Club—locale MS-4
Shady Oaks Lake—reservoir IN-6
Shady Oaks Lake—reservoir MS-4
Shady Oaks Lake Dam—dam IN-6
Shady Oaks Lake Dam—dam MS-4
Shady Oaks Mall—locale FL-3
Shady Oaks Marsh—swamp MD-2
Shady Oaks Rsvr—reservoir AR-4
Shady Park—park OH-6
Shady Park Sch—school PA-2
**Shady Park (trailer park)**—pop pl DE-2
Shady Pass—gap WA-9
**Shady Pine**—pop pl OR-9
Shady Pine Ch—church PA-2
Shady Pines Southern Baptist Ch—church AL-4
**Shady Plain**—pop pl PA-2
Shadypoint OK-5
**Shady Point**—pop pl OK-5
Shady Point Creek—stream OR-9
Shady Point Sch—hist pl OK-5
Shady Post Office TN-4
Shady Ranch Trailer Lodge—locale AZ-5
Shady Rest—hist pl KY-4
Shady Rest—locale (2) FL-3
**Shady Rest**—pop pl CT-1
**Shady Rest**—pop pl (2) TN-4
Shady Rest—uninc pl SC-3
Shady Rest Camp—locale MT-8
Shady Rest Cem—cemetery FL-3
Shady Rest Cem—cemetery MI-6
Shady Rest Cem—cemetery VA-3
Shady Rest Cemetery AL-4
Shady Rest Golf Course—other NJ-2
Shady Rest Mobile Home Park—locale AZ-5
Shady Rest Park—park KS-7
**Shady Rest Park (subdivision)**—pop pl DE-2
Shady Rest Rsvr—reservoir MT-8
Shady Ridge Ch—church AL-4
**Shady Ridge (subdivision)**—pop pl DE-2
**Shady Rill**—pop pl VT-1
Shady Run NV-8
Shady Run—stream IN-6
Shady Run—stream TX-5
Shady Run Canyon—valley NV-8
Shady Sch—school KY-4
Shady Sea Ch—church FL-3
**Shady Shores**—pop pl MI-6
**Shady Shores**—pop pl TX-5
Shady Side—hist pl KY-4
Shadyside—hist pl MS-4
Shadyside—locale MI-6
Shadyside—locale VA-3
Shadyside—locale WV-2
**Shadyside**—pop pl LA-4
**Shady Side**—pop pl MD-2
**Shadyside**—pop pl (2) OH-6
**Shadyside**—pop pl PA-2
**Shady Side**—pop pl WV-2
Shady Side Acad—school PA-2
Shadyside Cem—cemetery GA-3
Shadyside Cem—cemetery OH-6
Shadyside-Fairfax Cem—cemetery LA-4
**Shady Side (historical)**—pop pl MS-4
Shadyside Hosp—hospital PA-2
Shady Side Lake—reservoir PA-2
Shadyside Landing—locale MS-4
Shady Side MS—school PA-2
Shady Side Park—park GA-3
Shadyside Park—park IN-6
Shadyside Park—park MI-6
Shady Side Park—park MI-6
Shadyside Park—park OH-6
Shadyside Presbyterian Ch—church PA-2
Shadyside Presbyterian Church—hist pl PA-2
Shadyside Rec Area—locale MD-2
Shadyside Sch—school IL-6
Shady Side Sch—school KS-7
Shadyside Sch—school MD-2
Shadyside Sch (abandoned)—school PA-2
Shadyside Shop Ctr—locale PA-2
Shadyside Station—building PA-2
**Shady Side (subdivision)**—pop pl DE-2
**Shady Side (subdivision)**—pop pl IN-6
Shady Side (Trailer Court) IN-6
Shady Slash Branch—stream SC-3
Shady Spring—CDP WV-2
Shady Spring—spring ID-8
Shady Spring—spring NM-5
Shady Spring—spring (2) OR-9
Shady Spring—spring UT-8
Shady Spring—spring WV-2
Shady Spring Mtn—summit WV-2
Shady Springs Baptist Church TN-4
Shady Springs Ch—church TN-4
Shady Springs Tabernacle—church IN-6
Shady Tank—reservoir TX-5
Shady Tower—tower FL-3
Shady Trees—uninc pl TX-5
Shady Vale Ch—church TN-4
**Shady Valley**—pop pl TN-4
Shady Valley—valley TN-4
Shady Valley (CCD)—cens area TN-4
Shady Valley Ch—church MS-4
Shady Valley Ch—church TN-4
Shady Valley Country Club—other TX-5
Shady Valley Division—civil TN-4
Shady Valley Elementary School TN-4
Shady Valley Post Office—building TN-4
Shady Valley Sch—school NE-7
Shady Valley Sch—school TN-4
Shadyview Lakes—lake OH-6
Shadyview Mission—church TN-4
**Shadywood**—pop pl AL-4
Shadywood Point—cape MN-6
Shadywood Sch—school MI-6
**Shaefer**—pop pl FL-3
Shaefer Creek—stream ID-8
Shaefer Creek—stream SD-7
Shaefermeyer Creek—stream CO-8
Shaefermeyer Rsvr No. 1—reservoir CO-8
Shaefermeyer Rsvr No. 4—reservoir CO-8
Shaefer Mtn—summit CO-8
Shaefer Overlook—locale PA-2
Shaefer Ranch—locale TX-5
Shaefers Peak—summit NM-5
Shaefers Treasure Mine—mine AZ-5
Shaeffer Butte Rsvr—reservoir OR-9
Shaeffer Cem—cemetery AR-4
Shaeffer Cem—cemetery (2) IL-6
Shaeffer Cem—cemetery IA-7
Shaeffer Cem—cemetery NY-2
Shaeffer Cem—cemetery OH-6
Shaeffer Cem—cemetery PA-2
Shaeffer Chapel—church MS-4
Shaeffer Hollow—valley VA-3
Shaeffer Mountain CA-9
Shaeffer Ranch—locale TX-5
Shaeffer Run—stream PA-2
Shaeffer Sch—school (3) PA-2
Shaefferstown PA-2
Shaeffertown PA-2
Shaeirn Lake—lake CA-9
Shaeirn Ranch—locale CA-9
Shafer—locale WV-2
**Shafer**—pop pl MN-6
Shafer, Joseph, Farm—hist pl IN-6
Shafer, Lake—reservoir IN-6
Shafer Basin—basin UT-8
Shafer Butte—summit ID-8
Shafer Canyon—valley KS-7
Shafer Canyon—valley NM-5
Shafer Canyon—valley UT-8
Shafer Cem—cemetery MO-7
Shafer Cem—cemetery NY-2
Shafer Cem—cemetery VA-3
Shafer Cem—cemetery (3) WV-2
Shafer Creek—stream CA-9
Shafer Creek—stream CO-8
Shafer Creek—stream ID-8
Shafer Creek—stream KS-7
Shafer Creek—stream MT-8
Shafer Creek—stream OR-9
Shafer Creek—stream VA-3
Shafer Creek—stream WY-8
Shafer Ditch—canal CO-8
Shafer Ditch—canal (2) WY-8
Shafer Farm Cem—cemetery OH-6
Shafer Flat—flat CA-9
Shafer Hill—summit KY-4
Shafer Hollow—valley MO-7
Shafer Knob—summit WV-2
Shafer Lake—lake KS-7
Shafer Lake—lake MI-6
Shafer Lake—lake (2) MN-6
Shafer Location—locale MI-6
Shafer Memorial Grounds—locale PA-2
Shafer Memorial Park—park MD-2
Shafer Mine—mine MI-6
Shafer Mine (surface)—mine TN-4
Shafer Ranch—locale AZ-5
Shafer Ranch—locale CO-8
Shafer Ranch—locale TX-5
Shafer Ridge—ridge IN-6
Shafer Ridge Ch—church IN-6
Shafer Run—stream (2) PA-2
Shafer Run Cave—cave PA-2
Shafers—locale PA-2
Shafers Brook—stream NY-2
Shafer Sch—school MI-6
Shafers Chapel MS-4
Shafer Sch (historical)—school PA-2
Shafer School PA-2
Shafer Schoolhouse (abandoned)—school PA-2
Shafers Church Cem—cemetery OH-6
Shafer's Grocery and Residence—hist pl MI-6
Shafer Site—hist pl NY-2
Shafer Slough—gut MO-7
Shafer's Mill—hist pl MD-2
Shafers Point—cape WA-9
Shafers Run—stream (2) PA-2
**Shafer (Township of)**—pop pl MN-6
Shafer Trail—trail UT-8
Shaferville IL-6
Shaferville—other IL-6
Shaff—locale OR-9
Shaff Cem—cemetery IN-6
Shaffer—locale PA-2
**Shaffer**—pop pl KS-7
**Shaffer**—pop pl VA-3
Shaffer, Bayou—stream LA-4
Shaffer, Enoch, House—hist pl MI-6
Shaffer Bluff—cliff AR-4
Shaffer Bridge—bridge CA-9
Shaffer Bridge—bridge IN-6
Shaffer Camp—locale AZ-5
Shaffer Cem—cemetery IN-6
Shaffer Cem—cemetery (2) KS-7
Shaffer Cem—cemetery LA-4
Shaffer Cem—cemetery MI-6
Shaffer Cem—cemetery MS-4
Shaffer Cem—cemetery MO-7
Shaffer Cem—cemetery OH-6
Shaffer Cem—cemetery (2) PA-2
Shaffer Cem—cemetery (2) VA-3
Shaffer Cem—cemetery (2) WV-2
Shaffer Ch—church (2) PA-2
Shaffer Creek—stream IL-6
Shaffer Creek—stream MO-7
Shaffer Creek—stream PA-2
Shaffer Ditch—canal (2) IN-6
Shaffer Draft—valley PA-2
Shaffer Drain—canal MI-6
Shaffer Fork—stream UT-8
Shaffer Hill—summit CO-8
Shaffer Hollow—valley IL-6
Shaffer Hollow—valley (2) VA-3
Shaffer Hollow—valley WV-2
Shaffer Hotel—hist pl NM-5
Shaffer Lake—lake MN-6
Shaffer Memorial Cem—cemetery PA-2
Shaffer Memorial Cem—cemetery VA-3
Shaffer Mountain AL-4
Shaffer Mountain AR-4
Shaffer Mtn—summit CA-9
Shaffer Mtn—summit WV-2
Shaffer Park—park PA-2
**Shaffer Property (subdivision)**—pop pl DE-2
Shaffer Ranch—locale AZ-5
Shaffer Ranch—locale CO-8
Shaffer Reservoir CO-8
Shaffer Reservoir—summit CO-8
Shaffer Rsvr—reservoir WY-8
Shaffers—locale PA-2
Shaffer's Bridge—hist pl PA-2
Shaffers Canyon—valley UT-8
Shaffer Sch—school CA-9
Shaffer Sch—school WY-8
Shaffer Sch (abandoned)—school PA-2
Shaffer Sch (historical)—school SD-7
**Shaffers Corner**—pop pl PA-2
**Shaffers Corners**—pop pl PA-2
Shaffers Crossing—locale CO-8
Shaffers Draw—valley CO-8
Shaffers Knob—summit PA-2
Shaffers Path Lookout Tower—other PA-2
Shaffers Path Tower PA-2
Shaffer Spring—spring AZ-5
Shaffer's Reservoir CO-8
Shaffers Run—stream OH-6
Shaffers Run—stream PA-2
Shaffers Trail—trail PA-2
**Shaffersville**—pop pl PA-2
Shaffer Swamp—swamp PA-2
Shaffer Wash—stream AZ-5
Shaffer Well—well CA-9
Shaffer Well—well NV-8
Shaffer Windmill—locale NM-5
Shaffner and Major Drain—stream MI-6
Shaffner Branch—canal NV-8
Shaffner Bridge TN-4
Shaffner Creek ND-7
Shaffner Creek—stream OR-9
Shaffner Drain—canal NV-8
Shafford Memorial Park—park NY-2
Shaffton—locale IA-7
Shaffton Cem—cemetery IA-7
Shafords Lake—reservoir NC-3
Shafor Park—park OH-6
**Shaft**—pop pl PA-2
Shaft Branch—stream WV-2
Shaft Creek—stream AK-9
Shaft Draw—valley CO-8
Shaften DE-2
Shafter MS-4
Shafter—locale CA-9
Shafter—locale IL-6
Shafter—locale KY-4
Shafter—locale TX-5
**Shafter**—pop pl CA-9
**Shafter**—pop pl MO-7
**Shafter**—pop pl NV-8
Shafter Canyon—valley TX-5
Shafter (CCD)—cens area CA-9
Shafter Cem—cemetery CA-9
Shafter Cem—cemetery MI-6
Shafter Creek—stream WA-9
Shafter Ditch—canal CA-9
Shafter Draw—valley TX-5
Shafter Hills—summit TX-5
Shafter Historic Mining District—hist pl TX-5
Shafter Interchange—crossing NV-8
Shafter Knoll—summit NV-8
Shafter Lake—lake TX-5
Shafter Lake Cem—cemetery TX-5
Shafter Lake Gas Field—oilfield TX-5
Shafter Lake Oil Field—other TX-5
Shafter Mine—mine CO-8
Shafter Mine—mine TX-5
Shafter Run—stream WV-2
Shafter Sch—school CA-9
Shafter Sch—school HI-9
**Shafter (Township of)**—pop pl IL-6
Shafter Well—well NV-8
Shafter Well—well TX-5
Shafter Well Number Four—well NV-8
Shafter Well Number One—well NV-8
Shafter Well Number Three—well NV-8
Shafter Well Number Two—well NV-8
Shaftey Ditch—canal IN-6
Shaft Gulch—valley CO-8
Shaft House (LA 5660)—hist pl NM-5
Shaft Mtn—summit TX-5
Shaft No 7—mine KY-4
Shafto Corners—locale NJ-2
**Shafton**—pop pl PA-2
Shaft Ox Corner—locale DE-2
Shaft Peak—summit AK-9
Shaft Point—cape AR-4
Shaft Pond—lake IL-6
Shaft Ridge—ridge NC-3
Shaft Rock—island AK-9
Shaft Rock—pillar CA-9
**Shaftsburg**—pop pl MI-6
**Shaftsbury**—pop pl VT-1
Shaftsbury, Lake—lake VT-1
**Shaftsbury Center**—pop pl VT-1
Shaftsbury Hollow—valley NY-2
Shaftsbury Hollow—valley VT-1
**Shaftsbury (Town of)**—pop pl VT-1
Shaft Sch—school MI-6
Shaft Sch (historical)—school PA-2
Shaftville NJ-2
**Shaft (William Penn)**—pop pl PA-2
Shagafoot Lake—lake LA-4
Shagak Bay—bay AK-9
Shagalog Brook RI-1
Shagalog River MA-1
Shagalog River RI-1
Shagaloo (historical)—locale MS-4
Shagawa Lake—lake MN-6
Shagawa River—stream MN-6
Shagback Mtn—summit VT-1
Shagbark Lake—lake IL-6
Shag Bluff—cliff AK-9
Shag Cove—bay AK-9
**Shageluk**—pop pl AK-9
Shageluk Lake—lake AK-9
Shageluk Slough—stream AK-9
Shagg Pond—lake ME-1
Shaggy Bald NC-3
Shaggy Canyon—valley TX-5
Shaggy Cypress Swamp—swamp FL-3
Shaggy Peak—summit NM-5
Shaggy Peak—summit TX-5
Shaggy Peak—summit UT-8
Shag Hole—bay OR-9
Shag Hollow—valley (2) UT-8
Shag Island—island AK-9
Shag Island—island IN-6
Shag Island—island ME-1
Shag Lake—lake MI-6
Shag Lake—lake OR-9
Shag Ledge—bar (2) ME-1
Shag Ledge—island (2) ME-1
Shag Ledges—bar ME-1
Shagnasty—summit NV-8
Shagnasty Basin—basin NV-8
Shagnasty Lake—lake MI-6
Shagoopah Falls CA-9
Shag Rock—bar (2) AK-9
Shag Rock—bar ME-1
Shag Rock—island (2) CA-9
Shag Rock—island (3) ME-1
Shag Rock—island WA-9
Shag Rock—pillar AK-9
Shag Rocks—bar AK-9
Shag Rocks—bar CA-9
Shag Rocks—bar (2) MA-1
Shag Roost—summit ME-1
Shag Slough—gut (2) CA-9
Shagwa Lake—lake CO-8
Shagwamigon Bay WI-6
Shagwamigon Point WI-6
Shagwong Point—cape NY-2
Shagwong Reef—bar NY-2
Shagwong Rock—bar NY-2
Shaha Cem—cemetery NM-5
Shahafka Cove—bay AK-9
Shahan—locale WV-2
Shahan Cem—cemetery WV-2
Shahan Ch—church OK-5
Shahan (historical)—locale AL-4
Shahan Hollow—valley TN-4
Shahan Ridge—ridge MO-7
Shahan Slough—bay TN-4
Shahans Mill (historical)—locale AL-4
Shahan Spring—spring AL-4
Shahaska Creek MN-6
Shah-bush-kung Bay—bay MN-6
Shah-bush-kung Point—cape MN-6
Shaheen Creek—stream AK-9
Shaheeya Lake—lake MT-8
Shaheeya Peak—summit MT-8
Shahghai Well—well NV-8
Shaiak Island—island AK-9
Shailer Pond—lake CT-1
Shailer Sch—school ME-1
**Shailerville**—pop pl CT-1
Shailerville Tylerville Cem—cemetery CT-1
Shain Cem—cemetery KY-4
Shain Creek—stream IA-7
Shain Creek—stream MO-7
Shain Drain—canal CA-9
Shainin Lake—lake AK-9
**Shainline**—pop pl PA-2
Shainline Station—locale PA-2
Shaishnikof River—stream AK-9
Shakamak, Lake—reservoir IN-6
Shakamak Airp—airport IN-6
Shakamak Elem Sch—school IN-6
Shakamak HS—school IN-6
Shakamak Lake Dam—dam IN-6
Shakamak MS—school IN-6
Shakan—locale AK-9
Shakan Bay—bay AK-9
Shakan Creek—stream AK-9
Shakan Island—island AK-9
Shakbatina Baleli Creek MS-4
Shake Butte—summit OR-9
Shake Cabin—locale CA-9
Shake Cabin—locale ID-8
Shake Cabin Flat—flat CA-9
Shakecabin Flat—flat CA-9
Shake Cabin Ravine—valley CA-9
Shake Camp—locale CA-9
Shake Camp—locale OR-9
Shake Camp Spring—spring OR-9
Shake Canyon AZ-5
Shake Canyon—valley (3) CA-9
Shake City—locale CA-9
Shake Creek AZ-5
Shake Creek—stream (3) CA-9
Shake Creek—stream (4) ID-8
Shake Creek—stream OR-9
Shake Creek—stream WA-9
Shake Creek Ranger Station—locale ID-8
Shake Den Harbor—bay NY-2
Shakeflat Creek—stream CA-9
Shake Gulch OR-9
Shake Gulch—valley AZ-5
Shake Gulch—valley CA-9
Shake Gulch—valley ID-8
**Shake (historical)**—pop pl OR-9
Shake House—locale CA-9
Shakelford Cem—cemetery OK-5
Shakelford Cow Camp—locale MT-8
Shakelford's VA-3
Shake Meadow—flat ID-8
Shake Meadow Creek—stream ID-8
Shaken—locale NC-3
Shaken Creek—stream NC-3
Shake Pile Tank—reservoir AZ-5
Shaker MA-1
Shaker NY-2
Shakerag VA-3
Shake Rag—locale (2) GA-3
**Shakerag**—pop pl IL-6
**Shakerag**—pop pl VA-3
Shake Rag Branch AL-4
Shakerag Branch—stream AL-4
Shake Rag Branch—stream GA-3
Shake Rag Branch—stream NC-3
Shakerag Branch—stream (2) TN-4
Shake Rag Branch—stream VA-3
Shakerag Cave—cave AL-4
Shake Rag Cem—cemetery AL-4
Shakerag Creek—stream AR-4
Shakerag Creek—stream MO-7
Shake Rag Hills—range KY-4
**Shake Rag (historical)**—pop pl MS-4
Shake Rag Hollow—valley AR-4
Shakerag Hollow—valley (2) TN-4
Shakerag Hollow Mine (underground)—mine TN-4
Shakerag Ridge—ridge TN-4
Shakerag Sch—school IL-6
Shake Rag Sch—school TN-4
Shake Ravine—valley CA-9
Shaker Bog—swamp ME-1
Shaker Branch—stream NH-1
Shaker Bro MA-1
Shaker Brook MA-1
Shaker Brook—stream ME-1
Shaker Brook—stream MA-1
Shaker Brook—stream NH-1
Shaker Cem—cemetery OH-6
Shaker Creek—stream KY-4
Shaker Creek—stream OH-6
Shaker Crossing OH-6
Shaker Crossing—locale NY-2
Shaker Day Camp—locale OH-6
Shaker Forms Country Club—locale MA-1
Shaker Glen—valley MA-1
Shaker Glen Brook—stream MA-1
**Shaker Heights**—pop pl OH-6
Shaker Heights Country Club—other OH-6
Shaker Heights Park—park OH-6
**Shakerhill**—pop pl MA-1
Shaker Hill—ridge NH-1
Shaker Hill—summit ME-1
Shaker Hill—summit MA-1
Shaker Hill—summit NH-1
Shaker Hollow—valley KY-4
Shake Ridge—ridge AZ-5
Shake Ridge Tank—reservoir AZ-5
Shaker Lane Sch—school MA-1
Shaker Mill Brook MA-1
Shaker Mill Brook—stream MA-1
Shaker Mill Dam—dam MA-1
Shaker Mill Pond MA-1
Shaker Mill Pond—lake MA-1
Shaker Millpond—reservoir MA-1
Shaker Mill Pond—reservoir MA-1
Shaker Mill Pond Dam—dam MA-1
Shaker Mountain—ridge NH-1
Shaker Mtn—summit MA-1
Shaker Mtn—summit (2) NY-2
Shaker Mtn—summit VT-1
Shaker Museum—building NY-2
Shaker Place—locale NY-2
Shaker Pond—lake CT-1
Shaker Pond—lake ME-1
Shaker Pond—reservoir MA-1
Shaker Pond Dam—dam MA-1
Shaker Ponds—lake NH-1
Shaker Prairie—flat IN-6
Shaker Prairie Ch—church IN-6
Shaker Prairie Ditch—canal IN-6
Shaker Ridge Country Club—other NY-2
Shaker Rsvr—reservoir MA-1
Shaker Run—stream IN-6
Shakers—locale NY-2
Shakers Creek—stream NY-2
Shakers Island MA-1
Shaker Spring—spring UT-8
Shaker Square—hist pl OH-6
Shaker Square Hist Dist (Boundary Increase)—hist pl OH-6
Shaker State For—forest NH-1
Shaker Swamp—swamp NY-2
Shakertown—locale AR-4
**Shakertown**—pop pl KY-4

Shakertown at Pleasant Hill Hist Dist—*hist pl* KY-4
Shakertown Ch—*church* KY-4
Shakertowne—*CDP* MO-7
Shakertown Sch—*school* KY-4
Shaker Village—*hist pl* ME-1
**Shaker Village**—*pop pl* ME-1
**Shaker Village**—*pop pl* (3) MA-1
**Shaker Village**—*pop pl* NH-1
Shaker Village Hist Dist—*hist pl* OH-6
*Shakerville* VA-3
Shaker West Lot Farm—*hist pl* KY-4
Shakes, Mount—*summit* AK-9
Shakes Glacier—*glacier* AK-9
Shakes Lake—*lake* AK-9
Shakespare, Mount—*summit* CA-9
Shakespare Cem—*cemetery* WY-8
Shakespeare—*locale* NM-5
Shakespeare Arroyo—*stream* NM-5
Shakespeare Canyon—*valley* NM-5
**Shakespeare Club**—*pop pl* PA-2
Shakespeare Garden—*hist pl* IL-6
Shakespeare Garden and Shay House—*hist pl* SD-7
Shakespeare Ghost Town—*hist pl* NM-5
Shakespeare Glacier—*glacier* AK-9
Shakespeare Hall—*hist pl* RI-1
Shakespeare Hollow—*valley* UT-8
Shakespeare Mine—*mine* UT-8
*Shakespeare Point* UT-8
Shakespeare Point—*summit* NV-8
Shakespeare Sch—*school* IL-6
Shakespeare Tanks—*reservoir* TX-5
Shakespear Point—*cliff* UT-8
Shakespere Sch—*school* ME-1
Shake Spring—*spring* (3) AZ-5
Shake Spring—*spring* CA-9
Shake Spring—*spring* MT-8
Shakes Run—*stream* KY-4
Shakes Slough—*gut* AK-9
**Shakesville**—*pop pl* VA-3
Shake Table—*summit* OR-9
*Shake Table Mtn* OR-9
Shake Tree Canyon—*valley* AZ-5
Shake Tree Gulch—*valley* CA-9
Shake Tree Trail—*trail* AZ-5
Shakett Creek—*stream* FL-3
Shake Well Cave—*cave* AL-4
Shakey Lake—*lake* IN-6
Shakey Lakes—*reservoir* MI-6
Shakey River—*stream* MI-6
Shaking Bog—*swamp* ME-1
Shaklee Windmill—*locale* CO-8
**Shaklefords Fork**—*pop pl* VA-3
Shakley Cem—*cemetery* PA-2
Shakmanof Cove—*bay* AK-9
Shakmanof Point—*cape* AK-9
**Shakopee**—*pop pl* MN-6
Shakopee Community (Indian Reservation)—*reserve* MN-6
Shakopee Creek—*stream* MN-6
Shakopee Hist Dist—*hist pl* MN-6
Shakopee Lake—*lake* (3) MN-6
Shaktolik (Shaktoolik)—*other* AK-9
**Shaktoolik**—*pop pl* AK-9
Shaktoolik Bay—*bay* AK-9
Shaktoolik River—*stream* AK-9
Shaktoolik Roadhouse—*locale* AK-9
*Shakum Brook* MA-1
*Shakum Pond* MA-1
Shakun Islets—*island* AK-9
Shakun Rock—*island* AK-9
Shakuseyi Creek—*stream* AK-9
Shaky Bay—*swamp* NC-3
Shakybog Lake—*lake* AR-4
Shaky Canyon—*valley* NM-5
Shaky Joe Branch—*stream* FL-3
Shaky Joe Swamp—*swamp* FL-3
Shaky Lake—*lake* FL-3
Shaky Lake—*lake* WI-6
Shaky Pond—*lake* NH-1
Shaky Pond—*swamp* FL-3
*Shaky River* MI-6
Shaky Spring—*spring* MT-8
Shalagoco Country Club—*other* WI-6
Shalako—*summit* AZ-5
**Shalamar Subdivision**—*pop pl* UT-8
Shalango—*hist pl* VA-3
*Shalanos Creek* ND-7
Shalda Creek—*stream* MI-6
Shaldas Corner—*locale* MI-6
Shald Ranch—*locale* NE-7
Shale—*locale* CO-8
**Shale Brick**—*pop pl* NC-3
Shale Butte—*summit* ID-8
Shale Butte—*summit* OR-9
Shale Butte Lake—*lake* ID-8
Shale Butte Trappers Cabin—*locale* ID-8
**Shale City**—*pop pl* IL-6
**Shale City**—*pop pl* OR-9
Shale Creek—*stream* AK-9
Shale Creek—*stream* ID-8
Shale Creek—*stream* (2) MT-8
Shale Creek—*stream* OR-9
Shale Creek—*stream* (2) UT-8
Shale Creek—*stream* WA-9
Shale Creek—*stream* (2) WY-8
Shale Creek Bridge—*bridge* UT-8
*Shale Cut Spring* NV-8
Shalecut Spring—*spring* NV-8
Shale Draw—*valley* WY-8
Shale Dugway—*trail* UT-8
**Shaleh Estates Subdivision**—*pop pl* UT-8
Shale Hill—*summit* MO-7
Shale Hill—*summit* (2) WY-8
Shale Hills—*other* CA-9
Shale Hills—*range* CO-8
Shale Hollow—*valley* WY-8
Shale Island—*island* AK-9
Shale Lake—*lake* OR-9
Shale Lake—*lake* UT-8
Shalem Bridge—*other* NM-5
Shalem Drain—*canal* NM-5
Shale Mtn—*summit* ID-8
Shale Mtn—*summit* MT-8
Shale Mtn—*summit* WY-8
Shale Peak—*summit* MT-8
*Shale Pit Hill* TX-5
Shale Point—*cape* CA-9
Shale Point—*summit* (2) ID-8
Shaler Branch—*stream* SC-3
**Shalercrest**—*pop pl* PA-2
Shaler HS—*school* PA-2
Shale Ridge—*ridge* UT-8
Shaler JHS—*school* PA-2
Shaler Lake—*lake* UT-8
Shaler Mountains—*other* AK-9
Shale Rock Pond—*reservoir* AZ-5
Shaler Plateau—*plain* AZ-5
Shaler Sch—*school* NJ-2
*Shalers Run* OH-6
**Shalersville**—*pop pl* OH-6
Shalersville (Township of)—*civ div* OH-6
Shale Rsvr—*reservoir* MT-8
Shaler Township—*CDP* PA-2
**Shaler (Township of)**—*pop pl* PA-2
Shaleruckik Mtn—*summit* AK-9
Shale Run—*stream* PA-2
Shales Brook—*stream* MA-1
*Shales Creek* CA-9
*Shales Creek* MO-7
Shale Slough—*stream* WA-9
Shale Spring—*spring* NM-5
Shale Spring—*spring* UT-8
Shale Spring Canyon—*valley* CA-9
Shale Tank—*reservoir* (2) AZ-5
**Shaleton (Kendricks)**—*pop pl* NC-3
Shaleton Sch—*school* NY-2
Shaleville—*locale* NC-3
Shale Wall Bluff—*cliff* AK-9
Shaley Baygall—*swamp* TX-5
Shaley Creek—*stream* TX-5
Shaley Lake—*lake* SC-3
*Shaley Peak* NV-8
**Shalimar**—*pop pl* FL-3
**Shalimar**—*pop pl* NC-3
Shalimar Country Club Golf Course—*other* AZ-5
Shalimar Sch—*school* FL-3
Shalit, Samuel, House—*hist pl* NM-5
Shallcross—*hist pl* KY-4
Shallcross, Sereck, House—*hist pl* DE-2
Shallcross Lake—*reservoir* DE-2
Shallcross Lake Dam—*dam* DE-2
Shallenberger Spring—*spring* NV-8
Shallmar—*locale* MD-2
*Shallmer* MD-2
Shallop Creek—*stream* NC-3
Shallop Creek Sch—*school* NC-3
*Shallop Pond* MA-1
*Shallops Landing* NC-3
**Shallotte**—*pop pl* NC-3
Shallotte Creek—*stream* NC-3
Shallotte Inlet—*channel* NC-3
Shallotte Lookout Tower—*locale* NC-3
*Shallotte Point* NC-3
**Shallotte Point**—*pop pl* NC-3
Shallotte River—*stream* NC-3
Shallotte Sound—*bay* NC-3
Shallotte (Township of)—*fmr MCD* NC-3
Shallow, Lake—*lake* LA-4
Shallow Alkali Lake—*lake* ND-7
**Shallowater**—*pop pl* TX-5
Shallowater (CCD)—*cens area* TX-5
Shallowater Sch—*school* TX-5
Shallowater Water Field—*other* TX-5
Shallowbag Bay—*bay* NC-3
Shallow Bay—*bay* VA-3
Shallow Bay—*bay* WA-9
Shallow Bayou—*bay* LA-4
Shallow Bayou—*stream* LA-4
Shallow Brook—*stream* NJ-2
Shallow Brook—*stream* NY-2
Shallow Ch—*church* MS-4
Shallow Creek—*bay* MD-2
Shallow Creek—*stream* CO-8
Shallow Creek—*stream* (2) WY-8
Shallow Cutoff—*channel* FL-3
**Shallowell**—*pop pl* NC-3
Shallow Ford—*locale* NC-3
**Shallowford**—*pop pl* TN-4
Shallowford Airp—*airport* NC-3
*Shallow Ford Baptist Church* TN-4
*Shallowford Bridge* GA-3
Shallow Ford Bridge—*bridge* GA-3
Shallow Ford Bridge—*bridge* NC-3
Shallow Ford Bridge—*bridge* SC-3
Shallow Ford Bridge—*bridge* VA-3
Shallowford Ch—*church* TN-4
Shallow Ford Hill—*summit* TN-4
**Shallowford Hills (subdivision)**—*pop pl* TN-4
Shallowford Lakes—*reservoir* NC-3
Shallowford Lakes Dam Number One—*dam* NC-3
Shallowford Road United Methodist Ch—*church* TN-4
Shallow Fork Creek—*stream* KY-4
Shallow Gilkey Lake—*lake* MI-6
*Shallow Lake* MI-6
*Shallow Lake* MN-6
*Shallow Lake* SD-7
Shallow Lake—*flat* NV-8
Shallow Lake—*lake* (2) AK-9
Shallow Lake—*lake* CA-9
Shallow Lake—*lake* (2) CO-8
Shallow Lake—*lake* ID-8
Shallow Lake—*lake* IN-6
Shallow Lake—*lake* ME-1
Shallow Lake—*lake* (3) MI-6
Shallow Lake—*lake* (5) MN-6
Shallow Lake—*lake* NY-2
Shallow Lake—*lake* (2) ND-7
Shallow Lake—*lake* OR-9
Shallow Lake—*lake* UT-8
Shallow Lake—*lake* (4) WI-6
Shallow Mouth—*gut* FL-3
Shallow Point—*cape* MS-4
Shallow Pond—*lake* (2) ME-1
Shallow Pond—*lake* (3) MA-1
Shallow Pond—*lake* NY-2
**Shallow Pond**—*pop pl* MA-1
Shallow Pond—*swamp* MN-6
Shallow Pond Lake—*lake* MN-6
Shallow Pond Mtn—*summit* ME-1
Shallow Prong Lake—*lake* TX-5
Shallow Rapids—*rapids* AZ-5
Shallow Rapids—*rapids* NV-8
*Shallow River* NE-7
Shallow Run—*stream* IN-6
*Shallows* MI-6
**Shallows**—*pop pl* MI-6
Shallow Shoal Branch—*stream* KY-4
Shallow Spring—*spring* NV-8
Shallow Stream—*stream* ME-1
**Shallow Water**—*pop pl* KS-7
Shallow Water Elem Sch—*school* KS-7
Shallow Water Windmill—*locale* TX-5
Shallow Well—*well* (2) NM-5
Shallow Well Ch—*church* NC-3
Shallow Well Draw—*valley* NM-5
*Shalls School* PA-2
Shalney Branch—*stream* VT-1
Shalom Cem—*cemetery* NJ-2
Shalom Memorial Park (Cemetery)—*cemetery* IL-6
Shalona Lake—*lake* CO-8
*Shaloon River* CA-9
Shalow Beach—*beach* CA-9
Shalow Memorial Park—*cemetery* FL-3
Shalters Ch—*church* PA-2
Shalters Grove—*flat* PA-2
Shaly Peak—*summit* NV-8
*Shalz Field* KS-7
Shaman Island—*island* AK-9
Shaman Lake—*lake* MN-6
**Shamballa Ashrama**—*pop pl* CO-8
**Shamballah-Ashrama**—*pop pl* CO-8
**Shambaugh**—*pop pl* IA-7
Shambaugh, George, House—*hist pl* OH-6
Shambaugh Cem—*cemetery* IN-6
Shambaugh Cem—*cemetery* OH-6
Shambaugh Creek—*stream* WI-6
Shambaugh Hollow—*valley* WV-2
Shambaugh Run—*stream* IN-6
*Shambaugh School* IN-6
**Shambaugh Siding**—*pop pl* IN-6
Shambeau Lake—*lake* WI-6
Shamberger Cem—*cemetery* MO-7
Shamblen Cem—*cemetery* WV-2
Shamblen Run—*stream* WV-2
*Shamblers Knob* TN-4
Shambley Creek—*stream* AL-4
Shambo Coulee—*valley* MT-8
Shambo Island—*island* NY-2
Shambolee Golf Club—*other* IL-6
Shambo Mtn—*summit* MT-8
Shambo Ranch Landing Field—*airport* SD-7
Shambo Sch—*school* MT-8
Shambo Springs—*locale* MT-8
Shambow Creek—*stream* MT-8
Shambow Pond—*lake* MT-8
Shamburg—*locale* (2) PA-2
Shamburger Cem—*cemetery* (2) AL-4
Shamburger Cem—*cemetery* MS-4
Shamburger Cem—*cemetery* NC-3
Shamburger Cem—*cemetery* TX-5
Shamburger Lake—*reservoir* TX-5
Shamburg Oil Field—*oilfield* PA-2
*Shamcook* RI-1
Shamel Creek—*stream* WA-9
Shamel Park—*park* CA-9
Shamineau Lake—*lake* MN-6
*Sham Lake* MN-6
Sham Lake—*lake* MN-6
Shamley Cove—*valley* AL-4
Shamlin Cem—*cemetery* WV-2
Shamlin Windmill—*locale* TX-5
Shammack Creek Structure 2 Dam—*dam* MS-4
Shammels Mound Landing (historical)—*locale* TN-4
Shammon Branch—*stream* WV-2
Shammos Sch (abandoned)—*school* PA-2
Shammrock Mine—*mine* CO-8
**Shamokin**—*pop pl* PA-2
**Shamokin**—*pop pl* SC-3
Shamokin, Lake—*reservoir* SC-3
*Shamokin Airfield* PA-2
Shamokin City—*civil* PA-2
Shamokin Creek—*stream* PA-2
**Shamokin Dam**—*pop pl* PA-2
Shamokin Dam Borough—*civil* PA-2
Shamokin Filler Plant Station—*locale* PA-2
Shamokin Hill—*summit* PA-2
*Shamokin Island* PA-2
Shamokin Mtn—*summit* PA-2
Shamokin Rod and Gun Club—*locale* PA-2
Shamokin Rsvr—*reservoir* PA-2
Shamokin State Hosp—*hospital* PA-2
**Shamokin (Township of)**—*pop pl* PA-2
*Shamokin Valley Church* PA-2
Shamokin Valley Country Club—*other* PA-2
Shamona Creek—*stream* PA-2
Shamona Creek Elem Sch—*school* PA-2
*Shamong* NJ-2
Shamong Hotel—*hist pl* NJ-2
**Shamong (Township of)**—*pop pl* NJ-2
*Shamrock* PA-2
Shamrock—*locale* CO-8
Shamrock—*locale* IL-6
Shamrock—*locale* KS-7
Shamrock—*locale* NY-2
Shamrock—*locale* (2) PA-2
Shamrock—*other* PA-2
**Shamrock**—*pop pl* FL-3
**Shamrock**—*pop pl* KY-4
**Shamrock**—*pop pl* LA-4
**Shamrock**—*pop pl* MO-7
**Shamrock**—*pop pl* OK-5
**Shamrock**—*pop pl* (2) PA-2
**Shamrock**—*pop pl* (2) TX-5
**Shamrock**—*pop pl* WV-2
**Shamrock**—*pop pl* WI-6
Shamrock, Lake—*lake* WY-8
Shamrock Airp—*airport* IN-6
Shamrock Bay—*bay* AK-9
Shamrock Branch—*stream* IN-6
Shamrock Campground—*locale* MT-8
Shamrock Canyon—*valley* (2) NV-8
Shamrock (CCD)—*cens area* TX-5
Shamrock Cem—*cemetery* MS-4
Shamrock Cem—*cemetery* OK-5
Shamrock Cem—*cemetery* TX-5
Shamrock Ch—*church* AR-4
Shamrock Ch—*church* SC-3
Shamrock Cove—*bay* TX-5
Shamrock Creek—*stream* (4) AK-9
Shamrock Creek—*stream* ID-8
Shamrock Creek—*stream* (2) OR-9
Shamrock Creek—*stream* (2) WI-6
Shamrock Diggings—*mine* NV-8
Shamrock Dock—*locale* TN-4
**Shamrock Drive Subdivision**—*pop pl* UT-8
Shamrock Farm Dam—*dam* NC-3
Shamrock Gardens Sch—*school* NC-3
Shamrock Glacier—*glacier* AK-9
Shamrock Golf Course—*locale* NC-3
Shamrock Golf Course Lake—*reservoir* NC-3
Shamrock Golf Course Lake Dam—*dam* NC-3
Shamrock Gulch—*valley* ID-8
Shamrock Gulch—*valley* (3) MT-8
Shamrock-Heyburn Lake (CCD)—*cens area* OK-5
Shamrock Hill—*summit* NV-8
Shamrock Hills—*range* WY-8
Shamrock Island—*island* TX-5
Shamrock Lake—*lake* AK-9
Shamrock Lake—*lake* (2) CA-9
Shamrock Lake—*lake* CO-8
Shamrock Lake—*lake* KY-4
Shamrock Lake—*lake* MI-6
Shamrock Lake—*lake* (2) MN-6
Shamrock Lake—*lake* UT-8
Shamrock Lake—*lake* WA-9
Shamrock Lake—*lake* WI-6
**Shamrock Lake**—*pop pl* IN-6
Shamrock Lake—*reservoir* GA-3
**Shamrock Lakes**—*pop pl* IN-6
Shamrock Mesa—*summit* CO-8
Shamrock Mill—*other* LA-4
Shamrock Mills—*hist pl* NC-3
Shamrock Mine—*mine* AZ-5
Shamrock Mine—*mine* (3) CO-8
Shamrock Mine—*mine* ID-8
Shamrock Mine—*mine* MT-8
Shamrock Mine—*mine* NV-8
Shamrock Mine—*mine* TN-4
Shamrock Mine—*mine* WA-9
Shamrock Mines—*mine* (2) CO-8
Shamrock Mobile Home Park—*locale* AZ-5
Shamrock Number 1 Lode Mine—*mine* SD-7
Shamrock Park—*park* MN-6
Shamrock Park—*park* TX-5
Shamrock Point—*cape* TX-5
Shamrock Point—*summit* MT-8
Shamrock Point Light—*locale* TX-5
Shamrock Public Golf Course—*locale* PA-2
Shamrock Pumping Station—*other* NM-5
Shamrock Ranch—*locale* (3) CO-8
Shamrock Ranch—*locale* WY-8
Shamrock Resort—*locale* TN-4
Shamrock Sch—*school* MA-1
Shamrock Shaft—*mine* AZ-5
**Shamrock (Shamrock Mill)**—*pop pl* LA-4
**Shamrock Shores**—*pop pl* TX-5
Shamrock Spring—*spring* ID-8
Shamrock Spring—*spring* NV-8
Shamrock Spring—*spring* OR-9
Shamrock Spring—*spring* WA-9
**Shamrock Station**—*pop pl* PA-2
Shamrock Station (historical)—*building* PA-2
**Shamrock Station (Shamrock)**—*pop pl* PA-2
**Shamrock Subdivision**—*pop pl* UT-8
Shamrock Tank—*reservoir* AZ-5
**Shamrock Terrace (subdivision)**—*pop pl* NC-3
Shamrock Township—*civil* MO-7
**Shamrock Township**—*pop pl* NE-7
**Shamrock (Township of)**—*pop pl* MN-6
**Shamrock Village (subdivision)**—*pop pl* NC-3
*Shamrod Spring* AZ-5
Shamrod Spring—*spring* AZ-5
*Shamrod Springs* AZ-5
Shamual Manor Nursing Home—*building* IL-6
Shanafelt Field—*park* OH-6
Shanafelt Sch—*school* IL-6
**Shanagolden**—*pop pl* WI-6
**Shanagolden (Town of)**—*pop pl* WI-6
Shanahan Ch—*church* OK-5
Shanahan Drain—*canal* MI-6
Shanahan Drain—*stream* MI-6
Shanahan Flat—*flat* CA-9
Shanahan Hill—*summit* CO-8
Shanahan Hill—*summit* MI-6
Shanahan Place—*locale* OR-9
Shanango Sch (historical)—*school* PA-2
Shanaska Creek—*stream* MN-6
Shanatee Sch (historical)—*school* TN-4
Shanborne Branch—*stream* TN-4
Shan Creek—*stream* OK-5
Shan Creek—*stream* OR-9
Shan Creek Viewpoint—*locale* OR-9
Shand, Mount—*summit* AK-9
**Shandaken**—*pop pl* NY-2
Shandaken Brook—*stream* NY-2
Shandaken Rural Cem—*cemetery* NY-2
**Shandaken (Town of)**—*pop pl* NY-2
Shand Creek—*stream* VA-3
**Shandelee**—*pop pl* NY-2
Shandelee Brook—*stream* NY-2
Shandelee Lake—*lake* NY-2
Shandin Hills—*range* CA-9
**Shandon**—*pop pl* CA-9
**Shandon**—*pop pl* (2) OH-6
Shandon—*uninc pl* SC-3
Shandon Cem—*cemetery* CA-9
Shandon Flat—*flat* CA-9
Shandon Station—*locale* OH-6
Shandow Lake—*lake* VT-1
Shandrew Island—*island* IL-6
**Shands**—*pop pl* FL-3
Shands Branch—*stream* SC-3
Shands Bridge—*bridge* FL-3
Shands Teaching Hosp and Clinic—*hospital* FL-3
**Shandy**—*pop pl* TN-4
Shandy Baptist Ch—*church* TN-4
Shandy Hall—*hist pl* OH-6
Shandy Sch—*school* MO-7
Shane—*locale* OH-6
**Shane**—*pop pl* MD-2
Shane Bldg—*hist pl* ID-8
Shane Branch—*stream* NJ-2
Shane Cem—*cemetery* IL-6
Shane Cem—*cemetery* TN-4
*Shane Creek* MO-7
Shane Creek—*stream* MI-6
Shane Creek—*stream* MT-8
Shane Creek Sch—*school* MT-8
Shane Ditch—*canal* MT-8
Shane Gulch—*valley* CO-8
Shane Lake—*lake* NE-7
**Shaner**—*pop pl* PA-2
Shanerburg Run—*stream* PA-2
Shaner Cem—*cemetery* MO-7
Shaner Cem—*cemetery* OH-6
Shane Ridge—*ridge* MT-8
**Shaners Crossroads**—*pop pl* PA-2
Shaner Spring—*spring* OR-9
Shaner Township—*civil* SD-7
Shane Saddle—*gap* OR-9
*Shanes Branch* NJ-2
Shanes Cem—*cemetery* TN-4
*Shanes Fork* TN-4
Shane Spring—*spring* NM-5
*Shanesville* OH-6
Shanesville—*locale* PA-2
**Shanesville**—*pop pl* OH-6
Shanesville Chapel—*church* PA-2
Shanetoh Spring—*spring* AZ-5
Shaney Brook—*stream* PA-2
Shaney Brook Trail—*trail* PA-2
Shanghai—*locale* AL-4
Shanghai—*locale* NC-3
Shanghai—*locale* VA-3
**Shanghai**—*pop pl* IL-6
**Shanghai**—*pop pl* IN-6
**Shanghai**—*pop pl* NC-3
**Shanghai**—*pop pl* WV-2
**Shanghai**—*pop pl* PR-3
Shanghai Bend—*bend* CA-9
Shanghai Branch—*stream* TN-4
Shanghai Canyon—*valley* NV-8
Shanghai Cem—*cemetery* AL-4
Shanghai Cem—*cemetery* MI-6
Shanghai Cemeteries—*cemetery* TN-4
Shanghai Ch—*church* (2) AL-4
**Shanghai City**—*pop pl* IL-6
**Shanghai Corners**—*pop pl* MI-6
Shanghai Creek—*stream* CA-9
Shanghai Creek—*stream* ID-8
Shanghai Creek—*stream* IA-7
Shanghai Creek—*stream* KS-7
Shanghai Creek—*stream* OR-9
Shanghai Creek—*stream* UT-8
Shanghai Creek—*stream* WA-9
Shanghai Creek No 1 Mine—*mine* UT-8
Shanghai Dock—*locale* TN-4
Shanghai Hollow—*valley* MO-7
Shanghai Lake—*lake* MN-6
Shanghai Lake State Wildlife Mngmt Area—*park* MN-6
Shanghai Lookout—*locale* ID-8
Shanghai Mine—*mine* CA-9
Shanghai Resort—*locale* TN-4
Shanghai Ridge—*ridge* CA-9
Shanghai Ridge—*ridge* WI-6
Shanghai Sch—*school* IL-6
Shanghai Sch—*school* OR-9
Shanghai Sch (historical)—*school* (2) AL-4
Shanghai Spring—*spring* MO-7
*Shanghi Baptist Church* AL-4
Shanghi Ch—*church* MO-7
*Shanghi Church* AL-4
*Shanghi Creek* KS-7
Shanghi Sch—*school* NC-3
Shang Hollow—*valley* PA-2
Shang Hollow Trail—*trail* PA-2
Shangin Bay—*bay* AK-9
Shangin Islet—*island* AK-9
**Shangrala**—*pop pl* TN-4
Shangri-La—*locale* HI-9
**Shangrila**—*pop pl* AL-4
Shangri-la—*uninc pl* FL-3
Shangrila, Lake—*lake* WI-6
Shangri La Airp—*airport* PA-2
*Shangri La Creek* OR-9
Shangrila Creek—*stream* OR-9
Shangri-La Dam—*dam* PA-2
Shangri La Dam—*dam* TN-4
*Shangrila Lake* WI-6
Shangri-La Lake—*reservoir* TN-4
Shangrila Meadows—*flat* WY-8
**Shangri-La Mill**—*pop pl* OR-9
**Shangri-La Mobile Home Park (subdivision)**—*pop pl* NC-3
**Shangri La Point**—*pop pl* WI-6
Shangri La Ranch—*locale* AZ-5
Shangri-La Ranch—*locale* TX-5
Shangri-La Rsvr—*reservoir* PA-2
Shangri-la Sch—*school* OR-9
**Shangrila Subdivision**—*pop pl* UT-8
*Shanha River* SD-7
**Shaniko**—*pop pl* OR-9
Shaniko Butte—*summit* OR-9
Shaniko Flats—*flat* OR-9
Shaniko Hist Dist—*hist pl* OR-9
Shaniko Junction—*locale* OR-9
Shaniko Summit—*summit* OR-9
Shaningarok Creek—*stream* AK-9
Shaningarok Ridge—*ridge* AK-9
Shank, Mount—*summit* NY-2
Shankatank Creek—*stream* IN-6
Shank Creek—*stream* IN-6
Shank Ditch—*canal* OH-6
Shank Draw—*valley* WY-8
Shankel Cem—*cemetery* VA-3
Shankel Grove Ch—*church* NC-3
Shanker Lake—*lake* MS-4
Shankers Bend—*bend* WA-9
Shankey Branch—*stream* TN-4
Shankey Branch Cave—*cave* TN-4
*Shankey Creek* IN-6
Shank Hill—*summit* KS-7
Shank (historical)—*locale* SD-7
*Shankitunk Creek* IN-6
Shank Lake—*lake* MI-6
Shank Lake—*lake* TX-5
Shank Lake—*lake* WI-6
Shank Lake Creek—*stream* MI-6
Shankland Ditch—*canal* IN-6
Shankland Hill Cem—*cemetery* IN-6
Shankle—*locale* NC-3
Shankle, Seaborn M., House—*hist pl* GA-3
Shankle Branch—*stream* AL-4
Shankle Branch—*stream* GA-3
Shankle Cem—*cemetery* (2) VA-3
Shankle Ridge—*ridge* GA-3
Shanklerville—*locale* TX-5
**Shanklerville (Enterprise)**—*pop pl* TX-5
Shankles—*post sta* PA-2
Shankles Creek—*stream* GA-3
**Shankletown**—*pop pl* NC-3
Shankletown Sch—*school* NC-3
Shankley Mtn—*summit* NY-2
Shanklin Bluff—*cliff* NE-7
Shanklin Branch—*stream* TN-4
Shanklin Creek—*stream* KY-4
Shanklin Creek—*stream* SC-3
Shanklin House—*hist pl* KY-4
Shanklins Cem—*cemetery* KY-4
Shanklin Sch—*school* IL-6
Shanklins Ferry Camp—*locale* WV-2
*Shank Painted Pond* MA-1
Shank Painter Bar—*bar* MA-1
Shank Painter Pond—*lake* MA-1
*Shank-painters Pond* MA-1
Shank Park—*park* PA-2
*Shank Pooder Pond* MA-1
**Shanks**—*pop pl* WV-2
Shanks Basin—*valley* MT-8
Shanks Cem—*cemetery* KS-7
Shanks Cem—*cemetery* (2) LA-4
Shanks Cem—*cemetery* MO-7
Shanks Cem—*cemetery* OH-6
Shanks Cem—*cemetery* TN-4
Shanks Cem—*cemetery* TX-5
Shanks Cem—*cemetery* WI-6
Shank Sch—*school* IL-6
Shank Sch—*school* IA-7
*Shank School* IN-6
Shanks Cove—*basin* CA-9
Shanks Creek—*bay* MD-2
Shanks Creek—*stream* ID-8
Shanks Creek—*stream* OR-9
Shanks Creek—*stream* SC-3
Shanks Creek—*stream* VA-3
Shanks Gulch—*valley* SD-7
Shanks Hill—*summit* IL-6
*Shanks Island* TN-4
Shanks Island—*island* VA-3
Shanks Mill—*locale* PA-2
Shanks Park—*park* KS-7
Shanks Ranch—*locale* NM-5
Shanks Ripple—*rapids* TN-4
Shanks Run—*stream* (2) PA-2
Shanks Run Cave—*cave* PA-2
Shanks Shoals—*bar* TN-4
Shanks Spring—*spring* TN-4
Shankstown Creek—*stream* MS-4
**Shankstown (historical)**—*pop pl* MS-4
**Shanksville**—*pop pl* PA-2
Shanksville Borough—*civil* PA-2
Shanksville Post Office (historical)—*building* PA-2
Shanksville-Stonycreek Sch—*school* PA-2
Shanks Windmill—*locale* NM-5
**Shanktown**—*pop pl* PA-2
Shank Township (historical)—*civil* SD-7
**Shankweilers**—*pop pl* PA-2
**Shanky Branch**—*pop pl* TN-4
Shanky Branch Ch of God—*church* TN-4
*Shanky Creek* MT-8
*Shankytank Creek* IN-6
*Shanley* ND-7
Shanley Bldg—*hist pl* MO-7
Shanley Creek—*stream* MT-8
Shanley Ditch—*canal* IN-6
Shanley Eddy—*bay* PA-2
Shanley HS—*school* ND-7
Shanley Ranch—*locale* NE-7
Shanley Spring—*spring* AZ-5
Shanley Tank—*reservoir* (2) AZ-5
*Shannac Brook* NJ-2
*Shannack Brook* NJ-2
*Shannae Brook* NJ-2
Shannahan Valley—*valley* WI-6
Shanna House—*hist pl* PA-2
*Shannandale* AR-4
Shannandale—*locale* VA-3
S Hanna Ranch—*locale* NE-7
**Shanna Subdivision**—*pop pl* UT-8
*Shanndy Brook* NJ-2
Shanneck Sch—*school* MI-6
*Shannerville* PA-2
Shannoc Brook—*stream* NJ-2
**Shannock**—*pop pl* RI-1
*Shannock Dam* RI-1
Shannock Hill—*summit* RI-1
Shannock Hist Dist—*hist pl* RI-1
*Shannock Mills* RI-1
Shannock Valley Elem Sch—*school* PA-2
Shannock Valley HS—*school* PA-2
*Shannon* KS-7
*Shannon* OH-6
Shannon—*locale* NV-8
Shannon—*locale* OR-9
Shannon—*locale* PA-2
**Shannon**—*pop pl* AL-4
**Shannon**—*pop pl* (2) AR-4
**Shannon**—*pop pl* GA-3
**Shannon**—*pop pl* IL-6
**Shannon**—*pop pl* KS-7
**Shannon**—*pop pl* KY-4
**Shannon**—*pop pl* MS-4
**Shannon**—*pop pl* NC-3
**Shannon**—*pop pl* (2) OH-6
**Shannon**—*pop pl* TX-5
**Shannon**—*pop pl* WV-2
Shannon, Lake—*lake* FL-3
Shannon, Lake—*lake* WI-6
Shannon, Lake—*reservoir* VA-3
Shannon, Lake—*reservoir* WA-9
Shannon, Mount—*summit* AK-9
*Shannon Airport* PA-2
Shannon Basin—*basin* AZ-5
**Shannon Bee Estates Subdivision**—*pop pl* UT-8
*Shannon Branch* TN-4
*Shannon Branch* VA-3
Shannon Branch—*stream* (2) KY-4
Shannon Branch—*stream* MS-4
Shannon Branch—*stream* (2) TN-4
Shannon Branch—*stream* VA-3
Shannon Branch—*stream* WV-2
Shannon Bridge—*bridge* MT-8
Shannon Brook—*stream* ME-1
Shannon Brook—*stream* NH-1

Shannon Butte—summit CA-9
Shannon Campground—park AZ-5
Shannon Canyon—valley CA-9
Shannon Canyon—valley NM-5
Shannon Cave—cave TN-4
Shannon (CCD)—cens area GA-3
Shannon Cem—cemetery (2) MS-4
Shannon Cem—cemetery MO-7
Shannon Cem—cemetery NH-1
Shannon Cem—cemetery (7) TN-4
Shannon Cem—cemetery (2) TX-5
Shannon Cem—cemetery VA-3
Shannon Cem—cemetery WV-2
Shannon Ch—church AR-4
Shannon Ch—church KY-4
Shannon Ch—church NC-3
Shannon Ch—church TX-5
**Shannon City**—pop pl IA-7
Shannon Corners—locale NY-2
Shannon Corral—locale ID-8
Shannon Coulee—valley MT-8
Shannon County—civil MO-7
Shannon County—civil SD-7
**Shannon (County)**—pop pl MO-7
Shannon Creek KS-7
Shannon Creek MT-8
Shannon Creek—stream KS-7
Shannon Creek—stream (2) KY-4
Shannon Creek—stream MI-6
Shannon Creek—stream (2) MT-8
Shannon Creek—stream SC-3
Shannon Creek—stream TN-4
Shannon Creek—stream TX-5
Shannon Creek—stream (2) WA-9
Shannondale—locale MO-7
Shannondale—locale PA-2
**Shannondale**—pop pl AR-4
**Shannondale**—pop pl IN-6
**Shannondale**—pop pl MO-7
**Shannondale**—pop pl TN-4
**Shannondale**—pop pl WV-2
Shannondale Branch—stream MO-7
Shannondale Ch—church TN-4
Shannondale Elem Sch—school TN-4
Shannondale Fire Tower MO-7
Shannondale Homes—other TN-4
Shannondale Landing (historical)—locale MS-4
Shannondale Lookout Tower—locale MO-7
Shannondale Presbyterian Church TN-4
Shannondale State For—forest MO-7
**Shannondoah Estates (subdivision)**—pop pl UT-8
Shannon Draw—valley NM-5
Shannon Elem Sch—school AL-4
Shannon Elem Sch—school MS-4
**Shannon Forest (subdivision)**—pop pl NC-3
Shannon Friends Ch—church KS-7
Shannon Gap—gap VA-3
**Shannon Glen (subdivision)**—pop pl AL-4
Shannon Gulch—valley AZ-5
Shannon Gulch—valley (2) MT-8
**Shannon Heights**—pop pl PA-2
Shannon Hill—locale PA-2
Shannon Hill—locale VA-3
**Shannon Hill**—pop pl SC-3
Shannon Hill—summit AK-9
**Shannon Hills**—pop pl AR-4
**Shannon Hills**—pop pl TN-4
**Shannon Hills**—pop pl VA-3
Shannon Hill Sch—school KS-7
**Shannon Hills (subdivision)**—pop pl NC-3
Shannon (historical)—locale AL-4
Shannon Hollow—valley AR-4
Shannon Hollow—valley MO-7
Shannon Hollow—valley TN-4
Shannon Hollow—valley UT-8
Shannon Hotel—hist pl MN-6
Shannon-King Cem—cemetery VA-3
Shannon Knob—summit TN-4
Shannon Lake—lake IN-6
Shannon Lake—lake MN-6
Shannon Lake—lake (2) MT-8
Shannon Lake—lake WI-6
Shannon Lake—reservoir AL-4
Shannon Lake—reservoir MI-6
Shannon Lake Dam—dam AL-4
Shannon Landing—locale TN-4
Shannon Marsh—swamp WA-9
Shannon Memorial Airp—airport PA-2
Shannon Memorial Field PA-2
Shannon Methodist Ch—church MS-4
Shannon Mill Creek—stream WV-2
Shannon Mine—mine AL-4
Shannon Mine—mine AZ-5
Shannon Mine—mine CA-9
Shannon Mine—mine MT-8
Shannon Mtn—summit AZ-5
Shannon Oil Field—oilfield KS-7
Shannon Oil Field—oilfield TX-5
Shannon Park—park AZ-5
Shannon Park—park TX-5
**Shannon Park (subdivision)**—pop pl (3) NC-3
Shannon Pass—gap WY-8
Shannon Pass Trail—trail WY-8
Shannon Place—locale CA-9
Shannon Point—cape AK-9
Shannon Point—cape WA-9
Shannon Pool Oil Field—oilfield WY-8
Shannon Ranch—locale CA-9
Shannon Ravine—valley CA-9
Shannon Rec Area—park AZ-5
Shannon River—stream MN-6
Shannon Road Ch—church AR-4
Shannon Run—stream KY-4
Shannon Run—stream OH-6
Shannon Run—stream (4) PA-2
Shannon Run Ch—church PA-2
Shannon Run Sch (abandoned)—school PA-2
Shannon Sch—school AR-4
Shannon Sch—school IL-6
Shannon Sch—school KS-7
Shannon Sch—school LA-4
Shannon Sch—school MI-6
Shannon Sch—school MS-4
Shannon Sch—school MO-7
Shannon Sch—school SC-3
Shannon Sch—school TN-4
Shannon Sch (historical)—school TN-4
Shannon School AL-4
Shannons Creek SD-7
Shannon Slough—gut CA-9
Shannon Smokeless Mine Station—locale PA-2
Shannon Spring—spring MO-7
Shannon Spring—spring TN-4
Shannon Springs Park—park OK-5
Shannon Store TN-4
**Shannon Tank**—pop pl AR-4
Shannon Tanks—reservoir NM-5
**Shannontown**—pop pl SC-3
**Shannon Township**—pop pl (2) KS-7
Shannon (Township of)—fmr MCD NC-3
Shannon (Township of)—other IL-6
Shannon Tunnel—tunnel VA-3
Shannon Valley—basin CA-9
Shannon Village Shop Ctr—locale NC-3
**Shannonville**—pop pl AR-4
Shannon-Williamson Ranch—hist pl CA-9
Shannon Wood—locale FL-3
**Shannon Woods (subdivision)**—pop pl NC-3
Shannopin PA-2
Shannopin Country Club—other PA-2
Shannopin Station (historical)—locale PA-2
Shano—locale WA-9
Shanokin Dam PA-2
**Shanor Heights**—pop pl PA-2
Shano Siphon—other WA-9
Shansfield Branch—stream NC-3
Shantaky Hollow—valley IN-6
Shantatalik Creek—stream AK-9
Shant Branch—stream WV-2
Shantee Creek—stream (2) OH-6
Shanter PA-2
Shanti—locale CA-9
Shantie Spring—spring NM-5
Shantituck Brook RI-1
Shanto AZ-5
Shanto Canyon AZ-5
Shantok Brook—stream CT-1
Shanton Creek—stream WY-8
Shanton Ditch—canal IN-6
Shanto Plateau AZ-5
Shan-to Spring AZ-5
Shanto Stream AZ-5
Shanto Trading Post AZ-5
Shanty AL-4
Shanty Bay WI-6
Shanty Bay—bay NY-2
Shanty Bay—swamp NC-3
Shanty Bottom Brook—stream NY-2
Shanty Bottom Lake—lake WI-6
Shanty Branch—stream (2) AL-4
Shanty Branch—stream (2) GA-3
Shanty Branch—stream (3) KY-4
Shanty Branch—stream NC-3
Shanty Branch—stream PA-2
Shanty Branch—stream SC-3
Shanty Branch—stream (2) TN-4
Shanty Bridge Creek—stream VA-3
Shanty Brook—stream MI-6
Shanty Brook—stream (5) NY-2
Shanty Canyon—valley UT-8
Shanty Cove—valley NC-3
Shanty Creek IN-6
Shanty Creek VA-3
Shanty Creek—stream CA-9
Shanty Creek—stream GA-3
Shanty Creek—stream IN-6
Shanty Creek—stream MI-6
Shanty Creek—stream NY-2
Shanty Creek—stream OH-6
Shanty Creek—stream PA-2
Shanty Creek—stream VA-3
Shanty Creek—stream WA-9
Shanty Falls—falls IN-6
Shanty Ford Branch—stream FL-3
Shanty Gap—gap NC-3
Shanty Hollow—valley AR-4
Shanty Hollow—valley (2) KY-4
Shanty Hollow—valley MO-7
Shanty Hollow—valley NY-2
Shanty Hollow—valley PA-2
Shanty Hollow—valley (2) TN-4
Shanty Hollow—valley VA-3
Shanty Hollow—valley WV-2
Shanty Hollow Lake—reservoir KY-4
Shanty Lake MI-6
Shanty Lake WI-6
Shanty Lake—lake LA-4
Shanty Lake—lake MN-6
Shanty Mountain Brook—stream ME-1
Shanty Mtn—summit NC-3
Shanty Point Trail—trail PA-2
Shanty Ridge—ridge VA-3
Shanty Ridge—ridge WY-8
Shanty Rock Flow—bay NY-2
Shanty Run—stream (4) PA-2
Shanty Run—stream WV-2
Shanty Spring—spring UT-8
Shanty Spring Branch—stream NC-3
Shanty Town—locale MN-6
Shantytown—locale WI-6
**Shantytown**—pop pl MO-7
**Shantytown**—pop pl NV-8
**Shanty Town**—pop pl NV-8
Shanty Town Ch—church GA-3
Shantytown Lake WI-6
Shanub Point—cliff AZ-5
Shanwappum River WA-9
Shanz Island MP-9
Shanz Islands MP-9
Shanz-Stockman Spring—spring MO-7
Shaokatan, Lake—lake MN-6
Shaokatan Cem—cemetery MN-6
Shaokatan State Wildlife Mngmt Area—park MN-6
**Shaokatan (Township of)**—pop pl MN-6
Shaomet MA-1
Shaot Kam AZ-5
**Shaotkam**—pop pl AZ-5
Sha-pah-la AZ-5
Sha-pah-lah-lwee AZ-5
Shapely Draw WY-8
Shapely Island NH-1
Shape of a Breast MH-9
Shapira Hotel—hist pl TX-5
Shapka Island—island AK-9
**Shapleigh**—pop pl ME-1
Shapleigh Island—island NH-1
Shapleigh Memorial Sch—school ME-1
Shapleigh Pond—lake ME-1
Shapleigh Sch—school ME-1
**Shapleigh (Town of)**—pop pl ME-1
Shapley Brook—stream NY-2
Shapley Cem—cemetery MO-7
Shapley Cem—cemetery NY-2
Shapley Draw—valley WY-8
Shapley Gas And Oil Field—oilfield TX-5
Shapley Hill MA-1
Shapley Island NH-1
Shapleys Island NH-1
Shapley Town House—hist pl NH-1
Shaplish Canyon—valley OR-9
Shapnack Island—island PA-2
Shapps Lake—lake TX-5
Shapre-Monte House—hist pl AL-4
Shapville IL-6
**Sharal Park Subdivision**—pop pl UT-8
Sharapiku FM-9
Sharapuku FM-9
Sharatin Bay—bay AK-9
Sharatin Mtn—summit AK-9
Sharber Creek—stream CA-9
Sharbers Cem—cemetery KY-4
Sharbert Well—well CO-8
Sharborn MA-1
Sharby Creek—stream MS-4
Sharecropper Ridge—ridge MO-7
Sharer—locale KY-4
Shares Basin—basin ID-8
Shares Snout—summit ID-8
Sharethora Cem—cemetery OH-6
Sharett Cem—cemetery VA-3
Sharette Butte—summit MT-8
Sharewell Cem—cemetery MS-4
**Sharewood Acres**—pop pl MD-2
**Shari**—pop pl MS-4
Sharing the Ch of Jesus Christ—church FL-3
Shariton River IA-7
Sharit Shoals—bar AL-4
Shark—locale AR-4
Shark Bank—bar SC-3
Shark Bay—bay TX-5
Shark Bay—lake LA-4
Shark Bayou—stream LA-4
Shark Channel—channel FL-3
Shark Cove—bay (2) ME-1
Shark Creek TN-4
Shark Creek—stream NJ-2
Shark Creek—stream OR-9
Shark Cutoff—channel FL-3
Shark Edge Mtn—summit AK-9
Sharkey—locale KY-4
Sharkey—locale LA-4
**Sharkey**—pop pl MS-4
Sharkey Bayou—gut MS-4
Sharkey Branch—stream WV-2
Sharkey Cem—cemetery LA-4
Sharkey Ch—church IN-6
**Sharkey County**—pop pl MS-4
Sharkey Creek—stream (3) ID-8
Sharkey Creek—stream MS-4
Sharkey Hot Spring—spring ID-8
Sharkey-Issaquena Community Hosp—hospital MS-4
Sharkey Mine—mine CO-8
Sharkey Mound Group—hist pl MO-7
Sharkey Pate Cem—cemetery MS-4
Sharkey Plantation MS-4
Sharkeys MS-4
Sharkey Sch—school IL-6
Sharkeys Landing—locale MS-4
Sharkeyville Creek—stream ME-1
Shark Hole—cove MA-1
Shark Inlet NJ-2
Shark Island CA-9
Shark Island—island LA-4
Shark Island—island ME-1
Shark Island—island VI-3
Shark Key—island FL-3
Sharknose Ridge—ridge CA-9
Shark Point FL-3
Shark Point—cape AK-9
Shark Point—cape (3) FL-3
Shark Point—cape MD-2
Shark Reef—bar WA-9
Shark River—stream FL-3
Shark River—stream NJ-2
Shark River Bay FL-3
Shark River Bluff—cliff FL-3
**Shark River Hills**—pop pl NJ-2
Shark River Inlet—gut NJ-2
Shark River Island—island FL-3
Shark River Island—island NJ-2
**Shark River Manor**—pop pl NJ-2
Shark River Park—park NJ-2
Sharkriverville NJ-2
Shark Rock WA-9
Shark Rock—summit WA-9
Shark Run—stream PA-2
Sharks Nose—cliff WY-8
Sharkstooth CO-8
Sharkstooth, The—summit CO-8
Sharkstooth Peak—summit CO-8
Sharkstown—locale PA-2
Sharktooth Creek—stream CA-9
Shark Tooth Hill—summit AK-9
Sharktooth Lake—lake CA-9
Sharktooth Oil Field CA-9
Sharktooth Peak—summit CA-9
Shark Valley Lookout Tower—tower FL-3
Shark Valley Slough—gut FL-3
Sharlot Hall Museum—building AZ-5
Sharlow—locale ND-7
Sharlow—locale WV-2
Sharlow Town Hall—building ND-7
**Sharlow Township**—pop pl ND-7
Sharman—locale AR-4
Sharman Cem—cemetery AR-4
Sharman Ch—church AR-4
Sharman Creek—stream ID-8
Sharman Park—park FL-3
Sharmans Branch—stream MD-2
Sharman (Showman Station)—locale MD-2
Sharon AL-4
Sharon NJ-2
Sharon OH-6
Sharon—locale CA-9
Sharon—locale (2) IA-7
Sharon—locale MD-2
Sharon—locale MO-7
Sharon—locale NC-3
Sharon—locale OH-6
Sharon—locale VA-3
**Sharon**—pop pl CT-1
**Sharon**—pop pl GA-3
**Sharon**—pop pl ID-8
**Sharon**—pop pl IN-6
**Sharon**—pop pl IA-7
**Sharon**—pop pl KS-7
**Sharon**—pop pl KY-4
**Sharon**—pop pl LA-4
**Sharon**—pop pl MA-1
**Sharon**—pop pl MI-6
**Sharon**—pop pl (2) MS-4
**Sharon**—pop pl NH-1
**Sharon**—pop pl NJ-2
**Sharon**—pop pl (2) NY-2
**Sharon**—pop pl (3) NC-3
**Sharon**—pop pl ND-7
**Sharon**—pop pl (2) OH-6
**Sharon**—pop pl OK-5
**Sharon**—pop pl PA-2
**Sharon**—pop pl SC-3
**Sharon**—pop pl (2) TN-4
**Sharon**—pop pl TX-5
**Sharon**—pop pl VT-1
**Sharon**—pop pl WA-9
**Sharon**—pop pl WV-2
**Sharon**—pop pl WI-6
Sharon, Fred B., House—hist pl IA-7
Sharon, Lake—lake FL-3
Sharon, Lake—lake WI-6
Sharon, Lake—reservoir TX-5
Sharon Acres Ch—church NC-3
**Sharon Acres (subdivision)**—pop pl MS-4
Sharon Airp—airport NC-3
Sharon Airp—airport PA-2
Sharon Baptist Ch—church KS-7
Sharon Baptist Church MS-4
Sharon Bethel Ch—church IA-7
Sharon Bluffs State Park—park IA-7
Sharon Branch—stream KY-4
Sharon Broad Brook Sch—school VT-1
**Sharonbrook**—pop pl NC-3
Sharon Brook—stream IN-6
Sharon (CCD)—cens area GA-3
Sharon (CCD)—cens area TN-4
Sharon Cem MS-4
Sharon Cem—cemetery AL-4
Sharon Cem—cemetery (2) IL-6
Sharon Cem—cemetery (2) IN-6
Sharon Cem—cemetery (2) IA-7
Sharon Cem—cemetery KS-7
Sharon Cem—cemetery KY-4
Sharon Cem—cemetery (2) MN-6
Sharon Cem—cemetery (2) MS-4
Sharon Cem—cemetery MO-7
Sharon Cem—cemetery NC-3
Sharon Cem—cemetery (2) ND-7
Sharon Cem—cemetery OH-6
Sharon Cem—cemetery SC-3
Sharon Cem—cemetery (2) VA-3
Sharon Cem—cemetery WA-9
**Sharon Center**—pop pl IA-7
**Sharon Center**—pop pl NY-2
**Sharon Center**—pop pl OH-6
**Sharon Center**—pop pl PA-2
Sharon Center Public Square Hist Dist—hist pl OH-6
**Sharon Center (Township name Sharon)**—pop pl PA-2
Sharon Ch GA-3
Sharon Ch—church (4) AL-4
Sharon Ch—church (3) AR-4
Sharon Ch—church (2) FL-3
Sharon Ch—church (12) GA-3
Sharon Ch—church (4) IL-6
Sharon Ch—church (3) IN-6
Sharon Ch—church (4) IA-7
Sharon Ch—church KS-7
Sharon Ch—church (4) KY-4
Sharon Ch—church (4) LA-4
Sharon Ch—church MD-2
Sharon Ch—church MN-6
Sharon Ch—church (5) MS-4
Sharon Ch—church (2) MO-7
Sharon Ch—church (15) NC-3
Sharon Ch—church (4) OH-6
Sharon Ch—church OK-5
Sharon Ch—church (5) SC-3
Sharon Ch—church (2) TN-4
Sharon Ch—church (2) TX-5
Sharon Ch—church (15) VA-3
Sharon Chapel—church IN-6
Sharon Chapel—church IA-7
Sharon Ch (historical)—church AL-4
Sharon Ch (historical)—church (3) TN-4
Sharon Ch of Christ—church TN-4
Sharon Christian Acad—school FL-3
Sharon City—civil PA-2
Sharon City Hall—building TN-4
**Sharon Colony (subdivision)**—pop pl NC-3
Sharon Country Club—locale MA-1
Sharon Country Club—other CT-1
Sharon Creek—stream OH-6
Sharon Creek—stream OR-9
Sharondale—locale KY-4
**Sharondale**—pop pl TN-4
Sharon-Dawes Consolidated Sch—school WV-2
Sharon Division—civil TN-4
Sharon Eastside Cem—cemetery CT-1
Sharon Elem Sch—school MS-4
Sharon Elem Sch—school NC-3
Sharon Forest Ch—church NC-3
**Sharon Forest (subdivision)**—pop pl NC-3
Sharon Fork—stream OH-6
Sharon Gardens Memorial Park—cemetery FL-3
Sharon Golf Course—locale NC-3
Sharon Grange—locale WA-9
**Sharon Grove**—pop pl KY-4
Sharon Grove Ch—church AL-4
Sharon Grove Ch—church VA-3
Sharon Grove Methodist Ch AL-4
**Sharon Heights**—pop pl MA-1
**Sharon Heights**—pop pl WV-2
Sharon Heights—uninc pl CA-9
Sharon Heights Sch—school MA-1
Sharon Heights Shop Ctr—locale MA-1
**Sharon Hill**—pop pl PA-2
Sharon Hill Borough—civil PA-2
Sharon Hill Cem—cemetery IA-7
Sharon Hill Ch—church IN-6
Sharon Hill Congregational Holiness Ch AL-4
Sharon Hill Elem Sch—school PA-2
**Sharon Hills**—pop pl LA-4
**Sharon Hills**—pop pl OH-6
Sharon Hill Sch—school MI-6
**Sharon Hills (subdivision)**—pop pl MS-4
Sharon Hill Station—building PA-2
Sharon Hist Dist—hist pl MA-1
Sharon (historical)—locale SD-7
Sharon (historical P.O.)—locale IA-7
**Sharon Hollow**—pop pl MI-6
Sharon HS—school MA-1
Sharon HS—school PA-2
Sharon Independent Sch—school IA-7
Sharon Johnson Park—park AL-4
Sharon Lake CA-9
Sharon Lake—lake OH-6
Sharon Lake—reservoir FL-3
Sharon Lake—reservoir TX-5
Sharon Lateral—canal CA-9
Sharon Lodge No. 28 IOOF—hist pl WV-2
Sharon Lutheran Church and Cemetery—hist pl VA-3
Sharon (Magisterial District)—fmr MCD VA-3
Sharon Memorial Park—cemetery MA-1
Sharon Memorial Park (Cemetery)—cemetery NC-3
Sharon Methodist Ch—church MS-4
Sharon Methodist Episcopal Ch (historical)—church AL-4
Sharon Mtn—summit (2) CT-1
Sharon North—CDP PA-2
Sharon Oil And Gas Field—church PA-2
Sharon Oil And Gas Field—oilfield PA-2
Sharon Oil Field—oilfield MS-4
**Sharon Park**—pop pl GA-3
**Sharon Park**—pop pl (2) OH-6
**Sharon Park**—pop pl SC-3
**Sharon Park**—pop pl TN-4
Sharon Park—uninc pl PA-2
Sharon Post Office—building TN-4
Sharon Presbyterian Church MS-4
Sharon Ridge Oil Field—oilfield TX-5
Sharon Run OH-6
Sharon Run—stream WV-2
Sharon Sch—school FL-3
Sharon Sch—school GA-3
Sharon Sch—school IL-6
Sharon Sch—school KS-7
Sharon Sch—school (3) NC-3
Sharon Sch—school OH-6
Sharon Sch—school SC-3
Sharon Sch—school TN-4
Sharon Sch—school UT-8
Sharon Sch—school VA-3
Sharon Sch (historical)—school TN-4
Sharon Shop Ctr—locale MA-1
Sharon Shop Ctr—locale NC-3
Sharon Short Hills—ridge MI-6
Sharons Mexican Mission—church KS-7
Sharon Speedway—other OH-6
Sharon Springs—locale VA-3
**Sharon Springs**—pop pl KS-7
**Sharon Springs**—pop pl NY-2
Sharon Springs—spring VA-3
Sharon Springs Cem—cemetery KS-7
**Sharon Springs Township**—pop pl KS-7
**Sharon Station**—pop pl NY-2
Sharon Temple—church DE-2
Sharon Temple Junior Acad—school DE-2
**Sharon (Town of)**—pop pl CT-1
**Sharon (Town of)**—pop pl MA-1
**Sharon (Town of)**—pop pl NH-1
**Sharon (Town of)**—pop pl NY-2
**Sharon (Town of)**—pop pl VT-1
**Sharon (Town of)**—pop pl (2) WI-6
Sharon Township—fmr MCD (4) IA-7
**Sharon Township**—pop pl KS-7
**Sharon Township**—pop pl NE-7
**Sharon Township**—pop pl ND-7
**Sharon Township**—pop pl SD-7
Sharon Township (historical)—civil SD-7
**Sharon (Township of)**—pop pl IL-6
**Sharon (Township of)**—pop pl MI-6
**Sharon (Township of)**—pop pl MN-6
**Sharon (Township of)**—pop pl (4) OH-6
**Sharon (Township of)**—pop pl PA-2
Sharon Township Town Hall—hist pl OH-6
Sharon Training Sch (historical)—school TN-4
Sharon Valley—locale CA-9
**Sharon Valley**—pop pl CT-1
Sharon Valley—valley (2) OH-6
Sharon Valley Hist Dist—hist pl CT-1
Sharon Valley Sch—school CA-9
**Sharonville**—pop pl MD-2
**Sharonville**—pop pl OH-6
Sharonville Depot U. S. Reservation—locale OH-6
**Sharon West**—pop pl OH-6
Sharon Woods—area OH-6
Sharon Woods Metropolitan Park—park OH-6
Sharp—locale SC-3
Sharp—locale UT-8
**Sharp**—pop pl (2) LA-4
**Sharp**—pop pl ME-1
**Sharp**—pop pl MS-4
**Sharp**—pop pl NJ-2
**Sharp**—pop pl TX-5
Sharp, Edward, House—hist pl NJ-2
Sharp, Elisha, House—hist pl TN-4
Sharp, Ella, House—hist pl MI-6
Sharp, James, House—hist pl WA-9
Sharp, John C., House—hist pl UT-8
Sharp, Mathias, House—hist pl IN-6
Sharp, Morris, House—hist pl OH-6
Sharp, Mount—summit AK-9
Sharp, Mount—summit TX-5
Sharp, Samuel, House—hist pl OH-6
Sharp, Stephen, House—hist pl OH-6
Sharparoon Pond—lake NY-2
Sharp Ave Sch—school CA-9
Sharpback Mtn—summit PA-2
Sharpback Trail—trail PA-2
Sharp Bayou—stream MS-4
Sharp Branch—stream (2) AL-4
Sharp Branch—stream MS-4
Sharp Branch—stream NC-3
Sharp Branch—stream (5) TN-4
Sharp Branch—stream VA-3
Sharp Branch Dam—dam AL-4
Sharp Branch Lake—reservoir AL-4
Sharp Bridge—bridge MS-4
Sharp Brothers House—hist pl NY-2
Sharp Butte—summit AZ-5
Sharp Butte—summit WY-8
Sharp Canal—canal LA-4
Sharp Canyon—valley (2) CO-8
Sharp Canyon Stock Trail—trail CO-8
Sharp Cape—cape AK-9
Sharp Cem TN-4
Sharp Cem—cemetery (3) AL-4
Sharp Cem—cemetery (4) AR-4
Sharp Cem—cemetery (3) GA-3
Sharp Cem—cemetery IL-6
Sharp Cem—cemetery (4) IN-6
Sharp Cem—cemetery (3) KY-4
Sharp Cem—cemetery LA-4
Sharp Cem—cemetery MS-4
Sharp Cem—cemetery (3) MO-7
Sharp Cem—cemetery (2) OH-6
Sharp Cem—cemetery OK-5
Sharp Cem—cemetery (14) TN-4
Sharp Cem—cemetery TX-5
Sharp Ch—church AR-4
Sharp Ch—church (2) LA-4
Sharp Ch—church MD-2
Sharp Ch—church NC-3
Sharp Chapel—church LA-4
Sharp Corner Ch—church TN-4
Sharp Corner Sch—school IL-6
**Sharp (County)**—pop pl AR-4
Sharp Cove—valley AL-4
Sharp Creek AZ-5
Sharp Creek OR-9
Sharp Creek TN-4
Sharp Creek—stream (2) AZ-5
Sharp Creek—stream MI-6
Sharp Creek—stream MT-8
Sharp Creek—stream NV-8
Sharp Creek—stream NC-3
Sharp Creek—stream OK-5
Sharp Creek—stream OR-9
Sharp Ditch—canal CA-9
Sharp Ditch—canal ID-8
Sharp Ditch—canal (2) IN-6
Sharp Ditch—canal OH-6
Sharp Ditch—canal OR-9
Sharp Drain—canal (2) MI-6
Sharpe—locale GA-3
Sharpe—locale KS-7
Sharpe—locale PA-2
**Sharpe**—pop pl KY-4
Sharpe, Col. Silas Alexander, House—hist pl NC-3
Sharpe, Lake—reservoir SD-7
Sharpe Army Depot (Field Annex)—military CA-9
Sharpe Bay—bay MI-6
Sharpe Cem—cemetery (2) GA-3
Sharpe Cem—cemetery MO-7
Sharpe Cove—bay WA-9
Sharpe Creek KS-7
Sharpe Creek—stream GA-3
Sharpe Creek—stream IN-6
Sharpe Ditch—canal IN-6
Sharpee Cem—cemetery IN-6
Sharpee Sch—school WI-6
Sharpe Farms Airp—airport MO-7
Sharpe Field (airport)—airport AL-4
Sharpe General Depot—other CA-9
Sharpe General Depot (Tracy-Annex)—building CA-9
**Sharpe Hill**—pop pl PA-2
Sharpe Hill—summit CT-1
Sharpe Hollow—valley MO-7
Sharpe Lake Number 2—reservoir AL-4
Sharpenburg Ditch—canal IN-6
Sharpe Number One Lake—reservoir AL-4
Sharpe Number 1 Dam—dam AL-4
Sharpe Number 2 Dam—dam AL-4
Sharpe Pond—lake PA-2
Sharpe Pond Dam—dam PA-2
Sharpe Pond Lake PA-2
Sharper Branch—stream IN-4
Sharper Creek—stream OK-5
Sharper Island NJ-2
Sharperville—locale MD-2
**Sharpes**—pop pl FL-3
Sharpesburg (Township of)—fmr MCD NC-3
Sharpes Cem—cemetery MD-2
Sharpe Sch—school KY-4
Sharpe Sch—school TN-4
Sharpes Chapel—church GA-3
Sharpes Corner—locale WA-9
Sharpes Creek KS-7
Sharpes Creek—stream KS-7
Sharpes Ferry AL-4
Sharpes Ferry Landing (historical)—locale AL-4
Sharpes Hill—locale SC-3
Sharpes Lake MI-6
Sharpes Lake—lake FL-3
Sharpes Lake—reservoir AL-4
Sharpes Pond PA-2
**Sharp Estates**—pop pl TN-4
Sharpes (Township of)—fmr MCD NC-3
Sharpes Valley—valley UT-8
Sharpetown MD-2
Sharpe Trail—trail PA-2
**Sharpeye**—pop pl OH-6
Sharp Farmhouse—hist pl NY-2
Sharp Farm Site—locale MO-7
Sharp Ford—locale AL-4
Sharp Ford—locale AR-4
Sharp Gap—gap GA-3
Sharp Gap—gap (2) TN-4
Sharp Gin—locale TX-5
**Sharphagen**—pop pl GA-3
Sharp Hardy Homestead—locale FL-3
Sharp Hill—summit CT-1
Sharp Hill—summit GA-3
Sharp Hill—summit NH-1
Sharp Hill—summit WY-8
Sharp Hill Cem—cemetery CT-1
Sharp Hill Cem—cemetery VA-3
Sharp Hills—range NY-2
**Sharp (historical)**—pop pl NC-3

Sharp Hollow—*valley* AL-4
Sharp Hollow—*valley* AZ-5
Sharp Hollow—*valley* OK-5
Sharp Hollow—*valley* (5) TN-4
Sharp Hollow—*valley* (2) WV-2
Sharp Hollow Tank—*reservoir* AZ-5
Sharp Hollow Trick Tank—*reservoir* AZ-5
Sharp House—*hist pl* KY-4
Sharp House—*hist pl* TX-5
Sharping Lake—*lake* SD-7
*Sharpings Lake* SD-7
Sharpings Lake Dam—*dam* SD-7
Sharp Knob—*summit* WV-2
*Sharp Lake* AR-4
Sharp Lake—*lake* CO-8
Sharp Lake—*lake* (2) MI-6
Sharp Lake—*lake* MN-6
Sharp Lake—*lake* MT-8
Sharp Lake Dam—*dam* MS-4
Sharp Ledge—*other* AK-9
**Sharples**—*pop pl* WV-2
Sharples Camp—*locale* CO-8
Sharples Homestead—*hist pl* PA-2
Sharples HS—*school* OH-6
Sharples HS—*school* WV-2
Sharpless, William C., House—*hist pl* PA-2
Sharples Separator Works—*hist pl* PA-2
Sharpless Lake—*lake* PA-2
Sharpless Lake Dam—*dam* PA-2
Sharpless Pond—*lake* FL-3
Sharpless Ranch—*locale* CA-9
**Sharpley**—*pop pl* DE-2
Sharp Lumberyard—*hist pl* OK-5
Sharp Memorial Ch—*church* MS-4
Sharp Mine—*mine* TN-4
Sharp Mine (underground)—*mine* TN-4
*Sharp Mountain* NC-3
*Sharp Mountain* PA-2
Sharp Mountain Ch—*church* GA-3
Sharp Mountain Creek—*stream* GA-3
Sharp Mtn—*summit* AL-4
Sharp Mtn—*summit* AK-9
Sharp Mtn—*summit* CA-9
Sharp Mtn—*summit* GA-3
Sharp Mtn—*summit* MT-8
Sharp Mtn—*summit* TN-4
Sharp Mtn—*summit* TX-5
Sharp Mtn—*summit* (2) UT-8
Sharp Muskrat Lake—*lake* MN-6
Sharpners Pond—*lake* MA-1
Sharp Nose Drain—*canal* WY-8
Sharp Nose Draw—*valley* WY-8
Sharp Note Lake—*lake* CA-9
Sharp-Page House—*hist pl* OH-6
*Sharp Park* CA-9
Sharp Park—*park* CA-9
Sharp Park—*park* MI-6
**Sharp Park**—*pop pl* CA-9
Sharp Park Golf Course—*other* CA-9
Sharp Park Sch—*school* MI-6
Sharp Peak—*summit* AK-9
Sharp Peak—*summit* AZ-5
Sharp Peak—*summit* CA-9
Sharp Peak—*summit* (3) NV-8
Sharp Peak—*summit* OR-9
Sharp Place—*locale* TN-4
Sharp Place Cem—*cemetery* TN-4
Sharp Plantation (historical)—*locale* MS-4
Sharp Point—*cape* (3) AK-9
Sharp Point—*cape* CA-9
Sharp Point—*cape* FL-3
Sharp Point—*cape* VA-3
Sharp Point—*cliff* NM-5
**Sharp Point**—*pop pl* NC-3
Sharp Point Cem—*cemetery* IN-6
Sharp Pond—*lake* AL-4
Sharp Ranch—*locale* CO-8
Sharp Ranch—*locale* NM-5
Sharp Ranch—*locale* OR-9
Sharp Ranch—*locale* SD-7
Sharp Ranch—*locale* TX-5
Sharp Reservation—*reservoir* NY-2
Sharp Ridge—*ridge* OR-9
Sharp Ridge—*ridge* PA-2
Sharp Ridge—*ridge* TN-4
Sharp Ridge—*ridge* WV-2
Sharp Ridge Cem—*cemetery* PA-2
Sharp Ridge Ch (historical)—*church* PA-2
Sharp Ridge Memorial Park—*park* TN-4
Sharp Rock—*island* CA-9
Sharp Run—*stream* IN-6
Sharp Run—*stream* PA-2
Sharp Run—*stream* WV-2
**Sharps**—*pop pl* NC-3
**Sharps**—*pop pl* VA-3
Sharp's, Jay, Store—*hist pl* MT-8
Sharpsboro—*locale* MO-7
Sharpsboro—*other* GA-3
Sharps Branch—*stream* (3) KY-4
Sharps Branch—*stream* (3) NJ-2
Sharps Branch—*stream* SC-3
Sharps Branch—*stream* TN-4
Sharps Branch—*stream* TX-5
Sharps Branch—*stream* WV-2
Sharps Brook—*stream* CT-1
*Sharpsburg* PA-2
Sharpsburg—*locale* MS-4
Sharpsburg—*locale* PA-2
**Sharpsburg**—*pop pl* GA-3
**Sharpsburg**—*pop pl* IL-6
**Sharpsburg**—*pop pl* IA-7
**Sharpsburg**—*pop pl* KY-4
**Sharpsburg**—*pop pl* MD-2
**Sharpsburg**—*pop pl* NC-3
**Sharpsburg**—*pop pl* (3) OH-6
**Sharpsburg**—*pop pl* PA-2
Sharpsburg Borough—*civil* PA-2
Sharpsburg Branch—*stream* MO-7
Sharpsburg (CCD)—*cens area* KY-4
Sharpsburg Ch—*church* MO-7
Sharpsburg Ch—*church* PA-2
Sharpsburg Post Office
(historical)—*building* MS-4
Sharpsburg Sch—*school* IL-6
Sharpsburg Sch—*school* OH-6
**Sharpsburg (Sharpsboro)**—*pop pl* GA-3
Sharps Canyon—*valley* (2) CA-9
Sharps Canyon—*valley* ID-8
Sharps Canyon—*valley* NV-8
*Sharps Cem* TN-4
Sharps Cem—*cemetery* TN-4
Sharp Sch—*school* MN-6
Sharp Sch—*school* MS-4
Sharp Sch—*school* MO-7
Sharp Sch—*school* (2) NJ-2
Sharp Sch—*school* TN-4
Sharps Chapel—*church* AR-4
Sharps Chapel—*church* TN-4
**Sharps Chapel**—*pop pl* TN-4
Sharps Chapel (CCD)—*cens area* TN-4
Sharps Chapel Division—*civil* TN-4
Sharps Chapel Elem Sch—*school* TN-4
Sharps Chapel Post Office—*building* TN-4
Sharps Chapel Sch (historical)—*school* TN-4
*Sharp School* SD-7
Sharp School—*locale* IL-6
Sharps Corner—*locale* NJ-2
Sharps Corner—*locale* SD-7
**Sharps Corner**—*pop pl* OR-9
Sharps Corners—*locale* PA-2
**Sharps Corners**—*pop pl* MI-6
*Sharps Creek* KS-7
Sharps Creek—*stream* KS-7
Sharps Creek—*stream* MD-2
Sharps Creek—*stream* MI-6
Sharps Creek—*stream* MS-4
Sharps Creek—*stream* NV-8
Sharps Creek—*stream* OH-6
Sharps Creek—*stream* OR-9
Sharps Creek—*stream* SC-3
Sharps Creek—*stream* TN-4
Sharps Creek—*stream* (2) VA-3
Sharps Creek Archeol Site—*hist pl* KS-7
Sharps Creek Crossing Site—*hist pl* OK-5
Sharpscreek (historical)—*locale* KS-7
Sharps Creek Rec Area—*area* OR-9
Sharps Creek Wayside—*locale* OR-9
**Sharps Crossing**—*pop pl* OH-6
Sharpsdale—*locale* CO-8
Sharps Drain—*canal* (2) MI-6
Sharps Draw—*valley* CO-8
*Sharps Eye* OH-6
*Sharps Ferry* TN-4
Sharps Ferry—*locale* FL-3
Sharps Ferry—*locale* TN-4
Sharps Ford Bridge—*bridge* AL-4
Sharps Ford (historical)—*crossing* TN-4
Sharps Fork Federal Creek—*stream* OH-6
Sharps Gap—*gap* AR-4
Sharps Gulch—*valley* CA-9
**Sharps Hill**—*pop pl* PA-2
Sharps Hill—*summit* (2) NY-2
Sharps Hill—*summit* OH-6
Sharps Hill—*summit* VT-1
Sharp Shin—*ridge* KY-4
Sharpshin Island—*island* MD-2
Sharps (historical)—*locale* IA-7
Sharps (historical)—*locale* MS-4
Sharps Hollow—*valley* AL-4
Sharps Hollow—*valley* PA-2
Sharps Hollow—*valley* UT-8
Sharp Sinks—*basin* AL-4
*Sharp's Island* MD-2
Sharps Island—*island* MD-2
Sharps Island Light—*hist pl* MD-2
*Sharps Lake* MI-6
Sharps Lake—*lake* NC-3
Sharps Lake—*lake* TX-5
Sharps Lake—*reservoir* NC-3
Sharps Lake Dam—*dam* NC-3
Sharps Landing (historical)—*locale* NC-3
**Sharps Lane**—*pop pl* CA-9
Sharps Lodge—*locale* NC-3
Sharps Meadows Creek—*stream* WY-8
Sharps Mill—*locale* AL-4
Sharps Mill Dam—*dam* AL-4
Sharps Mill (historical P.O.)—*locale* IN-6
Sharps Mill Pond—*lake* CT-1
Sharps Mill Pond—*reservoir* AL-4
*Sharps Mountain* AL-4
Sharps Mtn—*summit* NJ-2
Sharps Mtn—*summit* VA-3
Sharps Point—*cape* (2) MD-2
Sharps Point—*cape* NJ-2
Sharps Pond—*lake* NY-2
Sharps Pond—*swamp* DE-2
Sharps Prairie—*area* OR-9
Sharp Spring—*spring* AL-4
Sharp Spring—*spring* (2) NV-8
Sharp Springs—*spring* ID-8
Sharp Springs Cem—*cemetery* TN-4
Sharps Ravine—*valley* CA-9
Sharps Ridge—*ridge* NY-2
Sharps Rocks—*bar* ME-1
Sharps Run—*stream* NJ-2
Sharps Run—*stream* (2) OH-6
Sharps Run—*stream* PA-2
Sharps Run—*stream* (2) WV-2
Sharps Sch—*school* IL-6
Sharps Sch (abandoned)—*school* PA-2
**Sharps Shores (subdivision)**—*pop pl* AL-4
**Sharps Spur**—*pop pl* AL-4
**Sharps Spur**—*pop pl* GA-3
Sharps Station—*locale* MO-7
Sharps Store (historical)—*locale* MS-4
Sharp State Public Shooting Area—*park* SD-7
Sharpstein Sch—*school* WA-9
Sharp Stick Mine—*mine* CA-9
Sharp Store (historical)—*locale* MS-4
*Sharpstown* NJ-2
Sharpstown—*locale* FL-3
**Sharpstown**—*pop pl* MD-2
Sharpstown—*post sta* TX-5
Sharpstown Country Club—*other* TX-5
Sharpstown HS—*school* TX-5
Sharpstown Park—*park* TX-5
Sharpstown Shop Ctr—*locale* TX-5
Sharps Trail—*trail* PA-2
Sharp Street Memorial United Methodist Church
and Community House—*hist pl* MD-2
**Sharp Subdivision**—*pop pl* UT-8
*Sharp Sugar Hollow* TN-4
Sharpsville—*locale* KY-4
**Sharpsville**—*pop pl* IN-6
**Sharpsville**—*pop pl* PA-2
**Sharpsville**—*pop pl* TN-4
Sharpsville Borough—*civil* PA-2
Sharpsville Ch—*church* TN-4
*Sharpsville Ch of Christ* TN-4
Sharpsville Sch—*school* MI-6
Sharps Well—*well* NV-8
Sharps Windmill—*locale* TX-5
Sharptail Flowage—*reservoir* WI-6
Sharptail Lake—*lake* MI-6
*Sharpton Creek* SC-3
*Sharp Top* TN-4
Sharp Top—*locale* GA-3
Sharptop—*summit* GA-3
Sharp Top—*summit* GA-3
Sharp Top—*summit* ID-8
Sharptop—*summit* NC-3
Sharp Top—*summit* (2) NC-3
Sharp Top—*summit* OR-9
Sharp Top—*summit* PA-2
Sharp Top—*summit* VA-3
Sharptop Cem—*cemetery* TN-4
Sharp Top Ch—*church* GA-3
*Sharp Top Mtn* GA-3
Sharp Top Mtn—*summit* AR-4
Sharp Top Mtn—*summit* GA-3
Sharptop Mtn—*summit* GA-3
Sharp Top Mtn—*summit* NY-2
Sharp Top Mtn—*summit* SC-3
Sharp Top Mtn—*summit* VA-3
Sharp Top Overlook—*locale* VA-3
Sharptop Ridge—*ridge* NC-3
Sharp Top Vista—*summit* PA-2
**Sharptown**—*pop pl* IN-6
**Sharptown**—*pop pl* MD-2
**Sharptown**—*pop pl* NJ-2
Sharpville-Prairie Elem Sch—*school* IN-6
Sharpy Jim Ridge—*ridge* AR-4
Sharpy Mtn—*summit* NC-3
Sharp 47 Ranch—*locale* WY-8
Sharrard Park—*flat* CO-8
**Sharrertown**—*pop pl* PA-2
Sharretts Airp—*airport* PA-2
*Sharrodsville* OH-6
Sharron Cem—*cemetery* AR-4
Sharron Chapel CME Ch—*church* MS-4
Sharron Creek—*stream* NC-3
Sharron Hill Ch—*church* AL-4
Sharrott Creek—*stream* MT-8
Sharswood, George, Sch—*hist pl* PA-2
Sharswood Sch—*school* PA-2
Shart Chapel—*church* VA-3
Shart Draw—*valley* CO-8
Shartel—*uninc pl* OK-5
Shartell Canyon—*valley* CA-9
**Shartlesville**—*pop pl* PA-2
**Shartz Road**—*pop pl* OH-6
Sharum—*locale* AR-4
*Sharutoniichi-to* MP-9
Sharvers Run—*stream* VA-3
Sharyer Spring—*spring* WA-9
Sharyland—*locale* TX-5
Sharyland Gas Field—*oilfield* TX-5
*Shaser Creek* WA-9
Shashamund Lake—*lake* AK-9
Sha Sha Point—*cape* MN-6
*Shashene River* MA-1
*Shashine River* MA-1
*Shashin River* MA-1
Shasket Creek—*stream* WA-9
**Shasta**—*pop pl* CA-9
Shasta, Mount—*summit* AK-9
Shasta, Mount—*summit* CA-9
Shasta Alpine Lodge (Horse
Camp)—*locale* CA-9
Shasta Bally—*summit* CA-9
Shasta Butte—*summit* ID-8
Shasta Butte—*summit* OR-9
Shasta Christian Day Sch—*school* CA-9
*Shasta City* CA-9
Shasta Costa Bar—*bar* OR-9
Shasta Costa Creek—*stream* OR-9
Shasta Costa Riffle—*rapids* OR-9
**Shasta (County)**—*pop pl* CA-9
*Shasta Creek* OR-9
*Shasta Creek* WA-9
Shasta Creek—*stream* (2) AK-9
Shasta Creek—*stream* ID-8
Shasta Dam—*dam* CA-9
Shasta District Fairgrounds—*locale* CA-9
Shasta Gap—*gap* OR-9
Shasta Gulch—*valley* OR-9
Shasta HS—*school* CA-9
Shasta Inn and Week Lumber Company
Boarding House—*hist pl* CA-9
Shasta Iron Mine—*mine* CA-9
Shasta JHS—*school* OR-9
Shasta Junior Coll—*school* CA-9
Shasta Lake—*lake* ID-8
Shasta Lake—*reservoir* CA-9
Shasta Marina—*locale* CA-9
Shasta Meadows Sch—*school* CA-9
Shasta Mine—*mine* CA-9
Shasta Point—*cliff* ID-8
*Shasta Reservoir* CA-9
**Shasta Retreat**—*pop pl* CA-9
Shasta River—*stream* CA-9
Shasta Sch—*school* OR-9
Shasta Spring—*spring* CA-9
Shasta Spring—*spring* OR-9
**Shasta Springs**—*pop pl* CA-9
Shasta State Historical Monmt—*park* CA-9
Shasta State Historic Park—*hist pl* CA-9
Shasta Union Sch—*school* CA-9
Shasta Valley—*valley* CA-9
Shasteen Bend—*bend* TN-4
Shasteen Cem—*cemetery* (2) TN-4
Shasteens Mill (historical)—*locale* TN-4
Shastina—*summit* CA-9
Shastina, Lake—*reservoir* CA-9
Shastine Crater—*crater* CA-9
Shateen Branch—*stream* NC-3
Shateen Gap—*gap* NC-3
**Shatley Springs**—*pop pl* NC-3
Shatluck Brook—*stream* VT-1
Shatney Mountain—*ridge* NH-1
*Shato* AZ-5
*Shato Canyon* AZ-5
Shato Canyon—*valley* AZ-5
*Shato Creek* AZ-5
*Shato Plateau* AZ-5
**Sha-to-She**—*pop pl* OK-5
*Sha-to Spring* AZ-5
Shato Spring—*spring* AZ-5
*Shato Stream* AZ-5
Shato Stream (historical)—*stream* AZ-5
Shatswell Sch—*school* MA-1
Shattalon Lake—*reservoir* NC-3
Shattalon Lake Dam—*dam* NC-3
*Shatter* NC-3
Shatterack Brook—*stream* MA-1
Shatterack Mtn—*summit* MA-1
Shatterack Mtn—*summit* (2) VT-1
Shatterack Pond—*lake* MA-1
Shattered Peak—*summit* AK-9
Shatters Bayou—*stream* LA-4
*Shattersburg* TN-4
Shattles Cem—*cemetery* GA-3
Shatt Mine—*mine* OR-9
Shatto—*locale* WV-2
Shatto Cem—*cemetery* MO-7
Shatto Ditch—*canal* IN-6
**Shattuc**—*pop pl* IL-6
Shattuck—*mine* AZ-5
**Shattuck**—*pop pl* OK-5
Shattuck, Franklyn C., House—*hist pl* WI-6
Shattuck, Moody, House—*hist pl* MA-1
Shattuck, Ralph W., House—*hist pl* MA-1
Shattuck Branch—*stream* GA-3
Shattuck Brook—*stream* CT-1
Shattuck Brook—*stream* (2) MA-1
Shattuck Brook—*stream* NH-1
Shattuck Butte—*summit* (2) ID-8
Shattuck Cem—*cemetery* IN-6
Shattuck Clearing—*flat* NY-2
Shattuck Creek—*stream* ID-8
Shattuck Creek—*stream* MN-6
Shattuck Gulch—*valley* CO-8
Shattuck Hill—*summit* VT-1
Shattuck Hist Dist—*hist pl* MN-6
Shattuck Lake—*lake* ME-1
Shattuck Mtn—*summit* ID-8
Shattuck Mtn—*summit* VT-1
Shattuck Natl Bank Bldg—*hist pl* OK-5
Shattuck Park—*park* CA-9
Shattuck Park—*park* MA-1
Shattuck Point—*cape* ME-1
Shattuck Pond—*lake* NH-1
Shattuck Sch—*school* MA-1
Shattuck Sch—*school* MN-6
Shattuck Sch—*school* OR-9
Shattucks Grove Cem—*cemetery* IL-6
Shattuck Street Sch—*school* MA-1
**Shattuckville**—*pop pl* MA-1
**Shattuckville**—*pop pl* MI-6
Shattuck Well—*well* NM-5
Shattuck West Tank—*reservoir* NM-5
Shattuc Oil Field—*other* IL-6
**Shauano Vista**—*pop pl* CO-8
Shaub, Martin, Mill Site/House—*hist pl* OH-6
Shaubach Ranch—*locale* CA-9
Shauck Cem—*cemetery* OH-6
**Shauck (Johnsville)**—*pop pl* OH-6
*Shaucks* OH-6
Shaue Gulch—*stream* MT-8
Shaue Gulch Creek—*stream* MT-8
*Shauer Lake* MN-6
Shauer Lake—*lake* MN-6
Shaufler—*locale* TX-5
Shauger Hill—*summit* MI-6
Shaughnessy Creek—*stream* MT-8
Shaughnessy Hill—*summit* MT-8
Shaughnessy Ravine—*valley* CA-9
Shaughnessy Run—*stream* PA-2
Shaughnessy Sch—*school* MA-1
Shaughnessy Swamp—*swamp* MA-1
Shaui Koli Creek—*stream* MS-4
*Shaulak* FM-9
Shaul Cem—*cemetery* IA-7
Shaulis Sch (historical)—*school* PA-2
Shaull Elem Sch—*school* PA-2
*Shaull Sch* PA-2
Shaul Ranch—*locale* NE-7
Shaul Ranch—*locale* WY-8
Shaul Valley—*basin* CA-9
Shauntie—*locale* UT-8
Shauntie Hills—*summit* UT-8
Shauntie Wash—*valley* UT-8
Shauntie Well—*well* UT-8
Shaupeneak Mtn—*summit* NY-2
Shaup Lake—*lake* NE-7
Shaupps Sch—*school* NE-7
Shaurai Shomayim Cem—*cemetery* PA-2
*Shavanah Valley* CO-8
Shavano—*locale* CO-8
Shavano, Mount—*summit* CO-8
Shavano Creek—*stream* CO-8
**Shavano Park**—*pop pl* TX-5
*Shavanough Lake* MI-6
Shavano Valley—*valley* CO-8
Shavano Valley Ditch—*canal* CO-8
Shavedhead Creek—*stream* MT-8
Shave Gulch—*valley* MT-8
Shavehead Cem—*cemetery* MI-6
Shavehead Lake—*lake* MI-6
Shavehead Sch—*school* MI-6
Shave Hill—*summit* ME-1
Shavenaugh Lake—*lake* MI-6
Shaven Crown Hill—*summit* MA-1
*Shaveneau* MI-6
*Shaveneu* MI-6
*Shaver* IA-7
Shaver, Charles W., House—*hist pl* AR-4
Shaver, John W., House—*hist pl* AR-4
Shaver, Judge Benjamin, House—*hist pl* AR-4
Shaver Branch—*stream* GA-3
Shaver Cem—*cemetery* AR-4
Shaver Cem—*cemetery* IL-6
Shaver Cem—*cemetery* MO-7
Shaver Cem—*cemetery* (3) TN-4
Shaver Cem—*cemetery* VA-3
Shaver Cem—*cemetery* (2) WV-2
Shaver Ch—*church* AR-4
*Shaver Creek* SC-3
Shaver Creek—*stream* (2) AR-4
Shaver Creek—*stream* MO-7
Shaver Creek—*stream* (2) NY-2
Shaver Creek—*stream* PA-2
*Shaver Creek Dam* PA-2
Shaver Creek Dam—*reservoir* PA-2
Shaver Drain—*canal* MI-6
Shaver Ford—*locale* MO-7
Shaver Fork—*stream* (2) WV-2
Shaver Gap—*gap* AL-4
Shaver Hollow—*valley* AL-4
Shaver Hollow—*valley* NY-2
Shaver Hollow—*valley* PA-2
Shaver Hollow—*valley* TN-4
Shaver Hollow—*valley* VA-3
Shaver Hollow Shelter—*locale* VA-3
*Shaver Lake* MN-6
Shaver Lake—*lake* AR-4
Shaver Lake—*lake* MN-6
Shaver Lake—*lake* WA-9
**Shaver Lake**—*pop pl* CA-9
Shaver Lake—*reservoir* CA-9
*Shaver Lake Heights* CA-9
**Shaver Lake Heights**—*pop pl* CA-9
Shaver Lake Point—*cape* CA-9
**Shaver Lake Point**—*pop pl* CA-9
Shaver Mill (historical)—*locale* TN-4
Shaver Mooring—*locale* OR-9
Shaver Mtn—*summit* PA-2
Shaver Mtn—*summit* VA-3
Shaver Park—*park* IA-7
Shaver Pond—*lake* NY-2
Shaver Pond—*reservoir* AL-4
Shaver Pond—*reservoir* NY-2
Shaver Ranch—*locale* MT-8
Shaver Rental Houses District—*hist pl* NC-3
Shaver Run—*stream* WV-2
Shavers Cem—*cemetery* KY-4
Shavers Cem—*cemetery* WV-2
Shaver Sch—*school* NY-2
Shaver Sch—*school* OR-9
Shavers Chapel—*church* KY-4
*Shavers Creek* PA-2
Shavers Fork—*stream* WV-2
**Shavers (historical)**—*pop pl* MS-4
Shavers Lick Run—*stream* WV-2
Shavers Mountain—*ridge* WV-2
Shavers Mountain Trail—*trail* WV-2
Shavers Run—*stream* WV-2
Shavers Sch—*school* SC-3
*Shavers Summit* CA-9
Shavers Valley—*area* CA-9
Shavers Well—*well* CA-9
Shaver Town—*locale* TN-4
Shavertown—*locale* VA-3
**Shavertown**—*pop pl* PA-2
Shavertown—*uninc pl* PA-2
Shavertown Bridge—*bridge* NY-2
Shavertown Ch—*church* NY-2
Shaver Trail—*trail* CA-9
Shavetail Creek—*stream* IL-6
Shavetail Park—*flat* CO-8
Shavetail Rsvr—*reservoir* CO-8
Shavetail Wash—*stream* CO-8
Shaving Brook—*stream* MA-1
Shavings Creek—*stream* MT-8
Shavins Bayou—*gut* LA-4
Shavins Lake—*lake* LA-4
Shaviovik River—*stream* AK-9
**Shavox**—*pop pl* MD-2
Shavrer Lateral—*canal* ID-8
Shavrey Branch—*stream* NC-3
*Shaw* WA-9
Shaw—*locale* CO-8
Shaw—*locale* IL-6
Shaw—*locale* KY-4
Shaw—*locale* MN-6
Shaw—*locale* TN-4
Shaw—*locale* TX-5
**Shaw**—*pop pl* AL-4
**Shaw**—*pop pl* AR-4
**Shaw**—*pop pl* IL-6
**Shaw**—*pop pl* KS-7
**Shaw**—*pop pl* LA-4
**Shaw**—*pop pl* ME-1
**Shaw**—*pop pl* MS-4
**Shaw**—*pop pl* MO-7
**Shaw**—*pop pl* NC-3
**Shaw**—*pop pl* OR-9
**Shaw**—*pop pl* WV-2
Shaw, Abner T., House—*hist pl* TN-4
Shaw, Anna Howard, JHS—*hist pl* PA-2
Shaw, Cal, Adobe Duplex—*hist pl* NV-8
Shaw, Cal, Stone Row House—*hist pl* NV-8
Shaw, E. A., House—*hist pl* IA-7
Shaw, Mount—*summit* NH-1
Shaw, M. W., Bldg—*hist pl* TX-5
Shaw, Samuel, Residence—*hist pl* OH-6
Shaw, Sylvester, Residence—*hist pl* OH-6
Shaw, Thomas Mott, Estate—*hist pl* MA-1
Shaw, Tillman, House—*hist pl* AR-4
*Sha-wa-cas-kah River* KS-7
Shaw AFB—*military* SC-3
*Shawamet Neck* MA-1
Shawan—*locale* MD-2
**Shawan**—*pop pl* MO-7
**Shawanee**—*pop pl* TN-4
Shawanee Baptist Ch—*church* TN-4
Shawanee Post Office—*building* TN-4
Shawanee Sch (historical)—*school* TN-4
**Shawanese**—*pop pl* PA-2
*Shawangunk* NY-2
Shawangunk Kill—*stream* NY-2
Shawangunk Lake—*reservoir* NY-2
Shawangunk Mountains—*range* NY-2
**Shawangunk (Town of)**—*pop pl* NY-2
Shawanni, Lake—*reservoir* NJ-2
Shawano—*locale* FL-3
**Shawano**—*pop pl* WI-6
**Shawano (County)**—*pop pl* WI-6
Shawano Creek—*stream* WI-6
Shawano Lake—*lake* WI-6
Shawano Lake Outlet—*stream* WI-6
Shawano Lake State Fishery Area—*park* WI-6
**Shawano North Beach**—*pop pl* WI-6
Shawano Ridge—*ridge* NC-3
Shawan Run—*stream* WV-2
Shaw Arch—*arch* UT-8
*Shawaukema* MA-1
*Shawaukema Hills* MA-1
*Shawaukemo Hills* MA-1
*Shawave Mountains* NV-8
Shaw Ave Place—*hist pl* MO-7
Shaw Ave Sch—*school* NY-2
Shawawa Creek—*stream* CO-8
Shawback Sch—*school* IL-6
Shaw Basin—*basin* MT-8
Shaw Bay—*bay* KY-4
Shaw Bay—*bay* MD-2
Shaw Bend—*bend* TX-5
**Shaw Bend**—*pop pl* TX-5
Shaw Bend Cem—*cemetery* TX-5
Shaw Bluff—*cliff* KY-4
Shaw Bluff—*cliff* MO-7
Shaw Bog Reservoir Dam—*dam* MA-1
Shaw Bog Rsvr—*reservoir* MA-1
Shaw Bogs—*swamp* MA-1
Shawbonee Girl Scout Camp—*locale* IL-6
**Shawboro**—*pop pl* NC-3
Shaw Brake—*lake* AR-4
Shaw Brakes—*area* NM-5
Shaw Branch—*stream* (2) AL-4
Shaw Branch—*stream* (2) GA-3
Shaw Branch—*stream* KY-4
Shaw Branch—*stream* MI-6
Shaw Branch—*stream* MS-4
Shaw Branch—*stream* (3) MO-7
Shaw Branch—*stream* NJ-2
Shaw Branch—*stream* (4) TN-4
Shaw Branch—*stream* (5) TX-5
Shaw Branch—*stream* WV-2
Shaw Brant Ditch—*canal* OR-9
*Shaw Brook* WI-6
Shaw Brook—*stream* (3) ME-1
Shaw Brook—*stream* (2) MA-1
Shaw Brook—*stream* (2) NH-1
Shaw Brook—*stream* (4) NY-2
Shaw Brook—*stream* WI-6
Shaw Burn—*area* OR-9
*Shaw Butte* AZ-5
Shaw Butte—*summit* AZ-5
Shaw Butte—*summit* MT-8
Shaw Butte Microwave Relay
Station—*tower* AZ-5
Shaw Butte Sch—*school* AZ-5
Shaw Cabin Hollow—*valley* PA-2
Shaw Camp—*locale* ME-1
Shaw Canyon—*valley* AZ-5
Shaw Canyon—*valley* CA-9
Shaw Canyon—*valley* OR-9
Shaw Catholic Cem—*cemetery* OR-9
*Shaw Cem* AL-4
Shaw Cem—*cemetery* (2) AL-4
Shaw Cem—*cemetery* (2) AR-4
Shaw Cem—*cemetery* (2) GA-3
Shaw Cem—*cemetery* IL-6
Shaw Cem—*cemetery* (2) KS-7
Shaw Cem—*cemetery* KY-4
Shaw Cem—*cemetery* (2) ME-1
Shaw Cem—*cemetery* MA-1
Shaw Cem—*cemetery* MS-4
Shaw Cem—*cemetery* MO-7
Shaw Cem—*cemetery* NE-7
Shaw Cem—*cemetery* (2) NH-1
Shaw Cem—*cemetery* NY-2
Shaw Cem—*cemetery* (2) OH-6
Shaw Cem—*cemetery* PA-2
Shaw Cem—*cemetery* (11) TN-4
Shaw Cem—*cemetery* (2) TX-5
Shaw Cem—*cemetery* (2) WV-2
Shaw Corners—*locale* NY-2
**Shaw Corners**—*pop pl* NY-2
Shaw Coulee—*valley* (2) MT-8
Shaw County Park—*park* WA-9
Shaw Cove—*bay* CT-1
*Shaw Creek* OK-5
*Shaw Creek* WI-6
Shaw Creek—*stream* AL-4
Shaw Creek—*stream* (2) AK-9
Shaw Creek—*stream* AR-4
Shaw Creek—*stream* (2) CA-9
Shaw Creek—*stream* (2) CO-8
Shaw Creek—*stream* FL-3
Shaw Creek—*stream* GA-3
Shaw Creek—*stream* ID-8
Shaw Creek—*stream* (2) IL-6
Shaw Creek—*stream* (4) KS-7
Shaw Creek—*stream* (4) KY-4
Shaw Creek—*stream* LA-4
Shaw Creek—*stream* MI-6
Shaw Creek—*stream* (3) MS-4
Shaw Creek—*stream* (3) MT-8
Shaw Creek—*stream* NE-7
Shaw Creek—*stream* NY-2
Shaw Creek—*stream* (2) NC-3
Shaw Creek—*stream* OH-6
Shaw Creek—*stream* (8) OR-9
Shaw Creek—*stream* SC-3
Shaw Creek—*stream* (2) SD-7
Shaw Creek—*stream* (4) TX-5
Shaw Creek—*stream* (5) WA-9
Shaw Creek—*stream* WI-6
Shaw Creek—*stream* WY-8
Shaw Creek Ch—*church* (2) NC-3
Shaw Creek Dome—*summit* AK-9
Shaw Creek Flats—*flat* AK-9
Shaw Creek Guard Station—*locale* MT-8
Shaw Creek Lodge—*locale* AK-9
Shaw Creek Rec Area—*park* SD-7
**Shawcrest**—*pop pl* NJ-2
**Shaw Crest (Trailer Camp)**—*pop pl* NJ-2
Shawcroft Cow Camp—*locale* CO-8
Shaw-Cude House—*hist pl* NC-3
Shaw Cutoff—*channel* NJ-2
Shaw Dairy Farm Airp—*airport* PA-2
Shaw Dam—*dam* OR-9
Shaw Ditch—*canal* (2) IN-6
Shaw Ditch—*canal* OR-9
Shaw Drain—*stream* MI-6
Shaw Draw—*valley* WY-8
Shaw Elem Sch—*school* FL-3
Shawe Memorial HS—*school* IN-6
*Shawe Memorial Sch* IN-6
Shaw Family Cem—*cemetery* MS-4
Shaw Family Farms—*hist pl* NC-3
Shaw Farm—*hist pl* OH-6
Shaw Farm—*hist pl* WI-6
Shaw Farm Cem—*cemetery* PA-2
Shaw Flat—*flat* CA-9
Shaw Fly—*swamp* NY-2
*Shaw Fork* VA-3
Shaw Gap—*gap* GA-3
Shaw Gap—*gap* VA-3
Shawger Sch—*school* NJ-2
Shaw Grove Branch—*stream* TN-4
Shaw Grove Gap—*gap* TN-4
Shaw Gulch—*valley* (2) CA-9
Shaw Gulch—*valley* CO-8
Shaw Gulch—*valley* MT-8
Shaw Gulch—*valley* OR-9
Shaw-Hammons House—*hist pl* MN-6
**Shawhan**—*pop pl* KY-4

*Sheba* ... MS-4
Sheba Mine—*mine* ... AZ-5
Shebang Creek—*stream* ... ID-8
Sheba Temple—*summit* ... AZ-5
Shebear Hollow—*valley* ... OH-6
*Shebear Lake* ... MI-6
She-Bear Mtn—*summit* ... WY-8
*She-be-ku* ... AZ-5
Shebeon Creek—*stream* ... MI-6
Shebeon Drain—*canal* ... MI-6
*Shebeon River* ... MI-6
**Sheboygan**—*pop pl* ... WI-6
Sheboygan Bay—*bay* ... WI-6
Sheboygan Cem—*cemetery* ... WI-6
**Sheboygan (County)**—*pop pl* ... WI-6
Sheboygan County Courthouse—*hist pl* ... WI-6
Sheboygan Drain—*canal* ... MI-6
**Sheboygan Falls**—*pop pl* ... WI-6
Sheboygan Falls Cem—*cemetery* ... WI-6
**Sheboygan Falls (Town of)**—*pop pl* ... WI-6
Sheboygan Lake—*lake* ... WI-6
Sheboygan Marsh State Wildlife Area—*park* ... WI-6
Sheboygan Point—*cape* ... WI-6
Sheboygan Reef—*bar* ... WI-6
Sheboygan River—*stream* ... WI-6
**Sheboygan South**—*pop pl* ... WI-6
**Sheboygan (Town of)**—*pop pl* ... WI-6
**Sheboygan West**—*pop pl* ... WI-6
She Branch—*stream* ... VA-3
Sheby Prospect—*mine* ... NV-8
*She Canyon* ... UT-8
She Canyon—*valley* ... UT-8
Shechi Lake Dam—*dam* ... AL-4
Shechi Lake Dam Number Two—*dam* ... AL-4
Shechi Lake Number One—*reservoir* ... AL-4
Shechi Lake Number Two—*reservoir* ... AL-4
Shechi Lakes—*reservoir* ... AL-4
Sheckard Lateral—*canal* ... ID-8
Sheckell Cem—*cemetery* ... IN-6
Sheckels Run—*stream* ... KY-4
Sheckler Community Center—*locale* ... NV-8
Sheckler Reservoir (Aban'd)—*locale* ... NV-8
Sheckler Rsvr—*reservoir* ... NV-8
*Sheco Creek* ... MS-4
She Creek—*stream* ... GA-3
She Creek—*stream* ... ID-8
Shedaker Sch—*school* ... NJ-2
Shedaker Station—*locale* ... NJ-2
Shed Branch—*stream* ... AL-4
Shed Brook—*stream* ... NY-2
Shed Brook—*stream* ... PA-2
Shed Camp—*locale* ... OR-9
Shed Cem—*cemetery* ... AR-4
Shed Cem—*cemetery* ... IL-6
Shed Coulee—*valley* ... MT-8
*Shed Creek* ... GA-3
Shed Creek—*stream* ... GA-3
Shed Creek—*stream* (3) ... MT-8
Shed Creek—*stream* ... OR-9
**Shedd**—*pop pl* ... OR-9
Shedd, John G., Aquarium—*hist pl* ... IL-6
Shedd and Marshall Store—*hist pl* ... KS-7
Shedd Aquarium—*building* ... IL-6
*Shedd Brook* ... MA-1
Shedd Brook—*stream* ... NH-1
Shedd Canyon—*valley* ... CA-9
Shedd Cem—*cemetery* ... AL-4
Shedd Cem—*cemetery* ... MI-6
Shedd Corners—*locale* ... NY-2
Shedd-Dunn House—*hist pl* ... OH-6
Shedden Brook—*stream* ... NY-2
*Sheddfield* ... IN-6
Shedd Hill—*summit* ... NH-1
Shedd Hill—*summit* ... VT-1
Shedd Hill Cem—*cemetery* ... AL-4
Shedd Park—*park* ... IL-6
Shedd Park—*park* ... MA-1
Shedd Park Fieldhouse—*hist pl* ... IL-6
*Shedds* ... OR-9
Shedd Sch—*school* ... IL-6
Shedd Slough—*stream* ... OR-9
**Sheddsville**—*pop pl* ... VT-1
Sheddsville Hill—*summit* ... VT-1
Shed Gulch Creek—*stream* ... MT-8
Shed Hill—*summit* ... NY-2
Shed Hollow—*valley* ... KY-4
Shed Hollow—*valley* ... UT-8
Shedhorn Creek—*stream* ... MT-8
Shedhorn Mtn—*summit* ... MT-8
Shed Island—*island* ... GA-3
Shed Lake—*lake* ... MT-8
Shed Mtn—*summit* ... AK-9
Shedowin Creek—*stream* ... MI-6
Shed Pond—*lake* ... ME-1
Shed Ridge—*ridge* ... TN-4
Shedroof Mtn—*summit* ... WA-9
Shedrow Ditch—*canal* ... IN-6
**Sheds**—*pop pl* ... NY-2
*Sheds, The* ... CO-8
Sheds Bridge—*bridge* ... MT-8
Sheds Camp—*locale* ... CO-8
Sheds Corners—*locale* ... NY-2
Sheds Gulch—*valley* ... NV-8
Shed Tank—*reservoir* ... AZ-5
Shed Valley—*valley* ... AZ-5
Shed Valley Tank—*reservoir* ... AZ-5
**Shedville**—*pop pl* ... IN-6
Shedville Cem—*cemetery* ... IL-6
Shedwick, John, Development Houses—*hist pl* ... PA-2
Sheean Brook—*stream* ... ME-1
Sheeder—*locale* ... PA-2
Sheeder Prairie State Preserve—*park* ... IA-7
Sheeds Creek—*stream* ... TN-4
Sheeds Creek Checking Station—*locale* ... TN-4
Sheedy Branch—*stream* ... MS-4
Sheehan—*locale* ... CO-8
Sheehan Branch—*stream* ... TN-4
Sheehan Bridge—*bridge* ... KY-4
Sheehan Brook—*stream* ... ME-1
Sheehan Coulee—*valley* ... MT-8
Sheehan Creek—*stream* ... NC-3
Sheehan House—*hist pl* ... KY-4
Sheehan Island—*island* ... IL-6
Sheehan Lake—*lake* ... WA-9
Sheehan Lateral—*canal* ... UT-8
*Sheehan Point* ... MD-2
Sheehan Point—*cape* ... MD-2
Sheehan Spring—*spring* ... NV-8
Sheehee Spring—*spring* ... CA-9
Sheehy Canyon—*valley* ... AZ-5
Sheehy Creek—*stream* ... CA-9
Sheehy Drain—*stream* ... MI-6
Sheehy Hollow—*valley* ... TN-4
Sheehy Sch—*school* ... CA-9
Sheehys (historical)—*locale* ... AZ-5
Sheehy Spring—*spring* ... AZ-5
Sheek Cem—*cemetery* ... CO-8
Sheek Cem—*cemetery* ... MO-7
Sheek Creek—*stream* ... NC-3
Sheek Creek—*stream* ... TX-5
Sheek Rsvr—*reservoir* ... CO-8
Sheeks—*locale* ... TX-5
Sheeks Cem—*cemetery* ... IN-6
Sheeks House—*hist pl* ... AR-4
Sheeks Lake—*lake* ... IN-6
Sheeks-Robertson House—*hist pl* ... TX-5
Sheelar Lake—*lake* ... FL-3
Sheele Creek—*stream* ... KS-7
Sheeles Camp—*locale* ... CA-9
Sheeley Cem—*cemetery* ... OH-6
Sheeley Creek—*stream* ... WY-8
Sheeley House—*hist pl* ... WI-6
Sheeley Mtn—*summit* ... NY-2
Sheeley Tank—*reservoir* ... NM-5
Sheeley Trail—*trail* ... CO-8
Sheelite Mine—*mine* ... ID-8
Sheelite Mine—*mine* ... NV-8
Sheely Bridge—*hist pl* ... CO-8
Sheely Cem—*cemetery* ... MO-7
**Sheely Hills (subdivision)**—*pop pl* ... MS-4
Sheely Lake—*lake* ... IN-6
Sheelys Sch—*school* ... PA-2
Sheen, Lake—*lake* ... FL-3
Sheen Creek—*stream* ... MI-6
Sheen Draw—*valley* ... TX-5
Sheen Island—*island* ... MN-6
Sheenjek Lake—*lake* ... AK-9
Sheenjek River—*stream* ... AK-9
*Sheen Lake* ... WI-6
*Sheen Point* ... MN-6
Sheen Point—*cape* ... MN-6
Sheen Ranch—*locale* ... TX-5
Sheepback Knob—*summit* ... NC-3
Sheepback Mtn—*summit* ... NC-3
Sheep Barn Brook—*stream* ... CT-1
Sheep Basin—*basin* ... AZ-5
Sheep Basin—*basin* ... CO-8
Sheep Basin—*basin* ... NV-8
Sheep Basin—*basin* (2) ... NM-5
Sheep Basin Canyon—*valley* ... NM-5
Sheep Basin Divide—*ridge* ... NM-5
Sheep Basin Mtn—*summit* ... AZ-5
Sheep Basin Tank—*reservoir* ... NM-5
Sheep Bay—*bay* ... AK-9
Sheepbed Mtn—*summit* ... TN-4
Sheep Bluff—*cliff* ... AL-4
Sheep Bottom—*bend* ... UT-8
Sheep Branch—*stream* ... AL-4
Sheep Branch—*stream* ... IN-6
Sheep Branch—*stream* ... KY-4
Sheep Bridge—*bridge* (2) ... AZ-5
Sheep Bridge—*bridge* ... ID-8
Sheep Bridge—*bridge* ... UT-8
Sheep Bridge—*bridge* (2) ... WY-8
Sheepbridge Branch—*stream* ... SC-3
Sheep Bridge Campground—*locale* ... OR-9
Sheep Butte—*summit* ... AZ-5
Sheep Butte—*summit* ... ID-8
Sheep Butte—*summit* ... ND-7
Sheep Butte—*summit* ... WA-9
*Sheep Buttes* ... SD-7
Sheep Buttes—*summit* ... NV-8
Sheep Butte Spring—*spring* ... ND-7
*Sheep Butte 2* ... ND-7
Sheep Cabin Creek—*stream* ... CO-8
Sheep Camp—*locale* (2) ... AZ-5
Sheep Camp—*locale* (5) ... CA-9
Sheep Camp—*locale* ... NV-8
Sheep Camp—*locale* ... OR-9
Sheep Camp Butte—*summit* ... CA-9
Sheep Camp Canyon—*valley* ... CA-9
Sheep Camp Canyon—*valley* ... NM-5
Sheep Camp Canyon—*valley* ... TX-5
Sheep Camp Corral—*locale* ... UT-8
Sheep Camp Coulee—*valley* (2) ... MT-8
Sheep Camp Creek—*stream* (2) ... CA-9
Sheepcamp Creek—*stream* (2) ... CA-9
Sheep Camp Creek—*stream* ... MT-8
Sheep Camp Creek—*stream* ... WY-8
Sheep Camp Drain—*canal* ... WY-8
Sheepcamp Draw—*valley* ... MT-8
Sheep Camp Draw—*valley* ... NM-5
Sheep Camp Draw—*valley* ... SD-7
Sheep Camp Draw—*valley* ... WY-8
Sheep Camp Glacier—*valley* ... ID-8
Sheep Camp Glades—*flat* ... OR-9
Sheep Camp Lake—*lake* ... CA-9
Sheep Camp Lakes—*lake* ... CA-9
Sheep Camp Meadow—*flat* ... CA-9
Sheep Camp Mtn—*summit* ... TX-5
Sheep Camp Rsvr—*reservoir* ... OR-9
Sheep Camp Rsvr—*reservoir* ... WY-8
Sheep Camp Spring—*spring* (2) ... AZ-5
Sheepcamp Spring—*spring* ... AZ-5
Sheep Camp Spring—*spring* (2) ... CA-9
Sheepcamp Spring—*spring* ... CA-9
Sheep Camp Spring—*spring* (2) ... CA-9
Sheep Camp Spring—*spring* ... NV-8
Sheep Camp Spring—*spring* (2) ... OR-9
Sheep Camp Springs—*spring* ... AZ-5
Sheep Camp Springs—*spring* ... NM-5
Sheep Camp Tank—*reservoir* ... AZ-5
Sheep Camp Tank—*reservoir* ... NM-5
Sheep Camp Wash—*stream* ... AZ-5
Sheep Camp Windmill—*locale* (3) ... TX-5
*Sheep Canyon* ... AZ-5
*Sheep Canyon* ... CO-8
Sheep Canyon—*valley* ... AZ-5
Sheep Canyon—*valley* (6) ... CA-9
Sheep Canyon—*valley* (6) ... CO-8
Sheep Canyon—*valley* (2) ... ID-8
Sheep Canyon—*valley* ... MT-8
Sheep Canyon—*valley* (10) ... NV-8
Sheep Canyon—*valley* (3) ... NM-5
Sheep Canyon—*valley* ... SD-7
Sheep Canyon—*valley* (8) ... UT-8
Sheep Canyon—*valley* (4) ... WA-9
Sheep Canyon—*valley* (2) ... WY-8
Sheep Canyon Arroyo—*stream* ... CO-8
Sheep Canyon Creek—*stream* ... WY-8
Sheep Canyon Ranger Station—*locale* ... CA-9
Sheep Canyon Rsvr—*reservoir* ... NV-8
Sheep Canyon Spring—*spring* (2) ... AZ-5
Sheep Canyon Well—*well* ... NV-8
*Sheep Cave* ... AL-4
Sheep Cave—*cave* ... AR-4
Sheep Cave—*cave* (2) ... TN-4
Sheep Cave—*hist pl* ... TX-5
Sheep Cave Hollow—*valley* ... TN-4
Sheep Cienega—*flat* ... AZ-5
Sheep Cienega—*swamp* ... AZ-5
Sheep Cliff—*cliff* ... GA-3
Sheep Cliff—*cliff* ... NC-3
Sheep Cliff Creek—*stream* ... NC-3
Sheep Corral—*locale* ... CA-9
Sheep Corral Canyon—*valley* ... CA-9
Sheep Corral Canyon—*valley* ... NV-8
Sheep Corral Canyon—*valley* ... NM-5
Sheep Corral Canyon—*valley* ... UT-8
Sheep Corral Creek—*stream* ... CA-9
Sheep Corral Creek—*stream* ... OR-9
Sheep Corral Draw—*valley* ... NM-5
Sheep Corral Gulch—*valley* ... CO-8
Sheep Corral Gulch—*valley* ... MT-8
Sheep Corral Mine—*mine* ... NV-8
Sheep Corral Rsvr—*reservoir* ... OR-9
Sheep Corrals—*locale* ... OR-9
Sheep Corral Spring—*spring* ... AZ-5
Sheep Corral Spring—*spring* ... CO-8
Sheep Corral Spring—*spring* ... NV-8
Sheep Corral Spring—*spring* ... OR-9
Sheep Corral Springs—*spring* ... OR-9
Sheep Corral Tank—*reservoir* ... AZ-5
Sheep Coulee—*valley* (6) ... MT-8
Sheep Coulee—*valley* ... ND-7
Sheep Coulee Spring—*spring* ... MT-8
Sheep Cove—*bay* ... ME-1
*Sheep Creek* ... CA-9
*Sheep Creek* ... ID-8
*Sheep Creek* ... MT-8
*Sheep Creek* ... NE-7
*Sheep Creek* ... OR-9
*Sheep Creek* ... UT-8
*Sheep Creek* ... WA-9
*Sheep Creek* ... WV-2
*Sheep Creek* ... WY-8
Sheep Creek—*fmr MCD* ... NE-7
Sheep Creek—*stream* ... AL-4
Sheep Creek—*stream* (10) ... AK-9
Sheep Creek—*stream* (3) ... AZ-5
Sheep Creek—*stream* (11) ... CA-9
Sheep Creek—*stream* (15) ... CO-8
Sheep Creek—*stream* ... GA-3
Sheep Creek—*stream* (48) ... ID-8
Sheep Creek—*stream* ... IN-6
Sheep Creek—*stream* ... KS-7
Sheep Creek—*stream* ... KY-4
Sheep Creek—*stream* ... MO-7
Sheep Creek—*stream* (44) ... MT-8
Sheep Creek—*stream* (2) ... NE-7
Sheep Creek—*stream* (17) ... NV-8
Sheep Creek—*stream* (2) ... NM-5
Sheep Creek—*stream* ... NC-3
Sheep Creek—*stream* (6) ... ND-7
Sheep Creek—*stream* ... OK-5
Sheep Creek—*stream* (29) ... OR-9
Sheep Creek—*stream* (3) ... SD-7
Sheep Creek—*stream* (4) ... TX-5
Sheep Creek—*stream* (9) ... UT-8
Sheep Creek—*stream* (2) ... VA-3
Sheep Creek—*stream* (12) ... WA-9
Sheep Creek—*stream* (29) ... WY-8
Sheep Creek Bar—*bar* ... ID-8
Sheep Creek Bar—*bench* ... MT-8
Sheep Creek Bay—*bay* ... UT-8
Sheep Creek Bay Campground—*park* ... UT-8
Sheep Creek Butte—*summit* (2) ... OR-9
Sheep Creek Cabin—*locale* ... AZ-5
Sheep Creek Camp—*locale* ... MT-8
Sheep Creek Canal—*canal* ... UT-8
Sheep Creek Canal—*canal* ... WY-8
Sheep Creek Canyon—*valley* (2) ... NV-8
Sheep Creek Canyon Geological Area—*area* ... UT-8
Sheep Creek Connecting Trail—*trail* ... UT-8
Sheep Creek Dam—*dam* ... ND-7
Sheep Creek Dam—*dam* ... UT-8
Sheep Creek Dam State Rec Area—*park* ... ND-7
Sheep Creek Divide—*ridge* ... OR-9
Sheep Creek Falls—*falls* ... WA-9
Sheep Creek Flat—*flat* ... UT-8
Sheep Creek Gap—*gap* ... UT-8
Sheep Creek Hill—*summit* ... UT-8
Sheep Creek Hills—*range* ... ID-8
Sheep Creek Hill Summit—*summit* ... OR-9
Sheep Creek Irrigation Canal—*canal* ... WY-8
Sheep Creek Lake—*reservoir* ... UT-8
Sheep Creek Oil Field—*oilfield* ... WY-8
Sheep Creek Park—*flat* ... UT-8
Sheep Creek Park—*flat* ... WY-8
Sheep Creek Peak—*summit* ... ID-8
Sheep Creek Point—*cape* ... AZ-5
Sheep Creek Pond—*lake* ... ID-8
*Sheep Creek Range* ... NV-8
Sheep Creek Range—*range* ... NV-8
Sheep Creek Rapids—*rapids* ... ID-8
Sheep Creek Rapids—*rapids* ... OR-9
Sheep Creek Rsvr—*reservoir* ... ID-8
Sheep Creek Rsvr—*reservoir* ... MT-8
Sheep Creek Rsvr—*reservoir* ... NV-8
Sheep Creek Rsvr—*reservoir* (2) ... UT-8
Sheep Creek Seep—*spring* ... AZ-5
Sheep Creek Siphon—*other* ... OR-9
Sheep Creek Slough—*stream* ... AK-9
Sheep Creek Spring—*spring* ... CA-9
Sheep Creek Spring—*spring* (2) ... CO-8
Sheep Creek Spring—*spring* ... ID-8
Sheep Creek Spring—*spring* (2) ... NV-8
Sheep Creek Spring—*spring* ... OR-9
Sheep Creek Spring—*spring* ... UT-8
Sheep Creek Spring—*spring* ... WA-9
Sheep Creek Trail—*trail* ... CA-9
Sheep Creek Trail—*trail* ... CO-8
Sheep Creek Trail—*trail* ... MT-8
Sheep Creek Well—*well* ... NV-8
Sheep Creek Wickiup Cave—*hist pl* ... MT-8
Sheep Creek Windmill—*locale* ... NV-8
Sheep Crossing/Baldy Ninetyfour Trail—*trail* ... AZ-5
Sheep Crossing Campground—*locale* ... NM-5
Sheep Crossing Campground—*park* ... AZ-5
Sheep Den Hollow—*valley* ... OH-6
Sheep Dip Canyon—*valley* ... AZ-5
Sheep Dip Canyon—*valley* ... OR-9
Sheep Dip Creek—*stream* ... AZ-5
Sheep Dip Creek—*stream* ... WY-8
*Sheepdip Hollow* ... ID-8
Sheep Dip Hollow—*valley* (2) ... ID-8
Sheep Dip Hollow—*valley* ... UT-8
Sheep Dip Mtn—*summit* ... ID-8
Sheep Dip Mtn—*summit* ... UT-8
Sheep Dip Trough—*locale* ... UT-8
Sheep Dip Well—*well* ... AZ-5
Sheep Ditch—*canal* ... IN-6
Sheep Ditch—*canal* ... OR-9
Sheep Ditch—*canal* ... WY-8
Sheep Draw—*valley* (3) ... CO-8
Sheep Draw—*valley* ... MT-8
Sheep Draw—*valley* ... NV-8
Sheep Draw—*valley* (2) ... NM-5
Sheep Draw—*valley* (3) ... SD-7
Sheep Draw—*valley* (5) ... WY-8
Sheep Draw Tank—*reservoir* ... NM-5
Sheep Draw Well—*well* ... NM-5
Sheep Drive Ridge—*ridge* ... ID-8
Sheep Drive Rsvr—*reservoir* ... CO-8
Sheep Drive Trail—*trail* ... CO-8
Sheep Drive Trail—*trail* ... ID-8
Sheepeater Canyon—*valley* ... WY-8
Sheepeater Canyon Bridge—*bridge* ... WY-8
*Sheepeater Cliff* ... WY-8
Sheepeater Cliffs—*cliff* ... WY-8
Sheepeater Creek—*stream* ... WY-8
Sheepeater Hot Springs—*spring* ... ID-8
Sheepeater Lake—*lake* (2) ... ID-8
Sheepeater Mtn—*summit* ... ID-8
Sheepeater Point—*cliff* ... ID-8
Sheepeater Ridge—*ridge* ... ID-8
Sheepeater Trail—*trail* ... ID-8
*Sheepen Creek* ... DE-2
Sheepen Creek—*stream* ... NY-2
*Sheepen Ditch* ... DE-2
Sheep Fall Brook—*stream* ... MA-1
Sheep Falls—*falls* (2) ... ID-8
Sheep Falls Branch—*stream* ... KY-4
Sheep Fence Windmill—*locale* ... NM-5
Sheep Fish Pond—*lake* ... NM-5
Sheep Flat—*flat* (2) ... CA-9
Sheep Flat—*flat* (2) ... NV-8
Sheep Flat—*flat* ... OR-9
Sheep Flat—*flat* ... UT-8
Sheep Flat Rsvr—*reservoir* ... NV-8
Sheep Flats—*flat* ... CO-8
Sheep Flats—*flat* ... MT-8
Sheep Flats (historical)—*locale* ... SD-7
Sheepfold Cem—*cemetery* ... NY-2
Sheepford Branch—*stream* ... SC-3
*Sheepford Creek* ... SC-3
Sheep Fork—*stream* ... AK-9
Sheep Fork—*stream* ... KY-4
Sheep Gap—*gap* ... CA-9
Sheep Gap—*gap* ... NC-3
Sheep Gap—*gap* ... WA-9
Sheep Gap Mtn—*summit* ... WA-9
Sheep Glacier—*glacier* ... AK-9
Sheep Gulch—*valley* ... AK-9
Sheep Gulch—*valley* (2) ... AZ-5
Sheep Gulch—*valley* (3) ... CA-9
Sheep Gulch—*valley* (6) ... CO-8
Sheep Gulch—*valley* (3) ... ID-8
Sheep Gulch—*valley* (13) ... MT-8
Sheep Gulch—*valley* (3) ... OR-9
Sheep Gulch—*valley* ... UT-8
Sheep Gulch—*valley* (3) ... WA-9
Sheep Gulch—*valley* ... WY-8
Sheep Gulch Spring—*spring* ... AZ-5
Sheep Gulch Spring—*spring* ... WA-9
Sheep Gully—*stream* ... LA-4
*Sheep Hammock* ... DE-2
Sheep Hammock—*island* (2) ... FL-3
Sheep-Harney Elem Sch—*school* ... NC-3
Sheephead Basin—*basin* (2) ... CO-8
Sheephead Basin—*basin* ... OR-9
Sheephead Bayou—*bay* (2) ... FL-3
Sheephead Bayou—*stream* ... LA-4
Sheephead Bend—*bend* ... TX-5
*Sheephead Canyon* ... AZ-5
Sheephead Corral—*locale* ... WA-9
Sheephead Cove—*bay* ... MD-2
Sheephead Cove Marsh—*swamp* ... MD-2
Sheephead Creek—*bay* ... NC-3
Sheephead Creek—*gut* ... SC-3
Sheephead Creek—*stream* (2) ... FL-3
Sheephead Creek—*stream* ... ID-8
Sheephead Creek—*stream* ... MT-8
Sheephead Creek—*stream* ... WY-8
Sheephead Cut—*channel* ... FL-3
Sheephead Gulch—*valley* ... CO-8
Sheephead Island—*island* ... ME-1
Sheephead Key—*island* ... FL-3
Sheephead Lake—*lake* ... MI-6
Sheephead Marsh—*swamp* ... NC-3
Sheephead Mountain Spring—*spring* ... OR-9
Sheephead Mtn—*summit* (3) ... CA-9
Sheephead Mtn—*summit* ... OR-9
Sheephead Mtn—*summit* ... WY-8
Sheephead Pass—*gap* ... CA-9
*Sheephead Peak* ... ID-8
*Sheep Head Peak* ... TX-5
Sheephead Point—*cape* ... AL-4
Sheephead Point—*cape* ... NY-2
Sheephead Ridge—*ridge* ... OR-9
**Sheephead Rock**—*pop pl* ... NC-3
*Sheep Head Rsvr* ... OR-9
Sheephead Rsvr—*reservoir* (2) ... OR-9
Sheep Heads Mtn—*summit* ... OR-9
Sheephead Spring—*spring* ... CA-9
Sheep Head Spring—*spring* ... NV-8
Sheephead Spring—*spring* ... OR-9
Sheephead Spring—*spring* ... WA-9
*Sheep Heads Ridge* ... OR-9
*Sheep Heads Spring* ... OR-9
Sheep Heaven—*summit* ... PA-2
Sheepheaven Butte—*summit* ... CA-9
Sheepheaven Spring—*spring* ... CA-9
Sheep Herd Creek—*stream* ... UT-8
Sheepherder Creek—*stream* ... MT-8
Sheep Herder Creek—*stream* ... OR-9
Sheepherder Hill—*summit* ... MT-8
Sheepherder Hill—*summit* ... UT-8
Sheepherder Hill—*summit* ... WY-8
Sheepherder Lake—*lake* ... ID-8
Sheepherder Lake—*lake* ... WA-9
Sheepherder Lake—*lake* (2) ... WY-8
Sheepherder Monument Butte—*summit* ... ID-8
Sheepherder Mtn—*summit* ... MT-8
Sheepherder Peak—*summit* ... MT-8
Sheepherder Point—*cape* ... ID-8
Sheepherders Baseball Park—*flat* ... NM-5
Sheepherder Spring—*spring* ... CO-8
Sheepherder Spring—*spring* ... NV-8
Sheepherder Spring—*spring* (2) ... OR-9
Sheepherder Springs—*spring* ... NV-8
Sheepherder Springs Draw—*valley* ... CO-8
*Sheepherd Island* ... ME-1
*Sheep Hill* ... AZ-5
*Sheep Hill* ... CO-8
Sheep Hill—*ridge* ... MA-1
Sheep Hill—*summit* (2) ... AZ-5
Sheep Hill—*summit* ... FL-3
Sheep Hill—*summit* (2) ... ID-8
Sheep Hill—*summit* ... NH-1
Sheep Hill—*summit* ... NJ-2
Sheep Hill—*summit* (2) ... OR-9
Sheep Hill—*summit* (4) ... PA-2
Sheep Hill—*summit* ... VT-1
Sheep Hill Park—*park* ... NJ-2
Sheep Hills—*range* ... CA-9
Sheep Hills—*range* ... ID-8
Sheep Hill Sch (historical)—*school* ... TN-4
Sheep Hill Tank—*reservoir* ... AZ-5
Sheephole Hollow—*valley* ... KY-4
Sheep Hole Mountains—*range* ... CA-9
Sheep Hole Oasis—*spring* ... CA-9
Sheep Hole Pass—*summit* ... CA-9
*Sheep Hollow* ... ID-8
Sheep Hollow—*valley* ... AR-4
Sheep Hollow—*valley* ... CA-9
Sheep Hollow—*valley* ... ID-8
Sheep Hollow—*valley* ... NC-3
Sheep Hollow—*valley* (2) ... OR-9
Sheep Hollow—*valley* (5) ... TN-4
Sheep Hollow—*valley* ... TX-5
Sheep Hollow—*valley* (2) ... UT-8
Sheep Hollow—*valley* ... WV-2
*Sheephorn* ... ID-8
Sheephorn—*locale* ... CO-8
Sheephorn Creek—*stream* ... CO-8
Sheephorn Mtn—*summit* ... CO-8
Sheephorn Mtn—*summit* ... ID-8
Sheep Horn Mtn—*summit* ... ID-8
Sheephorn Peak—*summit* ... ID-8
Sheephorn Spring—*spring* ... ID-8
Sheephouse Creek—*stream* ... CA-9
Sheep House Hollow—*valley* ... OH-6
Sheep House Knob—*summit* ... WV-2
*Sheep Island* ... CA-9
*Sheep Island* ... ME-1
*Sheep Island* ... NV-8
*Sheep Island* ... WA-9
*Sheep Island* ... FM-9
Sheep Island—*island* (3) ... AK-9
Sheep Island—*island* (2) ... FL-3
Sheep Island—*island* (16) ... ME-1
Sheep Island—*island* (2) ... MA-1
Sheep Island—*island* ... NE-7
Sheep Island—*island* ... NH-1
Sheep Island—*island* (3) ... NC-3
Sheep Island—*island* ... SC-3
Sheep Island—*island* ... VA-3
Sheep Island—*island* ... WI-6
Sheep Island Bar—*bar* ... ME-1
Sheep Island (historical)—*island* ... AL-4
Sheep Island Ledge—*bar* (3) ... ME-1
Sheep Island North Ledges—*bar* ... ME-1
Sheep Island Point—*cape* ... MD-2
Sheep Islands—*island* ... FL-3
Sheep Islands—*island* ... MN-6
Sheep Islands—*island* ... NC-3
Sheep Island Shoals—*bar* ... ME-1
Sheep Island Slue—*channel* ... NC-3
Sheep Island Slue Light—*tower* ... NC-3
Sheep Kill Gulch—*valley* ... CO-8
Sheepkill Pond—*lake* ... NJ-2
Sheep Knob—*summit* ... CO-8
Sheep Knob—*summit* (6) ... GA-3
Sheep Knob—*summit* (5) ... NC-3
Sheep Knob—*summit* ... VA-3
Sheep Knob—*summit* ... WV-2
Sheep Knoll—*summit* ... UT-8
Sheep Knolls—*summit* ... UT-8
*Sheep Lake* ... MT-8
*Sheep Lake* ... WY-8
Sheep Lake—*lake* (4) ... AK-9
Sheep Lake—*lake* ... CO-8
Sheep Lake—*lake* (2) ... ID-8
Sheep Lake—*lake* ... MN-6
Sheep Lake—*lake* ... MT-8
Sheep Lake—*lake* (2) ... OR-9
Sheep Lake—*lake* (6) ... WA-9
Sheep Lake—*lake* (3) ... WY-8
Sheep Lake—*reservoir* ... CO-8
Sheep Lake—*reservoir* ... ID-8
Sheep Lake—*swamp* ... ND-7
Sheep Lake Rsvr—*reservoir* ... ID-8
Sheep Lakes—*lake* ... CO-8
Sheep Lakes—*lake* ... WA-9
Sheep Lake Trail—*trail* ... WA-9
Sheep L. Ditch—*canal* ... OR-9
*Sheep Lick* ... CO-8
*Sheep Lick Draw* ... OR-9
Sheeplick Draw—*valley* ... OR-9
Sheeplick Point—*cliff* ... TN-4
Sheep Lot Hollow—*valley* ... OH-6
*Sheep Low* ... MS-4
*Sheep L. Reservoir* ... WY-8
Sheep Meadow—*flat* ... CA-9
Sheepmens Little Valley—*valley* ... UT-8
*Sheep Mesa* ... AZ-5
Sheep Mesa—*summit* ... AZ-5
Sheep Mesa—*summit* ... WY-8
Sheep Mine—*mine* (2) ... AZ-5
*Sheep Mountain* ... ID-8
*Sheep Mountain* ... NV-8
Sheep Mountain—*ridge* ... OR-9
Sheep Mountain—*ridge* ... WY-8
Sheep Mountain Creek—*stream* ... ID-8
*Sheep Mountain Dry Lake* ... NV-8
*Sheep Mountain Lake* ... NV-8
Sheep Mountain Lodge—*locale* ... AK-9
Sheep Mountain Ranch—*locale* ... MT-8
Sheep Mountain Range Archeol District—*hist pl* ... NV-8
Sheep Mountain Rsvr—*reservoir* ... WY-8
Sheep Mountain Saddle—*gap* ... ID-8
Sheep Mountain Spring—*spring* ... AZ-5
Sheep Mountain Spring—*spring* ... NM-5
Sheep Mountain Trail—*trail* ... CO-8
Sheep Mountain Work Center—*locale* ... ID-8
Sheep Mounts Well—*well* ... AZ-5
*Sheep Mtn* ... CA-9
*Sheep Mtn* ... CO-8
Sheep Mtn—*range* ... WY-8
Sheep Mtn—*summit* (5) ... AK-9
Sheep Mtn—*summit* (7) ... AZ-5
Sheep Mtn—*summit* (4) ... CA-9
Sheep Mtn—*summit* (19) ... CO-8
Sheep Mtn—*summit* (11) ... ID-8
Sheep Mtn—*summit* (24) ... MT-8
Sheep Mtn—*summit* ... NE-7
Sheep Mtn—*summit* (3) ... NV-8
Sheep Mtn—*summit* ... NH-1
Sheep Mtn—*summit* (3) ... NM-5
Sheep Mtn—*summit* (2) ... NY-2
Sheep Mtn—*summit* (3) ... NC-3
Sheep Mtn—*summit* (6) ... OR-9
Sheep Mtn—*summit* (2) ... SD-7
Sheep Mtn—*summit* ... UT-8
Sheep Mtn—*summit* (4) ... WA-9
Sheep Mtn—*summit* (8) ... WY-8
Sheep Mtn Range—*range* ... ID-8
Sheep Mtn Table—*summit* ... SD-7
Sheep Neck, The—*cape* ... TN-4
Sheepneck Branch—*stream* ... AL-4
Sheepneck Branch—*stream* ... VA-3
Sheepneck Creek—*stream* ... NC-3
Sheepneck Creek—*stream* ... TN-4
Sheepneck Hollow—*valley* ... TN-4
Sheep Nose—*cliff* ... GA-3
Sheep Nose—*summit* ... CO-8
Sheepnose Mtn—*summit* ... TN-4
Sheep Park—*flat* (2) ... CO-8
Sheep Park—*flat* ... MT-8
Sheep Pass—*gap* ... CA-9
Sheep Pass—*gap* (2) ... NV-8
Sheep Pass—*gap* ... WY-8
Sheep Pass Camp—*locale* ... CA-9
Sheep Pass Canyon—*valley* ... NV-8
Sheep Pass Corral—*locale* ... NV-8
Sheep Pass Guzzler—*reservoir* ... NV-8
Sheep Pass Spring—*spring* ... NV-8
Sheep Pass Well—*well* ... NV-8
Sheep Pasture Bluff—*cliff* ... WI-6
Sheep Pasture Hill—*summit* ... MA-1
Sheep Pasture Mtn—*summit* ... TX-5
Sheep Peak—*summit* ... AZ-5
Sheep Peak—*summit* ... CA-9
Sheep Peak—*summit* ... ID-8
Sheep Peak—*summit* ... NV-8
Sheep Peak—*summit* ... TX-5
Sheep Peaks—*summit* ... NV-8
Sheep Pelt Camp—*locale* ... CA-9
Sheep Pelt Well—*well* ... AZ-5
Sheep Pen Basin—*basin* ... ID-8
Sheep Pen Bluff—*cliff* ... TN-4
Sheep Pen Branch—*stream* ... KY-4
Sheep Pen Branch—*stream* ... MS-4
Sheep Pen Branch—*stream* ... SC-3
Sheep Pen Branch—*stream* ... TN-4
*Sheep Pen Canon* ... CO-8
Sheep Pen Canyon—*valley* ... CO-8
Sheeppen Canyon—*valley* ... NM-5
Sheep Pen Canyon—*valley* ... NM-5
Sheep Pen Canyon—*valley* ... TX-5
Sheep Pen Cem—*cemetery* ... OH-6
Sheep Pen Cove—*bay* ... RI-1
*Sheeppen Creek* ... NC-3
Sheeppen Creek—*bay* ... NC-3
Sheep Pen Creek—*gut* ... NC-3
Sheep Pen Creek—*stream* ... CA-9
Sheep Pen Creek—*stream* ... NJ-2
Sheep Pen Creek—*stream* ... NC-3
Sheeppen Creek—*stream* ... UT-8
Sheep Pen Ditch—*stream* ... DE-2
Sheep Pen Draw—*valley* ... SD-7
Sheep Pen Gap—*gap* ... NC-3
Sheep Pen Gap—*gap* ... TN-4
Sheep Pen Gully—*stream* ... LA-4
Sheep Pen Gut—*gut* ... MD-2
Sheep Pen Harbor—*cove* ... MA-1
Sheeppen Hollow—*valley* ... TN-4
Sheep Pen Landing—*locale* ... DE-2
Sheep Pen Marsh—*swamp* ... FL-3
Sheeppen Point—*cape* ... NC-3
Sheep Pen Point—*cape* ... NC-3
Sheep Pen Rock—*pillar* ... RI-1
Sheep Pens—*basin* ... UT-8
Sheep Pen Spring—*spring* ... PA-2
Sheeppen Spring—*spring* ... UT-8
Sheep Pen Spring—*spring* ... UT-8
Sheep Pen Swamp—*swamp* ... RI-1
Sheep Pen Tank—*reservoir* ... TX-5
Sheep Pockets Rsvr—*reservoir* ... AZ-5
Sheep Pockets Trough—*reservoir* ... AZ-5
Sheep Point—*cape* ... AK-9
Sheep Point—*cape* ... RI-1
Sheep Point—*cape* ... WA-9
Sheep Point—*cliff* ... AZ-5
Sheep Point—*locale* ... VA-3
Sheep Point—*summit* ... ID-8
Sheep Point—*summit* ... WY-8
Sheep Point Canyon—*valley* ... AZ-5
Sheep Point Cove—*bay* ... RI-1
Sheep Pond—*lake* (2) ... MA-1
Sheep Ponds—*lake* ... MA-1
Sheep Porcupine Island—*island* ... ME-1
Sheep Prairie—*flat* ... OR-9
Sheep Queen Hill—*summit* ... NM-5
Sheep Ranch—*locale* ... NV-8
Sheep Ranch—*locale* ... OR-9
**Sheepranch**—*pop pl* ... CA-9
Sheep Ranch Canyon—*valley* ... AZ-5
Sheep Ranch Canyon—*valley* ... NV-8
Sheep Ranch Creek—*stream* ... OR-9
Sheep Ranch Creek—*stream* ... WI-6
Sheep Ranch Flat—*flat* ... NV-8
Sheep Ranch Fortified House—*hist pl* ... OR-9

Shelton Camp—*locale* CA-9
Shelton Canyon—*valley* NM-5
Shelton Cave—*cave* MO-7
Shelton (CCD)—*cens area* WA-9
Shelton Cem—*cemetery* (4) AL-4
Shelton Cem—*cemetery* AR-4
Shelton Cem—*cemetery* GA-3
Shelton Cem—*cemetery* (2) IL-6
Shelton Cem—*cemetery* KS-7
Shelton Cem—*cemetery* (4) KY-4
Shelton Cem—*cemetery* (3) MS-4
Shelton Cem—*cemetery* (4) MO-7
Shelton Cem—*cemetery* NE-7
Shelton Cem—*cemetery* (2) NC-3
Shelton Cem—*cemetery* (10) TN-4
Shelton Cem—*cemetery* (2) VA-3
Shelton Chapel—*church* AL-4
Shelton Chapel—*church* GA-3
Sholton Chapol *church* KY-4
Shelton Chapel—*church* TN-4
Shelton Coll—*school* FL-3
Shelton Coll—*school* NJ-2
*Shelton Creek* WA-9
Shelton Creek—*stream* AL-4
Shelton Creek—*stream* AR-4
Shelton Creek—*stream* CA-9
Shelton Creek—*stream* CO-8
Shelton Creek—*stream* IL-6
Shelton Creek—*stream* (2) KY-4
Shelton Creek—*stream* (2) MS-4
Shelton Creek—*stream* MO-7
Shelton Creek—*stream* (2) NC-3
Shelton Creek—*stream* (3) TN-4
Shelton Creek—*stream* (2) WA-9
Shelton Dam—*dam* (2) AL-4
Shelton Ditch—*canal* CO-8
Shelton Ditch—*canal* OR-9
Shelton Draw—*valley* WY-8
**Shelton Estates**—*pop pl* TN-4
Shelton Ford—*locale* MO-7
*Shelton Gap* TN-4
Shelton Grove Ch—*church* AL-4
Shelton Grove Ch—*church* MS-4
Shelton Grove Ch—*church* TN-4
*Shelton Grove Missionary Baptist Ch* AL-4
Shelton Hill—*ridge* MN-6
Shelton Hollow—*valley* IN-6
Shelton Hollow—*valley* (2) MO-7
Shelton Hollow—*valley* OH-6
Shelton Hollow—*valley* (4) TN-4
Shelton Hollow—*valley* TX-5
Shelton-Houghton House—*hist pl* TX-5
Shelton House—*hist pl* MS-4
Shelton House—*hist pl* NC-3
Sheltonia Landing (historical)—*locale* MS-4
Shelton Island—*island* SC-3
Shelton Lake—*lake* WY-8
Shelton Lake—*reservoir* (3) AL-4
Shelton Lake—*reservoir* MS-4
Shelton Lake—*reservoir* TX-5
Shelton Lake Dam—*dam* (2) AL-4
Shelton Lakes—*reservoir* AL-4
**Shelton Lake Shores (subdivision)**—*pop pl* AL-4
Shelton Laurel—*locale* NC-3
Shelton Laurel Chapel—*church* NC-3
Shelton Laurel Creek—*stream* NC-3
Shelton L.D.S. Ward Chapel—*hist pl* ID-8
Shelton Lookout Tower—*locale* WI-6
Shelton-McMurphey House and Grounds—*hist pl* OR-9
Shelton Memorial Cem—*cemetery* TN-4
Shelton Memorial Ch—*church* VA-3
Shelton Memorial Chapel (historical)—*church* TN-4
Shelton Mill Branch—*stream* TX-5
Shelton Mine—*mine* NV-8
Shelton Mission—*church* TN-4
Shelton Mtn—*summit* NC-3
Shelton Park—*park* AL-4
Shelton Park—*park* TN-4
Shelton Park Ch—*church* MI-6
Shelton Park Sch—*school* VA-3
Shelton Peak—*summit* WY-8
Shelton Pisgah Mtn—*summit* NC-3
Shelton Plantation House—*hist pl* NC-3
Shelton Prairie—*area* CA-9
Shelton Public Library and Town Hall—*hist pl* WA-9
Shelton Ranch—*locale* (2) CO-8
Shelton Ridge—*ridge* CA-9
Shelton Ridge—*ridge* (2) TN-4
*Shelton Rock* CA-9
*Shelton Rsvr* CT-1
Shelton Rsvr—*reservoir* CT-1
**Sheltons**—*pop pl* LA-4
Shelton Sch—*school* CT-1
Sheltons Ford (historical)—*crossing* (3) TN-4
Sheltons Ford Post Office (historical)—*building* TN-4
Shelton (Site)—*locale* AK-9
Sheltons Landing—*locale* TN-4
Sheltons Point—*cape* VA-3
Shelton Spring—*spring* MO-7
Sheltons Sch (historical)—*school* TN-4
Sheltons Shoals—*bar* TN-4
Sheltons Shop—*locale* VA-3
Shelton State Community Coll—*school* AL-4
Shelton State Technical Institute—*school* AL-4
Shelton State Wayside—*park* OR-9
**Shelton Store**—*pop pl* NC-3
Shelton Tank—*reservoir* AZ-5
Shelton Tank—*reservoir* TX-5
**Shelton Town**—*pop pl* NC-3
**Sheltontown**—*pop pl* NC-3
Shelton (Town of)—*civ div* CT-1
Shelton Township—*civil* MO-7
**Shelton Township**—*pop pl* NE-7
Shelton Trail—*trail* PA-2
Shelton Valley—*valley* WA-9
Shelton Ward Ch—*church* ID-8
**Shelton Woods (subdivision)**—*pop pl* AL-4
Shelvey—*locale* PA-2
*Shelving Church* AL-4
*Shelving Rock* TX-5
Shelving Rock—*locale* NY-2
*Shelving Rock Baptist Church* AL-4
Shelving Rock Bay—*bay* NY-2
Shelving Rock Bluff—*cliff* TX-5
Shelving Rock Brook—*stream* NY-2
Shelving Rock Creek—*stream* CA-9
Shelving Rock Hollow—*valley* TN-4
Shelving Rock Mtn—*summit* NY-2
Shelving Rock Run—*stream* WV-2
Shelving Rock Sch (historical)—*school* AL-4
Shelvin Rock Ch—*church* AL-4
Shely Peaks—*summit* TX-5
Shem—*locale* UT-8
Shemahgun, Lake—*lake* MN-6
Shemariah Ch—*church* VA-3
Shem Creek—*stream* SC-3
Shemonie Lake—*reservoir* FL-3
*Shemo Point* MA-1
Shemwell Cem—*cemetery* TN-4
Shemya—*other* AK-9
Shemya Island—*island* AK-9
Shemya Island—*other* AK-9
Shemya Pass—*channel* AK-9
Shemya Station/Air Force Station—*mil airp* AK-9
*She-nah-nam* WA-9
Shenandoah—*locale* NY-2
**Shenandoah**—*pop pl* FL-3
**Shenandoah**—*pop pl* GA-3
**Shenandoah**—*pop pl* IA-7
**Shenandoah**—*pop pl* OH-6
**Shenandoah**—*pop pl* PA-2
**Shenandoah**—*pop pl* TN-4
**Shenandoah**—*pop pl* TX-5
**Shenandoah**—*pop pl* VA-3
Shenandoah—*uninc pl* VA-3
Shenandoah, Lake—*reservoir* NJ-2
Shenandoah, Lake—*reservoir* VA-3
Shenandoah Acres—*locale* VA-3
Shenandoah Alum Springs—*spring* VA-3
Shenandoah Borough—*civil* PA-2
Shenandoah Caverns—*cave* VA-3
**Shenandoah Caverns**—*pop pl* VA-3
Shenandoah Cem—*cemetery* CA-9
Shenandoah Ch—*church* FL-3
Shenandoah Coll—*school* VA-3
**Shenandoah (County)**—*pop pl* VA-3
Shenandoah County Courthouse—*hist pl* VA-3
Shenandoah Creek—*stream* PA-2
Shenandoah Creek Dam—*dam* PA-2
Shenandoah Downs—*other* WV-2
Shenandoah Elem Sch—*school* FL-3
Shenandoah Elem Sch—*school* PA-2
**Shenandoah Estates**—*pop pl* (2) TN-4
*Shenandoah Falls* WV-2
**Shenandoah Farms**—*pop pl* VA-3
Shenandoah Flying Field Airp—*airport* IN-6
Shenandoah Golf Club—*other* MI-6
**Shenandoah Heights**—*pop pl* PA-2
**Shenandoah Heights (subdivision)**—*pop pl* TN-4
**Shenandoah Hills**—*pop pl* VA-3
Shenandoah Hosp—*hospital* VA-3
Shenandoah Industrial Park—*facility* GA-3
Shenandoah Iron Works (Magisterial District)—*fmr MCD* VA-3
Shenandoah JHS—*school* FL-3
**Shenandoah Junction**—*pop pl* PA-2
**Shenandoah Junction**—*pop pl* WV-2
Shenandoah Land and Improvement Company Office—*hist pl* VA-3
Shenandoah (Magisterial District)—*fmr MCD* VA-3
Shenandoah Memorial Cem—*cemetery* VA-3
Shenandoah Mill—*locale* NV-8
Shenandoah Mine—*mine* CA-9
Shenandoah Mine—*mine* CO-8
Shenandoah Mine—*mine* NV-8
Shenandoah Mine (Abandoned)—*mine* CA-9
*Shenandoah Mountain* NV-8
*Shenandoah Mountains* VA-3
*Shenandoah Mountains* WV-2
Shenandoah Mountain Trail—*trail* VA-3
Shenandoah Mtn—*range* VA-3
Shenandoah Mtn—*range* WV-2
Shenandoah Mtn—*summit* NY-2
Shenandoah Natl Park—*park* VA-3
Shenandoah Park—*park* FL-3
Shenandoah Peak—*summit* NV-8
**Shenandoah Place**—*pop pl* VA-3
Shenandoah River—*stream* VA-3
Shenandoah River—*stream* WV-2
Shenandoah River Lodge—*building* VA-3
Shenandoah Rsvr—*reservoir* PA-2
Shenandoah Sch—*school* CA-9
Shenandoah Sch—*school* FL-3
**Shenandoah Shores**—*pop pl* VA-3
Shenandoah Street Sch—*school* CA-9
**Shenandoah (subdivision)**—*pop pl* DE-2
**Shenandoah (subdivision)**—*pop pl* NC-3
Shenandoah Valley—*flat* CA-9
Shenandoah Valley—*valley* OH-6
Shenandoah Valley Acad—*school* VA-3
Shenandoah Valley Golf Club—*other* VA-3
Shenandoah Valley Overlook—*locale* (3) VA-3
*Shenando Creek* WA-9
**Shenango**—*pop pl* PA-2
Shenango Ch—*church* PA-2
Shenango Creek—*stream* MT-8
Shenango Creek—*stream* PA-2
Shenango Creek—*stream* WV-2
Shenango Mine—*mine* MN-6
Shenango Public Use Area—*locale* PA-2
*Shenango Reservoir* OH-6
*Shenango Reservoir* PA-2
Shenango River—*stream* OH-6
Shenango River—*stream* PA-2
Shenango River Dam—*dam* PA-2
Shenango River Lake—*reservoir* OH-6
Shenango River Lake—*reservoir* PA-2
*Shenango River Rsvr* OH-6
*Shenango River Rsvr* PA-2
**Shenango (Township of)**—*pop pl* (2) PA-2
Shenango Valley Bible Ch—*church* PA-2
Shenango Valley Cem—*cemetery* PA-2
Shenanigan Flat—*flat* CA-9
Shenanigan Mine—*mine* CA-9
Shenanigan Ridge—*ridge* CA-9
Shenbergers Ch—*church* PA-2
Shenecoy Field—*locale* PA-2
Shenendehowa Central Sch—*school* NY-2
Shenendoah City—*locale* UT-8
Shenes Ledge—*bench* NY-2
*Shenewemedy* MA-1
*Shenford* ND-7
Shenford (historical)—*locale* ND-7
**Shenford Township**—*pop pl* ND-7
Shenipsit Dam—*dam* CT-1
Shenipsit Lake—*reservoir* CT-1
Shenipsit State For—*forest* CT-1
Shenk Airp—*airport* IN-6
Shenk Airp—*airport* PA-2
**Shenkel**—*pop pl* PA-2
Shenkel Hill—*summit* PA-2
Shenkel Island—*island* CA-9
Shenkenbeger Park—*park* FL-3
Shenks—*locale* FL-3
*Shenks Church* PA-2
*Shenks Ferry* PA-2
**Shenks Ferry**—*pop pl* PA-2
Shenks Ferry Site (36LA2)—*hist pl* PA-2
Shenks Hollow—*valley* VA-3
Shenk's Mill Covered Bridge—*hist pl* PA-2
Shenky Creek—*stream* MI-6
Shennecossett Beach—*beach* CT-1
Shennecossett Country Club—*other* CT-1
**Shennington**—*pop pl* WI-6
**Shennon Village**—*pop pl* TN-4
Shenoah Campground—*locale* UT-8
Shenon Creek—*stream* MT-8
**Shenorock**—*pop pl* NY-2
Shenorock, Lake—*reservoir* NY-2
**Shenorock (Lake Shenorock)**—*pop pl* NY-2
Shenship Lake—*swamp* AR-4
Shenton Creek—*stream* MD-2
Shenukdei Island—*island* FM-9
Sheomet Lake—*reservoir* MA-1
Sheomet Lake Dam—*dam* MA-1
Sheosh Creek—*stream* WI-6
Shep—*locale* TX-5
Shep, Mount—*summit* OR-9
*Shepahard's Creek* PA-2
*Shepang* CT-1
*Shepard* OH-6
Shepard—*locale* ND-7
**Shepard**—*pop pl* SC-3
Shepard—*uninc pl* NC-3
Shepard, John, House—*hist pl* CT-1
Shepard, L. Fay, House—*hist pl* ID-8
Shepard, Thomas, House—*hist pl* MA-1
Shepard, William T., House—*hist pl* AL-4
Shepard Block—*hist pl* MA-1
Shepard Branch—*stream* NC-3
Shepard Branch—*stream* TN-4
Shepard Branch—*stream* TX-5
*Shepard Brook* MA-1
Shepard Brook—*stream* CT-1
Shepard Brook—*stream* VT-1
Shepard Camp—*locale* OR-9
Shepard Cem—*cemetery* (2) AL-4
Shepard Cem—*cemetery* GA-3
Shepard Cem—*cemetery* (5) TN-4
Shepard Cem—*cemetery* TX-5
Shepard Cem—*cemetery* WV-2
Shepard Chapel—*church* TN-4
Shepard Church, The—*church* MS-4
Shepard Company Bldg—*hist pl* RI-1
Shepard Corners—*locale* NY-2
*Shepard Creek* CA-9
*Shepard Creek* NE-7
*Shepard Creek* WI-6
Shepard Creek—*stream* AK-9
Shepard Creek—*stream* TN-4
Shepard Creek—*stream* UT-8
Shepard Creek—*stream* WY-8
Shepard Drain—*canal* MI-6
Shepard Elem Sch—*school* PA-2
Shepard Glacier—*glacier* MT-8
Shepard Graveyard—*cemetery* AL-4
Shepard Grove Cem—*cemetery* MS-4
Shepard Hill—*summit* IN-6
Shepard Hill—*summit* MA-1
Shepard Hill—*summit* (2) NH-1
Shepard Hill—*summit* NY-2
Shepard Hill—*summit* TX-5
**Shepard (historical)**—*pop pl* IA-7
Shepard Hollow—*valley* AL-4
Shepard Hollow—*valley* NY-2
Shepard HS—*school* NC-3
Shepard JHS—*school* NC-3
Shepard Lake—*lake* TN-4
Shepard Lake—*lake* UT-8
Shepard Lake—*lake* WI-6
Shepard Lake—*reservoir* TX-5
Shepard Lake Creek—*stream* WI-6
Shepard Millpond Dam—*dam* NC-3
*Shepard Morris Reservoir* PA-2
*Shepard Mountain* MO-7
Shepard MS—*school* TX-5
Shepard Mtn—*summit* MT-8
Shepard Park—*park* MO-7
Shepard Point—*cape* AK-9
*Shepard Pond* MA-1
Shepard Ranch—*locale* NE-7
Shepard Rsvr—*reservoir* WY-8
*Shepard Run* PA-2
Shepard Run—*stream* PA-2
*Shepards Bayou* MS-4
*Shepards Bend* AL-4
Shepards Brook—*stream* MA-1
Shepards Brook—*stream* NY-2
*Shepards Cem* MS-4
Shepard Sch—*school* CA-9
Shepard Sch—*school* IL-6
Shepard Sch—*school* MO-7
Shepard Sch—*school* OH-6
Shepard Sch—*school* PA-2
Shepard Sch (abandoned)—*school* MO-7
Shepards Corner—*locale* NY-2
Shepards Corners—*locale* NY-2
*Shepards Creek* NY-2
*Shepards Creek* PA-2
Shepards Creek—*stream* MI-6
Shepard Settlement—*locale* NY-2
Shepards Hill—*summit* ME-1
Shepard Slough—*stream* CA-9
Shepards Millpond—*reservoir* FL-3
Shepardson Brook—*stream* ME-1
Shepardson Brook—*stream* MA-1
Shepardson Sch—*school* CT-1
Shepardson Sch—*school* VT-1
Shepards Point—*cape* NC-3
Shepards Point—*cape* OR-9
*Shepards Pond* MA-1
Shepards River—*stream* ME-1
Shepards River—*stream* NH-1
*Shepards Run* KY-4
Shepard State Park—*park* MS-4
Shepard Street Sch—*hist pl* OH-6
*Shepardsville* AL-4
**Shepardsville**—*pop pl* IN-6
**Shepardsville**—*pop pl* MI-6
Shepard Swamp—*swamp* NY-2
*Shepardville* AL-4
**Shepardville**—*pop pl* MA-1
*Shepardville Reservoir* MA-1
Shepard Well—*well* CO-8
*Shepaug River* CT-1
Shepaug River—*stream* CT-1
*Shepaug Rsvr* CT-1
Shepaug Rsvr—*reservoir* CT-1
Shep Cem—*cemetery* TX-5
Shep Creek—*stream* (3) ID-8
Sheperd Knapp Sch—*school* MA-1
*Sheperds* NC-3
Sheperds Run—*stream* OH-6
*Sheperdstown* PA-2
**Shephard**—*pop pl* MN-6
Shephard Branch—*stream* AL-4
Shephard Branch—*stream* (2) KY-4
Shephard Brook—*stream* ME-1
*Shephard Butte* ND-7
Shephard Cabin—*locale* CO-8
Shephard Cem—*cemetery* IL-6
Shephard Ch—*church* MS-4
Shephard Ch—*church* MO-7
Shephard Creek—*stream* CA-9
Shephard Creek—*stream* NE-7
Shephard Creek—*stream* TX-5
Shephard Gap—*gap* AL-4
Shephard Glacier—*glacier* AK-9
Shephard Hollow—*valley* TN-4
Shephard Lake—*lake* FL-3
Shephard Lake—*reservoir* NC-3
Shephard Lake Dam—*dam* MS-4
Shephard Lake Dam—*dam* NC-3
Shephard Landing—*locale* AL-4
Shephard Mesa—*summit* CA-9
Shephard Mine—*mine* CO-8
Shephard Peak—*summit* ID-8
Shephard Point—*cape* NY-2
Shephard Pond—*reservoir* MA-1
Shephard Pond Dam—*dam* MA-1
Shephard Ranch—*locale* SD-7
Shephard Rips—*rapids* ME-1
*Shephards* NC-3
**Shephards**—*pop pl* NC-3
*Shephard's Creek* NY-2
Shephard Slough—*gut* FL-3
*Shephardsville* IN-6
Shepherd—*locale* AL-4
Shepherd—*locale* IL-6
Shepherd—*locale* MS-4
Shepherd—*locale* PA-2
**Shepherd**—*pop pl* GA-3
**Shepherd**—*pop pl* IN-6
**Shepherd**—*pop pl* MI-6
**Shepherd**—*pop pl* MT-8
**Shepherd**—*pop pl* TN-4
**Shepherd**—*pop pl* TX-5
Shepherd, Bayou—*stream* LA-4
Shepherd, Dr. Warren, House—*hist pl* UT-8
Shepherd, Earl, Bungalow—*hist pl* ID-8
Shepherd, Harriet S., House—*hist pl* UT-8
Shepherd, John J., House—*hist pl* OH-6
Shepherd, J. R., House—*hist pl* ID-8
Shepherd, Lake—*lake* FL-3
Shepherd, Les and Hazel, Bungalow—*hist pl* ID-8
Shepherd, Ted, Cottage—*hist pl* ID-8
Shepherd, William, House—*hist pl* NY-2
Shepherd Acad—*school* (2) FL-3
Shepherd Airp—*airport* MO-7
Shepherd Bald—*summit* NC-3
Shepherd Baptist Ch—*church* TN-4
*Shepherd Baptist Church* AL-4
Shepherd Bend—*bend* AL-4
Shepherd Bldg—*hist pl* AL-4
Shepherd Bluff—*cliff* AR-4
Shepherd Branch—*stream* AL-4
Shepherd Branch—*stream* FL-3
Shepherd Branch—*stream* (3) KY-4
Shepherd Branch—*stream* NC-3
Shepherd Branch—*stream* (2) TN-4
Shepherd Brook—*stream* ME-1
Shepherd Brook—*stream* MA-1
Shepherd Brook—*stream* NH-1
Shepherd Brook—*stream* VT-1
Shepherd Brook Mtn—*summit* (2) ME-1
Shepherd Bungalow—*hist pl* ID-8
Shepherd Butte—*summit* MT-8
Shepherd Butte Sch—*school* MT-8
Shepherd Camp Hollow—*valley* TN-4
*Shepherd Canyon* NM-5
Shepherd Canyon—*valley* (2) CA-9
Shepherd Cave—*cave* MO-7
*Shepherd Cem* AL-4
Shepherd Cem—*cemetery* (2) AL-4
Shepherd Cem—*cemetery* IL-6
Shepherd Cem—*cemetery* (2) KY-4
Shepherd Cem—*cemetery* ME-1
Shepherd Cem—*cemetery* MS-4
Shepherd Cem—*cemetery* (2) MO-7
Shepherd Cem—*cemetery* (3) NC-3
Shepherd Cem—*cemetery* OH-6
Shepherd Cem—*cemetery* (4) TN-4
Shepherd Cem—*cemetery* (2) WV-2
Shepherd Ch—*church* AL-4
Shepherd Ch—*church* MI-6
Shepherd Ch—*church* SC-3
Shepherd Ch—*church* WV-2
Shepherd Chapel—*church* WV-2
Shepherd Coll—*school* WV-2
*Shepherd Cove* MA-1
Shepherd Cove—*basin* CA-9
Shepherd Cove—*bay* MO-7
*Shepherd Creek* FL-3
*Shepherd Creek* NY-2
*Shepherd Creek* PA-2
Shepherd Creek—*stream* (2) AK-9
Shepherd Creek—*stream* AR-4
Shepherd Creek—*stream* (2) CA-9
Shepherd Creek—*stream* KY-4
Shepherd Creek—*stream* LA-4
Shepherd Creek—*stream* (4) NC-3
Shepherd Creek—*stream* OR-9
Shepherd Creek—*stream* (2) TX-5
Shepherd Creek—*stream* VA-3
**Shepherd Creek County Estates Subdivision**—*pop pl* UT-8
Shepherd Crest—*summit* CA-9
Shepherd Crossing—*locale* MT-8
Shepherd Crossing Spring—*spring* AR-4
Shepherd Dam—*dam* AL-4
Shepherd Drive Sch—*school* GA-3
Shepherd-Evergreen (CCD)—*cens area* TX-5
Shepherd Field—*other* VA-3
Shepherd Field—*park* CA-9
Shepherd Flat—*flat* SD-7
**Shepherd Forest**—*pop pl* TN-4
Shepherd Fork Dry Creek—*stream* OH-6
Shepherd Gas And Oil Field—*oilfield* TX-5
Shepherd Grove Cem—*cemetery* SC-3
Shepherd Grove Ch—*church* AR-4
Shepherd Gulch—*valley* OR-9
Shepherd Gulch—*valley* WY-8
Shepherd Hall—*hist pl* WV-2
Shepherd Hardware—*hist pl* ID-8
Shepherd Hill—*locale* AL-4
**Shepherd Hill**—*pop pl* VA-3
Shepherd Hill—*summit* CT-1
Shepherd Hill—*summit* NY-2
Shepherd Hill—*summit* WV-2
**Shepherd Hills (subdivision)**—*pop pl* TN-4
Shepherd Hollow—*valley* AL-4
Shepherd Hollow—*valley* AR-4
Shepherd Hollow—*valley* TN-4
Shepherd Island—*island* ME-1
Shepherd Island—*island* MA-1
Shepherd Island—*island* SC-3
Shepherd JHS—*school* IL-6
*Shepherd Junction* DC-2
Shepherd Knob—*summit* NC-3
*Shepherd Lake* CT-1
Shepherd Lake—*lake* CA-9
Shepherd Lake—*lake* CO-8
Shepherd Lake—*lake* FL-3
Shepherd Lake—*lake* ID-8
Shepherd Lake—*lake* OK-5
Shepherd Mall—*post sta* OK-5
Shepherd Memorial Park—*cemetery* NC-3
*Shepherd Millpond* NC-3
Shepherd Millpond—*reservoir* NC-3
Shepherd Mountain Lake—*reservoir* MO-7
Shepherd Mountains—*summit* AK-9
Shepherd Mtn—*summit* AR-4
Shepherd Mtn—*summit* MO-7
Shepherd Mtn—*summit* MT-8
Shepherd Mtn—*summit* (2) NC-3
Shepherd Mtn—*summit* TX-5
Shepherd of the Glades Lutheran Ch—*church* FL-3
Shepherd of the Hills Cem—*cemetery* MO-7
Shepherd of the Hills Ch—*church* (2) CO-8
Shepherd of the Hills Ch—*church* MN-6
Shepherd of the Hills Fish Hatchery—*other* MO-7
Shepherd of the Hills Homestead—*building* MO-7
*Shepherd of the Hills Museum* MO-7
Shepherd of the Hills State Fish Hatchery—*other* MO-7
Shepherd of the Lake Ch—*church* MN-6
Shepherd of the Lakes Ch—*church* WI-6
*Shepherd of the Mountains Lutheran Church* UT-8
Shepherd of the Springs EV Lutheran Ch—*church* FL-3
Shepherd Parkway—*park* DC-2
Shepherd Pass—*gap* CA-9
Shepherd Peak—*summit* CA-9
Shepherd Point—*cape* UT-8
*Shepherd Pond* NJ-2
Shepherd Pond—*lake* ME-1
Shepherd Pond—*reservoir* MA-1
Shepherd Ridge—*ridge* CA-9
*Shepherd Run* VA-3
Shepherd Run—*stream* NC-3
**Shepherds**—*pop pl* NC-3
Shepherds Bayou—*stream* MS-4
Shepherds Branch—*stream* TX-5
*Shepherd's Brook* CT-1
*Shepherds Brook* MA-1
Shepherds Ch—*church* NC-3
Shepherds Ch—*church* VA-3
Shepherd Sch—*school* CA-9
Shepherd Sch—*school* DC-2
Shepherd Sch—*school* FL-3
Shepherd Sch—*school* (2) KY-4
Shepherd Sch—*school* MI-6
Shepherd Sch—*school* MO-7
Shepherd Sch—*school* NY-2
Shepherd Sch (historical)—*school* MO-7
*Shepherd School* PA-2
Shepherds Corners—*locale* PA-2
Shepherds Cove—*cove* MA-1
*Shepherds Creek* ND-7
Shepherd's Delight—*hist pl* MD-2
Shepherd (Shepherd Junction)—*uninc pl* DC-2
**Shepherds Hill**—*pop pl* ME-1
**Shepherds Hill**—*pop pl* VA-3
Shepherds Hill Cove—*bay* ME-1
*Shepherds Island* MA-1
Shepherds Island—*island* MD-2
Shepherd Site—*hist pl* KY-4
*Shepherds Lake* WA-9
Shepherds Lake—*reservoir* AL-4
Shepherds Landing—*locale* DC-2
Shepherd's Mill—*hist pl* WV-2
Shepherds Mtn—*summit* OH-6
Shepherd's Plain—*hist pl* VA-3
*Shepherds Point* NC-3
Shepherds Point—*summit* WY-8
Shepherds Pond—*lake* CT-1
Shepherd Spring—*spring* OR-9
Shepherd Spring Creek—*stream* FL-3
Shepherd Springs—*spring* WY-8
Shepherd Springs, Lake—*reservoir* AR-4
*Shepherds Run* PA-2
Shepherds Run—*stream* KY-4
Shepherds Store—*locale* VA-3
Shepherd Statue—*park* DC-2
**Shepherdstown**—*pop pl* OH-6
**Shepherdstown**—*pop pl* PA-2
**Shepherdstown**—*pop pl* WV-2
Shepherdstown Elem Sch—*school* PA-2
Shepherdstown Hist Dist—*hist pl* WV-2
Shepherdstown Hist Dist (Boundary Increase)—*hist pl* WV-2
Shepherdstown (Magisterial District)—*fmr MCD* WV-2
Shepherd Street Sch—*school* TN-4
Shepherds Valley—*valley* WV-2
*Shepherdsville* IN-6
**Shepherdsville**—*pop pl* KY-4
Shepherdsville Ch—*church* KY-4
Shepherdsville Ch—*church* VA-3
Shepherdsville Northwest (CCD)—*cens area* KY-4
Shepherdsville Southeast (CCD)—*cens area* KY-4
Shepherds White Oak Creek—*stream* OH-6
**Shepherdtown**—*pop pl* KY-4
Shepherd Town Hall—*building* ND-7
**Shepherd Township**—*pop pl* ND-7
Shepherd (Township of)—*fmr MCD* AR-4
Shephered Post Office (historical)—*building* TN-4
Shep Hollow—*valley* KY-4
Shepis Bldg—*hist pl* LA-4
Shepler Cem—*cemetery* OH-6
Shepler Ch—*church* (2) OH-6
*Shepler Hill* WV-2
Shepler Hollow—*valley* KY-4
**Shepley**—*pop pl* WI-6
Shepley Hill—*summit* MA-1
Shepley Hollow—*valley* MO-7
Shepleys Hill—*summit* MA-1
Shepman Run—*stream* PA-2
*Shepmans Run* PA-2
Shep Meadow—*flat* VT-1
Shepola—*locale* KY-4
Shepo Lake—*lake* MN-6
*Sheppard* GA-3
**Sheppard**—*pop pl* AL-4
**Sheppard**—*pop pl* AR-4
**Sheppard**—*pop pl* CA-9
**Sheppard**—*pop pl* WI-6
Sheppard AFB—*military* TX-5
Sheppard AFB/Wichita Falls Municipal Airport—*mil airp* TX-5
Sheppard Air Force Base Sch—*school* TX-5
Sheppard and Enoch Pratt Hosp and Gatehouse—*hist pl* MD-2
Sheppard Bay—*bay* MI-6
Sheppard Branch—*stream* AR-4
Sheppard Branch—*stream* GA-3
Sheppard Branch—*stream* NC-3
Sheppard Branch—*stream* TN-4
*Sheppard Brook* CT-1
Sheppard Burkburnett Sch—*school* TX-5
Sheppard Canyon—*valley* (2) NM-5
*Sheppard Cem* AL-4
Sheppard Cem—*cemetery* (2) AL-4
Sheppard Cem—*cemetery* AR-4
Sheppard Cem—*cemetery* IL-6
Sheppard Cem—*cemetery* IN-6
Sheppard Cem—*cemetery* IA-7
Sheppard Cem—*cemetery* MS-4
Sheppard Cem—*cemetery* (2) MO-7
Sheppard Cem—*cemetery* NC-3
Sheppard Cem—*cemetery* OH-6
Sheppard Cem—*cemetery* WV-2
Sheppard Ch—*church* MO-7
Sheppard Cottage—*hist pl* AL-4
Sheppard Creek—*stream* AL-4
Sheppard Creek—*stream* GA-3
Sheppard Creek—*stream* MT-8
Sheppard Creek—*stream* TX-5
Sheppard Crossroads—*locale* SC-3
Sheppard Dam—*dam* PA-2
Sheppard Draw—*valley* WY-8
*Sheppard Hollow* AL-4
*Sheppard Hollow* TN-4
Sheppard Island—*flat* AR-4
Sheppard Island Public Use Area—*park* AR-4
Sheppard Lake—*lake* AL-4
Sheppard Lake—*lake* (2) FL-3
Sheppard Landing—*locale* AL-4
Sheppard Landing (historical)—*locale* MS-4
Sheppard Ledges—*bar* MA-1
Sheppard-Meyers Dam—*dam* PA-2
Sheppard-Meyers Rsvr—*reservoir* PA-2
Sheppard Millpond—*reservoir* NC-3
Sheppard Mtn—*summit* MT-8
*Sheppard Myers Rsvr* PA-2
**Sheppard Park**—*pop pl* SC-3
Sheppard Place Cem—*cemetery* GA-3
Sheppard Plaza (Shop Ctr)—*locale* (2) FL-3
Sheppard Point—*locale* AR-4
Sheppard Point—*summit* MO-7
*Sheppard Pond* MA-1
Sheppard Pond—*lake* NJ-2
Sheppard Pond Dam—*dam* AL-4
Sheppard-Pratt Hosp—*hospital* MD-2
Sheppard Ranch—*locale* CO-8
Sheppard Ranch—*locale* NV-8
Sheppard Ridge—*ridge* AR-4
Sheppard Ridge—*ridge* (2) MO-7
Sheppard Run—*stream* NC-3
Sheppard Run—*stream* PA-2
Sheppard Run Canal—*canal* NC-3
Sheppards—*locale* GA-3
Sheppards—*locale* VA-3
Sheppards Branch—*stream* NJ-2
Sheppard Sch—*school* (2) CA-9
Sheppard Sch—*school* FL-3
Sheppard Sch—*school* MI-6
Sheppard Sch—*school* (2) MO-7
Sheppard Sch—*school* PA-2
Sheppard Sch—*school* TN-4
Sheppards Factory Pond—*lake* MA-1
Sheppards Island—*island* DE-2
Sheppards Lake—*lake* LA-4
Sheppards Landing—*locale* MS-4
Sheppards Mill—*locale* NJ-2
Sheppards Mill—*locale* VA-3
Sheppards Millpond—*reservoir* NJ-2
Sheppards Millpond Dam—*dam* NJ-2
Sheppards Run—*stream* PA-2
Sheppards Run—*stream* WV-2
Sheppards Store (historical)—*locale* MS-4
Sheppards Store (historical)—*locale* TN-4
*Sheppardston Landing* MS-4
Sheppard Tank—*reservoir* NM-5
Sheppardtown—*locale* MS-4

Sheppardtown Post Office
(historical)—building ... MS-4
Sheppard Wash—stream ... AZ-5
Sheppard Well—well ... NV-8
Sheppard Windmill—locale ... AZ-5
Sheppard Windmill—locale ... NM-5
Sheppe Pond—lake ... VA-3
Shepperd—locale ... MD-2
Shepperd Crossing—locale ... AR-4
Shepperd Sch—school ... MD-2
Shepperds Dell State Park—park ... OR-9
Shepperson House—hist pl ... TX-5
Shepperson Ranch—locale ... WY-8
Sheppersons Creek ... VA-3
**Shepphard**—pop pl ... TX-5
Sheppler Hill—summit ... PA-2
Shepp Post Office (historical)—building ... TN-4
Shepp Ranch—locale ... ID-8
Shepp Sch (historical)—school ... TN-4
**Shepp (Shepards Station)**—pop pl ... TN-4
**Sheppton**—pop pl ... PA-2
Shep Ranch ... ID-8
Sheps Canyon—valley ... SD-7
Sheps Canyon Sch—school ... SD-7
Sheps Creek—stream ... TX-5
**Sheps End**—pop pl ... VA-3
Sheps Gulch—valley ... MT-8
Shep Shoal—bar ... NC-3
Sheps Ridge—ridge ... UT-8
Shepton—locale ... TX-5
Shequaga Creek—stream ... NY-2
Shequaga Falls—falls ... NY-2
Sherack—locale ... MN-6
**Sheraden**—pop pl ... PA-2
Sheraden Elem Sch—school ... PA-2
Sheraden Park—park ... PA-2
Sheradon—uninc pl ... PA-2
Sheram Cem—cemetery ... GA-3
**Sherando**—pop pl ... VA-3
Sherando Camp—locale ... VA-3
Sherando Ch—church ... VA-3
Sherando Lake—reservoir ... VA-3
Sherar—locale ... OR-9
Sherar Burn—area ... OR-9
**Sherard**—pop pl ... MS-4
Sherard Church ... MS-4
Sherard Elementary School ... MS-4
Sherard Lake—lake ... SC-3
Sherard Sch—school ... MS-4
**Sherar Grabe (historical)**—pop pl ... OR-9
Sherars Bridge—locale ... OR-9
Sherars Falls—falls ... OR-9
Sherar Springs Creek—stream ... OR-9
Sheratakku ... FM-9
Sheraton Flats—flat ... CA-9
Sheraton Inn-Gettysburg Airp—airport ... PA-2
Sheraton Inn Greensburg Airp—airport ... PA-2
**Sheraton Place (subdivision)**—pop pl ... NC-3
Sheraug Dam—dam ... CT-1
Sherb Brook—stream ... ME-1
Sherbert Cem—cemetery ... AL-4
Sherbine Cem—cemetery ... PA-2
Sherbino Draw ... TX-5
Sherbino Mesa—summit ... TX-5
Sherbino Ranch—locale ... TX-5
Sherbondy Park—park ... FL-3
Sherbondy Park—park ... OH-6
Sherborn ... MA-1
**Sherborn**—pop pl ... MA-1
Sherborn Center Hist Dist—hist pl ... MA-1
Sherborn Centre ... MA-1
Sherborn Post Office—building ... MA-1
**Sherborn (Town of)**—pop pl ... MA-1
Sherbourne ... MA-1
Sherbourne Sch—school ... MI-6
**Sherbrooke**—pop pl ... ND-7
Sherbrooke Cem—cemetery ... ND-7
**Sherbrook Estates**—pop pl ... NJ-2
Sherbrooke Town Hall—building ... ND-7
**Sherbrooke Township**—pop pl ... ND-7
Sherburn ... MA-1
**Sherburn**—pop pl ... MN-6
Sherburn, Town of ... MA-1
Sherburn Brook ... ME-1
Sherburn Commercial Hist Dist—hist pl ... MN-6
Sherburne ... MA-1
Sherburne ... MN-6
Sherburne—locale ... LA-4
**Sherburne**—pop pl ... KY-4
**Sherburne**—pop pl ... NY-2
Sherburne, Henry, House—hist pl ... NH-1
Sherburne, Lake—reservoir ... MT-8
Sherburne, Town of ... MA-1
Sherburne, Warren E., House—hist pl ... MA-1
Sherburne Brook—stream ... NH-1
Sherburne Cem—cemetery ... MA-1
**Sherburne Center**—pop pl ... VT-1
Sherburne (corporate name Sherburn) ... MN-6
**Sherburne (County)**—pop pl ... MN-6
Sherburne County Courthouse—hist pl ... MN-6
Sherburne Covered Suspension
Bridge—hist pl ... KY-4
**Sherburne Four Corners**—pop pl ... NY-2
Sherburne Gas and Oil Field—oilfield ... LA-4
Sherburne Hill—summit ... NH-1
Sherburne Hills—range ... CA-9
Sherburne Hist Dist—hist pl ... NY-2
Sherburne HS—hist pl ... NY-2
Sherburne Lake ... MT-8
Sherburne Natl Wildlife Ref—park ... MN-6
Sherburne Pass—gap ... VT-1
Sherburne Peak—summit ... MT-8
Sherburne Ranger Station Hist
Dist—hist pl ... MT-8
Sherburne Sch—school (2) ... NH-1
Sherburne Sch—school ... VT-1
**Sherburne (Town of)**—pop pl ... NY-2
**Sherburne (Town of)**—pop pl ... VT-1
Sherburne Valley Sch—school ... VT-1
Sherburne West Hill Cem—cemetery ... NY-2
Sherburn Hills ... CA-9
Sherburn Lake—lake ... IN-6
**Sherburnville**—pop pl ... IL-6
Sherdahl—locale ... KS-7
Sherd Cem—cemetery ... MO-7
Sherd Lake—lake ... WY-8
Sherd Sch—school ... MI-6
Shereau Branch—stream ... SC-3
Sherell Pond—reservoir ... AL-4
Sherell Pond Dam—dam ... AL-4
Sheren Gulch ... WY-8
Sherer Canyon—valley ... CA-9
Sherer Cem—cemetery ... OH-6
Sherer Creek—stream ... CA-9
Sherer Creek—stream ... TX-5
Sherer Creek—stream ... WA-9
Sherer Ditch—canal ... OH-6
Sherer Island ... IL-6
Sherer Ridge—ridge ... CA-9
Sherer Sch—school ... NE-7
Sherer Spring—spring ... CA-9
Sherersville ... PA-2
**Sherersville**—pop pl ... PA-2
Sherett Lake—lake ... MI-6
Sherex Chemical Company—facility ... IL-6
Sherfey-Boyer Cemetery ... TN-4
Sherfick Stream—stream ... IN-6
Sherfield Bend—bend ... FL-3
Sheriaton River ... IA-7
Sheridan ... IN-6
Sheridan ... KS-7
Sheridan ... PA-2
Sheridan—fmr MCD ... NE-7
Sheridan—locale ... CA-9
Sheridan—locale ... IA-7
Sheridan—locale ... KY-4
Sheridan—locale ... NM-5
Sheridan—locale ... OH-6
**Sheridan**—pop pl ... AR-4
**Sheridan**—pop pl ... CA-9
**Sheridan**—pop pl ... CO-8
**Sheridan**—pop pl ... IL-6
**Sheridan**—pop pl ... IN-6
**Sheridan**—pop pl ... LA-4
**Sheridan**—pop pl ... ME-1
**Sheridan**—pop pl ... MD-2
**Sheridan**—pop pl ... MI-6
**Sheridan**—pop pl ... MO-7
**Sheridan**—pop pl ... MT-8
**Sheridan**—pop pl ... NV-8
**Sheridan**—pop pl ... NY-2
**Sheridan**—pop pl ... OR-9
**Sheridan**—pop pl (2) ... PA-2
**Sheridan**—pop pl ... TX-5
**Sheridan**—pop pl ... WV-2
**Sheridan**—pop pl ... WI-6
**Sheridan**—pop pl ... WY-8
Sheridan—post sta ... OK-5
Sheridan—uninc pl ... OK-5
Sheridan, Lake—lake ... PA-2
Sheridan, Mount—summit ... CO-8
Sheridan, Mount—summit ... OK-5
Sheridan, Mount—summit ... WY-8
Sheridan, Philip H., Sch—hist pl ... PA-2
Sheridan Airfield—airport ... OR-9
Sheridan Airp—airport ... IN-6
Sheridan-Alameda Shop Ctr—other ... CO-8
Sheridan Apartments—hist pl ... TX-5
Sheridan Beach—locale ... WA-9
Sheridan Bend—bend ... FL-3
Sheridan Branch—stream ... IL-6
Sheridan Branch—stream ... TX-5
Sheridan Branch—stream ... WV-2
Sheridan Bridge—bridge ... FL-3
Sheridan Brook—stream ... PA-2
Sheridan Brook—stream ... VT-1
Sheridan Butte—summit ... MT-8
Sheridan Campground—locale ... MT-8
Sheridan Canyon—valley ... NV-8
Sheridan Canyon—valley (2) ... NM-5
Sheridan (CCD)—cens area ... OR-9
Sheridan Cem—cemetery ... IA-7
Sheridan Cem—cemetery (3) ... LA-4
Sheridan Cem—cemetery ... MO-7
Sheridan Cem—cemetery ... MT-8
Sheridan Cem—cemetery ... NE-7
Sheridan Cem—cemetery ... OK-5
Sheridan Ch—church ... IA-7
Sheridan Ch—church ... LA-4
Sheridan Ch—church ... MI-6
Sheridan Ch—church ... PA-2
Sheridan Circle—locale ... DC-2
Sheridan Corners—locale ... PA-2
Sheridan County—civil ... KS-7
Sheridan County—civil ... ND-7
Sheridan County Airport—airport ... WY-8
Sheridan County Courthouse—hist pl ... ND-7
Sheridan County Courthouse—hist pl ... WY-8
Sheridan County Elk Winter
Pasture—park ... WY-8
Sheridan County State Lake—reservoir ... KS-7
Sheridan County State Lake Dam—dam ... KS-7
Sheridan Creek ... WI-6
Sheridan Creek—stream ... AK-9
Sheridan Creek—stream (4) ... CA-9
Sheridan Creek—stream ... ID-8
Sheridan Creek—stream ... IL-6
Sheridan Creek—stream ... MI-6
Sheridan Creek—stream (2) ... MT-8
Sheridan Creek—stream ... NV-8
Sheridan Creek—stream ... WI-6
Sheridan Creek—stream ... WY-8
Sheridan Creek Guard Station—locale ... WY-8
Sheridan Creek Trail—trail ... ID-8
Sheridan Drain ... MI-6
Sheridan Drain—canal ... MI-6
Sheridan Drive Ch—church ... MI-6
Sheridan Elem Sch—school ... PA-2
Sheridan Filtration Plant—other ... WY-8
**Sheridan Forest (subdivision)**—pop pl ... NC-3
Sheridan Fork ... WY-8
Sheridan Gables Shop Ctr—other ... CO-8
**Sheridan Gardens**—pop pl ... WY-8
Sheridan Gas Field—oilfield ... TX-5
Sheridan Gates—gap ... NE-7
Sheridan Glacier—glacier ... AK-9
Sheridan Graves—cemetery ... TX-5
Sheridan Grove Cem—cemetery ... MO-7
Sheridan Gulch—valley ... CA-9
Sheridan Gulch—valley ... MT-8
Sheridan Gulch—valley ... NV-8
Sheridan Gulch—valley ... NM-5
Sheridan Gulch—valley ... UT-8
Sheridan Heights Draw—valley ... WY-8
Sheridan Heights Park—park ... AL-4
**Sheridan Heights
(subdivision)**—pop pl ... AL-4
**Sheridan Heights Subdivision**—pop pl ... UT-8
Sheridan Hill—summit ... CO-8
Sheridan Hill—summit ... KY-4
Sheridan Hill—summit ... MI-6
Sheridan Hills ... AZ-5
Sheridan Hills Baptist Ch—church ... FL-3
Sheridan Hill Sch—school ... NY-2
Sheridan Hills Christian Sch—school ... FL-3
Sheridan Hills Elem Sch—school ... FL-3
Sheridan (historical)—locale ... KS-7
**Sheridan (historical)**—pop pl ... SD-7
Sheridan Hollow—valley ... PA-2
Sheridan House—hist pl ... OH-6
Sheridan HS—school ... OH-6
Sheridan Inn—hist pl ... WY-8
Sheridan Inn Natl Historical
Landmark—park ... WY-8
Sheridan JHS—school ... CT-1
Sheridan JHS—school ... MN-6
Sheridan Junior Coll—school ... WY-8
Sheridan Lake—lake ... CO-8
Sheridan Lake—lake ... LA-4
Sheridan Lake—lake ... MN-6
Sheridan Lake—lake ... MT-8
Sheridan Lake—lake ... WY-8
**Sheridan Lake**—pop pl ... CO-8
Sheridan Lake—reservoir ... SD-7
Sheridan Lake Cem—cemetery ... CO-8
Sheridan Lake Dam—dam ... SD-7
Sheridan Lake (dry)—lake ... AZ-5
Sheridan Lookout Tower—locale ... LA-4
Sheridan (Magisterial District)—fmr MCD
(2) ... WV-2
Sheridan Main Street Hist Dist—hist pl ... WY-8
Sheridan Mall—locale ... FL-3
Sheridan Mountains ... AZ-5
Sheridan Mountains—summit ... AZ-5
Sheridan Mtn—summit ... AZ-5
Sheridan Mtn—summit ... CO-8
Sheridan Mtn—summit ... NM-5
Sheridan Mtn—summit ... NY-2
Sheridan Mtn—summit ... OR-9
Sheridan Mtn—summit ... VT-1
Sheridan North Ditch—canal ... CO-8
Sheridan Oaks Plaza (Shop Ctr)—locale ... FL-3
Sheridan Park—park ... IL-6
Sheridan Park—park ... IN-6
Sheridan Park—park ... MN-6
Sheridan Park—park ... NY-2
Sheridan Park—park (2) ... WI-6
**Sheridan Park**—pop pl ... WA-9
Sheridan Park—uninc pl ... NY-2
Sheridan Park Elem Sch—school ... FL-3
Sheridan Park Hist Dist—hist pl ... IL-6
Sheridan Pass—gap ... WY-8
Sheridan Peak—summit ... AK-9
Sheridan Peak—summit ... OR-9
Sheridan Plaza Hotel—hist pl ... IL-6
Sheridan Point—cape ... MD-2
Sheridan Point—cape ... MT-8
Sheridan Point—cape ... VA-3
Sheridan Point—cape ... WA-9
Sheridan Point—cliff ... KS-7
Sheridan Ranch—locale ... CO-8
Sheridan Range ... AZ-5
Sheridan Ridge—ridge ... ID-8
Sheridan Road Chapel—church ... OK-5
Sheridan Road Sch—school ... MI-6
Sheridan Road Sch—school ... WI-6
Sheridan Rsvr—reservoir ... ID-8
Sheridan Sch—school ... CA-9
Sheridan Sch—school ... CT-1
Sheridan Sch—school ... DC-2
Sheridan Sch—school (6) ... IL-6
Sheridan Sch—school ... MA-1
Sheridan Sch—school (2) ... MI-6
Sheridan Sch—school (2) ... MN-6
Sheridan Sch—school (3) ... NE-7
Sheridan Sch—school ... NY-2
Sheridan Sch—school (2) ... OH-6
Sheridan Sch—school (2) ... PA-2
Sheridan Sch—school (3) ... WA-9
Sheridan Sch—school ... WI-6
Sheridan Sch (abandoned)—school ... MO-7
Sheridan Sch (abandoned)—school ... PA-2
Sheridan School—locale ... ID-8
Sheridan Shop Ctr—other ... CO-8
Sheridan Shore Yacht Club—other ... IL-6
Sheridan South—cens area ... WY-8
Sheridan South Ditch—canal ... CO-8
Sheridan Spring—spring ... WA-9
**Sheridan Square**—pop pl ... DE-2
Sheridan Square Apartments—hist pl ... IL-6
Sheridan State Fishing Lake—park ... KS-7
Sheridan State Game Mngmt Area ... KS-7
Sheridan Station (historical)—locale ... KS-7
Sheridan Statue—park ... DC-2
Sheridan Street Sch—school ... CA-9
Sheridan Street Sch—school ... MA-1
**Sheridan Subdivision**—pop pl ... UT-8
Sheridan Tank—reservoir ... AZ-5
**Sheridan (Town of)**—pop pl ... NY-2
**Sheridan (Town of)**—pop pl ... WI-6
Sheridan Township—civil (2) ... MO-7
Sheridan Township—fmr MCD (5) ... IA-7
**Sheridan Township**—pop pl (7) ... KS-7
**Sheridan Township**—pop pl ... MO-7
**Sheridan Township**—pop pl (3) ... NE-7
**Sheridan Township**—pop pl ... ND-7
**Sheridan Township**—pop pl ... SD-7
Sheridan (Township of)—civ div ... MI-6
**Sheridan (Township of)**—pop pl ... IL-6
**Sheridan (Township of)**—pop pl (6) ... MI-6
**Sheridan (Township of)**—pop pl ... MN-6
Sheridan Trail—trail ... WY-8
Sheridan Valley Ski Area—area ... MI-6
Sheridan Village ... IL-6
Sheridan Vocational Center—school ... FL-3
Sheridan Way Sch—school ... CA-9
Sheridan Wells—other ... NM-5
Sheridan West—cens area ... WY-8
Sheridan Wildlife Area—park ... KS-7
Sheridan Wilson Canal—canal ... NE-7
Sheriden Lake—lake ... MI-6
Sheriff Cem—cemetery ... KY-4
Sheriff Creek—stream ... CO-8
Sheriff Dam—dam ... SD-7
Sheriff Gulch—valley (2) ... MT-8
Sheriff Gulch—valley ... WA-9
Sheriff Hollow—valley ... MO-7
Sheriff Knob—summit ... GA-3
Sheriff Lake—lake ... MN-6
Sheriff Lake—lake ... NY-2
Sheriff Lake Cem—cemetery ... MN-6
Sheriff Lake Outlet—stream ... NY-2
Sheriff Lake Tabernacle—church ... MN-6
Sheriff Mill Complex—hist pl ... SC-3
Sheriff Mtn—summit ... MT-8
Sheriff Number 1 Dam—dam ... SD-7
Sheriff Ridge Sch (historical)—school ... MS-4
Sheriff Rsvr—reservoir ... CO-8
Sheriff Rsvr—reservoir ... SD-7
Sheriffs Acad—school ... CA-9
Sheriffs Camp—locale ... MI-6
Sheriffs Draw—valley ... AZ-5
Sheriffs Mesa—summit ... AZ-5
Sheriffs Posse Arena—building ... AZ-5
Sheriffs Posse Rodeo and Roping
Area—park ... AZ-5
Sheriff Spring—spring ... WA-9
Sheriff Springs Branch—stream ... AR-4
Sheriff Trail—trail ... PA-2
Sheriff White Bay—bay ... NC-3
**Sherill Gardens (subdivision)**—pop pl ... AL-4
Sherill Mountain ... NY-2
Sheril Mountain ... NY-2
Sherilton Valley Ranch—locale ... CA-9
Sheritt Cem—cemetery ... AL-4
Sherk Creek—stream ... ND-7
Sherklock Station ... TX-5
Sherks Sch—school ... PA-2
Sherley Mansion—hist pl ... KY-4
Sherley Township—civil ... MO-7
Sherley (Township of) ... MO-7
Sherling Lake—reservoir ... AL-4
Sherling Lake Number One ... AL-4
Sherling Lake Number Two ... AL-4
Sherling Lake Number 1 Dam—dam ... AL-4
Sherlock ... KS-7
Sherlock—locale ... TX-5
**Sherlock Corners**—pop pl ... NY-2
Sherlock Creek—stream ... CA-9
Sherlock Creek—stream ... ID-8
Sherlock Creek—stream ... MI-6
Sherlock Creek—stream ... WA-9
Sherlock Dipping Vat Spring—spring ... OR-9
Sherlock Draw—valley ... AZ-5
Sherlock Draw Tank Number
One—reservoir ... AZ-5
Sherlock Draw Tank Number
Two—reservoir ... AZ-5
Sherlock Grove—woods ... CA-9
Sherlock Gulch Dam—dam ... OR-9
Sherlock Gulch Rsvr—reservoir ... OR-9
Sherlock Homestead
(abandoned)—locale ... WY-8
Sherlock Park—park ... MN-6
Sherlock Peak—summit ... ID-8
Sherlock Peak—summit ... WA-9
Sherlock Rsvr—reservoir ... WY-8
Sherlock Sch—school ... IL-6
Sherlock Shearing Pens—locale ... WY-8
Sherlock Spring—spring ... CA-9
Sherlock Tank—reservoir ... AZ-5
**Sherlock Township**—pop pl ... KS-7
Sherlynd Ch—church ... VA-3
Sherman ... KS-7
Sherman ... ME-1
Sherman ... ND-7
Sherman (2) ... OH-6
Sherman ... SD-7
Sherman—fmr MCD (3) ... NE-7
Sherman—locale ... AL-4
Sherman—locale ... AK-9
Sherman—locale ... CO-8
Sherman—locale ... CT-1
Sherman—locale ... FL-3
Sherman—locale ... IA-7
Sherman—locale ... KS-7
Sherman—locale ... MN-6
Sherman—locale ... NM-5
Sherman—locale ... NC-3
Sherman—locale ... WA-9
**Sherman**—pop pl ... IL-6
**Sherman**—pop pl ... KY-4
**Sherman**—pop pl ... ME-1
**Sherman**—pop pl ... MI-6
**Sherman**—pop pl ... MS-4
**Sherman**—pop pl ... MO-7
**Sherman**—pop pl ... NY-2
**Sherman**—pop pl ... PA-2
**Sherman**—pop pl ... SD-7
**Sherman**—pop pl ... TX-5
**Sherman**—pop pl ... WV-2
**Sherman**—pop pl ... WY-8
Sherman—uninc pl ... AL-4
Sherman, Bayou—stream (2) ... LA-4
Sherman, Byron R., House—hist pl ... MT-8
Sherman, Eber, Farm—hist pl ... MA-1
Sherman, Elijah, Farm—hist pl ... NC-3
Sherman, Hoyt, Place—hist pl ... IA-7
Sherman, John, Birthplace—hist pl ... OH-6
Sherman, John, Memorial
Gateway—hist pl ... OH-6
Sherman, Lake—lake ... OH-6
Sherman, Lampson P., House—hist pl ... IA-7
Sherman, Mount—summit ... CO-8
Sherman, Point—cape ... AK-9
Sherman, The—hist pl ... NE-7
Sherman, William B., Farm—hist pl ... MA-1
Sherman, William Watts, House—hist pl ... RI-1
**Sherman Acres**—pop pl ... CA-9
Sherman Air Field ... KS-7
Sherman Archeol Site—hist pl ... KY-4
Sherman Army Airfield—airport ... KS-7
Sherman Ave Hist Dist—hist pl ... WI-6
Sherman Ballard Rec Area—park ... WV-2
Sherman Baptist Ch—church ... MS-4
Sherman Bar—bar ... CA-9
Sherman Bay—bay ... WI-6
Sherman Bldg—hist pl ... IN-6
Sherman Bog Rsvr—reservoir ... MA-1
Sherman Branch—stream ... NC-3
Sherman Bridge—bridge ... MA-1
Sherman Bridge—other ... MI-6
Sherman Brook—stream ... CT-1
Sherman Brook—stream (2) ... MA-1
Sherman Brook—stream (2) ... NY-2
Sherman Brook—stream ... RI-1
Sherman Canyon—valley ... CA-9
Sherman Canyon—valley ... CO-8
Sherman Canyon—valley ... WA-9
Sherman Canyon—valley ... WY-8
Sherman Cem—cemetery ... AR-4
Sherman Cem—cemetery ... IA-7
Sherman Cem—cemetery (2) ... KS-7
Sherman Cem—cemetery (2) ... MS-4
Sherman Cem—cemetery ... NY-2
Sherman Cem—cemetery ... NC-3
Sherman Cem—cemetery (2) ... OH-6
Sherman Cem—cemetery ... SD-7
Sherman Cem—cemetery ... TX-5
Sherman Cem—cemetery ... VT-1
Sherman Cem—cemetery ... WI-6
Sherman Center ... KS-7
Sherman Center—locale ... WI-6
Sherman Center Sch—school ... NE-7
Sherman Center Sch (historical)—school ... MO-7
Sherman Centre—locale ... IA-7
Sherman Ch—church ... CT-1
Sherman Ch—church ... KY-4
Sherman Ch—church (2) ... MS-4
Sherman Ch—church ... PA-2
Sherman Chapel—church ... IA-7
Sherman Chapel—church ... KS-7
Sherman Chapel—church ... TX-5
Sherman Ch of Christ—church ... MS-4
Sherman Circle—locale ... DC-2
Sherman City ... KS-7
**Sherman City**—pop pl ... MI-6
Sherman City Cem—cemetery ... MI-6
Sherman Cliffs—cliff ... AL-4
Sherman Corner ... MN-6
**Sherman Corner**—pop pl (2) ... CT-1
**Sherman Corner**—pop pl ... MA-1
Sherman Corners—locale ... WI-6
**Sherman Corners**—pop pl ... OH-6
Sherman Coulee—valley ... MT-8
Sherman County—civil ... KS-7
**Sherman County**—pop pl ... OR-9
**Sherman (County)**—pop pl ... TX-5
Sherman County Park ... KS-7
Sherman County State Lake—reservoir ... KS-7
Sherman County State Lake Dam—dam ... KS-7
Sherman Cove—bay ... FL-3
Sherman Cove—bay ... ME-1
Sherman Cove—valley ... UT-8
Sherman Crater—crater ... WA-9
Sherman Creek—stream ... AK-9
Sherman Creek—stream ... AR-4
Sherman Creek—stream (2) ... CA-9
Sherman Creek—stream ... CO-8
Sherman Creek—stream ... FL-3
Sherman Creek—stream ... ID-8
Sherman Creek—stream (2) ... MI-6
Sherman Creek—stream ... MS-4
Sherman Creek—stream ... MT-8
Sherman Creek—stream (2) ... NV-8
Sherman Creek—stream ... NY-2
Sherman Creek—stream ... OR-9
Sherman Creek—stream (2) ... PA-2
Sherman Creek—stream (3) ... WA-9
Sherman Creek—stream (2) ... WI-6
Sherman Creek Campground—locale ... WA-9
Sherman Creek Park—park ... WI-6
Sherman Creek Pass ... WA-9
Sherman Creek Point—cape ... WA-9
Sherman Creek Sch—school ... MS-4
Sherman Creek Spring ... NV-8
Shermandale ... PA-2
Sherman Dam ... MA-1
Sherman Dam—dam ... MA-1
Sherman Ditch—canal ... IA-7
Sherman Drain—canal ... MI-6
Sherman Drain—stream ... MI-6
Sherman Emmons Ditch—canal ... IN-6
Sherman Experiment Station—other ... OR-9
Sherman Ferry (historical)—locale ... MS-4
Sherman Flat—flat ... CA-9
Sherman Flats—flat ... CA-9
Sherman Fork—stream ... PA-2
Sherman F Owen Lake ... TN-4
Sherman Glacier—glacier ... AK-9
**Sherman Grove**—pop pl ... FL-3
Sherman Guard Station—locale ... WY-8
Sherman Gulch—valley ... CA-9
Sherman Gulch—valley ... MT-8
Sherman Gulch Beacon—other ... MT-8
Sherman Gulf—valley ... NY-2
Sherman Heights—cliff ... KS-7
**Sherman Heights**—pop pl (2) ... AL-4
Sherman Heights Sch—school ... AL-4
Sherman Heneman Park—park ... OH-6
Sherman Hill—summit ... CT-1
Sherman Hill—summit (2) ... MA-1
Sherman Hill—summit ... MS-4
Sherman Hill—summit ... NH-1
Sherman Hill—summit ... NY-2
Sherman Hill—summit ... RI-1
Sherman Hill—summit ... WY-8
Sherman Hill Ch—church ... TN-4
Sherman Hill Hist Dist—hist pl ... IA-7
Sherman Hill Sch—school ... MS-4
Sherman (historical P.O.)—locale ... IA-7
Sherman Hollow—valley ... IL-6
Sherman Hollow—valley ... KY-4
Sherman Hollow—valley ... NY-2
Sherman Hollow—valley ... TN-4
Sherman Hosp—hospital ... IL-6
Sherman Hosp—hospital ... IN-6
Sherman House—hist pl ... NY-2
Sherman House—hist pl ... WI-6
Sherman-Howe Mine—mine ... ID-8
Sherman Indian Institute—other ... CA-9
Sherman Inlet—bay ... FL-3
Sherman Institute (historical)—school ... AL-4
Sherman Island—island ... CA-9
Sherman Island—island ... OH-6
**Sherman Island**—pop pl ... CA-9
Sherman Island Gas Field ... CA-9
Sherman Island Powerplant—other ... NY-2
Sherman Island Waterfowl Mngmt
Area—park ... CA-9
Sherman Junction—locale ... TX-5
Sherman Knob—summit ... KY-4
Sherman Lake—lake ... CA-9
Sherman Lake—lake ... ME-1
Sherman Lake—lake (2) ... MI-6
Sherman Lake—lake (2) ... MN-6
Sherman Lake—lake ... WA-9
Sherman Lake—lake (3) ... NY-2
Sherman Lake—lake (3) ... WI-6
**Sherman Lake**—pop pl ... MI-6
Sherman Lake—reservoir ... CO-8
Sherman Lake—reservoir ... VA-3
Sherman Machine and Iron Works
Bldg—hist pl ... OK-5
Sherman (Magisterial District)—fmr MCD
(3) ... WV-2
Sherman Manor ... MI-6
Sherman Mill Creek—stream ... MI-6
**Sherman Mills**—pop pl ... ME-1
Sherman Mills Cem—cemetery ... ME-1
Sherman Mine—mine ... MN-6
Sherman Minton Bridge—bridge ... IN-6
Sherman Minton Bridge—bridge ... KY-4
Sherman Missionary Baptist Ch—church ... MS-4
Sherman Mountains ... WY-8
Sherman Mtn—summit ... AR-4
Sherman Mtn—summit ... CO-8
Sherman Mtn—summit ... NV-8
Sherman Mtn—summit ... NM-5
Sherman Mtn—summit ... NY-2
Sherman Mtn—summit ... PA-2
Sherman Mtns—range ... WY-8
**Sherman Oaks**—pop pl ... CA-9
Sherman Oaks Circle—other ... CA-9
Sherman Oaks Sch—school (2) ... CA-9
Sherman Oil Field—oilfield ... TX-5
Sherman Oil Field—other ... MI-6
Sherman Park—park ... AR-4
Sherman Park—park ... IL-6
Sherman Park—park ... IN-6
Sherman Park—park ... MD-2
Sherman Park—park ... MO-7
Sherman Park—park ... SD-7
Sherman Park—park ... WI-6
**Sherman Park**—pop pl ... MI-6
**Sherman Park**—pop pl ... NY-2
Sherman Park Mounds—locale ... SD-7
Sherman Parkway—park ... AZ-5
Sherman Park Zoo—locale ... MI-6
Sherman Pass—gap ... WA-9
Sherman Peak—summit ... AK-9
Sherman Peak—summit (2) ... CA-9
Sherman Peak—summit (3) ... ID-8
Sherman Peak—summit (2) ... NV-8
Sherman Peak—summit (3) ... WA-9
Sherman Peak—summit ... WY-8
Sherman Place—locale ... NV-8
Sherman Place—locale ... NM-5
Sherman Point—cape (2) ... FL-3
Sherman Point—cape ... ME-1
Sherman Pond ... NY-2
Sherman Pond—lake ... AL-4
Sherman Pond—lake ... MA-1
Sherman Pond—lake (2) ... MI-6
Sherman Pond—lake ... NE-7
Sherman Pond—reservoir ... SC-3
Sherman Ranch—locale ... NE-7
Sherman Ranch—locale ... NM-5
Sherman Ranch—locale ... OR-9
Sherman Ranch Slough—stream ... CO-8
Sherman Reservoir Dam—dam ... MA-1
Sherman Ridge—ridge ... CA-9
Sherman Ridge—ridge ... ID-8
Sherman Ridge—ridge ... PA-2
Sherman Riffle—rapids ... OR-9
Sherman Rock—other ... AK-9
Sherman (RR name for Sherman
Station)—other ... ME-1
Sherman Rsvr—reservoir ... MA-1
Sherman Rsvr—reservoir ... NE-7
Sherman Rsvr—reservoir ... OR-9
Sherman Rsvr—reservoir ... VT-1
Sherman Run—stream ... OH-6
Sherman Run—stream ... PA-2
Sherman Saddle—gap ... ID-8
Shermans Bay—bay ... NY-2
**Shermans Bay**—pop pl ... NY-2
Shermans Bridge ... MA-1
Sherman Camp (historical)—locale ... MS-4
Sherman Sch—school (3) ... CA-9
Sherman Sch—school ... CO-8
Sherman Sch—school (3) ... CT-1
Sherman Sch—school (8) ... IL-6
Sherman Sch—school ... IA-7
Sherman Sch—school ... KS-7
Sherman Sch—school (3) ... MI-6
Sherman Sch—school ... NE-7
Sherman Sch—school ... NJ-2
Sherman Sch—school ... NY-2
Sherman Sch—school (2) ... OH-6
Sherman Sch—school ... PA-2
Sherman Sch—school ... SD-7
Sherman Sch—school ... TX-5
Sherman Sch—school ... UT-8
Sherman Sch—school ... WA-9
Sherman Sch—school (4) ... WI-6
Sherman Sch (abandoned)—school (2) ... PA-2
Sherman Sch (historical)—school ... MS-4
Sherman School—locale ... MI-6
Shermans Corner—locale ... ME-1
**Shermans Corner**—pop pl ... ME-1
**Shermans Corner**—pop pl ... MN-6
Shermans Corner (historical)—locale ... MA-1
Shermans Cove ... AL-4
Sherman's Cove ... ME-1
Shermans Creek ... PA-2
Shermansdale ... PA-2
**Shermans Dale**—pop pl ... PA-2
Shermans Dale Sch (abandoned)—school ... PA-2
Sherman Shady Spring—spring ... CA-9
Shermans Mill—locale ... ME-1
Shermans Mill Post Office
(historical)—building ... TN-4
Shermans Pond ... MA-1
Sherman Spring—spring (2) ... AZ-5
Sherman Spring—spring ... OR-9
Sherman Springs—spring ... ID-8
Shermans Run ... PA-2
Sherman State Fishing Lake and Wildlife
Area—park ... KS-7
**Sherman Station**—pop pl ... ME-1
Shermans Tower—tower ... PA-2
Shermans Trail—trail ... PA-2
Sherman Street Historic Residential
District—hist pl ... CO-8
Shermansville ... KS-7
**Shermansville**—pop pl ... PA-2
Sherman Tavern—hist pl ... KY-4
Shermantown—locale ... NV-8
Shermantown Canyon—valley ... NV-8

Sherman Townhall—building ... IA-7
Sherman (Town of)—pop pl ... CT-1
Sherman (Town of)—pop pl ... ME-1
Sherman (Town of)—pop pl ... NY-2
Sherman (Town of)—pop pl (4) ... WI-6
Sherman Township ... SD-7
Sherman Township—civil ... KS-7
Sherman Township—civil (2) ... MO-7
Sherman Township—civil ... SD-7
Sherman Township—fmr MCD (9) ... IA-7
Sherman Township—pop pl (11) ... KS-7
Sherman Township—pop pl (3) ... MO-7
Sherman Township—pop pl (5) ... NE-7
Sherman Township—pop pl ... ND-7
Sherman Township—pop pl (3) ... SD-7
Sherman Township Cem—cemetery ... IA-7
Sherman (Township of)—fmr MCD ... AR-4
Sherman (Township of)—pop pl ... IL-6
Sherman (Township of)—pop pl (9) ... MI-6
Sherman (Township of)—pop pl ... MN-6
Sherman (Township of)—pop pl ... OH-6
Sherman United Methodist Ch—church ... MS-4
Sherman Valley—basin ... OR-9
Sherman Valley—valley ... PA-2
Sherman Valley—valley ... WA-9
Sherman Valley—valley ... WI-6
Sherman Valley Ch—church ... PA-2
Sherman Valley Run—stream ... PA-2
Shermanville Township—pop pl ... KS-7
Sherman Wash—arroyo ... AZ-5
Sherman Wash—valley ... UT-8
Sherman Well—well ... NM-5
Sherman Wilson Drain—stream ... MI-6
Sherman Woods ... MI-6
Shermar Hill ... RI-1
Sherm Chitwood Rsvr—reservoir ... CA-9
Shermerhorn Landing—pop pl ... NY-2
Shermer Park—park ... IL-6
Shermer Pond—reservoir ... NC-3
Shermer Pond Dam—dam ... NC-3
Sherm Siding—pop pl ... GA-3
Shernertown ... PA-2
Shernerville—pop pl ... PA-2
Sherobee Ch—church ... LA-4
Sherod Creek—stream ... OH-6
Sherod Meadows—flat ... OR-9
Sherod Park—park ... OH-6
Sherod Ranch—locale ... MT-8
Sherodsville ... OH-6
Sheron ... NJ-2
Sheron Cem—cemetery ... OH-6
She Ross Ch—church ... TN-4
Sherpa Glacier—glacier ... WA-9
Sherpa Peak—summit ... WA-9
Sherrard—pop pl ... IL-6
Sherrard—pop pl ... WV-2
Sherrard Cem—cemetery ... IL-6
Sherrard Hill—summit ... WY-8
Sherrard Point—summit ... OR-9
Sherrard Sch—school ... MI-6
Sherrards Old Landing—locale ... MS-4
Sherrars Gap—gap ... NC-3
Sherrat Post Office (historical)—building ... PA-2
Sherratt Point—cape ... UT-8
Sherred Hill Sch (abandoned)—school ... PA-2
Sherred Sch (historical)—school ... PA-2
Sherre HS—school ... LA-4
Sherrell Hollow—valley ... TN-4
Sherrelwood—CDP ... CO-8
Sherrelwood Estates—pop pl ... CO-8
Sherrer Lake—reservoir ... AL-4
Sherret ... PA-2
Sherret Branch—stream ... AL-4
Sherrett—pop pl ... PA-2
Sherrette Creek—stream ... AK-9
Sherrick Run—stream ... OH-6
Sherrie Run ... OH-6
Sherril Cem—cemetery ... IN-6
Sherril Creek—stream ... AR-4
Sherril Ditch ... IN-6
Sherril Heights—pop pl ... TN-4
Sherril Hollow—valley ... IN-6
Sherrill—pop pl ... AR-4
Sherrill—pop pl ... IA-7
Sherrill—pop pl ... MO-7
Sherrill—pop pl ... NY-2
Sherrill Branch—stream ... TN-4
Sherrill Cem—cemetery (2) ... NC-3
Sherrill Cem—cemetery (2) ... TN-4
Sherrill Cove—valley ... TN-4
Sherrill Cove Branch—stream ... NC-3
Sherrill Cove Tunnel—tunnel ... NC-3
Sherrill Creek—stream ... MO-7
Sherrill Ditch ... IN-6
Sherrill Ditch—canal ... NC-3
Sherrill Ford ... NC-3
Sherrill Gap—gap ... NC-3
Sherrill Hill Cem—cemetery ... NC-3
Sherrill Hills—range ... WY-8
Sherrill Hollow—valley ... MO-7
Sherrill Hollow—valley ... TN-4
Sherrill Lake—lake ... MS-4
Sherrill Mound—summit ... IA-7
Sherrill Park—park ... TX-5
Sherrill Post Office (historical)—building ... TN-4
Sherrill Rsvr—reservoir ... NY-2
Sherrill Sch—school ... AR-4
Sherrill Sch—school ... MI-6
Sherrills Creek—stream ... GA-3
Sherrills Ford—pop pl ... NC-3
Sherrill's Inn—hist pl ... NC-3
Sherrills Springs ... MS-4
Sherrilltown—locale ... TN-4
Sherrill Township—pop pl ... MO-7
Sherrils Lake Dam—dam ... MS-4
Sherrin School ... AL-4
Sherrit Drain—stream ... MI-6
Sherrits—locale ... OH-6
Sherritt Cem—cemetery ... IN-6
Sherritt Drain—stream ... IN-6
Sherritts—pop pl ... OH-6
Sherrod Ave Ch of Christ—church ... AL-4
Sherrod Cem—cemetery (3) ... AL-4
Sherrod Cem—cemetery ... GA-3
Sherrod Cem—cemetery (4) ... TN-4
Sherrod Cem—cemetery ... TX-5
Sherrod Ch of Christ (historical)—church ... AL-4
Sherrod Farm—hist pl ... NC-3
Sherrod Hill Cem—cemetery ... PA-2
Sherrod (historical)—locale ... AL-4
Sherrod Lake (historical)—lake ... AL-4
Sherrod Quarters—locale ... AL-4
Sherrod Rsvr—reservoir ... WY-8
Sherrods Chapel—church ... OH-6
Sherrod Sch (historical)—school ... AL-4
Sherrodsville—pop pl ... OH-6
Sherrod Valley Church of Christ ... AL-4
Sherrod Valley Sch ... AL-4
Sherrod-Williams Cem—cemetery ... TN-4
Sherrod Windmill—locale ... TX-5
Sherrold Lake—lake ... CA-9
Sherron Acres—uninc pl ... NC-3
Sherron Cem—cemetery ... TN-4
Sherron Ch—church ... MS-4
Sherrouse Sch—school ... LA-4
Sherrow Sch (abandoned)—school ... MO-7
Sherruck Brook—stream ... NY-2
Sherry—locale ... TX-5
Sherry—pop pl ... AR-4
Sherry—pop pl ... WI-6
Sherry Arm Bay—bay ... MN-6
Sherry Branch—stream ... MO-7
Sherry Cem—cemetery ... IN-6
Sherry Cem—cemetery ... KY-4
Sherry Cem—cemetery ... WI-6
Sherry Coulee—valley ... MT-8
Sherry Creek—stream ... IL-6
Sherry Creek—stream ... WI-6
Sherry Grade—trail ... WA-9
Sherry Hollow—valley ... MO-7
Sherry Junction—locale ... WI-6
Sherryl—pop pl ... MT-8
Sherry Lake—lake ... MN-6
Sherry Lake—lake ... PA-2
Sherry Lake—lake ... WA-9
Sherry One—locale ... MT-8
Sherry Park—pop pl ... VA-3
Sherry Rapids—rapids ... WI-6
Sherrys Brook—stream ... FL-3
Sherry's Ranch—locale ... MT-8
Sherry (sta.) (RR name for Blenker)—other ... WI-6
Sherry (Town of)—pop pl ... WI-6
Sherstad Slough—lake ... MN-6
Shertz Creek—stream ... ID-8
Shertz Trail—trail ... ID-8
Shervettes Corner—pop pl ... MD-2
Sherwill—locale ... VA-3
Sherwill Community Center—building ... VA-3
Sherwin—locale ... ID-8
Sherwin—locale ... KS-7
Sherwin—pop pl ... PA-2
Sherwin Bar—bar ... ID-8
Sherwin Bay—bay ... NY-2
Sherwin Bay Cem—cemetery ... NY-2
Sherwin Creek—stream ... CA-9
Sherwin Creek—stream ... ID-8
Sherwin Creek—stream ... NY-2
Sherwin Grade—slope ... CA-9
Sherwin Hill—ridge ... CA-9
Sherwin Island—island ... MD-2
Sherwin Junction ... KS-7
Sherwin Lake—reservoir ... CO-8
Sherwin Lakes—lake ... CA-9
Sherwin Meadow ... CA-9
Sherwin Meadow—flat ... CA-9
Sherwin Plaza—post sta ... CA-9
Sherwin Point—summit ... ID-8
Sherwin Ravine—valley ... CA-9
Sherwin Summit—summit ... CA-9
Sherwood ... IL-6
Sherwood—locale ... IA-7
Sherwood—locale ... LA-4
Sherwood—locale ... MN-6
Sherwood—locale ... OK-5
Sherwood—locale ... WV-2
Sherwood—pop pl ... AR-4
Sherwood—pop pl ... DE-2
Sherwood—pop pl ... GA-3
Sherwood—pop pl ... IL-6
Sherwood—pop pl ... MD-2
Sherwood—pop pl ... MI-6
Sherwood—pop pl ... MS-4
Sherwood—pop pl ... NY-2
Sherwood—pop pl ... NC-3
Sherwood—pop pl ... ND-7
Sherwood—pop pl ... OH-6
Sherwood—pop pl ... OR-9
Sherwood—pop pl ... TN-4
Sherwood—pop pl ... TX-5
Sherwood—pop pl ... VA-3
Sherwood—pop pl (2) ... WI-6
Sherwood—post sta ... CA-9
Sherwood—uninc pl ... AZ-5
Sherwood, James Noble, House—hist pl ... MI-6
Sherwood, Lake—lake ... FL-3
Sherwood, Lake—lake ... MI-6
Sherwood, Lake—reservoir ... AL-4
Sherwood, Lake—reservoir ... AR-4
Sherwood, Lake—reservoir ... CA-9
Sherwood, Lake—reservoir ... MO-7
Sherwood, Lake—reservoir ... TN-4
Sherwood, Lake—reservoir ... WV-2
Sherwood, Lake—reservoir ... WI-6
Sherwood, Michael, House—hist pl ... NC-3
Sherwood Acres—pop pl ... DE-2
Sherwood Acres—pop pl ... ME-1
Sherwood Acres (subdivision)—pop pl ... NC-3
Sherwood Archer—pop pl ... SC-3
Sherwood Baptist Church ... AL-4
Sherwood-Bates Sch—school ... NC-3
Sherwood Beach—pop pl ... ID-8
Sherwood Burial Park—park ... VA-3
Sherwood Butte—summit ... OR-9
Sherwood Buttes ... OR-9
Sherwood Campground—park ... OR-9
Sherwood Canyon—valley ... OR-9
Sherwood Canyon—valley ... SD-7
Sherwood Canyon—valley ... WY-8
Sherwood (CCD)—cens area ... TN-4
Sherwood Cem—cemetery ... KS-7
Sherwood Cem—cemetery ... MN-6
Sherwood Cem—cemetery (3) ... MO-7
Sherwood Cem—cemetery ... SC-3
Sherwood Cem—cemetery ... TN-4
Sherwood Cem—cemetery ... TX-5
Sherwood Cem—cemetery ... VT-1
Sherwood Ch—church ... AL-4
Sherwood Ch—church (2) ... GA-3
Sherwood Ch—church ... IN-6
Sherwood Ch—church ... NC-3
Sherwood Ch—church ... SC-3
Sherwood Corners—locale ... MI-6
Sherwood Corners—locale ... PA-2
Sherwood Creek—stream ... AL-4
Sherwood Creek—stream (2) ... CA-9
Sherwood Creek—stream ... CO-8
Sherwood Creek—stream ... GA-3
Sherwood Creek—stream ... MI-6
Sherwood Creek—stream (2) ... OR-9
Sherwood Creek—stream (3) ... WA-9
Sherwood Creek—stream ... WY-8
Sherwood Dam—dam ... TN-4
Sherwood-Davidson And Buckingham Houses—hist pl ... OH-6
Sherwood Ditch—canal ... CO-8
Sherwood Ditch—canal ... OH-6
Sherwood Division—civil ... TN-4
Sherwood Drain—canal ... MI-6
Sherwood Elem Sch—school ... FL-3
Sherwood Elem Sch—school ... TN-4
Sherwood Estates—pop pl ... KS-7
Sherwood Estates—pop pl (2) ... TN-4
Sherwood Estates (subdivision)—pop pl ... TN-4
Sherwood Farm—pop pl ... TN-4
Sherwood Farms—pop pl ... VA-3
Sherwood Flat—flat ... CO-8
Sherwood For—forest ... WA-9
Sherwood Forest (2) ... IL-6
Sherwood Forest ... IN-6
Sherwood Forest—locale ... GA-3
Sherwood Forest—locale ... VA-3
Sherwood Forest—pop pl ... AL-4
Sherwood Forest—pop pl ... CA-9
Sherwood Forest—pop pl ... DE-2
Sherwood Forest—pop pl ... FL-3
Sherwood Forest—pop pl ... GA-3
Sherwood Forest—pop pl ... IN-6
Sherwood Forest—pop pl (3) ... MD-2
Sherwood Forest—pop pl (2) ... MA-1
Sherwood Forest—pop pl ... MS-4
Sherwood Forest—pop pl (2) ... NC-3
Sherwood Forest—pop pl ... SC-3
Sherwood Forest—pop pl ... TN-4
Sherwood Forest—pop pl (2) ... VA-3
Sherwood Forest—uninc pl ... GA-3
Sherwood Forest—uninc pl ... LA-4
Sherwood Forest—uninc pl ... SC-3
Sherwood Forest—uninc pl ... TN-4
Sherwood Forest—uninc pl ... WA-9
Sherwood Forest Addition (subdivision)—pop pl ... UT-8
Sherwood Forest Ch—church ... FL-3
Sherwood Forest Country Club—other ... LA-4
Sherwood Forest Elem Sch—school ... NC-3
Sherwood Forest Estates—pop pl ... AZ-5
Sherwood Forest Lake—lake ... FL-3
Sherwood Forest Lodge Complex—hist pl ... MN-6
Sherwood Forest (Mobile Home Park)—pop pl ... NH-1
Sherwood Forest Park—park ... CA-9
Sherwood Forest Park—park ... NC-3
Sherwood Forest Sch—school ... FL-3
Sherwood Forest Sch—school ... LA-4
Sherwood Forest Sch—school ... VA-3
Sherwood Forest Sch—school ... WA-9
Sherwood Forest Shop Ctr—locale ... AZ-5
Sherwood Forest (subdivision)—pop pl (4) ... AL-4
Sherwood Forest (subdivision)—pop pl (4) ... MS-4
Sherwood Forest (subdivision)—pop pl (10) ... NC-3
Sherwood Forest (subdivision)—pop pl (3) ... TN-4
Sherwood Forest (trailer park)—pop pl ... DE-2
Sherwood Gardens ... MI-6
Sherwood Golf Course—locale ... ND-7
Sherwood Green—pop pl ... NJ-2
Sherwood Hall—pop pl ... VA-3
Sherwood Heights Ch—church ... OH-6
Sherwood Heights Sch—school ... ME-1
Sherwood Heights Sch—school ... OR-9
Sherwood Hills (2) ... AR-4
Sherwood Hills—pop pl ... VA-3
Sherwood Hills Condo—pop pl ... UT-8
Sherwood Hills (subdivision)—pop pl ... AL-4
Sherwood Hills Subdivision—pop pl ... UT-8
Sherwood (historical)—locale ... KS-7
Sherwood (historical)—locale ... MA-1
Sherwood Hollow—valley ... NY-2
Sherwood Hollow—valley ... PA-2
Sherwood Hollow—valley ... WV-2
Sher-Wood Hosp—hospital ... CA-9
Sherwood House—hist pl ... NY-2
Sherwood HS—school ... MD-2
Sherwood HS—school ... OR-9
Sherwood Island State Park—park ... CT-1
Sherwood JHS—school ... TN-4
Sherwood-Kinney Divide—ridge ... SD-7
Sherwood Knolls—pop pl ... NY-2
Sherwood Lake—lake (2) ... MI-6
Sherwood Lake—lake ... OR-9
Sherwood Lake—reservoir ... GA-3
Sherwood Lake—reservoir ... KS-7
Sherwood Lake—reservoir ... NC-3
Sherwood Lake—reservoir ... WI-6
Sherwood Lateral—canal ... CO-8
Sherwood Manor—CDP ... CT-1
Sherwood Manor—hist pl ... MD-2
Sherwood Manor—pop pl (2) ... MD-2
Sherwood Mansion—building ... TN-4
Sherwood Meadow—flat ... OR-9
Sherwood Meadows Subdivision—pop pl ... UT-8
Sherwood Memorial Gardens—cemetery ... TN-4
Sherwood Mesa Plaza Shop Ctr—locale ... AZ-5
Sherwood Millpond—lake ... CT-1
Sherwood Millpond—reservoir ... CT-1
Sherwood Mine—mine ... CA-9
Sherwood Mine—mine ... MI-6
Sherwood Mountain Pot—cave ... TN-4
Sherwood Mtn—summit ... ME-1
Sherwood Mtn—summit ... WA-9
Sherwood Municipal Airp—airport ... ND-7
Sherwood Oaks Condominium—pop pl ... UT-8
Sherwood Oil Field—oilfield ... WY-8
Sherwood on the Fox ... IL-6
Sherwood Park—park ... AZ-5
Sherwood Park—park ... CA-9
Sherwood Park—park ... CO-8
Sherwood Park—park ... IL-6
Sherwood Park—park ... MI-6
Sherwood Park—park ... OK-5
Sherwood Park—park (2) ... TX-5
Sherwood Park—park ... UT-8
Sherwood Park—park ... WI-6
Sherwood Park—pop pl ... AL-4
Sherwood Park—pop pl (2) ... DE-2
Sherwood Park—pop pl ... FL-3
Sherwood Park—pop pl ... MI-6
Sherwood Park—pop pl ... NY-2
Sherwood Park—pop pl ... NC-3
Sherwood Park—pop pl ... VA-3
Sherwood Park Addition (subdivision)—pop pl ... UT-8
Sherwood Park Cem—cemetery ... NY-2
Sherwood Park Elem Sch—school ... NC-3
Sherwood Park Golf Course—locale ... FL-3
Sherwood Park (subdivision)—pop pl ... NC-3
Sherwood Park (subdivision)—pop pl ... PA-2
Sherwood Park Subdivision—pop pl (2) ... UT-8
Sherwood Path—trail ... NY-2
Sherwood Peak—summit ... CA-9
Sherwood Place—pop pl ... TX-5
Sherwood Plaza—locale ... MA-1
Sherwood Plaza Shop Ctr—locale ... AL-4
Sherwood Plaza Shop Ctr—locale ... NC-3
Sherwood Point—cape ... CT-1
Sherwood Point—cape ... WI-6
Sherwood Point Light Station—hist pl ... WI-6
Sherwood Point Shoal—bar ... WI-6
Sherwood Pond ... CT-1
Sherwood Pond—lake ... MI-6
Sherwood Post Office—building ... AZ-5
Sherwood Post Office—building ... TN-4
Sherwood Rancheria—locale ... CA-9
Sherwood Reese Ranch—locale ... MO-7
Sherwood Ridge—ridge ... CA-9
Sherwood Ridge (subdivision)—pop pl ... NC-3
Sherwood Robbins Cem—cemetery ... NY-2
Sherwood Run—stream ... OH-6
Sherwood Run—stream ... PA-2
Sherwood Sch—school ... AL-4
Sherwood Sch—school (2) ... CA-9
Sherwood Sch—school ... CO-8
Sherwood Sch—school ... FL-3
Sherwood Sch—school (3) ... IL-6
Sherwood Sch—school (3) ... MI-6
Sherwood Sch—school (2) ... MO-7
Sherwood Sch—school ... NY-2
Sherwood Sch—school ... NC-3
Sherwood Sch—school ... OR-9
Sherwood Sch—school (2) ... TN-4
Sherwood Sch—school (2) ... TX-5
Sherwood Sch (abandoned)—school ... PA-2
Sherwood Shop Ctr—locale ... AL-4
Sherwood Shop Ctr—locale ... AZ-5
Sherwood Shop Ctr—locale ... TX-5
Sherwood Shores—pop pl ... KY-4
Sherwood Shores—pop pl ... TX-5
Sherwood Shores Ch—church ... TX-5
Sherwood Shores (subdivision)—pop pl ... AL-4
Sherwood's Point ... CT-1
Sherwood Spring—spring ... OR-9
Sherwood State Public Shooting Area—park ... SD-7
Sherwood Station (historical)—locale ... PA-2
Sherwood (subdivision)—pop pl (3) ... AL-4
Sherwood Terrace—pop pl ... NC-3
Sherwood (Town of)—pop pl ... WI-6
Sherwood (Township of)—pop pl ... MI-6
Sherwood Valley—valley ... CA-9
Sherwood Valley Rancheria (Indian Reservation)—pop pl ... CA-9
Sherwood Village—pop pl ... NC-3
Sherwood Village—pop pl ... OH-6
Sherwood Village—uninc pl ... AZ-5
Sherwood Wash—stream ... NV-8
Sherzberg Bayou ... NE-7
Sheser Creek—stream ... MT-8
Shesett Lake ... MI-6
Sheshabee ... MN-6
Sheshalik—pop pl ... AK-9
Sheshalik Spit—bar ... AK-9
Sheshebee—pop pl ... MN-6
Sheshequin—pop pl ... PA-2
Sheshequin (Township of)—pop pl ... PA-2
Sheshequin Valley—valley ... PA-2
Sheshequin Valley Cem—cemetery ... PA-2
Sheshok Creek—stream ... AK-9
Shesky Branch—stream ... TX-5
Shesler Lake ... MI-6
Shestak—locale ... NE-7
Shetek, Lake—lake ... MN-6
Shetek Church Camp—locale ... MN-6
Shetek State Wildlife Mngmt Area—park ... MN-6
Shetek (Township of)—pop pl ... MN-6
Shetipo Creek—stream ... WA-9
Shetland—locale ... KY-4
Shetland Creek—stream ... KY-4
Shetland Creek—stream ... MI-6
Shetland Divide—gap ... MT-8
Shetland Hills—pop pl ... MD-2
Shetland Well—well ... TX-5
Shetlerville—pop pl ... IL-6
Shetley Creek—stream ... GA-3
Shetley Creek—stream ... MO-7
Shetley Creek Ch—church ... MO-7
Shetley Creek Sch (historical)—school ... MO-7
Shetly Creek ... MO-7
Shetterly Ditch—canal ... IN-6
Shetterly Spring—spring ... TN-4
Shetter Quarry—mine ... TN-4
Shetters Grove—pop pl ... PA-2
Shettler Sch—school ... MI-6
Shettleston—locale ... PA-2
Shettleworth Bayou—stream ... LA-4
Shetty Creek—stream ... AR-4
Shetucket River—stream ... CT-1
Sheuy Well—well ... AZ-5
Sheva—locale ... VA-3
Shevlin—pop pl ... MN-6
Shevlin—pop pl ... OR-9
Shevlin Cem—cemetery ... MN-6
Shevling, L. W., Ranch—hist pl ... SD-7
Shevlin (historical)—pop pl (2) ... OR-9
Shevlin-Moose Cem—cemetery ... MN-6
Shevlin Park—park ... OR-9
Shevlin (Township of)—pop pl ... MN-6
Shevlin Well—well ... OR-9
Shevlon ... AZ-5
Shevlon Creek ... AZ-5
Shevlons Butte ... AZ-5
Shewag Lake—lake ... ID-8
Shewalter Ranch—locale ... CO-8
Shewamet Purchase ... MA-1
Shewartzwalder Mine—mine ... CO-8
Shewbird Mtn—summit ... NC-3
Shewbridge Field—park ... IL-6
Shew Cem—cemetery ... NY-2
Shewey Cem—cemetery ... VA-3
Shewey Valley—valley ... VA-3
Shewhart-Gard Settling Basin—basin ... IL-6
Shewhart Hollow—valley ... IL-6
Shew Hollow—valley ... NY-2
Shewmake—locale ... GA-3
Shewmaker Cem—cemetery ... IL-6
Shewmaker Ditch—canal ... MT-8
Shewmaker Sch—school ... IL-6
Shewmake Tank—reservoir ... TX-5
Shewmake Windmill—locale ... TX-5
Shew Pond—reservoir ... NY-2
Shewville—pop pl ... CT-1
Shewville Brook ... CT-1
Shewville Brook—stream ... CT-1
Shexnayder—pop pl ... LA-4
Sheybogan—pop pl ... TN-4
Sheyenne ... ND-7
Sheyenne—pop pl ... ND-7
Sheyenne Ch—church ... ND-7
Sheyenne Dam—dam ... ND-7
Sheyenne Lake—reservoir ... ND-7
Sheyenne River ... SD-7
Sheyenne River ... WY-8
Sheyenne River—stream ... ND-7
Sheyenne River Acad—school ... ND-7
Sheyenne River Diversion Dam—dam ... ND-7
Sheyenne Stockyards ... ND-7
Sheyenne Township—pop pl ... ND-7
Sheyenne Township Hall—building ... ND-7
Sheyenne Township (historical)—civil ... ND-7
Sheyenne Valley Ch—church (2) ... ND-7
Sheythe Creek—stream ... OR-9
Sheza Butte—summit ... AZ-5
Shiawassee (County)—pop pl ... MI-6
Shiawassee County Courthouse—hist pl ... MI-6
Shiawassee Lake—lake (2) ... MI-6
Shiawassee Natl Wildlife Ref—park ... MI-6
Shiawassee Oil Field—other ... MI-6
Shiawassee Pond—reservoir ... MI-6
Shiawassee River—stream ... MI-6
Shiawassee River State Game Area—park ... MI-6
Shiawassee Sch—school ... MI-6
Shiawasseetown—pop pl ... MI-6
Shiawassee (Township of)—pop pl ... MI-6
Shiawassetown—pop pl ... MI-6
Shibboleth—pop pl ... MO-7
Shibboleth Branch—stream ... MO-7
Shibboleth Cem—cemetery ... KS-7
Shibboleth (historical)—locale ... KS-7
Shib Branch—stream ... KY-4
Shibell, Mount—summit ... AZ-5
Shible Lake—lake ... MN-6
Shible Lake State Wildlife Mngmt Area—park ... MN-6
Shibles, Capt. Peter, House—hist pl ... WA-9
Shible (Township of)—pop pl ... MN-6
Shibley—locale ... AR-4
Shibley Ch—church ... AR-4
Shibley Point ... MO-7
Shibley Point School ... MO-7
Shibley Pond—reservoir ... PA-2
Shibleys Point—locale ... MO-7
Shibleys Point Cem—cemetery ... MO-7
Shibleys Point Sch (abandoned)—school ... MO-7
Shiboley Ch—church ... KY-4
Shichah River ... SD-7
Shichiyo Islands ... FM-9
Shichiyo Shoto ... FM-9
Shickasheen Brook ... RI-1
Shick Cem—cemetery ... OH-6
Shick Creek—stream ... OR-9
Shickley—pop pl ... NE-7
Shickley Cem—cemetery ... NE-7
Shick Ranch—locale ... SD-7
Shick River ... SD-7
Shick Shack Hill—summit ... IL-6
Shickshinny—pop pl ... PA-2
Shickshinny Borough—civil ... PA-2
Shickshinny Creek—stream ... PA-2
Shickshinny Fire Tower—tower ... PA-2
Shickshinny Lake—reservoir ... PA-2
Shickshinny Lake Dam—dam ... PA-2
Shickshinny Mtn—summit ... PA-2
Shideler—pop pl ... IN-6
Shideler Cem—cemetery ... IN-6
Shider Pond—reservoir ... GA-3
Shidler—pop pl ... OK-5
Shidler Ditch ... IN-6
Shidler Hoffman Ditch—canal ... IN-6
Shidler Sch—school ... OK-5
Shidoni ... MP-9
Shiekuk Creek—stream ... AK-9
Shield ... ND-7
Shield—locale ... AK-9
Shield Canyon—valley ... ID-8
Shield Cem—cemetery (2) ... MS-4
Shield Cem—cemetery ... NC-3
Shield Gulch—valley ... ID-8
Shield Lake—lake ... NM-5
Shield Lake—lake ... WA-9
Shield Lake—reservoir ... TX-5
Shield Mill (historical)—locale ... AL-4
Shield Mtn—summit ... CO-8
Shield Oil Field—oilfield ... TX-5
Shield Point ... FL-3
Shield Ranch—locale ... TX-5
Shield River ... MT-8
Shields ... IN-6
Shields ... OH-6
Shields—locale ... MT-8
Shields—locale ... NC-3
Shields—locale ... TX-5
Shields—locale (2) ... VA-3
Shields—pop pl ... IL-6
Shields—pop pl ... IN-6
Shields—pop pl ... KS-7
Shields—pop pl ... KY-4
Shields—pop pl ... MI-6
Shields—pop pl ... ND-7
Shields—pop pl ... PA-2
Shields, David, House—hist pl ... PA-2
Shield's, Edwin M., House—hist pl ... OH-6
Shields, E. R., House—hist pl ... NV-8
Shields, Mount—summit ... MT-8
Shields Bar—bar ... TN-4
Shield's Block—hist pl ... OH-6
Shields Bloomery Forge (historical)—locale ... TN-4
Shieldsboro ... MS-4
Shieldsboro Oil Field—oilfield ... MS-4
Shields Branch—stream ... IL-6
Shields Branch—stream ... ME-1
Shields Branch—stream ... TN-4
Shields Bridge—bridge ... AL-4
Shields Brook—stream (2) ... ME-1
Shields Brook—stream ... NH-1
Shieldsburg—locale ... PA-2
Shields Butte—summit ... OR-9
Shields Butte Lake ... OR-9
Shields Camp—locale ... CA-9
Shields Canyon—valley (2) ... CA-9
Shields Canyon—valley ... NM-5
Shields Cem—cemetery ... AL-4
Shields Cem—cemetery ... CA-9
Shields Cem—cemetery (3) ... IL-6
Shields Cem—cemetery ... IN-6
Shields Cem—cemetery ... IA-7
Shields Cem—cemetery (3) ... KS-7
Shields Cem—cemetery (2) ... KY-4
Shields Cem—cemetery (3) ... MS-4
Shields Cem—cemetery ... OH-6
Shields Cem—cemetery ... OR-9
Shields Cem—cemetery (3) ... TN-4
Shields Cem—cemetery ... VA-3
Shields Ch—church ... MO-7
Shield Sch—school ... NC-3
Shields Chapel—church ... IL-6
Shields Commissary—locale ... NC-3
Shields Community ... TX-5
Shields-Corinth Cem—cemetery ... MO-7
Shields Corners ... MI-6
Shields Cove—bay ... VA-3
Shields Cove—valley ... TN-4
Shields Creek—stream ... AR-4
Shields Creek—stream (2) ... CA-9
Shields Creek—stream (2) ... MT-8
Shields Creek—stream (2) ... OR-9
Shields Creek—stream ... TN-4
Shields Creek—stream ... VA-3
Shields Creek—stream ... WA-9
Shields Crossing—locale ... MT-8
Shields Crossroads—pop pl ... GA-3
Shields Dam—dam ... NM-5
Shields Dam (historical)—dam ... TN-4
Shields Elem Sch—school ... KS-7
Shields Flat—flat ... CA-9
Shields Gap—gap ... VA-3
Shields Gin (historical)—locale ... TN-4
Shields Gulch—valley ... CA-9
Shields Gulch—valley ... CO-8
Shields-Harris Cem—cemetery ... TN-4
Shields Heights Sch—school ... OK-5
Shields Hill—summit ... MO-7
Shields Hills—range ... AR-4
Shields Hollow ... TN-4
Shields HS—school ... IL-6
Shields JHS—school ... IN-6
Shields Knob—summit ... AR-4
Shields Lake—lake (2) ... MN-6
Shields Lake—lake ... NM-5
Shields Lake—reservoir ... VA-3
Shields Lateral—canal ... AZ-5
Shields Memorial Ch—church ... WV-2
Shields Mill (historical)—locale ... TN-4
Shields Mine—mine ... WY-8
Shields Mtn—summit ... TN-4
Shields Park—park ... IN-6
Shields Peak—summit ... CA-9
Shields Point—cape ... AK-9
Shields Point—cape ... FL-3
Shields Point—cape ... VA-3
Shields Pond—reservoir ... GA-3
Shields Prong—stream ... DE-2
Shields Prong—stream ... MD-2
Shields Ridge—ridge ... NC-3
Shields Ridge—ridge ... TN-4
Shields River—stream ... MT-8
Shields Run—stream ... MD-2
Shields Sch—school ... AL-4
Shields Sch—school (2) ... CA-9
Shields Sch—school ... MI-6
Shields Sch (historical)—school ... AL-4
Shields School—locale ... MI-6
Shields Spring—spring ... OR-9
Shields Spring—spring ... TN-4
Shields' Station—hist pl ... TN-4
Shields Tank—reservoir ... NM-5
Shields (Town of)—pop pl (2) ... WI-6
Shields Township—obs name ... ND-7
Shields Township—pop pl ... NE-7
Shields (Township of)—pop pl ... IL-6
Shields Valley—cens area ... MT-8
Shieldsville—pop pl ... MN-6
Shieldsville (Township of)—civ div ... MN-6
Shields-Wakins Field—park ... TN-4
Shields Woolen Mill—hist pl ... IA-7
Shiell Gulch—valley (2) ... CA-9
Shiell Ranch—locale (2) ... CA-9
Shiells Canyon—valley ... CA-9
Shiels, Mount—summit ... AK-9
Shiels Glacier—glacier ... AK-9
Shielsville ... IN-6
Shier, Carl H., Barn—hist pl ... OH-6
Shier, Carl H., Chicken House—hist pl ... OH-6
Shier, Carl H., House—hist pl ... OH-6
Shieratakku ... FM-9
Shier Drain—canal ... MI-6
Shiershke Spring ... CA-9
Shiess Creek ... ID-8

Shifflet Corner—locale ... VA-3
Shifflett Cem—cemetery ... MO-7
Shiffman Cave—cave ... AL-4
Shiflet Cem—cemetery ... TN-4
Shiflet Field—airport ... NC-3
Shiflet Ridge—ridge ... TN-4
Shiflett, G. W., Barn—hist pl ... TN-4
Shiflett, H. C., Barn—hist pl ... TN-4
Shiflett Pond—reservoir ... GA-3
Shiftail Canal—canal ... LA-4
Shifting Sands—area ... CA-9
Shift Lake—lake ... MN-6
Shiggin Creek—stream ... OK-5
Shigh Creek ... OR-9
Shigley Lake—lake ... NE-7
Shikel Lake—lake ... GA-3
Shikellamy HS—school (2) ... PA-2
Shikellamy JHS—school ... PA-2
Shikellamy Overlook—locale ... PA-2
Shikellamy Scout Camp—locale ... PA-2
Shikellamy State Park—park ... PA-2
Shikellimy Trail—trail ... PA-2
Shiki Islands ... FM-9
Shiki-Shoto ... FM-9
Shikosi Island—island ... AK-9
Shilake Ch—church ... LA-4
Shilch ... NC-3
Shilchin Bito Canyon ... AZ-5
Shilcotts Bayou—stream ... AR-4
Shiles Creek—stream ... MD-2
Shiley East Oil Field—oilfield ... KS-7
Shiley North Oil Field—oilfield ... KS-7
Shiley Oil Field—oilfield ... KS-7
**Shiley Township**—pop pl ... KS-7
Shiliak Creek—stream ... AK-9
S Hill—summit ... TN-4
Shillalah Creek—stream ... KY-4
Shillalah Pond—lake ... ME-1
Shillam Flat—flat ... ID-8
Shillapoo Lake—flat ... WA-9
Shillerville Cem—cemetery ... TX-5
**Shilling**—pop pl ... CA-9
Shilling Ave Hist Dist—hist pl ... ID-8
Shilling Bridge ... ND-7
Shillingburg Mine—mine ... NM-5
Shilling Creek—stream ... ID-8
Shilling Dam—dam ... MN-6
Shilling-Lamb House—hist pl ... CO-8
Shilling Mill ... OH-6
Shillings Branch—stream ... LA-4
Shillings Cem—cemetery ... TN-4
Shilling Sch (historical)—school ... PA-2
Shillings Flat—flat ... WV-2
Shillings Mill—locale ... OH-6
Shilling Spring ... CO-8
Shillings Spring—spring ... CO-8
Shillings Springs ... CO-8
Shillings Trail—trail ... VA-3
**Shillington**—pop pl ... PA-2
Shillington Borough—civil ... PA-2
Shillington Park—park ... PA-2
Shillington Shop Ctr—locale ... PA-2
Shillpot Creek ... DE-2
Shilo ... NC-3
Shiloah ... NJ-2
Shiloah Ch—church ... MO-7
Shiloah Church ... AL-4
Shiloah Church ... WV-2
Shiloah Mineral Springs—spring ... CA-9
Shiloah Sch (historical)—school ... TN-4
Shilo Baptist Ch—church ... AL-4
Shilo Cem—cemetery ... AR-4
Shilo Cem—cemetery ... GA-3
Shilo Cem—cemetery ... IL-6
Shilo Cem—cemetery ... IN-6
Shilo Cem—cemetery (2) ... OH-6
Shilo Cem—cemetery (2) ... TX-5
Shilo Ch ... AL-4
Shilo Ch—church ... CA-9
Shilo Ch—church (2) ... MO-7
Shilo Ch—church ... NC-3
Shilo Ch—church ... OK-5
Shilo Ch—church ... TX-5
Shiloh ... AL-4
Shiloh ... KS-7
Shiloh ... MS-4
Shiloh ... TN-4
Shiloh—locale (3) ... AL-4
Shiloh—locale (3) ... AR-4
Shiloh—locale ... CA-9
Shiloh—locale ... FL-3
Shiloh—locale (3) ... GA-3
Shiloh—locale ... IA-7
Shiloh—locale ... LA-4
Shiloh—locale ... MD-2
Shiloh—locale ... MS-4
Shiloh—locale ... NJ-2
Shiloh—locale ... OH-6
Shiloh—locale ... OK-5
Shiloh—locale ... PA-2
Shiloh—locale ... SC-3
Shiloh—locale (2) ... TN-4
Shiloh—locale (4) ... TX-5
Shiloh—locale (5) ... VA-3
Shiloh—locale ... WV-2
**Shiloh**—pop pl (4) ... AL-4
**Shiloh**—pop pl ... AR-4
**Shiloh**—pop pl ... FL-3
**Shiloh**—pop pl ... GA-3
**Shiloh**—pop pl ... ID-8
**Shiloh**—pop pl ... IL-6
**Shiloh**—pop pl (2) ... IN-6
**Shiloh**—pop pl ... KY-4
**Shiloh**—pop pl ... LA-4
**Shiloh**—pop pl ... ME-1
**Shiloh**—pop pl (2) ... MD-2
**Shiloh**—pop pl ... MI-6
**Shiloh**—pop pl (2) ... MS-4
**Shiloh**—pop pl ... NJ-2
**Shiloh**—pop pl (4) ... NC-3
**Shiloh**—pop pl (3) ... OH-6
**Shiloh**—pop pl ... PA-2
**Shiloh**—pop pl (3) ... SC-3
**Shiloh**—pop pl (9) ... TN-4
**Shiloh**—pop pl (4) ... TX-5
**Shiloh**—pop pl ... WV-2
Shiloh Acad—school ... IL-6
Shiloh Acad (historical)—school ... TN-4
Shiloh Apostolic Overcoming Holiness Ch of God—church ... IN-6
Shiloh Baptist Ch ... AL-4
Shiloh Baptist Ch ... MS-4
Shiloh Baptist Ch—church (13) ... AL-4
Shiloh Baptist Ch—church ... FL-3
Shiloh Baptist Ch—church ... IN-6
Shiloh Baptist Ch—church ... KS-7
Shiloh Baptist Ch—church ... LA-4
Shiloh Baptist Ch—church (2) ... MS-4
Shiloh Baptist Ch—church ... TN-4
Shiloh Baptist Ch—church ... UT-8
Shiloh Baptist Ch (historical)—church ... AL-4
Shiloh Baptist Ch (historical)—church ... MS-4
Shiloh Baptist Church—hist pl ... OH-6
Shiloh Baptist Church—hist pl ... TN-4
Shiloh Baptist Temple—church ... KS-7
Shiloh Basin—basin ... OR-9
**Shiloh Basin**—pop pl ... OR-9
Shiloh Basin Cem—cemetery ... OR-9
Shiloh Basin Sch—school ... OR-9
Shiloh Branch—stream (3) ... AL-4
Shiloh Branch—stream ... AR-4
Shiloh Branch—stream ... MO-7
Shiloh Branch—stream ... OK-5
Shiloh Branch—stream (2) ... SC-3
Shiloh Branch—stream (3) ... TN-4
Shiloh Branch—stream (4) ... TX-5
Shiloh Branch Cave—cave ... TN-4
Shiloh Bridge—bridge ... CA-9
Shiloh Bridge—bridge ... TN-4
Shiloh Camp—locale ... FL-3
Shiloh Camp—locale ... LA-4
Shiloh Camp—locale ... MO-7
Shiloh Camp Ground ... MS-4
Shiloh Canal—canal ... NC-3
**Shiloh Canyon (subdivision)**—pop pl (2) ... AZ-5
Shiloh Cave—cave ... IN-6
Shiloh (CCD)—cens area ... GA-3
Shiloh (CCD)—cens area ... KY-4
Shiloh (CCD)—cens area ... SC-3
Shiloh Cem—cemetery (25) ... AL-4
Shiloh Cem—cemetery (14) ... AR-4
Shiloh Cem—cemetery ... CA-9
Shiloh Cem—cemetery (4) ... FL-3
Shiloh Cem—cemetery (7) ... GA-3
Shiloh Cem—cemetery (8) ... IL-6
Shiloh Cem—cemetery (9) ... IN-6
Shiloh Cem—cemetery ... IA-7
Shiloh Cem—cemetery (3) ... KS-7
Shiloh Cem—cemetery ... KY-4
Shiloh Cem—cemetery (4) ... LA-4
Shiloh Cem—cemetery (2) ... MD-2
Shiloh Cem—cemetery (23) ... MS-4
Shiloh Cem—cemetery (9) ... MO-7
Shiloh Cem—cemetery ... NE-7
Shiloh Cem—cemetery ... NC-3
Shiloh Cem—cemetery (3) ... OK-5
Shiloh Cem—cemetery ... PA-2
Shiloh Cem—cemetery (2) ... SC-3
Shiloh Cem—cemetery (18) ... TN-4
Shiloh Cem—cemetery (19) ... TX-5
Shiloh Cem—cemetery (3) ... VA-3
Shiloh Ch ... AL-4
Shiloh Ch ... GA-3
Shiloh Ch ... MS-4
Shiloh Ch—church (74) ... AL-4
Shiloh Ch—church (28) ... AR-4
Shiloh Ch—church ... DE-2
Shiloh Ch—church (15) ... FL-3
Shiloh Ch—church (50) ... GA-3
Shiloh Ch—church (16) ... IL-6
Shiloh Ch—church (18) ... IN-6
Shiloh Ch—church ... IA-7
Shiloh Ch—church (17) ... KY-4
Shiloh Ch—church (11) ... LA-4
Shiloh Ch—church (4) ... MD-2
Shiloh Ch—church (41) ... MS-4
Shiloh Ch—church (15) ... MO-7
Shiloh Ch—church (2) ... NJ-2
Shiloh Ch—church (2) ... NY-2
Shiloh Ch—church (46) ... NC-3
Shiloh Ch—church (8) ... OH-6
Shiloh Ch—church (3) ... OK-5
Shiloh Ch—church (4) ... PA-2
Shiloh Ch—church (28) ... SC-3
Shiloh Ch—church (26) ... TN-4
Shiloh Ch—church (36) ... TX-5
Shiloh Ch—church (39) ... VA-3
Shiloh Ch—church (10) ... WV-2
Shiloh Ch—church ... WI-6
Shiloh Ch (abandoned)—church ... MO-7
Shiloh Chapel—church ... AL-4
Shiloh Chapel—church ... IL-6
Shiloh Chapel—church ... MO-7
Shiloh Chapel Ch ... AL-4
Shiloh Ch (historical)—church (4) ... AL-4
Shiloh Ch (historical)—church (3) ... MS-4
Shiloh Ch (historical)—church ... MO-7
Shiloh Ch (historical)—church (4) ... TN-4
Shiloh Ch of Christ ... AL-4
Shiloh Ch of Christ ... MS-4
Shiloh Church—hist pl ... AR-4
Shiloh Church—hist pl ... RI-1
Shiloh Church Cem—cemetery ... NC-3
Shiloh CME Ch ... AL-4
Shiloh CME Ch—church ... MS-4
Shiloh Creek—stream ... AL-4
Shiloh Creek—stream (3) ... AR-4
Shiloh Creek—stream ... GA-3
Shiloh Creek—stream ... IN-6
Shiloh Creek—stream ... KS-7
Shiloh Creek—stream ... KY-4
Shiloh Creek—stream ... LA-4
Shiloh Creek—stream (4) ... MS-4
Shiloh Creek—stream ... MO-7
Shiloh Creek—stream (2) ... TX-5
Shiloh Crossing—uninc pl ... NJ-2
Shiloh Cumberland Ch—church ... TX-5
Shiloh Cumberland Presbyterian Church ... AL-4
Shiloh-Deovolente Ch—church ... MS-4
Shiloh Drain—stream ... IN-6
Shiloh Draw—valley ... NM-5
**Shiloh East**—pop pl ... PA-2
Shiloh Elem Sch—school ... NC-3
Shiloh Elem Sch (historical)—school ... AL-4
Shiloh Fork—stream ... GA-3
Shiloh Gulch—valley ... TN-4
**Shiloh Hill**—pop pl (2) ... IL-6
Shiloh Hills—range ... NM-5
Shiloh Hill Sch (historical)—school ... MS-4
Shiloh Hist Dist—hist pl ... AR-4
Shiloh (historical)—locale ... AL-4
Shiloh (historical)—locale ... MS-4
**Shiloh (historical)**—pop pl ... MS-4
Shiloh Hollow—valley ... AR-4
Shiloh Hollow—valley ... IL-6
Shiloh Hollow—valley ... MO-7
Shiloh Hollow—valley ... TN-4
Shiloh House—hist pl ... AR-4
Shiloh House—hist pl ... IL-6
Shiloh House—hist pl ... MI-6
Shiloh HS—school ... AL-4
Shiloh JHS—school (2) ... AL-4
Shiloh Lake—lake ... AL-4
Shiloh Lake—lake ... WI-6
Shiloh Lake—reservoir ... TX-5
Shiloh Landing—locale ... MS-4
Shiloh Landing (historical)—locale ... LA-4
Shiloh Lookout Tower—locale (2) ... AL-4
Shiloh Lookout Tower—locale ... AR-4
Shiloh Lookout Tower—locale ... MS-4
Shiloh (Magisterial District)—fmr MCD ... VA-3
Shiloh Marina—locale ... AR-4
Shiloh-Marion Baptist Church and Cemetery—hist pl ... GA-3
Shiloh-Marion-Church Hill Ch—church ... GA-3
Shiloh Meeting House and Cemetery—hist pl ... IN-6
Shiloh Memorial Cem—cemetery ... TN-4
Shiloh Methodist Ch—church ... LA-4
Shiloh Methodist Ch—church ... MS-4
Shiloh Methodist Church ... AL-4
Shiloh Metropolitan Baptist Ch—church ... FL-3
**Shiloh Mills**—pop pl ... NC-3
Shiloh Missionary Baptist Ch ... AL-4
Shiloh Missionary Baptist Ch ... MS-4
Shiloh Missionary Baptist Ch—church ... AL-4
Shiloh Mountain Chain—ridge ... TX-5
Shiloh Mtn—summit ... AR-4
Shiloh Mtn—summit ... VA-3
Shiloh Natl Military Park—hist pl ... TN-4
Shiloh North ... AL-4
Shiloh North Ch ... AL-4
Shiloh No. 3 Drainage Ditch ... IL-6
Shiloh No 3 Drainage Ditch—canal ... IL-6
Shiloh Oil And Gas Field—oilfield ... AR-4
Shiloh Park—park ... IL-6
Shiloh Park Ch—church ... MD-2
**Shiloh (Pittsburg Landing)**—pop pl ... TN-4
Shiloh Plaza Shop Ctr—locale ... TN-4
Shiloh Pond—lake ... ME-1
Shiloh Post Office (historical)—building ... MS-4
Shiloh Post Office (historical)—building ... SD-7
Shiloh Post Office (historical)—building ... TN-4
Shiloh Primitive Baptist Ch ... AL-4
Shiloh Primitive Baptist Ch—church ... AL-4
Shiloh Primitive Baptist Ch (historical)—church ... TN-4
Shiloh Primitive Baptist Church ... MS-4
Shiloh Rec Area—park ... AR-4
Shiloh Ridge—ridge ... TN-4
Shiloh Road Ch—church ... TX-5
Shiloh Sch ... AL-4
Shiloh Sch—school (3) ... AL-4
Shiloh Sch—school ... AR-4
Shiloh Sch—school ... CA-9
Shiloh Sch—school (2) ... FL-3
Shiloh Sch—school ... GA-3
Shiloh Sch—school (3) ... IL-6
Shiloh Sch—school (2) ... IA-7
Shiloh Sch—school ... KS-7
Shiloh Sch—school ... KY-4
Shiloh Sch—school ... LA-4
Shiloh Sch—school (3) ... MS-4
Shiloh Sch—school (5) ... MO-7
Shiloh Sch—school ... MT-8
Shiloh Sch—school (2) ... NE-7
Shiloh Sch—school ... NC-3
Shiloh Sch—school (3) ... SC-3
Shiloh Sch—school (3) ... TN-4
Shiloh Sch—school (2) ... TX-5
Shiloh Sch (abandoned)—school (2) ... MO-7
Shiloh Sch (historical)—school (6) ... AL-4
Shiloh Sch (historical)—school (4) ... MS-4
Shiloh Sch (historical)—school (4) ... MO-7
Shiloh Sch (historical)—school (8) ... TN-4
Shiloh Sch (reduced usage)—school ... TX-5
Shiloh Special Drainage Ditch—canal ... IL-6
Shiloh Spring—spring (2) ... TN-4
Shiloh Springs—spring ... AL-4
Shiloh Springs Sch—school ... OH-6
**Shiloh Station**—pop pl ... IL-6
**Shiloh Subdivision**—pop pl ... UT-8
Shiloh Tanks—reservoir ... NM-5
Shiloh Temple—church ... IN-6
Shiloh Temple—hist pl ... ME-1
Shiloh Township—fmr MCD ... IA-7
**Shiloh Township**—pop pl ... KS-7
Shiloh (Township of)—fmr MCD ... AR-4
Shiloh (Township of)—fmr MCD (2) ... NC-3
**Shiloh (Township of)**—pop pl (2) ... IL-6
Shiloh United Methodist Church ... AL-4
Shiloh Valley Grange—locale ... IL-6
Shiloh Valley (Township of)—civ div ... IL-6
**Shiloh Village**—pop pl ... IN-6
Shiloh Well—well ... WY-8
Shiloh Wonder Ch—church ... NC-3
Shiloh Zion Ch—church ... AL-4
Shilolt Cem—cemetery ... GA-3
Shilo Tank—reservoir ... AZ-5
**Shilow**—pop pl ... FL-3
**Shilow**—pop pl ... SC-3
Shilo Well—well ... NM-5
Shilow Hollow ... TN-4
Shilshole Bay ... WA-9
Shilshole Bay—bay ... WA-9
Shilshole Bay Moorage—harbor ... WA-9
Shilsons Corner—locale ... VA-3
Shiltos Creek—stream ... CA-9
Shiltown—locale ... OH-6
Shilts Ditch—canal ... OH-6
Shima Bend—bend ... CA-9
**Shimada Acres Subdivision**—pop pl ... UT-8
Shima Tract—civil ... CA-9
Shimek Cem—cemetery ... TX-5
Shimek Forest Dam Three—dam ... IA-7
Shimek Forest Pond Two—reservoir ... IA-7
Shimek State For—forest ... IA-7
Shimel Run—stream ... PA-2
Shimels Run ... PA-2
Shimer—civil ... KS-7
**Shimer**—pop pl ... PA-2
Shimerfield Airp—airport ... PA-2
**Shimer Manor**—pop pl ... NJ-2
Shimer Run—stream ... OH-6
Shimers ... PA-2
Shimers Brook—stream ... NJ-2
Shimer Sch—school ... NJ-2
Shimers Mtn—summit ... PA-2
Shimers Rock Cut—gap ... PA-2
Shimersville ... PA-2
**Shimersville**—pop pl ... PA-2
Shimertown ... PA-2
Shimer Township ... KS-7
**Shimerville**—pop pl (2) ... PA-2
Shimhi—slope ... UT-8
Shimmell Sch—school ... PA-2
Shimmerhorn, The ... OR-9
Shimmerhorn Creek ... OR-9
Shimmiehorn ... OR-9
Shimmiehorn, The—summit ... OR-9
Shimmiehorn Creek—stream ... OR-9
Shimmiehorn Ridge ... OR-9
Shimmin Canyon—valley ... CA-9
Shimmin Ranch—locale ... NE-7
Shimmin Ridge—ridge ... CA-9
Shimmins Camp—locale ... CO-8
Shimmins Lake—lake ... NE-7
Shimmins Sch—school ... NE-7
**Shimmo**—pop pl ... MA-1
Shimmoah ... MA-1
Shimmo Creek—cove ... MA-1
Shimmoh ... MA-1
Shimmo Point ... MA-1
Shimmo Pond—lake ... MA-1
Shimmy Lake—lake ... CA-9
Shimmys Pond—lake ... SC-3
Shimoon Lake—lake ... OK-5
Shi-mo-pavi ... AZ-5
Shi-mo-pavi Spring ... AZ-5
Shimopovi ... AZ-5
Shimopovi Spring ... AZ-5
Shimo-Sudien ... MH-9
Shimo-Suiden ... MH-9
Shimps Run ... NJ-2
Shimps Town ... PA-2
**Shimpstown**—pop pl ... PA-2
Shimpstown Sch—school ... PA-2
Shimwell Howwow ... NY-2
Shinaberry Cem—cemetery (2) ... WV-2
Shinaku Creek—stream ... AK-9
Shinaku Inlet—bay ... AK-9
Shinall Cem—cemetery ... GA-3
Shinall Mtn—summit ... AR-4
Shinando Creek—stream ... WA-9
Shinanguag Lake—lake ... MI-6
Shinapaaru ... MH-9
Shinaparu ... MH-9
Shinapzru ... MH-9
Shinar Creek—stream ... CA-9
Shinar Sch (abandoned)—school ... MO-7
Shin-ar-ump Cliffs ... AZ-5
Shinarump Cliffs—cliff ... AZ-5
Shinarump Cliffs—cliff ... UT-8
Shinarump Point—cliff ... AZ-5
Shinawl Branch—stream ... VA-3
Shinbines Drain—canal ... MI-6
Shinbone ... PA-2
Shin Bone, The—bend ... AL-4
Shinbone, The—cliff ... TN-4
Shinbone, The—ridge ... TN-4
Shinbone, The—summit ... TN-4
Shinbone Branch—stream ... KY-4
Shinbone Cliff—cliff ... KY-4
Shinbone Creek—stream ... AL-4
Shinbone Creek—stream ... NC-3
Shinbone Creek—stream ... UT-8
Shinbone Gin (historical)—locale ... AL-4
Shinbone (historical)—locale ... AL-4
Shinbone Hollow ... TN-4
Shinbone Hollow Branch ... TN-4
Shin Bone Lake—lake ... ND-7
Shinbone Mountain ... AL-4
Shinbone Mtn—summit ... TN-4
Shinbone Ridge—ridge ... AL-4
Shinbone Ridge—ridge ... CA-9
Shinbone Ridge—ridge ... GA-3
Shinbone Ridge—ridge (2) ... NC-3
Shinbone Ridge—ridge (2) ... TN-4
Shinbone Rock—pillar ... TN-4
Shinbone Valley—valley (2) ... AL-4
Shinbone Valley—valley ... GA-3
Shin Brook—stream (2) ... ME-1
Shin Creek—stream ... MT-8
Shin Creek—stream ... NY-2
Shin Creek—stream ... OR-9
Shindagin Hollow—valley ... NY-2
Shindagin Hollow State For—forest ... NY-2
Shindata Creek—stream ... AK-9
Shindel ... PA-2
Shindeldecker Cem—cemetery ... OH-6
**Shindle**—pop pl ... PA-2
Shindledecker Ditch—canal ... CO-8
Shindle Gap—gap ... PA-2
Shindler—locale ... SD-7
Shindler Riffle—rapids ... OR-9
Shindler Sch—school ... SD-7
Shindy Draw—valley ... UT-8
Shindy Hollow Picnic Site—park ... UT-8
Shindy Spring—spring ... UT-8
Shine—locale ... NC-3
Shine—locale ... WA-9
Shine, Jere, Site—hist pl ... AL-4
Shineberger Creek—stream (2) ... MT-8
**Shinebone**—pop pl ... AL-4
Shine Branch—stream ... TX-5
Shine Cave—cave ... AL-4
Shine Creek—stream ... AK-9
Shine Creek—stream ... FL-3
Shine Creek—stream ... MT-8
Shine Island—island ... FL-3
Shine Lake—lake ... MN-6
Shine Lake—lake ... WI-6
Shine Lookout—locale ... WA-9
Shine Pond—lake ... FL-3
**Shiner**—pop pl ... TX-5
Shiner (CCD)—cens area ... TX-5
Shiner Cem—cemetery ... TX-5
Shiner Ch—church ... KY-4
Shiner Drain—canal ... MI-6
Shiner Hole—lake ... MA-1
Shiner Lake—lake ... MI-6
Shiner Lake—lake ... WA-9
Shiner Lake—lake ... WI-6
Shiner Pond—lake ... MA-1
Shiner Pond—lake ... NY-2
Shiner Pond—lake ... TX-5
Shiner Ranch—locale ... TX-5
Shiner Ranch (historical)—locale ... AZ-5
Shiner Rsvr—reservoir ... UT-8
Shinersburg Cem—cemetery ... OH-6
Shinersville ... PA-2
Shiner Tank—reservoir ... AZ-5
**Shinerville**—pop pl ... PA-2
Shiner Windmill—locale ... TX-5
Shines Bridge—bridge ... NC-3
Shines Crossroads ... NC-3
**Shines Crossroads**—pop pl ... NC-3
Shines Mill (historical)—locale ... AL-4
Shine (Township of)—fmr MCD ... NC-3
Shinewell—locale ... OK-5
Shiney Rock Cem—cemetery ... AL-4
Shiney Town—locale ... FL-3
Shin Falls—falls ... ME-1
Shingas Town ... PA-2
Shingiss—locale ... PA-2
**Shingle**—pop pl ... AL-4
Shingle Bay—bay ... ID-8
Shingle Bay—bay ... MI-6
Shingle Bay—bay ... NY-2
Shingle Bay—swamp ... GA-3
Shingle Bay Mtn—summit ... NY-2
Shingle Bayou—gut ... LA-4
Shinglebelt Creek ... MI-6
Shingle Block Hollow—valley ... VA-3
Shingleblock Ridge—ridge ... VA-3
Shingleblock Run—stream ... WV-2
Shinglebolt Creek—stream ... MI-6
Shinglebolt Hollow—valley ... PA-2
Shingle Branch—stream ... AL-4
Shingle Branch—stream ... FL-3
Shingle Branch—stream (2) ... KY-4
Shingle Branch—stream ... NC-3
Shingle Branch—stream ... PA-2
Shingle Branch—stream ... TX-5
Shingle Branch—stream ... WV-2
Shingle Brook—stream ... ME-1
Shingle Brook—stream ... MA-1
Shingle Brook—stream (2) ... NY-2
Shinglebury—locale ... PA-2
Shingle Butte—summit ... MT-8
Shingle Buttes—summit ... NV-8
Shingle Cabin Brook—stream ... PA-2
Shingle Cabin Hill—summit ... PA-2
Shingle Camp Hollow—valley ... MD-2
Shingle Camp Lake—lake ... WI-6
Shingle Canyon ... AZ-5
Shingle Canyon ... UT-8
Shingle Canyon—valley (2) ... AZ-5
Shingle Canyon—valley ... CA-9
Shingle Canyon—valley ... NM-5
Shingle Canyon Shaft (Active)—mine ... NM-5
Shingle Cove—valley ... NC-3
Shingle Creek ... CA-9
Shingle Creek ... UT-8
Shingle Creek—bay ... NC-3
**Shingle Creek**—pop pl ... FL-3
Shingle Creek—spring ... OR-9
Shingle Creek—stream (5) ... CA-9
Shingle Creek—stream ... CO-8
Shingle Creek—stream (2) ... FL-3
Shingle Creek—stream (4) ... ID-8
Shingle Creek—stream ... IN-6
Shingle Creek—stream ... MI-6
Shingle Creek—stream (2) ... MN-6
Shingle Creek—stream ... MT-8
Shingle Creek—stream ... NE-7
Shingle Creek—stream ... NV-8
Shingle Creek—stream (2) ... NY-2
Shingle Creek—stream ... NC-3
Shingle Creek—stream (2) ... OR-9
Shingle Creek—stream ... SC-3
Shingle Creek—stream ... SD-7
Shingle Creek—stream (4) ... UT-8
Shingle Creek—stream ... VA-3
Shingle Creek—stream ... WI-6
Shingle Creek—stream ... WY-8
Shingle Creek Campground—locale ... UT-8
Shingle Creek Ch—church ... FL-3
Shingle Creek Meadows—flat ... UT-8
Shingle Creek Narrows—channel ... UT-8
Shingle Creek Park—park ... MN-6
Shingle Creek Parkway—TRAIL ... MN-6
Shingle Creek Ranger Station—locale ... UT-8
Shingle Creek Recreation Site—park ... UT-8
Shingle Creek Sch—school ... MN-6
Shingle Creek United Methodist Ch—church ... FL-3
Shingle Flat—flat ... CA-9
Shingle Flat—flat ... ID-8
Shingleford Crossing—locale ... NC-3
Shingle Gap—gap ... KY-4
Shingle Gulch—valley ... OR-9
Shingle Gulch—valley ... UT-8
Shingle Gulf—valley ... NY-2
Shingle Gully—stream ... NY-2
Shingle Hill—summit ... CA-9
Shingle Hill—summit ... CT-1
Shingle Hill—summit (2) ... MA-1
Shingle Hill—summit ... VT-1
Shingle Hill—summit ... VA-3
Shingle Hills—summit ... TX-5
**Shingle Hollow**—pop pl ... NC-3
Shingle Hollow—valley ... MO-7
Shingle Hollow—valley ... NY-2
Shingle Hollow—valley (2) ... PA-2
Shingle Hollow—valley (2) ... TN-4
Shingle Hollow—valley ... UT-8
Shingle Hollow—valley (3) ... VA-3
Shingle House ... PA-2
**Shinglehouse**—pop pl ... PA-2
Shinglehouse Borough—civil ... PA-2
Shinglehouse Slough—stream ... OR-9
Shingle Island—island ... AK-9
Shingle Island—island ... ME-1
Shingle Island River—stream ... MA-1
Shingle Island Swamp—swamp ... MA-1
Shingle Kill—stream (2) ... NY-2
Shingle Knife Hollow—valley ... AR-4
Shingle Knife Shingle Mill (historical)—building ... TX-5
Shingle Knob—summit ... KY-4
Shingle Lake—lake (2) ... CO-8
Shingle Lake—lake ... MI-6
Shingle Lake—lake ... MS-4
Shingle Lake—lake ... TN-4
Shingle Landing—locale ... DE-2
Shingle Landing—locale ... FL-3
Shingle Landing—locale ... MD-2
Shingle Landing Creek—stream ... NC-3
Shingle Landing Prong—bay ... MD-2
Shingle Machine Branch—stream ... KY-4
Shingle Machine Branch—stream ... TX-5
Shingle Mill—locale (2) ... WA-9
Shingle Mill Bench—bench ... CA-9
Shinglemill Branch—stream ... LA-4
Shingle Mill Branch—stream ... PA-2
Shingle Mill Branch—stream ... SC-3
Shingle Mill Branch—stream ... TN-4
Shingle Mill Bridge—other ... MI-6
Shingle Mill Brook—stream ... CT-1
Shinglemill Brook—stream ... MA-1
Shinglemill Brook—stream ... NH-1
Shingle Mill Butte—summit ... OR-9
Shingle Mill Canyon—valley ... AZ-5
Shingle Mill Canyon—valley ... NM-5
Shingle Mill Canyon—valley (3) ... UT-8
Shingle Mill Corner—locale ... NH-1
Shingle Mill Creek—stream (3) ... CA-9
Shinglemill Creek—stream ... CO-8
Shingle Mill Creek—stream ... MT-8
Shingle Mill Creek—stream (2) ... OR-9
Shingle Mill Creek—stream (3) ... UT-8
Shingle Mill Creek—stream ... WY-8
Shingle Mill Draw—valley ... UT-8
Shingle Mill Flat—flat ... CA-9
Shingle Mill Flat—flat ... UT-8
Shingle Mill Flat—locale ... CA-9
Shingle Mill Fork ... UT-8
Shingle Mill Fork—stream ... UT-8
Shingle Mill Gap—gap ... GA-3
Shingle Mill Gulch—valley ... CA-9
Shinglemill Gulch—valley ... CA-9
Shingle Mill Gulch—valley ... CA-9
Shingle Mill Gulch—valley ... CO-8
Shinglemill Hollow—valley ... AL-4
Shingle Mill Hollow—valley ... MO-7
Shingle Mill Hollow—valley (2) ... PA-2
Shingle Mill Hollow—valley (2) ... TN-4
Shingle Mill Hollow—valley (3) ... UT-8
Shingle Mill Hollow Trail—trail ... PA-2
Shingle Mill Lake—lake ... MI-6
Shingle Mill Lake—lake ... MN-6
Shingle Mill Lake—lake ... UT-8
Shingle Mill Lake—lake ... WI-6
Shingle Mill Lake—swamp ... AR-4
Shingle Mill Mesa Thirty Five Trail—trail ... AZ-5
Shingle Mill Mtn—summit ... AZ-5
Shingle Mill Picnic Area—locale ... UT-8
Shingle Mill Pond—lake (2) ... CT-1
Shinglemill Pond—lake ... MA-1
Shingle Mill Pond—reservoir ... RI-1
Shingle Mill Run—stream (2) ... PA-2
Shinglemill Slough—stream ... TX-5
Shingle Mill Spring—spring ... CA-9
Shinglemill Swale—valley ... UT-8
Shingle Mtn—summit ... NY-2
Shingle Mtn—summit ... TN-4
Shingle Mtn—summit ... WA-9
Shingle Pass—gap ... NV-8
Shingle Path Trail—trail ... PA-2
Shingle Peak—summit ... CO-8
Shinglepen Branch—stream ... KY-4
Shinglepile Branch—stream ... AL-4
Shingle Pile Creek—stream ... NC-3
Shingle Place Hill—summit ... MA-1
Shingle P.O. (historical)—locale ... AL-4
Shingle Point—cape ... AK-9
Shingle Point—cape ... LA-4
Shingle Point—cape ... MI-6
Shingle Point—cape ... NC-3
Shingle Point—locale ... DE-2
Shingle Pond—lake ... NH-1
Shingle Pond—lake (2) ... NY-2
Shingle Pond Trail—trail ... NH-1
**Shingler**—pop pl ... GA-3
Shingle Ridge—ridge ... PA-2
Shingle Ridge—ridge ... TN-4
Shingle Roof Branch—stream ... KY-4
Shingle Roof Campground—locale ... GA-3
Shingle Rsvr—reservoir ... OR-9
Shingle Run—stream (4) ... PA-2
Shingle Run—stream ... VA-3
Shingle Shanty—locale ... CA-9
Shingle Shanty Brook—stream ... NY-2
Shingle Shanty Hollow—valley ... PA-2
Shingle Shanty Pond—lake ... NY-2
Shingleside—hist pl ... NY-2
Shingles Landing—locale ... TN-4
Shingle Spring—spring ... AZ-5
Shingle Spring—spring (2) ... CA-9
Shingle Spring—spring (2) ... NV-8
Shingle Spring—spring ... UT-8
**Shingle Springs**—pop pl ... CA-9
Shingle Springs—spring ... CA-9
**Shingle Springs Rancheria (Indian Reservation)**—pop pl ... CA-9
Shingle Swamp—swamp ... GA-3
Shingle Swamp—swamp ... MA-1
Shingle Swamp—swamp ... SC-3
Shingle Swamp Brook—stream ... MA-1
Shingle Swamp Island—island ... GA-3
**Shingleton**—pop pl ... MI-6
**Shingleton**—pop pl ... TN-4
Shingleton Dam—dam ... IN-6
Shingleton Gap ... PA-2
Shingleton Gap Stream ... PA-2
**Shingletown**—pop pl ... CA-9
**Shingletown**—pop pl ... PA-2
**Shingletown**—pop pl ... TN-4
Shingletown Branch—stream ... PA-2
Shingletown Branch—stream ... TN-4
Shingletown Gap—gap ... PA-2
Shingletown Gap Stream ... PA-2
Shingle Town (historical)—locale ... AL-4
Shingletown Ridge—ridge ... CA-9
Shingletown Sch—school ... MI-6
Shingle Trap Mtn—summit ... NC-3
Shingletree Bay—swamp ... NC-3

Shingletree Branch—*stream* NC-3
Shingletree Branch—*stream* TN-4
Shingletree Bridges—*bridge* NC-3
Shingle Tree Hollow—*valley* VA-3
Shingletree Pond—*lake* NY-2
Shingle Tree Run—*stream* WV-2
Shingletree Run—*stream* WV-2
Shingle Tree Run Trail—*trail* WV-2
Shingletree Swamp—*stream* NC-3
Shingle Valley—*valley* CA-9
Shingle Yard Hollow—*valley* AL-4
Shingle Yard Hollow—*valley* MS-4
Shingobee Bay—*bay* MN-6
Shin-Go-Beek Scout Camp—*locale* WI-6
Shingobee Lake—*lake* MN-6
Shingobee River—*stream* MN-6
Shingobee Ski Area—*locale* MN-6
**Shingobee (Township of)**—*pop pl* MN-6
Shin Hammock—*island* FL-3
Shin Hammock Marsh—*swamp* FL-3
Shin Hollow—*locale* NY-2
Shin Hollow—*valley* PA-2
Shin Hollow—*valley* TX-5
**Shinhopple**—*pop pl* NY-2
Shiniliaok Creek—*stream* AK-9
Shinilikrok Creek—*stream* AK-9
Shining Butte—*summit* ID-8
Shining Cloud Falls—*falls* MI-6
Shining Creek—*stream* NC-3
Shining Creek—*stream* VA-3
Shining Creek Gap—*gap* NC-3
Shining Dome—*summit* AK-9
Shining Hours Acad—*school* FL-3
*Shining Lake* ME-1
Shining Lake—*lake* ID-8
Shining Lake—*lake* OR-9
Shining Light Ch—*church* NC-3
Shining Rock—*locale* TN-4
Shining Rock—*summit* MA-1
Shining Rock—*summit* NC-3
Shining Rock Creek—*stream* NC-3
Shining Rock Gap—*gap* NC-3
Shining Rock Ledge—*ridge* NC-3
Shining Rock Wilderness Area—*park* NC-3
Shining Star Ch—*church* MD-2
*Shin Islands* CT-1
Shin Kee Tract—*civil* CA-9
Shinker Lake—*lake* MN-6
Shinkle, Amos, Summer Residence—*hist pl* KY-4
Shinkle Creek—*stream* KY-4
Shinkles Ridge—*ridge* OH-6
Shinkles Ridge Ch—*church* OH-6
Shinks Branch—*stream* KY-4
Shinlever Cem—*cemetery* TN-4
Shinliver Sch—*school* TN-4
Shinliver Spring—*spring* TN-4
Shinn—*locale* CA-9
Shinn—*locale* IL-6
Shinn, Joseph, House—*hist pl* NJ-2
Shinn, Levi, House—*hist pl* WV-2
Shinn, Mount—*summit* CA-9
Shinn Bone Lane Airp—*airport* IN-6
Shinn Cemetary—*cemetery* AR-4
Shinn Covered Bridge—*hist pl* OH-6
Shinn Creek—*gut* NC-3
Shinn Ditch—*canal* IN-6
Shinnebarger Bridge—*other* IL-6
Shinnecock Canal—*canal* NY-2
Shinnecock Hills—*locale* NY-2
Shinnecock Hills—*summit* NY-2
Shinnecock Hills Golf Course—*other* NY-2
Shinnecock Indian Cem—*cemetery* NY-2
Shinnecock Ind Res—*194 (1980)* NY-2
Shinnecock Inlet—*channel* NY-2
Shinnecock Light—*locale* NY-2
Shinnecock Sch—*school* NY-2
*Shinner Gulch* MT-8
Shinners English Spring—*spring* OR-9
*Shinners Neck* VA-3
Shinnery Bend—*bend* TX-5
Shinnery Cem—*cemetery* TX-5
Shinnery Creek—*stream* TX-5
Shinnery Draw—*valley* (3) TX-5
Shinnery Flats—*flat* TX-5
Shinnery Lake Community Hall—*building* TX-5
Shinnery Springs—*spring* TX-5
Shinnery Windmill—*locale* TX-5
Shinney Creek—*stream* FL-3
Shinney Tank—*reservoir* TX-5
Shinn Family Barn—*hist pl* OK-5
Shinn Mtn—*summit* (2) AR-4
Shinn Mtn—*summit* CA-9
Shinn Northeast Oil Field—*oilfield* KS-7
Shinn Park—*flat* CO-8
Shinn Peaks—*summit* CA-9
Shinn Point—*cape* NC-3
Shinn Ranch—*locale* CA-9
Shinn Ridge—*ridge* WV-2
Shinn Run—*stream* (2) WV-2
Shinns Branch—*stream* NJ-2
Shinns Branch—*stream* WI-6
Shinn Sch—*school* (2) IL-6
Shinns Creek—*stream* NC-3
Shinn Spring—*spring* AR-4
*Shinns Run* NJ-2
Shinns Run—*stream* WV-2
Shinns Run Ch—*church* WV-2
*Shinns Spring* MS-4
**Shinnston**—*pop pl* WV-2
*Shinnsville* NC-3
*Shinntown* KS-7
*Shinntown* NJ-2
Shinntown—*locale* NJ-2
**Shinnville**—*pop pl* NC-3
Shinnville Ch—*church* NC-3
Shinny Creek—*stream* NC-3
Shinny Lake—*lake* TX-5
*Shinny Run* KY-4
Shinoak Branch—*stream* TX-5
Shin Oak Creek—*stream* (2) TX-5
Shin Oak Mtn—*summit* (2) TX-5
Shin Oak Spring—*spring* TX-5
Shinob Kibe—*summit* UT-8
*Shinondo Creek* WA-9
Shinpaugh Ridge—*ridge* MO-7
*Shin Point* VT-1
Shin Point—*summit* AL-4
Shin Point—*summit* ID-8
Shin Point Trail—*trail* ID-8
**Shin Pond**—*pop pl* ME-1
**Shinrock**—*pop pl* OH-6
Shinscot Brook—*stream* RI-1
*Shins Island* NE-7
Shin Skin Ridge—*ridge* CA-9
*Shinsville* NC-3
**Shintown**—*pop pl* PA-2
Shintown Run—*stream* PA-2
Shintown Run Trail—*trail* PA-2
*Shinuk Kaha* MS-4
*Shinuma Altar* AZ-5
Shinumo Altar—*summit* AZ-5
Shinumo Amphitheater—*basin* AZ-5
Shinumo Camp—*locale* AZ-5
*Shinumo Creek* AZ-5
Shinumo Creek—*stream* AZ-5
Shinumo Rapids—*rapids* AZ-5
Shinumo Wash—*stream* AZ-5
Shiny Creek—*stream* NC-3
Shiny Lake—*lake* ME-1
**Shiny Rock**—*pop pl* VA-3
Shiny Rock—*rock* AL-4
*Shiny Run* KY-4
*Shioc River* WI-6
Shioc River—*stream* WI-6
**Shiocton**—*pop pl* WI-6
*Shiocton River* WI-6
Shiola Creek—*stream* MS-4
Ship Ashore Race Track—*other* CA-9
*Shi-paui-i-luvi* AZ-5
*Shi-pau-i-luvi* AZ-5
*Ship Bar Channel* MS-4
Ship Bay—*bay* WA-9
**Ship Bottom**—*pop pl* NJ-2
*Ship Bottom Beach* NJ-2
*Ship Branch* MS-4
Ship Branch—*stream* AR-4
Ship Branch—*stream* MS-4
Ship Cave—*cave* TN-4
Ship Cem—*cemetery* MS-4
*Ship Chandlery* MA-1
*Ship Channel* FL-3
*Ship Channel* NC-3
Ship Channel—*channel* AK-9
Ship Channel—*channel* NJ-2
Ship Channel—*channel* UT-8
Ship Channel (not verified)—*channel* MP-9
Ship Cove—*bay* AK-9
Ship Cove—*bay* ME-1
*Ship Creek* MT-8
*Ship Creek* TX-5
Ship Creek—*stream* (2) AK-9
Ship Creek—*stream* (2) CA-9
Ship Creek—*stream* MD-2
Ship Creek—*stream* NC-3
*Ship Dam Tank* AZ-5
Shipe, Col. Monroe M., House—*hist pl* TX-5
Shipe Cem—*cemetery* (2) TN-4
Shipe Creek—*stream* IL-6
Shipe Hollow—*valley* WV-2
Shipe Playground—*park* TX-5
Shipe Run—*stream* PA-2
Shipes Canal—*canal* AL-4
Shipes Hill—*summit* AL-4
Shipetaukin Creek—*stream* NJ-2
**Shipetown**—*pop pl* TN-4
Ship Harbor—*bay* ME-1
Ship Harbor—*bay* WA-9
Ship Hollow—*valley* (2) TX-5
*Shiphouse Point* NY-2
Ship Inn—*hist pl* PA-2
*Ship Island* ME-1
*Ship Island* VT-1
Ship Island—*island* (2) AK-9
Ship Island—*island* ID-8
Ship Island—*island* (2) ME-1
Ship Island—*island* (2) MS-4
Ship Island—*island* NH-1
Ship Island—*island* NY-2
Ship Island Bar—*bar* MS-4
Ship Island Bar Channel—*channel* MS-4
Ship Island Bend—*bend* MS-4
Ship Island Channel—*channel* MS-4
Ship Island Creek—*stream* ID-8
Ship Island Flats—*bar* MS-4
Ship Island Harbor—*bay* MS-4
Ship Island Hole—*island* ME-1
Ship Island Lake—*lake* ID-8
Ship Island Lighthouse—*locale* MS-4
Ship Island Pass—*channel* MS-4
Ship Island Passage—*channel* AK-9
Ship Islands—*area* AK-9
Ship Island Trail—*trail* ID-8
Shipjack Island—*island* WA-9
Ship John Shoal—*bar* NJ-2
Ship John Shoal Light—*locale* NJ-2
*Ship Keel Beach* MH-9
Ship Lake—*lake* MT-8
*Shipland* MS-4
Shipland Plantation Landing—*locale* MS-4
Shipler Mtn—*summit* CO-8
Shipler Park—*flat* CO-8
Shipley—*locale* OR-9
**Shipley**—*pop pl* IA-7
**Shipley**—*pop pl* KY-4
**Shipley**—*pop pl* MD-2
**Shipley**—*pop pl* TN-4
Shipley, C. P., House—*hist pl* IA-7
Shipley Bay—*bay* AK-9
Shipley Branch—*stream* GA-3
Shipley Branch—*stream* KY-4
Shipley Branch—*stream* PA-2
Shipley Bridge—*bridge* ND-7
Shipley Bridge—*bridge* OR-9
**Shipley Brothers Mine**—*pop pl* PA-2
Shipley Cem—*cemetery* (2) IL-6
Shipley Cem—*cemetery* KY-4
Shipley Cem—*cemetery* MS-4
Shipley Cem—*cemetery* MO-7
Shipley Cem—*cemetery* NE-7
Shipley Cem—*cemetery* (4) TN-4
Shipley Cem—*cemetery* TX-5
Shipley Ch—*church* TN-4
**Shipley Corner**—*pop pl* MD-2
*Shipley Creek* NV-8
Shipley Creek—*stream* OR-9
Shipley Draw—*valley* WY-8
Shipley Grove Ch—*church* TN-4
**Shipley Heights**—*pop pl* DE-2
Shipley Hill—*summit* MA-1
Shipley Hill—*summit* NH-1
Shipley Hollow—*valley* MO-7
Shipley Hollow—*valley* TN-4
Shipley Hollow—*valley* VA-3
Shipley Hot Spring—*spring* NV-8
Shipley Knob—*summit* KY-4
Shipley Lake—*lake* AK-9
Shipley Oil Field—*oilfield* TX-5
Shipley Point—*cape* MD-2
Shipley Pool—*lake* OR-9
Shipley Ranch—*locale* WY-8
**Shipley Ridge (subdivision)**—*pop pl* DE-2
Shipley Run Hist Dist—*hist pl* DE-2
Shipley Sch—*school* DE-2
Shipley Sch—*school* PA-2
Shipley Sch (historical)—*school* (2) TN-4
Shipley Sch Number 3—*school* ND-7
Shipley Sch Number 4—*school* ND-7
Shipley Slough—*canal* MO-7
Shipley Spring—*spring* MO-7
Shipley Spring—*spring* OR-9
Shipley Springs—*spring* OR-9
Shipley Tank—*reservoir* AZ-5
Shipley Well—*well* (2) AZ-5
**Shipley Woods**—*pop pl* DE-2
Shipman—*locale* MS-4
**Shipman**—*pop pl* IL-6
**Shipman**—*pop pl* VA-3
Shipman, W. H., House—*hist pl* HI-9
Shipman Bass Lake—*lake* MN-6
Shipman Branch—*stream* NC-3
Shipman Brook—*stream* NH-1
Shipman Canyon—*valley* NM-5
Shipman Cave—*cave* TN-4
Shipman Cem—*cemetery* MS-4
Shipman Cem—*cemetery* MO-7
Shipman Cem—*cemetery* OH-6
*Shipman Cove* AL-4
Shipman Creek—*stream* AR-4
Shipman Creek—*stream* CA-9
Shipman Creek—*stream* (2) TN-4
Shipman Creek Cave—*cave* TN-4
**Shipman Hill**—*pop pl* VT-1
Shipman Hole—*reservoir* MO-7
Shipman Hollow—*valley* NY-2
Shipman Hollow—*valley* (3) TN-4
Shipman Island—*island* MN-6
Shipman Lake—*lake* MN-6
Shipman Lookout Tower—*tower* MS-4
Shipman Mtn—*summit* CO-8
Shipman Park—*flat* CO-8
Shipman Park—*park* IL-6
Shipman Point—*cape* NY-2
Shipman Pond—*lake* NY-2
Shipman Post Office (historical)—*building* MS-4
Shipman Post Office (historical)—*building* TN-4
Shipman Ridge—*ridge* IN-6
Shipmans Chapel—*church* MS-4
*Shipmans Chapel Methodist Ch* MS-4
Shipmans Creek Sch (historical)—*school* TN-4
**Shipmans Eddy**—*pop pl* PA-2
Shipmans Pond—*reservoir* AL-4
**Shipman (Township of)**—*pop pl* IL-6
Shipman Trap Tank—*reservoir* TX-5
Shipman United Methodist Ch—*church* MS-4
Shipman Well—*well* NM-5
Ship Mountain Point—*ridge* UT-8
Ship Mountains—*range* CA-9
Ship Mountain Trail—*trail* CA-9
Ship Mtn—*summit* AK-9
Ship Mtn—*summit* CA-9
Shipoke Park—*park* PA-2
**Shipolovi**—*pop pl* AZ-5
Shipolovi Community Bldg—*building* AZ-5
Shipp—*locale* AR-4
Shipp—*locale* OH-6
**Shipp**—*pop pl* LA-4
Shipp, Laban, House—*hist pl* KY-4
Shipp, Lake—*lake* FL-3
*Shippan Point* CT-1
Shippan Point—*cape* CT-1
**Shippan Point**—*pop pl* CT-1
Shipp Bend—*bend* TN-4
Shipp Bend Ch—*church* TN-4
Shipp Bottom—*bend* TN-4
Shipp Cem—*cemetery* (2) AL-4
Shipp Cem—*cemetery* (2) TN-4
*Shipp Cemetery* MS-4
Shipp Chapel—*church* AL-4
Shipp Chapel—*church* GA-3
Shipp Creek—*stream* MS-4
Shipp Creek—*stream* OH-6
Shipp Ditch—*canal* IN-6
Ship Peak—*pillar* WA-9
Shippe Canyon—*valley* MT-8
Shippee—*locale* CA-9
**Shippee**—*pop pl* NE-7
Shippee Brook—*stream* MA-1
Shippee Brook—*stream* RI-1
Shippeeburg Cem—*cemetery* IN-6
Shippee Corner—*locale* RI-1
*Shippee Saw Mill Pond* RI-1
Shippee Sawmill Pond—*lake* RI-1
Shippees Draw—*valley* CO-8
**Shippen**—*pop pl* AR-4
Shippen, Judge Henry, House—*hist pl* PA-2
Shippen Creek—*stream* MD-2
Shippen House—*hist pl* PA-2
Shippen Manor—*hist pl* NJ-2
Shippenport—*locale* NJ-2
Shippen Run—*stream* (3) PA-2
**Shippensburg**—*pop pl* PA-2
Shippensburg Airp—*airport* PA-2
Shippensburg Area JHS—*school* PA-2
Shippensburg Area Senior HS—*school* PA-2
Shippensburg Borough—*civil* (2) PA-2
Shippensburg Hist Dist—*hist pl* PA-2
Shippensburg Rsvr—*reservoir* PA-2
Shippensburg State Coll—*school* PA-2
**Shippensburg (Township of)**—*pop pl* PA-2
Shippen Sch—*school* PA-2
Shippens Run—*stream* PA-2
Shippen Station—*locale* PA-2
*Shippensville* PA-2
**Shippen (Township of)**—*pop pl* (2) PA-2
**Shippenville**—*pop pl* PA-2
Shippenville Borough—*civil* PA-2
Shippenville Station—*locale* PA-2
Shipper Pen Windmill—*locale* NM-5
Shippey Lake—*lake* FL-3
Shipp Hollow—*valley* AR-4
Shipp Hollow—*valley* (2) TN-4
Shipp House—*hist pl* KY-4
Shipping Creek—*stream* MD-2
Shipping Creek—*stream* VA-3
Shipping Pasture Spring—*spring* NM-5
Shipping Pasture Tank—*reservoir* (4) AZ-5
Shipping Pasture Well—*well* TX-5
Shipping Pasture Windmill—*locale* (5) TX-5
Shipping Pens Well—*well* TX-5
Shipping Pen Well—*well* NM-5
Shipping Point—*cape* (2) MD-2
Shipping Point—*cape* VA-3
**Shippingport**—*pop pl* PA-2
Shippingport Borough—*civil* PA-2
Shippingport Island—*island* KY-4
Shippingport Nuclear Powerplant (historical)—*building* PA-2
Shippingport Post Office (historical)—*building* TN-4
Shipping Tank—*reservoir* (2) AZ-5
Shipping Tank—*reservoir* NM-5
Shipping Trap Tank—*reservoir* TX-5
Shipping Trap Windmill—*locale* NM-5
Shipping Trap Windmill—*locale* (2) TX-5
Shipp Lake—*lake* MI-6
Shipp Lake—*reservoir* TX-5
Shipp Lake Dam—*dam* MS-4
Shippley Drain—*canal* MI-6
Ship Point—*cape* (2) MD-2
Ship Point—*cape* (2) NC-3
Ship Point—*cape* VA-3
Ship Point—*island* VT-1
*Ship Pond* ME-1
Ship Pond—*lake* MA-1
*Ship Pond Cove* RI-1
Ship Pond Stream—*stream* ME-1
Ship Post Office (historical)—*building* MS-4
Shipp Park Ch—*church* AL-4
Shipp Ranch—*locale* AZ-5
Shipp Ranch—*locale* TX-5
Shipps Bay—*bay* VA-3
**Shipps Bend**—*pop pl* TN-4
Shipps Bend Sch (historical)—*school* TN-4
Shipp Sch—*school* MO-7
Shipps Creek—*stream* AL-4
Shipps Ferry—*locale* AR-4
*Shipps Lake* TX-5
Shipps Lake—*reservoir* TX-5
Shipps Landing (historical)—*locale* MS-4
Shipps Landing (historical)—*locale* TN-4
Shipps Landing Post Office (historical)—*building* TN-4
Shipps Mtn—*summit* AR-4
Shipps Pond—*lake* AL-4
**Shipps Spur**—*pop pl* GA-3
Shipps Yards—*locale* TN-4
Shippy Branch—*stream* NC-3
Shippy Cem—*cemetery* MI-6
Shippy Creek—*stream* MS-4
Shippy Hill—*summit* CT-1
Shippy Salem Cem—*cemetery* IL-6
Shippy Sch—*school* MI-6
**Ship Road**—*pop pl* PA-2
Ship Road Station—*locale* PA-2
Ship Rock—*bar* AK-9
Ship Rock—*bar* CA-9
Ship Rock—*island* AK-9
Ship Rock—*island* AZ-5
Ship Rock—*island* FL-3
Shiprock—*locale* WY-8
Shiprock—*other* NM-5
Ship Rock—*pillar* (2) CO-8
Ship Rock—*pillar* MT-8
Ship Rock—*pillar* UT-8
Ship Rock—*pillar* WY-8
**Shiprock**—*pop pl* NM-5
Ship Rock—*rock* MA-1
Shiprock—*summit* AZ-5
Ship Rock—*summit* NM-5
Ship Rock—*summit* WI-6
Ship Rock Campground—*locale* NM-5
Shiprock Gallup Oil Field—*other* NM-5
Shiprock-Sanostee (CCD)—*cens area* NM-5
Shiprock Substation—*other* NM-5
Shiprock Wash—*stream* NM-5
Ships Bay—*bay* NC-3
Ships Branch—*stream* KY-4
*Ships Canal* AL-4
*Ships Church* AL-4
Ships Corner—*locale* VA-3
**Ships Corner**—*pop pl* VA-3
Shipsee Cem—*cemetery* KS-7
Shipshead Creek—*bay* MD-2
**Shipshewana**—*pop pl* IN-6
Shipshewana Lake—*lake* IN-6
Shipshewana-Scott Elem Sch—*school* IN-6
Ship Shoal Inlet—*gut* VA-3
Ship Shoal Island—*island* NC-3
Ship Shoal Island—*island* VA-3
Ships Prow—*cliff* CO-8
Shipstead Coulee—*valley* MT-8
Shipstern Island—*island* ME-1
**Shipswatch (subdivision)**—*pop pl* NC-3
Ship Tank—*reservoir* TX-5
Shipton—*locale* KS-7
Shipton Coulee—*valley* ND-7
Ship Windmill—*locale* NM-5
Shipwreck Point—*cape* AK-9
Shipwreck Point—*cape* WA-9
*Shipyard* NC-3
Shipyard Acres—*locale* CA-9
Shipyard Bar—*area* NC-3
Shipyard Bay—*bay* AK-9
Shipyard Canal—*canal* FL-3
Shipyard Cove—*bay* AK-9
Shipyard Cove—*bay* ME-1
Shipyard Creek—*gut* VA-3
Shipyard Creek—*stream* FL-3
Shipyard Creek—*stream* GA-3
Shipyard Creek—*stream* (2) MD-2
Shipyard Creek—*stream* SC-3
Shipyard Island—*island* FL-3
Shipyard Landing—*locale* MD-2
Shipyard Landing—*locale* NC-3
Shipyard Landing—*locale* VA-3
Shipyard Plantations—*uninc pl* SC-3
Shipyard Point—*cape* (2) ME-1
Shipyard Point—*cape* MA-1
Shipyard Point—*cape* MS-4
*Shipyard River* SC-3
Shipyard Tank—*reservoir* AZ-5
*Shira Gake* MH-9
*Shirard Gray Cemetery* MS-4
*Shiras* AL-4
Shiras Creek—*stream* MI-6
Shiras Number 1 Drift Mine (underground)—*mine* AL-4
Shiras Park—*park* MI-6
Shiras Pond—*lake* NY-2
Shiras Pool—*lake* MI-6
Shiras Run—*stream* WV-2
Shira Temple—*summit* AZ-5
Shircliff Hollow—*valley* IN-6
**Shire**—*pop pl* TX-5
Shired Creek—*stream* FL-3
**Shirod Island** *pop pl* FL-3
*Shire Gake* MH-9
Shire Gulch—*valley* CO-8
Shireman Hill—*summit* IN-6
*Shiremans* PA-2
**Shiremanstown**—*pop pl* PA-2
Shiremanstown Borough—*civil* PA-2
Shiremanstown Elem Sch—*school* PA-2
Shire Oaks—*locale* PA-2
Shirer Branch—*stream* FL-3
Shires Cem—*cemetery* TN-4
Shires Run—*stream* PA-2
Shirey Bay—*bay* AR-4
Shirey Bay-Rainey Brake State Game Management Area—*park* AR-4
Shirey Cem—*cemetery* PA-2
Shirey Mtn—*summit* AR-4
Shirey Run—*stream* PA-2
Shireys Mill Ch—*church* AL-4
Shireys Mill Creek—*stream* AL-4
Shirfs Run Dam—*dam* PA-2
**Shirk**—*pop pl* OK-5
Shirk, W. W., Bldg—*hist pl* IN-6
Shirk Bayou—*bay* FL-3
Shirk Cem—*cemetery* (2) IN-6
Shirk Creek—*stream* WA-9
Shirk Draw—*valley* WY-8
Shirkey Branch—*stream* WV-2
Shirkey Mill Branch—*stream* VA-3
Shirk Gap—*gap* WV-2
Shirkie Mine Pond—*lake* IN-6
**Shirkieville**—*pop pl* IN-6
Shirk Lake—*reservoir* OR-9
**Shirkleville**—*pop pl* IN-6
Shirk Oil Field—*oilfield* TX-5
*Shirk Point* FL-3
Shirk Point—*cape* FL-3
Shirk Rim—*cliff* OR-9
Shirks Ch—*church* (2) PA-2
Shirks Corner—*locale* PA-2
**Shirkshire**—*pop pl* MA-1
Shirks Hollow—*valley* IN-6
Shirks Lookout—*summit* OR-9
Shirks Run—*stream* (2) PA-2
Shirksville—*locale* PA-2
Shirksville Ch—*church* PA-2
Shirk Votaw Ditch—*canal* IN-6
**Shirland**—*pop pl* IL-6
Shirland Canal—*canal* CA-9
Shirland Cem—*cemetery* IL-6
Shirland (Township 993f)—*civ div* IL-6
*Shirley* KS-7
Shirley—*hist pl* VA-3
Shirley—*locale* CA-9
Shirley—*locale* (2) CO-8
Shirley—*locale* IL-6
Shirley—*locale* IA-7
Shirley—*locale* MN-6
Shirley—*locale* MT-8
Shirley—*locale* NJ-2
Shirley—*locale* TN-4
Shirley—*locale* (2) TX-5
Shirley—*locale* VA-3
Shirley—*locale* WY-8
**Shirley**—*pop pl* AL-4
**Shirley**—*pop pl* AR-4
**Shirley**—*pop pl* CA-9
**Shirley**—*pop pl* IL-6
**Shirley**—*pop pl* IN-6
**Shirley**—*pop pl* KY-4
**Shirley**—*pop pl* MA-1
**Shirley**—*pop pl* MO-7
**Shirley**—*pop pl* (2) NY-2
**Shirley**—*pop pl* PA-2
**Shirley**—*pop pl* SC-3
**Shirley**—*pop pl* WV-2
**Shirley**—*pop pl* WI-6
Shirley, James, House—*hist pl* AL-4
Shirley, Lake—*reservoir* AL-4
Shirley, Lake—*reservoir* MA-1
Shirley, Point—*cape* MA-1
Shirley, Point—*point* MA-1
**Shirley Acres**—*pop pl* VA-3
Shirley Ave Sch—*school* CA-9
Shirley Barbara Oil Field—*oilfield* TX-5
Shirley Basin—*basin* (2) WY-8
**Shirley Basin**—*pop pl* WY-8
Shirley Basin Rsvr—*reservoir* WY-8
Shirley Bluff—*cliff* GA-3
Shirley Branch—*stream* AL-4
Shirley Branch—*stream* (2) KY-4
Shirley Branch—*stream* SC-3
Shirley Branch—*stream* TX-5
Shirley Bridge—*bridge* AL-4
Shirley Brook—*stream* ME-1
Shirley Cem—*cemetery* (2) AL-4
Shirley Cem—*cemetery* GA-3
Shirley Cem—*cemetery* IN-6
Shirley Cem—*cemetery* KS-7
Shirley Cem—*cemetery* MS-4
Shirley Cem—*cemetery* (3) MO-7
Shirley Cem—*cemetery* OK-5
Shirley Cem—*cemetery* TN-4
Shirley (census name for Shirley Compact)—*CDP* MA-1
**Shirley Center**—*pop pl* MA-1
Shirley Center Hist Dist—*hist pl* MA-1
Shirley Center Sch—*school* MA-1
*Shirley Centre* MA-1
Shirley Ch—*church* MS-4
Shirley Ch—*church* TX-5
*Shirley City* (2) IN-6
Shirley Compact (census name Shirley)—*other* MA-1
*Shirley County* KS-7
Shirley Creek—*stream* AR-4
Shirley Creek—*stream* (3) CA-9
Shirley Creek—*stream* (2) ID-8
Shirley Creek—*stream* IL-6
Shirley Creek—*stream* IN-6
Shirley Creek—*stream* KS-7
Shirley Creek—*stream* OR-9
Shirley Creek—*stream* SC-3
Shirley Creek—*stream* TX-5
Shirley Crossing—*locale* TN-4
Shirley Dam—*dam* AL-4
Shirley Drain—*stream* IN-6
**Shirley Duke**—*pop pl* VA-3
Shirley-Eustis House—*hist pl* MA-1
Shirley Ferry (historical)—*locale* TN-4
Shirley Field—*airport* PA-2
Shirley Field—*hist pl* LA-4
*Shirley Fort* MA-1
Shirley Gap Lookout—*locale* OR-9
**Shirley Gate Park**—*pop pl* VA-3
Shirley Grove—*locale* GA-3
Shirley G Spring—*spring* ID-8
Shirley Gulch—*valley* CA-9
Shirley Gut—*locale* MA-1
*Shirley Hill* NH-1
**Shirley Hill**—*pop pl* NH-1
Shirley Hill—*summit* NH-1
Shirley Hill Ch—*church* AL-4
Shirley Hills—*uninc pl* GA-3
Shirley Hills Sch—*school* GA-3
Shirley Hole—*bay* VA-3
Shirley Hollow—*valley* AL-4
Shirley Hollow—*valley* TN-4
Shirley Home For The Aged—*building* PA-2
Shirley-Ismay—*cens area* MT-8
Shirley Knob—*summit* PA-2
Shirley Knobs—*summit* PA-2
Shirley Lake—*lake* AK-9
Shirley Lake—*lake* (2) CA-9
Shirley Lake—*lake* FL-3
Shirley Lake—*lake* ND-7
Shirley Lake—*lake* OR-9
Shirley Lake—*lake* WI-6
Shirley Lake—*lake* WY-8
Shirley Lake—*reservoir* AL-4
Shirley Lower Bend—*bend* AR-4
Shirley Main Canal—*canal* MT-8
**Shirley Meadows**—*pop pl* CA-9
Shirley Miller Dam—*dam* SD-7
Shirley Millpond—*reservoir* VA-3
**Shirley Mills**—*pop pl* ME-1
Shirley Mine (underground)—*mine* AL-4
*Shirley Mountains* WY-8
Shirley Mtn—*summit* CA-9
Shirley Mtn—*summit* MT-8
Shirley Mtns—*range* WY-8
**Shirley Park**—*pop pl* GA-3
Shirley Peak—*summit* CA-9
Shirley Picnic Area—*locale* MO-7
**Shirley Place**—*pop pl* FL-3
Shirley Place Cem—*cemetery* MS-4
Shirley P. O. (historical)—*locale* AL-4
Shirley Pond—*lake* ME-1
Shirley Pond—*lake* TN-4
Shirley Pond—*reservoir* AL-4
Shirley Post Office (historical)—*building* TN-4
Shirley Queen Mine—*mine* CA-9
Shirley Ranch—*locale* NM-5
*Shirley Ranges* WY-8
*Shirley Reservoir* MA-1
Shirley Ridge—*ridge* MO-7
Shirley Run—*stream* (2) PA-2
Shirleys Bar—*bar* DE-2
**Shirleysburg**—*pop pl* PA-2
Shirleysburg Borough—*civil* PA-2
Shirley Sch—*school* MO-7
Shirley Sch—*school* TX-5
Shirley Sch (abandoned)—*school* MO-7
Shirleys Crossroads—*locale* AL-4
Shirley Shaker Village—*hist pl* MA-1
Shirley Slough—*gut* IL-6
Shirley Spring—*spring* AL-4
Shirley Spring—*spring* ID-8
Shirley Spring—*spring* UT-8
**Shirley Springs**—*pop pl* VA-3
*Shirleys Run* PA-2
Shirley Station (historical)—*locale* MA-1
Shirley Tank—*reservoir* NM-5
Shirleyton—*locale* TN-4
Shirleyton Post Office (historical)—*building* TN-4
**Shirley (Town of)**—*pop pl* ME-1
**Shirley (Town of)**—*pop pl* MA-1
**Shirley Township**—*pop pl* KS-7
Shirley (Township of)—*fmr MCD* MO-7
**Shirley (Township of)**—*pop pl* PA-2
Shirley United Baptist Ch—*church* TN-4
*Shirley Village* MA-1
Shirley Well—*well* AZ-5
**Shirlington**—*pop pl* VA-3
*Shirmanstown* PA-2
**Shiro**—*pop pl* TX-5
Shiro Cem—*cemetery* TX-5
Shirpser Sch—*school* CA-9
Shir-Roy Campground—*locale* NH-1
Shirtail Creek—*stream* CO-8
*Shirt Creek* OR-9
Shirtee Creek—*stream* AL-4
Shirt Lake—*lake* MN-6
Shirtpond Cove—*bay* MD-2
*Shirts Canon* UT-8
Shirts Canyon—*valley* UT-8
Shirts Creek—*stream* (2) ID-8
Shirts Creek—*stream* OR-9
Shirts Creek—*stream* UT-8
*Shirts Lake* UT-8
Shirts Lake—*lake* ID-8
*Shirt Tail Bend* MS-4
Shirttail Bend—*bend* WI-6
Shirttail Branch—*stream* FL-3
Shirttail Branch—*stream* TX-5
Shirttail Butte—*summit* WY-8
Shirttail Canyon—*valley* (3) CA-9
Shirttail Canyon—*valley* NV-8
Shirttail Canyon—*valley* SD-7
Shirttail Canyon—*valley* TX-5
Shirttail Creek—*stream* (2) OR-9

Shirttail Fork—stream WV-2
Shirttail Gulch—valley (2) CA-9
Shirttail Gulch—valley (2) ID-8
Shirttail Gulch—valley SD-7
Shirttail Hills—summit AZ-5
Shirt Tail Lake—lake FL-3
Shirttail Mesa—summit AZ-5
Shirttail Park—flat MT-8
Shirttail Peak—summit (2) CA-9
Shirttail Peak—summit CO-8
Shirttail Point—cape AK-9
Shirttail Point—cape MA-1
Shirttail Spring—spring AZ-5
Shirttail Well—well NV-8
Shirtz Canyon UT-8
Shirtz Creek UT-8
Shirukak Lake—lake AK-9
Shisebogama Lake WI-6
Shishakshinovik Pass—gap AK-9
Shishaldin Volcano—summit AK-9
Shishebagama Lake WI-6
Shishebogama Lake—lake WI-6
Shishebogomo Lake WI-6
Shi-Shi Beach—beach WA-9
Shishkof Pond—lake AK-9
**Shishmaref**—pop pl AK-9
Shishmaref Inlet—bay AK-9
Shishmarev Strait—channel MP-9
Shisler Cem—cemetery NE-7
Shisler Ditch—canal OH-6
Shisler Lake—lake MI-6
Shisloiso Hills—other AK-9
Shisnona Lake—lake AK-9
Shisnona River—stream AK-9
Shissler Creek—stream ID-8
Shissler Peak—cliff ID-8
Shitamaring Creek—stream UT-8
Shite Creek—stream ID-8
Shitepoke Creek—stream OR-9
Shitepoke Trail—trail OR-9
Shith Cem—cemetery MO-7
Shitike Butte—summit OR-9
Shitike Creek—stream OR-9
Shitten Creek—stream OR-9
Shittim Gulch—valley WA-9
Shittum Wash—valley UT-8
Shiva Mountain OR-9
Shivar Springs Bottling Company Cisterns—hist pl SC-3
Shiva Temple—summit AZ-5
**Shive**—pop pl TX-5
Shivelear Hollow—valley AR-4
Shiveley CA-9
Shiveley Cem—cemetery OH-6
Shiveleys Lake—reservoir OH-6
Shively—locale OH-6
Shively—locale WV-2
**Shively**—pop pl CA-9
**Shively**—pop pl KY-4
Shively Branch—stream VA-3
Shively Cem—cemetery KY-4
Shively Ch—church KY-4
**Shively Corners**—pop pl OH-6
Shively Creek—stream CA-9
Shively Creek—stream MT-8
Shively Creek—stream OR-9
Shively Flat—flat CA-9
Shively Gulch MT-8
Shively Park—park IN-6
Shively Park—park KY-4
Shively Park—park OR-9
Shively Sch—school IL-6
Shively Slough—stream WI-6
Shiver—locale GA-3
Shiver Branch—stream GA-3
Shiver Creek—stream MN-6
Shiver Creek—stream UT-8
Shiverette Island—island MI-6
Shiver Grove Ch—church GA-3
Shiver Hole—cave TN-4
Shiverices Pond MA-1
Shiverick Shipyard—locale MA-1
Shivericks Pond—lake MA-1
Shivering Mtn—summit AK-9
Shivering Sands Creek—stream WI-6
Shiver Millpond—lake SC-3
**Shivers**—pop pl MS-4
Shivers, The—bar ME-1
Shivers Bay—bay FL-3
Shivers Branch—stream AL-4
Shivers Cem—cemetery MS-4
Shiver Sch—school GA-3
Shivers Corners—locale NY-2
Shivers HS—school MS-4
Shivers JHS MS-4
Shivers Lookout Tower—locale MS-4
Shivers Mill—locale GA-3
Shivers Mill Creek—stream GA-3
Shivers Mill (historical)—locale AL-4
Shivers Post Office (historical)—building MS-4
Shivers-Simpson House—hist pl GA-3
Shivers Trap Spring—spring AZ-5
Shives—locale AR-4
Shivigny Creek—stream OR-9
Shivigny Mtn—summit OR-9
Shivugak Bluff—cliff AK-9
Shivwits—locale UT-8
Shivwits Cem—cemetery UT-8
Shivwits Plateau—plain AZ-5
Shiwits Plateau AZ-5
Shiwitz Plateau AZ-5
Shiyainowaru FM-9
Shiyarapuku FM-9
Shlenker House—hist pl MS-4
Shloh Well—well AZ-5
Shlokovik Point—cape AK-9
S H Mesa—summit AZ-5
Shmithfield PA-2
S H Mountains AZ-5
**Shoaf**—pop pl PA-2
Shoaf, Henry, Farm—hist pl NC-3
Shoaf, John H., House—hist pl TX-5
Shoaf Creek—stream MS-4
Shoaff Dawson Ditch—canal IN-6
Shoaff Lake—lake IN-6
Shoaff Park—park IN-6
Shoaf Lake—reservoir NC-3
Shoaf Ovens—other PA-2
Shoafs Landing TN-4
Shoal—locale KY-4
**Shoal**—pop pl MO-7
**Shoal**—pop pl NC-3
Shoal Alke MN-6
Shoal Bay WA-9
Shoal Bay—bay AK-9
Shoal Bay—bay WA-9
Shoal Bayou FL-3
Shoal Bight—bay WA-9
Shoal Bluff Cem—cemetery TN-4
Shoal Bluff Ch—church TN-4
Shoal Branch—stream (4) GA-3
Shoal Branch—stream NJ-2
Shoal Branch—stream (4) NC-3
Shoal Branch—stream TN-4
Shoal Branch—stream WV-2
Shoal Cast—bay AK-9
Shoal Cemetery TN-4
**Shoal Cove**—pop pl AK-9
Shoal Creek AL-4
Shoal Creek AR-4
Shoal Creek GA-3
Shoal Creek IN-6
Shoal Creek NC-3
Shoal Creek UT-8
Shoal Creek—gut GA-3
Shoal Creek—locale AR-4
Shoal Creek—locale GA-3
**Shoal Creek**—pop pl NC-3
Shoal Creek—stream (16) AL-4
Shoal Creek—stream AK-9
Shoal Creek—stream AR-4
Shoal Creek—stream (22) GA-3
Shoal Creek—stream (4) IL-6
Shoal Creek*—stream IA-7
Shoal Creek—stream KS-7
Shoal Creek—stream KY-4
Shoal Creek—stream MD-2
Shoal Creek—stream (6) MO-7
Shoal Creek—stream (11) NC-3
Shoal Creek—stream OH-6
Shoal Creek—stream (3) SC-3
Shoal Creek—stream (9) TN-4
Shoal Creek—stream (4) TX-5
Shoal Creek—stream UT-8
Shoal Creek—stream VA-3
Shoal Creek—stream WY-8
Shoal Creek Aqueduct (historical)—canal AL-4
Shoal Creek Baptist Church AL-4
Shoal Creek Cem—cemetery (2) AL-4
Shoal Creek Ch—church (4) AL-4
Shoal Creek Ch—church (9) GA-3
Shoal Creek Ch—church (5) NC-3
Shoal Creek Ch—church SC-3
Shoal Creek Ch (historical)—church AL-4
Shoal Creek Church—hist pl AL-4
Shoal Creek Country Club—locale AL-4
Shoal Creek Drainage Ditch—canal MO-7
**Shoal Creek Drive**—pop pl MO-7
**Shoal Creek Estates**—pop pl MO-7
Shoal Creek Falls—falls NC-3
Shoal Creek Gap—gap NC-3
Shoal Creek Golf Course—locale AL-4
Shoal Creek (historical)—locale AL-4
Shoal Creek Island—island AR-4
Shoal Creek Mountains—ridge AL-4
Shoal Creek Mtn—summit AL-4
Shoal Creek Narrows—channel AR-4
Shoal Creek Picnic Area—park AL-4
Shoal Creek Sch—school GA-3
Shoal Creek Sch—school (2) IL-6
Shoal Creek Spring—spring AL-4
Shoal Creek Township—civil MO-7
Shoal Creek (Township of)—fmr MCD AR-4
Shoal Creek (Township of)—fmr MCD NC-3
**Shoal Creek (Township of)**—pop pl IL-6
Shoal Creek Valley—valley AL-4
Shoal Creek Valley Church AL-4
Shoal Dam—dam WV-2
Shoaler Mountain ME-1
Shoal Falls—falls WY-8
Shoalford P. O. (historical)—locale AL-4
Shoal Harbor NJ-2
Shoal Hill—summit MO-7
Shoal Hill—summit VA-3
Shoal Hill Ch—church NC-3
Shoaling Point—cape VA-3
Shoaling Rock RI-1
Shoal Inlet NC-3
Shoal Lake—lake (2) MN-6
Shoal Lake—lake WA-9
Shoal Lake—lake WI-6
Shoal Lake—lake WY-8
Shoally Creek SC-3
Shoal Mtn—summit (2) NC-3
Shoal Point CA-9
Shoal Point—cape (3) AK-9
Shoal Point—cape CT-1
Shoal Point—cape (2) FL-3
Shoal Point—cape MI-6
Shoal Point Bayou FL-3
Shoal Pond—lake MA-1
Shoal Pond—lake NH-1
Shoal Pond Brook—stream NH-1
Shoal Pond Trail—trail NH-1
Shoal Ridge—ridge GA-3
Shoal Ridge—ridge (2) NC-3
Shoal River AL-4
Shoal River—stream FL-3
Shoal Rock Creek—stream NC-3
Shoal Run—stream IN-6
Shoals—locale GA-3
**Shoals**—pop pl GA-3
**Shoals**—pop pl IN-6
**Shoals**—pop pl NC-3
**Shoals**—pop pl OK-5
**Shoals**—pop pl WV-2
Shoals, Isles Of—island ME-1
Shoals,Isles of—island NH-1
Shoals, The AL-4
Shoals, The—bar GA-3
**Shoals, The**—pop pl DE-2
**Shoals Acres**—pop pl AL-4
Shoals Bible Baptist Ch—church AL-4
Shoals Branch—stream DE-2
Shoals Branch—stream KY-4
Shoals Branch Sch—school TN-4
Shoals Ch—church OK-5
Shoals Chapel Sch—school OK-5
Shoals Community Elem Sch—school IN-6
Shoals Community HS—school IN-6
Shoals Community MS—school IN-6
Shoals Creek GA-3
Shoals Creek SC-3
Shoals Creek—stream CA-9
Shoals Creek—stream GA-3
Shoals Creek Bridge—bridge AL-4
Shoals Elementary School NC-3
Shoals Hosp—hospital AL-4
**Shoals Junction**—pop pl SC-3
**Shoals Overlook**—pop pl IN-6
Shoals Plaza Shop Ctr—locale AL-4
Shoals Point—cape AK-9
Shoals Pond SC-3
Shoal Spring TN-4
Shoal Spring—spring OR-9
Shoals Sch—school NC-3
Shoals Sch—school OK-5
Shoals (Township of)—fmr MCD NC-3
Shoal Township—civil MO-7
Shoalwater, Cape—cape WA-9
Shoalwater Bay WA-9
Shoalwater Bay—bay LA-4
Shoalwater Bay—bay OR-9
Shoalwater Bay—bay TX-5
Shoalwater Bay—bay WA-9
Shoalwater Bay Marsh—swamp OR-9
**Shoalwater Ind Res**—pop pl WA-9
Shoalwater Pass—channel AK-9
Shoaly Branch—stream TN-4
Shoaly Branch Ch—church NC-3
Shoap Spring—spring UT-8
Shoat, Hazel, House—hist pl MO-7
Shoat Branch—stream AR-4
Shoat Creek—stream OK-5
Shoat Creek—stream TX-5
Shoates—locale NC-3
Shoat Lake Sch—school OK-5
Shoat Lick Hollow—valley TN-4
Shoat Mill Branch—stream (2) AL-4
Shoat Mtn—summit OK-5
Shoats Creek—stream LA-4
Shoats Creek—stream TX-5
Shoats Mill Branch AL-4
Shoat Springs Cem—cemetery OK-5
Shoat Springs Sch—school OK-5
Shoat Tank—reservoir AZ-5
Shoat Tank Wash—stream AZ-5
Shoaty Creek—stream AK-9
Shoaty Mtn—summit AK-9
Shoban Lake—lake ID-8
Shobar Canyon—valley NE-7
Shobe, Moses, House—hist pl KY-4
Shobe Canyon—valley OR-9
Shobe Cem—cemetery MO-7
Shobe Creek—stream OR-9
Shobei Sho FM-9
Shobelful Shoal—bar MA-1
Shobe-Morrison House—hist pl MO-7
**Shober**—pop pl PA-2
Shoberg Lake—lake WI-6
Shober Number One Drain—stream MI-6
Shobers Run—stream PA-2
Shobert, William Henry, House—hist pl WA-9
Shobes Branch—stream MO-7
Shobes Grove—locale IA-7
Shobe Spring—spring WA-9
**Shobon**—pop pl WY-8
**Shobonier**—pop pl IL-6
Shobonier Sch—school IL-6
Shoboti Creek MS-4
Shocco MS-4
Shocco Ch—church NC-3
Shocco Creek—stream NC-3
**Shoccoe**—pop pl MS-4
Shoccoe Post Office (historical)—building MS-4
Shocco Mtn—summit AL-4
**Shocco Springs**—pop pl AL-4
Shocco Station (historical)—locale AL-4
Shocco (Township of)—fmr MCD NC-3
Shochary Ridge—ridge PA-2
Shock—locale WV-2
Shockalo Church MS-4
Shockaloe Base Camp Number One MS-4
Shockaloe Base Camp Number Two MS-4
Shockaloe Creek MS-4
Shockaloe Natl Recreation Trail MS-4
Shockaloe Trail—trail MS-4
Shockaloo Creek—stream MS-4
Shock Cem—cemetery OH-6
Shock Creek—stream CA-9
Shockey Cem—cemetery KS-7
Shockey Cem—cemetery (2) OH-6
Shockey Fork—stream KY-4
Shockey (historical)—locale KS-7
Shockey Run—stream WV-2
Shockey Sch (abandoned)—school MO-7
Shockeys Knob—summit VA-3
Shockeys Knob—summit WV-2
Shockeysville—locale VA-3
Shockeyville KS-7
Shock Ford—locale MO-7
Shock Gully TX-5
Shock Hill ME-1
Shock Hill—summit CO-8
Shock Hollow—valley OH-6
Shock Hollow—valley WV-2
Shock Lake—lake IN-6
Shockley Branch—stream AR-4
Shockley Branch—stream WV-2
Shockley Cem—cemetery FL-3
Shockley Cem—cemetery IL-6
Shockley Cem—cemetery KS-7
Shockley Cem—cemetery TN-4
Shockley Cem—cemetery VA-3
Shockley Ch—church TN-4
Shockley Creek—stream TX-5
**Shockley Heights (subdivision)**—pop pl DE-2
Shockley Hill—summit MA-1
Shockley Hill Ch—church WV-2
Shockley Lake—lake NM-5
**Shockley Manor**—pop pl DE-2
Shockley-Ross Cem—cemetery OH-6
Shockley Rsvr—reservoir OR-9
Shockley Sch (abandoned)—school MO-7
Shockleys Chapel Sch (historical)—school TN-4
Shockley Slough—stream ND-7
Shockney Cem—cemetery IN-6
Shockney Ditch—canal IN-6
Shockoe—locale VA-3
Shockoe Creek—stream (3) VA-3
Shockoe Hill Cem—cemetery VA-3
Shockoe Sch—school VA-3
Shockoe Slip Hist Dist—hist pl VA-3
Shockoe Slip Hist Dist (Boundary Increase)—hist pl VA-3
Shockoe Valley and Tobacco Row Hist Dist—hist pl VA-3
Shock Run—stream WV-2
Shocks (historical P.O.)—locale IA-7
Shocks Mills PA-2
**Shocks Mills (Rowenna)**—pop pl PA-2
Shocks Station (historical)—locale IA-7
Shockum Mountains—other AK-9
Shocky Hill—summit PA-2
Sho Creek—stream ID-8
Shodach Stream NY-2
Shodack Landing NY-2
Shoddy Mill Pond—lake CT-1
Shoddy Springs—spring MT-8
Shoddyville TN-4
Shodie Creek KY-4
Shoe—locale NC-3
Shoe, The—arch UT-8
Shoe and Stocking Campground—locale CO-8
Shoe and Stocking Creek—stream CO-8
Shoe Bar Oil Field—other NM-5
Shoe Bar Ranch—locale TX-5
Shoe Basin Mine—mine CO-8
Shoe Bayou—stream LA-4
Shoebeck Gulch—valley CO-8
Shoebox Well—well NV-8
Shoe Branch—stream NC-3
Shoebridge Bonanza—mine UT-8
Shoe Buckle Canyon—valley AZ-5
Shoe Buckle Rsvr—reservoir AZ-5
Shoecraft, Lake—lake WA-9
Shoecraft, Matthew, House—hist pl NY-2
Shoecraft Creek—stream ID-8
Shoecraft Hill—summit NY-2
Shoe Craft Hollow—valley IA-7
Shoe Creek SD-7
Shoe Creek—stream AK-9
Shoe Creek—stream IL-6
Shoe Creek—stream VA-3
Shoe Factory Pond MA-1
Shoefelt Corners—locale NY-2
Shoefelt Gulch—valley MT-8
Shoeffer Rsvr—reservoir OR-9
Shoeffler Butte—summit ID-8
Shoefly Canyon AZ-5
Shoe Game Wash—stream AZ-5
Shoe Game Wash—stream NM-5
Shoehammer Sch—school KY-4
Shoeheart Ridge CA-9
Shoe Heel NC-3
Shoeheel Cemetery—cemetery NC-3
Shoeheel Creek NC-3
Shoeheel Creek SC-3
Shoe Heel Creek—stream NC-3
Shoe Heel Creek—stream SC-3
Shoeheel Lake—lake AK-9
Shoe Hole NC-3
Shoehole, The NC-3
Shoehole Bay NC-3
Shoe Hole Bay—bay NC-3
Shoehorn Mtn—summit AK-9
Shoe House Sch—school WA-9
Shoeinhorse Mtn—summit CA-9
Shoe Inlet—bay AK-9
Shoe Island—island AK-9
Shoe Island—island GA-3
Shoe Island—island MI-6
Shoe Lake MI-6
Shoe Lake MN-6
Shoe Lake—lake IN-6
Shoe Lake—lake MI-6
Shoe Lake—lake (2) MN-6
Shoe Lake—lake SC-3
Shoe Lake—lake (2) WA-9
Shoe Lake—lake (2) WI-6
Shoe Lake—lake WY-8
**Shoe Lake**—pop pl IN-6
Shoe Lakes MI-6
Shoe Lake Trail—trail WA-9
Shoeleather Creek—stream AK-9
Shoemake, John H., House—hist pl IA-7
Shoemake Branch—stream TX-5
Shoemake Creek—stream TX-5
Shoemake Hollow—valley TN-4
Shoemake Opening—gap CA-9
Shoemaker—locale NM-5
Shoemaker—locale PA-2
Shoemaker, Capt. Jacob, House—hist pl PA-2
Shoemaker, Mount—summit MT-8
Shoemaker, William, JHS—hist pl PA-2
Shoemaker Bally—summit CA-9
Shoemaker Bay—bay AK-9
Shoemaker Bluff—cliff TX-5
Shoemaker Branch PA-2
Shoemaker Branch—stream (2) GA-3
Shoemaker Branch—stream KY-4
Shoemaker Branch—stream PA-2
Shoemaker Branch—stream TN-4
Shoemaker Branch Baker Run - in part PA-2
Shoemaker Bridge—bridge CA-9
Shoemaker Bridge—bridge PA-2
Shoemaker Butte—summit WA-9
Shoemaker Canyon—valley (2) CA-9
Shoemaker Canyon—valley NE-7
Shoemaker Canyon—valley NM-5
Shoemaker Cem—cemetery AL-4
Shoemaker Cem—cemetery IL-6
Shoemaker Cem—cemetery (5) IN-6
Shoemaker Cem—cemetery MS-4
Shoemaker Cem—cemetery (3) MO-7
Shoemaker Cem—cemetery (2) OH-6
Shoemaker Cem—cemetery PA-2
Shoemaker Cem—cemetery VA-3
Shoemaker Covered Bridge—hist pl PA-2
Shoemaker Creek—stream ID-8
Shoemaker Creek—stream MI-6
Shoemaker Creek—stream NC-3
Shoemaker Creek—stream OR-9
Shoemaker Dam—dam SD-7
Shoemaker Ditch—canal (4) IN-6
Shoemaker Ditch—canal OR-9
Shoemaker Drain—stream MI-6
Shoemaker Elem Sch—school PA-2
Shoemaker Flat—flat UT-8
Shoemaker Gap—gap MT-8
Shoemaker Gulch—stream CA-9
Shoemaker Gulch—valley (3) CA-9
Shoemaker Hill—summit CA-9
Shoemaker Hill—summit NM-5
Shoemaker Hill—summit NY-2
Shoemaker Hill—summit PA-2
Shoemaker Hollow UT-8
Shoemaker Hollow—valley OH-6
Shoemaker Hollow—valley WV-2
Shoemaker-Houck Farm—hist pl NJ-2
Shoemaker III Village Site—hist pl MD-2
Shoemaker Island—island NE-7
Shoemaker JHS—school PA-2
Shoemaker Knob—summit PA-2
Shoemaker Knob—summit VA-3
Shoemaker Lake—lake (2) MN-6
Shoemaker Lake—reservoir GA-3
Shoemaker Mine—mine MT-8
Shoemaker Mine—mine WA-9
Shoemaker Mtn—summit NY-2
Shoemaker Place—locale TX-5
**Shoemaker Point**—pop pl WI-6
Shoemaker Ranch—locale NM-5
Shoemaker Ridge—ridge PA-2
Shoemaker River—stream VA-3
Shoemaker Run PA-2
Shoemaker Run—stream (2) PA-2
Shoemakers—locale PA-2
**Shoemakers**—pop pl PA-2
Shoemaker Sch—school CA-9
Shoemaker Sch—school MA-1
Shoemaker Sch—school NJ-2
Shoemaker Spring—spring AL-4
Shoemaker Spring—spring AZ-5
Shoemaker Spring—spring (2) CA-9
Shoemaker Spring—spring CO-8
Shoemaker Spring—spring IL-6
Shoemaker Spring—spring NV-8
Shoemaker Spring—spring NM-5
Shoemaker Springs (historical)—locale AL-4
Shoemakers Run PA-2
**Shoemakersville**—pop pl PA-2
Shoemakersville Borough—civil PA-2
Shoemaker Tank—reservoir CO-8
Shoemakertown PA-2
Shoemaker Trail—trail PA-2
Shoemaker Valley—valley CA-9
Shoemaker Wash—valley UT-8
Shoemaker Windmill—locale NM-5
Shoemake Windmill—locale NM-5
**Shoemak Village**—pop pl PA-2
Shoemate-Augustine Ranch—locale CO-8
Shoemate Gap—gap TN-4
Shoe Mtn—summit OK-5
Shoenberger—locale PA-2
Shoenbrun OH-6
Shoeneck PA-2
Shoeneck Creek—stream PA-2
Shoenersville PA-2
**Shoenersville**—pop pl PA-2
**Shoentown**—pop pl PA-2
Shoepack Creek—stream ID-8
Shoe Pack Lake MN-6
Shoepack Lake—lake MI-6
Shoepack Lake—lake (3) MN-6
Shoepack Lookout Tower—locale MN-6
Shoepack Point—summit ID-8
Shoepac Lake—lake AK-9
Shoepac Lake—lake MI-6
Shoe Pac Lake—lake (2) MI-6
Shoepac Lake—lake (2) MI-6
Shoepac River—stream MI-6
Shoe Peg Mtn—summit TX-5
Shoe Peg Valley—valley ID-8
Shoe Pond—reservoir MA-1
Shoe Pond Dam—dam MA-1
Shoe Rock—other AK-9
Shoeshine Cave—cave AL-4
Shoe Shop-Doucette Ten Footer—hist pl MA-1
Shoesmith Sch—school IL-6
Shoesole Creek—stream MS-4
Shoesole Flat—flat OR-9
Shoesole Lake—lake FL-3
Shoestring Branch—stream TN-4
Shoestring Brook MA-1
Shoestring Butte—summit OR-9
Shoestring Cove—bay AK-9
Shoe String Creek OR-9
Shoestring Creek—stream MT-8
Shoestring Creek—stream (4) OR-9
Shoestring Creek Bear Wallow Creek Trail—trail MT-8
Shoestring Draw—valley CA-9
Shoestring Falls—falls ID-8
Shoestring Glacier—glacier WA-9
Shoestring Glade—flat OR-9
Shoestring Grade—cliff OR-9
Shoe String Hill MA-1
Shoestring Hill—summit MA-1
Shoestring Hollow—valley MO-7
Shoestring Lake—lake CO-8
Shoestring Lake—lake UT-8
Shoestring Lake—lake WA-9
Shoestring Lake—lake WI-6
Shoestring Lake—lake WY-8
Shoestring Ridge—ridge OH-6
Shoestring Ridge—ridge (2) OR-9
Shoestring Ridge—ridge WV-2
Shoestring Sch—school ID-8
Shoestring Spring—spring (2) OR-9
Shoestring Trail—trail OR-9
Shoestring Valley—basin OR-9
Shoestring Valley—valley NV-8
Shoe Sugar Pond—lake TX-5
Shoe Tank—reservoir AZ-5
Shoe Tank—reservoir TX-5
Shoethread RI-1
Shofapotofa Creek MS-4
**Shoffner**—pop pl AR-4
Shoffner Branch—stream TN-4
Shoffner Cem—cemetery TN-4
Shoffners Bridge TN-4
Shofner—locale TN-4
Shofner Bridge—bridge TN-4
Shofner Cem—cemetery (2) TN-4
Shofner Cem—cemetery TX-5
Shofner Ch—church TN-4
Shofner Creek—stream TX-5
Shogvik Lake—lake AK-9
**Shohola**—pop pl PA-2
Shohola Creek—stream MN-6
Shohola Creek—stream PA-2
Shohola Elem Sch—school PA-2
Shohola Falls—falls PA-2
**Shohola Falls**—pop pl PA-2
Shohola Falls Dam PA-2
Shohola Falls Trails End—locale PA-2
Shohola Lake—lake MN-6
Shohola Marsh Dam—dam PA-2
Shohola Marsh Rsvr—reservoir PA-2
Shohola Sch—school PA-2
**Shohola (Township of)**—pop pl PA-2
**Shokan**—pop pl NY-2
Shok Bar—bar IL-6
Shokie Country Club—other IL-6
Shokokluk Creek AK-9
**Shokokon**—pop pl IL-6
Shokokon Slough—gut IL-6
Shoko Lake—lake MN-6
Shokum Creek—stream AK-9
**Sholam**—pop pl NY-2
Sholan Park—park MA-1
Sholan Point—cape MA-1
Sholar Bridge Cem—cemetery MS-4
Sholar Pond—reservoir GA-3
Sholars Crossroads—locale NC-3
Sholars Mill Creek—stream MS-4
Sholden Pond—swamp AR-4
Shole Inlet NC-3
Sholem Cem—cemetery NJ-2
Sholer Branch—stream GA-3
**Sholes**—pop pl NE-7
Sholes, Albert S., House—hist pl OR-9
Sholes Creek MD-2
Sholes Creek—stream CA-9
Sholes Creek—stream WA-9
Sholes Glacier—glacier WA-9
Sholey Branch GA-3
Sholey Branch (historical)—stream TN-4
Sholin Island—island AK-9
Sholler Mtn—summit ME-1
Sholom Cem—cemetery MA-1
Sholom Memorial Park (Cemetery)—cemetery CA-9
Sholom Sch—school MA-1
Sholow AZ-5
Sholts Cem—cemetery IN-6
Shome Sho FM-9
Shomin Airp—airport KS-7
Shomo Cem—cemetery AL-4
Shomo Creek—stream AL-4
Shomo Takali MS-4
Shomushon—locale MH-9
Shonagana Rsvr—reservoir NM-5
Shone-Charley House—hist pl OR-9
Shonenya Lake—lake MI-6
Shones Creek UT-8
Shones Hollow UT-8
Shones Mill Pond MS-4
Shone Spring—spring OR-9
Shonessy Building/Don Chun Wo Store—hist pl AZ-5
Shonessy House—hist pl AZ-5
Shoney Cem—cemetery MO-7
Shongalo Creek MS-4
Shongalo (historical)—locale MS-4
**Shongaloo**—pop pl LA-4
Shongaloo Lookout Tower—locale LA-4
Shongaloo Oil Field—oilfield LA-4
Shongelo—locale MS-4
Shongelo Creek—stream MS-4
Shongelo Creek Oil Field—oilfield MS-4
Shongelo Lake—lake MS-4
Shongelo Post Office (historical)—building MS-4
Shongelo Sch (historical)—school MS-4
Shongo—locale NY-2
**Shongo**—pop pl NY-2
Shongo Creek—stream NY-2
Shongola MS-4
Shongola Cem—cemetery MS-4
Shongola Creek MS-4
Shongopavi Community Bldg—building AZ-5
Shongopovi AZ-5
**Shongopovi**—pop pl AZ-5
Shongopovi Spring—spring AZ-5
Shongum—locale NJ-2
Shongum Lake—reservoir NJ-2
Shongum Lake Dam—dam NJ-2
Shongum Mountain Sanatorium—hospital NJ-2
Shonian Harbor PW-9
Shoniktok Point—cape AK-9
Shonip Creek—stream ID-8
Shonka Ditch—canal NE-7
Shonkin—locale MT-8
Shonkin Bar—island MT-8
Shonkin Coulee MT-8
Shonkin Cow Camp—locale MT-8
Shonkin Creek MT-8
Shonkin Creek—stream MT-8
Shonkin Lake—lake MT-8
Shonkiron FM-9
Shonnard, Eugenie, House—hist pl NM-5
Shonny Branch—stream KY-4
Shonsy Draw—valley WY-8
**Shont**—pop pl ID-8
**Shonto**—pop pl AZ-5
Shonto Airp—airport AZ-5
Shonto Boarding Sch—school AZ-5
Shonto Butte—summit AZ-5
**Shonto (Navajo Boarding School)**—pop pl AZ-5
Shonto Plateau—plain AZ-5
Shonto Spring—spring (5) AZ-5
Shonto Trading Post AZ-5
Shonto Wash—valley AZ-5
Shonto Well—well AZ-5
Shont Siding—locale ID-8
Shontz Airp—airport PA-2
Shonya Hill—summit VT-1
Shoo Bird NC-3
Shoock Gap WV-2
Shoof Lake—reservoir TN-4
Shoof Lake Dam—dam TN-4
Shoo Fly—locale CA-9
**Shoofly**—pop pl NC-3
Shoo Fly Bar—bar MS-4
Shoofly Canal—canal ID-8
Shoofly Canyon—valley AZ-5

Short Line Junction—locale OH-6
Short Line Junction—uninc pl WV-2
Short Line Park—locale MN-6
Short Lots Sch—school NY-2
Short Low Ditch—canal WA-9
Shortly—locale DE-2
Short Marsh DE-2
Short Marsh—swamp DE-2
Short Marsh Cove DE-2
Short Mesa—summit CO-8
Short Mountain—locale KY-4
Short Mountain—locale TN-4
Short Mountain—ridge AR-4
Short Mountain—ridge (2) PA-2
Short Mountain Camp—locale TN-4
Short Mountain Cem—cemetery OK-5
Short Mountain Ch—church TN-4
Short Mountain Creek—stream AR-4
Short Mountain Post Office (historical)—building (2) TN-4
Short Mountain Public Hunting Area—park WV-2
Short Mountain Reservoir OK-5
Short Mountain Sch—school TN-4
Short Mountain (Township of)—fmr MCD AR-4
Short Mtn PA-2
Short Mtn—summit (5) AR-4
Short Mtn—summit CT-1
Short Mtn—summit KY-4
Short Mtn—summit (4) OK-5
Short Mtn—summit (2) OR-9
Short Mtn—summit (6) PA-2
Short Mtn—summit (12) TN-4
Short Mtn—summit (9) VA-3
Short Mtn—summit WA-9
Short Mtn—summit (3) WV-2
Short Neck—cape UT-8
**Short Off**—pop pl NC-3
Shortoff Ch—church NC-3
Shortoff Creek—stream NC-3
Shortoff Gap—gap NC-3
Shortoff Knob—summit NC-3
Shortoff Mountain Trail—trail NC-3
Shortoff Mtn—summit (2) NC-3
Short Park—park NM-5
Short Park—park WA-9
Short Pass—channel AK-9
Short Peak—summit MT-8
Short Pine Canyon—valley TX-5
Short Pine Cem—cemetery SD-7
Short Pine Creek—stream NE-7
Short Pines SD-7
Short Pines Gas Field—locale SD-7
Short Place—locale CA-9
Short Point—cape AK-9
Short Point—cape LA-4
Short Point—cape ME-1
Short Point—cape MD-2
Short Point—cape (2) NY-2
Short Point—cape (2) NC-3
Short Point—cape (2) RI-1
Short Point—cape UT-8
Short Point—cliff CO-8
Short Point—summit ID-8
Short Point Bay—bay NY-2
Short Point Creek—stream (2) IL-6
Short Point Sch—school IL-6
Short Point Trail—trail CO-8
Shortpole Branch—stream WV-2
Short Pond—lake ME-1
Short-Poynor Cem—cemetery TN-4
Short Prong—gut VA-3
Short Prong—stream LA-4
Short Prong Marsh—swamp VA-3
Short Prong Prairie Creek—stream WY-8
Short Prong West Frio River—stream TX-5
**Short Pump**—pop pl VA-3
Short Ranch—locale CA-9
Short Ranch—locale ND-7
Short Ranch—locale WY-8
Short Ridge—ridge (5) CA-9
Short Ridge—ridge CO-8
Short Ridge—ridge IN-6
Short Ridge—ridge KY-4
Short Ridge—ridge NC-3
Short Ridge—ridge OH-6
Short Ridge—ridge (2) OR-9
Short Ridge—ridge (3) TN-4
Short Ridge—ridge VA-3
Short Ridge—ridge WA-9
Shortridge Branch—stream VA-3
Shortridge Butte—summit OR-9
Shortridge Cem—cemetery VA-3
Short Ridge Ch—church WV-2
Short Ridge Creek OR-9
Shortridge Creek—stream OR-9
Short Ridge Creek—stream TN-4
Shortridge Farm Cem—cemetery OH-6
Shortridge Fork—stream KY-4
Shortridge HS—hist pl IN-6
Shortridge HS—school IN-6
Shortridge Ranch—locale MT-8
Short Ridges—ridge VA-3
Short River—stream AK-9
Short Run—locale PA-2
Short Run—stream (3) IN-6
Short Run—stream MD-2
Short Run—stream (4) PA-2
Short Run—stream (10) WV-2
Short Run Ch—church MD-2
Short Run Trail—trail PA-2
Shorts KY-4
Shorts—locale AL-4
Short Sand Beach—beach OR-9
Short Sand Beach Creek OR-9
Short Sand Beach State Park OR-9
Short Sand Creek—stream OR-9
Short Sands—beach ME-1
Shorts Bar—bar ID-8
Shorts Beach (2) DE-2
Shorts Brook—stream MA-1
Shorts Cem—cemetery WV-2
Shorts Ch—church AL-4
Short Sch—school CA-9
Short Sch—school MO-7
Shorts Chapel—church MS-4
Short School Hollow—valley MO-7
Shorts Corner—locale DE-2
**Shorts Corner**—pop pl IN-6
**Shorts Corner**—pop pl TX-5
Shorts Creek—locale VA-3
Shorts Creek—stream ID-8
Shorts Creek—stream KS-7
Shorts Creek—stream VA-3
Shorts Creek Pond—lake MD-2
Shorts Ditch—stream DE-2
Shorts Gap—gap VA-3
Short's Hill—hist pl MS-4
Short's Hotel—hist pl PA-2
Shorts Lake—reservoir NC-3
Shorts Lake Dam—dam NC-3
Shorts Landing—locale DE-2
Shorts Landing (historical)—locale AL-4
Short's Landing Hotel Complex—hist pl DE-2
Short Slope—cliff MT-8
Short Slough—gut CA-9
Short Slough—lake IL-6
Shorts Meadow—flat MT-8
Shorts Mill—locale GA-3
Shorts Mill (historical)—locale TN-4
Shorts Pond—lake NY-2
Short Spring—spring OR-9
Short Spring—spring TN-4
Short Spring Branch—stream TX-5
Short Springs Cem—cemetery OK-5
Short Squaw Creek—stream MT-8
Shorts Sch (historical)—school TN-4
Shorts Station—locale KY-4
**Shorts Store**—pop pl VA-3
Shorts Store (historical)—locale TN-4
Short Stop Cave—cave AL-4
Short Street Sch—school PA-2
Shorts Valley—valley UT-8
Shortsville—locale PA-2
Shortsville—locale VA-3
**Shortsville**—pop pl NY-2
Shortsville Sch—school IL-6
Short Swamp—stream NC-3
Short Swing Trail—trail NY-2
Shorts Woods Golf Course—area OH-6
Shorttail Gulch—valley CA-9
**Short Tail Springs**—pop pl TN-4
Short Tail Springs—spring TN-4
Short Tank—reservoir NM-5
Shortt Gap—gap VA-3
Shortt Gap—locale VA-3
**Short Town**—pop pl KY-4
**Short Tract**—pop pl NY-2
Short Tract Cem—cemetery NY-2
Short Trail—trail (2) PA-2
Short Trail Camp—locale WA-9
Short Tree Ch—church LA-4
Shortts Knob—summit VA-3
Short Turn—gut VA-3
**Shortville**—pop pl WI-6
Short Wash—stream CA-9
Short Wash Rsvr—reservoir WY-8
Short Water—stream CO-8
Shortway Bayou—gut LA-4
Short Well—well NM-5
Short Wharf Creek—stream MA-1
Short Wiley Creek—stream OR-9
Short Windmill—locale NM-5
Short Woods—swamp CT-1
Short Woods Brook—stream CT-1
Short Woods Park Mound—hist pl OH-6
Shorty Camp Spring—spring AZ-5
Shorty Canyon—valley ID-8
Shorty Canyon—valley NM-5
Shorty Cove—bay AK-9
Shorty Cox Hollow—valley OK-5
Shorty Creek—stream (4) AK-9
Shorty Creek—stream CO-8
Shorty Creek—stream ID-8
Shorty Creek—stream (4) MT-8
Shorty Creek—stream NV-8
Shorty Creek—stream OK-5
Shorty Creek—stream TX-5
Shorty Creek—stream (2) WY-8
Shorty Creek Rsvr—reservoir MT-8
Shorty Davis Ranch—locale OR-9
Shorty Davis Tank—reservoir AZ-5
Shorty Draw—valley SD-7
Shorty Gulch—valley CO-8
Shorty Gulch—valley MT-8
Shorty Harris Canyon—valley CA-9
Shorty Hollow—valley AR-4
Shorty Lake—lake CA-9
Shorty Lrke—lake MN-6
Shorty Lovelace Hist Dist—hist pl CA-9
Shorty Miller—locale NM-5
Shorty Millers Lower Ranch—locale NM-5
Shorty Mtn—summit GA-3
Shorty Peak—summit ID-8
Shorty Ridge Rsvr—reservoir MT-8
Shorty Ridge Well—well MT-8
Shorty Rsvr—reservoir OR-9
Shortys Banks—bar FL-3
Shortys Cabin—locale CO-8
Shortys Cabin—park CA-9
Shortys Canyon—valley AZ-5
**Shortys Corner**—pop pl OR-9
Shortys Gulch—valley ID-8
Shortys Hill—summit MT-8
Shorty Smock Windmill—locale TX-5
**Shortys Place**—pop pl PA-2
Shortys Pocket—bay FL-3
Shorty Spring—spring CO-8
Shortys Reef—bar MN-6
Shortys Rsvr—reservoir WY-8
Shortys Slough—gut FL-3
Shortys Tank—reservoir NM-5
Shortys Well—well AZ-5
Shortys Well—well CA-9
Shorty Swope Tank—reservoir NM-5
Shorty Tank—reservoir (2) AZ-5
Shorty Tank—reservoir (2) NM-5
Shorty Top—summit NC-3
Shorty Well—locale NM-5
Shorty Windmill—locale NM-5
Shorty Windmill—locale TX-5
Shortz Lake—flat CA-9
Shoshoko Falls—falls WY-8
Shoshone—locale CO-8
**Shoshone**—pop pl CA-9
**Shoshone**—pop pl ID-8
**Shoshone**—pop pl NV-8
Shoshone, Mount—summit WY-8
Shoshone Basin—basin ID-8
Shoshone Basin—basin WY-8
Shoshone Bay—bay ID-8
Shoshone Cabin—locale ID-8
Shoshone Campground—locale NV-8
Shoshone Canyon—valley NV-8
Shoshone Canyon—valley WY-8
Shoshone Country Club—other ID-8
Shoshone Creek CO-8
Shoshone Creek ID-8
Shoshone Creek—stream (2) ID-8
Shoshone Creek—stream (4) NV-8
Shoshone Creek—stream (3) WY-8
Shoshone Dam—dam CO-8
Shoshone-Episcopal Mission—hist pl WY-8
Shoshone Falls—falls ID-8
Shoshone Falls Park—park ID-8
Shoshone Falls Power Plant Caretaker's House—hist pl ID-8
Shoshone Forest Camp—locale ID-8
Shoshone Forest Service Recreation Site NV-8
Shoshone Forest Service Station—locale ID-8
Shoshone Geyser Basin—basin WY-8
**Shoshone Hills Subdivision**—pop pl UT-8
Shoshone Hist Dist—hist pl ID-8
Shoshone Ice Caves—cave ID-8
Shoshone Jeep Trail—trail NV-8
Shoshone Lake—lake (3) WY-8
Shoshone Lake Trail—trail WY-8
Shoshone Meadows—flat NV-8
Shoshone Mountains NV-8
Shoshone Mtn—summit (2) NV-8
Shoshone Mtns—range NV-8
Shoshone Natl For—forest WY-8
Shoshone Opportunity Sch—school ID-8
Shoshone Park—park AZ-5
Shoshone Park—park ID-8
Shoshone Pass—gap NV-8
Shoshone Pass—gap WY-8
Shoshone Peak CO-8
Shoshone Peak—summit ID-8
Shoshone Peak—summit NV-8
Shoshone Peak North NV-8
Shoshone Peak South NV-8
Shoshone Plateau—area WY-8
Shoshone P O—locale NV-8
Shoshone Point—cliff AZ-5
Shoshone Point—summit NV-8
Shoshone Ponds—swamp NV-8
Shoshone Powerplant—other CO-8
Shoshone Ranch—locale WY-8
Shoshone Range NV-8
Shoshone Range—range ID-8
Shoshone Range—range NV-8
Shoshone Reservoir WY-8
Shoshone River ID-8
Shoshone River NV-8
Shoshone River OR-9
Shoshone River WA-9
Shoshone River WY-8
Shoshone River—stream WY-8
Shoshone Rsvr—reservoir ID-8
Shoshone Spring—spring CA-9
Shoshone Spring—spring ID-8
Shoshone Springs—spring NV-8
Shoshone Stock Driveway—trail WY-8
Shoshone Trail—trail WY-8
**Shoshoni**—pop pl WY-8
Shoshoni Peak—summit CO-8
Shosky Creek—stream AK-9
Shosta Costa Creek OR-9
Shot Bag Branch—stream GA-3
Shotbag Creek—stream AL-4
Shotbag Creek—stream GA-3
Shotbag Creek—stream MS-4
Shotbag Island NY-2
Shotbag Sch—school MS-4
Shot Beech Ridge—ridge NC-3
Shot Branch—stream TN-4
Shot Canyon—valley UT-8
Shot Coulee—valley MT-8
Shot Creek ID-8
Shot Creek—stream ID-8
Shotgold Creek—stream AK-9
Shotgun at 1206 Canterbury Street—hist pl TX-5
Shotgun Bench—bench WY-8
Shotgun Bend—locale CA-9
Shotgun Butte—summit WY-8
Shotgun Canyon—valley (2) NM-5
Shotgun Canyon—valley OR-9
Shotgun Corners—locale MI-6
Shotgun Coulee—valley MT-8
Shotgun Cove—bay AK-9
Shotgun Creek CA-9
Shotgun Creek—stream (2) AK-9
Shotgun Creek—stream (4) CA-9
Shotgun Creek—stream (2) ID-8
Shotgun Creek—stream MI-6
Shotgun Creek—stream MT-8
Shotgun Creek—stream (4) OR-9
Shotgun Creek—stream WA-9
Shotgun Creek—stream WY-8
Shotgun Crossing—locale TX-5
Shotgun Draw—valley UT-8
Shotgun Eddy Rapids—rapids WI-6
Shotgun Gulch—valley CA-9
Shotgun Hill—summit VA-3
Shotgun Hill Branch—stream VA-3
Shotgun Hills—other AK-9
Shotgun Hollow—valley OR-9
Shotgun Hollow—valley WV-2
Shotgun Knoll—summit UT-8
Shotgun Lake—lake CA-9
Shotgun Lake—reservoir KY-4
Shotgun Mtn—summit CO-8
Shotgun Pass—gap CA-9
Shotgun Peak—summit CA-9
Shotgun Ranch—locale WY-8
Shotgun Recreational Site—park OR-9
Shotgun Rsvr—reservoir MT-8
Shotguns at 1203–1205 Bob Harrison—hist pl TX-5
Shotgun Slough—basin MT-8
Shotgun Tank—reservoir TX-5
Shotgun Trail—trail PA-2
Shotgun Valley—valley ID-8
Shotgun Well—well ID-8
Shothole Branch—stream LA-4
Shot Hole Spring—spring WY-8
Shot Hollow—valley TX-5
Shot Islands ME-1
Shotley—locale MN-6
Shotley Brook—stream MN-6
Shotley Brook (Unorganized Territory of)—unorg MN-6
Shotley State Wildlife Mngmt Area—park MN-6
**Shotley (Township of)**—pop pl MN-6
Shotly MN-6
Shot Mine—mine OR-9
Shotnick Basin—basin UT-8
**Shoto**—pop pl WI-6
Shoto Lake—reservoir WI-6
Shotoverin Lake—lake CA-9
Shot Point—cape MI-6
Shot Pouch Branch—stream SC-3
Shot Pouch Butte—summit OR-9
Shot Pouch Creek—stream KY-4
Shot Pouch Creek—stream NC-3
Shotpouch Creek—stream OR-9
Shot Pouch Creek—stream OR-9
Shot Pouch Run—stream OH-6
Shots Creek—stream MS-4
Shott Brothers Ranch—locale CO-8
Shott Cem—cemetery IL-6
Shottenkirk Lake—reservoir SD-7
Shotto Spring—spring MI-6
Shot Tower—hist pl IA-7
Shot Tower—hist pl MD-2
Shot Tower—hist pl VA-3
Shot Tower—hist pl WI-6
Shot Tower State Historical Park—park VA-3
Shotts Bridge—bridge OH-6
Shotts Cem—cemetery PA-2
Shott Sch (historical)—school MO-7
Shotts Creek MS-4
Shott Spring—spring OR-9
Shotts Sch—school PA-2
Shotts School MS-4
**Shottsville**—pop pl AL-4
Shottsville Cem—cemetery AL-4
Shottsville Ch—church AL-4
Shottsville Methodist Ch AL-4
Shotuih Hill—summit AK-9
Shot Up Tank—reservoir AZ-5
Shot Up Well—well AZ-5
Shotwell—locale NC-3
**Shotwell**—pop pl AL-4
Shotwell, Benjamin, House—hist pl NJ-2
Shotwell Cem—cemetery MO-7
Shotwell Ditch—canal WA-9
Shotwell Point—cape NY-2
Shotwell Run—stream VA-3
Shot Windmill—locale TX-5
Shoub Cem—cemetery NY-2
Shoue Gulch MT-8
Shoue Gulch Creek MT-8
Shoulder, The—gap CO-8
Shoulderblade—locale KY-4
Shoulder Blade Camp—locale MT-8
Shoulderblade Ch—church KY-4
Shoulderblade Creek—stream KY-4
Shoulder Blade Creek—stream MT-8
Shoulderblade Island—island AK-9
**Shoulderbone**—pop pl GA-3
Shoulder Bone Branch—stream SC-3
Shoulderbone Creek—stream GA-3
Shoulder Branch Cem—cemetery NC-3
Shoulder Branch Ch—church NC-3
Shoulder Creek—stream MT-8
Shoulder Creek—stream WI-6
Shoulder Hollow—valley TN-4
Shoulder Lake CA-9
Shoulder Mtn—summit AK-9
Shoulder Run—stream VA-3
Shoulders Hill—locale VA-3
Shoulder Strap Branch—stream TN-4
**Shoultes**—pop pl WA-9
Shoultes Sch—school WA-9
Shoults Cem—cemetery OH-6
Shoumberg Hollow—valley OH-6
Shoun Branch—stream TN-4
Shoun Mine—mine TN-4
**Shouns**—pop pl TN-4
Shouns Chapel Sch—school TN-4
Shouns Cross Roads Post Office TN-4
Shouns Elem Sch—school TN-4
Shouns Mines TN-4
Shouns Post Office (historical)—building TN-4
Shouns Prospect—mine TN-4
Shoup—locale ID-8
**Shoup**—pop pl MI-6
Shoup Bay—bay AK-9
Shoup Bldg—hist pl ID-8
Shoup Boardinghouse—hist pl NM-5
Shoup Creek—stream MT-8
Shoup Creek—stream OR-9
Shoup Glacier—glacier AK-9
Shoup Lake—lake MT-8
Shouplina, Mount—summit AK-9
Shoup Mill Sch—school OH-6
Shoup Park—park CA-9
Shoup Rock Shelters—hist pl ID-8
Shoup Run—stream PA-2
Shoups NC-3
**Shoups Ford**—pop pl NC-3
Shoups Grove Ch—church NC-3
Shoups Run PA-2
Shouse Cem—cemetery (2) TN-4
Shouse Chapel—church IL-6
Shouse Ford Public Use Area—park AR-4
Shouse Hollow—valley TN-4
Shouse Run—stream PA-2
Shouse Temple—church NC-3
Shousetown PA-2
Shousetown—other PA-2
Shouteau MT-8
Shouting Ridge—ridge NC-3
Shouting Rock MA-1
Shove Creek PA-2
Shove Creek—stream ID-8
Shove Creek (historical)—stream PA-2
Shovehaven Golf Course—other CT-1
Shovel Basin—basin OR-9
Shovel Creek—stream (6) AK-9
Shovel Creek—stream CA-9
Shovel Creek—stream (2) ID-8
Shovel Creek—stream (2) MT-8
Shovel Creek—stream OR-9
Shovel Creek—stream (3) WA-9
Shovel Creek Guard Station—locale CA-9
Shovel Creek Meadow—flat CA-9
Shovel Creek Rapids—rapids ID-8
Shovel Creek Rapids—rapids WA-9
Shoveler Pool—reservoir UT-8
Shovelfull Shoal MA-1
Shovelful Shoal—bar MA-1
Shovel Grave—summit CA-9
Shovel Gulch—valley AK-9
Shovel Handle Creek—stream CA-9
Shovel Hollow—valley MO-7
Shovel Hollow—valley NY-2
Shovel Hollow—valley VA-3
Shovel Lake—lake AK-9
Shovel Lake—lake MN-6
Shovel Lake—lake (2) WA-9
Shovel Lake—locale MN-6
Shoveller Lake—lake MN-6
Shovel Mountain—locale TX-5
Shovel Mtn—summit TX-5
Shovel Mtn Community TX-5
Shovel Point—cape MN-6
Shovel Point Horn—summit AK-9
Shovel Shop MA-1
Shovelshop Pond—reservoir MA-1
Shovelshop Pond Dam—dam MA-1
Shovel Spring—spring AZ-5
Shovel Spring—spring MT-8
Shovel Spring—spring NV-8
Shovel Spring—spring OR-9
Shovel Spring Canyon—valley NV-8
**Shoveltown**—pop pl MO-7
Shove Ridge—ridge IN-6
**Shover Springs**—pop pl AR-4
Shoves Neck—cape MA-1
Shovun Lake—lake AK-9
Showalter Bench—bench UT-8
Showalter Cem—cemetery (2) KY-4
Showalter Creek—stream OR-9
Showalter Creek—stream UT-8
Showalter Gap—gap PA-2
Showalter House—hist pl KY-4
Showalter Junior High School PA-2
Showalter MS—school PA-2
Showalter Mtn—summit UT-8
Show Ave Sch—school PA-2
Showboat Camp—locale AL-4
SHOWBOAT MAJESTIC—hist pl OH-6
Showboat Park—park MI-6
Showboat Theatre—hist pl WA-9
Show Bridge—bridge CA-9
Show Ch—church MI-6
Show Creek TX-5
Show Creek—stream IA-7
**Showell**—pop pl MD-2
Showell Pond—lake NH-1
Showell Sch DE-2
Showens Run—stream WV-2
Showerbath Branch—stream SC-3
Showerbath Canyon—valley UT-8
Showerbath Spring—spring AZ-5
Showerbath Spring—spring UT-8
Shower Bath Springs—spring ID-8
Shower Branch—stream CA-9
Shower Creek—stream MT-8
Shower Creek—stream OR-9
Shower Falls—falls MT-8
Shower Gulch—valley AK-9
Shower Point Campground—park AZ-5
Showers PA-2
Showers—mine UT-8
Showers Creek—stream CA-9
Showers Creek—stream MT-8
Showers Lake—lake CA-9
Showers Mine and Headframe—hist pl UT-8
Showers Mtn—summit CA-9
Showers Pass—gap CA-9
Showers Post Office (historical)—building PA-2
Shower Spring—spring AZ-5
Showers Rock—pillar CA-9
Show Gulch OR-9
Show Hope Ch—church MS-4
**Show Low**—pop pl AZ-5
Show Low City Park—park AZ-5
Showlow Creek AZ-5
Show Low Creek—stream AZ-5
Show Low Creek Bridge—bridge AZ-5
Show Low Dam AZ-5
Show Low Elem Sch—school AZ-5
Show Low HS—school AZ-5
Show Low JHS—school AZ-5
Show Low Lake—reservoir AZ-5
Show Low Library—building AZ-5
Show Low Municipal Airp—airport AZ-5
Show Low Post Office—building AZ-5
Show Low Town Hall—building AZ-5
Show Low Well—well AZ-5
Showman Park—park TX-5
Showman Run—stream PA-2
Showmans Rest Cem—cemetery FL-3
Show Me Creek—stream AK-9
Shown Cem—cemetery KY-4
Shown Hollow—valley TN-4
Shown Springs—spring TN-4
Shown Troughs—spring OR-9
Show Place Estates—locale PA-2
Show Pockets Tank—reservoir AZ-5
Show Run—stream IN-6
Shows Cem MS-4
Shows Cem—cemetery (3) MS-4
**Shows Field**—pop pl MS-4
**Shoys**—pop pl VI-3
S H Peak—summit AZ-5
Shrader—locale AL-4
**Shrader**—pop pl PA-2
Shrader, Henry, House—hist pl TX-5
Shrader Branch—stream AL-4
Shrader Branch—stream AR-4
Shrader Branch Towanda Creek PA-2
Shrader Cem—cemetery TN-4
Shrader Cem—cemetery VA-3
Shrader Cem—cemetery (2) WV-2
Shrader Grove Ch—church PA-2
Shrader Hollow—valley WV-2
Shrader Lake—reservoir VA-3
Shrader Mill Creek AL-4
Shrader Run—stream OH-6
**Shraders**—pop pl PA-2
Shrader Sch (historical)—school AL-4
**Shraders Siding**—pop pl WV-2
**Shraderville**—pop pl MS-4
Shraderville Post Office (historical)—building MS-4
Shram Creek—stream UT-8
S H Ranch—locale AZ-5
Shrank Sch—school SD-7
Shrank School SD-7
Shrapnel Creek—stream ID-8
Shrapnell Drain—canal MI-6
Shrawder Mtn—summit PA-2
Shrawn Creek MO-7
Shreck—locale WA-9
Shreck Cem—cemetery CO-8
Shreeves Run PA-2
Shreffler Cem—cemetery IL-6
Shreiner PA-2
Shreiners—locale (2) PA-2
Shreiners Cem—cemetery PA-2
Shreve—locale AL-4
Shreve—locale KY-4
**Shreve**—pop pl OH-6
Shreve Branch—stream NJ-2
Shreve (CCD)—cens area AL-4
Shreve Cem—cemetery KY-4
Shreve Cem—cemetery OH-6
Shreve Cem—cemetery WI-6
Shreve Church PA-2
Shreve Creek—stream OH-6
Shreve Division—civil AL-4
Shreve Island—uninc pl LA-4
Shreve Lake—lake OH-6
Shreve Lake Wildlife Area—park OH-6
Shreveport LA-4
**Shreveport**—pop pl LA-4
Shreveport Commercial Hist Dist—hist pl LA-4
Shreveport-Footlight Ranch Airp—airport PA-2
**Shreveport Junction**—pop pl AR-4
**Shreveport Junction**—pop pl LA-4
Shreveport Municipal Bldg—hist pl LA-4
Shreveport Oil Field—oilfield LA-4
**Shreveport Park**—pop pl VA-3
Shreveport Regional Airp—airport LA-4
Shreveport Water Works Company, Pump Station—hist pl LA-4
Shreveport Woman's Department Club Bldg—hist pl LA-4
Shreve Ridge—ridge PA-2
Shreve Ridge Cem—cemetery PA-2
Shreve Ridge Ch (historical)—church PA-2
Shreves Bar—bar LA-4
Shreve Sch—school PA-2
Shreve Sch (abandoned)—school PA-2
Shreves Chapel—church PA-2
Shreves Cutoff—bend (2) LA-4
Shreves Island—island LA-4
Shreves Island Sch—school LA-4
Shreves Landing LA-4
Shreves Mill (historical)—locale AL-4
Shreves Mills NJ-2
Shreves Run PA-2
Shreves Run—stream PA-2
Shreves Tank—reservoir NM-5
**Shrevewood**—pop pl VA-3
Shrewbird NC-3
Shrew Creek—stream WA-9
Shrew Creek Trail—trail WA-9
Shrewder—locale OK-5
Shrew Lake—lake AK-9
Shrewsburg Spring—spring CA-9
Shrewsbury—locale LA-4
**Shrewsbury**—pop pl KY-4
**Shrewsbury**—pop pl MA-1
**Shrewsbury**—pop pl MO-7
**Shrewsbury**—pop pl (2) NJ-2
**Shrewsbury**—pop pl PA-2
**Shrewsbury**—pop pl VT-1
**Shrewsbury**—pop pl WV-2
Shrewsbury, Samuel, Sr., House—hist pl WV-2
Shrewsbury Bay—bay NJ-2
Shrewsbury Borough—civil PA-2
Shrewsbury Branch—stream WV-2
Shrewsbury Cem—cemetery IL-6
Shrewsbury Centre MA-1
Shrewsbury Ch—church MD-2
Shrewsbury Church—hist pl MD-2
Shrewsbury Gulch—valley CO-8
Shrewsbury Hist Dist—hist pl MA-1
Shrewsbury Hist Dist—hist pl NJ-2
Shrewsbury Hist Dist—hist pl PA-2
Shrewsbury Hollow—valley WV-2
Shrewsbury HS—school MA-1
Shrewsbury JHS—school MA-1
Shrewsbury Neck—cape MD-2
Shrewsbury Peak—summit VT-1
Shrewsbury River NJ-2
Shrewsbury River—stream NJ-2
**Shrewsbury Road**—pop pl NJ-2
Shrewsbury Rocks—bar NJ-2
Shrewsbury Round Barn—hist pl ME-1
Shrewsbury Sch—school NJ-2
**Shrewsbury Station**—pop pl PA-2
**Shrewsbury Street (subdivision)**—pop pl MA-1
**Shrewsbury (Town of)**—pop pl MA-1
**Shrewsbury (Town of)**—pop pl VT-1
Shrewsbury Township—civil PA-2
Shrewsbury Township Hall—hist pl NJ-2
**Shrewsbury (Township of)**—pop pl NJ-2
**Shrewsbury (Township of)**—pop pl (3) PA-2
Shride House—hist pl AZ-5
Shriek Dam—dam ND-7
Shrike Lake—lake MN-6
Shrikes Branch IN-6
Shrimp Bay—bay AK-9
Shrimp Bayou—stream LA-4
Shrimp Bayou—stream MS-4
Shrimp Creek—stream GA-3
Shrimp Hill—summit PA-2
Shrimp Lagoon—lake LA-4
Shrimp Lake—lake MT-8
Shrimp Lake—lake WY-8
Shrimplin Creek—stream OH-6
Shrine, The—locale RI-1
Shrine and Lawler Schools—school TN-4
Shrine Auditorium—building CA-9
**Shrine Beach**—pop pl WA-9
Shrine Bldg—hist pl TN-4
Shrine Club Lake Dam—dam MS-4
Shrine Creek—stream AK-9
Shrine Hill Park—park VA-3
Shrine HS—school MI-6

*Shrine Lake* ... FL-3
Shrine Mine—*mine* ... NM-5
Shrine Mont Church Camp—*locale* ... VA-3
Shrine Mtn—*summit* ... CO-8
Shrine Of Maria-Poch—*other* ... OH-6
Shrine of Memorial Mausoleum—*cemetery* ... UT-8
Shrine of Our Lady of Sorrows—*hist pl* ... MO-7
Shrine of Saint Jude Catholic Ch—*church* ... DE-2
Shrine of Saint Patrick—*church* ... MO-7
Shrine of Saint Terese—*church* ... AK-9
Shrine of the Immaculate Conception—*church* ... DC-2
Shrine of the Immaculate Conception—*hist pl* ... GA-3
Shrine of the Little Flower Sch—*school* ... MD-2
Shrine of the Little Flower Sch—*school* ... MI-6
Shrine of the Sacred Heart—*church* ... DC-2
Shrine Park—*park* ... KS-7
Shrine Park—*park* ... NE-7
Shrine Park—*park* ... OH-6
Shrine Pass—*gap* ... CO-8
Shriner Ditch—*canal* ... OH-6
Shriner Draw—*valley* ... WY-8
Shriner Hosp—*hospital* ... MO-7
Shriner-Ketcham House—*hist pl* ... MI-6
Shriner Knob—*summit* ... WV-2
Shriner Lake—*lake* ... CA-9
Shriner Lake—*lake* ... IN-6
Shriner Lake—*lake* ... WA-9
Shriner Mtn—*summit* ... PA-2
Shriner Peak—*summit* ... WA-9
Shriner Sch—*school* ... IL-6
*Shriners Crippled Childrens Hospital* ... UT-8
Shriners Hosp—*hospital* ... CA-9
Shriners Hosp—*hospital* ... KY-4
Shriners Hosp—*hospital* ... MA-1
Shriners Hosp—*hospital* ... MO-7
Shriners Hosp—*hospital* ... PA-2
Shriners Hosp—*hospital* ... UT-8
Shriners Hosp for Crippled Children—*hospital* ... FL-3
Shriners Knob—*summit* ... PA-2
Shrine Sch—*school* ... AL-4
Shrink Hollow—*valley* ... PA-2
*Shriock Run* ... PA-2
**Shriver**—*pop pl* ... WV-2
Shriver Airp—*airport* ... PA-2
Shriver Cem—*cemetery* ... IA-7
Shriver Cem—*cemetery* ... PA-2
Shriver Cem—*cemetery* (3) ... WV-2
Shriver Covered Bridge—*hist pl* ... PA-2
Shriver Creek—*stream* ... GA-3
Shriver Farmstead—*hist pl* ... IL-6
Shriver House—*hist pl* ... IL-6
Shriver-Johnson Bldg—*hist pl* ... SD-7
Shriver Ridge—*ridge* ... MD-2
Shriver Ridge—*ridge* (2) ... PA-2
Shriver Run—*stream* (3) ... WV-2
**Shrivers Corners**—*pop pl* ... PA-2
Shrivers Run—*stream* ... WV-2
*Shrives* ... AR-4
Shrives Spring—*spring* ... ID-8
*Shrock* ... IN-6
Shrock—*locale* ... OR-9
Shrock Cem—*cemetery* ... IN-6
Shrock Ch—*church* ... MS-4
Shrock Creek—*stream* ... IN-6
*Shrock Ditch* ... IN-6
Shrock Ditch—*canal* ... IN-6
Shrock Draw—*valley* ... WA-9
**Shrock (historical)**—*pop pl* ... MS-4
Shrock House—*hist pl* ... MS-4
*Shrock Methodist Church* ... MS-4
Shrock Post Office (historical)—*building* ... MS-4
Shrock Sch (historical)—*school* ... MS-4
Shroder Creek—*stream* ... MT-8
Shroder Rsvr—*reservoir* ... OR-9
Shroder Tank—*reservoir* ... AZ-5
Shroder Waterhole—*lake* ... OR-9
*Shroeder Rsvr* ... OR-9
*Shroenrock Lake* ... WI-6
Shrontz Cem—*cemetery* ... IL-6
Shropshire Cem—*cemetery* ... MS-4
Shropshire Cem—*cemetery* ... TN-4
Shropshire Ditch—*canal* ... CO-8
Shropshire Farm—*hist pl* ... KY-4
Shropshire Hollow—*valley* ... TN-4
Shropshire House—*hist pl* ... KY-4
Shropshire Valley—*valley* ... OK-5
Shroud Ridge—*ridge* ... WV-2
Shrouds Creek—*stream* ... VA-3
Shrout Cem—*cemetery* ... KY-4
Shrout Hollow—*valley* ... KY-4
Shroyer—*locale* ... KS-7
Shroyer Lake—*lake* ... ND-7
Shroyer Mtn—*summit* ... CA-9
Shroyer Ranch—*locale* ... TX-5
Shroyer Ridge—*ridge* ... OR-9
Shroy Meadows—*swamp* ... OR-9
Shrub—*locale* ... CA-9
Shrub Branch—*stream* ... MS-4
Shrub Branch—*stream* ... SC-3
Shrub Branch Ch—*church* ... SC-3
Shrubby Island—*island* ... AK-9
Shrub Hill—*summit* ... RI-1
Shrub Islet—*island* ... AK-9
**Shrub Oak**—*pop pl* ... NY-2
Shrub Oak Brook—*stream* ... NY-2
Shrub Pocosin—*swamp* ... VA-3
*Shrug Nakya* ... AZ-5
Shrum—*locale* ... MO-7
*Shrum Branch* ... TN-4
Shrum Branch—*stream* ... MO-7
Shrum Cem—*cemetery* ... MO-7
Shrum Cem—*cemetery* ... TN-4
Shrum Creek—*stream* ... MO-7
Shrum Hollow—*valley* ... TN-4
Shrum Sch (abandoned)—*school* ... MO-7
Shryack, Frederick, House—*hist pl* ... KY-4
Shryack Sch—*school* ... WY-8
Shryers Bluff—*cliff* ... MO-7
**Shryock**—*pop pl* ... WV-2
Shryock Run—*stream* ... PA-2
Shryock Sch—*school* ... KY-4
Shuart Drain—*stream* ... MI-6
Shubael Pond—*lake* ... MA-1
*Shubart Pond* ... MA-1
**Shubel (historical)**—*pop pl* ... OR-9
Shubelik Mountains—*range* ... AK-9
Shubell Park—*park* ... MI-6
Shubel Sch—*school* ... OR-9
**Shubert**—*pop pl* ... NE-7
**Shubert**—*pop pl* ... TN-4
Shubert, Sam S., Theatre—*hist pl* ... MA-1
Shubert Lake—*lake* ... NE-7
Shubert Post Office (historical)—*building* ... TN-4
Shubert Sch—*school* ... NY-2
Shuberts Lake—*lake* ... MI-6
Shubert Theatre—*building* ... MA-1
Shublik Island—*island* ... AK-9
Shublik Mountains—*range* ... AK-9
Shubra Canal—*canal* ... SC-3
Shubrick Peak—*summit* ... CA-9
Shubrick Rock—*island* ... CA-9
**Shubuta**—*pop pl* ... MS-4
Shubuta Bridge—*hist pl* ... MS-4
Shubuta Cem—*cemetery* ... MS-4
Shubuta Creek—*stream* ... MS-4
Shubuta Oil Field—*oilfield* ... MS-4
Shubuta Sch—*school* ... MS-4
*Shuceelah Creek* ... MS-4
*Shuch Creek* ... PA-2
Shuck Cem—*cemetery* ... IN-6
Shuck Cem—*cemetery* ... WV-2
*Shuck Creek* ... PA-2
Shuck Creek—*stream* ... ID-8
Shuck Creek—*stream* ... KY-4
Shuck Creek Sch—*school* ... KY-4
Shuckhart Lake—*lake* ... MN-6
Shucking Tank—*reservoir* ... AZ-5
Shuck Island—*island* ... IL-6
Shuckleford Run—*stream* ... WV-2
Shuckman Canyon—*valley* ... CA-9
Shuck Mtn—*summit* ... OR-9
Shuckpen Gap—*gap* ... NC-3
Shuck Ridge—*ridge* ... NC-3
Shuck Ridge Creek—*stream* ... NC-3
Shuck Saddle—*gap* ... ID-8
Shuckstack—*summit* ... NC-3
Shuckstack Ridge—*ridge* ... NC-3
Shuck State Wildlife Mngmt Area—*park* ... MN-6
Shucktown—*locale* ... MS-4
**Shucktown**—*pop pl* ... MS-4
Shucky Bean Hollow—*valley* ... KY-4
Shudlick Park—*park* ... WI-6
Shueble Creek—*stream* ... OR-9
Shue Creek—*stream* ... SD-7
Shue Creek Cem—*cemetery* ... SD-7
Shue Creek Township (historical)—*civil* ... SD-7
Shuemate Cem—*cemetery* ... TN-4
Shues Bluff Ch—*church* ... WV-2
Shuetown—*locale* ... NY-2
Shuey, Lewis, House—*hist pl* ... VA-3
Shuey Ditch—*canal* ... IN-6
Shuey Lake—*reservoir* ... PA-2
Shuey Lake Dam—*dam* ... PA-2
Shuey's Mill—*hist pl* ... OH-6
**Shueyville**—*pop pl* ... IA-7
Shueyville Cem—*cemetery* ... IA-7
Shufeldt Lake—*lake* ... NM-5
Shufeldt Ridge—*ridge* ... MT-8
Shufelt Hollow—*valley* ... PA-2
*Shuferville* ... MS-4
Shuff Branch—*stream* ... KY-4
**Shuffelt Acres (subdivision)**—*pop pl* ... DE-2
Shuff Hollow—*valley* ... WV-2
Shuffield Lake—*lake* ... AR-4
*Shuff Lake* ... AL-4
Shuffle Branch—*stream* ... VA-3
*Shuffle Creek* ... TN-4
Shuffle Creek—*stream* ... IN-6
Shuffle Creek—*stream* ... TX-5
Shuffle Ridge—*ridge* ... VA-3
**Shuffletown**—*pop pl* ... NC-3
*Shuffordville* ... MS-4
Shuffs Tank—*reservoir* ... AZ-5
*Shu Fly* ... AL-4
**Shuford**—*pop pl* ... MS-4
**Shuford**—*pop pl* ... NC-3
Shuford Creek—*stream* ... NC-3
Shuford House—*hist pl* ... NC-3
Shuford Mills Dam—*dam* ... NC-3
Shuford Mills Lake—*reservoir* ... NC-3
Shuford Mtn—*summit* ... NC-3
Shuford Pond—*reservoir* ... NC-3
Shuford Post Office (historical)—*building* ... MS-4
Shuford Sch—*school* ... NC-3
Shufords Fishing Lake—*reservoir* ... NC-3
Shufords Lake Dam—*dam* ... NC-3
*Shufordsville* ... MS-4
Shufordsville Cem—*cemetery* ... MS-4
Shugars Ditch—*canal* ... OH-6
Shugart JHS—*school* ... MD-2
Shugart Springs—*spring* ... AL-4
Shug Mtn—*summit* ... TN-4
Shugnaurohu Island—*island* ... FM-9
*Shugrud Coulee* ... WI-6
Shugru Hill—*summit* ... CA-9
Shugru Rsvr—*reservoir* ... CA-9
Shuhart Creek—*stream* ... IL-6
*Shukamutcha River* ... MS-4
Shukash Butte—*summit* ... OR-9
Shukok Creek—*stream* ... AK-9
*Shukoklu Creek* ... AK-9
Shukokluk Creek—*stream* ... AK-9
Shuksan, Mount—*summit* ... WA-9
Shuksan Arm—*bay* ... WA-9
Shuksan Creek—*stream* ... WA-9
Shuksan Lake—*lake* ... WA-9
Shuktusa Creek—*stream* ... AK-9
**Shula Grove (historical)**—*pop pl* ... MS-4
Shulakpachak Peak—*summit* ... AK-9
Shular Canyon—*valley* ... TX-5
Shular Hollow—*valley* ... VA-3
Shuld Branch—*stream* ... MO-7
Shule, Peter Paul, Barn—*hist pl* ... TN-4
Shuler—*locale* ... AR-4
**Shuler**—*pop pl* ... SC-3
Shuler Bay—*swamp* ... FL-3
Shuler Bend—*bend* ... OK-5
Shuler Branch—*stream* ... FL-3
Shuler Branch—*stream* ... NC-3
Shuler Branch—*stream* ... TN-4
Shuler Canyon—*valley* ... CA-9
Shuler Cem—*cemetery* ... VA-3
Shuler Cove—*valley* ... NC-3
Shuler Creek—*stream* ... NC-3
Shuler Creek—*stream* ... TN-4
Shuler Drain—*canal* ... MI-6
Shuler Draw—*valley* ... WY-8
Shuler Gap—*gap* ... GA-3
Shuler Gap—*gap* ... NC-3
Shuler Hollow—*valley* ... KY-4
Shuler Island—*island* ... VA-3
Shuler JHS—*school* ... OH-6
*Shuler Lake* ... NC-3
Shuler Lake—*lake* ... MI-6
*Shuler Lake Dam* ... NC-3
Shuler Mtn—*summit* ... NC-3
Shuler Oil And Gas Field—*oilfield* ... AR-4
Shulers Ruby Mine—*mine* ... NC-3
Shulerville—*locale* ... SC-3
Shule Sch—*school* ... IL-6
Shulin Lake—*lake* ... AK-9
Shull, Henry, Farmhouse Inn—*hist pl* ... IN-6
Shullbred Point—*cape* ... SC-3
Shull Cem—*cemetery* ... MO-7
Shull Cem—*cemetery* (2) ... NC-3
Shull Cem—*cemetery* ... TN-4
*Shull Creek* ... OK-5
Shull Creek—*stream* ... WA-9
Shull-David Elem Sch—*school* ... PA-2
Shull Drain—*stream* ... MI-6
Shull House—*hist pl* ... AR-4
Shull Island—*island* ... SC-3
Shull Lake—*lake* ... WA-9
Shull Lateral—*canal* ... ID-8
Shull-Lugenbuhl Farm—*hist pl* ... OH-6
Shull Mtn—*summit* ... WA-9
Shull Run—*stream* ... PA-2
*Shulls* ... NC-3
Shulls Airp—*airport* ... PA-2
**Shullsburg**—*pop pl* ... WI-6
Shullsburg Branch—*stream* ... WI-6
**Shullsburg (Town of)**—*pop pl* ... WI-6
Shull Sch—*school* ... IL-6
**Shulls Mill**—*pop pl* ... NC-3
*Shulls Mills* ... NC-3
**Shulls Mills**—*pop pl* ... NC-3
Shulls Pond—*reservoir* ... SC-3
*Shulls Run* ... PA-2
*Shull's Urban Estates* ... IL-6
Shulough Post Office (historical)—*building* ... AL-4
Shultas Cem—*cemetery* ... NY-2
Shulte Cem—*cemetery* ... MO-7
Shulte Creek—*stream* ... OR-9
Shulters and Stubbs Drain—*canal* ... MI-6
Shulte Spring—*spring* ... AZ-5
**Shultis Corners**—*pop pl* ... NY-2
**Shults**—*pop pl* ... OK-5
Shults Cem—*cemetery* ... NY-2
*Shults Ditch* ... IN-6
Shults Grove Ch—*church* ... TN-4
Shults Hill—*summit* ... NY-2
Shults Memorial Chapel—*church* ... IN-6
Shults Ranch—*locale* ... CA-9
Shults Spring—*spring* ... AZ-5
*Shultys Landing* ... AL-4
*Shultz* ... AZ-5
*Shultz* ... MI-6
*Shultz* ... WI-6
Shultz Cem—*cemetery* ... PA-2
Shultz Cem—*cemetery* ... TN-4
*Shultz Creek* ... AL-4
*Shultz Creek* ... IN-6
Shultz Creek—*stream* (2) ... OR-9
Shultz Creek—*stream* ... PA-2
Shultz Creek—*stream* ... WA-9
Shultz Creek—*stream* ... WI-6
Shultz Ford—*locale* ... MO-7
Shultz-Funk Site (36LA7 and 36LA9)—*hist pl* ... PA-2
Shultz-Lewis Childrens Home—*school* ... IN-6
*Shultz Mine* ... AZ-5
Shultz Mtn—*summit* ... CA-9
Shultz Pond—*lake* ... CT-1
Shultz Ranch—*locale* ... WY-8
Shultz Ridge—*ridge* ... PA-2
Shultz Sch—*school* ... MI-6
Shultz Sch Number 2 (historical)—*school* ... SD-7
Shultz Shoemaker Shop—*building* ... NC-3
Shultz Spring—*spring* ... AZ-5
Shultztown—*locale* ... KY-4
Shultztown Cem—*cemetery* ... KY-4
*Shultzville* ... PA-2
Shulunuruk Creek—*stream* ... AK-9
Shumac Ch—*church* ... VA-3
*Shumacher Creek* ... TX-5
Shumacher Ditch—*canal* ... IN-6
Shumacher Rsvr Number Five—*reservoir* ... OR-9
Shumacher Sch—*school* ... OH-6
Shumagin Bank—*other* ... AK-9
Shumagin Islands—*island* ... AK-9
Shumake Knoll—*summit* ... CA-9
Shumaker—*locale* ... AR-4
Shumaker Branch—*stream* (2) ... AL-4
Shumaker Branch—*stream* ... AR-4
Shumaker Branch—*stream* ... TN-4
Shumaker Cem—*cemetery* ... IN-6
Shumaker Cem—*cemetery* ... PA-2
Shumaker Cem—*cemetery* ... TN-4
Shumaker Creek—*stream* ... WA-9
Shumaker Crossing—*locale* ... NY-2
*Shumaker Dam* ... SD-7
Shumaker Hill—*summit* ... IN-6
Shumaker Hollow—*valley* ... TN-4
Shumaker-Lewis House—*hist pl* ... WV-2
Shumaker Mtn—*summit* ... NC-3
*Shumaker Park* ... AR-4
Shumaker Ridge—*ridge* ... IN-6
Shumaker Ridge—*ridge* ... KY-4
Shumaker Sch—*school* ... OH-6
Shumaker (Unorganized Territory of)—*unorg* ... AR-4
Shuman—*locale* ... CA-9
Shuman, Mount—*summit* ... AK-9
Shuman Canyon—*valley* ... CA-9
Shuman Canyon—*valley* ... OR-9
Shuman Cem—*cemetery* ... NY-2
Shuman Cem—*cemetery* ... ND-7
Shuman Cem—*cemetery* ... WV-2
Shuman Gulch—*valley* ... UT-8
Shuman House—*locale* ... AK-9
Shuman Lake—*lake* (2) ... AK-9
Shuman Point—*locale* ... PA-2
Shuman Pond—*reservoir* ... GA-3
Shuman Run—*stream* ... PA-2
Shuman Run—*stream* ... WV-2
**Shumans**—*pop pl* ... PA-2
Shumans Lake—*lake* ... PA-2
Shumans Run—*stream* ... PA-2
Shumans Store—*locale* ... SC-3
Shumansville—*locale* ... VA-3
*Shumantown* ... PA-2
Shuman Town Hall—*building* ... ND-7
**Shuman Township**—*pop pl* ... ND-7
Shumard Canyon—*valley* ... TX-5
Shumard Peak—*summit* ... TX-5
Shumate—*locale* ... VA-3
Shumate Branch—*stream* ... KY-4
Shumate Branch—*stream* ... MO-7
Shumate Branch—*stream* ... SC-3
Shumate Cem—*cemetery* ... AR-4
Shumate Cem—*cemetery* ... KY-4
Shumate Cem—*cemetery* ... MO-7
Shumate Cem—*cemetery* ... NC-3
Shumate Cem—*cemetery* ... WV-2
Shumate Chapel—*church* ... WV-2
Shumate Creek—*stream* ... AR-4
Shumate Creek—*stream* ... WV-2
Shumate Gap—*gap* ... VA-3
Shumate Gap—*gap* ... WV-2
Shumate Hollow—*valley* ... WV-2
Shumate Mtn—*summit* ... AL-4
Shumate Sch—*school* ... WV-2
Shumatuscacant River—*stream* ... MA-1
*Shumay* ... AZ-5
*Shumbola Creek* ... AL-4
Shumla—*locale* ... TX-5
**Shumla**—*pop pl* ... NY-2
Shumla Bend—*bend* ... TX-5
Shumla Falls—*falls* ... NY-2
Shumocher Creek—*stream* ... WA-9
Shumold Lake—*lake* ... FL-3
*Shumold Pond* ... FL-3
Shumont—*locale* ... NC-3
Shumont Mtn—*summit* ... NC-3
Shumpert Cem—*cemetery* ... MS-4
Shumpert Pond—*reservoir* ... SC-3
*Shumperts Millpond* ... SC-3
Shump Gulch—*valley* ... OR-9
*Shumula Creek* ... AL-4
Shumulla Creek—*stream* ... AL-4
*Shumullah Creek* ... AL-4
*Shumultah Creek* ... AL-4
Shumunkanuc Hill—*summit* ... RI-1
*Shumunkanug Hill* ... RI-1
*Shumunkauvg Hill* ... RI-1
*Shumuthpa* ... AZ-5
*Shumuthpa Spring* ... AZ-5
Shumway—*locale* ... CA-9
**Shumway**—*pop pl* ... AZ-5
**Shumway**—*pop pl* ... IL-6
Shumway Arroyo—*stream* ... NM-5
Shumway Block—*hist pl* ... MA-1
Shumway Butte—*summit* ... AZ-5
*Shumway Canyon* ... UT-8
Shumway Canyon—*valley* ... UT-8
Shumway Cem—*cemetery* ... AZ-5
Shumway Cem—*cemetery* ... KS-7
Shumway Cem—*cemetery* ... PA-2
Shumway Creek—*stream* ... OR-9
Shumway Dam—*dam* ... OR-9
Shumway Flat—*flat* ... CA-9
Shumway Hall and Morgan Refectory-Shattuck Sch—*hist pl* ... MN-6
Shumway Hill—*summit* ... NY-2
Shumway Hill—*summit* ... PA-2
Shumway Hollow—*valley* ... OH-6
Shumway JHS—*school* ... WA-9
Shumway Lake—*lake* ... MN-6
Shumway Lake—*lake* ... WI-6
Shumway Lake—*reservoir* ... OR-9
Shumway Meadow—*flat* ... OR-9
Shumway Oil Field—*oilfield* ... KS-7
Shumway Point—*ridge* ... UT-8
Shumway Ranch—*locale* ... CA-9
Shumway Ranch—*locale* ... OR-9
*Shumway Ridge* ... UT-8
Shumway Rsvr—*reservoir* ... OR-9
Shumway Sch—*hist pl* ... AZ-5
Shumway Sch—*school* ... WI-6
Shumway Tank—*reservoir* ... AZ-5
Shunck Run—*stream* ... PA-2
Shunem—*locale* ... IA-7
Shunem Cem—*cemetery* ... IA-7
Shunem Ch (historical)—*church* ... TN-4
Shunenberg Creek—*stream* ... WI-6
Shunenberg Lake—*lake* ... WI-6
Shunenberg Springs—*spring* ... WI-6
Shunesburg—*locale* ... UT-8
Shunesburg Mail Trail—*trail* ... UT-8
Shunesburg Mtn—*summit* ... UT-8
Shunes Creek—*stream* ... UT-8
Shunes Hollow—*valley* ... UT-8
Shunga Glen Park—*park* ... KS-7
Shunganunga Creek—*stream* ... KS-7
**Shungnak**—*pop pl* ... AK-9
Shungnak Mtn—*summit* ... AK-9
Shungnak River—*stream* ... AK-9
Shungnak Village—*other* ... AK-9
*Shungopovi* ... AZ-5
*Shungopovi Spring* ... AZ-5
**Shunk**—*pop pl* ... OH-6
**Shunk**—*pop pl* ... PA-2
Shunk (abandoned)—*school* ... PA-2
*Shunka Creek* ... ND-7
*Shunock Branch* ... CT-1
Shunock River—*stream* ... CT-1
Shunpike—*locale* ... NY-2
*Shun-ta-nesh-nanga* ... KS-7
Shuntavi Butte—*summit* ... UT-8
Shunway Brook—*stream* ... CT-1
Shupac Lake—*lake* ... MI-6
Shupak Ditch—*canal* ... MT-8
Shupak Ponds—*reservoir* ... MT-8
Shupe—*locale* ... VA-3
Shupe Airp—*airport* ... KS-7
Shupe Ave Sch—*school* ... OH-6
Shupe Branch—*stream* ... VA-3
Shupe Creek—*stream* ... VA-3
Shupe Drain—*canal* ... MI-6
Shupe Hollow—*valley* ... KY-4
Shupe Hollow—*valley* ... VA-3
*Shupe Raymond Addition Subdivision* ... UT-8
Shupe Run—*stream* ... PA-2
Shupe-Williams Candy Company Factory—*hist pl* ... UT-8
**Shupings Mill**—*pop pl* ... NC-3
Shuping's Mill Complex—*hist pl* ... NC-3
Shupp Hill—*summit* ... PA-2
Shuppy Cem—*cemetery* ... IA-7
**Shuqualak**—*pop pl* ... MS-4
Shuqualak Cem—*cemetery* ... MS-4
Shuqualak Creek—*stream* ... MS-4
Shuqualak Female Acad (historical)—*school* ... MS-4
**Shuqualak (RR name Shuqulak)**—*pop pl* ... MS-4
Shuqulak (RR name for Shuqualak)—*other* ... MS-4
Shurdan Creek—*stream* ... KY-4
Shurd Lakes—*lake* ... MN-6
Shuree Creek—*stream* ... NM-5
Shuree Lodge—*locale* ... NM-5
Shurin Cem—*cemetery* ... MS-4
Shurley Cem—*cemetery* ... AR-4
Shurley Draw—*valley* ... TX-5
Shurley Oil Field—*oilfield* ... WY-8
Shurlington—*uninc pl* ... GA-3
Shurls Pond Dam—*dam* ... MS-4
Shurly Sch—*school* ... MI-6
Shurn Creek—*stream* ... IN-6
*Shurongan Island* ... MP-9
Shurongan Island—*island* ... MP-9
Shurr Cem—*cemetery* ... IN-6
Shurtleff—*locale* ... NY-2
Shurtleff, Jonas R., House—*hist pl* ... ME-1
Shurtleff Brook—*stream* ... MA-1
Shurtleff Corners—*locale* ... NY-2
Shurtleff Creek—*stream* ... WY-8
Shurtleff Park—*park* ... MA-1
Shurtleff Sch (Chelsea)—*school* ... MA-1
Shurtleff Sch (Revere)—*school* ... MA-1
Shurtlett Spring—*spring* ... AZ-5
Shurtliff Canyon—*valley* ... ID-8
Shurtliff Spring—*spring* ... WY-8
Shurts Sch—*school* ... IL-6
Shurtz Bush—*area* ... UT-8
Shurtz Bush Creek—*stream* ... UT-8
*Shurtz Canyon* ... UT-8
Shurtz Canyon—*valley* ... UT-8
*Shurtz Creek* ... UT-8
Shurtzer Drain—*stream* ... MI-6
Shurtz Field—*flat* ... OR-9
Shurtz Lake—*lake* ... UT-8
Shushalluk Creek—*stream* ... AK-9
**Shushan**—*pop pl* ... NY-2
Shushan Covered Bridge—*hist pl* ... NY-2
Shush Be Tou—*reservoir* ... AZ-5
Shush Be Tou Campgrounds—*park* ... AZ-5
Shush Be Tou Dam—*dam* ... AZ-5
Shush Bezahze—*reservoir* ... AZ-5
Shush Bezahze Campgrounds—*park* ... AZ-5
Shush Bezahze Dam—*dam* ... AZ-5
Shushuskin Canyon—*valley* ... WA-9
*Shuster* ... AL-4
*Shuster* ... OR-9
Shuster Pond—*lake* ... NJ-2
*Shuster Ranch* ... OR-9
*Shuster Spring* ... OR-9
Shuster Spring—*spring* ... NM-5
Shusters Sch—*school* ... PA-2
Shu Swamp—*swamp* ... NY-2
Shutdown Mtn—*summit* ... ME-1
Shute, Thomas, House—*hist pl* ... TN-4
Shute Airp—*airport* ... KS-7
Shute Branch—*stream* ... NC-3
Shute Cove—*valley* ... NC-3
Shute Creek—*stream* ... WY-8
Shute Creek Lake—*lake* ... WY-8
*Shute Island* ... MD-2
Shute Mtn—*summit* ... CA-9
Shute Octagon House—*hist pl* ... NY-2
Shute Park—*park* ... OR-9
Shute Point—*cape* ... UT-8
Shuter Cem—*cemetery* ... OH-6
Shute Road Well—*well* ... AZ-5
*Shuters Hill* ... VA-3
**Shutersville (historical)**—*pop pl* ... MS-4
*Shutes Branch* ... TN-4
Shutes Branch Access Area—*park* ... TN-4
Shutes Branch Rec Area—*park* ... TN-4
**Shutesbury**—*pop pl* ... MA-1
Shutesbury Center Sch—*school* ... MA-1
*Shutesbury Centre* ... MA-1
Shutesbury State For—*forest* ... MA-1
**Shutesbury (Town of)**—*pop pl* ... MA-1
Shutes Cem—*cemetery* ... MS-4
Shute Sch—*school* ... IL-6
Shutes Folly Island—*island* ... SC-3
*Shute Spring* ... AZ-5
Shute Springs—*spring* ... AZ-5
Shute Springs Creek—*stream* ... AZ-5
Shutes Run—*stream* ... PA-2
**Shuteston**—*pop pl* ... LA-4
Shuteston Oil and Gas Field—*oilfield* ... LA-4
Shute Tank—*reservoir* ... AZ-5
Shute Tank Number Two—*reservoir* ... AZ-5
Shutetown Creek—*stream* ... CO-8
Shuteye Creek—*stream* ... CA-9
Shut Eye Creek—*stream* ... MS-4
Shuteye Creek—*stream* ... MO-7
Shuteye Pass—*gap* ... CA-9
Shuteye Peak—*summit* ... CA-9
Shutgart Spring—*spring* ... PA-2
Shut Hollow—*valley* ... TN-4
Shut-In, The—*summit* ... TX-5
Shut-in Branch—*stream* ... AR-4
Shut-In Branch—*stream* ... KY-4
Shut-in Branch—*stream* ... NC-3
Shut-in Canyon—*valley* ... ID-8
Shut-in Creek—*stream* ... GA-3
Shutin Creek—*stream* ... MO-7
Shut-in Creek—*stream* ... MO-7
Shut-In Creek—*stream* (2) ... NC-3
Shut-in Creek—*stream* ... TN-4
Shut-In Gap—*gap* ... NC-3
Shut In Gap—*gap* ... TN-4
Shut-In Hollow—*valley* ... MO-7
Shut-in Hollow—*valley* ... TX-5
Shut-In Mtn—*summit* ... AR-4
Shut-In Mtn—*summit* ... MO-7
Shut-in Ridge—*ridge* (2) ... NC-3
Shut-Ins—*other* (2) ... MO-7
Shut In Shoals—*bar* ... TN-4
Shutispear Creek—*stream* ... MS-4
**Shutleff Corner**—*pop pl* ... MA-1
Shutler—*locale* ... OR-9
Shutler Flat—*flat* ... OR-9
*Shutlers* ... OR-9
Shutman Path—*trail* ... PA-2
Shutoff, The—*gap* ... UT-8
Shutt Cem—*cemetery* ... KY-4
Shutter Arm—*bay* ... OR-9
**Shutter Corners**—*pop pl* ... NY-2
Shutter Creek—*stream* ... OR-9
Shutter Landing—*locale* ... OR-9
Shutterly Mill—*other* ... VA-3
Shutters Cem—*cemetery* ... VA-3
Shuttle Meadow Golf Club—*other* ... CT-1
Shuttle Meadow Pond—*lake* ... CT-1
Shuttle Meadow Rsvr—*reservoir* ... CT-1
*Shuttler* ... OR-9
Shuttlesworth Cem—*cemetery* ... AL-4
*Shuttleton* ... PA-2
Shuttleworth Corners—*locale* ... NY-2
Shuttpelz Lake—*lake* ... OR-9
Shutts Cem—*cemetery* ... IN-6
Shutts Chapel—*church* ... KY-4
Shutts Corners—*locale* ... NY-2
Shutts Flats—*flat* ... WY-8
Shutts Hill—*summit* ... NY-2
Shutts Prong—*stream* ... TN-4
Shutz Sch—*school* ... PA-2
*Shuunakia* ... AZ-5
Shuwah—*locale* ... WA-9
Shuwah Creek—*stream* ... WA-9
Shuyak Harbor—*bay* ... AK-9
Shuyak Island—*island* ... AK-9
Shuyak Radio Communication Center—*locale* ... AK-9
Shuyak Strait—*channel* ... AK-9
Shuyler Creek—*stream* ... MO-7
Shwab House—*hist pl* ... KY-4
Shwab Sch—*school* ... TN-4
Shweeash Creek—*stream* ... OR-9
Shwin Ranch—*locale* ... NV-8
*Shy Beaver* ... PA-2
**Shy Beaver**—*pop pl* ... PA-2
Shy Beaver Access Area—*area* ... PA-2
Shy Beaver Creek—*stream* ... PA-2
Shy Beaver Pond—*lake* ... ME-1
*Shy Bever Boat Launch* ... PA-2
Shy Cem—*cemetery* ... MO-7
Shy Corner—*locale* ... ME-1
Shy Creek—*stream* ... OR-9
*Shy Ditch* ... IN-6
*Shyenne River* ... SD-7
*Shyenne River* ... WY-8
Shyes Cem—*cemetery* ... TN-4
Shyflat Cem—*cemetery* ... KY-4
Shy Hammock Creek—*stream* ... AL-4
Shy Hammock Creek—*stream* ... MS-4
Shyhawks Island—*island* ... NJ-2
*Shyld Gulch* ... MT-8
Shylock Bar—*bar* ... AL-4
Shylock Mine—*mine* ... AZ-5
Shylock Shoals—*bar* ... AL-4
Shylo Creek—*stream* ... MT-8
Shy Mtn—*summit* ... MO-7
Shy Mug Branch—*stream* ... KY-4
Shyne Lake—*reservoir* ... SD-7
Shyne No. 27 Township—*civ div* ... SD-7
Shyne Township—*civil* ... SD-7
Shyne 1 Dam—*dam* ... SD-7
Shypkowski Ranch—*locale* ... ND-7
Shypoke State Wildlife Mngmt Area—*park* ... MN-6
Shy Pond—*lake* ... TX-5
Shyrock Gulch—*valley* ... MT-8
Shy Rsvr—*reservoir* ... MT-8
Shyster Butte—*summit* ... NV-8
Shyster Creek—*stream* ... NV-8
Shyster Spring—*spring* ... NV-8
Shyville—*locale* ... OH-6
SH 21 Bridge—*bridge* ... TX-5
Si, Mount—*summit* ... WA-9
Siah Butte—*summit* ... OR-9
Siah Creek—*stream* ... ID-8
Siah Lake—*lake* ... ID-8
Siahs Swamp—*lake* ... RI-1
*Siah Swamp* ... RI-1
Siaktak Hills—*summit* ... AK-9
**Sialat**—*pop pl* ... FM-9
Sialat, Infal—*stream* ... FM-9
*Sialatuk* ... AZ-5
Siam—*locale* ... TN-4
**Siam**—*pop pl* ... IA-7
**Siam**—*pop pl* ... OH-6
Siam Cem—*cemetery* ... IA-7
Siam Ch—*church* ... TN-4
Siam Creek—*stream* ... ID-8
Siamental Cem—*cemetery* ... SD-7
Siamese Brook—*stream* ... NY-2
Siamese Creek—*stream* ... ID-8
Siamese Lakes—*lake* ... AK-9
Siamese Lakes—*lake* ... MN-6
Siamese Lakes—*lake* ... MT-8
Siamese Legation Bldg—*building* ... DC-2
Siamese Mtn—*summit* ... NY-2
Siamese Ponds—*lake* ... NY-2
Siamese Spring—*spring* ... OR-9
Siam Hollow—*valley* ... KY-4
Siam Post Office (historical)—*building* ... TN-4
Siam Prospect—*mine* ... TN-4
Siam Sch—*school* ... MI-6
Siam Sch—*school* ... TN-4
Siam Valley—*valley* ... TN-4
*Siani* ... MS-4
Siant Gabriel Gas and Oil Field—*oilfield* ... LA-4
Siapapa Stream—*stream* ... AS-9
Siard, Bayou—*stream* ... LA-4
Siard Cabin—*locale* ... NV-8
Siard Canyon—*valley* ... NV-8
Siard Creek—*stream* ... NV-8
Siard Ranch—*locale* ... NV-8
Sias—*locale* ... WV-2
Sias Cem—*cemetery* (2) ... WV-2
**Siasconset**—*pop pl* ... MA-1
*Siasconsett* ... MA-1
Sias Point—*cape* ... MA-1
Sias Sch—*school* ... WV-2
*Siater Creek* ... AL-4
Siavlat Mtn—*summit* ... AK-9
Sibal Ranch—*locale* ... NE-7
Sibbald Corral—*locale* ... NV-8
Sibbald Run—*stream* ... PA-2

Sibbie—locale GA-3
Sibbitt Cem—cemetery NC-3
Sibeal Creek WY-8
Siberia—locale CA-9
Siberia—locale ME-1
Siberia—pop pl IN-6
Siberia—summit CA-9
Siberia Ch—church KY-4
Siberia Creek—stream CA-9
Siberia Creek—stream ID-8
Siberia Creek—stream WA-9
Siberia Creek Campground—locale CA-9
Siberia Creek Trail—trail CA-9
Siberia Creek Trail (Pack)—trail CA-9
Siberia Lake—lake CO-8
Siberia Meadows—flat ME-1
Siberian Outpost—basin CA-9
Siberian Pass—gap CA-9
Siberian Pass Creek—stream CA-9
Siberia Ridge—ridge WY-8
Sibert AL-4
Sibert—locale AL-4
Sibert—pop pl AL-4
Sibert—pop pl KY-4
Sibert-Hima (CCD)—cens area KY-4
Sibert Island—island KY-4
Sibert Lake—lake MN-6
Sibert Methodist Ch—church AL-4
Siberton—pop pl AL-4
Siberton Baptist Ch—church AL-4
Siberton Park—park AL-4
Siberts Mill (historical)—locale AL-4
Sibilant Lake—lake MN-6
Sibille Creek WY-8
Sibille-Insel MP-9
Sibilles Creek WY-8
Sibkey Spring—spring MO-7
Sibles Creek—stream IA-7
Sibleton (Sibleyton)—pop pl MS-4
Sibley MI-6
Sibley—locale GA-3
Sibley—locale TN-4
Sibley—pop pl IL-6
Sibley—pop pl IA-7
Sibley—pop pl (2) LA-4
Sibley—pop pl MS-4
Sibley—pop pl MO-7
Sibley—pop pl ND-7
Sibley, Henry H., House—hist pl MN-6
Sibley, Hiram, Homestead—hist pl NY-2
Sibley, Lake—lake IL-6
Sibley Blvd Interchange—other IL-6
Sibley Branch—stream LA-4
Sibley Branch—stream TN-4
Sibley Brook—stream CT-1
Sibley Brook—stream ME-1
Sibley Butte—summit ND-7
Sibley Butte Township—pop pl ND-7
Sibley Canyon—valley NM-5
Sibley Cem—cemetery (2) AL-4
Sibley Cem—cemetery CT-1
Sibley Cem—cemetery KS-7
Sibley Cem—cemetery (2) LA-4
Sibley Cem—cemetery ME-1
Sibley Cem—cemetery MI-6
Sibley Cem—cemetery NY-2
Sibley Cem—cemetery (2) ND-7
Sibley City AL-4
Sibley-Corcoran House—hist pl MA-1
Sibley Corner—locale ME-1
Sibley (County)—pop pl MN-6
Sibley County Courthouse and Sheriff's Residence and Jail—hist pl MN-6
Sibley County Courthouse-1879—hist pl MN-6
Sibley Creek—stream (2) AL-4
Sibley Creek—stream ID-8
Sibley Creek—stream KY-4
Sibley Creek—stream MS-4
Sibley Creek—stream OH-6
Sibley Creek—stream OR-9
Sibley Creek—stream TX-5
Sibley Creek—stream VA-3
Sibley Creek—stream WA-9
Sibley Creek—stream WY-8
Sibley Draw—valley CA-9
Sibley Draw—valley OR-9
Sibley Field—park MN-6
Sibley Ford SD-7
Sibley Gap—gap NM-5
Sibley Gas and Oil Field—oilfield LA-4
Sibley (historical)—locale KS-7
Sibley Hole—lake NM-5
Sibley Hollow—valley AR-4
Sibley Hosp—hospital DC-2
Sibley House—hist pl MI-6
Sibley HS—school MN-6
Sibley Island—island ME-1
Sibley Island Dam ND-7
Sibley Island (historical)—island ND-7
Sibley Lake—lake AL-4
Sibley Lake—lake MN-6
Sibley Lake—lake (2) ND-7
Sibley Lake—lake WY-8
Sibley Lake—reservoir KY-4
Sibley Lake—reservoir LA-4
Sibley Lake Natl Wildlife Ref—park ND-7
Sibley Memorial Hosp—hospital DC-2
Sibley Millpond—reservoir GA-3
Sibley Mtn—summit NM-5
Sibley Nature Park—park ND-7
Sibley Oil Field—oilfield MS-4
Sibley Park—park MN-6
Sibley Peak—summit WY-8
Sibley Pond—lake (2) ME-1
Sibley Pond—reservoir AL-4
Sibley Pond Dam AL-4
Sibley Ponds—reservoir MA-1
Sibley Quarry—mine MI-6
Sibley Rsvr—reservoir MA-1
Sibley Sands—bar OR-9
Sibley Sch—school IL-6
Sibley Sch—school KS-7
Sibley Sch—school (2) MI-6
Sibley Sch—school (2) MN-6
Sibley Sch (historical)—school MS-4
Sibleys Corner—pop pl MA-1
Sibleys Mill (historical)—locale AL-4
Sibley Spring—spring ID-8
Sibley State Park—park MN-6
Sibleys Trail Resort ND-7
Sibley Swamp—swamp MA-1
Sibleyton—pop pl MS-4
Sibleyton Post Office (historical)—building MS-4
Sibley Township—pop pl KS-7
Sibley Township—pop pl ND-7
Sibley (Township of)—pop pl (2) MN-6
Sibley Trail Ch—church ND-7
Sibley Trail Town Hall—building ND-7
Sibley Trail Township—pop pl ND-7
Sibley Triangle Bldg—hist pl NY-2
Sibleyville—locale KS-7
Sibleyville—pop pl NY-2
Sibleyville—pop pl PA-2
Sibleyville Corners PA-2
Sibleyville Creek—stream AL-4
Sibley Well—well NM-5
Sibley Windmill—locale NM-5
Sibo Brake—swamp TX-5
Siboco—locale OR-9
Sibole, George, Store—hist pl NM-5
Sibyl—locale AZ-5
Sibylee—locale WY-8
Sibylee Creek WY-8
Sibyl (historical)—pop pl IA-7
Sibyl Interchange—crossing AZ-5
Sibylla Atoll MP-9
Sibylla Island—island MP-9
Sibylles Creek WY-8
Sibyl RR Station—building AZ-5
Sibyl Rsvr—reservoir WY-8
Siby Spring—spring OK-5
Sicans Pond—lake NY-2
Sicard—pop pl LA-4
Sicard Flat—locale CA-9
Sicard Flat Ditch—canal CA-9
Siccowee Branch—stream TN-4
Sicely Run PA-2
Sichar Cem—cemetery OK-5
Sichimovi AZ-5
Sichomivi AZ-5
Sichomovi—pop pl AZ-5
Siciegottit—summit NV-8
Sicily—island PA-2
Sicily—pop pl IL-6
Sicily, Isle of—island FL-3
Sicily Creek—stream NE-7
Sicily Island—area LA-4
Sicily Island—pop pl LA-4
Sicily Island Cem—cemetery LA-4
Sicily Island Ch—church LA-4
Sicily Mine—mine CA-9
Sicily Run—stream PA-2
Sicily Township—pop pl NE-7
Sick Cow Spring—spring UT-8
Sick Doe Gulch—valley CA-9
Sickels Ranch (historical)—locale SD-7
Sicker Cem—cemetery NY-2
Sickfoot Creek—stream OR-9
Sickik Creek—stream AK-9
Sick Island—island (2) FL-3
Sickkibunkiaut Hill—summit RI-1
Sick Lake—lake FL-3
Sicklebar Spring—spring OR-9
Sickle Creek WY-8
Sickle Creek—stream MI-6
Sickle Creek—stream WY-8
Sickle Hill—summit WV-2
Sickle Lake WI-6
Sickle Lake—lake IN-6
Sickle Lake—lake MI-6
Sickle Pond NJ-2
Sickler Creek—stream MT-8
Sickler Dam—dam PA-2
Sickler Hill—pop pl PA-2
Sickle Ridge—ridge AL-4
Sickle Ridge Sch (abandoned)—school PA-2
Sickler Pond PA-2
Sicklers Cem—cemetery PA-2
Sicklers Mtn—summit NY-2
Sicklers Pond—reservoir PA-2
Sicklertown NJ-2
Sicklerville—pop pl NJ-2
Sicklerville (Sicklertown)—pop pl NJ-2
Sickles—pop pl MI-6
Sickles—pop pl OK-5
Sickles Corner—pop pl PA-2
Sickles Creek—stream NY-2
Sickles Drain—canal (2) MI-6
Sickles Lake—lake WI-6
Sickle Spring—spring UT-8
Sickles Tavern—hist pl MO-7
Sickley NE-7
Sickleys Corners—locale NY-2
Sickman Sch—school PA-2
Sick Rock Hollow—valley AR-4
Sicks Stadium—other WA-9
Siclehema AZ-5
Sico (historical)—locale AL-4
Sicolocco Creek—stream AL-4
Sicomac Ch—church NJ-2
S.I.C. Rsvr—reservoir OR-9
Sicseequa Creek OR-9
Sicseekqua Creek OR-9
Sicsicqua Creek OR-9
Sid KS-7
Sid—pop pl KS-7
Sid—pop pl TX-5
Sid and Charley—summit UT-8
Sid Anderson Branch—stream KY-4
Sidbert Run VA-3
Sidbury,Charlotte,House—hist pl TX-5
Sidbury Landing—locale NC-3
Sid Butte—summit ID-8
Sid Calk Lake—lake KY-4
Sid Carter Hollow—valley UT-8
Sid Creek—stream MS-4
Siddall Cem—cemetery OH-6
Siddensburg PA-2
Siddens Valley—valley AK-9
Sidderth Branch NC-3
Sid Dodd Plantation (historical)—locale MS-4
Sid Dodd Sch (historical)—school MS-4
Siddon—locale VA-3
Siddons—locale WY-8
Siddonsburg—pop pl PA-2
Siddonsville—pop pl AL-4
Siddoway Canal—canal ID-8
Siddoway Fork—stream ID-8
Siddoway Fork—stream WY-8
Siddoways Rsvr—reservoir UT-8
Sidds Landing—locale CA-9
Sideboard Bank—bar FL-3
Sidebottom Cem—cemetery KY-4
Sidebottom Cem—cemetery (2) MO-7
Sidebottom Island—island KY-4
Sideburn—locale VA-3
Sideburn Branch—stream VA-3
Side Camp—pop pl OR-9
Side Camp Spring—spring SD-7
Side Canyon—valley ID-8
Side Canyon—valley NV-8
Side Canyon—valley (3) UT-8
Side Canyon Ridge—ridge UT-8
Side Canyon Wash—arroyo NV-8
Side Channel—channel ME-1
Side Creek—stream AK-9
Side Cut Park—park OH-6
Side Ditch—canal MO-7
Sidehill Canal—canal ID-8
Sidehill Canyon—valley CO-8
Side Hill Claim—mine AZ-5
Sidehill Ditch—canal ID-8
Sidehill Ditch—canal UT-8
Sidehill Meadow—flat CA-9
Sidehill Pass—gap NV-8
Sidehill Prairie—area CA-9
Sidehill Prairie—flat CA-9
Sidehill Rsvr—reservoir CO-8
Sidehill Rsvr—reservoir OR-9
Side Hill Siphon—canal CA-9
Sidehill Spring CO-8
Side Hill Spring NV-8
Sidehill Spring—spring AZ-5
Side Hill Spring—spring CA-9
Sidehill Spring—spring CO-8
Sidehill Spring—spring (7) NV-8
Sidehill Spring—spring (3) OR-9
Sidehill Spring—spring (4) UT-8
Side Hill Spring—spring WY-8
Sidehill Spring Number Two—spring OR-9
Side Hill Springs—spring UT-8
Sidehill Tank—reservoir AZ-5
Sidehill Trail—trail ID-8
Sidehill Trail—trail MT-8
Side Hill Trail—trail NC-3
Side Hollow—valley UT-8
Side Lake—lake LA-4
Side Lake—lake MI-6
Side Lake—lake (3) MN-6
Side Lake—pop pl MN-6
Side Lake—reservoir NC-3
Side Lake Bayou—gut AL-4
Side Lake Dam—dam NC-3
Side Landing—locale VA-3
Sidel Drain—canal MI-6
Sideling Hill—ridge WV-2
Sideling Hill—summit MD-2
Sideling Hill—summit PA-2
Sideling Hill—summit VA-3
Sideling Hill Ch—church PA-2
Sideling Hill Creek PA-2
Sideling Hill Creek—stream MD-2
Sideling Hill Creek—stream (2) PA-2
Sideling Hill Plaza—locale PA-2
Sideling Hill Run—stream PA-2
Sideling Hill Tunnel—tunnel PA-2
Sideling Run WV-2
Sidell KS-7
Sidell—locale KY-4
Sidell—pop pl FL-3
Sidell—pop pl IL-6
Sidell—pop pl PA-2
Sidell Junction—pop pl IL-6
Sidell (Township of)—pop pl IL-6
Side Mtn—summit AZ-5
Sidener Cem—cemetery (3) IN-6
Sidener School Number 59 IN-6
Sidenfaden, William, House—hist pl ID-8
Sidenor Well—well NM-5
Sidensparker Pond—lake ME-1
Sidenstricker Branch—stream WV-2
Side Oat Tank—reservoir AZ-5
Side-of-Mountain Creek—stream SC-3
Side O' Th' Bay NJ-2
Side O'th' Bay—bay NJ-2
Side Pistol Lake—lake ME-1
Side Pocket Lake—lake TX-5
Side Rock Campground—park AZ-5
Side Rock Well—well AZ-5
Side Rod Camp—locale CA-9
Siders Cem—cemetery WV-2
Siders Estates—pop pl UT-8
Siders Pond—lake MA-1
Sides—pop pl PA-2
Sides Branch—stream NC-3
Sides Cem—cemetery AR-4
Sides Cem—cemetery MO-7
Sides Knoll—summit AZ-5
Sides Lake—lake AZ-5
Sides Mine (underground)—mine AL-4
Sides Place—locale TN-4
Side Spring—spring AL-4
Sides Run—stream PA-2
Sides Sch—school AL-4
Sidestown—pop pl NC-3
Sideview—locale KY-4
Sideview (historical)—pop pl TN-4
Sideview Post Office (historical)—building TN-4
Sidewalk Clock at 1501 3rd Avenue, Manhattan—hist pl NY-2
Sidewalk Clock at 161-11 Jamaica Avenue, New York, NY—hist pl NY-2
Sidewalk Clock at 200 5th Avenue, Manhattan—hist pl NY-2
Sidewalk Clock at 519 3rd Avenue, Manhattan—hist pl NY-2
Sidewalk Clock at 522 5th Avenue, Manhattan—hist pl NY-2
Sidewalk Clock at 783 5th Avenue, Manhattan—hist pl NY-2
Sidewalk Creek—stream OR-9
Sideway—locale KY-4
Sidewinder Mine—mine CA-9
Sidewinder Mtn—summit CA-9
Sidewinder Valley—valley CA-9
Sidewinder Waterhole—reservoir OR-9
Sidewinder Well—well (2) CA-9
Sidey Windmill—locale NM-5
Sidfrieds Ferry PA-2
Sid Hill—summit NC-3
Sid Hollow—valley MO-7
Sidie Hollow—valley (2) WI-6
Sidie Valley WI-6
Sidik Lake—lake AK-9
Siding CO-8
Siding A—pop pl IA-7
Siding Eleven SD-7
Siding Number 4—locale MI-6
Siding Number 5—locale MI-6
Sid Key—island FL-3
Sid Lake—lake ID-8
Sid Lake—lake MI-6
Sid Lake No 1—lake ID-8
Sid Lake No 2—lake ID-8
Sid Larson Bay—bay AK-9
Sidle Canyon—valley NM-5
Sidle Canyon—valley TX-5
Sidle Cem—cemetery OH-6
Sidle Spring—spring TX-5
Sidley—locale PA-2
Sidley Lake WA-9
Sidley Lake—lake WA-9
Sidley Lakes WA-9
Sidling Hill VA-3
Sidling Hill Sch—school OH-6
Sidling Mtn VA-3
Sid Loose Rsvr OR-9
Sid Luce Rsvr—reservoir OR-9
Sidman Cem—cemetery PA-2
Sidman (Lovett Station)—pop pl PA-2
Sidman Post Office (historical)—building PA-2
Sidman (RR name Lovett)—uninc pl PA-2
Sidmans Hill—summit NY-2
Sid-Mar—hist pl IN-6
Sidnaw—pop pl MI-6
Sidnaw Creek—stream MI-6
Sidnaw Lookout Tower—locale MI-6
Sidner Draw—valley WY-8
Sidner Flats—flat WY-8
Sidney IN-6
Sidney KS-7
Sidney NC-3
Sidney—locale AL-4
Sidney—locale CO-8
Sidney—locale KY-4
Sidney—locale MO-7
Sidney—locale NC-3
Sidney—locale PA-2
Sidney—locale SC-3
Sidney—locale TX-5
Sidney—locale WV-2
Sidney—pop pl AL-4
Sidney—pop pl AR-4
Sidney—pop pl IL-6
Sidney—pop pl IN-6
Sidney—pop pl IA-7
Sidney—pop pl ME-1
Sidney—pop pl MI-6
Sidney—pop pl MT-8
Sidney—pop pl NE-7
Sidney—pop pl NJ-2
Sidney—pop pl NY-2
Sidney—pop pl NC-3
Sidney—pop pl OH-6
Sidney—pop pl OR-9
Sidney—pop pl WI-6
Sidney, Lake—lake FL-3
Sidney, Mount—summit VA-3
Sidney Basin—basin CO-8
Sidney Bog Brook—stream ME-1
Sidney Branch—stream IN-6
Sidney Branch—stream TN-4
Sidney Branch Cem—cemetery IN-6
Sidney (CCD)—cens area KY-4
Sidney Cem—cemetery IA-7
Sidney Cem—cemetery MT-8
Sidney Center (Maywood Station)—pop pl NY-2
Sidney Ch—church ME-1
Sidney Ch—church VA-3
Sidney C Lewis Highway Bridge—bridge TN-4
Sidney Corner—other ME-1
Sidney Corners—locale NY-2
Sidney Courthouse Square Hist Dist—hist pl OH-6
Sidney C Phillips JHS—school AL-4
Sidney Creek—stream (2) AK-9
Sidney Creek—stream (2) AR-4
Sidney Creek—stream MT-8
Sidney Creek—stream NC-3
Sidney Creek—stream SD-7
Sidney Creek—stream VA-3
Sidney Creek—stream WI-6
Sidney Crossroad NC-3
Sidney Crossroads—locale NC-3
Sidney Ditch—canal OR-9
Sidney Draw—valley CO-8
Sidney Draw—valley (2) NE-7
Sidney Elem Sch—school IN-6
Sidney Flat—flat CA-9
Sidney Gulch—valley CA-9
Sidney Hill Country Club—locale MA-1
Sidney (historical)—locale KS-7
Sidney (historical)—locale ND-7
Sidney Lake—lake FL-3
Sidney Lake—lake MI-6
Sidney Lake—lake MT-8
Sidney Lanier, Lake—reservoir GA-3
Sidney Lanier Bridge—bridge (2) GA-3
Sidney Lanier Sch—school FL-3
Sidney Mine—mine MN-6
Sidney Mtn—summit NY-2
Sidney Mtn—summit TX-5
Sidney Municipal Airp—airport NE-7
Sidney Peak—summit CA-9
Sidney Peaks—summit UT-8
Sidney Potters Town NJ-2
Sidney Power Ditch—canal OR-9
Sidney Rsvr—reservoir NY-2
Sidney Run NJ-2
Sidney Rural—fmr MCD NE-7
Sidney Sch—school MO-7
Sidney Sch—school SD-7
Sidney Sch—school VA-3
Sidney (siding)—locale OR-9
Sidneys Knob—summit PA-2
Sidneys Pond—lake MA-1
Sidney (sta)—pop pl OR-9
Sidney Station OR-9
Sidney Stockdale (historical)—locale SD-7
Sidney Swamp—swamp MI-6
Sidney Top—summit NC-3
Sidney (Town of)—pop pl ME-1
Sidney (Town of)—pop pl NY-2
Sidney Township—fmr MCD IA-7
Sidney Township—pop pl ND-7
Sidney Township—pop pl SD-7
Sidney (Township of)—pop pl IL-6
Sidney (Township of)—pop pl MI-6
Sidney Tunnel—mine CO-8
Sidney Valley—basin UT-8
Sidneyville—locale WV-2
Sidney Walnut Ave Hist Dist—hist pl OH-6
Sidney Waterworks And Electric Light Bldg—hist pl OH-6
Sidnors Stand (historical)—locale TN-4
Sido—pop pl MO-7
Sidon—pop pl AR-4
Sidon—pop pl MS-4
Sidon Canal—canal WY-8
Sidon Cem—cemetery AR-4
Sidon Cut-Off—bend MS-4
Sidon Cutoff Lake—lake MS-4
Sidonia—pop pl TN-4
Sidonia Baptist Ch—church TN-4
Sidonia Sch—school ND-7
Sidonia Sch (historical)—school TN-4
Sidonia Township—pop pl ND-7
Sidon Landing Number One (historical)—locale MS-4
Sidon Landing Number Three (historical)—locale MS-4
Sidon Landing Number Two (historical)—locale MS-4
Sid Ormsbee Lookout—locale CA-9
Sid Place—locale NM-5
Sid Place—locale TX-5
Sid Richardson—locale TX-5
Sid Rsvr—reservoir ID-8
Sids UT-8
Sids Brook—stream MA-1
Sids Canyon—valley UT-8
Sids Draw—valley (2) UT-8
Sids Flat—flat MT-8
Sids Holes—spring UT-8
Sid Simpson Spring—spring AZ-5
Sid Simpson State Park—park IL-6
Sid Smith Ranch—locale CA-9
Sids Mtn—summit UT-8
Sids Notch—gap NY-2
Sids Pass—gap AK-9
Sids Prong—stream NM-5
Sids Rsvr—reservoir UT-8
Sid Town—pop pl MI-6
Sidville—locale KY-4
Sidwalter Buttes—summit OR-9
Sidwalter Corral—locale OR-9
Sidway Sch—school NY-2
Sidwell and Mills Drain—canal MI-6
Sidwell Creek—stream TN-4
Sidwell Friends Sch—school MD-2
Sidwell Lake—lake NY-2
Sidwell Park—park TX-5
Sidwell Well—well NM-5
Sieard Mine (underground)—mine AL-4
Siebecker Pond—reservoir PA-2
Siebecker Pond Dam—dam PA-2
Siebeck Island—island MT-8
Siebell Lake—lake MN-6
Sieben—locale MT-8
Sieben—locale VI-3
Sieben Ranch—locale (2) MT-8
Sieben Ranch Ditch—canal MT-8
Sieber—mine NV-8
Sieber Canyon—valley CO-8
Sieberg Mine—mine CO-8
Sieberi Ditch—canal OH-6
Sieber Lake—lake IA-7
Sieber's Creek MN-6
Siebert Bottom Hollow—valley MO-7
Siebert Creek—stream CO-8
Siebert Creek—stream WA-9
Siebert Creek Trail—trail CO-8
Siebert Drain—canal MI-6
Siebert Lake—lake PA-2
Siebert Mtn—summit NV-8
Siebert Park—park (2) PA-2
Siebert Pond Dam—dam NJ-2
Siebert Sch—school MI-6
Siebert Sch—school OH-6
Sieberts Creek MI-6
Siebold Farm/Ruehle (Realy) Farm—hist pl MI-6
Siebold Lake—swamp ND-7
Siebolt Creek—stream WY-8
Siebzig Inseln PW-9
Sieche Hollow—valley SD-7
Sieche Hollow State Park—park SD-7
Sieden Prairie Sch—school IL-6
Siedenstricker—locale AR-4
Siefer Run—stream PA-2
Siefert Airp—airport IN-6
Siefert Hollow—valley IN-6
Siefert Sch—school MI-6
Siefert Sch—school WI-6
Siefort Mountain CA-9
Siegal Lake—lake WI-6
Siegal Mountain MT-8
Sieg Cem—cemetery OH-6
Siegel—locale MN-6
Siegel—locale NV-8
Siegel, Mount—summit NV-8
Siegel Creek—stream ID-8
Siegel Creek—stream MT-8
Siegel Creek—stream NV-8
Siegells Store NC-3
Siegel Marsh Dam—dam PA-2
Siegel Marsh Number 1 Dam PA-2
Siegel Marsh Rsvr—reservoir PA-2
Siegel Mines—mine NV-8
Siegel Mtn—summit MT-8
Siegel Pass—gap MT-8
Siegel Ranch—locale NV-8
Siegel Saint Paul Ch—church IA-7
Siegel's Department Store—hist pl IN-6
Siegels Slough—gut WA-9
Siegen—pop pl LA-4
Siegersville PA-2
Siegfield Park—pop pl NY-2
Siegfried—uninc pl PA-2
Siegfried, Mount—summit AK-9
Siegfried Canyon—valley CA-9
Siegfried Creek—stream MN-6
Siegfried Pyre—summit AZ-5
Siegfrieds PA-2
Siegfrieds Bridge PA-2
Siegfrieds Bridge - in part PA-2
Siegfried Sch (historical)—school PA-2
Siegfried's Dale Farm—hist pl PA-2
Siegfriedsdale Sch (abandoned)—school PA-2
Siegfrieds - in part PA-2
Siegle—pop pl LA-4
Siegle Creek MT-8
Siegle Ditch—canal OR-9
Siegler Canyon CA-9
Siegler Creek CA-9
Siegler Sch—school FL-3
Siegler Springs CA-9
Siegmund Rsvr—reservoir OR-9
Siegner, George V., House—hist pl WI-6
Siegrest Draw—valley NM-5
Sie Hollow—valley AR-4
Siekrest Gulch—valley MT-8
Sieler—locale WA-9
Sieler Creek—stream UT-8
Sieler Dam—dam SD-7
Sieler Meadow—flat UT-8
Sieler Siding WA-9
Siemens—locale MI-6
Siemens Creek—stream MI-6
Siemer House—hist pl IA-7
Siemer Lake—lake WI-6
Siemer Silo and Barn—hist pl MN-6
Sieminski Creek—stream MT-8
Siemion Ranch—locale MT-8
Siemond Ranch—locale AZ-5
Siemon Park—park CA-9
Siemp—other VA-3
Siempre Verde Park—park CA-9
Siena Coll—school NY-2
Siena Coll—school TN-4
Siena Heights Cem—cemetery MI-6
Siena Heights Coll—school MI-6
Siena HS—school IL-6
Siena Sisters Of Mercy Rest Home, The—locale OH-6
Siena (St. Bernadine of Siena College)—pop pl NY-2
Sienega Del Gabilan CA-9
Sienna, Lake—lake TX-5
Siep, Bayou—stream TX-5
Sieper—pop pl LA-4
Sieper Creek—stream LA-4
Sieps—pop pl LA-4
Sier Hill—summit PA-2
Sierks—locale NY-2
Sierra CA-9
Sierra NV-8
Sierra—locale CA-9
Sierra—locale CO-8
Sierra—uninc pl CA-9
Sierra Abajo UT-8
Sierra Almagre CO-8
Sierra Alta—summit NM-5
Sierra Alta (Barrio)—fmr MCD PR-3
Sierra Alta Ranch—locale NM-5
Sierra Ancha Experimental For—forest AZ-5
Sierra Ancha Mountains AZ-5
Sierra Ancha Wilderness Area—park AZ-5
Sierra Apache AZ-5
Sierra Arida—ridge AZ-5
Sierra Army Depot—military CA-9
Sierra Arteza AZ-5
Sierra Ave Sch—school CA-9
Sierra Babquqvar AZ-5
Sierra Baja (Barrio)—fmr MCD PR-3
Sierra Bayamon—pop pl (2) PR-3
Sierra Bermeja—range PR-3
Sierra Blanca NM-5
Sierra Blanca—pop pl TX-5
Sierra Blanca—ridge CO-8
Sierra Blanca—ridge NM-5
Sierra Blanca, Lake—lake AZ-5
Sierra Blanca Canyon—valley AZ-5
Sierra Blanca (CCD)—cens area TX-5
Sierra Blanca Creek—stream CO-8
Sierra Blanca Dam—dam AZ-5
Sierra Blanca Mountains AZ-5
Sierra Blanca Peak CO-8
Sierra Blanca Peak—summit NM-5
Sierra Blanca River, The AZ-5
Sierra Blanca (Ski Area)—pop pl NM-5
Sierra Blanca Spring—spring AZ-5
Sierra Blanco AZ-5
Sierra Blanco CO-8
Sierra Bonita—pop pl AZ-5
Sierra Bonita Ranch—hist pl AZ-5
Sierra Bonita Ranch—locale AZ-5
Sierra Brava—pop pl PR-3
Sierra Buttes—summit CA-9
Sierra Buttes Mine—mine CA-9
Sierra Campground—locale (2) CA-9
Sierra Canyon—valley AZ-5
Sierra Canyon—valley NV-8
Sierra Castellan TX-5
Sierra (CCD)—cens area CA-9
Sierra Chino—locale TX-5
Sierra City—pop pl CA-9
Sierra Club Guymon Lodge—locale CA-9
Sierra Coll—school CA-9
Sierra Colorado AZ-5
Sierra Conservation Center—pop pl CA-9
Sierra (County)—pop pl CA-9
Sierra (County)—pop pl NM-5
Sierra Creek—stream (2) CA-9
Sierra Creek—stream CO-8
Sierra Cuchillo—ridge NM-5
Sierra Dawn Condominium—pop pl UT-8
Sierra de AZ-5
Sierra de Cayey—range PR-3
Sierra De Cristo Rey—summit NM-5
Sierra de Don Fernando—summit NM-5
Sierra de Guardarraya—range PR-3
Sierra de Jajome—range PR-3
Sierra de la Cabeza Prieta AZ-5
Sierra de la Cruz—summit NM-5
Sierra de la Espuma AZ-5
Sierra de la Frente Negna AZ-5

**Silerton**—*pop pl* TN-4
Silerton Baptist Ch—*church* TN-4
Silerton Post Office—*building* TN-4
Silerton Sch (historical)—*school* TN-4
*Silerville* KY-4
Silerville Ch—*church* KY-4
**Silerville (Strunk Post Office)**—*pop pl* KY-4
Siles—*locale* PA-2
Silesca Guard Station—*locale* CO-8
Silesca Pond—*lake* CO-8
Siles Gap—*gap* NC-3
**Silesia**—*pop pl* MD-2
**Silesia**—*pop pl* MT-8
*Silesia Creek* MT-8
Silesia Creek—*stream* WA-9
Silesia Creek Shelter—*locale* WA-9
Siles Mtn—*summit* KY-4
**Siletz**—*pop pl* OR-9
Siletz Agency Site—*hist pl* OR-9
Siletz Airp—*airport* OR-9
Siletz Bay—*bay* OR-9
Siletz Bay Airp—*airport* OR-9
Siletz Bay State Airp—*airport* OR-9
Siletz (CCD)—*cens area* OR-9
Siletz Hill—*summit* OR-9
**Siletz Ind Res**—*pop pl* OR-9
Siletz Keys—*island* OR-9
*Siletz River* OR-9
Siletz River—*stream* OR-9
*Siletz River Fish Hatchery* OR-9
Siletz Rsvr—*reservoir* OR-9
*Silex* SD-7
Silex—*locale* AR-4
**Silex**—*pop pl* IN-6
**Silex**—*pop pl* MO-7
Silex, Lake—*lake* CO-8
Silex, Mount—*summit* CO-8
Silex (historical)—*locale* SD-7
Silex Hollow—*valley* OH-6
Silex Pond—*lake* CT-1
Silfis Run—*stream* PA-2
Silge Creek—*stream* ID-8
*Silh-Tusayan* AZ-5
Sili—*locale* AS-9
Siliaga Point—*cape* AS-9
Siliataligalu Point—*cape* AS-9
*Silica* MT-8
Silica—*locale* KS-7
Silica—*locale* MN-6
Silica—*locale* TN-4
Silica—*locale* VA-3
Silica—*locale* WV-2
**Silica**—*pop pl* MO-7
**Silica**—*pop pl* OH-6
**Silica**—*pop pl* SC-3
**Silica**—*pop pl* WI-6
Silica Butte—*summit* MT-8
Silica Camp—*locale* OR-9
Silica Dome—*summit* NV-8
**Silica Hills**—*pop pl* GA-3
Silica Mine—*mine* IL-6
Silica Mtn—*summit* OR-9
Silica Mtn—*summit* WA-9
Silica Trail—*trail* OR-9
*Silicia Creek* WA-9
Silicon Mine—*mine* NV-8
Silicosaska Park—*park* WA-9
Siligin Spring—*spring* GU-9
Siligo Meadows—*flat* CA-9
Siligo Peak—*summit* CA-9
*Silimok* AZ-5
*Silinakik* AZ-5
Silio—*locale* NM-5
Silka Lateral—*canal* UT-8
Silk Covered Bridge—*hist pl* VT-1
Silk Creek—*stream* OR-9
Silk Creek Cem—*cemetery* OR-9
Silk Creek Sch—*school* OR-9
Silken Skein Falls—*falls* MT-8
Silket Branch—*stream* WV-2
Silk Exchange Bldg—*hist pl* MO-7
Silk Fork—*stream* WV-2
**Silk Hope**—*pop pl* GA-3
**Silk Hope**—*pop pl* NC-3
Silk Hope Elem Sch—*school* NC-3
Silk Knob—*summit* KY-4
Silk Lake—*lake* MI-6
Silkman House—*hist pl* PA-2
Silkmans Swamp—*swamp* PA-2
*Silk Mill Dam* MA-1
Silkmill Run—*stream* PA-2
**Silk Mills**—*pop pl* GA-3
Silk Run—*stream* WV-2
Silks Basin—*valley* UT-8
Silk Stocking District—*hist pl* AL-4
Silkville—*hist pl* KS-7
Silkville—*locale* KS-7
Silkworm Mine—*mine* NV-8
**Silkworth**—*pop pl* PA-2
Silkworth, Lake—*lake* PA-2
Silky Hollow—*valley* TN-4
Sill, Mount—*summit* CA-9
*Sillacogga* AL-4
Sillars Bayou—*gut* LA-4
Sill Basin—*basin* WA-9
Sillbaugh Ch—*church* PA-2
Sill Branch—*stream* KY-4
Sill Branch—*stream* MS-4
Sill Branch—*stream* TN-4
Sill (CCD)—*cens area* OK-5
Sill Creek—*stream* ID-8
Sill Creek—*stream* NY-2
Sill Ditch—*canal* WY-8
Sillem Ridge—*ridge* WY-8
Siller Coliseum—*building* MS-4
Sillerud Ch—*church* MN-6
Sillery Bay—*bay* MD-2
Sill Hill—*summit* CA-9
**Sill (historical)**—*pop pl* TN-4
Silliasen Valley—*basin* NE-7
Silliman, Arthur, House—*hist pl* MI-6
Silliman, Mount—*summit* CA-9
Silliman, Mount—*summit* NV-8
Silliman Creek—*stream* CA-9
Silliman Institute—*hist pl* LA-4
Silliman Lake—*lake* CA-9
Silliman Meadow—*flat* CA-9
Silliman Memorial Presbyterian
Church—*hist pl* NY-2
Silliman Pass—*gap* CA-9
Sillimans Corners—*locale* NY-2
Sillimans Creek—*stream* IN-6
Sill Lake—*lake* MN-6
Sill Lake—*lake* WY-8
Sillman Hollow—*valley* WV-2
Sillman Memorial Library—*hist pl* IA-7
Sill Mine—*mine* CO-8
Sill Ranch—*locale* MT-8
Sill Rock—*bar* NY-2
Sill Run—*stream* PA-2
Sills—*locale* AR-4
Sills—*locale* FL-3
Sills Air Park—*airport* KS-7
Sills Branch—*stream* GA-3
Sills Cem—*cemetery* AL-4
Sills Cem—*cemetery* OH-6
Sills Cem—*cemetery* TN-4
Sills Ch—*church* NC-3
Sill Sch—*school* MI-6
Sill Sch—*school* OH-6
Sills Creek—*stream* NC-3
Sills Ditch—*canal* IN-6
Sills Lake—*lake* CA-9
Sills Sch (abandoned)—*school* PA-2
*Sills Store* NC-3
Sillsville—*locale* CO-8
Sillure, A. W., House—*hist pl* TX-5
Sillusi Butte—*summit* WA-9
Sillyasheen Mtn—*summit* AK-9
Sillycook Mtn—*summit* GA-3
*Silma* CO-8
Silman Lake—*lake* NM-5
Silman Spring—*spring* TX-5
Silmares Landing (historical)—*locale* AL-4
Silm Drain—*canal* MI-6
**Sil Murk (Papago)**—*pop pl* AZ-5
**Sil Nakaya**—*pop pl* AZ-5
*Sil Nakya* AZ-5
**Sil Nakya**—*pop pl* AZ-5
Sil Nakya Hills—*summit* AZ-5
Sil Nakya Pass—*gap* AZ-5
Sil Nakya Valley—*valley* AZ-5
Sil Nakya Wash—*stream* AZ-5
Silo—*locale* OH-6
**Silo**—*pop pl* MN-6
**Silo**—*pop pl* OK-5
Siloa Cem—*cemetery* NE-7
Siloa Ch—*church* MN-6
Siloah Ch—*church* MN-6
Siloam—*locale* AL-4
Siloam—*locale* CO-8
Siloam—*locale* IL-6
Siloam—*locale* KY-4
Siloam—*locale* (2) TX-5
Siloam—*locale* VA-3
Siloam—*other* TN-4
**Siloam**—*pop pl* GA-3
**Siloam**—*pop pl* MD-2
**Siloam**—*pop pl* MS-4
**Siloam**—*pop pl* NJ-2
**Siloam**—*pop pl* NY-2
**Siloam**—*pop pl* NC-3
**Siloam**—*pop pl* TN-4
**Siloam**—*pop pl* TX-5
*Siloam Baptist Ch* MS-4
Siloam Baptist Ch—*church* AL-4
Siloam Baptist Ch—*church* MS-4
Siloam Baptist Ch—*church* TN-4
*Siloam Baptist Church* AL-4
Siloam Baptist Church—*hist pl* AL-4
Siloam Bayou—*stream* MS-4
Siloam Branch—*stream* KY-4
Siloam (CCD)—*cens area* GA-3
Siloam (CCD)—*cens area* TN-4
Siloam Cem—*cemetery* LA-4
Siloam Cem—*cemetery* (3) MS-4
Siloam Cem—*cemetery* NJ-2
Siloam Cem—*cemetery* NY-2
Siloam Cem—*cemetery* NC-3
Siloam Cem—*cemetery* (2) OH-6
Siloam Cem—*cemetery* TN-4
Siloam Cem—*cemetery* TX-5
Siloam Cemeteries—*cemetery* NC-3
*Siloam Ch* AL-4
Siloam Ch—*church* (7) AL-4
Siloam Ch—*church* AR-4
Siloam Ch—*church* DE-2
Siloam Ch—*church* (2) FL-3
Siloam Ch—*church* (3) GA-3
Siloam Ch—*church* IL-6
Siloam Ch—*church* (3) KY-4
Siloam Ch—*church* LA-4
Siloam Ch—*church* (5) MS-4
Siloam Ch—*church* (2) MO-7
Siloam Ch—*church* NJ-2
Siloam Ch—*church* (4) NC-3
Siloam Ch—*church* (2) PA-2
Siloam Ch—*church* (4) SC-3
Siloam Ch—*church* TN-4
Siloam Ch—*church* (2) TX-5
Siloam Ch—*church* (2) VA-3
Siloam Ch—*church* WV-2
Siloam Chapel—*church* WI-6
*Siloam City* MO-7
Siloam Creek—*stream* AL-4
Siloam Division—*civil* TN-4
Siloam Gas Field—*oilfield* MS-4
Siloam Lookout Tower—*locale* MO-7
*Siloam Methodist Ch* MS-4
Siloam Methodist Ch—*church* MS-4
Siloam Park—*park* MO-7
Siloam Sch—*school* NC-3
Siloam Sch (historical)—*school* AL-4
Siloam Sch (historical)—*school* MS-4
*Siloam School* PA-2
Siloam Spring—*spring* MO-7
Siloam Spring Ch—*church* OK-5
Siloam Spring Hollow—*valley* MO-7
Siloam Springs—*locale* MO-7
**Siloam Springs**—*pop pl* AR-4
**Siloam Springs**—*pop pl* (2) MO-7
Siloam Springs Cem—*cemetery* MO-7
Siloam Springs Golf Course—*other* AR-4
Siloam Springs Lake—*reservoir* AR-4
Siloam Springs Township—*civil* MO-7
Siloam Springs Train Station—*hist pl* AR-4
Siloam (Township of)—*fmr MCD* AR-4
Siloam (Township of)—*fmr MCD* NC-3
Siloan Baptist Ch—*church* FL-3
Siloan Ch—*church* KY-4
Siloan Ch—*church* NC-3
Silobaro Windmill—*locale* TX-5
Silo Canyon—*valley* NV-8
Silo Cove—*bay* OK-5
Siloem Ch—*church* KY-4
Siloem Sch—*school* KY-4
Silo Hollow—*valley* (2) MO-7
Silo Hollow—*valley* TN-4
Siloma Ch—*church* AL-4
*Silom Ch* AL-4
Silom Ch (historical)—*church* AL-4
*Silom Church* MS-4
Silome Cem—*cemetery* MS-4
Silome Ch—*church* GA-3
Silome Sch—*school* AL-4
*Silon* AL-4
Silon Cem—*cemetery* IN-6
*Silon Church* AL-4
Silon Creek—*stream* IN-6
Silone Ch—*church* GA-3
Silo Spring—*spring* NV-8
Silo Tank—*reservoir* AZ-5
Silsbee—*locale* UT-8
**Silsbee**—*pop pl* TX-5
Silsbee (CCD)—*cens area* TX-5
Silsbee Oil Field—*oilfield* TX-5
Silsbee Sch—*school* CA-9
Silsby, Col. William H., House—*hist pl* OR-9
Silsby Hill—*summit* ME-1
Silsby Mtn—*summit* VT-1
Silsby Plain—*flat* ME-1
Silsby Ranch—*locale* NM-5
Silt—*locale* CA-9
**Silt**—*pop pl* CO-8
Silta Draw—*valley* ID-8
**Siltcoos**—*pop pl* OR-9
Siltcoos Forest Camp—*locale* OR-9
Siltcoos Lake—*lake* OR-9
Siltcoos Lake—*reservoir* OR-9
Siltcoos Lake Dam—*dam* OR-9
Siltcoos Lookout—*locale* OR-9
Siltcoos River—*stream* OR-9
Silt Creek—*stream* WA-9
Silted Rsvr—*reservoir* WY-8
Silted Tank—*reservoir* AZ-5
Silted Up Tank—*reservoir* NM-5
**Siltix**—*pop pl* WV-2
Silt Lakes—*lake* MT-8
Silt Pond A—*reservoir* PA-2
Silt Pond A Dam—*dam* PA-2
Silt Pond B—*reservoir* PA-2
Silt Pond B Dam—*dam* PA-2
Silt Rsvr—*reservoir* WY-8
Silt Tank—*reservoir* (2) AZ-5
Silt Tank—*reservoir* (2) NM-5
Silt Tank—*reservoir* TX-5
**Siluria**—*pop pl* AL-4
Siluria Cem—*cemetery* AL-4
Silurian Hills—*other* CA-9
Silurian Lake—*flat* CA-9
Silurian Mineral Springhouse—*hist pl* WI-6
Silurian Valley—*valley* CA-9
*Silush* WV-2
*Silva* VA-3
**Silva**—*pop pl* MO-7
**Silva**—*pop pl* ND-7
**Silva**—*pop pl* VA-3
Silva, Arthur D., Flume—*hist pl* ID-8
Silva, Arthur D., Ranch—*hist pl* ID-8
Silva, Arthur D., Water Tank—*hist pl* ID-8
Silva, Manuel, Barn—*hist pl* ID-8
Silva-Benejan House—*hist pl* PR-3
Silva Canyon—*valley* (3) NM-5
Silvacola—*locale* TN-4
*Silva Creek* NV-8
*Silva Creek* WA-9
Silva Creek—*stream* NM-5
Silva Drain—*canal* CA-9
Silva Draw—*valley* CO-8
Silva Field—*park* CA-9
Silva Flat Rsvr—*reservoir* CA-9
Silvagni Ranch—*locale* UT-8
Silva (historical)—*locale* AZ-5
Silva Island—*island* CA-9
Silvan, Loma—*summit* TX-5
**Silvana**—*pop pl* WA-9
Silvana Terraces—*locale* WA-9
Silvan Lake—*reservoir* GA-3
Silva Park—*park* TX-5
**Silvara**—*pop pl* PA-2
Silva Ranch—*locale* NM-5
Silva Ravine—*valley* CA-9
Silva Sch—*school* CA-9
Silvas Creek—*stream* WA-9
*Silva Spring* NV-8
Silva Spring—*spring* (2) NM-5
*Silva Springs* NV-8
Silva State Wildlife Mngmt Area—*park* MO-7
Silva Tank—*reservoir* NM-5
Silva Tank—*reservoir* (2) TX-5
Silve Coulee—*valley* MT-8
Silvenhall Cem—*cemetery* MS-4
*Silver* MI-6
**Silver**—*pop pl* AR-4
**Silver**—*pop pl* SC-3
**Silver**—*pop pl* TX-5
**Silver**—*pop pl* UT-8
**Silver**—*pop pl* WI-6
Silver, Lake—*lake* (3) FL-3
Silver, Lake—*lake* ND-7
**Silver Acres**—*pop pl* CA-9
**Silver Acres Subdivision**—*pop pl* UT-8
**Silverado**—*pop pl* CA-9
Silverado Canyon—*valley* (2) CA-9
Silverado Canyon—*valley* NV-8
Silverado Canyon—*valley* UT-8
Silverado Country Club—*other* CA-9
Silverado Creek—*stream* CA-9
Silverado JHS—*school* CA-9
Silverado Mine—*mine* CA-9
Silverado Mtn—*summit* NV-8
Silverado Park—*park* CA-9
Silverado Ridge—*ridge* AZ-5
Silverado Sch—*school* CA-9
Silverado Station—*other* CA-9
Silverado Truck Trail—*trail* CA-9
Silverado Wash—*stream* AZ-5
Silver Age Mine—*mine* AZ-5
Silver Arrow Sch—*school* KS-7
Silver Bar Canyon—*valley* NM-5
Silver Basin—*basin* AZ-5
Silver Basin—*basin* (4) CO-8
Silver Basin—*basin* (2) MT-8
Silver Basin Creek—*stream* AZ-5
*Silver Bass Lake* MI-6
Silver Bass Lake—*lake* WI-6
Silverbass Lake—*lake* WI-6
Silver Bay—*bay* AK-9
Silver Bay—*bay* NJ-2
Silver Bay—*bay* NY-2
**Silver Bay**—*pop pl* MN-6
**Silver Bay**—*pop pl* NJ-2
**Silver Bay**—*pop pl* NY-2
Silver Bay Association Complex—*hist pl* NY-2
*Silver Bay Harbor* MN-6
Silver Bayou—*stream* MS-4
Silver Bay Trail—*trail* AK-9
*Silver Beach* CT-1
Silver Beach—*beach* ID-8
Silver Beach—*beach* MA-1
Silver Beach—*beach* NY-2
**Silver Beach**—*pop pl* CT-1
**Silver Beach**—*pop pl* ID-8
**Silver Beach**—*pop pl* MA-1
**Silver Beach**—*pop pl* MI-6
**Silver Beach**—*pop pl* NJ-2
**Silver Beach**—*pop pl* NY-2
**Silver Beach**—*pop pl* VA-3
**Silver Beach**—*pop pl* WA-9
Silver Beach Baptist Ch—*church* FL-3
Silver Beach Harbor—*cove* MA-1
Silver Beach Heights—*locale* FL-3
Silver Beach Lodge—*locale* MI-6
Silver Bear—*mine* AZ-5
Silver Bear Gulch—*valley* AZ-5
*Silverbell* AZ-5
Silverbell—*locale* AZ-5
**Silver Bell**—*pop pl* AZ-5
Silver Bell Cem—*cemetery* AZ-5
*Silver Belle* AZ-5
**Silver Bell Estates**
**Subdivision**—*pop pl* UT-8
Silverbell Golf Course—*other* AZ-5
Silver Bell Mine—*mine* AZ-5
Silver Bell Mine—*mine* CA-9
Silver Bell Mine—*mine* (2) CO-8
Silver Bell Mine—*mine* (2) ID-8
Silverbell Mine—*mine* ID-8
Silver Bell Mine—*mine* (2) MT-8
Silver Bell Mine—*mine* (4) NV-8
Silver Bell Mine—*mine* NM-5
Silver Bell Mine—*mine* (2) UT-8
Silver Bell Mine—*mine* WA-9
*Silverbell Mountains* AZ-5
Silver Bell Mountains—*summit* AZ-5
Silverbell Number One Dam—*dam* AZ-5
Silverbell Number Two Dam—*dam* AZ-5
Silver Bell Peak—*summit* AZ-5
Silver Bell Post Office—*building* AZ-5
Silverbell Regional Park—*park* AZ-5
Silver Bell Run—*stream* MD-2
Silver Bell Tailing Dam—*dam* AZ-5
Silver Bell Tailings Pond—*reservoir* AZ-5
Silver Bell Trailer Park—*locale* AZ-5
Silver Bell Wash—*stream* AZ-5
Silver Belt Mine—*mine* MT-8
Silver Belt Shaft—*mine* AZ-5
*Silver Birch* WI-6
*Silver Birch Camp* MA-1
Silver Birch Lake—*lake* WI-6
Silver Birch Park—*park* WI-6
Silver Birch Pond—*lake* CT-1
Silver Birch Sch—*school* MN-6
Silver Blue Lake—*lake* FL-3
Silver Bluff—*cliff* GA-3
Silver Bluff—*cliff* SC-3
Silver Bluff—*hist pl* SC-3
**Silver Bluff**—*pop pl* NC-3
Silver Bluff Ch—*church* SC-3
**Silver Bluff Estates**—*pop pl* FL-3
*Silver Bluff Landing* SC-3
Silver Bluff Sch—*school* FL-3
*Silverboro* NC-3
*Silver Botton* TN-4
*Silverbow* MT-8
Silver Bow—*locale* MT-8
Silverbow—*locale* NV-8
Silverbow Basin—*basin* AK-9
Silver Bow Brewery Malt House—*hist pl* MT-8
Silverbow Corral—*locale* NV-8
**Silver Bow County**—*pop pl* MT-8
Silver Bow County Poor Farm
Hosp—*hist pl* MT-8
*Silverbow Creek* MT-8
Silverbow Creek—*stream* (2) AK-9
Silver Bow Creek—*stream* AK-9
Silver Bow Creek—*stream* (2) MT-8
*Silverbow Lake* MT-8
Silver Bow Lake—*lake* MT-8
Silver Bow Mine—*mine* CA-9
Silver Bow Mine—*mine* UT-8
Silver Bow Northwest—*cens area* MT-8
**Silver Bow Park**—*pop pl* MT-8
Silver Bow Ranch—*locale* MT-8
*Silverbow River* ID-8
Silver Bow Siding—*locale* MT-8
Silver Bow South—*cens area* MT-8
Silverbow Springs (historical)—*spring* NV-8
Silver Branch—*stream* GA-3
Silver Branch—*stream* IN-6
Silver Branch—*stream* MS-4
Silver Branch—*stream* PA-2
Silver Bridge—*bridge* CA-9
Silverbrook—*other* PA-2
**Silverbrook**—*pop pl* DE-2
**Silver Brook**—*pop pl* DE-2
**Silver Brook**—*pop pl* WA-9
Silver Brook—*stream* (2) CT-1
Silver Brook—*stream* IN-6
Silver Brook—*stream* ME-1
Silver Brook—*stream* (3) MA-1
Silver Brook—*stream* MI-6
Silver Brook—*stream* (2) NH-1
Silver Brook—*stream* (3) NY-2
Silver Brook—*stream* VA-3
Silverbrook Cem—*cemetery* DE-2
Silver Brook Cem—*cemetery* GA-3
Silver Brook Cem—*cemetery* SC-3
Silver Brook Ch—*church* VA-3
Silver Brook Colliery—*building* PA-2
**Silverbrook Gardens**—*pop pl* DE-2
Silver Brook Junction—*locale* PA-2
**Silver Brook (Silverbrook)**—*pop pl* PA-2
Silver Brook (Township of)—*civ div* MN-6
Silverbrook United Methodist Ch—*church* DE-2
Silver Buckle Ranch—*locale* MT-8
*Silver Bun Church* AL-4
Silver Butte—*summit* AZ-5
Silver Butte—*summit* ID-8
Silver Butte—*summit* (3) OR-9
Silver Butte Creek—*stream* MT-8
Silver Butte Creek—*stream* OR-9
*Silver Butte Fisher Pass* MT-8
Silver Butte Fisher River—*stream* MT-8
Silver Butte Mine—*mine* NV-8
Silver Butte Mtn—*summit* MT-8
Silver Butte Pass—*gap* MT-8
Silver Butte Spring—*spring* AZ-5
Silver Butte Trail—*trail* MT-8
Silver Butte Trail—*trail* OR-9
Silver Cable Mine—*mine* MT-8
Silver Camp Canyon—*valley* AZ-5
Silver Camp Divide—*gap* AZ-5
Silver Campground—*locale* ID-8
Silver Campground—*locale* NM-5
*Silver Canon Mountains* NV-8
Silver Canyon—*valley* (2) CA-9
Silver Canyon—*valley* (3) NV-8
Silver Canyon—*valley* (2) NM-5
Silver Canyon—*valley* UT-8
Silver Canyon Landing—*locale* CA-9
Silver Cascade—*stream* NH-1
Silver Cascade Falls—*falls* CO-8
Silver Cave—*cave* AL-4
Silver Cave—*cave* AZ-5
Silver Cave—*cave* MO-7
Silver Cave Mine—*mine* NM-5
Silver Cem—*cemetery* GA-3
Silver Cem—*cemetery* IA-7
Silver Cem—*cemetery* (3) NC-3
Silver Chapel—*church* NC-3
Silver Chapel—*church* TN-4
Silver Chapel (historical)—*church* AL-4
Silver Chief Canyon—*valley* NV-8
Silver Christmas Mine—*mine* AZ-5
*Silver Church* MS-4
Silver Circle—*flat* CO-8
Silver Circle Trail—*trail* CO-8
Silver City—*locale* KY-4
Silver City—*locale* MT-8
Silver City—*locale* TN-4
Silver City—*locale* (4) TX-5
Silver City—*locale* UT-8
**Silver City**—*pop pl* CA-9
**Silver City**—*pop pl* (2) GA-3
**Silver City**—*pop pl* ID-8
**Silver City**—*pop pl* IA-7
**Silver City**—*pop pl* MI-6
**Silver City**—*pop pl* MS-4
**Silver City**—*pop pl* NV-8
**Silver City**—*pop pl* NM-5
**Silver City**—*pop pl* NC-3
**Silver City**—*pop pl* OK-5
**Silver City**—*pop pl* SD-7
Silver City Branch—*stream* TN-4
Silver City (CCD)—*cens area* GA-3
Silver City (CCD)—*cens area* NM-5
Silver City Cem—*cemetery* MT-8
Silver City Cem—*cemetery* UT-8
Silver City Cemetery—*hist pl* UT-8
Silver City Country Club—*locale* MS-4
Silver City Creek—*stream* CO-8
Silver City Dome—*summit* KS-7
Silver City Draw—*valley* NM-5
Silver City Elem Sch (historical)—*school* MS-4
Silver City Hist Dist—*hist pl* ID-8
Silver City Hist Dist—*hist pl* NM-5
Silver City Hist Dist North
Addition—*hist pl* NM-5
Silver City Landing (historical)—*locale* MS-4
Silver City Mine—*mine* ID-8
Silver City Oil Field—*oilfield* KS-7
*Silver City Range* ID-8
*Silver City Range* OR-9
Silver City Range—*other* NM-5
Silver City Range—*range* ID-8
Silver City Sch—*school* LA-4
Silver City Water Wells—*well* NM-5
Silver City Water Works Bldg—*hist pl* NM-5
Silver Cliff—*cliff* MN-6
**Silver Cliff**—*pop pl* CO-8
Silver Cliff Cem—*cemetery* CO-8
Silver Cliff Cem—*cemetery* KS-7
Silver Cliff Plateau—*summit* CO-8
*Silver Cliffs* CO-8
Silver Cliffs Mine—*mine* CA-9
**Silver Cliff (Town of)**—*pop pl* WI-6
*Silver Clip Claim* AZ-5
Silver Cloud Ch—*church* MS-4
Silver Cloud Mine—*mine* (2) CO-8
Silver Cloud Mine—*mine* NV-8
Silver Coin Gulch—*valley* CO-8
Silver Coin Mine—*mine* AZ-5
Silver Coin Mine—*mine* NV-8
Silver Cord Cascade—*falls* WY-8
Silver Cord Gulch—*valley* ID-8
Silver Cord Mine—*mine* AZ-5
Silver Corners—*locale* MN-6
*Silver Creek* AL-4
*Silver Creek* AZ-5
*Silver Creek* CA-9
*Silver Creek* CT-1
*Silver Creek* DE-2
*Silver Creek* ID-8
*Silver Creek* IN-6
*Silver Creek* KS-7
*Silver Creek* MI-6
*Silver Creek* MN-6
*Silver Creek* MO-7
*Silver Creek* NV-8
*Silver Creek* NC-3
*Silver Creek* PA-2
*Silver Creek* TN-4
*Silver Creek* TX-5
*Silver Creek* VA-3
*Silver Creek* WY-8
Silver Creek—*bay* AK-9
Silver Creek—*gut* MI-6
Silver Creek—*locale* GA-3
Silver Creek—*locale* KY-4
Silver Creek—*locale* MI-6
Silver Creek—*locale* MN-6
Silver Creek—*locale* OH-6
Silver Creek—*locale* TN-4
**Silver Creek**—*pop pl* AL-4
**Silver Creek**—*pop pl* AZ-5
**Silver Creek**—*pop pl* MN-6
**Silver Creek**—*pop pl* MS-4
**Silver Creek**—*pop pl* MO-7
**Silver Creek**—*pop pl* NE-7
**Silver Creek**—*pop pl* NY-2
**Silver Creek**—*pop pl* OH-6
**Silver Creek**—*pop pl* PA-2
**Silver Creek**—*pop pl* WA-9
**Silver Creek**—*pop pl* WI-6
**Silvercreek**—*pop pl* WI-6
Silver Creek—*reservoir* PA-2
Silver Creek—*stream* (5) AL-4
Silver Creek—*stream* (7) AK-9
Silver Creek—*stream* (8) AZ-5
Silver Creek—*stream* AR-4
Silver Creek—*stream* (20) CA-9
Silver Creek—*stream* (18) CO-8
Silver Creek—*stream* (2) FL-3
Silver Creek—*stream* (2) GA-3
Silver Creek—*stream* (20) ID-8
Silver Creek—*stream* (7) IL-6
Silver Creek—*stream* (6) IN-6
Silver Creek—*stream* (16) IA-7
Silver Creek—*stream* (13) KS-7
Silver Creek—*stream* (2) KY-4
Silver Creek—*stream* (2) LA-4
Silver Creek—*stream* (38) MI-6
Silver Creek—*stream* (15) MN-6
Silver Creek—*stream* (9) MS-4
Silver Creek—*stream* (6) MO-7
Silver Creek—*stream* (6) MT-8
Silver Creek—*stream* (13) NE-7
Silver Creek—*stream* (6) NV-8
Silver Creek—*stream* (3) NM-5
Silver Creek—*stream* (4) NY-2
Silver Creek—*stream* (5) NC-3
Silver Creek—*stream* (2) ND-7
Silver Creek—*stream* (10) OH-6
Silver Creek—*stream* (3) OK-5
Silver Creek—*stream* (16) OR-9
Silver Creek—*stream* (7) PA-2
Silver Creek—*stream* RI-1
Silver Creek—*stream* (2) SC-3
Silver Creek—*stream* (6) SD-7
Silver Creek—*stream* (2) TN-4
Silver Creek—*stream* (10) TX-5
Silver Creek—*stream* (5) UT-8
Silver Creek—*stream* (4) VA-3
Silver Creek—*stream* (20) WA-9
Silver Creek—*stream* WV-2
Silver Creek—*stream* (25) WI-6
Silver Creek—*stream* (5) WY-8
**Silver Creek Acres**—*pop pl* MS-4
Silver Creek Airp—*airport* NC-3
Silver Creek Attendance Center
(historical)—*school* MS-4
Silver Creek Bridge—*hist pl* KS-7
Silver Creek Camp—*locale* MI-6
Silver Creek Camp—*locale* NM-5
Silver Creek Camp—*locale* OR-9
Silver Creek Camp—*locale* PA-2
Silver Creek Camp Ground—*locale* CA-9
Silver Creek Campground—*locale* (2) CA-9
Silver Creek Campground—*locale* ID-8
Silver Creek Campground—*locale* WA-9
Silver Creek Canyon—*valley* NM-5
Silver Creek Canyon—*valley* WY-8
Silver Creek Cem—*cemetery* IL-6
Silver Creek Cem—*cemetery* IN-6
Silver Creek Cem—*cemetery* KS-7
Silver Creek Cem—*cemetery* KY-4
Silver Creek Cem—*cemetery* LA-4
Silver Creek Cem—*cemetery* (3) MN-6
Silver Creek Cem—*cemetery* MS-4
Silver Creek Cem—*cemetery* (4) NE-7
Silver Creek Cem—*cemetery* OH-6
Silver Creek Cem—*cemetery* SD-7
Silver Creek Cem—*cemetery* WA-9
Silver Creek Center Sch—*school* IL-6
Silver Creek Ch—*church* GA-3
Silver Creek Ch—*church* (3) IN-6
Silver Creek Ch—*church* (3) IA-7
Silver Creek Ch—*church* KY-4
Silver Creek Ch—*church* (2) LA-4
Silver Creek Ch—*church* (2) MN-6
Silver Creek Ch—*church* MS-4
Silver Creek Ch—*church* (3) NC-3
Silver Creek Ch—*church* OH-6
Silver Creek Ch—*church* OK-5
Silver Creek Ch—*church* TN-4
Silver Creek Ch—*church* TX-5
Silver Creek Ch—*church* VA-3
Silver Creek Ch—*church* WI-6
**Silver Creek Church**—*pop pl* CA-9
Silver Creek Conservation Club—*other* IN-6
*Silver Creek Dam* PA-2
Silver Creek Dam—*dam* (2) OR-9
Silver Creek Dam—*dam* PA-2
Silver Creek Ditch—*canal* CO-8
Silver Creek Ditch—*canal* UT-8
Silver Creek Diversion Dam—*dam* OR-9
Silver Creek Divide—*gap* NM-5
Silver Creek Drain—*stream* MI-6
Silver Creek Drainage Ditch—*canal* IL-6
Silver Creek Falls Rec Area—*park* OR-9
Silver Creek Falls State Park—*park* OR-9
Silver Creek Fish Hatchery—*locale* TX-5
Silver Creek Gap—*gap* NC-3
*Silver Creek Guard Station* ID-8
Silver Creek Guard Station—*locale* WA-9
Silver Creek (historical)—*locale* IA-7
Silver Creek (historical P.O.)—*locale* IA-7
Silver Creek HS—*school* IN-6
Silver Creek JHS—*school* IN-6
Silver Creek Junction—*locale* UT-8
Silver Creek Knob—*summit* NC-3
Silver Creek Lake—*lake* MO-7
Silver Creek Lakes—*lake* CO-8
Silver Creek Landing—*locale* OR-9
Silver Creek Landing (historical)—*locale* MS-4
Silver Creek Lodge—*locale* MI-6
Silver Creek Lookout—*locale* ID-8
Silver Creek Lookout Tower
(historical)—*locale* MI-6

Silver Creek Marsh—*swamp* OR-9
Silver Creek Meadows—*flat* CA-9
Silver Creek Mine—*mine* AZ-5
*Silver Creek Number One* MS-4
*Silver Creek Number Three* MS-4
*Silver Creek Number Two* MS-4
Silver Creek Park—*park* AL-4
Silver Creek Park—*park* WI-6
Silver Creek Pass—*gap* WA-9
**Silver Creek Plunge**—*pop pl* ID-8
Silver Creek Pond—*lake* (2) MI-6
Silver Creek Pond—*reservoir* MI-6
*Silver Creek Post Office* TN-4
Silvercreek Post Office (historical)—*building* TN-4
Silver Creek Ranch—*locale* (2) NV-8
*Silver Creek Reservoir* AZ-5
*Silver Creek Reservoir* UT-8
Silver Creek Riffle—*rapids* (2) OR-9
Silver Creek Rsvr—*reservoir* NV-8
Silver Creek Rsvr—*reservoir* NY-2
Silver Creek Rsvr—*reservoir* (2) OR-9
Silver Creek Rsvr—*reservoir* (2) PA-2
Silver Creek Rsvr—*reservoir* WY-8
Silver Creek Sch—*hist pl* MT-8
Silver Creek Sch—*school* IL-6
Silver Creek Sch—*school* KY-4
Silver Creek Sch—*school* NV-8
Silver Creek Sch—*school* (2) WI-6
Silver Creek Sch (historical)—*school* MS-4
Silver Creek Sch (historical)—*school* MO-7
Silver Creek Shoal—*bar* AL-4
Silver Creek Shoals—*bar* TN-4
*Silver Creek Spring* AZ-5
Silver Creek Spring—*spring* (2) AZ-5
Silver Creek Summit—*summit* ID-8
Silver Creek Tank—*reservoir* AZ-5
Silver Creek Townhall—*building* IA-7
*Silver Creek Township* KS-7
Silver Creek Township—*civil* MO-7
Silver Creek Township—*fmr MCD* (3) IA-7
**Silver Creek Township**—*pop pl* KS-7
**Silver Creek Township**—*pop pl* (3) NE-7
**Silver Creek Township**—*pop pl* SD-7
Silver Creek (Township of)—*civ div* IL-6
Silver Creek (Township of)—*civ div* IN-6
Silver Creek (Township of)—*civ div* MI-6
Silver Creek (Township of)—*civ div* (2) MN-6
Silver Creek (Township of)—*civ div* OH-6
Silver Creek (Township of)—*fmr MCD* NC-3
Silver Creek Trail—*trail* (2) CO-8
Silver Creek Trail—*trail* ID-8
Silver Creek Trail—*trail* WA-9
Silver Creek Valley—*valley* OR-9
Silver Creek Wash—*stream* AZ-5
Silver Creek Work Center—*locale* ID-8
Silver Crescent Mine—*mine* CA-9
**Silvercrest Mesa Subdivision**—*pop pl* UT-8
**Silvercrest Park Subdivision**—*pop pl* UT-8
Silvercrest Run—*stream* IN-6
Silvercrest Sch—*school* OR-9
Silvercrest State Hosp—*hospital* IN-6
Silver Cross—*locale* AL-4
Silver Cross Cem—*cemetery* LA-4
**Silver Crown**—*pop pl* WY-8
Silver Crown Lake—*lake* WA-9
Silver Crown Mine—*mine* AZ-5
Silver Crown Mine—*mine* CO-8
Silver Crown Mtn—*summit* WA-9
Silver Cut Meadows—*flat* AZ-5
Silverdaale Sch—*school* NC-3
Silverdale—*locale* CO-8
Silverdale—*locale* MN-6
**Silverdale**—*pop pl* IN-6
**Silverdale**—*pop pl* KS-7
**Silverdale**—*pop pl* NC-3
**Silverdale**—*pop pl* PA-2
**Silverdale**—*pop pl* TN-4
**Silverdale**—*pop pl* WA-9
Silverdale Baptist Ch—*church* TN-4
Silverdale Borough—*civil* PA-2
Silver Dale Canyon—*valley* NM-5
Silverdale Cem—*cemetery* KS-7
Silverdale Cem—*cemetery* MN-6
Silverdale Cem—*cemetery* MO-7
Silverdale Cem—*cemetery* TN-4
Silverdale Ch—*church* MO-7
Silverdale Cumberland Presbyterian Ch—*church* TN-4
Silverdale Lookout Tower Cem—*cemetery* TN-4
Silverdale Post Office (historical)—*building* PA-2
Silverdale Sch—*school* MN-6
Silverdale Sch—*school* NE-7
Silverdale Sch—*school* WI-6
Silverdale Sch (historical)—*school* PA-2
Silverdale Siding—*locale* WA-9
Silver Dale Spring—*spring* NM-5
**Silverdale Township**—*pop pl* KS-7
Silver Dawn Creek—*stream* NY-2
Silver Dawn Lake—*lake* NY-2
Silver Dick Mine—*mine* OR-9
Silver Dime Mine—*mine* AZ-5
Silver Divide—*ridge* CA-9
Silver Dollar Beach—*locale* MT-8
Silver Dollar Cafe—*hist pl* TX-5
Silver Dollar City—*park* MO-7
**Silver Dollar City**—*pop pl* MO-7
Silver Dollar Flat—*flat* OR-9
Silver Dollar Island—*island* CO-8
Silver Dollar Lake—*lake* CO-8
Silverdollar Lake—*lake* WI-6
Silver Dollar Mine—*mine* AZ-5
Silver Dollar Mine—*mine* CA-9
Silver Dollar Mine—*mine* NM-5
Silver Dollar Mine—*mine* UT-8
Silver Dollar Peak—*summit* ID-8
Silver Dollar Pond—*lake* CO-8
Silver Dollar Pond—*lake* NY-2
Silver Dollar Shop Ctr—*locale* TN-4
Silver Dollar Spring—*spring* AZ-5
Silver Dome—*summit* ID-8
Silver Drain—*stream* MI-6
Silver Draw—*valley* CO-8
Silver Drip Trail (Pack)—*trail* NM-5
Silver Drum Mine—*mine* UT-8
Silver Dyke Canyon—*valley* NV-8
Silver Dyke Mine—*mine* MT-8
Silver Dyke Mine—*mine* NV-8
Silver Eagle Peak—*summit* WA-9
Silver Eagle Shaft—*mine* NV-8
Silver Eel Cove—*bay* NY-2
*Silver Eel Pond* NY-2
Silverena Cem—*cemetery* MS-4
*Silverena Church* MS-4
Silverena Sch (historical)—*school* MS-4
Silverene Ch—*church* AL-4
Silver Falls—*falls* AK-9
Silver Falls—*falls* CA-9
Silver Falls—*falls* CO-8
Silver Falls—*falls* CT-1
Silver Falls—*falls* (2) MI-6
Silver Falls—*falls* (3) OR-9
Silver Falls—*falls* TX-5
Silver Falls—*falls* (2) WA-9
Silver Falls Bench—*bench* UT-8
Silver Falls Campground—*locale* WA-9
*Silver Falls Canyon* UT-8
Silver Falls City—*locale* OR-9
Silver Falls Creek—*stream* MT-8
Silver Falls Creek—*stream* UT-8
Silver Falls Guard Station—*locale* CO-8
Silver Falls State Park—*park* OR-9
Silver Falls State Park Concession Bldg Area—*hist pl* OR-9
Silverfalls Timber Co. Dam—*dam* OR-9
Silver Fir Campground—*locale* WA-9
Silver Fire Tower—*tower* PA-2
Silver Flat—*flat* CA-9
**Silver Ford Heights**—*pop pl* PA-2
**Silver Fork**—*pop pl* CA-9
**Silver Fork**—*pop pl* UT-8
Silver Fork—*stream* CA-9
Silver Fork—*stream* MO-7
Silver Fork—*stream* OR-9
Silver Fork—*stream* UT-8
Silver Fork American River—*stream* CA-9
*Silver Fork Creek* MO-7
Silver Fork Gap—*gap* OR-9
Silver Fork Sch—*school* CA-9
Silver Fox Campground—*park* UT-8
Silver Fox Lodge—*locale* AK-9
Silver Fox Ridge—*ridge* WI-6
Silver Gage Ditch—*canal* CO-8
Silver Gap—*gap* AL-4
Silver Gap—*gap* WV-2
**Silver Gap**—*pop pl* WV-2
Silver Gate—*gap* WY-8
**Silver Gate**—*pop pl* MT-8
**Silvergate II (subdivision)**—*pop pl* (2) AZ-5
Silver Gate Sch—*school* CA-9
**Silvergate Trails (subdivision)**—*pop pl* (2) AZ-5
Silver Glacier—*glacier* AK-9
Silver Glance Lake—*lake* UT-8
Silver Glance Mine—*mine* (2) CO-8
Silver Glenn Springs—*spring* FL-3
Silver Glenn Springs Run—*stream* FL-3
Silver Glyn Chapel—*church* FL-3
Silver Grange Ditch—*canal* OR-9
Silver Green Cem—*cemetery* FL-3
Silver Grey Mine—*mine* CA-9
Silver Grouse Mine—*mine* MT-8
*Silver Grove* IN-6
Silver Grove—*locale* TN-4
**Silver Grove**—*pop pl* KY-4
**Silver Grove**—*pop pl* MD-2
**Silver Grove**—*pop pl* WV-2
Silver Grove Cem—*cemetery* VA-3
Silver Grove Ch—*church* OH-6
Silver Grove Ch—*church* VA-3
**Silver Grove (RR name Stevens)**—*pop pl* KY-4
Silver Gulch—*stream* WA-9
Silver Gulch—*valley* AK-9
Silver Gulch—*valley* CA-9
Silver Gulch—*valley* (4) CO-8
Silver Gulch—*valley* MT-8
Silver Gulch—*valley* NE-7
Silver Gulch—*valley* OR-9
Silver Gulch Mine—*mine* NV-8
*Silverheel Gulch* CO-8
SILVER HEEL (log canoe)—*hist pl* MD-2
Silverheels, Mount—*summit* CO-8
*Silverheels Creek* CO-8
Silverheels Creek—*stream* CO-8
*Silverheels Gulch* CO-8
Silverheels Gulch—*valley* CO-8
Silverheels Mine—*mine* CO-8
**Silver Heights**—*pop pl* CO-8
*Silver Hill* AL-4
*Silver Hill* IN-6
*Silver Hill* MA-1
Silver Hill—*locale* (2) GA-3
Silverhill—*locale* KY-4
Silver Hill—*locale* VA-3
Silver Hill—*locale* WV-2
**Silverhill**—*pop pl* AL-4
**Silver Hill**—*pop pl* AR-4
**Silver Hill**—*pop pl* MD-2
**Silver Hill**—*pop pl* MA-1
**Silver Hill**—*pop pl* (3) NC-3
**Silverhill**—*pop pl* TN-4
**Silver Hill**—*pop pl* TN-4
Silver Hill—*summit* (2) AZ-5
Silver Hill—*summit* (3) CA-9
Silver Hill—*summit* CO-8
Silver Hill—*summit* CT-1
Silver Hill—*summit* ID-8
Silver Hill—*summit* (3) MA-1
Silver Hill—*summit* MS-4
Silver Hill—*summit* MT-8
Silver Hill—*summit* (2) NV-8
Silver Hill—*summit* (3) NH-1
Silver Hill—*summit* NJ-2
Silver Hill—*summit* NM-5
Silver Hill—*summit* (2) NY-2
Silver Hill—*summit* PA-2
Silver Hill—*summit* (2) WA-9
Silver Hill Boulder Cave—*cave* PA-2
Silver Hill Canyon—*valley* (2) NV-8
Silverhill Cem—*cemetery* AL-4
Silver Hill Cem—*cemetery* AR-4
Silver Hill Cem—*cemetery* IA-7
Silver Hill Cem—*cemetery* TX-5
Silver Hill Ch—*church* AL-4
Silver Hill Ch—*church* AR-4
Silver Hill Ch—*church* (2) GA-3
Silver Hill Ch—*church* MD-2
Silver Hill Ch—*church* NC-3
*Silverhill Creek* AL-4
Silverhill Elem Sch—*school* AL-4
Silver Hill Hist Dist—*hist pl* NM-5
Silver Hill Mine—*mine* (2) AZ-5
Silver Hill Mine—*mine* NM-5
Silver Hill Mine—*mine* UT-8
**Silver Hill Park**—*pop pl* MD-2
*Silver Hills* IN-6
**Silver Hills**—*pop pl* IN-6
Silver Hills—*range* (2) IN-6
Silver Hill Sch—*school* MD-2
Silver Hill (site)—*locale* NV-8
Silver Hills Mine—*mine* ID-8
Silver Hills Sch—*school* UT-8
Silver Hill State For—*forest* NY-2
Silver Hill (Township of)—*fmr MCD* NC-3
Silver Hill Trail—*trail* OR-9
Silver (historical)—*locale* NC-3
Silver Hole Marsh—*swamp* NY-2
Silver Hollow—*valley* AR-4
Silver Hollow—*valley* MO-7
Silver Hollow—*valley* NY-2
Silver Hollow Notch—*gap* NY-2
Silver Hook—*bend* RI-1
**Silver Hook**—*pop pl* RI-1
Silver Hook Lake—*reservoir* IN-6
Silver Hook Lake Dam—*dam* IN-6
Silver Horn—*bay* AK-9
Silverhorn Creek—*stream* CA-9
Silverhorn Mine—*mine* NV-8
Silverhorn Ski Area—*locale* ID-8
Silverhorn Wash—*stream* NV-8
Silver Houses Hist Dist—*hist pl* MD-2
*Silver island* UT-8
Silver Island—*cape* SC-3
Silver Island—*island* MD-2
Silver Island—*island* MI-6
Silver Island—*summit* UT-8
Silver Island Canyon—*valley* UT-8
Silver Island Cem—*cemetery* IN-6
Silver Island Lake—*lake* MN-6
*Silver Island Mountain* UT-8
Silver Island Mtns—*range* UT-8
Silver Island Pass—*gap* UT-8
*Silver Island Range* UT-8
*Silver Islet Range* UT-8
Silver Jack Mine—*mine* CO-8
Silver Key—*island* (2) FL-3
**Silver King**—*pop pl* ID-8
Silver King—*ridge* MT-8
Silver King Canyon—*valley* TX-5
Silver King Consolidated—*mine* UT-8
Silver King Creek—*stream* CA-9
Silver King Extension—*mine* UT-8
Silver King Falls—*falls* OR-9
Silver King Lake—*lake* CO-8
Silver King Lake—*lake* MT-8
Silver King Mine—*mine* AK-9
Silver King Mine—*mine* (3) AZ-5
Silver King Mine—*mine* (2) CA-9
Silver King Mine—*mine* (2) CO-8
Silver King Mine—*mine* (2) ID-8
Silver King Mine—*mine* (6) MT-8
Silver King Mine—*mine* (4) NV-8
Silver King Mine—*mine* NM-5
Silver King Mine—*mine* (2) UT-8
Silver King Mine—*mine* WA-9
Silver King Mtn—*summit* (2) MT-8
Silver King Mtn—*summit* NV-8
Silver King Mtn—*summit* OR-9
Silver King Ore Loading Station—*hist pl* UT-8
Silver King Pass—*gap* NV-8
Silver King Ranch—*locale* MT-8
Silver King Trail—*trail* CA-9
Silver King Trail—*trail* MT-8
Silver King Valley—*flat* CA-9
Silver King Wash—*stream* AZ-5
Silver King Well—*well* NV-8
Silver King Windmill—*well* AZ-5
Silver Knob—*summit* CA-9
Silver Knob—*summit* NC-3
Silver Knoll Ch—*church* MS-4
*Silver Lake* AL-4
*Silver Lake* AZ-5
*Silver Lake* CA-9
*Silver Lake* CO-8
*Silver Lake* CT-1
*Silver Lake* FL-3
*Silver Lake* GA-3
*Silverlake* IN-6
*Silver Lake* MI-6
*Silver Lake* MN-6
*Silver Lake* NJ-2
*Silver Lake* ND-7
*Silver Lake* OR-9
*Silver Lake* RI-1
*Silver Lake* UT-8
*Silverlake* UT-8
*Silver Lake* VT-1
*Silverlake* WA-9
*Silver Lake* WI-6
Silver Lake—*flat* CA-9
Silver Lake—*flat* NV-8
Silver Lake—*flat* OR-9
Silver Lake—*lake* (2) AL-4
Silver Lake—*lake* (2) AK-9
Silver Lake—*lake* AR-4
Silver Lake—*lake* (6) CA-9
Silver Lake—*lake* (3) CO-8
Silver Lake—*lake* CT-1
Silver Lake—*lake* DE-2
Silver Lake—*lake* (21) FL-3
Silver Lake—*lake* GA-3
Silver Lake—*lake* (2) ID-8
Silver Lake—*lake* (4) IL-6
Silver Lake—*lake* (4) IN-6
Silver Lake—*lake* (2) IA-7
Silver Lake—*lake* (2) KS-7
Silver Lake—*lake* (2) KY-4
Silver Lake—*lake* LA-4
Silver Lake—*lake* (6) ME-1
Silver Lake—*lake* (5) MA-1
Silver Lake—*lake* (25) MI-6
Silver Lake—*lake* (24) MN-6
Silver Lake—*lake* (2) MS-4
Silver Lake—*lake* (2) MO-7
Silver Lake—*lake* (4) MT-8
Silver Lake—*lake* NE-7
Silver Lake—*lake* NV-8
Silver Lake—*lake* (4) NH-1
Silver Lake—*lake* (4) NJ-2
Silver Lake—*lake* (14) NY-2
Silver Lake—*lake* (3) NC-3
Silver Lake—*lake* (3) ND-7
Silver Lake—*lake* (5) OH-6
Silver Lake—*lake* (2) OK-5
Silver Lake—*lake* OR-9
Silver Lake—*lake* (5) PA-2
Silver Lake—*lake* RI-1
Silver Lake—*lake* SC-3
Silver Lake—*lake* (4) SD-7
Silver Lake—*lake* (4) TX-5
Silver Lake—*lake* (2) UT-8
Silver Lake—*lake* (3) VT-1
Silver Lake—*lake* (2) VA-3
Silver Lake—*lake* (12) WA-9
Silver Lake—*lake* (28) WI-6
Silver Lake—*lake* (1) WY-0
Silver Lake—*locale* CA-9
Silver Lake—*locale* TN-4
Silver Lake—*locale* TX-5
**Silver Lake**—*pop pl* FL-3
**Silver Lake**—*pop pl* IL-6
**Silver Lake**—*pop pl* IN-6
**Silver Lake**—*pop pl* IA-7
**Silver Lake**—*pop pl* KS-7
**Silver Lake**—*pop pl* (2) MA-1
**Silver Lake**—*pop pl* MI-6
**Silver Lake**—*pop pl* MN-6
**Silver Lake**—*pop pl* MO-7
**Silver Lake**—*pop pl* NJ-2
**Silver Lake**—*pop pl* (3) NY-2
**Silver Lake**—*pop pl* NC-3
**Silver Lake**—*pop pl* (2) OH-6
**Silver Lake**—*pop pl* OR-9
**Silver Lake**—*pop pl* (3) PA-2
**Silver Lake**—*pop pl* WA-9
**Silverlake**—*pop pl* WA-9
**Silver Lake**—*pop pl* WV-2
**Silver Lake**—*pop pl* (2) WI-6
Silver Lake—*reservoir* (2) CA-9
Silver Lake—*reservoir* (3) CO-8
Silver Lake—*reservoir* CT-1
Silver Lake—*reservoir* (4) DE-2
Silver Lake—*reservoir* FL-3
Silver Lake—*reservoir* GA-3
Silver Lake—*reservoir* ID-8
Silver Lake—*reservoir* IA-7
Silver Lake—*reservoir* ME-1
Silver Lake—*reservoir* MD-2
Silver Lake—*reservoir* (3) MA-1
Silver Lake—*reservoir* MI-6
Silver Lake—*reservoir* (2) MO-7
Silver Lake—*reservoir* MT-8
Silver Lake—*reservoir* (7) NJ-2
Silver Lake—*reservoir* (3) NY-2
Silver Lake—*reservoir* (3) NC-3
Silver Lake—*reservoir* ND-7
Silver Lake—*reservoir* OK-5
Silver Lake—*reservoir* (5) PA-2
Silver Lake—*reservoir* (2) SC-3
Silver Lake—*reservoir* TN-4
Silver Lake—*reservoir* (2) TX-5
Silver Lake—*reservoir* (3) UT-8
Silver Lake—*reservoir* VA-3
Silver Lake—*reservoir* WV-2
Silver Lake—*reservoir* WI-6
Silver Lake—*swamp* AR-4
Silver Lake—*swamp* MO-7
Silver Lake—*uninc pl* NJ-2
Silver Lake—*uninc pl* WA-9
Silver Lake Airstrip—*airport* OR-9
Silver Lake Assembly—*other* NY-2
Silver Lake Bank—*hist pl* PA-2
*Silver Lake Basin* CO-8
Silver Lake Basin—*basin* CO-8
Silver Lake Basin—*reservoir* MI-6
Silver Lake Branch—*stream* MO-7
Silver Lake Branch—*stream* TX-5
Silver Lake Brook—*stream* NY-2
Silver Lake Campground—*locale* CA-9
Silver Lake Campground—*locale* WY-8
Silver Lake Cem—*cemetery* FL-3
Silver Lake Cem—*cemetery* (2) IA-7
Silver Lake Cem—*cemetery* KS-7
Silver Lake Cem—*cemetery* ME-1
Silver Lake Cem—*cemetery* MA-1
Silver Lake Cem—*cemetery* MI-6
Silver Lake Cem—*cemetery* NE-7
Silver Lake Cem—*cemetery* NY-2
Silver Lake Cem—*cemetery* OK-5
Silver Lake Cem—*cemetery* OR-9
Silver Lake Cem—*cemetery* WA-9
Silver Lake Ch—*church* IA-7
Silver Lake Ch—*church* MS-4
Silver Lake Ch—*church* NJ-2
Silver Lake Ch—*church* NC-3
Silver Lake Ch—*church* SD-7
Silver Lake Chapel—*church* IN-6
Silver Lake Country Club—*other* IL-6
Silver Lake Country Club—*other* MI-6
Silver Lake Country Club—*other* OH-6
Silver Lake County Park—*park* PA-2
*Silver Lake Creek* PA-2
Silver Lake Creek—*stream* LA-4
Silver Lake Dam—*dam* (3) DE-2
Silver Lake Dam—*dam* (2) MA-1
Silver Lake Dam—*dam* (3) NJ-2
Silver Lake Dam—*dam* NC-3
Silver Lake Dam—*dam* ND-7
Silver Lake Dam—*dam* (4) PA-2
Silver Lake Dam—*dam* (2) UT-8
Silver Lake District—*hist pl* NH-1
Silver Lake Ditch—*canal* CO-8
Silver Lake Ditch—*canal* OR-9
Silver Lake Elem Sch—*school* DE-2
Silver Lake Elem Sch—*school* IN-6
Silver Lake Elem Sch—*school* KS-7
Silver Lake Elem Sch—*school* OR-9
**Silver Lake Estates Subdivision**—*pop pl* UT-8
Silver Lake Farm—*hist pl* NH-1
Silver Lake-Fircrest—*CDP* WA-9
Silver Lake Flat—*flat* UT-8
Silver Lake Flat—*reservoir* UT-8
Silver Lake Flat Dam—*dam* UT-8
Silver Lake Forest Service Strip—*airport* OR-9
Silver Lake Fork—*gut* NJ-2
Silver Lake-Fort Rock (CCD)—*cens area* OR-9
Silver Lake Golf Course—*other* MI-6
Silver Lake (historical)—*lake* IA-7
Silver Lake (historical)—*locale* CA-9
Silver Lake (historical)—*locale* SD-7
**Silver Lake (historical)**—*pop pl* MS-4
Silver Lake (historical P.O.)—*locale* IA-7
Silver Lake (historical P.O.)—*locale* MA-1
Silver Lake HS—*school* KS-7
Silver Lake HS—*school* MA-1
Silver Lake Inlet—*stream* NY-2
Silver Lake Institute Hist Dist—*hist pl* NY-2
Silver Lake Islet—*reservoir* UT-8
Silver Lake Islet Dam—*dam* UT-8
Silver Lake JHS—*school* MA-1
*Silver Lake Junction* IN-6
*Silver Lake Junction* OH-6
Silver Lake Junction—*locale* NY-2
Silver Lake Junction—*uninc pl* LA-4
Silver Lake Lean-to—*locale* NY-2
Silver Lake Lookout Tower—*locale* MI-6
**Silver Lake (Madison Station)**—*pop pl* NH-1
**Silver Lake Manor (subdivision)**—*pop pl* DE-2
Silver Lake Meadow—*flat* NJ-2
Silver Lake Mine—*mine* CA-9
Silver Lake Mine—*mine* CO-8
Silver Lake Mine—*mine* TN-4
*Silver Lake Mountains* NY-2
Silver Lake Mountains—*ridge* NY-2
Silver Lake Mountain Trail—*trail* NY-2
Silver Lake Mtn—*summit* (2) NY-2
Silver Lake Natl Wildlife Ref—*park* ND-7
Silver Lake Outlet—*stream* (2) NY-2
Silver Lake Park—*park* DE-2
Silver Lake Park—*park* IA-7
Silver Lake Park—*park* MN-6
Silver Lake Park—*park* (3) NY-2
Silver Lake Park—*park* WA-9
Silver Lake Pioneer Cem—*cemetery* MN-6
**Silver Lake (Plasse)**—*pop pl* CA-9
Silver Lake Public Hunting Area—*area* IA-7
Silver Lake Ranch—*locale* FL-3
Silver Lake Ranch—*locale* TX-5
Silver Lake Ranger Station—*locale* OR-9
Silver Lake Rec Area—*park* FL-3
Silver Lake Recreation Center—*park* CA-9
Silver Lake Rsvr—*reservoir* CA-9
Silver Lake Rsvr—*reservoir* MA-1
Silver Lake Rsvr—*reservoir* NY-2
Silver Lakes—*lake* IN-6
Silver Lakes—*lake* LA-4
Silver Lake Sch—*school* FL-3
Silver Lake Sch—*school* IL-6
Silver Lake Sch—*school* MI-6
Silver Lake Sch—*school* (2) MN-6
Silver Lake Sch—*school* SD-7
Silver Lake Sch—*school* WA-9
**Silver Lakes Estates (Trailer Park)**—*pop pl* IN-6
**Silver Lake Shores (subdivision)**—*pop pl* DE-2
Silverlakes MS—*school* FL-3
Silver Lake Spring—*spring* (2) TN-4
**Silver Lake (sta.)**—*pop pl* MN-6
Silver Lake State Game Mngmt Area—*park* (2) IA-7
Silver Lake State Park—*park* MI-6
Silver Lake State Park—*park* NH-1
Silver Lake State Park—*park* NY-2
Silver Lake State Park—*park* VT-1
Silver Lake Station—*locale* NJ-2
Silver Lake Station (historical)—*locale* MA-1
**Silver Lake Summer Home Area**—*pop pl* UT-8
**Silver Lake Summer Resort**—*pop pl* UT-8
Silver Lake Tank—*reservoir* TX-5
Silver Lake Township—*fmr MCD* (3) IA-7
**Silver Lake Township**—*pop pl* KS-7
**Silver Lake Township**—*pop pl* NE-7
**Silver Lake Township**—*pop pl* ND-7
**Silver Lake Township**—*pop pl* SD-7
Silver Lake Township (historical)—*civil* SD-7
Silver Lake (Township of)—*fmr MCD* AR-4
**Silver Lake (Township of)**—*pop pl* MN-6
**Silver Lake (Township of)**—*pop pl* PA-2
**Silver Lake Village**—*pop pl* NY-2
*Silver Lakeville* IN-6
**Silver Lake ( within PMSA's 1120 and 4560 )**—*pop pl* MA-1
Silver Landing—*locale* AL-4
Silver Lane—*post sta* CT-1
Silver Lane Sch—*school* CT-1
Silver L Canal—*canal* OR-9
*Silver Lead Creek* ID-8
Silver Lead Creek—*stream* MI-6
Silver-Lead Mine—*mine* CA-9
Silver Lead Mine Lake—*lake* MI-6
Silver Lead Spring—*spring* CA-9
**Silverleaf**—*pop pl* ND-7
Silverleaf Branch—*stream* VA-3
Silver Leaf Ch—*church* GA-3
Silverleaf Ch—*church* VA-3
Silver Leaf Ch—*church* VA-3
Silverleaf Ch—*church* VA-3
*Silver Leaf Creek* NC-3
Silverleaf Creek—*stream* NC-3
Silverleaf Creek—*stream* VA-3
Silver Leaf Mine—*mine* ID-8
Silver Leaf Mine—*mine* NV-8
Silver Leaf Mine—*mine* WA-9
*Silver Leaf Pond* NY-2
Silver Leaf Pond—*lake* NY-2
Silver Leaf Sch—*school* IL-6
*Silver Leaf Station* ND-7
**Silver Leaf (Township of)**—*pop pl* MN-6
Silver Lea Sch—*school* OR-9
Silver Ledge—*bench* VT-1
Silver Ledge Mine—*mine* CO-8
Silver Lick Hollow—*valley* KY-4
Silver Lick Mine—*mine* NV-8
Silver L I. D. Rsvr—*reservoir* OR-9
*Silver Lookout Tower* PA-2
Silverly Creek—*stream* WA-9
Silverman, Morris, House—*hist pl* MT-8
Silverman Lake—*lake* WY-8
Silverman Springs Coulee—*valley* MT-8
Silver Maple Cem—*cemetery* NY-2
Silver Maple Sch—*school* MN-6
Silver Maple Sch—*school* WI-6
Silver Meadow—*flat* UT-8
**Silver Meadows (subdivision)**—*pop pl* AL-4
**Silver Meadows Subdivision**—*pop pl* UT-8
Silver Mesa—*summit* CO-8
Silver Mesa Sch—*school* UT-8
Silver Mill Hollow—*valley* PA-2
Silvermill Hollow Run—*stream* PA-2
Silver Mills—*locale* PA-2
*Silvermine* CT-1
Silver Mine—*locale* MO-7
**Silvermine**—*pop pl* CT-1
Silvermine Arch—*arch* KY-4
Silvermine Arch Trail—*trail* KY-4
Silvermine Bald—*summit* NC-3
Silvermine Branch—*stream* (2) KY-4
Silvermine Branch—*stream* (2) NC-3
Silvermine Branch—*stream* TN-4
Silvermine Brook—*stream* (2) CT-1
Silvermine Ch—*church* NC-3
Silvermine Cliff—*cliff* KY-4
Silver Mine Creek—*stream* CA-9
Silvermine Creek—*stream* GA-3
Silver Mine Creek—*stream* NC-3
Silvermine Creek—*stream* NC-3
Silvermine Creek—*stream* TN-4
Silver Mine Creek—*stream* TX-5
Silvermine Creek—*stream* TX-5
Silver Mine Creek—*stream* WY-8
Silver Mine Dam—*dam* MO-7
Silvermine Gap—*gap* NC-3
Silvermine Hall—*hospital* CT-1
Silvermine Hill—*summit* CT-1
Silver Mine Hill—*summit* MA-1
*Silver Mine Hollow* PA-2
Silver Mine Hollow—*valley* KY-4
Silvermine Hollow—*valley* KY-4
Silver Mine Hollow—*valley* OH-6
Silvermine Hollow—*valley* TN-4
Silver Mine Hollow—*valley* UT-8
Silver Mine Hollow—*valley* VA-3
Silver Mine Knob—*summit* KY-4
Silver Mine Knob—*summit* PA-2
Silver Mine Lake—*reservoir* NY-2
Silver Mine Lakes—*lake* MI-6
Silver Mine Pass—*gap* TX-5
Silvermine Pond—*lake* CT-1
Silvermine Ridge—*ridge* GA-3
Silver Mine Ridge—*ridge* SC-3
Silvermine River—*stream* CT-1
Silvermine River—*stream* NY-2
Silver Mine Run—*stream* PA-2
Silver Mines Branch—*stream* KY-4
Silvermine Sch—*school* KY-4
Silver Mine Sink—*basin* MO-7
Silvermont—*hist pl* NC-3
Silver Monument Mine (Inactive)—*mine* NM-5
Silver Moon Ch—*church* MO-7
Silver Moon Creek—*stream* ID-8
Silver Moon Gulch—*valley* ID-8
Silver Moon Lake—*lake* IL-6
Silver Moon Lake—*lake* TN-4
Silver Moon Mine—*mine* (2) NV-8
Silver Mound—*summit* (2) WI-6
Silver Mound Archeol District—*hist pl* WI-6
Silver Mound Ch—*church* AR-4
Silver Mound Trail—*trail* WI-6
Silver Mount—*summit* MI-6
Silver Mountain Ch—*church* MS-4
**Silver Mountain Estates Subdivision**—*pop pl* UT-8
Silver Mountain Mine—*mine* CO-8
Silver Mountain Mine—*mine* UT-8
Silver Mountain Mine—*mine* WA-9
Silver Mountain Mineral Monmt—*pillar* CA-9
*Silver Mountains* ID-8
*Silver Mountains* NV-8
*Silver Mountains* OR-9
Silver Mountain Sch—*school* MS-4
Silver Mountain (Site)—*locale* CA-9
Silver Mount Cem—*cemetery* NY-2
Silver Mount Ch—*church* MS-4
Silvermount Ch—*church* NC-3
Silver Mtn—*summit* (2) AZ-5
Silver Mtn—*summit* (3) CA-9
Silver Mtn—*summit* (6) CO-8
Silver Mtn—*summit* (2) ID-8
Silver Mtn—*summit* NH-1
Silver Mtn—*summit* NY-2
Silver Mtn—*summit* SD-7
Silvernagel Creek—*stream* WI-6
Silvernail Drain—*canal* MI-6
Silvernail Drain—*stream* NE-7
Silver Nail Lake—*lake* WA-9
**Silvernails**—*pop pl* NY-2
Silvernail State Wildlife Area—*park* WI-6
Silver Oak Sch—*school* MN-6
Silveropolis Hill—*summit* UT-8
**Silver Palm**—*pop pl* FL-3
Silver Palm Park—*park* FL-3
Silver Palm Sch—*school* FL-3
Silver Palm Schoolhouse—*hist pl* FL-3
Silver Palm United Methodist Ch—*church* FL-3
Silver Park—*flat* (2) CO-8
Silver Park—*locale* NV-8
Silver Park—*park* OH-6
Silver Park Ch—*church* OH-6
Silver Park Creek—*stream* CO-8
Silver Park Sch—*school* CO-8
Silver Park Springs—*spring* NV-8
**Silver Park Subdivision**—*pop pl* UT-8
Silver Pass—*gap* CA-9
Silver Pass—*gap* CO-8
Silver Pass—*gap* MT-8
Silver Pass—*gap* UT-8
Silver Pass—*gap* WA-9
Silver Pass Canyon—*valley* UT-8
Silver Pass Creek—*stream* CA-9
Silver Pass Gulch—*valley* UT-8
Silver Pass Lake—*lake* CA-9
*Silver Peak* CO-8
*Silverpeak* NV-8
*Silver Peak* UT-8
*Silver Peak* WY-8
**Silver Peak**—*pop pl* NV-8
**Silverpeak**—*pop pl* NV-8
Silver Peak—*summit* (2) AZ-5
Silver Peak—*summit* (10) CA-9
Silver Peak—*summit* ID-8
Silver Peak—*summit* MT-8
Silver Peak—*summit* NV-8
Silver Peak—*summit* NM-5

Silver Peak—*summit* ... OR-9
Silver Peak—*summit* ... SD-7
Silver Peak—*summit* ... TX-5
Silver Peak—*summit* ... UT-8
Silver Peak—*summit* ... VA-3
Silver Peak—*summit* ... WA-9
Silver Peak Lookout Complex—*hist pl* ... AZ-5
*Silver Peak Mountains* ... NV-8
Silver Peak Range—*range* ... NV-8
Silver Peak Tank—*reservoir* ... NM-5
Silver Pick Basin—*basin* ... CO-8
Silver Pick Mill—*locale* ... CO-8
Silver Pick Mine—*mine* ... CO-8
Silver Pick Mine—*mine* ... NV-8
**Silver Pines**—*pop pl* ... GA-3
Silver Pine Sch—*school* ... TN-4
Silver Pines Village (Shop Ctr)—*locale* ... FL-3
Silver Pipe Dam—*dam* ... NM-5
**Silver Plume**—*pop pl* ... CO-8
Silver Plume Depot—*hist pl* ... CO-8
Silver Plume Mine—*mine* ... CO-8
Silver Plume Mtn—*summit* ... CO-8
Silver Point—*cape* ... AK-9
Silver Point—*cape* ... IN-6
Silver Point—*cape* ... NY-2
Silver Point—*cape* ... OR-9
Silver Point—*cape* ... WA-9
**Silver Point**—*pop pl* ... IN-6
**Silver Point**—*pop pl* ... TN-4
Silver Point Baptist Ch—*church* ... TN-4
Silver Point Ch—*church* ... MO-7
Silver Point Mine—*mine* ... CO-8
*Silverpoint Post Office* ... TN-4
Silver Point Post Office—*building* ... TN-4
Silverpoint Sch (historical)—*school* ... TN-4
Silver Pond—*lake* ... FL-3
Silver Prairie—*flat* ... OR-9
Silver Prince Creek—*stream* ... CO-8
Silver Prince Mine—*mine* (2) ... AZ-5
Silver Pug Lake—*lake* ... ME-1
*Silver Queen Mine* ... AZ-5
Silver Queen Mine—*mine* (2) ... AZ-5
Silver Queen Mine—*mine* ... CO-8
Silver Queen Mine—*mine* ... ID-8
Silver Queen Mine—*mine* (2) ... MT-8
Silver Queen Mine—*mine* ... SD-7
Silver Queen Mine—*mine* ... WA-9
Silver Range Mine—*mine* ... NV-8
**Silver Rapids**—*pop pl* ... MN-6
Silver Reef—*locale* ... UT-8
Silver Reef Mine—*mine* ... AZ-5
Silver Reef Mine—*mine* (2) ... CA-9
Silver Reef Mine—*mine* ... NV-8
*Silver Reef Mountains* ... AZ-5
Silver Reef Mountains—*summit* ... AZ-5
Silver Reef Pass—*gap* ... AZ-5
Silver Reef Valley—*valley* ... AZ-5
Silver Reef Wash—*stream* ... AZ-5
Silver Ridge—*locale* ... AR-4
Silver Ridge—*locale* ... ME-1
**Silver Ridge**—*pop pl* ... NJ-2
**Silver Ridge**—*pop pl* ... TN-4
Silver Ridge—*ridge* ... AL-4
Silver Ridge—*ridge* ... ID-8
Silver Ridge—*ridge* ... OH-6
Silver Ridge—*ridge* ... TN-4
Silver Ridge—*ridge* ... WA-9
Silver Ridge Baptist Ch—*church* ... TN-4
Silver Ridge Cem—*cemetery* ... ME-1
Silver Ridge Cem—*cemetery* ... NE-7
Silver Ridge Cem—*cemetery* ... SD-7
Silver Ridge Ch—*church* ... MS-4
Silver Ridge Peninsula—*cape* ... AR-4
**Silver Ridge Subdivision**—*pop pl* ... UT-8
Silver Ridge (Township of)—*unorg* ... ME-1
Silver Ripple Cascade—*falls* ... ME-1
*Silver River* ... NH-1
Silver River—*stream* ... FL-3
Silver River—*stream* (3) ... MI-6
Silver Rock—*pillar* ... OR-9
**Silver Rock**—*pop pl* ... MD-2
Silver Rock Mine—*mine* ... ID-8
Silverrona Spring—*spring* ... AZ-5
Silver Row—*hist pl* ... UT-8
Silver Rule Creek—*stream* ... ID-8
Silver Rule Mine—*mine* ... MT-8
*Silver Run* ... FL-3
*Silver Run* ... MT-8
*Silver Run* ... PA-2
*Silver Run* ... WV-2
Silver Run—*locale* ... MS-4
**Silver Run**—*pop pl* ... AL-4
**Silver Run**—*pop pl* ... MD-2
**Silver Run**—*pop pl* ... OH-6
**Silver Run**—*pop pl* ... WV-2
Silver Run—*stream* ... AL-4
Silver Run—*stream* ... DE-2
Silver Run—*stream* ... ID-8
Silver Run—*stream* ... KY-4
Silver Run—*stream* (2) ... MD-2
Silver Run—*stream* ... MS-4
Silver Run—*stream* ... NY-2
Silver Run—*stream* (2) ... NC-3
Silver Run—*stream* ... OH-6
Silver Run—*stream* (3) ... PA-2
Silver Run—*stream* (2) ... SC-3
Silver Run—*stream* (2) ... WV-2
Silver Run Branch—*stream* ... GA-3
Silver Run Branch—*stream* ... MS-4
Silver Run Branch—*stream* ... TX-5
Silver Run Cem—*cemetery* ... SC-3
Silver Run Ch—*church* ... AL-4
Silver Run Ch—*church* (2) ... GA-3
Silver Run Ch—*church* ... NC-3
*Silver Run Creek* ... AL-4
Silver Run Creek—*stream* ... AL-4
Silver Run Creek—*stream* (2) ... MT-8
Silver Run Creek—*stream* (2) ... NC-3
Silver Run Creek—*stream* ... WY-8
Silver Run Grange—*locale* ... WA-9
Silver Run Lake—*lake* ... WY-8
Silver Run Lake—*reservoir* ... MS-4
Silver Run Lake—*reservoir* ... NC-3
Silver Run Lake Dam—*dam* ... MS-4
Silver Run Lake Dam—*dam* ... NC-3
Silver Run Lakes—*reservoir* ... MS-4
Silver Run Peak—*summit* ... MT-8
Silver Run Plateau—*plain* ... MT-8
Silver Run Sch—*school* ... AL-4
Silver Run Sch (historical)—*school* ... MS-4
Silver Run Station—*locale* ... WV-2
Silver Run Wildlife Area—*park* ... DE-2
Silver Rute Mine—*mine* ... ID-8
Silvers, John, Barn—*hist pl* ... KS-7
Silversack Lake—*lake* ... MN-6
Silver Sack Lake—*lake* ... WI-6
Silver Sage Girl Scout Camp—*locale* ... ID-8
Silver Sage Ranch—*locale* ... MT-8
**Silver Sage Subdivision**—*pop pl* ... UT-8
Silver Salmon Creek—*stream* (2) ... AK-9
Silver Salmon Falls—*falls* ... AK-9
Silver Salmon Lake—*lake* ... AK-9
Silver Salmon Lakes—*lake* ... AK-9
Silver Salmon Rapids—*rapids* ... AK-9
*Silver Sands* ... FL-3
Silver Sands—*uninc pl* ... FL-3
*Silver Sands Bay* ... MI-6
Silver Sands Beach—*beach* ... CT-1
Silver Sands Beach—*beach* ... UT-8
**Silver Sands Beach**—*pop pl* ... ID-8
Silver Sands Junior High—*school* ... FL-3
Silver Sands Sch—*school* ... FL-3
Silver Scarf Falls—*falls* ... WY-8
Silvers Cem—*cemetery* ... MO-7
Silvers Cem—*cemetery* ... NC-3
Silver School Branch—*stream* ... WI-6
Silvers Cove—*valley* ... NC-3
Silvers Cove Creek—*stream* ... NC-3
Silvers Creek—*stream* ... SC-3
*Silvers Fork* ... MO-7
Silver Shade Ch (abandoned)—*church* ... MO-7
Silver Shade Sch (historical)—*school* (2) ... MO-7
**Silver Shadow Estates**—*pop pl* ... UT-8
**Silver Shadows Subdivision**—*pop pl* ... UT-8
**Silver Shell Beach**—*pop pl* ... MA-1
Silver Shield Lake—*reservoir* ... MA-1
Silvershield Mill—*locale* ... CO-8
Silver Shield Mine—*mine* ... AZ-5
Silver Shoal—*locale* ... GA-3
Silver Shoal Ch—*church* ... GA-3
Silver Shoals Bridge—*bridge* ... GA-3
Silver Shoals Ch—*church* ... GA-3
Silvers Hollow—*valley* ... KY-4
Silvers Hollow—*valley* ... TN-4
**Silver Shores**—*pop pl* ... FL-3
Silver Shores Dock—*locale* ... AL-4
*Silver Side* ... DE-2
Silverside—*locale* ... DE-2
**Silverside Heights**—*pop pl* ... DE-2
Silverside Sch—*school* ... DE-2
Silvers Lake—*lake* ... MI-6
Silvers Lake—*reservoir* ... NC-3
**Silvers Mills**—*pop pl* ... ME-1
Silvers Mine—*mine* ... OR-9
Silversmith Branch—*stream* ... AR-4
Silversmith Creek—*stream* ... FL-3
**Silversmith Estates**—*pop pl* ... UT-8
**Silver Smith Subdivision**—*pop pl* ... UT-8
Silver Spar—*mine* ... UT-8
Silver Spear Mine—*mine* ... CA-9
Silverspoon Mine—*mine* ... CA-9
Silver Spoon Mine—*mine* ... CO-8
Silver Spoon Rsvr—*reservoir* ... WY-8
Silver Spray Falls—*falls* ... CA-9
*Silver Spray Spring* ... AZ-5
Silver Spree Ch—*church* ... MS-4
*Silver Spree Methodist Ch* ... MS-4
*Silver Spree School* ... MS-4
**Silver Spring**—*pop pl* ... MD-2
**Silver Spring**—*pop pl* ... NC-3
**Silver Spring**—*pop pl* (2) ... PA-2
**Silver Spring**—*pop pl* ... RI-1
Silver Spring—*spring* (2) ... AZ-5
Silver Spring—*spring* ... CA-9
Silver Spring—*spring* ... MT-8
Silver Spring—*spring* (2) ... NV-8
Silver Spring—*spring* ... NM-5
Silver Spring—*spring* (2) ... OR-9
Silver Spring—*spring* ... PA-2
Silver Spring—*spring* ... SD-7
Silver Spring—*spring* ... TN-4
Silver Spring—*spring* ... WA-9
Silver Spring—*spring* ... WV-2
Silver Spring—*spring* ... WI-6
*Silver Spring Beach* ... MA-1
Silver Spring Beach—*beach* ... NV-8
**Silver Spring Beach**—*pop pl* ... MA-1
Silver Spring Brook—*stream* ... CT-1
Silver Spring Brook—*stream* ... ME-1
Silver Spring Brook—*stream* (2) ... MA-1
Silver Spring Brook Marshes—*swamp* ... MA-1
Silver Spring Camp—*locale* ... OR-9
Silver Spring Cem—*cemetery* ... IL-6
Silver Spring Ch—*church* ... OK-5
Silver Spring Ch—*church* ... SC-3
*Silver Spring Church* ... PA-2
Silver Spring Country Club—*other* ... CT-1
Silver Spring Cove—*bay* ... RI-1
Silver Spring Creek—*stream* ... MN-6
Silver Spring Creek—*stream* ... WI-6
Silver Spring Elem Sch—*school* ... PA-2
Silver Spring Golf Course—*locale* ... PA-2
Silver Spring Gulch—*valley* ... AZ-5
Silver Spring Harbor—*bay* ... MA-1
**Silver Spring Heights**—*pop pl* ... MD-2
Silver Spring Intermediate Sch—*school* ... MD-2
Silver Spring Lake—*lake* ... RI-1
Silver Spring Lake—*reservoir* ... RI-1
Silver Spring Lake—*reservoir* ... VA-3
Silver Spring Lake Dam—*dam* ... RI-1
Silver Spring Meeting House—*building* ... PA-2
Silver Spring Mine—*mine* ... CA-9
Silver Spring Park—*park* ... WI-6
**Silver Spring Park**—*pop pl* ... MD-2
*Silver Spring Peak* ... NH-1
*Silver Spring Pond* ... RI-1
Silver Spring Post Office (historical)—*building* ... PA-2
Silver Spring Post Office (historical)—*building* ... TN-4
**Silver Spring (RR name Bruckarts)**—*pop pl* ... PA-2
*Silver Springs* ... PA-2
Silver Springs—*locale* ... FL-3
Silver Springs—*locale* ... MO-7
Silver Springs—*locale* ... NC-3
**Silver Springs**—*pop pl* (2) ... CO-8
**Silver Springs**—*pop pl* ... FL-3
**Silver Springs**—*pop pl* ... MS-4
**Silver Springs**—*pop pl* ... NV-8
**Silver Springs**—*pop pl* ... NJ-2
**Silver Springs**—*pop pl* ... NY-2
**Silver Springs**—*pop pl* ... NC-3
**Silver Springs**—*pop pl* ... TN-4
**Silver Springs**—*pop pl* ... UT-8
**Silver Springs**—*pop pl* ... VA-3
Silver Springs—*spring* ... AZ-5
Silver Springs—*spring* ... FL-3
Silver Springs—*spring* ... NV-8
Silver Springs—*spring* ... PA-2
Silver Springs—*spring* (2) ... WA-9
Silver Springs—*spring* ... WY-8
Silver Springs Acad (historical)—*school* ... TN-4
Silver Springs Airp—*airport* ... NV-8
Silver Springs Baptist Ch—*church* ... TN-4
*Silver Springs Baptist Church* ... MS-4
Silver Springs Branch—*stream* ... TN-4
*Silver Springs Brook* ... MA-1
Silver Springs Camp—*locale* ... FL-3
Silver Springs Canyon—*valley* ... NM-5
Silver Springs Cem—*cemetery* ... MS-4
Silver Springs Cem—*cemetery* ... NC-3
Silver Springs Ch—*church* ... AR-4
Silver Springs Ch—*church* ... MS-4
Silver Springs Ch—*church* ... MO-7
Silver Springs Ch—*church* ... NC-3
Silver Spring Sch—*school* (2) ... WI-6
*Silver Springs Creek* ... LA-4
*Silver Springs Creek* ... MS-4
Silver Springs Creek—*stream* ... MS-4
Silver Springs Creek—*stream* ... NM-5
Silver Springs Creek—*stream* (2) ... WY-8
Silver Springs Hill—*summit* ... MS-4
Silver Springs Lake—*reservoir* ... PA-2
Silver Springs Ranch—*locale* ... CO-8
*Silver Springs River* ... FL-3
*Silver Springs Run* ... FL-3
Silver Springs Sch—*school* ... TN-4
Silver Springs Sch—*school* ... WV-2
Silver Springs Sch (historical)—*school* ... TN-4
**Silver Springs Shores (subdivision)**—*pop pl* ... FL-3
Silver Springs State Park—*park* ... IL-6
*Silver Springs Station* ... MD-2
**Silver Springs (subdivision)**—*pop pl* ... DE-2
**Silver Spring (Township of)**—*pop pl* ... PA-2
**Silver Spruce**—*pop pl* ... CO-8
Silver Spruce Lodge—*locale* ... WY-8
Silver Spruce Mill—*locale* ... CO-8
Silver Spruce Mine—*mine* ... AZ-5
Silver Spruce Mine—*mine* ... CO-8
Silver Spruce Trail—*trail* ... CO-8
Silver Spur—*ridge* ... CA-9
Silver Spur Creek—*stream* ... ID-8
Silver Spur Mine—*mine* ... NM-5
Silver Spur Ranch—*locale* ... CO-8
Silver Spur Ranch—*locale* ... WY-8
Silver Spur Ranch (trailer park)—*locale* ... AZ-5
**Silver Spur Ranch (trailer park)**—*pop pl* ... AZ-5
Silver Spur Ridge—*ridge* ... ID-8
Silver Spur Sch—*school* ... CA-9
Silver Spur Spring—*spring* ... AZ-5
Silver Spur Village (trailer park)—*locale* ... AZ-5
**Silver Spur Village (trailer park)**—*pop pl* ... AZ-5
Silvers Station—*locale* ... ID-8
Silver Stairs—*trail* ... UT-8
Silverstairs Creek—*stream* ... OR-9
*Silverstar* ... MT-8
**Silver Star**—*pop pl* ... MT-8
Silver Star Cem—*cemetery* ... OK-5
Silver Star Ch—*church* ... LA-4
Silver Star Ch—*church* ... MS-4
Silver Star Creek—*stream* ... WA-9
Silver Star Fishing Access—*locale* ... MT-8
Silver Star Hall—*locale* ... MT-8
Silver Star Mine—*mine* ... ID-8
Silver Star Mine—*mine* (2) ... NV-8
Silver Star Mine—*mine* ... OR-9
Silver Star Mine—*mine* ... WA-9
Silver Star Mtn—*summit* (2) ... WA-9
Silver Star Plaza (Shop Ctr)—*locale* ... FL-3
Silver Star Queen—*mine* ... ID-8
*Silver Star Ridge* ... WA-9
Silver Star Sch—*school* ... KY-4
Silver State Ditch No 1—*canal* ... WY-8
Silver State Draw—*arroyo* ... NV-8
Silver State Flour Mill—*hist pl* ... NV-8
Silver State Mine—*mine* ... NV-8
Silver State Spring—*spring* ... NV-8
Silver State Valley—*valley* ... NV-8
Silver State Youth Camp—*locale* ... CO-8
Silver Station Brook—*stream* ... IN-6
**Silverstone**—*pop pl* ... NC-3
**Silverstone (subdivision)**—*pop pl* ... NC-3
Silver Strand—*cape* ... CA-9
**Silver Strand**—*pop pl* ... CA-9
Silver Strand Falls—*falls* ... CA-9
Silver Strand Mine—*mine* ... CA-9
Silver Strand Sch—*school* ... CA-9
Silver Strand (Sliver Strand Beach)—*uninc pl* ... CA-9
Silver Strand State Beach—*park* ... CA-9
Silver Stream—*stream* ... ME-1
Silver Stream—*stream* ... NH-1
Silver Stream—*stream* (2) ... NY-2
*Silver Street* ... SC-3
**Silverstreet**—*pop pl* ... SC-3
Silver Street Cem—*cemetery* ... CT-1
Silver Street Ch—*church* ... IN-6
Silver Street Elem Sch—*school* ... IN-6
Silver Street (historical)—*locale* ... IA-7
Silverstreet Lookout Tower—*locale* ... SC-3
Silver Street Sch—*school* ... OH-6
**Silverstreet (Silver Stret)**—*pop pl* ... SC-3
*Silver Street (Sliverstreet)* ... SC-3
Silverstrike Mine—*mine* ... AZ-5
Silverstrike Spring—*spring* ... AZ-5
*Silver Strip* ... ND-7
Silver Suck Trail—*trail* ... OK-5
Silver Summit Mine—*mine* ... ID-8
Silver Summit Mine—*mine* ... WA-9
Silver Swan Mine—*mine* ... CO-8
Silversword Inn—*locale* ... HI-9
Silversword Loop—*trail* ... HI-9
Silvertail Canyon—*valley* ... NM-5
Silvertail Mine—*mine* ... NM-5
Silver Tank—*reservoir* (2) ... AZ-5
Silver Tank—*reservoir* ... NV-8
Silver Tank—*reservoir* ... TX-5
Silver Terrace Playground—*park* ... CA-9
Silverthorn—*locale* ... CA-9
Silverthorn Creek—*stream* ... MT-8
**Silverthorne**—*pop pl* ... CO-8
Silverthorne Cem—*cemetery* ... NE-7
Silverthorne Sch—*school* ... WI-6
Silverthorn Lake—*lake* ... WI-6
Silverthorn Point—*cape* ... NC-3
Silverthorn Sch (abandoned)—*school* ... PA-2
Silver Thread Falls—*falls* ... NY-2
Silverthread Falls—*falls* ... PA-2
Silverthrone, Mount—*summit* ... AK-9
Silverthrone Col—*gap* ... AK-9
Silvertip—*locale* ... AK-9
Silver Tip—*locale* ... WY-8
**Silver Tip**—*pop pl* ... AK-9
Silvertip, Mount—*summit* ... AK-9
Silvertip Basin—*basin* ... WY-8
Silver Tip Camp—*locale* ... OR-9
Silvertip Campground—*locale* ... CA-9
*Silvertip Creek* ... MT-8
Silvertip Creek—*stream* ... AK-9
Silvertip Creek—*stream* ... ID-8
Silvertip Creek—*stream* ... MT-8
Silver Tip Creek—*stream* ... MT-8
Silvertip Creek—*stream* ... MT-8
Silvertip Creek—*stream* ... WA-9
Silver Tip Creek—*stream* ... WY-8
Silvertip Creek—*stream* ... WY-8
Silver Tip Creek—*stream* ... WY-8
Silver Tip Ditch—*canal* ... MT-8
Silvertip Guard Station—*locale* ... MT-8
*Silvertip Gulch* ... MT-8
*Silvertip Gulch* ... WY-8
Silvertip Landing—*locale* ... ID-8
Silvertip Mine—*mine* ... AZ-5
Silver Tip Mine—*mine* ... OR-9
Silvertip Mine—*mine* ... WA-9
Silvertip Mtn—*summit* ... MT-8
Silver Tip Oil Field—*oilfield* ... WY-8
Silvertip Peak—*summit* ... WA-9
Silvertip Peak—*summit* ... WY-8
Silver Tip Ranch—*locale* ... MT-8
Silvertip Rsvr—*reservoir* ... MT-8
Silvertip Spring—*spring* ... UT-8
*Silverton* ... KS-7
*Silverton* ... SC-3
Silverton—*locale* ... PA-2
Silverton—*locale* ... TN-4
Silverton—*locale* ... WA-9
**Silverton**—*pop pl* ... CO-8
**Silverton**—*pop pl* ... ID-8
**Silverton**—*pop pl* ... NJ-2
**Silverton**—*pop pl* ... OH-6
**Silverton**—*pop pl* ... OR-9
**Silverton**—*pop pl* ... TX-5
**Silverton**—*pop pl* ... WV-2
Silverton Airfield—*airport* ... OR-9
Silverton (CCD)—*cens area* ... OR-9
Silverton (CCD)—*cens area* ... TX-5
Silverton Cem—*cemetery* ... OR-9
Silverton Ch—*church* ... MN-6
Silverton Commercial Hist Dist—*hist pl* ... OR-9
Silverton Creek—*stream* ... ID-8
**Silverton Estates**—*pop pl* ... NJ-2
Silverton Field—*park* ... OH-6
Silverton Hills—*summit* ... OR-9
Silverton Hills Grange—*locale* ... OR-9
Silverton Hist Dist—*hist pl* ... CO-8
**Silverton Pine Terrace**—*pop pl* ... NJ-2
Silverton Sch—*school* ... KS-7
**Silverton (subdivision)**—*pop pl* ... NC-3
**Silverton (Township of)**—*pop pl* ... MN-6
Silvertooth Cave—*cave* ... TN-4
**Silvertop**—*pop pl* ... TN-4
Silver Top Mtn—*summit* ... NM-5
Silvertop Post Office (historical)—*building* ... TN-4
Silvertop Sch (historical)—*school* ... TN-4
*Silvertop Towhead* ... TN-4
Silvertown—*locale* ... GA-3
**Silvertown**—*pop pl* ... GA-3
Silvertown Sch—*school* ... VT-1
Silver Township—*fmr MCD* ... IA-7
**Silver (Township of)**—*pop pl* ... MN-6
Silver Trail Mine—*mine* ... WA-9
Silver Trails Camp—*locale* ... MI-6
Silver Tree Mine—*mine* ... NM-5
Silvervale Falls—*falls* ... NC-3
Silver Valley—*locale* ... TX-5
**Silver Valley**—*pop pl* ... NC-3
Silver Valley—*stream* ... WV-2
**Silver Valley Addition (subdivision)**—*pop pl* ... SD-7
Silver Valley Campground—*locale* ... CA-9
Silver Valley Campground—*locale* ... MI-6
Silver Valley Cem—*cemetery* ... IA-7
Silver Valley Cem—*cemetery* ... TX-5
Silver Valley Community Hall—*locale* ... AR-4
Silver Valley Creek—*stream* ... NE-7
Silver Valley Sch—*school* ... NC-3
Silver Valley Sch—*school* ... WV-2
Silver Vault Mine (historical)—*mine* ... ID-8
**Silver View Farm (subdivision)**—*pop pl* ... DE-2
**Silverville**—*pop pl* ... IN-6
**Silverville**—*pop pl* ... PA-2
Silverville Branch—*stream* ... IN-6
Silver Water Tank—*other* ... MD-2
Silver Wave Mine—*mine* ... CO-8
Silver Well—*well* ... NM-5
*Silver Wood* ... IN-6
**Silverwood**—*pop pl* ... IN-6
**Silverwood**—*pop pl* ... LA-4
**Silverwood**—*pop pl* ... MI-6
**Silverwood**—*pop pl* ... MN-6
**Silverwood**—*pop pl* ... VA-3
Silverwood Falls—*falls* ... CA-9
Silverwood Lake—*reservoir* ... CA-9
Silvery Cem—*cemetery* ... LA-4
Silver Zone—*locale* ... NV-8
Silver Zone Basin—*basin* ... NV-8
Silver Zone Pass—*gap* ... NV-8
Silver Zone Well—*well* ... NV-8
Silvesta Cem—*cemetery* ... ND-7
**Silvesta Township**—*pop pl* ... ND-7
Silvester Cem—*cemetery* ... TN-4
Silvester Point—*cape* ... AK-9
Silvestre Overlook—*cliff* ... UT-8
Silvests Pond—*reservoir* ... AL-4
Silveus Ditch—*canal* ... IN-6
Silvey Branch—*stream* ... MO-7
Silvey Cem—*cemetery* (3) ... MO-7
Silvey Flats—*flat* ... CO-8
Silvey Gap—*gap* ... TN-4
Silvey Hollow—*valley* ... OH-6
Silveys Pocket—*basin* ... CO-8
Silvia Creek—*stream* ... AK-9
Silvia Ditch—*canal* ... CA-9
Silvia Hill Ch—*church* ... GA-3
Silvia Hollow—*valley* ... UT-8
Silvia Place Pond Dam—*dam* ... MA-1
Silvia Ranch—*locale* ... NM-5
*Silvias Creek* ... WA-9
Silvias Pond—*reservoir* ... CT-1
Silvias Sch—*school* ... FL-3
*Silvicola* ... TN-4
Silvie Bend—*bend* ... LA-4
Silvie Bend—*bend* ... TX-5
Silvies—*locale* ... OR-9
Silvies Canyon—*valley* ... OR-9
*Silvies Creek* ... OR-9
*Silvies Creek* ... WA-9
Silvies Landing—*locale* ... OR-9
*Silvies River* ... OR-9
Silvies River—*stream* ... OR-9
Silvies Valley—*valley* ... OR-9
Silvies Valley Ranch—*locale* ... OR-9
**Silview**—*pop pl* ... DE-2
**Silvis**—*pop pl* ... IL-6
**Silvis Heights**—*pop pl* ... IL-6
Silvis Lake—*lake* ... MI-6
Silvista (historical)—*locale* ... ND-7
Silvis Trail—*trail* ... PA-2
Silvola Ranch—*locale* ... WA-9
Sil Vous Plait—*falls* ... MT-8
*Silynarki* ... AZ-5
Simalusa Creek—*stream* ... LA-4
Simanola Valley—*valley* ... NM-5
Simar—*locale* ... MN-6
**Simar**—*pop pl* ... MI-6
Simas Lake—*lake* ... CA-9
Simax Bay—*bay* ... OR-9
Simax Beach Campgrounds—*park* ... OR-9
*Simboro* ... TX-5
Sim Chapel—*church* ... KY-4
Sim Chapel—*church* ... MS-4
*Sim Chapel Missionary Baptist Ch* ... MS-4
Simcock House—*hist pl* ... KS-7
**Simcoe**—*pop pl* ... AL-4
**Simcoe**—*pop pl* ... MO-7
**Simcoe**—*pop pl* ... ND-7
Simcoe Butte—*summit* ... WA-9
Simcoe (CCD)—*cens area* ... AL-4
Simcoe Ch—*church* ... AL-4
Simcoe Creek—*stream* ... WA-9
Simcoe Division—*civil* ... AL-4
Simcoe Mountains—*range* ... WA-9
Simcoe Post Office (historical)—*building* ... AL-4
Simcoe Post Office (historical)—*building* ... TN-4
Simcoe Sch—*school* ... AL-4
Simco Farm—*locale* ... IL-6
Simcox Branch—*stream* ... TN-4
Simcox Mtn—*summit* ... PA-2
Si Meade Hollow—*valley* ... NY-2
Sime Lake—*lake* ... TX-5
Sime Lake—*lake* ... WI-6
Sim Elem Sch—*school* ... KS-7
Simeling Run—*stream* ... PA-2
Simels (Abandoned)—*locale* ... AK-9
Si Melton Cem—*cemetery* ... TN-4
*Simeneaux Ponds* ... LA-4
**Simensen**—*pop pl* ... WA-9
Simenson—*locale* ... WA-9
Simentons Store—*locale* ... VA-3
Simeon—*locale* ... NE-7
Simeon—*locale* ... VA-3
Simeon, Mount—*summit* ... AK-9
Simeon Bay—*bay* ... AK-9
Simeon Branch—*stream* ... LA-4
Simeon Creek—*stream* ... AK-9
Simeon Lake—*lake* ... AK-9
Simeon Mills Hist Dist—*hist pl* ... WI-6
Simeonof Harbor—*bay* ... AK-9
Simeonof Island—*island* ... AK-9
Simeonof Natl Wildlife Ref—*park* ... AK-9
Simeon Pass—*gap* ... AK-9
Simeon PO—*locale* ... NE-7
Simeons Pond—*gut* ... LA-4
Sime Ridge—*ridge* ... WI-6
Simerly Cem—*cemetery* (3) ... TN-4
Simerly Creek—*stream* (2) ... TN-4
Simerly Lookout Tower—*locale* ... AL-4
Si Merrell Slough—*swamp* ... MT-8
**Simers**—*pop pl* ... KY-4
Simerson Creek—*stream* ... NC-3
Simerson Spring—*spring* ... OR-9
Simerwell Cem—*cemetery* ... KS-7
Simes Creek—*stream* ... TX-5
Simes Creek—*stream* ... WI-6
Simes Creek Flowage—*reservoir* ... WI-6
Simes Landing (historical)—*locale* ... AL-4
Simfield Ch—*church* ... NC-3
Sim Hill Ch—*church* ... TN-4
*Simi* ... CA-9
Simi—*civil* ... CA-9
Simi—*locale* ... CA-9
Simi, Arroyo—*stream* ... CA-9
Simi Adobe-Strathearn House—*hist pl* ... CA-9
*Simiahmoo Bay* ... WA-9
Simian Lake—*lake* ... MN-6
Simi Civic Center—*building* ... CA-9
Simi Hills—*range* ... CA-9
Simik Mtn—*summit* ... AK-9
Similar Sound—*bay* ... FL-3
Similin Cem—*cemetery* ... MO-7
Similin Creek—*stream* ... MO-7
*Similkameen Dam* ... WA-9
Similkameen River—*stream* ... WA-9
Similk Bay—*bay* ... WA-9
**Similk Beach**—*pop pl* ... WA-9
*Simindson Lake* ... NE-7
Siminmin—*summit* ... FM-9
*Simi Oil Field* ... CA-9
*Simions Creek* ... MI-6
Simi Peak—*summit* ... CA-9
Simi Sch—*school* ... CA-9
**Simi (Simi Valley)**—*pop pl* ... CA-9
Simison-Hale Cem—*cemetery* ... OR-9
Simis Sch—*school* ... AZ-5
Simi Station—*locale* ... CA-9
**Simi Valley**—*pop pl* ... CA-9
Simi Valley—*valley* ... CA-9
Simi Valley (CCD)—*cens area* ... CA-9
Simi Valley HS—*school* ... CA-9
**Simi Valley (Simi)**—*pop pl* ... CA-9
Simkin Cem—*cemetery* ... SC-3
Simkins, Paris, House—*hist pl* ... SC-3
Simkins Draw—*valley* ... SD-7
Simkins Point—*summit* ... AR-4
Simkins Sch—*school* ... MA-1
Simkins Thorofare—*channel* ... NJ-2
**Simla**—*pop pl* ... CO-8
Sim Langdon Sch—*school* ... KY-4
Sim Layton Sch (abandoned)—*school* ... MO-7
**Simler**—*pop pl* ... MO-7
Simley HS—*school* ... MN-6
Sim Long Branch—*stream* ... KY-4
*Simmans Creek* ... AL-4
*Simmasho* ... OR-9
Sim Memorial Park—*park* ... KS-7
Simmering Lookout Tower—*locale* ... OH-6
Simmering Park—*park* ... OK-5
Simmering Ridge—*ridge* ... OH-6
Simmerley Flat—*flat* ... CA-9
Simmerly Creek—*stream* ... CA-9
Simmerly Slough—*stream* ... CA-9
Simmerlys Mill (historical)—*locale* ... TN-4
Simmerman—*locale* ... VA-3
Simmerman Ditch—*canal* ... IN-6
Simmers Hollow—*valley* ... VA-3
Simmerson Place—*locale* ... WY-8
**Simmesport**—*pop pl* ... LA-4
*Simmino Creek* ... VA-3
Simmler—*locale* ... CA-9
*Simmo Creek* ... OR-9
Simmon Branch—*stream* ... AL-4
Simmon Chapel—*church* ... AL-4
*Simmon Creek* ... ID-8
*Simmond Creek* ... OR-9
Simmond Creek—*stream* ... NY-2
*Simmonds Creek* ... NV-8
Simmonds Creek—*stream* ... OR-9
*Simmonds Crossroads* ... AL-4
Simmonds Gap—*gap* ... VA-3
*Simmonds Island* ... TN-4
*Simmon Grove Ch* ... MS-4
Simmon Grove Ch—*church* ... NC-3
Simmon Hill Ch—*church* ... GA-3
Simmon Hollow—*valley* ... AR-4
Simmon Lake—*lake* ... SD-7
Simmon Lake—*lake* ... TX-5
Simmon Pond—*lake* ... FL-3
Simmon Ridge Ch—*church* ... SC-3
Simmon Rsvr—*reservoir* ... WY-8
*Simmons* ... FL-3
*Simmons* ... NC-3
Simmons—*locale* ... AR-4
Simmons—*locale* ... KY-4
Simmons—*locale* ... MI-6
Simmons—*locale* ... TX-5
**Simmons**—*pop pl* ... MO-7
**Simmons**—*pop pl* ... WV-2
Simmons, Gilbert M., Memorial Library—*hist pl* ... WI-6
Simmons, James B., House—*hist pl* ... GA-3
Simmons, John P., House—*hist pl* ... IA-7
Simmons, Lake—*lake* (2) ... FL-3
Simmons, Peter, House—*hist pl* ... TN-4
Simmons, Robert, House—*hist pl* ... SC-3
Simmons, William S., Plantation—*hist pl* ... GA-3
Simmons Airp—*airport* ... AL-4
Simmons Airp—*airport* ... MS-4
Simmons Airp—*airport* ... NC-3
Simmons Attendance Center—*school* ... MS-4
Simmons Bay—*bay* ... MN-6
Simmons Bay—*locale* ... NC-3
Simmons Bay—*swamp* ... GA-3
Simmons Bay—*swamp* ... NC-3
Simmons Bay—*swamp* ... SC-3
Simmons Bay Bridge—*bridge* ... NC-3
Simmons Bay Creek—*gut* ... NC-3
Simmons Bay Creek—*stream* ... NC-3
Simmons Bayou—*stream* ... LA-4
Simmons Bayou—*stream* ... MS-4
Simmons Block—*hist pl* ... MA-1
Simmons Bluff—*cliff* ... GA-3
Simmons Bluff Post Office (historical)—*building* ... TN-4
Simmons Bottom—*locale* ... TX-5
*Simmons Branch* ... AL-4
Simmons Branch—*stream* (4) ... AL-4
Simmons Branch—*stream* (3) ... GA-3
Simmons Branch—*stream* ... KY-4
Simmons Branch—*stream* (4) ... MS-4
Simmons Branch—*stream* ... MO-7
Simmons Branch—*stream* (6) ... NC-3
Simmons Branch—*stream* (10) ... TN-4
Simmons Branch—*stream* ... TX-5
Simmons Branch—*stream* ... WV-2
Simmons Branch—*stream* ... WI-6
Simmons Branch Cem—*cemetery* ... GA-3
Simmons Branch Ch—*church* ... GA-3
Simmons Branch Industrial Site—*locale* ... TN-4
Simmons Branch Mine—*mine* ... TN-4
Simmons Branch Mines—*mine* ... TN-4
Simmons Brook—*stream* ... ME-1
Simmons Brook—*stream* ... RI-1
Simmons Brothers Pond Dam—*dam* ... MS-4
Simmons Canyon—*valley* (2) ... CA-9
Simmons Canyon—*valley* ... NM-5
Simmons Canyon—*valley* ... OR-9
Simmons Canyon—*valley* ... UT-8
Simmons Canyon—*valley* ... WY-8
Simmons Cave—*cave* ... MO-7
*Simmons Cem* ... AL-4
*Simmons Cem* ... TN-4
Simmons Cem—*cemetery* (3) ... AL-4
Simmons Cem—*cemetery* (2) ... AR-4
Simmons Cem—*cemetery* ... FL-3
Simmons Cem—*cemetery* (3) ... GA-3
Simmons Cem—*cemetery* (3) ... IL-6
Simmons Cem—*cemetery* (4) ... IN-6
Simmons Cem—*cemetery* ... KS-7
Simmons Cem—*cemetery* (2) ... KY-4
Simmons Cem—*cemetery* (3) ... LA-4
Simmons Cem—*cemetery* ... ME-1
Simmons Cem—*cemetery* ... MA-1
Simmons Cem—*cemetery* ... MI-6
Simmons Cem—*cemetery* (5) ... MS-4

Simmons Cem—cemetery (2) MO-7
Simmons Cem—cemetery (3) NC-3
Simmons Cem—cemetery OH-6
Simmons Cem—cemetery OK-5
Simmons Cem—cemetery OR-9
Simmons Cem—cemetery (19) TN-4
Simmons Cem—cemetery (8) TX-5
Simmons Cem—cemetery (4) VA-3
Simmons Cem—cemetery (3) WV-2
Simmons Ch—church AR-4
Simmons Ch—church FL-3
Simmons Ch—church TN-4
Simmons Ch—church TX-5
Simmons Chapel—church NC-3
Simmons Chapel—church OK-5
Simmons Chapel—church (3) TN-4
**Simmons Chapel**—pop pl TN-4
Simmons Chapel Cem—cemetery TX-5
Simmons Chapel Sch—school TN-4
Simmons Ch (historical)—church MS-4
Simmon Sch (historical)—school TN-4
Simmons City TX-5
Simmons Corner—locale NC-3
Simmons Corner—locale RI-1
Simmons Corners—locale NY-2
Simmons Coulee MT-8
Simmons Coulee—valley MT-8
Simmons Creek AL-4
Simmons Creek IN-6
Simmons Creek MS-4
Simmons Creek OR-9
Simmons Creek—stream (4) AL-4
Simmons Creek—stream AR-4
Simmons Creek—stream (2) CA-9
Simmons Creek—stream FL-3
Simmons Creek—stream (3) ID-8
Simmons Creek—stream (2) IL-6
Simmons Creek—stream IN-6
Simmons Creek—stream (3) IA-7
Simmons Creek—stream KS-7
Simmons Creek—stream KY-4
Simmons Creek—stream (2) LA-4
Simmons Creek—stream (2) MI-6
Simmons Creek—stream (3) MS-4
Simmons Creek—stream (2) MT-8
Simmons Creek—stream (3) OR-9
Simmons Creek—stream PA-2
Simmons Creek—stream (3) SC-3
Simmons Creek—stream (2) TN-4
Simmons Creek—stream (2) TX-5
Simmons Creek—stream VA-3
Simmons Creek—stream (3) WA-9
Simmons Creek—stream (2) WV-2
Simmons Creek—stream WY-8
Simmons Creek Ch—church WV-2
Simmons Creek Sch—school WV-2
Simmons Crossing—locale FL-3
Simmons Crossroads—locale AL-4
Simmonsdale VA-3
Simmons Dam—dam AL-4
Simmons Dam—dam PA-2
Simmons Ditch—canal WY-8
Simmons Drain—canal MI-6
Simmons Draw—valley ID-8
Simmons Draw—valley OR-9
Simmons Draw—valley WY-8
Simmons-Edwards House—hist pl SC-3
Simmons Elementary School MS-4
Simmons Elementary School PA-2
Simmonsen's House—hist pl MT-8
Simmons Family Cem—cemetery AL-4
Simmons Flat—flat CA-9
Simmons Ford—locale AR-4
Simmons Ford (historical)—locale NC-3
Simmons Ford Public Access—locale MO-7
Simmons Fork—stream (3) WV-2
Simmons Gap—gap TN-4
Simmons Gap—gap VA-3
Simmons Gap Ranger Station—locale VA-3
Simmons Gin Branch—stream TN-4
Simmons Grove Ch—church LA-4
Simmons Grove Ch—church (2) NC-3
Simmons Grove Church MS-4
Simmons Gulch CO-8
Simmons Gulch—valley AZ-5
Simmons Gulch—valley CO-8
Simmons Gulch—valley OR-9
Simmons Gully—stream LA-4
Simmons Gurnet ME-1
Simmons-Harth House—hist pl SC-3
Simmons Hassock—island NY-2
Simmons High School MS-4
Simmons Hill VT-1
**Simmons Hill**—pop pl VT-1
Simmons Hill—summit (2) ME-1
Simmons Hill—summit RI-1
Simmons Hill Ch—church GA-3
Simmons Hill Mine—mine MO-7
**Simmons (historical)**—pop pl OR-9
Simmons Hollow TN-4
Simmons Hollow—valley AR-4
Simmons Hollow—valley MO-7
Simmons Hollow—valley (6) TN-4
Simmons Homestead—locale WY-8
Simmons House—hist pl GA-3
Simmons House—hist pl MS-4
Simmons House—hist pl SD-7
Simmons HS—school KY-4
Simmons Institute—school CA-9
Simmons Island—island CA-9
Simmons Island—island NY-2
Simmons Island Bridge TN-4
Simmons Island Park—park WI-6
Simmons JHS—school AL-4
Simmons JHS—school IL-6
Simmons JHS—school SD-7
Simmons Knob—summit KY-4
Simmons Lake—lake (3) MI-6
Simmons Lake—lake MS-4
Simmons Lake—lake OK-5
Simmons Lake—lake WA-9
Simmons Lake—reservoir AL-4
Simmons Lake—reservoir GA-3
Simmons Lake—reservoir NC-3
Simmons Lake—reservoir TN-4
Simmons Lake Dam—dam (2) MS-4
Simmons Lake Dam—dam TN-4
Simmons Lakeside Resort—locale MI-6
Simmons Landing AL-4
Simmons Landing—locale NC-3
Simmons Landing (historical)—locale (2) AL-4
Simmons Lateral—canal NM-5
Simmons Ledges—bench NH-1
Simmons Lookout—locale ID-8
Simmons Lower RI-1
Simmons Lower Reservoir Dam—dam RI-1
Simmons Lower Rsvr—reservoir RI-1
Simmons Meadow—flat MT-8
Simmons Memorial Baptist Ch—church MS-4
Simmons Mill Ch—church LA-4
Simmons Mill (historical)—locale TN-4
Simmons Mill Pond RI-1
Simmons Mill Pond—swamp NC-3
Simmons Mound—summit IL-6
Simmons Mtn—summit AL-4
Simmons Mtn—summit OK-5
Simmons Mtn—summit VA-3
Simmons Mtn—summit (2) WV-2
Simmons Mtn Lake AL-4
Simmons Nott Airp—airport NC-3
Simmons Park—flat MT-8
Simmons Peak—summit (2) AZ-5
Simmons Peak—summit CA-9
Simmons Peak—summit CO-8
Simmons Peak—summit ID-8
Simmons Peak Trail—trail CO-8
Simmons Plantation—locale AR-4
Simmons Plantation (historical)—locale MS-4
Simmons Playground—park CA-9
Simmons Point—cape AK-9
Simmons Point—cape CA-9
Simmons Point—cape FL-3
Simmons Point—cape MN-6
Simmons Point—cape NY-2
Simmons Point—cliff GA-3
Simmons Point—summit CA-9
Simmons Pond—dam MS-4
Simmons Pond—lake (2) FL-3
Simmons Pond—lake GA-3
Simmons Pond—lake ME-1
Simmons Pond—lake MA-1
Simmons Pond—lake NH-1
Simmons Pond—lake NY-2
Simmons Pond—lake RI-1
Simmons Pond—reservoir NJ-2
Simmons Pond—reservoir RI-1
Simmons Pond Dam—dam RI-1
Simmons Ponds—lake MA-1
Simmons Post Camp—locale CA-9
Simmons Prairie Lake—lake FL-3
Simmons Ranch—locale CO-8
Simmons Ranch—locale FL-3
Simmons Ranch—locale NM-5
Simmons Ranch—locale (2) OR-9
Simmons Ranch—locale (2) TX-5
Simmons Rapids—rapids WI-6
Simmons Ridge TN-4
Simmons Ridge—ridge ID-8
Simmons Ridge—ridge MO-7
Simmons Ridge—ridge (2) NC-3
Simmons Ridge—ridge OH-6
Simmons Ridge—ridge TN-4
Simmons Ridge Cem—cemetery OH-6
Simmons (RR name for Freeman)—other WV-2
Simmons Run—stream OH-6
Simmons Run—stream PA-2
Simmons Run—stream VA-3
Simmons Run—stream (3) WV-2
Simmons Saddle—gap NM-5
Simmons Sch—school CA-9
Simmons Sch—school FL-3
Simmons Sch—school GA-3
Simmons Sch—school IL-6
Simmons Sch—school IA-7
Simmons Sch—school MI-6
Simmons Sch—school MS-4
Simmons Sch—school (2) MO-7
Simmons Sch—school PA-2
Simmons Sch—school (2) SD-7
Simmons Sch (abandoned)—school (2) PA-2
Simmons Sch (historical)—school (2) AL-4
Simmons Sch Number 3 (historical)—school SD-7
Simmons Settlement—locale LA-4
Simmons (site)—locale AZ-5
Simmons Slough—stream OR-9
Simmons Spring—spring (2) AZ-5
Simmons Spring—spring CO-8
Simmons Spring—spring OR-9
Simmons Springs Branch—stream MS-4
Simmons Spur—ridge OR-9
Simmons Stone House—hist pl NY-2
**Simmons Subdivision**—pop pl (2) UT-8
Simmons Temple—church AL-4
Simmonstown—locale PA-2
Simmons Trail—trail WY-8
Simmons Trout Lake—reservoir CA-9
Simmons Univ—school KY-4
Simmons Upper Reservoir Dam—dam RI-1
Simmons Upper Rsvr—reservoir RI-1
Simmonsville MS-4
Simmonsville—locale SC-3
Simmonsville—locale TX-5
**Simmonsville**—pop pl MS-4
**Simmonsville**—pop pl RI-1
**Simmonsville**—pop pl SC-3
**Simmonsville**—pop pl TX-5
**Simmonsville**—pop pl VA-3
Simmonsville (Magisterial District)—fmr MCD VA-3
Simmons Windmill—locale NM-5
Simmons Windmill—locale TX-5
Simmon Town AL-4
Simm Point VT-1
Simms OH-6
Simms WV-2
Simms—locale LA-4
Simms—locale (2) TX-5
**Simms**—pop pl CA-9
**Simms**—pop pl MT-8
**Simms**—pop pl TX-5
Simms—post sta CA-9
Simms, Lake—lake WA-9
Simms Bayou TX-5
Simms Branch—stream KY-4
Simms Branch—stream TN-4
Simms Branch—stream TX-5
Simms Branch—stream VA-3
Simms Branch Cave—cave TN-4
Simms Bridge—bridge TN-4
Simms Camp—locale CA-9
Simms Cem TN-4
Simms Cem—cemetery (3) AL-4
Simms Cem—cemetery AR-4
Simms Cem—cemetery GA-3
Simms Cem—cemetery IL-6
Simms Cem—cemetery (2) TN-4
Simms Chapel—church GA-3
Simms Creek CO-8
Simms Creek—stream FL-3
Simms Creek—stream LA-4
Simms Creek—stream MS-4
Simms Creek—stream MO-7
Simms Creek—stream MT-8
Simms Creek—stream OR-9
Simms Creek—stream SD-7
Simms Creek—stream TX-5
Simms Dam—dam OR-9
Simms Draw—valley WY-8
Simms-Ellis House—hist pl LA-4
Simms Flat—flat MO-7
Simms Footbridge—other TX-5
Simms Fork—stream NC-3
Simms-Franklin Ditch IN-6
Simms Gulley—stream TX-5
Simms Gut—gut VA-3
Simms Hill—locale VT-1
Simms Hill—summit NY-2
Simms Hill—summit NC-3
Simms Hollow—valley IL-6
Simms Hollow—valley TN-4
Simms Island—island CA-9
Simms Lake—lake TX-5
Simms Lake—lake WI-6
Simms Landing—locale FL-3
Simms Landing—locale MD-2
Simms Mtn—summit GA-3
Simms Mtn—summit MO-7
Simms Park—park CA-9
Simms Park—park MN-6
Simms Pit—cave MO-7
Simms Point VA-3
Simms Point—cape VT-1
Simms Point—cape VA-3
Simms Pond—lake GA-3
Simms Pond—lake PA-2
Simms Ranch NM-5
Simms Ranch—locale NM-5
Simms Ranch—locale OR-9
Simms Rock—bar ME-1
Simms (RR name for Sims)—other NC-3
Simms Rsvr—reservoir (2) OR-9
Simms Run—stream WV-2
Simms Sch—school MI-6
Simms Sch—school MO-7
Simms Sch—school WV-2
Simms Spring—spring TX-5
Simms Stream—stream NH-1
Simms Tank—reservoir TX-5
Simms Valley MO-7
Simms Valley Sch (abandoned)—school MO-7
Simmsville—locale AL-4
Simmsville Chapel—church AL-4
Simmsville Chapel Ch AL-4
Simms Wharf MD-2
Simms Wharf—locale MD-2
Simms Windmill—locale TX-5
Simm Valley MO-7
**Simnasho**—pop pl OR-9
Simnasho Butte—summit OR-9
Simnasho Cem—cemetery OR-9
Simnioniw Ranch—locale ND-7
Simoda—locale WV-2
Simon—locale WV-2
**Simon**—pop pl OK-5
Simon, Herman, House—hist pl PA-2
Simon, Lake—lake MN-6
Simon, Mount—summit CO-8
Simon, Mount—summit WI-6
Simon (Abandoned)—locale NV-8
Simona Creek MI-6
Simona Tank—reservoir TX-5
Simon Bldg—hist pl TX-5
Simon Bolivar Park—park CA-9
Simon Bottom—bend TX-5
Simon Branch—stream AR-4
Simon Branch—stream GA-3
Simon Branch—stream MI-6
Simon Branch—stream (3) NC-3
Simon Branch—stream TN-4
Simon Branch—stream TX-5
Simon Bridge—bridge LA-4
Simon Brook—stream MA-1
Simon Butte—summit ND-7
Simon Butte—summit WA-9
Simon Cabin—locale AK-9
Simon Canyon—valley (2) NM-5
Simon Canyon (LA 5047)—hist pl NM-5
Simon Cem—cemetery (2) LA-4
Simon Cem—cemetery OK-5
Simon Cem—cemetery (2) TX-5
Simon Chapel Number 1—church MS-4
Simon Chapel Number 1 Cem—cemetery MS-4
Simon Chapel Number 1 Sch—school MS-4
Simon Chapel Number 2—church MS-4
Simon Chapel Number 2 Cem—cemetery MS-4
Simon Ch (historical)—church PA-2
Simon Creek IN-6
Simon Creek—stream AK-9
Simon Creek—stream GA-3
Simon Creek—stream MS-4
Simon Creek—stream NV-8
Simon Creek—stream (2) OK-5
Simon Creek—stream WV-2
Simond, Col. Benjamin, House—hist pl MA-1
Simondale VA-3
Simon Dam—dam SD-7
Simon Draw—valley CO-8
Simonds—locale MS-4
Simonds Bridge—bridge MD-2
Simonds Brook—stream NH-1
Simonds Chapel—church NC-3
Simonds Creek IN-6
**Simonds Gardens**—pop pl DE-2
Simonds Hill—summit MA-1
Simonds Hill—summit VT-1
Simondson Lake—lake NE-7
Simonds Park—park MA-1
Simonds Pond NY-2
Simonds Pond—reservoir MA-1
Simonds Pond Dam—dam MA-1
Simonds Reservoir—lake VT-1
Simonds Run—stream OH-6
Simonds Run—stream PA-2
Simonds Sch—school CA-9
Simonds Sch—school MI-6
Simonds Tavern—hist pl MA-1
Simoneaus Island SD-7
Simoneaux Ponds—lake LA-4
Simone Grove CA-9
Simone Island—island FL-3
Simonet Cave—cave AL-4
Simonetter Sch—school CA-9
Simonetti Spring—spring OR-9
Simonfield MS-4
Simon Fish Pond—lake WV-2
Simon Flat—flat OR-9
Simon Glade—flat DE-2
Simon Gulch—valley UT-8
Simon Gurnet ME-1
Simon Hill—summit MA-1
Simon Hill Cem—cemetery WI-6
Simon Hill Ch—church MS-4
Simon Hollow—valley KY-4
Simon Hollow—valley TN-4
Simonia Ch—church GA-3
Simonin Ditch—canal IN-6
Simonis Gulch—valley OR-9
Simon Island—island VA-3
Simonis Spring—spring OR-9
Simon Kenton Sch—school (2) OH-6
Simon Lake—lake MN-6
Simon Lake—lake OR-9
Simon Lake Sch—school CT-1
Simon Landing—locale OR-9
Simon Mine—mine CA-9
Simon Mtn—summit NV-8
Simono—island PW-9
Simonof Island—island AK-9
Simono Island PW-9
Simono To PW-9
Simon Pass—channel LA-4
Simon Pass Gas Field—oilfield LA-4
Simon Peter Bend—bend TX-5
Simon Pocket—bay TN-4
Simon Point—cape AK-9
Simon Point—cape MA-1
Simon Pond MA-1
Simon Pond—lake ME-1
Simon Pond—lake NY-2
Simon Ravine—valley CA-9
Simon Rsvr—reservoir MT-8
Simon Run—stream WV-2
Simons SC-3
Simons—locale OH-6
**Simons**—pop pl KY-4
Simon's, M. H., Undertaking Chapel—hist pl CA-9
Simons Bldg and Livery Barn—hist pl MN-6
Simons Branch—stream GA-3
Simons Branch—stream NC-3
Simons Branch—stream WV-2
Simons Brook—stream ME-1
Simons Brothers Dam—dam SD-7
Simons Cabin—locale AK-9
Simons Cap FL-3
Simons Cem—cemetery KY-4
Simons Cem—cemetery OH-6
Simon Sch—school DC-2
Simon Sch—school SD-7
Simons Chapel—church GA-3
Simons Chapel—church TN-4
Simons Chapel (historical)—church TN-4
**Simons Corner**—pop pl VA-3
Simons Coulee—valley MT-8
Simons Creek IN-6
Simons Creek—stream UT-8
**Simonsdale**—pop pl VA-3
Simonsdale Sch—school VA-3
Simons Dale Shop Ctr—locale VA-3
Simons Dam—dam SD-7
Simons Ditch DE-2
Simons Ditch—canal MD-2
Simons Draw—valley MT-8
Simonsen, Soren, House—hist pl UT-8
Simons Fork—stream WV-2
Simons General Store—hist pl NY-2
simons Gurnet ME-1
Simons Hill MA-1
Simons Hollow—valley PA-2
Simons' Inn—hist pl VT-1
Simons Island—island NC-3
Simons JHS—school CA-9
Simons Kiddie Kastle Christian Day Care—school FL-3
Simons Lake—lake MI-6
Simons Lake—lake WI-6
Simons Lake—reservoir SC-3
Simons Mine—mine WA-9
Simons Mtn—summit WA-9
**Simonson**—pop pl VA-3
Simonson and Lowe Ranch—locale NE-7
Simonson Brook—stream NJ-2
Simonson Canyon—valley UT-8
Simonson Coulee—valley WI-6
Simonson Farmstead—hist pl SD-7
Simonson Lake—lake MI-6
Simonson Lake—lake MN-6
Simonson Meadow—flat CO-8
Simonson Ranch—locale NE-7
Simonson Slough—swamp MN-6
Simons Park—park IL-6
Simons Pocket TN-4
Simons Pond MA-1
Simons Pond NY-2
Simons Pond—reservoir GA-3
Simons Pond Dam—dam SD-7
Simon Spring—spring NV-8
Simon Springs—spring AZ-5
Simons Rapids—rapids WI-6
Simons Recreation Center—park PA-2
Simons River—stream DE-2
Simons Rock Early Coll—school MA-1
Simons Sch—school MI-6
Simons Siding—locale SC-3
Simons Spring—spring CA-9
Simonstown Sch (abandoned)—school PA-2
Simons Trail—trail AK-9
**Simonsville**—pop pl VT-1
Simonton—locale FL-3
**Simonton**—pop pl TN-4
**Simonton**—pop pl TX-5
Simonton Assembly of God Church TN-4
Simonton Ch—church TN-4
**Simonton Corners**—pop pl ME-1
Simonton Cove—bay CA-9
Simonton Cove—bay ME-1
Simonton Creek—stream IN-6
Simonton Ditch—canal IN-6
Simonton Flat—flat AZ-5
Simonton Fork TN-4
Simonton Lake—lake IN-6
**Simonton Lake**—pop pl IN-6
Simonton Point—cape AK-9
Simontons Creek IN-6
Simon Well—well NV-8
**Simoran Park Addition (subdivision)**—pop pl UT-8
Sim Park—park CA-9
Simpatico, Lake—reservoir CO-8
Simp Gap—gap NC-3
Simp Hollow—valley KY-4
Simpkins—locale VA-3
Simpkins Corner—locale VA-3
Simpkins Creek AR-4
Simpkins Creek—stream OK-5
Simpkins Creek—stream TX-5
Simpkins Drain—canal MI-6
Simpkins Hollow—valley KY-4
Simpkins Place—locale MT-8
Simpkins Sch—school PA-2
Simpkins Spring—spring ID-8
Simpkins Spring—spring UT-8
Simpkinstown—locale VA-3
Simpkinsville (historical)—locale AL-4
Sim Place—locale NJ-2
Simple Branch—stream IN-6
Simpler Branch—stream DE-2
Simplex Creek—stream AK-9
Simplicity—locale VA-3
Simplot—locale ID-8
Simplot Airstrip—airport UT-8
Simplot Campground—locale ID-8
Simplot Silica Sand Mine—mine NV-8
Simpson PA-2
Simpson—locale AL-4
Simpson—locale (2) AR-4
Simpson—locale CO-8
Simpson—locale GA-3
Simpson—locale KY-4
Simpson—locale MT-8
Simpson—locale NV-8
Simpson—locale OR-9
**Simpson**—pop pl CO-8
**Simpson**—pop pl (2) IL-6
**Simpson**—pop pl IN-6
**Simpson**—pop pl KS-7
**Simpson**—pop pl (2) LA-4
**Simpson**—pop pl MN-6
**Simpson**—pop pl MS-4
**Simpson**—pop pl (2) MO-7
**Simpson**—pop pl NC-3
**Simpson**—pop pl OK-5
**Simpson**—pop pl (3) PA-2
**Simpson**—pop pl SC-3
**Simpson**—pop pl WV-2
Simpson, Bayou—gut LA-4
Simpson, Charles A., House—hist pl HI-9
Simpson, Charles S., House—hist pl IA-7
Simpson, James E., House—hist pl MA-1
Simpson, Mount—summit AK-9
Simpson, Samuel, House—hist pl CT-1
Simpson, W. A., House—hist pl ID-8
Simpson, Walter, House—hist pl OH-6
Simpson, William A., House—hist pl OH-6
Simpson, William Dunlap, House—hist pl SC-3
Simpson Acad—school MS-4
Simpson Access Point—locale GA-3
Simpson Arroyo—valley CO-8
Simpson Bay—bay AK-9
Simpson Bend—bend VA-3
Simpson Bible Sch—school CA-9
Simpson Brake—swamp AR-4
Simpson Brake—swamp LA-4
Simpson Branch—stream AL-4
Simpson Branch—stream AR-4
Simpson Branch—stream IA-7
Simpson Branch—stream (4) KY-4
Simpson Branch—stream MS-4
Simpson Branch—stream (2) MO-7
Simpson Branch—stream NC-3
Simpson Branch—stream SC-3
Simpson Branch—stream (3) TN-4
Simpson Branch—stream TX-5
Simpson Branch—stream VA-3
Simpson Branch—stream WV-2
Simpson Branch Sch—school KY-4
Simpson Brook—stream ME-1
Simpson Brook—stream (3) VT-1
Simpson Brothers Dam—dam SD-7
Simpson Buttes—summit UT-8
Simpson Cabin—locale AK-9
Simpson Cabins—locale AZ-5
Simpson-Cain Cem—cemetery AL-4
Simpson Canyon—valley CA-9
Simpson Canyon—valley OR-9
Simpson Canyon—valley TX-5
Simpson Canyon—valley UT-8
Simpson Cem—cemetery AL-4
Simpson Cem—cemetery CO-8
Simpson Cem—cemetery DE-2
Simpson Cem—cemetery FL-3
Simpson Cem—cemetery (2) GA-3
Simpson Cem—cemetery (4) IL-6
Simpson Cem—cemetery (3) IN-6
Simpson Cem—cemetery (2) KS-7
Simpson Cem—cemetery (4) KY-4
Simpson Cem—cemetery (5) MS-4
Simpson Cem—cemetery (2) MO-7
Simpson Cem—cemetery NE-7
Simpson Cem—cemetery NY-2
Simpson Cem—cemetery NC-3
Simpson Cem—cemetery SC-3
Simpson Cem—cemetery (9) TN-4
Simpson Cem—cemetery (4) TX-5
Simpson Cem—cemetery VA-3
Simpson Cem—cemetery (2) WV-2
Simpson Ch—church (2) IL-6
Simpson Ch—church IN-6
Simpson Ch—church OH-6
Simpson Ch—church PA-2
Simpson Ch—church (2) WV-2
Simpson-Chaco (CCD)—cens area NM-5
Simpson Chapel—church AL-4
Simpson Chapel—church (2) IN-6
Simpson Chapel—church MO-7
Simpson Chapel—church WV-2
Simpson Chapel—church WI-6
Simpson Chapel Cem—cemetery TN-4
Simpson Chapel Ch AL-4
Simpson Chapel Hollow—valley TN-4
Simpson Coll—school IA-7
Simpson Colliery Breaker—building PA-2
**Simpson Corner**—pop pl IN-6
Simpson Corners—locale ME-1
**Simpson (County)**—pop pl KY-4
**Simpson County**—pop pl MS-4
Simpson County Courthouse—hist pl KY-4
Simpson County Courthouse—hist pl MS-4
Simpson County General Hosp—hospital MS-4
Simpson Cove—bay AK-9
Simpson Cove—lake PA-2
Simpson Creek AZ-5
Simpson Creek CO-8
Simpson Creek NM-5
Simpson Creek OR-9
Simpson Creek TX-5
Simpson Creek—gut FL-3
Simpson Creek—stream AL-4
Simpson Creek—stream AK-9
Simpson Creek—stream AR-4
Simpson Creek—stream CA-9
Simpson Creek—stream (2) CO-8
Simpson Creek—stream GA-3
Simpson Creek—stream IN-6
Simpson Creek—stream (2) IA-7
Simpson Creek—stream KY-4
Simpson Creek—stream MI-6
Simpson Creek—stream MN-6
Simpson Creek—stream MS-4
Simpson Creek—stream MO-7
Simpson Creek—stream (2) MT-8
Simpson Creek—stream NE-7
Simpson Creek—stream NV-8
Simpson Creek—stream NY-2
Simpson Creek—stream (2) NC-3
Simpson Creek—stream OH-6
Simpson Creek—stream (10) OR-9
Simpson Creek—stream (2) SC-3
Simpson Creek—stream TN-4
Simpson Creek—stream (4) TX-5
Simpson Creek—stream WV-2
Simpson Creek—stream (2) WI-6
Simpson Creek Covered Bridge—hist pl WV-2
Simpson Creek Sch—school SC-3
Simpson Creek Sch (abandoned)—school MO-7
**Simpson Crossing**—pop pl SC-3
Simpson Crossroads—locale GA-3
Simpson Cyclone Post Office PA-2
Simpson Dam—dam OR-9
Simpson Ditch—canal IN-6
Simpson Ditch—canal WY-8
Simpson Draw—valley NM-5
Simpson Draw—valley WY-8
Simpson East (CCD)—cens area KY-4
Simpson (Election Precinct)—fmr MCD IL-6
Simpson Elem Sch—school KS-7
Simpson Ferry—locale PA-2
Simpson Fork—stream WV-2
Simpson Gap—gap NC-3
Simpson Gap—gap WY-8
Simpson Gulch—valley CA-9
Simpson Gulch—valley WY-8
Simpson Hill—summit IN-6
Simpson Hill—summit ME-1
Simpson Hill—summit VT-1
Simpson (historical)—locale MS-4
Simpson Hollow—valley AL-4
Simpson Hollow—valley IL-6
Simpson Hollow—valley KY-4
Simpson Hollow—valley PA-2
Simpson Hollow—valley VA-3
Simpson Hollow—valley WV-2
Simpson Hollow—valley WI-6
Simpson House—hist pl MA-1
Simpson Island ME-1
Simpson Island MA-1
Simpson Island—island ME-1
Simpson Island—island TN-4
Simpson Island—island (2) VA-3
Simpson Island (historical)—island TN-4
Simpson JHS—school MI-6
Simpson JHS—school NY-2
Simpson JHS—school OH-6
Simpson Knob—summit WV-2
Simpson Lagoon—bay AK-9
Simpson Lake MN-6
Simpson Lake WA-9
Simpson Lake WY-8
Simpson Lake—lake AR-4
Simpson Lake—lake CO-8
Simpson Lake—lake (2) MI-6
Simpson Lake—lake MN-6
Simpson Lake—lake WA-9
Simpson Lake—lake (3) WI-6
Simpson Lake—lake WY-8
Simpson Lake—reservoir AZ-5
Simpson Lake—reservoir FL-3
Simpson Lake—reservoir MS-4
Simpson Lake—reservoir NC-3
Simpson Lake—reservoir TX-5
Simpson Lake Dam—dam NC-3
Simpson Lake (historical)—lake SD-7
Simpson Lake Oil and Gas Field—oilfield LA-4
Simpson Lakes WA-9
Simpson Lakes—lake MI-6
Simpson Lakes—reservoir GA-3
Simpson Lateral—canal ID-8
Simpson Legion Lake Dam—dam MS-4
Simpson Legion State Fishing Lake—reservoir MS-4
Simpson Logging Company Locomotive No. 7 and Peninsular Railway Caboose No. 700—hist pl WA-9
Simpson Log House—hist pl KY-4
Simpson Lookout—locale WA-9
Simpson Lookout Tower—locale MS-4
Simpson Lookout Tower—locale SC-3
Simpson Meadow—flat CA-9
Simpson Memorial Trail (Pack)—trail NM-5

Simpson Memorial United Methodist Ch—*church* FL-3
Simpson Mesa—*summit* CO-8
*Simpson Methodist Church* AL-4
Simpson Methodist Episcopal Church—*hist pl* MN-6
Simpson Mine—*mine* MO-7
Simpson Mtn—*summit* (2) CO-8
Simpson Mtn—*summit* MO-7
Simpson Mtn—*summit* TX-5
Simpson Mtn—*summit* VA-3
Simpson Mtns—*range* UT-8
Simpson Neck—*cape* NC-3
Simpson Neck—*cape* VA-3
Simpson Nursery Pond—*lake* FL-3
Simpson Oil Field—*oilfield* TX-5
Simpson Park—*park* CA-9
Simpson Park—*park* (2) FL-3
Simpson Park—*park* OR-9
Simpson Park Campground—*locale* MI-6
Simpson Park Canyon—*valley* NV-8
*Simpson Park Mountains* NV-8
Simpson Park Range—*range* NV-8
Simpson Pass—*gap* AK-9
Simpson Pass—*gap* NV-8
Simpson Peak—*summit* AK-9
Simpson Peak—*summit* NM-5
Simpson Peaks—*summit* WY-8
Simpson Place—*locale* OR-9
Simpson Point—*cape* AL-4
Simpson Point—*cape* ME-1
Simpson Point—*cape* UT-8
Simpson Point—*cape* VA-3
Simpson Point—*cliff* AR-4
Simpson Point Ch—*church* AL-4
Simpson Point Sch (historical)—*school* AL-4
Simpson Pond—*lake* CT-1
Simpson Pond—*reservoir* NH-1
Simpson Pond—*reservoir* TN-4
Simpson Post Office (historical)—*building* AL-4
Simpson-Raborn Cem—*cemetery* MS-4
Simpson Ranch—*locale* AZ-5
Simpson Ranch—*locale* MT-8
Simpson Ranch—*locale* (3) NM-5
Simpson Reef—*bar* OR-9
*Simpson Ridge* WA-9
Simpson Ridge—*ridge* (2) KY-4
Simpson Ridge—*ridge* WA-9
Simpson Ridge—*ridge* WY-8
Simpson Ridges—*ridge* VA-3
Simpson River—*stream* FL-3
Simpson Rock—*other* AK-9
Simpson Rsvr—*reservoir* OR-9
Simpson Run—*stream* (2) OH-6
Simpson Run—*stream* (2) PA-2
Simpson Run—*stream* WV-2
**Simpsons**—*pop pl* ME-1
**Simpsons**—*pop pl* TN-4
**Simpsons**—*pop pl* VA-3
*Simpsons Brook* MA-1
Simpsons Camp—*locale* OR-9
Simpsons Cem—*cemetery* FL-3
*Simpson Sch* TN-4
Simpson Sch—*school* AZ-5
Simpson Sch—*school* CT-1
Simpson Sch—*school* IL-6
Simpson Sch—*school* (2) OK-5
Simpson Sch—*school* TN-4
Simpsons Chapel—*church* AL-4
Simpson Sch (historical)—*school* (2) MS-4
Simpson Sch (historical)—*school* TN-4
Simpson's College—*hist pl* MO-7
Simpsons Corner—*locale* ME-1
*Simpsons Creek* OH-6
Simpsons Creek—*stream* AR-4
Simpsons Creek—*stream* VA-3
Simpsons Draw—*valley* CO-8
*Simpsons Ferry* TN-4
Simpsons Ford (historical)—*crossing* TN-4
Simpson Shop Ctr—*locale* TN-4
*Simpsons Island* TN-4
Simpsons Lake—*reservoir* NC-3
Simpsons Lake Dam—*dam* NC-3
*Simpson Slough* AR-4
*Simpson Slough* OR-9
Simpson Slough—*stream* AR-4
Simpsons Mill—*locale* MD-2
*Simpsons Mills Post Office* TN-4
Simpsons Mission—*church* VA-3
*Simpson's Mountains* UT-8
*Simpsons Pond* MA-1
Simpsons Post Office (historical)—*building* TN-4
*Simpson Spring* TN-4
Simpson Spring—*spring* AL-4
Simpson Spring—*spring* (2) AZ-5
Simpson Spring—*spring* KY-4
Simpson Spring—*spring* MO-7
Simpson Spring—*spring* NV-8
Simpson Spring—*spring* (2) TN-4
Simpson Springs—*spring* NV-8
Simpson Springs—*spring* TX-5
Simpson Springs—*spring* UT-8
Simpson Springs—*spring* WY-8
Simpson Springs Campground—*park* UT-8
Simpson Springs Creek—*stream* WY-8
Simpson Springs Mtn—*summit* TX-5
*Simpson Springs Pony Express and Stage Station* UT-8
Simpsons Resort—*locale* MI-6
Simpsons Rest—*summit* CO-8
Simpsons Rsvr—*reservoir* CO-8
Simpsons Sch (historical)—*school* TN-4
Simpsons Shop (historical)—*locale* MS-4
*Simpson Stage Route* NV-8
Simpson State Fish Hatchery—*other* WA-9
Simpson State Wayside—*locale* OR-9
*Simpson Station* KS-7
Simpson Store—*locale* SC-3
**Simpson Store**—*pop pl* (2) PA-2
Simpson Store (historical)—*locale* MS-4
Simpson Street Sch—*hist pl* PA-2
**Simpson (subdivision)**—*pop pl* AL-4
**Simpson Subdivision (subdivision)**—*pop pl* AL-4
Simpson Switch—*locale* IL-6
Simpson Tank—*reservoir* AZ-5
Simpson Test Well No 1 (Approximate Location)—*well* AK-9
Simpson Township—*civil* MO-7
Simpson (Township of)—*fmr MCD* AR-4
Simpson Tunnel—*tunnel* PA-2
Simpson United Methodist Church—*hist pl* NJ-2
Simpson-Vance House—*hist pl* CA-9
*Simpsonville* TX-5
**Simpsonville**—*pop pl* KY-4
**Simpsonville**—*pop pl* MD-2
**Simpsonville**—*pop pl* NY-2
**Simpsonville**—*pop pl* SC-3
**Simpsonville**—*pop pl* TX-5
**Simpsonville**—*pop pl* VT-1
Simpsonville (CCD)—*cens area* KY-4
Simpsonville (CCD)—*cens area* SC-3
Simpsonville Cem—*cemetery* TX-5
Simpsonville Christian Church—*hist pl* KY-4
Simpsonville Methodist Church—*hist pl* KY-4
Simpsonville Stone Arch Bridge—*hist pl* VT-1
Simpsonville (Township of)—*fmr MCD* NC-3
Simpson Well—*well* NM-5
Simpson Windmill—*locale* TX-5
*Simpson Yard* (2) FL-3
Simpson-Yeomans-Country Side Hist Dist—*hist pl* MO-7
Simpton, Point—*cape* CA-9
*Simpton Point* CA-9
Simp West Farm Cem—*cemetery* TN-4
**Simrall**—*pop pl* MS-4
Simrall-Warfield House—*hist pl* KY-4
Simrell Cem—*cemetery* MO-7
Simrell Cem—*cemetery* TN-4
Simroe Ch—*church* NC-3
*Sims* MS-4
Sims—*locale* CA-9
Sims—*locale* ND-7
Sims—*locale* SC-3
Sims—*locale* TX-5
Sims—*locale* WV-2
**Sims**—*pop pl* AR-4
**Sims**—*pop pl* IL-6
**Sims**—*pop pl* (2) IN-6
**Sims**—*pop pl* NC-3
Sims—*reservoir* AR-4
Sims, Capt. William, House—*hist pl* TN-4
Sims, John Green, House—*hist pl* TN-4
Sims, Lake—*lake* FL-3
Sims, O. B., House—*hist pl* TX-5
*Sims-Allen Cemetery* AL-4
Sims Bayou—*stream* LA-4
Sims Bayou—*stream* TX-5
Sims Bayou Park—*park* TX-5
Sims Bend—*bend* KY-4
Simsberry Draw—*valley* CO-8
Sims Bluff—*cliff* AL-4
Simsboro—*locale* TX-5
**Simsboro**—*pop pl* AR-4
**Simsboro**—*pop pl* LA-4
*Sims Branch* KY-4
Sims Branch—*gut* FL-3
Sims Branch—*stream* AL-4
Sims Branch—*stream* AR-4
Sims Branch—*stream* (2) GA-3
Sims Branch—*stream* KY-4
Sims Branch—*stream* MO-7
Sims Branch—*stream* NC-3
Sims Branch—*stream* (2) TN-4
Sims Branch—*stream* TX-5
Sims Branch—*stream* VA-3
Sims Branch—*stream* (2) WV-2
Sims Bridge—*bridge* TN-4
*Simsbury* PA-2
**Simsbury**—*pop pl* CT-1
Simsbury Bank and Trust Company Bldg—*hist pl* CT-1
Simsbury Cem—*cemetery* VT-1
**Simsbury Center (census name Simsbury)**—*pop pl* CT-1
Simsbury RR Depot—*hist pl* CT-1
Simsbury Rsvr—*reservoir* CT-1
**Simsbury (Town of)**—*pop pl* CT-1
Sims Butte—*summit* OR-9
Sims Canyon—*valley* NV-8
Sims Canyon—*valley* (2) UT-8
Sims Canyon—*valley* WY-8
Sims Cave—*cave* AL-4
Sims Cem—*cemetery* (5) AL-4
Sims Cem—*cemetery* AR-4
Sims Cem—*cemetery* FL-3
Sims Cem—*cemetery* (2) GA-3
Sims Cem—*cemetery* IL-6
Sims Cem—*cemetery* IN-6
Sims Cem—*cemetery* IA-7
Sims Cem—*cemetery* (2) KY-4
Sims Cem—*cemetery* LA-4
Sims Cem—*cemetery* MI-6
Sims Cem—*cemetery* (6) MS-4
Sims Cem—*cemetery* (2) MO-7
Sims Cem—*cemetery* ND-7
Sims Cem—*cemetery* (7) TN-4
Sims Cem Number Two—*cemetery* TN-4
Sims Ch—*church* LA-4
Sims Ch—*church* TN-4
Sims Chapel—*church* (2) AL-4
Sims Chapel—*church* AR-4
Sims Chapel—*church* MS-4
**Sims Chapel**—*pop pl* AL-4
Sims Chapel Ch—*church* AL-4
*Sims Chapel Methodist Ch* AL-4
*Sims Chapel Primitive Baptist Ch* AL-4
Sims Chapel Sch—*school* AL-4
Sims Chapel Sch—*school* SC-3
*Sims Chapel United Methodist Church* AL-4
Sims Corner—*locale* WA-9
Sims Corner Rsvr—*reservoir* WA-9
Sims Cove—*valley* AR-4
Sims Cove—*valley* CA-9
*Sims Creek* LA-4
Sims Creek—*stream* AL-4
Sims Creek—*stream* (3) CA-9
Sims Creek—*stream* CO-8
Sims Creek—*stream* (2) KY-4
Sims Creek—*stream* LA-4
Sims Creek—*stream* MI-6
Sims Creek—*stream* MT-8
Sims Creek—*stream* NC-3
Sims Creek—*stream* ND-7
Sims Creek—*stream* (2) TX-5
Sims Ditch—*stream* GA-3
Sims Drain—*stream* IN-6
Sims Ford—*locale* TN-4
**Sims Fork**—*pop pl* KY-4
Sims Fork—*stream* KY-4
Sims Fork—*stream* WV-2
Sims Franklin Ditch—*canal* IN-6
Sims Gap—*gap* CA-9
Sims Gap—*gap* GA-3
Sims-Garfield Ranch—*hist pl* MT-8
Sims Gulch—*valley* CA-9
Sims Hill—*summit* AR-4
Sims Hollow—*valley* KY-4
Sims Hollow—*valley* (2) TN-4
Sims Hotel—*hist pl* AR-4
Sims House—*hist pl* MS-4
Sims House—*hist pl* TX-5
Sims HS—*school* MS-4
Sims HS—*school* SC-3
Sims Lake—*lake* LA-4
Sims Lake—*lake* (2) MS-4
Sims Lake—*lake* WA-9
Sims Lake—*reservoir* AL-4
Sims Lake—*swamp* MO-7
Sims Lake Dam—*dam* AL-4
Sims Lake Number One—*reservoir* AL-4
Sims Lake Number Two—*reservoir* AL-4
Sims Landing—*locale* GA-3
Sims Lookout—*locale* CA-9
Sims Memorial Ch—*church* AL-4
Sims Mesa—*summit* CO-8
Sims Mill Creek—*stream* AL-4
Sims Mill Pond—*lake* MS-4
Sims Mine—*mine* ID-8
Sim Smith Bridge—*hist pl* IN-6
Sims Mtn—*summit* CA-9
Sims Mtn—*summit* WV-2
Sims Neck—*cape* TN-4
Sims Number 1 Dam—*dam* AL-4
Sims Number 2 Dam—*dam* AL-4
Sims Oil Field—*other* IL-6
*Simson Gluch* WY-8
Sims Park—*park* KS-7
Sims Park—*park* NC-3
Sims Park—*park* SC-3
Sims Peak—*summit* UT-8
Sims Point—*cape* MI-6
Sims Point—*cliff* AR-4
*Sims Pond* PA-2
Sims Pond—*dam* NC-3
Sims Pond—*lake* AZ-5
Sims Pond—*lake* NC-3
Sims Pond—*reservoir* (2) AL-4
Sims Pond—*reservoir* GA-3
Sims Pond—*reservoir* NC-3
Sims Pond Bay—*swamp* NC-3
Sims Ponds—*lake* AL-4
*Simsport* LA-4
Sims Post Office (historical)—*building* MS-4
Simsquish Brook—*stream* ME-1
Simsquish Lake—*lake* ME-1
Sims Ranch—*locale* NM-5
Sims Ranch—*locale* (2) WY-8
Sims Ridge—*locale* TN-4
Sims Ridge Cem—*cemetery* TN-4
Sims Ridge Ch of Christ—*church* TN-4
Sims Ridge Sch (historical)—*school* TN-4
Sims Rogers Ditch—*canal* IN-6
**Sims (RR name Simms)**—*pop pl* NC-3
Sims Rsvr—*reservoir* AZ-5
Sims Run—*stream* (2) OH-6
Sims Run—*stream* (2) WV-2
Sims Sch—*school* AL-4
Sims Sch—*school* MS-4
Sims Sch—*school* NC-3
Sims Sch—*school* OK-5
Sims Sch—*school* SD-7
Sims Sch—*school* (2) TX-5
Sims Sch (historical)—*school* AL-4
Sims Slough—*gut* TX-5
Sims Spring—*locale* TN-4
Sims Spring—*spring* GA-3
Sims Spring—*spring* (2) TN-4
Sims Spring Branch—*stream* GA-3
Sims Spring Branch—*stream* TN-4
**Sims Station**—*pop pl* OH-6
*Sims Store* TN-4
*Sims Switch* MS-4
*Sims Tank* AZ-5
Sims Tank—*reservoir* AZ-5
**Simstown**—*pop pl* KY-4
**Sims (Township of)**—*pop pl* IN-6
**Sims (Township of)**—*pop pl* MI-6
*Sims Trap* AL-4
Sims Valley—*valley* MO-7
Sims Valley State Community Lake—*reservoir* MO-7
Simsville—*locale* FL-3
**Simsville**—*pop pl* AL-4
Simsville Ch—*church* GA-3
Simtag Farms Airstrip—*airport* OR-9
Simtustus, Lake—*reservoir* OR-9
Simual Ch—*church* MS-4
Sim Yaten Canyon—*valley* NM-5
Sim Yaten Hills—*summit* NM-5
Sim Yaten Tank—*reservoir* NM-5
Sina, Lake—*lake* MN-6
Sina Branch—*stream* TN-4
Sina Creek—*stream* AL-4
Sina Fall—*falls* AS-9
Sinagoso—*area* GU-9
Sin Agua Tank—*reservoir* AZ-5
Sinagua Valley—*valley* AZ-5
*Sinahomis River* WA-9
Sinai—*locale* FL-3
Sinai—*locale* MS-4
Sinai—*locale* VA-3
**Sinai**—*pop pl* KY-4
**Sinai**—*pop pl* SD-7
Sinai, Lake—*lake* SD-7
Sinai, Mount—*summit* TX-5
Sinai Cem—*cemetery* AR-4
Sinai Cem—*cemetery* FL-3
Sinai Cem—*cemetery* (2) MS-4
Sinai Cem—*cemetery* SD-7
*Sinai Ch* AL-4
Sinai Ch—*church* AL-4
Sinai Ch—*church* (2) MS-4
Sinai Ch—*church* NC-3
Sinai Ch—*church* (2) SC-3
Sinai Ch—*church* TN-4
Sinai Ch—*church* VA-3
Sinai Cove—*bay* MD-2
Sinai Elem Sch—*school* KS-7
Sinai Hall—*locale* AL-4
Sinai Hosp—*hospital* MI-6
Sinai Memorial Park—*cemetery* MA-1
Sinai Sch—*school* NJ-2
Sinai Sch—*school* VA-3
Sinai Sch (historical)—*school* AL-4
Sinai Spring—*spring* FL-3
Sinaiville Ch—*church* WV-2
Sinaiville Sch—*school* WV-2
**Sinajana**—*pop pl* GU-9
Sinajana (Election District)—*fmr MCD* GU-9
Sinaje—*area* GU-9
Sinaloa JHS—*school* CA-9
Sinamanoo Point—*cape* AS-9
Sinamox—*locale* OR-9
Sin and Flesh Brook—*stream* RI-1
*Sinapalo* MH-9
Sinapalu—*summit* MH-9
Sinapioa Mtn—*summit* AS-9
Sinapoto Point—*cape* AS-9
Sinapoto Stream—*stream* AS-9
Sina Ridge—*ridge* AS-9
Sinaruruk River—*stream* AK-9
Sina Stream—*stream* AS-9
Sinatau Point—*cape* AS-9
Sinavevela Stream—*stream* AS-9
Sin-av-to-weap—*area* UT-8
Sinawava, Temple of—*basin* UT-8
Sinawik Park—*park* IL-6
Sinbad Canyon—*valley* UT-8
Sinbad Country—*area* UT-8
Sinbad Creek—*stream* CA-9
Sinbad Interchange—*locale* UT-8
Sinbad Ridge—*ridge* CO-8
Sinbad Ridge—*ridge* UT-8
Sinbad Spring—*spring* UT-8
Sinbad Valley—*area* UT-8
Sinbad Valley—*basin* CO-8
Sinca Dam—*dam* PA-2
Sincavage Lumber Company Dam—*dam* PA-2
Sincer, Louis, House—*hist pl* LA-4
Sincere Ch—*church* IL-6
Sincere Creek—*stream* OK-5
Sincerity—*locale* WV-2
Sin City—*locale* AZ-5
Sinclair—*locale* ID-8
Sinclair—*locale* IA-7
Sinclair—*locale* WV-2
**Sinclair**—*pop pl* IL-6
**Sinclair**—*pop pl* ME-1
**Sinclair**—*pop pl* PA-2
**Sinclair**—*pop pl* WY-8
Sinclair, Dr. Archibald Neil, House—*hist pl* HI-9
Sinclair, Harry F., House—*hist pl* NY-2
Sinclair, Lake—*reservoir* GA-3
Sinclair, T. M., Mansion—*hist pl* IA-7
Sinclair, Upton, House—*hist pl* CA-9
Sinclair Brook—*stream* (3) ME-1
Sinclair Cem—*cemetery* (2) MN-6
Sinclair Cem—*cemetery* MS-4
Sinclair Cem—*cemetery* TN-4
Sinclair Cem—*cemetery* (2) TX-5
Sinclair Cem—*cemetery* VA-3
Sinclair Cem—*cemetery* WV-2
Sinclair Ch—*church* GA-3
Sinclair Ch—*church* TX-5
Sinclair Circle—*locale* VA-3
Sinclair City—*locale* TX-5
Sinclair Coll—*school* OH-6
Sinclair Corner—*locale* NY-2
Sinclair Creek—*stream* AR-4
Sinclair Creek—*stream* (3) MT-8
Sinclair Creek—*stream* NY-2
Sinclair Creek—*stream* VA-3
Sinclair Crossroads—*locale* SC-3
Sinclair (Election Precinct)—*fmr MCD* IL-6
Sinclaire Point—*cape* NY-2
Sinclair Falls—*falls* NY-2
**Sinclair Farms**—*pop pl* VA-3
Sinclair Hill—*summit* NY-2
Sinclair (historical)—*locale* MT-8
Sinclair Hollow—*valley* AR-4
Sinclair Hollow—*valley* TX-5
Sinclair Hollow—*valley* VA-3
Sinclair Inlet—*bay* WA-9
*Sinclair Island* MA-1
Sinclair Island—*island* WA-9
Sinclair Island Light—*locale* WA-9
Sinclair JHS—*school* CO-8
*Sinclair Lake* GA-3
Sinclair Lake—*lake* AK-9
Sinclair Lake—*lake* ID-8
Sinclair Lake—*lake* MI-6
Sinclair Lake—*lake* ND-7
Sinclair Lake—*lake* TX-5
Sinclair Lake—*reservoir* KS-7
Sinclair Lake—*reservoir* NC-3
Sinclair Lake—*reservoir* TN-4
Sinclair Lake Dam—*dam* NC-3
Sinclair Lake Dam—*dam* TN-4
Sinclair Lake Rec Area—*locale* GA-3
Sinclair Lewis Park—*park* MN-6
Sinclair Loading Rack—*hist pl* OK-5
Sinclair Lookout—*locale* FL-3
Sinclair Mine (Inactive)—*mine* FL-3
Sinclair Mtn—*summit* AK-9
Sinclair Park—*park* OH-6
Sinclair Recreation Park—*park* WY-8
*Sinclair Reservoir* GA-3
Sinclair Ridge—*ridge* WV-2
Sinclair River—*stream* AK-9
Sinclair Sch—*school* ME-1
Sinclair Sch—*school* TX-5
Sinclair Sch—*school* (2) VA-3
Sinclair Slough—*lake* ND-7
Sinclair Station, (Old)—*hist pl* TX-5
Sinclair Tank—*reservoir* AZ-5
Sinclair Town Hall—*building* ND-7
Sinclair Township—*civil* KS-7
**Sinclair Township**—*pop pl* KS-7
**Sinclair Township**—*pop pl* ND-7
**Sinclair (Township of)**—*pop pl* MN-6
Sinclair Trail—*trail* NH-1
**Sinclairville**—*pop pl* NY-2
Sinclair Wash—*stream* AZ-5
Sinclair Windmill—*locale* TX-5
**Sinco**—*pop pl* TX-5
Sinco Branch—*stream* AR-4
Sin Creek—*stream* CO-8
Sin Creek—*stream* IA-7
Sindeldecker Branch—*stream* PA-2
Sindel Gulch—*valley* CA-9
Sindicich Lagoons—*lake* CA-9
Sindion Point—*summit* VA-3
Sindt Point—*cape* NE-7
Sine—*locale* WA-9
Sineak River—*stream* AK-9
*Sineasha* MS-4
*Sineasha Methodist Church* MS-4
*Sineflesh River* RI-1
Sinei—*spring* FM-9
Sine Mtn—*summit* VA-3
Sinengsong—*area* GU-9
Sinenjaya—*area* GU-9
Sinepuxent—*locale* MD-2
Sinepuxent Bay—*bay* MD-2
**Sinepuxent (sta.)**—*pop pl* MD-2
Sine Run—*stream* WV-2
Sines Ditch—*canal* IN-6
Sines Drain—*stream* MI-6
Sin Fin Mine—*mine* AZ-5
**Singac**—*pop pl* NJ-2
Singac Brook—*stream* NJ-2
Singa Island—*island* AK-9
Singaruak Creek—*stream* AK-9
Singas Creek—*stream* NV-8
Singatse Peak—*summit* NV-8
Singatse Range—*range* NV-8
*Singatze Range* NV-8
Singauk Entrance—*gut* AK-9
Singauruk Point—*cape* AK-9
Singauruk River—*stream* AK-9
Singauruk Shelter Cabin—*locale* AK-9
*Singawateen* ID-8
Singayoak Creek—*stream* AK-9
Singeak—*locale* AK-9
Singeakpuk River—*stream* AK-9
Singecat Branch—*stream* NC-3
Singecat Ridge—*ridge* NC-3
Singe Creek—*stream* OR-9
Singed Pig Bay—*swamp* NC-3
Singepole Mtn—*summit* ME-1
**Singer**—*pop pl* LA-4
**Singer**—*pop pl* MD-2
**Singer**—*pop pl* VA-3
Singer, John F., House—*hist pl* PA-2
Singer Bldg—*hist pl* CA-9
Singer Bldg—*hist pl* IL-6
Singer Cem—*cemetery* KS-7
*Singer Cemetery* MO-7
Singer Creek—*stream* CA-9
Singer Creek—*stream* OR-9
Singer Ditch—*canal* (2) IN-6
Singer Ditch Dam—*dam* IN-6
Singer Drain—*canal* OR-9
Singer Health Center—*hospital* IL-6
Singer Hill Ch—*church* PA-2
Singer Island—*island* FL-3
Singer Island—*uninc pl* FL-3
Singer Lake—*lake* MI-6
Singer Lake—*lake* NM-5
Singer Lake—*lake* OH-6
Singer Lake Draw—*valley* NM-5
Singerly—*locale* MD-2
**Singerly**—*pop pl* VA-3
Singer Mine—*mine* NV-8
Singer-Moye Archeol Site—*hist pl* GA-3
Singer Peak—*summit* WY-8
Singer Pond—*lake* GA-3
Singer Run—*stream* KY-4
Singer Run—*stream* OH-6
Singer Run—*stream* PA-2
Singers Cem—*cemetery* IL-6
Singer Sewing Company—*hist pl* TX-5
Singers Gap—*gap* PA-2
Singers Gap Rsvr—*reservoir* PA-2
Singers Gap Run—*stream* PA-2
**Singers Glen**—*pop pl* VA-3
Singers Glen Hist Dist—*hist pl* VA-3
Singers Hill—*summit* GA-3
*Singers Island* FL-3
**Singersville**—*pop pl* PA-2
Singer Wash—*stream* NV-8
Singgood Cem—*cemetery* MT-8
Singheiser Mine—*mine* ID-8
Singheiser Trail—*trail* ID-8
Singigrak Spit—*bar* AK-9
Singigyak—*locale* AK-9
Singikpak Point—*cape* AK-9
Singikpo Cape—*cape* AK-9
Singik Point—*cape* AK-9
Singiluk—*locale* AK-9
Singing Beach—*beach* MA-1
Singing Bridge—*other* IL-6
Singing Brook—*stream* WY-8
**Singing Hills**—*pop pl* OH-6
Singing Hills Golf Course—*other* CA-9
*Singing Mountain* NV-8
Singing Pines Ranch—*locale* CO-8
*Singing River* TX-5
Singing River—*stream* MS-4
Singing River Baptist Ch—*church* MS-4
Singing River Bridge—*bridge* MS-4
*Singing River Elementary School* MS-4
Singing River Hosp—*hospital* MS-4
Singing River Hospital Airp—*airport* MS-4
Singing River Island—*island* MS-4
Singing River Mall Shop Ctr—*locale* MS-4
Singing River Ranch—*locale* (2) CO-8
Singing River Sch—*school* MS-4
Singing Springs—*locale* CA-9
**Singing Springs (subdivision)**—*pop pl* NC-3
Singing Spur Mobile Park—*locale* AZ-5
*Singing Tower* FL-3
Singing Waters Park—*park* NY-2
Singing Wind Ranch—*locale* AZ-5
*Singiser* TX-5
Single, Benjamin, House—*hist pl* WI-6
Single Brothers House—*building* NC-3
Single Brothers' House—*hist pl* NC-3
Single Brothers Industrial Complex Site—*hist pl* NC-3
Single Creek—*stream* IN-6
Single Creek—*stream* OR-9
Sing Lee Creek—*stream* ID-8
Single Hill—*summit* VT-1
Single Lake—*lake* MN-6
Single Mill Draw—*valley* NM-5
Single Mill Well—*well* NM-5
Single Run—*stream* IN-6
Singleshot—*locale* MT-8
Singleshot Mtn—*summit* MT-8
Single Spring Cem—*cemetery* AL-4
Single Spring Ch—*church* (2) AL-4
*Single Springs Cemetery* AL-4
Single Standard Mine—*mine* AZ-5
Single Swamp—*swamp* MA-1
Single Tank Spring—*spring* NV-8
Singletar Cem—*cemetery* LA-4
**Singletary**—*pop pl* GA-3
Singletary Bridge—*bridge* NC-3
Singletary Brook—*stream* MA-1
Singletary Cem—*cemetery* MS-4
Singletary Cem—*cemetery* (2) NC-3
Singletary Ch—*church* SC-3
Singletary Creek—*stream* MS-4
Singletary Cross Roads Ch—*church* NC-3
Singletary Forks—*locale* SC-3
Singletary Islands—*island* SC-3
Singletary Lake—*lake* TX-5
Singletary Lake—*reservoir* NC-3
Singletary Lake State Park—*park* NC-3
*Singletary Millpond* SC-3
Singletary Millpond—*reservoir* NC-3
Singletary Pond—*reservoir* GA-3
Singletary Pond—*reservoir* MA-1
Singletary Pond Dam—*dam* MA-1
Singletary Sch—*school* SC-3
Singletarys Pond—*lake* AL-4
Singletary Swamp—*swamp* NC-3
*Singleton* MS-4
Singleton—*locale* PA-2
Singleton—*locale* TN-4
**Singleton**—*pop pl* CO-8
**Singleton**—*pop pl* MS-4
**Singleton**—*pop pl* SC-3
**Singleton**—*pop pl* TN-4
**Singleton**—*pop pl* TX-5
Singleton, Capt. William E., House—*hist pl* TX-5
Singleton, Samuel, House—*hist pl* UT-8
Singleton Bar—*bar* AL-4
Singleton Bend—*bend* TN-4
Singleton Branch—*stream* MO-7
Singleton Butte—*summit* CA-9
Singleton Cem—*cemetery* AR-4
Singleton Cem—*cemetery* (2) KY-4
Singleton Cem—*cemetery* (2) MS-4
Singleton Cem—*cemetery* SC-3
Singleton Cem—*cemetery* TN-4
Singleton Cem—*cemetery* TX-5
Singleton Ch—*church* (2) MS-4
Singleton Ch—*church* VA-3
Singleton Chapel (historical)—*church* MS-4
Singleton Creek—*stream* AR-4
Singleton Creek—*stream* CA-9
Singleton Creek—*stream* GA-3
Singleton Creek—*stream* (3) SC-3
Singleton Creek—*stream* TN-4
Singleton Creek—*stream* UT-8
Singleton Crossroads—*locale* SC-3
Singleton Ditch—*canal* IL-6
Singleton Ditch—*canal* IN-6
Singleton Drain—*canal* MI-6
Singleton Farm—*locale* TX-5
Singleton Flat—*flat* UT-8
Singleton-Hall Cem—*cemetery* MS-4
Singleton Hill—*summit* GA-3
Singleton Hill—*summit* PA-2
Singleton (historical)—*locale* AL-4
**Singleton (historical)**—*pop pl* MS-4
Singleton Hollow—*valley* AL-4
Singleton Hollow—*valley* VA-3
Singleton House—*hist pl* GA-3
Singleton Island—*island* SC-3
Singleton JHS—*school* GA-3
Singleton Lake—*lake* AL-4
Singleton Landing—*locale* AL-4
Singleton-Lathem-Large House—*hist pl* NJ-2
*Singleton Methodist Church* MS-4
Singleton Mine (underground)—*mine* AL-4
Singleton Park—*park* OR-9
Singleton Plantation—*locale* AL-4
Singleton Post Office (historical)—*building* MS-4
Singleton Post Office (historical)—*building* TN-4
Singleton Ranch—*locale* CA-9
Singleton Ridge—*ridge* MO-7
*Singletons Bar* AL-4
Singletons Bay—*swamp* NC-3
Singleton Sch—*school* KY-4
Singleton Sch (historical)—*school* MS-4
Singleton Sch (historical)—*school* TN-4
Singleton Settlement—*locale* MS-4
Singleton's Graveyard—*hist pl* SC-3
Singletons Landing (historical)—*locale* AL-4
Singletons Landing Strip—*airport* IN-6
*Singleton Spring* AL-4
Singleton Spring—*spring* WA-9
*Singleton Swamp* NC-3
Singleton Swamp—*stream* SC-3
Singleton Swash—*beach* SC-3
Singleton Tank—*reservoir* TX-5
Singleton Terminal—*locale* TN-4
Singleton Valley—*valley* OR-9
*Singletown Run* PA-2
Singletree Campground—*park* UT-8
Singletree Creek—*stream* NV-8
Singletree Creek—*stream* UT-8
Singletree Gulch—*valley* OR-9
Single Tree Hill—*summit* MA-1
Single Tree Ranch—*locale* NV-8
Single Tree Tank—*reservoir* NM-5
Single Trough Spring—*spring* UT-8
Singley Bar—*bar* CA-9
Singley Cem—*cemetery* AL-4
Singley Cem—*cemetery* LA-4
Singley Cem—*cemetery* MS-4
Singley Creek—*stream* CA-9
Singley Lake Dam—*dam* (2) MS-4
Singley Landing (historical)—*locale* AL-4
Singley Ponds Dam—*dam* MS-4
Singley Sch—*school* IL-6
Singoalik Lagoon—*lake* AK-9
Singoalik River—*stream* AK-9
Sing Peak—*summit* CA-9
Singrey Sch (abandoned)—*school* MO-7
Singsaas Ch—*church* SD-7

Singsaas Slough State Wildlife Mngmt Area—*park* ... SD-7
*Singsass Lutheran Church* ... SD-7
Sings Creek—*stream* ... NC-3
*Singsing Creek* ... NY-2
Sing Sing Creek—*stream* ... NY-2
Sing Sing Pond—*lake* ... ME-1
Sing Sing Prison—*other* ... NY-2
*Sington* ... TN-4
*Singtown* ... TN-4
**Singtown**—*pop pl* ... TN-4
*Singular Rocks* ... PA-2
Sing Windmill—*locale* ... TX-5
*Siniaquoteen* ... ID-8
Siniard Cave—*cave* ... AL-4
Siniard Lake—*reservoir* ... NC-3
Siniard Lower Dam—*dam* ... NC-3
Sinia Sch (historical)—*school* ... MO-7
Sinifa—*other* ... GU-9
Sinigrok Point—*cape* ... AK-9
Siniktaneyak Creek—*stream* ... AK-9
Siniktanneyak Mtn—*summit* ... AK-9
Sininger Lagoon—*swamp* ... NE-7
Sin-I-Rock—*other* ... AK-9
Sinissippi Lake—*reservoir* ... WI-6
Sinister Peak—*summit* ... WA-9
Sinita Tank—*reservoir* ... AZ-5
Sinitsin Cove—*bay* ... AK-9
Sinitsin Island—*island* ... AK-9
Sink, The—*basin* (2) ... AL-4
Sink, The—*basin* ... CA-9
Sink, The—*basin* (2) ... KY-4
Sink, The—*basin* ... PA-2
Sink, The—*basin* ... TN-4
Sink, The—*basin* (2) ... UT-8
Sink Branch—*stream* ... FL-3
Sink Branch—*stream* ... TN-4
Sink Cem—*cemetery* ... IN-6
Sink Cem—*cemetery* ... TN-4
Sink Ch—*church* ... TN-4
Sink Creek—*gut* ... FL-3
**Sink Creek**—*pop pl* ... FL-3
Sink Creek—*stream* (3) ... CO-8
Sink Creek—*stream* ... FL-3
Sink Creek—*stream* (2) ... ID-8
Sink Creek—*stream* ... IN-6
Sink Creek—*stream* ... IA-7
Sink Creek—*stream* ... MI-6
Sink Creek—*stream* ... MO-7
Sink Creek—*stream* (4) ... MT-8
Sink Creek—*stream* ... OH-6
Sink Creek—*stream* (3) ... OR-9
Sink Creek—*stream* ... TN-4
Sink Creek—*stream* (2) ... TX-5
Sink Creek—*stream* ... WI-6
Sink Ditch—*canal* ... UT-8
Sink Draw—*valley* ... UT-8
Sinke Hill—*summit* ... MI-6
Sinker Butte—*summit* ... ID-8
Sinker Canyon—*valley* ... ID-8
Sinker Creek—*stream* (2) ... ID-8
Sinker Creek—*stream* ... IN-6
Sinker Creek—*stream* (2) ... OR-9
Sinker Creek Butte—*summit* ... ID-8
Sinker Fork—*stream* ... WV-2
Sinker Mtn—*summit* ... ID-8
Sinker Mtn—*summit* ... OR-9
Sinker Rock—*pillar* ... RI-1
Sinker Tunnel—*tunnel* ... ID-8
Sinkford Cem—*cemetery* ... VA-3
**Sink (historical)**—*pop pl* ... TN-4
Sink Hole—*basin* ... UT-8
Sinkhole, The—*basin* ... UT-8
Sinkhole, The—*lake* ... ME-1
Sinkhole Cave—*cave* ... TN-4
Sinkhole Creek—*gut* ... TN-4
Sink Hole Creek—*stream* ... NC-3
Sinkhole Creek—*stream* ... TN-4
Sinkhole Flat—*flat* ... NM-5
Sink Hole Flat—*flat* ... TX-5
Sinkhole Flat—*flat* ... UT-8
Sinkhole Hill—*summit* ... KY-4
Sinkhole Hill—*summit* ... MI-6
Sink Hole Hollow—*valley* ... MO-7
Sinkhole Hollow—*valley* ... MO-7
Sink Hole Hollow—*valley* ... OH-6
Sinkhole Hollow—*valley* (3) ... TN-4
*Sinkhole Lake* ... MI-6
Sink Hole Lake—*lake* ... AK-9
Sinkhole Lateral—*canal* ... ID-8
Sink Hole Mine—*mine* ... NC-3
Sinkhole Mtn—*summit* ... TN-4
Sink Hole Number One Tank—*reservoir* ... AZ-5
Sinkhole Pond—*lake* (2) ... AZ-5
Sinkhole Pond—*reservoir* ... AZ-5
Sink Hole Ponds—*lake* ... FL-3
Sink Hole Ridge—*ridge* ... MO-7
Sinkhole Ridge—*ridge* ... MO-7
Sinkhole Ridge—*ridge* (2) ... TN-4
*Sink Hole Rsvr* ... AZ-5
Sinkhole Rsvr—*reservoir* ... AZ-5
Sinkhole Rsvr—*reservoir* ... UT-8
Sink Holes—*bend* ... UT-8
Sinkhole Swamp—*lake* ... PA-2
Sinkhole Tank—*reservoir* (2) ... AZ-5
Sink Hole Tank—*reservoir* ... AZ-5
Sinkhole Tank—*reservoir* (4) ... AZ-5
Sink Hole Tank—*reservoir* ... NM-5
Sink Hole Tank—*reservoir* ... TX-5
Sinkhole Trap Windmill—*locale* ... NM-5
Sinkhole Valley—*valley* ... VA-3
Sink Hollow—*valley* ... ID-8
Sink Hollow—*valley* (2) ... UT-8
Sinkin Experimental Forest—*park* ... MO-7
Sinking Branch—*stream* (3) ... KY-4
Sinking Branch—*stream* ... TN-4
*Sinking Branch Bear Meadow Run* ... PA-2
*Sinking Branch Hollow* ... MO-7
*Sinking Branch Penns Creek* ... PA-2
Sinking Cane Hollow—*valley* ... TN-4
Sinking Canyon—*valley* ... ID-8
Sinking Cove—*locale* ... TN-4
Sinking Cove—*valley* ... TN-4
Sinking Cove Cave—*cave* ... TN-4
Sinking Cove Sch—*school* ... TN-4
*Sinking Creek* ... AL-4
*Sinking Creek* ... KY-4
*Sinking Creek* ... MO-7
*Sinking Creek* ... PA-2
*Sinking Creek* ... TN-4
**Sinking Creek**—*pop pl* ... TN-4
**Sinking Creek**—*pop pl* ... VA-3
Sinking Creek—*stream* (2) ... AL-4
Sinking Creek—*stream* ... AK-9
Sinking Creek—*stream* ... AR-4
Sinking Creek—*stream* ... ID-8
Sinking Creek—*stream* (2) ... IN-6
Sinking Creek—*stream* (9) ... KY-4
Sinking Creek—*stream* (5) ... MO-7
Sinking Creek—*stream* ... NC-3
Sinking Creek—*stream* ... OH-6
Sinking Creek—*stream* ... PA-2
Sinking Creek—*stream* (17) ... TN-4
Sinking Creek—*stream* (6) ... VA-3
Sinking Creek—*stream* ... WA-9
Sinking Creek—*stream* (2) ... WV-2
Sinking Creek—*stream* ... WI-6
Sinking Creek Cave—*cave* ... TN-4
Sinking Creek Cave System—*hist pl* ... KY-4
Sinking Creek Ch—*church* ... KY-4
Sinking Creek Ch—*church* ... MO-7
Sinking Creek Ch—*church* ... OH-6
Sinking Creek Ch—*church* (3) ... TN-4
Sinking Creek Ch—*church* ... VA-3
Sinking Creek Ch—*church* ... WV-2
*Sinking Creek Gap* ... PA-2
Sinking Creek Hill—*summit* ... AL-4
Sinking Creek Hill—*summit* ... KY-4
Sinking Creek Lookout Tower—*locale* ... MO-7
Sinking Creek Mtn—*summit* ... VA-3
Sinking Creek Sch (historical)—*school* (2) . TN-4
Sinking Creek Shoals—*bar* ... TN-4
Sinking Creek Trail—*trail* ... PA-2
*Sinking Fork* ... TN-4
**Sinking Fork**—*pop pl* ... KY-4
Sinking Fork—*stream* ... IN-6
Sinking Fork—*stream* (4) ... KY-4
Sinking Fork—*stream* ... TN-4
Sinking Fork Ch—*church* ... KY-4
Sinking Fork Livingston Creek—*stream* ... KY-4
Sinking Hollow—*valley* ... MO-7
Sinking Lake Cave—*cave* ... AL-4
Sinking Pond—*swamp* ... TN-4
Sinking Rock Hole—*lake* ... KY-4
*Sinking Run* ... PA-2
Sinking Run—*stream* (4) ... PA-2
Sinking Ship—*summit* ... AZ-5
Sinking Ship—*summit* ... UT-8
*Sinking Ship Butte* ... AZ-5
**Sinking Spring**—*pop pl* ... OH-6
**Sinking Spring**—*pop pl* ... PA-2
Sinking Spring—*spring* ... VA-3
Sinking Spring Borough—*civil* ... PA-2
Sinking Spring Branch—*stream* ... PA-2
Sinking Spring Cave—*cave* ... AL-4
Sinking Spring Cem—*cemetery* ... IN-6
Sinking Spring Cem—*cemetery* ... VA-3
Sinking Spring Ch—*church* ... KY-4
Sinking Spring Ch—*church* ... TN-4
Sinking Spring Ch—*church* ... VA-3
Sinking Spring Ch (historical)—*church* ... TN-4
Sinking Spring Run—*stream* ... WV-2
Sinking Springs—*spring* ... TN-4
Sinking Springs Cave Number 1—*cave* ... TN-4
Sinking Springs Cave Number 2—*cave* ... TN-4
Sinking Springs Ch—*church* (2) ... TN-4
Sinking Spring Sch—*school* ... KY-4
Sinking Spring Sch (historical)—*school* ... TN-4
Sinking Springs Overlook—*locale* ... PA-2
*Sinking Springs Sch* ... TN-4
Sinking Springs Sch—*school* ... TN-4
Sinking Springs Sch (historical)—*school* (2) ... TN-4
Sinking Spring Trail—*trail* ... PA-2
Sinking Streams Cave—*cave* ... TN-4
Sinking Township—*civil* ... MO-7
Sinking Valley—*locale* ... KY-4
**Sinking Valley**—*pop pl* ... PA-2
Sinking Valley—*valley* (2) ... KY-4
Sinking Valley—*valley* ... PA-2
Sinking Valley Ch—*church* ... KY-4
Sinking Valley Ch—*church* ... PA-2
Sinking Valley Country Club—*other* ... PA-2
Sinking Valley Lead Zinc Mines—*mine* ... PA-2
Sinking Valley Sch—*school* ... KY-4
Sinking Water Branch—*stream* ... TN-4
Sinking Waters—*basin* ... VA-3
Sink Lake—*lake* ... MI-6
Sink Lake—*lake* ... MN-6
Sink Lake—*lake* ... ND-7
Sink Lake—*lake* ... TX-5
Sink Lake—*lake* ... WA-9
Sinklear Cem—*cemetery* ... MO-7
Sinkler Branch—*stream* ... AR-4
Sinkler Branch—*stream* ... MS-4
Sinkler Cem—*cemetery* ... WV-2
*Sinkler Creek* ... MS-4
Sinkler Dam—*dam* ... PA-2
Sinkler Lake—*reservoir* ... PA-2
Sink Moountain Prospect—*mine* ... TN-4
Sink Mountain Rec Area—*park* ... TN-4
Sink Mtn—*summit* (2) ... TN-4
*Sink of Mohave* ... CA-9
Sink Of The Creek—*lake* ... GA-3
Sinkola Cem—*cemetery* ... GA-3
Sink Pond—*lake* ... AL-4
Sink Pond Hollow—*valley* ... VA-3
Sink Post Office (historical)—*building* ... TN-4
Sinkpot Brook—*stream* ... MA-1
Sink Ridge—*ridge* ... UT-8
Sink Rsvr—*reservoir* ... NV-8
Sink Run—*stream* ... PA-2
*Sink Run Dam* ... PA-2
Sinks—*locale* ... KY-4
Sinks, The—*area* ... AZ-5
Sinks, The—*basin* (3) ... AL-4
Sinks, The—*basin* ... AZ-5
Sinks, The—*basin* ... CA-9
Sinks, The—*basin* ... GA-3
Sinks, The—*basin* ... ID-8
Sinks, The—*basin* (2) ... KY-4
Sinks, The—*basin* (2) ... MO-7
Sinks, The—*basin* (2) ... TN-4
Sinks, The—*basin* ... UT-8
Sinks, The—*basin* (2) ... VA-3
Sinks, The—*basin* ... WY-8
Sinks, The—*lake* ... WY-8
Sinks Canyon—*valley* ... WY-8
*Sinks Cave* ... AL-4
Sinks Cave—*cave* ... AL-4
Sinks Cem—*cemetery* (2) ... TN-4
Sink Sch—*school* ... TN-4
Sink Sch (historical)—*school* ... OR-9
**Sinks Grove**—*pop pl* ... WV-2
Sinks Hill—*summit* ... TX-5
**Sinks (historical)**—*pop pl* ... OR-9
Sinks Hollow—*valley* ... TN-4
Sinks Lake—*lake* ... ID-8
Sinks of Dove Creek—*basin* ... UT-8
Sinks Of Gandy—*basin* ... WV-2
Sinks Of Little Brush, The—*basin* ... KY-4
Sink Spring—*spring* ... ID-8
Sink Spring Branch—*stream* ... TN-4
Sinks Sch—*school* ... KY-4
Sinks Shaft—*mine* ... NM-5
Sinks Tank—*reservoir* ... NM-5
Sink Tank—*reservoir* (2) ... AZ-5
Sink Three Cave—*cave* ... AL-4
*Sink Valley* ... UT-8
Sink Valley—*valley* ... AZ-5
Sink Valley—*valley* ... UT-8
Sink Valley Ch—*church* ... TN-4
Sink Valley Sch (historical)—*school* ... TN-4
Sink Valley Wash—*valley* ... UT-8
*Sinlahegan Creek* ... WA-9
*Sinlahekim Creek* ... WA-9
Sinlahekin Creek—*stream* ... WA-9
Sinlahekin Valley—*valley* ... WA-9
*Sinlehekin Creek* ... WA-9
*Sinnahamis River* ... WA-9
*Sinnamahoning* ... PA-2
**Sinnamahoning (RR name Sinnemahoning)**—*pop pl* ... PA-2
Sinnamon Cut—*gap* ... CA-9
Sinnamon Meadow—*flat* ... CA-9
Sinnard—*locale* ... CO-8
Sinnard Ditch—*canal* ... WY-8
Sinnard Rsvr—*reservoir* ... WY-8
*Sinneeg* ... MN-6
Sinneeg Creek—*stream* ... MN-6
Sinneeg Lake—*lake* ... MN-6
*Sinne-hanna* ... PA-2
**Sinnemahoning**—*pop pl* ... PA-2
Sinnemahoning Creek—*stream* ... PA-2
*Sinnemahoning Creek - in part* ... PA-2
Sinnemahoning Portage Creek—*stream* ... PA-2
Sinnemahoning Post Office (historical)—*building* ... PA-2
Sinnemahoning (RR name for Sinnamahoning)—*other* ... PA-2
Sinnemahoning State Park—*park* ... PA-2
Sinnema Ranch—*locale* ... MT-8
*Sinnenahoning Creek* ... PA-2
Sinners Creek Sch—*school* ... WI-6
Sinners Friend Ch—*church* ... GA-3
Sinners Friend Ch (historical)—*church* ... AL-4
Sinne Sawmill (historical)—*locale* ... PA-2
Sinnett Branch—*stream* ... WV-2
Sinnett Cem—*cemetery* ... OK-5
Sinnett Chapel—*church* ... IL-6
Sinnett Hollow—*valley* ... WV-2
Sinnett Octagon House—*hist pl* ... IA-7
Sinnett Run—*stream* ... WV-2
Sinnickson—*locale* ... VA-3
**Sinnickson Landing**—*pop pl* (2) ... NJ-2
*Sinning Flesh Brook* ... RI-1
Sinnipee Cem—*cemetery* ... WI-6
Sinnipee Creek—*stream* ... WI-6
Sinnipee Sch—*school* ... WI-6
Sinnissippi Park—*park* ... IL-6
Sinnissippi Site—*hist pl* ... IL-6
Sinnot Creek—*stream* ... AK-9
Sinnott, Joseph, Mansion—*hist pl* ... PA-2
**Sinnott (historical)**—*pop pl* ... OR-9
Sinnott Memorial—*other* ... OR-9
Sinnott Memorial Bldg No. 67—*hist pl* ... OR-9
**Sinnott (Township of)**—*pop pl* ... MN-6
Sinona Creek—*stream* ... AK-9
Sinona Lake—*lake* ... AK-9
Sinopah Mtn—*summit* ... MT-8
Sinopoulo, John, House—*hist pl* ... OK-5
Sinoski Mine—*mine* ... AZ-5
Sino Spring—*spring* ... NM-5
Sinrazat Shelter Cabin—*locale* ... AK-9
Sinsabaugh—*locale* ... MO-7
Sinsheim—*locale* ... PA-2
Sinsheimer Sch—*school* ... CA-9
*Sin-sin-ah-wah* ... WI-6
*Sin-sin-ah-wah River* ... IL-6
*Sin-sin-ah-wah River* ... WI-6
**Sinsinawa**—*pop pl* ... WI-6
Sinsinawa Mound—*summit* ... WI-6
Sinsinawa River—*stream* ... IL-6
Sinsinawa River—*stream* ... WI-6
*Sinsinaway* ... WI-6
*Sinsinaway River* ... IL-6
*Sinsinaway River* ... WI-6
*Sinsiniwaw* ... WI-6
*Sinsiniwaw River* ... IL-6
*Sinsiniwaw River* ... WI-6
*Sinsinnewa* ... WI-6
*Sinsinnewa River* ... IL-6
*Sinsinnewa River* ... WI-6
*Sinta Bogue Ch* ... AL-4
Sintas Windmill—*locale* ... NM-5
Sinter Plain—*flat* ... WY-8
*Sinthlick Branch* ... WV-2
**Sinton**—*pop pl* ... TX-5
Sinton-Odem (CCD)—*cens area* ... TX-5
Sinton Oil Field—*oilfield* ... TX-5
Sinton Siding—*locale* ... TX-5
Sintorosa Country Club—*other* ... CA-9
*Sint Sink* ... NY-2
*Sint Sink Bay* ... NY-2
*Sint Sink Neck* ... NY-2
Sinuk—*channel* ... AK-9
**Sinuk**—*pop pl* ... AK-9
Sinuk Creek—*stream* ... AK-9
Sinuk (Sinrock) River—*stream* ... AK-9
*Sinyakwateen* ... ID-8
*Sinyala Canyon* ... AZ-5
Sinyalak Creek—*stream* ... AK-9
*Sinyala Mesa* ... AZ-5
*Sinyala Rapids* ... AZ-5
Sinyala Tank—*reservoir* ... AZ-5
*Sinyalemin Lake* ... MT-8
*Sinyalemin Ridge* ... MT-8
Sinyard Hollow—*valley* ... AR-4
Sinyella, Mount—*summit* ... AZ-5
Sinyella Canyon—*valley* ... AZ-5
Sinyella Mesa—*summit* ... AZ-5
Sinyella Rapids—*rapids* ... AZ-5
Sinyella Spring—*spring* ... AZ-5
*Siog Pond* ... MA-1
Siona Mtn—*summit* ... AS-9
Sion Ch—*church* ... IA-7
**Sion Farm**—*pop pl* ... VI-3
Sion Farm (Census Subdistrict)—*cens area* . VI-3
Sion Hill—*hist pl* ... VI-3
Sion Hill—*locale* ... VI-3
Siotukuyuk Bluff—*cliff* ... AK-9
Siouan Scout Reservation—*park* ... VA-3
*Sioug Pond* ... MA-1
**Siousca**—*pop pl* ... PA-2
*Sioux* ... OH-6
Sioux—*locale* ... NC-3
Sioux—*locale* ... WI-6
Sioux Agency (Township of)—*civ div* ... MN-6
Sioux Ajax Tunnel—*mine* ... UT-8
*Sioux Bayou* ... WI-6
Sioux Bayou—*stream* ... MS-4
Sioux Bend Public Hunting Area—*area* ... IA-7
Sioux Cem—*cemetery* ... IA-7
**Sioux Center**—*pop pl* ... IA-7
Sioux Charley Lake—*lake* ... MT-8
**Sioux City**—*pop pl* ... IA-7
Sioux City and St. Paul RR Section House—*hist pl* ... MN-6
Sioux City Baptist Church—*hist pl* ... IA-7
Sioux City Central HS—*hist pl* ... IA-7
Sioux City City Hall—*building* ... IA-7
Sioux City Mine—*mine* ... MT-8
Sioux City Municipal Airp—*airport* ... IA-7
Sioux City Public Library (Smith Villa Branch)—*hist pl* ... IA-7
Sioux Coulee—*valley* ... WI-6
Sioux Council Boy Scout Reservation—*park* ... SD-7
Sioux County—*civil* ... ND-7
Sioux County Courthouse—*hist pl* ... IA-7
Sioux County Home—*locale* ... IA-7
Sioux Creek—*stream* ... MT-8
Sioux Creek—*stream* ... NE-7
Sioux Creek—*stream* ... SD-7
Sioux Creek—*stream* ... WI-6
Sioux Creek—*stream* ... WY-8
Sioux Creek Cem—*cemetery* ... WI-6
**Sioux Creek (Town of)**—*pop pl* ... WI-6
Sioux Crossing—*locale* ... MT-8
Sioux Ditch—*canal* ... WY-8
Sioux Empire Coll—*school* ... IA-7
Sioux Falls—*falls* ... MN-6
Sioux Falls—*falls* ... SD-7
**Sioux Falls**—*pop pl* ... SD-7
Sioux Falls Coll—*school* ... SD-7
Sioux Falls Diversion Channel—*reservoir* ... SD-7
Sioux Falls Diversion Dam and Weir—*dam* ... SD-7
Sioux Falls Hist Dist—*hist pl* ... SD-7
Sioux Falls Junction—*locale* ... SD-7
*Sioux Falls Municipal Airport* ... SD-7
Sioux Falls Natl Bank Bldg—*hist pl* ... SD-7
Sioux Falls Township—*civil* ... SD-7
Sioux Lake—*lake* (2) ... MN-6
Sioux Lateral—*canal* ... CA-9
Sioux Lookout Historical Monmt—*park* ... NE-7
Sioux Lookout Sch—*school* ... NE-7
Sioux Lookout State Wildlife Mngmt Area—*park* ... MN-6
*Sioux Mountain* ... CO-8
Sioux Nation State Wildlife Mngmt Area—*park* ... MN-6
Siouxon Creek—*stream* ... WA-9
Siouxon Peak—*summit* ... WA-9
Siouxon Trail—*trail* ... WA-9
Sioux Park—*park* ... SD-7
Sioux Pass—*gap* ... MT-8
Sioux Pass—*gap* ... UT-8
Sioux Pass—*gap* (2) ... WY-8
Sioux Pass—*locale* ... MT-8
Sioux Passage Park Archeol Site—*hist pl* ... MO-7
Sioux Pass Creek—*stream* ... MT-8
Sioux Pass Trail—*trail* ... WY-8
Sioux Peak—*summit* ... UT-8
Sioux Pine Island—*island* ... MN-6
Sioux Portage Creek—*stream* ... WI-6
**Sioux Rapids**—*pop pl* ... IA-7
Sioux Ridge—*ridge* ... KY-4
*Sioux River* ... MN-6
Sioux River—*other* ... WI-6
Sioux River—*stream* ... WI-6
Sioux River Campground—*locale* ... MN-6
Sioux River Lookout Tower—*locale* ... MN-6
Sioux River Slough—*gut* ... WI-6
Sioux Rsvr—*reservoir* ... MT-8
Sioux Sanitorium—*hospital* ... SD-7
Sioux Sch—*school* ... SD-7
Sioux Shaft—*mine* ... UT-8
Sioux Townhall—*building* ... IA-7
Sioux Township—*civil* ... MO-7
Sioux Township—*fmr MCD* (5) ... IA-7
**Sioux Township**—*pop pl* ... ND-7
**Sioux Township**—*pop pl* ... SD-7
Sioux Trail Camp—*locale* ... NM-5
Sioux Trail Sch—*school* ... ND-7
**Sioux Trail Township**—*pop pl* ... ND-7
Sioux Tunnel—*mine* ... UT-8
**Sioux Valley**—*pop pl* ... MN-6
Sioux Valley Cem—*cemetery* ... MN-6
Sioux Valley Ch—*church* ... SD-7
Sioux Valley Hosp—*hospital* ... SD-7
**Sioux Valley Junction**—*pop pl* ... SD-7
Sioux Valley Landing Strip—*airport* ... SD-7
Sioux Valley Sch—*school* ... MN-6
Sioux Valley Sch—*school* ... SD-7
**Sioux Valley Township**—*pop pl* ... SD-7
Sioux Valley (Township of)—*civ div* ... MN-6
**Sioux Village (subdivision)**—*pop pl* ... SD-7
*Sioux Wood River* ... MN-6
*Sioux Wood River* ... ND-7
*Sioux Wood River* ... SD-7
*Siovi Shuatak* ... AZ-5
Siovi Shuatak—*locale* ... AZ-5
Siovi Shuatak Pass—*gap* ... AZ-5
Siovi Shuatak Wash—*stream* ... AZ-5
Sip—*locale* ... KY-4
**Sipapu**—*pop pl* ... NM-5
Sipapu Bridge—*bridge* ... UT-8
Sipapu Ski Area—*locale* ... NM-5
Siparyann Creek—*stream* ... MT-8
Siparyann Ridge—*ridge* ... MT-8
Sipau Branch—*stream* ... AL-4
**Sipaulovi**—*pop pl* ... AZ-5
Sip Branch—*stream* ... LA-4
Sipe Ditch—*canal* ... IN-6
**Sipes**—*pop pl* ... FL-3
Sipes Bed—*basin* ... IN-6
Sipes Branch—*stream* ... PA-2
Sipes Canyon—*valley* ... NM-5
Sipe Sch—*school* ... WV-2
Sipes Club—*locale* ... MO-7
Sipes Creek—*stream* ... MT-8
Sipes Creek—*stream* ... WI-6
Sipes Creek Trail—*trail* ... MT-8
Sipes Hollow—*valley* ... IN-6
Sipes Mill—*locale* ... PA-2
Sipe Springs—*locale* ... TX-5
Sipe Springs Cem—*cemetery* ... TX-5
Sipe Springs Creek—*stream* ... TX-5
Sipes RR Station—*locale* ... FL-3
Sipes Run—*stream* ... PA-2
Sipes Sch—*school* ... IL-6
Sipes Spring—*spring* ... WI-6
**Sipesville**—*pop pl* ... PA-2
Sipesville Elem Sch—*school* ... PA-2
Sipesville Post Office (historical)—*building* ... PA-2
Sipesville Station—*building* ... PA-2
Sip Hole—*lake* ... SC-3
Siphon Basin—*basin* ... AZ-5
Siphon Canyon—*valley* (2) ... AZ-5
Siphon Canyon—*valley* ... CA-9
Siphon Cave—*cave* ... AL-4
Siphon Cave—*cave* ... MO-7
Siphon Cem—*cemetery* ... OR-9
Siphon Creek—*stream* ... WI-6
Siphon Ditch—*canal* ... CA-9
Siphon Ditch—*canal* ... NM-5
Siphon Draw—*valley* ... AZ-5
Siphon Eight—*canal* ... CA-9
Siphon Eighteen—*canal* ... CA-9
Siphon Eleven—*canal* ... CA-9
Siphon Fifteen—*canal* ... CA-9
Siphon Five—*canal* ... CA-9
Siphon Four—*canal* ... CA-9
Siphon Fourteen—*canal* ... CA-9
*Siphon Lake* ... WI-6
Siphon Lake—*lake* ... CA-9
Siphon Lakes—*lake* ... ID-8
Siphon Lateral—*canal* ... NM-5
Siphon Nine—*canal* ... CA-9
Siphon Ninteen—*canal* ... CA-9
Siphon One—*canal* ... CA-9
Siphon Rsvr—*reservoir* ... CA-9
Siphon Seven—*canal* ... CA-9
Siphon Seventeen—*canal* ... CA-9
Siphon Six—*canal* ... CA-9
Siphon Sixteen—*canal* ... CA-9
Siphon Spring—*spring* ... CO-8
Siphon Springs—*spring* ... WI-6
Siphon Ten—*canal* ... CA-9
Siphon Thirteen—*canal* ... CA-9
Siphon Three—*canal* ... CA-9
Siphon Twelve—*canal* ... CA-9
Siphon Twenty—*canal* ... CA-9
Siphon Twentyone—*canal* ... CA-9
Siphon Twentythree—*canal* ... CA-9
Siphon Twentytwo—*canal* ... CA-9
Siphon Two—*canal* ... CA-9
Siphon Well—*well* ... AZ-5
Siphorien Bayou—*stream* ... LA-4
Sip Lake—*lake* ... LA-4
Siple Cem—*cemetery* ... MI-6
Siple Mtn—*summit* ... WV-2
Siple Sch—*school* ... MI-6
Siple Tank—*reservoir* ... AZ-5
Sipp Bay—*bay* ... ME-1
Sipp Brook—*stream* ... ME-1
*Sippehaw* ... NC-3
Sipperly Hill—*summit* ... CT-1
Sipperly Lown Farmhouse—*hist pl* ... NY-2
**Sippewisset**—*pop pl* ... MA-1
*Sippican, Town of* ... MA-1
Sippican Bog—*swamp* ... MA-1
Sippican Harbor—*harbor* ... MA-1
Sippican Harbor Marshes—*swamp* ... MA-1
Sippican Historical Society Bldg—*building* ... MA-1
Sippican Neck—*cape* ... MA-1
Sippican River—*stream* ... MA-1
Sippican River Marshes—*swamp* ... MA-1
*Sippican Village* ... MA-1
*Sippicon River* ... MA-1
Sippie Mine—*mine* ... WY-8
Sippihaw Country Club—*locale* ... NC-3
Sipple—*locale* ... MT-8
Sipple, Thomas, House—*hist pl* ... DE-2
Sipple and Smith Mine—*mine* ... WY-8
Sipple Cem—*cemetery* ... KY-4
Sipple Hill—*summit* ... WY-8
Sipple House—*hist pl* ... DE-2
Sipple Slough—*stream* ... IL-6
**Sippo**—*pop pl* ... OH-6
Sippo Creek—*stream* ... OH-6
**Sippo Heights**—*pop pl* ... OH-6
Sippo Lake—*reservoir* ... OH-6
Sip Pond—*lake* ... NH-1
*Sip Pond Brook* ... MA-1
Sip Pond Brook—*stream* ... NH-1
*Sippowisset* ... MA-1
Sipp Sch—*school* ... IL-6
Sipps Point—*cape* ... DE-2
Sips Creek—*stream* ... WY-8
*Sipsey* (2) ... AL-4
**Sipsey**—*pop pl* ... AL-4
Sipsey Bar—*bar* ... AL-4
Sipsey (CCD)—*cens area* ... AL-4
Sipsey Ch—*church* ... AL-4
*Sipsey Creek* ... AL-4
Sipsey Creek—*stream* ... AL-4
Sipsey Creek—*stream* ... GA-3
Sipsey Creek—*stream* (2) ... MS-4
Sipsey Division—*civil* ... AL-4
**Sipsey Fork**—*pop pl* ... MS-4
Sipsey Fork—*stream* ... AL-4
*Sipsey Fork Black Warrior River* ... AL-4
*Sipsey Fork Church* ... AL-4
Sipsey Island (historical)—*island* ... AL-4
Sipsey JHS—*school* ... AL-4
*Sipsey Mill Bridge* ... AL-4
Sipsey Mills (historical)—*locale* ... AL-4
*Sipsey Mine* ... AL-4
Sipsey Mine (surface)—*mine* ... AL-4
Sipsey Mine (underground)—*mine* ... AL-4
*Sipsey River* ... AL-4
*Sipsey River* ... MS-4
Sipsey River—*stream* ... AL-4
*Sipsey River Forest Camp* ... AL-4
Sipsey River Hunting Club—*locale* ... AL-4
Sipsey River Rec Area—*locale* ... AL-4
Sipsey Swamp—*swamp* ... AL-4
*Sipsey Turnpike* ... AL-4
Sipsey Valley Sch (historical)—*school* ... AL-4
*Sipsie River* ... AL-4
*Sipsie River* ... MS-4
Sipson Island—*island* ... MA-1
*Sipsons Island* ... MA-1
*Sipsons Meadow* ... MA-1
Sips Spring—*spring* ... WY-8
Siput—*summit* ... GU-9
Sipyen—*locale* ... FM-9
Sipy Hollow—*valley* ... TX-5
**Siracusaville**—*pop pl* ... LA-4
Sir Alec Gap—*gap* ... AR-4
Sir Alec Mtn—*summit* ... AR-4
Sir Alexander Nevsky Chapel—*hist pl* ... AK-9
SI Ranch—*locale* ... NM-5
Sirard Camp—*locale* ... MI-6
Siras Hill—*summit* ... ME-1
Sircy Ridge—*ridge* ... TN-4
**Siren**—*pop pl* ... WI-6
Sirena, Lake—*lake* ... FL-3
*Sirenburgh* ... TN-4
**Sirenburg (historical)**—*pop pl* ... TN-4
Sirenburgh Post Office (historical)—*building* ... TN-4
Siren Lake—*lake* (2) ... MN-6
Siren Lookout Tower—*locale* ... WI-6
**Siren (Town of)**—*pop pl* ... WI-6
Sir Francis Drake Historical Monmt—*park* . CA-9
Sir Francis Drake HS—*school* ... CA-9
Siria Cem—*cemetery* ... KS-7
Siria Ranch—*locale* ... MT-8
Siri Ranch—*locale* ... NV-8
Siri Ranch Spring—*spring* ... NV-8
Sirius, Bayou—*stream* ... LA-4
Sirius Point—*cape* ... AK-9
**Sir Johns Run**—*pop pl* ... WV-2
Sir Johns Run—*stream* ... WV-2
Sirks Run—*stream* ... VA-3
*Sirmans* ... FL-3
Sirmans—*locale* ... GA-3
**Sirmans**—*pop pl* ... FL-3
**Sirmans (Ebb)**—*pop pl* ... FL-3
Sirocco—*locale* ... KY-4
Sirons Mill—*locale* ... VA-3
Sirr Creek—*stream* ... AK-9
Sirretta Meadows—*flat* ... CA-9
Sirretta Peak—*summit* ... CA-9
Sirrine Ditch—*canal* ... MT-8
Sirrine Ditch—*canal* ... WY-8
Sirrine Stadium—*other* ... SC-3
Sirr Mtn—*summit* ... AK-9
*Sirson Island* ... MA-1
*Sirsons Island* ... MA-1
Siruk Creek—*stream* ... AK-9
Sir William Johnson State Park—*park* ... NY-2
*Sis* ... FM-9
Sisabagamah Creek—*stream* ... MN-6
Sisabagamah Lake—*lake* ... MN-6
Sisal Creek—*stream* ... TX-5
Sisar Canyon—*valley* ... CA-9
Sisar Creek—*stream* ... CA-9
Sischu Creek—*stream* ... AK-9
Sischu Mountains—*range* ... AK-9
Sischu Mtn—*summit* ... AK-9
Sisco—*locale* ... FL-3
Sisco—*locale* ... WA-9
Sisco Brook—*stream* ... VT-1
Sisco Cem—*cemetery* ... AL-4
Sisco Cem—*cemetery* ... AR-4
Sisco Cem—*cemetery* ... TN-4
Sisco Chapel—*church* ... KY-4
Siscoe Branch—*stream* ... IN-6
**Sisco Heights**—*pop pl* ... WA-9
Sisco Hollow—*valley* ... MO-7
*Sisco Lake* ... NE-7
Sisco Lake—*lake* ... NE-7
Sisco Mtn—*summit* ... TN-4
Sisco Sch—*school* ... MI-6
Sisco Spring—*spring* ... MO-7
Siscowit Rsvr—*reservoir* ... CT-1
Siscowit Rsvr—*reservoir* ... NY-2
Siseebakwet Lake—*lake* ... MN-6
Sisek Cove—*bay* ... AK-9
Sisemore—*locale* ... AR-4
Sisemore Creek—*stream* ... OK-5
Sisemore Landing Public Use Area—*park* .. OK-5
Sisgravik Lake—*lake* ... AK-9
Sis Hollow—*valley* ... AR-4
Sisiak Creek—*stream* (2) ... AK-9
Sisi Butte—*summit* ... OR-9
Sisi Creek—*stream* ... OR-9
*Sisio* ... MH-9
Sisi Ridge—*ridge* ... WA-9
*Siskawit Bay* ... MI-6
Sisk Cem—*cemetery* ... AL-4
Sisk Cem—*cemetery* ... MO-7
*Sisken Lake* ... MI-6
**Siskeyville**—*pop pl* ... OR-9
Sisk Gap—*gap* ... AL-4
Sisk Gap—*gap* ... NC-3
Siskin Lake—*lake* ... MI-6
Sisk Island—*island* ... TN-4
*Siskivit Bay* ... WI-6
Siskiwit, Mount—*summit* ... MI-6
Siskiwit Bay—*bay* ... MI-6
Siskiwit Bay—*bay* ... WI-6
Siskiwit Bay Campground—*locale* ... MI-6
Siskiwit Falls—*falls* ... MI-6
Siskiwit Islands—*island* ... MI-6
Siskiwit Lake—*lake* ... MI-6
Siskiwit Lake—*lake* ... WI-6
Siskiwit River—*stream* ... WI-6
Siskiyou—*locale* ... OR-9
**Siskiyou (County)**—*pop pl* ... CA-9
*Siskiyou Fork* ... CA-9
Siskiyou Fork—*stream* ... CA-9
*Siskiyou Fork Middle Fork River* ... CA-9

Skate Point—cape (2) ... NC-3
Skaters Lake—lake ... AK-9
Skates Canyon—valley ... NM-5
Skates Hill—summit ... NY-2
Skates (historical)—locale ... MS-4
Skates Post Office (historical)—building ... TN-4
Skating Lake—lake ... WA-9
Skating Pond—lake ... UT-8
Skating Rink Canyon—valley ... NM-5
Skattaboe Block—hist pl ... ID-8
Skatutakee Lake—lake ... NH-1
Skatutakee Mtn—summit ... NH-1
Skatvold Cem—cemetery ... MN-6
Skawomet ... MA-1
Skeahan Bar—bar ... CA-9
Skeantocks River ... CT-1
Skeantocoke River ... CT-1
Skeater Park—park ... WI-6
Skedaddle Cove—bay ... ME-1
Skedaddle Creek—stream ... CA-9
Skedaddle Creek—stream ... NV-8
Skedaddle Dam (historical)—dam ... NV-8
Skedaddle Mountains—summit ... CA-9
Skedaddle Ranch—locale ... CA-9
Skedaddle Spring—spring ... CA-9
Skedaddle Spring—spring ... OR-9
Skedee—pop pl ... OK-5
Skedee Cem—cemetery ... OK-5
Skedee Creek ... NE-7
Skedee Creek—stream ... OK-5
Skedgell Sch—school ... ME-1
Skeebo Branch—stream ... NC-3
Skeebo Branch—stream ... SC-3
Skeedee Cem—cemetery ... NE-7
Skeedee Creek—stream ... NE-7
Skeedee Sch—school ... NE-7
Skeedee View Sch—school ... NE-7
Skeedskeedee-agie River ... WY-8
Skee Glacier—glacier ... AK-9
Skeekah Cove—valley ... NC-3
Skeel Creek—stream ... MI-6
Skeele, Capt. J. S., House—hist pl ... OH-6
Skeel Gulch—valley ... ID-8
Skeel Lake ... MI-6
Skeel Rsvr—reservoir ... CO-8
Skeel Rsvr No 1—reservoir ... CO-8
Skeels—pop pl ... MI-6
Skeel School—locale ... IL-6
Skeels Corner—pop pl ... VT-1
Skeels Crossroads—pop pl ... OH-6
Skeels Lake ... MI-6
Skeels Lake—lake ... MI-6
Skeels Oil Field—other ... MI-6
Skeels Pond—lake ... MI-6
Skeel Spur—locale ... MI-6
Skeelter Shelter—locale ... WA-9
Skeen—pop pl ... TX-5
Skeen, William D., House—hist pl ... UT-8
Skeenah Creek—stream ... GA-3
Skeenah Creek—stream ... NC-3
Skeenah Creek Mill—locale ... GA-3
Skeenah Gap—gap ... GA-3
Skeenah Gap—gap ... NC-3
Skeen Cem—cemetery ... MS-4
Skeen Cem—cemetery ... OH-6
Skeen Cem—cemetery ... TN-4
Skeen Cem—cemetery (6) ... VA-3
Skeen Cem—cemetery ... WV-2
Skeen Creek—stream ... VA-3
Skeen Creek—stream ... WY-8
Skeen Elem Sch—school ... FL-3
Skeen Lake—lake ... TX-5
Skeen Mtn ... NY-2
Skeen Peak—summit ... TX-5
Skeen Ranch—locale ... OR-9
Skeens Cem—cemetery ... KY-4
Skeens Cem—cemetery ... WV-2
Skeen Sch—school ... VA-3
Skeens Ferry ... NC-3
Skeen's Mill Covered Bridge—hist pl ... NC-3
Skeens Ridge—ridge ... VA-3
Skeens Sch (historical)—school ... TN-4
Skeen Union Ch—church ... VA-3
Skees, Richard, House—hist pl ... KY-4
Skees, William, House—hist pl ... KY-4
Skees Spring—spring ... KY-4
Skeeter Butte—summit ... OR-9
Skeetercake Creek ... AK-9
Skeeter Camp—locale ... OR-9
Skeeter Camp Trail—trail ... OR-9
Skeeter Cem—cemetery ... VA-3
Skeeter Creek ... OR-9
Skeeter Creek—stream ... KS-7
Skeeter Creek—stream ... MT-8
Skeeter Creek—stream ... WA-9
Skeeter Crossing ... VA-3
Skeeter Island—island ... NJ-2
Skeeter Island Creek—stream ... NJ-2
Skeeter Lake—lake ... LA-4
Skeeter Lake—lake ... MN-6
Skeeters Camp—locale ... OR-9
Skeeters Cem—cemetery ... KS-7
Skeeters Creek ... VA-3
Skeeters Creek—stream ... OR-9
Skeeters Flat ... OR-9
Skeeters Swamp—swamp ... OR-9
Skeetersville—pop pl ... WV-2
Skeeter Swamp ... OR-9
Skeetertown—locale ... VA-3
Skeeterville—locale ... TX-5
Skeet Key—island ... FL-3
Skeetkill Creek—stream ... NJ-2
Skeet Ridge—ridge ... TN-4
Skeetrock—locale ... VA-3
Skeet Rock Branch—stream ... VA-3
Skeetrock Ch—church ... VA-3
Skeet Rock Knob—summit ... KY-4
Skeet Rock Knob—summit ... VA-3
Skeets Wash—stream ... NM-5
Skeff Creek—stream ... CO-8
Skegemog, Lake—lake ... MI-6
Skegemog Point—cape ... MI-6
Skegemog Point Site—hist pl ... MI-6
Skegg Branch—stream ... VA-3
Skegg Creek—stream ... KY-4
Skegg Creek Ch—church ... KY-4
Skegg Crossroads—pop pl ... AL-4
Skegg Gap—gap ... KY-4
Skegg Gap—gap ... VA-3
Skegg Hole—bay ... VA-3
Skegg Knob—summit ... KY-4
Skegg Knob—summit ... VA-3
Skeggs—locale ... VA-3
Skeggs Branch—stream ... VA-3
Skeggs Creek ... KY-4
Skeggs Crossroads—locale ... AL-4
Skeggs Point—summit ... CA-9
Skeggs Spring ... MO-7
Skegg Tunnel—tunnel ... VA-3
Skeinah Creek ... GA-3
Skeinah Gap ... GA-3
Skein Lake—lake ... ID-8
Skein Mesa—summit ... CO-8
Skein Mesa Rsvr—reservoir ... CO-8
Skein Spring—spring ... CO-8
Skeleton Bluff—cliff ... TN-4
Skeleton Bone Tank—reservoir ... AZ-5
Skeleton Butte—summit ... AK-9
Skeleton Butte—summit ... ID-8
Skeleton Camp—locale ... CA-9
Skeleton Campground—locale ... ID-8
Skeleton Canyon—valley (3) ... AZ-5
Skeleton Canyon—valley (2) ... CA-9
Skeleton Canyon—valley (2) ... NM-5
Skeleton Canyon—valley ... WA-9
Skeleton Cave ... AZ-5
Skeleton Cave—cave ... OR-9
Skeleton Cliff—cliff ... MT-8
Skeleton Creek ... MT-8
Skeleton Creek—stream ... CA-9
Skeleton Creek—stream (2) ... ID-8
Skeleton Creek—stream ... MD-2
Skeleton Creek—stream (2) ... MT-8
Skeleton Creek—stream ... OK-5
Skeleton Creek—stream ... WA-9
Skeleton Creek Mine
(underground)—mine ... AL-4
Skeleton Flat—flat ... CA-9
Skeleton Glade—flat ... CA-9
Skeleton Gulch—valley ... CO-8
Skeleton Hills—summit ... NV-8
Skeleton Island—island ... SD-7
Skeleton Key—island ... FL-3
Skeleton Lake—lake ... MN-6
Skeleton Mesa—summit ... AZ-5
Skeleton Mine (underground)—mine ... AL-4
Skeleton Mountains—summit ... AL-4
Skeleton Mtn—summit ... MT-8
Skeleton Mtn—summit ... OR-9
Skeleton Park Tank—reservoir ... AZ-5
Skeleton Pass—gap ... CA-9
Skeleton Ridge—ridge ... AZ-5
Skeleton Ridge—ridge (2) ... NM-5
Skeleton Ridge Trail (Pack)—trail ... NM-5
Skeleton Spring—spring ... CA-9
Skeleton Spring—spring ... NM-5
Skeleton Tank—reservoir (3) ... AZ-5
Skell Channel—channel ... OR-9
Skelley ... OH-6
Skelley—locale ... OR-9
Skelley Creek ... OH-6
Skell Head—cliff ... OR-9
Skellinger Dam—dam ... NJ-2
Skellinger Lake ... NJ-2
Skellock Draw—valley ... OR-9
Skellock Guard Station—locale ... OR-9
Skelly ... OH-6
Skelly, William G., House—hist pl ... OK-5
Skelly Branch—stream ... TN-4
Skelly Creek ... OH-6
Skelly Creek—stream ... MT-8
Skelly Elem Sch—school ... KS-7
Skelly Field—park ... AL-4
Skelly Field—park ... OK-5
Skelly Gulch—valley ... MT-8
Skelly Hill—summit ... ID-8
Skelly Hollow—valley ... OK-5
Skelly JHS—school ... OK-5
Skelly Lake—lake ... MN-6
Skelly Sch (historical)—school ... PA-2
Skellys Spring—spring ... UT-8
Skellytown—pop pl ... TX-5
Skellyville—locale ... KS-7
Skelp—pop pl ... PA-2
Skelt—locale ... WV-2
Skeltcher Creek—stream ... CO-8
Skelt Mtn—summit ... VA-3
Skelton ... AL-4
Skelton ... KS-7
Skelton—locale ... IL-6
Skelton—pop pl ... IN-6
Skelton—pop pl ... WV-2
Skelton, Alexander Stephens,
House—hist pl ... GA-3
Skelton, Thomas, House—hist pl ... ME-1
Skelton Bend—bend ... AL-4
Skelton Bend Estates
(subdivision)—pop pl ... AL-4
Skelton Branch—stream ... AL-4
Skelton Branch—stream ... IN-6
Skelton Branch—stream ... TN-4
Skelton Cave—cave ... TN-4
Skelton Cem—cemetery ... IN-6
Skelton Cem—cemetery (3) ... TN-4
Skelton Creek—stream ... AL-4
Skelton Creek—stream ... AR-4
Skelton Creek—stream ... CA-9
Skelton Creek—stream ... IN-6
Skelton Creek—stream ... KS-7
Skelton Creek—stream ... SC-3
Skelton Gulch—valley ... ID-8
Skelton Hollow ... TN-4
Skelton Hollow—valley ... AL-4
Skelton Hollow—valley ... AR-4
Skelton Lake—lake ... CA-9
Skelton Lake—reservoir ... TX-5
Skelton Lakes—lake ... CA-9
Skelton Landing Strip—airport ... MO-7
Skelton Mtn—summit ... AR-4
Skelton Number 1 Dam—dam ... AL-4
Skelton Prospect—mine ... TN-4
Skelton (RR name for Forksville)—other ... VA-3
Skelton Rsvr—reservoir ... CT-1
Skelton Run—stream ... WV-2
Skelton Sch (historical)—school ... AL-4
Skelton Sch (historical)—school ... TN-4
Skelton Spring—spring (2) ... OR-9
Skeltontown—pop pl ... PA-2
Skelton (Township of)—pop pl ... IN-6
Skelton (Township of)—pop pl ... MN-6
Skelton Twin Lakes—reservoir ... NC-3
Skelt Run—stream ... WV-2
Skelts Run—stream ... WV-2
Skemonto, Lake—reservoir ... NY-2
Skena Creek ... GA-3
Skena Gap ... GA-3
Skene—pop pl ... MS-4
Skene Mtn—summit ... NY-2
Skene Post Office (historical)—building ... TN-4
Skene Sch—school ... MS-4
Skeniah Creek ... GA-3
Skeniah Gap ... GA-3
Skenks ... OH-6
Skeokum Mine—mine ... NV-8
Skeppernawin River ... OR-9
Skepton Airp—airport ... PA-2
Skepton Construction Airp—airport ... PA-2
Skern Creek—stream ... ID-8
Skerrey Point—cape ... NY-2
Skerrob Brook ... CT-1
Skerrob Brook ... MA-1
Skerry—locale ... ME-1
Skerry—locale ... NY-2
Skerry Brook—stream ... MA-1
Sketo Bridge—bridge ... KY-4
Skevington Ranch—locale ... TX-5
Skewarky ... NC-3
Skew Falls—falls ... ME-1
Ski, Lake—reservoir ... MO-7
Ski-a-took ... OK-5
Skiatook—pop pl ... OK-5
Skiatook Cem—cemetery ... OK-5
Skiatook Oil Field—oilfield ... OK-5
Skibby Bottom—bay ... MT-8
Ski Beach—beach ... CA-9
Skibo—pop pl ... MN-6
Skibo—pop pl ... NC-3
Skibo Lookout Tower—locale ... MN-6
Skibo (Luzerne)—pop pl ... KY-4
Skibo Mill—locale ... MN-6
Ski Boot Hill—locale ... AK-9
Skibvedt Cem—cemetery ... MN-6
Skice Lake—lake ... WI-6
Ski Creek—stream ... AK-9
Ski Creek—stream (2) ... ID-8
Skidaway Institute of
Oceanography—school ... GA-3
Skidaway Island—CDP ... GA-3
Skidaway Island—island ... GA-3
Skidaway Island State Park—park ... GA-3
Skidaway Narrows—channel ... GA-3
Skidaway River—channel ... GA-3
Skidaway Road—post sta ... GA-3
Skid Camp Pond—reservoir ... NM-5
Skid Canyon—valley ... NM-5
Skid Creek—stream ... MT-8
Skid Creek—stream ... OR-9
Skiddaway Island ... GA-3
Skiddaway Narrows ... GA-3
Skiddaway River ... GA-3
Skidder—locale ... LA-4
Skidder Branch—stream ... NC-3
Skiddoo Gulch—valley ... MT-8
Skiddy—pop pl ... KS-7
Skiddy Canyon—valley ... AZ-5
Skiddy Cem—cemetery ... KS-7
Skiddy Ridge—ridge ... AZ-5
Skiddy Tank—reservoir ... AZ-5
Skid Gulch—valley ... CA-9
Skid Island—island ... SC-3
Skidl Hill—summit ... AL-4
Skidmore ... KS-7
Skidmore ... PA-2
Skidmore—locale ... KS-7
Skidmore—locale ... WV-2
Skidmore—pop pl ... MD-2
Skidmore—pop pl ... MI-6
Skidmore—pop pl ... MO-7
Skidmore—pop pl ... PA-2
Skidmore—pop pl ... TX-5
Skidmore Bluff—cliff ... WI-6
Skidmore Branch—stream ... KY-4
Skidmore Cave—cave ... AL-4
Skidmore (CCD)—cens area ... TX-5
Skidmore Cem—cemetery ... AL-4
Skidmore Cem—cemetery ... IN-6
Skidmore Cem—cemetery ... KY-4
Skidmore Cem—cemetery ... ME-1
Skidmore Cem—cemetery ... MO-7
Skidmore Cem—cemetery ... TN-4
Skidmore Chapel—church ... AL-4
Skidmore Coll—school ... NY-2
Skidmore Corner—locale ... VA-3
Skidmore Creek—stream ... CA-9
Skidmore Creek—stream ... KY-4
Skidmore Creek—stream ... MI-6
Skidmore Crossing—locale ... WV-2
Skidmore Fork—stream (2) ... VA-3
Skidmore Hollow—valley ... OH-6
Skidmore Island—island ... VA-3
Skidmore Mtn—summit ... WV-2
Skidmore Park—park ... MN-6
Skidmore Ridge—ridge ... AR-4
Skidmore Ridge—ridge (2) ... CA-9
Skidmore Run ... VA-3
Skidmore Run—stream ... OH-6
Skidmore Run—stream ... WV-2
Skidmore Sch—school ... WV-2
Skidmore Sch (historical)—school ... MO-7
Skidmore Slough—stream ... WA-9
Skidmore Spring—spring (2) ... AL-4
Skid Mtn—summit ... TX-5
Skidoo—hist pl ... CA-9
Skidoo—locale ... CA-9
Skidoo Bay—bay ... MT-8
Skidoo Creek—stream ... MT-8
Skidoo Spring—spring ... OR-9
Skid Point ... DE-2
Skid Point—cape ... DE-2
Skid Road Creek—stream ... ID-8
Skid Tank—reservoir ... AZ-5
Skidway Campground—locale ... MT-8
Skidway Lake—lake ... MI-6
Skidway Lake—lake ... MN-6
Skidway Lake—pop pl ... MI-6
Skie Air Service Landing Field—airport ... SD-7
Skienah Creek ... GA-3
Skienah Gap ... GA-3
Skiera Sch—school ... MI-6
Skiermo Lake ... ND-7
Skiffa Tank—reservoir ... TX-5
Skiff Cove—bay ... AK-9
Skiff Creek ... VA-3
Skiffer Creek—stream ... MS-4
Skiffe's Creek ... VA-3
Skiffes Creek—stream ... VA-3
Skiffes Creek Annex—other ... VA-3
Skiffes Creek Rsvr—reservoir ... VA-3
Skiffes Creek Sand Spit Site—hist pl ... VA-3
Skiffington Creek—stream ... WA-9
Skiff Island ... MA-1
Skiff Island—island ... AK-9
Skiff Island—island ... LA-4
Skiff Lake—lake ... LA-4
Skiff Lake—lake ... MI-6
Skiff Lake—lake ... MS-4
Skiff Lake Ch—church ... MI-6
Skiffley Creek—stream ... NC-3
Skiffly Branch—stream ... NC-3
Skiff Mountain—locale ... CT-1
Skiff Mountain Cem—cemetery ... CT-1
Skiff Mtn—summit ... CT-1
Skiff Mtn—summit (2) ... NY-2
Skiff Passage—channel ... AK-9
Skiff Point—cape ... WA-9
Skiff Sch—school ... AZ-5
Skiffs Creek ... VA-3
Skiffs Island (historical)—island ... MA-1
Skifstrom Lake ... MN-6
Skift Mountain ... CT-1
Ski Haven Estates
Subdivision—pop pl ... UT-8
Ski Haven Lake Estates—pop pl ... PA-2
Ski Heil Peak—summit ... CA-9
Ski Hi—locale ... CA-9
Skihi Creek—stream ... AK-9
Ski Hill—pop pl ... IL-6
Ski Hill—summit (2) ... CA-9
Ski Hill—summit ... MT-8
Skihi Peak—summit (2) ... MT-8
Ski Hi Ranch—locale ... CO-8
Ski Hi Retreat Tank—reservoir ... AZ-5
Ski Island—island ... CA-9
Ski Island Lake—reservoir ... OK-5
Ski Islands—island ... CA-9
Ski Lake—lake ... AK-9
Ski Lake—lake ... CA-9
Ski Lake—lake ... WY-8
Ski Lake—reservoir ... AL-4
Ski Lake—reservoir ... NC-3
Ski Lake Dam—dam ... NC-3
Ski Lake Number Three ... AL-4
Ski/Lake Village
Condominium—pop pl ... UT-8
Skilak Glacier—glacier ... AK-9
Skilak Guard Station—locale ... AK-9
Skilak Lake—lake ... AK-9
Skilak River—stream ... AK-9
Skiles Branch—stream ... IL-6
Skiles Branch—stream (2) ... TN-4
Skiles Cem—cemetery ... MO-7
Skiles Creek—stream ... TN-4
Skiles Draw—valley ... WY-8
Skiles Falls—falls ... TX-5
Skiles Ferry ... NC-3
Skiles (historical)—pop pl ... TN-4
Skiles JHS—school ... IL-6
Skiles Rsvr—reservoir ... WY-8
Skiles Sch (historical)—school ... TN-4
Skiles Spring—spring ... MO-7
Skiles Test Elem Sch—school ... IN-6
Skilesville—locale ... KY-4
Ski Liberty (ski area)—locale ... PA-2
Skilkantin Creek ... WA-9
Skillagalee Light Station—hist pl ... MI-6
Skillakalia Bayou Landing
(historical)—locale ... MS-4
Skill Center—school ... LA-4
Skillen Ditch—canal ... IN-6
Skillen School Number 34 ... IN-6
Skillern, John, House—hist pl ... ID-8
Skillern Cove—valley ... TN-4
Skillern Creek—stream ... ID-8
Skillern Creek—stream ... TN-4
Skillern Hot Springs—spring ... ID-8
Skillern House—hist pl ... AR-4
Skillern Mtn—summit ... VA-3
Skillern Peak—summit ... ID-8
Skillet, The ... MS-4
Skillet, The—area ... TN-4
Skillet Branch ... TN-4
Skillet Branch—stream ... KY-4
Skillet Branch—stream ... VA-3
Skillet Creek ... IA-7
Skillet Creek—stream ... IA-7
Skillet Creek—stream ... MT-8
Skillet Creek—stream ... OR-9
Skillet Creek—stream ... TN-4
Skillet Creek—stream ... TX-5
Skillet Creek—stream ... WV-2
Skillet Creek—stream ... WI-6
Skillet Ditch—canal ... AR-4
Skilleteliah Creek ... MS-4
Skillet Falls—falls ... WI-6
Skillet Fork—stream ... IL-6
Skillet Fork Drainage Ditch—canal ... IL-6
Skillet Fork Lagoon—stream ... IL-6
Skillet Gap—gap ... TN-4
Skillet Glacier—glacier ... WY-8
Skillet Goliah Bayou ... MS-4
Skillet Handle—cape ... OR-9
Skillet Handle—summit ... AL-4
Skillet Handle Branch—stream ... KY-4
Skillet Handle Hollow—valley ... OH-6
Skillet Hollow—valley ... MO-7
Skillet Hollow—valley ... VA-3
Skillet Knob—summit ... NM-5
Skillet Knob—summit ... TX-5
Skillet Lake—lake ... CO-8
Skillet Mesa—ridge ... NM-5
Skillet Mtn—summit ... MT-8
Skillet Point—cape ... MD-2
Skillet Strand—swamp ... FL-3
Skilligallee ... MI-6
Skillikalia Bayou—stream ... MS-4
Skillings ... ME-1
Skillings Corner—pop pl ... ME-1
Skillings Hill—summit ... ME-1
Skillings River—stream ... ME-1
Skillingston Cem—cemetery ... ME-1
Skilling Well—well ... CA-9
Skillion Creek—stream ... MT-8
Skillman—locale ... KY-4
Skillman—pop pl ... MO-7
Skillman—pop pl ... NJ-2
Skillman Ave Ch—church ... TX-5
Skillman Branch—stream ... TN-4
Skillman Cem—cemetery ... IN-6
Skillman Dam—dam ... NJ-2
Skillman Flat—flat ... CA-9
Skillman Gulch—valley ... CO-8
Skillman House—hist pl ... KY-4
Skillman Ranch—locale ... MT-8
Skillman Spring—spring ... TN-4
Skillpot Island—island ... NY-2
Skilly Brook—stream ... ME-1
Skilly Hills—summit ... ME-1
Ski Lodge Spring—spring ... OR-9
Skilpot Lake—lake ... NC-3
Skime—locale ... MN-6
Skimerhorn Creek—stream ... MN-6
Skimerhorn Lake—lake ... MN-6
Skimiehan Cem—cemetery ... TN-4
Skimino—locale ... VA-3
Skimino Creek—stream ... VA-3
Skiminoe—pop pl ... VA-3
Skimino Farms—pop pl ... VA-3
Skimino Pond—reservoir ... VA-3
Skim Lake—lake ... FL-3
Skim Lake—lake ... NY-2
Skimmed Milk Rsvr—reservoir ... CO-8
Skimmer Creek—stream ... VA-3
Skimmerhorn Creek ... OR-9
Skimmerhorn Creek—stream ... MT-8
Skimmerhorn Creek—stream ... OR-9
Skim Milk Basin—basin ... CO-8
Skimo Creek—stream ... AK-9
Ski Mountain (subdivision)—pop pl ... NC-3
Skimpah ... UT-8
Skinall Gap—gap ... PA-2
Skinamadink ... MS-4
Skinaway Creek—stream (2) ... IA-7
Skinaway Lake—lake ... MN-6
Skinaway Lake—lake ... WI-6
Skin Bayou ... OK-5
Skin Cabin Creek—stream ... NC-3
Skin Corner—locale ... NJ-2
Skin Creek—stream ... ID-8
Skin Creek—stream ... MT-8
Skin Creek—stream (2) ... OH-6
Skin Creek—stream ... OR-9
Skin Creek—stream ... WV-2
Skin Creek (Magisterial
District)—fmr MCD ... WV-2
Skindance Lake—lake ... MN-6
Skinem—pop pl ... AL-4
Skinem—pop pl ... TN-4
Skinequit Pond—lake ... MA-1
Skinflint Fork—stream ... VA-3
Skinfoot Ridge—ridge ... TN-4
Skin Fork—stream (2) ... WV-2
Skinframe Creek ... KY-4
Skinframe Creek—stream (2) ... KY-4
Skin Gulch—valley ... CO-8
Skinhead ... AL-4
Skinhouse Branch—stream ... KY-4
Skin Island—island ... AK-9
Skin-it Gulch—valley ... OR-9
Skinker Neck ... VA-3
Skinkers Corner—locale ... VA-3
Skinkers Creek—stream ... VA-3
Skinkers Neck—cape ... VA-3
Skink Hollow—valley ... NY-2
Skinkle Landing Strip—airport ... CO-8
Skinnawah Creek—stream ... KS-7
Skinned Ash Creek—stream ... TN-4
Skinned Chestnut Branch—stream ... KY-4
Skinned Horse Rsvr—reservoir ... CO-8
Skinned Pine Ridge—ridge ... SC-3
Skinned Poplar Branch—stream ... WV-2
Skinned Poplar Gap—gap ... WV-2
Skinned Sapling Creek—stream ... FL-3
Skinnels Creek—stream ... VA-3
Skinner—locale ... ME-1
Skinner—locale ... MO-7
Skinner, Horace A., House—hist pl ... UT-8
Skinner, Jason, House—hist pl ... CT-1
Skinner, Marcus Meyer, House—hist pl ... AL-4
Skinner, Richard M., House—hist pl ... IL-6
Skinner Bay—bay ... ID-8
Skinner Bay—swamp ... FL-3
Skinner Bay—swamp ... GA-3
Skinner Bldg—hist pl ... NM-5
Skinner Bldg—hist pl ... WA-9
Skinner Bog—swamp ... ME-1
Skinner Branch—stream ... AL-4
Skinner Branch—stream ... IN-6
Skinner Branch—stream (2) ... KY-4
Skinner Branch—stream ... VA-3
Skinner Bridge—bridge ... MO-7
Skinner Brook ... NY-2
Skinner Brook—stream ... CT-1
Skinner Brook—stream (2) ... NH-1
Skinner Butte—summit ... OR-9
Skinner Canyon—valley ... NV-8
Skinner Canyon—valley ... NM-5
Skinner Canyon—valley ... TX-5
Skinner Canyon—valley ... UT-8
Skinner Cem—cemetery ... ID-8
Skinner Cem—cemetery (6) ... KY-4
Skinner Cem—cemetery ... MA-1
Skinner Cem—cemetery (2) ... MI-6
Skinner Cem—cemetery (2) ... MO-7
Skinner Cem—cemetery ... NY-2
Skinner Cem—cemetery ... OH-6
Skinner Cem—cemetery (2) ... TX-5
Skinner Ch—church ... IN-6
Skinner Chapel—church ... GA-3
Skinner Corners—locale ... NY-2
Skinner Creek ... ID-8
Skinner Creek ... MI-6
Skinner Creek ... WI-6
Skinner Creek—stream ... AL-4
Skinner Creek—stream (2) ... CA-9
Skinner Creek—stream ... ID-8
Skinner Creek—stream ... IN-6
Skinner Creek—stream ... KY-4
Skinner Creek—stream ... LA-4
Skinner Creek—stream ... MI-6
Skinner Creek—stream (2) ... MS-4
Skinner Creek—stream ... MO-7
Skinner Creek—stream (2) ... NY-2
Skinner Creek—stream ... OK-5
Skinner Creek—stream (2) ... OR-9
Skinner Creek—stream ... PA-2
Skinner Creek—stream (2) ... WI-6
Skinner Creek Flowage—reservoir ... WI-6
Skinner Crossroad—locale ... TN-4
Skinner Crossroads—pop pl ... TN-4
Skinner Cutoff Trail—trail ... UT-8
Skinner Dam—dam ... OR-9
Skinner Ditch—canal (2) ... IN-6
Skinner Drain ... MI-6
Skinner Drain—canal ... MI-6
Skinner Draw—valley ... CO-8
Skinner Draw—valley ... TX-5
Skinner Extension Drain—stream ... MI-6
Skinner Flat—flat (2) ... CA-9
Skinner Fork—stream ... WV-2
Skinner Gap—gap ... PA-2
Skinner Glacier—glacier ... OR-9
Skinner Grove ... CA-9
Skinner Gulch ... OR-9
Skinner Gulch—valley ... CO-8
Skinner Gulch—valley ... MT-8
Skinner Gulch Spring Number
One—spring ... MT-8
Skinner Gulch Spring Number
Two—spring ... MT-8
Skinner Head—cape ... MA-1
Skinner Hill—summit ... AR-4
Skinner Hill—summit ... CO-8
Skinner Hill—summit ... MA-1
Skinner Hill—summit ... NH-1
Skinner Hill—summit ... NY-2
Skinner Hill—summit ... ND-7
Skinner Hill—summit ... PA-2
Skinner Hill—summit ... TN-4
Skinner (historical)—pop pl ... OR-9
Skinner Hollow—valley ... AR-4
Skinner Hollow—valley ... NY-2
Skinner Hollow—valley ... PA-2
Skinner Hollow—valley (2) ... TN-4
Skinner Hollow—valley ... UT-8
Skinner Hollow—valley ... VT-1
Skinner Hollow—valley ... WV-2
Skinner Island—island ... AK-9
Skinner Island—island ... IL-6
Skinner JHS—school ... CO-8
Skinner Lake ... LA-4
Skinner Lake—lake (2) ... FL-3
Skinner Lake—lake ... IN-6
Skinner Lake—lake (2) ... LA-4
Skinner Lake—lake (3) ... MI-6
Skinner Lake—lake ... MT-8
Skinner Lake—lake ... WI-6
Skinner Lake—pop pl ... IN-6
Skinner Lake—reservoir ... AL-4
Skinner Lake—swamp ... AR-4
Skinner Meadows—flat ... MT-8
Skinner Memorial Chapel—hist pl ... MN-6
Skinner Mill Place—locale ... CA-9
Skinner Mine—mine ... OR-9
Skinner Mtn—summit ... TN-4
Skinner Park—park ... IL-6
Skinner Park—park ... NJ-2
Skinner Pasture Tank—reservoir ... AZ-5
Skinner Peak—summit ... CA-9
Skinner Peaks—summit ... UT-8
Skinner Ranch—locale (2) ... TX-5
Skinner Ranch—locale ... WY-8
Skinner Ridge—ridge ... AZ-5
Skinner Ridge—ridge ... CA-9
Skinner Ridge—ridge ... CO-8
Skinner Ridge—ridge ... OH-6
Skinner Ridge—ridge ... PA-2
Skinner Ridge—ridge ... VA-3
Skinner Ridge Trail—trail ... CA-9
Skinner Road Sch—school ... CT-1
Skinner Rsvr—reservoir ... CA-9
Skinners ... NC-3
Skinners—locale ... CA-9
Skinners—locale ... CO-8
Skinners Bar—bar ... OR-9
Skinners Bay—swamp ... GA-3
Skinners Branch—stream ... AR-4
Skinners Branch—stream ... NC-3
Skinners Bridge Landing
(historical)—locale ... NC-3
Skinnersburg—pop pl ... KY-4
Skinners Canal—canal ... NC-3
Skinners Cem—cemetery ... MS-4
Skinner Sch—school (2) ... IL-6
Skinner Sch—school ... TX-5
Skinner Sch (historical)—school ... MO-7
Skinner School (Abandoned)—locale ... TX-5
Skinners Corners—locale ... NY-2
Skinners Creek—stream ... IA-7
Skinners Eddy—pop pl ... PA-2
Skinners Falls—locale ... NY-2
Skinners Fork—stream ... OR-9
Skinners Head ... MA-1
Skinners Island—island ... MT-8
Skinners Lake—lake ... MT-8
Skinners Lake—reservoir ... AL-4
Skinners Landing—locale ... AL-4
Skinners Neck—cape ... MD-2
Skinner Spring—spring ... OR-9
Skinner Spring—spring ... TX-5
Skinner Spring—spring (2) ... UT-8
Skinner Springs—spring ... UT-8
Skinners Ridge ... CA-9
Skinners Run—stream ... MD-2
Skinners Store (historical)—locale ... AL-4
Skinners Swamp—swamp ... SC-3
Skinners Switch ... MS-4
Skinners Switch—locale ... NY-2
Skinner State Park—park ... MA-1
Skinner Subdivision
(subdivision)—pop pl ... AL-4
Skinnersville—locale ... NC-3
Skinnersville (Township of)—fmr MCD ... NC-3
Skinner Tank—reservoir (2) ... AZ-5
Skinner Tank—reservoir ... TX-5
Skinnerton—pop pl ... AL-4
Skinnerton Ch—church ... AL-4
Skinnerton (Skinnertown)—pop pl ... AL-4
Skinner Town—locale ... TX-5
Skinner (Township of)—unorg ... ME-1
Skinner Village ... AZ-5

**Sky Lakes Estates (subdivision)**—pop pl NC-3
Sky Lake Swamp—swamp MS-4
Skyland—locale VA-3
**Skyland**—pop pl CA-9
**Skyland**—pop pl GA-3
**Skyland**—pop pl MA-1
**Skyland**—pop pl NV-8
**Skyland**—pop pl NC-3
**Skyland**—pop pl OR-9
**Skyland**—pop pl SC-3
Skyland Airp—airport NC-3
Skyland Blvd Baptist Ch—church AL-4
Skyland Camp—locale CO-8
Skyland Camp—locale NC-3
Skyland Camp-Bowman Lake Ranger Station—hist pl MT-8
Skyland Cem—cemetery NC-3
Skyland Ch—church FL-3
Skyland Ch—church NC-3
Skyland Creek—stream MT-8
*Skyland Elementary School* AL-4
Skyland Estates—locale VA-3
Skyland Heights—uninc pl FL-3
Skyland Lake—lake ID-8
Skyland Lakes—locale VA-3
**Skyland Manor (subdivision)**—pop pl AL-4
Skyland-Morrison Creek Trail—trail MT-8
Skyland Park—park AL-4
Skyland Park—park CO-8
Skyland Park—park NC-3
**Skyland Park Estates (subdivision)**—pop pl AL-4
**Skyland Park (subdivision)**—pop pl AL-4
Skyland Plaza Shop Ctr—locale AL-4
Skyland-Puzzle Creek Trail—trail MT-8
Skyland Ridge—ridge CA-9
**Skylands**—pop pl NJ-2
Skyland Sch—school AL-4
Skyland Sch—school GA-3
Skyland Sch—school KS-7
Skyland Sch—school NC-3
Skyland Shop Ctr—locale AL-4
**Skyland Terrace**—pop pl GA-3
*Skyland Village* CO-8
Skylane Airp—airport IN-6
Skylark Airpark—airport CT-1
Skylark Creek—stream CO-8
Skylark Lake—lake MT-8
Skylark Mine—mine (2) ID-8
Skylark Mine—mine UT-8
Skylark Sch—school CA-9
Sky Lateral—canal NV-8
Skylawn Memorial Gardens—cemetery CA-9
Skyles Creek—stream WV-2
Skyles Lake—lake MT-8
Skyles Spring—spring TN-4
Sky Lift Shop Ctr—locale TN-4
Skylight—locale AR-4
**Skylight**—pop pl KY-4
Skylight, Mount—summit NY-2
Skylight Arch—arch UT-8
Skylight Brook—stream NY-2
Skylight Canyon—stream OR-9
Skylight Cave—cave AL-4
Skylight Cave—cave OR-9
Skylight Mtn—summit AR-4
Skylight Pond—lake VT-1
Skylight Pond Trail—trail VT-1
Skylight Ridge—ridge CA-9
Skylight Spring—spring OR-9
*Skyline* ID-8
Skyline—locale KY-4
Skyline—locale MT-8
**Skyline**—pop pl AL-4
**Skyline**—pop pl CO-8
**Skyline**—pop pl MD-2
**Skyline**—pop pl MN-6
**Skyline**—pop pl MS-4
**Skyline**—pop pl NC-3
**Skyline**—pop pl WV-2
Skyline—uninc pl CO-8
**Skyline Acres**—pop pl AL-4
**Skyline Acres**—pop pl OH-6
**Skyline Additions**—pop pl MD-2
**Skyline Addition Subdivision**—pop pl UT-8
Skyline Alternate Trail—trail OR-9
Skyline Arch—arch UT-8
**Skyline Bel Aire Estates**—pop pl AZ-5
Skyline Bible Ranch—locale TN-4
Skyline Campground—locale CO-8
Skyline Caverns—cave VA-3
Skyline (CCD)—cens area OR-9
Skyline Cem—cemetery AL-4
Skyline Ch—church AL-4
Skyline Ch—church MO-7
Skyline Ch—church VA-3
Skyline Country Club—locale AL-4
Skyline Country Club—other AZ-5
Sky Line Country Club—other NE-7
Skyline Country Club—other NY-2
Skyline Country Club—other TX-5
Skyline Creek—stream OR-9
**Skyline Crest**—pop pl DE-2
Skyline Ditch—canal CO-8
Skyline Divide—ridge WA-9
Skyline Drive Ch—church AL-4
Skyline Elem Sch—school KS-7
**Skyline Estates**—pop pl AL-4
**Skyline Estates**—pop pl MD-2
**Skyline Estates Subdivision**—pop pl (2) UT-8
Skyline Golf Course—other CA-9
Skyline Golf Course—other OH-6
**Skyline Heights**—pop pl PA-2
Skyline Heights Baptist Ch—church TN-4
Skyline Heights Sch—school AR-4
**Skyline Heights (subdivision)**—pop pl (2) AZ-5
**Skyline Heights (subdivision)**—pop pl FL-3
**Skyline Heights (subdivision)**—pop pl SD-7
**Skyline Heights (subdivision)**—pop pl TN-4
Skyline HS—school CA-9
Skyline HS—school KS-7
Skyline HS—school MO-7
Skyline HS—school UT-8
Skyline Interchange—crossing AZ-5
Skyline Junior Coll—school CA-9
Skyline Lake—lake IL-6
Skyline Lake—lake MI-6
Skyline Lake—lake WA-9
Sky Line Lake—uninc pl NJ-2
Skyline Lakes—reservoir NJ-2
**Skyline Manor Subdivision**—pop pl UT-8
Skyline Memorial Garden—cemetery NC-3
Skyline Memorial Gardens—cemetery OR-9
Skyline Mine—mine CA-9
Skyline Mine—mine CO-8
Skyline Mine—mine OR-9
Skyline Mine—mine UT-8
Skyline Missionary Baptist Ch—church AL-4
Skyline Mtn—summit MT-8
Skyline North Sch—school CA-9
**Skyline Orchard**—pop pl DE-2
Skyline Park—park CA-9
Skyline Park—park KS-7
Skyline Park—park MN-6
Skyline Park—park OK-5
Skyline Park—park OR-9
Skyline Park—park PA-2
Skyline Park—park TX-5
**Skyline Park**—pop pl TN-4
**Skyline Park Subdivision**—pop pl UT-8
Skyline Peak—summit WY-8
Skyline Plaza Shop Ctr—locale AL-4
Skyline Ranch—locale (3) CA-9
Skyline Ranch—locale CO-8
Skyline Ranch—locale WY-8
Skyline Ranch (Site)—locale CA-9
**Skyline Ridge**—pop pl DE-2
Skyline Ridge—ridge CA-9
Skyline Ridge—ridge MT-8
Skyline Rim—cliff UT-8
Skyliners Park—park OR-9
Skyline Rsvr—reservoir CO-8
Skyline Rsvr—reservoir OR-9
Skyline Rsvr No. 2—reservoir CO-8
Skyline Rsvr No. 3—reservoir CO-8
Skyline Rsvrs—reservoir OR-9
Skyline Sch—school AL-4
Skyline Sch—school (2) CA-9
Skyline Sch—school KS-7
Skyline Sch—school MN-6
Skyline Sch—school MO-7
Skyline Sch—school OR-9
Skyline Seaplane Base—airport WA-9
Skyline Shop Ctr—locale AL-4
Skyline Shop Ctr—locale UT-8
**Skyline Shores (subdivision)**—pop pl AL-4
Skyline Ski Slide—other MI-6
*Skyline Towers* UT-8
*Skyline Trail* OR-9
Skyline Trail—trail CO-8
Skyline Trail—trail (2) MT-8
Skyline Trail—trail OR-9
Skyline Trail—trail (2) UT-8
Skyline Trail—trail (2) WA-9
**Skyline View**—pop pl PA-2
Skyline Village—locale MI-6
Skyline Vista Sch—school CO-8
Skyline Wildlife Mngmt Area—park AL-4
Sky Lode Mine—mine SD-7
**Sky Londa**—pop pl CA-9
Sky Manor—airport NJ-2
**Sky Manor**—pop pl NJ-2
Sky Manor Airp—airport NC-3
**Sky Meadow Farms**—pop pl NY-2
Sky Meadow Ranch—locale CA-9
Sky Meadow Ranch—locale WA-9
Sky Meadows—flat CA-9
Skymo Creek—stream WA-9
Skymo Lake—lake WA-9
**Skymont**—pop pl VA-3
Skymont Lake Dam Number One—dam TN-4
Skymont Lake Number One—reservoir TN-4
Sky Mountain Ranch—locale MT-8
Skymount Lake Dam Number Two—dam TN-4
Skymount Lake Number Two—reservoir TN-4
Skyo Mtn—summit WA-9
*Skypark* UT-8
Sky Park Fishing Lodge—building TN-4
Skypark Golf Course—other AL-4
Skypark Industrial Park—locale UT-8
**Sky Park (subdivision)**—pop pl AL-4
**Skypark T Hanger Subdivision**—pop pl UT-8
Sky Parlor Meadow—flat CA-9
Sky Peak—summit MT-8
Sky Pilot—summit ID-8
Sky Pilot—summit MT-8
Sky Pilot Harbor—locale KY-4
Sky Pilot Pass—gap WA-9
Sky Pilot Peak—summit WY-8
*Sky Piolet Peak* MT-8
Sky Point—cape TX-5
Sky Point Park—park TX-5
*Sky Pond* MA-1
Sky Pond—lake CO-8
Sky Pond—lake NH-1
Sky Pond State Forest—park NH-1
Skyport Airp—airport OR-9
*Sky Ranch* SD-7
Sky Ranch—locale CA-9
Sky Ranch—locale CO-8
Sky Ranch—locale OR-9
Sky Ranch—locale TX-5
**Sky Ranch**—pop pl AL-4
**Sky Ranch**—pop pl NY-2
**Sky Ranch**—pop pl SD-7
Sky Ranch Airp—airport CO-8
Sky Ranch Airp—airport PA-2
Sky Ranch Estates Airp—airport NV-8
Sky Ranch Flat—flat ID-8
Sky Ranch for Boys—locale SD-7
Sky Ranch for Boys Airstrip—airport SD-7
Sky Ranch II Airp—airport MO-7
Skyranch Landing Strip—airport KS-7
Sky Ranch Pond—lake NH-1
Sky Ranch Rsvr Number Four—reservoir OR-9
Sky Ranch Rsvr Number Three—reservoir OR-9
**Sky Ranch (subdivision)**—pop pl AL-4
Skyriders Airp—airport MO-7
*Skyriders Landing Strip* MO-7
Skyridge Camp—locale NM-5
Sky Ridge Mobile Homes—locale AZ-5
Sky Rock—summit CA-9
Skyrocket Creek—stream CO-8
Skyrocket Hills—range WA-9
Skyrocket Mine—mine CA-9
Skyrud Skyway—airport ND-7
Sky Run—stream IN-6
Skyscraper Hill—summit ME-1
Skyscraper Mtn—summit AK-9
Skyscraper Mtn—summit WA-9
Skyscraper Peak—summit AK-9
Skyscraper Peak—summit TX-5
**Skyscraper Shadows**—pop pl TX-5
Sky Spring—spring NM-5
Skytop—locale CA-9
Skytop—locale FL-3
**Skytop**—pop pl NY-2
**Skytop**—pop pl PA-2
Sky Top Creek—stream MT-8
Skytop Dam—dam PA-2
Sky Top Glacier—glacier MT-8
Skytop Lake—lake (2) MT-8
Sky Top Lakes—lake MT-8
Skytop Lower Lake—reservoir PA-2
Skytop Lower Lake Dam—dam PA-2
Sky Trail—trail CA-9
Skyuka Creek—stream NC-3
Skyuka Spring—spring GA-3
Skyuka Trail—trail GA-3
Skyuka Trail—trail TN-4
**Sky Valley**—pop pl CA-9
**Sky Valley**—pop pl GA-3
Sky Valley—valley CA-9
Sky Valley Pioneer Camp—locale NC-3
Sky Valley Ranch—locale CO-8
Sky View—locale UT-8
**Skyview**—pop pl AL-4
**Sky View Acres**—pop pl PA-2
Skyview Airp—airport MO-7
Skyview Ch—church FL-3
Sky View Ch—church MS-4
Sky View Ch—church TN-4
Sky View Ch—church VA-3
Skyview Elem Sch—school FL-3
**Skyview Estates (subdivision)**—pop pl NC-3
**Skyview Estates (subdivision)**—pop pl TN-4
Sky View Hosp—hospital CT-1
Sky View HS—school UT-8
Skyview Lake—lake FL-3
**Sky View Lake**—pop pl PA-2
Skyview Lake—reservoir (2) AL-4
Skyview Lake—reservoir NC-3
Sky View Lake—reservoir NC-3
*Skyview Lake Dam* AL-4
Sky View Lake Dam—dam NC-3
Skyview Lake Dam Lower—dam NC-3
Skyview Lake Dam Upper—dam NC-3
Skyview Lake Lower—reservoir NC-3
Skyview Lake Lower Dam—dam NC-3
Skyview Lake Upper—reservoir NC-3
**Sky View Manor**—pop pl NJ-2
Skyview Memorial Park—park OR-9
Skyview Memorial Park—park PA-2
**Skyview Mobile Home Park**—pop pl PA-2
Sky View Park—park KY-4
**Skyview Park**—pop pl NC-3
**Sky View Park**—pop pl VA-3
Sky View Sch—school CO-8
Skyview Sch—school IL-6
**Skyview Subdivision**—pop pl UT-8
**Skyview Terrace**—pop pl SC-3
Sky Village—locale CO-8
**Sky Village**—pop pl NC-3
Sky Village (Ruins)—locale NM-5
Skyvue Memorial Gardens (Cemetery)—cemetery TX-5
*Skyway* CO-8
**Skyway**—pop pl (2) CO-8
**Skyway**—pop pl SD-7
Skyway—uninc pl WA-9
Skyway Airp—airport IN-6
Skyway Campground—locale CO-8
*Skyway Channel* FL-3
Skyway Elem Sch—school FL-3
Skyway Estates—uninc pl CO-8
Skyway Hills Baptist Ch—church MS-4
Skyway Hills Ch of Christ—church MS-4
**Skyway Hills (subdivision)**—pop pl MS-4
Skyway Memorial Gardens—cemetery (2) FL-3
Skyway Park—uninc pl CO-8
Skyway Point—locale CO-8
Skyway Ranch—locale CO-8
Skyway Ranch Landing Strip—airport MO-7
Skyway Sch—school CO-8
Skyway Shop Ctr, The—locale FL-3
**Skyway Terrace**—pop pl NC-3
**Skyway Village**—pop pl AZ-5
**Sky West Estates Subdivision**—pop pl UT-8
Skywest Golf Course—other CA-9
*Skywood Dam No.1* AL-4
*Skywood Dam No.3* AL-4
*Skywood Dam Number 1* AL-4
*Skywood Dam Number 3* AL-4
Skywood Lake Number One—reservoir AL-4
Skywood Lake Number Three—reservoir AL-4
Skywood Lake Number Two—reservoir AL-4
*Skywood No.2 Dam* AL-4
*Skywood Number 2 Dam* AL-4
Sky Y Camp—locale AZ-5
Slab—locale PA-2
Slab—locale WV-2
Slab Barn Lake—lake ID-8
Slabbery Pond—swamp MA-1
Slab Branch—stream AL-4
Slab Branch—stream MS-4
Slab Branch—stream NJ-2
Slab Bridge—bridge NY-2
Slab Bridge Branch—stream NJ-2
Slab Bridge Brook—stream VT-1
Slab Bridge Creek—stream MD-2
Slab Bridge Prong—stream MD-2
*Slab Brook* MA-1
Slab Brook—stream MA-1
Slab Butte—summit ID-8
*Slab Cabin Branch Spring Creek* PA-2
Slab Cabin Cem—cemetery PA-2
*Slab Cabin Creek* PA-2
Slab Cabin Gulch—valley ID-8
Slab Cabin Run—stream PA-2
*Slab Cabin Spring Creek* PA-2
Slab Camp Branch—stream KY-4
Slabcamp Branch—stream KY-4
Slab Camp Branch—stream (3) KY-4
Slab Camp Branch—stream NC-3
Slabcamp Branch—stream WV-2
Slab Camp Cem—cemetery WV-2
Slabcamp Ch—church KY-4
*Slabcamp Creek* WV-2
Slab Camp Creek—stream GA-3
Slab Camp Creek—stream IN-6
Slab Camp Creek—stream KY-4
Slabcamp Creek—stream KY-4
Slabcamp Creek—stream OH-6
Slab Camp Creek—stream WA-9
Slab Camp Fork—stream WV-2
Slab Camp Guard Station—locale WA-9
Slabcamp Hollow—valley WV-2
Slab Camp Hollow—valley WV-2
Slabcamp Mtn—summit WV-2
Slabcamp Ridge—ridge WV-2
Slabcamp Run—stream (2) OH-6
Slab Camp Run—stream OH-6
Slabcamp Run—stream VA-3
Slabcamp Run—stream (2) WV-2
Slab Camp Run—stream WV-2
Slabcamp Run—stream WV-2
Slab Camp Run—stream WV-2
Slabcamp Run—stream (2) WV-2
Slab Camp Run—stream WV-2
Slabcamp Run—stream (5) WV-2
Slabcamp Trail—trail WV-2
*Slab Cane Creek* IN-6
*Slab Canyon* UT-8
Slab Canyon—valley (2) UT-8
Slab Canyon Wash—valley CO-8
Slab Causeway Branch—stream NJ-2
Slab Cave—cave AL-4
*Slab City* KS-7
Slab City—locale (2) ME-1
**Slab City**—pop pl ME-1
**Slab City**—pop pl NH-1
**Slab City**—pop pl (3) NY-2
**Slab City**—pop pl WI-6
Slab City Cem—cemetery ME-1
Slab City Creek—stream NY-2
Slab City Creek—stream WI-6
Slab Cliffs—cliff NV-8
Slab Coll (historical)—school TN-4
Slab Coll Sch (historical)—school AL-4
Slab Cove—valley NC-3
*Slab Creek* OR-9
Slab Creek—gut NJ-2
Slab Creek—stream AL-4
Slab Creek—stream CA-9
Slab Creek—stream OR-9
Slab Creek—stream UT-8
Slab Creek—stream (2) WV-2
Slab Creek—stream WY-8
Slab Creek Rsvr—reservoir CA-9
Slab Crossing—locale MT-8
Slab Crossing—locale TX-5
*Slab Fork* WV-2
**Slab Fork**—pop pl WV-2
Slab Fork—stream (6) WV-2
Slab Fork Cem—cemetery WV-2
Slab Fork Ch—church OH-6
Slab Fork Ch—church (2) WV-2
Slab Fork Johns Creek—stream OH-6
Slab Fork (Magisterial District)—fmr MCD WV-2
Slab Gulch—valley MT-8
Slab Gut Brook—stream CT-1
Slab Hollow—valley OH-6
Slab Hollow—valley PA-2
Slab Hollow—valley WV-2
Slab Hollow Cem—cemetery OH-6
Slabhouse Springs—spring OR-9
Slab Lake—lake MI-6
Slab Lakes—lake CA-9
Slab Landing Bridge—bridge SC-3
Slab Landing (historical)—locale NC-3
Slab Lick Branch—stream KY-4
Slab Meadow Brook—stream CT-1
Slab Mill Gulch—valley CO-8
*Slab Mountain* ID-8
Slab Park—flat CO-8
Slab Park—flat WY-8
Slab Park—park WY-8
Slab Pile Spring—spring UT-8
Slab Point—cape AK-9
Slab Run—stream KY-4
Slab Run—stream NC-3
Slab Run—stream (3) OH-6
Slab Run—stream (2) PA-2
Slab Run Ch—church OH-6
Slab Run Swamp—swamp PA-2
*Slab Run Trail* PA-2
Slab Sch—school WI-6
*Slabtown* CA-9
*Slabtown* IN-6
*Slabtown* MS-4
*Slabtown* MO-7
*Slabtown* NJ-2
*Slab Town* TN-4
*Slabtown* WI-6
Slabtown—locale KY-4
Slabtown—locale MO-7
Slabtown—locale NJ-2
Slabtown—locale TX-5
Slabtown—locale VA-3
Slabtown—locale WI-6
Slabtown—other MO-7
**Slabtown**—pop pl IN-6
**Slabtown**—pop pl (2) MD-2
**Slabtown**—pop pl NY-2
**Slabtown**—pop pl OH-6
**Slabtown**—pop pl (5) PA-2
**Slabtown**—pop pl TN-4
**Slabtown**—pop pl (3) VA-3
**Slabtown**—pop pl WV-2
*Slabtown Branch* TN-4
Slabtown Branch—stream MO-7
Slabtown Branch—stream TN-4
Slabtown Branch—stream (2) VA-3
Slabtown Cem—cemetery TX-5
Slabtown (historical)—locale AL-4
Slabtown (historical)—locale SD-7
Slabtown Hollow—valley PA-2
Slabtown Hollow—valley TN-4
**Slabtown (Ira)**—pop pl PA-2
Slabtown Lake—reservoir NJ-2
Slabtown Pond—swamp WI-6
Slabtown Sch—school WI-6
Slab Town Sch (historical)—school TN-4
Slabtown Spring—spring MO-7
Slab Trail Rsvr—reservoir WY-8
Slack Acad (historical)—school AL-4
Slack Airp—airport PA-2
Slack Branch—stream WV-2
Slack Canyon—valley CA-9
Slack Canyon—valley OR-9
Slack Canyon—valley WA-9
Slack Canyon Conservation Camp—locale CA-9
Slack Cem—cemetery WA-9
*Slack Creek* MI-6
Slack Creek—stream AL-4
Slack Creek—stream ID-8
Slack Creek—stream KS-7
Slack Creek—stream WY-8
Slack Ditch—canal CO-8
Slack Drain—canal MI-6
Slack Hill—summit VT-1
Slack Hollow—valley KY-4
Slack Hollow—valley PA-2
Slack Hollow—valley WV-2
Slack Lake—lake MI-6
**Slackland**—pop pl AL-4
Slackland Ch—church AL-4
Slackland Post Office (historical)—building AL-4
Slack Mtn—summit ID-8
Slack Reach—channel (2) SC-3
Slack Reservoir Dam—dam RI-1
Slack Ridge Ch (historical)—church MS-4
Slack Rsvr—reservoir RI-1
**Slacks**—pop pl LA-4
Slacks Branch—stream MO-7
Slacks Cem—cemetery TN-4
Slack Sch—school MI-6
Slack Sch—school WY-8
Slack Sch (abandoned)—school MO-7
Slacks Chapel (historical)—church TN-4
Slacks Corner—locale ID-8
Slacks Corner—locale MD-2
Slacks Creek—stream ID-8
Slacks Lake—reservoir NC-3
Slacks Lake Dam—dam NC-3
Slacks Mtn—summit ID-8
Slacks Overlook, The—locale VA-3
Slacks Ravine—valley CA-9
Slacks Run—stream PA-2
Slacks Valley—valley CA-9
*Slackville, Town of* MA-1
Slackwater—locale PA-2
Slack-Weiss Ditch—canal CO-8
Slack-Weiss Rsvr—reservoir CO-8
*Slackwood* NJ-2
**Slackwood**—pop pl NJ-2
**Slackwoods**—pop pl NJ-2
Sladden Park—park OR-9
Slade—locale KY-4
**Slade**—pop pl FL-3
**Slade**—pop pl KS-7
Slade Branch—stream IL-6
Slade Branch—stream WV-2
Slade Cem—cemetery (2) GA-3
Slade Cem—cemetery IL-6
Slade Cem—cemetery MA-1
Slade Cem—cemetery (4) MS-4
Slade Cem—cemetery NH-1
Slade Ch—church MS-4
*Slade Creek* MT-8
Slade Creek—stream MT-8
Slade Creek—stream NY-2
Slade Creek—stream NC-3
Slade Flat—flat ID-8
Slade Gut—stream NC-3
Slade Hotel—hist pl MN-6
Slade Interchange—other KY-4
Sladek Dam—dam SD-7
Slade Lake—lake MN-6
Slade Lake—reservoir SC-3
Slade Landing Creek—stream NC-3
Slade Natl Wildlife Ref—park ND-7
Slade Pond—lake NY-2
Slade Pond—reservoir VA-3
Slade Ranch—locale AZ-5
Slader Basin—basin UT-8
Slader Creek—stream NY-2
Slader Creek—stream UT-8
Slader Ridge—ridge UT-8
Slade Rsvr—reservoir AZ-5
Slade Run—stream MD-2
Slades Branch—stream GA-3
Slade Sch—school MD-2
Slade Sch—school MA-1
Slade Sch—school WY-8
**Slades Corner**—pop pl MA-1
**Slades Corner**—pop pl WI-6
**Slades Corners**—pop pl WI-6
*Slade'S Ferry* MA-1
**Slades Ferry**—pop pl MA-1
Slades Ferry Bridge—bridge MA-1
*Slade's Pond* CT-1
*Slades Station* AL-4
Slades Swamp—stream NC-3
**Sladesville**—pop pl NC-3
Slade Twin Arches—arch KY-4
Slafter Lake—lake WI-6
Slag-a-melt Creek—stream MT-8
Slag-a-melt Lakes—lake MT-8
Slag-a-melt Mine—mine MT-8
Slagel Canyon—valley NM-5
Slagel Cem—cemetery IA-7
Slagel Hollow—valley KY-4
Slager Lake—lake TX-5
Slagger—locale CA-9
Slagger Camp—locale CA-9
Slagger Spring—spring CA-9
*Slaght Drain* MI-6
Slaght Drain—canal MI-6
**Slagle**—pop pl LA-4
**Slagle**—pop pl MO-7
**Slagle**—pop pl WV-2
Slagle, Lake—lake OH-6
Slagle Basin—basin CO-8
Slagle Branch—stream TN-4
Slagle Cem—cemetery NC-3
Slagle Cem—cemetery OH-6
Slagle Cem—cemetery TN-4
Slagle Cem—cemetery VA-3
Slagle Ch—church MO-7
Slagle Ch—church TN-4
Slagle Creek—stream MI-6
Slagle Creek—stream (2) MO-7
Slagle Creek—stream (2) OR-9
Slagle Creek—stream TN-4
Slagle Ditch—canal FL-3
Slagle Draw—valley WY-8
Slagle Farm Cem—cemetery OH-6
Slagle Gap—gap VA-3
Slagle Hollow—valley TN-4
*Slagle Lake* VA-3
Slagle Memorial Ch—church NC-3
Slagle Pass—gap CO-8
Slagle Sch—school NC-3
Slagle Sch (historical)—school MO-7
Slagles Lake—reservoir VA-3
*Slagles Millpond* VA-3
**Slagle (Township of)**—pop pl MI-6
Slagley Hollow—valley AR-4
*Slago Ch* MS-4
Slagowski Ranch—locale NV-8
Slagowski Ranch—locale WY-8
**Slag Pile**—pop pl WI-6
Slag Pile Pond—lake TN-4
Slag Point—cape AK-9
Slaigo Brook—stream ME-1
*S Lake* MI-6
S Lake—lake AK-9
S Lake—lake OR-9
Slalom Cabin—locale AK-9
Slana—locale AK-9
Slana ANV945—reserve AK-9
Slana River—stream AK-9
Slana Slough—stream AK-9
Sland Canyon—valley CO-8
Slands Bridge—bridge SC-3
**Slandsville**—pop pl SC-3
Slane Canyon—valley NM-5
Slane Chapel—church MO-7
Slane Creek—stream CO-8
Slane Knob—summit NM-5
Slanes Flat—flat CA-9
Slanes Flat Ridge—ridge CA-9
Slanes Knob—summit WV-2
**Slanesville**—pop pl WV-2
Slang Pond—lake NY-2
Slank Ridge—ridge GA-3
Slanley Cem—cemetery NM-5
Slann Island—island SC-3
*Slanns Bridge* SC-3
*Slanns Island* SC-3
**Slansville**—pop pl SC-3
Slant—other VA-3
Slant Ch—church VA-3
Slanted Buttes—summit (2) NV-8
Slanting Misery—cliff TN-4
Slanting Peak—summit AK-9
Slanting Shoals Branch—stream TN-4
Slant Rock—bar WA-9
Slant Rock—summit NY-2
Slap Branch—stream NC-3
Slapes Corner—locale NJ-2
Slapjack Butte—summit OR-9
Slapjack Creek—stream (2) CA-9
Slapjack Spring—spring CA-9
Slapneck—locale MI-6
Slapneck Creek—stream MI-6
*Slapout* AL-4
**Slapout**—pop pl OK-5
**Slap Out (Spurgeon)**—pop pl IL-6
Slapover Ridge—ridge OK-5
Slap Swamp—stream NC-3
**Slaseman Mobile Home Park**—pop pl PA-2
Slash—locale VA-3
Slash, The—flat VA-3
Slash, The—gut NC-3
Slash, The—swamp FL-3
Slash Bay Hollow—valley MO-7
Slash Bayou—stream LA-4
Slash Branch—stream KY-4
Slash Branch—stream NC-3
Slash Branch—stream TN-4
Slash Branch—stream WV-2
Slash Ch—church VA-3
Slash Church—hist pl VA-3
Slash Creek—stream GA-3
Slash Creek—stream IN-6
Slash Creek—stream OK-5
*Slash Ditch* IN-6
Slashers Ledges—bench CT-1
Slash Five Spring—spring SD-7
Slash F Tank—reservoir NM-5
Slash Hill—summit NY-2
Slash Hollow—valley KY-4
Slash-h Ranch—locale NM-5
Slash J Slash Ranch—locale CO-8
Slash Lick Run—stream WV-2
Slash-Loesch Ditch—stream IN-6
Slash Pond—lake GA-3
Slash Ranch—locale NM-5
Slash Ranch—locale TX-5
Slash Ridge—ridge WY-8
Slash Ridge Lookout—locale WY-8
Slash Run Stream (historical)—stream DC-2
Slash Spring—spring OR-9
Slash S Ranch—locale AZ-5
Slash Well—well AZ-5
Slash 6 Ranch—locale CO-8
Slassoh Cem—cemetery CT-1
Slat—locale KY-4
*Slat Creek* ID-8
Slat Creek—stream CA-9
Slate—locale VA-3
**Slate**—pop pl WV-2
Slate Archeol Site—hist pl MS-4
Slate Basin—basin ID-8
Slate Bluff—cliff OK-5
Slate Bottom Creek—stream NY-2
Slate Branch—stream AR-4
Slate Branch—stream (7) KY-4
Slate Branch—stream LA-4
Slate Branch—stream OK-5
Slate Branch—stream (2) TN-4
Slate Branch—stream (3) VA-3
Slate Branch—stream WV-2
Slate Branch Cem—cemetery AR-4
Slate Branch Ch—church KY-4
Slatecamp Run—stream WV-2
Slate Canyon—valley (2) CA-9
Slate Canyon—valley UT-8
Slate Castle—pillar CA-9
Slate Castle Creek—stream CA-9
Slate Cem—cemetery AR-4
Slate Cem—cemetery GA-3

Slate Cem—cemetery KS-7
Slate Ch—church (2) WV-2
Slate Covered Bridge—hist pl NH-1
Slate Creek CA-9
Slate Creek UT-8
Slate Creek WA-9
Slate Creek WY-8
Slate Creek—locale AK-9
**Slate Creek**—pop pl ID-8
Slate Creek—stream AL-4
Slate Creek—stream (10) AK-9
Slate Creek—stream (4) AZ-5
Slate Creek—stream (2) AR-4
Slate Creek—stream (19) CA-9
Slate Creek—stream (5) CO-8
Slate Creek—stream (6) ID-8
Slate Creek—stream IL-6
Slate Creek—stream (2) IN-6
Slate Creek—stream (3) KS-7
Slate Creek—stream (4) KY-4
Slate Creek—stream MO-7
Slate Creek—stream (2) MT-8
Slate Creek—stream NV-8
Slate Creek—stream NM-5
Slate Creek—stream (2) NY-2
Slate Creek—stream NC-3
Slate Creek—stream (2) OK-5
Slate Creek—stream (8) OR-9
Slate Creek—stream (2) PA-2
Slate Creek—stream (2) SD-7
Slate Creek—stream (4) TN-4
Slate Creek—stream (3) UT-8
Slate Creek—stream VA-3
Slate Creek—stream (5) WA-9
Slate Creek—stream WV-2
Slate Creek—stream (5) WY-8
Slate Creek Bridge—hist pl CO-8
Slate Creek Butte—summit CA-9
Slate Creek Butte—summit WY-8
Slate Creek Cabin—locale ID-8
Slate Creek Camp—locale NM-5
Slate Creek Cem—cemetery TN-4
Slate Creek Ch—church KY-4
Slate Creek Dam—dam SD-7
Slate Creek Hot Spring—spring ID-8
Slate Creek Mine—mine AK-9
Slate Creek Ranger Station—locale CO-8
Slate Creek Recreation Site—locale ID-8
Slate Creek Ridge—ridge WY-8
Slate Creek Saddle—gap ID-8
Slate Creek Sch—school AL-4
Slate Creek Sch—school CA-9
Slate Creek School—locale WY-8
Slate Creek Springs—spring CA-9
**Slatecut**—pop pl IN-6
**Slatedale**—pop pl PA-2
Slatedale Cem—cemetery PA-2
Slate Dam PA-2
Slate Divide Trail—trail ID-8
Slate Draw—valley WY-8
Slate-Dunn Peak Trail—trail ID-8
Slate Field PA-2
Slatefield—locale PA-2
Slate Flat—flat UT-8
Slate Ford PA-2
Slate Ford—locale MO-7
Slateford—locale WI-6
**Slateford**—pop pl PA-2
Slate Ford Creek PA-2
Slateford Creek—stream PA-2
Slate Fork—stream KY-4
Slate Fork—stream WV-2
Slate Fork Churn Creek—stream OH-6
Slate Gap—gap AR-4
Slate Gap—gap (2) CA-9
Slate Gap—gap MO-7
Slategoat Mtn—summit MT-8
Slate Gorge—valley UT-8
Slate Gorge Overlook—locale UT-8
Slate Gulch—valley (2) CA-9
Slate Gulch—valley OR-9
Slate Hill—locale PA-2
Slate Hill—locale VA-3
**Slate Hill**—pop pl NY-2
Slate Hill—summit (2) AR-4
Slate Hill—summit ME-1
Slate Hill—summit NM-5
Slate Hill—summit (2) OH-6
Slate Hill—summit (2) RI-1
Slate Hill Cem—cemetery (2) NY-2
Slate Hill Ch PA-2
Slate Hill Ch—church IN-6
Slate Hill Ch—church KY-4
Slate Hill Ch—church PA-2
Slate Hill Ch—church TN-4
Slate Hill Ch—church (2) VA-3
Slate Hill Sch (abandoned)—school PA-2
Slate Hill Sch (historical)—school AL-4
Slate Hill Sch (historical)—school TN-4
Slate (historical)—locale AL-4
Slate (historical)—locale KS-7
Slate (historical P.O.)—locale IN-6
Slate Hole—lake GA-3
Slate Hollow—valley (3) KY-4
Slate Hollow—valley OH-6
Slate House—hist pl GA-3
Slate Island—island AK-9
Slate Island—island FL-3
Slate Island—island ME-1
Slate Island—island MA-1
Slate Island Cove—bay ME-1
Slate Islands—area AK-9
Slate Islets—area AK-9
Slate Jack Canyon—valley UT-8
Slate Jack Spring—spring UT-8
Slate Knobs—summit TN-4
Slate Lake—lake AK-9
Slate Lake—lake CO-8
Slate Lake—lake ID-8
Slate Lake—lake MN-6
Slate Lake—lake (2) MT-8
Slate Lake—lake WA-9
Slate Lakes—lake AZ-5
Slate Lakes Cove—cove AZ-5
Slate Ledge—bench NH-1
**Slate Lick**—pop pl KY-4
**Slate Lick**—pop pl PA-2
Slate Lick—stream (2) KY-4
Slate Lick—stream OH-6
Slate Lick Branch—stream (2) KY-4
Slatelick Branch—stream KY-4
Slate Lick Branch—stream VA-3
Slate Lick Ch—church KY-4
Slatelick Hollow—valley WV-2
Slate Lick Knob—summit (2) WV-2
Slate Lick Run VA-3
Slate Lick Run—stream PA-2
Slate (Magisterial District)—fmr MCD WV-2
Slate Mills—locale VA-3
**Slate Mills**—pop pl OH-6
Slate Mine—mine CA-9
Slate Mine—mine NV-8
Slate Mountain Ch—church NC-3
Slate Mountain Ch—church VA-3
Slate Mountain Mine (Inactive)—mine CA-9
Slate Mountains CA-9
Slate Mountains—range AZ-5
Slate Mountains—ridge CA-9
Slate Mountain Well Seventy-one—well AZ-5
Slate Mtn—summit AZ-5
Slate Mtn—summit (3) CA-9
Slate Mtn—summit CO-8
Slate Mtn—summit ID-8
Slate Mtn—summit NV-8
Slate Mtn—summit NC-3
Slate Mtn—summit (2) VA-3
Slate Mtn—summit WA-9
Slate Mtn Mine AZ-5
Slate Pass—gap WA-9
Slate Peak CO-8
Slate Peak NV-8
Slate Peak—summit AK-9
Slate Peak—summit ID-8
Slate Peak—summit WA-9
Slatepile Mtn—summit AK-9
Slate Point—cape MT-8
Slate Point—cliff KY-4
Slate Point—summit ID-8
Slate Pond—lake NY-2
Slate Port PA-2
Slate Post Office (historical)—building TN-4
Slate Prairie—flat FL-3
Slate Prairie—flat SD-7
Slate Prairie Ch—church SD-7
Slate Prairie Sch—school SD-7
Slate Quarry Brook—stream ME-1
Slate Quarry Hollow—valley TN-4
Slate Quarry Road Dutch Barn—hist pl NY-2
Slater—locale AL-4
Slater—locale CA-9
Slater—locale FL-3
Slater—locale KY-4
Slater—locale OH-6
Slater—locale TX-5
Slater—locale WA-9
Slater—locale WY-8
**Slater**—pop pl CO-8
**Slater**—pop pl IA-7
**Slater**—pop pl MO-7
**Slater**—pop pl SC-3
S Lateral—canal CA-9
Slate Range—range CA-9
Slate Range Bar—bar CA-9
Slater Bible Chapel—church FL-3
Slater Bldg—hist pl MA-1
Slater Bldg—hist pl OR-9
Slater Branch—stream AL-4
Slater Branch—stream GA-3
Slater Branch—stream KY-4
Slater Branch—stream (3) MO-7
Slater Branch—stream VA-3
Slater Brook—stream CT-1
Slater Butte—summit CA-9
Slater Cabin—locale NM-5
Slater Canyon—valley CA-9
Slater (CCD)—cens area SC-3
Slater Cem—cemetery IA-7
Slater Cem—cemetery NY-2
Slater Cem—cemetery TN-4
Slater Cem—cemetery WV-2
Slater Chapel Cem—cemetery TX-5
Slater CME Church AL-4
Slater Cox Bridge—bridge FL-3
Slater Creek CA-9
Slater Creek ID-8
Slater Creek—stream AK-9
Slater Creek—stream CA-9
Slater Creek—stream (2) CO-8
Slater Creek—stream (2) ID-8
Slater Creek—stream (2) IL-6
Slater Creek—stream IA-7
Slater Creek—stream MI-6
Slater Creek—stream NY-2
Slater Creek—stream OR-9
Slater Creek—stream TX-5
Slater Creek—stream (2) WV-2
Slater Creek—stream WY-8
Slater Creek Lake—lake CO-8
Slater Ditch—canal CO-8
Slater Ditch—canal OH-6
Slater Ferry (historical)—locale MS-4
Slater Flats—flat WY-8
Slater Hill—summit CT-1
Slater Hill—summit ME-1
**Slater (historical)**—pop pl OR-9
Slater Hollow—valley AL-4
Slater Hollow—valley MO-7
Slater Hollow—valley PA-2
Slater Hollow—valley WV-2
Slate Ridge—locale PA-2
Slate Ridge—ridge ID-8
Slate Ridge—ridge NV-8
Slate Ridge—ridge PA-2
Slate Ridge—ridge VA-3
Slate Ridge—ridge WY-8
Slate Ridge Bible Ch—church KY-4
Slate Ridge Cem—cemetery PA-2
Slate Ridge Sch—hist pl MD-2
Slate Ridge Sch—school MD-2
Slate Ridge Trail—trail CA-9
Slater Island—island CA-9
Slate River CO-8
Slate River—stream CO-8
Slate River—stream (2) MI-6
Slate River—stream VA-3
Slate River Ch—church VA-3
Slate River (Magisterial District)—fmr MCD VA-3
Slate River Mills—locale VA-3
Slater Lake MN-6
Slater Lake—lake CO-8
Slater-Marietta—CDP SC-3
Slater Memorial Airp—airport MO-7
Slater Mill Creek—stream GA-3
Slater Mine—mine NV-8
Slate Rock—pillar OR-9
Slate Rock Branch—stream AL-4
Slate Rock Branch—stream TN-4
Slate Rock Ch—church TX-5
Slate Rock Creek NC-3
Slaterock Creek—stream NV-8
Slate Rock Creek—stream NC-3
Slate Rock Creek—stream TN-4
Slate Rock Hollow—valley UT-8
Slate Rock Peak—summit UT-8
Slate Rock Ridge—ridge NC-3
Slate Rock Run—stream WV-2
Slate Rock Spring—spring ID-8
Slater Park—flat CO-8
Slater Park—hist pl RI-1
Slater Pond—lake MO-7
Slater Ranch—locale NM-5
Slater Red Tank—reservoir NM-5
Slaterrock Creek NC-3
Slater Run—stream OH-6
Slater Run—stream (3) PA-2
Slater Run Trail—trail PA-2
**Slaters**—pop pl OH-6
Slaters Ch AL-4
Slater Sch—school CA-9
Slater Sch—school CO-8
Slater Sch—school GA-3
Slater Sch—school TN-4
Slater Sch (abandoned)—school MO-7
Slaters Chapel—church AL-4
Slaters Chapel—church TN-4
Slater Sch (historical)—school PA-2
Slaters Corner VA-3
Slaters Creek ID-8
Slaters Creek—stream TN-4
Slaters Flat—flat ID-8
Slaters Fork—stream KY-4
Slater's Lake MN-6
Slaters Landing (historical)—locale AL-4
Slater Slough—stream WA-9
Slater's Mill—hist pl NJ-2
Slaters Mine—mine NV-8
Slaters Mtn—summit VA-3
Slaters Pond MA-1
Slater Spring—spring MO-7
Slater Spring—spring UT-8
Slaters Reservoir MA-1
**Slatersville**—pop pl RI-1
Slatersville Hist Dist—hist pl RI-1
Slatersville Pond RI-1
Slatersville Reservoir RI-1
Slatersville Reservoir Lower Dam—dam RI-1
Slatersville Reservoir Middle Dam—dam RI-1
Slatersville Reservoirs—reservoir RI-1
Slatersville Reservoir Upper Dam—dam RI-1
Slatersville Rsvr Upper—reservoir RI-1
Slate Rsvr—reservoir CO-8
Slate Rsvr—reservoir ID-8
Slate Rsvr—reservoir OR-9
Slater Tank—reservoir NM-5
**Slater (Township of)**—pop pl MN-6
**Slate Run**—pop pl PA-2
Slate Run—stream (2) IN-6
Slate Run—stream (2) KY-4
Slate Run—stream (7) OH-6
Slate Run—stream (2) PA-2
Slate Run—stream (2) VA-3
Slate Run—stream (5) WV-2
Slate Run Elem Sch—school IN-6
Slate Run Park—park OH-6
Slaterville—locale VA-3
**Slaterville**—pop pl AK-9
**Slaterville**—pop pl UT-8
Slaterville Diversion Dam—dam UT-8
Slaterville Springs—locale NY-2
Slate Sch—school WV-2
**Slates Corner**—pop pl VA-3
Slates Creek—stream (2) MI-6
**Slate Shoals**—pop pl TX-5
Slates Hot Springs—spring CA-9
Slates Island—island MA-1
Slate Slide Riffle—rapids OR-9
Slate Slide Shelter (historical)—locale OR-9
Slates Memorial Ch—church NC-3
Slates Pond—reservoir VA-3
Slate Spring AZ-5
**Slate Spring**—pop pl MS-4
Slate Spring—spring AZ-5
Slate Spring—spring CA-9
Slate Spring—spring WY-8
Slate Spring Branch—stream VA-3
**Slate Spring (corporate name for Slate Springs)**—pop pl MS-4
Slate Spring Draw—valley SD-7
Slate Spring Ridge—ridge CA-9
Slate Springs MS-4
**Slate Springs**—pop pl TN-4
Slate Springs Baptist Ch—church TN-4
Slate Springs Cem—cemetery TN-4
Slate Springs (corporate name Slate Spring) MS-4
Slate Springs Mountain Trail—trail (2) VA-3
Slate Springs Mtn—summit VA-3
Slate Springs Sch (historical)—school TN-4
Slate Springs Trail A—trail VA-3
Slate Springs Trail AA—trail VA-3
Slate Springs Trail B—trail VA-3
Slates Store (historical)—locale MS-4
Slatestone—locale TN-4
**Slatestone**—pop pl NC-3
Slatestone Branch—stream TN-4
Slatestone Creek—stream MI-6
Slatestone Creek—stream SC-3
Slatestone Creek—stream TN-4
Slatestone Hollow—valley TN-4
Slatestone Mine—mine TN-4
**Slatesville**—pop pl TN-4
Slate Tank—reservoir AZ-5
Slate Valley—locale KY-4
**Slate Valley**—pop pl PA-2
Slate Valley Ch—church KS-7
Slate Valley Sch—school KS-7
Slate Valley Sch (abandoned)—school PA-2
Slateville OR-9
Slateville—locale NY-2
Slateville—locale PA-2
Slateville Ch—church PA-2
Slate Well—well AZ-5
Slatey Branch—stream TN-4
Slatey Branch (historical)—stream TN-4
Slatey Ch—church KY-4
Slatey Cove—valley NC-3
Slatey Creek (historical)—stream TN-4
Slat Fence Hollow—valley TN-4
Slather Slough—swamp SD-7
Slather Slough State Wildlife Mngmt Area—park SD-7
Slathtouka Creek—stream AK-9
Slating Lake—lake MI-6
**Slatington**—pop pl PA-2
Slatington Airp—airport PA-2
Slatington Borough—civil PA-2
Slatington Elem Sch—school PA-2
Slatington HS PA-2
Slatka Creek—stream AK-9
**Slaton**—pop pl TX-5
Slaton, James E., House—hist pl KY-4
Slaton Branch—stream AL-4
Slaton (CCD)—cens area TX-5
Slaton Cem—cemetery TX-5
Slaton Draw—valley TX-5
Slaton JHS—school TX-5
Slaton Lake—lake TX-5
Slaton Ranch—locale NM-5
Slaton Sch—school GA-3
Slatons Pit—cave TN-4
Slator Ranch—locale (2) TX-5
Slats Tank—reservoir AZ-5
Slatten Branch—stream NC-3
Slatten Branch—stream SC-3
Slatten Falls—falls NC-3
Slatten House—hist pl MO-7
Slatten Ridge—ridge SC-3
Slatter Cem—cemetery TX-5
Slatter Creek ID-8
Slatterly Cabin—locale NV-8
Slatterly Park—park MN-6
Slattersville Rsvr—reservoir RI-1
Slattery Drain—canal MI-6
Slattery Gulch—valley CA-9
Slattery Mine—mine NV-8
Slattery Oil Field—oilfield WY-8
Slattery Pond—lake CA-9
Slaty Bluff—cliff AR-4
Slaty Branch—stream KY-4
Slaty Branch—stream (2) NC-3
Slaty Branch—stream (2) TN-4
Slaty Creek—stream AR-4
Slaty Creek—stream KY-4
Slaty Creek Cem—cemetery KY-4
Slaty Creek Ch—church KY-4
Slaty Crossing Ch—church AR-4
Slatyfork WV-2
**Slaty Fork**—pop pl WV-2
Slaty Fork—stream WV-2
**Slatyfork (RR name Laurel Bank)**—pop pl WV-2
Slaty Gap—gap VA-3
Slaty Hollow—valley OH-6
Slaty Hollow—valley WV-2
Slaty Knob—summit NC-3
Slaty Knob—summit TN-4
Slaty Lick Draft—valley VA-3
Slaty Mtn—summit VA-3
Slaty Ridge—ridge WV-2
Slaubaugh Run—stream MD-2
Slauchs Run (historical)—stream PA-2
Slaughter FL-3
Slaughter VA-3
Slaughter MH-9
Slaughter—locale DE-2
Slaughter—other VA-3
**Slaughter**—pop pl FL-3
**Slaughter**—pop pl LA-4
Slaughterback Hill—summit PA-2
Slaughter Bay—bay WI-6
Slaughter Beach—beach DE-2
**Slaughter Beach**—pop pl DE-2
Slaughter Beach Canal DE-2
Slaughter Bend—bend TX-5
Slaughter Branch—stream AL-4
Slaughter Branch—stream KY-4
Slaughter Branch—stream LA-4
Slaughter Branch—stream (2) MO-7
Slaughter Branch—stream (2) TX-5
Slaughter Brook—stream (2) ME-1
Slaughter Brook—stream NH-1
Slaughter Camp—locale AZ-5
Slaughter Canyon CA-9
Slaughter Canyon—valley (3) CA-9
Slaughter Canyon—valley NV-8
Slaughter Canyon—valley (2) NM-5
Slaughter Canyon—valley UT-8
Slaughter Cem—cemetery IN-6
Slaughter Cem—cemetery IA-7
Slaughter Cem—cemetery KY-4
Slaughter Cem—cemetery LA-4
Slaughter Cem—cemetery MS-4
Slaughter Cem—cemetery (2) TN-4
Slaughter Cove—valley TN-4
Slaughter Cove Creek—stream TN-4
Slaughter Creek DE-2
Slaughter Creek ID-8
Slaughter Creek—stream (3) AL-4
Slaughter Creek—stream AK-9
Slaughter Creek—stream DE-2
Slaughter Creek—stream (4) GA-3
Slaughter Creek—stream (2) ID-8
Slaughter Creek—stream IA-7
Slaughter Creek—stream MD-2
Slaughter Creek—stream (2) MT-8
Slaughter Creek—stream SD-7
Slaughter Creek—stream (2) TX-5
Slaughter Creek—stream UT-8
Slaughter Creek—stream WV-2
Slaughter Creek—stream WY-8
Slaughter Creek Broods—channel MD-2
Slaughter Creek Cem—cemetery GA-3
Slaughter Creek Cem—cemetery WV-2
Slaughter Creek Narrows—channel MD-2
Slaughter Dam—dam AL-4
Slaughter Draw—valley AZ-5
Slaughter Flat Landing—locale MS-4
Slaughter Flats—flat UT-8
Slaughter Gap—gap GA-3
Slaughter Gap—gap TX-5
Slaughter Gulch—stream OR-9
Slaughter Gulch—valley CO-8
Slaughter Gulch—valley (2) ID-8
Slaughter Gulch—valley (2) OR-9
Slaughter Gulch Rapids—rapids OR-9
Slaughter Gulch Rsvr—reservoir OR-9
Slaughter Gut—gut NJ-2
Slaughter Hill—summit FL-3
Slaughter Hill—summit MT-8
Slaughter Hill—summit NY-2
Slaughter Hill—summit TN-4
Slaughter-Hill Ranch—hist pl NM-5
**Slaughter (historical)**—pop pl TN-4
Slaughter Hollow—valley CO-8
Slaughter Hollow—valley MO-7
Slaughter Hollow—valley PA-2
Slaughter Hollow—valley (3) TN-4
Slaughter Hollow—valley TX-5
Slaughterhouse—locale OR-9
Slaughterhouse Bay—bay ND-7
Slaughterhouse Bend—bend MO-7
Slaughterhouse Branch—stream MD-2
Slaughter House Canyon NV-8
Slaughterhouse Canyon UT-8
Slaughterhouse Canyon—valley AZ-5
Slaughterhouse Canyon—valley (2) CA-9
Slaughterhouse Canyon—valley ID-8
Slaughterhouse Canyon—valley (5) NV-8
Slaughterhouse Canyon—valley SD-7
Slaughter House Canyon—valley UT-8
Slaughterhouse Covered Bridge—hist pl VT-1
Slaughterhouse Creek CO-8
Slaughterhouse Creek—stream (2) CO-8
Slaughterhouse Creek—stream (3) ID-8
Slaughterhouse Creek—stream MI-6
Slaughterhouse Creek—stream (2) MT-8
Slaughter House Creek—stream MT-8
Slaughterhouse Creek—stream MT-8
Slaughterhouse Creek—stream NV-8
Slaughterhouse Creek—stream ND-7
Slaughterhouse Creek—stream UT-8
Slaughterhouse Creek—stream (2) WI-6
Slaughterhouse Draw—valley ID-8
Slaughterhouse Draw—valley TX-5
Slaughterhouse Gulch—valley AZ-5
Slaughterhouse Gulch—valley (4) CA-9
Slaughterhouse Gulch—valley (6) CO-8
Slaughterhouse Gulch—valley (8) ID-8
Slaughterhouse Gulch—valley (3) MT-8
Slaughterhouse Gulch—valley NV-8
Slaughterhouse Gulch—valley (2) OR-9
Slaughterhouse Gulch—valley SD-7
Slaughterhouse Gulch—valley (2) WY-8
Slaughterhouse Hill—summit IN-6
Slaughterhouse Hollow—valley PA-2
Slaughter House Hollow—valley PA-2
Slaughterhouse Island—island CA-9
Slaughterhouse Lake MI-6
Slaughterhouse Lake—lake (2) WA-9
Slaughterhouse Point—cape CA-9
Slaughterhouse Pond—reservoir MA-1
Slaughterhouse Range—ridge OR-9
Slaughterhouse Run—stream OH-6
Slaughterhouse Run—stream (2) WV-2
Slaughter House Spring AZ-5
Slaughterhouse Spring—spring AZ-5
Slaughterhouse Spring—spring CA-9
Slaughterhouse Spring—spring ID-8
Slaughterhouse Spring—spring (2) NV-8
Slaughterhouse Spring—spring NM-5
Slaughterhouse Spring—spring OR-9
Slaughterhouse Springs—spring ID-8
Slaughter House Wash—stream AZ-5
Slaughterhouse Well—well TX-5
Slaughtering Ground Trail—trail PA-2
Slaughter Island—island AK-9
Slaughter Island (historical)—island TN-4
Slaughter Lake—lake TX-5
Slaughter Lake—reservoir AL-4
Slaughter Lake Dam—dam MS-4
Slaughter Landing—locale AL-4
Slaughter Meso—summit NM-5
Slaughter Mill (historical)—locale AL-4
Slaughter Mtn—summit AZ-5
Slaughter Mtn—summit GA-3
Slaughter Mtn—summit TX-5
Slaughter Mtn—summit VA-3
Slaughter Neck—cape DE-2
Slaughter Neck Cem—cemetery DE-2
Slaughter Neck Ch—church DE-2
Slaughter Neck Ditch DE-2
Slaughter Neck Sch—school DE-2
Slaughter Peaks—summit NV-8
Slaughter Pen Bay—bay WA-9
Slaughter Pen Branch—stream GA-3
Slaughterpen Creek VA-3
Slaughter Pen Hollow—valley KY-4
Slaughter Pen Hollow—valley (2) TN-4
Slaughterpen Hollow—valley VA-3
Slaughter Pen Pond—lake WA-9
Slaughter Pen Slough—gut AR-4
Slaughter Pole Creek—stream CA-9
Slaughter Pond—lake CO-8
Slaughter Pond—lake ME-1
Slaughter Pond—reservoir NC-3
Slaughter Pond Dam—dam NC-3
Slaughter Post Office (historical)—building TN-4
Slaughter Pumping Station—other TX-5
Slaughter Ranch—locale NM-5
Slaughter Ranch—locale (2) TX-5
Slaughter Ravine—valley CA-9
Slaughter Rsvr—reservoir SD-7
Slaughter Run—stream PA-2
Slaughter Run—stream WV-2
Slaughters—locale AL-4
**Slaughters**—pop pl KY-4
Slaughter Sand Pond—lake FL-3
Slaughters Cem—cemetery AL-4
Slaughter Sch—school KY-4
Slaughters Channel—channel OR-9
Slaughters (corporate name Slaughtersville) KY-4
Slaughters Creek—stream OR-9
Slaughters Dock—locale TN-4
Slaughter Sink—basin MO-7
Slaughters Lake—lake AR-4
Slaughters Lake—reservoir KY-4
Slaughters Landing AL-4
Slaughter Slopes—slope UT-8
Slaughter Slopes Rsvr—reservoir UT-8
Slaughter Slough—swamp MN-6
Slaughter's Pond NY-2
Slaughter Spring—spring NM-5
Slaughter Spring Gulch—valley CO-8
Slaughters Run PA-2
Slaughter Station DE-2
Slaughtersville KY-4
**Slaughtersville (corporate name for Slaughters)**—pop pl KY-4
Slaughter Tank—locale AZ-5
Slaughter Tank—reservoir AZ-5
Slaughter Tree Wash—valley CA-9
Slaughterville KY-4
**Slaughterville**—pop pl OK-5
Slaughter Windmill—locale TX-5
Slaunch Branch—stream WV-2
Slaunch Fork—stream WV-2
Slausen Sch—school CA-9
Slauson JHS—school MI-6
Slauson Lake—lake MN-6
Slauson Playground—park CA-9
Slavans—locale KY-4
Slavans Sch—school KY-4
Slave Cave—cave KY-4
Slave Cem—cemetery AL-4
Slave Cem—cemetery NC-3
Slave Cem—cemetery SC-3
Slave Cem—cemetery (8) TN-4
Slave Houses, Gregg Plantation—hist pl SC-3
Slaven, Frank, Roadhouse—hist pl AK-9
Slaven Cabin—locale AK-9
Slaven Canyon—valley NV-8
Slaven Cem MS-4
Slaven Cem—cemetery MS-4
Slaven Cem—cemetery WV-2
Slaven Dome—summit AK-9
Slaven Mtn—summit AR-4
Slavens Branch—stream KY-4
Slavens Branch—stream TN-4
Slavens Cem—cemetery MO-7
Slavens Cem—cemetery OH-6
Slavens Cem—cemetery TN-4
Slavens Creek—stream AR-4
Slavens Creek—stream TN-4
Slavens Knob—summit TN-4
Slavens Sch—school CO-8
Slavens Sch (historical)—school PA-2
Slave Street, Smokehouse, and Allee, Boone Hall Plantation—hist pl SC-3
Slavey Hollow—valley KY-4
**Slavia**—pop pl FL-3
Slavia Cem—cemetery FL-3
Slavic Cem—cemetery PA-2
Slavin Gulch—valley AZ-5
Slavin Hollow—valley WV-2
Slavin Wash—stream AZ-5
Slavin Well—well AZ-5
Slavna Point—cape AK-9
**Slavonia (historical)**—pop pl MS-4
Slavonia Mine CO-8
Slavonian Ditch—canal CA-9
Slavonian Hall—hist pl WA-9
Slavonian Mine—mine SD-7
Slavonic Cem—cemetery (2) TX-5
Slawson IN-6
Slawson Canyon—valley WA-9
Slawson Cem—cemetery IN-6
Slawson Lake—swamp MN-6
Slawson Mtn—summit NY-2
Slawther Creek WI-6
**Slay**—pop pl TX-5
Slayback Ditch—canal NM-5
Slay Bacon Branch—stream NC-3
Slay Bacon Hollow—valley TN-4
Slaybaugh Corner—locale MI-6
Slaybaugh Creek—stream WY-8
Slay Bend—bend AR-4
Slay Branch—stream AL-4
Slay Bridge—bridge MS-4
Slay Camp—locale TX-5
Slay Cem—cemetery AR-4
Slay Cem—cemetery (3) MS-4
Slay Creek—stream MS-4
Slay Creek—stream TX-5
Slay Dam—dam AL-4
**Slayden**—pop pl MS-4
**Slayden**—pop pl TN-4
**Slayden**—pop pl TX-5
Slayden Baptist Ch—church MS-4
Slayden Cem—cemetery MS-4
Slayden Cem—cemetery TN-4
Slayden Creek—stream VA-3
Slayden Hollow—valley TN-4
Slayden Sch (historical)—school MS-4
Slaydens Crossing MS-4
Slayden Swamp VA-3
Slaydon Cem—cemetery NC-3
Slaydons Creek—stream TX-5
Slaydons Slough—gut TX-5
Slay Lake—reservoir AL-4
Slaymaker, Stephen, House—hist pl WI-6
**Slaymakersville**—pop pl PA-2
Slayter Creek—stream TX-5
**Slayton**—pop pl MN-6
Slayton Branch—stream AR-4
Slayton Cem—cemetery AL-4
Slayton Cem—cemetery GA-3
Slayton Cem—cemetery MN-6
Slayton Corral—locale OR-9
Slayton Creek—stream MS-4
Slayton Field—park NJ-2
Slayton Ford—locale MO-7
Slayton Gap—gap GA-3
Slayton Hill—summit AL-4
Slayton Junction—locale MT-8
Slayton Lake—lake MI-6
Slayton Pond VT-1
Slayton Pond—lake NY-2
Slayton Pond—lake VT-1
Slayton Sch—school OK-5
Slayton Sch (historical)—school MO-7
Slaytons Fork—stream TN-4
**Slayton (Township of)**—pop pl MN-6
**Slaytonville**—pop pl AR-4
**Slaytonville**—pop pl DE-2
Slayton Well—well OR-9
S Lazy U Reservoirs—reservoir CO-8
S L Creek—stream MT-8
Sleadd, William, Farm—hist pl KY-4

Sleater Hill—*summit* NY-2
Sled Camp—*locale* WA-9
Sled Canyon—*valley* SD-7
*Sled Creek* KY-4
Sled Creek—*stream* CA-9
Sled Creek—*stream* (2) ID-8
Sled Creek—*stream* ND-7
Sled Creek—*stream* (2) OR-9
Sled Creek—*stream* VA-3
Sled Creek—*stream* WY-8
Sledd—*locale* MO-7
Sledd Branch—*stream* KY-4
Sledd Creek—*stream* (2) KY-4
Sledd Creek Cabin Area—*locale* KY-4
Sledds Lake—*reservoir* VA-3
Sledds Point—*cape* MD-2
**Sledds Point**—*pop pl* MD-2
Sledge—*locale* (2) AL-4
**Sledge**—*pop pl* MS-4
Sledge, James A., House—*hist pl* GA-3
Sledge Bayou—*stream* MS-4
Sledge Canal—*canal* LA-4
Sledge Cem—*cemetery* GA-3
Sledge Creek—*stream* AL-4
Sledge Creek—*stream* AK-9
Sledge Creek—*stream* WY-8
Sledge Crevasse—*lake* MS-4
*Sledge Crossing* AL-4
Sledge Elem Sch—*school* MS-4
Sledge Ford—*locale* AL-4
Sledge Ford Bridge—*bridge* AL-4
Sledge Hammer Gulch—*valley* CO-8
Sledge Hammer Point—*cape* WA-9
Sledge-Hayley House—*hist pl* NC-3
Sledge HS—*school* MS-4
Sledge Island—*island* AK-9
Sledge Island—*island* NC-3
Sledge Length Ridge—*ridge* VT-1
Sledge Oil Field—*oilfield* OK-5
*Sledges Station* AL-4
Sledgeville (historical)—*locale* MS-4
Sled Harbor—*locale* NY-2
Sled Haul Brook—*stream* CT-1
Sled Lake—*lake* MN-6
Sled Pass—*gap* AK-9
Sled Ridge—*ridge* CA-9
Sled Road Branch—*stream* KY-4
Sled Road Hollow—*valley* PA-2
Sled Run—*stream* KY-4
Sled Run—*stream* WV-2
Sled Runner Creek—*stream* WY-8
Sled Runner Gap—*gap* NC-3
Sled Runner Gap—*gap* TN-4
Sled Runner Ridge—*ridge* NC-3
Sled Saddle—*gap* NM-5
Sled Springs—*spring* OR-9
Sled Springs Guard Station—*locale* OR-9
Slee Lake—*lake* MT-8
Sleeley-Wick Oil Field—*oilfield* KS-7
Sleeman Creek—*stream* MT-8
Sleeman Well—*well* NV-8
Sleepcamp Run—*stream* WV-2
**Sleeper**—*pop pl* MO-7
Sleeper, Albert E., House—*hist pl* MI-6
Sleeper Airfield—*airport* KS-7
Sleeper Branch—*stream* NJ-2
Sleeper Branch—*stream* SC-3
Sleeper Brook—*stream* (2) NH-1
Sleeper Brook—*stream* VT-1
Sleeper Canyon—*valley* CA-9
Sleeper Canyon—*valley* NM-5
Sleeper Cem—*cemetery* MN-6
Sleeper Cem—*cemetery* MS-4
Sleeper Coulee—*valley* MT-8
Sleeper Creek—*stream* MS-4
Sleeper Creek—*stream* NY-2
Sleeper Gulch—*valley* CA-9
Sleeper Hollow—*valley* OK-5
Sleeper Lake—*lake* (2) MI-6
*Sleeper-McCann House* MA-1
Sleeper Peak—*summit* CA-9
Sleepers, The—*summit* NH-1
Sleepers Bend—*bend* AZ-5
Sleepers Island—*island* NH-1
Sleepers Point—*cape* NH-1
Sleeper's Ranch—*locale* WY-8
Sleepers River—*stream* VT-1
Sleeper Tank—*reservoir* NM-5
Sleeper Trail—*trail* NH-1
Sleep Gulch—*valley* CO-8
*Sleep Hill* MA-1
**Sleep Hollow Manor**—*pop pl* VA-3
Sleep Hollow Sch—*school* NE-7
Sleeping Bay—*bay* MI-6
Sleeping Bear, The—*summit* MI-6
Sleeping Bear Bay—*bay* MI-6
Sleeping Bear Creek—*stream* OK-5
*Sleeping Bear Dune* MI-6
Sleeping Bear Dunes—*summit* MI-6
Sleeping Bear Dunes Natl
Lakeshore—*park* MI-6
*Sleeping Bear Dunes Natl Rec Area* MI-6
*Sleeping Bear-Glen Lake State Park* MI-6
Sleeping Bear Inn—*hist pl* MI-6
*Sleeping Bear Natl Seashore* MI-6
Sleeping Bear Point—*cape* MI-6
Sleeping Bear Point Life Saving
Station—*hist pl* MI-6
Sleeping Bear Shoal—*bar* MI-6
*Sleeping Beauty* AZ-5
Sleeping Beauty—*summit* CA-9
Sleeping Beauty—*summit* NY-2
Sleeping Beauty—*summit* WA-9
Sleeping Beauty Mine—*mine* AK-9
Sleeping Beauty Mine—*mine* CA-9
*Sleeping Beauty Mtn* AZ-5
Sleeping Beauty Mtn—*summit* AZ-5
Sleeping Beauty Peak—*summit* AZ-5
Sleeping Beauty Shaft—*mine* NM-5
Sleeping Beauty Spring—*spring* AZ-5
Sleeping Beauty Tank—*reservoir* AZ-5
Sleeping Cave—*cave* HI-9
Sleeping Child Creek—*stream* MT-8
Sleeping Child Hot Springs—*spring* MT-8
Sleeping Column Canyon—*valley* NV-8
Sleeping Deer Mtn—*summit* ID-8
Sleeping Duck—*flat* AZ-5
Sleeping Duck Pond—*lake* IA-7
Sleeping Elephant Mtn—*summit* CO-8
Sleeping Elk Lake—*lake* MT-8
Sleeping Giant—*ridge* AL-4
Sleeping Giant—*summit* HI-9
Sleeping Giant, The—*summit* CO-8
Sleeping Giant Campground—*locale* WY-8
Sleeping Giant JHS—*school* CT-1
Sleeping Giant Mtn—*summit* MT-8
Sleeping Giant Mtn—*summit* WY-8
*Sleeping Giants* AL-4
Sleeping Giant State Park—*park* CT-1
Sleeping Giant Tower—*hist pl* CT-1
Sleeping Giant Winter Sports
Area—*park* WY-8
Sleeping Lady Hills—*other* NM-5
Sleeping Lion Mtn—*summit* TX-5
*Sleeping Sea Bird Islet* MH-9
Sleeping Sister Mtn—*summit* AK-9
Sleeping Spring—*spring* TX-5
Sleeping Spring Draw—*valley* TX-5
Sleeping Tom Summer Homes—*locale* CO-8
Sleeping Ute Mtn—*summit* CO-8
Sleepy Bay—*bay* AK-9
Sleepy Bill Fork—*stream* OR-9
Sleepy Canyon—*valley* KS-7
Sleepy Cat Peak—*summit* CO-8
Sleepy Cat Trail—*trail* CO-8
Sleepy Cem—*cemetery* AL-4
*Sleepy Creek* CA-9
**Sleepy Creek**—*pop pl* NC-3
**Sleepy Creek**—*pop pl* WV-2
Sleepy Creek—*stream* AL-4
Sleepy Creek—*stream* (2) AK-9
Sleepy Creek—*stream* CO-8
Sleepy Creek—*stream* ID-8
Sleepy Creek—*stream* (2) MI-6
Sleepy Creek—*stream* (2) NC-3
Sleepy Creek—*stream* OR-9
Sleepy Creek—*stream* SC-3
Sleepy Creek—*stream* VA-3
Sleepy Creek—*stream* (2) WV-2
Sleepy Creek Lake—*reservoir* WV-2
Sleepy Creek Lake Lower—*reservoir* NC-3
Sleepy Creek Lake Lower Dam—*dam* NC-3
Sleepy Creek Lake Upper—*reservoir* NC-3
Sleepy Creek Lake Upper Dam—*dam* NC-3
Sleepy Creek Lookout Tower—*locale* WV-2
Sleepy Creek (Magisterial
District)—*fmr MCD* WV-2
Sleepy Creek Mtn—*summit* WV-2
Sleepy Creek Public Hunting And Fishing
Area—*park* WV-2
Sleepy Dam—*dam* MI-6
**Sleepy Eye**—*pop pl* MN-6
Sleepy Eye Creek—*stream* MN-6
Sleepy Eye Lake—*lake* (2) MN-6
Sleepy Eye Lake—*lake* WI-6
Sleepy Eye State Park—*park* MN-6
Sleepy Gap—*gap* NC-3
Sleepy Grass Campground—*locale* NM-5
Sleepy Grass Canyon—*valley* NM-5
Sleepy Grass Dam—*dam* NM-5
*Sleepy Gulch* CO-8
Sleepy Gulch—*valley* MT-8
Sleepy Gulch—*valley* UT-8
Sleepy He Branch—*stream* WV-2
Sleepy Hill Windmill—*locale* AZ-5
Sleepy Hole—*locale* VA-3
Sleepy Hole Borough—*civil* VA-3
Sleepy Hole Point—*cape* VA-3
*Sleepy Hollow* TN-4
Sleepy Hollow—*basin* CA-9
Sleepy Hollow—*basin* WA-9
Sleepy Hollow—*gap* ID-8
Sleepy Hollow—*locale* PA-2
Sleepy Hollow—*locale* WA-9
**Sleepy Hollow**—*pop pl* (2) CA-9
**Sleepy Hollow**—*pop pl* IL-6
**Sleepy Hollow**—*pop pl* IN-6
**Sleepy Hollow**—*pop pl* MI-6
**Sleepy Hollow**—*pop pl* MS-4
**Sleepy Hollow**—*pop pl* VA-3
Sleepy Hollow—*valley* AL-4
Sleepy Hollow—*valley* (6) CA-9
Sleepy Hollow—*valley* IN-6
Sleepy Hollow—*valley* KY-4
Sleepy Hollow—*valley* MA-1
Sleepy Hollow—*valley* (3) MO-7
Sleepy Hollow—*valley* MT-8
Sleepy Hollow—*valley* (2) NY-2
Sleepy Hollow—*valley* OH-6
Sleepy Hollow—*valley* PA-2
Sleepy Hollow—*valley* (4) TN-4
Sleepy Hollow—*valley* TX-5
Sleepy Hollow—*valley* (3) UT-8
Sleepy Hollow—*valley* VT-1
Sleepy Hollow—*valley* WA-9
Sleepy Hollow—*valley* WV-2
Sleepy Hollow—*valley* WI-6
Sleepy Hollow, Lake—*lake* OH-6
Sleepy Hollow Boys Camp—*other* PA-2
Sleepy Hollow Brook—*stream* MA-1
Sleepy Hollow Cave—*cave* PA-2
Sleepy Hollow Cem—*cemetery* MA-1
Sleepy Hollow Cem—*cemetery* NE-7
Sleepy Hollow Cem—*cemetery* NY-2
Sleepy Hollow Country Club—*other* NY-2
Sleepy Hollow Country Club—*other* WV-2
Sleepy Hollow Creek—*stream* CA-9
Sleepy Hollow Creek—*stream* (2) NE-7
Sleepy Hollow Creek—*stream* OR-9
Sleepy Hollow Creek—*stream* WA-9
Sleepy Hollow Ditch—*stream* IL-6
Sleepy Hollow Drain—*canal* ID-8
**Sleepy Hollow Estates**—*pop pl* (2) VA-3
*Sleepy Hollow Farms* PA-2
Sleepy Hollow Golf Course—*other* PA-2
Sleepy Hollow Golf Course—*other* WV-2
Sleepy Hollow Hall—*hist pl* PA-2
Sleepy Hollow HS—*school* NY-2
*Sleepy Hollow - in part* PA-2
*Sleepy Hollow Lake* MA-1
Sleepy Hollow Lake—*lake* GA-3
Sleepy Hollow Lake—*reservoir* IN-6
Sleepy Hollow Lake—*reservoir* KY-4
Sleepy Hollow Lakes—*reservoir* MO-7
**Sleepy Hollow Lane
Subdivision**—*pop pl* UT-8
**Sleepy Hollow Manor**—*pop pl* NY-2
**Sleepy Hollow Manor**—*pop pl* VA-3
Sleepy Hollow Park—*park* IL-6
Sleepy Hollow Pond—*lake* MA-1
**Sleepy Hollow Run**—*pop pl* VA-3
Sleepy Hollow Run—*stream* PA-2
Sleepy Hollow Sch—*school* (2) CA-9
Sleepy Hollow Sch—*school* IL-6
Sleepy Hollow Sch—*school* SC-3
Sleepy Hollow Sch—*school* VA-3
Sleepy Hollow State Park—*park* MI-6
**Sleepy Hollow (subdivision)**—*pop pl* MS-4
**Sleepy Hollow Subdivision**—*pop pl* UT-8
**Sleepy Hollow Subdivision
Two**—*pop pl* UT-8
Sleepy Hollow Trailer Village—*locale* AZ-5
Sleepy Hollow Windmill—*locale* AZ-5
**Sleepy Hollow Woods**—*pop pl* VA-3
Sleepy Island Lake—*lake* MN-6
Sleepy Jack Creek—*stream* WY-8
Sleepy John Creek—*stream* OK-5
*Sleepy Lagoon* WA-9
Sleepy Lake—*reservoir* VA-3
Sleepy Mtn—*summit* AL-4
Sleepy Park Meadow—*flat* WA-9
Sleepy Pond—*swamp* MI-6
*Sleepy Ridge* OR-9
Sleepy Ridge—*ridge* OR-9
Sleepy Ridge—*stream* CO-8
Sleepy Run—*stream* KY-4
Sleepy Saddle—*gap* ID-8
Sleepy Tom Gulch—*valley* MT-8
**Sleepy Valley**—*pop pl* CA-9
Sleepy Valley—*valley* WI-6
S Lees Saw Mills—*locale* NC-3
Sleet Brook—*stream* IN-6
Sleeter Lake—*lake* VA-3
**Sleeth**—*pop pl* IN-6
Sleeth Site—*hist pl* IL-6
Sleeths Run—*stream* WV-2
**Sleetmute**—*pop pl* AK-9
Sleetmute ANV946—*reserve* AK-9
Sleets Shop—*locale* VA-3
Sleezer Creek—*stream* OR-9
**Sleggs Landing**—*pop pl* NY-2
Slegman Spring—*spring* OR-9
Sleighbell Slough—*gut* WI-6
Sleigh Canyon—*valley* UT-8
Sleigh Creek—*stream* AK-9
*Sleighrunner Lake* MI-6
Sleighrunner Lake—*lake* MI-6
Sleight, Thomas, Cabin—*hist pl* ID-8
Sleight Canyon—*valley* ID-8
Sleight Drain—*canal* MI-6
Sleighton Branch—*stream* AL-4
Sleighton Creek—*stream* WI-6
Sleighton Creek Sch—*school* WI-6
Sleighton Farm Sch—*school* PA-2
Sleighton Spring—*spring* AL-4
Sleight Pond—*lake* IL-6
**Sleightsburg**—*pop pl* NY-2
*Sleights Canyon* ID-8
Sleight Sch—*school* MI-6
Sleights Creek—*stream* NC-3
Sleighville Creek—*stream* CA-9
Sleighville House—*locale* CA-9
Sleighville Ridge—*ridge* CA-9
Sleigo Presbyterian Ch—*church* MS-4
Sleiman North (Shop Ctr)—*locale* FL-3
Sleiman South (Shop Ctr)—*locale* FL-3
Sleitat Mtn—*summit* AK-9
*Sleith Fork* WV-2
*Sleith Run* WV-2
Slemmons Creek—*stream* OH-6
Slemp—*locale* KY-4
Slemp Cem—*cemetery* (3) VA-3
Slemp Creek—*stream* VA-3
Slemp Pond—*lake* VA-3
Slender Bay—*swamp* NC-3
Slender Branch—*stream* NC-3
*Slenderdale Ridge* PA-2
Slender Pond—*lake* NY-2
Sleoca Mine (underground)—*mine* AL-4
Sleping Elephant Campground—*locale* CO-8
Sleppy Mine—*mine* OR-9
Slettebak Grocercies, Hardware and Opera
House—*hist pl* SD-7
**Sletten**—*pop pl* MN-6
Sletten Lake—*lake* MN-6
Sletten Lake—*lake* ND-7
Sletten Sch—*school* (2) SD-7
**Sletten (Township of)**—*pop pl* MN-6
Sleuter Hollow—*valley* MO-7
Slew Creek—*stream* MT-8
Slewgundy Ridge—*ridge* ME-1
Slew Spring—*spring* UT-8
Sleyster Cem—*cemetery* MO-7
Sleyster Sch—*school* MO-7
Slezak Mine—*mine* MT-8
**Slick**—*pop pl* OK-5
Slickaway—*locale* OH-6
Slickaway Hollow—*valley* OH-6
Slickaway Run—*stream* (2) OH-6
*Slick Bayou* OK-5
Slick Branch—*stream* VA-3
Slick Bridge—*bridge* ID-8
Slick-Carson Oil Field—*oilfield* KS-7
*Slick Creek* MT-8
*Slick Creek* OR-9
*Slick Creek* SD-7
Slick Creek—*stream* ID-8
Slick Creek—*stream* KY-4
Slick Creek—*stream* MS-4
Slick Creek—*stream* (2) MT-8
Slick Creek—*stream* ND-7
Slick Creek—*stream* (3) OR-9
Slick Creek—*stream* (2) SD-7
Slick Creek—*stream* WY-8
Slick Ditch—*canal* IN-6
Slickear Canyon—*valley* OR-9
Slick Ear Creek—*stream* ID-8
Slickear Creek—*stream* ID-8
Slickear Creek—*stream* OR-9
Slick Ear Creek—*stream* OR-9
Slick Ear Creek—*stream* WA-9
Slickear Mtn—*summit* OR-9
Slickens Creek—*stream* NC-3
Slickenside Creek—*stream* ID-8
Slickensides Arch—*arch* UT-8
Slicker Bar—*bar* ID-8
Slicker Creek—*stream* (2) OK-5
Slicker Creek—*stream* OR-9
Slicker Sch—*school* AR-4
Slickey Lake—*flat* OR-9
Slick Falls Branch—*stream* NC-3
Slickford—*locale* KY-4
**Slick Ford**—*pop pl* AL-4
Slickford Sch—*school* KY-4
Slick Fork Sch—*school* KY-4
Slick Gulch—*valley* MT-8
Slick Hill—*summit* TX-5
Slick Hill—*summit* UT-8
*Slick Hill Hollow* UT-8
Slick Hill Hollow—*valley* UT-8
Slick Hill Sch (historical)—*school* TN-4
Slick Hollow—*valley* OR-9
Slick Hollow—*valley* PA-2
Slick Hollow—*valley* TN-4
Slick Horn—*summit* UT-8
*Slick Horn Canyon* UT-8
Slickhorn Canyon—*valley* UT-8
*Slickhorn Gulch* UT-8
Slickhorn Pasture—*flat* UT-8
Slickhorn Rapids—*rapids* UT-8
*Slickhorn Wash* UT-8
Slicking Creek—*stream* SC-3
Slicking Falls—*falls* SC-3
Slicking Gap—*gap* NC-3
Slicking Gap—*gap* SC-3
Slicking Mtn—*summit* SC-3
Slick Limb Branch—*stream* TN-4
**Slicklizzard**—*pop pl* AL-4
Slick Mtn—*summit* TX-5
Slick Mtn—*summit* WY-8
Slicknasty Creek—*stream* TX-5
Slicknasty Windmill—*locale* TX-5
Slick Oil Field—*oilfield* TX-5
Slickpoo—*locale* ID-8
**Slickport**—*pop pl* PA-2
Slick Rock—*cliff* AZ-5
Slick Rock—*cliff* ID-8
Slick Rock—*locale* CO-8
Slick Rock—*locale* KY-4
Slick Rock—*locale* TN-4
Slick Rock—*other* NM-5
Slick Rock—*pillar* CA-9
Slickrock—*pillar* UT-8
Slick Rock—*pillar* WY-8
Slick Rock—*summit* CA-9
Slick Rock—*summit* MT-8
Slick Rock—*summit* (2) NC-3
Slick Rock Baptist Ch—*church* TN-4
Slick Rock Basin—*basin* AZ-5
Slickrock Bench—*bench* UT-8
Slick Rock Bluff—*cliff* AR-4
*Slickrock Branch* NC-3
Slickrock Branch—*stream* (4) KY-4
Slick Rock Branch—*stream* (2) KY-4
Slick Rock Branch—*stream* MS-4
Slickrock Branch—*stream* MO-7
Slick Rock Branch—*stream* NC-3
Slickrock Branch—*stream* (3) NC-3
Slick Rock Branch—*stream* TN-4
Slickrock Branch—*stream* TN-4
Slick Rock Branch—*stream* TN-4
Slickrock Branch—*stream* VA-3
Slickrock Branch—*stream* (2) WV-2
Slick Rock Branch—*stream* WV-2
*Slick-Rock Branch Catawba River* NC-3
Slick Rock Bridge—*bridge* CO-8
Slickrock Canyon—*valley* CA-9
Slick Rock Canyon—*valley* CA-9
Slick Rock Canyon—*valley* (2) NM-5
Slick Rock Canyon—*valley* TX-5
Slick Rock Canyon—*valley* UT-8
Slickrock Canyon—*valley* UT-8
Slick Rock Canyon—*valley* UT-8
Slick Rock Ch—*church* KY-4
Slickrock Country Camp—*park* UT-8
*Slick Rock Creek* OR-9
*Slickrock Creek* TX-5
Slick Rock Creek—*stream* AR-4
Slick Rock Creek—*stream* (2) CA-9
Slickrock Creek—*stream* (2) CA-9
Slickrock Creek—*stream* NC-3
Slick Rock Creek—*stream* (2) OR-9
Slickrock Creek—*stream* OR-9
Slick Rock Creek—*stream* (2) OR-9
Slickrock Creek—*stream* TN-4
Slickrock Creek—*stream* TX-5
Slickrock Creek—*stream* WA-9
Slick Rock Detention Dam—*dam* AZ-5
Slick Rock Falls—*falls* NC-3
Slickrock Ford—*locale* AL-4
Slick Rock Ford—*locale* (2) AR-4
Slickrock Ford—*locale* NC-3
Slickrock Ford—*locale* TN-4
Slickrock Fork—*stream* KY-4
Slick Rock Hollow—*valley* AL-4
Slickrock Hollow—*valley* AR-4
Slickrock Hollow—*valley* MO-7
Slick Rock Hollow—*valley* MO-7
Slickrock Hollow—*valley* MO-7
Slick Rock Hollow—*valley* (2) MO-7
Slickrock Hollow—*valley* MO-7
Slickrock Hollow—*valley* (3) TN-4
Slick Rock Hollow—*valley* TN-4
Slickrock Hollow—*valley* WV-2
Slickrock Knob—*summit* NC-3
Slick Rock Mesa—*summit* NM-5
Slick Rock Mountain Dam—*dam* NC-3
Slick Rock Mountain Lake—*reservoir* NC-3
Slickrock Mtn—*summit* NC-3
Slick Rock Mtn—*summit* NC-3
Slickrock Mtn—*summit* TX-5
Slick Rock Run—*stream* WV-2
Slickrock Saddle—*gap* UT-8
*Slick Rock Saddle Bench* UT-8
Slickrock Saddle Bench—*bench* UT-8
Slick Rock Sch—*school* (3) KY-4
Slick Rock Sch (historical)—*school* TN-4
Slick Rock Spring—*spring* (3) AZ-5
**Slick Rock (subdivision)**—*pop pl* NC-3
Slick Rock Tank—*reservoir* (3) AZ-5
*Slick Rock Wash* AZ-5
Slick Rock Wash—*stream* AZ-5
Slick Rock Wash—*stream* NM-5
Slick Rock Wash—*valley* AZ-5
Slickrock Water—*lake* UT-8
Slick Rsvr—*reservoir* ID-8
Slick Run—*stream* IN-6
**Slicks**—*pop pl* OH-6
Slick Sch—*school* IL-6
Slick Shoal Creek—*stream* GA-3
Slick Shoal Hollow—*valley* MO-7
Slick Shoals—*bar* KY-4
Slick Shoals Branch—*stream* KY-4
Slick Shoals Island—*island* TN-4
Slick Taw Gulch—*valley* OR-9
Slick Top Mtn—*summit* AR-4
Slickum Branch—*stream* AL-4
Slickum Slough—*stream* TX-5
Slickup Creek—*stream* TN-4
*Slickville* PA-2
**Slickville**—*pop pl* PA-2
Slickway—*locale* KY-4
Slickway Branch—*stream* KY-4
Slick Windmills—*locale* NM-5
Slide—*locale* TN-4
Slide—*locale* TX-5
Slide, The—*cape* UT-8
Slide, The—*cliff* OR-9
Slide, The—*cliff* (2) WA-9
Slide, The—*slope* (2) CA-9
Slide, The—*slope* UT-8
Slide, The—*valley* CO-8
Slide Basin Trail—*trail* OR-9
Slide Bluffs—*cliff* CA-9
Slide Branch—*stream* NC-3
Slide Branch—*stream* WV-2
Slide Brook—*stream* (4) NH-1
Slide Brook—*stream* (5) NY-2
Slide Brook—*stream* VT-1
Slide Butte—*summit* ND-7
Slide Camp—*locale* (2) WA-9
Slide Campground—*park* OR-9
*Slide Canyon* CA-9
*Slide Canyon* UT-8
Slide Canyon—*valley* AZ-5
Slide Canyon—*valley* CA-9
Slide Canyon—*valley* CO-8
Slide Canyon—*valley* (4) ID-8
Slide Canyon—*valley* TX-5
Slide Canyon—*valley* (5) UT-8
Slide Canyon—*valley* WA-9
Slide Canyon—*valley* WY-8
Slide Canyon Spring—*spring* UT-8
Slide Coulee—*valley* MT-8
*Slide Cove* NV-8
Slide Cove—*bay* AZ-5
*Slide Creek* CA-9
*Slide Creek* ID-8
Slide Creek—*stream* (4) AK-9
Slide Creek—*stream* AZ-5
Slide Creek—*stream* (16) CA-9
Slide Creek—*stream* (3) CO-8
Slide Creek—*stream* (17) ID-8
Slide Creek—*stream* (3) MT-8
Slide Creek—*stream* NV-8
Slide Creek—*stream* NY-2
Slide Creek—*stream* (31) OR-9
Slide Creek—*stream* (13) WA-9
Slide Creek—*stream* (3) WY-8
Slide Creek Campground—*locale* CA-9
Slide Creek Campground—*locale* OR-9
Slide Creek Dam—*dam* OR-9
Slide Creek Falls—*falls* WY-8
Slide Creek Riffle—*rapids* OR-9
Slide Creek Rsvr—*reservoir* OR-9
Slide Creek Trailhead—*locale* NV-8
Slide Ditch—*canal* OR-9
Slide Down—*summit* CO-8
Slidedown Mtn—*summit* (2) ME-1
Slidedown Valley—*valley* ME-1
Slide Draw—*valley* WY-8
Slide Elbow Tank—*reservoir* AZ-5
*Slide Fall* CA-9
Slide Falls—*falls* OR-9
Slide Fork—*stream* UT-8
Slide Glacier—*glacier* AK-9
*Slide Gulch* ID-8
Slide Gulch—*valley* (2) CA-9
Slide Gulch—*valley* (2) CO-8
Slide Gulch—*valley* (3) ID-8
Slide Gulch—*valley* OR-9
Slide Hill—*summit* CA-9
Slide (historical), The—*cliff* ND-7
Slide Hollow—*valley* NY-2
Slide Hollow—*valley* (7) PA-2
Slide Hollow—*valley* (5) TN-4
Slide Hollow—*valley* (3) UT-8
Slide Hollow—*valley* WV-2
Slide Hollow Creek—*stream* PA-2
Slide Hollow Trail—*trail* (3) PA-2
Slide Hollow Trail (in part)—*trail* PA-2
**Slide Inn**—*pop pl* CA-9
Slide Island Draft—*valley* PA-2
*Slide Lake* WY-8
Slide Lake—*lake* AK-9
Slide Lake—*lake* CA-9
Slide Lake—*lake* (5) CO-8
Slide Lake—*lake* (3) ID-8
Slide Lake—*lake* MI-6
Slide Lake—*lake* (2) MT-8
Slide Lake—*lake* (2) OR-9
Slide Lake—*lake* (3) UT-8
Slide Lake—*lake* WA-9
Slide Lake—*lake* (2) WY-8
Slide Lake Campground—*locale* CA-9
Slide Lake-Otatso Creek Patrol Cabin and
Woodshed—*hist pl* MT-8
Slide Lakes—*lake* CA-9
Slide Lakes—*reservoir* OR-9
Slidell—*locale* MD-2
**Slidell**—*pop pl* LA-4
**Slidell**—*pop pl* TX-5
Slidell Radar Site—*military* LA-4
Slidell Sch (historical)—*school* MS-4
Slidell Temple—*church* LA-4
Slide Mandall Lake—*lake* CO-8
Slide Mine—*mine* CO-8
*Slide Mountain* ID-8
Slide Mountain Brook—*stream* NY-2
Slide Mountain Creek—*stream* OR-9
Slide Mountain Geological Area—*park* OR-9
Slide Mtn—*summit* AK-9
Slide Mtn—*summit* AZ-5
Slide Mtn—*summit* (2) CA-9
Slide Mtn—*summit* (4) CO-8
Slide Mtn—*summit* ID-8
Slide Mtn—*summit* ME-1
Slide Mtn—*summit* MT-8
Slide Mtn—*summit* NV-8
Slide Mtn—*summit* (4) NY-2
Slide Mtn—*summit* (5) OR-9
Slide Mtn—*summit* PA-2
Slide Mtn—*summit* (2) WA-9
Slide Mtn—*summit* WY-8
Slide Notch—*gap* MA-1
Slideoff Creek—*stream* TX-5
Slide Off Mtn—*summit* NY-2
Slideout Canyon—*valley* UT-8
Slide Out Coulee—*valley* MT-8
Slideout Creek—*stream* OR-9
Slide Out Creek—*stream* OR-9
Slideout Creek—*stream* OR-9
Slideout Lake—*lake* OR-9
Slideout Peak—*summit* MT-8
Slide Peak—*summit* CA-9
Slide Peak—*summit* (2) WA-9
Slide Point—*cape* AZ-5
Slide Point Trail—*trail* CA-9
Slide Post Office (historical)—*building* TN-4
Slide Ravine—*valley* (2) CA-9
Slider Cave—*cave* IN-6
Slide Reef—*bar* AK-9
Slide Ridge—*ridge* CA-9
Slide Ridge—*ridge* OR-9
Slide Ridge—*ridge* WA-9
Slide Ridge—*summit* AK-9
Sliderock Basin—*basin* CO-8
Slide Rock Canyon—*valley* CO-8
Sliderock Canyon—*valley* CO-8
Slide Rock Canyon—*valley* ID-8
Sliderock Creek—*stream* WY-8
Slide Rock Gulch—*valley* MT-8
Slide Rock Hollow—*valley* UT-8
Sliderock Lake—*lake* ID-8
Slide Rock Lake—*lake* ID-8
Sliderock Lake—*lake* MT-8
*Sliderock Mountain* MT-8
Slide Rock Mountain Trail—*trail* MT-8
Sliderock Mtn—*summit* CO-8
Slide Rock Mtn—*summit* CO-8
Sliderock Mtn—*summit* MT-8
Slide Rock Mtn—*summit* MT-8
Sliderock Mtn—*summit* (2) MT-8
Slide Rock Point—*summit* MT-8
Sliderock Ridge—*ridge* CO-8
Sliderock Ridge—*ridge* ID-8
Slide Rock Ridge—*ridge* NV-8
Slide Rock Rsvr—*reservoir* CO-8
Slide Rock Swim Area—*park* AZ-5
Slider Run—*stream* WV-2
Sliders—*locale* VA-3
Sliders Branch—*stream* PA-2
Sliders Dam—*dam* PA-2
Sliders Knob—*summit* TN-4
Slide Rsvr—*reservoir* WY-8
Slide Run—*stream* (2) PA-2
Slide Run—*stream* (2) WV-2
Slides, The—*cliff* CO-8
Slides, The—*slope* CA-9
Slides Creek—*stream* CA-9
Slides Downes Brook Trail—*trail* NH-1
Slides Glade—*flat* CA-9
Slide Spring—*spring* (2) AZ-5
Slide Spring—*spring* (2) ID-8
Slide Spring—*spring* NV-8
Slide Spring—*spring* (2) OR-9
Slide Spring—*spring* UT-8
Slides Ridge—*ridge* CA-9
Slide Tank—*reservoir* AZ-5
Slide Trail—*trail* NH-1
Slide Waterhole—*lake* OR-9
Slide Windmill—*locale* WY-8
Slidex Mine—*mine* MT-8
Sliding Bluff (historical)—*cliff* ND-7
Sliding Falls—*falls* NY-2
Sliding Hill—*summit* VA-3
Sliding Hill Creek—*stream* WV-2
*Slidinghill Run* WV-2
Sliding Knob—*summit* NC-3
Sliding Knob Branch—*stream* NC-3
*Sliding Mountain* MT-8
Sliding Mtn—*summit* MT-8
Sliding Rock Mtn—*summit* PA-2
Sliding Rock Overlook—*locale* AZ-5
Sliding Rock Recreation Site—*locale* NC-3
Sliding Rock Ruins—*locale* AZ-5
Sliding Rocks Valley—*valley* AZ-5
Sliding Run—*stream* WV-2
Sliding Sands Trail—*trail* HI-9
Sliding Towhead—*island* MO-7
Slidre Cem—*cemetery* WI-6
Slidy Mtn—*summit* NV-8
Slifer—*locale* IA-7
Slifer House—*hist pl* PA-2
Slifers Ch—*church* OH-6
*Slife Run* PA-2
Sliger Cem—*cemetery* AR-4
Sliger Cem—*cemetery* MO-7
Sliger Cem—*cemetery* TN-4
Sliger Mine—*mine* CA-9
Sliggins Brothers Ranch—*locale* WY-8
Sligh JHS—*school* FL-3
**Slighs**—*pop pl* SC-3
*Slight Canyon* ID-8
*Slights Canyon* ID-8
Slights Sch—*school* MI-6
*Sligo* MS-4
Sligo—*locale* NC-3
Sligo—*locale* PA-2
Sligo—*locale* TX-5
**Sligo**—*pop pl* (2) KY-4
**Sligo**—*pop pl* LA-4
**Sligo**—*pop pl* MO-7
**Sligo**—*pop pl* OH-6
**Sligo**—*pop pl* PA-2
Sligo Borough—*civil* PA-2
Sligo Bridge—*bridge* TN-4
Sligo Brook—*stream* NH-1
Sligo Creek—*stream* MD-2
Sligo Creek Park—*park* MD-2
Sligo Dock—*locale* TN-4
Sligo Hill—*summit* MA-1
**Sligo (historical)**—*pop pl* TN-4
Sligo JHS—*school* MD-2
Sligo Oil and Gas Field—*oilfield* LA-4
**Sligo Park Hills**—*pop pl* MD-2
Sligo Plantation (historical)—*locale* MS-4
Sligo Post Office (historical)—*building* TN-4
Sligos Ferry (historical)—*crossing* TN-4
**Sligo Woods**—*pop pl* MD-2

Sliker Hill—summit AZ-5
Sliker Strip—airport NJ-2
Sliker Tank—reservoir AZ-5
Slikok Creek—stream AK-9
Slikok Lake—lake AK-9
Slim—locale OK-5
Slim and Fatty Rsvr—reservoir OR-9
Slim and Fatty Spring—spring OR-9
Sliman Rsvr—reservoir ID-8
Slim Butte—locale SD-7
Slim Butte—summit SD-7
Slim Butte Creek—stream SD-7
Slim Butte Monmt—park SD-7
Slim Buttes—range SD-7
Slim Buttes Ch—church SD-7
Slim Buttes Township (historical)—civil SD-7
Slim Butte Township—civil SD-7
Slim Canyon—valley AZ-5
Slim Chance Campground—park OR-9
Slim Chute—stream MO-7
Slim Cove—bay NY-2
Slim Creek MT-8
Slim Creek—stream (3) ID-8
Slim Creek—stream (2) MT-8
Slim Creek—stream NV-8
Slim Creek—stream NC-3
Slim Creek—stream OH-6
Slim Creek—stream (2) OR-9
Slim Creek—stream WI-6
Slim Creek Flowage—lake WI-6
Slime Bank—bar AK-9
Slime Creek—stream AK-9
Slime Meadow Brook—stream ME-1
Slime Pond—reservoir MO-7
Slime Wash—stream NV-8
Slim Glacier—glacier AK-9
Slim Gulch—valley MT-8
Slim Hollow—valley VA-3
Slim Island—island (2) AK-9
Slim Island—island (2) KY-4
Slim Island—island LA-4
Slim Island—island (2) MO-7
Slim Jim Canyon—valley AZ-5
Slim Jim Creek—stream AZ-5
Slim Jim Creek—stream MT-8
Slim Jim Gulch—valley CO-8
Slim Jimmy Branch—stream KY-4
Slim Jim Ridge—ridge AZ-5
Slim Lake—lake AK-9
Slim Lake—lake CA-9
Slim Lake—lake IL-6
Slim Lake—lake (3) MN-6
Slim Lake—lake WA-9
Slim Lake—lake (2) WI-6
Slimmer Creek—stream MT-8
Slimmer Creek Trail—trail MT-8
Slimp Branch—stream TN-4
Slimp Hollow—valley TN-4
Slim Pickens Rapid OR-9
Slim Pickings Rapid OR-9
Slim Pickins Rapid—rapids OR-9
Slim Pickins Rapids—rapids OR-9
Slim Pines—woods FL-3
Slim Pit—cave AL-4
Slimp Lake—lake OK-5
Slim Point—cape (2) NY-2
Slim Pond—lake IN-6
Slim Pond—lake (3) NY-2
Slim Pond—reservoir NY-2
Slim Pond Slough—stream KY-4
Slim Prairie—flat OR-9
Slim Ridge—ridge NC-3
Slim Ridge—ridge VA-3
Slim Ridge Branch—stream VA-3
Slim Ridge Hollow—valley VA-3
Slim Sam Basin—basin MT-8
Slim Sam Creek—stream (2) MT-8
Slims Campground—locale ID-8
Slims Cem—cemetery IL-6
Slims Coulee—valley MT-8
Slims Draw—valley WY-8
Slims Peak—summit CA-9
Slims Spring—spring AZ-5
Slims Tank—reservoir AZ-5
Slim Tank—reservoir AZ-5
Slim Valley—basin (2) PA-2
Slim Valley—valley PA-2
Slim Valley Ridge—ridge PA-2
Slimwater Creek—stream OR-9
S Line Rsvr—reservoir NV-8
**Slinger**—pop pl WI-6
Slingerland NY-2
Slingerland's NY-2
**Slingerlands**—pop pl NY-2
Slingerlands Station NY-2
Sling Hollow—valley TX-5
Slings Gap—gap VA-3
Slings Gap Overlook—locale VA-3
Slinkard Airfield Airp—airport WA-9
Slinkard Cem—cemetery IN-6
Slinkard Cem—cemetery MO-7
Slinkard Creek—stream CA-9
Slinkard Peak—summit CA-9
Slinkards Creek IN-6
Slinkard Spring—spring AZ-5
Slinkard Valley—valley CA-9
Slink Branch—stream NC-3
Slinkerd Cem—cemetery MO-7
Slink Shoals Ford—locale TN-4
Slink Shoal Sluice and Wing Dams—hist pl NC-3
Slins Island—island ME-1
**Sliocco Springs**—pop pl AL-4
Slip, The—gap WY-8
Slip and Slide Creek—stream MT-8
Slip Bluff County Park—park IA-7
Slip Canyon—valley UT-8
Slip Creek—stream OR-9
Slip Creek—stream TN-4
Slipdown Mtn—summit TX-5
Slip Easy Mine—mine ID-8
Slipe Pond—swamp MA-1
Slipfield Branch—stream KY-4
Slip Gulch—valley MT-8
Slip Hill—summit (2) TN-4
Sliphill Sch—school WV-2
Slip Hollow—valley KY-4
Slip Hollow—valley PA-2
Slip Hollow—valley WV-2
Slip Lake—lake MN-6
Slip Mtn—summit (2) NY-2
Slip Number Five—harbor CA-9
Slip Number One—harbor CA-9
Slipoff, The—cliff AL-4
Slipoff Branch—stream AL-4
Slipoff Branch—stream NC-3
Slipoff Hollow—valley (2) AL-4
Slipoff Hollow—valley TN-4
Slipoff Knob—summit NC-3
Slipout Creek—stream OR-9
Slipper Creek—stream OR-9
Slipper Hollow—valley UT-8
Slipper Lake—lake AK-9
Slipper Lake—lake OR-9
Slipper Point—cape AK-9
Slipper Pole Cave—cave AL-4
Slipper Rock—pillar WY-8
Slipper Rsvr—reservoir OR-9
Slipper Run—stream OH-6
Slipper Spur—ridge TN-4
Slipper Spur Gap—gap TN-4
Slippery Ann Creek MT-8
Slippery Bill Mtn—summit MT-8
Slippery Branch—stream TN-4
Slippery Branch—stream VA-3
Slippery Brook—stream NH-1
Slippery Brook Trail—trail NH-1
Slippery Ch—church TN-4
Slippery Creek—gut FL-3
Slippery Creek—stream (3) AK-9
Slippery Creek—stream CA-9
Slippery Creek—stream (2) ID-8
Slippery Creek—stream MT-8
Slippery Creek—stream (3) TX-5
Slippery Creek—stream (2) WA-9
Slippery Elm Hollow—valley (2) PA-2
Slippery Falls—falls OK-5
Slippery Ford—locale AL-4
Slippery Gut Branch—stream WV-2
Slippery Hill Cem—cemetery NC-3
Slippery Hill Ridge—ridge NC-3
Slippery Hoof Creek—stream MT-8
Slippery Hoof Lake—lake MT-8
Slippery Jim Canyon—valley WY-8
Slippery Jim Spring—spring CO-8
Slippery John Creek—stream MT-8
Slippery Lake—lake AR-4
Slippery Moss Shelter—hist pl OK-5
Slippery Point Cem—cemetery IN-6
Slippery Rock—locale PA-2
**Slippery Rock**—pop pl PA-2
Slippery Rock—stream (2) PA-2
Slippery Rock—summit KY-4
Slippery Rock Area Elem Sch—school PA-2
Slippery Rock Area HS—school PA-2
Slippery Rock Area MS—school PA-2
Slippery Rock Borough—civil PA-2
Slippery Rock Brook—stream NJ-2
Slippery Rock Creek—stream KY-4
Slippery Rock Creek—stream NY-2
Slippery Rock Creek—stream PA-2
Slippery Rock Creek Gorge—valley PA-2
**Slippery Rock Park**—pop pl PA-2
Slippery Rock Picnic Area—locale CA-9
Slippery Rock State Normal School PA-2
**Slippery Rock (Township of)**—pop pl (2) PA-2
Slippery Rock Univ—school PA-2
Slippery Sch (historical)—school TN-4
Slippery Sides Mtn—summit CO-8
Slippery Slough—gut FL-3
Slippery Well—well AZ-5
Slip Point—cape WA-9
Slippy Branch—stream VA-3
Slippy Creek—stream ID-8
Slip Ridge Branch—stream WV-2
Slip Run—stream PA-2
Slip Run—stream WV-2
Slipshuck Ridge—ridge TN-4
Slip Top—summit TN-4
Slip Up Creek—stream OR-9
Slip-up Creek—stream SD-7
Slipup Post Office AL-4
Slit Cave—cave AL-4
Sliter Butte—summit OR-9
**Sliters**—pop pl NY-2
Slit Rock—arch AZ-5
Sliver Cave—cave AL-4
Sliver Creek—stream ID-8
Sliver Creek Trail—trail ID-8
Sliver Mine—mine MN-6
Slivers Point—cape WI-6
SL Lateral—canal TX-5
Sloan PA-2
Sloan—locale AL-4
Sloan—locale AR-4
Sloan—locale CO-8
Sloan—locale KY-4
Sloan—locale MT-8
**Sloan**—pop pl IL-6
**Sloan**—pop pl IN-6
**Sloan**—pop pl IA-7
**Sloan**—pop pl MS-4
**Sloan**—pop pl NV-8
**Sloan**—pop pl NY-2
**Sloan**—pop pl NC-3
Sloan, Dr. David Dickson, Farm—hist pl NC-3
Sloan, Dr. Earl S., House—hist pl NC-3
Sloan, George B., Estate—hist pl NY-2
Sloan, John, Homestead—hist pl SD-7
Sloan, Samuel, House—hist pl NJ-2
Sloan, William P., House—hist pl WI-6
Sloan Branch—stream AR-4
Sloan Branch—stream IN-6
Sloan Branch—stream (2) KY-4
Sloan Branch—stream SC-3
Sloan Branch—stream (3) TN-4
Sloan Branch—stream (2) VA-3
Sloan Bridge—bridge GA-3
Sloan Bridge—bridge MT-8
Sloan Bridge—bridge TN-4
Sloan Bridge Boat Launching Ramp—locale TN-4
Sloan Brothers Ranch—locale SD-7
Sloan Butte CA-9
Sloan Butte—summit CA-9
Sloan Buttes—summit MT-8
Sloan Canyon—valley CA-9
Sloan Canyon—valley NM-5
Sloan Cave—cave TN-4
Sloan Cem—cemetery AR-4
Sloan Cem—cemetery IL-6
Sloan Cem—cemetery (2) IN-6
Sloan Cem—cemetery IA-7
Sloan Cem—cemetery KY-4
Sloan Cem—cemetery (5) MO-7
Sloan Cem—cemetery (2) OH-6
Sloan Cem—cemetery OK-5
Sloan Cem—cemetery OR-9
Sloan Cem—cemetery TN-4
Sloan Cem—cemetery VA-3
Sloan Cem—cemetery (2) WV-2
Sloan Coulee—valley MT-8
Sloan Cove—bay DE-2
Sloan Cow Camp—locale MT-8
Sloan Creek NV-8
Sloan Creek—stream AL-4
Sloan Creek—stream AZ-5
Sloan Creek—stream (2) AR-4
Sloan Creek—stream MI-6
Sloan Creek—stream MS-4
Sloan Creek—stream MO-7
Sloan Creek—stream NM-5
Sloan Creek—stream OR-9
Sloan Creek—stream (2) TX-5
Sloan Creek—stream VA-3
Sloan Creek—stream WA-9
Sloan Creek Campground—locale WA-9
Sloan Ditch—canal (5) IN-6
Sloan Ditch—canal (2) MT-8
Sloane, Rush R., House—hist pl OH-6
Sloan-Easley Cem—cemetery TX-5
Sloane Branch—stream KY-4
Sloan Elem Sch—school PA-2
Sloane Peak—summit CO-8
Sloanes Peak CO-8
Sloan Ford—locale MO-7
Sloan Fork—stream KY-4
Sloan Gap—gap PA-2
Sloan Gap—gap (2) TN-4
Sloan Gulch—valley MT-8
Sloan Gulch—valley OR-9
Sloan Hill Ch—church GA-3
**Sloan (historical)**—pop pl OR-9
Sloan Hollow—valley (2) MO-7
Sloan Hollow—valley PA-2
Sloan Hollow—valley (3) TN-4
Sloan Hollow Ch—church PA-2
Sloan Hollow Sch (historical)—school PA-2
Sloan House—hist pl AZ-5
Sloan Island—island AR-4
Sloan Knob—summit AR-4
Sloan Lake IN-6
Sloan Lake MN-6
Sloan Lake—lake CO-8
Sloan Lake—lake MN-6
Sloan Lake—lake MT-8
Sloan Lake—lake WY-8
Sloan Lake—reservoir MI-6
Sloan Landing—locale DE-2
Sloan Mill AL-4
Sloan Mill Creek AL-4
Sloan Mtn—summit AL-4
Sloan Mtn—summit OR-9
Sloan Museum—building MI-6
Sloan-Parker House—hist pl WV-2
Sloan Peak—summit WA-9
Sloan Petroglyph Site—hist pl NV-8
Sloan Pond—lake MI-6
Sloan Prospect—mine TN-4
Sloan Pumping Station—locale PA-2
Sloan Ranch—locale AZ-5
Sloan Ranch—locale CA-9
Sloan Ranch—locale (3) MT-8
Sloan Ranch—locale TX-5
Sloan-Raymond-Fitch House—hist pl CT-1
Sloan Ridge—ridge TN-4
Sloan Run—stream OH-6
Sloan Run—stream PA-2
Sloans Airp—airport MO-7
Sloans Bay—swamp NC-3
Sloans Canyon—valley CA-9
Sloan Sch PA-2
Sloan Sch—school IN-6
Sloan Sch—school IA-7
Sloan Sch—school PA-2
Sloan Sch—school TX-5
Sloans Chapel—church KY-4
Sloans Chapel—church NC-3
Sloan Sch (historical)—school AL-4
Sloans Creek GA-3
Sloans Creek—stream GA-3
Sloans Creek—stream ID-8
Sloans Creek—stream NC-3
Sloans Creek—stream TX-5
Sloans Crossing—locale KY-4
Sloans Gap PA-2
Sloans Gulch—valley ID-8
Sloan Shaft—mine PA-2
Sloan Sisters Ranch—locale TX-5
Sloans Lake—lake CO-8
Sloans Lake Park—park CO-8
Sloans Point—summit ID-8
Sloans Point Cem—cemetery MO-7
Sloans Point Fire Trail (historical)—trail ID-8
Sloans Point Sch (abandoned)—school MO-7
Sloan Springs—spring OR-9
**Sloans Ridge**—pop pl FL-3
Sloans Ridge—ridge OR-9
Sloans Springs Canyon—valley TX-5
Sloans Valley—basin KY-4
**Sloans Valley**—pop pl KY-4
**Sloansville**—pop pl NY-2
Sloansville Valley Cem—cemetery NY-2
Sloantown—locale VA-3
Sloan Township—fmr MCD IA-7
**Sloanville**—pop pl TN-4
Sloan Wells Camp—locale NM-5
Sloan Yelverton Cem—cemetery OH-6
**Sloat**—pop pl CA-9
Sloat Brook—stream PA-2
Sloat Creek AL-4
Sloat Drain—canal MI-6
Sloat-Horn-Rossell House—hist pl WV-2
Sloat House—hist pl NY-2
**Sloatsburg**—pop pl NY-2
Sloat Sch—school (2) CA-9
**Slob**—pop pl VI-3
Slob Hist Dist—hist pl VI-3
**Slocomb**—pop pl AL-4
**Slocomb**—pop pl NC-3
Slocomb (CCD)—cens area AL-4
Slocomb Cross-roa NC-3
Slocomb Division—civil AL-4
Slocum PA-2
Slocum RI-1
Slocum—locale LA-4
**Slocum**—pop pl MI-6
**Slocum**—pop pl NC-3
**Slocum**—pop pl OH-6
**Slocum**—pop pl PA-2
**Slocum**—pop pl RI-1
**Slocum**—pop pl TX-5
Slocum, Joseph, House—hist pl RI-1
Slocum, Point—cape AK-9
Slocum Arm—bay AK-9
Slocumb Branch—stream GA-3
Slocumb Monmt—park NC-3
Slocum Brook—stream CT-1
Slocum Brook—stream MA-1
Slocumbs Lake—reservoir GA-3
Slocum Camp—locale CA-9
Slocum Canyon—valley CA-9
Slocum Cem—cemetery AR-4
Slocum Cem—cemetery IN-6
Slocum Cem—cemetery (2) LA-4
Slocum Cem—cemetery OH-6
Slocum Ch—church PA-2
Slocum Corner MA-1
**Slocum Corners**—pop pl PA-2
Slocum Creek—stream IA-7
Slocum Creek—stream (2) MT-8
Slocum Creek—stream (2) NY-2
Slocum Creek—stream NC-3
Slocum Creek—stream OR-9
Slocum Creek—stream WY-8
Slocum Dam RI-1
Slocum Ditch—canal (3) IN-6
Slocum Drain—canal MI-6
Slocum Draw—valley TX-5
Slocum - Gibbs Dam Number 2—dam MA-1
Slocum - Gibbs Number 1 Dam—dam MA-1
Slocum Gulch—valley CA-9
Slocum Hall—hist pl OH-6
**Slocum Heights**—pop pl OH-6
Slocum Highway—channel MI-6
Slocum Hill—summit (2) PA-2
Slocum Hollow—valley NY-2
Slocum House—hist pl CA-9
Slocum House—hist pl WA-9
Slocum HS—school LA-4
Slocum Inlet—bay AK-9
Slocum Lake MI-6
Slocum Lake—lake IL-6
Slocum Ledge—bar RI-1
Slocum Meadow—swamp MA-1
Slocum Mtn—summit CA-9
Slocum Neck MA-1
Slocum Ranch—locale CO-8
Slocum Reservoir Dam—dam RI-1
Slocum River MA-1
Slocum Rsvr—reservoir RI-1
Slocum's MI-6
Slocums RI-1
**Slocums**—pop pl OH-6
Slocum Sch IN-6
Slocum Sch—school CT-1
Slocum Sch—school IN-6
Slocum Sch—school NY-2
Slocum Sch—school OH-6
Slocums Corner RI-1
**Slocums Corner**—pop pl MA-1
Slocums Ledge RI-1
Slocums Ledge—rock MA-1
Slocums Neck—cape MA-1
Slocum Spring—spring AR-4
Slocum Spring—spring PA-2
Slocums River—bay (2) MA-1
Slocums (Slocum) RI-1
Slocum Station—locale PA-2
Slocum Station Ch—church OH-6
Slocum Street Sch—school IL-6
Slocums Tunnel (historical)—tunnel PA-2
Slocumsville RI-1
Slocum Tower—pillar LA-4
**Slocum (Township of)**—pop pl PA-2
Slocum Truax JHS—school MI-6
Slocum Village—uninc pl NC-3
Slocum Village Shop Ctr—locale NC-3
Slocumville RI-1
Slocum Well—well CA-9
**Slocun Village (subdivision)**—pop pl NC-3
Slo Duc Creek—stream AK-9
Sloey KS-7
Slokhenjikh Creek—stream AK-9
Slokhenjikh Hills—other AK-9
Slokums Island MA-1
Sloman Branch—stream FL-3
Slomann Park—park WI-6
Slome Mountain WA-9
Slonaker—locale PA-2
Slonaker Cem—cemetery PA-2
Slonaker Cem—cemetery TN-4
Slonaker Ditch—canal IN-6
Slonaker Lake—lake NE-7
Slonaker Sch—school CA-9
Slone—locale LA-4
Slone Branch—stream (2) KY-4
Slone Cem—cemetery (2) KY-4
Slone Ch—church LA-4
Slone Coal Creek IN-6
Slone Fork—stream KY-4
**Slone's Branch**—pop pl KY-4
Slones Branch—stream KY-4
Slones Branch Station—locale KY-4
Slone Sch—school KY-4
**Slones Ridge**—pop pl FL-3
**Slonikers Mill**—pop pl AR-4
Slooch Ditch—canal DE-2
Sloon Hill—summit NY-2
Sloop Bay—bay NY-2
Sloop Channel—channel NY-2
Sloop Channel—channel (2) VA-3
Sloop Chapel—church NC-3
Sloop Cove—bay MD-2
Sloop Creek—stream NJ-2
Sloop Creek—stream OR-9
Sloop Creek—stream TX-5
Sloop Creek—stream (2) VA-3
**Sloop Creek Estates**—pop pl NJ-2
Sloop Dam—dam NC-3
Sloop Gut—gut VA-3
Sloop Island—island ME-1
Sloop Island—island NC-3
Sloop Island—island VT-1
Sloop Island Ledge—bar ME-1
Sloop Ledge—bar ME-1
Sloop Point—cape NJ-2
Sloop Point—cape NC-3
Sloop Point—cape (2) VA-3
Sloop Point—hist pl NC-3
Sloop Pond—lake TX-5
Sloop Sedge—island NJ-2
Sloop Thorofare—channel (2) NJ-2
Sloopys Double Drop Cave—cave AL-4
Slop Bowl—swamp TX-5
Slop Branch—stream TN-4
Slop Creek KY-4
Slop Ditch KY-4
Slop Ditch—canal KY-4
Slope Brook—stream NJ-2
**Slope Center Township**—pop pl ND-7
Slope Ch—church OH-6
Slope County—civil ND-7
Slope Creek—stream (2) AK-9
Slope Creek—stream OH-6
Slope Glacier—glacier AK-9
Slope Hollow—valley KY-4
Slope Hollow—valley OH-6
Slope Lake—lake MI-6
Slope Mtn—summit AK-9
Slope Mtn—summit NH-1
Slope Peak—summit AK-9
Slope Point—cape (3) AK-9
Sloper Mine—mine ID-8
Sloper Pond CT-1
Sloper Sch—school WI-6
Slopers Pond—reservoir CT-1
Slope Spring—spring (2) UT-8
Slope Trail—trail UT-8
Slope Well—well NM-5
Slop Hollow—valley AL-4
Sloping Cliffs MH-9
**Sloping Hills**—pop pl NJ-2
Sloping Meadow—area NM-5
Sloppy Gulch—valley NV-8
Sloppy Hollow—valley TX-5
Slop Spring—spring OR-9
Slo Run—stream IN-6
Slosh Dam—dam AL-4
Slosh Lake—reservoir AL-4
Slosh Lake Strip Mine Dam AL-4
**Sloss**—pop pl AL-4
**Sloss**—pop pl CO-8
Sloss, John, House—hist pl KY-4
Sloss and Ganong Drain—stream MI-6
Sloss Blast Furnace Site—hist pl AL-4
Sloss Creek—stream CA-9
Sloss Lake—reservoir AL-4
Sloss Lake Dam—dam AL-4
Sloss Mines (underground)—mine AL-4
Sloss Mine (underground)—mine AL-4
Sloss Quarry—mine AL-4
Slot, The—area CA-9
Slot, The—locale CA-9
Slotin Bldg—hist pl GA-3
Slotsye Lake—lake MN-6
Slotted Pen Creek—stream OR-9
Slouch Pond—lake NY-2
Slough—fmr MCD NE-7
Slough—locale OH-6
Slough, The—channel AK-9
Slough, The—channel MD-2
Slough, The—gut WY-8
Slough, The—stream (3) CO-8
Slough, The—stream (2) IL-6
Slough, The—stream (2) NV-8
Slough, The—stream NC-3
Slough, The—stream OR-9
Slough, The—stream UT-8
Slough, The—stream WV-2
Slough Bench—bench UT-8
Slough Bend—bend TN-4
Slough Bond MA-1
Slough Branch—stream AL-4
Slough Branch—stream GA-3
Slough Branch—stream MO-7
Slough Bridge—bridge AR-4
Slough Bridge—bridge WI-6
Slough Bridge Branch—stream TX-5
Slough Brook—stream NJ-2
Slough Campground—park OR-9
Slough Canyon—valley (2) NM-5
Slough Canyon—valley UT-8
Slough Canyon Point—summit UT-8
Slough Canyon Spring—spring UT-8
Slough Cem—cemetery OH-6
Slough Cove—bay MA-1
Slough Creek IN-6
Slough Creek KS-7
Slough Creek—stream AR-4
Slough Creek—stream CO-8
Slough Creek—stream ID-8
Slough Creek—stream (2) IN-6
Slough Creek—stream (2) IA-7
Slough Creek—stream (3) KS-7
Slough Creek—stream MO-7
Slough Creek—stream (2) MT-8
Slough Creek—stream NV-8
Slough Creek—stream OK-5
Slough Creek—stream (2) TX-5
Slough Creek—stream VA-3
Slough Creek—stream WA-9
Slough Creek—stream WI-6
Slough Creek—stream WY-8
Slough Creek Ditch—canal CO-8
Slough Creek Guard Station—locale MT-8
Slough Creek Patrol Cabins—locale WY-8
Slough Creek Public Use Area—locale KS-7
Slough Creek Public Use Area—park KS-7
Slough Drainage Ditch—canal AR-4
Slough Grass—bar UT-8
Slough Grass Creek—stream MT-8
Slough Grass Rsvr—reservoir MT-8
Slough Hollow—valley MO-7
**Sloughhouse**—pop pl CA-9
Sloughhouse (CCD)—cens area CA-9
Slough Island—island FL-3
Slough Island—island TN-4
Slough Lake MN-6
Slough Lake ND-7
Slough Lake—lake IL-6
Slough Lake—lake MI-6
Slough Lake—lake (5) MN-6
Slough Lake—lake MT-8
Slough Lake—swamp MN-6
Slough Landing Neck—cape TN-4
Slough Landing Neck Revetment—levee TN-4
Slough Point—cape CA-9
Slough Point—cape MA-1
Slough Pond—lake (2) MA-1
Slough Pond—lake NY-2
Slough Pond—reservoir CO-8
Slough Ridge—ridge TX-5
Sloughs, The—stream CO-8
Slough Sch—school CA-9
Sloughs Gut—gut DE-2
Slough Spring—spring (2) NM-5
Sloughs Wildlife Mngmt Area—park KY-4
Slough Tank—reservoir NM-5
Slough Tank—reservoir TX-5
Sloughters Creek AL-4
Slought Hollow MO-7
Slough Wash—valley UT-8
Sloulin Field International Airp—airport ND-7
Sloutier Cem—cemetery WA-9
Sloux Creek Sch—school NE-7
Slovac AR-4
**Slovac**—pop pl AR-4
**Slovak**—pop pl AR-4
Slovak Cem—cemetery NY-2
Slovak Cem—cemetery (2) PA-2
Slovak Cem—cemetery TX-5
Slovak Sokol Camp—locale NJ-2
**Slovan**—pop pl PA-2
**Slovan**—pop pl WI-6
Slovan Well—well AZ-5
Slover—locale GA-3
Slover-Bradham House—hist pl NC-3
Slover Canyon—valley CA-9
Slover Cemetery—cemetery AR-4
Slover Ch—church KY-4
Slover Creek—stream AR-4
Slover Creek—stream KY-4
Slover Flat Creek KY-4
Slover Hollow—valley MO-7
Slover Memorial Park—park MO-7
Slover Mtn—summit CA-9
Slover Sch—school CA-9
Slover Sch—school NJ-2
Slovers Creek—stream KY-4
Slover Spring—spring TN-4
Slovic Academy PA-2
Slovik Branch CT-1
Slovik Brook—stream CT-1
Sloway Campground—locale MT-8
Sloway Gulch MT-8
Slow Bayou LA-4
Slow Cem—cemetery IN-6
**Slow Creek**—pop pl NC-3
Slow Creek—stream AK-9
Slow Creek—stream MN-6
Slow Creek—stream MT-8
Slow Creek—stream NC-3
Slow Creek—stream ND-7
Slow Creek—stream OK-5
Slow Creek—stream OR-9
Slow Creek Sch—school NC-3
Slow Ditch OH-6
Slow Elk Hills—range UT-8
Slow Elk Wash—valley (2) UT-8
Slowenski School (historical)—locale MO-7
Slowers Branch WV-2
Slowe Sch—school DC-2
Slowey, Patrick, House—hist pl MA-1
Slowey Gulch—valley MT-8
Slowey's Gulch MT-8
Slowfoot Lake—lake MI-6
Slowfoot Lake—lake MN-6
Slow Fork Hills—other AK-9
Slow Fork Kuskokwim River—stream AK-9
Slow Gulch—valley ID-8
Slow Motion Creek—stream AR-4
Slow Run—stream (2) IN-6
Slow Run Creek—stream GA-3
Slow Springs Rsvr—reservoir OR-9
Slow Tom Hollow—valley AR-4
Slow Trail Gulch—valley CO-8
Slow Trail Ridge—ridge CO-8
S L Ranch—locale NV-8
S L Reed Lake Dam—dam MS-4
Sluce Gut DE-2
Sluder Branch—stream NC-3
Sluder Cem—cemetery AR-4
Sluder Cem—cemetery MO-7
Sluder Cem—cemetery NC-3
Sluder Gap—gap TN-4
Sludge Pond One—reservoir PA-2
Sludge Pond 1 PA-2
Slug Canyon—valley CA-9
Slug Creek—stream CA-9
Slug Creek—stream ID-8
Sluggs Dam—dam AL-4
Sluggs Fish Pond AL-4
Sluggs Lake—reservoir AL-4
Slug Gulch CA-9
Slug Gulch—flat CA-9
Slug Gulch—valley (5) CA-9
Slug Gulch Mine—mine CA-9
Slug Mtn—summit AK-9
Slug River—stream AK-9
Slug Run—stream (2) IL-6
Sluicebox Creek—stream AK-9
Sluice Boxes—basin MT-8
Sluice Brook—stream MA-1
Sluice Canyon—valley OR-9
Sluice Creek—stream CT-1
Sluice Creek—stream ID-8
Sluice Creek—stream MT-8
Sluice Creek—stream NJ-2
Sluice Creek—stream (3) OR-9
Sluice Creek—stream VA-3
Sluice Creek Rapids—rapids OR-9
Sluice Creek Saddle—gap OR-9
Sluice Ditch—canal DE-2
Sluice Gulch—valley MT-8
Sluice Gut DE-2
Sluice Millpond—reservoir VA-3
Sluice Pond—reservoir MA-1
Sluice Pond Dam—dam MA-1
Sluice Race—channel DE-2

Sluiceway, The—*channel* NY-2
Sluiceway Falls—*falls* WY-8
Sluiskin Falls—*falls* WA-9
Sluiskin Mtn—*summit* WA-9
Sluiter Drain—*stream* SD-7
Sluitkill Neck—*cape* VA-3
Sluka Park—*park* MI-6
Slumber Creek—*stream* WA-9
Slumber Falls—*falls* TX-5
Slumbering Hills—*summit* NV-8
Slumber Lake—*lake* MN-6
Slumber Peak—*summit* WA-9
Slum Creek—*stream* PA-2
Slumgullion Creek—*stream* (2) CO-8
Slumgullion Creek—*stream* NV-8
Slumgullion Earthflow—*other* CO-8
*Slumgullion Gulch* CO-8
Slumgullion Pass—*gap* AZ-5
Slumgullion Pass—*gap* CO-8
Slumgullion Pass Campground—*locale* CO-8
*Slumgullion Slide* CO-8
Slunger Bay—*bay* AR-4
Slunger Creek—*stream* AR-4
Slurry Impoundment - Johns Washer—*reservoir* AL-4
Slurry Impoundment - Johns Washer Dam—*dam* AL-4
Slurry Pond Number One—*reservoir* AZ-5
Slurry Pond Number One Dam—*dam* AZ-5
Slush Branch—*stream* VA-3
Slusher Branch—*stream* KY-4
Slusher Canal—*canal* OR-9
Slusher Canyon—*valley* OR-9
Slusher Cem—*cemetery* (2) KY-4
Slusher Cem—*cemetery* MO-7
Slusher Creek—*stream* OR-9
Slusher Hollow—*valley* AR-4
Slusher Lake—*lake* OR-9
Slusher Sch—*school* KY-4
Slusher Sch—*school* MO-7
Slushers Point—*cape* MT-8
Slusher Spring—*spring* OR-9
Slusher Windmill—*locale* NM-5
Slushman Creek—*stream* MT-8
Slüsh Pond—*lake* (2) NY-2
Slush Pond Mtn—*summit* NY-2
Slush Run—*stream* IN-6
Sluss Cem—*cemetery* VA-3
*Slusser* VA-3
Slusser Ditch—*canal* IN-6
Slussers Chapel—*church* VA-3
Slussers Gulch—*valley* MT-8
Sluss Sch—*school* VA-3
Sluter Mine—*mine* OR-9
Sluter Ridge—*ridge* TN-4
*Slutkill Neck* VA-3
**Slutter**—*pop pl* TX-5
Slutz Cem—*cemetery* OH-6
Slybac E O C Airp—*airport* PA-2
Slyboro—*locale* NY-2
Sly Branch—*stream* KY-4
Sly Brook—*stream* (2) ME-1
Sly Brook Lakes—*lake* ME-1
Sly Canyon—*valley* NM-5
Sly Creek—*stream* (2) CA-9
Sly Creek—*stream* OR-9
Sly Creek Rsvr—*reservoir* CA-9
Slye Sch—*school* CT-1
**Sly Farms**—*pop pl* MI-6
Sly Fork—*stream* IN-6
Slygo Ch—*church* GA-3
*Slygo Hill* MA-1
Slygo Ridge—*ridge* GA-3
Slygo Valley—*valley* GA-3
Sly Hill—*summit* SD-7
**Slykerville**—*pop pl* PA-2
Sly Lake—*lake* PA-2
Sly Meadows—*flat* ID-8
Sly Mtn—*summit* NC-3
Sly Number 1 Dam—*dam* SD-7
Sly Park Creek—*stream* CA-9
Sly Park Dam—*dam* CA-9
Sly Park Guard Station—*locale* CA-9
*Sly Park Reservoir* CA-9
*Sly Pond* PA-2
Sly Pond—*lake* (3) NY-2
Sly Ponds—*lake* MA-1
Sly Ridge—*ridge* ID-8
Sly Sch—*school* NY-2
Smackass Gap—*gap* NC-3
*Smack Bayou* FL-3
Smack Bayou—*bay* FL-3
Smack Cem—*cemetery* IL-6
Smack Channel—*channel* LA-4
Smacker—*locale* OK-5
*Smackout* MO-7
Smackout Camp—*locale* WA-9
Smackout Creek—*stream* WA-9
Smackout Pass—*gap* WA-9
Smackout Valley—*valley* WA-9
**Smackover**—*pop pl* AR-4
Smackover Creek—*stream* (2) AR-4
Smackover Creek—*stream* TX-5
Smackover Oil And Gas Field—*oilfield* (2) AR-4
Smackover (Township of)—*fmr MCD* (2) AR-4
Smackover Training Sch—*school* AR-4
Smack Point—*cape* FL-3
Smacks Bayou—*bay* FL-3
Smacks Creek—*stream* VA-3
Smada—*locale* TX-5
Smafield Drain—*canal* MI-6
Smail Creek—*stream* MI-6
Smailes Cem—*cemetery* WV-2
Smaill, David, House—*hist pl* NV-8
S Main Drain—*canal* ID-8
*Smake Creek* SD-7
*Smal* PA-2
**Smalco**—*pop pl* MS-4
Smale—*inactive* AR-4
**Smale**—*pop pl* AR-4
Smales Branch—*stream* WV-2
Small—*locale* CA-9
Small—*locale* ID-8
Small—*locale* NJ-2
Small—*locale* (2) TX-5
**Small**—*pop pl* NC-3
**Small**—*pop pl* TX-5
Small, Cape—*cape* ME-1
Small, Lake—*lake* FL-3
Small Arm—*bay* AK-9
*Small Bass Lakes* WI-6
Small Bass Lakes—*lake* WI-6
Small Bay—*bay* AK-9
Small Bayou La Pointe—*stream* LA-4
Small Bear Creek—*stream* MI-6
Small Boat Lagoon—*bay* CA-9
Small Bones Cave—*cave* AL-4
Small Branch—*stream* (3) IN-6
Small Branch—*stream* NJ-2
*Small Brook* MA-1
Small Brook—*stream* IN-6
Small Brook—*stream* ME-1
Small Butte—*summit* AZ-5
Small Butte—*summit* CA-9
Small Canyon—*valley* AZ-5
Small Cave—*cave* (3) AL-4
Small Cave—*cave* TN-4
*Small Cem* TN-4
Small Cem—*cemetery* (2) IN-6
Small Cem—*cemetery* IA-7
Small Cem—*cemetery* TN-4
Small Cem—*cemetery* WV-2
Small Change Ch (historical)—*church* TN-4
Small Chapel—*church* NC-3
**Small Corners**—*pop pl* NY-2
*Small Creek* MO-7
*Small Creek* NV-8
Small Creek—*stream* (3) AK-9
Small Creek—*stream* ID-8
Small Creek—*stream* MT-8
Small Creek—*stream* (9) OR-9
Small Creek—*stream* VA-3
Small Creek—*stream* (2) WA-9
Small Creek Well—*well* AZ-5
**Small Cross Roads**—*pop pl* NC-3
Smalldon Drain—*canal* MI-6
Small Drain—*stream* IN-6
Small Dyke—*ridge* CO-8
*Smalle Creek* WA-9
Small-Elliott House—*hist pl* WA-9
Smallen Hollow—*valley* MO-7
**Smallett**—*pop pl* MO-7
Smallett Cave—*cave* MO-7
Smalley, Lewis, Homestead—*hist pl* PA-2
Smalley Bar—*bar* MA-1
Smalley Bogs—*swamp* MA-1
Smalley Branch—*stream* TX-5
Smalley Cem—*cemetery* AR-4
Smalley Cem—*cemetery* IN-6
Smalley Cem—*cemetery* TX-5
Smalley Creek—*stream* KY-4
Smalley Creek—*stream* NC-3
Smalley Creek—*stream* TX-5
Smalley Ditch—*canal* IN-6
Smalley Drain—*gut* VA-3
Smalley Falls—*falls* WI-6
Smalley Gulch—*valley* CO-8
Smalley (historical)—*locale* SD-7
Smalley Lake—*lake* MI-6
Smalley Lake—*reservoir* IN-6
Smalley Ridge—*ridge* TN-4
Smalley Sch—*school* NJ-2
*Smalleys Corner* MO-7
**Smalleys Corner**—*pop pl* MO-7
*Smalleys Creek* PA-2
*Smalleys Island* PA-2
Smalleys Pond—*reservoir* DE-2
Smalley Swamp—*swamp* VT-1
**Smalleytown**—*pop pl* NJ-2
Smalley (Township of)—*fmr MCD* AR-4
Smalley-Wormser House—*hist pl* NJ-2
Smallfelt Ditch—*canal* IN-6
Smallfoot Sch—*school* NE-7
Small Fry Day Care Center (5th Campus)—*school* FL-3
Small Fry Day Care (4th Campus)—*school* FL-3
Small Fry Educational Day Care Sch—*school* FL-3
Small Fry Educational Day Care (3rd Campus)—*school* FL-3
Small Fry Lake—*lake* OR-9
Small Fry Mine—*mine* UT-8
Small Fry Sch (1st Campus)—*school* FL-3
Small Fry Sch (2nd Campus)—*school* FL-3
*Small Grasslands* MH-9
*Small Grasslands Point* MH-9
Small Greens Creek—*stream* TX-5
Small Gulch—*valley* OR-9
Small Heiau—*hist pl* HI-9
Small Henry Lake—*lake* MN-6
*Small Hill* MA-1
*Small Hill* OR-9
Small Hill—*summit* ME-1
Small Hill Rsvr—*reservoir* AZ-5
Small Hope Mine—*mine* CA-9
Small Horn Canyon—*valley* MT-8
Smallhous—*locale* KY-4
Smallhous Ch—*church* KY-4
Small House—*hist pl* GA-3
Small House—*hist pl* PA-2
Smallhous Shell Mound (15OH10)—*hist pl* KY-4
Smallidge Point—*cape* ME-1
Smallin Cave—*cave* MO-7
Smalling Bridge—*bridge* TN-4
Smalling Crossroads—*locale* TN-4
Smalling Post Office (historical)—*building* TN-4
Smalling Spring—*spring* TN-4
*Small Island* RI-1
*Small Island* FM-9
Small Island—*island* WA-9
*Small islet* FM-9
Small Lake—*lake* (2) MN-6
Small Lake—*reservoir* MO-7
Smallman Creek—*stream* OR-9
Smallman Post Office (historical)—*building* TN-4
Smallmans Branch—*stream* VA-3
*Small Marpo* MH-9
Small Marsh—*swamp* SC-3
Small Middle Run—*stream* OH-6
Small Mine—*mine* TN-4
Small Mound—*summit* WI-6
Small Oil Well Tank—*reservoir* AZ-5
Small Paint Creek—*stream* AK-9
Small Point—*cape* ME-1
Small Point—*cape* MA-1
Small Point—*cliff* AZ-5
Small Point—*locale* ME-1
**Small Point Beach**—*pop pl* ME-1
Small Point Ch—*church* ME-1
Small Point Harbor—*bay* ME-1
Small Point Hill—*summit* ME-1
*Small Pond* MA-1
Small Pond—*lake* MA-1
Small Pond—*reservoir* SC-3
Smallpox Bay—*bay* WA-9
Smallpox Cem—*cemetery* MO-7
Smallpox Creek—*stream* IL-6
Smallpox Creek—*stream* MT-8
Smallpox Creek—*stream* WI-6
Smallpox Creek—*stream* WY-8
Smallpox Gulch—*valley* CO-8
Smallpox Hosp—*hist pl* NY-2
*Small Pox Island* RI-1
*Smallpox Spring* TX-5
Smallpox Spring—*spring* MO-7
Smallpox Tommies Camp—*locale* FL-3
Smallpox Tommies Old Place—*locale* FL-3
Smallpox Tommies Seminole Village—*locale* FL-3
Smallpox Well—*well* TX-5
Small Ranch—*locale* WY-8
Small Run—*stream* IN-6
Small Run—*stream* PA-2
Small Rush Creek—*stream* IN-6
Smalls, Robert, House—*hist pl* SC-3
Small Salt Creek—*stream* UT-8
Small Salt Well Tank—*reservoir* AZ-5
Smalls Bush Sch—*school* NY-2
Smalls Canyon—*valley* CA-9
Small Sch—*school* MA-1
Small Sch—*school* SC-3
Smalls Cove—*bay* (2) ME-1
Smalls Cove—*bay* NH-1
*Small's Creek* WA-9
Smalls Creek—*stream* IN-6
Smalls Creek—*stream* MO-7
**Smalls Crossroads**—*pop pl* NC-3
Smalls Falls—*falls* ME-1
Smalls Grove Ch—*church* KY-4
Smalls Hill—*summit* (2) ME-1
Smalls Hill—*summit* MA-1
Smalls Island—*island* ME-1
*Small Sister Island* FM-9
Smalls Mtn—*summit* ME-1
*Smalls Point* ME-1
Smalls Pond—*lake* MA-1
Smalls Pond—*lake* NH-1
Small Spot Mine—*mine* CO-8
Small Spring—*spring* NV-8
Small Spring—*spring* OR-9
Small Spring Cave—*cave* AL-4
Smalls River—*stream* AK-9
Smalls Sch (abandoned)—*school* PA-2
Small Tank—*reservoir* (6) AZ-5
Small Tank—*reservoir* TX-5
Small Timber Lake—*lake* AK-9
*Small Town* MA-1
**Smalltown**—*pop pl* MA-1
Small Twin Canyon—*valley* AZ-5
Small Twin Lake—*lake* CA-9
Small White Mesa—*summit* AZ-5
Small White Mesa Flat—*flat* AZ-5
Small Wide Mesa—*summit* AZ-5
Small Windmill—*locale* NM-5
*Smallwood* AL-4
**Smallwood**—*pop pl* MD-2
**Smallwood**—*pop pl* NY-2
**Smallwood**—*pop pl* PA-2
**Smallwood**—*pop pl* SC-3
Smallwood, Benjamin Franklin, House—*hist pl* OK-5
Smallwood, Eli, House—*hist pl* NC-3
Smallwood, Ted, Store—*hist pl* FL-3
*Smallwood Branch* MS-4
Smallwood Branch—*stream* (2) KY-4
Smallwood Branch—*stream* TN-4
Smallwood Cem—*cemetery* IN-6
Smallwood Cem—*cemetery* MS-4
Smallwood Cem—*cemetery* TX-5
Smallwood Ch—*church* MS-4
Smallwood Creek—*stream* AK-9
Smallwood Creek—*stream* AR-4
Smallwood Creek—*stream* OR-9
Smallwood Dam—*dam* MI-6
Smallwood Ditch—*canal* IN-6
Smallwood Drive Sch—*school* NY-2
Smallwood Gulch—*valley* CA-9
Smallwood Hills—*summit* MS-4
Smallwood Island—*island* FL-3
*Smallwood Lake* NY-2
Smallwood Lake—*reservoir* MI-6
Smallwood Landing—*locale* MS-4
Smallwood Re-Education Center—*school* TN-4
Smallwood Sch—*school* VA-3
Smallwoods Sch (historical)—*school* MS-4
Smallwood State Park—*park* MD-2
**Smallwood (subdivision)**—*pop pl* NC-3
**Smallwood (Township of)**—*pop pl* IL-6
Small World Learning Center—*school* FL-3
Smally Cem—*cemetery* NJ-2
Smally Creek—*stream* AK-9
*Smally Gulch* CO-8
Smally Spring Branch—*stream* PA-2
Smaltz Brothers Dam—*dam* SD-7
Smarden—*locale* TN-4
Smarden Post Office (historical)—*building* TN-4
Smarr—*locale* GA-3
Smarsh Branch—*stream* SC-3
Smart, Fred, House—*hist pl* NY-2
Smart, Lake—*lake* FL-3
Smart Bay—*bay* MN-6
Smart Bldg—*hist pl* OH-6
Smart Branch—*stream* AL-4
Smart Branch—*stream* (2) NC-3
Smart Brook—*stream* (2) ME-1
Smart Cem—*cemetery* AR-4
Smart Cem—*cemetery* IL-6
Smart Cem—*cemetery* (2) LA-4
Smart Cem—*cemetery* (2) ME-1
Smart Cem—*cemetery* MO-7
Smart Cem—*cemetery* (2) TX-5
Smart Cemeteries—*cemetery* SC-3
Smart Creek—*stream* MT-8
Smart Creek—*stream* TN-4
Smart Creek—*stream* WA-9
Smart Ditch—*canal* CO-8
Smart Ditch—*canal* IN-6
Smart Fork—*stream* MT-8
Smart-Griffin House—*hist pl* MS-4
Smart Grove Ch—*church* NC-3
Smart JHS—*school* IA-7
Smart JHS—*school* MI-6
Smart Mtn—*summit* ME-1
Smart Mtn—*summit* NC-3
Smart Oil And Gas Field—*oilfield* AR-4
Smart Ranch—*locale* NM-5
*Smarts* TN-4
Smarts Bluff—*cliff* WI-6
Smarts Brook Trail—*trail* NH-1
**Smartsburg**—*pop pl* IN-6
Smart Sch—*school* IN-6
Smart Sch—*school* ME-1
Smart Sch—*school* TX-5
Smart School Fire Lookout Tower—*locale* TX-5
Smarts Corner—*locale* ME-1
Smarts Creek—*stream* VA-3
Smarts Gulch—*valley* CA-9
Smarts Hill—*summit* ME-1
*Smarts Mill Brook* NH-1
Smarts Mtn—*summit* NH-1
Smarts Pond—*lake* ME-1
Smarts Pond—*reservoir* NY-2
Smart Spring—*spring* CA-9
Smarts Rsvr—*reservoir* OR-9
*Smartsville* CA-9
**Smartt**—*pop pl* TN-4
Smartt Mountain Mine (surface)—*mine* TN-4
Smartt Mtn—*summit* TN-4
Smart (Township of)—*fmr MCD* AR-4
Smartt Post Office—*building* TN-4
**Smartt (RR name Smartts)**—*pop pl* TN-4
Smartts (RR Name For Smartt)—*other* TN-4
Smart View Overlook—*locale* VA-3
Smart View Rec Area—*park* VA-3
Smartville—*locale* NY-2
**Smartville**—*pop pl* CA-9
Smarty Creek—*stream* WA-9
Smary Branch—*stream* LA-4
**Smathers**—*pop pl* PA-2
Smathers Beach—*beach* FL-3
Smathers Cem—*cemetery* NC-3
Smathers Cem—*cemetery* PA-2
Smathers Cemeteries—*cemetery* NC-3
Smathers-Demorse House—*hist pl* TX-5
Smathers Ditch—*canal* IN-6
*Smathers Mountain* NC-3
Smathers Run—*stream* PA-2
Smathers View—*summit* NC-3
Smauder Hill—*summit* NY-2
Smay Creek—*stream* WA-9
Smays Run—*stream* PA-2
Smays Trail—*trail* PA-2
S McKnight—*locale* TX-5
SMC Lake—*lake* WA-9
Smead—*locale* AR-4
Smead, David, House—*hist pl* OH-6
Smead Brook—*stream* MA-1
Smead Canyon—*valley* ID-8
Smead Ch—*church* AR-4
Smead House—*hist pl* OH-6
Smead Island—*island* MA-1
Smeads Bench—*bench* MT-8
*Smeads Brook* MA-1
Smeads Creek—*stream* MT-8
*Smeads Island* MA-1
Smead Well—*well* ID-8
Smear Bayou—*stream* MS-4
Smear Lake—*lake* WI-6
Smearl Creek—*stream* MT-8
**Smearney**—*pop pl* AR-4
Smearny—*locale* AR-4
Smears Creek—*stream* NY-2
*Smeathers Creek* TX-5
Smeathers Lateral—*stream* KY-4
Smedberg Lake—*lake* CA-9
*Smede* MS-4
**Smedes**—*pop pl* MS-4
Smedes Plantation (historical)—*locale* MS-4
Smedes Post Office (historical)—*building* MS-4
Smedley—*locale* VA-3
**Smedley**—*pop pl* IN-6
Smedley, Franklin, Sch—*hist pl* PA-2
Smedley, Thomas, House—*hist pl* ID-8
**Smedley Acres Subdivision**—*pop pl* UT-8
Smedley Ch—*church* IN-6
Smedley Creek—*stream* OK-5
Smedley JHS—*school* CA-9
Smedley MS—*school* PA-2
*Smedley Sch* PA-2
Smedley Sch—*school* CO-8
Smedley Sch—*school* PA-2
Smedley Sch (abandoned)—*school* PA-2
*Smedleys Station* IN-6
Smedly Cem—*cemetery* IL-6
*Smedrick Ledge* ME-1
Smeed Cem—*cemetery* AR-4
Smeede Hotel—*hist pl* OR-9
Smelcer Cem—*cemetery* IN-6
Smelker Drain—*canal* MI-6
Smellage Cem—*cemetery* TN-4
Smell Brook—*stream* ME-1
Smell Creek—*stream* GA-3
Smeller Creek—*stream* MT-8
Smeller Lake—*lake* MT-8
**Smelley**—*pop pl* AL-4
Smelley Creek—*stream* AL-4
Smelley Hollow—*valley* AR-4
*Smelley P.O.* AL-4
Smelling Lake—*lake* WA-9
Smell Well Cave—*cave* AL-4
Smelly Creek—*stream* AL-4
Smelser Cem—*cemetery* TN-4
Smelser Cem—*cemetery* WI-6
Smelser Creek—*stream* MO-7
Smelser Creek—*stream* SD-7
Smelser Pass—*gap* NV-8
Smelser Sch (abandoned)—*school* MO-7
Smelser Spring—*spring* AL-4
Smelser Spring Branch—*stream* AL-4
**Smelser (Town of)**—*pop pl* WI-6
Smelt Brook—*bay* ME-1
Smelt Brook—*stream* (4) ME-1
Smelt Brook—*stream* (3) MA-1
Smelt Brook—*stream* RI-1
Smelt Brook Cove—*bay* RI-1
Smelt Brook Dam—*dam* MA-1
Smelt Creek—*stream* AK-9
Smelter Basin—*basin* CO-8
Smelter Butte—*summit* ID-8
Smelter Canyon—*valley* AZ-5
Smelter Canyon—*valley* ID-8
Smelter Canyon—*valley* (2) TX-5
Smelter City—*uninc pl* AZ-5
Smelter Creek—*stream* TX-5
Smelter Creek—*stream* UT-8
*Smelter Gulch* CO-8
Smelter Gulch—*valley* CO-8
Smelter Gulch—*valley* ID-8
**Smelter Heights**—*pop pl* ID-8
*Smelter Hill* MO-7
**Smelter Hill**—*pop pl* MT-8
Smelter Hill—*summit* (2) AZ-5
Smelter Hill—*summit* (2) CO-8
Smelter Hill—*summit* MT-8
Smelter Hills—*summit* UT-8
Smelter Hollow—*valley* (2) MO-7
Smelter Knolls—*summit* (2) UT-8
Smelter Knolls Rsvr—*reservoir* UT-8
Smelter Machine Shop—*hist pl* AZ-5
Smelter Mtn—*summit* CO-8
Smelter Mtn—*summit* MT-8
Smelter Place—*locale* CO-8
**Smelter Prairie**—*pop pl* OK-5
Smelter Rock—*island* WA-9
Smelter Ruins—*locale* NM-5
Smelter Sch—*school* KS-7
Smelter Spring—*spring* UT-8
Smelter Town—*locale* AZ-5
**Smeltertown**—*pop pl* CO-8
**Smeltertown**—*pop pl* TX-5
**Smelterville**—*pop pl* ID-8
Smelter Wash—*stream* AZ-5
Smelter Well—*well* UT-8
Smelt Island—*island* AK-9
Smelt Pond—*lake* MA-1
Smelt Road Ridge—*ridge* CA-9
Smelt Sands Wayside—*park* OR-9
Smeltz—*locale* OR-9
Smeltzer—*locale* AR-4
Smeltzer—*locale* CA-9
**Smeltzer**—*pop pl* PA-2
Smeltzer Canyon—*valley* WA-9
Smeltzer Cem—*cemetery* OH-6
Smeltzer Creek—*stream* SC-3
Smeltzer Mtn—*summit* SC-3
Smeltzer Packing Company—*facility* MI-6
Smeltz Pond Trail—*trail* PA-2
Smelzer Lake—*lake* MO-7
Smerney Cem—*cemetery* MS-4
Smetana—*locale* TX-5
*Smethers Creek* IN-6
**Smethport**—*pop pl* NC-3
**Smethport**—*pop pl* PA-2
Smethport Area Junior Senior HS—*school* PA-2
Smethport Borough—*civil* PA-2
Smethport Elem Sch—*school* PA-2
Smethurst Mine—*mine* CA-9
**Smicksburg**—*pop pl* PA-2
Smicksburg Borough—*civil* PA-2
Smicksburg Cem—*cemetery* PA-2
Smicksburg Station—*locale* PA-2
Smikrud Coulee—*valley* WI-6
Smilax—*locale* KY-4
Smilax Branch—*stream* VA-3
Smilax Canal—*canal* CA-9
Smilax Lateral One—*canal* CA-9
Smilax Sch—*school* KY-4
Smile—*locale* KY-4
*Smile A While Lake* WI-6
Smiley—*locale* PA-2
Smiley—*locale* VA-3
**Smiley**—*pop pl* PA-2
**Smiley**—*pop pl* TX-5
Smiley, Lake—*lake* AK-9
Smiley, Samuel, House—*hist pl* WI-6
Smiley Arroyo—*stream* NM-5
Smiley Bayou—*stream* AR-4
*Smileyberg* KS-7
*Smileybery* KS-7
Smiley Branch—*stream* MO-7
Smiley Camp—*locale* CA-9
Smiley Canyon—*valley* NE-7
Smiley Canyon—*valley* NV-8
Smiley Canyon Creek—*stream* NE-7
Smiley (CCD)—*cens area* TX-5
Smiley Cem—*cemetery* IN-6
Smiley Cem—*cemetery* LA-4
Smiley Cem—*cemetery* (2) MS-4
Smiley Cem—*cemetery* MO-7
Smiley Cem—*cemetery* OH-6
*Smiley Cemetery* KS-7
Smiley Coulee—*valley* MT-8
Smiley Creek—*stream* (2) ID-8
Smiley Creek—*stream* MO-7
Smiley Creek—*stream* MT-8
Smiley Creek—*stream* NV-8
Smiley Creek—*stream* SD-7
Smiley Crossroads—*locale* GA-3
Smiley Ditch—*canal* OH-6
Smiley Ditch No 2—*canal* WY-8
Smiley Ditch No 3—*canal* WY-8
Smiley Draw—*valley* (2) WY-8
**Smiley Heights**—*pop pl* LA-4
Smiley Heights—*uninc pl* CA-9
Smiley Hollow—*valley* VA-3
Smiley HS—*school* TX-5
Smiley JHS—*school* CO-8
*Smiley Lake* MN-6
Smiley Lake—*lake* MN-6
Smiley Meadow—*flat* WY-8
Smiley Meadows—*flat* ID-8
Smiley Mtn—*summit* CA-9
Smiley Mtn—*summit* ID-8
Smiley Park—*park* CA-9
**Smiley Park**—*pop pl* CA-9
Smiley Pond—*reservoir* GA-3
Smiley Ridge—*ridge* WA-9
Smiley Run—*stream* (2) PA-2
Smiley Sch—*school* CA-9
Smiley Sch—*school* PA-2
Smiley Sch—*school* TX-5
Smiley Sch—*school* VT-1
Smiley Sch—*school* WI-6
Smiley Sewage Lagoon Dam—*dam* MS-4
Smileys Point—*summit* NV-8
Smiley Spring—*spring* TX-5
Smiley Spring—*spring* WY-8
Smiley Springs—*spring* WY-8
Smiley Tank—*reservoir* AZ-5
**Smiley (Township of)**—*pop pl* MN-6
Smileyville—*locale* MO-7
**Smileyville**—*pop pl* KS-7
Smiley Young Park—*park* AL-4
Smilie Cem—*cemetery* KS-7
Smilies Mill Creek—*stream* AL-4
Smilin Creek—*stream* NC-3
Smiling River Forest Camp—*locale* OR-9
Smiling Tiger Ranch—*locale* AZ-5
Smilty Creek Lodge—*locale* ID-8
Smina Cem—*cemetery* WA-9
**S Minnewaukan**—*pop pl* ND-7
Smishek Lake—*lake* ND-7
Smishek Lake Dam—*dam* ND-7
*Smishick Lake* ND-7
*Smitana* TX-5
Smit Cem—*cemetery* CO-8
Smite Lake—*lake* MN-6
*Smith* MA-1
*Smith* MS-4
Smith—*cemetery* OK-5
Smith—*locale* AR-4
Smith—*locale* FL-3
Smith—*locale* KY-4
Smith—*locale* (2) MS-4
Smith—*locale* TX-5
**Smith**—*pop pl* FL-3
**Smith**—*pop pl* IN-6
**Smith**—*pop pl* NV-8
**Smith**—*pop pl* NC-3
**Smith**—*pop pl* PA-2
**Smith**—*pop pl* (3) SC-3
**Smith**—*pop pl* TN-4
Smith, Abigail Adams, Museum—*hist pl* NY-2
Smith, Adon, House—*hist pl* NY-2
Smith, A. L., House—*hist pl* MS-4
Smith, Albert, House—*hist pl* NY-2
Smith, Albert, House—*hist pl* UT-8
Smith, Alexander, Carpet Mills Hist Dist—*hist pl* NY-2
Smith, Alfred E., House—*hist pl* NY-2
Smith, Alvin T., House—*hist pl* OR-9
Smith, Alvord I., House—*hist pl* IA-7
Smith, Andrew, House—*hist pl* OR-9
Smith, Arthur A., Covered Bridge—*hist pl* MA-1
Smith, Asa, Homestead—*hist pl* ME-1
Smith, Beecher, House—*hist pl* KY-4
Smith, Benjamin, House—*hist pl* NC-3
Smith, Benjamin, House—*hist pl* OH-6
Smith, Bernard Pitzer, House—*hist pl* OR-9
Smith, B. J., House—*hist pl* TX-5
Smith, Bradford, Bldg—*hist pl* MA-1
Smith, Camillia, House—*hist pl* WI-6
Smith, Charles R., House—*hist pl* WI-6
Smith, C. Harvey, House—*hist pl* ID-8
Smith, Chesebro, House—*hist pl* ND-7
Smith, Christopher H., House—*hist pl* TN-4
Smith, C. L., & Son General Store—*hist pl* AR-4
Smith, Curtis S., House—*hist pl* MA-1
Smith, Daniel, House—*hist pl* NY-2
Smith, Daniel, House—*hist pl* WI-6
Smith, David V., House—*hist pl* NJ-2
Smith, Dr. Robert, House—*hist pl* OH-6
Smith, Dr. William Addison, House—*hist pl* KY-4
Smith, Edward, Jr., Farm—*hist pl* OH-6
Smith, Edwin, House—*hist pl* OH-6
Smith, Edwin A., House—*hist pl* WA-9
Smith, Ellen, House—*hist pl* UT-8
Smith, Elliot, House—*hist pl* MA-1
Smith, Enoch, House—*hist pl* KY-4
Smith, Ephraim, House—*hist pl* IL-6
Smith, Ernest W., House—*hist pl* CA-9
Smith, F. A., House—*hist pl* KY-4
Smith, Fleming, Warehouse—*hist pl* NY-2
Smith, F.O.J., Tomb—*hist pl* ME-1
Smith, Francis Marion, House—*hist pl* NC-3
Smith, Francis West, House—*hist pl* WI-6
Smith, F.W., Silver Company—*hist pl* MA-1
Smith, George W., Homestead—*hist pl* ME-1
Smith, George W., House—*hist pl* KY-4
Smith, George W., House—*hist pl* NE-7
Smith, H. Alden, House—*hist pl* MN-6
Smith, Hannah Maria Libby, House—*hist pl* UT-8
Smith, H. D., Company Bldg—*hist pl* CT-1
Smith, Henry, Farm—*hist pl* PA-2
Smith, Henry, Farmstead—*hist pl* NY-2
Smith, Henry, House—*hist pl* ID-8
Smith, Henry H./J.H. Murphy House—*hist pl* IA-7
Smith, Henry Spencer, House—*hist pl* WI-6
Smith, Henry Tunis, Farm—*hist pl* NY-2
Smith, Henry W., House—*hist pl* IN-6
Smith, Herbert and Katherine, House—*hist pl* OR-9
Smith, Hiram C., House—*hist pl* IA-7
Smith, Hiram C., Milking Shed—*hist pl* IA-7
Smith, Hiram F., Orchard—*hist pl* WA-9
Smith, Jabez, House—*hist pl* CT-1
Smith, Jacob, House—*hist pl* NY-2
Smith, James, Homestead—*hist pl* ME-1
Smith, James, House—*hist pl* IA-7
Smith, James, House—*hist pl* MA-1
Smith, James, House—*hist pl* MO-7
Smith, James, Tanyard—*hist pl* KY-4
Smith, Jay Dayton, House—*hist pl* NV-8
Smith, J. E., Stone Duplex—*hist pl* NV-8
Smith, Jesse N., House—*hist pl* AZ-5
Smith, Jesse N., House—*hist pl* UT-8
Smith, Jessie, Farmstead—*hist pl* SD-7
Smith, Jessie B., House—*hist pl* AR-4
Smith, J. Homer, House—*hist pl* AZ-5
Smith, John, House—*hist pl* IA-7
Smith, John, House—*hist pl* (2) NJ-2
Smith, John, House—*hist pl* WI-6
Smith, John Mace, House—*hist pl* MA-1
Smith, John Sterling, Jr., House—*hist pl* TX-5
Smith, John T., House—*hist pl* OR-9
Smith, John W., House—*hist pl* IN-6
Smith, Joseph, House—*hist pl* RI-1
Smith, Joseph Riley, Hist Dist—*hist pl* AL-4
Smith, J. P., Shoe Company Plant—*hist pl* IL-6
Smith, Lake—*lake* FL-3
Smith, Lake—*lake* IA-7

Smith, Lake—reservoir VA-3
Smith, Lansing T., House—hist pl AL-4
Smith, Lauritz, House—hist pl UT-8
Smith, Lawrence, House—hist pl MO-7
Smith, Lloyd R., House—hist pl WI-6
Smith, Maj. Hampden, House—hist pl KY-4
Smith, Mary J. G., House—hist pl OR-9
Smith, Matthias, House—hist pl MA-1
Smith, Milton W., House—hist pl OR-9
Smith, Mitchell Baker, Company Bldg—hist pl KY-4
Smith, Mount—summit TX-5
Smith, Nat, House—hist pl WA-9
Smith, Nathan, House—hist pl ID-8
Smith, Nelson and Clifton Rodes, House—hist pl KY-4
Smith, N. P., Pioneer Hardware Store—hist pl OR-9
Smith, Parson, House—hist pl ME-1
Smith, Pierce T., House—hist pl CO-8
Smith, Professor George E. P., House—hist pl AZ-5
Smith, Reuel E., House—hist pl NY-2
Smith, Richard C., House—hist pl WI-6
Smith, Robert, Mortuary—hist pl IN-6
Smith, Robert H., Law Office—hist pl TN-4
Smith, Rowland B., House—hist pl AR-4
Smith, Samuel, House—hist pl CT-1
Smith, Samuel, House And Tannery—hist pl OH-6
Smith, Samuel, Tavern Site—hist pl MA-1
Smith, Samuel G., Farm—hist pl IN-6
Smith, Samuel L., House—hist pl MI-6
Smith, S. C., House—hist pl NJ-2
Smith, Seth W., House—hist pl UT-8
Smith, S. G., House—hist pl AR-4
Smith, Simeon, House—hist pl VT-1
Smith, Simeon P., House—hist pl NH-1
Smith, T. C., House—hist pl WI-6
Smith, Thomas, House—hist pl KY-4
Smith, Tullie, House—hist pl GA-3
Smith, T. W., House—hist pl MT-8
Smith, Walker and Johnson Lake—reservoir AL-4
Smith, Walker and Johnson Lake Dam—dam AL-4
Smith, Walter George, Sch—hist pl PA-2
Smith, Warren B., House—hist pl UT-8
Smith, Watters, Farm on Duck Creek—hist pl WV-2
Smith, W. D., House—hist pl TX-5
Smith, W. E., House—hist pl GA-3
Smith, W. F., and Sons Leaf House & Brown Brothers Company Bldg—hist pl NC-3
Smith, William, House—hist pl CO-8
Smith, William, House—hist pl PA-2
Smith, William E., House—hist pl NC-3
Smith, William F., House—hist pl MO-7
Smith, William G., House—hist pl IA-7
Smith, William G., House—hist pl NC-3
Smith, William McNeil, House—hist pl UT-8
Smith, William P., House—hist pl UT-8
Smith, William R., House—hist pl OH-6
Smith, Woral C., Lime Kiln and Limestone House—hist pl NE-7
Smith, W. W., House—hist pl MN-6
Smith, Zebulon, House—hist pl ME-1
Smith Acad—school MA-1
Smith Academy AL-4
**Smith Acres (subdivision)**—pop pl AL-4
**Smith Acres (subdivision)**—pop pl NC-3
Smith Agricultural Sch—school MA-1
Smith Airp—airport PA-2
Smith-Alston House—hist pl GA-3
Smith Alumnae Gymnasium—hist pl MA-1
Smith and Brost Number 1 Dam—dam SD-7
Smith and Clark Brothers Ranch and Grounds—hist pl CA-9
Smith and Evans Tank—reservoir AZ-5
Smith and Failing Meadow—flat CA-9
Smith and Helwig Drain—canal MI-6
Smith and Leland Hill—summit NY-2
Smith And Merchant Drain—canal MI-6
Smith and Moorehouse Creek UT-8
Smith and Morehouse Campground—park UT-8
Smith and Morehouse Creek—stream UT-8
Smith and Morehouse Dam—dam UT-8
Smith and Morehouse Rsvr—reservoir UT-8
Smith and Norred Lake—reservoir AL-4
Smith and Rex Ditch—canal CO-8
Smith and Sayles Reservoir Dam—dam RI-1
Smith and Sayles Rsvr—reservoir RI-1
Smith and Smith Ranch Lake Dam—dam MS-4
Smith And Sutton Drain—canal MI-6
Smith and Thomas Mill (historical)—locale AL-4
Smith and Williams Cem—cemetery MS-4
Smith Andy Number 1 Dam—dam SD-7
Smith-Appleby House—hist pl RI-1
Smith Arroyo—valley CO-8
Smith Ave Ch—church KY-4
Smith Ave Sch—school CT-1
Smithback Sch—school WI-6
Smith-Bailey Drug Company Bldg—hist pl UT-8
Smith Bank Number One Prospect—mine TN-4
Smith Bank Number Three Prospect—mine TN-4
Smith Bar—bar UT-8
Smith Bar Ditch—canal CA-9
Smith Barn—hist pl SC-3
Smith-Barnard Cem—cemetery MS-4
Smith-Barnes Sch—school GA-3
Smith-Barron House—hist pl TX-5
Smith Basin—basin UT-8
Smith Basin—basin WA-9
Smith Bay—bay AK-9
Smith Bay—bay IA-7
Smith Bay—bay KY-4
Smith Bay—bay MN-6
Smith Bay—bay (2) NY-2
Smith Bay—bay SD-7
Smith Bay—bay VA-3
Smith Bay—cape VI-3
Smith Bay—lake LA-4
Smith Bay—swamp FL-3
Smith Bay—swamp NC-3
Smith Bayou—bay FL-3
Smith Bayou—bay MI-6
Smith Bayou—gut (2) LA-4
Smith Bayou—gut TX-5
Smith Bayou—stream AL-4
Smith Bayou—stream (3) LA-4
Smith Bay Tumps—cape VA-3
Smith Beach RI-1
**Smith Beach**—pop pl VA-3
Smith Bed Mine (underground)—mine AL-4
Smith Bend—bend AL-4
Smith Bend—bend GA-3
Smith Bend—bend MO-7
Smith Bend—bend (4) TN-4
Smith Bend Sch—school MO-7
Smith Bend Sch (historical)—school TN-4
Smith-Benning House—hist pl GA-3
Smith-Bethel Cem—cemetery IN-6
Smith Birch Spring—spring OR-9
Smith Bldg—hist pl WV-2
Smith Bluff—cliff (2) MO-7
Smith Bluff—cliff TX-5
Smith Bluff Cut-Off TX-5
Smith Bluff Cutoff—channel TX-5
Smithboro—locale GA-3
**Smithboro**—pop pl IL-6
**Smithboro**—pop pl NY-2
**Smithboro**—pop pl SC-3
Smith Bottom—basin AL-4
Smith Bottom Cem—cemetery AL-4
Smith Bottom Ch—church TN-4
Smith Branch AL-4
Smith Branch AR-4
Smith Branch MS-4
Smith Branch TN-4
Smith Branch WV-2
Smith Branch—stream (16) AL-4
Smith Branch—stream (2) FL-3
Smith Branch—stream (5) GA-3
Smith Branch—stream IL-6
Smith Branch—stream IN-6
Smith Branch—stream KS-7
Smith Branch—stream (17) KY-4
Smith Branch—stream (3) LA-4
Smith Branch—stream (7) MS-4
Smith Branch—stream (11) MO-7
Smith Branch—stream (9) NC-3
Smith Branch—stream OH-6
Smith Branch—stream (7) SC-3
Smith Branch—stream (25) TN-4
Smith Branch—stream (12) TX-5
Smith Branch—stream (6) VA-3
Smith Branch—stream (6) WV-2
Smith Branch Rec Area—park TN-4
Smith Branch Sch—school KY-4
Smith Break—swamp TX-5
Smith Bridge—bridge DE-2
Smith Bridge—bridge GA-3
Smith Bridge—bridge MS-4
Smith Bridge—bridge MT-8
Smith Bridge—bridge NC-3
Smith Bridge—bridge (2) VA-3
Smith Bridge—locale PA-2
Smith Bridge—other IL-6
Smith Bridge—other MI-6
Smith Bridges—bridge NC-3
Smith Brook PA-2
Smith Brook—stream (2) CT-1
Smith Brook—stream (20) ME-1
Smith Brook—stream (6) MA-1
Smith Brook—stream (7) NH-1
Smith Brook—stream (4) NY-2
Smith Brook—stream (5) VT-1
Smith Brook—stream WA-9
Smith Brook Bog—swamp ME-1
Smith Brook Campsite—locale ME-1
Smith Brook Deadwater—lake ME-1
Smith Brook Deadwater—stream ME-1
Smith Brook Pond—lake (2) ME-1
Smith Brook Ridge—ridge ME-1
Smith Brothers Airp—airport IN-6
Smith Brothers Bar UT-8
Smith Brothers Landing MS-4
Smith Brothers Landing Strip SD-7
Smith Brothers Pond—reservoir AL-4
Smith Brothers Pond Dam—dam AL-4
Smith Brown Ditch—canal CO-8
Smith Brown Hollow—valley MO-7
Smith-Buntura-Evans House—hist pl MS-4
Smithburg TN-4
Smithburg—locale MS-4
**Smithburg**—pop pl NJ-2
**Smithburg**—pop pl WV-2
Smith Butte AZ-5
Smith Butte OR-9
Smith Butte—summit (2) AZ-5
Smith Butte—summit ID-8
Smith Butte—summit ND-7
Smith Butte—summit OR-9
Smith Butte—summit (2) WA-9
Smith Cabin—locale AZ-5
Smith Cabin—locale (2) CA-9
Smith Cabin—locale ID-8
Smith Cabin—locale NM-5
Smith Cabin—locale (2) UT-8
Smith Cabin—locale WY-8
Smith Cabin Run—stream PA-2
Smith Cabins—locale WY-8
Smith Camp—locale CA-9
Smith Campbell Sch (abandoned)—school MO-7
Smith Campground Ch—church IN-6
Smith Canal—canal (2) CA-9
Smith Canal—canal WA-9
Smith-Cannon House—hist pl SC-3
Smith Canyon AZ-5
Smith Canyon ID-8
Smith Canyon—valley (6) AZ-5
Smith Canyon—valley (9) CA-9
Smith Canyon—valley (2) CO-8
Smith Canyon—valley (8) ID-8
Smith Canyon—valley NE-7
Smith Canyon—valley (3) NV-8
Smith Canyon—valley (6) NM-5
Smith Canyon—valley (7) OR-9
Smith Canyon—valley TX-5
Smith Canyon—valley (3) UT-8
Smith Canyon—valley (2) WA-9
Smith Canyon—valley (3) WY-8
Smith Canyon Trail—trail UT-8
Smith Carriage Company District—hist pl MA-1
Smith Cave—cave AL-4
Smith Cave—cave (3) TN-4
Smith Cem AL-4
Smith Cem MS-4
Smith Cem—cemetery (28) AL-4
Smith Cem—cemetery (12) AR-4
Smith Cem—cemetery (8) FL-3
Smith Cem—cemetery (24) GA-3
Smith Cem—cemetery (16) IL-6
Smith Cem—cemetery (12) IN-6
Smith Cem—cemetery (10) IA-7
Smith Cem—cemetery (31) KY-4
Smith Cem—cemetery (13) LA-4
Smith Cem—cemetery (5) ME-1
Smith Cem—cemetery (3) MI-6
Smith Cem—cemetery MN-6
Smith Cem—cemetery (28) MS-4
Smith Cem—cemetery (25) MO-7
Smith Cem—cemetery NE-7
Smith Cem—cemetery NV-8
Smith Cem—cemetery (10) NY-2
Smith Cem—cemetery (20) NC-3
Smith Cem—cemetery (15) OH-6
Smith Cem—cemetery (3) OK-5
Smith Cem—cemetery OR-9
Smith Cem—cemetery (8) PA-2
Smith Cem—cemetery (2) SC-3
Smith Cem—cemetery (79) TN-4
Smith Cem—cemetery (27) TX-5
Smith Cem—cemetery (2) VT-1
Smith Cem—cemetery (20) VA-3
Smith Cem—cemetery (19) WV-2
Smith Cemeteries—cemetery NC-3
Smith Cem Number 2 AL-4
**Smith Center**—pop pl KS-7
Smith Center Elem Sch—school KS-7
Smith Center HS—school KS-7
Smith Center Municipal Airp—airport KS-7
Smith Ch AL-4
Smith Ch MS-4
Smith Ch—church AL-4
Smith Ch—church AR-4
Smith Ch—church IL-6
Smith Ch—church MS-4
Smith Ch—church MO-7
Smith Ch—church (3) VA-3
Smith Ch—church (2) WV-2
Smith Channel—channel TX-5
Smith Chapel AL-4
Smith Chapel—church (6) AL-4
Smith Chapel—church (5) AR-4
Smith Chapel—church (6) GA-3
Smith Chapel—church IL-6
Smith Chapel—church (4) KY-4
Smith Chapel—church LA-4
Smith Chapel—church (2) MD-2
Smith Chapel—church MI-6
Smith Chapel—church (7) MS-4
Smith Chapel—church (7) MO-7
Smith Chapel—church (8) NC-3
Smith Chapel—church (3) OH-6
Smith Chapel—church OK-5
Smith Chapel—church SC-3
Smith Chapel—church (12) TN-4
Smith Chapel—church (6) TX-5
Smith Chapel—church (3) VA-3
Smith Chapel—church (5) WV-2
**Smith Chapel**—pop pl (3) TN-4
Smith Chapel Cem—cemetery (2) AL-4
Smith Chapel Cem—cemetery (2) AR-4
Smith Chapel Cem—cemetery (3) GA-3
Smith Chapel Cem—cemetery KY-4
Smith Chapel Cem—cemetery (3) TN-4
Smith Chapel Cem—cemetery WV-2
Smith Chapel Ch—church GA-3
Smith Chapel Ch—church TN-4
Smith Chapel Ch of God—church AL-4
Smith Chapel Church AL-4
Smith Chapel Freewill Baptist Ch—church MS-4
Smith Chapel (historical)—church TN-4
Smith Chapel Sch (historical)—school (2) TN-4
Smith Chitwood Hosp—hospital TN-4
Smith Church TN-4
Smith Cienega—flat AZ-5
Smith-Clark and Smith-Bickler Houses—hist pl TX-5
Smith Clove Meetinghouse—hist pl NY-2
Smith Club Lake—reservoir TX-5
Smith Coll—school MA-1
Smith Coll (historical)—school TN-4
**Smith Colony**—pop pl NH-1
Smith Community Center—locale MO-7
Smith-Condon Creek—stream WA-9
Smith Conley Creek—stream WI-6
Smith-Cooper Cem—cemetery MS-4
Smith Corner—locale AR-4
Smith Corner—locale CT-1
Smith Corner—locale NY-2
Smith Corner—locale PA-2
Smith Corner—locale VT-1
**Smith Corner**—pop pl CA-9
**Smith Corner**—pop pl NH-1
Smith Corners—locale MI-6
Smith Corners—locale (5) NY-2
Smith Corners—locale (2) OH-6
Smith Corners—locale (3) PA-2
**Smith Corners**—pop pl NY-2
**Smith Corners**—pop pl (2) OH-6
**Smith Corners**—pop pl PA-2
Smith Corners Cem—cemetery MI-6
Smith Corrals—locale ID-8
Smith-Cosgrove House—hist pl MN-6
Smith Cotton HS—school MO-7
Smith Coulee—valley (10) MT-8
Smith Coulee—valley ND-7
Smith Coulee—valley WI-6
Smith County—civil KS-7
**Smith County**—pop pl MS-4
**Smith County**—pop pl TN-4
**Smith (County)**—pop pl TX-5
Smith County Airp—airport MS-4
Smith County Courthouse—building TN-4
Smith County Courthouse—hist pl TN-4
Smith County Fairgrounds*—locale KS-7
Smith County General Hosp—hospital MS-4
Smith County HS—school TN-4
Smith County Memorial Hosp—hospital TN-4
Smith County Training Center—school MS-4
Smith County Training HS MS-4
Smith County Vocational Center—school TN-4
Smith Court Residences—park MA-1
Smith Cove CT-1
Smith Cove ME-1
Smith Cove—bay (3) CT-1
Smith Cove—bay FL-3
Smith Cove—bay (5) ME-1
Smith Cove—bay (2) MD-2
Smith Cove—bay (2) NH-1
Smith Cove—bay NY-2
Smith Cove—bay RI-1
Smith Cove—bay WA-9
Smith Cove—cove MA-1
Smith Cove—stream TN-4
Smith Cove—valley NC-3
Smith Covered Bridge—hist pl IN-6
Smith Cove Waterway—bay WA-9
Smith Cow Camp—locale CA-9
Smith-Cox Well—well NM-5
Smith Creek CA-9
Smith Creek KY-4
Smith Creek MS-4
Smith Creek MO-7
Smith Creek MT-8
Smith Creek NV-8
Smith Creek NC-3
Smith Creek OR-9
Smith Creek TN-4
Smith Creek TX-5
Smith Creek UT-8
Smith Creek WA-9
Smith Creek—bay MD-2
Smith Creek—bay NY-2
Smith Creek—gut NC-3
**Smith Creek**—pop pl FL-3
**Smith Creek**—pop pl TN-4
Smith Creek—stream (6) AL-4
Smith Creek—stream (5) AK-9
Smith Creek—stream AZ-5
Smith Creek—stream (8) AR-4
Smith Creek—stream (21) CA-9
Smith Creek—stream (10) CO-8
Smith Creek—stream (4) FL-3
Smith Creek—stream (4) GA-3
Smith Creek—stream (23) ID-8
Smith Creek—stream IL-6
Smith Creek—stream (3) IN-6
Smith Creek—stream (5) IA-7
Smith Creek—stream (3) KS-7
Smith Creek—stream (9) KY-4
Smith Creek—stream (3) LA-4
Smith Creek—stream MD-2
Smith Creek—stream MA-1
Smith Creek—stream (10) MI-6
Smith Creek—stream (2) MN-6
Smith Creek—stream (13) MS-4
Smith Creek—stream (5) MO-7
Smith Creek—stream (20) MT-8
Smith Creek—stream (3) NE-7
Smith Creek—stream (7) NV-8
Smith Creek—stream NH-1
Smith Creek—stream NJ-2
Smith Creek—stream NM-5
Smith Creek—stream (2) NY-2
Smith Creek—stream (13) NC-3
Smith Creek—stream ND-7
Smith Creek—stream (2) OK-5
Smith Creek—stream (28) OR-9
Smith Creek—stream (3) PA-2
Smith Creek—stream (3) SC-3
Smith Creek—stream (3) SD-7
Smith Creek—stream (6) TN-4
Smith Creek—stream (19) TX-5
Smith Creek—stream (5) UT-8
Smith Creek—stream (13) VA-3
Smith Creek—stream (15) WA-9
Smith Creek—stream (3) WV-2
Smith Creek—stream (6) WI-6
Smith Creek—stream (7) WY-8
Smith Creek Basin—basin NV-8
Smith Creek Butte—summit WA-9
Smith Creek Butte Trail—trail WA-9
Smith Creek Campground—locale CO-8
Smith Creek Cem—cemetery MO-7
Smith Creek Ch—church AR-4
Smith Creek Ch—church FL-3
Smith Creek Ch—church KY-4
Smith Creek Ch—church MO-7
Smith Creek Ch—church WV-2
Smith Creek Creamery (historical)—locale SD-7
Smith Creek Dome—summit AK-9
Smith Creek Guard Station—locale ID-8
Smith Creek Lake—lake ID-8
Smith Creek Lakes—lake UT-8
Smith Creek Landing—locale FL-3
Smith Creek Marsh—swamp MD-2
Smith Creek Mountains - in part NV-8
Smith Creek Pass—gap MT-8
Smith Creek Point—cape (2) NC-3
Smith Creek Public Use Area—park ND-7
Smith Creek Ranch—locale (2) NV-8
Smith Creek Ranger Station—locale CA-9
Smith Creek Rim—cliff WY-8
Smith Creek Sch—school FL-3
Smith Creek Sch—school IA-7
Smith Creek Sch—school KY-4
Smith Creek Sch—school NV-8
Smith Creek Sch—school WV-2
Smith Creek Site—hist pl MS-4
Smith Creek (Summit)—gap NV-8
Smith Creek (Township of)—fmr MCD NC-3
Smith Creek Trail—trail (2) MT-8
Smith Creek Trail—trail NV-8
Smith Creek Trail—trail WA-9
Smith Creek Valley (Depression)—basin NV-8
Smith Creek Well Number Fifty Six—well NV-8
Smith Creek Work Center—locale ID-8
Smith Creek Youth Camp—locale OR-9
Smith Crossing—locale MI-6
Smith Crossing—locale WV-2
**Smith Crossing**—pop pl ME-1
**Smith Crossing**—pop pl NC-3
Smith Crossroads—locale DE-2
Smith Crossroads—locale FL-3
Smith Crossroads—locale WV-2
**Smith Crossroads**—pop pl NC-3
Smith Crossroads (historical)—locale AL-4
Smith Cut Anticline—cliff WY-8
Smith Cutoff—gut MS-4
Smithdale—locale IL-6
Smithdale—locale PA-2
Smithdale—locale TX-5
**Smithdale**—pop pl AL-4
**Smithdale**—pop pl AR-4
**Smithdale**—pop pl MS-4
Smithdale Field—other MS-4
Smithdale Oil Field—oilfield MS-4
Smithdale P.O. MS-4
Smithdale Sch—school IL-6
Smithdale Spur AR-4
Smith Dam—dam (2) AL-4
Smith Dam—dam MN-6
Smith Dam—dam (4) OR-9
Smith Dam—dam SD-7
Smith-Davis House—hist pl OH-6
Smith Dead River—gut MS-4
Smith Detention Dam—dam AZ-5
Smith Ditch IN-6
Smith Ditch—canal (2) CA-9
Smith Ditch—canal (4) CO-8
Smith Ditch—canal HI-9
Smith Ditch—canal IL-6
Smith Ditch—canal (15) IN-6
Smith Ditch—canal KY-4
Smith Ditch—canal MI-6
Smith Ditch—canal (2) MT-8
Smith Ditch—canal NJ-2
Smith Ditch—canal (4) OH-6
Smith Ditch—canal (4) OR-9
Smith Ditch—canal (2) WY-8
Smith Ditch—stream AL-4
Smith Ditch—valley MS-4
Smith Ditch No 1—canal WY-8
Smith Drain—canal (9) MI-6
Smith Drain—stream (2) MI-6
Smith Drain—stream SC-3
Smith Draw—valley CO-8
Smith Draw—valley ID-8
Smith Draw—valley NM-5
Smith Draw—valley (2) SD-7
Smith Draw—valley TX-5
Smith Draw—valley WA-9
Smith Draw—valley (6) WY-8
Smithee Cem—cemetery AR-4
Smithee Jack Creek—stream GA-3
Smith Elementary School AZ-5
Smith Elementary School MS-4
Smith Elementary School PA-2
Smith Elem Sch—school NC-3
Smith Elem Sch—school TN-4
Smith-Ellis Cem—cemetery MO-7
Smithe Redwoods State Res—park CA-9
Smither Farm—locale TX-5
Smitherman Branch—stream TX-5
Smitherman Mill Pond—reservoir NC-3
Smitherman Millpond Dam—dam NC-3
Smither Memorial Cem—cemetery VA-3
Smithern Fork—stream KY-4
Smithern Knob—summit KY-4
Smither Prison Farm—other TX-5
**Smithers**—pop pl WV-2
Smithers Cave—cave AL-4
Smithers Creek IN-6
Smithers Creek NV-8
Smithers Creek—stream WV-2
Smithers Lake—lake TX-5
**Smithers Lake**—pop pl TX-5
Smithers Mtn AL-4
Smithers Mtn—summit AL-4
Smithers Riffle—rapids OR-9
Smithers Spring—spring AL-4
Smithers Windmill—locale NM-5
Smith Estate—hist pl CA-9
Smith Estate—hist pl NY-2
**Smith Estates Subdivision**—pop pl UT-8
Smith Esteb Memorial Home—building IN-6
Smithey Branch GA-3
Smithey Branch—stream GA-3
Smithey Hollow—valley AL-4
Smitheys Creek—stream NC-3
Smitheys Creek Public Use Area—park NC-3
Smith Falls—falls (2) ID-8
Smith Falls—falls NE-7
Smith Falls—falls OR-9
Smith Family Cem—cemetery GA-3
Smith Family Cem—cemetery MS-4
Smith Family Farmstead—hist pl PA-2
Smith Farm Cem—cemetery OH-6
Smith Farmhouse—hist pl TN-4
Smith Ferry MA-1
Smith Ferry TN-4
Smith Ferry—locale NJ-2
Smith Ferry—locale TX-5
Smith Ferry Canal—canal CA-9
Smith Ferry (historical)—crossing TN-4
Smith Ferry (historical)—locale OR-9
Smith Ferry Lookout Tower—locale TX-5
Smithfield MD-2
Smithfield (2) OR-9
Smithfield VA-3
Smith Field—airport KS-7
Smithfield—hist pl VA-3
Smithfield—locale KS-7
Smithfield—locale NY-2
Smithfield—locale OR-9
Smithfield—locale TN-4
Smith Field—park (2) MA-1
**Smithfield**—pop pl AL-4
**Smithfield**—pop pl IL-6
**Smithfield**—pop pl IN-6
**Smithfield**—pop pl KY-4
**Smithfield**—pop pl LA-4
**Smithfield**—pop pl ME-1
**Smithfield**—pop pl MO-7
**Smithfield**—pop pl NE-7
**Smithfield**—pop pl NC-3
**Smithfield**—pop pl OH-6
**Smithfield**—pop pl PA-2
**Smithfield**—pop pl TX-5
**Smithfield**—pop pl UT-8
**Smithfield**—pop pl (2) VA-3
**Smithfield**—pop pl WV-2
**Smithfield**—pop pl VI-3
**Smithfield Acres (subdivision)**—pop pl DE-2
Smith Field Airp—airport IN-6
Smithfield Borough—civil PA-2
Smithfield Canal—canal UT-8
Smithfield Canyon—valley UT-8
Smithfield Canyon Campground UT-8
Smithfield Cem—cemetery IA-7
Smithfield Cem—cemetery PA-2
Smithfield Center—uninc pl PA-2
Smithfield Ch—church NC-3
Smithfield Ch—church PA-2
Smithfield Ch—church (2) VA-3
Smithfield City Cem—cemetery UT-8
Smithfield Creek VA-3
Smithfield Division—civil UT-8
Smithfield Elem Sch—school NC-3
Smithfield Elem Sch—school (2) PA-2
Smithfield Friends Meeting House, Parsonage & Cemetery—hist pl RI-1
Smithfield Hist Dist—hist pl AL-4
Smithfield Hist Dist—hist pl VA-3
Smithfield JHS—school NC-3
Smithfield Juniata Elem Sch—school PA-2
Smithfield (Magisterial District)—fmr MCD WV-2
**Smithfield (Middleway)**—pop pl WV-2
Smithfield Park—park MI-6
Smithfield Picnic Area—park UT-8
Smithfield Public Library—hist pl UT-8
Smithfield Road Hist Dist—hist pl RI-1
Smithfield Sch—school MI-6
Smithfield Sch (historical)—school TN-4
Smithfield-Selma MS NC-3
Smithfield-Selma Senior HS—school NC-3
Smithfield Shop Ctr—locale FL-3
Smithfield Site—hist pl MS-4
**Smithfield (South Huntingdon)**—pop pl PA-2
**Smithfield (sta.) (Weems)**—pop pl OH-6
Smithfield Street Bridge—hist pl PA-2
Smithfield Street United Methodist Ch—church PA-2
**Smithfield (subdivision)**—pop pl AL-4
**Smithfield Subdivision**—pop pl UT-8
Smithfield Summit—locale PA-2
Smithfield Tithing Office—hist pl UT-8
**Smithfield (Town of)**—pop pl ME-1
**Smithfield (Town of)**—pop pl NY-2
**Smithfield (Town of)**—pop pl RI-1
Smithfield Township—fmr MCD IA-7
Smithfield (Township of)—fmr MCD NC-3
**Smithfield (Township of)**—pop pl IN-6
**Smithfield (Township of)**—pop pl OH-6
**Smithfield (Township of)**—pop pl (3) PA-2
Smith Fire Tower AL-4
Smith Fire Tower—tower FL-3
Smith Fire Tower—tower PA-2
Smith Flat—flat (6) CA-9
Smith Flat—flat NV-8
Smith Flat—flat OR-9
**Smithflat**—pop pl CA-9
Smith Flats—flat MT-8
Smith Flats—flat VA-3
Smith Flats—flat WY-8
Smith Flats—hist pl NY-2
Smith Flat (Smithflat) CA-9
**Smithflat (Smith Flat)**—pop pl CA-9
Smith Ford—locale (2) AL-4
Smith Ford—locale KY-4
Smith Ford—locale SC-3
Smith Ford Ditch—canal CO-8
Smith Ford (historical)—locale (2) MO-7
Smith Fork TN-4
Smith Fork—stream (2) CA-9
Smith Fork—stream CO-8
Smith Fork—stream IN-6
Smith Fork—stream (5) KY-4
Smith Fork—stream MO-7
Smith Fork—stream MT-8
Smith Fork—stream TN-4
Smith Fork—stream UT-8
Smith Fork Campground—locale CO-8
Smith Fork Ch—church MO-7
Smith Fork Ch—church TN-4
Smith Fork Creek IN-6
Smith Fork Creek—stream TN-4
Smith Fork Mtn—summit CO-8
Smith Fork Sch—school KY-4
Smith Fort—locale VA-3
**Smith Four Corners**—pop pl VT-1
Smith-Frazier Cem—cemetery TX-5
Smith-Fry Ditch—canal IN-6
Smith-Gallego House—hist pl CO-8
Smith Gap—gap (2) AL-4
Smith Gap—gap GA-3
Smith Gap—gap NC-3
Smith Gap—gap (3) PA-2
Smith Gap—gap TN-4
Smith Gap—gap TX-5
Smith Gap—gap (2) VA-3
Smith Gap—gap WA-9
Smith Gap—locale PA-2
Smith Gap Creek—stream TN-4
Smith Gap Sch (abandoned)—school PA-2
**Smith Gardens**—pop pl PA-2
Smith Gate—gap OR-9
Smith-Gilmer Cem—cemetery LA-4
Smith Glacier WA-9
Smith Glacier—glacier AK-9
Smith Golf Course—other MO-7
Smith-Gordon Ditch—canal CA-9
Smithgrove NC-3
Smith Grove—locale TX-5
**Smith Grove**—pop pl NC-3
Smith Grove Cave Number Four—cave TN-4
Smith Grove Cave Number One—cave TN-4
Smith Grove CAve Number Two—cave TN-4
Smith Grove Cem—cemetery MS-4
Smith Grove Ch—church (7) GA-3
Smith Grove Ch—church IL-6
Smith Grove Ch—church KY-4
Smith Grove Ch—church MS-4
Smith Grove Ch—church (5) NC-3
Smith Grove Ch—church SC-3
Smith Grove Ch—church (2) TN-4
Smith Grove Ch—church VA-3
Smith Grove Ch of Christ—church TX-5
Smith Grove Ridge—ridge KY-4
Smith Grove Sch TN-4
Smith Grove Sch—school KY-4
Smith Grove Sch—school NC-3
Smith Grove Sch—school TN-4
Smith Gulch ID-8
Smith Gulch—valley AZ-5
Smith Gulch—valley (5) CA-9

**Smiths Corner**—pop pl PA-2
Smith's Corner Hist Dist—hist pl NH-1
Smiths Corners OR-9
**Smiths Corners**—pop pl NY-2
**Smiths Corners**—pop pl PA-2
Smith's Cove NY-2
Smiths Cove RI-1
Smiths Cove—valley TN-4
Smiths Creek AL-4
Smiths Creek AR-4
Smiths Creek ID-8
Smiths Creek MS-4
Smiths Creek MO-7
Smiths Creek NV-8
Smiths Creek NC-3
Smiths Creek PA-2
Smith's Creek VA-3
Smiths Creek—locale KY-4
**Smiths Creek**—pop pl MI-6
Smiths Creek—stream AL-4
Smiths Creek—stream CA-9
Smiths Creek—stream MI-6
Smiths Creek—stream NV-8
Smiths Creek—stream NC-3
Smiths Creek Valley NV-8
Smiths Crossing MI-6
Smiths Crossing—other MI-6
**Smiths Crossing**—pop pl IN-6
Smiths Crossroad—locale GA-3
Smiths Crossroads GA-3
Smiths Crossroads—locale GA-3
Smiths Crossroads—locale (2) VA-3
**Smiths Crossroads**—pop pl AL-4
**Smiths Crossroads**—pop pl FL-3
**Smiths Crossroads**—pop pl NC-3
Smiths Cross Roads Post Office TN-4
Smiths Cross Roads Post Office (historical)—building TN-4
**Smiths Cross Roads (Radcliffe)**—pop pl VA-3
Smiths Cross Roads Sch (historical)—school TN-4
Smiths Dam—dam AL-4
Smiths Dam—dam UT-8
Smiths Ferry AL-4
Smiths Ferry TN-4
**Smiths Ferry**—pop pl ID-8
**Smiths Ferry**—pop pl MA-1
**Smiths Ferry**—pop pl PA-2
Smiths Ferry (historical)—locale (2) AL-4
Smiths Ferry (historical)—locale KS-7
Smiths Ferry (historical)—locale MS-4
Smiths Flat CA-9
Smiths Flat OR-9
Smiths Ford—locale (2) AL-4
Smiths Ford—locale OR-9
Smiths Forge (historical)—locale TN-4
**Smiths Fork**—pop pl TN-4
Smiths Fork—stream (3) WY-8
Smiths Fork Creek WY-8
Smiths Fork Guard Station—locale WY-8
Smiths Fork Pass—gap UT-8
Smiths Fork Pass Lake—lake UT-8
Smith's Fort—hist pl VA-3
Smiths Gap PA-2
Smiths Grove NC-3
**Smiths Grove**—pop pl KY-4
Smiths Grove Baptist Church—hist pl KY-4
Smiths Grove (CCD)—cens area KY-4
Smiths Grove Ch—church GA-3
Smiths Grove Ch—church KY-4
Smiths Grove Ch—church (3) NC-3
Smiths Grove Ch—church TN-4
Smiths Grove District—hist pl KY-4
Smiths Grove Hist Dist (Boundary Increase)—hist pl KY-4
Smiths Grove Presbyterian Church—hist pl KY-4
Smiths Grove Sch (historical)—school TN-4
Smith Shaft Mine (underground)—mine AL-4
Smith Harbor—bay WA-9
Smith-Shelton Cem—cemetery TN-4
Smiths Hill—summit MA-1
Smiths Hill—summit NJ-2
**Smithshire**—pop pl IL-6
**Smiths (historical)**—pop pl MA-1
Smith Shoal—bar (2) FL-3
Smith Shoal Bridge TN-4
Smith Shoals—bar TN-4
**Smith Shoals Subdivision**—pop pl TN-4
Smith Shoemaker Ditch—canal IN-6
Smith Shoe Shop—hist pl MA-1
**Smith Shores (subdivision)**—pop pl AL-4
Smith-Short and Willin Ditch—stream DE-2
Smiths Siding—locale TX-5
Smith Siding—locale UT-8
Smith's Irrigation Ditch—hist pl CO-8
Smiths Island AL-4
Smiths Island NH-1
Smiths Island NC-3
Smiths Island PA-2
Smith's Island VA-3
Smith's Island WA-9
Smiths Island—island FL-3
Smiths Island—island ID-8
Smiths Islands (historical)—island TN-4
Smiths Knob—summit PA-2
Smiths Knob Vista—summit PA-2
Smiths Ladder Cave—cave PA-2
Smiths Lake MI-6
Smiths Lake MS-4
Smiths Lake—lake CA-9
Smiths Lake—lake NC-3
**Smiths Lake**—pop pl NM-5
Smiths Lake—reservoir (2) AL-4
Smiths Lake—reservoir GA-3
Smiths Lake—reservoir (4) NC-3
Smiths Lake Dam AL-4
Smiths Lake Dam—dam (3) NC-3
Smiths Landing AL-4
Smith's Landing WI-6
Smiths Landing—locale AL-4
Smiths Landing—locale GA-3
Smiths Landing (historical)—locale AL-4
Smiths Ledge—bar ME-1
Smith Slope Mine (underground)—mine AL-4
Smith Slough CA-9
Smith Slough—bay TN-4
Smith Slough—gut CA-9
Smith Slough—gut WI-6
Smith Slough—lake MI-6
Smith Slough—stream MT-8
Smith Slough—stream WI-6
Smiths Mill AL-4
Smiths Mill AZ-5
Smiths Mill MS-4
Smiths Mill NY-2
Smiths Mill—locale AL-4
Smiths Mill—locale GA-3
Smiths Mill—locale VA-3
**Smiths Mill**—pop pl MN-6
**Smiths Mill**—pop pl MS-4
Smiths Mill Bay—swamp NC-3
Smiths Mill Bridge—bridge VA-3
Smiths Mill (historical)—locale (4) AL-4
Smiths Mill (historical)—locale (2) MS-4
Smiths Mill (historical)—locale (2) TN-4
Smiths Millpond—lake ME-1
Smiths Millpond—reservoir NC-3
Smiths Millpond—reservoir SC-3
Smiths Millpond Bog—swamp ME-1
Smiths Mills MA-1
Smiths Mills—locale NJ-2
**Smiths Mills**—pop pl ME-1
**Smiths Mills**—pop pl NY-2
Smiths Mine SD-7
Smiths Mtn—summit CO-8
Smiths Neck MA-1
Smiths Neck—cape CT-1
Smiths Old Mill (historical)—locale TN-4
Smithson—locale AL-4
**Smithson**—pop pl IN-6
Smithson, Nathaniel, House—hist pl TN-4
Smithson and McKay Brothers Blocks—hist pl OR-9
Smithson Branch—stream (3) TN-4
Smithson Cem—cemetery AL-4
Smithson Cem—cemetery KY-4
Smithson Cem—cemetery (3) TN-4
Smithsonia GA-3
Smithsonia—locale AL-4
Smithsonia—locale GA-3
Smithsonia (alternate name Smithonia)—inactive GA-3
Smithsonia (Bibb County Home for Aged)—hospital GA-3
Smithsonia Cave—cave AL-4
Smithsonia Ch—church AL-4
Smithsonia Landing (historical)—locale AL-4
Smithsonian Astrophysical Observatory—building AZ-5
Smithsonian Bldg—hist pl DC-2
Smithsonian Butte—summit UT-8
Smithsonian Institution—other DC-2
Smithsonian Institution Shelter—hist pl CA-9
Smithsonian Metro Station—locale DC-2
Smithsonian Observatory—building CA-9
Smithsonia Sch (historical)—school AL-4
Smithsonite Mine—mine NV-8
Smithson Lake—reservoir OK-5
Smithson Lake Dam—dam MS-4
Smithson Landing—locale NC-3
Smithson Sch—school CA-9
Smithson Stadium TN-4
Smithsons Valley TX-5
Smithson Valley—locale TX-5
Smithson Valley Cem—cemetery TX-5
**Smiths Park**—pop pl SD-7
Smiths Pasture—flat MA-1
Smiths Pinnacle AR-4
Smith's Point MA-1
Smiths Point NC-3
Smiths Point OR-9
Smiths Point—cape FL-3
Smiths Point—cape NY-2
**Smiths Point**—pop pl NH-1
Smiths Point—ridge CA-9
Smiths Pond MA-1
Smiths Pond NJ-2
Smiths Pond NC-3
Smiths Pond—lake FL-3
Smiths Pond—lake GA-3
Smiths Pond—lake NH-1
Smiths Pond—reservoir (4) AL-4
Smiths Pond—reservoir MA-1
Smiths Pond—reservoir NC-3
Smiths Pond Dam—dam NC-3
Smiths Pond (historical)—lake AL-4
Smiths Ponds—reservoir AL-4
Smiths Prairie—lake FL-3
Smith Spreader Dam—dam SD-7
Smith Spring—spring (3) AL-4
Smith Spring—spring (3) AZ-5
Smith Spring—spring CA-9
Smith Spring—spring (2) CO-8
Smith Spring—spring ID-8
Smith Spring—spring (2) MO-7
Smith Spring—spring MT-8
Smith Spring—spring NV-8
Smith Spring—spring (2) NM-5
Smith Spring—spring (4) OR-9
Smith Spring—spring (2) TN-4
Smith Spring—spring TX-5
Smith Spring—spring (2) UT-8
Smith Spring—spring (2) WA-9
Smith Spring Branch—stream TX-5
Smith Spring Hollow—valley MO-7
Smith Springs—locale ID-8
**Smith Springs**—pop pl TX-5
Smith Springs—spring CO-8
Smith Springs—spring WA-9
Smith Springs—uninc pl TN-4
Smith Springs Branch—stream AR-4
Smith Springs Campground—park OR-9
Smith Springs Cem—cemetery TX-5
Smith Springs Creek—stream TN-4
Smith Springs Hollow—valley WA-9
Smith Springs Sch—school TX-5
**Smith Spur**—pop pl MT-8
Smiths Ranch CA-9
Smiths Ranch—locale WY-8
Smiths Ridge—ridge CA-9
Smiths River CA-9
Smith's Rock CT-1
Smiths Rsvr—reservoir (2) UT-8
Smiths Run PA-2
Smiths Run—stream PA-2
Smithsrund Lake—lake ND-7
Smiths Run Trail—trail (2) PA-2
Smiths-Salem (CCD)—cens area AL-4
Smiths-Salem Division—civil AL-4
Smiths Sch (historical)—school (2) AL-4
Smiths School AL-4
Smiths School TN-4
Smiths Shoals—bar TN-4
Smiths Shops MS-4
Smiths Slope Mine (underground)—mine AL-4
Smiths Slough—gut TX-5
Smiths Slough—swamp IA-7
Smiths Slough State Game Mngmt Area—park IA-7
**Smiths (Smiths Station)**—pop pl PA-2
Smiths Springs TN-4
Smiths Spur MS-4
Smiths Station AZ-5
Smiths Station MS-4
**Smiths Station**—pop pl AL-4
**Smiths Station**—pop pl PA-2
Smiths Station HS—school AL-4
Smiths Store—locale NC-3
Smiths Store (historical)—locale AL-4
Smiths Store (historical)—locale (3) MS-4
**Smiths Subdivision**—pop pl FL-3
**Smiths Subdivision**—pop pl UT-8
Smiths Sulphur Spring MS-4
Smiths Swamp—stream NC-3
Smiths Swamp—swamp PA-2
Smiths Swamp Branch—stream NC-3
Smith State For—forest NH-1
Smith Station AZ-5
Smith Station—locale CA-9
Smith's Tavern—hist pl SC-3
Smiths Temple Holiness Ch—church AL-4
Smith Store (historical)—locale MS-4
Smiths (Township of)—fmr MCD NC-3
Smith Street Park—park NC-3
Smith Street Primary Sch—hist pl RI-1
Smith Street Sch—school NY-2
Smith Sturdy Cem—cemetery MO-7
Smiths Turnout SC-3
**Smiths Turnout**—pop pl SC-3
**Smith Subdivision**—pop pl TN-4
**Smith Subdivision**—pop pl UT-8
Smith Summit—locale PA-2
Smiths Valley NV-8
Smiths Valley PA-2
Smithsville PA-2
Smith Swamp—stream (2) SC-3
Smith Swamp—stream VA-3
Smith Swamp—swamp NY-2
Smith Swamp—swamp (3) SC-3
Smith Swamp (Carolina Bay)—swamp NC-3
Smith Swamp Sch—school SC-3
Smiths Well—well OR-9
Smith Switch—locale NY-2
Smith Tabernacle CME Ch—church AL-4
Smith Tank AZ-5
Smith Tank—lake TX-5
Smith Tank—reservoir (10) AZ-5
Smith Tank—reservoir (6) NM-5
Smith Tank—reservoir TX-5
Smith Tanks—reservoir AZ-5
Smith Tavern—hist pl NY-2
Smith Temple Ch—church AL-4
Smith-Thaxter-Merrifield House—hist pl MA-1
Smithton WV-2
Smithton—locale ME-1
**Smithton**—pop pl AR-4
**Smithton**—pop pl IL-6
**Smithton**—pop pl MO-7
**Smithton**—pop pl PA-2
Smithton Borough—civil PA-2
Smithton Branch—stream AR-4
Smithton Cem—cemetery ME-1
Smithton Cem—cemetery (2) MO-7
Smithton-Franklin Cem—cemetery IL-6
Smithton (historical)—locale (2) KS-7
**Smithton (historical)**—pop pl MO-7
Smithton Sch (historical)—school MO-7
Smithton Township—civil MO-7
**Smithton (Township of)**—pop pl IL-6
Smith Tower—locale LA-4
Smithtown MS-4
Smithtown—locale MS-4
Smithtown—locale (2) PA-2
Smithtown—locale (2) TN-4
**Smithtown**—pop pl AL-4
**Smithtown**—pop pl KY-4
**Smith Town**—pop pl MS-4
**Smithtown**—pop pl NH-1
**Smithtown**—pop pl NJ-2
**Smithtown**—pop pl NY-2
**Smithtown**—pop pl (2) NC-3
**Smithtown**—pop pl PA-2
**Smithtown**—pop pl WV-2
Smithtown Baptist Ch—church AL-4
Smithtown Bay—bay MN-6
Smithtown Bay—bay NY-2
**Smithtown Branch**—pop pl NY-2
Smithtown Cem—cemetery NH-1
Smithtown Central HS—school NY-2
Smithtown Ch—church IA-7
Smithtown Creek—stream PA-2
Smithtown Gap—gap PA-2
Smithtown General Hosp—hospital NY-2
Smithtown Landing Country Club—other NY-2
**Smithtown Pines**—pop pl NY-2
Smithtown (P.O.)—uninc pl NY-2
Smithtown Sch (abandoned)—school PA-2
Smith Township—civil (2) MO-7
**Smith Township**—pop pl KS-7
**Smith Township**—pop pl MO-7
**Smith Township**—pop pl ND-7
**Smith Township**—pop pl SD-7
Smith (Township of)—fmr MCD (5) AR-4
Smith (Township of)—fmr MCD NC-3
**Smith (Township of)**—pop pl (3) IN-6
**Smith (Township of)**—pop pl (2) OH-6
**Smith (Township of)**—pop pl PA-2
Smith Township Sch—school PA-2
**Smithtown (Town of)**—pop pl NY-2
**Smith Tract**—pop pl NJ-2
Smith Trail—trail (4) PA-2
Smith-Turner House—hist pl MI-6
Smith-Tuthill Funeral Parlors—hist pl CA-9
Smith Valley—basin KY-4
Smith Valley—basin NV-8
Smith Valley—locale NY-2
**Smith Valley**—pop pl IN-6
Smith Valley—valley MT-8
Smith Valley—valley NV-8
Smith Valley—valley (2) PA-2
Smith Valley—valley TN-4
Smith Valley—valley WI-6
Smith Valley Mine—mine NV-8
Smith Valley Sch—hist pl WI-6
Smith Valley Sch—school WI-6
Smith Valley Township—inact MCD NV-8
**Smithview**—pop pl KY-4
Smith Village MA-1
**Smith Village**—pop pl OK-5
**Smith Village Subdivision**—pop pl UT-8
Smithville AL-4
Smithville AZ-5
Smithville MD-2
Smithville MN-6
Smithville NC-3
Smithville PA-2
Smithville RI-1
Smithville VA-3
Smithville—locale (2) AR-4
Smithville—locale IL-6
Smithville—locale MD-2
Smithville—locale (2) PA-2
Smithville—locale TX-5
Smithville—locale VA-3
**Smithville**—pop pl AR-4
**Smithville**—pop pl GA-3
**Smithville**—pop pl IL-6
**Smithville**—pop pl (2) IN-6
**Smithville**—pop pl KY-4
**Smithville**—pop pl LA-4
**Smithville**—pop pl ME-1
**Smithville**—pop pl (2) MD-2
**Smithville**—pop pl MA-1
**Smithville**—pop pl MI-6
**Smithville**—pop pl MN-6
**Smithville**—pop pl MS-4
**Smithville**—pop pl MO-7
**Smithville**—pop pl NH-1
**Smithville**—pop pl (2) NJ-2
**Smithville**—pop pl NY-2
**Smithville**—pop pl NC-3
**Smithville**—pop pl (2) OH-6
**Smithville**—pop pl OK-5
**Smithville**—pop pl PA-2
**Smithville**—pop pl TN-4
**Smithville**—pop pl TX-5
**Smithville**—pop pl VT-1
**Smithville**—pop pl WA-9
**Smithville**—pop pl (2) WV-2
Smithville Acad—school GA-3
Smithville Airfield—airport NJ-2
Smithville Apothecary—hist pl NJ-2
Smithville Attendance Center—school MS-4
Smithville Baptist Ch—church AL-4
Smithville Baptist Ch—church MS-4
Smithville Canal—canal AZ-5
Smithville (CCD)—cens area GA-3
Smithville (CCD)—cens area TN-4
Smithville (CCD)—cens area TX-5
Smithville Cem—cemetery IL-6
Smithville Cem—cemetery MS-4
Smithville Cem—cemetery NH-1
Smithville Cem—cemetery SC-3
Smithville Cem—cemetery TX-5
Smithville Center—locale NY-2
Smithville Ch—church AL-4
Smithville Ch—church GA-3
Smithville Ch—church MS-4
Smithville Ch—church OH-6
Smithville Ch—church SC-3
Smithville Ch (historical)—church AL-4
Smithville Ch of Christ—church MS-4
Smithville Commercial Hist Dist—hist pl TX-5
Smithville Cumberland Presbyterian Ch—church TN-4
Smithville Dam—dam MO-7
Smithville Dam—dam NJ-2
Smithville Dam—locale MI-6
Smithville Ditch—stream MD-2
Smithville Division—civil TN-4
Smithville Female Acad (historical)—school TN-4
**Smithville Flats**—pop pl NY-2
Smithville Freewill Baptist Ch—church MS-4
Smithville High School MS-4
Smithville Hist Dist—hist pl NJ-2
Smithville (historical P.O.)—locale MA-1
Smithville Lake—reservoir MD-2
Smithville Lake—reservoir MO-7
Smithville Lake—reservoir NJ-2
Smithville Lake State Wildlife Area—park MO-7
Smithville Lookout Tower—locale GA-3
Smithville Methodist Ch—church MS-4
Smithville Municipal Airp—airport TN-4
Smithville-North Scituate—hist pl RI-1
Smithville Pond NJ-2
Smithville Post Office—building TN-4
Smithville Post Office (historical)—building AL-4
Smithville Post Office (historical)—building PA-2
Smithville Rec Area—park MS-4
Smithville Sch—school SC-3
Smithville Sch—school TN-4
Smithville Seminary—hist pl RI-1
Smithville (Site)—locale UT-8
**Smithville (sta.) (Weilersville)**—pop pl OH-6
**Smithville (Town of)**—pop pl NY-2
**Smithville Township**—pop pl SD-7
Smithville (Township of)—fmr MCD NC-3
Smithville United Methodist Ch—church TN-4
Smith Warehouse—hist pl TX-5
Smith Wash—stream (4) AZ-5
Smith Water Canyon—valley CA-9
Smith Waterhole—reservoir NM-5
Smith Watershed AL-4
Smith Well—locale NM-5
Smith Well—well (2) AZ-5
Smith Well—well NV-8
Smith Well—well (5) NM-5
Smith Well—well OR-9
Smith Wells—well OR-9
Smith-Whitford House—hist pl NC-3
Smithwick—locale NC-3
Smithwick—locale TX-5
**Smithwick**—pop pl SD-7
Smithwick Cem—cemetery SD-7
Smithwick Channel—channel MI-6
Smithwick Creek—stream GA-3
Smithwick Creek—stream NC-3
Smithwick Island—island MI-6
Smithwick Landing—locale NC-3
Smithwicks Lake—lake MN-6
Smithwick Township—civil SD-7
Smith-Wilkey Cem—cemetery TN-4
Smith-Wills Stadium—park MS-4
Smith Windmill—locale CO-8
Smith Windmill—locale (8) NM-5
Smith Windmill—locale (2) TX-5
**Smithwood**—pop pl TN-4
Smithwood Baptist Ch—church TN-4
Smith Wood Brook NY-2
Smithwood Ch—church NC-3
Smith Woods—woods IL-6
Smithwood Sch—school TN-4
Smithy Cem—cemetery SC-3
Smithy Creek—stream (2) ID-8
Smithy Mtn—summit CO-8
Smithys Lake NE-7
Smitt Cem—cemetery MO-7
Smittie Ridge—ridge OR-9
Smittle Cave—cave MO-7
Smittle Creek—stream CA-9
Smittle Sch—school MO-7
Smitty—uninc pl TX-5
Smitty Branch—stream TN-4
Smitty Coulee—valley MT-8
Smitty Hollow AL-4
Smitty Spring—spring AZ-5
Smitty Windmill—locale TX-5
Smiy Lake MN-6
Smizer Gulch—valley CO-8
Smoak Bridge—bridge GA-3
Smoak Cem—cemetery GA-3
**Smooks**—pop pl SC-3
Smooks (CCD)—cens area SC-3
Smoot Island MN-6
**Smock**—pop pl PA-2
Smock, Matthias, House—hist pl NJ-2
Smock Creek—stream IN-6
Smock Creek—stream KY-4
Smock Creek—stream WI-6
**Smock (historical)**—pop pl OR-9
Smock Memorial Bridge—bridge PA-2
Smock Prairie—flat OR-9
Smocks Ch—church KY-4
Smock Sch—school OR-9
**Smocks Corners**—pop pl NJ-2
Smock-Sluss Oil Field—oilfield KS-7
**Smockville**—pop pl IN-6
**Smoke Bend**—pop pl LA-4
Smoke Camp Knob—summit WV-2
Smoke Camp Run—stream WV-2
**Smoke Corner**—pop pl IN-6
Smoke Creek CO-8
Smoke Creek MT-8
Smoke Creek SD-7
**Smoke Creek**—pop pl NV-8
Smoke Creek—stream AK-9
Smoke Creek—stream CA-9
Smoke Creek—stream (4) MT-8
Smoke Creek—stream NV-8
Smoke Creek—stream NY-2
Smoke Creek—stream WY-8
Smoke Creek Airstrip—airport NV-8
Smoke Creek Desert—plain NV-8
Smoke Creek Ranch—locale NV-8
Smoke Creek Rsvr—reservoir CA-9
Smoke Creek Rsvr—reservoir NV-8
Smoke Creek Spring—spring OR-9
Smoke Creek Station—locale NV-8
Smoke Ditch IN-6
Smoke Draft—valley (2) PA-2
Smoke Hill—summit MA-1
**Smoke Hole**—pop pl WV-2
Smoke Hole—valley WV-2
Smoke Hole Cave—cave WV-2
Smoke Hole Caverns—cave WV-2
Smoke Hole Ch—church WV-2
Smoke Hole Run—stream PA-2
Smoke Hole Tank—reservoir AZ-5
Smokehouse—locale ID-8
Smokehouse Bay—bay (2) FL-3
Smokehouse Bluff—cliff AR-4
Smokehouse Branch—stream GA-3
Smokehouse Branch—stream WV-2
Smokehouse Campground—locale CO-8
Smokehouse Cove—bay MD-2
Smokehouse Cove—bay NC-3
Smokehouse Creek—gut FL-3
Smokehouse Creek—stream (3) CA-9
Smokehouse Creek—stream (4) FL-3
Smokehouse Creek—stream NC-3
Smokehouse Creek—stream TX-5
Smokehouse Crossing—locale FL-3
Smokehouse Fork—stream WV-2
Smokehouse Hollow—valley MO-7
Smokehouse Hollow Trail—trail PA-2
Smokehouse Island—island FL-3
Smokehouse Jam—flat GA-3
Smokehouse Knob—summit GA-3
Smokehouse Lake—lake FL-3
Smokehouse Mtn—summit WY-8
Smokehouse on Riverside Creek—hist pl KY-4
Smokehouse Point—cape GA-3
Smokehouse Pond—lake FL-3
Smokehouse Ridge—ridge CA-9
Smokehouse Ridge—ridge WV-2
Smokehouse Run—stream PA-2
Smoke-in-Hole Creek—stream MT-8
Smoke Jumper Hot Springs—spring WY-8
Smoke Lake WI-6
Smoke Lake—lake MN-6
Smoke Lake—lake WI-6
Smoke Lateral—canal ID-8
Smokeless PA-2
Smokeless—locale WV-2
**Smokeless**—pop pl PA-2
Smokeless Post Office (historical)—building PA-2
Smokemont (Campground)—locale NC-3
Smoke Mtn—summit AK-9
Smoke Mtn—summit NC-3
Smoke Neck AL-4
Smokeout Canyon Rsvr—reservoir OR-9
Smoke Point—cape MD-2
Smoke Point—cape TX-5
Smoker Canyon—valley CA-9
Smoker Gulch—valley SD-7
**Smoke Rise**—pop pl AL-4
**Smoke Rise**—pop pl NJ-2
**Smokerise**—pop pl TN-4
**Smoke Rise**—pop pl TN-4
Smoke Rise Park—park AZ-5
**Smoke Rise (subdivision)**—pop pl AL-4
**Smokerise (subdivision)**—pop pl NC-3
Smoke Rock Creek—stream AR-4
Smoke Rock Mtn—summit AR-4
Smokers Canyon—valley OR-9
Smokers Point—cape MI-6
Smoke Run—locale PA-2
Smokerun Post Office (historical)—building PA-2
Smoke Run (RR name for Smokerun) other PA-2
**Smokerun (RR name Smoke Run)**—pop pl PA-2
Smoke Sch (abandoned)—school PA-2
Smokes Corners—locale SC-3
Smokes Creek NY-2
Smokeshire Cem—cemetery VT-1
**Smoke Signal**—pop pl AZ-5
Smoke Signal Point—cliff AZ-5
Smoke Signal Spring—spring AZ-5
Smoke Spring OR-9
Smokestack Hollow—valley OK-5
Smokestack Hollow—valley PA-2
Smokestack Rock—pillar NE-7
Smoketown MD-2
Smoketown PA-2
Smoketown—locale OH-6
Smoketown—locale (3) PA-2
**Smoketown**—pop pl MD-2
**Smoketown**—pop pl (2) PA-2
Smoketown Airp—airport PA-2
Smoketown Elem Sch—school PA-2
Smoketown Sch—school PA-2
**Smoke Tree**—pop pl CA-9
Smoke Tree—uninc pl CA-9
Smoke Tree Canyon—valley CA-9
Smoketree Elem Sch—school AZ-5
Smoke Tree Forest—locale CA-9
Smoke Tree Sch—school CA-9
Smoketree Valley—valley CA-9
Smoketree Wash—stream AZ-5
Smoke Tree Wash—stream AZ-5
Smoke Tree Wash—stream (2) CA-9
Smoke Tree Well—well CA-9
Smokey KS-7
Smokey Bear Hill—summit NM-5
Smokey Bear Spring—spring OR-9
Smokey Bear State For—forest MN-6
Smokey Branch MO-7
Smokey Butte—summit ND-7
Smokey Butte Creek MT-8
Smokey Canyon—valley NV-8
Smokey Creek—stream ID-8
Smokey Creek—stream KY-4
Smokey Creek—stream MT-8
Smokey Dome ID-8
Smokey Hill KS-7
Smokey Hole Cave—cave AL-4
Smokey Hollow—valley OH-6
Smokey Hollow Swamp—swamp MI-6
Smokey Lake ND-7
Smokey Lake—lake AK-9
Smokey Lake—lake CA-9
Smokey Lake—lake ID-8
Smokey Lake—lake SC-3
Smokey Lake—reservoir OR-9
Smokey Mountain UT-8
Smokey Mountain WA-9
Smokey Mtn—summit PA-2
Smokey Point NY-2
**Smokey Point**—pop pl WA-9
Smokey Post Office (historical)—building TN-4
Smokey Row TN-4
Smokey Spring—spring (2) NV-8
Smokey Spring—spring UT-8
Smokeys Vega—flat TX-5
Smokey Tank—reservoir AZ-5
Smokey Valley—valley WA-9
Smoki Museum—building AZ-5
Smoking Point—cape NY-2
Smoky KS-7
Smoky Bear Campground—locale ID-8
Smoky Bear Lodge—locale ID-8
Smoky Bend—bend TN-4
Smoky Bend—bend TX-5
Smoky (blast center)—locale NV-8
Smoky Branch MO-7
Smoky Branch—stream (3) TN-4
Smoky Branch—stream WV-2
Smoky Branch Boat Launching Ramp—locale TN-4
Smoky Butte—summit MT-8
Smoky Butte—summit ND-7
Smoky Butte—summit OR-9
Smoky Butte Creek MT-8
Smoky Butte Creek—stream MT-8
**Smoky Butte Township**—pop pl ND-7
Smoky Cabin—locale CA-9
Smoky Camp Brook—stream NH-1
Smoky Camp Creek—stream CA-9
Smoky Canyon—valley ID-8
Smoky Canyon—valley NV-8
Smoky Cave—cave AL-4
Smoky Corners—locale OH-6
Smoky Cove—valley NC-3
Smoky Cove Ch—church LA-4
Smoky Creek CO-8
Smoky Creek ID-8
Smoky Creek TN-4
Smoky Creek—stream (2) CA-9
Smoky Creek—stream ID-8
Smoky Creek—stream KY-4
Smoky Creek—stream MO-7
Smoky Creek—stream (2) MT-8
Smoky Creek—stream NC-3
Smoky Creek—stream OH-6
Smoky Creek—stream (2) OR-9
Smoky Creek—stream TN-4
Smoky Creek—stream TX-5
Smoky Creek—stream WA-9
Smoky Creek Campground—locale WA-9
Smoky Creek Ch—church TN-4
Smoky Creek Sch—school TN-4

Smoky Creek (Site)—*locale* TX-5
Smoky Creek (Township of)—*fmr MCD* NC-3
Smoky Dome—*summit* ID-8
Smoky Dome Canyon—*valley* ID-8
Smoky Dome Lakes—*lake* ID-8
Smoky Drain—*stream* WV-2
Smoky Draw—*valley* TX-5
Smoky Forest Camp—*locale* ID-8
*Smoky Fork* WV-2
Smoky Fork—*stream* KY-4
Smoky Gap—*gap* NC-3
Smoky Gap—*gap* WY-8
Smoky Gap Oil Field—*oilfield* WY-8
Smoky Hammock—*island* FL-3
*Smoky Hill* KS-7
**Smoky Hill**—*pop pl* KS-7
Smoky Hill—*summit* (2) WI-6
Smoky Hill AFB—*military* KS-7
Smoky Hill AFB Bombing Range—*military* KS-7
*Smoky Hill Bluffs* KS-7
*Smoky Hill Buttes* KS-7
Smoky Hill Buttes—*range* KS-7
Smoky Hill Cem—*cemetery* (2) KS-7
Smoky Hill Flowage—*reservoir* WI-6
Smoky Hill River—*stream* CO-8
Smoky Hill River—*stream* KS-7
Smoky Hills—*range* KS-7
Smoky Hills—*ridge* NV-8
Smoky Hill Sch—*school* CO-8
Smoky Hill Sch—*school* PA-2
Smoky Hill Sch—*school* WI-6
Smoky Hills Lookout Tower—*locale* MN-6
Smoky Hills State For—*forest* MN-6
**Smoky Hill Township**—*pop pl* (3) KS-7
Smoky Hill Trail—*trail* CO-8
*Smoky Hollow* NY-2
*Smoky Hollow* UT-8
Smoky Hollow—*area* AK-9
Smoky Hollow—*bay* WA-9
**Smoky Hollow**—*pop pl* MO-7
Smoky Hollow—*valley* AZ-5
Smoky Hollow—*valley* AR-4
Smoky Hollow—*valley* IN-6
Smoky Hollow—*valley* IA-7
Smoky Hollow—*valley* (3) KY-4
Smoky Hollow—*valley* (3) MO-7
Smoky Hollow—*valley* (3) NY-2
Smoky Hollow—*valley* OR-9
Smoky Hollow—*valley* TN-4
Smoky Hollow—*valley* (2) UT-8
Smoky Hollow—*valley* WV-2
Smoky Hollow—*valley* WI-6
Smoky Hollow—*valley* WY-8
Smoky Hollow Lake—*lake* MN-6
Smoky Hollow Lake—*reservoir* GA-3
Smoky Hollow Mine—*mine* IA-7
Smoky Hollow Peak—*summit* WY-8
Smoky Hollow Rim—*cliff* OR-9
Smoky Hollow Tank—*reservoir* AZ-5
Smoky Hollow (Township of)—*civ div* MN-6
Smoky Island—*island* TN-4
Smoky Jack Campground—*locale* CA-9
Smoky Johnson Hill—*summit* MT-8
**Smoky Junction**—*pop pl* TN-4
Smoky Junior Radio Tower—*tower* NV-8
Smoky Knob—*summit* KY-4
*Smoky Lake* CA-9
Smoky Lake—*lake* ID-8
Smoky Lake—*lake* MI-6
Smoky Lake—*lake* ND-7
Smoky Lake—*lake* SC-3
Smoky Lake—*lake* WI-6
Smoky Lake Sch Number 1—*school* ND-7
Smoky Lake Sch Number 2—*school* ND-7
Smoky Landing Dock—*locale* TN-4
Smoky Lane Ch—*church* AR-4
Smoky Lookout Tower—*locale* MT-8
Smoky Mountain Acad—*school* TN-4
*Smoky Mountain Caverns* TN-4
Smoky Mountain Christian Camp Lake—*reservoir* TN-4
Smoky Mountain Christian Camp Lake Dam—*dam* TN-4
Smoky Mountain Elem Sch—*school* NC-3
Smoky Mountain Elem Sch—*school* TN-4
Smoky Mountain Golf Course—*locale* TN-4
Smoky Mountain Ranch—*locale* TX-5
*Smoky Mountains* NV-8
Smoky Mountain Sch (historical)—*school* TN-4
Smoky Mtn—*summit* CA-9
Smoky Mtn—*summit* ID-8
Smoky Mtn—*summit* MT-8
Smoky Mtn—*summit* NC-3
Smoky Mtn—*summit* TN-4
Smoky Mtn—*summit* UT-8
Smoky Mtn—*summit* WA-9
Smoky Mtns—*range* ID-8
Smoky Ordinary—*locale* VA-3
Smoky Peak—*summit* (2) ID-8
Smoky Point—*cape* AK-9
Smoky Point—*cape* NY-2
Smoky Point—*cape* VA-3
Smoky Range—*range* MT-8
Smoky Ravine—*valley* CA-9
*Smoky Row Branch* KY-4
Smoky Row Ch—*church* VA-3
Smoky Row Creek—*stream* VA-3
Smokyrow Run—*stream* OH-6
Smoky Row Sch—*school* IL-6
Smoky Row Sch—*school* MO-7
Smoky Run—*stream* OH-6
Smoky Run—*stream* PA-2
Smoky Run—*stream* SD-7
Smoky Run—*stream* (2) TN-4
Smoky Senior Radio Tower—*tower* NV-8
Smoky Shoals—*bar* TN-4
**Smoky (Smoky Ordinary)**—*pop pl* VA-3
Smoky Spring—*spring* ID-8
Smoky Spring—*spring* NM-5
Smoky Spring—*spring* OR-9
Smoky Spring—*spring* TX-5
**Smoky Township**—*pop pl* KS-7
*Smoky Valley* NV-8
Smoky Valley—*locale* KY-4
Smoky Valley—*valley* PA-2
Smoky Valley—*valley* TN-4
Smoky Valley Cem—*cemetery* KY-4
Smoky Valley Ch—*church* KY-4
Smoky Valley Chapel—*church* NC-3
Smoky Valley Forest Service Facility—*locale* NV-8
Smoky Valley Fork—*stream* KY-4
Smoky Valley Lake—*reservoir* KY-4
*Smoky Valley N. E. Summit* NV-8
Smoky Valley Roller Mill—*hist pl* KS-7
Smoky Valley Sch (historical)—*school* NV-8
Smoky View Campground—*locale* TN-4
**Smoky View Estates**—*pop pl* TN-4
**Smoky View Township**—*pop pl* KS-7
**Smolan**—*pop pl* KS-7
Smolan Cem—*cemetery* KS-7
**Smolan Township**—*pop pl* KS-7
Smole Sawmill—*locale* CO-8
Smolich Island—*island* MN-6
Smolloron Spring—*spring* CA-9
Smook Cem—*cemetery* NC-3
Smoot—*locale* TX-5
**Smoot**—*pop pl* UT-8
**Smoot**—*pop pl* WV-2
**Smoot**—*pop pl* WY-8
Smoot, Reed, House—*hist pl* UT-8
Smoot, Richmond Kelley, House—*hist pl* TX-5
Smoot Bluff—*cliff* TN-4
Smoot Branch—*stream* AL-4
Smoot Branch—*stream* WV-2
Smoot Cem—*cemetery* IL-6
Smoot Cem—*cemetery* MO-7
Smoot Cem—*cemetery* WY-8
Smootch Branch—*stream* VA-3
*Smoot Creek* OR-9
Smoot Creek—*stream* KY-4
Smoot Creek—*stream* MT-8
Smoot Ditch—*canal* MT-8
*Smoot Farm Estates* UT-8
**Smoot Farm Estates (Plat A)**—*pop pl* UT-8
**Smoot Farm Estates (Plat B-D)**—*pop pl* UT-8
Smooth Butte—*summit* AZ-5
Smooth Canyon—*valley* CO-8
Smooth Canyon—*valley* NV-8
Smooth Canyon—*valley* (3) UT-8
Smooth Canyon—*valley* WY-8
Smooth Canyon Spring—*spring* NV-8
Smooth Channel—*channel* AK-9
*Smoothers Creek* IN-6
Smoothface Mtn—*summit* AK-9
Smooth Gulch—*valley* (2) OR-9
Smooth Gulch—*valley* WA-9
Smooth Hollow—*valley* OR-9
Smooth Hollow—*valley* UT-8
**Smooth Hummocks**—*pop pl* MA-1
Smoot Hill—*summit* WA-9
Smoothingiron Branch—*stream* TX-5
Smoothing Iron Camp—*locale* NM-5
Smoothingiron Cem—*cemetery* TX-5
Smoothing Iron Mesa—*summit* NM-5
Smoothing Iron Mtn—*summit* TX-5
Smoothingiron Mtn—*summit* TX-5
Smoothing Iron Ridge—*ridge* WA-9
Smoothing Iron Rsvr—*reservoir* CO-8
Smooth Iron Pond—*lake* FL-3
Smooth Knoll—*summit* AZ-5
Smooth Knoll—*summit* UT-8
Smooth Knoll Rsvr—*reservoir* UT-8
Smooth Mtn—*summit* AK-9
Smoot Hollow—*valley* MO-7
*Smooth Pond* MA-1
Smooth Ridge—*ridge* VA-3
Smooth Ridge—*ridge* WA-9
Smooth Ridge Trail—*trail* WA-9
Smoothrock Creek—*stream* WA-9
Smooth Rock Falls—*falls* UT-8
Smoothrock Hollow—*valley* KY-4
Smooth Rock Lick Run—*stream* WV-2
Smoothwire Creek—*stream* CA-9
Smoot Island—*island* MN-6
Smoot Lake—*lake* AZ-5
Smoot Lake—*lake* OH-6
Smoot Park—*park* NC-3
Smoot Park—*park* UT-8
Smoot Ranch—*locale* TX-5
Smoots—*locale* VA-3
Smoots Creek—*stream* KS-7
*Smootsdell* IN-6
Smoots Landing—*locale* VA-3
Smoots Mill (historical)—*locale* AL-4
Smoots Mill Run—*stream* VA-3
Smoots Point—*cape* MD-2
Smoots Pond—*reservoir* MD-2
Smoots Pond—*reservoir* VA-3
Smoots Pond Run—*stream* MD-2
Smoots Run—*stream* VA-3
Smoot Tank—*reservoir* TX-5
Smoot Theater—*hist pl* WV-2
Smorgasbord Creek—*stream* ID-8
Smotherman Cem—*cemetery* (3) TN-4
Smothers—*locale* VA-3
Smothers Cem—*cemetery* IL-6
*Smothers Creek* WV-2
Smothers Creek—*stream* IN-6
Smothers Creek—*stream* TX-5
Smothers Creek Cutoff—*canal* IN-6
Smothers Hill—*summit* FL-3
Smothers Lake—*reservoir* NC-3
Smothers Lake Dam—*dam* NC-3
Smothers Sch—*school* DC-2
Smouse, Winfield, House—*hist pl* IA-7
Smouse Mesa—*summit* NM-5
Smouse Mines—*mine* NM-5
Smouse Sch—*school* (2) IA-7
Smout Creek—*stream* ID-8
**Smout Subdivision**—*pop pl* UT-8
S Mowai—*area* HI-9
SMS Bldg—*hist pl* TX-5
SMS CORMORAN—*hist pl* GU-9
S M S Dam No. 1—*dam* OR-9
*S M S Rsvr* OR-9
S M S Rsvr Number One—*reservoir* OR-9
Smth Grove CAve Number Three—*cave* TN-4
S Mtn—*summit* AZ-5
Smudge Spring—*spring* NV-8
Smuggler Canyon—*valley* AZ-5
Smuggler Canyon—*valley* CA-9
*Smuggler Cove* HI-9
Smuggler Cove—*bay* AK-9
Smuggler Cove—*bay* OR-9
Smuggler Gulch—*valley* CA-9
Smuggler Gulch—*valley* WY-8
Smuggler Gulch Trail—*trail* WY-8
Smuggler Harbor—*bay* NY-2
Smuggler Mine—*hist pl* CO-8
Smuggler Mine—*mine* AZ-5
Smuggler Mine—*mine* (2) CO-8
Smuggler Mine—*mine* MT-8
Smuggler Mine—*mine* OR-9
Smuggler Mine—*mine* WY-8
Smuggler Mtn—*summit* CO-8
Smugglers Arroyo—*valley* TX-5
Smugglers Bayou—*bay* TX-5
Smugglers Canyon—*valley* AZ-5
Smugglers Cave—*cave* CA-9
Smugglers Cave—*cave* VT-1
*Smugglers Cove* HI-9
*Smugglers Cove* OR-9
Smugglers Cove—*bay* (2) AK-9
Smugglers Cove—*bay* CA-9
Smugglers Cove—*bay* ME-1
Smugglers Cove—*bay* MS-4
Smugglers Cove—*bay* (2) WA-9
Smugglers Creek—*stream* AK-9
Smugglers Ditch—*canal* CO-8
Smugglers Gap—*gap* (3) TX-5
Smuggler Shaft—*mine* CO-8
Smugglers Lake—*lake* AK-9
Smuggler Slough—*stream* WA-9
Smugglers Notch—*gap* VT-1
Smugglers Pass—*gap* TX-5
*Smugglers Point* CA-9
Smuggler Tunnel—*tunnel* UT-8
Smuggler-Union Hydroelectric Power Plant—*hist pl* CO-8
Smuggles Notch—*other* VT-1
Smugs Ria—*stream* MA-1
Smuin Gulch—*valley* CO-8
**Smullton**—*pop pl* PA-2
Smullton Gap—*gap* PA-2
*Smulton* PA-2
Smumey—*locale* LA-4
Smurr—*locale* AZ-5
S Murray Ridge Cem—*cemetery* OH-6
Smut Branch—*stream* GA-3
Smute Canyon—*valley* KS-7
*Smut Eye* AL-4
Smuteye—*locale* AL-4
**Smut Eye**—*pop pl* AL-4
Smuteye Lake—*reservoir* AL-4
Smuteye Pond—*dam* AL-4
Smuthers Creek—*stream* TN-4
Smuthers Ravine—*valley* CA-9
Smut Hollow—*valley* NY-2
Smut Hollow—*valley* PA-2
Smutty Bay—*swamp* FL-3
Smutty Hollow—*valley* NH-1
*Smutty Nose Island* ME-1
Smutty Nose Island—*island* ME-1
Smuttynose Island—*island* (2) ME-1
Smutty Sweet Gum Creek—*stream* FL-3
Smutz Canyon—*valley* NE-7
Smutzlar Siding—*locale* IL-6
Smyer—*locale* AL-4
**Smyer**—*pop pl* TX-5
Smyer Lake Dam Number Two—*dam* AL-4
Smyer Oil Field—*oilfield* TX-5
Smyers Lake Dam Number One—*dam* AL-4
**Smyerstown**—*pop pl* PA-2
Smylie Cem—*cemetery* MS-4
*Smyna Church* AL-4
**Smyre**—*pop pl* NC-3
Smyre Creek—*stream* NC-3
Smyres Cem—*cemetery* NC-3
Smyres Chapel—*church* NC-3
Smyrles Cem—*cemetery* SC-3
Smyrna—*locale* (2) AR-4
Smyrna—*locale* (2) MS-4
Smyrna—*locale* NE-7
Smyrna—*locale* PA-2
Smyrna—*locale* TN-4
Smyrna—*locale* (2) TX-5
Smyrna—*locale* WA-9
**Smyrna**—*pop pl* (2) AL-4
**Smyrna**—*pop pl* DE-2
**Smyrna**—*pop pl* FL-3
**Smyrna**—*pop pl* GA-3
**Smyrna**—*pop pl* (2) IN-6
**Smyrna**—*pop pl* IA-7
**Smyrna**—*pop pl* KY-4
**Smyrna**—*pop pl* MI-6
**Smyrna**—*pop pl* NY-2
**Smyrna**—*pop pl* NC-3
**Smyrna**—*pop pl* OH-6
**Smyrna**—*pop pl* (2) SC-3
**Smyrna**—*pop pl* (4) TN-4
**Smyrna**—*pop pl* TX-5
Smyrna Airp—*airport* DE-2
Smyrna Airp—*airport* TN-4
*Smyrna Baptist Ch* TN-4
Smyrna Baptist Ch—*church* (2) FL-3
Smyrna Baptist Ch—*church* TN-4
Smyrna Baptist Ch (historical)—*church* AL-4
*Smyrna Baptist Church* AL-4
*Smyrna Baptist Church* MS-4
Smyrna Baptist Church—*hist pl* SC-3
Smyrna Bench—*bench* WA-9
Smyrna Branch—*stream* AR-4
Smyrna Branch—*stream* NC-3
Smyrna Branch Sch—*school* NC-3
Smyrna (CCD)—*cens area* DE-2
Smyrna (CCD)—*cens area* GA-3
Smyrna (CCD)—*cens area* TN-4
*Smyrna Cem* MS-4
Smyrna Cem—*cemetery* (2) AL-4
Smyrna Cem—*cemetery* AR-4
Smyrna Cem—*cemetery* IL-6
Smyrna Cem—*cemetery* IA-7
Smyrna Cem—*cemetery* KY-4
Smyrna Cem—*cemetery* (7) MS-4
Smyrna Cem—*cemetery* OH-6
Smyrna Cem—*cemetery* OR-9
Smyrna Cem—*cemetery* SC-3
Smyrna Cem—*cemetery* (6) TN-4
Smyrna Cem—*cemetery* (3) TX-5
Smyrna Center—*locale* ME-1
*Smyrna Ch* AL-4
Smyrna Ch—*church* (7) AL-4
Smyrna Ch—*church* (8) AR-4
Smyrna Ch—*church* (12) GA-3
Smyrna Ch—*church* (2) IN-6
Smyrna Ch—*church* IA-7
Smyrna Ch—*church* KY-4
Smyrna Ch—*church* (2) LA-4
Smyrna Ch—*church* (5) MS-4
Smyrna Ch—*church* (3) MO-7
Smyrna Ch—*church* (10) NC-3
Smyrna Ch—*church* OR-9
Smyrna Ch—*church* PA-2
Smyrna Ch—*church* (8) SC-3
Smyrna Ch—*church* (10) TN-4
Smyrna Ch—*church* (2) TX-5
Smyrna Ch—*church* (4) VA-3
Smyrna Ch (historical)—*church* MS-4
Smyrna Ch (historical)—*church* TN-4
Smyrna Ch of Christ—*church* TN-4
Smyrna Christian Sch—*school* DE-2
Smyrna Church Cem—*cemetery* TX-5
Smyrna Community Center—*locale* AL-4
Smyrna Creek—*stream* FL-3
Smyrna Creek—*stream* KY-4
Smyrna Creek—*stream* NC-3
Smyrna Division—*civil* TN-4
Smyrna Elem Sch—*school* DE-2
Smyrna Elem Sch—*school* NC-3
Smyrna Grove Ch—*church* NC-3
Smyrna Hill—*summit* AL-4
Smyrna Hist Dist—*hist pl* DE-2
Smyrna HS—*school* DE-2
Smyrna HS (historical)—*school* MS-4
Smyrna Landing—*locale* DE-2
Smyrna Lookout Tower—*locale* TN-4
Smyrna Methodist Ch (historical)—*church* (2) AL-4
Smyrna Methodist Ch (historical)—*church* MS-4
*Smyrna Methodist Church* AL-4
**Smyrna Mills**—*pop pl* ME-1
Smyrna MS—*school* DE-2
Smyrna North Elem Sch—*school* DE-2
*Smyrna Presbyterian Ch* MS-4
Smyrna Presbyterian Ch—*church* MS-4
Smyrna Primitive Baptist Ch (historical)—*church* MS-4
*Smyrna River* DE-2
Smyrna River—*stream* DE-2
**Smyrna Road Homes (subdivision)**—*pop pl* TN-4
Smyrna Sch—*school* AR-4
Smyrna Sch—*school* KY-4
Smyrna Sch (historical)—*school* MO-7
Smyrna Sch (historical)—*school* (6) TN-4
*Smyrna School* AL-4
Smyrna Shop Ctr—*locale* FL-3
Smyrna Spring Branch—*stream* TN-4
*Smyrna Station* DE-2
Smyrna Substation—*other* CA-9
**Smyrna (Town of)**—*pop pl* ME-1
**Smyrna (Town of)**—*pop pl* NY-2
Smyrna (Township of)—*fmr MCD* AR-4
Smyrna (Township of)—*fmr MCD* (2) NC-3
**Smyrna (Township of)**—*pop pl* IN-6
Smyser Elem Sch (abandoned)—*school* PA-2
Smyser (RR name for Seven Valleys)—*other* PA-2
Smyser Sch—*school* IL-6
*Smyser School* PA-2
Smyser Station—*locale* PA-2
Smysor Sch—*school* IL-6
**Smyth**—*pop pl* TX-5
Smyth, Andrew, House—*hist pl* TX-5
Smyth, Dennis A., House—*hist pl* UT-8
Smyth Branch—*stream* VA-3
Smyth Cem—*cemetery* KY-4
Smyth Cem—*cemetery* OR-9
Smyth Cem—*cemetery* TN-4
Smyth Chapel—*church* VA-3
**Smyth (County)**—*pop pl* VA-3
Smyth Creek—*stream* OR-9
Smyth Crossing—*locale* TX-5
Smyth Dam—*dam* OR-9
*Smythe* IN-6
**Smythe**—*pop pl* IN-6
Smythe (historical)—*locale* AL-4
Smythe Ranch—*locale* TX-5
*Smythers Creek* WV-2
Smythe Sch—*school* CA-9
Smythe Sch—*school* IL-6
Smythe Sch—*school* TX-5
Smythe Trail—*trail* ID-8
Smyth Gap—*gap* VA-3
Smyth Hill—*summit* GA-3
*Smyth-Inseln* MP-9
*Smyth Islands* MP-9
Smyth Lake—*lake* MN-6
*Smyth Point* ME-1
Smyth Quarry—*mine* TX-5
Smyth Ranch—*locale* OR-9
Smyth Road Sch—*school* NH-1
Smyth (RR name for Balfour)—*other* NC-3
Smyth Rsvr—*reservoir* OR-9
**Smyths**—*pop pl* UT-8
Smyth Sch—*school* SD-7
Smyths Chapel—*church* NC-3
Smyth Station—*locale* NC-3
Smyth Station—*locale* TX-5
Smyth Tank—*reservoir* TX-5
Smyth Tower—*hist pl* NH-1
Smyth Wells (flowing)—*well* OR-9
Snabel Creek—*stream* OR-9
Snable, Andrew, House—*hist pl* NJ-2
Snackenbury Creek—*stream* CA-9
Snack Lake—*lake* MN-6
*Snacks* IN-6
**Snacks**—*pop pl* IN-6
Snaden Island—*island* CA-9
Snaden Slough—*stream* CA-9
Snadon Bluff—*cliff* MO-7
Snadon Ford—*locale* MO-7
Snadon Hollow—*valley* MO-7
*Snady Creek* TX-5
Snafi Tank—*reservoir* NM-5
Snafu Tank—*reservoir* AZ-5
Snag Boat Bend—*bend* OR-9
Snag Branch—*stream* MO-7
Snag Branch—*stream* TN-4
Snag Canyon—*valley* WA-9
Snag Cove Campground—*locale* WA-9
*Snag Creek* WY-8
Snag Creek—*stream* (2) AK-9
Snag Creek—*stream* ID-8
Snag Creek—*stream* IL-6
Snag Creek—*stream* IA-7
Snag Creek—*stream* KY-4
Snag Creek—*stream* (2) WA-9
Snag Creek—*stream* WV-2
Snag Creek—*stream* WY-8
Snag Creek Site (15BK2)—*hist pl* KY-4
Snag Creek Trail—*trail* WA-9
Snage Canyon—*valley* UT-8
Snag Fork—*stream* KY-4
Snaggletooth—*summit* CA-9
Snag Gulch—*valley* MT-8
Snaggy Bald—*summit* NC-3
Snaggy Bald Ridge—*ridge* NC-3
Snaggy Bar—*bar* TN-4
Snaggy Basin—*bay* TN-4
Snaggy Bend—*bend* OR-9
Snaggy Bend—*bend* WI-6
Snaggy Bend Bar—*bar* OR-9
Snaggy Gulch—*valley* MT-8
Snaggy Island—*island* TN-4
Snaggy Lake—*lake* AR-4
Snaggy Lake—*lake* LA-4
Snaggy Lake—*swamp* LA-4
Snaggy Lead—*ridge* GA-3
Snaggy Mtn—*summit* MD-2
Snaggy Mtn—*summit* NC-3
Snaggy Mtn—*summit* TN-4
Snaggy Mtn—*summit* WV-2
Snaggy Opening—*locale* TN-4
Snaggy Point—*summit* NC-3
Snaggy Ridge—*ridge* PA-2
Snaggy Towhead—*island* TN-4
Snag Harbor—*bay* FL-3
Snag Hill—*summit* (2) CA-9
Snag Hollow—*valley* KS-7
Snag Hollow—*valley* MT-8
Snag Hollow—*valley* VA-3
*Snag Island* OR-9
Snag Island—*island* (2) AK-9
Snag Island—*island* CA-9
Snag Island Jetty—*dam* OR-9
Snag Islands—*island* OR-9
Snag Islands—*island* WA-9
*Snag Island Spit* OR-9
*Snag Lake* TX-5
Snag Lake—*lake* AL-4
Snag Lake—*lake* (2) AK-9
Snag Lake—*lake* AR-4
Snag Lake—*lake* (3) CA-9
Snag Lake—*lake* IL-6
Snag Lake—*lake* (2) LA-4
Snag Lake—*lake* NY-2
Snag Lake—*lake* OK-5
Snag Lake—*lake* OR-9
Snag Lake—*lake* (4) TX-5
Snag Lake—*lake* (2) WI-6
Snag Lake Campground—*locale* CA-9
Snag Lake Dam—*dam* AL-4
Snag Mtn—*summit* TN-4
Snag Point—*cape* AK-9
Snag Point—*cape* FL-3
*Snag Pond* ME-1
Snag Pond—*lake* TX-5
Snag Pond—*reservoir* PA-2
Snag Ridge Fork—*stream* KY-4
Snag Rsvr—*reservoir* CO-8
Snag Slough—*stream* IA-7
Snag Spring—*spring* AZ-5
Snag Spring—*spring* (2) OR-9
Snagtooth Creek—*stream* WA-9
Snagtooth Mtn—*summit* WA-9
Snagtooth Ridge—*ridge* WA-9
Snahapish River—*stream* WA-9
Snailback Creek—*stream* OR-9
Snail Bay—*bay* LA-4
Snail Bayou—*gut* LA-4
Snail Canyon—*valley* (2) CA-9
Snail Canyon—*valley* OR-9
Snail Cave—*cave* (2) AL-4
Snail Creek—*stream* (2) IN-6
Snail Creek—*stream* OK-5
Snail Creek—*stream* OR-9
Snail Creek—*stream* VA-3
Snail Creek—*stream* WY-8
Snail Head—*summit* CA-9
Snail Hollow—*valley* UT-8
Snail Lake—*lake* (2) MN-6
Snail Lake Sch—*school* MN-6
Snail Point—*cape* AK-9
Snail Pond—*lake* ME-1
Snail Rock—*island* AK-9
Snail Shell Harbor—*bay* MI-6
Snailum Creek—*stream* TX-5
*Snairs Hollow* PA-2
Snake Alley—*hist pl* IA-7
Snake Alley Hist Dist—*hist pl* IA-7
Snake Arroyo—*stream* CO-8
Snake Bayou—*gut* (2) LA-4
Snake Bayou—*gut* MS-4
Snake Bayou—*gut* TX-5
Snake Bayou—*stream* FL-3
Snake Bayou—*stream* MS-4
Snake Bench—*bench* SD-7
Snake Bight—*bay* FL-3
Snake Bight Canal—*canal* FL-3
Snake Bight Channel—*channel* FL-3
Snake Bite (Township of)—*fmr MCD* NC-3
Snake Bluff—*cliff* MO-7
Snake Bluff Ch—*church* MO-7
Snake Bog—*swamp* ME-1
*Snake Branch* SC-3
*Snake Branch* TX-5
Snake Branch—*stream* AL-4
Snake Branch—*stream* AR-4
Snake Branch—*stream* GA-3
Snake Branch—*stream* IN-6
Snake Branch—*stream* (3) KY-4
Snake Branch—*stream* (4) NC-3
Snake Branch—*stream* (2) SC-3
Snake Branch—*stream* (2) TN-4
Snake Branch—*stream* TX-5
Snake Branch—*stream* VA-3
Snake Brook—*stream* (3) ME-1
Snake Brook—*stream* MA-1
Snake Brook—*stream* NY-2
Snake Brook Dam—*dam* MA-1
*Snake Brook Reservoir* MA-1
Snake Butte—*summit* AZ-5
Snake Butte—*summit* (2) MT-8
Snake Butte—*summit* (4) SD-7
*Snake Buttes* ND-7
Snake Butte Sch—*school* MT-8
Snake Butte Sch—*school* SD-7
Snake Butte Township (historical)—*civil* SD-7
*Snake Canal* FL-3
*Snake Canyon* CA-9
Snake Canyon—*valley* CO-8
Snake Canyon—*valley* NV-8
Snake Canyon—*valley* (2) UT-8
Snake Cave—*cave* AL-4
Snake Charmer Draw—*valley* WY-8
*Snake Coulee* MT-8
Snake Coulee—*valley* MT-8
*Snake Creek* AL-4
*Snake Creek* AR-4
*Snake Creek* CO-8
*Snake Creek* FL-3
*Snake Creek* GA-3
*Snake Creek* ID-8
*Snake Creek* KS-7
*Snake Creek* LA-4
*Snake Creek* NE-7
*Snake Creek* OK-5
*Snake Creek* OR-9
*Snake Creek* TX-5
Snake Creek—*fmr MCD* NE-7
Snake Creek—*gut* (3) FL-3
Snake Creek—*locale* SD-7
**Snake Creek**—*pop pl* VA-3
Snake Creek—*stream* (6) AL-4
Snake Creek—*stream* AK-9
Snake Creek—*stream* (2) AZ-5
Snake Creek—*stream* (4) AR-4
Snake Creek—*stream* (3) CA-9
Snake Creek—*stream* FL-3
Snake Creek—*stream* (2) GA-3
Snake Creek—*stream* (5) ID-8
Snake Creek—*stream* (4) IL-6
Snake Creek—*stream* (3) IN-6
Snake Creek—*stream* (3) IA-7
Snake Creek—*stream* (7) KS-7
Snake Creek—*stream* (3) KY-4
Snake Creek—*stream* LA-4
Snake Creek—*stream* (3) MI-6
Snake Creek—*stream* (3) MN-6
Snake Creek—*stream* (6) MS-4
Snake Creek—*stream* MO-7
Snake Creek—*stream* (4) MT-8
Snake Creek—*stream* (4) NE-7
Snake Creek*—*stream* NE-7
Snake Creek—*stream* NV-8
Snake Creek—*stream* NJ-2
Snake Creek—*stream* (4) NY-2
Snake Creek—*stream* (5) ND-7
Snake Creek—*stream* (10) OK-5
Snake Creek—*stream* (7) OR-9
Snake Creek—*stream* PA-2
Snake Creek—*stream* (6) SD-7
Snake Creek—*stream* (4) TN-4
Snake Creek—*stream* (11) TX-5
Snake Creek—*stream* (3) UT-8
Snake Creek—*stream* (2) VA-3
Snake Creek—*stream* WA-9
Snake Creek—*stream* (4) WI-6
Snake Creek—*stream* WY-8
Snake Creek—*uninc pl* FL-3
Snake Creek Brake—*swamp* MS-4
*Snake Creek Canal* FL-3
Snake Creek Canal—*canal* FL-3
Snake Creek Cave—*cave* NV-8
Snake Creek Cem—*cemetery* TX-5
Snake Creek Ch—*church* (3) OK-5
Snake Creek Cove Public Use Area—*park* OK-5
*Snake Creek Crossing* SD-7
Snake Creek Cutoff—*channel* FL-3
Snake Creek Ditch—*canal* MT-8
Snake Creek Forest Service Recreation Site—*locale* NV-8
Snake Creek Gap—*gap* GA-3
Snake Creek (historical)—*locale* AL-4
*Snake Creek - in part* SD-7
Snake Creek Loop—*trail* MT-8
*Snake Creek Marsh Public Hunting Area* IA-7
Snake Creek Natl Wildlife Ref—*park* ND-7
*Snake Creek Natl Wildlife Refuge* ND-7
Snake Creek Park—*park* (2) FL-3
Snake Creek Pass—*gap* MT-8
Snake Creek Pumping Station—*locale* ND-7
*Snake Creek Reservoir* ND-7
Snake Creek State Game Mngmt Area—*area* IA-7
Snake Creek State Public Fishing Area—*park* WI-6
Snake Creek Tank Number One—*reservoir* AZ-5
**Snake Creek Township**—*pop pl* ND-7
Snake Creek Tunnel—*tunnel* UT-8
*Snake Creek White River* AZ-5
Snake Dance—*locale* FL-3
Snake Den—*summit* RI-1
Snake Den—*valley* OR-9
Snake Den Bluff—*cliff* OK-5
Snakeden Branch—*stream* (2) IL-6
Snakeden Branch—*stream* MD-2
Snake Den Branch—*stream* TN-4
Snakeden Branch—*stream* VA-3
Snake Den Cem—*cemetery* TX-5
Snakeden Creek—*stream* TN-4
Snakeden Hollow—*valley* IL-6
Snake Den Hollow—*valley* MO-7
Snakeden Knob—*summit* NC-3
Snake Den Lake—*lake* OK-5
*Snake Den Ledge* RI-1
Snakeden Mtn—*summit* (2) NC-3
Snake Den Mtn—*summit* TN-4
Snake Den Mtn—*summit* VA-3
Snakeden Mtn—*summit* WV-2
Snake Den Point—*cliff* AZ-5
Snakeden Ridge—*ridge* NC-3
Snake Den Ridge—*ridge* NC-3
Snakeden Ridge—*ridge* (4) NC-3
Snake Den Ridge—*ridge* NC-3
Snakeden Ridge—*ridge* (2) TN-4
Snakeden Ridge—*ridge* VA-3
Snake Den Sch—*school* KS-7
Snake Den Tank—*reservoir* TX-5
Snakeden Top—*summit* NC-3
Snakeden Trail—*trail* WV-2
Snake Ditch—*canal* WY-8
Snake Division—*forest* NV-8
Snake Draw—*valley* AZ-5

Snake Draw—*valley* TX-5
Snake Eyes Spring—*spring* OR-9
Snakefeeder Branch—*stream* TN-4
Snake Flat—*flat* AZ-5
Snake Fork—*stream* WV-2
Snake Gap—*gap* AL-4
Snake Gulch—*valley* AZ-5
Snake Gulch—*valley* (2) CA-9
Snake Gulch—*valley* CO-8
Snake Gulch—*valley* MT-8
Snake Gulch—*valley* NM-5
Snake Gut—*gut* NC-3
Snakehead Creek—*stream* OR-9
Snakehead Point—*summit* CA-9
Snake Highway—*channel* MI-6
*Snake Hill* MA-1
*Snake Hill* NJ-2
*Snake Hill* VT-1
**Snake Hill**—*pop pl* NY-2
Snake Hill—*summit* (5) MA-1
Snake Hill—*summit* NJ-2
Snake Hill—*summit* (2) NM-5
Snake Hill—*summit* (6) NY-2
Snake Hill—*summit* ND-7
Snake Hill—*summit* OR-9
Snake Hill—*summit* PA-2
Snake Hill—*summit* (2) RI-1
Snake Hill—*summit* TX-5
Snake Hill—*summit* WY-8
Snakehill Channel—*channel* NY-2
Snake Hills—*other* NM-5
Snake Hills—*summit* MA-1
Snake Hole Creek—*stream* AR-4
Snake Hole Creek—*stream* NY-2
*Snake Hollow* IN-6
Snake Hollow—*valley* KY-4
Snake Hollow—*valley* NV-8
Snake Hollow—*valley* (3) OH-6
Snake Hollow—*valley* (2) TN-4
Snake Hollow—*valley* (2) TX-5
Snake Hollow—*valley* (2) VA-3
Snake Hollow—*valley* WV-2
Snake Hollow Mtn—*summit* VA-3
Snake Hollow Sch—*school* IA-7
Snake Hot Springs—*spring* WY-8
*Snake Island* NY-2
*Snake Island* NC-3
*Snake Island* FM-9
Snake Island—*island* AR-4
Snake Island—*island* CA-9
Snake Island—*island* (4) FL-3
Snake Island—*island* (2) LA-4
Snake Island—*island* (2) ME-1
Snake Island—*island* (2) MD-2
Snake Island—*island* MA-1
Snake Island—*island* (2) MI-6
Snake Island—*island* (2) MN-6
Snake Island—*island* (2) NY-2
Snake Island—*island* NC-3
Snake Island—*island* OH-6
Snake Island—*island* OK-5
Snake Island—*island* RI-1
Snake Island—*island* SC-3
Snake Island—*island* (3) TX-5
Snake Island—*island* VA-3
Snake Island—*island* (2) WI-6
Snake Island Branch—*stream* TN-4
Snake Island Ch—*church* AR-4
Snake Island Cove—*bay* TX-5
Snake Island Flat—*swamp* AR-4
Snake John Reef—*ridge* CO-8
Snake John Reef—*ridge* UT-8
Snake John Spring—*spring* UT-8
Snake John Wash—*valley* UT-8
Snake Key—*island* (3) FL-3
Snake Knob—*summit* AR-4
Snake Knob—*summit* GA-3
Snake Knob—*summit* (2) NC-3
Snake Knob—*summit* WV-2
*Snake Lake* CA-9
*Snake Lake* MN-6
Snake Lake—*lake* (2) AR-4
Snake Lake—*lake* (4) CA-9
Snake Lake—*lake* LA-4
Snake Lake—*lake* MN-6
Snake Lake—*lake* MT-8
Snake Lake—*lake* WA-9
Snake Lake—*lake* (5) WI-6
Snake Lake—*lake* WY-8
Snake Lake—*reservoir* CO-8
Snake Lake—*reservoir* KS-7
Snake Lake Park—*park* WA-9
Snake Lake Trail—*trail* WY-8
Snake Lake Valley—*valley* CA-9
Snake Lick Creek—*stream* KY-4
Snakel Ranch—*locale* TX-5
*Snakelum Point* WA-9
Snake Meadow—*flat* CA-9
Snake Meadow Brook—*stream* CT-1
Snake Meadow Brook—*stream* MA-1
Snake Meadow Hill—*summit* MA-1
Snake Meadow Pond—*lake* CT-1
Snake Mine (underground)—*mine* AL-4
*Snake Mountain* NV-8
Snake Mountain—*ridge* TN-4
Snake Mountain Tank—*reservoir* TX-5
Snake Mtn—*summit* AR-4
Snake Mtn—*summit* NY-2
Snake Mtn—*summit* NC-3
Snake Mtn—*summit* (2) OK-5
Snake Mtn—*summit* TX-5
Snake Mtn—*summit* VT-1
Snake Mtns—*range* NV-8
Snake Nation—*locale* GA-3
Snake Nation Mtn—*summit* GA-3
Snake Nation Sch—*school* GA-3
Snake Number Two Dam—*dam* AZ-5
Snake Oil Island—*island* NY-2
Snakeoil Island—*island* NY-2
Snake Pass—*gap* UT-8
Snake Pit—*basin* MT-8
Snake Point—*cape* FL-3
Snake Point—*cape* (2) ME-1
Snake Point—*cape* MI-6
Snakepoint Post Office (historical)—*building* TN-4
Snake Pond—*lake* (3) ME-1
Snake Pond—*lake* (3) MA-1
Snake Pond—*lake* (2) NH-1
Snake Pond—*lake* (3) NY-2
Snake Pond—*lake* TN-4
Snake Pond—*reservoir* AZ-5
Snake Pond Beach—*beach* MA-1
Snake Pond Ridge—*ridge* KY-4
Snake Ranch—*locale* NM-5
Snake Range—*range* NV-8
Snake Rapids—*rapids* MI-6
Snake Ravine—*valley* CA-9
Snake Ridge—*ridge* (3) AZ-5
Snake Ridge—*ridge* CA-9
Snake Ridge—*ridge* CO-8
Snake Ridge—*ridge* KY-4
Snake Ridge—*ridge* LA-4
Snake Ridge—*ridge* NY-2
Snake Ridge—*ridge* NC-3
Snake Ridge—*ridge* PA-2
Snake Ridge—*ridge* (2) TN-4
Snake Ridge—*ridge* WV-2
Snake Ridge Tank—*reservoir* (2) AZ-5
*Snake River* FL-3
*Snake River* WY-8
Snake River—*locale* WA-9
Snake River—*stream* (2) AK-9
Snake River—*stream* CA-9
Snake River—*stream* CO-8
Snake River—*stream* FL-3
Snake River—*stream* ID-8
Snake River—*stream* MA-1
Snake River—*stream* MI-6
Snake River—*stream* (4) MN-6
Snake River—*stream* NE-7
Snake River—*stream* OR-9
Snake River—*stream* WA-9
Snake River—*stream* WY-8
Snake River Archeol District—*hist pl* WA-9
Snake River Arm—*bay* CO-8
Snake River Bird of Prey Natural Area—*park* ID-8
Snake River Birds of Prey Area—*park* ID-8
Snake River Bridge—*hist pl* WA-9
*Snake River Canyon* OR-9
Snake River (CCD)—*cens area* WA-9
Snake River Ch—*church* MN-6
Snake River County Park—*park* MN-6
Snake River Falls—*falls* CO-8
Snake River Falls—*falls* NE-7
Snake River Fish Hatchery (Private)—*other* ID-8
Snake River HS—*school* ID-8
Snake River JHS—*school* ID-8
**Snake River Junction**—*pop pl* WA-9
Snake River Lookout Station—*locale* WY-8
Snake River Mine—*mine* OR-9
*Snake River Mountains* ID-8
Snake River Overlook—*locale* WY-8
Snake River Plain—*flat* ID-8
Snake River Plain—*plain* OR-9
*Snake River Range* ID-8
Snake River Range—*range* ID-8
Snake River Range—*range* WY-8
Snake River Ranger Station—*hist pl* ID-8
Snake River Ranger Station—*locale* ID-8
Snake River Ranger Station—*locale* WY-8
Snake River Recreation Site—*locale* WY-8
Snake River Slides Safety Rest Area—*locale* OR-9
Snake River State For—*forest* MN-6
Snake River Trail—*trail* WY-8
Snake River Valley Canal—*canal* ID-8
Snake Rock—*bar* WA-9
Snake Rock—*summit* CT-1
Snake Rocks—*summit* NY-2
Snakeroot Branch—*stream* WV-2
Snakeroot Cem—*cemetery* WV-2
Snake Rsvr—*reservoir* ID-8
Snake Run—*stream* IN-6
Snake Run—*stream* (2) KY-4
Snake Run—*stream* OH-6
Snake Run—*stream* (3) PA-2
Snake Run—*stream* (2) VA-3
Snake Run—*stream* (4) WV-2
Snake Run Ridge—*ridge* VA-3
Snake Run Sch—*school* NE-7
*Snake Slough* AR-4
Snake Slough—*gut* AR-4
Snake Slough—*gut* (2) CA-9
Snake Slough—*gut* KY-4
Snake Slough—*stream* TX-5
Snakes Pit—*cave* AL-4
Snake Spring—*spring* AZ-5
Snake Spring—*spring* (2) CA-9
Snake Spring—*spring* MA-1
Snake Spring—*spring* OR-9
Snake Spring Elem Sch—*school* PA-2
Snake Springs—*spring* AZ-5
Snake Springs—*spring* TX-5
Snake Springs Rest Area—*park* AZ-5
**Snake Spring (Township of)**—*pop pl* PA-2
Snake Spring Valley Ch—*church* PA-2
*Snakespring Valley Run* PA-2
Snake Spring Valley Run—*stream* PA-2
Snake Spring Valley Township—*civil* PA-2
Snake Spring Wash—*stream* AZ-5
Snake Spur—*ridge* TN-4
Snake Swamp—*stream* SC-3
Snake Swamp—*swamp* NY-2
Snake Tank—*reservoir* (3) AZ-5
Snake Tank—*reservoir* (4) NM-5
Snake Tank—*reservoir* (2) TX-5
Snake Tank Number One—*reservoir* AZ-5
Snake Tank Number Two—*reservoir* AZ-5
Snake Tongue—*stream* TN-4
Snaketooth Butte—*summit* OR-9
Snaketooth Way—*trail* OR-9
*Snaketown* AZ-5
Snaketown—*locale* AZ-5
Snake Track Tank—*reservoir* AZ-5
Snake Trail—*trail* MN-6
*Snake Valley* UT-8
Snake Valley—*basin* NV-8
Snake Valley—*valley* UT-8
Snake Valley—*valley* WV-2
Snake Well—*well* NM-5
Snake Well—*well* TX-5
Snake Windmill—*locale* NM-5
Snakey Futch Windmill—*locale* TX-5
Snakey Lake—*lake* MI-6
Snaking Road Gulch—*valley* CO-8
*Snaklum Point* WA-9
Snaky Canyon—*valley* ID-8
Snaky Windmill—*locale* NM-5
*Sna-nul-kwo* WA-9
Snap—*locale* KY-4
Snap—*locale* TX-5
Snap Balds—*summit* MO-7
*Snap Branch* WV-2
Snap Branch—*stream* NC-3
Snap Branch—*stream* SC-3
Snap Branch—*stream* TN-4
Snap Canyon—*valley* AZ-5
Snap Canyon—*valley* NM-5
Snap Canyon—*valley* UT-8
Snap Canyon Rapids—*rapids* UT-8
Snap Cem—*cemetery* TN-4
Snap Cem—*cemetery* TX-5
Snap Creek—*stream* MT-8
Snap Creek—*stream* WV-2
**Snap Creek Junction**—*pop pl* WV-2
Snap Draw—*valley* AZ-5
Snapfinger—*locale* GA-3
Snap Finger Branch—*stream* GA-3
Snapfinger Creek—*stream* GA-3
Snap Jack Creek—*stream* MI-6
Snap Jack Lake—*lake* MI-6
Snap Lodge Branch—*stream* VA-3
Snapneck Creek—*stream* KY-4
Snapneck Creek—*stream* TN-4
**Snap-N-Fox Farms Subdivision**—*pop pl* UT-8
*Snapp* NC-3
Snapp Branch—*stream* TN-4
Snapp Bridge—*bridge* TN-4
Snapp Cem—*cemetery* MO-7
Snapp Cem—*cemetery* (2) TN-4
Snapp Creek—*stream* IN-6
Snapp Creek—*stream* VA-3
Snapp Ditch Number Two—*canal* MT-8
Snapp Donegan Ditch—*canal* MT-8
Snapper Creek—*post sta* FL-3
Snapper Creek—*stream* AL-4
*Snapper Creek Canal* FL-3
Snapper Creek Canal Number C-100—*canal* FL-3
Snapper Creek Elem Sch—*school* FL-3
Snapper Creek Lake—*lake* FL-3
Snapper Creek Park—*park* FL-3
Snapper Cut—*channel* FL-3
*Snapper Number 1 Mine* AL-4
Snapper Point—*cape* FL-3
Snapper Ski Trail—*trail* NH-1
*Snappet* MA-1
**Snapp (Fleet)**—*pop pl* VA-3
Snapp House—*hist pl* KY-4
Snapp House—*hist pl* VA-3
Snapping Shoals—*locale* GA-3
Snapping Shoals Creek—*stream* GA-3
*Snapping Turtle Eggs Creek* IN-6
Snapping Turtle Run—*stream* OH-6
Snapp JHS—*school* NY-2
Snap Point—*cliff* AZ-5
Snap Point—*summit* OR-9
Snapps Branch—*stream* MO-7
Snapps Forge (historical)—*locale* TN-4
Snapp Spring—*spring* OR-9
Snapps Run—*stream* VA-3
Snap Rsvr—*reservoir* WY-8
Snapsburg Cem—*cemetery* MN-6
Snap Seep Tank—*reservoir* AZ-5
Snaps Island—*island* KY-4
Snap Spring—*spring* AZ-5
Snaptail Lake—*lake* MN-6
Snap Tank—*reservoir* AZ-5
Snare Brook—*stream* (2) ME-1
Snare Canyon—*valley* AZ-5
Snare Canyon—*valley* NM-5
Snare Cove—*bay* ME-1
Snare Creek—*stream* AK-9
Snare Creek—*stream* CO-8
Snare Creek—*stream* ME-1
Snare Mesa—*bench* NM-5
Snare Point—*cape* OR-9
Snarepole Gut—*gut* MD-2
Snare Run—*stream* PA-2
Snareville Sch—*school* IL-6
Snark Creek—*stream* OR-9
**Snark (historical)**—*pop pl* OR-9
Snass Creek—*stream* WA-9
*Snatch* TN-4
Snatch Creek—*stream* KY-4
Snatch Creek—*stream* SD-7
Snatch Creek Rec Area—*park* SD-7
*Snatchett* TN-4
Snatch Lake—*lake* MN-6
Snatelum Point—*cape* WA-9
**Snave**—*pop pl* MS-4
Snavely Branch—*stream* VA-3
Snavely Cem—*cemetery* PA-2
Snavely Cem—*cemetery* VA-3
Snavelys Sch (abandoned)—*school* PA-2
Snead—*locale* GA-3
**Snead**—*pop pl* AL-4
Snead Beach—*beach* VA-3
Snead Beach Channel—*channel* VA-3
Snead Branch—*stream* NC-3
Snead Branch—*stream* VA-3
Snead Cem—*cemetery* AR-4
Snead Cem—*cemetery* (2) NC-3
Snead Cem—*cemetery* (2) VA-3
Snead Chapel—*church* AL-4
Snead Chapel—*church* VA-3
Snead Coll—*school* AL-4
Snead Creek—*stream* FL-3
*Snead Crossroads* AL-4
**Snead Crossroads**—*pop pl* AL-4
Snead Hill—*summit* KY-4
Snead Hollow—*valley* TN-4
Snead Hollow—*valley* VA-3
Snead Hol Trail—*trail* PA-2
Snead Island—*island* FL-3
*Snead Island Cut Off* FL-3
Snead Island Cutoff—*channel* FL-3
Snead JHS—*school* AL-4
Snead Lake One—*reservoir* AL-4
Snead Lake Two—*reservoir* AL-4
Snead-Lampkin Cem—*cemetery* MS-4
Snead Manufacturing Bldg—*hist pl* KY-4
*Snead Memorial Church* AL-4
Snead Mound—*hist pl* OH-6
*Snead Point* FL-3
*Sneads* GA-3
**Sneads**—*pop pl* FL-3
*Sneadsborough* NC-3
Sneads (CCD)—*cens area* FL-3
Sneads Ch—*church* VA-3
Snead Sch—*school* VA-3
*Sneads Chapel Church* AL-4
Sneads Corner—*locale* VA-3
*Sneads Creek* FL-3
Sneads Creek—*stream* AL-4
Sneads Creek—*stream* NC-3
Sneads Elem Sch—*school* FL-3
*Snead Seminary* AL-4
**Sneads Ferry**—*pop pl* NC-3
Sneads Ferry Bridge—*bridge* NC-3
**Sneads Grove**—*pop pl* NC-3
Sneads Grove Sch—*school* NC-3
Sneads HS—*school* FL-3
*Sneads Island* FL-3
Snead Slough—*stream* TX-5
*Sneads Point* FL-3
Sneads Smokehouse Lake—*lake* FL-3
Sneads Spring—*locale* VA-3
*Snead State Junior College* AL-4
Sneadview Ch—*church* AL-4
Sneak Creek—*stream* ID-8
Sneaker Lake—*lake* MN-6
Sneakfoot Meadows—*flat* ID-8
Sneaking Creek—*stream* GA-3
Sneaking Creek—*stream* NC-3
Sneaking Island (historical)—*island* TN-4
Sneaking Island Shoals—*bar* TN-4
Sneakover Pass—*gap* UT-8
Sneak Point—*pillar* ID-8
Sneaky Prospect—*mine* UT-8
Sneaky Valley—*valley* MI-6
Sneath Bottom—*bend* MT-8
Sneckerberger Sch—*school* PA-2
Snedaker Basin—*basin* MT-8
Snedaker Divide—*ridge* MT-8
Snedden Creek—*stream* OR-9
Snedden Ranch—*locale* CA-9
Snedegar Pond—*lake* KY-4
*Snedekers Ferry* AL-4
Snedekerville—*locale* PA-2
**Sneden Landing**—*pop pl* NY-2
*Sneden's* NY-2
Snederker Gut—*stream* NC-3
Snedigar Branch—*stream* KY-4
Snedigar Lateral—*canal* CA-9
*Sneech Brook* RI-1
Sneech Pond—*lake* RI-1
*Sneechteconnet Pond* RI-1
**Sneed**—*pop pl* TX-5
Sneed, Constantine, House—*hist pl* TN-4
**Sneed Acres**—*pop pl* OK-5
Sneed Branch—*stream* NC-3
Sneed Camp—*locale* TX-5
Sneed Cem—*cemetery* GA-3
Sneed Cem—*cemetery* IL-6
Sneed Cem—*cemetery* MS-4
Sneed Cem—*cemetery* NC-3
Sneed Cem—*cemetery* TN-4
Sneed Ch—*church* IL-6
*Sneed Creek* WI-6
Sneed Creek—*stream* (2) LA-4
Sneed Creek—*stream* TX-5
Sneed Creek—*stream* WI-6
**Sneed Forest Estates**—*pop pl* TN-4
**Sneed Glen**—*pop pl* TN-4
Sneed Hollow—*valley* AL-4
Sneed Lake—*lake* TX-5
Sneed Mtn—*summit* TX-5
Sneed Mtn—*summit* WA-9
Sneed Ranch—*locale* TX-5
*Sneedsboro* NC-3
Sneeds Brake—*swamp* AR-4
Sneeds Bridge—*other* MO-7
Sneeds Cem—*cemetery* FL-3
Sneed Sch (historical)—*school* MO-7
*Sneeds Creek* AL-4
Sneeds Creek—*stream* (2) AR-4
*Sneeds Mountain* TX-5
Sneed Spring—*spring* AL-4
Sneed Spring—*spring* TN-4
Sneed Spring Cave—*cave* AL-4
Sneed's Ranch—*locale* MT-8
Sneeds South Camp—*locale* TX-5
Sneedville—*locale* TX-5
**Sneedville**—*pop pl* TN-4
Sneedville (CCD)—*cens area* TN-4
Sneedville Division—*civil* TN-4
Sneedville First Baptist Ch—*church* TN-4
Sneedville Post Office—*building* TN-4
Sneed Windmill—*locale* TX-5
Snee Farm—*hist pl* SC-3
Sneen Lake—*lake* WI-6
Snee-oosh Beach—*locale* WA-9
**Snee-oosh-Beach**—*pop pl* WA-9
Snee-oosh Point—*cape* WA-9
Sneep Gillespie Ditch—*canal* IN-6
Sneffels—*locale* CO-8
Sneffels, Mount—*summit* CO-8
Sneffels Creek—*stream* CO-8
*Sneffels Peak* CO-8
**Snefs**—*pop pl* IA-7
Sneftens Draw—*valley* WY-8
Snehumption Creek—*stream* WA-9
Snell—*locale* VA-3
Snell—*locale* WI-6
**Snell**—*pop pl* KY-4
**Snell**—*pop pl* MS-4
**Snell**—*pop pl* TN-4
Snell, Levi, House—*hist pl* NY-2
Snell, Perry, Hall—*hist pl* KY-4
Snell Apostolic Ch—*church* MS-4
Snell Arcade—*hist pl* FL-3
Snellbank Reef—*bar* TX-5
Snell Branch—*stream* LA-4
Snell Branch—*stream* SC-3
Snell Bridge—*bridge* AL-4
Snell Brook—*stream* ME-1
Snell Butte—*summit* CA-9
Snell Canyon—*valley* NE-7
Snell Canyon—*valley* UT-8
Snell Canyon—*valley* WY-8
Snell Cem—*cemetery* AR-4
Snell Cem—*cemetery* GA-3
Snell Cem—*cemetery* MO-7
Snell Cem—*cemetery* OH-6
Snell Cem—*cemetery* OK-5
Snell-Chrisenberry Cem—*cemetery* TN-4
**Snell Corner**—*pop pl* MA-1
*Snell Creek* GA-3
Snell Creek—*stream* CA-9
Snell Creek—*stream* CO-8
Snell Creek—*stream* FL-3
Snell Creek—*stream* MA-1
Snell Creek—*stream* MS-4
Snell Creek—*stream* (2) MT-8
Snell Creek—*stream* NV-8
Snell Creek—*stream* NC-3
Snell Creek—*stream* (2) OR-9
Snell Creek—*stream* PA-2
Snell Creek—*stream* TX-5
Snell Creek—*stream* WA-9
Snellenbarger Cem—*cemetery* OH-6
Snellenburg's Clothing Factory—*hist pl* PA-2
Snellen Cem—*cemetery* KY-4
Snellen Hollow—*valley* KY-4
Snell Hill—*summit* ME-1
Snell Hill—*summit* NY-2
Snell Hollow—*valley* MO-7
Snell Hollow—*valley* OR-9
Snell Hollow—*valley* UT-8
**Snelling**—*pop pl* CA-9
**Snelling**—*pop pl* SC-3
*Snelling Branch* TN-4
Snelling (CCD)—*cens area* CA-9
Snelling Diversion Dam—*dam* CA-9
Snelling Lake—*lake* MN-6
Snelling Merced Falls Sch—*school* CA-9
Snelling Pond—*reservoir* GA-3
Snelling Pond—*swamp* FL-3
Snellings Memorial Acre (Cemetery)—*cemetery* GA-3
Snell Island—*uninc pl* FL-3
Snell Island Harbor—*bay* FL-3
Snell Isle—*island* FL-3
Snell Isle Center (Shop Ctr)—*locale* FL-3
Snell Lake—*lake* KY-4
Snell Lake—*lake* OR-9
Snell Lake—*lake* WA-9
Snell Lock—*pillar* NY-2
Snell Lodge—*locale* NC-3
**Snellman**—*pop pl* MN-6
Snellman Cem—*cemetery* MN-6
Snellman Island—*island* MN-6
Snell Mill Branch—*stream* AL-4
Snell Mtn—*summit* CO-8
Snell Peak—*summit* CA-9
Snell Post Office (historical)—*building* MS-4
Snell Prong—*stream* KY-4
Snell Ranch—*locale* UT-8
Snell Rock—*pillar* CO-8
Snell Rock Creek—*stream* CO-8
Snells—*locale* WI-6
*Snells Bayou* FL-3
Snells Bridge—*bridge* VA-3
Snell Sch (historical)—*school* MS-4
*Snells Creek* MA-1
**Snells Crossroads**—*pop pl* AL-4
**Snells Crossroads**—*pop pl* NC-3
Snells Island—*island* ID-8
*Snells Meadow Brook* MA-1
Snell Spring—*spring* CA-9
Snell Spring—*spring* MT-8
Snells Siding Site (historical)—*locale* NC-3
Snell Valley—*valley* CA-9
**Snellville**—*pop pl* GA-3
Snellville-Grayson (CCD)—*cens area* GA-3
**Snellville (historical)**—*pop pl* MA-1
Snellville Mtn—*summit* GA-3
Snelly Peak—*summit* CA-9
Snelson Branch—*stream* NC-3
Snelson Creek—*stream* CO-8
Snelson Creek—*stream* VA-3
Snelsons Crossroads—*locale* GA-3
Snethen Cem—*cemetery* MO-7
Snetsinger Lake—*lake* MN-6
Snettisham—*locale* AK-9
Snettisham Peninsula—*cape* AK-9
Sneva Ditch—*canal* CO-8
Sneva Mtn—*summit* CO-8
Sneve Gulch—*valley* CO-8
Sngall—*ridge* PW-9
Sngelokl—*bay* PW-9
*Sngelokl Bay* PW-9
Snglin Creek—*stream* KY-4
Sni-A-Bar—*locale* MO-7
*Sniabar Creek* MO-7
Sni-A-Bar Creek—*stream* MO-7
Sni-A-Bar Township—*civil* (2) MO-7
**Snicarte**—*pop pl* IL-6
Snicarte Island—*island* IL-6
Snicarte Slough—*gut* IL-6
S Nicholas Ranch—*locale* SD-7
Snickers Gap—*gap* VA-3
*Snickersville* VA-3
Snidecar Drain—*stream* MI-6
*Snider* WV-2
Snider—*locale* IL-6
**Snider**—*pop pl* KY-4
**Snider**—*pop pl* MT-8
**Snider**—*pop pl* TN-4
**Snider**—*pop pl* WV-2
Snider Airp—*airport* PA-2
Snider Basin—*basin* (2) WY-8
Snider Basin—*bay* TN-4
Snider Basin Guard Station—*locale* WY-8
Snider Bend—*bend* TX-5
Snider Bottom—*bend* UT-8
Snider Branch—*stream* IN-6
Snider Branch—*stream* NC-3
Snider Branch—*stream* TX-5
Snider Branch—*stream* VA-3
Snider Brook—*stream* VT-1
Snider Canyon—*valley* UT-8
Snider Cem—*cemetery* IL-6
Snider Cem—*cemetery* IN-6
Snider Cem—*cemetery* MS-4
Snider Cem—*cemetery* (3) MO-7
Snider Cem—*cemetery* OH-6
Snider Cem—*cemetery* OK-5
Snider Cem—*cemetery* TN-4
Snider Cem—*cemetery* VA-3
Snider Cem—*cemetery* (3) WV-2
Snider Ch—*church* WV-2
*Snider Creek* ID-8
*Snider Creek* OR-9
*Snider Creek* TX-5
*Snider Creek* WA-9
Snider Creek—*stream* (2) MT-8
Snider Creek—*stream* OR-9
Snider Creek—*stream* (2) WA-9
Snider Flat—*flat* WA-9
Snider Hall—*hist pl* TX-5
Snider Hill—*summit* VA-3
Snider Hill Cem—*cemetery* IL-6
Snider (historical)—*locale* AL-4
**Snider (historical)**—*pop pl* TN-4
Snider Hollow—*valley* (2) MO-7
Snider Hollow—*valley* TN-4
Snider Island—*island* NY-2
Snider Lake—*lake* CA-9
Snider Lake—*lake* IL-6
Snider Lake—*lake* IA-7
Snider Lake—*lake* MN-6
Snider Lateral—*canal* ID-8
*Snider Meadow Creek* OR-9
Snider Mill—*locale* NC-3
Snider Peak—*summit* AK-9
Snider Peak—*summit* WA-9
Snider Pond—*lake* NY-2
Snider Post Office (historical)—*building* TN-4
Snider Ranger Station—*locale* WA-9
Snider Run—*stream* PA-2
Snider Run—*stream* WV-2
*Sniders* SC-3
Snider Sch—*school* WY-8
Snider Sch (historical)—*school* IA-7
Snider School—*locale* MT-8
**Sniders Crossroads**—*pop pl* SC-3
**Sniders Estates**—*pop pl* MD-2
*Snider Shoal* AL-4
Sniders Lake—*reservoir* (2) AL-4
Sniders Mill (historical)—*locale* AL-4
Sniders Mills (historical)—*locale* TN-4
Snider Spring—*spring* OR-9
Snider Spring—*spring* UT-8
Sniders Shoal (historical)—*bar* AL-4
Sniders Spring Branch—*stream* AL-4
Snider Temple—*church* WV-2
*Snidertown* NJ-2
Sniderville—*locale* WI-6
Snider Waterhole—*lake* CA-9
Snieder's Ranch—*locale* MT-8
Snif Creek—*stream* CO-8
Sniffel, Mount—*summit* WY-8
Sniffen Court Hist Dist—*hist pl* NY-2
Sniffens Point—*cape* CT-1
Sniff Lake—*lake* MN-6
Snikey Branch—*stream* LA-4
Sniktau, Mount—*summit* CO-8
Sniktaw Creek—*stream* CA-9
Sniktaw Meadow—*flat* CA-9
*Sniktaw Meadows* CA-9
**Sni Mills**—*pop pl* MO-7
Sni Mills Ch—*church* MO-7
*Snipatuet Brook* MA-1
*Snipatuet Pond* MA-1
Snipatuit Brook—*stream* MA-1
Snipatuit Pond—*lake* MA-1
Snipe—*locale* AR-4
Snipe—*locale* TX-5
Snipe Bay—*bay* AK-9
Snipe Branch—*stream* WV-2
*Snipe Creek* OR-9
Snipe Creek—*stream* AR-4
Snipe Creek—*stream* CO-8
Snipe Creek—*stream* FL-3
Snipe Creek—*stream* IA-7
Snipe Creek—*stream* KS-7
Snipe Creek—*stream* KY-4
Snipe Creek—*stream* NJ-2
Snipe Creek—*stream* NC-3
Snipe Creek—*stream* (2) OR-9
Snipe Gulch—*valley* CA-9
Snipe Head—*summit* AK-9
Snipe Hollow—*valley* AZ-5
Snipe Hollow—*valley* IL-6
Snipe Island—*island* (3) AK-9
Snipe Island—*island* FL-3
Snipe Island—*island* (2) NY-2
Snipe Island Brook—*stream* VT-1
Snipe Keys—*island* (2) FL-3
*Snipe Lake* MI-6
Snipe Lake—*lake* (2) AK-9
Snipe Lake—*lake* AZ-5
Snipe Lake—*lake* (2) MI-6
Snipe Lake—*lake* MN-6
Snipe Lake—*lake* (3) WI-6
Snipe Mtn—*summit* CO-8
Snipe Point—*cape* (2) AK-9
Snipe Point—*cape* FL-3
Snipe Point—*cliff* WY-8
*Snipers Creek* WA-9
Snipers Point—*cape* AK-9
Snipes Cem—*cemetery* NC-3
Snipe Sch—*school* SC-3
Snipes Corral—*locale* CO-8
Snipes Cove—*valley* TX-5
Snipes Creek—*stream* NC-3
Snipes Creek—*stream* WA-9
Snipes Grave Rock—*summit* GA-3
Snipes Grove Ch—*church* TN-4
Snipes Grove Sch (historical)—*school* TN-4
Snipe Slough—*stream* MO-7
Snipes Mountain Lateral—*canal* WA-9
Snipes Mtn—*summit* (2) WA-9
Snipes Pond—*reservoir* SC-3
Snipe Spring—*spring* ID-8
Snipes Shoals—*bar* GA-3
Snipes Tunnel—*tunnel* NC-3
**Snipesville**—*pop pl* GA-3
Snip Islands—*area* AK-9
*Snipituet Pond* MA-1
Snip Lake—*lake* MN-6
*Snippatuit Pond* MA-1
Snippershan Ledge—*bar* ME-1
Sniption Canyon—*valley* OR-9
*Sniptuett Brook* MA-1
*Sniptuett Pond* MA-1
Snip Waterhole—*lake* OR-9
Snite Run—*stream* PA-2
Snitz Creek—*stream* (2) PA-2
*Snitz Run* PA-2
Snively—*locale* OH-6
Snively Basin—*basin* WA-9
Snively Canyon Archeol District—*hist pl* WA-9
Snively Cem—*cemetery* PA-2

**Snively Corners**—pop pl PA-2
Snively Farm—hist pl MD-2
Snively Gulch—valley OR-9
Snively Gulch—valley WA-9
Snively Hot Spring—spring OR-9
Snively Park—park MN-6
Snively Ranch—locale WA-9
Snively Siphon—canal OR-9
Snively Spring—spring WA-9
Snivley OH-6
Snivley Chapel—church KY-4
Snivleys Ridge—ridge CA-9
S N Junction—locale TX-5
Snoad Branch NC-3
Snobel Valley—valley CA-9
Snoboy—locale CA-9
Snock Cem—cemetery TX-5
Snockey Pond—lake IL-6
Snodale Rec Area—park OK-5
Snodderly Cem—cemetery TN-4
Snodderly Sch—school TN-4
Snoddy—locale AL-4
**Snoddy**—pop pl SC-3
Snoddy Cem—cemetery IN-6
Snoddy Ch—church IN-6
Snoddy Chapel—church AL-4
Snoddy Chapel Nazarene Ch AL-4
Snoddyville TN-4
Snoddyville Post Office TN-4
Snode Creek—stream NC-3
Snoden Creek—stream ID-8
Snoderley Cem—cemetery AR-4
Snoderly Post Office (historical)—building TN-4
**Snodes**—pop pl OH-6
Snodes Creek NC-3
Snodgrass—locale TN-4
Snodgrass Branch TN-4
Snodgrass Branch—stream VA-3
Snodgrass Cem—cemetery KY-4
Snodgrass Cem—cemetery MO-7
Snodgrass Cem—cemetery (2) TN-4
Snodgrass Cem—cemetery (2) TX-5
Snodgrass Cem—cemetery VA-3
Snodgrass Cem—cemetery (3) WV-2
Snodgrass Creek WY-8
Snodgrass Creek—stream CA-9
Snodgrass Ditch—canal IN-6
Snodgrass Ferry (historical)—locale AL-4
Snodgrass Field—locale GA-3
Snodgrass Ford—locale (2) VA-3
Snodgrass Hollow—valley MO-7
Snodgrass House—building GA-3
Snodgrass Island—island FL-3
Snodgrass Lake LA-4
Snodgrass Lake—lake AK-9
Snodgrass Lake—lake LA-4
Snodgrass Lake—lake MN-6
Snodgrass Landing (historical)—locale AL-4
Snodgrass Mtn—summit CO-8
Snodgrass Post Office (historical)—building TN-4
Snodgrass Run—stream PA-2
Snodgrass Run—stream WV-2
Snodgrass Run Trail—trail WV-2
Snodgrass Sch (abandoned)—school MO-7
Snodgrass Slough—stream CA-9
Snodgrass Tank—reservoir AZ-5
Snodgrass Tavern—hist pl WV-2
Snodgrass Union Cem—cemetery MO-7
Snody Dock—locale NY-2
Snoffers Lake—reservoir NC-3
Snoffers Lake Dam—dam NC-3
**Snohomish**—pop pl WA-9
Snohomish, Lake—lake AK-9
Snohomish (CCD)—cens area WA-9
**Snohomish County**—pop pl WA-9
Snohomish County Courthouse—hist pl WA-9
Snohomish County (Paine Fld) Airp—airport WA-9
Snohomish Hills—other AK-9
Snohomish Hist Dist—hist pl WA-9
Snohomish River—stream WA-9
Snoke Lake—lake IN-6
Snokomo Creek—stream KS-7
Snoline Sch—school WA-9
Snomac OK-5
Snoma Cem—cemetery SD-7
Snoma Finnish Cemetery—hist pl SD-7
Snoma Sch—school SD-7
Snoody Creek—stream MS-4
**Snook**—pop pl PA-2
**Snook**—pop pl TX-5
Snook, Van B., House—hist pl KY-4
Snook Canyon—valley WA-9
Snook Dam—dam SD-7
Snook Hole Channel—channel FL-3
Snook House—hist pl KY-4
Snook Kill—stream NY-2
Snook Mtn—summit CA-9
Snook Ranch—locale WY-8
Snook Rsvr—reservoir NE-7
Snooks Cave PA-2
Snooks Cem—cemetery NY-2
Snooks Corners—locale NY-2
Snooks Covered Bridge—hist pl PA-2
Snooks Highway—channel MI-6
Snooks Hollow—valley KS-7
Snooks Lake—lake SC-3
Snooks Nose—summit NC-3
Snooks Pond—lake NY-2
Snooks Run—stream OH-6
Snooks Trail—trail PA-2
Snookum Lode Mine SD-7
Snooky Spring—spring CA-9
Snoopy Rsvr—reservoir WY-8
Snoopys Airp—airport KS-7
Snoopys Mills IN-6
Snoosebox Lake—lake MN-6
Snoose Coulee—valley MT-8
Snoose Creek—stream ID-8
Snoose Creek—stream WI-6
Snoose Junction—locale WA-9
Snoose Lake—lake WI-6
Snoose Mine—mine ID-8
Snooseville Corner—locale OR-9
Snoot Creek—stream OR-9
Snooter Spring—spring NM-5
Snoozer Mine—mine CA-9
Snoozer Ridge—ridge CA-9
Snoppersons Creek VA-3
Snoqualme WA-9
Snoqualme Pass WA-9
Snoqualme River WA-9
**Snoqualmie**—pop pl WA-9
Snoqualmie Depot—hist pl WA-9
Snoqualmie Falls—falls WA-9
**Snoqualmie Falls**—pop pl WA-9
Snoqualmie Falls Cavity Generating Station—hist pl WA-9
Snoqualmie Gulch—valley CA-9
Snoqualmie Lake—lake WA-9
Snoqualmie Lake Potholes—lake WA-9
Snoqualmie Mtn—summit WA-9
Snoqualmie Natl Forest (CCD)—cens area WA-9
Snoqualmie Pass—flat WA-9
**Snoqualmie Pass (Recreational Area)**—pop pl WA-9
Snoqualmie River WA-9
Snoqualmie River—stream WA-9
Snoqualmie Tunnel—tunnel WA-9
Snoqualmine Natl For—forest WA-9
Snoquera—locale WA-9
Snores Rocks—pillar RI-1
Snorgrass Cem—cemetery MO-7
Snoring Bay—bay WA-9
Snoring Inn—locale AK-9
Snoring Spring—spring CA-9
Snort Creek—stream IA-7
Snort Creek—stream MT-8
Snorting Buck Hollow—valley PA-2
Snorting Lick Run—stream WV-2
Snort Lake—lake MN-6
Snort Lake—lake WI-6
Snortland Dam—dam ND-7
Snoshoe Mine—mine MN-6
Snout Creek—stream OR-9
Snoveltown PA-2
**Snover**—pop pl MI-6
Snover Canyon—valley CA-9
Snover Drain—canal MI-6
Snover Memorial Park—cemetery MI-6
Snow UT-8
Snow—locale KY-4
Snow—locale ND-7
Snow—locale OK-5
**Snow**—pop pl AR-4
**Snow**—pop pl MI-6
**Snow**—pop pl TX-5
**Snow**—pop pl UT-8
Snow, Dudley, House—hist pl AL-4
Snow, John, House—hist pl OH-6
Snow, Mount—summit VT-1
Snow, Russ and Holland, Houses—hist pl OH-6
Snow Acad Bldg—hist pl UT-8
Snowal Creek WA-9
Snowall Creek—stream WA-9
Snow Angel Ranch—locale CO-8
Snowater Springs CO-8
**Snowball**—pop pl AR-4
Snowball Branch—stream AR-4
Snowball Cem—cemetery PA-2
Snowball Creek—stream AK-9
Snowball Creek—stream CO-8
Snowball Creek—stream MN-6
Snowball Creek—stream NV-8
Snowball Extension Ditch—canal CO-8
Snowball Gap—gap NC-3
**Snowball Gate**—pop pl PA-2
Snowball Hill—summit MO-7
Snowball Hollow Creek—stream NY-2
Snowball Lake—lake MN-6
Snowball Mine—mine AZ-5
Snowball Mine—mine NV-8
Snowball Mine—mine UT-8
Snowball Mtn—summit CA-9
Snowball Mtn—summit NC-3
Snowball Ranch—locale NV-8
Snowball Sch (historical)—school (2) MO-7
Snowband Lake—lake WY-8
Snowbank—cliff UT-8
Snowbank Campground—locale MT-8
Snow Bank Canyon NV-8
Snowbank Canyon—valley NV-8
Snowbank Creek—stream AK-9
Snowbank Creek—stream MT-8
Snow Bank Creek—stream NV-8
Snowbank Glacier—glacier MT-8
Snowbank Lake—lake CO-8
Snowbank Lake—lake ID-8
Snowbank Lake—lake MN-6
Snowbank Lake—lake MT-8
Snowbank Mine—mine MT-8
Snowbank Mtn—summit ID-8
Snowbank Mtn—summit MT-8
Snowbank Ridge—ridge MT-8
Snow Bank Rsvr—reservoir WY-8
Snowbank Spring—spring UT-8
Snowbank Trail—trail ID-8
Snowbank Trail—trail MT-8
Snow Basin—basin CA-9
Snow Basin—basin NV-8
Snow Basin—basin (2) OR-9
Snow Basin—basin UT-8
Snow Basin Creek—stream CA-9
Snow Basin Heliport—airport UT-8
Snow Basin Rec Area UT-8
Snowbasin Ski Area UT-8
Snow Basin Ski Area—locale UT-8
Snow Bay—bay MN-6
Snow Bench—bench UT-8
Snow Bend AL-4
Snow Bend—locale CA-9
Snowbird—post sta UT-8
Snowbird Canyon—valley AZ-5
Snowbird Canyon—valley NV-8
Snowbird Chapel—church ND-7
Snowbird Cherokee Indian Sch—school NC-3
Snowbird Creek—stream ID-8
Snowbird Creek—stream (2) NC-3
Snowbird Gap—gap (3) NC-3
Snowbird Hollow—valley TN-4
Snowbird Lake—lake NM-5
Snowbird Lake—lake SC-3
**Snowbird Lodge Subdivision**—pop pl UT-8
Snowbird Meadows—flat ID-8
Snowbird Mesa—summit NM-5
Snowbird Mine—mine AK-9
Snow Bird Mine—mine CA-9
Snowbird Mine—mine CA-9
Snowbird Mountains—ridge NC-3
Snowbird Mtn—summit (2) NC-3
Snowbird Mtn—summit OR-9
Snowbird Mtn—summit TN-4
Snowbird Rec Area—park UT-8
Snowbird Sch—school NC-3
Snowbird Shelter—locale OR-9
Snowbird Ski Area UT-8
Snowbird Ski Resort Heliport—airport UT-8
Snowbirds Point—summit KY-4
Snowbird Spring—spring AZ-5
Snowbird Spring—spring NV-8
Snowbird Top—summit NC-3
Snow Board Ridge—ridge OR-9
Snowbound Mine—mine CO-8
Snow Brake—swamp AR-4
Snow Brake—swamp MS-4
Snow Brake Lake—lake MS-4
Snow Branch—stream (2) AR-4
Snow Branch—stream MO-7
Snow Branch—stream SC-3
Snow Branch—stream (2) TN-4
Snowbridge Lake—lake WY-8
Snow Brook—stream (2) ME-1
Snow Brook—stream (2) NH-1
Snow Brook—stream NY-2
Snow Brook—stream VT-1
Snowbrush Gulch—valley OR-9
Snowbrush Mine—mine CA-9
Snow Brushy Creek—stream WA-9
Snow Bunny Lodge—building OR-9
Snow Cabin—locale ID-8
Snow Cabin—locale OR-9
Snow Cabin—locale UT-8
Snow Camp—locale CA-9
**Snow Camp**—pop pl NC-3
Snow Camp Branch—stream TN-4
Snow Camp Creek—stream (2) CA-9
Snow Camp Lake—lake CA-9
Snow Camp Meadow—flat OR-9
Snow Camp Mtn—summit CA-9
Snow Camp Mtn—summit OR-9
Snow Camp Trail—trail OR-9
Snow Canyon—valley (5) CA-9
Snow Canyon—valley (2) NV-8
Snow Canyon—valley (3) NM-5
Snow Canyon—valley (4) UT-8
Snow Canyon Campground—park UT-8
Snow Canyon State Park—park UT-8
**Snow Canyon Subdivision**—pop pl UT-8
Snow Canyon Tank—reservoir NM-5
Snow Cap Creek—stream WA-9
Snowcap Mtn—summit AK-9
Snowcaps Mine—mine CA-9
Snow Cattle Co Ditch No 4—canal WY-8
Snow Cave—cave AL-4
Snow Cave Ridge—ridge WY-8
Snow Cem—cemetery AL-4
Snow Cem—cemetery (2) AR-4
Snow Cem—cemetery IL-6
Snow Cem—cemetery (3) IN-6
Snow Cem—cemetery KY-4
Snow Cem—cemetery ME-1
Snow Cem—cemetery MA-1
Snow Cem—cemetery MS-4
Snow Cem—cemetery OH-6
Snow Cem—cemetery (5) TN-4
Snow Cem—cemetery VT-1
Snow Cem—cemetery WA-9
Snow Ch—church AR-4
Snow Ch—church GA-3
Snow Ch—church MI-6
Snow Chapel—church TN-4
Snow Chapel Cem—cemetery TN-4
Snow Cloud Mine—mine CA-9
Snow Coll—school UT-8
Snow Coll Field Station—school UT-8
Snow Cone—summit ID-8
**Snow Corner**—pop pl ME-1
Snow Corral Creek—stream CA-9
Snow Corral Meadow—flat CA-9
Snow Corral Ridge—ridge UT-8
Snow Coulee—valley (2) MT-8
Snow Cove—bay ME-1
Snow Creek AL-4
Snow Creek CA-9
Snow Creek ID-8
Snow Creek MS-4
Snow Creek MT-8
Snow Creek OH-6
Snow Creek OK-5
Snow Creek TN-4
Snow Creek WI-6
Snow Creek WY-8
Snow Creek—locale VA-3
**Snow Creek**—pop pl CA-9
Snow Creek—stream (4) AK-9
Snow Creek—stream AR-4
Snow Creek—stream (11) CA-9
Snow Creek—stream GA-3
Snow Creek—stream (14) ID-8
Snow Creek—stream IL-6
Snow Creek—stream KS-7
Snow Creek—stream KY-4
Snow Creek—stream LA-4
Snow Creek—stream MI-6
Snow Creek—stream MS-4
Snow Creek—stream MO-7
Snow Creek—stream (9) MT-8
Snow Creek—stream (3) NV-8
Snow Creek—stream NM-5
Snow Creek—stream (5) NC-3
Snow Creek—stream (2) OK-5
Snow Creek—stream (12) OR-9
Snow Creek—stream PA-2
Snow Creek—stream SC-3
Snow Creek—stream (3) TN-4
Snow Creek—stream (2) TX-5
Snow Creek—stream UT-8
Snow Creek—stream (3) VA-3
Snow Creek—stream (7) WA-9
Snow Creek—stream WI-6
Snow Creek—stream (4) WY-8
Snow Creek Butte—summit ID-8
Snow Creek Cabin—locale NM-5
Snow Creek Ch—church NC-3
Snow Creek Ch—church SC-3
Snow Creek Ch—church VA-3
Snow Creek Ditch—canal OR-9
Snow Creek Falls—falls CA-9
Snow Creek Glacier—glacier WA-9
Snow Creek (historical)—locale MS-4
**Snow Creek (historical)**—pop pl NC-3
Snow Creek (Magisterial District)—fmr MCD VA-3
Snow Creek Methodist Church and Burying Ground—hist pl NC-3
Snow Creek Placer Claim No. 1—hist pl AK-9
Snow Creek Post Office TN-4
Snow Creek Project Camp—locale OR-9
Snow Creek Ranch—locale NV-8
Snow Creek Rec Area—park VA-3
Snow Creek Spring—spring ID-8
**Snow Creek Subdivision**—pop pl UT-8
Snow Creek (Township of)—fmr MCD (2) NC-3
Snow Creek Wall—cliff WA-9
Snowcrest HS—school UT-8
Snowcrest Mtn—summit MT-8
Snowcrest Range—range MT-8
Snow Crest Ski Area—area WI-6
Snowcrest Trail—trail MT-8
Snow Dam—dam SD-7
Snowd Branch—stream NC-3
Snowd Branch Ch—church NC-3
Snowden MS-4
Snowden—locale (2) CA-9
Snowden—locale MN-6
Snowden—locale MT-8
Snowden—locale NC-3
Snowden—locale VA-3
Snowden—locale WV-2
**Snowden**—pop pl MS-4
**Snowden**—pop pl NY-2
**Snowden**—pop pl PA-2
**Snowden**—pop pl SC-3
**Snowden**—pop pl VA-3
**Snowden**—pop pl WA-9
Snowden, Lake—reservoir OH-6
Snowden Bay—swamp FL-3
Snowden Branch—stream AL-4
Snowden Branch—stream KY-4
Snowden Branch—stream MO-7
Snowden Branch—stream WI-6
Snowden Cem—cemetery KY-4
Snowden Cem—cemetery LA-4
Snowden Cem—cemetery MD-2
Snowden Cem—cemetery OH-6
Snowden Cem (historical)—cemetery MO-7
Snowden Chapel (historical)—church MS-4
Snowden Coulee—valley MT-8
Snowden Creek—stream AK-9
Snowden Creek—stream FL-3
Snowden Hill—summit CA-9
Snowden House—hist pl IA-7
Snowden Lake—lake AR-4
Snowden Lake—lake WI-6
Snowden Lake—reservoir CO-8
**Snowden Manor**—pop pl MD-2
Snowden-Mc Sweeney Oil Field—oilfield KS-7
Snowden Mtn—summit AK-9
**Snowden Oaks**—pop pl MD-2
Snowden Park—park FL-3
Snowden Peak—summit VT-1
Snowden Plantation—locale AR-4
Snowden Pond—reservoir MD-2
Snowden Sch—school AR-4
Snowden Sch—school LA-4
Snowden Sch—school TN-4
Snowden Spring Branch—stream TX-5
Snowdens Saw mill Branch MD-2
Snowden (Township of)—other PA-2
Snowdenville—locale PA-2
Snowdenville Sch (abandoned)—school MO-7
Snow Ditch—canal IN-6
Snow Ditch—canal MT-8
Snow Dome—summit AK-9
Snow Dome—summit WA-9
Snowdon CA-9
Snowdon—locale NY-2
**Snowdon**—pop pl CA-9
Snowdon Peak—summit CO-8
Snowdoun—building MS-4
Snowdoun—hist pl MS-4
**Snowdoun**—pop pl AL-4
Snowdoun Baptist Church AL-4
Snowdoun Ch—church AL-4
Snowdoun Community Center—building AL-4
Snowdoun Valley Ch—church AL-4
Snowdown AL-4
Snowdown Cem—cemetery MS-4
Snowdown Ch—church AL-4
Snowdown Ch—church (2) MS-4
Snowdown Ch of Christ MS-4
Snowdown Public School MS-4
Snowdown Sch—school MS-4
Snow Drain—stream IN-6
Snow Drain—stream MI-6
Snow Draw—valley WY-8
Snowdrift Crater—crater ID-8
Snowdrift Creek—stream MT-8
Snowdrift Creek—stream WY-8
Snowdrift Draw—valley WY-8
Snowdrift Gulch—valley CO-8
Snowdrift Lake—lake CO-8
Snowdrift Lake—lake WY-8
Snowdrift Mine—mine AZ-5
Snowdrift Mine—mine CO-8
Snowdrift Mine—mine NV-8
Snowdrift Mtn—range ID-8
Snowdrift Mtn—summit CO-8
Snowdrift Peak—summit AK-9
Snowdrift Peak—summit CO-8
Snowdrift Rsvr—reservoir ID-8
Snower Sch—school AL-4
Snow Falls—falls TN-4
Snow Falls—locale ME-1
Snow Falls Creek—stream WI-6
Snow Fence Pond—lake UT-8
Snow Ferry (historical)—locale AL-4
Snowfield Creek—stream WA-9
Snowfield Lake—lake CO-8
Snowfield Peak—summit WA-9
Snowfield Trail—trail PA-2
Snowflake TN-4
Snow Flake—locale TN-4
Snowflake—locale VA-3
Snowflake—mine UT-8
**Snowflake**—pop pl AZ-5
**Snowflake**—pop pl WV-2
**Snow Flake**—pop pl WV-2
Snowflake Canyon—valley NM-5
Snowflake (CCD)—cens area AZ-5
Snowflake Creek—stream ND-7
Snowflake Elem Sch—school AZ-5
Snowflake JHS—school AZ-5
Snowflake Lake—lake AK-9
Snowflake Lake—lake WA-9
Snowflake Mine—mine (2) NV-8
Snowflake Municipal Airp—airport AZ-5
Snowflake Ridge—ridge MT-8
Snowflake Springs—spring MT-8
Snowflake Stake Acad Bldg—hist pl AZ-5
Snow Flake Talc Mine—mine CA-9
Snowflake Taylor Elem Sch—school AZ-5
Snowflake Tunnel—tunnel NM-5
Snow Flat—flat AZ-5
Snow Flat—flat (2) CA-9
Snow Flat—flat UT-8
Snow Flat Boy Scout Camp—park AZ-5
Snow Flat Spring Cave—cave UT-8
Snowflower Mine—mine CA-9
Snowflower Mtn—summit NV-8
Snow Flower Pit—cave AL-4
Snowford Ch—church AL-4
Snow Fork—stream CA-9
Snow Fork—stream OH-6
Snow Fork Creek—stream OR-9
Snow Fork Hollow OH-6
Snow Fountain and Clock—hist pl MA-1
Snow Gap—gap AR-4
Snow Gap—gap CA-9
Snow Gap—gap NM-5
Snow Gate WY-8
**Snow Geese Dunes (subdivision)**—pop pl NC-3
**Snow Geese South (subdivision)**—pop pl NC-3
Snow Glacier Mountain MT-8
Snow Glade—flat CA-9
Snow Goose Pool—lake MO-7
Snowgrass Flat—flat WA-9
Snowgrass Mtn—summit WA-9
Snow Grove Canyon—valley CO-8
Snow Gulch—valley (6) AK-9
Snow Gulch—valley (2) CA-9
Snow Gulch—valley MT-8
Snow Gulch—valley NV-8
Snow Gulch—valley OR-9
Snow Gulch—valley WA-9
Snow Hall—building OK-5
Snowhall Inn—locale MT-8
Snow Haven Ski Area—locale ID-8
Snowheel Mtn—summit AK-9
Snow Heights Sch—school TX-5
Snow Hill NJ-2
Snow Hill—hist pl MD-2
Snow Hill—hist pl VA-3
Snow Hill—locale AL-4
Snow Hill—locale IA-7
Snowhill—locale NC-3
Snow Hill—locale (2) NC-3
Snow Hill—locale TN-4
Snow Hill—locale (2) TX-5
Snow Hill—locale WV-2
**Snow Hill**—pop pl AL-4
**Snow Hill**—pop pl AR-4
**Snow Hill**—pop pl FL-3
**Snow Hill**—pop pl (2) IN-6
**Snow Hill**—pop pl KY-4
**Snow Hill**—pop pl MD-2
**Snow Hill**—pop pl NJ-2
**Snow Hill**—pop pl (3) NC-3
**Snow Hill**—pop pl TX-5
**Snow Hill**—pop pl VA-3
**Snow Hill**—pop pl WV-2
Snow Hill—summit AL-4
Snow Hill—summit AR-4
Snow Hill—summit (2) CT-1
Snow Hill—summit (2) IN-6
Snow Hill—summit (3) MA-1
Snow Hill—summit NC-3
Snow Hill—summit PA-2
Snow Hill—summit TX-5
Snow Hill—summit VT-1
Snow Hill—summit WI-6
Snow Hill Branch—stream AL-4
Snow Hill Branch—stream MD-2
Snow Hill Brook—stream CT-1
Snow Hill Cave—cave TN-4
Snow Hill (CCD)—cens area TN-4
Snow Hill Cem—cemetery AL-4
Snow Hill Cem—cemetery GA-3
Snow Hill Cem—cemetery IA-7
Snow Hill Cem—cemetery (2) NC-3
Snowhill Cem—cemetery OH-6
Snowhill Cem—cemetery SC-3
Snow Hill Cem—cemetery WI-6
Snowhill Ch—church AL-4
Snow Hill Ch—church (3) GA-3
Snowhill Ch—church GA-3
Snowhill Ch—church IL-6
Snow Hill Ch—church MD-2
Snow Hill Ch—church MS-4
Snow Hill Ch—church (6) NC-3
Snowhill Ch—church NC-3
Snow Hill Ch—church (6) NC-3
Snow Hill Ch—church OK-5
Snow Hill Ch—church (3) SC-3
Snow Hill Ch—church (4) TX-5
Snow Hill Ch—church VA-3
Snow Hill Ch—church WV-2
Snow Hill Colored Sch (historical)—school TN-4
Snow Hill Country Club—other OH-6
Snow Hill Division—civil TN-4
Snow Hill Elem Sch—school NC-3
Snow Hill Elem Sch—school TN-4
Snow Hill Falls—falls PA-2
**Snow Hill Falls**—pop pl PA-2
Snow Hill (historical)—locale KS-7
Snowhill Institute AL-4
Snow Hill Institute—school AL-4
Snow Hill Landing MD-2
**Snow Hill Manor**—pop pl MD-2
Snow Hill Marina—locale MD-2
Snow Hill Picnic Area—area PA-2
Snow Hill Post Office (historical)—building TN-4
Snow Hill Public Landing MD-2
Snow Hill Sch—school AL-4
Snow Hill Sch—school FL-3
Snow Hill Sch—school OH-6
Snow Hill Sch—school SC-3
Snow Hill Sch (historical)—school AL-4
Snow Hill Site—hist pl MD-2
Snow Hill Township—civil MO-7
Snow Hill (Township of)—fmr MCD NC-3
Snow Hole—cave AL-4
Snow Hole, The—summit NY-2
Snow Hole Rapids—rapids ID-8
Snow Hollow—valley (2) ID-8
Snow Hollow—valley (2) MO-7
Snow Hollow—valley (2) TN-4
Snow Hollow—valley UT-8
Snow Hollow—valley WY-8
**Snow Hollow Lake**—pop pl MO-7
Snow Hollow Lake—reservoir MO-7
Snow Island OH-6
Snow Island FM-9
Snow Island—island (2) ME-1
Snow Island—island SC-3
Snow Junction—locale SC-3
Snowking Lake—lake WA-9
Snowking Mtn—summit WA-9
Snow King Mtn—summit WY-8
Snow Knob—summit AR-4
Snow Lake MT-8
Snow Lake—lake AK-9
Snow Lake—lake AR-4
Snow Lake—lake (4) CA-9
Snow Lake—lake (2) CO-8
Snow Lake—lake (2) ID-8
Snow Lake—lake IN-6
Snow Lake—lake (5) MI-6
Snow Lake—lake MN-6
Snow Lake—lake MS-4
Snow Lake—lake MT-8
Snow Lake—lake NE-7
Snow Lake—lake OH-6
Snow Lake—lake (4) UT-8
Snow Lake—lake (4) WA-9
Snow Lake—lake (2) WY-8
**Snow Lake**—pop pl AR-4
Snow Lake—reservoir MS-4
Snow Lake—swamp SD-7
Snow Lakebed—flat AR-4
Snow Lakebed—flat MN-6
Snow Lake Creek—stream WY-8
Snowlake Peak—summit NV-8
Snow Lakes—lake CA-9
Snow Lakes—lake MN-6
Snow Lakes—lake MT-8
Snow Lakes—lake OR-9
Snow Lakes—lake UT-8
Snow Lakes—lake WA-9
**Snow Lake Shores**—pop pl MS-4
Snow Lakes Trail—trail WA-9
Snowland—hist pl DE-2
Snowland—park DE-2
Snowland Ski Area—locale UT-8
Snowlick Mtn—summit AR-4
Snowline—locale MT-8
Snowline Camp—locale CA-9
Snowline Fox Farm—locale CA-9
Snowline Lake—reservoir CO-8
Snowline Ranch—locale MT-8
Snowline Ridge—ridge CO-8
Snowline Station MT-8
Snowmaker Spring—spring ID-8
Snowman Brook—stream ME-1
Snowman Sch—school ME-1
Snowmans Hill—summit CA-9
Snow Marsh NC-3
**Snowmass**—pop pl CO-8
Snowmass-At-aspen CO-8
Snowmass Creek—stream CO-8
Snowmass Ditch—canal CO-8
Snowmass Divide Ditch—canal CO-8
Snowmass Falls Ranch—locale CO-8
Snowmass Lake—lake CO-8
Snowmass Mtn—summit CO-8
Snowmass Peak—summit CO-8
**Snowmass Village**—pop pl CO-8
**Snow Mayberry Subdivision**—pop pl TN-4
Snow Meadow—flat CA-9
Snow Mesa—summit CO-8
Snow Mill Pond MA-1
Snow Mine AL-4
Snowmoody Ridge—ridge OR-9
Snow Moon Lake—lake MT-8
Snow Mound Sch (historical)—school SD-7
Snow Mountain—ridge VA-3
Snow Mountain Brook—stream ME-1
Snow Mountain Ditch—canal CA-9
Snow Mountain Gulch—valley AK-9
Snow Mountain House—locale CA-9
Snow Mountain Pond—lake ME-1
Snow Mountains MT-8
Snow Mountains OR-9
Snow Mountains WY-8
Snow Mountain Spring—spring OR-9
Snow Mtn NY-2
Snow Mtn OR-9
Snow Mtn—summit AZ-5
Snow Mtn—summit (5) CA-9
Snow Mtn—summit KY-4
Snow Mtn—summit (4) ME-1
Snow Mtn—summit (2) MA-1
Snow Mtn—summit NY-2
Snow Mtn—summit OR-9
Snow Mtn—summit TX-5
Snow Mtn East—summit CA-9
Snow Mtn West—summit CA-9
Snow Park—flat NM-5
Snow Park—park IL-6
Snow Park Ski Area—park MT-8
Snow Park Ski Lifts—other UT-8
Snow Pass—gap WY-8
Snow Passage—channel AK-9
Snowpatch Craig—summit AK-9
Snow Peak—summit (2) CA-9
Snow Peak—summit (3) ID-8
Snow Peak—summit MT-8
Snow Peak—summit NM-5
Snow Peak—summit (2) OR-9
Snow Peak—summit (2) WA-9
Snow Peak Camp—locale OR-9
Snow Peak Log Pond—reservoir OR-9
Snow Peak Mill City Trail—trail OR-9
Snow Plow—ridge UT-8
Snowplow Lake—lake MI-6

Snowplow Mtn—summit ... WA-9
Snow Point ... MA-1
Snow Point ... NC-3
Snow Point—cape ... MA-1
Snow Point—cape ... SC-3
Snow Point—cape ... TX-5
Snow Point—summit ... AL-4
Snow Point—summit ... OR-9
Snow Point Canyon—valley ... CA-9
Snow Pond ... MA-1
Snow Pond—lake ... MA-1
Snow Pond—lake ... NH-1
Snow Pond—lake ... NY-2
Snow Pond—reservoir (2) ... MA-1
Snow Pond Dam—dam (2) ... MA-1
Snow Prairie—flat ... CA-9
Snow Prairie Cem—cemetery ... MI-6
Snow Prairie Sch—school ... MI-6
Snowquarter Creek—stream ... VA-3
Snow Ranch—locale ... CA-9
Snow Ranch—locale (3) ... NM-5
Snow Ranch—locale ... UT-8
Snow Ranch—locale ... WY-8
Snow Ridge—ridge ... CA-9
Snow Ridge—ridge ... ID-8
Snow Ridge—ridge ... OK-5
Snow Ridge—ridge ... TN-4
Snow Ridge—ridge ... UT-8
Snow River ... TX-5
Snow River—stream ... AK-9
Snow River Pass—gap ... AK-9
Snow Road Sch—school ... MI-6
Snow Roberts Sch—school ... AL-4
Snow Rock—rock ... MA-1
Snow Rogers Elem Sch ... AL-4
Snow Run—stream ... IN-6
Snow Run—stream ... OH-6
Snow Run—stream ... PA-2
Snow Run Brook—stream ... IN-6
Snows Bend—bend ... AL-4
Snows Branch—stream ... AL-4
Snows Branch—stream ... DE-2
Snows Brook—stream (2) ... MA-1
Snows Brook—stream ... NH-1
Snows Brook—stream ... VT-1
Snows Brook Trail—trail ... NH-1
Snows Camp Dock—locale ... TN-4
Snows Canyon—valley ... UT-8
Snows Cem—cemetery ... MI-6
Snow Sch—hist pl ... OK-5
Snow Sch—school (2) ... CA-9
Snow Sch—school ... CT-1
Snow Sch—school ... KS-7
Snow Sch—school ... ME-1
Snow Sch—school ... MI-6
Snow Sch—school ... ND-7
Snow Sch—school ... VT-1
Snow Sch (abandoned)—school ... PA-2
Snows Chapel—church ... AL-4
Snow Sch (historical)—school ... AL-4
Snow Sch (historical)—school ... TN-4
Snow Sch 8—school ... ND-7
Snows Corner—locale ... FL-3
Snows Corner—locale ... WI-6
Snows Corners ... WI-6
Snows Creek ... AL-4
Snows Creek—stream ... MA-1
Snows Creek—stream ... MS-4
Snows Cut—channel ... NC-3
Snows Dam—dam ... AL-4
**Snow Settlement**—pop pl ... ME-1
Snows Falls ... ME-1
Snows Field—park ... MA-1
Snow Shanty Trail—trail ... PA-2
Snow Shed—building ... UT-8
Snowshed Mtn—summit ... MT-8
Snowshed Peak—summit ... AZ-5
Snowshed Trail—trail ... AZ-5
Snows Hill ... MA-1
**Snows Hill**—pop pl ... TN-4
Snows Hill—summit ... ME-1
**Snows Hill (Blend)**—pop pl ... TN-4
Snowshoe—locale ... MI-6
**Snow Shoe**—pop pl ... PA-2
**Snowshoe**—pop pl ... WV-2
Snowshoe Bay—bay ... MN-6
Snowshoe Bay—bay ... NY-2
Snow Shoe Borough—civil ... PA-2
Snowshoe Brook—stream ... MN-6
Snowshoe Butte—summit ... ID-8
Snowshoe Butte—summit ... OR-9
Snowshoe Butte—summit ... WA-9
Snowshoe Butte Trail—trail ... WA-9
Snowshoe Cabin—locale ... CO-8
Snowshoe Camp—locale ... WA-9
Snowshoe Canyon—valley ... CO-8
Snowshoe Canyon—valley ... UT-8
Snowshoe Canyon—valley (2) ... WY-8
Snowshoe Cave—cave ... ID-8
Snow Shoe City ... PA-2
Snowshoe Creek ... CO-8
Snowshoe Creek ... WA-9
Snowshoe Creek—stream (5) ... AK-9
Snowshoe Creek—stream ... AZ-5
Snowshoe Creek—stream ... CA-9
Snowshoe Creek—stream ... CO-8
Snowshoe Creek—stream (4) ... ID-8
Snowshoe Creek—stream (3) ... MT-8
Snowshoe Creek—stream (2) ... OR-9
Snowshoe Creek—stream (2) ... WA-9
Snowshoe Creek—stream (3) ... WY-8
Snowshoe Creek Trail—trail ... OR-9
Snowshoe Falls—falls ... MT-8
Snowshoe Falls—falls ... WA-9
Snow Shoe Fire Tower—tower ... PA-2
Snowshoe Flat—flat ... OR-9
Snowshoe Forest Camp—locale ... OR-9
Snowshoe Gulch—valley ... AK-9
Snowshoe Gulch—valley ... ID-8
Snowshoe Gulch—valley ... MT-8
Snowshoe Gulch—valley ... NV-8
Snowshoe Gulch—valley ... OR-9
Snowshoe Intersection ... PA-2
Snowshoe Island—island ... NY-2
Snowshoe Lake ... MN-6
Snowshoe Lake ... MT-8
Snowshoe Lake—lake (2) ... AK-9
Snowshoe Lake—lake ... ME-1
Snowshoe Lake—lake ... MI-6
Snowshoe Lake—lake (4) ... MN-6
Snowshoe Lake—lake ... MT-8
Snowshoe Lake—lake ... OR-9
Snowshoe Lake—lake (2) ... WI-6
Snowshoe Lake Road—trail ... ME-1
Snowshoe Lakes—lake ... MT-8
Snowshoe Lake Trail—trail ... OR-9
Snowshoe Mesa—summit ... CO-8
Snowshoe Mine—mine ... ID-8
Snowshoe Mine—mine ... MT-8
Snowshoe Mtn—summit ... CO-8
Snowshoe Mtn—summit (2) ... ME-1
Snowshoe Mtn—summit ... WA-9
Snowshoe Mtn—summit ... WY-8
Snowshoe Pass—gap ... AK-9
Snowshoe Pass—gap ... MT-8
Snowshoe Pass—gap (2) ... WY-8
Snowshoe Peak—summit ... MT-8
Snowshoe Point—summit ... OR-9
Snowshoe Pond—lake (3) ... ME-1
Snowshoe Pond—lake ... NY-2
Snowshoe Ranch—locale (2) ... CO-8
Snowshoe Ranch—locale ... WY-8
Snowshoe Ridge—ridge ... AZ-5
Snowshoe Ridge—ridge ... UT-8
Snowshoe Ridge—ridge (2) ... WA-9
Snow Shoe Rsvr—reservoir ... PA-2
Snowshoes Cabin—locale ... ID-8
Snowshoe Ski Area—other ... WV-2
Snowshoe Spring—spring ... MT-8
Snowshoe Spring—spring (3) ... OR-9
Snowshoe Spring—spring ... WA-9
Snowshoe Springs Campground—locale ... CA-9
Snow Shoe (sta.) (RR name for Clarence)—other ... PA-2
Snowshoe Summit—summit ... ID-8
Snowshoe Thompson—pillar ... CA-9
Snowshoe Thompson Ditch Number Two—canal ... CA-9
Snowshoe Thompson Historical Monmnt—park ... CA-9
**Snow Shoe (Township of)**—pop pl ... PA-2
Snowshoe Trail—trail ... CO-8
Snow Shop Station—locale ... PA-2
Snowside Canyon—valley ... ID-8
Snowside Point—cliff ... ID-8
Snows Island ... SC-3
Snow's Island—hist pl ... SC-3
Snows Lake—lake ... CA-9
Snows Lake—reservoir ... AL-4
Snows Lake—reservoir ... SC-3
Snowslide Canyon ... UT-8
Snowslide Canyon—valley (4) ... CA-9
Snowslide Canyon—valley ... CO-8
Snowslide Canyon—valley ... ID-8
Snowslide Canyon—valley ... OR-9
Snowslide Canyon—valley ... UT-8
Snow Slide Canyon—valley ... UT-8
Snowslide Creek ... MT-8
Snowslide Creek—stream (2) ... AK-9
Snowslide Creek—stream (2) ... CA-9
Snowslide Creek—stream (2) ... CO-8
Snowslide Creek—stream (7) ... ID-8
Snowslide Creek—stream (5) ... MT-8
Snowslide Creek—stream ... WA-9
Snowslide Creek—stream ... WY-8
Snowslide Gulch—valley ... AK-9
Snowslide Gulch—valley (6) ... CA-9
Snowslide Gulch—valley (3) ... CO-8
Snowslide Gulch—valley (3) ... ID-8
Snowslide Gulch—valley ... MT-8
Snowslide Gulch—valley ... NV-8
Snowslide Gulch—valley ... UT-8
Snowslide Gulch—valley ... WA-9
Snowslide Lake—lake ... CA-9
Snowslide Lake—lake ... ID-8
Snowslide Lakes—lake ... ID-8
Snowslide Mountain ... ID-8
Snowslide Mtn—summit ... CO-8
Snowslide Mtn—summit ... MT-8
Snowslide Park—flat ... CO-8
Snowslide Peak—summit ... CA-9
Snowslide Peak—summit (2) ... ID-8
Snowslide Spring—spring ... AZ-5
Snow Slide Spring—spring ... CA-9
Snowslide Summit—summit ... ID-8
Snowslide Trail—trail ... CO-8
Snowslide Trailhead—locale ... NV-8
**Snowslip**—pop pl ... MT-8
Snowslip Mtn—summit ... MT-8
Snow Slough—gut ... OR-9
Snows Marsh—swamp ... NC-3
Snows Marshes ... NC-3
Snows Mill—locale ... GA-3
Snows Mill—locale ... PA-2
Snows Mill Creek ... AL-4
Snows Mill (historical)—locale ... AL-4
Snows Mill Pond ... MA-1
Snows Millpond—reservoir ... MA-1
Snows Mill Pond Dam—dam ... MA-1
Snows Mountain—ridge ... NH-1
Snows Neck—cape ... DE-2
Snows Point—cape ... MA-1
Snows Point—cape ... NC-3
Snows Pond ... MA-1
Snows Pond—lake (2) ... MA-1
Snows Pond—reservoir ... GA-3
Snows Pond—swamp ... MA-1
Snow Spring ... AZ-5
Snow Spring ... OR-9
Snow Spring—locale ... GA-3
Snow Spring—spring ... AL-4
Snow Spring—spring ... CA-9
Snow Spring—spring ... CO-8
Snow Spring—spring ... NV-8
Snow Spring—spring ... NM-5
Snow Spring—spring (2) ... OR-9
Snow Spring—spring ... UT-8
Snow Spring—spring ... WA-9
Snow Spring Creek—stream ... WY-8
Snow Spring Mountain ... GA-3
Snow Springs—locale ... GA-3
Snow Springs Ch—church ... GA-3
Snow Springs Mtn—summit ... GA-3
Snow Spring Wash—stream ... NV-8
Snow Spring Wash—valley ... UT-8
Snow Spur Creek ... CO-8
Snow Spur Creek—stream ... CO-8
Snows Rock—island ... ME-1
Snows School ... TN-4
Snows Swamp Branch—stream ... NC-3
Snow Stake Creek—stream ... AZ-5
Snowstorm Creek ... NV-8
Snowstorm Creek—stream ... CA-9
Snowstorm Creek—stream ... NV-8
Snowstorm Flat—flat ... NV-8
Snowstorm Lake—lake ... CO-8
Snowstorm Mine—mine ... MT-8
Snow Storm Mine—mine ... NV-8
Snowstorm Mine—mine ... NV-8
Snowstorm Mine (historical)—mine ... SD-7
Snowstorm Mines—mine ... ID-8
Snowstorm Mtn—summit ... AZ-5
Snowstorm Mtn—summit ... CA-9
Snowstorm Mtn—summit ... MT-8
Snowstorm Mtn—summit ... NV-8
Snowstorm Mtns—summit ... NV-8
Snowstorm Peak—summit ... CO-8
Snowstorm Peak—summit ... ID-8
Snowstorm Ranch—locale ... CA-9
Snow Storm Rsvr—reservoir ... OR-9
Snowstorm Tank—reservoir ... AZ-5
**Snow Subdivision**—pop pl ... UT-8
Snow Summit—summit ... CA-9
Snow Summit Ranch—locale ... UT-8
Snow Survey Cabin—locale ... CA-9
Snow Tank—reservoir (2) ... AZ-5
Snow Tank—reservoir (2) ... NM-5
Snow Tank—reservoir ... TX-5
Snowtent Spring—spring ... CA-9
**Snow Terrace (subdivision)**—pop pl ... AL-4
Snow Top—summit ... AK-9
Snow Tower—summit ... AK-9
Snow Towers, The—summit ... AK-9
**Snowtown**—pop pl ... AL-4
**Snow Town**—pop pl ... SC-3
Snowtown Ch ... MS-4
Snowtown Ch—church ... AL-4
Snow Town Ch—church ... MS-4
**Snow Township**—pop pl ... ND-7
Snow Valley—flat ... ID-8
Snow Valley—valley (2) ... CA-9
Snow Valley—valley ... NV-8
Snow Valley—valley ... OK-5
Snow Valley Peak—summit ... NV-8
Snow Valley Pond—reservoir ... NJ-2
Snow Valley Rec Area—locale ... CA-9
Snow Valley Residential Hist Dist—hist pl ... AL-4
Snow Valley Ski Area—area ... VT-1
Snow Valley Ski Club—other ... MI-6
Snowview Sch—school ... OH-6
Snowville ... AL-4
**Snowville**—pop pl ... MI-6
**Snowville**—pop pl ... NH-1
**Snowville**—pop pl ... OH-6
**Snowville**—pop pl ... UT-8
**Snowville**—pop pl ... VA-3
Snowville Cem—cemetery ... UT-8
Snowville Ch—church ... VA-3
Snowville Christian Church—hist pl ... VA-3
Snowville Hist Dist—hist pl ... VA-3
Snowville Sch—school ... SC-3
Snowville Sch—school ... UT-8
Snowville Sch—school ... VA-3
Snow Water Canyon—valley ... NV-8
Snow Water Creek ... ID-8
Snow Water Creek—stream ... ID-8
Snow Water Lake—lake ... NV-8
Snow Water Springs—locale ... CO-8
Snow White—summit ... AK-9
Snow White Mine—mine ... CA-9
Snowy, Mount—summit ... MT-8
Snowy Butte ... OR-9
Snowy Butte Flour Mill—hist pl ... OR-9
Snowy Creek—stream ... CA-9
Snowy Creek—stream ... MD-2
Snowy Creek—stream ... WA-9
Snowy Creek—stream ... WV-2
Snowy Creek Trail—trail ... CA-9
Snowy Forest Camp—locale ... CA-9
Snowy Gulch—valley ... MT-8
Snowy Lake—lake ... AK-9
Snowy Lakes Pass—gap ... WA-9
Snowy Mountain ... WY-8
Snowy Mountain Fire Tower—tower ... PA-2
Snowy Mountains ... MT-8
Snowy Mountains ... WY-8
Snowy Mountain Vista—locale ... PA-2
Snowy Mtn—summit ... AK-9
Snowy Mtn—summit ... NY-2
Snowy Mtn—summit ... PA-2
Snowy Mtn—summit ... VA-3
Snowy Mtn—summit ... WV-2
Snowy Peak—summit ... CA-9
Snowy Peak—summit ... MT-8
Snowy Point—summit ... WV-2
Snowy Range ... MT-8
Snowy Range ... WY-8
Snowy Range—range ... WY-8
Snowy Range Pass—gap ... WY-8
Snowy Range Ranch—locale ... MT-8
Snowyside Lake ... ID-8
Snowyside Lakes ... ID-8
Snowyside Peak—summit ... ID-8
Snowy Summit—summit ... ID-8
Snowy Top—summit ... ID-8
Snowy Top Mountain ... ID-8
**S.N.P.J.**—pop pl ... PA-2
S. N. P. J. Borough—civil ... PA-2
S N Smith Grant—civil ... FL-3
Snub Brook—stream ... ME-1
Snub Lake—lake ... MN-6
Snub Pitch—cliff ... ME-1
Snuff Box Canal—canal ... GA-3
Snuffbox Creek—stream ... MI-6
Snuff Box Swamp—swamp (2) ... GA-3
Snuff Branch—stream ... TN-4
Snuff Creek—stream ... OH-6
Snuffer Cem—cemetery ... KY-4
Snuffer Cem—cemetery (2) ... WV-2
Snuffers Ridge—ridge ... VA-3
Snuff Gap—gap ... MT-8
Snuffins Creek—stream ... CA-9
Snuff Lake—lake ... MN-6
**Snuff Ridge**—pop pl ... TX-5
Snuff Shelter—locale ... OR-9
Snufftown ... NJ-2
Snufftown ... PA-2
**Snufftown**—pop pl ... NY-2
**Snufftown**—pop pl ... PA-2
Snuffy Smith Cave ... AL-4
Snug Anchorage—bay ... AK-9
Snug Corner Cove—bay ... AK-9
Snug Cove ... MI-6
Snug Cove—bay (2) ... AK-9
Snuggedy Swamp—swamp ... SC-3
Snug Harbor—bay (3) ... AK-9
Snug Harbor—bay (4) ... MI-6
Snug Harbor—bay ... NJ-2
Snug Harbor—cove ... MA-1
Snug Harbor—harbor ... MD-2
Snug Harbor—harbor ... MI-6
Snug Harbor—harbor ... NJ-2
Snug Harbor—locale ... AK-9
**Snug Harbor**—pop pl ... CT-1
**Snug Harbor**—pop pl ... DE-2
**Snug Harbor**—pop pl ... FL-3
**Snug Harbor**—pop pl (2) ... MD-2
**Snug Harbor**—pop pl ... MA-1
**Snug Harbor**—pop pl (2) ... MI-6
**Snug Harbor**—pop pl ... NJ-2
**Snug Harbor**—pop pl ... NC-3
**Snug Harbor**—pop pl ... RI-1
**Snug Harbor**—pop pl ... VA-3
**Snug Harbor**—pop pl ... WA-9
Snug Harbor Cave—cave ... AL-4
Snug Harbor Marina—other ... GA-3
Snug Harbor Marsh—swamp ... MD-2
Snug Harbor Public Use Area—park ... OK-5
Snug Harbor Sch—school ... AL-4
Snug Harbor Sch—school ... MA-1
Snug Harbor Shop Ctr—locale ... VA-3
**Snug Harbor (subdivision)**—pop pl ... NC-3
**Snug Hill**—pop pl ... DE-2
**Snumshire**—pop pl ... NH-1
Snure Tank—reservoir ... AZ-5
Snusbox Lake—lake ... MN-6
Snus Lake—lake ... NE-7
Snowslide Creek—stream ... AK-9
Sny, The—stream ... IL-6
Snydam Creek—stream ... NY-2
Snyden Hill ... NY-2
Snyder—locale ... IA-7
Snyder—locale ... TX-5
Snyder—locale ... UT-8
Snyder—locale ... VA-3
**Snyder**—pop pl ... AR-4
**Snyder**—pop pl ... CO-8
**Snyder**—pop pl ... IL-6
**Snyder**—pop pl ... IA-7
**Snyder**—pop pl ... MO-7
**Snyder**—pop pl ... NE-7
**Snyder**—pop pl ... NY-2
**Snyder**—pop pl ... NC-3
**Snyder**—pop pl ... OK-5
**Snyder**—pop pl ... PA-2
**Snyder**—pop pl ... TX-5
Snyder, Gov. Simon, Mansion—hist pl ... PA-2
Snyder, H. E., House—hist pl ... NE-7
Snyder, Noah, Farm—hist pl ... WV-2
Snyder, William Penn, House—hist pl ... PA-2
Snyder, Wilson I., House—hist pl ... UT-8
Snyder Airp—airport ... PA-2
Snyder Bay—bay ... MN-6
Snyder Bluff—cliff ... KY-4
Snyder Branch ... TX-5
Snyder Branch—stream ... IN-6
Snyder Branch—stream ... IA-7
Snyder Branch—stream ... KY-4
Snyder Branch—stream ... NC-3
Snyder Branch—stream (2) ... TN-4
Snyder Branch—stream ... TX-5
Snyder Branch—stream ... VA-3
Snyder Bridge—locale ... IA-7
Snyder Brook—stream ... NH-1
Snyder Brook—stream ... NY-2
Snyderburg ... PA-2
Snyder Camp—locale ... CA-9
Snyder Camp—locale ... MI-6
Snyder Canal—canal ... CO-8
Snyder Canyon—valley ... CA-9
Snyder Canyon—valley ... CO-8
Snyder Canyon—valley ... ID-8
Snyder Canyon—valley (2) ... OR-9
Snyder Canyon—valley ... WA-9
Snyder Caves—cave ... PA-2
Snyder (CCD)—cens area ... OK-5
Snyder (CCD)—cens area ... TX-5
Snyder Cem—cemetery ... IL-6
Snyder Cem—cemetery (2) ... IN-6
Snyder Cem—cemetery (2) ... MO-7
Snyder Cem—cemetery ... NE-7
Snyder Cem—cemetery (4) ... NY-2
Snyder Cem—cemetery ... NC-3
Snyder Cem—cemetery (3) ... OH-6
Snyder Cem—cemetery ... OK-5
Snyder Cem—cemetery (3) ... PA-2
Snyder Cem—cemetery ... SC-3
Snyder Cem—cemetery (3) ... TN-4
Snyder Cem—cemetery ... TX-5
Snyder Cem—cemetery ... WV-2
Snyder Cemetery—cemetery ... AR-4
Snyder Ch—church ... NJ-2
Snyder Chapel—church ... WV-2
Snyder Chapel (historical)—church ... TN-4
Snyder Consolidated Sch—school ... KY-4
Snyder Corner—locale ... PA-2
**Snyder County**—pop pl ... PA-2
Snyder Cove—bay ... WA-9
Snyder Covered Bridge No. 17—hist pl ... PA-2
Snyder Creek ... ID-8
Snyder Creek ... NC-3
Snyder Creek—stream ... AK-9
Snyder Creek—stream (3) ... CO-8
Snyder Creek—stream (4) ... ID-8
Snyder Creek—stream ... IL-6
Snyder Creek—stream (2) ... IA-7
Snyder Creek—stream ... KS-7
Snyder Creek—stream (3) ... MI-6
Snyder Creek—stream ... MO-7
Snyder Creek—stream (2) ... MT-8
Snyder Creek—stream ... NY-2
Snyder Creek—stream (2) ... NC-3
Snyder Creek—stream (2) ... OR-9
Snyder Creek—stream ... PA-2
Snyder Creek—stream ... TN-4
Snyder Creek—stream (2) ... WA-9
Snyder Creek—stream (2) ... WY-8
**Snyder Crossing**—pop pl ... NY-2
Snyder Dam—dam ... PA-2
Snyder Ditch—canal (2) ... IN-6
Snyder Ditch—canal ... MO-7
Snyder Ditch—canal ... OH-6
Snyder Ditch Ch—church ... MO-7
Snyder Drain ... MI-6
Snyder Drain—canal ... MI-6
Snyder Draw—valley ... CO-8
Snyder Elem Sch—school ... PA-2
Snyder Falls—falls ... CO-8
Snyder Falls Creek—stream ... AK-9
Snyder Flats—flat ... CO-8
Snyder Gap—gap ... NC-3
Snyder Gap—gap ... TN-4
Snyder Guard Station Historical District—hist pl ... ID-8
Snyder Gulch—valley ... CA-9
Snyder Gulch—valley (3) ... CO-8
Snyder Gulch—valley ... MT-8
Snyder Hill—summit ... AZ-5
Snyder Hill—summit ... IN-6
Snyder Hill—summit (3) ... NY-2
Snyder Hill—summit ... PA-2
Snyder Hill—summit ... WA-9
Snyder Hill—summit ... WV-2
Snyder Hill Cem—cemetery (2) ... NY-2
Snyder (historical)—locale ... AL-4
Snyder (historical)—locale ... KS-7
Snyder (historical P.O.)—locale ... IA-7
Snyder Hollow ... MO-7
Snyder Hollow—valley ... MO-7
Snyder Hollow—valley ... OH-6
Snyder Hollow—valley (2) ... WV-2
Snyder House—hist pl ... AR-4
Snyder HS—school ... NJ-2
Snyder JHS—school ... PA-2
Snyder Knob—summit (2) ... WV-2
Snyder Knoll—summit ... AZ-5
Snyder Lake ... MI-6
Snyder Lake—lake ... CA-9
Snyder Lake—lake ... CO-8
Snyder Lake—lake ... IL-6
Snyder Lake—lake (3) ... MI-6
Snyder Lake—lake ... MN-6
Snyder Lake—lake ... MT-8
Snyder Lake—lake ... NE-7
Snyder Lake—lake ... NM-5
Snyder Lake—lake (2) ... NY-2
Snyder Lake—lake ... TX-5
Snyder Lake—lake ... WA-9
Snyder Lake—lake ... WI-6
Snyder Lake—lake ... WY-8
Snyder Lake—reservoir ... NM-5
Snyder Lake—reservoir ... ND-7
Snyder Lake—reservoir ... TX-5
Snyder Lake—reservoir ... WI-6
Snyder Lake Dam—dam ... ND-7
Snyder Lake Natl Wildlife Ref—park ... ND-7
Snyder Lake Trail—trail ... MT-8
Snyder Lateral—canal ... ID-8
Snyder Meadow—flat ... OR-9
Snyder Meadow Creek—stream ... OR-9
Snyder Memory Gardens—cemetery ... TN-4
Snyder Mesa—summit ... UT-8
Snyder Middleswarth Natural Area—area ... PA-2
Snyder-Middleswarth State For Park ... PA-2
Snyder-Middleswarth State Park—park ... PA-2
Snyder Mine—mine (2) ... AZ-5
Snyder Mine—mine ... MN-6
Snyder Mtn—summit ... AK-9
Snyder Mtn—summit ... AR-4
Snyder Mtn—summit ... CO-8
Snyder Mtn—summit ... WA-9
Snyder Number Two Dam—dam ... UT-8
Snyder Oil Field—oilfield ... TX-5
Snyder Park—park ... OH-6
Snyder Park—park ... WI-6
Snyder Park Sch—school ... OH-6
Snyder Pasture—flat ... WA-9
Snyder Place—locale ... WY-8
Snyder Pond—lake ... IN-6
Snyder Pond—lake (2) ... NY-2
Snyder Pond—lake ... PA-2
Snyder Pond—swamp ... IL-6
Snyder Pond Dam—dam ... AL-4
Snyder Prospect—mine ... TN-4
Snyder Ranch—locale ... CA-9
Snyder Ranch—locale ... NE-7
Snyder Ranch—locale ... NM-5
Snyder Ranch—locale ... WY-8
Snyder Ranch Airp—airport ... PA-2
Snyder Ranch Airstrip—airport ... OR-9
Snyder Recreation Center—park ... CA-9
Snyder Ridge—ridge ... CA-9
Snyder Ridge—ridge ... MO-7
Snyder Ridge—ridge ... MT-8
Snyder Ridge Trail—trail ... MT-8
Snyder Roton Aqueduct—canal ... TX-5
Snyder Rsvr—reservoir ... MT-8
Snyder Rsvr—reservoir ... UT-8
Snyder Rsvr—reservoir ... WY-8
Snyder Rsvr Number Two—reservoir ... UT-8
Snyder Run ... WV-2
Snyder Run—stream (2) ... PA-2
Snyder Run—stream (4) ... WV-2
Snyder Run Access Area—area ... PA-2
Snyder Run Boat Launch ... PA-2
Snyders ... AL-4
**Snyders**—pop pl ... PA-2
Snyders Airp—airport ... PA-2
Snyders Bluff—cliff ... MS-4
Snyder's Bluff—hist pl ... MS-4
Snyders Bluff Landing (historical)—locale ... MS-4
Snyders Bluff Sch (historical)—school ... MS-4
**Snydersburg**—pop pl ... MD-2
**Snydersburg**—pop pl ... PA-2
Snyders Ch—church ... WV-2
Snyder Sch—school ... CA-9
Snyder Sch—school ... IA-7
Snyder Sch—school ... MI-6
Snyder Sch—school ... MO-7
Snyder Sch—school ... NY-2
Snyder Sch—school (3) ... PA-2
Snyder Sch (abandoned)—school ... MO-7
Snyder Sch (abandoned)—school (3) ... PA-2
Snyders Chapel—church ... IN-6
Snyder Sch (historical)—school (3) ... PA-2
Snyder Sch (historical)—school ... TN-4
**Snyders Corner**—pop pl ... WA-9
Snyders Corners—locale ... NY-2
**Snyders Corners**—pop pl (2) ... NY-2
Snyders Ditch—canal ... OH-6
Snyders Ditch—canal ... WY-8
Snyder Seeps—lake ... UT-8
Snyders Ferry ... PA-2
Snyders Grove—locale ... IA-7
Snyder Shaft—mine ... NV-8
**Snyders Hill**—pop pl ... NH-1
Snyders Hill—summit ... PA-2
Snyders Hole—valley ... ID-8
Snyders Lake—lake ... NY-2
**Snyders Lake**—pop pl ... NY-2
Snyders Lake—reservoir ... NC-3
Snyders Lake Dam—dam ... NC-3
Snyders Landing—locale ... MD-2
Snyder Slough—stream ... WA-9
Snyders Mill ... AL-4
**Snyders Mill**—pop pl ... OH-6
Snyders Mine—mine ... MT-8
Snyders Pond—reservoir ... NY-2
Snyder Spring—spring (2) ... CO-8
Snyder Spring—spring ... OR-9
Snyder Spring—spring ... UT-8
Snyder Spring—spring ... WY-8
Snyder Springs—spring ... ID-8
Snyder Square—locale ... PA-2
Snyders Ranch (historical)—locale ... SD-7
Snyders (RR name for Laona)—other ... WI-6
Snyders Run ... PA-2
Snyders Run—stream (3) ... PA-2
Snyders Sch—school ... PA-2
Snyders Sch (historical)—school ... TN-4
Snyders Shool ... AL-4
Snyder's Super Service Station—hist pl ... OK-5
Snydersville ... PA-2
**Snydersville**—pop pl (2) ... PA-2
Snyder Swale—flat ... WA-9
Snyder Swale—valley ... WA-9
Snyder Swamp—swamp ... NY-2
Snyder Swamp—swamp ... PA-2
Snyder Tank—reservoir (2) ... AZ-5
Snyder Tennis Complex—park ... FL-3
Snydertown—locale ... NJ-2
Snydertown—locale ... PA-2
**Snydertown**—pop pl (6) ... PA-2
Snydertown Borough—civil ... PA-2
**Snyder (Township of)**—pop pl (2) ... PA-2
Snyder Trail—trail ... WA-9
Snyder Valley—basin ... NE-7
Snyderville ... PA-2
Snyderville—locale ... UT-8
**Snyderville**—pop pl ... MI-6
**Snyderville**—pop pl ... NY-2
**Snyderville**—pop pl ... OH-6
**Snyderville (Muff)**—pop pl ... PA-2
Snyder Water Canyon—valley ... UT-8
Snyder Waterhole ... CA-9
Snyder Well—well (2) ... AZ-5
Snyder Well—well ... NM-5
Snyder Well—well ... TX-5
Snyder Well No 20—well ... WY-8
Snyer Knoll ... AZ-5
Sny Magill Creek—stream ... IA-7
Soacson ... AZ-5
Soadabscook Stream ... ME-1
Soakas Creek—stream ... NC-3
Soak Ash Creek—stream ... TN-4
Soak Creek—stream ... TN-4
Soak Creek—stream ... WV-2
Soaked Lake—lake ... MN-6
Soakem Mtn—summit ... MT-8
Soakhide Brook—stream ... RI-1
Soakie Creek—stream ... MO-7
Soaking Gully—swamp ... FL-3
Soakingwater Creek—stream ... AL-4
Soakpak Mtn—summit ... AK-9
Soap And Tallow Branch—stream ... LA-4
Soap Basin—basin ... CO-8
Soapberry Draw—valley ... NM-5
Soapberry Mtn—summit ... AK-9
Soapbox Canyon—valley ... AZ-5
Soap Box Derby Track—locale ... TN-4
Soap Butte—summit ... CA-9
Soap Canyon—valley ... AZ-5
Soap Creek ... GA-3
Soap Creek ... MO-7
Soap Creek ... MT-8
Soap Creek—stream ... AL-4
Soap Creek—stream (2) ... AZ-5
Soap Creek—stream (5) ... CA-9
Soap Creek—stream (2) ... CO-8
Soap Creek—stream ... FL-3
Soap Creek—stream (2) ... GA-3
Soap Creek—stream ... ID-8
Soap Creek—stream (2) ... IA-7
Soap Creek—stream ... LA-4
Soap Creek—stream ... MI-6
Soap Creek—stream (4) ... MO-7
Soap Creek—stream (3) ... MT-8
Soap Creek—stream (2) ... NE-7
Soap Creek—stream ... NV-8
Soap Creek—stream (2) ... OR-9
Soap Creek—stream (2) ... TX-5
Soap Creek—stream ... VA-3
Soap Creek—stream ... WA-9
Soap Creek—stream (2) ... WY-8
Soap Creek Campground—locale ... CO-8
Soap Creek Canyon—valley ... MT-8
**Soap Creek (Cliff Dwellers Lodge)**—pop pl ... AZ-5
Soap Creek Ditch—canal ... MT-8
Soap Creek Lodge—locale ... GA-3
Soap Creek Mesa ... CO-8
Soap Creek Number One Tank—reservoir ... AZ-5
Soap Creek Number Two Tank—reservoir ... AZ-5
Soap Creek Oilfield—oilfield ... MT-8
Soap Creek Pass—locale ... CA-9
Soap Creek Pasture ... AZ-5
Soap Creek Pasture—flat ... AZ-5
Soap Creek Rapids—rapids ... AZ-5
Soap Creek Ridge—ridge ... CA-9
Soap Creek School (abandoned)—locale ... OR-9
Soap Creek Township—fmr MCD ... IA-7
Soap Creek Trail—trail ... AZ-5
Soap Dam Creek—stream ... TN-4
Soap Flat—flat ... OR-9
Soap Flat—flat ... UT-8
Soap Gap—gap ... AL-4
Soapgrass Mtn—summit ... OR-9
Soap Gulch—valley ... MT-8
Soap Hill—summit ... AL-4
Soap Hill—summit ... NY-2

Soap Hole Basin—basin WY-8
Soap Hole Branch—stream AL-4
Soaphole Bridge—bridge WY-8
Soap Hole Ditch—canal WY-8
Soap Hole Draw—valley WY-8
Soap Holes—basin WY-8
Soap Holes—bend WY-8
Soap Holes—lake WY-8
Soap Hole Spring—spring SD-7
Soaphole Spring—spring WY-8
Soap Holes Rsvr—reservoir WY-8
Soap Hole Wash—valley WY-8
Soap Hollow—valley PA-2
Soap Hollow—valley UT-8
Soap Hollow Rsvr—reservoir UT-8
Soap Lake—lake CA-9
Soap Lake—lake MN-6
Soap Lake—lake ND-7
Soap Lake—lake (2) WA-9
**Soap Lake**—pop pl WA-9
Soap Lake Hill WA-9
Soap Lake Mtn—summit WA-9
**Soap Lake (sta.)**—pop pl WA-9
Soap Mesa—summit CO-8
Soap Mtn—summit OK-5
Soaproot Flat—flat CA-9
Soaproot Saddle—gap CA-9
Soap Run—stream MI-6
Soaps Ford—locale TN-4
Soap Spring—spring CO-8
Soap Spring—spring MT-8
Soap Spring—spring (2) OR-9
Soapstick—locale GA-3
Soapstone—locale VA-3
Soapstone Basin—basin UT-8
Soapstone Branch—stream (2) AL-4
Soapstone Branch—stream FL-3
Soapstone Branch—stream (3) GA-3
Soapstone Branch—stream MD-2
Soapstone Branch—stream (4) NC-3
Soapstone Branch—stream VA-3
Soapstone Camp—locale CO-8
Soapstone Campground—locale UT-8
Soapstone Ch—church AL-4
Soapstone Ch—church NC-3
Soapstone Ch—church SC-3
Soapstone Cove—bay AK-9
Soapstone Creek OR-9
Soapstone Creek—stream (2) AL-4
Soapstone Creek—stream (2) CA-9
Soapstone Creek—stream (2) GA-3
Soapstone Creek—stream IN-6
Soapstone Creek—stream LA-4
Soapstone Creek—stream NY-2
Soapstone Creek—stream NC-3
Soapstone Creek—stream OR-9
Soapstone Creek—stream UT-8
Soapstone Creek—stream WY-8
Soapstone Forest Service Station UT-8
Soapstone Gap—gap GA-3
Soapstone Gap—gap (4) NC-3
Soapstone Guard Station—locale UT-8
Soapstone Gulch—valley (2) CA-9
Soapstone Hill—summit AR-4
Soapstone Hill—summit (2) CA-9
Soapstone Hill—summit MA-1
Soapstone Hill—summit TN-4
Soapstone (historical)—locale AL-4
Soapstone Hollow—valley KY-4
Soapstone Island—island FL-3
Soapstone Knob—summit NC-3
Soapstone Lake CA-9
Soapstone Lake—lake WY-8
Soapstone Lake—reservoir OR-9
**Soapstone Mountain**—pop pl NC-3
Soapstone Mountain—ridge GA-3
Soapstone Mtn—summit CT-1
Soapstone Mtn—summit NC-3
Soapstone Mtn—summit UT-8
Soapstone Mtn State Forest CT-1
Soapstone Pass—gap UT-8
Soapstone Pit—basin WI-6
Soapstone Point—cape AK-9
Soapstone Pond—lake CA-9
Soapstone Ranger Station UT-8
Soapstone Ridge—hist pl GA-3
Soapstone Ridge—ridge (2) CA-9
Soapstone Ridge—ridge (2) NC-3
Soapstone Spring—spring ID-8
Soapstone Springs—spring CO-8
**Soapstone Summer Home Area**—pop pl UT-8
Soapstone Valley Park—park DC-2
Soapston Mountain UT-8
Soaptown—locale OH-6
Soaptown Hollow—valley OH-6
Soapville IN-6
Soap Wash—valley (2) UT-8
Soap Wash Rsvr—reservoir UT-8
Soapweed—locale CA-9
Soapweed Creek—stream CA-9
Soapweed Tank—reservoir AZ-5
Soapy Dale Peak—summit WY-8
Soapy Hill—summit CO-8
Soard Cave TN-4
Soard Flat—flat ID-8
Soards Gulch—valley ID-8
Soares Gulch—valley CA-9
Soaring Eagle Campground—locale TN-4
Soar Memorial Park—park FL-3
So-Bahli-Alhi Glacier—glacier WA-9
Sobaka Rock—island AK-9
Sobak Cem—cemetery ND-7
Sob Canyon AZ-5
S O B Canyon—valley AZ-5
Sob Canyon—valley ID-8
Sob Creek—stream (2) ID-8
Sob Creek—stream WY-8
Sobek Lake—reservoir SD-7
Sobel Post Office (historical)—building TN-4
Sober PA-2
**Sober**—pop pl PA-2
Soberanes Creek—stream CA-9
Soberanes Point—cape CA-9
Sober Lake—lake MN-6
Sober Up Coulee—valley MT-8
Sober-Up Gulch—valley NV-8
Soberup Ranch—locale MT-8
Soberville Hollow—valley UT-8
Sobey Creek—stream CA-9
Sobey Sch—school MI-6
S.O.B. Hill—summit UT-8
**Sobieski**—pop pl MN-6
**Sobieski**—pop pl WI-6
**Sobieski Corners**—pop pl WI-6
Sobieskie Mountain WA-9
Sobieski Mtn—summit WA-9
Sobieski Park—park MN-6
Sobiesky Creek—stream MI-6
SOB Lake—lake NV-8
**Soboba Hot Springs**—pop pl CA-9
**Soboba Ind Res**—pop pl CA-9
Sobol—locale OK-5
Sobola MS-4
Sobol Cem—cemetery OK-5
Sobol Ch—church OK-5
Sobol Lookout Tower—locale OK-5
Sobota FM-9
Sobotka Mill (historical)—locale AL-4
Sobou FM-9
Sobou Mission FM-9
Sob Point—cape MD-2
Sob Point—summit ID-8
Sobrante—locale CA-9
Sobrante Park Sch—school CA-9
Sobrante Ridge—ridge CA-9
Sobrante Rsvr—reservoir CA-9
S O B Rapids—rapids UT-8
SOB Spring—spring OR-9
Sobuk FM-9
Sobu Reef FM-9
Sobu Riff FM-9
Soby Tank—reservoir TX-5
Socagee Bayou TX-5
Socagee Creek TX-5
Socagee Creek—stream TX-5
Socagie Creek TX-5
Socapartoy AL-4
Socapatoy—locale AL-4
Socapatoy, Lake—reservoir (2) AL-4
Socapatoy Cem—cemetery AL-4
Socapatoy Ch—church AL-4
Socapatoy Creek AL-4
Socapatoy Creek—stream AL-4
Socapatoyo Creek AL-4
Socareda Camp—locale NC-3
**Socastee**—pop pl SC-3
Socastee Creek—stream SC-3
Socastee Swamp—stream SC-3
Socatean Bay—bay ME-1
Socatean Point—cape ME-1
Socatean Ponds—lake ME-1
Socatean Stream—stream ME-1
Soccee Swamp—stream SC-3
Soccer Park—park FL-3
Soccopotoy AL-4
S'Ocholis Canyon—valley OR-9
S'Ocholis Picnic Ground—park OR-9
Socia Branch—stream LA-4
Social RI-1
**Social**—pop pl RI-1
Social Bend TN-4
**Social Circle**—pop pl GA-3
Social Circle (CCD)—cens area GA-3
Social Circle Hist Dist—hist pl GA-3
Social Hall Creek—stream SC-3
**Social Hill**—pop pl AR-4
Social Hill Ch—church (2) AR-4
**Social Island**—pop pl PA-2
Socialist Park—park PA-2
Socialist Valley—basin OR-9
**Social Plains**—pop pl NC-3
Social Plains Sch—school IA-7
Social Point Ch—church TX-5
Social Pond—lake RI-1
Social Ridge—ridge OR-9
Social Science House—hist pl OH-6
Social Springs Ch—church LA-4
Social Town—locale AL-4
Social Union Ch—church NC-3
**Socialville**—pop pl OH-6
Socias Lake—lake MS-4
Sociedad Cem—cemetery TX-5
Society Ch—church NC-3
Society for Savings Bldg—hist pl OH-6
Society for the Lying-In Hosp—hist pl NY-2
Society Hall (historical)—locale TN-4
Society Hill—locale MS-4
**Society Hill**—pop pl AL-4
**Society Hill**—pop pl MD-2
**Society Hill**—pop pl SC-3
Society Hill—summit KY-4
Society Hill Baptist Ch—church MS-4
Society Hill (CCD)—cens area SC-3
Society Hill Cem—cemetery AL-4
Society Hill Cem—cemetery MS-4
Society Hill Ch—church AL-4
Society Hill Ch—church GA-3
Society Hill Ch—church KY-4
Society Hill Ch—church (2) SC-3
Society Hill Hist Dist—hist pl PA-2
Society Hill Post Office (historical)—building AL-4
Society of African Missions Ch—church NJ-2
Society of Friends Hall—hist pl NY-2
Society of Friends Meeting House—church PA-2
Society of Friends Quaker Meeting House DE-2
Society Ridge Baptist Church MS-4
Society Ridge Ch—church MS-4
Society Sons of Truth Cemetery KS-7
Society Turn—locale CO-8
**Socio**—pop pl GU-9
Sockannosset RI-1
Sockanosset RI-1
**Sockanosset**—pop pl RI-1
Sockanosset Hill—summit RI-1
Sock Branch—stream TX-5
Sock Creek—stream MS-4
Sock Creek—stream OR-9
Sockdolager Rapids—rapids AZ-5
Socket Waterhole—lake OR-9
Sockeye Creek—stream (2) AK-9
Sockeye Lake—lake AK-9
Sockeye Lake—lake MN-6
Sockfoot—summit AL-4
Sock Hollow—valley MO-7
Sock Hollow—valley OR-9
Sock-it-to-Me Rapids—rapids UT-8
Sock Lake—lake (3) MN-6
Sock Lake—lake MT-8
Sockomatchie Creek MS-4
Sockorockets Ditch—stream DE-2
Sockorockits Ditch DE-2
Sockrider Peak—summit CO-8
Socks Island—island ME-1
Socktown AL-4
Sockum Creek DE-2
Sockum Creek—stream CA-9
Sockum Ridge Park—park IA-7
Sockumtown DE-2
Sockwa Creek—stream WA-9
Sockwell Baptist Church AL-4
Sockwell Sch (historical)—school AL-4
Soco Bald—summit NC-3
Soco Community Center—locale NC-3
Soco Creek—stream NC-3
Socoe Creek—stream NC-3
Soco Falls—falls NC-3
Soco Gap—gap NC-3
Soco Gap Parking Area—locale NC-3
Socogna—summit GU-9
**Socola**—pop pl LA-4
Socola Canal—canal LA-4
Socola Canal Number Two—canal LA-4
Socom Branch DE-2
Socom Creek DE-2
Socona Ch—church NC-3
Socopatoy AL-4
Soco Ridge—ridge NC-3
Socorra Mine—mine AZ-5
**Socorro**—pop pl NM-5
**Socorro**—pop pl TX-5
Socorro Canyon—valley NM-5
**Socorro (County)**—pop pl NM-5
Socorro Ditch—canal NM-5
Socorro Lateral—canal TX-5
Socorro Main Canal—canal NM-5
Socorro Mines Mining Company Mill, Fannie Hill—hist pl NM-5
Socorro Mission—hist pl TX-5
Socorro Mountains—range NM-5
Socorro Peak—summit AZ-5
Socorro Peak—summit NM-5
Socorro Riverside Drain—canal NM-5
Socorro Riverside Sub Drain—canal NM-5
Socorro Sch—school TX-5
Socorro Spring—spring NM-5
Socrates Mine—mine CA-9
Socrates Mtn—summit WV-2
Socrum—locale FL-3
Socs Island—island ME-1
Soctahoma Creek—stream MS-4
Soctish Creek—stream CA-9
Soctish Point—summit CA-9
Soctum Creek—stream AL-4
Soctum Fire Tower (historical)—tower AL-4
Soctum Hill—summit AL-4
**Sod**—pop pl WV-2
Sod, Mount—summit MA-1
**Soda**—pop pl TX-5
Soda Ash Wells—well WY-8
Soda Bar (historical P.O.)—locale IA-7
Soda Basin—basin CA-9
Soda Basin—basin UT-8
Soda Bay CA-9
Soda Bay—bay AK-9
Soda Bay—bay CA-9
**Soda Bay**—pop pl CA-9
Soda Butte—locale WY-8
Soda Butte—summit CA-9
Soda Butte—summit WY-8
Soda Butte Canyon WY-8
Soda Butte Creek—stream MT-8
Soda Butte Creek—stream WY-8
Soda Canal—canal ID-8
Soda Canyon—valley AZ-5
Soda Canyon—valley (3) CA-9
Soda Canyon—valley CO-8
Soda Canyon Overlook—locale CO-8
Soda Canyon Sch—school CA-9
Soda Ch—church TX-5
Soda Cone—summit CA-9
Soda Creek CA-9
Soda Creek WA-9
Soda Creek WY-8
Soda Creek—stream (5) AK-9
Soda Creek—stream AR-4
Soda Creek—stream (19) CA-9
Soda Creek—stream (8) CO-8
Soda Creek—stream (5) ID-8
Soda Creek—stream MA-1
Soda Creek—stream (3) MT-8
Soda Creek—stream ND-7
Soda Creek—stream (6) OR-9
Soda Creek—stream (2) WA-9
Soda Creek—stream WI-6
Soda Creek—stream (2) WY-8
Soda Creek Forest Camp—locale OR-9
Soda Creek Point—cliff ID-8
Soda Creek Ridge—ridge CA-9
Soda Creek Station—locale CA-9
Soda Creek Trail—trail CA-9
Soda Dam—dam NM-5
Sodafield Cem—cemetery FL-3
Soda Flat—flat CA-9
Soda Fork OR-9
Soda Fork—stream CA-9
Soda Fork—stream OR-9
Soda Fork—stream WY-8
Soda Fork Meadows—flat WY-8
Soda Gulch—valley (3) CA-9
Soda Gulch—valley (3) CO-8
Soda Gulch—valley (2) OR-9
Soda Hill—locale NC-3
Soda Hollow—valley AR-4
Soda Hollow—valley WY-8
Sodak Mill—locale MT-8
Sodak Mine—mine MT-8
So Dak Park SD-7
**So Dak Park**—pop pl SD-7
Soda Lake AZ-5
Soda Lake CA-9
Soda Lake—flat AZ-5
Soda Lake—flat CA-9
Soda Lake—lake AK-9
Soda Lake—lake (3) CA-9
Soda Lake—lake MN-6
Soda Lake—lake NE-7
Soda Lake—lake NV-8
Soda Lake—lake (2) OR-9
Soda Lake—lake (3) TX-5
Soda Lake—lake (2) WA-9
Soda Lake—lake (9) WY-8
Soda Lake—reservoir AZ-5
Soda Lake Bed—flat LA-4
Soda Lake Drain—canal NV-8
Soda Lakes—lake MT-8
Soda Lakes—lake (3) WY-8
Soda Lakes—reservoir CO-8
Soda Lakes Clubhouse—other CO-8
Sodalite Creek—stream MT-8
Sodalite Lake—lake MT-8
Sodality Chapel—hist pl AL-4
Soda Mine—mine OR-9
Soda Mountains—other CA-9
Soda Mtn—summit AR-4
Soda Mtn—summit OR-9
Soda Mtn—summit WY-8
Soda Peak—summit ID-8
Soda Peak—summit WA-9
Soda Peaks—summit WA-9
Soda Peaks Lake—lake WA-9
Soda Peaks Trail—trail WA-9
Soda Pocket Creek—stream NM-5
Soda Point—cliff CO-8
Soda Point—cliff ID-8
Soda Point Reservoir ID-8
Soda Pond—lake NY-2
Soda Range—range NY-2
Soda Ravine—valley CA-9
Soda Ridge—ridge CA-9
Sodarisi Canyon—valley NV-8
Soda Rock—pillar CA-9
Soda Sink CA-9
Soda Slide—other UT-8
Soda Smith Spring—spring OR-9
Soda Spar Mine—mine SD-7
Soda Spring WA-9
Soda Spring—spring (5) AZ-5
Soda Spring—spring (18) CA-9
Soda Spring—spring (4) CO-8
Soda Spring—spring ID-8
Soda Spring—spring MT-8
Soda Spring—spring (3) NV-8
Soda Spring—spring NM-5
Soda Spring—spring (6) OR-9
Soda Spring—spring TX-5
Soda Spring—spring (3) UT-8
Soda Spring—spring (4) WA-9
Soda Spring Campground—locale WA-9
Soda Spring Canyon—valley CA-9
Soda Spring Coulee—valley MT-8
Soda Spring Creek AZ-5
Soda Spring Creek—stream (4) CA-9
Soda Spring Creek—stream WA-9
Soda Spring Dome CA-9
Soda Spring Gulch—valley CA-9
Soda Spring Gulch—valley CO-8
Soda Spring (historical)—spring UT-8
Soda Spring Lake CA-9
Soda Spring Meadow—flat WA-9
Soda Spring Number One—spring AZ-5
Soda Spring Number Two—spring AZ-5
Soda Spring Ranch—locale AZ-5
Soda Springs CA-9
Soda Springs—locale (3) CA-9
Soda Springs—locale MT-8
Soda Springs—locale TX-5
**Soda Springs**—pop pl CA-9
**Soda Springs**—pop pl ID-8
**Soda Springs**—pop pl TX-5
Soda Springs—spring AZ-5
Soda Springs—spring (5) CA-9
Soda Springs—spring (4) CO-8
Soda Springs—spring MA-1
Soda Springs—spring MT-8
Soda Springs—spring (2) NV-8
Soda Springs—spring (2) OR-9
Soda Springs—spring (3) WA-9
Soda Springs—spring WY-8
Soda Springs Basin—basin UT-8
Soda Springs Butte CA-9
Soda Springs Cabin—hist pl CA-9
Soda Springs Campground—locale CA-9
Soda Springs Campground—locale (4) WA-9
Soda Springs Canyon—valley CA-9
Soda Springs Canyon—valley CO-8
Soda Springs Canyon—valley UT-8
Soda Springs Canyon—valley WA-9
Soda Springs Ch—church TX-5
Soda Springs Community Hall—locale TX-5
Soda Springs Creek AZ-5
Soda Springs Creek—stream AZ-5
Soda Springs Creek—stream (2) CA-9
Soda Springs Creek—stream MT-8
Soda Springs Creek—stream TX-5
Soda Springs Dam—dam OR-9
Soda Springs Guard Station—locale CA-9
Soda Springs Gulch AZ-5
Soda Springs Gulch CO-8
Soda Springs Hills—range ID-8
**Soda Springs (historical)**—pop pl OR-9
Soda Springs Park—flat CO-8
Soda Springs Rsvr—reservoir OR-9
Soda Springs (Site)—locale CA-9
Soda Spring Valley—basin NV-8
Soda Straw Cave TN-4
Soda Top—summit AL-4
Soda Valley—valley AR-4
Soda Valley—valley CA-9
Soda Valley—valley OR-9
Soda Valley Ch—church AR-4
Sodaville—locale NV-8
**Sodaville**—pop pl OR-9
Sodaville Mineral Springs—spring OR-9
Sodaville Springs State Park—park OR-9
Soda Water Spring—spring AZ-5
**Soda Well**—pop pl WY-8
Soda Well—well TX-5
Soda Well—well WY-8
Soda Windmill—locale (2) NM-5
Soda Windmill—locale (3) TX-5
Soda Windmills—locale TX-5
Sod Cem—cemetery OK-5
Sod Ch—church WV-2
Sodden Brook MA-1
Soddy TN-4
**Soddy**—pop pl TN-4
Soddy Branch TX-5
Soddy Cem—cemetery TN-4
Soddy Ch of Christ—church TN-4
Soddy Ch of God—church TN-4
Soddy Creek—stream TN-4
**Soddy-Daisy**—pop pl TN-4
Soddy-Daisy (CCD)—cens area TN-4
Soddy-Daisy City Hall—building TN-4
Soddy-Daisy Division—civil TN-4
Soddy-Daisy JHS—school TN-4
Soddy Elem Sch—school TN-4
**Soddy Lake Heights**—pop pl TN-4
Soddy Marine Park—park TN-4
Soddy Meadow Brook—stream ME-1
Soddy Municipal Park—park TN-4
Soddy Number One Mine—mine TN-4
Soddy Post Office—building TN-4
Soddy Shoals—bar TN-4
Sodeberg Cem—cemetery ND-7
Sodem Pond—reservoir MA-1
Soden, Hallie B., House—hist pl KS-7
Soden Dam—dam KS-7
Soden Park—park KS-7
Soden's Grove Bridge—hist pl KS-7
Sodergreen High Line Ditch—canal WY-8
Sodergreen Lake—lake WY-8
Sodergreen Ranch—locale WY-8
Sodergren Lake WY-8
Soderman, John, Farmhouse—hist pl MI-6
Soderman Lakes—lake MN-6
Soderquist Rsvr—reservoir CO-8
Soderstrom Ranch—locale CO-8
Soderstrom Sch—school KS-7
Soderville MN-6
**Soderville**—pop pl MN-6
Sod Hammac Cem—cemetery AL-4
Sod House—hist pl OK-5
Sod House—locale NV-8
Sod House Creek—stream NV-8
Sod House Dam—dam OR-9
Sod House Draw TX-5
Sod House Point—summit NV-8
Sod House - Quinn River Well—well NV-8
Sod House Ranch—hist pl OR-9
Sod House Sch—school OR-9
Sodhouse Spring—spring OR-9
Sod House Station NV-8
Sodium—locale WY-8
Sodom IN-6
Sodom NJ-2
Sodom—locale ME-1
Sodom—locale PA-2
**Sodom**—pop pl CT-1
**Sodom**—pop pl ME-1
**Sodom**—pop pl (2) NY-2
**Sodom**—pop pl NC-3
**Sodom**—pop pl OH-6
**Sodom**—pop pl VT-1
**Sodom**—pop pl WV-2
Sodom Branch—stream (2) NC-3
Sodom Brook ME-1
Sodom Brook—stream (2) MA-1
Sodom Brook—stream RI-1
Sodom Cem—cemetery AL-4
Sodom Cem—cemetery GA-3
Sodom Cem—cemetery IN-6
Sodom Cem—cemetery MN-6
Sodom Cem—cemetery NY-2
Sodom Cem—cemetery (2) OH-6
Sodom Creek—stream KY-4
Sodom Dam—dam OR-9
Sodom Ditch—canal OR-9
Sodom Hill—summit CT-1
Sodom Hill—summit NH-1
Sodom Hollow—valley NC-3
Sodom Mill Historic and Archeol District—hist pl RI-1
Sodom Mountain Ski Area—locale MA-1
Sodom Mtn—summit MA-1
Sodom Mtn—summit NC-3
Sodom Pond—lake VT-1
Sodom Pond Brook—stream VT-1
Sodom Rocks—pillar CT-1
Sodom Sch—school IL-6
Sodom Sch—school PA-2
Sodom Schoolhouse—hist pl PA-2
Sodom Schoolhouse State Historic Site PA-2
Sodom Swamp—swamp FL-3
Sodon Lake—lake MI-6
Sodrac Park—park SD-7
Sodre Revir DE-2
Sod Run—stream IN-6
Sod Run—stream MD-2
Sod Thorofare—channel NJ-2
Sodtown KS-7
Sodtown Cem—cemetery NE-7
**Sodus**—pop pl MI-6
**Sodus**—pop pl NY-2
Sodus Bay—bay NY-2
**Sodus Center**—pop pl NY-2
Sodus Creek—stream IA-7
Sodus Creek—stream NY-2
Sodus Ditch—canal NY-2
**Sodus Point**—pop pl NY-2
Sodus Point Lighthouse—hist pl NY-2
Sodus Sch—school IA-7
**Sodus (Town of)**—pop pl NY-2
**Sodus (Township of)**—pop pl MI-6
**Sodus (Township of)**—pop pl MN-6
Sodville—locale TX-5
Sodville Cem—cemetery KS-7
Sodville (historical)—locale KS-7
**Sodville Township**—pop pl KS-7
**Sodyeco**—pop pl NC-3
Sodyeco Junction NC-3
Sodyeco Lagoon—reservoir NC-3
Sodyeco Lagoon Dam—dam NC-3
**Sodyeco (Southern Chemicals Corp.)**—pop pl NC-3
Soegaard (historical)—locale MS-4
Soehls Lake—lake NE-7
Soelberg Ranch—locale ID-8
Soell Creek—stream TX-5
Soestrom Brook CT-1
Soestrum Brook CT-1
**Soffe Subdivision**—pop pl UT-8
Sofia—locale NM-5
Sofia Cem—cemetery NM-5
Sofia Warehouse—hist pl NY-2
Sofie Lake—lake MN-6
Sofkahatchee Creek—stream AL-4
**Sofkee**—pop pl GA-3
Sofkee Creek—stream GA-3
Sofkee Hatchee Creek AL-4
Soft Boil Bar—bar ID-8
Softing Lake—lake MN-6
Softkee Branch GA-3
Soft Maple—locale NY-2
Soft Maple Creek WI-6
Soft Maple Creek—stream WI-6
Soft Maple Rsvr—reservoir NY-2
Soft Pit—cave AL-4
Soft Prairie—flat FL-3
Soft Rock Creek—stream MT-8
Soft Run—stream PA-2
Soft Shell—locale KY-4
Softuk Bar—bar AK-9
Softuk Lagoon—bay AK-9
Soft Water Canyon—valley NM-5
Soft Water Creek SD-7
Softwater Creek—stream NY-2
Soft Water Creek—stream SD-7
Softwater Creek—stream WY-8
Soft Water Draw—valley SD-7
Soft Water Draw—valley (2) WY-8
Softwater Lake MI-6
Soft Water Lake—lake MI-6
Softwater Lake—lake (2) MI-6
Soft Water Spring—spring CA-9
Soft Water Spring—spring CO-8
Softwater Spring—spring MT-8
Softwater Spring—spring ND-7
Softwater Spring—spring OR-9
Soft Water Township (historical)—civil SD-7
Soft Water Wash—stream NM-5
Softwood Hollow—valley WV-2
Sogany Lake IN-6
Soggy Hill Branch—stream NC-3
Soggy Lake—flat CA-9
Soggy Run—stream OH-6
Sogi—locale AS-9
Sogie MS-4
Soginese Creek—stream MA-1
**Sogn**—pop pl MN-6
Sogonosh Valley Sch—school MI-6
**Soham**—pop pl NM-5
Sohare Creek—stream WY-8
Sohn Creek—stream MI-6
Soh Nting FM-9
Soho—other WV-2
**Soho**—pop pl PA-2
Soho—uninc pl NJ-2
Soho Cottage—hist pl MA-1
Soho Hist Dist—hist pl NY-2
Soholt Draw—valley SD-7
Soholt Ranch—locale SD-7
Sohoma Lake OK-5
Sohon—locale MT-8
Sohon's Pass ID-8
Sohorn Creek TN-4
Sohs-Cohen Sch—school PA-2
Sohu Park—park AZ-5
Soil and Water Conservancy District Dam—dam IN-6
Soil Bank Well—well TX-5
**Soileau**—pop pl LA-4
Soileau Ch—church LA-4
Sojourner Oil Field—oilfield TX-5
Sojourner Sch—school TX-5
Sojourner Truth Sch—school MD-2
**Sokaogan Chippewa Community (Indian Reservation)**—pop pl WI-6
Sokas FM-9
Sokehs Harbor—harbor FM-9
Sokehs Island FM-9
Sokehs Mass Grave Site—hist pl FM-9
Sokehs (Municipality)—civ div FM-9
**Sokehs Pah**—pop pl FM-9
Sokehs Passage—channel FM-9
Sokehs Powe—slope FM-9
Sokey Branch—stream TN-4
Sokey Creek—stream TN-4
Sokno Lake—lake NM-5
Sokokis Brook—stream NH-1
Sokokis Lake—lake ME-1
**Sokol Camp**—pop pl MI-6
Sokolof Island—island AK-9
Sokones MA-1
Sokos FM-9
Sokota State Wildlife Mngmt Area—park MN-6
Sokulk—locale WA-9
Sol MS-4
Sol, Isla del—island FL-3
Solace Camp—locale OR-9
Solace Mine—mine ID-8
Solace Ranch—locale CO-8
Sol Adams Cem—cemetery WV-2
Solambo Mine—mine CA-9
Solam Creek WI-6
Solana NM-5
Solana—locale MN-6
**Solana**—pop pl FL-3
**Solana Beach**—pop pl CA-9
Solana Beach County Park—park CA-9
Solana Ranch—locale TX-5
Solana State For—forest MN-6
Solander Creek—stream MT-8
**Solano**—pop pl NM-5
Solano, Rancho—locale AZ-5
Solano Ave Sch—school CA-9
Solano Cem—cemetery NM-5
**Solano (County)**—pop pl CA-9
Solano Cove—bay FL-3
Solano Park—park AZ-5
Solano Point—cape FL-3
Solano Sch—school AZ-5
Solano Wash—stream AZ-5
Solano Well—well AZ-5
**Solar**—pop pl UT-8
Solar Camera Tower—other CA-9
Solar Lake—lake WY-8
Solar Mine—mine CO-8
Solar Mine—mine MT-8
Solar Mine—mine NV-8
Sola Rock—other AK-9
Solar Pass—channel LA-4
Solars Mine—mine AK-9
Solars Sawmill—locale AK-9
Solary Wharf—locale FL-3
Solarz Lake—lake MN-6

Sola Sch—school ... MN-6
Solberg—locale ... VI-3
**Solberg**—pop pl ... IA-7
Solberg Butte—summit ... ND-7
Solberg Cem—cemetery ... SD-7
Solberg Creek—stream ... WA-9
Solberg Dam—dam ... WI-6
Solberg-Hunterdon—airport ... NJ-2
Solberg Lake—lake ... MI-6
Solberg Lake—lake (2) ... MN-6
Solberg Lake—lake ... WA-9
Solberg Lake—reservoir ... WI-6
Solberg Lakebed—flat ... MN-6
Solberg Point—cape ... MN-6
Solberg Ranch—locale ... CO-8
Solberg Sch Number 1 (historical)—school ... SD-7
Solberg Slough—gut ... ND-7
Solbery Lake—lake ... MN-6
Sol Brook—stream ... ME-1
Solburn Oil Field—oilfield ... KS-7
Solchenberger Cem—cemetery ... WI-6
Sol Creek ... TX-5
Soldado Crossing—locale ... TX-5
Soldado Tank—reservoir ... AZ-5
Soldan HS—school ... MO-7
Soldani—locale ... OK-5
Soldani Mansion—hist pl ... OK-5
Soldatna (Soldotna)—other ... AK-9
Sold Canyon—valley ... CA-9
Solder Canyon ... CO-8
Solders Canyon—valley ... OR-9
Solders Canyon Rsvr—reservoir ... OR-9
Solders Spring—spring ... OR-9
**Soldier**—pop pl ... ID-8
**Soldier**—pop pl ... IA-7
**Soldier**—pop pl ... KS-7
**Soldier**—pop pl ... KY-4
**Soldier**—pop pl ... PA-2
Soldier And Sailor Memorial Park—park ... PA-2
Soldier Annex Canal—canal ... AZ-5
Soldier Annex Dam—dam ... AZ-5
Soldier Annex Lake—reservoir ... AZ-5
Soldier Bar—bar ... ID-8
Soldier Basin—basin ... AZ-5
Soldier Basin—basin ... CA-9
Soldier Basin Trail—trail ... CA-9
Soldier Bay—swamp ... NC-3
Soldier Bay Ch—church ... NC-3
Soldier Bench—bench (2) ... UT-8
Soldier Boy Creek—stream ... WA-9
Soldier Brook—stream ... ME-1
Soldier Butte—summit ... AZ-5
Soldier Camp—locale (2) ... AZ-5
Soldier Camp—locale ... OR-9
**Soldier Camp**—pop pl ... AZ-5
Soldier Camp Creek—stream ... AZ-5
Soldier Camp Island ... GA-3
Soldier Camp Mtn—summit ... AZ-5
Soldier Camp Mtn—summit ... OR-9
Soldier Camp Trail—trail ... AZ-5
Soldier Camp Wash ... AZ-5
Soldier Camp Wash—stream ... AZ-5
Soldier Canyon—valley ... AZ-5
Soldier Canyon—valley ... CA-9
Soldier Canyon—valley (3) ... CO-8
Soldier Canyon—valley ... TX-5
Soldier Canyon—valley (3) ... UT-8
Soldier Canyon Cove—bay ... CO-8
Soldier Canyon Dam—dam ... CO-8
Soldier Canyon Dam No 1—dam ... UT-8
Soldier Canyon Dam No 2—dam ... UT-8
Soldier Canyon Rsvr—reservoir ... CO-8
Soldier Cap—summit ... ID-8
Soldier Cap—summit ... NV-8
Soldier Cap Butte ... ID-8
Soldier Cap Mound—summit ... KS-7
Soldier Ch—church ... IA-7
Soldier Creek ... AZ-5
Soldier Creek ... KS-7
Soldier Creek ... NV-8
Soldier Creek—locale ... SD-7
Soldier Creek—stream ... AL-4
Soldier Creek—stream ... AK-9
Soldier Creek—stream (4) ... AZ-5
Soldier Creek—stream (12) ... CA-9
Soldier Creek—stream (2) ... CO-8
Soldier Creek—stream ... FL-3
Soldier Creek—stream (9) ... ID-8
Soldier Creek—stream ... IL-6
Soldier Creek—stream (3) ... IA-7
Soldier Creek—stream (3) ... KS-7
Soldier Creek—stream ... KY-4
Soldier Creek—stream (5) ... MT-8
Soldier Creek—stream (2) ... NE-7
Soldier Creek—stream (4) ... NV-8
Soldier Creek—stream ... NM-5
Soldier Creek—stream (9) ... OK-5
Soldier Creek—stream (8) ... OR-9
Soldier Creek—stream (3) ... SD-7
Soldier Creek—stream (4) ... UT-8
Soldier Creek—stream ... WA-9
Soldier Creek—stream (9) ... WY-8
Soldier Creek Bay Fisherman Access (proposed)—locale ... UT-8
Soldier Creek Camp—locale ... WY-8
Soldier Creek Campground—park ... AZ-5
Soldier Creek Campground—park ... UT-8
Soldier Creek Campground Loop Trail—trail ... UT-8
Soldier Creek Canyon ... CO-8
Soldier Creek Ch—church ... KY-4
Soldier Creek Dam—dam ... UT-8
Soldier Creek Dam Day Use Area—park ... UT-8
Soldier Creek Ditch—canal ... WY-8
Soldier Creek Kilns—hist pl ... UT-8
Soldier Creek Overlook—locale ... UT-8
Soldier Creek Rec Area—park ... AZ-5
Soldier Creek Recreation Complex—park ... UT-8
Soldier Creek Rsvr—reservoir ... UT-8
Soldier Creek Rsvr—reservoir ... WY-8
Soldier Creek Sch—school ... OK-5
Soldier Crossing—locale ... UT-8
Soldier Drain—swamp ... GA-3
Soldier Field—hist pl ... IL-6
Soldier Field—other ... IL-6
Soldier Forest Camp—locale ... ID-8
Soldier Fork ... UT-8
Soldier Fork—stream ... KY-4
Soldier Fork—stream ... UT-8
Soldier Frank Hill—summit ... CA-9
Soldier Frank Point—cape ... CA-9
Soldier Gap—summit ... NV-8
Soldier Gulch—valley ... CA-9
Soldier Gulch—valley ... CO-8
Soldier Gulch—valley ... MT-8
Soldier Gulch—valley ... OR-9
Soldier Hill—summit ... CT-1
Soldier Hill—summit (2) ... NM-5
Soldier Hill Cem—cemetery ... PA-2
Soldier (historical P.O.)—locale ... IA-7
Soldier Hole—bay ... FL-3
Soldier Hole Creek ... AZ-5
Soldier Hole Creek—stream ... AZ-5
Soldier Hole Spring—spring ... AZ-5
Soldier Hole Tank—reservoir ... AZ-5
Soldier Hollow—valley ... OK-5
Soldier Hollow—valley ... UT-8
Soldier Key ... FL-3
Soldier Key—island ... FL-3
Soldier Lake—lake ... CA-9
Soldier Lake—lake ... MI-6
Soldier Lake—lake ... MT-8
Soldier Lake—lake ... OR-9
Soldier Lake—lake ... TX-5
Soldier Lake—reservoir ... AZ-5
Soldier Lake—reservoir ... MD-2
Soldier Lakes—lake ... ID-8
Soldier Lakes—lake ... NV-8
Soldier Lake Tank—reservoir ... AZ-5
Soldier Ledge—bar ... ME-1
Soldier Meadow—flat (2) ... CA-9
Soldier Meadow—flat ... NV-8
Soldier Meadow Number One Airp—airport ... NV-8
Soldier Meadow Number Two Airp—airport ... NV-8
Soldier Meadow Ranch—locale ... NV-8
Soldier Meadows—flat ... CA-9
Soldier Meadows—flat ... ID-8
Soldier Meadows Creek ... CA-9
Soldier Meadows Creek—stream ... OR-9
Soldier Mesa—summit ... AZ-5
Soldier Mesa—summit ... TX-5
Soldier Mesa Tank—reservoir ... AZ-5
Soldier Mound—summit ... TX-5
Soldier Mountain Rsvr—reservoir ... CA-9
Soldier Mtn—summit ... CA-9
Soldier Mtn—summit ... CO-8
Soldier Mtn—summit (2) ... MT-8
Soldier Mtn—summit ... NM-5
Soldier Mtns—range ... ID-8
Soldier Park—flat ... CO-8
Soldier Park—flat ... UT-8
Soldier Park—flat ... WY-8
Soldier Pass—gap ... AZ-5
Soldier Pass—gap ... CA-9
Soldier Pass—gap ... UT-8
Soldier Pass Canyon—valley ... CA-9
Soldier Peak—summit ... NV-8
Soldier Point—cape ... CA-9
Soldier Point—cape ... ME-1
Soldier Point—cape ... MN-6
Soldier Pond—lake ... ME-1
**Soldier Pond**—pop pl ... ME-1
Soldier Pond Bay—swamp ... FL-3
Soldier Ridge—ridge ... CA-9
Soldier River—locale ... IA-7
Soldier River—stream ... IA-7
Soldier River Cutoff—canal ... IA-7
Soldier Run ... PA-2
Soldier Run—stream ... PA-2
Soldiers And Sailors Cem—cemetery ... NE-7
Soldiers and Sailors Memorial Auditorium—hist pl ... TN-4
Soldiers and Sailors Memorial Bldg—hist pl ... KS-7
Soldiers and Sailors Memorial Bldg and Madison Theater—hist pl ... OH-6
Soldiers and Sailors Memorial Bridge—hist pl ... PA-2
Soldiers and Sailors Memorial Coliseum—hist pl ... IN-6
Soldiers and Sailors Memorial Gymnasium—hist pl ... KY-4
Soldiers And Sailors Memorial Hall—building ... PA-2
Soldiers and Sailors Memorial Hall—hist pl ... IL-6
Soldiers and Sailors Memorial Hall—hist pl ... PA-2
Soldiers and Sailors Monmt—hist pl ... OH-6
Soldiers and Sailors Monmt—hist pl ... PA-2
Soldiers And Sailors Orphans Home—building ... OH-6
Soldiers Bluff—cliff ... TX-5
Soldiers Bluff Park—park ... TX-5
Soldiers Camp Creek—stream ... AL-4
Soldiers Camp Island—island ... GA-3
Soldiers Canyon—valley ... ID-8
Soldiers Canyon—valley ... NM-5
Soldiers Cove—cave ... AL-4
Soldiers Cem—cemetery ... MA-1
Soldiers Cem—cemetery ... MO-7
Soldiers Cem—cemetery ... NH-1
Soldiers Cem—cemetery ... TX-5
Soldiers Claim Canyon—valley ... NV-8
Soldiers Creek ... NE-7
Soldiers Creek—stream ... FL-3
Soldiers Creek—stream ... TX-5
Soldiers Delight—ridge ... MD-2
Soldiers Draw—valley ... CO-8
Soldiers Farewell—summit ... NM-5
Soldiers Farewell Stage Station (Site)—locale ... NM-5
Soldiers Field—locale ... MA-1
Soldiers Field—other ... GA-3
Soldiers Field Cem—cemetery ... CT-1
Soldiers Field Park—park ... MN-6
Soldiers Gap—gap ... TX-5
**Soldiers Grove**—pop pl ... WI-6
Soldiers Grove—woods ... CA-9
Soldiers Gulch—valley ... NM-5
Soldiers Hole—channel ... NJ-2
Soldiers Hollow—valley ... UT-8
Soldiers Home ... ID-8
Soldiers Home—hospital ... MA-1
**Soldiers Home**—pop pl ... IL-6
Soldiers Home Camp (historical)—locale ... PA-2
Soldiers Home Creek—stream ... ID-8
Soldiers Home Dam—dam ... ND-7
Soldiers Home Ditch—canal ... CO-8
Soldiers Home (Ohio Soldiers and Sailors Home)—hospital ... OH-6
Soldiers Home Spring—spring ... CA-9
Soldiers Island—island ... MN-6
Soldiers Island—island ... NJ-2
Soldier's Joy—hist pl ... VA-3
Soldiers Key ... FL-3
Soldier's Lake ... MN-6
Soldiers Lake—lake ... MT-8
Soldier Slough—stream ... AK-9
Soldier Slough—stream ... TX-5
Soldiers Meadow Rsvr—reservoir ... ID-8
Soldiers Meadows Creek ... CA-9
Soldiers Memorial County Park—park ... KS-7
Soldiers Memorial Hall—building ... CT-1
Soldiers Memorial MS—school ... TN-4
Soldiers Memorial Park—park ... IN-6
Soldiers Memorial Park—park ... MN-6
Soldiers Memorial Park—park ... WI-6
Soldiers Memorial Sch ... TN-4
Soldier's Monmt—hist pl ... IL-6
Soldiers Monmt—park ... MA-1
Soldiers Mount—summit ... MT-8
Soldiers Orphan Sch—school ... PA-2
Soldiers Park—flat ... CO-8
Soldiers Pass—gap ... NV-8
Soldiers Pass—gap ... UT-8
Soldiers Peak—summit ... OK-5
Soldiers Place—locale ... NY-2
Soldiers Point—cape ... MN-6
Soldier Spring—spring (2) ... AZ-5
Soldier Spring—spring ... CO-8
Soldier Spring—spring (2) ... ID-8
Soldier Spring—spring (2) ... NV-8
Soldier Spring—spring ... NM-5
Soldier Spring—spring (3) ... OR-9
Soldier Spring—spring (2) ... TX-5
Soldier Spring—spring (2) ... WY-8
Soldier Spring Creek—stream ... NE-7
Soldier Springs—spring ... UT-8
Soldiers Retreat—hist pl ... KY-4
Soldiers Retreat Valley—valley ... VA-3
Soldiers Run—stream ... OH-6
Soldiers & Sailors World War Memorial—hist pl ... SD-7
Soldiers Spring—spring ... SD-7
Soldiers Spring—spring ... TX-5
Soldiers Spring Creek—stream ... TX-5
Soldiers Tank—reservoir ... AZ-5
**Soldier Summit**—pop pl (2) ... UT-8
Soldier Summit Division—civil ... UT-8
Soldiers Waterhole Historical Monmt—park ... TX-5
Soldiers Well—well ... WY-8
Soldiers Widows Home—building ... IL-6
Soldier Tank—reservoir ... NM-5
Soldier Township—civil ... KS-7
Soldier Township—fmr MCD (2) ... IA-7
**Soldier Township**—pop pl ... KS-7
Soldiertown (Township of)—unorg (2) ... ME-1
Soldier Trail—trail ... AZ-5
Soldier Trail—trail ... MT-8
Soldier Trail Tank—reservoir ... AZ-5
Soldier Valley—locale ... IA-7
Soldier Valley Cem—cemetery ... IA-7
Soldier Wash—stream ... AZ-5
Soldier Well—well (2) ... AZ-5
Soldier Well—well ... CA-9
Soldier Well—well ... NM-5
Soldier Wells—well ... CA-9
Soldier Well Tank—reservoir ... AZ-5
Soldier Windmill—locale ... TX-5
**Soldotna**—pop pl ... AK-9
Soldotna Creek—stream ... AK-9
Sol Duc Hot Springs—locale ... WA-9
Solduc River ... WA-9
Sole, Tollef, House—hist pl ... WA-9
**Solebury**—pop pl ... PA-2
Solebury Cem—cemetery ... PA-2
Solebury Ch—church ... PA-2
Solebury Farm Dam—dam ... PA-2
Solebury Mtn—summit ... PA-2
Solebury Post Office (historical)—building ... PA-2
Solebury Sch—school ... PA-2
**Solebury (Township of)**—pop pl ... PA-2
**Soledad**—pop pl ... CA-9
Soledad, Canada —valley ... CA-9
Soledad-Agua Dulce Union Sch—school ... CA-9
Soledad Artesian Well—well ... TX-5
Soledad Banco Number 120—levee ... TX-5
Soledad Campground—locale ... CA-9
Soledad Canyon—valley (2) ... CA-9
Soledad Canyon—valley ... NM-5
Soledad (CCD)—cens area ... CA-9
Soledad Cem—cemetery ... NM-5
Soledad Cem—cemetery ... TX-5
Soledad Creek—stream ... TX-5
Soledad Guard Station—locale ... CA-9
Soledad Mtn—summit (2) ... CA-9
Soledad Park—park ... CA-9
Soledad Pass—gap ... CA-9
Soledad Peak—summit ... NM-5
Soledad Sch—school ... CA-9
Soledad Siphon—canal ... CA-9
Soledad State Prison—other ... CA-9
Soledad Valley—valley ... CA-9
Soledad Windmill—locale (4) ... TX-5
**Soledi**—pop pl ... FM-9
Soleduck Falls—falls ... WA-9
Soleduck Lake ... WA-9
Soleduck Lake—lake ... WA-9
Soleduck Park—flat ... WA-9
Soleduck Ranger Station—locale ... WA-9
Soleduck River—stream ... WA-9
Soleduck Trail—trail ... WA-9
Soleduck Valley—valley ... WA-9
Sole-ee-tuck River ... WA-9
Soleit Lake—lake ... WI-6
Sole Lake ... MI-6
Solemar Hosp—hospital ... MA-1
Solem Ch—church (2) ... MN-6
**Solemint**—pop pl ... CA-9
Solem Lake—lake (2) ... MN-6
**Solem (Township of)**—pop pl ... MN-6
**Solen**—pop pl ... ND-7
Soleng Shop Ctr—locale ... AZ-5
Solen Township Road Dam—dam ... ND-7
Soleo—locale ... AL-4
**Soleo (Soleco)**—pop pl ... AL-4
Soleratus Creek ... UT-8
**Soler (Township of)**—pop pl ... MN-6
Soles—locale ... VA-3
Soles Cem—cemetery ... AL-4
Soles Cem—cemetery (2) ... NC-3
Sole Sch—school ... IL-6
Soles Rest Creek—stream ... ID-8
Soles Tunnel—tunnel ... WV-2
Solete ... FM-9
Solfatara Creek—stream ... WY-8
Solfatara Plateau—area ... WY-8
Solf Cem—cemetery ... OK-5
Solf Cove—bay ... AK-9
Solferino Creek—stream ... IA-7
Solfisburg Memorial Park—cemetery ... IL-6
**Solgohachia**—pop pl ... AR-4
Solhaug Spring—spring ... MT-8
Solheim Sch (abandoned)—school ... SD-7
Sol Hollow—valley ... KY-4
Sol Hollow—valley ... TN-4
Solida Ch—church ... OH-6
Solida Creek—stream ... OH-6
Solider Spring ... NV-8
Solid Rock Cem—cemetery ... MO-7
Solid Rock Ch—church ... AL-4
Solid Rock Ch—church ... GA-3
Solid Rock Ch—church ... MS-4
Solid Rock Ch—church (2) ... MO-7
Solid Rock Ch—church (2) ... NC-3
Solid Rock Ch—church (3) ... TN-4
Solid Rock Ch—church ... VA-3
Solid Rock Christian Sch—school ... FL-3
Solid Rock First United Evangelistic Baptist Ch—church ... FL-3
Solid Rock Holiness Ch—church ... DE-2
Solid Rock Primitive Baptist Ch—church ... AL-4
Solid Rock Spiritual Ch—church ... AL-4
Solid Silver Creek—stream ... NV-8
Solid Silver Mine—mine ... NV-8
Solier, Lake—lake ... LA-4
Solino—locale ... TX-5
Solinsky Crossing—locale ... CA-9
Solis—civil ... CA-9
Solis—locale ... TX-5
Solisa ... MD-2
Solis Canyon—valley ... NM-5
Solisenito Banco Number 81—levee ... TX-5
Soliseno Banco Number 23—levee ... TX-5
Sol Island—island ... FM-9
Solis Landing—locale ... TX-5
Solis Spring—spring ... TX-5
Solitaire Bay ... ID-8
Solitaire Butte ... AZ-5
Solitaire Creek—stream ... ID-8
Solitaire Lake—lake ... UT-8
Solitare Bay ... ID-8
Solitare Saddle—gap ... ID-8
Solitario, The—summit ... TX-5
Solitario Canyon—valley ... NV-8
Solitario Peak—summit ... TX-5
Solitario Wash—arroyo ... NV-8
Solitary Island ... SD-7
Solitary Lake—lake ... CO-8
Solite ... FL-3
**Solite**—pop pl ... NC-3
Solitrock Pond ... NJ-2
Solitrock Reservoir ... NJ-2
Solitude ... TN-4
Solitude—locale ... KY-4
Solitude—locale ... UT-8
Solitude—locale ... VA-3
Solitude—locale ... VI-3
**Solitude**—pop pl ... IN-6
**Solitude**—pop pl ... LA-4
**Solitude**—pop pl ... UT-8
Solitude, Cape—cliff ... AZ-5
Solitude, Lake—lake ... CO-8
Solitude, Lake—lake ... MI-6
Solitude, Lake—lake ... MT-8
Solitude, Lake—lake ... NH-1
Solitude, Lake—lake (3) ... WY-8
Solitude, Lake—reservoir ... NJ-2
Solitude, Lake—reservoir ... UT-8
Solitude, Mount—summit ... WY-8
Solitude Bar—bar ... OR-9
Solitude Bay—bay ... VI-3
Solitude Bend—bend ... IN-4
Solitude Canyon—valley ... OR-9
Solitude Ch—church ... AL-4
**Solitude Condominium**—pop pl ... UT-8
Solitude Creek ... MD-2
Solitude Creek—bay ... MD-2
Solitude Creek—stream ... CO-8
Solitude Farm—hist pl ... PA-2
Solitude Ford—locale ... TN-4
Solitude Guard Station—locale ... UT-8
Solitude Gulch—valley ... AZ-5
Solitude Gulch Tank—reservoir ... AZ-5
Solitude (historical P.O.)—locale ... IN-6
Solitude Lake—lake ... CO-8
Solitude Lake—lake ... MN-6
Solitude Plantation House—hist pl ... LA-4
Solitude Point—cape ... LA-4
Solitude Point—summit ... MT-8
Solitude Post Office ... TN-4
Solitude Riffle—rapids ... OR-9
Solitude Run—stream ... IN-6
Solitude Sch (historical)—school ... AL-4
Solitude Sch (historical)—school ... TN-4
Solitude Ski Area—locale ... UT-8
Solitude Ski Area Heliport—airport ... UT-8
Solitude Tailings Dam—dam ... AZ-5
Solitude Tailings Pond—reservoir ... AZ-5
Solitude Trail—trail ... WY-8
Solitude Tunnel—mine ... UT-8
Solitude Wash—valley ... UT-8
Solivik Island—island ... AK-9
Soliz-Baca House—hist pl ... NM-5
Solizes Cem—cemetery ... TX-5
Sollars Cem—cemetery ... OH-6
Sollars Point ... MD-2
Sollars Rsvr—reservoir ... AR-4
**Sollberg**—pop pl ... IA-7
Sol Legare Island—island ... SC-3
**Sol Legare Island**—pop pl ... SC-3
Solleks Creek—stream ... WA-9
Solleks River—stream ... WA-9
Solle Ponds—lake ... OR-9
Soller ... MD-2
Soller Point ... MD-2
Sollers—locale ... MD-2
Sollers Ch—church ... MD-2
Sollers Cove ... MD-2
**Sollers Homes**—pop pl ... MD-2
Sollers Point—cape ... MD-2
**Sollers Point**—pop pl ... MD-2
Solley—locale ... MD-2
**Solley Hill**—pop pl ... LA-4
Solleys Cem—cemetery ... MD-2
Solleys Cove—bay ... MD-2
Sollid Sch—school ... MT-8
**Sollitt**—pop pl ... IL-6
Solly ... MD-2
Sollys Knob—summit ... AR-4
Sol Martin Branch—stream ... AL-4
Sol Messer Mtn—summit ... TN-4
**Solms**—pop pl ... TX-5
Solo—locale ... AR-4
Solo—locale ... MO-7
Solo—locale ... NM-5
Solo—locale ... NC-3
Solo—locale ... TX-5
**Solo**—pop pl ... TN-4
Solo, Mount—summit ... WA-9
Soloa Peak—summit ... ID-8
Solo Creek—stream (2) ... AK-9
Solo Creek—stream ... ID-8
Solo Creek—stream ... WA-9
Solo Flats—flat ... AK-9
Solo Joe Creek—stream ... MT-8
Solo Lake—lake ... AK-9
Solola Valley—locale ... NC-3
Soloma Flat—flat ... AK-9
Soloman Branch—stream ... TN-4
Soloman Butte—summit ... OR-9
Soloman Chapel Ch—church ... MS-4
Soloman Chapel Sch—school ... MS-4
Soloman Creek—stream ... MS-4
Soloman Creek—stream ... OR-9
Soloman Creek—stream ... VA-3
Soloman Flat—flat ... OR-9
Soloman Lake—lake ... AK-9
Soloman Lake—reservoir ... NC-3
Soloman Lake Dam—dam ... NC-3
Soloman Ridge ... MD-2
Solomans Chapel—church ... WV-2
Solomans Run ... PA-2
Soloma Point—cape ... AK-9
**Solomar**—pop pl ... CA-9
Solomon—locale ... IL-6
Solomon—locale ... IA-7
**Solomon**—pop pl ... AK-9
**Solomon**—pop pl ... AZ-5
**Solomon**—pop pl ... KS-7
Solomon, Mount—summit ... CA-9
Solomon Allen Cem—cemetery ... AR-4
Solomon ANV948—reserve ... AK-9
Solomon Basin—basin ... UT-8
Solomon Branch—stream (2) ... KY-4
Solomon Branch—stream ... TN-4
Solomon Branch—stream ... VA-3
Solomon Bridge—bridge ... GA-3
Solomon Bryant Hill—summit ... IN-6
Solomon Butte ... OR-9
Solomon Butte—summit ... AZ-5
Solomon Canyon—valley ... CA-9
Solomon Canyon—valley ... OR-9
Solomon Canyon—valley ... TX-5
Solomon Canyon Rsvr—reservoir ... OR-9
Solomon Cem—cemetery ... AL-4
Solomon Cem—cemetery ... IL-6
Solomon Cem—cemetery (2) ... TN-4
Solomon Ch—church ... AL-4
Solomon Ch—church ... LA-4
Solomon Ch—church ... MD-2
Solomon Chapel—church ... NC-3
Solomon Chapel—church ... TN-4
Solomon Christian Ch—church ... MS-4
Solomon City ... KS-7
Solomon Creek—stream (2) ... AK-9
Solomon Creek—stream ... ID-8
Solomon Creek—stream ... IL-6
Solomon Creek—stream ... IN-6
Solomon Creek—stream ... KY-4
Solomon Creek—stream ... MT-8
Solomon Creek—stream ... OK-5
Solomon Creek—stream ... OR-9
Solomon Creek—stream ... UT-8
Solomon Creek—stream ... WA-9
Solomon Creek—stream ... WY-8
Solomon Creek Ch—church ... IN-6
Solomon-Curd House—hist pl ... GA-3
Solomon Dam—dam ... AL-4
Solomon-District Three Township—civil ... KS-7
Solomon Ditch—canal ... IN-6
Solomon Drain—canal ... ID-8
Solomon Elementary School ... AZ-5
Solomoneno Creek ... TX-5
Solomon Ferry (historical)—locale ... TN-4
Solomon Flat ... OR-9
Solomon Fork—stream ... KY-4
Solomon Gap—gap ... PA-2
**Solomon Gap**—pop pl ... PA-2
Solomon Grove Ch—church ... AR-4
Solomon Grove Ch—church ... GA-3
Solomon Grove Sch—school ... AR-4
Solomon Gulch—valley ... AK-9
Solomon Gulch—valley (2) ... CA-9
Solomon Gulch—valley ... SD-7
**Solomon Heights (subdivision)**—pop pl ... AL-4
Solomon Hill—summit ... AL-4
Solomon Hill—summit ... ND-7
Solomon Hills—summit ... CA-9
Solomon Hollow—valley ... MO-7
Solomon Hollow—valley (3) ... TN-4
Solomon House—hist pl ... PA-2
Solomon Island—island ... TN-4
Solomon JHS—school ... MS-4
Solomon Johnson Park—park ... TX-5
Solomon Lake—lake ... AK-9
Solomon Lake—lake ... ID-8
Solomon Lake—lake ... MN-6
Solomon Lake—lake ... SC-3
Solomon Lake Ch—church ... MN-6
Solomon Mine—mine ... CO-8
Solomon Mtn—summit ... ID-8
Solomon Mtn—summit ... MT-8
Solomon Mtn—summit ... TX-5
Solomon Park—park ... AL-4
Solomon Pass—gap ... AZ-5
Solomon Peak—summit ... CA-9
Solomon Pond—lake ... MA-1
Solomon Post Office—building ... AZ-5
**Solomon Rapids**—pop pl ... KS-7
Solomon Rapids Sch—school ... KS-7
Solomon Rapids Station ... KS-7
**Solomon Rapids Township**—pop pl ... KS-7
Solomon Ridge—ridge ... MD-2
Solomon Ridge—ridge ... MT-8
Solomon Ridge Trail—trail ... MT-8
Solomon River—stream ... AK-9
Solomon River—stream ... KS-7
Solomon Roadhouse—hist pl ... AK-9
Solomon RR—other ... AK-9
Solomon Rsvr—reservoir ... UT-8
Solomon Run—stream ... OH-6
Solomon Run—stream (2) ... PA-2
Solomons ... HI-9
**Solomons**—pop pl ... MD-2
Solomons, Mount—summit ... CA-9
Solomon Saltpeter Cave—cave ... TN-4
Solomons Cem—cemetery ... SC-3
Solomons Ch—church ... PA-2
Solomons Ch—church ... VA-3
Solomon Sch—school ... AZ-5
Solomon Sch—school ... IL-6
Solomon Sch—school ... MI-6
Solomons Chapel (historical)—church ... TN-4
Solomon Sch (historical)—school ... AL-4
Solomon Sch (historical)—school ... MO-7
Solomon Sch (historical)—school ... TN-4
Solomons Cove—bay ... MD-2
Solomons Creek—stream ... NC-3
Solomons Creek—stream ... VA-3
Solomons Crossroads—locale ... SC-3
Solomons Fork ... KS-7
Solomons Gap ... PA-2
**Solomons Gap**—pop pl ... PA-2
Solomons Gap Station—locale ... PA-2
Solomons Graveyard—cemetery ... NJ-2
Solomons Hollow—valley ... UT-8
Solomon Siding—locale ... AZ-5
Solomon Simmons Cemetery ... MS-4
Solomons Island—island ... MD-2
Solomons Knob—summit ... CA-9
Solomons Lake ... ID-8
Solomons Lake—reservoir ... AL-4
Solomon Slough—lake ... SD-7
Solomons Lump Lighthouse—locale ... MD-2
Solomons Mill (historical)—locale ... AL-4
Solomon-Smith-Martin House—hist pl ... GA-3
Solomon Springs—spring ... WY-8
Solomons Run ... PA-2
Solomons Run—stream ... VA-3
**Solomons Store**—pop pl ... VA-3
Solomons Temple—cave ... TN-4
Solomons Temple—church ... AL-4
Solomons Temple—summit ... CA-9
Solomons Temple—summit ... UT-8
Solomons Temple Baptist Ch—church ... TN-4
Solomon's Temple Ch—church ... AR-4
Solomons Temple Sch (historical)—school ... TN-4
Solomonsville ... AZ-5
Solomonsville Cem—cemetery ... AZ-5
Solomons Waterhole—lake ... HI-9
Solomon Temple—church ... GA-3
Solomon Temple—church ... LA-4
Solomon Temple—church ... PA-2
Solomon Temple—church ... SC-3
Solomon Temple—church ... TX-5
Solomon Temple—summit ... AZ-5
Solomon Temple Church ... TN-4
Solomon Temple Sch ... TN-4
Solomon Township ... KS-7
**Solomon Township**—pop pl (5) ... KS-7
Solomon Valley Airpark—airport ... KS-7
Solomon Valley Airport ... KS-7
Solomon Valley Sch—school ... KS-7
Solomonville ... AZ-5
Solomonville Pass ... AZ-5
Solomonville Road Overpass—hist pl ... AZ-5
Solomon Windmill—locale ... NM-5
Solo Mtn—summit ... AK-9
Solon ... IN-6
Solon ... TN-4
Solon—locale ... MI-6
**Solon**—pop pl ... IA-7
**Solon**—pop pl ... ME-1
**Solon**—pop pl ... NY-2
**Solon**—pop pl ... OH-6
Solon, John, House—hist pl ... TX-5
Solon Cem—cemetery ... MI-6
Solon Cem—cemetery ... NE-7
**Solon Center**—pop pl ... MI-6
Solon Dam—dam ... NM-5
Solon Ditch—canal ... IN-6
**Solon Mills**—pop pl ... IL-6
Solon Pond—lake ... NY-2
Solon Pond Sch—school ... NY-2
Solon Post Office (historical)—building ... TN-4
Solon Robinson Elem Sch—school ... IN-6
**Solon Springs**—pop pl ... WI-6
**Solon Springs (Town of)**—pop pl ... WI-6
Solonsville Ch—church ... TX-5
Solon Swamp—swamp ... MI-6
**Solon (Town of)**—pop pl ... ME-1
**Solon (Town of)**—pop pl ... NY-2
**Solon Township**—pop pl ... ND-7
**Solon (Township of)**—pop pl (2) ... MI-6
Solo Peak—summit ... AZ-5
Solo Peak—summit ... CA-9
Solo Point—cape ... WA-9
Solo Point—cape ... AS-9
Solo Ranch—locale ... TX-5
Solor Ch—church ... MN-6
Solo Slough ... WA-9
Solo Spring—spring ... AZ-5
Solo Springs ... AZ-5
Sol Pogue Hollow—valley ... IN-6
Sol Post Office (historical)—building ... MS-4
Sol Ray Gap—gap ... NC-3
Sol Ray Spring ... AZ-5
Sol Rhea Saddle—gap ... AZ-5
Sol Rhea Spring—spring ... AZ-5
Sol Ridge—ridge ... ME-1
Sol Ridge—ridge ... NC-3
**Solromar**—pop pl ... CA-9
**Solsberry**—pop pl ... IN-6

Solsberry Cem—*cemetery* IN-6
Solsburg—*locale* VA-3
Sols Canyon—*valley* UT-8
Sols Cliff—*cliff* ME-1
Sols Creek—*gut* NC-3
Sols Creek—*stream* NC-3
Sols Creek Cem—*cemetery* NC-3
Sols Creek Ch—*church* NC-3
Sol se Mete Canyon—*valley* NM-5
Sol se Mete Peak—*summit* NM-5
Sol se Mete Spring—*spring* NM-5
Sol Shank Ditch—*canal* IN-6
Sols Island—*island* NY-2
Sols Island—*island* NC-3
Sols Knob—*summit* VA-3
Sols Knoll—*summit* UT-8
*Sols Lake* MI-6
Sols Mtn—*summit* NC-3
Solsmunket Lake—*lake* AK-9
Solso Sch—*school* NE-7
Sols Point—*cape* MD-2
Sols Point Gut—*gut* MD-2
Sols Pond—*lake* MA-1
Sols Rapids—*rapids* NY-2
Sols Spring—*spring* UT-8
Solstice Canyon—*valley* CA-9
**Solsville**—*pop pl* NY-2
Sols Wash—*stream* AZ-5
Sols Wash Tank—*reservoir* AZ-5
Soltera Cove—*bay* AZ-5
Solters Creek—*stream* NJ-2
Sol Thumb—*ridge* AK-9
Soltudus Mtn—*summit* VT-1
Soluka Creek—*stream* AK-9
Solum Cem—*cemetery* WI-6
Solum Creek—*stream* WI-6
Solum Lake—*lake* MN-6
Solution Creek—*stream* WY-8
Solution Rift—*cave* TN-4
**Solvang**—*pop pl* CA-9
*Solvay* IL-6
*Solvay* MI-6
**Solvay**—*pop pl* NY-2
Solvie Slough—*lake* MN-6
Solwald Lake—*lake* MN-6
Solway—*locale* KY-4
**Solway**—*pop pl* MN-6
**Solway**—*pop pl* TN-4
Solway Bridge—*bridge* TN-4
Solway Cem—*cemetery* (2) MN-6
Solway Ch—*church* TN-4
Solway Sch—*school* TN-4
**Solway (Township of)**—*pop pl* MN-6
Solyanka Point—*cape* AK-9
Solyo—*locale* CA-9
Soma—*locale* UT-8
*Somasick Mountain* CT-1
Somavia Sch—*school* CA-9
**Somber**—*pop pl* IA-7
Somber Ch—*church* IA-7
Somber Creek—*stream* AK-9
Somber Hill—*summit* WY-8
Sombodoro Mesa—*summit* NM-5
Sombra del Monte Ch—*church* NM-5
Sombra del Monte Sch—*school* NM-5
*Sombreretillo Creek* TX-5
Sombrerito Creek—*stream* TX-5
**Sombrero Acres (subdivision)**—*pop pl* AL-4
Sombrero Alto—*summit* NM-5
*Sombrero Butte* AZ-5
Sombrero Butte—*locale* AZ-5
Sombrero Butte—*summit* AZ-5
Sombrero Butte—*summit* NM-5
Sombrero Butte Tank—*reservoir* AZ-5
Sombrero Canyon—*valley* CA-9
Sombrero Country Club—*locale* FL-3
Sombrero Creek—*stream* FL-3
Sombrero Island—*island* AK-9
Sombrero Key—*island* FL-3
Sombrero Peak—*summit* AZ-5
Sombrero Peak—*summit* CA-9
Sombrero Peak—*summit* NV-8
Sombrero Peak—*summit* TX-5
Sombrero Peak Palm Grove—*locale* CA-9
Sombrero Peak Ranch—*locale* TX-5
Sombrero Point—*cape* AK-9
Sombrero Tank—*reservoir* NM-5
Sombrero Windmill—*locale* TX-5
**Sombrillo**—*pop pl* NM-5
Sombrillo Ditch—*canal* NM-5
Sombrio Cem—*cemetery* NM-5
Somdahl Lake—*lake* MN-6
Some Chance Pond—*lake* OR-9
Some Creek—*stream* MT-8
Someday Ranch Airp—*airport* MO-7
Someman Lake—*lake* MN-6
Someone Creek—*stream* AK-9
*Somer* NC-3
Somer Brook—*stream* PA-2
**Somerdale**—*pop pl* NJ-2
**Somerdale**—*pop pl* OH-6
Somerdale Park Sch—*school* NJ-2
Somerdale Sch—*school* NJ-2
*Somerfied* PA-2
**Somerfield**—*pop pl* PA-2
*Somerford* OH-6
Somerford Cem—*cemetery* NE-7
Somerford Cem—*cemetery* OH-6
Somerford Old Cem—*cemetery* OH-6
Somerford Sch—*school* NE-7
**Somerford (Township of)**—*pop pl* OH-6
Somerford Valley—*valley* NE-7
Somerlid Sch—*school* CO-8
Somero, Arroyo—*stream* CA-9
Somers—*locale* VA-3
**Somers**—*pop pl* CT-1
**Somers**—*pop pl* IA-7
**Somers**—*pop pl* MT-8
**Somers**—*pop pl* NY-2
**Somers**—*pop pl* WI-6
Somers Bay—*bay* NJ-2
*Somers Brook* PA-2
Somers Cem—*cemetery* TN-4
*Somers Center* CT-1
**Somers Center (census name Somers)**—*pop pl* CT-1
Somers Corner—*locale* ME-1
Somers Cove—*bay* MD-2
Somers Cove—*bay* NJ-2
Somers Creek—*stream* OR-9
Somers Creek—*stream* WI-6
Somers Creek Rapids—*rapids* OR-9
Somers Crossroads—*locale* NC-3
*Somerset* (2) IL-6
*Somerset* IN-6
*Somerset* MD-2
Somerset—*airport* NJ-2
Somerset—*locale* (2) CA-9
Somerset—*locale* NE-7
Somerset—*locale* NC-3
Somerset—*locale* VT-1
**Somerset**—*pop pl* AL-4
**Somerset**—*pop pl* CO-8
**Somerset**—*pop pl* IL-6
**Somerset**—*pop pl* IN-6
**Somerset**—*pop pl* KS-7
**Somerset**—*pop pl* KY-4
**Somerset**—*pop pl* LA-4
**Somerset**—*pop pl* MD-2
**Somerset**—*pop pl* MA-1
**Somerset**—*pop pl* MI-6
**Somerset**—*pop pl* NJ-2
**Somerset**—*pop pl* NY-2
**Somerset**—*pop pl* NC-3
**Somerset**—*pop pl* OH-6
**Somerset**—*pop pl* PA-2
**Somerset**—*pop pl* TX-5
**Somerset**—*pop pl* VA-3
**Somerset**—*pop pl* WI-6
Somerset, Lake—*lake* FL-3
Somerset, Lake—*lake* MI-6
Somerset, Lake—*reservoir* GA-3
Somerset, Lake—*reservoir* PA-2
Somerset Acad—*hist pl* ME-1
Somerset Acad—*hist pl* MD-2
Somerset Acad—*school* ME-1
Somerset Airp—*airport* KS-7
Somerset Apartments—*hist pl* MI-6
Somerset Area JHS—*school* PA-2
Somerset Area Senior HS—*school* PA-2
Somerset Beach—*locale* VA-3
Somerset Borough—*civil* PA-2
Somerset (CCD)—*cens area* KY-4
Somerset Cem—*cemetery* KS-7
Somerset Cem—*cemetery* LA-4
Somerset Cem—*cemetery* NY-2
**Somerset Center**—*pop pl* MI-6
**Somerset Centre**—*pop pl* MA-1
Somerset Ch—*church* IN-6
Somerset Ch—*church* KY-4
Somerset Ch—*church* MD-2
Somerset Ch—*church* OH-6
Somerset Christian Church—*hist pl* VA-3
Somerset City Sch and Carnegie Library—*hist pl* KY-4
Somerset Country Club—*other* MN-6
Somerset Country Club—*other* PA-2
**Somerset (County)**—*pop pl* ME-1
**Somerset (County)**—*pop pl* MD-2
**Somerset County**—*pop pl* NJ-2
**Somerset County**—*pop pl* PA-2
Somerset County Airp—*airport* PA-2
Somerset County Courthouse—*hist pl* ME-1
Somerset County Courthouse—*hist pl* PA-2
*Somerset Court House* NJ-2
*Somerset Creek* OH-6
Somerset Creek—*stream* (2) KY-4
Somerset Creek—*stream* MD-2
Somerset Creek—*stream* OH-6
Somerset Downtown Commercial District—*hist pl* KY-4
Somerset Elem Sch—*school* KS-7
**Somerset Estates Place Subdivision**—*pop pl* UT-8
**Somerset Farm Subdivision**—*pop pl* UT-8
**Somerset Garden Condominium**—*pop pl* UT-8
**Somerset Heights**—*pop pl* MD-2
Somerset Heights Sch—*school* MN-6
Somerset Hills—*airport* NJ-2
**Somerset Hills**—*pop pl* NC-3
Somerset Hills Cem—*cemetery* NJ-2
Somerset Hills Golf Course—*other* NJ-2
Somerset Hist Dist—*hist pl* OH-6
Somerset Hosp—*hospital* NJ-2
Somerset HS—*school* MA-1
Somersetin—*locale* NJ-2
*Somerset Interchange* PA-2
Somerset JHS—*school* MD-2
Somerset JHS—*school* MA-1
Somerset Junction—*locale* ME-1
Somerset Knob—*summit* KY-4
Somerset Lake—*lake* NY-2
Somerset Lake—*reservoir* IN-6
Somerset Lake Dam—*dam* IN-6
Somerset Mall—*locale* MA-1
Somerset Mall—*locale* PA-2
Somerset Number Sixty Dam—*dam* PA-2
Somerset Number Sixty Pond E Dam—*dam* PA-2
Somerset Oil Field—*oilfield* TX-5
Somerset Park—*park* CA-9
**Somerset Park**—*pop pl* NJ-2
Somerset Park—*uninc pl* GA-3
*Somerset Place* NC-3
**Somerset Place Condominium**—*pop pl* UT-8
Somerset Place State Historical Site—*locale* NC-3
Somerset Place State Historic Site—*hist pl* NC-3
Somerset Plaza—*locale* KS-7
Somerset Plaza—*locale* PA-2
Somerset Pumping Station—*locale* MA-1
Somerset Reservoir Dam—*dam* MA-1
Somerset Roller Mills—*hist pl* NJ-2
Somerset Rsvr—*reservoir* MA-1
Somerset Rsvr—*reservoir* OH-6
Somerset Rsvr—*reservoir* VT-1
Somerset Sch—*school* CA-9
Somerset Sch—*school* (2) MD-2
Somerset Sch—*school* NJ-2
Somerset Sch (abandoned)—*school* PA-2
Somerset State Hosp—*hospital* PA-2
**Somerset (Town of)**—*pop pl* MA-1
**Somerset (Town of)**—*pop pl* NY-2
**Somerset (Town of)**—*pop pl* WI-6
**Somerset Township**—*pop pl* MO-7
**Somerset (Township of)**—*pop pl* IL-6
**Somerset (Township of)**—*pop pl* MI-6
**Somerset (Township of)**—*pop pl* MN-6
**Somerset (Township of)**—*pop pl* OH-6
**Somerset (Township of)**—*pop pl* (2) PA-2
Somerset Township Sch—*school* PA-2
*Somerset Village* MA-1
**Somerset West**—*pop pl* OR-9
Somerset West-Rock Creek (CCD)—*cens area* OR-9
Somers Fire Tower—*tower* CT-1
Somers Hist Dist—*hist pl* CT-1
Somer Shoal—*bar* NJ-2
Somers House—*hist pl* VA-3
Somers HS—*school* CT-1
Somers Lake—*lake* MI-6
Somers Lake—*lake* MN-6
Somers Lake—*lake* WI-6
Somers Lane—*locale* PA-2
Somers Mansion—*hist pl* NJ-2
Somers Park—*park* IN-6
Somers Point—*cape* OR-9
**Somers Point**—*pop pl* NJ-2
Somers Ranch—*locale* OR-9
Somers (RR name for Pricedale)—*other* PA-2
Somers Sch—*school* MT-8
Somers Sch—*school* OH-6
Somers Sch—*school* WI-6
*Somers Street* CT-1
**Somers Town**—*pop pl* NY-2
Somers Town House—*hist pl* NY-2
**Somers (Town of)**—*pop pl* CT-1
**Somers (Town of)**—*pop pl* NY-2
**Somers (Town of)**—*pop pl* WI-6
Somers (Township of)—*fmr MCD* NC-3
**Somers (Township of)**—*pop pl* OH-6
*Somersville* OH-6
Somersville—*locale* CA-9
Somersville—*other* ME-1
**Somersville**—*pop pl* CT-1
Somersville Elem Sch—*school* CT-1
*Somersville Mill Pond* CT-1
Somersville Pond—*lake* CT-1
**Somersworth**—*pop pl* NH-1
Somerton—*locale* VA-3
**Somerton**—*pop pl* AZ-5
**Somerton**—*pop pl* OH-6
**Somerton**—*pop pl* PA-2
Somerton Airp—*airport* AZ-5
Somerton Canal—*canal* AZ-5
Somerton (CCD)—*cens area* AZ-5
Somerton City Hall—*building* AZ-5
Somerton Creek—*stream* NC-3
Somerton Creek—*stream* VA-3
Somerton Elem Sch—*school* AZ-5
Somerton Friends Meeting House—*church* VA-3
Somerton Lateral—*canal* AZ-5
Somerton Lateral Wasteway—*canal* AZ-5
Somerton Park—*park* AZ-5
Somerton Post Office—*building* AZ-5
Somerton Siding—*locale* AZ-5
Somerton Springs Country Club—*other* PA-2
*Somerton Springs Golf Course* PA-2
**Somerton (sta.)**—*pop pl* AZ-5
**Somer (Township of)**—*pop pl* IL-6
**Somervell (County)**—*pop pl* TX-5
Somervell County Courthouse—*hist pl* TX-5
*Somerville* CT-1
*Somerville* PA-2
Somerville—*hist pl* DE-2
Somerville—*locale* VA-3
**Somerville**—*pop pl* AL-4
**Somerville**—*pop pl* IN-6
**Somerville**—*pop pl* ME-1
**Somerville**—*pop pl* MA-1
**Somerville**—*pop pl* MS-4
**Somerville**—*pop pl* NJ-2
**Somerville**—*pop pl* NY-2
**Somerville**—*pop pl* OH-6
**Somerville**—*pop pl* (2) PA-2
**Somerville**—*pop pl* TN-4
**Somerville**—*pop pl* TX-5
**Somerville**—*pop pl* WV-2
Somerville, City of—*civil* MA-1
Somerville Branch—*stream* TN-4
Somerville (CCD)—*cens area* AL-4
Somerville (CCD)—*cens area* TN-4
Somerville (CCD)—*cens area* TX-5
Somerville Cem—*cemetery* AL-4
Somerville Cem—*cemetery* NJ-2
Somerville Cem—*cemetery* (3) TN-4
Somerville Central Hosp—*hospital* MA-1
Somerville Ch—*church* AL-4
Somerville Church Cem—*cemetery* AL-4
*Somerville Church of God* AL-4
Somerville City Hall—*building* MA-1
Somerville Courthouse—*hist pl* AL-4
Somerville Creek—*stream* CA-9
Somerville Dam—*dam* TX-5
Somerville Division—*civil* AL-4
Somerville Division—*civil* TN-4
Somerville Draw—*valley* WY-8
Somerville Elem Sch—*school* IN-6
Somerville Elem Sch—*school* TN-4
Somerville First Baptist Ch—*church* TN-4
Somerville Flats—*flat* WY-8
Somerville Fork—*stream* WV-2
Somerville Hist Dist—*hist pl* TN-4
Somerville Hotel—*hist pl* CA-9
Somerville HS—*school* MA-1
**Somerville in Draper Subdivision**—*pop pl* UT-8
Somerville Junction—*uninc pl* MA-1
Somerville Lake—*reservoir* TX-5
Somerville Mine—*mine* IN-6
Somerville Post Office—*building* AL-4
Somerville Post Office—*building* TN-4
Somerville Road Ch of Christ—*church* AL-4
*Somerville Road Elementary School* AL-4
Somerville Road Sch—*school* AL-4
*Somerville Rsvr* OR-9
*Somerville Rsvr* TX-5
Somerville Sch—*school* AL-4
Somerville Sch—*school* NJ-2
**Somerville (Town of)**—*pop pl* ME-1
**Somesbar**—*pop pl* CA-9
**Somes Bar**—*pop pl* CA-9
Somes Cove—*bay* ME-1
Somes Creek—*stream* CA-9
Somes Harbor—*bay* ME-1
Somes Mtn—*summit* CA-9
Somes Pond—*lake* ME-1
Somes Sound—*bay* ME-1
Somesville Hist Dist—*hist pl* ME-1
**Somesville (Mount Desert Post Office)**—*pop pl* ME-1
*Sometime Creek* GA-3
Sometime Rsvr—*reservoir* OR-9
*Somey Creek* NC-3
Somey Creek—*stream* NC-3
**Somis**—*pop pl* CA-9
**Sommer**—*pop pl* IL-6
Sommer, August, House—*hist pl* IN-6
Sommer, Morris, House—*hist pl* ID-8
Sommercamp, Mary Elizabeth, House—*hist pl* ID-8
Sommercamp Basin—*basin* ID-8
Sommercamp Flat (historical)—*flat* ID-8
Sommercamp Mine (historical)—*mine* ID-8
Sommercamp Pit—*mine* ID-8
Sommercamp Spring—*spring* ID-8
Sommer Ditch—*canal* IN-6
Sommerford Cem—*cemetery* TX-5
Sommerheim Park Archeol District—*hist pl* PA-2
Sommer Lake—*lake* MN-6
Sommerlotte Cem—*cemetery* TX-5
**Sommers**—*pop pl* CO-8
Sommers Airp—*airport* KS-7
Sommers Butte—*summit* ID-8
Sommers Cem—*cemetery* IA-7
Sommers Cem—*cemetery* TX-5
Sommer Sch—*school* OH-6
Sommers Ditch—*canal* NV-8
Sommers Draw—*valley* WY-8
**Sommerset Hollow Subdivision**—*pop pl* UT-8
**Sommerset South Place Subdivision**—*pop pl* UT-8
Sommers Flat—*flat* WY-8
Sommers Hill—*summit* WY-8
Sommers Lake—*lake* IN-6
Sommers Lake—*lake* MI-6
Sommers Mill—*locale* TX-5
Sommers Prospect—*mine* CA-9
Sommers Ranch—*locale* (2) WY-8
Sommers Sch (historical)—*school* AL-4
Sommers-Shockley Sch—*school* WY-8
**Sommers South (subdivision)**—*pop pl* AL-4
*Sommerton* VA-3
*Sommerton Creek* NC-3
*Sommerton Creek* VA-3
*Sommerville* CA-9
**Sommerville**—*pop pl* AL-4
**Sommerville**—*pop pl* SD-7
Sommerville, Edgar, House—*hist pl* OR-9
Sommerville Baptist Ch—*church* AL-4
Sommerville Basin—*bay* NY-2
Sommerville Bayou—*gut* TX-5
Sommerville Dam—*dam* OR-9
Sommerville Farms—*locale* CA-9
Sommerville-Kearney House—*hist pl* LA-4
Sommerville Methodist Ch—*church* AL-4
Sommerville Valley—*valley* NY-2
Somme Woods—*woods* IL-6
Sommey Flat—*flat* CA-9
Somnac—*area* GU-9
Somo—*locale* KY-4
Somo Cem—*cemetery* WI-6
Somo Creek—*stream* WI-6
**Somo Junction**—*pop pl* WI-6
Somo Lake—*lake* WI-6
**Somonauk**—*pop pl* IL-6
Somonauk Ch—*church* IL-6
Somonauk Creek—*stream* IL-6
**Somonauk (Township of)**—*pop pl* IL-6
Somo River—*stream* WI-6
**Somo (Town of)**—*pop pl* WI-6
*Soms Knob* OH-6
*Son* MS-4
*Son* FM-9
Sonadora (Barrio)—*fmr MCD* (2) PR-3
Sonador (Barrio)—*fmr MCD* PR-3
*Sonanoxet Island* RI-1
Sonans—*locale* VA-3
Sonans Sch—*school* VA-3
*Sonar* NV-8
Sonar Pit—*cave* AL-4
Sonata Lake—*reservoir* NC-3
*Sona Villa Park* UT-8
Son Chapman Draw—*valley* TX-5
Soncy—*locale* TX-5
**Sondheimer**—*pop pl* LA-4
*Sondia Creek* TX-5
Sondogardy Pond—*lake* NH-1
Sondreagger Lake—*reservoir* KS-7
S-One Canal—*canal* NV-8
Sones Chapel—*church* MS-4
Sones Lake—*lake* LA-4
*Sonesome Tree Coulee* MT-8
Sones Pond—*reservoir* PA-2
Sones Pond Dam—*dam* PA-2
**Sonestown**—*pop pl* PA-2
Sonestown Covered Bridge—*hist pl* PA-2
Song—*island* FM-9
Songadeewin Camp—*locale* VT-1
Songbird Creek—*stream* NC-3
Songbird Creek—*stream* VA-3
Songbird Island—*island* WA-9
Songbird Sch—*school* PA-2
Song Branch—*stream* NC-3
Song Creek—*stream* MI-6
*Songel A Lise Lagoon* PW-9
Songen Gap—*gap* OR-9
Songer Airp—*airport* IN-6
Songer Butte—*summit* OR-9
Songer Cem—*cemetery* (3) IL-6
Songer Hill—*summit* PA-2
**Songer (Township of)**—*pop pl* IL-6
Songetigech—*island* FM-9
*Songhalum* MH-9
*Songhalum Reede* MH-9
Song Hawk Lake—*lake* SD-7
Song Lake—*lake* NY-2
Songo Branch—*stream* TN-4
Songo Cem—*cemetery* ME-1
Songo Lock—*hist pl* ME-1
**Songo Lock**—*pop pl* ME-1
Songo Pond—*lake* ME-1
Songo River—*stream* ME-1
**Songsong**—*pop pl* MH-9
Songstad Ranch—*locale* MT-8
Songster Butte—*summit* MT-8
Songton—*slope* MH-9
Soni, Unun En—*cape* FM-9
Sonia—*other* KY-4
Soniat Canal—*canal* LA-4
**Soniat (Cedar Grove Plantation)**—*pop pl* LA-4
Sonickson Creek—*stream* AK-9
Soniekkei—*bar* FM-9
Sonielem Lake—*lake* MT-8
Sonielem Ridge—*ridge* MT-8
Sonju Lake—*lake* MN-6
*Sonkey Branch* TN-4
Sonlight Ch—*church* GA-3
Sonman—*locale* PA-2
Sonna—*locale* ID-8
Sonneborn Bldg—*hist pl* MD-2
Sonneman Mine—*mine* ID-8
Sonnenberg Gardens—*hist pl* NY-2
Sonnenberg Sch—*school* OH-6
Sonnenschein Number 1 Dam—*dam* SD-7
Sonnenschein Number 2 Dam—*dam* SD-7
Sonnenschein Number 3 Dam—*dam* SD-7
Sonner Cem—*cemetery* OH-6
Sonner Hall—*hist pl* VA-3
Sonners Flat—*flat* ID-8
Sonnesyn Sch—*school* MN-6
Sonnet Mine—*mine* CA-9
Sonnett Creek—*stream* LA-4
Sonnette—*locale* MT-8
Sonnicant Lake—*lake* WY-8
Sonnickson Butte—*summit* ID-8
Sonnier Bayou—*stream* LA-4
Sonnier Cem—*cemetery* LA-4
Sonnies Pond—*lake* MI-6
Sonntag Cem—*cemetery* TX-5
Sonntag Hill—*summit* CA-9
*Sonnuuk* FM-9
**Sonny**—*pop pl* OR-9
Sonny Bay Creek—*stream* WA-9
Sonny Boy Lakes—*lake* WA-9
Sonny Boy Lode Mine—*mine* SD-7
Sonny Boy Mine—*mine* UT-8
Sonny Boy Prospect—*mine* CA-9
*Sonnybrook Baptist Church* AL-4
Sonny Coulee—*valley* MT-8
Sonny Gile Hollow—*valley* OK-5
**Sonny (historical)**—*pop pl* OR-9
Sonny Jernigen Dam—*dam* TN-4
Sonny Jernigen Lake—*reservoir* TN-4
Sonny Lake—*lake* UT-8
Sonny Meadow—*flat* CA-9
Sonny Montgomery Recreation Park—*park* MS-4
Sonny Tank—*reservoir* AZ-5
Sono—*bar* FM-9
**Sono**—*pop pl* WI-6
Son-of-a-Gun Gulch—*valley* CO-8
Son of Zion Cem—*cemetery* TN-4
*Sonoita* AZ-5
Sonoita—*locale* AZ-5
Sonoita Creek—*stream* AZ-5
Sonoita District Number Twenty-Fiver Sch—*school* AZ-5
*Sonoita Mountains* AZ-5
*Sonoita Range* AZ-5
*Sonoita Valley* AZ-5
Sono Junction—*locale* WI-6
*Sonoma* TX-5
Sonoma—*locale* AL-4
**Sonoma**—*pop pl* CA-9
**Sonoma**—*pop pl* MD-2
**Sonoma**—*pop pl* MI-6
**Sonoma**—*pop pl* TX-5
Sonoma, Lake—*reservoir* CA-9
Sonoma, Lake—*reservoir* NJ-2
Sonoma Canyon—*valley* (2) NV-8
Sonoma (CCD)—*cens area* CA-9
Sonoma Coast State Beach—*park* CA-9
**Sonoma (County)**—*pop pl* CA-9
Sonoma Creek—*stream* (2) CA-9
Sonoma Creek—*stream* NV-8
Sonoma Depot—*hist pl* CA-9
Sonoma Drive Sch—*school* CA-9
Sonoma Golf and Country Club—*other* CA-9
Sonoma Grammar Sch—*hist pl* CA-9
Sonoma Lake—*lake* MI-6
Sonoma Lake—*lake* NV-8
Sonoma Mine—*mine* CA-9
Sonoma Mine—*mine* NV-8
Sonoma Mission—*church* CA-9
Sonoma Mountains—*range* CA-9
Sonoma Mtn—*summit* CA-9
Sonoma Peak—*summit* NV-8
Sonoma Plaza—*hist pl* CA-9
*Sonoma Range* NV-8
Sonoma Range—*range* NV-8
Sonoma State Coll—*school* CA-9
Sonoma State Home (Eldridge P O)—*building* CA-9
Sonoma Valley—*valley* CA-9
Sonoma Valley Club—*other* CA-9
Sonoma Valley Hosp—*hospital* CA-9
**Sonoma Vista**—*pop pl* CA-9
Sonom Beach—*beach* AK-9
Sonome Canyon—*valley* CA-9
Sonome (Site)—*locale* NV-8
Sonongei—*cape* FM-9
*Sonora* GA-3
**Sonora**—*pop pl* AZ-5
**Sonora**—*pop pl* AR-4
**Sonora**—*pop pl* CA-9
**Sonora**—*pop pl* KY-4
**Sonora**—*pop pl* MS-4
**Sonora**—*pop pl* NY-2
**Sonora**—*pop pl* ND-7
**Sonora**—*pop pl* OH-6
**Sonora**—*pop pl* TX-5
Sonora, Caverns of—*cave* TX-5
Sonora Bridge Campground—*locale* CA-9
Sonora (CCD)—*cens area* CA-9
Sonora (CCD)—*cens area* KY-4
Sonora (CCD)—*cens area* TX-5
Sonora Cem—*cemetery* MO-7
Sonora Cem—*cemetery* NY-2
Sonora Cem—*cemetery* TX-5
Sonora Ch—*church* MS-4
Sonora Community Hall—*building* AL-4
Sonora Creek—*stream* (2) AK-9
Sonora Creek—*stream* CA-9
*Sonora Desert* AZ-5
Sonora Gulch—*valley* ID-8
Sonora Gulch—*valley* MT-8
Sonora Hill—*summit* AZ-5
Sonora (historical)—*locale* IA-7
Sonora (historical)—*locale* KS-7
Sonora Island—*island* AK-9
Sonora Junction—*locale* CA-9
Sonoran Desert—*plain* AZ-5
Sonora Passage—*channel* AK-9
Sonora Peak—*summit* CA-9
Sonora Post Office (historical)—*building* MS-4
Sonora Reef—*bar* WA-9
Sonora Rural (CCD)—*cens area* TX-5
Sonora Sch—*school* CA-9
Sonora Sch—*school* MS-4
**Sonora Town**—*pop pl* AZ-5
**Sonora (Township of)**—*pop pl* IL-6
**Sonoraville**—*pop pl* GA-3
Sonoraville Sch—*school* GA-3
Sonoreno Draw—*valley* NM-5
*Sonorian Dunes* CA-9
Sonovista Park—*park* SC-3
*Sonoyta* AZ-5
*Sonoyta Creek* AZ-5
*Sonoyta Mountain* AZ-5
Sonoyta Mountains—*range* AZ-5
Sonoyta Valley—*valley* AZ-5
Son Pond—*bay* LA-4
Son Prong—*stream* MT-8
Sonrisa Park—*park* AZ-5
Sonrise Baptist Ch—*church* UT-8
Son Run—*stream* IN-6
Sons Acad (historical)—*school* MS-4
Sons Airp—*airport* PA-2
*Sonsala* AZ-5
*Sonsan Spring* MH-9
Sons Branch—*stream* KY-4
Sons Bridge—*bridge* KY-4
Sons Chapel—*church* AR-4
Sons Creek—*stream* MO-7
Sonsela Buttes—*summit* AZ-5
*Sonsela Mtn* AZ-5
*Sonsella Buttes* AZ-5
Sons of Herman Cem—*cemetery* ND-7
Sons of Herman Cem—*cemetery* TX-5
Sons of Israel Cem—*cemetery* MA-1
Sons of Italy Hall—*hist pl* MN-6
Sons of Jacob Cem—*cemetery* CT-1
Sons of Jacob Cem—*cemetery* IA-7
Sons of Jacob Cem—*cemetery* MA-1
Sons of Mary Seminary—*school* MA-1
Sons of Norway Hall—*hist pl* AK-9
Sons of Poland Camp—*locale* NJ-2
Sons of the American Revolution Bldg—*building* DC-2
*Sons of Truth Cemetery* KS-7
*Sonsola* AZ-5
*Sonson* MH-9
*Sonson Bay* MH-9
*Sonsonhiya* MH-9
Sonsorol (County-equivalent)—*civil* PW-9
Sons Tank—*reservoir* NM-5
Sons Well—*well* TX-5
Sontag—*locale* VA-3
**Sontag**—*pop pl* MS-4
*Sontag Creek* AZ-5
Sontag Creek—*stream* AZ-5
Sontag Ditch—*canal* CA-9
*Sontag Hill* CA-9
Sontag Mesa—*summit* AZ-5
Sontag Point—*summit* CA-9
Sontag Post Office—*building* MS-4
Sontag Sch—*school* VA-3
Sontags Spring—*spring* MO-7
Sonth Lancaster—*locale* NH-1
Sontimer Airp—*airport* MO-7
*Sontiska* FL-3
*Sonton* MH-9
Son Vine Lake Dam—*dam* MS-4
Sonya, Lake—*lake* OR-9
Sonya Creek—*stream* AK-9
Sonyakay Ridge—*ridge* AK-9
Sony Draw—*valley* WY-8
**Sonyea**—*pop pl* NY-2
Sonyok Mtn—*summit* MT-8
*Soo Canals* MI-6
*Soo Creek* MI-6
Soo Creek—*stream* SD-7
Soocup Canyon—*valley* OR-9
*Sooes Mountain* WA-9
Sooes Peak—*summit* WA-9
Sooes River—*stream* WA-9
Sooey, Lake—*lake* NJ-2
*Soofield Creek* MT-8
Sooghmeghat—*locale* AK-9
Soo Hill Sch—*school* MI-6
Soo Hotel—*hist pl* ND-7
Soo Hunting Club—*locale* MI-6
Soo Junction—*locale* MI-6
**Soo Junction**—*pop pl* MN-6
*Sookalena* MS-4
*Sookalena Creek* MS-4
*Sookanatchie Creek* MS-4
*Sookee River* GA-3
Sookeys Creek—*stream* KY-4
*Sook Hanatcha River* AL-4
*Sookhanatcha River* MS-4
Sookie Creek—*stream* TX-5
Sooks Branch—*stream* SC-3
Sook Spring—*spring* AR-4
*Sooktaloosa Bluff* AL-4
Sooky Creek—*stream* NC-3
Sooky Gap—*gap* GA-3
Soo Lake—*lake* WI-6
Soo Line Depot—*hist pl* (2) MN-6
Soo Line Depot—*hist pl* ND-7
Soo Line Depot—*hist pl* (2) WI-6
Soo Line High Bridge—*hist pl* MN-6
Soo Line High Bridge—*hist pl* WI-6
*Soo Line Junction* MN-6
Soo Line Passenger Depot—*hist pl* ND-7
Soo Locks—*dam* MI-6
Soo Machine Club—*locale* MI-6
Soomaghat Mtn—*summit* AK-9
Soonapule Stream—*stream* AS-9
Sooner—*locale* OK-5
Sooner Bench—*bench* UT-8
Sooner Creek—*stream* NV-8
Sooner Ditch—*canal* CO-8
Sooner HS—*school* OK-5

Sooner Park—park ... OK-5
Sooner River—stream ... AK-9
Sooner Rocks—summit ... UT-8
Sooner Rsvr—reservoir ... WY-8
Sooner Sch—school ... OK-5
Sooner Slide—other ... UT-8
Sooner Theater Bldg—hist pl ... OK-5
Sooner Trend Oil Field—oilfield ... OK-5
Soonerville—locale ... OK-5
Sooner Wash—valley ... UT-8
Sooner Water—spring ... UT-8
Soo Nipi ... NH-1
**Soo Nipi**—pop pl ... NH-1
Soo Nipi Park—locale ... NH-1
Soonkakat River—stream ... AK-9
Soonnuuk ... FM-9
Soo Prong—stream ... MT-8
Soopwu ... FM-9
Sooquee River ... GA-3
Soosap Peak—summit ... OR-9
Soos Creek—stream ... WA-9
Soo Ship Canals ... MI-6
Soot Creek—stream ... MS-4
Soot Creek Mine (underground)—mine ... AL-4
**Soo Township**—pop pl ... ND-7
**Soo (Township of)**—pop pl ... MI-6
Sooty Creek—stream ... MI-6
**Sooy Place**—pop pl ... NJ-2
Sop Canyon—valley ... UT-8
**Sopchoppy**—pop pl ... FL-3
Sopchoppy Elem Sch—school ... FL-3
Sopchoppy-Panacea United Methodist Ch—church ... FL-3
Sopchoppy River—stream ... FL-3
Sope Creek—stream ... GA-3
Sope Creek Ruins—hist pl ... GA-3
**Soper**—pop pl ... OK-5
Soper Bay—swamp ... AL-4
Soper Branch—stream ... AL-4
Soper Branch—stream ... MD-2
Soper Brook—stream (3) ... ME-1
Soper Cem—cemetery ... ME-1
Soper Cem—cemetery ... MI-6
Soper Cem—cemetery ... MO-7
Soper Cem—cemetery ... NY-2
Soper Cem—cemetery ... ND-7
Soper Cem—cemetery ... OK-5
Soper Ch—church ... ND-7
Soper Creek—stream ... MI-6
Soper Creek—stream ... NY-2
Soper Creek—stream ... WI-6
Soper Drain—canal ... MI-6
Soper Hollow ... PA-2
Soper Lake—lake ... MN-6
Soper Logan—lake ... ME-1
Soper Mill Brook—stream ... ME-1
Soper Mountain (Township of)—unorg ... ME-1
Soper Mtn—summit ... ME-1
Soper Point ... NY-2
Soper Pond—lake ... ME-1
Soper Ranch—locale ... SD-7
Sopers Mill Access Area—park ... IA-7
Soper's Mill Bridge—hist pl ... IA-7
Sopers Ranch—locale ... CA-9
Sopers Sch—school ... KY-4
**Soperton**—pop pl ... GA-3
**Soperton**—pop pl ... WI-6
Soperton (CCD)—cens area ... GA-3
Sopertown—locale ... PA-2
**Soperville**—pop pl ... IL-6
**Sopha (historical)**—pop pl ... TN-4
Sopha Post Office (historical)—building ... TN-4
Sopher Ridge—ridge ... OR-9
Sophi—locale ... KY-4
Sophia ... TN-4
**Sophia**—pop pl ... NC-3
**Sophia**—pop pl ... OK-5
**Sophia**—pop pl ... WV-2
Sophia, Lake—reservoir ... PA-2
Sophia, Mount—summit ... PA-2
Sophia Cem—cemetery ... OK-5
Sophia Creek—stream ... SD-7
Sophia Ditch—canal ... WY-8
Sophian Plaza—hist pl ... MO-7
Sophia Post Office ... TN-4
Sophia's Dairy—hist pl ... MD-2
Sophia Sutton Mission—church ... MS-4
Sophia Swamp—swamp ... SC-3
Sophia Valley—basin ... NE-7
Sophie, Mount—summit ... MN-6
Sophie Creek—stream ... MT-8
Sophie Gap—gap ... TN-4
Sophie Hill—summit ... TN-4
Sophie Hole—cave ... AL-4
Sophie Island—island ... NC-3
Sophie Island Creek—bay ... NC-3
Sophie Lake—lake ... MT-8
Sophies Dam ... PA-2
Sophio Canyon—valley ... NM-5
Sophio Spring—spring ... NM-5
Sophio Well—well (2) ... NM-5
Sophio Windmill—locale ... NM-5
Sophy Lake ... MI-6
Sophys Meadows—range ... WA-9
Sopi—well ... FM-9
Sopiago Creek—stream ... CA-9
Sopinfou, Unun En—cape ... FM-9
Sopiram ... FM-9
Sopiram, Unun En—cape ... FM-9
Sopo, Ununen—bar ... FM-9
Sopori ... AZ-5
Sopori Ranch—locale ... AZ-5
Sopori Sch—school ... AZ-5
Sopori Wash—stream ... AZ-5
Sopou ... FM-9
**Sopris**—pop pl ... CO-8
Sopris, Mount—summit ... CO-8
Sopris Creek—stream ... CO-8
Sopris Lake—lake ... CO-8
Sopris Mine—mine ... CO-8
Sopris Peak ... CO-8
**Sopris Plaza**—pop pl ... CO-8
Sop Spring—spring ... UT-8
Sopuia, Oror En—locale ... FM-9
Sopuk ... FM-9
Sopun Ufou, Anangen—bar ... FM-9
Sopunur—island ... FM-9
**Sopuo**—pop pl ... FM-9
Sopweerd ... FM-9
Sopweru—island ... FM-9
Sopweru, Mochun—channel ... FM-9
Sopwiram ... FM-9
Sopwlong—locale ... FM-9
Sopwonog ... FM-9
Sopwota ... FM-9
Sopwotiw ... FM-9
Sopwu ... FM-9
Soque ... CA-9
Soque ... GA-3
Soque Branch ... GA-3
Soque Branch—stream ... GA-3
Soque Cove ... CA-9
Soque Creek ... CA-9
Soquee Branch ... GA-3
Soquee River—stream ... GA-3
**Soquel**—pop pl ... CA-9
Soquel Campground—locale ... CA-9
Soquel Canyon—valley ... CA-9
Soquel Cove—bay ... CA-9
Soquel Creek—stream ... CA-9
Soquel Meadow—flat ... CA-9
Soquel Meadow Ranch—locale ... CA-9
Soquel Point—cape ... CA-9
Soque Point ... CA-9
Soque River ... GA-3
**Soradoville**—pop pl ... PA-2
Sorag Pond—swamp ... MA-1
Sora Lake—lake ... MN-6
S-O Ranch—locale ... AZ-5
SO Ranch—locale ... NM-5
Sorber Cem—cemetery ... PA-2
Sorber Mtn—summit ... PA-2
Sorber Pond—lake ... PA-2
Sorber Run—stream ... PA-2
Sorberton Cem—cemetery ... PA-2
Sorbet Canal—canal ... LA-4
Sorby Hill—summit ... ND-7
**Sorby (historical)**—pop pl ... TN-4
Sorby Lake—lake ... MN-6
Sorby Post Office (historical)—building ... TN-4
Sorden Cem—cemetery ... IA-7
Sordo Well—well ... TX-5
Sordo Well (Windmill)—locale ... TX-5
Sordo Windmill—locale ... TX-5
Sore Eye Point—cliff ... AR-4
Sore Finger Cove—bay ... AK-9
Sore Finger Creek—stream ... TX-5
Sore Finger Point—ridge ... CA-9
Sore Finger Rsvr—reservoir ... WY-8
Sore Fingers—summit ... AZ-5
Sorefoot Creek—stream ... OR-9
Sorefoot Ranch—locale ... OR-9
Sore Head ... WA-9
Sorehead Creek—stream ... WA-9
Sorehead Tunnel—mine ... NV-8
Sorel ... LA-4
SoRelle Lake—reservoir ... TX-5
Sorelle Ranch—locale ... TX-5
SoRelle Windmill—locale ... NM-5
Sorell Peak ... CA-9
Sorel River ... VT-1
Sorenleng—island ... FM-9
Soren Peterson Meadow—flat ... UT-8
Sorens Cove—valley ... UT-8
Sorensdale Park—park ... CA-9
Sorensen—uninc pl ... CA-9
Sorensen, Dykes, House—hist pl ... UT-8
Sorensen, Fredrick Christian, House—hist pl ... UT-8
Sorensen, Severin, House—hist pl ... NE-7
Sorensen Ave Drain—canal ... CA-9
Sorensen Canyon—valley ... UT-8
Sorensen Creek—stream ... ID-8
Sorensen Creek—stream ... WY-8
Sorensen Hill—summit ... CA-9
Sorensen Lake—lake ... MN-6
Sorensen Ranch—locale ... MT-8
**Sorensens**—pop pl ... CA-9
Sorensen Sch—school (2) ... CA-9
Sorensen Sch—school ... TX-5
**Sorensen Subdivision**—pop pl ... UT-8
Sorensen Well—well ... NV-8
Sorenson, Mount—summit ... AK-9
Sorenson Canyon—valley ... WA-9
Sorenson Cem—cemetery ... MN-6
Sorenson Cem—cemetery ... WI-6
Sorenson Creek—stream ... MN-6
Sorenson Creek—stream (2) ... OR-9
Sorenson Creek—stream ... WA-9
Sorenson Ditch—canal ... CO-8
Sorenson Draw—valley ... UT-8
Sorenson Draw—valley ... WY-8
Sorenson Lake—lake ... AZ-5
Sorenson Lake—lake ... ND-7
Sorenson Lateral—canal ... SD-7
Sorenson Park—park ... UT-8
Sorenson Ranch—locale ... CO-8
Sorenson Rsvr—reservoir ... CO-8
Sorenson Spring—spring ... ID-8
Sorenson Spring—spring ... WA-9
**Sorenson Township**—pop pl ... ND-7
**Sorento**—pop pl ... IL-6
Sorepaw Creek—stream ... AK-9
Sore Paw Rsvr—reservoir ... WY-8
Sore Spring—spring ... AZ-5
Sore Thumb—summit ... WA-9
Soreye Tank—reservoir ... AZ-5
Sorge Cem—cemetery ... OK-5
Sorgen Ditch—canal ... IN-6
Sorgenfrei Creek—stream ... WA-9
Sorgenfri—locale ... VI-3
**Sorgho**—pop pl ... KY-4
Sorgho Cem—cemetery ... KY-4
Sorgho Sch—school ... KY-4
Sorghum ... KS-7
Sorghum Branch—stream ... IL-6
Sorghum Branch—stream ... MS-4
Sorghum Branch—stream ... SC-3
Sorghum Branch—stream (2) ... TN-4
Sorghum Canyon—valley ... AZ-5
Sorghum Creek—stream ... MS-4
Sorghum Flat—flat ... OR-9
Sorghum Flat—flat ... SD-7
Sorghum Gulch—valley ... CO-8
Sorghum Hill—summit ... AZ-5
Sorghum Hollow—valley ... AR-4
Sorghum Hollow—valley ... KS-7
Sorghum Hollow—valley ... MS-4
Sorghum Hollow—valley ... TN-4
Sorghum Hollow—valley ... WA-9
Sorghum Lake—lake ... MS-4
Sorghum Lake—locale ... MS-4
Sorghum Mill Lake—lake ... MS-4
Sorghum Patch Hollow—valley ... TN-4
Sorghum Ridge—ridge ... WV-2
Sorghumville—locale ... TX-5
Sorghumville Sch (historical)—school ... TX-5
Sorgs Arroyo—stream ... CO-8
Sorholus Tank—reservoir ... CA-9
Soria City Sch—school ... MS-4
Sorillo Windmill—locale ... TX-5
Sorin Camp—locale ... AZ-5
Sorins Bluff—cliff ... MN-6
Sorio Windmill—locale ... TX-5
**Sorkness Township**—pop pl ... ND-7
Sorlen—island ... FM-9
Sorman Cem—cemetery ... LA-4
Sorocco—uninc pl ... VA-3
**Soroco**—pop pl ... PR-3
**Soroka Shores**—pop pl ... FL-3
Sorol—island ... FM-9
Sorol Atoll—island ... FM-9
Sorol (Municipality)—civ div ... FM-9
Soro Park—flat ... CO-8
Soroptomists Crippled Childrens Camp—locale ... TX-5
Sorosis Park—park ... OR-9
Sorosis Rsvr—reservoir ... OR-9
**Sorrel**—pop pl ... LA-4
Sorrel, Bayou—stream ... LA-4
Sorrel Bay—stream ... LA-4
Sorrel Cave—cave ... IA-7
Sorrel Creek—stream ... TX-5
Sorrel Creek—stream ... VA-3
Sorrel Gulch—valley ... MT-8
Sorrel Hill—summit ... NY-2
**Sorrelhorse**—pop pl ... PA-2
Sorrel Horse, The ... PA-2
Sorrel Horse Canyon—valley ... AZ-5
Sorrel Horse Canyon—valley ... CA-9
Sorrel Horse Creek—stream ... MT-8
Sorrelhorse Hotel—building ... PA-2
Sorrel Horse Mesa—summit ... AZ-5
Sorrel Horse Sch—school ... MT-8
Sorrell ... LA-4
Sorrell—locale ... MO-7
Sorrell—locale ... VA-3
**Sorrell**—pop pl ... LA-4
Sorrell Airp—airport ... WA-9
Sorrel Lake ... LA-4
Sorrell Branch—stream ... AL-4
Sorrell Cem—cemetery ... MO-7
Sorrell Cem—cemetery ... NC-3
Sorrell Cem—cemetery ... TN-4
Sorrell Chapel—church ... TN-4
Sorrell Chapel Cem—cemetery ... TN-4
Sorrell Creek—stream ... NC-3
Sorrell Dam—dam ... AL-4
Sorrelle—locale ... TX-5
Sorrell Guest Resort—locale ... MT-8
Sorrell Lake—reservoir ... AL-4
Sorrell Lake Dam—dam ... AL-4
Sorrell Peak—summit ... CA-9
Sorrell Post Office (historical)—building ... MS-4
Sorrell Ranch—locale ... TX-5
Sorrell Ridge—ridge ... MD-2
Sorrell Rsvr—reservoir ... MT-8
Sorrells—locale ... AR-4
Sorrells, Walter B., Cottage—hist pl ... AR-4
Sorrells Branch—stream ... GA-3
Sorrells Branch—stream ... KY-4
Sorrells Cem—cemetery ... TN-4
Sorrells Creek—stream ... AR-4
Sorrells Creek—stream ... TX-5
Sorrells Dock—locale ... TN-4
Sorrells Hollow—valley ... TN-4
Sorrells Springs Ch—church ... GA-3
Sorrell Station ... LA-4
Sorrell Windmill—locale ... TX-5
Sorrel Peak ... CA-9
Sorrel Point Ridge—ridge ... VA-3
Sorrel Rsvr—reservoir ... ID-8
Sorrels—locale ... OK-5
**Sorrels**—pop pl ... TX-5
Sorrels Branch—stream ... GA-3
Sorrels Cem—cemetery ... AR-4
Sorrels Cove—valley ... NC-3
Sorrels Creek—stream ... AK-9
Sorrels Grove Ch—church ... NC-3
Sorrel Spring—spring ... ID-8
Sorrel Spring—spring ... OR-9
Sorrenson Dam ... ND-7
Sorrento—locale ... CA-9
Sorrento—locale ... CO-8
**Sorrento**—pop pl ... FL-3
**Sorrento**—pop pl ... LA-4
**Sorrento**—pop pl ... ME-1
Sorrento Cem—cemetery ... FL-3
**Sorrento Estates Subdivision**—pop pl ... UT-8
Sorrento Gas and Oil Field—oilfield ... LA-4
Sorrento Harbor—bay ... ME-1
**Sorrento Shores**—pop pl ... FL-3
**Sorrento Shores South**—pop pl ... FL-3
**Sorrento Skies (subdivision)**—pop pl ... NC-3
**Sorrento (Town of)**—pop pl ... ME-1
Sorrento Tunnel—tunnel ... ID-8
Sorrento Valley Site—hist pl ... CA-9
Sorrick Cemetery ... TN-4
Sorrier Branch—stream ... GA-3
Sorroca—locale ... CA-9
Sorro Park ... CO-8
Sorrow—spring ... FM-9
Sorrow, Bayou—stream ... LA-4
Sorrowfull Mother Shrine—other ... OH-6
Sorrowful Mother Shrine—church ... IN-6
Sortan Wash—stream ... CA-9
Sorter Creek—stream ... OK-5
Sorter Lake—lake ... MI-6
**Sorters**—pop pl ... TX-5
Sorters Bluff—cliff ... MO-7
Sorters Cross Roads School ... AL-4
Sorters Sch—school ... MI-6
Sortor Drain—stream ... MI-6
Sortore Cem—cemetery ... NY-2
Sortorstorm's Ranch—locale ... MT-8
Sorule Homestead—locale ... NM-5
**Sorum**—pop pl ... SD-7
**Sorum Addition (subdivision)**—pop pl ... SD-7
Sorum Cem—cemetery ... MN-6
Sorum Cooperative Store—hist pl ... SD-7
Sorum Dam—dam ... SD-7
**Sorum Heights (subdivision)**—pop pl ... SD-7
Sorum Hotel—hist pl ... SD-7
Sorum Sch—school ... SD-7
Sory and Towery Lake Dam—dam ... MS-4
Sosa—locale ... PR-3
Sosbee Bay—bay ... AK-9
Sosby Pond—reservoir ... GA-3
Sosebee Cove—valley ... GA-3
Sosei ... FM-9
So Sela ... AZ-5
Sosela Buttes ... AZ-5
Sosile ... AZ-5
Soske Dam—dam ... SD-7
Sosnik-Morris-Early Commercial Block—hist pl ... NC-3
Sosnovoi Island—island ... AK-9
**Soso**—pop pl ... MS-4
Soso Bayou—gut ... AR-4
Soso Elem Sch—school ... MS-4
Soso Methodist Ch—church ... MS-4
Sosonhiya ... MH-9
Sosonjaya ... MH-9
Soso Oil And Gas Field—oilfield ... MS-4
Sossamon Field—airport ... NC-3
Sossamon Industrial Park—locale ... NC-3
Sosthenes Gulch—valley ... CO-8
Sosthenes Mine—mine ... CO-8
Sotak Flowage—reservoir ... WI-6
Sotano Blanco—basin ... NM-5
Sotano Saddle—gap ... NM-5
Sotcher Farmhouse—hist pl ... PA-2
Sotcher Lake—lake ... CA-9
Sotelo Cem—cemetery ... TX-5
Sothell ... WA-9
Sothman Draw—valley ... WY-8
Sotin Creek—stream ... ID-8
Soto—uninc pl ... CA-9
Soto, Pablo, House—hist pl ... AZ-5
Soto Canyon—valley ... CA-9
Soto Canyon—valley ... TX-5
Soto Dam—dam ... AZ-5
Soto Dam Tank—reservoir ... AZ-5
Soto Jima ... FM-9
Soto Lake—reservoir ... CA-9
Sotol Basin—basin ... NM-5
Sotol Creek—stream ... NM-5
Sotol Draw—valley ... TX-5
Sotol Hill—summit ... TX-5
Sotol Vista Overlook—locale ... TX-5
Soto Mtn—summit ... TX-5
Soto Peak ... AZ-5
Soto Peak—summit ... AZ-5
Soto Ranch—locale ... CA-9
Soto Saint Junction—locale ... CA-9
Soto Saline Slough—gut ... LA-4
Sotos Crossing (historical)—locale ... AZ-5
Soto Spring—spring ... CA-9
Soto Street Sch—school ... CA-9
Soto Tank—reservoir (2) ... AZ-5
Soto Tank—reservoir ... TX-5
Soto Wash—stream ... AZ-5
Sotoyome—civil ... CA-9
Sotoyome Sch—school ... CA-9
Sotsin Point—cape ... CA-9
Sotter Creek—stream ... ID-8
Sotterley—hist pl ... MD-2
Sotterley—locale ... MD-2
Sotterley Point—cape ... MD-2
Sotterly ... MD-2
Sotterly Point ... MD-2
Souadabscook Stream—stream ... ME-1
Souas Corner—locale ... CA-9
Soubunge Mtn—summit ... ME-1
Soucada Creek ... TX-5
Sou Canyon—valley ... NV-8
Soucier Bog—swamp ... ME-1
Soucier Camp—locale ... ME-1
Soucook River—stream ... NH-1
Soucook River State For—forest ... NH-1
Soucys Camp—locale ... ME-1
Soudan ... MN-6
Soudan—locale ... MT-8
Soudan—locale ... VA-3
**Soudan**—pop pl ... AR-4
**Soudan**—pop pl ... MN-6
Soudan Cem—cemetery ... AR-4
Soudan (historical)—locale ... KS-7
Soudan Iron Mine—hist pl ... MN-6
Soudan Mine—mine ... MN-6
Souder—locale ... MO-7
Souder Cem—cemetery ... KY-4
Souder Ch—church ... MO-7
Souder Creek ... KY-4
Souder Creek—stream ... MO-7
Souder Lake—lake ... IN-6
Souders Branch—stream ... IN-6
Souders Branch—stream ... KY-4
**Soudersburg**—pop pl ... PA-2
Soudersburg Post Office (historical)—building ... PA-2
Souders Lake—reservoir ... IN-6
**Souderton**—pop pl ... PA-2
Souderton Airp—airport ... PA-2
Souderton Area Senior HS—school ... PA-2
Souderton Borough—civil ... PA-2
Souderton Shop Ctr—locale ... PA-2
Souderton Square—locale ... PA-2
Souenlovie Creek—stream ... MS-4
Sougahatchee Ch—church ... AL-4
Sougahatchee Creek—stream ... AL-4
Sougahatchee Dam—dam ... AL-4
Sougahatchee Lake—reservoir (2) ... AL-4
Sougahatchee Lookout Tower—locale ... AL-4
Sougahatchee Reservoir ... AL-4
Sougan Branch—stream ... TN-4
Sougan Hollow—valley ... TN-4
Souga Stream—stream ... AS-9
Sought For Pond ... MA-1
Sou-go-hat-che Creek ... AL-4
Souhegan East ... NH-1
Souhegan River ... MA-1
Souhegan River—stream ... NH-1
Sou Hills—summit ... NV-8
Souhna—locale ... FM-9
Sou Hot Springs—spring ... NV-8
Souiak—bar ... FM-9
Souilpa Creek ... AL-4
Souinlovey Creek ... MS-4
**Soukesburg**—pop pl ... PA-2
Soukop Dam ... ND-7
Soukup Draw—valley ... WY-8
Soulajule (Brackett)—civil ... CA-9
Soulajule (Cornwall)—civil ... CA-9
Soulajule (Gormley)—civil ... CA-9
Soulajule (Vasquez)—civil ... CA-9
Soulajule (Watkins)—civil ... CA-9
Soulard ... MO-7
Soulard Neighborhood Hist Dist—hist pl ... MO-7
Soulard-Page District—hist pl ... MO-7
Soul Chapel ... MS-4
Soul Chapel—church ... KY-4
Soul Chapel Branch—stream ... KY-4
Soul Chapel Cem—cemetery ... MS-4
Soul Chapel (historical)—church ... MS-4
Soul City—locale ... NC-3
Soul City House of God—church ... MS-4
Soule ... KS-7
Soule, C. S., House—hist pl ... IL-6
Soule, Lawrence, House—hist pl ... MA-1
Soule Brook—stream ... ME-1
Soule Cem—cemetery (2) ... NY-2
Soule Cem—cemetery ... NC-3
Soule Ch—church ... NC-3
Soule Chapel—church ... KY-4
Soule Chapel—church (2) ... MS-4
Soule Chapel—church ... WV-2
Soule Chapel Cem—cemetery ... MS-4
Soule Chapel Ch—church ... SC-3
Soule Chapel Methodist Church ... MS-4
Soule Coll—school ... LA-4
Soule Creek—stream ... AK-9
Soule Glacier—glacier ... AK-9
Soule Mill—locale ... ME-1
Soulen Rsvr—reservoir ... ID-8
Soule Pond—lake ... ME-1
Soule Ranch—locale ... CA-9
Soule Ridge—ridge ... ME-1
Soule Road Sch—school ... NY-2
Soules Cem—cemetery ... SC-3
Soule Sch—school ... NH-1
Soule Sch—school ... VT-1
Soules Chapel ... MS-4
Soules Chapel—church ... GA-3
Soules Chapel—church ... MS-4
Soules Chapel—church ... TN-4
Soules Chapel—locale ... TX-5
Soules Chapel Cemetery ... MS-4
Soules Chapel Church ... AL-4
Soules Creek—stream (2) ... WI-6
Soules Creek Cem—cemetery ... WI-6
Soules Pond—lake ... MA-1
Soules Swamp—stream ... NC-3
Soules Swamp—swamp ... NC-3
Soulia Mtn—summit ... NY-2
**Soulouque**—pop pl ... LA-4
Soulsby Mine—mine ... CA-9
**Soulsbyville**—pop pl ... CA-9
Soulsbyville Ditch—canal ... CA-9
Souls Canal ... LA-4
Souls Chapel—church (2) ... AL-4
Souls Chapel—church ... AR-4
Souls Chapel—church ... MO-7
Souls Chapel—church ... SC-3
Souls Chapel Cem—cemetery ... AL-4
Souls Chapel (historical)—church ... MS-4
Souls Chapel (historical)—locale ... MO-7
Souls Chapel Sch (historical)—school ... AL-4
Souls Harbor Ch—church (2) ... AL-4
Souls Harbor Ch—church ... IN-6
Souls Harbor Ch—church ... MS-4
Souls Harbor Ch—church ... WV-2
Souls Harbour Free Will Baptist Ch—church ... FL-3
Souls Haven Ch—church ... MS-4
Soulth Center Sch—school ... WI-6
Soulville Cem—cemetery ... NE-7
Soumethun—uninc pl ... TX-5
Soumi Lake ... MN-6
Sounahntel—bar ... FM-9
Sounamw—locale ... FM-9
Sound ... NJ-2
Sound—locale ... ME-1
Sound, Lake—lake ... NY-2
Sound, The ... ME-1
Soundau—unknown ... FM-9
Soundau, Dauen—gut ... FM-9
Soundau, Pillap En—stream ... FM-9
Sound Bay—bay ... NC-3
Sound Beach—beach ... VA-3
**Sound Beach**—pop pl ... NY-2
Sound Ch—church ... DE-2
Sounders Lake ... AR-4
Sounders Pond—reservoir ... VA-3
Sound Gut—stream ... MD-2
Sound (historical)—locale ... NC-3
Sounding Knob—summit ... VA-3
Sound Islands—area ... AK-9
Sound Landing—locale (2) ... NC-3
Sound Neck—area ... NC-3
**Sound of the Sea (subdivision)**—pop pl ... NC-3
Sound Point—cape ... FL-3
Sound Point—cape (2) ... NC-3
Sound Shore—beach ... MD-2
**Sound Shores (subdivision)**—pop pl ... NC-3
Soundside—locale ... NC-3
**Sound Side**—pop pl (2) ... NC-3
**Sound View**—pop pl ... CT-1
Soundview—uninc pl ... NY-2
Sound View Cem—cemetery ... WA-9
Soundview Ch—church ... NC-3
Soundview Logging Camp 17—locale ... WA-9
Sound View Park—park ... NY-2
Sounkioul—bar ... FM-9
Soun Kiroun—civil ... FM-9
Sounkroun ... FM-9
Soun Lierpwater—bar ... FM-9
Sounmwas—bar ... FM-9
Soun Nankengkeng—bar ... FM-9
Sounpwong, Dolen—summit ... FM-9
Sounting—locale ... FM-9
Soup Bean Branch—stream ... NC-3
Soup Bowl—reservoir ... UT-8
Soup Bowl Creek—stream ... CA-9
Soup Creek—stream ... CA-9
Soup Creek—stream (2) ... MT-8
Soup Creek—stream (2) ... OR-9
Soup Creek—stream ... WA-9
Soup Creek Campground—locale ... MT-8
Soup Hole—lake ... WA-9
Souphouse Flat—flat ... VT-1
Soupihr—locale ... FM-9
Soup Lake—lake ... AK-9
Soup Lakes—lake ... OR-9
Soup Lake Waterhole—reservoir ... OR-9
Souporuk—bar ... FM-9
Soup Rock—pillar ... UT-8
Soup Spring—spring ... CA-9
Soup Spring—spring (2) ... OR-9
Sour Apple Flat—flat ... OR-9
Sour Branch—stream ... AL-4
Sour Branch—stream (2) ... TN-4
Sour Branch—stream (3) ... TX-5
Sourbunge Mountain ... ME-1
Source Lake—lake ... MN-6
Source Lake—lake ... WA-9
Source Of Light Ch—church ... GA-3
Source of the River District—hist pl ... TX-5
Source Point—summit ... CA-9
Sour Creek—stream ... WI-6
Sour Creek—stream ... WY-8
Sour Creek Trail—trail ... WY-8
Sourdnahunk Field Campground—summit ... ME-1
Sourdnahunk Lake ... ME-1
Sourdnahunk Stream ... ME-1
Sourdough—locale ... AK-9
Sourdough—locale ... MT-8
Sourdough Basin—basin ... OR-9
Sourdough Camp—locale ... AK-9
Sourdough Camp—locale ... OR-9
Sourdough Campground—locale ... WY-8
Sourdough Camp (historical)—locale ... OR-9
Sourdough Canyon—valley ... CA-9
Sourdough Canyon—valley ... OR-9
Sourdough Canyon—valley ... WA-9
Sourdough Cave—cave ... MT-8
Sourdough Creek ... MT-8
Sour Dough Creek ... WY-8
Sourdough Creek—stream (3) ... AK-9
Sourdough Creek—stream ... CO-8
Sourdough Creek—stream (5) ... ID-8
Sourdough Creek—stream (2) ... MT-8
Sour Dough Creek—stream ... MT-8
Sourdough Creek—stream (5) ... MT-8
Sourdough Creek—stream ... OK-5
Sourdough Creek—stream ... OR-9
Sourdough Creek—stream ... TX-5
Sourdough Creek—stream (3) ... WA-9
Sourdough Creek—stream (4) ... WY-8
Sourdough Draw—valley ... SD-7
Sourdough Flat—flat ... OR-9
Sourdough Flats—flat ... SD-7
Sourdough Flats—flat ... WA-9
Sourdough Gap—gap ... WA-9
Sourdough Glacier—glacier ... WY-8
Sourdough Gulch—valley ... AK-9
Sourdough Gulch—valley (2) ... ID-8
Sourdough Gulch—valley (3) ... OR-9
Sourdough Gulch—valley ... WA-9
Sourdough Gulch—valley ... WY-8
Sourdough Hill—summit ... AK-9
Sourdough Hill—summit ... CA-9
Sourdough Island—island ... MT-8
Sourdough Lake—lake ... MN-6
Sourdough Lake—lake ... WA-9
Sourdough Lakes—lake ... CO-8
Sourdough Lodge—hist pl ... AK-9
Sourdough Lookout Trail—trail ... WA-9
Sourdough Mine—mine ... MT-8
Sourdough Mountains—summit ... WA-9
Sourdough Mtn—summit ... OR-9
Sourdough Mtn—summit (3) ... WA-9
Sourdough Peak—summit ... AK-9
Sourdough Peak—summit ... ID-8
Sourdough Peak—summit ... MT-8
Sourdough Pit—mine ... CA-9
Sourdough Point—cape ... ID-8
Sourdough Point—cape ... MT-8
Sourdough Ridge—ridge ... ID-8
Sourdough Ridge—ridge ... OR-9
Sourdough Ridge—ridge ... WA-9
Sourdough Sch—school ... MT-8
Sourdough Spring—spring (2) ... CA-9
Sourdough Spring—spring ... CO-8
Sourdough Spring—spring ... MT-8
Sourdough Spring—spring (2) ... OR-9
Sourdough Tank—reservoir ... TX-5
Sourdough Well—well ... AZ-5
Soureirei—bar ... FM-9
Sourgrass Camp—locale ... OR-9
Sour Grass Creek—stream ... CA-9
Sourgrass Creek—stream (2) ... OR-9
Sourgrass Flat—flat ... AZ-5
Sourgrass Flat Windmill—locale ... AZ-5
Sour Grass Gulch—valley ... CA-9
Sourgrass Lake—lake ... CA-9
Sourgrass Meadow—flat ... CA-9
Sourgrass Mtn—summit ... OR-9
Sourgrass Summit—gap ... OR-9
Sourgrass Trail—trail ... OR-9
Sourhouet Springs—spring ... NV-8
**Souris**—pop pl ... ND-7
Souris, Bayou—stream ... LA-4
Souris River*—stream ... ND-7
Souris Valley Golf Course—locale ... ND-7
Sour Lake—lake ... GA-3
**Sour Lake**—pop pl ... TX-5
Sour Lake (CCD)—cens area ... TX-5
**Sour Lake (corporate name for Sourlake)**—pop pl ... TX-5
Sourlake (corporate name Sour Lake) ... TX-5
Sour Lake Dome Oil Field—oilfield ... TX-5
Sour Lake Prairie—flat ... TX-5
Sour Lakes, The—lake ... TX-5
Sourland Mtn—summit ... NJ-2
Sour Moose Creek—stream ... WY-8
Sour Orange Hammock—island ... FL-3
Sour Pine Pond—swamp ... TX-5
Sour Run—stream ... OH-6
Sours Cem—cemetery ... OH-6
Sours Lateral—canal ... NM-5
**Sours Mills**—pop pl ... PA-2
Sour Spring—spring ... MO-7
Sours Run—stream ... IN-6
Sours Run—stream ... OH-6
Sours Run—stream ... VA-3
Sours Run—stream ... WV-2
Sour Water Canyon—valley ... AZ-5
Sour Water Spring—spring ... AZ-5

Sour Water Wash—stream (2) AZ-5
Sour Well—well TX-5
Sourwood—locale KY-4
Sourwood Branch—stream KY-4
Sourwood Branch—stream SC-3
Sourwood Creek—stream MS-4
Sourwood Creek—stream TN-4
Sourwood Gap—gap NC-3
Sourwood Mountain—ridge VA-3
Sourwood Mtn—summit TN-4
Sourwood Ridge—ridge WV-2
Sourwood Spring—spring AL-4
Sousa, John Philip, House—hist pl NY-2
Sousa Bridge—bridge DC-2
Sousa JHS—school DC-2
Sousa JHS—school NY-2
Sous Creek—stream TX-5
Souse Creek—stream MT-8
Souse Creek—stream TX-5
Sousek Cem—cemetery NE-7
Souser Creek TX-5
Souse Ridge—ridge MT-8
Souse Springs (Hatch Water Supply)—spring NM-5
Sousie Creek—stream ID-8
Sousley, Franklin R., Birthplace—hist pl KY-4
Sousley Lake—lake IN-6
Sousleys Lake IN-6
Souslin Cem—cemetery OH-6
Sou Springs NV-8
Souteast Sch—school NY-2
Soutel Drive and Norfolk Road Shop Ctr—locale FL-3
Souters Bend—bend OK-5
South IL-6
South MS-4
South—locale AL-4
**South**—pop pl KY-4
South—post sta AL-4
South—post sta AK-9
South—post sta NJ-2
South—post sta SC-3
South—post sta TN-4
South—uninc pl MD-2
South—uninc pl MA-1
South—uninc pl NJ-2
South—uninc pl NY-2
South—uninc pl TN-4
South—uninc pl TX-5
South, George W., Memorial Protestant Episcopal Church of the Advocate—hist pl PA-2
South, Rsvr—reservoir IN-6
**South Aberdeen**—pop pl WA-9
South Aberdeen Junction—uninc pl WA-9
South Abeyta Creek—stream CO-8
South Abington MA-1
South Abington, Town of MA-1
South Abington Elem Sch—school PA-2
**South Abington (Township of)**—pop pl PA-2
South Abington Village MA-1
South Abutment Public Use Area—park (2) MS-4
South Accomack Sch—school VA-3
South Acme Oil Field—oilfield TX-5
**South Acres (census name for Sulphur South)**—pop pl LA-4
**South Action**—pop pl ME-1
South Acton—locale ME-1
**South Acton**—pop pl MA-1
South Acton Swamp—swamp MA-1
**South Acworth**—pop pl NH-1
South Addison IL-6
**South Addison**—pop pl IL-6
**South Addison**—pop pl ME-1
**South Addison**—pop pl NY-2
South Adobe Tank—reservoir NM-5
**South Adrian**—pop pl MI-6
South Agnew Mine—mine MN-6
South Airport Draw—valley WY-8
South Akron OH-6
**South Akron**—pop pl OH-6
**South Alabama**—pop pl NY-2
South Alabama Infirmary (historical)—hospital AL-4
South Alabama Motor Speedway—locale AL-4
South Alabama Oil And Gas Field—oilfield OK-5
South Alameda Sch—school CO-8
South Alamo Canal—canal CA-9
South Alamo Creek—stream TX-5
South Alamo Drain—canal CA-9
South Alamo Street-South Mary's Street Hist Dist—hist pl TX-5
South Albany—cens area WY-8
**South Albany**—pop pl GA-3
**South Albany**—pop pl NY-2
**South Albany**—pop pl VT-1
South Albany HS—school OR-9
South Albany Point—cape MI-6
South Albemarle—locale NC-3
South Albemarle Park—park NC-3
South Albemarle (Township of)—fmr MCD NC-3
South Albion—locale ME-1
**South Albion**—pop pl NY-2
**South Alburg**—pop pl VT-1
South Alder Brook—stream VT-1
South Alder Creek—stream CA-9
South Alexandria—locale NH-1
**South Alexandria**—pop pl NH-1
South Alexandria Schools—school LA-4
South Alhambra—uninc pl CA-9
South Alkali Creek—stream OR-9
South Alkali Drain—canal OR-9
South Alkali Flat—flat NM-5
**Southall**—pop pl TN-4
**South Allapattah**—pop pl FL-3
Southall Cem—cemetery VA-3
Southall Cem—cemetery WV-2
Southall Chapel—church VA-3
Southall Drugs—hist pl AL-4
South Allegheny Elem Sch—school PA-2
South Alligator Bayou—stream AR-4
Southall Lake—reservoir MS-4
Southall Lake Dam—dam (2) MS-4
South All Night Creek—stream WY-8
Southall Post Office (historical)—building TN-4
Southall Ridge—ridge WV-2
**Southall (subdivision)**—pop pl MS-4
Southall (Township of)—fmr MCD AR-4
South Altamaha River—stream GA-3
**South Altoona**—pop pl PA-2
South Aluk Hill—summit AK-9
South Alum Creek—stream AR-4
**Southam**—pop pl ND-7
South Amador Tank—reservoir NM-5
**South Amana**—pop pl IA-7
South Amana Pond—lake IA-7
South Amarillo—uninc pl TX-5
South Amazon Park—park OR-9
South Ambo Channel—channel MP-9
**South Amboy**—pop pl NJ-2
South Amboy Junction—locale NJ-2
South Amboy Reach—channel NJ-2
Southam Canyon—valley UT-8
South Amelia River—stream FL-3
South Amelong Creek—stream MT-8
**South Amenia**—pop pl NY-2
South Amenia Cem—cemetery NY-2
South America, Lake—lake CA-9
South America Ch—church IL-6
South America Island—island AK-9
South American Canyon—valley NV-8
South American Lake CA-9
South American Point—cape AZ-5
South American Pond—lake VT-1
South America Park—flat MT-8
**South Americus**—pop pl GA-3
South Amesbury MA-1
**South Amherst**—pop pl MA-1
**South Amherst**—pop pl OH-6
**South Amity**—pop pl ME-1
South Amity Creek—stream OR-9
South Amity Sch (abandoned)—school ME-1
South Amory—uninc pl MS-4
**Southampton**—pop pl MA-1
**Southampton**—pop pl NY-2
**Southampton**—pop pl PA-2
**Southampton**—pop pl VA-3
Southampton—uninc pl VA-3
Southampton Baptist Church and Cemetery—hist pl PA-2
Southampton Beach—beach NY-2
Southampton Cem—cemetery NY-2
Southampton Correctional Center—building VA-3
**Southampton (County)**—pop pl VA-3
Southampton Creek—stream PA-2
Southampton Golf Course—other NY-2
Southampton HS—school VA-3
Southampton Memorial Hosp—hospital VA-3
Southampton Memorial Park—cemetery VA-3
Southampton Mills—locale PA-2
**Southampton (PC RR name Street Road)**—pop pl PA-2
Southampton Road Sch—school MA-1
Southampton Sch—school IL-6
Southampton Sch—school VA-3
Southampton Sch (abandoned)—school PA-2
Southampton Shoal—bar CA-9
Southampton Shoal Channel—channel CA-9
Southampton State Correctional Farm—other VA-3
**Southampton Subdivision**—pop pl UT-8
**Southampton (Town of)**—pop pl MA-1
**Southampton (Township of)**—pop pl NJ-2
**Southampton (Township of)**—pop pl NY-2
**Southampton (Township of)**—pop pl (4) PA-2
Southampton Village Hist Dist—hist pl NY-2
Southamptonville PA-2
**South Amsterdam**—pop pl NY-2
**South Anaheim**—pop pl CA-9
South Anchorage—bay AK-9
South Anclote FL-3
South Anclote Key FL-3
South And East Junction—uninc pl FL-3
South and East Osceola (CCD)—cens area FL-3
**South Anderson**—pop pl SC-3
South Andover—locale ME-1
South Angosta Well—well NM-5
South Animas Canyon—valley NM-5
South Ankle Creek—stream OR-9
South Anna—locale (2) VA-3
**Southanna**—pop pl VA-3
South Anna Ch—church VA-3
South Anna (Magisterial District)—fmr MCD VA-3
South Anna River—stream VA-3
South Ann Mine—mine MN-6
South Annville Ch—church PA-2
**South Annville (Township of)**—pop pl PA-2
South Ant Basin—basin ID-8
South Ant Canyon—valley ID-8
South Antelope Campground—locale CA-9
South Antelope Canal—canal OR-9
South Antelope Creek NE-7
South Antelope Creek WY-8
South Antelope Creek—stream NE-7
South Antelope Draw—valley WY-8
South Antelope Spring—spring SD-7
South Antelope Tank—reservoir TX-5
South Antelope Valley (CCD)—cens area CA-9
South Antler Creek*—stream ND-7
South Antrim Elem Sch—school PA-2
South Apache Creek—stream CO-8
**South Apalachin**—pop pl NY-2
South Apex Hill—summit UT-8
South Apopka—CDP FL-3
South Apperson Creek—stream WY-8
South Appleton—uninc pl WI-6
South Arapaho Peak—summit CO-8
South Arapaho Rsvr—reservoir CO-8
South Arbor—locale WA-9
Southard—locale MO-7
**Southard**—pop pl NJ-2
**Southard**—pop pl OK-5
Southard Block—hist pl ME-1
Southard Branch—stream KY-4
Southard Cem—cemetery (2) KY-4
Southard Cem—cemetery MO-7
Southard Cem—cemetery OH-6
Southard Ch—church KY-4
Southard Ch—church NJ-2
Southard Hollow—valley AR-4
Southard Lake—lake MI-6
Southard Lake—lake OR-9
**South Ardmore**—pop pl AL-4
**South Ardmore**—pop pl PA-2
Southard Point—cape ME-1
Southard Sch—school NY-2
Southards Creek—stream KY-4
Southards Pond—lake NY-2
South Area Alternative Center—school FL-3
South Area Alternative Sch—school FL-3
**South Argyle**—pop pl NY-2
South Argyle Cem—cemetery NY-2
South Arkansas River—stream CO-8
South Arkdale Cem—cemetery WI-6
South Arlington OH-6
South Arlington—other VA-3
South Arlington—post sta FL-3
South Arm MN-6
South Arm—bay (2) AK-9
South Arm—bay CA-9
South Arm—bay MI-6
South Arm—bay NJ-2
South Arm—bay WY-8
South Arm—locale ME-1
South Arm Bay of Isles—bay AK-9
South Arm Beck Ditch—canal IN-6
South Arm Campground—park UT-8
South Arm Cholmondeley Sound—bay AK-9
South Arm Dam—dam OR-9
South Arm Ditch—canal IN-6
South Arm Great Salt Lake UT-8
South Arm Hood Bay—bay AK-9
South Arm Hoonah Sound—channel AK-9
South Arm Kelp Bay—bay AK-9
South Arm Knife Lake—lake MN-6
South Arm Lake Lida—lake MN-6
South Arm Lower Richardson Lake—bay ME-1
South Arm Moira Sound—bay AK-9
South Arm Of Knife Lake MN-6
South Arm Rice Creek—stream CA-9
South Arm Rsvr—reservoir OR-9
South Arm Sand Arroyo Bay—bay MT-8
South Arm Spring—spring OR-9
South Armstrong Sch—school MN-6
South Arm Three Arm Bay—bay AK-9
**South Arm (Township of)**—pop pl MI-6
South Arm Uganik Bay—bay AK-9
South Arm Yokum Valley—valley OR-9
South Arndell Well—well TX-5
South Aroostook (Unorganized Territory of)—unorg ME-1
South Arrastre Creek—stream CO-8
South Arrowhead River MN-6
South Asbury Ridge—ridge WI-6
**South Ashburnham**—pop pl MA-1
South Ash Creek—stream UT-8
South Ashe—uninc pl NC-3
**South Ashfield**—pop pl MA-1
South Ashford Cem—cemetery CT-1
South Ash Lake MN-6
South Ashland Ch—church MS-4
South Ashley Creek—stream MO-7
South Asylum Bay—bay WI-6
**South Athol**—pop pl MA-1
South Athol Pond—reservoir MA-1
South Athol Pond Dam—dam MA-1
**South Atlanta**—pop pl GA-3
South Atlanta Ch—church GA-3
South Atlanta Sch—school GA-3
South Atlantic City NJ-2
South Atlantic Seventh Day Adventist Camp—locale FL-3
South Attica—locale NY-2
South Attica Cem—cemetery MI-6
**South Attleboro**—pop pl MA-1
South Attleboro JHS—school MA-1
South Attleborough MA-1
**South Auburn**—pop pl PA-2
South Augusta—CDP GA-3
**South Augusta**—pop pl IA-7
South Aulander Sch—school NC-3
South Aunts Creek—stream MO-7
South Aurora—cens area CO-8
South Au Sable River MI-6
South Austin—uninc pl TX-5
**Southaven**—pop pl MS-4
Southaven Church of Christ MS-4
Southaven City Hall—building MS-4
Southaven Elem Sch—school MS-4
Southaven HS—school MS-4
Southaven Post Office—building MS-4
**Southaven (subdivision)**—pop pl TN-4
South Avery Creek—stream IA-7
South Ave Sch—school NY-2
South Ave Sch—school WV-2
South Avis Sch—school PA-2
South Avon—locale NY-2
South Avondale Sch—school OH-6
South Babb Creek—stream CA-9
South Badger Creek—stream ID-8
South Badger Creek—stream MT-8
South Badger Creek—stream WY-8
South Badger Lake—lake MN-6
South Baffle Dam—dam MA-1
South Bainard Creek—stream CO-8
**South Baker (historical)**—pop pl OR-9
South Baker Sch—school OR-9
South Bald Eagle Creek PA-2
South Baldface—summit NH-1
South Bald Mountain NV-8
South Bald Mountain Tank—reservoir AZ-5
South Bald Mtn—summit CO-8
South Baldy CO-8
South Baldy—summit CO-8
South Baldy—summit NM-5
South Baldy—summit OR-9
South Baldy—summit WA-9
South Baldy Mtn—summit CO-8
South Baldy Mtn—summit MT-8
South Ballard Tank—reservoir NM-5
South Baltimore MD-2
**South Baltimore**—pop pl MD-2
South Bancroft—locale ME-1
South Bank—bar AL-4
South Bank—bar FL-3
South Banks—bar FL-3
South Bank Sch—school PA-2
South Banner Lake—lake WY-8
South Banner Mine—mine CA-9
South Bannock—cens area ID-8
South Bar—cape WY-8
South Barataria Oil and Gas Field—oilfield LA-4
South Barber Creek—stream CA-9
South Barber Elem Sch—school (2) KS-7
South Barber HS—school KS-7
South Barber Lake—lake WI-6
South Bar Channel—channel FL-3
South Bar Creek—stream WY-8
South Bar Lake—lake MI-6
South Bar Light FL-3
South Barnes Lake—lake MN-6
South Barnsdall Oil Field—oilfield OK-5
**South Barnstead**—pop pl NH-1
South Bar Point—cape MD-2
South Barre—locale NY-2
**South Barre**—pop pl MA-1
**South Barre**—pop pl VT-1
South Barrel Spring—spring WY-8
South Barrel Springs Draw—valley WY-8
South Barrett Creek WY-8
South Barrington—locale NH-1
**South Barrington**—pop pl IL-6
South Barton—other VT-1
South Barton Gulch—valley CO-8
South Bartonville IL-6
South Base—military CA-9
South Base—uninc pl GA-3
South Base Creek FL-3
**South Basehor**—pop pl KS-7
South Basehor—uninc pl KS-7
South Basin—basin ME-1
South Basin—basin MD-2
South Basin—basin UT-8
South Basin—basin WA-9
South Basin—bay CA-9
South Basin—bay FL-3
South Basin—bay NJ-2
South Basin—reservoir CA-9
South Bass Island—island OH-6
South Bass Island State Park—park OH-6
South Bass Lake—lake FL-3
South Bass Lake—lake WI-6
South Bastian Spring—spring NV-8
South Battle Creek—stream CO-8
South Baxter—locale WY-8
South Baxter Basin—basin WY-8
South Bay MA-1
South Bay MI-6
South Bay NY-2
South Bay NC-3
South Bay WA-9
South Bay—bay (2) AK-9
South Bay—bay AZ-5
South Bay—bay (2) CA-9
South Bay—bay CT-1
South Bay—bay FL-3
South Bay—bay IA-7
South Bay—bay (3) ME-1
South Bay—bay MA-1
South Bay—bay (4) MI-6
South Bay—bay MN-6
South Bay—bay (11) NY-2
South Bay—bay NC-3
South Bay—bay (2) TX-5
South Bay—bay VT-1
South Bay—bay VA-3
South Bay—bay (2) WA-9
South Bay—cove MA-1
South Bay—lake WI-6
South Bay—other NY-2
**South Bay**—pop pl FL-3
**South Bay**—pop pl (2) NY-2
**South Bay**—pop pl OH-6
**South Bay**—pop pl WA-9
South Bay—reservoir UT-8
South Bay—swamp NY-2
South Bay Aqueduct—canal CA-9
South Bayard—locale NE-7
South Bay Cities (CCD)—cens area CA-9
South Bay City MI-6
**South Bay City**—pop pl TX-5
South Bay Creek—stream NY-2
**South Bay Estates**—pop pl FL-3
South Bay (Fields Landing) CA-9
South Bay (historical)—bay MA-1
South Bay Hosp—hospital CA-9
South Bay Lake WI-6
South Baylor Creek—stream TX-5
South Bay Mini Plaza (Shop Ctr)—locale FL-3
South Bayou—gut LA-4
South Bayou—lake MI-6
South Bayou—stream AR-4
South Bayou Blue—stream TX-5
South Bayou Mallet Oil and Gas Field—oilfield LA-4
South Bay Park—park CA-9
South Bay Pass—channel TX-5
South Bay Pumping Plant—other CA-9
South Bay Sch—school (2) NY-2
South Bay Sch—school WA-9
South Bay Shop Ctr—locale CA-9
South Bay Union Sch—school CA-9
**South Bayview**—pop pl VA-3
**South Bay Village**—pop pl NY-2
South Bay Vista Park—park FL-3
Southbeach OR-9
South Beach RI-1
South Beach—beach MA-1
South Beach—beach (2) NY-2
South Beach—beach WA-9
South Beach—locale OH-6
**South Beach**—pop pl NY-2
**South Beach**—pop pl OR-9
**Southbeach**—pop pl OR-9
**South Beach**—pop pl (2) WA-9
South Beach Park—park (4) FL-3
South Beach Sch (historical)—school FL-3
South Beach State Park—park OR-9
South Beach Street Hist Dist—hist pl FL-3
South Beach Wayside—park OR-9
South Beacon Mtn—summit NY-2
South Bean Blossom Creek IN-6
South Bean Lake—lake MN-6
South Bear Branch—swamp FL-3
South Bear Butte Tank—reservoir AZ-5
South Bear Creek—stream CA-9
South Bear Creek—stream CO-8
South Bear Creek—stream IA-7
South Bear Creek—stream MT-8
South Bear Creek—stream TX-5
South Bear Creek—stream WI-6
South Bear Creek—stream WY-8
South Beardstown Drainage Ditch—canal IL-6
South Beardstown Pumping Station—locale IL-6
South Bear Lake—lake FL-3
South Bear Lake—lake MT-8
South Bear Park—park IA-7
South Beaver (CCD)—cens area OK-5
South Beaver Creek NE-7
South Beaver Creek SD-7
South Beaver Creek WI-6
South Beaver Creek—stream AK-9
South Beaver Creek—stream (5) CO-8
South Beaver Creek—stream (2) IA-7
South Beaver Creek—stream KS-7
South Beaver Creek—stream MI-6
South Beaver Creek—stream NC-3
South Beaver Creek—stream OR-9
South Beaver Creek—stream (2) SD-7
South Beaver Creek—stream TX-5
South Beaver Creek—stream (5) WY-8
South Beaver Creek Ch—church NC-3
South Beaver Creek Ch—church WI-6
South Beaver Creek Township KS-7
**South Beaver Dam**—pop pl WI-6
South Beaverdam Creek GA-3
South Beaverdam Lake—lake ME-1
South Beaver Mesa—summit UT-8
South Beaver Rsvr—reservoir MT-8
South Beaver Sch—hist pl AZ-5
South Beaver Sch—school AZ-5
South Beaverton Oil Field—other MI-6
**South Beaver (Township of)**—pop pl PA-2
South Beaver Valley Cem—cemetery SD-7
South Bedias Creek—stream TX-5
South Bedke Spring—spring UT-8
South Beebe Spring—spring WA-9
South Beede Rsvr—reservoir OR-9
South Beef River Ch—church WI-6
South Bee House Creek—stream TX-5
South Beeman Tank—reservoir TX-5
South Beheimer Ditch—canal NM-5
**South Bel Air (subdivision)**—pop pl MD-2
South Belfast Cem—cemetery ME-1
South Belingham Station MA-1
South Bell (CCD)—cens area TX-5
South Bell City Gas Field—oilfield LA-4
**South Bellingham**—pop pl MA-1
**South Bellingham**—pop pl WA-9
South Bellingham (historical P.O.)—locale MA-1
South Bell Sch—school MI-6
**South Belmar**—pop pl (2) NJ-2
South Belmont—CDP NC-3
**South Belmont**—pop pl NC-3
South Belmont Cem—cemetery ME-1
**South Beloit**—pop pl IL-6
South Beloit Municipal Park—park IL-6
**South Belridge**—pop pl CA-9
South Belridge Oil Field CA-9
South Bench—bench MT-8
South Bench Creek—stream UT-8
South Benches Spring—spring AZ-5
South Benches Tank—reservoir AZ-5
South Bench Rsvr—reservoir ID-8
South Bench Trail—trail CO-8
Southbend NE-7
South Bend—bend MO-7
South Bend—locale LA-4
**South Bend**—pop pl IN-6
**South Bend**—pop pl MN-6
**South Bend**—pop pl NE-7
**South Bend**—pop pl PA-2
**South Bend**—pop pl TX-5
**South Bend**—pop pl WA-9
South Bend Canal—canal UT-8
South Bend Carnegie Public Library—hist pl WA-9
South Bend Cem—cemetery IL-6
South Bend Cem—cemetery KS-7
South Bend Cem—cemetery LA-4
South Bend Cem—cemetery TX-5
South Bend Ch—church AR-4
South Bend Ch—church GA-3
South Bend Ch—church IL-6
South Bend Coll—school IN-6
South Bend Country Club—other IN-6
South Bend (historical)—locale SD-7
Southbend Mine—mine CA-9
South Bend Motor Speedway—other IN-6
South Bend Mtn—summit OR-9
South Bend Park—park GA-3
South Bend Plaza—locale IN-6
South Bend Remedy Company—hist pl IN-6
**South Bend Township**—pop pl KS-7
**South Bend (Township of)**—pop pl MN-6
**South Bend (Township of)**—pop pl PA-2
South Benedict Windmill—locale TX-5
South Bennett Creek—stream TX-5
South Bennettsville—CDP SC-3
South Benson Creek—stream KY-4
South Benton (CCD)—cens area WA-9
South Benton Township—civil (2) MO-7
South Berkeley—uninc pl CA-9
South Berkeley Springs—other WV-2
**South Berlin**—pop pl MA-1
**South Berlin**—pop pl TN-4
South Berlin Post Office (historical)—building TN-4
**South Berne**—pop pl NY-2
South Berry Creek—stream TX-5
South Berry Windmill—locale NM-5
**South Berwick**—pop pl ME-1
South Berwick Center (census name South Berwick)—other ME-1
**South Berwick (Town of)**—pop pl ME-1
South Berwick-Wells Ch—church ME-1
South Bethany IN-6
**South Bethany**—pop pl DE-2
**South Bethany (Bethany)**—pop pl IN-6
South Bethany Cem—cemetery MN-6
South Bethel Cem—cemetery ME-1
South Bethel Cem—cemetery (2) MO-7
South Bethel Cem—cemetery OK-5
South Bethel Ch—church IA-7
South Bethel Sch—school TX-5
**South Bethlehem**—pop pl NY-2
**South Bethlehem**—pop pl (2) PA-2
South Bethlehem Borough—civil PA-2
South Bidwell Hill—summit CA-9
South Bierremark—other AK-9
South Big Creek—stream AR-4
South Big Creek—stream KS-7
South Big Creek—stream MO-7
South Big Creek Oil Field—oilfield LA-4
South Big Creek Rsvr No 2—reservoir UT-8
South Big Flat Windmill—locale NM-5
South Big Horn County Hosp—hospital WY-8
South Big Horn Creek—stream MT-8
South Bight—bay (2) AK-9
South Big Rock (Township of)—fmr MCD AR-4
South Big Saddle Point—cape AZ-5
South Big Spring—spring AZ-5
South Big Spring Canyon AZ-5
South Big Springs Rsvr—reservoir ID-8
**South Billerica**—pop pl MA-1
South Billings—unorg reg ND-7
South Billings Oil Field—other MI-6
South Bills Creek—stream TX-5
South Biltmore—uninc pl NC-3
South Bingham Ch—church MI-6
South Bingham Creek—stream TX-5
South Bird Creek—stream OK-5
South Bird Island TX-5
South Bird Island—island TX-5
South Birdville Sch—school TX-5
**South Bisbee**—pop pl AZ-5
South Bitch Creek—stream WY-8
South Bitter Lake Oil Field—other NM-5
South Bitterswash Creek—stream NC-3
South Black Banks NY-2
South Black Banks Hassock—island NY-2
South Blackbird Creek—stream MO-7
South Blackbird Creek—stream NE-7
South Black Lake—lake MI-6
South Black Rock—bar ME-1
South Black Rocks—summit UT-8
South Black Wolf Sch—school KS-7
South Blanconia Oil Field—oilfield TX-5
**South Blendon**—pop pl MI-6
South Blendon Ch—church MI-6
South Blind Creek—gut FL-3
South Block—summit UT-8
**South Bloomfield**—pop pl NY-2
**South Bloomfield**—pop pl OH-6
South Bloomfield (Township of)—civ div OH-6
**South Bloomingville**—pop pl OH-6
South Bloomingville Sch—school OH-6
South Bloom Lateral—canal CA-9
South Blow Down Tank—reservoir AZ-5
**South Bluefield**—pop pl WV-2
South Bluehill ME-1
**South Blue Hill**—pop pl ME-1
South Blue Hole—lake MS-4
South Blue Lake—lake WI-6
South Blue Lake Group—lake OR-9
South Bluff—cliff AR-4
South Bluff—cliff MA-1
South Bluff—cliff MI-6
South Bluff—cliff WI-6
South Bluff—ridge NE-7
South Bluff—summit WI-6
South Bluff Country Club—other IL-6
South Bluff Creek—stream MN-6
**South Bluff Estates Subdivision**—pop pl UT-8
South Bluffs Warehouse Hist Dist—hist pl TN-4
**South Blvd Subdivision**—pop pl UT-8
South Blye Tank—reservoir AZ-5
**South Boardman**—pop pl MI-6
South Boat Ditch—canal AR-4
South Boat Lake—lake FL-3
South Boca Grande FL-3
**South Boca Grande**—pop pl FL-3
South Bog—swamp ME-1
South Boggy Creek—stream OK-5
South Boggy Creek—stream TX-5
South Bog Islands—island ME-1
South Bog Lake—lake MN-6
South Bog Stream—stream (2) ME-1
South Bogus Jim Creek—stream SD-7
South Boise ID-8
South Boise Drain—canal ID-8
South Boise Fire Station—hist pl ID-8
South Boise Historic Mining District—hist pl ID-8
South Boktuklo Creek—stream OK-5
South Bolivar—locale NY-2
**South Bolton**—pop pl MA-1
**South Bombay**—pop pl NY-2
South Bombsite Windmill—locale TX-5
South Boneta Canal—canal UT-8
South Bonfield Branch—stream IL-6
South Bon Homme State Public Shooting Area—park SD-7
South Bonnet Pond—lake FL-3
South Bonnie Brae Tract Hist Dist—hist pl CA-9
South Boone Creek—stream WY-8
South Bootlegger Picnic Area—park MT-8
South Boquet Mtn—summit NY-2
South Bordenstake Notch—channel VA-3
Southboro MA-1
Southboro—uninc pl FL-3
Southboro, Town of MA-1
Southboro Elem Sch—school FL-3
Southboro (RR name for Southborough)—other MA-1
**Southborough**—pop pl MA-1
**Southborough (RR name Southboro)**—pop pl MA-1
Southborough Sch—school MA-1
**Southborough (Town of)**—pop pl MA-1
South Bosco Oil and Gas Field—oilfield LA-4
**South Bosque**—pop pl TX-5
South Bosque River TX-5
South Bosque River—stream TX-5
**South Boston**—pop pl IN-6
South Boston Ch—church MI-6
South Boston Hist Dist—hist pl VA-3
**South Boston (ind. city)**—pop pl VA-3
South Boston Speedway—other VA-3
South Boston Station (historical)—locale MA-1
**South Boston (subdivision)**—pop pl MA-1
South Bottle Hollow Dam—dam UT-8
South Bottleneck Ravine MH-9
South Bottoms Hist Dist—hist pl NE-7
South Bouie Ch—church TX-5
South Boulder CO-8
South Boulder Canyon—canal CO-8
South Boulder Canyon Ditch—canal CO-8
South Boulder Cem—cemetery MT-8
South Boulder Creek MT-8

South Boulder Creek WA-9
South Boulder Creek—stream CO-8
South Boulder Creek—stream ID-8
South Boulder Creek—Stream MT-8
South Boulder Creek Trail—trail CO-8
South Boulder Diversion Canal—canal CO-8
South Boulder Foothills Ditch—canal CO-8
South Boulder Peak—summit CO-8
South Boulder River—stream MT-8
South Boulevard-Park Row Hist Dist—hist pl TX-5
South Boundary Lake—lake WY-8
South Boundary Pond—lake ME-1
South Boundary Spring—spring OR-9
South Boundary Trail—trail MT-8
South Boundary Trail—trail UT-8
South Boundary Trail—trail WV-2
South Boundary Trail—trail WY-8
South Boundbrook NJ-2
**South Bound Brook—pop pl (2)** NJ-2
South Bound Brook (sta.)—uninc pl NJ-2
South Bountiful Sch—school UT-8
South Bouquet Mtn NY-2
**Southbourne (subdivision)—pop pl** NC-3
South Bourn Shelter—locale VT-1
South Bow—locale NH-1
South Bow Creek—stream KS-7
**South Bowers—pop pl** DE-2
South Boxelder Creek—stream SD-7
**South Boyette—pop pl** FL-3
South Boyette RR Station—locale FL-3
South Boyle Lake MI-6
South Bradenton—CDP FL-3
**South Bradford—pop pl** NY-2
**South Bradford—pop pl** PA-2
South Bradford Cem—cemetery NY-2
South Bradford Ch—church VT-1
South Bradley (CCD)—cens area TN-4
South Bradley Division—civil TN-4
South Brady Creek—stream TX-5
**South Brainerd (subdivision)—pop pl** TN-4
**South Braintree (subdivision)—pop pl** MA-1
South Branch CO-8
South Branch IL-6
South Branch IN-6
South Branch KS-7
South Branch LA-4
South Branch ME-1
South Branch MD-2
South Branch MA-1
South Branch MI-6
South Branch MO-7
South Branch NJ-2
South Branch NY-2
South Branch PA-2
South Branch VT-1
South Branch VA-3
South Branch WA-9
South Branch—fmr MCD (2) NE-7
South Branch—locale PA-2
Southbranch—other MI-6
**South Branch—pop pl** MI-6
**South Branch—pop pl** MN-6
**South Branch—pop pl** NJ-2
South Branch—stream IL-6
South Branch—stream KS-7
South Branch—stream MO-7
South Branch—stream WV-2
South Branch Absecon Creek—stream NJ-2
South Branch Alder Stream ME-1
South Branch Alder Stream—stream ME-1
South Branch Allagash Stream—stream ME-1
South Branch American Colony Canal—canal CA-9
South Branch Amity Creek MN-6
South Branch Amos Palmer Drain—stream MI-6
South Branch Anclote River—stream FL-3
South Branch Antelope Creek—stream CA-9
South Branch Antelope Creek—stream ND-7
South Branch Arroyo Conejo—stream CA-9
South Branch Ashuelot River—stream NH-1
South Branch Ashwaubenon Creek—stream WI-6
South Branch Au Sable River MI-6
South Branch Au Sable River—stream MI-6
South Branch Austin Stream—stream ME-1
South Branch Bad Creek—stream OH-6
South Branch Baker River—stream NH-1
South Branch Bald Eagle Creek PA-2
South Branch Baraboo River WI-6
South Branch Battle River—stream MN-6
South Branch Bayou Biloxi LA-4
South Branch Bear Brook—stream (2) NY-2
South Branch Bear Creek LA-4
South Branch Bear Creek—stream MD-2
South Branch Bear Creek—stream MI-6
South Branch Bear Creek—stream PA-2
South Branch Bear River CA-9
South Branch Bear Run—stream PA-2
South Branch Beaver Brook—stream WI-6
South Branch Beaver Creek—stream MT-8
South Branch Beaver Creek—stream NY-2
South Branch Beaver Creek—stream ND-7
South Branch Beaver Creek—stream WI-6
South Branch Beaver Creek—stream WY-8
South Branch Bee Fork—stream MO-7
South Branch Bell Creek—stream CA-9
South Branch Bennett Branch—stream PA-2
South Branch Betsy River MI-6
South Branch Big Creek—stream WA-9
South Branch Big Mineral Creek—stream TX-5
South Branch Big Ox Creek—stream IN-6
South Branch Big Swamp Creek—stream MT-8
South Branch Big Timber Creek—stream NJ-2
South Branch Birch River—stream ME-1
South Branch Black Cat Brook—stream ME-1
South Branch Black Creek—stream MI-6
South Branch Blacklick Creek—stream PA-2
South Branch Black River MI-6
South Branch Black River—stream MI-6
South Branch Black River—stream NY-2
South Branch Blacktail Creek—stream SD-7
South Branch Black Valley—valley WI-6
South Branch Blackwater River—stream ME-1
South Branch Boardman River—stream MI-6
South Branch Bowline Creek—stream ND-7
South Branch Bowman Creek—stream PA-2
South Branch Box Butte Creek—stream NE-7
South Branch Boxelder Creek—stream CO-8
South Branch Boyne River—stream MI-6
South Branch Brady Run—stream PA-2
South Branch Brassua Stream—stream ME-1
South Branch Brayley Brook—stream ME-1
South Branch Brook RI-1
South Branch Brook—stream (2) ME-1
South Branch Browns Run—stream PA-2
South Branch Brule River MN-6
South Branch Brushy Canyon—valley CA-9
South Branch Buffalo River MN-6
South Branch Buffalo River—stream MN-6
South Branch Bullet Hill Brook—stream CT-1
South Branch Bunnell Brook—stream CT-1
South Branch Burrs Mill Brook—stream NJ-2
South Branch Caesar Creek—stream OH-6
South Branch Calkins Creek—stream PA-2
South Branch Camp—locale ME-1
South Branch Camp Creek—stream NE-7
South Branch Campground—locale MI-6
South Branch Camp Kettle Creek—stream OR-9
South Branch Canada Run—stream PA-2
South Branch Canal—canal WA-9
South Branch Canawacta Creek—stream PA-2
South Branch Cane Creek—stream AL-4
South Branch Caney Creek—stream TX-5
South Branch Caribou Stream—stream ME-1
South Branch Carl Creek MI-6
South Branch Carp River—stream MI-6
South Branch Carrabasset River—stream ME-1
South Branch Carroll Creek MI-6
South Branch Carry Brook—stream ME-1
South Branch Carson River—stream NV-8
South Branch Casselman River—stream MD-2
South Branch Cass River—stream MI-6
South Branch Catatonk Creek—stream NY-2
South Branch Catca Creek—stream LA-4
South Branch Cattail Creek—stream ND-7
South Branch Cattaraugus Creek—stream NY-2
South Branch Cave Gulch—valley (2) WY-8
South Branch Cedar Creek—stream IL-6
South Branch Cedar Creek—stream SD-7
South Branch Cedar Creek—stream VA-3
South Branch Cedar Spring Canyon—valley TX-5
South Branch Ch—church MI-6
South Branch Ch—church WV-2
South Branch Champion Run PA-2
South Branch Charlotte River MI-6
South Branch Chicago River—stream IL-6
South Branch Chico Creek—stream CO-8
South Branch Chippewa River MI-6
South Branch Choctaw Creek—stream TX-5
South Branch Chopawamsic Creek—stream VA-3
South Branch Clear Creek IL-6
South Branch Cleveland Canal—canal UT-8
South Branch Clifty Creek—stream IN-6
South Branch Clovis Ditch—canal CA-9
South Branch Coal Creek—stream TX-5
South Branch Cobscook River ME-1
South Branch Codorus Creek—stream PA-2
South Branch Cold Brook NY-2
South Branch Cole Creek—stream MI-6
South Branch Cole Creek—stream PA-2
South Branch Conewago Creek—stream PA-2
South Branch Coon Creek OH-6
South Branch Copper Creek—stream WI-6
South Branch Cormorant River MN-6
South Branch Corrumpa Creek—stream NM-5
South Branch Cottonwood Creek—stream NV-8
South Branch Coulee—valley MT-8
South Branch Coulee—valley ND-7
South Branch Cove Creek—stream OR-9
South Branch Cowanshannock Creek—stream PA-2
South Branch Creek DE-2
South Branch Creek—stream UT-8
South Branch Creek—stream WI-6
South Branch Crooked Creek—stream NE-7
South Branch Crow Creek—stream IL-6
South Branch Crow Creek—stream WY-8
South Branch Crow River MN-6
South Branch Crystal Creek—stream NY-2
South Branch Cut Creek—stream OR-9
South Branch Dead River—stream ME-1
South Branch Deep Creek—stream KS-7
South Branch Deer Creek—stream NE-7
South Branch Deerfield River—stream VT-1
South Branch Devil River MI-6
South Branch Devils River—stream MI-6
South Branch Devils Trackriver MN-6
South Branch Dog Creek—stream CA-9
South Branch Double Springs Creek—stream OK-5
South Branch Dry Creek MT-8
South Branch Dry Creek—stream SD-7
South Branch Dry Fork La Prele Creek WY-8
South Branch Duck Creek—stream SD-7
South Branch East Branch Waiska River—stream MI-6
South Branch East Cem—cemetery WV-2
South Branch Echo Brook—stream ME-1
South Branch Ecorse River—stream MI-6
South Branch Edgerton Creek—stream CO-8
South Branch Edwards River IL-6
South Branch Eighteenmile Creek—stream NY-2
South Branch Elk Creek PA-2
South Branch Elk Creek—stream VA-3
South Branch Elkhart River—stream IN-6
South Branch Elk River—stream KS-7
South Branch Ellen Creek—stream WA-9
South Branch Elm Creek KS-7
South Branch Elm Creek—stream OK-5
South Branch Elm River—stream MI-6
South Branch Elm River—stream ND-7
South Branch Embarrass River WI-6
South Branch Embarrass River—stream WI-6
South Branch Equinunk Creek—stream PA-2
South Branch Extension—canal WA-9
South Branch Fall River Canal—canal ID-8
South Branch Farmers Creek—stream MI-6
South Branch Feather River CA-9
South Branch Fellows Creek—stream MI-6
South Branch Fishing Creek—stream MD-2
South Branch Fivemile Creek KS-7
South Branch Flint River—stream MI-6
South Branch Ford Brook—stream NY-2
South Branch Ford River—stream MI-6
South Branch Forest River—stream ND-7
South Branch Fork Creek—stream VA-3
South Branch Forked Creek—stream IL-6
South Branch Forked River—stream NJ-2
South Branch Fourmile Creek—stream AL-4
South Branch Fox Brook—stream ME-1
South Branch Frazier Creek—stream OK-5
South Branch French Creek—stream (2) PA-2
South Branch (French Station)—locale WV-2
South Branch Gale River—stream NH-1
South Branch Galien River—stream MI-6
South Branch Garner Creek ND-7
South Branch Garrison Creek—stream IN-6
South Branch Genesee Creek—stream WI-6
South Branch Gilbert Creek—stream WI-6
South Branch Glade Run PA-2
South Branch Glendening Creek—stream NY-2
South Branch Gogomain River—stream MI-6
South Branch Gold Creek—stream MI-6
South Branch Good Luck Ditch—canal ID-8
South Branch Goose River—stream ND-7
South Branch Grass River—stream NY-2
South Branch Grassy Creek IN-6
South Branch Green Creek—stream SD-7
South Branch Grindstone Creek—stream NY-2
South Branch Grindstone River—stream MN-6
South Branch Grouse Creek—stream CA-9
South Branch Grummit Canyon Creek—stream SD-7
South Branch Grummit Canyon Creek—stream WY-8
South Branch Gunpowder Falls—stream MD-2
South Branch Hackberry Creek—stream KS-7
South Branch Haddix Run—stream WV-2
South Branch Hamilton Run—stream PA-2
South Branch Hamlin Brook—stream CT-1
South Branch Hansen Canal—canal CA-9
South Branch Harrison Canal—canal ID-8
South Branch Harvey Creek—stream WI-6
South Branch Heart River—stream ND-7
South Branch Hefty Creek—stream WI-6
South Branch Helm Colonial Ditch—canal CA-9
South Branch Hendrie River—stream MI-6
South Branch Hickory Creek—stream KS-7
South Branch Hickory Creek—stream OK-5
South Branch Highland Canal—canal AZ-5
South Branch Hist Dist—hist pl NJ-2
South Branch Hog Creek—stream MI-6
South Branch Horne Brook—stream NH-1
South Branch Humbug Creek—stream NE-7
South Branch Hurricane Creek—stream MS-4
South Branch Hursey Ditch—canal IN-6
South Branch Indian Creek—stream VA-3
South Branch Indian Run—stream PA-2
South Branch Ingles Draw—valley MI-6
South Branch - in part PA-2
South Branch Iron River—stream MI-6
South Branch Island Canal—canal (2) CA-9
South Branch Island Run—stream OH-6
South Branch Island Run—stream PA-2
South Branch Israel River—stream NH-1
South Branch Jacobs Brook—stream NH-1
South Branch Johnson Creek PA-2
South Branch Jordan Creek—stream MO-7
South Branch Kalamazoo River—stream MI-6
South Branch Kayaderosseras Creek—stream NY-2
South Branch Kettle Creek—stream NJ-2
South Branch King Creek—stream MS-4
South Branch Kings Creek—stream KS-7
South Branch Kinnickinnic River—stream WI-6
South Branch Kinzua Creek—stream PA-2
South Branch Kishwaukee River—stream (2) IL-6
South Branch Knapp Creek—stream PA-2
South Branch Kochville And Frankenlust Drain—stream MI-6
South Branch Kokosing River—stream OH-6
South Branch Lagrange Creek—stream VA-3
South Branch LaGrue Bayou—stream AR-4
South Branch Lake—lake CO-8
South Branch Lake—lake ME-1
South Branch Lamoille Creek—stream NV-8
South Branch La Moine River—stream IL-6
South Branch Lampee Canal—canal CA-9
South Branch La Plaisance Creek—stream MI-6
South Branch Larry Creek—stream IL-6
South Branch Laurel Run—stream MD-2
South Branch Laurel Run—stream (2) PA-2
South Branch Laurel Run—stream WV-2
South Branch Leach Creek—stream PA-2
South Branch Legionville Run—stream PA-2
South Branch Ley Creek—stream NY-2
South Branch Library—hist pl WI-6
South Branch Lincoln River—stream MI-6
South Branch Lindsey Creek—stream NY-2
South Branch Linton Creek—stream MI-6
South Branch Little Aughwick Creek—stream PA-2
South Branch Little Dead Diamond River—stream NH-1
South Branch Little Deep Creek WA-9
South Branch Little Elk River—stream MN-6
South Branch Little Floyd River—stream IA-7
South Branch Little Fork River MN-6
South Branch Little Heart River—stream ND-7
South Branch Little Medicine River WY-8
South Branch Little Musquash Stream ME-1
South Branch Little Musquash Stream—stream ME-1
South Branch Little Piasa Creek—stream IL-6
South Branch Little Popple River—stream WI-6
South Branch Little Portage Creek—stream PA-2
South Branch Little River WI-6
South Branch Little River—stream NY-2
South Branch Little River—stream WA-9
South Branch Little Salmon River—stream NY-2
South Branch Little Sugar Creek—stream MO-7
South Branch Little Sugar River—stream MI-6
South Branch Little Tippo Bayou - in part MS-4
South Branch Little Walnut River—stream KS-7
South Branch Little White Oak Creek—stream NC-3
South Branch Little Wolf River WI-6
South Branch Little Wolf River—stream WI-6
South Branch Lizard Creek—stream IA-7
South Branch Lonetree Creek—stream SD-7
South Branch Looking Glass River MI-6
South Branch Lyman Brook—stream NH-1
South Branch Macatawa River—stream MI-6
South Branch Machias River—stream ME-1
South Branch Macon Creek—stream MI-6
South Branch Macon River MI-6
South Branch Mad River—stream ME-1
South Branch Mad River—stream NH-1
South Branch Mad River—stream NY-2
South Branch Maggie Creek—stream NV-8
South Branch Magowah Creek—stream MS-4
South Branch Manistee River MI-6
South Branch Manitou River—stream MN-6
South Branch Manitowoc River—stream WI-6
South Branch Maple Creek—stream PA-2
South Branch Maple River—stream ND-7
South Branch Marie DeLarme Creek—stream IN-6
South Branch Marie DeLarme Creek—stream OH-6
South Branch Marsh Creek PA-2
South Branch Marsh River—stream ME-1
South Branch Marten Creek—stream MT-8
South Branch Massey Creek—stream VA-3
South Branch Massies Creek OH-6
South Branch McConnell Brook—stream ME-1
South Branch McDermitt Creek NV-8
South Branch McDermitt Creek OR-9
South Branch McDowell Creek—stream TX-5
South Branch McKinstry Drain—stream MI-6
South Branch Medicine Lodge River—stream KS-7
South Branch Medunkeunk Stream—stream ME-1
South Branch Meduxnekeag River ME-1
South Branch Meduxnekeag River—stream ME-1
South Branch Meduxnekeag Stream—stream ME-1
South Branch Memorial Gardens—cemetery WV-2
South Branch Merriweather Creek MI-6
South Branch Metedeconk River—stream NJ-2
South Branch Metetecunk River NJ-2
South Branch Middlebury River—stream VT-1
South Branch Middle Creek—stream NE-7
South Branch Middle Creek—stream PA-2
South Branch Middle Fork Feather River—stream CA-9
South Branch Middle Fork Owl Creek—stream WY-8
South Branch Middle Fork Zumbro River MN-6
South Branch Middle Fork Zumbro River—stream MN-6
South Branch Middle Loup River—stream NE-7
South Branch Middle Thompson Creek—stream CO-8
South Branch Mill Creek KS-7
South Branch Mill Creek—stream CA-9
South Branch Mill Creek—stream KS-7
South Branch Mill Creek—stream MI-6
South Branch Mill Creek—stream NJ-2
South Branch Mill Creek—stream OR-9
South Branch Mill River—stream MA-1
South Branch Mineral Creek TX-5
South Branch Miner Creek—stream MT-8
South Branch Minisceongo Creek—stream NY-2
South Branch Mira Creek—stream NE-7
South Branch Miry Creek NE-7
South Branch Miscauno Creek—stream WI-6
South Branch Mission Creek—stream KS-7
South Branch Moose River—stream ME-1
South Branch Moose River—stream NY-2
South Branch Mosquito Creek—stream CA-9
South Branch Mouillee Creek—stream MI-6
South Branch Mountain—ridge WV-2
South Branch Mountains ME-1
South Branch Mount Misery Brook—stream NJ-2
South Branch Mtn—summit WV-2
South Branch Mud Creek OR-9
South Branch Mud Creek WA-9
South Branch Mud Creek—stream IN-6
South Branch Mud Creek—stream MN-6
South Branch Mud Creek—stream NE-7
South Branch Muddy Creek PA-2
South Branch Muddy Creek—stream OH-6
South Branch Muddy Creek—stream (2) PA-2
South Branch Mud Run—stream PA-2
South Branch Naaman Creek—stream DE-2
South Branch Naaman Creek—stream PA-2
South Branch Naked Creek—stream VA-3
South Branch Navarro River CA-9
South Branch Neenah Creek—stream WI-6
South Branch Newport Creek—stream PA-2
South Branch Nibb Creek—stream VA-3
South Branch Norris Brook—stream ME-1
South Branch North Brush Creek—stream CO-8
South Branch North County Drain—canal MI-6
South Branch North Creek—stream IN-6
South Branch North Fork Elk River—stream CA-9
South Branch North Fork Hardware River—stream VA-3
South Branch North Fork Navarro River—stream CA-9
South Branch North Fork New River—stream NC-3
South Branch North Fork Redbank Creek—stream PA-2
South Branch North Fork Stillaguamish River—stream WA-9
South Branch Oconto River—stream WI-6
South Branch Oconto River State Wildlife Area—park WI-6
South Branch Of Big Blue RIVER NE-7
south Branch Of The Little Fork Of Rainy River MN-6
South Branch of the Pawtuxet River RI-1
South Branch Of Toms River NJ-2
South Branch Oleander Canal—canal CA-9
South Branch Onancock Creek—stream VA-3
South Branch O'Neill Creek—stream WI-6
South Branch Ontonagon River—stream MI-6
South Branch Opalescent River NY-2
South Branch Orrs Creek—stream MI-6
South Branch Oswayo Creek—stream PA-2
South Branch Otter Brook—stream ME-1
South Branch Otter Creek IN-6
South Branch Otter Creek—stream (2) IL-6
South Branch Otter Creek—stream KS-7
South Branch Otter Creek—stream MI-6
South Branch Otter Creek—stream UT-8
South Branch Owl Creek—stream CA-9
South Branch Paint River—stream MI-6
South Branch Pakanasink Creek—stream NY-2
South Branch Palmer Stream—stream ME-1
South Branch Park—park OH-6
South Branch Park Gulch—valley CO-8
South Branch Park River—stream CT-1
South Branch Park River—stream ND-7
South Branch Patapsco River—stream MD-2
South Branch Pawpaw Creek—stream TN-4
South Branch Paw Paw River—stream MI-6
South Branch Pawtuxet River—stream RI-1
South Branch Pebble Creek—stream NE-7
South Branch Pelican River WI-6
South Branch Pemebonwon River—stream WI-6
South Branch Pennsauken Creek—stream NJ-2
South Branch Penobscot River—stream ME-1
South Branch Pentwater River—stream MI-6
South Branch Peoples Creek—stream MT-8
South Branch Peshtigo River—stream WI-6
South Branch Phelps Creek—stream OH-6
South Branch Piedmont Creek—stream CA-9
South Branch Pigeon Creek—stream PA-2
South Branch Pigeon River WI-6
South Branch Pigeon River—stream MI-6
South Branch Pigeon River—stream WI-6
South Branch Pike River—stream WI-6
South Branch Pinconning River—stream MI-6
South Branch Pine Creek IN-6
South Branch Pine Creek—stream IN-6
South Branch Pine Creek—stream PA-2
South Branch Pine Creek—stream SD-7
South Branch Pine Creek—stream TX-5
South Branch Pine River—stream (4) MI-6
South Branch Pin Oak Creek—stream MO-7
South Branch Pipestone Creek—stream MN-6
South Branch Piscataquog River—stream NH-1
South Branch Pleasant Run—stream IN-6
South Branch Plum Creek NE-7
South Branch Plum Creek—stream PA-2
South Branch Point of Rocks Creek—stream NE-7
South Branch Point Of Rocks Creek—stream NE-7
South Branch Pond Campground—locale ME-1
South Branch Ponds Brook—stream ME-1
South Branch Popple River—stream WI-6
South Branch Portage River—stream OH-6
South Branch Portfield Creek—stream CA-9
South Branch Potomac River—stream VA-3
South Branch Potomac River—stream WV-2
South Branch Prairie Creek—stream SD-7
South Branch Presque Isle River—stream MI-6
South Branch Presque Isle River—stream WI-6
South Branch Queens Creek OR-9
South Branch Raccoon Creek—stream NJ-2
South Branch Rahway River—stream NJ-2
South Branch Ranch—locale MI-6
South Branch Rancocas Creek—stream NJ-2
South Branch Rapid RiA VAR Miller Creek MN-6
South Branch Rapid River MN-6
South Branch Raritan River—stream NJ-2
South Branch Rattlesnake Creek—stream KS-7
South Branch Red Creek—stream MS-4
South Branch Red River WI-6
South Branch Rexburg Canal—canal ID-8
South Branch Rice Creek—stream MI-6
South Branch Rio San Antonio—channel CO-8
South Branch River—stream MI-6
South Branch River Raisin—stream MI-6
South Branch River Raisin Creek MI-6
South Branch Roaring Creek—stream PA-2
South Branch Roaring Run—stream PA-2
South Branch Robinson Creek—stream CA-9
South Branch Rockaway Creek—stream NJ-2
South Branch Rock Creek—stream IL-6
South Branch Rockhouse Fork—stream WV-2
South Branch Rock River—stream WI-6
South Branch Rock Run—stream PA-2
South Branch Rolfe Brook—stream ME-1
South Branch Root River—stream MN-6
South Branch Rosin Camp Fork—stream VA-3
South Branch Rush Drain—canal MI-6
South Branch Rush River—stream MN-6
South Branch Russell Brook—stream ME-1
South Branch Salt Creek—stream IN-6
South Branch Salt Creek—stream IA-7
South Branch Salt River—stream MI-6
South Branch Sand Canyon—valley NE-7
South Branch Sand Creek—stream CA-9
South Branch Sand Creek—stream (2) NE-7
South Branch Sandy Creek NY-2
South Branch Sandy Creek—stream MI-6
South Branch Sandy River—stream ME-1
South Branch Sawmill Run—stream NY-2
South Branch Saxtons River—stream VT-1
South Branch Scammon Creek—stream WA-9
South Branch Sch—school (2) VT-1
South Branch Sch (abandoned)—school PA-2
South Branch Settlement Branch—stream TX-5
South Branch Shelldrake River—stream MI-6
South Branch Shepards Creek—stream MI-6
South Branch Shiawassee River—stream MI-6
South Branch Shoal Creek IA-7
South Branch Shunganunga Creek—stream KS-7
South Branch Silver Brook—stream MA-1
South Branch Slapneck Creek—stream MI-6
South Branch Slate Creek—stream KS-7
South Branch Slater Creek—stream MT-8
South Branch Slater Creek—stream WY-8
South Branch Slippery Rock Creek—stream PA-2
South Branch Smoke Creek—stream NY-2
South Branch Snake Creek—stream NE-7
South Branch Snake River—stream MN-6
South Branch Snowy Creek—stream WV-2
South Branch Soldier Creek—stream KS-7
South Branch Soper Brook—stream ME-1
South Branch Souhegan River—stream MA-1
South Branch Souhegan River—stream NH-1
South Branch South Altamaha River—channel GA-3
South Branch South Branch Kishwaukee River—stream IL-6
South Branch South Branch Tule River—stream CA-9
South Branch South Creek—stream MO-7
South Branch South Fork Ogden River—stream UT-8
South Branch South Fork Panther Creek—stream KY-4
South Branch South Fork Pine Creek—stream PA-2
South Branch Spillman Creek—stream KS-7
South Branch Spring Brook—stream MI-6
South Branch Spring Creek IN-6
South Branch Spring Creek MI-6
South Branch Spring Creek—stream VA-3
South Branch Spruce Brook—stream ME-1
South Branch State Line Run—stream NY-2
South Branch State Line Run—stream PA-2
South Branch Stearns Brook—stream NH-1
South Branch Stony Creek—stream MI-6
South Branch Stouts Creek—stream NJ-2
South Branch Stream—stream ME-1
South Branch Stroudwater River—stream ME-1
South Branch Stutts Creek—stream MI-6
South Branch Suamico River—stream WI-6
South Branch Sugar Creek IL-6
South Branch Sugar Creek—stream IN-6
South Branch Sugar Creek—stream PA-2
South Branch Sugar River—stream NH-1
South Branch Sugar Run - in part PA-2
South Branch Summit Lake Ditch—canal CA-9
South Branch Sunday River—stream ME-1
South Branch Sunrise River MN-6
South Branch Sunrise River—stream MN-6
South Branch Sutter Creek—stream CA-9
South Branch Swan Creek MI-6
South Branch Symmes Creek—stream OH-6
South Branch Tenmile Creek—stream WI-6
South Branch Tequa Creek—stream KS-7
South Branch Teton River ID-8
South Branch Thornbottom Creek - in part PA-2
South Branch Three Brooks—stream ME-1
South Branch Three Mile Creek—stream MI-6
South Branch Thunder Bay River MI-6
South Branch Timber Creek—stream NE-7
South Branch Timber Swamp Brook—stream NJ-2
South Branch Tionesta Creek PA-2
South Branch Tionesta Creek—stream PA-2
South Branch Tobacco River—stream MI-6
South Branch Tonquish Creek—stream MI-6
South Branch Toomey Gulch OR-9
South Branch Towanda Creek—stream PA-2
South Branch Townline Creek—stream MI-6
South Branch Town Line Creek—stream MI-6
**South Branch Township—pop pl** NE-7
South Branch (Township of)—civ div (2) MI-6
South Branch (Township of)—civ div MN-6
South Branch Trade River—stream WI-6
South Branch Trail—trail ME-1
South Branch Trempealeau River—stream WI-6
South Branch Trimble Glacier—glacier AK-9
South Branch Trout Brook—stream CT-1
South Branch Trout Brook—stream ME-1
South Branch Trout River—stream VT-1
South Branch Tularcitos Creek—stream CA-9
South Branch Tule River—stream CA-9
South Branch Tunkhannock Creek—stream PA-2
South Branch Turkey Creek—stream GA-3
South Branch Turkey Creek—stream IN-6
South Branch Turkey River IA-7
South Branch Turkey River—stream IA-7
South Branch Turtle Creek—stream NE-7
South Branch Turtle Creek—stream OH-6
South Branch Turtle River—stream ND-7
South Branch Tuscarora Creek—stream NY-2
South Branch Tweed River—stream VT-1
South Branch Twin Creek—stream MI-6
South Branch Twin Creek—stream WI-6
South Branch Two Hearted River—stream MI-6
South Branch Two Lick Creek—stream PA-2
South Branch Twomile Brook—stream ME-1
South Branch Two RiveA VAR South Branch Two Rivers River MN-6
South Branch Two Rivers MN-6
South Branch Two Rivers—stream MN-6
South Branch Two Rivers River MN-6
South Branch Union Ditch—canal CO-8
South Branch Van Campen Creek—stream NY-2
South Branch Vaughns Creek—stream MS-4
South Branch Verdigre Creek—stream NE-7
South Branch Verdigris River—stream KS-7
South Branch Vermillion River—stream MN-6
South Branch Vickery Brook—stream ME-1
South Branch Wadleigh Brook—stream ME-1
South Branch Waiska River—stream MI-6
South Branch Waits River—stream VT-1
South Branch Wakarusa River—stream KS-7
South Branch Ward Creek—stream CA-9
South Branch Warehouse Creek—stream AK-9
South Branch Warren Canal—canal UT-8
South Branch Washington Colony Canal—canal CA-9
South Branch Wassataquoik Stream—stream ME-1
South Branch Water Gap Wash—valley WY-8
South Branch Water Hen Creek—stream MN-6
South Branch Watonwan River MN-6
South Branch Wedde Creek—stream WI-6
South Branch Weeping Water Creek—stream NE-7
South Branch Wells River—stream VT-1
South Branch West Canada Creek—stream NY-2
South Branch West Fork Trout Creek—stream MT-8
South Branch West Nodaway River—stream IA-7
South Branch West Twin Brook—stream ME-1
South Branch West Weber Canal—canal UT-8
South Branch White Bear Creek—stream MT-8
South Branch White Creek—stream MI-6
South Branch White Deer Creek PA-2
South Branch Whiteface River—stream MN-6
South Branch White River—stream MI-6
South Branch Whitman Coulee—valley MT-8
South Branch Whitney Brook—stream ME-1
South Branch Who Who Creek—stream CA-9
South Branch Wildcat Creek IN-6
South Branch Wildcat Creek—stream SC-3

South Branch Wild Rice River—stream MN-6
South Branch Wilford Canal—canal ID-8
South Branch Wilhite Creek—stream MS-4
South Branch Williams River—stream VT-1
South Branch Willow Creek—stream MI-6
South Branch Willow Creek—stream PA-2
South Branch Willow Creek—stream TX-5
South Branch Wilson Canal—canal UT-8
South Branch Wolf Creek—stream OH-6
South Branch Wolf Run—stream WV-2
South Branch Wyalusing Creek—stream PA-2
South Branch Wyomanock Creek—stream NY-2
South Branch Yankee Run—stream OH-6
South Branch Yellow Creek IN-6
South Branch Yellow Medicine River—stream MN-6
South Branch Yellow River—stream (2) WI-6
South Branch Zippel Creek—stream MN-6
South Branch Zipple Creek MN-6
South Branch Zumbro River MN-6
South Brandywine MS—school PA-2
South Bratton Creek—stream AR-4
South Brazos (CCD)—cens area TX-5
South Breaker—bar (2) ME-1
South Breeze Elem Sch—school KS-7
South Breitenbush Trail—trail OR-9
South Brenton Sch—school IL-6
South Brewer ME-1
**South Brewer**—pop pl ME-1
**South Brewster**—pop pl MA-1
**South Brice**—pop pl TX-5
South Bridge—bridge FL-3
South Bridge—bridge ME-1
South-Bridge—locale PA-2
South Bridge—other MO-7
**Southbridge**—pop pl MA-1
**Southbridge Center**—pop pl MA-1
Southbridge Centre MA-1
South Bridge Cove—bay TX-5
South Bridge (historical)—bridge TN-4
Southbridge HS—school MA-1
**South Bridge Plat A**—pop pl UT-8
Southbridge Plaza—locale MA-1
South Bridger Creek—stream WY-8
Southbridge-Sargent Manufacturing District—hist pl MA-1
South Bridge Sch—school WV-2
South Bridges Creek—stream MO-7
South Bridges Creek - in part MO-7
South Bridge Street Hist Dist—hist pl TX-5
**Southbridge (subdivision)**—pop pl NC-3
Southbridge Townhall—building MA-1
Southbridge Town Hall—hist pl MA-1
**Southbridge (Town of)**—pop pl MA-1
**South Bridgeview**—pop pl IL-6
**South Bridgewater**—pop pl MA-1
**South Bridgton**—pop pl ME-1
South Bridgton Congregational Church—hist pl ME-1
South Brighton—uninc pl CA-9
South Brimfield, Town of MA-1
South Bristol—locale NY-2
**South Bristol**—pop pl ME-1
South Bristol Cem—cemetery WI-6
South Bristol Sch—school WI-6
**South Bristol (Town of)**—pop pl ME-1
**South Bristol (Town of)**—pop pl NY-2
**South Britain**—pop pl CT-1
South Britain Consolidated Sch—school CT-1
South Britain Hist Dist—hist pl CT-1
South Broad Creek—gut FL-3
South Broad River GA-3
South Broad Street Hist Dist—hist pl (2) GA-3
South Broad Street Row—hist pl NC-3
South Broadway—CDP WA-9
South Broadway Hist Dist—hist pl MN-6
South Broadway Sch—school KY-4
South Broadway Sch—school MN-6
South Brock Spring—spring NV-8
South Brokenback Creek WY-8
South Brook MA-1
South Brook NJ-2
**Southbrook**—pop pl OH-6
**Southbrook**—pop pl TN-4
South Brook—stream CT-1
South Brook—stream (7) ME-1
South Brook—stream (3) MA-1
South Brook—stream NH-1
South Brook—stream (3) NY-2
South Brook—stream PA-2
South Brook—stream VT-1
Southbrook Ch—church MN-6
**South Brookfield**—pop pl NY-2
South Brookley Ch—church AL-4
South Brookley Methodist Ch—church AL-4
South Brookley Sch—school AL-4
**South Brookline**—pop pl NH-1
South Brooklyn OH-6
**South Brooklyn**—pop pl NY-2
Southbrook Park—park OH-6
South Brooks Slough—lake ND-7
South Brooksville—CDP FL-3
**South Brooksville**—pop pl ME-1
**Southbrook (Township of)**—pop pl MN-6
South Brook Troups Creek—stream PA-2
South Brook West Branch Red Clay Creek—stream PA-2
South Broons Canyon—valley UT-8
South Brother—island CT-1
South Brother—summit ME-1
South Brother Island—island NY-2
South Brother Island Channel—channel NY-2
South Brother Mtn ME-1
South Broward Cradle Nursery—school FL-3
South Broward HS—school FL-3
South Brown Creek TX-5
South Brownie Creek—stream UT-8
South Brown Sch—school KS-7
South Browns Creek—stream TX-5
South Browns Pass TX-5
South Brownsville—uninc pl PA-2
**South Brown Township**—pop pl KS-7
South Bruff Creek—stream CO-8
South Brule River—stream MN-6
South Brunner Canyon AZ-5
South Bruno Canyon—valley AZ-5
South Brunswick River—channel GA-3
**South Brunswick Terrace**—pop pl NJ-2
**South Brunswick (Township of)**—pop pl NJ-2
South Brush Creek—stream (2) CO-8
South Brush Creek—stream MO-7
South Brush Creek—stream (2) WY-8
South Brushy Creek—stream AR-4
South Brushy Creek—stream NE-7
South Brushy Creek—stream TX-5
South Brushy Draw—valley TX-5
South Brushy Tank—reservoir NM-5
South Brushy Windmill—locale TX-5
South Bryan (CCD)—cens area OK-5
South Buckball Peak—summit VT-1
South Buck Creek—stream OK-5
South Buck Creek—stream TX-5
South Buck Creek—stream WI-6
South Buck Creek—stream WY-8
South Buckeye Oil Field—other MI-6
South Buckley Draw—valley TX-5
South Buckley Lake—lake MN-6
South Buck Mtn—summit PA-2
South Buck Shoals (Township of)—fmr MCD NC-3
South Buckskin Creek—stream VA-3
South Buena Vista Sch—school CO-8
**South Buffalo**—pop pl KY-4
South Buffalo—uninc pl NY-2
South Buffalo Cem—cemetery PA-2
South Buffalo Creek NC-3
South Buffalo Creek—stream NC-3
South Buffalo Creek—stream SC-3
South Buffalo Creek—stream VA-3
South Buffalo Fork—stream WY-8
South Buffalo North Side Light—hist pl NY-2
South Buffalo Prairie Sch—school IL-6
South Buffalo River WI-6
**South Buffalo (Township of)**—pop pl PA-2
South Bulgar—locale PA-2
South Bull Canyon—valley OR-9
South Bull Canyon Rsvr—reservoir OR-9
South Bull Creek—stream SD-7
South Bull Pond—lake FL-3
South Bullwhack Spring—spring NV-8
South Bully Creek—stream OR-9
South Bunk Clay Well—locale NM-5
South Bunker Ledge—bar ME-1
**Southburg**—pop pl NY-2
South Burgettstown—uninc pl PA-2
South Burgoon Gap PA-2
South Burgoon Gap—locale PA-2
South Burkett Windmill—locale TX-5
**South Burlington**—pop pl VT-1
South Burlington Cem—cemetery IL-6
South Burned Timber Mtn—summit NM-5
South Burnett Island—island AK-9
South Burn Guard Station—locale OR-9
South Burnham Creek—stream WA-9
South Burno Mtn—summit CO-8
South Burns Cem—cemetery OK-5
South Burns Ch—church OK-5
South Burnside Cem—cemetery MI-6
South Burnt Corral Point—cliff AZ-5
South Burnt Fork Creek—stream MT-8
South Burnt Timber Creek—stream CO-8
South Burris Island—island NC-3
South Burr Oak Cem—cemetery WI-6
South Burro Peak—summit UT-8
South Burrus Island NC-3
**Southbury**—pop pl CT-1
Southbury Hist Dist No. 1—hist pl CT-1
Southbury HS—school CT-1
South Burying Ground—cemetery CT-1
**Southbury (Town of)**—pop pl CT-1
Southbury Training Sch—school CT-1
South Bushwick Reformed Protestant Dutch Church Complex—hist pl NY-2
**South Butler**—pop pl MI-6
**South Butler**—pop pl NY-2
South Butler Acad—school AL-4
South Butler Cem—cemetery AL-4
South Butler (historical)—locale AL-4
South Butte—summit (2) AZ-5
South Butte—summit CA-9
South Butte—summit ID-8
South Butte—summit NM-5
South Butte—summit UT-8
South Butte—summit (2) WA-9
South Butte—summit (2) WY-8
South Butte Creek—stream MT-8
South Butte Creek—stream ND-7
South Butte Mine—mine ID-8
South Butterly Oil Field—oilfield OK-5
South Butte Sch—school CO-8
South Buttes Dam—dam SD-7
South Butte Well—well NV-8
South Buttress—ridge AK-9
South Buttress—summit AK-9
**South Buxton**—pop pl (2) ME-1
South Buzan Canyon—valley NM-5
South Buzzard Roost Mesa Tank—reservoir AZ-5
**South Byfield**—pop pl MA-1
South Byfield Ch—church MA-1
South Bypass Interchange—other AR-4
South Bypass Lift Ditch—canal CA-9
**South Byron**—pop pl NY-2
**South Byron**—pop pl WI-6
South Cabin Creek—stream WY-8
**South Cabot**—pop pl VT-1
South Cache Creek—stream WY-8
South Cache Creek Oil Field—oilfield OK-5
South Cache HS—school UT-8
South Cache Middle School UT-8
South Cactus Tank—reservoir AZ-5
South Cactus Windmill—locale TX-5
South Caineville Mesa—summit UT-8
**South Cairo**—pop pl NY-2
South Caldwell HS—school NC-3
South Calera—locale AL-4
South Calhoun Sch—school IN-6
South Callahan Creek—stream ID-8
South Callahan Creek—stream MT-8
South Calumet Avenue IN-6
**South Cambridge**—pop pl NY-2
**South Cambridge**—pop pl VT-1
**South Camden**—pop pl MI-6
South Camden—uninc pl NJ-2
South Cameron—locale NY-2
South Camp—locale NE-7
South Camp—locale NM-5
South Camp—locale (3) TX-5
South Camp—locale UT-8
South Camp—locale WY-8
South Campbell—unorg reg SD-7
**South Campbellsville**—pop pl KY-4
South Campbell Tank—reservoir AZ-5
South Camp Canyon—valley NV-8
South Campground—locale MT-8
South Campground—locale UT-8
South Campground—locale WA-9
South Campground—park OR-9
South Campground Amphitheater—hist pl UT-8
South Campground Comfort Station—hist pl UT-8
South Camp Hollow—valley TX-5
South Camp Peak—summit NV-8
South Camp Tank—reservoir NM-5
South Camp Well—well AZ-5
South Camp Windmill—locale NM-5
South Camp Windmill—locale (2) TX-5
South Camp Wood Creek—stream TX-5
South Canaan—locale CT-1
**South Canaan**—pop pl PA-2
South Canaan Cem—cemetery OH-6
South Canaan Cem—cemetery PA-2
South Canaan Ch—church MO-7
South Canaan Ch—church OH-6
South Canaan Congregational Church—hist pl CT-1
**South Canaan (Township of)**—pop pl PA-2
South Canadian OK-5
South Canadian River CO-8
South Canadian River OK-5
South Canadian River TX-5
South Canal—canal (2) CA-9
South Canal—canal CO-8
South Canal—canal FL-3
South Canal—canal ID-8
South Canal—canal LA-4
South Canal—canal MA-1
South Canal—canal MI-6
South Canal—canal (2) MS-4
South Canal—canal NC-3
South Canal—canal (2) OR-9
South Canal—canal SD-7
South Canal—canal WY-8
South Caney Creek—stream AR-4
South Caney Creek—stream OK-5
**South Canisteo**—pop pl NY-2
South Cannan CT-1
South Cannon (CCD)—cens area TN-4
South Cannon Division—civil TN-4
South Canon CO-8
South Canon Bridge—hist pl CO-8
South Canon Ditch—canal CO-8
South Canon Medio—valley NM-5
**South Canterbury**—pop pl CT-1
South Canton MA-1
**South Canton**—pop pl GA-3
South Canton Community Ch—church OH-6
South Canyon AZ-5
South Canyon ID-8
South Canyon UT-8
South Canyon—valley AZ-5
South Canyon—valley CA-9
South Canyon—valley (3) CO-8
South Canyon—valley (4) ID-8
South Canyon—valley NV-8
South Canyon—valley (5) NM-5
South Canyon—valley (3) OR-9
South Canyon—valley SD-7
South Canyon—valley (2) TX-5
South Canyon—valley (9) UT-8
**South Canyon Country Estates (subdivision)**—pop pl SD-7
South Canyon Creek CA-9
South Canyon Creek ID-8
South Canyon Creek—stream CO-8
South Canyon Creek Falls CA-9
South Canyon Dam Tank—reservoir AZ-5
South Canyon Gulch CO-8
South Canyon Lake—lake CO-8
South Canyon Mine—mine CO-8
South Canyon Point—cape UT-8
South Canyon Point—cliff AZ-5
South Canyon Rsvr—reservoir NV-8
South Canyon Sch—school SD-7
South Canyon Spring—spring AZ-5
South Canyon Spring—spring ID-8
South Canyon Spring—spring NV-8
South Canyon Tank—reservoir AZ-5
South Canyon Well—well TX-5
South Cape FL-3
South Cape HI-9
South Cape—cape AK-9
South Cape—cape FM-9
South Cape Beach—beach MA-1
South Caperton—locale WV-2
South Caprock Oil Field—other NM-5
South Carbon Mine (underground)—mine AL-4
South Carbon (RR name for Carbon)—other WV-2
South Caribou—summit CA-9
South Carizozo Creek OK-5
South Carl Drain—canal MI-6
South Carlsbad State Beach—beach CA-9
South Carlton Oil Field—oilfield AL-4
**South Carmen**—pop pl NM-5
South Carmen Oil Field—oilfield OK-5
**South Carnegie**—pop pl PA-2
South Carolina Baptist Church AL-4
South Carolina Campground Ch—church GA-3
South Carolina Ch—church AL-4
South Carolina Dispensary Office Bldg—hist pl SC-3
South Carolina Governors Mansion—building SC-3
South Carolina Governor's Mansion—hist pl SC-3
South Carolina Gun Club—other SC-3
South Carolina Natl Bank of Charleston—hist pl SC-3
South Carolina Penitentiary State Farm—other SC-3
South Carolina State Arsenal—hist pl SC-3
South Carolina State Capitol—building SC-3
South Carolina State Hospital, Mills Bldg—hist pl SC-3
South Carolina Statehouse—hist pl SC-3
South Carolina Western Railway Station—hist pl SC-3
South Carriaoao Creek OK-5
South Carrizo Creek—stream NM-5
South Carrizo Creek—stream OK-5
South Carrizo Draw—valley TX-5
South Carrizzo Creek OK-5
South Carroll Post Office (historical)—building TN-4
South Carrollton—locale NY-2
**South Carrollton**—pop pl KY-4
**South Carrollton**—pop pl MO-7
South Carrollton Residential Hist Dist—hist pl GA-3
South Carson Creek—stream ID-8
South Carson Creek—stream LA-4
South Cart Creek—stream WY-8
South Carter Creek—stream OK-5
South Carter Mtn—summit NH-1
**South Carthage**—pop pl TN-4
South Carthage Cave—cave TN-4
South Carthage (CCD)—cens area TN-4
South Carthage Division—civil TN-4
**South Carver**—pop pl MA-1
South Casa Blanca Windmill—locale NM-5
South Cascade Glacier—glacier WA-9
South Cascade Lake—lake WA-9
**South Casco**—pop pl ME-1
South Casnovia Cem—cemetery MI-6
South Cass House Creek—stream NV-8
South Castleberry Creek—stream AR-4
South Castle Creek—stream CO-8
South Castle Lake WA-9
South Catahoula Oil Field—oilfield LA-4
South Catamount Creek—stream CO-8
South Catamount Creek Reservoir CO-8
South Catamount Rsvr—reservoir CO-8
South Catherine Ditch—canal OR-9
South Catnip Creek—stream NV-8
South Causeway Isles—island FL-3
South Cave Hills—range SD-7
**South Cecil (subdivision)**—pop pl NC-3
South Cedar Cem—cemetery KS-7
South Cedar Cem—cemetery OK-5
South Cedar City MO-7
South Cedar Creek IA-7
South Cedar Creek—stream IA-7
South Cedar Creek—stream (2) KS-7
South Cedar Creek—stream NE-7
South Cedar Creek—stream ND-7
South Cedar Creek—stream OK-5
South Cedar Creek—stream TX-5
South Cedar Creek—stream WY-8
South Cedar Gulch—valley CO-8
South Cedar (historical)—locale KS-7
South Cedar Ridge Canyon—valley UT-8
South Cedar Sch—school KS-7
South Cedar Street Annex MI-6
**South Cedar Township**—pop pl NE-7
South Cedar Wash—valley UT-8
South Cedar Wash Rsvr—reservoir UT-8
South Cem—cemetery AL-4
South Cem—cemetery (8) CT-1
South Cem—cemetery GA-3
South Cem—cemetery (3) IL-6
South Cem—cemetery IN-6
South Cem—cemetery IA-7
South Cem—cemetery KS-7
South Cem—cemetery ME-1
South Cem—cemetery (13) MA-1
South Cem—cemetery MN-6
South Cem—cemetery (2) MO-7
South Cem—cemetery (2) NH-1
South Cem—cemetery NM-5
South Cem—cemetery NY-2
South Cem—cemetery ND-7
South Cem—cemetery (2) PA-2
South Cem—cemetery TN-4
South Cem—cemetery VT-1
South Cement Well—well TX-5
**South Center**—pop pl IN-6
South Center Cem—cemetery KS-7
South Center Lake—lake MN-6
South Center Ridge Oil Field—oilfield MS-4
South Center Sch—school MO-7
South Center Sch House—hist pl MA-1
**South Centerville**—pop pl NY-2
South Center Windmill—locale TX-5
South Central—locale AR-4
South Central—uninc pl AZ-5
South Central Aberdeen Hist Dist—hist pl MS-4
South Central Area Vocational Sch—school IN-6
South Central Ave Elem Sch—school PA-2
South Central Bell Company Office Bldg—hist pl KY-4
South Central Canal—canal CA-9
Southcentral (Census Subdistrict)—cens area VI-3
South Central Drain—canal CA-9
South Central Drain Five—canal CA-9
South Central Drain Four—canal CA-9
South Central Drain One—canal CA-9
South Central Drain Six—canal CA-9
South Central Drain Two—canal CA-9
South Central Drain Two A—canal CA-9
South Central Elem Sch—school IN-6
South Central Elem Sch—school TN-4
South Central Fairgrounds—locale VA-3
South Central Junior and HS—school IN-6
South Central Junior-Senior HS—school IN-6
South Central Park—park KY-4
South Central Pontotoc (CCD)—cens area OK-5
South Central Post Office—building AZ-5
South Central Sch IN-6
South Central Sch TN-4
**South Centre (Township of)**—pop pl PA-2
South Ceta Canyon TX-5
South Ch—church AL-4
South Ch—church IL-6
South Ch—church KY-4
South Ch—church VA-3
South Chagrin Reservation—park OH-6
South Chain Lake—lake IN-6
South Chain Lake—lake OR-9
South Chalone Peak—summit CA-9
South Champion Cem—cemetery NY-2
South Chandler Creek—stream CO-8
South Chaney Ditch—canal OH-6
South Channel CA-9
South Channel MA-1
South Channel—channel CA-9
South Channel—channel FL-3
South Channel—channel MA-1
South Channel—channel (2) MI-6
South Channel—channel MS-4
South Channel—channel (2) NJ-2
South Channel—channel (2) NC-3
South Channel—channel (5) OR-9
South Channel—channel SC-3
South Channel—channel WA-9
South Channel—channel (2) WI-6
South Channel—channel FM-9
South Channel—channel (2) MP-9
South Channel—gut FL-3
South Channel Bear Creek—stream MT-8
South Channel Columbia River—channel WA-9
South Channel Ditch—canal MT-8
South Channel Mystic River MA-1
South Channel Platte River—channel NE-7
South Channel Platte River—stream (3) NE-7
South Channel Range B—channel OR-9
South Channel Range C—channel OR-9
South Channel Range Light—locale MA-1
South Channel Saint Clair River—channel MI-6
South Channel Savannah River—channel GA-3
South Channel Yakataga River—stream AK-9
South Chapel—church (2) TN-4
South Chapelle Creek—stream SD-7
South Chapin Mtn—summit ID-8
**South Chaplin**—pop pl CT-1
South Chaplin Cem—cemetery CT-1
**South Charleston**—pop pl OH-6
**South Charleston**—pop pl WV-2
South Charleston Hist Dist—hist pl OH-6
South Charleston Mound—hist pl WV-2
**South Charlestown**—pop pl NH-1
**South Charlton**—pop pl MA-1
South Charlton Rsvr MA-1
South Charlton Rsvr—reservoir MA-1
South Chase—locale WI-6
**South Chatham**—pop pl MA-1
**South Chatham**—pop pl NH-1
South Chatham Station (historical)—building MA-1
South Chattanooga—uninc pl TN-4
South Chatten- Muncy Ranch—locale NM-5
South Chaves—locale NM-5
South Cheatbeck Basin—basin ID-8
South Cheatham JHS—school TN-4
**South Chehalis**—pop pl WA-9
**South Chelmsford**—pop pl MA-1
South Cheney—locale WA-9
South Cheniere Creek—stream LA-4
South Chequest Creek—stream IA-7
South Cherokee (CCD)—cens area OK-5
South Cherry Creek CO-8
South Cherry Creek—stream ID-8
South Cherry Hollow—valley TX-5
South Cherry Lake—lake NE-7
South Cherry Street Hist Dist—hist pl KY-4
South Chesapeake City Hist Dist—hist pl MD-2
**South Chesconessex**—pop pl VA-3
**South Chester (subdivision)**—pop pl PA-2
South Chestuee Creek—stream TN-4
**South Cheverly Forest**—pop pl MD-2
South Cheyenne Canyon—valley CO-8
South Cheyenne Creek—stream CO-8
South Chicago IL-6
**South Chicago**—pop pl IL-6
South Chicago Community Hosp—hospital IL-6
South Chicago Creek—stream CO-8
South Chicago Harbor IN-6
**South Chicago Heights**—pop pl IL-6
South Chickamaga Creek GA-3
South Chickamauga Creek—stream GA-3
South Chickamauga Creek—stream TN-4
South Chickamauga Shoals—bar TN-4
South Chicolete Creek—stream TX-5
South Chicosa Creek—stream CO-8
South Chilco Mtn—summit ID-8
South Chili—locale NY-2
South Chilli Lake—reservoir MS-4
South Chimney Peak—summit MT-8
South Chimney Rock—pillar WY-8
**South China**—pop pl ME-1
South China Meeting House—hist pl ME-1
South China Mtn—summit CA-9
South China Oil Field—oilfield TX-5
South China Sch—school TX-5
South China Spring—spring OR-9
South China Windmill—locale TX-5
South Chinitna Mtn—summit AK-9
South Chipmunk Coulee—valley WI-6
South Chipmunk Ridge WI-6
South Chipola Creek—stream AL-4
South Chippen Hill Sch—school CT-1
South Chippewa—uninc pl WI-6
South Chism Brook—stream CT-1
South Chiva Windmill—locale TX-5
South Choate Creek—stream TN-4
South Choctaw Acad—school AL-4
South Chollas Canyon CA-9
South Chollas Valley—valley CA-9
South Choudrant Creek—stream LA-4
South Choyas CA-9
South Christian Sch—school KY-4
South Christian Sch—school MI-6
South Chuctanunda Creek—stream NY-2
South Chugwater Creek WY-8
South Chugwater Creek—stream WY-8
**South Church Heights Subdivision**—pop pl UT-8
South Church Manse—hist pl NJ-2
South Church Point Oil and Gas Field—oilfield LA-4
South Church Street Hist Dist—hist pl WV-2
South Cicero Cem—cemetery WI-6
South Cienega Creek—stream AZ-5
South Cienega Spring—spring AZ-5
South Cinder Butte—summit CO-8
South Cinder Peak—summit OR-9
South Cita Canyon—valley TX-5
South Cita Creek—stream TX-5
South City—uninc pl FL-3
South City Baptist Ch—church KS-7
South City Center—locale KS-7
South City Plaza—locale KS-7
South City View Sch—school MO-7
South Clarksburg (Magisterial District)—fmr MCD WV-2
South Clark Sch—school SD-7
South Clarksfield Cem—cemetery OH-6
**South Clarksville**—pop pl PA-2
South Clear Creek—stream (2) CO-8
South Clear Creek—stream WY-8
South Clear Creek Falls—falls CO-8
South Clearfield—uninc pl PA-2
South Clearfield Sch—school UT-8
South Clear Lake—lake IN-6
South Clear Lake—lake MI-6
South Clearwater (Unorganized Territory of)—unorg MN-6
**South Cle Elum**—pop pl WA-9
South Cle Elum Ridge—ridge WA-9
South Clermont—locale FL-3
**South Cleveland**—pop pl TN-4
South Cleveland (census name for Cleveland South)—CDP TN-4
South Cleveland Community Center—building TN-4
South Cleveland Oil Field—oilfield TX-5
South Cleveland Sch—school NC-3
South Clewiston—locale FL-3
South Clifford Drain—canal MI-6
**South Clinchfield**—pop pl VA-3
South Clinton IL-6
South Clinton SC-3
**South Clinton**—pop pl TN-4
South Clinton Baptist Ch—church TN-4
South Clinton Elem Sch—school TN-4
**South Clinton Heights**—pop pl FL-3
South Clinton Sewage Lagoon Dam—dam MS-4
South Clinton (Township of)—fmr MCD NC-3
South Clippinger OH-6
**South Clippinger**—pop pl OH-6
South Clover Creek OR-9
South Clover Creek—stream OR-9
South Clyde—uninc pl NY-2
South Clyde Sch—school IL-6
South Coal Creek IA-7
South Coal Creek WY-8
South Coantag Creek—stream WY-8
**South Coast**—pop pl LA-4
South Coast Agriculture Field Station (Univ of Cal.)—school CA-9
South Coast (CCD)—cens area CA-9
South Coast Gun Club—other CA-9
South Coastside (CCD)—cens area CA-9
**South Coatesville**—pop pl PA-2
South Coatesville Borough—civil PA-2
**South Cobb**—pop pl GA-3
South Cobb HS—school GA-3
**South Cocoa Beach**—pop pl FL-3
South Coconut Bayou—bay FL-3
**South Coffeyville**—pop pl OK-5
South Coffeyville-Wann (CCD)—cens area OK-5
South Coffman Windmill—locale NM-5
South Coggins Creek—stream TX-5
South Cohutta Ch—church GA-3
**South Colby**—pop pl WA-9
South Cold Water Canyon—valley UT-8
South Coldwater Creek—stream WA-9
South Cole Creek Unit (Oil Field)—oilfield WY-8
South Coleman Canyon—valley UT-8
South Coles Levee Oil Field CA-9
South Collge Peak—summit AZ-5
South Coll Sch—school IL-6
South Colon Cem—cemetery MI-6
South Colony Creek—stream CO-8
South Colony Lakes—lake CO-8
South Colorado Tank—reservoir TX-5
**South Colton**—pop pl NY-2
South Colton Rsvr—reservoir NY-2
**South Columbia**—pop pl NY-2
South Columbia—uninc pl TN-4
South Columbia Sch—school NH-1
South Columbus—locale KY-4
**South Columbus**—pop pl GA-3
**South Columbus**—pop pl OH-6
South Columbus Hist Dist—hist pl MS-4
South Columbus Sch—school GA-3
South Colwell Pond—lake NY-2
South Comanche Creek—stream MT-8
South Common Hist Dist—hist pl MA-1
South Common Park—park MA-1
**South Commons**—pop pl MA-1
South Community Ch—church MI-6
South Comobabi Mountains—range AZ-5
South Comobavi Mountains AZ-5
South Company Ditch—canal NM-5
South Comstock Mine—mine NV-8
South Concho Draw—valley TX-5
South Concho Irrigation Canal—canal TX-5
South Concho River—stream TX-5
**South Condit**—pop pl OH-6
South Cone Lake—lake MN-6
**South Congaree**—pop pl SC-3
South Congregational Ch—church MA-1
South Congregational Church—hist pl MA-1
South Congregational Church—hist pl NY-2
South Connection Lake—lake MN-6
**South Connellsville**—pop pl PA-2
South Connellsville Borough—civil PA-2
**South Conway**—pop pl NH-1
South Cooksey Windmill—locale TX-5
South Cooney Hills—ridge WY-8
South Coon Lake—lake MN-6
South Copano Bay Oil Field—oilfield TX-5
South COPE Center—school FL-3
South Copperas Creek—stream TX-5
South Copper Canyon—valley NM-5
South Copper Creek—stream IA-7
South Copper Fork Tank—reservoir AZ-5
South Corbin—uninc pl KY-4
South Corbin Oil Field—other NM-5
South Corinth—locale ME-1
**South Corinth**—pop pl NY-2
**South Corinth**—pop pl VT-1
South Corinth Baptist Ch—church MS-4
South Corinth Elementary School MS-4
South Cormorant River—stream MN-6
**South Corning**—pop pl NY-2
South Corning Gas Field CA-9
**South Cornish**—pop pl NH-1
South Corona—uninc pl CA-9
South Corral Canyon—valley UT-8
South Corral Lake—lake OR-9
South Corral Spring—spring OR-9
**South Cortland**—pop pl NY-2

South Coteau Lake—*lake* ... SD-7
South Cotton Lake Oil Field—*oilfield* ... TX-5
**South Cottonwodd Heights Subdivision**—*pop pl* ... UT-8
**South Cottonwood**—*pop pl* ... ND-7
**South Cottonwood**—*pop pl* ... UT-8
**South Cottonwood Acres Subdivision**—*pop pl* ... UT-8
South Cottonwood Canyon—*valley* ... UT-8
*South Cottonwood Creek* ... ID-8
*South Cottonwood Creek* ... MT-8
*South Cottonwood Creek* ... WY-8
South Cottonwood Creek—*stream* ... CO-8
South Cottonwood Creek—*stream* ... ID-8
South Cottonwood Creek—*stream* (3) ... MT-8
South Cottonwood Creek—*stream* ... NM-5
South Cottonwood Creek—*stream* ... SD-7
South Cottonwood Creek—*stream* (3) ... WY-8
South Cottonwood River—*stream* ... KS-7
South Cottonwood Rsvr—*reservoir* ... OR-9
South Cottonwood Spring—*spring* ... ID-8
South Cottonwood Spring—*spring* ... MT-8
*South Cotuit Pond* ... MA-1
South Country Line Creek—*stream* ... NC-3
South Country Sch—*school* ... NY-2
South County—*airport* ... NJ-2
South County Center (Shop Ctr)—*locale* ... MO-7
South County Hosp—*hospital* ... MS-4
South County Hospital Airp—*airport* ... RI-1
South County Line Ch—*church* ... IL-6
South County Regional Park—*park* ... FL-3
South County Triplex Park—*park* ... FL-3
South Courthouse Square Hist Dist—*hist pl* ... KY-4
South Court Street Bridge—*bridge* ... MS-4
South Cove—*bay* ... AK-9
South Cove—*bay* ... AZ-5
South Cove—*bay* ... CA-9
South Cove—*bay* (2) ... CT-1
South Cove—*bay* ... FL-3
South Cove—*bay* (3) ... ME-1
South Cove—*bay* ... OR-9
**South Cove**—*pop pl* ... AZ-5
*South Coventry* ... CT-1
South Coventry (census name for Coventry)—*CDP* ... CT-1
*South Coventry Lake* ... CT-1
**South Coventry Station**—*pop pl* ... CT-1
**South Coventry (Township of)**—*pop pl* ... PA-2
South Cove Point—*cape* ... ME-1
South Covington—*uninc pl* ... TN-4
South Covington Ch—*church* ... VA-3
South Cow Bayou—*stream* ... TX-5
South Cow Creek—*stream* ... CA-9
South Cow Creek Campground—*locale* ... CA-9
South Cowden Oil Field—*oilfield* (2) ... TX-5
South Cowden Ranch—*locale* ... TX-5
South Cox Creek—*stream* ... NC-3
South Cox Hollow—*valley* ... TX-5
South Cox Well—*well* ... NM-5
South Coyote—*locale* ... CA-9
South Coyote Canyon—*valley* ... OR-9
South Coyote Creek—*stream* ... OR-9
South Coyote Draw—*valley* ... WY-8
South Coyote Oil Field—*oilfield* ... WY-8
*South Craig Highlands* ... CO-8
South Craig Point—*cape* ... AK-9
*South Crane Creek* ... NC-3
South Crane Creek—*stream* ... ID-8
South Crane Sch—*school* ... ID-8
South Crawford—*fmr MCD* ... NE-7
South Crawford Sch (abandoned)—*school* ... MO-7
*South Creek* ... CA-9
*South Creek* ... CO-8
*South Creek* ... MO-7
*South Creek* ... MT-8
*South Creek* ... OH-6
*South Creek* ... OR-9
*South Creek* ... PA-2
*South Creek* ... UT-8
South Creek—*bay* ... MD-2
South Creek—*gut* ... FL-3
**South Creek**—*pop pl* ... NC-3
**South Creek**—*pop pl* ... TN-4
South Creek—*stream* ... AK-9
South Creek—*stream* ... AR-4
South Creek—*stream* (2) ... CA-9
South Creek—*stream* (2) ... CO-8
South Creek—*stream* (4) ... FL-3
South Creek—*stream* ... GA-3
South Creek—*stream* (3) ... ID-8
South Creek—*stream* (2) ... IN-6
South Creek—*stream* ... IA-7
South Creek—*stream* ... KS-7
South Creek—*stream* ... MI-6
South Creek—*stream* ... MN-6
South Creek—*stream* ... MO-7
South Creek—*stream* (5) ... MT-8
South Creek—*stream* (2) ... NE-7
South Creek—*stream* (2) ... NV-8
South Creek—*stream* (2) ... NJ-2
South Creek—*stream* ... NM-5
South Creek—*stream* (2) ... NY-2
South Creek—*stream* (2) ... NC-3
South Creek—*stream* (2) ... OH-6
South Creek—*stream* (5) ... OR-9
South Creek—*stream* (4) ... PA-2
South Creek—*stream* (2) ... SC-3
South Creek—*stream* (2) ... SD-7
South Creek—*stream* ... TN-4
South Creek—*stream* (2) ... TX-5
South Creek—*stream* (7) ... UT-8
South Creek—*stream* ... VA-3
South Creek—*stream* (4) ... WA-9
South Creek—*stream* (3) ... WY-8
South Creek Butte—*summit* ... WA-9
South Creek Campground—*locale* ... WA-9
South Creek Ch—*church* ... NY-2
South Creek Ch—*church* ... SD-7
South Creek Falls—*falls* ... CA-9
South Creek Ridge—*ridge* ... UT-8
South Creek Rsvr—*reservoir* ... OR-9
South Creek Sch—*school* ... NE-7
South Creek Sch—*school* ... SD-7
**South Creek Township**—*pop pl* ... SD-7
**South Creek (Township of)**—*pop pl* ... PA-2
South Creek Windmill—*locale* ... NM-5
South Creighton Sch—*school* ... SD-7
Southcrest Ch—*church* ... TX-5
South Crestone Creek—*stream* ... CO-8
South Crestone Ditch—*canal* ... CO-8
South Crestone Lake—*lake* ... CO-8
South Crest Park—*park* ... CA-9
Southcrest Park—*park* ... TX-5
**Southcrest Subdivision**—*pop pl* ... TN-4
**Southcrest Subdivision**—*pop pl* ... UT-8
South Crillon Glacier—*glacier* ... AK-9
South Crocker Mtn—*summit* ... ME-1
South Cromwell Oil Field—*oilfield* ... OK-5
South Crooked Brook—*stream* ... ME-1
South Crooked Canyon—*valley* ... NM-5
South Crooked Creek—*stream* ... CO-8
South Crooked Creek—*stream* ... NC-3
South Crooked Hollow—*valley* ... MO-7
South Crooked Lake—*lake* ... MI-6
South Crosby Peak—*summit* ... NM-5
South Cross Creek—*stream* ... TN-4
**South Crossett**—*pop pl* ... AR-4
Southcross JHS—*school* ... TX-5
Southcross Park—*park* ... TX-5
South Crossroads Cem—*cemetery* ... MS-4
South Cross Roads Sch—*school* ... MO-7
South Crouch (Township of)—*civ div* ... IL-6
*South Crow Creek* ... WY-8
South Crow Creek—*stream* ... MT-8
South Crow Creek—*stream* (2) ... WY-8
South Crow Creek Rsvr—*reservoir* ... WY-8
South Crowders Creek—*stream* ... NC-3
South Crow Windmill—*locale* ... TX-5
South Crystal Creek—*stream* ... CO-8
South Crystal Lake—*lake* ... FL-3
**South Cuba**—*pop pl* ... NY-2
**South Cumberland**—*pop pl* ... MD-2
*South Cumberland Elementary School* ... TN-4
South Cumberland Rec Area—*park* ... TN-4
South Cumberland Sch—*school* ... TN-4
South Cummings Lake—*lake* ... WI-6
South Cunningham Creek—*stream* ... CO-8
South Currant Creek—*stream* ... AK-9
South Cushing—*locale* ... ME-1
*South Cuyama Oil Field* ... CA-9
South Cypress Creek—*stream* ... AR-4
South Cypress Creek Oil Field—*oilfield* ... MS-4
South Dade Alliance Ch—*church* ... FL-3
South Dade Ch—*church* ... FL-3
South Dade Christian Ch—*church* ... FL-3
South Dade Community Health Center—*hospital* ... FL-3
South Dade Government Center—*building* ... FL-3
South Dade Hebrew Acad—*school* ... FL-3
South Dade HS—*school* ... FL-3
South Dade Park—*park* ... FL-3
South Dade Sch—*school* ... FL-3
South Dade Sewage Treatment Facility—*building* ... FL-3
South Dade Skill Center—*school* ... FL-3
South Dagus Rsvr—*reservoir* ... OR-9
South Daisy—*uninc pl* ... TN-4
South Daisy Ch—*church* ... TN-4
South Dakota Hand Grazing Association Dam—*dam* ... SD-7
**South Dakota Human Services Center**—*pop pl* ... SD-7
South Dakota Komes 1 Dam—*dam* ... SD-7
**South Dakota Park**—*pop pl* ... SD-7
South Dakota Sch for the Blind—*hist pl* ... SD-7
South Dakota Sch for the Blind—*school* ... SD-7
South Dakota Sch for the Deaf—*hist pl* ... SD-7
South Dakota Sch Of Mines—*school* ... SD-7
South Dakota State Capitol and Governor's House—*hist pl* ... SD-7
South Dakota State Penitentiary Historic Buildings—*hist pl* ... SD-7
South Dakota State Univ—*school* ... SD-7
South Dakota State Univ Pasture Research Center—*school* ... SD-7
*Southdale* ... MN-6
*Southdale* ... OH-6
Southdale—*locale* ... PA-2
**Southdale**—*pop pl* ... UT-8
Southdale Ch—*church* ... MS-4
*Southdale Missionary Baptist Ch* ... MS-4
Southdale Picnic Area—*park* ... MI-6
Southdale Sch—*school* ... IA-7
Southdale Sch—*school* ... OH-6
South Dale Sch (historical)—*school* ... MO-7
Southdale Shop Ctr—*locale* ... FL-3
Southdale Shop Ctr—*locale* ... MN-6
Southdale Shop Ctr—*locale* ... MS-4
**Southdale (subdivision)**—*pop pl* ... MS-4
**South Dale Subdivision**—*pop pl* ... UT-8
South Dallas—*uninc pl* ... TX-5
*South Dam* ... WA-9
South Dam—*dam* ... SD-7
South Dam Canyon—*valley* ... NM-5
South Dam Tailings Pond—*reservoir* ... AZ-5
South Danbury Christian Church—*hist pl* ... NH-1
**South Danbury (Converse Station)**—*pop pl* ... NH-1
**South Danby**—*pop pl* ... NY-2
South Daniels Gulch Spring—*spring* ... AZ-5
**South Dansville**—*pop pl* ... NY-2
*South Danvers* ... MA-1
*South Danvers, Town of* ... MA-1
*South Danville* ... IL-6
South Danville—*locale* ... VT-1
**South Danville**—*pop pl* ... IL-6
**South Danville**—*pop pl* ... NH-1
**South Danville**—*pop pl* ... PA-2
South Danville (RR name for Riverside)—*other* ... PA-2
South Danville Station—*locale* ... PA-2
South Darrs Creek—*stream* ... TX-5
**South Dartmouth**—*pop pl* ... MA-1
South Davidson Windmill—*locale* ... TX-5
South Davie JHS—*school* ... NC-3
South Davis—*cens area* ... UT-8
South Davis Community Hosp—*hospital* ... UT-8
South Davis Creek—*stream* ... MO-7
South Davis Division—*civil* ... UT-8
South Davis JHS—*school* ... UT-8
*South Davis Junior High School* ... UT-8
South Davis Millpond Branch—*stream* ... MD-2
South Davis Sch—*school* ... TX-5
South Davis Tank—*reservoir* ... TX-5
*South Dayton* ... OH-6
**South Dayton**—*pop pl* ... NY-2
**South Dayton**—*pop pl* ... TN-4
**South Dayton**—*pop pl* ... TX-5
**South Daytona**—*pop pl* ... FL-3
South Daytona Christian Ch—*church* ... FL-3
South Daytona Elem Sch—*school* ... FL-3
**South Daytona (RR name Blake)**—*pop pl* ... FL-3
**South Daytona West**—*pop pl* ... FL-3
South Dayton Ch—*church* ... TX-5
*South Dayton Oil Field* ... TX-5
South Deadman Canyon—*valley* ... CO-8
*South Deadman Creek* ... WY-8
South Deadman Creek—*stream* ... WA-9
South Deadman Gulch—*valley* ... ID-8
South Dearborn HS—*school* ... IN-6
South Dearborn Street-Printing House Row Hist Dist—*hist pl* ... IL-6
South Dease Lake—*lake* ... MI-6
**South Decatur**—*pop pl* ... GA-3
South Deception Lake—*lake* ... AK-9
South Decker Creek—*stream* ... CO-8
South Deep Creek—*stream* ... CA-9
South Deep Creek—*stream* ... NC-3
South Deepwater Creek—*stream* ... MO-7
South Deer Creek—*stream* ... OK-5
South Deer Creek—*stream* ... WY-8
South Deer Creek Grange—*locale* ... OR-9
South Deer Creek Oil Field—*oilfield* ... OK-5
**South Deerfield**—*pop pl* ... MA-1
**South Deerfield**—*pop pl* ... NH-1
South Deerfield Oil Field—*oilfield* ... MS-4
South Deerfield Water Supply Dam—*dam* ... MA-1
South Deer Flat Tank—*reservoir* ... AZ-5
*South Deering* ... IL-6
South Deering—*locale* ... IL-6
South Deer Island—*island* ... TX-5
**South Deer Island**—*pop pl* ... ME-1
**South Deer Isle**—*pop pl* ... ME-1
South Delaney Lake—*lake* ... CO-8
South Dell Sch (historical)—*school* ... MO-7
**South Delta**—*pop pl* ... OH-6
South Denison Cem—*cemetery* ... KS-7
South Denmark Cem—*cemetery* ... OH-6
**South Dennis**—*pop pl* ... MA-1
**South Dennis**—*pop pl* ... NJ-2
South Dennis Cem—*cemetery* ... MA-1
South Dennis Station—*building* ... MA-1
*South Dennisville* ... NJ-2
*South Denver* ... CO-8
South Depoe Bay Creek—*stream* ... OR-9
South Derby Ditch—*canal* ... CO-8
South Derby Trail—*trail* ... CO-8
South Desert—*plain* ... UT-8
South Desert Mountain Rsvr—*reservoir* ... UT-8
South Desert Overlook—*locale* ... UT-8
South Desert Spring—*spring* ... UT-8
*South Des Moines* ... IA-7
**South Detroit Township**—*pop pl* ... SD-7
*South Devils Track* ... MN-6
*South Devil Track* ... MN-6
South Devon Sch—*school* ... MT-8
**South Devonshire Estates (subdivision)**—*pop pl* ... PA-2
South Dewey—*unorg reg* ... SD-7
South Dewey Sch—*school* ... WI-6
South Diamond Canal—*canal* ... OR-9
South Diamond Creek—*stream* ... NM-5
*South Diamond Gulch* ... UT-8
*South Digger Creek* ... CA-9
South Dike—*levee* ... NV-8
South Dillon Sch—*school* ... SC-3
South District Sch—*school* ... NY-2
South Ditch—*canal* (4) ... CA-9
South Ditch—*canal* (2) ... OR-9
South Ditch—*canal* (4) ... UT-8
South Ditch—*canal* ... WA-9
South Ditch—*canal* ... WI-6
South Divide—*cens area* ... CO-8
South Divide Lake—*lake* ... CA-9
South Division HS—*school* ... WI-6
South Dix—*summit* ... NY-2
**South Dixie**—*pop pl* ... KY-4
South Dixie Ditch—*canal* ... OR-9
South Dixie Lake—*lake* ... OR-9
**South Dixon (Township of)**—*pop pl* ... IL-6
South Dobbyn Creek—*stream* ... CA-9
South Dock—*locale* ... NY-2
South Dock (Marina)—*locale* ... NM-5
**South Dodge**—*pop pl* ... KS-7
South Dodge—*uninc pl* ... KS-7
South Doe Creek—*stream* ... WY-8
South Dokegood Creek—*stream* ... TX-5
South Dome—*ridge* ... CA-9
South Dome—*summit* ... AK-9
South Dona Ana (CCD)—*cens area* ... NM-5
South Donaldson Well—*well* ... NM-5
South Donna Sch—*school* ... TX-5
South Donnelly Peak—*summit* ... NV-8
**South Dorset**—*pop pl* ... VT-1
**South Dos Palos (Dos Palos Station)**—*pop pl* ... CA-9
South Double Barrel Creek—*stream* ... FL-3
South Double Branch—*stream* ... MO-7
South Double Creek—*stream* ... AL-4
South Double Creek—*stream* ... NC-3
South Doublehead—*summit* ... NH-1
South Double R Creek—*stream* ... SD-7
South Douglas Cem—*cemetery* ... MA-1
South Dove Oil Field—*oilfield* ... TX-5
South Dover—*locale* ... ME-1
South Dover—*locale* ... NY-2
South Dover Acres—*uninc pl* ... DE-2
South Dover Cem—*cemetery* ... MI-6
Southdown—*locale* ... KY-4
Southdown—*locale* ... LA-4
South Downey—*uninc pl* ... CA-9
Southdown Fork Stout Run—*stream* ... OH-6
Southdown HS—*school* ... LA-4
*Southdown Island* ... ME-1
Southdown Plantation—*hist pl* ... LA-4
**Southdown Plantation**—*pop pl* ... LA-4
Southdown Sch—*school* ... LA-4
Southdown Sch—*school* ... NY-2
**South Down Shores**—*pop pl* ... MD-2
South Downs Sch—*school* ... IL-6
South Drain—*canal* ... AZ-5
South Drain—*canal* ... ID-8
South Drain—*canal* ... MI-6
South Drain—*canal* ... WA-9
South Drain Ditch—*canal* ... NM-5
South Draw—*valley* ... CO-8
South Draw—*valley* ... TX-5
South Draw—*valley* ... UT-8
South Draw—*valley* (4) ... WY-8
**South Dresden**—*pop pl* ... ME-1
**South Dresden Township**—*pop pl* ... ND-7
*South Drews Canal* ... OR-9
South Drew Tank—*reservoir* ... NM-5
South Dry Creek—*fmr MCD* ... NE-7
South Dry Creek—*stream* ... CO-8
South Dry Creek—*stream* (2) ... MT-8
South Dry Creek—*stream* ... WY-8
South Dry Creek Rsvr—*reservoir* ... OR-9
South Dryden Pioneer Cem—*cemetery* ... MI-6
South Dry Fork—*stream* ... CO-8
South Dry Run—*stream* ... PA-2
*South Dry Sac Creek* ... MO-7
South Dry Sac River—*stream* ... MO-7
South Dubakella Mtn—*summit* ... CA-9
South Duchesne—*cens area* ... UT-8
South Duchesne Division—*civil* ... UT-8
South Duck Creek—*stream* ... KS-7
South Duck Creek—*stream* ... OK-5
South Dugway Canyon—*valley* ... NM-5
South Duke Street Mall—*locale* ... PA-2
South Dumpling—*island* ... NY-2
South Dunbury (historical P.O.)—*locale* ... MA-1
South Dunbury Station (historical)—*locale* ... MA-1
South Duncan Branch—*stream* ... TN-4
South Dunham Cem—*cemetery* ... IL-6
South Dunn—*unorg reg* ... ND-7
South Duquesne—*uninc pl* ... PA-2
South Durbin Creek—*stream* ... SC-3
**South Durham**—*pop pl* ... ME-1
**South Durham**—*pop pl* ... NY-2
South Durham—*uninc pl* ... NC-3
**South Duxbury**—*pop pl* ... MA-1
**South Duxbury**—*pop pl* ... VT-1
South Dyer Creek—*stream* ... CO-8
**South Dyersburg**—*pop pl* ... TN-4
South Eagle Ch—*church* ... MO-7
South Eagle Creek—*stream* ... KS-7
South Eaglenest Creek—*stream* ... WY-8
South Eagle Pointe—*cape* ... LA-4
South Easken Windmill—*locale* ... TX-5
*Southeast* ... MO-7
Southeast—*post sta* ... MD-2
Southeast—*post sta* ... OK-5
Southeast—*post sta* ... TX-5
Southeast—*uninc pl* ... FL-3
Southeast—*uninc pl* ... KS-7
Southeast—*uninc pl* ... LA-4
Southeast—*uninc pl* ... OK-5
Southeast Aitkin (Unorganized Territory of)—*unorg* ... MN-6
*Southeast Alabama General Hospital* ... AL-4
Southeast Alabama Med Ctr—*hospital* ... AL-4
Southeast Alabama Med Ctr Airp—*airport* ... AL-4
*Southeast Alabama Rehabilitation Center* ... AL-4
Southeast Anchorage—*bay* ... CA-9
Southeast Antelope Tank—*reservoir* ... TX-5
Southeast Arm—*bay* ... WY-8
Southeast Aylesworth Oil Field—*oilfield* ... OK-5
Southeast Baptist Ch—*church* ... UT-8
Southeast Basin—*harbor* ... CA-9
South East Bay—*bay* ... UT-8
Southeast Bay—*cove* ... MA-1
Southeast Benton (CCD)—*cens area* ... OR-9
Southeast Bexar (CCD)—*cens area* ... TX-5
Southeast Bight—*bay* ... AK-9
Southeast Black Rock—*island* ... OR-9
Southeast Blakely Oil Field—*oilfield* ... OK-5
Southeast Bon Homme—*unorg reg* ... SD-7
Southeast Bradley (CCD)—*cens area* ... TN-4
Southeast Bradley Division—*civil* ... TN-4
*Southeast Branch* ... ME-1
Southeast Branch Fishing Creek—*stream* ... MD-2
Southeast Branch Little Heart River—*stream* ... ND-7
*Southeast Branch Sand Spring Run* ... PA-2
Southeast Branch Severn River—*stream* ... VA-3
Southeast Breaker—*bar* (2) ... ME-1
Southeast Breakers—*bar* ... MA-1
Southeast Bryan (CCD)—*cens area* ... OK-5
Southeast Bryant Oil And Gas Field—*oilfield* ... OK-5
Southeast Buffalo—*unorg reg* ... SD-7
Southeast Bullock HS—*school* ... GA-3
Southeast Bullock JHS—*school* ... GA-3
Southeast Bull Tank—*reservoir* ... TX-5
Southeast Burying Ground—*cemetery* ... CT-1
Southeast Cape—*cape* ... AK-9
Southeast (CCD)—*cens area* ... CA-9
Southeast Cem—*cemetery* ... CT-1
Southeast Center Sch—*school* ... IN-6
Southeast Chaney Dell Oil Field—*oilfield* ... OK-5
Southeast Channel—*channel* ... FL-3
Southeast Chaves (CCD)—*cens area* ... NM-5
Southeast Christian Ch—*church* ... UT-8
Southeast Closman Workings—*mine* ... TN-4
Southeast Colorado Fairgrounds—*locale* ... CO-8
Southeast Comanche (CCD)—*cens area* ... OK-5
Southeast Corner Spring—*spring* ... ND-7
Southeast Cove—*bay* ... AK-9
Southeast Creek—*stream* ... MD-2
Southeast Creek—*stream* ... NJ-2
**Southeast Crossing**—*pop pl* ... TX-5
Southeast Curty Oil Field—*oilfield* ... OK-5
Southeast District Sing Convention Ch—*church* ... AL-4
Southeast Ditch—*canal* ... VA-3
Southeast Drain—*canal* ... AZ-5
South East Eileen State No 1—*other* ... AK-9
*Southeast Elementary School* ... PA-2
Southeast Elem Sch—*school* ... AL-4
Southeast Elem Sch—*school* ... IN-6
Southeast Ellislie Oil Field—*oilfield* ... MS-4
Southeast End—*other* ... AK-9
Southeastern—*post sta* ... PA-2
Southeastern—*uninc pl* ... CA-9
Southeastern Baptist Coll—*school* ... MS-4
Southeastern Bible Coll—*school* ... AL-4
South Eastern Bible Coll—*school* ... FL-3
Southeastern Christian Coll—*school* ... KY-4
Southeastern Coll At Burlington—*school* ... IA-7
Southeastern Coll of Osteopathic Medicine—*school* ... FL-3
Southeastern Colorado Branch Experimental Station—*other* ... CO-8
Southeastern Cove—*bay* ... AK-9
Southeastern District of the Christian and Missionary Alliance—*church* ... FL-3
Southeastern Elem Sch—*school* ... AL-4
Southeastern El Paso—*cens area* ... CO-8
Southeastern Facility—*post sta* ... PA-2
*Southeastern Fish Cultural Research Laboratory* ... AL-4
**Southeastern Hills**—*pop pl* ... KY-4
Southeastern Holiness Institute—*hist pl* ... GA-3
Southeastern HS—*school* ... MI-6
Southeastern JHS—*school* ... NC-3
Southeastern Louisiana College—*other* ... LA-4
Southeastern Louisiana Univ—*school* ... LA-4
Southeastern Massachusetts Univ—*school* ... MA-1
Southeastern Med Ctr—*hospital* ... FL-3
Southeastern Sch—*school* ... OH-6
Southeastern Sch—*school* (2) ... VA-3
Southeastern Sch (abandoned)—*school* ... PA-2
Southeastern State Coll—*school* ... OK-5
Southeastern Technical Institute—*school* ... MA-1
Southeastern Theological Seminary—*school* ... NC-3
*Southeast Fairbanks (Census Area)* ... AK-9
**Southeast Fairbanks (Census Subarea)**—*pop pl* ... AK-9
Southeast Fairview Oil Field—*oilfield* ... MS-4
Southeast Farallon—*island* ... CA-9
Southeast Fork County Line Creek—*stream* ... KS-7
Southeast Fork Kahiltna Glacier—*glacier* ... AK-9
Southeast Gainesville Residential District—*hist pl* ... FL-3
Southeast Greensboro Airp—*airport* ... NC-3
Southeast Gregory—*unorg reg* ... SD-7
**Southeast Grove**—*pop pl* ... IN-6
Southeast Harbor—*bay* ... MA-1
Southeast Harbor—*harbor* ... ME-1
Southeast Harris (CCD)—*cens area* ... TX-5
Southeast Hartsgrove Cem—*cemetery* ... OH-6
Southeast Head—*cape* (2) ... FL-3
Southeast Hidalgo (CCD)—*cens area* ... TX-5
*Southeast High School* ... KS-7
Southeast Hill Sch—*school* ... VT-1
Southeast Hollow—*valley* ... NY-2
Southeast Hollow Trail—*trail* ... NY-2
Southeast Hoover Oil Field—*oilfield* ... OK-5
Southeast HS—*school* ... AR-4
Southeast HS—*school* ... FL-3
Southeast HS—*school* (2) ... KS-7
Southeast HS—*school* ... MO-7
Southeast HS—*school* ... NE-7
Southeast HS—*school* (2) ... NC-3
Southeast HS—*school* ... OH-6
Southeast HS—*school* ... OK-5
Southeast Hunter Oil Field—*oilfield* ... OK-5
Southeast Iron Chapel Oil Field—*oilfield* ... OK-5
Southeast Jackson (CCD)—*cens area* ... OR-9
Southeast Jack Williams Bay—*bay* ... LA-4
Southeast JHS—*school* ... IA-7
Southeast JHS—*school* (2) ... MI-6
Southeast JHS—*school* ... MO-7
Southeast JHS—*school* ... NC-3
Southeast Kansas Agricultural Experiment—*other* ... KS-7
Southeast Laffoon Oil Field—*oilfield* ... OK-5
*South East Lake MS* ... AL-4
*southeast Lake Nellie* ... FL-3
Southeast Lake Nellie—*lake* ... FL-3
South East Lake Sch—*school* ... AL-4
Southeast Landing—*locale* ... MD-2
Southeast Laterals Watershed Number Six—*reservoir* ... TX-5
Southeast Laterals Watershed Rsvr No 1—*reservoir* ... TX-5
Southeast Laterals Watershed Rsvr No 10—*reservoir* ... TX-5
Southeast Laterals Watershed Rsvr No 2—*reservoir* ... TX-5
Southeast Laterals Watershed Rsvr No 3—*reservoir* ... TX-5
Southeast Laterals Watershed Rsvr No 4—*reservoir* ... TX-5
Southeast Laterals Watershed Rsvr No 5—*reservoir* ... TX-5
Southeast Laterals Watershed Rsvr No 7—*reservoir* ... TX-5
Southeast Laterals Watershed Rsvr No 8—*reservoir* ... TX-5
Southeast Laterals Watershed Rsvr No 9—*reservoir* ... TX-5
Southeast Lauderdale Elem Sch—*school* ... MS-4
Southeast Lauderdale HS—*school* ... MS-4
Southeast Lauderdale JHS—*school* ... MS-4
Southeast Ledge—*bar* ... ME-1
Southeast Ledge—*bar* ... RI-1
Southeast Lexington Residential and Commercial District—*hist pl* ... KY-4
Southeast Loch—*bay* ... HI-9
Southeast Lonsdale Mine—*mine* ... TN-4
Southeast Louisiana Hosp—*hospital* ... LA-4
Southeast Lyon (CCD)—*cens area* ... KY-4
Southeast (Magisterial District)—*fmr MCD* ... WV-2
Southeast Mahnomen (Unorganized Territory of)—*unorg* ... MN-6
**Southeast Manor**—*pop pl* ... IN-6
Southeast Marin (CCD)—*cens area* ... CA-9
Southeast Marion Township—*civil* ... MO-7
Southeast McCurtain (CCD)—*cens area* ... OK-5
Southeast Mesa—*summit* ... AZ-5
Southeast Missouri Hospital Heliport—*airport* ... MO-7
Southeast Missouri State Coll—*school* ... MO-7
Southeast Montgomery (CCD)—*cens area* ... TX-5
Southeast Moss Hill Oil Field—*oilfield* ... MS-4
Southeast Mounds Rsvr—*reservoir* ... UT-8
Southeast Newcastle Oil Field—*oilfield* ... OK-5
Southeast Nolichucky (CCD)—*cens area* ... TN-4
Southeast Nolichucky Division—*civil* ... TN-4
Southeast Norman Oil Field—*oilfield* ... OK-5
Southeast Oil And Gas Field—*oilfield* ... OK-5
**South Easton**—*pop pl* ... MA-1
**South Easton**—*pop pl* ... NY-2
South Easton Cem—*cemetery* ... PA-2
South Easton (historical P.O.)—*locale* ... MA-1
South Easton Station (historical)—*locale* ... MA-1
**South Easton (subdivision)**—*pop pl* ... PA-2
Southeast Osage (CCD)—*cens area* ... OK-5
Southeast Otero (CCD)—*cens area* ... NM-5
**Southeast Owasco**—*pop pl* ... NY-2
Southeast Paradise Oil Field—*oilfield* ... OK-5
Southeast Park—*park* ... FL-3
Southeast Park—*park* ... IL-6
Southeast Park—*park* ... NC-3
Southeast Park Sch—*school* ... MO-7
Southeast Pass—*channel* ... AK-9
Southeast Pass—*channel* ... LA-4
Southeast Pass—*channel* ... MP-9
Southeast Pass Oil Field—*oilfield* ... LA-4
Southeast Pauls Valley Oil Field—*oilfield* ... OK-5
Southeast Piscataquis (Unorganized Territory of)—*unorg* ... ME-1
Southeast Plaza Shop Ctr—*locale* ... AL-4
*South East Point* ... FM-9
Southeast Point—*cape* ... AK-9
Southeast Point—*cape* ... FL-3
Southeast Point—*cape* ... NJ-2
Southeast Point—*cape* ... RI-1
Southeast Point—*cape* ... WA-9
Southeast Point—*cape* (2) ... MP-9
Southeast Point—*summit* ... TX-5
Southeast Polk Fourmile Sch—*school* ... IA-7
Southeast Polk HS—*school* ... IA-7
Southeast Pond—*lake* ... ME-1
Southeast Pond—*lake* ... MA-1
Southeast Pontotoc (CCD)—*cens area* ... OK-5
Southeast Prong Beaverdam Creek—*stream* ... NC-3
Southeast (Quadrant)—*fmr MCD* ... DC-2
**Southeast Quarter**—*pop pl* ... MA-1
South East Quarter (historical)—*civil* ... MA-1
Southeast Red Springs Oil Field—*oilfield* ... OK-5
*Southeast Reef* ... CA-9
Southeast Renfrow Oil Field—*oilfield* ... OK-5
Southeast Reservoirs—*reservoir* ... NV-8
Southeast Ridge—*ridge* ... MA-1
Southeast River Windmill—*locale* ... TX-5
Southeast Rock—*bar* ... AK-9
Southeast Rock—*bar* ... ME-1
Southeast Rock Auxiliary—*island* ... CA-9
South East Rollo Pasture—*flat* ... KS-7
Southeast Roseau (Unorganized Territory of)—*unorg* ... MN-6
Southeast Rsvr—*reservoir* ... CO-8
South East Sacramento State Wildlife Mgt Are—*park* ... NE-7
Southeast Salt Fork Oil Field—*oilfield* ... OK-5
South East Sch—*school* ... AR-4
Southeast Sch—*school* ... CO-8
Southeast Sch—*school* ... CT-1
Southeast Sch—*school* ... GA-3
Southeast Sch—*school* (2) ... IL-6
Southeast Sch—*school* ... IA-7
Southeast Sch—*school* ... LA-4
Southeast Sch—*school* ... MI-6
Southeast Sch—*school* (3) ... MO-7
Southeast Sch—*school* ... OK-5
Southeast Sch—*school* ... PA-2
Southeast Sch—*school* (2) ... TX-5
Southeast Sch—*school* ... VT-1
Southeast Shoal—*bar* ... AL-4
Southeast Shoal—*bar* (2) ... ME-1
Southeast Shop Ctr—*locale* ... FL-3
South East Spit—*bar* ... MS-4
Southeast Spring—*spring* ... ID-8
Southeast Spur—*ridge* ... AK-9
Southeast Station Post Office—*building* ... AZ-5
Southeast Stratford Oil Field—*oilfield* ... OK-5
Southeast Tank—*reservoir* (2) ... AZ-5
Southeast Tank—*reservoir* (2) ... NM-5
Southeast Tank—*reservoir* ... TX-5
South East Thief Hollow Windmill—*locale* ... TX-5
Southeast Tomball Oil Field—*oilfield* ... TX-5
**Southeast (Town of)**—*pop pl* ... NY-2
**Southeast (Township of)**—*pop pl* ... IN-6
Southeast Washita (CCD)—*cens area* ... OK-5
Southeast Water Trough—*hist pl* ... IA-7
Southeast Well—*well* ... NM-5
Southeast Well—*well* ... TX-5
South East Wilberton Pasture—*flat* ... KS-7
Southeast Williams—*unorg reg* ... ND-7
Southeast Windmill—*locale* (2) ... NM-5
Southeast Windmill—*locale* (4) ... TX-5
Southeast Woodlands Oil Field—*oilfield* ... MS-4
Southeast Yankton—*unorg reg* ... SD-7
Southeast Yeager Tank—*reservoir* ... TX-5
**South Eaton**—*pop pl* ... PA-2
South Eaton Cem—*cemetery* ... MI-6
**South Ebervale**—*pop pl* ... PA-2
South Eddy Creek—*stream* ... MI-6
South Eden Canyon—*valley* ... UT-8
South Eden Rsvr—*reservoir* ... UT-8
South Edgecombe JHS—*school* ... NC-3
Southedge JHS—*school* ... NY-2
*South Edgewood* ... IN-6
**South Edgewood**—*pop pl* ... IN-6
*South Edisto River* ... SC-3
South Edisto River—*stream* ... SC-3
**South Edmeston**—*pop pl* ... NY-2
South Edna Peak—*summit* ... UT-8
South Edwards—*locale* ... NY-2
South Edwards River—*stream* ... IL-6
South Eel Creek Campground—*park* ... OR-9
**South Effingham**—*pop pl* ... ME-1
**South Effingham**—*pop pl* ... NH-1
*South Egan Range* ... NV-8
South Egg Creek—*stream* ... ND-7
**South Egg Harbor**—*pop pl* ... NJ-2
**South Egremont**—*pop pl* ... MA-1
South Egremont Village Hist Dist—*hist pl* ... MA-1
South Eighth Ave City Park—*park* ... AL-4
South Eighth Street Hist Dist—*hist pl* ... ID-8
South Eighth Street Sch—*school* ... NJ-2
South Eight Sch—*school* ... OK-5
South Elbow Hollow—*valley* ... ID-8
South Elder Mine—*mine* ... CA-9
South El Dorado (CCD)—*cens area* ... CA-9
*South Elementary School* ... MS-4
South Elem Sch—*school* ... DE-2
South Elem Sch—*school* ... IN-6
South Elem Sch—*school* (3) ... KS-7
South Elem Sch—*school* (2) ... NC-3
South Elem Sch—*school* ... TX-5
South Eleventh Street Baptist Ch—*church* ... AL-4
**South Elgin**—*pop pl* ... IL-6
**South Eliot**—*pop pl* ... ME-1
South Elizabeth—*uninc pl* ... NJ-2
South Elk Basin Oil Field—*oilfield* ... WY-8

South Elk Creek—*stream* CO-8
South Elk Creek—*stream* KS-7
South Elkhorn—*locale* KY-4
**South Elkhorn**—*pop pl* IL-6
South Elkhorn Ch—*church* KY-4
South Elkhorn Creek—*stream* KY-4
South Elkhorn Township—*civil* MO-7
South Elk Ridge—*ridge* UT-8
South Ellis (CCD)—*cens area* OK-5
South Ellsworth—*locale* CT-1
South Elm—*locale* TX-5
South Elma—*locale* WA-9
South Elm Creek—*stream* KS-7
South Elm Creek—*stream* TX-5
South Elmdale Ch—*church* MN-6
**South El Monte**—*pop pl* CA-9
*South Elora Lake* MN-6
**South El Rancho Subdivision**—*pop pl* UT-8
South Elrod Cem—*cemetery* SD-7
South Elsmere Sch—*school* NE-7
South Elton Oil and Gas Field—*oilfield* LA-4
**South Elwood**—*pop pl* IN-6
South Embleton Coulee—*valley* MT-8
South Emerson Ave Ch of God—*church* IN-6
South Emerson Lake—*lake* CA-9
South Emmons—*unorg reg* ND-7
South Emory Creek—*stream* MO-7
*South End* CT-1
South End—*bay* WA-9
South End—*locale* SD-7
**South End**—*pop pl* (2) CT-1
**South End**—*pop pl* VT-1
South End—*uninc pl* TX-5
South End Bridge—*bridge* NH-1
South End Cem—*cemetery* MA-1
South End Cem—*cemetery* VT-1
South End Ch—*church* KY-4
South End Community Hall—*locale* NV-8
*South End Creek* GA-3
South End District—*hist pl* MA-1
South End Ditch—*canal* ID-8
South End Drain—*canal* CA-9
South End Field—*park* GA-3
South End-Groesbeckville Hist Dist—*hist pl* NY-2
South End Hist Dist—*hist pl* CT-1
South End Lake—*lake* ID-8
South End Park—*park* MN-6
South End Park—*park* PA-2
South End Point—*cape* CT-1
South End Pond—*lake* MA-1
South End Sch—*school* CT-1
South End Sch—*school* MA-1
South End Sch—*school* NJ-2
South End Sch—*school* NC-3
South End Sch—*school* OR-9
Southend Sportsman Club—*other* CA-9
**South End (subdivision)**—*pop pl* MA-1
South End Tank—*reservoir* NM-5
**South English**—*pop pl* IA-7
South English Cem—*cemetery* IA-7
South English River—*stream* IA-7
**South Enola**—*pop pl* PA-2
*South Enon Estates* OH-6
South Ensley Ch—*church* MI-6
South Entering Rock—*rock* MA-1
South Entrance—*channel* AK-9
South Entrance—*locale* WY-8
South Entrance—*other* UT-8
South Entrance Sign—*hist pl* UT-8
South Entrance Station—*locale* AZ-5
South Entrance Station—*locale* CA-9
South Entrance Trail—*trail* WY-8
South Ephraim Ditch—*canal* UT-8
South Epps Gas Field—*oilfield* LA-4
Souther, Abe, House—*hist pl* KY-4
Souther, John, House—*hist pl* MA-1
Souther Creek—*stream* WA-9
Southerd Homestead—*locale* MT-8
South Erickson Lake—*lake* UT-8
South Erie—*post sta* PA-2
South Erin—*locale* NY-2
*Southerland* IA-7
Southerland Bottom—*bend* LA-4
Southerland-Burnette House—*hist pl* NC-3
Southerland Canyon—*valley* TX-5
Southerland Cem—*cemetery* KY-4
Southerland Cem—*cemetery* MO-7
Southerland Cem—*cemetery* TN-4
Southerland Coulee—*valley* MT-8
Southerland Hill—*summit* MS-4
Southerland Mtn—*summit* NY-2
Southerland Park Golf Course—*locale* AR-4
Southerland Sch—*school* MT-8
Southerland Sch—*school* TX-5
**Southerlands Crossroads**—*pop pl* AR-4
Southerlands Pond—*lake* NC-3
Southerlands Pond Dam—*dam* NC-3
Southerlandss Pond—*reservoir* NC-3
Southerland Well—*locale* NM-5
Southerly Breakwater—*other* IL-6
Southerly Island—*island* AK-9
Southerly Run—*stream* VA-3
Southern—*locale* CA-9
Southern Acad—*school* AL-4
Southern Acres Mobile Home Park—*locale* AZ-5
**Southern Acres Subdivision**—*pop pl* UT-8
Southern Adams County Heliport—*airport* PA-2
Southern Aid Society-Dunbar Theater Bldg—*hist pl* DC-2
*Southern Aire* MO-7
Southernaire Dock—*locale* TN-4
Southernaire Resort—*locale* TN-4
Southern Alameda Yard—*locale* CA-9
*Southern and Western Theological Seminary* TN-4
Southern Arizona Mental Health Center—*hospital* AZ-5
Southern Arizona Sch for Boys—*school* AZ-5
Southern Artery Shop Ctr—*locale* MA-1
Southern Ave Sch—*school* PA-2
Southern Baptist Coll—*school* AR-4
Southern Baptist Seminary—*church* KY-4
*Southern Bay Channel* FL-3
Southern Belle Mine—*mine* AZ-5
Southern Belle Mine—*mine* CA-9
Southern Bell Telephone Company Bldg—*hist pl* GA-3
Southern Belting Company Bldg—*hist pl* GA-3
*Southern Bench* NV-8
Southern Bible Coll—*school* TX-5
Southern Blvd Bridge—*bridge* FL-3
Southern Blvd Ch of Christ—*church* AL-4
Southern Branch—*stream* VA-3
Southern Branch Elizabeth River—*stream* VA-3
Southern Calif Gas Camp—*locale* CA-9
Southern California Bible Coll—*school* CA-9
Southern California Military Acad—*school* CA-9
*Southern California Peak* CA-9
Southern California Sch of Theology—*school* CA-9
Southern Canal—*canal* AZ-5
Southern Canal—*canal* (2) NM-5
Southern Cayuga HS—*school* NY-2
Southern Cem—*cemetery* MD-2
Southern Cem—*cemetery* MI-6
Southern Cem—*cemetery* NC-3
Southern Cem—*cemetery* OH-6
Southern Cem—*cemetery* (2) TN-4
Southern Ch—*church* NC-3
Southern Ch—*church* TN-4
*Southern Channel* FL-3
**Southern Charm Subdivision**—*pop pl* UT-8
Southern Choctaw HS—*school* AL-4
Southern Christian Home For Children—*building* GA-3
*Southern Christian Institute* MS-4
Southern Connecticut State Coll—*school* CT-1
Southern Cotton Oil Co.—*hist pl* GA-3
Southern Counties Gas Co.—*hist pl* CA-9
Southern Cove—*bay* (2) ME-1
Southern Creek—*stream* AK-9
Southern Creek—*stream* AR-4
Southern Cross—*locale* MT-8
Southern Cross Mine—*mine* AZ-5
Southern Cross Mine—*mine* CA-9
Southern Cross Mine—*mine* CO-8
*Southern Crossroads* MS-4
Southern Cross Spring—*spring* MT-8
Southern Ditch—*canal* KY-4
Southern Dock—*locale* TN-4
Southern Dolomite Company RR Station—*locale* FL-3
Southern Dunes—*summit* FL-3
Southern Dutchess Country Club—*other* NY-2
Southern (Election Precinct)—*fmr MCD* IL-6
Southern Estates Park—*park* FL-3
**Southern Estates (subdivision)**—*pop pl* AL-4
Southern Eureka—*mine* UT-8
*Southern Female University* AL-4
Southern Glacier—*glacier* AK-9
Southern Gold Mine—*mine* SC-3
Southern Grove Ch—*church* AR-4
Southern Grove Ch—*church* (2) NC-3
Southern Guilford HS—*school* NC-3
Southern Harbor—*bay* ME-1
**Southern Heights**—*pop pl* KY-4
**Southern Heights**—*pop pl* WA-9
Southern Heights-Beechmont District—*hist pl* KY-4
Southern Heights Ch—*church* MO-7
Southern Heights Elem Sch—*school* IN-6
Southern Heights Ridge—*ridge* CA-9
Southern Heights Sch—*school* NM-5
Southern Heights Sch—*school* TN-4
**Southern Heights (subdivision)**—*pop pl* TN-4
Southern Hill—*summit* AR-4
*Southern Hills* (2) OH-6
**Southern Hills**—*pop pl* TN-4
Southern Hills—*uninc pl* LA-4
*Southern Hills Baptist Ch* MS-4
Southern Hills Baptist Ch—*church* MS-4
Southern Hills Ch—*church* MS-4
Southern Hills Ch—*church* MO-7
Southern Hills Country Club—*other* NE-7
Southern Hills Country Club—*other* OK-5
Southern Hills JHS—*school* CO-8
Southern Hills Lake Dam—*dam* IN-6
Southern Hills Mennonite Ch—*church* KS-7
Southern Hills Park—*uninc pl* LA-4
Southern Hills Sch—*school* LA-4
Southern Hills Sch—*school* OK-5
Southern Hills Shop Ctr—*locale* (2) MO-7
Southern (historical)—*locale* AL-4
Southern Home Ch—*church* FL-3
Southern Hotel—*hist pl* MT-8
Southern Hotel—*hist pl* OK-5
Southern Hotel—*hist pl* TX-5
Southern HS—*school* KY-4
Southern HS—*school* (2) MD-2
Southern HS—*school* (2) NC-3
Southern Huntingdon County HS—*school* PA-2
*Southern Huntingdon County Junior Senior HS* PA-2
Southern Ice and Cold Storage Company—*hist pl* OK-5
Southern Illinois Country Club—*other* IL-6
Southern Illinois Univ—*school* IL-6
Southern Illinois Univ (Edwardsville)—*school* IL-6
Southern Illnois Univ (School of Tech)—*school* IL-6
Southern Indiana Gas & Electric (Brown Station)—*facility* IN-6
Southern Indiana Purdue Agriculture Center—*school* IN-6
*Southern Industrial Institute* AL-4
Southern Infirmary (historical)—*hospital* AL-4
Southern Inlet—*stream* ME-1
Southern Island—*island* ME-1
Southern JHS—*school* (3) KY-4
Southern JHS—*school* MA-1
Southern JHS—*school* NC-3
Southern JHS—*school* PA-2
**Southern Junction**—*pop pl* AL-4
**Southern Junction**—*pop pl* CO-8
**Southern Junction**—*pop pl* GA-3
Southern Key Cem—*cemetery* FL-3
Southern Keys Cem—*cemetery* FL-3
*Southern Knoll* OH-6
Southern Lake—*lake* AK-9
Southern Lake—*reservoir* AR-4
Southern Lateral—*canal* ID-8
Southern Lehigh HS—*school* PA-2
Southern Lehigh MS—*school* PA-2
Southern Local HS—*school* OH-6
Southern Manor Country Club—*locale* FL-3
Southern Mark Island—*island* ME-1
Southern Maryland Public Works Camp—*locale* MD-2
**Southern Meadows (subdivision)**—*pop pl* AL-4
Southern Memorial Gardens—*cemetery* LA-4
Southern Memorial Hosp—*hospital* NV-8
Southern Memorial Park—*cemetery* FL-3
Southern Memorial Park—*cemetery* MS-4
*Southern Methodist Ch* AL-4
Southern Methodist Ch—*church* AL-4
Southern Methodist Ch of Waynesboro—*church* MS-4
Southern Methodist Publishing House—*hist pl* TN-4
Southern Methodist Univ—*school* TX-5
Southern Michigan State For Nursery—*forest* MI-6
Southern Michigan State Prison—*other* MI-6
Southern Military Acad (historical)—*school* AL-4
Southern Minnesota Depot—*hist pl* MN-6
Southern Missionary Coll—*school* (2) TN-4
Southern Mississippi Retardation Center—*hospital* MS-4
*Southern Mountain* AZ-5
*Southern Mountains* ID-8
Southern Mtn—*summit* NC-3
Southern Nantahala Wilderness—*park* GA-3
Southern Nash HS—*school* NC-3
Southern Nash JHS—*school* NC-3
Southern Natl Bank—*hist pl* KY-4
Southern Neck—*cape* ME-1
Southern Nevada Vocational Technical Center—*school* NV-8
Southern Normal Sch—*school* AL-4
Southern Ocean County Hospital—*airport* NJ-2
Southern Ohio Lunatic Asylum—*hist pl* OH-6
*Southern Ohmia Drain* MI-6
Southern Oregon Coll—*school* OR-9
*Southern Pacific Basin* CA-9
Southern Pacific Bridge—*bridge* CA-9
Southern Pacific Causeway—*bridge* UT-8
Southern Pacific Depot—*hist pl* (2) CA-9
Southern Pacific Depot Hist Dist—*hist pl* TX-5
Southern Pacific Freight Depot—*hist pl* AZ-5
Southern Pacific Hosp—*hospital* CA-9
Southern Pacific Hosp—*hospital* TX-5
Southern Pacific Passenger Depot—*hist pl* CA-9
Southern Pacific Railroad: Ogden-Lucin Cut-Off Trestle—*hist pl* UT-8
Southern Pacific RR Company's Sacramento Depot—*hist pl* CA-9
Southern Pacific RR Depot—*hist pl* (2) AZ-5
Southern Pacific RR Depot—*hist pl* LA-4
Southern Pacific RR Passenger Depot—*hist pl* TX-5
Southern Pacific RR Passenger Station—*hist pl* TX-5
Southern Pacific RR Station—*hist pl* (2) CA-9
Southern Pacific Shops—*other* (2) CA-9
Southern Pacific Spring—*spring* NV-8
Southern Pacific Station—*locale* (4) CA-9
Southern Pacific Station—*locale* TX-5
Southern Paiute Archeol District—*hist pl* UT-8
Southern Paiute Ind Res—*reserve* UT-8
Southern Palms Shop Ctr—*locale* AZ-5
Southern Palms Trailer Park—*locale* AZ-5
Southern Park Stable—*hist pl* OH-6
*Southern Peak* CA-9
Southern Pilgrim Coll—*school* NC-3
**Southern Pine**—*pop pl* VA-3
Southern Pine Hills—*area* AL-4
Southern Pine Hills—*area* MS-4
**Southern Pines**—*pop pl* NC-3
Southern Pines Elem Sch—*school* NC-3
Southern Pines Golf Course—*locale* NC-3
Southern Pines Lookout Tower—*locale* NC-3
Southern Pines MS—*school* NC-3
Southern Pines Waterworks—*locale* NC-3
Southern Pines Waterworks—*reservoir* NC-3
Southern Pines Waterworks Dam—*dam* NC-3
Southern Plaza (Shop Ctr)—*locale* FL-3
Southern Plaza Shop Ctr—*locale* IN-6
**Southern Points**—*pop pl* VA-3
Southern Pond—*lake* FL-3
Southern Prong Saint Jerome Creek—*bay* MD-2
Southern Railway Depot—*hist pl* (2) AL-4
Southern Railway Depot—*hist pl* SC-3
Southern Railway Freight Depot—*hist pl* TN-4
Southern Railway Passenger Depot—*hist pl* KY-4
Southern Railway Passenger Depot—*hist pl* NC-3
Southern Railway Passenger Depot—*hist pl* SC-3
Southern Railway Passenger Station—*hist pl* NC-3
Southern Railway Passenger Station—*hist pl* SC-3
Southern Railway Spencer Shops—*hist pl* NC-3
Southern Railway System Depot—*hist pl* AL-4
Southern Railway Terminal Station—*hist pl* AL-4
Southern RR Depot—*hist pl* AL-4
Southern Sch—*school* (2) KY-4
Southern Sch—*school* MO-7
Southern Schoolhouse Ch—*church* AL-4
Southern Seminary Junior Coll—*school* VA-3
Southern Seminary Main Bldg—*hist pl* VA-3
Southern Shop Ctr—*locale* VA-3
Southern Shops (Lone Oak)—*CDP* SC-3
**Southern Shores**—*pop pl* (2) NC-3
Southern Simmons Pond—*lake* MA-1
Southern Slopes (CCD)—*cens area* WA-9
**Southern (Southern University)**—*pop pl* LA-4
Southern Sportsman Lodge—*building* AL-4
Southern State Coll—*school* AR-4
Southern State Coll (Agricultural School)—*school* AR-4
Southern States Fairgrounds (historical)—*locale* NC-3
Southern Station—*locale* TN-4
Southern Substation—*locale* AZ-5
Southern Tank—*reservoir* AZ-5
Southern Tech (Southern Technical Institute)—*uninc pl* GA-3
*Southern Temple Church* TN-4
Southern Terminal, Susquehanna and Tidewater Canal—*hist pl* MD-2
Southern Terminal and Warehouse Hist Dist—*hist pl* TN-4
Southern Terminal Redoubt—*hist pl* VA-3
**Southern Terrace (subdivision)**—*pop pl* NC-3
**Southern Trailer Park**—*pop pl* UT-8
Southern Triangles—*bar* ME-1
Southern Trinity HS—*school* CA-9
Southern Union State Coll—*school* AL-4
Southern Univ—*school* LA-4
Southern Univ Archives Bldg—*hist pl* LA-4
Southern (University of Southern Mississippi)—*school* MS-4
Southern Univ (historical)—*school* AL-4
Southern Univ (New Orleans Branch)—*school* LA-4
*Southern Utah State College* UT-8
Southern Ute Agency—*locale* CO-8
**Southern Ute Ind Res**—*pop pl* CO-8
Southern Vermont Art Center—*building* VT-1
**Southern View**—*pop pl* IL-6
Southern View Sch—*school* IL-6
**Southern View (subdivision)**—*pop pl* TN-4
Southern Wayne HS—*school* NC-3
Southern Wisconsin Colony and Training School—*other* WI-6
*Southern Woods* TN-4
Southern Yards—*locale* VA-3
Southers Cem—*cemetery* IL-6
Southerwood—*locale* PA-2
**Southerwood**—*pop pl* PA-2
Southerwood Ch—*church* PA-2
**South Essex**—*pop pl* MA-1
South Essex Cem—*cemetery* IL-6
South Essex (historical P.O.)—*locale* MA-1
South Estatoe Ch—*church* NC-3
South Estes Windmill—*locale* TX-5
**South Etna**—*pop pl* ME-1
**South Etowah**—*pop pl* TN-4
**South Euclid**—*pop pl* OH-6
South Eugene HS—*school* OR-9
South Eureka Mine—*mine* CA-9
South Evans Ch—*church* MO-7
South Evans Gulch—*valley* CO-8
South Evart Cem—*cemetery* MI-6
South Evart Ch—*church* MI-6
**South Excello**—*pop pl* OH-6
South Exeter—*locale* ME-1
South Extension Canal—*canal* AZ-5
South Extension Old Field Canal—*canal* UT-8
*South Fabius River* MO-7
South Fabius River—*stream* MO-7
**South Factory Village**—*pop pl* MA-1
*South Fahang Valley* MH-9
South Fairbanks—*uninc pl* AK-9
South Fairfield—*locale* MI-6
South Fairlee—*other* VT-1
**South Fairlington**—*pop pl* VA-3
**South Fairview**—*pop pl* VA-3
South Fairview Ch—*church* PA-2
South Fairview Community Hall—*building* KS-7
South Fairview Run—*stream* IN-6
South Fairview Sch—*school* MT-8
South Falcon Creek—*stream* TX-5
*South Fall Creek* WY-8
South Fall Creek (Township of)—*fmr MCD* NC-3
South Falls—*falls* OR-9
South Fallsburg (census name for South Fallsburgh)—*CDP* NY-2
*South Fallsburgh* NY-2
South Fallsburgh (census name South Fallsburg)—*other* NY-2
*South Fanaganam Valley* MH-9
South Fant Street Sch—*school* SC-3
South Fariston Ch—*church* KY-4
**South Farmingdale**—*pop pl* NY-2
South Farmingdale (sta.)—*uninc pl* NY-2
South Farmington Chapel—*church* NY-2
South Farm Lake—*lake* MN-6
South Farm Meadow Ditch—*canal* CO-8
*South Farms* CT-1
South Farms—*locale* CT-1
**South Farms**—*pop pl* CT-1
South Fayette—*locale* WV-2
**South Fayette (Township of)**—*pop pl* PA-2
South Fayetteville (sta.)—*uninc pl* NC-3
South Fayston Cem—*cemetery* VT-1
South Federal—*post sta* FL-3
South Ferron Rsvr—*reservoir* UT-8
**South ferry**—*pop pl* RI-1
South Ferry Point—*cape* MD-2
South Field—*flat* NV-8
South Field—*park* MI-6
**Southfield**—*pop pl* MA-1
**Southfield**—*pop pl* MI-6
Southfield—*uninc pl* LA-4
South Field Area—*mine* CO-8
Southfield Canal—*canal* GA-3
South Field Canal—*canal* UT-8
South Field Canyon—*valley* AZ-5
South Field Canyon Tank—*reservoir* AZ-5
Southfield Cem—*cemetery* MI-6
*Southfield Center* MI-6
South Field Ditch—*canal* UT-8
Southfield Furnace Ruin—*hist pl* NY-2
Southfield Lake—*lake* AL-4
Southfield-Lathrup HS—*school* MI-6
Southfield Number 10 Sch—*school* MI-6
*Southfield Park* OH-6
Southfield Park—*park* CT-1
Southfield Park—*park* (2) MI-6
**Southfields**—*pop pl* NY-2
Southfield Sch—*school* LA-4
**Southfield (Township of)**—*pop pl* MI-6
South Fillmore (Township of)—*civ div* IL-6
South Finegayan Latte Stone Park—*hist pl* GU-9
South Finger Islands—*island* WA-9
South First and Second Street Hist Dist—*hist pl* WI-6
South First Creek Sch—*school* MT-8
South First Natl Bank Block—*hist pl* OR-9
South Fish Creek—*stream* TX-5
South Fish Creek—*stream* WI-6
South Fish Creek—*stream* WY-8
South Fish Lake—*lake* WI-6
South Fishtail Bay—*bay* MI-6
**South Fitchburg**—*pop pl* MA-1
South Fitch Plaza—*locale* MA-1
South Five Ch—*church* MO-7
South Flannigan (Township of)—*civ div* IL-6
South Flat—*flat* (2) OR-9
South Flat—*flat* UT-8
South Flat—*flat* WY-8
South Flat—*other* AK-9
South Flat Ch—*church* OK-5
South Flat Creek—*stream* MO-7
South Flat Ditch—*canal* CO-8
*South Flathead River* MT-8
South Flat River—*stream* NC-3
South Flats—*flat* KS-7
South Flat Sch—*school* WY-8
South Flat Top Lake—*reservoir* TX-5
South Flint Plaza Shop Ctr—*locale* MI-6
*South Flint River* AL-4
South Flint River Bar (historical)—*bar* AL-4
South Flint Sch—*school* IL-6
South Floater Ditch—*canal* WI-6
**South Flomaton**—*pop pl* FL-3
**South Floral Park**—*pop pl* NY-2
**South Floral Park (Jamaica Square)**—*pop pl* NY-2
**South Florence**—*pop pl* AL-4
South Florida Ave Ch—*church* FL-3
South Florida Baptist Hosp—*hospital* FL-3
South Florida Evaluation and Treatment Center (state)—*locale* FL-3
South Florida Heights Ch—*church* FL-3
South Florida Junior Coll—*school* FL-3
South Florida Military Acad—*school* (2) FL-3
South Florida Military College—*hist pl* FL-3
South Florida Reception Center—*building* FL-3
South Florida State Hosp—*hospital* (2) FL-3
South Florida Youth Conservation Camp—*locale* FL-3
South Flow—*bay* NY-2
**South Fontana**—*pop pl* CA-9
*South Foose Creek* CO-8
South Fooses Creek—*stream* CO-8
South Ford—*locale* TN-4
**Southford**—*pop pl* CT-1
Southford Falls State Park—*park* CT-1
South Ford River Cem—*cemetery* MI-6
South Forest City Township—*civil* SD-7
**South Forest Estates**—*pop pl* SC-3
*South Fork* AZ-5
*South Fork* AR-4
*South Fork* CA-9
*South Fork* CO-8
*South Fork* GA-3
*South Fork* HI-9
*South Fork* ID-8
*South Fork* IL-6
*South Fork* IN-6
*South Fork* KS-7
*South Fork* KY-4
*South Fork* MT-8
*South Fork* NC-3
*South Fork* OR-9
*South Fork* PA-2
*South Fork* SD-7
*South Fork* TN-4
*South Fork* VA-3
*South Fork* WA-9
*South Fork* WY-8
South Fork—*canal* OH-6
South Fork—*cens area* MT-8
South Fork—*fmr MCD* NE-7
South Fork—*locale* (3) CA-9
South Fork—*locale* TN-4
**South Fork**—*pop pl* CA-9
**South Fork**—*pop pl* CO-8
**South Fork**—*pop pl* (2) KY-4
**Southfork**—*pop pl* KY-4
**South Fork**—*pop pl* MO-7
**South Fork**—*pop pl* NC-3
**South Fork**—*pop pl* PA-2
South Fork—*stream* AK-9
South Fork—*stream* CA-9
South Fork—*stream* OH-6
South Fork—*stream* SC-3
South Fork—*stream* (2) WY-8
South Fork Abbot Creek—*stream* MT-8
South Fork Agnes Creek—*stream* WA-9
South Fork Ah Pah Creek—*stream* CA-9
South Fork Ahtanum Creek—*stream* WA-9
South Fork Alamito Creek—*stream* TX-5
South Fork Alamo de Cesanio Creek—*stream* TX-5
South Fork Albion River—*stream* CA-9
South Fork Alder Canyon—*valley* CA-9
*South Fork Alder Creek* ID-8
South Fork Alder Creek—*stream* ID-8
South Fork Alderson Creek—*stream* MT-8
South Fork Alkali Creek—*stream* CO-8
South Fork Alkali Creek—*stream* (2) MT-8
South Fork Allen Creek—*stream* MT-8
South Fork Allison Creek—*stream* NV-8
South Fork Alsea River—*stream* OR-9
South Fork American Fork—*stream* MT-8
South Fork American Fork Canyon—*valley* UT-8
South Fork American River—*stream* CA-9
South Fork Ames Branch—*stream* WI-6
South Fork Anderson Creek—*stream* OR-9
South Fork Anderson Creek—*stream* (2) WY-8
South Fork Andrew Creek—*stream* AK-9
South Fork Andrus Creek—*stream* MT-8
South Fork Angel Creek—*stream* NV-8
South Fork Animas River—*stream* CO-8
South Fork Annie Creek—*stream* NV-8
*South Fork Antelope Creek* ID-8
South Fork Antelope Creek—*stream* CA-9
South Fork Antelope Creek—*stream* ID-8
South Fork Antelope Creek—*stream* (2) MT-8
South Fork Antelope Creek—*stream* OR-9
South Fork Antelope Creek—*stream* WY-8
South Fork Apache Tear Canyon—*valley* NV-8
South Fork Apperson Creek—*stream* CA-9
South Fork Apple Creek—*stream* MO-7
South Fork Apple River—*stream* IL-6
South Fork Appomattox River—*stream* VA-3
**South Fork (Arabia)**—*pop pl* KY-4
South Fork Arapaho Creek—*stream* CO-8
South Fork Argo Creek—*stream* OR-9
*South Fork Arikaree River* CO-8
*South Fork Arikaree River* KS-7
*South Fork Arkansas Creek* WA-9
*South Fork Arkansas River* CO-8
South Fork Arm—*bay* MT-8
South Fork Arolik River—*stream* AK-9
South Fork Arroyo de los Pinos—*stream* NM-5
South Fork Arroyo Leon—*stream* NM-5
South Fork Ash Canyon—*valley* AZ-5
South Fork Ash Creek—*stream* (2) AZ-5
South Fork Ash Creek—*stream* CA-9
South Fork Ash Creek—*stream* MT-8
South Fork Ash Creek—*stream* OR-9
South Fork Ashley Creek—*stream* UT-8
South Fork Asotin Creek—*stream* WA-9
South Fork Atchison Branch—*stream* TN-4
South Fork Avalanche Canyon—*valley* WY-8
South Fork Avintaquin Creek—*stream* UT-8
South Fork Babbs Canyon—*valley* CA-9
South Fork Bachelor Creek—*stream* MT-8
South Fork Backbone Creek—*stream* CA-9
South Fork Back Creek—*stream* VA-3
South Fork Bacon Creek—*stream* ID-8
*South Fork Bad Axe River* WI-6
South Fork Bad Axe River—*stream* WI-6
*South Fork Badger Creek* ID-8
South Fork Badger Creek—*stream* WY-8
South Fork Bad River—*stream* MI-6
South Fork Bad River—*stream* SD-7
South Fork Badwater Creek—*stream* WY-8
*South Fork Bail Creek* NV-8
South Fork Baker Branch—*stream* GA-3
South Fork Baker Canyon—*valley* UT-8
*South Fork Baker Canyon - in part* UT-8
South Fork Baker Creek—*stream* CO-8
South Fork Baker Creek—*stream* ID-8
South Fork Baker Creek—*stream* NV-8
South Fork Baker Gulch—*valley* ID-8
South Fork Baking Powder Creek—*stream* MT-8
South Fork Bald Mountain Creek—*stream* OR-9
South Fork Ballenger Draw—*valley* WY-8
*South Fork Balleus Creek* NC-3
South Fork Baptist Ch (historical)—*church* TN-4
*South Fork Baraboo River* WI-6
South Fork Barber Creek—*stream* MT-8
South Fork Bare Creek—*stream* WY-8
South Fork Barnaby Creek—*stream* WA-9
South Fork Barrett Canyon—*valley* NV-8
South Fork Barron Creek—*stream* OR-9
South Fork Bartlett Creek—*stream* CA-9
South Fork Barton Creek—*stream* TX-5
South Fork Basin—*basin* OR-9
South Fork Basin Creek—*stream* MT-8
South Fork Basin Creek—*stream* TN-4
South Fork Battle Butte Creek—*stream* MT-8
South Fork Battle Creek—*stream* CA-9
South Fork Battle Creek—*stream* NV-8
South Fork Battle Creek—*stream* OR-9
South Fork Bayou Dan—*stream* LA-4
South Fork Bayou de Chien—*stream* KY-4
*South Fork Bayou du Chien* KY-4
*South Fork Bayou Pierre* MS-4
*South Fork Bean Blossom Creek* IN-6
South Fork Bean Brook—*stream* WI-6
South Fork Bean Creek—*stream* OR-9
*South Fork Bear Creek* CO-8
*South Fork Bear Creek* WA-9
*South Fork Bear Creek* WY-8
South Fork Bear Creek—*stream* (4) CA-9
South Fork Bear Creek—*stream* CO-8
South Fork Bear Creek—*stream* FL-3
South Fork Bear Creek—*stream* (2) ID-8
South Fork Bear Creek—*stream* IL-6
South Fork Bear Creek—*stream* MN-6
South Fork Bear Creek—*stream* MS-4
South Fork Bear Creek—*stream* (2) MT-8
South Fork Bear Creek—*stream* NM-5
South Fork Bear Creek—*stream* (2) OR-9
South Fork Bear Creek—*stream* PA-2
South Fork Bear Creek—*stream* TN-4
South Fork Bear Creek—*stream* (3) WA-9
South Fork Bear Creek—*stream* (2) WY-8
South Fork Beargrass Creek—*stream* KY-4
South Fork Bear Gulch—*valley* SD-7
South Fork Bear Gulch—*valley* WY-8
South Fork Bear Haven Creek—*stream* CA-9
South Fork Bear River—*stream* CA-9
South Fork Bear Wallow Creek—*stream* AZ-5
South Fork Beason Creek—*stream* TN-4
*South Fork Beaver Creek* CO-8
*South Fork Beaver Creek* KS-7
South Fork Beaver Creek MT-8
*South Fork Beaver Creek* NE-7
*South Fork Beaver Creek* SD-7
*South Fork Beaver Creek* TN-4
*South Fork Beaver Creek* UT-8
South Fork Beaver Creek—*stream* CO-8
South Fork Beaver Creek—*stream* (2) ID-8
South Fork Beaver Creek—*stream* IN-6
South Fork Beaver Creek—*stream* KY-4
South Fork Beaver Creek—*stream* LA-4
South Fork Beaver Creek—*stream* (4) MT-8
South Fork Beaver Creek—*stream* (7) OR-9
South Fork Beaver Creek—*stream* TN-4
South Fork Beaver Creek—*stream* UT-8
South Fork Beaver Creek—*stream* (3) WA-9
South Fork Beaver Creek—*stream* WI-6
*South Fork Beaver Creek Township* KS-7
South Fork Beaverdam Creek—*stream* PA-2
South Fork Beaver River—*stream* UT-8
South Fork Bee Bayou—*stream* AR-4
South Fork Beech Creek—*stream* NC-3
South Fork Beech Creek—*stream* PA-2
*South Fork Beef River* WI-6
South Fork Beegum Creek—*stream* CA-9
South Fork Beeman Branch—*stream* MO-7
*South Fork Belly River* MT-8
South Fork Bennetts Run—*stream* VA-3
South Fork Bens Creek—*stream* PA-2
South Fork Benson Creek—*stream* WA-9
South Fork Berry Creek—*stream* CA-9
South Fork Berry Creek—*stream* OR-9
South Fork Berry Creek—*stream* WA-9
*South Fork Berry Creek - in part* NV-8
South Fork Bieberstedt Creek—*stream* OR-9
South Fork Big Bear Creek—*stream* UT-8
South Fork Big Bear Hollow—*valley* UT-8
South Fork Big Beaver Creek—*stream* PA-2
South Fork Big Beaver Creek—*stream* TN-4
South Fork Big Brushy Creek—*stream* MO-7
South Fork Big Butte Creek—*stream* OR-9
*South Fork Big Canyon* TX-5

South Fork Big Clear Creek—stream ........ WV-2
South Fork Big Coulee Creek—stream ....... MT-8
South Fork Big Creek ........ AL-4
South Fork Big Creek ........ IN-6
South Fork Big Creek ........ KS-7
South fork Big Creek ........ UT-8
South Fork Big Creek—stream ........ AR-4
South Fork Big Creek—stream ........ CA-9
South Fork Big Creek—stream ........ CO-8
South Fork Big Creek—stream (3) ........ ID-8
South Fork Big Creek—stream (2) ........ MT-8
South Fork Big Creek—stream ........ NV-8
South Fork Big Creek—stream ........ OR-9
South Fork Big Creek—stream ........ WY-8
South Fork Big Deer Creek—stream ........ ID-8
South Fork Big Mallard Creek—stream ........ ID-8
South Fork Big Nemaha River—stream ........ NE-7
South Fork Big Pine Creek—stream ........ CA-9
South Fork Big Pine Creek—stream ........ NC-3
South Fork Big River—stream ........ AK-9
South Fork Big River—stream ........ CA-9
South Fork Big Rock Creek—stream ........ CA-9
South Fork Big Sandy Creek—stream ........ NE-7
South Fork Big Sheep Creek—stream ........ OR-9
South Fork Big Slough—stream ........ KS-7
South Fork Big Spring Canyon—valley ........ AZ-5
South Fork Big Sur River—stream ........ CA-9
South Fork Big Timber Creek—stream ........ MT-8
South Fork Big Wall Creek—stream ........ OR-9
South Fork Big Wash—stream ........ NV-8
South Fork Big Willow Creek—stream ........ NC-3
South Fork Billy Creek—stream ........ OR-9
South Fork Birch Creek ........ WY-8
South Fork Birch Creek—stream ........ AK-9
South Fork Birch Creek—stream ........ CA-9
South Fork Birch Creek—stream ........ ID-8
South Fork Birch Creek—stream ........ MT-8
South Fork Birch Creek—stream (3) ........ UT-8
South Fork Birch Creek—stream ........ WY-8
South Fork Bird Creek—stream ........ CA-9
South Fork Bishop Creek—stream (2) ........ CA-9
South Fork Bitch Creek ........ WY-8
South Fork Bitter Creek ........ MT-8
South Fork Bitter Creek—stream ........ MT-8
South Fork Black Bayou—stream ........ LA-4
South Fork Black Birch Canyon—valley ........ UT-8
South Fork Black Creek—stream ........ FL-3
South Fork Black Creek—stream ........ OR-9
South Fork Blackhawk Creek—stream ........ IA-7
South Fork Blacklick Creek ........ PA-2
South Fork Blackmare Creek—stream ........ ID-8
South Fork Blackmare Cutoff—trail ........ ID-8
South Fork Blackoak Creek—stream ........ AL-4
South Fork Black River ........ MI-6
South Fork Black River—stream ........ MN-6
South Fork Black Rock Creek—stream ........ CA-9
South Fork Blacktail Creek ........ MT-8
South Fork Blacktail Creek—stream (2) ........ MT-8
South Fork Blacktail Creek—stream ........ SD-7
South Fork Black Valley Creek—stream ........ MO-7
South Fork Black Vermillion River ........ KS-7
South Fork Blackwater River—stream (2) ........ MO-7
South Fork Blackwater River—stream ........ VA-3
South Fork Black Wolf Creek—stream ........ CO-8
South Fork Blair Creek—stream ........ NC-3
South Fork Blake Creek—stream ........ WI-6
South Fork Blanco River—stream ........ TX-5
South Fork Blitzen River ........ OR-9
South Fork Blood River—stream ........ TN-4
South Fork Blood River Drainage Ditch—canal ........ TN-4
South Fork Bloom Creek—stream ........ MT-8
South Fork Bloomington Creek—stream ........ ID-8
South Fork Blowing Springs Creek—stream ........ TN-4
South Fork Blue Branch—stream ........ MO-7
South Fork Blue Creek—stream ........ CA-9
South Fork Blue Creek—stream (3) ........ TN-4
South Fork Blue River—stream ........ IN-6
South Fork Bluewater Creek—stream ........ MT-8
South Fork Bluffs—cliff ........ CA-9
South Fork Blunt Creek—stream ........ TN-4
South Fork Bob Creek—stream ........ WI-6
South Fork Bogard Creek—stream ........ TN-4
South Fork Boil Creek ........ ID-8
South Fork Boise River—stream ........ ID-8
South Fork Boll Creek ........ ID-8
South Fork Boll Creek ........ NV-8
South Fork Bonanza Creek ........ MT-8
South Fork Bonanza Creek—stream ........ AK-9
South Fork Bonanza Creek—stream ........ MT-8
South Fork Bonito Creek—stream ........ AZ-5
**South Fork Boquet River**—pop pl ........ NY-2
South Fork Boquet River—stream ........ NY-2
South Fork Borough—civil ........ PA-2
South Fork Borrego Palm Canyon—valley . CA-9
South Fork Borrow Creek—stream ........ AL-4
South Fork Bougher Run—stream ........ PA-2
South Fork Boulder Creek ........ ID-8
South Fork Boulder Creek ........ OR-9
South Fork Boulder Creek ........ WA-9
South Fork Boulder Creek—stream (2) ........ OR-9
South Fork Boulder Creek—stream (2) ........ WA-9
South Fork Boulder Creek—stream ........ WY-8
South Fork Boulder River—stream ........ MT-8
South Fork Bouquet River ........ NY-2
South Fork Box Canyon ........ NV-8
South Fork Box Creek ........ MT-8
South Fork Box Creek—stream ........ MT-8
South Fork Box Creek—stream ........ UT-8
South Fork Box Creek—stream ........ WY-8
South Fork Box Creek - in part ........ UT-8
South Fork Boyle Creek—stream ........ ID-8
South Fork Boyle Creek—stream ........ NV-8
South Fork Bozeman Creek—stream ........ MT-8
South Fork Brackett Creek—stream ........ MT-8
South Fork Bradbury Brook—stream ........ MN-6
South Fork Bradford Creek—stream ........ OH-6
South Fork Branch—stream ........ KY-4
South Fork Bratten Spring Creek—stream ........ MO-7
South Fork Breakfast Creek—stream ........ ID-8
South Fork Breitenbush River—stream ........ OR-9
South Fork Bremner River—stream ........ AK-9
South Fork Bridge—bridge ........ CA-9
South Fork Bridge Creek ........ MT-8
South Fork Bridge Creek ........ OR-9
South Fork Bridge Creek—stream ........ MT-8
South Fork Bridge Creek—stream ........ OR-9
South Fork Bridge Creek—stream ........ WA-9
South Fork Bristow Creek—stream ........ MT-8
South Fork Broad River—stream ........ GA-3
South Fork Broad Run—stream ........ VA-3
South Fork Brokenback Creek—stream ........ WY-8
South Fork Brouilletts Creek—stream ........ IL-6
South Fork Brown Creek—stream ........ AR-4
South Fork Brownie Creek—stream ........ OR-9
South Fork Bruce Creek—stream ........ WA-9
South Fork Brush Creek ........ CO-8
South Fork Brush Creek—stream ........ AR-4
South Fork Brush Creek—stream ........ CA-9
South Fork Brush Creek—stream ........ ID-8
South Fork Brush Creek—stream (4) ........ MO-7
South Fork Brush Creek—stream ........ WV-2
South Fork Brushy Creek—stream (2) ........ TX-5
South Fork Brushy Creek—stream ........ WA-9
South Fork Brushy Fork—stream ........ OH-6
South Fork Buck Creek—stream ........ AK-9
South Fork Buck Creek—stream ........ IN-6
South Fork Buck Creek—stream ........ NM-5
South Fork Buck Creek—stream (3) ........ OR-9
South Fork Buck Creek—stream ........ TX-5
South Fork Buckeye Creek—stream (2) ........ CA-9
South Fork Buckhorn Creek—stream ........ ID-8
South Fork Buckhorn Summit—summit ........ ID-8
South Fork Buckhorn Trail—trail ........ ID-8
South Fork Buckland River—stream ........ AK-9
South Fork Buckner Creek—stream ........ KS-7
South Fork Buffalo Creek—stream ........ CO-8
South Fork Buffalo Creek—stream ........ MO-7
South Fork Buffalo Creek—stream ........ MT-8
South Fork Buffalo Creek—stream ........ OH-6
South Fork Buffalo Creek—stream ........ TX-5
South Fork Buffalo Creek—stream ........ WV-2
South Fork Buffalo Creek—stream ........ WY-8
South Fork Buffalo River—stream ........ TN-4
South Fork Buffalo River—stream ........ VA-3
South Fork Buffalo River—stream ........ WI-6
South Fork Buffalo River - in part ........ MS-4
South Fork Buford Canyon—valley ........ AZ-5
South Fork Bull Canyon—valley ........ ID-8
South Fork Bull Creek—stream (2) ........ MT-8
South Fork Bull Creek—stream ........ ND-7
South Fork Bull Creek—stream ........ WY-8
South Fork Bull Lake Creek—stream ........ WY-8
South Fork Bull River—stream ........ MT-8
South Fork Bull Run River—stream ........ OR-9
South Fork Burls Creek—stream ........ AK-9
South Fork Burns Creek ........ MT-8
South Fork Burnt River—stream ........ OR-9
South Fork Burwell Creek—stream ........ WY-8
South Fork Busby Creek—stream ........ MT-8
South Fork Butano Creek—stream ........ CA-9
South Fork Butte Creek—stream ........ OR-9
South Fork Butter Creek ........ OR-9
South Fork Buzzard Canyon—valley ........ NM-5
South Fork Cabin—locale ........ CA-9
South Fork Cabin Creek—stream (2) ........ ID-8
South Fork Cabin Creek—stream ........ MT-8
South Fork Cabin Creek—stream ........ OR-9
South Fork Cable Creek—stream ........ OR-9
South Fork Cache Creek ........ MT-8
South Fork Cache Creek—stream ........ MT-8
South Fork Cache La Poudre River—stream ........ CO-8
South Fork Caddo River—stream ........ AR-4
South Fork Cadet Creek—stream ........ MO-7
South Fork Calamus River—stream ........ NE-7
South Fork Calapooya Creek—stream ........ OR-9
South Fork Calaveras River—stream ........ CA-9
South Fork Calawah River—stream ........ WA-9
South Fork Calf Creek—stream ........ CA-9
South Fork California Creek—stream ........ NV-8
South Fork Calispell Creek—stream ........ WA-9
South Fork Camas Creek—stream ........ ID-8
South Fork Camas Creek—stream ........ OR-9
South Fork Camp—locale ........ CA-9
South Fork Camp—locale ........ MT-8
South Fork Camp—locale (4) ........ OR-9
South Fork Camp—locale ........ WA-9
South Fork Campbell Canyon—stream ........ ID-8
South Fork Campbell Creek—stream ........ AK-9
South Fork Camp Branch—stream ........ TN-4
South Fork Camp Creek ........ OR-9
South Fork Camp Creek—stream ........ CA-9
South Fork Camp Creek—stream ........ IL-6
South Fork Camp Creek—stream (2) ........ KY-4
South Fork Camp Creek—stream ........ OR-9
South Fork Camp Creek—stream ........ TX-5
South Fork Camp Creek Campground—park ........ OR-9
South Fork Campground ........ UT-8
South Fork Campground—locale (2) ........ CA-9
South Fork Camp Ground—locale ........ CA-9
South Fork Campground—locale ........ CO-8
South Fork Campground—locale ........ ID-8
South Fork Campground—locale ........ UT-8
South Fork Campground—locale ........ WA-9
South Fork Campground—locale ........ WY-8
South Fork Campground—park ........ AZ-5
South Fork Campground—park (3) ........ OR-9
South Fork Campgrounds—locale ........ CO-8
South Fork Camp Rader Run—stream ........ VA-3
South Fork Canada del Agua—stream ........ NM-5
South Fork Canadian River—stream ........ CO-8
South Fork Cane Creek—stream ........ NC-3
South Fork Cane Creek—stream (2) ........ TN-4
South Fork Caney Creek—stream ........ AL-4
South Fork Caney Creek—stream ........ KY-4
South Fork Canyon—valley (2) ........ AZ-5
South Fork Canyon—valley ........ CO-8
South Fork Canyon—valley ........ NM-5
South Fork Canyon Creek ........ ID-8
South Fork Canyon Creek—stream (3) ........ CA-9
South Fork Canyon Creek—stream (2) ........ ID-8
South Fork Canyon Creek—stream (3) ........ MT-8
South Fork Canyon Creek—stream (2) ........ NV-8
South Fork Canyon Creek—stream ........ OR-9
South Fork Canyon Creek—stream ........ WA-9
South Fork Canyon Creek—stream (2) ........ WY-8
South Fork Canyon Trail Two Hundred Fortythree—trail ........ AZ-5
South Fork Captain John Creek—stream ........ ID-8
South Fork Captina Creek—stream ........ OH-6
South Fork Cap Winn Creek—stream ........ NV-8
South Fork Carl Creek ........ MI-6
South Fork Carnero Creek—stream ........ CO-8
South Fork Carrol Creek—stream ........ MT-8
South Fork Carter Creek—stream ........ OR-9
South Fork Cartridge Creek—stream ........ CA-9
South Fork Cascade Canyon—valley ........ WY-8
South Fork Cascade Creek—stream ........ CO-8
South Fork Cascade River—stream ........ WA-9
South Fork Casper Creek—stream ........ WY-8
South Fork Cass House Creek ........ NV-8
South Fork Cass River—stream ........ MI-6
South Fork Castle Canyon—valley ........ AZ-5
South Fork Castle Creek ........ WA-9
South Fork Castle Creek—stream ........ CA-9
South Fork Castle Creek—stream ........ ID-8
South Fork Castle Creek—stream ........ SD-7
South Fork Castle Creek—stream ........ WA-9
South Fork Castle Creek—stream ........ WY-8
South Fork Catawba River—stream ........ NC-3
South Fork Catching Creek—stream ........ OR-9
South Fork Cat Creek—stream ........ CO-8
South Fork Cat Creek—stream ........ ID-8
South Fork Cat Creek—stream ........ NV-8
South Fork Catfish Creek—stream ........ IA-7
South Fork Cathedral Creek—stream ........ CA-9
South Fork Catherine Creek—stream ........ OR-9
South Fork Catoctin Creek—stream ........ VA-3
South Fork Catron Wash—stream ........ NM-5
South Fork Cattail Creek—stream ........ NC-3
South Fork Cattaraugus Creek ........ NY-2
South Fork Cavalry Creek—stream ........ OK-5
South Fork Cave Creek ........ AZ-5
South Fork Cave Creek—stream ........ AZ-5
South Fork Cave Creek—stream ........ NV-8
South Fork (CCD)—cens area ........ KY-4
South Fork Cedar Creek—stream ........ AL-4
South Fork Cedar Creek—stream ........ CO-8
South Fork Cedar Creek—stream ........ ID-8
South Fork Cedar Creek—stream (2) ........ MT-8
South Fork Cedar Creek—stream ........ NM-5
South Fork Cedar Creek—stream ........ ND-7
South Fork Cedar Creek—stream (2) ........ OR-9
South Fork Cedar Creek—stream ........ SD-7
South Fork Cedar Creek—stream (2) ........ TN-4
South Fork Cedar Creek—stream ........ TX-5
South Fork Cedar Creek—stream (2) ........ WA-9
South Fork Cedar Creek—stream ........ WY-8
South Fork Cedar River ........ IA-7
South Fork Cedar River—stream ........ WA-9
South Fork Cedar Wash—stream ........ NV-8
South Fork Cellar Springs Creek—stream ........ AZ-5
South Fork Cem—cemetery ........ MO-7
South Fork Cem—cemetery ........ NE-7
South Fork Cem—cemetery ........ OH-6
South Fork Cem—cemetery ........ OR-9
South Fork Cem—cemetery ........ PA-2
South Fork Cem—cemetery ........ VA-3
South Fork Cement Creek—stream ........ CO-8
South Fork Ch—church ........ AR-4
South Fork Ch—church (2) ........ IL-6
South Fork Ch—church ........ KS-7
South Fork Ch—church (7) ........ KY-4
Southfork Ch—church ........ KY-4
South Fork Ch—church ........ KY-4
South Fork Ch—church (2) ........ MO-7
South Fork Ch—church (4) ........ NC-3
South Fork Ch—church (2) ........ TN-4
South Fork Ch—church ........ VA-3
South Fork Chalk Creek—stream (2) ........ UT-8
South Fork Chalk Run—stream ........ VA-3
South Fork Chall Creek—stream ........ WY-8
South Fork Chamberlain Creek ........ ID-8
South Fork Chamberlain Creek—stream ........ ID-8
South Fork Chambers Creek—stream ........ TX-5
South Fork Chamokane Creek—stream ........ WA-9
South Fork Champion Creek—stream ........ ID-8
South Fork Champion Creek—stream ........ TX-5
South Fork Chaos Creek—stream ........ NV-8
South Fork Chariton River—stream ........ IA-7
South Fork Chatterdown Creek—stream ........ CA-9
South Fork Chatworth Creek—stream ........ CA-9
South Fork Cheaha Creek ........ AL-4
South Fork Chehalis River—stream ........ WA-9
South Fork Chena River—stream ........ AK-9
South Fork Cheney Creek—stream ........ UT-8
South Fork Cherokee Creek—stream ........ WY-8
South Fork Cherry Creek ........ MT-8
South Fork Cherry Creek—stream (3) ........ MT-8
South Fork Cherry Creek—stream ........ OR-9
South Fork Cherry Creek—stream ........ WY-8
South Fork Cherry River—stream ........ WV-2
South Fork Chesnimnus Creek—stream ........ OR-9
South Fork Chetco River—stream ........ OR-9
South Fork Chewelah Creek—stream ........ WA-9
South Fork Cheyenne River ........ SD-7
South Fork Cheyenne River ........ WY-8
South Fork Chiatovich Creek—stream ........ NV-8
South Fork Chickamin River—stream ........ AK-9
South Fork Chikamin Creek—stream ........ WA-9
South Fork Chilcoot Creek—stream ........ OR-9
South Fork Chilli Creek—stream ........ MS-4
South Fork Chimney Rock Canyon—valley ........ UT-8
South Fork China Creek—stream ........ CA-9
South Fork China Gulch—valley ........ CA-9
South Fork Chiwaukum Creek—stream ........ WA-9
South Fork Chloride Canyon—valley ........ UT-8
South Fork Chokecherry Creek—stream ........ NV-8
South Fork Christie Creek—stream ........ ID-8
South Fork Chugwater Creek ........ WY-8
South Fork Cienega Creek—stream ........ TX-5
South Fork Cimarroncito Creek—stream ........ NM-5
South Fork Citico Creek—stream ........ TN-4
South Fork Citico Trail—trail ........ TN-4
South Fork City Creek—stream ........ UT-8
South Fork Clackamas River—stream ........ OR-9
South Fork Claiborne Creek—stream ........ CA-9
South Fork Clam River—stream ........ WI-6
South Fork Clanton Creek—stream ........ IA-7
South Fork Clarence Creek—stream ........ MT-8
South Fork Clark Branch—stream ........ KY-4
South Fork Clark Canyon—valley ........ NM-5
South Fork Clark Creek—stream ........ OR-9
South Fork Clark Fork—stream ........ ID-8
South Fork Clarks Fork Creek—stream ........ OR-9
South Fork Clark Wash—stream ........ AZ-5
South Fork Claybank Creek—stream ........ MO-7
South Fork Clay Creek—stream ........ CO-8
South Fork Clear Creek ........ CO-8
South Fork Clear Creek ........ WA-9
South Fork Clear Creek ........ WY-8
South Fork Clear Creek—stream ........ AR-4
South Fork Clear Creek—stream (3) ........ CA-9
South Fork Clear Creek—stream ........ CO-8
South Fork Clear Creek—stream (2) ........ ID-8
South Fork Clear Creek—stream ........ MO-7
South Fork Clear Creek—stream ........ MT-8
South Fork Clear Creek—stream ........ OK-5
South Fork Clear Creek—stream ........ OR-9
South Fork Clear Creek—stream ........ TN-4
South Fork Clear Creek—stream ........ TX-5
South Fork Clear Creek—stream ........ WA-9
South Fork Clearwater River—stream ........ ID-8
South Fork Clearwater Station—locale ........ ID-8
South Fork Cliff Creek—stream ........ OR-9
South Fork Clinch River—stream ........ VA-3
South Fork Clugston Creek—stream ........ WA-9
South Fork Coal Bank Creek—stream ........ MT-8
South Fork Coal Creek—stream ........ IL-6
South Fork Coal Creek—stream ........ MT-8
South Fork Coal Draw—valley ........ WY-8
South Fork Coal Fork—stream ........ UT-8
South Fork Coal Wash—valley ........ UT-8
South Fork Cochino Bayou—stream ........ TX-5
South Fork Coeur d'Alene River—stream ........ ID-8
South Fork Coffee Creek—stream ........ CA-9
South Fork Coffeepot Creek—stream ........ OR-9
South Fork Cogswell Creek—stream ........ OR-9
South Fork Cold Creek—stream ........ CA-9
South Fork Cold Creek—stream ........ ID-8
South Fork Cold Creek—stream ........ MT-8
South Fork Cold Creek—stream ........ NV-8
South Fork Cold Spring Creek—stream ........ OR-9
South Fork Cold Springs Canyon—valley ........ OR-9
South Fork Coles Creek—stream ........ MS-4
South Fork Collier Creek—stream ........ KY-4
South Fork Collier Creek—stream ........ OR-9
South Fork Colockum Creek—stream ........ WA-9
South Fork Conejos River—stream ........ CO-8
South Fork Conemaugh River ........ PA-2
South Fork Conley Creek—stream ........ CA-9
South Fork Contrary Creek—stream ........ MO-7
South Fork Cook Creek—stream ........ OR-9
South Fork Cooks Creek—stream ........ MT-8
South Fork Coon Creek—stream ........ MN-6
South Fork Coon Creek—stream ........ TN-4
South Fork Coon Creek—stream ........ WY-8
South Fork Cooper Creek—stream ........ WY-8
South Fork Cooper Forks—stream ........ AZ-5
South Fork Coos River—stream ........ OR-9
South Fork Copeland Creek—stream ........ OR-9
South Fork Coppei Creek—stream ........ WA-9
South Fork Copper River—stream ........ WI-6
South Fork Coquille River—stream ........ OR-9
South Fork Corbus Creek—stream ........ ID-8
South Fork Core Creek ........ UT-8
South Fork Corn Creek ........ AZ-5
South Fork Corner Canyon—valley ........ UT-8
South Fork Corn Wash ........ AZ-5
South Fork Corral Canyon—valley ........ NM-5
South Fork Corral Creek—stream (2) ........ MT-8
South Fork Corral Creek—stream ........ OR-9
South Fork Corral Creek—stream ........ WY-8
South Fork Cortina Creek—stream ........ CA-9
South Fork Cosumnes River ........ CA-9
South Fork Cosumnes River—stream ........ CA-9
South Fork Cotaco Creek ........ AL-4
South Fork Cottaneva Creek—stream ........ CA-9
South Fork Cottoneva Creek ........ CA-9
South Fork Cottonwood Canyon—valley ........ NV-8
South Fork Cottonwood Canyon—valley ........ UT-8
South Fork Cottonwood Creek ........ CO-8
South Fork Cottonwood Creek ........ UT-8
South Fork Cottonwood Creek—stream (6) ........ CA-9
South Fork Cottonwood Creek—stream ........ CO-8
South Fork Cottonwood Creek—stream (3) ........ ID-8
South Fork Cottonwood Creek—stream (9) ........ MT-8
South Fork Cottonwood Creek—stream (4) ........ NV-8
South Fork Cottonwood Creek—stream (3) ........ OR-9
South Fork Cottonwood Creek—stream ........ UT-8
South Fork Cottonwood Creek—stream (3) ........ WY-8
South Fork Cottonwood Draw—valley ........ WY-8
South Fork Cottonwood River—stream ........ KS-7
South Fork Cottonwood Slough—gut ........ CA-9
South Fork Cougar Creek—stream ........ ID-8
South Fork Countryman Creek—stream ........ MT-8
South Fork Courtneys Creek—stream ........ MT-8
South Fork Cow Bayou ........ TX-5
South Fork Cow Creek ........ CA-9
South Fork Cow Creek ........ OR-9
South Fork Cow Creek—stream ........ ID-8
South Fork Cow Creek—stream (2) ........ MT-8
South Fork Cow Creek—stream ........ NV-8
South Fork Cow Creek—stream ........ OR-9
South Fork Cow Creek—stream ........ WA-9
South Fork Cowee Creek—stream ........ AK-9
South Fork Cowiche Creek—stream ........ WA-9
South Fork Cowikee Creek—stream ........ AL-4
South Fork Coxit Creek—stream ........ WA-9
South Fork Coyote Wash—stream ........ CA-9
South Fork Crab Creek—stream ........ WA-9
South Fork Crabtree Creek—stream ........ MD-2
South Fork Crabtree Creek—stream ........ OR-9
South Fork Craig River—stream ........ AK-9
South Fork Cranberry River—stream ........ WV-2
South Fork Crane Creek ........ ID-8
South Fork Crawford Creek—stream ........ IN-6
South Fork Crawley Creek—stream ........ WV-2
South Fork Crazy Woman Creek—stream . WY-8
South Fork Creek ........ AZ-5
South Fork Creek ........ CA-9
South Fork Creek ........ CO-8
South Fork Creek ........ KS-7
South Fork Creek ........ NV-8
South Fork Creek ........ ND-7
South Fork Creek ........ OR-9
South Fork Creek ........ PA-2
South Fork Creek ........ WA-9
South Fork Creek—stream ........ IL-6
South Fork Creek—stream ........ IN-6
South Fork Creek—stream ........ KY-4
South Fork Cripple Creek—stream ........ OR-9
South Fork Cripple Horse Creek—stream ........ MT-8
South Fork Cronin Creek—stream ........ OR-9
South Fork Crooked Creek—stream ........ AL-4
South Fork Crooked Creek—stream ........ CA-9
South Fork Crooked Creek—stream ........ MN-6
South Fork Crooked Creek—stream ........ MO-7
South Fork Crooked Creek—stream ........ NC-3
South Fork Crooked Creek—stream ........ OR-9
South Fork Crooked Creek—stream ........ SD-7
South Fork Crooked Creek—stream (2) ........ TN-4
South Fork Crooked Creek—stream (2) ........ WA-9
South Fork Crooked River—stream ........ OR-9
South Fork Cross Creek—stream ........ PA-2
South Fork Crow Creek ........ WY-8
South Fork Crow Creek—stream ........ MT-8
South Fork Crowders Creek—stream ........ NC-3
South Fork Crowders Creek—stream ........ SC-3
South Fork Crow River—stream ........ MN-6
South Fork Crystal Creek—stream ........ CO-8
South Fork Crystal River—stream ........ CO-8
South Fork Cub Creek—stream ........ ID-8
South Fork Cub Creek—stream ........ TN-4
South Fork Cub Creek—stream ........ UT-8
South Fork Cucharas River—stream ........ CO-8
South Fork Cuchillo Negro Creek—stream ........ NM-5
South Fork Culebra Creek ........ CO-8
South Fork Cumberland River—stream ........ KY-4
South Fork Cumberland River—stream ........ TN-4
South Fork Cuneo Creek—stream ........ CA-9
South Fork Cunningham Creek—stream ........ VA-3
South Fork Curley Creek—stream ........ WA-9
South Fork Currant Creek—stream ........ NV-8
South Fork Currant Creek—stream ........ UT-8
South Fork Currant Creek—stream ........ WA-9
South Fork Curreys Fork ........ KY-4
South Fork Currys Fork—stream ........ KY-4
South Fork Cut Bank Creek—stream ........ MT-8
South Fork Cut Creek ........ MT-8
South Fork Cypress Bayou—stream ........ AR-4
South Fork Dabbs Creek—stream ........ TN-4
South Fork Daggett Creek—stream ........ NV-8
South Fork Daisy Dean Creek—stream ........ MT-8
South Fork Dakota Creek—stream ........ WA-9
South Fork Dale Creek—stream ........ MT-8
South Fork Daly Creek ........ OR-9
South Fork Dam—dam ........ NM-5
South Fork Dam—dam ........ OR-9
South Fork Daniels Creek—stream ........ ID-8
South Fork Darby Creek—stream ........ KY-4
South Fork Darby Creek—stream ........ WY-8
South Fork Date Creek—stream ........ AZ-5
South Fork Davis Creek—stream ........ CA-9
South Fork Davis Gulch—valley ........ CO-8
South Fork Day Creek—stream ........ WA-9
South Fork Deadman Creek ........ WY-8
South Fork Deadman Creek—stream ........ AZ-5
South Fork Deadman Creek—stream (2) ........ MT-8
South Fork Deadman Creek—stream ........ WA-9
South Fork Deadman Gulch—valley ........ WA-9
South Fork Deadwood Creek—stream ........ CA-9
South Fork Dearborn River—stream ........ MT-8
South Fork Deardorff Creek—stream ........ OR-9
South Fork Deep Creek—stream ........ AK-9
South Fork Deep Creek—stream ........ CA-9
South Fork Deep Creek—stream ........ CO-8
South Fork Deep Creek—stream (2) ........ ID-8
South Fork Deep Creek—stream (4) ........ MT-8
South Fork Deep Creek—stream ........ NV-8
South Fork Deep Creek—stream ........ OR-9
South Fork Deep Creek—stream ........ TX-5
South Fork Deep Creek—stream ........ UT-8
South Fork Deep Creek—stream (2) ........ WA-9
South Fork Deer Creek ........ MT-8
South Fork Deer Creek ........ WY-8
South Fork Deer Creek—stream ........ AZ-5
South Fork Deer Creek—stream ........ CA-9
South Fork Deer Creek—stream (2) ........ CO-8
South Fork Deer Creek—stream (4) ........ ID-8
South Fork Deer Creek—stream ........ IL-6
South Fork Deer Creek—stream ........ IN-6
South Fork Deer Creek—stream (2) ........ MT-8
South Fork Deer Creek—stream ........ OK-5
South Fork Deer Creek—stream (3) ........ OR-9
South Fork Deer Creek—stream ........ TN-4
South Fork Deer Creek—stream (2) ........ UT-8
South Fork Deer Creek—stream ........ WY-8
South Fork Deering Creek—stream ........ NV-8
South Fork Deer Lake Canyon—valley ........ AZ-5
South Fork Deer River—stream ........ AL-4
South Fork DeGarmo Canyon—valley ........ OR-9
South Fork Dempsey Creek—stream ........ WY-8
South Fork Denny Creek ........ MT-8
South Fork Derby Creek—stream ........ CO-8
South Fork Desolation Creek—stream ........ OR-9
South Fork Devils Canyon—valley ........ CA-9
South Fork Devils Gulch—valley ........ CA-9
South Fork Diamond Gulch ........ UT-8
South Fork Dibble Creek—stream ........ CA-9
South Fork Dick Creek—stream ........ WY-8
South Fork Dickey Creek—stream ........ MT-8
South Fork Dicks Creek—stream ........ ID-8
South Fork Dickson Creek—stream ........ CO-8
South Fork Digger Creek—stream ........ CA-9
South Fork Dillinger Creek—stream ........ ID-8
South Fork Dirty Creek ........ OK-5
South Fork Dirty Creek—stream ........ OK-5
South Fork Dismal River—stream ........ NE-7
South Fork Ditch ........ IN-6
South Fork Ditch—canal ........ CA-9
South Fork Ditch—canal ........ IL-6
South Fork Ditch—canal ........ WY-8
South Fork Ditch Creek—stream ........ WY-8
South Fork Divide—ridge ........ WA-9
South Fork Divide Creek—stream (2) ........ MT-8
South Fork Dixie Creek—stream ........ OR-9
South Fork Doame River—stream ........ AK-9
South Fork Dobbins Creek ........ CA-9
South Fork Dodge Creek—stream ........ ID-8
South Fork Dodge Creek—stream ........ MT-8
South Fork Dodson Creek—stream ........ OH-6
South Fork Dog Slaughter Creek—stream ........ KY-4
South Fork Domingo Creek—stream ........ CA-9
South Fork Doolittle Creek—stream ........ MT-8
South Fork Dorsey Creek—stream ........ WY-8
South Fork Double Branch—stream ........ GA-3
South Fork Double Canyon—valley ........ CA-9
South Fork Double Creek—stream (2) ........ OK-5
South Fork Douglas Creek ........ MT-8
South Fork Douglas Creek—stream ........ MT-8
South Fork Drake Branch—stream ........ TN-4
South Fork Driftwood Creek—stream ........ KS-7
South Fork Driftwood Creek—stream ........ NE-7
South Fork Dry Blood Creek—stream ........ MT-8
South Fork Dry Cottonwood Creek—stream ........ MT-8
South Fork Dry Creek ........ MT-8
South Fork Dry Creek ........ TX-5
South Fork Dry Creek ........ WY-8
South Fork Dry Creek—stream ........ AL-4
South Fork Dry Creek—stream ........ AR-4
South Fork Dry Creek—stream (4) ........ CA-9
South Fork Dry Creek—stream ........ ID-8
South Fork Dry Creek—stream ........ MO-7
South Fork Dry Creek—stream (4) ........ MT-8
South Fork Dry Creek—stream ........ NE-7
South Fork Dry Creek—stream ........ OK-5
South Fork Dry Creek—stream (2) ........ UT-8
South Fork Dry Creek—stream (2) ........ WA-9
South Fork Dry Creek—stream (2) ........ WY-8
South Fork Dryden Creek—stream ........ KY-4
South Fork Dry Fork—stream ........ UT-8
South Fork Dry Fork Cheyenne River—stream (2) ........ WY-8
South Fork Dry Fork Marias River—stream ........ MT-8
South Fork Dry Gulch—valley ........ MT-8
South Fork Dry Gulch Canal—canal ........ UT-8
South Fork Dry Park Creek—stream ........ MT-8
South Fork Dry Run—stream ........ VA-3
South Fork Dry Willow Creek—stream ........ CO-8
South Fork Duchesne River ........ UT-8
South Fork Duck Creek—stream ........ ID-8
South Fork Duck Creek—stream ........ KS-7
South Fork Duck Creek—stream (2) ........ MT-8
South Fork Duck Creek—stream ........ WY-8
South Fork Dump Creek—stream ........ ID-8
South Fork Duncan Creek—stream ........ CA-9
South Fork Duncan Creek—stream ........ KY-4
South Fork Duncan Creek—stream ........ SC-3
South Fork Duncans Creek ........ SC-3
South Fork Dunkard Fork—stream ........ PA-2
South Fork Dunkard Fork Wheeling Creek ........ PA-2
South Fork Dunkard Wheeling Creek ........ PA-2
South Fork Dupuyer Creek—stream ........ MT-8
South Fork Durham Creek—stream ........ OR-9
South Fork Durse Canyon—valley ........ UT-8
South Fork Dutch John Creek—stream ........ NV-8
South Fork Eagle Creek—stream ........ NM-5
South Fork Eagle Creek—stream ........ OH-6
South Fork Eagle Creek—stream ........ OR-9
South Fork Eagle Creek—stream ........ TN-4
South Fork Eagle Creek—stream ........ WY-8
South Fork Eagle River—stream ........ AK-9
South Fork Eagle River—stream ........ CO-8
South Fork Earley Creek—stream ........ WY-8
South Fork East Creek—stream ........ CA-9
South Fork East Creek—stream ........ VT-1
South Fork East Fork King Hill Creek—stream ........ ID-8
South Fork East Fork Mill Creek—stream ........ NV-8
South Fork East Fork New River—stream ........ CA-9
South Fork East Fork Salmon River—stream ........ ID-8
South Fork East Government Creek—stream ........ UT-8
South Fork Eastman Gulch—valley ........ CA-9
South Fork Eau Claire River—stream ........ WI-6
South Fork Eccles Canyon—valley ........ UT-8
South Fork Eddington Creek—stream ........ OR-9
South Fork Edisto River—stream ........ SC-3
South Fork Edwards Creek—stream ........ MT-8
South Fork Eel River—stream ........ CA-9
South Fork Eel River—stream ........ IN-6
South Fork Eightmile Canyon—valley ........ ID-8
South Fork Eight Mile Creek ........ MT-8
South Fork Eightmile Creek—stream (2) ........ MT-8
South Fork Eightmile Creek—stream ........ NV-8
South Fork Elder Creek—stream ........ CA-9
South Fork Elementary School ........ NC-3
South Fork Elk Creek—stream ........ CA-9
South Fork Elk Creek—stream ........ ID-8
South Fork Elk Creek—stream (3) ........ MT-8
South Fork Elk Creek—stream ........ OR-9
South Fork Elk Creek—stream ........ WI-6
South Fork Elk Creek—stream (2) ........ WY-8
South Fork Elkhead Creek ........ CO-8
South Fork Elkhorn Creek—stream ........ CO-8
South Fork Elkhorn River*—stream ........ NE-7
South Fork Elkhorn River—stream (2) ........ NE-7
South Fork Elkhorn River*—stream ........ NE-7
South Fork Elkhorn River—stream (2) ........ NE-7
South Fork Elk River—stream ........ CA-9
South Fork Elk River—stream ........ CO-8
South Fork Elk River—stream ........ OR-9
South Fork Ellejoy Creek—stream ........ TN-4
South Fork Ellison Branch—stream ........ NC-3
South Fork Elm Creek—stream ........ MN-6
South Fork Elm Creek—stream ........ OK-5
South Fork Elmore Creek—stream ........ TN-4
South Fork Emerson Creek—stream ........ CA-9
South Fork Emigrant Canyon—valley ........ NV-8
South Fork English Creek—stream ........ CA-9
South Fork English River ........ IA-7
South Fork Erskine Creek—stream ........ CA-9
South Fork Eureka Creek—stream ........ WA-9
South Fork Evans Creek—stream ........ ID-8
South Fork Everson Creek—stream ........ MT-8
South Fork Fairfield Creek—stream ........ NE-7
South Fork Fall Creek—stream ........ CO-8
South Fork Fall Creek—stream ........ ID-8
South Fork Fall Creek—stream ........ KS-7
South Fork Fall Creek—stream ........ WY-8
South Fork Falling River—stream ........ VA-3
South Fork Falls—falls ........ CO-8
South Fork Falls—falls ........ WY-8
South Fork Falls Creek—stream ........ ID-8
South Fork Falls Creek—stream ........ WA-9
South Fork Fawn Creek—stream ........ ID-8
South Fork Feather River—stream ........ CA-9
South Fork Ferguson Creek—stream ........ OR-9
South Fork Fiddler Gulch—stream ........ OR-9
South Fork Fifteenmile Creek—stream ........ WY-8
South Fork Fish Creek ........ MT-8
South Fork Fish Creek ........ UT-8
South Fork Fish Creek ........ WY-8
South Fork Fish Creek—stream ........ MT-8
South Fork Fish Creek—stream ........ UT-8
South Fork Fish Creek—stream ........ WY-8
South Fork Fisherman Creek—stream ........ WY-8
South Fork Fishing and Hunting Club Hist Dist—hist pl ........ PA-2
South Fork Fishing Creek ........ SC-3
South Fork Fishing Creek—stream ........ SC-3
South Fork Fishing Creek—stream ........ WV-2
South Fork Fitsum Creek—stream ........ ID-8
South Fork Fitzhugh Creek—stream ........ CA-9
South Fork Fitzhugh Creek—stream ........ NV-8

South Fork Fivemile Creek—*stream* ... ID-8
South Fork Fivemile Creek—*stream* (2) ... MT-8
South Fork Fivemile Creek—*stream* ... OR-9
South Fork Fivemile Creek—*stream* ... WY-8
South Fork Flagler Creek—*stream* ... OR-9
South Fork Flambeau River—*stream* ... WI-6
*South Fork Flat Creek* ... AL-4
South Fork Flat Creek—*stream* ... NV-8
South Fork Flat Creek—*stream* ... NC-3
South Fork Flat Creek—*stream* ... TN-4
South Fork Flat Creek—*stream* ... WA-9
South Fork Flathead Creek—*stream* ... MT-8
South Fork Flathead River—*stream* ... MT-8
South Fork Flats—*flat* ... AK-9
South Fork Flatwillow Creek—*stream* ... MT-8
South Fork Floras Creek—*stream* ... OR-9
South Fork Flower Creek—*stream* ... MT-8
South Fork Flume Creek—*stream* ... WA-9
South Fork Folger Creek—*stream* ... AK-9
South Fork Fontenelle Creek—*stream* ... WY-8
South Fork Forest Camp—*locale* ... AZ-5
South Fork Forked Deer River—*stream* ... TN-4
South Fork Forman Ravine—*valley* ... CA-9
South Fork Fortification Creek—*stream* ... CO-8
South Fork Fortune Creek—*stream* ... WA-9
South Fork Fortymile River—*stream* ... AK-9
South Fork Foster Creek—*stream* ... MT-8
South Fork Foundation Creek—*stream* ... WA-9
South Fork Fountain Creek—*stream* ... TN-4
South Fork Fourbit Creek—*stream* ... OR-9
South Fork Fourmile Creek—*stream* ... ID-8
South Fork Fourmile Creek—*stream* ... MT-8
South Fork Fourmile Creek—*stream* ... OR-9
South Fork Fourmile Creek—*stream* ... WY-8
*South Fork Fourteen Mile Creek* ... MT-8
South Fork Fowkes Canyon
Creek—*stream* ... WY-8
*South Fork Fox Creek* ... MT-8
South Fork Fox Creek—*stream* ... MT-8
South Fork Francis Canyon—*valley* ... UT-8
South Fork Freeman Creek—*stream* ... MT-8
South Fork French Cabin Creek—*stream* ... WA-9
*South Fork French Creek* ... ID-8
*South Fork French Creek* ... WA-9
*South Fork French Creek* ... WY-8
South Fork French Creek—*stream* ... CO-8
South Fork French Creek—*stream* (2) ... SD-7
South Fork Frenchie Draw—*valley* ... WY-8
South Fork Frenchman Creek—*stream* ... CO-8
*South Fork Frenchman River* ... CO-8
South Fork Freshwater Creek—*stream* ... CA-9
South Fork Fresno River—*stream* ... CA-9
South Fork Fritz Creek—*stream* ... ID-8
South Fork Frog Creek—*stream* ... NV-8
South Fork Fryingpan River—*stream* ... CO-8
South Fork Fuller Creek—*stream* ... CA-9
South Fork Fulton Creek—*stream* ... WA-9
South Fork Furnace Creek—*stream* ... TN-4
*South Fork Gabori Creek* ... MO-7
South Fork Gage Creek—*stream* ... TX-5
South Fork Gale Creek—*stream* ... WA-9
South Fork Gales Creek—*stream* ... OR-9
South Fork Galice Creek—*stream* ... OR-9
South Fork Gallinas Creek—*stream* ... CA-9
South Fork Game Creek—*stream* ... WY-8
South Fork Garcia River—*stream* ... CA-9
South Fork Garrard Creek—*stream* ... WA-9
South Fork Gate Creek—*stream* (2) ... OR-9
*South Fork Gato Creek* ... CO-8
South Fork Gauley River—*stream* ... WV-2
South Fork Gees Creek—*stream* ... MO-7
South Fork Geise Creek—*stream* ... TN-4
South Fork George Creek—*stream* ... UT-8
South Fork George River—*stream* ... AK-9
South Fork Gettings Creek—*stream* ... OR-9
*South Fork Gibson Jack Creek* ... ID-8
South Fork Gilbert Creek—*stream* ... MT-8
South Fork Gilbert Run—*stream* ... OH-6
South Fork Gilmore Creek—*stream* ... ID-8
South Fork Gimlet Creek—*stream* ... OR-9
South Fork Glenn Creek—*stream* ... MT-8
South Fork Goat Creek—*stream* ... ID-8
South Fork Goble Creek—*stream* ... OR-9
South Fork Goetz Creek—*stream* ... WY-8
South Fork Gold Creek—*stream* ... ID-8
South Fork Gold Creek—*stream* ... WA-9
South Fork Gold Fork River—*stream* ... ID-8
*South Fork Gold River* ... ID-8
South Fork Goldsborough Creek—*stream* ... WA-9
South Fork Goodale Coulee—*valley* ... MT-8
South Fork Good Luck Creek—*stream* ... MT-8
South Fork Goodnews River—*stream* ... AK-9
South Fork Goodpaster River—*stream* ... AK-9
South Fork Goods Creek—*stream* ... CA-9
South Fork Goodwin Canyon—*valley* ... AZ-5
South Fork Goose Creek—*stream* ... VA-3
South Fork Gopher Canyon—*valley* ... CA-9
South Fork Gordon Creek—*stream* ... CA-9
South Fork Gordon Creek—*stream* ... OH-6
South Fork Gordon Creek—*stream* ... OR-9
South Fork Gordon Creek—*stream* ... UT-8
South Fork Grace Creek—*stream* ... CO-8
*South Fork Grand River* ... SD-7
South Fork Grand River—*stream* ... SD-7
South Fork Grange—*locale* ... WA-9
South Fork Granite Creek—*stream* ... ID-8
South Fork Granite Creek—*stream* ... NV-8
South Fork Granite Creek—*stream* ... WA-9
South Fork Granite Creek—*stream* ... WY-8
South Fork Grapevine Creek—*stream* ... MT-8
South Fork Grapevine Creek—*stream* (2) ... TX-5
South Fork Grassy Creek—*stream* ... KY-4
South Fork Grays Canyon—*valley* ... WA-9
*South Fork Grays Creek* ... ID-8
South Fork Grays Creek—*stream* ... ID-8
South Fork Grays River—*stream* ... WA-9
South Fork Greasewood Creek—*stream* ... MT-8
South Fork Great Miami River—*stream* ... OH-6
South Fork Greenhorn Creek—*stream* ... CA-9
South Fork Greenhorn Creek—*stream* ... MT-8
*South Fork Greenleaf Creek* ... CO-8
*South Fork Green Mountain Canon Creek* ... NV-8
South Fork Green Mountain
Creek—*stream* ... NV-8
South Fork Green River—*stream* (2) ... KY-4
South Fork Green River—*stream* ... ND-7
South Fork Green Run—*stream* ... MD-2
South Fork Greens Run—*stream* ... WV-2
South Fork Green Timber Creek—*stream* ... OR-9
South Fork Greenwich Creek—*stream* ... UT-8

South Fork Greenwood Creek—*stream* ... CA-9
South Fork Grindstone Creek—*stream* ... MO-7
South Fork Griswold Creek—*stream* ... CA-9
South Fork Groundhog Creek—*stream* ... OR-9
South Fork Groundhouse River—*stream* ... MN-6
South Fork Grouse Creek—*stream* (3) ... ID-8
South Fork Grove—*woods* ... CA-9
South Fork Grove Creek—*stream* (2) ... MT-8
South Fork Guadalupe River—*stream* ... TX-5
South Fork Gualala River—*stream* ... CA-9
South Fork Guard Station—*locale* ... CA-9
South Fork Guard Station—*locale* ... CO-8
South Fork Guard Station—*locale* ... OR-9
South Fork Guinns Creek—*stream* ... MO-7
South Fork Gulch—*valley* ... ID-8
South Fork Gunpowder Creek—*stream* ... KY-4
South Fork Guyre Creek—*stream* ... CA-9
South Fork Guzzlers Gulch—*valley* ... KS-7
South Fork Gypsum Creek—*stream* ... WY-8
South Fork Hackberry Creek—*stream* (2) ... TX-5
South Fork Halfway Coulee—*valley* ... MT-8
South Fork Hall Creek—*stream* ... CA-9
South Fork Hall Creek—*stream* ... WY-8
South Fork Halls Creek—*stream* ... WI-6
South Fork Hams Fork—*stream* ... WY-8
South Fork Hanaupah Canyon—*valley* ... CA-9
South Fork Hancock Branch—*stream* ... NH-1
South Fork Hand Creek—*stream* ... MT-8
South Fork Hanks Creek—*stream* ... NV-8
South Fork Hanson Creek—*stream* ... NV-8
South Fork Happy Canyon—*valley* ... UT-8
South Fork Hardesty Creek—*stream* ... UT-8
South Fork Hardware River—*stream* ... VA-3
South Fork Hardy Creek—*stream* ... CA-9
South Fork Hare Creek—*stream* ... CA-9
South Fork Harmon Creek—*stream* ... TN-4
South Fork Harper Draw—*valley* ... WY-8
South Fork Harris Creek—*stream* ... TN-4
South Fork Harrison Creek—*stream* ... AK-9
South Fork Harrods Creek—*stream* ... KY-4
South Fork Harvey Creek—*stream* ... WA-9
South Fork Haskins Creek—*stream* ... CA-9
South Fork Hawk Branch—*stream* ... NC-3
South Fork Hawkins Creek—*stream* ... ID-8
South Fork Hawkins Creek—*stream* ... MT-8
South Fork Hay Coulee—*valley* ... MT-8
South Fork Hay Creek—*stream* ... WY-8
South Fork Hayes Creek—*stream* ... MT-8
South Fork Hay Hollow—*valley* ... NM-5
South Fork Hay Hollow—*valley* ... TX-5
South Fork Hay River—*stream* ... WI-6
South Fork Hayworth Creek—*stream* ... MI-6
South Fork Hazel Creek—*stream* ... CA-9
South Fork Heiners Creek—*stream* ... UT-8
*South Fork Helen Creek* ... MT-8
South Fork Hellhole Canyon—*valley* ... CA-9
South Fork Hell Roaring Creek—*stream* ... MT-8
South Fork Hells Gulch—*valley* ... ID-8
South Fork Hemler Creek—*stream* ... MT-8
South Fork Hemlock Creek—*stream* ... WI-6
South Fork Hemmert Canyon—*valley* ... WY-8
South Fork Hendrys Creek—*stream* ... NV-8
South Fork Hensley Creek—*stream* ... CA-9
South Fork Herder Creek—*stream* ... NV-8
South Fork Hermosa Creek—*stream* ... CO-8
South Fork Hess Creek—*stream* ... AK-9
*South Fork Hickahala Creek* ... MS-4
South Fork Hickory Creek—*stream* ... VA-3
South Fork High Creek—*stream* ... UT-8
South Fork Highline Ditch—*canal* ... CO-8
South Fork Hilgard Creek—*stream* ... MT-8
South Fork Hill—*summit* ... MT-8
South Fork Hill—*summit* ... OR-9
South Fork Hill Creek—*stream* ... OR-9
South Fork Hill Creek—*stream* ... TX-5
South Fork Hill Creek—*stream* ... WY-8
South Fork Hinch Creek—*stream* ... MT-8
South Fork Hinkle Creek—*stream* ... OR-9
South Fork Hoback River—*stream* ... WY-8
South Fork Hockanum River—*stream* ... CT-1
South Fork Hog Canyon—*valley* ... UT-8
South Fork Hog Creek—*stream* ... TX-5
South Fork Hog Park Creek—*stream* ... CO-8
South Fork Hog Park Creek—*stream* ... WY-8
South Fork Hoholitna River—*stream* ... AK-9
South Fork Hoh River—*stream* ... WA-9
South Fork Hollow—*valley* ... MO-7
South Fork Holly Creek—*stream* ... OK-5
South Fork Holston River—*stream* ... TN-4
South Fork Holston River—*stream* ... VA-3
South Fork Holy Terror Creek—*stream* ... ID-8
South Fork Homochitto River—*stream* ... MS-4
*South Fork Honey Creek* ... OR-9
South Fork Honey Locust Creek—*stream* ... KY-4
South Fork Hooper Canyon—*valley* ... UT-8
South Fork Hoopers Creek—*stream* ... NC-3
South Fork Hoover Creek—*stream* ... MT-8
South Fork Hoppers Creek—*stream* ... NC-3
South Fork Horse Canyon—*valley* ... NV-8
South Fork Horse Canyon—*valley* (2) ... UT-8
South Fork Horse Creek—*stream* ... IL-6
South Fork Horse Creek—*stream* (4) ... MT-8
South Fork Horse Creek—*stream* ... NM-5
South Fork Horse Creek—*stream* ... NC-3
South Fork Horse Creek—*stream* ... TX-5
South Fork Horse Creek—*stream* ... WY-8
South Fork Horsefly Creek—*stream* ... CO-8
South Fork Horseshoe Creek—*stream* ... ID-8
South Fork Horsley Creek—*stream* ... VA-3
South Fork Hot Springs Creek—*stream* ... MT-8
South Fork Howard Creek—*stream* ... OR-9
South Fork Howell Creek—*stream* ... MO-7
South Fork HS—*school* ... CA-9
South Fork HS—*school* ... FL-3
South Fork Huckleberry Creek—*stream* ... WA-9
South Fork Huerfano River—*stream* ... CO-8
South Fork Hughes River—*stream* ... WV-2
South Fork Hull Creek—*stream* ... ID-8
South Fork Humboldt River—*stream* ... NV-8
South Fork Humbug Creek—*stream* ... CA-9
South Fork Humbug Creek—*stream* ... MT-8
South Fork Hunt Creek—*stream* ... ID-8
South Fork Hunt Creek—*stream* ... WA-9
*South Fork Hunter Creek* ... CO-8
South Fork Hunter Creek—*stream* ... WA-9
*South Fork Hunters Creek* ... WA-9
South Fork Hu-Pwi Wash—*stream* ... NV-8
South Fork Hurricane Creek—*stream* ... TN-4
South Fork Huslia River—*stream* ... AK-9
South Fork Hyde Creek—*stream* ... MT-8

South Fork Imnaha River—*stream* ... OR-9
South Fork Indian Canyon—*valley* ... UT-8
South Fork Indian Coulee—*valley* ... MT-8
South Fork Indian Creek—*stream* (2) ... CA-9
South Fork Indian Creek—*stream* (2) ... ID-8
South Fork Indian Creek—*stream* ... IL-6
South Fork Indian Creek—*stream* (2) ... KY-4
South Fork Indian Creek—*stream* (2) ... MT-8
South Fork Indian Creek—*stream* ... NV-8
South Fork Indian Creek—*stream* ... OR-9
South Fork Indian Creek—*stream* (2) ... TN-4
South Fork Indian Creek—*stream* ... UT-8
South Fork Indian Creek—*stream* (2) ... WY-8
South Fork Indian River—*stream* ... AK-9
South Fork Indian Run—*stream* ... OH-6
South Fork Indian Run—*stream* ... VA-3
South Fork Indian Run—*stream* ... WV-2
South Fork Indian Valley—*valley* ... CA-9
South Fork Ind Res—*reserve* ... NV-8
South Fork Inman Creek—*stream* ... ID-8
South Fork Iowa River—*stream* ... IA-7
South Fork Iron Creek—*stream* ... ID-8
South Fork Iron Creek—*stream* ... OR-9
South Fork Iron Fork—*stream* ... CA-9
South Fork Irwin Canyon—*valley* ... NV-8
South Fork Isle du Bois Creek—*stream* ... MO-7
South Fork Jackass Creek—*stream* ... OR-9
South Fork Jack Canyon—*valley* ... CO-8
South Fork Jack Creek—*stream* ... MT-8
South Fork Jack Fork Creek—*stream* ... OK-5
*South Fork Jacks Fork* ... MO-7
*South Fork Jackson Creek* ... OR-9
South Fork Jackson Creek—*stream* ... CA-9
South Fork Jackson Creek—*stream* ... MT-8
South Fork Jackson Creek—*stream* ... OR-9
South Fork Jacks River—*stream* ... GA-3
South Fork Jacobsen Gulch—*valley* ... OR-9
South Fork Jakes Creek—*stream* ... NV-8
South Fork James Creek—*stream* ... AK-9
South Fork James Creek—*stream* ... MO-7
South Fork Janes Creek—*stream* ... AR-4
South Fork Janes Creek—*stream* ... MO-7
South Fork Jaycox Creek—*stream* ... NY-2
South Fork Jay Creek—*stream* ... WY-8
South Fork Jebo Canyon—*valley* ... UT-8
South Fork Jennings Creek—*stream* ... TN-4
South Fork Jenny Branch—*stream* ... LA-4
*South Fork Jensen Wash* ... UT-8
South Fork Jensen Wash—*valley* ... UT-8
South Fork Jim Creek—*stream* ... CO-8
South Fork Jim Creek—*stream* ... OR-9
South Fork Jim Creek—*stream* ... WA-9
South Fork Jim Ned Creek—*stream* ... TX-5
South Fork Jocko River—*stream* ... MT-8
South Fork Joe Creek—*stream* ... ID-8
South Fork Joe Ney Slough—*stream* ... OR-9
South Fork John Creek—*stream* ... WA-9
South Fork John Day Creek—*stream* ... ID-8
South Fork John Day River—*stream* ... OR-9
*South Fork Johns Creek* ... WA-9
South Fork Johnson Canyon—*valley* ... CA-9
South Fork Johnson Creek—*stream* ... NE-7
South Fork Johnson Creek—*stream* (2) ... UT-8
South Fork Johns River—*stream* ... WA-9
South Fork Jonca Creek—*stream* ... MO-7
South Fork Jones Creek—*stream* ... AK-9
South Fork Jones Creek—*stream* ... MT-8
South Fork Jones Creek—*stream* ... NC-3
South Fork Jordan Creek—*stream* ... OR-9
*South Fork Jordan River* ... VA-3
*South Fork Jordon River* ... VA-3
South Fork Juan Creek—*stream* ... CA-9
South Fork Judith River—*stream* ... MT-8
South Fork Jump River—*stream* ... WI-6
**South Fork Junction**—*pop pl* ... WV-2
South Fork Junction Creek—*stream* ... UT-8
South Fork Juniper Canyon—*valley* ... OR-9
South Fork Juniper Creek—*stream* ... CA-9
South Fork Kalamazoo Creek—*stream* ... NV-8
South Fork Kamishak River—*stream* ... AK-9
South Fork Kanaka Creek—*stream* ... CA-9
South Fork Kane Canyon—*valley* ... UT-8
South Fork Kaskaskia River—*stream* ... IL-6
South Fork Kate Creek—*stream* ... MT-8
South Fork Kaukonahua Stream—*stream* ... HI-9
South Fork Kaunakakai Gulch—*valley* ... HI-9
*South Fork Kaweah River* ... CA-9
South Fork Kaweah River—*stream* ... CA-9
South Fork Kays Creek—*stream* ... UT-8
South Fork Keating Creek—*stream* ... AZ-5
South Fork Keeler Creek—*stream* ... MT-8
South Fork Keene Creek—*stream* ... OR-9
South Fork Kellerman Gulch—*valley* ... WY-8
South Fork Kelly Creek—*stream* ... ID-8
South Fork Kelsey Creek—*stream* ... CA-9
South Fork Kennally Creek—*stream* ... ID-8
*South Fork Kennedy Creek* ... MT-8
South Fork Kent Creek—*stream* ... IL-6
South Fork Kentucky River—*stream* ... KY-4
South Fork Kern River—*stream* ... CA-9
South Fork Ketron Branch—*stream* ... VA-3
South Fork Kilchis River—*stream* ... OR-9
South Fork Kimta Creek—*stream* ... WA-9
South Fork King Creek—*stream* ... OR-9
South Fork King Creek—*stream* ... WY-8
South Fork Kings Creek—*stream* ... SC-3
South Fork Kings Creek—*stream* ... WA-9
South Fork Kings River—*stream* (2) ... CA-9
South Fork Kinnickinnic River—*stream* ... WI-6
South Fork Kinnikinnick Creek—*stream* ... OH-6
*South Fork Kirby Creek* ... WY-8
South Fork Kitchen Creek—*stream* ... ID-8
South Fork Kittikaski Branch—*stream* ... AL-4
South Fork Kiutuestia Creek—*stream* ... GA-3
South Fork Klaskanine River—*stream* ... OR-9
South Fork Koger Creek—*stream* ... KY-4
South Fork Koyukuk River—*stream* ... AK-9
South Fork Kuskokwim River—*stream* ... AK-9
South Fork Kusshi Creek—*stream* ... WA-9
South Fork Kuyukutuk River—*stream* ... AK-9
South Fork Kuzitrin River—*stream* ... AK-9
South Fork Kyle Canyon—*stream* ... ID-8
South Fork La Bonte Creek—*stream* ... WY-8
South Fork La Brea Creek—*stream* ... CA-9
*South Fork Lac Qui Parle River* ... MN-6
South Fork Lacy Fork—*stream* ... TX-5
*South Fork Ladder Creek* ... KS-7
South Fork Ladue River—*stream* ... AK-9
South Fork La Garde Creek—*stream* ... CO-8
*South Fork Laird Creek* ... MT-8

South Fork Lake—*lake* ... AK-9
South Fork Lake—*lake* ... ID-8
South Fork Lake—*lake* ... MN-6
South Fork Lake—*lake* ... MT-8
South Fork Lake—*lake* ... WY-8
South Fork Lake Canyon—*valley* ... UT-8
*South Fork Lake Creek* ... OR-9
South Fork Lake Creek—*stream* ... CO-8
South Fork Lake Creek—*stream* ... KS-7
South Fork Lake Creek—*stream* ... OR-9
South Fork Lake Creek—*stream* ... WY-8
South Fork Lake Fork—*stream* ... ID-8
South Fork Lake Fork—*stream* ... IL-6
South Fork Lakes—*lake* (2) ... CA-9
South Fork Lakes—*lake* (2) ... MT-8
South Fork Lakes—*lake* ... WY-8
South Fork Lame Deer Creek—*stream* ... MT-8
South Fork Lame Johnny Creek—*stream* ... SD-7
South Fork Las Cruces Arroyo—*stream* ... NM-5
South Fork Lassen Creek—*stream* ... WY-8
South Fork Laughery Creek—*stream* ... IN-6
*South Fork Lauramie Creek* ... IN-6
South Fork Laurel Creek—*stream* ... NC-3
South Fork Laurel Run—*stream* ... OH-6
South Fork Lava Creek—*stream* ... ID-8
South Fork Lawrence Creek—*stream* ... KY-4
South Fork Lawrence Creek—*stream* ... OR-9
South Fork Lawson Creek—*stream* ... ID-8
South Fork Lawson Creek—*stream* ... OR-9
South Fork Lay Creek—*stream* ... MT-8
South Fork Leaf Rock Creek—*stream* ... MT-8
South Fork Leary Creek—*stream* ... CA-9
South Fork Leatherwood Creek—*stream* ... IN-6
South Fork Lee Creek—*stream* ... MT-8
South Fork Lee Creek—*stream* ... WV-2
South Fork Leeds Creek—*stream* ... WY-8
South Fork Lees Creek—*stream* ... OH-6
South Fork Left Hand Creek—*stream* ... WY-8
*South Fork Leigh Creek* ... ID-8
South Fork Lemiti Creek—*stream* ... OR-9
South Fork Lemoigne Canyon—*valley* ... CA-9
South Fork Lemonweir River—*stream* ... WI-6
South Fork Lena Creek—*stream* ... MT-8
South Fork Leon Creek—*stream* ... NM-5
South Fork Leon River—*stream* ... TX-5
South Fork Lewis And Clark
River—*stream* ... OR-9
South Fork Lewis Creek—*stream* ... IN-6
*South Fork Lewis River* ... WA-9
South Fork Lexington Creek—*stream* ... NV-8
South Fork Libby Creek—*stream* ... WA-9
South Fork Lick Creek—*stream* ... IL-6
South Fork Lick Creek—*stream* ... MT-8
South Fork Lick Creek—*stream* ... TN-4
South Fork Lick Creek Branch—*stream* ... KY-4
South Fork Licking River—*stream* ... KY-4
South Fork Licking River—*stream* ... OH-6
South Fork Lightner Creek—*stream* ... CO-8
*South Fork Lightning Creek* ... ID-8
*South Fork Lightning Creek* ... WA-9
South Fork Lightning Creek—*stream* ... OR-9
South Fork Limber Jim Creek—*stream* ... OR-9
*South Fork Lime Creek* ... MI-6
South Fork Lime Creek—*stream* ... ID-8
South Fork Limekiln Creek—*stream* ... UT-8
South Fork Lincoln Creek—*stream* ... WA-9
South Fork Lindsay Creek—*stream* ... NV-8
South Fork Line Creek—*stream* ... UT-8
South Fork Linganore Creek—*stream* ... MD-2
South Fork Linn Creek—*stream* ... MO-7
South Fork Lion Creek—*stream* ... ID-8
South Fork Lion Creek—*stream* ... MT-8
South Fork Lisk Creek—*stream* ... MT-8
South Fork Little Badger Creek—*stream* ... MT-8
South Fork Little Barren Creek—*stream* ... MO-7
South Fork Little Barren River—*stream* ... KY-4
South Fork Little Bear Creek—*stream* ... WY-8
South Fork Little Bear River—*stream* ... UT-8
*South Fork Little Beaver Creek* ... MT-8
South Fork Little Belt Creek—*stream* ... MT-8
South Fork Little Boulder Creek—*stream* ... WA-9
South Fork Little Butte Creek—*stream* ... OR-9
South Fork Little Cacapon River—*stream* ... WV-2
*South Fork little Calispell Creek* ... WA-9
South Fork Little Canyon Creek—*stream* ... WY-8
South Fork Little Chestnut Creek—*stream* ... VA-3
South Fork Little Colorado River—*stream* ... AZ-5
South Fork Little Conemaugh
River—*stream* ... PA-2
South Fork Little Copper Creek—*stream* ... ID-8
South Fork Little Coyote Creek—*stream* ... NM-5
South Fork Little Deep Creek—*stream* ... WA-9
South Fork Little Difficult Run—*stream* ... VA-3
*South Fork Little Elk River* ... MN-6
South Fork Little Falls Creek—*stream* ... WA-9
South Fork Little Green Creek—*stream* ... TX-5
South Fork Little Greys River—*stream* ... WY-8
South Fork Little Houston Creek—*stream* ... WY-8
South Fork Little Humboldt
River—*stream* ... NV-8
South Fork Little Hurricane
Creek—*stream* ... AR-4
South Fork Little Joe Creek—*stream* ... MT-8
South Fork Little Laramie River—*stream* ... WY-8
South Fork Little Lick Creek—*stream* ... CA-9
South Fork Little Manatee River—*stream* ... FL-3
*South Fork Little Mazarn Creek* ... AR-4
South Fork Little Medicine Bow
River—*stream* ... WY-8
*South Fork Little Meramac River* ... MO-7
South Fork Little Mill Creek—*stream* ... CA-9
South Fork Little Mud Creek—*stream* ... GA-3
South Fork Little Naches River—*stream* ... WA-9
South Fork Little Nemaha River—*stream* ... NE-7
South Fork Little Nestucca River—*stream* ... OR-9
South Fork Little Osage River—*stream* ... KS-7
South Fork Little Panoche Creek—*stream* ... CA-9
South Fork Little Peoples Creek—*stream* ... MT-8
South Fork Little Piney Creek—*stream* ... ID-8
*South Fork Little Prickly Pear Creek* ... MT-8
South Fork Little Prickly Pear
Creek—*stream* ... MT-8
South Fork Little Raccoon Creek—*stream* ... IN-6
South Fork Little Red River—*stream* ... AR-4
*South Fork Little River* ... AL-4
*South Fork Little River* ... GA-3
South Fork Little River—*stream* ... CA-9
South Fork Little River—*stream* ... GA-3
South Fork Little River—*stream* ... KY-4
South Fork Little River—*stream* ... MA-1

South Fork Little River—*stream* ... NC-3
South Fork Little River—*stream* ... VA-3
South Fork Little Rock Coulee—*valley* ... MT-8
South Fork Little Rock Creek—*stream* ... CA-9
South Fork Little Salt Creek—*stream* ... IN-6
South Fork Little Scrubgrass
Creek—*stream* ... PA-2
South Fork Little Sewee Creek—*stream* ... TN-4
South Fork Little Sleeping Child
Creek—*stream* ... MT-8
South Fork Little Snake River—*stream* ... CO-8
South Fork Little Sugar Creek—*stream* ... KS-7
South Fork Little Sur River—*stream* ... CA-9
South Fork Little Tongue River—*stream* ... WY-8
*South Fork Little Wichita River* ... TX-5
South Fork Little Wichita River—*stream* ... TX-5
South Fork Little Willow Creek—*stream* ... OR-9
South Fork Little Wind River—*stream* ... WY-8
*South Fork Llano River* ... TX-5
South Fork Lobster Creek—*stream* (2) ... OR-9
South Fork Lodge—*locale* ... AK-9
South Fork Lodge—*locale* ... NM-5
*South Fork Lodgepole Creek* ... WY-8
South Fork Lodgepole Creek—*stream* ... MT-8
South Fork Logan Creek—*stream* ... MT-8
South Fork Logy Creek—*stream* ... WA-9
*South Fork Lolo Creek* ... ID-8
South Fork Lolo Creek—*stream* ... MT-8
South Fork Lone Bear Creek—*stream* ... WY-8
*South Fork Lone Cabin Creek* ... ID-8
*South Fork Lone Creek* ... OR-9
*South Fork Lone Pine Creek* ... CO-8
South Fork Lone Rock Draw—*valley* ... CO-8
*South Fork Lone Tree Creek* ... MT-8
South Fork Lone Tree Creek—*stream* (2) ... MT-8
South Fork Lone Tree Creek—*stream* ... WY-8
South Fork Lone Tree Gulch—*valley* ... WY-8
South Fork Long Canyon—*valley* (2) ... CA-9
South Fork Long Canyon—*valley* ... NV-8
South Fork Long Creek—*stream* ... IA-7
South Fork Long Creek—*stream* ... OR-9
South Fork Long Run—*stream* ... WV-2
South Fork Long Valley Creek—*stream*
(2) ... CA-9
*South Fork Lookout creek* ... OR-9
South Fork Lookout Creek—*stream* ... ID-8
South Fork Los Banos Creek—*stream* ... CA-9
South Fork Lost Creek—*stream* ... CO-8
South Fork Lost Creek—*stream* ... IA-7
South Fork Lost Creek—*stream* ... MT-8
South Fork Lost Creek—*stream* ... WA-9
*South Fork Lost Fork Judith River* ... MT-8
South Fork Lost Fork Judith
River—*stream* ... MT-8
South Fork Lost River—*stream* ... IN-6
*South Fork Loup River* ... NE-7
South Fork Louse Creek—*stream* ... OR-9
South Fork Lower Pine Creek—*stream* ... WI-6
South Fork Lower Willow Creek—*stream* ... MT-8
South Fork Lubken Creek—*stream* ... CA-9
*South Fork Lubkin Creek* ... CA-9
*South Fork Luffenholtz Creek* ... CA-9
South Fork Lunice Creek—*stream* ... WV-2
South Fork Lyons Creek—*stream* ... MT-8
South Fork Lytle Creek—*stream* ... CA-9
South Fork Macks Creek—*stream* ... ID-8
South Fork Mad Creek—*stream* ... CO-8
South Fork Madden Brook—*stream* ... VT-1
South Fork Madison River—*stream* ... MT-8
*South Fork Mad River* ... WA-9
South Fork Mad River—*stream* ... CA-9
South Fork Maggodee Creek—*stream* ... VA-3
South Fork (Magisterial
District)—*fmr MCD* ... WV-2
South Fork Mahogany Creek—*stream* ... ID-8
South Fork Maiden Creek—*stream* ... MT-8
South Fork Main Creek—*stream* ... WI-6
South Fork Malheur River—*stream* ... OR-9
South Fork Manastash Creek—*stream* ... WA-9
*South Fork Mancos River* ... CO-8
South Fork Manor Creek—*stream* ... WA-9
South Fork Manti Canyon—*valley* ... UT-8
*South Fork Maquoketa River* ... IA-7
South Fork Maquoketa River—*stream* ... IA-7
South Fork Marsh Coulee—*valley* ... MT-8
*South Fork Marsh Creek* ... ID-8
South Fork Marten Creek—*stream* ... MT-8
South Fork Martin Creek—*stream* ... AK-9
South Fork Martins Creek—*stream* ... AR-4
South Fork Marys Creek—*stream* ... TX-5
*South Fork Massie Creek* ... OH-6
South Fork Massies Creek—*stream* ... OH-6
South Fork Matanuska River—*stream* ... AK-9
South Fork Matanzas Creek—*stream* ... CA-9
South Fork Maverick Canyon—*valley* ... NV-8
South Fork Maxfield Creek—*stream* ... WA-9
South Fork McAfee Creek—*stream* ... CA-9
South Fork McCann Branch—*stream* ... TN-4
*South Fork McClellans Creek* ... NV-8
South Fork McCools Creek—*stream* ... KY-4
South Fork McDonald Creek—*stream* (2) ... MT-8
South Fork McDowell Creek—*stream* ... OR-9
South Fork McHenry Creek—*stream* ... VA-3
*South Fork McKay Creek* ... OR-9
South Fork McKee Creek—*stream* ... IL-6
South Fork McKenzie River—*stream* ... OR-9
*South Fork McKittricks Branch* ... VA-3
South Fork Meadow—*flat* ... WA-9
South Fork Meadow Canyon—*valley* ... ID-8
South Fork Meadow Creek—*stream* ... MT-8
South Fork Meadow Creek—*stream* ... OR-9
South Fork Meadow Creek—*stream* ... WY-8
*South Fork Meadows* ... CA-9
South Fork Meadows—*flat* (3) ... CA-9
South Fork Meadows—*flat* ... MT-8
South Fork Meadows—*flat* ... WA-9
*South Fork Medicine Creek* ... SD-7
South Fork Medicine Knoll Creek—*stream* ... SD-7
South Fork Merced River—*stream* ... CA-9
South Fork Mercy Creek—*stream* ... CA-9
South Fork Mesa Creek—*stream* ... CO-8
South Fork Mexican Creek—*stream* ... CO-8
South Fork Meyers Creek—*stream* ... MT-8
*South Fork Miami River* ... OH-6
South Fork Miami River—*stream* ... FL-3
South Fork Mica Creek—*stream* ... ID-8
South Fork Michigan River—*stream* ... CO-8
South Fork Middle Beaver
Creek—*stream* ... WY-8
South Fork Middle Boone Creek—*stream* ... WY-8

South Fork Middle Boulder
Creek—*stream* ... CO-8
South Fork Middle Canyon—*valley* ... AZ-5
South Fork Middle Creek—*stream* ... OR-9
South Fork Middle Creek—*stream* ... WA-9
South Fork Middle Crow Creek—*stream* ... WY-8
*South Fork Middle Fabius River* ... MO-7
South Fork Middle Fabius River—*stream* ... MO-7
South Fork Middle Fork Imhaha
River—*stream* ... OR-9
South Fork Middle Fork Tule
River—*stream* ... CA-9
South Fork Middle Ladder Creek—*stream* ... KS-7
*South Fork Middle Piney Creek* ... WY-8
South Fork Middle River—*stream* ... FL-3
South Fork Middle River—*stream* ... IA-7
*South Fork Milk Creek* ... WY-8
South Fork Milk Creek—*stream* ... MT-8
South Fork Milkhouse Creek—*stream* ... NV-8
South Fork Milk River—*stream* ... MT-8
*South Fork Mill Creek* ... CA-9
*South Fork Mill Creek* ... IL-6
*South Fork Mill Creek* ... NV-8
*South Fork Mill Creek* ... OR-9
*South Fork Mill Creek* ... WA-9
South Fork Mill Creek—*stream* (4) ... CA-9
South Fork Mill Creek—*stream* ... ID-8
South Fork Mill Creek—*stream* ... KS-7
South Fork Mill Creek—*stream* ... MS-4
South Fork Mill Creek—*stream* ... MO-7
South Fork Mill Creek—*stream* ... MT-8
South Fork Mill Creek—*stream* ... NV-8
South Fork Mill Creek—*stream* (3) ... OR-9
South Fork Mill Creek—*stream* ... PA-2
South Fork Mill Creek—*stream* ... WA-9
South Fork Mill Creek—*stream* (2) ... WY-8
South Fork Miller Creek—*stream* ... ID-8
South Fork Miller Creek—*stream* ... MT-8
South Fork Miller Creek—*stream* ... WY-8
South Fork Mills River—*stream* ... NC-3
South Fork Millville Canyon—*valley* ... UT-8
South Fork Mimbres River—*stream* ... NM-5
South Fork Mine—*mine* ... ID-8
South Fork Mineral Canyon—*valley* ... UT-8
South Fork Mineral Creek—*stream* ... CO-8
South Fork Mineral Creek—*stream* ... NM-5
South Fork Mineral Creek—*stream* ... OR-9
South Fork Miner Creek—*stream* ... WY-8
South Fork Mink Creek—*stream* ... ID-8
South Fork Minneha Creek—*stream* ... ID-8
*South Fork Minnesota Creek* ... CO-8
South Fork Minnesota Creek—*stream* ... CO-8
South Fork Minnie Creek—*stream* ... CA-9
South Fork Mission Creek—*stream* ... CA-9
South Fork Mission Creek—*stream* (2) ... MT-8
South Fork Missouri Ditch—*canal* ... MT-8
South Fork Missouri Gulch—*valley* ... CO-8
South Fork Mitchell River—*stream* ... NC-3
South Fork Moccasin Creek—*stream* ... GA-3
South Fork Moccasin Creek—*stream* ... VA-3
South Fork Mogollow Creek—*stream* ... NM-5
South Fork Mohawk River—*stream* ... OR-9
*South Fork Mokelumne River* ... CA-9
South Fork Mokelumne River—*stream* ... CA-9
South Fork Monroe Creek—*stream* ... UT-8
South Fork Montana Creek—*stream* ... AK-9
South Fork Montgomery Creek—*stream* ... CA-9
South Fork Montgomery Fork—*stream* ... TN-4
South Fork Montgomery Gulch—*valley* ... MT-8
South Fork Montour Run—*stream* ... PA-2
South Fork Monument Creek—*stream* ... MT-8
*South Fork Moores Creek* ... NV-8
South Fork Moormans River—*stream* ... VA-3
South Fork Moosa Canyon—*valley* ... CA-9
South Fork Moquitch Canyon—*valley* ... AZ-5
South Fork Moran Creek—*stream* ... WY-8
South Fork Moreau River—*stream* ... SD-7
*South Fork Morgan Creek* ... MT-8
South Fork Morgan Creek—*stream* ... TX-5
*South Fork Mosquito Creek* ... NV-8
South Fork Mosquito Creek—*stream* ... AK-9
South Fork Mosquito Creek—*stream* ... NV-8
South Fork Mosquito Creek—*stream* ... OR-9
South Fork Moss Agate Creek—*stream* ... SD-7
South Fork Moss Agate Creek—*stream* ... WY-8
South Fork Motion Creek—*stream* ... CA-9
South Fork Mountain—*ridge* ... CA-9
South Fork Mountain—*ridge* ... WV-2
South Fork Mountain Creek—*stream* ... NC-3
South Fork Mountains—*ridge* ... AR-4
South Fork Mountain Trail—*trail* ... OR-9
South Fork Mouse Creek—*stream* ... WA-9
South Fork Moyer Creek—*stream* ... ID-8
*South Fork Mtn* ... CA-9
South Fork Mtn—*summit* (2) ... CA-9
South Fork Mtn—*summit* ... WA-9
South Fork Mtn—*summit* ... WV-2
South Fork Mtn—*summit* ... WY-8
*South Fork Mud Creek* ... WA-9
South Fork Mud Creek—*stream* ... GA-3
South Fork Mud Creek—*stream* ... IL-6
South Fork Mud Creek—*stream* (2) ... TN-4
South Fork Mud Creek—*stream* ... TX-5
South Fork Mud Creek—*stream* ... WA-9
South Fork Mud Creek—*stream* ... WY-8
South Fork Mud Creek Spring—*spring* ... WA-9
*South Fork Muddy Creek* ... MT-8
*South Fork Muddy Creek* ... UT-8
South Fork Muddy Creek—*stream* ... KY-4
South Fork Muddy Creek—*stream* ... MD-2
South Fork Muddy Creek—*stream* ... MT-8
South Fork Muddy Creek—*stream* ... NC-3
South Fork Muddy Creek—*stream* ... UT-8
South Fork Muddy Creek Marsh—*swamp* ... MD-2
South Fork Mud Spring Creek—*stream* ... AZ-5
*South Fork Mud Springs Creek* ... AZ-5
South Fork Mule Canyon—*valley* ... NV-8
South Fork Mule Creek—*stream* ... CA-9
*South Fork Mullen Creek* ... WY-8
South Fork Murderers Creek—*stream* ... OR-9
*South Fork Murphy Creek* ... WY-8
South Fork Murray Creek—*stream* ... ID-8
*South Fork Muscatatuck River* ... IN-6
South Fork Mussel Creek—*stream* ... AL-4
*South Fork Musselshell River* ... MT-8
South Fork Musselshell River—*stream* ... MT-8
South Fork Mustang Creek—*stream* ... CO-8
South Fork Mustang Creek—*stream* (2) ... TX-5
*South Fork Naches River* ... WA-9
South Fork Narrows Creek—*stream* ... ID-8

South Fork Nash Creek ... AZ-5
South Fork Natl Creek—stream ... OR-9
South Fork Neal Creek—stream ... OR-9
South Fork Necanicum River—stream ... OR-9
South Fork Negrito Creek—stream ... NM-5
South Fork Negro Creek—stream ... NV-8
South Fork Nehalem River—stream ... OR-9
South Fork Neils Creek—stream ... TX-5
South Fork Nemadji River—stream ... MN-6
South Fork Nemadji River—stream ... WI-6
South Fork Nemaha River ... NE-7
South Fork Nemaha River—stream ... KS-7
South Fork Nemote Creek—stream ... MT-8
South Fork Newaukum River—stream ... WA-9
South Fork New River—stream ... FL-3
South Fork New River—stream ... NC-3
South Fork Nichols Branch—stream ... MO-7
South Fork Ninemile Creek—stream ... MN-6
South Fork Ninemile Creek—stream (2) ... WA-9
South Fork Ninemile Creek—stream ... WY-8
South Fork Ninnescah River—stream ... KS-7
South Fork Ninuluk Creek—stream ... AK-9
South Fork Noland Creek—stream ... KY-4
South Fork Nolin River ... KY-4
South Fork Nolin River—stream ... KY-4
South Fork Nooksack River—stream ... WA-9
South Fork North Boone Creek—stream ... WY-8
South Fork North Bosque River—stream ... TX-5
South Fork North Buffalo Creek—stream ... WY-8
South Fork North Canyon—valley ... ID-8
South Fork North Cobb Creek—stream ... MO-7
South Fork North Creek—stream ... NV-8
South Fork North Creek—stream (2) ... UT-8
South Fork North Cross Creek—stream ... TN-4
South Fork North Eden Canyon—valley ... UT-8
South Fork North Fabius River—stream ... MO-7
South Fork North Fork Ahtanum Creek ... WA-9
South Fork North Fork Asotin Creek—stream ... WA-9
South Fork North Fork Breitenbush River—stream ... OR-9
South Fork North Fork Divide Creek—stream ... MT-8
South Fork North Fork Little Missouri River ... WY-8
South Fork North Fork Owl Creek—stream ... WY-8
South Fork North Fork Quitchupah Creek—stream ... UT-8
South Fork North Fork Sun River ... MT-8
South Fork North French Creek ... CO-8
South Fork North Hardscrabble Creek—stream ... CO-8
South Fork North Horse Creek—stream ... WY-8
South Fork North Prong Medina River—stream ... TX-5
South Fork North River ... MO-7
South Fork North River—stream ... MO-7
South Fork North Seco Creek—stream ... NM-5
South Fork North Wash—valley ... UT-8
South Fork Norton Creek—stream ... ID-8
South Fork Norton Creek—stream ... OR-9
South Fork Noyo River—stream ... CA-9
South Fork Nulato River—stream ... AK-9
South Fork Nuluk River—stream ... AK-9
South Fork Oak Canyon—valley ... AZ-5
South Fork Oak Creek—stream ... CA-9
South Fork Oak Creek—stream (2) ... UT-8
South Fork Oak Creek—stream ... WA-9
South Fork Oat Creek—stream ... CA-9
South Fork Obion River—stream ... TN-4
South Fork O'Brien Creek—stream ... WA-9
South Fork of Antelope Creek ... ID-8
South Fork of Big Creek ... IN-6
South Fork of Blackfoot River ... ID-8
South Fork of Buck Creek ... IN-6
South Fork Of Cabin Creek ... CO-8
South Fork of Cannon Ball River ... ND-7
South Fork of Clear Fork of Trinity River ... TX-5
South Fork Of Dolores River ... CO-8
South Fork of East Fork of Bitterroot River ... MT-8
South Fork of East Fork of Hayfork River ... CA-9
South Fork of East Fork Salmon River ... ID-8
South Fork of Fourche LaFave River ... AR-4
South Fork Of Grand River ... CO-8
South Fork of Kaweah River ... CA-9
South Fork of Little Creek ... IN-6
South Fork of Malheur River ... OR-9
South Fork of Meadow Creek ... ID-8
South Fork of Middle Fork Eel River ... CA-9
South Fork of Montezuma Creek ... UT-8
South Fork of North Fork Ahtanum Creek ... WA-9
South Fork of North Fork Yuba River ... CA-9
South Fork Of Salmo River ... ID-8
South Fork Of Salmo River ... WA-9
South Fork of Scappoose Creek ... OR-9
South Fork Of Seneca Fork ... OH-6
South Fork of Silent Canyon ... NV-8
South Fork of Snake River ... ID-8
South Fork of Snake River ... OR-9
South Fork of Snake River ... WA-9
South Fork of Snake River ... WY-8
South Fork Of South B ... VA-3
South Fork Of South Branch Of Potomac River ... VA-3
South Fork Of South Branch Of The Potomac River ... VA-3
South Fork of South Branch of the Potomac River ... WV-2
South Fork Of South Branch Potomac ... VA-3
South Fork of South Fork Cosumnes River ... CA-9
South Fork of South Umpqua River ... OR-9
South Fork of Stillwater River ... MT-8
South Fork of the Catawbaw River ... NC-3
South Fork of the Republican River ... KS-7
South Fork Of The Republican River ... NE-7
South Fork of the Trinity River ... CA-9
South Fork of the Yadkin River ... NC-3
South Fork of Trinity River ... CA-9
South Fork of Walkers Creek ... CA-9
South Fork Ogden Creek—stream ... WY-8
South Fork Ogden River ... UT-8
South Fork Ogden River—stream ... UT-8
South Fork Ogeechee Creek—stream ... GA-3
South Fork Ogeechee River—stream ... GA-3
South Fork Ogilvy Ditch—canal ... CO-8
South Fork Ogle Creek—stream ... VA-3
South Fork Ojitos Canyon—valley ... NM-5
South Fork Olmstead Creek—stream ... WY-8
South Fork One Eye Creek—stream ... CA-9
South Fork Open Creek—stream ... MT-8
South Fork Ophir Canyon—valley ... UT-8
South Fork Oregon Creek—stream ... CA-9
South Fork Orestimba Creek—stream ... CA-9
South Fork Orogrande Creek ... ID-8
South Fork Osage Creek ... AR-4
South Fork Ostrander Creek—stream ... WA-9
South Fork Otis Canyon—valley ... CA-9
South Fork Otter Creek—stream ... AK-9
South Fork Otter Creek—stream ... IL-6
South Fork Otter Creek—stream ... PA-2
South Fork Otter Creek—stream ... WY-8
South Fork Ouachita River—stream ... AR-4
South Fork Overton Creek ... NV-8
South Fork Overton Wash—stream ... NV-8
South Fork Owens Creek—stream ... CA-9
South Fork Owl Creek—stream ... SD-7
South Fork Owl Creek—stream ... TN-4
South Fork Owl Creek—stream ... WA-9
South Fork Owl Creek—stream (2) ... WY-8
South Fork Owyhee River ... ID-8
South Fork Owyhee River ... NV-8
South Fork Owyhee River ... OR-9
South Fork Owyhee River—stream ... ID-8
South Fork Owyhee River—stream ... NV-8
South Fork Oxford Creek—stream ... TN-4
South Fork Ozan Creek—stream ... AR-4
South Fork Pacheco Creek—stream ... CA-9
South Fork Packsaddle Creek—stream ... ID-8
South Fork Pacoima Canyon—valley ... CA-9
South Fork Pads Creek—stream ... VA-3
South Fork Paine Creek—stream ... WA-9
South Fork Paint Creek—stream ... WI-6
South Fork Painter Creek—stream ... TN-4
South Fork Paint River—stream ... AK-9
South Fork Palix River—stream ... WA-9
South Fork Palm Wash—stream ... CA-9
South Fork Palomas Creek—stream ... NM-5
South Fork Palo Pinto Creek—stream ... TX-5
South Fork Palouse River—stream ... ID-8
South Fork Palouse River—stream ... WA-9
South Fork Panhandle Creek—stream ... CO-8
South Fork Panther Creek ... KY-4
South Fork Panther Creek—stream ... AL-4
South Fork Panther Creek—stream ... AR-4
South Fork Panther Creek—stream ... KY-4
South Fork Panther Creek—stream ... TN-4
South Fork Papoose Creek—stream ... CA-9
South Fork Paris Canyon—valley ... ID-8
South Fork Paris Creek—stream ... WA-9
South Fork Park—flat ... CO-8
South Fork Park Creek—stream ... OR-9
South Fork Parker Branch—stream ... VA-3
South Fork Parker Creek—stream ... AZ-5
South Fork Parker Creek—stream ... CA-9
South Fork Parmenter Creek—stream ... MT-8
South Fork Parsnip Creek—stream ... OR-9
South Fork Parsnip Wash—stream ... NV-8
South Fork Partridge Creek—stream ... ID-8
Southfork Pass—gap ... CA-9
South Fork Pass—gap ... CO-8
South Fork Pass—gap ... NV-8
South Fork Pass Creek—stream ... AK-9
South Fork Pass Creek—stream ... ID-8
South Fork Pass Creek—stream ... MT-8
South Fork Pass Creek—stream ... WA-9
South Fork Pat Ford Creek—stream ... CA-9
South Fork Patoka River—stream ... IN-6
South Fork Patterson Creek—stream ... CA-9
South Fork Patterson Creek—stream ... MO-7
South Fork Pauline Creek—stream ... MT-8
South Fork Payette River ... ID-8
South Fork Payette River—stream ... ID-8
South Fork Peachtree Creek—stream ... GA-3
South Fork Peak—summit ... NM-5
South Fork Pearch Creek—stream ... CA-9
South Fork Pea Ridge Creek—stream ... MO-7
South Fork Pearl Creek—stream ... SD-7
South Fork Pebble Creek—stream ... ID-8
South Fork Pedee Creek—stream ... OR-9
South Fork Pemberton Branch ... DE-2
South Fork Peoples Creek—stream ... MT-8
South Fork Perch Creek ... CA-9
South Fork Perry Aiken Creek—stream ... CA-9
South Fork Persian Ditch—canal ... CA-9
South Fork Pete Canyon—valley ... NV-8
South Fork Pete Enyart Canyon—valley ... OR-9
South Fork Petty Creek—stream ... MT-8
South Fork Phelan Creek—stream ... ID-8
South Fork Phelps Brook—stream ... UT-8
South Fork Philips Lick ... VA-3
South Fork Pickett Creek—stream ... ID-8
South Fork Picnic Ground—locale ... UT-8
South Fork Pico Creek—stream ... CA-9
South Fork Pigeon Creek ... PA-2
South Fork Pilgrim Creek—stream ... MT-8
South Fork Pine Canyon—valley ... NM-5
South Fork Pine Creek ... NV-8
South Fork Pine Creek ... WA-9
South Fork Pine Creek—stream ... CA-9
South Fork Pine Creek—stream (2) ... ID-8
South Fork Pine Creek—stream ... IN-6
South Fork Pine Creek—stream ... MT-8
South Fork Pine Creek—stream (2) ... NV-8
South Fork Pine Creek—stream ... PA-2
South Fork Pine Creek—stream (3) ... UT-8
South Fork Pine Creek—stream (2) ... WA-9
South Fork Pine Creek—stream ... WY-8
South Fork Pine Hollow Creek—stream ... WY-8
South Fork Pine River—stream ... MN-6
South Fork Piney Creek ... CO-8
South Fork Piney Creek ... TN-4
South Fork Piney River—stream ... CO-8
South Fork Piney River—stream ... VA-3
South Fork Pinto Creek—stream ... UT-8
South Fork Pinto Creek—stream ... WY-8
South Fork Piru Creek—stream ... CA-9
South Fork Pismire Wash—valley ... UT-8
South Fork Pistol Creek—stream ... UT-8
South Fork Pistol River—stream ... OR-9
South Fork Pit River—stream ... CA-9
South Fork Placer Creek—stream ... CO-8
South Fork Plum Creek—stream ... NE-7
South Fork Pocatello Creek—stream ... ID-8
South Fork Pocket Creek—stream ... MT-8
South Fork Poison Creek—stream ... ID-8
South Fork Poker Jim Creek—stream ... MT-8
South Fork Pole Creek ... WY-8
South Fork Pole Creek—stream (2) ... MT-8
South Fork Pole Creek—stream ... OR-9
South Fork Polvadera Creek—stream ... NM-5
South Fork Pomme de Terre River—stream ... MO-7
South Fork Pond Creek—stream ... OK-5
South Fork Ponderosa Canyon—valley ... UT-8
South Fork Ponds—lake ... WY-8
South Fork Poorman Creek—stream (2) ... CA-9
South Fork Poorman Creek—stream ... MT-8
South Fork Poplar River ... WI-6
South Fork Poplar Swamp—stream ... VA-3
South Fork Popple River—stream ... WI-6
South Fork Popular River ... WI-6
South Fork Porcupine Creek—stream ... ID-8
South Fork Porphyry Creek—stream ... ID-8
South Fork Porter Canyon—valley ... NV-8
South Fork Porter Creek—stream ... WA-9
South Fork Potlach River ... ID-8
South Fork Potlatch Creek ... ID-8
South Fork Pottawatomie Creek—stream ... KS-7
South Fork Potter Creek—stream ... ID-8
South Fork Pottinger Creek—stream ... KY-4
South Fork Potts Creek—stream ... WV-2
South Fork Pound River—stream ... VA-3
South Fork Powderhorn Canyon—valley ... NM-5
South Fork Powder River—stream ... WY-8
South Fork Powell Creek—stream ... PA-2
South Fork Powell River—stream ... VA-3
South Fork Prairie—flat ... IN-6
South Fork Prairie Creek—stream ... IN-6
South Fork Prairie Dog Creek—stream ... KS-7
South Fork Preston Creek—stream ... WA-9
South Fork Prewitt Creek—stream ... CA-9
South Fork Prospect Creek—stream ... UT-8
South Fork Prosser Creek—stream ... CA-9
South Fork Provo River ... UT-8
South Fork Provo River—stream (2) ... UT-8
South Fork Pudding River—stream ... OR-9
South Fork Puerco River—stream ... NM-5
South Fork Pumpkin Draw—valley ... WY-8
South Fork Purgatoire River—stream ... CO-8
South Fork Putah Creek—stream ... CA-9
South Fork Pysht River—stream ... WA-9
South Fork Quail Creek—stream ... AK-9
South Fork Quantico Creek—stream ... VA-3
South Fork Quartz Creek—stream ... MT-8
South Fork Quartz Creek—stream ... OR-9
South Fork Quartz Creek—stream ... WA-9
South Fork Quealy Creek—stream ... WY-8
South Fork Queen Gulch—valley ... MT-8
South Fork Queens Creek ... OR-9
South Fork Quicksand Creek—stream ... KY-4
South Fork Quinault River ... WA-9
South Fork Quinn River—stream ... NV-8
South Fork Rabbit Creek—stream ... CO-8
South Fork Rabbit Creek—stream (2) ... ID-8
South Fork Rabbit River—stream ... MN-6
South Fork Raccoon Creek—stream ... IL-6
South Fork Race Creek—stream ... ID-8
South Fork Raft River—stream ... WA-9
South Fork Raider Creek—stream ... CA-9
South Fork Rainey Creek—stream ... ID-8
South Fork Rainy Creek ... ID-8
South Fork Rainy Creek—stream ... SD-7
South Fork Ramelli Creek—stream ... CA-9
South Fork Ramey Creek ... ID-8
South Fork Ramshorn Creek—stream ... CA-9
South Fork Ranch—locale ... TX-5
South Fork Ranch Creek—stream ... CO-8
**South Fork Ranchettes Subdivision**—pop pl ... UT-8
South Fork Ranger Station—locale ... CA-9
South Fork Ranger Station—locale ... WY-8
South Fork Rapid Creek—stream ... CO-8
South Fork Rapid Creek—stream ... SD-7
South Fork Rapier Mill Creek—stream ... GA-3
South Fork Rapier Mill Creek—stream ... NC-3
South Fork Raton Creek—stream ... CO-8
South Fork Rattlesnake Creek—stream ... CA-9
South Fork Rattlesnake Creek—stream ... ID-8
South Fork Rattlesnake Creek—stream ... NC-3
South Fork Rattlesnake Creek—stream ... OH-6
South Fork Raven Creek—stream ... KY-4
South Fork Raymond Creek—stream ... WY-8
South Fork Rec Area—locale ... AR-4
South Fork Rec Area—park ... MO-7
South Fork Red Bud Creek—stream ... MS-4
South Fork Red Butte Creek—stream ... UT-8
South Fork Red Canyon—valley ... UT-8
South Fork Red Cap Creek—stream ... CA-9
South Fork Red Creek—stream ... UT-8
South Fork Red Creek—stream ... WV-2
South Fork Reddies River—stream ... NC-3
South Fork Red Fork Powder River—stream ... WY-8
South Fork Red Meadow Creek—stream ... MT-8
South Fork Red River ... OK-5
South Fork Red River—stream ... ID-8
South Fork Red River—stream (2) ... KY-4
South Fork Red River—stream ... TN-4
South Fork Red Rock Creek—stream ... MT-8
South Fork Red Run—stream ... WV-2
South Fork Red Sandstone Creek—stream ... CO-8
South Fork Red Shale Creek—stream ... MT-8
South Fork Redwood Creek—stream ... CA-9
South Fork Reed Canyon—valley ... ID-8
South Fork Reed Creek—stream ... VA-3
South Fork Reeds Creek—stream ... ID-8
South Fork Reese Creek—stream ... ID-8
South Fork Reese Creek—stream ... OR-9
South Fork Reno Creek—stream ... MT-8
South Fork Republican River—stream ... CO-8
South Fork Republican River—stream ... KS-7
South Fork Republican River—stream ... NE-7
South Fork Reservoir Dam Site—other ... PA-2
South Fork Rex Creek—stream ... AK-9
South Fork Rickard Coulee—valley ... MT-8
South Fork Rickeall Creek—stream ... OR-9
South Fork Ridge—ridge ... ID-8
South Fork Ridge—ridge ... KY-4
South Fork Ridge—ridge ... WA-9
South Fork Ridge Trail—trail ... OR-9
South Fork Riley Creek—stream ... OR-9
South Fork Rio Bonito—stream ... NM-5
South Fork Rio de la Casa—stream ... NM-5
South Fork Rio Grande—stream ... CO-8
South Fork Rio Hondo—stream ... NM-5
South Fork Rio Quemado—stream ... NM-5
South Fork Rio Ruidoso—stream ... NM-5
South Fork Rito Azul—stream ... NM-5
South Fork Rivanna River—stream ... VA-3
South Fork Rivanna River Dam—dam ... VA-3
South Fork Rivanna River Rsvr—reservoir ... VA-3
South Fork River ... NC-3
South Fork River Cem—cemetery ... MI-6
South Fork River Run—stream ... WV-2
South Fork Road Canyon—valley ... NM-5
South Fork Roanoke River—stream ... VA-3
South Fork Roaring Branch—stream ... VT-1
South Fork Roaring Fork—stream ... TN-4
South Fork Roaring River—stream ... OR-9
South Fork Robbers Roost Canyon—valley ... UT-8
South Fork Robie Creek—stream ... ID-8
South Fork Robinson Creek—stream ... ID-8
South Fork Robinson Creek—stream ... NV-8
South Fork Rock Canyon—valley ... AZ-5
South Fork Rock Canyon—valley ... UT-8
South Fork Rockcastle River—stream ... KY-4
South Fork Rock Creek ... ID-8
South Fork Rock Creek ... MT-8
South Fork Rock Creek ... NV-8
South Fork Rock Creek ... OK-5
South Fork Rock Creek ... OR-9
South Fork Rock Creek ... WA-9
South Fork Rock Creek ... WY-8
South Fork Rock Creek—stream ... AZ-5
South Fork Rock Creek—stream (2) ... CA-9
South Fork Rock Creek—stream ... CO-8
South Fork Rock Creek—stream (3) ... ID-8
South Fork Rock Creek—stream (3) ... MT-8
South Fork Rock Creek—stream (4) ... OR-9
South Fork Rock Creek—stream ... UT-8
South Fork Rock Creek—stream ... WY-8
South Fork Rock Creek - in part ... NV-8
South Fork Rockfish River—stream ... VA-3
South Fork Rock Run—stream ... WV-2
South Fork Rock Springs Creek—stream ... MT-8
South Fork Rocky Arroyo—stream ... NM-5
South Fork Rocky Creek ... TX-5
South Fork Rocky Creek—stream ... TX-5
South Fork Rocky Draw ... NM-5
South Fork Rocky Draw—valley ... NM-5
South Fork Rocky Fork—stream ... OH-6
South Fork Rocky Gulch—stream ... OR-9
South Fork Rogers Creek—stream ... WA-9
South Fork Rogue River—stream ... OR-9
South Fork Romy Creek—stream ... MT-8
South Fork Root River—stream ... MN-6
South Fork Roper Creek—stream ... WA-9
South Fork Roseau River—stream ... MN-6
South Fork Rosebud Creek—stream ... MT-8
South Fork Roses Creek—stream ... NC-3
South Fork Ross Creek ... ID-8
South Fork Ross Creek—stream (2) ... MT-8
South Fork Ross Fork—stream (2) ... ID-8
South Fork Rough and Ready Creek—stream ... OR-9
South Fork Round Prairie Creek—stream ... OR-9
South Fork Rowdy Creek—stream ... CA-9
South Fork RR Creek—stream ... MT-8
South Fork Rsvr—reservoir ... CA-9
South Fork Rsvr—reservoir (2) ... MT-8
South Fork Rsvr—reservoir ... NV-8
South Fork Rsvr—reservoir ... OR-9
South Fork Rubicon River—stream ... CA-9
South Fork Ruby Creek—stream ... MT-8
South Fork Ruby Creek—stream ... OR-9
South Fork Rumble Creek—stream ... MT-8
South Fork Running Creek—stream ... ID-8
South Fork Running Wolf Creek—stream ... MT-8
South Fork Rush Creek—stream ... ID-8
South Fork Rush Creek—stream ... MN-6
South Fork Rush Creek—stream ... TX-5
South Fork Rushing Creek ... TN-4
South Fork Rush River ... MN-6
South Fork Russell Creek—stream ... KY-4
South Fork Russian Creek—stream ... WA-9
South Fork Ryegrass Creek—stream ... OR-9
South Fork Sabine River—stream ... TX-5
South Fork Sac Branch—stream ... KS-7
South Fork Sacramento River—stream ... CA-9
South Fork Saddle Gulch—valley ... ID-8
South Fork Sage Creek—stream ... ID-8
South Fork Sage Creek—stream ... MT-8
South Fork Sage Creek—stream ... SD-7
South Fork Sage Creek—stream (4) ... WY-8
South Fork Saquache Creek—stream ... CO-8
South Fork Saguache River ... CO-8
South Fork Saint Charles Creek—stream ... ID-8
South Fork Saint Lawrence Creek—stream ... WY-8
South Fork Saint Lucie River—stream ... FL-3
South Fork Saint Peter Creek—stream ... WA-9
South Fork Salado Creek—stream ... NM-5
South Fork Salcha River—stream ... AK-9
South Fork Saline Creek—stream ... MO-7
South Fork Saline River—stream (2) ... AR-4
South Fork Saline River—stream ... IL-6
South Fork Saline River—stream ... KS-7
South Fork Salmonberry Creek—stream ... OR-9
South Fork Salmonberry River—stream ... OR-9
South Fork Salmon Creek—stream ... CA-9
South Fork Salmon Creek—stream (2) ... WA-9
South Fork Salmon Falls Creek ... NV-8
South Fork Salmon Falls Creek—stream ... NV-8
South Fork Salmon River ... ID-8
South Fork Salmon River ... WA-9
South Fork Salmon River—stream ... CA-9
South Fork Salmon River—stream ... ID-8
South Fork Salmon River—stream ... OR-9
South Fork Salmon River—stream ... WA-9
south Fork Salmo River ... ID-8
south Fork Salmo River ... WA-9
South Fork Salt Branch—stream ... TX-5
South Fork Salt Creek—stream ... CO-8
South Fork Salt Creek—stream ... IN-6
South Fork Salt Creek—stream ... OR-9
South Fork Salt Creek - in part ... MO-7
South Fork Salt Fork—stream ... MO-7
South Fork Salt River ... AZ-5
South Fork Salt River—stream ... MO-7
South Fork Salt Well Creek—stream ... KY-4
South Fork Salvador Canyon—valley ... CA-9
South Fork Sand Arroyo—stream ... CO-8
South Fork Sand Arroyo—valley ... MT-8
South Fork Sand Canyon—valley ... CA-9
South Fork Sand Creek ... OR-9
South Fork Sand Creek—stream ... WY-8
South Fork Sand Draw—valley ... WY-8
South Fork Sand Run—stream ... MD-2
South Fork Sandstone Creek—stream ... MT-8
South Fork Sandy Creek ... AL-4
South Fork San Fernando Creek—stream ... TX-5
South Fork Sanford Creek ... UT-8
South Fork San Gabriel River—stream ... TX-5
South Fork Sangamon River—stream ... IL-6
South Fork Sangeronimo Creek—stream ... TX-5
South Fork San Jacinto River—stream ... CA-9
South Fork San Joaquin River—stream ... CA-9
South Fork San Miguel River—stream ... CO-8
South Fork San Onofre Canyon—valley ... CA-9
South Fork San Pedro Creek—stream ... CA-9
South Fork San Pedro Creek—stream ... TX-5
South Fork Sanpoil River—stream ... WA-9
South Fork San Simeon Creek—stream ... CA-9
South Fork Santa Ana River—stream ... CA-9
South Fork Santa Clara River—stream ... CA-9
South Fork Santa Creek—stream ... ID-8
South Fork Santa Lucia Creek—stream ... CA-9
South Fork Santa Maria River—stream ... AZ-5
South Fork Santa Rita Creek—stream ... CA-9
South Fork Sappa Creek—stream ... KS-7
South Fork Sauk River—stream ... WA-9
South Fork Saw Creek—stream ... TN-4
South Fork Sawyer Creek—stream ... NC-3
South Fork Sayles Creek—stream ... WY-8
South Fork Scappoose Creek ... OR-9
South Fork Scarce Creek—stream ... TN-4
South Fork Scarham Creek—stream ... AL-4
South Fork Scenery Creek—stream ... AK-9
South Fork Sch—school ... CA-9
South Fork Sch—school ... IL-6
South Fork Sch—school ... KY-4
South Fork Sch—school ... MT-8
South Fork Sch—school ... NC-3
South Fork Sch—school ... ND-7
South Fork Sch (abandoned)—school ... SD-7
SouthFork Sch (historical)—school ... TN-4
South Fork Schoolhouse Gulch—valley ... SD-7
South Fork Schooner Creek—stream ... OR-9
South Fork Scioto Brush Creek—stream ... OH-6
South Fork Scott Creek—stream ... ID-8
South Fork Scott Creek—stream ... OR-9
South Fork Scott River—stream ... CA-9
South Fork Scotts Creek—stream ... CA-9
South Fork Second Creek ... NC-3
South Fork Second Creek—stream ... MT-8
South Fork Second Creek—stream ... NC-3
South Fork Seekseequa Creek—stream ... OR-9
South Fork Sekiu River—stream ... WA-9
South Fork Sellars Creek—stream ... ID-8
South Fork Serpentine River—stream ... AK-9
South Fork Seven Mile Canyon ... UT-8
South Fork Sevenmile Canyon—valley ... UT-8
South Fork Sevenmile Creek—stream ... CO-8
South Forks Falls Creek—stream ... OR-9
South Fork Shade Creek—stream ... MT-8
South Fork Shafer Canyon—valley ... UT-8
South Fork Shale Creek—stream ... OR-9
South Fork Shannon Canyon—valley ... CA-9
South Fork Shaw Creek—stream ... IL-6
South Fork Sheats Creek ... TN-4
South Fork Sheeds Creek—stream ... TN-4
South Fork Sheep Canyon—valley ... CA-9
South Fork Sheep Coulee—valley ... MT-8
South Fork Sheep Creek—stream ... AZ-5
South Fork Sheep Creek—stream (5) ... ID-8
South Fork Sheep Creek—stream (3) ... MT-8
South Fork Sheep Creek—stream ... NV-8
South Fork Sheep Creek—stream ... UT-8
South Fork Sheep Creek—stream ... WY-8
South Fork Sheep Creek Trail—trail ... ID-8
South Fork Shelby Creek—stream ... IL-6
South Fork Shell Creek—stream ... WY-8
South Fork Shelter—locale ... OR-9
South Fork Shelter—locale ... WV-2
South Fork Shelton Creek ... WA-9
South Fork Shenandoah River—stream ... VA-3
South Fork Sherman Creek—stream ... WA-9
South Fork Shields Creek—stream ... CA-9
South Fork Shields River—stream ... MT-8
South Fork Shingle Creek—stream ... ID-8
South Fork Short Creek—stream ... OH-6
South Fork Shorty Creek—stream ... MT-8
South Fork Shoshone Canyon—valley ... NV-8
South Fork Shoshone Creek—stream ... ID-8
South Fork Shoshone Creek—stream ... NV-8
South Fork Shoshone River—stream ... WY-8
South Fork Shotgun Creek—stream ... CA-9
South Fork Shute Creek—stream ... WY-8
South Fork Siletz River—stream ... OR-9
South Fork Sill Branch—stream ... TN-4
South Fork Silver Creek—stream ... CA-9
South Fork Silver Creek—stream (2) ... CO-8
South Fork Silver Creek—stream ... NV-8
South Fork Silver Creek—stream ... NM-5
South Fork Silver Creek—stream (2) ... OR-9
South Fork Silver Creek—stream ... WA-9
South Fork Silver Creek—stream (2) ... WY-8
South Fork Simcoe Creek—stream ... WA-9
South Fork Simms Creek—stream ... MT-8
South Fork Simpson Creek—stream ... OR-9
South Fork Singer Creek—stream ... CA-9
South Fork Sinker Creek—stream ... ID-8
South Fork Sinnemahoning Creek ... PA-2
South Fork Sisquoc River—stream ... CA-9
South Fork Siuslaw River—stream ... OR-9
South Fork Siwash Creek—stream ... WA-9
South Fork Sixes River—stream ... OR-9
South Fork Sixmile Canyon—valley ... UT-8
South Fork Sixmile Creek—stream ... UT-8
South Fork Sixteenmile Creek—stream ... MT-8
South Fork Skagit River—stream ... WA-9
South Fork Skalkaho Creek ... MT-8
South Fork Skeenah Creek—stream ... NC-3
South Fork Skeleton Canyon—valley ... AZ-5
South Fork Skirum Creek ... AL-4
South Fork Skokomish River—stream ... WA-9
South Fork Skookumchuck Creek—stream ... ID-8
South Fork Skookum Creek—stream ... WA-9
South Fork Skunk Creek—stream ... ND-7
South Fork Skykomish River—stream ... WA-9
South Fork Slate Creek—stream ... CA-9
South Fork Slate Creek—stream (2) ... WA-9
South Fork Slate Creek—stream ... WY-8
South Fork Slater Creek—stream ... CO-8
South Fork Sleeman Creek—stream ... MT-8
South Fork Sleeping Child Creek—stream ... MT-8
South Fork Sleepy Creek—stream ... WV-2
South Fork Slim Sam Creek—stream ... MT-8
South Fork Small Creek—stream ... WA-9
South Fork Smalls Creek—stream ... IN-6
South Fork Smith Canyon—valley ... ID-8
South Fork Smith Creek—stream (2) ... ID-8
South Fork Smith Creek—stream ... NV-8
South Fork Smith Creek—stream ... ND-7
South Fork Smith Creek—stream ... UT-8
South Fork Smith River—stream ... CA-9
South Fork Smith River—stream ... MT-8
South Fork Smith River—stream ... OR-9
South Fork Smiths Fork—stream ... WY-8
South Fork Snake Creek—stream ... SD-7
South Fork Snoqualmie River—stream ... WA-9
South Fork Snow Creek—stream ... MT-8
South Fork Snow River—stream ... AK-9
South Fork Snowshoe Canyon—valley ... WY-8
South Fork Snowshoe Creek ... CO-8
South Fork Snyder Creek—stream ... OR-9
South Fork Soap Creek—stream ... AZ-5
South Fork Soda Creek—stream ... CO-8
South Fork Soldier Creek ... UT-8
South Fork Soldier Creek—stream ... CA-9
South Fork Soldier Creek—stream ... ID-8
South Fork Soldier Creek—stream ... KY-4
South Fork Soldier Creek—stream ... NE-7
South Fork Soldier Creek—stream ... UT-8
South Fork Soleduck River—stream ... WA-9
South Fork Solomon River—stream ... KS-7
South Fork Sorrel Horse Creek—stream ... MT-8
South Fork South Beaver Creek ... IA-7
South Fork South Bedias Creek—stream ... TX-5
South Fork South Branch Chicago River—stream ... IL-6
South Fork South Branch Potomac River—stream ... VA-3
South Fork South Branch Potomac River—stream ... WV-2
South Fork South Branch Wolf Creek—stream ... OH-6
South Fork South Canyon—valley ... ID-8
South Fork South Cottonwood Creek—stream ... WY-8
South Fork South Creek—stream ... UT-8
South Fork South Creek—stream ... WA-9
South Fork South Crow Creek—stream ... WY-8
South Fork South Eden Canyon—valley ... UT-8
South Fork South Fabius River—stream ... MO-7
South Fork South Fork Chambers Creek—stream ... TX-5
South Fork South Fork Sultan River—stream ... WA-9
South Fork South Fork Teton River—stream ... MT-8
South Fork South Grand River—stream ... MO-7
South Fork South Henderson Creek—stream ... IL-6
South Fork South Platte River—stream ... CO-8
South Fork South Prairie Creek—stream ... WA-9
South Fork South Twin River—stream ... NV-8
South Fork Spade Creek—stream ... MT-8
South Fork Spanish Canyon—valley ... CA-9
South Fork Spanish Creek—stream ... CA-9
South Fork Spanish Creek—stream ... MT-8
South Fork Spencer Creek—stream (2) ... OR-9
South Fork Split Creek—stream ... ID-8
South Fork Spotted Dog Creek—stream ... MT-8
South Fork Sprague River—stream ... OR-9
South Fork Spread Creek—stream ... WY-8
South Fork Spring—spring ... AZ-5
South Fork Spring—spring (2) ... ID-8
South Fork Spring—spring (3) ... NV-8
South Fork Spring—spring ... OR-9
South Fork Spring—spring ... UT-8
South Fork Spring Branch Creek—stream ... ID-8
South Fork Spring Canyon—valley ... CO-8
South Fork Spring Coulee—valley ... MT-8
South Fork Spring Creek ... MO-7
South Fork Spring Creek ... WA-9
South Fork Spring Creek—stream ... AZ-5
South Fork Spring Creek—stream ... CA-9
South Fork Spring Creek—stream ... MO-7
South Fork Spring Creek—stream (2) ... MT-8
South Fork Spring Creek—stream (3) ... OR-9
South Fork Spring Creek—stream ... WA-9
South Fork Spring Creek—stream (2) ... WY-8
South Fork Spring Gulch—valley ... CA-9
South Fork Spring River—stream ... AR-4
South Fork Spring River—stream ... MO-7
South Fork Spruce Creek—stream ... ID-8
South Fork Spruce Run Creek—stream ... OR-9
South Fork Squally Creek—stream ... NC-3
South Fork Squaw Creek ... MT-8
South Fork Squaw Creek—stream ... AZ-5
South Fork Squaw Creek—stream ... CA-9
South Fork Squaw Creek—stream ... ID-8
South Fork Squaw Creek—stream (2) ... MT-8
South Fork Squaw Creek—stream ... NV-8
South Fork Squaw Creek—stream (3) ... OR-9
South Fork Squaw Creek—stream ... WY-8
South Fork Stacey Creek—stream ... CA-9
South Fork Staley Creek—stream ... OR-9
South Fork Standard Creek—stream ... MT-8
South Fork Stanislaus River—stream ... CA-9
South Fork Starkey Gulch—valley ... CO-8
South Fork State Creek—stream ... MT-8
South Fork Station Camp Creek—stream ... KY-4
South Fork Steel Creek—stream ... MT-8
South Fork Steele Creek—stream ... NV-8
South Fork Steelhead Creek ... CA-9
South Fork Steelhead Creek—stream ... OR-9
South Fork Stell Creek—stream ... OR-9
South Fork Stewarts Creek—stream ... VA-3
South Fork Stickney Creek—stream ... MT-8
South Fork Stillaguamish River—stream ... WA-9
South Fork Stillwater River ... MT-8
South Fork Stillwater River—stream ... OH-6
South Fork St. Joe River ... ID-8
South Fork Stoner Creek—stream ... WY-8
South Fork Stony Creek—stream ... CA-9
South Fork Stony Creek—stream ... WA-9
South Fork Storm Creek—stream ... ID-8
South Fork Stovall Creek—stream ... VA-3
South Fork Straight Canyon—valley ... NV-8
South Fork Straight Creek—stream ... PA-2
South Fork Street Creek—stream ... OR-9
South Fork Strouds Creek—stream ... TX-5
**Southfork Subdivision**—pop pl ... UT-8
South Fork Sublett Creek—stream ... ID-8
South Fork Sublette Canyon—valley ... ID-8
South Fork Sublette Creek—stream ... WY-8

*South Fork Sugar Creek* ... PA-2
South Fork Sugar Creek—*stream* ... ID-8
South Fork Sugar Creek—*stream* ... KS-7
South Fork Sugar Creek—*stream* ... KY-4
South Fork Sugar Creek—*stream* ... OH-6
South Fork Sugar Creek—*stream* ... TN-4
South Fork Sugar Creek—*stream* ... WV-2
South Fork Sugar Creek—*stream* ... WI-6
South Fork Sugarloaf Creek—*stream* ... CA-9
South Fork Sugarloaf Creek—*stream* ... NC-3
South Fork Sulatna River—*stream* ... AK-9
South Fork Sullivan Creek—*stream* ... MT-8
*South Fork Sulman Creek* ... OR-9
*South Fork Sulmon Creek* ... OR-9
South Fork Sulphur Creek—*stream* ... WY-8
South Fork Sulphur Creek Trail—*trail* ... ID-8
South Fork Sulphur Draw—*valley* ... TX-5
*South Fork Sultan River* ... WA-9
South Fork Sultan River—*stream* ... WA-9
South Fork Summit Creek—*stream* ... OR-9
South Fork Summit Creek—*stream* ... UT-8
*South Fork Sunday Creek* ... MT-8
*South Fork Sun River* ... MT-8
South Fork Sun River—*stream* ... MT-8
South Fork Surprise Creek—*stream* ... ID-8
*South Fork Sur River* ... CA-9
South Fork Swamp Creek—*stream* ... MT-8
South Fork Swan Creek—*stream* ... MT-8
South Fork Swan Creek—*stream* ... NE-7
South Fork Swan River—*stream* ... CO-8
South Fork Swasey Creek—*stream* ... UT-8
South Fork Sweeney Creek—*stream* ... MT-8
South Fork Sweet Creek—*stream* ... OR-9
South Fork Sweet Grass Creek—*stream* ... MT-8
South Fork Swensons Canyon—*valley* ... UT-8
South Fork Swett Creek—*stream* ... UT-8
South Fork Sybille Creek—*stream* ... WY-8
*South Fork Sycamore Creek* ... AZ-5
South Fork Sycamore Creek—*stream* ... NM-5
South Fork Sycamore Creek—*stream* (2) ... TN-4
South Fork Sycan River—*stream* ... OR-9
South Fork Sycolin Creek—*stream* ... VA-3
South Fork Tacoma Creek—*stream* ... WA-9
South Fork Talala Creek—*stream* ... OK-5
South Fork Tamarack Creek—*stream* ... CA-9
South Fork Tamarack Creek—*stream* ... MT-8
South Fork Taneum Creek—*stream* ... WA-9
South Fork Tank—*reservoir* (2) ... AZ-5
South Fork Tarpiscan Creek—*stream* ... WA-9
*South Fork Tarryall Creek* ... CO-8
South Fork Taylor Bayou—*stream* ... TX-5
South Fork Taylor Canyon—*valley* ... MT-8
South Fork Taylor Creek—*stream* ... CA-9
South Fork Taylor Creek—*stream* ... FL-3
South Fork Taylor Creek—*stream* ... MT-8
South Fork Taylor Creek—*stream* ... OR-9
South Fork Taylor Creek—*stream* ... UT-8
South Fork Taylor Creek—*stream* ... WA-9
South Fork Teal Creek—*stream* ... OR-9
South Fork Tenderfoot Creek—*stream* ... MT-8
South Fork Tenmile Creek—*stream* ... MT-8
South Fork Tenmile Creek—*stream* ... OR-9
South Fork Tenmile Creek—*stream* ... PA-2
South Fork Ten Mile River—*stream* ... CA-9
South Fork Terrapin Creek—*stream* ... AL-4
South Fork Terre Noire Creek—*stream* ... AR-4
South Fork Tesuque Creek—*stream* ... NM-5
South Fork Teton Creek—*stream* ... WY-8
*South Fork Teton River* ... ID-8
South Fork Teton River—*stream* ... MT-8
South Fork Texas Creek—*stream* (2) ... CO-8
South Fork Thief Creek—*stream* ... MT-8
South Fork Thistle Creek—*stream* ... UT-8
*South Fork Thomas Fork* ... WY-8
*South Fork Thomas Fork Creek* ... WY-8
South Fork Thorn Creek—*stream* ... ID-8
South Fork Thrashers Creek—*stream* ... VA-3
South Fork Three Bar Creek—*stream* ... MT-8
South Fork Three Bar Creek—*stream* ... WY-8
South Fork Three Creeks—*stream* ... UT-8
South Fork Three Forks—*valley* ... UT-8
South Fork Threemile Creek—*stream* ... ID-8
South Fork Threemile Creek—*stream* ... MT-8
South Fork Threemile Creek—*stream* ... UT-8
South Fork Threemile Creek—*stream* ... WA-9
South Fork Thriteenmile Creek—*stream* ... MT-8
South Fork Thunder Creek—*stream* ... WA-9
South Fork Thunder River—*stream* ... WI-6
South Fork Ticaboo Creek—*stream* ... UT-8
South Fork Tickle Creek—*stream* ... OR-9
South Fork Tie Creek—*stream* ... MT-8
*South Fork Tietion River* ... WA-9
*South Fork Ticton River* ... WA 9
South Fork Tieton River—*stream* ... WA-9
*South Fork Tillatoba Creek* ... MS-4
South Fork Tillatoba Creek—*stream* ... MS-4
South Fork Tilton Creek—*stream* ... WA-9
South Fork Timber Creek—*stream* ... ID-8
South Fork Timber Swamp Brook—*stream* ... NJ-2
South Fork Tincup Creek—*stream* ... ID-8
South Fork Tish Tang a Tang Creek—*stream* ... CA-9
South Fork Toats Coulee Creek—*stream* ... WA-9
South Fork Tobannee Creek—*stream* ... GA-3
South Fork Tolt River—*stream* ... WA-9
South Fork Tolt Watershed—*area* ... WA-9
*South Fork Tombeal Creek* ... ID-8
South Fork Tom Beall Creek—*stream* ... ID-8
*South Fork Tom Bell Creek* ... ID-8
*South Fork Tom Creek* ... NC-3
South Fork Tomlinson Run—*stream* ... WV-2
South Fork Toms Creek—*stream* ... NC-3
South Fork Toms Creek—*stream* ... TN-4
South Fork Topia Creek—*stream* ... NV-8
South Fork Toponce Creek—*stream* ... ID-8
South Fork Toppenish Creek—*stream* ... WA-9
South Fork Toquop Wash—*stream* ... NV-8
*South Fork Toroda creek* ... WA-9
*South Fork Touchet River* ... WA-9
South Fork Touchet River—*stream* ... WA-9
South Fork Toutle River—*stream* ... WA-9
**South Fork (Town of)**—*pop pl* ... WI-6
South Fork Township—*civil* (3) ... MO-7
South Fork Township—*fmr MCD* (3) ... IA-7
**South Fork Township**—*pop pl* ... ND-7
South Fork (Township of)—*fmr MCD* (2) ... AR-4
South Fork (Township of)—*fmr MCD* (2) ... NC-3
**South Fork (Township of)**—*pop pl* ... IL-6
**South Fork (Township of)**—*pop pl* ... MN-6
South Fork Trace Branch—*stream* ... AL-4
South Fork Trail—*trail* (3) ... CA-9
South Fork Trail—*trail* (2) ... CO-8
South Fork Trail—*trail* ... ID-8
South Fork Trail—*trail* ... MT-8
South Fork Trail—*trail* (2) ... OR-9
South Fork Trail—*trail* (2) ... WA-9
South Fork Trail—*trail* (2) ... WY-8
South Fork Trail Canyon—*valley* ... CA-9
*South Fork Trail Creek* ... MT-8
South Fork Trail Creek—*stream* (2) ... MT-8
South Fork Trail (Pack)—*trail* ... CA-9
South Fork Trail (Pack)—*trail* ... NM-5
South Fork Trap Creek—*stream* ... ID-8
South Fork Trask River—*stream* ... OR-9
South Fork Tree Draw—*valley* ... WY-8
South Fork Trigger Branch—*stream* ... MS-4
*South Fork Trinity River* ... TX-5
South Fork Trinity River—*stream* ... CA-9
South Fork Trinity River—*stream* ... TX-5
South Fork Tripod Creek—*stream* ... ID-8
South Fork Trout Creek—*stream* ... CA-9
South Fork Trout Creek—*stream* ... MT-8
South Fork Trout Creek—*stream* ... NV-8
South Fork Trout Creek—*stream* (2) ... OR-9
South Fork Trout Creek—*stream* (3) ... WA-9
South Fork Trout Creek—*stream* ... WI-6
South Fork Troy Creek—*stream* ... NV-8
*South Fork Trujillo Creek* ... CO-8
South Fork Trujillo Creek—*stream* ... CO-8
*South Fork Tualatin River* ... OR-9
South Fork Tucker Creek—*stream* ... MT-8
South Fork Tufts Creek—*stream* ... UT-8
South Fork Tug Fork—*stream* ... WV-2
South Fork Tularosa Canyon—*valley* ... NM-5
South Fork Tule River—*stream* ... CA-9
South Fork Tully Canyon—*valley* ... CA-9
South Fork Tumalo Creek—*stream* ... OR-9
South Fork Tumbling Run—*stream* ... VA-3
South Fork Tuolumne River—*stream* ... CA-9
*South Fork Turkey Creek* ... CO-8
*South Fork Turkey Creek* ... NC-3
*South Fork Turkey Creek* ... TN-4
South Fork Turkey Creek—*stream* (3) ... MO-7
South Fork Turkey Creek—*stream* ... NE-7
South Fork Turkey Creek—*stream* ... TN-4
South Fork Tuskeegee Creek—*stream* ... NC-3
*South Fork Twelvemile Creek* ... CA-9
*South Fork Twelvemile Creek* ... OR-9
South Fork Twelvemile Creek—*stream* ... AK-9
South Fork Twelvemile Creek—*stream* ... CA-9
South Fork Twelvemile Creek—*stream* ... SD-7
South Fork Twelvemile Creek—*stream* ... UT-8
*South Fork Twentymile Creek* ... WA-9
South Fork Twentymile Creek—*stream* ... WA-9
South Fork Twin Creek—*stream* ... KY-4
South Fork Twin Creek—*stream* ... NV-8
South Fork Twin Creek—*stream* ... WY-8
South Fork Twisp River—*stream* ... WA-9
South Fork Two Calf Creek—*stream* ... MT-8
South Fork Two Leggins Creek—*stream* ... MT-8
*South Fork Two Medicine Creek* ... MT-8
South Fork Two Medicine River—*stream* ... MT-8
South Fork Tye River—*stream* ... VA-3
South Fork Umatilla River—*stream* ... OR-9
South Fork Union Creek—*stream* ... NE-7
South Fork Upatoi Creek—*stream* ... GA-3
South Fork Upper Carmen River—*stream* ... AK-9
South Fork Upper Creek—*stream* ... NC-3
South Fork Upper Spruce Creek—*stream* ... KY-4
South Fork Urraca Creek—*stream* ... NM-5
South Fork Usal Creek—*stream* ... CA-9
South Fork Valentine Creek—*stream* ... MT-8
South Fork Valentine Creek—*stream* ... OR-9
South Fork Valley—*valley* ... CA-9
South Fork Valley Creek—*stream* ... MT-8
South Fork Valley Creek—*stream* ... TX-5
South Fork Vance Creek—*stream* ... OR-9
*South Fork Van Duzen River* ... CA-9
South Fork Vermilion River—*stream* ... IL-6
*South Fork Vernon Fork Muscatatuck* ... IN-6
South Fork Vine Maple Creek—*stream* ... OR-9
South Fork Visher Creek—*stream* ... OR-9
South Fork Wade Creek—*stream* ... OR-9
South Fork Wages Creek—*stream* ... CA-9
South Fork Wailua River—*stream* ... HI-9
*South Fork Wailua Stream* ... HI-9
South Fork Walker Branch—*stream* ... IA-7
South Fork Walker Creek—*stream* ... CA-9
South Fork Walker Creek—*stream* ... ID-8
South Fork Walker Creek—*stream* ... WY-8
South Fork Walla Walla River—*stream* ... OR-9
South Fork Waller Creek—*stream* ... CA-9
South Fork Wallowa Crook—*stream* ... OR-9
*South Fork Wallowa River* ... OR-9
South Fork Walnut Canyon—*valley* ... NM-5
South Fork Walnut Creek—*stream* ... AZ-5
South Fork Walnut Creek—*stream* ... IA-7
South Fork Walnut Creek—*stream* ... KS-7
South Fork Walnut Creek—*stream* ... OK-5
South Fork Wanderers Creek—*stream* ... TX-5
South Fork War Canyon—*valley* ... NV-8
South Fork War Creek—*stream* ... WA-9
South Fork Ward Branch—*stream* ... MO-7
South Fork Warm Spring Creek—*stream* ... WY-8
South Fork Warm Springs Creek—*stream* ... ID-8
South Fork Warm Springs Creek—*stream* (2) ... MT-8
South Fork Warm Springs Creek—*stream* ... WY-8
South Fork Warm Springs River—*stream* ... OR-9
*South Fork Warner Creek* ... OR-9
*South Fork Wash* ... NV-8
South Fork Watab River—*stream* ... MN-6
South Fork Watch Creek—*stream* ... KY-4
South Fork Waterfall Creek—*stream* ... ID-8
South Fork Waterhole—*lake* ... OR-9
*South Fork Watonwan River* ... MN-6
South Fork Watonwan River—*stream* ... MN-6
South Fork Watson Creek—*stream* ... MT-8
South Fork Way—*trail* ... OR-9
South Fork Weaubleau Creek—*stream* ... MO-7
South Fork Webb Creek—*stream* ... MO-7
South Fork Webber Creek—*stream* ... ID-8
South Fork Weber Creek—*stream* ... CA-9
South Fork Weber River—*stream* (2) ... UT-8
*South Fork Weirgor Creek* ... WI-6
South Fork Weist Creek—*stream* ... OR-9
South Fork Well—*well* ... NV-8
South Fork Wellington Creek—*stream* ... ID-8
South Fork Wenaha River—*stream* ... OR-9
*South Fork Wenas Creek* ... WA-9
South Fork Wenas Creek—*stream* ... WA-9
South Fork West Branch Potato Creek—*stream* ... PA-2
South Fork West Camp Creek—*stream* ... OR-9
South Fork West Creek—*stream* ... PA-2
South Fork West Fork Blacktail Deer Creek—*stream* ... MT-8
South Fork West Fork Canyon—*valley* ... ID-8
South Fork West Fork Creek—*stream* ... ID-8
South Fork West Fork Gallatin River—*stream* ... MT-8
South Fork West Fork Miller Creek—*stream* ... WY-8
South Fork West Indian Creek—*stream* ... CO-8
South Fork West Pass Creek—*stream* ... WY-8
South Fork West Soap Creek—*stream* ... MT-8
*South Fork West Tennessee Creek* ... CO-8
South Fork West Virginia Fork Dunkard Creek—*stream* ... WV-2
South Fork Whalehead Creek—*stream* ... OR-9
South Fork Whaley Gulch—*valley* ... SD-7
South Fork Whetstone Creek—*stream* ... MT-8
South Fork Whetstone Creek—*stream* ... SD-7
South Fork Whetstone River—*stream* ... SD-7
South Fork Whimstick Creek—*stream* ... ID-8
*South Fork Whiskey Creek* ... OR-9
South Fork Whiskey Jack Creek—*stream* ... ID-8
South Fork Whisky Creek—*stream* ... OR-9
South Fork Whitcomb Creek—*stream* ... WI-6
*South Fork Whitebird Creek* ... ID-8
South Fork White Bird Creek—*stream* ... ID-8
*South Fork White Creek* ... IN-6
South Fork White Creek—*stream* ... IN-6
South Fork White Creek—*stream* ... MT-8
South Fork White Draw—*valley* ... NM-5
*South Fork White Oak Bayou* ... TX-5
South Fork White Oak Creek—*stream* ... AR-4
*South Fork White River* ... SD-7
South Fork White River—*stream* ... CO-8
South Fork White River—*stream* ... MT-8
South Fork White River—*stream* ... WI-6
South Fork White Rock Branch—*stream* ... VA-3
South Fork Whites Branch—*stream* ... KY-4
South Fork Whitetail Creek—*stream* (3) ... MT-8
South Fork Whitewater Creek—*stream* ... NM-5
South Fork Whitewater River—*stream* ... CA-9
South Fork Whitewater River—*stream* ... MN-6
South Fork White Woman Creek—*stream* ... CO-8
South Fork White Woman Creek—*stream* ... KS-7
South Fork Wildcat Canyon—*valley* ... NV-8
*South Fork Wild Cat Creek* ... IN-6
South Fork Wildcat Creek—*stream* ... CA-9
South Fork Wildcat Creek—*stream* ... IN-6
South Fork Wildcat Creek—*stream* (2) ... KS-7
South Fork Wild Cherry Creek—*stream* ... CO-8
South Fork Wild Cow Creek—*stream* ... WY-8
South Fork Wilkes Creek—*stream* ... MT-8
South Fork Wilkins Creek—*stream* ... OR-9
South Fork Willame Creek—*stream* ... WA-9
*South Fork Willamina Creek* ... OR-9
South Fork Willapa River—*stream* ... WA-9
South Fork Willard Creek—*stream* ... NV-8
South Fork Williams Creek—*stream* ... ID-8
South Fork Williams Fork—*stream* (2) ... CO-8
*South Fork Williams Fork River* ... CO-8
*South Fork Willians river* ... CO-8
South Fork Willis Canyon—*valley* ... AZ-5
South Fork Willis Canyon—*valley* ... UT-8
South Fork Willoughby Creek—*stream* ... MT-8
South Fork Willow Canyon—*valley* ... CA-9
*South Fork Willow Creek* ... CA-9
*South Fork Willow Creek* ... MT-8
*South Fork Willow Creek* ... NV-8
*South Fork Willow Creek* ... PA-2
*South Fork Willow Creek* ... WY-8
South Fork Willow Creek—*stream* (7) ... CA-9
South Fork Willow Creek—*stream* (2) ... ID-8
South Fork Willow Creek—*stream* (5) ... MT-8
South Fork Willow Creek—*stream* (5) ... NV-8
South Fork Willow Creek—*stream* (2) ... OR-9
South Fork Willow Creek—*stream* (2) ... UT-8
South Fork Willow Creek—*stream* ... WY-8
South Fork Willow Creek Canyon—*valley* ... UT-8
South Fork Willow Creek (historical)—*stream* ... OR-9
South Fork Willow River—*stream* ... MN-6
South Fork Willow River—*stream* ... WI-6
South Fork Willow Slough—*stream* ... CA-9
*South Fork Wills Creek* ... OH-6
South Fork Wilson Creek—*stream* ... CO-8
South Fork Wilson River—*stream* ... OR-9
*South Fork Winberry Creek* ... OR-9
South Fork Winberry Creek—*stream* ... OR-9
South Fork Winchuck River—*stream* ... CA-9
*South Fork Wind Creek* ... OR-9
South Fork Wind Creek—*stream* (2) ... OR-9
South Fork Wind Creek—*stream* ... WY-8
South Fork Winston Creek—*stream* ... WA-9
*South Fork Wisconsin Creek* ... MT-8
South Fork Withrow Creek—*stream* ... NC-3
South Fork Wolf Creek—*stream* (2) ... CA-9
South Fork Wolf Creek—*stream* ... GA-3
South Fork Wolf Creek—*stream* ... OK-5
South Fork Wolf Creek—*stream* ... UT-8
South Fork Wolf Creek—*stream* ... WA-9
South Fork Wolf Fang Creek—*stream* ... ID-8
South Fork Wolf River—*stream* ... KS-7
South Fork Woodall Creek—*stream* ... AR-4
South Fork Wood Canyon—*valley* ... AZ-5
South Fork Wood River—*stream* ... WY-8
South Fork Woods Creek—*stream* ... CA-9
South Fork Woods Gulch Creek—*stream* ... MT-8
*South Fork Woody Creek* ... MT-8
South Fork Woody Creek—*stream* ... MT-8
South Fork Wooley Creek—*stream* ... CA-9
South Fork Worthing Canyon—*valley* ... ID-8
South Fork Wounded Man Creek—*stream* ... MT-8
South Fork Wright Creek—*stream* ... MO-7
South Fork Wright Creek—*stream* ... MT-8
South Fork Yaak River—*stream* ... MT-8
South Fork Yager Creek—*stream* ... CA-9
South Fork Yancy Creek—*stream* ... TX-5
South Fork Yankee Creek—*stream* ... AK-9
South Fork Yatama Creek—*stream* ... WA-9
South Fork Yearian Creek—*stream* ... ID-8
South Fork Yellow Bank River—*stream* ... MN-6
South Fork Yellow Bank River—*stream* ... SD-7
*South Fork Yellowleaf Creek* ... AL-4
South Fork Yellowleaf Creek—*stream* ... AL-4
*South Fork Yellow Medicine River* ... MN-6
South Fork Yellow River—*stream* ... WI-6
South Fork Yellowstone Creek—*stream* ... CO-8
South Fork Yellowstone River—*stream* ... WY-8
South Fork Young Branch—*stream* ... TN-4
South Fork Young Creek—*stream* ... MT-8
South Fork Youngs River—*stream* ... OR-9
*South Fork Yuba River* ... CA-9
South Fork Zumbro River—*stream* ... MN-6
South Forrest Attendance Center—*school* ... MS-4
South Fort—*locale* ... AZ-5
Southfort—*locale* ... FL-3
South Fort (historical)—*locale* ... MS-4
**South Fort Mitchell**—*pop pl* ... KY-4
South Fort Myers—*uninc pl* ... FL-3
South Fort Plain (RR name for Fort Plain P.O.)—*other* ... NY-2
South Fort Polk—*uninc pl* ... LA-4
**South Fort Smith**—*pop pl* ... AR-4
South Fort Smith Municipal Airp—*airport* ... AR-4
South Fort Worth—*uninc pl* ... TX-5
South Fort Worth Sch—*school* ... TX-5
**South Forty**—*pop pl* ... CO-8
**South Foster**—*pop pl* ... RI-1
South Foster Coulee—*valley* ... MT-8
South Fountain Ave Hist Dist—*hist pl* ... OH-6
*South Fourche La Fave River* ... AR-4
South Fourche LaFave River—*stream* ... AR-4
South Fourche Roadside Park—*park* ... AR-4
South Fourteen Ditch—*canal* ... NM-5
South Fourteen Tank—*reservoir* ... AZ-5
South Fourteenth Shop Ctr—*locale* ... FL-3
South Fowler Tank—*reservoir* ... TX-5
South Fowl Lake—*lake* ... MN-6
**South Foxboro**—*pop pl* ... MA-1
*South Foxborough* ... MA-1
*South Fox Creek* ... WY-8
South Fox Creek—*stream* ... IA-7
South Fox Island—*island* ... MI-6
South Fox Island Lighthouse—*locale* ... MI-6
South Fox Island Shoals—*bar* ... MI-6
South Fox Lake Sch—*school* ... MN-6
South Fox Rsvr—*reservoir* ... OR-9
South Fox Spring—*spring* ... NV-8
South Fox Well (flowing)—*well* ... NV-8
*South Framingham* ... MA-1
**South Framingham**—*pop pl* ... MA-1
South Fram Sch—*school* ... ND-7
**South Franconia**—*pop pl* ... VA-3
South Frankfort Neighborhood Hist Dist—*hist pl* ... KY-4
**South Franklin**—*pop pl* ... VT-1
South Franklin Cem—*cemetery* ... VT-1
South Franklin CSD Number 20 Sch—*school* ... TX-5
South Franklin Mtn—*summit* ... TX-5
*South Franklin Peak* ... TX-5
South Franklin Presbyterian Ch—*church* ... AL-4
South Franklin Sch—*school* ... OH-6
**South Franklin (Township of)**—*pop pl* ... PA-2
South Franklin (Unorganized Territory of)—*unorg* ... ME-1
South Franks Canyon—*valley* ... UT-8
South Franz Creek—*stream* ... CO-8
South Frasier Branch—*stream* ... AL-4
South Freedom Ch—*church* ... IL-6
South Freedom Ch—*church* ... NC-3
South Freeport—*locale* ... IL-6
**South Freeport**—*pop pl* ... ME-1
South Freeport Cem—*cemetery* ... ME-1
*South French Creek* ... CO-8
South French Creek—*stream* ... WY-8
South Friborg Cem—*cemetery* ... MN-6
South Fritz Island—*island* ... MO-7
South Front Street Hist Dist—*hist pl* ... PA-2
South Frying Pan Creek—*stream* ... MT-8
South Fullingim Draw—*valley* ... NM-5
**South Fulton**—*pop pl* ... TN-4
South Fulton Baptist Ch—*church* ... TN-4
South Fulton (CCD)—*cens area* ... TN-4
South Fulton City Hall—*building* ... TN-4
South Fulton Division—*civil* ... TN-4
South Fulton Elem Sch—*school* ... TN-4
South Fulton HS—*school* ... TN-4
South Fulton Industrial Park—*locale* ... TN-4
South Fulton Shopping Plaza—*locale* ... TN-4
*South Furnace Hill* ... PA-2
*South Gabori Creek* ... MO-7
South Gabouri Creek—*stream* ... MO-7
South Gabriel Cem—*cemetery* ... TX-5
**South Gadsden**—*pop pl* ... AL-4
South Gadsden Baptist Ch—*church* ... AL-4
South Gadsden Ch of God—*church* ... AL-4
South Gadsden Sch—*school* ... AL-4
South Gaines Creek—*stream* ... OK-5
South Gale—*locale* ... TX-5
South Gale School (historical)—*locale* ... MO-7
South Gallagher Flowage—*reservoir* ... WI-6
South Galloway Township—*civil* ... MO-7
**South Galway Corner**—*pop pl* ... NY-2
South Gandy Channel—*channel* ... FL-3
South Gap—*gap* ... NM-5
South Gap—*locale* ... VA-3
South Gap Creek—*stream* ... MT-8
South Gap Lake—*lake* ... WY-8
South Garber Creek—*stream* ... CO-8
South Garcia—*locale* ... NM-5
South Garcia Well—*well* ... NM-5
South Garden—*locale* ... VA-3
South Gardena—*uninc pl* ... CA-9
South Garden Canyon—*valley* ... NV-8
South Garden Oil And Gas Field—*oilfield* ... OK-5
South Garden Sch—*school* ... KS-7
*South Gardiner* ... ME-1
**South Gardiner**—*pop pl* ... ME-1
**South Gardner**—*pop pl* ... MA-1
*South Gardner Pond* ... MA-1
*South Gardner Reservoir* ... MA-1
*South Gardner Village* ... MA-1
South Garfield—*cens area* ... MT-8
South Garfield (CCD)—*cens area* ... OK-5
South Garfield Sch—*school* ... MI-6
*South Gargathy Creek* ... VA-3
South Garrison Branch—*stream* ... TN-4
**South Garry Owen**—*pop pl* ... IA-7
*South Gary* ... IN-6
South Gasconades Creek—*stream* ... TX-5
South Gash Creek—*stream* ... MT-8
**South Gastonia**—*pop pl* ... NC-3
South Gastonia (census name for Gastonia South)—*CDP* ... NC-3
South Gastonia Elem Sch—*school* ... NC-3
*Southgate* ... IL-6
*Southgate* ... IN-6
South Gate—*CDP* ... MD-2
South Gate—*locale* ... CA-9
South Gate—*locale* ... NV-8
**South Gate**—*pop pl* ... CA-9
**South Gate**—*pop pl* ... IN-6
**Southgate**—*pop pl* ... KY-4
**Southgate**—*pop pl* ... MI-6
**Southgate**—*pop pl* ... WA-9
Southgate—*post sta* ... OR-9
Southgate—*post sta* ... WA-9
Southgate (alternate name for Sarasota Southeast)—*CDP* ... FL-3
Southgate Baptist Ch—*church* ... MS-4
South Gate Brook—*stream* ... ME-1
South Gate Cem—*cemetery* ... IN-6
Southgate Crossing Shop Ctr—*locale* ... TN-4
**Southgate Estates (subdivision)**—*pop pl* ... NC-3
Southgate Financial Center—*building* ... KS-7
South Gate Hill—*summit* ... IN-6
Southgate House—*hist pl* ... KY-4
South Gate HS—*school* ... CA-9
Southgate HS—*school* ... MI-6
Southgate Industrial Park—*locale* ... DE-2
South Gate JHS—*school* ... CA-9
Southgate-Lewis House—*hist pl* ... TX-5
Southgate Mall—*locale* ... AZ-5
Southgate Mall Shop Ctr—*locale* ... AL-4
Southgate Mtn—*summit* ... VT-1
South Gate Park—*park* ... CA-9
Southgate-Parker-Maddux House—*hist pl* ... KY-4
**Southgate Park Subdivision**—*pop pl* ... UT-8
Southgate Plaza—*locale* ... VA-3
South Gate Plaza—*post sta* ... ID-8
South Gate Plaza (Shop Ctr)—*locale* (2) ... FL-3
Southgate Plaza (Shop Ctr)—*locale* ... MA-1
Southgate Plaza Shop Ctr—*locale* ... NY-2
Southgate Pond—*lake* ... VI-3
South Gate Ridge—*CDP* ... FL-3
Southgate Sch—*school* ... CA-9
Southgate Sch—*school* ... NY-2
Southgate Sch—*school* ... TX-5
Southgate Sch—*school* ... WA-9
*Southgate Shop Ctr* ... TN-4
South Gate Shop Ctr—*locale* ... AL-4
Southgate Shop Ctr—*locale* (2) ... AZ-5
Southgate Shop Ctr—*locale* ... AR-4
Southgate Shop Ctr—*locale* ... CA-9
Southgate Shop Ctr—*locale* (4) ... FL-3
Southgate (Shop Ctr)—*locale* ... FL-3
South Gate Shop Ctr—*locale* ... FL-3
Southgate Shop Ctr—*locale* (3) ... KS-7
Southgate Shop Ctr—*locale* ... MI-6
Southgate Shop Ctr—*locale* (2) ... MS-4
Southgate Shop Ctr—*locale* ... MO-7
Southgate Shop Ctr—*locale* ... NC-3
Southgate Shop Ctr—*locale* ... OH-6
Southgate Shop Ctr—*locale* (2) ... SD-7
South Gate Shop Ctr—*locale* ... TN-4
Southgate Shop Ctr—*locale* ... UT-8
South Gate Shopping Mall—*locale* ... PA-2
Southgate Shopping Plaza—*locale* ... MA-1
**South Gate (subdivision)**—*pop pl* ... AL-4
**Southgate (subdivision)**—*pop pl* ... AL-4
**Southgate (subdivision)**—*pop pl* (2) ... NC-3
**Southgate Subdivision**—*pop pl* ... TN-4
**South Gate (subdivision)**—*pop pl* ... TN-4
**South Gate Village (subdivision)**—*pop pl* ... TN-4
South Gatlin Creek—*stream* ... TX-5
South Gavilan Windmill—*locale* ... NM-5
South Gawley Ridge—*ridge* ... OR-9
South Geddis Canyon—*valley* ... TX-5
South Geen Mtn—*summit* ... OR-9
**South Georgetown**—*pop pl* ... MA-1
South Georgia Coll—*school* ... GA-3
South Georgia College Administration Bldg—*hist pl* ... GA-3
South Georgia Mine—*mine* ... AZ-5
South Georgia State College—*building* ... GA-3
South Georiga Home For The Aged—*building* ... GA-3
South Georiga Technical Sch—*school* ... GA-3
South German Park—*park* ... MN-6
South German Street Hist Dist—*hist pl* ... MN-6
South Getaway Coulee—*valley* ... MT-8
**South Gibson**—*pop pl* ... PA-2
South Gibson Cem—*cemetery* ... PA-2
**South Gifford**—*pop pl* ... MO-7
South Gila Ditch—*canal* ... AZ-5
South Gila Valley—*valley* ... AZ-5
South Gila Valley Main Canal—*canal* ... AZ-5
South Gilbert Sch—*school* ... MI-6
**South Gilboa**—*pop pl* ... NY-2
**South Gilboa (Station)**—*pop pl* ... NY-2
*South Gildford* ... MT-8
South Gililland Well—*well* ... NM-5
South Girard HS—*school* ... AL-4
South Glacier—*glacier* ... AK-9
South Glacier—*glacier* ... WA-9
*South Glacier Lake* ... WA-9
South Glade Creek—*stream* ... PA-2
South Glassboro—*uninc pl* ... NJ-2
**South Glastonbury**—*pop pl* ... CT-1
South Glastonbury Hist Dist—*hist pl* ... CT-1
South Glen Aubin Oil Field—*oilfield* ... MS-4
**South Glendale Subdivision**—*pop pl* ... UT-8
Southglenn—*CDP* ... CO-8
South Glenn Ch of God—*church* ... KS-7
Southglenn Shop Ctr—*other* ... CO-8
South Glen Playground—*park* ... MN-6
**South Glens Falls**—*pop pl* ... NY-2
South Glens Falls HS—*school* ... NY-2
South Glenwood Landing—*locale* ... NY-2
**South Glenwoods**—*pop pl* ... CT-1
South Glory Hole—*bay* ... GA-3
South Godwin Sch—*school* ... MI-6
*South Gold Creek* ... ID-8
South Gold Creek—*stream* ... MT-8
South Golden Valley—*unorg reg* ... ND-7
**South Goldsboro**—*pop pl* ... NC-3
South Goldsboro (census name for Goldsboro South)—*CDP* ... NC-3
South Golf Course—*other* ... AZ-5
South Gooding Main Canal—*canal* ... ID-8
South Gooding Siphon—*other* ... ID-8
South Goodland Sch—*school* ... SC-3
South Goodwin Spring—*spring* ... AZ-5
South Goodwin Tank—*reservoir* ... AZ-5
South Gooseberry Island—*island* ... MA-1
South Goose Creek—*stream* ... KY-4
*South Goose Lake* ... WA-9
**South Gorham**—*pop pl* ... ME-1
*South Gorin* ... MO-7
**South Gorin (census name for Gorin)**—*pop pl* ... MO-7
South Goucher Creek—*stream* ... SC-3
South Gouge Eye Well—*well* ... NV-8
**South Gouldsboro**—*pop pl* ... ME-1
South Government Island—*island* ... MI-6
South Grade Rsvr—*reservoir* ... OR-9
South Grade Sch—*school* ... MT-8
South Grade Sch—*school* ... NE-7
South Grade Sch Bldg—*hist pl* ... IN-6
*South Grafton* ... MA-1
**South Grafton**—*pop pl* ... MA-1
**South Grafton**—*pop pl* ... WV-2
**South Grafton Street (subdivision)**—*pop pl* ... MA-1
South Graham Sch—*school* ... NC-3
South Graham Shoal—*bar* ... MI-6
South Granada Ditch—*canal* ... CO-8
**South Granby**—*pop pl* ... NY-2
South Grand Ave Interchange—*other* ... IL-6
South Grand Blanc Cem—*cemetery* ... MI-6
South Grand Chenier Gas Field—*oilfield* ... LA-4
South Grand Island Bridge—*bridge* ... NY-2
South Grand River—*stream* ... MO-7
South Granger (historical P.O.)—*locale* ... IN-6
**South Grants Pass**—*pop pl* ... OR-9
**South Granville**—*pop pl* ... NY-2
South Granville Sch—*school* ... NC-3
South Grape Creek—*stream* ... TX-5
South Grape Creek Sch—*school* ... TX-5
South Grasshopper Lake—*lake* ... FL-3
**South Gray**—*pop pl* ... ME-1
South Gray Rsvr—*reservoir* ... CO-8
South Graysport Public Use Area—*park* ... MS-4
South Greasewood Creek—*stream* ... WY-8
South Greasy Creek—*stream* ... TX-5
**South Greece**—*pop pl* ... NY-2
South Greek Lake—*lake* ... NY-2
South Green Baptist Ch—*church* ... MS-4
South Greenbriar Creek—*stream* ... TX-5
South Greene HS—*school* ... TN-4
South Greene Township—*civil* ... MO-7
**South Greenfield**—*pop pl* ... MO-7
**South Greenfield**—*pop pl* ... NY-2
South Green Hist Dist—*hist pl* ... MA-1
South Green Lake Cem—*cemetery* ... MN-6
South Greenleaf Creek—*stream* ... CO-8
South Greensboro—*uninc pl* ... NC-3
**South Greensburg**—*pop pl* ... PA-2
South Greensburg Borough—*civil* ... PA-2
South Green Sedge—*swamp* ... NY-2
South Green (Township of)—*fmr MCD* ... MO-7
South Greentree Rsvr—*reservoir* ... MS-4
South Greenup District—*hist pl* ... KY-4
**South Greenville**—*pop pl* ... SC-3
*South Greenville Elementary School* ... NC-3
South Greenville Hist Dist—*hist pl* ... AL-4
South Greenville Park—*park* ... NC-3
South Greenville Sch—*school* ... LA-4
South Greenville Sch—*school* ... NC-3
South Greenwood—*locale* ... MI-6
**South Greenwood**—*pop pl* ... SC-3
South Greenwood Creek—*stream* ... MN-6
South Gregory Creek Rsvr—*reservoir* ... OR-9
South Griffith Well—*well* ... NM-5
South Grizzly Creek—*stream* ... CO-8
South Groesbeck Creek—*stream* ... TX-5
South Grotto—*cave* ... ID-8
*South Grove* ... MN-6
South Grove—*woods* ... CA-9
South Grove Cem—*cemetery* ... IL-6
South Grove Cem—*cemetery* ... IA-7
South Grove Cem—*cemetery* ... WI-6
South Grove Creek—*stream* ... TX-5
South Grove Elem Sch—*school* ... IN-6
South Grove Hollow—*valley* ... UT-8
**South Groveland**—*pop pl* ... MA-1
South Grove Sch—*school* ... MN-6
South Grove Sch—*school* ... MO-7
South Grove Sch—*school* ... NY-2
South Grove Sch (historical)—*school* ... PA-2
South Grove Spring—*spring* ... UT-8
South Groveton—*uninc pl* ... TX-5
**South Grove (Township of)**—*pop pl* ... IL-6
South Grundy (Magisterial District)—*fmr MCD* ... VA-3
South Guadalupe River—*stream* ... TX-5
South Guam—*locale* ... NM-5
South Guard—*summit* ... CA-9
South Guardian Angel—*summit* ... UT-8
South Guardian Rock—*pillar* ... WA-9
South Guard Lake—*lake* ... CA-9
South Guffy Creek—*stream* ... MO-7
South Gulch—*valley* ... CA-9
South Gulch—*valley* ... CO-8
South Gulch—*valley* ... ID-8
South Gulch Ditch—*canal* ... CA-9
South Gully—*stream* ... NY-2
South Gully—*valley* ... NY-2
South Guntersville—*uninc pl* ... AL-4
South Guth Park—*park* ... TX-5
South Guzzler Waterhole—*reservoir* ... OR-9
South Gypsum Creek—*stream* ... KS-7
South Habersham HS—*school* ... GA-3
South Hackberry Draw—*valley* ... NM-5
**South Hackensack**—*pop pl* ... NJ-2
**South Hackensack (Township of)**—*pop pl* ... NJ-2
**South Hadley**—*pop pl* ... MA-1
South Hadley Canal—*canal* ... MA-1
South Hadley Cem—*cemetery* ... MI-6
South Hadley Center Sch—*school* ... MA-1
South Hadley Ch—*church* ... MI-6
South Hadley Falls—*falls* ... MA-1
**South Hadley Falls**—*pop pl* ... MA-1
South Hadley Falls HS—*school* ... MA-1
South Hadley Falls Townhall—*building* ... MA-1
South Hadley Sch—*school* ... MA-1
**South Hadley (Town of)**—*pop pl* ... MA-1
*South Halawa Gulch* ... HI-9
South Halawa Stream—*stream* ... HI-9
**South Haleyville**—*pop pl* ... AL-4
South Haleyville—*uninc pl* ... AL-4

South Haleyville Baptist Ch—*church* ... AL-4
South Haleyville Ch of Christ—*church* ... AL-4
South Haleyville Grammer Sch (historical)—*school* ... AL-4
South Halfmoon Creek—*stream* ... CO-8
**South Halifax**—*pop pl* ... MA-1
South Hall—*hist pl* ... CA-9
**South Hall**—*pop pl* ... TN-4
South Hall—*valley* ... UT-8
South Hall, River Falls State Normal Sch—*hist pl* ... WI-6
South Hall Landing—*locale* ... AL-4
South Hall Sch—*school* ... GA-3
*South Hamilton* ... OH-6
**South Hamilton**—*pop pl* ... MA-1
**South Hamilton**—*pop pl* ... NY-2
*South Hamilton Elem Sch* ... PA-2
South Hamilton Elem Sch—*school* ... FL-3
South Hamilton HS—*school* ... MA-1
**South Hamilton (RR name Hamilton and Wenham)**—*pop pl* ... MA-1
South Hamilton Sch—*school* ... PA-2
South Hamilton Street Row—*hist pl* ... NY-2
South Hamlin Sch—*school* ... MI-6
South Hamma Hamma River Bridge—*hist pl* ... WA-9
South Hammock Canyon—*valley* ... NM-5
South Hammocks—*island* ... MD-2
*South Hammond* ... IN-6
**South Hammond**—*pop pl* ... NY-2
South Hammond Brook—*stream* ... ME-1
*South Hampton* ... NJ-2
**Southhampton**—*pop pl* ... MO-7
**South Hampton**—*pop pl* ... NH-1
**South Hampton**—*pop pl* ... VA-3
Southhampton Bay—*bay* ... CA-9
South Hampton Ch—*church* ... KY-4
South Hampton Creek—*stream* ... GA-3
South Hampton Oil and Gas Field—*oilfield* ... TX-5
*South Hampton Oil Field* ... TX-5
Southhampton Speedway—*other* ... VA-3
**South Hampton (Town of)**—*pop pl* ... NH-1
South Hanaford Creek—*stream* ... WA-9
**South Hancock**—*pop pl* ... ME-1
South Hand Grazing Association Dam—*dam* ... SD-7
South Hanksville Airp—*airport* ... UT-8
South Hanlon—*locale* ... TX-5
South Hannahs Fork—*stream* ... ID-8
**South Hannibal**—*pop pl* ... NY-2
*South Hanover* ... NJ-2
**South Hanover**—*pop pl* ... MA-1
*South Hanover Elementary School* ... PA-2
South Hanover (historical P.O.)—*locale* ... MA-1
South Hanover Sch—*school* ... PA-2
**South Hanover (Township of)**—*pop pl* ... PA-2
**South Hanson**—*pop pl* ... MA-1
South Hanson (historical P.O.)—*locale* ... MA-1
South Hanson (RR name for Hanson)—*other* ... MA-1
South Hanson Station (historical)—*locale* . MA-1
South Happytown Oil and Gas Field—*oilfield* ... LA-4
*South Harbor* ... IN-6
*South Harbor* ... WA-9
South Harbor—*bay* ... NJ-2
South Harborcreek Ch—*church* ... PA-2
South Harbor Park—*park* ... NY-2
South Harbor (Township of)—*civ div* ... MN-6
South Harding—*unorg reg* ... SD-7
South Harding (CCD)—*cens area* ... NM-5
South Hardscrabble Creek—*stream* ... CO-8
South Hardscrabble Park—*flat* ... CO-8
*South Hardwick* ... VT-1
*South Hare Creek* ... WY-8
South Harford Cem—*cemetery* ... PA-2
South Harkins Well—*well* ... MT-8
South Harmony Oil Field—*oilfield* ... MS-4
South Harnett Sch—*school* ... NC-3
South Harper Hist Dist—*hist pl* ... SC-3
South Harper Lake—*lake* ... WI-6
South Harpersfield Ch—*church* ... OH-6
South Harpeth Ch—*church* ... TN-4
*South Harpeth Creek* ... TN-4
South Harpeth Creek—*stream* ... TN-4
*South Harpeth River* ... TN 4
South Harpeth River—*stream* ... TN-4
South Harpeth Sch (historical)—*school* ... TN-4
**South Harpswell**—*pop pl* ... ME-1
**South Harriman**—*pop pl* ... TN-4
South Harriman Baptist Ch—*church* ... TN-4
South Harriman MS—*school* ... TN-4
South Harrison Cem—*cemetery* ... ME-1
South Harrison Lake—*reservoir* ... IN-6
South Harrison Sch—*school* ... ME-1
South Harrison (Township of)—*fmr MCD* ... AR-4
**South Harrison (Township of)**—*pop pl* ... NJ-2
South Harris Trail—*trail* ... OK-5
South Hart Cem—*cemetery* ... MI-6
**South Hartford**—*pop pl* (2) ... NY-2
South Hartland Cem—*cemetery* ... MN-6
South Hartsville—*CDP* ... SC-3
South Hartsville Ch—*church* ... SC-3
**South Hartwick**—*pop pl* ... NY-2
South Harvey Ch—*church* ... OH-6
**South Harwich**—*pop pl* ... MA-1
South Harwich Methodist Church—*hist pl* . MA-1
*South Haskell Creek* ... NV-8
South Hatch Canyon—*valley* ... UT-8
South Haulover Creek—*stream* ... SC-3
**South Haven**—*pop pl* (2) ... IN-6
**South Haven**—*pop pl* ... KS-7
**South Haven**—*pop pl* ... MD-2
**South Haven**—*pop pl* ... MI-6
**South Haven**—*pop pl* ... MN-6
**Southhaven**—*pop pl* ... MS-4
**South Haven**—*pop pl* ... NY-2
**South Haven**—*pop pl* ... OK-5
**South Haven**—*pop pl* ... TX-5
*South Haven Beach* ... MD-2
South Haven Ch—*church* ... MS-4
South-Haven Christian Ch—*church* ... FL-3
*Southhaven Elem Sch* ... TN-4
South Haven Elem Sch—*school* ... IN-6
South Haven Elem Sch—*school* ... TN-4
South Haven Golf Course—*other* ... AR-4
**South Haven Highlands**—*pop pl* ... MI-6
South Haven HS—*school* ... KS-7
South Haven Oil Field—*oilfield* ... KS-7
South Haven Sch—*school* ... MS-4
South Haven Sch—*school* ... NY-2
**Southhaven (subdivision)**—*pop pl* ... MS-4
**South Haven (subdivision)**—*pop pl* ... NC-3
**South Haven Township**—*pop pl* ... KS-7
**South Haven (Township of)**—*pop pl* ... MI-6
**South Hawley**—*pop pl* ... MA-1
South Haynes Lake—*lake* ... MN-6
*South Hazelhurst Attendance Center* ... MS-4
South Head—*cape* ... AK-9
South Head—*cliff* ... AK-9
South Head—*cliff* ... WA-9
**South Heart**—*pop pl* ... ND-7
South Heater Sch—*school* ... IL-6
South Heather Creek—*stream* ... WY-8
**South Heberton (subdivision)**—*pop pl* ... PA-2
South Hebron Cem—*cemetery* ... IL-6
South Hecla Mine—*mine* ... UT-8
South Heglar Canyon—*valley* ... ID-8
South Hegman Lake—*lake* ... MN-6
**South Heidelberg (Township of)**—*pop pl* ... PA-2
**South Heights**—*pop pl* ... PA-2
**South Heights Addition (subdivision)**—*pop pl* ... UT-8
South Heights Borough—*civil* ... PA-2
South Heights Cem—*cemetery* ... OK-5
South Heights Ch of the Nazarene—*church* ... FL-3
South Heights Sch—*school* ... KY-4
South Heights Sch—*school* ... OK-5
South Hell Creek—*stream* ... NV-8
South Helmer Lake—*lake* ... MI-6
South Helms Creek—*stream* ... TX-5
South Hemlock—*locale* ... NH-1
South Hemlock Lake—*reservoir* ... IN-6
**South Hempstead**—*pop pl* ... NY-2
**South Henderson**—*pop pl* ... NC-3
South Henderson Cem—*cemetery* ... IL-6
South Henderson (census name for Henderson South)—*CDP* ... NC-3
South Henderson Church and Cemetery—*hist pl* ... IL-6
South Henderson Creek—*stream* (2) ... IL-6
South Henderson Sch—*school* ... IL-6
South Henderson Well—*well* ... TX-5
South Hermitage—*locale* ... PA-2
South Hermitage Post Office (historical)—*building* ... PA-2
**South Hero**—*pop pl* ... VT-1
South Hero Cem—*cemetery* ... VT-1
South Hero Inn—*hist pl* ... VT-1
South Hero Island—*island* ... VT-1
South Heron Lake—*lake* ... MN-6
**South Hero (Town of)**—*pop pl* ... VT-1
South Herrick Cem—*cemetery* ... PA-2
South Hialeah Sch—*school* ... FL-3
South Hickory Creek—*stream* ... TX-5
South Hickory Hill Ch—*church* ... IL-6
South Hidalgo (CCD)—*cens area* ... NM-5
South Higginsport—*locale* ... KY-4
**South Highland**—*pop pl* ... KY-4
**South Highland**—*pop pl* ... NY-2
South Highland Baptist Ch—*church* ... AL-4
South Highland Ch—*church* ... AL-4
South Highland Ch—*church* ... GA-3
South Highland Presbyterian Ch—*church* ... AL-4
*South Highlands* ... OH-6
**South Highlands**—*pop pl* ... AL-4
**South Highlands**—*pop pl* ... OH-6
**South Highlands**—*pop pl* ... WA-9
South Highlands—*uninc pl* ... LA-4
South Highlands Baptist Ch—*church* ... AL-4
South Highland Sch—*school* (3) ... AL-4
South Highland Sch—*school* ... SD-7
*South Highlands Elem Sch* ... AL-4
South Highlands Hosp—*hospital* ... AL-4
*South Highlands Middle School* ... AL-4
South Highlands Sch—*school* ... LA-4
South Highline Lateral Canal—*canal* ... AZ-5
South High Lonesome Oil Field—*other* ... NM-5
*South High School* ... KS-7
South High Springs RR Station—*locale* ... FL-3
South High Street Commercial Grouping—*hist pl* ... OH-6
*South Hill* ... UT-8
South Hill—*locale* ... AL-4
South Hill—*locale* ... KY-4
South Hill—*locale* ... PA-2
**South Hill**—*pop pl* ... NY-2
**South Hill**—*pop pl* ... VA-3
**South Hill**—*pop pl* ... WA-9
South Hill—*summit* ... CA-9
South Hill—*summit* ... ID-8
South Hill—*summit* ... ME-1
South Hill—*summit* (2) ... NV-8
South Hill—*summit* (2) ... NH-1
South Hill—*summit* (13) ... NY-2
South Hill—*summit* ... PA-2
South Hill—*summit* (3) ... VT-1
South Hill Cem—*cemetery* ... IL-6
South Hill Cem—*cemetery* ... NY-2
South Hill Cem—*cemetery* (3) ... VT-1
**South Hill Crest Subdivision**—*pop pl* ... UT-8
South Hill Hist Dist—*hist pl* ... KY-4
South Hill (Magisterial District)—*fmr MCD* . VA-3
**South Hill Park**—*pop pl* ... OH-6
South Hills—*other* ... CA-9
**South Hills**—*pop pl* ... PA-2
**South Hills**—*pop pl* ... SC-3
**South Hills**—*pop pl* ... TN-4
**South Hills**—*pop pl* (2) ... WV-2
South Hills—*range* ... OK-5
South Hills—*summit* (3) ... UT-8
South Hills—*uninc pl* ... KY-4
South Hills Acad—*school* ... CA-9
South Hills Ch—*church* ... NY-2
South Hill Sch—*school* ... NH-1
South Hill Sch—*school* ... NM-5
South Hill Sch—*school* ... NY-2
South Hills Country Club—*other* ... CA-9
South Hills Country Club—*other* ... PA-2
South Hills Golf Club—*locale* ... TN-4
South Hills Golf Course—*locale* ... PA-2
South Hills Golf Course—*locale* ... TN-4
South Hills HS—*school* ... CA-9
South Hills HS—*school* ... PA-2
South Hillside Ch—*church* ... TX-5
South Hillside Elem Sch—*school* ... KS-7
South Hills Sch—*school* ... TX-5
South Hills Sch (abandoned)—*school* ... PA-2
South Hills Shop Ctr—*locale* ... CA-9
**South Hills (subdivision)**—*pop pl* ... NC-3
**South Hills (subdivision)**—*pop pl* ... TN-4
**South Hill (subdivision)**—*pop pl* ... VA-3
South Hilmar Cem—*cemetery* ... CA-9
South Hi-Mount Sch—*school* ... TX-5
South Hinckley Canal—*canal* ... UT-8
**South Hinesburg**—*pop pl* ... VT-1
**South Hingham**—*pop pl* ... MA-1
South Hingham (historical P.O.)—*locale* ... MA-1
**South Hiram**—*pop pl* ... ME-1
South Hobart Well—*well* ... NM-5
South Hodges Drain—*canal* ... CA-9
South Hogan Creek—*stream* ... IN-6
South Hog Canyon—*valley* ... NV-8
South Hog Creek—*stream* ... AR-4
**South Hoisington**—*pop pl* ... KS-7
South Hoiston Ch—*church* ... TN-4
South Hoke Elem Sch—*school* ... NC-3
**South Holbrook**—*pop pl* ... NY-2
South Hole—*basin* ... AZ-5
South Hole—*gut* ... FL-3
South Hole—*valley* ... CO-8
South Hole Spring—*spring* ... AZ-5
**South Holland**—*pop pl* ... IL-6
South Hollandale—*locale* ... MN-6
South Holley Tank—*reservoir* ... TX-5
South Hollis—*locale* ... ME-1
South Hollow—*valley* ... IN-6
South Hollow—*valley* ... MO-7
South Hollow—*valley* (2) ... PA-2
South Hollow—*valley* ... TN-4
South Hollow—*valley* (3) ... UT-8
South Hollow—*valley* ... WV-2
South Hollow Brook—*stream* ... NY-2
South Hollow Cem—*cemetery* ... VT-1
South Holly Branch—*stream* ... AR-4
South Holly Creek—*stream* (2) ... OK-5
South Holston Boat Dock—*locale* ... VA-3
South Holston Dam—*dam* ... TN-4
South Holston Lake—*reservoir* ... TN-4
South Holston Lake—*reservoir* ... VA-3
**South Holt**—*pop pl* ... AL-4
**South Holt Highlands (subdivision)**—*pop pl* ... AL-4
South Holton Sch—*school* ... KS-7
South Home Lake—*lake* ... NM-5
**South Homer (Township of)**—*pop pl* ... IL-6
**South Homestead Township**—*pop pl* ... KS-7
**South Hominy**—*pop pl* ... NC-3
South Hominy Creek—*stream* ... NC-3
South Honcut Creek—*stream* ... CA-9
South Honeycutt Windmill—*locale* ... NM-5
*South Honeysuckle Lake* ... MI-6
**South Hooksett**—*pop pl* ... NH-1
South Hoosier Creek—*stream* ... IA-7
**South Hope**—*pop pl* ... ME-1
South Hope Creek—*stream* ... CO-8
South Hope Lake—*lake* ... MN-6
South Hopewell Ch—*church* ... MS-4
South Hopewell Ch (historical)—*church* ... MS-4
South Hopkins Sch—*school* ... KY-4
**South Hopkinton**—*pop pl* ... RI-1
**South Horicon**—*pop pl* ... NY-2
South Horn Branch—*stream* ... MO-7
**South Hornell**—*pop pl* ... NY-2
*South Horn Mountain* ... UT-8
South Horn Mtn—*summit* ... UT-8
South Horse Camp Spring—*spring* ... NV-8
South Horse Creek—*stream* ... CO-8
South Horse Creek—*stream* ... WY-8
South Horse Creek Ditch—*canal* ... WY-8
South Horse Creek Lateral—*canal* ... NE-7
South Horse Creek Lateral—*canal* ... WY-8
South Horse Hollow Rsvr—*reservoir* ... UT-8
South Horse Mountain Tank—*reservoir* ... AZ-5
*South Horseneck Shoal* ... FL-3
South Horseshoe Creek—*stream* ... WY-8
South Horse Spring—*spring* ... NV-8
**South Hot Springs**—*pop pl* ... AR-4
South Houma Oil and Gas Field—*oilfield* ... LA-4
South House Pasture Well—*well* ... NM-5
South House Windmill—*locale* ... NM-5
**South Houston**—*pop pl* ... TX-5
**South Houston (RR name Dumont)**—*pop pl* ... TX-5
South Howland Cove—*bay* ... AZ-5
South Hoyt Sch—*school* ... KS-7
South HQ—*locale* ... TX-5
South HQ Tank—*reservoir* ... AZ-5
South HS—*school* (2) ... CA-9
South HS—*school* (2) ... CO-8
South HS—*school* ... KS-7
South HS—*school* ... MA-1
South HS—*school* ... MI-6
South HS—*school* ... NE-7
South HS—*school* ... NY-2
South HS—*school* (6) ... OH-6
South HS—*school* ... PA-2
South HS—*school* ... UT-8
South HS—*school* ... WI-6
South Huckleberry Mtn—*summit* ... WA-9
South Hudson Falls—*CDP* ... NY-2
*South Huerfano Creek* ... CO-8
*South Huerfano River* ... CO-8
South Hughes Canyon—*valley* ... UT-8
South Hughes (CCD)—*cens area* ... OK-5
South Hume Sch—*school* ... IL-6
South Humphreys Gas Field—*oilfield* ... LA-4
*South Hunt* ... IN-6
South Hunt Creek—*stream* ... CO-8
South Hunter Oil And Gas Field—*oilfield* ... OK-5
South Huntingdon—*other* ... PA-2
South Huntingdon Township HS—*school* ... PA-2
**South Huntingdon (Township of)**—*pop pl* ... PA-2
**South Huntington**—*pop pl* ... NY-2
South Hunton Creek—*stream* ... WY-8
South Huntsville Airp—*airport* ... AL-4
South Hurricane (Township of)—*civ div* ... IL-6
**South Hutchinson**—*pop pl* ... KS-7
South Hutchinson Elem Sch—*school* ... KS-7
**South Hyannis**—*pop pl* ... MA-1
South Hyco Creek—*stream* ... NC-3
South Ice Cave—*cave* ... OR-9
South Ideal Shop Ctr—*locale* ... KS-7
**South Idylwild (subdivision)**—*pop pl* ... FL-3
**South Ilion**—*pop pl* ... NY-2
South Illinois Sch—*school* ... KS-7
South Illinois Sch—*school* ... SD-7
South Immanuel Ch—*church* ... MN-6
South Indian Cem—*cemetery* ... OK-5
*South Indian Creek* ... CA-9
*South Indian Creek* ... SD-7
South Indian Creek—*stream* ... MO-7
South Indian Creek—*stream* ... MT-8
South Indian Creek—*stream* ... SD-7
South Indian Creek—*stream* ... TN-4
South Indian Creek—*stream* ... WY-8
South Indian Field—*island* ... FL-3
South Indian Rsvr—*reservoir* ... OR-9
South Industrial Park—*locale* ... TN-4
**Southington**—*pop pl* ... CT-1
**Southington**—*pop pl* ... OH-6
Southington Country Club—*other* ... CT-1
Southington Mtn—*summit* ... CT-1
Southington Rsvr No 1—*reservoir* ... CT-1
Southington Rsvr No 2—*reservoir* ... CT-1
Southington Rsvr No 3—*reservoir* ... CT-1
**Southington (Town of)**—*pop pl* ... CT-1
**Southington (Township of)**—*pop pl* ... OH-6
South Inian Pass—*channel* ... AK-9
*South Inlet* ... FL-3
South Inlet—*bay* ... NY-2
South Inlet—*bay* ... OR-9
South Inlet—*gut* ... VA-3
South Inlet—*stream* (2) ... ME-1
South Inlet—*stream* (3) ... NY-2
South Inlet Brook—*stream* ... ME-1
**South International Falls**—*pop pl* ... MN-6
**South Ionia**—*pop pl* ... MI-6
South Iredell HS—*school* ... NC-3
South Iron Blossom—*mine* ... UT-8
South Iron Blossom Headframe—*hist pl* ... UT-8
South Iron Gate Tank—*reservoir* ... AZ-5
South Ironwood Creek—*stream* ... SD-7
**South Irvine**—*pop pl* ... KY-4
South Islamorada Underwater Coral Gardens—*bar* ... FL-3
*South Island* ... MD-2
*South Island* ... NY-2
*South Island* ... FM-9
*South Island* ... MP-9
South Island—*island* ... AL-4
South Island—*island* (4) ... AK-9
South Island—*island* ... FL-3
South Island—*island* (2) ... MA-1
South Island—*island* ... MI-6
South Island—*island* ... NC-3
South Island—*island* ... SC-3
South Island—*island* ... VA-3
South Island—*island* ... MP-9
South Island Campground—*park* ... OR-9
South Island Lake—*lake* ... MN-6
*South Islands* ... FM-9
*South Islesboro* ... ME-1
South Italian Creek—*stream* ... CO-8
South Itasca—*locale* ... WI-6
South Itasca—*uninc pl* ... WI-6
South Itasca (Unorganized Territory of)—*unorg* ... MN-6
South Jack Creek—*stream* ... SD-7
South Jackson—*locale* ... VA-3
**South Jackson**—*pop pl* ... MI-6
South Jackson Canyon—*valley* ... CA-9
South Jackson Mine—*mine* ... CA-9
South Jackson Public Shooting Area—*park* ... SD-7
South Jackson Sch—*school* ... GA-3
South Jackson Street Ch of Christ—*church* ... MS-4
South Jackson United Pentecostal Ch—*church* ... MS-4
**South Jacksonville**—*pop pl* ... FL-3
**South Jacksonville**—*pop pl* ... IL-6
South Jacksonville—*uninc pl* ... AR-4
South Jacktar Hollow—*valley* ... MO-7
South Jacobsen Rsvr—*reservoir* ... OR-9
**South Jamesport**—*pop pl* ... NY-2
South James Windmill—*locale* ... TX-5
South Janesville—*uninc pl* ... WI-6
South Jeannette Oil Field—*oilfield* ... MS-4
South Jefferson—*cens area* ... CO-8
South Jefferson—*locale* ... ME-1
South Jefferson—*locale* ... NY-2
South Jefferson Ave Hist Dist—*hist pl* ... MI-6
South Jefferson (CCD)—*cens area* ... OK-5
South Jefferson Cem—*cemetery* ... KY-4
South Jefferson Creek—*stream* ... MT-8
South Jefferson Sch—*school* ... WV-2
South Jennings Oil and Gas Field—*oilfield* ... LA-4
South Jenny Lake Junction—*locale* ... WY-8
South Jersey Ch—*church* ... NJ-2
South Jersey Facility—*post sta* ... NJ-2
South Jersey Nazarene Camp—*locale* ... NJ-2
South Jett Windmill—*locale* ... NM-5
South Jetty—*cliff* ... CA-9
South Jetty—*dam* ... CA-9
South Jetty—*dam* ... FL-3
South Jetty—*dam* (3) ... OR-9
South Jetty—*dam* (2) ... TX-5
South Jetty—*locale* ... TX-5
South Jetty—*locale* ... WA-9
South Jetty—*other* ... GA-3
South Jetty County Park—*park* ... OR-9
South Jetty Light—*locale* ... NJ-2
South Jetty Light—*other* ... DE-2
South Jetty Nehalem Bay—*dam* ... OR-9
**South Jewett**—*pop pl* ... NY-2
South JHS—*school* (2) ... CA-9
South JHS—*school* (2) ... CO-8
South JHS—*school* ... ID-8
South JHS—*school* (2) ... IL-6
South JHS—*school* ... KS-7
South JHS—*school* (3) ... MA-1
South JHS—*school* (3) ... MI-6
South JHS—*school* (2) ... MN-6
South JHS—*school* ... MO-7
South JHS—*school* ... NY-2
South JHS—*school* ... ND-7
South JHS—*school* ... OH-6
South JHS—*school* ... OK-5
South JHS—*school* ... SC-3
South JHS—*school* ... SD-7
South JHS—*school* (2) ... TN-4
South JHS—*school* ... TX-5
South JHS—*school* ... WA-9
South Jim Hogg (CCD)—*cens area* ... TX-5
South Jogg Windmill—*locale* ... TX-5
South Jog Well—*well* ... TX-5
South Johns Gulch—*valley* ... CO-8
**South Johnson City**—*pop pl* ... TN-4
South Johnson Oil Field—*other* ... IL-6
South Johnson Tank—*reservoir* ... NM-5
South Johnston HS—*school* ... NC-3
South Jones Canyon—*valley* ... NM-5
South Jones HS—*school* ... MS-4
South Jones Prairie—*flat* ... OR-9
South Jones Tank—*reservoir* ... TX-5
South Jonestown Ch—*church* ... TX-5
**South Jonestown Hills**—*pop pl* ... TX-5
**South Jordan**—*pop pl* ... UT-8
South Jordan Canal—*canal* ... UT-8
South Jordan Cem—*cemetery* ... UT-8
*South Jordan Creek* ... MO-7
**South Jordan Heights Subdivision**—*pop pl* ... UT-8
South Jordan Sch—*school* ... UT-8
South J Street Hist Dist—*hist pl* ... WA-9
South Judd Mine—*mine* ... MN-6
South Jug Creek—*stream* ... WI-6
South Jump Creek—*stream* ... ID-8
South Junction—*locale* ... NY-2
South Junction—*locale* ... OR-9
**South Junction**—*pop pl* ... CO-8
South Junction—*uninc pl* ... KS-7
*South Junction Creek* ... UT-8
*South Junior High School* ... UT-8
South Junior High School—*summit* ... MA-1
South Junipers—*range* ... ID-8
South Juniper Spring—*spring* ... NV-8
South Juniper Wash—*valley* ... UT-8
South Jupiter Narrows—*channel* ... FL-3
South Kaibab Trail—*trail* ... AZ-5
South Kaigani Harbor—*bay* ... AK-9
*South Kalabera Cliffs* ... MH-9
*South Kaukinehua* ... HI-9
South Kawishiwi River—*stream* ... MN-6
South Kawishiwi River Camp—*locale* ... MN-6
South Kaw Oil Field—*oilfield* ... OK-5
South Kearns Sch—*school* ... UT-8
South Kearny—*uninc pl* ... NJ-2
*South Keene* ... NH-1
**South Keene**—*pop pl* ... NH-1
South Kelly Canyon—*valley* ... NM-5
South Kelly Windmill—*locale* ... TX-5
South Kelsey Peak—*summit* ... CA-9
**South Kenner**—*pop pl* ... LA-4
**South Kenosha**—*pop pl* ... WI-6
South Kensington—*CDP* ... MD-2
*Southkent* ... MI-6
South Kent—*locale* ... CT-1
South Kent Sch—*school* ... CT-1
South Keokuk Ch Of Brethren—*church* ... IA-7
*South Kettle Creek* ... NJ-2
South Key West Spring—*spring* ... NV-8
South Kickapoo Creek—*stream* ... IL-6
South Kidder—*unorg reg* ... ND-7
South Kidney Butte—*summit* ... NV-8
South Kieschnick Tank—*reservoir* ... TX-5
South Kight Tank—*reservoir* ... NM-5
South Kilbourne Sch—*school* ... SC-3
South Kildee Windmill—*locale* ... TX-5
**South Killingly**—*pop pl* ... CT-1
**South Kingman**—*pop pl* ... OH-6
South King Sch—*school* ... SD-7
South Kings Peak—*summit* ... UT-8
**South Kingston**—*pop pl* ... NH-1
South Kingston Cem—*cemetery* ... MN-6
South Kingston Ch—*church* ... MN-6
South Kingston Oil Field—*oilfield* ... MS-4
**South Kingstown (Town of)**—*pop pl* ... RI-1
South King Street Hist Dist—*hist pl* ... NC-3
South Kinnikinnick Creek—*stream* ... IL-6
South Kirby Coulee—*valley* ... MT-8
South Kirby Sch—*school* ... VT-1
South Kirkwood—*locale* ... GA-3
South Kirwood—*uninc pl* ... GA-3
South Kitsap HS—*school* ... WA-9
South Kiwanis Park—*park* ... MI-6
**South Klamath (historical)**—*pop pl* ... OR-9
South Knappie Canyon—*valley* ... SD-7
South Knob—*summit* ... CA-9
South Knob—*summit* ... KY-4
South Knob—*summit* ... PA-2
South Knobs (Township of)—*fmr MCD* ... NC-3
South Knollwood Baptist Ch—*church* ... KS-7
South Knox Elem Sch—*school* ... IN-6
South Knox Elem Sch—*school* ... TN-4
*South Knox HS* ... IN-6
South Knox Junior and Senior HS—*school* .. IN-6
**South Knoxville**—*pop pl* ... TN-4
South Knoxville Optimist Park—*park* ... TN-4
South Knoxville Post Office—*building* ... TN-4
South Knoxville Quarry—*mine* ... TN-4
South Koffer Hollow—*valley* ... MO-7
South Kohala (CCD)—*cens area* ... HI-9
*South Kokomo* ... IN-6
South Komelik—*locale* ... AZ-5
South Kona (CCD)—*cens area* ... HI-9
South Kona For Res—*forest* ... HI-9
South Koochiching (Unorganized Territory of)—*unorg* ... MN-6
South Kootenai Lake—*lake* ... MT-8
South Koronis Park—*park* ... MN-6
**South Kortright**—*pop pl* ... NY-2
South Kortright Central Sch—*school* ... NY-2
South Kuykendall Draw—*valley* ... NM-5
South La Barge Creek—*stream* ... WY-8
South Lacy Creek—*stream* ... TX-5
*South Ladder Creek* ... KS-7
South Ladder Creek—*stream* ... CO-8
South Ladder Creek—*stream* ... KS-7
South Lafayette Street Creole Cottages—*hist pl* ... AL-4
**South Lafourche**—*pop pl* ... LA-4
South Lagoon—*lake* (2) ... IL-6
**South Lagrange**—*pop pl* ... ME-1
South Lagrange Oil Field—*oilfield* ... MS-4
*South Lagua Point* ... MH-9
**South Laguna**—*pop pl* ... CA-9
South Laguna Lateral—*canal* ... NM-5
South Laguna Mines—*mine* ... NM-5
*South Lake* ... IN-6
*South Lake* ... MA-1
*South Lake* ... MI-6
*South Lake* ... WI-6
South Lake—*gut* ... AL-4
South Lake—*lake* ... AK-9
South Lake—*lake* ... AR-4
South Lake—*lake* (2) ... CA-9
South Lake—*lake* (8) ... FL-3
South Lake—*lake* ... GA-3
South Lake—*lake* (2) ... ID-8
South Lake—*lake* (2) ... IN-6
South Lake—*lake* (2) ... LA-4
South Lake—*lake* (7) ... MI-6
South Lake—*lake* (3) ... MN-6
South Lake—*lake* (2) ... MS-4
South Lake—*lake* ... MO-7
South Lake—*lake* (2) ... NM-5
South Lake—*lake* ... NY-2
South Lake—*lake* ... NC-3
South Lake—*lake* ... ND-7
South Lake—*lake* ... OK-5
South Lake—*lake* (2) ... OR-9
South Lake—*lake* ... UT-8
South Lake—*lake* (2) ... WA-9
South Lake—*lake* (3) ... WI-6
**South Lake**—*pop pl* ... CA-9
**South Lake**—*pop pl* ... IN-6
**South Lake**—*pop pl* ... NY-2
**Southlake**—*pop pl* ... TX-5
South Lake—*reservoir* ... CA-9
South Lake—*reservoir* ... CO-8
South Lake—*reservoir* ... KS-7
South Lake—*reservoir* ... MO-7
South Lake—*reservoir* (3) ... NY-2
South Lake—*reservoir* ... NC-3
South Lake—*reservoir* (3) ... TX-5
South Lake—*swamp* ... MI-6
South Lake Bayou—*stream* ... MS-4
South Lake Campbell Cem—*cemetery* ... SD-7
South Lake Campground—*park* (2) ... OR-9
South Lake Canyon—*valley* ... UT-8
South Lake Canyon—*valley* ... WY-8
South Lake Charles Gas Field—*oilfield* ... LA-4
South Lake Creek—*stream* ... CO-8
South Lake Creek—*stream* ... WA-9
South Lake Dam—*dam* ... NC-3
South Lake Dillman—*reservoir* ... IN-6
South Lake Dillman Dam—*dam* ... IN-6
South Lake Elem Sch—*school* ... FL-3
South Lake Farms—*locale* ... CA-9
South Lake HS—*school* ... MI-6
South Lake Johanna Ch—*church* ... MN-6
Southlake Mall—*locale* ... IN-6
South Lake Memorial Hosp—*hospital* ... FL-3
*South Lake Metigoshe* ... ND-7
**South Lakemont**—*pop pl* ... PA-2
South Lake Morton Hist Dist—*hist pl* ... FL-3
**South Lake Oswego**—*pop pl* ... OR-9
South Lake Plaza (Shop Ctr)—*locale* ... FL-3
*South Lakes* ... MI-6
South Lakes Church—*lake* ... WI-6
Southlake Shop Ctr—*locale* ... UT-8
**South Lake Tahoe**—*pop pl* ... CA-9
South Lake Tahoe (CCD)—*cens area* ... CA-9
South Lake Talmadge—*lake* ... FL-3
*South Laketon* ... IN-6
South Lake Valley Well Number One—*well* ... NV-8
South Lakeview Plaza (Shop Ctr)—*locale* ... MO-7
**South Lakeville**—*pop pl* ... MA-1
South Lakeville Sch—*school* ... MA-1
South Lake Waterhole—*lake* ... OR-9
**South Lakewood**—*pop pl* (2) ... NJ-2
South Lakewood Cottage Sch—*school* ... CO-8
South Lakewood Sch—*school* ... CO-8
*South Lake Worth Inlet* ... FL-3
South Lamar HS—*school* ... AL-4
South Lambert Rsvr—*reservoir* ... ID-8
South Lamoose Creek—*stream* ... MT-8
South Lampasas River—*stream* ... TX-5
**South Lancaster**—*pop pl* ... MA-1
**South Lancaster**—*pop pl* ... NH-1
South Lancaster Acad—*school* ... MA-1
South Lancaster Engine House—*hist pl* ... MA-1
South Lancaster (RR name Thayer)—*CDP* . MA-1
**South Lancaster (Town of)**—*pop pl* ... WI-6
Southland—*locale* ... GA-3
**Southland**—*pop pl* (2) ... AR-4
**Southland**—*pop pl* ... GA-3
**Southland**—*pop pl* (2) ... KY-4
**Southland**—*pop pl* (2) ... MI-6
**Southland**—*pop pl* (2) ... TX-5
Southland Acad—*school* ... GA-3
**Southland Acres**—*pop pl* ... TX-5
**Southland Acres**—*pop pl* ... VA-3
Southland Acres Ch—*church* ... TX-5
**Southland Acres Subdivision**—*pop pl* ... UT-8
Southland Ch—*church* ... FL-3
Southland Estate Winery—*locale* ... NC-3
Southland Flying Service Airp—*airport* ... MS-4
**Southland Hills**—*pop pl* ... MD-2
Southland Industrial Park—*locale* ... NC-3
South Landing—*locale* ... CA-9
South Landing—*locale* ... WY-8
Southland Memorial Gardens—*cemetery* ... SC-3
Southland Memorial Park (Cemetery)—*cemetery* ... TX-5
Southland Mission—*church* ... OH-6
Southland Park—*park* ... TX-5
Southland Park—*uninc pl* ... LA-4
Southland Park Racetrack—*other* ... AR-4
**Southland Park (subdivision)**—*pop pl* ... MS-4
Southland (RR name for El Jobean)—*other* ... FL-3
Southland Sch—*school* ... TX-5
Southland Sch—*school* ... UT-8
Southland Shop Ctr—*locale* ... FL-3
Southland (Shop Ctr)—*locale* ... FL-3
Southland Shop Ctr—*locale* ... NC-3
Southland Shop Ctr—*locale* ... TN-4
Southland Station RR Station—*locale* ... FL-3
**Southland Terrace Subdivision**—*pop pl* ... UT-8
South Laney Creek—*stream* ... MT-8
South Langhorne—*other* ... PA-2
Southlan Shop Ctr—*locale* ... FL-3
**South Lansing**—*pop pl* ... NY-2
South Lansing Sch for Girls—*school* ... NY-2
South Lapile Creek—*stream* ... AR-4
South La Pine Roadside Rest—*park* ... OR-9
**South LaPorte**—*pop pl* ... IN-6
**South Laramie**—*pop pl* ... WY-8
South Laredo—*uninc pl* ... TX-5

South Larsen Canyon—*valley* ... CO-8
South Larto Lake Oil Field—*oilfield* ... LA-4
South Last Chance Creek—*stream* ... UT-8
*South Lateral* ... CO-8
South Lateral—*canal* ... CA-9
South Lateral—*canal* ... CO-8
South Lateral—*canal* ... TX-5
South Lateral—*canal* ... UT-8
South Lateral Bench Canal—*canal* ... WY-8
South Lateral C Canal—*canal* ... UT-8
South Lateral Ditch—*canal* ... CO-8
South Lateral Lake Fork Canal—*canal* ... UT-8
South Lateral Moraine—*ridge* ... CO-8
South Lateral Tunnel—*tunnel* ... NV-8
South Latimer (CCD)—*cens area* ... OK-5
South Laurel—*CDP* ... MD-2
South Laurel Baptist Ch—*church* ... MS-4
South Lava Butte—*summit* ... NM-5
South Lava Creek—*stream* ... ID-8
*South La Veta Creek* ... CO-8
**Southlawn**—*pop pl* ... IL-6
**Southlawn**—*pop pl* ... MD-2
**South Lawn**—*pop pl* ... MD-2
**South Lawn**—*pop pl* ... TX-5
Southlawn Baptist Ch—*church* ... AL-4
Southlawn Cem—*cemetery* (2) ... IN-6
South Lawn Cem—*cemetery* ... IN-6
Southlawn Cem—*cemetery* ... IA-7
South Lawn Cem—*cemetery* ... KS-7
South Lawn Cem—*cemetery* ... NH-1
South Lawn Cem—*cemetery* (2) ... OH-6
**Southlawn Cemetery**—*pop pl* ... MA-1
South Lawn Ch—*church* ... TX-5
Southlawn Ch of Christ—*church* ... AL-4
**Southlawn East (subdivision)**—*pop pl* ... AL-4
Southlawn Elem Sch—*school* ... AL-4
Southlawn Elem Sch—*school* ... KS-7
South Lawn Memorial Cem—*cemetery* ... AZ-5
Southlawn Memorial Gardens—*cemetery* ... IA-7
Southlawn Memorial Park—*cemetery* ... VA-3
South Lawn Park—*park* ... TX-5
Southlawn Sch—*school* ... NY-2
South Lawn Sch—*school* ... OH-6
South Lawn Sch—*school* ... TX-5
Southlawn Shop Ctr—*locale* ... AL-4
**Southlawn (subdivision)**—*pop pl* ... AL-4
South Lawrence—*unorg reg* ... SD-7
South Lawrence Cem—*cemetery* (2) ... WI-6
South Lawrence Ch—*church* ... WI-6
South Lawrence Elem Sch—*school* ... TN-4
South Lawrence Plaza—*locale* ... MA-1
**South Lawrence (subdivision)**—*pop pl* ... MA-1
**South Layhill**—*pop pl* ... MD-2
*South Lazy U Reservoirs* ... CO-8
**South Lead Hill**—*pop pl* ... AR-4
South Lead Lake—*reservoir* ... NV-8
*South Leake Attendance Center* ... MS-4
South Leake Sch—*school* ... MS-4
South Lease Windmill—*locale* ... TX-5
South Lebanon—*CDP* ... OR-9
**South Lebanon**—*pop pl* ... ME-1
**South Lebanon**—*pop pl* ... NY-2
**South Lebanon**—*pop pl* ... OH-6
**South Lebanon**—*pop pl* ... PA-2
South Lebanon Brook—*stream* ... NY-2
South Lebanon (Township of)—*fmr MCD* ... AR-4
**South Lebanon (Township of)**—*pop pl* ... PA-2
South Ledge—*bar* (2) ... ME-1
South Ledge—*other* ... AK-9
South Ledge Ditch—*canal* ... CO-8
South Ledges—*bar* ... ME-1
South Lee—*locale* ... MO-7
**South Lee**—*pop pl* ... MA-1
**South Lee**—*pop pl* ... NH-1
South Lee Cem—*cemetery* ... MA-1
South Leeds—*locale* ... ME-1
South Lees—*locale* ... NC-3
South Le Flore (CCD)—*cens area* ... OK-5
South Leggett—*locale* ... CA-9
South Leigh Creek—*stream* ... ID-8
South Leigh Creek—*stream* ... WY-8
South Leigh Creek Trail—*trail* ... WY-8
South Leigh Lakes—*lake* ... WY-8
South Lemmerhirt Lake—*lake* ... MN-6
South Lena Baptist Ch—*church* ... AL-4
South Lenoir HS—*school* ... NC-3
*South Leon Creek* ... TX-5
South Leon River—*stream* ... TX-5
South Leopard Creek—*bay* ... NC-3
*South Leora Lake* ... MN-6
South Leroy Meetinghouse—*hist pl* ... OH-6
South Levant—*locale* ... ME-1
*South Leverett* ... MA-1
South Lewisburg Oil and Gas Field—*oilfield* ... LA-4
South Lewis HS—*school* ... NY-2
*South Lewiston* ... ME-1
**South Lewiston**—*pop pl* ... ME-1
South Lexington—*uninc pl* ... KY-4
South Lexington—*uninc pl* ... NC-3
South Lexington Primary Sch—*school* ... NC-3
*South Liberty* ... MO-7
South Liberty—*locale* ... TN-4
South Liberty—*locale* ... TX-5
**South Liberty**—*pop pl* ... ME-1
**South Liberty**—*pop pl* ... MO-7
South Liberty Ch—*church* (3) ... IN-6
South Liberty Ch—*church* ... KY-4
South Liberty Ch—*church* (2) ... OH-6
South Liberty Ch—*church* ... TN-4
South Liberty Church Cem—*cemetery* ... GA-3
South Liberty Oil Field—*oilfield* ... TX-5
South Liberty Sch—*school* ... IL-6
South Liberty Sch—*school* ... MT-8
South Liberty Sch—*school* ... OH-6
South Liberty Sch—*school* ... SD-7
South Liberty (Township of)—*fmr MCD* ... NC-3
South Lick Branch—*stream* ... KY-4
South Lick Creek Branch—*stream* ... TN-4
*South Lightning Creek* ... WA-9
South Lilly Creek—*stream* ... TX-5
**South Lima**—*pop pl* ... NY-2
South Lime Lake—*lake* ... AK-9
South Limestone Sch—*school* ... OK-5
**South Limington**—*pop pl* ... ME-1
South Limpy Prairie—*flat* ... OR-9
**South Lincoln**—*pop pl* (2) ... ME-1
**South Lincoln**—*pop pl* ... MA-1
**South Lincoln**—*pop pl* ... VT-1
South Lincoln Sch—*school* ... NE-7
South Lincoln Sch—*school* ... OH-6
South Lincoln Sch—*school* ... SD-7
**South Lincolnton**—*pop pl* ... NC-3
South Lincolnton (CCD)—*cens area* ... GA-3
South Lindstrom Lake—*lake* ... MN-6
South Line Island—*island* ... NY-2
South Line Tank—*reservoir* ... TX-5
**South Lineville**—*pop pl* ... MO-7
South Lineville Cem—*cemetery* ... MO-7
South Linger Draw—*valley* ... TX-5
South Linger Windmill—*locale* ... TX-5
South Linn Creek—*stream* ... MO-7
South Linn Township—*civil* ... MO-7
South Linson Creek—*stream* ... OK-5
South Lisbon Windmill—*locale* ... NM-5
South Litchfield Ch—*church* ... MI-6
South Litchfield (Township of)—*civ div* ... IL-6
*South Lito Sink* ... MH-9
South Little Kincaid Creek—*stream* ... KY-4
South Little Lake—*lake* ... IN-6
South Little Springs—*spring* ... NV-8
South Litton Well—*locale* ... NM-5
South Liveoak Draw—*valley* ... TX-5
**South Livermore**—*pop pl* ... ME-1
**South Liverpool**—*pop pl* ... IL-6
**South Livingston**—*pop pl* ... NJ-2
**South Livonia**—*pop pl* ... NY-2
South Llano River—*stream* ... TX-5
South Lobe Creek—*stream* ... CO-8
*South Lockport* ... IL-6
**South Lockport**—*pop pl* ... IL-6
**South Lockport**—*pop pl* ... NY-2
*South Lodge Pole Creek* ... WY-8
South Lodgepole Creek—*stream* ... WY-8
South Lodi Cem—*cemetery* ... SD-7
*South Logan* ... OH-6
**South Logan**—*pop pl* ... OH-6
South Logan Benson Canal—*canal* ... UT-8
South Logan Creek—*stream* ... NE-7
*South Loi Island* ... MP-9
*South Londo Lake* ... MI-6
**South Londonderry**—*pop pl* ... VT-1
**South Londonderry (Township of)**—*pop pl* ... PA-2
South Londonderry Village Hist Dist—*hist pl* ... VT-1
South London Mine—*mine* ... CO-8
South Lone Elm Oil Field—*oilfield* ... OK-5
South Lone Lake—*lake* ... ID-8
South Lone Pine Creek—*stream* ... CO-8
*South Long Branch* ... MO-7
South Long Canyon—*valley* ... CA-9
South Long Creek—*stream* (2) ... OK-5
South Long Dry Creek—*stream* ... TX-5
South Long Lake—*lake* (2) ... MN-6
South Long Lake Ch—*church* ... MN-6
South Long Point—*cape* ... UT-8
South Long Point—*ridge* ... CA-9
South Long Pond—*lake* ... NY-2
South Long Run—*stream* ... KY-4
South Lookout—*locale* ... PA-2
South Lookout Peak—*summit* ... CO-8
South Loon Lake—*lake* ... ND-7
South Loon Mtn—*summit* ... ID-8
South Loop—*trail* ... NV-8
*South Loop Cove* ... AZ-5
South Loop Printing House District—*hist pl* ... IL-6
**South Lorain**—*pop pl* ... OH-6
*South Lorain (P.O.)* ... OH-6
**South Los Angeles**—*pop pl* ... CA-9
South Los Tanos Tank—*reservoir* ... NM-5
South Lost Creek—*stream* ... UT-8
South Lost Hollow—*valley* ... UT-8
South Lost Horse Creek—*stream* ... MT-8
*South Lottis Creek* ... CO-8
South Lottis Creek—*stream* ... CO-8
South Louisville—*uninc pl* ... KY-4
*South Louisville Baptist Church* ... MS-4
South Louisville Ch—*church* ... MS-4
South Louisville Reformed Church—*hist pl* ... KY-4
South Louisville Yards—*locale* ... KY-4
South Loup River—*stream* ... NE-7
**South Loup Township**—*pop pl* ... NE-7
South Love Mesa Bench—*bench* ... CO-8
**South Lowell**—*pop pl* ... AL-4
**South Lowell**—*pop pl* ... NC-3
South Lowell Cem—*cemetery* ... AL-4
South Lowell Post Office (historical)—*building* ... AL-4
**South Lowell (subdivision)**—*pop pl* ... MA-1
South Lowe Pasture—*flat* ... KS-7
South Lowville Sch—*school* ... WI-6
South Loxa Sch—*school* ... IL-6
**South Lubec**—*pop pl* ... ME-1
South Lumberton—*uninc pl* ... NC-3
**South Lunenburg**—*pop pl* ... VT-1
South Lunenburg Sch—*school* ... VT-1
South Lutheran Cem—*cemetery* ... NE-7
**South Luxemburg**—*pop pl* ... WI-6
South Lygay Oil Field—*oilfield* ... TX-5
South Lyman—*unorg reg* ... SD-7
**South Lyme**—*pop pl* ... CT-1
**South Lynchburg**—*pop pl* ... SC-3
**South Lyndeboro**—*pop pl* ... NH-1
**South Lyndeborough**—*pop pl* ... NH-1
South Lyndeborough Cem—*cemetery* ... NH-1
**South Lynnfield**—*pop pl* ... MA-1
Southlyn Sch—*school* ... OH-6
**South Lyon**—*pop pl* ... MI-6
South Lyons Cem—*cemetery* ... NY-2
South Mabry Manor Park—*park* ... FL-3
South Macomb Oil Field—*oilfield* ... OK-5
South Macon—*uninc pl* ... GA-3
*South Macon Creek* ... MI-6
South Macon HS—*school* ... AL-4
**South Macon (Township of)**—*pop pl* ... IL-6
**South Madison**—*pop pl* ... OH-6
**South Madison**—*pop pl* ... WV-2
South Madison Avenue-Pannell Road Hist Dist—*hist pl* ... GA-3
South Madison MS—*school* ... GA-3
South (Magisterial District)—*fmr MCD* ... WV-2
South Magnolia Sewage Lagoon Dam—*dam* ... MS-4
South Mahogany Rsvr—*reservoir* ... NV-8
**South Mahoning (Township of)**—*pop pl* ... PA-2
South Maid Hill—*summit* ... VT-1
South Main—*uninc pl* ... CA-9
South Main and Washington Streets Hist Dist—*hist pl* ... CT-1
South Main and Washington Streets Hist Dist (Boundary Increase)—*hist pl* ... CT-1
South Main Canal—*canal* (2) ... CA-9
South Main Ch—*church* ... IL-6
South Main Ditch—*canal* ... CO-8
South Maine Ch—*church* ... WI-6
South Main Golf Club—*other* ... TX-5
South Main Hist Dist—*hist pl* ... MS-4
South Main Hist Dist—*hist pl* ... SC-3
South Main Marketplace—*locale* ... MA-1
South Main Sch—*school* ... OH-6
South Main Square—*locale* ... UT-8
**South Main Street Addition (subdivision)**—*pop pl* ... UT-8
South Main Street Commercial Hist Dist—*hist pl* ... OR-9
South Main Street District—*hist pl* (2) ... OH-6
South Main Street District (Boundary Increase)—*hist pl* ... OH-6
South Main Street Hist Dist—*hist pl* ... GA-3
South Main Street Hist Dist—*hist pl* ... KY-4
South Main Street Hist Dist—*hist pl* ... NY-2
South Main Street Hist Dist—*hist pl* ... NC-3
South Main Street Hist Dist—*hist pl* (2) ... RI-1
South Main Street Hist Dist—*hist pl* ... TN-4
South Main Street Sch—*hist pl* ... MA-1
**South Main Townhouses (subdivision)**—*pop pl* ... UT-8
South Maktak Hills—*other* ... AK-9
South Malakoff Oil Field—*oilfield* ... TX-5
**South Malden**—*pop pl* ... WV-2
South Mall—*post sta* ... MO-7
South Mamm Peak—*summit* ... CO-8
*South Mam Peak* ... CO-8
*Southman Canyon* ... UT-8
Southman Canyon Gas Field—*oilfield* ... UT-8
**South Manchester**—*pop pl* ... CT-1
Southman Creek—*stream* ... OR-9
South Mangrove Point—*cape* ... FL-3
**South Manheim (Township of)**—*pop pl* ... PA-2
South Manila Oil Field—*oilfield* ... TX-5
South Manistique Lake—*lake* ... MI-6
South Manistique Lake Campground—*locale* ... MI-6
**South Manitou**—*pop pl* ... MI-6
South Manitou Island—*island* ... MI-6
South Manitou Island Cem—*cemetery* ... MI-6
South Manitou Island Light—*locale* ... MI-6
South Manitou Island Lighthouse Complex and Life Saving Station Hist Dist—*hist pl* ... MI-6
South Manitou Island School—*locale* ... MI-6
South Manitou Park Trail—*trail* ... CO-8
**South Manor**—*pop pl* ... NY-2
**South Mansfield**—*pop pl* ... LA-4
**South Mantoloking Beach**—*pop pl* ... NJ-2
South Maple Canyon—*valley* ... UT-8
South Maple Grove Cem—*cemetery* ... MI-6
South Maple Lake—*lake* ... MN-6
South Maple Ridge Ch—*church* ... MN-6
**South Mapleton Hills**—*pop pl* ... TN-4
South Marais River—*stream* ... ND-7
South Marble Gulch—*valley* ... OR-9
South Marble Island—*island* ... AK-9
South Marengo Hist Dist—*hist pl* ... CA-9
*South Marion* ... IN-6
**South Marion**—*pop pl* ... IN-6
South Marion Cem—*cemetery* ... IA-7
South Marion Ch—*church* ... IA-7
South Marion Ch—*church* ... NC-3
South Marion Street Parkway—*hist pl* ... CO-8
South Markel Windmill—*locale* ... NM-5
South Market—*locale* ... MA-1
*South Marlborough* ... MA-1
South Marlow Cem—*cemetery* ... AR-4
*South Marsh* ... MD-2
South Marshall—*locale* ... KY-4
South Marshall—*summit* ... VA-3
South Marshall (CCD)—*cens area* ... OK-5
South Marshall HS—*school* ... KY-4
South Marshall Sch—*school* ... TX-5
South Marsh Creek—*stream* ... FL-3
*South Marshfield* ... MA-1
South Marsh Gulch—*valley* ... CO-8
South Marsh Island—*island* ... MD-2
South Marsh Lake—*lake* (2) ... NE-7
South Martha Washington Ditch—*canal* ... NC-3
**South Martin**—*pop pl* ... IN-6
South Martin Cem—*cemetery* ... MI-6
South Martin Ch—*church* ... IN-6
South Martin Creek—*stream* ... KS-7
South Martinsville—*uninc pl* ... VA-3
South Martinsville Sch—*school* ... VA-3
South Marys Creek—*stream* ... TX-5
South Mary Well—*well* ... SD-7
**South Masaryktown**—*pop pl* ... FL-3
**South Mashpee**—*pop pl* ... MA-1
South Matchless Mtn—*summit* ... CO-8
South Mattieu Lake—*lake* ... OR-9
South Matubba Street Ch of Christ—*church* ... MS-4
South Maxie Canyon—*valley* ... UT-8
South May Creek—*stream* ... CO-8
*Southmayde* ... TX-5
South Mayde Creek—*stream* ... TX-5
Southmayd Park—*park* ... TX-5
Southmayd Ridge—*ridge* ... CA-9
Southmayd Sch—*school* ... TX-5
**Southmayd (Southmayde Station)**—*pop pl* ... TX-5
South Mayo River—*stream* ... NC-3
South Mayo River—*stream* ... VA-3
*South McAdoo Creek* ... TN-4
*South McAlester* ... OK-5
South McBryde Pond—*reservoir* ... AZ-5
South McCabe Lake—*lake* ... CO-8
South McCauley Ditch—*canal* ... MT-8
South McComb—*uninc pl* ... MS-4
South McComb Baptist Ch—*church* ... MS-4
South McCormick Ch—*church* ... AR-4
South McElroy Cave—*cave* ... TN-4
South McKay Ditch No 2—*canal* ... WY-8
South McKittrick Canyon—*valley* ... TX-5
South Mclean—*unorg reg* ... ND-7
South McNally Canal—*canal* ... CA-9
South Meadow—*swamp* ... NY-2
*South Meadow Brook* ... MA-1
South Meadow Brook—*stream* (3) ... MA-1
South Meadow Brook—*stream* ... NY-2
South Meadow Brook Rsvr—*reservoir* ... MA-1
South Meadow Ch—*church* ... VT-1
South Meadow Creek—*stream* ... MT-8
South Meadow Creek—*stream* ... WA-9
South Meadow Creek Lake—*lake* ... MT-8
South Meadow Creek Ranger Station—*locale* ... MT-8
South Meadow Gulch—*valley* ... CA-9
South Meadow Lake—*lake* ... AK-9
South Meadow Pond—*lake* ... MA-1
South Meadow Pond—*reservoir* ... MA-1
South Meadow Pond Dam—*dam* ... MA-1
South Meadows—*flat* ... MA-1
**South Meadow Township**—*pop pl* ... ND-7
**South Meadville (Franklin Pike Corners)**—*pop pl* ... PA-2
South Mebane Sch—*school* ... NC-3
South Mecca Cem—*cemetery* ... OH-6
*South Mechumps Creek* ... VA-3
South Mecklenburg HS—*school* ... NC-3
South Medford—*CDP* ... OR-9
**South Media**—*pop pl* ... PA-2
*South Medicine Creek* ... SD-7
South Medicine Creek—*stream* ... WA-9
South Meetinghouse—*hist pl* ... NH-1
South Meherrin River—*stream* ... VA-3
South Memorial Plaza Shop Ctr—*locale* ... AL-4
South Mendoza Wash—*stream* ... AZ-5
South Mercer JHS—*school* ... WA-9
South Merchantville—*uninc pl* ... NJ-2
Southmere—*locale* ... FL-3
*South Meriden* ... CT-1
**South Meriden**—*pop pl* ... CT-1
South Mermentau Gas Field—*oilfield* ... LA-4
**South Merrimack**—*pop pl* ... NH-1
South Mesa—*summit* (2) ... AZ-5
South Mesa—*summit* ... CA-9
South Mesa—*summit* ... NV-8
South Mesa—*summit* (4) ... NM-5
South Mesa—*summit* ... TX-5
South Mesa—*summit* ... UT-8
South Mesa Lake—*lake* ... CO-8
South Mesa Sch—*school* ... CO-8
South Mesa Tank—*reservoir* ... AZ-5
South Mesa Tank—*reservoir* ... NM-5
South Mesquite Creek—*stream* (3) ... TX-5
South Messier Lake—*lake* ... ND-7
South Metter Residential Hist Dist—*hist pl* ... GA-3
*South Metz Lake* ... IN-6
**South Miami**—*pop pl* ... FL-3
South Miami Elem Sch—*school* ... FL-3
**South Miami Heights**—*pop pl* ... FL-3
South Miami Heights Ch—*church* ... FL-3
South Miami Heights Elem Sch—*school* ... FL-3
South Miami Heights Preschool—*school* ... FL-3
South Miami Heights Shop Ctr—*locale* ... FL-3
South Miami Hosp—*hospital* ... FL-3
South Miami JHS—*school* ... FL-3
South Miami Lutheran Preschool—*school* ... FL-3
South Miami Rec Area—*park* ... FL-3
South Miami Senior HS—*school* ... FL-3
South Miami Shop Ctr—*locale* ... FL-3
South Michigan Ave Hist Dist—*hist pl* ... MI-6
South Mickey Ridge—*ridge* ... CA-9
**South Middleboro**—*pop pl* ... MA-1
*South Middleborough* ... MA-1
South Middleborough (historical P.O.)—*locale* ... MA-1
South Middleborough Station (historical)—*locale* ... MA-1
*South Middle Branch ZA VAR Rice Lake Branch Zumbro River* ... MN-6
*South Middle Branch Zumbro River* ... MN-6
South Middlebush Cem—*cemetery* ... NJ-2
South Middle Butte—*summit* ... WY-8
*South Middle Creek* ... CO-8
South Middle Creek—*stream* ... CO-8
*South Middle Fork Coquille River* ... OR-9
*South Middle Fork Zumbro River* ... MN-6
**South Middleton**—*pop pl* ... MA-1
*South Middleton Consolidated School* ... PA-2
South Middleton Drain—*canal* ... ID-8
*South Middleton Junior-Senior High School* ... PA-2
**South Middleton (Township of)**—*pop pl* ... PA-2
South Mifflin Sch—*school* ... OH-6
*South Milan* ... IN-6
*South Milford* ... OH-6
**South Milford**—*pop pl* ... IN-6
**South Milford**—*pop pl* ... MA-1
**South Milford**—*pop pl* ... NH-1
**South Milford**—*pop pl* ... OH-6
**South Milford**—*pop pl* ... VA-3
South Milford Cem—*cemetery* ... IN-6
South Milford Hist Dist—*hist pl* ... DE-2
South Military Hill—*summit* ... MI-6
South Milk Ranch Well—*well* ... NV-8
South Mill—*locale* ... NM-5
**South Millbrook**—*pop pl* ... NY-2
*South Mill Creek* ... TN-4
South Mill Creek—*stream* ... LA-4
South Mill Creek—*stream* ... WV-2
South Mill Creek Ch—*church* ... TX-5
South Mill Creek Ch—*church* ... WV-2
South Mill Creek Sch—*school* ... KY-4
South Miller Creek—*stream* ... MT-8
South Millick Spring—*spring* ... NV-8
South Mill Pond—*lake* ... NH-1
**South Mills**—*pop pl* ... NC-3
South Mills (Township of)—*fmr MCD* ... NC-3
South Mill Well—*well* ... NM-5
South Milton Cem—*cemetery* ... MI-6
South Milton Community Hall—*locale* ... MI-6
**South Milwaukee**—*pop pl* ... WI-6
South Milwaukee Passenger Station—*hist pl* ... WI-6
*South Minden* ... NE-7
South Mineral Campground—*locale* ... CO-8
South Mineral Cem—*cemetery* ... IA-7
*South Mineral Creek* ... TX-5
South Mineral Creek—*stream* ... TX-5
South Minerva Creek—*stream* ... IA-7
*South Mineshas Island* ... MI-6
**Southminister Woods (subdivision)**—*pop pl* ... NC-3
*South Minneapolis* ... MN-6
Southminster Presbyterian Ch—*church* ... FL-3
South Minton Ch—*church* ... GA-3
*South Mississippi Charity Hospital* ... MS-4
South Mississippi Electric Power Association Dam—*dam* ... MS-4
South Mississippi State Hosp—*hospital* ... MS-4
South Mitchell—*locale* ... NE-7
South Mitchell Creek—*stream* ... MI-6
South Mizell Windmill—*locale* ... NM-5
South Mize Well—*well* ... NM-5
South Moat Mtn—*summit* ... NH-1
*South Moccasin Mountain* ... MT-8
South Moccasin Mountains—*spring* ... MT-8
South Moccasin Wash—*stream* ... AZ-5
South Modesto—*CDP* ... CA-9
South Mokelumne River—*stream* ... CA-9
**South Moline**—*pop pl* ... IL-6
**South Moline Gardens**—*pop pl* ... IL-6
South Moline (Township of)—*civ div* ... IL-6
*South Monistique Lake* ... MI-6
South Moniteau Township—*civil* ... MO-7
**South Monmouth**—*pop pl* ... ME-1
South Monoosnoc Hill—*summit* ... MA-1
South Monroe—*CDP* ... MI-6
South Monroe JHS—*school* ... LA-4
South Monroe Sch—*school* ... MI-6
**South Monson**—*pop pl* ... MA-1
**Southmont**—*pop pl* ... AL-4
**Southmont**—*pop pl* ... NC-3
**Southmont**—*pop pl* ... PA-2
Southmont Borough—*civil* ... PA-2
Southmont Elem Sch—*school* ... NC-3
**South Monterey**—*pop pl* ... MI-6
South Monterey Ch—*church* ... MI-6
South Montesano—*locale* ... WA-9
South Montgomery County Acad—*school* ... AL-4
South Monticello Point—*cape* ... NM-5
**South Montrose**—*pop pl* ... PA-2
**Southmont (subdivision)**—*pop pl* ... NC-3
**South Montville**—*pop pl* ... ME-1
South Monumental Springs—*spring* ... NV-8
South Moody Creek—*stream* ... ID-8
South Moon Lake—*lake* ... FL-3
*Southmoor* ... IN-6
**Southmoor**—*pop pl* (2) ... IL-6
South Moore Hollow—*valley* ... TN-4
South Moore Oil Field—*oilfield* ... OK-5
Southmoor Golf Course—*other* ... MO-7
**Southmoor Park**—*pop pl* ... IN-6
**Southmore**—*pop pl* ... IL-6
Southmore—*uninc pl* ... TX-5
South Moreau Creek—*stream* ... MO-7
Southmore Hosp—*hospital* ... TX-5
South Moreland Park—*park* ... MO-7
Southmore Sch—*school* ... TX-5
South Morgan Cem—*cemetery* ... UT-8
South Morgan Township—*civil* ... MO-7
**South Morningside Heights**—*pop pl* ... UT-8
South Morrill—*locale* ... NE-7
South Morrison Sch—*school* ... VA-3
South Morris Well—*well* ... NM-5
South Mortar Creek—*stream* ... AL-4
South Mosley Canyon—*valley* ... NM-5
South Mosquito Creek—*stream* ... CO-8
South Mosquito Creek—*stream* ... FL-3
Southmost Cem—*cemetery* ... TX-5
Southmost Coll—*school* ... TX-5
Southmost Ranch—*locale* ... TX-5
**South Moultrie**—*pop pl* ... GA-3
**South Mound**—*pop pl* ... KS-7
South Mound—*summit* ... KS-7
South Mound—*summit* ... WI-6
South Mound Cem—*cemetery* ... IN-6
*South Mounds* ... IL-6
South Mound Spring—*spring* ... OR-9
South Mount—*summit* ... AK-9
*South Mountain* ... ID-8
South Mountain—*locale* ... ID-8
**South Mountain**—*pop pl* (2) ... PA-2
**South Mountain**—*pop pl* ... TX-5
South Mountain—*ridge* ... NM-5
South Mountain Cem—*cemetery* ... MA-1
South Mountain Ch—*church* ... AR-4
South Mountain Ch—*church* ... NC-3
South Mountain Chapel—*church* ... PA-2
South Mountain Concert Hall—*hist pl* ... MA-1
South Mountain Creek—*stream* ... CO-8
South Mountain Creek—*stream* ... ID-8
South Mountaineer Creek—*stream* ... CA-9
South Mountain HS—*school* ... AZ-5
South Mountain Institute—*school* ... NC-3
*South Mountain Junior High School* ... PA-2
South Mountain MS—*school* ... PA-2
South Mountain Park—*park* (2) ... PA-2
South Mountain Pass—*gap* ... NY-2
South Mountain Reservation—*park* ... NJ-2
South Mountain Restoration Center—*hospital* ... PA-2
South Mountain Rsvr—*reservoir* ... CA-9
South Mountain Rsvr—*reservoir* ... OR-9
South Mountain Rsvr—*reservoir* ... PA-2
*South Mountains* ... PA-2
*South Mountains* ... UT-8
South Mountains—*range* ... NC-3
South Mountains—*ridge* ... AZ-5
South Mountain Sch—*school* ... NJ-2
South Mountain Springs—*spring* ... CA-9
*South Mountain State Sanatorium* ... PA-2
South Mountain Trailer Park—*locale* ... AZ-5
South Mount Carmel Sch—*school* ... IA-7
South Mount Hawkins—*summit* ... CA-9
South Mount Hope Sch—*school* ... OH-6
*South Mount School* ... PA-2
**South Mount Vernon**—*pop pl* ... OH-6
South Mount Zion Ch—*church* ... GA-3
South Mount Zion Ch—*church* ... OH-6
South Mouse Creek—*stream* ... TN-4
South Mouth—*stream* ... FL-3
South Mouth Arolik River—*stream* ... AK-9
South Mowich Glacier—*glacier* ... WA-9
South Mowich River—*stream* ... WA-9
South MS—*school* ... OR-9
South MS—*school* ... TX-5
*South Mtn* ... CT-1
*South Mtn* ... MA-1
*South Mtn* ... PA-2
South Mtn—*range* ... MD-2
South Mtn—*range* (3) ... PA-2
South Mtn—*summit* (3) ... AZ-5
South Mtn—*summit* (2) ... AR-4
South Mtn—*summit* (2) ... CA-9
South Mtn—*summit* (2) ... CO-8
South Mtn—*summit* (2) ... CT-1
South Mtn—*summit* ... ID-8
South Mtn—*summit* (3) ... ME-1
South Mtn—*summit* (3) ... MA-1
South Mtn—*summit* (2) ... NH-1
South Mtn—*summit* ... NM-5
South Mtn—*summit* (8) ... NY-2
South Mtn—*summit* (2) ... NC-3
South Mtn—*summit* (2) ... OR-9
South Mtn—*summit* (2) ... PA-2
South Mtn—*summit* ... TX-5
South Mtn—*summit* (6) ... UT-8
South Mtn—*summit* (2) ... VT-1
South Mtn—*summit* ... VA-3
South Mtn—*summit* ... WA-9
South Mtn—*summit* ... WY-8
*South Mtn Brook* ... CT-1
South Mtn Manor—*summit* ... PA-2
South Mtns—*range* ... NV-8
*South Mud Creek* ... OR-9
*South Mud Creek* ... WA-9
South Mud Creek—*stream* ... MO-7
South Muddy Ch—*church* ... IL-6
*South Muddy Creek* ... CO-8
South Muddy Creek—*stream* (2) ... CO-8
South Muddy Creek—*stream* ... NC-3
South Muddy Creek—*stream* (2) ... WY-8
*South Muddy Mountains* ... NV-8
**South Muddy (Township of)**—*pop pl* ... IL-6
South Mud Lake—*lake* ... IN-6
**South Mud Lake**—*pop pl* ... IN-6
South Mudlick Branch—*stream* ... WV-2
South Mud Spring—*spring* ... NV-8
**South Mulberry**—*pop pl* ... FL-3
South Mule Creek—*stream* ... CO-8
South Mullen Creek—*stream* ... WY-8
South Mullins—*uninc pl* ... SC-3
South Mundy Ch—*church* ... MI-6
South Murderkill Hundred—*civil* ... DE-2
*South Muscatine* ... IA-7
South Mustang Draw—*valley* ... TX-5
South Mustang Windmill—*locale* ... TX-5
South Myrtle Creek—*stream* ... OR-9
South Myton Bench—*bench* ... UT-8
**South Naknek**—*pop pl* ... AK-9
South Naknek ANV950—*reserve* ... AK-9
South Nampa Lateral—*canal* ... ID-8
South Nanamkin Creek—*stream* ... WA-9
*South Nanapkin Creek* ... WA-9
South Naples—*locale* ... ME-1
South Naselle River—*stream* ... WA-9
South Nassau Communities Hosp—*hospital* ... NY-2
South Natchez HS—*school* ... MS-4
**South Natick**—*pop pl* ... MA-1
*South Natick Reservoir* ... MA-1
South Navarre Campground—*locale* ... WA-9
South Navarre Peak—*summit* ... WA-9
South Neba Wildlife Mngmt Area—*park* ... UT-8
South Nebraska City Hist Dist—*hist pl* ... NE-7
South Necedah—*uninc pl* ... WI-6
South Needham Creek—*stream* ... AL-4
South Needles Compressor Station—*other* ... CA-9
South Negro Canyon—*valley* ... AZ-5
**South Nellieville**—*pop pl* ... GA-3
South Nemah River—*stream* ... WA-9
South Nepaug Brook—*stream* ... CT-1
*South Net Point* ... MH-9
South Nettleton Baptist Ch—*church* ... MS-4
South Neva Lake—*lake* ... WI-6
*South Newark* ... OH-6
South New Bedford HS—*school* ... MA-1
**South New Berlin**—*pop pl* ... NY-2
*South Newburg* ... ME-1
**South Newburgh**—*pop pl* ... ME-1
**South Newbury**—*pop pl* ... NH-1
**South Newbury**—*pop pl* ... OH-6
**South Newbury**—*pop pl* ... VT-1
South Newbury Village Hist Dist—*hist pl* ... VT-1
**South Newcastle**—*pop pl* ... ME-1
**South New Castle**—*pop pl* ... PA-2
South New Castle Borough—*civil* ... PA-2
**South Newfane**—*pop pl* ... VT-1
South Newhall Sch—*school* ... MO-7
**South New Haven**—*pop pl* ... NY-2
South New Home Cem—*cemetery* ... MO-7
South New Hope Ch—*church* ... WI-6
South Newington Ch—*church* ... GA-3
South Newlin Creek—*stream* ... CO-8
South Newlin Gulch—*valley* ... CO-8
**South New Lyme**—*pop pl* ... OH-6
South Newport—*locale* ... GA-3
South Newport—*locale* ... VT-1
South Newport Ch—*church* ... GA-3
South Newport Cut—*channel* ... GA-3
South Newport River—*stream* ... GA-3
South New River Canal—*canal* ... FL-3
**South Newstead**—*pop pl* ... NY-2
South Newton—*uninc pl* ... NC-3
South Newton Junior and Senior HS—*school* ... IN-6
South Newton Sch—*school* ... NC-3
**South Newton (Township of)**—*pop pl* ... PA-2
South New Well Windmill—*locale* ... TX-5
South Nichols Mtn—*summit* ... MA-1
South Ninemile Point—*cape* ... MI-6
South Ninemile Windmill—*locale* ... NM-5
South Nine Section Tank—*reservoir* ... AZ-5
**South Nineveh**—*pop pl* ... NY-2
South Nipple Gulch—*valley* ... CO-8
South Nix Oil Field—*oilfield* ... TX-5
South Noble Oil Field—*oilfield* ... OK-5
South Nolan Creek—*stream* ... TX-5
South Nonations—*bar* ... NY-2
*South Norfolk* ... VA-3
South Norfolk—*locale* ... CT-1
South Norfolk—*uninc pl* ... VA-3
South Norfolk Airp—*airport* ... VA-3
South Norfolk Borough—*civil* ... VA-3
**South Northfield**—*pop pl* ... VT-1
South Norton Tank—*reservoir* ... TX-5
*South Norwalk* ... CT-1
**South Norwalk**—*pop pl* ... CT-1
South Norwalk Rsvr—*reservoir* ... CT-1
*South Norwood Canyon* ... UT-8
South Notch—*gap* ... NY-2
South Notch Interchange—*other* ... NH-1
South No 1 Tank—*reservoir* ... NM-5

South Number 1 Mine (underground)—*mine* AL-4
South Nutgrass—*reservoir* NV-8
South Nuttall—*locale* WV-2
South Nutter Rsvr—*reservoir* AZ-5
**South Nyack**—*pop pl* NY-2
South Oak Brush Canyon—*valley* UT-8
*South Oak Brush Creek* UT-8
South Oak Brush Wash—*valley* UT-8
South Oak Canyon Mesa—*summit* NM-5
South Oak Cliff—*uninc pl* TX-5
South Oak Cliff HS—*school* TX-5
South Oak Creek—*stream* AZ-5
South Oak Creek—*stream* (2) CO-8
South Oak Creek Cem—*cemetery* KS-7
South Oakdale Hist Dist—*hist pl* OR-9
*South Oak Grove Baptist Church* AL-4
South Oak Grove Cem—*cemetery* AL-4
South Oak Grove Ch—*church* AL-4
South Oak Grove School (abandoned)—*locale* OR-9
South Oakland Sch—*school* KS-7
South Oakland Sch (historical)—*school* MO-7
*South Oak Park* IL-6
South Oak Points—*summit* AZ-5
South Oak Ridge Ch—*church* NC-3
South Oak Ridge Sch—*school* IL-6
South Oaks Square (Shop Ctr)—*locale* FL-3
South Oat Creek—*stream* WY-8
South Oberlin Oil Field—*oilfield* LA-4
**South Ocala**—*pop pl* FL-3
South Ocala Baptist Ch—*church* FL-3
South Ocala Sch—*school* FL-3
**South Oceanside**—*pop pl* CA-9
South Odom Windmill—*locale* TX-5
South of Bar T Tank—*reservoir* AZ-5
South Of Dan Sch—*school* VA-3
South Of Shooters Island Reach—*channel* NY-2
South of the Border—*post sta* SC-3
South Of The Yellowstone—*cens area* MT-8
South Ogallala—*fmr MCD* NE-7
**South Ogden**—*pop pl* UT-8
South Ogden Highline Canal—*canal* UT-8
South Ogden JHS—*school* UT-8
South Ogdensburg—*locale* NJ-2
South Ogeechee (CCD)—*cens area* GA-3
South Oil City—*uninc pl* PA-2
**Southold**—*pop pl* NY-2
Southold Bay—*bay* NY-2
**South Old Bridge**—*pop pl* NJ-2
South Old Dock—*locale* NC-3
**Southold (Town of)**—*pop pl* NY-2
Southold Yacht Club—*other* NY-2
**South Olean**—*pop pl* NY-2
**South Oleander (subdivision)**—*pop pl* NC-3
South Olean Yards—*locale* NY-2
South Ole Creek—*stream* ID-8
South Ole Creek—*stream* WA-9
South Olga Lakes—*lake* AK-9
**South Olga Township**—*pop pl* ND-7
**South Olive**—*pop pl* (2) OH-6
South Olive Elem Sch—*school* FL-3
South Olive Park—*park* FL-3
South Olohena—*civil* HI-9
South Olsen Creek—*stream* OR-9
**South Olympus Heights Subdivision**—*pop pl* UT-8
**South Omaha**—*pop pl* NE-7
South Omaha Creek—*stream* NE-7
South One Horse Lake—*lake* MT-8
South Onion Creek—*stream* IA-7
South Onion Creek—*stream* TX-5
**South Onondaga**—*pop pl* NY-2
South Open Hollow—*valley* TX-5
South Opening—*channel* (2) MP-9
*South Orange* NJ-2
**South Orange**—*pop pl* VA-3
South Orange—*post sta* NJ-2
South Orange Station—*hist pl* NJ-2
South Orange Station—*locale* NJ-2
South Orangetown JHS—*school* NY-2
**South Orange Village**—*pop pl* NJ-2
South Orange Village Hall—*hist pl* NJ-2
**South Orange Village (Township of)**—*pop pl* NJ-2
**South Orchard**—*pop pl* AL-4
*South Orchards* AL 4
**South Orchards**—*pop pl* AL-4
South Ordway Lateral—*canal* CO-8
South Ore Creek—*stream* MI-6
**South Orland**—*pop pl* ME-1
South Orlando Seventh Day Adventist Sch—*school* FL-3
South Orla Oil Field—*oilfield* TX-5
**South Orleans**—*pop pl* MA-1
**South Oroville**—*pop pl* CA-9
South Orphan Well—*well* NM-5
**South Orrington**—*pop pl* ME-1
South Orwell Cem—*cemetery* OH-6
South Oshkosh—*uninc pl* WI-6
*South Oswego* OR-9
**South Oswego**—*pop pl* OR-9
**South Otselic**—*pop pl* NY-2
South Otselic Hist Dist—*hist pl* NY-2
**South Ottawa**—*pop pl* IL-6
South Ottawa (Township of)—*civ div* IL-6
*South Otter Creek* KS-7
South Otter Creek—*stream* IA-7
**South Otter (Township of)**—*pop pl* IL-6
*South Ottumwa* IA-7
**Southover**—*pop pl* GA-3
Southover Park—*park* PA-2
South Ovid Cem—*cemetery* MI-6
**South Owego**—*pop pl* NY-2
South Owl Creek—*stream* KS-7
South Oxbow Lake—*lake* MI-6
South Oxford—*locale* NY-2
South Oxford Cem—*cemetery* MS-4
South Oxford Ch—*church* MS-4
*South Oxford Congregational Ch* MS-4
South Oxford (Unorganized Territory of)—*unorg* ME-1
South Oyster Bay—*bay* NY-2
South Oyster Island—*island* FL-3
**South Ozark**—*pop pl* AR-4
South Ozark Sch (historical)—*school* MO-7
**South Ozone Park**—*pop pl* NY-2
South Pacific Ocean—*sea* AS-9
South Packsaddle Canyon—*valley* WY-8
South Pacolet River—*stream* SC-3
South Pacolet River Rsvr Number One—*reservoir* SC-3
South Paddy Creek—*stream* CA-9
**South Padre Island**—*pop pl* TX-5
South Pahroc Range—*range* NV-8
*South Pahroc Range - in part* NV-8
South Paint Rock Creek—*stream* WY-8
South Paint Rock Rsvr—*reservoir* WY-8
South Palm Acad—*school* FL-3
**South Palm Beach**—*pop pl* FL-3
South Palm Gardens Sch—*school* TX-5
**South Palmyra**—*pop pl* NY-2
South Palmyra (Township of)—*civ div* IL-6
*South Paloduro Creek* TX-5
South Palo Duro Creek—*stream* TX-5
*South Palo Pinto Creek* TX-5
*South Paluxy Creek* TX-5
South Paluxy River—*stream* TX-5
*South Panola Community Hospital* MS-4
South Panola HS—*school* MS-4
South Panther Skin Creek—*stream* AR-4
South Papillion Creek—*stream* NE-7
*South Parawa Creek* OR-9
**South Paris**—*pop pl* ME-1
South Parish—*hist pl* NH-1
South Parish Cem—*cemetery* NH-1
South Parish Congregational Church and Parish House—*hist pl* ME-1
*South Park* MI-6
*South Park* NC-3
*South Park* (2) OH-6
South Park—*basin* CA-9
South Park—*flat* (2) CO-8
South Park—*flat* WY-8
South Park—*park* (4) CA-9
South Park—*park* FL-3
South Park—*park* GA-3
South Park—*park* (5) IL-6
South Park—*park* KS-7
South Park—*park* MI-6
South Park—*park* (2) MN-6
South Park—*park* (2) MO-7
South Park—*park* MT-8
South Park—*park* (2) NE-7
South Park—*park* NY-2
South Park—*park* NC-3
South Park—*park* (2) OH-6
South Park—*park* OK-5
South Park—*park* TN-4
South Park—*park* TX-5
South Park—*park* WA-9
South Park—*park* (3) WI-6
**South Park**—*pop pl* (2) CA-9
**South Park**—*pop pl* IL-6
**South Park**—*pop pl* IN-6
**South Park**—*pop pl* KY-4
**South Park**—*pop pl* MI-6
**South Park**—*pop pl* NJ-2
**South Park**—*pop pl* OH-6
**South Park**—*pop pl* WA-9
**South Park**—*pop pl* (2) WV-2
South Park—*post sta* LA-4
South Park—*post sta* SC-3
South Park—*uninc pl* KS-7
South Park—*uninc pl* LA-4
South Park—*uninc pl* TX-5
**South Park Addition (subdivision)**—*pop pl* UT-8
South Park Ave Trailhead—*locale* UT-8
South Park Calvary United Presbyterian Church—*hist pl* NJ-2
South Park Canyon—*valley* CA-9
South Park Cem—*cemetery* (2) IN-6
South Park Cem—*cemetery* NM-5
South Park Ch—*church* KY-4
South Park Ch—*church* NY-2
South Park Ch—*church* NC-3
South Park Ch—*church* TX-5
South Park City—*uninc pl* CO-8
South Park Community Church—*hist pl* CO-8
*South Park Creek* WY-8
South Park Creek—*stream* WY-8
South Park Elem Sch—*school* KS-7
**South Parkersburg**—*pop pl* WV-2
South Parker Tank—*reservoir* TX-5
**South Park Estates (subdivision)**—*pop pl* AL-4
South Park Fishing Club—*other* KY-4
South Park Golf Course—*locale* PA-2
*South Park High School* NC-3
South Park Hills—*range* KY-4
South Park Hist Dist—*hist pl* OH-6
South Park Hist Dist (Boundary Increase)—*hist pl* OH-6
South Park Historical Monmt—*pillar* CO-8
South Park HS—*school* TX-5
South Park JHS—*school* TX-5
*South Park Junction* CO-8
South Park Lager Beer Brewery—*hist pl* CO-8
**South Parkland**—*pop pl* KY-4
Southpark Mall—*locale* NC-3
Southpark Mall (Shop Ctr)—*locale* IA-7
South Park MS—*school* PA-2
South Park Peak—*summit* CA-9
South Park Sch—*school* (2) CA-9
South Park Sch—*school* IL-6
South Park Sch—*school* KS-7
South Park Sch—*school* KY-4
South Park Sch—*school* MO-7
South Park Sch—*school* NY-2
South Park Sch—*school* NC-3
South Park Sch—*school* TN-4
South Park Sch—*school* WV-2
South Park Sch—*school* WI-6
South Park Senior HS—*school* PA-2
South Park Shoal—*bar* IL-6
South Park Shop Ctr—*locale* NC-3
South Park Site—*hist pl* OH-6
South Parks Lewisville Canal—*canal* ID-8
South Park Stadium—*other* NY-2
**South Park (subdivision)**—*pop pl* AL-4
**Southpark (subdivision)**—*pop pl* NC-3
**South Park (Township of)**—*pop pl* PA-2
South Park Trailer Court—*uninc pl* LA-4
**South Park View**—*pop pl* KY-4
South Park Village—*post sta* WA-9
South Parkway-Heiskell Farm Hist Dist—*hist pl* TN-4
South Parkway Sch—*school* NY-2
South Park Well—*well* ID-8
*South Parsonfield* ME-1
**South Parsonsfield**—*pop pl* ME-1
Southpart Cem—*cemetery* MA-1
*South PartridA VAR Lower Partridge Lake* MN-6
*South Partridge Lake* MN-6
**South Pasadena**—*pop pl* CA-9
**South Pasadena**—*pop pl* FL-3
South Pasadena Hist Dist—*hist pl* CA-9
South Pasadena HS—*school* CA-9
South Pasadena JHS—*school* CA-9
**South Pascagoula**—*pop pl* MS-4
*South Pass* FL-3
*South Pass* FM-9
*South Pass* MP-9
South Pass—*channel* (2) AK-9
South Pass—*channel* FL-3
South Pass—*channel* (2) LA-4
South Pass—*channel* MS-4
South Pass—*channel* TX-5
South Pass—*channel* WA-9
South Pass—*channel* FM-9
South Pass—*channel* (4) MP-9
South Pass—*fmr MCD* NE-7
South Pass—*gap* AZ-5
South Pass—*gap* OR-9
South Pass—*gap* (2) WA-9
South Pass—*gap* WY-8
South Pass—*hist pl* WY-8
South Pass—*locale* CA-9
**South Pass**—*pop pl* LA-4
South Passage—*area* NM-5
South Passage—*channel* (2) AK-9
South Passage—*channel* OH-6
South Passage Point—*cape* AK-9
South Passage Reservoirs—*reservoir* NM-5
South Pass City—*hist pl* WY-8
**South Pass City**—*pop pl* WY-8
South Pass Island—*island* TX-5
South Pass Lake—*bay* TX-5
South Pass Lake—*lake* OR-9
South Pass Lake Trail—*trail* OR-9
South Pass Ski Tow—*other* WY-8
South Pass Spring—*spring* AZ-5
South Pasture—*flat* KS-7
South Pasture (historical)—*civil* MA-1
South Pasture Pond—*reservoir* CO-8
South Pasture Spring—*spring* TX-5
South Pasture Tank—*reservoir* (2) AZ-5
South Pasture Tank—*reservoir* TX-5
South Pasture Tank no 1—*reservoir* NM-5
South Pasture Tank no 2—*reservoir* NM-5
South Pasture Tanks—*reservoir* TX-5
South Pasture Well—*well* NM-5
South Pasture Windmill—*locale* (3) NM-5
South Pasture Windmill—*locale* (3) TX-5
South Patawa Creek—*stream* OR-9
South Patch—*bar* FM-9
South Paterson—*uninc pl* NJ-2
South Paterson Station—*locale* NJ-2
*South Patoka* IN-6
South Patoka River—*stream* IN-6
**South Patrick**—*pop pl* FL-3
South Patrick Shop Ctr—*locale* FL-3
South Patrick Shores (Amherst)—*CDP* FL-3
South Patten Sch—*school* ME-1
South Patterfore Canyon—*valley* UT-8
South Patterson Park—*park* TN-4
South Patterson Spring—*spring* UT-8
South Pawnee Creek—*stream* CO-8
South Paw Paw Cemtery—*cemetery* IL-6
**South Peabody (subdivision)**—*pop pl* MA-1
**South Peacham**—*pop pl* VT-1
South Peacham Brook—*stream* VT-1
South Peachland Creek—*stream* OK-5
South Peacock Mine—*mine* ID-8
*South Peak* NV-8
South Peak—*summit* AK-9
South Peak—*summit* (2) CA-9
South Peak—*summit* CO-8
South Peak—*summit* (2) ME-1
South Peak—*summit* MT-8
South Peak—*summit* (5) NH-1
South Peak—*summit* (2) NM-5
South Peak—*summit* (2) OR-9
South Peak—*summit* (2) UT-8
South Peak—*summit* WA-9
South Peak Kinsman Mtn—*summit* NH-1
*South Peak Of Baldpate* ME-1
South Peak White Mtn—*summit* CA-9
South Peapod—*island* WA-9
*South Pease River* TX-5
South Pecan Lake Oil and Gas Field—*oilfield* LA-4
South Peck Spring—*spring* CO-8
South Pecos Sch—*school* TX-5
South Peddy Draw—*valley* WY-8
**South Pekin**—*pop pl* IL-6
**South Pelzer**—*pop pl* SC-3
**South Pemberton**—*pop pl* NJ-2
South Pembina Cem—*cemetery* ND-7
South Pembina Ch—*church* ND-7
*South Pembina River* ND-7
**South Peninsula**—*pop pl* FL-3
South Peninsula (CCD)—*cens area* FL-3
South Penn Run—*stream* PA-2
**South Penns Grove**—*pop pl* NJ-2
**South Penobscot**—*pop pl* ME-1
*South Peno School* SD-7
South Peoples Spring—*spring* AZ-5
**South Pepperell**—*pop pl* MA-1
South Percha Creek—*stream* NM-5
South Perinton Ch—*church* NY-2
*South Perkasie* PA-2
**South Perkasie**—*pop pl* PA-2
South Perkasie Covered Bridge—*hist pl* PA-2
South Perkins—*unorg reg* SD-7
South Perkins Windmill—*locale* TX-5
South Perley Brook—*stream* ME-1
South Perrin Canal—*canal* CA-9
**South Perry**—*pop pl* OH-6
South Perry Street Hist Dist—*hist pl* AL-4
South Persimmon Ch—*church* OK-5
South Persimmon Creek—*stream* OK-5
*South Peru* IN-6
**South Peru**—*pop pl* IN-6
South Petaca—*locale* NM-5
South Peterboro Street Commercial Hist Dist—*hist pl* NY-2
South Peterboro Street Residential Hist Dist—*hist pl* NY-2
**South Philipsburg**—*pop pl* PA-2
South Philipsburg Borough—*civil* PA-2
**South Phoenix**—*pop pl* AZ-5
South Phoenix Adult Center—*building* AZ-5
South Picayune Creek—*stream* IA-7
South Pick Anderson Lift Ditch—*canal* CA-9
South Picket House Draw—*valley* OK-5
South Pier—*bar* MA-1
South Pier—*locale* PA-2
South Pier—*other* IL-6
South Pierce—*unorg reg* ND-7
South Pierce Branch—*stream* TN-4
South Pigpen Creek—*stream* NM-5
South Pike Bay Campground—*locale* MN-6
South Pike HS—*school* MS-4
South Pike JHS—*school* MS-4
South Pine—*fmr MCD* NE-7
**South Pine Bluff**—*pop pl* AR-4
South Pine Canyon—*valley* UT-8
South Pine Canyon Tank—*reservoir* NM-5
South Pine Channel—*channel* FL-3
*South Pine Creek* OR-9
*South Pine Creek* UT-8
*South Pine Creek* WY-8
South Pine Creek—*stream* CO-8
South Pine Creek—*stream* ID-8
South Pine Creek—*stream* OR-9
South Pine Creek—*stream* UT-8
South Pine Creek Trail—*trail* CO-8
South Pine Draw—*valley* WY-8
South Pine Grove Sch—*school* FL-3
South Pine Lake—*lake* WI-6
South Pine Lakes—*locale* FL-3
South Pine River Lateral—*canal* CO-8
South Pine Sch (historical)—*school* MO-7
South Pines Sch—*school* WA-9
South Pine Supply Ditch—*canal* CO-8
South Pine Wash—*valley* UT-8
South Piney Creek—*stream* CO-8
South Piney Creek—*stream* MO-7
South Piney Creek—*stream* TN-4
South Piney Creek—*stream* (2) WY-8
South Piney Ditch—*canal* WY-8
South Piney Mountain Trail—*trail* VA-3
South Piney Trail—*trail* WY-8
South Pinhead Butte—*summit* OR-9
South Pinnacle Rock—*island* AK-9
South Pinon Hills—*summit* CO-8
South Pinto Hills—*summit* UT-8
South Pioa Mtn—*summit* AS-9
**South Piscataway**—*pop pl* MD-2
South Pit—*crater* HI-9
South Pit Chino Mine—*mine* NM-5
**South Pittsburg**—*pop pl* TN-4
South Pittsburg Ch of Christ—*church* TN-4
South Pittsburg Ch of the Nazarene—*church* TN-4
South Pittsburg City Hall—*building* TN-4
South Pittsburg Cumberland Presbyterian Ch—*church* TN-4
South Pittsburg Ferry (historical)—*locale* TN-4
South Pittsburg First Baptist Ch—*church* TN-4
South Pittsburg HS—*school* TN-4
South Pittsburgh Water Company Station—*building* PA-2
South Pittsburg Municipal Hosp—*hospital* TN-4
South Pittsburg Municipal Park—*park* TN-4
South Pittsburg Pit—*cave* TN-4
South Pittsburg Post Office—*building* TN-4
South Pittsburg Primitive Baptist Ch—*church* TN-4
South Pittsburg Sch—*school* TN-4
**South Pittsfield**—*pop pl* NH-1
South Pittsford Ch—*church* MI-6
South Pitts Windmill—*locale* NM-5
South Placer Fire Station—*building* CA-9
**South Plainedge**—*pop pl* NY-2
**South Plainfield**—*pop pl* NJ-2
South Plainfield Ch—*church* NC-3
South Plainfield HS—*school* NJ-2
South Plainfield OMS Helistop—*airport* NJ-2
South Plainfield Station—*locale* NJ-2
South Plains—*plain* MA-1
**South Plains**—*pop pl* TX-5
**South Plains**—*pop pl* VA-3
South Plains Ch—*church* VA-3
South Plains Fairground—*locale* TX-5
South Plains Junior Coll—*school* TX-5
South Plainview Sch—*school* CO-8
South Plantation HS—*school* FL-3
South Platte—*fmr MCD* NE-7
**South Platte**—*pop pl* CO-8
South Platte Ch—*church* MO-7
South Platte Ditch—*canal* CO-8
*South Platte River* CO-8
South Platte River—*stream* CO-8
South Platte River—*stream* NE-7
South Platte River Supply Canal—*canal* NE-7
**South Platte Township**—*pop pl* NE-7
**South Plattsburgh**—*pop pl* NY-2
South Plaza Industrial Park—*locale* AL-4
South Plaza Shop Ctr—*locale* AZ-5
South Plaza (Shop Ctr)—*locale* (2) FL-3
South Plaza Shop Ctr—*locale* MA-1
South Plaza Shop Ctr—*locale* OH-6
South Pleasant Cem—*cemetery* ND-7
South Pleasant Ch—*church* IN-6
South Pleasant Ch—*church* ND-7
South Pleasant Grove Ch—*church* KY-4
South Pleasant View Sch—*school* SD-7
*South Pleasureville* KY-4
South Plum Creek—*stream* CO-8
South Plum Creek—*stream* TX-5
*South Plymouth* MA-1
**South Plymouth**—*pop pl* NY-2
**South Plymouth**—*pop pl* OH-6
South Plymouth Cem—*cemetery* NY-2
**South Pocasset**—*pop pl* MA-1
South Pocket—*basin* AZ-5
South Pocket—*valley* CA-9
South Pocket—*valley* WY-8
South Pocket Hollow—*valley* MO-7
South Pocket Tank—*reservoir* AZ-5
*South Podunk Pond* MA-1
South Pogy Mtn—*summit* ME-1
South Poinsett Access Area—*park* SD-7
*South Point* DE-2
*South Point* HI-9
*South Point* MO-7
*South Point* VA-3
South Point—*cape* (3) AK-9
South Point—*cape* (3) CA-9
South Point—*cape* (5) FL-3
South Point—*cape* (2) LA-4
South Point—*cape* ME-1
South Point—*cape* (2) MD-2
South Point—*cape* (2) MI-6
South Point—*cape* NV-8
South Point—*cape* NH-1
South Point—*cape* NJ-2
South Point—*cape* (2) NC-3
South Point—*cape* OR-9
South Point—*cape* SC-3
South Point—*cape* UT-8
South Point—*cape* (2) VA-3
South Point—*cape* WA-9
South Point—*cape* WI-6
South Point—*cape* MH-9
South Point—*cape* MP-9
South Point—*cliff* (2) WA-9
South Point—*island* FL-3
South Point—*locale* LA-4
South Point—*locale* WA-9
**South Point**—*pop pl* OH-6
South Point—*summit* OR-9
South Point Cem—*cemetery* MO-7
South Point Cem—*cemetery* TN-4
South Point Ch—*church* NC-3
South Point Ch—*church* TN-4
South Point Ch—*church* TX-5
South Point Ch—*church* WV-2
South Point Complex—*hist pl* HI-9
*South Point Creek* FL-3
South Pointe Center (Shop Ctr)—*locale* FL-3
South Pointe Park—*park* FL-3
South Point Gut—*gut* VA-3
South Point HS—*school* NC-3
South Point Marsh—*swamp* VA-3
South Point Mesa—*summit* NM-5
South Point Road Substation—*other* HI-9
South Point (Township of)—*fmr MCD* NC-3
South Point Trail—*trail* WA-9
**South Poland**—*pop pl* ME-1
South Pole—*post sta* NY-2
South Pole Canyon—*valley* TX-5
South Pole Creek—*stream* MT-8
South Pole Mine—*mine* OR-9
South Polk Elem Sch—*school* TN-4
South Pollack Well—*well* TX-5
**South Pomfret**—*pop pl* VT-1
*South Pond* MA-1
*South Pond* OH-6
*South Pond* PA-2
South Pond—*lake* CT-1
South Pond—*lake* GA-3
South Pond—*lake* IL-6
South Pond—*lake* (6) ME-1
South Pond—*lake* (2) MA-1
South Pond—*lake* (2) MI-6
South Pond—*lake* NJ-2
South Pond—*lake* (8) NY-2
South Pond—*lake* UT-8
South Pond—*lake* (4) VT-1
**South Pond**—*pop pl* MA-1
South Pond—*reservoir* AR-4
South Pond—*reservoir* CT-1
South Pond—*reservoir* PA-2
South Pond—*reservoir* TX-5
South Pond—*reservoir* VA-3
South Pond Brook—*stream* VT-1
South Pond Cem—*cemetery* MA-1
South Pond Dam—*dam* PA-2
South Pondera Coulee—*valley* MT-8
South Pond Mtn—*summit* NY-2
South Pond Outlet—*stream* NY-2
South Ponds—*lake* NH-1
South Pond Trail—*trail* VT-1
South Ponil Creek—*stream* NM-5
South Ponte Vedra Beach—*locale* FL-3
South Pontotoc Attendance Center—*school* MS-4
*South Pontotoc HS* MS-4
South Pool—*reservoir* MN-6
**South Pooler**—*pop pl* GA-3
South Pool Well—*well* NM-5
South Pope Park—*park* TX-5
South Poplar Branch—*stream* IN-6
South Poplar Run—*stream* PA-2
South Poplar Springs Ch—*church* GA-3
South Popplestone Ledge—*bar* ME-1
*South Port* AL-4
*South Port* IN-6
South Port—*locale* FL-3
Southport—*locale* IL-6
Southport—*locale* OR-9
Southport—*locale* TN-4
Southport—*park* WI-6
**Southport**—*pop pl* CA-9
**Southport**—*pop pl* CT-1
**Southport**—*pop pl* FL-3
**Southport**—*pop pl* (2) IN-6
**Southport**—*pop pl* LA-4
**Southport**—*pop pl* ME-1
**Southport**—*pop pl* MI-6
**Southport**—*pop pl* (2) NY-2
**Southport**—*pop pl* NC-3
**Southport**—*pop pl* VA-3
South Portal—*tunnel* (2) CA-9
South Portal Campground—*locale* CA-9
South Portal Canyon—*valley* CA-9
South Portal Elizabeth Tunnel—*tunnel* CA-9
South Portal Number Four—*other* CA-9
South Portal Outlet—*other* CO-8
Southport Baptist Ch—*church* IN-6
*South Port Canal* FL-3
South Port Canal—*canal* FL-3
Southport (CCD)—*cens area* FL-3
Southport Cem—*cemetery* IL-6
Southport Channel—*channel* CA-9
Southport Creek—*stream* OR-9
Southport Elem Sch—*school* FL-3
Southport Elem Sch—*school* IN-6
South Porter Cem—*cemetery* WI-6
Southport Gulch—*valley* UT-8
Southport Harbor—*bay* CT-1
Southport Hist Dist—*hist pl* CT-1
Southport Hist Dist—*hist pl* NC-3
Southport HS—*school* IN-6
Southport Island—*island* ME-1
**Southport Junction**—*pop pl* LA-4
**South Portland**—*pop pl* ME-1
South Portland Air Natl Guard Station—*building* ME-1
South Portland Coast Guard Base—*military* ME-1
*South Portland Gardens* ME-1
**South Portland Gardens**—*pop pl* ME-1
*South Portland Heights* ME-1
Southport Landing—*locale* CA-9
Southport Light One—*tower* NC-3
Southport Mall Shop Ctr—*locale* MS-4
Southport Mine—*mine* OR-9
**South Port Saint Lucie**—*pop pl* FL-3
Southport Sch—*school* WI-6
Southport Shop Ctr—*locale* FL-3
Southport (Shop Ctr)—*locale* FL-3
**South Portsmouth**—*pop pl* KY-4
**South Portsmouth**—*pop pl* RI-1
South Portsmouth Sch—*school* KY-4
Southport (sta.)—*uninc pl* NY-2
**Southport (Town of)**—*pop pl* ME-1
**Southport (Town of)**—*pop pl* NY-2
Southport United Methodist Ch—*church* IN-6
South Posey Creek—*stream* WY-8
South Post Oak—*uninc pl* TX-5
South Pothole—*lake* NM-5
South Potomac JHS—*school* MD-2
South Potsdam Cem—*cemetery* NY-2
South Potts Creek—*stream* NC-3
**South Pottstown**—*pop pl* PA-2
**South Poultney**—*pop pl* VT-1
South Powell Creek—*stream* OH-6
South Powellhurst Sch—*school* OR-9
South Powerhouse—*other* CA-9
South Power Lateral—*canal* ID-8
South Prairie—*flat* OR-9
South Prairie—*flat* WA-9
South Prairie—*locale* ND-7
**South Prairie**—*pop pl* OR-9
**South Prairie**—*pop pl* WA-9
South Prairie Cem—*cemetery* IL-6
South Prairie Cem—*cemetery* IA-7
South Prairie Cem—*cemetery* ND-7
South Prairie Cem—*cemetery* TX-5
South Prairie Creek—*stream* IN-6
South Prairie Creek—*stream* WA-9
South Prairie Grange Hall—*locale* IA-7
South Prairie Lee Park—*park* MO-7
South Prairie Park—*park* CA-9
South Prairie Sch—*school* (2) IL-6
South Prairie Sch—*school* OR-9
South Prentiss Ch—*church* MS-4
South Prentiss Sch (historical)—*school* MS-4
South Preston Sch (abandoned)—*school* PA-2
South Princeton—*locale* ME-1
South Privo Tank—*reservoir* NM-5
South Privo Windmill—*locale* NM-5
*South Prong* GA-3
*South Prong* MD-2
*South Prong* TN-4
*South Prong* TX-5
*South Prong* VA-3
South Prong—*stream* (2) CO-8
South Prong Alafia River—*stream* FL-3
South Prong Alligator Creek—*stream* FL-3
South Prong Anderson Creek—*stream* NC-3
*South Prong Antelope Creek* NE-7
*South Prong Antelope Creek* WY-8
South Prong Barber Creek—*stream* WY-8
South Prong Barbours Creek—*stream* VA-3
*South Prong Barren Fork* TN-4
South Prong Barren Fork—*stream* TN-4
South Prong Bayou Cocodrie—*stream* LA-4
South Prong Bay River—*stream* NC-3
South Prong Big Creek—*stream* AR-4
South Prong Big Creek—*stream* GA-3
*South Prong Big Sandy Creek* TX-5
South Prong Bingham Branch—*stream* KY-4
South Prong Black Canyon Creek—*stream* OR-9
South Prong Black Coulee—*valley* MT-8
South Prong Blue Creek—*stream* WY-8
South Prong Buck Creek—*stream* GA-3
South Prong Buckhorn Creek—*stream* VA-3
South Prong Buffalo Creek—*stream* NC-3
South Prong Caballo Creek—*stream* WY-8
South Prong Camp Creek—*stream* SC-3
South Prong Canoochee Creek—*stream* GA-3
South Prong Cartledge Creek—*stream* NC-3
South Prong Cedar Bluff Creek—*stream* MO-7
South Prong Cem—*cemetery* FL-3
South Prong Chestnut Creek—*stream* AL-4
South Prong Chinners Swamp—*stream* SC-3
*South Prong Chugwater Creek* WY-8
South Prong Clark Creek—*stream* NC-3
South Prong Clear Creek—*stream* OR-9
South Prong Clear Fork—*stream* TN-4
South Prong College Creek—*stream* GA-3
South Prong Coon Creek—*stream* TX-5
South Prong Cottonwood Creek—*stream* TX-5
South Prong Cottonwood Creek—*stream* WY-8
South Prong Cox Creek—*stream* AL-4
South Prong Cox Creek—*stream* NC-3
*South Prong Coxs Creek* NC-3
South Prong Creek—*stream* (2) GA-3
South Prong Creek—*stream* (2) TX-5
South Prong Crooked River—*stream* MO-7
South Prong Cypress Creek—*stream* TX-5
South Prong Deadman Creek—*stream* WY-8
South Prong Double Branch—*stream* FL-3
South Prong Double Branch—*stream* TN-4
South Prong Dry Fork Powder River—*stream* WY-8
South Prong Elko Creek—*stream* GA-3
South Prong Falling Creek—*stream* NC-3
South Prong Fort Godsden Creek—*stream* FL-3
South Prong Glady Fork—*stream* NC-3
South Prong Goose Pond Bayou—*stream* LA-4
South Prong Goshen Creek—*stream* GA-3
South Prong Green River—*stream* NC-3
South Prong Hannahs Creek—*stream* NC-3
South Prong Horse Creek—*stream* TN-4
South Prong Horse Creek—*stream* TX-5
South Prong House Creek—*stream* GA-3
South Prong Indian Creek—*stream* TX-5
South Prong Irish Hollow—*valley* IL-6
South Prong Jacks Fork—*stream* MO-7
*South Prong Jacks Fork River* MO-7
South Prong Leatherwood Creek—*stream* MO-7

South Prong Leonard Pond Run—stream MD-2
South Prong Lewis Fork—stream NC-3
South Prong Lewis Fork Creek NC-3
South Prong Little Pine Creek—stream NC-3
South Prong Little Racoon Creek IN-6
South Prong Little Red River—stream TX-5
South Prong Little River—stream (2) NC-3
South Prong Little Rock Creek—stream TN-4
South Prong Long Creek—stream TX-5
South Prong Long Draw—valley NM-5
South Prong Lostland Run—stream MD-2
South Prong Marler Creek—stream TX-5
South Prong Marshall Creek—stream GA-3
South Prong McLeod Creek—stream NC-3
South Prong Meridan Creek—stream TX-5
South Prong Michael Hollow—valley IL-6
South Prong Middle Creek—stream AR-4
South Prong Mill Creek AL-4
South Prong Moss Creek—stream TX-5
South Prong of Grand Bayou—stream LA-4
South Prong Pecan Bayou—stream TX-5
South Prong Pigg River—stream VA-3
South Prong Pine Creek—stream OR-9
South Prong Pond FL-3
South Prong Poor Fork—stream TN-4
South Prong Pumpkin Creek—stream WY-8
South Prong Reeds Creek—stream AR-4
South Prong Richland Creek TN-4
South Prong Richland Creek—stream NC-3
South Prong Roasting Ear Creek—stream AR-4
South Prong Rsvr—reservoir OR-9
South Prong Saint Marys River—stream FL-3
South Prong Saint Sebastian River—stream FL-3
South Prong Salt creek IN-6
South Prong Sand Creek—stream TX-5
South Prong Sandy River—stream VA-3
South Prong Sebastian Creek FL-3
South Prong Shining Creek—stream NC-3
South Prong Sons Creek—stream MO-7
South Prong South Antelope Creek—stream NE-7
South Prong South Antelope Creek—stream WY-8
South Prong South Fork Little Medicine—stream WY-8
South Prong Spavinaw Creek—stream AR-4
South Prong Spotted Horse Creek—stream WY-8
South Prong Spring Creek—stream IL-6
South Prong Stanley Creek NC-3
South Prong Steritt Swamp—stream SC-3
South Prong Stinking Quarter Creek—stream NC-3
South Prong Stotts Creek—stream IN-6
South Prong Swamp—swamp FL-3
South Prong Swift Creek—stream SC-3
South Prong Sycamore Creek—stream AZ-5
South Prong Tauler Creek—stream AL-4
South Prong Taylors Creek—stream AL-4
South Prong Thickhead Mountain PA-2
South Prong Thick Mountain—cape PA-2
South Prong Trail—trail WV-2
South Prong Trail (pack)—trail OR-9
South Prong Troughs—spring OR-9
South Prong Turkey Creek—stream NC-3
South Prong Walden Creek—stream TN-4
South Prong Wallows Creek—stream WY-8
South Prong West Branch Rocky River—stream NC-3
South Prong West Spring Draw—valley WY-8
South Prong Wet Ash Swamp—stream NC-3
South Prong White Oak River—stream NC-3
South Prong Wicomico River—stream MD-2
South Prong Wild Horse Creek—stream WY-8
South Prong Wolf Creek*—stream NE-7
South Prong Wolf Creek—stream SD-7
South Prong Wright Creek—stream NC-3
South Prong Wrights Creek NC-3
South Prospect Heights Sch—school IL-6
South Prospect Street Hist Dist—hist pl MD-2
South Providence RI-1
South Public Sch—school NM-5
South Puddle Valley Well—well UT-8
South Pueblo—uninc pl CO-8
South Pulantat Site—hist pl GU-9
South Pulaski Hist Dist—hist pl TN-4
**South Pulteney**—pop pl NY-2
South Punished Womans State Public Shooting Area—park SD-7
**South Punta Gorda Heights**—pop pl FL-3
South Purchase Swamp—swamp MA-1
**South Purmela**—pop pl TX-5
South Putman Peak ID-8
South Putnam HS—school IN-6
South Putnam Mtn—summit ID-8
South Putnam Peak ID-8
South Putnam Sch IN-6
South Puyallup River—stream WA-9
**South Pymatuning (Township of)**—pop pl PA-2
South Pyramid—summit OR-9
South Pyramid Creek—stream OR-9
South Pyramid Creek—stream WA-9
South Pyramid Draw—valley NM-5
South Pyramid Peak—summit NM-5
South Quacumquasit Pond MA-1
South Quadra Mtn—summit AK-9
South Quaker Cem—cemetery NH-1
South Quapaw Creek—stream OK-5
**South Quarter**—pop pl MA-1
South Quarter Cem—cemetery MA-1
South Quartz Creek—stream CO-8
South Quartz Mountain Rsvr—reservoir OR-9
South Quay—locale VA-3
South Quay Ch—church VA-3
**South Quincy (subdivision)**—pop pl MA-1
South Rabbit Ears Pass CO-8
South Rabon Creek—stream SC-3
South Raccoon Creek IA-7
South Raccoon River—stream IA-7
South Race—channel NY-2
**South Radley**—pop pl KS-7
South Radnor Cem—cemetery OH-6
South Rail Canyon—valley CA-9
South Rainbow Peak—summit CA-9
South Raker—summit ID-8
South Raleigh—uninc pl NC-3
South Raleigh Airport NC-3
South Ramp Creek—stream IN-6

South Ranch—locale NM-5
South Ranchito Sch—school CA-9
**South Randall Township**—pop pl KS-7
**South Randolph**—pop pl VT-1
**South Randolph**—pop pl WI-6
**South Range**—pop pl MI-6
**South Range**—pop pl WI-6
South Range—range WI-6
South Range—summit MI-6
South Range Community Bldg—hist pl MI-6
**South Rangeley**—pop pl ME-1
South Rapides Acad—school LA-4
South Rat Hole Canyon—valley CO-8
South Rat Hole Canyon—valley UT-8
South Rattlesnake Butte—summit CO-8
South Rattlesnake Canyon—valley NM-5
**South Raub**—pop pl IN-6
South Rawah Peak—summit CO-8
South Rays Fork—stream KY-4
South Reach—channel NJ-2
South Reading MA-1
**South Reading**—pop pl VT-1
South Reading, Town of MA-1
South Reading Schoolhouse—hist pl VT-1
South Rec Area—park UT-8
South Rector Canyon—valley TX-5
South Red Canyon—valley CO-8
South Red Creek—stream CO-8
South Red Hill—summit AZ-5
South Red Hill—summit WY-8
South Red Iron Lake—lake SD-7
South Red Mtn—summit CA-9
South Red River (Township of)—civ div MN-6
South Red Wash—valley UT-8
South Redwater Creek—stream WY-8
South Reed Ch—church OH-6
South Reed Well—well NM-5
South Reelfoot Creek—stream TN-4
**South Rehoboth**—pop pl MA-1
South Reiradon Hill—summit CO-8
South Relief Canyon—valley NV-8
**South Renovo**—pop pl PA-2
South Renovo Borough—civil PA-2
South Renovo Rsvr—reservoir PA-2
South Republican Mngmt Area—park CO-8
South Reservation Ditch—canal CO-8
South Reservoir Dam—dam MA-1
South Reservoir Dam—dam UT-8
South Reservoir East Dike—dam MA-1
South Reservoir West Dike—dam MA-1
South Rice Lake—lake WI-6
South Richeau Creek—stream WY-8
**South Richford**—pop pl VT-1
South Rich High School UT-8
South Richland Cem—cemetery NY-2
South Richland Sch—school MO-7
**South Richmond**—pop pl IN-6
South Richmond—uninc pl VA-3
South Richmond Corners—locale PA-2
South Richmond Hill—uninc pl NY-2
South Richmond Sch—school PA-2
South Rich Sch—school UT-8
South Ridge WA-9
South Ridge—locale MN-6
**Southridge**—pop pl FL-3
**Southridge**—pop pl VA-3
South Ridge—ridge AL-4
South Ridge—ridge (5) CA-9
South Ridge—ridge NH-1
South Ridge—ridge NY-2
South Ridge—ridge OH-6
South Ridge—ridge (2) UT-8
South Ridge—ridge WA-9
South Ridge—ridge (3) WI-6
South Ridge—summit ME-1
South Ridge—summit NV-8
South Ridge—uninc pl LA-4
South Ridge Cem—cemetery OH-6
Southridge Ch—church FL-3
South Ridge Ch—church MN-6
South Ridge Ch—church OH-6
South Ridge East Cem—cemetery OH-6
Southridge Elem Sch—school IN-6
**South Ridge Estates**—pop pl PA-2
South Ridgefield Park Station—locale NJ-2
Southridge HS—school IN-6
Southridge Park—park FL-3
Southridge Plaza—post sta TX-5
South Ridge Sch—school ME-1
South Ridge Sch—school NY-2
South Ridge Sch—school WI-6
Southridge Sch—school WY-8
South Ridge Schoolhouse—hist pl OH-6
Southridge Shop Ctr—locale MO-7
**Southridge (subdivision)**—pop pl AL-4
**Southridge Subdivision**—pop pl UT-8
**Southridge Subdivision Eight**—pop pl UT-8
**Southridge Subdivision (1-6)**—pop pl UT-8
**Southridge Subdivision (9)**—pop pl UT-8
**Southridge 76 Subdivision**—pop pl UT-8
South Rigby Canal—canal ID-8
South Riggs Canyon—valley WA-9
South Rigolets—gut MS-4
South Rigolets Island—island AL-4
South Rigolets Island—island MS-4
**South Riley**—pop pl MI-6
South Riley Cem—cemetery MI-6
South Riley Sch—school MI-6
South Rim—cliff AZ-5
South Rim—cliff CA-9
South Rim—cliff TX-5
South Rim—cliff UT-8
South Rim—cliff (2) WY-8
South Rim Campgrounds—park AZ-5
South Rim Ranger Station—locale CO-8
South Rinconada Canyon—valley NM-5
South Rio Arriba (CCD)—cens area NM-5
South Ripley—locale KY-4
**South Ripley**—pop pl NY-2
South Ripley Ch—church NY-2
South Ripley Junior and Senior HS—school IN-6
South Ripple Hollow—valley IL-6
South River CO-8
South River MA-1
South River MO-7
South River NJ-2
South River NY-2
South River NC-3
South River—bay MA-1

South River—channel GA-3
South River—locale MO-7
**South River**—pop pl MD-2
**South River**—pop pl NJ-2
**South River**—pop pl NC-3
**South River**—pop pl VA-3
South River—stream AK-9
South River—stream GA-3
South River—stream IA-7
South River—stream ME-1
South River—stream MD-2
South River—stream (2) MA-1
South River—stream MO-7
South River—stream NH-1
South River—stream (2) NJ-2
South River—stream (2) NC-3
South River—stream (4) VA-3
South River Bay—bay MI-6
South River Bridge—bridge MD-2
South River (CCD)—cens area KY-4
South River Cem—cemetery VA-3
South River Ch—church GA-3
South River Ch—church (3) NC-3
South River Ch—church VA-3
South River Club—hist pl MD-2
**South River Crossing (historical)**—pop pl IA-7
South River Ditch—canal IA-7
South River Drive Hist Dist—hist pl FL-3
South River Falls—falls VA-3
South River Falls Trail—trail VA-3
South River Friends Meetinghouse—hist pl VA-3
South River Headwaters Marsh—swamp MD-2
South River Light—tower NC-3
South River (Magisterial District)—fmr MCD (3) VA-3
**South River Manor**—pop pl MD-2
South River Marshes—swamp MA-1
South River Overlook—locale VA-3
South River Park—park MD-2
South River Park Cem—cemetery AL-4
South River Park Ch—church AL-4
South River Peak—summit CO-8
South River Picnic Area—park VA-3
South River Reservoir Dam—dam MA-1
South River Road Cem—cemetery OH-6
South River Rsvr—reservoir MA-1
South River Sch—school IA-7
South River Sch—school MA-1
South River Sch—school MI-6
South River Shelter—locale VA-3
South Riverside—civ div SD-7
South Riverside Baptist Ch—church KS-7
South Riverside Cabin—locale MT-8
South Riverside Park—park KS-7
South Riverside Sch—school NE-7
South Riverside Township—civil SD-7
South River Slope—flat WY-8
South River State For—forest MA-1
South Riverton AL-4
South Riverton Sch (historical)—school AL-4
South River Township—civil MO-7
South River (Township of)—fmr MCD NC-3
South River Windmill—locale TX-5
South River Yacht Club—other MD-2
South Road—post sta NY-2
South Road Cem—cemetery WI-6
South Road Ch—church KY-4
South Road Sch—school MI-6
South Road Sch—school NH-1
South Roanoke—uninc pl VA-3
South Roanoke Park—park VA-3
South Roaring Creek OK-5
South Roaring River—stream OR-9
**South Robbinston**—pop pl ME-1
South Robbinston Ridge Sch—school ME-1
South Robb Spring—spring NM-5
South Robeson Sch—school NC-3
South Rock—bar (2) AK-9
South Rock—bar MI-6
South Rock—bar WA-9
South Rock—island (2) AK-9
South Rock—island FL-3
South Rock—other AK-9
South Rock—rock MA-1
South Rock Branch—stream MO-7
South Rock Creek KS-7
South Rock Creek—stream (2) CO-8
South Rock Creek—stream IA-7
South Rock Creek—stream WY-8
South Rock Creek Sch—school OK-5
South Rockdale (CCD)—cens area GA-3
**South Rockford (Childsdale)**—pop pl MI-6
South Rockford Post Office (historical)—building TN-4
South Rockhouse Mtn—summit MA-1
**South Rock Island**—pop pl IL-6
South Rock Island (Township of)—civ div IL-6
South Rocks—area (2) AK-9
South Rocks—island AK-9
South Rocks—pillar PA-2
South Rock Spring—spring NV-8
South Rock Tank—reservoir AZ-5
South Rock Tank—reservoir TX-5
South Rockwall (CCD)—cens area TX-5
South Rockwell Lake MN-6
South Rockwood—other PA-2
**South Rockwood**—pop pl MI-6
South Rockwood Sch—school OR-9
South Rocky Creek—stream TX-5
**South Rocky Mount**—pop pl NC-3
**South Rodanthe**—pop pl NC-3
South Roger Mills (CCD)—cens area OK-5
South Roggen—locale CO-8
South Rolette—unorg reg ND-7
South Rolling Fork KY-4
**South Rolling Hills (subdivision)**—pop pl TN-4
**South Rome**—pop pl IL-6
South Romero Windmill—locale TX-5
**South Roscoe Township**—pop pl KS-7
**South Ross (Township of)**—pop pl IL-6
South Rossville—locale GA-3
South Rothwell Lake—lake MN-6
South Round Lake MN-6
South Roundout NY-2
South Route of Old Nez Perce Trail—trail MT-8
South Route Old Nez Perce Trail—trail ID-8

**South Row**—pop pl MA-1
South Rowan HS—school NC-3
South Row Sch—school MA-1
**South Roxana**—pop pl IL-6
South Roxbury Oil Field—oilfield KS-7
**South Royalston**—pop pl MA-1
**South Royalton**—pop pl VT-1
South Royalton Hist Dist—hist pl VT-1
South Roy Creek—stream OR-9
South RR Hist Dist—hist pl GA-3
South RR Lateral—canal ID-8
South Rsvr—reservoir CA-9
South Rsvr—reservoir MA-1
South Rsvr—reservoir NY-2
South Rsvr—reservoir (2) OR-9
South Rsvr—reservoir TX-5
South Rsvr—reservoir UT-8
South Rsvr—reservoir (2) WY-8
South Ruckels Branch—stream NJ-2
**South Ruffner**—pop pl WV-2
South Ruin Creek—stream KY-4
**South Rumford**—pop pl ME-1
South Rumsey Creek—stream TX-5
South Run—stream NJ-2
South Run—stream PA-2
South Run—stream (4) VA-3
South Runway—other GU-9
South Rush Creek—stream CO-8
South Rushford MN-6
**South Rushford**—pop pl MN-6
South Rushing Creek—stream TN-4
South Rush River Cem—cemetery WI-6
South Rushville—fmr MCD NE-7
South Rusk Windmill—locale TX-5
**South Russell**—pop pl NY-2
**South Russell**—pop pl OH-6
South Russell Cem—cemetery OH-6
South Russell Mine—mine MN-6
South Russian Creek—stream CA-9
**South Rutland (local name Tylerville)**—pop pl NY-2
South Ruxton Creek—stream CO-8
South Ryder Peak—summit CO-8
**South Ryegate**—pop pl VT-1
South Sabula Lakes Park—park IA-7
South Sacramento—uninc pl CA-9
South Sacramento State Wildlife Mgt Area—park NE-7
South Saddle Lake—lake AK-9
South Saddle Mtn—summit OR-9
South Saddle Peak—summit CO-8
South Sage Creek—stream TX-5
South Sage Flat—flat UT-8
South Sage Spring Creek Oil Field—oilfield WY-8
South Saginaw MI-6
South Saint Clair Sch—school AL-4
South Saint Johns Cem—cemetery MN-6
South Saint Johns Ch—church NE-7
**South Saint Johnsville**—pop pl NY-2
South Saint Joseph MO-7
South Saint Nicholas Lake—lake TX-5
South Saint Olaf Ch—church (2) ND-7
**South Saint Paul**—pop pl MN-6
South Saint Petri Cem—cemetery IA-7
South Saint Sch—school LA-4
South Saint Vrain Creek—stream CO-8
South Saint Vrain Trail—trail CO-8
South Salado Creek—stream TX-5
South Salado Peak—summit NM-5
South Salado Peak Tank—reservoir NM-5
South Salem—locale TX-5
**South Salem**—pop pl IN-6
**South Salem**—pop pl NY-2
**South Salem**—pop pl OH-6
**South Salem**—pop pl VA-3
South Salem Acad—hist pl OH-6
South Salem Cem—cemetery ND-7
South Salem Ch—church IN-6
South Salem Covered Bridge—hist pl OH-6
South Salem Dam—dam NM-5
South Salem Hills OR-9
South Salem HS—school OR-9
South Salem Run—stream IN-6
South Salem Sch—school NY-2
South Salem Sch—school VA-3
**South Salem (subdivision)**—pop pl MA-1
**South Salem Township**—pop pl KS-7
South Saleratus Creek UT-8
South Salina Street Hist Dist—hist pl NY-2
South Saline Creek—stream TX-5
**South Salisbury**—pop pl NC-3
South Salisbury—uninc pl MD-2
South Salmon Creek Beach—beach CA-9
South Salmo River—stream ID-8
South Salmo River—stream WA-9
South Salt Creek—stream IN-6
South Salt Creek—stream KS-7
South Salt Lagoon—lake AK-9
**South Salt Lake**—pop pl UT-8
South Salt Lake Branch Post Office—building UT-8
**South Salt Lake Subdivision**—pop pl UT-8
South Salt Wash—valley UT-8
South Saluda Ch—church SC-3
South Saluda River—stream SC-3
South Sammy Creek Oil Field—oilfield MS-4
South Samples Well—well NM-5
South Sampson Well—well TX-5
South San Antonio—uninc pl TX-5
South San Antonio HS—school TX-5
South San Antonio HS West Campus—school TX-5
South Sand Bench—bench UT-8
South Sand Branch—stream WV-2
South Sand Canyon—valley NM-5
South Sand Creek—stream CO-8
South Sand Creek—stream MT-8
South Sand Creek—stream SD-7
South Sand Hills (CCD)—cens area TX-5
South Sandhills Tank—reservoir NM-5
South Sand Hill Well—well NM-5
South Sandia Peak—summit NM-5
South Sandia Spring—spring NM-5
**South San Diego**—pop pl CA-9
**South Sandisfield**—pop pl MA-1
South Sand Lake—lake MI-6
South Sand Point Trail—trail WA-9
South Sand Rsvr—reservoir UT-8
South Sandusky Ave Hist Dist—hist pl OH-6

South Sand Wash—valley CO-8
South Sand Wash Creek CO-8
South Sand Well—well TX-5
**South Sandwich**—pop pl MA-1
South Sand Windmill—locale TX-5
South Sandy Beach—beach ME-1
South Sandy Branch—stream OK-5
South Sandy Cem—cemetery AL-4
South Sandy Ch (historical)—church AL-4
South Sandy Creek AL-4
South Sandy Creek NY-2
South Sandy Creek—stream AL-4
South Sandy Creek—stream GA-3
South Sandy Creek—stream NY-2
South Sandy Creek—stream PA-2
South Sandy Hunter Camp—locale AL-4
South Sandy Run—stream LA-4
**South Sanford**—pop pl ME-1
**South Sanford Heights (subdivision)**—pop pl FL-3
**South San Francisco**—pop pl CA-9
South San Francisco (CCD)—cens area CA-9
South San Francisco HS—school CA-9
**South San Gabriel**—pop pl CA-9
South San Joaquin Main Canal—canal CA-9
South San Jose Creek—stream CA-9
South San Jose Hills—CDP CA-9
South San Jose Sch—school FL-3
South San Leandro—uninc pl CA-9
South San Park—park TX-5
South San Pedro—CDP TX-5
South San Pitch Canyon—valley UT-8
South San Pitch River - in part UT-8
South San Ramon Creek—stream CA-9
**South Santa Ana**—pop pl CA-9
South Santa Clara Creek—stream CO-8
South Santa Fe Oil Field—oilfield TX-5
South Santa Fe Windmill—locale TX-5
South Santan—locale AZ-5
South Santee—locale SC-3
South Santee River—stream SC-3
South Santiago Cem—cemetery MN-6
South Santiago Ch—church MN-6
**South Santiam (historical)**—pop pl OR-9
South Santiam River—stream OR-9
**South San Ysidro**—pop pl NM-5
South Sappa Creek KS-7
South Sarasota—CDP FL-3
South Saunders Oil Field—other NM-5
South Sauty Ch—church AL-4
South Sauty Creek—stream AL-4
South Sauty Point Cabin Site Area—locale AL-4
South Sauty Point Subdivision AL-4
**South Sauty Subdivision (subdivision)**—pop pl AL-4
South Sawmill Creek WY-8
South Sawmill Creek—stream MT-8
South Sawmill Creek—stream WY-8
South Sawtooth Mtn—summit WY-8
South Sawyer Glacier—glacier AK-9
South Sayles Creek WY-8
South Scales Well—well NM-5
South Scalp Creek—stream SD-7
South Scalp Creek Rec Area—park SD-7
**South Scappoose**—pop pl OR-9
South Scappoose Creek—stream OR-9
South Scatterwood Lake SD-7
South Scatterwood Lake—lake SD-7
South Sch—hist pl CT-1
South Sch—hist pl MA-1
South Sch—hist pl WI-6
South Sch—school (2) AZ-5
South Sch—school AR-4
South Sch—school (3) CA-9
South Sch—school (2) CO-8
South Sch—school (7) CT-1
South Sch—school GA-3
South Sch—school (11) IL-6
South Sch—school IN-6
South Sch—school (3) IA-7
South Sch—school (2) KS-7
South Sch—school LA-4
South Sch—school (7) MA-1
South Sch—school (5) MI-6
South Sch—school (2) MS-4
South Sch—school (5) MO-7
South Sch—school (3) NE-7
South Sch—school (3) NY-2
South Sch—school (2) NC-3
South Sch—school (8) OH-6
South Sch—school OK-5
South Sch—school TN-4
South Sch—school (6) TX-5
South Sch—school VT-1
South Sch—school VA-3
South Sch—school (4) WI-6
South Schelling Windmill—locale NM-5
South Schell Peak—summit NV-8
**South Schenectady**—pop pl NY-2
South Schenectady (RR name for Rotterdam)—other NY-2
South Schneider Ditch—canal CO-8
South Sch No 135—school NE-7
South Sch No 165—school NE-7
South Sch No 28—school NE-7
South Sch No 71—school NE-7
South Sch No 92—school NE-7
South Sch No 93—school NE-7
**South Schodack**—pop pl NY-2
South School KS-7
South School Cem—cemetery NY-2
South School Section Lake MN-6
South School Section Well—well NM-5
South Schraalenburgh Church—hist pl NJ-2
**South Schroon**—pop pl NY-2
South Scituate MA-1
South Scituate, Town of MA-1
**South Scituate (historical)**—pop pl RI-1
South Scotland Sch—school NC-3
South Scott Ch—church IN-6
South Scott Lake—lake MI-6
South Scotty Creek—stream OR-9
South Scranton—uninc pl PA-2
South Scranton HS—school PA-2
South Scranton Station—locale PA-2
**South Scriba**—pop pl NY-2
South Sea Bird Ravine MH-9
**South Seabrook**—pop pl NH-1
South Sealy Oil Field—oilfield TX-5

**South Seaside Park**—pop pl NJ-2
**South Seattle**—pop pl WA-9
**South Seaville**—pop pl NJ-2
South Sebago Sch (historical)—school MO-7
South Sebec—locale ME-1
South Seco Canyon—valley NM-5
South Seco Creek—stream NM-5
South Seco Windmill—locale NM-5
South Security Sch—school CO-8
**South Seekonk**—pop pl MA-1
South Selkirk Lake—lake MI-6
South Seminary—locale TX-5
South Seminole Ch—church TN-4
South Seminole Community Hosp—hospital FL-3
South Seminole Sch—school FL-3
South Senator Tank—reservoir AZ-5
South Seneca Ch of Christ—church KS-7
**South Seneca Gardens**—pop pl KS-7
South Seneca Gardens—uninc pl KS-7
South Serrano Ave Hist Dist—hist pl CA-9
**South Setauket**—pop pl NY-2
South Settlement Branch TX-5
South Seven Rivers—stream NM-5
South Seventeenmile Creek—stream WA-9
South Seventeenmile Mtn—summit WA-9
South Seventeenth Street Sch—school NJ-2
South Sevier MS—school UT-8
**South Seward Township**—pop pl KS-7
South Shady Grove Ch—church MS-4
South Shady Grove Ch of God MS-4
South Shaft—mine CA-9
**South Shafter (Smith Corner)**—pop pl CA-9
**South Shaftsbury**—pop pl VT-1
South Shale Ridge—ridge CO-8
South Sharon PA-2
South Sharpe Creek KS-7
South Sharps Creek—stream KS-7
**South Sharps Creek Township**—pop pl KS-7
South Shaser Creek—stream WA-9
South Shattuck Lake—lake WI-6
South Shaver Sch—school TX-5
South Sheba Crater—crater AZ-5
South Shed Lake—lake MI-6
South Sheep Creek—stream OR-9
South Sheep Creek Rsvr—reservoir OR-9
South Sheephead Spring—spring OR-9
South Sheep Mtn—summit CO-8
South Sheep Mtn—summit WY-8
**South Sheffield**—pop pl AL-4
South Sheldon Gulch—valley WY-8
South Shell Bank Flats—bar LA-4
South Shell Rock Cem—cemetery IA-7
South Shellstone Creek—stream GA-3
South Shelton Rock—summit TX-5
South Shelving Rock TX-5
South Shenango Ch—church PA-2
**South Shenango (Township of)**—pop pl PA-2
**South Sherborn**—pop pl MA-1
South Sherborn Cem—cemetery MA-1
South Sherburne—other VT-1
**South Sheridan**—pop pl AR-4
South Sheridan—unorg reg ND-7
South Sherwood—post sta LA-4
South Shinnery Windmill—locale TX-5
South Shoal—bar OH-6
South Shoal Creek IA-7
South Shoal Creek—stream NC-3
South Shooter Flat Tank—reservoir AZ-5
South Shoppe Well—locale NM-5
South Shore IL-6
South Shore LA-4
South Shore—beach MA-1
South Shore—locale TX-5
**South Shore**—pop pl KY-4
**South Shore**—pop pl MO-7
**South Shore**—pop pl SD-7
South Shore Beach—locale RI-1
South Shore Beach Apartments—hist pl IL-6
South Shore Camp—locale OR-9
South Shore Campground—park AZ-5
South Shore (CCD)—cens area (2) WA-9
South Shore Community Center—locale FL-3
South Shore Consumers Mall (Shop Ctr)—locale MA-1
South Shore Country Club—hist pl IL-6
South Shore Country Club—locale MA-1
South Shore Country Club—other IL-6
South Shore Country Club—other IN-6
South Shore Country Club—other NY-2
South Shore Forest Camp—locale OR-9
South Shore Golf Club—other IN-6
South Shore Hosp—hospital IL-6
South Shore Hosp and Med Ctr—hospital FL-3
South Shore HS—school IL-6
**South Shore (Labor Camp)**—pop pl FL-3
Southshore Landing—locale NC-3
South Shore Marina—locale CA-9
South Shore Marshes Wildlife Mngmt Area—park MA-1
South Shore Park OH-6
South Shore Park—park IL-6
South Shore Park—park WI-6
**South Shore Park**—pop pl OH-6
South Shore Park (historical)—park FL-3
South Shore Picnic Ground—park OR-9
South Shore Plaza (Shop Ctr)—locale MA-1
South Shore (railroad station)—locale FL-3
South Shore Rec Area—park NE-7
South Shore Rec Area—park SD-7
**South Shore (RR name Taylor)**—pop pl KY-4
**South Shores**—pop pl CA-9
South Shore Sch—school OR-9
South Shores JHS—school MI-6
South Shores Park—park IL-6
South Shores Sch—school CA-9
South Shores Sch—school IL-6
South Shore State Park—park IL-6
South Shore Trail—trail MT-8
South Shoshone Oil Field—oilfield WY-8
South Shoshone Peak—summit NV-8
South Shotgun Coulee—valley MT-8
**South Shrewsbury**—pop pl MA-1
South Shrewsbury River NJ-2
South Shunganunga Creek KS-7
South Shuteston Gas Field—oilfield LA-4
South Shyster Creek—stream NV-8
South Sibley Well—well NM-5

Southside ... ID-8
South Side ... MO-7
South Side (3) ... OH-6
South Side ... TN-4
Southside—locale ... AR-4
Southside—locale ... PA-2
Southside—locale ... TN-4
**Southside—pop pl** ... AL-4
**South Side—pop pl** ... AR-4
**Southside—pop pl** ... AR-4
**Southside—pop pl** ... FL-3
**South Side—pop pl** ... FL-3
**Southside—pop pl** ... FL-3
**South Side—pop pl** ... ME-1
**Southside—pop pl** ... MS-4
**Southside—pop pl** ... NC-3
**South Side—pop pl** ... NC-3
**South Side pop pl (2)** ... OH 6
**Southside—pop pl** ... SC-3
**Southside—pop pl** ... TN-4
**Southside—pop pl** ... WV-2
Southside—post sta ... GA-3
Southside—post sta ... LA-4
Southside—post sta ... PA-2
South Side—post sta ... WI-6
South Side—uninc pl ... AR-4
Southside—uninc pl (2) ... FL-3
South Side—uninc pl ... NY-2
Southside—uninc pl ... NC-3
Southside—uninc pl ... OK-5
Southside—uninc pl ... OR-9
South Side—uninc pl (2) ... PA-2
Southside—uninc pl ... TN-4
Southside—uninc pl ... VA-3
Southside Acad—school ... VA-3
**Southside Acres (subdivision)—pop pl** ... AL-4
Southside Alliance Bible Ch—church ... FL-3
Southside Assembly of God Ch—church ... FL-3
Southside Assembly of God Ch—church ... MS-4
South Side-Baker Hist Dist—hist pl ... CO-8
South Side Ball Field—park ... AL-4
Southside Baptist Ch ... AL-4
Southside Baptist Ch ... MS-4
Southside Baptist Ch—church (12) ... AL-4
Southside Baptist Ch—church (6) ... FL-3
Southside Baptist Ch—church ... KS-7
South Side Baptist Ch—church ... MS-4
Southside Baptist Ch—church (2) ... MS-4
Southside Baptist Ch—church ... MS-4
Southside Baptist Ch—church (3) ... MS-4
Southside Baptist Ch—church ... TN-4
South Side Blvd Sch—school ... ID-8
South Side Bridge—bridge ... PA-2
Southside Brook—stream ... ME-1
South Side Canal—canal ... AZ-5
Southside Canal—canal ... AZ-5
South Side Canal—canal ... CO-8
South Side Canal—canal ... FL-3
South Side Canal—canal ... ID-8
South Side Canal—canal ... MT-8
South Side Canal—canal ... OR-9
South Side Canal—canal ... TX-5
Southside Cem—cemetery ... AL-4
Southside Cem—cemetery ... FL-3
South Side Cem—cemetery ... GA-3
South Side Cem—cemetery ... IN-6
South Side Cem—cemetery ... ME-1
Southside Cem—cemetery ... MA-1
South Side Cem—cemetery ... MN-6
South Side Cem—cemetery ... MS-4
South Side Cem—cemetery ... MO-7
Southside Cem—cemetery ... MO-7
Southside Cem—cemetery ... NY-2
South Side Cem—cemetery ... NY-2
Southside Cem—cemetery ... NC-3
South Side Cem—cemetery ... ND-7
Southside Cem—cemetery ... OH-6
South Side Cem—cemetery ... OK-5
South Side Cem—cemetery ... PA-2
Southside Cem—cemetery ... PA-2
Southside Cem—cemetery ... SD-7
South Side Cem—cemetery ... TX-5
South Side Cem—cemetery ... WA-9
Southside Cem—cemetery ... WI-6
Southside (Census Subdistrict)—cens area ... VI-3
Southside Ch—church (5) ... AL-4
South Side Ch—church ... AL-4
Southside Ch—church (2) ... AL-4
Southside Ch—church ... AR-4
South Side Ch—church ... AR-4
Southside Ch—church ... AR-4
Southside Ch—church (7) ... FL-3
South Side Ch—church ... GA-3
Southside Ch—church (3) ... GA-3
Southside Ch—church (2) ... IN-6
South Side Ch—church ... IN-6
Southside Ch—church ... KY-4
South Side Ch—church ... KY-4
South Side Ch—church ... LA-4
Southside Ch—church ... MS-4
Southside Ch—church ... MO-7
South Side Ch—church ... NE-7
Southside Ch—church ... NY-2
South Side Ch—church ... NC-3
Southside Ch—church (5) ... NC-3
Southside Ch—church (2) ... OK-5
Southside Ch—church (4) ... SC-3
South Side Ch—church ... SC-3
Southside Ch—church ... SC-3
Southside Ch—church (4) ... TN-4
Southside Ch—church ... TX-5
Southside Ch—church ... VA-3
Southside Ch (historical)—church ... MS-4
Southside Ch of Christ—church (2) ... AL-4
Southside Ch of Christ—church (2) ... MS-4
Southside Ch of Christ—church ... TN-4
Southside Ch of Christ—church ... UT-8
Southside Ch of God—church ... MS-4
Southside Ch of God in Christ—church ... FL-3
Southside Ch of the Nazarene—church ... AL-4
Southside Christian Ch—church ... AL-4
Southside Christian Ch—church (2) ... FL-3
Southside Christian Sch—school ... IN-6
South Side Christian Sch—school ... MI-6
South Side Colored Methodist Ch (historical)—church ... AL-4
South Side Commercial Center—locale ... NC-3
South Side Community Park—park ... TX-5
Southside Congregational Holiness Ch—church ... AL-4
South Side Country Club—other ... IL-6
South Side County Park—park ... OR-9
Southside Creek—stream ... MI-6
Southside District Hosp—hospital ... AZ-5
South Side Ditch ... HI-9
South Side Ditch—canal (2) ... CO-8
Southside Ditch—canal ... KS-7
South Side Ditch—canal ... SD-7
South Side Ditch—canal (4) ... WY-8
South Side Draw—valley ... WY-8
Southside Elem Sch ... AL-4
South Side Elem Sch ... MS-4
South Side Elem Sch ... TN-4
Southside Elem Sch—school (3) ... AL-4
Southside Elem Sch—school (2) ... FL-3
Southside Elem Sch—school ... IN-6
South Side Elem Sch—school ... IN-6
Southside Elem Sch—school ... MS-4
South Side Elem Sch—school ... PA-2
Southside Elem Sch—school ... TN-4
**Southside Estates—pop pl** ... FL-3
Southside Estates—uninc pl ... TX-5
Southside Estates Acad—school ... FL-3
Southside Estates Ch—church ... FL-3
Southside Estates Elem Sch—school ... FL-3
Southside Estates Plaza (Shop Ctr)—locale ... FL-3
South Side Estates Shop Ctr—locale ... FL-3
South Side Feeder Lateral—canal ... TX-5
South Side Fire Station No. 3—hist pl ... SD-7
Southside First Baptist Ch—church ... AL-4
South Side Hist Dist—hist pl ... MO-7
South Side Hist Dist—hist pl ... WA-9
Southside Hist Dist—hist pl ... WI-6
Southside Hosp—hospital ... NY-2
South Side Hospital—building ... PA-2
Southside HS ... IN-6
South Side HS—hist pl ... PA-2
Southside HS—school (2) ... AL-4
South Side HS—school ... AL-4
Southside HS—school ... AR-4
South Side HS—school ... IN-6
South Side HS—school ... MS-4
South Side HS—school ... NY-2
Southside HS—school ... NY-2
South Side HS—school ... PA-2
South Side HS—school (2) ... TN-4
South Side HS—school ... TX-5
Southside HS—school (2) ... VA-3
Southside Industrial Park—locale ... PA-2
South Side JHS ... IN-6
Southside JHS—school (2) ... FL-3
South Side JHS—school ... IL-6
Southside JHS—school ... NH-1
South Side JHS—school ... NY-2
Southside JHS—school ... NY-2
Southside JHS—school ... SC-3
South Side JHS—school ... TN-4
South Side Junction—uninc pl ... WV-2
South Side Lake Cem—cemetery ... NY-2
**Southside (Lincoln Cotton Mills)—pop pl** ... NC-3
South Side Lions Park—park ... TX-5
South Side Lions Park East—park ... TX-5
Southside Lookout Tower—tower ... FL-3
Southside (Magisterial District)—fmr MCD ... VA-3
South Side Market Bldg—hist pl ... PA-2
South Side Masonic Lodge No. 1114—hist pl ... TX-5
Southside Methodist Ch—church ... AL-4
Southside Methodist Ch—church ... MS-4
South Side Missionary Baptist Ch—church ... MS-4
South Side MS—school ... IN-6
Southside MS and HS—school ... PA-2
South Side Park—flat ... UT-8
Southside Park—park ... AL-4
Southside Park—park ... AR-4
South Side Park—park ... CA-9
Southside Park—park ... FL-3
South Side Park—park ... IL-6
South Side Park—park (3) ... IN-6
Southside Park—park ... NY-2
South Side Park—park ... OH-6
South Side Park—park ... OK-5
Southside Park—park ... TN-4
South Side Park—park ... TN-4
South Side Park—park ... WI-6
**Southside Park (subdivision)—pop pl** ... NC-3
South Side Place ... TX-5
**Southside Place—pop pl** ... TX-5
Southside Plantation (historical)—locale ... MS-4
Southside Playground—park ... MI-6
Southside Plaza Shop Ctr—locale ... VA-3
Southside Plaza Shopping Center ... TN-4
Southside P.O. (historical)—building ... MS-4
Southside Pond—lake ... VI-3
Southside Post Office—building ... TN-4
Southside Reservoirs—reservoir ... CO-8
Southside Reservoirs—reservoir ... NV-8
Southside Ridge—ridge ... VA-3
Southsider Sch—school ... AL-4
South Side Rsvr—reservoir ... MT-8
Southside Rsvr—reservoir ... NY-2
Southside Sch ... FL-3
Southside Sch ... IN-6
South Side Sch—hist pl ... FL-3
South Side Sch—hist pl ... IL-6
Southside Sch—school (7) ... AL-4
Southside Sch—school ... AR-4
South Side Sch—school ... AR-4
Southside Sch—school ... CA-9
South Side Sch—school ... CT-1
Southside Sch—school (6) ... FL-3
Southside Sch—school (3) ... GA-3
South Side Sch—school ... GA-3
Southside Sch—school (2) ... GA-3
Southside Sch—school ... ID-8
South Side Sch—school ... ID-8
South Side Sch—school (2) ... IL-6
Southside Sch—school (2) ... IL-6
South Side Sch—school ... IL-6
South Side Sch—school (2) ... IN-6
Southside Sch—school ... IN-6
South Side Sch—school ... IN-6
South Side Sch—school (3) ... KY-4
South Side Sch—school ... KY-4
South Side Sch—school (5) ... LA-4
Southside Sch—school ... MD-2
South Side Sch—school ... MI-6
South Side Sch—school (2) ... MN-6
South Side Sch—school ... MS-4
Southside Sch—school ... MS-4
Southside Sch—school ... MO-7
Southside Sch—school ... MT-8
South Side Sch—school ... MT-8
South Side Sch—school ... NJ-2
Southside Sch—school ... NY-2
Southside Sch—school (2) ... NC-3
South Side Sch—school ... OH-6
Southside Sch—school (2) ... OH-6
South Side Sch—school ... OK-5
Southside Sch—school ... OK-5
South Side Sch—school (2) ... PA-2
Southside Sch—school (6) ... SC-3
Southside Sch—school ... TN-4
South Side Sch—school (2) ... TN-4
Southside Sch—school ... TN-4
South Side Sch—school (4) ... TX-5
Southside Sch—school ... TX-5
South Side Sch—school ... TX-5
Southside Sch—school (3) ... TX-5
Southside Sch—school ... VA-3
Southside Sch—school ... WA-9
South Side Sch—school ... WI-6
South Side Sch—school ... WY-8
South Side Sch (abandoned)—school ... PA-2
Southside Sch (historical)—school (2) ... MS-4
Southside Sch (historical)—school ... TN-4
Southside Schools—school ... AR-4
South Side Second Presbyterian Ch (historical)—church ... AL-4
Southside Senior HS—school ... IN-6
Southside Shop Ctr—locale (2) ... AL-4
South Side Shop Ctr—locale ... FL-3
Southside Shop Ctr—locale (2) ... FL-3
South Side Shop Ctr—locale ... IA-7
Southside Shop Ctr—locale ... ND-7
Southside Shop Ctr—locale (2) ... TN-4
Southside Shopping Plaza—locale ... FL-3
Southside Skills Center—school ... FL-3
Southside Speedway—other ... VA-3
Southside Sportsmens Club District—hist pl ... NY-2
**Southside (subdivision)—pop pl** ... AL-4
South Side Tabernacle Baptist Ch—church ... FL-3
South Side Tank—reservoir ... AZ-5
**Southside Township—pop pl** ... KS-7
**Southside (Township of)—pop pl** ... MN-6
Southside Trail—trail ... NY-2
South Side Trail—trail ... WA-9
Southside United Methodist Ch—church ... AL-4
Southside University Plaza (Shop Ctr)—locale ... FL-3
Southside Vocational Sch—school ... VA-3
South Side Waikapu Ditch—canal ... HI-9
**South Siding—pop pl** ... AZ-5
South Signal Mtn—summit ... CO-8
South Silent Canyon—valley ... NV-8
South Silver Creek—stream ... IA-7
South Silver Creek Youth Camp—locale ... OR-9
South Silver Lake—lake ... MN-6
**South Silver Lake—pop pl** ... MN-6
South Similkameen River ... WA-9
South Simmons Creek—stream ... TX-5
South Sink—basin ... UT-8
**South Sioux City—pop pl** ... NE-7
South Sioux Sch—school ... SD-7
South Sippo Park—park ... OH-6
South Siskiyou Fork—stream ... CA-9
South Siskiyou Fork Middle Smith River ... CA-9
South Siskiyou Fork Smith River ... CA-9
South Sister ... OR-9
South Sister—summit ... CA-9
South Sister—summit ... OR-9
South Sister Creek—stream (2) ... OR-9
South Sister Island—island ... FL-3
South Sister Knob—summit ... VA-3
South Sisters ... OR-9
South Siuslow (CCD)—cens area ... OR-9
South Sixmile Canyon—valley ... NV-8
South Sixmile Canyon Spring—spring ... NV-8
South Sixmile Draw—valley ... TX-5
South Sixmile Wash—stream ... NV-8
South Six-shooter Peak ... UT-8
South Sixshooter Peak—summit ... UT-8
South Six Windmill—locale ... TX-5
South Skinner Creek—stream ... ID-8
South Skitty Branch—stream ... NC-3
South Skookum Lake—lake ... WA-9
South Skull Cliffs ... MH-9
South Skunk River—stream ... IA-7
South Skunk River Wildlife Area—park ... IA-7
South Slang Creek—stream ... VT-1
South Slash—lake ... MO-7
South Slate Creek—stream ... SD-7
South Slater Run—stream ... PA-2
South Slaterville Canal—canal ... UT-8
South Slate Sch—school ... SD-7
South Slick Creek ... MT-8
South Slick Creek ... SD-7
South Slick Rock Tank—reservoir ... AZ-5
South Slide—trail ... NH-1
South Slope Sch—school ... ID-8
South Slough ... OR-9
South Slough ... WA-9
South Slough—gut (2) ... CA-9
South Slough—gut (2) ... OR-9
South Slough—lake ... SD-7
South Slough—stream ... CA-9
South Slough—stream ... ID-8
South Slough—stream ... LA-4
South Slough—stream ... MI-6
South Slough—stream ... WA-9
South Slough Cem—cemetery ... OR-9
South Slough Pond (duck pond)—reservoir ... OR-9
South Smith Canyon—valley ... AZ-5
South Smith Fork—stream ... CO-8
South Smith Lake—lake ... MN-6
South Smith River ... MT-8
South Smiths Fork ... WY-8
South Snag Harbor—bay ... FL-3
South Snohomish—locale ... WA-9
South Snowshoe Creek—stream ... CO-8
South Snyder Creek—stream ... WY-8
South Soap Creek—stream ... IA-7
South Soda Creek—stream ... CA-9
**South Sodus—pop pl** ... NY-2
South Sokehs Island ... FM-9
South Soldier Creek—stream ... WY-8
South Solomon Cem—cemetery ... KS-7
South Solon—locale ... ME-1
**South Solon—pop pl** ... OH-6
South Solon Meetinghouse—hist pl ... ME-1
South Somerset Sch—school ... MA-1
South SoRelle Windmill—locale ... NM-5
South Sound Creek—stream ... FL-3
**South (South Arlington)—pop pl** ... VA-3
South South Branch Mountain ... ME-1
South Spafford—locale ... NY-2
South Spanish Creek—stream ... CO-8
South Sparta Cem—cemetery ... NY-2
South Sparta Ch—church ... IN-6
South Spectacle Butte—summit ... WA-9
South Spectacle Pond—lake ... CT-1
South Spectacle Pond—lake ... MA-1
**South Spencer—pop pl** ... MA-1
South Spencer Creek—stream ... MO-7
South Spencer Draw—valley ... NM-5
South Spencer-Robinson Ditch—canal ... WI-6
South Spillway—dam ... CA-9
South Spit—bar (3) ... AK-9
South Spit—bar ... CA-9
South Spit—bar ... MS-4
South Spit—cape ... AK-9
South Spring—locale ... NM-5
South Spring—spring ... ID-8
South Spring—spring ... IA-7
South Spring—spring (6) ... NV-8
South Spring—spring ... NM-5
South Spring—spring (2) ... OR-9
South Spring—spring (4) ... UT-8
South Spring—spring ... WY-8
South Spring Acres—locale ... NM-5
South Spring Branch—stream ... IA-7
South Spring Canyon—valley ... NV-8
South Spring Canyon—valley ... UT-8
South Spring Creek ... UT-8
South Spring Creek ... WA-9
South Spring Creek—stream ... MO-7
South Spring Creek—stream ... MT-8
South Spring Creek—stream (2) ... WY-8
South Spring Creek Lake—lake ... WY-8
South Spring Draw—valley ... WY-8
**South Springfield—pop pl** ... ME-1
South Springfield—uninc pl ... MA-1
South Spring Gulch ... CO-8
South Spring Hill Mine—mine ... CA-9
South Spring Point—cape ... NV-8
South Spring Ranch—locale ... NM-5
South Spring River—stream ... NM-5
South Spring Rsvr—reservoir ... OR-9
South Springs—spring (2) ... NV-8
South Springs—spring ... NM-5
South Springs—spring ... UT-8
**South Springs Acres—pop pl** ... NM-5
South Spring Top—summit ... NC-3
South Spring Well—well ... OR-9
South Sprng—spring ... NV-8
South Spronks Creek—stream ... CO-8
South Spruce Ridge—ridge ... AZ-5
South Spruce Run ... PA-2
South Spruce Well—well ... NV-8
South Spud Island Rec Area—park ... CA-9
South Squankum Brook ... NJ-2
South Square—post sta ... NC-3
South Square Shop Ctr—locale ... FL-3
South Squaw Creek—stream ... IA-7
South Squaw Creek—stream ... WY-8
South Squaw Tip—summit ... OR-9
South Squirrel Spring—spring ... AZ-5
South Squirrel Springs Canyon—valley ... NM-5
South Stacey Sch—school ... MT-8
South Stacey Spring—spring ... MT-8
South Stadium—park ... TN-4
South Stagebarn Canyon—valley ... SD-7
South Stanchfield Lake—lake ... MN-6
South Standard ... IL-6
South Standard—mine ... UT-8
South Standard (corporate and RR name Standard City) ... IL-6
**South Standish—pop pl** ... ME-1
South Standish Sch—school ... ME-1
South Stanley—unorg reg ... SD-7
South Stanley Creek—stream ... NC-3
South Stanly Ch—church ... NC-3
South Stanly HS—school ... NC-3
South Star Cem—cemetery ... KS-7
South Starksboro—locale ... VT-1
South Starksboro Friends Meeting House and Cemetery—hist pl ... VT-1
South Starkville Sch—school ... CO-8
South Star Mine—mine ... CA-9
South Star Sch—school ... KS-7
South Star Sch—school ... NE-7
South Star Spring—spring ... OR-9
South State Street Sch—school ... WV-2
South Station—locale ... NJ-2
**South Station—pop pl** ... VA-3
South Station Chattanooga Post Office—building ... TN-4
South Station Headhouse—hist pl ... MA-1
South Stauffer Creek—stream ... ID-8
South Steely Creek—stream ... CA-9
South Steer Draw—valley ... WY-8
South Steptoe Fence Well—well ... NV-8
**South Sterling—pop pl (2)** ... PA-2
South Stewart Canyon—valley ... ID-8
South Stickney—other ... IL-6
South Stirrup Run—stream ... MD-2
South Stocking Lake—lake ... MN-6
South Stock Pen Tank—reservoir ... AZ-5
**South Stockton—pop pl** ... NY-2
**South Stoddard—pop pl** ... NH-1
South Stokes HS—school ... NC-3
South Stone County Fire Station Number Two—building ... MO-7
**South Stony Brook—pop pl** ... NY-2
South Stop—bay ... FL-3
**South Stoughton—pop pl** ... MA-1
South Stowell Oil Field—oilfield ... TX-5
**South St. Paul—pop pl** ... MN-6
**South Strabane—pop pl** ... PA-2
**South Strabane (Township of)—pop pl** ... PA-2
**South Strafford—pop pl** ... VT-1
South Stream—stream ... VT-1
**South Streator (subdivision)—pop pl** ... IL-6
South Street AME Ch (historical)—church ... AL-4
South Street Bridge—bridge ... DE-2
South Street-Broad Street-Main Street-Laurel Street Hist Dist—hist pl ... GA-3
South Street Brook ... CT-1
South Street Cem—cemetery ... CT-1
South Street Cem—cemetery ... NH-1
South Street Hist Dist—hist pl ... AL-4
South Street Hist Dist—hist pl ... ME-1
South Street Hist Dist—hist pl ... MA-1
South Street Hist Dist—hist pl ... MI-6
South Street Hist Dist—hist pl ... NY-2
South Street Hist Dist—hist pl ... RI-1
South Street Hist Dist—hist pl ... SC-3
South Street Sch—school (2) ... CT-1
South Street Sch—school ... GA-3
South Street Sch—school (3) ... MA-1
South Street Sch—school ... NJ-2
South Street Sch—school ... NY-2
South Street Sch—school (2) ... OH-6
South Street Sch—school ... PA-2
South Street Seaport—hist pl ... NY-2
South Street Seaport Hist Dist—hist pl ... NY-2
South Street Station—locale ... NJ-2
South Strong—locale ... ME-1
South Studebaker Rsvr—reservoir ... CO-8
South Sturgeon Lake—lake ... MN-6
South Suck Creek—stream ... TN-4
**South Sudbury—pop pl** ... MA-1
South Sudbury (RR name for Sudbury)—other ... MA-1
South Suffolk—uninc pl ... VA-3
South Sugar Creek—stream ... GA-3
South Sugar Creek—stream ... MO-7
South Sugar Creek Township—civil ... MO-7
South Sugar Lake—lake ... CA-9
South Sugar Loaf ... MA-1
South Sugarloaf—summit ... NH-1
South Sugarloaf—summit ... OR-9
South Sugar Loaf Hill ... MA-1
South Sugarloaf Island—island ... ME-1
South Sugarloaf Mtn—summit ... MA-1
**South Sulphur—pop pl** ... TX-5
South Sulphur Canyon—valley ... ID-8
South Sulphur Creek—stream ... SD-7
South Sulphur River—stream ... TX-5
South Sulphur River (Old Channel)—stream ... TX-5
South Sulphur Spring—spring ... UT-8
South Summerour Well—well ... TX-5
South Summit—summit ... NV-8
South Summit Canyon—valley ... ID-8
South Summit HS—school ... UT-8
South Summit Ridge—ridge ... UT-8
South Summit Sch—school ... MI-6
South Summit Street District—hist pl ... IA-7
South Summit Tank—reservoir ... AZ-5
South Sump ... NV-8
South Sumter—CDP ... SC-3
South Sumter HS—school ... FL-3
South Sumter MS—school ... FL-3
South Sumter Plaza (Shop Ctr)—locale ... FL-3
South Sunday Creek—stream ... MT-8
South Sunflower County Hosp—hospital ... MS-4
South Sunrise Oil and Gas Field—oilfield ... LA-4
**South Superior—pop pl** ... WI-6
**South Superior—pop pl** ... WY-8
South Superior—uninc pl ... WI-6
South Superior Union Hall—hist pl ... WY-8
South Supply Creek—stream ... CO-8
South Surry—locale ... ME-1
South Surry Cem—cemetery ... ME-1
South Survey Sch—school ... WI-6
South Sutter (CCD)—cens area ... CA-9
South Sutter Ditch—canal ... CA-9
**South Sutton—pop pl** ... MA-1
**South Sutton—pop pl** ... NH-1
South Sutton Cem—cemetery ... MA-1
South Swag—basin ... UT-8
South Swamp—swamp ... MA-1
South Swamp—swamp ... MI-6
South Swamp—swamp ... OR-9
South Swamp Creek—stream ... MT-8
South Swan Creek ... OH-6
South Swan Landing—locale ... NV-8
**South Swansea—pop pl** ... MA-1
**South Switch Junction—pop pl** ... IA-7
South Sybille Sch—school ... WY-8
South Sycamore Mesa Tank—reservoir ... NM-5
South Sylamore Creek—stream ... AR-4
South Syracuse—fmr MCD ... NE-7
South Tablan Valley ... MH-9
South Table Creek—stream ... NE-7
South Table Draw—valley ... WY-8
South Table Mesa ... WY-8
South Table Mtn—summit ... CA-9
South Table Mtn—summit ... CO-8
South Table Mtn—summit ... OR-9
South Table Mtn—summit ... WY-8
South Table Ravine ... MH-9
**South Tacoma—pop pl** ... WA-9
South Tacoma State Game Ref—park ... WA-9
South Tacoma Swamp—swamp ... WA-9
**South Taft—pop pl** ... CA-9
South Taft Creek—stream ... NV-8
South Tahoe HS—school ... CA-9
South Tahoe Sch—school ... CA-9
South Tahoe Senior HS—school ... CA-9
South Tahoma Glacier—glacier ... WA-9
South Tailholt Tank—reservoir ... AZ-5
South Tallahassee Creek—stream ... CO-8
South Talmadge, Lake—lake ... FL-3
South Talofofo Site—hist pl ... GU-9
South Tama HS—school ... IA-7
**South Tamaqua—pop pl** ... PA-2
South Tamarind Sch—school ... CA-9
**South Tampa—pop pl** ... FL-3
**South Tamworth—pop pl** ... NH-1
South Tank ... AZ-5
South Tank—lake ... TX-5
South Tank—reservoir (16) ... AZ-5
South Tank—reservoir (16) ... NM-5
South Tank—reservoir (7) ... TX-5
South Tank Canyon—valley ... NM-5
South Tapo Canyon Oil Field ... CA-9
South Tarkio River ... IA-7
South Tarryall Creek—stream ... CO-8
South Tarryall Peak—summit ... CO-8
South Tate Creek—stream ... CO-8
South Taylor Canyon—valley ... AZ-5
South Taylor Canyon—valley ... NM-5
South Taylor Creek—stream ... CO-8
South Taylor Spring—spring ... AZ-5
South Taylor Spring—spring ... NV-8
South Taylor Tank—reservoir ... NM-5
South Taylor Wash ... AZ-5
South Taylor Wash—stream ... AZ-5
South Teal Lake—lake ... WA-9
South Technical Education Center—school ... FL-3
South Temperance Lake—lake ... MN-6
**South Temple—pop pl** ... PA-2
South Temple—uninc pl ... TX-5
South Temple Ch—church ... TX-5
South Temple Creek—stream ... WY-8
South Temple Hist Dist—hist pl ... UT-8
South Temple Wash—valley ... UT-8
South Tenmile Creek—stream ... AR-4
South Tenmile Lake ... OR-9
South Tenth Street Bridge—hist pl ... PA-2
South Tenth Street Sch—school ... NJ-2
South Tent Mtn—summit ... UT-8
South Tent Peak ... UT-8
South Teoctalia Creek ... MS-4
South Terrace Elem Sch—school ... IN-6
South Terrace Plaza Shop Ctr—locale ... TN-4
**South Terrace (subdivision)—pop pl** ... PA-2
South Terrapin Lake ... MN-6
South Terrebonne HS—school ... LA-4
South Teton—summit ... WY-8
South Teton River—stream ... ID-8
**South Texarkana—pop pl** ... TX-5
South Texas Childrens Home—other ... TX-5
South Texas Creek—stream ... CO-8
South Texas Hill Canyon—valley ... NM-5
South Texas Med Ctr—uninc pl ... TX-5
South Texas Natl Bank—hist pl ... TX-5
South Texas State Fairground—locale ... TX-5
South Texas Water Company Canal—canal ... TX-5
South Thimble Island—island ... VA-3
South Thomas Canyon—valley ... NM-5
**South Thomaston—pop pl** ... ME-1
**South Thomaston (Town of)—pop pl** ... ME-1
South Thompson—locale ... GA-3
South Thompson Creek—stream ... CO-8
South Thompson Creek Cow Camp—locale ... CO-8
South Thompson Creek Oil Field—oilfield ... MS-4
South Thornwell Gas Field—oilfield ... LA-4
South Three Forks Creek—stream ... WY-8
South Three Forks Lakes—lake ... WY-8
South Three Links Lakes—lake ... ID-8
South Thurston—locale ... NY-2
South Thurston Spring ... NV-8
South Tiffany Creek—stream ... WI-6
**South Tifton—pop pl** ... GA-3
South Tiger Mtn—summit ... WA-9
South Tiger River ... SC-3
South Tigre Lagoon Gas Field—oilfield ... LA-4
South Timber Cave—cave ... AL-4
South Timber Creek—stream ... IA-7
South Timber Peak—summit ... NV-8
**South Tipalao—pop pl** ... GU-9
South Tippah Creek—stream ... MS-4
South Tishomingo Sch (historical)—school ... MS-4
South Tit—summit ... ID-8
**South Titusville (subdivision)—pop pl** ... FL-3
South Tobiason Lake ... ND-7
South Toe River—stream ... NC-3
South Toe River Sch—school ... NC-3
South Toe Sch ... NC-3
South Toe (Township of)—fmr MCD ... NC-3
South Toiyabe Peak—summit ... NV-8
South Tomhicken Creek ... PA-2
South Tomlinson Run—stream ... PA-2
South Tomoka Wildlife Mngmt Area—park ... FL-3
South Toms Prairie Cem—cemetery ... IL-6
**South Toms River—pop pl** ... NJ-2
**Southton—pop pl** ... TX-5
South Tongue Campground—locale ... WY-8
South Tongue River—stream ... WY-8
South Tonkawa Gas Field—oilfield ... OK-5
South Tonk Branch—stream ... TX-5
Southton Oil Field—oilfield ... TX-5
Southton Sanitorium—hospital ... TX-5
South Toole—cens area ... MT-8
South Toomey Gulch ... OR-9
South Topeka Interchange—locale ... KS-7
**South Torrington—pop pl** ... WY-8
South Torrington Union Pacific Depot—hist pl ... WY-8
South Toutle Glacier ... WA-9
South Towanda—locale ... PA-2
South Tower—locale ... MI-6
South Tower—tower ... FL-3
South Tower Center Light—locale ... WA-9
Southtown—locale ... NJ-2
**Southtown—pop pl** ... AL-4
Southtown Center Shop Ctr—locale ... TN-4
Southtown Creek—stream ... MI-6
Southtown Ditch—canal ... ID-8
South Towne Mall—locale ... UT-8
Southtown Hist Dist—hist pl ... MS-4
South Town Mall—locale ... SD-7
South Town Park—park ... IA-7
South Township—fmr MCD ... IA-7
**South Township—pop pl** ... MO-7
Southtown Shop Ctr—locale ... MN-6
**Southtown Village (subdivision)—pop pl** ... TN-4
South Trabajo Creek—stream ... NM-5
South Track Canal—canal ... UT-8
South Tracy Ave Hist Dist—hist pl ... MT-8
South Tracy-South Black Hist Dist—hist pl ... MT-8
South Trade Street Houses—hist pl ... NC-3
South Trafford—locale ... PA-2
**South Trail—pop pl** ... FL-3
South Trail—trail ... FL-3
South Trail—trail ... MD-2
South Trail Creek—stream (2) ... OR-9
South Trail Shop Ctr—locale ... FL-3
South Trails Shop Ctr—locale ... MO-7
South Trail Village (Shop Ctr)—locale ... FL-3
South Trapper Creek—stream ... WY-8
South Trap Windmill—locale (2) ... TX-5
South Traveler Mtn—summit ... ME-1
South Treasure—cens area ... MT-8
South Tree Ch—church ... KY-4
South Trent Creek—stream ... WY-8

South Trenton—pop pl ... NY-2
South Trescott—pop pl ... ME-1
South Triangle Pond—lake ... MA-1
South Triangle Windmill—locale ... WY-8
South Trick Lake—lake ... AK-9
South Trigo Peaks—summit ... AZ-5
South Trimble Memorial Bridge—bridge ... KY-4
South Trinity Canyon—valley ... NV-8
South Trinity Cem—cemetery ... SD-7
South Trinity Ch—church ... ND-7
South Trona—pop pl ... CA-9
South Troost ... MO-7
South Troupsburg—locale ... NY-2
South Trout Lake ... MN-6
South Troy—locale ... MN-6
South Troy—pop pl ... MO-7
South Truro—pop pl ... MA-1
South Tucson—pop pl ... AZ-5
South Tule Canyon—valley ... CA-9
South Tule Ditch—canal ... CA-9
South Tule Draw—valley ... TX-5
South Tule Spring—spring ... UT-8
South Tulip Creek—stream ... MS-4
South Tulsa (CCD)—cens area ... OK-5
South Tuman Point—cape ... AK-9
South Tunbridge—pop pl ... VT-1
South Tunis—pop pl ... NC-3
South Tunnel—pop pl ... TN-4
South Tunnel Post Office (historical)—building ... TN-4
South Tupawek Bayou—stream ... LA-4
South Turkey Creek—stream ... CO-8
South Turkey Creek—stream ... NC-3
South Turkey Creek—stream ... OK-5
South Turkey Creek—stream (2) ... TX-5
South Turkey Creek Community Center—locale ... CO-8
South Turkeyfoot Creek ... OH-6
South Turkeyfoot Creek—stream ... OH-6
South Turknett Well—well ... NM-5
South Turlock—CDP ... CA-9
South Turner—locale ... ME-1
South Turner Brook—stream ... ME-1
South Turner Mtn—summit ... ME-1
South Turtle Lake—lake ... MN-6
South Turtle Lake—lake ... WI-6
South Twentyeighth Ave Baptist Ch—church ... MS-4
South Twentymile Meadows—range ... WA-9
South Twentymile Peak—summit ... WA-9
South Twentymile Trail—trail ... WA-9
South Twigg (Township of)—pop pl ... IL-6
South Twilight Peak—summit ... CO-8
South Twin ... MI-6
South Twin—summit ... AK-9
South Twin—summit ... WA-9
South Twin Bay—bay ... AK-9
South Twin Brook—stream ... ME-1
South Twin Cone Peak—summit ... CO-8
South Twin Creek ... NV-8
South Twin Creek ... TX-5
South Twin Creek—stream ... AK-9
South Twin Creek—stream (2) ... CO-8
South Twin Creek—stream (2) ... ID-8
South Twin Creek—stream ... TX-5
South Twin Creek—stream ... UT-8
South Twin Creek—stream (3) ... WY-8
South Twin Flat Mtn—summit ... UT-8
South Twin Glacier—glacier ... AK-9
South Twin Gulch—valley ... CA-9
South Twin Hollow—valley ... UT-8
South Twin Island—island ... WI-6
South Twin Lake ... IL-6
South Twin Lake ... MI-6
South Twin Lake ... MN-6
South Twin Lake ... WI-6
South Twin Lake—lake (2) ... FL-3
South Twin Lake—lake ... IN-6
South Twin Lake—lake ... ME-1
South Twin Lake—lake (2) ... MI-6
South Twin Lakes—lake (7) ... MN-6
South Twin Lake—lake (3) ... NE-7
South Twin Lake—lake ... ND-7
South Twin Lake—lake ... OR-9
South Twin Lake—lake ... WA-9
South Twin Lake—lake (2) ... WI-6
South Twin Lake—lake ... WY-8
South Twin Lake—reservoir ... IA-7
South Twin Lake Campground—park ... OR-9
South Twin Lakes ... IL-6
South Twin Lakes ... MI-6
South Twin Lakes ... WI-6
South Twin Mtn—summit ... ME-1
South Twin Mtn—summit ... NH-1
South Twin Pasture—flat ... NV-8
South Twin Peak—summit ... AK-9
South Twin Peak—summit ... UT-8
South Twin River—stream ... NV-8
South Twin Wash—stream ... NM-5
South Twistwood Creek—stream ... MS-4
South Twitchell Point—cape ... MT-8
South Two Lakes—lake ... WI-6
South Twomile Creek—stream ... OR-9
South Twomile Windmill—locale ... TX-5
South Two Ocean Creek—stream ... WY-8
South Two River—stream ... MN-6
South Tyger River—stream ... SC-3
South Tyrol Park—park ... MN-6
South Ugly Creek—stream ... NC-3
South Uhl Draw—valley ... NM-5
South Uhl Tank—reservoir ... NM-5
South Umpqua (CCD)—cens area ... OR-9
South Umpqua Falls—falls ... OR-9
South Umpqua Falls Picnic Ground—park ... OR-9
South Umpqua Guard Station—locale ... OR-9
South Umpqua River—stream ... OR-9
South Umpqua Safety Rest Area—locale ... OR-9
South Unadilla—locale ... NY-2
South Union ... PA-2
South Union—locale ... PA-2
South Union—locale ... SC-3
South Union—locale ... WA-9
South Union—pop pl ... KY-4
South Union—pop pl ... ME-1
South Union Cem—cemetery ... IN-6
South Union Cem—cemetery (2) ... MS-4
South Union Cem—cemetery ... TX-5
South Union Ch—church ... IN-6
South Union Ch—church (3) ... KY-4
South Union Ch—church ... LA-4
South Union Ch—church (2) ... MS-4
South Union Ch—church ... OH-6
South Union Ch—church ... SC-3
South Union Chapel—church ... IN-6
South Union Creek—stream ... TX-5
South Union (historical)—locale ... AL-4
South Union Methodist Ch ... MS-4
South Union Sch—school ... MA-1
South Union Sch—school ... PA-2
South Union Shaker Center House and Preservatory—hist pl ... KY-4
South Union Shakertown Hist Dist—hist pl ... KY-4
South Union Street Hist Dist—hist pl ... NC-3
South Union Street Hist Dist—hist pl ... VT-1
South Uniontown—pop pl ... PA-2
South Union (Township of)—fmr MCD ... AR-4
South Union (Township of)—pop pl ... PA-2
South Unitarian—hist pl ... MA-1
South Upton—pop pl ... IL-6
South Ute Creek ... CO-8
South Utica—uninc pl ... NY-2
South Utoy Creek—stream ... GA-3
South Uxbridge—pop pl ... MA-1
South Valdosta—pop pl ... GA-3
South Vallenar Point—cape ... AK-9
South Valley—basin ... CO-8
South Valley—basin (2) ... UT-8
South Valley—CDP ... NM-5
South Valley—cens area ... MT-8
South Valley—pop pl ... NY-2
South Valley—valley ... UT-8
South Valley Brook—stream ... NH-1
South Valley Canal—canal ... UT-8
South Valley Cem—cemetery ... KS-7
South Valley Ch—church ... GA-3
South Valley Ch—church ... MT-8
South Valley Chapel—church ... KS-7
South Valley Estates Subdivision—pop pl ... UT-8
South Valley Hills—range ... PA-2
South Valley River Park—park ... IA-7
South Valley Sch—school ... NJ-2
South Valley Stream—CDP ... NY-2
South Valley (Town of)—pop pl ... NY-2
South Valley Township—pop pl ... ND-7
South Valley Trail—trail ... VA-3
South Valley View Subdivision—pop pl ... UT-8
South Van Buren—pop pl ... MO-7
South Vandailia—pop pl ... NY-2
South Van Eaton Ranch—locale ... NM-5
South Vargas Windmill—locale ... TX-5
South Vassalboro—locale ... ME-1
South Vaya Dam—dam ... CO-8
South Vekol Well—well ... AZ-5
South Venice—pop pl ... FL-3
South Venice Ch—church ... FL-3
South Ventana ... CA-9
South Ventana Cone—summit ... CA-9
South Verde Creek ... TX-5
South Verdigris River ... KS-7
South Vernon ... MA-1
South Vernon—pop pl ... VT-1
South Vernon (census name South Mount Vernon)—pop pl ... OH-6
South Vernon Elem Sch—school ... KS-7
South Versailles (Township of)—pop pl ... PA-2
South Vershire—locale ... VT-1
South Vestal—pop pl ... NY-2
South Vestavia Hills (subdivision)—pop pl ... AL-4
South Veta Creek ... CO-8
South Vicksburg ... MS-4
South Vicksburg Public Sch No. 200—hist pl ... MS-4
South Victoria Creek—stream ... SD-7
South Victory Sch (abandoned)—school ... MO-7
South Vienna—pop pl ... OH-6
South Vienna Cem—cemetery ... OH-6
Southview—pop pl ... PA-2
Southview—uninc pl ... NY-2
South View Acres—pop pl ... PA-2
Southview Cem—cemetery ... GA-3
South View Cem—cemetery (4) ... GA-3
Southview Cem—cemetery ... GA-3
South View Cem—cemetery ... IN-6
Southview Cem—cemetery ... MA-1
Southview Cem—cemetery ... NC-3
Southview Cem—cemetery ... OH-6
South View Ch—church ... AR-4
Southview Ch—church ... MO-7
Southview Country Club—other ... MN-6
South View Estates—pop pl ... TN-4
Southview Hosp—hospital ... WI-6
Southview JHS—school ... MN-6
South View JHS—school ... NC-3
Southview Manor (subdivision)—pop pl ... AL-4
Southview Park—park ... OH-6
Southview Park—park ... UT-8
Southview Park Subdivision—pop pl ... UT-8
South View PUD (subdivision)—pop pl ... UT-8
Southview Sch—school ... GA-3
Southview Sch—school ... MN-6
Southview Sch—school ... OK-5
Southview Sch—school ... PA-2
Southview Sch—school ... VA-3
South View Sch (abandoned)—school ... MO-7
South View Senior HS—school ... NC-3
Southview Shop Ctr—locale (2) ... AL-4
Southview Subdivision—pop pl ... UT-8
Southview Townhouses (subdivision)—pop pl ... NC-3
South Viking Township—pop pl ... ND-7
South Village ... MA-1
South Village—locale ... OK-5
South Village—pop pl ... MA-1
South Village Cem—cemetery ... VT-1
South Village Green—park ... NY-2
South Village Park—park ... OR-9
South Village Pond—lake ... VT-1
South Village Pond Dam—dam ... MA-1
Southville ... MA-1
Southville—locale ... NY-2
Southville—pop pl ... KY-4
Southville—pop pl ... MA-1
South Vineland—pop pl ... NJ-2
South Vinemont—pop pl ... AL-4
South Virgin Mtns—range ... NV-8
South Virgin Peak Ridge—ridge ... NV-8
South Vista—pop pl ... CA-9
Southvogtsberger-Strawn Oil Field—oilfield ... TX-5
South Volney—pop pl ... NY-2
South Vo Tech Sch—school ... PA-2
South Wachusett Brook—stream ... MA-1
South Waco JHS—school ... TX-5
South Waco Sch—school (2) ... TX-5
South Wadesboro—pop pl ... NC-3
South Wagner Sch—school ... MT-8
South Wagon Creek—stream ... TX-5
South Wagoner (CCD)—cens area ... OK-5
South Waiehu Stream—stream ... HI-9
South Waikapu Ditch ... HI-9
South Walden—locale ... VT-1
South Waldoboro—pop pl ... ME-1
South Waldo Shelter—locale ... OR-9
South Wales—pop pl ... NY-2
South Walker Canyon—valley ... UT-8
South Walker Cem—cemetery ... IA-7
South Walker Spring—spring ... OR-9
South Wallace Canyon—valley ... CA-9
South Wallace Well—well ... NM-5
South Wallingford—pop pl ... VT-1
South Wallins—pop pl ... KY-4
South Wall Lake Cem—cemetery ... IA-7
South Wall Rock Rsvr—reservoir ... OR-9
South Walnut Creek ... KS-7
South Walnut Creek—stream ... IA-7
South Walnut Creek—stream ... TX-5
South Walnut Isle—island ... OH-6
South Walnut Lake—reservoir ... MN-6
South Walnut Spring—spring ... AZ-5
South Walnut Street Hist Dist—hist pl ... GA-3
South Walpole—pop pl ... MA-1
South Walrus Peak—summit ... AK-9
South Waltham—uninc pl ... MA-1
South Wanatah—pop pl ... IN-6
South Wanette Oil Field—oilfield ... OK-5
Southward—locale ... GA-3
Southward Bay—bay ... NC-3
Southward Bridge—bridge ... MS-4
South Ward Elem Sch—school ... PA-2
Southward Lake—lake ... MI-6
South Ward Oil Field—oilfield ... TX-5
South Wardsboro—pop pl ... VT-1
South Ward Sch—hist pl ... FL-3
South Ward Sch—hist pl ... IA-7
South Ward Sch—hist pl ... PA-2
South Ward Sch—school ... FL-3
South Ward Sch—school ... IN-6
South Ward Sch—school ... KY-4
South Ward Sch—school ... MO-7
South Ward Sch—school (2) ... NE-7
South Ward Sch—school ... OH-6
South Ward Sch—school (7) ... TX-5
South Ward Sch (abandoned)—school ... MO-7
South Ward Sch (abandoned)—school ... PA-2
Southwards Marsh ... RI-1
South Wareham—pop pl ... MA-1
South Wareham (historical P.O.)—locale ... MA-1
South Wareham Station (historical)—locale ... MA-1
Southwark—uninc pl ... PA-2
Southwark District—hist pl ... PA-2
Southwark Sch—hist pl ... PA-2
South Warm Springs Creek ... OR-9
South Warm Springs Creek—stream (2) ... OR-9
South Warner Rim—ridge ... OR-9
South Warren—locale ... PA-2
South Warren—pop pl ... ME-1
South Warren—pop pl ... PA-2
South Warren—pop pl ... RI-1
South Warren Cem—cemetery ... ME-1
South Warren Sch—school ... NC-3
South Warsaw—pop pl ... NY-2
South Warsaw—pop pl ... OH-6
South Wash—valley (2) ... UT-8
South Washington ... NC-3
South Washington ... ND-7
South Washington—locale ... VT-1
South Washington—pop pl ... IN-6
South Washington—pop pl ... VA-3
South Washington Addition (subdivision)—pop pl ... UT-8
South Washington County Hosp—hospital ... MS-4
South Washington Lake—lake ... ND-7
South Washington Street Hist Dist—hist pl ... GA-3
South Washington Street Parabolic Bridge—hist pl ... NY-2
Southwater—lake ... FL-3
South Water Canyon—valley ... NM-5
South Waterford—pop pl ... ME-1
South Water Hollow—valley ... UT-8
South Water Street Hist Dist—hist pl ... WV-2
South Watson Creek—stream ... OK-5
South Watuppa Pond—lake ... MA-1
South Waubay Lake—lake ... SD-7
South Waukegan ... IL-6
South Waveland ... IN-6
South Waverly—pop pl ... PA-2
South Waverly Borough—civil ... PA-2
South Wawona—pop pl ... CA-9
Southway Baptist Ch—church ... MS-4
South Wayne—pop pl ... WI-6
Southway Plaza—locale ... IN-6
Southway Plaza (Shop Ctr)—locale ... FL-3
South Wea Creek—stream ... KS-7
South Weare—pop pl ... NH-1
South Weber—pop pl ... UT-8
South Weber Cem—cemetery ... UT-8
South Weber Sch—school ... UT-8
South Weber Valley Estates Subdivision—pop pl ... UT-8
South Webster—pop pl ... OH-6
South Webster Park—flat ... CO-8
South Weeki Wachee—CDP ... FL-3
South Weldon—pop pl ... NC-3
South Well ... AZ-5
South Well—locale (6) ... NM-5
South Well—well (3) ... AZ-5
South Well—well (3) ... NV-8
South Well—well (24) ... NM-5
South Well—well (9) ... TX-5
Southwell Branch—stream ... GA-3
South Well Canyon—valley (2) ... NM-5
Southwell Drain—canal ... MI-6
South Well Draw ... TX-5
South Well Draw—valley ... TX-5
South Wellfleet—pop pl ... MA-1
South Wellfleet Cem—cemetery ... MA-1
Southwell Lake—lake ... MI-6
South Well Number Three—well ... NV-8
South Wenatchee ... WA-9
South Wenatchee—uninc pl ... WA-9
South Wenatchee Sch—school ... WA-9
South Wendell—pop pl ... MA-1
Southwest ... MO-7
Southwest ... OH-6
Southwest—pop pl ... FL-3
Southwest—pop pl ... IN-6
South West—pop pl ... IN-6
Southwest—pop pl ... NC-3
Southwest—pop pl ... PA-2
Southwest—uninc pl ... OK-5
Southwest Acad—school ... MS-4
Southwest Addition (subdivision)—pop pl ... TN-4
Southwest Alabama Oil Field—oilfield ... OK-5
Southwest Alliance Ch—church ... FL-3
Southwest Anchorage—bay ... AK-9
Southwest Antelope Tank—reservoir ... TX-5
Southwest Arapahoe—cens area ... CO-8
Southwest Archeol Center—building ... AZ-5
Southwest Avondale Sch—school ... KS-7
Southwest Baptist Ch—church ... AL-4
Southwest Baptist Ch—church ... FL-3
Southwest Baptist Ch—church (2) ... KS-7
Southwest Baptist Coll—school ... MO-7
Southwest Barton Cem—cemetery ... ND-7
Southwest Bay—bay ... NC-3
Southwest Bay—cove ... MA-1
Southwest Bayou—stream ... LA-4
Southwest Bayou—stream ... MS-4
Southwest Beach—beach ... MA-1
Southwest Bell (CCD)—cens area ... TX-5
Southwest Bend ... ME-1
South West Bend—pop pl ... ME-1
Southwest Benton (CCD)—cens area ... OR-9
Southwest Bluff—cliff ... ME-1
Southwest Bon Homme—unorg reg ... SD-7
Southwest Branch ... OH-6
Southwest Branch—gut ... LA-4
Southwest Branch Back River—stream ... VA-3
Southwest Branch Big Papillion Creek—stream ... NE-7
Southwest Branch Campsite—locale ... ME-1
Southwest Branch Charles Branch—stream ... MD-2
Southwest Branch Fishdam River—stream ... MI-6
Southwest Branch Housatonic River—stream ... MA-1
Southwest Branch Indian River—stream ... ME-1
Southwest Branch Manhan River ... MA-1
South West Branch of Pawtuxet River ... RI-1
Southwest Branch Of Roncocas Creek ... NJ-2
Southwest Branch Saint John River—stream ... ME-1
Southwest Branch South Branch Rancocas Creek—stream ... NJ-2
Southwest Branch Taku Glacier—glacier ... AK-9
Southwest Branch Vermilion River—stream ... OH-6
Southwest Branch Western Branch Patuxent Riv—stream ... MD-2
Southwest Breaker—island ... ME-1
Southwest Breakers—bar ... MA-1
Southwest Brook—stream ... ME-1
Southwest Broward Junior Athletic Association—park ... FL-3
Southwest Bull Tank—reservoir ... TX-5
South Westbury—CDP ... NY-2
Southwest Butte—summit ... ID-8
Southwest Canyon—valley ... NM-5
South West Cape ... FL-3
South West Cape ... FM-9
Southwest Cape—cape ... AK-9
Southwest Cape—cape ... FL-3
Southwest Cape Light—locale ... VI-3
Southwest Castle Oil Field—oilfield ... OK-5
Southwest (CCD)—cens area ... TX-5
Southwest Cem—cemetery (3) ... CT-1
Southwest Cem—cemetery ... IL-6
Southwest Cem—cemetery ... MA-1
Southwest Cem—cemetery ... MO-7
Southwest Cem—cemetery ... NC-3
Southwest Cem—cemetery ... OK-5
Southwest (Census Subdistrict)—cens area ... VI-3
Southwest Ch—church ... NC-3
South West Chadron—fmr MCD ... NE-7
Southwest Channel—channel ... FL-3
Southwest Chaves (CCD)—cens area ... NM-5
Southwest Chicago Christian Sch—school ... IL-6
Southwest Ch of the Nazarene—church ... AL-4
South West City—pop pl ... MO-7
South West City Cem—cemetery ... MO-7
Southwest Comanche (CCD)—cens area ... OK-5
Southwest Community Ch—church ... FL-3
Southwest Cotton (CCD)—cens area ... OK-5
Southwest Country Day Sch—school ... FL-3
Southwest Cove—bay ... AK-9
Southwest Cove—bay (3) ... ME-1
Southwest Cove—bay ... NJ-2
South West Cove Point ... NJ-2
Southwest Cove Point—cape ... NJ-2
Southwest Cranfield Oil Field—oilfield ... MS-4
Southwest Creek—stream ... ME-1
Southwest Creek—stream (4) ... NC-3
Southwest Criner Oil Field—oilfield ... OK-5
Southwest Delhi Oil Field—oilfield ... LA-4
Southwest District Sch—hist pl ... CT-1
Southwest Edgecombe HS—school ... NC-3
Southwest Elementary School ... PA-2
Southwest Elem Sch—school ... AL-4
Southwest Elem Sch—school (2) ... NC-3
Southwest Elem Sch—school ... TN-4
South Westerlo—pop pl ... NY-2
Southwestern Acad—school ... CA-9
Southwestern At Memphis Coll—school ... TN-4
Southwestern at Memphis Hist Dist—hist pl ... TN-4
Southwestern Baptist Theological Semi ... TX-5
Southwestern Baptist Theological Seminary—school ... TX-5
Southwestern Bell Main Dial Bldg—hist pl ... OK-5
Southwestern Bell Telephone Bldg—hist pl ... OK-5
Southwestern Bible Baptist College ... AZ-5
Southwestern Bible Institute—school ... TX-5
Southwestern Brewery and Ice Company—hist pl ... NM-5
Southwestern Canal—canal ... LA-4
Southwestern Central Sch—school ... NY-2
Southwestern Christian Coll—school ... TX-5
Southwestern Coll—school ... AZ-5
Southwestern Coll—school ... CA-9
Southwestern Coll—school ... KS-7
Southwestern Elem Sch—school (2) ... IN-6
Southwestern Heights HS—school ... KS-7
Southwestern Hosp—hospital ... OK-5
Southwestern HS—school (2) ... IN-6
Southwestern HS—school (2) ... MI-6
Southwestern HS—school ... OH-6
Southwestern HS—school ... VA-3
Southwestern JHS ... IN-6
Southwestern JHS—school ... IN-6
Southwestern Junior Coll—school ... TX-5
Southwestern Louisiana Canal—canal ... LA-4
Southwestern Mine—mine ... CO-8
Southwestern Mountains ... VA-3
Southwestern New Mexico State Fairgrounds—other ... NM-5
Southwestern Oregon Community Coll—school ... OR-9
Southwestern Proving Ground—pop pl ... AR-4
Southwestern Randolph HS—school ... NC-3
Southwestern Research Station—building ... AZ-5
Southwestern Sch—school (2) ... GA-3
Southwestern Sch—school ... PA-2
Southwestern Sch—school ... VA-3
Southwestern Seventh Grade Center—school ... FL-3
Southwestern (Southwestern University)—uninc pl ... LA-4
Southwestern State Coll—school ... OK-5
Southwestern State Hosp—hospital ... GA-3
Southwestern State Hosp—hospital ... VA-3
Southwestern State Technical Coll—school ... AL-4
Southwestern Technical Sch—school ... OH-6
Southwestern Telegraph and Telephone Bldg—hist pl ... TX-5
Southwestern Training Sch—school ... LA-4
Southwestern Univ Administration Bldg and Mood Hall—hist pl ... TX-5
Southwest Fall River—unorg reg ... SD-7
South West Fargo ... ND-7
South West Fargo—pop pl ... ND-7
Southwest Faulk—unorg reg ... SD-7
South Westfield (Township of)—fmr MCD ... NC-3
Southwest Fork ... NC-3
Southwest Fork Alligator River—stream ... NC-3
Southwest Fork County Line Creek—stream ... KS-7
Southwest Fork Loxahatchee River—stream ... FL-3
Southwest Fork South Branch Wolf Creek—stream ... OH-6
Southwest Fork Trent Creek—stream ... NC-3
Southwest Foundation for Research and Education—other ... TX-5
Southwest Freeway—post sta ... TX-5
Southwest Gardens—uninc pl ... KS-7
Southwest Gas Site Mini Park—park ... AZ-5
Southwest Gate—channel ... FL-3
Southwest General Hosp—hospital ... TX-5
Southwest Georgia Acad—school ... GA-3
Southwest Glades (CCD)—cens area ... FL-3
Southwest Glasgow Residential District—hist pl ... KY-4
Southwest Grant (CCD)—cens area ... OK-5
Southwest Grayson (CCD)—cens area ... TX-5
Southwest Greensburg—pop pl ... PA-2
Southwest Greensburg Borough—civil ... PA-2
Southwest Ground—bar ... MA-1
Southwest Grove—woods ... CA-9
Southwest Gut—gut ... VA-3
South West Harbor ... ME-1
Southwest Harbor—bay ... ME-1
Southwest Harbor—pop pl ... ME-1
Southwest Harbor Coast Guard Base—military ... ME-1
Southwest Harbor (Town of)—civ div ... ME-1
Southwest (Hecla)—pop pl ... PA-2
Southwest Hist Dist—hist pl ... VA-3
Southwest Holly Springs Hist Dist—hist pl ... MS-4
Southwest Hoosick—pop pl ... NY-2
Southwest HS ... IN-6
Southwest HS—school ... GA-3
Southwest HS—school ... MN-6
Southwest HS—school (2) ... MO-7
Southwest HS—school ... NC-3
Southwest HS—school ... TX-5
South West Hubbard—pop pl ... OH-6
Southwest Indian Sch—school ... AZ-5
Southwest Islands—island (2) ... AK-9
Southwest Jackson (CCD)—cens area ... OR-9
Southwest JHS—school (3) ... AR-4
Southwest JHS—school ... FL-3
South West JHS—school ... MI-6
Southwest JHS—school (2) ... NC-3
Southwest JHS—school ... PA-2
Southwest JHS—school ... TX-5
Southwest JHS—school ... WI-6
Southwest Junior College ... MS-4
Southwest Junoir HS—school ... CA-9
Southwest Kansas Area Vocational-Technical Sch—school ... KS-7
Southwest Key ... FL-3
Southwest Lake—lake ... WI-6
Southwest Lateral—canal ... AZ-5
Southwest Lateral—canal ... CA-9
Southwest Laurens MS—school ... GA-3
Southwest Ledge ... ME-1
Southwest Ledge—bar ... ME-1
Southwest Ledge—rock ... MA-1
Southwest Ledge Lighthouse—locale ... CT-1
Southwest Ledge Quarries—mine ... TX-5
Southwest Ledges—bar ... ME-1
Southwest Lewis Oil Field—oilfield ... OK-5
Southwest Lewiston Canal—canal ... UT-8
Southwest Little Rock—pop pl ... AR-4
Southwest Lonsdale Mine—mine ... TN-4
Southwest Louisiana Boys Village—locale ... LA-4
Southwest Lyon (CCD)—cens area ... KY-4
Southwest Madison (Township of)—pop pl ... PA-2
Southwest (Magisterial District)—fmr MCD (2) ... WV-2
Southwest Marin (CCD)—cens area ... CA-9
Southwest Marion Township—civil ... MO-7
Southwest McCord Oil Field—oilfield ... OK-5
Southwest Mcintosh—unorg reg ... ND-7
Southwest Mckenzie—unorg reg ... ND-7
Southwest Meade—unorg reg ... SD-7
Southwest Memorial Park—park ... OH-6
Southwest Mermentau Gas Field—oilfield ... LA-4
Southwest Mesa—summit ... TX-5
Southwest Miami Senior HS—school ... FL-3
South Westminster (historical P.O.)—locale ... MA-1
Southwest Mississippi Junior Coll—school ... MS-4
Southwest Mississippi Mental Health Complex—hospital ... MS-4
Southwest Mississippi Regional Med Ctr—hospital ... MS-4
Southwest Missouri State Univ—school ... MO-7
Southwest Missouri State Univ (West Plains Campus)—school ... MO-7
Southwest Moloka'i Archeol District—hist pl ... HI-9
Southwest Mountains—ridge ... VA-3
Southwest Mountrail—unorg reg ... ND-7
Southwest Muldoon Oil Field—oilfield ... TX-5
Southwest Museum—building ... CA-9
South Westnedge ... MI-6
South Westnedge Park—park ... MI-6
South Westnedge Sch—school ... MI-6
Southwest Nolichucky (CCD)—cens area ... TN-4
Southwest Nolichucky Division—civil ... TN-4
Southwest Oakdale Gas Field—oilfield ... OK-5
Southwest Orange (CCD)—cens area ... FL-3
Southwest Oswego—pop pl ... NY-2
Southwest Paden Oil Field—oilfield ... OK-5
Southwest Palermo Cem—cemetery ... NY-2
South West Park—park ... MT-8
Southwest Pass ... FL-3
South West Pass ... LA-4
Southwest Pass—channel (2) ... LA-4
Southwest Pass—channel ... TX-5
Southwest Pass—channel ... MP-9
Southwest Pass—gap ... LA-4
Southwest Passage—channel ... MP-9
Southwest Passage—gap ... NM-5
Southwest Perkins—unorg reg ... SD-7
Southwest Peter Lake Tank—reservoir ... TX-5
Southwest Plaza—locale ... KS-7
Southwest Plaza—locale ... MO-7
Southwest Plaza—summit ... NM-5
Southwest Plaza (Shop Ctr)—locale ... MO-7
Southwest Pleasant Valley Gas And Oil Field—oilfield ... OK-5
Southwest Point ... RI-1
Southwest Point—cape ... AK-9
Southwest Point—cape ... DE-2
Southwest Point—cape ... FL-3
Southwest Point—cape ... LA-4
Southwest Point—cape (3) ... ME-1
Southwest Point—cape ... NC-3
Southwest Point—cape (3) ... RI-1
South West Point—cape ... TN-4
Southwest Point—hist pl ... TN-4
South West Point Ferry ... TN-4
Southwest Point Golf Course—locale ... TN-4
Southwest Point Park—park ... TN-4
Southwest Ponca City Oil Field—oilfield ... OK-5
Southwest Pond—lake ... DE-2
Southwest Pond—lake (2) ... ME-1
Southwest Pontotoc (CCD)—cens area ... OK-5
South Westport—pop pl ... MA-1
Southwest Poultry Experiment Station—locale ... AZ-5
Southwest Prairie Ch—church ... WI-6
Southwest Prong—stream ... NC-3
Southwest Prong Beaverdam Creek—stream ... NC-3
Southwest Prong Newport River—stream ... NC-3
Southwest Prong Slocum Creek—stream ... NC-3
Southwest (Quadrant)—fmr MCD ... DC-2
Southwest Randlett Oil Field—oilfield ... OK-5
Southwest Regional Education Center—building ... NC-3
Southwest Research Institute—school ... TX-5
Southwest Rift Zone—area ... HI-9
Southwest Road—channel ... VI-3
Southwest Roberts Branch Mine—mine ... TN-4
Southwest Rock—bar ... MA-1
South West Rock—rock (2) ... MA-1
Southwest Rocks—bar ... ME-1
Southwest Rsvr—reservoir ... CO-8
Southwest Sandy Creek Oil Field—oilfield ... OK-5
Southwest San Felipe Ditch—canal ... NM-5
Southwest San Gabriel Valley (CCD)—cens area ... CA-9
Southwest Sch ... IN-6
Southwest Sch ... NC-3
Southwest Sch—school (2) ... CT-1
Southwest Sch—school ... FL-3
Southwest Sch—school (2) ... GA-3
Southwest Sch—school ... ID-8
Southwest Sch—school ... IL-6
Southwest Sch—school ... KS-7
Southwest Sch—school ... LA-4
Southwest Sch—school (3) ... MI-6
Southwest Sch—school (3) ... MO-7
Southwest Sch—school ... NJ-2
Southwest Sch—school ... NY-2
Southwest Sch—school ... NC-3
Southwest Sch—school (2) ... OK-5
Southwest Sch—school ... PA-2
Southwest Sch—school ... SD-7
Southwest Sch—school (2) ... TX-5
Southwest Sch Number 2—school ... TX-5
Southwest Sharon Cem—cemetery ... OH-6
Southwest Shasta (CCD)—cens area ... CA-9
Southwest Shop Ctr—locale ... MS-4
South Westside (CCD)—cens area ... FL-3
Southwest Sioux—unorg reg ... ND-7
Southwest Slip—harbor ... CA-9
Southwest Sportsman Park—park ... CA-9
Southwest Spring—spring ... NM-5
Southwest State Coll—school ... TX-5
Southwest Swamp—stream ... VA-3

Spanishburg—*locale* WV-2
Spanishburg Ch—*church* WV-2
**Spanish B Village**—*pop pl* HI-9
Spanish Cabin Creek—*stream* CA-9
*Spanish Camp* HI-9
Spanish Camp—*locale* CA-9
Spanish Camp—*locale* TX-5
Spanish Camp Creek—*stream* WA-9
Spanish Camp Oil Field—*oilfield* TX-5
Spanish Canyon—*valley* (3) CA-9
Spanish Canyon—*valley* (2) NV-8
Spanish Canyon—*valley* OK-5
Spanish Cem—*cemetery* LA-4
Spanish Charlie Basin—*basin* OR-9
**Spanish Colony**—*pop pl* CO-8
Spanish Coquina Quarries—*hist pl* FL-3
Spanish Coulee—*valley* MT-8
Spanish Coulee Sch—*school* MT-8
*Spanish Court* IL-6
*Spanish Creek* MT-8
*Spanish Creek* OK-5
*Spanish Creek* WA-9
Spanish Creek—*locale* CA-9
Spanish Creek—*stream* (7) CA-9
Spanish Creek—*stream* CO-8
Spanish Creek—*stream* FL-3
Spanish Creek—*stream* GA-3
Spanish Creek—*stream* ID-8
Spanish Creek—*stream* MT-8
Spanish Creek—*stream* WA-9
Spanish Creek—*stream* WY-8
Spanish Creek Basin—*basin* MT-8
Spanish Creek Ranch—*locale* MT-8
Spanish Creek Ranger Station—*locale* MT-8
Spanish Creek Recreation Site—*locale* MT-8
Spanish Creek Sch—*hist pl* MT-8
Spanish Cut—*stream* GA-3
Spanish Diggings—*mine* WY-8
Spanish Dikes—*hist pl* GU-9
Spanish Dry Diggings—*locale* CA-9
Spanish Embassy Bldg—*building* DC-2
Spanish Flat—*flat* (2) CA-9
Spanish Flat—*flat* NV-8
Spanish Flat—*flat* OR-9
Spanish Flat—*locale* (2) CA-9
**Spanish Flat Resort**—*pop pl* CA-9
Spanish Flat Rsvr—*reservoir* NV-8
Spanish Flats—*flat* CA-9
Spanish Fleet Survivors and Salvors Camp Site—*hist pl* FL-3
*Spanish Fork* UT-8
**Spanish Fork**—*pop pl* UT-8
Spanish Fork—*stream* ID-8
Spanish Fork—*stream* UT-8
*Spanish Fork Airport* UT-8
Spanish Fork Canyon—*valley* UT-8
*Spanish Fork City* UT-8
Spanish Fork City Cem—*cemetery* UT-8
Spanish Fork Fire Station—*hist pl* UT-8
Spanish Fork HS—*school* UT-8
Spanish Fork HS Gymnasium—*hist pl* UT-8
Spanish Fork Intermediate Sch—*school* UT-8
Spanish Fork Natl Guard Armory—*hist pl* UT-8
Spanish Fork-Payson—*cens area* UT-8
Spanish Fork-Payson Division—*civil* UT-8
Spanish Fork Peak—*summit* UT-8
Spanish Fork Post Office—*building* UT-8
Spanish Fork-Springville Airp—*airport* UT-8
Spanish Fork Station—*locale* UT-8
Spanish Fort—*hist pl* FM-9
Spanish Fort—*locale* AL-4
**Spanish Fort**—*pop pl* LA-4
**Spanish Fort**—*pop pl* MS-4
**Spanish Fort**—*pop pl* TX-5
Spanish Fort Branch—*stream* AL-4
Spanish Fort Cem—*cemetery* MO-7
Spanish Fort Cemeteries—*cemetery* TX-5
Spanish Fort Ch—*church* AL-4
Spanish Fort Elem Sch—*school* AL-4
Spanish Fort Landing—*locale* MS-4
Spanish Fort Ruins—*locale* LA-4
Spanish Fort Shop Ctr—*locale* AL-4
Spanish Fort Site—*hist pl* TX-5
Spanish Fort Site (22SH500)—*hist pl* MS-4
Spanish George Spring—*spring* UT-8
Spanish Girl Mine—*mine* NV-8
Spanish Governor's Palace—*hist pl* TX-5
Spanish Grove—*locale* VA-3
Spanish Grove Ch—*church* VA-3
Spanish Grove Community Center—*locale* TN-4
Spanish Grove Sch (historical)—*school* TN-4
Spanish Gulch—*valley* (3) CA-9
Spanish Gulch—*valley* CO-8
Spanish Gulch—*valley* NV-8
Spanish Gulch—*valley* (2) OR-9
Spanish Gulch Cem—*cemetery* OR-9
Spanish Gulch Spring—*spring* NV-8
Spanish Hammock—*island* GA-3
Spanish Harbor—*bay* FL-3
Spanish Harbor Channel—*channel* FL-3
*Spanish Harbor Key* FL-3
Spanish Harbor Keys—*island* FL-3
Spanish Hill—*summit* CA-9
Spanish Hill—*summit* PA-2
*Spanish Hollow* OR-9
Spanish Hollow—*valley* OR-9
Spanish Hollow—*valley* UT-8
*Spanish Hollow Canyon* OR-9
Spanish House, The—*hist pl* CT-1
Spanish Island—*island* LA-4
Spanish Islands—*area* AK-9
Spanish King No 1 Mine—*mine* CO-8
Spanish Lake—*lake* (2) CA-9
Spanish Lake—*lake* (4) LA-4
Spanish Lake—*lake* MO-7
Spanish Lake—*lake* (2) OR-9
**Spanish Lake**—*pop pl* MO-7
Spanish Lake Bayou—*stream* LA-4
Spanish Lakes—*lake* MT-8
Spanish Lake Township—*civil* MO-7
Spanish Landing—*locale* FL-3
Spanish Landing Park—*park* CA-9
*Spanish Lot* TX-5
Spanish Meadow—*flat* CA-9
Spanish Mill Creek—*stream* FL-3
Spanish Mine—*mine* CA-9
Spanish Mine—*mine* WY-8
Spanish Mine (Inactive)—*mine* CA-9
*Spanish Mission Bautista* UT-8
Spanish Moss Bend—*bend* MS-4
Spanish Mound—*summit* LA-4
Spanish Mount Point—*hist pl* SC-3
Spanish Mtn—*summit* CA-9
Spanish Mtn—*summit* NV-8
Spanish Needle Community Center—*locale* IL-6
Spanish Needle Creek—*stream* CA-9
Spanish Needle Creek—*stream* IL-6
Spanish Needle Knob—*summit* TN-4
Spanish Needles Sch—*school* MO-7
Spanish Oak Branch—*stream* (2) NC-3
Spanish Oak Branch—*stream* (2) WV-2
Spanish Oak Ch—*church* MS-4
Spanish Oak Creek—*stream* (5) TX-5
Spanish Oak Gap—*gap* GA-3
Spanish Oak Gap—*gap* KY-4
Spanish Oak Gap—*gap* NC-3
Spanish Oak Mtn—*summit* NC-3
Spanish Oak Ridge—*ridge* AR-4
Spanish Park—*park* TX-5
Spanish Pass—*channel* LA-4
Spanish Pass—*gap* TX-5
Spanish Pass—*gut* LA-4
Spanish Peak—*summit* CA-9
Spanish Peak—*summit* NV-8
Spanish Peak—*summit* OK-5
Spanish Peak—*summit* OR-9
Spanish Peaks—*range* MT-8
Spanish Peaks—*spring* MT-8
Spanish Peaks Ditch—*canal* CO-8
Spanish Peaks State Wildlife Area—*park* CO-8
Spanish Pipeline Well—*well* NV-8
Spanish Point—*cape* (2) FL-3
Spanish Point—*cape* LA-4
Spanish Point—*cape* MS-4
Spanish Point—*cape* SC-3
Spanish Point—*cliff* WY-8
Spanish Point (historical)—*cape* ND-7
Spanish Queen Mine—*mine* NM-5
Spanish Ranch—*locale* (2) CA-9
Spanish Ranch—*locale* NV-8
**Spanish Ranch**—*pop pl* CA-9
Spanish Ranch Canyon—*valley* NV-8
Spanish Ranch Creek—*stream* CA-9
Spanish Ravine—*valley* (3) CA-9
Spanish Ravine—*valley* NV-8
Spanish Ridge—*ridge* (3) CA-9
*Spanish River* CO-8
*Spanish River* UT-8
*Spanish River* WY-8
Spanish River—*post sta* FL-3
Spanish River—*stream* AL-4
Spanish River Community HS—*school* FL-3
Spanish River Park—*park* FL-3
Spanish R Mine—*mine* SD-7
Spanish Rocks—*bar* GU-9
Spanish Shanty Point—*cape* FL-3
Spanish Spring—*spring* (2) CA-9
Spanish Spring—*spring* (2) NV-8
Spanish Springs—*reservoir* NV-8
Spanish Springs—*spring* CA-9
Spanish Springs Canyon—*valley* NV-8
Spanish Springs Peak—*summit* CA-9
Spanish Springs Peak—*summit* NV-8
Spanish Springs Ranch—*locale* NV-8
Spanish Springs Valley—*valley* NV-8
*Spanish Spring Valley* NV-8
Spanish Stirrup Ranch—*locale* NM-5
*Spanish Town* CA-9
Spanish Town—*hist pl* LA-4
Spanish Town—*locale* ID-8
Spanish Town—*locale* VI-3
**Spanish Trace (subdivision)**—*pop pl* AL-4
Spanish Trail—*trail* AZ-5
Spanish Trail Baptist Ch—*church* FL-3
Spanish Trail Ch—*church* MS-4
Spanish Trail Crossing at Warm Creek (inundated)—*locale* UT-8
**Spanish Trails**—*pop pl* TN-4
Spanish Treasure Cave—*cave* AR-4
*Spanish Treasure Wash* UT-8
Spanish Valley—*flat* UT-8
Spanish Valley—*valley* CA-9
*Spanish Valley Creek* CA-9
Spanish Village—*locale* CO-8
Spanish Village—*locale* TX-5
Spanish Village Hist Dist—*hist pl* OK-5
Spanish Wall—*hist pl* FM-9
Spanish War Memorial Park—*park* TN-4
**Spanish Wells**—*pop pl* SC-3
*Span Island* IL-6
Spankem Branch—*stream* KY-4
Spankem Branch—*stream* TN-4
**Spanker**—*pop pl* OH-6
Spanker Branch—*stream* AR-4
Spanker Branch—*stream* IL-6
Spanker Branch—*stream* IN-6
Spanker Branch—*stream* WV-2
Spanker Creek—*stream* AR-4
Spankey—*locale* IL-6
Spankey Hill—*summit* IL-6
*Spanking Jack Creek* NC-3
Spanking Slump Branch—*stream* TN-4
Spanking Stump Trail—*trail* TN-4
Spankum Branch—*stream* KY-4
Spann—*locale* GA-3
Spann—*locale* KY-4
Spannabone Lake (dry)—*lake* AZ-5
Spannaus Gulch—*valley* CA-9
Spannaus Spring—*spring* CA-9
*Spann Branch* AL-4
Spann Branch—*stream* AL-4
Spann Branch—*stream* (2) SC-3
**Spann Brothers Estates (subdivision)**—*pop pl* AL-4
Spann Cabin—*locale* CO-8
Spann Cem—*cemetery* MS-4
Spann Cem—*cemetery* (2) TN-4
Spann Ch—*church* SC-3
Spann Ch—*church* TX-5
*Spann Elementary School* MS-4
Spann Hosp—*hospital* TX-5
*Spann Lake* SC-3
Spann Ponds—*reservoir* AL-4
Spann Sch—*school* AL-4
Spann Sch—*school* MS-4
Spann Sch (historical)—*school* TN-4
Spannus Ranch—*locale* CA-9
*Spannus Spring* CA-9
Spannuth Sch—*school* NE-7
Spanoak Corners—*locale* WV-2
Span Oak Run—*stream* WV-2
Span Oak Trail—*trail* WV-2
Sparague-Deaver House—*hist pl* OH-6
Spar Bed Hill—*summit* NY-2
Spar Branch—*stream* TN-4
Spar Canyon—*valley* ID-8
Spar Canyon—*valley* NM-5
**Spar City**—*pop pl* CO-8
Spar Cove—*bay* (2) ME-1
*Spar Creek* MD-2
Spar Creek—*stream* MT-8
Spar Creek—*stream* WY-8
*Sparcy Run* OH-6
Spare Creek—*stream* ID-8
*Spare Island* NY-2
Sparenberg—*locale* TX-5
*Sparenburg* TX-5
*Sparerib Creek* TX-5
Sparerib Creek—*stream* TX-5
Spare Tank—*reservoir* AZ-5
Sparger Gulf—*valley* GA-3
Spargo Branch—*stream* MO-7
Spargo Creek—*stream* MI-6
Spar Gulch—*valley* CO-8
Spargur Hill—*summit* OH-6
**Spargursville**—*pop pl* OH-6
Sparhawk Lake—*lake* WY-8
Spar Hill Mine—*mine* NM-5
*Spar Island* SD-7
Spar Island—*island* IL-6
Spar Island—*island* ME-1
Spar Island—*island* RI-1
Spark Brook—*stream* MA-1
Spark Chapel—*church* KY-4
Sparke Sch—*school* NY-2
*Spark Hill* MA-1
Sparkhule Mtn—*summit* CA-9
**Sparkill**—*pop pl* NY-2
*Sparkill Brook* NJ-2
Sparkill Brook—*stream* NY-2
Sparkill Creek—*stream* NJ-2
Sparkill Creek—*stream* NY-2
Sparkill Creek Drawbridge—*hist pl* NY-2
Sparkill Sch—*school* NY-2
Spark Lake—*lake* MN-6
**Sparkle**—*pop pl* CA-9
Sparkleberry Lake—*lake* FL-3
Sparkleberry Landing—*locale* NC-3
*Sparkleberry Pond* FL-3
Sparkle Brook Sch (abandoned)—*school* MO-7
Sparkle Creek—*stream* AK-9
Sparkle Lake—*lake* NY-2
**Sparkle Lake**—*pop pl* NY-2
Sparkle Plenty Pit—*cave* AL-4
Spark Level Ch—*church* FL-3
Sparklin Cem—*cemetery* IN-6
Sparkling Creek—*stream* MI-6
Sparkling Hollow—*valley* MO-7
Sparkling Lake—*lake* WI-6
*Sparkling Spring* AL-4
*Sparkling Spring* VA-3
Sparkling Springs—*locale* AL-4
**Sparkling Springs**—*pop pl* VA-3
Sparkling Water Lake—*lake* FL-3
Sparkman—*locale* TN-4
**Sparkman**—*pop pl* AR-4
**Sparkman**—*pop pl* FL-3
*Sparkman Bay* FL-3
Sparkman Bay—*swamp* FL-3
Sparkman Branch—*stream* KY-4
Sparkman Branch—*stream* TN-4
Sparkman Cave—*cave* TN-4
Sparkman Cem—*cemetery* (2) AR-4
Sparkman Cem—*cemetery* MO-7
Sparkman Cem—*cemetery* (3) TN-4
Sparkman Channel—*channel* FL-3
Sparkman Creek—*stream* (2) GA-3
Sparkman (historical)—*locale* AL-4
Sparkman Hollow—*valley* MO-7
Sparkman Hollow—*valley* (2) TN-4
Sparkman HS—*school* AL-4
Sparkman Lake—*lake* AR-4
Sparkman Lake—*lake* FL-3
Sparkman Lake—*reservoir* TN-4
Sparkman Lake Dam—*dam* MS-4
Sparkman Mine (underground)—*mine* AL-4
Sparkman Post Office (historical)—*building* TN-4
Sparkman Sch (historical)—*school* TN-4
Sparkman Seminary (historical)—*school* TN-4
*Sparkmantown Sch* TN-4
Spark Plug Lake—*lake* WA-9
Spark Plug Mtn—*summit* WA-9
Sparkplug Tank—*reservoir* AZ-5
Sparks—*locale* CO-8
Sparks—*locale* GA-3
Sparks—*locale* LA-4
Sparks—*locale* OR-9
**Sparks**—*pop pl* GA-3
**Sparks**—*pop pl* KS-7
**Sparks**—*pop pl* MD-2
**Sparks**—*pop pl* NE-7
**Sparks**—*pop pl* NV-8
**Sparks**—*pop pl* OK-5
**Sparks**—*pop pl* TX-5
Sparks, Gov. Chauncy, House—*hist pl* AL-4
Sparks, G. P., House—*hist pl* MI-6
Sparks, James, House—*hist pl* AR-4
Sparks Branch—*stream* (2) AL-4
Sparks Branch—*stream* GA-3
Sparks Branch—*stream* (4) KY-4
Sparks Branch—*stream* OK-5
Sparks Branch—*stream* (2) TX-5
Sparks Brook—*stream* VT-1
Sparks Canyon—*valley* CO-8
Sparks Canyon—*valley* WY-8
Sparks Cem—*cemetery* (2) AL-4
Sparks Cem—*cemetery* (4) IN-6
Sparks Cem—*cemetery* IA-7
Sparks Cem—*cemetery* (9) KY-4
Sparks Cem—*cemetery* MI-6
Sparks Cem—*cemetery* (3) MO-7
Sparks Cem—*cemetery* NE-7
Sparks Cem—*cemetery* (4) TN-4
Sparks Cem—*cemetery* TX-5
Sparks Cem—*cemetery* VA-3
Sparks Cem—*cemetery* WV-2
Sparks Ch—*church* AL-4
Sparks Chapel Sch (historical)—*school* TN-4
Sparks Creek—*stream* AL-4
Sparks Creek—*stream* GA-3
Sparks Creek—*stream* MT-8
Sparks Creek—*stream* NM-5
Sparks Creek—*stream* NC-3
Sparks Creek—*stream* OR-9
Sparks Creek—*stream* SC-3
Sparks Crossing—*locale* (2) TX-5
Sparks Family Hospital Heliport—*airport* NV-8
Sparks Ferry (historical)—*locale* IN-6
Sparks Foundation County Park—*park* MI-6
Sparks Gap—*gap* GA-3
Sparks Gap—*locale* AL-4
**Sparks Glencoe**—*pop pl* MD-2
Sparks Gulch—*valley* OR-9
Sparks Hall—*hist pl* NE-7
Sparks Hill—*locale* IL-6
Sparks Hill—*summit* MA-1
Sparks Hollow—*valley* KY-4
Sparks Hollow—*valley* TN-4
Sparks HS—*school* MD-2
Sparks HS—*school* NV-8
Sparks Island—*island* ME-1
Sparks JHS—*school* NV-8
Sparks Kindergarten and Day Care—*school* FL-3
Sparks Lake—*lake* MI-6
Sparks Lake—*lake* OR-9
Sparks Landing—*locale* TN-4
Sparks Mill—*locale* GA-3
Sparks Mtn—*summit* KY-4
Sparks Park—*park* FL-3
Sparks Park—*park* TX-5
Sparks Place—*locale* AZ-5
*Spark's Point* ME-1
Spark Spring—*spring* MO-7
Sparks Ranch—*locale* NM-5
Sparks Ridge—*ridge* TN-4
Sparks Rsvr—*reservoir* WY-8
Sparks Sch—*school* (2) KY-4
Sparks Sch (historical)—*school* AL-4
Sparks Schools—*school* CA-9
Sparks Shelter Archeol Site—*hist pl* KY-4
Sparks (Site)—*locale* AK-9
Sparks Slough—*stream* UT-8
Sparks Spring—*spring* ID-8
Sparks Spring—*spring* MO-7
Sparks Spring—*spring* OR-9
Sparks Spring—*spring* UT-8
Sparks Spring Ch—*church* TX-5
Sparks Station—*locale* MD-2
Sparks Tank—*reservoir* AZ-5
Sparks Township—*inact MCD* NV-8
Sparksville—*locale* KY-4
**Sparksville**—*pop pl* IN-6
Sparks Vocational Sch—*school* KY-4
Sparks Well (Dry)—*well* ID-8
Sparks Windmill—*locale* NM-5
Sparks Windmill—*locale* TX-5
Sparky Spring—*spring* AZ-5
Spar Lake—*lake* GA-3
Spar Lake—*lake* MT-8
Spar Lake Campground—*locale* MT-8
**Sparland**—*pop pl* IL-6
Sparlin Cem—*cemetery* OR-9
Sparling, Lake—*lake* FL-3
Sparling Cem—*cemetery* MO-7
Sparling Drain—*canal* MI-6
Sparling Gulch—*valley* CO-8
Sparling Lake—*lake* FL-3
Sparling Ranch—*locale* CA-9
**Sparlingville**—*pop pl* MI-6
Sparlingville Drain—*canal* MI-6
Sparlingville Sch—*school* MI-6
Sparlin Island—*island* ID-8
Spar Mill Bay—*bay* NY-2
Spar Mine—*mine* AZ-5
Spar Mine—*mine* MT-8
Spar Mine—*mine* NY-2
Spar Mountain Spring—*spring* ID-8
Spar Mtn—*summit* WY-8
Spar Peak—*summit* MT-8
Spar Point—*cape* ME-1
Spar Point—*cape* RI-1
Spar Pole Hill—*summit* WA-9
Sparr—*locale* MI-6
Sparr—*locale* PA-2
**Sparr**—*pop pl* FL-3
Sparr Baptist Ch—*church* FL-3
Sparr Cem—*cemetery* IN-6
Sparr Ditch—*canal* MT-8
Sparre Barn—*hist pl* MN-6
Sparr Elem Sch—*school* FL-3
Sparrevohn (Air Force) Station—*military* AK-9
Sparrow—*locale* KY-4
Sparrow, Richard, House—*hist pl* MA-1
Sparrow Bay—*bay* NC-3
Sparrow Brook—*stream* ME-1
**Sparrow Bush**—*pop pl* NY-2
Sparrow Cem—*cemetery* IL-6
Sparrow Cem—*cemetery* ME-1
Sparrow Creek—*stream* ID-8
Sparrow Creek—*stream* IL-6
Sparrow Creek—*stream* IN-6
Sparrow Creek—*stream* MO-7
Sparrow Creek—*stream* NJ-2
Sparrow Creek—*stream* WV-2
Sparrow Creek Cem—*cemetery* IN-6
Sparrow Foot Creek—*stream* MO-7
Sparrowfoot Public Use Area—*locale* MO-7
Sparrow Gulch—*valley* MT-8
Sparrowhawk Brook—*stream* NY-2
Sparrowhawk Mtn—*summit* ME-1
Sparrow Hawk Mtn—*summit* OK-5
Sparrowhawk Point—*cape* NY-2
Sparrow Hill—*summit* ME-1
Sparrow Hill—*summit* MA-1
Sparrow Hollow—*valley* IN-6
Sparrow House—*hist pl* ME-1
*Sparrow Island* RI-1
*Sparrow Island* FM-9
Sparrow Island—*island* ME-1
Sparrow Nest Creek—*stream* SC-3
Sparrow Point—*cape* (2) VA-3
Sparrow Point—*summit* ID-8
Sparrow Rapids—*rapids* MI-6
Sparrow Rsvr—*reservoir* ID-8
Sparrow Run—*stream* PA-2
Sparrows Beach—*beach* MD-2
Sparrows Cem—*cemetery* NC-3
Sparrows Gut—*gut* NC-3
*Sparrows Hill* MA-1
*Sparrows Lake* MA-1
Sparrow Slough—*stream* MT-8
Sparrows Point—*cape* MD-2
**Sparrows Point**—*pop pl* MD-2
**Sparrows Point (Br. P.O.)**—*pop pl* MD-2
Sparrows Point Channel—*channel* MD-2
Sparrows Point Country Club—*other* MD-2
Sparrows Point HS—*school* MD-2
Sparrows Point Junction—*uninc pl* MD-2
Sparrow Springs Lake—*reservoir* NC-3
Sparrow Springs Lake Dam—*dam* NC-3
Sparrow Swamp—*stream* SC-3
Sparrow Swamp Ch—*church* SC-3
Sparrow Waste Ditch—*canal* MT-8
Sparr Spring—*spring* MD-2
Spar Spring—*spring* SD-7
*Sparta* AL-4
Sparta—*locale* LA-4
Sparta—*locale* NE-7
Sparta—*locale* PA-2
Sparta—*locale* VA-3
**Sparta**—*pop pl* GA-3
**Sparta**—*pop pl* IL-6
**Sparta**—*pop pl* IN-6
**Sparta**—*pop pl* KY-4
**Sparta**—*pop pl* MI-6
**Sparta**—*pop pl* MN-6
**Sparta**—*pop pl* MS-4
**Sparta**—*pop pl* MO-7
**Sparta**—*pop pl* NJ-2
**Sparta**—*pop pl* NY-2
**Sparta**—*pop pl* NC-3
**Sparta**—*pop pl* OH-6
**Sparta**—*pop pl* OR-9
**Sparta**—*pop pl* TN-4
**Sparta**—*pop pl* WI-6
Sparta Acad—*school* AL-4
Sparta Brook—*stream* NY-2
Sparta Butte—*summit* OR-9
Sparta (CCD)—*cens area* GA-3
Sparta (CCD)—*cens area* TN-4
Sparta Cem—*cemetery* AL-4
Sparta Cem—*cemetery* LA-4
Sparta Cem—*cemetery* MS-4
Sparta Cem—*cemetery* MO-7
Sparta Cem—*cemetery* NY-2
Sparta Cem—*cemetery* WI-6
**Sparta (census name Lake Mohawk)**—*pop pl* NJ-2
Sparta Center Ch—*church* NY-2
Sparta Ch—*church* MS-4
Sparta Ch—*church* MO-7
Sparta City Hall—*building* TN-4
Sparta Creek—*stream* WI-6
Sparta Devils Hole—*cave* TN-4
Sparta Division—*civil* TN-4
Sparta (Election Precinct)—*fmr MCD* IL-6
Sparta Free Library—*hist pl* WI-6
Sparta Glen—*valley* NJ-2
Sparta Glen Park—*park* NJ-2
Sparta Golf and Country Club—*locale* TN-4
**Sparta Heights (subdivision)**—*pop pl* TN-4
Sparta Hill Ch—*church* AL-4
**Sparta Hills (subdivision)**—*pop pl* TN-4
Sparta Hist Dist—*hist pl* GA-3
Sparta Hist Dist—*hist pl* IL-6
Sparta (historical)—*locale* AL-4
Sparta (historical)—*locale* KS-7
Sparta Industrial Park—*locale* TN-4
Sparta Junction—*locale* NJ-2
Sparta Lake—*lake* IN-6
**Sparta Lake**—*pop pl* NJ-2
Sparta Lake—*reservoir* NJ-2
Sparta Lake Dam—*dam* NJ-2
Sparta Lake Ditch—*canal* IN-6
Sparta Masonic Temple—*hist pl* WI-6
Sparta-Matta Mine—*mine* MN-6
Sparta Methodist Ch—*church* MS-4
Sparta Mountains—*range* NJ-2
Sparta Mtn—*summit* TX-5
**Spartanburg**—*pop pl* IN-6
**Spartanburg**—*pop pl* SC-3
Spartanburg (CCD)—*cens area* SC-3
Spartanburg Country Club—*other* SC-3
**Spartanburg (County)**—*pop pl* SC-3
Spartanburg Creek—*stream* IN-6
*Spartanburgh* IN-6
Spartanburg Hist Dist—*hist pl* SC-3
*Spartanburg Municipal Reservoir* SC-3
Spartan Creek—*stream* MT-8
Spartan Field—*flat* CA-9
Spar Tank—*reservoir* AZ-5
Spartan Oil Field—*oilfield* TX-5
Spartan Reef—*bar* HI-9
**Spartansburg**—*pop pl* PA-2
Spartansburg Borough—*civil* PA-2
Spartan Sch—*school* OK-5
Spartan Stadium—*other* CA-9
Spartan State Wildlife Mngmt Area—*park* MN-6
Spartan Stores Warehouse—*facility* MI-6
Spartan Village Sch—*school* MI-6
Sparta Post Office—*building* TN-4
Sparta Post Office (historical)—*building* MS-4
Sparta Post Office (historical)—*building* PA-2
Sparta Rock House—*hist pl* TN-4
Sparta Sch (historical)—*school* MS-4
Sparta Shop Ctr—*locale* TN-4
Sparta Spring (historical)—*spring* OR-9
Sparta Station—*locale* NJ-2
**Sparta (Town of)**—*pop pl* NY-2
**Sparta (Town of)**—*pop pl* WI-6
Sparta Township—*civil* MO-7
**Sparta Township**—*pop pl* NE-7
**Sparta (Township of)**—*pop pl* IL-6
**Sparta (Township of)**—*pop pl* (2) IN-6
**Sparta (Township of)**—*pop pl* MI-6
**Sparta (Township of)**—*pop pl* MN-6
**Sparta (Township of)**—*pop pl* NJ-2
**Sparta (Township of)**—*pop pl* PA-2
Sparta-White County Airp—*airport* TN-4
Sparte Lookout Tower—*locale* LA-4
Spartman Branch—*stream* FL-3
**Sparton Marshfield (subdivision)**—*pop pl* PA-2
Spar Tree Trail—*trail* WA-9
*Spa Run* WV-2
*Spa Spring* WV-2
Spa Spring Creek—*stream* NJ-2
Spasski Bay—*bay* AK-9
Spasski Creek—*stream* AK-9
Spasski Island—*island* AK-9
Spasski Trail—*trail* AK-9
Spastic Sch—*school* KY-4
**Spasticville**—*pop pl* KS-7
Spate Lake—*lake* LA-4
Spath Rsvr—*reservoir* WY-8
Spatter Cone—*summit* HI-9
Spatterdock Lake—*lake* IL-6
Spatterdock Lake—*lake* MI-6
Spatterdock Lake—*lake* MO-7
Spatterdock Lake—*lake* OR-9
Spatterdock Pond—*lake* DE-2
Spaugh Cem—*cemetery* IN-6
Spaugh JHS—*school* NC-3
Spaugh Pond—*lake* MO-7
*Spaulding* CA-9
Spaulding—*locale* AL-4
Spaulding—*locale* FL-3
Spaulding—*locale* IL-6
Spaulding—*locale* IA-7
Spaulding—*locale* ME-1
Spaulding—*locale* MN-6
**Spaulding**—*pop pl* FL-3
**Spaulding**—*pop pl* IL-6
**Spaulding**—*pop pl* IA-7
**Spaulding**—*pop pl* LA-4
**Spaulding**—*pop pl* OK-5
**Spaulding**—*pop pl* TX-5
**Spaulding**—*pop pl* WV-2
**Spaulding**—*pop pl* WI-6
Spaulding—*stream* TX-5
Spaulding, Henry F., Coachman's House—*hist pl* NY-2
Spaulding, Joseph, House—*hist pl* RI-1
Spaulding, Lake—*reservoir* CA-9
Spaulding Basin—*flat* ID-8
Spaulding Bay—*bay* MN-6
Spaulding Bay—*bay* VT-1
*Spaulding Bight* TX-5
Spaulding Block—*hist pl* MA-1
Spaulding Branch—*stream* KY-4
Spaulding Bridge—*bridge* WI-6
*Spaulding Brook* MA-1
Spaulding Brook—*stream* CT-1
Spaulding Brook—*stream* (4) ME-1
Spaulding Brook—*stream* (2) MA-1
Spaulding Brook—*stream* (2) NH-1
Spaulding Brook—*stream* NY-2
Spaulding Brook—*stream* (2) VT-1
Spaulding Butte—*summit* CA-9
Spaulding Canyon—*valley* NV-8
Spaulding Cem—*cemetery* (3) MI-6
Spaulding Cem—*cemetery* MO-7
Spaulding Cem—*cemetery* (2) WV-2
*Spaulding Church* AL-4
*Spaulding Corner* CA-9
Spaulding Corner—*locale* NY-2
**Spaulding Corners**—*pop pl* IL-6
Spaulding Cove—*bay* ME-1
*Spaulding Creek* OR-9
Spaulding Creek—*stream* CA-9
Spaulding Creek—*stream* MT-8
Spaulding Creek—*stream* OR-9
Spaulding Creek—*stream* PA-2
Spaulding Creek—*stream* WI-6
*Spaulding Dam* MA-1
Spaulding Dam—*dam* IL-6
Spaulding Drain—*stream* (2) MI-6
Spaulding Draw—*valley* AZ-5
*Spaulding Elementary School* AL-4
Spaulding Furnace—*locale* NY-2
Spaulding Gulch—*valley* CO-8
Spaulding Gulch—*valley* OR-9
**Spaulding Heights**—*pop pl* MD-2
*Spaulding Hill* MA-1
Spaulding Hill—*summit* (3) NH-1
Spaulding Hill—*summit* (2) VT-1
Spaulding (historical)—*locale* SD-7
Spaulding Hollow—*valley* NY-2
Spaulding House—*hist pl* ME-1
Spaulding HS—*school* SC-3
Spaulding Island—*island* ME-1
Spaulding JHS—*school* MD-2
*Spaulding Junction* AL-4
*Spaulding Lake* MN-6
Spaulding Lake—*lake* ME-1
Spaulding Lake—*lake* MN-6
Spaulding Lake—*lake* NH-1
Spaulding Lake—*lake* WA-9
Spaulding Manufacturing Company—*hist pl* IA-7
Spaulding Memorial Sch—*school* MA-1
Spaulding Mill (site)—*locale* OR-9
Spaulding Monroe MS—*school* NC-3
Spaulding MS—*school* NC-3
Spaulding Mtn—*summit* ME-1
Spaulding North Sch—*school* IL-6
Spaulding-Olive House—*hist pl* OK-5
Spaulding Park—*park* OK-5
Spaulding Peak—*summit* CO-8
Spaulding Point—*cape* AK-9
Spaulding Point—*cape* ME-1
Spaulding Point—*summit* CA-9
*Spaulding Pond* CT-1
Spaulding Pond—*lake* (2) ME-1
Spaulding Pond—*lake* NH-1
Spaulding Pond—*reservoir* (2) CT-1
Spaulding Pond—*reservoir* ME-1
Spaulding Ponds—*lake* ME-1
Spaulding Ranch—*locale* ID-8
Spaulding Ridge—*ridge* ME-1
Spaulding Ridge—*ridge* OR-9
*Spaulding Rsvr* OR-9
Spaulding Rsvr—*reservoir* CA-9
Spaulding Salt Marsh—*flat* NV-8
Spaulding Sch—*school* AL-4
Spaulding Sch—*school* CT-1
Spaulding Sch—*school* MA-1
Spaulding Sch—*school* MI-6
Spaulding Sch—*school* NC-3
Spaulding Sch Gymnasium-Auditorium—*hist pl* OK-5
Spauldings Incorporated Airp—*airport* PA-2
Spauldings Pond—*lake* WI-6
Spaulding Spring—*spring* AZ-5
Spaulding Swamp—*swamp* NY-2
Spaulding Tank—*reservoir* AZ-5

Spencer Branch—*stream* (3) ... NC-3
Spencer Branch—*stream* (2) ... SC-3
Spencer Branch—*stream* (2) ... TN-4
Spencer Branch—*stream* (2) ... VA-3
Spencer Branch—*stream* (2) ... WV-2
Spencer Bridge—*bridge* ... OR-9
*Spencer Brook* ... CT-1
Spencer Brook—*locale* ... MN-6
Spencer Brook—*stream* ... CT-1
Spencer Brook—*stream* (4) ... ME-1
Spencer Brook—*stream* ... MA-1
Spencer Brook—*stream* ... MN-6
Spencer Brook—*stream* ... NH-1
Spencer Brook—*stream* (2) ... NY-2
Spencer Brook—*stream* ... VT-1
Spencer Brook Cem—*cemetery* ... MN-6
*Spencer Brook Dam* ... MA-1
Spencer Brook (Township of)—*civ div* ... MN-6
**Spencerburg**—*pop pl* ... MO-7
Spencer Butte—*summit* ... ID-8
Spencer Butte—*summit* ... OR-9
Spencer Butte—*summit* ... WA-9
Spencer Butte JHS—*school* ... OR-9
Spencer Camp—*locale* ... ID-8
Spencer Camp—*locale* ... UT-8
Spencer Camp—*locale* ... WA-9
Spencer Canal—*canal* ... ID-8
Spencer Canal—*canal* ... LA-4
Spencer Canyon—*valley* (2) ... AZ-5
Spencer Canyon—*valley* (2) ... CA-9
Spencer Canyon—*valley* ... NM-5
Spencer Canyon—*valley* (3) ... UT-8
Spencer Canyon—*valley* ... WA-9
Spencer Canyon Campground—*park* ... AZ-5
Spencer Cave—*cave* ... AL-4
Spencer Cave—*cave* ... MO-7
Spencer (CCD)—*cens area* ... TN-4
*Spencer Cem* ... AL-4
Spencer Cem—*cemetery* (2) ... AL-4
Spencer Cem—*cemetery* (4) ... AR-4
Spencer Cem—*cemetery* ... ID-8
Spencer Cem—*cemetery* ... IL-6
Spencer Cem—*cemetery* (6) ... IN-6
Spencer Cem—*cemetery* ... IA-7
Spencer Cem—*cemetery* (4) ... KY-4
Spencer Cem—*cemetery* ... LA-4
Spencer Cem—*cemetery* ... MN-6
Spencer Cem—*cemetery* (2) ... MS-4
Spencer Cem—*cemetery* (2) ... MO-7
Spencer Cem—*cemetery* ... OR-9
Spencer Cem—*cemetery* ... SC-3
Spencer Cem—*cemetery* ... SD-7
Spencer Cem—*cemetery* ... TN-4
Spencer Cem—*cemetery* ... TX-5
Spencer Cem—*cemetery* ... UT-8
Spencer (census name for Spencer Center)—*CDP* ... MA-1
Spencer Center (census name Spencer)—*other* ... MA-1
*Spencer Centre* ... MA-1
Spencer Ch—*church* ... AL-4
Spencer Ch—*church* ... KY-4
Spencer Ch—*church* ... NY-2
Spencer Ch—*church* ... OH-6
Spencer Ch—*church* ... TX-5
Spencer Chapel—*church* ... KY-4
Spencer Chapel—*church* ... MI-6
Spencer Chapel—*church* ... OK-5
Spencer Chapel Cem—*cemetery* ... MO-7
Spencer Corner—*locale* ... RI-1
**Spencer Corner**—*pop pl* ... PA-2
**Spencer Corners**—*pop pl* ... NY-2
*Spencer Coulee* ... MT-8
Spencer Coulee—*valley* ... MT-8
Spencer Coulee—*valley* ... ND-7
Spencer Country Club—*other* ... IA-7
*Spencer County* ... TN-4
**Spencer County**—*pop pl* ... IN-6
**Spencer (County)**—*pop pl* ... KY-4
**Spencer County Farm**—*pop pl* ... IN-6
Spencer County State For—*forest* ... IN-6
Spencer Cove—*bay* ... ME-1
*Spencer Creek* ... MD-2
*Spencer Creek* ... MI-6
Spencer Creek—*bay* ... MD-2
Spencer Creek—*locale* ... OR-9
Spencer Creek—*stream* ... AZ-5
Spencer Creek—*stream* (2) ... AR-4
Spencer Creek—*stream* (3) ... CA-9
Spencer Creek—*stream* ... IN-6
Spencer Creek—*stream* ... IA-7
Spencer Creek—*stream* (2) ... KY-4
Spencer Creek—*stream* (2) ... MI-6
Spencer Creek—*stream* ... MS-4
Spencer Creek—*stream* (4) ... MO-7
Spencer Creek—*stream* (3) ... NC-3
Spencer Creek—*stream* ... OH-6
Spencer Creek—*stream* (3) ... OK-5
Spencer Creek—*stream* (8) ... OR-9
Spencer Creek—*stream* ... PA-2
Spencer Creek—*stream* (3) ... TN-4
Spencer Creek—*stream* ... TX-5
Spencer Creek—*stream* (2) ... VA-3
Spencer Creek—*stream* (5) ... WA-9
Spencer Creek—*stream* (3) ... WI-6
Spencer Creek Ch—*church* ... MO-7
Spencer Creek Cove Public Use Area—*park* ... OK-5
Spencer Dam—*dam* ... AL-4
Spencer Dam—*dam* ... ME-1
Spencer Dam—*dam* ... NE-7
Spencer Dam—*dam* ... NM-5
Spencer Dam Number Two—*dam* ... AL-4
Spencer Ditch—*canal* ... MT-8
Spencer Ditch—*canal* ... WY-8
Spencer Division—*civil* ... TN-4
Spencer Drain—*canal* ... MI-6
Spencer Drain—*stream* ... MI-6
Spencer Draw—*valley* ... CO-8
Spencer Draw—*valley* ... MO-7
Spencer Draw—*valley* ... NM-5
Spencer Draw—*valley* ... TX-5
Spencer Draw—*valley* (4) ... WY-8
Spencer Elem Sch—*school* ... TN-4
**Spencer Estates Subdivision**—*pop pl* ... UT-8
Spencer Family Cem—*cemetery* ... MS-4
Spencer Field (airport)—*airport* ... TN-4
Spencer Flat—*flat* ... UT-8
Spencer Flats—*flat* ... FL-3
Spencer Fork—*stream* ... KY-4
Spencer Fork—*stream* ... VA-3
Spencer Fork Wildlife Mngmt Area—*park* ... UT-8
Spencer Gap—*gap* ... KY-4
Spencer Glacier—*glacier* ... AK-9
Spencer Golf Club—*other* ... WV-2
Spencer Gulch—*valley* ... CO-8
Spencer Gulch—*valley* ... OR-9
Spencer Gut—*gut* ... ME-1
Spencer Harris Hollow—*valley* ... MO-7
Spencer Heights—*locale* ... CO-8
**Spencer Heights**—*pop pl* ... IL-6
Spencer Heights Memorial Cem—*cemetery* ... IL-6
Spencer Hill—*locale* ... TN-4
Spencer Hill—*summit* (2) ... CT-1
Spencer Hill—*summit* ... MS-4
Spencer Hill—*summit* ... NY-2
Spencer Hill—*summit* ... OH-6
Spencer Hill—*summit* ... RI-1
Spencer Hill—*summit* ... VT-1
Spencer Hill Cem—*cemetery* ... AL-4
Spencer Hill Ch—*church* ... AL-4
Spencer-Hill Memorial Ch—*church* ... NC-3
Spencer Hill Post Office (historical)—*building* ... TN-4
**Spencer Hills**—*pop pl* ... GA-3
Spencer Hill Sch (historical)—*school* ... AL-4
Spencer Hist Dist—*hist pl* ... NC-3
*Spencer Hollow* ... MO-7
Spencer Hollow—*valley* ... AL-4
Spencer Hollow—*valley* ... AR-4
Spencer Hollow—*valley* ... OH-6
Spencer Hollow—*valley* (2) ... TN-4
Spencer Hollow—*valley* ... TX-5
Spencer Hollow—*valley* ... WV-2
Spencer Hosp—*hospital* ... PA-2
Spencer Hot Springs—*spring* ... NV-8
Spencer House—*hist pl* ... CT-1
Spencer House—*hist pl* ... SC-3
Spencer HS—*school* ... IA-7
Spencer HS—*school* ... MS-4
Spencerian Coll—*school* ... WI-6
Spencer Industrial Center—*locale* ... AL-4
Spencer Island—*island* ... MD-2
Spencer Island—*island* ... NH-1
Spencer Island—*island* ... WA-9
Spencer JHS—*school* ... GA-3
Spencer JHS—*school* ... IA-7
Spencer Knob—*summit* ... GA-3
Spencer Knoll—*summit* ... AZ-5
Spencer Lake—*lake* (2) ... CO-8
Spencer Lake—*lake* ... ID-8
Spencer Lake—*lake* ... ME-1
Spencer Lake—*lake* ... MI-6
Spencer Lake—*lake* ... MN-6
Spencer Lake—*lake* ... MT-8
Spencer Lake—*lake* ... NE-7
Spencer Lake—*lake* ... NY-2
Spencer Lake—*lake* ... OH-6
Spencer Lake—*lake* ... TX-5
Spencer Lake—*lake* (3) ... WA-9
Spencer Lake—*lake* (3) ... WI-6
Spencer Lake—*reservoir* ... AL-4
Spencer Lake—*reservoir* ... KS-7
Spencer Lake—*reservoir* ... TX-5
Spencer Lake Bible Camp—*locale* ... WI-6
Spencer Lake Camps—*locale* ... ME-1
Spencer Lake Dam—*dam* ... MS-4
Spencer Lake Memorial Cem—*cemetery* ... WI-6
Spencer Lakes—*lake* ... CA-9
Spencer Lake State Wildlife Area—*reservoir* ... OH-6
Spencer Lake Two—*reservoir* ... AL-4
*Spencer (Magisterial District)* ... WV-2
Spencer (Magisterial District)—*fmr MCD* ... VA-3
Spencer Marsh—*swamp* ... WI-6
Spencer Meadow—*flat* ... CA-9
Spencer Meadow—*flat* ... WA-9
Spencer Meadow—*swamp* ... ME-1
Spencer Memorial Baptist—*school* ... FL-3
Spencer Memorial Baptist Ch—*church* ... MS-4
Spencer Memorial Cem—*cemetery* ... WV-2
Spencer Memorial Park—*park* ... WV-2
Spencer Mill Creek—*stream* ... SC-3
Spencer Mill Lake—*lake* ... LA-4
Spencer Mills Ch—*church* ... MI-6
**Spencer Mountain**—*pop pl* ... NC-3
*Spencer Mountains* ... ME-1
Spencer Mtn—*summit* ... CO-8
Spencer Mtn—*summit* ... ME-1
Spencer Mtn—*summit* (2) ... MA-1
Spencer Mtn—*summit* ... NC-3
Spencer Mtn—*summit* ... TN-4
Spencer Mtn—*summit* (2) ... TX-5
Spencer No. 2 Site—*hist pl* ... OK-5
Spencer Number Two Dam—*dam* ... UT-8
Spencer Number Two Rsvr—*reservoir* ... UT-8
Spencer Oil Field—*oilfield* ... TX-5
*Spencer Park* ... NE-7
Spencer Park—*park* ... HI-9
Spencer Park—*park* ... IL-6
Spencer Park—*park* (2) ... IN-6
Spencer Park—*park* ... NC-3
Spencer Park Chapel—*church* ... TX-5
Spencer Park Dentzel Carousel—*hist pl* ... IN-6
Spencer Park Sch—*school* ... NE-7
Spencer Peak—*summit* ... AK-9
Spencer Peak—*summit* ... AZ-5
Spencer Peak—*summit* ... WA-9
Spencer-Penn Sch—*school* ... VA-3
Spencer-Pierce-Little House—*hist pl* ... MA-1
Spencer Place—*locale* ... AR-4
*Spencer Plateau* ... AZ-5
Spencer Point—*cape* ... NY-2
Spencer Point—*cape* (2) ... NC-3
Spencer Point—*cape* ... UT-8
Spencer Point—*summit* ... WA-9
Spencer Point Ch (historical)—*church* ... TN-4
Spencer Pond—*lake* ... CT-1
Spencer Pond—*lake* (4) ... ME-1
Spencer Pond—*lake* ... MA-1
Spencer Pond—*lake* ... NH-1
Spencer Pond—*reservoir* ... CT-1
Spencer Pond—*reservoir* ... PA-2
Spencer Pool Creek—*stream* ... TX-5
**Spencerport**—*pop pl* ... NY-2
Spencer Post Office—*building* ... TN-4
Spencer Post Office (historical)—*building* ... MS-4
Spencer Ranch—*locale* ... ID-8
Spencer Ranch—*locale* ... MT-8
Spencer Ranch—*locale* (2) ... NE-7
Spencer Ranch—*locale* (2) ... NM-5
**Spencer Ridge**—*pop pl* ... KY-4
Spencer Ridge—*ridge* ... AR-4
Spencer Ridge—*ridge* ... GA-3
Spencer Ridge—*ridge* ... KY-4
Spencer Ridge—*ridge* ... OH-6
Spencer Ridge—*ridge* ... WV-2
Spencer Ridge Ch—*church* ... KY-4
Spencer Ridge Ch—*church* ... OH-6
Spencer Rips—*rapids* (3) ... ME-1
Spencer-Robinson Ditch—*canal* ... WI-6
Spencer Rock—*pillar* ... TN-4
Spencer Rsvr—*reservoir* ... ID-8
Spencer Rsvr—*reservoir* ... NV-8
Spencer Rsvr—*reservoir* ... OH-6
*Spencer Run* ... WV-2
Spencer Run—*stream* (2) ... OH-6
Spencer Run—*stream* (3) ... PA-2
*Spencers* ... NC-3
**Spencers Annex Subdivision**—*pop pl* ... UT-8
Spencers Branch—*stream* ... KY-4
**Spencers Butte (historical)**—*pop pl* ... OR-9
Spencers Cem—*cemetery* ... AL-4
Spencer Sch—*school* ... CT-1
Spencer Sch—*school* ... GA-3
Spencer Sch—*school* (4) ... IL-6
Spencer Sch—*school* (2) ... IA-7
Spencer Sch—*school* ... LA-4
Spencer Sch—*school* ... MI-6
Spencer Sch—*school* ... ND-7
Spencer Sch—*school* ... OH-6
Spencer Sch—*school* ... UT-8
Spencer Sch (abandoned)—*school* ... PA-2
*Spencers Chapel Church* ... AL-4
Spencer Sch (historical)—*school* ... MO-7
**Spencers Corners**—*pop pl* ... PA-2
Spencers Creek—*stream* ... AL-4
**Spencer Settlement**—*pop pl* ... NY-2
Spencers Grove—*locale* ... IA-7
Spencers Grove (historical P.O.)—*locale* ... IA-7
Spencer Shaft—*mine* ... PA-2
Spencer Shop Ctr—*locale* ... MA-1
*Spencers Hot Spring* ... NV-8
Spencers Ledge—*cliff* ... NY-2
**Spencers Mill**—*pop pl* ... TN-4
*Spencers Mill Creek* ... AL-4
Spencers Mill Creek—*stream* ... VA-3
Spencer Spit—*bar* ... WA-9
Spencer Spit State Park—*park* ... WA-9
Spencers Pond—*reservoir* ... AL-4
Spencer Spring—*spring* (2) ... AZ-5
Spencer Spring—*spring* ... NM-5
Spencer Spring—*spring* ... OK-5
Spencer Spring—*spring* ... PA-2
Spencer Spring—*spring* ... UT-8
Spencer Spring Creek—*stream* ... AZ-5
Spencer Springs—*spring* ... AZ-5
Spencer Springs—*spring* ... MT-8
Spencer Square Shop Ctr—*locale* ... TN-4
Spencers Rock Cave—*cave* ... TN-4
*Spencers Run* ... PA-2
Spencers Shower—*cave* ... TN-4
*Spencers Station* ... OH-6
Spencer State For—*forest* ... MA-1
Spencer State Public Shooting Area—*park* (2) ... SD-7
*Spencer Station* ... MA-1
**Spencer Station**—*pop pl* ... OH-6
Spencer Store—*locale* ... MO-7
**Spencer Store**—*pop pl* ... AL-4
Spencer Stream—*stream* (2) ... ME-1
Spence Rsvr—*reservoir* ... OR-9
Spencers Well—*locale* ... AZ-5
Spencer Tank—*reservoir* ... AZ-5
Spencer Temple—*church* ... WV-2
Spencer Terrace—*bench* ... AZ-5
Spencertown—*locale* ... PA-2
**Spencertown**—*pop pl* ... NY-2
Spencertown Acad—*hist pl* ... NY-2
Spencer Town Center Hist Dist—*hist pl* ... MA-1
Spencer Town Hall—*hist pl* ... OH-6
Spencer Town Hall and Fire Station—*hist pl* ... IN-6
**Spencer (Town of)**—*pop pl* ... MA-1
**Spencer (Town of)**—*pop pl* ... NY-2
**Spencer (Town of)**—*pop pl* ... WI-6
Spencer Township—*civil* (3) ... MO-7
**Spencer Township**—*pop pl* ... NE-7
**Spencer Township**—*pop pl* ... ND-7
**Spencer (Township of)**—*pop pl* (3) ... IN-6
**Spencer (Township of)**—*pop pl* ... MI-6
**Spencer (Township of)**—*pop pl* ... MN-6
**Spencer (Township of)**—*pop pl* (4) ... OH-6
Spencer Valley—*valley* ... CA-9
Spencer Valley Sch—*school* ... CA-9
**Spencerville**—*pop pl* ... MD-2
**Spencerville**—*pop pl* ... NM-5
**Spencerville**—*pop pl* ... OH-6
**Spencerville**—*pop pl* ... OK-5
Spencerville—*post sta* ... IN-6
Spencerville Cem—*cemetery* ... OH-6
Spencerville Cem—*cemetery* ... OK-5
Spencerville Covered Bridge—*hist pl* ... IN-6
Spencerville Junior Acad—*school* ... MD-2
Spencerville P. O. (historical)—*locale* ... AL-4
Spencerville Rsvr—*reservoir* ... OH-6
Spencerville Sch Campus—*hist pl* ... OK-5
Spencer Water Supply Dam—*dam* ... TN-4
Spencer Water Supply Lake—*reservoir* ... TN-4
Spencer Well—*well* ... AZ-5
Spencer Well—*well* (2) ... NM-5
Spencer Well—*well* ... OR-9
Spencer West (CCD)—*cens area* ... KY-4
Spencer Windmill—*locale* ... NM-5
Spence Sch—*school* ... TN-4
Spences Corner—*locale* ... NC-3
Spences Corner—*other* ... NC-3
Spences Creek—*stream* ... VA-3
*Spences Ferry* ... TN-4
Spences Lake—*lake* ... GA-3
Spence's Point—*hist pl* ... VA-3
Spence Spring—*spring* (2) ... AZ-5
Spence Spring—*spring* ... CO-8
*Spencess Landing* ... MD-2
*Spences Spring* ... AL-4
Spences Store—*locale* ... TN-4
Spenceville (Site)—*locale* ... CA-9
Spendlove Knoll—*summit* ... UT-8
Spendlove Tank—*reservoir* ... AZ-5
Spendthrift Site (22CO520)—*hist pl* ... MS-4
Spengler Bridge—*hist pl* ... NY-2
Spengler Cem—*cemetery* ... OH-6
Spengler's Corner—*hist pl* ... MS-4
Spengler's Corner Hist Dist—*hist pl* ... MS-4
Spen Lake—*lake* ... MN-6
Speno Lake—*lake* ... MO-7
*Spenser Station* ... OH-6
Spenser Wash—*stream* ... AZ-5
**Speonk**—*pop pl* ... NY-2
Speonk Point—*cape* ... NY-2
Speonk River—*stream* ... NY-2
Sperati Point—*cape* ... ND-7
Sperl Hollow—*valley* ... PA-2
Sperling, Frederick, House—*hist pl* ... WI-6
Sperling Oil Field—*oilfield* ... KS-7
Sperling Sch—*school* ... OK-5
*Sperlin Point* ... ME-1
*Sperlin's Point* ... ME-1
Spermaceti Cove—*bay* ... NJ-2
**Spero**—*pop pl* ... NC-3
*Sperry* ... ND-7
Sperry—*locale* ... CA-9
Sperry—*locale* ... WA-9
**Sperry**—*pop pl* ... IA-7
**Sperry**—*pop pl* ... MO-7
**Sperry**—*pop pl* ... OK-5
**Sperry**—*pop pl* ... TX-5
Sperry, Lake—*lake* ... FL-3
Sperry Brook—*stream* (2) ... NY-2
Sperry Brook—*stream* ... VT-1
Sperry Cabin Run—*stream* ... WV-2
Sperry Cem—*cemetery* ... CT-1
Sperry Cem—*cemetery* ... OK-5
Sperry Cem—*cemetery* ... TN-4
Sperry Chalets—*hist pl* ... MT-8
Sperry Chalets—*locale* ... MT-8
*Sperry Creek* ... MT-8
Sperry Creek—*stream* ... OH-6
Sperry Creek—*stream* (2) ... OR-9
Sperry Dam—*dam* ... ND-7
Sperry Fork—*stream* ... OH-6
Sperry Glacier—*glacier* ... MT-8
Sperry Hill—*summit* ... CT-1
Sperry Hill—*summit* ... NY-2
Sperry Hills—*other* ... CA-9
**Sperry (historical)**—*pop pl* ... OR-9
Sperry Hollow—*valley* ... NY-2
Sperry Hollow—*valley* ... WV-2
Sperry HS—*school* ... NY-2
Sperry Lake—*lake* ... MN-6
Sperry Lake—*lake* ... ND-7
Sperry Lateral—*canal* ... CA-9
Sperry Mtn—*summit* ... CO-8
Sperry Office Bldg—*hist pl* ... CA-9
Sperry Park—*park* ... NY-2
Sperry Peak—*summit* ... WA-9
Sperry Pond—*lake* ... CT-1
Sperry Pond—*lake* ... ME-1
Sperry Pond—*lake* ... OH-6
Sperry Pond—*reservoir* ... CT-1
Sperry Pond—*reservoir* ... NY-2
Sperry Ranch—*locale* ... MT-8
Sperry Run—*stream* ... WV-2
Sperry Run Ch—*church* ... WV-2
*Sperrys Pond* ... CT-1
Sperrys Pond—*lake* ... MA-1
Sperry Spring—*spring* (2) ... OR-9
**Sperry Springs**—*pop pl* ... NJ-2
Sperry Springs—*spring* ... CA-9
Sperry Township—*fmr MCD* ... IA-7
Sperry Union Flour Mill—*hist pl* ... CA-9
Sperryville—*locale* ... NY-2
**Sperryville**—*pop pl* ... VA-3
Sperryville Hist Dist—*hist pl* ... VA-3
Spesard Knob—*summit* ... VA-3
Spessard Cem—*cemetery* ... VA-3
Spessard Holland Park—*park* ... FL-3
Spessard L Holland Bridge—*bridge* ... FL-3
Spessard L Holland Elem Sch—*school* ... FL-3
Spessard Mill (historical)—*locale* ... TN-4
Spessard Sch (historical)—*school* ... MO-7
*Spesutia Island* ... MD-2
*Spesutia Narrows* ... MD-2
Spesutie Ch—*church* ... MD-2
Spesutie Island—*island* ... MD-2
Spesutie Narrows—*channel* ... MD-2
*Spetch Rim* ... OR-9
Spettel Cove—*bay* ... TX-5
S Petty or A Hantan Grant—*civil* ... FL-3
Spewing Camp Branch—*stream* ... KY-4
Spewing Camp Sch—*school* ... KY-4
Spewmarrow Creek—*stream* ... NC-3
Spewrell Bluff—*cliff* ... GA-3
Spex Arth Creek—*stream* ... WA-9
Speyers Homestead—*locale* ... WY-8
Speyers Rsvr—*reservoir* ... WY-8
Spezzano Gully—*valley* ... NY-2
*Sphaghnum Lake* ... MN-6
Sphagnum Bog—*swamp* ... OR-9
Sphagnum Creek—*stream* ... MN-6
Sphagnum Lake—*lake* ... MI-6
Sphagnum Lake—*lake* ... MN-6
Sphagnum Pond—*reservoir* ... NY-2
S P Hill—*summit* ... AZ-5
Sphinx—*locale* ... MT-8
Sphinx—*locale* ... UT-8
*Sphinx, The* ... AK-9
*Sphinx, The* ... UT-8
Sphinx, The—*pillar* ... CA-9
Sphinx, The—*pillar* ... UT-8
Sphinx, The—*summit* ... WY-8
Sphinx Butte—*summit* ... OR-9
*Sphinx Creek* ... CO-8
Sphinx Creek—*stream* ... AK-9
Sphinx Creek—*stream* ... CA-9
Sphinx Creek—*stream* ... MT-8
Sphinx Creek—*stream* ... OR-9
Sphinx Crest—*ridge* ... CA-9
Sphinx Island—*island* ... AK-9
Sphinx Lakes—*lake* ... CA-9
*Sphinx Mtn* ... AK-9
Sphinx Mtn—*summit* ... AK-9
Sphinx Mtn—*summit* ... MT-8
**Sphinx Park**—*pop pl* ... CO-8
Sphinx Peak—*summit* ... MT-8
Sphinx Rock—*pillar* ... UT-8
Sphinx Rock, The—*pillar* ... NC-3
Sphinx Trail—*trail* ... NH-1
Sphunge Islands—*island* ... MN-6
Spica—*locale* ... KS-7
Spice—*locale* (2) ... WV-2
Spice Bayou—*gut* ... LA-4
Spice Bottom Creek—*stream* ... NC-3
Spice Branch—*stream* ... KY-4
Spice Branch—*stream* ... NC-3
Spice Branch—*stream* ... TN-4
Spice Branch—*stream* ... WV-2
Spice Branch Prospect—*mine* ... TN-4
Spice Brook—*stream* ... CT-1
Spicebush Creek—*stream* ... MI-6
Spice Cove—*valley* (2) ... NC-3
Spice Cove Mtn—*summit* ... NC-3
Spice Creek—*stream* ... MD-2
Spice Creek—*stream* ... NC-3
Spice Creek—*stream* ... TX-5
Spice Creek—*stream* (3) ... WV-2
Spice Hollow—*valley* ... TN-4
Spice Key—*island* ... FL-3
Spice Knob—*locale* ... KY-4
Spice Knob—*summit* ... KY-4
Spice Lake—*lake* ... MN-6
Spice Lake—*lake* ... WI-6
**Spiceland**—*pop pl* ... IN-6
Spiceland Elem Sch—*school* ... IN-6
**Spiceland (Township of)**—*pop pl* ... IN-6
Spice Laurel Branch—*stream* ... WV-2
Spice Lick—*stream* ... KY-4
Spice Lick Bottoms—*flat* ... TN-4
Spice Lick Branch—*stream* ... KY-4
Spicelick Branch—*stream* ... KY-4
Spice Lick Branch—*valley* ... KY-4
Spicelick Creek—*stream* ... WV-2
Spicelick Fork—*stream* ... WV-2
Spice Lick Hollow—*valley* ... KY-4
Spicelick Run—*stream* ... WV-2
Spice Lick Run—*stream* ... WV-2
Spice Mortar Branch—*stream* ... KY-4
Spice Mtn—*summit* ... VT-1
Spice Pond Creek—*stream* ... MS-4
Spicer—*locale* ... CO-8
Spicer—*locale* ... OR-9
**Spicer**—*pop pl* ... MN-6
Spicer, John M., House—*hist pl* ... MN-6
Spicer, John M., Summer House and Farm—*hist pl* ... MN-6
Spicer Basin—*basin* ... CO-8
Spicer Bay—*bay* ... NY-2
Spicer Bay—*bay* ... NC-3
Spicer Branch—*stream* ... KY-4
Spicer Branch—*stream* ... TN-4
*Spicer Brook* ... MA-1
Spicer Brook—*stream* ... PA-2
Spicer Brook—*stream* ... VT-1
Spicer Canyon—*valley* ... CA-9
Spicer Cem—*cemetery* ... KY-4
Spicer Cem—*cemetery* ... WI-6
Spicer Ch—*church* ... KY-4
**Spicer City**—*pop pl* ... CA-9
Spicer Cove—*valley* ... NC-3
Spicer Creek—*channel* ... MD-2
Spicer Creek—*stream* ... AK-9
Spicer Creek—*stream* ... CA-9
Spicer Creek—*stream* ... MI-6
Spicer Creek—*stream* ... NJ-2
Spicer Creek—*stream* ... NY-2
Spicer Creek—*stream* (2) ... OH-6
Spicer Creek—*stream* ... TX-5
Spicer Ditch—*canal* ... CO-8
Spicer Falls—*falls* ... NY-2
Spicer Fork—*stream* ... KY-4
Spicer Hollow—*valley* ... TN-4
*Spicer Ice Pond* ... CT-1
Spice Ridge—*ridge* ... WV-2
Spice Ridge Trail—*trail* ... WV-2
*Spice River* ... OH-6
Spicer Lake—*lake* ... IN-6
Spicer Lake—*lake* ... KS-7
Spicer Lake—*swamp* ... MN-6
Spicer Ledge—*bench* ... CT-1
Spicer Meadow—*flat* ... CA-9
Spicer Meadow Rsvr—*reservoir* ... CA-9
*Spice-Root* ... MH-9
*Spice-Root Beach* ... MH-9
*Spice-Root Stream* ... MH-9
Spicer Peak—*summit* ... CO-8
Spicer Pond—*lake* ... ME-1
*Spicer Prong* ... DE-2
*Spicers* ... NJ-2
Spicers Airp—*airport* ... NC-3
Spicer Sch—*school* ... CO-8
Spicer Sch—*school* ... OH-6
Spicers Cove—*bay* ... ME-1
Spicers Island—*island* ... VA-3
Spicers Lake—*reservoir* ... VA-3
*Spicers Meadow Rsvr* ... CA-9
*Spice Run* ... WV-2
Spice Run—*stream* ... OH-6
Spice Run—*stream* ... VA-3
Spice Run—*stream* (7) ... WV-2
Spicerville Sch—*school* ... MI-6
Spicer Well No 2—*well* ... WY-8
Spices Creek—*stream* ... NC-3
Spice Valley Ch—*church* ... IN-6
Spice Valley (Township of)—*civ div* ... IN-6
**Spicewood**—*pop pl* ... TX-5
**Spicewood Acres (subdivision)**—*pop pl* ... NC-3
Spicewood Branch—*stream* (5) ... KY-4
Spicewood Branch—*stream* (4) ... TN-4
Spicewood Branch—*stream* ... VA-3
Spicewood Branch—*stream* (2) ... WV-2
Spicewood Canyon—*valley* ... TX-5
Spicewood Cem—*cemetery* ... IN-6
Spicewood Creek—*stream* ... AR-4
Spicewood Creek—*stream* ... MS-4
Spicewood Creek—*stream* ... TX-5
Spicewood Flat—*flat* ... KY-4
Spicewood Fork—*stream* (2) ... KY-4
Spicewood Hollow—*valley* ... AR-4
Spicewood Hollow—*valley* (2) ... MO-7
Spicewood Hollow—*valley* (3) ... TN-4
Spicewood Hollow—*valley* ... VA-3
Spicewood Run—*stream* ... PA-2
**Spicewood (subdivision)**—*pop pl* ... NC-3
**Spickard**—*pop pl* ... MO-7
Spickard, Mount—*summit* ... WA-9
Spickard Cem—*cemetery* ... OH-6
*Spickards* ... MO-7
*Spickardsville* ... MO-7
*Spickardsville Spickard Post Office* ... MO-7
**Spickardsville Spickard Post Office**—*pop pl* ... MO-7
Spicker, Peter, House—*hist pl* ... PA-2
Spickert Knob—*summit* ... IN-6
Spicket Falls Hist Dist—*hist pl* ... MA-1
Spicket Hill—*summit* ... MA-1
Spicket Hill—*summit* ... NH-1
Spicket River—*stream* ... MA-1
Spicket River—*stream* ... NH-1
Spicket River At Lowell Street Dam—*dam* ... MA-1
Spicket River Rsvr—*reservoir* ... MA-1
Spickett, Mount—*summit* ... MA-1
*Spickett River* ... MA-1
*Spickett River* ... NH-1
Spickler—*locale* ... MD-2
Spicy Branch—*stream* ... KY-4
Spicy Gap—*gap* ... TN-4
Spicy Run—*stream* ... OH-6
Spider—*locale* ... KY-4
Spider Bay—*bay* ... MI-6
Spider Branch—*stream* ... IL-6
Spider Bridge—*bridge* ... NH-1
Spider Cave—*cave* (2) ... AL-4
Spider Cave—*cave* (3) ... PA-2
Spider Cave—*hist pl* ... MI-6
Spidercrab Bay—*bay* ... VA-3
*Spider Creek* ... WY-8
Spider Creek—*stream* ... AK-9
Spider Creek—*stream* (3) ... AR-4
Spider Creek—*stream* (2) ... ID-8
Spider Creek—*stream* ... KY-4
Spider Creek—*stream* ... MN-6
Spider Creek—*stream* ... NM-5
Spider Creek—*stream* ... OR-9
Spider Creek—*stream* ... VA-3
Spider Creek—*stream* ... WA-9
Spider Creek—*stream* ... WV-2
Spider Creek—*stream* (3) ... WI-6
Spider Creek—*stream* ... WY-8
Spider Creek Flowage—*lake* ... WI-6
Spider Gas Field—*oilfield* ... LA-4
Spider Glacier—*glacier* (2) ... WA-9
Spider Hill Cem—*cemetery* ... IN-6
Spider Island—*island* ... AK-9
Spider Island—*island* (2) ... ME-1
Spider Island—*island* (2) ... MN-6
Spider Island—*island* ... WI-6
*Spider Lake* ... MI-6
*Spider Lake* ... WA-9
*Spider Lake* ... WI-6
Spider Lake—*lake* ... CA-9
Spider Lake—*lake* ... ME-1
Spider Lake—*lake* (2) ... MI-6
Spider Lake—*lake* (9) ... MN-6
Spider Lake—*lake* (2) ... MT-8
Spider Lake—*lake* ... UT-8
Spider Lake—*lake* (4) ... WA-9
Spider Lake—*lake* (10) ... WI-6
Spider Lake—*lake* ... WY-8
Spider Lake Ch—*church* ... WI-6
Spider Lake Lookout Tower—*locale* ... MN-6
*Spider Lakes* ... WA-9
Spider Lake Shelter—*locale* ... WA-9
**Spider Lake (Town of)**—*pop pl* ... WI-6
Spider Meadow—*flat* ... WA-9
Spider Mtn—*summit* ... TX-5
Spider Mtn—*summit* ... WA-9
Spider Peak—*summit* ... WY-8
*Spider Point* ... DE-2
Spider Pond—*lake* ... NY-2
Spider Ponds—*lake* ... MI-6
Spider Ranch—*locale* ... AZ-5
Spider Ridge—*ridge* ... GA-3
Spider Ridge—*ridge* (2) ... WV-2
Spider Rock—*pillar* ... AZ-5
Spider Rock Overlook—*locale* ... AZ-5
Spider Rsvr—*reservoir* ... UT-8
Spider Spring—*spring* (2) ... AZ-5
Spider Spring—*spring* ... NM-5
Spider Tank—*reservoir* ... AZ-5
Spider Valley Creek—*stream* ... SC-3
**Spiderweb**—*pop pl* ... SC-3
Spider Web Ranch—*locale* ... AZ-5
Spider Windmill—*locale* ... NM-5
Spieden Bluff—*cliff* ... WA-9
Spieden Channel—*channel* ... WA-9
Spieden Island—*island* ... WA-9
Spiegelberg House—*hist pl* ... NM-5
Spiegel Grove State Park—*park* ... OH-6
*Spieglemoyer Gap* ... PA-2
*Spieglemoyer Run* ... PA-2
*Spieglemyer Trail* ... PA-2
Spieker Ditch—*canal* ... MT-8
Spie Knob—*summit* ... TX-5
Spielman—*locale* ... MD-2
Spielman, H. M. S., House—*hist pl* ... NE-7
Spielman Sch—*school* ... MI-6
*Spien Kopj* ... IN-6
Spier, Lake—*lake* ... FL-3
Spier Creek—*stream* ... AK-9
Spier Falls—*falls* ... NY-2
Spiering Rsvr—*reservoir* ... OR-9
Spier Lake—*lake* ... MN-6
Spiers Branch—*stream* ... TN-4
Spiers Cem—*cemetery* ... MS-4
Spiers Gulch—*valley* ... CA-9
Spiers Island—*island* ... IL-6
Spiers Pond—*reservoir* ... VA-3
Spiers Sch—*school* ... SD-7
Spiers Stand—*rock* ... MA-1
**Spies**—*pop pl* ... NC-3
Spies Boardinghouse—*hist pl* ... MI-6
Spies Church—*locale* ... PA-2
*Spies Hill* ... PA-2
Spies Hill Sch—*school* ... GA-3
Spies Lake—*lake* ... MI-6
Spies Lake—*lake* ... TX-5
Spies Lake—*lake* (2) ... WI-6
Spies Mine—*mine* ... MI-6
Spies Run—*stream* ... PA-2
Spiess—*locale* ... NM-5
*Spiess Lake* ... MI-6
Spieth and Krug Brewery—*hist pl* ... MT-8
Spieth Houses—*hist pl* ... MT-8
Spigelmyer Gap—*gap* ... PA-2
Spigelmyer Run—*stream* ... PA-2
*Spiggot River* ... MA-1
Spight (historical)—*locale* ... MS-4
Spight Post Office (historical)—*building* ... MS-4

Spigner Cem—cemetery OK-5
Spigners AL-4
Spignet Butte—summit OR-9
Spignet Creek—stream OR-9
Spigot Lake—lake MN-6
Spike—locale KY-4
Spike Bay—gut LA-4
Spike Brook—stream IN-6
Spike Buck—locale CO-8
**Spikebuck**—pop pl CO-8
Spike Buck Butte—summit OR-9
Spike Buck Camp—locale PA-2
Spike Buck Creek—stream (2) CA-9
Spike Buck Creek—stream MS-4
Spike Buck Gulch CO-8
Spike Buck Gulch—valley CA-9
Spike Buck Gulch—valley CO-8
Spike Buck Hollow—valley PA-2
Spike Buck Mtn—summit CA-9
Spikebuck Town Mound and Village Site—hist pl NC-3
Spike Buck Trail—trail PA-2
Spike Camp Spring—spring MT-8
Spike Cem—cemetery AL-4
Spike Creek—stream AK-9
Spike Creek—stream ID-8
Spike Creek—stream MT-8
Spike E Hills—range AZ-5
Spike Hollow—valley PA-2
Spike Hollow—valley UT-8
Spike Hollow Draw—valley CO-8
Spike Horn Creek—stream MI-6
Spikehorn Creek—stream MI-6
Spike Horn Creek—stream MI-6
Spike Horn Creek—stream MN-6
Spikehorn Creek—stream WI-6
Spike Horn Swamp—swamp MI-6
Spike Island—island AK-9
Spike Island—island NY-2
**Spike Island**—pop pl (2) PA-2
Spike Lake—lake (3) MN-6
Spikeman Creek—stream WA-9
Spike Mtn—summit AK-9
Spikenard Creek—stream CA-9
**Spikenard (historical)**—pop pl OR-9
Spiken Ridge—ridge SD-7
Spiker IN-6
Spiker—locale NE-7
Spiker Brook PA-2
Spiker Cem—cemetery IN-6
Spiker Creek—stream NC-3
Spiker Lake—lake IN-6
Spike Rock—bar WA-9
Spike Rock—other AK-9
Spiker Run—stream MD-2
Spikes Canyon—valley NM-5
Spikes Cem—cemetery AR-4
Spikes Cem—cemetery LA-4
Spikes Creek—gut NC-3
Spikes Creek—stream NM-5
Spikes Gulch—valley OR-9
Spikes Peak—summit CA-9
Spike Spring—spring WA-9
Spikes Sch—school AR-4
Spiketown Sch—school IL-6
Spiket River Spricket River MA-1
Spikey Arroyo—stream NM-5
Spikner Cem—cemetery LA-4
Spikner HS—school TX-5
Spilde Creek—stream OR-9
Spile Lake—lake MO-7
Spiler Canyon—valley CO-8
Spiler Cem—cemetery AL-4
Spiler Lake—lake CO-8
Spilieberg Creek WI-6
Spilieberg Lake WI-6
Spilker Lateral—canal CA-9
Spillar Ranch—locale TX-5
Spillcorn—locale NC-3
Spillcorn Creek—stream NC-3
Spill Creek—stream MO-7
Spilleburg Creek WI-6
Spilleburg Lake WI-6
Spiller—locale OH-6
Spillerberg Creek—stream WI-6
Spillerberg Lake—lake WI-6
Spiller Branch VA-3
Spiller Branch—stream LA-4
Spiller Canyon—valley NM-5
Spiller Canyon—valley UT-8
Spiller Cem—cemetery IL-6
Spiller Cem—cemetery TX-5
Spiller Creek—stream AR-4
Spiller Creek—stream CA-9
Spiller Creek—stream WI-6
Spiller Hollow—valley TX-5
Spiller Lake—lake CA-9
Spiller Mine—mine TX-5
Spiller Oil Field—oilfield TX-5
Spiller Peak—summit CO-8
Spiller Ranch—locale TX-5
Spillers Branch—stream TX-5
Spillers Cem—cemetery LA-4
Spillers Cem—cemetery TX-5
Spiller Sch—school VA-3
Spillers Creek—stream LA-4
Spillers Store—locale TX-5
**Spillertown**—pop pl IL-6
Spillerville Cem—cemetery TX-5
Spill Hollow—valley AR-4
Spilliens Cem—cemetery MO-7
Spilling Gulch—valley MT-8
Spill Lake—lake MT-8
Spillman—locale LA-4
Spillman Brook—stream NH-1
Spillman Cem—cemetery KS-7
Spillman Cem—cemetery LA-4
Spillman Cem—cemetery MO-7
Spillman Cem—cemetery NM-5
Spillman Chapel—church KY-4
Spillman Cove—bay ME-1
Spillman Creek FL-3
Spillman Creek—stream IL-6
Spillman Creek—stream KS-7
Spillman Draw—valley WY-8
Spillman Field Airp—airport MO-7
Spillman Hollow—valley TX-5
Spillman Mound—summit MO-7
Spillman Mtn—summit WV-2
Spillman Run—stream WV-2
Spillmans Hole—lake KY-4
Spillmans Island TX-5
Spillmans Landing—locale VA-3
Spillover, The—area WA-9
Spillsbury Ranch—locale UT-8
**Spillville**—pop pl IA-7
Spillway TN-4
Spillway Bay—bay TX-5
Spillway Bayou—gut LA-4
Spillway Beaverhead Lodge—locale AZ-5
Spillway Boat Ramp—locale UT-8
Spillway Campground—locale MT-8
Spillway Campground—park AL-4
Spillway Canal—canal LA-4
Spillway Canyon—valley CA-9
Spillway Ditch—canal MO-7
Spillway Falls—falls PA-2
Spillway Hollow—valley UT-8
Spillway Lake—lake CA-9
Spillway Lake—reservoir LA-4
Spillway Lake—reservoir PA-2
Spillway Landing—locale AR-4
Spillway Rec Area—park (2) MO-7
Spillway State Park KS-7
Spillway State Park—park KS-7
Spilman Ch—church WV-2
Spilmans Island—island TX-5
**Spilo**—pop pl GA-3
**Spilona**—pop pl NC-3
Spilsers Lake MN-6
**Spilt Rock**—pop pl PA-2
Spinach Creek—stream AK-9
Spina Hotel—hist pl MN-6
Spinaly City PA-2
Spino Trail—trail MN-6
Spincely Creek WI-6
Spincich Lake—lake MI-6
**Spindale**—pop pl NC-3
Spindale Elem Sch—school NC-3
**Spindle**—pop pl NM-5
Spindle, The—island MA-1
Spindle, The—pillar MA-1
Spindle, The—rock MA-1
Spindle Creek—stream ID-8
Spindle Creek Bar—bar ID-8
Spindle Hill CT-1
Spindle Hill—summit MA-1
Spindle Point—cape NH-1
Spindle Pond—reservoir VA-3
Spindler Cem—cemetery OH-6
Spindler Ditch—canal (2) IN-6
Spindler Lake MN-6
Spindler Lake—lake MN-6
Spindle Rock—bar NY-2
Spindle Rock—bar WA-9
Spindle Rock—rock MA-1
Spindlers Run—stream VA-3
Spindletop—uninc pl TX-5
Spindletop Bayou—stream TX-5
Spindletop Ditch—canal TX-5
Spindletop Estates—locale KY-4
Spindle Top Hill—summit OK-5
Spindletop Marsh—swamp TX-5
Spindletop Oil Field—oilfield TX-5
Spindle Top Oil Field—oilfield WY-8
Spindletop Sch—school TX-5
Spindle Top Windmill—locale TX-5
Spindletown—locale PA-2
**Spindleville**—pop pl MA-1
Spindleville Pond—reservoir MA-1
Spindleville Pond Dam—dam MA-1
**Spindley City**—pop pl PA-2
Spindlove UT-8
SPINDRIFT SAILING YACHT—hist pl NJ-2
Spine, The—ridge AZ-5
Spine Cob Butte—summit OR-9
Spine Creek—stream CO-8
Spinecup Ridge—ridge CA-9
Spinelli Sch—school CA-9
Spine Mtn—summit AK-9
Spingarn HS—school DC-2
Spink—hist pl IN-6
**Spink**—pop pl SD-7
Spink Barker Ditch—canal ID-8
Spink Canyon—valley CO-8
Spink Cem—cemetery ID-8
**Spink Colony**—pop pl SD-7
Spink County—civil SD-7
Spink Creek—stream AK-9
Spink Farm—hist pl RI-1
Spink Lake—lake AK-9
Spink Neck—cape RI-1
Spink Point—summit MT-8
Spink Ranch—locale WY-8
**Spinks**—pop pl AL-4
**Spinks**—pop pl TN-4
Spinks Brook—stream NY-2
Spinks Canyon—valley CA-9
Spinks Cem—cemetery AL-4
Spinks Cem—cemetery MS-4
Spink Sch—school SD-7
Spinks Chapel (historical)—church AL-4
Spinks Corner—locale CA-9
**Spinks Corners**—pop pl MI-6
Spinks Creek—stream TX-5
**Spinks (historical)**—pop pl MS-4
Spinks Lake TX-5
Spinks Neck RI-1
Spinks P.O. (historical)—building MS-4
Spinks Pond Dam—dam MS-4
Spinks Spur—locale TN-4
**Spink Township**—pop pl SD-7
**Spin Lake**—pop pl IL-6
Spin Lake—reservoir IL-6
Spinnaker Island—island MA-1
Spinnan Lake—lake MN-6
Spinnell Udden (historical)—cape DE-2
Spinner Brook—stream PA-2
Spinner House—hist pl PA-2
Spinner Island—island CA-9
Spinner Park—park AL-4
Spinners Dam—dam UT-8
Spinners Rsvr—reservoir UT-8
Spinners Town PA-2
**Spinnerstown**—pop pl PA-2
**Spinnerville**—pop pl NY-2
Spinnerville Gulf—valley NY-2
Spinnet Lake—lake WI-6
Spinney Brook—stream ME-1
Spinney Ch—church NH-1
Spinney Cove—bay ME-1
Spinney Creek—stream ME-1
Spinney Creek—stream TX-5
Spinney Island—island ME-1
Spinney Mtn—summit CO-8
Spinney Ranch—locale CO-8
Spinning Lake—lake OR-9
Spinning Lake—reservoir OR-9
Spinning Mill Brook—stream (2) CT-1
Spinning Ranch—locale MT-8
Spinning Sch—school WA-9
Spinning Wheel Branch—stream PA-2
Spinningwheel Trail—trail PA-2
Spinnler Point—cape PA-2
Spinola Creek—stream WA-9
Spinola Sch (historical)—school MS-4
Spino Spring—spring OR-9
Spiny Ridge—ridge AK-9
Spio (historical)—locale AL-4
Spion Copp—summit OR-9
Spion Kapp Ditch—canal CO-8
Spion Kop AZ-5
Spion Kop—locale MT-8
Spion Kop—summit ID-8
Spion Kop Creek—stream ID-8
Spion Kop Rock—pillar ID-8
Spipen River WA-9
**Spiral**—pop pl ND-7
Spiral Butte—summit WA-9
Spiral Cave—cave AL-4
Spiral Creek—stream AK-9
Spiral Park—park MN-6
Spirea Creek—stream WY-8
Spire Creek—stream ID-8
Spire Creek—stream WA-9
Spire Glacier—glacier WA-9
Spire Island—island AK-9
Spire Island Reef—bar AK-9
Spire Lake—lake CA-9
Spire Lake—lake WA-9
Spire Mtn—summit MT-8
Spire Mtn—summit WA-9
Spire Point—cliff WA-9
Spire Point—pillar UT-8
Spire Rock—locale MT-8
Spire Rock—pillar AK-9
Spire Rock—pillar OR-9
Spire Rock—summit (2) MT-8
Spire Rock Flats—flat MT-8
Spire Rock Viaduct—other MT-8
Spires—locale IL-6
**Spires**—pop pl IL-6
Spires Cem—cemetery AR-4
Spires Ch—church SC-3
Spires Chapel—church TN-4
Spires Creek—stream ID-8
Spires Creek—stream (2) TX-5
Spires Hollow—valley OH-6
Spires Lake—lake IA-7
Spires Lake—reservoir UT-8
Spires Pond—lake SC-3
Spires Ranch—locale NM-5
Spires Store AL-4
Spiridon Bay—bay AK-9
Spiridon Lake—lake AK-9
Spirit—locale WA-9
**Spirit**—pop pl WI-6
Spirit Branch—stream GA-3
Spirit Brook—stream ME-1
Spirit Canyon SD-7
Spirit Canyon—valley UT-8
Spirit Creek AR-4
Spirit Creek—stream (2) GA-3
Spirit Creek—stream ID-8
Spirit Creek—stream MI-6
Spirit Creek—stream UT-8
Spirit Falls—falls MA-1
Spirit Falls—falls OR-9
**Spirit Falls**—pop pl WI-6
Spirit Gulch—valley CO-8
Spirit Hill—summit OR-9
Spirit Island WA-9
Spirit Island—island (4) MN-6
Spirit Lake MN-6
Spirit Lake—lake AK-9
Spirit Lake—lake AR-4
Spirit Lake—lake CA-9
Spirit Lake—lake CO-8
Spirit Lake—lake FL-3
Spirit Lake—lake ID-8
Spirit Lake—lake IA-7
Spirit Lake—lake (2) MI-6
Spirit Lake—lake (5) MN-6
Spirit Lake—lake NM-5
Spirit Lake—lake (3) OR-9
Spirit Lake—lake SD-7
Spirit Lake—lake UT-8
Spirit Lake—lake (2) WA-9
Spirit Lake—lake (5) WI-6
**Spirit Lake**—pop pl AR-4
**Spirit Lake**—pop pl ID-8
**Spirit Lake**—pop pl IA-7
**Spirit Lake**—pop pl WA-9
Spirit Lake—reservoir UT-8
Spirit Lake-Athol—cens area ID-8
Spirit Lake Campground—park UT-8
Spirit Lake Ch—church SD-7
Spirit Lake Dam—dam UT-8
Spirit Lake Forest Camp—locale WA-9
Spirit Lake Hist Dist—hist pl ID-8
Spirit Lake HS—school IA-7
Spirit Lake Lodge—locale UT-8
Spirit Lake Lodge—locale WA-9
Spirit Lake Massacre Log Cabin—hist pl IA-7
Spirit Lake Public Library—hist pl IA-7
Spirit Lake Ranger Station—locale WA-9
Spirit Lake Sch—school WI-6
Spirit Lake State Game Mngmt Area—park IA-7
Spirit Lake Township—fmr MCD IA-7
**Spirit Lake Township**—pop pl SD-7
Spiritland Cem—cemetery WI-6
Spirit Ledge—bar ME-1
Spirit Mound—hist pl SD-7
Spirit Mound—summit SD-7
Spirit Mound Cem—cemetery SD-7
**Spirit Mound Township**—pop pl SD-7
Spirit Mountain CA-9
Spirit Mountain Caverns—cave WY-8
Spirit Mtn—summit AK-9
Spirit Mtn—summit NV-8
Spirit Mtn—summit OR-9
Spirit Mtn—summit WA-9
Spirit of Saint Louis Airp—airport MO-7
Spirito Santo Bay FL-3
Spirit Park—park WI-6
Spirit Peak—summit UT-8
Spirit Point—cape MN-6
Spirit Pond—lake ME-1
Spirit Range—summit AK-9
Spirit River—stream WI-6
Spirit River Flowage—reservoir WI-6
Spirit Rock Historic Marker—park WI-6
Spirit Sch—school WA-9
Spirits Creek—stream AR-4
Spirit Spring—spring UT-8
Spirit Square—building NC-3
**Spirit (Town of)**—pop pl WI-6
Spiritual Assembly of the Baha'is of Wichita—church KS-7
Spiritual Guidance Society—church FL-3
Spiritualist Cem—cemetery WI-6
Spiritual Power Ch—church (2) AL-4
Spirit Valley—valley ID-8
**Spiritwood**—pop pl ND-7
Spiritwood Cem—cemetery ND-7
Spiritwood Lake—lake ND-7
**Spiritwood Lake**—pop pl ND-7
**Spiritwood Township**—pop pl ND-7
Spiro—locale KY-4
**Spiro**—pop pl OK-5
Spiro (CCD)—cens area OK-5
Spiro Mound Group—hist pl OK-5
Spiro Tunnel—mine UT-8
Spirt Island—island ME-1
Spirt Lake Cem—cemetery SD-7
Spiry Place—locale ID-8
Spit, The DE-2
Spit, The—bar AL-4
Spit, The—cape NC-3
Spit Bay—bay NC-3
Spit Brook—stream NH-1
Spit Cove MS-4
Spite House—hist pl ME-1
Spitfire Lake—lake NY-2
Spithaler Sch—school PA-2
Spithead Towhead—area MS-4
Spit House NC-3
Spitler, Samuel, House—hist pl OH-6
Spitler Ditch—canal IN-6
Spitler Hill—summit VA-3
Spitler Knoll Overlook—locale VA-3
**Spitler (Long) (Longs Store)**—pop pl VA-3
Spitler Peak—summit CA-9
Spitler Sch—school PA-2
Spitlers Creek IN-6
Spitler Woods State Park—park IL-6
Spitlog MO-7
Spit Neck—cape MD-2
Spitover, The—other AK-9
Spit Point—cape AK-9
Spit Point—cape MD-2
Spitt, The DE-2
Spitz, Berthold, House—hist pl NM-5
Spitzbergen Marsh—swamp MI-6
Spitzberg Hill—summit PA-2
Spitzburg Hill PA-2
**Spitzenberg**—pop pl OR-9
Spitzenberg Hill—summit PA-2
Spitzenberg Mtn—summit NY-2
Spitzenberg Spring—spring UT-8
Spitzenburg OR-9
Spitzer and Sons Airp—airport ND-7
Spitzer Bldg—hist pl OH-6
Spitzer Cem—cemetery OH-6
Spitzer Cem—cemetery TN-4
Spitzer Lake—lake MN-6
Spitzer Lake—reservoir CO-8
Spitz Gulch CO-8
Spitz Hill—summit AZ-5
Spitzi Creek—stream WY-8
Spitzie Bottom—bend CO-8
Spitzie Draw—valley CO-8
Spitzie Place—locale CO-8
Spitzie Spring—spring CO-8
Spitz Island—island AK-9
Spitzi Spring—spring WY-8
Spitznagel Cemetery AL-4
Spitznagl Cem—cemetery AL-4
Spitznogle Lake—lake IA-7
Spitz Spring—spring AZ-5
Spitz Spring Overpass—crossing AZ-5
Spitz Spring Underpass—crossing AZ-5
Spiva Branch—stream GA-3
Spiva Butte—summit WA-9
Spivak—locale CO-8
Spiva Park—park MO-7
Spivey TN-4
Spivey—locale TN-4
**Spivey**—pop pl FL-3
**Spivey**—pop pl KS-7
Spivey, Lake—reservoir GA-3
Spivey-Baxter Cem—cemetery TX-5
Spivey Branch—stream KY-4
Spivey Cem—cemetery MO-7
Spivey Cem—cemetery NC-3
Spivey Cem—cemetery (2) TN-4
Spivey Cem—cemetery TX-5
Spivey Cem—cemetery VA-3
Spivey Ch—church TN-4
Spivey Cove Rec Area—park TN-4
Spivey Creek—stream AL-4
Spivey Creek—stream (2) TN-4
Spivey Crossing—locale TX-5
Spivey Falls—falls TN-4
Spivey Ford—locale VA-3
Spivey Gap—gap (2) NC-3
**Spivey Hill Siding**—pop pl NC-3
Spivey Hollow—valley TN-4
Spivey Lake—lake AR-4
Spivey Lake—lake FL-3
Spivey Lake—reservoir NC-3
Spivey Mill—locale VA-3
Spivey Mill Creek—stream AL-4
Spivey Mtn—summit NC-3
Spivey Pond—reservoir AL-4
Spivey Post Office TN-4
Spiveys Cem—cemetery SC-3
Spivey Sch—school KY-4
Spivey Sch—school TN-4
Spiveys Corner NC-3
**Spiveys Corner**—pop pl NC-3
Spivey Site—hist pl MS-4
Spiveys Millpond—reservoir SC-3
**Spivey Store**—pop pl VA-3
Spivey Swamp—stream VA-3
Spivey Tabernacle—church AL-4
Spivy Twin Pits—cave AL-4
Splain Coulee—valley MT-8
Splains Gulch—valley CO-8
S P Lakes—reservoir CA-9
Splane Place—uninc pl LA-4
Splan Springs—spring MT-8
Splash Dam—dam (3) PA-2
Splash Dam—locale PA-2
Splashdam—locale VA-3
**Splashdam, (Splash Dam)**—pop pl VA-3
Splashdam Ch—church VA-3
Splash Dam Hollow—valley (2) PA-2
Splashdam Hollow—valley WV-2
Splash Dam Lake—lake UT-8
Splash Dam Pond—reservoir (2) PA-2
Splash Dam Run—stream PA-2
Splash Dam Trail—trail PA-2
Splashing Water Canyon—valley AZ-5
Splash Lake—lake MN-6
Splatter Branch—stream KY-4
Splatter Branch—stream TN-4
Splatter Canyon—valley UT-8
Splatter Creek—stream TN-4
Splatter Drip Canyon—valley UT-8
Splawn—locale TX-5
Splawn Branch—stream AL-4
Splawn Mtn—summit CA-9
Splawn Mtn—summit WA-9
Splawn Ridge Sch (abandoned)—school MO-7
**Splendora**—pop pl TX-5
Splendora Cem—cemetery TX-5
Splendora Oil Field—oilfield TX-5
Spletts Creek—stream ID-8
Splettstosser Ranch—locale ID-8
Splice Creek—stream MO-7
Splice Creek Ch—church MO-7
Splice Island—island LA-4
Splice Island Chute—stream LA-4
Splinler MS-4
**Splinter**—pop pl MS-4
Splinterback Ch—church MS-4
Splinter Brook—stream ME-1
Splintercat Creek—stream OR-9
Splinter Creek—stream MS-4
Splinter Creek—stream WI-6
Splinter Post Office (historical)—building MS-4
Splinter Ridge—ridge IN-6
Splinter Ridge Cem—cemetery IN-6
Splinter Ridge Sch—school IN-6
Splinter Sch (historical)—school MS-4
Splint Sch—school KY-4
Split, Cape—cape ME-1
Split, The—lake GA-3
Split Branch—stream TN-4
Split Brook—stream (2) ME-1
Split Butte—summit (3) ID-8
Split Butte Lake—lake ID-8
Split Chestnut Hollow—valley TN-4
Split Creek—stream (3) AK-9
Split Creek—stream (3) ID-8
Split Creek—stream UT-8
Split Creek—stream WA-9
Split Creek Bridge—bridge ID-8
Split Creek Point—cliff ID-8
Split Creek Point—summit ID-8
Split Creek Ridge—ridge ID-8
Split Ear Spring—spring WY-8
Split Falls—falls OR-9
Split Fork—stream WV-2
Split Gap—gap TN-4
Split Glacier—glacier AK-9
Split Hand Creek—stream MN-6
Split Hand Lake—reservoir MN-6
**Splithand (Township of)**—pop pl MN-6
**Split Hill**—pop pl ME-1
Split Hill—summit WY-8
Split Island—island AK-9
Split Island—island MI-6
Split Lake—lake CA-9
Split Lake—lake NE-7
Split Level Ruin—locale UT-8
Split Limb Sch—school MO-7
Split Lip Flats—flat NM-5
**Splitlog**—pop pl MO-7
Splitlog Branch—stream KY-4
Split Log Branch—stream KY-4
Splitlog Church—hist pl OK-5
Splitlog Hollow—valley MO-7
Split Log Spring—spring SD-7
Split Mesa—summit NM-5
Split Mountain Campground UT-8
Split Mountain Canyon—valley UT-8
Split Mountain Gorge Campground—locale UT-8
Split Mountain Landing—airport UT-8
Split Mountain Overlook—locale UT-8
Split Mtn—summit (3) CA-9
Split Mtn—summit (2) MT-8
Split Mtn—summit NV-8
Split Mtn—summit NC-3
Split Mtn—summit (2) TX-5
Split Mtn—summit UT-8
Split Mtn—summit WY-8
Split Oak Spring—spring CA-9
Splitoff, The—summit WA-9
Split Peak—summit NV-8
Split Peaks NV-8
Split Peak Windmill—locale TX-5
Split Pine Hollow—valley NV-8
Split Pine Hollow—valley UT-8
Split Pine Spring—spring SD-7
Split Pinnacle—pillar CA-9
Split Pit—cave TN-4
Split Point—cape AK-9
Split Point—cape MD-2
Split Point—cape UT-8
Split Poplar Fork—stream KY-4
Split Ridge—ridge NV-8
Split Road Lake—lake ID-8
Split Rock—bar AK-9
Split Rock—cliff AL-4
Split Rock—cliff CA-9
Split Rock—island CA-9
Split Rock—island WA-9
Split Rock—other CA-9
Split Rock—pillar (3) CA-9
Split Rock—pillar ID-8
Split Rock—pillar KY-4
Split Rock—pillar OR-9
Split Rock—pillar PA-2
**Split Rock**—pop pl NY-2
**Split Rock**—pop pl PA-2
**Split Rock**—pop pl WI-6
Split Rock—rock MA-1
Split Rock—summit AZ-5
Split Rock—summit (3) CA-9
Split Rock—summit CO-8
Split Rock—summit CT-1
Split Rock—summit ID-8
Split Rock—summit (2) WY-8
Split Rock, Twin Peaks—hist pl WY-8
Split Rock Bay—bay UT-8
Split Rock Canyon—valley AZ-5
Splitrock Canyon—valley CA-9
Split Rock Canyon—valley ID-8
Split Rock Canyon—valley WY-8
Split Rock Ch—church SD-7
Split Rock County Park—park IA-7
Split Rock Cove—bay RI-1
Split Rock Creek—stream CA-9
Split Rock Creek—stream MN-6
Split Rock Creek—stream MT-8
Split Rock Creek—stream OR-9
Split Rock Creek—stream SD-7
Split Rock Creek—stream WI-6
Split Rock Creek—stream (2) WY-8
Split Rock Creek State Park—park MN-6
Split Rock Falls—falls NY-2
Split Rock Furnace—hist pl NJ-2
Split Rock Gulf—stream NY-2
**Split Rock Heights (subdivision)**—pop pl SD-7
Split Rock (historical)—locale SD-7
Split Rock Junction—locale MT-8
Split Rock Lake—lake IL-6
Split Rock Lake—lake MN-6
Split Rock Lake—lake MT-8
Split Rock Lake—lake NY-2
Split Rock Lake—reservoir IA-7
Split Rock Lake—reservoir MN-6
Split Rock Lake Dam—dam IA-7
Split Rock Lighthouse—hist pl MN-6
Split Rock Lighthouse—locale MN-6
Split Rock Lutheran Church SD-7
Split Rock Mountain Pit—cave AL-4
Split Rock Mtn AL-4
Splitrock Mtn—summit AL-4
Split Rock Mtn—summit (2) NY-2
Split Rock Park—park SD-7
Split Rock Point—cape AL-4
Splitrock Point—cape AK-9
Split Rock Point—cape MN-6
Split Rock Point—cape (2) NY-2
Splitrock Pond NJ-2
Split Rock Pond—lake ME-1
Split Rock Pond—lake NY-2
Splitrock Pond Dam—dam NJ-2
Split Rock Prehistoric Site (48FR1484)—hist pl WY-8
Split Rock Ranch—locale WY-8
Split Rock Rapids—rapids ID-8
Split Rock Ridge—ridge NY-2
Split Rock Ridge—ridge NC-3
Split Rock Rips—rapids ME-1
Split Rock River—stream MN-6
Splitrock Rsvr—reservoir NJ-2
Split Rock Ruin (LA 5664)—hist pl NM-5
Split Rock Run—stream WV-2
Split Rock Sch—school NY-2
Split Rock Sch—school WY-8
Split Rock (ski area)—locale PA-2
Splitrock Spring—spring CA-9
Split Rock Spring—spring MT-8
Split Rock Spring—spring WY-8
Split Rock Tank—reservoir NM-5
**Split Rock Township**—pop pl SD-7
**Split Rock (Township of)**—pop pl MN-6
Split Rsvr—reservoir MT-8
Splits, The—other AK-9
Splits Creek—stream SD-7
Splits Hole—cave AL-4
Split Silk—locale GA-3
Split Spring—spring UT-8
Split Tank—reservoir (8) AZ-5
Split Tank—reservoir NM-5
Split Tank—reservoir TX-5
Split Thumb—summit AK-9
Split Thumb Icefall—other AK-9
Splitting Knife—bar MA-1
Splitting Knife Channel Range Light—locale MA-1
Split Top—summit AK-9
Split Top—summit ID-8
Split Top Mtn—summit AK-9
Split Tree Branch—stream WV-2
Split Tree Rsvr—reservoir OR-9
Split Trough Spring—spring CO-8
Split Whiteoak Branch—stream NC-3
Split Whiteoak Gap—gap NC-3
Split Whiteoak Ridge—ridge NC-3
Splitwood Branch—stream KY-4
Splitwood Branch—stream TN-4
S P Lookout—locale CA-9
**Splunge**—pop pl MS-4
Splunge Baptist Church MS-4
Splunge Ch—church MS-4
Splunge Creek—stream AL-4
Splunge Creek—stream IN-6
Splunge Creek—stream (2) MS-4
Splunge Lookout Tower—locale MS-4
S P Mtn—summit AZ-5
Spocari—locale AL-4
Spodue Mtn—summit OR-9
Spoede Sch—school MO-7
Spofford—locale OR-9
**Spofford**—pop pl NH-1
**Spofford**—pop pl TX-5
Spofford-Barnes House—hist pl MA-1
Spofford Gap—gap NH-1
Spofford Hill—summit TX-5
Spofford Lake—lake NH-1
**Spofford Lake**—pop pl NH-1
Spofford Pond—lake MA-1

Spofford Ridge—*ridge* ME-1
Spofford Sch—*school* MA-1
*Spoffords Pond* MA-1
Spogett Bay—*swamp* MS-4
Spogie Ditch—*canal* KS-7
Spohn Canal—*canal* NE-7
Spohn Hosp—*hospital* TX-5
*Spohn Middle School* IN-6
Spohn Ranch—*locale* TX-5
Spohrer Cem—*cemetery* MO-7
Spohr Mine—*mine* NV-8
Spoilcane Creek—*stream* GA-3
Spoil Island—*island* TX-5
Spokage Creek—*stream* AL-4
Spokana Gulch—*valley* WA-9
Spokane—*locale* SD-7
**Spokane**—*pop pl* LA-4
**Spokane**—*pop pl* MO-7
**Spokane**—*pop pl* NC-3
**Spokane**—*pop pl* OH-6
**Spokane**—*pop pl* WA-9
Spokane, Mount—*summit* WA-9
**Spokane, Portland & Seattle Junction**—*pop pl* WA-9
Spokane Bar—*bar* MT-8
Spokane Battlefield State Park—*park* WA-9
Spokane Bridge—*locale* WA-9
Spokane (CCD)—*cens area* WA-9
Spokane City Hall Bldg—*hist pl* WA-9
Spokane Community Coll—*school* WA-9
Spokane Country Club—*other* WA-9
**Spokane County**—*pop pl* WA-9
Spokane County Courthouse—*hist pl* WA-9
Spokane Cove—*bay* AK-9
Spokane Creek—*stream* AK-9
Spokane Creek—*stream* (2) MT-8
Spokane Creek—*stream* OR-9
Spokane Creek—*stream* SD-7
Spokane Creek Sch—*school* MT-8
Spokane Evergreen Cem—*cemetery* WA-9
Spokane Falls—*falls* WA-9
Spokane Falls Community Coll—*school* WA-9
Spokane Flour Mill—*hist pl* WA-9
Spokane Hills—*range* MT-8
Spokane House Historic Site—*locale* WA-9
**Spokane Ind Res**—*pop pl* WA-9
Spokane Industrial Park—*locale* WA-9
Spokane International Airp—*airport* WA-9
Spokane Junior Acad—*school* WA-9
Spokane Meadows—*flat* ID-8
Spokane Memorial Gardens Cem—*cemetery* WA-9
Spokane Mine—*mine* SD-7
Spokane Mine—*mine* WA-9
Spokane Molybdenum Mine—*mine* WA-9
Spokane Mount—*summit* WA-9
Spokane Mtn—*summit* WA-9
Spokane Point—*cape* ID-8
Spokane Public Library—*hist pl* WA-9
Spokane Ranch—*locale* MT-8
Spokane Reservation (CCD)—*cens area* WA-9
Spokane River—*stream* ID-8
Spokane River—*stream* WA-9
Spokane State Game Farm—*other* WA-9
Spokane Valley—*valley* WA-9
Spokane Valley Hosp—*hospital* WA-9
Spoke Factory Sch (abandoned)—*school* PA-2
Spokelay Ch (historical)—*church* TN-4
Spokelay Sch (historical)—*school* TN-4
Spoken Word Christian Sch—*school* FL-3
Spoken Word Church-Apostolic Faith—*church* FL-3
Spoke Pile Creek—*stream* TX-5
Spoke Plant—*locale* AR-4
Spoke Plant Hollow—*valley* AR-4
Spoke Run—*stream* IN-6
Spokes Hill—*summit* WI-6
Spokeville—*locale* WI-6
Spoll Cem—*cemetery* MS-4
Spomer Lakes—*reservoir* CO-8
Sponable Creek—*stream* NY-2
Sponable Gully—*valley* NY-2
Sponcil Hollow—*valley* KY-4
Sponenbergh Creek—*stream* WA-9
Sponge Crawl Creek—*stream* FL-3
*Sponge Creek* IN-6
Sponge Creek—*stream* ID-8
Sponge Creek—*stream* OR-9
Sponge Creek Camp—*locale* OR-9
Sponge Exchange (Shop Ctr)—*locale* FL-3
Sponge Harbor Point—*cape* FL-3
Sponge Lake—*lake* ID-8
Sponge Meadows—*flat* ID-8
Sponge Mtn—*summit* ID-8
Sponge Point—*cape* FL-3
**Sponge Rocks**—*pop pl* FL-3
Sponge Spring—*spring* OR-9
Spongs Bar—*bar* OR-9
Spong Sch—*school* VA-3
Spongs Landing—*locale* OR-9
Sponsa State Wildlife Mngmt Area—*park* MN-6
Sponseller—*locale* AZ-5
Sponseller Ditch—*canal* OH-6
Sponseller Lake—*lake* AZ-5
Sponseller Mtn—*summit* AZ-5
Sponseller Tank—*reservoir* AZ-5
Sponsel Rsvr—*reservoir* CO-8
**Sponsler**—*pop pl* IN-6
Sponyers Knob—*summit* OH-6
Spook Canyon—*valley* AZ-5
Spook Canyon—*valley* CA-9
Spook Canyon—*valley* NE-7
Spook Cave—*cave* AL-4
Spook Cave—*cave* IA-7
Spook City—*locale* CO-8
Spook Creek—*stream* ID-8
Spook Creek—*stream* SD-7
Spook Hill—*summit* AZ-5
Spook Hill—*summit* MD-2
Spook Hill—*summit* NM-5
Spook Hill—*summit* PA-2
Spook Hill Dam—*dam* AZ-5
Spook Hill Rec Area—*park* AZ-5
Spook Hollow—*valley* (2) PA-2
Spook Island—*island* AK-9
*Spook Lake* WI-6
Spook Lake—*lake* (2) MT-8
Spook Rock—*summit* NY-2
Spook Run—*stream* PA-2
Spooks Branch—*stream* NC-3
Spooks Knoll Rsvr—*reservoir* AZ-5
Spook Swamp—*swamp* PA-2
Spook Tank—*reservoir* AZ-5
Spook Woods—*woods* NY-2
Spooky Bay Creek—*bay* WI-6
Spooky Brook Dam—*dam* NJ-2
Spooky Brook Pond—*reservoir* NJ-2
Spooky Butte—*summit* ID-8
Spooky Canyon—*valley* ID-8
Spooky Hollow—*valley* KY-4
Spooky Meadow—*flat* CA-9
Spooky Mtn—*summit* CO-8
Spooky Valley—*basin* AK-9
Spooler Swamp—*swamp* SC-3
Spoolsville—*locale* MD-2
Spoonamore Canyon—*valley* WA-9
Spoonamore Creek—*stream* TX-5
Spoon Bay—*bay* NY-2
Spoonbill—*locale* CA-9
Spoonbill Bay—*lake* LA-4
Spoonbill Creek—*stream* CA-9
Spoonbill Pass State Public Shooting Area—*park* SD-7
Spoon Branch—*stream* KY-4
Spoon Branch—*stream* MO-7
Spoon Butte—*summit* WY-8
Spoon Cem—*cemetery* OH-6
Spoon Creek—*stream* AK-9
Spoon Creek—*stream* IL-6
Spoon Creek—*stream* KS-7
Spoon Creek—*stream* MT-8
Spoon Creek—*stream* OH-6
Spoon Creek—*stream* (2) OR-9
Spoon Creek—*stream* UT-8
Spoon Creek—*stream* VA-3
Spoon Creek—*stream* WA-9
Spoon Creek—*stream* WI-6
Spoon Creek—*stream* WY-8
Spoon Creek Ch—*church* (2) VA-3
Spoon Draw—*valley* TX-5
Spooner—*locale* GA-3
**Spooner**—*pop pl* MN-6
**Spooner**—*pop pl* WI-6
Spooner—*uninc pl* TX-5
Spooner Branch—*stream* AR-4
Spooner Brook—*stream* NY-2
Spooner Corners—*locale* NY-2
*Spooner Creek* MT-8
Spooner Creek—*stream* CA-9
Spooner Creek—*stream* (2) MT-8
Spooner Creek—*stream* NY-2
Spooner Creek—*stream* NC-3
Spooner Creek—*stream* WI-6
Spooner Ditch—*canal* IA-7
Spooner Flat—*flat* NY-2
Spooner Hall, Univ of Kansas—*hist pl* KS-7
Spooner Hill—*summit* (2) CT-1
Spooner Hill—*summit* NH-1
Spooner Hill—*summit* VT-1
Spooner Hollow—*valley* UT-8
Spooner Junction—*locale* NV-8
Spooner Lake—*lake* WI-6
Spooner Lake—*reservoir* NV-8
Spooner Point—*cape* ME-1
Spooner Pond—*lake* MA-1
Spooner Public Sch—*hist pl* MN-6
Spooner Ridge—*ridge* OR-9
Spooner Rsvr—*reservoir* CA-9
**Spooners Creek East Harbor (subdivision)**—*pop pl* NC-3
**Spooners Creek Harbor (subdivision)**—*pop pl* NC-3
Spooners Creek Marina—*building* NC-3
**Spooners Creek North (subdivision)**—*pop pl* NC-3
Spooner Slough—*lake* MN-6
Spooners Mesa—*summit* CA-9
**Spooners Mill**—*pop pl* ME-1
*Spooners Pond* MA-1
Spooner Springs—*spring* GA-3
Spooner Summit—*gap* NV-8
**Spooner (Town of)**—*pop pl* WI-6
Spooner Trough Canyon—*valley* CA-9
Spoonerville—*locale* VT-1
Spoonerville Cem—*cemetery* VT-1
Spoon Fish Lake—*lake* AK-9
Spoon Gap Ch—*church* VA-3
Spoon Gap Creek—*stream* VA-3
Spoon Gap Hollow—*valley* VA-3
Spoon Glacier—*glacier* AK-9
Spoonhead, Mount—*summit* AZ-5
*Spoonhead Butte* AZ-5
Spoon Hill—*summit* MA-1
Spoon Hill—*summit* NY-2
Spoon Hollow—*valley* MO-7
Spoon Hollow—*valley* TN-4
Spoon Hollow—*valley* WV-2
Spoon Lake—*lake* AR-4
Spoon Lake—*lake* MN-6
Spoon Lake—*lake* MT-8
Spoon Lake—*lake* NY-2
Spoon Lake—*lake* OR-9
Spoon Ledge—*bar* ME-1
Spoon Mine—*mine* CA-9
Spoon Mtn—*summit* ME-1
Spoon Mtn—*summit* NV-8
Spoon Mtn—*summit* VT-1
Spoon Mtn—*summit* VA-3
Spoon Ravine—*valley* CA-9
Spoon River—*stream* (2) IL-6
Spoon River—*stream* (2) OH-6
Spoon River Junior Coll—*school* IL-6
Spoon River Valley HS—*school* IL-6
Spoons Chapel—*church* NC-3
*Spoonseller Tank* AZ-5
Spoon Shop Brook—*stream* CT-1
Spoon Spring—*spring* (2) MO-7
Spoon Spring—*spring* OR-9
Spoon Spring—*spring* WA-9
*Spoon Springs* OR-9
Spoon Tank—*reservoir* AZ-5
Spoonville Bridge—*bridge* CT-1
Spoonville Site—*hist pl* MI-6
Spoonwood Pond—*lake* NH-1
Spoor Canyon—*valley* (2) CA-9
Spoor Hollow—*valley* PA-2
Spoor Sch—*school* WI-6
Spoos Mill—*locale* OR-9
**Spore**—*pop pl* OH-6
Spores, Jacob C., House—*hist pl* OR-9
Spores Creek—*stream* OR-9
**Spores (historical)**—*pop pl* OR-9
Spores Point—*cape* OR-9
Spori Canyon—*valley* ID-8
Sporley Lake—*lake* MI-6
Spor Mtn—*summit* UT-8
*Spors Mountain* UT-8
Sport Creek—*stream* MT-8
Sportfish Lake—*lake* AK-9
Sport Haven Landing—*locale* AR-4
Sport Hill—*locale* PA-2
**Sport Hill**—*pop pl* CT-1
Sport Hill—*summit* CT-1
Sport Hill Sch Number 9—*school* SD-7
**Sporting Hill**—*pop pl* (2) PA-2
Sporting Hill—*summit* NY-2
Sporting Hill Elem Sch—*school* PA-2
Sporting Hill Post Office (historical)—*building* PA-2
Sporting Hill Sch—*school* PA-2
Sport Lake—*lake* WI-6
Sportland Park—*park* IN-6
Sportman Dam—*dam* MT-8
*Sportman Dock* TN-4
Sportman Lake—*reservoir* AL-4
Sport Point—*cape* OH-6
Sports—*locale* AL-4
**Sport Sales Plaza Subdivision**—*pop pl* UT-8
Sports Arena—*building* CA-9
Sports Bldg—*hist pl* CT-1
**Sportsburg**—*pop pl* PA-2
Sportshaven—*locale* CA-9
Sports Lake—*lake* AK-9
Sports Lake—*reservoir* IN-6
Sports Lake—*reservoir* VA-3
Sports Lake Dam—*dam* IN-6
Sportsman Airpark—*airport* OR-9
Sportsman Center—*locale* WI-6
Sportsman Club—*locale* MA-1
Sportsman Club Lake—*reservoir* (2) KY-4
Sportsman Club Lake Dam—*dam* (3) MS-4
Sportsman Club Park—*park* WI-6
Sportsman Country Club—*other* IL-6
Sportsman Creek—*stream* CA-9
Sportsman Dock—*locale* TN-4
Sportsman Glade—*flat* CA-9
*Sportsman Lake* KY-4
Sportsman Lake—*lake* CA-9
Sportsman Lake—*lake* IL-6
Sportsman Lake—*lake* LA-4
Sportsman Lake—*lake* MO-7
Sportsman Lake—*lake* MT-8
Sportsman Lake—*lake* WY-8
**Sportsman Lake**—*pop pl* IL-6
Sportsman Lake—*reservoir* (3) IL-6
Sportsman Lake—*reservoir* IA-7
Sportsman Lake—*reservoir* (3) KY-4
Sportsman Lake—*reservoir* (2) MS-4
Sportsman Lake—*reservoir* (2) OK-5
Sportsman Lake—*reservoir* VA-3
Sportsman Lake Dam—*dam* AL-4
Sportsman Lake Dam—*dam* MS-4
Sportsman Lakes—*reservoir* OR-9
Sportsman Lake Trail—*trail* MT-8
Sportsman Lake Trail—*trail* WY-8
Sportsman Lodge—*locale* AK-9
Sportsman Lodge—*locale* CO-8
Sportsman Marina—*locale* AL-4
Sportsman Paradise County Campground—*locale* NV-8
Sportsman Park—*building* OH-6
Sportsman Park—*park* IA-7
Sportsman Park—*park* (2) MN-6
Sportsman Park—*park* MS-4
Sportsman Park—*park* PA-2
Sportsman Park—*park* TX-5
Sportsman Park—*park* WA-9
Sportsman Park—*park* WI-6
Sportsman Park Racetrack—*other* IA-7
Sportsman Patrol Cabin—*locale* MT-8
Sportsman Pond—*lake* WA-9
Sportsman Pond—*reservoir* LA-4
Sportsman Pond—*reservoir* NH-1
Sportsman Pond—*stream* SC-3
Sportsman Pond—*swamp* SC-3
Sportsman Ranch—*locale* CA-9
Sportsman Ridge—*ridge* WY-8
Sportsmans Club Lake—*reservoir* IN-6
Sportsmans Club Lake Dam—*dam* IN-6
*Sportsmans Golf Course* PA-2
Sportsman Shop Dock—*locale* TN-4
*Sportsman's Lake* WA-9
Sportsmans Lake—*lake* WA-9
Sportsmans Lake—*reservoir* KS-7
Sportsmans Lake—*reservoir* PA-2
Sportsmans Lake—*reservoir* TN-4
*Sportsmans Lake Dam* AL-4
Sportsmans Lake Dam—*dam* TN-4
Sportsmans Park Drag Strip—*locale* NC-3
Sportsmans Park Fish Camp—*locale* AL-4
Sportsmans Park Racetrack—*other* IL-6
Sportsmans Pond—*reservoir* MA-1
Sportsmans Pond Dam—*dam* MA-1
Sportsman Spring—*spring* NV-8
**Sportsmans Village (subdivision)**—*pop pl* NC-3
**Sportsmen Acres**—*pop pl* OK-5
Sportsmen Club—*other* IN-6
Sportsmen Club Dam—*dam* AL-4
Sportsmen Club Dan—*dam* MA-1
Sportsmen Club Lake—*reservoir* AL-4
Sportsmen Club Lake Dam—*dam* AL-4
Sportsmen Dam—*dam* MI-6
Sportsmen Lake—*lake* MI-6
Sportsmen Outdoor Chapel—*church* MO-7
Sportsmen Park—*park* MN-6
Sportsmens Gun Club—*other* CA-9
**Sportsmens Paradise**—*pop pl* KY-4
Sportsmens Park—*flat* OH-6
Sportsmens Park—*park* ID-8
Sports Run—*stream* IN-6
Sport Valley—*valley* WI-6
Sport Valley Creek—*stream* WI-6
**Spot**—*pop pl* NC-3
**Spot**—*pop pl* TN-4
Spot Canyon—*valley* NV-8
Spot Cem—*cemetery* TN-4
Spot Ch—*church* TN-4
Spot Creek—*stream* CA-9
Spot Creek—*stream* (2) OR-9
Spot Hollow—*valley* OH-6
Spot Hollow—*valley* (2) TN-4
Spotico Creek—*stream* VA-3
Spot Interchange—*crossing* AZ-5
Spot Knob—*summit* NC-3
Spot Lake—*lake* (4) MI-6
Spot Lake—*lake* (3) MN-6
Spot Lake—*lake* WI-6
Spotlight Well—*well* NV-8
Spot Meadow Brook—*stream* NH-1
Spot Mill Creek—*stream* SC-3
**Spot Mobile Home Park**—*pop pl* PA-2
Spot Mtn—*summit* AK-9
Spot Mtn—*summit* ID-8
Spot Mtn—*summit* MT-8
Spot Pond—*lake* MA-1
Spot Pond Brook—*stream* MA-1
Spot Post Office (historical)—*building* TN-4
Spotsa Swamp—*swamp* MA-1
Spots Branch—*stream* FL-3
Spots Branch—*stream* TN-4
Spot Sch (historical)—*school* TN-4
Spots Point—*cape* ME-1
**Spotswood**—*pop pl* NJ-2
Spotswood Ch—*church* VA-3
Spotswood Country Club—*other* VA-3
Spotswood Furnace Ruins—*locale* VA-3
Spotswood (Magisterial District)—*fmr MCD* VA-3
**Spotswood Manor**—*pop pl* NJ-2
Spotswood Mine—*mine* CA-9
Spotswood Sch—*school* (2) VA-3
**Spotsylvania**—*pop pl* VA-3
**Spotsylvania (County)**—*pop pl* VA-3
Spotsylvania Court House Hist Dist—*hist pl* VA-3
Spotsylvania Lookout Tower—*locale* VA-3
Spot Taylor Sch—*school* TX-5
*Spotted Bear Creek* SD-7
Spotted Bear Creek—*stream* SD-7
Spotted Bear Lake—*lake* MT-8
Spotted Bear Mountain Trail—*trail* MT-8
Spotted Bear Mtn—*summit* MT-8
Spotted Bear Pass—*gap* MT-8
Spotted Bear Ranger Station—*locale* MT-8
Spotted Bear River—*stream* MT-8
Spotted Bear River Trail—*trail* MT-8
Spotted Bear Schafer Trail—*trail* MT-8
Spotted Buck Mtn—*summit* WA-9
*Spotted Creek* MT-8
Spotted Creek—*stream* WA-9
Spotted Deer Creek—*stream* OK-5
Spotted Deer Mtn—*summit* WA-9
Spotted Dog Creek—*stream* MT-8
Spotted Eagle Lake—*reservoir* MT-8
Spotted Eagle Mission (historical)—*church* SD-7
Spotted Eagle Mtn—*summit* MT-8
Spotted Elk Creek—*stream* MT-8
Spotted Fawn Canyon—*valley* UT-8
Spotted Fawn Lake—*lake* CA-9
Spotted Fawn Mine—*mine* OR-9
Spotted Glacier—*glacier* AK-9
Spotted Horn—*locale* ND-7
Spotted Horn Creek—*stream* ND-7
Spotted Horse—*locale* WY-8
Spotted Horse Creek—*stream* WY-8
Spotted Horse Mine—*mine* MT-8
Spotted Horse Valley—*basin* NE-7
Spotted Lake—*lake* CO-8
Spotted Lakes—*lake* CA-9
Spotted Louis Creek—*stream* ID-8
Spotted Louis Point—*summit* ID-8
Spotted Mountain Tank—*reservoir* AZ-5
Spotted Mtn—*summit* AZ-5
Spotted Mtn—*summit* ME-1
Spotted Mtn—*summit* NY-2
Spotted Oak Canyon—*valley* TX-5
Spotted Oak Spring—*spring* TX-5
Spotted Range—*range* NV-8
*Spotted Ridge* CA-9
Spotted Robe—*locale* MT-8
Spotted Rock—*pillar* CA-9
Spotted Spruce Mtn—*summit* ME-1
Spotted Tail Campground—*locale* NE-7
Spotted Tail Cem—*cemetery* NE-7
Spotted Tail Cem—*cemetery* SD-7
Spottedtail Community Hall—*locale* NE-7
Spotted Tail Coulee—*valley* MT-8
Spotted Tail Creek—*stream* NE-7
Spottedtail Creek—*stream* NE-7
Spotted Tail Gravesite—*hist pl* SD-7
Spotted Tail Picnic Ground—*locale* WY-8
Spottedtail Run—*stream* PA-2
Spottedtail Run—*stream* WV-2
Spotted Tail Sch—*school* NE-7
Spotted Tank—*reservoir* NM-5
Spottedtrail Gulch—*valley* WY-8
Spotted Wolf Canyon—*valley* UT-8
Spottlewood Creek—*stream* CO-8
Spottlewood Creek—*stream* WY-8
Spotts Cem—*cemetery* AR-4
Spotts Gulch—*valley* MT-8
Spotts Knob—*summit* PA-2
Spotts Park—*park* TX-5
Spotts Ridge—*ridge* WV-2
Spotts Round Barn—*hist pl* IA-7
**Spottsville**—*pop pl* KY-4
Spottsville (CCD)—*cens area* KY-4
Spottswood—*locale* SD-7
**Spottswood**—*pop pl* VA-3
Spottswood Sch—*school* VA-3
*Spottsylvania* VA-3
**Spotville**—*pop pl* AR-4
Spotwood Creek—*stream* CO-8
Spotwood Creek—*stream* WY-8
Spout Creek—*stream* ID-8
Spout Creek—*stream* OR-9
*Spouting Cave* RI-1
Spouting Horn—*cape* MA-1
Spouting Horn Park—*park* HI-9
Spouting Rock—*pillar* RI-1
Spouting Spring—*spring* WY-8
Spouting Spring Branch—*stream* AL-4
Spout Lake—*lake* CO-8
Spout Run—*stream* (3) VA-3
Spout Shoal—*bar* ME-1
Spout Spr Hollow—*valley* MO-7
Spout Spring—*locale* VA-3
Spout Spring—*spring* (7) AL-4
Spout Spring—*spring* AZ-5
Spout Spring—*spring* AR-4
Spout Spring—*spring* CA-9
Spout Spring—*spring* IN-6
Spout Spring—*spring* KY-4
Spout Spring—*spring* (6) MO-7
Spout Spring—*spring* (2) OR-9
Spout Spring—*spring* (11) TN-4
Spout Spring—*spring* VA-3
Spout Spring—*spring* WA-9
Spout Spring Branch—*stream* MS-4
Spout Spring Branch—*stream* SC-3
Spout Spring Branch—*stream* (2) TN-4
Spout Spring Cave—*cave* MO-7
Spout Spring Crossroads—*locale* GA-3
Spout Spring Gap—*gap* AL-4
Spout Spring Hill—*summit* TN-4
Spout Spring Hollow—*valley* AL-4
Spout Spring Hollow—*valley* MO-7
Spout Spring Hollow—*valley* (2) TN-4
Spoutspring Post Office (historical)—*building* TN-4
Spout Springs—*locale* KY-4
Spout Springs—*locale* TN-4
**Spout Springs**—*pop pl* NC-3
Spout Springs—*spring* OR-9
Spout Springs—*spring* WY-8
Spout Springs Branch—*stream* KY-4
Spout Springs Cem—*cemetery* MS-4
Spout Springs Hollow—*valley* AR-4
Spout Springs Lookout Tower—*locale* OR-9
Spout Springs Presbyterian Ch—*church* MS-4
Spout Springs Sch—*school* MS-4
Spout Springs Ski Area—*locale* OR-9
Spraberry—*locale* TX-5
Spraberry Ch—*church* TX-5
Spraberry Gas Plant—*oilfield* TX-5
Spraberry Oil Field—*oilfield* TX-5
Spraberry Trend Oil Field—*oilfield* TX-5
Spracklen Ranch—*locale* WY-8
Spracklin Branch—*stream* WY-8
*Spracklin Ranch* WY-8
Spraddle Creek—*stream* CO-8
Sprading Cem—*cemetery* KS-7
Spradley Branch—*stream* AL-4
Spradley Hollow—*valley* AR-4
Spradlin Branch—*stream* KY-4
Spradlin Branch Sch—*school* KY-4
Spradlin Cem—*cemetery* MO-7
Spradlin Creek—*stream* MO-7
Spradling Branch—*stream* TN-4
Spradling Cem—*cemetery* IL-6
Spradling Cem—*cemetery* TN-4
Spradling Ridge—*ridge* TN-4
Spradling Sch—*school* AR-4
Spradling Spring—*spring* UT-8
Spradlin Lake—*lake* AR-4
Spradlin Park—*flat* CO-8
Spradlin Pond—*reservoir* AL-4
Sprager Creek—*stream* WY-8
Spragg-Alcorn-Bewley Ditch—*canal* NV-8
Spraggans Ch—*church* IN-6
Spraggen Sch—*school* KY-4
Spraggins—*locale* MS-4
Spraggins Lake Dam—*dam* MS-4
Spragg Rsvr—*reservoir* WY-8
Spraggs—*locale* PA-2
Spragg-Woodcock Ditch—*canal* NV-8
Sprague—*locale* OH-6
**Sprague**—*pop pl* AL-4
**Sprague**—*pop pl* MO-7
**Sprague**—*pop pl* NE-7
**Sprague**—*pop pl* WA-9
**Sprague**—*pop pl* WV-2
**Sprague**—*pop pl* WI-6
Sprague, Brown, and Knowlton Store—*hist pl* IA-7
Sprague, David, House—*hist pl* RI-1
Sprague, David R. and Ellsworth A., Houses—*hist pl* MN-6
Sprague, Elias, House—*hist pl* CT-1
Sprague, Gov. William, Mansion—*hist pl* RI-1
Sprague, Jonathan, House—*hist pl* OH-6
Sprague, Thomas S., House—*hist pl* MI-6
Sprague Bldg—*hist pl* WA-9
Sprague Branch—*stream* KY-4
Sprague Brook—*stream* MA-1
Sprague Brook—*stream* (2) NH-1
Sprague Brook—*stream* (3) NY-2
Sprague Brook—*stream* VT-1
Sprague Brothers Ditch—*canal* CO-8
Sprague Cabin—*locale* CA-9
Sprague Camp—*locale* ME-1
Sprague Canyon—*valley* NM-5
Sprague Cem—*cemetery* AL-4
Sprague Cem—*cemetery* ME-1
Sprague Cem—*cemetery* NY-2
Sprague Cem—*cemetery* OH-6
Sprague Cem—*cemetery* OR-9
Sprague City—*locale* ME-1
Sprague Corner—*locale* ME-1
Sprague Cove—*bay* ME-1
Sprague Creek—*stream* ID-8
Sprague Creek—*stream* (2) MI-6
Sprague Creek—*stream* MN-6
Sprague Creek—*stream* (2) MT-8
Sprague Creek—*stream* (2) WY-8
Sprague Creek Campground—*locale* MT-8
Sprague Drain—*canal* (2) MI-6
Sprague Draw—*valley* WA-9
*Sprague Flowage* WI-6
Sprague Glacier—*glacier* CO-8
Sprague Gulch—*valley* CO-8
Sprague Gulch—*valley* MT-8
Sprague Gulch—*valley* OR-9
*Sprague Hill* MA-1
Sprague Hill—*summit* ME-1
Sprague Hill—*summit* RI-1
Sprague Hill—*summit* VT-1
Sprague Hollow—*valley* PA-2
Sprague House—*hist pl* MA-1
Sprague House—*hist pl* OH-6
Sprague Island—*island* FL-3
Sprague Lake—*lake* MI-6
Sprague Lake—*lake* MN-6
Sprague Lake—*lake* ND-7
Sprague Lake—*lake* OR-9
Sprague Lake—*lake* (2) WA-9
Sprague Landing—*locale* AL-4
Sprague Lane Sch—*school* WY-8
Sprague Ledge—*bar* (2) ME-1
Sprague Lower Reservoir Dam—*dam* RI-1
Sprague Lower Rsvr—*reservoir* RI-1
Sprague-Marshall-Bowie House—*hist pl* OR-9
Sprague-Mather Flowage—*reservoir* WI-6
*Sprague-Mathers Flowage* WI-6
Sprague Meadow Brook—*stream* ME-1
Sprague Mill—*locale* ME-1
Sprague Mtn—*summit* CO-8
Sprague Neck—*cape* ME-1
Sprague Neck Bar—*bar* ME-1
**Sprague Park**—*pop pl* RI-1
Sprague Pass—*gap* CO-8
Sprague Point—*cape* FL-3
*Sprague Pond* RI-1
Sprague Pond—*lake* ME-1
Sprague Pond—*lake* MA-1
Sprague Pond—*lake* NY-2
Sprague Pond—*lake* RI-1
Sprague Ranch—*locale* WY-8
**Sprague River**—*pop pl* OR-9
Sprague River—*stream* ME-1
Sprague River—*stream* OR-9
*Sprague River Campgrounds* OR-9
Sprague River Picnic Area—*park* OR-9
Sprague River Valley—*valley* OR-9
Spragues Beach—*beach* ME-1
Sprague Sch—*school* CT-1
Sprague Sch—*school* GA-3
Sprague Sch—*school* ME-1
Sprague Sch—*school* MA-1
Sprague Sch—*school* MT-8
Spragues Corner—*locale* NY-2
Spragues Hill—*summit* MA-1
*Spragues Lower Reservoir* RI-1
**Spragues Mill**—*pop pl* ME-1
*Spragues Pond* RI-1
Sprague Street Houses—*hist pl* LA-4
Sprague Street Park—*park* NC-3
*Spragues Upper Reservoir* RI-1
Spraguetown—*locale* NJ-2
Spraguetown—*locale* NY-2
**Sprague (Town of)**—*pop pl* CT-1
Sprague Upper Rsvr—*reservoir* RI-1
*Spragueville* ME-1
**Spragueville**—*pop pl* IA-7
**Spragueville**—*pop pl* ME-1
**Spragueville**—*pop pl* NH-1
**Spragueville**—*pop pl* NY-2
**Spragueville**—*pop pl* RI-1
Sprain Brook—*stream* CT-1
Sprain Brook—*stream* NY-2
Sprain Ridge House of Rest—*building* NY-2
Sprain Ridge Park—*park* NY-2
Spraker Lateral—*canal* ID-8
**Sprakers**—*pop pl* NY-2
Spraklin Island—*island* MT-8
Spranger Creek—*stream* WI-6
Sprangs Point—*cape* MI-6
**Sprankle Mills**—*pop pl* PA-2
Spranklin Creek—*stream* WV-2
Spra Run—*stream* PA-2
Sprat Bay—*bay* VI-3
Sprat Branch—*stream* KY-4
Sprat Hall—*locale* VI-3
Sprat Hole—*bay* VI-3
Spratlen-Anderson Wholesale Grocery Company-Davis Brothers Warehouse—*hist pl* CO-8
Spratley Cem—*cemetery* VA-3
Spratleys Mill—*locale* VA-3
Spratling Cem—*cemetery* AL-4
Spratling Commercial Park—*locale* UT-8
Spratling Field (airport)—*airport* AL-4
Spratling Well—*well* NV-8
Sprat Point—*cape* VI-3
Spratt—*locale* MI-6
Spratt—*locale* OH-6
Spratt Branch—*stream* AL-4
Spratt Branch—*stream* WV-2
Spratt Cem—*cemetery* MI-6
Spratt Ch—*church* MI-6
Spratt Creek—*gut* FL-3
Spratt Creek—*stream* CA-9
Spratt Creek—*stream* MI-6
Spratt Creek—*stream* TX-5
Spratt Creek—*stream* WA-9
Spratt Lake—*reservoir* NC-3
Spratt Mtn—*summit* WA-9
Spratt Park—*park* NY-2
Spratt Point—*cape* FL-3
Spratt Rsvr—*reservoir* WY-8
Spratts Cove—*bay* VA-3
Spratts Lake—*lake* IL-6
**Sprattsville**—*pop pl* WV-2
Sprauge Cem—*cemetery* WI-6
Sprauling Grove Ch—*church* GA-3
*Sprawling* TN-4
*Sprawling Branch* TX-5
Sprawls Mill Creek—*stream* LA-4
*Spray* NC-3
Spray—*locale* FL-3
**Spray**—*pop pl* NC-3
**Spray**—*pop pl* OR-9
Spray Airstrip—*airport* OR-9
**Spray Beach**—*pop pl* NJ-2
Sprayberry Bend—*bend* AL-4
Sprayberry HS—*school* GA-3
Spray Canyon—*valley* WA-9
Spray Cape—*cape* AK-9
Spray Cem—*cemetery* OR-9
Spray Creek—*stream* AK-9
Spray Creek—*stream* ID-8
Spray Creek—*stream* IN-6
Spray Creek—*stream* MI-6
Spray Creek—*stream* OR-9
Spray Creek—*stream* WA-9
Spray Falls—*falls* MI-6
Spray Falls—*falls* (2) WA-9
Spray Garwin Ditch—*canal* MT-8
Spray Geyser—*geyser* WY-8
Spray Industrial Hist Dist—*hist pl* NC-3
Spray Island—*island* AK-9
Spray Island—*island* MN-6
Spray Park—*flat* WA-9
Spray Resrvoir—*reservoir* UT-8
Spray Ridge—*ridge* NC-3
Spray Rsvr No 2—*reservoir* ID-8
Spray Station (historical P.O.)—*locale* IN-6

Spring Creek Lake—reservoir OK-5
Spring Creek Lake—reservoir (2) TN-4
Spring Creek Lake—reservoir VA-3
Spring Creek Lakes—lake CO-8
Spring Creek (Magisterial District)—fmr MCD WV-2
Spring Creek Manor (subdivision)—pop pl PA-2
Spring Creek Manor Subdivision—pop pl UT-8
Spring Creek Marina—locale AL-4
Spring Creek Meadow—flat OR-9
Spring Creek Memorial Cem—cemetery OK-5
Spring Creek Mesa—summit CO-8
Spring Creek Mills Post Office (historical)—building TN-4
Spring Creek Mine—mine AZ-5
Spring Creek Mine—mine ID-8
Spring Creek Missionary Baptist Church AL-4
Spring Creek MS—school UT-8
Spring Creek Mtn—summit NV-8
Spring Creek Mtn—summit NC-3
Spring Creek Mtn—summit UT-8
Spring Creek Natl Wildlife Area—park WI-6
Spring Creek OFDBA 88-2 Dam—dam TN-4
Spring Creek Oil Field—oilfield TN-4
Spring Creek Oil Field—oilfield WY-8
Spring Creek Park—flat WY-8
Spring Creek Park—park KS-7
Spring Creek Park—park NY-2
Spring Creek Pass—gap CO-8
Spring Creek Point—cliff UT-8
Spring Creek Point Rsvr—reservoir CO-8
Spring Creek Pond—reservoir GA-3
Springcreek Post Office TN-4
Spring Creek Post Office—building TN-4
Spring Creek Post Office (historical)—building MS-4
Spring Creek Presbyterian Ch (historical)—church MS-4
Spring Creek (Public Use Area)—park MO-7
Spring Creek Ranch—locale AZ-5
Spring Creek Ranch—locale CO-8
Spring Creek Ranch—locale MT-8
Spring Creek Ranch—locale NV-8
Spring Creek Ranch—locale (3) TX-5
Spring Creek Ranch—locale UT-8
Spring Creek Ranch—locale WY-8
Spring Creek Ranch Lake Number One—reservoir TN-4
Spring Creek Ranch Lake Number One Dam—dam TN-4
Spring Creek Ranch Lake Number Two—reservoir TN-4
Spring Creek Ranch Lake Number Two Dam—dam TN-4
Spring Creek Rearing Station—locale NV-8
Spring Creek Rec Area—park NE-7
Spring Creek Rec Area—park OK-5
Spring Creek Rec Area—park (2) SD-7
Spring Creek Ridge TN-4
Spring Creek Ridge—ridge TN-4
Spring Creek Ridge—ridge UT-8
Spring Creek Road Baptist Ch—church TN-4
Spring Creek Rsvr OR-9
Spring Creek Rsvr—reservoir (3) CO-8
Spring Creek Rsvr—reservoir ID-8
Spring Creek Rsvr—reservoir MT-8
Spring Creek Rsvr No. 1—reservoir CO-8
Spring Creek Sch—hist pl SD-7
Spring Creek Sch—school (2) CA-9
Spring Creek Sch—school (2) IL-6
Spring Creek Sch—school (2) KS-7
Spring Creek Sch—school MS-4
Spring Creek Sch—school MO-7
Spring Creek Sch—school (7) MT-8
Spring Creek Sch—school (3) NE-7
Spring Creek Sch—school NC-3
Spring Creek Sch—school OK-5
Spring Creek Sch—school OR-9
Spring Creek Sch—school PA-2
Spring Creek Sch—school (2) SD-7
Spring Creek Sch—school TN-4
Spring Creek Sch—school TX-5
Spring Creek Sch—school (2) WI-6
Spring Creek Sch (abandoned)—school MO-7
Spring Creek Sch (historical)—school AL-4
Spring Creek Sch (historical)—school (5) TN-4
Spring Creek Sch No 19—school NE-7
Spring Creek Sch No 21—school NE-7
Spring Creek Sch Number 2—school ND-7
Spring Creek School (abandoned)—locale MO-7
Spring Creek Site—hist pl MI-6
Spring Creek Spring MO-7
Spring Creek Spring—spring MT-8
Spring Creek Spring—spring NV-8
Spring Creek Spring—spring OR-9
Spring Creek Spring—spring TX-5
Springcreek (Spring Creek)—pop pl LA-4
Spring Creek Springs—spring PA-2
Spring Creek State Wildlife Mngmt Area—park MN-6
Spring Creek Subdivision—pop pl UT-8
Spring Creek Summit PA-2
Spring Creek Township—civil (7) MO-7
Spring Creek Township—civil SD-7
Spring Creek Township—fmr MCD (3) IA-7
Spring Creek Township—pop pl (6) KS-7
Spring Creek Township—pop pl NE-7
Spring Creek Township—pop pl ND-7
Spring Creek Township—pop pl SD-7
Spring Creek (Township of)—civ div IL-6
Spring Creek (Township of)—civ div (2) MN-6
Spring Creek (Township of)—fmr MCD (2) AR-4
Springcreek (Township of)—pop pl OH-6
Spring Creek (Township of)—pop pl (2) PA-2
Spring Creek Trail—trail (2) CO-8
Spring Creek Tributary Bridge—hist pl KS-7
Spring Creek Trout Pond—lake MI-6
Spring Creek Valley For Preserve—forest IL-6
Spring Creek Windmill—locale TX-5
Springcrest—pop pl TN-4
Springcrest Meadows (subdivision)—pop pl NC-3
Springdale CT-1
Spring Dale MS-4
Spring Dale OH-6
Springdale PA-2
Springdale SD-7
Springdale—CDP SC-3
Springdale—locale CO-8
Springdale—locale ID-8
Springdale—locale (2) KY-4
Springdale—locale NV-8
Springdale—locale (2) NJ-2
Springdale—locale (2) TX-5
Springdale—locale VA-3
Springdale—pop pl (2) AL-4
Springdale—pop pl AR-4
Springdale—pop pl CT-1
Springdale—pop pl FL-3
Springdale—pop pl (2) IA-7
Springdale—pop pl (2) KS-7
Springdale—pop pl KY-4
Springdale—pop pl MA-1
Springdale—pop pl (2) MS-4
Springdale—pop pl MT-8
Springdale—pop pl NJ-2
Springdale—pop pl NC-3
Springdale—pop pl OH-6
Springdale—pop pl OR-9
Springdale—pop pl PA-2
Springdale—pop pl (2) SC-3
Springdale—pop pl (2) TN-4
Springdale—pop pl UT-8
Springdale—pop pl (2) VA-3
Springdale—pop pl WA-9
Springdale—pop pl WV-2
Spring Dale—pop pl WV-2
Springdale—uninc pl CA-9
Springdale—uninc pl OK-5
Springdale Acres (subdivision)—pop pl NC-3
Springdale Baptist Ch—church TN-4
Springdale Baptist Church AL-4
Springdale Baptist Church MS-4
Springdale Borough—civil PA-2
Springdale Branch—stream TX-5
Springdale Branch—stream WI-6
Springdale Brook—stream CT-1
Springdale Campground—locale CO-8
Springdale Canyon—valley NV-8
Springdale (CCD)—cens area WA-9
Springdale Cem—cemetery CT-1
Springdale Cem—cemetery IL-6
Springdale Cem—cemetery (2) IN-6
Springdale Cem—cemetery (2) IA-7
Springdale Cem—cemetery KS-7
Springdale Cem—cemetery KY-4
Springdale Cem—cemetery MA-1
Springdale Cem—cemetery (3) MS-4
Springdale Cem—cemetery OH-6
Springdale Cem—cemetery OK-5
Springdale Cem—cemetery PA-2
Springdale Cem—cemetery UT-8
Springdale Ch—church AL-4
Springdale Ch—church KY-4
Springdale Ch—church MI-6
Springdale Ch—church (4) MS-4
Springdale Ch—church (2) NC-3
Springdale Ch—church (2) OH-6
Springdale Ch—church OK-5
Springdale Ch—church PA-2
Springdale Ch—church SC-3
Springdale Ch—church SD-7
Springdale Ch—church TX-5
Springdale Ch—church VA-3
Springdale Ch—church WI-6
Springdale Colony—pop pl MT-8
Springdale Creek—stream CO-8
Springdale Ditch—canal CO-8
Springdale Elem Sch—school TN-4
Springdale Farm—hist pl PA-2
Springdale Gardens—locale MD-2
Springdale Golf Club—other NJ-2
Springdale Golf Course—locale PA-2
Springdale Hist Dist—hist pl PA-2
Springdale (historical)—locale SD-7
Springdale Institute (historical)—school TN-4
Springdale Junior-Senior HS—school PA-2
Springdale Lake—lake OH-6
Springdale Lake—reservoir GA-3
Springdale Lake—reservoir PA-2
Springdale Lake Dam—dam MS-4
Springdale Lakes—lake MS-4
Springdale Mall—locale MA-1
Springdale Mall Shop Ctr—locale AL-4
Springdale Methodist Ch (historical)—church MS-4
Springdale Mill Complex—hist pl VA-3
Springdale Mills—hist pl PA-2
Springdale Park—park GA-3
Springdale Park—park MI-6
Springdale Park—park MO-7
Springdale Playground—park OK-5
Springdale Plaza and Mall Shop Ctr AL-4
Springdale Plaza Shop Ctr—locale AL-4
Springdale P.O. (historical)—building AL-4
Springdale Pond—lake CT-1
Springdale Pond—reservoir MA-1
Spring Dale Post Office TN-4
Springdale Post Office (historical)—building TN-4
Springdale Presbyterian Ch—church AL-4
Springdale Ranch—locale MT-8
Springdale (RR name for Spring Dale)—other WV-2
Spring Dale (RR name Springdale)—pop pl WV-2
Springdale Run—stream IN-6
Springdale Sch—school CA-9
Springdale Sch—school CT-1
Springdale Sch—school GA-3
Springdale Sch—school (2) ID-8
Spring Dale Sch—school IL-6
Springdale Sch—school IL-6
Springdale Sch—school KS-7
Springdale Sch—school KY-4
Springdale Sch—school NE-7
Springdale Sch—school NC-3
Springdale Sch—school (3) OK-5
Springdale Sch—school OR-9
Springdale Sch—school SC-3
Springdale Sch—school (2) SD-7
Springdale Sch—school TN-4
Springdale Sch—school TX-5
Springdale Sch—school UT-8
Springdale Sch—school WI-6
Springdale Sch (abandoned)—school PA-2
Spring Dale Sch (abandoned)—school PA-2
Springdale Sch (historical)—school AL-4
Springdale Sch (historical)—school MS-4
Springdale Sch (historical)—school (2) TN-4
Springdale Sewage Disposal—other AR-4
Springdale Spring—spring CO-8
Springdale Station MA-1
Springdale (subdivision)—pop pl (2) AL-4
Springdale (subdivision)—pop pl MA-1
Springdale (subdivision)—pop pl PA-2
Springdale (subdivision)—pop pl (2) TN-4
Spring Dale Subdivision—pop pl UT-8
Springdale (Town of)—pop pl WI-6
Springdale Township—civ div NE-7
Springdale Township—fmr MCD IA-7
Springdale Township—pop pl KS-7
Springdale Township—pop pl (2) SD-7
Springdale (Township of)—fmr MCD AR-4
Springdale (Township of)—pop pl MI-6
Springdale (Township of)—pop pl MN-6
Springdale (Township of)—pop pl PA-2
Springdale Valley Sch—school CO-8
Spring Dam—dam CO-8
Spring Dam—reservoir TX-5
Spring Dam Pond—lake CT-1
Spring Day Island FM-9
Springdell—locale PA-2
Springdell—locale SC-3
Springdell—pop pl UT-8
Springdell Ch—church SC-3
Spring Dell Sch (historical)—school SD-7
Spring Depot MS-4
Spring Ditch—canal AZ-5
Spring Ditch—canal KY-4
Spring Ditch—canal MT-8
Spring Ditch—canal (3) UT-8
Spring Ditch—canal WY-8
Spring Drain—canal MI-6
Spring Draw UT-8
Spring Draw—valley CO-8
Spring Draw—valley KS-7
Spring Draw—valley (3) MT-8
Spring Draw—valley OR-9
Spring Draw—valley (3) SD-7
Spring Draw—valley (2) TX-5
Spring Draw—valley (23) WY-8
Spring Draw Rsvr—reservoir WY-8
Spring Draw 1—valley CO-8
Spring Draw 2—valley CO-8
Springen Ranch—locale WY-8
Springen Ranch Oil Field—oilfield WY-8
Springer OH-6
Springer—locale MI-6
Springer—pop pl NM-5
Springer—pop pl OK-5
Springer, Judge Francis, House—hist pl IA-7
Springer Arroyo—stream NM-5
Springer Bldg—hist pl NM-5
Springer Canyon—valley NV-8
Springer (CCD)—cens area NM-5
Springer Cem—cemetery AL-4
Springer Cem—cemetery GA-3
Springer Cem—cemetery (3) IL-6
Springer Cem—cemetery (3) IN-6
Springer Cem—cemetery ME-1
Springer Cem—cemetery MO-7
Springer Cem—cemetery OH-6
Springer Cem—cemetery (3) TN-4
Springer Ch—church AL-4
Springer Ch—church IL-6
Springer Chapel—church MO-7
Springer Corners—locale PA-2
Springer Creek—stream CO-8
Springer Creek—stream MI-6
Springer Creek—stream MT-8
Springer Creek—stream (2) OR-9
Springer Ditch—canal NM-5
Springer Ditch—canal OR-9
Springer Ditch—canal WY-8
Springer Farm—hist pl DE-2
Springer Farm—hist pl PA-2
Springer Flat—flat CA-9
Springer Gap—gap TX-5
Springer Glade—valley MS-4
Springer Gulch—valley CO-8
Springer Hill—summit KY-4
Springer Hill—summit ME-1
Springer Hill—summit NV-8
Springer Hollow—valley OH-6
Springer Hollow—valley TN-4
Springer Hollow—valley UT-8
Springer Intensive Learning Center—school DE-2
Springer JHS DE-2
Springer Lake—lake MN-6
Springer Lake—lake WA-9
Springer Lake—lake WI-6
Springer Lake—reservoir NM-5
Springer Lake—reservoir NC-3
Springer Lake Dam—dam NC-3
Springer Lateral—canal WY-8
Springer Main Lateral—canal WY-8
Springer McGaughey Ditch—canal IN-6
Springer Mtn—summit AZ-5
Springer Mtn—summit GA-3
Springer Mtn—summit NY-2
Springer Mtn—summit OR-9
Springer Opera House—hist pl GA-3
Springer Pit—mine CO-8
Springer Ranch—locale NE-7
Springer Reservoir WY-8
Springer Ridge—ridge OR-9
Springer Ridge Ch—church TN-4
Springer Ridge (historical)—pop pl TN-4
Springer Road Ch of Christ—church TN-4
Springer (RR name for Springerton) IL-6
Springers TN-4
Springers Brook—stream NJ-2
Springer Sch—school CA-9
Springer Sch—school (2) IL-6
Springer Sch—school PA-2
Springer Sch (abandoned)—school PA-2
Springer Sch (historical)—school TN-4
Springers Creek NJ-2
Springer Slough—stream AL-4
Springers Point—cape NC-3
Springer Spring—spring NV-8
Springers Station—pop pl TN-4
Springersville—pop pl IN-6
Springers Wharf—locale NJ-2
Springerton—pop pl IL-6
Springer Town Hall—building ND-7
Springer Township—pop pl ND-7
Springerville IN-6
Springerville—pop pl AZ-5
Springerville-Eagar Municipal Airp—airport AZ-5
Springer Well—well CO-8
Springer Wildlife Mangement Unit—park WY-8
Springettsbury Elem Sch (abandoned)—school PA-2
Springettsbury (Township of)—pop pl PA-2
Spring Falls—falls TX-5
Spring Falls Branch—stream TN-4
Spring Farm—locale ME-1
Spring Farm Brook—stream NH-1
Spring Farm School PA-2
Spring Farms Elem Sch PA-2
Spring Farms Elem Sch—school PA-2
Springfellor Hill—summit AR-4
Springfield DE-2
Springfield IN-6
Springfield KS-7
Springfield MS-4
Springfield PA-2
Springfield—CDP SC-3
Springfield—hist pl VA-3
Springfield—locale (4) AL-4
Springfield—locale CA-9
Springfield—locale (2) GA-3
Springfield—locale (2) IA-7
Springfield—locale NJ-2
Springfield—locale (2) PA-2
Springfield—locale (2) TX-5
Springfield—locale (2) VA-3
Springfield—locale VI-3
Springfield—pop pl AL-4
Springfield—pop pl AR-4
Springfield—pop pl CO-8
Springfield—pop pl (2) FL-3
Springfield—pop pl GA-3
Springfield—pop pl (2) ID-8
Springfield—pop pl IL-6
Springfield—pop pl (2) IN-6
Springfield—pop pl KY-4
Springfield—pop pl LA-4
Springfield—pop pl ME-1
Springfield—pop pl (2) MD-2
Springfield—pop pl MA-1
Springfield—pop pl (2) MI-6
Springfield—pop pl MN-6
Springfield—pop pl MO-7
Springfield—pop pl NE-7
Springfield—pop pl NH-1
Springfield—pop pl NJ-2
Springfield—pop pl NY-2
Springfield—pop pl (3) NC-3
Springfield—pop pl OH-6
Springfield—pop pl OR-9
Springfield—pop pl PA-2
Springfield—pop pl SC-3
Springfield—pop pl SD-7
Springfield—pop pl TN-4
Springfield—pop pl TX-5
Springfield—pop pl VT-1
Springfield—pop pl VA-3
Springfield—pop pl WV-2
Springfield—pop pl WI-6
Springfield, City of—civil MA-1
Springfield, Lake—reservoir IL-6
Springfield, Lake—reservoir MO-7
Springfield, Town of MA-1
Springfield Acres—pop pl TN-4
Springfield Airp—airport CO-8
Springfield Airp—airport OR-9
Springfield Aqueduct—canal MA-1
Springfield Armory—hist pl MA-1
Springfield Armory—locale MA-1
Springfield Armory Natl Historic Site—park MA-1
Springfield Baptist Ch—church FL-3
Springfield Baptist Ch—church TN-4
Springfield Baptist Church MS-4
Springfield Baptist Church—hist pl (2) GA-3
Springfield (Big Spring)—pop pl PA-2
Springfield Bird Haven—park ID-8
Springfield Boys Camp—locale MA-1
Springfield Boys Camp—pop pl MA-1
Springfield Branch—stream AL-4
Springfield Branch—stream TN-4
Springfield Branch—stream VA-3
Springfield Bridge—hist pl AR-4
Springfield Bridge (historical)—bridge PA-2
Springfield Canal—canal GA-3
Springfield (CCD)—cens area KY-4
Springfield (CCD)—cens area SC-3
Springfield Cem—cemetery AL-4
Springfield Cem—cemetery CO-8
Springfield Cem—cemetery GA-3
Springfield Cem—cemetery IN-6
Springfield Cem—cemetery (2) IA-7
Springfield Cem—cemetery (3) KS-7
Springfield Cem—cemetery KY-4
Springfield Cem—cemetery LA-4
Springfield Cem—cemetery MA-1
Springfield Cem—cemetery (2) MN-6
Springfield Cem—cemetery (2) MS-4
Springfield Cem—cemetery NY-2
Springfield Cem—cemetery (2) OH-6
Springfield Cem—cemetery (3) PA-2
Springfield Cem—cemetery (2) SC-3
Springfield Cem—cemetery SD-7
Springfield Cem—cemetery (3) TN-4
Springfield Cem—cemetery TX-5
Springfield Center—pop pl NY-2
Springfield Center (census name for Springfield)—other VT-1
Springfield Center (Springfield)—pop pl NY-2
Spring Field Ch AL-4
Springfield Ch—church (11) AL-4
Springfield Ch—church (3) AR-4
Springfield Ch—church FL-3
Springfield Ch—church (15) GA-3
Springfield Ch—church IN-6
Springfield Ch—church IA-7
Springfield Ch—church (3) LA-4
Springfield Ch—church MI-6
Springfield Ch—church (12) MS-4
Springfield Ch—church (3) NC-3
Springfield Ch—church OH-6
Springfield Ch—church OK-5
Springfield Ch—church PA-2
Springfield Ch—church (14) SC-3
Springfield Ch—church (3) TX-5
Springfield Ch—church (11) VA-3
Springfield Ch—church WV-2
Springfield Chapel—church OH-6
Springfield Chapel Cem—cemetery OH-6
Springfield Ch (historical)—church AL-4
Springfield City MA-1
Springfield City Hall—building TN-4
Springfield Coll—school MA-1
Springfield Community Ch—church FL-3
Springfield Community Hospital Heliport—airport MO-7
Springfield Congregational Church—hist pl ME-1
Spring Field Corners—locale PA-2
Springfield Corners—locale WI-6
Springfield Corners—pop pl WI-6
Springfield Country Club—locale TN-4
Springfield Country Club—other MN-6
Springfield Country Club—other OH-6
Springfield Country Club—other PA-2
Springfield Country Club—other VA-3
Springfield Country Club Dam—dam MA-1
Springfield Creek—stream AL-4
Springfield Creek—stream ID-8
Springfield Creek—stream NE-7
Springfield Creek—stream SC-3
Springfield Crossroads—locale DE-2
Springfield District Court—hist pl MA-1
Springfield Downtown Hist Dist—hist pl VT-1
Springfield Downtown Hist Dist (Boundary Increase)—hist pl VT-1
Springfield Elem Sch—school AZ-5
Springfield Elem Sch—school IN-6
Springfield Elem Sch—school PA-2
Springfield Estates—pop pl VA-3
Springfield Estates Sch—school VA-3
Springfield Falls—falls PA-2
Springfield Falls—pop pl PA-2
Springfield Farm—hist pl MD-2
Springfield Farm—hist pl WA-9
Springfield Farms—locale VA-3
Springfield Farms Addition (subdivision)—pop pl DE-2
Springfield Fire & Marine Insurance Co.—hist pl MA-1
Springfield Forest—pop pl VA-3
Springfield Four Corners—pop pl NY-2
Springfield Furnace PA-2
Springfield Gardens—pop pl NY-2
Springfield Gardens HS—school NY-2
Springfield General Hosp—hist pl OR-9
Springfield Girls Camp—pop pl MA-1
Springfield Golf Course PA-2
Springfield-Greenbrier (CCD)—cens area TN-4
Springfield-Greenbrier Division—civil TN-4
Springfield Hill—summit KY-4
Springfield Hist Dist—hist pl FL-3
Springfield (historical)—locale KS-7
Springfield (historical)—locale MS-4
Springfield (historical)—pop pl MS-4
Springfield (historical P.O.)—locale IN-6
Springfield Hollow—valley MO-7
Springfield Hosp—hospital MA-1
Springfield HS—school MA-1
Springfield HS—school (3) OH-6
Springfield HS—school (2) PA-2
Springfield HS—school TN-4
Springfield HSs—school MA-1
Springfield HS (south)—school MA-1
Springfield HS (west)—school MA-1
Springfield Island—island SC-3
Springfield JHS—school MA-1
Springfield Junction—locale NH-1
Springfield Junction—pop pl OR-9
Springfield Junction—pop pl PA-2
Springfield Junior Coll—school IL-6
Springfield Lake—lake OH-6
Springfield Lake—reservoir PA-2
Springfield Lake—reservoir TX-5
Springfield Lake Outlet—stream OH-6
Springfield Landing Strip—airport CO-8
Springfield Lookout Tower—locale AL-4
Springfield (Magisterial District)—fmr MCD (2) VA-3
Springfield (Magisterial District)—fmr MCD (2) WV-2
Springfield Memorial Cem—cemetery NE-7
Springfield Memorial Cem—cemetery OR-9
Springfield Memorial Ch—church NC-3
Springfield Memorial Gardens—cemetery TN-4
Springfield Memorial Park—park PA-2
Springfield Memorial Sch—school MA-1
Springfield Methodist Protestant Church AL-4
Springfield Mill—hist pl PA-2
Springfield Mills—pop pl NC-3
Springfield Mine—mine AZ-5
Springfield Mine—mine CA-9
Springfield Mine—mine ID-8
Springfield Missionary Baptist Church MS-4
Springfield Mountains MA-1
Springfield MS—school TN-4
Springfield Municipal Airp—airport SD-7
Springfield Municipal Airp—airport TN-4
Springfield Municipal Hosp—hospital MA-1
Springfield Natl Cem—cemetery MO-7
Springfield No. 1—fmr MCD NE-7
Springfield Oil Field—oilfield MS-4
Springfield Park—park FL-3
Springfield Park—park NY-2
Springfield Park—pop pl PA-2
Springfield Place—pop pl MI-6
Springfield Plains Cem—cemetery MI-6
Springfield Plantation—hist pl MS-4
Springfield Plantation House—hist pl SC-3
Springfield Plaza—locale MA-1
Springfield Plaza (Shop Ctr)—locale FL-3
Springfield P. O. MS-4
Springfield Point—cape NH-1
Springfield Pond—lake TN-4
Springfield Post Office—building TN-4
Springfield Presbyterian Church—hist pl KY-4
Springfield Presbyterian Church—hist pl MD-2
Springfield Public Sch—hist pl PA-2
Springfield Pumping Station—other CO-8
Springfield Rec Area—park SD-7
Springfield Regional Airp—airport MO-7
Springfield Rosenwall Sch—school SC-3
Springfield Rsvr—reservoir KY-4
Springfield Rsvr—reservoir MA-1
Springfield Rsvr—reservoir VT-1
Springfields AL-4
Springfield Sch—school (2) FL-3
Springfield Sch—school IL-6
Springfield Sch—school IA-7
Springfield Sch—school MI-6
Springfield Sch—school (3) NC-3
Springfield Sch—school OH-6
Springfield Sch—school PA-2
Springfield Sch—school TN-4
Springfield Sch—school VA-3
Springfield Sch—school WI-6
Springfield Sch (abandoned)—school PA-2
Springfield Sch (historical)—school (3) AL-4
Springfield Schoolhouse—hist pl CO-8
Springfield Shopping Mall—locale MA-1
Springfield Special Sch—school TN-4
Springfield Spring—spring CA-9
Springfield Springs—spring TX-5
Springfield (sta.) (RR name for North Springfield)—other PA-2
Springfield State Hosp—hospital MD-2
Springfield Station—locale NJ-2
Springfield Station—locale VA-3
Springfield Steam Power Company Block—hist pl MA-1
Springfield (subdivision)—pop pl NC-3
Springfield (subdivision)—pop pl TN-4
Springfield Tank—reservoir AZ-5
Springfield Terrace Sch—school GA-3
Springfield Town Hall and Howard Memorial Methodist Church—hist pl NH-1
Springfield (Town of)—pop pl ME-1
Springfield (Town of)—pop pl NH-1
Springfield (Town of)—pop pl NY-2
Springfield (Town of)—pop pl VT-1
Springfield (Town of)—pop pl (4) WI-6
Springfield Township—CDP PA-2
Springfield Township—civil MO-7
Springfield Township—civil SD-7
Springfield Township—fmr MCD (3) IA-7
Springfield Township—pop pl MO-7
Springfield Township—pop pl ND-7
Springfield Township Elem Sch—school PA-2
Springfield Township (historical)—civil SD-7
Springfield (Township of)—pop pl IL-6
Springfield (Township of)—pop pl (4) IN-6
Springfield (Township of)—pop pl (2) MI-6
Springfield (Township of)—pop pl MN-6
Springfield (Township of)—pop pl (2) NJ-2
Springfield (Township of)—pop pl (11) OH-6
Springfield (Township of)—pop pl (9) PA-2
Springfield Township Sch Number 1 (abandoned)—school PA-2
Springfield Township Senior HS PA-2
Springfield Town Square Hist Dist—hist pl TN-4
Springfield Valley—valley WV-2
Springfield Water Works Intake Dam—dam MA-1
Springfield Water Works Intake Rsvr—reservoir MA-1
Springfield Woods—pop pl VA-3
Springfiled Ch—church AL-4
Spring Flat—flat CA-9
Spring Flat—flat (2) OR-9
Spring Flat—flat WA-9
Spring Flat Campground—locale CA-9
Spring Flat Canyon—valley ID-8
Spring Flat Creek—stream WA-9
Spring Flats—flat UT-8
Spring Ford Country Club—other PA-2
Spring-Ford HS—school PA-2
Spring-Ford JHS—school PA-2
Spring Ford MS—school PA-2
Spring Ford Senior HS PA-2
Springford Village (subdivision)—pop pl PA-2
Spring Forest—pop pl MO-7
Spring Forest Camp—locale OR-9
Spring Forest Cem—cemetery NY-2
Spring Forest JHS—school TX-5
Spring Fork VA-3
Spring Fork—locale MO-7
Spring Fork—pop pl WV-2
Spring Fork—stream (3) KY-4
Spring Fork—stream MO-7
Spring Fork—stream OH-6
Spring Fork—stream VA-3
Spring Fork—stream (4) WV-2
Spring Fork Branch—stream TN-4
Spring Fork Ch—church MO-7
Spring Fork Creek MO-7
Spring Fork Lake—reservoir MO-7
Spring Fork Quicksand Creek—stream KY-4
Spring Fork Sch—school KY-4
Spring Fountain—locale IA-7
Spring Gap—gap AL-4
Spring Gap—gap TX-5
Spring Gap—gap VA-3
Spring Gap—gap WV-2
Spring Gap—gap WY-8
Spring Gap—locale CA-9
Spring Gap—locale MD-2
Spring Gap—pop pl WV-2
Spring Gap Branch—stream KY-4
Spring Gap Ch—church WV-2
Spring Gap Creek—stream VA-3
Spring Gap Mtn—summit WV-2
Spring Gap Powerhouse—other CA-9
Spring Garden FL-3
Spring Garden NJ-2
Spring Garden NC-3
Spring Garden—hist pl DE-2
Spring Garden—locale GA-3
Spring Garden—locale PA-2
Springgarden—locale VI-3
Spring Garden—pop pl AL-4
Spring Garden—pop pl CA-9
Spring Garden—pop pl IL-6
Spring Garden—pop pl MO-7
Spring Garden—pop pl NC-3
Spring Garden—pop pl (3) PA-2

**Spring Lake Park**—*pop pl* ... MN-6
Spring Lake Park Sch—*school* ... MN-6
Spring Lake Park Sch—*school* ... TX-5
Spring Lake Prairie—*lake* ... FL-3
*Spring Lake Reservoir* ... RI-1
*Spring Lake Reservoir Number 2* ... RI-1
*Spring Lake Reservvoir Number 1* ... RI-1
Spring Lake Rsvr—*reservoir* ... OR-9
*Spring Lakes* ... UT-8
Spring Lakes—*area* ... AK-9
Spring Lakes—*lake* (2) ... MI-6
Spring Lakes—*lake* ... MT-8
Spring Lakes—*lake* ... NY-2
Spring Lakes—*lake* ... WA-9
Spring Lakes—*reservoir* ... MS-4
Spring Lakes—*reservoir* ... MO-7
Spring Lakes—*reservoir* ... OH-6
Spring Lake Sch—*school* ... KY-4
Spring Lake Sch—*school* ... PA-2
Spring Lake Sch—*school* (2) ... SD-7
Springlake Sch—*school* ... TX-5
Spring Lake Slough—*stream* ... MS-4
Spring Lake Spring—*spring* ... PA-2
**Spring Lake (Spring Lake Beach)**—*pop pl* ... NJ-2
*Spring Lake State Park* ... MS-4
Spring Lake State Park—*park* ... IL-6
Spring Lake State Park—*park* ... IA-7
Spring Lake State Public Shooting Area—*park* ... SD-7
**Spring Lake (subdivision)**—*pop pl* ... DE-2
**Spring Lake (subdivision)**—*pop pl* (2) ... NC-3
**Spring Lake (Town of)**—*pop pl* ... WI-6
Spring Lake Township—*civil* (2) ... SD-7
**Spring Lake Township**—*pop pl* ... ND-7
**Spring Lake Township**—*pop pl* (3) ... SD-7
**Spring Lake (Township of)**—*pop pl* ... IL-6
**Spring Lake (Township of)**—*pop pl* ... MI-6
**Spring Lake (Township of)**—*pop pl* ... MN-6
Spring Lake Valley—*valley* ... OR-9
Spring Landing—*locale* ... AL-4
Spring Landing—*locale* ... CA-9
Spring Landing—*locale* ... NC-3
**Spring Lane Condominium**—*pop pl* ... UT-8
Spring Lane Sch—*school* ... PA-2
Springlawn—*locale* ... PA-2
Spring Lawn Cem—*cemetery* ... OH-6
Springlawn Cem—*cemetery* ... OH-6
Spring Leaf Ch (historical)—*church* ... MS-4
Spring Leaf Sch (historical)—*school* ... MS-4
Springle Creek—*stream* ... IN-6
Spring Ledge Country Club—*other* ... IN-6
**Springlee**—*pop pl* ... KY-4
Springley Cem—*cemetery* ... IL-6
**Spring Lick**—*pop pl* ... KY-4
Springlick Branch—*stream* ... KY-4
Spring Lick Hollow—*valley* ... MD-2
Spring Lick Run—*stream* ... MD-2
Spring Lodge—*locale* ... NC-3
Spring Logan—*swamp* ... ME-1
Spring Lot Brook—*stream* ... CT-1
**Springmaid Beach**—*pop pl* ... SC-3
Spring Mall Park Lake—*reservoir* ... IN-6
Spring Mall Park Lake Dam—*dam* ... IN-6
Springman Creek—*stream* ... WY-8
Spring Meadow—*flat* ... CA-9
Spring Meadow—*flat* ... OR-9
Spring Meadow—*flat* ... WA-9
**Spring Meadow**—*pop pl* ... PA-2
Spring Meadow Branch—*stream* ... VA-3
Spring Meadow Creek—*stream* ... MT-8
Spring Meadow Creek—*stream* ... WI-6
Spring Meadow Post Office (historical)—*building* ... PA-2
**Spring Meadows**—*pop pl* ... OH-6
**Spring Meadows**—*pop pl* ... VA-3
Spring Meadows Childrens Home—*building* ... KY-4
Spring Meadows Country Club—*other* ... NJ-2
Spring Meadow Spring—*spring* ... PA-2
**Spring Meadow Subdivision**—*pop pl* ... UT-8
Spring Methodist Ch (historical)—*church* ... MS-4
Springmeyer Sch—*school* ... OH-6
*Spring Mill* ... PA-2
Spring Mill—*building* ... IN-6
Spring Mill—*hist pl* ... AR-4
**Spring Mill**—*pop pl* ... KY-4
**Spring Mill**—*pop pl* ... NJ-2
**Spring Mill**—*pop pl* ... OH-6
**Spring Mill**—*pop pl* ... PA-2
Spring Mill Branch—*stream* ... GA-3
Spring Mill Complex—*hist pl* ... PA-2
Spring Mill County Park—*park* ... PA-2
Spring Mill Creek—*stream* ... MI-6
Spring Mill Dam—*dam* ... PA-2
Spring Mill Elem Sch—*school* ... IN-6
*Spring Mill Estates* ... IN-6
**Spring Mill Estates**—*pop pl* ... IN-6
Spring Mill Golf Course—*locale* ... PA-2
Spring Mill Impounding—*basin* ... PA-2
Spring Mill Pond—*lake* ... MI-6
Spring Mill Run—*stream* ... IN-6
*Spring Mills* ... NJ-2
*Springmills* ... WV-2
Spring Mills—*CDP* ... SC-3
Spring Mills—*locale* ... MD-2
Spring Mills—*locale* ... NY-2
Spring Mills—*locale* ... VA-3
Spring Mills—*locale* ... WV-2
**Spring Mills**—*pop pl* ... NJ-2
**Spring Mills**—*pop pl* ... PA-2
Spring Mill Sch—*school* ... MD-2
Spring Mill Sch—*school* ... PA-2
*Spring Mills Creek* ... PA-2
Spring Mills Creek—*stream* ... NY-2
Spring Mills Post Office (historical)—*building* ... TN-4
**Spring Mills (RR name Rising Springs)**—*pop pl* ... PA-2
Spring Mill State Park—*park* ... IN-6
Spring Mill Station—*building* ... PA-2
**Spring Mill Village**—*pop pl* ... IN-6
**Spring Mill Woods**—*pop pl* ... IN-6
Spring Mine—*mine* ... AZ-5
Spring Mine—*mine* ... CO-8
Spring Mine—*mine* ... KY-4
Spring Mine Creek—*stream* ... MN-6
Spring Mine Lake—*lake* ... MN-6
**Springmont**—*pop pl* ... PA-2
**Springmont**—*pop pl* ... TN-4
Springmore Sch—*school* ... IL-6
**Spring Mount**—*pop pl* (2) ... PA-2
*Spring Mountain* ... ID-8
**Spring Mountain**—*pop pl* ... OH-6
Spring Mountain—*ridge* ... OR-9
Spring Mountain—*ridge* ... WY-8
Spring Mountain Branch—*stream* ... NC-3
Spring Mountain Canyon—*valley* ... ID-8
Spring Mountain Ch—*church* ... AL-4
Spring Mountain Ch—*church* ... NC-3
Spring Mountain Cow Camp—*locale* ... WY-8
*Spring Mountain Creek* ... CA-9
Spring Mountain Divide Trail—*trail* ... NV-8
Spring Mountain Gulch—*valley* ... CA-9
Spring Mountain Lookout Tower—*locale* ... WV-2
Spring Mountain Ranch—*locale* ... NV-8
**Spring Mountain Ranchettes Subdivision**—*pop pl* ... UT-8
Spring Mountain Trail Shelter—*locale* ... NC-3
Spring Mountain Way—*trail* ... OR-9
Spring Mountain Youth Camp—*locale* ... NV-8
Spring Mtn—*summit* ... AZ-5
Spring Mtn—*summit* (2) ... AR-4
Spring Mtn—*summit* ... CO-8
Spring Mtn—*summit* ... GA-3
Spring Mtn—*summit* (2) ... ID-8
Spring Mtn—*summit* (3) ... NM-5
Spring Mtn—*summit* (5) ... NC-3
Spring Mtn—*summit* (2) ... OK-5
Spring Mtn—*summit* (2) ... OR-9
Spring Mtn—*summit* ... PA-2
Spring Mtn—*summit* (2) ... TX-5
Spring Mtn—*summit* ... UT-8
Spring Mtn—*summit* ... VA-3
Spring Mtn—*summit* ... WA-9
Spring Mtn—*summit* (4) ... WV-2
Spring Mtn—*summit* ... WY-8
Spring Mtns—*range* ... NV-8
*Spring Mtn Trail* ... PA-2
Spring Number One—*spring* (2) ... MT-8
Spring Number Two—*spring* (2) ... MT-8
Spring Oaks JHS—*school* ... TX-5
Spring of Contention—*spring* ... NM-5
Spring on the Hill (historical)—*locale* ... SD-7
Spring on the Right (historical)—*locale* ... SD-7
Spring Park—*park* ... AL-4
**Spring Park**—*pop pl* ... MN-6
Spring Park—*uninc pl* ... FL-3
Spring Park Bay—*bay* ... MN-6
Spring Park Butte—*summit* ... MT-8
Spring Park Ch—*church* (2) ... FL-3
Spring Park Creek—*stream* ... MT-8
Spring Park Flat—*flat* ... MT-8
Spring Park Lake—*reservoir* ... TX-5
Spring Park Rsvr—*reservoir* ... CO-8
Spring Park Sch—*school* ... FL-3
**Spring Park (subdivision)**—*pop pl* ... AL-4
Spring Passage—*channel* ... WA-9
*Spring Peak* ... NV-8
Spring Peak—*summit* ... AZ-5
Spring Peak—*summit* ... NV-8
Spring Picnic Area—*locale* ... UT-8
*Spring Place* ... KS-7
Spring Place—*hist pl* ... TN-4
**Spring Place**—*pop pl* ... GA-3
**Spring Place**—*pop pl* ... TN-4
Spring Place Ch—*church* ... GA-3
Spring Place Ch—*church* (2) ... TN-4
**Spring Plains**—*pop pl* ... PA-2
**Spring Plains (historical)**—*pop pl* ... MS-4
Spring Plaza—*locale* ... UT-8
Spring Plaza (Shop Ctr)—*locale* ... FL-3
Spring Point—*cape* ... AK-9
Spring Point—*cape* ... IN-6
Spring Point—*cape* ... ME-1
Spring Point—*cape* ... MD-2
Spring Point—*cape* ... NC-3
Spring Point—*cape* ... OR-9
Spring Point—*cape* ... TX-5
Spring Point—*cape* ... UT-8
Spring Point—*cape* ... VI-3
Spring Point—*ridge* ... UT-8
Spring Point Canyon—*ridge* ... UT-8
Spring Point Creek—*stream* ... IL-6
Spring Point Ledge Lighthouse—*locale* ... ME-1
Spring Point Ledge Light Station—*hist pl* ... ME-1
Spring Point Sch—*school* ... IL-6
Spring Point (Township of)—*civ div* ... IL-6
*Spring Polk Branch* ... AL-4
*Spring Pond* ... FL-3
*Spring Pond* ... MA-1
*Spring Pond* ... PA-2
Spring Pond—*bay* ... NY-2
Spring Pond—*lake* ... CT-1
Spring Pond—*lake* (2) ... FL-3
Spring Pond—*lake* ... GA-3
Spring Pond—*lake* ... IA-7
Spring Pond—*lake* (2) ... ME-1
Spring Pond—*lake* (2) ... MA-1
Spring Pond—*lake* (3) ... MI-6
Spring Pond—*lake* ... NJ-2
Spring Pond—*lake* (4) ... NY-2
Spring Pond—*lake* ... OH-6
Spring Pond—*lake* ... RI-1
Spring Pond—*lake* ... VT-1
Spring Pond—*lake* (2) ... WI-6
Spring Pond—*reservoir* ... CO-8
Spring Pond—*reservoir* ... FL-3
Spring Pond—*reservoir* (2) ... MA-1
Spring Pond—*reservoir* ... PA-2
Spring Pond Dam—*dam* ... MA-1
Spring Pond Lake—*lake* ... CT-1
Spring Pond Oil Field—*oilfield* ... MS-4
*Springport* ... NY-2
**Springport**—*pop pl* ... IN-6
**Springport**—*pop pl* (2) ... MI-6
Springport Cem—*cemetery* ... MI-6
Spring Port (historical)—*locale* ... MS-4
**Springport (Town of)**—*pop pl* ... NY-2
**Springport (Township of)**—*pop pl* ... MI-6
Spring Prairie—*area* ... CA-9
Spring Prairie—*flat* ... OR-9
**Spring Prairie**—*pop pl* ... WI-6
Spring Prairie Cem—*cemetery* ... MN-6
**Spring Prairie (Town of)**—*pop pl* ... WI-6
Spring Prairie (Township of)—*civ div* ... MN-6
Spring Ranch—*locale* ... ID-8
Spring Ranch—*locale* ... MT-8
Spring Ranch—*locale* ... NE-7
Spring Ranch Spring—*spring* ... ID-8
**Spring Ranch Township**—*pop pl* ... NE-7
Spring Rapids—*rapids* ... WI-6
Spring Ravine—*valley* ... CA-9
Spring Recreation Site—*park* ... OR-9
Spring Reef Creek—*stream* ... MT-8
*Spring Ridge* ... GA-3
*Spring Ridge* ... TN-4
**Spring Ridge**—*pop pl* ... LA-4
**Springridge**—*pop pl* ... LA-4
**Spring Ridge**—*pop pl* ... LA-4
**Spring Ridge**—*pop pl* ... MS-4
Spring Ridge—*ridge* (2) ... AZ-5
Spring Ridge—*ridge* ... CA-9
Spring Ridge—*ridge* ... GA-3
Spring Ridge—*ridge* ... ID-8
Spring Ridge—*ridge* ... NV-8
Spring Ridge—*ridge* (2) ... TN-4
Spring Ridge—*ridge* ... UT-8
Spring Ridge—*ridge* ... VA-3
Spring Ridge—*ridge* ... WV-2
Spring Ridge—*ridge* ... WI-6
Spring Ridge—*ridge* ... WY-8
Spring Ridge Administrative Site—*locale* ... UT-8
Spring Ridge Cem—*cemetery* (2) ... MS-4
Spring Ridge Cem—*cemetery* ... TX-5
Spring Ridge Ch—*church* ... KS-7
Spring Ridge Ch—*church* ... LA-4
Spring Ridge Ch—*church* (4) ... MS-4
Spring Ridge Ch—*church* ... TX-5
Springridge Lake Dam—*dam* ... MS-4
*Spring Ridge Plantation* ... MS-4
Spring Ridge Sch—*school* ... KY-4
Spring Ridge Sch (historical)—*school* (2) ... MS-4
Springridge Shop Ctr—*locale* ... MS-4
*Spring River* ... AR-4
*Spring River* ... MO-7
*Spring River* ... WI-6
Spring River—*stream* ... AR-4
Spring River—*stream* ... KS-7
Spring River—*stream* ... ME-1
Spring River—*stream* ... MO-7
Spring River—*stream* ... OK-5
Spring River—*stream* (2) ... OR-9
Spring River Cem—*cemetery* ... MO-7
Spring River Ch—*church* ... AR-4
Spring River Ch—*church* ... MO-7
Spring River Lake—*lake* ... ME-1
Spring River Mtn—*summit* ... ME-1
Spring River Shoal—*bar* ... AR-4
Spring River Township—*civil* ... MO-7
Spring River (Township of)—*fmr MCD* (2) ... AR-4
Spring Road Ch—*church* ... VA-3
Spring Road Sch—*school* ... WI-6
Spring Rock—*pillar* ... CA-9
Spring Rock—*pillar* ... RI-1
Spring Rockhouse Branch—*stream* ... TN-4
Spring Rock Township—*fmr MCD* ... IA-7
Spring Rsvr—*reservoir* (3) ... OR-9
Spring Rsvr—*reservoir* ... UT-8
*Spring Run* ... OH-6
*Spring Run* ... PA-2
*Spring Run* ... UT-8
*Spring Run* ... WV-2
Spring Run—*locale* ... WV-2
**Spring Run**—*pop pl* ... PA-2
Spring Run—*stream* ... CO-8
Spring Run—*stream* (2) ... FL-3
Spring Run—*stream* ... ID-8
Spring Run—*stream* (3) ... IL-6
Spring Run—*stream* (4) ... IN-6
Spring Run—*stream* ... MI-6
Spring Run—*stream* ... NY-2
Spring Run—*stream* (8) ... OH-6
Spring Run—*stream* (23) ... PA-2
Spring Run—*stream* (5) ... VA-3
Spring Run—*stream* (18) ... WV-2
Spring Run—*stream* (2) ... WY-8
Spring Run—*swamp* ... SC-3
**Spring Run Acres (subdivision)**—*pop pl* ... PA-2
Spring Run Branch—*stream* ... SC-3
Spring Run Camp—*locale* ... PA-2
Spring Run Canyon—*valley* ... ID-8
Spring Run Ch—*church* ... PA-2
Spring Run Fish Hatchery—*other* ... WV-2
Spring Run Gulch—*valley* ... UT-8
Spring Run Hollow—*valley* ... VA-3
Spring Run Landing—*locale* ... FL-3
**Spring Run Manor (subdivision)**—*pop pl* ... PA-2
Spring Run Park—*park* ... PA-2
Spring Run State Game Mngmt Area—*park* ... IA-7
Spring Run State Game Mngmt Areas—*park* ... IA-7
**Spring Run Subdivision**—*pop pl* ... UT-8
*Springs* ... MS-4
**Springs**—*pop pl* ... PA-2
Springs, Isle Of—*island* ... ME-1
Springs, Leroy, House—*hist pl* ... SC-3
Springs, The—*CDP* ... NY-2
Springs, The—*lake* ... NY-2
**Springs, The**—*pop pl* ... MA-1
Springs Assembly of God Ch—*church* ... FL-3
Springs Boat Dock—*locale* ... TN-4
*Springsboro* ... OH-6
*Springs Branch* ... IL-6
*Springs Branch* ... SC-3
*Springs Branch* ... WY-8
Springs Branch—*stream* ... KS-7
Springs Branch—*stream* ... TN-4
Springs Branch Creek—*stream* ... IA-7
Springs Camp—*locale* ... WA-9
Springs Cem—*cemetery* ... AL-4
Springs Cem—*cemetery* ... GA-3
Springs Cem—*cemetery* ... OK-5
Springs Ch—*church* ... NC-3
Spring Sch—*school* ... CA-9
Spring Sch—*school* ... OH-6
Spring Sch—*school* ... SC-3
Spring Sch (abandoned)—*school* ... PA-2
Springs Chapel—*church* ... TN-4
Springs Chapel Cem—*cemetery* ... TN-4
*Springs Chapel Cemetery* ... MS-4
Spring School (Aban'd)—*locale* ... CA-9
Springs Church, The—*church* ... VA-3
*Springs Creek* ... ID-8
*Springs Creek* ... WY-8
Springs Creek—*stream* ... NE-7
Springs Creek—*stream* ... NV-8
Springs Creek—*stream* ... ND-7
Springs Creek—*stream* ... TX-5
Springs Creek—*stream* ... WY-8
Springs Drain—*canal* ... WY-8
*Springs Draw* ... WY-8
Spring Seat—*locale* ... TX-5
Spring Seat Ch—*church* ... TX-5
Springs Forest Service Station—*building* ... AZ-5
*Springs Gulch* ... MT-8
Springs Gulch—*valley* ... MT-8
Springs Gulch Creek—*stream* ... MT-8
Spring Shadows—*uninc pl* ... TX-5
Spring Shadows Sch—*school* ... TX-5
Springside—*locale* ... FL-3
**Springside**—*pop pl* ... NJ-2
**Springside**—*pop pl* ... OH-6
Springside Cem—*cemetery* ... KS-7
Springside (historical)—*locale* ... KS-7
Springside JHS—*school* ... PA-2
Springside Park—*park* ... MA-1
**Springside Park (subdivision)**—*pop pl* ... FL-3
Springside Par 3 Golf Course—*locale* ... PA-2
Springside Ranch—*locale* ... MT-8
Springside Sch—*school* ... PA-2
**Springs Inn Estates (subdivision)**—*pop pl* ... TN-4
Springs Island—*island* ... ME-1
Springs Junction—*locale* ... AL-4
Springs Lake—*reservoir* ... NC-3
Springs Lake Dam—*dam* ... NC-3
Spring Slide Mtn—*summit* ... MT-8
Spring Slough—*gut* (2) ... AR-4
Spring Slough—*lake* ... ND-7
Spring Slough—*stream* ... AR-4
Spring Slough—*stream* ... ID-8
Spring Slough—*stream* ... IL-6
Spring Slough—*stream* ... OR-9
**Springs Mill**—*pop pl* ... MD-2
Springs Park—*park* ... GA-3
Springs Park—*park* ... OK-5
Springs Park—*park* ... WI-6
**Springs Park**—*pop pl* ... SC-3
Springs Plaza—*post sta* ... FL-3
Springs Plaza (Shop Ctr)—*locale* ... FL-3
Springs Post Office (historical)—*building* ... MS-4
Springs Post Office (historical)—*building* ... SD-7
Springs Run—*stream* ... IN-6
Springs Sch—*school* ... IL-6
*Springs Station* ... IN-6
*Spring Station* ... IN-6
Spring Station—*hist pl* ... KY-4
Spring Station—*locale* ... KY-4
Springstead—*locale* ... WI-6
Springstead Creek—*stream* ... WI-6
*Springstead Lakes* ... WI-6
Springstead Landing—*locale* ... WI-6
Springstead Lookout Tower—*locale* ... WI-6
**Springstead Trading Post**—*pop pl* ... NM-5
Springsteel Island—*island* ... MN-6
**Springsteel Island**—*pop pl* ... MN-6
*Springsteel Point* ... MN-6
Springsteen Lake—*lake* ... WA-9
Springsteen Ranch—*locale* ... WY-8
Springston—*locale* ... ID-8
Springston Canyon—*valley* ... OR-9
Springston Cem—*cemetery* ... WV-2
Springstone Run—*stream* ... WV-2
Springston Knob—*summit* ... MO-7
Springstowne—*post sta* ... CA-9
Springstown JHS—*school* ... CA-9
Spring Street Cem—*cemetery* ... MA-1
Spring Street Financial District—*hist pl* ... CA-9
Spring Street Hist Dist—*hist pl* ... ME-1
Spring Street Sch—*school* ... MA-1
Spring Street Sch—*school* ... OH-6
Spring Street Station (historical)—*locale* ... MA-1
Springstude Cem—*cemetery* ... MO-7
Springs Valley Community HS—*school* ... IN-6
Springs Valley Elem Sch—*school* ... IN-6
Springs Valley State Fish and Wildlife Area—*park* ... IN-6
Springs Valley Structure Number F-3 Dam—*dam* ... IN-6
**Springsville (historical)**—*pop pl* ... NC-3
Spring Swamp—*stream* ... SC-3
Spring Swamp—*swamp* ... PA-2
Spring Tabernacle—*church* ... TX-5
Spring Tank—*reservoir* (9) ... AZ-5
Spring Tank—*reservoir* (7) ... NM-5
Spring Tank—*reservoir* (4) ... TX-5
Spring Tanque de Caballos—*spring* ... NM-5
Spring Ten—*spring* ... NM-5
Springtime—*locale* ... MT-8
Springtime Campground—*locale* ... NM-5
Springtime Canyon—*valley* ... NM-5
Springtime Flat—*flat* ... CA-9
Springtime Mine—*mine* ... MT-8
**Spring Time (subdivision)**—*pop pl* ... NC-3
Springtime Tunnel—*mine* ... NV-8
Springton—*locale* ... PA-2
**Springton**—*pop pl* ... WV-2
Springton Lake MS—*school* ... PA-2
Springton Manor Farm—*hist pl* ... PA-2
Springton Rsvr—*reservoir* ... PA-2
Springton Station—*building* ... PA-2
*Springtown* ... MO-7
*Springtown* ... TN-4
Springtown—*locale* ... MT-8
Springtown—*locale* ... NJ-2
Springtown—*locale* (2) ... PA-2
Springtown—*locale* ... TX-5
**Springtown**—*pop pl* ... AR-4
**Springtown**—*pop pl* ... IN-6
**Springtown**—*pop pl* ... MO-7
**Springtown**—*pop pl* (2) ... NJ-2
**Springtown**—*pop pl* ... NY-2
**Springtown**—*pop pl* (3) ... PA-2
**Springtown**—*pop pl* ... TX-5
Springtown Baptist Ch—*church* ... TN-4
Springtown Boulder Cave—*cave* ... PA-2
Springtown Branch—*stream* ... TN-4
Springtown (CCD)—*cens area* ... TX-5
Springtown Cem—*cemetery* ... IL-6
Springtown Cem—*cemetery* ... OK-5
Springtown Ch—*church* ... OK-5
Springtown Ch—*church* (2) ... SC-3
*Springtown Church* ... AL-4
*Springtown Gulch* ... WA-9
Springtown Oil Field—*oilfield* ... TX-5
*Springtown Post Office* ... TN-4
Springtown Sch—*school* ... IL-6
Springtown Sch—*school* ... SC-3
*Spring Township* ... KS-7
Spring Township—*civil* (2) ... SD-7
Spring Township—*fmr MCD* ... IA-7
**Spring Township**—*pop pl* ... KS-7
**Spring Township**—*pop pl* ... SD-7
Spring (Township of)—*fmr MCD* (3) ... AR-4
**Spring (Township of)**—*pop pl* ... IL-6
**Spring (Township of)**—*pop pl* (5) ... PA-2
Springtown (Site)—*locale* ... ID-8
Spring Trail—*trail* ... MA-1
Spring Trail Spring—*spring* ... AZ-5
**Springtree Condominium**—*pop pl* ... UT-8
*Springvale* ... IA-7
Springvale—*locale* ... KS-7
Springvale—*locale* ... MN-6
Springvale—*locale* ... NY-2
Springvale—*locale* ... TN-4
Springvale—*locale* ... VA-3
**Springvale**—*pop pl* ... GA-3
**Springvale**—*pop pl* ... ME-1
**Springvale**—*pop pl* ... OH-6
**Springvale**—*pop pl* ... PA-2
**Springvale**—*pop pl* ... TN-4
**Springvale**—*pop pl* ... VA-3
Spring Vale Acad—*school* ... MI-6
Springvale Cem—*cemetery* ... GA-3
Springvale Cem—*cemetery* ... IN-6
Springvale Ch—*church* ... KS-7
Springvale Ch—*church* ... MN-6
Spring Vale Country Club—*other* ... OH-6
Springvale Ditch—*canal* ... WY-8
Springvale No 1 Ditch—*canal* ... WY-8
Springvale No 2 Ditch—*canal* ... WY-8
Springvale Park—*park* ... GA-3
Springvale Post Office (historical)—*building* ... TN-4
Springvale Sch—*school* ... CA-9
*Springvale State Fish Hatchery* ... TN-4
Springvale Station—*locale* ... GA-3
**Springvale (Town of)**—*pop pl* (2) ... WI-6
Springvale Township—*civ div* ... KS-7
Springvale Township—*civil* ... SD-7
**Springvale Township**—*pop pl* ... ND-7
**Springvale (Township of)**—*pop pl* ... MI-6
**Springvale (Township of)**—*pop pl* ... MN-6
*Springvalle* ... OH-6
*Springvalley* ... AL-4
*Spring Valley* ... MO-7
*Spring Valley* ... NV-8
*Spring Valley* ... ND-7
*Spring Valley* (2) ... OH-6
*Spring Valley* ... UT-8
Spring Valley—*basin* ... NE-7
Spring Valley—*basin* (2) ... NV-8
Spring Valley—*locale* ... AZ-5
Spring Valley—*locale* ... CA-9
Spring Valley—*locale* ... IA-7
Spring Valley—*locale* (2) ... NJ-2
Spring Valley—*locale* ... PA-2
Spring Valley—*locale* ... TX-5
Spring Valley—*locale* ... VA-3
Spring Valley—*locale* ... WA-9
Spring Valley—*locale* ... WY-8
**Spring Valley**—*pop pl* ... AL-4
**Spring Valley**—*pop pl* (2) ... AR-4
**Spring Valley**—*pop pl* ... CA-9
**Spring Valley**—*pop pl* ... CO-8
**Spring Valley**—*pop pl* ... DE-2
**Spring Valley**—*pop pl* ... DC-2
**Spring Valley**—*pop pl* ... IL-6
**Spring Valley**—*pop pl* ... KY-4
**Spring Valley**—*pop pl* ... MD-2
**Spring Valley**—*pop pl* ... MN-6
**Spring Valley**—*pop pl* ... MS-4
**Spring Valley**—*pop pl* ... MO-7
**Spring Valley**—*pop pl* (2) ... NY-2
**Spring Valley**—*pop pl* (3) ... OH-6
**Spring Valley**—*pop pl* ... OR-9
**Spring Valley**—*pop pl* (3) ... PA-2
**Spring Valley**—*pop pl* ... SD-7
**Spring Valley**—*pop pl* (2) ... TN-4
**Spring Valley**—*pop pl* ... TX-5
**Spring Valley**—*pop pl* ... VA-3
**Spring Valley**—*pop pl* ... WV-2
**Spring Valley**—*pop pl* (2) ... WI-6
Spring Valley—*post sta* ... TX-5
Spring Valley—*stream* ... NV-8
Spring Valley—*valley* (2) ... AZ-5
Spring Valley—*valley* (4) ... CA-9
Spring Valley—*valley* (2) ... CO-8
Spring Valley—*valley* ... ID-8
Spring Valley—*valley* ... KS-7
Spring Valley—*valley* (3) ... MO-7
Spring Valley—*valley* (2) ... NV-8
Spring Valley—*valley* ... OH-6
Spring Valley—*valley* ... OR-9
Spring Valley—*valley* (2) ... VA-3
Spring Valley—*valley* (2) ... WA-9
Spring Valley—*valley* (7) ... WI-6
**Spring Valley Acres (subdivision)**—*pop pl* ... AL-4
Spring Valley Athletic Club—*other* ... TX-5
Spring Valley Baptist Ch—*church* ... AL-4
*Spring Valley Baptist Church* ... MS-4
Spring Valley Branch—*stream* ... CA-9
Spring Valley Branch—*stream* ... VA-3
Spring Valley Branch—*stream* ... WV-2
Spring Valley Canal—*canal* ... MT-8
*Spring Valley Canyon* ... NV-8
Spring Valley Canyon—*valley* (2) ... NV-8
Spring Valley Carnegie Library—*hist pl* ... MN-6
Spring Valley Cem—*cemetery* ... AR-4
Spring Valley Cem—*cemetery* ... CO-8
Spring Valley Cem—*cemetery* (2) ... IL-6
Spring Valley Cem—*cemetery* ... IA-7
Spring Valley Cem—*cemetery* ... KS-7
Spring Valley Cem—*cemetery* ... MN-6
Spring Valley Cem—*cemetery* ... MS-4
Spring Valley Cem—*cemetery* (2) ... MO-7
Spring Valley Cem—*cemetery* ... OK-5
Spring Valley Cem—*cemetery* (2) ... SD-7
Spring Valley Cem—*cemetery* ... WY-8
Spring Valley Ch—*church* ... AL-4
Spring Valley Ch—*church* (2) ... AR-4
Spring Valley Ch—*church* ... IL-6
Spring Valley Ch—*church* (2) ... KS-7
Spring Valley Ch—*church* ... KY-4
Spring Valley Ch—*church* ... MI-6
Spring Valley Ch—*church* (2) ... MS-4
Spring Valley Ch—*church* (4) ... MO-7
Spring Valley Ch—*church* ... NE-7
Spring Valley Ch—*church* ... NC-3
Spring Valley Ch—*church* ... OH-6
Spring Valley Ch—*church* (2) ... SD-7
Spring Valley Ch—*church* ... TX-5
Spring Valley Ch—*church* (3) ... VA-3
Spring Valley Ch—*church* ... WA-9
Spring Valley Ch—*church* ... WV-2
Spring Valley Ch—*church* (2) ... WI-6
Spring Valley Ch (abandoned)—*church* ... MO-7
Spring Valley Ch (historical)—*church* ... MS-4
*Spring Valley Church* ... TN-4
Spring Valley Church—*school* ... KS-7
**Spring Valley Colony**—*pop pl* ... SD-7
Spring Valley Colony Ch—*church* ... SD-7
Spring Valley Community Center—*locale* ... OR-9
Spring Valley Country Club—*locale* ... MA-1
Spring Valley Country Club—*other* ... KY-4
Spring Valley Country Club—*other* ... SC-3
Spring Valley Country Club—*other* ... WV-2
*Spring Valley Creek* ... MO-7
Spring Valley Creek—*stream* (2) ... CA-9
Spring Valley Creek—*stream* (2) ... ID-8
Spring Valley Creek—*stream* ... IL-6
Spring Valley Creek—*stream* ... IA-7
Spring Valley Creek—*stream* ... MN-6
Spring Valley Creek—*stream* (4) ... MO-7
Spring Valley Creek—*stream* ... NV-8
Spring Valley Creek—*stream* ... ND-7
Spring Valley Creek—*stream* (2) ... OR-9
Spring Valley Creek—*stream* ... WA-9
Spring Valley Creek—*stream* (2) ... WI-6
Spring Valley Dam—*dam* ... NJ-2
Spring Valley Dock—*locale* ... AL-4
Spring Valley Drain—*stream* ... MI-6
Spring Valley Drop—*canal* ... MT-8
**Spring Valley Estates**—*pop pl* ... AL-4
**Spring Valley Estates**—*pop pl* ... IN-6
**Spring Valley Estates**—*pop pl* ... PA-2
Spring Valley Farm—*hist pl* ... WV-2
Spring Valley Farms Ponds—*reservoir* ... AL-4
Spring Valley General Hosp—*hospital* ... NY-2
Spring Valley Golf Club—*other* ... CA-9
Spring Valley Golf Club—*other* ... OH-6
Spring Valley Guard Station—*locale* ... AZ-5
Spring Valley Gulch—*valley* ... CA-9
Spring Valley Hist Dist—*hist pl* ... PA-2
Spring Valley (historical)—*locale* ... IA-7
Spring Valley (historical)—*locale* ... KS-7
Spring Valley (historical)—*locale* ... SD-7
**Spring Valley (historical)**—*pop pl* ... OR-9
Spring Valley House-Sulfur Springs Hotel—*hist pl* ... IL-6
Spring Valley HS—*school* ... SC-3
Spring Valley JHS—*school* ... CA-9
Spring Valley Knolls—*summit* ... AZ-5
*Spring Valley Lake* ... WI-6
Spring Valley Lake—*lake* ... CA-9
Spring Valley Lake—*lake* ... NE-7
Spring Valley Lake—*lake* ... NC-3
Spring Valley Lake—*lake* (2) ... OH-6
Spring Valley Lake—*post sta* ... CA-9
Spring Valley Lake—*reservoir* ... MO-7
Spring Valley Lake—*reservoir* ... NJ-2
Spring Valley Lake—*reservoir* ... NC-3
Spring Valley Lake—*reservoir* (2) ... OH-6
Spring Valley Lake—*reservoir* ... PA-2
Spring Valley Lake Dam—*dam* ... NC-3
Spring Valley Lake Dam—*dam* ... PA-2
Spring Valley Lakes—*reservoir* ... AL-4
Spring Valley Mausoleum—*hist pl* ... MN-6
Spring Valley Meadow—*flat* ... OR-9
**Spring Valley (Mechanics Valley)**—*pop pl* ... PA-2
Spring Valley Methodist Episcopal Church—*hist pl* ... MN-6
Spring Valley Mtn—*summit* ... CA-9
Spring Valley Oil Field—*oilfield* ... KS-7
Spring Valley Park—*park* ... MI-6
Spring Valley Park—*park* ... MO-7
Spring Valley Park—*park* ... NV-8
Spring Valley Park—*park* ... PA-2
Spring Valley Pass—*gap* ... NV-8
*Spring Valley Ponds* ... AL-4
Spring Valley Ponds Dam—*dam* ... AL-4
Spring Valley Post Office (historical)—*building* ... SD-7
Spring Valley Presbyterian Church—*hist pl* ... OR-9
*Spring Valley Ranch* ... SD-7
Spring Valley Ranch—*locale* ... CA-9
Spring Valley Ranch—*locale* ... CO-8
Spring Valley Ranch—*locale* ... KS-7
Spring Valley Ranch Landing Strip—*airport* ... AR-4
Spring Valley Ridge—*ridge* ... CA-9
Spring Valley Rsvr—*reservoir* ... CA-9
Spring Valley Sch—*hist pl* ... CO-8
Spring Valley Sch—*school* ... AL-4
Spring Valley Sch—*school* (5) ... CA-9
Spring Valley Sch—*school* (3) ... IL-6
Spring Valley Sch—*school* ... IA-7
Spring Valley Sch—*school* (3) ... KS-7
Spring Valley Sch—*school* (2) ... MI-6
Spring Valley Sch—*school* (4) ... MO-7
Spring Valley Sch—*school* ... NE-7
Spring Valley Sch—*school* ... NJ-2
Spring Valley Sch—*school* (2) ... OH-6
Spring Valley Sch—*school* (2) ... OK-5
Spring Valley Sch—*school* (3) ... SD-7
Spring Valley Sch—*school* (5) ... WI-6
Spring Valley Sch (historical)—*school* ... MO-7
Spring Valley Sch (historical)—*school* ... TN-4
Spring Valley School—*locale* ... CO-8
Spring Valley School—*locale* ... KS-7
Spring Valley Shop Ctr—*locale* ... TX-5
Spring Valley State Public Shooting Area—*park* ... SD-7
Spring Valley Station—*locale* ... AL-4
**Spring Valley (subdivision)**—*pop pl* (3) ... AL-4
**Spring Valley (subdivision)**—*pop pl* (4) ... NC-3
**Spring Valley (subdivision)**—*pop pl* ... PA-2
**Spring Valley (subdivision)**—*pop pl* ... TN-4
**Spring Valley Subdivision**—*pop pl* ... UT-8
Spring Valley Summit—*gap* ... NV-8

Spring Valley Swamp—swamp SC-3
Spring Valley Tank—reservoir AZ-5
Spring Valley Town Hall—building ND-7
**Spring Valley (Town of)**—pop pl WI-6
Spring Valley Township—civil MO-7
Spring Valley Township—civil (2) SD-7
Spring Valley Township—fmr MCD (2) IA-7
**Spring Valley Township**—pop pl (2) KS-7
**Spring Valley Township**—pop pl ND-7
**Spring Valley Township**—pop pl (3) SD-7
Spring Valley Township Hall—building SD-7
Spring Valley (Township of)—civ div MN-6
Spring Valley (Township of)—civ div OH-6
Spring Valley Wash NV-8
Spring Valley Wash—arroyo AZ-5
Spring Valley Wash—arroyo NV-8
Spring Valley Wildlife Area—park OH-6
Spring Veiw NE 7
**Springview**—pop pl NE-7
**Springview**—pop pl (2) TN-4
**Spring View Acres**—pop pl GA-3
Spring View Ch—church TN-4
Springview Hosp—hospital OH-6
Springview Lake—reservoir TX-5
Spring View Sch—school CA-9
Springview Sch—school FL-3
Springview Sch—school GA-3
Springview Sch—school MI-6
Spring View Sch—school NE-7
Springview Sch—school SD-7
Spring Villa—hist pl AL-4
Spring Villa—locale AL-4
Spring Villa Camping and Rec
Area—park AL-4
Spring Village Pond MA-1
Spring Villa State Park AL-4
Springville MA-1
Springville PA-2
Springville—locale CA-9
Springville—locale FL-3
Springville—locale IL-6
Springville—locale IA-7
Springville—locale (2) PA-2
Springville—locale VA-3
**Springville**—pop pl AL-4
**Springville**—pop pl CA-9
**Springville**—pop pl (3) IN-6
**Springville**—pop pl IA-7
**Springville**—pop pl (2) LA-4
**Springville**—pop pl MI-6
**Springville**—pop pl MS-4
**Springville**—pop pl NJ-2
**Springville**—pop pl (2) NY-2
**Springville**—pop pl (2) OH-6
**Springville**—pop pl (5) PA-2
**Springville**—pop pl TN-4
**Springville**—pop pl UT-8
**Springville**—pop pl WI-6
Springville Assembly of God Church MS-4
Springville Branch WI-6
Springville Branch—stream TN-4
Springville Branch Bad Axe
River—stream WI-6
Springville Brook WI-6
Springville (CCD)—cens area AL-4
Springville (CCD)—cens area TN-4
Springville Cem—cemetery IA-7
Springville Cem—cemetery (2) PA-2
Springville Cem—cemetery SC-3
Springville Ch—church AL-4
Springville Ch—church FL-3
Springville Ch—church (2) MS-4
Springville Ch—church PA-2
Springville Ch—church TN-4
Springville Ch—church VA-3
Springville Chapel Missionary Baptist
Ch—church MS-4
Springville City Cem—cemetery UT-8
Springville Community Presbyterian
Ch—church UT-8
Springville Creek—stream NY-2
Springville Crossing UT-8
Springville Crossings—locale UT-8
Springville Division—civil AL-4
Springville Division—civil TN-4
Springville Elem Sch—school IN-6
Springville Elem Sch (historical)—school AL-4
Springville Estate Dam—dam AL-4
**Springville (historical)**—pop pl OR-9
Springville HS—school AL-4
Springville HS—school UT-8
Springville HS Art Gallery—hist pl UT-8
Springville JHS—school UT-8
Springville-Johnsondale (CCD)—cens area CA-9
Springville Lake—reservoir AL-4
Springville Lake Estates—locale AL-4
Springville Lookout Tower—locale LA-4
Springville-Mapleton—cens area UT-8
Springville-Mapleton Division—civil UT-8
Springville Missionary Baptist Ch MS-4
Springville MS—school UT-8
Springville Pond—reservoir WI-6
Springville Post Office—building TN-4
Springville Post Office—building UT-8
Springville Presbyterian Church—hist pl UT-8
Springville Sch—school NE-7
Springville Sch—school PA-2
Springville Sch—school SC-3
Springville Sch—school TN-4
Springville Sportsman Dam—dam AL-4
Springville Sportsmen Lake—reservoir AL-4
Springville Station—locale UT-8
**Springville (subdivision)**—pop pl PA-2
**Springville (Town of)**—pop pl WI-6
**Springville (Township of)**—pop pl MI-6
**Springville (Township of)**—pop pl PA-2
Springwagon Creek—stream NM-5
Spring Warrior Camp—locale FL-3
Spring Warrior Ch—church FL-3
Spring Warrior Creek—stream FL-3
Spring Warriors—locale FL-3
Spring Wash AZ-5
Spring Wash UT-8
Spring Wash—stream AZ-5
Spring Wash Canyon—valley UT-8
**Springwater**—pop pl IA-7
**Springwater**—pop pl NY-2
**Springwater**—pop pl OR-9
Spring Water Camp—locale HI-9
Spring Water Canyon—valley AZ-5
Springwater Cem—cemetery IA-7
Springwater Cem—cemetery MN-6
Springwater Cem—cemetery WI-6
Springwater Ch—church IA-7
Springwater Creek—stream MN-6
Springwater Creek—stream NY-2
Springwater Creek—stream SD-7
Springwater Dam—reservoir ND-7
Spring Water Lake—lake AK-9
Spring Water Lake Dam—dam ND-7
Springwater Nursing Home—hospital WI-6
Springwater Run—stream OH-6
**Springwater (Town of)**—pop pl NY-2
**Springwater (Town of)**—pop pl WI-6
**Springwater (Township of)**—pop pl MN-6
Springwater Valley—valley NY-2
Springway Ch—church GA-3
Springway Creek stream AK 9
Spring Well—locale NM-5
Spring Well—well (2) NM-5
Springwell Cem—cemetery NE-7
**Springwell Heights**—pop pl MI-6
Springwells MI-6
Spring Wheeler Creek—stream CA-9
Spring Willow Coulee—valley MT-8
Spring Windmill—locale NM-5
Spring Windmill—locale TX-5
**Springwood**—pop pl IN-6
**Springwood**—pop pl MD-2
**Springwood**—pop pl NC-3
**Springwood**—pop pl OH-6
**Springwood**—pop pl SC-3
**Springwood**—pop pl VA-3
Springwood Cem—cemetery SC-3
Springwood Ch—church NC-3
Springwood Lakes—lake MI-6
Springwood Landing (historical)—locale MS-4
Springwood Manor—hist pl NY-2
Springwood Plantation—locale SC-3
Spring Woods HS—school TX-5
Springwoods JHS—school TX-5
Springwood Truss Bridge—hist pl VA-3
**Springwood Village**—pop pl NY-2
Spring Yard Hill—summit AL-4
Springy Brook—stream ME-1
Springy Brook Mtn—summit ME-1
Springy Pond ME-1
Springy Pond—lake MA-1
Sprinkle—locale TX-5
Sprinkle Branch—stream KY-4
Sprinkle Branch—stream NC-3
Sprinkle Cem—cemetery AL-4
Sprinkle Cem—cemetery (2) IN-6
Sprinkle Cem—cemetery NC-3
Sprinkle Cem—cemetery VA-3
Sprinkle Coulee—valley MT-8
Sprinkle Creek—stream IN-6
Sprinkle Creek—stream NC-3
Sprinkle Lake—lake OH-6
Sprinkler Branch—stream NC-3
Sprinkler Lake—lake (3) MI-6
Sprinkles Branch—stream TN-4
Sprinkling Canal Hollow—valley PA-2
Sprite—locale GA-3
Sprite Creek—stream (2) NY-2
Sprite Island—island CT-1
Sprite Lake—lake MN-6
Sprite Lake—lake (2) WA-9
Sprite Lakelet WA-9
Spritzer Ranch—locale MT-8
Sprive Run—stream WV-2
Sproat Cem—cemetery OH-6
Sproat Sch—school MI-6
Sproats Meadow—swamp OR-9
Sproat Spring—spring ID-8
Sproat Trail—trail PA-2
Sproch Cem—cemetery CO-8
Sprogels Run—stream PA-2
Sprole—locale MT-8
Sprole Ranch—locale NM-5
Sproles Cem—cemetery MS-4
Sproles Cem—cemetery TN-4
Sproles Cem—cemetery (2) VA-3
Sproles (historical)—locale MS-4
Sprolls Hollow—valley TN-4
Spromberg Canyon—valley WA-9
Sprong Bluff—cliff NY-2
Sprong Lake—lake MI-6
Spronks Creek—stream CO-8
Spross Park—park MO-7
Sprotsmens Lakes—reservoir MS-4
**Sprott**—pop pl AL-4
**Sprott**—pop pl MO-7
Sprott (CCD)—cens area AL-4
Sprott Cem—cemetery TN-4
Sprott Division—civil AL-4
Sprott's Hill Mounds Site—hist pl OH-6
**Sprotville**—pop pl AR-4
Sproul—locale WV-2
**Sproul**—pop pl PA-2
Sproul, Mesa—summit TX-5
Sproul, The—crater AZ-5
Sproul Bend—bend KY-4
Sproul Canyon—valley OR-9
Sproul Cem—cemetery PA-2
Sproul Dam—dam OR-9
Sproule Cabin—locale NV-8
Sproule Creek CA-9
Sproule Creek—stream CA-9
Sproule Flat—flat ID-8
Sproul Homestead—hist pl ME-1
Sproul Lake—lake MN-6
Sproul Lateral—canal CA-9
Sproull Mtn—summit GA-3
Sproul Point—cape ME-1
Sproul Point—summit OR-9
Sproul Rsvr—reservoir OR-9
Sproul Rsvr—reservoir TX-5
Sproul's Cafe—hist pl ME-1
Sproul Sch—school CO-8
Sprouls Point ME-1
Sproul Spring—spring OR-9
Sproul State For—forest PA-2
Sprouse Branch—stream NC-3
Sprouse Cem—cemetery NC-3
Sprouse Cem—cemetery TX-5
Sprouse Creek—stream WV-2
Sprouse Gap—gap NC-3
Sprouse Hollow—valley TX-5
Sprouse Hollow—valley VA-3
Sprouse Mine—mine NM-5
Sprouse Mtn—summit VA-3
Sprouse Ridge—ridge KY-4
Sprouses VA-3
**Sprouses Corner**—pop pl VA-3
Sprouse Spring—spring UT-8
Sprout—locale KY-4
Sprout Branch—stream KY-4
Sprout Branch—stream MS-4
**Sprout Brook**—pop pl NY-2
Sprout Brook—stream NJ-2
Sprout Cem—cemetery MI-6
Sprout Creek—stream CA-9
Sprout Creek—stream ID-8
Sprout Creek—stream NY-2
Sprout Hill—summit NY-2
Sprout Lake—lake NY-2
Sprout Mtn summit ID 8
Sprout Point—cape PA-2
Sprout Point Fire Tower—tower PA-2
Sprouts Creek—stream VA-3
Sprout Spring—spring UT-8
Sprout Springs KY-4
Sprouts Run—stream VA-3
Sprout Tunnel—tunnel WV-2
Sproutville—CDP NY-2
Sprowl Cem—cemetery MS-4
Sprowl's Covered Bridge—hist pl PA-2
**Spruance City**—pop pl DE-2
Spruance Pond—lake ME-1
Spruances Branch—stream DE-2
Spruance Sch—school PA-2
Spruances Neck—cape DE-2
Spruca Lake MI-6
Spruce NC-3
Spruce PA-2
Spruce—locale CO-8
Spruce—locale MI-6
Spruce—locale MN-6
Spruce—locale NV-8
Spruce—locale PA-2
Spruce—locale WV-2
Spruce—other PA-2
**Spruce**—pop pl MI-6
**Spruce**—pop pl MO-7
**Spruce**—pop pl PA-2
**Spruce**—pop pl WI-6
Spruce Bank Sch (abandoned)—school PA-2
Spruce Bluff—cliff FL-3
Spruce Bottom Shelter—locale WA-9
Spruce Branch—stream (4) KY-4
Spruce Branch—stream NC-3
Spruce Branch—stream TN-4
Spruce Branch—stream WV-2
Spruce Brook AZ-5
Spruce Brook—stream (9) CT-1
Spruce Brook—stream (2) ME-1
Spruce Brook—stream (4) NH-1
Spruce Brook—stream RI-1
Spruce Cabin Falls—falls PA-2
Spruce Cabin Pond—reservoir PA-2
Spruce Cabin Run—stream PA-2
Spruce Campground—locale (2) CO-8
Spruce Canyon—valley AZ-5
Spruce Canyon—valley (3) CA-9
Spruce Canyon—valley (2) CO-8
Spruce Canyon—valley (3) NM-5
Spruce Canyon—valley UT-8
Spruce Canyon Spring—spring AZ-5
Spruce Canyon Youth Camp—locale WA-9
Spruce Cape—cape AK-9
Spruce Cem—cemetery (2) MN-6
Spruce Cem—cemetery WI-6
Spruce Center—locale MN-6
Spruce Ch—church KY-4
Spruce Ch—church MN-6
**Spruce Corner**—pop pl MA-1
Spruce Cove—bay ME-1
Spruce Creek CO-8
Spruce Creek ID-8
Spruce Creek IA-7
Spruce Creek MO-7
Spruce Creek MT-8
Spruce Creek OR-9
Spruce Creek PA-2
Spruce Creek WV-2
**Spruce Creek**—pop pl PA-2
Spruce Creek—stream (10) AK-9
Spruce Creek—stream (3) CA-9
Spruce Creek—stream (11) CO-8
Spruce Creek—stream FL-3
Spruce Creek—stream (11) ID-8
Spruce Creek—stream IA-7
Spruce Creek—stream (3) KY-4
Spruce Creek—stream ME-1
Spruce Creek—stream MI-6
Spruce Creek—stream (2) MN-6
Spruce Creek—stream (12) MT-8
Spruce Creek—stream NM-5
Spruce Creek—stream (3) NY-2
Spruce Creek—stream OH-6
Spruce Creek—stream (3) OR-9
Spruce Creek—stream PA-2
Spruce Creek—stream (2) TN-4
Spruce Creek—stream UT-8
Spruce Creek—stream VA-3
Spruce Creek—stream (4) WA-9
Spruce Creek—stream WV-2
Spruce Creek—stream (7) WY-8
Spruce Creek Airp—airport FL-3
Spruce Creek Baptist Ch—church FL-3
Spruce Creek Cabin—locale NM-5
Spruce Creek Ch—church WV-2
Spruce Creek Elem Sch—school FL-3
Spruce Creek Lakes—lake ID-8
Spruce Creek Park—park IA-7
Spruce Creek Senior HS—school FL-3
Spruce Creek Spring—spring AZ-5
**Spruce Creek (Spruce)**—pop pl PA-2
Spruce Creek State Wildlife Mngmt
Area—park MN-6
Spruce Creek Swamp—swamp FL-3
**Spruce Creek (Township of)**—pop pl PA-2
Spruce Crossing Gulch—valley CO-8
Sprucedale—locale AZ-5
**Sprucedale**—pop pl CO-8
Spruce Double—summit TN-4
Spruce Double Branch—stream TN-4
Spruce Drain—canal CA-9
Spruce Drain No 2—canal CA-9
Spruce Drain Number One—canal CA-9
Spruce Drain Number One B—canal CA-9
Spruce Drain 2—canal CA-9
Spruce Draw—valley CA-9
Spruce Draw—valley CO-8
Sprucefish Lake—lake AK-9
Spruce Flats—flat TN-4
Spruce Flats—flat WV-2
Spruce Flats Branch—stream TN-4
Spruce Fork WV-2
Spruce Fork—stream (4) KY-4
Spruce Fork—stream NC-3
Spruce Fork—stream (17) WV-2
Spruce Fork Ch—church (2) WV-2
Spruce Four Drain—canal CA-9
Spruce Gap—gap (2) PA-2
**Spruce Gardens**—pop pl NJ-2
**Spruce Glen Brook** stream CT 1
Spruce Grouse Pond NY-2
Spruce Grove—locale PA-2
Spruce Grove—woods CA-9
Spruce Grove Campground—locale (2) CA-9
Spruce Grove Campground—locale CO-8
Spruce Grove Cem—cemetery MN-6
Spruce Grove Ch—church MN-6
Spruce Grove Ch—church NC-3
Spruce Grove Ch—church PA-2
Spruce Grove Ch—church (4) WV-2
Spruce Grove Sch—hist pl PA-2
Spruce Grove (Township of)—civ div (2) MN-6
Spruce Gulch—valley CA-9
Spruce Gulch—valley (7) CO-8
Spruce Gulch—valley (3) ID-8
Spruce Gulch—valley MT-8
Spruce Gulch—valley OR-9
Spruce Gulch—valley (2) SD-7
Spruce Gulch—valley WY-8
Spruce Gulch Lake—lake ID-8
Spruce Gut ME-1
Spruce Hall—hist pl CO-8
Spruce Haven Camp—locale CO-8
Sprucehead ME-1
Spruce Head—cape ME-1
Spruce Head—cliff ME-1
**Spruce Head**—pop pl ME-1
Spruce Head Island ME-1
Sprucehead Island—island ME-1
**Spruce Head Island**—pop pl ME-1
Spruce Hill MA-1
Spruce Hill NY-2
**Spruce Hill**—pop pl (2) PA-2
Spruce Hill—ridge OH-6
Spruce Hill—summit CO-8
Spruce Hill—summit ME-1
Spruce Hill—summit (4) MA-1
Spruce Hill—summit NH-1
Spruce Hill—summit NM-5
Spruce Hill—summit (4) NY-2
Spruce Hill—summit PA-2
Spruce Hill—summit VT-1
Spruce Hill Acres—locale PA-2
Spruce Hill Brook—stream NY-2
Spruce Hill Cem—cemetery MN-6
Spruce Hill Cem—cemetery NY-2
Spruce Hill Ch—church MN-6
Spruce Hills—summit ME-1
Spruce Hills—summit MT-8
Spruce Hill Sch (abandoned)—school PA-2
Spruce Hill Sch Number 1—school ND-7
Spruce Hill Sch Number 2—school ND-7
**Spruce Hill (Township of)**—pop pl MN-6
**Spruce Hill (Township of)**—pop pl PA-2
Spruce Hill Trail—trail ME-1
Spruce Hill Trail—trail MA-1
Spruce Hill Works—hist pl OH-6
**Spruce (historical)**—pop pl OR-9
Spruce Hole—basin CO-8
Spruce Hole—basin NH-1
Spruce Hole Trail—trail CO-8
Spruce Hollow—valley (4) KY-4
Spruce Hollow—valley MD-2
Spruce Hollow—valley OR-9
Spruce Hollow—valley (2) PA-2
Spruce Hollow—valley (3) WV-2
Spruce Hollow—valley WY-8
Spruce Hollow Run—stream PA-2
Spruce Island—island (2) AK-9
Spruce Island—island (3) ME-1
Spruce Island—island NY-2
Spruce Island Gut ME-1
Spruce Island Lake—lake MN-6
Spruce Knob—summit PA-2
Spruce Knob—summit VT-1
Spruce Knob—summit (3) WV-2
Spruce Knob Lake—reservoir WV-2
Spruce Knob Lake Campground—locale WV-2
Spruce Knoll—summit VT-1
Spruce Lake MI-6
Spruce Lake MN-6
Spruce Lake WA-9
Spruce Lake WI-6
Spruce Lake—lake (3) AK-9
Spruce Lake—lake (2) CO-8
Spruce Lake—lake (2) FL-3
Spruce Lake—lake (2) ID-8
Spruce Lake—lake (9) MI-6
Spruce Lake—lake (12) MN-6
Spruce Lake—lake (3) MT-8
Spruce Lake—lake NY-2
Spruce Lake—lake OH-6
Spruce Lake—lake (2) OR-9
Spruce Lake—lake PA-2
Spruce Lake—lake (11) WI-6
Spruce Lake—lake WY-8
Spruce Lake—reservoir CO-8
Spruce Lake—reservoir NJ-2
Spruce Lake—reservoir NY-2
Spruce Lake—reservoir WI-6
Spruce Lake Bog Natl Landmark—locale WI-6
Spruce Lake Dam—dam NJ-2
Spruce Lake Mtn—summit NY-2
Spruce Lakes WI-6
Spruce Lakes—lake CO-8
Spruce Lakes—lake NH-1
Spruceland Camps—locale NH-1
Spruce Lateral Five—canal CA-9
Spruce Lateral Four—canal CA-9
Spruce Lateral One—canal CA-9
Spruce Lateral Three—canal CA-9
Spruce Laurel Ch—church WV-2
Spruce Laurel Fork—stream WV-2
Spruce Lawn Ditch—canal CO-8
Spruce Lick—stream (2) WV-2
Spruce Lick Branch—stream TN-4
Spruce Lick Branch—stream (2) VA-3
Spruce Lick Ch—church WV-2
Spruce Lick Creek—stream TN-4
Spruce Lick Fork—stream WV-2
Spruce Lick Fresh Water Dam—dam TN-4
Spruce Lick Hollow—valley WV-2
Spruce Lick Run—stream VA-3
Spruce Lick Run—stream WV-2
Spruce Lick Slurry Refuse Dam—dam TN-4
Spruce Lick Slurry Refuse
Impound—reservoir TN-4
Spruce Lodge Campground—locale CO-8
Spruce Log Trail—trail OR-9
**Spruce Lookout**—locale MT 8
Spruce Low Gap—gap WV-2
Spruce Meadow—flat OR-9
Spruce Mill Brook—stream NY-2
Spruce Mill Park—park CO-8
Spruce Mine—mine MN-6
Sprucemont—locale NV-8
Sprucemont Mountains NV-8
Spruce Mountain Brook—stream ME-1
Spruce Mountain Cove—bay ME-1
Spruce Mountain Lake—lake ME-1
Spruce Mountain Lake Brook—stream ME-1
Spruce Mountain Lookout Family Picnic
Area—park AZ-5
Spruce Mountain Pond—lake ME-1
Spruce Mountain Ridge—ridge NV-8
Spruce Mountain Ridge—ridge NC-3
Spruce Mountain Run—stream (2) PA-2
Spruce Mountain Trail—trail PA-2
Spruce Mountain Trail—trail WV-2
Spruce Mtn—summit (2) AZ-5
Spruce Mtn—summit (8) CO-8
Spruce Mtn—summit CT-1
Spruce Mtn—summit ID-8
Spruce Mtn—summit (10) ME-1
Spruce Mtn—summit MA-1
Spruce Mtn—summit MT-8
Spruce Mtn—summit NV-8
Spruce Mtn—summit (2) NH-1
Spruce Mtn—summit (12) NY-2
Spruce Mtn—summit NC-3
Spruce Mtn—summit (2) PA-2
Spruce Mtn—summit (2) VT-1
Spruce Mtn—summit WA-9
Spruce Mtn—summit (3) WV-2
Spruce Mtn—summit WY-8
Spruce Mtn Brook CT-1
Spruce Narrows—valley WV-2
Spruce One Drain—canal CA-9
Spruce Park—flat MT-8
Spruce Park—flat NM-5
Spruce Park—park MN-6
Spruce Park Ch—church MN-6
Spruce Park Hist Dist—hist pl NM-5
Spruce Park Moose Lake Trail—trail MT-8
Spruce Peak—summit AK-9
Spruce Peak—summit (4) VT-1
Spruce Picnic Area—locale CO-8
Spruce Pine—locale KY-4
Spruce Pine—locale TN-4
**Spruce Pine**—pop pl AL-4
**Spruce Pine**—pop pl NC-3
Spruce Pine Baptist Ch—church AL-4
Spruce Pine Branch VA-3
Sprucepine Branch—stream KY-4
Spruce Pine Branch—stream (4) KY-4
Sprucepine Branch—stream TN-4
Spruce Pine Branch—stream (2) VA-3
Sprucepine Branch—stream VA-3
Spruce Pine Campground—locale NC-3
Spruce Pine Cem—cemetery AL-4
Spruce Pine Ch—church TN-4
Spruce Pine Ch—church VA-3
Spruce Pine Ch of Christ—church AL-4
Sprucepine Creek VA-3
Spruce Pine Creek—stream GA-3
Spruce Pine Creek—stream (2) KY-4
Spruce Pine Creek—stream VA-3
Sprucepine Fork—stream KY-4
Spruce Pine Fork—stream (5) KY-4
Spruce Pine Gap—gap VA-3
Spruce Pine Golf Course—locale NC-3
Spruce Pine Hollow—valley KY-4
Spruce Pine Hollow—valley (2) VA-3
Spruce Pine Island—island KY-4
Spruce Pine Lake—lake KY-4
Spruce Pine Lookout Tower—locale NC-3
Spruce Pine Memorial Cem—cemetery NC-3
Sprucepine Ridge—ridge NC-3
Spruce Pine Rsvr—reservoir NC-3
Spruce Pine Sch—school KY-4
Spruce Pine Sch (historical)—school AL-4
Spruce Pine Sch (historical)—school TN-4
Spruce Pine United Methodist Ch—church AL-4
Spruce Pinnacle—summit NC-3
Spruce Point ME-1
Spruce Point—cape (2) AK-9
Spruce Point—cape (5) ME-1
Spruce Point—cape MI-6
Spruce Point—cape NV-8
Spruce Point—cape OR-9
Spruce Point—cliff CO-8
**Spruce Point**—pop pl CA-9
**Spruce Point**—pop pl ME-1
Spruce Point—summit MT-8
Spruce Point Cem—cemetery OR-9
Spruce Point Chapel—church ME-1
Spruce Point Cove—bay ME-1
Spruce Point Ledges—bar ME-1
Spruce Point Trail—trail CO-8
Spruce Pond—lake CT-1
Spruce Pond—lake (2) ME-1
Spruce Pond—lake (3) MA-1
Spruce Pond—lake NH-1
Spruce Pond—lake (3) NY-2
Spruce Pond—lake PA-2
Spruce Pond—lake VT-1
Spruce Pond Camp (BSA)—locale NY-2
Spruce Ponds—lake NH-1
Spruce Ranch—locale TX-5
Spruce Reservoir Dam—dam PA-2
Spruce Ridge NC-3
Spruce Ridge—ridge CA-9
Spruce Ridge—ridge (2) CO-8
Spruce Ridge—ridge ME-1
Spruce Ridge—ridge NH-1
Spruce Ridge—ridge NY-2
Spruce Ridge—ridge NC-3
Spruce Ridge—ridge WV-2
Spruce Ridge Branch—stream KY-4
Spruce Ridge Camp—locale NY-2
Spruce River—stream MI-6
Spruce River—stream WI-6
Spruce Rock AK-9
Spruce Rsvr—reservoir CO-8
Spruce Run PA-2
Spruce Run WV-2
**Spruce Run**—pop pl NJ-2
Spruce Run—stream MD-2
Spruce Run—stream NJ-2
Spruce Run—stream (3) OH-6
Spruce Run—stream (19) PA-2
Spruce Run—stream (3) VA-3
Spruce Run—stream (21) WV-2
Spruce Run Ch—church NJ-2
Spruce Run Ch—church VA-3
Spruce Run Ch—church (2) WV-2
Spruce Run County Park—park OR-9
Spruce Run Creek—stream OR-9
Spruce Run Earthworks—hist pl OH-6
Spruce Run Lake—lake OR-9
Spruce Run Mtn—summit VA-3
Spruce Run Rsvr—reservoir NJ-2
Spruce Run Rsvr—reservoir PA-2
Spruce Run State Park—park NJ-2
Spruce Run Trail—trail (2) PA-2
Spruce Run Vista—locale PA-2
**Spruces**—pop pl PA-2
Spruce Saint Sch—school WI-6
Spruces Campground—park UT-8
Spruces Campground, The—locale UT-8
Spruce Sch—school CA-9
Spruce Sch—school NY-2
Spruce Sch—school WA-9
Spruce Sch—school WV-2
Spruce Shafter Fence—locale NV-8
**Spruce Shores**—pop pl ME-1
Spruce Spring—spring AZ-5
Spruce Spring—spring (3) CO-8
Spruce Spring—spring NV-8
Spruce Spring—spring NM-5
Spruce Spring—spring (3) OR-9
Spruce Spring—spring (3) UT-8
Spruce Spring—spring WA-9
Spruce Spring Campground—locale WA-9
Spruce Springs—spring MT-8
Spruce Springs Rsvr—reservoir UT-8
Spruces Rec Area UT-8
Spruce Stomp—flat CO-8
Spruce Street Sch—school MA-1
Spruce Street Sch—school PA-2
Spruce Street YMCA—hist pl NC-3
Spruce Swamp—swamp CT-1
Spruce Swamp—swamp (4) MA-1
Spruce Swamp—swamp MI-6
Spruce Swamp—swamp (2) NH-1
Spruce Swamp—swamp NJ-2
Spruce Swamp—swamp (2) NY-2
Spruce Swamp—swamp (2) PA-2
Spruce Swamp Brook MA-1
Spruce Swamp Brook—stream MA-1
Spruce Swamp Creek—stream CT-1
Spruce Tabernacle—church WV-2
Spruce Tank—reservoir (2) AZ-5
Spruce Thicket Trail—trail TN-4
Spruce Three Drain—canal CA-9
Spruceton—locale NY-2
Spruceton Trail—trail NY-2
Spruce Top—summit ME-1
Spruce Top—summit (2) NY-2
Spruce Top—summit VT-1
Sprucetown PA-2
**Sprucetown**—pop pl PA-2
Sprucetown Ch—church PA-2
**Spruce (Town of)**—pop pl WI-6
**Spruce Township**—pop pl MO-7
**Spruce (Township of)**—pop pl MN-6
Spruce Trail—trail UT-8
Spruce Tree Campground—locale ID-8
Spruce Tree House—locale CO-8
Spruce Tree Point—cliff CO-8
**Sprucevale**—pop pl OH-6
**Spruce Valley**—pop pl WV-2
Spruce Valley Cem—cemetery MN-6
Spruce Valley (Township of)—civ div MN-6
Spruce Water Canyon—valley CO-8
Spruce Well—well (2) NV-8
**Sprucewood**—pop pl CO-8
Sprucewood Sch—school UT-8
**Sprucewood Subdivision**—pop pl UT-8
Sprucey Branch—stream KY-4
Sprucy Sch—school KY-4
Sprudel—locale AR-4
Spruell Drift Mine (underground)—mine AL-4
Spruell Lake Dam—dam MS-4
Spruiell Branch—stream AL-4
Spruiell Cem—cemetery AL-4
Spruill Ranch—locale NM-5
Spruills Bridge—bridge NC-3
Sprule—locale KY-4
Sprule Sch—school KY-4
Sprule Windmill—locale NM-5
Sprunger Ditch—canal IN-6
Sprungers South Adams County
Airstrip—airport IN-6
Sprung Spring—spring AZ-5
Sprunica Ch—church IN-6
Sprunica Sch—school IN-6
Spruoa Lake MN-6
Spry UT-8
Spry—locale UT-8
**Spry**—pop pl PA-2
**Spry**—pop pl UT-8
Spry, Mount—summit UT-8
Spry Branch—stream WV-2
Spry Cem—cemetery IA-7
Spry Cem—cemetery UT-8
Spry Cem—cemetery WV-2
Spry Hollow—valley MO-7
Spry Island MD-2
Spry Island Shoal—bar MD-2
Spry JHS—school NY-2
Spry Landing—locale MD-2

Spry Sch—school IL-6
S P Snyder Park—park FL-3
S P Tank—reservoir (2) AZ-5
Spud Basin—basin ID-8
Spud Brook—stream MA-1
Spud Butte—summit ID-8
Spud Canyon—valley WA-9
Spud Creek—stream AZ-5
Spud Creek—stream (3) ID-8
Spud Creek—stream MT-8
Spudder Flats—flat TX-5
Spudder Park—park TX-5
Spud Gulch—valley CO-8
Spud Hill—summit AZ-5
Spud Hill—summit CO-8
Spud Hill—summit WA-9
Spud Hollow—valley MO-7
Spud Island—island CA-9
Spud Lake MT-8
Spud Lake—lake MI-6
Spud Lake—lake MN-6
Spud Mtn—summit AZ-5
Spud Mtn—summit OR-9
Spud Mtn—summit (2) WA-9
Spud Patch—area NM-5
Spud Patch, The—flat CO-8
Spud Patch Camp—locale CO-8
Spud Patch Canyon—valley (2) NM-5
Spud Patch Creek—stream NM-5
Spud Patch Flat—flat ID-8
Spud Patch Ridge—ridge NM-5
Spud Patch Spring—spring ID-8
Spud Patch Tank—reservoir AZ-5
Spud Point—cape CA-9
Spud Point—summit MT-8
Spud Rock—summit AZ-5
Spud Rock Cabin (site)—locale AZ-5
Spud Rock Spring—spring AZ-5
Spud Run—stream IN-6
Spud Run—stream OH-6
Spud Run Ch—church OH-6
Spuds—locale FL-3
Spud Spring—spring OR-9
Spud Town Branch—stream TN-4
Spudville Clubhouse—building MN-6
Spuhler Gulch—valley MT-8
Spuhler Peak—summit MT-8
Spuhler Saddle—gap MT-8
Spuhn Island—island AK-9
Spuhn Point—cape AK-9
Spukwush Creek—stream WA-9
Spuller Lake—lake CA-9
Spundulic Mine—mine AZ-5
Spunk Branch—stream MN-6
Spunk Brook MN-6
Spunk Cem—cemetery OH-6
Spunk Creek—stream MN-6
Spunk Lake MN-6
Spunk Run—stream OH-6
Spunky Canyon—valley CA-9
Spunky Canyon Campground—locale CA-9
Spunky Creek—stream OK-5
Spunky Ridge—ridge IL-6
Spur NE-7
Spur—locale WI-6
**Spur**—pop pl TX-5
Spur, Lake—lake AR-4
Spur, The—ridge TN-4
Spur, The—ridge UT-8
Spur, The—summit (2) WY-8
Spur Branch—stream SC-3
Spur Branch—stream TX-5
Spur Branch—stream VA-3
Spur Branch Sch—school VA-3
Spur Brook—stream MA-1
Spur Brook—stream NH-1
Spur Butte—summit OR-9
Spur Canal Number 1—canal FL-3
Spur Canal Number 4—canal FL-3
Spur Canyon UT-8
Spur Canyon—valley WY-8
Spur (CCD)—cens area TX-5
Spur Creek—stream (2) ID-8
Spur Creek—stream KY-4
Spur Creek—stream SC-3
Spur Creek—stream SD-7
Spur Creek—stream (2) TX-5
Spur Creek—stream WA-9
Spur Creek—stream WI-6
Spur Cross—locale AZ-5
Spur Ditch—canal MI-6
Spur End Creek—stream MN-6
Spur Five AR-4
Spur Fork—valley UT-8
**Spur Four**—pop pl AR-4
Spur Gasoline Station—hist pl KY-4
Spurgeon—locale WV-2
**Spurgeon**—pop pl IN-6
**Spurgeon**—pop pl MO-7
**Spurgeon**—pop pl NC-3
**Spurgeon**—pop pl TN-4
Spurgeon—uninc pl CA-9
Spurgeon and Myers Ranch—locale ND-7
Spurgeon Baptist Bible Coll—school FL-3
Spurgeon Block—hist pl CA-9
Spurgeon Cem—cemetery IN-6
Spurgeon Cem—cemetery IA-7
Spurgeon Cem—cemetery OH-6
Spurgeon Cem—cemetery TN-4
Spurgeon Ch—church TN-4
Spurgeon Creek—stream NC-3
Spurgeon Creek—stream WA-9
Spurgeon Ditch—canal IN-6
Spurgeon Draw—valley NM-5
Spurgeon Draw Tank—reservoir NM-5
Spurgeon Gulch—valley SD-7
Spurgeon Hollow—valley IN-6
Spurgeon Hollow—valley MO-7
Spurgeon Hollow—valley (3) TN-4
Spurgeon House—hist pl NC-3
Spurgeon Island—island TN-4
Spurgeon Knob—summit TN-4
Spurgeon Mesa—summit NM-5
Spurgeon Prairie—area MO-7
Spurgeon Sch—school CA-9
**Spurgeons Corner**—pop pl IN-6
Spurgeon Smith Mine (underground)—mine TN-4
Spurgeon Tank No 1—reservoir NM-5
Spurgeon Tank No 2—reservoir NM-5

**Spurger**—pop pl TX-5
Spurger (CCD)—cens area TX-5
Spurger Lookout—locale TX-5
Spurgion Cabin—locale CO-8
Spur Glacier—glacier AK-9
Spur (historical)—locale AL-4
Spur Hollow—valley MO-7
Spur House—hist pl NH-1
Spurior Place—locale NE-7
Spur Island—island GA-3
Spur Lake MA-1
Spur Lake—lake (2) MN-6
Spur Lake—lake (4) WI-6
Spur Lake—locale NM-5
Spur Lake Basin—basin NM-5
Spur Lake Cem—cemetery NM-5
Spur Lake Draw—valley NM-5
Spur Lakes—lake MN-6
Spur Lake Well—well NM-5
Spurlark Circle Subdivision UT-8
Spurler Creek—stream TX-5
Spurlin—locale TX-5
Spurlin Cem—cemetery AR-4
Spurlin Cem—cemetery TN-4
Spurling—locale MT-8
Spurling Branch—stream TN-4
Spurling Cem—cemetery KY-4
Spurling Cem—cemetery OH-6
Spurling Cem—cemetery TN-4
Spurling Point—cape ME-1
Spurling's Point ME-1
**Spurlington**—pop pl KY-4
Spurlin Mesa—summit CO-8
Spurlin Sch—school FL-3
Spurlins Hollow—valley KY-4
Spurlock—locale AZ-5
Spurlock—locale KY-4
Spurlock Branch—stream KY-4
Spurlock Branch—stream LA-4
Spurlock Branch—stream TN-4
Spurlock Branch—stream TX-5
Spurlock Branch—stream VA-3
Spurlock Cave—cave MO-7
Spurlock Cave—cave VA-3
Spurlock Cem—cemetery WV-2
Spurlock Ch—church WV-2
Spurlock Chapel—church TX-5
**Spurlock Circle Subdivision**—pop pl UT-8
Spurlock Creek AR-4
Spurlock Creek—stream (2) KY-4
Spurlock Creek—stream VA-3
Spurlock Creek—stream WV-2
Spurlock Creek Ch—church KY-4
Spurlock Creek Ch—church WV-2
Spurlock Fork—stream (2) KY-4
Spurlock Gap—gap KY-4
Spurlock Hollow—valley AR-4
Spurlock Hollow—valley MO-7
Spurlock Hollow—valley (2) TN-4
Spurlock Lake—reservoir TX-5
Spurlock Post Office (historical)—building TN-4
Spurlock Ranch—locale CO-8
Spurlock Ranch—locale NM-5
Spurlock Ranch—locale OR-9
Spurlocks (historical)—locale MS-4
Spurlock Spring—spring AL-4
**Spurlock Subdivision**—pop pl UT-8
Spurlock Tank—reservoir AZ-5
Spurlockville—locale WV-2
Spurlockville Sch—school WV-2
Spurlop Mtn—summit OK-5
Spur Meadow—flat CA-9
Spur Mtn—summit AK-9
Spur Mtn—summit MT-8
Spur Mtn—summit TX-5
Spur Mtn—summit WA-9
Spur Park—flat MT-8
Spur Path—trail NH-1
Spur Peak—summit NM-5
Spur Peak—summit WA-9
Spur Pond MA-1
Spur Pond—lake FL-3
Spur Pool—reservoir MI-6
Spurr, Eliphalet, House—hist pl MA-1
Spurr, John, House—hist pl MA-1
Spurr, Mount—summit AK-9
Spurrier TN-4
Spurrier—locale KY-4
Spurrier Field—park TN-4
Spurrier Gardens KS-7
Spurrier Post Office (historical)—building TN-4
**Spurrier Subdivision**—pop pl UT-8
Spurr Lake—lake MA-1
Spurrler Ridge—ridge OH-6
Spurr Pond MA-1
Spurr River—stream MI-6
**Spurrs Corner**—pop pl ME-1
Spur Rsvr—reservoir CO-8
**Spurr (Township of)**—pop pl MI-6
Spurs, The—ridge VA-3
Spur Tank—reservoir (3) AZ-5
Spur Tank—reservoir NM-5
Spurt Point—cape AK-9
Spurt Point Lake—lake AK-9
Spur Trail Draw—valley NM-5
Spurt Run—stream IN-6
Spurville—locale NE-7
Spur Well—well NM-5
Spur Windmill—locale TX-5
Spurwink Ch—church ME-1
Spurwink Congregational Church—hist pl ME-1
Spurwink Hill—summit ME-1
Spurwink River—stream ME-1
Spurxem Creek MN-6
Spurxem Lake MN-6
Spuryer Cem—cemetery VA-3
Spurzem Creek—stream MN-6
Spurzem Lake—lake MN-6
Spurzen Lake MN-6
Spur 10 Gate—locale WA-9
Spute Lake—lake WI-6
Sputter Branch—stream KY-4
Sputzman Creek—stream KY-4
Spuytenduivel Brook—stream NY-2
**Spuyten Duyvil**—pop pl NY-2
Spuyten Duyvil Creek—gut NY-2
Spy Branch—stream AR-4
Spy Buck Creek AR-4
Spybuck Creek—stream AR-4
Spybuck Drainage Canal—canal AR-4

Spychalskis Pond—reservoir IN-6
Spy Creek—stream ID-8
Spy Creek—stream MT-8
Spygalls Hill—summit AK-9
Spyglass Hill—summit MS-4
Spy Glass Hill—summit WY-8
Spyglass Hill Golf Course—other CA-9
Spyglass Island—island MD-2
Spyglass Miners Trail—trail ID-8
Spyglass Peak—summit ID-8
Spy Hill—summit NY-2
Spy Hill Cem—cemetery VA-3
Spy Island Historical Site—locale NY-2
Spy Islands—island AK-9
Spyker—locale LA-4
Spy Key—island FL-3
Spy Knob—summit TX-5
Spy Lake—lake NY-2
Spy Lake—lake OR-9
Spy Mound—summit MO-7
Spy Mountain—ridge CA-9
Spy Mountain Trail—trail MT-8
Spy Mtn—summit MT-8
Spy Mtn—summit TX-5
Spy Point—summit ID-8
Spy Pond—lake MA-1
Spy Pond—lake NY-2
Spy Pond Field—park MA-1
Spyrock—locale CA-9
Spy Rock—pillar AR-4
Spy Rock—rock WV-2
Spyrock—summit CA-9
Spy Rock—summit CT-1
Spy Rock—summit MA-1
Spy Rock—summit NY-2
Spy Rock—summit TX-5
Spy Rock—summit VA-3
Spy Rock Creek—stream SC-3
Spy Rock Hollow AR-4
Spy Rock Hollow—valley AR-4
Spy Rock Ridge AR-4
Spy Run IN-6
Spy Run—stream KY-4
Spy Run—stream VA-3
Spy Run Creek—stream IN-6
Spy Run Sch—school KY-4
Sqam Pond MA-1
Sqaw Buttes—summit MT-8
SQ Lateral—canal TX-5
Squab—locale CA-9
Squabble Brook—stream CT-1
Squabble Creek—stream KY-4
Squabble Creek—stream MT-8
Squabble Creek—stream TX-5
Squabble Hollow—valley VT-1
Squabble Hollow Sch—school VT-1
Squabble Mine—mine AZ-5
Squabbletown NJ-2
Squabbletown—locale CA-9
Squabetter Hill MA-1
**Squab Hollow**—pop pl PA-2
Squab Hollow—valley NY-2
Squab Hollow—valley PA-2
Squab Island—island AK-9
Squaconning Creek—stream MI-6
Squag City—locale NH-1
Squak WA-9
Squakeag Plantation MA-1
Squak Glacier—glacier WA-9
Squakheag MA-1
Squak Island—island WI-6
Squak Mtn—summit WA-9
Squalicum Creek—stream WA-9
Squalicum Lake—lake WA-9
Squalicum Mall—locale WA-9
Squalicum Mtn—summit WA-9
Squalicum Waterway—channel WA-9
Squall Creek—stream VA-3
Squalliamish River WA-9
Squalling Bluff—cliff NC-3
Squalling Bluff Cove—bay NC-3
Squally Creek—stream NC-3
Squally Creek—stream WA-9
Squally Jim—summit WA-9
Squally Point—cape OR-9
Squally Point—cape RI-1
Squam MA-1
**Squam**—pop pl MA-1
Squam, Mount—summit NH-1
Squamanagonic Camp—locale NH-1
Squam Bank MA-1
Squam Beach MA-1
Squam Brook—stream MA-1
Squam Creek—stream ME-1
Squam Head MA-1
Squam Head—cliff MA-1
Squam (historical)—civil MA-1
Squamish Harbor—bay WA-9
Squam Lake—lake NH-1
Squam Mountains—ridge NH-1
Squam Pond—lake MA-1
Squam River MA-1
Squam River—stream NH-1
Squamscot Bog—swamp NH-1
Squamscott River—stream NH-1
Squam Swamp—swamp MA-1
Squan NJ-2
Squancum Branch NJ-2
Squanish Harbor WA-9
Squankin Pond—lake ME-1
Squankum NJ-2
**Squankum**—pop pl NJ-2
Squankum Branch—stream NJ-2
Squankum Brook—stream NJ-2
Squannaconk Swamp MA-1
Squannacook Hill MA-1
Squannacook Hill—summit MA-1
Squannacook River—stream MA-1
Squannacook River Dam—dam MA-1
Squannacook River Rsvr—reservoir (2) MA-1
Squannahonk Swamp MA-1
Squannakonk Swamp—swamp MA-1
Squannakouk Swamp MA-1
Squan River NJ-2
Squantum (2) RI-1
Squantum—cliff MA-1
**Squantum**—pop pl NH-1
Squantum Association—hist pl RI-1
Squantum Channel—channel MA-1
Squantum Marshes—swamp MA-1

Squantum Point—cape ME-1
Squantum Point—cape MA-1
Squantum Point—cape RI-1
**Squantum (subdivision)**—pop pl MA-1
Squantz Cove—bay CT-1
Squantz Pond—reservoir CT-1
Squantz Pond State Park—park CT-1
Squapan ME-1
**Squa Pan**—pop pl ME-1
Squa Pan Fire Tower—locale ME-1
Squapan Inlet ME-1
Squa Pan Inlet—stream ME-1
Squa Pan Inlet Stream ME-1
Squa Pan Knob—summit ME-1
Squapan Lake ME-1
Squa Pan Lake—reservoir ME-1
Squa Pan Mtn—summit ME-1
Squapan Stream ME-1
Squa Pan Stream—stream ME-1
Squapan (Township of)—unorg ME-1
Squa-quid WA-9
Square MI-6
Square Barn Corners—locale NY-2
Square Bay WA-9
Square Bay—bay AK-9
Square Bay—bay MI-6
Square Bay—bay NY-2
Square Black Rock—island CA-9
Square Bluff—summit WI-6
Squareboat Lake—lake MN-6
Square Brook—stream NH-1
Square Brook—stream VT-1
Square Butte ND-7
Square Butte WY-8
Square Butte—pillar MT-8
**Square Butte**—pop pl MT-8
Square Butte—summit (2) AZ-5
Square Butte—summit (10) MT-8
Square Butte—summit (2) ND-7
Square Butte Bench—bench MT-8
Square Butte Bench Cem—cemetery MT-8
Square Butte Creek—stream ND-7
Square Butte Number 4 Dam—dam ND-7
Square Butte Number 5 Dam—dam ND-7
Square Buttes—summit ND-7
Square Butte Sch Number 1—school ND-7
Square Butte Sch Number 2—school ND-7
Square Butte Sch Number 3—school ND-7
Square Butte Spring—spring AZ-5
Square Butte Wash—valley AZ-5
Square Butte 2 Dam—dam ND-7
Square Cedar Cem—cemetery OK-5
Square Cemetery, The—cemetery NY-2
Square Corner—locale PA-2
Square Corral Spring—spring CA-9
Square Cove—bay AK-9
Square Creek—stream (2) MT-8
Square Creek—stream WA-9
Square D Company—facility NC-3
Square D Company—facility SC-3
Square Deal Mine—mine MT-8
Square Dock Mtn—summit ME-1
Square Falls Mtn—summit NY-2
Square Fort MS-4
Square Gulch—valley CO-8
Square Handkerchief Shoal—bar MS-4
Square Harbor WA-9
Square Head—cliff AS-9
Squarehead Cove—bay AK-9
Square Hill—summit NE-7
Square Island—island AK-9
Square Island Lake—lake TX-5
Square Lake MN-6
Square Lake—lake (4) AK-9
Square Lake—lake (2) CA-9
Square Lake—lake (3) FL-3
Square Lake—lake GA-3
Square Lake—lake (2) ID-8
Square Lake—lake ME-1
Square Lake—lake (5) MI-6
Square Lake—lake (4) MN-6
Square Lake—lake (2) MT-8
Square Lake—lake NE-7
Square Lake—lake ND-7
Square Lake—lake (2) OR-9
Square Lake—lake (2) WA-9
Square Lake—lake (2) WI-6
Square Lake—lake WY-8
Square Lake—swamp MS-4
Square Lake Cem—cemetery MI-6
Square Lake Oil Field—other NM-5
Square Lake Ridge—ridge ME-1
Square Lake Test Well—well AK-9
Square Lake (Unorganized Territory of)—unorg ME-1
Square Ledge—bench NH-1
Square Mesa—summit TX-5
Square Mountain Creek—stream ID-8
Square Mountain Creek—stream OR-9
Square Mountain Rsvr OR-9
Square Mtn AZ-5
Square Mtn—summit AZ-5
Square Mtn—summit (2) ID-8
Square Mtn—summit MT-8
Square Mtn—summit NH-1
Square Mtn—summit NY-2
Square Mtn—summit (2) OR-9
Square Mtn—summit UT-8
Square Oak Ch—church KY-4
Square Park—flat WY-8
Square Peak—summit MT-8
Square Point—cape (2) AK-9
Square Pond CT-1
Square Pond—lake ME-1
Square Pond—lake (2) NY-2
Square Pond—reservoir AZ-5
Square Prairie Sch—school MO-7
Square Ranch—locale CT-1
Square Rib PA-2
Square Rock—other AK-9
Square Rock—pillar NH-1
Square Rock—summit ID-8
Square Rock Ch—church AR-4
Square Rock Creek—stream AR-4
Square Rock Draw—valley WY-8
Square Rock Lake—lake ID-8
Square Rock Ridge—ridge AR-4
Square Rsvr—reservoir UT-8
Square Run—stream (2) IN-6
Square Schoolhouse—hist pl NH-1

Square S Ranch—locale CO-8
Squares Tunnel—mine CA-9
Square Tank—reservoir (2) AZ-5
Square Tank Well—well NM-5
Square Tank Windmill—locale TX-5
Square Tavern—hist pl PA-2
Square Timber Run—stream PA-2
Square Top ID-8
**Squaretop**—pop pl OK-5
Square Top—summit (2) ID-8
Square Top—summit (2) NV-8
Square Top—summit ND-7
Square Top—summit OR-9
Square Top—summit PA-2
Square Top—summit UT-8
Square Top—summit WY-8
Square Top Butte SD-7
Squaretop Butte—summit ND-7
Square Top Butte—summit SD-7
Square Top Butte—summit WY-8
Square Top Drift Fence—other WY-8
Squaretop Guard Station—locale CO-8
Squaretop Hills—summit AZ-5
Square Top Lake—lake ID-8
Square Top Lakes—lake CO-8
Squaretop Mtn—summit CO-8
Square Top Mtn—summit (2) CO-8
Square Top Mtn—summit TX-5
Square Top Mtn—summit (2) UT-8
Squaretop Mtn—summit WY-8
Square Top Mtn—summit WY-8
Square Top Rsvr—reservoir WY-8
Square Top Rsvr No 6—reservoir WY-8
Square Top Well No 1—well WY-8
Square Top Well No 2—well WY-8
Square Tower Canon—valley UT-8
Square Tower Group Ruins—locale UT-8
Square Tower House UT-8
Square Tower House—locale CO-8
Square Tower Ruin Campgroung UT-8
Square Tower (ruins)—locale UT-8
Square Tower Ruins Campground—park UT-8
Squaretown (Township of)—unorg ME-1
Square Well—well OR-9
Square Well Slough—stream OR-9
Square White Rock—island OR-9
Square 13 Hist Dist—hist pl OH-6
Squarno Drain—canal MI-6
Squar River NJ-2
Squashan Creek—stream CA-9
Squash Canyon—valley NM-5
Squash Hollow—valley WV-2
Squash Hollow Brook—stream CT-1
Squash Island ME-1
Squash Lake—lake MN-6
Squash Lake—lake (2) WI-6
Squash Meadow—bar MA-1
Squash Meadow Lake MA-1
Squash Meadow Pond MA-1
Squash Pond—lake NY-2
**Squassux Landing**—pop pl NY-2
Squat Lake—lake MN-6
Squatter Flat—flat OR-9
Squatter's Cabin—hist pl CA-9
Squatters Creek—stream MI-6
Squattingdown Creek—stream GA-3
Squatty CA-9
Squatty Butte—summit CA-9
Squatty Tank—reservoir NM-5
Squaw—pillar CO-8
Squaw, The WY-8
Squaw and Papoose Rock—pillar UT-8
Squaw Back Ridge—ridge OR-9
Squawbally Hill MA-1
Squaw Bar—bar ID-8
Squaw Basin—basin UT-8
Squaw Basin—basin WY-8
Squaw Basin Creek—stream UT-8
Squaw Basin Tank—reservoir AZ-5
Squaw Bay ID-8
Squaw Bay—bay AK-9
Squaw Bay—bay (2) ID-8
Squaw Bay—bay ME-1
Squaw Bay—bay MI-6
Squaw Bay—bay MN-6
Squaw Bay—bay WA-9
Squaw Bay—bay (4) WI-6
**Squaw Bay**—pop pl ID-8
Squaw Bayou—stream LA-4
Squaw Beach—beach AZ-5
Squaw Beach—beach MI-6
Squaw Bench—bench (2) UT-8
Squaw Bend—bend MO-7
**Squawberry**—pop pl TN-4
Squawberry Spring—spring ID-8
Squawbetty Hill—summit MA-1
Squawboard Meadow—flat ID-8
Squaw Branch—stream IN-6
Squaw Branch—stream KS-7
Squaw Branch—stream TN-4
Squaw Breast CO-8
Squaw Brook—locale ME-1
Squaw Brook—stream ME-1
Squaw Brook—stream NJ-2
Squaw Brook—stream NY-2
Squaw Butte AZ-5
Squaw Butte—summit AZ-5
Squaw Butte—summit (2) ID-8
Squaw Butte—summit (3) MT-8
Squaw Butte—summit (2) NV-8
Squaw Butte—summit (11) OR-9
Squaw Butte—summit (2) UT-8
Squaw Butte—summit (2) WA-9
Squaw Butte—summit (3) WY-8
Squaw Butte Creek—stream OR-9
Squaw Buttes—spring MT-8
Squaw Buttes—summit WY-8
Squaw Butte Sch—school SD-7
Squaw Butte Trail—trail OR-9
Squaw Camp—locale (2) CA-9
Squaw Camp—locale ID-8
Squaw Camp Creek—stream ID-8
Squaw Canyon UT-8
Squaw Canyon WA-9
Squaw Canyon—locale WA-9
Squaw Canyon—valley (4) AZ-5
Squaw Canyon—valley (3) CA-9
Squaw Canyon—valley (2) CO-8
Squaw Canyon—valley NM-5
Squaw Canyon—valley OR-9

Squaw Canyon—valley (4) UT-8
Squaw Canyon—valley WA-9
Squaw Canyon—valley (2) WY-8
Squaw Canyon Well—well AZ-5
Squaw Cap—summit ME-1
Squaw Center Sch—school IA-7
Squaw Coulee—valley (2) MT-8
Squaw Cove—bay NH-1
Squaw Coxcombs—summit AZ-5
Squaw Creek AZ-5
Squaw Creek CA-9
Squaw Creek CO-8
Squaw Creek ID-8
Squaw Creek MI-6
Squaw Creek MT-8
Squaw Creek NV-8
Squaw Creek OR-9
Squaw Creek SD-7
Squaw Creek TX-5
Squaw Creek UT-8
Squaw Creek WI-6
Squaw Creek—canal MI-6
Squaw Creek—stream AL-4
Squaw Creek—stream (5) AK-9
Squaw Creek—stream (7) AZ-5
Squaw Creek—stream (13) CA-9
Squaw Creek—stream (8) CO-8
Squaw Creek—stream (33) ID-8
Squaw Creek—stream IL-6
Squaw Creek—stream (3) IN-6
Squaw Creek—stream (7) IA-7
Squaw Creek—stream (6) KS-7
Squaw Creek—stream (10) MI-6
Squaw Creek—stream (4) MN-6
Squaw Creek—stream MO-7
Squaw Creek—stream (21) MT-8
Squaw Creek—stream NE-7
Squaw Creek*—stream NE-7
Squaw Creek—stream (8) NE-7
Squaw Creek—stream (4) NV-8
Squaw Creek—stream (3) NM-5
Squaw Creek—stream NY-2
Squaw Creek—stream (3) ND-7
Squaw Creek—stream OH-6
Squaw Creek—stream (6) OK-5
Squaw Creek—stream (47) OR-9
Squaw Creek—stream (7) SD-7
Squaw Creek—stream (7) TX-5
Squaw Creek—stream (5) UT-8
Squaw Creek—stream (12) WA-9
Squaw Creek—stream (13) WI-6
Squaw Creek—stream (14) WY-8
Squaw Creek Archeol Site—hist pl CA-9
Squaw Creek Arm—bay CA-9
Squaw Creek Bay—bay ND-7
Squaw Creek Campground—locale ID-8
Squaw Creek Campground—locale ND-7
Squaw Creek Canal—canal OR-9
Squaw Creek Canyon—valley OR-9
Squaw Creek Cem—cemetery (2) TX-5
Squaw Creek Ch—church TX-5
Squaw Creek Ch—church WI-6
Squaw Creek Coal Company—facility IN-6
Squaw Creek Country Club—other OH-6
Squaw Creek Cove North Public Use Area—park KS-7
Squaw Creek Cove South Public Use Area—park KS-7
Squaw Creek Dam—dam ND-7
Squaw Creek Dam—dam OR-9
Squaw Creek Ditch—canal MO-7
Squaw Creek Drain—canal MI-6
Squaw Creek Falls—falls OR-9
Squaw Creek Fire Control Station—locale CA-9
Squaw Creek - in part MO-7
Squaw Creek - in part UT-8
Squaw Creek Irrigation District Dam—dam OR-9
Squaw Creek Irrigation District Rsvr—reservoir OR-9
Squaw Creek Lakes ID-8
Squaw Creek Mesa—summit AZ-5
Squaw Creek Municipal Golf Course—other IA-7
Squaw Creek Natl Wildlife Ref—park MO-7
Squaw Creek Overlook—locale OR-9
Squaw Creek Park—park IA-7
Squaw Creek Ranch—locale MT-8
Squaw Creek Ranch—locale NV-8
Squaw Creek Ranch—locale WY-8
Squaw Creek Ranger Station—locale MT-8
Squaw Creek Regional Park—park IA-7
Squaw Creek Ridge—ridge CA-9
Squaw Creek Ridge—ridge WA-9
Squaw Creek Rim—cliff OR-9
Squaw Creek Rsvr—reservoir ID-8
Squaw Creek Rsvr—reservoir (3) OR-9
Squaw Creek Rsvr—reservoir SD-7
Squaw Creek Sawmill—locale ID-8
Squaw Creek Sch—school MO-7
Squaw Creek Sch—school MT-8
Squaw Creek Sch—school SD-7
Squaw Creek Sch—school WI-6
Squaw Creek Sch (historical)—school AL-4
Squaw Creek South Branch UT-8
Squaw Creek Spring—spring ID-8
Squaw Creek Spring—spring MT-8
Squaw Creek Spring—spring (3) OR-9
Squaw Creek State Wayside—locale OR-9
Squaw Creek Tank—reservoir (2) AZ-5
Squaw Creek Trail—trail (2) WY-8
Squaw Creek Valley—valley NV-8
Squaw Creek Vee—area OR-9
Squaw Crossing—locale UT-8
Squaw Crossing—other AK-9
Squaw Crossing Slough—stream AK-9
Squaw Dance Valley—valley AZ-5
Squaw Dome—summit CA-9
Squaw Dress Ridge—ridge AZ-5
Squaw Falls—falls OR-9
Squaw Fill—valley UT-8
Squaw Fingers—pillar CO-8
Squaw Flat—flat (2) AZ-5
Squaw Flat—flat (7) CA-9
Squaw Flat—flat (3) ID-8
Squaw Flat—flat MT-8
Squaw Flat—flat NV-8
Squaw Flat—flat (9) OR-9
Squaw Flat—flat SD-7
Squaw Flat—flat (4) UT-8

Stack Spring—*spring* CA-9
Stacks Run—*stream* WV-2
Stacks Slough—*gut* ND-7
Stackstown Cave—*cave* PA-2
**Stack Town**—*pop pl* PA-2
**Stacktown**—*pop pl* PA-2
*Stackwood* NJ-2
Stackyard Hollow—*valley* WV-2
Stack Yards—*summit* OR-9
Staco Cem—*cemetery* NY-2
*Stacy* NC-3
Stacy—*locale* CA-9
Stacy—*locale* LA-4
Stacy—*locale* TN-4
Stacy—*locale* TX-5
Stacy—*locale* VA-3
**Stacy**—*pop pl* (2) AR-4
**Stacy**—*pop pl* MN-6
**Stacy**—*pop pl* NC-3
Stacy, George O., House—*hist pl* MA-1
**Stacy Basin**—*pop pl* NY-2
Stacy Bldg—*hist pl* MA-1
Stacy Bluff—*cliff* NY-2
Stacy Branch—*stream* GA-3
Stacy Branch—*stream* (3) KY-4
Stacy Branch—*stream* (2) VA-3
Stacy Branch—*stream* WV-2
Stacy Brook—*stream* NY-2
Stacy Brook—*stream* VT-1
Stacy Cem—*cemetery* KY-4
Stacy Cem—*cemetery* MN-6
Stacy Cem—*cemetery* NC-3
Stacy Cem—*cemetery* TN-4
Stacy Cem—*cemetery* VA-3
Stacy Cem—*cemetery* (2) WV-2
Stacy Creek—*channel* MA-1
Stacy Creek—*stream* ID-8
Stacy Creek—*stream* LA-4
Stacy Creek—*stream* ME-1
Stacy Creek—*stream* NC-3
Stacy Crossroads—*locale* VT-1
Stacy Ditch—*canal* NM-5
Stacy Drain—*stream* MI-6
Stacy Falls—*falls* KY-4
Stacy Fork—*locale* KY-4
Stacy Fork—*stream* KY-4
Stacy Hill—*summit* ME-1
Stacy Hill—*summit* NH-1
Stacy Hollow—*valley* MO-7
Stacy Knob—*locale* PA-2
*Stacy Lake* NH-1
Stacy Lake Dam—*dam* MS-4
Stacy Lakes—*lake* CO-8
Stacy Lakes Draw—*valley* CO-8
**Stacy Landing**—*pop pl* LA-4
Stacy Mill Branch—*stream* LA-4
Stacy Mtn—*summit* AR-4
Stacy Mtn—*summit* MA-1
Stacy Mtn—*summit* NH-1
Stacy Mtn—*summit* (2) NY-2
Stacy Park—*park* IL-6
Stacy Park—*park* MO-7
Stacy Park—*park* NJ-2
Stacy Post Office (historical)—*building* AL-4
Stacy Post Office (historical)—*building* TN-4
Stacy Ranch—*locale* AZ-5
Stacy Ridge—*ridge* TN-4
**Stacy (Rowdy Post Office)**—*pop pl* KY-4
Stacy Russell Lake Dam—*dam* MS-4
Stacy Sch—*school* MA-1
Stacy Sch—*school* NC-3
Stacy Slough—*lake* ND-7
*Stacys Mountain* MA-1
Stacy Spring—*spring* AZ-5
Stacy Spring—*spring* TN-4
Stacy Springs—*spring* AR-4
Stacy's Tavern—*hist pl* IL-6
*Stacy Store* AR-4
Stacy (Township of)—*fmr MCD* NC-3
*Stacyville* NC-3
**Stacyville**—*pop pl* IA-7
**Stacyville**—*pop pl* ME-1
Stacyville Cem—*cemetery* IA-7
Stacyville Junction—*locale* IA-7
**Stacyville (Post Office)**—*pop pl* ME-1
**Stacyville (Town of)**—*pop pl* ME-1
Stacyville Township—*fmr MCD* IA-7
Stadden Ditch—*canal* IN-6
Staddle Brook—*stream* CT-1
Staddle Hill—*summit* CT-1
Staddle Hill Sch—*school* CT-1
Stadeli Rsvr—*reservoir* OR-9
Stadel Mtn—*summit* NY-2
Stadem Slough State Public Shooting Area—*park* SD-7
Stader Cem—*cemetery* KY-4
Stader Cem—*cemetery* OH-6
Stader Hotel—*hist pl* KY-4
Stadia Rock—*other* AK-9
Stadish Monmt—*park* MA-1
Stadium—*hist pl* KY-4
Stadium—*locale* WA-9
**Stadium**—*pop pl* WI-6
Stadium—*uninc pl* NY-2
Stadium Bldg—*hist pl* RI-1
Stadium Creek—*stream* ID-8
Stadium Creek—*stream* MT-8
Stadium Drive Sch—*school* OH-6
Stadium Field House—*building* PA-2
Stadium-Hilton Airp—*airport* PA-2
Stadium Hosp—*hospital* CA-9
Stadium HS—*school* WA-9
Stadium Lake—*lake* WA-9
Stadium Park Canal—*canal* NY-2
Stadium Peak—*summit* MT-8
**Stadium Place (subdivision)**—*pop pl* AL-4
Stadium Plaza—*locale* MA-1
Stadium Sch—*school* OH-6
Stadium-Seminary Hist Dist—*hist pl* WA-9
Stadler Creek—*stream* MT-8
Stadler Drain—*canal* MI-6
Stadler Drain—*stream* MI-6
Stadon Creek—*stream* VA-3
Stadtler Drain—*canal* CA-9
Stadtman Mesa—*summit* CO-8
Stadtmuller House—*hist pl* CA-9
**Stady**—*pop pl* ND-7
*Staeers* IN-6
Stae Game Rsvr Number Two—*reservoir* OR-9
*Staege Bay* MN-6
Staege Bay—*bay* MN-6
Staehle Cemeteries—*cemetery* TX-5
Staehly Mtn—*summit* WA-9
Staehly Ranch—*locale* WA-9
Staen Hole—*lake* TN-4
Staff—*locale* TX-5
*Staffa Mountain* CA-9
Staff Branch—*stream* WV-2
Staff Creek—*stream* IA-7
Staffers Sch—*school* PA-2
Staff Lake—*lake* MI-6
Staffon Flowage—*reservoir* WI-6
*Staffon School Flowage* WI-6
*Stafford* AZ-5
*Stafford* MO-7
Stafford—*locale* AL-4
Stafford—*locale* AR-4
Stafford—*locale* GA-3
Stafford—*locale* NE-7
**Stafford**—*pop pl* CA-9
**Stafford**—*pop pl* CT-1
**Stafford**—*pop pl* KS-7
**Stafford**—*pop pl* (2) MD-2
**Stafford**—*pop pl* NY-2
**Stafford**—*pop pl* OH-6
**Stafford**—*pop pl* OK-5
**Stafford**—*pop pl* OR-9
**Stafford**—*pop pl* SC-3
**Stafford**—*pop pl* TX-5
**Stafford**—*pop pl* VA-3
Stafford, Francis M., House—*hist pl* KY-4
Stafford, Frederick H. and Elizabeth, House—*hist pl* MI-6
Stafford, John, Hist Dist—*hist pl* NJ-2
Stafford, John, House—*hist pl* TX-5
Stafford, Lake—*lake* FL-3
Stafford, W. R., Flour Mill and Elevator—*hist pl* MI-6
Stafford, W. R., Planing Mill Site—*hist pl* MI-6
Stafford, W. R., Saw Mill Site—*hist pl* MI-6
Stafford, W. R., Worker's House—*hist pl* MI-6
Stafford Airp—*airport* MO-7
Stafford Bank and Opera House—*hist pl* TX-5
Stafford Bluff—*summit* IL-6
Stafford Branch—*stream* GA-3
Stafford Branch—*stream* WV-2
Stafford Bridge—*bridge* MD-2
Stafford Bridge—*bridge* SC-3
Stafford Brook—*stream* ME-1
Stafford Brook—*stream* MA-1
Stafford Brook—*stream* NY-2
Stafford Cabin—*hist pl* AZ-5
Stafford Cem—*cemetery* AR-4
Stafford Cem—*cemetery* IL-6
Stafford Cem—*cemetery* KS-7
Stafford Cem—*cemetery* (3) KY-4
Stafford Cem—*cemetery* (4) LA-4
Stafford Cem—*cemetery* MS-4
Stafford Cem—*cemetery* (2) MO-7
Stafford Cem—*cemetery* (3) NY-2
Stafford Cem—*cemetery* NC-3
Stafford Cem—*cemetery* OR-9
Stafford Cem—*cemetery* (6) TN-4
Stafford Cem—*cemetery* WV-2
Stafford Center—*locale* NC-3
**Stafford Center**—*pop pl* IN-6
Stafford Ch—*church* AL-4
Stafford Ch—*church* FL-3
Stafford Ch—*church* IN-6
Stafford Ch—*church* MN-6
*Stafford Congregational Methodist Ch* AL-4
Stafford Corners—*locale* NY-2
Stafford Country Club—*other* KS-7
Stafford County—*civil* KS-7
**Stafford (County)**—*pop pl* VA-3
Stafford County Park—*park* MI-6
*Stafford Creek* WI-6
Stafford Creek—*stream* CA-9
Stafford Creek—*stream* CO-8
Stafford Creek—*stream* FL-3
Stafford Creek—*stream* KY-4
Stafford Creek—*stream* MI-6
Stafford Creek—*stream* MS-4
Stafford Creek—*stream* MT-8
Stafford Creek—*stream* NC-3
Stafford Creek—*stream* OR-9
Stafford Creek—*stream* TN-4
Stafford Creek—*stream* (2) WA-9
Stafford-Crimmons Cem—*cemetery* IL-6
Stafford-Cummings House—*building* MA-1
Stafford Dam—*reservoir* SD-7
Stafford Dam State Public Shooting Area—*park* SD-7
Stafford Ditch—*canal* DE-2
Stafford Draw—*valley* MT-8
*Stafford Elementary School* AL-4
Stafford Falls—*falls* WA-9
**Stafford Forest (subdivision)**—*pop pl* NC-3
Stafford Forge—*locale* NJ-2
Stafford Forge Dam—*dam* NJ-2
Stafford Forge Fish and Wildlife Mngmt Area—*park* NJ-2
Stafford Fork—*stream* KY-4
Stafford Fork Ch—*church* KY-4
Stafford Gap—*gap* NC-3
Stafford Gulch—*valley* CO-8
**Stafford Heights (subdivision)**—*pop pl* PA-2
Stafford Hill—*summit* (2) ME-1
Stafford Hill—*summit* MA-1
Stafford Hill—*summit* MI-6
Stafford Hill Ch—*church* VA-3
Stafford Hill Memorial—*hist pl* MA-1
Stafford Hill Sch—*school* KY-4
Stafford Hill Wildlife Mngmt Area—*park* MA-1
*Stafford Hollow* CT-1
Stafford Hollow Hist Dist—*hist pl* CT-1
Stafford House—*hist pl* MI-6
Stafford HS—*school* KS-7
Stafford HS—*school* VA-3
Stafford Island—*island* GA-3
Stafford Knob—*summit* NC-3
*Stafford Lake* TN-4
Stafford Lake—*lake* FL-3
Stafford Lake—*lake* GA-3
Stafford Lake—*lake* IL-6
Stafford Lake—*lake* IN-6
Stafford Lake—*lake* LA-4
Stafford Lake—*lake* MI-6
Stafford Lake—*lake* TX-5
Stafford Lake—*reservoir* CA-9
Stafford Lake Dam—*dam* SD-7
Stafford Lookout—*locale* WA-9
Stafford (Magisterial District)—*fmr MCD* WV-2
Stafford Meadow Brook—*stream* PA-2
Stafford Mills—*hist pl* MA-1
Stafford-Missouri City (CCD)—*cens area* TX-5
Stafford Mtn—*summit* CA-9
Stafford Municipal Airp—*airport* KS-7
Stafford Park—*park* CA-9
Stafford Plantation Hist Dist—*hist pl* GA-3
Stafford Point—*cape* LA-4
Stafford Point Ch—*church* LA-4
Stafford Pond—*lake* FL-3
Stafford Pond—*lake* ME-1
Stafford Pond—*lake* RI-1
Stafford Ranch—*locale* WY-8
Stafford Ravine—*valley* CA-9
*Stafford Ridge* MD-2
Stafford Run—*stream* TX-5
*Staffords* MA-1
Stafford Saint Cem—*cemetery* CT-1
Staffords Bridge—*bridge* NY-2
Staffordsburg—*locale* KY-4
*Stafford Sch* AL-4
Stafford Sch—*school* AL-4
Stafford Sch—*school* CT-1
Stafford Sch—*school* NJ-2
Stafford Sch—*school* OH-6
Stafford Sch—*school* OR-9
Stafford Sch—*school* TN-4
Stafford Sch—*school* (2) TX-5
Stafford Sch Number 1—*school* ND-7
Stafford Sch Number 2—*school* ND-7
Stafford Sch Number 5—*school* ND-7
Stafford Sch Number 6—*school* ND-7
*Staffords Creek* PA-2
Stafford Shaft—*mine* NV-8
Stafford Shaft—*mine* PA-2
**Staffordshire**—*pop pl* VA-3
Stafford Siding—*locale* FL-3
Staffords Island—*island* FL-3
Stafford Spring—*spring* MT-8
Stafford Spring—*spring* TN-4
**Stafford Springs**—*pop pl* CT-1
**Stafford Springs**—*pop pl* MS-4
Stafford Springs—*spring* MS-4
*Stafford Springs Methodist Church* AL-4
*Staffords Station* TN-4
**Staffords Store**—*pop pl* TN-4
**Staffords (subdivision), The**—*pop pl* AL-4
Stafford Station—*locale* NY-2
**Staffordsville**—*pop pl* KY-4
**Staffordsville**—*pop pl* VA-3
**Staffordtown**—*pop pl* TN-4
**Stafford (Town of)**—*pop pl* CT-1
**Stafford (Town of)**—*pop pl* NY-2
**Stafford Township**—*pop pl* KS-7
**Stafford Township**—*pop pl* ND-7
**Stafford (Township of)**—*pop pl* (2) IN-6
**Stafford (Township of)**—*pop pl* MN-6
**Stafford (Township of)**—*pop pl* NJ-2
Stafford Trace—*stream* WV-2
Stafford Village Four Corners Hist Dist—*hist pl* NY-2
**Staffordville**—*pop pl* CT-1
**Staffordville**—*pop pl* NJ-2
Staffordville Public Landing—*locale* NJ-2
Staffordville Rsvr—*reservoir* CT-1
Stafford Wayside—*park* VA-3
Stafford Well—*well* MT-8
Staff Row and Old Post Area-Fort McPherson—*hist pl* GA-3
**Stafore Estates**—*pop pl* PA-2
Stag Bay—*bay* AK-9
Stag Branch—*stream* FL-3
Stag Branch—*stream* TX-5
*Stag Brook* MA-1
Stag Brook—*stream* ME-1
Stag Brook—*stream* MN-6
Stag Brook—*stream* NJ-2
Stag Canyon—*valley* (3) CA-9
Stag Canyon—*valley* CO-8
Stag Canyon—*valley* NV-8
Stag Canyon—*valley* NM-5
Stag Canyon—*valley* OR-9
Stag Canyon—*valley* (2) UT-8
Stag Cove—*valley* CA-9
Stag Creek—*locale* TX-5
Stag Creek—*stream* CA-9
Stag Creek—*stream* ID-8
Stag Creek—*stream* KS-7
Stag Creek—*stream* MI-6
Stag Creek—*stream* MT-8
Stag Creek—*stream* NV-8
Stag Creek—*stream* TX-5
Stag Creek Community Center—*locale* TX-5
Stag Creek Sch—*school* KS-7
Stag Dome—*summit* CA-9
Stag Draw—*valley* CO-8
Stage—*locale* CO-8
**Stage**—*pop pl* MS-4
Stage and Pony Express Station Site—*locale* WY-8
Stagebarn Canyon—*valley* SD-7
Stagebarn Caverns—*cave* SD-7
*Stagebarn Crystal Cavern* SD-7
Stage Barn (historical)—*locale* SD-7
Stagebarn Ridge—*ridge* SD-7
Stage Bridge—*bridge* VA-3
**Stage Bridge**—*pop pl* VA-3
Stage Brook—*stream* MA-1
Stage Canyon—*valley* CO-8
Stage Canyon—*valley* NV-8
**Stagecoach**—*pop pl* NV-8
**Stagecoach**—*pop pl* TX-5
Stagecoach—*summit* UT-8
Stagecoach Canyon—*valley* ID-8
Stagecoach Canyon—*valley* NM-5
Stagecoach Draw—*valley* WY-8
**Stagecoach Forest (subdivision)**—*pop pl* NC-3
Stagecoach Gap—*gap* NM-5
Stagecoach Hollow—*valley* WY-8
Stagecoach House—*building* NC-3
Stage Coach Inn—*hist pl* LA-4
Stagecoach Inn—*hist pl* TN-4
Stagecoach Inn—*hist pl* TX-5
Stage Coach Inn—*hist pl* TX-5
Stagecoach Inn—*hist pl* UT-8
Stagecoach Inn—*hist pl* VT-1
Stage Coach Inn State Historical Site—*locale* UT-8
Stagecoach Lake—*reservoir* NE-7
Stagecoach Pass—*gap* AZ-5
Stagecoach Road—*hist pl* TN-4
Stagecoach Road Oil Field—*oilfield* MS-4
**Stagecoach Run (subdivision)**—*pop pl* NC-3
Stagecoach Ski Area—*other* CO-8
Stagecoach Spring—*spring* CA-9
Stagecoach Trailer Park—*locale* AZ-5
**Stagecoach Trail (subdivision)**—*pop pl* NC-3
Stagecoach Valley—*basin* NV-8
Stagecoach Wash—*valley* UT-8
Stagecoach Waterhole—*lake* TX-5
**Stage Coach Woods (subdivision)**—*pop pl* AL-4
*Stage Creek* SD-7
Stage Creek—*stream* NE-7
Stage Creek—*stream* ND-7
Stage Creek—*stream* TN-4
**Stagecrest (subdivision)**—*pop pl* NC-3
Stage Gulch—*valley* (2) CA-9
Stage Gulch—*valley* (2) OR-9
Stage Harbor—*harbor* MA-1
Stage Harbor Light—*locale* MA-1
Stage Head—*cliff* MA-1
Stage Hill—*summit* SD-7
Stage Hill—*summit* VA-3
Stage Hollow—*valley* TX-5
Stage House Inn—*hist pl* NJ-2
Stage Island—*cape* MA-1
Stage Island—*island* (3) ME-1
Stage Island—*island* MA-1
Stage Island—*island* MI-6
Stage Island—*summit* MA-1
Stage Island Bay—*bay* ME-1
Stage Island Harbor—*bay* ME-1
Stage Island Pool—*lake* MA-1
Stage Junction—*locale* VA-3
Stage Lake—*lake* MI-6
**Stage Mobile Home Village (trailer park)**—*pop pl* DE-2
Stage Mound Hill—*summit* OH-6
Stage Neck—*cape* ME-1
Stage Point—*cape* MA-1
Stage Pond—*lake* FL-3
Stage Pond Cem—*cemetery* FL-3
Stager—*locale* MI-6
Stager-Beckwith House—*hist pl* OH-6
Stager Creek—*stream* MI-6
Stager Lake—*lake* MI-6
**Stage Road Development (subdivision)**—*pop pl* DE-2
Stage Road Gulch—*valley* OR-9
Stage Road Monmt—*park* NC-3
Stage Road Pass—*gap* OR-9
Stage Road Rsvr—*reservoir* UT-8
Stageroad Spring—*spring* ID-8
Stageroad Spring—*spring* NV-8
Stage Road Tank—*reservoir* TX-5
Stagerweed Fork—*stream* KY-4
Stage Stand Branch—*stream* AL-4
Stage Stand Branch—*stream* FL-3
Stagestand Branch—*stream* TX-5
Stage Stand Cem—*cemetery* FL-3
Stagestand Creek—*stream* LA-4
Stage Stand Creek—*stream* OK-5
Stage Stand Creek—*stream* TX-5
Stage Station—*locale* AZ-5
Stage Station—*locale* CA-9
Stage Station Flat—*flat* CO-8
Stage Station Historical Marker—*locale* CA-9
Stage Station Springs—*spring* WY-8
Stage Stop—*hist pl* CA-9
Stage Stop Windmill—*locale* NM-5
Stage Tank—*reservoir* AZ-5
Stage Valley—*valley* WI-6
Stag Flat—*flat* CA-9
**Stagg**—*pop pl* KY-4
Stagg, John C., House—*hist pl* NJ-2
Stagg Cem—*cemetery* IN-6
Stagg Cem—*cemetery* MS-4
*Stagg Creek* TX-5
Stagg Creek—*stream* MD-2
Stagg Creek—*stream* (2) NC-3
Stagg Creek—*stream* VA-3
Stagger Branch—*stream* (2) VA-3
Stagger Creek—*stream* FL-3
Stagger Fork—*stream* (2) KY-4
Stagger Hollow—*valley* VA-3
Stagger Inn Campground—*locale* WA-9
Stagger Mud Lake—*lake* FL-3
Stagger Ranch—*locale* MT-8
Staggers Cem—*cemetery* PA-2
Staggerweed Branch—*stream* (2) KY-4
Stagger Weed Creek—*stream* NC-3
Staggerweed Creek—*stream* VA-3
Stagg Hall—*hist pl* MD-2
Stagg Hill—*summit* KS-7
Stagg Hill Golf Course—*other* KS-7
Stagg House—*hist pl* NC-3
Stagg HS—*school* CA-9
Stagg HS—*school* IL-6
Stagg Lake—*reservoir* TX-5
Stagg Lake Dam—*dam* MS-4
*Stagg Pond* NY-2
Stagg Ranch—*locale* AZ-5
Staggs Airp—*airport* MO-7
Staggs Branch—*stream* KY-4
Staggs Branch—*stream* TN-4
Staggs Bridge—*bridge* AL-4
Staggs Cem—*cemetery* (2) AR-4
Staggs Cem—*cemetery* (2) TN-4
Staggs Hollow—*valley* (3) TN-4
Staggs Mine (underground)—*mine* TN-4
Staggs Prairie Cem—*cemetery* TX-5
Staggs Run—*stream* WV-2
Staggs Spring—*spring* TN-4
Stagg Street Sch—*school* CA-9
**Stagg Subdivision**—*pop pl* UT-8
Stagg Tank—*reservoir* AZ-5
Stag Gulch—*valley* (2) CO-8
Stag Gulch Spring—*spring* CO-8
Stag Hill—*summit* NJ-2
Stag Hollow—*valley* TX-5
Stag Hollow Brook—*stream* NH-1
Stag Hollow Creek—*stream* OR-9
Stag Hollow Ditch—*canal* WY-8
Staghorn Mtn—*summit* WA-9
Stag Horn Point—*cape* NY-2
Stag Hound Butte—*summit* AZ-5
Stagies Point—*cape* MN-6
Stag Island—*island* AK-9
Stag Island—*island* MO-7
Stag Lake—*lake* (2) MI-6
Stag Lake—*lake* OR-9
Stag Lake—*lake* WI-6
Stagman Butte—*summit* WA-9
Stagman Ridge—*ridge* WA-9
Stag Mesa—*summit* CO-8
Stagmire Draw—*valley* MT-8
Stag Mtn—*summit* NV-8
Stagnant Lake—*lake* OR-9
Stagner Branch—*stream* TX-5
Stagner Cem—*cemetery* MO-7
Stagner Ch—*church* TX-5
Stagner Creek—*stream* WY-8
Stagner Landing (historical)—*locale* TN-4
Stagner Mtn—*summit* WY-8
Stagner Ridge—*ridge* WY-8
Stagner Sch—*school* MO-7
Stagners Lake—*lake* TX-5
St. Agnes Catholic Church—*hist pl* ID-8
Stago Canyon—*valley* AZ-5
**Stag Park**—*pop pl* NC-3
Stag Point—*cape* CA-9
Stag Pond—*lake* NJ-2
Stag River—*stream* AK-9
Stag Rock—*summit* MT-8
Stag Rock Creek—*stream* MT-8
Stag Rock Mtn—*summit* MT-8
Stag Rock Spring—*spring* MT-8
Stag Rock Spring Number Two—*spring* MT-8
Stag Run—*gap* MT-8
Stag Run—*stream* OH-6
**Stag Run (subdivision)**—*pop pl* AL-4
Stag Saddle—*gap* CA-9
Stag Shelter—*locale* OR-9
Stags Leap—*cliff* CA-9
Stag Spring—*spring* CA-9
Stag Spring—*spring* NV-8
Stag Spring—*spring* (2) UT-8
Stag Thicket Spring—*spring* CA-9
Stag Trail—*trail* OR-9
Stagville—*hist pl* NC-3
Stahahe, Lake—*reservoir* NY-2
Stahahe Brook—*stream* NY-2
Stahineckers Pond—*lake* PA-2
Stahis Ravine—*valley* CA-9
Stahl—*locale* MO-7
Stahl, Lake—*lake* FL-3
Stahl Bayou—*bay* MI-6
Stahlbusch Island—*island* OR-9
Stahl Canyon—*valley* OR-9
Stahl Cem—*cemetery* IL-6
Stahl Cem—*cemetery* IN-6
Stahl Cem—*cemetery* KY-4
Stahl Cem—*cemetery* MO-7
Stahl Ch—*church* MN-6
Stahl Ch—*church* PA-2
Stahl Creek—*stream* MO-7
Stahl Creek—*stream* MT-8
*Stahl Ditch* IN-6
Stahl Ditch—*canal* CA-9
Stahl Ditch—*canal* (2) IN-6
Stahl Ditch—*canal* OH-6
Stahl Drain—*canal* CA-9
Stahler Cem—*cemetery* NY-2
*Stahlers* PA-2
Stahle Run—*stream* PA-2
*Stahley Mountain* WA-9
*Stahley Ranch* WA-9
*Stahl Hill* ME-1
Stahl Lake—*lake* MN-6
Stahl Lake—*lake* TX-5
Stahl Lake Sch—*school* MN-6
Stahlman—*uninc pl* TN-4
Stahlman Creek—*stream* OR-9
Stahlman Point—*summit* OR-9
Stahlman Roundtop—*summit* PA-2
Stahl Mtn—*summit* WA-9
Stahl Peak—*summit* MT-8
Stahl Point—*cape* MD-2
**Stahl Point**—*pop pl* MD-2
Stahl Ranch—*locale* CO-8
Stahls—*locale* PA-2
Stahls Hill—*summit* ME-1
Stahls Mountain Airp—*airport* PA-2
Stahls Park—*park* IA-7
**Stahlstown**—*pop pl* PA-2
Stainaker Cem—*cemetery* WV-2
Stainback Cem—*cemetery* TN-4
Stainback Cem—*cemetery* VA-3
Staines River—*stream* AK-9
Stains Cem—*cemetery* MO-7
Stains Sch—*school* MO-7
*Stainton Elementary School* MS-4
Stainton Sch—*school* MS-4
Stainville—*locale* TN-4
Stainville Post Office (historical)—*building* TN-4
Stair Bluff—*cliff* AR-4
Stair Canyon—*valley* (2) UT-8
Staircase Canyon—*valley* CA-9
Staircase Falls—*falls* CA-9
Staircase Mtn—*summit* NC-3
Staircase Rapids—*rapids* WA-9
Stair Cem—*cemetery* TN-4
Stair Creek—*stream* OR-9
Stair Creek Falls—*falls* OR-9
Staire Branch—*stream* NC-3
Stair Falls—*falls* (3) ME-1
Stair Mtn—*summit* AK-9
Stairs, The—*slope* UT-8
Stairs Brook Trail—*trail* NH-1
Stairs Col Trail—*trail* NH-1
**Stairs Corners**—*pop pl* NY-2
Stairs Gulch—*valley* UT-8
Stairs Mtn—*summit* NH-1
Stairs Mtn—*summit* NC-3
Stairs Powerplant—*other* UT-8
Stairs Slope—*slope* UT-8
Stairs Slough State Public Shooting Area—*park* SD-7
Stairstep Hill—*summit* TN-4
Stair Steps—*bench* CO-8
Stairsteps Hollow—*valley* TN-4
Stairstep Spring—*spring* OR-9
**Stairtown**—*pop pl* TX-5
Stair Trail—*trail* UT-8
**Stairville**—*pop pl* PA-2
Stairway Canyon—*valley* AZ-5
Stairway Creek—*stream* CA-9
Stairway Glacier—*glacier* AK-9
Stairway Hunt Club Dam—*dam* PA-2
Stairway Icefall—*falls* AK-9
Stairway Lake—*reservoir* (2) PA-2
Stairway Meadow—*flat* CA-9
Stairway Mtn—*summit* TX-5
Stairway Portage—*trail* MN-6
Stake Cem—*cemetery* OK-5
Stake Ch—*church* PA-2
Stake Creek—*stream* FL-3
Stake Creek Point—*cape* FL-3
Staked Waterhole—*reservoir* OR-9
*Stake Gap* FL-3
*Stake Island* WA-9
Stake Islands—*island* LA-4
Stake Key—*island* FL-3
*Stake Knob* GA-3
Stakely Mill—*locale* TN-4
Stakely Spring—*spring* OR-9
Stake Point—*cape* CA-9
Stake Point—*cape* (2) FL-3
Staker, Alma, House—*hist pl* UT-8
Staker, James B., House—*hist pl* UT-8
Staker Canyon—*valley* UT-8
Staker Ridge—*ridge* OH-6
*Staker School* IN-6
Staker Spring—*spring* UT-8
Stakes, Mount—*summit* CA-9
Stake Slough—*stream* TN-4
Stake Springs—*spring* CO-8
Stake Springs Draw—*valley* CO-8
Stake Tank—*reservoir* AZ-5
*Stake Thorofare* NJ-2
Stake Thorofare—*channel* NJ-2
Stakke Lake—*lake* MN-6
Stalactite Cave—*cave* MO-7
Stalanaker Lake—*lake* TX-5
St. Albans Hist Dist—*hist pl* VT-1
*Stalbaum* IN-6
Stalbaum Hershman Ditch—*canal* IN-6
St. Albertus Roman Catholic Church—*hist pl* MI-6
Stalbird—*locale* NY-2
Stalbird Brook—*stream* NH-1
**Stalco**—*pop pl* GA-3
Stalcup—*locale* KY-4
Stalcup Bend—*bend* AR-4
Stalcup Branch—*stream* IN-6
Stalcup Branch—*stream* TN-4
Stalcup Cem—*cemetery* IN-6
Stalcup Cem—*cemetery* TN-4
**Stalcup Corner**—*pop pl* IN-6
Stalcup Hollow—*valley* MO-7
Stalcup Prospect—*mine* TN-4
Stalcup Top—*summit* NC-3
Stalder Creek—*stream* OR-9
Stalder Slough—*stream* OR-9
Stalding Creek—*stream* WA-9
Staley—*locale* IL-6
Staley—*locale* OK-5
Staley—*locale* WA-9
**Staley**—*pop pl* CA-9
**Staley**—*pop pl* NC-3
Staley Airp—*airport* WA-9
Staley Branch—*stream* KY-4
Staley Branch—*stream* MO-7
Staley Bridge—*other* IL-6
Staley Cem—*cemetery* OH-6
Staley Cem—*cemetery* TX-5
Staley Corral—*locale* WY-8
Staley Corral Rsvr—*reservoir* WY-8
Staley Coulee—*valley* WA-9
Staley Creek—*stream* NC-3
Staley Creek—*stream* OR-9
Staley Creek—*stream* VA-3
Staley Crossroads—*locale* VA-3
**Staley Crossroads**—*pop pl* SC-3
Staley (Embryfield)—*locale* TX-5
Staley Farm—*hist pl* OH-6
Staley-Gordon Mine—*mine* CO-8
**Staley Heights**—*pop pl* GA-3
Staley Hollow—*valley* MO-7
Staley JHS—*school* GA-3
*Staley Junction* OR-9
Staley Knob—*summit* OH-6
Staley Knob—*summit* VA-3
Staley Lake—*lake* MI-6
Staley Lake—*reservoir* IN-6
Staley Lake—*reservoir* NC-3
Staley Lake Dam—*dam* IN-6
Staley Lake Dam—*dam* NC-3
Staley Memorial Gardens—*cemetery* GA-3
Staley Mill Dam—*dam* NC-3
Staley Mill Lake—*reservoir* NC-3
Staley Mound—*summit* MO-7
Staley Mound Cem—*cemetery* MO-7
Staley Pasture—*flat* UT-8
Staley Place—*locale* MT-8
Staley Ridge—*ridge* OH-6
Staley Ridge—*ridge* OR-9
Staley Ridge Trail—*trail* OR-9
Staley Rsvr—*reservoir* UT-8
Staley Run—*stream* OH-6
**Staleys**—*pop pl* IL-6
Staley Sch—*school* IL-6
**Staleys Cross Roads**—*pop pl* VA-3
Staley Siding—*locale* WA-9
Staleys Junction—*locale* OR-9
Staley Spring—*spring* CA-9
**Staley Springs**—*pop pl* ID-8
**Staleyville**—*pop pl* NY-2
Staley Well—*well* WY-8
*Stalin Lake* MI-6
Staliper Cave—*cave* PA-2
Stalker—*locale* PA-2
Stalker Elem Sch—*school* IN-6
Stalker Lake—*lake* MN-6
Stalker Lake—*reservoir* CO-8
Stalker Sch—*school* MI-6
Stalking Head Creek—*stream* GA-3
Stallard Bay—*swamp* GA-3
Stallard Branch—*stream* VA-3
Stallard Cem—*cemetery* (7) VA-3
Stallard Dam—*dam* OR-9
Stallard Lake—*lake* WA-9

Stallard Memorial Ch—church ... VA-3
Stallard Ranch—locale ... NM-5
Stallard Rsvr—reservoir ... OR-9
**Stallard Subdivision—pop pl** ... UT-8
Stall Branch—stream ... MS-4
Stall Brook—stream ... MA-1
Stall Cem—cemetery ... TN-4
Stallcop Cem—cemetery ... MN-6
Stallcop Lake—swamp ... MN-6
*Stallcopp Lake* ... MN-6
Stall Creek—stream ... KY-4
Stall Creek—stream ... WA-9
Stallcup Cave—cave ... MO-7
Stallcup Island—island ... KY-4
Staller Lake—reservoir ... IN-6
Staller Lake Dam—dam ... IN-6
Stalley Bay—bay ... VI-3
Stall Hollow—valley ... MO-7
*Stallicap Lake* ... MN-6
Stallin Cem—cemetery ... MS-4
Stalling Bend—bend ... AR-4
Stalling Butte—summit ... OR-9
Stalling Butte Spring—spring ... OR-9
Stallings—other ... NC-3
**Stallings—pop pl** ... IL-6
**Stallings—pop pl** ... NC-3
**Stallings—pop pl** ... TX-5
*Stallings Butte* ... OR-9
Stallings-Carpenter House—hist pl ... NC-3
Stallings Cem—cemetery ... GA-3
Stallings Cem—cemetery (2) ... IN-6
Stallings Cem—cemetery ... KY-4
Stallings Cem—cemetery ... TN-4
*Stallings Creek* ... AL-4
Stallings Creek—stream ... AL-4
Stallings Creek—stream ... VA-3
Stallings Crossroad—locale ... GA-3
Stallings Crossroads—locale ... NC-3
**Stallings Crossroads—pop pl** ... NC-3
Stallings Dam—dam ... AL-4
Stallings Ferry (historical)—locale ... MS-4
Stallings Island—hist pl ... GA-3
Stallings Lake—reservoir ... AL-4
Stallings Lake—reservoir ... NC-3
Stallings Lake Dam—dam ... NC-3
Stallings Memorial Park—cemetery ... NC-3
Stallings Pond—reservoir ... SC-3
Stallings Ranch—locale ... NM-5
*Stallings River* ... VA-3
*Stallings Station* ... NC-3
Stallings Store (historical)—locale ... MS-4
Stallings Tank—reservoir ... NM-5
Stalling Tank—reservoir (2) ... NM-5
Stallins Cem—cemetery ... KY-4
Stallion Bay—bay ... FL-3
Stallion Branch—stream ... TN-4
Stallion Branch—stream ... VA-3
*Stallion Cliff Mountain* ... VA-3
Stallion Fork—stream ... KY-4
Stallion Hammock—island ... FL-3
Stallion Head Branch—stream ... DE-2
Stallion Hill—summit ... CT-1
Stallion Hollow—valley ... AR-4
Stallion Ledge—bar ... ME-1
Stallion Mtn—summit ... TN-4
Stallion Sch (historical)—school ... MO-7
Stallion Tank—reservoir ... AZ-5
Stallion Waterhole—lake ... OR-9
Stallman Bridge—bridge ... IN-6
Stallman Corners—locale ... CA-9
Stallman Sch—school ... MO-7
Stallo—locale ... MS-4
*Stallona* ... MS-4
Stallone—airport ... NJ-2
Stall Run—stream ... OH-6
**Stalls—pop pl** ... TX-5
Stalls Corner—locale ... MI-6
*Stalls Falls* ... OR-9
Stalls Landing (historical)—locale ... TN-4
*Stall Spring* ... TN-4
**Stallsville—pop pl** ... SC-3
Stallwitz Lake—locale ... TX-5
Stallworth Cem—cemetery ... TX-5
Stallworth Dam—dam (2) ... AL-4
*Stallworth Lake* ... AL-4
Stallworth Lake—reservoir ... AL-4
Stallworth Pond—reservoir ... AL-4
Stallworths Black Pond—reservoir ... AL-4
Stallworths Black Pond Dam—dam ... AL-4
Stallworths Shadow Lake—reservoir ... AL-4
Stalman Cem—cemetery ... WV-2
**Stalmuke—pop pl** ... MS-4
Stalnaker Cem—cemetery ... WV-2
Stalnaker Hall—hist pl ... WV-2
Stalnaker Run—stream (4) ... WV-2
Stalnaker Sch—school ... WV-2
St. Aloysius Catholic Church—hist pl ... OH-6
St. Alphonsus' Hosp Nurses' Home and Heating Plant/Laundry—hist pl ... ID-8
Stalsby Creek—stream ... GA-3
Stalsworth Cem—cemetery ... TN-4
Stalter Branch—stream ... KS-7
Stalter Canyon—valley ... OR-9
Stalter Cem—cemetery ... KS-7
Stalter Mine—mine ... OR-9
*Sta-lu-kaho-mish Lake* ... WA-9
*Stalukahamish River* ... WA-9
**Stalvey—pop pl** ... SC-3
Stalvey Bay—swamp ... GA-3
Stalwart—locale ... MI-6
Stalwart Cem—cemetery ... MI-6
Stalworth Camp—locale ... MS-4
Stalworth Lake—lake ... FL-3
Stamans Run—stream ... PA-2
**Stambaugh—pop pl** ... KY-4
**Stambaugh—pop pl** ... MI-6
Stambaugh, Henry H., Memorial Auditorium—hist pl ... OH-6
Stambaugh Bldg—hist pl ... OH-6
Stambaugh Branch—stream ... KY-4
Stambaugh Camp—locale ... OH-6
Stambaugh Cem—cemetery ... KY-4
*Stambaugh Corner* ... MI-6
Stambaugh Creek—stream ... WY-8
*Stambaugh Hollow* ... PA-2
Stambaugh Rsvr—reservoir ... CO-8
Stambaugh Sch—school ... OH-6
**Stambaugh (Township of)—pop pl** ... MI-6
**Stambaugh (Youngstown)—pop pl** ... PA-2
Stamboul Gulch—valley ... CO-8
STAMBOUL (Whaling Bark)—hist pl ... CA-9
*Stambro* ... NY-2
St. Ambrose Cathedral and Rectory—hist pl ... IA-7
Stamen Bilingual Learning Center—school ... FL-3
Stamen Sch Number 1—school ... ND-7
Stamen Sch Number 2—school ... ND-7
**Stamey Branch—pop pl** ... NC-3
Stamey Branch—stream (2) ... NC-3
Stamey Cove—valley ... NC-3
Stamey Cove Branch—stream ... NC-3
Stamey Cove Gap—gap ... NC-3
Stamey Knob—summit ... NC-3
**Stamey Town—pop pl** ... NC-3
*Stamfers Wharf* ... VA-3
Stamford—locale ... SD-7
**Stamford—pop pl** ... CT-1
**Stamford—pop pl** ... NE-7
**Stamford—pop pl** ... NY-2
**Stamford—pop pl** ... TX-5
**Stamford—pop pl** ... VT-1
Stamford, Lake—reservoir ... TX-5
Stamford (CCD)—cens area ... TX-5
Stamford Cem—cemetery ... NE-7
Stamford Cem—cemetery ... NY-2
Stamford Cem—cemetery ... TX-5
Stamford City Hall—hist pl ... TX-5
Stamford Country Club—other ... TX-5
Stamford Harbor—bay ... CT-1
Stamford Meadows—swamp ... VT-1
Stamford Pond—lake ... VT-1
Stamford Rsvr—reservoir ... NY-2
Stamford Stream—stream ... VT-1
Stamford (Town of)—civ div ... CT-1
**Stamford (Town of)—pop pl** ... NY-2
**Stamford (Town of)—pop pl** ... VT-1
Stamhaugh Hollow—valley ... PA-2
Stamill Canyon—valley ... WA-9
Stamill Flat—flat ... WA-9
Stammer Creek—stream ... NY-2
Stammer Creek State For—forest ... NY-2
Stamm Fork—stream ... KY-4
Stamm Sch—school ... IL-6
Stamm Sch—school ... OH-6
Stamm Sch—school ... PA-2
Stamm Trail—trail ... PA-2
**Stamp—pop pl** ... AL-4
Stamp, The—summit ... VA-3
Stamp Act Island—island ... NH-1
Stamp Branch Ch—church ... GA-3
*Stamp Creek* ... SC-3
Stamp Creek—stream (2) ... GA-3
Stamp Creek—stream ... SC-3
Stamp Creek—stream ... TN-4
Stamp Creek Ch—church ... GA-3
Stamp Creek Ch—church ... SC-3
Stamp Creek Ridge—ridge ... TN-4
Stamp Creek Valley—valley ... TN-4
Stamp Dance Creek—stream ... OK-5
Stamp Ditch—canal ... IN-6
Stamped Canyon—valley ... NM-5
Stampede—locale ... TX-5
Stampede—locale ... WA-9
**Stampede—pop pl** ... ND-7
Stampede Bog—swamp ... WY-8
Stampede Canyon—valley ... CA-9
*Stampede Creek* ... NV-8
Stampede Creek—stream ... AK-9
Stampede Creek—stream ... OR-9
Stampede Creek—stream (2) ... TX-5
Stampede Creek—stream ... WA-9
Stampede Dam—dam ... CA-9
Stampede Gap—gap ... NV-8
Stampede Lake—lake ... ID-8
Stampede Meadow—flat ... WY-8
Stampede Mountain—summit ... TX-5
Stampede Pass—gap ... WA-9
Stampede Ranch—locale ... NV-8
Stampede Rsvr—reservoir ... CA-9
Stampede Site—hist pl ... CA-9
Stampede Tunnel—tunnel ... WA-9
Stampede Valley—valley ... CA-9
Stamper Branch—stream (6) ... KY-4
Stamper Cem—cemetery ... KY-4
Stamper Cem—cemetery ... MO-7
Stamper Cem—cemetery (2) ... NC-3
*Stamper Creek* ... IN-6
Stamper Fork—stream ... KY-4
**Stamper (historical)—pop pl** ... MS-4
Stamper Hollow—valley ... KY-4
Stamper Pond—lake ... MS-4
Stamper Post Office (historical)—building ... MS-4
Stamper Post Office (historical)—building ... TN-4
**Stampers—pop pl** ... VA-3
Stampers Branch—stream ... KY-4
Stamper Sch—school ... KY-4
Stampers Chapel (historical)—church ... TN-4
*Stampers Creek* ... IN-6
**Stampers Creek—pop pl** ... IN-6
Stampers Creek—stream ... IN-6
Stampers Creek Ch—church ... IN-6
Stampers Creek Sinks—basin ... IN-6
Stampers Creek (Township of)—civ div ... IN-6
Stamper Site—hist pl ... OK-5
*Stampers Landing* ... VA-3
Stampers Mill (historical)—locale ... TN-4
Stampers Wharf—locale ... VA-3
Stampfler Sch—school ... MI-6
Stamp Gap—gap (2) ... TN-4
Stamp Hill—summit ... TN-4
Stamping Creek—stream ... WV-2
**Stamping Ground—pop pl** ... KY-4
Stamping Ground (CCD)—cens area ... KY-4
Stamping Ground Hollow—valley ... VA-3
Stamping Ground Mtn—summit ... VA-3
Stamping Ground Ridge—ridge ... TN-4
Stamping Ground Run—stream ... WV-2
Stamping Ground Trail—trail ... TN-4
Stamp Knob—summit ... GA-3
**Stampley—pop pl** ... LA-4
**Stampley—pop pl** ... MS-4
Stampley Cem—cemetery ... MS-4
Stampley Creek—stream ... MS-4
Stampley Post Office (historical)—building ... MS-4
Stamp Meadows—flat ... ID-8
Stamp Mill Lake—lake ... WY-8
Stamp Ridge—ridge ... GA-3
Stamp Ridge—ridge ... TN-4
Stamps—locale ... TX-5
**Stamps—pop pl** ... AR-4
Stamps Branch—stream ... TX-5
Stamps Cem—cemetery (2) ... AL-4
Stamps Cem—cemetery ... TN-4
*Stamps Chapel* ... AL-4
Stamps Chapel—church ... GA-3
Stamps Cove—valley ... TN-4
Stamps Hollow—valley ... TN-4
Stamps Hollow Creek—stream ... TN-4
Stamps Island—island ... IA-7
Stamps Lake—lake ... MS-4
Stamps Landing—locale ... MS-4
Stamps Oil And Gas Field—oilfield ... AR-4
Stamps Plantation (historical)—locale ... MS-4
Stamps Quarry—mine ... TN-4
Stamps Spring—spring ... AZ-5
Stamps Star Quarry—mine ... TN-4
Stamps Well—well (2) ... AZ-5
*Stampus Creek* ... IN-6
*Stamp Well* ... AZ-5
Stams Mtn—summit ... OR-9
Stamukhi Shoal—bar ... AK-9
Stamy, Mount—summit ... AK-9
Stamy Rsvr—reservoir ... OR-9
**Stanaford—pop pl** ... WV-2
Stanaford Branch—stream ... WV-2
Stanaford Road Ch—church ... WV-2
Stanafork Station—locale ... WV-2
*Stanaker Draw* ... UT-8
*Stanard* ... NY-2
Stanard Sch—school ... OH-6
Stanards Mill—locale ... VA-3
**Stanardsville—pop pl** ... VA-3
Stanardsville (Magisterial District)—fmr MCD ... VA-3
Stanardsville Run—stream ... VA-3
Stanardsville Sch—school ... VA-3
Stanbaugh Drain—canal ... MI-6
**Stanberry—pop pl** ... MO-7
**Stanberry—pop pl** ... WI-6
Stanberry Lake—lake ... WI-6
Stanberry Park—park ... OH-6
**Stanberry Park—pop pl** ... OH-6
Stanberry Ranch—locale ... AZ-5
*Stanbery* ... WI-6
**Stanbery—pop pl** ... WI-6
Stanbery, Edwin, Office—hist pl ... OH-6
*Stanbery Park* ... OH-6
Stan Branch—stream ... KY-4
Stanbro—locale ... NY-2
**Stanbrook—pop pl** ... MD-2
Stanbro Rsvr—reservoir ... OR-9
Stanburn Park—park ... TX-5
*Stanbury* ... NC-3
*Stanbury* ... WI-6
*Stance Brook* ... WI-6
*Stance Creek* ... WI-6
Stancel Cem—cemetery ... TX-5
Stancel Creek—stream ... TX-5
Stancell—locale ... NC-3
Stancel Spring—spring ... AL-4
Stancers Pond—lake ... MI-6
**Stanchfield—pop pl** ... MN-6
Stanchfield Corner—locale ... MN-6
Stanchfield Creek—stream ... MN-6
Stanchfield Lake—lake ... MN-6
**Stanchfield (Township of)—pop pl** ... MN-6
Stanchion Creek—stream ... OR-9
Stanciels Pond—reservoir ... NC-3
Stanciels Pond Dam—dam ... NC-3
Stancil Bayou—gut ... MO-7
Stancil Cem—cemetery ... MO-7
Stancil Chapel—church ... NC-3
Stancil Grove Ch—church ... GA-3
Stancil Lakes—lake ... SC-3
Stancil Ridge—ridge ... GA-3
**Stancils Chapel—pop pl** ... NC-3
Stancils Landing (historical)—locale ... MS-4
Stancioff House—hist pl ... MD-2
Stancliffe Creek—stream ... OR-9
Stancliff Sch (abandoned)—school ... PA-2
**Stanco—pop pl** ... SC-3
Stan Coffin Lake—lake ... WA-9
*Stancos Creek* ... CA-9
Stan Creek—stream ... OR-9
**Stand—pop pl** ... MO-7
*Standale* ... MI-6
**Standale—pop pl** ... MI-6
*Standard* ... NC-3
Standard—locale ... AL-4
Standard—locale ... AK-9
Standard—locale ... LA-4
Standard—locale ... MD-2
Standard—locale ... WA-9
**Standard—pop pl** ... AL-4
**Standard—pop pl** ... AK-9
**Standard—pop pl** ... CA-9
**Standard—pop pl** ... IL-6
**Standard—pop pl** ... IN-6
**Standard—pop pl** ... LA-4
**Standard—pop pl** ... MS-4
**Standard—pop pl** ... NC-3
**Standard—pop pl** ... PA-2
**Standard—pop pl** ... TX-5
**Standard—pop pl** ... WV-2
Standard Branch—stream ... AL-4
Standard Canal—canal ... LA-4
Standard Cem—cemetery ... IL-6
Standard Cem—cemetery ... KY-4
Standard Church, The—church ... VT-1
**Standard City (South Standard PO)—pop pl** ... IL-6
Standard Country Club—locale ... AL-4
Standard Country Club—other ... KY-4
Standard Creek—stream (2) ... AK-9
Standard Creek—stream ... GA-3
Standard Creek—stream (2) ... MT-8
Standard Creek—stream ... OR-9
Standard Creek—stream ... WA-9
*Standard Crossroad* ... NC-3
Standard Ditch—canal ... CO-8
Standard Drain—canal ... CA-9
Standard Draw—valley ... WY-8
Standard Furnace (40HI145)—hist pl ... TN-4
Standard Gulch—valley ... AZ-5
Standard Gun Club—other ... CA-9
Standard Heights—uninc pl ... LA-4
Standard Heights Sch—school ... LA-4
Standard Hill—summit ... CA-9
Standard Hollow—valley ... OR-9
Standard Ice Company Bldg—hist pl ... AR-4
Standard Lake—lake ... MI-6
Standard Lake—lake ... MT-8
Standard Lakes—lake ... ID-8
Standard Lateral—canal ... CA-9
Standard Liquors, Incorporated (Plant)—facility ... IN-6
Standard Mammoth Mine—mine ... ID-8
Standard Mine—mine ... AZ-5
Standard Mine—mine (3) ... CA-9
Standard Mine—mine ... CO-8
Standard Mine—mine ... ID-8
Standard Mine—mine (2) ... NV-8
Standard Mine—mine ... NM-5
Standard Mine—mine (2) ... OR-9
Standard Mine—mine ... UT-8
Standard Mine—mine ... WY-8
Standard Mine Number One—mine ... CA-9
Standard Mine Number Two—mine ... CA-9
Standard Mineral Mine—mine ... AZ-5
Standard Mine (underground)—mine (2) ... AL-4
*Standard Oil* ... CA-9
Standard Oil Bldg—hist pl ... CA-9
Standard Oil Camp Eleven-C—locale ... CA-9
Standard Oil Camp Five-D—locale ... CA-9
Standard Oil Camp Nine-D—locale ... CA-9
Standard Oil Camp One-C—locale ... CA-9
Standard Oil Company Bldg of Nebraska—hist pl ... NE-7
Standard Oil Gasoline Station—hist pl ... IL-6
Standard Oil Signa Station—locale ... CA-9
*Standard Oil Tank Farm* ... CA-9
Standard Park—park ... CA-9
Standard Park—park ... WY-8
Standard Pass Creek School—locale ... WY-8
Standard Peak—summit ... MT-8
Standard Peak—summit ... WY-8
Standard Pit—basin ... WY-8
Standard Plaza Shop Ctr—locale ... FL-3
Standard Printing Company—hist pl ... MO-7
Standard Rsvr—reservoir ... WY-8
**Standardsburg—pop pl** ... OH-6
Standard Sch—school ... CA-9
Standard Sch—school (3) ... IL-6
Standard Sch—school (2) ... MI-6
Standard Sch—school (3) ... MT-8
Standard Sch—school (4) ... NE-7
Standard Sch—school ... WA-9
**Standard Shaft—pop pl** ... PA-2
**Standard Shaft (Moline)—pop pl** ... PA-2
Standard (site)—locale ... AZ-5
**Standard Spur—pop pl** ... ND-7
Standard Theatre—hist pl ... MO-7
Standard Town And Country Club—other ... GA-3
Standard Tungsten Mine—mine ... AZ-5
**Standard-Umsted—pop pl** ... AR-4
Standardville—locale ... UT-8
Standard Wash—stream ... AZ-5
Standard Wells—well ... NM-5
Standart—locale ... TX-5
**Standart—pop pl** ... WI-6
Standart Ch—church ... WI-6
Standart Mine—mine ... CA-9
Standart-Simmons Hardware Company—hist pl ... OH-6
*Standbacks Ferry* ... NC-3
Standby Creek—stream ... MT-8
Standby Mine—mine ... SD-7
Standcliff Creek—stream ... OR-9
*Standcliff Rsvr* ... OR-9
Stand Cove—bay ... ME-1
Standefer Ranch—locale ... NM-5
Standerson Island—island ... MI-6
Standfast Creek—stream ... SD-7
Standfield Cem—cemetery ... TN-4
Standfield Ch—church ... TN-4
Standfield Hollow—valley ... TN-4
Standfield Meadow—flat ... OR-9
Standford PO (historical)—building ... PA-2
*Standfords Branch* ... WV-2
Standford Spring—spring ... AL-4
Standford Springs—spring ... AL-4
Standhill Mtn—summit ... NC-3
Standhope Peak—summit ... ID-8
**Standia Subdivision—pop pl** ... UT-8
Standifer Branch—stream ... TN-4
Standifer Bridge—bridge ... TN-4
Standifer Cem—cemetery (2) ... TN-4
Standifer Creek—stream ... MS-4
Standifer Creek—stream ... TN-4
Standifer Gap—gap ... TN-4
Standifer Gap—gap ... TX-5
Standifer Gap Ch—church ... TN-4
Standiford Cem—cemetery ... KY-4
Standiford Cem—cemetery (2) ... MO-7
Standiford Creek—stream ... VA-3
Standiford Field (Airport)—airport ... KY-4
Standiford (historical)—locale ... AL-4
Standiford Sch—school ... CA-9
Standifred Creek—stream ... KS-7
Standing Bar Tank—reservoir ... AZ-5
Standing Bear Lake—reservoir ... NE-7
Standing Boy Creek—stream ... GA-3
Standing Circle R Ranch Airp—airport ... WA-9
Standing Cloud Creek—stream ... SD-7
Standing Cow Ruins—locale ... AZ-5
Standing Cypress Creek—stream ... MS-4
Standing Cypress Point—cape ... AL-4
Standing Elk Creek—stream ... MT-8
Standing Elk Mine—mine ... NV-8
Standing Fall House—hist pl ... AZ-5
Standing Gap—gap ... NC-3
*Standing Hickory Creek* ... MS-4
Standing Horse Mesa—summit ... AZ-5
Standing Indian Wildlife Mngmt Area—park ... NC-3
**Standing Pine—pop pl** ... MS-4
Standing Pine Cem—cemetery ... MS-4
Standing Pine Ch—church ... MS-4
Standing Pine Creek—stream ... MS-4
Standing Pine Sch—school ... MS-4
Standing Pine Watershed Structure 5 Dam—dam ... MS-4
Standing Pine Watershed Structure 9 Dam—dam ... MS-4
Standing Pond—lake ... NJ-2
Standing Pond—lake ... VT-1
*Standing Red Rock Creek* ... AZ-5
Standing Redrock Creek—stream ... AZ-5
Standing Reed Creek—stream ... MS-4
Standing Rock—cliff ... NM-5
Standing Rock—locale ... KY-4
Standing Rock—locale ... NM-5
Standing Rock—locale ... TN-4
Standingrock—locale ... WV-2
Standing Rock—pillar ... AZ-5
Standing Rock—pillar ... AR-4
Standing Rock—pillar ... ID-8
Standing Rock—pillar ... MO-7
Standing Rock—pillar (3) ... TN-4
Standing Rock—pillar ... UT-8
**Standing Rock—pop pl** ... AL-4
Standing Rock—summit (2) ... AZ-5
Standing Rock—summit ... MT-8
Standing Rock—summit (2) ... NM-5
Standing Rock—summit ... UT-8
Standing Rock—summit ... WY-8
Standing Rock Airp—airport ... ND-7
*Standing Rock Basin* ... UT-8
Standing Rock Branch—stream ... TN-4
Standing Rock Bridge—bridge ... TN-4
Standing Rock Catchment Basin—reservoir ... AZ-5
Standing Rock Cem—cemetery ... ND-7
Standing Rock Cem—cemetery ... OH-6
Standing Rock Cem—cemetery ... OK-5
Standing Rock Ch—church ... AL-4
Standing Rock Ch—church ... KY-4
Standing Rock Ch—church ... OK-5
Standing Rock Ch—church ... TN-4
Standing Rock Creek—stream ... MO-7
Standing Rock Creek—stream ... TN-4
Standing Rock Creek—stream ... WY-8
Standing Rock Dock—locale ... TN-4
Standing Rock Hill—summit ... ND-7
Standing Rock (historical)—locale ... ND-7
Standing Rock Hollow—valley (2) ... MO-7
Standing Rock Hollow—valley ... TN-4
**Standing Rock Ind Res—pop pl** ... ND-7
Standing Rock Ind Res—reserve ... SD-7
Standing Rock Lake—lake ... AK-9
Standing Rock Landing Public Use Area—park ... OK-5
Standing Rock Mtn—summit ... OK-5
Standing Rock Park—park ... WI-6
Standing Rock Post Office (historical)—building ... TN-4
Standing Rock Pumping Station—other ... NM-5
Standingrock Run—stream ... WV-2
*Standing Rocks* ... UT-8
Standing Rocks—pillar (2) ... AZ-5
Standing Rocks—summit ... AR-4
Standing Rock Sch (historical)—school ... TN-4
Standing Rock Tank—reservoir ... AZ-5
Standing Rock Tribe Dam—dam (5) ... SD-7
Standing Rock Wash—stream ... NM-5
Standing Rock Well—well ... AZ-5
Standing Snake Pinnacle—pillar ... NV-8
Standing Springs Ch—church ... SC-3
*Standing Stone* ... TN-4
**Standing Stone—pop pl** ... PA-2
**Standingstone—pop pl** ... TN-4
Standing Stone—summit ... TN-4
Standing Stone Ch—church ... PA-2
Standingstone Ch—church ... WV-2
*Standing Stone Creek* ... MS-4
Standing Stone Creek—stream ... PA-2
Standingstone Creek—stream ... WV-2
Standing Stone Dam—dam ... TN-4
Standingstone Fork—stream ... OH-6
Standing Stone Golf Course—locale ... PA-2
Standing Stone Lake—reservoir ... TN-4
Standingstone Lake—reservoir ... TN-4
Standingstone Mtn—summit ... NC-3
Standing Stone Mtn—summit ... SC-3
Standing Stone Post Office (historical)—building ... TN-4
Standingstone Run—stream ... OH-6
Standing Stone Run—stream ... PA-2
Standingstone Run—stream (2) ... WV-2
Standing Stone Rustic Park Hist Dist—hist pl ... TN-4
Standing Stone State Park And Forest—park ... TN-4
Standing Stone State Rustic Park—park ... TN-4
**Standing Stone (Township of)—pop pl** ... PA-2
Standing Stump—area ... MS-4
Standing Stump Bayou—stream ... MS-4
*Standing Tree* ... AZ-5
Standing Twin Peak—summit ... NM-5
Stand in Point—cape ... ME-1
**Standish—pop pl** ... CA-9
**Standish—pop pl** ... ME-1
**Standish—pop pl** ... MA-1
**Standish—pop pl** ... MI-6
**Standish—pop pl** ... MO-7
**Standish—pop pl** ... NY-2
Standish—uninc pl ... MA-1
Standish, Alexander, House—hist pl ... MA-1
Standish, James H., House—hist pl ... MA-1
Standish, Lake—lake ... FL-3
Standish Brook—stream ... CT-1
Standish Brook—stream ... NY-2
Standish Cem—cemetery ... OH-6
Standish Creek—stream ... MT-8
Standish Ditch—canal (2) ... WY-8
Standish Gravel Pit—mine ... CA-9
Standish-Hickey State Rec Area—park ... CA-9
*Standish Hill* ... MA-1
Standish Hill—summit ... CT-1
Standish Lake—lake ... MI-6
Standish Lake—lake ... ND-7
Standish Mill Pond Dam—dam ... MA-1
Standish Monument—school ... MA-1
Standish Pond—lake ... CT-1
Standish Pond—lake ... MI-6
Standish Sch—school ... MI-6
Standish Sch—school ... MN-6
Standish Sch—school ... MO-7
Standish Sch—school ... OH-6
Standish Shore—beach ... MA-1
*Standish Shores* ... MA-1
**Standish (Town of)—pop pl** ... ME-1
**Standish (Township of)—pop pl** ... MI-6
Standish Village Plaza (Shop Ctr)—locale ... MA-1
Standlee Chapel—church ... TX-5
**Standley—pop pl** ... OH-6
Standley, Capt. James S., House—hist pl ... OK-5
Standley Branch—stream ... MO-7
Standley Cabin—locale ... OR-9
Standley Ch—church ... AR-4
Standley Creek—stream ... CA-9
Standley Creek—stream ... GA-3
Standley Creek—stream ... OR-9
Standley Guard Station—locale ... OR-9
Standley Hill—summit ... CO-8
Standley House—hist pl ... TX-5
Standley Lake—reservoir ... CO-8
Standley Mtn—summit (2) ... AR-4
Standley Park—park ... CA-9
Standley Spring—spring ... OR-9
Standleys Store—locale ... GA-3
*Standover Creek* ... NC-3
Stand Peak—summit ... AK-9
Standpine Park—park ... ME-1
Standpipe Draw—valley ... WY-8
Standpipe Hill—summit ... OK-5
Standpipe Hill—summit ... WA-9
Standpipe Spring—spring ... WY-8
St. Andrews Apartments—hist pl ... GA-3
St. Andrew's Church—hist pl ... ME-1
St. Andrews Episcopal Chapel—hist pl ... RI-1
St. Andrews Episcopal Church—hist pl ... CO-8
St. Andrew's Episcopal Church—hist pl ... OH-6
St. Andrews Episcopal Church—hist pl ... SC-3
St. Andrew's Protestant Episcopal Church—hist pl ... CT-1
**St. Andrews Township—pop pl** ... ND-7
Standridge Bend—bend ... AL-4
**Standridge (subdivision)—pop pl** ... AL-4
Stand Rock—pillar ... WI-6
Standrock Branch—stream ... VA-3
Standrod—locale ... ID-8
Standrod—locale ... UT-8
Standrod Bank—hist pl ... ID-8
Standrod House—hist pl ... ID-8
Stands Basin—basin ... MT-8
Standsbury Ranch—locale ... AZ-5
Standstill, Lake—lake ... WA-9
*Standt Eddy* ... PA-2
Standup Creek—stream ... WA-9
Standup Gulch—valley ... CO-8
Staney Cone—summit ... AK-9
Staney Creek—stream ... AK-9
Staney Island—island ... AK-9
*Stanfer Wharf* ... VA-3
Stanfford Hill Wildlife Mngmt Area—park ... MA-1
*Stanfiel* ... AL-4
*Stanfield* ... AL-4
Stanfield—locale ... TX-5
**Stanfield—pop pl** ... AZ-5
**Stanfield—pop pl** ... NC-3
**Stanfield—pop pl** ... OR-9
**Stanfield—pop pl** ... TN-4
*Stanfield Branch* ... OR-9
Stanfield Branch—stream ... AR-4
Stanfield Branch—stream ... GA-3
Stanfield Branch—stream ... NC-3
Stanfield Branch—stream (2) ... TN-4
Stanfield Branch Furnish Ditch—canal ... OR-9
Stanfield Cem—cemetery ... KY-4
Stanfield Cem—cemetery ... OH-6
Stanfield Cem—cemetery ... TX-5
Stanfield Ch—church ... MO-7
Stanfield Creek—stream ... MS-4
Stanfield Drain—canal ... OR-9
Stanfield General Ch (historical)—church ... MO-7
Stanfield Hill—locale ... CA-9
Stanfield Hill—summit ... CA-9
Stanfield (historical)—locale ... AL-4
Stanfield Hollow—valley (2) ... TN-4
Stanfield Junction—locale ... OR-9
Stanfield Park—park ... TX-5
Stanfield Road Interchange—crossing ... AZ-5
Stanfield Rsvr—reservoir ... OR-9
Stanfield Sch—school ... AZ-5
Stanfield Sch—school ... NC-3
Stanfill—locale ... TN-4
**Stanfill—pop pl** ... KY-4
Stanfill Cem—cemetery ... TN-4
Stanfill Ch—church ... AR-4
Stanfill-Oaklawn Cem—cemetery ... KY-4
Stanfill Sch (historical)—school (2) ... TN-4
Stanfold Ch—church ... WI-6
**Stanfold (Town of)—pop pl** ... WI-6
*Stanford* ... KS-7
*Stanford* ... MS-4
Stanford—CDP ... CA-9
Stanford—locale ... ID-8
Stanford—locale ... IA-7
**Stanford—pop pl** ... AR-4
**Stanford—pop pl** ... IL-6
**Stanford—pop pl** ... IN-6
**Stanford—pop pl** ... KY-4
**Stanford—pop pl** ... MT-8
Stanford, George, Farm—hist pl ... OH-6
Stanford, Mount—summit (2) ... CA-9
Stanford Ave Sch—school (2) ... CA-9
Stanford Ave Stormwater Retention Pond—dam ... PA-2
Stanford Branch—stream (2) ... AL-4
Stanford Branch—stream ... TN-4
Stanford Canyon—valley ... AZ-5
Stanford (CCD)—cens area ... KY-4
Stanford Cem—cemetery (2) ... AL-4
Stanford Cem—cemetery ... IN-6
Stanford Cem—cemetery ... LA-4
Stanford Cem—cemetery ... MN-6
Stanford Cem—cemetery (2) ... NY-2
Stanford Cem—cemetery ... TX-5
Stanford Cem—cemetery ... WI-6
Stanford Ch—church ... AR-4
Stanford Ch—church ... NC-3
Stanford Chapel—church ... NC-3
Stanford Commercial District—hist pl ... KY-4
*Stanford Creek* ... AL-4
Stanford Creek—stream ... AZ-5
Stanford Creek—stream ... TX-5
Stanford Dam No 1—dam ... NM-5
Stanford Draw—valley ... NM-5
Stanford Furniture Co. Bldg—hist pl ... OK-5
Stanford Golf Course—other ... CA-9
Stanford Golf Course—other ... NY-2
**Stanford Heights—pop pl** ... NY-2
Stanford (historical P.O.)—locale ... IA-7
Stanford Hollow—valley ... AL-4
Stanford HQ (Site)—locale ... CA-9

Stanford JHS—school CA-9
Stanford Lake AL-4
Stanford Lake—lake CA-9
Stanford Lake Dam—dam MS-4
Stanford Lakes—lake CA-9
Stanford-Lathrop House—hist pl CA-9
Stanford Linear Accelerator—other CA-9
Stanford Park—park TX-5
Stanford Peak CA-9
Stanford Playground—park CA-9
Stanford Point—cliff CA-9
Stanford Point—summit ID-8
Stanford Pond—lake NH-1
Stanford Post Office (historical)—building AL-4
Stanford Ranch AZ-5
Stanford Ranch—locale AZ-5
Stanford Rock—pillar CA-9
Stanford Rsvr—reservoir KY-4
Stanford Russell Ranch—locale MT-8
Stanfordsburg KY-4
Stanford Sch—school (2) CA-9
Stanford Sch—school SD-7
Stanford Sch—school TN-4
Stanford Sch (historical)—school PA-2
Stanfords Creek—stream NC-3
Stanford Spring—spring AZ-5
Stanford Spring—spring CA-9
Stanford Spring—spring (2) ID-8
Stanford (subdivision)—pop pl MS-4
Stanford Tank—reservoir AZ-5
Stanford (Town of)—pop pl NY-2
Stanford (Township of)—pop pl IL-6
Stanford (Township of)—pop pl MN-6
Stanford Trough—spring CA-9
Stanford Univ—school CA-9
Stanford University CA-9
Stanford Valley—valley TX-5
Stanfordville—locale GA-3
Stanfordville—pop pl NY-2
Stanfordville—pop pl PA-2
Stanfordville (Stanford)—pop pl NY-2
Stanforth JHS—school NY-2
Stang, John, House—hist pl OH-6
Stangelville—pop pl WI-6
Stanger Springs Ch—church TX-5
Stange Sch—school NE-7
Stangland Airp—airport IN-6
Stangland Slough—lake SD-7
Stangler Ditch IN-6
Stang Lookout Tower—locale WI-6
Stango Cem—cemetery LA-4
Stanholt-Elmore HS—school AL-4
Stanhope—locale MO-7
Stanhope—locale OH-6
Stanhope—locale PA-2
Stanhope—pop pl IA-7
Stanhope—pop pl KY-4
Stanhope—pop pl NJ-2
Stanhope—pop pl NC-3
Stanhope Brook—stream VT-1
Stanhope Ch—church KY-4
Stanhope Hill—summit VT-1
Stanhope Island—island AK-9
Stanhope Meadow—swamp ME-1
Stanhope Oil Field—oilfield KS-7
Stanhope Union Cem—cemetery NJ-2
Stan Hywet Hall-Frank A. Seiberling House—hist pl OH-6
Stanifer Branch—stream TX-5
Stanifer Pond—lake TN-4
Stanifird Mtn—summit OK-5
Staniford Hollow—valley KY-4
Stanislaus—pop pl CA-9
Stanislaus County CA-9
Stanislaus (County)—pop pl CA-9
Stanislaus County Park—park CA-9
Stanislaus County Ranch—locale CA-9
Stanislaus Grove Big Trees (South Calavera)—woods CA-9
Stanislaus Meadow—flat CA-9
Stanislaus Memorial Hosp—hospital CA-9
Stanislaus Peak—summit CA-9
Stanislaus Pit—pop pl CA-9
Stanislaus River—stream CA-9
Stanislaus River Campground—locale CA-9
Stanislaus Sch—school CA-9
Stanislaus Sch—school IL-6
Stanislaus State Coll—school CA-9
Stanislaus Tunnel—tunnel CA-9
Stanislaus-Yosemite (CCD)—cens area CA-9
Staniukovich Mtn—summit AK-9
Stank Canyon—valley NV-8
Stankey Creek—stream WA-9
Stank Hill—summit NV-8
Stankie Valley WI-6
Stanko Draw—valley WY-8
Stanko Lake—lake MI-6
Stankul Drain—canal MI-6
Stanland Bay—swamp NC-3
Stanland Branch—stream NC-3
Stanley—locale AL-4
Stanley—locale CA-9
Stanley—locale MN-6
Stanley—locale OH-6
Stanley—locale OK-5
Stanley—locale PA-2
Stanley—locale WV-2
Stanley—pop pl ID-8
Stanley—pop pl IN-6
Stanley—pop pl IA-7
Stanley—pop pl KS-7
Stanley—pop pl KY-4
Stanley—pop pl (2) LA-4
Stanley—pop pl MA-1
Stanley—pop pl MI-6
Stanley—pop pl MO-7
Stanley—pop pl NM-5
Stanley—pop pl NY-2
Stanley—pop pl NC-3
Stanley—pop pl ND-7
Stanley—pop pl (2) OR-9
Stanley—pop pl TN-4
Stanley—pop pl VA-3
Stanley—pop pl WI-6
Stanley, Lake—lake (2) FL-3
Stanley Addition—locale KY-4
Stanley and Card Ranch—locale NM-5
Stanley Basin—basin ID-8
Stanley Bay—lake GA-3
Stanley-Boyd Sch—school WI-6
Stanley Branch AR-4
Stanley Branch—stream AL-4
Stanley Branch—stream FL-3
Stanley Branch—stream (2) GA-3
Stanley Branch—stream KS-7
Stanley Branch—stream LA-4
Stanley Branch—stream MO-7
Stanley Branch—stream (2) NC-3
Stanley Branch—stream SC-3
Stanley Branch—stream TN-4
Stanley Bridge—bridge FL-3
Stanley Brook—stream IN-6
Stanley Brook—stream ME-1
Stanley Brook—stream NH-1
Stanley Brook—stream NY-2
Stanley Brook—stream (2) VT-1
Stanley B Springs—spring NV-8
Stanley Butte—summit AZ-5
Stanley Butte—summit ID-8
Stanley Cabin OR-9
Stanley Cabin—locale OR-9
Stanley Camp—locale NV-8
Stanley Canal—canal CA-9
Stanley Canyon—valley CO-8
Stanley Canyon—valley (2) WA-9
Stanley Cave—cave TN-4
Stanley Cem—cemetery (2) AL-4
Stanley Cem—cemetery (3) AR-4
Stanley Cem—cemetery (3) GA-3
Stanley Cem—cemetery ID-8
Stanley Cem—cemetery IL-6
Stanley Cem—cemetery IN-6
Stanley Cem—cemetery IA-7
Stanley Cem—cemetery (3) KY-4
Stanley Cem—cemetery LA-4
Stanley Cem—cemetery ME-1
Stanley Cem—cemetery MO-7
Stanley Cem—cemetery NE-7
Stanley Cem—cemetery NH-1
Stanley Cem—cemetery NC-3
Stanley Cem—cemetery (3) OH-6
Stanley Cem—cemetery OK-5
Stanley Cem—cemetery (4) TN-4
Stanley Cem—cemetery (5) VA-3
Stanley Cem—cemetery (3) WV-2
Stanley Cemeteries—cemetery WV-2
Stanley Center NC-3
Stanley Ch—church GA-3
Stanley Ch—church MO-7
Stanley Channel—channel WA-9
Stanley Chapel—church NC-3
Stanley Circle Subdivision—pop pl UT-8
Stanley Cliff—cliff TN-4
Stanley Corner—pop pl SD-7
Stanley Corners—pop pl MI-6
Stanley Coulee—valley MT-8
Stanley County—civil NC-3
Stanley County—civil SD-7
Stanley Cove—bay ME-1
Stanley Creek CA-9
Stanley Creek NC-3
Stanley Creek—stream (2) CA-9
Stanley Creek—stream CO-8
Stanley Creek—stream (2) GA-3
Stanley Creek—stream (2) ID-8
Stanley Creek—stream LA-4
Stanley Creek—stream (2) MI-6
Stanley Creek—stream MN-6
Stanley Creek—stream MO-7
Stanley Creek—stream (4) MT-8
Stanley Creek—stream NC-3
Stanley Creek—stream (5) OR-9
Stanley Creek—stream SC-3
Stanley Creek—stream (3) TN-4
Stanley Creek—stream (2) TX-5
Stanley Creek—stream WY-8
Stanley Creek Sch—school GA-3
Stanley Crossroads—locale AL-4
Stanley Dam—dam MA-1
Stanley Dam—dam ND-7
Stanley Dam—dam OR-9
Stanley Ditch CO-8
Stanley Ditch—canal CO-8
Stanley Ditch—canal IN-6
Stanley Ditch—canal MT-8
Stanley Draper Lake—reservoir OK-5
Stanley Draper Rsvr OK-5
Stanley Elem Sch—school (2) KS-7
Stanley Fish Hole—lake FL-3
Stanley Ford Bridge—bridge NC-3
Stanley Fork—stream (3) WV-2
Stanley Franks Camp—locale FL-3
Stanley Gap—gap AR-4
Stanley Gap—gap GA-3
Stanley Gas Pool—oilfield MS-4
Stanley Graves—cemetery TX-5
Stanley Grove Cem—cemetery AR-4
Stanley Grove Ch—church GA-3
Stanley Gulch—valley CO-8
Stanley Hall Sch—school IL-6
Stanley Hall Sch—school IN-6
Stanley Heights Baptist Church TN-4
Stanley Heights Ch—church TN-4
Stanley Hill—ridge WI-6
Stanley Hill—summit AL-4
Stanley Hill—summit ME-1
Stanley Hill—summit NH-1
Stanley (historical)—locale AL-4
Stanley (historical)—locale SD-7
Stanley Hollow TN-4
Stanley Hollow—valley OH-6
Stanley Hollow—valley (2) TN-4
Stanley Hollow Creek—stream NY-2
Stanley Hotel—hist pl CO-8
Stanley Hotel District—hist pl CO-8
Stanley Hot Springs—spring ID-8
Stanley Institute—hist pl MD-2
Stanley Island NC-3
Stanley Island—island MA-1
Stanley Island—island MO-7
Stanley Island (historical)—island SD-7
Stanley JHS—school NC-3
Stanley Junction—locale TN-4
Stanley Knobs—summit TN-4
Stanley Lake—lake CO-8
Stanley Lake—lake ID-8
Stanley Lake—lake (2) MI-6
Stanley Lake—lake (2) MN-6
Stanley Lake—lake MO-7
Stanley Lake—lake OR-9
Stanley Lake—lake PA-2
Stanley Lake—lake WI-6
Stanley Lake—reservoir OK-5
Stanley Lake—reservoir TX-5
Stanley Lake Campground—locale (2) ID-8
Stanley Lake Campground—locale MI-6
Stanley Lake Creek—stream ID-8
Stanley Lake Dam—dam PA-2
Stanley Landing—locale GA-3
Stanley Landing—locale KY-4
Stanley Lateral Ditch—canal CO-8
Stanley Lateral 1—canal CA-9
Stanley Ledge—island ME-1
Stanley Manor—pop pl DE-2
Stanley Manor—pop pl NY-2
Stanley McGraw Bay—bay UT-8
Stanley Meadows—flat OR-9
Stanley Mill Creek—stream AL-4
Stanley-Miller Mine—mine CA-9
Stanley Mill (historical)—locale GA-3
Stanley Mill (historical)—locale MS-4
Stanley Mine—mine (2) CO-8
Stanley Mission—church NC-3
Stanley Mound—summit WI-6
Stanley Mtn—summit AR-4
Stanley Mtn—summit CA-9
Stanley Mtn—summit CO-8
Stanley Mtn—summit MT-8
Stanley Municipal Airp—airport ND-7
Stanley Neck—cape MD-2
STANLEY NORMAN—hist pl MD-2
Stanley Park—flat CO-8
Stanley Park—flat WY-8
Stanley Park—park CT-1
Stanley Park—park MA-1
Stanley Park—park MN-6
Stanley Park—park NC-3
Stanley Park—pop pl CO-8
Stanley Peak—summit MT-8
Stanley Peak—summit OR-9
Stanley Peninsula—cape WA-9
Stanley Point ME-1
Stanley Point—cape CT-1
Stanley Point—cape (2) ME-1
Stanley Point—cape WA-9
Stanley Pond PA-2
Stanley Pond—reservoir ME-1
Stanley Post Office (historical)—building TN-4
Stanley Prairie—swamp FL-3
Stanley Quarter Park—park CT-1
Stanley Ranch—locale CA-9
Stanley Ranch—locale ID-8
Stanley Ranger Station—hist pl ID-8
Stanley Ridge—ridge CA-9
Stanley Ridge—ridge MI-6
Stanley Rock—pillar OR-9
Stanley Run—stream MD-2
Stanley Sch—school (2) CA-9
Stanley Sch—school CT-1
Stanley Sch—school IA-7
Stanley Sch—school MA-1
Stanley Sch—school NY-2
Stanley Sch—school TX-5
Stanley Sch—school WA-9
Stanleys Chapel—church TN-4
Stanley Sch (historical)—school TN-4
Stanleys Corner VA-3
Stanleys Corner—pop pl PA-2
Stanleys Corners PA-2
Stanleys Crossroads AL-4
Stanleys Island MA-1
Stanleys Island MO-7
Stanley Slide Brook—stream NH-1
Stanley Smeenk Dam Number 1—dam SD-7
Stanley Sog—swamp FL-3
Stanley Spring—spring AR-4
Stanley Spring—spring MT-8
Stanley Spring—spring NM-5
Stanley Spring—spring UT-8
Stanley Spring—spring WA-9
Stanleys Store—locale GA-3
Stanleys Store—pop pl NC-3
Stanley (Stanley Jct.)—pop pl PA-2
Stanley Station Center—locale KS-7
Stanley Store—locale NC-3
Stanley Stream—stream ME-1
Stanley Theater—hist pl NJ-2
Stanley Theater—hist pl NY-2
Stanley Theater and Clark Bldg—hist pl PA-2
Stanleytown—pop pl (2) VA-3
Stanley (Town of)—pop pl WI-6
Stanley Township—pop pl ND-7
Stanley (Township of)—fmr MCD AR-4
Stanley (Township of)—pop pl MN-6
Stanley Trap Tank—reservoir AZ-5
Stanley United Methodist Ch—church TN-4
Stanley Valley ID-8
Stanley Valley—valley TN-4
Stanley Valley—valley VA-3
Stanley Valley Creek—stream TN-4
Stanley Valley Creek—stream VA-3
Stanleyville—pop pl NC-3
Stanleyville—pop pl OH-6
Stanley Walker Mine—mine TN-4
Stanley-Whitman House—hist pl CT-1
Stanley-Woodruff-Allen House—hist pl CT-1
Stanley Woods Camp—locale NY-2
Stanley Yard—locale OH-6
Stanly, Edward R., House—hist pl NC-3
Stanly, John Wright, House—hist pl NC-3
Stanly County—pop pl NC-3
Stanly County Airfield NC-3
Stanly County Airp—airport NC-3
Stanly County Country Club—locale NC-3
Stanly County Court House—building NC-3
Stanly County Fairgrounds—locale NC-3
Stanly County Hosp—hospital NC-3
Stanly Gardens Cem—cemetery NC-3
Stanly State Prison NC-3
Stanly Technical Institute—school NC-3
Stanmire Lake—lake TX-5
Stanmyer Cem—cemetery AL-4
Stannard NY-2
Stannard—pop pl VT-1
Stannard Beach—beach CT-1
Stannard Brook—stream VT-1
Stannard Corners NY-2
Stannard Creek—stream MT-8
Stannard Mtn—summit VT-1
Stannard Pond—lake CT-1
Stannard Pond—lake VT-1
Stannard Rock Lighthouse—hist pl MI-6
Stannards—pop pl NY-2
Stannard Schoolhouse—hist pl VT-1
Stannards Corners NY-2
Stannard (Town of)—pop pl VT-1
Stannard (Township of)—pop pl MI-6
St. Anna Township—pop pl ND-7
St. Anne Church—hist pl NH-1
St. Anne's Church and Mission Site—hist pl ME-1
St. Anne's Church and Parish Complex—hist pl MA-1
St. Anne's Episcopal Church—hist pl ME-1
Stannett Creek—stream MO-7
Stanniger Creek—stream MI-6
St. Ann Roman Catholic Church Complex—hist pl OH-6
St. Ann's Church Complex—hist pl RI-1
Stano—locale KS-7
Stanocola—pop pl AR-4
Stanolind Canal—canal LA-4
Stanolind-Luby Camp Refinery—other TX-5
Stanolind Rsvr—reservoir TX-5
Stan-Penn Lodge Mine—mine SD-7
Stanridge Hill—summit WA-9
Stanrod Cem—cemetery UT-8
Stansberry Cave—cave MO-7
Stansberry Cem—cemetery MS-4
Stansberry Cem—cemetery NC-3
Stansberry Cem—cemetery TN-4
Stansberry Creek MD-2
Stansberry Creek—stream CA-9
Stansberry Creek—stream MO-7
Stansberry Lake—lake WA-9
Stansberry Number Four Tank—reservoir AZ-5
Stansberry Number Three Tank—reservoir AZ-5
Stansberry Point MD-2
Stansberry Ranch—locale TX-5
Stansbery Cem—cemetery OH-6
Stansbury UT-8
Stansbury—locale WY-8
Stansbury Bar UT-8
Stansbury Bay—bay UT-8
Stansbury Cem—cemetery TN-4
Stansbury Creek—stream ID-8
Stansbury Creek—stream MD-2
Stansbury Ditch IN-6
Stansbury Ditch—canal IN-6
Stansbury Estates—pop pl MD-2
Stansbury Gap—gap TN-4
Stansbury Gulch—valley UT-8
Stansbury Hollow—valley TN-4
Stansbury House—hist pl CA-9
Stansbury Island—island UT-8
Stansbury Island Bar—bar UT-8
Stansbury Junction—locale WY-8
Stansbury Lake WA-9
Stansbury Lake—lake UT-8
Stansbury Manor—pop pl MD-2
Stansbury Mtn—summit TN-4
Stansbury Mtns—range UT-8
Stansbury Number Four Mine (surface)—mine TN-4
Stansbury park—pop pl UT-8
Stansbury Point—cape MD-2
Stansbury Post Office (historical)—building AL-4
Stansbury Sch—school (2) UT-8
Stansbury Siding—locale TN-4
Stansbury Spring—spring CA-9
Stansbury Subdivision—pop pl UT-8
Stansbury Well—locale NM-5
Stansel—locale AL-4
Stansel Ch—church AL-4
Stansell Branch—stream GA-3
Stansel Plantation (historical)—locale MS-4
Stansfield Airp—airport CO-8
Stansfield Lake—reservoir MT-8
St. Ansgar—pop pl IA-7
St. Ansgar Township—fmr MCD IA-7
Stanshaw Creek—stream CA-9
Stanshaw Meadows—flat CA-9
Stan Shuatuk—locale AZ-5
Stansil Bridge—bridge GA-3
Stansons Lake—reservoir AL-4
Stanstead, The—hist pl MA-1
Stanstrom Creek—stream AK-9
Stan Tank—locale AZ-5
St. Anthony—pop pl IA-7
St. Anthony—pop pl ND-7
St. Anthony Catholic Church, Padua—hist pl OH-6
St. Anthony Falls MN-6
St. Anthony Falls Hist Dist—hist pl MN-6
St. Anthony Park Branch Library—hist pl MN-6
St. Anthony's Roman Catholic Church—hist pl CO-8
St. Anthony's Roman Catholic Church Complex—hist pl IA-7
Stantial Bog—swamp ME-1
Stantial Brook—stream ME-1
Stanton KS-7
Stanton—fmr MCD NE-7
Stanton—locale AZ-5
Stanton—locale OR-9
Stanton—locale WI-6
Stanton—pop pl AL-4
Stanton—pop pl CA-9
Stanton—pop pl DE-2
Stanton—pop pl FL-3
Stanton—pop pl (2) IA-7
Stanton—pop pl KS-7
Stanton—pop pl KY-4
Stanton—pop pl LA-4
Stanton—pop pl MI-6
Stanton—pop pl MN-6
Stanton—pop pl MS-4
Stanton—pop pl MO-7
Stanton—pop pl NE-7
Stanton—pop pl NJ-2
Stanton—pop pl ND-7
Stanton—pop pl (2) PA-2
Stanton—pop pl TN-4
Stanton—pop pl TX-5
Stanton, Edmin M., Sch—hist pl FL-3
Stanton, Edwin M., Sch—hist pl PA-2
Stanton, Elizabeth Cady, House—hist pl NJ-2
Stanton, Elizabeth Cady, House—hist pl NY-2
Stanton, Joseph, House—hist pl RI-1
Stanton, Lewis H., House—hist pl MN-6
Stanton, Mount—summit NH-1
Stanton, Phillip Ackley, House—hist pl CA-9
Stanton, Robert, House—hist pl CT-1
Stanton Baptist Ch—church MS-4
Stanton Bay—bay IL-6
Stanton Bay—swamp FL-3
Stanton Brook—stream NH-1
Stanton Brook—stream PA-2
Stanton Brothers Lake Dam—dam MS-4
Stanton Canyon—valley UT-8
Stanton (CCD)—cens area KY-4
Stanton (CCD)—cens area TN-4
Stanton (CCD)—cens area TX-5
Stanton Cem—cemetery AL-4
Stanton Cem—cemetery FL-3
Stanton Cem—cemetery IL-6
Stanton Cem—cemetery IA-7
Stanton Cem—cemetery MO-7
Stanton Cem—cemetery (2) NY-2
Stanton Cem—cemetery ND-7
Stanton Cem—cemetery (2) TN-4
Stanton Center—hist pl MD-2
Stanton Center Sch—school IL-6
Stanton Ch—church AL-4
Stanton Ch—church IA-7
Stanton Ch—church MS-4
Stanton Chapel—church TN-4
Stanton Christian Sch—school AL-4
Stanton Coll (historical)—school MS-4
Stanton Corner—locale PA-2
Stanton Coulee—valley MT-8
Stanton County—civil KS-7
Stanton County Municipal Airp—airport KS-7
Stanton Creek—stream AL-4
Stanton Creek—stream CA-9
Stanton Creek—stream (2) CO-8
Stanton Creek—stream (2) FL-3
Stanton Creek—stream ID-8
Stanton Creek—stream IL-6
Stanton Creek—stream MI-6
Stanton Creek—stream MT-8
Stanton Creek—stream NY-2
Stanton Creek—stream WI-6
Stanton Crossing—locale ID-8
Stanton Depot Post Office TN-4
Stanton Division—civil TN-4
Stanton Drain—canal MI-6
Stanton Draw—valley WY-8
Stanton Dredge UT-8
Stanton Elem Sch—school DE-2
Stanton Estates—pop pl DE-2
Stanton Farm—hist pl OH-6
Stanton Florence Sch—school WA-9
Stanton Full Gospel Ch—church DE-2
Stanton Glacier—glacier MT-8
Stanton Glade—flat CA-9
Stanton Griffith Ridge—ridge WV-2
Stanton Gulch—valley MT-8
Stanton Hall—hist pl MS-4
Stanton Heights—locale PA-2
Stanton Heights—pop pl PA-2
Stanton Hill—summit AL-4
Stanton Hill—summit (2) NY-2
Stanton Hill Cem—cemetery NY-2
Stanton Hollow—valley NY-2
Stanton Hollow—valley TN-4
Stanton Interchange—other KY-4
Stanton JHS—school TX-5
Stanton Junior High School DE-2
Stanton Lake—lake IN-6
Stanton Lake—lake MT-8
Stanton Lake—lake NE-7
Stanton Lakes—lake MI-6
Stanton Masonic Lodge and Sch—hist pl TN-4
Stanton Memorial Cem—cemetery NY-2
Stanton Memorial North Shore Ch—church FL-3
Stanton Mills—locale PA-2
Stanton Mine—mine UT-8
Stanton MS—school DE-2
Stanton Mtn—summit SC-3
Stanton Oil Field—oilfield MS-4
Stanton Oil Field—other MI-6
Stanton Park—park DC-2
Stanton Park—park IL-6
Stanton Park—park IN-6
Stanton Park—park (2) MI-6
Stanton Park—park NE-7
Stanton Pass—gap UT-8
Stanton Peak—summit AK-9
Stanton Peak—summit CA-9
Stanton Point—cape IL-6
Stanton Point—cliff AZ-5
Stanton Point—pop pl IL-6
Stanton Pond PA-2
Stanton Pond—lake CT-1
Stanton Post Office—building TN-4
Stanton Prospect—mine TN-4
Stanton Ranch—locale CA-9
Stanton Ranch—locale TX-5
Stanton Road Elem Sch—school AL-4
Stanton Run PA-2
Stantonsburg—pop pl NC-3
Stantonsburg Elem Sch—school NC-3
Stantonsburg (Township of)—fmr MCD NC-3
Stanton Sch—school (2) CA-9
Stanton Sch—school DC-2
Stanton Sch—school FL-3
Stanton Sch—school GA-3
Stanton Sch—school ID-8
Stanton Sch—school MO-7
Stanton Sch—school NH-1
Stanton Sch—school OH-6
Stanton Sch—school PA-2
Stanton Sch—school VT-1
Stanton Sch—school WY-8
Stanton Sch (historical)—school TN-4
Stanton's Mill—hist pl MD-2
Stanton Special Drainage Ditch—canal IL-6
Stanton (sta.)—pop pl DE-2
Stanton State Game Area—park MI-6
Stanton Station NJ-2
Stanton Station—locale NJ-2
Stanton Station—locale PA-2
Stanton Storm Channel—canal CA-9
Stanton Storm Drain—canal CA-9
Stantontown—other OH-6
Stantontown Cem—cemetery OH-6
Stanton (Town of)—pop pl (2) WI-6
Stanton Township—civil KS-7
Stanton Township—fmr MCD IA-7
Stanton Township—pop pl (3) KS-7
Stanton Township—pop pl (2) NE-7
Stanton (Township of)—fmr MCD NC-3
Stanton (Township of)—pop pl IL-6
Stanton (Township of)—pop pl MI-6
Stanton (Township of)—pop pl MN-6
Stantontown Swamp—swamp PA-2
Stantonville—pop pl TN-4
Stantonville (CCD)—cens area TN-4
Stantonville Cem—cemetery TN-4
Stantonville Division—civil TN-4
Stantonville Post Office—building TN-4
Stantonville Sch (historical)—school TN-4
Stanton Weir Point—cape CT-1
Stanville—pop pl KY-4
Stanville Ch—church TN-4
Stanvix Hall AZ-5
Stanwich—pop pl CT-1
Stanwich Ch—church CT-1
Stanwick—pop pl NJ-2
Stanwick Glen—pop pl NJ-2
Stanwick Sch—school NJ-2
Stanwix AZ-5
Stanwix—locale AZ-5
Stanwix—pop pl NY-2
Stanwix Flats—flat AZ-5
Stanwix Heights—pop pl NY-2
Stanwixs Station AZ-5
Stanwood—pop pl IA-7
Stanwood—pop pl MI-6
Stanwood—pop pl NY-2
Stanwood—pop pl OH-6
Stanwood—pop pl PA-2
Stanwood—pop pl WA-9
Stanwood (CCD)—cens area WA-9
Stanwood Cem—cemetery IA-7
Stanwood Ch—church KS-7
Stanwood Gardens PA-2
Stanwood Gardens—pop pl PA-2
Stanwood (historical)—locale KS-7
Stanwood (historical)—pop pl OR-9
Stanwood Homestead—hist pl ME-1
Stanwood Park ME-1
Stanwood Park—pop pl ME-1
Stanwood Point—cape MA-1
Stanwood Saddle—gap CA-9
Stanwood Sch—school KS-7
Stanza Creek—stream CA-9
Stanzel—locale IA-7
Stapaloop Creek—stream WA-9
Stapeloop Creek WA-9
Stapely Knoll—summit NV-8
Staple Bend Tunnel—tunnel PA-2
Staple Branch VA-3
Staple Cove ME-1
Staple D Ranch—locale CO-8
Stapleford Drain—canal MI-6
Staple Hollow VA-3
Staplehurst—pop pl NE-7
Staplehurst Cem—cemetery NE-7
Staple Lake—lake SC-3
Staple Point ME-1
Staple Pond ME-1
Stapler Cem—cemetery GA-3
Stapler Ford—locale AL-4
Staple Ridge—ridge ME-1
Stapler Park—park DE-2
Staples—locale LA-4
Staples—pop pl MN-6
Staples—pop pl TX-5
Staples, Norris, House—hist pl OR-9
Staples, Sylvanus N., House—hist pl MA-1
Staples Brook ME-1
Staples Brook—stream ME-1
Staples Brook—stream MA-1
Staples Canyon—valley NE-7
Staples Cem—cemetery ME-1
Staples Cem—cemetery MN-6
Staples Cem—cemetery MS-4
Staples Cem—cemetery TX-5
Staples Cem—cemetery VT-1
Staples Cem—cemetery WI-6
Staples Corner—pop pl IL-6
Staples Corner—pop pl MA-1
Staples Corners—locale MD-2
Staples' Cove ME-1
Staples Cove—bay (3) ME-1
Staples Covered Bridge—bridge OR-9
Staples-Crafts-Wiswall Farm—hist pl MA-1
Staples Creek—stream ID-8
Staples Creek—stream OR-9
Staples Creek—stream WI-6
Staples Ditch No 1—canal CO-8
Staples Ditch No 2—canal CO-8
Staples Draft VA-3
Staples Ford—pop pl IN-6
Staples Hill—summit ME-1
Staples Hollow—valley AL-4
Staples Hollow—valley MO-7
Staples Hollow—valley VA-3
Staples HS—school CT-1
Staples Inn—hist pl ME-1
Staples Lake—lake MN-6
Staples Lake—lake (2) WI-6
Staples Landing (historical)—locale AL-4
Staples Mill—pop pl VA-3
Staples Millpond—reservoir VA-3
Staples Mtn—summit ME-1
Staples Point—cape (2) ME-1
Staples Pond—lake (2) ME-1
Staples Pond—lake VT-1
Staples Run—stream VA-3
Staples Sch—school CT-1
Staples Sch—school ME-1
Staples Shore—pop pl MA-1
Staples Spring—spring UT-8
Staples Spring Branch—stream TN-4
Staples State Wildlife Mngmt Area—park MN-6
Staples (Township of)—pop pl MN-6
Staples Trail—trail VT-1
Stapleton IN-6
Stapleton—locale CO-8
Stapleton—locale VA-3
Stapleton—pop pl AL-4
Stapleton—pop pl GA-3
Stapleton—pop pl IN-6
Stapleton—pop pl NE-7

Stapleton—pop pl ..... NY-2
Stapleton—pop pl ..... OR-9
Stapleton Bldg—hist pl ..... CT-1
Stapleton (CCD)—cens area ..... GA-3
Stapleton Cem—cemetery ..... AL-4
Stapleton Cem—cemetery ..... IN-6
Stapleton Cem—cemetery (2) ..... VA-3
Stapleton Creek—stream ..... FL-3
Stapleton Elem Sch—school ..... AL-4
Stapleton Farm—hist pl ..... KY-4
Stapleton (historical P.O.)—locale ..... IA-7
Stapleton International Airp—airport ..... CO-8
Stapleton Mill Pond—reservoir ..... GA-3
Stapleton No. 1—fmr MCD ..... NE-7
Stapleton No. 2—fmr MCD ..... NE-7
Stapleton Post Office ..... TN-4
Stapleton Run—stream ..... IN-6
Stapleton Sch—school ..... GA-3
Stapletons Crossroads—locale ..... GA-3
Stapleton Township—fmr MCD ..... IA-7
Stapleton Township Cem—cemetery ..... IA-7
Stapleton Well—well ..... NM-5
Stapletown (historical)—pop pl ..... MO-7
Stapley Hall Special Sch—school ..... AZ-5
Stapley Park—park ..... AZ-5
Stapley Point—cape ..... UT-8
Staplin Corners—locale ..... NY-2
Staplin Creek—stream ..... CO-8
Staplin Creek—stream ..... NY-2
Stapp—locale ..... OK-5
Stapp Branch—stream ..... TX-5
Stapp Canyon—valley ..... TX-5
Stapp Cem—cemetery (2) ..... KY-4
Stapp Creek—stream ..... AL-4
Stapp Creek—stream ..... CA-9
Stappers Cem—cemetery ..... TX-5
Stapp Gas Field—oilfield ..... TX-5
Stapp Homeplace—hist pl ..... KY-4
Stapp Lakes—lake ..... CO-8
Stapp Lakes Lodge—locale ..... CO-8
Stapp Lake Trail—trail ..... CO-8
Stapplehurst ..... NE-7
Stapp Quarry—mine ..... SD-7
Stapp Ranch—locale ..... CA-9
Stapps Branch—stream ..... NC-3
Stapp Sch—school ..... KY-4
Stapps Hollow—valley ..... AR-4
Star ..... IN-6
Star ..... NC-3
Star—locale ..... IA-7
Star—locale ..... MI-6
Star—locale ..... MO-7
Star—locale ..... NY-2
Star—locale (2) ..... OK-5
Star—locale ..... WV-2
Star—mine ..... CA-9
Star—other ..... VA-3
Star—pop pl ..... AL-4
Star—pop pl ..... FL-3
Star—pop pl ..... ID-8
Star—pop pl ..... LA-4
Star—pop pl ..... MS-4
Star—pop pl ..... NE-7
Star—pop pl ..... NC-3
Star—pop pl ..... TX-5
Star—pop pl ..... WV-2
Star, Lake—lake ..... FL-3
Star and Blue Bonnet Claims Mine—mine ..... SD-7
Staraya Bay—bay ..... AK-9
Star Bay—bay ..... CA-9
Star Bayou—gut ..... TX-5
Star Bend—bend ..... CA-9
Star Bethel Ch—church (2) ..... AL-4
Star Bethel Ch—church ..... GA-3
Starbird Corner—locale ..... ME-1
Starbird Pond—lake ..... ME-1
Starbird Ridge—ridge ..... VT-1
Starbirds—locale ..... ME-1
Starbird Sch—school ..... ME-1
Star Bldg—hist pl ..... IN-6
Star Bluff—cliff ..... OK-5
Star Bluff—cliff ..... SC-3
Star Bluff Crossroads—pop pl ..... SC-3
Starboard—pop pl ..... ME-1
Starboard Cove—bay ..... ME-1
Starboard Creek—stream ..... ME-1
Starboard Creek—stream ..... NY-2
Starboard Creek—stream ..... PA-2
Starboard Island—island ..... ME-1
Starboard Island Bar—bar ..... ME-1
Starboard Island Ledge—bar ..... ME-1
Starboard Rock—summit ..... ME-1
Star Branch—stream ..... AL-4
Star Branch—stream ..... KY-4
Star Branch—stream ..... NC-3
Star Branch—stream ..... TN-4
Star Branch—stream (2) ..... VA-3
Starbrick—pop pl ..... PA-2
Star Bridge—bridge ..... ID-8
Star Bridge—other ..... IL-6
Star Brook—stream ..... NY-2
Starbuch Mine—mine ..... WA-9
Starbuck—pop pl ..... MN-6
Starbuck—pop pl ..... WA-9
Starbuck (CCD)—cens area ..... WA-9
Starbuck Cem—cemetery ..... TN-4
Starbuckhill Cem—cemetery ..... NY-2
Starbuck Island—island ..... NY-2
Starbuck Lake—reservoir ..... CO-8
Starbuck Mtn—summit ..... NY-2
Starbuck Sch—school ..... CA-9
Starbuck Sch—school ..... NY-2
Starbucks Island ..... NY-2
Starbucktown—pop pl ..... OH-6
Starbuck Township—pop pl ..... ND-7
Starbuckville—pop pl ..... NY-2
Starbuck Well—well ..... CO-8
Star Butte—summit ..... CA-9
Star Butte—summit ..... ID-8
Star Butte—summit ..... WY-8
Star Butte Creek—stream ..... ID-8
Star Camp—locale (2) ..... TX-5
Star Canyon—valley ..... CA-9
Star Canyon—valley ..... UT-8
Star (CCD)—cens area ..... TX-5
Star Cem—cemetery ..... IN-6
Star Cem—cemetery (5) ..... KS-7
Star Cem—cemetery ..... LA-4
Star Cem—cemetery ..... MI-6
Star Cem—cemetery ..... MN-6
Star Cem—cemetery ..... MS-4
Star Cem—cemetery ..... NE-7
Star Cem—cemetery ..... OK-5
Star Cem—cemetery ..... SD-7
Star Cem—cemetery ..... WI-6
Star Center Cem—cemetery ..... KS-7
Star Center Sch—school ..... WI-6
Star Center Sch Number 4—school ..... WI-6
Star Ch—church ..... IL-6
Star Ch—church ..... IN-6
Star Ch—church ..... MO-7
Star Ch—church ..... NE-7
Star Ch—church ..... WV-2
Star Chapel—church ..... MO-7
Starch Creek—stream ..... AR-4
Starcher Fork—stream ..... WV-2
Starcher (historical)—locale ..... SD-7
Starcher Rocks—summit ..... WV-2
Starch Factory Creek—stream ..... NY-2
Starch Factory Springs ..... MH-9
Star City—locale ..... IL-6
Star City—locale ..... MI-6
Star City—pop pl ..... AR-4
Star City—pop pl ..... IN-6
Star City—pop pl ..... MO-7
Star City—pop pl ..... WV-2
Star City Cem—cemetery ..... MI-6
Star City Creek—stream ..... CA-9
Star City Lookout Tower—locale ..... AR-4
Star City Meadow ..... CA-9
Star City (Site)—locale ..... CA-9
Starcke, Richard, House—hist pl ..... TX-5
Starck Hollow—valley ..... MS-4
Star-Clipper-Canfield Bldg and Winding Stairway—hist pl ..... IA-7
Star Community Center—building ..... KS-7
Star Community Center—locale ..... CO-8
Star Corner (historical)—pop pl ..... SD-7
Star Corners—locale (2) ..... MI-6
Star Corner Sch (historical)—school ..... SD-7
Star Coulee—valley ..... MT-8
Star Creek ..... OR-9
Star Creek—stream (3) ..... AK-9
Star Creek—stream ..... AZ-5
Star Creek—stream ..... AR-4
Star Creek—stream (2) ..... CA-9
Star Creek—stream ..... GA-3
Star Creek—stream (3) ..... ID-8
Star Creek—stream ..... IN-6
Star Creek—stream ..... KY-4
Star Creek—stream ..... MI-6
Star Creek—stream (6) ..... MT-8
Star Creek—stream ..... NV-8
Star Creek—stream ..... OR-9
Star Creek—stream ..... PA-2
Star Creek—stream (2) ..... TX-5
Star Creek—stream ..... UT-8
Star Creek—stream ..... VA-3
Star Creek—stream (2) ..... WA-9
Star Creek—stream ..... WI-6
Star Creek—stream ..... WY-8
Star Creek Benches—bench ..... UT-8
Star Creek Camp—locale ..... ID-8
Star Creek Ch—church ..... GA-3
Star Creek Dam—dam ..... OR-9
Star Creek Ranch—locale ..... NV-8
Star Creek Rsvr—reservoir ..... OR-9
Star Creek School ..... GA-3
Star Cross—pop pl ..... NJ-2
Star District Sch—school ..... NY-2
Star Ditch—canal (3) ..... CO-8
Star Ditch—canal ..... NM-5
Star Ditch—canal ..... WY-8
Star Divide Windmill—locale ..... TX-5
Star Drug Store—hist pl ..... TX-5
Stardust Country Club—locale ..... NV-8
Stardust Country Club—other ..... CA-9
Star Dust Dock—locale ..... TN-4
Stardust Golf Course—other ..... AZ-5
Stardust Helispot—airport ..... NV-8
Stardust International Raceway—locale ..... NV-8
Stardust Mine—mine ..... AZ-5
Stardust Mine—mine ..... UT-8
Stardust Tungsten Mine—mine ..... WY-8
Stardust Village—pop pl ..... IN-6
Starens Branch—stream ..... NC-3
Starey Draft—valley ..... VA-3
Star Falls—falls ..... MT-8
Starfield—locale ..... MO-7
Starfire—pop pl ..... KY-4
Starfish Bluff—cliff ..... AK-9
Starfish Cove—bay ..... OR-9
Star Flat—flat ..... AZ-5
Star Flat—flat ..... CA-9
Star Flat—flat ..... NV-8
Star Flat—flat ..... OR-9
Star Flat—flat ..... UT-8
Starford—pop pl ..... PA-2
Star Fork—stream (2) ..... WV-2
Star Fork Branch—stream ..... SC-3
Star Fort—locale ..... VA-3
Star Gap—gap ..... AR-4
Star Gap—gap ..... NC-3
Star Gap—gap ..... TN-4
Star Gap Arch—arch ..... KY-4
Star Gap Branch—stream ..... KY-4
Star Garage—hist pl ..... FL-3
Star Glade—flat ..... OR-9
Stargo—pop pl ..... AZ-5
Stargo Creek—stream ..... NV-8
Stargo Gulch—valley ..... AZ-5
Star Grove Cem—cemetery ..... IL-6
Star Gulch—valley ..... AK-9
Star Gulch—valley ..... CA-9
Star Gulch—valley (2) ..... ID-8
Star Gulch—valley ..... MT-8
Star Gulch—valley (2) ..... OR-9
Star Gulch Sulphur Camp—locale ..... OR-9
Star Harbor—pop pl ..... TX-5
Star Harmony Sch—school ..... WI-6
Star Heights Subdivision—pop pl ..... UT-8
Star Hill—locale ..... AL-4
Starhill—locale ..... LA-4
Star Hill—pop pl ..... DE-2
Star Hill—summit ..... VT-1
Star Hill—summit ..... WY-8
Star Hill African Methodist Episcopal Ch—church ..... DE-2
Star Hill Airp—airport ..... NC-3
Star Hill Branch—stream ..... VA-3
Star Hill-Briar Park—CDP ..... DE-2
Starhill Cem—cemetery ..... LA-4
Star Hill Cem—cemetery ..... MS-4
Star Hill Cem—cemetery ..... TX-5
Star Hill Ch—church ..... DE-2
Star Hill Ch—church ..... LA-4
Starhill Ch—church ..... LA-4
Star Hill Ch—church (2) ..... MS-4
Star Hill Elem Sch—school ..... DE-2
Star Hill Golf and Country Club—locale ..... NC-3
Star Hill Village—pop pl ..... DE-2
Star (historical)—locale ..... KS-7
Star (historical)—pop pl ..... OR-9
Star (historical)—pop pl ..... TN-4
Star (historical P.O.)—locale ..... IA-7
Star Hollow—valley ..... AL-4
Star Hollow—valley ..... KY-4
Star Hollow—valley ..... MO-7
Star Hollow Creek—stream ..... TX-5
Star Hope Camp—locale ..... ID-8
Star Hope Cem—cemetery ..... VA-3
Star Hope Ch—church ..... AL-4
Star Hope Ch—church ..... MO-7
Star Hope Creek—stream ..... ID-8
Star Hope Gulch—valley ..... ID-8
Star Hope Mine—mine ..... ID-8
Star Hope Sch (historical)—school ..... AL-4
Star Hope School (historical)—locale ..... MO-7
Starichkof Reef—bar ..... AK-9
Staring Lake—lake ..... MN-6
Staring's Lake ..... MN-6
Starin Park—park ..... WI-6
Stariski Campground—locale ..... AK-9
Stariski Creek—stream ..... AK-9
Star Island ..... FM-9
Star Island—island ..... FL-3
Star Island—island ..... MI-6
Star Island—island ..... MN-6
Star Island—island (2) ..... NH-1
Star Island—island ..... NY-2
Star Island Campground—locale ..... MN-6
Star Journal Model Home—hist pl ..... CO-8
Starjunction ..... PA-2
Star Junction—pop pl (2) ..... PA-2
Star Junction Number One Dam—dam ..... PA-2
Star Junction Number Two Dam—dam ..... PA-2
Star Junction Rsvr—reservoir ..... PA-2
Stark ..... TX-5
Stark—locale ..... AZ-5
Stark—locale ..... IL-6
Stark—locale ..... KY-4
Stark—locale ..... MI-6
Stark—locale ..... MN-6
Stark—locale ..... MT-8
Stark—locale ..... NY-2
Stark—locale ..... TX-5
Stark—locale ..... WV-2
Stark—pop pl ..... AR-4
Stark—pop pl ..... GA-3
Stark—pop pl ..... KS-7
Stark—pop pl ..... MN-6
Stark—pop pl ..... MO-7
Stark—pop pl ..... NH-1
Stark—pop pl ..... WI-6
Stark, Edward, House—hist pl ..... MA-1
Stark, Gen. George, House—hist pl ..... NH-1
Stark, Gen. John, House—hist pl ..... NH-1
Stark, Gov. Lloyd Crow, House and Carriage House—hist pl ..... MO-7
Stark, W. H., House—hist pl ..... TX-5
Stark Airp—airport ..... KS-7
Stark-Baldwin Cem—cemetery ..... TN-4
Stark Bayou—stream ..... MS-4
Stark Bend—bend ..... AR-4
Stark Brook—stream (2) ..... NH-1
Stark Brook—stream ..... VT-1
Stark Canyon—valley ..... ID-8
Stark Caverns ..... MO-7
Stark Cem—cemetery (2) ..... AR-4
Stark Cem—cemetery ..... FL-3
Stark Cem—cemetery ..... GA-3
Stark Cem—cemetery ..... IN-6
Stark Cem—cemetery (2) ..... MO-7
Stark Cem—cemetery ..... NE-7
Stark Cem—cemetery ..... NH-1
Stark Cem—cemetery ..... PA-2
Stark Cem—cemetery ..... TX-5
Stark Cem—cemetery ..... VT-1
Stark Ch—church ..... GA-3
Stark City—pop pl ..... AR-4
Stark City—pop pl ..... MO-7
Stark-Clint House—hist pl ..... WI-6
Stark Corners—pop pl ..... OH-6
Stark County—civil ..... ND-7
Stark (County)—pop pl ..... IL-6
Stark (County)—pop pl ..... OH-6
Stark County Courthouse—hist pl ..... ND-7
Stark County Courthouse and Annex—hist pl ..... OH-6
Stark Covered Bridge—hist pl ..... NH-1
Stark Creek—stream ..... CA-9
Stark Creek—stream (2) ..... CO-8
Stark Creek—stream ..... MT-8
Stark Creek—stream ..... TX-5
Stark Dam—dam ..... PA-2
Stark Drain—stream ..... MI-6
Starke—pop pl ..... FL-3
Starke (CCD)—cens area ..... FL-3
Starke Cem—cemetery ..... VA-3
Starke County—pop pl ..... IN-6
Starke County Airp—airport ..... IN-6
Starke County Courthouse—hist pl ..... IN-6
Starke Elem Sch—school ..... FL-3
Starke Lake—lake ..... FL-3
Starke Lake Baptist Ch—church ..... FL-3
Stark Elem Sch—school ..... KS-7
Starkenburg—locale ..... MO-7
Starke Plaza (Shop Ctr)—locale ..... FL-3
Starker-Leopold Hist Dist—hist pl ..... IA-7
Starke Round Barn—hist pl ..... NE-7
Starke Sch—school ..... IL-6
Starkes Creek ..... MO-7
Starke Seventh Day Adventist Christian Acad—school ..... FL-3
Starkes Ferry—pop pl ..... FL-3
Starke Univ Sch—school ..... AL-4
Starkey—fmr MCD ..... NE-7
Starkey—locale ..... ID-8
Starkey—locale ..... OR-9
Starkey—pop pl ..... NY-2
Starkey—pop pl (2) ..... VA-3
Starkey, Otis, House—hist pl ..... NY-2
Starkey and Erwin Ranch—locale ..... CA-9
Starkey Branch ..... MO-7
Starkey Branch—stream ..... IN-6
Starkey (CCD)—cens area ..... OR-9
Starkey Cem—cemetery (2) ..... AR-4
Starkey Cem—cemetery ..... IL-6
Starkey Cem—cemetery ..... OR-9
Starkey Cem—cemetery ..... TX-5
Starkey Cem—cemetery ..... VA-3
Starkey Corner—locale ..... OR-9
Starkey Corner—pop pl ..... MD-2
Starkey Corners—locale ..... ME-1
Starkey Creek ..... NC-3
Starkey Creek—stream ..... AR-4
Starkey Creek—stream ..... NC-3
Starkey Creek—stream ..... OR-9
Starkey Creek—stream ..... TN-4
Starkey Creek—stream ..... TX-5
Starkey Developmental Center—school ..... KS-7
Starkey Experimental For—forest ..... OR-9
Starkey Gap—gap ..... NC-3
Starkey Gap—gap (2) ..... TN-4
Starkey Gulch—valley ..... CO-8
Starkey Hill—summit ..... AR-4
Starkey (historical)—locale ..... SD-7
Starkey (historical)—pop pl ..... TN-4
Starkey Hollow—valley ..... AL-4
Starkey Hollow—valley (2) ..... AR-4
Starkey Hollow—valley (2) ..... MO-7
Starkey Hollow—valley ..... TN-4
Starkey Lake—lake ..... MI-6
Starkey Lake—lake ..... WI-6
Starkey-McCully Block—hist pl ..... OR-9
Starkey Mine—mine ..... NM-5
Starkey Mine (historical)—mine ..... MO-7
Starkey Mtn—summit ..... AR-4
Starkey Point—cape ..... NY-2
Starkey Public Use Area—park ..... AR-4
Starkey Ranch—locale ..... NE-7
Starkey Ridge—ridge ..... NC-3
Starkey Ridge—ridge ..... WV-2
Starkey Road Baptist Ch—church ..... FL-3
Starkey Rock—pillar ..... TN-4
Starkey Run—stream ..... WV-2
Starkeys Airp—airport ..... IN-6
Starkey Sch—school ..... FL-3
Starkey Sch—school ..... IL-6
Starkey Sch—school ..... TX-5
Starkeys Corner—pop pl ..... MD-2
Starkeytown—locale ..... TN-4
Starkey (Town of)—pop pl ..... NY-2
Starkey Township—pop pl ..... ND-7
Stark Falls Brook—stream ..... NH-1
Stark Falls Dam—dam ..... NY-2
Stark Falls Rsvr—reservoir ..... NY-2
Stark Field—area ..... CA-9
Stark Gate—locale ..... AR-4
Stark Hills—summit ..... NY-2
Stark Hollow—valley ..... OK-5
Stark Hollow—valley ..... VA-3
Stark House—hist pl ..... KY-4
Stark HS—school ..... TX-5
Starkie Gap—gap ..... TX-5
Starkille Lagoon Dam—dam ..... MS-4
Star Killer Hollow—valley ..... OK-5
Stark Knob—summit ..... KY-4
Stark Knob Access Area—park ..... TN-4
Stark Knob Ch—church ..... TN-4
Stark Lake—lake ..... MN-6
Starkley Corner ..... MD-2
Stark Mtn—summit ..... MT-8
Stark Mtn—summit ..... VT-1
Stark North Well—well ..... TX-5
Stark Nursery—other ..... MO-7
Stark Overpass—crossing ..... AZ-5
Stark Park—park ..... NH-1
Stark Park—park ..... TX-5
Stark Patent Bottom—bend ..... OH-6
Stark Point ..... MT-8
Stark Point—cape ..... NY-2
Stark Pond—lake ..... NY-2
Stark Pond—lake ..... VA-3
Stark Pond—reservoir ..... NH-1
Stark Pond Marsh—swamp ..... NH-1
Stark Pond Rec Area—park ..... NH-1
Stark Post Office—locale ..... KY-4
Stark Ridge—ridge ..... UT-8
Stark Ridge—ridge ..... WV-2
Stark RR Station—building ..... AZ-5
Stark Rsvr—reservoir (2) ..... OR-9
Stark Rsvr—reservoir ..... PA-2
Stark Rsvr—reservoir ..... WY-8
Stark Run—stream ..... WV-2
Starks—locale ..... IL-6
Starks—pop pl ..... LA-4
Starks—pop pl ..... ME-1
Starks—pop pl ..... PA-2
Starks—pop pl ..... WI-6
Starks, Samuel, House—hist pl ..... WV-2
Starks Bayou—stream (3) ..... LA-4
Starks Bldg—hist pl ..... KY-4
Starksboro—pop pl ..... VT-1
Starksboro (Town of)—pop pl ..... VT-1
Starksboro Village Meeting House—hist pl ..... VT-1
Starks Branch—stream ..... TX-5
Starks Canal ..... LA-4
Starks Canal—canal ..... LA-4
Starks Cem—cemetery ..... TN-4
Stark Sch—school ..... CT-1
Stark Sch—school (2) ..... IL-6
Stark Sch—school (2) ..... MI-6
Stark Sch—school ..... MO-7
Stark Sch—school (2) ..... OH-6
Stark Sch—school ..... VT-1
Starks Chapel—church ..... TX-5
Stark Sch Number 1 (historical)—school ..... SD-7
Stark School Corner—locale ..... NY-2
Starks Creek—stream ..... MO-7
Starks Creek—stream ..... OR-9
Starks Creek—stream ..... WI-6
Starks Cutoff—channel ..... FL-3
Starks Hill—summit ..... NH-1
Starks Hill Camp—locale ..... LA-4
Starks Hollow—valley ..... UT-8
Starks Knob—pop pl ..... NY-2
Starks Landing—locale ..... FL-3
Starks Landing—locale ..... NY-2
Starks Mill Branch—stream ..... VA-3
Starks Mound—summit ..... WI-6
Starks Mtn—summit ..... ME-1
Starks North Canal—canal ..... LA-4
Starks Oil Field—oilfield ..... LA-4
Starks Prairie—lake ..... FL-3
Stark Spring—spring ..... AR-4
Stark Spring—spring ..... OR-9
Stark Springs—spring ..... WA-9
Starks School ..... AL-4
Starks Spring—spring ..... WI-6
Starks Springs—spring ..... WI-6
Starks Switch ..... TX-5
Starks Thicket—woods ..... TX-5
Starks (Town of)—pop pl ..... ME-1
Starks Twin Oaks Airpark—airport ..... OR-9
Starksville—locale ..... GA-3
Stark Swamp—swamp ..... PA-2
Starks Windmill—locale ..... TX-5
Stark Tank—reservoir ..... NM-5
Stark Terrace—pop pl ..... SC-3
Stark (Town of)—pop pl ..... NH-1
Stark (Town of)—pop pl ..... NY-2
Stark (Town of)—pop pl ..... WI-6
Stark Township—civil ..... MO-7
Stark (Township of)—pop pl ..... MN-6
Stark Union Church—hist pl ..... NH-1
Stark Valley Cem—cemetery ..... NE-7
Stark Valley Ch—church ..... NE-7
Stark Valley Sch—school ..... WI-6
Starkville—pop pl ..... CO-8
Starkville—pop pl ..... MS-4
Starkville—pop pl ..... NY-2
Starkville—pop pl ..... PA-2
Starkville Acad—school ..... MS-4
Starkville Cem—cemetery ..... CO-8
Starkville City Hall—building ..... MS-4
Starkville Country Club—locale ..... MS-4
Starkville Gun Club Lake Dam—dam ..... MS-4
Starkville (historical)—locale ..... AL-4
Starkville HS—school ..... MS-4
Starkville Lagoon Dam—dam ..... MS-4
Starkville Middle School ..... MS-4
Starkville Mine—mine ..... CO-8
Starkville Mines—mine ..... CO-8
Starkville No 1 Coal Mine—mine ..... CO-8
Starkville Post Office (historical)—building ..... AL-4
Starkville Public Library—building ..... MS-4
Starkville Sewage Lagoon Dam—dam ..... MS-4
Starkville (Stark)—pop pl ..... NY-2
Starkville United Methodist Church ..... MS-4
Starkweather—pop pl ..... ND-7
Starkweather Canyon—valley ..... NM-5
Starkweather Coulee—valley ..... ND-7
Starkweather Creek—stream ..... WI-6
Starkweather Hill—summit ..... NY-2
Starkweather Lake—lake ..... CA-9
Starkweather Pond—lake ..... NY-2
Starkweather Religious Center—hist pl ..... MI-6
Starkweather Sch—school ..... MI-6
Starkweather Spring—spring ..... NM-5
Starkweather Tank—reservoir ..... AZ-5
Stark Well—well ..... AZ-5
Stark Windmill—locale ..... NM-5
Starky Mill Branch—stream ..... AL-4
Starkys Creek—stream ..... NC-3
Star Lake ..... CO-8
Star Lake ..... MI-6
Star Lake ..... MN-6
Star Lake ..... ND-7
Star Lake ..... WA-9
Star Lake ..... WI-6
Star Lake—lake (4) ..... AK-9
Star Lake—lake ..... AR-4
Star Lake—lake (2) ..... CA-9
Star Lake—lake ..... CO-8
Star Lake—lake ..... CT-1
Star Lake—lake (2) ..... FL-3
Star Lake—lake ..... ID-8
Star Lake—lake (2) ..... MI-6
Star Lake—lake (8) ..... MN-6
Star Lake—lake ..... MT-8
Star Lake—lake (2) ..... NH-1
Star Lake—lake (2) ..... NM-5
Star Lake—lake ..... NY-2
Star Lake—lake ..... OK-5
Star Lake—lake ..... TX-5
Star Lake—lake ..... VT-1
Star Lake—lake (2) ..... WA-9
Star Lake—lake (9) ..... WI-6
Star Lake—lake (2) ..... WY-8
Star Lake—pop pl ..... NM-5
Star Lake—pop pl ..... NY-2
Star Lake—pop pl ..... WA-9
Star Lake—pop pl ..... WI-6
Star Lake—reservoir ..... CO-8
Star Lake—reservoir ..... FL-3
Star Lake—reservoir ..... NJ-2
Star Lake—reservoir ..... SD-7
Star Lake—reservoir ..... UT-8
Star Lake—reservoir ..... WI-6
Star Lakebed—flat ..... MN-6
Star Lake Cem—cemetery ..... OH-6
Star Lake Chapel—church ..... MN-6
Star Lake Dam—dam ..... OR-9
Star Lake Dam—dam ..... SD-7
Star Lake Dam—dam ..... UT-8
Star Lake Lookout Tower—locale ..... MI-6
Star Lake Pumping Station—other ..... NM-5
Star Lake Ranch—locale ..... ID-8
Star Lake Rsvr—reservoir ..... OR-9
Star Lakes—lake ..... CA-9
Starlake (Star Lake)—pop pl ..... WI-6
Star Lake State Wildlife Mngmt Area—park ..... MN-6
Star Lake (Township of)—pop pl ..... MN-6
Star Lake Trading Post—locale ..... NM-5
Star Lake Upper Dam—dam ..... NJ-2
Star Lake Well No 1—locale ..... ID-8
Starland—locale ..... MO-7
Starland Branch—stream ..... GA-3
Star Landing ..... MO-7
Star Landing—locale ..... DE-2
Starl House—hist pl ..... DE-2
Starlight—locale ..... NC-3
Starlight—pop pl ..... IN-6
Starlight—pop pl ..... PA-2
Starlight Arch—arch ..... UT-8
Starlight Baptist Ch—church ..... AL-4
Starlight Camp—locale ..... PA-2
Starlight Canyon—valley ..... AZ-5
Starlight Canyon—valley ..... UT-8
Starlight Cem—cemetery ..... GA-3
Starlight Center—school ..... CA-9
Starlight Ch—church (2) ..... AL-4
Starlight Ch—church (2) ..... GA-3
Starlight Ch—church (3) ..... LA-4
Star Light Ch—church ..... LA-4
Starlight Ch—church ..... LA-4
Starlight Ch—church ..... MO-7
Starlight Ch—church ..... OH-6
Starlight Ch—church ..... TX-5
Starlight Ch—church ..... VA-3
Starlight Ch (historical)—church ..... MS-4
Starlight Creek—stream ..... ID-8
Starlight Lake—lake ..... MN-6
Starlight Lake—reservoir ..... PA-2
Starlight Lake Dam—dam ..... PA-2
Starlight Memorial Garden—cemetery ..... NC-3
Starlight Mine—mine (2) ..... AZ-5
Starlight Mine—mine ..... CA-9
Starlight Mine—mine ..... NV-8
Starlight Mtn—summit ..... MT-8
Starlight No 7 Mine—mine ..... CO-8
Starlight Park—park ..... AZ-5
Starlight Park Sch—school ..... AZ-5
Starlight Sch—school ..... AL-4
Starlight Sch—school ..... LA-4
Starlight Sch—school ..... WI-6
Starlight Sch (historical)—school ..... AL-4
Starlight Sch (historical)—school ..... MO-7
Starlight Well—well ..... AZ-5
Starline Elem Sch—school ..... AZ-5
Starling ..... AL-4
Starling—locale ..... NC-3
Starling Branch—stream ..... GA-3
Starling Branch—stream ..... KY-4
Starling Cem—cemetery ..... AL-4
Starling Cem—cemetery ..... MS-4
Starling Cem—cemetery ..... VA-3
Starling Ch (historical)—church ..... AL-4
Starling Creek—stream ..... AR-4
Starling Creek—stream ..... VA-3
Starling Ford—locale ..... GA-3
Starling Gap—gap ..... AL-4
Starling JHS—school ..... OH-6
Starling Lake—lake ..... MN-6
Starling Mill (historical)—locale ..... MS-4
Starling Run—stream ..... OH-6
Starlings Crossroads—locale ..... VA-3
Starlings Pond—reservoir ..... AL-4
Starling Spring—spring ..... MO-7
Starlington—pop pl ..... AL-4
Starlington Ch—church ..... AL-4
Starlington Lookout Tower—locale ..... AL-4
Starlington Sch (historical)—school ..... AL-4
Starlins Swamp—stream ..... NC-3
Starlite Mine—mine ..... CA-9
Starlite Trailer Park—locale ..... AZ-5
Star Lode Mine—mine ..... SD-7
Star Market Shop Ctr—locale ..... MA-1
Star Marsh—swamp ..... MI-6
Star Meadow—flat ..... MT-8
Star Meadow Guard Station—locale ..... MT-8
Star Meadow Ranch—locale ..... MT-8
Star Meadows—flat ..... ID-8
Star Memorial Cem—cemetery ..... TX-5
Star Mesa—summit ..... CO-8
Star Mesa—summit ..... TX-5
Star Mill—pop pl ..... IN-6
Star Mill Creek—stream ..... ID-8
Star Mills—pop pl ..... KY-4
Star Mills (Warner)—pop pl ..... KY-4
Star Mine—mine (4) ..... CA-9
Star Mine—mine (2) ..... CO-8
Star Mine—mine ..... ID-8
Star Mine—mine ..... MT-8
Star Mine—mine (4) ..... NV-8
Star Mine—mine (2) ..... OR-9
Star Mines ..... PA-2
Star Mines—mine ..... MT-8
Starmont Sch—school ..... IA-7
Starmont (subdivision)—pop pl ..... NC-3
Star Mountain ..... WY-8
Star Mountain Pond—lake ..... NY-2
Star Mountain Windmill—locale ..... TX-5
Starmount Forest—pop pl ..... NC-3
Starmount Forest Country Club—locale ..... NC-3
Starmount HS—school ..... NC-3
Starmount Sch—school ..... NC-3
Starmount Shop Ctr—locale ..... NC-3
Starmount (subdivision)—pop pl (2) ..... NC-3
Star MS—school ..... NC-3
Star Mtn—summit ..... AZ-5
Star Mtn—summit ..... AR-4
Star Mtn—summit ..... CA-9
Star Mtn—summit ..... CO-8
Star Mtn—summit ..... ID-8
Star Mtn—summit ..... NY-2
Star Mtn—summit ..... OH-6
Star Mtn—summit ..... OR-9
Star Mtn—summit (3) ..... TX-5
Starne—locale ..... IL-6
Starne Branch—stream ..... SC-3
Starnee Ch—church ..... LA-4
Star Nelson Airp—airport ..... CO-8
Star Nelson Ranch—locale ..... CO-8
Starner Hill—summit ..... MD-2
Starners—locale ..... PA-2
Starners Dam—dam ..... MD-2
Starners Station—pop pl ..... PA-2
Starnes Bend—bend ..... VA-3
Starnes Bluff Ch—church ..... VA-3
Starnes Branch—stream ..... IN-6
Starnes Bridge—other ..... KY-4
Starnes Cavern—cave ..... VA-3
Starnes Cem—cemetery ..... OK-5
Starnes Cem—cemetery (2) ..... TN-4
Starnes Cem—cemetery (3) ..... VA-3
Starnes Chapel—church ..... AL-4
Starnes Cove—valley ..... NC-3
Starnes Cove Ch—church ..... NC-3
Starnes Cove Fishing Lake—reservoir ..... NC-3
Starnes Cove Fishing Lake Dam—dam ..... NC-3
Starnes Cove Lakes—reservoir ..... NC-3
Starnes Creek—stream ..... TN-4
Starnes (historical)—locale ..... MS-4
Starnes (historical)—pop pl ..... TN-4

Starnes Hollow—*valley* TN-4
Starnes Island—*island* TX-5
Starnes Lake—*reservoir* TX-5
Starnes Mine—*mine* TN-4
Starnes Post Office (historical)—*building* TN-4
Starnes Ridge—*ridge* NC-3
**Starnes (Slant)**—*pop pl* VA-3
**Starnes Slant Post Office**—*pop pl* VA-3
Starnes Spring—*spring* AR-4
Starnes Spring Cem—*cemetery* AR-4
**Starnes (Starne)**—*pop pl* IL-6
Starns—*locale* LA-4
Starns Cem—*cemetery* LA-4
*Starns Chapel* AL-4
*Starns Chapel Ch* AL-4
Star Number One Mine—*mine* NV-8
Star of Bethelhem Ch—*church* GA-3
Star of Bethlehem Baptist Ch—*church* MS-4
Star of Bethlehem Cem—*cemetery* AL-4
Star of Bethlehem Ch—*church* AL-4
Star of Bethlehem Ch—*church* AR-4
Star Of Bethlehem Ch—*church* KY-4
Star of Bethlehem Ch—*church* LA-4
Star of Bethlehem Ch—*church* TN-4
Star of Bethlehem Ch—*church* VA-3
Star Of Bethlehem Ch—*church* VA-3
Star of Bethlehem Ch—*church* VA-3
*Star of David Cemetery* FL-3
Star of David Memorial Gardens—*cemetery* FL-3
Star of David Memorial Park—*cemetery* FL-3
Star of Hope Cem—*cemetery* IN-6
Star of Hope Lodge—*hist pl* ME-1
STAR OF INDIA—*hist pl* CA-9
Star of the Sea Catholic Ch—*church* MA-1
Star of the Sea Chapel—*church* MA-1
Star of the Sea Chapel—*church* TX-5
Star of the Sea Sch—*school* CA-9
Star of the Sea Sch—*school* HI-9
Star of the Sea Sch—*school* MA-1
Star of the Sea Sch—*school* VA-3
STAR OF THE WEST—*hist pl* MS-4
Star of the West Mine—*mine* CA-9
Star of the West Mine—*mine* CO-8
Star of the West Mine—*mine* NV-8
Star of the West Public Use Area—*park* AR-4
Star of the West Sch—*school* MO-7
Star of Zion AME Zion Ch—*church* AL-4
*Staronard Creek* MI-6
Star Park—*flat* MT-8
Star Park—*park* CA-9
Star Park—*park* IA-7
Star Park—*park* TX-5
Star Peak—*summit* (2) CO-8
Star Peak—*summit* NV-8
Star Peak—*summit* NM-5
Star Peak—*summit* NC-3
Star Peak—*summit* WA-9
Star Peaks—*ridge* WY-8
Star Peak Springs—*spring* AZ-5
Star Place (historical)—*locale* MS-4
Star Place-Shiloh Cem—*cemetery* MS-4
Star Plaza Shop Ctr—*locale* AZ-5
*Starpoint* TN-4
Star Point—*cape* AK-9
Star Point—*cape* TX-5
Star Point—*locale* GA-3
**Star Point**—*pop pl* TN-4
Star Point—*summit* UT-8
Starpoint Central Sch—*school* NY-2
Star Point Ch—*church* LA-4
Star Point Dock—*locale* TN-4
Star Point Mine—*mine* NV-8
Star Point Post Office (historical)—*building* TN-4
Star Point Sch—*school* IL-6
**Star Point Subdivision (subdivision)**—*pop pl* AL-4
Star Pond—*lake* PA-2
Star Pool Windmill—*locale* TX-5
Star Post Office (historical)—*building* AL-4
**Star Praire**—*pop pl* WI-6
**Star Prairie**—*pop pl* WI-6
Star Prairie Sch (abandoned)—*school* MO-7
**Star Prairie (Town of)**—*pop pl* WI-6
**Star Prairie Township**—*pop pl* SD-7
*Starr* FL-3
Starr—*locale* FL-3
Starr—*locale* NV-8
Starr—*locale* (2) PA-2
Starr—*locale* UT-8
Starr—*locale* WA-9
**Starr**—*pop pl* MD-2
**Starr**—*pop pl* OH-6
**Starr**—*pop pl* SC-3
Starr, C. J., Barn and Carriage House—*hist pl* CT-1
Starr, Edwin and Anna, House—*hist pl* OR-9
Starr, Horace C., House and Carriage Barns—*hist pl* OH-6
Starr, Lake—*lake* FL-3
Starr, Mount—*summit* CA-9
Star Ranch—*locale* CO-8
Star Ranch—*locale* (2) ID-8
Star Ranch—*locale* MT-8
Star Ranch—*locale* (2) NE-7
Star Ranch—*locale* OR-9
Star Ranch—*locale* TX-5
Star Ranch (abandoned)—*locale* AZ-5
Star Ranch Spring—*spring* ID-8
Star Ranch Table—*summit* ID-8
Starr and Blakely Drug Store—*hist pl* OR-9
Star Range—*range* UT-8
Star Ranger Station—*locale* OR-9
Starr Bogs—*swamp* MA-1
Starr Branch—*stream* GA-3
Starr Branch—*stream* VA-3
Starr Bridge Lake—*reservoir* GA-3
Starr Butte—*summit* WA-9
Starr Camp—*locale* NE-7
Starr Campground—*park* OR-9
Starr Canyon—*valley* CO-8
Starr Canyon—*valley* NV-8
Starr Canyon—*valley* NM-5
Starr (CCD)—*cens area* SC-3
Starr Cem—*cemetery* CT-1
Starr Cem—*cemetery* GA-3
Starr Cem—*cemetery* IN-6
Starr Cem—*cemetery* NE-7
Starr Cem—*cemetery* OH-6
Starr Cem—*cemetery* (3) OK-5
Starr Cem—*cemetery* PA-2
Starr Ch—*church* TX-5
Starr Chapel—*church* VA-3
**Starrco**—*pop pl* TX-5
Starr Commonwealth Sch—*school* MI-6
**Starr (County)**—*pop pl* TX-5
Starr Creek—*stream* AK-9
Starr Creek—*stream* GA-3
Starr Creek—*stream* NV-8
Starr Creek—*stream* (5) OR-9
Starr Crossing—*locale* PA-2
Starr Ditch—*canal* CO-8
Starr Ditch—*canal* IN-6
Starr Ditch—*canal* TX-5
Star Redoubt Number One—*locale* PA-2
Starr Elem Sch—*school* IN-6
Starret Knob—*summit* NC-3
*Starret Pond* CT-1
Starrett Branch—*stream* TX-5
Starrett Corners—*locale* NY-2
Starrett Creek—*channel* FL-3
Starrett Creek—*stream* OH-6
Starrett House—*hist pl* WA-9
Starrett Lackey Ditch—*canal* OH-6
*Starrett Lake* WI-6
Starrett Lake—*lake* WI-6
*Starrett Pond* CT-1
Starrett Ridge—*ridge* OH-6
Starrett Run—*stream* OH-6
*Starretts Creek* FL-3
Starretts Meadows—*flat* NC-3
*Star Revetment - in part* MS-4
**Starr Farm**—*pop pl* GA-3
**Starr Farm Beach**—*pop pl* VT-1
Starr Garden Recreation Center—*park* PA-2
Starr Gulch—*valley* CO-8
*Starr Hill* DE-2
Starr Hill—*summit* MA-1
Starr Hill—*summit* NY-2
Starr Hill—*summit* WA-9
Starr Hill (Township of)—*fmr MCD* AR-4
Starr Hist Dist—*hist pl* IN-6
Starr (historical)—*locale* SD-7
Starr Hollow—*valley* OH-6
*Starr Hope Creek* ID-8
Starr House—*hist pl* DE-2
Starr House—*hist pl* TX-5
Starrhs Ferry—*locale* ID-8
Star Ridge—*ridge* CA-9
Star Ridge—*ridge* TN-4
Star Ridge Ch—*church* MO-7
Star Ridge Sch—*school* MO-7
Starrigavan Bay—*bay* AK-9
Starrigavan Campground—*locale* AK-9
*Starring Lake* MN-6
*Starrings Lake* MN-6
**Starr King**—*pop pl* NH-1
Starr King, Mount—*summit* CA-9
Starr King, Mount—*summit* NH-1
Starr King (historical)—*locale* NV-8
Starr King Lake—*lake* CA-9
Starr King Meadow—*flat* CA-9
*Starr King Mtn* NH-1
Starr King Sch—*school* (2) CA-9
*Starr Lake* MN-6
*Starr Lake* WI-6
Starr Lake—*lake* AK-9
Starr Manor—*hist pl* CO-8
Starr Millpond—*lake* CT-1
Starr Mountain Trail—*trail* TN-4
Starr Mtn—*summit* TN-4
Starr Mtn—*summit* VT-1
Star Road Cem—*cemetery* NY-2
Star Rock—*other* (2) AK-9
Star Rock—*pillar* NY-2
**Star Rock**—*pop pl* PA-2
Star Rock Refuge (LA 55838)—*hist pl* NM-5
Star Rocks—*bar* AK-9
Star Route—*locale* TX-5
Starrow Park—*park* MA-1
Starr Park—*park* CT-1
Starr Park—*park* IN-6
Starr Park—*park* MI-6
Starr Park Ranch—*locale* CA-9
Starr Peak—*summit* CO-8
Starr Piano Company Warehouse and Administration Bldg—*hist pl* IN-6
*Starr Point* UT-8
Starr Point—*cape* AK-9
Starr Pond—*reservoir* GA-3
Starr Ranch—*hist pl* UT-8
Starr Ranch—*locale* CA-9
Starr Ranch—*locale* NE-7
Starr Ravine—*valley* CA-9
Starr Ridge—*ridge* NY-2
Starr Ridge—*ridge* OR-9
Starr Rock—*bar* WA-9
Starr Rsvr—*reservoir* OR-9
Starr Sch—*school* IL-6
Starr Sch—*school* (2) MI-6
Starr Sch—*school* NE-7
Starr Sch—*school* OH-6
Starr Sch—*school* WI-6
**Starr School**—*pop pl* MT-8
Starr School Flat—*flat* MT-8
**Starrs Corners**—*pop pl* OH-6
Starrs Mill—*locale* GA-3
**Starr's Mill (Nyson)**—*pop pl* GA-3
Starrs Millpond—*lake* GA-3
**Starrs Point (historical)**—*pop pl* OR-9
Starr Spring—*spring* NM-5
Starr Spring—*spring* (2) OR-9
*Starr Springs Campground* UT-8
*Starr Springs Rec Area* UT-8
Starr Street Baptist Ch—*church* AL-4
Starrsville—*locale* GA-3
Starrsville Ch—*church* GA-3
Star Rsvr—*reservoir* ID-8
**Starr Township**—*pop pl* KS-7
**Starr Township**—*pop pl* SD-7
**Starr (Township of)**—*pop pl* OH-6
Starr-Truscott House—*hist pl* OH-6
**Starrucca**—*pop pl* (2) PA-2
Starrucca Borough—*civil* PA-2
Starrucca Creek—*stream* PA-2
Starrucca Station—*locale* PA-2
Starrucca Viaduct—*hist pl* PA-2
*Starr Valley* WY-8
Starr Valley—*basin* NV-8
Starr Valley Cem—*cemetery* NV-8
Starr Valley Community Hall—*locale* NV-8
Starrville—*locale* TX-5
Starrville Ch—*church* TX-5
Starrville Mtn—*summit* TX-5
Starrville Rodeo Ground—*locale* TX-5
Starry Lake—*lake* MN-6
Starry Sch—*school* IA-7
Starr 8—*locale* UT-8
Stars, Lake of the—*lake* MT-8
Star Sch—*school* CO-8
Star Sch—*school* (6) IL-6
Star Sch—*school* (3) KS-7
Star Sch—*school* KY-4
Star Sch—*school* (4) MI-6
Star Sch—*school* (7) MO-7
Star Sch—*school* (7) NE-7
Star Sch—*school* ND-7
Star Sch—*school* (2) OK-5
Star Sch—*school* PA-2
Star Sch—*school* SD-7
Star Sch—*school* VT-1
Star Sch—*school* WA-9
Star Sch (abandoned)—*school* (2) MO-7
Star Sch (abandoned)—*school* PA-2
Star Sch (historical)—*school* (3) MO-7
Star Sch (historical)—*school* SD-7
Star Sch Number 3—*school* MI-6
*Star School* SD-7
Star Sch 13—*school* MI-6
Star Seep—*area* UT-8
**Star Shaft**—*pop pl* NM-5
Star Shaft (Active)—*mine* NM-5
Starshire Farm Airp—*airport* KS-7
*Stars Mountain* TN-4
Star Spencer HS—*school* OK-5
*Star Spring* OR-9
Star Spring—*spring* OR-9
Star Spring—*spring* UT-8
Starspring Hollow—*valley* TN-4
Star Springs Campground—*park* UT-8
Star Stanton Hill—*summit* NY-2
Star Store—*locale* MO-7
**Start**—*pop pl* LA-4
Star Tannery—*locale* VA-3
Start Cem—*cemetery* LA-4
Start Creek—*stream* MI-6
**Startex**—*pop pl* SC-3
**Start (Goff)**—*pop pl* LA-4
Star Theatre—*hist pl* UT-8
Star Theatre—*hist pl* WI-6
Start HS—*school* OH-6
Starting of the Water Spring—*spring* AZ-5
Starting Water Wash—*stream* AZ-5
**Startown**—*pop pl* NC-3
Startown Elem Sch—*school* NC-3
Star Town Mine—*mine* CA-9
**Star Township**—*pop pl* KS-7
**Star Township**—*pop pl* ND-7
**Star Township**—*pop pl* SD-7
Star (Township of)—*fmr MCD* NC-3
**Star (Township of)**—*pop pl* MI-6
**Star (Township of)**—*pop pl* MN-6
Star Town (Site)—*locale* CA-9
Star Trail—*trail* CO-8
*Starts Point* MD-2
*Star Tungsten Mine* NV-8
Star Tunnel—*mine* CO-8
Star Tunnel—*mine* UT-8
**Startup**—*pop pl* WA-9
Startup Candy Factory—*hist pl* UT-8
Startup Creek—*stream* AK-9
Startup Lakes—*lake* AK-9
**Startup Subdivision**—*pop pl* UT-8
Startzell Sch (historical)—*school* PA-2
Startz Hill—*summit* TX-5
**Startzville**—*pop pl* TX-5
*Starucca* PA-2
Starvacre Ford—*locale* AL-4
Starvale (historical)—*locale* KS-7
*Star Valley* KS-7
Star Valley—*basin* CA-9
**Star Valley**—*pop pl* AZ-5
**Star Valley**—*pop pl* WI-6
Star Valley—*valley* AZ-5
Star Valley—*valley* ID-8
Star Valley—*valley* OK-5
Star Valley—*valley* WI-6
Star Valley—*valley* WY-8
Star Valley Cabin—*locale* NV-8
Star Valley Cem—*cemetery* KS-7
Star Valley Cem—*cemetery* OK-5
Star Valley Elem Sch—*school* WY-8
Star Valley HS—*school* WY-8
Star Valley JHS—*school* WY-8
Star Valley Latter Day Saints Hosp—*hospital* WY-8
Star Valley Ranch—*locale* ID-8
Star Valley Ridge—*ridge* NV-8
Star Valley Sch—*school* MO-7
Star Valley School—*locale* KS-7
**Star Valley Township**—*pop pl* (2) SD-7
Starvation Bar—*bar* CA-9
Starvation Branch—*stream* FL-3
Starvation Branch—*stream* ME-1
Starvation Campground—*park* UT-8
Starvation Canyon—*valley* AZ-5
Starvation Canyon—*valley* CA-9
Starvation Canyon—*valley* (2) NV-8
Starvation Canyon—*valley* NM-5
Starvation Canyon—*valley* (2) UT-8
Starvation Cove—*gut* TX-5
Starvation Creek—*stream* AK-9
Starvation Creek—*stream* CA-9
Starvation Creek—*stream* (2) CO-8
Starvation Creek—*stream* ID-8
Starvation Creek—*stream* KS-7
Starvation Creek—*stream* (3) MT-8
Starvation Creek—*stream* NV-8
Starvation Creek—*stream* OK-5
Starvation Creek—*stream* OR-9
Starvation Creek—*stream* UT-8
Starvation Creek—*stream* WY-8
Starvation Creek Grove—*woods* CA-9
Starvation Creek State Park—*park* OR-9
Starvation Dam—*dam* UT-8
Starvation Draw—*valley* NM-5
Starvation Draw—*valley* WY-8
Starvation Draw Detention Dam No 3—*dam* NM-5
Starvation Draw Detention Dam No 4—*dam* NM-5
*Starvation Flat* ID-8
Starvation Flat—*flat* AZ-5
Starvation Flat—*flat* CA-9
Starvation Flat—*flat* NV-8
Starvation Flat—*flat* WA-9
Starvation Flats—*flat* FL-3
Starvation Flats—*flat* WA-9
Starvation Gulch—*valley* CA-9
Starvation Gulch—*valley* CO-8
Starvation Gulch*—*valley* NE-7
**Starvation Heights**—*pop pl* OR-9
Starvation Hollow—*valley* TX-5
Starvation Key—*island* (2) FL-3
*Starvation Lake* WI-6
Starvation Lake—*lake* CA-9
Starvation Lake—*lake* FL-3
Starvation Lake—*lake* MI-6
Starvation Lake—*lake* (2) MN-6
Starvation Lake—*lake* WA-9
Starvation Mtn—*summit* CA-9
Starvation Mtn—*summit* WA-9
Starvation Opening—*flat* CA-9
Starvation Peak—*summit* NM-5
Starvation Peak—*summit* WY-8
Starvation Point—*cape* FL-3
Starvation Point—*cape* MI-6
Starvation Point—*cape* TX-5
Starvation Point—*cape* (2) UT-8
Starvation Point—*cliff* AZ-5
Starvation Point—*hist pl* LA-4
Starvation Point—*ridge* OR-9
Starvation Point—*summit* CO-8
Starvation Prairie—*flat* FL-3
Starvation Ridge—*ridge* MT-8
Starvation Ridge—*ridge* OR-9
Starvation Rock—*cape* OR-9
Starvation Rsvr—*reservoir* UT-8
Starvation Slough—*stream* FL-3
Starvation Spring—*spring* (2) OR-9
Starvation Spring—*spring* UT-8
*Starvation Springs* OR-9
*Starvation State Beach* UT-8
Starvation State Park—*park* UT-8
Starvation Tank—*locale* AZ-5
Starvation Trail—*trail* OR-9
Starvation Valley—*valley* AL-4
Starvation Valley—*valley* CO-8
Starvation Wash—*valley* WY-8
Starvation Wildlife Mngmt Area—*park* UT-8
Starvation Windmill—*locale* NM-5
Starved Rock—*hist pl* IL-6
Starved Rock—*summit* IL-6
Starved Rock Lock and Dam—*dam* IL-6
Starved Rock Lodge and Cabins—*hist pl* IL-6
Starved Rock State Park—*park* IL-6
Starved to Death Creek—*stream* MT-8
Starve Goat Island (historical)—*island* RI-1
Starve Hollow—*valley* IN-6
*Starve Hollow Beach* IN-6
**Starve Hollow Lake**—*pop pl* IN-6
Starve Hollow Lake—*reservoir* IN-6
Starve Hollow Lake Dam—*dam* IN-6
Starve Hollow State Beach—*park* IN-6
Starve Island—*island* OH-6
Starve Island Reef—*bar* OH-6
Starveout—*valley* OR-9
Starve Out Branch—*stream* TX-5
Starve Out Canyon—*valley* NM-5
*Starve Out Creek* OR-9
Starveout Creek—*stream* ID-8
Starveout Creek—*stream* (2) OR-9
Starve Out Creek—*stream* SD-7
Starve Out Creek Airstrip—*airport* OR-9
Starve Out Flat—*flat* MT-8
Starveout Island (historical)—*island* PA-2
Starveout Mine—*mine* CA-9
Starveout Spring—*spring* OR-9
Starve-Out Trap—*reservoir* NM-5
Starve Out Well—*well* AZ-5
Starve Pond—*lake* TN-4
Starve-to-Death Ridge—*ridge* OR-9
Starvey Creek—*stream* MO-7
**Starview**—*pop pl* PA-2
Starview Ch—*church* AL-4
**Starview Heights**—*pop pl* PA-2
Star View Sch—*school* CA-9
Starvilla Creek—*stream* OK-5
**Star Village**—*pop pl* PA-2
**Starville**—*pop pl* MI-6
Starville Ch—*church* TX-5
Starvout—*locale* OR-9
Starvout Creek—*stream* OR-9
Starvout Creek Mines—*mine* OR-9
Starvout Ridge—*ridge* WA-9
Starwano Way—*trail* OR-9
Star Wash—*stream* AZ-5
Starweather Cem—*cemetery* ND-7
Starwein Flat—*flat* CA-9
Starwein Ridge—*ridge* CA-9
Star Well—*well* AZ-5
Star Well—*well* NM-5
Star Windmill—*locale* (2) NM-5
Star Windmill—*locale* (5) TX-5
**Staryeacre Ford**—*pop pl* AL-4
Star Zion Ch—*church* NC-3
Starzman Lake—*lake* WA-9
Stasch Brothers Ranch—*locale* NE-7
Stasek Slough—*stream* OR-9
*Stasel Falls* OR-9
Stasel Falls—*falls* OR-9
*Staser* IN-6
*Stasers* IN-6
Stassen Arm—*canal* IN-6
Stassen Lake—*lake* MN-6
*State* DC-2
State—*post sta* TN-4
State Agricultural And Industrial Sch—*school* NY-2
State Agricultural Experimental Station—*building* UT-8
State Agricultural Experiment Station—*other* TX-5
*State And Colling Drain* MI-6
State And Indian Creek Drain—*canal* MI-6
State and Prospect District—*hist pl* IN-6
State Area Vocational Technical Sch—*school* TN-4
State Armory—*hist pl* MA-1
State Arsenal—*hist pl* NE-7
State Arsenal—*hist pl* RI-1
State Asylum for the Deaf,Dumb and Blind—*hist pl* CA-9
**State Asylum (Spring Grove State Hospital)**—*pop pl* MD-2
State Ave Center—*locale* KS-7
State Bank—*hist pl* IL-6
State Bank and Trust Company—*hist pl* NV-8
State Bank Building, Decatur Branch—*hist pl* AL-4
State Bank of Antler—*hist pl* ND-7
State Bank of Hammond Bldg—*hist pl* IN-6
State Bank of Holton—*hist pl* KS-7
State Bank of Indiana, Branch of (Memorial Hall)—*hist pl* IN-6
State Bank of Kamiah—*hist pl* ID-8
State Bank of Kooskia—*hist pl* ID-8
State Bank of Ladysmith—*hist pl* WI-6
State Bank of North Carolina—*hist pl* NC-3
State Bank of Stratford—*hist pl* IA-7
State Bank of Tennessee—*hist pl* TN-4
State Bank of Wisconsin—*hist pl* WI-6
*State Barge Canal* NY-2
State Barge Canal—*canal* NY-2
State Barn Wash—*valley* UT-8
*State Bayou* LA-4
State Blvd Baptist Ch—*church* MS-4
State Blvd Plaza—*locale* IN-6
*State Boat Channel* NY-2
State Bogs—*swamp* MA-1
State Boundary Reference Monument—*locale* TX-5
State Boys Sch—*school* MO-7
State Boys Sch Area 1—*school* NM-5
State Boys Sch Area 2—*school* NM-5
State Branch—*stream* AL-4
State Branch—*stream* (2) KY-4
State Bridge—*hist pl* CO-8
**State Bridge**—*pop pl* CO-8
**State Bridge**—*pop pl* NY-2
State Bridge Draw—*valley* CO-8
State Brook—*stream* NY-2
State Brook Mtn—*summit* NY-2
Stateburg—*locale* SC-3
Stateburg Hist Dist—*hist pl* SC-3
Stateburg Sch—*school* SC-3
**Stateburg (sta.)**—*pop pl* SC-3
*State Camp* WA-9
State Camp—*locale* (2) PA-2
**State Camp**—*pop pl* WA-9
*State Canal* UT-8
State Canal—*canal* LA-4
State Canal—*canal* UT-8
State Capital—*uninc pl* AR-4
State Capitol—*building* IN-6
State Capitol—*building* MD-2
State Capitol—*building* NJ-2
State Capitol—*building* OK-5
State Capitol—*building* VA-3
State Capitol—*locale* ID-8
State Capitol—*locale* WY-8
State Capitol—*other* NE-7
State Capitol—*uninc pl* CA-9
State Capitol—*uninc pl* MT-8
State Capitol Bldg—*hist pl* PA-2
State Capitol Heliport—*airport* UT-8
State Cattle Ranch Dam Number 1—*dam* AL-4
State Cattle Ranch Dam Number 2—*dam* AL-4
State Cattle Ranch Dam Number 3—*dam* AL-4
State Cattle Ranch Dam Number 4—*dam* AL-4
State Cattle Ranch Dam Number 5—*dam* AL-4
State Cattle Ranch Dam Number 6—*dam* AL-4
State Cattle Ranch Dam Number 7—*dam* AL-4
State Cattle Ranch Dam Number 8—*dam* AL-4
State Cattle Ranch Lakes—*reservoir* AL-4
State Cem—*cemetery* OH-6
State Cem—*cemetery* SC-3
State Cemetery of Texas—*hist pl* TX-5
**State Center**—*pop pl* IA-7
**State Center Junction**—*pop pl* IA-7
State Center Township—*fmr MCD* IA-7
State Ch—*church* SC-3
State Coal Mine Junction—*locale* CO-8
State Coll Area JHS—*school* PA-2
State College—*locale* MS-4
**State College**—*pop pl* PA-2
State College—*uninc pl* SC-3
State College Air Depot—*airport* PA-2
State College Airp—*airport* PA-2
State College Borough—*civil* PA-2
*State College Camp* PA-2
State College Experimental Station—*other* NY-2
*State College Forest* NC-3
State College Sewage Lagoon Dam—*dam* MS-4
State Coll (Mississippi State University)—*school* MS-4
State Coll Of Arkansas—*school* AR-4
State Coll (Savannah State College)—*school* GA-3
State Colony for Negroes (historical)—*locale* AL-4
State Correctional Center for Women—*building* MO-7
State Correctional Institute—*locale* MA-1
State Correctional Institution—*school* MA-1
State Correctional Institution at Graterford—*locale* PA-2
*State Creek* IN-6
*State Creek* MO-7
State Creek—*stream* (4) ID-8
State Creek—*stream* KS-7
State Creek—*stream* MT-8
State Creek—*stream* NE-7
State Creek—*stream* OR-9
State Creek—*stream* (2) WA-9
State Dam—*dam* UT-8
*State Ditch* IN-6
*State Ditch* MI-6
State Ditch—*canal* IN-6
State Ditch—*canal* MI-6
State Ditch—*canal* OR-9
State Ditch—*canal* WY-8
State Ditch Number Eightyfive—*canal* MN-6
State Ditch Number Eightyfour—*canal* MN-6
State Ditch Number Fifteen—*canal* MN-6
State Ditch Number Fifty—*canal* MN-6
State Ditch Number Fiftyone—*canal* MN-6
State Ditch Number Forty-eight—*canal* MN-6
State Ditch Number Fortynine—*canal* MN-6
State Ditch Number Ninty—*canal* MN-6
State Ditch Number Nintyone—*canal* MN-6
State Ditch Number One—*canal* MN-6
State Ditch Number Seventytwo—*canal* MN-6
State Ditch Number Sixtyeight—*canal* MN-6
State Ditch Number Sixtynine—*canal* MN-6
State Ditch Number Sixtyone—*canal* MN-6
State Ditch Number Three—*canal* MN-6
State Ditch Number Two—*canal* MN-6
State Division of Forestry—*locale* CA-9
State Dock—*locale* KY-4
State Drain—*canal* MI-6
State Draw—*valley* CO-8
State Experiment Farm And Antelope Res—*park* SD-7
State Fair Community Coll—*school* MO-7
**State Fair Grounds**—*pop pl* MO-7
State Fair Park—*park* WI-6
State Fair Shop Ctr—*locale* MO-7
State Farm—*locale* VA-3
State Farmers Market—*locale* FL-3
State Farm (Penal Institution)—*building* VA-3
State Farm Show Bldg—*building* PA-2
State Farm (Wateree River Correctional Institution)—*building* SC-3
State Ferry (historical)—*locale* TX-5
*State Ferry Landing* SC-3
State Fish Hatchery—*locale* FL-3
State Fish Hatchery—*locale* PA-2
State Fish Hatchery—*other* NE-7
*State Fish Hatchery-Corry Number 1* PA-2
*State Fish Hatchery Corry Number 2* PA-2
State Fish Hatchery Number 1—*other* TX-5
State Fish Hatchery Number 2—*other* TX-5
State Forest HQ—*locale* CO-8
State Foresty Guard Station—*locale* CA-9
State For Rensselaer Number 3—*forest* NY-2
State Fort Park—*park* MA-1
State Game Lands No 63—*park* PA-2
State Game Lands Number 100—*park* PA-2
State Game Lands Number 101—*park* PA-2
State Game Lands Number 102—*park* PA-2
State Game Lands Number 103—*park* PA-2
State Game Lands Number 104—*park* PA-2
State Game Lands Number 105—*park* PA-2
State Game Lands Number 106—*park* PA-2
State Game Lands Number 107—*park* PA-2
State Game Lands Number 108—*park* PA-2
State Game Lands Number 109—*park* PA-2
State Game Lands Number 111—*park* PA-2
State Game Lands Number 112—*park* PA-2
State Game Lands Number 113—*park* PA-2
State Game Lands Number 114—*park* PA-2
State Game Lands Number 115—*park* PA-2
State Game Lands Number 116—*park* PA-2
State Game Lands Number 118—*park* PA-2
State Game Lands Number 12—*park* PA-2
State Game Lands Number 120—*park* PA-2
State Game Lands Number 121—*park* PA-2
State Game Lands Number 122—*park* PA-2
State Game Lands Number 123—*park* PA-2
State Game Lands Number 124—*park* PA-2
State Game Lands Number 126—*park* PA-2
State Game Lands Number 127—*park* PA-2
State Game Lands Number 128—*park* PA-2
State Game Lands Number 13—*park* PA-2
State Game Lands Number 130—*park* PA-2
State Game Lands Number 131—*park* PA-2
State Game Lands Number 132—*park* PA-2
State Game Lands Number 133—*park* PA-2
State Game Lands Number 134—*park* PA-2
State Game Lands Number 135—*park* PA-2
State Game Lands Number 136—*park* PA-2
State Game Lands Number 137—*park* PA-2
State Game Lands Number 138—*park* PA-2
State Game Lands Number 14—*park* PA-2
State Game Lands Number 141—*park* PA-2
State Game Lands Number 142—*park* PA-2
State Game Lands Number 143—*park* PA-2
State Game Lands Number 144—*park* PA-2
State Game Lands Number 145—*park* PA-2
State Game Lands Number 147—*park* PA-2
State Game Lands Number 148—*park* PA-2
State Game Lands Number 150—*park* PA-2
State Game Lands Number 151—*park* PA-2
State Game Lands Number 152—*park* PA-2
State Game Lands Number 153—*park* PA-2
State Game Lands Number 154—*park* PA-2
State Game Lands Number 155—*park* PA-2
State Game Lands Number 156—*park* PA-2
State Game Lands Number 157—*park* PA-2
State Game Lands Number 158—*park* PA-2
State Game Lands Number 159—*park* PA-2
State Game Lands Number 161—*park* PA-2
State Game Lands Number 162—*park* PA-2
State Game Lands Number 164—*park* PA-2
State Game Lands Number 165—*park* PA-2
State Game Lands Number 166—*park* PA-2
State Game Lands Number 167—*park* PA-2
State Game Lands Number 168—*park* PA-2
State Game Lands Number 169—*park* PA-2
State Game Lands Number 170—*park* PA-2
State Game Lands Number 171—*park* PA-2
State Game Lands Number 172—*park* PA-2
State Game Lands Number 173—*park* PA-2
State Game Lands Number 174—*park* PA-2
State Game Lands Number 175—*park* PA-2
State Game Lands Number 176—*park* PA-2
State Game Lands Number 178—*park* PA-2
State Game Lands Number 179—*park* PA-2
State Game Lands Number 180—*park* PA-2
State Game Lands Number 182—*park* PA-2
State Game Lands Number 183—*park* PA-2
State Game Lands Number 184—*park* PA-2
State Game Lands Number 185—*park* PA-2
State Game Lands Number 188—*park* PA-2
State Game Lands Number 189—*park* PA-2
State Game Lands Number 190—*park* PA-2
State Game Lands Number 191—*park* PA-2
State Game Lands Number 192—*park* PA-2
State Game Lands Number 193—*park* PA-2
State Game Lands Number 194—*park* PA-2
State Game Lands Number 195—*park* PA-2
State Game Lands Number 196—*park* PA-2
State Game Lands Number 197—*park* PA-2
State Game Lands Number 198—*park* PA-2
State Game Lands Number 199—*park* PA-2
State Game Lands Number 201—*park* PA-2

**Station**—*pop pl* NC-3
Station Ave Sch—*school* OH-6
Station Bay—*bay* AK-9
Station Bay—*swamp* NC-3
*Station Branch* GA-3
Station Branch—*stream* FL-3
Station Branch—*stream* GA-3
Station Branch—*stream* KY-4
Station Branch—*stream* NC-3
Station Branch—*stream* TX-5
Station Brook—*stream* VT-1
*Station Butte* WY-8
Station Butte—*summit* NV-8
Station Butte—*summit* OR-9
Station Camp—*locale* KY-4
Station Camp (CCD)—*cens area* KY-4
Station Camp Ch—*church* KY-4
Station Camp Ch—*church* TN-4
Station Camp Creek—*stream* KY-4
Station Camp Creek—*stream* (2) TN-4
**Station Camp (historical)**—*pop pl* TN-4
Station Camp Post Office (historical)—*building* TN-4
Stationcamp Run—*stream* WV-2
Station Camp Sch—*school* KY-4
Station Camp Sch—*school* TN-4
Station Canyon—*valley* ID-8
Station Canyon—*valley* OR-9
Station Cem—*cemetery* KY-4
Station Ch—*church* KY-4
Station Cove—*bay* DE-2
*Station Creek* ID-8
*Station Creek* MT-8
*Station Creek* OR-9
Station Creek—*channel* SC-3
**Station Creek**—*pop pl* MS-4
Station Creek—*stream* AK-9
Station Creek—*stream* (2) CA-9
Station Creek—*stream* (8) ID-8
Station Creek—*stream* MS-4
Station Creek—*stream* (4) MT-8
Station Creek—*stream* OK-5
Station Creek—*stream* (5) OR-9
Station Creek—*stream* SC-3
Station Creek—*stream* TN-4
Station Creek—*stream* (2) TX-5
Station Creek—*stream* UT-8
Station Creek—*stream* (2) VA-3
Station Creek—*stream* WA-9
Station Creek—*stream* (3) WY-8
Station Creek Campground—*locale* WY-8
Station Creek Cave—*cave* TN-4
Station Creek Cem—*cemetery* TX-5
Station Creek Ch—*church* MS-4
Station Creek Ch—*church* VA-3
Station Creek (historical)—*locale* MS-4
*Station Creek Missionary Baptist Church* MS-4
Station Creek Sch (historical)—*school* MS-4
Station Creek Tunnel—*tunnel* ID-8
Station Draw—*valley* WY-8
Station Eleven—*summit* CO-8
Station Elm Creek—*stream* SD-7
**Station Fifteen**—*pop pl* OH-6
Station Fork—*stream* ID-8
Station Gap—*gap* WV-2
Station Gulch—*valley* (2) CA-9
Station Gulch—*valley* CO-8
Station Gulch—*valley* ID-8
Station Harbor—*harbor* PW-9
**Station Hills**—*pop pl* VA-3
Station Hollow—*valley* IN-6
Station Hollow—*valley* TN-4
Station Hollow—*valley* UT-8
Station Hollow—*valley* WV-2
*Station Island* OH-6
Station Island—*island* (4) AK-9
Station L Airstrip—*airport* OR-9
Station Lake—*lake* FL-3
Station Mall—*locale* PA-2
Stationmaster's House—*hist pl* NH-1
Station Mtn—*summit* SC-3
*Station Number 3* AL-4
*Station Number 4* AL-4
Station Peak—*summit* CA-9
Station Point—*cape* AK-9
*Station Pond* NH-1
Station Pond—*lake* FL-3
Station Pond Marsh—*swamp* MA-1
Station Ranch—*locale* CO-8
Station Road Bridge—*hist pl* OH-6
Station Rock—*pillar* NJ-2
Station Rock—*rock* NY-2
Station Rocks—*bar* AK-9
Station Run—*stream* KY-4
Station Run—*stream* PA-2
Station Sch (historical)—*school* TN-4
*Stations Hafen* PW-9
Station Spring—*spring* (2) ID-8
Station Spring—*spring* MT-8
Station Spring—*spring* NV-8
Station Spring—*spring* (3) OR-9
Station Spring—*spring* VA-3
Station Spring Creek—*stream* (2) VA-3
Station Square—*locale* PA-2
Station Square Shop Ctr—*locale* NC-3
Station Tank—*reservoir* (2) AZ-5
**Station West**—*pop pl* TN-4
**Station 15 (Philadelphia Road Station)**—*pop pl* OH-6
*Station 50* SD-7
Station 8—*locale* WY-8
*Station 88* SD-7
Statler Cem—*cemetery* MO-7
Statler Cem—*cemetery* OH-6
Statler Ditch—*canal* OH-6
Statler Draw—*valley* WY-8
Statler Hill Lookout Tower—*locale* PA-2
*Statler Run* WV-2
**Statler Run**—*pop pl* WV-2
Statler Sch—*school* IL-6
Statlers Par 3 Golf Course—*locale* PA-2
Statlers Run—*stream* KY-4
Staton—*locale* MT-8
**Staton**—*pop pl* NC-3
Staton and Cissna Ditch—*canal* CO-8
Staton-Biggs Cem—*cemetery* NC-3
Staton Branch—*stream* WV-2
Staton Cem—*cemetery* NC-3
Staton Cem—*cemetery* TX-5
Staton Coulee—*valley* MT-8
Staton Gap—*gap* AL-4
Staton Hill—*summit* PA-2
*Statonic* AZ-5
Staton Mtn—*summit* MT-8
Statons Creek—*stream* VA-3
**Statonville**—*pop pl* TN-4
Statonville Branch—*stream* TN-4
Statts Mills—*locale* WV-2
Statuary Mtn—*summit* MT-8
Statue Hills—*summit* ID-8
Statue Lake—*lake* CA-9
Statue of Liberty Natl Monmt (Also NJ)—*park* NY-2
Statue of Liberty Natl Monmt (Also NY)—*park* NJ-2
Statue of Liberty Natl Monument, Ellis Island and Liberty Island—*hist pl* NJ-2
Statue of Liberty Natl Monument, Ellis Island and Liberty Island—*hist pl* NY-2
Statue Spring—*spring* NM-5
*Statum Creek* CA-9
*Statum Meadow* CA-9
Statzer Draw—*valley* WY-8
Statzer Point—*cliff* WY-8
Statz Spring—*spring* OR-9
Staubach Creek—*stream* MT-8
Stauber, Samuel B., Farm—*hist pl* NC-3
Staub Run—*stream* MD-2
Staubus Cem—*cemetery* TN-4
*Stauch Ranch* OR-9
Staudaher Bishop Ditch—*canal* MT-8
Staudaher Ditch—*canal* MT-8
Staudaher East Side Ditch—*canal* MT-8
Staudaher West Side Ditch—*canal* MT-8
Staude Cem—*cemetery* IL-6
Staudenmeyer Ranch—*locale* MT-8
Staudher Rsvr—*reservoir* CO-8
Stauduhar House—*hist pl* IL-6
Staufer Sch—*school* SD-7
Stauffer—*locale* CA-9
Stauffer—*locale* OR-9
**Stauffer**—*pop pl* WY-8
Stauffer—*uninc pl* CA-9
Stauffer, Christian, House—*hist pl* PA-2
Stauffer, Dr. B., House—*hist pl* PA-2
Stauffer, John, House and Barn—*hist pl* OR-9
Stauffer Canyon—*valley* UT-8
Stauffer Cem—*cemetery* OH-6
Stauffer Ch—*church* MD-2
Stauffer Ch—*church* PA-2
Stauffer Chemical Dike Number Nineteen—*dam* TN-4
Stauffer Chemical Dike Number Seventeen—*dam* TN-4
Stauffer Chemical Tailings Pond—*reservoir* TN-4
Stauffer Chemical Tailings Pond North—*reservoir* UT-8
Stauffer Chemical Tailings Pond North Dam—*dam* UT-8
*Stauffer Creek* ID-8
Stauffer Creek—*stream* ID-8
Stauffer Ditch—*canal* IN-6
Stauffer Flat—*flat* ID-8
Stauffer Globe Pond Dam Number Twenty-one—*dam* TN-4
Stauffer Globe Pond Number Twenty-one—*reservoir* TN-4
Stauffer Industrial Park—*locale* PA-2
Stauffer Lake—*lake* MN-6
Stauffer Lake—*lake* WI-6
**Stauffer Mine**—*pop pl* WY-8
Stauffer Park—*park* CA-9
Stauffer Park—*park* IN-6
Stauffer Park—*park* PA-2
Stauffer Pond Number Twenty—*reservoir* TN-4
Stauffer Run—*stream* (2) PA-2
Stauffers Ch—*church* PA-2
Stauffer Sch (abandoned)—*school* (2) PA-2
Stauffer Sch (historical)—*school* MO-7
Stauffers Sch—*school* PA-2
Stauffer Turning Basin—*basin* TX-5
Stauffles Run—*stream* WV-2
Staughter Creek—*stream* LA-4
St. Augustine's Catholic Church—*hist pl* (2) OH-6
St. Augustine's Roman Catholic Church—*hist pl* MO-7
Staulkinghead Creek—*stream* LA-4
Staum Dam—*reservoir* SD-7
Staum Dam State Public Shooting Area—*park* SD-7
Staums Dam—*dam* SD-7
Staunch Point—*cape* AK-9
*Staunton* NJ-2
**Staunton**—*pop pl* GA-3
**Staunton**—*pop pl* IL-6
**Staunton**—*pop pl* IN-6
**Staunton**—*pop pl* NM-5
**Staunton**—*pop pl* (2) OH-6
Staunton Branch—*stream* VA-3
Staunton Ch—*church* (2) VA-3
Staunton Country Club—*other* IL-6
Staunton Creek—*stream* VA-3
Staunton Dam—*dam* VA-3
Staunton Elem Sch—*school* IN-6
Staunton Hill—*hist pl* VA-3
Staunton HS—*school* IN-6
**Staunton (ind. city)**—*pop pl* VA-3
Staunton (Magisterial District)—*fmr MCD* VA-3
Staunton Military Acad—*school* VA-3
**Staunton Mill**—*pop pl* TN-4
Staunton Natl Cem—*cemetery* VA-3
**Staunton Park**—*pop pl* VA-3
Staunton Ranch—*locale* MT-8
Staunton Ridge—*ridge* NV-8
*Staunton River* NC-3
Staunton River—*stream* VA-3
Staunton River Ch—*church* VA-3
Staunton River HS—*school* VA-3
Staunton River (Magisterial District)—*fmr MCD* VA-3
Staunton River State Park—*park* VA-3
Staunton River Trail—*trail* VA-3
Staunton Rsvr—*reservoir* IL-6
Staunton Sch—*school* OH-6
Staunton Sch—*school* WV-2
**Staunton (sta.)**—*pop pl* IN-6
Staunton Street Sch—*school* OH-6
**Staunton (Township of)**—*pop pl* IL-6
**Staunton (Township of)**—*pop pl* OH-6
Staunton View Public Use Area—*park* VA-3
Staunton West Oil Field—*other* IL-6
*Staups Pond* SC-3
Stauter Creek—*stream* AL-4
*Stauton* IN-6
*Stauvers Run* VA-3
**Stavanger**—*pop pl* IL-6
Stavanger Cem—*cemetery* IL-6
Stavanger Cem—*cemetery* (3) IA-7
Stavanger Cem—*cemetery* SD-7
Stavanger Ch—*church* (2) IA-7
Stavanger Ch—*church* MN-6
Stavanger Ch—*church* ND-7
Stavanger Ch—*church* SD-7
Stavanger Town Hall—*building* ND-7
**Stavanger Township**—*pop pl* ND-7
Stave Bluff—*cliff* AL-4
Stave Bluff Landing—*locale* AL-4
**Stavebolt Landing (historical)**—*pop pl* OR-9
Stave Branch—*stream* FL-3
Stave Branch—*stream* KY-4
Stave Branch—*stream* WV-2
Stave Brook—*stream* VT-1
**Stave Creek**—*pop pl* AL-4
Stave Creek—*stream* AL-4
*Stave Creek Baptist Church* AL-4
Stave Creek Ch—*church* AL-4
Stavefield Trail—*trail* PA-2
Stave Hollow—*valley* AL-4
Stave Hollow—*valley* KY-4
Stave Hollow—*valley* TN-4
Stave Island—*island* AR-4
Stave Island—*island* (3) ME-1
Stave Island—*island* VT-1
Stave Island Bar—*bar* ME-1
*Stave Island Harbor* ME-1
Stave Island Harbor—*bay* ME-1
Stave Island Ledge—*bar* ME-1
Stave Island Ledge—*bar* VT-1
Stave Lake—*lake* AR-4
Stave Lake—*reservoir* KS-7
Stave Landing—*locale* DE-2
Stave Landing—*locale* GA-3
Stave Landing—*locale* NC-3
Stave Landing—*locale* SC-3
Stave Landing—*locale* VA-3
Stavely Hollow—*valley* TN-4
Stavely-Kunz-Johnson House—*hist pl* TX-5
Stave Mill Branch—*stream* MS-4
Stave Mill Branch—*stream* TN-4
Stavemill Branch—*stream* TN-4
Stavemill Hollow—*valley* AL-4
Stave Mill Hollow—*valley* AL-4
Stave Mill Hollow—*valley* AR-4
Stavens Memorial Cem—*cemetery* ND-7
Stave Point—*cape* FL-3
Staver Ditch—*canal* IN-6
Staver Run—*stream* PA-2
Stavers Ch—*church* WI-6
Stave Run—*stream* VA-3
Stave Run—*stream* WV-2
Staves—*locale* AR-4
*Staves Island* HI-9
Stave Spring—*spring* UT-8
**Stavetown**—*pop pl* IN-6
**Stave Township**—*pop pl* ND-7
Staveyard Bend—*bend* AR-4
Staveyard Branch—*stream* TX-5
Staveyard Hollow—*valley* TN-4
Stavis Bay—*bay* WA-9
Stavis Creek—*stream* WA-9
Stavley Creek—*stream* ID-8
Stavley Pond—*lake* MD-2
**Stavo**—*pop pl* AL-4
Stawberry Hill—*summit* WY-8
*Stawton* DE-2
Stay—*locale* KY-4
Stay—*locale* LA-4
Stay, Lake—*lake* MN-6
*Stay-a-while Spring* WA-9
Stayawhile Spring—*spring* WA-9
Stayback Hill—*summit* NY-2
Stay Creek—*stream* KY-4
Stay House—*hist pl* AL-4
Stayman—*locale* WA-9
**Stayton**—*pop pl* OR-9
**Stayton**—*pop pl* TN-4
Stayton (CCD)—*cens area* OR-9
Stayton Cem—*cemetery* KY-4
Stayton Elem Sch—*school* OR-9
Stayton Gap—*gap* KY-4
*Stayton Island* OR-9
Stayton Island—*island* OR-9
Stayton Island County Park—*park* OR-9
Stayton Meadows Golf Club—*other* MO-7
Stayton Mine—*mine* CA-9
Stayton MS—*school* OR-9
Stayton South Oil Field—*oilfield* KS-7
Staytonville—*locale* DE-2
St. Bartholomew's Episcopal Church—*hist pl* VT-1
**St. Benedict**—*pop pl* IA-7
**St. Benedict**—*pop pl* ND-7
**St Benedict Manor Condominiums**—*pop pl* UT-8
St. Benedict's Catholic Church—*hist pl* NE-7
St. Benedict's Catholic Sch—*hist pl* MT-8
St. Benedict's Church—*hist pl* CT-1
St. Benedict's Mission Sch—*hist pl* MN-6
**St. Bernard**—*pop pl* NE-7
St. Bernard Catholic Church and Rectory—*hist pl* OH-6
**St. Bernard Township**—*pop pl* NE-7
St. Bonaventure Church Complex—*hist pl* NE-7
St. Bonaventure Monastery—*hist pl* MI-6
St. Boniface Catholic Church Complex—*hist pl* NE-7
St. Boniface Church—*hist pl* IN-6
St. Boniface Roman Catholic Church, School, Rectory, and Convent—*hist pl* OH-6
S-T Canal—*canal* MT-8
**St. Catherines**—*pop pl* IA-7
St. Cecilia's Cathedral—*hist pl* NE-7
St. Cecilia Society Bldg—*hist pl* MI-6
**St. Charles**—*pop pl* IA-7
**St. Charles**—*pop pl* MT-8
St. Charles Apartments—*hist pl* NE-7
St. Charles Borromeo Church Complex—*hist pl* RI-1
St. Charles Bridge—*hist pl* CO-8
St. Charles City Bakery—*hist pl* MN-6
St. Charles Hist Dist—*hist pl* MO-7
St. Charles Hist Dist (Boundary Increase)—*hist pl* MO-7
St. Charles-Muller's Hotel—*hist pl* NV-8
St. Charles Odd Fellows Hall—*hist pl* MO-7
St. Charles of the Valley Catholic Church and Rectory—*hist pl* ID-8
St. Charles Seminary and Chapel—*hist pl* OH-6
St. Charles Township—*fmr MCD* IA-7
**St. Charles Township**—*pop pl* NE-7
St. Christopher Catholic Ch—*church* UT-8
*St. Clair* MN-6
St. Clair—*hist pl* IN-6
St. Clair River Tunnel—*hist pl* MI-6
St. Clair Street Bridge—*hist pl* OH-6
St. Clair Street Hist Dist—*hist pl* OH-6
St. Clair Township—*fmr MCD* (2) IA-7
St. Columba Mission Site—*hist pl* MN-6
**St. Columbans**—*pop pl* NE-7
St. Cornelia's Episcopal Church—*hist pl* MN-6
St Cornelius Cem—*cemetery* NE-7
St. Croix Boom Company House and Barn—*hist pl* MN-6
St. Croix Boom Site—*hist pl* MN-6
St. Croix Island International Historic Site—*hist pl* ME-1
*St. Croix Junction* MN-6
St. Croix Lumber Mills-Stillwater Manufacturing Company—*hist pl* MN-6
St. Croix River Access Site—*hist pl* MN-6
**St. Croix Township**—*pop pl* ND-7
St. Cyril and St. Methodius Church—*hist pl* ME-1
St. David Catholic Church—*hist pl* ME-1
St. David's Episcopal Church and Cemetery—*hist pl* SC-3
St. Denis Catholic Church—*hist pl* ME-1
St Dominic-Jackson Memorial Hospital Airp—*airport* MS-4
**St. Donatus**—*pop pl* IA-7
**Stead**—*pop pl* NM-5
*Stead Canyon* WY-8
Stead Cem—*cemetery* AL-4
Stead Dead River—*lake* MS-4
Stead Flat—*flat* AZ-5
Stead Golf Course—*locale* NV-8
Steadham Cem—*cemetery* (3) AL-4
Steadham Mission Cem—*cemetery* AL-4
Steadhams Store—*locale* GA-3
**Steadman**—*pop pl* GA-3
Steadman, Foy, Site—*hist pl* TX-5
**Steadman Acres Subdivision**—*pop pl* UT-8
Steadman Cem—*cemetery* GA-3
Steadman Cem—*cemetery* TN-4
Steadman Chapel Ch—*church* AL-4
**Steadman Estates - Numbers 2-5**—*pop pl* UT-8
Steadman Hill—*summit* VT-1
Steadman Island—*island* GA-3
Steadman Landing—*locale* ME-1
Steadman Missionary Ch—*church* GA-3
Steadman Pond—*reservoir* MA-1
Steadman Pond Dam—*dam* MA-1
Steadman Ridge—*ridge* (2) TN-4
Steadman Sch (historical)—*school* MS-4
*Steadmans Island* GA-3
Stead Sch—*school* NV-8
Steadwell Cem—*cemetery* PA-2
Steady Run—*stream* IA-7
Steady Run Township—*fmr MCD* IA-7
Steagall Spring—*spring* OR-9
Steak Bake Creek—*stream* KS-7
Steak Creek—*stream* AK-9
Steak Lake—*lake* MN-6
Steakman Branch—*stream* VA-3
Steaky Sch (historical)—*school* TN-4
Steal Chapel—*church* MS-4
Steal Easy Mtn—*summit* TX-5
**Stealey**—*pop pl* WV-2
Stealey-Goff-Vance House—*hist pl* WV-2
Stealey Mtn—*summit* CO-8
Stealing Lake—*lake* FL-3
Stealy—*locale* OK-5
Steam—*locale* AZ-5
**Steam**—*pop pl* KY-4
Steam Beer Placer—*mine* OR-9
*Steamboat* AZ-5
Steamboat—*locale* NV-8
Steamboat—*locale* (2) OR-9
Steamboat—*summit* ID-8
Steamboat—*summit* UT-8
Steamboat Bay—*bay* (2) AK-9
Steamboat Bay—*bay* ID-8
Steamboat Bay—*bay* (2) MN-6
Steamboat Bay—*bay* SD-7
Steamboat Bay Lake—*lake* MN-6
Steamboat Bayou—*stream* LA-4
Steamboat Bayou—*stream* MS-4
Steamboat Bend Shop Ctr—*locale* MO-7
Steamboat Butte—*summit* (3) MT-8
Steamboat Butte—*summit* NM-5
Steamboat Butte—*summit* WY-8
Steamboat Butte Oil Field—*oilfield* WY-8
Steamboat Cabin Slough—*lake* AK-9
Steamboat Camp—*locale* ID-8
**Steamboat Canyon**—*pop pl* AZ-5
Steamboat Canyon—*valley* AZ-5
Steamboat Canyon—*valley* (2) CA-9
Steamboat Canyon—*valley* NM-5
**Steamboat Canyon Trading Post**—*pop pl* AZ-5
Steamboat Channel—*channel* FL-3
Steamboat Cove—*bay* AZ-5
Steamboat Cove—*bay* ME-1
*Steamboat Creek* OR-9
Steamboat Creek—*channel* FL-3
Steamboat Creek—*stream* (3) AK-9
Steamboat Creek—*stream* AR-4
Steamboat Creek—*stream* CA-9
Steamboat Creek—*stream* (3) ID-8
Steamboat Creek—*stream* NV-8
Steamboat Creek—*stream* (4) OR-9
Steamboat Creek—*stream* SC-3
Steamboat Creek—*stream* SD-7
Steamboat Creek—*stream* VA-3
Steamboat Creek—*stream* (2) WA-9
Steamboat Ditch—*canal* NV-8
Steamboat Dock Site—*hist pl* CT-1
Steamboat Eddy—*rapids* GA-3
Steamboat Falls—*falls* OR-9
Steamboat Falls Campground—*park* OR-9
Steamboat Gap—*channel* FL-3
Steamboat Gulch—*valley* CA-9
Steamboat Gulch—*valley* ID-8
Steamboat Hill—*summit* CO-8
Steamboat Hills—*summit* NV-8
Steamboat Hollow—*valley* KY-4
Steamboat House—*hist pl* AR-4
Steamboat House—*hist pl* LA-4
Steamboat Island—*island* (2) MI-6
Steamboat Island—*island* (2) MN-6
Steamboat Island—*island* (2) MT-8
Steamboat Island—*island* NH-1
Steamboat Island—*island* NY-2
Steamboat Island—*island* OR-9
Steamboat Island—*island* TX-5
Steamboat Island—*island* (2) WA-9
Steamboat Island—*island* (2) WI-6
Steamboat Island (historical)—*island* AL-4
Steamboat Lake—*lake* AK-9
Steamboat Lake—*lake* CO-8
Steamboat Lake—*lake* (3) ID-8
Steamboat Lake—*lake* (2) MN-6
Steamboat Lake—*lake* OR-9
Steamboat Lake—*lake* WA-9
Steamboat Lake—*lake* (3) WY-8
Steamboat Landing—*locale* CA-9
Steamboat Landing—*locale* SC-3
Steamboat Landing (historical)—*locale* SD-7
Steamboat Lookout Pass (pack)—*trail* MT-8
Steamboat Mesa—*summit* CO-8
Steamboat Mesa—*summit* UT-8
Steamboat Mine—*mine* OR-9
Steamboat Mound—*summit* OK-5
Steamboat Mountain Lookout—*locale* MT-8
Steamboat Mtn—*summit* AK-9
Steamboat Mtn—*summit* (2) AZ-5
Steamboat Mtn—*summit* (2) CA-9
Steamboat Mtn—*summit* CO-8
Steamboat Mtn—*summit* (2) MT-8
Steamboat Mtn—*summit* (2) OR-9
Steamboat Mtn—*summit* (2) TX-5
Steamboat Mtn—*summit* (3) UT-8
Steamboat Mtn—*summit* WA-9
Steamboat Mtn—*summit* WY-8
Steamboat Old River Slough—*stream* GA-3
Steamboat Pass—*channel* TX-5
Steamboat Pass—*gap* UT-8
Steamboat Peak—*summit* ID-8
Steamboat Peak—*summit* WY-8
Steamboat Plaza—*post sta* CO-8
Steamboat Point—*cape* AK-9
Steamboat Point—*cape* OR-9
Steamboat Point—*cape* (3) UT-8
Steamboat Point—*cape* WI-6
Steamboat Point—*cape* WY-8
Steamboat Point—*cliff* CA-9
Steamboat Point—*cliff* WY-8
Steamboat Point—*summit* OR-9
Steamboat Prow—*summit* WA-9
Steamboat Ridge—*ridge* OR-9
Steamboat Rim—*cliff* WY-8
*Steamboat River* MN-6
Steamboat River—*stream* GA-3
Steamboat River—*stream* MN-6
Steamboat River (Township of)—*civ div* MN-6
Steamboat Rock—*cape* CO-8
Steamboat Rock—*cape* ID-8
Steamboat Rock—*cape* OR-9
Steamboat Rock—*cliff* IA-7
Steamboat Rock—*island* AZ-5
Steamboat Rock—*island* (2) CA-9
Steamboat Rock—*island* OR-9
Steamboat Rock—*island* WA-9
Steamboat Rock—*locale* ID-8
Steamboat Rock—*pillar* AZ-5
Steamboat Rock—*pillar* CA-9
Steamboat Rock—*pillar* ID-8
Steamboat Rock—*pillar* (2) MT-8
Steamboat Rock—*pillar* NE-7
Steamboat Rock—*pillar* OR-9
Steamboat Rock—*pillar* SD-7
Steamboat Rock—*pillar* UT-8
Steamboat Rock—*pillar* WA-9
Steamboat Rock—*pillar* (2) WI-6
Steamboat Rock—*pillar* (2) WY-8
**Steamboat Rock**—*pop pl* IA-7
Steamboat Rock—*ridge* OR-9
Steamboat Rock—*summit* (2) AZ-5
Steamboat Rock—*summit* CA-9
Steamboat Rock—*summit* CO-8
Steamboat Rock—*summit* IA-7
Steamboat Rock—*summit* MT-8
Steamboat Rock—*summit* TN-4
Steamboat Rock—*summit* WA-9
Steamboat Rock—*summit* (5) WY-8
Steamboat Rock Campground—*locale* CO-8
Steamboat Rocks—*locale* ID-8
Steamboat Rock Wayside State Park—*park* IA-7
Steamboat Ski Area—*other* CO-8
Steamboat Slough—*gut* (2) CA-9
Steamboat Slough—*stream* (4) AK-9
Steamboat Slough—*stream* CA-9
Steamboat Slough—*stream* (3) WA-9
Steamboat Spring—*spring* AZ-5
Steamboat Spring—*spring* CO-8
Steamboat Spring—*spring* (2) OR-9
*Steamboat Springs* NV-8
**Steamboat Springs**—*pop pl* CO-8
Steamboat Springs Airp—*airport* CO-8
Steamboat Springs Depot—*hist pl* CO-8
Steamboat Springs (Hot)—*spring* NV-8
Steamboat Summit—*beach* ID-8
Steamboat Tank—*reservoir* (2) AZ-5
Steamboat Tank—*reservoir* NM-5
*Steamboat Trading Post* AZ-5
Steamboat Trail—*trail* (2) CA-9
Steamboat Trail—*trail* OR-9
Steamboat Tunnel—*mine* UT-8
Steamboat Valley—*basin* NV-8
Steamboat Village—*uninc pl* CO-8
Steamboat Wash—*stream* AZ-5
Steamboat Wash—*valley* AZ-5
Steamboat Wash—*valley* UT-8
*Steamburg* NY-2
Steamburg—*locale* OH-6
Steamburg—*locale* PA-2
**Steamburg**—*pop pl* (2) MI-6
**Steamburg**—*pop pl* NY-2
Steamburg Brook—*stream* MA-1
Steamburg Cem—*cemetery* NY-2
**Steam Corner**—*pop pl* IN-6
*Steam Corners* IN-6
**Steam Corners**—*pop pl* OH-6
Steam Engine Canyon—*valley* WY-8
Steam Engine Company No. 10—*hist pl* KY-4
Steam Engine Company No. 11—*hist pl* KY-4
Steam Engine Company No. 18—*hist pl* KY-4
Steam Engine Company No. 2—*hist pl* KY-4
Steam Engine Company No. 20—*hist pl* KY-4
Steam Engine Company No. 21—*hist pl* KY-4
Steam Engine Company No. 22—*hist pl* KY-4
Steam Engine Company No. 3—*hist pl* KY-4
Steam Engine Company No.4—*hist pl* KY-4
Steam Engine Company No. 7—*hist pl* KY-4
Steamer Bay—*bay* AK-9
Steamer Knoll—*summit* AK-9
Steamer Point—*cape* AK-9
Steamer Point Light—*locale* AK-9
Steamer Rocks—*area* AK-9
Steam Furnace Cem—*cemetery* OH-6
Steam Geyser—*geyser* NV-8
Steamhaul Lake—*lake* MN-6
Steam Hole Ridge—*ridge* NC-3
Steam Hollow—*valley* VA-3
Steaming Bluff—*cliff* HI-9
Steaming Cone—*summit* HI-9
Steam Island—*island* LA-4
Steam Lake—*lake* MN-6
Steam Mill—*locale* GA-3
Steam Mill Bend—*bend* KY-4
Steam Mill Branch—*stream* AR-4
Steammill Branch—*stream* KY-4
Steam Mill Branch—*stream* KY-4
Steammill Branch—*stream* MS-4
Steam Mill Branch—*stream* NY-2
Steam Mill Branch—*stream* PA-2
Steam Mill Brook—*stream* MA-1
Steam Mill Brook—*stream* NH-1
Steam Mill Brook—*stream* VT-1
Steam Mill Canyon—*valley* UT-8
Steam Mill (CCD)—*cens area* GA-3
Steam Mill Ch—*church* MS-4
Steam Mill Creek—*stream* GA-3
Steam Mill Creek—*stream* PA-2
Steam Mill Creek—*stream* TX-5
Steam Mill Hollow—*valley* MS-4
Steam Mill Hollow—*valley* (3) MO-7
Steam Mill Hollow—*valley* (4) TN-4
Steam Mill Hollow—*valley* WV-2
Steam Mill Lake—*lake* UT-8
Steam Mill Landing—*locale* AL-4
Steam Mill Peak—*summit* UT-8
Steam Mill Pond—*lake* NY-2
Steam Mill Run—*stream* PA-2
Steam Mill Sch (abandoned)—*school* PA-2
Steam Mill Swamp—*swamp* PA-2
Steam Mill Trail—*trail* PA-2
Steam Plant Cove—*cave* AL-4
Steam Plant Road Industrial Area—*locale* TN-4
Steamport Hill—*summit* KY-4
Steamport Landing—*locale* KY-4
Steampot Creek—*stream* OR-9
Steampot Saddle—*gap* OR-9
*Steam Pump* AZ-5
Steam Pump Dam—*dam* PA-2
Steam Pump Ranch—*locale* AZ-5
*Steam Pump Village* AZ-5
Steam Pump Well—*locale* NM-5
Steam Sawmill Hill—*summit* NY-2
*Steamship Beach* MH-9
*Steamship Point* MH-9
Steamship Rock—*pillar* WY-8
Steamship TENNESSEE Remains—*hist pl* CA-9
Steam Shovel Draw—*valley* WY-8
Steam Shovel Hill—*summit* WA-9
Steam Shovel Mtn—*summit* TX-5
Steamtown—*locale* OH-6
Steamtown Creek—*stream* NY-2
Steam Valley—*locale* PA-2
**Steam Valley**—*pop pl* NY-2
*Steam Valley Branch* PA-2
Steam Valley Ch—*church* PA-2
Steam Valley Run—*stream* (2) PA-2
Steam Well—*well* CA-9
Steam Well—*well* NM-5
Steam Wells—*well* NV-8
Steamy Gap—*gap* GA-3
Stean Cem—*cemetery* TX-5
*Stean Creek* MO-7
Ste. Anne Roman Catholic Church Complex—*hist pl* MI-6
Steans Creek—*stream* UT-8
*Steans Island* AL-4
*Stearleys* IN-6
**Stearleyville**—*pop pl* IN-6
Stearman Elem Sch—*school* KS-7
Stearn Cem—*cemetery* OR-9
Stearnes—*locale* VA-3
Stearns—*locale* NC-3
Stearns—*locale* OR-9
Stearns—*locale* WI-6
**Stearns**—*pop pl* KY-4
Stearns, C. S., House—*hist pl* IA-7
Stearns, Edward R., House—*hist pl* OH-6
Stearns, Frederick, Bldg—*hist pl* MI-6
Stearns, Frederick K., House—*hist pl* MI-6
Stearns, Lyman, Farm—*hist pl* OH-6
Stearns, R. H., House—*hist pl* MA-1
Stearns, William, House—*hist pl* OH-6
Stearns Administrative and Commercial District—*hist pl* KY-4
Stearns Bayou—*bay* MI-6
Stearns Bldg—*hist pl* MA-1
Stearns Bluff—*cliff* WA-9
*Stearns Branch* GA-3
Stearns Brook—*stream* ME-1
Stearns Brook—*stream* NH-1
Stearns Brook—*stream* VT-1
Stearns Butte—*summit* OR-9
*Stearns Camp* NH-1
Stearns Cem—*cemetery* AR-4
Stearns Cem—*cemetery* (3) IL-6
Stearns Cem—*cemetery* ME-1

Steep Creek—stream (5) ... OR-9
Steep Creek—stream ... TX-5
Steep Creek—stream ... UT-8
Steep Creek—stream (2) ... WA-9
Steep Creek—stream (2) ... WY-8
Steep Creek Bench—bench ... UT-8
Steep Creek Ch—church ... AL-4
Steep Creek Lake—lake ... UT-8
Steep Creek Sch—school ... AL-4
Steep Cut Creek—stream ... AR-4
Steep Draw—valley ... TX-5
Steeper Creek ... UT-8
**Steep Falls**—pop pl ... ME-1
Steep Gap—valley ... OH-6
Steep Gulch ... CA-9
Steep Gulch—valley ... AK-9
Steep Gulch—valley ... CA-9
Steep Gulch—valley (3) ... ID-8
Steep Gully—valley ... AR-4
Steep Gully—valley (2) ... LA-4
Steep Gully—valley ... TX-5
Steep Gully Branch—stream ... LA-4
Steep Gut Bayou—gut ... AR-4
**Steep Gut Hollow**—pop pl ... WV-2
Steep Gut Hollow—valley ... TN-4
Steepgut Hollow—valley ... WV-2
Steep Gutter Brook—stream ... MA-1
Steep Head—stream ... FL-3
Steep Head—valley (3) ... FL-3
Steep Head Branch—stream (3) ... FL-3
Steephead Creek ... AL-4
Steep Head Creek—stream ... AL-4
Steephill—hist pl ... VA-3
Steep Hill—summit ... MA-1
Steep Hill Branch—stream ... GA-3
Steep Hill Branch—stream ... NC-3
Steep Hill Brook—stream ... MA-1
Steep Hill Canyon—valley ... CA-9
Steep Hill Cem—cemetery ... AR-4
Steep Hill Ch—church ... GA-3
Steep Hill Creek—stream ... LA-4
Steep Hill Creek—stream ... MS-4
Steep Hollow—locale ... TX-5
Steep Hollow—valley ... AL-4
Steep Hollow—valley ... AR-4
Steep Hollow—valley (3) ... CA-9
Steep Hollow—valley (3) ... KY-4
Steep Hollow—valley ... MS-4
Steep Hollow—valley ... MO-7
Steep Hollow—valley ... NM-5
Steep Hollow—valley ... OH-6
Steep Hollow—valley (3) ... TN-4
Steep Hollow—valley (2) ... TX-5
Steep Hollow—valley ... UT-8
Steep Hollow—valley ... VA-3
Steep Hollow Baptist Church ... MS-4
Steep Hollow Branch—stream ... AL-4
Steep Hollow Branch—stream ... KY-4
Steep Hollow Branch—stream ... TN-4
Steep Hollow Branch—stream (3) ... TX-5
Steep Hollow Cem—cemetery ... IN-6
Steep Hollow Cem—cemetery ... MS-4
Steep Hollow Ch—church ... MS-4
Steephollow Creek—stream ... CA-9
Steep Hollow Hill—summit ... FL-3
Steep Hollow Sch (historical)—school ... MS-4
Steep Hollow Tank—reservoir ... NM-5
Steep Island—island ... AK-9
Steep Lake—lake ... MN-6
Steep Landing—locale ... ME-1
**Steeple**—pop pl ... NC-3
Steeple Canyon—valley ... AZ-5
Steeple Canyon—valley ... NM-5
Steeplechase—post sta ... TX-5
**Steeple Chase Farms**—pop pl ... TN-4
Steeplechase Pier—locale ... NJ-2
Steeplechase Pier—locale ... NY-2
**Steeplechase (subdivision)**—pop pl (2) ... AZ-5
Steeple Creek—stream ... AZ-5
Steeplehollow Crossing—locale ... CA-9
Steeple Island ... MP-9
Steeple Mesa—summit ... AZ-5
Steeple Mesa Seventy-Three Trail—trail ... AZ-5
Steeple Pasture—flat ... WY-8
Steeple Peak—summit ... AK-9
Steeple Point—cape ... AK-9
Steeple Ranch—locale ... NM-5
Steeple Rock ... CA-9
Steeple Rock—pillar ... OR-9
Steeple Rock—pillar ... WA-9
Steeple Rock—summit ... NM-5
Steeple Rock Canyon—valley ... NM-5
**Steeple Run**—pop pl ... IL-6
Steeple Sch—school ... MA-1
Steeple Sch—school ... MI-6
Steepleton Branch—stream ... TX-5
Steepletop—hist pl ... NY-2
Steeple U Ranch—locale ... NM-5
Steeple U Tank—reservoir ... NM-5
**Steeple View Subdivision**—pop pl ... UT-8
Steep Mile Creek—stream ... TX-5
Steep Mound Site (22LK26)—hist pl ... MS-4
Steep Mtn—summit (2) ... CO-8
Steep Mtn—summit ... MT-8
Steep Mtn—summit ... UT-8
Steep Pinch Ridge—ridge ... VA-3
**Steep Pines Fork**—pop pl ... NC-3
Steep Point—cape (2) ... AK-9
Steep Point—cape (2) ... NC-3
Steep Point—cape ... WA-9
Steep Point Channel—channel ... NC-3
Steep Ravine Canyon—valley ... CA-9
Steep Rock—summit ... CT-1
Steep Rock Hill—summit ... MA-1
Steeprock Island—island ... MN-6
Steep Rock Mtn—summit ... NC-3
Steep Run—stream ... IN-6
Steep Run—stream ... MD-2
Steep Run—stream ... NJ-2
Steep Run—stream ... NC-3
Steep Run—stream ... OH-6
Steep Run—stream ... PA-2
Steeps, The—cliff ... UT-8
Steep Shoals Creek—stream ... AR-4
Steep Slope Spring—spring ... OR-9
Steep Spring—spring ... OR-9
Steep Tank—reservoir (2) ... AZ-5
Steepto ... MP-9
Steep-to Island ... MP-9
Steep Trail Creek—stream ... CA-9
Steepy Mtn—summit ... CO-8
Steer, Lake—lake ... FL-3
Steerage Rock—summit ... MA-1
Steer Basin—basin ... ID-8
Steer Basin Campground—locale ... ID-8
Steer Branch—stream ... NC-3
Steer Branch—stream ... VA-3
Steer Brook ... PA-2
Steer Canyon—valley ... NV-8
Steer Canyon—valley ... OR-9
Steer Canyon—valley ... TX-5
Steer Canyon—valley (2) ... UT-8
Steer Coulee—valley ... MT-8
Steer Creek—stream (2) ... CA-9
Steer Creek—stream ... CO-8
Steer Creek—stream ... IL-6
Steer Creek—stream ... IA-7
Steer Creek—stream ... KY-4
Steer Creek—stream ... MN-6
Steer Creek—stream ... MO-7
Steer Creek—stream ... NE-7
Steer Creek—stream (3) ... OR-9
Steer Creek—stream ... TN-4
Steer Creek—stream ... WV-2
Steer Creek—stream (2) ... WY-8
Steer Creek Camp—locale ... NE-7
Steer Creek Trail—trail ... CA-9
Steer Dam—dam ... AZ-5
Steerdown Branch—stream ... TN-4
Steer Draw—valley ... WY-8
Steere Creek ... OR-9
Steere Hill—summit ... RI-1
Steere Island—island ... NY-2
Steere Sch—school ... LA-4
Steeres Pond—reservoir ... RI-1
Steer Flat—flat ... NV-8
Steer Fork ... SC-3
Steer Fork—stream (3) ... KY-4
Steer Fork—stream ... WV-2
Steer Gulch—valley (3) ... UT-8
Steer Hollow—valley ... TN-4
Steer Hollow—valley ... UT-8
Steer Hollow—valley ... WV-2
Steer Island—island ... NC-3
Steer Island—island ... WV-2
Steer Knob—summit ... VA-3
Steer Lake—lake ... CO-8
Steer Lake—lake ... MN-6
Steer Lake—lake ... MT-8
Steer Lake—lake ... NV-8
Steerlick Run—stream ... WV-2
Steer Meadow—swamp ... MT-8
Steer Mesa—summit ... UT-8
Steer Mesa Tank—reservoir ... NM-5
Steer Mtn—summit ... AZ-5
Steer Pasture—flat ... KS-7
Steer Pasture Canyon—valley ... UT-8
Steer Pasture Spring—spring ... AZ-5
Steer Pasture Tank—reservoir (4) ... AZ-5
Steer Pasture Tank—reservoir ... NM-5
Steer Pasture Well—well ... AZ-5
Steer Pen Slough—lake ... FL-3
Steer Point—cape ... UT-8
Steer Pond—lake ... NY-2
Steer Ridge—ridge ... AZ-5
Steer Ridge—ridge (4) ... UT-8
Steer Ridge Bottom—flat ... UT-8
Steer Ridge Canyon—valley ... UT-8
Steer Ridge Rapids—rapids ... UT-8
Steer Ridge Rsvr—reservoir ... OR-9
Steer Run—stream (2) ... PA-2
Steer Run—stream (2) ... WV-2
Steer Run Ch—church ... WV-2
Steers ... IN-6
Steers Canyon—valley (2) ... OR-9
Steers Creek ... OR-9
Steers Gulch—valley ... CO-8
Steers Millpond—reservoir ... VA-3
Steers Mine—mine ... AK-9
Steer Spring—spring ... AZ-5
Steer Spring—spring ... UT-8
Steer Spring Canyon—valley (2) ... AZ-5
Steer Springs—spring ... AZ-5
Steer Springs Canyon—valley ... AZ-5
Steers Stadium—other ... TX-5
Steer Stall Hollow—valley ... MO-7
Steer Tank—reservoir (4) ... AZ-5
Steer Tank—reservoir ... TX-5
Steer Unit Tank—reservoir ... AZ-5
Steer Unit Twenty Three Tank ... AZ-5
Steer Wells—well ... TX-5
Steer Windmill—locale (2) ... TX-5
Steese—post sta ... AK-9
Steestachee Bald—summit ... NC-3
Steestachee Branch—stream ... NC-3
Steet Canyon—valley ... OR-9
Steet Mtn—summit ... OR-9
Steets Ledge—bar ... ME-1
Steever Park—park ... KS-7
Steeves Ranch—locale ... MT-8
Steezers Farm—locale ... AL-4
Stefan Gollob Park—park ... AZ-5
Stefanik Airp—airport ... PA-2
Stefanik Sch—school ... MA-1
Stefan Park—park ... IA-7
Steffan Creek ... WA-9
Steffan Manor Sch—school ... CA-9
Steffee Elementary School ... PA-2
Steffee Sch—school ... PA-2
Steffel Ditch—canal ... IN-6
Steffen Bridge—bridge ... MO-7
Steffen Brothers Rsvr—reservoir ... WA-9
Steffen Creek—stream ... WA-9
Steffen Hill—summit ... WY-8
Steffen Oil Field—oilfield ... KS-7
Steffen Point—cape ... WI-6
Steffens, Ephraim, House—hist pl ... MN-6
Steffens, Joseph, House—hist pl ... IL-6
Steffens Creek ... WA-9
Steffens-Drewa House Complex—hist pl ... TX-5
**Steffensen Heights Subdivision**—pop pl ... UT-8
Steffens Hill—summit ... PA-2
**Steffenville**—pop pl ... MO-7
Steffen West Oil Field—oilfield ... KS-7
Steffey Cem—cemetery (2) ... VA-3
Steffey Sch (abandoned)—school ... PA-2
**Steff (Goffs)**—pop pl ... KY-4
Steffin Meadow—flat ... OR-9
**Steffins Hill**—pop pl ... PA-2
Steff (RR name for Gray)—other ... KY-4
Steffy Cem—cemetery ... VA-3
Steffy Chapel—church ... PA-2
Steffy Ditch—canal ... IN-6
Stefko Blvd Shop Ctr—locale ... PA-2
Stefonic Ranch—locale ... MT-8
Stegall—locale ... LA-4
Stegall—locale ... TN-4
Stegall—locale ... TX-5
**Stegall**—pop pl ... AR-4
**Stegall**—pop pl ... NE-7
Stegall Branch—stream ... NC-3
Stegall Cem—cemetery ... TN-4
Stegall Church ... MS-4
Stegall General Store—hist pl ... AR-4
Stegall Lake—reservoir ... NC-3
Stegall Lake Dam—dam ... NC-3
Stegall Mtn ... MO-7
Stegall Mtn—summit ... MO-7
Stegall Post Office (historical)—building ... TN-4
Stegall Ranch—locale ... TX-5
Stegalls Mill Creek ... MS-4
Stegal Tank—reservoir ... AZ-5
Stegar Bluff—cliff ... KY-4
Stegar Hollow—valley ... IA-7
Stege—locale ... CA-9
Stegell Station ... LA-4
Stegeman—locale ... CA-9
Stegeman Canyon—valley ... WA-9
Stegeman Creek ... MI-6
**Ste. Genevieve**—pop pl ... MO-7
**Ste Genevieve**—pop pl ... MO-7
Ste. Genevieve (County)—civil ... MO-7
Ste. Genevieve Hist Dist—hist pl ... MO-7
Ste. Genevieve (Township of)—fmr MCD ... MO-7
**Steger**—pop pl ... IL-6
Steger Cem—cemetery ... KY-4
Steger House—hist pl ... AL-4
Stegers Creek—stream ... VA-3
Stegers Store—locale ... AL-4
Stegerwald, Andrew, House—hist pl ... WA-9
Stege Sch—school ... CA-9
Stegmaier Brewery—hist pl ... PA-2
Stegman Creek—stream ... MI-6
Stegmiller Mine—mine ... MI-6
**Stehekin**—pop pl ... WA-9
Stehekin (CCD)—cens area ... WA-9
Stehekin River—stream ... WA-9
Stehekin Sch—hist pl ... WA-9
Stehekin State Airp—airport ... WA-9
Stehle Oil Field—oilfield ... TX-5
Stehli Beach—beach ... NY-2
Stehl Tank—reservoir ... TX-5
Stehman Ch—church ... PA-2
Stehman Run—stream ... PA-2
Stehr Lake—reservoir ... AZ-5
Stehr Lake Dam—dam ... AZ-5
Stehr Tank—reservoir ... AZ-5
**Steiber Township**—pop pl ... ND-7
Steichen Sch Number 3 (historical)—school ... SD-7
Steichens Ponds—lake ... CT-1
Steidley Branch—stream ... IL-6
Steie Ranch—locale ... MT-8
Steifer Mine—mine ... CA-9
Steig Coulee—valley ... WI-6
Steigelmier State Public Shooting Area—park ... SD-7
Steigel Valley Air Park—airport ... PA-2
Steiger Butte—summit ... OR-9
Steiger Creek—stream ... MT-8
Steiger Hill—summit ... CA-9
Steiger Lake—reservoir ... IN-6
Steiger Lake Dam—dam ... IN-6
Steiger Ridge—ridge ... OH-6
Steiger Spring—spring ... OR-9
Steiger Tank—reservoir ... AZ-5
Steigerwald Lake—lake ... WA-9
Steigerwalds Lake ... WA-9
Steigerwald Slough ... WA-9
Steigerwalts Sch—school ... PA-2
Steigmeyer Mill—locale ... NV-8
Steig Well ... MT-8
**Steilacoom**—pop pl ... WA-9
Steilacoom Catholic Church—hist pl ... WA-9
Steilacoom Hist Dist—hist pl ... WA-9
Steilacoom Lake—lake ... WA-9
Steilaguamish Lake ... WA-9
Steilaguamish River ... WA-9
Steimel Lake ... MI-6
Stein—locale ... LA-4
Stein, Daniel, House—hist pl ... LA-4
Stein, L. L., House—hist pl ... OK-5
Steinacher Creek—stream ... CA-9
Steinacher Lake—lake ... CA-9
Steinacher Ridge—ridge ... CA-9
Steinacker Draw ... UT-8
Steinake Lake State Rec Area ... UT-8
Steinaker Campground—park ... UT-8
Steinaker Dam—dam ... UT-8
Steinaker Ditch—canal ... UT-8
Steinaker Draw—valley ... UT-8
Steinaker Feeder Canal—canal ... UT-8
Steinaker Lake State Park ... UT-8
Steinaker Rsvr—reservoir ... UT-8
Steinaker Service Canal—canal ... UT-8
Steinaker State Park—park ... UT-8
Steinaker State Rec Area ... UT-8
**Steinauer**—pop pl ... NE-7
Steinauer Opera House—hist pl ... NE-7
Steinbach Canyon—valley ... CA-9
Steinbach-Cookman Bldg—hist pl ... NJ-2
Steinbach Ranch—locale ... MT-8
Steinbachs Corners—locale ... PA-2
Steinback Canyon—valley ... CA-9
Steinbarger Lake—lake ... IN-6
**Steinbarger Lake**—pop pl ... IN-6
Stein Basin—basin ... OR-9
Steinbauer Lake—swamp ... MI-6
Steinbaugh Cem—cemetery ... KY-4
Steinbaugh Windmill—locale ... NM-5
Steinbeck—post sta ... CA-9
Steinbeck Bend—bend ... TX-5
**Steinbeck Corners**—pop pl ... NY-2
Steinberg Cem—cemetery ... IN-6
Steinbergen Creek ... CA-9
Steinbergen Ranch—locale ... CO-8
Steinbergen Slough ... CA-9
Steinbergens Slough ... CA-9
Steinberger Creek ... CA-9
Steinberger Slough—gut ... CA-9
Steinberg Ridge—ridge ... OR-9
Stein Branch—stream ... KY-4
Stein Branch—stream ... NC-3
Stein Branch—stream (2) ... TX-5
Steinbrink Drain—stream ... MI-6
Stein Brothers Bldg—hist pl ... NE-7
Stein Butte—summit ... OR-9
Stein Canyon—valley ... NM-5
Stein Cem—cemetery ... IL-6
Stein Creek—stream ... CA-9
Stein Creek—stream ... IA-7
Steindam House—hist pl ... OH-6
Stein Ditch—canal ... IN-6
Steindler Sch—school ... IL-6
**Steindorf School**—pop pl ... CA-9
Stein Drain—canal ... MI-6
Steinegger Lodging House—hist pl ... AZ-5
**Steiner**—pop pl ... AL-4
**Steiner**—pop pl ... MI-6
**Steiner**—pop pl ... MS-4
Steiner, John, Store—hist pl ... WI-6
Steiner Bank Bldg—hist pl ... AL-4
Steiner Bend—bend ... CA-9
Steiner Branch ... GA-3
Steiner Branch—stream ... GA-3
Steiner Branch—stream ... WI-6
Steiner Canal—canal ... LA-4
Steiner Canyon—valley ... CA-9
Steiner Cem—cemetery ... GA-3
Steiner Ch—church ... TX-5
Steiner Community Hall—locale ... MN-6
Steiner Creek—stream ... CA-9
Steiner Creek—stream ... NV-8
Steiner Dam—dam ... ND-7
Steiner Drain—canal ... CA-9
Steiner Flat—flat ... CA-9
Steiner Grove Ch—church ... GA-3
Steiner Lake—reservoir ... AL-4
Steiner Lake—reservoir ... IL-6
Steiner Lake Dam—dam ... AL-4
Steiner Lateral—canal ... CA-9
Steiner-Lobman and Teague Hardware Buildings—hist pl ... AL-4
Steiner Post Office (historical)—building ... MS-4
Steiner Ranch—locale ... CO-8
Steiner Ranch—locale ... NV-8
Steiners Canyon—valley ... WA-9
Steiner Sch—school ... NM-5
Steiners Fishing Camp—locale ... TN-4
Steiners Flat ... CA-9
Steiners Lake ... MN-6
Steiners Landing—locale ... AL-4
Steiner Spring—spring ... NV-8
Steiners Ranch ... CA-9
Steiners Sch—school ... PA-2
Steiners Skyview Lake Dam ... AL-4
Steiners Store (historical)—locale ... AL-4
**Steinersville**—pop pl ... OH-6
Steinersville Park ... OH-6
Steiners Wharf—locale ... MD-2
**Steiner Township**—pop pl ... ND-7
Steinerts Lake—lake ... MN-6
Steiner Valley—bend ... TX-5
Steiner Valley Cem—cemetery ... TX-5
Steiner Valley Park—park ... TX-5
Steinerville ... CA-9
Stein Falls—falls ... OR-9
Stein Gulch—valley ... CA-9
Stein Gulch—valley ... ID-8
Stein Gulch—valley (2) ... OR-9
Steinhagen Ch—church ... MO-7
Steinham Store ... GA-3
Steinhart Park—park ... NE-7
**Steinhatchee**—pop pl ... FL-3
Steinhatchee Cem—cemetery ... FL-3
Steinhatchee Elem Sch—school ... FL-3
Steinhatchee River—stream ... FL-3
Steinhatchee Spring—spring ... FL-3
Steinhatchee Wildlife Mngmt Area—park ... FL-3
Steinhauer Branch—stream ... MO-7
Steinhauer Creek—stream ... OR-9
Steinhauer Dam—dam ... PA-2
Steinhauser Gut—gut ... MD-2
Steinhauser Park—park ... MI-6
Steinheim, Alfred, Museum—hist pl ... NY-2
Steinhilber Creek—stream ... OR-9
Steinhilber Rsvr—reservoir ... MT-8
Steinhoff Oil Field—oilfield ... KS-7
Steinhopper Hollow—valley ... PA-2
Steinige ... MP-9
Stein Island ... AL-4
Steinke, Max, Barn—hist pl ... WA-9
Steinke Creek—stream ... WI-6
Steinke Ditch—canal ... IN-6
Steinke Pond—lake ... WI-6
Steinke Valley—valley ... WI-6
Stein Lake—lake ... MN-6
Stein Lake—lake ... ND-7
Steinle Ranch—locale (2) ... WY-8
Steinman—locale ... OR-9
Steinman—locale ... VA-3
Steinman Creek—stream ... OR-9
Steinman Hardware Store—hist pl ... PA-2
Steinman Hollow—valley ... TX-5
Steinmeir Estates ... IN-6
Steinmetz—locale ... MO-7
Steinmetz Bridge—bridge ... WA-9
Steinmetz Ch—church ... PA-2
Steinmetz Creek—stream ... OR-9
Steinmetz HS—school ... IL-6
Steinmetz Park—park ... NY-2
Steinmetz Sch (historical)—school ... PA-2
Steinmeyer, William, House—hist pl ... WI-6
Steinmeyer Cem—cemetery ... IA-7
Stein Mine—mine ... MN-6
Stein Mtn—summit (2) ... ID-8
Stein Mtn—summit ... PA-2
Steinnon Creek—stream ... OR-9
Stein Playground—park ... MI-6
Steinrich Ch—church ... KS-7
Steins—locale ... NM-5
Steins—locale ... PA-2
Steins, Jacob, House—hist pl ... MO-7
**Steinsburg**—pop pl ... PA-2
Stein Sch—school ... IL-6
Steins Corner ... PA-2
Steins Creek—stream ... MO-7
Steins Creek—stream ... NM-5
Steinshouer Branch—stream ... MO-7
Steins Island—island ... AL-4
Steins Mountain ... OR-9
Steins Mtn—summit ... NM-5
Steins Peak—summit ... NM-5
Steins Pillar—pillar ... OR-9
Steins Street District—hist pl ... MO-7
**Stein Subdivision**—pop pl ... UT-8
Steinsville—locale ... PA-2
Stein Swamp—swamp ... PA-2
Steinthal—locale ... WI-6
**Steinway**—pop pl ... NY-2
Steinway Creek—stream ... NY-2
Steinway House—hist pl ... NY-2
Steiny Hill—summit ... NY-2
**Steirman**—pop pl ... ID-8
Steiwer Hill—summit ... OR-9
Steiwer Peaks—summit ... OR-9
Stekel Rsvr—reservoir ... OR-9
**Stekey**—pop pl ... LA-4
Stekey Creek ... TN-4
Stekl Sch (abandoned)—school ... SD-7
Stekoa Creek—stream ... GA-3
Stekoah ... NC-3
**Stekoll Camp**—pop pl ... TX-5
Stel, Lake—reservoir ... NC-3
Stelbar Grizzly Creek Ranch—locale ... CO-8
Stelbars Connor Ranch—locale ... CO-8
**Stelbars Lindland**—pop pl ... CO-8
Stelbars Michigan River Ranch—locale ... CO-8
St. Elena Patent—mine ... NV-8
Steliko Canyon—valley ... WA-9
St. Elizabeth ... ND-7
St Elizabeths Cem—cemetery ... NE-7
St. Elizabeth's Church—hist pl ... CO-8
St. Elizabeth's Magyar Roman Catholic Church—hist pl ... OH-6
St. Elizabeth's Retreat Chapel—hist pl ... CO-8
Stella—CDP ... PR-3
Stella—locale (2) ... KY-4
Stella—locale ... MS-4
Stella—locale ... OH-6
Stella—locale ... OK-5
Stella—locale ... VA-3
Stella—locale ... WA-9
**Stella**—pop pl ... AR-4
**Stella**—pop pl ... FL-3
**Stella**—pop pl ... LA-4
**Stella**—pop pl ... MO-7
**Stella**—pop pl ... NE-7
**Stella**—pop pl ... NY-2
**Stella**—pop pl ... NC-3
**Stella**—pop pl ... TN-4
Stella—uninc pl ... TX-5
Stella, Lake—lake ... FL-3
Stella, Lake—lake ... MI-6
Stella, Lake—lake (2) ... MN-6
Stella, Mount—summit ... OR-9
Stella Blacksmith Shop—hist pl ... WA-9
Stella Bridge—bridge ... NC-3
Stella Canal—canal ... LA-4
Stella Cem—cemetery ... NE-7
Stella Cem—cemetery ... OK-5
Stella Cem—cemetery ... TN-4
Stella Ch—church ... VA-3
Stella Creek—stream (2) ... AK-9
Stella Creek—stream ... ID-8
Stella Creek—stream ... MT-8
Stella Creek—stream ... WI-6
Stella Dam—dam ... MT-8
Stella Ditch—canal ... CO-8
Stellafane Observatory—hist pl ... VT-1
Stella Friends Academy Cem—cemetery ... OK-5
Stella (historical)—locale ... KS-7
Stella Lake ... WI-6
Stella Lake—lake ... CA-9
Stella Lake—lake ... FL-3
Stella Lake—lake ... NV-8
Stella Lake—lake ... ND-7
Stella Lake—lake (2) ... WI-6
Stella Lake—swamp ... GA-3
Stella Landing—locale (2) ... MS-4
Stellamaris, Lake—reservoir ... KS-7
Stella Maris Ch—church ... SC-3
Stella Maris Chapel—church ... MN-6
Stella Maris Convent—school ... ME-1
Stella Maris Hospice—hospital ... MD-2
Stella Maris Sch ... PA-2
Stella Mine—mine ... MT-8
Stella Mtn—summit ... CO-8
**Stella Niagara**—pop pl ... NY-2
Stella Niagara Seminary—school ... NY-2
Stella Oil and Gas Field—oilfield ... LA-4
Stella Plantation (historical)—locale ... MS-4
Stellar—locale ... TX-5
Stellar, Mount—summit ... AK-9
Stellar Airpark—airport ... AZ-5
Stella Range—channel ... OR-9
Stella Range—channel ... WA-9
Stellar Creek—stream ... AK-9
Stellar Creek—stream ... MT-8
Stellaria Creek—stream ... WY-8
Stellar Lake—reservoir ... MT-8
Stella RR Station—locale ... FL-3
Stella Ruth Community Center—locale ... TN-4
Stella Ruth Sch (historical)—school ... TN-4
Stella Sch—school ... WI-6
Stella Sch (historical)—school ... TN-4
**Stella (Town of)**—pop pl ... WI-6
Stellaville—locale ... NY-2
**Stellaville**—pop pl ... GA-3
Stell Branch—stream ... TN-4
Stell Creek—stream ... OR-9
**Stelle**—pop pl ... IL-6
Stelle Cemeteries—cemetery ... KY-4
Stelle Hollow ... CO-8
Steller, Mount—summit ... AK-9
Steller Cove—bay ... AK-9
Steller Glacier—glacier ... AK-9
Steller River—stream ... AK-9
Stelley Tabernacle—church ... NC-3
Stellhorn Bridge—bridge ... IN-6
Stelljes House—hist pl ... NH-1
Stell Lake—reservoir ... CO-8
Stell-Lind Banco Number 128—levee ... TX-5
Stellnaker Lake ... WI-6
Stellner Coulee—valley ... MT-8
Stellrecht Point—cape ... FL-3
**Stelltown**—pop pl ... AR-4
Stellwagen Ledges—bar ... MA-1
Stell wagen Rock—rock ... MA-1
Stellwagen Sch—school ... MI-6
Stellwagon Draw—valley ... WY-8
St. Elmo Hist Dist—hist pl ... CO-8
Stels Pond ... DE-2
Stelter Ditch—canal ... IN-6
Stelters Ranch—locale ... AK-9
Stelting Ridge—ridge ... WI-6
**Stelton**—pop pl ... NJ-2
**Stelvideo**—pop pl ... OH-6
Stelvideo Cem—cemetery ... OH-6
**Stem**—pop pl ... NC-3
Ste Marie ... IL-6
**Ste Marie**—pop pl ... IL-6
Ste Marie Public Use Area—park ... AR-4
**Stem Beach**—pop pl ... CO-8
Stember Creek—stream ... WA-9
Stembersville ... PA-2
Stem Branch—stream ... TX-5
Stem Cem—cemetery ... TN-4
Stemeni Ford (historical)—locale ... AL-4
Stemilt Basin—basin ... WA-9
Stemilt Creek—stream ... WA-9
Stemilt Hill—summit ... WA-9
Stemilt Hill Cem—cemetery ... WA-9
Stemilt Project Rsvr—reservoir ... WA-9
Steminis Ferry ... AL-4
Steminis Ford ... AL-4
Stem Lake—lake ... MN-6
Stemler Basin—basin ... OR-9
Stemler Cave—cave ... IL-6
Stemler Draw—valley ... WY-8
Stemler Ridge—ridge ... OR-9
Stemler Ridge Rsvr—reservoir ... OR-9
Stemlersville—locale ... PA-2
Stemlerville ... PA-2
Stemley—locale ... AL-4
Stemley Baptist Ch—church ... AL-4
Stemley Bridge (historical)—bridge ... AL-4
**Stemley Cove**—pop pl ... AL-4
Stemley Rock Ch—church ... AL-4
Stemleyton ... AL-4
Stemley United Methodist Ch ... AL-4
Stemly ... AL-4
**Stemm**—pop pl ... IN-6
Stemmer, J. C., House—hist pl ... IA-7
Stemmer Ditch—canal ... CO-8
Stemmer Lake—lake ... MN-6
Stemmer Run ... MD-2
**Stemmers Run**—pop pl ... MD-2
**Stemmer's Run**—pop pl ... MD-2
Stemmers Run—stream ... MD-2
Stemmers Run JHS—school ... MD-2
Stemons Cem—cemetery ... MO-7
**Stemper**—pop pl ... FL-3
Stemper, Lake—lake ... FL-3
Stemphleytown—locale ... VA-3
**Stemple**—pop pl ... MT-8
**Stemple**—pop pl ... OH-6
Stemple Canyon—valley ... CA-9
Stemple Creek ... CA-9
Stemple Creek—stream ... CA-9
Stemple Creek—stream ... MT-8
Stemple Pass—gap ... MT-8
Stemple Ridge—ridge ... WV-2
Stemple Ridge Ch—church ... WV-2
Stemple Ridge Sch—school ... WV-2
Stemple Sch—school ... IA-7
Stem Pond—reservoir ... VA-3
Stemp Spring—spring ... WY-8
Stemp Spring Gulch—valley ... WY-8
Stem Run—stream ... IN-6
Stems—locale ... AL-4
Stems Store ... TN-4
Stemwinder Hill—summit ... MT-8
Stemwinder Minne—mine ... CO-8
Sten, Lake—lake ... FL-3
**Stena Township**—pop pl ... SD-7
Stencer Ridge—ridge ... MO-7
**Stendal**—pop pl ... IN-6
Stender Cem—cemetery ... WV-2
Stender Sch—school ... NE-7
Stendorf Sch—school ... CA-9
Stener Mine—mine ... NV-8
Stenerson Lake—lake ... MN-6
Stenerson Mtn—summit ... MT-8
Stengel, John S., House—hist pl ... OH-6
Stenger—locale ... PA-2
Stenger Hill—summit ... KS-7
Stengle Cem—cemetery ... MI-6
Stenis Cem—cemetery ... MS-4
Stenkil ... DE-2
Stenlund Lake—lake ... MN-6
Stenner Creek—stream ... CA-9
Stennett—locale ... IA-7
Stennett Butte—summit ... OR-9
Stennett Junction ... SD-7
Stennick Cem—cemetery ... AR-4
Stennis International Airp—airport ... MS-4
Stennitt Creek—stream ... AR-4
Stensgar Creek—stream ... WA-9
Stensgar Mtn—summit ... WA-9
Stenso Cem—cemetery ... ND-7
Stenson Creek ... WI-6
Stenson Lake—lake ... WI-6
Stenson Mine—mine ... NM-5
Stenson Sch—school ... IL-6
Stenson Sch (historical)—school ... AL-4
Stenstrom Sch (abandoned)—school ... PA-2
Stensvad Oil Field—oilfield ... MT-8
Stensven Coulee—valley ... WI-6
**Stent**—pop pl ... CA-9
Stenton—hist pl ... PA-2
Stenton—uninc pl ... PA-2
Stenton Child Center—building ... PA-2
Stenton Park—park ... PA-2
Stentz Spring—locale ... WA-9
Stentz Spring—spring ... WA-9
Stenulson Coulee—valley ... WI-6
Stenwood Sch—school ... VA-3
Step, The—ridge ... UT-8
Stepanek Crossing—locale ... MO-7
Stepan Lake—lake ... AK-9
Stepanof Cove—bay ... AK-9
Stepanof Flats—flat ... AK-9
Step Canyon—valley ... UT-8
Step Church Cem—cemetery ... OH-6
Step Creek—stream ... AK-9
Step Creek—stream ... ID-8
Step Creek—stream (2) ... OR-9

Step Creek—stream PA-2
Stepens Spring OR-9
Step Flats—flat UT-8
Step Gap—gap TN-4
Step Gulch—valley AK-9
**Stephan**—pop pl SD-7
Stephan, Louis, House—hist pl ID-8
Stephan Drive Ch—church KY-4
Stephan F Austin Sch—school TX-5
Stephan Foster Memorial—building PA-2
**Stephanie Estates Subdivision**—pop pl UT-8
Stephanie Lake—lake IL-6
Stephan Lake—lake AK-9
Stephan Mission Dam—dam SD-7
Stephan Post Office (historical)—building SD-7
Stephan Reef—bar PW-9
Stephan Rural School SD-7
Stephans Bridge—other MI-6
Stephan Sch—school SD-7
Stephans Pond—reservoir GA-3
Stephansville School MS-4
Stephany Ridge—ridge TN-4
Stephen—locale MS-4
**Stephen**—pop pl MN-6
Stephen, Adam, House—hist pl WV-2
Stephen A Forbes State Park—park IL-6
Stephen Aisle—gap AZ-5
Stephen AME Ch—church AL-4
Stephen Brook MA-1
Stephen Butte—summit AZ-5
Stephen Cem—cemetery VA-3
Stephen Chapel—church GA-3
Stephen Chapel—church TN-4
Stephen Chapel—church TX-5
Stephen Chapel Ford—crossing TN-4
Stephen Chapel United Methodist Ch—church TN-4
Stephen Collins Foster Elem Sch—school IN-6
Stephen Creek—locale TX-5
Stephen Creek—stream NJ-2
Stephen Creek—stream TX-5
Stephen Decatur Elem Sch—school IN-6
Stephen Decatur HS—school IL-6
Stephen Decatur HS—school MD-2
Stephen Decatur Monmt—park MD-2
Stephen Decatur Sch—school CA-9
Stephen Decatur Sch—school PA-2
Stephen Eubanks Grant—civil FL-3
Stephen F Austin Coll—school TX-5
Stephen F. Austin College—uninc pl TX-5
Stephen F. Austin HS—school TX-5
Stephen F Austin Sch—school (5) TX-5
Stephen F. Austin State Park—park TX-5
Stephen Fernandez and other Heirs of D Fernandez Grant—civil FL-3
Stephen Fernandez Grant—civil FL-3
Stephen Foster Dam—dam PA-2
Stephen Foster Sch—school CA-9
Stephen Foster Sch—school FL-3
Stephen Foster Sch—school KY-4
Stephen Foster Sch—school PA-2
Stephen Foster Sch—school VA-3
Stephen Foster State Memorial—park FL-3
**Stephen Heights**—pop pl PA-2
Stephen (historical)—locale KS-7
Stephen Holston—post sta TN-4
Stephenhouse Run—stream PA-2
Stephen H Taft Elem Sch—school IA-7
**Stephen Knolls**—pop pl MD-2
Stephen Knolls Sch—school MD-2
Stephen Lake—reservoir NJ-2
Stephen Lake Dam—dam NJ-2
Stephen Memorial Ch AL-4
Stephen Mills Cem—cemetery GA-3
Stephen Mission Dam—dam SD-7
Stephen Park—park AZ-5
Stephen Park—park IL-6
Stephen Peak—summit WA-9
Stephen Riff PW-9
Stephens—locale GA-3
Stephens—locale KY-4
Stephens—locale OR-9
**Stephens**—pop pl AR-4
**Stephens**—pop pl (2) MO-7
**Stephens**—pop pl TN-4
**Stephens**—pop pl VA-3
Stephens—uninc pl CA-9
Stephens, A. J., House—hist pl IA-7
Stephens, Joseph L., House—hist pl KY-4
Stephens, Judge Nelson T., House—hist pl KS-7
Stephens, Lake—reservoir MS-4
Stephens, Mitchell M., House—hist pl UT-8
Stephens and Akeman Airp—airport MO-7
Stephens Bluff—cliff AL-4
Stephens Bluff—cliff TX-5
Stephens Bluff Landing (historical)—locale AL-4
Stephens Branch MS-4
Stephens Branch VT-1
Stephens Branch—stream (4) GA-3
Stephens Branch—stream (3) KY-4
Stephens Branch—stream MD-2
Stephens Branch—stream MO-7
Stephens Branch—stream NC-3
Stephens Branch—stream OK-5
Stephens Branch—stream SC-3
Stephens Branch—stream (2) TN-4
Stephens Branch—stream WV-2
Stephens Branch Sch—school KY-4
Stephens Bridge—bridge AL-4
Stephens Brook—stream NJ-2
Stephens Brook—stream NY-2
Stephens Brothers Ranch—locale CO-8
**Stephensburg**—pop pl KY-4
**Stephensburg**—pop pl NJ-2
Stephensburg Brook—stream NJ-2
Stephensburgh NJ-2
Stephensburg Lake—reservoir KY-4
**Stephensburg (Old Stephensburg)**—pop pl KY-4
Stephens Butte—summit CA-9
Stephens Campground—locale CA-9
Stephens Canyon WA-9
Stephens Canyon—valley CA-9
Stephens Canyon—valley (2) UT-8
Stephens Cem TN-4
Stephens Cem—cemetery AL-4
Stephens Cem—cemetery AR-4
Stephens Cem—cemetery FL-3
Stephens Cem—cemetery (3) GA-3
Stephens Cem—cemetery (4) IN-6
Stephens Cem—cemetery (3) KY-4
Stephens Cem—cemetery LA-4
Stephens Cem—cemetery (3) MS-4
Stephens Cem—cemetery (5) MO-7
Stephens Cem—cemetery NY-2
Stephens Cem—cemetery NC-3
Stephens Cem—cemetery OH-6
Stephens Cem—cemetery PA-2
Stephens Cem—cemetery (12) TN-4
Stephens Cem—cemetery TX-5
Stephens Cem—cemetery (3) WV-2
Stephens Ch—church AL-4
Stephens Ch—church MS-4
Stephens Ch—church MO-7
Stephens Ch—church TX-5
Stephen Sch (abandoned)—school MO-7
Stephens Chapel—church (2) GA-3
Stephens Chapel Baptist Ch—church MS-4
Stephens Chapel Post Office (historical)—building TN-4
**Stephens City**—pop pl VA-3
Stephens Coll—school MO-7
Stephens Community Hist Dist—hist pl OR-9
**Stephens (County)**—pop pl GA-3
**Stephens (County)**—pop pl OK-5
**Stephens (County)**—pop pl TX-5
Stephens County Courthouse—hist pl GA-3
Stephens County Memorial Gardens—cemetery GA-3
Stephens Creek FL-3
Stephens Creek MO-7
Stephens Creek NV-8
Stephens Creek TX-5
Stephens Creek VA-3
Stephens Creek—stream AL-4
Stephens Creek—stream AK-9
Stephens Creek—stream AR-4
Stephens Creek—stream CA-9
Stephens Creek—stream (3) GA-3
Stephens Creek—stream (3) ID-8
Stephens Creek—stream IN-6
Stephens Creek—stream KY-4
Stephens Creek—stream MN-6
Stephens Creek—stream MT-8
Stephens Creek—stream (2) NV-8
Stephens Creek—stream (2) NY-2
Stephens Creek—stream NC-3
Stephens Creek—stream OK-5
Stephens Creek—stream (2) TN-4
Stephens Creek—stream WY-8
Stephens Crossing—locale TX-5
**Stephens Crossing**—pop pl IN-6
**Stephens Crossroads**—pop pl NC-3
**Stephens Crossroads**—pop pl SC-3
Stephens Dam—dam AL-4
Stephens Dam—dam MA-1
Stephens Ditch—canal OH-6
Stephens Ferry Bridge—bridge AL-4
**Stephens First Addition (subdivision)**—pop pl UT-8
Stephens Fish Creek Ranch—locale ID-8
Stephens Forest Pond—reservoir IA-7
Stephens Forest Pond Dam—dam IA-7
Stephens Fork—stream VA-3
Stephens Fork—stream WV-2
Stephens Fort—locale VA-3
Stephens Gap—gap (2) AL-4
Stephens Gap—gap TN-4
Stephens Gap Cave—cave AL-4
Stephens Gap Ch—church TN-4
Stephens Glacier—glacier AK-9
Stephens Grove—woods CA-9
Stephens Gulch—valley ID-8
Stephens Head—cape ME-1
Stephens Hill—summit AK-9
Stephens Hill—summit MT-8
**Stephens (historical)**—pop pl MS-4
Stephens Holding Mines—mine CA-9
Stephens Hollow—valley KY-4
Stephens Hollow—valley (2) MO-7
Stephens Hollow—valley (2) TN-4
Stephens HS—school LA-4
Stephens Institute—school GA-3
Stephens JHS—school CA-9
Stephens Knob—summit KY-4
Stephens Knob—summit WV-2
Stephens Lake—lake KY-4
Stephens Lake—lake MN-6
Stephens Lake—lake NJ-2
Stephens Lake—lake NY-2
Stephens Lake—lake TX-5
Stephens Lake—reservoir AL-4
Stephens Lake—reservoir GA-3
Stephens Lake—reservoir MS-4
Stephens Lake—reservoir MO-7
Stephens Lake—reservoir TN-4
Stephens Lake—reservoir WV-2
Stephens Lakes—lake ID-8
Stephens Lee HS—school NC-3
Stephens-Lucas House—hist pl SD-7
Stephens Memorial Baptist Church AL-4
Stephens Memorial Ch—church AL-4
Stephens Memorial Ch—church NC-3
Stephens Memorial Hosp—hospital TX-5
Stephens Memorial Park—park OK-5
Stephens Mill Dam—dam AL-4
Stephens Mill (historical)—locale AL-4
Stephens Mill Pond—reservoir AL-4
Stephens Mills NY-2
**Stephens Mills**—pop pl NY-2
Stephens Mine—mine MN-6
Stephens Mine—mine MO-7
Stephens Oil And Gas Field—oilfield AR-4
Stephenson IN-6
Stephenson MS-4
Stephenson—cave VA-3
Stephenson—locale TN-4
**Stephenson**—pop pl MI-6
**Stephenson**—pop pl MS-4
**Stephenson**—pop pl VA-3
**Stephenson**—pop pl WV-2
Stephenson, Benjamin, House—hist pl IL-6
Stephenson, Lake—lake TX-5
Stephenson Airp—airport IN-6
Stephenson-Allen House—hist pl MS-4
Stephenson Branch—stream KY-4
Stephenson Branch—stream TX-5
Stephenson Brook—stream NY-2
Stephenson Cem—cemetery AL-4
Stephenson Cem—cemetery FL-3
Stephenson Cem—cemetery IN-6
Stephenson Cem—cemetery KS-7
Stephenson Cem—cemetery LA-4
Stephenson Cem—cemetery MI-6
Stephenson Cem—cemetery MS-4
Stephenson Cem—cemetery (2) MO-7
Stephenson Cem—cemetery (4) NC-3
Stephenson Cem—cemetery OH-6
Stephenson Cem—cemetery (2) TN-4
Stephenson Cem—cemetery TX-5
Stephenson Ch—church MD-2
Stephenson Ch—church NC-3
Stephenson Ch—church TN-4
Stephenson Chapel AL-4
**Stephenson (County)**—pop pl IL-6
Stephenson County Courthouse—hist pl IL-6
Stephenson Creek AL-4
Stephenson Creek FL-3
Stephenson Creek MS-4
Stephenson Creek—stream GA-3
Stephenson Creek—stream OR-9
Stephenson Creek—stream TX-5
Stephenson Crossing—locale AL-4
Stephenson Dock—locale TN-4
Stephenson Family Cem—cemetery MS-4
Stephenson Gap—gap GA-3
Stephenson Hill—summit CA-9
Stephenson (historical)—locale AL-4
Stephenson House—hist pl AL-4
Stephenson Institute (historical)—school TN-4
Stephenson Island—island GA-3
Stephenson Island—island WI-6
Stephenson Lake—lake MI-6
Stephenson Lake—lake TX-5
Stephenson Lake—lake WI-6
Stephenson Lake—reservoir OR-9
Stephenson Lookout Tower—locale MI-6
Stephenson Lookout Tower—locale MS-4
Stephenson Lookout Tower—tower MS-4
Stephenson Mine—mine MI-6
Stephenson Mtn—summit AR-4
Stephenson Mtn—summit OR-9
Stephenson Peak—summit CA-9
Stephenson Place MS-4
Stephenson Point—cape TX-5
Stephenson Point—cape VT-1
Stephenson Ranch—locale AZ-5
Stephenson Ranch—locale WY-8
Stephenson Range—range NY-2
Stephenson Sch—school IL-6
Stephenson Sch—school NY-2
Stephenson Sch—school OR-9
Stephenson Sch—school WI-6
Stephenson Sch (historical)—school TN-4
Stephensons Landing—locale ME-1
Stephensons Point MD-2
Stephensons Stream—stream AK-9
**Stephenson (Town of)**—pop pl WI-6
**Stephenson (Township of)**—pop pl MI-6
Stephen S. Palmer MS—school PA-2
Stephens Park—park MI-6
Stephens Park—park (2) MO-7
Stephens Pass—channel AK-9
Stephens Pass—gap CA-9
Stephens Passage—channel AK-9
Stephens Pass Camp—locale CA-9
Stephens Point—cape (2) FL-3
Stephens Point—cliff TN-4
Stephens Pond—lake NY-2
Stephens Pond—reservoir AL-4
Stephens Pond—reservoir GA-3
Stephens Ponds—lake NJ-2
**Stephensport**—pop pl KY-4
Stephens Ranch—locale CA-9
Stephens Ranch—locale MT-8
Stephens Ranch—locale TX-5
Stephens Ridge—ridge CA-9
Stephens Ridge—ridge GA-3
Stephens Ridge—ridge KY-4
Stephens Ridge—ridge TN-4
Stephens Ridge—ridge WV-2
Stephens Rsvr—reservoir MT-8
Stephens Rsvr—reservoir OR-9
Stephens Run—stream IN-6
Stephens Run—stream PA-2
Stephens Run—stream VA-3
Stephens Run—stream WV-2
Stephens Sch—school AR-4
Stephens Sch—school CA-9
Stephens Sch—school (2) GA-3
Stephens Sch—school MI-6
Stephens Sch—school MS-4
Stephens Sch—school SC-3
Stephens Sch—school TN-4
Stephens Sch—school WI-6
Stephens Sch (abandoned)—school PA-2
Stephens Spring—spring CO-8
Stephens Spring—spring OR-9
Stephens Spring—spring TN-4
Stephens Spur AL-4
Stephens S. S. Heirs Cem—cemetery OR-9
Stephens State For—forest IA-7
Stephens State Park—park NJ-2
**Stephens Subdivision**—pop pl (2) UT-8
Stephens Tanks—reservoir NM-5
Stephenston IN-6
Stephensville (2) FL-3
**Stephensville**—pop pl GA-3
**Stephensville**—pop pl WI-6
Stephensville Sch (historical)—school MS-4
Stephens Well—well AZ-5
Stephens Well—well NM-5
Stephens Windmill—locale CO-8
STEPHEN TABER (schooner)—hist pl ME-1
**Stephentown**—pop pl NY-2
**Stephentown Center**—pop pl NY-2
**Stephentown (Town of)**—pop pl NY-2
**Stephenville**—pop pl LA-4
**Stephenville**—pop pl MS-4
**Stephenville**—pop pl NJ-2
**Stephenville**—pop pl TX-5
Stephenville (CCD)—cens area TX-5
Stephenville Country Lake—reservoir TX-5
Stephenville P.O. (historical)—building MS-4
Stephenville South (CCD)—cens area TX-5
Stephen Wilkinson Cemetery MS-4
Stephen Wintworth Claim—civil MS-4
Stepherson Windmill—locale TX-5
Stephey Cem—cemetery CT-1
Step Hollow—valley KY-4
Stephons Cem—cemetery MS-4
Step House—locale CO-8
Stepladder Creek—stream WA-9
Stepladder Mountains—range CA-9
Stepladder Trough—flat UT-8
Step Lake AL-4
Step Mountains—other AK-9
Step Mtn—summit AK-9
Step Mtn—summit OK-5
Step Mtn—summit UT-8
**Stepney**—pop pl CT-1
**Stepney**—pop pl MD-2
Stepney Depot CT-1
Stepney Sch—school CT-1
Stepo, Mount—summit AK-9
Stepovak Bay—bay AK-9
Stepp Branch—stream (2) KY-4
Stepp Branch—stream NC-3
Stepp Branch—stream WV-2
Stepp Cem—cemetery IN-6
Stepp Cem—cemetery (3) KY-4
Stepp Cem—cemetery MO-7
Stepp Cem—cemetery NC-3
Stepp Cem—cemetery WV-2
Stepp Creek—stream AR-4
Stepp Creek—stream WY-8
Steppe Creek TX-5
Steppe Creek—stream ID-8
Steppe Mine—mine AZ-5
Steppes Creek—stream TX-5
Steppig Lake—lake IL-6
Stepping Rock—pillar KY-4
Stepping Rock Ridge—ridge KY-4
Stepping Stone Hollow—valley PA-2
Stepping Stones—bar NY-2
Stepping Stones—island ME-1
Stepping Stones Light—locale NY-2
Stepping Stones Nursery Sch—school FL-3
Stepping Stones Park—park NY-2
Stepp Knob—summit TN-4
Stepp Lake—lake AL-4
Stepp Mtn—summit TX-5
Step Point—cape AL-4
Step Point—ridge UT-8
Step Post Office (historical)—building AL-4
Stepps Ford Bridge—bridge OK-5
Stepps Gap—gap (2) NC-3
**Steppsville**—pop pl TN-4
Steppsville Post Office (historical)—building TN-4
**Stepptown**—pop pl WV-2
**Steppville**—pop pl AL-4
Steppville Post Office (historical)—building AL-4
**Steprock**—pop pl AR-4
Steprock Ch—church AR-4
Steprock Hill—summit TN-4
Step Rsvr—reservoir UT-8
Step Run—stream PA-2
Steps, The WA-9
Steps, The—cliff CO-8
Steps Gap Run—stream WV-2
Steps Lake—lake AL-4
Steps Mtn—summit SC-3
Steps Point—cape AS-9
Step Spring—spring OR-9
Step Spring—spring UT-8
Steps Run—stream WV-2
Stepstone—locale KY-4
Stepstone Creek—stream (2) KY-4
Stepstone Creek—stream WA-9
Stepstone Falls—falls RI-1
Steptoe NV-8
Steptoe—locale (2) NV-8
**Steptoe**—pop pl WA-9
Steptoe Battlefield Site—hist pl WA-9
Steptoe Branch—stream TX-5
Steptoe Butte—summit WA-9
Steptoe Butte State Park—park WA-9
Steptoe Canyon—valley WA-9
Steptoe (CCD)—cens area WA-9
Steptoe City NV-8
Steptoe Creek—stream NV-8
Steptoe Creek—stream WA-9
Steptoe Hill—summit VA-3
Steptoe Historical Marker—park UT-8
Steptoe Memorial State Park—park WA-9
Steptoe Mountain WA-9
Steptoe Ranch—locale NV-8
Steptoe Sch—school (2) SD-7
Steptoe Siding—locale NV-8
Steptoe Slough—swamp NV-8
Steptoe Spring—spring NV-8
Steptoe Valley NV-8
Steptoe Valley—basin NV-8
Steptoe Valley Hosp—hospital NV-8
Steptoe Waterhole—lake NV-8
**Steptown**—pop pl WV-2
Step Valley—valley WI-6
Stequaleho Creek—stream WA-9
Sterchi Sch—school TN-4
Sterck School DE-2
Sterenouville—locale PA-2
Sterett Creek—stream (2) MO-7
Sterett Creek Dike—levee MO-7
Sterett Creek Public Use Area—park MO-7
Stergan Lake—lake FL-3
Stergeon Creek GA-3
Sterick Bldg—hist pl TN-4
Steriner Pond—lake OH-6
Steritt Swamp—stream SC-3
Sterley—locale TX-5
Sterling (2) IN-6
Sterling NJ-2
Sterling PA-2
Sterling TN-4
Sterling—locale AK-9
Sterling—locale IA-7
Sterling—locale MT-8
Sterling—locale PA-2
Sterling—locale VA-3
Sterling—locale WA-9
**Sterling**—pop pl CO-8
**Sterling**—pop pl CT-1
**Sterling**—pop pl FL-3
**Sterling**—pop pl GA-3
**Sterling**—pop pl (2) ID-8
**Sterling**—pop pl IL-6
**Sterling**—pop pl KS-7
**Sterling**—pop pl LA-4
**Sterling**—pop pl MA-1
**Sterling**—pop pl MI-6
**Sterling**—pop pl MS-4
**Sterling**—pop pl MO-7
**Sterling**—pop pl NE-7
**Sterling**—pop pl NY-2
**Sterling**—pop pl NC-3
**Sterling**—pop pl ND-7
**Sterling**—pop pl OH-6
**Sterling**—pop pl OK-5
**Sterling**—pop pl PA-2
**Sterling**—pop pl TN-4
**Sterling**—pop pl UT-8
**Sterling**—pop pl VA-3
Sterling, Bayou—stream LA-4
Sterling, Ella Mahalla Cutter, House—hist pl MA-1
Sterling, Fred T., House—hist pl MT-8
Sterling, Lake—reservoir CA-9
Sterling, Mount—summit MA-1
Sterling, Mount—summit MT-8
Sterling, Ross,S., House—hist pl TX-5
Sterling Airp—airport KS-7
Sterling and Francine Clark Art Institute—building MA-1
Sterling Bayou—gut LA-4
Sterling-Berry House—hist pl TX-5
Sterling Block-Bishop Arcade—hist pl CT-1
Sterling Branch—stream AR-4
Sterling Brook ME-1
Sterling Brook—stream ME-1
Sterling Brook—stream PA-2
Sterling Brook—stream VT-1
**Sterling Camp Grounds**—pop pl MA-1
Sterling Canyon—valley (2) AZ-5
Sterling Canyon—valley CO-8
Sterling Canyon Tank—reservoir AZ-5
Sterling Cem—cemetery AL-4
Sterling Cem—cemetery CT-1
Sterling Cem—cemetery IA-7
Sterling Cem—cemetery KS-7
Sterling Cem—cemetery MI-6
Sterling Cem—cemetery NE-7
Sterling Cem—cemetery NY-2
Sterling Cem—cemetery ND-7
Sterling Cem—cemetery OK-5
Sterling Cem—cemetery OR-9
Sterling Cem—cemetery TX-5
Sterling Cem—cemetery UT-8
Sterling Cem—cemetery VT-1
**Sterling (census name Sterling Park)**—pop pl VA-3
Sterling Center—other NY-2
**Sterling Center**—pop pl MN-6
Sterling Center Hist Dist—hist pl MA-1
Sterling Centre MA-1
Sterling Ch—church GA-3
Sterling Ch—church KS-7
Sterling Ch—church MN-6
Sterling Ch—church SD-7
Sterling Cherry Farm Dam—dam AL-4
Sterling Cherry Farm Pond—reservoir AL-4
Sterling Christian Sch—school CA-9
**Sterling City**—pop pl TX-5
Sterling City (CCD)—cens area TX-5
Sterling Close—locale PA-2
Sterling Coll—school KS-7
Sterling Congregational Church—hist pl MN-6
**Sterling (County)**—pop pl TX-5
Sterling Creek—stream (2) AK-9
Sterling Creek—stream GA-3
Sterling Creek—stream MN-6
Sterling Creek—stream MT-8
Sterling Creek—stream (2) NY-2
Sterling Creek—stream OR-9
Sterling Creek—stream TX-5
Sterling Creek—stream VA-3
Sterling Creek—stream WI-6
Sterling Dam—dam ND-7
Sterling Ditch—canal MT-8
Sterling Ditch—canal OR-9
Sterling Elem Sch—school KS-7
Sterling Elem Sch—school NC-3
Sterling Farmer Dam—dam TN-4
Sterling Farmer Lake—reservoir TN-4
Sterling Field—park OH-6
**Sterling Forest**—pop pl NY-2
Sterling Forest Lake—reservoir NY-2
Sterling Forest Station—locale OR-9
Sterling Free Public Carnegie Library—hist pl KS-7
Sterling Grove Cem—cemetery MI-6
Sterling Grove Hist Dist—hist pl LA-4
Sterling G.S. OR-9
Sterling Gulch—valley (2) CO-8
Sterling Gulch—valley MT-8
Sterling Gulch—valley OR-9
Sterling Harris Sch—school UT-8
**Sterling Heights**—pop pl IN-6
**Sterling Heights**—pop pl MI-6
**Sterling Heights**—pop pl OH-6
**Sterling Hill**—pop pl CT-1
Sterling Hill—summit CT-1
Sterling Hill—summit NJ-2
Sterling Hill—summit WA-9
Sterling Hill Hist Dist—hist pl CT-1
Sterling (historical)—locale AL-4
Sterling Hollow—valley MO-7
Sterling Hollow—valley TN-4
Sterling Hollow—valley (2) UT-8
Sterling Homestead—hist pl CT-1
Sterling HS—school KS-7
Sterling HS—school NJ-2
Sterling HS—school SC-3
Sterling HS—school TX-5
Sterling Island—island MI-6
Sterling Island—island MO-7
Sterling JHS—school WA-9
**Sterling Junction**—pop pl LA-4
**Sterling Junction**—pop pl MA-1
Sterling Junior Coll—school CO-8
Sterling Lake AL-4
Sterling Lake—lake (2) MN-6
Sterling Lake—lake NY-2
Sterling Lake—reservoir AL-4
Sterling Landing—locale MO-7
**Sterling Landing**—pop pl AK-9
Sterling Lateral No 1—canal CO-8
Sterling Lookout Tower—locale MO-7
Sterling Lookout Tower—locale WI-6
Sterling (Magisterial District)—fmr MCD VA-3
Sterling Marsh—swamp MI-6
Sterling Mine—mine CA-9
Sterling Mine—mine CO-8
Sterling Mine—mine MT-8
Sterling Mine (underground)—mine AL-4
Sterling Mount—summit NC-3
Sterling Mtn—summit CA-9
Sterling Mtn—summit VT-1
Sterling No 2 Ditch—canal CO-8
Sterling Oil Field—oilfield KS-7
Sterling Oil Field—other MI-6
Sterling Opera House—hist pl CT-1
**Sterling Park**—pop pl CA-9
**Sterling Park**—pop pl TN-4
**Sterling Park**—pop pl VA-3
Sterling Park (census name for Sterling)—CDP VA-3
Sterling Park Elem Sch—school FL-3
Sterling Place IL-6
Sterling Place—locale CO-8
**Sterling Place**—pop pl IL-6
Sterling Plaza (Shop Ctr)—locale FL-3
Sterling Point—cape WA-9
**Sterling Point**—pop pl VA-3
Sterling Pond—lake ME-1
Sterling Pond—lake (2) NY-2
Sterling Pond—lake VT-1
Sterling Pond—reservoir CT-1
Sterling Pond Outlet—stream NY-2
Sterling Post Office (historical)—building AL-4
Sterling Price Community Lake—reservoir MO-7
Sterling Queen Mine—mine CA-9
Sterling Ranch—locale NM-5
Sterling Range—range VT-1
Sterling Reservoir CO-8
Sterling Ridge—ridge ME-1
Sterling Ridge Shop Ctr—locale MO-7
Sterling RR Station—locale FL-3
Sterling Rsvr—reservoir ND-7
Sterling Run PA-2
**Sterling Run**—pop pl PA-2
Sterling Run—stream IN-6
Sterling Run—stream OH-6
Sterling Run—stream (2) PA-2
Sterlings Camps—locale ME-1
Sterling Sch—school AL-4
Sterling Sch—school CA-9
Sterling Sch—school CT-1
Sterling Sch—school (2) IL-6
Sterling Sch—school OH-6
Sterling Sch—school VA-3
Sterling Sch—school WI-6
**Sterling Scott**—pop pl TN-4
Sterling Shoal—bar AK-9
Sterling Siding—locale TN-4
Sterling Southwest Oil Field—oilfield KS-7
**Sterling Spring**—pop pl AR-4
Sterling Spring—spring AZ-5
Sterling Spring—spring (2) CO-8
**Sterling Springs**—pop pl AR-4
Sterling State Park—park MI-6
Sterling Station—locale NY-2
**Sterling (Sterling Center)**—pop pl NY-2
**Sterling (Sterling Station)**—pop pl NY-2
Sterlings (Township of)—fmr MCD NC-3
Sterlington—locale NY-2
**Sterlington**—pop pl LA-4
**Sterling (Town of)**—pop pl CT-1
**Sterling (Town of)**—pop pl MA-1
**Sterling (Town of)**—pop pl NY-2
**Sterling (Town of)**—pop pl (2) WI-6
**Sterling Township**—pop pl (2) KS-7
**Sterling Township**—pop pl ND-7
**Sterling Township**—pop pl SD-7
Sterling Township Hall—building SD-7
Sterling (Township of)—other MI-6
**Sterling (Township of)**—pop pl IL-6
**Sterling (Township of)**—pop pl IN-6
**Sterling (Township of)**—pop pl MN-6
**Sterling (Township of)**—pop pl OH-6
**Sterling (Township of)**—pop pl PA-2
Sterling Truck Trail—trail MI-6
Sterling Union Cem—cemetery OH-6
Sterling Union Pacific RR Depot—hist pl CO-8
Sterling Valley—locale WA-9
**Sterling Valley**—pop pl NY-2
Sterling Valley Creek—stream NY-2
Sterlingville—locale NY-2
Sterlingville Cemetery OR-9
**Sterlingville (historical)**—pop pl OR-9
Sterling Wells—well CO-8
**Sterling West**—pop pl IL-6
**Sterling Woods**—pop pl NJ-2
**Sterlingworth**—pop pl PA-2
Sterman Branch—stream KY-4
Sterman Canyon—valley TX-5
Sterman Windmill—locale TX-5
Stermer Ridge—ridge AZ-5
Stermer Tank—reservoir AZ-5
Stermer Trick Tank—reservoir AZ-5
**Stern**—pop pl FL-3
Stern, Gottlieb, House—hist pl SD-7
Sternberg Cem—cemetery TX-5
Sternberger Hosp—hospital NC-3
Sternberger Sch—school NC-3
Sternbergh House—hist pl NY-2
Stern Coll Yeshiva Univ—school NY-2
Sterne, Adolphus, House—hist pl TX-5
Sterne Branch—stream AL-4
Sterne Brunson Sch—school MI-6
Sterne Cem—cemetery AL-4
Sterne Cem—cemetery IL-6
Sterne Park—park CO-8
Sterner Cem—cemetery IA-7
Sterner Gulch—valley CO-8
Sterner Rsvr—reservoir CO-8
Sterner Sch (abandoned)—school PA-2
Sterners Run—stream PA-2
Sternerton (historical)—locale KS-7
Sternes Cem—cemetery VT-1
Stern Gulch—valley AK-9
Stern Lake Dam—dam NC-3
Stern Ranch—locale NM-5
Stern Sch—school MS-4
Sterns Creek—stream VA-3
Sterns Drain—canal MI-6

Sterns Number 1 Dam—dam SD-7
Sterns Number 2 Dam—dam SD-7
Sterns Pond—lake CT-1
Sterns Ranch—locale (2) NE-7
Sterret Island—island MD-2
Sterrett—pop pl AL-4
Sterrett—pop pl TX-5
Sterrettania—pop pl PA-2
Sterrett Cem—cemetery AL-4
Sterrett Ch—church AL-4
Sterrett Classical Acad—school PA-2
Sterrett Elem Sch (historical)—school AL-4
Sterrett Gap PA-2
Sterrett-Hassinger House—hist pl PA-2
Sterrett Hill—locale TX-5
Sterrett House—hist pl KY-4
Sterrett Knob—summit OH-6
Sterrett Mesa—summit AZ-5
Sterrett Sch PA-2
Sterretts Creek FL-3
Sterretts Gap—gap PA-2
Sterretts Pond CT-1
Sterrett Sub-District Sch—hist pl PA-2
Sterrits Gap PA-2
Sterritt Peak—summit NV-8
Sterr Park—park WI-6
Sterry Creek—stream PA-2
Sterry Hall—hist pl ID-8
Sterry Lake—lake CO-8
Sterry Sch—school CA-9
Stet—pop pl MO-7
Stetattle Creek—stream WA-9
Stetler Lakes—lake MT-8
Stetler Ranch (Abandoned)—locale MT-8
Stetlersville—locale PA-2
Stetonic AZ-5
Stet Sch—school MO-7
Stetser Sch—school PA-2
Stetson—locale ID-8
Stetson—pop pl ME-1
Stetson—uninc pl FL-3
Stetson, John B., House—hist pl FL-3
Stetson Brook—stream ME-1
Stetson Brook—stream (2) MA-1
Stetson Brook—stream VT-1
Stetson Cem—cemetery (2) ME-1
Stetson Cem—cemetery NM-5
Stetson Ch—church FL-3
Stetson Chapel MS-4
Stetson Corner—pop pl CT-1
Stetson Cove—cove MA-1
Stetson Creek—stream AK-9
Stetson Creek—stream (2) CA-9
Stetson Creek—stream ID-8
Stetson (historical)—locale SD-7
Stetson Hosp—hospital PA-2
Stetson House—hist pl MA-1
Stetson JHS—school PA-2
Stetson Mtn—summit ME-1
Stetson Plaza Shop Ctr—locale AZ-5
Stetson Pond—lake ME-1
Stetson Pond—lake MA-1
Stetson Pond—reservoir MA-1
Stetson Ridge—ridge ME-1
Stetson Road—pop pl MA-1
Stetson Rocks—bar ME-1
Stetson Sch—school (4) ME-1
Stetson Sch—school MA-1
Stetson Sch—school NH-1
Stetson Sch Number 76—school IN-6
Stetsons Cove MA-1
Stetson Seep—spring NM-5
Stetsons Pond MA-1
Stetson Stream—stream ME-1
Stetson (Town of)—pop pl ME-1
Stetsontown (Township of)—unorg ME-1
Stetson Union Church—hist pl ME-1
Stetson Univ—school FL-3
Stetsonville—pop pl NY-2
Stetsonville—pop pl WI-6
Stettin (historical)—pop pl WI-6
Stettin Sch—school WI-6
Stettin (Town of)—pop pl WI-6
Stettler Ch—church OH-6
Stettler Subdivision—pop pl UT-8
Stettlersville PA-2
Steuart Corner—locale MD-2
Steuart Lake—lake CO-8
Steuart Level—pop pl MD-2
Steuben—locale IA-7
Steuben—locale (2) PA-2
Steuben—pop pl ME-1
STeuben—pop pl MI-6
Steuben—pop pl NY-2
Steuben—pop pl OH-6
Steuben—pop pl WI-6
Steuben Cenetery—cemetery NY-2
Steuben Corners—locale PA-2
Steuben County—pop pl IN-6
Steuben (County)—pop pl NY-2
Steuben County Courthouse—hist pl IN-6
Steuben County Jail—hist pl IN-6
Steuben Creek—stream CO-8
Steuben Creek—stream NY-2
Steuben Estate Complex—hist pl NJ-2
Steuben Harbor—bay ME-1
Steuben Hill—summit NY-2
Steuben House—hist pl NJ-2
Steuben JHS—school WI-6
Steuben Lake—lake MI-6
Steuben Lookout Tower—locale MI-6
Steuben Park—park NY-2
Steuben Place—locale CA-9
Steuben Ranch—locale CO-8
Steuben Sch—school (2) IL-6
Steuben Sch—school NJ-2
Steuben Sch—school PA-2
Steuben Station PA-2
Steuben Town PA-2
Steuben (Town of)—pop pl ME-1
Steuben (Town of)—pop pl NY-2
Steuben (Township of)—pop pl IL-6
Steuben (Township of)—pop pl (2) IN-6
Steuben (Township of)—pop pl PA-2
Steuben Valley—pop pl NY-2
Steubenville—pop pl IN-6
Steubenville—pop pl KY-4
Steubenville—pop pl OH-6
Steubenville Cem—cemetery IN-6
Steubenville Commercial Hist Dist—hist pl OH-6
Steubenville Country Club—other OH-6
Steubenville (Township of)—civ div OH-6
Steubenville YMCA Bldg—hist pl OH-6
Steuber Hollow—valley MO-7
Steuber Station PA-2
Steubertown PA-2
Steuck Ponds—lake MO-7
Steunenberg, A. K., House—hist pl ID-8
Steusser Lake—lake MI-6
Stevans IN-6
Stevans Tank—reservoir AZ-5
Steve—locale AR-4
Steveale Creek—stream CA-9
Steveale Meadow—flat CA-9
Steve and Kens Pit—cave AL-4
Steve Barton Point—cape CA-9
Steve Bay—swamp GA-3
Steve Bigle Mtn—summit NY-2
Steve Branch—stream KY-4
Steve Branch—stream LA-4
Steve Branch—stream (2) NC-3
Steve Branch—stream WV-2
Steve Canyon—valley CO-8
Steve Ch—church AR-4
Steve Creek—stream CA-9
Steve Creek—stream ID-8
Steve Creek—stream IL-6
Steve Creek—stream KY-4
Steve Creek—stream OR-9
Steve Creek—stream TN-4
Steve Creek—stream TX-5
Steve Creek—stream WI-6
Steve Creek Flowage—reservoir WI-6
Steve Dunagan—locale NM-5
Steve Fitzpatrick Branch—stream KY-4
Steve Fork—stream CA-9
Steve Fork—stream OR-9
Steve Forks—locale MT-8
Steve Forks—stream MT-8
Steve Fork Trail—trail CA-9
Steve Fork Trail—trail OR-9
Stevegaddy (historical)—locale MS-4
Steve Gap—gap NC-3
Steve Hills—ridge MS-4
Steve Horn Branch—stream VA-3
Steve Horn Gap—gap VA-3
Steve Island—island ME-1
Steve Kemp Draw—valley TX-5
Steve Lake—lake AK-9
Steve Lake—lake ID-8
Steve Lake—lake NE-7
Stevely Cem—cemetery OH-6
Steven—locale LA-4
Steven, Lake—lake FL-3
Steven, Lake—lake MI-6
Steve Napier Branch—stream KY-4
Steven Brook MA-1
Steven Brook—stream MA-1
Stevenburg—pop pl WV-2
Steven Cay—island VI-3
Steven Chapel—church TN-4
Stevendale Ch—church LA-4
Steven Gap—gap GA-3
Steven Hollow AR-4
Steven House—hist pl WI-6
Steven Larson Ditch—canal ID-8
Stevenot Camp—locale CA-9
Stevenot Lateral—canal CA-9
Steven Place PA-2
Steven Pond MA-1
Stevens CA-9
Stevens IN-6
Stevens—locale CA-9
Stevens—locale ID-8
Stevens—locale IA-7
Stevens—locale TX-5
Stevens—locale VT-1
Stevens—pop pl AL-4
Stevens—pop pl MS-4
Stevens—pop pl NJ-2
Stevens—pop pl (2) PA-2
Stevens, Abiel, House—hist pl MA-1
Stevens, Andrew J., House—hist pl MI-6
Stevens, Arnold, House—hist pl ID-8
Stevens, Charles, House—hist pl OR-9
Stevens, Daniel, House—hist pl MA-1
Stevens, Dominic, House—hist pl MT-8
Stevens, Elisha, House—hist pl TX-5
Stevens, Everitt P., House—hist pl NC-3
Stevens, John, House—hist pl NY-2
Stevens, John Calvin, House—hist pl ME-1
Stevens, Lake—lake NY-2
Stevens, Lake—lake WA-9
Stevens, Linton, Covered Bridge—hist pl PA-2
Stevens, Sherman, House—hist pl CA-9
Stevens, Sidney, House—hist pl UT-8
Stevens, Thaddeus, Sch of Observation—hist pl PA-2
Stevens, Wes, Site—hist pl NE-7
Stevens, William, House—hist pl CT-1
Stevens, William, House—hist pl DE-2
Stevens Airfield—airport CO-8
Stevens Arbor Sch (historical)—school MS-4
Stevens Arch UT-8
Stevens Arroyo—stream (2) NM-5
Stevens Ave Ch of Christ—church AL-4
Stevens Banner Cem—cemetery MO-7
Stevens Bay—bay GA-3
Stevens Bay—bay VT-1
Stevens Bend—bend AL-4
Stevens' Bldg—hist pl MA-1
Stevens Bldg—hist pl TX-5
Stevens Bluff AL-4
Stevensboro WV-2
Stevens Branch DE-2
Steven's Branch VT-1
Stevens Branch WV-2
Stevens Branch—stream AR-4
Stevens Branch—stream FL-3
Stevens Branch—stream GA-3
Stevens Branch—stream (3) KY-4
Stevens Branch—stream LA-4
Stevens Branch—stream MA-1
Stevens Branch—stream MS-4
Stevens Branch—stream MO-7
Stevens Branch—stream OH-6
Stevens Branch—stream (2) TN-4
Stevens Branch—stream TX-5
Stevens Branch—stream VT-1
Stevens Branch—stream (2) VA-3
Stevens Branch—stream WV-2
Stevens Bridge—bridge NC-3
Stevens Bridge—bridge OK-5
Stevens Brook MA-1
Stevens Brook—stream CT-1
Stevens Brook—stream (4) ME-1
Stevens Brook—stream MA-1
Stevens Brook—stream MN-6
Stevens Brook—stream (3) NH-1
Stevens Brook—stream NY-2
Stevens Brook—stream (3) VT-1
Stevens Brook Trail—trail NH-1
Stevens-Buchanan House—hist pl MS-4
Stevensburg—locale WV-2
Stevensburg—pop pl VA-3
Stevensburg (Magisterial District)—fmr MCD VA-3
Stevens Cabin—locale UT-8
Stevens Camp—locale CA-9
Stevens Camp—locale NV-8
Stevens Camp—locale NJ-2
Stevens Canal—canal CA-9
Stevens Canal—canal NC-3
Stevens Canyon—valley AZ-5
Stevens Canyon—valley CO-8
Stevens Canyon—valley (2) OR-9
Stevens Canyon—valley (4) UT-8
Stevens Canyon—valley (2) WA-9
Stevens Canyon Arch UT-8
Stevens Canyon Entrance—locale WA-9
Stevens-Cason Cem—cemetery GA-3
Stevens Cem MO-7
Stevens Cem—cemetery AR-4
Stevens Cem—cemetery CT-1
Stevens Cem—cemetery (2) GA-3
Stevens Cem—cemetery (2) IL-6
Stevens Cem—cemetery (2) KY-4
Stevens Cem—cemetery (4) LA-4
Stevens Cem—cemetery (2) ME-1
Stevens Cem—cemetery MN-6
Stevens Cem—cemetery (5) MS-4
Stevens Cem—cemetery (3) MO-7
Stevens Cem—cemetery NE-7
Stevens Cem—cemetery (3) NY-2
Stevens Cem—cemetery OH-6
Stevens Cem—cemetery (4) TN-4
Stevens Cem—cemetery TX-5
Stevens Cem—cemetery UT-8
Stevens Cem—cemetery (3) VA-3
Stevens Cem—cemetery WV-2
Stevens Ch—church NC-3
Stevens Chapel—church KS-7
Stevens Chapel—church (3) NC-3
Stevens Chapel—church PA-2
Stevens Chapel—church VA-3
Stevens Chapel—church WV-2
Stevens Chapel Cem—cemetery MO-7
Stevens Chapel United Methodist Ch—church MS-4
Stevens Clinic Hosp—hospital WV-2
Stevens Corner—locale (2) ME-1
Stevens Corner—locale MD-2
Stevens Corner—pop pl MA-1
Stevens Corner Cem—cemetery MA-1
Stevens Corners MA-1
Stevens Corners—locale MD-2
Stevens Corners—locale (2) NY-2
Stevens Corners—locale PA-2
Stevens County—civil KS-7
Stevens (County)—pop pl MN-6
Stevens County—pop pl WA-9
Stevens County Fairgrounds—locale KS-7
Stevens Cove—bay ME-1
Stevens Cove—bay RI-1
Stevens Cove—valley NC-3
Stevens Cove—valley VA-3
Stevens Cove Cem—cemetery VA-3
Stevens Creek FL-3
Stevens Creek MN-6
Stevens Creek MT-8
Stevens Creek NJ-2
Stevens Creek PA-2
Stevens Creek TX-5
Stevens Creek WI-6
Stevens Creek—fmr MCD NE-7
Stevens Creek—locale AR-4
Stevens Creek—pop pl VA-3
Stevens Creek—stream AL-4
Stevens Creek—stream (2) AK-9
Stevens Creek—stream AR-4
Stevens Creek—stream (2) CA-9
Stevens Creek—stream (3) CO-8
Stevens Creek—stream (4) ID-8
Stevens Creek—stream (2) IL-6
Stevens Creek—stream (3) KY-4
Stevens Creek—stream (3) MI-6
Stevens Creek—stream MN-6
Stevens Creek—stream (2) MT-8
Stevens Creek—stream NE-7
Stevens Creek—stream NM-5
Stevens Creek—stream (3) NC-3
Stevens Creek—stream OK-5
Stevens Creek—stream (2) OR-9
Stevens Creek—stream (2) PA-2
Stevens Creek—stream (2) SC-3
Stevens Creek—stream (4) TX-5
Stevens Creek—stream UT-8
Stevens Creek—stream VA-3
Stevens Creek—stream (5) WA-9
Stevens Creek—stream (2) WI-6
Stevens Creek (CCD)—cens area SC-3
Stevens Creek Dam—dam GA-3
Stevens Creek Dam—dam SC-3
Stevens Creek Park—park CA-9
Stevens Creek Rsvr—reservoir CA-9
Stevens Creek Sch—school CA-9
Stevens Creek Trail—trail MT-8
Stevens-Crosby Airp—airport NV-8
Stevens Crossing—locale GA-3
Stevens Crossing—pop pl MA-1
Stevens Crossing Station (historical)—locale MA-1
Stevensdale—pop pl (2) LA-4
Stevens Dam WA-9
Stevens Dam—dam ND-7
Stevens Ditch—canal (2) IN-6
Stevens Ditch—canal MT-8
Stevens Ditch—canal OH-6
Stevens Drain—canal CA-9
Stevens Drain—canal (2) MI-6
Stevens Draw—valley (2) CO-8
Stevens Draw—valley MT-8
Stevens Draw—valley NM-5
Stevens Draw—valley (2) WY-8
Stevens Elem Sch—school MS-4
Stevens Elem Sch—school PA-2
Stevens Estates Subdivision—pop pl UT-8
Stevens Ferry Bridge AL-4
Stevens Ferry Bridge—bridge AL-4
Stevens Flat—flat WY-8
Stevens Fork—stream (2) KY-4
Stevens Gap Branch OK-5
Stevens Glacier WA-9
Stevens Gorge—valley AZ-5
Stevens Grove Cem—cemetery GA-3
Stevens Grove Ch—church GA-3
Stevens Gulch—valley AK-9
Stevens Gulch—valley (5) CO-8
Stevens Gulch—valley ID-8
Stevens Gulch—valley MT-8
Stevens Gulch—valley OR-9
Stevens Hall—hist pl WA-9
Stevens Hill—pop pl WI-6
Stevens Hill—summit (2) ME-1
Stevens Hill—summit MA-1
Stevens Hill—summit (4) NH-1
Stevens Hill—summit SC-3
Stevens Hill—summit TX-5
Stevens Hill Ch—church PA-2
Stevens Hole Run—stream WV-2
Stevens Hollow—valley AL-4
Stevens Hollow—valley AR-4
Stevens Hollow—valley KY-4
Stevens Hollow—valley TN-4
Stevens Hollow—valley UT-8
Stevens HS—hist pl PA-2
Stevens Industrial Sch—school PA-2
Stevens Institute of Technology—school NJ-2
Stevens Island RI-1
Stevens Island—island (2) ME-1
Stevens Island—island MN-6
Stevens Island—island NH-1
Stevens Island—island RI-1
Stevens Island—summit NJ-2
Stevens JHS—school WA-9
Stevens Knob—summit KY-4
Stevens Knob—summit VA-3
Stevens Knob—summit WV-2
Stevens Knoll—summit WI-6
Stevens Lake SD-7
Stevens Lake WI-6
Stevens Lake—lake AK-9
Stevens Lake—lake FL-3
Stevens Lake—lake IN-6
Stevens Lake—lake KY-4
Stevens Lake—lake (4) MI-6
Stevens Lake—lake (10) MN-6
Stevens Lake—lake (2) NM-5
Stevens Lake—lake (4) WA-9
Stevens Lake—lake WI-6
Stevens Lake—pop pl WA-9
Stevens Lake—reservoir CA-9
Stevens Lake—reservoir GA-3
Stevens Lake—reservoir WI-6
Stevens Lake Campground—locale WI-6
Stevens Lake Dam—dam MS-4
Stevens Lake Dam—dam PA-2
Stevens Lakes—lake AK-9
Stevens Landing—locale AR-4
Stevens Landing—pop pl NY-2
Stevens Lateral—canal ID-8
Stevens-Mayo HS—school TX-5
Stevens Memorial Hospital Heliport—airport WA-9
Stevens Mesa—summit UT-8
Stevens Mill—pop pl ME-1
Stevens Mill—pop pl NC-3
Stevens Millpond—lake SC-3
Stevens Mill Run VA-3
Stevens Mill Run—stream VA-3
Stevens Mills—pop pl (2) VT-1
Stevens Mine—mine AZ-5
Stevens Mine—mine (3) CO-8
Stevens Mtn—summit AZ-5
Stevens Mtn—summit CA-9
Stevens Mtn—summit (2) NY-2
Stevens Narrow UT-8
Stevens Narrows—gap UT-8
Stevens Natural Arch—arch UT-8
Stevenson—locale KY-4
Stevenson—locale LA-4
Stevenson—locale MN-6
Stevenson—locale PA-2
Stevenson—pop pl AL-4
Stevenson—pop pl CT-1
Stevenson—pop pl IN-6
Stevenson—pop pl MD-2
Stevenson—pop pl WA-9
Stevenson, Adlai E., I, House—hist pl IL-6
Stevenson, Henry, House—hist pl KY-4
Stevenson, Mount—summit CA-9
Stevenson, Mount—summit WY-8
Stevenson, Robert Louis, Branch—hist pl CA-9
Stevenson, Samuel A. and Margaret, House—hist pl IA-7
Stevenson Airp—airport (2) KS-7
Stevenson Bay—bay MI-6
Stevenson Bay—bay NY-2
Stevenson Bayou—stream MO-7
Stevenson Beach—beach NY-2
Stevenson Bluff AL-4
Stevenson Branch—stream KY-4
Stevenson Branch—stream NC-3
Stevenson Branch—stream TN-4
Stevenson Branch—stream TX-5
Stevenson-Bridgeport Municipal Airp—airport AL-4
Stevenson Brook—stream VT-1
Stevenson Canyon UT-8
Stevenson Canyon—valley AZ-5
Stevenson Canyon—valley NE-7
Stevenson (CCD)—cens area AL-4
Stevenson (CCD)—cens area WA-9
Stevenson Cem—cemetery (2) AR-4
Stevenson Cem—cemetery IL-6
Stevenson Cem—cemetery IN-6
Stevenson Cem—cemetery (2) KS-7
Stevenson Cem—cemetery KY-4
Stevenson Cem—cemetery (2) LA-4
Stevenson Cem—cemetery MS-4
Stevenson Cem—cemetery MO-7
Stevenson Cem—cemetery NH-1
Stevenson Cem—cemetery NY-2
Stevenson Cem—cemetery (2) NC-3
Stevenson Cem—cemetery OH-6
Stevenson Cem—cemetery OK-5
Stevenson Cem—cemetery PA-2
Stevenson Cem—cemetery VA-3
Stevenson Cem—cemetery WI-6
Stevenson Ch—church KY-4
Stevenson Chapel—church KY-4
Stevenson Chapel (historical)—church AL-4
Stevenson County Park—park OR-9
Stevenson Cove ME-1
Stevenson Cove—valley NC-3
Stevenson Creek AL-4
Stevenson Creek CA-9
Stevenson Creek—stream AL-4
Stevenson Creek—stream (2) CA-9
Stevenson Creek—stream (2) FL-3
Stevenson Creek—stream MO-7
Stevenson Creek—stream MT-8
Stevenson Creek—stream OR-9
Stevenson Creek—stream WI-6
Stevenson Dam—dam CT-1
Stevenson Detention Center—locale DE-2
Stevenson Ditch—canal MT-8
Stevenson Ditch No 2—canal CO-8
Stevenson Division—civil AL-4
Stevenson Drain—canal MI-6
Stevenson Drain—stream MI-6
Stevenson Draw—valley WY-8
Stevenson Elem Sch—school AZ-5
Stevenson Entrance—channel AK-9
Stevenson Gulch—valley CA-9
Stevenson Hill—summit GA-3
Stevenson Hill—summit ME-1
Stevenson Hill—summit WY-8
Stevenson Hist Dist—hist pl AL-4
Stevenson Hollow—valley AL-4
Stevenson Hollow—valley (2) MO-7
Stevenson Hollow—valley TN-4
Stevenson Hosp—hospital CA-9
Stevenson House—hist pl CA-9
Stevenson House—hist pl IL-6
Stevenson House—hist pl LA-4
Stevenson House—hist pl NC-3
Stevenson House and Brickyard—hist pl GA-3
Stevenson HS—school AL-4
Stevenson HS—school (2) MI-6
Stevenson Island WI-6
Stevenson Island—island AK-9
Stevenson Island—island WY-8
Stevenson Island—pop pl UT-8
Stevenson JHS—school CA-9
Stevenson JHS—school MI-6
Stevenson Lake OR-9
Stevenson Lake—lake LA-4
Stevenson Lake—lake (2) MI-6
Stevenson Lake—lake NE-7
Stevenson Lateral—canal AZ-5
Stevenson Lookout Tower—locale LA-4
Stevenson Meadow—flat CA-9
Stevenson Mine—mine MN-6
Stevenson Mountain OR-9
Stevenson MS—school TX-5
Stevenson Mtn—summit (2) AR-4
Stevenson Municipal Park—park AL-4
Stevenson Park—park SC-3
Stevenson Park—park TX-5
Stevenson Peak—summit (2) CA-9
Stevenson Pier Sch—school WI-6
Stevenson Playground—park IL-6
Stevenson Point TX-5
Stevenson Point—cape MI-6
Stevenson Point—cape NC-3
Stevenson Pond—lake IL-6
Stevenson Pond—lake PA-2
Stevenson Pond—reservoir NC-3
Stevenson Pond Dam—dam NC-3
Stevenson Primary Sch—hist pl MS-4
Stevenson Ranch—locale MT-8
Stevenson Ranch—locale NM-5
Stevenson Ridge Trail—trail WA-9
Stevenson RR Depot and Hotel—hist pl AL-4
Stevensons CA-9
Stevenson Sch—school (2) AZ-5
Stevenson Sch—school (4) CA-9
Stevenson Sch—school (3) IL-6
Stevenson Sch—school IN-6
Stevenson Sch—school (2) MI-6
Stevenson Sch—school ND-7
Stevenson Sch—school OH-6
Stevenson Sch—school OK-5
Stevenson Sch—school SD-7
Stevenson Sch—school TX-5
Stevenson Sch—school WA-9
Stevensons Chapel—church MS-4
Stevensons Chapel Cem—cemetery MS-4
Stevenson Sch (historical)—school MS-4
Stevenson Sch (historical)—school PA-2
Stevenson School MS-4
Stevenson School (Abandoned)—locale AR-4
Stevensons Lake—reservoir KS-7
Stevensons Lake—reservoir SC-3
Stevensons Landing AR-4
Stevensons Mill (historical)—locale AL-4
Stevensons Point MD-2
Stevenson Tank—reservoir TX-5
Stevenson (Township of)—pop pl IL-6
Stevens Opera Block—hist pl SD-7
Stevens Paper Company Lower Dam—dam MA-1
Stevens Paper Company Upper Dam—dam MA-1
Stevens Park—park OH-6
Stevens Park Golf Course—other TX-5
Stevens Park Sch—school TX-5
Stevens Pass—gap WA-9
Stevens Pass Hist Dist—hist pl WA-9
Stevens Peak—summit CA-9
Stevens Peak—summit (2) ID-8
Stevens Peak—summit MT-8
Stevens Peak—summit WA-9
Stevens Playground—park IL-6
Stevens Point—cape AR-4
Stevens Point—cape (2) ID-8
Stevens Point—cape (2) ME-1
Stevens Point—cape MO-7
Stevens Point—cape OR-9
Stevens Point—cape VA-3
Stevens Point—pop pl PA-2
Stevens Point—pop pl WI-6
Stevens Point—summit NH-1
Stevens Point Country Club—other WI-6
Stevens Point HS—school WI-6
Stevens Point Plaza (Shop Ctr)—locale FL-3
Stevens Point State Normal Sch—hist pl WI-6
Stevens Pond MA-1
Stevens Pond—lake FL-3
Stevens Pond—lake (4) MA-1
Stevens Pond—lake NH-1
Stevens Pond—lake NY-2
Stevens Pond—lake VT-1
Stevens Pond—lake WI-6
Stevens Pond—reservoir ME-1
Stevens Pond—reservoir (3) MA-1
Stevens Pond—reservoir NC-3
Stevens Pond Dam—dam (2) MA-1
Stevens Pond Outlet Dam—dam MA-1
Stevens Pond Park—park NH-1
Stevensport IN-6
Stevens Pottery—locale GA-3
Stevens Prairie—area CA-9
Stevens Ranch—hist pl SD-7
Stevens Ranch—locale (3) AZ-5
Stevens Ranch—locale CA-9
Stevens Ranch—locale CO-8
Stevens Ranch—locale NE-7
Stevens Ranch—locale NV-8
Stevens Ranch—locale (3) NM-5
Stevens Ranch—locale (2) TX-5
Stevens Ranch—locale UT-8
Stevens Ravine—valley CA-9
Stevens Reef—bar WI-6
Stevens Reservation—park AL-4
Stevens Ridge GA-3
Stevens Ridge—ridge (2) WA-9
Stevens Ridge Trail—trail MT-8
Stevens River ME-1
Stevens River—stream VT-1
Stevens Rock—bar ME-1
Stevens Rock—bar NY-2
Stevens (RR name for Silver Grove)—other KY-4
Stevens RR Station (historical)—locale FL-3
Stevens Rsvr—reservoir CO-8
Stevens Rsvr—reservoir NY-2
Stevens Rsvr—reservoir OR-9
Stevens Run—stream KY-4
Stevens Run—stream (2) PA-2
Stevens Run—stream VA-3
Stevens Run—stream WV-2
Stevens Saddle—gap ID-8
Stevens Sch PA-2
Stevens Sch—hist pl PA-2
Stevens Sch—school CO-8
Stevens Sch—school (4) CT-1
Stevens Sch—school DC-2
Stevens Sch—school (3) KY-4
Stevens Sch—school ME-1
Stevens Sch—school ND-7
Stevens Sch—school (8) PA-2
Stevens Sch—school TX-5
Stevens Sch—school VT-1
Stevens Sch—school (3) WA-9
Stevens Sch—school WV-2
Stevens Slough—gut ND-7
Stevens Slough—gut WI-6
Stevens Slough—lake ND-7
Stevens Slough—stream MT-8
Stevens Spring—spring AZ-5
Stevens Spring—spring MO-7
Stevens Spring—spring (2) NV-8
Stevens Spring—spring OR-9
Stevens Spring—spring UT-8
Stevens Spring—spring WI-6
Stevens Springs—spring NV-8
Stevens Spur—locale AL-4
Stevens Square—park MA-1
Stevens Square—park MN-6
Stevens State Sch of Technology PA-2
Stevens Station NJ-2
Stevens (Stevens Village)—other AK-9
Stevens Store—locale AR-4
Stevens Store (historical)—locale TN-4
Stevens Street Baptist Ch—church TN-4
Stevens Subdivision—pop pl UT-8
Stevens Swamp—swamp MA-1
Stevens Tank AZ-5
Stevens Tank—reservoir (3) AZ-5
Stevens Tank—reservoir (2) NM-5
Stevens Tank—reservoir TX-5
Stevenston IN-6
Stevenstown KS-7
Stevenstown—pop pl PA-2
Stevenstown—pop pl WI-6
Stevenstown Mine—mine AK-9
Stevens Township—pop pl ND-7
Stevens Township Hall—locale WA-9
Stevens (Township of)—pop pl MN-6
Stevens (Township of)—pop pl PA-2
Stevens Valley—valley PA-2
Stevens Valley—valley WI-6
Stevens-Van Trump Historical Monmt—park WA-9
Stevens Village—pop pl AK-9
Stevens Village ANV953—reserve AK-9
Stevensville NY-2
Stevensville—locale UT-8
Stevensville—pop pl ME-1
Stevensville—pop pl MD-2
Stevensville—pop pl MI-6
Stevensville—pop pl MT-8
Stevensville—pop pl PA-2
Stevensville—pop pl VT-1
Stevensville—pop pl VA-3
Stevensville Bank—hist pl MD-2
Stevensville Brook—stream VT-1
Stevensville Cem—cemetery MI-6
Stevensville Golf Course—other MT-8
Stevensville Hist Dist—hist pl MD-2
Stevensville (Magisterial District)—fmr MCD VA-3
Stevensville Rsvr—reservoir MT-8
Stevensville Station NJ-2
Stevens Wash—stream AZ-5
Stevens Wash—valley UT-8

Stick Gulch—valley ... MT-8
Stick Lake—lake ... CA-9
Stick Lake Canyon—valley ... CA-9
Stickland Chapel Cem—cemetery ... MS-4
Stickleback Lake—lake ... MI-6
Stickle Cattle Farms Airp—airport ... MO-7
Stickle Creek—stream ... MN-6
Stickle Hollow ... PA-2
Stickle Pond—reservoir (2) ... NJ-2
Stickle Pond Dam—dam (2) ... NJ-2
Stickler-Miller Cemetery ... PA-2
Stickler Run—stream ... WV-2
Stickler Spring—spring ... OR-9
Sticklerville—locale ... MO-7
Stickles Hollow—valley ... PA-2
Sticklestad Ch—church ... MN-6
Stickley—locale ... MI-6
Stickley, Gustav, House—hist pl ... NY-2
Stickley Cem—cemetery ... VA-3
Stickley House—hist pl ... TN-4
Stickley Lake—lake ... MI-6
Stickley Run—stream ... VA-3
**Stickleys—pop pl** ... VA-3
**Stickleyville—pop pl** ... VA-3
Sticklin Creek ... MT-8
Stickmeyer Bridge—bridge ... AL-4
Stickmeyer Mtn—summit ... AL-4
Stickney ... OH-6
Stickney—locale ... KS-7
Stickney—locale ... MO-7
**Stickney—pop pl** ... IL-6
**Stickney—pop pl** ... PA-2
**Stickney—pop pl** ... SD-7
**Stickney—pop pl** ... WV-2
Stickney, Charles H., House—hist pl ... CO-8
Stickney, George, House—hist pl ... IL-6
Stickney, Lake—lake ... WA-9
Stickney, Mount—summit ... NH-1
Stickney, Mount—summit ... WA-9
Stickney Airp—airport ... SD-7
Stickney Bridge—bridge ... NY-2
Stickney Brook—stream ... ME-1
Stickney Brook—stream ... NH-1
Stickney Brook—stream ... VT-1
**Stickney Corner—pop pl** ... ME-1
Stickney Creek—stream ... MT-8
Stickney Dam—dam ... SD-7
Stickney Glacier—valley ... ID-8
Stickney Gulch—valley ... ID-8
Stickney Gulch—valley ... OR-9
Stickney Hill—summit ... CT-1
Stickney Hill—summit (2) ... ME-1
Stickney Hill—summit ... VT-1
Stickney Hill Brook—stream ... CT-1
Stickney Lake—lake ... MN-6
Stickney Lake—lake ... NE-7
Stickney Lake—lake ... WA-9
Stickney Lake—reservoir (2) ... SD-7
Stickney Lake Dam—dam ... SD-7
Stickney Lateral—canal ... CA-9
Stickney Point—cape ... FL-3
Stickneys—locale ... NY-2
Stickney Sch—school ... MI-6
Stickney Sch—school ... OH-6
Stickney-Shepard House—hist pl ... MA-1
Stickney Slough—gut ... WA-9
**Stickney (Township of)—pop pl** ... IL-6
Stickpile Tunnel—tunnel ... MD-2
Stickpin Hill—summit ... WA-9
Stick Post Office (historical)—building ... TN-4
Stick Rock Creek—stream ... OR-9
Stick Ross Mtn—summit ... OK-5
Stick Run—stream ... IN-6
**Sticks—pop pl** ... PA-2
Stick Style House at Stony Creek—hist pl ... CT-1
Stick To It ... AL-4
Stickwan Creek—stream ... AK-9
Stickweed Pond—lake ... DE-2
Sticky Branch—stream ... IN-6
Sticky Branch—stream ... TX-5
Sticky Creek—stream ... MS-4
Sticky Creek—stream ... WY-8
Sticky Joe Spring—spring ... OR-9
Sticky River—stream ... ME-1
Stidam Creek ... OK-5
S Tidball Dam—dam ... SD-7
Stidham—locale ... KY-4
**Stidham—pop pl** ... OK-5
Stidham Bend—bend ... KY-4
Stidham Branch—stream ... KY-4
Stidham Cem—cemetery ... AL-4
Stidham Cem—cemetery ... OH-6
Stidham Cem—cemetery ... VA-3
Stidham Ch—church ... IN-6
Stidham Creek—stream ... OK-5
Stidham Fork—stream ... KY-4
Stidham Fork—stream (2) ... VA-3
Stidham Lake—lake ... WA-9
Stidham Post Office—locale ... KY-4
Stidham Ranch—locale ... AZ-5
Stidham Sch—school ... OK-5
Stid Hill—summit ... NY-2
Stidman Branch—stream ... TN-4
Stidmon Gap—gap ... GA-3
**Stiebels Corner—pop pl** ... WA-9
Stiefelmeyer's—hist pl ... AL-4
**Stiefeltown—pop pl** ... SC-3
Stiefler Cem—cemetery ... PA-2
Stiefler Corner—locale ... PA-2
Stiefler Hill—summit ... PA-2
Stiegel-Coleman House—hist pl ... PA-2
Stiegel Elem Sch—school ... PA-2
Stieger Lake—lake ... MN-6
Stieg Well—well ... MT-8
Stiehl Field—airport ... ND-7
Stiefeltown ... SC-3
Stieneke Area County Park—park ... IA-7
Stienhart Lakes—lake ... CA-9
Stienman ... OR-9
Stiens Creek ... ID-8
Stiens Pass ... ID-8
Stier ... PA-2
**Stier—pop pl** ... AR-4
**Stier—pop pl** ... PA-2
**Stieren—pop pl** ... TX-5
**Stier (Johnsonville)—pop pl** ... PA-2
Stierley Airp—airport ... IN-6
Stierman Gulch—valley ... ID-8
Stiemberg Cem—cemetery ... TX-5
Stiers ... PA-2
Stiers Cem—cemetery ... OH-6
**Stier Station—pop pl** ... PA-2
Stierwalt Cem—cemetery ... IN-6
Sties Canyon—valley ... WA-9
Stifel Creek—stream ... CO-8
Stiff, Bayou—stream ... LA-4
Stiffarm Coulee—valley ... MT-8
Stiff Creek—stream ... TX-5
Stiffknee Top—summit ... TN-4
Stiffknee Trail—trail ... TN-4
**Stiffler—pop pl** ... PA-2
Stiffler Drain—canal ... MI-6
Stiffler Ridge—ridge ... PA-2
**Stifflertown—pop pl** ... PA-2
Stiff Tree Draw—valley ... ID-8
Stiffy Hollow—valley ... TX-5
Stigall Elem Sch—school ... TN-4
Stigall Lake Number One—reservoir ... TX-5
Stigall Lake Number Two—reservoir ... TX-5
Stiger Cem—cemetery ... TX-5
Stigers Island—island ... KS-7
Stigerwalt, John, House—hist pl ... NC-3
Stiggall Cem—cemetery ... KY-4
Stigger Creek—stream ... VA-3
Stiggins Lake—lake ... AL-4
**Stigler—pop pl** ... OK-5
Stigler (CCD)—cens area ... OK-5
Stigler Cem—cemetery ... MS-4
Stigler Lake—reservoir ... OK-5
Stigler Sch
Gymnasium-Auditorium—hist pl ... OK-5
St. Ignace Mission—hist pl ... MI-6
**St. Ignatius—pop pl** ... MT-8
Stignatius Cem—cemetery ... VT-1
St. Ignatius College—hist pl ... IL-6
St. Ignatius HS—hist pl ... OH-6
St. Ignatius Mission—hist pl ... MT-8
Stikine River—stream ... AK-9
Stikine Strait—channel ... AK-9
Stiklestad Cem—cemetery ... ND-7
Stiklestad United Lutheran
Church—hist pl ... MN-6
Stilaguamish Lake ... WA-9
Stilaguamish River ... WA-9
Stile Pond ... MA-1
Stile Ranch—locale ... CA-9
Stile Reservoir ... MA-1
Stiles ... AZ-5
Stiles—locale ... KY-4
Stiles—locale ... NC-3
Stiles—locale ... ND-7
Stiles—locale ... TX-5
**Stiles—pop pl** ... IA-7
**Stiles—pop pl** ... NY-2
**Stiles—pop pl** ... PA-2
**Stiles—pop pl** ... WI-6
Stiles, Ezra, House—hist pl ... RI-1
Stilesboro—locale ... GA-3
Stiles Branch—stream ... NC-3
Stiles Brook—stream (2) ... CT-1
Stiles Brook—stream (2) ... VT-1
Stiles Canyon—valley ... CA-9
Stiles Cem—cemetery ... GA-3
Stiles Cem—cemetery ... IA-7
Stiles Cem—cemetery ... MI-6
Stiles Cem—cemetery (2) ... NC-3
Stiles Cem—cemetery ... OH-6
Stiles Cem—cemetery (2) ... TN-4
Stiles Cem—cemetery ... TX-5
Stiles Cem—cemetery ... VT-1
Stiles Chapel—church ... AL-4
Stiles Creek—stream ... AK-9
Stiles Creek—stream ... GA-3
Stiles Creek—stream ... TN-4
Stiles Crossing—locale ... KY-4
Stiles Crossing—locale ... PA-2
Stiles Flowage ... WI-6
Stiles Ford—locale ... TN-4
Stiles Hill ... AZ-5
Stiles Hill ... MA-1
Stiles Hill—summit ... MA-1
Stiles Hill—summit ... NY-2
Stiles Hill—summit ... PA-2
Stiles Hill—summit ... VT-1
Stiles-Hinson House—hist pl ... SC-3
Stiles (historical P.O.)—locale ... IA-7
Stiles Hollow—valley ... WV-2
Stiles Junction—locale ... WI-6
Stiles Lake—lake ... ME-1
Stiles Lookout Tower—locale ... WI-6
Stiles Memorial Cem—cemetery ... CT-1
Stiles Mtn—summit ... ME-1
Stiles Mtn—summit ... VT-1
Stiles Oil Field—oilfield ... TX-5
Stiles Pond ... WI-6
Stiles Pond—lake ... CT-1
Stiles Pond—lake ... VT-1
Stiles Pond—reservoir ... MA-1
Stiles Pond Outlet Dam—dam ... MA-1
Stiles Post Office (historical)—building ... AL-4
Stiles Reservoir Dam—dam ... MA-1
Stiles Rsvr—reservoir ... MA-1
Stiles Rsvr—reservoir ... NM-5
Stiles Rsvr—reservoir ... OR-9
Stiles Sch—school ... IL-6
Stiles Sch—school ... MI-6
Stiles Sch—school ... OH-6
Stiles Spring—spring ... KY-4
Stiles Spring—spring ... OR-9
**Stiles (Town of)—pop pl** ... WI-6
**Stilesville—pop pl** ... IN-6
**Stilesville—pop pl** ... NY-2
Stilesville Elem Sch—school ... IN-6
Stiletto Peak—summit ... WA-9
Stilhouse Hollow—valley ... PA-2
Stilke Lake—lake ... MN-6
Still—locale ... ND-7
Still—locale ... OR-9
Stillaguamish Country Club—other ... WA-9
Stillaguamish Grange—locale ... WA-9
stillaguamish Lake ... WA-9
Stillaguamish Peak—summit ... WA-9
Stillaguamish River ... WA-9
Stillaguamish River—stream ... WA-9
Stillaguamish River ... WA-9
Still Bay—bay ... NY-2
Still Bay—swamp ... FL-3
Still Bay—swamp (2) ... GA-3
**Still Bluff—pop pl** ... NC-3
Still Branch—stream (3) ... AL-4
Still Branch—stream (2) ... AR-4
Still Branch—stream (3) ... FL-3
Still Branch—stream (6) ... GA-3
Still Branch—stream ... KY-4
Still Branch—stream ... LA-4
Still Branch—stream ... MS-4
Still Branch—stream ... NC-3
Still Branch—stream ... SC-3
Still Branch—stream (2) ... TN-4
Still Branch—stream ... TX-5
Still Branch—stream ... VA-3
Still Branch Church ... MS-4
**Still Brook—pop pl** ... TN-4
Still Brook—stream (3) ... CT-1
Still Brook—stream (2) ... MA-1
Still Brook—stream ... NH-1
Still Brook—stream ... NY-2
Still Brook—stream ... VT-1
Still Camp Branch—stream (2) ... TN-4
Stillcamp Ch—church ... MO-7
Stillcamp Ditch—canal ... MO-7
Still Canyon—valley ... AZ-5
Still Canyon—valley ... CA-9
Still Canyon—valley ... CO-8
Still Canyon—valley ... NV-8
Still Canyon—valley (2) ... NM-5
Still Canyon—valley ... TX-5
Still Canyon Tank—reservoir ... AZ-5
Still Cave—cave (2) ... AL-4
Still Cem—cemetery ... AL-4
Still Cem—cemetery ... FL-3
Still Cem—cemetery ... GA-3
Still Cem—cemetery ... MS-4
Still Cem—cemetery ... MO-7
Still Cem—cemetery ... OK-5
Still Cem—cemetery ... TN-4
Still Corner Brook—stream ... MA-1
Still Corners—locale ... NY-2
Still Creek ... IN-6
Still Creek—gut (2) ... NC-3
Still Creek—gut ... SC-3
**Still Creek—pop pl** ... PA-2
Still Creek—stream ... AL-4
Still Creek—stream ... CA-9
Still Creek—stream ... CO-8
Still Creek—stream ... FL-3
Still Creek—stream (2) ... MT-8
Still Creek—stream ... NY-2
Still Creek—stream ... OK-5
Still Creek—stream (3) ... OR-9
Still Creek—stream ... PA-2
Still Creek—stream ... SC-3
Still Creek—stream ... TN-4
Still Creek—stream ... TX-5
Still Creek—stream (3) ... WA-9
Still Creek Campground—park ... OR-9
Still Creek Dam—dam ... PA-2
Still Creek Rsvr—reservoir ... PA-2
Still Creek Trail—trail ... OR-9
Stille—locale ... LA-4
**Stille—pop pl** ... LA-4
Stille Ranch—locale ... NE-7
Stilley—locale ... NC-3
Stilley Cem—cemetery ... IL-6
Stilley Cem—cemetery ... KY-4
Stilley House—hist pl ... KY-4
**Stilleys Crossroads—pop pl** ... NC-3
Stilleys Siding—uninc pl ... PA-2
Still Fork—stream ... OH-6
Still Fork Ch—church ... OH-6
Still Fork Church Cem—cemetery ... OH-6
Still Fork Creek—stream ... NC-3
Still Gulch—valley ... CA-9
Still Gulch—valley ... MT-8
Still Gulch—valley ... OR-9
Still Gut—stream ... NC-3
**Stillham—pop pl** ... NY-2
Still Harbor—bay ... AK-9
Still Harbor—bay ... WA-9
Still Head—swamp ... FL-3
Still Hill—summit ... NY-2
Still Hill—summit ... VT-1
Still Hill Cem—cemetery ... CT-1
Still Hollow—valley (4) ... AR-4
Still Hollow—valley ... KY-4
Still Hollow—valley (2) ... TN-4
Still Hollow—valley ... UT-8
Still Hollow—valley ... WV-2
Still Hollow Trail—trail ... AR-4
Still Hopes—hist pl ... SC-3
Still Hosp—hospital ... MO-7
Stillhouse Bayou—gut ... AR-4
Stillhouse Bayou—stream ... AR-4
Stillhouse Bayou—stream ... LA-4
Stillhouse Bottom—valley ... NC-3
Stillhouse Branch ... GA-3
Still House Branch ... TN-4
Stillhouse Branch—stream (3) ... AL-4
Stillhouse Branch—stream (3) ... AR-4
Stillhouse Branch—stream (4) ... GA-3
Stillhouse Branch—stream ... IL-6
Stillhouse Branch—stream (19) ... KY-4
Stillhouse Branch—stream ... MS-4
Still House Branch—stream ... MS-4
Stillhouse Branch—stream (2) ... MS-4
Stillhouse Branch—stream (2) ... MO-7
Stillhouse Branch—stream (16) ... NC-3
Stillhouse Branch—stream ... OH-6
Stillhouse Branch—stream (5) ... SC-3
Stillhouse Branch—stream (16) ... TN-4
Stillhouse Branch—stream (2) ... TX-5
Stillhouse Branch—stream (5) ... VA-3
Stillhouse Branch—stream (2) ... WV-2
Still House Brook—stream ... NJ-2
Stillhouse Cave ... MO-7
Stillhouse Cave—cave ... AL-4
Stillhouse Cave—cave ... MO-7
Stillhouse Cave—cave (2) ... TN-4
Stillhouse Cove—basin ... GA-3
Stillhouse Creek ... GA-3
Stillhouse Creek ... KY-4
Stillhouse Creek ... TX-5
Stillhouse Creek—stream (2) ... AR-4
Stillhouse Creek—stream (2) ... GA-3
Stillhouse Creek—stream ... LA-4
Stillhouse Creek—stream (2) ... TN-4
Stillhouse Creek—stream (2) ... TX-5
Stillhouse Creek—stream (2) ... VA-3
Stillhouse Creek Dam—dam ... TN-4
Stillhouse Creek (historical)—stream ... TN-4
Stillhouse Creek Lake—reservoir ... TN-4
Stillhouse Draft ... VA-3
Stillhouse Ferry—locale ... TX-5
Stillhouse Ford—locale ... MO-7
Stillhouse Gap—gap ... GA-3
Stillhouse Gap—gap ... NC-3
Stillhouse Gap—gap ... WV-2
Stillhouse Hill—summit ... KY-4
Stillhouse Hole—other ... TN-4
Stillhouse Hollow ... MO-7
Stillhouse Hollow—valley (9) ... AL-4
Stillhouse Hollow—valley (9) ... AR-4
Stillhouse Hollow—valley ... IL-6
Stillhouse Hollow—valley ... IN-6
Stillhouse Hollow—valley (2) ... KY-4
Still House Hollow—valley ... KY-4
Stillhouse Hollow—valley (11) ... KY-4
Stillhouse Hollow—valley (12) ... MO-7
Stillhouse Hollow—valley ... NC-3
Stillhouse Hollow—valley (3) ... PA-2
Stillhouse Hollow—valley (9) ... TN-4
Still House Hollow—valley ... TN-4
Stillhouse Hollow—valley (20) ... TN-4
Stillhouse Hollow—valley (2) ... TX-5
Stillhouse Hollow—valley (8) ... VA-3
Stillhouse Hollow—valley ... WV-2
Stillhouse Hollow Lake—reservoir ... TX-5
Stillhouse Hollow Parking Area—locale ... VA-3
Stillhouse Knob—summit ... GA-3
Stillhouse Knob—summit ... PA-2
Stillhouse Mtn—summit ... VA-3
Stillhouse Point—cape ... TN-4
Stillhouse Rock—cliff ... TN-4
Still House Run ... PA-2
Stillhouse Run—stream (2) ... OH-6
Stillhouse Run—stream (2) ... PA-2
Stillhouse Run—stream (3) ... VA-3
Stillhouse Run—stream (3) ... WV-2
Stillhouse Sch—school ... LA-4
Still House Shoals ... TN-4
Stillhouse Shoals—bar ... TN-4
Stillhouse Spring—spring ... AR-4
Stillhouse Spring—spring ... KY-4
Stillhouse Spring—spring ... MS-4
Stillhouse Spring—spring (2) ... MO-7
Stillhouse Spring—spring (2) ... TN-4
Stillhouse Springs—lake ... WI-6
**Stillhouse Springs—pop pl** ... MO-7
Stilling Basin Public Use Area—park ... OK-5
Stillings—locale ... MO-7
Stillings Cem—cemetery ... MO-7
Stillions—locale ... AR-4
Still Island—island ... AK-9
Still Island—island ... GA-3
Still JHS—school ... CA-9
Still Lake ... WI-6
Still Lake—lake ... CA-9
Still Lake—lake ... ID-8
Still Lake—lake ... IN-6
Still Lake—lake ... MI-6
Still Lake—lake ... MN-6
Still Lake—lake ... SD-7
Still Lake—reservoir ... NY-2
Still Landing—locale ... NC-3
Stillma Island ... MO-7
Stillman ... AR-4
Stillman ... WV-2
Stillman—locale ... MI-6
**Stillman—pop pl** ... WV-2
Stillman, Charles, House—hist pl ... TX-5
Stillman Bay—bay ... NY-2
Stillman Brook—stream ... NY-2
Stillman Coll—school ... AL-4
Stillman Creek—stream ... ID-8
Stillman Creek—stream ... IL-6
Stillman Creek—stream ... KS-7
Stillman Creek—stream ... NJ-2
Stillman Creek—stream ... NY-2
Stillman Creek—stream ... UT-8
Stillman Creek—stream ... WA-9
Stillman Ditch—canal ... AL-4
Stillman Glade—gut ... DE-2
Stillman Heights Elementary School ... AL-4
Stillman Heights Sch—school ... AL-4
Stillman Hollow ... VA-3
Stillman Institute ... AL-4
Stillman Lake—lake ... ID-8
Stillman Loading Pens—locale ... TX-5
Stillman Park—park ... OR-9
Stillman Park—park ... TX-5
Stillman Point—cliff ... ID-8
Stillman Pond—lake ... CT-1
Stillmans Branch ... KS-7
Stillman Sch—school ... AR-4
Stillman Sch—school ... CT-1
Stillman Sch—school (2) ... NJ-2
**Stillmans Corner—pop pl** ... CT-1
Stillman's Run Battle Site—hist pl ... IL-6
**Stillman Valley—pop pl** ... IL-6
Stillman Valley—valley ... TX-5
Stillman Valley Creek—stream ... TX-5
**Stillman Village—pop pl** ... NY-2
**Stillmanville—pop pl** ... RI-1
**Still Meadow—pop pl** ... NE-7
**Stillmeadows—pop pl** ... MD-2
**Still Meadows (subdivision)—pop pl** ... NC-3
Still Memorial Cem—cemetery ... AL-4
Stillmett Creek ... WA-9
Stillmore—locale ... MS-4
**Stillmore—pop pl** ... GA-3
Stillmore Cem—cemetery ... GA-3
**Stillons (historical)—pop pl** ... MS-4
Stillpond ... MD-2
Still Pond—inlet ... NJ-2
Still Pond—bay ... MD-2
Still Pond—lake (4) ... FL-3
Still Pond—lake ... NH-1
**Still Pond—pop pl** ... MD-2
Still Pond—swamp ... AL-4
Stillpond Creek ... MD-2
Still Pond Creek—stream ... MD-2
Stillpond Neck ... MD-2
Still Pond Neck—cape ... MD-2
Still Pond Station—locale ... MD-2
Still Ridge—ridge ... NM-5
Still River ... MA-1
Still River—locale ... CT-1
**Still River—pop pl** ... MA-1
Still River—stream (3) ... CT-1
Still River—stream ... MA-1
Still River Village ... MA-1
Stillrock Branch—stream ... KY-4
Still Run ... VA-3
Still Run ... WV-2
Still Run—stream (2) ... NJ-2
Still Run—stream (3) ... VA-3
Still Run—stream ... WV-2
Stills Cem—cemetery ... AL-4
Stills Cem—cemetery (2) ... TN-4
Still Sch (historical)—school ... PA-2
Stills Creek—stream ... TX-5
Stills Cross Road ... AL-4
**Stills Cross Road—pop pl** ... AL-4
Stills Crossroads—locale ... AL-4
Stills Landing (Ruins)—locale ... CA-9
Stills Mtn—summit ... VA-3
Stillson Creek—stream ... WI-6
Stillson Hill—summit ... CT-1
Stillson Hill Sch—school ... PA-2
Stillson Hill Sch (abandoned)—school ... PA-2
Stillson Pond—lake ... NY-2
Stillson Sch—school ... WI-6
Stills Point—cape ... ME-1
Still Spring—spring ... AZ-5
Still Spring—spring ... MO-7
Still Spring—spring (2) ... OR-9
Still Spring—spring ... UT-8
Still Spring Branch—stream ... AR-4
Still Spring Creek—stream ... OR-9
Still Spring Hollow—valley ... MO-7
Still Station ... OR-9
Still Swamp—swamp ... PA-2
Still Tank—reservoir ... AZ-5
Still Tank—reservoir ... NM-5
**Still Valley—pop pl** ... NJ-2
Stillwagon Mine—mine ... CA-9
Stillwater ... ME-1
Stillwater—locale ... AR-4
Stillwater—locale ... KY-4
Stillwater—locale ... NH-1
Stillwater—locale (2) ... NY-2
Stillwater—locale ... OH-6
Stillwater—locale ... RI-1
Stillwater—locale ... WA-9
**Stillwater—pop pl** ... ME-1
**Stillwater—pop pl** ... MN-6
**Stillwater—pop pl** ... NV-8
**Stillwater—pop pl** ... NJ-2
**Stillwater—pop pl (3)** ... NY-2
**Stillwater—pop pl** ... OK-5
**Stillwater—pop pl** ... PA-2
Stillwater—swamp ... NY-2
Stillwater, The—stream ... NY-2
Stillwater Anchorage—bay ... AK-9
**Stillwater Ave—pop pl** ... ME-1
Stillwater Basin—bay ... MA-1
Still Water Bay—bay ... MO-7
Stillwater Bay—bay ... TX-5
Stillwater Bayou—stream ... MS-4
Stillwater Borough—civil ... PA-2
Stillwater Branch—stream ... NC-3
Stillwater Bridge—bridge ... MA-1
Stillwater Brook—stream (2) ... NY-2
Stillwater Brook—stream ... VT-1
Stillwater Butte—summit ... CA-9
Stillwater By-Pass—trail ... NH-1
Stillwater Campground—locale ... CO-8
Stillwater Campground—locale ... UT-8
Stillwater Canon ... UT-8
Stillwater Canyon—valley ... UT-8
Stillwater (CCD)—cens area ... OK-5
Stillwater Cem—cemetery ... IA-7
Stillwater Cem—cemetery ... NY-2
Stillwater Cem—cemetery ... OH-6
Stillwater Ch—church ... MT-8
Stillwater Country Club—other ... OK-5
Stillwater Cove—bay (2) ... CA-9
Stillwater Cove County Park—park ... CA-9
Stillwater Covered Bridge No.
134—hist pl ... PA-2
Stillwater Creek ... NC-3
Stillwater Creek ... OH-6
Still Water Creek ... PA-2
Stillwater Creek—stream ... AK-9
Stillwater Creek—stream ... CA-9
Stillwater Creek—stream ... CO-8
Stillwater Creek—stream ... IN-6
Stillwater Creek—stream ... KY-4
Stillwater Creek—stream ... NY-2
Stillwater Creek—stream ... OH-6
Stillwater Creek—stream ... OK-5
Stillwater Creek—stream ... PA-2
Stillwater Creek—stream ... VA-3
Stillwater Creek—stream (2) ... WA-9
Stillwater Dam—dam ... PA-2
Stillwater Ditch ... CO-8
Stillwater Ditch—canal ... CO-8
Stillwater Ditch—canal ... MT-8
Stillwater Dump—flat ... NV-8
Stillwater Fork—stream ... UT-8
Stillwater Grange—locale ... MT-8
Stillwater Harbor ... CA-9
Stillwater Heliport—airport ... UT-8
**Stillwater Hill—pop pl** ... NY-2
Stillwater (historical P.O.)—locale ... IA-7
Stillwater Inlet—stream ... NY-2
**Stillwater Junction—pop pl** ... NY-2
**Stillwater Junction—pop pl** ... OH-6
Stillwater Lake—reservoir (3) ... PA-2
Stillwater Lake Dam—dam ... PA-2
**Stillwater Lake Estates—pop pl** ... PA-2
Stillwater Lakes ... NV-8
Stillwater Marsh—hist pl ... NV-8
Stillwater Marsh—swamp ... NV-8
Stillwater Meadows—flat ... CA-9
Stillwater Mountains ... NV-8
Stillwater Mtn—summit ... NY-2
Stillwater Natl Wildlife Ref—park ... NV-8
Stillwater Natural Area—area ... PA-2
Stillwater North—cens area ... MT-8
Stillwater Oil Field—oilfield ... OK-5
Stillwater Park—flat ... CO-8
Stillwater Park—flat ... WY-8
Stillwater Park Playground—park ... ME-1
Stillwater Plains—plain ... CA-9
Stillwater Plateau—plain ... MT-8
Stillwater Point—cliff ... NV-8
Stillwater Point Rsvr—reservoir ... NV-8
Stillwater Pond—lake ... CT-1
Stillwater Pond—lake (2) ... MA-1
Stillwater Pond—lake ... NY-2
Stillwater Pond—lake ... VT-1
Stillwater Pond—reservoir ... CT-1
Stillwater Pond—reservoir ... RI-1
Stillwater Pond Dam—dam ... RI-1
Stillwater Range—range ... NV-8
Stillwater Ranger Station—locale ... MT-8
Stillwater Ranger Station Hist
Dist—hist pl ... MT-8
Stillwater Reservoir ... MA-1
Stillwater Reservoir ... PA-2
Stillwater Reservoir Dam—dam ... PA-2
Stillwater Reservoir Dam—dam ... RI-1
Stillwater Reservoir Diversion
Canal—canal ... NV-8
Stillwater River ... MA-1
Stillwater River ... RI-1
Stillwater River—stream ... ME-1
Stillwater River—stream ... MA-1
Stillwater River—stream (2) ... MT-8
Stillwater River—stream ... OH-6
Stillwater River—stream ... RI-1
Stillwater Rsvr ... RI-1
Stillwater Rsvr—reservoir ... CO-8
Stillwater Rsvr—reservoir ... NY-2
Stillwater Rsvr—reservoir ... RI-1
Still Waters—lake ... CO-8
**Still Waters—pop pl** ... AL-4
Stillwater Sanitorium—hospital ... OH-6
Stillwater Santa Fe Depot—hist pl ... OK-5
Stillwater Sch—school ... NV-8
Still Waters Dam—dam ... AL-4
Stillwater Slough—stream ... NV-8
Stillwater Slough Cutoff—canal ... NV-8
Still Waters Marina—locale ... AL-4
Stillwater State For—forest ... MT-8
Stillwater State Game Perserve—park ... MT-8
Stillwater Station—locale ... NJ-2
Stillwater Swamp—swamp ... VT-1
**Stillwater (Town of)—pop pl** ... NY-2
**Stillwater Township—pop pl** ... ND-7
**Stillwater (Township of)—pop pl** ... MN-6
**Stillwater (Township of)—pop pl** ... NJ-2
Stillwater Trail—trail ... NH-1
Stillwater Truck Trail—trail ... WA-9
Stillwater Union Cem—cemetery ... NY-2
Stillwater Valley—valley ... CO-8
Stillwater Wildlife Mngmt Area—park ... NV-8
Stillwell ... KS-7
Stillwell—locale ... AK-9
Stillwell—locale ... WV-2
**Stillwell—pop pl** ... GA-3
**Stillwell—pop pl** ... IL-6
**Stillwell—pop pl** ... IN-6
**Stillwell—pop pl** ... IA-7
**Stillwell—pop pl** ... OH-6
Stillwell Branch—stream ... GA-3
Stillwell Branch—stream ... KY-4
Stillwell Branch—stream ... NC-3
Stillwell Cem—cemetery ... GA-3
Stillwell Cem—cemetery (2) ... IN-6
Stillwell Cem—cemetery ... MO-7
Stillwell Cem—cemetery ... NC-3
Stillwell Ch—church ... WV-2
Stillwell Cove ... MD-2
Stillwell Creek—stream ... NC-3
Stillwell Creek—stream ... OR-9
Stillwell Creek—stream ... TX-5
Stillwell Creek—stream ... WA-9
Stillwell Creek—stream ... WV-2
Stillwell Creek—stream ... WI-6
Stillwell Crossing—locale ... TX-5
Stillwell Dam—dam ... WI-6
Stillwell Elem Sch—school ... IN-6
Stillwell Hollow—valley (2) ... MO-7
Stillwell Hollow—valley ... WV-2
Stillwell Lake ... NY-2
Stillwell Lake—lake ... MI-6
Stillwell Lake—lake ... NC-3
Stillwell Lake Trail—trail ... NY-2
Stillwell Mtn—summit ... AR-4
Stillwell Mtn—summit ... TX-5
Stillwell Point—cape ... CA-9
Stillwell-Preston House—hist pl ... NJ-2
Stillwell Ranch—locale ... CA-9
Stillwell Ranch—locale ... SD-7
Stillwell Ranch—locale ... TX-5
Stillwell Ridge ... PA-2
Stillwell Run—stream ... VA-3
Stillwell Sch—school ... AR-4
Stillwell Sch—school ... KS-7
Stillwell Sch—school ... WV-2
Stillwell Shelter—locale ... WA-9
Stillwells Mill (historical)—locale ... AL-4
Stillwell's Ranch ... TX-5
Stillwell Tower—locale ... LA-4
Stillwell Tunnel—mine ... CO-8
**Stillwood (subdivision)—pop pl** ... NC-3
Stillwright Point ... FL-3
Stilly Hollow—valley ... TN-4
Stilson—locale ... TX-5
**Stilson—pop pl** ... GA-3
**Stilson—pop pl** ... IA-7
Stilson Cem—cemetery ... MI-6
Stilson Creek—stream ... OR-9
Stilson (historical)—locale ... KS-7
Stilson Pond—lake ... NY-2
Stils Pond ... MA-1
Stiltner—locale ... WV-2
Stiltner Branch—stream ... VA-3
Stiltner Cem—cemetery ... WV-2
Stiltner Creek—stream ... OR-9
Stiltner Creek—stream ... VA-3
**Stilton—pop pl** ... SC-3
Stilton Branch—stream ... VA-3
Stilton Creek ... VA-3
Stilton Valley ... MO-7
Stiltz—locale ... PA-2
**Stiltz—pop pl** ... MD-2
**Stilwell—pop pl** ... KS-7
**Stilwell—pop pl** ... OK-5
Stilwell, Lake—lake ... WA-9
Stilwell, Thomas, House—hist pl ... NY-2
Stilwell Ch—church ... ND-7
Stilwell City Lake—reservoir ... OK-5
Stilwell East (CCD)—cens area ... OK-5
Stilwell Elem Sch—school ... KS-7
Stilwell Hollow—valley ... VA-3
Stilwell Lake—reservoir ... NY-2
Stilwell Park—park ... OK-5

St. Mary's Roman Catholic Church Complex—*hist pl* ... IA-7
St Marys Run—*stream* ... IN-6
St. Mary's Sch—*hist pl* ... OH-6
St. Marys Township—*fmr MCD* ... IA-7
**St. Marys Township**—*pop pl* ... ND-7
*St. Marys Transfer* ... MI-6
**St. Mary Township**—*pop pl* ... ND-7
St Mattews Ch—*church* ... MO-7
St. Matthews—*hist pl* ... MA-1
St. Matthew's Cathedral Close—*hist pl* ... WY-8
St. Matthew's Church—*hist pl* ... RI-1
St. Matthews Episcopal Ch—*church* ... UT-8
St. Matthew's Sch—*hist pl* ... MN-6
St. Matthias' Episcopal Church—*hist pl* ... NE-7
**St. Michael**—*pop pl* ... NE-7
**St. Michael**—*pop pl* ... ND-7
St. Michael Catholic Church—*hist pl* ... OH-6
St. Michael Catholic Church Complex—*hist pl* ... OH-6
St. Michael's Catholic Church Complex—*hist pl* ... NE-7
St. Michael's Church—*hist pl* ... MA-1
St. Michael's Church—*hist pl* ... ND-7
St. Michael's Church, Cemetery, Rectory and Ancient Order of Hibernians Hall—*hist pl* ... IA-7
St. Michaels Episcopal Ch—*church* ... UT-8
St. Michael's Episcopal Church—*hist pl* ... SC-3
St. Michael's Mission—*hist pl* ... WY-8
St. Michael's Roman Catholic Church, Convent, Rectory, and School—*hist pl* ... RI-1
St. Michael's Sch and Convent—*hist pl* ... MN-6
St. Michael the Archangel Catholic Church—*hist pl* ... OH-6
Stnenkjer Cem—*cemetery* ... ND-7
St. Nicholas Catholic Church and Rectory—*hist pl* ... OH-6
St. Nicholas Hotel—*hist pl* ... IL-6
St. Nicholas Orthodox Church—*hist pl* ... MN-6
St. Nicholas's Catholic Church—*hist pl* ... OH-6
Stoak Creek—*stream* ... MO-7
Stoakes Creek—*stream* ... VA-3
Stoakley—*locale* ... MD-2
*Stoap Creek* ... CA-9
*Stoapit* ... AZ-5
**Stoa Pitk**—*pop pl* ... AZ-5
Stoa Sch—*school* ... MN-6
Stoa Slough—*swamp* ... SD-7
Stoa Tontk Well—*well* ... AZ-5
Stoa Vaya (site)—*locale* ... AZ-5
Stobaugh House—*hist pl* ... AR-4
Stob Gap—*gap* ... AR-4
Stob Gap Hollow—*valley* ... AR-4
Stobie Gulch—*valley* ... ID-8
Stobie Ranch—*locale* ... MT-8
Stob Lake—*lake* ... GA-3
**Stobo**—*pop pl* ... PA-2
Stobtown Ch—*church* ... OK-5
*Stobual* ... MP-9
*Stobual Island* ... MP-9
*Stoby Creek* ... NC-3
*Stocemouo Point* ... ME-1
Stoch Ditch—*canal* ... IN-6
Stockade—*locale* ... FL-3
Stockade, The—*hist pl* ... SC-3
Stockade, The—*summit* ... SC-3
Stockade Beaver Creek—*stream* ... SD-7
Stockade Beaver Creek—*stream* ... WY-8
Stockade Buttes—*summit* ... OR-9
Stockade Canyon—*valley* ... NV-8
Stockade Cem—*cemetery* ... MS-4
Stockade Creek—*stream* (3) ... OR-9
Stockade Creek—*stream* ... WY-8
Stockade Draw—*valley* ... SD-7
Stockade Flat—*flat* ... CA-9
Stockade Hist Dist—*hist pl* ... NY-2
Stockade Hist Dist (Boundary Increase)—*hist pl* ... NY-2
Stockade Lake—*lake* ... WY-8
Stockade Lake Dam—*dam* ... SD-7
Stockade Mtn—*summit* ... NC-3
Stockade Mtn—*summit* ... OR-9
Stockade Point—*cape* ... AK-9
Stockade Redan (historical)—*locale* ... MS-4
Stockade Sch—*school* ... MT-8
Stockade Spring—*spring* (3) ... NV-8
Stockade Spring Campground—*locale* ... WA-9
Stockade Springs—*spring* ... NV-8
Stockade Springs—*spring* ... OR-9
Stockade Tank—*reservoir* ... NM-5
Stockade Wash—*stream* ... NV-8
*Stockaloa Creek* ... MS-4
Stockard—*locale* ... TX-5
Stockard Branch—*stream* ... TN-4
Stockard Cem—*cemetery* ... TN-4
Stockard Ford—*locale* ... TN-4
Stockard Hollow—*valley* ... TN-4
Stockard JHS—*school* ... TX-5
Stockard Prospect—*mine* ... TN-4
Stockards Store (historical)—*locale* ... MS-4
Stockberger Well—*well* ... NV-8
Stock Branch—*stream* ... VA-3
Stockbrands and Kemmerer Department Store—*hist pl* ... KS-7
**Stockbridge**—*pop pl* ... GA-3
**Stockbridge**—*pop pl* ... MA-1
**Stockbridge**—*pop pl* ... MI-6
**Stockbridge**—*pop pl* ... NY-2
**Stockbridge**—*pop pl* ... VT-1
**Stockbridge**—*pop pl* (2) ... WI-6
*Stockbridge, Town of* ... MA-1
Stockbridge Apartment Bldg—*hist pl* ... OH-6
Stockbridge Bowl—*reservoir* ... MA-1
Stockbridge Bowl Dam—*dam* ... MA-1
Stockbridge Branch—*stream* ... ME-1
Stockbridge Casino—*hist pl* ... MA-1
Stockbridge (CCD)—*cens area* ... GA-3
Stockbridge Cem—*cemetery* ... ME-1
Stockbridge Cem—*cemetery* (2) ... MA-1
Stockbridge Cem—*cemetery* ... NY-2
Stockbridge (census name for Stockbridge Center)—*CDP* ... MA-1
Stockbridge Center (census name Stockbridge)—*other* ... MA-1
Stockbridge Ch—*church* ... WI-6
Stockbridge Corner—*locale* ... NH-1
**Stockbridge Corners**—*pop pl* ... NH-1
Stockbridge Falls—*falls* ... NY-2
Stockbridge Gap—*gap* ... VT-1
Stockbridge Harbor—*bay* ... WI-6
Stockbridge Hill—*summit* ... ME-1
Stockbridge (historical)—*locale* ... MO-7
Stockbridge House—*hist pl* ... CO-8
**Stockbridge Ind Res**—*pop pl* ... WI-6
Stockbridge Knoll—*summit* ... TX-5
*Stockbridge Mountain* ... MA-1
Stockbridge Mtn—*summit* ... NY-2
Stockbridge Plains Sch—*school* ... MA-1
Stockbridge Point—*cape* ... ME-1
Stockbridge Pond—*lake* ... ME-1
Stockbridge Quarry—*facility* ... GA-3
Stockbridge Sch—*school* ... MA-1
Stockbridge Sch—*school* ... OH-6
Stockbridge Town Hall—*hist pl* ... MI-6
**Stockbridge (Town of)**—*pop pl* ... MA-1
**Stockbridge (Town of)**—*pop pl* ... NY-2
**Stockbridge (Town of)**—*pop pl* ... VT-1
**Stockbridge (Town of)**—*pop pl* ... WI-6
**Stockbridge (Township of)**—*pop pl* ... MI-6
Stockbridge Valley—*valley* ... NY-2
Stockbridge Valley HS—*school* ... NY-2
Stockburger Ridge—*ridge* ... GA-3
Stock Cabin—*locale* ... WY-8
Stock Canyon—*valley* ... CO-8
Stock Canyon—*valley* ... WA-9
Stock Cem—*cemetery* ... MO-7
Stock Center—*hist pl* ... WY-8
**Stock Creek**—*pop pl* ... TN-4
Stock Creek—*stream* ... MD-2
Stock Creek—*stream* ... MT-8
Stock Creek—*stream* (2) ... TN-4
Stock Creek—*stream* (2) ... VA-3
Stock Creek—*stream* ... WA-9
Stock Creek Ch—*church* ... TN-4
Stock Creek Dock—*locale* ... TN-4
*Stock Creek Ridge* ... TN-4
Stockdale—*locale* ... IL-6
Stockdale—*locale* ... MO-7
**Stockdale**—*pop pl* ... AL-4
**Stockdale**—*pop pl* ... CA-9
**Stockdale**—*pop pl* ... DE-2
**Stockdale**—*pop pl* (2) ... IN-6
**Stockdale**—*pop pl* ... OH-6
**Stockdale**—*pop pl* ... PA-2
**Stockdale**—*pop pl* ... TX-5
Stockdale Baptist Ch—*church* ... AL-4
Stockdale Borough—*civil* ... PA-2
Stockdale (CCD)—*cens area* ... TX-5
Stockdale Ch—*church* ... OH-6
Stockdale Country Club—*other* ... CA-9
Stockdale Creek—*stream* ... CO-8
Stockdale Creek—*stream* ... OR-9
Stockdale Creek—*stream* ... WY-8
Stockdale Harbor—*harbor* ... AK-9
Stockdale (historical)—*locale* ... KS-7
Stockdale Lake—*lake* ... NE-7
Stockdale Lake—*reservoir* ... SD-7
Stockdale Mine Supply Airp—*airport* ... PA-2
Stockdale Mtn—*summit* ... CA-9
Stockdale Point—*summit* ... CO-8
Stockdale Ranch—*locale* (2) ... CA-9
Stockdale Rec Area—*park* ... KS-7
Stockdale Rsvr—*reservoir* ... CO-8
Stockdale School (historical)—*locale* ... MO-7
Stockdale Siding—*locale* ... OH-6
Stock Dam P10 A1 Rsvr—*reservoir* ... ND-7
Stockdate Cem—*cemetery* ... TN-4
Stock Ditch—*canal* ... IN-6
Stock Ditch—*canal* ... OR-9
Stock Drive Trail—*trail* ... MT-8
Stock Driveway Canyon—*valley* ... NM-5
Stock Driveway Rsvr—*reservoir* ... AZ-5
Stocke Butte—*summit* ... ND-7
Stockel Creek—*stream* ... OR-9
Stocker Branch—*stream* ... MT-8
Stocker Brook—*stream* ... NH-1
Stocker Coulee—*valley* ... MT-8
Stocker Creek—*stream* ... MT-8
Stocker Ditch—*canal* ... MT-8
Stocker Draw—*valley* ... MT-8
Stocker Hill—*summit* ... TN-4
Stocker Island—*island* ... PA-2
Stocker Knob—*summit* ... VA-3
Stocker Pond—*lake* ... NH-1
Stocker Ridge—*ridge* ... OH-6
Stocker Run—*stream* ... OH-6
Stockers Knob—*summit* ... VA-3
*Stockersville* ... PA-2
**Stockertown**—*pop pl* ... PA-2
Stockertown Borough—*civil* ... PA-2
Stockerts (Site)—*locale* ... WV-2
**Stockett**—*pop pl* ... MT-8
Stocketts Run—*stream* ... MD-2
Stock Exchange Bank—*hist pl* ... OK-5
Stockey Sch—*school* ... MI-6
Stockfarm Creek—*stream* ... LA-4
Stockfarm Creek—*stream* ... MS-4
Stock Farm Ditch—*canal* ... IN-6
Stock Farm Mtn—*summit* ... NH-1
Stockfarm Sch—*school* ... MS-4
Stockfeldt Cem—*cemetery* ... NE-7
Stockfleith Ditch—*canal* ... IN-6
Stockgrowers Bank—*hist pl* ... WY-8
Stockgrowers Bank Bldg—*hist pl* ... SD-7
Stockgrowers State Bank—*hist pl* ... KS-7
**Stockham**—*pop pl* ... AZ-5
**Stockham**—*pop pl* ... NE-7
**Stockham**—*pop pl* ... OH-6
Stockham Cem—*cemetery* ... NE-7
Stockham Hill—*summit* ... NY-2
Stockham Park—*park* ... AL-4
Stockham RR Station—*building* ... AZ-5
Stockhaven Lake—*lake* ... MN-6
Stock Hill—*locale* ... GA-3
Stockhoff Creek—*stream* ... CA-9
Stockhoff Rsvr—*reservoir* ... OR-9
Stock Hollow—*valley* ... TN-4
**Stockholm**—*pop pl* ... KY-4
**Stockholm**—*pop pl* ... ME-1
**Stockholm**—*pop pl* ... MN-6
**Stockholm**—*pop pl* ... NJ-2
**Stockholm**—*pop pl* ... SD-7
**Stockholm**—*pop pl* ... TX-5
**Stockholm**—*pop pl* ... WI-6
Stockholm, Lake—*reservoir* ... NJ-2
Stockholm Bay—*bay* ... AK-9
Stockholm Brook—*stream* ... NY-2
Stockholm Cem—*cemetery* ... KS-7
Stockholm Cem—*cemetery* ... SD-7
**Stockholm Center**—*pop pl* ... NY-2
Stockholm Ch—*church* ... KY-4
Stockholm Ch—*church* ... NE-7
Stockholm Ch—*church* ... WI-6
Stockholm Creek—*stream* ... KY-4
Stockholm-DeKalb-Hart Hist Dist—*hist pl* ... NY-2
Stockholm Hollow—*valley* ... KY-4
Stockholm Lake—*lake* ... NE-7
Stockholm Mtn—*summit* ... ME-1
Stockholm Point—*cape* ... AK-9
**Stockholm (Town of)**—*pop pl* ... ME-1
**Stockholm (Town of)**—*pop pl* ... NY-2
**Stockholm (Town of)**—*pop pl* ... WI-6
Stockholm Township—*fmr MCD* ... IA-7
**Stockholm Township**—*pop pl* ... SD-7
**Stockholm (Township of)**—*pop pl* ... MN-6
Stockholm United Methodist Church—*hist pl* ... NJ-2
Stockhousen Lake—*lake* ... MN-6
Stocking, Samuel, House—*hist pl* ... NY-2
Stocking Brook—*stream* (2) ... CT-1
Stocking Creek—*stream* ... MN-6
Stocking Creek—*stream* ... NY-2
Stocking Head Creek—*stream* ... GA-3
Stocking Head Creek—*stream* ... NC-3
Stocking Hill—*summit* ... NY-2
*Stocking Lake* ... MN-6
Stocking Lake—*lake* ... CA-9
Stocking Lake—*lake* ... MI-6
Stocking Lake—*lake* (3) ... MN-6
Stockingleg Fork—*stream* ... WV-2
Stocking Leg Hollow—*valley* ... OH-6
Stocking Meadow Lookout—*locale* ... ID-8
Stocking Meadows—*flat* ... ID-8
Stocking Mill Dam—*dam* ... MA-1
Stocking Point—*cape* ... MN-6
Stocking Ranch—*locale* ... ID-8
Stocking Range—*locale* ... ID-8
Stocking Run—*stream* ... WV-2
Stocking Sch—*school* ... MI-6
Stockings Fork—*valley* ... UT-8
Stockington—*locale* ... NJ-2
*Stocking Town* ... NJ-2
**Stocking Township**—*pop pl* ... NE-7
Stock Island—*CDP* ... FL-3
Stock Island—*island* ... FL-3
Stock Island—*island* ... LA-4
Stock Island Channel—*channel* ... FL-3
Stock Judging Pavilion—*hist pl* ... IA-7
Stock Judging Pavilion—*hist pl* ... SD-7
**Stockland**—*pop pl* ... IL-6
Stockland Rsvr—*reservoir* ... NV-8
**Stockland (Township of)**—*pop pl* ... IL-6
Stockley—*locale* ... DE-2
*Stockley Branch* ... DE-2
Stockley Branch—*stream* ... DE-2
Stockley Creek—*stream* ... AK-9
Stockley Creek—*stream* ... DE-2
Stockley Creek—*stream* ... WI-6
Stockley Gut—*gut* ... DE-2
*Stockley Hill* ... TX-5
Stocklmeir Sch—*school* ... CA-9
**Stockly**—*pop pl* ... DE-2
Stockly Bay—*bay* ... MI-6
*Stockman* ... SC-3
Stockman—*locale* ... TX-5
**Stockman**—*pop pl* ... SC-3
Stockman, Dr. G. C., House—*hist pl* ... IA-7
*Stockman Branch* ... SC-3
Stockman Branch—*stream* (2) ... SC-3
Stockman Cem—*cemetery* ... OH-6
Stockman Creek—*stream* ... TX-5
*Stockman Ditch* ... IN-6
Stockman Hollow—*valley* ... TX-5
Stockman Island—*island* ... ME-1
Stockman Park—*park* ... SC-3
Stockman Rsvr—*reservoir* ... MT-8
Stockman Run—*stream* ... PA-2
Stockmans Inn (historical)—*locale* ... TN-4
*Stockmans Island* ... ME-1
Stockman Spring—*spring* ... AZ-5
Stockman Station—*locale* (2) ... AZ-5
Stockman Trail—*trail* ... MT-8
Stockmens Association Cabin—*locale* ... MT-8
*Stockmore Forest Service Station* ... UT-8
Stockmore Ranger Station—*locale* ... UT-8
Stockney Creek—*stream* ... ID-8
Stock Number Two Tank—*reservoir* ... AZ-5
Stock Park—*park* ... ID-8
Stock Pass Gulch—*valley* ... CO-8
Stock Pavilion—*hist pl* ... WI-6
Stock Pen Canyon—*valley* ... AZ-5
Stock Pen Lake—*lake* ... TX-5
Stockpen Prairie—*flat* ... TX-5
Stock Pen Tank—*reservoir* ... AZ-5
Stock Pond—*lake* ... AZ-5
Stock Pond—*lake* ... UT-8
Stockpond Tank—*reservoir* ... AZ-5
Stockport—*locale* ... PA-2
**Stockport**—*pop pl* ... IN-6
**Stockport**—*pop pl* ... IA-7
**Stockport**—*pop pl* (2) ... NY-2
**Stockport**—*pop pl* ... OH-6
Stockport Creek—*stream* ... NY-2
Stockport Creek—*stream* ... PA-2
Stockport Middle Ground—*island* ... NY-2
Stockport Station—*locale* ... NY-2
**Stockport (Town of)**—*pop pl* ... NY-2
Stock Post Office (historical)—*building* ... SD-7
*Stock Range* ... KS-7
Stockrange (historical)—*locale* ... KS-7
Stockrest Well—*well* ... WY-8
*Stock Rider Peak* ... CO-8
Stockridge Indian Cemetery—*hist pl* ... WI-6
**Stocks**—*pop pl* ... GA-3
Stocks Canyon—*valley* ... AZ-5
Stocks Creek—*stream* ... MI-6
Stocks Creek—*stream* ... NV-8
Stocks Farming Company Ranch—*locale* ... NV-8
Stocks Hill—*summit* ... AL-4
Stock Slough—*stream* ... OR-9
*Stocks Mills* ... AL-4
*Stocks Mills Post Office* ... AL-4
Stocks Mine (underground)—*mine* ... AL-4
Stocks Pond—*lake* ... GA-3
Stocks Ranch—*locale* ... TX-5
Stockstill Creek—*stream* ... TN-4
Stockstill Lake—*lake* ... LA-4
**Stocksville**—*pop pl* ... NC-3
Stocks Well Number One—*well* ... TX-5
Stock Tank Number Three—*reservoir* ... AZ-5
*Stockton* ... IN-6
*Stockton* ... NJ-2
*Stockton* ... OH-6
*Stockton* ... TN-4
*Stockton* ... UT-8
*Stockton* ... VA-3
Stockton—*fmr MCD* ... NE-7
Stockton—*hist pl* ... NC-3
Stockton—*locale* ... AZ-5
Stockton—*locale* ... AR-4
Stockton—*locale* ... TN-4
**Stockton**—*pop pl* ... AL-4
**Stockton**—*pop pl* ... CA-9
**Stockton**—*pop pl* ... GA-3
**Stockton**—*pop pl* ... IL-6
**Stockton**—*pop pl* ... IN-6
**Stockton**—*pop pl* ... IA-7
**Stockton**—*pop pl* ... KS-7
**Stockton**—*pop pl* (2) ... MD-2
**Stockton**—*pop pl* ... MN-6
**Stockton**—*pop pl* ... MO-7
**Stockton**—*pop pl* ... NJ-2
**Stockton**—*pop pl* ... NY-2
**Stockton**—*pop pl* ... OH-6
**Stockton**—*pop pl* ... PA-2
**Stockton**—*pop pl* ... UT-8
**Stockton**—*pop pl* ... VA-3
**Stockton**—*pop pl* ... WI-6
Stockton, Lake—*reservoir* ... CA-9
Stockton, Lake—*reservoir* ... KS-7
Stockton, Robert Henry, House—*hist pl* ... MO-7
Stockton Bar—*ridge* ... UT-8
Stockton Bend—*bend* ... TX-5
Stockton Bldg—*hist pl* ... AR-4
Stockton Bottom—*flat* ... AR-4
*Stockton Branch* ... AL-4
Stockton Branch—*stream* ... MO-7
Stockton Cabin—*locale* ... CA-9
*Stockton Canyon* ... CA-9
Stockton Canyon—*valley* ... OK-5
Stockton Canyon—*valley* ... TX-5
Stockton (CCD)—*cens area* ... AL-4
Stockton (CCD)—*cens area* ... CA-9
Stockton Cem—*cemetery* ... AL-4
Stockton Cem—*cemetery* ... KY-4
Stockton Cem—*cemetery* ... NY-2
Stockton Cem—*cemetery* ... TN-4
Stockton Cem—*cemetery* ... TX-5
Stockton Cem—*cemetery* ... UT-8
Stockton Ch—*church* (2) ... AL-4
Stockton Chapel—*church* ... TX-5
Stockton Consolidated Sch—*school* ... IA-7
Stockton Corners—*locale* ... PA-2
Stockton Country Club—*other* ... CA-9
Stockton Cove—*valley* ... NC-3
*Stockton Creek* ... TN-4
Stockton Creek—*stream* ... CA-9
Stockton Creek—*stream* ... ID-8
Stockton Creek—*stream* ... KY-4
Stockton Creek—*stream* ... VA-3
Stockton-Curry House—*hist pl* ... FL-3
Stockton Deep Water Channel—*channel* ... CA-9
Stockton Ditch—*canal* ... CA-9
Stockton Diverting Canal—*canal* ... CA-9
Stockton Division—*civil* ... AL-4
Stockton Draw—*valley* ... AZ-5
Stockton Drift Mine (underground)—*mine* ... AL-4
**Stockton Estates**—*pop pl* ... TN-4
*Stockton Flat* ... CA-9
Stockton Flat—*flat* (2) ... CA-9
Stockton Flats Sch—*school* ... AL-4
Stockton Flat Well—*well* ... NV-8
*Stockton Fork* ... VA-3
Stockton Gap—*gap* ... AZ-5
Stockton Golf Course—*other* ... IL-6
Stockton Harbor—*bay* ... ME-1
Stockton Hill—*summit* (2) ... AZ-5
Stockton Hill—*summit* ... CA-9
Stockton Hill—*summit* ... MN-6
Stockton Hill Ditch—*canal* ... CA-9
Stockton Hill Mine—*mine* ... CA-9
Stockton (historical)—*locale* ... AL-4
Stockton HS—*school* ... KS-7
Stockton Island—*island* ... WI-6
Stockton Islands—*area* ... AK-9
Stockton Jail—*hist pl* ... UT-8
Stockton JHS—*school* ... KS-7
Stockton Lake—*lake* ... NJ-2
Stockton Lake—*lake* ... TX-5
Stockton Lake—*reservoir* ... IN-6
Stockton Lake—*reservoir* ... MO-7
Stockton Lake—*reservoir* ... VA-3
Stockton Lake Dam—*dam* ... IN-6
Stockton Lake Dam—*dam* ... MO-7
Stockton Memorial Cem—*cemetery* ... AL-4
Stockton Methodist Church—*hist pl* ... AL-4
Stockton Metropolitan Airp—*airport* ... CA-9
Stockton Mill—*hist pl* ... MN-6
Stockton Mill Creek—*stream* ... VA-3
Stockton Mine—*mine* ... AZ-5
Stockton Mtn—*summit* ... NY-2
Stockton Municipal Airp—*airport* ... KS-7
Stockton Municipal Airp—*airport* ... MO-7
Stockton Naval Communications Station—*military* ... CA-9
Stockton Number 1 Dam—*dam* ... SD-7
**Stockton Number 6**—*pop pl* ... PA-2
**Stockton Number 7**—*pop pl* ... PA-2
**Stockton Number 8**—*pop pl* ... PA-2
Stockton Park—*park* ... FL-3
Stockton Pass—*gap* ... AZ-5
Stockton Pass Campground—*park* ... AZ-5
Stockton Pass Dam—*dam* ... AZ-5
Stockton Pass Wash—*stream* ... AZ-5
Stockton Place—*locale* ... NM-5
Stockton Pond—*reservoir* ... GA-3
Stockton Post Office (historical)—*building* ... TN-4
Stockton Public Use Area—*park* ... MO-7
Stockton Ranch—*locale* ... CA-9
Stockton Ridge—*ridge* ... CA-9
Stockton Rural Cem—*cemetery* ... CA-9
Stockton Savings and Loan Society Bank—*hist pl* ... CA-9
Stockton Sch—*school* ... AL-4
Stockton Sch—*school* ... CA-9
Stockton Sch—*school* ... FL-3
Stockton Sch—*school* ... IL-6
Stockton Sch—*school* ... NJ-2
Stockton Sch—*school* ... TN-4
*Stocktons Creek* ... TN-4
Stockton Spring—*spring* ... OR-9
**Stockton Springs**—*pop pl* ... ME-1
Stockton Springs Community Church—*hist pl* ... ME-1
Stockton Springs (Town of)—*civ div* ... ME-1
Stockton State Park—*park* ... MO-7
**Stockton (subdivision)**—*pop pl* ... DE-2
Stockton Tank—*reservoir* ... TX-5
**Stockton (Town of)**—*pop pl* ... NY-2
**Stockton (Town of)**—*pop pl* ... WI-6
*Stockton Township* ... KS-7
**Stockton (Township of)**—*pop pl* ... IL-6
**Stockton (Township of)**—*pop pl* ... IN-6
**Stockton Valley**—*pop pl* ... TN-4
Stockton Valley—*valley* ... MN-6
Stockton Valley—*valley* ... TN-4
Stockton Valley Acad (historical)—*school* ... TN-4
Stockton Valley Ch—*church* ... TN-4
Stockton Valley Creek—*stream* ... MN-6
Stockton Wash—*stream* ... AZ-5
*Stockton Wash Dam* ... AZ-5
Stockton Wash Retarding Dam—*dam* ... AZ-5
Stockton Well—*well* ... AZ-5
*Stock Town* ... KS-7
**Stock (Township of)**—*pop pl* (2) ... OH-6
Stock Trail Rsvr No 4—*reservoir* ... WY-8
*Stock Trial Point* ... CO-8
Stock Valley—*valley* ... ID-8
**Stockville**—*pop pl* ... NE-7
**Stockville (historical)**—*pop pl* ... TN-4
Stockwater Ditch—*canal* ... OR-9
**Stockwell**—*pop pl* ... IN-6
**Stockwell**—*pop pl* ... NY-2
Stockwell, Lake—*reservoir* ... NJ-2
Stockwell Bluff—*cliff* ... GA-3
Stockwell Brook—*stream* ... MA-1
Stockwell Brook—*stream* ... NH-1
Stockwell Brook—*stream* ... VT-1
*Stockwell Creek* ... WI-6
Stockwell Creek—*stream* ... WY-8
Stockwell Elem Sch—*school* ... IN-6
Stockwell Mine—*mine* ... CA-9
Stockwell Mtn—*summit* ... NY-2
Stockwell Pond—*lake* ... NY-2
Stockwell Ponds—*reservoir* ... MA-1
Stockwell Sch—*school* ... KS-7
Stockwell Swamp—*swamp* ... CT-1
Stockwisch Ditch—*canal* ... IN-6
**Stockwood (subdivision)**—*pop pl* ... NC-3
Stockyard Creek—*stream* ... ND-7
Stockyard Gulch—*valley* ... CO-8
*Stockyards* ... CO-8
*Stock Yards* ... IA-7
*Stockyards* (2) ... MO-7
*Stock Yards* ... NE-7
*Stock Yards* ... OH-6
Stock Yards—*uninc pl* ... CA-9
Stockyards—*uninc pl* ... OK-5
Stock Yards—*uninc pl* ... TX-5
Stockyards City Hist Dist—*hist pl* ... OK-5
Stockyards Exchange—*hist pl* ... MN-6
*Stock Yards (RR name Union Stock Yards)* ... IL-6
Stockyard Tank—*reservoir* ... AZ-5
Stoco HS—*school* ... WV-2
Stoco Jr HS—*school* ... WV-2
*Stocton Canyon* ... CA-9
Stoddard—*locale* ... MO-7
**Stoddard**—*pop pl* ... ID-8
**Stoddard**—*pop pl* ... NH-1
**Stoddard**—*pop pl* ... UT-8
**Stoddard**—*pop pl* ... WI-6
Stoddard, Mount—*summit* ... NH-1
Stoddard Bridge—*bridge* ... ID-8
Stoddard Brook—*stream* ... VT-1
Stoddard Cabin—*locale* ... CA-9
Stoddard Canyon—*valley* ... CA-9
Stoddard Canyon—*valley* (3) ... UT-8
Stoddard County—*civil* ... MO-7
**Stoddard (County)**—*pop pl* ... MO-7
Stoddard County Courthouse—*hist pl* ... MO-7
Stoddard Creek—*stream* (2) ... ID-8
Stoddard Creek—*stream* ... NE-7
Stoddard Creek—*stream* ... NV-8
Stoddard Creek—*stream* ... NY-2
Stoddard Creek—*stream* ... SC-3
Stoddard Creek Campground—*locale* ... ID-8
Stoddard Creek Lookout—*locale* ... ID-8
Stoddard Creek Point—*summit* ... ID-8
Stoddard Creek Trail—*trail* ... ID-8
Stoddard Ditch—*canal* ... IN-6
Stoddard Diversion Dam—*dam* ... UT-8
Stoddard Drain—*stream* ... MI-6
Stoddard Flat—*flat* ... CA-9
Stoddard Gulch—*valley* ... ID-8
*Stoddard Hill* ... MA-1
Stoddard Hill—*summit* (2) ... MA-1
Stoddard Hill—*summit* ... UT-8
Stoddard Hill State Park—*park* ... CT-1
Stoddard (historical)—*locale* ... AL-4
Stoddard Hollow—*valley* (2) ... NY-2
Stoddard Lake—*lake* ... CA-9
Stoddard Lake—*lake* ... ID-8
Stoddard Lake—*lake* ... MI-6
*Stoddard Lakes* ... ID-8
Stoddard Lateral—*canal* ... CA-9
Stoddard Meadow—*flat* ... CA-9
Stoddard Mine—*mine* ... AZ-5
Stoddard Mtn—*summit* ... CA-9
Stoddard Mtn—*summit* ... UT-8
Stoddard Mtn—*summit* ... WA-9
Stoddard Park—*park* ... MA-1
Stoddard Peak—*summit* ... CA-9
Stoddard Point—*cape* ... MD-2
Stoddard Point—*cape* ... UT-8
Stoddard Pond—*reservoir* ... MA-1
Stoddard Pond Dam—*dam* ... MA-1
Stoddard Ranch—*locale* ... AZ-5
Stoddard Ranch—*locale* ... CA-9
Stoddard Ranch—*locale* ... NE-7
Stoddard Ridge—*ridge* ... CA-9
Stoddard Ridge—*ridge* ... WI-6
Stoddard Rips—*rapids* ... ME-1
Stoddard Rocks—*summit* ... NH-1
Stoddard Rsvr—*reservoir* ... OR-9
Stoddard Sch—*school* (2) ... MI-6
Stoddard Sch—*school* ... NE-7
Stoddard Sch—*school* ... SD-7
Stoddard Slough—*gut* ... UT-8
*Stoddards Pond* ... MA-1
Stoddard Spring—*spring* ... AZ-5
Stoddard Spring—*spring* ... CA-9
*Stoddards Town* ... MA-1
*Stoddardsville* ... PA-2
**Stoddard (Town of)**—*pop pl* ... NH-1
Stoddard Trail—*trail* ... ID-8
Stoddard Valley—*valley* ... CA-9
Stoddard Well—*well* ... CA-9
Stoddart Island—*island* ... ME-1
**Stoddartsville**—*pop pl* ... PA-2
*Stoddartsville Falls* ... PA-2
Stodden Ditch—*canal* ... MT-8
Stodden Slough—*stream* ... MT-8
Stodders Neck—*cape* ... MA-1
Stoddert—*locale* ... VA-3
**Stoddert**—*pop pl* ... VA-3
Stoddert JHS—*school* ... MD-2
Stoddert Sch—*school* ... DC-2
Stoder Cem—*cemetery* ... MO-7
Stodge Meadow Pond—*reservoir* ... MA-1
Stodge Meadow Pond Dam—*dam* ... MA-1
Stodghill Lake—*reservoir* ... TX-5
Stoeball Branch—*stream* ... TN-4
Stoebuck Mtn—*summit* ... AR-4
Stoeck, Mount—*summit* ... AK-9
Stoeckel, Robbins, House—*hist pl* ... CT-1
Stoecklin Cem—*cemetery* ... MO-7
*Stoe Creek* ... NJ-2
Stoe Creek—*stream* ... IA-7
Stoehrs—*locale* ... IL-6
*Stoelting Ridge* ... WI-6
Stoeltzing Cem—*cemetery* ... KS-7
Stoepel Park—*park* ... MI-6
Stoepel Park Number 2—*park* ... MI-6
Stoer Island—*island* ... FL-3
Stoesser Block and Annex—*hist pl* ... CA-9
Stoever, John Casper, Log House—*hist pl* ... PA-2
Stofella Lateral—*canal* ... AZ-5
Stofer Hill—*summit* ... MI-6
*Stoffel* ... WV-2
Stoffel, Henry, Blacksmith Shop—*hist pl* ... OH-6
Stoffela Store/Railroad Exchange—*hist pl* ... AZ-5
Stoffel Creek—*stream* ... VA-3
Stoffels Point—*cape* ... MN-6
Stofferan Creek—*stream* ... IA-7
Stoffer Ridge—*ridge* ... WY-8
Stogdon Creek—*stream* ... MO-7
Stoggnang Creek—*stream* ... AK-9
Stogner Cem—*cemetery* (3) ... MS-4
Stogner House—*hist pl* ... MS-4
Stogner Lake Dam—*dam* ... MS-4
Stogsdill Cove—*valley* ... AL-4
Stogsdill Point—*cape* ... AL-4
Stogsdill Sink—*basin* ... AL-4
Stogspill Cem—*cemetery* ... AL-4
Stohlman Cem—*cemetery* ... CA-9
*Stoh-luk-whahmpsh River* ... WA-9
Stohman Windmill—*locale* ... NM-5
Stohr Creek—*stream* ... MT-8
**Stohrs Cross Roads**—*pop pl* ... WV-2
**Stohrs Crossroads**—*pop pl* ... WV-2
Stohrville Oil Field—*oilfield* ... KS-7
*Stohrville Township* ... KS-7
Stoil—*locale* ... CA-9
Stoke—*locale* ... VA-3
Stokeley—*uninc pl* ... AL-4
**Stokely**—*pop pl* ... MS-4
Stokely, William J., Sch—*hist pl* ... PA-2
Stokely Athletic Center—*building* ... TN-4
Stokely Chapel—*church* (2) ... TN-4
Stokely Dam—*dam* ... TN-4
Stokely Hollow—*valley* ... NC-3
Stokely Lake—*reservoir* ... TN-4
Stokely Post Office (historical)—*building* ... MS-4
Stokely Prospect—*mine* ... TN-4
Stokelys Ferry (historical)—*locale* ... MS-4
Stokelys Island (historical)—*island* ... TN-4
Stokely-Van Camp Industrial Complex—*hist pl* ... NJ-2
Stokenbury Cem—*cemetery* ... AR-4
Stoken Cem—*cemetery* ... IN-6
Stoke Park—*locale* ... PA-2
**Stoker**—*pop pl* ... KY-4
Stoker, Henry, House and Outbuildings—*hist pl* ... ID-8
Stoker Branch—*stream* ... LA-4
Stoker Branch—*stream* ... TX-5
Stoker Canyon—*valley* ... CA-9
Stoker Cem—*cemetery* ... AL-4
Stoker Cem—*cemetery* ... IL-6
Stoker Cem—*cemetery* ... KY-4
Stoker Cem—*cemetery* ... TX-5
Stoker Ditch—*canal* ... IN-6
Stoker House—*hist pl* ... LA-4
Stoker Mine—*mine* ... WA-9
Stoker Ranch—*locale* ... TX-5
Stoker Sch—*school* ... UT-8
Stoker Spring—*spring* ... NV-8
Stoker Spring Number One—*spring* ... NV-8
Stoker-Stampfli Farm—*hist pl* ... TN-4
Stokes—*locale* ... AL-4
Stokes—*locale* (2) ... SC-3
Stokes—*locale* ... TN-4
**Stokes**—*pop pl* ... AL-4
**Stokes**—*pop pl* ... AR-4
**Stokes**—*pop pl* ... MS-4
**Stokes**—*pop pl* ... NC-3
**Stokes**—*pop pl* ... SC-3
Stokes, Benjamin A., House—*hist pl* ... OH-6
Stokes, Oliver O., House—*hist pl* ... SD-7
Stokes Bayou—*gut* ... LA-4
Stokes Bayou—*stream* (2) ... MS-4
*Stokes-Beard Elementary School* ... MS-4
Stokes-Beard Sch—*school* ... MS-4
Stokes Bluff Landing—*locale* ... SC-3
Stokes Branch—*stream* ... AL-4
Stokes Branch—*stream* ... AR-4
Stokes Branch—*stream* ... FL-3
Stokes Branch—*stream* ... TN-4
Stokes Branch—*stream* ... VA-3
Stokes Bridge—*bridge* ... FL-3
Stokes Bridge—*bridge* ... GA-3
Stokes Bridge—*bridge* ... SC-3
Stokes Bridge—*locale* ... SC-3
Stokes Bridge-Cypress (CCD)—*cens area* ... SC-3
Stokesburg Ch—*church* ... NC-3
Stokes Canyon—*valley* ... CA-9
Stokes Canyon—*valley* ... UT-8
Stokes Castle—*pillar* ... NV-8
Stokes Cem—*cemetery* ... AL-4

Stokes Cem—cemetery ... IL-6
Stokes Cem—cemetery (2) ... MS-4
Stokes Cem—cemetery (2) ... MO-7
Stokes Cem—cemetery (3) ... TN-4
Stokes Cem—cemetery ... TX-5
Stokes Chapel—church ... IL-6
Stokes Chapel—church ... KY-4
Stokes Chapel—church ... MI-6
Stokes Chapel—church ... NC-3
**Stokes Corner**—pop pl ... NY-2
Stokes County ... NC-3
Stokes County—civil ... NC-3
Stokes County Courthouse—hist pl ... NC-3
Stokes Creek ... AR-4
Stokes Creek—stream (3) ... AR-4
Stokes Creek—stream ... FL-3
Stokes Creek—stream ... LA-4
Stokes Creek—stream ... MS-4
Stokes Creek—stream (2) ... TN-4
Stokes Creek—stream ... TX-5
Stokes Creek—stream (2) ... VA-3
**Stokes Crossing**—pop pl ... TN-4
Stokesdale—locale ... PA-2
**Stokesdale**—pop pl ... NC-3
Stokesdale Elem Sch—school ... NC-3
Stokesdale Junction ... PA-2
Stokes (Election Precinct)—fmr MCD ... IL-6
Stokes Elem Sch—school ... IN-6
Stokes Elem Sch—school ... NC-3
Stokes Ferry—locale ... FL-3
Stokes Ferry Bridge—bridge ... NC-3
**Stokes Ferry (historical)**—pop pl ... NC-3
Stokes Flat—flat ... FL-3
Stokes Flat—flat ... NV-8
Stokes Gulch—valley ... CO-8
Stokes Hill—summit ... FL-3
Stokes Hill—summit ... TN-4
Stokes Hill Sch—school ... NY-2
**Stokes (historical)**—pop pl ... MS-4
**Stokes (historical)**—pop pl ... NC-3
Stokes Hollow—valley ... TN-4
Stokes House—hist pl ... AR-4
Stokes Iron Mine ... NV-8
Stokes Island—island ... FL-3
Stokes Lake—lake ... FL-3
Stokesland—locale ... VA-3
Stokesland—uninc pl ... VA-3
Stokes Landing—locale ... FL-3
Stokes Landing—locale ... MS-4
Stokes-Lee House—hist pl ... NJ-2
Stokes Lookout Tower—locale ... MN-6
Stokes-Mayfield House—hist pl ... SC-3
Stokes Meadow ... PA-2
Stokes Memorial Sch—school ... NJ-2
Stokes Mill—locale ... TN-4
Stokes Mine—mine ... NV-8
Stokes Mound—summit ... MO-7
Stokes Mound Sch—school ... MO-7
Stokes Mound Township—civil ... MO-7
Stokes Mtn—summit ... CA-9
Stokes Park—park ... FL-3
Stokes Plantation ... MS-4
Stokes Post Office (historical)—building ... MS-4
Stokes Post Office (historical)—building ... TN-4
**Stokes Ranch**—pop pl ... NE-7
Stokes RR Station—locale ... FL-3
Stokes Sch—school ... AL-4
Stokes Sch—school ... NE-7
Stokes Sch—school ... NY-2
Stokes Sch—school ... TN-4
Stokes Sch—school ... WI-6
Stokes Sch (historical)—school ... NC-3
Stokes Siding—locale ... WY-8
Stokes Spring ... AZ-5
Stokes State For—forest ... NJ-2
**Stokes (Stokes Corner)**—pop pl ... NY-2
Stokes Stringer—stream ... CA-9
**Stokestown**—pop pl ... NC-3
**Stokes (Township of)**—pop pl (2) ... MN-6
**Stokes (Township of)**—pop pl (2) ... OH-6
Stokes Tract ... PA-2
Stokes Valley—valley ... CA-9
Stokesville—locale (2) ... GA-3
Stokesville—locale ... VA-3
Stokesville Cem—cemetery ... ND-7
Stokesville Ch—church ... GA-3
Stokes Well—well ... AZ-5
Stokes Well—well ... TX-5
Stokes Windmill—locale ... TX-5
Stokey Lake—lake ... MN-6
Stokey Ridge—ridge ... IN-6
Stokke State Wildlife Mngmt Area—park ... MN-6
Stokley—locale ... MO-7
**Stokley**—pop pl ... AL-4
Stokley Ferry (historical)—crossing ... TN-4
Stokley Hill—summit ... TX-5
Stokley Landing—locale ... FL-3
Stokley Sch—school ... PA-2
Stokman State Wildlife Mngmt Area—park ... MN-6
**St. Olaf**—pop pl ... IA-7
St. Olafs Catholic Ch—church ... UT-8
Stolberg, Charles, House—hist pl ... MI-6
Stolbi Rocks—bar ... AK-9
Stole Creek—stream ... MT-8
Stolen Creek—stream ... ID-8
Stolen Tank—reservoir ... AZ-5
Stolen Tank Number Two—reservoir ... AZ-5
Stoler Creek—stream ... IN-6
Stoley Branch ... GA-3
Stoll, Adam J., House—hist pl ... OH-6
Stollberg Ditch—canal ... IN-6
Stoll Cem—cemetery (2) ... IN-6
Stoll Cem—cemetery ... MI-6
**Stolle**—pop pl ... IL-6
Stolle Dam—dam ... AL-4
Stolle Lake—reservoir ... AL-4
Stolle Meadows—flat ... ID-8
Stoller Sch (abandoned)—school ... SD-7
Stolles Creek—stream ... TX-5
**Stolletown**—pop pl ... IL-6
Stolley, William, Homestead & Site of Fort Independence (Boundary)—hist pl ... NE-7
Stolley Homestead Site—hist pl ... NE-7
Stolley State Park—park ... NE-7
Stolling Cem—cemetery (2) ... WV-2
Stolling Fork—stream ... WV-2
**Stollings**—pop pl ... WV-2
Stollings Branch—stream ... WV-2
Stollings Creek ... AL-4
Stoll Lake—lake ... MN-6
Stoll Mtn—summit ... CO-8
Stolls Point—cape ... AL-4
Stollsteimer—locale ... CO-8
Stollsteimer Creek—stream ... CO-8
Stolmes House—hist pl ... CO-8
Stolp Creek—stream ... KS-7
Stolp Island—island ... IL-6
Stolp Island Hist Dist—hist pl ... IL-6
Stolp Woolen Mill Store—hist pl ... IL-6
Stolte, William, Jr., House—hist pl ... WI-6
Stolte, William, Sr., House—hist pl ... WI-6
Stoltenberg Oil Field—oilfield ... KS-7
Stoltz Arm—canal ... IN-6
Stoltz Cem—cemetery ... IL-6
Stoltz Cem—cemetery ... OH-6
Stoltzfus Airp—airport ... PA-2
Stoltzfus Cem—cemetery ... PA-2
Sto-luck-wamish River ... WA-9
Stolz—locale ... TX-5
Stolz Cem—cemetery ... MN-6
Stolz Cem—cemetery ... PA-2
Stolzenback (historical)—locale ... KS-7
Stolzenberg Mtn—summit ... WA-9
Stolz Field Airp—airport ... IN-6
Stolzfus Spring—spring ... PA-2
Stomar—locale ... CA-9
Stomner House—hist pl ... ND-7
**Stomp Springs**—pop pl ... SC-3
Stomy Island—island ... NY-2
Stone—canal ... MT-8
Stone—locale ... CA-9
Stone—locale ... ID-8
Stone—locale ... KS-7
Stone—locale ... KY-4
Stone—locale ... MT-8
Stone—locale ... OH-6
Stone—locale ... WI-6
**Stone**—pop pl ... IN-6
**Stone**—pop pl ... KY-4
**Stone**—pop pl ... SC-3
**Stone**—pop pl ... TN-4
**Stone**—pop pl ... WA-9
Stone, Capt. Jonathan, House—hist pl ... OH-6
Stone, Daniel, Plank House—hist pl ... NC-3
Stone, Elisha F., House—hist pl ... ME-1
Stone, Gen. Asahel, Mansion—hist pl ... IN-6
Stone, John, House—hist pl ... KY-4
Stone, John M., Cotton Mill—hist pl ... MS-4
Stone, Joseph, House—hist pl ... MA-1
Stone, Joseph B., House—hist pl ... NC-3
Stone, Joseph L., House—hist pl ... MA-1
Stone, Judge Earl S., House—hist pl ... IN-6
Stone, Lake—reservoir ... FL-3
Stone, Mount—summit ... WA-9
Stone, Robert and Lula, House—hist pl ... TX-5
Stone, Roy C., House—hist pl ... TX-5
Stone, Valerius C., House—hist pl ... OH-6
Stone and Log Bldg—hist pl ... ID-8
Stone and Timber Draw—valley ... WY-8
**Stone Arabia**—pop pl ... NY-2
Stone Arch Bridge—hist pl (2) ... IL-6
Stone Arch Bridge—hist pl ... NY-2
Stone Arch Lake—reservoir ... IN-6
Stone Arch Underpass—hist pl ... NH-1
Stone A Ruins—locale ... NM-5
Stone Ave Underpass—hist pl ... AZ-5
Stone Axe Lake—lake ... MN-6
Stone Bald Mountain ... NC-3
**Stonebank**—pop pl ... WI-6
Stonebank Creek—stream ... NJ-2
Stone Barn—hist pl ... IA-7
Stone Barn Camp—locale ... WY-8
Stone Barn on Brushy Creek—hist pl ... KY-4
Stone Barn on Lee's Creek—hist pl ... KY-4
Stone Barn Spring—spring ... WY-8
Stone Basin—basin ... CA-9
Stone Basin—basin ... CO-8
Stone Basin Rsvr—reservoir ... CO-8
Stone Bay ... NC-3
Stone Bayou—stream ... LA-4
Stone Beach Gardner Cabin—building ... IA-7
Stone Bend—bend ... TN-4
Stoneberger Basin—basin ... NV-8
Stoneberger Creek—stream ... NV-8
Stone Bldg—hist pl ... ID-8
Stone Bldg—hist pl ... MA-1
Stone Bldg—hist pl ... NE-7
Stonebluff ... IN-6
Stone Bluff ... OK-5
Stone Bluff—cliff ... WI-6
**Stonebluff**—pop pl ... IN-6
**Stone Bluff**—pop pl ... IN-6
**Stonebluff**—pop pl ... OK-5
Stone Bluff Bridge—bridge ... TN-4
Stoneboro—locale ... SC-3
**Stoneboro**—pop pl ... PA-2
Stoneboro Borough—civil ... PA-2
Stoneborough Hollow—valley ... TN-4
Stone Boy Creek—stream ... AK-9
Stone Boys Tent Creek—stream ... AK-9
**Stonebraker**—pop pl ... MD-2
Stonebraker Branch—stream ... IN-6
Stonebraker Cem—cemetery ... IN-6
Stonebraker Cem—cemetery ... MO-7
Stonebraker Ranch—locale ... ID-8
Stonebraker Sch—school ... IL-6
**Stone Branch**—pop pl ... WV-2
Stone Branch—stream (3) ... AL-4
Stone Branch—stream ... GA-3
Stone Branch—stream (4) ... IN-6
Stone Branch—stream (2) ... KY-4
Stone Branch—stream ... LA-4
Stone Branch—stream ... OH-6
Stone Branch—stream (3) ... TN-4
Stone Branch—stream (3) ... VA-3
Stone Branch—stream ... WV-2
Stone Branch Ch—church ... WV-2
Stonebreaker Creek—stream ... CA-9
Stonebreaker Crossing—locale ... CA-9
Stone Breastwork Indian Battlesite—locale ... MT-8
Stonebridge ... IL-6
Stone Bridge—bridge (2) ... OR-9
Stone Bridge—bridge ... VA-3
Stone Bridge—hist pl ... CT-1
Stone Bridge—locale ... PA-2
Stonebridge—locale ... PA-2
Stone Bridge—locale ... PA-2
Stone Bridge—locale ... VA-3
**Stonebridge**—pop pl ... OR-9
**Stone Bridge**—pop pl ... SD-7
Stone Bridge and the Oregon Central Military Wagon Road—hist pl ... OR-9
Stone Bridge Branch—stream ... NJ-2
Stone Bridge Brook—stream ... VT-1
Stone Bridge Cem—cemetery ... NY-2
Stone Bridge Ch—church ... MD-2
**Stonebridge Condo**—pop pl (2) ... UT-8
Stone Bridge Creek ... TX-5
Stonebridge Dam—dam ... NC-3
Stone Bridge Draw—valley ... UT-8
**Stonebridge Estates (subdivision)**—pop pl ... AL-4
**Stone Bridge (historical)**—pop pl ... TN-4
Stonebridge Hollow—valley ... VA-3
Stonebridge Lake—reservoir ... NC-3
Stone Bridge Pond—lake ... MA-1
Stone Bridge Pond—lake ... NY-2
Stone Bridge Rsvr—reservoir ... WY-8
Stone Brook ... MA-1
**Stonebrook**—pop pl (2) ... TN-4
Stone Brook—stream (2) ... ME-1
Stone Brook—stream ... MA-1
Stone Brook—stream ... NH-1
Stonebrook and Harlow Drain—canal ... MI-6
**Stone Brook (subdivision)**—pop pl ... NC-3
Stone Bruise—locale ... VA-3
Stone Bungalow—hist pl ... AZ-5
**Stoneburg**—pop pl ... TX-5
**Stoneburner Landing**—pop pl ... IN-6
Stone Butte—summit ... OR-9
Stone Cabin ... NV-8
Stone Cabin—locale ... AZ-5
Stone Cabin—locale (2) ... NV-8
Stone Cabin—locale ... NM-5
Stone Cabin—locale ... WY-8
Stone Cabin—mine ... NV-8
Stone Cabin Basin—basin ... NV-8
Stone Cabin Box Spring—spring ... AZ-5
Stone Cabin Brook—stream ... NY-2
Stone Cabin Canyon ... AZ-5
Stone Cabin Canyon ... UT-8
Stone Cabin Canyon—valley ... AZ-5
Stone Cabin Canyon—valley (2) ... NV-8
Stone Cabin Creek—stream ... NV-8
Stone Cabin Creek—stream ... OR-9
Stone Cabin Creek—stream ... UT-8
Stone Cabin Creek—stream ... WY-8
Stone Cabin Dam—dam ... AZ-5
Stone Cabin Draw—valley ... UT-8
Stone Cabin Flat—flat ... CA-9
Stone Cabin Gap—gap ... MD-2
Stone Cabin Gap Wash—valley ... AZ-5
Stone Cabin Gas Field—oilfield ... UT-8
Stone Cabin Gulch—valley ... NM-5
Stone Cabin Mtn—summit ... AZ-5
Stone Cabin Ranch—locale ... NV-8
Stone Cabin Run—stream ... PA-2
Stone Cabin Spring—spring (2) ... AZ-5
Stone Cabin Spring—spring ... NV-8
Stone Cabin Valley—valley ... NV-8
Stone Cabin Wash—stream ... AZ-5
Stone Camp—locale ... ME-1
Stone Camp—locale ... PA-2
Stone Camp Branch—stream ... TN-4
Stone Camp Mountain—ridge ... WV-2
Stone Camp Run—stream ... WV-2
Stone Camp Spring—spring ... AZ-5
Stone Canyon—valley (5) ... CA-9
Stone Canyon—valley (2) ... CO-8
Stone Canyon—valley ... NV-8
Stone Canyon—valley (7) ... NM-5
Stone Canyon—valley ... WA-9
Stone Canyon Mine—mine ... CA-9
Stone Canyon Rsvr—reservoir ... CA-9
Stone Canyon Trail—trail ... CA-9
Stone Castle Motel Airp—airport ... PA-2
Stone Cave—cave ... TN-4
Stone Cave Hill—summit ... PA-2
Stone Cave Spring—spring ... TN-4
Stone Cellar—locale ... CA-9
Stone Cellar Campground—locale ... CO-8
Stone Cellar Guard Station—locale ... CO-8
Stone Cellar on Cabin Creek—hist pl ... KY-4
Stone Cem—cemetery (4) ... AL-4
Stone Cem—cemetery ... AR-4
Stone Cem—cemetery ... GA-3
Stone Cem—cemetery ... IL-6
Stone Cem—cemetery (2) ... IN-6
Stone Cem—cemetery ... KS-7
Stone Cem—cemetery (4) ... KY-4
Stone Cem—cemetery ... ME-1
Stone Cem—cemetery (3) ... MS-4
Stone Cem—cemetery (7) ... MO-7
Stone Cem—cemetery (3) ... NY-2
Stone Cem—cemetery ... NC-3
Stone Cem—cemetery ... PA-2
Stone Cem—cemetery ... SC-3
Stone Cem—cemetery (12) ... TN-4
Stone Cem—cemetery (2) ... TX-5
Stone Cem—cemetery (2) ... VA-3
Stone Cem—cemetery (3) ... WV-2
Stone Cem—cemetery ... WI-6
Stone Ch ... MO-7
Stone Ch—church ... AR-4
Stone Ch—church ... GA-3
Stone Ch—church ... MI-6
Stone Ch—church ... MO-7
Stone Ch—church ... NJ-2
Stone Ch—church (2) ... NY-2
Stone Ch—church ... ND-7
Stone Ch—church (2) ... OH-6
Stone Ch—church (4) ... PA-2
Stone Ch—church ... WI-6
Stone Chapel—church ... GA-3
Stone Chapel—church (2) ... MD-2
Stone Chapel—church ... MO-7
Stone Chapel—church ... OH-6
Stone Chapel—church ... SC-3
Stone Chapel—hist pl ... MO-7
Stone Chapel Cem—cemetery ... TX-5
Stone Chapel Ch—church ... WV-2
Stone Chapel Church ... AL-4
Stone Chapel Sch—school ... OK-5
Stone Chimney Creek—stream ... TX-5
Stone Chimney Hollow—valley (2) ... PA-2
Stone Church—hist pl ... GA-3
**Stone Church**—pop pl ... IL-6
**Stone Church**—pop pl ... NJ-2
**Stone Church**—pop pl ... NY-2
**Stone Church**—pop pl ... PA-2
Stone Church, The—summit ... NY-2
Stone Church Brook—stream (2) ... NY-2
Stone Church Cem—cemetery ... CT-1
Stone Church Cem—cemetery ... MO-7
Stone Church Cem—cemetery ... WV-2
**Stone Church (Centerville)**—pop pl ... PA-2
Stone Church Corner—locale ... NY-2
Stone Church (Election Precinct)—fmr MCD ... IL-6
Stone Church Hollow Creek ... PA-2
Stone Church Sch (historical)—school ... MO-7
Stonecipher Branch—stream ... TN-4
Stone City—locale ... TX-5
**Stone City**—pop pl ... CO-8
**Stone City**—pop pl ... IA-7
Stone Cliff—locale ... WV-2
Stonecliffe Rec Area—area ... PA-2
Stoneco ... NY-2
**Stonecoal**—pop pl ... WV-2
Stone Coalbank Creek—stream ... TN-4
Stonecoal Block Sch—school ... WV-2
Stonecoal Branch ... WV-2
Stonecoal Branch—stream (3) ... KY-4
Stone Coal Branch—stream ... KY-4
Stonecoal Branch—stream (2) ... KY-4
Stone Coal Branch—stream ... KY-4
Stonecoal Branch—stream (6) ... KY-4
Stone Coal Branch—stream (2) ... TN-4
Stonecoal Branch—stream (2) ... VA-3
Stonecoal Branch—stream (6) ... WV-2
Stonecoal Cem—cemetery ... KY-4
Stonecoal Ch—church (2) ... KY-4
Stonecoal Chapel—church ... WV-2
Stone Coal Creek—stream ... CA-9
Stonecoal Creek—stream ... KY-4
Stone Coal Creek—stream ... VA-3
Stonecoal Creek—stream ... VA-3
Stonecoal Creek—stream (3) ... WV-2
Stonecoal Fork ... WV-2
Stonecoal Fork—stream (2) ... KY-4
Stone Coal Fork—stream ... KY-4
Stonecoal Fork—stream ... KY-4
Stone Coal Hollow—valley (2) ... KY-4
Stonecoal Hollow—valley (2) ... KY-4
Stone Coal Hollow—valley ... VA-3
Stone Coal Hollow—valley ... WV-2
**Stonecoal Junction**—pop pl ... WV-2
**Stone Coal Junction**—pop pl ... WV-2
Stone Coal Mtn—summit ... CA-9
Stonecoal Rsvr—reservoir ... WV-2
Stone Coal Run—stream ... OH-6
Stone Coal Run—stream ... PA-2
Stonecoal Run—stream (3) ... WV-2
Stone Coal Run—stream ... WV-2
Stonecoal Run—stream (3) ... WV-2
Stonecoal Sch—school (2) ... KY-4
Stonecoal Sch—school ... VA-3
Stonecoal Sch—school (2) ... WV-2
Stonecoal Trail—trail ... WV-2
Stone Coal Valley—stream ... CA-9
Stone Coe Creek—stream ... IN-6
Stone Coal Branch—stream ... KY-4
Stone Corner Sch—school ... MN-6
Stone Corral ... AZ-5
Stone Corral—locale (3) ... CA-9
Stone Corral—locale (2) ... NV-8
Stone Corral—locale ... OR-9
Stone Corral—other ... ID-8
Stone Corral Canyon—valley ... AZ-5
Stone Corral Canyon—valley (2) ... CA-9
Stone Corral Creek—stream (3) ... CA-9
Stone Corral Creek—stream ... OR-9
Stone Corral Flats—flat ... CA-9
Stone Corral Hollow—valley ... CA-9
Stone Corral Lake—lake ... OR-9
Stone Corral Ranch—locale ... CA-9
Stone Corral (Site)—locale ... CA-9
Stone Corrals No. 1-6 (41OL250)—hist pl ... TX-5
Stone Corral Spring—spring ... AZ-5
Stone Corral Spring—spring ... NM-5
Stone Corral Springs—spring ... AZ-5
Stone Corral Well—well ... NV-8
Stone County—civil ... MO-7
**Stone (County)**—pop pl ... AR-4
**Stone County**—pop pl ... MS-4
**Stone (County)**—pop pl ... MO-7
Stone County Courthouse—building ... MS-4
Stone County Courthouse—hist pl ... AR-4
Stone County Courthouse—hist pl ... MO-7
Stone County Recorder Bldg—hist pl ... AR-4
Stone Cove—stream ... TN-4
Stone Cove Branch ... WV-2
Stone Cove Branch—stream ... KY-4
Stone Cove Ridge—ridge ... VA-3
Stone Creek ... CO-8
Stone Creek ... IN-6
Stone Creek ... MS-4
Stone Creek ... NC-3
Stone Creek ... PA-2
Stone Creek ... SD-7
Stone Creek ... TX-5
Stone Creek—bay ... NY-2
Stone Creek—channel ... NY-2
**Stone Creek**—pop pl ... OH-6
**Stone Creek**—pop pl ... VA-3
Stone Creek—stream ... AL-4
Stone Creek—stream (2) ... AK-9
Stone Creek—stream (2) ... AZ-5
Stone Creek—stream ... AR-4
Stone Creek—stream (3) ... CA-9
Stone Creek—stream ... CO-8
Stone Creek—stream (2) ... GA-3
Stone Creek—stream ... IL-6
Stone Creek—stream ... IN-6
Stone Creek—stream (2) ... KY-4
Stone Creek—stream ... MD-2
Stone Creek—stream ... MN-6
Stone Creek—stream (4) ... MT-8
Stone Creek—stream ... NE-7
Stone Creek—stream ... NM-5
Stone Creek—stream (2) ... NC-3
Stone Creek—stream ... ND-7
Stone Creek—stream ... OH-6
Stone Creek—stream (2) ... OR-9
Stone Creek—stream (2) ... PA-2
Stone Creek—stream (2) ... TN-4
Stone Creek—stream (2) ... TX-5
Stone Creek—stream ... UT-8
Stone Creek—stream (2) ... VA-3
Stone Creek—stream ... WA-9
Stone Creek—stream ... WI-6
Stone Creek—stream ... WY-8
Stone Creek Cem—cemetery ... GA-3
Stone Creek Ch—church ... GA-3
Stone Creek Ch—church ... NC-3
Stone Creek Ch—church ... PA-2
Stone Creek Dam—dam ... PA-2
**Stone Creek PUD (subdivision)**—pop pl ... UT-8
Stone Creek Ridge—ridge ... PA-2
**Stone Creek Subdivision**—pop pl (2) ... UT-8
**Stone Creek Township**—pop pl ... ND-7
Stone Creek Valley Park—park ... PA-2
Stonecrest—hist pl ... NY-2
**Stonecrest**—pop pl ... MD-2
Stonecrest Golf Course—locale ... PA-2
Stone Crest Mall—locale ... MO-7
Stone Crest Mall (Shop Ctr)—locale ... MO-7
**Stonecrest (Trailer Park)**—pop pl ... IN-6
Stonecrop Hill—summit ... PA-2
Stone Cross—locale ... MD-2
Stonecrusher Drain—canal ... MI-6
Stonecup Lake—lake ... WY-8
Stonecutter Creek—stream ... NC-3
Stonecutter Mill—locale ... NC-3
Stonecyphen Cem—cemetery ... GA-3
Stonecypher Lake—reservoir ... GA-3
Stone Dairy Cabin—locale ... CA-9
**Stonedale**—pop pl ... PA-2
Stone Dam—dam ... AZ-5
Stone Dam—dam ... VT-1
**Stonedam**—pop pl ... NY-2
Stonedam Bloomary Forge (historical)—locale ... TN-4
Stone Dam Ch—church ... TN-4
Stone Dam Creek—stream ... AR-4
Stone Dam Creek—stream ... NY-2
Stonedam Island—island ... NH-1
Stone Dam Lake—lake ... NY-2
Stone Dam Lake Camp—locale ... NY-2
Stone Dam Mtn—summit ... NY-2
Stone Dam Pond—reservoir ... RI-1
Stone Dam Rsvr—reservoir ... CA-9
Stone Dam Trail—trail ... NY-2
Stone-Darracott House—hist pl ... NH-1
Stone Deavours Sch—school ... MS-4
Stone Dilts Ditch—canal ... IN-6
Stone Ditch—canal ... CA-9
Stone Ditch—canal ... IN-6
Stone Ditch—canal ... OH-6
Stonedive Creek—stream ... TX-5
Stone Diversion Dam—dam ... MA-1
Stone Dock Hollow—valley ... PA-2
Stone Door—pillar ... TN-4
Stone Drain—canal ... MI-6
Stone Draw—valley ... WY-8
Stoned Well Cave—cave ... AL-4
Stone Dye Branch—stream ... KY-4
Stone Dye Hills—ridge ... TN-4
Stone Eagles—hist pl ... NJ-2
Stone East Plaza Shop Ctr—locale ... TN-4
Stone Elem Sch ... MS-4
Stone Elem Sch—school ... MS-4
Stone Face—cliff ... IL-6
Stone Falls—falls ... NY-2
Stone Farm—hist pl ... NH-1
Stonefield—hist pl ... VA-3
Stonefield—hist pl ... WI-6
Stonefield Ch—church ... LA-4
Stonefield Ch—church ... MS-4
Stone Ford—locale ... MO-7
Stone Fork Sch—school ... KY-4
Stone Fort—locale ... IL-6
**Stonefort**—pop pl ... IL-6
Stonefort Bluff—cliff ... IL-6
Stonefort (Election Precinct)—fmr MCD ... IL-6
**Stonefort (Township of)**—pop pl ... IL-6
Stonega—locale ... IA-7
**Stonega**—pop pl ... VA-3
Stonega Gap—gap ... VA-3
Stonega Lookout Tower—locale ... VA-3
Stone Gap—gap ... PA-2
**Stonegate**—pop pl ... MD-2
**Stone Gate**—pop pl ... NY-2
**Stonegate**—pop pl ... TN-4
Stonegate—uninc pl ... CA-9
**Stonegate Crossing (subdivision)**—pop pl (2) ... AZ-5
Stonegate Park—park ... TX-5
Stone Gate Sch—school ... MO-7
Stonegate Sch—school ... OK-5
Stonegate Square ... IN-6
**Stonegate (subdivision)**—pop pl ... AL-4
**Stonegate (subdivision)**—pop pl (2) ... MS-4
Stoneger ... IA-7
**Stone Glen**—pop pl ... PA-2
Stone-Grant House—hist pl ... KY-4
Stone Grove Ch—church ... NC-3
Stone Gulch ... OR-9
Stone Gulch—valley ... AK-9
Stone Gulch—valley ... CA-9
Stone Gulch—valley (2) ... CO-8
Stone Gulch—valley (2) ... OR-9
Stone Hall—hist pl ... MD-2
Stonehall—hist pl ... MI-6
Stone Hall—hist pl ... NY-2
Stone Hall, Atlanta Univ—hist pl ... GA-3
Stoneham—locale ... TX-5
**Stoneham**—pop pl ... CO-8
**Stoneham**—pop pl ... GA-3
**Stoneham**—pop pl ... MA-1
**Stoneham**—pop pl ... PA-2
Stoneham Cem—cemetery (2) ... TX-5
Stoneham Corners—locale ... NH-1
Stoneham Firestation—hist pl ... MA-1
Stoneham HS—school ... MA-1
Stoneham JHS—school ... MA-1
Stonehammer Lake—reservoir ... WY-8
Stoneham Mtn—summit ... VT-1
Stoneham Public Library—hist pl ... MA-1
Stoneham Station (historical)—locale ... MA-1
Stoneham Townhall—building ... MA-1
**Stoneham (Town of)**—pop pl ... ME-1
**Stoneham (Town of)**—pop pl ... MA-1
**Stoneham (Township of)**—pop pl ... MN-6
Stonehamville Ch—church ... TX-5
Stonehan Lake—reservoir ... TX-5
Stoneharbor ... NJ-2
Stone Harbor—bay ... NJ-2
**Stone Harbor**—pop pl ... NJ-2
Stone Harbor Bird Sanctuary—park ... NJ-2
Stone Harbor Bridge—bridge ... NJ-2
Stone Harbor Canal—gut ... NJ-2
Stone Harbor Creek—stream ... NJ-2
Stone Harbor Hole—gut ... NJ-2
**Stone Harbor Manor**—pop pl ... NJ-2
**Stonehaven**—pop pl ... DE-2
**Stone Haven**—pop pl ... MA-1
Stone Haven Camp—locale ... PA-2
**Stonehaven (historical)**—pop pl ... MA-1
**Stonehaven (subdivision)**—pop pl ... NC-3
**Stone Head**—pop pl ... IN-6
Stone Head—summit ... PA-2
Stonehead Cave—cave ... TN-4
Stonehead (L-7)—hist pl ... CA-9
**Stonehedge Cliffs (subdivision)**—pop pl ... AL-4
Stone Hedges Country Club—other ... NY-2
**Stonehedge (subdivision)**—pop pl ... AL-4
Stonehenge—hist pl ... NH-1
Stonehenge Memorial—park ... WA-9
Stone Hill—cliff ... MT-8
Stonehill—locale (2) ... MT-8
Stone Hill—locale ... PA-2
Stone Hill—locale ... SD-7
**Stone Hill**—pop pl ... MO-7
Stone Hill—summit ... AR-4
Stone Hill—summit ... CT-1
Stone Hill—summit ... KY-4
Stone Hill—summit (3) ... ME-1
Stone Hill—summit (2) ... MA-1
Stone Hill—summit ... NJ-2
Stone Hill—summit (2) ... NY-2
Stone Hill—summit ... PA-2
Stone Hill—summit ... TN-4
Stone Hill—summit ... VT-1
Stone Hill—summit ... WI-6
Stone Hill Branch—stream ... MO-7
Stonehill Coll—school ... MA-1
Stone Hill (historical)—locale ... AL-4
Stone Hill River—stream ... NY-2
Stone Hill Rsvr—reservoir ... CT-1
Stone Hill Rsvr—reservoir ... OR-9
Stone Hills—range ... ID-8
Stone Hill Sch—school ... MO-7
Stone Hill Sch—school ... SC-3
Stone Hinds Ditch—canal ... IN-6
**Stone (historical)**—pop pl ... OR-9
Stonehocker Creek—stream ... AK-9
Stone Hoe, Canal (historical)—canal ... AZ-5
Stone Hollow ... TN-4
Stone Hollow—valley ... AL-4
Stone Hollow—valley ... AR-4
Stone Hollow—valley (3) ... PA-2
Stone Hollow—valley (2) ... WV-2
**Stone Hollow Condo**—pop pl ... UT-8
**Stone Hollow Condominium**—pop pl ... UT-8
Stoneholm—hist pl ... MA-1
Stone Horse Creek—stream ... KS-7
Stone Horse Creek—stream ... VA-3
Stone Horse Ledge—bar ... ME-1
Stone Horse Rocks—bar ... MA-1
Stonehorse Shoal ... MA-1
Stone Horse Shoal—bar ... MA-1
Stone House ... NV-8
Stone House ... PA-2
Stone House—building ... VA-3
Stone House—hist pl ... AR-4
Stone House—hist pl ... CA-9
Stone House—hist pl ... CO-8
Stone House—hist pl ... IA-7
Stone House—hist pl ... ME-1
Stone House—hist pl ... MA-1
Stone House—hist pl ... VA-3
Stone House—locale (2) ... AZ-5
Stonehouse—locale ... CA-9
Stone House—locale ... CA-9
Stonehouse—locale ... CA-9
Stone House—locale ... CA-9
Stone House—locale ... NV-8
Stonehouse—locale ... NV-8
Stone House—locale ... NJ-2
Stonehouse—locale ... PA-2
Stone House—locale ... PA-2
Stonehouse—other ... NY-2
**Stone House**—pop pl ... PA-2
Stonehouse, The—locale ... NH-1
Stone House at Fisher's Mill—hist pl ... KY-4
Stonehouse Branch—stream ... SC-3
Stonehouse Brook—stream ... CT-1
Stonehouse Brook—stream (2) ... NH-1
Stone House Brook—stream ... NJ-2
Stonehouse Butte—summit ... ND-7
Stonehouse Canyon—valley (2) ... NV-8
Stonehouse Canyon—valley (2) ... OR-9
Stone House Cem—cemetery ... CT-1
Stone House Corner—locale ... PA-2
Stonehouse Cove—bay ... MD-2
Stone House Creek ... OR-9
Stonehouse Creek—stream ... AK-9
Stonehouse Creek—stream ... ID-8
Stonehouse Creek—stream ... MO-7
Stone House Creek—stream ... NV-8
Stonehouse Creek—stream (3) ... OR-9
Stone House Creek—stream ... SC-3
Stonehouse Creek—stream ... VA-3
Stonehouse Farm—hist pl ... NY-2
Stonehouse Gulch—valley ... CA-9
Stonehouse Gulch—valley ... CO-8
Stonehouse Gulch—valley ... MT-8
Stone House Hill ... MA-1
Stonehouse Hill—summit (2) ... MA-1
Stone House Hill—summit ... NH-1
Stonehouse Interchange—locale ... NV-8
Stonehouse Island—island ... MI-6
Stone House Lake—lake ... AK-9
Stone House Lake—lake ... SD-7
Stonehouse (Magisterial District)—fmr MCD ... VA-3
Stonehouse Mtn—summit ... MT-8
Stonehouse Mtn—summit ... NH-1
Stone House of Indian Creek—hist pl ... KY-4
Stone House on Beale's Run—hist pl ... KY-4
Stone House on Bracken Creek—hist pl ... KY-4
Stone House on Brooklyn Hill—hist pl ... KY-4
Stone House on Buffalo Creek—hist pl ... KY-4
Stone House on Clear Creek—hist pl ... KY-4

Stone House on Clifton Pike—*hist pl* KY-4
Stone House on Kentucky River—*hist pl* KY-4
Stone House on Old Stage Road—*hist pl* KY-4
Stone House on Plum Creek—*hist pl* KY-4
Stone House on Steele's Grant—*hist pl* KY-4
Stone House on Tanner's Creek—*hist pl* KY-4
Stone House on West Hickman—*hist pl* KY-4
Stonehouse Pond—*reservoir* NH-1
Stone House Ranch—*locale* NV-8
Stonehouse Rec Area—*park* AR-4
Stone Houses—*hist pl* MO-7
Stone House Sch—*school* NY-2
Stone House Site—*hist pl* VA-3
Stonehouse Spring—*spring* NV-8
Stone House Trail—*trail* ME-1
Stone House Wash—*stream* AZ-5
Stone HS—*school* MS-4
Stonehurst—*hist pl* OH-6
**Stonehurst**—*pop pl* CA-9
**Stonehurst**—*pop pl* (2) PA-2
Stonehurst Ave Sch—*school* CA-9
**Stonehurst East**—*pop pl* NJ-2
**Stonehurst Hills**—*pop pl* PA-2
Stonehurst Hills Elem Sch—*school* PA-2
*Stonehurst Hills Sch* PA-2
Stonehurst Recreation Center—*park* CA-9
Stonehurst Sch—*school* CA-9
**Stonehurst West**—*pop pl* NJ-2
Stone Institute—*school* MA-1
*Stone Island* NC-3
Stone Island—*island* AK-9
Stone Island—*island* CA-9
Stone Island—*island* CT-1
Stone Island—*island* (2) FL-3
Stone Island—*island* LA-4
Stone Island—*island* (3) ME-1
Stone Island—*island* WI-6
Stone Island Ledge—*bar* ME-1
Stone Islands—*area* AK-9
Stone Jail Bldg and Row House—*hist pl* NV-8
Stone Jar Hollow—*valley* AR-4
Stone JHS—*school* MS-4
Stone JHS—*school* NC-3
*Stone Johnnie* ID-8
Stone Johnny—*summit* ID-8
Stone Johnny Coulee—*valley* ND-7
Stone Johnny Hill—*summit* ND-7
Stone Jug—*hist pl* NY-2
Stone Jug Hill—*summit* PA-2
Stoneking Cem—*cemetery* (2) IL-6
Stoneking Cem—*cemetery* WV-2
Stone Knife Cave—*cave* PA-2
Stone Lagoon—*lake* CA-9
**Stone Lagoon**—*pop pl* CA-9
*Stonelake* IL-6
*Stone Lake* MN-6
*Stone Lake* WI-6
Stone Lake—*lake* AZ-5
Stone Lake—*lake* CA-9
Stone Lake—*lake* CO-8
Stone Lake—*lake* IN-6
Stone Lake—*lake* IA-7
Stone Lake—*lake* (3) MI-6
Stone Lake—*lake* (9) MN-6
Stone Lake—*lake* NM-5
Stone Lake—*lake* ND-7
Stone Lake—*lake* OK-5
Stone Lake—*lake* SC-3
Stone Lake—*lake* SD-7
Stone Lake—*lake* WA-9
Stone Lake—*lake* (9) WI-6
**Stone Lake**—*pop pl* SC-3
**Stone Lake**—*pop pl* WI-6
Stone Lake—*reservoir* IL-6
Stone Lake—*reservoir* MD-2
Stone Lake—*reservoir* MO-7
Stone Lake—*reservoir* NM-5
Stone Lake—*reservoir* SC-3
Stone Lake—*reservoir* TN-4
Stone Lake—*swamp* MN-6
Stonelake Bridge—*hist pl* SD-7
Stone Lake Community Ch—*church* IN-6
Stone Lake Dam—*dam* PA-2
Stone Lakes—*lake* MT-8
Stone Lakes—*reservoir* TN-4
Stone Lake State Public Shooting Area—*park* SD-7
**Stone Lake (Town of)**—*pop pl* WI-6
Stone Lateral—*canal* ID-8
Stone Ledge—*rock* MA-1
Stone Ledge Lake—*lake* MI-6
Stoneleigh—*hist pl* VA-3
Stoneleigh—*hist pl* WV-2
**Stoneleigh**—*pop pl* MD-2
Stoneleigh-Burnham Sch—*school* MA-1
Stoneleigh Manor—*hist pl* IL-6
Stoneleigh Park Hist Dist—*hist pl* NJ-2
*Stone Lick* OH-6
Stonelick—*locale* OH-6
Stone Lick—*stream* KY-4
Stone Lick—*stream* WV-2
Stone Lick Branch—*stream* (2) KY-4
Stonelick Branch—*stream* WV-2
Stonelick Cem—*cemetery* OH-6
Stone Lick Ch—*church* KY-4
Stonelick Ch—*church* OH-6
Stonelick Ch—*church* WV-2
Stonelick Covered Bridge—*hist pl* OH-6
*Stonelick Creek* WV-2
Stonelick Creek—*stream* KY-4
Stonelick Creek—*stream* OH-6
Stone Lick Creek—*stream* PA-2
Stonelick Creek—*stream* WV-2
Stone Lick Hollow—*valley* VA-3
Stonelick Knob—*summit* WV-2
Stonelick Lake—*reservoir* OH-6
Stonelick Lake State Park—*park* OH-6
Stonelick Run—*stream* (3) WV-2
**Stonelick (Township of)**—*pop pl* OH-6
Stonelick Valley Missionary Ch—*church* OH-6
Stone Lions Shrine—*summit* NM-5
Stone Lookout Tower—*tower* MS-4
Stoneman—*locale* CA-9
Stoneman, Joseph, House—*hist pl* OH-6
Stoneman Creek—*stream* ID-8
Stone Man Creek—*stream* ND-7
Stoneman Creek Spring—*spring* ID-8
Stone Man Dam—*dam* ND-7
Stoneman Hill—*summit* VA-3
Stoneman Lake—*lake* AZ-5
**Stoneman Lake**—*pop pl* AZ-5
Stoneman Lake Interchange—*crossing* AZ-5
Stoneman Mtn—*summit* NC-3
Stone Manor—*hist pl* IL-6
Stone Man Pass—*gap* CO-8
Stoneman Sch—*school* CA-9
Stoneman Spring—*spring* ID-8
Stone Memorial Baptist Ch—*church* AL-4
Stone Memorial Zoo—*park* MA-1
Stonemen's Row Hist Dist—*hist pl* CO-8
Stone Mill—*hist pl* VT-1
Stone Mill—*locale* NJ-2
Stone Mill—*locale* VA-3
Stone Mill Brook—*stream* NY-2
Stone Mill Creek—*stream* FL-3
Stonemill Creek—*stream* VA-3
Stone Mill Hollow—*valley* TN-4
*Stone Mill Hollow Branch* TN-4
Stone Mill Plaza—*locale* PA-2
Stone Mill Pond—*lake* NY-2
Stone Mill Run—*stream* OH-6
**Stone Mills**—*pop pl* NY-2
Stone Mills Creek—*stream* NY-2
Stone Mill Spring—*spring* MO-7
Stone Mills Union Church—*hist pl* NY-2
Stone Mine—*mine* TN-4
Stonemont—*locale* PA-2
*Stone Mountain* WV-2
Stone Mountain—*locale* VA-3
Stone Mountain—*pillar* AZ-5
**Stone Mountain**—*pop pl* GA-3
Stone Mountain—*ridge* (2) TN-4
Stone Mountain Branch—*stream* (2) NC-3
Stone Mountain Branch—*stream* TN-4
Stone Mountain (CCD)—*cens area* GA-3
Stone Mountain Ch—*church* TN-4
Stone Mountain Ch—*church* VA-3
Stone Mountain Chapel—*church* VA-3
Stone Mountain Creek—*stream* GA-3
Stone Mountain Creek—*stream* NC-3
Stone Mountain Creek—*stream* VA-3
Stone Mountain Gap—*gap* TN-4
Stone Mountain Memorial—*park* GA-3
Stone Mountain Overlook—*locale* NC-3
Stone Mountain Park—*park* KY-4
*Stone Mountains* NC-3
Stone Mountains—*ridge* TN-4
Stone Mountain Sch—*school* TN-4
Stone Mountain State Memorial Park—*park* GA-3
Stone Mountain Trail—*trail* (2) TN-4
Stone MS—*school* AL-4
Stone MS—*school* FL-3
*Stone Mtn* TN-4
Stone Mtn—*range* VA-3
Stone Mtn—*summit* AK-9
Stone Mtn—*summit* CO-8
Stone Mtn—*summit* GA-3
Stone Mtn—*summit* ME-1
Stone Mtn—*summit* (2) MA-1
Stone Mtn—*summit* NH-1
Stone Mtn—*summit* NJ-2
Stone Mtn—*summit* (8) NC-3
Stone Mtn—*summit* OR-9
Stone Mtn—*summit* (4) PA-2
Stone Mtn—*summit* (3) TN-4
Stone Mtn—*summit* VT-1
Stone Mtn—*summit* (4) VA-3
Stone Mtn—*summit* WA-9
Stone Mtn—*summit* (2) WY-8
Stone Opening—*flat* CA-9
Stone Palace Camp—*locale* PA-2
Stone Park—*park* AZ-5
Stone Park—*park* IA-7
Stone Park—*park* MS-4
**Stone Park**—*pop pl* IL-6
**Stone Park**—*pop pl* SC-3
Stone Peak—*summit* AZ-5
Stone-Pennebaker House—*hist pl* TN-4
Stone-Penn House—*hist pl* TN-4
Stonepile Ch—*church* GA-3
Stonepile Creek—*stream* WY-8
*Stone Pile Gap* GA-3
Stone Pile Gap—*gap* GA-3
Stonepile Gap—*gap* GA-3
Stone Pile Gap—*gap* TN-4
Stone Pile Ridge—*ridge* TN-4
Stone Pillar Pass—*gap* WY-8
Stone Place (Ruins)—*locale* CA-9
Stone Plantation (historical)—*locale* MS-4
*Stone Point* ME-1
*Stone Point* MD-2
Stone Point—*cape* NC-3
Stone Point—*cape* (2) TX-5
Stone Point—*cape* VA-3
Stone Pond—*bay* LA-4
Stone Pond—*lake* FL-3
Stone Pond—*lake* MA-1
Stone Pond—*lake* MO-7
Stone Pond—*lake* (3) NH-1
Stone Pond—*lake* PA-2
Stone Pond—*lake* RI-1
Stone Pond—*reservoir* NY-2
Stone Pond—*reservoir* NC-3
Stone Pond Brook—*stream* NH-1
Stone Pond Dam—*dam* NC-3
Stone Pond (historical)—*lake* IN-6
Stoneport—*locale* MI-6
Stone Post Office—*hist pl* MI-6
Stonepot Run—*stream* WV-2
Stone Quarry, The—*summit* UT-8
Stone Quarry Bay—*bay* MT-8
Stone Quarry Bayou—*gut* AL-4
Stone Quarry Branch—*stream* IN-6
Stone Quarry Branch—*stream* (2) KY-4
Stone Quarry Bridge—*hist pl* IL-6
Stone Quarry Canyon—*valley* SD-7
Stone Quarry Canyon—*valley* WA-9
Stone Quarry Chapel—*church* OH-6
*Stone Quarry Creek* IL-6
Stone Quarry Creek—*stream* AR-4
Stonequarry Creek—*stream* KY-4
Stone Quarry Creek—*stream* KY-4
Stone Quarry Creek—*stream* MO-7
Stonequarry Creek—*stream* TN-4
Stone Quarry Ditch—*canal* UT-8
Stone Quarry Gulch—*valley* CO-8
Stone Quarry Gulch—*valley* ID-8
Stone Quarry Gulch—*valley* OR-9
Stone Quarry Hill—*summit* (2) NY-2
Stone Quarry Hollow—*valley* AL-4
Stone Quarry Hollow—*valley* PA-2
Stone Quarry Hollow—*valley* TN-4
Stone Quarry Hollow—*valley* TX-5
Stone Quarry Lake—*lake* MI-6
**Stone Quarry Mills**—*pop pl* IN-6
Stone Quarry Ridge—*ridge* MD-2
Stone Quarry Ridge—*ridge* OH-6
Stone Quarry Run—*stream* (2) PA-2
Stonequarry Sch—*school* OH-6
Stone Quarry Sch (abandoned)—*school* PA-2
Stone Quarry Spring—*spring* OR-9
Stone Quarry Trail—*trail* PA-2
Stone Quarters on Burgin Road—*hist pl* KY-4
Stoner—*locale* PA-2
**Stoner**—*pop pl* CO-8
Stoner, Joseph J., House—*hist pl* WI-6
Stoner, Lycurgus, House—*hist pl* IN-6
Stoner, Samuel, Homestead—*hist pl* PA-2
Stone Ranch—*locale* CA-9
Stone Ranch—*locale* CO-8
Stone Ranch—*locale* (2) TX-5
Stone Ranch—*locale* WY-8
Stone Ranch Mil Res Conn Natl Guard—*other* CT-1
Stone Ranch Stage Station—*hist pl* WY-8
Stone Ranch Well—*well* NM-5
Stoner Rapids—*rapids* MI-6
Stoner Ave Sch—*school* CA-9
Stoner Branch—*stream* KY-4
Stoner Bridge—*other* MO-7
Stoner Cave—*cave* MO-7
Stoner Cem—*cemetery* IL-6
Stoner Cem—*cemetery* IN-6
Stoner Cem—*cemetery* (3) MO-7
Stoner Cem—*cemetery* (2) OH-6
Stoner Cem—*cemetery* OK-5
Stoner Chapel—*church* GA-3
*Stoner Creek* CO-8
*Stoner Creek* TN-4
Stoner Creek—*stream* CA-9
Stoner Creek—*stream* CO-8
Stoner Creek—*stream* (2) KY-4
Stoner Creek—*stream* MD-2
Stoner Creek—*stream* MI-6
Stoner Creek—*stream* (2) MT-8
Stoner Creek—*stream* NM-5
Stoner Creek—*stream* WY-8
Stoner Creek Ch—*church* KY-4
Stoner Creek Elem Sch—*school* TN-4
Stoner Ditch—*canal* IN-6
*Stone Reservoir* CA-9
Stoner Field—*park* AL-4
Stoner Guard Station—*locale* CO-8
Stoner Gulch—*valley* CA-9
Stoner Hill Sch—*school* LA-4
Stoner House—*hist pl* CA-9
*Stone Ridge* PA-2
**Stoneridge**—*pop pl* DE-2
**Stoneridge**—*pop pl* MO-7
**Stone Ridge**—*pop pl* (2) NY-2
Stone Ridge—*ridge* AZ-5
Stone Ridge—*ridge* AR-4
Stone Ridge—*ridge* CA-9
Stone Ridge—*ridge* (2) PA-2
Stone Ridge—*ridge* TN-4
Stone Ridge—*ridge* (2) VA-3
Stone Ridge—*ridge* WV-2
Stone Ridge Pond—*reservoir* NY-2
Stone Ridge Sch (abandoned)—*school* PA-2
**Stone Ridge (subdivision)**—*pop pl* AL-4
**Stoneridge (subdivision)**—*pop pl* (2) NC-3
**Stoneridge (subdivision)**—*pop pl* TN-4
Stone Ring Creek—*stream* AK-9
*Stoner Island* MO-7
Stoner Island—*island* NY-2
*Stone River* TN-4
Stone River—*uninc pl* TN-4
Stone River Estates—*uninc pl* TN-4
Stoner Lake—*lake* CO-8
Stoner Lake—*lake* (2) MI-6
Stoner Lake—*lake* MN-6
Stoner Lake—*lake* MT-8
Stoner Lake—*lake* WA-9
Stoner Lakes—*lake* NY-2
Stoner Mesa—*summit* CO-8
Stoner Mesa Rsvr—*reservoir* CO-8
Stoner Mtn—*summit* NM-5
Stoner Mtn—*summit* TN-4
Stone-Nelson Wheelock Ditch—*canal* WY-8
Stone Road Mtn—*summit* VA-3
Stone Road Trail—*trail* PA-2
Stone-Robinson Sch—*school* VA-3
Stone Rock—*island* AK-9
Stone Rock—*rock* MA-1
Stone Rock Bay—*bay* AK-9
Stonerook Cem—*cemetery* PA-2
Stone Row—*hist pl* MO-7
**Stone Row**—*pop pl* PA-2
Stoner Place—*locale* MT-8
Stoner Point Rsvr—*reservoir* CO-8
Stoner Point Rsvr No. 2—*reservoir* CO-8
Stoner Point Rsvr No. 3—*reservoir* CO-8
Stoner Pond—*lake* MI-6
Stoner Ranch—*locale* TX-5
Stoner Recreation Center—*park* CA-9
*Stoners* MT-8
Stoners Bay—*bay* WI-6
Stoner Sch—*school* (2) MI-6
Stoner Sch—*school* WI-6
Stoners Creek—*stream* TN-4
Stoner Site—*hist pl* IL-6
Stoner Ski Area—*other* CO-8
Stoner Spring—*spring* CO-8
Stoner Stock Trail—*trail* CO-8
**Stonerstown**—*pop pl* PA-2
**Stonersville**—*pop pl* PA-2
Stone Rsvr—*reservoir* (2) ID-8
Stone Rsvr—*reservoir* OR-9
Stone Run—*stream* MD-2
Stone Run—*stream* OH-6
Stone Run—*stream* (5) PA-2
Stone Run—*stream* WV-2
Stone Run Ch—*church* WV-2
Stone Run - in part PA-2
Stonerville—*locale* PA-2
Stoner Well—*well* NM-5
**Stones**—*pop pl* AL-4
Stones Bay—*bay* NC-3
Stone's Block—*hist pl* OH-6
Stones Bog—*swamp* MA-1
Stonesboro Post Office (historical)—*building* TN-4
Stones Bottom—*flat* TN-4
Stones Branch—*stream* MO-7
Stones Bridge—*bridge* MD-2
Stones Bridge—*bridge* MA-1
Stones Bridge—*bridge* WI-6
*Stones Bridge Branch* GA-3
*Stones Brook* MA-1
Stones Brook—*stream* CT-1
Stones Brook—*stream* MA-1
Stones Brook—*stream* VT-1
Stones Cabins—*locale* AK-9
Stones Canyon—*valley* CA-9
Stones Cem—*cemetery* AL-4
Stone Sch—*hist pl* IA-7
Stone Sch—*hist pl* NH-1
Stone Sch—*school* CO-8
Stone Sch—*school* (4) IL-6
Stone Sch—*school* IA-7
Stone Sch—*school* (4) KS-7
Stone Sch—*school* (2) ME-1
Stone Sch—*school* MD-2
Stone Sch—*school* (3) MA-1
Stone Sch—*school* (7) MI-6
Stone Sch—*school* MS-4
Stone Sch—*school* (2) MO-7
Stone Sch—*school* NE-7
Stone Sch—*school* NY-2
Stone Sch—*school* PA-2
Stone Sch—*school* (3) WI-6
Stone Sch (abandoned)—*school* PA-2
Stones Chapel—*church* AL-4
Stones Chapel—*church* MO-7
Stones Chapel—*church* (2) NC-3
Stones Chapel—*church* (2) VA-3
Stones Chapel Cem—*cemetery* MO-7
Stone Sch District Number 4—*school* MI-6
Stone Sch (historical)—*school* AL-4
Stone Sch (historical)—*school* TN-4
*Stone Sch House* PA-2
Stone School Cem—*cemetery* (2) IL-6
Stone Schoolhouse—*hist pl* ME-1
Stone Schoolhouse Cem—*cemetery* NY-2
*Stones Corner* MO-7
Stones Corner—*locale* ME-1
Stones Corner—*locale* OK-5
Stones Corner—*locale* VA-3
Stones Corner Cem—*cemetery* ME-1
*Stones Creek* TN-4
Stones Creek—*stream* NC-3
**Stones Crossing**—*pop pl* IN-6
Stones Crossroads—*locale* GA-3
Stone Seminary—*church* TN-4
Stone Serpent Mound—*hist pl* KY-4
Stones Ferry (historical)—*locale* AL-4
*Stones Hill* MA-1
Stones Hollow—*valley* KY-4
Stones HQ (Site)—*locale* CA-9
**Stone Siding**—*pop pl* MD-2
Stones Knob—*summit* NC-3
Stones Lake—*lake* MN-6
Stones Landing—*locale* LA-4
Stones Landing—*locale* NC-3
Stones Landing (historical)—*locale* MS-4
Stone Slough—*stream* IL-6
*Stones Mill* AL-4
Stones Mill—*locale* VA-3
**Stones Mill**—*pop pl* VA-3
Stones Mill (historical)—*locale* TN-4
**Stones Orchard Addition**—*pop pl* UT-8
Stones Peak—*summit* CO-8
Stones Point—*cape* ME-1
*Stones Pond* MA-1
Stones Pond—*reservoir* NY-2
**Stonesport (historical)**—*pop pl* MO-7
Stone Spring—*spring* CO-8
Stone Spring—*spring* ID-8
Stone Spring—*spring* MO-7
Stone Spring—*spring* NV-8
Stone Spring—*spring* NM-5
Stone Spring—*spring* OR-9
Stone Springfield Cem—*cemetery* GA-3
Stone Springfield Ch—*church* GA-3
Stone Springfield Sch—*school* GA-3
Stone Springs—*uninc pl* VA-3
*Stones River* TN-4
Stones River—*stream* TN-4
Stones River Ch—*church* TN-4
Stones River Country Club—*locale* TN-4
**Stones River Homes**—*pop pl* TN-4
Stones River Hosp—*hospital* TN-4
Stones River Natl Battlefield—*hist pl* TN-4
Stones Rock—*bar* ME-1
**Stones Store**—*pop pl* VA-3
Stones Store (historical)—*locale* MS-4
Stone State Park—*park* IA-7
**Stone Station**—*pop pl* SC-3
Stone Steps—*ridge* VA-3
Stone Steps—*summit* WV-2
**Stones Throw**—*pop pl* DE-2
Stonesthrow Lake—*lake* WA-9
**Stones Throw (subdivision)**—*pop pl* DE-2
**Stones Throw (subdivision)**—*pop pl* NC-3
Stonestown—*post sta* CA-9
Stone's Trace—*hist pl* IN-6
Stone Street Baptist Ch—*church* AL-4
Stone Street Baptist Church—*hist pl* AL-4
Stonestreet Cem—*cemetery* PA-2
Stonestreet Creek—*stream* PA-2
Stone Street Elem Sch—*school* NC-3
Stone Street Hist Dist—*hist pl* NY-2
Stone Street Sch—*school* IL-6
Stonestreet Sch—*school* KY-4
Stone Street Sch—*school* MS-4
Stones Valley—*valley* CA-9
Stones View Ch—*church* KY-4
Stone Tank—*reservoir* AZ-5
Stone Tank—*reservoir* (2) TX-5
Stone Tank—*well* AZ-5
*Stone Tavern* PA-2
Stone Tavern—*locale* NJ-2
Stone Technical Center—*school* FL-3
Stone-Tolan House—*hist pl* NY-2
Stonetop Mtn—*summit* WY-8
Stonetown—*locale* NJ-2
Stonetown—*locale* PA-2
*Stone Trail* PA-2
Stone Trough Canyon—*valley* CA-9
Stone Valley—*valley* (2) CA-9
*Stone Valley Lake* PA-2
Stone Valley Ranch—*locale* CA-9
Stone Valley Sch—*school* CA-9
Stone Valley Sch (abandoned)—*school* PA-2
Stone View Oil and Gas Field—*oilfield* ND-7
**Stoneview Township**—*pop pl* ND-7
**Stonevilla**—*pop pl* PA-2
Stone Village Hist Dist—*hist pl* VT-1
Stoneville—*locale* SD-7
**Stoneville**—*pop pl* (2) MA-1
**Stoneville**—*pop pl* MS-4
**Stoneville**—*pop pl* NC-3
**Stoneville**—*pop pl* OH-6
**Stoneville**—*pop pl* WV-2
Stoneville Brook—*stream* MA-1
Stoneville Cem—*cemetery* PA-2
Stoneville Flats—*flat* WY-8
Stoneville (historical)—*locale* SD-7
Stoneville HS—*school* MA-1
Stoneville-Leland Cem—*cemetery* MS-4
Stoneville Pond—*reservoir* MA-1
Stoneville Pond Dam—*dam* MA-1
Stoneville Rsvr—*reservoir* MA-1
*Stonewal* MS-4
*Stonewall* AL-4
*Stonewall* MS-4
*Stonewall* SD-7
Stonewall—*hist pl* NC-3
Stonewall—*locale* AL-4
Stonewall—*locale* (2) KY-4
Stonewall—*locale* MS-4
Stonewall—*locale* TX-5
Stonewall—*locale* VA-3
Stonewall—*other* AK-9
**Stonewall**—*pop pl* AL-4
**Stonewall**—*pop pl* AR-4
**Stonewall**—*pop pl* CO-8
**Stonewall**—*pop pl* GA-3
**Stonewall**—*pop pl* LA-4
**Stonewall**—*pop pl* (2) MS-4
**Stonewall**—*pop pl* NC-3
**Stonewall**—*pop pl* OK-5
**Stonewall**—*pop pl* TN-4
**Stonewall**—*pop pl* VA-3
Stonewall—*uninc pl* WV-2
Stone Wall, The—*cliff* AK-9
Stonewall, The—*ridge* CO-8
**Stonewall Acres**—*pop pl* VA-3
Stonewall Bank—*bar* OR-9
Stonewall Baptist Ch—*church* MS-4
*Stone Wall Beach* MA-1
Stonewall Beach—*beach* MA-1
Stonewall Canyon—*stream* CA-9
Stonewall Canyon—*valley* CA-9
Stone Wall Canyon—*valley* NV-8
Stonewall Cem—*cemetery* CO-8
Stonewall Cem—*cemetery* FL-3
Stonewall Cem—*cemetery* (2) MS-4
Stonewall Cem—*cemetery* OH-6
Stonewall Cem—*cemetery* (2) TX-5
Stonewall Ch—*church* KY-4
Stonewall Ch—*church* (3) MS-4
Stonewall Ch—*church* SC-3
Stonewall Ch—*church* TX-5
Stonewall Ch—*church* (2) VA-3
*Stonewall College* MS-4
**Stonewall (County)**—*pop pl* TX-5
*Stonewall Creek* VA-3
Stonewall Creek—*stream* CA-9
Stonewall Creek—*stream* CO-8
Stonewall Creek—*stream* GA-3
Stonewall Creek—*stream* MS-4
Stonewall Creek—*stream* (2) MT-8
Stonewall Creek—*stream* OR-9
Stonewall Creek—*stream* (2) VA-3
Stonewall Creek—*stream* WY-8
**Stonewall Estates**—*pop pl* KY-4
Stonewall Flat—*flat* NV-8
**Stonewall Gap**—*pop pl* CO-8
Stonewall Grange Hall—*locale* OH-6
Stonewall-Hawthorne (Magisterial District)—*fmr MCD* VA-3
Stonewall Hill—*summit* TX-5
Stonewall Jackson Campground—*locale* TX-5
Stonewall Jackson Elem Sch—*school* FL-3
**Stonewall Jackson Homes**—*pop pl* NC-3
Stonewall Jackson Hosp—*hospital* VA-3
Stonewall Jackson HS—*school* VA-3
Stonewall Jackson JHS—*school* TX-5
Stonewall Jackson JHS—*school* VA-3
Stonewall Jackson Monument—*other* WV-2
Stonewall Jackson Sch—*hist pl* VA-3
Stonewall Jackson Sch—*school* AL-4
Stonewall Jackson Sch—*school* (3) VA-3
Stonewall Jackson Training Sch Hist Dist—*hist pl* NC-3
**Stonewall Jackson Training School**—*pop pl* NC-3
Stonewall Knob—*summit* GA-3
Stonewall Lake—*lake* KY-4
Stonewall Landing (historical)—*locale* AL-4
Stonewall Landing (historical)—*locale* MS-4
Stonewall (Magisterial District)—*fmr MCD* (6) VA-3
Stonewall (Magisterial District)—*fmr MCD* WV-2
Stonewall Mall—*post sta* TX-5
Stonewall Mall Shop Ctr—*locale* TX-5
**Stonewall Manor**—*pop pl* VA-3
Stonewall Memorial Hosp—*hospital* TX-5
Stonewall Memory Gardens—*cemetery* VA-3
Stonewall Mills—*locale* VA-3
Stonewall Mine—*mine* CA-9
Stonewall Mine—*mine* WA-9
Stonewall Mtn—*summit* MT-8
Stonewall Mtn—*summit* NV-8
Stonewall Park Cem—*cemetery* WV-2
Stonewall Pass—*gap* CA-9
Stonewall Pass—*gap* NV-8
Stone Wall Pass—*gap* NM-5
Stonewall Peak—*summit* CA-9
Stonewall Place Hist Dist—*hist pl* TN-4
*Stonewall Plantation* MS-4
Stonewall Pond—*lake* MA-1
Stonewall Post Office (historical)—*school* TN-4
Stone Wall Ranch—*hist pl* WY-8
Stonewall Ridge—*ridge* WA-9
Stonewall Sch—*school* KY-4
Stonewall Sch—*school* MS-4
Stonewall Sch—*school* TX-5
Stonewall Sch—*school* (2) VA-3
Stonewall Sch (historical)—*school* AL-4
Stonewall Sch (historical)—*school* TN-4
Stonewall Spring—*spring* NV-8
*Stonewall Station* MS-4
Stonewall Taylor Sch—*school* AL-4
Stonewall (Township of)—*fmr MCD* AR-4
Stonewall (Township of)—*fmr MCD* NC-3
Stonewall Valley—*valley* CO-8
Stone Warehouse—*hist pl* AZ-5
Stone Wash—*stream* CA-9
Stone Watering Trough Hollow—*valley* PA-2
Stone Well—*well* NM-5
**Stonewell Plantation**—*pop pl* LA-4
Stone Windmill—*hist pl* NY-2
**Stonewood**—*pop pl* WV-2
**Stonewood Acres (subdivision)**—*pop pl* NC-3
**Stonewood Farms**—*pop pl* PA-2
*Stoney* TX-5
**Stoney**—*pop pl* KS-7
Stoney, Mount—*summit* AK-9
Stoney, Robert, House—*hist pl* UT-8
Stoney, Robert W., House—*hist pl* UT-8
Stoney Bar—*bar* CA-9
Stoney Bar—*bar* MN-6
Stoney Branch—*stream* AL-4
Stoney Branch—*stream* DE-2
Stoney Branch—*stream* GA-3
**Stoneybreak**—*pop pl* PA-2
*Stoney Brook* ME-1
*Stoney Brook* MA-1
*Stoney Brook* NJ-2
*Stoney Brook* NY-2
*Stoney Brook* RI-1
**Stoneybrook**—*pop pl* KY-4
**Stoney Brook**—*pop pl* MD-2
Stoney Brook—*stream* ME-1
Stoney Brook—*stream* MN-6
Stoney Brook—*stream* PA-2
Stoneybrook Ch—*church* OH-6
**Stoney Brook Estates**—*pop pl* MD-2
**Stoneybrook Estates**—*pop pl* MD-2
**Stoney Brook Estates**—*pop pl* NJ-2
**Stoney Brook Estates**—*pop pl* VA-3
**Stoneybrook Estates Subdivision**—*pop pl* UT-8
Stoney Brook Golf Course—*locale* AL-4
Stoneybrook Lake—*lake* SC-3
Stoney Brook Mtn—*summit* ME-1
*Stoney Brook River* MN-6
**Stoneybrook (subdivision)**—*pop pl* (4) NC-3
**Stoney Brook (subdivision)**—*pop pl* (2) NC-3
**Stoney Brook (subdivision)**—*pop pl* TN-4
**Stoney Brook Subdivision**—*pop pl* UT-8
Stoney Brook (Township of)—*civ div* MN-6
Stoney Butte Township—*civil* SD-7
Stoney Castle—*hist pl* KY-4
Stoney Cem—*cemetery* SC-3
Stoney Corner—*locale* MI-6
**Stoney Corners**—*pop pl* MI-6
Stoney Corners Trail—*trail* MN-6
*Stoney Creek* ID-8
*Stoney Creek* IN-6
*Stoney Creek* MI-6
*Stoney Creek* MN-6
*Stoney Creek* NV-8
*Stoney Creek* NC-3
*Stoney Creek* PA-2
*Stoney Creek* SC-3
*Stoney Creek* VA-3
*Stoney Creek* WI-6
Stoney Creek—*stream* (5) CA-9
Stoney Creek—*stream* DE-2
Stoney Creek—*stream* ID-8
Stoney Creek—*stream* (5) IN-6
Stoney Creek—*stream* (3) NC-3
Stoney Creek—*stream* PA-2
Stoney Creek—*stream* VA-3
Stoney Creek—*stream* WI-6
Stoney Creek—*stream* WY-8
Stoney Creek Baptist Ch—*church* TN-4
Stoney Creek Ch—*church* NC-3
Stoney Creek Ch—*church* WV-2
*Stoney Creek Dam* DE-2
Stoney Creek Sch—*school* IN-6
Stoney Creek (Township of)—*civ div* (2) IN-6
**Stoneycrest (subdivision)**—*pop pl* NC-3
Stoneycroft Point—*cape* MI-6
Stoney Cross Island (historical)—*island* TN-4
Stoney Face Mtn—*summit* CO-8
Stoney Field—*park* SC-3
Stoney Forest Lookout Tower—*locale* MD-2
*Stoney Fork* PA-2
**Stoney Fork**—*pop pl* KY-4
**Stoney Fork**—*pop pl* TN-4
Stoney Fork—*stream* KY-4
Stoney Fork Ch—*church* KY-4
*Stoney Fork Creek* NC-3
Stoney Fork Junction—*uninc pl* KY-4
**Stoney Gardens (subdivision)**—*pop pl* NC-3
Stoney Glacier—*glacier* AK-9
Stoney Gulch—*valley* OR-9
**Stoney Hill**—*pop pl* OH-6
**Stoney Hill**—*pop pl* SC-3
Stoney Hill Ch—*church* SC-3
Stoney Hill Ch—*church* WV-2
Stoney Hill Sch—*school* SC-3
Stoney Hollow—*valley* KY-4
Stoney Indian Lake—*lake* MT-8
Stoney Indian Pass—*gap* MT-8
Stoney Indian Pass Trail—*trail* MT-8
Stoney Indian Peaks—*summit* MT-8
Stoney Island Meadow—*swamp* NJ-2
*Stoney Kill* NY-2
**Stoney Knob**—*pop pl* NC-3
Stoney Knob—*summit* NC-3
*Stoney Lake* MN-6
*Stoney Lake* ND-7
Stoney Lick Sch (abandoned)—*school* PA-2
Stoney- Lonesome Cem—*cemetery* TN-4
*Stoney Man* VA-3
**Stoney Mountain Estate**—*pop pl* NC-3
Stoney Mountain Park—*park* AZ-5
Stoney Mountain Rest Home—*hospital* NC-3
Stoney Mtn—*summit* GA-3
Stoney Mtn—*summit* NC-3
Stoney Mtn—*summit* OR-9

Stop Brook ... MA-1
Stopes ... PA-2
Stopes Tank—reservoir ... AZ-5
Stophel Cem—cemetery ... TN-4
Stopher Creek—stream ... MT-8
Stopher Ditch ... IN-6
Stopher Gulch—valley ... MT-8
Stop Hollow—valley ... WV-2
Stop Island—island ... AK-9
Stop Island—island ... MN-6
Stop Keys—island ... FL-3
Stop Landing (historical)—locale ... MS-4
Stopover—locale ... KY-4
Stoppel Point—summit ... NY-2
Stopper Creek—stream ... FL-3
Stopper Key ... FL-3
Stopping Rocks—summit ... KY-4
Stopple, George, Farmstead—hist pl ... MN-6
Stop River ... MA-1
Stop River—stream ... MA-1
Stop Run—stream ... IN-6
Stop Shop Center—locale ... MO-7
Stop Table—summit ... NE-7
Stop Table Cem—cemetery ... NE-7
Stop Trail Spring—spring ... AZ-5
**Stop 0308**—pop pl ... OK-5
Stop 28 Hollow—valley ... WV-2
**Storage**—pop pl ... PA-2
Storage Area Number Two—reservoir ... NC-3
Storage Area Number Two Dam—dam ... NC-3
Storage Basin ... MI-6
Storage Dam—dam (2) ... PA-2
Storage Pond—reservoir ... AL-4
Storage Reservoir Number Two Dam—dam ... PA-2
Storage Tank Windmill—locale ... TX-5
Storage Warehouse—hist pl ... AZ-5
Storck—locale ... VA-3
Storckman Cem—cemetery ... IL-6
Storckman Creek—stream ... IL-6
Stordahl Bldg—hist pl ... MN-6
Stordahl Cem—cemetery ... SD-7
Stordahl Ch—church (2) ... ND-7
Stord Brook—stream ... NY-2
**Storden**—pop pl ... MN-6
Storden Cem—cemetery ... MN-6
**Storden (Township of)**—pop pl ... MN-6
Store ... MS-4
Store Branch—stream ... AL-4
Store Branch—stream ... TN-4
Store Cabin Run—stream ... PA-2
Store Creek ... OK-5
Store Creek—stream ... MN-6
Store Creek—stream ... OK-5
Store Creek—stream ... SC-3
Store Draw—valley ... WY-8
Store Gulch—valley ... CA-9
Store Gulch—valley ... OR-9
Store Gulch Guard Station—locale ... OR-9
Store Gulch Guard Station No. 1020—hist pl ... OR-9
Store Hollow—valley ... KY-4
Store Hollow—valley ... MO-7
Store Homes Church ... MS-4
Storehouse, State Lunatic Asylum—hist pl ... GA-3
Storehouse Branch—stream ... KY-4
Store House Branch—stream ... VA-3
Storehouse Brook—stream ... CT-1
Storehouse Hollow—valley ... KY-4
Store House Hollow—valley ... KY-4
Storehouse Hollow—valley ... TN-4
Storehouse No. 3—hist pl ... AK-9
Storehouse No. 4—hist pl ... AK-9
Storehouse Run—stream ... NY-2
Storehouse Run—stream ... PA-2
Store Island—island ... NH-1
Store Lake—lake ... MN-6
Storelvedalen Cem—cemetery ... MN-6
Store Point—cape ... NC-3
Store Quarry Trail—trail ... PA-2
Storer Cem—cemetery ... ME-1
Storer Cem—cemetery ... OH-6
Storer Creek—stream ... KS-7
Storer Creek—stream ... MN-6
Storer Hill—summit ... ME-1
Storer House—hist pl ... CA-9
Storer Junior High School ... IN-6
Storer MS—school ... IN-6
Storers Lake—lake ... AL-4
Stores—locale ... IL-6
Stores Corner—locale ... ME-1
Store Spring ... OR-9
Stores Run ... OH-6
Store Tank—reservoir ... NM-5
**Store Village**—pop pl ... HI-9
Storey—locale ... CA-9
**Storey**—pop pl ... FL-3
Storey, Ellsworth, Cottages Hist Dist—hist pl ... WA-9
Storey, Ellsworth, Residences—hist pl ... WA-9
Storey, George Lincoln, House—hist pl ... OR-9
Storey Bend—island ... FL-3
Storey Branch—stream ... AL-4
Storey Branch—stream ... KY-4
Storey Branch—stream ... NC-3
Storey Cem—cemetery ... TX-5
Storey County—civil ... NV-8
Storey Creek ... VA-3
Storey Creek—stream (2) ... OR-9
Storey Creek—stream ... TX-5
Storey Crossing—locale ... FL-3
Storey Ditch—canal ... MT-8
Storey Hill—summit ... NH-1
Storey Hollow—valley ... TN-4
Storey Island—island ... AK-9
Storey JHS—school ... TX-5
Storey Lake—lake ... MI-6
Storey Lake—reservoir ... TX-5
**Storeyland**—pop pl ... IL-6
Storey Mill Creek—stream ... GA-3
Storey Mine ... AL-4
Storey Peak—summit ... WA-9
Storey Ranch—locale ... MT-8
Storey Road Underpass—crossing ... AZ-5
Storeys Island ... NJ-2
Storey Slough—gut ... AK-9
Storey Trail—trail ... PA-2
Storff Creek—stream ... NV-8
**Storie**—pop pl ... TN-4
Storie, Lake—reservoir ... AL-4
Storie Cem—cemetery ... TN-4
Storie Dam—dam ... AL-4
Storie Gulch—valley ... OR-9
Stories Cem—cemetery ... AL-4
Stories Cem—cemetery ... MO-7
Storie Spring Number Two—spring ... OR-9
Stork, John Henry, Log House—hist pl ... NE-7
Stork Creek ... CA-9
Stork Drain—canal ... MI-6
Storke Portal—tunnel ... CO-8
Stork Island—island ... ME-1
Storks Ditch—canal ... IA-7
Storks Ferry—locale ... IN-6
**Storla**—pop pl ... SD-7
Storlie ... ND-7
Storlie Cem—cemetery ... ND-7
**Storlie Township**—pop pl ... ND-7
Storm-bordson State Wildlife Mngmt Area—park ... MN-6
Storm Branch—stream (2) ... GA-3
Storm Branch—stream ... KY-4
Storm Branch—stream (2) ... SC-3
Storm Branch—stream ... TX-5
Storm Canyon ... NV-8
Storm Canyon—valley ... AZ-5
Storm Canyon—valley (2) ... CA-9
Storm Canyon Spring—spring ... AZ-5
Storm Canyon Well—well ... AZ-5
Storm Castle—summit ... MT-8
Storm Creek—stream ... AK-9
Storm Creek—stream (4) ... ID-8
Storm Creek—stream ... IN-6
Storm Creek—stream ... IA-7
Storm Creek—stream ... MS-4
Storm Creek—stream (2) ... MT-8
Storm Creek—stream ... OR-9
Storm Creek Ditch—canal ... IN-6
Storm Creek Flat—flat ... ID-8
Storm Creek Lake—reservoir ... AR-4
Storm Creek Lake—reservoir ... ND-7
Storm Creek State Game Mngmt Area—park ... ND-7
Storm Draw—valley ... WY-8
Storm Hill—summit (2) ... SD-7
Storm Hill—summit ... WY-8
Storm (historical)—locale ... SD-7
Stormhole Bend—bend ... AR-4
Storm House—hist pl ... OK-5
Storm Islands—area ... AK-9
Stormitt Butte—summit ... MT-8
Storm Jade Mine—mine ... CA-9
Storm King—locale ... NY-2
**Stormking**—pop pl ... KY-4
Storm King—summit ... CO-8
Storm King—summit ... WA-9
Storm King, Mount—summit ... WA-9
Storm King Campground—locale ... CO-8
Storm King Creek—stream ... CO-8
Storm King Golf Club—other ... NY-2
Storm King Highway—hist pl ... NY-2
Storm King Mountain ... ID-8
Storm King Mtn—summit (2) ... CO-8
Storm King Mtn—summit ... NY-2
Storm King Mtn—summit (2) ... WA-9
Storm King Peak—summit ... CO-8
Storm King Trail—trail ... WA-9
Storm Lake ... AR-4
Storm Lake ... MN-6
Storm Lake—lake ... CO-8
Storm Lake—lake ... ID-8
Storm Lake—lake ... IA-7
Storm Lake—lake ... NE-7
Storm Lake—lake ... ND-7
Storm Lake—lake ... OR-9
Storm Lake—lake ... WA-9
Storm Lake—lake ... WI-6
**Storm Lake**—pop pl ... IA-7
Storm Lake—reservoir ... MT-8
Storm Lake City Hall—building ... IA-7
Storm Lake Creek—stream ... MT-8
Storm Lake HS—school ... IA-7
Storm Lake Natl Wildlife Ref—park ... ND-7
Storm Lake Pass—gap ... MT-8
Storm Lake Public Library—hist pl ... IA-7
Storm Lake Ranch—locale ... NE-7
Storm Lake State Wildlife Mngmt Area—park ... IA-7
Storm Mountain ... CO-8
Storm Mountain ... SD-7
Storm Mountain Picnic Ground—locale ... UT-8
Storm Mountain Retreat Center—building ... SD-7
**Storm Mountain Terrace**—pop pl ... UT-8
Storm Mountain Trail—trail ... CO-8
Storm Mtn—summit ... AK-9
Storm Mtn—summit ... CO-8
Storm Mtn—summit ... ID-8
Storm Mtn—summit ... MT-8
Storm Mtn—summit ... OR-9
Storm Mtn—summit ... UT-8
Stormont—locale ... VA-3
Stormont, David, House—hist pl ... OH-6
Stormont Ditch—canal ... IN-6
Stormont (historical)—locale ... KS-7
Stormont-Vail Hospital Airp—airport ... KS-7
Storm Park—park ... MT-8
Storm Park Creek—stream ... MT-8
Storm Pass—gap (2) ... CO-8
Storm Pass Trail—trail ... CO-8
Storm Peak ... CO-8
Storm Peak ... WY-8
Storm Peak—summit (4) ... CO-8
Storm Peak—summit ... ID-8
Storm Peak—summit (2) ... MT-8
Storm Peak Lake—lake ... ID-8
Storm Peak Trail—trail ... MT-8
Storm Point ... ID-8
Storm Point—cliff ... WY-8
Storm Point—pillar ... WY-8
Storm Pond—reservoir ... NJ-2
Storm Ranch—locale ... AZ-5
Storm Ranch—locale ... TX-5
Storm Ranch—locale (2) ... WY-8
Storm Ridge—ridge ... CO-8
Storm Ridge—ridge ... ID-8
Storm Ridge—ridge ... WA-9
Storm Roark Hollow—valley ... KY-4
Storms—locale ... OH-6
Storms Cem—cemetery ... OH-6
Storms Ch—church ... OH-6
Storm Sch—school ... TX-5
Storm Sch—school ... WY-8
Storm Sch (historical)—school ... SD-7
Storms Creek ... IN-6
Storms Creek—stream (2) ... OH-6
Storms Creek—stream ... TN-4
Storms Creek Ch—church ... OH-6
Storms Ditch—canal ... IN-6
Storm Seep—spring ... AZ-5
Storm Shelter Cabin No 2—locale ... WY-8
Storms House—hist pl ... AZ-5
Storms House—hist pl ... NJ-2
Storms Island—island ... NJ-2
Storms Lake—lake ... MI-6
Storms Mtn—summit ... TX-5
Storms Oil Field—other ... IL-6
Storm Spring—spring ... MT-8
Storm Spring—spring ... NV-8
**Stormstown**—pop pl ... PA-2
Storm Town ... MS-4
**Stormville**—pop pl ... NY-2
**Stormville**—pop pl ... PA-2
**Stormville**—pop pl ... TX-5
Stormville Ch—church ... TX-5
Stormville Mtn—summit ... NY-2
Stormy Canyon—valley (2) ... CA-9
Stormy Canyon—valley ... NV-8
Stormy Creek—stream ... AK-9
Stormy Creek—stream ... MN-6
Stormy Creek—stream ... NV-8
Stormy Creek—stream ... WA-9
Stormy Ditch—canal ... CO-8
Stormy Gap—gap ... VA-3
Stormy Gulch—valley ... CO-8
Stormy Hill—summit ... NJ-2
Stormy Lake—lake ... AK-9
Stormy Lake—lake ... OR-9
Stormy Lake—lake ... WI-6
Stormy Lease Trail—trail ... TX-5
Stormy Mtn—summit ... WA-9
Stormy Pass—gap ... ID-8
Stormy Pass—gap ... MT-8
Stormy Peak ... CO-8
Stormy Peak—summit ... ID-8
Stormy Peak—summit ... NV-8
Stormy Peaks—summit ... CO-8
Stormy Peaks Pass—gap ... CO-8
Stormy Peaks Trail—trail ... CO-8
Stormy Point ... ID-8
Stormy Point—cape ... AK-9
Stormy Point—cape ... WA-9
Stormy Point—summit ... ID-8
Stormy Rsvr—reservoir ... WY-8
Stormy Spring—spring ... WA-9
Stormy Stack—island ... CA-9
Stormy Treasure Mine—mine ... CO-8
Sto-Rox Junior High School ... PA-2
Sto-Rox Senior HS—school ... PA-2
Storrie—locale ... CA-9
Storrie Ch—church ... NM-5
Storrie Intake Canal—canal ... NM-5
Storrie Lake—reservoir ... NM-5
Storrie Lake—reservoir ... OK-5
Storrie Lake State Park—park ... NM-5
Storrie Project Irrigation Canal—canal ... NM-5
Storrow Camp—locale ... MA-1
Storrow Sch—school ... MA-1
Storrs ... OH-6
Storrs—locale ... UT-8
**Storrs**—pop pl ... CT-1
Storrs Creek ... PA-2
Storrs Creek—stream ... NY-2
Storr's Harbor ... NY-2
Storrs Hill—summit ... NH-1
Storrs Lake—lake ... WI-6
Storrs Mine—mine ... MT-8
Storrs Point—cape ... NY-2
Storrs Pond—lake ... NH-1
Storrs Shaft—mine ... PA-2
Storrs-Spring Canyon Site ... UT-8
Storter Bay—bay ... FL-3
**Storwest**—pop pl ... OR-9
Story ... AL-4
Story—locale ... MT-8
Story—locale ... NE-7
Story—locale ... VA-3
Story—locale ... WI-6
**Story**—pop pl ... AR-4
**Story**—pop pl ... IN-6
**Story**—pop pl ... OK-5
**Story**—pop pl ... WY-8
Story, F. Q., Neighborhood Hist Dist—hist pl ... AZ-5
Story, Jesse and Mary, House—hist pl ... TX-5
Story, Joseph, House—hist pl ... MA-1
Storybook—locale ... PA-2
**Story Book Acres (subdivision)**—pop pl ... TN-4
Story Branch—stream ... KY-4
Story Branch—stream ... SC-3
Story Branch—stream ... TX-5
Story Brook ... MN-6
**Storybrook**—pop pl ... IL-6
Story-Camp Rowhouses—hist pl ... IL-6
Story Canyon—valley ... CA-9
Story Cem ... AL-4
Story Cem—cemetery ... KY-4
Story Cem—cemetery (5) ... TN-4
Story Cem—cemetery ... TX-5
Story Cem—cemetery ... WI-6
Story Chapel—church ... KY-4
**Story City**—pop pl ... IA-7
Story County Home—building ... IA-7
Story Creek ... NC-3
Story Creek—stream ... AK-9
Story Creek—stream (2) ... AR-4
Story Creek—stream ... CA-9
Story Creek—stream ... CO-8
Story Creek—stream ... MT-8
Story Creek—stream ... VA-3
Story Creek—stream ... WA-9
Story Creek—stream ... WI-6
Story Creek—stream ... WY-8
Story East Tank—reservoir ... NM-5
Story Flat—flat ... CA-9
Story Ford—locale ... KY-4
Story Grammar Sch—hist pl ... MA-1
Story Gulch—valley ... CO-8
Story Hill—summit ... CT-1
Story Hill Fire Tower—locale ... ME-1
**Story (historical)**—pop pl ... MS-4
Story Island ... MA-1
Story Island—island ... NJ-2
Story Island Channel—channel ... NJ-2
Story Lake ... IN-6
Story Lake—lake ... FL-3
Story Lake—lake ... IN-6
Story Lake—lake ... MI-6
Story Lake—reservoir ... GA-3
Story Landing—locale ... FL-3
Story Mine—mine ... AZ-5
Story Motor Company—hist pl ... MT-8
Story Mound—hist pl ... OH-6
Story Mound State Memorial—hist pl ... OH-6
Story Mtn—summit ... AR-4
Story Mtn—summit ... TN-4
Story-Odum Cem—cemetery ... GA-3
Story Park—park ... CA-9
Story Penrose Trail—trail ... WY-8
Story Pond—lake ... GA-3
Story Post Office (historical)—building ... AL-4
Story Post Office (historical)—building ... MS-4
Story Ranch—locale ... NM-5
Story River—gut ... SC-3
/Storys ... NC-3
Storys ... VA-3
Storys—locale ... NC-3
Story Sch—school ... MA-1
Story Sch—school ... OK-5
Story Sch—school ... WI-6
Storys Creek ... VA-3
Storys Creek—stream ... MO-7
Storys Creek—stream ... NC-3
Storys Creek Ch—church ... NC-3
**Storys Crossroads**—pop pl ... NC-3
Storys Millpond—reservoir ... GA-3
Story Springs—stream ... TX-5
Story Spring Shelter—locale ... VT-1
Storys Run—stream ... OH-6
Storys Store (historical)—locale ... MS-4
Story Tank—reservoir ... NM-5
Story Well—well ... NM-5
Storz, Gottlieb, House—hist pl ... NE-7
Stossel Creek—stream ... WA-9
Stoten Lake—lake ... SD-7
Stoten Opening—flat ... CA-9
Stotesberry Point—cape ... NC-3
**Stotesbury**—pop pl ... MO-7
**Stotesbury**—pop pl ... WV-2
Stotesbury Club House—hist pl ... PA-2
Stotesville ... AL-4
**Stotesville**—pop pl ... AL-4
Stotler Ch—church ... KS-7
Stotler (historical)—locale ... KS-7
Stotlers Crossroads—locale ... WV-2
**Stotonic**—pop pl ... AZ-5
Stotonik ... AZ-5
Stotonyak ... AZ-5
Stotonyak—locale ... AZ-5
Stots Canyon—valley ... SD-7
Stots Canyon—valley ... WY-8
Stots Spring—spring ... SD-7
Stott ... VA-3
**Stott**—pop pl ... VA-3
Stott Airp (private)—airport ... PA-2
Stottard Gulch—valley ... CA-9
Stott Canyon—valley ... AZ-5
Stott Cem—cemetery ... AL-4
Stott Knob—summit ... NC-3
Stottlemeyer Sch—school ... MI-6
Stottlemire Run—stream ... WV-2
Stott Mountain—ridge ... OR-9
Stotts Cem—cemetery ... KY-4
Stotts Cem—cemetery ... MO-7
Stott Sch—school ... IL-6
**Stotts City**—pop pl ... MO-7
Stotts City (Station)—locale ... MO-7
Stotts Corners ... VA-3
Stotts Creek ... IN-6
Stotts Creek—stream ... IN-6
Stotts Crossroads—locale ... VA-3
**Stotts Cross Roads**—pop pl ... NC-3
**Stotts Crossroads**—pop pl ... NC-3
Stotts Draw—valley ... WY-8
Stotts Lake—reservoir ... TN-4
Stotts Lake Dam—dam ... TN-4
Stotts Ranch—locale ... NE-7
Stotts Run—stream ... WV-2
Stotts Sch (historical)—school ... AL-4
Stotts Spring—spring ... WY-8
Stottsville—locale ... PA-2
Stotts Windmill—locale ... TX-5
**Stottville**—pop pl ... NY-2
Stotz Canyon ... AZ-5
**Stouchsburg**—pop pl ... PA-2
Stouchsburg Hist Dist—hist pl ... PA-2
Stoud Brook—stream ... CT-1
Stoudemire Cem—cemetery ... AL-4
Stouder Memorial Hosp—hospital ... OH-6
**Stoudertown**—pop pl ... OH-6
Stoudts Bridge (historical)—bridge ... PA-2
Stouffer Lake—reservoir ... PA-2
Stouffer Lake Dam—dam ... PA-2
Stouffer Reservoirs—reservoir ... CO-8
Stouffer Rsvr No 1—reservoir ... CO-8
Stouffer Rsvr No 2—reservoir ... CO-8
Stouffer Rsvr No 3—reservoir ... CO-8
Stouffer Rsvr No 4—reservoir ... CO-8
Stouffers Cem—cemetery ... MD-2
Stouffers Ch—church ... MD-2
Stouffers Heliport—airport ... MO-7
**Stoufferstown**—pop pl ... PA-2
**Stough**—pop pl ... AL-4
Stough Canyon—valley ... CA-9
Stough Cem—cemetery ... IN-6
Stough Creek—stream ... WY-8
Stough Creek Basin—basin ... WY-8
Stough Creek Basin Trail—trail ... WY-8
Stough Creek Lakes—lake ... WY-8
Stough Draw—valley ... CO-8
Stough Lake—lake ... WY-8
Stough Park—park ... CA-9
Stough Rsvr—reservoir ... CA-9
**Stoughstown**—pop pl ... PA-2
Stought Bayou—bay ... TX-5
Stoughten Creek—stream ... MT-8
**Stoughton**—pop pl ... MA-1
**Stoughton**—pop pl ... PA-2
**Stoughton**—pop pl ... WI-6
Stoughton, Ralph H., Estate—hist pl ... AZ-5
Stoughton, Town of ... MA-1
Stoughton Acres Golf Course—locale ... PA-2
Stoughton Brook—stream (3) ... CT-1
Stoughton Centre ... MA-1
**Stoughton Corners**—pop pl ... IN-6
Stoughton Creek—stream ... MI-6
Stoughtonham ... MA-1
Stoughtonham, Town of ... MA-1
Stoughtonham Furnace Site—hist pl ... MA-1
Stoughton HS—school ... MA-1
Stoughton JHS—school (2) ... MA-1
**Stoughton Junction**—pop pl ... MA-1
Stoughton Lake—reservoir ... PA-2
Stoughton Pond—lake ... VT-1
Stoughton RR Station—hist pl ... MA-1
Stoughton Sch—school ... SD-7
Stoughtons Pond—reservoir ... CT-1
Stoughton Townhall—building ... MA-1
**Stoughton (Town of)**—pop pl ... MA-1
Stoughton Universalist Church—hist pl ... WI-6
Stourbridge, Town of ... MA-1
Stourbridge Elem Sch—school ... PA-2
Stout ... IN-6
Stout ... NC-3
Stout—locale ... MS-4
Stout—locale ... TX-5
**Stout**—pop pl ... CA-9
**Stout**—pop pl ... IA-7
**Stout**—pop pl ... OH-6
**Stout**—pop pl ... TN-4
Stout, Ben, House—hist pl ... KY-4
Stout, Daniel, House—hist pl ... IN-6
Stout, John, House—hist pl ... MT-8
Stout, Joseph, House—hist pl ... NJ-2
Stoutameyer Branch—stream ... VA-3
Stoutamire Landing—locale ... FL-3
Stout Bottle Branch—stream ... MD-2
Stout Branch—stream (5) ... TN-4
Stout Branch—stream ... VA-3
Stout Bridge—other ... IL-6
Stout Campground—locale ... WA-9
Stout Canyon—valley ... NM-5
Stout Canyon—valley ... UT-8
Stout Cem—cemetery ... AZ-5
Stout Cem—cemetery ... IL-6
Stout Cem—cemetery ... IN-6
Stout Cem—cemetery ... NM-5
Stout Cem—cemetery (3) ... OH-6
Stout Cem—cemetery (9) ... TN-4
Stout Cem—cemetery ... WV-2
Stout (corporate name Rome) ... OH-6
Stout Creek ... KS-7
Stout Creek ... NJ-2
Stout Creek ... TX-5
Stout Creek—stream ... CO-8
Stout Creek—stream ... IN-6
Stout Creek—stream ... MI-6
Stout Creek—stream ... MS-4
Stout Creek—stream ... MO-7
Stout Creek—stream ... OR-9
Stout Creek—stream ... SC-3
Stout Creek—stream ... TN-4
Stout Creek—stream ... TX-5
Stout Creek—stream ... WV-2
Stout Creek Falls—falls ... OR-9
Stout Creek Lakes—lake ... CO-8
Stout Creek Sch—school ... CO-8
Stout Crossing—locale ... ID-8
Stout Ditch—canal ... IN-6
Stout Draw—valley ... WY-8
Stout Elem Sch—school ... IN-6
Stout Elem Sch—school ... KS-7
Stoutenberg Cem—cemetery ... NY-2
Stoutenburgh, William, House—hist pl ... NY-2
Stoutenburgh House—hist pl ... CA-9
Stoutenburgh-Minturn House—hist pl ... NJ-2
Stout Field—airport ... IN-6
Stout Gise Ditch—canal ... IN-6
Stout Grove—woods ... CA-9
Stout Hill—summit ... IN-6
Stout Hill—summit ... TN-4
Stout Hill Ch—church ... TN-4
Stout Hodge Ditch—canal ... IN-6
Stout Hollow—valley ... AL-4
Stout Hollow—valley ... KY-4
Stout Hollow—valley ... OH-6
Stout Hollow—valley ... PA-2
Stout Hollow—valley ... TN-4
Stout Hollow—valley ... WV-2
Stout Hollow Trail—trail ... PA-2
Stout House—hist pl ... MI-6
Stout Island—island ... AK-9
Stout Island—island ... WI-6
Stout Knob—summit ... TN-4
Stout Lake—lake ... NE-7
Stout Lake—lake ... TX-5
Stout Lake—lake ... WA-9
Stout Lake—reservoir ... IN-6
Stout Lake Dam—dam ... IN-6
**Stoutland**—pop pl ... MO-7
Stoutland Creek—stream ... MO-7
Stout Landing Strip—airport ... KS-7
Stout Mesa—summit ... NM-5
Stout Mesa Tank—reservoir ... NM-5
Stout Mountain Ch—church ... AL-4
Stout Mountain Missionary Baptist Ch ... AL-4
Stout Mtn—summit ... AL-4
Stout Mtn—summit ... OR-9
Stout Mtn—summit ... TN-4
Stout Post Office (historical)—building ... TN-4
Stout Prospect—mine ... TN-4
Stout Ranch—locale (2) ... WA-9
Stout Ranch—locale ... WY-8
Stout Ridge—ridge ... TN-4
Stout Run—stream ... KS-7
Stout Run—stream ... OH-6
Stout Run—stream ... WV-2
Stouts ... MS-4
Stout's ... OH-6
**Stouts**—pop pl ... NC-3
**Stouts**—pop pl ... PA-2
Stouts Bayou—stream ... LA-4
Stouts Bayou—stream ... MS-4
**Stoutsburg**—pop pl ... IN-6
**Stoutsburg**—pop pl ... NJ-2
Stouts Cem—cemetery ... WV-2
Stout Sch—school ... MO-7
Stouts Chapel—church ... IN-6
Stouts Chapel—church ... NC-3
Stouts Creek—stream ... MO-7
Stouts Creek—stream ... MT-8
Stouts Creek—stream ... NJ-2
Stouts Creek—stream ... OR-9
Stouts Creek—stream (2) ... TX-5
Stouts Creek—stream (2) ... VA-3
Stouts Creek Cem—cemetery ... TX-5
Stouts Creek Ch—church ... MO-7
Stouts Grove Cem—cemetery ... IL-6
Stouts Hollow—valley ... KY-4
Stouts Meadow—flat ... CA-9
**Stouts Mills**—pop pl ... WV-2
Stouts Mills Ch—church ... WV-2
Stouts Mountain ... AL-4
Stouts Mountain Post Office (historical)—building ... AL-4
Stouts Mtn—summit ... ID-8
Stoutson Quarry—mine ... TN-4
Stouts Pass—channel ... LA-4
Stouts P.O. (historical)—locale ... AL-4
Stouts Point—cliff ... AR-4
Stout Springs Sch (historical)—school ... TN-4
**Stout Spur**—pop pl ... AZ-5
Stout Spur—ridge ... AR-4
Stouts Run—stream (4) ... WV-2
Stouts Sch—school ... PA-2
Stouts Sch (abandoned)—school ... PA-2
Stouts Store (historical)—locale ... TN-4
Stout State Univ—school ... WI-6
Stouts Valley—valley ... PA-2
**Stoutsville**—pop pl ... MO-7
**Stoutsville**—pop pl ... OH-6
Stoutsville Rec Area—park ... MO-7
Stouts Well—well ... AZ-5
Stout Well—well ... AZ-5
Stoval—locale ... AZ-5
Stoval Airfield—airport ... AZ-5
Stoval Creek ... KY-4
Stovall—locale ... GA-3
Stovall—locale ... KY-4
Stovall—locale ... MS-4
Stovall—locale ... VA-3
**Stovall**—pop pl ... NC-3
Stovall—uninc pl ... GA-3
Stovall, John W., Farm—hist pl ... NC-3
Stovall Bayou—stream ... MS-4
Stovall Branch—stream ... AL-4
Stovall Branch—stream ... TN-4
Stovall Canyon—valley ... CA-9
Stovall Cem—cemetery ... AL-4
Stovall Cem—cemetery (2) ... MS-4
Stovall Cem—cemetery ... TN-4
Stovall Ch—church ... KY-4
Stovall Creek—stream ... AK-9
Stovall Creek—stream ... GA-3
Stovall Creek—stream ... KY-4
Stovall Creek—stream ... MS-4
Stovall Creek—stream ... TX-5
Stovall Creek—stream ... VA-3
Stovall Gap—gap ... TN-4
Stovall-George-Woodward House—hist pl ... GA-3
Stovall Hollow—valley ... AL-4
Stovall Hollow—valley ... TN-4
Stovall Homeplace—hist pl ... GA-3
Stovall House—hist pl ... FL-3
Stovall JHS—school ... TX-5
Stovall Lake—lake ... AK-9
Stovall Lake Dam—dam ... MS-4
Stovall Mill—locale ... GA-3
Stovall Mtn—summit ... AL-4
Stovall Mtn—summit ... AR-4
Stovall Mtn—summit ... TN-4
Stovall Pond—lake ... AL-4
Stovall Post Office (historical)—building ... MS-4
Stovall-Purcell House—hist pl ... GA-3
Stovall Ridge—ridge ... WV-2
Stovall Ridge Ch—church ... WV-2
Stovall Sch—school ... NC-3
Stovall-Shaw Sch—school ... NC-3
Stovall Windmill—locale ... TX-5
Stoval Spring—spring ... KY-4
Stovatt Bend—bend ... AL-4
Stoveall Mountain ... AL-4
Stove And Timber Creek—stream ... WY-8
Stove Basin—basin ... CO-8
Stove Camp—locale ... CA-9
Stove Canyon—valley (2) ... AZ-5
Stove Canyon—valley ... CA-9
Stove Canyon—valley ... CO-8
Stove Canyon—valley (2) ... TX-5
Stove Canyon Spring—spring ... AZ-5
Stove Creek ... NM-5
Stove Creek—fmr MCD ... NE-7
Stove Creek—stream ... AK-9
Stove Creek—stream ... CO-8
Stove Creek—stream (2) ... ID-8
Stove Creek—stream ... NE-7
Stove Creek—stream ... NM-5
Stove Creek—stream ... OR-9
Stove Creek—stream ... SD-7
Stove Creek—stream (3) ... WY-8
Stove Creek Bay—bay ... SD-7
Stove Creek Canyon—valley ... WY-8
Stove Draw—valley ... WY-8
Stove Flats—flat ... CA-9
Stove Glade—flat ... CA-9
Stove Gulch—valley (2) ... CO-8
Stove Gulch—valley ... ID-8
Stove Gulch—valley ... UT-8
Stove Gulch—valley ... WY-8
Stove Gulch Spring—spring ... ID-8
Stovehole Park—flat ... SD-7
Stove Hollow—valley ... TX-5
Stove Island—island ... NC-3
Stovekin Lake—lake ... WI-6
Stove Lake ... ID-8
Stove Lake—lake ... UT-8
Stoveleg Gap—gap ... CA-9
Stove Mtn—summit ... CO-8
Stovepipe Campground—locale ... CA-9
Stovepipe Canyon—valley (2) ... MT-8
Stovepipe Canyon—valley ... WY-8
Stove Pipe City—other ... NY-2
Stovepipe Creek—stream ... ID-8
Stovepipe Creek—stream ... MT-8
Stovepipe Creek—stream ... OK-5
Stovepipe Creek—stream ... WY-8
Stovepipe Flat—flat ... CA-9
Stovepipe Flat Tank—reservoir ... CA-9
Stovepipe Gulch—valley ... OR-9
Stovepipe Gulch—valley ... WY-8

Strange Cem—*cemetery* ... OH-6
Strange Cem—*cemetery* ... TN-4
**Strange Creek**—*pop pl* ... WV-2
Strange Creek—*stream* ... IN-6
Strange Creek—*stream* ... WV-2
Strange Hollow—*valley* (2) ... TN-4
Strange Island—*island* ... GA-3
Strange Library—*building* ... MS-4
*Strangenbergs Creek* ... NC-3
Strange Park—*park* ... MS-4
Strange Point—*cape* ... FL-3
Strange Post Office (historical)—*building* ... AL-4
*Stranger* ... KS-7
Stranger—*locale* ... TX-5
Stranger Cem—*cemetery* ... GA-3
Stranger Cem—*cemetery* ... MN-6
Stranger Creek—*stream* ... KS-7
Stranger Creek—*stream* ... SD-7
Stranger Creek—*stream* (3) ... WA-9
Stranger Creek Cem—*cemetery* ... WA-9
Stranger Hollow—*valley* ... PA-2
Stranger Mtn—*summit* ... WA-9
Stranger River—*stream* ... AK-9
*Strangers Branch* ... IN-6
*Strangers Brook* ... IN-6
Strangers Cem—*cemetery* ... GA-3
*Strangers Church* ... MS-4
**Strangers Home**—*pop pl* ... AR-4
Strangers Home Baptist Ch—*church* ... MS-4
Strangers Home Cem—*cemetery* ... AR-4
Strangers Home Cem—*cemetery* ... LA-4
Strangers Home Cem—*cemetery* ... MS-4
Strangers Home Ch—*church* ... AR-4
Strangers Home Ch—*church* ... LA-4
Strangers Home Ch—*church* (6) ... MS-4
Strangers Home Ch (historical)—*church* ... MS-4
*Strangers Hope Ch* ... MS-4
*Strangers Hope School* ... MS-4
Strangers Lake—*lake* ... WA-9
Strangers Rest Baptist Ch—*church* ... KS-7
Strangers Rest Cem—*cemetery* ... MS-4
Strangers Rest Ch—*church* (2) ... AR-4
Strangers Rest Ch—*church* ... MS-4
Strangers Rest Ch (historical)—*church* ... MS-4
**Stranger Township**—*pop pl* ... KS-7
*Stranges Branch* ... IN-6
Strange Sch—*school* ... MI-6
*Strange School* ... IN-6
Strange Siding—*locale* ... ND-7
**Strangeville**—*pop pl* ... SC-3
Strangeway Landing—*locale* ... VA-3
**Strangford**—*pop pl* ... PA-2
Strangford Cave—*cave* ... PA-2
Strang Hollow—*valley* ... PA-2
Strang Knob—*summit* ... KY-4
Strangle Woman Creek—*stream* ... AK-9
Strangman Pond—*reservoir* ... MA-1
Strangman Pond Dam—*dam* ... MA-1
Stranns Spring—*spring* ... OR-9
*Strap Creek* ... AL-4
St. Raphael Church—*hist pl* ... OH-6
Strap Iron Corral—*hist pl* ... WA-9
Strap Mill Hollow—*valley* ... PA-2
Strap Miner Creek—*stream* ... CA-9
Strapping Creek—*stream* ... OR-9
Strap Ravine—*valley* ... CA-9
Strap Ravine Nisenan Maidu Indian Site—*hist pl* ... CA-9
Strasbaugh Hill—*summit* ... PA-2
Strasbaugh Mine—*mine* ... CA-9
Strasbaugh Sch—*school* ... PA-2
*Strasbourg* ... OH-6
*Strasburg* ... AL-4
*Strasburg* ... PA-2
Strasburg—*CDP* ... CO-8
**Strasburg**—*pop pl* ... CO-8
**Strasburg**—*pop pl* ... IL-6
**Strasburg**—*pop pl* ... MI-6
**Strasburg**—*pop pl* ... MO-7
**Strasburg**—*pop pl* ... ND-7
**Strasburg**—*pop pl* ... OH-6
**Strasburg**—*pop pl* ... PA-2
**Strasburg**—*pop pl* ... VA-3
Strasburg, Herman, House—*hist pl* ... MI-6
Strasburg Borough—*civil* ... PA-2
Strasburg Cave—*cave* ... PA-2
Strasburg Cem—*cemetery* ... MO-7
Strasburg Cem—*cemetery* ... ND-7
Strasburg Elem Sch—*school* ... PA-2
Strasburg Hist Dist—*hist pl* ... PA-2
Strasburg Hist Dist—*hist pl* ... VA-3
Strasburg Jaycee Park—*park* ... PA-2
Strasburg Junction—*locale* ... VA-3
Strasburg Mine—*mine* ... OR-9
Strasburg Rsvr—*reservoir* ... PA-2
Strasburg Rsvr—*reservoir* ... VA-3
Strasburg Sch Number 1—*school* ... ND-7
Strasburg Sch Number 2—*school* ... ND-7
Strasburg Sch Number 3—*school* ... ND-7
Strasburg Sch Number 4—*school* ... ND-7
Strasburg Stone and Earthenware Manufacturing Company—*hist pl* ... VA-3
**Strasburg (Township of)**—*pop pl* ... PA-2
Strasia Meadow—*flat* ... CO-8
Strassberger's Conservatory—*hist pl* ... MO-7
Strassburg Cem—*cemetery* ... KS-7
Strassburg Cem—*cemetery* ... SD-7
Strassburg Ch—*church* ... KS-7
Strassburg Creek—*stream* ... WI-6
Strassburg Sch—*school* ... IL-6
Strassburg Sch Number 2—*school* ... ND-7
**Strassburg Township**—*pop pl* ... ND-7
Strassel—*locale* ... OR-9
Strassel Creek—*stream* ... OR-9
Strastrom Pond—*lake* ... CT-1
**Strata**—*pop pl* ... AL-4
Strata Ch—*church* ... AL-4
Strata Ch of Christ—*church* ... AL-4
Strata Sch (historical)—*school* ... AL-4
*Strate Creek* ... NC-3
*Strater* ... SD-7
Strater Hall—*locale* ... MT-8
**Stratfield**—*pop pl* ... CT-1
Stratfield Hist Dist—*hist pl* ... CT-1
Stratfield Sch—*school* ... CT-1
*Stratford* ... MO-7
*Stratford* ... VA-3
Stratford—*CDP* ... CT-1
Stratford—*locale* ... IL-6
Stratford—*locale* ... WA-9
**Stratford**—*pop pl* ... CA-9
**Stratford**—*pop pl* (2) ... CT-1
**Stratford**—*pop pl* ... DE-2
**Stratford**—*pop pl* ... GA-3
**Stratford**—*pop pl* ... IA-7
**Stratford**—*pop pl* ... MD-2
**Stratford**—*pop pl* ... NH-1
**Stratford**—*pop pl* ... NJ-2
**Stratford**—*pop pl* ... NY-2
**Stratford**—*pop pl* ... NC-3
**Stratford**—*pop pl* ... OH-6
**Stratford**—*pop pl* ... OK-5
**Stratford**—*pop pl* ... SD-7
**Stratford**—*pop pl* ... TX-5
**Stratford**—*pop pl* (2) ... VA-3
**Stratford**—*pop pl* ... WI-6
Stratford Acad—*school* ... NJ-2
Stratford Army Engine Plant—*military* ... CT-1
Stratford Ave Sch—*school* ... NY-2
Stratford Bldg—*hist pl* ... ND-7
Stratford Bog Brook—*stream* ... NH-1
Stratford Bog Pond—*lake* ... NH-1
Stratford Canal—*canal* ... CA-9
Stratford (CCD)—*cens area* ... CA-9
Stratford (CCD)—*cens area* ... OK-5
Stratford Cem—*cemetery* ... PA-2
Stratford Center Hist Dist—*hist pl* ... CT-1
Stratford Ch—*church* ... OH-6
Stratford Cliffs—*cliff* ... VA-3
Stratford Coll—*school* ... VA-3
Stratford East (CCD)—*cens area* ... TX-5
**Stratford Forest**—*pop pl* ... SC-3
Stratford Friends Sch—*school* ... PA-2
Stratford Hall—*hist pl* ... VA-3
**Stratford Hall**—*pop pl* ... VA-3
*Stratford Hill* ... CT-1
Stratford Hill—*summit* ... MT-8
*Stratford Hills* ... IL-6
*Stratford Hills* ... IN-6
**Stratford Hills**—*pop pl* (2) ... VA-3
Stratford Hills—*uninc pl* ... VA-3
**Stratford (historical)**—*pop pl* ... IN-6
*Stratford Hollow* ... NH-1
Stratford Hotel—*hist pl* ... UT-8
Stratford HS—*school* ... TN-4
Stratford Industrial Park—*locale* ... NC-3
Stratford JHS—*school* ... VA-3
Stratford Lake—*lake* ... TX-5
**Stratford Landing**—*pop pl* ... VA-3
Stratford Landing Sch—*school* ... VA-3
*Stratford Manor* ... OH-6
**Stratford Manor**—*pop pl* ... OH-6
Stratford Mill—*locale* ... VA-3
*Stratford Mill Run* ... VA-3
Stratford Mountain—*ridge* ... NH-1
Stratford Notch—*gap* ... NH-1
Stratford Oaks—*locale* ... NC-3
**Stratford On The Potomac**—*pop pl* ... VA-3
**Stratford-on-the-Potomac**—*pop pl* ... VA-3
**Stratford Park (subdivision)**—*pop pl* ... NC-3
Stratford Point—*cape* ... CT-1
Stratford Ranch—*locale* ... CA-9
Stratford Ridge—*ridge* ... MD-2
Stratford Sch—*school* ... MI-6
Stratford Sch—*school* ... NJ-2
**Stratford (subdivision)**—*pop pl* ... NC-3
**Stratford (Town of)**—*pop pl* ... NH-1
**Stratford (Town of)**—*pop pl* ... NY-2
**Stratford Village**—*pop pl* ... VA-3
Stratford West (CCD)—*cens area* ... TX-5
**Stratham**—*pop pl* ... NH-1
Stratham Ch—*church* ... NH-1
Stratham Heights—*summit* ... NH-1
Stratham Hill—*summit* ... NH-1
**Stratham Station**—*pop pl* ... NH-1
**Stratham (Town of)**—*pop pl* ... NH-1
**Strathcona**—*pop pl* ... MN-6
**Strathcona Hills**—*pop pl* ... PA-2
Strathearn—*locale* ... CA-9
Strathern Street Sch—*school* ... CA-9
Strathglass Bldg—*hist pl* ... ME-1
Strathglass Park District—*hist pl* ... ME-1
Strath Haven—*locale* ... PA-2
Strath Haven HS—*school* ... PA-2
**Strathmeade Springs**—*pop pl* ... VA-3
**Strathmere**—*pop pl* ... NJ-2
Strathmere Bay—*bay* ... NJ-2
*Strathmoor* ... MI-6
**Strathmoor Gardens**—*pop pl* ... KY-4
**Strathmoor Manor**—*pop pl* ... KY-4
**Strathmoor Village**—*pop pl* ... KY-4
**Strathmore**—*pop pl* ... CA-9
**Strathmore**—*pop pl* ... NJ-2
**Strathmore**—*pop pl* ... NY-2
**Strathmore**—*pop pl* ... VA-3
**Strathmore At Bel Pre**—*pop pl* ... MD-2
Strathmore (CCD)—*cens area* ... CA-9
*Strathmore Grove* ... IL-6
**Strathmore (historical)**—*pop pl* ... TN-4
Strathmore Ind Res—*reserve* ... CA-9
**Strathmore Junction**—*pop pl* ... CA-9
*Strathmore Landing* ... MS-4
Strathmore Paper Company Dam—*dam* ... MA-1
Strathmore Post Office (historical)—*building* ... TN-4
Strathmore Road Hist Dist—*hist pl* ... MA-1
Strathouse—*locale* ... VA-3
Strathy Hall—*hist pl* ... GA-3
Strathy Hall Cem—*cemetery* ... GA-3
Stratis Cave—*cave* ... AL-4
**Stratler Subdivision**—*pop pl* ... UT-8
Stratler Windmill—*locale* ... TX-5
Stratman Branch—*stream* ... LA-4
Stratman Chapel—*church* ... MO-7
Stratman Ditch—*canal* ... CO-8
Stratmoor—*CDP* ... CO-8
Stratmoor Golf Club—*other* ... CO-8
**Stratmoor Hills**—*pop pl* ... CO-8
*Strato* ... AL-4
*Strato Bowl* ... SD-7
Straton Falls—*falls* ... NY-2
*Straton Lake* ... TX-5
*Straton Ranch* ... NV-8
Strator Pond—*lake* ... IL-6
Stratosphere Bowl—*locale* ... SD-7
*Strattan* ... IA-7
**Strattanville**—*pop pl* ... PA-2
Strattanville Borough—*civil* ... PA-2
**Strattanville (RR name Strattonville)**—*pop pl* ... PA-2
Strattanville Tower (historical)—*tower* ... PA-2
*Stratten Island* ... ME-1
Stratter Point—*cape* ... VA-3
*Stratton* ... MS-4
Stratton—*locale* ... IL-6
Stratton—*locale* ... TX-5
**Stratton**—*pop pl* (2) ... CO-8
**Stratton**—*pop pl* ... ME-1
**Stratton**—*pop pl* ... MS-4
**Stratton**—*pop pl* ... NE-7
**Stratton**—*pop pl* ... NY-2
**Stratton**—*pop pl* ... OH-6
**Stratton**—*pop pl* ... VT-1
**Stratton**—*pop pl* ... VA-3
Stratton, C. C., House—*hist pl* ... OR-9
Stratton, Gov. Charles C., House—*hist pl* ... NJ-2
Stratton, Leslie M., YMCA—*hist pl* ... TN-4
Stratton, William B. and Mary Chase, House—*hist pl* ... MI-6
Stratton Bald—*summit* ... NC-3
Stratton Basin—*basin* ... ID-8
Stratton Branch—*stream* ... AL-4
Stratton Branch—*stream* (4) ... KY-4
Stratton Branch—*stream* ... NC-3
Stratton Branch—*stream* (3) ... TN-4
Stratton Brook—*stream* ... CT-1
Stratton Brook—*stream* (2) ... ME-1
Stratton Brook—*stream* ... VT-1
Stratton Brook Pond—*lake* ... ME-1
Stratton Brook State Park—*park* ... CT-1
*Stratton Butte* ... ID-8
Stratton Butte—*summit* ... ID-8
Stratton Butte—*summit* ... WA-9
Stratton Camp—*locale* ... WY-8
Stratton Camp Spring—*spring* ... AZ-5
Stratton Camp Well—*well* ... TX-5
Stratton Canyon—*valley* ... AZ-5
Stratton Canyon—*valley* ... CA-9
Stratton Cem—*cemetery* ... IN-6
Stratton Cem—*cemetery* (2) ... NE-7
Stratton Cem—*cemetery* ... TN-4
Stratton-Cornelius House—*hist pl* ... OR-9
Stratton Corral—*locale* ... WY-8
Stratton Creek—*stream* ... AR-4
Stratton Creek—*stream* (2) ... ID-8
Stratton Creek—*stream* ... IA-7
Stratton Creek—*stream* ... MT-8
Stratton Creek—*stream* ... NV-8
Stratton Creek—*stream* ... OH-6
Stratton Creek—*stream* ... OR-9
Stratton Creek—*stream* ... WY-8
Stratton Ditch—*canal* ... CO-8
Stratton Draw—*valley* ... WY-8
Stratton Fork—*stream* (3) ... KY-4
Stratton Gap—*gap* ... NC-3
Stratton Gap—*gap* ... TN-4
Stratton Hill—*summit* (2) ... MA-1
Stratton Hill—*summit* ... NY-2
Stratton Hill—*summit* ... VT-1
Stratton (historical)—*locale* ... SD-7
Stratton Hollow—*basin* ... WY-8
Stratton Hollow—*valley* ... WA-9
Stratton Hollow—*valley* ... WV-2
Stratton House—*hist pl* ... IA-7
Stratton Independence Mine—*mine* ... CO-8
Stratton Island—*island* (2) ... ME-1
Stratton JHS—*school* ... WV-2
Stratton Knob—*summit* ... KY-4
Stratton Knob—*summit* ... TN-4
Stratton Knoll—*summit* ... WY-8
Stratton Lake—*lake* ... CO-8
Stratton Lake—*lake* ... MN-6
Stratton Lake—*lake* ... WI-6
Stratton Lake—*reservoir* ... TX-5
Stratton Lakes—*lake* ... WY-8
Stratton Lookout Tower—*locale* ... VT-1
Stratton Manor—*hist pl* ... VA-3
Stratton Meadow—*flat* ... ID-8
Stratton Meadow—*flat* ... OR-9
Stratton Meadows—*flat* ... NC-3
Stratton Meadows—*flat* ... TN-4
**Stratton Meadows**—*pop pl* ... CO-8
Stratton Mill Creek—*stream* ... NY-2
Stratton Mine—*mine* ... AZ-5
**Stratton Mountain**—*pop pl* ... VT-1
Stratton Mountain Camp—*locale* ... VT-1
Stratton Mtn—*summit* ... MA-1
Stratton Mtn—*summit* ... VT-1
Stratton Oil Field—*oilfield* ... TX-5
Stratton Park—*flat* ... CO-8
Stratton Park—*park* ... IN-6
Stratton Park—*uninc pl* ... CO-8
Stratton Park Sch—*school* ... CO-8
Stratton Place—*locale* ... OR-9
Stratton Pond—*lake* ... ME-1
Stratton Pond—*lake* ... VT-1
Stratton Ponds—*lake* ... WI-6
*Strattonport Point* ... NY-2
Stratton Pumping Station—*other* ... TX-5
Stratton Ranch—*locale* ... NV-8
Stratton Ranch—*locale* (2) ... WY-8
Stratton Ridge—*locale* ... TX-5
Stratton Ridge Oil Field—*oilfield* ... TX-5
Stratton Rim—*cliff* ... WY-8
Stratton Rsvr—*reservoir* ... CO-8
Stratton Rsvr—*reservoir* ... MT-8
Stratton Saddle—*gap* ... AZ-5
Strattons Camp (historical)—*locale* ... AZ-5
Stratton Sch—*school* (2) ... CO-8
Stratton Sch—*school* ... KY-4
Stratton Sch—*school* ... MA-1
Stratton Sch—*school* ... TN-4
Stratton Shoals—*bar* ... TN-4
Stratton's Inn—*hist pl* ... VT-1
*Strattons Island* ... ME-1
Stratton Spring—*spring* ... CA-9
Stratton Spring—*spring* ... ID-8
Stratton Spring—*spring* ... NV-8
Stratton Spring—*spring* ... WY-8
**Stratton (Town of)**—*pop pl* ... VT-1
**Stratton (Township of)**—*pop pl* ... IL-6
*Strattonville* ... PA-2
Strattonville (RR name for Strattanville)—*other* ... PA-2
Stratton Wash—*stream* ... AZ-5
Stratton Well—*well* ... TX-5
**Stratton Woods**—*pop pl* ... MD-2
Straub, William Nichols, House—*hist pl* ... AR-4
Straub Canyon—*valley* ... WA-9
Straub Cem—*cemetery* ... KY-4
Straub Ch—*church* ... PA-2
Straube Creek—*stream* ... OR-9
Straub Mtn—*summit* ... CO-8
**Straubville**—*pop pl* ... ND-7
Strauch Sch—*school* ... CA-9
*Straud School* ... MS-4
**Straughn**—*pop pl* ... AL-4
**Straughn**—*pop pl* ... IN-6
Straughn Cem—*cemetery* ... AL-4
Straughn HS—*school* ... AL-4
*Straughn Station* ... IN-6
Straus, Jacob, House—*hist pl* ... IN-6
*Strausburg* ... OH-6
Straus Ditch No 2—*canal* ... WY-8
Strause, Lake—*reservoir* ... PA-2
Strause Gulch—*valley* ... CA-9
Straus Elem Sch—*school* ... NC-3
*Straus Hill* ... WY-8
Straus House—*hist pl* ... TX-5
Straus Lake—*reservoir* ... NC-3
Straus Lake Dam—*dam* ... NC-3
Straus Medina Ranch—*locale* ... TX-5
Strauss—*locale* ... KS-7
**Strauss**—*pop pl* ... NM-5
Strauss Canal—*canal* ... NC-3
Strauss Cem—*cemetery* ... LA-4
Straus Sch—*school* ... NC-3
Strauss Creek—*stream* ... WA-9
Strauss-Hamilton Airp—*airport* ... PA-2
*Strauss Hill* ... WY-8
Strauss House—*hist pl* ... AR-4
Strauss Mill—*locale* ... TN-4
Strauss Orchard—*locale* ... CA-9
Strauss Park—*park* ... TX-5
Straus Spring—*spring* ... OR-9
Strauss Quarry—*mine* ... CO-8
Strauss Ridge—*ridge* ... OH-6
Strauss Rock—*other* ... AK-9
Strauss Statue—*park* ... DC-2
Strauss Swamp—*swamp* ... NC-3
**Strausstown**—*pop pl* ... PA-2
Strausstown Borough—*civil* ... PA-2
Strauss Valley—*valley* ... PA-2
**Straussville**—*pop pl* ... NE-7
Straut—*locale* ... IL-6
Strauter Run—*stream* ... WV-2
**Straven**—*pop pl* ... AL-4
Stravens Mine (underground)—*mine* ... AL-4
*Stravon* ... AL-4
*Straw* ... NJ-2
Straw—*locale* ... KY-4
Straw—*locale* ... PA-2
**Straw**—*pop pl* ... MT-8
Straw, William Parker, House—*hist pl* ... NH-1
Strawbarn Ridge—*ridge* ... TN-4
Straw Bay Branch—*stream* ... FL-3
Straw Bay Islands—*island* ... FL-3
Strawberry—*locale* ... AL-4
Strawberry—*locale* ... AR-4
Strawberry—*locale* ... CA-9
Strawberry—*locale* ... KS-7
Strawberry—*locale* ... OR-9
Strawberry—*locale* (2) ... SC-3
**Strawberry**—*pop pl* ... AZ-5
**Strawberry**—*pop pl* ... AR-4
**Strawberry**—*pop pl* (2) ... CA-9
**Strawberry**—*pop pl* ... UT-8
Strawberry—*uninc pl* ... KY-4
Strawberry Acres Airp—*airport* ... PA-2
Strawberry Banke Hist Dist—*hist pl* ... NH-1
**Strawberry Banks (subdivision)**—*pop pl* ... NC-3
Strawberry Basin—*basin* ... ID-8
Strawberry Basin Trail—*trail* ... OR-9
Strawberry Bay—*bay* (2) ... WA-9
*Strawberry Bay Campground* ... UT-8
Strawberry Bay Recreation Complex—*park* ... UT-8
Strawberry Bench—*bench* ... CO-8
Strawberry Bottom—*bend* ... VA-3
Strawberry Bowl—*basin* ... UT-8
*Strawberry Branch* ... GA-3
*Strawberry Branch* ... VA-3
Strawberry Branch—*stream* ... GA-3
Strawberry Branch—*stream* ... MO-7
Strawberry Branch—*stream* ... NC-3
Strawberry Branch—*stream* ... TN-4
Strawberry Branch—*stream* ... VA-3
Strawberry Bridge—*bridge* ... PA-2
*Strawberry Butte* ... OR-9
Strawberry Butte—*summit* (3) ... MT-8
Strawberry Butte—*summit* ... NV-8
Strawberry Butte—*summit* ... OR-9
*Strawberry Camp* ... OR-9
Strawberry Camp—*locale* ... CA-9
Strawberry Campground—*locale* ... OR-9
Strawberry Canyon—*valley* ... AZ-5
Strawberry Canyon—*valley* ... CA-9
Strawberry Canyon—*valley* ... ID-8
Strawberry Canyon—*valley* ... NM-5
Strawberry Canyon—*valley* ... OR-9
Strawberry Canyon—*valley* (2) ... UT-8
Strawberry Cem—*cemetery* ... CO-8
Strawberry Cem—*cemetery* ... UT-8
Strawberry Cem—*cemetery* ... WI-6
Strawberry Ch—*church* ... GA-3
Strawberry Ch—*church* ... VA-3
Strawberry Channel—*channel* ... AK-9
Strawberry Channel—*channel* ... WI-6
Strawberry Chapel—*church* ... SC-3
Strawberry Chapel and Childsbury Town Site—*hist pl* ... SC-3
*Strawberry Church* ... MS-4
Strawberry Cienaga—*spring* ... CA-9
Strawberry Crater—*crater* ... AZ-5
*Strawberry Creek* ... CA-9
*Strawberry Creek* ... WA-9
Strawberry Creek—*stream* ... AZ-5
Strawberry Creek—*stream* ... AR-4
Strawberry Creek—*stream* (9) ... CA-9
Strawberry Creek—*stream* (3) ... CO-8
Strawberry Creek—*stream* ... FL-3
Strawberry Creek—*stream* ... GA-3
Strawberry Creek—*stream* (4) ... ID-8
Strawberry Creek—*stream* ... ME-1
Strawberry Creek—*stream* (2) ... MI-6
Strawberry Creek—*stream* ... MN-6
Strawberry Creek—*stream* (4) ... MT-8
Strawberry Creek—*stream* ... NV-8
Strawberry Creek—*stream* ... OK-5
Strawberry Creek—*stream* (4) ... OR-9
Strawberry Creek—*stream* ... SD-7
Strawberry Creek—*stream* (2) ... UT-8
Strawberry Creek—*stream* ... VA-3
Strawberry Creek—*stream* (2) ... WA-9
Strawberry Creek—*stream* (5) ... WY-8
Strawberry Dam (inundated)—*dam* ... UT-8
Strawberry Ditch—*canal* ... UT-8
Strawberry Dome—*summit* ... AK-9
Strawberry Falls—*falls* ... OR-9
Strawberry Ferry—*locale* ... AR-4
Strawberry Fields Site (22Md644)—*hist pl* ... MS-4
**Strawberry Fields (subdivision)**—*pop pl* ... TN-4
Strawberry Flat—*flat* (3) ... CA-9
Strawberry Flat—*flat* ... OR-9
Strawberry Flat—*flat* ... UT-8
Strawberry Gap—*gap* ... NC-3
Strawberry Glen Bridge—*bridge* ... ID-8
Strawberry Gulch—*valley* (2) ... CO-8
Strawberry Gulch—*valley* ... MT-8
Strawberry Gulch—*valley* (2) ... WY-8
Strawberry Harbor—*bay* ... AK-9
Strawberry Highline Canal—*canal* ... UT-8
*Strawberry Hi-Line Reservoir* ... UT-8
*Strawberry Hill* ... MA-1
*Strawberry Hill* ... NJ-2
Strawberry Hill—*hist pl* ... MD-2
Strawberry Hill—*hist pl* ... NY-2
Strawberry Hill—*hist pl* (2) ... NC-3
Strawberry Hill—*hist pl* ... VA-3
**Strawberry Hill**—*pop pl* ... VI-3
Strawberry Hill—*summit* ... AK-9
Strawberry Hill—*summit* ... CA-9
Strawberry Hill—*summit* ... CT-1
Strawberry Hill—*summit* ... MD-2
Strawberry Hill—*summit* (4) ... MA-1
Strawberry Hill—*summit* ... MT-8
Strawberry Hill—*summit* (2) ... NH-1
Strawberry Hill—*summit* ... NJ-2
Strawberry Hill—*summit* ... NY-2
Strawberry Hill—*summit* ... OR-9
Strawberry Hill—*summit* ... RI-1
Strawberry Hill—*summit* ... VT-1
Strawberry Hill Airp—*airport* ... NC-3
Strawberry Hill Campground—*park* ... SD-7
Strawberry Hill Hist Dist—*hist pl* ... VI-3
Strawberry Hill Landing—*locale* ... NC-3
Strawberry Hill Plantation—*locale* ... SC-3
Strawberry Hill Plantation (historical)—*locale* ... AL-4
Strawberry Hill Sch—*school* ... IA-7
**Strawberry Hills Estates**—*pop pl* ... MD-2
Strawberry Hill Station (historical)—*locale* ... MA-1
Strawberry Hollow—*valley* ... AZ-5
Strawberry Hollow—*valley* ... AR-4
Strawberry Hollow—*valley* ... IL-6
Strawberry Hollow—*valley* ... MO-7
*Strawberry Island* ... NH-1
*Strawberry Island* ... WI-6
Strawberry Island—*island* (2) ... AK-9
Strawberry Island—*island* (2) ... MI-6
Strawberry Islanc—*island* (2) ... MN-6
Strawberry Island—*island* (2) ... NY-2
Strawberry Island—*island* (3) ... WA-9
Strawberry Island—*island* (2) ... WI-6
Strawberry Island (historical)—*island* ... ND-7
Strawberry Islands—*island* ... WI-6
Strawberry Island Site—*hist pl* ... WI-6
Strawberry Island Village Archeol Site—*hist pl* ... WA-9
Strawberry Knob—*summit* (2) ... NC-3
Strawberry Knob—*summit* ... TN-4
Strawberry Knolls—*summit* ... UT-8
*Strawberry Lake* ... CA-9
*Strawberry Lake* ... FL-3
*Strawberry Lake* ... MI-6
Strawberry Lake—*lake* ... CA-9
Strawberry Lake—*lake* (2) ... CO-8
Strawberry Lake—*lake* (4) ... MI-6
Strawberry Lake—*lake* (4) ... MN-6
Strawberry Lake—*lake* ... MT-8
Strawberry Lake—*lake* (2) ... ND-7
Strawberry Lake—*lake* ... OR-9
Strawberry Lake—*lake* (2) ... WA-9
Strawberry Lake—*reservoir* ... ND-7
Strawberry Lake Ch—*church* ... MN-6
Strawberry Lake Dam—*dam* ... ND-7
Strawberry Lakes—*lake* ... CO-8
Strawberry Lake Sch—*school* ... MN-6
Strawberry Lake Sch Number 1—*school* ... ND-7
Strawberry Lake Sch Number 3—*school* ... ND-7
Strawberry Landing—*locale* ... DE-2
Strawberry Landing—*locale* ... SC-3
Strawberry Ledge—*bar* ... MA-1
Strawberry Lookout—*locale* ... WA-9
**Strawberry Manor**—*pop pl* ... CA-9
Strawberry Meadow—*swamp* ... MA-1
Strawberry Meadow Creek—*stream* ... CA-9
Strawberry Meadows—*flat* ... CA-9
Strawberry Meadows—*flat* ... WA-9
Strawberry Mine—*mine* (2) ... MT-8
Strawberry Mine—*mine* ... UT-8
Strawberry Mine Hist Dist—*hist pl* ... MT-8
*Strawberry Mountain* ... UT-8
*Strawberry Mountains* ... OR-9
Strawberry Mountain Wilderness—*park* ... OR-9
Strawberry Mtn—*summit* ... AZ-5
Strawberry Mtn—*summit* ... GA-3
Strawberry Mtn—*summit* ... ID-8
Strawberry Mtn—*summit* ... MN-6
Strawberry Mtn—*summit* (2) ... MT-8
Strawberry Mtn—*summit* ... OR-9
Strawberry Mtn—*summit* ... TN-4
Strawberry Mtn—*summit* (4) ... WA-9
Strawberry Mtn—*summit* ... WY-8
Strawberry North Summit—*summit* ... UT-8
Strawberry Park—*flat* ... CO-8
Strawberry Park—*park* ... TX-5
Strawberry Park Sch—*school* ... CA-9
Strawberry Patch-McKay House—*hist pl* ... MS-4
*Strawberry Peak* ... CA-9
Strawberry Peak—*summit* (4) ... CA-9
Strawberry Peak—*summit* ... CO-8
Strawberry Peak—*summit* (2) ... NM-5
Strawberry Peak—*summit* (3) ... UT-8
Strawberry Pinnacles—*pillar* ... UT-8
**Strawberry Plains**—*pop pl* ... TN-4
Strawberry Plains (CCD)—*cens area* ... TN-4
Strawberry Plains Ch—*church* ... MS-4
Strawberry Plains Division—*civil* ... TN-4
Strawberry Plains First Baptist Ch—*church* ... TN-4
Strawberry Plains Post Office—*building* ... TN-4
*Strawberry Point* ... MA-1
Strawberry Point—*cape* ... AK-9
Strawberry Point—*cape* ... CA-9
Strawberry Point—*cape* ... DE-2
Strawberry Point—*cape* ... MD-2
Strawberry Point—*cape* (2) ... MA-1
Strawberry Point—*cape* ... MN-6
Strawberry Point—*cape* ... NJ-2
Strawberry Point—*cape* ... UT-8
Strawberry Point—*cape* (3) ... WA-9
Strawberry Point—*cliff* ... UT-8
**Strawberry Point**—*pop pl* ... CA-9
**Strawberry Point**—*pop pl* ... IA-7
**Strawberry Point**—*pop pl* ... MI-6
Strawberry Point (Gustavus)—*other* ... AK-9
Strawberry Point Sch—*school* ... CA-9
Strawberry Point View Area—*locale* ... UT-8
Strawberry Ranch—*locale* ... NV-8
Strawberry Range—*range* ... OR-9
Strawberry Reef—*bar* ... AK-9
Strawberry Ridge—*locale* ... NC-3
**Strawberry Ridge**—*pop pl* ... PA-2
Strawberry Ridge—*ridge* ... MO-7
Strawberry Ridge—*ridge* (2) ... MT-8
Strawberry Ridge—*ridge* ... OR-9
Strawberry Ridge—*ridge* ... PA-2
Strawberry Ridge—*ridge* ... SD-7
Strawberry Ridge—*ridge* (2) ... UT-8
Strawberry Ridge—*ridge* ... WI-6
Strawberry Ridge—*ridge* ... WY-8
Strawberry Ridge—*summit* ... TN-4
Strawberry River—*stream* ... AR-4
Strawberry River—*stream* ... UT-8
Strawberry River Day Use Area—*park* ... UT-8
Strawberry Roan Mine—*mine* ... CO-8
Strawberry Rock—*bar* ... WA-9
Strawberry Rock—*pillar* ... CA-9
Strawberry Rsvr—*reservoir* ... OR-9
Strawberry Rsvr—*reservoir* (2) ... UT-8
Strawberry Run—*stream* ... MD-2
Strawberry Sch—*school* ... AR-4
Strawberry Sch—*school* ... ND-7
Strawberry Sch—*school* (2) ... WI-6
Strawberry Sch (historical)—*school* ... MS-4
*Strawberry Settlement* ... AR-4
Strawberry Spring—*locale* ... OK-5
Strawberry Spring—*spring* ... AZ-5
Strawberry Spring—*spring* (2) ... ID-8
Strawberry Spring—*spring* ... OK-5
Strawberry Spring—*spring* (4) ... OR-9
Strawberry Spur (historical)—*locale* ... SD-7
Strawberry Square—*locale* ... PA-2
Strawberry Top—*summit* ... GA-3
**Strawberry Township**—*pop pl* ... KS-7
Strawberry (Township of)—*fmr MCD* (4) ... AR-4
Strawberry Trail—*trail* (2) ... CO-8
Strawberry Tungsten Mine—*mine* ... CA-9
Strawberry Tunnel—*tunnel* ... UT-8
*Strawberry Valley* ... CO-8
Strawberry Valley—*basin* ... AZ-5
Strawberry Valley—*basin* ... KY-4
Strawberry Valley—*basin* (2) ... UT-8
**Strawberry Valley**—*pop pl* ... CA-9
Strawberry Valley—*valley* (2) ... CA-9
Strawberry Valley Creek—*stream* ... CA-9
Strawberry Valley Estates Airp—*airport* ... UT-8
*Strawberry West Summit* ... UT-8
Strawberry Yards—*locale* ... KY-4
*Strawbery Banke* ... NH-1
Straw Branch—*stream* ... IN-6
Straw Branch—*stream* ... KY-4
Strawbridge—*locale* ... PA-2
Strawbridge—*locale* ... WI-6
*Strawbridge and Clothier Distribution Center Airport* ... PA-2
*Strawbridge and Clothier Heliport* ... PA-2
Strawbridge and Clothier Store—*hist pl* ... PA-2
Strawbridge Cem—*cemetery* ... AL-4
Strawbridge Ch—*church* ... MD-2
Strawbridge Ch—*church* ... MS-4
Strawbridge Christiana Mall Airp—*airport* ... DE-2
*Strawbridge Hollow* ... VA-3
Strawbridge Home For Boys—*school* ... MD-2
Strawbridge Lake—*reservoir* ... NJ-2
Strawbridge Lake Upper Dam—*dam* ... NJ-2
Straw Brook—*stream* ... NH-1
Strawcamp Run—*stream* ... OH-6
Straw Creek—*stream* ... TX-5
Strawderman Hollow—*valley* ... WV-2
Straw Ditch—*canal* ... OH-6
Strawfield Creek—*stream* ... VA-3
Straw Floor Cem—*cemetery* ... AR-4
Straw Floor Ch—*church* ... AR-4
Straw Fork Butte Creek—*stream* ... OR-9
Strawhaker Corral—*locale* ... WY-8
Straw Hill—*summit* ... NH-1
Straw Hill Cem—*cemetery* ... TN-4
Straw Hollow—*swamp* ... MA-1
Strawhorn Creek—*gut* ... NC-3
Strawhorn Creek—*stream* ... NC-3
Strawhorn Creek—*stream* ... VA-3
Strawhorn Landing—*locale* ... NC-3
Strawhorn Swamp Cove—*swamp* ... NC-3
Straw House—*hist pl* ... ME-1
Strawhouse Trail—*trail* ... TX-5
Strawhun Cem—*cemetery* ... MO-7
Strawhun Sch (historical)—*school* ... MO-7
Straw Island—*island* ... MS-4
**Strawleigh**—*pop pl* ... MD-2
Strawman-fleming Ditch—*canal* ... OH-6
Straw Mtn—*summit* ... GA-3
*Strawn* (2) ... KS-7
Strawn—*locale* ... MD-2
**Strawn**—*pop pl* ... IL-6
**Strawn**—*pop pl* ... TX-5
Strawn Cem—*cemetery* ... AR-4
Strawn Cem—*cemetery* ... IL-6
Strawn Cem—*cemetery* ... IA-7
Strawn Cem—*cemetery* ... KS-7
Strawn Cem—*cemetery* ... OH-6
Strawn Creek—*stream* ... IL-6
Strawn-Gordon (CCD)—*cens area* ... TX-5
Strawn Hollow—*valley* ... PA-2
Strawn Lake—*reservoir* ... WV-2

Stroing Brook—*stream* NH-1
Stroing Ranch—*locale* CA-9
Strokes Cem—*cemetery* AL-4
Strole Ditch—*canal* IN-6
Stroller White Mtn—*summit* AK-9
*Strolling Fork* WV-2
Strol Township—*civil* SD-7
Strom—*locale* VA-3
Stroman, Lake—*reservoir* OH-6
Stroman Cem—*cemetery* TX-5
Strombeck Cem—*cemetery* MN-6
Stromberg Cabin—*locale* WA-9
*Stromberg Canyon* WA-9
Stromberg-Tetzloff Ditch—*canal* IN-6
*Stromburgh* NE-7
*Strombus Mountain* MH-9
*Strombus Point* MH-9
*Strombus Stream* MH-9
Strom Creek—*stream* MI-6
Strome County Park—*park* OR-9
Stromer Herman Number 1 Dam—*dam* SD-7
Stromer Herman Number 2 Dam—*dam* SD-7
Strom Field Airp—*airport* WA-9
Strom Lake—*lake* MN-6
Strom Ranch—*locale* WY-8
Strom Rsvr—*reservoir* WY-8
Stroms—*locale* MN-6
**Stromsburg**—*pop pl* NE-7
Stromsburg Cem—*cemetery* NE-7
**Stronach**—*pop pl* MI-6
**Stronach**—*pop pl* PA-2
Stronach Creek—*stream* MI-6
Stronach Dam—*dam* MI-6
**Stronach (Township of)**—*pop pl* MI-6
**Stroner**—*pop pl* WY-8
Strong—*locale* CO-8
Strong—*locale* UT-8
**Strong**—*pop pl* AR-4
**Strong**—*pop pl* KS-7
**Strong**—*pop pl* ME-1
**Strong**—*pop pl* MS-4
**Strong**—*pop pl* PA-2
Strong, Capt. Richard, House—*hist pl* NH-1
Strong, Gen. Samuel, House—*hist pl* VT-1
Strong, Jedediah, House—*hist pl* NY-2
Strong, Jedediah II, House—*hist pl* VT-1
Strong, John, House—*hist pl* VT-1
Strong, John Stoughton, House—*hist pl* OH-6
Strong, J. P., Store—*hist pl* NM-5
Strong, Richard, Cottage—*hist pl* NH-1
Strong, Samuel Paddock, House—*hist pl* VT-1
Strong, William, House—*hist pl* MN-6
Strong Arm Rsvr—*reservoir* ID-8
Strong Bldg—*hist pl* WI-6
Strong Branch—*stream* (4) KY-4
Strong Branch—*stream* MS-4
Strong Branch—*stream* VA-3
Strong Branch Sch—*school* KY-4
*Strong Brook* CT-1
Strong Butte Sch—*school* NE-7
Strong Canyon—*valley* NE-7
Strong Canyon—*valley* NM-5
Strong Cem—*cemetery* AL-4
Strong Cem—*cemetery* (2) AR-4
Strong Cem—*cemetery* GA-3
Strong Cem—*cemetery* IN-6
Strong Cem—*cemetery* KY-4
Strong Cem—*cemetery* MI-6
Strong Cem—*cemetery* (3) MS-4
Strong Cem—*cemetery* NM-5
Strong Cem—*cemetery* OH-6
Strong Cem—*cemetery* TN-4
Strong Cem—*cemetery* (2) TX-5
Strong Cem—*cemetery* VA-3
Strong Chapel—*church* MS-4
**Strong City**—*pop pl* OK-5
**Strong City (historical)**—*pop pl* KS-7
Strong Comstock Sch—*school* CT-1
Strong Creek—*stream* GA-3
Strong Creek—*stream* (3) ID-8
Strong Creek—*stream* OH-6
Strong Creek—*stream* SC-3
Strong Creek—*stream* TN-4
Strong Creek—*stream* WY-8
Strong Dam—*dam* OR-9
Strong Ditch—*canal* OH-6
Strong-Douglas Cem—*cemetery* AL-4
Strong Drain—*stream* MI-6
Strong Draw—*valley* ID-8
Strong Draw—*valley* WY-8
*Strongers Branch* IN-6
Strong Falls—*falls* WI-6
Strong Fork—*stream* KY-4
Strong Hill—*summit* NY-2
Stronghill Baptist Ch—*church* MS-4
Strong Hill Sch—*school* MS-4
Stronghold—*locale* CA-9
Stronghold—*locale* ME-1
Stronghold—*locale* MD-2
*Stronghold Canyon* AZ-5
Stronghold Canyon East—*valley* AZ-5
Stronghold Canyon West—*valley* AZ-5
Stronghold House (ruins)—*locale* UT-8
Stronghold Landing (historical)—*locale* MS-4
Stronghold Peak—*summit* AK-9
*Stronghold Table* SD-7
Stronghold Table—*bench* SD-7
Strong Hollow—*valley* MO-7
Strong Hollow—*valley* (2) TN-4
*Strong Hope* MS-4
**Stronghope**—*pop pl* MS-4
Stronghope Baptist Ch—*church* MS-4
Stronghope Cem—*cemetery* MS-4
Strong House—*hist pl* CT-1
Strong House—*hist pl* MA-1
**Stronghurst**—*pop pl* IL-6
Stronghurst Sch—*school* NM-5
**Stronghurst (Township of)**—*pop pl* IL-6
Strong Island—*island* CT-1
Strong Island—*island* ID-8
Strong Island—*island* MA-1
Strong Island—*island* MI-6
Strong Island Marshes—*swamp* MA-1
Strong JHS—*school* MI-6
**Strongknob**—*pop pl* UT-8
Strongknob—*summit* UT-8
*Strongknob Mountain* UT-8
Strong Lake—*lake* MI-6
Strong Lake—*lake* NE-7
Strong Lake Dam—*dam* MS-4
Strongman, Henry, House—*hist pl* NH-1
Strongman, William, House—*hist pl* NH-1
Strong Memorial Cem—*cemetery* TX-5
Strong Memorial Hosp—*hospital* NY-2
Strong Memorial Park—*park* TX-5
Strong Mtn—*summit* CA-9
Strong Mtn—*summit* PA-2
Strong Oil Field—*oilfield* TX-5
*Strong Point* MI-6
Strong Point—*cape* AK-9
Strong Point—*cape* TX-5
*Strong Pond* MA-1
Strong Pond—*lake* CT-1
Strong Pumping Station—*locale* AR-4
Strong Ranch—*locale* ID-8
Strong Ranch Slough—*stream* CA-9
Strong River—*stream* MS-4
Strong River Cem—*cemetery* MS-4
Strong River Ch—*church* MS-4
Strong Run—*stream* PA-2
*Strongs* MS-4
**Strongs**—*pop pl* MI-6
Strong's Block—*hist pl* MA-1
*Strongs Bluff* TX-5
*Strongs Brook* NY-2
Strongs Brook—*stream* CT-1
Strongs Brook—*stream* NY-2
Strongs Canyon—*valley* UT-8
Strong Sch—*school* (2) CT-1
Strong Sch—*school* KS-7
Strong Sch—*school* NY-2
Strong Sch—*school* TX-5
Strong Sch (abandoned)—*school* PA-2
**Strongs Corner**—*pop pl* MI-6
Strongs Corners—*locale* PA-2
**Strongs Corners**—*pop pl* MI-6
*Strongs Creek* NY-2
Strongs Creek—*stream* CA-9
Strongs Creek—*stream* NY-2
Strongs Fork—*stream* UT-8
Strongs Hill—*summit* PA-2
Strongs Island—*island* MI-6
*Strongs Knob* PA-2
Strongs Knob—*summit* UT-8
Strongs Lake—*lake* UT-8
Strongs Methodist Ch (historical)—*church* MS-4
Strongs Neck—*cape* NY-2
Strongs Peak—*summit* UT-8
Strongs Point—*cape* NY-2
*Strongs Pond* MA-1
Strongs Pond—*lake* MA-1
Strongs Prairie—*locale* WI-6
Strongs Prairie Cem—*cemetery* WI-6
**Strongs Prairie (Town of)**—*pop pl* WI-6
Strong Spring—*spring* CO-8
Strong Spring—*spring* MO-7
Strongs Ridge—*ridge* OH-6
Strongs Run—*stream* OH-6
*Strongs Station* MS-4
Strongs Station (Site)—*locale* CA-9
**Strongs (Strong)**—*pop pl* MS-4
**Strongstown**—*pop pl* PA-2
**Strongsville**—*pop pl* OH-6
Strong Swamp—*swamp* VT-1
Strong Tank—*reservoir* NM-5
**Strong (Town of)**—*pop pl* ME-1
**Strong Township**—*pop pl* KS-7
**Strong Township**—*pop pl* ND-7
*Strong Vincent High School* PA-2
*Strongwater Brook* MA-1
Strong Water Brook—*stream* MA-1
Strongwater Brook—*stream* MA-1
Strons Lake—*lake* SC-3
Strontia Spring—*spring* CO-8
**Strool**—*pop pl* SD-7
*Strool Dam* SD-7
Strool Sch—*school* SD-7
**Strool Township**—*pop pl* SD-7
Stroope Canyon—*valley* TX-5
Strop Butte—*summit* MT-8
Strope Creek—*stream* CA-9
Strop Hollow—*valley* MO-7
St. Rosa Church—*hist pl* OH-6
St. Rose Catholic Church Complex—*hist pl* OH-6
Strosnider Cem—*cemetery* PA-2
Strosnider East Ditch—*canal* NV-8
Strosnider Hill Cem—*cemetery* WV-2
Strosnider Ranch—*locale* NV-8
Strosnider West Ditch—*canal* NV-8
Strother—*locale* MO-7
**Strother**—*pop pl* SC-3
Strother Air Field Number Two—*airport* KS-7
*Strother Airport* KS-7
Strother Branch—*stream* TN-4
Strother Cem—*cemetery* TN-4
Strother Ch—*church* TN-4
Strother Creek—*stream* LA-4
Strother Creek—*stream* MO-7
Strother Field—*airport* KS-7
Strother-Mitchell Cem—*cemetery* TN-4
Strother Mtn—*summit* AR-4
Strother Run—*stream* VA-3
*Strothers Branch* VA-3
Strothers Branch—*stream* VA-3
Strother Sch—*school* MO-7
Strother Sch—*school* OK-5
Strother's Farm—*hist pl* GA-3
Stroube Ditch—*canal* IN-6
Stroube House—*hist pl* KY-4
*Strouble Ditch* IN-6
Strouble Lake—*lake* MI-6
Stroubles Creek—*stream* VA-3
Stroubs Mine—*mine* OR-9
Strouckel, John, House—*hist pl* SD-7
Stroud—*locale* KY-4
**Stroud**—*pop pl* AL-4
**Stroud**—*pop pl* OK-5
Stroud, James W., House—*hist pl* OK-5
Stroud Branch—*stream* LA-4
Stroud Branch—*stream* TX-5
Stroud Bridge—*bridge* KY-4
Stroud Cem—*cemetery* AL-4
Stroud Cem—*cemetery* (3) AR-4
Stroud Cem—*cemetery* IL-6
Stroud Cem—*cemetery* IN-6
Stroud Cem—*cemetery* MS-4
Stroud Cem—*cemetery* (3) SC-3
Stroud Cem—*cemetery* (2) TN-4
Stroud Cem—*cemetery* (2) WV-2
*Stroud Creek* WY-8
Stroud Creek—*stream* AL-4
Stroud Creek—*stream* AR-4
Stroud Creek—*stream* FL-3
Stroud Creek—*stream* GA-3
Stroud Creek—*stream* ID-8
Stroud Creek—*stream* MT-8
Stroud Dam—*dam* PA-2
Stroud Glacier—*glacier* WY-8
Stroud Gulch—*valley* ID-8
Stroud Hollow—*valley* TN-4
Stroud House—*hist pl* AR-4
Stroud Interchange—*other* OK-5
Stroud Lake—*lake* NM-5
Stroud Lake—*reservoir* OK-5
Stroud Line Sch (historical)—*school* MS-4
Stroud Mall—*locale* PA-2
Stroud Mansion—*hist pl* PA-2
Stroud Memorial Church Sch—*school* FL-3
Stroud Mine—*mine* NV-8
Stroud Mtn—*summit* GA-3
Stroud Mtn—*summit* TX-5
Stroud Peak—*summit* WY-8
Stroud Pond—*reservoir* NC-3
Stroud Ranch—*locale* TX-5
Stroud Rsvr—*reservoir* MT-8
Stroud Run State Park—*park* OH-6
Strouds—*locale* GA-3
Strouds—*locale* WV-2
Strouds—*locale* WY-8
Strouds Bay—*bay* NC-3
Strouds Branch—*stream* SC-3
**Stroudsburg**—*pop pl* PA-2
Stroudsburg Borough—*civil* PA-2
Stroudsburg HS—*school* PA-2
Stroudsburg-Pocono Airpark—*airport* PA-2
**Stroudsburg West**—*pop pl* PA-2
Stroud Sch—*school* GA-3
Stroud Sch—*school* OH-6
Stroud Sch (historical)—*school* SD-7
Strouds Creek—*stream* FL-3
Strouds Creek—*stream* GA-3
Strouds Creek—*stream* NC-3
Strouds Creek—*stream* TX-5
Strouds Creek—*stream* WV-2
Strouds Creek Cem—*cemetery* TX-5
Strouds Cross Road—*locale* AL-4
Strouds Knobs—*ridge* WV-2
Strouds Landing—*locale* FL-3
Stroud Springs—*spring* OR-9
Strouds Run—*stream* OH-6
Strouds Run Ch—*church* OH-6
**Stroudsville**—*pop pl* TN-4
**Stroud (Township of)**—*pop pl* PA-2
Stroud Trading Company Bldg—*hist pl* OK-5
**Stroudville**—*pop pl* TN-4
*Stroudwater* ME-1
**Stroudwater**—*pop pl* ME-1
Stroudwater Hist Dist—*hist pl* ME-1
Stroudwater River—*stream* ME-1
Strouf Island—*bench* MT-8
Strouf Pioneer Cem—*cemetery* MT-8
Strough Corners—*locale* NY-2
*Strough Crossing* NY-2
*Stroughs* NY-2
Stroughs Crossing—*locale* NY-2
Stroughton Lake—*reservoir* PA-2
Stroughton Lake Dam—*dam* PA-2
Stroup Cem—*cemetery* (2) AL-4
Stroup Cem—*cemetery* IN-6
Stroup Cem—*cemetery* OH-6
**Stroup Corners**—*pop pl* OH-6
*Stroup Creek* CA-9
Stroupe Creek—*stream* OR-9
Stroupe Gap—*gap* NC-3
Stroupes Store—*locale* VA-3
Stroup Park—*park* OK-5
Stroup Run—*stream* PA-2
Stroups—*locale* OH-6
*Stroups Crossroads* AL-4
**Stroups Crossroads**—*pop pl* AL-4
Stroup Spring—*spring* MO-7
**Strouptown**—*pop pl* PA-2
*Strouse* IN-6
Strouse—*other* IN-6
*Strouse Hill* WY-8
Strouseton (historical)—*locale* SD-7
Strouss Hill—*summit* WY-8
Strouss-Hirschberg Company—*hist pl* OH-6
Strout—*locale* MN-6
Strout, George A., House—*hist pl* CA-9
*Stroutamires Landing* FL-3
Strout Brook—*stream* (2) ME-1
Strout Camp—*locale* ME-1
Strout Cem—*cemetery* (2) ME-1
Strout Drain—*canal* CA-9
Strout Drain Two—*spring* CA-9
Strout Drain 2—*canal* CA-9
Strouth Cem—*cemetery* VA-3
Strout Island—*island* ME-1
Strout Island Ledges—*bar* ME-1
Strout Island Narrows—*channel* ME-1
Strout JHS—*school* MI-6
Strout Point—*cape* ME-1
Strout Spring—*spring* OR-9
*Strover Creek* MI-6
Strowbridge Cem—*cemetery* MA-1
Strowbridge Creek—*stream* KS-7
Strowbridge Dam—*dam* KS-7
Strowbridge Rsvr—*reservoir* KS-7
Strow Creek—*stream* VA-3
Strozier Branch—*stream* GA-3
Strozzi Ranch—*locale* NV-8
Strozzy Gulch—*valley* MT-8
Strube Dam—*dam* OR-9
Strube Lake—*reservoir* OR-9
Strubes Forest Camp (historical)—*locale* OR-9
Strubhar Ditch—*canal* IN-6
**Struble**—*pop pl* IA-7
**Struble**—*pop pl* PA-2
Struble Lake—*reservoir* PA-2
*Strubles* PA-2
Struby Creek—*stream* OR-9
Struby Creek Rsvr—*reservoir* OR-9
Struck, Dr. Kuno, House—*hist pl* IA-7
Struck Creek—*stream* MT-8
Struckmeyer Cem—*cemetery* TX-5
Struck Sch—*school* SD-7
**Structure**—*pop pl* TX-5
Structure at 490 E. 200 North—*hist pl* UT-8
Structure Number Eight—*dam* NC-3
Structure Number Eight Lake—*reservoir* NC-3
Structure Number Fifteen Dam—*dam* NC-3
Structure Number Fifteen Lake—*reservoir* NC-3
Structure Number Nineteen Dam—*dam* NC-3
Structure Number Nineteen Lake—*reservoir* NC-3
Structure Number Six B Dam—*dam* NC-3
Structure Number Six B Lake—*reservoir* NC-3
Structure Number Two C Dam—*dam* NC-3
Structure Number Two C Lake—*reservoir* NC-3
Struggle Gulch—*valley* ID-8
Struggle Lake—*lake* MN-6
Struggle Ranch (historical)—*locale* AL-4
**Strum**—*pop pl* PA-2
**Strum**—*pop pl* WI-6
Strum Bay—*swamp* GA-3
Strum Bay Cem—*cemetery* GA-3
Strum Creek—*stream* OR-9
Strum Lake—*reservoir* WI-6
Strump Sch (historical)—*school* MO-7
Strum Station (historical)—*building* PA-2
Strunce Cabin—*locale* CA-9
Strunger Bayou—*gut* MS-4
Strunk—*locale* KY-4
Strunk Branch—*stream* KY-4
Strunk Cem—*cemetery* MO-7
Strunk Cem—*cemetery* TN-4
*Strunkiln* DE-2
Strunk Lake—*lake* MN-6
Strunk-Nyssen House—*hist pl* MN-6
Strunk Ranch—*locale* NE-7
*Strunktown* PA-2
*Strunt Kill* DE-2
Strunz, Christian G., House—*hist pl* IN-6
Strup Lake—*lake* MN-6
Struple Coulee—*valley* MT-8
Strupp Sch—*school* WI-6
**Struthers**—*pop pl* OH-6
Struthers Library—*building* PA-2
Struthers Library Bldg—*hist pl* PA-2
Struthers Plaza Shop Ctr—*locale* OH-6
Strutman Field Airp—*airport* MO-7
Strutsell Sawmill—*locale* CO-8
Strutton Creek—*stream* NC-3
Struve Creek—*stream* WA-9
Struve-Hay Bldg—*hist pl* AL-4
Struve Slough—*stream* CA-9
Struya Point—*cape* AK-9
Strychnine Camp—*locale* NM-5
Strychnine Creek—*stream* ID-8
Strychnine Draw—*valley* NM-5
Strychnine Pond—*lake* UT-8
Strychnine Ridge—*ridge* ID-8
Strychnine Wash—*valley* UT-8
**Stryker**—*pop pl* MT-8
**Stryker**—*pop pl* OH-6
Stryker Cem—*cemetery* (2) TX-5
*Stryker Creek* TX-5
**Stryker Creek**—*pop pl* TX-5
Stryker Creek Junction—*locale* TX-5
*Stryker Creek Reservoir* TX-5
*Stryker Lake* MT-8
Stryker Peak—*summit* MT-8
Stryker Ridge—*ridge* MT-8
**Strykersville**—*pop pl* NY-2
Strykersville Cem—*cemetery* NY-2
**Stryker Village**—*pop pl* TN-4
Sts. Cyril and Methodius Church—*hist pl* CT-1
Sts. Cyril and Methodius Church—*hist pl* TX-5
St. Sebastian Catholic Church and Rectory—*hist pl* OH-6
*Stsiuck* FM-9
Sts. Peter and Paul Church—*hist pl* ME-1
Sts. Peter and Paul Russian Orthodox Church—*hist pl* MN-6
Sts. Peter & Paul Church and Rectory—*hist pl* OH-6
St. Stanislaus Catholic Church—*hist pl* ID-8
St. Stanislaus Church—*hist pl* OH-6
St. Stanislaus Church Hist Dist—*hist pl* ND-7
St. Stanislaus Kostka Church—*hist pl* MO-7
St. Stanislaus Kostka Mission—*hist pl* ID-8
St. Stanislaus Seminary—*hist pl* MO-7
St. Stephen Church—*hist pl* OH-6
St. Stephen Church and Rectory—*hist pl* OH-6
St. Stephenie Scandinavian Evangelical Lutheran Church—*hist pl* NE-7
**St. Stephens**—*pop pl* NE-7
**St. Stephens**—*pop pl* WY-8
St.Stephens' AME Church—*hist pl* OH-6
St. Stephen's Church—*hist pl* MA-1
St. Stephen's Church—*hist pl* RI-1
St. Stephen's Episcopal Church—*hist pl* IA-7
St. Stephen's Episcopal Church—*hist pl* NE-7
St. Stephen's Episcopal Church—*hist pl* (2) SC-3
St. Stephen's Episcopal Church, 1881—*hist pl* CO-8
St. Stephen's Memorial Church—*hist pl* MA-1
Sttep Spring—*spring* CO-8
**Stterwhite**—*pop pl* NC-3
St. Thaddeus Episcopal Church—*hist pl* SC-3
St. Theodosius Russian Orthodox Cathedral—*hist pl* OH-6
**St. Thomas**—*pop pl* ND-7
St. Thomas Aquinas Church—*hist pl* OH-6
St. Thomas Catholic Church—*hist pl* ID-8
St. Thomas Church and Convent—*hist pl* IL-6
St. Thomas Episcopal Church—*hist pl* IA-7
St. Thomas Episcopal Church—*hist pl* NH-1
St. Thomas Epsicopal Church—*hist pl* MA-1
**St. Thomas Township**—*pop pl* ND-7
St. Timothy's Protestant Episcopal Church—*hist pl* OH-6
Stuard Canyon—*valley* CA-9
*Stuart* NY-2
Stuart—*locale* AR-4
Stuart—*locale* CA-9
Stuart—*locale* CO-8
Stuart—*locale* MT-8
Stuart—*locale* WA-9
**Stuart**—*pop pl* FL-3
**Stuart**—*pop pl* IA-7
**Stuart**—*pop pl* NE-7
**Stuart**—*pop pl* OK-5
**Stuart**—*pop pl* VA-3
Stuart, Charles E., House—*hist pl* MI-6
Stuart, Col. John, House—*hist pl* SC-3
Stuart, Dr., House—*hist pl* OR-9
Stuart, Dr. Richard and Paulina, House—*hist pl* IA-7
Stuart, Gilbert, Birthplace—*hist pl* RI-1
Stuart, Jesse, House—*hist pl* KY-4
Stuart, J. M. Power Plant—*facility* OH-6
Stuart, John, House—*hist pl* KY-4
Stuart, Lake—*lake* WA-9
Stuart, Mount—*summit* WA-9
Stuart, Point—*cape* CA-9
Stuart, Robert, House—*hist pl* MI-6
Stuart Addition Hist Dist—*hist pl* VA-3
Stuart Bldg—*hist pl* KY-4
Stuart Branch—*stream* KY-4
Stuart Brook—*stream* (2) ME-1
Stuart Camp—*locale* CA-9
Stuart Canyon—*valley* CA-9
Stuart Canyon—*valley* WA-9
Stuart (CCD)—*cens area* FL-3
Stuart Cem—*cemetery* GA-3
Stuart Cem—*cemetery* IN-6
Stuart Cem—*cemetery* IA-7
Stuart Cem—*cemetery* ME-1
Stuart Cem—*cemetery* MS-4
Stuart Cem—*cemetery* (2) NC-3
Stuart Cem—*cemetery* OH-6
Stuart Cem—*cemetery* TN-4
Stuart Centre (Shop Ctr)—*locale* FL-3
Stuart Ch—*church* VA-3
Stuart Chapel—*church* GA-3
Stuart Chapel—*church* TN-4
Stuart Chapel—*church* VA-3
*Stuart Church* MO-7
Stuart Corner—*locale* VA-3
Stuart Corners—*locale* NY-2
Stuart Cove—*bay* FL-3
*Stuart Creek* MT-8
*Stuart Creek* NC-3
*Stuart Creek* OR-9
Stuart Creek—*stream* (3) AK-9
Stuart Creek—*stream* CA-9
Stuart Creek—*stream* CO-8
Stuart Creek—*stream* MT-8
Stuart Creek—*stream* NE-7
Stuart Creek—*stream* OR-9
Stuart Creek—*stream* VA-3
Stuart Creek—*stream* WY-8
Stuart Ditch No. 1—*canal* CO-8
Stuart Ditch No. 2—*canal* CO-8
Stuart Fork—*stream* CA-9
*Stuart Fork Creek* AR-4
*Stuart Fork Creek* CA-9
*Stuart Fork of Trinity River* CA-9
Stuart Gap—*gap* CA-9
Stuart Glacier—*glacier* WA-9
Stuart Guard Station—*locale* UT-8
*Stuart Gulch* ID-8
Stuart Hall Sch—*school* VA-3
**Stuart Heights**—*pop pl* TN-4
Stuart Heights Baptist Ch—*church* TN-4
Stuart Hill—*summit* CT-1
Stuart Hill Cem—*cemetery* MD-2
Stuart Hole—*gap* CO-8
Stuart Hollow—*valley* MO-7
Stuart Hollow—*valley* WV-2
Stuart Hotel—*hist pl* OK-5
Stuart Hot Springs—*spring* ID-8
Stuart House—*hist pl* TX-5
Stuart House—*hist pl* VA-3
Stuart House and Gardens—*hist pl* WA-9
Stuart HS—*school* KY-4
*Stuart Island* NY-2
Stuart Island—*island* AK-9
Stuart Island—*island* AR-4
Stuart Island—*island* WA-9
Stuart Island Airpark Airp—*airport* WA-9
Stuart Island Canal—*canal* AK-9
Stuart Island Reef—*bar* AK-9
Stuart JHS—*school* DC-2
Stuart Knob—*summit* WV-2
Stuart Lake—*lake* (5) MI-6
Stuart Lake—*lake* (3) MN-6
Stuart Lake—*lake* NY-2
**Stuart Lake**—*pop pl* MI-6
Stuart Lake Dam—*dam* MS-4
Stuart Lateral—*canal* ID-8
Stuart Manor—*hist pl* WV-2
**Stuart Manor**—*pop pl* OH-6
Stuart Mesa—*summit* CA-9
Stuart Mill Spring—*spring* MT-8
Stuart Motor Company—*hist pl* NC-3
Stuart MS—*school* FL-3
Stuart Mtn—*summit* AK-9
Stuart Mtn—*summit* OK-5
Stuart Mtn—*summit* VA-3
Stuart Neighborhood/Henderson Park Hist Dist—*hist pl* MI-6
Stuart Park Rec Area—*park* WV-2
Stuart Pass—*gap* WA-9
Stuart Peak—*summit* MT-8
Stuart Place—*locale* TX-5
**Stuart Place**—*pop pl* TX-5
Stuart Point—*cape* FL-3
Stuart Point—*cape* VA-3
**Stuart Point**—*pop pl* SC-3
Stuart Pond—*lake* ME-1
Stuart Pond—*lake* VT-1
Stuart Pond—*reservoir* MA-1
Stuart Pond Dam—*dam* MA-1
Stuart Portage—*trail* MN-6
Stuart Ranch—*locale* OK-5
Stuart Ranch—*locale* WY-8
Stuart Range—*range* WA-9
Stuart Ridge—*ridge* ME-1
Stuart River—*stream* MN-6
Stuart Run—*stream* VA-3
*Stuarts Branch* TN-4
*Stuarts Camp* AL-4
Stuart Sch—*school* IL-6
Stuart Sch—*school* IA-7
Stuart Sch—*school* LA-4
*Stuart School* TN-4
*Stuarts Creek* CA-9
*Stuarts Creek* NC-3
*Stuarts Creek* TX-5
**Stuarts Draft**—*pop pl* VA-3
Stuarts Hill—*summit* VA-3
Stuart Shop Ctr—*locale* FL-3
*Stuart Siding* WA-9
Stuarts Island (historical)—*island* TN-4
Stuarts Knob—*summit* VA-3
Stuarts Lake—*reservoir* GA-3
*Stuarts Landing* MS-4
Stuarts Lane Hollow—*valley* KY-4
Stuart Slough—*stream* WA-9
Stuarts Mill (historical)—*locale* TN-4
Stuart's Opera House—*hist pl* OH-6
Stuarts Peak—*summit* TX-5
*Stuarts Pond* AL-4
Stuart Spring—*spring* CA-9
Stuart Springs—*hist pl* AR-4
Stuarts Shoals—*bar* TN-4
Stuarts Springs—*spring* CO-8
Stuart Station Well—*well* NM-5
**Stuart Subdivision**—*pop pl* UT-8
Stuart Township—*fmr MCD* IA-7
**Stuart Township**—*pop pl* NE-7
Stuart Tunnel—*tunnel* WV-2
Stuart Union Ch—*church* MO-7
*Stuart Wash* CO-8
Stuart Well—*well* NM-5
Stuart Wharf—*locale* VA-3
Stubb Branch—*stream* MS-4
Stubb Cem—*cemetery* MS-4
Stubb Creek—*stream* CO-8
Stubbe Canyon—*valley* CA-9
Stubbe Spring—*spring* CA-9
*Stubb Gulch* AZ-5
Stubb Hollow—*valley* OR-9
Stubbins Gap—*gap* TX-5
Stubb Island—*island* ME-1
Stubblefield—*locale* IL-6
Stubblefield—*locale* KY-4
Stubblefield—*locale* TX-5
Stubblefield Arroyo—*stream* NM-5
Stubblefield Baptist Ch (historical)—*church* TX-5
Stubblefield Branch—*stream* MO-7
Stubblefield Canal—*canal* OR-9
Stubblefield Canyon—*valley* CA-9
Stubblefield Canyon—*valley* NM-5
Stubblefield Cem—*cemetery* AR-4
Stubblefield Cem—*cemetery* KY-4
Stubblefield Cem—*cemetery* MO-7
Stubblefield Cem—*cemetery* TN-4
Stubblefield Creek—*stream* TN-4
Stubblefield Eagle Tail Lateral—*canal* NM-5
Stubblefield Falls—*falls* MD-2
Stubblefield Fork—*stream* OR-9
Stubblefield Gas Storage Field—*other* IL-6
Stubblefield Hollow—*valley* (2) TN-4
Stubblefield Lake—*lake* IL-6
Stubblefield Lake—*lake* TX-5
Stubblefield Lake—*lake* WA-9
Stubblefield Lateral—*canal* NM-5
Stubblefield Mtn—*summit* AL-4
Stubblefield Mtn—*summit* OR-9
Stubblefield Point—*cliff* WA-9
Stubblefield Sch (historical)—*school* TX-5
**Stubblefields (historical)**—*pop pl* TN-4
Stubblefields Pit—*cave* TN-4
*Stubbs* (2) CA-9
Stubbs—*locale* KS-7
Stubbs—*locale* MO-7
Stubbs—*locale* TX-5
Stubbs—*locale* VA-3
**Stubbs**—*pop pl* NC-3
Stubbs, Elizabeth, House—*hist pl* DE-2
*Stubbs Bay* MN-6
Stubbs Bay—*bay* MN-6
**Stubbs Bay**—*pop pl* MN-6
Stubbs Bluff—*cliff* TN-4
Stubbs Brook—*stream* ME-1
Stubbs-Carter Cem—*cemetery* MS-4
Stubbs Cem—*cemetery* (2) GA-3
Stubbs Cem—*cemetery* LA-4
Stubbs Cem—*cemetery* (2) MS-4
Stubbs Cem—*cemetery* MO-7
Stubb Sch (historical)—*school* MS-4
Stubbs Corner—*locale* ME-1
Stubbs Creek—*stream* LA-4
Stubbs Creek—*stream* WY-8
Stubbs Draw—*valley* WY-8
Stubbs Earthworks—*hist pl* OH-6
Stubbs Fruedenberg Ditch—*canal* IN-6
Stubbs Gulch—*valley* AZ-5
Stubbs Gulch—*valley* CO-8
Stubbs Island—*island* CA-9
Stubbs Island—*island* MS-4
Stubbs Lake—*lake* FL-3
Stubbs Lake—*lake* TX-5
Stubbs Mill Cem—*cemetery* ME-1
Stubbs Mtn—*summit* AL-4
Stubbs Mtn—*summit* ME-1
Stubbs Park—*park* GA-3
Stubbs Park—*park* TX-5
Stubbs Point—*cape* AR-4
Stubbs Pond—*lake* VA-3
Stubbs Pond—*reservoir* SC-3
Stubbs Rapids—*rapids* WI-6
*Stubbs Sch* DE-2
Stubbs Sch—*school* MO-7
Stubbs Sch—*school* (2) TX-5
Stubbs Tank—*reservoir* (2) AZ-5
**Stubbs (Town of)**—*pop pl* WI-6
Stubbs Well—*well* (2) UT-8
*Stubb Tank* AZ-5
Stubby Plain Brook—*stream* CT-1
Stubby Point—*cape* MT-8
*Stubby Spring* CA-9
Stubby Well—*well* NM-5
Stub Canyon—*valley* UT-8
*Stub Creek* KS-7
Stub Creek—*stream* CO-8
Stub Creek—*stream* (2) ID-8
Stub Creek—*stream* KS-7
Stub Creek—*stream* OK-5
Stub Creek—*stream* OR-9
Stub Creek—*stream* (4) WA-9
Stub Creek—*stream* WY-8
Stub Creek Spring—*spring* ID-8
Stub Ditch—*canal* CO-8
Stub Draw—*valley* TX-5
Stuber Cem—*cemetery* IL-6
Stuber Lake—*reservoir* IN-6
Stuber Ranch—*locale* ND-7
Stuber Ranch Airp—*airport* KS-7
*Stubey Creek* WA-9
Stub Hill—*summit* NH-1
Stub Lake—*lake* CA-9
Stub Lake—*lake* (2) MN-6

Stub Lake—*lake* NE-7
Stub Lake—*lake* TX-5
Stub Lake—*reservoir* TX-5
Stub Lakes—*lake* MN-6
Stublefield Dam—*dam* NM-5
Stub Mine—*mine* NM-5
Stub Mine—*mine* OR-9
Stub Number One—*canal* AZ-5
Stub Number Two—*canal* AZ-5
Stub Pond—*reservoir* CT-1
Stubs Cabin—*locale* CO-8
Stubs Shoals—*bar* MN-6
Stubtoe Creek—*stream* ID-8
Stubtoe Peak—*summit* ID-8
**Stubtown**—*pop pl* MO-7
Stub Trail—*trail* NM-5
Stub Walsh Lake—*lake* WI-6
Stub Windmill—*locale* (3) TX-5
Stuby Cem—*cemetery* IL-6
Stucco—*locale* WY-8
Stuchell Sch (historical)—*school* PA-2
**Stuck**—*pop pl* WA-9
Stuck Cem—*cemetery* SC-3
Stuck Creek—*stream* CO-8
Stuck Creek Ditch—*canal* CO-8
Stuck Creek Ditch—*canal* WY-8
Stuckenhole Drain—*stream* NE-7
Stuckens Branch—*stream* TX-5
Stucker Cem—*cemetery* MO-7
Stucker Ditch—*canal* IN-6
Stucker Ditch—*stream* IN-6
*Stucker Fork* IN-6
Stucker Fork Structure Number 15—*dam* IN-6
Stucker Fork Structure Number 4—*dam* IN-6
Stucker Fork Structure Number 5—*dam* IN-6
Stucker Island—*island* PA-2
Stucker Mesa—*summit* CO-8
*Stuckers Fork* IN-6
*Stuckertown* PA-2
Stuckey—*locale* GA-3
**Stuckey**—*pop pl* SC-3
Stuckey Boone Lake—*reservoir* GA-3
Stuckey Butte—*summit* OR-9
Stuckey Butte Rsvr—*reservoir* OR-9
Stuckey Cem—*cemetery* AR-4
Stuckey Cem—*cemetery* (2) IN-6
Stuckey Cem—*cemetery* (2) OH-6
Stuckey Ditch—*canal* IN-6
*Stuckey Gin Branch* AL-4
Stuckey Hollow—*valley* PA-2
Stuckey Lake—*reservoir* AL-4
Stuckey Mill Creek—*stream* AL-4
Stuckey's Bridge—*hist pl* MS-4
Stuckeyville—*locale* PA-2
Stuck Hollow—*valley* PA-2
Stucki, J. U., House and
Outbuildings—*hist pl* ID-8
Stucki Debris Basin Dam—*dam* UT-8
Stucki Debris Basin Rsvr—*reservoir* UT-8
Stucki Spring—*spring* UT-8
Stuck Mtn—*summit* AK-9
*Stuck River* WA-9
Stuck Sch—*school* KS-7
Stuckslager, Harrison, House—*hist pl* IA-7
Stuckwisch Ditch—*canal* IN-6
Stucky Creek—*stream* NY-2
Stucky Ditch (historical)—*canal* NV-8
Stucky Gulch—*valley* MT-8
Stucky House—*hist pl* KY-4
Stucky Ridge—*ridge* MT-8
Stucky Sch—*school* IN-6
**Studa**—*pop pl* PA-2
Stud Creek—*stream* (2) ID-8
Stud Creek—*stream* NV-8
Stud Creek—*stream* OR-9
Stud Creek—*stream* WY-8
Studdard Cem—*cemetery* GA-3
Studdard Sch (historical)—*school* AL-4
**Studdards Crossroads**—*pop pl* AL-4
Studdards Cross Roads Ch
(historical)—*church* AL-4
Stud Duck Tank—*reservoir* TX-5
Studebaker—*locale* CA-9
Studebaker Bldg—*hist pl* FL-3
Studebaker Bldg—*hist pl* IL-6
Studebaker Cem—*cemetery* (2) IN-6
Studebaker Cem—*cemetery* OH-6
Studebaker Clubhouse and Tree
Sign—*hist pl* IN-6
Studebaker Creek—*stream* (2) WA-9
Studebaker Ditch—*canal* IN-6
Studebaker Draw—*valley* MT-8
Studebaker Flat—*flat* CA-9
Studebaker Hiatt Ditch—*canal* IN-6
Studebaker Hosp—*hospital* CA-9
Studebaker Park—*park* (3) IN-6
Studebaker Ridge—*ridge* WA-9
Studebaker Rsvr—*reservoir* CO-8
Studebaker Saddle—*gap* ID-8
Studebaker Sch—*school* CA-9
*Studebaker School* IN-6
Studebaker-Scott House And Beehive
Sch—*hist pl* OH-6
Studenberg Hollow—*valley* WI-6
Student Lake—*lake* ID-8
Students Home Acad (historical)—*school* TN-4
Students Island—*island* ME-1
Student Union—*uninc pl* AZ-5
Stude Park—*park* TX-5
Studer Creek—*stream* ID-8
Studer Ditch—*canal* OH-6
Studer Lake—*reservoir* TN-4
Studer Lake Dam—*dam* TN-4
Studer Ridge—*ridge* OR-9
Studevan Sch—*school* PA-2
Studevant Cem—*cemetery* OR-9
Stud Flat—*flat* UT-8
Stud Hill—*summit* CA-9
Stud Horse Butte—*summit* AZ-5
Studhorse Butte—*summit* MT-8
Studhorse Butte—*summit* OR-9
Stud Horse Butte—*summit* WY-8
Stud Horse Camp—*locale* CA-9
Studhorse Canyon—*valley* (3) CA-9
Stud Horse Canyon—*valley* NV-8
Studhorse Canyon—*valley* OR-9
Studhorse Canyon—*valley* UT-8
Studhorse Coulee—*valley* MT-8
Stud Horse Creek—*gut* GA-3
Studhorse Creek—*stream* AL-4
Studhorse Creek—*stream* CA-9
Studhorse Creek—*stream* CO-8
Stud Horse Creek—*stream* LA-4
Studhorse Creek—*stream* MT-8
Studhorse Creek—*stream* (2) OR-9
Studhorse Draw—*valley* UT-8
Studhorse Gulch—*valley* CA-9
Studhorse Lake—*lake* MN-6
Studhorse Meadow—*flat* CA-9
*Stud Horse Peaks* UT-8
Studhorse Peaks—*summit* UT-8
Stud Horse Point—*ridge* UT-8
Studhorse Ravine—*valley* CA-9
Stud Horse Rsvr—*reservoir* OR-9
Studhorse Seep—*spring* AZ-5
Studhorse Spring—*spring* NV-8
Studhorse Springs—*spring* UT-8
Stud Horse Tank—*reservoir* AZ-5
Studhorse Waterhole—*lake* OR-9
Studio Apartments—*hist pl* NY-2
Studio Bldg—*hist pl* CA-9
Studio Bldg—*hist pl* IA-7
**Studio City**—*pop pl* CA-9
Studio City Park—*park* CA-9
Studio Spring—*spring* CA-9
Stud Knoll—*summit* UT-8
Stud Lake—*lake* MN-6
Studley—*locale* VA-3
**Studley**—*pop pl* KS-7
Studley Bridge—*other* MI-6
Studley Cem—*cemetery* KS-7
Studley Hill—*summit* NY-2
Studley Sch—*school* MA-1
*Studleys Pond* MA-1
Studleys Pond—*reservoir* MA-1
Studleys Pond Dam—*dam* MA-1
Studley Spring—*spring* CA-9
Studman Branch—*stream* NC-3
Stud Mtn—*summit* CA-9
Studt Cem—*cemetery* IL-6
Study Butte—*locale* TX-5
**Study Butte**—*pop pl* TX-5
Study Butte—*summit* TX-5
Study Sch—*school* MO-7
*Study School* IN-6
Study Spring—*spring* ID-8
Stueber Branch—*stream* TX-5
Stuerman Branch—*stream* MO-7
Stuffle Cem—*cemetery* TN-4
Stuffle Run—*stream* VA-3
Stuffley Knob—*summit* KY-4
*Stugis Corners* PA-2
Stuhls Run—*stream* PA-2
Stuhr Park—*park* NE-7
Stujack Creek—*stream* WA-9
Stujack Pass—*gap* WA-9
Stuke Canyon—*valley* CA-9
Stukel—*locale* OR-9
Stukel Bridge—*bridge* OR-9
**Stukeley Hall Farms**—*pop pl* VA-3
Stukel Mtn—*summit* OR-9
*Stukel Peak* OR-9
Stukey Cem—*cemetery* MO-7
Stukey Creek—*stream* CO-8
Stukey Creek—*stream* WA-9
Stulce Prong—*stream* TN-4
Stulen Lake—*lake* WI-6
*Stuley* NC-3
Stull—*locale* ID-8
Stull—*locale* PA-2
**Stull**—*pop pl* KS-7
Stull Creek—*stream* ID-8
Stull Ditch—*canal* CO-8
Stull Ditch—*canal* OH-6
Stuller Cem—*cemetery* OH-6
Stull Gulch—*valley* MT-8
Stull Lakes—*lake* WY-8
Stull Mtn—*summit* CO-8
Stull Run—*stream* (2) VA-3
Stull Run—*stream* WV-2
Stull Sch—*school* NE-7
Stulls Corners—*locale* PA-2
Stulls Falls—*falls* OR-9
Stulls Ford—*locale* MD-2
*Stulls Pond* PA-2
*Stulls Run* WV-2
Stullz Branch—*stream* TN-4
Stulsaft Park—*park* CA-9
*Stults* MO-7
**Stults**—*pop pl* MO-7
Stults Branch—*stream* TN-4
Stults Cem—*cemetery* IN-6
Stults Cem—*cemetery* MO-7
Stults Prospect—*mine* TN-4
Stultz—*locale* MO-7
Stultz Cem—*cemetery* IL-6
Stultz Cem—*cemetery* NC-3
Stultz Ditch—*canal* IN-6
Stultz Gap—*gap* VA-3
Stultz Gulch—*valley* CO-8
Stultz Hill—*summit* OH-6
Stultz Lake—*lake* MO-7
Stultz Landing Field—*airport* CO-8
Stultz Mill—*locale* VA-3
Stultz Spring—*spring* AR-4
Stultz Trail—*trail* CO-8
Stuman Cem—*cemetery* AR-4
Stumbaugh Cem—*cemetery* IL-6
Stumbeaugh Mtn—*summit* MO-7
Stumberg, Dr. John H., House—*hist pl* MO-7
Stumble Creek—*stream* MN-6
Stumbler Lake—*reservoir* IN-6
Stumbler Lake Dam—*dam* IN-6
Stumble Run—*stream* WV-2
Stumble Run Cem—*cemetery* WV-2
Stumbo Branch—*stream* KY-4
Stumbo Memorial Hosp—*hospital* KY-4
Stumbough Ridge—*ridge* OR-9
Stumne Mounds—*hist pl* MN-6
Stumn Run—*stream* PA-2
Stump, Frederick, House—*hist pl* TN-4
Stump, John, House And Mill—*hist pl* OH-6
Stump Bay—*bay* NC-3
Stump Bayou—*gut* (3) LA-4
Stump Bayou—*stream* LA-4
Stump Beach—*beach* CA-9
Stump Branch—*stream* KY-4
Stump Branch—*stream* (2) SC-3
Stump Bridge (historical)—*bridge* MS-4
Stump Bridge P. O. (historical)—*locale* MS-4
Stump Brook—*stream* MA-1
Stump Campground—*locale* WA-9
Stump Canyon—*valley* AZ-5
Stump Canyon—*valley* CA-9
Stump Canyon—*valley* CO-8
Stump Canyon—*valley* ID-8
*Stump Canyon Lakes* CO-8
Stump Cave Branch—*stream* KY-4
Stump Cem—*cemetery* IL-6
Stump Cem—*cemetery* KY-4
Stump Cem—*cemetery* MD-2
Stump Cem—*cemetery* MO-7
Stump Cem—*cemetery* NE-7
Stump Cem—*cemetery* OH-6
Stump Cem—*cemetery* (2) PA-2
Stump Cem—*cemetery* VA-3
Stump Chapel—*church* WV-2
Stump City Sch—*school* AR-4
Stump Cove—*bay* AK-9
**Stump Creek**—*pop pl* PA-2
Stump Creek—*stream* CA-9
Stump Creek—*stream* DE-2
Stump Creek—*stream* FL-3
Stump Creek—*stream* (2) GA-3
Stump Creek—*stream* (3) ID-8
Stump Creek—*stream* IA-7
Stump Creek—*stream* MI-6
Stump Creek—*stream* MO-7
Stump Creek—*stream* MT-8
Stump Creek—*stream* NV-8
Stump Creek—*stream* NJ-2
Stump Creek—*stream* (3) OR-9
Stump Creek—*stream* PA-2
Stump Creek—*stream* WA-9
Stump Creek—*stream* WY-8
Stump Creek Butte—*summit* CA-9
Stump Creek Guard Station—*locale* ID-8
**Stump Creek (RR name
Cramer)**—*pop pl* PA-2
Stump Creek Trail—*trail* OR-9
Stump Ditch—*canal* (3) IN-6
Stump Ditch—*canal* NE-7
Stumpet Hill—*summit* CT-1
*Stumpey Point* NC-3
Stumpey Pond Upper Dam—*dam* MA-1
Stumpf, George, House—*hist pl* IN-6
Stumpf Brook—*stream* VT-1
Stumpf Cem—*cemetery* OH-6
Stumpfield Marsh—*swamp* NH-1
Stumpfield Mtn—*summit* CA-9
Stumpfield-Mudgett Rec Area—*park* NH-1
Stumpf Island—*island* WI-6
Stump Flat—*flat* UT-8
Stumpf Spring—*spring* WY-8
Stump Gap—*gap* NC-3
Stump Gulch—*valley* CO-8
Stump Gulch—*valley* (2) MT-8
Stump Gut—*stream* MD-2
Stump Hill—*summit* (2) MA-1
Stump Hill—*summit* RI-1
Stump Hill—*summit* TX-5
*Stump Hill Creek* OH-6
Stumph Oil and Gas Field—*oilfield* KS-7
*Stumphole* AL-4
Stump Hole—*lake* LA-4
Stump Hole—*lake* MO-7
Stumphole Bridge—*bridge* IN-6
Stump Hole (historical)—*lake* MO-7
Stump Hollow—*valley* ID-8
Stump Hollow—*valley* PA-2
Stump Hollow—*valley* (2) UT-8
Stump Hollow—*valley* WV-2
Stump Hollow—*valley* WY-8
Stump Hollow Campground—*locale* TN-4
Stump Hollow Canyon—*valley* ID-8
Stumphouse Mountain Tunnel—*tunnel* SC-3
Stumphouse Mtn—*summit* SC-3
Stumphouse Tunnel Complex—*hist pl* SC-3
Stumpie Arroyo—*valley* KS-7
Stump Inlet (historical)—*gut* NC-3
Stump Island—*island* AK-9
Stump Island—*island* LA-4
**Stumpke Corner**—*pop pl* IN-6
Stump Knob—*summit* TN-4
Stump Knob—*summit* WV-2
**Stump Knob (historical)**—*pop pl* TN-4
Stump Knob Post Office
(historical)—*building* IN-4
Stump Lagoon—*lake* (2) LA-4
*Stump Lake* MN-6
Stump Lake—*lake* AK-9
Stump Lake—*lake* AR-4
Stump Lake—*lake* GA-3
Stump Lake—*lake* ID-8
Stump Lake—*lake* IL-6
Stump Lake—*lake* (3) MI-6
Stump Lake—*lake* (6) MN-6
Stump Lake—*lake* MT-8
Stump Lake—*lake* ND-7
Stump Lake—*lake* WA-9
Stump Lake—*lake* (2) WI-6
Stump Lake—*lake* WY-8
Stump Lake—*reservoir* CO-8
Stump Lake—*reservoir* IN-6
Stump Lake—*reservoir* MN-6
Stump Lake—*reservoir* OR-9
Stump Lake Natl Wildlife Ref—*park* ND-7
Stump Lake Public Access Area—*locale* IL-6
Stump Lakes—*lake* CO-8
Stump Lake State Fish And Waterfowl Mngmt
Area—*park* IL-6
Stumple Lake—*lake* (2) MN-6
Stumplick Branch—*stream* NC-3
Stump Lick Run—*stream* PA-2
Stump Mtn—*summit* AR-4
Stump Neck—*cape* MD-2
Stump Park—*flat* (2) CO-8
Stump Pass—*channel* (2) FL-3
Stump Peak—*summit* ID-8
Stump Point—*cape* (3) MD-2
Stump Point—*cape* VA-3
Stump Point Marsh—*swamp* MD-2
*Stump Pond* MA-1
*Stump Pond* NY-2
*Stump Pond* RI-1
Stump Pond—*lake* AL-4
Stump Pond—*lake* CT-1
Stump Pond—*lake* (2) ME-1
Stump Pond—*lake* MA-1
Stump Pond—*lake* (2) NH-1
Stump Pond—*lake* (5) NY-2
Stump Pond—*lake* OR-9
Stump Pond—*lake* WI-6
Stump Pond—*reservoir* CO-8
Stump Pond—*reservoir* ME-1
Stump Pond—*reservoir* (4) MA-1
Stump Pond—*reservoir* NH-1
Stump Pond—*reservoir* (2) NY-2
Stump Pond—*reservoir* NC-3
Stump Pond—*reservoir* PA-2
Stump Pond—*reservoir* RI-1
*Stump Pond Dam* PA-2
*Stump Pond Dam* RI-1
Stump Pond Dam—*dam* (3) MA-1
Stump Pond Dam—*dam* NC-3
Stump Pond (historical)—*lake* MA-1
Stump Pond Stream—*stream* NY-2
Stump Post Office (historical)—*building* MS-4
Stump Prairie—*flat* OR-9
Stump Ranch—*swamp* CA-9
Stump Ridge Cem—*cemetery* MS-4
Stump Ridge Ch—*church* MS-4
Stump River—*stream* MN-6
Stump Rsvr—*reservoir* CO-8
Stump Rsvr—*reservoir* ID-8
Stump Run—*stream* (2) OH-6
Stump Run—*stream* (2) PA-2
Stump Run—*stream* (3) WV-2
Stump Run Ch—*church* OH-6
Stumps, The—*bay* WI-6
Stumps Bar—*bar* CA-9
Stumps Bluff—*cliff* KY-4
Stump Sch—*school* MI-6
Stumps Corners—*locale* DE-2
Stumps Creek—*stream* AL-4
Stumps Landing—*locale* TN-4
Stump Slough Ditch—*canal* IN-6
Stump Sound—*bay* NC-3
Stump Sound Ch—*church* NC-3
Stump Sound (Township of)—*fmr MCD* NC-3
Stump Spring—*spring* (2) AZ-5
Stump Spring—*spring* (3) CA-9
Stump Spring—*spring* CO-8
Stump Spring—*spring* (2) NV-8
Stump Spring—*spring* (3) OR-9
Stump Spring—*spring* TX-5
Stump Spring—*spring* UT-8
Stump Spring Butte—*summit* OR-9
Stump Spring Ch—*church* FL-3
Stump Springs—*spring* WA-9
Stumps Run—*stream* (2) KY-4
Stumps Run—*stream* PA-2
**Stump Station**—*pop pl* VT-1
Stump Tank—*reservoir* (3) AZ-5
Stump Tank—*reservoir* (2) NM-5
Stumptoe—*locale* AR-4
Stumptoe Sch (historical)—*school* TN-4
*Stumptown* MD-2
*Stump Town* TN-4
Stumptown—*locale* MD-2
Stump Town—*locale* MT-8
Stumptown—*locale* (2) PA-2
Stumptown—*locale* TX-5
Stumptown—*locale* (2) VA-3
**Stumptown**—*pop pl* IN-6
**Stumptown**—*pop pl* MD-2
**Stumptown**—*pop pl* NC-3
**Stumptown**—*pop pl* WV-2
Stumptown (historical)—*locale* AL-4
Stump Valley Sch—*school* IL-6
*Stumpville* CA-9
*Stumpville* TX-5
Stumpy Basin—*hist pl* OH-6
Stumpy Bay—*bay* VI-3
Stumpy Bayou—*gut* LA-4
Stumpy Bayou—*stream* (3) LA-4
Stumpy Bottom—*flat* WV-2
Stumpy Bottom Ch—*church* WV-2
Stumpy Cove—*bay* NC-3
Stumpy Creek—*stream* (2) CO-8
Stumpy Creek—*stream* (3) NC-3
Stumpy Creek Access Area—*area* NC-3
Stumpy Creek Bay—*bay* NC-3
*Stumpy Inlet* NC-3
Stumpy Lake—*lake* (3) LA-4
Stumpy Lake—*lake* MN-6
Stumpy Lake—*lake* (2) TX-5
Stumpy Lake—*reservoir* VA-3
Stumpy Lake—*swamp* LA-4
Stumpy Lake Country Club—*other* VA-3
Stumpy Lake Dam—*dam* VA-3
Stumpy Meadows Lake—*reservoir* CA-9
Stumpy Point—*cape* AR-4
Stumpy Point—*cape* NC-3
Stumpy Point—*cape* VI-3
**Stumpy Point**—*pop pl* NC-3
Stumpy Point Bay—*bay* NC-3
Stumpy Pond—*lake* MA-1
Stumpy Run—*stream* WV-2
Stumpy Slough—*gut* TX-5
Stumpy Strand—*swamp* FL-3
Stumpy Wood Field—*park* MS-4
*Stunce Brook* WI-6
Stunehean Creek—*stream* AK-9
Stunkard Cem—*cemetery* IL-6
Stunkard Cem—*cemetery* IN-6
Stunkard Run—*stream* IN-6
Stunkel Cem—*cemetery* IN-6
*Stunkel Ditch* IN-6
*Stunkle Dit* IN-6
Stunls Ranch—*locale* CA-9
Stunner Cabin—*locale* CO-8
Stunner Campground—*locale* CO-8
Stunner Pass—*gap* CO-8
Stuntson Cem—*cemetery* TN-4
Stuntz and Hochstetler Pines
Airp—*airport* IN-6
Stuntz Bay—*bay* MN-6
Stuntz Brook—*stream* WI-6
Stuntz Draw—*valley* UT-8
Stuntz Ridge—*ridge* CO-8
Stuntz Ridge—*ridge* UT-8
Stuntz Rsvr—*reservoir* CO-8
Stuntz (Township of)—*other* MN-6
Stuphin Cem—*cemetery* VA-3
Stupid Creek—*stream* OR-9
*Stuple Branch* VA-3
*Stuples Branch* VA-3
Stuples Hollow—*valley* VA-3
**Sturbridge**—*pop pl* MA-1
*Sturbridge, Town of* MA-1
Sturbridge Common Hist Dist—*hist pl* MA-1
Sturbridge Plaza—*locale* MA-1
**Sturbridge (Town of)**—*pop pl* MA-1
Sturbridge Village Pond Dam—*dam* MA-1
Sturdervant Cem—*cemetery* OR-9
*Sturdevant* AL-4
*Sturdevant Brook* NY-2
Sturdevant Chapel (historical)—*church* MS-4
*Sturdevant Creek* AL-4
Sturdevant Creek—*stream* NY-2
Sturdevant Ditch—*canal* WY-8
Sturdevant Hill—*summit* NY-2
Sturdevant Hill—*summit* PA-2
Sturdevant Point—*cliff* AZ-5
Sturdevant Pond—*lake* PA-2
Sturdevant Ridge—*ridge* CA-9
Sturdevant Rock—*island* AK-9
Sturdevant Spring—*spring* OR-9
Sturdivant—*locale* AL-4
Sturdivant—*locale* TX-5
**Sturdivant**—*pop pl* MO-7
Sturdivant Branch—*stream* TX-5
Sturdivant Canal—*canal* LA-4
Sturdivant Cem—*cemetery* AL-4
Sturdivant Cem—*cemetery* MO-7
Sturdivant Ch (historical)—*church* MS-4
Sturdivant Creek—*stream* (2) AL-4
Sturdivant Crossing—*locale* TN-4
Sturdivant Fishweir—*hist pl* MS-4
Sturdivant Hall—*hist pl* AL-4
**Sturdivant (historical)**—*pop pl* MS-4
*Sturdivant Island* ME-1
Sturdivant Island—*island* ME-1
Sturdivant Island Ledges—*bar* ME-1
Sturdivant Park—*park* OR-9
*Sturdivants* NC-3
Sturdivant-Sawyer House—*hist pl* IA-7
Sturdivants Crossroads—*locale* NC-3
*Sturduvants Crossroads* NC-3
*Sturdvant Creek* NY-2
Sturdy Creek—*stream* OR-9
Sturdy Memorial Hosp—*hospital* MA-1
Sturgell Cem—*cemetery* (2) WV-2
Sturgell Fork—*stream* WV-2
Sturgeon—*locale* ID-8
Sturgeon—*locale* KY-4
Sturgeon—*locale* MN-6
Sturgeon—*locale* TX-5
**Sturgeon**—*pop pl* MO-7
**Sturgeon**—*pop pl* PA-2
Sturgeon, Robert H., House—*hist pl* MI-6
Sturgeon Bar—*island* MI-6
*Sturgeon Bar Island* MI-6
*Sturgeon Bay* WI-6
Sturgeon Bay—*bay* IL-6
Sturgeon Bay—*bay* (3) MI-6
Sturgeon Bay—*bay* MT-8
Sturgeon Bay—*bay* (2) WI-6
**Sturgeon Bay**—*pop pl* WI-6
*Sturgeon Bay Canal* WI-6
Sturgeon Bay Canal Lighthouse—*hist pl* WI-6
Sturgeon Bay Point—*cape* MI-6
Sturgeon Bay Ship Canal—*canal* WI-6
**Sturgeon Bay (Town of)**—*pop pl* WI-6
Sturgeon Bend—*bend* CA-9
Sturgeon Branch—*stream* (2) KY-4
Sturgeon Branch—*stream* VA-3
Sturgeon Branch—*stream* (2) WV-2
Sturgeon Branch—*stream* WI-6
Sturgeon Branch Ch—*church* WV-2
Sturgeon (CCD)—*cens area* KY-4
Sturgeon Cem—*cemetery* IN-6
Sturgeon Cem—*cemetery* IA-7
Sturgeon Cem—*cemetery* MO-7
Sturgeon Channel—*channel* MN-6
*Sturgeon Creek* ME-1
*Sturgeon Creek* MT-8
*Sturgeon Creek* NH-1
Sturgeon Creek—*stream* GA-3
Sturgeon Creek—*stream* KY-4
Sturgeon Creek—*stream* ME-1
Sturgeon Creek—*stream* MI-6
Sturgeon Creek—*stream* MT-8
Sturgeon Creek—*stream* NC-3
Sturgeon Creek—*stream* TN-4
Sturgeon Creek—*stream* (3) VA-3
Sturgeon Creek—*stream* WA-9
Sturgeon Creek—*stream* WY-8
Sturgeon Creek Bridge—*bridge* NC-3
Sturgeon Drain—*stream* NE-7
Sturgeon Falls—*falls* MI-6
Sturgeon Flats—*area* MA-1
Sturgeon Flats—*flat* MA-1
Sturgeon Ford (historical)—*locale* TN-4
Sturgeon Fork—*stream* WV-2
Sturgeon-Gregg House—*hist pl* KY-4
Sturgeon Head—*cliff* AK-9
Sturgeon Hill—*summit* IL-6
Sturgeon Hole—*bay* GA-3
Sturgeon Hole—*channel* NJ-2
Sturgeon Hole—*lake* VA-3
Sturgeon Hole Creek—*stream* MI-6
Sturgeon Hole Slough—*stream* MI-6
*Sturgeon Hollow* KY-4
Sturgeon House—*hist pl* PA-2
Sturgeon Island—*island* IL-6
Sturgeon Island—*island* KY-4
Sturgeon Island—*island* ME-1
Sturgeon Island—*island* MT-8
Sturgeon Island—*island* NJ-2
Sturgeon Island—*island* SC-3
*Sturgeon Lake* WI-6
Sturgeon Lake—*lake* MI-6
Sturgeon Lake—*lake* (3) MN-6
Sturgeon Lake—*lake* NE-7
Sturgeon Lake—*lake* OR-9
**Sturgeon Lake**—*pop pl* MN-6
Sturgeon Lake Mission—*church* MN-6
Sturgeon Lake (Township of)—*civ div* MN-6
Sturgeon Lateral—*canal* ID-8
Sturgeon Lateral—*canal* NE-7
Sturgeon (Magisterial District)—*fmr MCD* VA-3
Sturgeon Mtn—*summit* MT-8
Sturgeon-Noblestown—*CDP* PA-2
Sturgeon Pen Slough—*stream* WA-9
Sturgeon Point—*cape* (2) MI-6
Sturgeon Point—*cape* NJ-2
Sturgeon Point—*cape* (3) NY-2
Sturgeon Point—*cape* VA-3
**Sturgeon Point**—*pop pl* MI-6
Sturgeon Point Light Station—*hist pl* MI-6
Sturgeon Point State Park—*park* MI-6
Sturgeon Pond—*reservoir* NJ-2
Sturgeon Pool—*reservoir* NY-2
Sturgeon Ranch—*locale* NM-5
Sturgeon Ranch—*locale* WY-8
Sturgeon Ridge—*summit* AK-9
*Sturgeon River* MA-1
**Sturgeon River**—*pop pl* MI-6
Sturgeon River—*stream* AK-9
Sturgeon River—*stream* (4) MI-6
Sturgeon River—*stream* (2) MN-6
Sturgeon River Chapel—*church* MN-6
Sturgeon River Landing—*locale* MN-6
Sturgeon River State For—*forest* MI-6
Sturgeon River State For—*forest* MN-6
Sturgeon Rock—*summit* WA-9
Sturgeon Rsvr No 1—*reservoir* WY-8
Sturgeon Rsvr No 2—*reservoir* WY-8
Sturgeon Rsvr No 3—*reservoir* WY-8
Sturgeon Run—*stream* OH-6
Sturgeon Sch—*school* IL-6
Sturgeon Swamp—*stream* VA-3
**Sturgeon (Township of)**—*pop pl* MN-6
Sturgeonville—*locale* VA-3
**Sturges**—*pop pl* MO-7
Sturges, Jonathan, House—*hist pl* CT-1
Sturges, Oliver, House—*hist pl* GA-3
Sturges, Susan, House—*hist pl* OH-6
**Sturges Corner**—*pop pl* NY-2
Sturges Creek—*stream* MD-2
*Sturges Fork* OR-9
Sturges Hill—*summit* NY-2
Sturges Hills—*other* NY-2
Sturges JHS—*school* CA-9
Sturges Ridge—*ridge* CT-1
Sturgess Island—*island* AK-9
Sturgill—*locale* OR-9
Sturgill Branch—*stream* (2) KY-4
Sturgill Branch—*stream* VA-3
Sturgill Cem—*cemetery* IL-6
Sturgill Cem—*cemetery* KY-4
Sturgill Cem—*cemetery* NC-3
Sturgill Cem—*cemetery* VA-3
Sturgill Ch—*church* NC-3
Sturgill Creek—*stream* ID-8
Sturgill Creek—*stream* OR-9
Sturgill Peak—*summit* ID-8
Sturgill Peak—*summit* OR-9
Sturgill Rapids—*rapids* ID-8
Sturgill Rapids—*rapids* OR-9
**Sturgills**—*pop pl* NC-3
Sturgis—*locale* OK-5
**Sturgis**—*pop pl* KY-4
**Sturgis**—*pop pl* MI-6
**Sturgis**—*pop pl* MS-4
**Sturgis**—*pop pl* PA-2
**Sturgis**—*pop pl* SD-7
Sturgis, Julius, Pretzel House—*hist pl* PA-2
Sturgis, William, House—*hist pl* WY-8
Sturgis and Haskell Bldg—*hist pl* ME-1
Sturgis Attendance Center—*school* MS-4
Sturgis Baptist Ch—*church* MS-4
Sturgis (CCD)—*cens area* KY-4
Sturgis Cem—*cemetery* MS-4
Sturgis Commercial Block—*hist pl* SD-7
Sturgis Corners—*locale* PA-2
Sturgis Creek—*stream* MI-6
Sturgis Dam—*dam* MI-6
*Sturgis Ditch* MI-6
Sturgis Drain—*canal* (3) MI-6
Sturgis Drain—*stream* MI-6
Sturgis Fork—*stream* OR-9
Sturgis Guard Station—*locale* OR-9
Sturgis Hill—*summit* AR-4
Sturgis Library—*building* MA-1
**Sturgis Mill**—*pop pl* TX-5
Sturgis Mine—*mine* OR-9
Sturgis Municipal Airp—*airport* SD-7
Sturgis Natl Bank—*hist pl* TX-5
Sturgis Pond—*reservoir* AR-4
Sturgis Prairie—*flat* FL-3
Sturgis Presbyterian Ch—*church* MS-4
Sturgis Reservoirs—*reservoir* SD-7
Sturgis Sandstone Quarry—*mine* SD-7
Sturgiss Ch—*church* WV-2
**Sturgisson**—*pop pl* WV-2
Sturgisson Ch—*church* WV-2
Sturgiss Sch—*school* WV-2
**Sturgis (Township of)**—*pop pl* MI-6
Sturgis Training Center—*school* MI-6
Sturgis United Methodist Ch—*church* MS-4
*Sturkee Creek* AL-4
Sturkey—*locale* FL-3
Sturkey, M. L. B., House—*hist pl* SC-3
Sturkie—*locale* AL-4
**Sturkie**—*pop pl* AR-4
Sturkie Cem—*cemetery* AL-4
Sturkie Ch—*church* AR-4
Sturkie Creek—*stream* AL-4
Sturlese Lake—*lake* LA-4
Sturley Windmill—*locale* NM-5
Sturm, Louis, House—*hist pl* MI-6
Sturm Cem—*cemetery* IL-6
Sturm Cem—*cemetery* OH-6
Sturm Cem—*cemetery* WV-2
Sturm Creek—*stream* WA-9
*Sturm Island* TN-4
Sturm Island—*island* FL-3
Sturm Ranch—*locale* SD-7
Sturms Mill—*locale* WV-2
S Turn, The—*bend* MO-7
Sturr Pond—*reservoir* NJ-2
*Sturrup Iron Creek* NC-3
**Sturtevant**—*pop pl* WI-6
Sturtevant, Leonard, House—*hist pl* MA-1
Sturtevant Bay—*bay* NH-1
Sturtevant Bridge—*bridge* MA-1
Sturtevant Brook—*stream* NH-1
Sturtevant Camp—*locale* CA-9
Sturtevant Cove—*bay* ME-1
Sturtevant Creek—*stream* OR-9
Sturtevant Falls—*falls* CA-9
Sturtevant Hall—*hist pl* ME-1
Sturtevant Hill—*locale* ME-1
Sturtevant Lake—*lake* WA-9
**Sturtevant Mill**—*pop pl* MA-1
Sturtevant Mtn—*summit* ME-1
*Sturtevant Pond* MA-1

Sturtevant Pond—*lake* ME-1
Sturtevant Sch—*school* MI-6
Sturtevant Stream—*stream* ME-1
Sturtz Ranch—*locale* NE-7
Sturtz Sch—*school* IL-6
Sturvesant Square—*park* NY-2
**Sturwood Hamlet**—*pop pl* NJ-2
Stussi, Henry, House—*hist pl* MN-6
Stussi Creek—*stream* OR-9
Stutheit Cem—*cemetery* NE-7
Stutler Canyon—*valley* CA-9
Stutler Canyon—*valley* NV-8
Stutler Fork—*stream* WV-2
Stutler Hollow—*valley* WV-2
Stutler Run—*stream* WV-2
Stutsman Cem—*cemetery* IN-6
Stutsman County—*civil* ND-7
Stutsman County Courthouse and Sheriff's Residence/Jail—*hist pl* ND-7
Stutsman County Rec Area—*park* ND-7
**Stutsmanville**—*pop pl* MI-6
Stutson Chapel—*church* MS-4
Stutter Spring—*spring* AZ-5
**Stuttgart**—*pop pl* AR-4
**Stuttgart**—*pop pl* KS-7
Stuttgart King Bayou—*canal* AR-4
Stutton, H. P., House—*hist pl* NE-7
**Stutts**—*pop pl* MO-7
Stutts Cem—*cemetery* (2) AL-4
Stutts Chapel—*church* MS-4
*Stutts Chapel Ch of Christ* MS-4
Stutts Creek—*stream* MI-6
Stutts (historical)—*locale* AL-4
*Stutts Road Church* AL-4
Stutts Sch (historical)—*school* AL-4
Stutts Spring Cave—*cave* AL-4
Stutz Ditch—*canal* IN-6
Stutzman Sch—*school* PA-2
Stutz Ranch—*locale* CA-9
Stutz Well—*well* AZ-5
Stuver, Mount—*summit* AK-9
Stuver Creek—*stream* AK-9
Stuyahok—*locale* AK-9
**Stuyahok**—*pop pl* (2) AK-9
Stuyahok Hills—*other* AK-9
Stuyahok Mine—*mine* AK-9
Stuyahok River—*stream* (2) AK-9
*Stuyvesant* NY-2
**Stuyvesant**—*pop pl* NY-2
Stuyvesant—*uninc pl* NY-2
Stuyvesant Brook—*stream* NY-2
**Stuyvesant Falls**—*pop pl* NY-2
Stuyvesant Falls Cem—*cemetery* NY-2
Stuyvesant Falls Mill District—*hist pl* NY-2
Stuyvesant Hall—*hist pl* OH-6
Stuyvesant Heights Hist Dist—*hist pl* NY-2
**Stuyvesant Hills**—*pop pl* DE-2
Stuyvesant Springs—*spring* NM-5
Stuyvesant Square Hist Dist—*hist pl* NY-2
**Stuyvesant (Town of)**—*pop pl* NY-2
St. Vincent De Paul Catholic Church—*hist pl* MO-7
St. Vincent's Hosp—*hist pl* MO-7
St. Wendelin Catholic Church, School, and Rectory—*hist pl* OH-6
S-Two Canal—*canal* NV-8
**St. Xavier**—*pop pl* MT-8
Stybr Rsvr No. 2—*reservoir* CO-8
Stygler Road Sch—*school* OH-6
Styler Ditch—*canal* UT-8
Styler Rsvr—*reservoir* UT-8
Styles Bayou—*stream* TX-5
Styles Brook—*stream* (2) NY-2
Styles Brook—*stream* VT-1
Styles Cem—*cemetery* ME-1
Styles Cem—*cemetery* TX-5
Styles Creek—*stream* FL-3
Styles Creek—*stream* TX-5
Styles Falls—*falls* VA-3
Styles Lake—*lake* WI-6
*Styles Mountain* ME-1
Styles Mtn—*summit* AR-4
Styles Number 1 Dam—*dam* SD-7
Styles Peak—*summit* VT-1
Styles Run—*stream* WV-2
Styllis Run—*stream* PA-2
**Stylon**—*pop pl* AL-4
Stylus Lake—*lake* MI-6
Stypes Branch—*stream* VA-3
*Styran Bay* NC-3
*Styrans Bay* NC-3
Styre Canyon—*valley* NE-7
Styron Airp—*airport* AL-4
Styron Bay—*bay* NC-3
Styron Creek—*stream* (2) NC-3
Styron Hills—*summit* NC-3
Styx—*locale* CA-9
Styx—*locale* TX-5
Styx, River—*stream* GA-3
Styx Branch—*stream* TN-4
Styx Canyon—*valley* OK-5
Styx Creek—*stream* WA-9
Styx Lake—*lake* AK-9
Styx River—*stream* AL-4
Styx River—*stream* AK-9
Styx River—*stream* FL-3
Styx River—*stream* KY-4
Styx River—*stream* OH-6
Styx River Ch—*church* AL-4
Styx State Fish Hatchery—*other* SC-3
Suaavamuli Ridge—*ridge* AS-9
Sua (County of)—*civ div* AS-9
*Suah Creek* TN-4
Suaia Stream—*stream* AS-9
**Suamico**—*pop pl* WI-6
*Suamico River* WI-6
Suamico River—*stream* WI-6
**Suamico (Town of)**—*pop pl* WI-6
Suamme Camp—*locale* PA-2
Suanee Creek—*stream* VA-3
Suappoa, Mount—*summit* AZ-5
Suarez—*CDP* PR-3
**Suarez**—*pop pl* PR-3
Suarez Point—*cape* AL-4
*Suavatooky* MS-4
Suazo Canyon—*valley* NM-5
Subaco—*locale* CA-9
Sub-Agency Ditch—*canal* WY-8
*Subeebeda* WA-9
*Subeebeeda* WA-9

Subeet—*locale* CA-9
Suber Cem—*cemetery* TN-4
Suber Memorial Gardens—*cemetery* FL-3
Subers Creek—*stream* SC-3
Sube Vaja Windmill—*locale* TX-5
Sub Howard Cem—*cemetery* KY-4
**Subiaco**—*pop pl* AR-4
Subiaco Rsvr—*reservoir* AR-4
Subia Ranch—*locale* AZ-5
Subira House—*hist pl* PR-3
*Sublet Creek* WY-8
Sublet Ditch—*canal* WY-8
*Sublet Ferry* AL-4
*Sublet Mountains* WY-8
Sublet Sch (historical)—*school* AL-4
*Sublets Ferry* AL-4
*Sublett* MO-7
Sublett—*locale* KY-4
Sublett—*locale* TX-5
**Sublett**—*pop pl* ID-8
Sublett Bluff—*cliff* AL-4
Sublett Bluff Cave—*cave* AL-4
Sublett Cave—*cave* AL-4
Sublett Cem—*cemetery* AL-4
Sublett Cem—*cemetery* TX-5
Sublett Creek—*stream* ID-8
Sublette—*locale* CO-8
Sublette—*locale* NM-5
**Sublette**—*pop pl* CO-8
**Sublette**—*pop pl* IL-6
**Sublette**—*pop pl* KS-7
**Sublette**—*pop pl* MO-7
Sublette and Campbell Post (historical)—*locale* SD-7
Sublette Canyon—*valley* ID-8
Sublette Creek—*stream* WY-8
Sublette Elem Sch—*school* KS-7
Sublette Flat—*flat* WY-8
Sublette Flying Club Land Strip—*airport* KS-7
Sublette HS—*school* KS-7
Sublette Mtn—*summit* WY-8
Sublette Park—*park* MO-7
Sublette Peak—*summit* WY-8
Sublette Range—*range* WY-8
Sublette Sch—*school* IL-6
Sublettes Flat—*flat* WY-8
**Sublette (Township of)**—*pop pl* IL-6
Sublette Well No 4—*well* WY-8
Sublette Well No 5—*well* WY-8
Sublett Ferry (historical)—*locale* AL-4
Sublett Forest Service Station—*locale* ID-8
Sublett Gap—*gap* AL-4
Sublett Gap Hollow—*valley* AL-4
Sublett Mill—*locale* AL-4
Sublett Point—*cape* AL-4
Sublett Range—*range* ID-8
Sublett Rsvr—*reservoir* ID-8
Subletts—*locale* VA-3
Subletts Cem—*cemetery* VA-3
Subletts Lake—*reservoir* KY-4
Sublett Troughs—*spring* ID-8
**Subligna**—*pop pl* GA-3
Subligna Cem—*cemetery* GA-3
**Sublime**—*pop pl* TX-5
Sublime, Point—*cape* AZ-5
*Sublime Point* AZ-5
**Sublimity**—*pop pl* OR-9
Sublimity Branch—*stream* KY-4
Sublimity Ch—*church* KY-4
**Sublimity City**—*pop pl* KY-4
Sublimity Elem Sch—*school* OR-9
Sublimity Hollow—*valley* KY-4
Sublimity Sch—*school* KY-4
*Submarine Base* HI-9
*Submarine Base (New London Naval Submarine Base)* CT-1
Submarine Creek—*stream* AK-9
Submarine Hole—*rapids* OR-9
Submarine Lake—*lake* AK-9
Submarine Lake—*lake* FL-3
Submarine Mine—*mine* WA-9
Submarine Point—*cape* NV-8
*Submarine Rock* AZ-5
Submarine Rock—*island* OR-9
Submissive Ch—*church* OH-6
Sub-Penitentiary Lake—*reservoir* OK-5
Sub Point—*cape* AK-9
Sub Rosa—*hist pl* MS-4
Sub Rosa Gulch—*valley* ID-8
Substitute Point—*cape* OR-9
Substitute Tank—*reservoir* AZ-5
Substitute Tank—*reservoir* NM-5
**Subtle**—*pop pl* KY-4
Suburb—*locale* NC-3
**Suburban**—*pop pl* NJ-2
**Suburban Acres**—*pop pl* VA-3
**Suburban Acres (subdivision)**—*pop pl* MS-4
**Suburban Apartments**—*pop pl* VA-3
Suburban Baptist Ch—*church* IN-6
Suburban Canal—*canal* LA-4
Suburban Canal—*canal* NE-7
*Suburban Ch* IN-6
Suburban Ch—*church* VA-3
Suburban Club Golf Course—*other* MD-2
Suburban Country Club—*other* VA-3
Suburban Ditch—*canal* MT-8
Suburban Enfield Mall—*locale* CT-1
Suburban Estates—*other* MD-2
**Suburban Estates**—*pop pl* IL-6
*Suburban Gardens* IN-6
Suburban General Hospital Airp—*airport* PA-2
Suburban Golf Course—*other* NJ-2
**Suburban Heights**—*pop pl* FL-3
Suburban Heights—*uninc pl* KS-7
**Suburban Heights (Baldwin Heights)**—*pop pl* IL-6
**Suburban Heights (subdivision)**—*pop pl* AL-4
**Suburban Heights Subdivision**—*pop pl* UT-8
Suburban Helistop—*airport* NJ-2
**Suburban Hills**—*pop pl* (2) TN-4
Suburban Hosp—*hospital* AL-4
Suburban Hosp—*hospital* MD-2
Suburban Hosp—*hospital* TN-4
Suburban Lake—*reservoir* PA-2
Suburban (Magisterial District)—*fmr MCD* WV-2
Suburban Memorial Gardens—*cemetery* PA-2
**Suburban Park**—*pop pl* MA-1

**Suburban Park**—*pop pl* NJ-2
**Suburban Park**—*pop pl* VA-3
Suburban Park Sch—*school* VA-3
Suburban Peak—*summit* ID-8
Suburban Sch—*school* VA-3
Suburban Shooping Center—*locale* TN-4
**Suburban Shores**—*pop pl* TN-4
Suburban Station Bldg—*hist pl* PA-2
**Suburban View Subdivision**—*pop pl* UT-8
**Suburban Village**—*pop pl* PA-2
**Suburban Woods (subdivision)**—*pop pl* NC-3
Suburba Post Office (historical)—*building* TN-4
Subway, The—*crossing* UT-8
Subway Cave—*cave* CA-9
*Sucanatchie River* MS-4
*Sucanochee* MS-4
S U Canyon—*valley* NM-5
*Sucapatova* AL-4
*Sucapatoya Creek* AL-4
Sucarbowa Creek—*stream* AL-4
**Sucarnochee**—*pop pl* MS-4
*Sucarnooche* MS-4
**Sucarnoochee**—*pop pl* MS-4
Sucarnoochee Post Office (historical)—*building* MS-4
Sucarnoochee River—*stream* AL-4
Sucarnoochee Sch (historical)—*school* MS-4
Sucarnoochie River—*stream* MS-4
*Sucarn River* AL-4
Sucatolba Creek—*stream* MS-4
*Succanesset Point* MA-1
*Succanesset Shoal* MA-1
**Succasunna**—*pop pl* NJ-2
Succasunna Brook—*stream* NJ-2
Succasunna-Kenvil—*CDP* NJ-2
Succasunna Plains—*flat* NJ-2
Success—*locale* MO-7
Success—*locale* NJ-2
Success—*locale* OK-5
Success—*locale* VA-3
**Success**—*pop pl* AR-4
**Success**—*pop pl* CA-9
**Success**—*pop pl* MS-4
**Success**—*pop pl* OH-6
Success, Lake—*lake* NY-2
Success, Lake—*lake* WA-9
Success, Lake—*reservoir* CA-9
Success, Lake—*reservoir* NJ-2
Success, Mount—*summit* NH-1
Success Baptist Ch—*church* MS-4
Success Branch—*stream* NJ-2
Success Cem—*cemetery* MS-4
Success Ch—*church* IL-6
Success Ch—*church* MO-7
Success Ch—*church* OH-6
Success Cleaver—*ridge* WA-9
Success Creek—*stream* WA-9
Success Dam—*dam* CA-9
Success Divide—*ridge* WA-9
**Success Estates**—*pop pl* UT-8
Successful Sales Company—*hist pl* OH-6
Success Glacier—*glacier* WA-9
Success Hill—*summit* CT-1
Success Hill—*summit* NH-1
Success (historical)—*locale* KS-7
**Success (historical)**—*pop pl* MS-4
**Success (historical)**—*pop pl* SD-7
Success Lake—*lake* CT-1
Success Lake—*reservoir* NJ-2
Success Lake Dam—*dam* NJ-2
Success Mine—*mine* CA-9
Success Mine—*mine* (2) NV-8
Success Mine—*mine* WA-9
Success Pond—*lake* NH-1
Success Post Office (historical)—*building* MS-4
*Success Reservoir* CA-9
Success Rock—*bar* NY-2
Success Sch—*school* MO-7
Success Sch (abandoned)—*school* (2) MO-7
Success Sch (historical)—*school* MS-4
Success Sch (historical)—*school* MO-7
Success Sch (historical)—*school* TN-4
Success School (historical)—*locale* MO-7
Success Spring (Dry)—*spring* ID-8
Success Summit—*gap* NV-8
Success (Township of)—*fmr MCD* NH-1
Success Trail—*trail* NH-1
*Succoneset Point* MA-1
*Succonessetts Shoal* MA-1
Succonnesset Point—*cape* MA-1
Succonnesset Shoal—*bar* MA-1
Succonnessett Pond—*lake* MA-1
*Succonnessett Ponds* MA-1
*Succonnessitt* MA-1
*Succonusset* MA-1
Succor Branch—*stream* NC-3
Succor Corners—*locale* DE-2
Succor Creek—*stream* ID-8
Succor Creek—*stream* OR-9
*Succor Creek Rec Area* OR-9
Succor Creek Siphon—*canal* OR-9
Succor Creek State Rec Area—*park* (2) OR-9
*Succor Creek Tunnel* OR-9
Succor Flat—*flat* CA-9
Succor Mine—*mine* NV-8
Succotash Point—*cape* RI-1
*Suce Creek* TN-4
Suce Creek—*stream* MT-8
Suce Creek Sch—*school* MT-8
Suches—*locale* GA-3
Suches (CCD)—*cens area* GA-3
Suches Creek—*stream* GA-3
Such Joja Rsvr—*reservoir* OR-9
**Suchville**—*pop pl* PR-3
Sucia Island—*island* WA-9
Sucia Island State Park—*park* WA-9
Sucia Ledge—*other* AK-9
*Sucio Island* WA-9
Suck, The—*area* TN-4
Suck, The—*bend* VA-3
*Suckanesset, Town of* MA-1
*Suckasunny* NJ-2
Suckatunkanuc Hill—*summit* RI-1
Suck Bar—*bar* TN-4
Suck Branch—*stream* (2) AL-4
Suck Branch—*stream* NC-3
Suck Branch—*stream* (2) TN-4
Suck Branch—*stream* VA-3
Suck Creek—*locale* WV-2

**Suck Creek**—*pop pl* TN-4
Suck Creek—*stream* (2) AL-4
Suck Creek—*stream* AR-4
Suck Creek—*stream* IL-6
Suck Creek—*stream* (3) NC-3
Suck Creek—*stream* SC-3
Suck Creek—*stream* TN-4
Suck Creek—*stream* VA-3
Suck Creek—*stream* WV-2
Suck Creek Ch—*church* SC-3
Suck Creek Ch—*church* TN-4
Suck Creek Sch—*school* TN-4
Suckegg Branch—*stream* VA-3
Suck-egg Hollow—*valley* TN-4
Suckell Pond—*lake* WA-9
*Sucker* MI-6
*Sucker* WI-6
Sucker Bay—*bay* MN-6
*Sucker Branch* WI-6
Sucker Branch—*stream* MD-2
Sucker Branch—*stream* MN-6
*Sucker Brook* MA-1
Sucker Brook—*locale* NY-2
Sucker Brook—*stream* (6) CT-1
Sucker Brook—*stream* (16) ME-1
Sucker Brook—*stream* (6) MA-1
Sucker Brook—*stream* MN-6
Sucker Brook—*stream* (5) NH-1
Sucker Brook—*stream* NJ-2
Sucker Brook—*stream* (17) NY-2
Sucker Brook—*stream* (2) RI-1
Sucker Brook—*stream* (7) VT-1
Sucker Brook Bay—*bay* NY-2
Sucker Brook Cove—*cove* MA-1
Sucker Brook Dam—*dam* CT-1
Sucker Brook Dam—*dam* VT-1
*Sucker Brook Falls* VT-1
Sucker Brook Hill—*summit* ME-1
Sucker Brook Pond—*lake* ME-1
Sucker Brook Shelter—*locale* VT-1
Sucker Brook Trail—*trail* NY-2
Sucker Brook Trail—*trail* VT-1
*Sucker Creek* ID-8
*Sucker Creek* MI-6
*Sucker Creek* OR-9
Sucker Creek—*stream* AL-4
Sucker Creek—*stream* AK-9
Sucker Creek—*stream* AR-4
Sucker Creek—*stream* CA-9
Sucker Creek—*stream* CO-8
Sucker Creek—*stream* (2) ID-8
Sucker Creek—*stream* (11) MI-6
Sucker Creek—*stream* (9) MN-6
Sucker Creek—*stream* (3) MT-8
Sucker Creek—*stream* NY-2
Sucker Creek—*stream* (5) OR-9
Sucker Creek—*stream* VT-1
Sucker Creek—*stream* WA-9
Sucker Creek—*stream* (8) WI-6
Sucker Creek—*stream* WY-8
Sucker Creek Drain—*canal* (2) MI-6
Sucker Creek Gap—*gap* OR-9
Sucker Creek Number One—*stream* MN-6
Sucker Creek Number Two—*stream* MN-6
Sucker Creek Shelter—*locale* OR-9
Sucker Creek Trail—*trail* OR-9
Sucker Dam—*dam* WY-8
*Sucker Flat* CA-9
Sucker Flat—*flat* ID-8
Sucker Flat—*locale* CA-9
Sucker Gulch—*valley* AZ-5
Sucker Gulch—*valley* ID-8
Sucker Gulch—*valley* MT-8
**Sucker (historical)**—*pop pl* OR-9
Sucker Hole Hill—*summit* NY-2
*Sucker Lake* ID-8
*Sucker Lake* MN-6
*Sucker Lake* WI-6
Sucker Lake—*lake* (3) AK-9
Sucker Lake—*lake* CA-9
Sucker Lake—*lake* GA-3
Sucker Lake—*lake* IN-6
Sucker Lake—*lake* ME-1
Sucker Lake—*lake* (5) MI-6
Sucker Lake—*lake* (4) MN-6
Sucker Lake—*lake* NY-2
Sucker Lake—*lake* ND-7
Sucker Lake—*lake* WI-6
Sucker Lake—*lake* WY-8
Sucker Lake—*reservoir* MN-6
*Sucker Lakes* MI-6
Sucker Lakes—*lake* MN-6
Sucker Point—*cape* MI-6
Sucker Point—*cape* PA-2
*Sucker Pond* NH-1
*Sucker Pond* NJ-2
*Sucker Pond* VT-1
Sucker Pond—*lake* MA-1
Sucker Pond—*lake* (2) NY-2
Sucker Pond—*reservoir* RI-1
*Sucker Pond Brook* RI-1
Sucker Pond Dam—*dam* RI-1
*Sucker Ponds* MI-6
*Sucker River* MN-6
Sucker River—*stream* AK-9
Sucker River—*stream* MI-6
Sucker Rsvr—*reservoir* WY-8
Sucker Run—*stream* CA-9
Sucker Run—*stream* (2) PA-2
Sucker Run Creek—*stream* OH-6
Sucker Slough—*stream* OR-9
Sucker Spring—*spring* OR-9
Sucker Spring—*spring* WY-8
Suckerville—*locale* ME-1
Suckerville Draw—*valley* NM-5
Suckerville Spring—*spring* CO-8
Suckey Lake—*lake* MI-6
Suck Gap—*gap* AL-4
Suck Hole—*bay* FL-3
Suck Hollow—*valley* (2) AR-4
Suck Hollow—*valley* TN-4
Suckik Creek—*stream* (2) AK-9
Suckles Lake—*lake* AR-4
Suck Lick Hollow—*valley* VA-3
Suck Lick Run—*stream* WV-2
Suckling Hills—*other* AK-9
Suck Mtn—*summit* (2) AR-4
Suck Mtn—*summit* VA-3
Suckow, Ruth, House—*hist pl* IA-7
Suck Point—*cape* TN-4

**Suckpoo**—*pop pl* ID-8
Suck Run—*stream* OH-6
Sucks, The—*area* TX-5
Sucksand Branch—*stream* SC-3
Sucks Fork—*stream* KY-4
Suck Shoals—*bar* TN-4
Suck Spring—*spring* UT-8
Suck Spring Ch—*church* VA-3
Suckstem Branch—*stream* TN-4
Suckstone Creek—*stream* TN-4
*Sucktaloosa Bluff* AL-4
*Suconeset Shoal Succonesset Shoal* MA-1
Suconnix State Wildlife Mngmt Area—*park* MN-6
Sucro—*locale* CA-9
Suction Butte—*summit* MT-8
Suction Creek—*stream* MT-8
Suction Point—*cliff* CO-8
Sudah Branch—*stream* WI-6
Sudall Ranch—*locale* CA-9
Sudan—*locale* PA-2
**Sudan**—*pop pl* TX-5
Sudan-Amherst (CCD)—*cens area* TX-5
Sudan Cem—*cemetery* TX-5
Sudan Creek—*stream* OR-9
Sudan Ditch—*canal* CA-9
Sudan Lake—*reservoir* TX-5
*Sudan Station* PA-2
Sud (Barrio)—*fmr MCD* PR-3
Sudberry Cem—*cemetery* TN-4
Sudbrook Ch—*church* MD-2
Sudbrook Park—*hist pl* MD-2
**Sudbrook Park**—*pop pl* MD-2
Sudbury—*locale* WA-9
**Sudbury**—*pop pl* MA-1
**Sudbury**—*pop pl* VT-1
**Sudbury Center**—*pop pl* MA-1
Sudbury Center Hist Dist—*hist pl* MA-1
*Sudbury Centre* MA-1
Sudbury Congregational Church—*hist pl* VT-1
Sudbury Dam—*dam* MA-1
Sudbury Plaza—*locale* MA-1
Sudbury Pond—*reservoir* MA-1
Sudbury Ranch—*locale* WY-8
Sudbury River—*stream* MA-1
Sudbury River Aqueduct (historical)—*canal* MA-1
Sudbury River Dam—*dam* (2) MA-1
Sudbury River Rsvr—*reservoir* (2) MA-1
Sudbury River Rsvr Number One—*reservoir* MA-1
Sudbury River Swamp—*swamp* MA-1
**Sudbury (RR name South Sudbury)**—*pop pl* MA-1
Sudbury Rsvr—*reservoir* MA-1
Sudbury Sch—*school* AR-4
Sudbury Sch No. 3—*hist pl* VT-1
**Sudbury (sta.)**—*pop pl* MA-1
**Sudbury (Town of)**—*pop pl* MA-1
**Sudbury (Town of)**—*pop pl* VT-1
Suddath Cem—*cemetery* TN-4
*Suddaths Ferry* TN-4
Suddawig Bottom—*bend* NC-3
Suddawig Branch—*stream* NC-3
Sudden—*locale* CA-9
Sudden Canyon—*valley* CA-9
Sudden Flats—*flat* CA-9
Sudden Lake—*lake* MI-6
Sudden Lake—*lake* MT-8
Sudden Peak—*summit* CA-9
Sudden Pond—*lake* MA-1
Sudden Stream—*stream* AK-9
Sudder Park—*park* AZ-5
Sudders Fork—*stream* KY-4
Sudderth Branch—*stream* NC-3
Suddeth Cem—*cemetery* AL-4
Suddruth Windmill—*locale* NM-5
*Sud-Durchfahrt* MP-9
Sudduth—*locale* IL-6
Sudduth—*locale* TX-5
Sudduth Branch—*stream* KY-4
Sudduth Cem—*cemetery* AL-4
Sudduth Cem—*cemetery* KY-4
Sudduth Cem—*cemetery* MS-4
Sudduth Cem—*cemetery* TX-5
Sudduth Coal Mine—*mine* CO-8
Sudduth Ditch No. 1—*canal* CO-8
Sudduth Draw—*valley* CO-8
*Sudduth Elementary School* MS-4
Sudduth Pond—*reservoir* SC-3
Sudduth Sch—*school* IL-6
Sudduth Sch—*school* (2) MS-4
*Sud-Einfahrt* MP-9
Sudekum Bldg—*hist pl* TN-4
Su-Dennie Dock—*locale* TN-4
Suder Sch—*school* IL-6
Sudheimer—*locale* MO-7
Sudie—*locale* GA-3
Sud Island—*island* AK-9
Sudith—*locale* KY-4
Sudler House—*hist pl* DE-2
Sudler's Conclusion—*hist pl* MD-2
**Sudlersville**—*pop pl* MD-2
*Sudlerville* MD-2
Sudley—*CDP* VA-3
Sudley—*hist pl* MD-2
Sudley—*locale* MD-2
Sudley Place—*hist pl* TN-4
*Sudley Spring* VA-3
Sudley Springs—*locale* VA-3
Sudlow Branch—*stream* NC-3
Sudlow JHS—*school* IA-7
Sudlow Lake—*lake* SC-3
Sudman Sch—*school* MI-6
*Sudost Durchfahrt* MP-9
*Sudost-Spitze* MP-9
*Sudse Creek* OR-9
Suds Run—*stream* WV-2
*Sudwest Durchfahrt* MP-9
Sudy, Lake—*reservoir* SC-3
Sue—*locale* TX-5
Sue—*locale* WV-2
Sue, Lake—*lake* FL-3
Sue, Lake—*reservoir* AR-4
Sue, Lake—*reservoir* TX-5
Sueann—*locale* AL-4
Sueann, Lake—*reservoir* AL-4
*Sueann Dam* AL-4
**Sue Ann Subdivision**—*pop pl* UT-8
Sue Bennett Coll—*school* KY-4

Sue City—*locale* MO-7
Sue City Cem—*cemetery* MO-7
Sue City Community Hall—*building* MO-7
Sue Creek—*stream* AK-9
Sue Creek—*stream* MD-2
**Suedberg**—*pop pl* PA-2
Suedberg Fossil Site—*locale* PA-2
**Suedburg (Suedberg)**—*pop pl* PA-2
Suedekum Cem—*cemetery* MO-7
*Suedeland* PA-2
Suedla Island—*island* AK-9
*Suee Creek* TN-4
*Suee Landing* TN-4
Sue Ellen Street Park—*park* MS-4
Sueet Slough—*lake* ND-7
Sue Hollow—*valley* KY-4
Sue Island—*island* MD-2
Suei-va Suei Va Spring—*spring* AZ-5
Sue Jane Coulee—*valley* MT-8
Sue Lake—*lake* MT-8
Suellen Cem—*cemetery* KY-4
Suelo, Puerto del—*gap* CA-9
Suelthaus Ford—*locale* MO-7
*Su Eltso Springs* AZ-5
**Sueltz Spur**—*pop pl* ND-7
Suemez Island—*island* AK-9
Sue Mine—*mine* AZ-5
Sueno Park—*park* AZ-5
Suent Lake—*reservoir* MS-4
Sue Peaks—*summit* TX-5
Sue Rudy Run—*stream* MD-2
Suesave Point—*cape* AS-9
Sues Branch—*stream* KY-4
Sues Draft—*valley* VA-3
Suesie Branch—*stream* KY-4
*Suess Creek* TN-4
Sues Spring—*spring* MO-7
Sues Spring Hollow—*valley* MO-7
Suess State Wildlife Mngmt Area—*park* MN-6
Sues Tank—*reservoir* AZ-5
Sue-Win Playground—*park* MI-6
Suey—*civil* CA-9
**Suey**—*pop pl* CA-9
Suey Canyon—*valley* CA-9
Suey Creek—*stream* CA-9
Suey Park—*park* CA-9
*Suez River* WA-9
**Suez (Township of)**—*pop pl* IL-6
Suffer Brake—*swamp* MS-4
Suffering Gulch—*valley* AZ-5
Suffering Wash—*stream* AZ-5
Sufferin Smith Spring—*spring* OR-9
**Suffern**—*pop pl* NY-2
Suffern-Bear Mountain Trail—*trail* NY-2
Suffern HS—*school* NY-2
**Suffern Park**—*pop pl* NY-2
**Suffield**—*pop pl* CT-1
**Suffield**—*pop pl* (2) OH-6
Suffield, Town of—*civil* CT-1
Suffield Acad—*school* CT-1
**Suffield Center**—*pop pl* CT-1
**Suffield Corner**—*pop pl* MA-1
*Suffield Equivalent Lands* MA-1
Suffield Hist Dist—*hist pl* CT-1
**Suffield Station**—*pop pl* OH-6
**Suffield (Town of)**—*pop pl* CT-1
**Suffield (Township of)**—*pop pl* OH-6
*Suffolk* PA-2
**Suffolk**—*pop pl* MS-4
**Suffolk**—*pop pl* MT-8
**Suffolk**—*pop pl* TX-5
Suffolk City—*civil* VA-3
**Suffolk County**—*pop pl* MA-1
**Suffolk (County)**—*pop pl* NY-2
Suffolk County AFB—*military* NY-2
Suffolk County Airport—*mil airp* NY-2
Suffolk County Almshouse Barn—*hist pl* NY-2
Suffolk County Community Coll—*school* NY-2
Suffolk County Courthouse—*hist pl* MA-1
Suffolk County Jail—*hist pl* MA-1
Suffolk County Park—*park* NY-2
**Suffolk Developmental Center**—*pop pl* NY-2
Suffolk Downs Park—*park* (2) MA-1
**Suffolk Downs Station**—*pop pl* MA-1
Suffolk Hills Sch—*school* AZ-5
Suffolk Hist Dist—*hist pl* VA-3
**Suffolk (ind. city)**—*pop pl* VA-3
Suffolk Manufacturing Company—*building* MA-1
Suffolk Mine—*mine* CO-8
Suffolk Park—*park* PA-2
Suffolk Resolves House—*hist pl* MA-1
Suffolk State Sch—*school* NY-2
Sufrett Creek—*stream* FL-3
Sufrett Cutoff—*bend* FL-3
Sufrido Tank—*reservoir* AZ-5
Sufrimiento Windmill—*locale* TX-5
Sufrosa Windmill—*locale* TX-5
Sugakuik Creek—*stream* AK-9
Sugan Branch—*stream* TN-4
*Sugar* UT-8
Sugar—*locale* CO-8
Sugar Ball—*basin* NH-1
Sugar Bar—*bar* AR-4
Sugar Bay—*bay* FL-3
Sugar Bay—*bay* KY-4
Sugar Bay—*bay* MN-6
Sugar Bay—*bay* PA-2
Sugar Bay—*bay* VI-3
**Sugar Bay (Jackson Landing)**—*pop pl* KY-4
**Sugar Beach**—*pop pl* MO-7
Sugarberry Lake—*reservoir* AL-4
Sugar Berth Pond—*lake* ME-1
Sugar Berth Ridge—*ridge* ME-1
Sugar Betty Hollow—*valley* KY-4
Sugar Bldg—*hist pl* CO-8
*Sugar Bluff* OH-6
Sugar-Bob Airp—*airport* PA-2
Sugar Bogue—*stream* MS-4
*Sugar Bogue Creek* MS-4
Sugar Bottom Cem—*cemetery* AL-4
Sugar Bottom Creek—*stream* MO-7
Sugar Bottom Hollow—*valley* VA-3
Sugar Bottoms Public Use Area—*park* IA-7
*Sugar Bowl* NH-1
Sugar Bowl—*basin* CA-9
Sugar Bowl—*basin* WA-9
Sugar Bowl—*basin* WI-6
Sugar Bowl—*summit* ID-8

Sugar Loaf Hill—*summit* NJ-2
Sugarloaf Hill—*summit* (3) NY-2
Sugarloaf Hill—*summit* OH-6
Sugarloaf Hill—*summit* OK-5
Sugarloaf Hill—*summit* RI-1
Sugarloaf Hill—*summit* SC-3
Sugar Loaf Hill—*summit* SD-7
Sugarloaf Hill—*summit* TX-5
Sugarloaf Hill—*summit* WA-9
Sugarloaf Hill—*summit* WI-6
Sugarloaf Hill—*summit* VI-3
Sugar Loaf (historical)—*locale* KS-7
Sugarloaf Island—*island* (2) AK-9
Sugarloaf Island—*island* CA-9
Sugarloaf Island—*island* NC-3
Sugarloaf Island—*island* WA-9
Sugarloaf Key—*island* FL-3
**Sugarloaf Key**—*pop pl* FL-3
Sugarloaf Knob—*bar* AK-9
Sugarloaf Knob—*summit* (2) AR-4
Sugarloaf Knob—*summit* ID-8
Sugarloaf Knob—*summit* (2) KY-4
Sugarloaf Knob—*summit* NV-8
Sugarloaf Knob—*summit* NC-3
Sugarloaf Knob—*summit* PA-2
Sugarloaf Knob—*summit* TN-4
Sugarloaf Knob—*summit* VA-3
Sugarloaf Knob—*summit* WV-2
Sugarloaf Lake—*lake* CO-8
Sugarloaf Lake—*lake* (2) MI-6
**Sugarloaf Lake**—*pop pl* AR-4
Sugarloaf Lake—*reservoir* AR-4
*Sugarloaf Landing* WA-9
Sugarloaf Marsh Creek—*stream* WY-8
Sugarloaf Meadow—*flat* (2) CA-9
Sugarloaf Mine—*mine* (2) CA-9
Sugar Loaf Mound—*hist pl* MO-7
Sugarloaf Mound—*summit* TX-5
Sugarloaf Mound—*summit* WI-6
*Sugar Loaf Mounds* TX-5
*Sugarloaf Mountain* CO-8
Sugarloaf Mountain—*ridge* OR-9
**Sugarloaf Mountain Park**—*pop pl* CA-9
Sugarloaf Mountain Rec Area—*park* SC-3
*Sugarloaf Mountains* AR-4
Sugar Loaf Mountains—*range* AR-4
Sugar Loaf Mountains—*range* OK-5
*Sugarloaf Mtn* AZ-5
*Sugarloaf Mtn* MD-2
*Sugarloaf Mtn* NY-2
*Sugarloaf Mtn* OR-9
*Sugarloaf Mtn* PA-2
*Sugarloaf Mtn* WA-9
Sugarloaf Mtn—*summit* (5) AK-9
Sugar Loaf Mtn—*summit* AK-9
Sugarloaf Mtn—*summit* (10) AZ-5
Sugar Loaf Mtn—*summit* (2) AR-4
Sugarloaf Mtn—*summit* (3) AR-4
Sugarloaf Mtn—*summit* (17) CA-9
Sugar Loaf Mtn—*summit* (2) CA-9
Sugarloaf Mtn—*summit* (5) CO-8
Sugar Loaf Mtn—*summit* CO-8
Sugarloaf Mtn—*summit* (5) CO-8
Sugarloaf Mtn—*summit* FL-3
Sugarloaf Mtn—*summit* (2) ID-8
Sugarloaf Mtn—*summit* (2) KY-4
Sugar Loaf Mtn—*summit* KY-4
Sugarloaf Mtn—*summit* (5) ME-1
Sugar Loaf Mtn—*summit* MD-2
Sugarloaf Mtn—*summit* (2) MI-6
Sugarloaf Mtn—*summit* (5) MT-8
Sugar Loaf Mtn—*summit* MT-8
Sugarloaf Mtn—*summit* (2) MT-8
Sugar Loaf Mtn—*summit* MT-8
Sugarloaf Mtn—*summit* (4) MT-8
Sugarloaf Mtn—*summit* NH-1
Sugarloaf Mtn—*summit* NM-5
Sugar Loaf Mtn—*summit* NM-5
Sugarloaf Mtn—*summit* (2) NM-5
Sugarloaf Mtn—*summit* (17) NY-2
Sugarloaf Mtn—*summit* (3) NC-3
Sugar Loaf Mtn—*summit* NC-3
Sugarloaf Mtn—*summit* (5) NC-3
Sugar Loaf Mtn—*summit* OK-5
Sugarloaf Mtn—*summit* (2) OK-5
Sugarloaf Mtn—*summit* (11) OR-9
Sugar Loaf Mtn—*summit* OR-9
Sugarloaf Mtn—*summit* (4) OR-9
Sugarloaf Mtn—*summit* (2) PA-2
Sugarloaf Mtn—*summit* SC-3
Sugarloaf Mtn—*summit* SD-7
Sugarloaf Mtn—*summit* (2) TN-4
Sugarloaf Mtn—*summit* (2) TX-5
Sugar Loaf Mtn—*summit* (2) TX-5
Sugarloaf Mtn—*summit* (4) TX-5
Sugar Loaf Mtn—*summit* TX-5
Sugarloaf Mtn—*summit* (4) UT-8
Sugarloaf Mtn—*summit* (2) VT-1
Sugarloaf Mtn—*summit* (5) VA-3
Sugarloaf Mtn—*summit* (2) WA-9
Sugar Loaf Mtn—*summit* WY-8
Sugarloaf Mtn—*summit* (5) WY-8
Sugarloaf Overlook—*locale* VA-3
Sugarloaf Park—*flat* CA-9
Sugarloaf Park—*locale* CA-9
*Sugarloaf Peak* CA-9
*Sugarloaf Peak* OR-9
*Sugar Loaf Peak* PA-2
Sugarloaf Peak—*summit* AK-9
Sugarloaf Peak—*summit* (3) AZ-5
Sugarloaf Peak—*summit* (10) CA-9
Sugarloaf Peak—*summit* (6) CO-8
Sugarloaf Peak—*summit* MT-8
Sugarloaf Peak—*summit* NV-8
Sugar Loaf Peak—*summit* (3) NV-8
Sugarloaf Peak—*summit* (3) NM-5
Sugarloaf Peak—*summit* WA-9
Sugarloaf Point—*cape* CA-9
Sugarloaf Pond—*lake* NH-1
Sugarloaf Prairie—*flat* AR-4
Sugarloaf Ranch—*locale* NM-5
Sugar Loaf Rec Area—*park* AR-4
Sugarloaf Rec Area—*park* ND-7
Sugarloaf Ridge—*ridge* CA-9
Sugarloaf Ridge—*ridge* NC-3
Sugarloaf Ridge State Park—*park* CA-9
Sugarloaf Rock—*pillar* CO-8
Sugar Loaf Rock—*pillar* MI-6
Sugar Loaf Rock—*pillar* MO-7
Sugarloaf Rock—*pillar* MT-8
Sugarloaf Rock—*summit* ID-8
Sugar Loaf Rock—*summit* UT-8
Sugar Loaf Rock (historical)—*summit* SD-7
**Sugarloaf (RR name Tomhicken)**—*pop pl* PA-2
Sugarloaf Rsvr—*reservoir* OR-9
Sugarloaf Rsvr—*reservoir* WY-8
Sugarloaf Sch—*hist pl* ID-8
Sugarloaf Sch—*school* FL-3
Sugarloaf Sch—*school* NC-3
Sugarloaf Sch—*school* OK-5
Sugarloaf Sch—*school* PA-2
Sugarloaf Sch (abandoned)—*school* PA-2
**Sugarloaf Shores**—*pop pl* FL-3
**Sugar Loaf Shores**—*pop pl* FL-3
Sugarloaf Spring—*spring* CO-8
Sugarloaf Spring—*spring* ID-8
Sugarloaf Spring—*spring* NM-5
Sugarloaf Spring—*spring* (2) OR-9
*Sugar Loaf (Sugar Loaf Heights)* IL-6
Sugarloaf Tank—*reservoir* (3) AZ-5
Sugarloaf Tank—*reservoir* NM-5
Sugarloaf Tank Number One—*reservoir* AZ-5
Sugarloaf Tank Number Two—*reservoir* AZ-5
*Sugar Loaf Township* KS-7
Sugarloaf (Township of)—*fmr MCD* (2) AR-4
Sugar Loaf (Township of)—*fmr MCD* (2) AR-4
Sugar Loaf (Township of)—*fmr MCD* NC-3
**Sugar Loaf (Township of)**—*pop pl* IL-6
**Sugarloaf (Township of)**—*pop pl* (2) PA-2
Sugar Loaf Trail—*trail* CO-8
Sugarloaf Valley—*basin* CA-9
Sugar Loaf Valley—*valley* WI-6
Sugarloaf Well—*well* NM-5
Sugar Loaf Well No 2—*well* WY-8
Sugarloaf Windmill—*locale* NM-5
Sugar Loaves—*bar* ME-1
Sugar Loaves—*summit* NV-8
*Sugarloof Mountain* OR-9
Sugarlump—*summit* CA-9
Sugar Maple Branch—*stream* TN-4
Sugar Maple Lake—*lake* WI-6
Sugar Mill Branch—*stream* FL-3
Sugar Mill Branch—*stream* TX-5
Sugar Mill Chute—*stream* LA-4
Sugar Mill Creek—*stream* IN-6
Sugar Mill Elem Sch—*school* FL-3
*Sugar Miller Creek* IN-6
Sugar Mill Historic Memorial—*park* FL-3
Sugar Mill Lake—*reservoir* IN-6
Sugar Mill Lake Dam—*dam* IN-6
Sugar Mill Mound—*summit* FL-3
Sugar Mill Pond—*lake* FL-3
**Sugarmill Woods**—*pop pl* FL-3
*Sugar Mound* KS-7
Sugar Mounds—*summit* TX-5
**Sugar Mountain**—*pop pl* NC-3
Sugar Mountain Ch—*church* NC-3
Sugar Mountain Lead—*ridge* TN-4
Sugar Mountain Trail—*trail* TN-4
Sugar Mountain Village—*locale* NC-3
Sugar Mtn—*summit* (3) AR-4
Sugar Mtn—*summit* ID-8
Sugar Mtn—*summit* MI-6
Sugar Mtn—*summit* NH-1
Sugar Mtn—*summit* NY-2
Sugar Mtn—*summit* NC-3
Sugar Mtn—*summit* (2) OK-5
Sugar Mtn—*summit* TN-4
*Sugarncane Branch* KY-4
Sugar Notch—*gap* PA-2
**Sugar Notch**—*pop pl* PA-2
Sugar Notch Borough—*civil* PA-2
Sugar Notch Run—*stream* PA-2
Sugar Oak Country Club—*other* LA-4
*Sugar Orchard* TN-4
Sugar Orchard Branch—*stream* TN-4
Sugar Orchard Creek—*stream* AR-4
Sugar Peak—*summit* NV-8
Sugar Peak—*summit* OR-9
**Sugar Pine**—*pop pl* (2) CA-9
Sugar Pine Basin—*basin* CA-9
Sugarpine Burn—*area* OR-9
Sugar Pine Butte—*summit* (2) CA-9
Sugar Pine Butte—*summit* OR-9
Sugar Pine Camp—*locale* CA-9
Sugar Pine Camp—*locale* OR-9
Sugar Pine Canyon—*valley* CA-9
Sugarpine Canyon—*valley* CA-9
Sugar Pine Canyon—*valley* CA-9
Sugar Pine Canyon—*valley* UT-8
*Sugar Pine Creek* CA-9
Sugarpine Creek—*stream* CA-9
Sugar Pine Creek—*stream* (3) CA-9
Sugarpine Creek—*stream* OR-9
Sugarpine Flat—*flat* CA-9
Sugar Pine Flat—*flat* (2) OR-9
Sugar Pine Gap—*gap* (2) CA-9
Sugarpine Gulch—*valley* CA-9
Sugarpine Gulch—*valley* OR-9
Sugarpine Hill—*summit* CA-9
Sugar Pine Lake—*lake* CA-9
Sugar Pine Mine—*mine* OR-9
Sugar Pine Mine (Inactive)—*mine* CA-9
Sugar Pine Mtn—*summit* (2) CA-9
Sugarpine Mtn—*summit* CA-9
Sugar Pine Mtn—*summit* CA-9
Sugarpine Mtn—*summit* OR-9
Sugar Pine Point—*cape* (2) CA-9
Sugar Pine Point—*locale* CA-9
Sugar Pine Point—*summit* CA-9
Sugar Pine Point State Park—*hist pl* CA-9
Sugar Pine Point State Park—*park* CA-9
Sugar Pine Point Trail—*trail* CA-9
Sugar Pine Ridge—*ridge* CA-9
Sugar Pine Ridge—*ridge* (3) OR-9
Sugar Pine Ridge Trail—*trail* OR-9
Sugar Pine Sheep Camp—*locale* CA-9
Sugarpine Shelter—*locale* OR-9
Sugarpine Spring—*spring* (2) CA-9
Sugar Pine Spring—*spring* CA-9
Sugarpine Spring—*spring* OR-9
Sugar Pine Spring—*spring* UT-8
Sugarplum Branch—*stream* KY-4
**Sugarplum Condominiums**—*pop pl* UT-8
**Sugarplum PUD Subdivision**—*pop pl* UT-8
Sugar Plum Tree Child Care Center—*school* FL-3
*Sugar Point* MN-6
Sugar Point—*cape* MD-2
Sugar Point—*cape* (2) MN-6
Sugar Point—*cliff* OH-6
Sugar Point—*summit* MD-2
Sugar Point Bog—*swamp* MN-6
Sugar Pond—*lake* AL-4
Sugar Pond—*reservoir* AZ-5
Sugar Pot Site—*hist pl* FL-3
Sugar Rapids—*locale* MI-6
Sugar Reef—*bar* OH-6
Sugar Reef Passage—*channel* RI-1
**Sugar Ridge**—*pop pl* OH-6
Sugar Ridge—*ridge* CA-9
Sugar Ridge—*ridge* KY-4
Sugar Ridge—*ridge* ME-1
Sugar Ridge—*ridge* OH-6
Sugar Ridge—*ridge* (3) PA-2
Sugar Ridge—*ridge* TN-4
Sugar Ridge Campground—*locale* AL-4
Sugar Ridge Cem—*cemetery* (3) IN-6
Sugar Ridge Cem—*cemetery* (2) OH-6
Sugar Ridge Ch—*church* AL-4
Sugar Ridge Ch—*church* IN-6
Sugar Ridge Ch—*church* MI-6
Sugar Ridge Ch—*church* OH-6
Sugar Ridge Ch—*church* PA-2
**Sugar Ridge (subdivision)**—*pop pl* NC-3
**Sugar Ridge (Township of)**—*pop pl* IN-6
*Sugar River* NH-1
Sugar River—*stream* IL-6
Sugar River—*stream* MI-6
Sugar River—*stream* NH-1
Sugar River—*stream* NY-2
Sugar River—*stream* WI-6
Sugar River For Preserve—*forest* IL-6
Sugar Rock—*locale* OH-6
Sugar Rock—*pillar* NM-5
*Sugar Run* OH-6
*Sugar Run* PA-2
*Sugar Run* WV-2
**Sugar Run**—*pop pl* PA-2
Sugar Run—*stream* IL-6
Sugar Run—*stream* (3) IN-6
Sugar Run—*stream* KY-4
Sugar Run—*stream* MS-4
Sugar Run—*stream* MT-8
Sugar Run—*stream* (17) OH-6
Sugar Run—*stream* (20) PA-2
Sugar Run—*stream* (8) VA-3
Sugar Run—*stream* (24) WV-2
Sugar Run Ch—*church* OH-6
Sugar Run Ch—*church* PA-2
Sugar Run Creek—*stream* PA-2
Sugar Run Dam—*dam* PA-2
Sugar Run Dam Number 103—*dam* PA-2
Sugar Run Falls—*falls* PA-2
Sugar Run Gap—*gap* PA-2
**Sugar Run (historical)**—*pop pl* PA-2
Sugar Run Mtn—*summit* VA-3
Sugar Run Rsvr—*reservoir* PA-2
Sugar Run Sch—*school* OH-6
Sugar Run Sch—*school* PA-2
Sugar Run Sch (abandoned)—*school* (3) PA-2
Sugar Sink—*basin* KY-4
Sugar Spot—*island* FL-3
Sugar Spring—*spring* (2) CA-9
Sugar Spring—*spring* OR-9
Sugar Spring Canyon—*valley* UT-8
Sugar Spring (historical)—*locale* TN-4
Sugar Springs Cove—*valley* NC-3
Sugar Springs Trail—*trail* PA-2
Sugar Square (Shop Ctr)—*locale* FL-3
Sugar Tail Spring—*spring* CA-9
**Sugartit**—*pop pl* KY-4
Sugarton—*locale* FL-3
Sugar Top—*summit* AK-9
Sugar Top—*summit* NC-3
*Sugar Town* NY-2
*Sugartown* NC-3
Sugartown—*locale* GA-3
**Sugartown**—*pop pl* LA-4
**Sugartown**—*pop pl* NY-2
**Sugar Town**—*pop pl* NC-3
**Sugartown**—*pop pl* PA-2
Sugartown Ch—*church* NY-2
Sugartown Ch—*church* NC-3
*Sugartown Creek* NC-3
Sugartown Hist Dist—*hist pl* PA-2
Sugartown Lookout Tower—*pillar* LA-4
Sugartown Ridge—*ridge* TN-4
**Sugartree**—*pop pl* (2) MO-7
**Sugar Tree**—*pop pl* TN-4
**Sugar Tree**—*pop pl* WV-2
Sugartree Airp—*airport* MO-7
Sugartree Bench Mtn—*summit* WV-2
Sugar Tree Branch—*stream* KY-4
Sugartree Branch—*stream* (3) KY-4
Sugar Tree Branch—*stream* KY-4
Sugar Tree Branch—*stream* MO-7
Sugartree Branch—*stream* NC-3
Sugar Tree Branch—*stream* NC-3
Sugartree Branch—*stream* NC-3
Sugartree Branch—*stream* (2) TN-4
Sugartree Branch—*stream* VA-3
Sugar Tree Branch—*stream* VA-3
Sugartree Branch—*stream* (2) WV-2
Sugartree Cem—*cemetery* OH-6
Sugar Tree Cem—*cemetery* OH-6
Sugar Tree Ch—*church* MO-7
Sugartree Ch—*church* VA-3
Sugar Tree Ch—*church* VA-3
*Sugar Tree Creek* IN-6
*Sugar Tree Creek* MO-7
*Sugar Tree Creek* NC-3
*Sugar Tree Creek* VA-3
Sugar Tree Creek—*stream* KY-4
Sugartree Creek—*stream* NC-3
Sugartree Creek—*stream* OH-6
Sugartree Creek—*stream* TN-4
Sugartree Creek—*stream* VA-3
Sugartree Creek—*stream* WV-2
Sugartree Ditch—*canal* MO-7
Sugar Tree Draft—*valley* VA-3
Sugartree Ford—*locale* KY-4
Sugartree Ford—*locale* TN-4
*Sugartree Fork* IN-6
Sugartree Fork—*stream* OH-6
Sugar Tree Fork—*stream* TN-4
Sugartree Fork—*stream* WV-2
Sugartree Gap—*gap* AR-4
Sugartree Gap—*gap* (2) NC-3
Sugar Tree Gap—*gap* TN-4
Sugartree Gap—*gap* (2) TN-4
Sugar Tree Gap—*gap* TN-4
Sugar Tree Grove Spring—*spring* MO-7
Sugar Tree Hollow—*valley* AL-4
Sugartree Hollow—*valley* AR-4
Sugar Tree Hollow—*valley* AR-4
Sugar Tree Hollow—*valley* KY-4
Sugartree Hollow—*valley* KY-4
Sugar Tree Hollow—*valley* KY-4
Sugar Tree Hollow—*valley* MO-7
Sugartree Hollow—*valley* (2) MO-7
Sugar Tree Hollow—*valley* (4) MO-7
Sugartree Hollow—*valley* (3) MO-7
Sugartree Hollow—*valley* (2) TN-4
Sugar Tree Hollow—*valley* TN-4
Sugartree Hollow—*valley* TN-4
Sugartree Hollow—*valley* VA-3
**Sugar Tree Knob**—*pop pl* TN-4
Sugar Tree Knob—*summit* AR-4
Sugartree Knob—*summit* TN-4
Sugar Tree Knob Ch—*church* TN-4
Sugar Tree Knob Sch (historical)—*school* TN-4
Sugartree Licks—*gap* NC-3
Sugar Tree Marina—*locale* TN-4
Sugar Tree Mtn—*summit* AR-4
Sugartree Mtn—*summit* (3) AR-4
Sugar Tree Point—*cape* AL-4
*Sugartree Post Office* TN-4
Sugar Tree Post Office—*building* TN-4
**Sugar Tree Ridge**—*pop pl* OH-6
Sugar Tree Ridge—*ridge* KY-4
Sugartree Ridge—*ridge* (2) NC-3
Sugar Tree Ridge Cem—*cemetery* MO-7
Sugar Tree Run—*stream* KY-4
Sugartree Run—*stream* KY-4
Sugartree Run—*stream* OH-6
Sugar Tree Run—*stream* WV-2
Sugar Tree Sch (abandoned)—*school* MO-7
Sugar Tree Sch (historical)—*school* MO-7
Sugar Tree Sch (historical)—*school* TN-4
Sugartree Spring—*spring* TN-4
**Sugar Tree (subdivision)**—*pop pl* AL-4
**Sugartree Township**—*pop pl* MO-7
Sugarvale (historical)—*locale* KS-7
*Sugar Valley* KS-7
*Sugar Valley* PA-2
**Sugar Valley**—*pop pl* GA-3
**Sugar Valley**—*pop pl* OH-6
**Sugar Valley**—*pop pl* (2) TX-5
**Sugar Valley**—*pop pl* (2) WV-2
Sugar Valley—*valley* ID-8
Sugar Valley—*valley* (2) PA-2
Sugar Valley Airp—*airport* NC-3
Sugar Valley Area Sch—*school* PA-2
Sugar Valley Cem—*cemetery* GA-3
Sugar Valley Cem—*cemetery* OH-6
Sugar Valley Ch—*church* GA-3
Sugar Valley Ch—*church* PA-2
Sugar Valley Ch—*church* VA-3
Sugar Valley Lakes—*lake* OH-6
*Sugar Valley Mtn* PA-2
Sugar Valley Mtn—*summit* PA-2
Sugar Valley Oil Field—*oilfield* TX-5
Sugar Valley-Resaca (CCD)—*cens area* GA-3
Sugar Valley Sch—*school* GA-3
Sugar Valley Shop Ctr—*locale* KS-7
Sugar Valley Wash—*valley* ID-8
Sugarville—*locale* UT-8
**Sugarville**—*pop pl* AL-4
**Sugarville**—*pop pl* TN-4
Sugarwood Park—*park* FL-3
*Sugar Works Run* PA-2
Sugar Works Run—*stream* PA-2
**Sugden**—*pop pl* OK-5
Sugden Cem—*cemetery* OK-5
Sugden Lake—*lake* MI-6
Sugden Reservoir Dam—*dam* MA-1
Sugden Rsvr—*reservoir* MA-1
Sugden Sch—*school* VA-3
*Sugdens Reservoir* MA-1
Sugerloaf Brook—*stream* MA-1
Sugermans Shopping Plaza—*locale* PA-2
Sugg Cem—*cemetery* AR-4
Sugg Cem—*cemetery* IL-6
Sugg Cem—*cemetery* KY-4
Sugg Cem—*cemetery* TN-4
Sugg Creek—*stream* KY-4
Suggett, John, House—*hist pl* KY-4
Suggett, William, Agricultural and Industrial District—*hist pl* KY-4
Suggetts Point—*cape* VA-3
Sugg Hill—*summit* TN-4
Sugg House—*hist pl* CA-9
Sugg Ranch—*locale* TX-5
*Suggs* TN-4
Suggs—*locale* TX-5
Suggs, Lake—*lake* FL-3
Suggs Bend—*bend* TN-4
Suggs Branch—*canal* NC-3
Suggs Branch—*stream* TN-4
Suggs Branch—*stream* TX-5
Suggs Cem—*cemetery* LA-4
Suggs Cem—*cemetery* (2) TN-4
Suggs Cem—*cemetery* (2) TX-5
Suggs Ch—*church* TN-4
Sugg Sch—*school* NC-3
*Suggs Creek* NC-3
**Suggs Creek**—*pop pl* TN-4
Suggs Creek—*stream* NC-3
Suggs Creek—*stream* TN-4
Suggs Creek Ch—*church* NC-3
Suggs Creek Presbyterian Ch—*church* TN-4
Suggs Crossroads—*locale* SC-3
**Suggs Crossroads**—*pop pl* NC-3
Suggs Dam—*dam* AL-4
Suggs Grove Ch—*church* NC-3
Suggs Head—*locale* FL-3
Suggs Head—*stream* FL-3
Suggs Hollow—*valley* TN-4
*Suggs Lake* AL-4
Suggs Lake—*lake* FL-3
Suggs Landing—*locale* NC-3
Suggs Mill Pond—*lake* NC-3
Suggs Millpond—*reservoir* GA-3
Suggs Mtn—*summit* AL-4
Suggs Mtn—*summit* AR-4
Suggs Pond—*reservoir* AL-4
Suggs Sch—*school* NC-3
Suggs Siding—*locale* NC-3
**Suggsville**—*pop pl* AL-4
Suggsville Female Acad (historical)—*school* AL-4
Suggsville Male Acad (historical)—*school* AL-4
Suggsville (sta.) (Allen)—*other* AL-4
*Suggy Creek* KY-4
Sugi Grove—*woods* HI-9
Sugnet Sch—*school* MI-6
**Sugrue**—*pop pl* LA-4
Sugtutlig Mtn—*summit* AK-9
Sugtutlik Peak—*summit* AK-9
Suhling Pond—*reservoir* IL-6
Suhr, John J., House—*hist pl* WI-6
Suhre Lake—*reservoir* IN-6
Suhre Lake Dam—*dam* IN-6
Suhre Sch—*school* IL-6
Suhrie Sch (historical)—*school* PA-2
Suhr State Wildlife Mngmt Area—*park* MN-6
*Suhuster Creek* UT-8
Suiattle Cem—*cemetery* WA-9
Suiattle Glacier—*glacier* WA-9
Suiattle Guard Station—*other* WA-9
Suiattle Mtn—*summit* WA-9
Suiattle Pass—*gap* WA-9
Suiattle River—*stream* WA-9
Suicide Bed Grounds Rsvr—*reservoir* WY-8
Suicide Bend—*bend* TX-5
Suicide Bluffs—*cliff* KS-7
Suicide Branch—*stream* SC-3
Suicide Cabin—*locale* CA-9
Suicide Cabin—*locale* MT-8
Suicide Canyon—*valley* AZ-5
Suicide Canyon—*valley* UT-8
Suicide Canyon—*valley* WA-9
Suicide Cave—*cave* IN-6
Suicide Cliff—*cliff* MH-9
Suicide Cliff—*hist pl* MH-9
**Suicide Corners**—*pop pl* NY-2
Suicide Cove—*bay* AK-9
*Suicide Creek* OR-9
Suicide Creek—*stream* OR-9
Suicide Falls—*falls* AK-9
Suicide Flat—*flat* TX-5
Suicide Gulch—*valley* CO-8
Suicide Hill—*summit* WY-8
Suicide Lake—*lake* WY-8
Suicide Mtn—*summit* CO-8
Suicide Park—*park* UT-8
Suicide Pass—*gap* ID-8
Suicide Pass—*gap* MT-8
*Suicide Peak* AK-9
*Suicide Peak* CA-9
Suicide Peaks—*summit* AK-9
Suicide Point—*cliff* AZ-5
Suicide Point—*cliff* WY-8
Suicide Ridge—*ridge* (2) AZ-5
Suicide Ridge—*ridge* CA-9
Suicide Rock—*pillar* CA-9
Suicide Rock—*pillar* ID-8
Suicide Rock—*pillar* NV-8
Suicide Rock—*summit* CA-9
Suicide Soda Lake—*lake* WY-8
Suicide Spring—*spring* AZ-5
Suicide Tank—*reservoir* (3) AZ-5
Suicide Tank Number One—*reservoir* AZ-5
Suicide Tank Number Two—*reservoir* AZ-5
Suicide Wash—*arroyo* AZ-5
Suicide Well—*well* OR-9
Suipe Creek—*stream* OR-9
Suire Cem—*cemetery* LA-4
*Suisun* CA-9
Suisun—*civil* CA-9
Suisun Bay—*bay* CA-9
**Suisun City**—*pop pl* CA-9
**Suisun City (Suisun-Fairfield)**—*pop pl* CA-9
Suisun Creek—*stream* CA-9
Suisun Cutoff—*channel* CA-9
*Suisun-Fairfield (Suisun City)* CA-9
Suisun Hill—*summit* CA-9
Suisun Masonic Lodge No. 55—*hist pl* CA-9
Suisun Point—*cape* CA-9
Suisun Point Channel—*channel* CA-9
Suisun Rsvr—*reservoir* CA-9
Suisun Slough—*stream* CA-9
Suisun Valley—*valley* CA-9
**Suit**—*pop pl* NC-3
Suit, Samuel Taylor, Cottage—*hist pl* WV-2
Suitcase Mine—*mine* CA-9
Suit Cem—*cemetery* NC-3
Suiter—*locale* OH-6
Suiter—*locale* VA-3
Suiter, Jacob, House—*hist pl* IA-7
Suiter, John H., House—*hist pl* IA-7
Suiter, William, House—*hist pl* IA-7
Suiters Branch—*stream* KY-4
Suiter-Williams Cem—*cemetery* OH-6
**Suitland**—*pop pl* MD-2
Suitland HS—*school* MD-2
Suitland JHS—*school* MD-2
**Suitland Manor**—*pop pl* MD-2
Suitland Sch—*school* MD-2
Suitland-Silver Hill—*CDP* MD-2
Suitor Brook—*stream* VT-1
Suitor Hollow—*valley* MO-7
Suits Ditch—*canal* IN-6
Suits Hill—*summit* TN-4
Suitter Creek—*stream* OR-9
Suitter Spring—*spring* OR-9
*Suiyo-To* FM-9
Suizo Mountains—*summit* AZ-5
Suizo Wash—*stream* AZ-5
Suizo Well—*well* AZ-5
Suk—*bar* FM-9
Sukakpak Mtn—*summit* AK-9
Suk and Cerney Flowage—*reservoir* WI-6
Suke Creek—*stream* WV-2
Sukes Pond—*lake* VT-1
Sukey Branch—*stream* KY-4
Sukey Fork—*stream* KY-4
Sukey Johnson Branch—*stream* VA-3
Sukey Ridge—*ridge* KY-4
Sukey Siler Hollow—*valley* KY-4
Sukhoi Lagoon—*bay* AK-9
Suki, Mount—*summit* AK-9
Sukik Island—*island* AK-9
*Sukimi To* MH-9
Sukkwan Island—*island* AK-9
Sukkwan Lake—*flat* AK-9
Sukkwan Narrows—*channel* AK-9
Sukkwan Strait—*channel* AK-9
S U Knolls—*summit* AZ-5
Sukoi Bay—*bay* AK-9
Sukoi Inlet—*bay* AK-9
Sukoi Islets—*area* AK-9
Sukoi Point—*cape* AK-9
Sukok Lake—*lake* AK-9
Suksdorf Ridge—*ridge* WA-9
**Sula**—*pop pl* MT-8
Sula Cay—*island* VI-3
Sula Cem—*cemetery* MT-8
Sula Creek—*stream* MT-8
Sula-Edwards—*cens area* MT-8
Sulakpoatokvik Creek—*stream* AK-9
Sulaney Branch—*stream* KY-4
Sula Peak—*summit* MT-8
Sula Ranger Station—*locale* MT-8
Sulatna Bluff—*cliff* AK-9
Sulatna Crossing—*locale* AK-9
Sulatna River—*stream* AK-9
Sulcer Spring—*spring* AL-4
Suldal Cem—*cemetery* WI-6
Suldal Valley—*valley* WI-6
Sulem Lake—*lake* MN-6
Sulfite Mine—*mine* AZ-5
Sulfur—*locale* NV-8
Sulfur Canyon—*valley* TX-5
Sulfur Creek—*stream* CA-9
Sulfur Creek—*stream* FL-3
Sulfur Creek—*stream* OK-5
Sulfur Creek—*stream* TX-5
*Sulfur Creek - in part* PA-2
Sulfur Draw—*valley* UT-8
Sulfur Hollow—*valley* MO-7
Sulfur Lick—*stream* KY-4
Sulfur Mine Hill—*summit* TX-5
Sulfur Run—*stream* WV-2
Sulfur Spring—*spring* (2) CA-9
Sulfur Spring—*spring* NM-5
Sulfur Spring—*spring* PA-2
Sulfur Spring—*spring* TN-4
Sulfur Spring—*spring* UT-8
Sulfur Spring Canyon—*valley* NM-5
Sulfur Springs—*spring* AR-4
Sulfur Springs—*spring* WY-8
Sulfur Springs Ch—*church* AL-4
Sulfur Springs Sch (historical)—*school* PA-2
Sulfur Springs Station—*locale* PA-2
Sulfur Trail—*trail* CO-8
Sulfur Well—*well* CO-8
Sulfur Well—*well* TX-5
Sulfur Well Branch—*stream* KY-4
Sulfur Well Draw—*valley* TX-5
Sulfur Windmill—*locale* NM-5
Sulfur Windmill—*locale* (5) TX-5
Sulger—*locale* PA-2
Sulgrave Club—*hist pl* DC-2
**Sulgrave Manor**—*pop pl* VA-3
Suliivan Center Cem—*cemetery* IL-6
Suli Knob—*summit* NC-3
Sulimar Oil Field—*other* NM-5
Suli Ridge—*ridge* NC-3
*Sull Creek* CO-8
Sullenburger Rsvr—*reservoir* CO-8
*sullen Creek* MI-6
Sullenger Bend—*bend* TN-4
Sullens Cem—*cemetery* AL-4
Sullens Cow Camp—*locale* OR-9
Sullens Creek—*stream* VA-3
Sullens Gap—*gap* KY-4
Sullens Hollow—*valley* MO-7
Sullers Cem—*cemetery* MS-4
Sullian Cem—*cemetery* IN-6
**Sulligent**—*pop pl* AL-4
Sulligent (CCD)—*cens area* AL-4
Sulligent Dam—*dam* AL-4
Sulligent Division—*civil* AL-4
Sulligent HS—*school* AL-4
Sulligent Lake—*reservoir* AL-4
Sulligent Post Office—*building* AL-4
Sullinger Bottom—*bend* MT-8
Sullinger Sch—*school* KY-4
Sullinger Windmill—*locale* NM-5
Sullin Hollow—*valley* TN-4
*Sullinis Church* AL-4
Sullins Branch—*stream* NC-3
Sullins Branch—*stream* TN-4
Sullins Cem—*cemetery* AL-4
Sullins Cem—*cemetery* TN-4
Sullins Coll—*school* VA-3
*Sullins Prong* KY-4
*Sullivan* NY-2
Sullivan—*locale* CA-9
Sullivan—*locale* CO-8
Sullivan—*locale* KS-7
Sullivan—*locale* WY-8
**Sullivan**—*pop pl* IL-6
**Sullivan**—*pop pl* IN-6
**Sullivan**—*pop pl* KY-4
**Sullivan**—*pop pl* ME-1
**Sullivan**—*pop pl* (2) MI-6
**Sullivan**—*pop pl* MO-7
**Sullivan**—*pop pl* NH-1
**Sullivan**—*pop pl* NY-2
**Sullivan**—*pop pl* OH-6
**Sullivan**—*pop pl* PA-2
**Sullivan**—*pop pl* TX-5
**Sullivan**—*pop pl* (2) WV-2
**Sullivan**—*pop pl* WI-6
Sullivan—*uninc pl* WI-6
Sullivan, Bayou—*stream* AL-4
Sullivan, Gen. John, House—*hist pl* NH-1
Sullivan, G. H., Lodging House—*hist pl* AZ-5
Sullivan, James J., Sch—*hist pl* PA-2
Sullivan, James R. and Mary E., House—*hist pl* UT-8
Sullivan, Lake—*lake* IN-6
Sullivan, Lake—*reservoir* IN-6
**Sullivan Acres Subdivision**—*pop pl* UT-8
Sullivan Airp—*airport* PA-2
Sullivan Ave Sch—*school* NY-2
Sullivan Bay—*bay* MN-6
Sullivan Bayou—*stream* LA-4
Sullivan Bend—*bend* TN-4
Sullivan Bluffs—*cliff* AK-9
Sullivan Branch—*stream* AL-4
Sullivan Branch—*stream* IL-6
Sullivan Branch—*stream* (2) MD-2
Sullivan Branch—*stream* MO-7
Sullivan Branch—*stream* OK-5
Sullivan Branch—*stream* PA-2

**Sulphur Springs (Quicks Mill)**—*pop pl* AL-4
Sulphur Springs Ranch—*locale* WY-8
*Sulphur Springs Range* NV-8
*Sulphur Springs Sch* AL-4
*Sulphur Springs Sch* TN-4
Sulphur Springs Sch—*school* AL-4
Sulphur Springs Sch—*school* (2) IL-6
Sulphur Springs Sch—*school* KY-4
Sulphur Springs Sch—*school* MS-4
Sulphur Springs Sch—*school* MO-7
Sulphur Springs Sch—*school* (2) TN-4
Sulphur Springs Sch—*school* VA-3
Sulphur Springs Sch (historical)—*school* AL-4
Sulphur Springs Sch (historical)—*school* (2) TN-4
Sulphur Springs Sch Number 4 (historical)—*school* TX-5
Sulphur Springs Slough—*gut* LA-4
**Sulphur Springs Station**—*pop pl* GA-3
Sulphur Springs (Township of)—*fmr MCD* (3) AR-4
Sulphur Springs (Township of)—*fmr MCD* NC-3
Sulphur Springs Union Chapel—*church* PA-2
Sulphur Springs Valley—*valley* AZ-5
**Sulphur Spring Terrace**—*pop pl* MD-2
*Sulphur Spring Valley* AZ-5
Sulphur Spring Valley—*valley* VA-3
*Sulphur Sprins Range* NV-8
Sulphur Tank—*reservoir* NM-5
Sulphur Tank—*reservoir* TX-5
Sulphur (Township of)—*fmr MCD* (3) AR-4
Sulphur Trail—*trail* AR-4
Sulphur Trap Windmill—*locale* TX-5
Sulphur Trestle Fort Site—*hist pl* AL-4
Sulphur Tunnel—*mine* CO-8
Sulphur Valley—*basin* CA-9
Sulphur Wash—*valley* UT-8
*Sulphur Well* IN-6
Sulphur Well—*locale* (2) KY-4
Sulphur Well—*locale* TN-4
Sulphur Well—*well* CA-9
Sulphur Well—*well* (2) NM-5
Sulphur Well—*well* (3) TX-5
Sulphur Well Academy Ch—*church* TN-4
Sulphur Well Acad (historical)—*school* TN-4
**Sulphur Well (Ambrose)**—*pop pl* KY-4
Sulphur Well Landing—*locale* TN-4
Sulphur Wells Ch—*church* KY-4
Sulphur Well Sch—*school* KY-4
Sulphur Well Spring—*spring* TN-4
Sulphur Well Swamp (historical)—*swamp* TN-4
Sulphur Windmill—*locale* NM-5
Sulphur Windmill—*locale* (7) TX-5
Sulphur Works—*locale* CA-9
Sul Ross Sch—*school* TX-5
Sul Ross State Univ—*school* TX-5
Sul Ross (Sul Ross State College)—*uninc pl* TX-5
Sultan—*locale* MN-6
**Sultan**—*pop pl* WA-9
**Sultana**—*pop pl* CA-9
Sultana-Arizona Mine—*mine* AZ-5
Sultana Sch—*school* CA-9
Sultan Basin—*basin* WA-9
Sultan Creek—*stream* CA-9
Sultan Creek—*stream* CO-8
Sultan Mine—*mine* AZ-5
Sultan Mine—*mine* NV-8
Sultan Mtn—*summit* CO-8
Sultan River—*stream* WA-9
Sultan Shaft—*mine* ID-8
*Sultan Subdivision* UT-8
**Sultan Subdivision, The**—*pop pl* UT-8
**Sultan Valley Downs Subdivision, The**—*pop pl* UT-8
Sulton Park—*park* MN-6
Sultz Swamp—*swamp* WI-6
Sulua Bay—*bay* AK-9
Suluak Creek—*stream* AK-9
Suluar Mesa—*summit* UT-8
Sulug Branch—*stream* WV-2
Sulugiak Creek—*stream* AK-9
Sulukna River—*stream* AK-9
Sulukpuk Creek—*stream* AK-9
Sulungatak Ridge—*ridge* AK-9
Sulupoagaktak Channel—*channel* AK-9
Sulutak Creek—*stream* AK-9
Sulven Creek—*stream* AK-9
Sulzberger, Mayer, JHS—*hist pl* PA-2
Sulzberger JHS—*school* PA-2
Sulzer—*locale* AK-9
Sulzer, Mount—*summit* AK-9
Sulzer Gulch—*valley* CO-8
Sulzer Passage—*channel* AK-9
Sulzer Portage—*trail* AK-9
Sumac—*locale* GA-3
**Sumac**—*pop pl* TN-4
Sumac Branch—*stream* TX-5
Sumac Canal—*canal* CA-9
Sumac Creek—*stream* AR-4
Sumac Creek—*stream* GA-3
Sumac Creek—*stream* ID-8
Sumac Creek—*stream* OR-9
Sumac Gulch—*valley* ID-8
*Sumach* GA-3
**Sumach**—*pop pl* GA-3
**Sumach**—*pop pl* MO-7
**Sumach**—*pop pl* WA-9
Sumach Cem—*cemetery* MO-7
Sumach Ch—*church* MO-7
Sumach-cumberland Ch—*church* GA-3
Sumach Hollow—*valley* AL-4
Sumach Hollow—*valley* TN-4
Sumac Hill—*summit* ME-1
Sumach Lake—*lake* WI-6
Sumac Hollow—*valley* TN-4
Sumac Hollow—*valley* UT-8
Sumach Sch (abandoned)—*school* MO-7
Sumac Island—*island* CT-1
Sumac Knob—*summit* WV-2
Sumac Lake—*lake* AR-4
Sumac Lake—*lake* MI-6
Sumac Lateral—*canal* CA-9
Sumac Lateral Two—*canal* CA-9
*Sumac Pond* MD-2
Sumac Post Office (historical)—*building* TN-4
Sumac Ridge—*ridge* GA-3
Sumac Run—*stream* VA-3
Sumac Spring—*spring* OR-9
Sumac Spring—*spring* WA-9
*Sumac Spring Canyon* AZ-5
*Sumac Springs Canyon* AZ-5
Sumac Valley—*valley* MO-7
**Suman**—*pop pl* IN-6
Suman Cem—*cemetery* IN-6
Suman Gate—*gap* TX-5
Suman Windmill—*locale* NM-5
**Sumas**—*pop pl* WA-9
Sumas (CCD)—*cens area* WA-9
Sumas Mtn—*summit* WA-9
Sumas River—*stream* WA-9
*Sumass River* WA-9
Sumatanga, Lake—*reservoir* AL-4
Sumatanga Dam—*dam* AL-4
Sumate Fork—*stream* WV-2
**Sumatra**—*pop pl* FL-3
**Sumatra**—*pop pl* MT-8
Sumatra Cem—*cemetery* MT-8
Sumatra Creek—*stream* AK-9
Sumatra Fire Tower—*tower* FL-3
**Sumava Resorts**—*pop pl* IN-6
**Sumay**—*pop pl* GU-9
Sumay Bay—*bay* GU-9
Sumay Cem—*cemetery* GU-9
Sumay Maleso—*area* GU-9
Sumay River—*stream* GU-9
Sumbax—*locale* MS-4
Sum Brook—*stream* IN-6
Sumbry Memorial Ch—*church* AL-4
Sum Creek—*stream* IN-6
Sumdum, Mount—*summit* AK-9
Sumdum (abandoned)—*locale* AK-9
Sumdum Glacier—*glacier* AK-9
Sumdum Island—*island* AK-9
Sumerall—*uninc pl* LA-4
**Sumerco**—*pop pl* WV-2
Sumerco Ch—*church* WV-2
Sumerduck—*locale* VA-3
Sumerduck Run—*stream* (2) VA-3
Sumerson—*locale* PA-2
*Sumers Reservoir* CO-8
*Sumersville* OH-6
*Sumervill Draw* WY-8
Sumida Park—*park* AZ-5
**Sumidero**—*pop pl* PR-3
Sumidero (Barrio)—*fmr MCD* PR-3
Sumido (Barrio)—*fmr MCD* PR-3
Suminit Ch—*church* VA-3
**Sumiton**—*pop pl* (2) AL-4
Sumiton Elem Sch—*school* AL-4
Sumiton Number Two Mine (underground)—*mine* AL-4
*Sumiyoshi Shima* FM-9
*Sumiyoshi To* FM-9
Sumlin Swamp—*swamp* GA-3
*Summan* IL-6
*Summer* NJ-2
**Summer**—*pop pl* NE-7
Summerall Lake—*lake* FL-3
Summerall Park—*park* FL-3
Summer Ave Ch—*church* TN-4
Summer Ave Sch—*school* NJ-2
Summer Bay—*bay* AK-9
*Summerberry River* ND-7
Summer Blossom—*gap* WA-9
Summer Bluff—*locale* AL-4
Summer Branch—*stream* (2) TX-5
Summer Brothers Stores—*hist pl* SC-3
Summerby Creek—*stream* MI-6
Summerby Swamp—*swamp* MI-6
Summer Camp—*locale* (2) NV-8
Summer Camp Canyon—*valley* NV-8
Summer Camp Creek—*stream* AK-9
Summer Camp Creek—*stream* CO-8
Summer Camp Creek—*stream* NV-8
Summer Camp Gulch—*valley* CO-8
Summer Camp Ridge—*ridge* NV-8
Summer Camp Spring—*spring* UT-8
Summer Cave—*cave* AL-4
Summer Cem—*cemetery* KS-7
Summer Cem—*cemetery* (2) MO-7
Summer Cem—*cemetery* NE-7
Summer Chapel, Prince Frederick's Episcopal Church—*hist pl* SC-3
Summer Chapel Rectory, Prince Frederick's Episcopal Church—*hist pl* SC-3
**Summer City**—*pop pl* TN-4
Summer City Baptist Ch—*church* TN-4
Summer City Cem—*cemetery* TN-4
Summer City Ch of God—*church* TN-4
Summer City Sch (historical)—*school* TN-4
*Summer Creek* CT-1
*Summer Creek* OR-9
*Summer Creek* SD-7
Summer Creek—*stream* (2) AK-9
Summer Creek—*stream* ID-8
Summer Creek—*stream* IA-7
Summer Creek—*stream* (2) OR-9
**Summer Crest Subdivision**—*pop pl* UT-8
*Summerdale* IL-6
**Summerdale**—*pop pl* AL-4
**Summerdale**—*pop pl* NY-2
**Summerdale**—*pop pl* PA-2
Summerdale—*uninc pl* PA-2
Summerdale Campground—*locale* CA-9
Summerdale (CCD)—*cens area* AL-4
Summerdale Cem—*cemetery* AL-4
Summerdale Division—*civil* AL-4
Summerdale HS—*school* AL-4
Summerdale JHS—*school* AL-4
Summerdale Plaza—*post sta* PA-2
Summerdale Sch—*school* IL-6
Summerdean—*locale* VA-3
Summerdean Ch—*church* VA-3
*Summerdear* VA-3
*Summerdeon* VA-3
**Summerdeon**—*pop pl* VA-3
*Summerduck* VA-3
*Summerduck Run* VA-3
**Summer Estates (subdivision)**—*pop pl* AL-4
Summer Falls—*falls* WA-9
*Summerfield* AL-4
Summerfield—*locale* LA-4
Summerfield—*locale* NJ-2
Summerfield—*locale* (2) TX-5
Summerfield—*other* TX-5
**Summerfield**—*pop pl* AL-4
**Summerfield**—*pop pl* FL-3
**Summerfield**—*pop pl* IL-6
**Summerfield**—*pop pl* KS-7
**Summerfield**—*pop pl* LA-4
**Summerfield**—*pop pl* MO-7
**Summerfield**—*pop pl* NC-3
**Summerfield**—*pop pl* (2) OH-6
**Summerfield**—*pop pl* OK-5
**Summerfield**—*pop pl* TN-4
**Summerfield**—*pop pl* TX-5
Summerfield Acad (historical)—*school* AL-4
Summerfield Airp—*airport* KS-7
Summerfield And Ida Drain—*stream* MI-6
Summerfield Branch—*stream* LA-4
Summerfield Branch—*stream* MO-7
Summerfield Canyon—*valley* OR-9
Summerfield Cem—*cemetery* IL-6
Summerfield Cem—*cemetery* IN-6
Summerfield Cem—*cemetery* KS-7
Summerfield Cem—*cemetery* (2) MI-6
Summerfield Cem—*cemetery* OK-5
Summerfield Cem—*cemetery* TN-4
Summerfield Cem—*cemetery* WV-2
Summerfield Ch—*church* AR-4
Summerfield Ch—*church* MS-4
Summerfield Ch—*church* TN-4
Summerfield Ch—*church* TX-5
Summerfield Ch—*church* VA-3
Summerfield Creek—*stream* OK-5
**Summerfield Crossing (subdivision)**—*pop pl* NC-3
Summerfield District—*hist pl* AL-4
Summerfield Elem Sch—*school* NC-3
**Summerfield Farms**—*pop pl* MD-2
Summerfield Hill—*summit* PA-2
Summerfield Lake—*lake* WI-6
Summerfield Ridge—*ridge* OR-9
Summerfield Run—*stream* WV-2
Summerfield Sch—*hist pl* OK-5
Summerfield Sch—*school* FL-3
Summerfield Sch—*school* SC-3
Summerfield Sch (historical)—*school* TN-4
Summerfield Street Row Hist Dist—*hist pl* NY-2
**Summerfield (subdivision)**—*pop pl* AL-4
**Summerfield (subdivision)**—*pop pl* (2) NC-3
**Summerfield Subdivision**—*pop pl* (2) UT-8
Summerfield Tank—*reservoir* AZ-5
**Summerfield (Township of)**—*pop pl* (2) MI-6
**Summerford**—*pop pl* OH-6
Summerford Branch—*stream* GA-3
Summer Fork—*stream* WV-2
**Summer Garden Townhouse Condominium**—*pop pl* UT-8
**Summer Grove**—*pop pl* LA-4
Summer Grove Acres—*uninc pl* LA-4
Summer Grove Ch—*church* SC-3
Summer Grove Estates—*uninc pl* LA-4
Summer Grove Hills—*uninc pl* LA-4
Summer Grove Sch—*school* LA-4
*Summer Gulch* CO-8
Summer Gulch—*valley* MT-8
Summer Harbor—*bay* ME-1
Summer Harbor—*bay* MI-6
Summer Harbor—*locale* ME-1
*Summer Haven* MI-6
Summer Haven—*locale* FL-3
Summerhaven—*locale* ME-1
**Summerhaven**—*pop pl* AZ-5
**Summerhaven**—*pop pl* NC-3
**Summer Haven**—*pop pl* TN-4
Summer Haven Lake—*lake* NE-7
*Summerhaze Subdivision* UT-8
**Summer Haze Subdivision**—*pop pl* UT-8
**Summer Heights**—*pop pl* MA-1
*Summerhill* IL-6
*Summerhill* NY-2
Summer Hill—*hist pl* MD-2
Summerhill—*locale* PA-2
**Summer Hill**—*pop pl* IL-6
**Summerhill**—*pop pl* PA-2
**Summer Hill**—*pop pl* PA-2
**Summer Hill**—*pop pl* SC-3
Summer Hill—*summit* CT-1
Summer Hill—*summit* MA-1
Summer Hill—*summit* NY-2
Summer Hill—*summit* (3) PA-2
Summerhill—*uninc pl* MD-2
Summer Hill Cem—*cemetery* (2) AL-4
Summer Hill Cem—*cemetery* CT-1
Summer Hill Cem—*cemetery* IA-7
Summer Hill Ch—*church* AL-4
Summer Hill Ch—*church* (3) GA-3
Summer Hill Ch—*church* NY-2
Summer Hill Ch—*church* PA-2
Summer Hill Ch (historical)—*church* (2) AL-4
Summerhill Childrens Center—*school* FL-3
**Summerhill Estates Subdivision**—*pop pl* UT-8
Summer Hill Lake—*lake* TX-5
**Summer Hills**—*pop pl* TN-4
Summer Hills Ch—*church* GA-3
Summer Hill Sch—*school* IL-6
Summer Hill Sch—*school* VA-3
Summer Hill Sch (historical)—*school* AL-4
Summer Hill State For—*forest* NY-2
**Summer Hill (subdivision)**—*pop pl* DE-2
**Summerhill (Summer Hill)**—*pop pl* NY-2
**Summerhill (Town of)**—*pop pl* NY-2
**Summerhill (Township of)**—*pop pl* (2) PA-2
**Summerhill Village Subdivision**—*pop pl* UT-8
Summer (historical P.O.)—*locale* IN-6
Summer Hollow—*valley* MO-7
Summer Hollow—*valley* TN-4
**Summer Home**—*pop pl* CA-9
**Summerhome**—*pop pl* CA-9
**Summerhome Park**—*pop pl* CA-9
Summerhouse Branch—*stream* TN-4
Summerhouse Canyon—*valley* ID-8
Summerhouse Canyon—*valley* UT-8
Summerhouse Creek—*stream* SC-3
Summer House Hollow—*valley* TN-4
Summerhouse Mountain Cave—*cave* AL-4
Summerhouse Mtn—*summit* AL-4
Summer House Mtn—*summit* AL-4
Summerhouse Mtn—*summit* AL-4
Summerhouse Pit—*cave* AL-4
*Summer House Point* SC-3
Summerhouse Point—*cape* SC-3
Summerhouse Ridge—*ridge* UT-8
Summerhouse Spring—*spring* UT-8
Summer HS—*school* KS-7
Summerhurst—*locale* WA-9
Summer Ice Lake—*lake* WY-8
*Summer Island* FM-9
Summer Island—*island* MI-6
Summer Island Site—*hist pl* MI-6
Summer Knob Cem—*cemetery* TN-4
Summerlain Institute—*school* FL-3
*Summer Lake* FL-3
Summer Lake—*lake* OR-9
**Summer Lake**—*pop pl* OR-9
Summer Lake (CCD)—*cens area* OR-9
Summer Lake Hot Spring—*locale* OR-9
Summer Lake Hot Springs—*spring* OR-9
Summer Lake I D Canal—*canal* OR-9
*Summerlakes* IL-6
*Summer Lake State Game Mngmt Area* OR-9
Summer Lake State Wildlife Area—*park* OR-9
*Summerland* AZ-5
Summer Land—*flat* WA-9
**Summerland**—*pop pl* CA-9
**Summerland**—*pop pl* (2) MS-4
Summerland—*uninc pl* SC-3
Summerland Baptist Ch—*church* MS-4
Summerland Cem—*cemetery* MS-4
Summerland Group—*island* NY-2
Summerland Island—*island* NY-2
Summerland Key—*island* FL-3
**Summerland Key**—*pop pl* FL-3
Summerland Oil And Gas Field—*oilfield* MS-4
Summerland Park—*flat* CO-8
Summerland Sch—*school* AR-4
Summerland Sch (historical)—*school* MS-4
Summerland Swamp—*swamp* FL-3
**Summerlee**—*pop pl* WV-2
*Summerlin* NC-3
*Summerlin Crossroads* NC-3
Summerlin Lake—*reservoir* GA-3
**Summerlins Crossroads**—*pop pl* NC-3
*Summer Meadow Creek* MI-6
Summer Meadow Creek—*stream* MI-6
**Summer Meadows Subdivision**—*pop pl* UT-8
**Summer Mesa (subdivision)**—*pop pl* AZ-5
Summer Mtn—*summit* PA-2
Summer Oaks County Park—*park* WI-6
**Summer Oaks Subdivision**—*pop pl* UT-8
**Summer Oaks Twin Homes Subdivision**—*pop pl* UT-8
**Summer Oak Subdivision**—*pop pl* UT-8
Summerour Ch—*church* GA-3
Summerow Cem—*cemetery* NC-3
Summer Pecka Ditch—*canal* IN-6
**Summerplace Green (subdivision)**—*pop pl* (2) AZ-5
Summer Place Sch—*school* NJ-2
**Summer Place Trails (subdivision)**—*pop pl* (2) AZ-5
**Summer Place Village (subdivision)**—*pop pl* (2) AZ-5
Summer Point—*cape* VT-1
**Summer Point**—*pop pl* VT-1
**Summerport Beach**—*pop pl* FL-3
Summer Ranch—*locale* UT-8
*Summer Ranch Mountains* UT-8
Summer Range Airp—*airport* PA-2
Summer Range Canyon—*valley* UT-8
Summer Resort Key—*island* FL-3
Summer Resort Tank—*reservoir* NM-5
*Summer Ridge* CA-9
Summers—*locale* WV-2
**Summers**—*pop pl* AR-4
**Summers**—*pop pl* ME-1
Summers Airp—*airport* PA-2
Summer Saloon—*hist pl* CO-8
Summers Branch—*stream* AL-4
Summers Branch—*stream* SC-3
Summers Branch—*stream* (2) TN-4
Summers Cem—*cemetery* AL-4
Summers Cem—*cemetery* AR-4
Summers Cem—*cemetery* MS-4
Summers Cem—*cemetery* (5) MO-7
Summers Cem—*cemetery* (2) OH-6
Summers Cem—*cemetery* (4) TN-4
Summers Cem—*cemetery* TX-5
Summers Cem—*cemetery* (3) WV-2
Summers Ch—*church* IL-6
Summers Ch—*church* WV-2
Summer Sch—*school* KS-7
Summers Chapel—*church* GA-3
Summers Chapel—*church* MS-4
Summers Chapel Sch—*school* OK-5
**Summers (County)**—*pop pl* WV-2
Summers County Courthouse—*hist pl* WV-2
Summers Creek—*stream* CA-9
Summers Creek—*stream* MO-7
Summers Creek—*stream* (2) OR-9
Summers Creek—*stream* PA-2
Summers Creek—*stream* TN-4
Summers Creek—*stream* VA-3
Summers Creek—*stream* WA-9
Summers Ditch—*canal* (2) IN-6
Summers Ditch—*canal* WY-8
Summers Double Pot Cave—*cave* AL-4
Summers Drain—*canal* MI-6
*Summers Dry Creek* WY-8
Summerseat—*hist pl* PA-2
Summer Seat Creek—*stream* MS-4
Summer Seat Knob—*summit* KY-4
Summerseat Sch—*school* PA-2
Summers Elem Sch—*school* FL-3
*Summerset* CO-8
Summerset—*locale* IA-7
Summerset, Lake—*reservoir* IL-6
Summerset Cem—*cemetery* MO-7
Summerset Ch—*church* VA-3
**Summerset Junction (historical)**—*pop pl* IA-7
Summerset Lake—*reservoir* MO-7
Summerset Township—*fmr MCD* IA-7
Summers Ford—*locale* AR-4
Summers Fork—*stream* (3) WV-2
**Summer Shade**—*pop pl* KY-4
**Summer Shade**—*pop pl* TN-4
Summer Shade (CCD)—*cens area* KY-4
Summer Shade Ch—*church* TN-4
Summershade Sch—*school* KY-4
Summer Shade Sch (historical)—*school* TN-4
Summer Shoals—*bar* KY-4
Summers Hollow—*valley* AL-4
Summers Hollow—*valley* MO-7
Summers Hollow—*valley* (2) TN-4
Summer Shop Ctr—*locale* TN-4
**Summerside**—*pop pl* OH-6
**Summerside Estates**—*pop pl* OH-6
Summerside Sch—*school* OH-6
**Summersill Estates (subdivision)**—*pop pl* NC-3
Summersill Sch—*school* NC-3
Summers Island—*swamp* LA-4
Summers Lake—*lake* TX-5
Summers Lake—*reservoir* AL-4
Summers Lake Dam—*dam* (2) MS-4
Summers-Longley House-Building—*hist pl* IN-6
Summer Slough—*stream* AK-9
Summers Mound—*summit* MO-7
Summers Mtn—*summit* VA-3
Summerson Cem—*cemetery* PA-2
Summerson Hollow—*valley* PA-2
Summerson Mtn—*summit* PA-2
Summerson Run—*stream* (2) PA-2
Summers Park—*park* OR-9
Summers Park—*park* TN-4
Summers Pit—*cave* AL-4
Summers Post Office (historical)—*building* AL-4
Summer Springs Coulee—*valley* MT-8
Summers Ranch—*locale* NE-7
Summers Ranch—*locale* NM-5
Summers Ranch—*locale* OR-9
*Summers Reservoir* CO-8
Summers Ridge—*ridge* CA-9
Summers Rsvr—*reservoir* CO-8
Summers Rsvr—*reservoir* MT-8
Summers Sch—*school* NY-2
Summers Sch—*school* WV-2
Summers Sch (historical)—*school* MO-7
*Summers Spring* AZ-5
Summers Spring—*spring* AZ-5
Summers Spring—*spring* TN-4
Summers State Wildlife Mngmt Area—*park* MN-6
Summers Street Hist Dist—*hist pl* GA-3
**Summers Subdivision**—*pop pl* UT-8
Summers Tank—*reservoir* NM-5
Summers Top—*summit* AL-4
**Summers Township**—*pop pl* KS-7
Summer Street Hist Dist—*hist pl* MA-1
Summer Street Rsvr—*reservoir* MA-1
Summer Street Sch—*school* (2) MA-1
**Summer (subdivision)**—*pop pl* NC-3
*Summersville* IL-6
*Summersville* MO-7
*Summersville* PA-2
**Summersville**—*pop pl* IL-6
**Summersville**—*pop pl* KY-4
**Summersville**—*pop pl* MO-7
**Summersville**—*pop pl* OH-6
**Summersville**—*pop pl* TN-4
**Summersville**—*pop pl* WV-2
Summersville (CCD)—*cens area* KY-4
Summersville Ch—*church* IN-6
Summersville Chapel—*church* NC-3
Summersville Dam—*dam* WV-2
Summersville Lake—*reservoir* WV-2
Summersville (Magisterial District)—*fmr MCD* WV-2
*Summersville Reservoir* WV-2
Summersville Towersite State Wildlife Area—*park* MO-7
**Summertime**—*pop pl* NC-3
*Summerton* VA-3
Summerton—*locale* MI-6
**Summerton**—*pop pl* SC-3
Summerton (CCD)—*cens area* SC-3
*Summertown* TN-4
**Summertown**—*pop pl* CA-9
**Summertown**—*pop pl* GA-3
**Summertown**—*pop pl* (2) TN-4
Summertown Baptist Ch—*church* TN-4
Summertown (CCD)—*cens area* GA-3
Summertown (CCD)—*cens area* TN-4
Summertown Cem—*cemetery* TN-4
Summertown Division—*civil* TN-4
Summertown Elem Sch—*school* TN-4
Summertown HS—*school* TN-4
Summertown Lookout Tower—*locale* TN-4
Summertown Nazarene Ch—*church* TN-4
Summertown Post Office—*building* TN-4
Summer Trees—*hist pl* MS-4
**Summertree (subdivision)**—*pop pl* MS-4
**Summertree Subdivision**—*pop pl* UT-8
Summerview Sch (historical)—*school* TN-4
Summer Villa and the McKay-Salmon House—*hist pl* NC-3
*Summerville* CA-9
*Summerville* MI-6
*Summerville* PA-2
Summerville—*locale* AR-4
Summerville—*locale* CA-9
**Summerville**—*pop pl* AL-4
**Summerville**—*pop pl* CO-8
**Summerville**—*pop pl* GA-3
**Summerville**—*pop pl* IL-6
**Summerville**—*pop pl* LA-4
**Summerville**—*pop pl* NY-2
**Summerville**—*pop pl* OR-9
**Summerville**—*pop pl* PA-2
**Summerville**—*pop pl* SC-3
**Summerville**—*pop pl* TX-5
Summerville Assembly of God Ch—*church* AL-4
Summerville Bar—*bar* AL-4
Summerville Borough—*civil* PA-2
Summerville (CCD)—*cens area* GA-3
Summerville (CCD)—*cens area* SC-3
Summerville Cem—*cemetery* SC-3
Summerville Cem—*cemetery* TN-4
*Summerville Ch* AL-4
Summerville Ch—*church* AL-4
Summerville Ch—*church* (2) NC-3
Summerville Chapel (historical)—*church* MS-4
Summerville Country Club—*other* SC-3
Summerville Creek—*stream* CO-8
Summerville Creek—*stream* MD-2
Summerville Cutoff Bar—*bar* AL-4
Summerville Ford—*locale* AR-4
Summerville Gap—*gap* PA-2
Summerville Hist Dist—*hist pl* GA-3
Summerville Hist Dist—*hist pl* SC-3
Summerville (historical)—*locale* AL-4
Summerville (historical)—*locale* KS-7
**Summerville (historical)**—*pop pl* MS-4
**Summerville (historical)**—*pop pl* MO-7
Summerville-Imbler Cem—*cemetery* OR-9
Summerville Institute (historical)—*school* MS-4
Summerville Lake—*lake* MT-8
*Summerville Mountain* MS-4
Summerville Oil Field—*oilfield* LA-4
Summerville Presbyterian Church and Cemetery—*hist pl* NC-3
Summerville Sch—*school* AL-4
Summerville Sch—*school* SC-3
Summerville Speedway—*other* SC-3
Summerville State Fish Hatchery—*locale* GA-3
**Summerville (Tingley)**—*pop pl* PA-2
Summerville Trail—*trail* CO-8
Summerville United Methodist Ch—*church* MS-4
Summerville Wash—*valley* UT-8
Summerville Water Plant—*other* SC-3
**Summerwinds (subdivision)**—*pop pl* NC-3
**Summerwood Estates (subdivision)**—*pop pl* UT-8
**Summerwood (subdivision)**—*pop pl* MS-4
**Summer Wood Subdivision**—*pop pl* UT-8
**Summerwood Subdivision**—*pop pl* UT-8
*Summes Pond* ME-1
Summey Bridge Ch—*church* TN-4
Summey Cove—*valley* NC-3
**Summey Subdivision**—*pop pl* TN-4
*Summit* KS-7
*Summit* NE-7
*Summit* ND-7
*Summit* OH-6
*Summit* PA-2
*Summit* WV-2
Summit—*fmr MCD* NE-7
Summit—*hist pl* MD-2
Summit—*locale* AL-4
Summit—*locale* (2) AK-9
Summit—*locale* AR-4
Summit—*locale* (6) CA-9
Summit—*locale* (2) ID-8
Summit—*locale* IL-6
Summit—*locale* (2) KS-7
Summit—*locale* (2) KY-4
Summit—*locale* LA-4
Summit—*locale* ME-1
Summit—*locale* MI-6
Summit—*locale* (2) MN-6
Summit—*locale* MT-8
Summit—*locale* NM-5
Summit—*locale* NY-2
Summit—*locale* (2) NC-3
Summit—*locale* OH-6
Summit—*locale* OR-9
Summit—*locale* (5) PA-2
Summit—*locale* RI-1
Summit—*locale* TN-4
Summit—*locale* (2) TX-5
Summit—*locale* VT-1
Summit—*locale* (2) VA-3
Summit—*locale* (2) WA-9
Summit—*locale* WV-2
**Summit**—*pop pl* AL-4
**Summit**—*pop pl* (2) AR-4
**Summit**—*pop pl* CA-9
**Summit**—*pop pl* CO-8
**Summit**—*pop pl* IL-6
**Summit**—*pop pl* (5) IN-6
**Summit**—*pop pl* (3) IA-7
**Summit**—*pop pl* KY-4
**Summit**—*pop pl* MS-4
**Summit**—*pop pl* MO-7
**Summit**—*pop pl* (2) MT-8
**Summit**—*pop pl* NJ-2
**Summit**—*pop pl* NY-2
**Summit**—*pop pl* (3) OH-6
**Summit**—*pop pl* OK-5
**Summit**—*pop pl* (2) OR-9
**Summit**—*pop pl* (2) PA-2
**Summit**—*pop pl* SC-3
**Summit**—*pop pl* SD-7
**Summit**—*pop pl* TN-4
**Summit**—*pop pl* UT-8
**Summit**—*pop pl* VT-1
**Summit**—*pop pl* VA-3
**Summit**—*pop pl* (2) WV-2
**Summit**—*pop pl* WI-6
Summit—*summit* NH-1
Summit—*summit* PA-2
Summit—*uninc pl* GA-3
Summit—*uninc pl* NC-3
Summit—*uninc pl* TN-4
Summit—*uninc pl* WI-6
Summit, Lake—*lake* FL-3
Summit, Lake—*reservoir* NC-3
*Summit, The* AZ-5
*Summit, The* IN-6
Summit, The—*cliff* AZ-5
Summit, The—*locale* WY-8
Summit, The—*other* AK-9
Summit, The—*summit* NV-8
Summit, The—*summit* UT-8
*Summit Airfield* DE-2
Summit Airpark—*airport* DE-2
Summit Apartment Bldg—*hist pl* IA-7
Summit Area—*flat* UT-8
Summit-Argo—*post sta* IL-6
Summit Ave—*uninc pl* NJ-2
Summit Ave Sch—*school* CA-9
Summit Ave Sch—*school* NJ-2
Summit Aviation—*locale* DE-2
Summit Baptist Ch—*church* MS-4
Summit Bench—*bench* NV-8
**Summit Bridge**—*pop pl* DE-2
Summit Brook—*stream* IN-6
Summit Brook—*stream* ME-1
Summit Brook—*stream* NY-2
Summit Butte—*summit* OR-9
Summit Cabin—*locale* MT-8
Summit Cabin—*locale* OR-9
Summit Camp—*locale* CA-9
Summit Camp—*locale* ID-8
Summit Camp—*locale* OR-9
*Summit Campground* ID-8
Summit Campground—*locale* CA-9
Summit Campground—*locale* ID-8

Summit Campground—*locale* UT-8
Summit Campground—*park* AZ-5
Summit Camp Lake—*reservoir* NC-3
Summit Camp Lake Lower Dam—*dam* NC-3
Summit Camp Lake Upper Dam—*dam* NC-3
*Summit Canyon* ID-8
Summit Canyon—*valley* (2) AZ-5
Summit Canyon—*valley* (3) CA-9
Summit Canyon—*valley* CO-8
Summit Canyon—*valley* NM-5
Summit Canyon—*valley* UT-8
*Summit Canyon Creek* ID-8
Summit Cascade Divide—*ridge* OR-9
Summit Cave—*cave* TN-4
Summit (CCD)—*cens area* KY-4
Summit Cem—*cemetery* AL-4
Summit Cem—*cemetery* GA-3
Summit Cem—*cemetery* (3) IA-7
Summit Cem—*cemetery* (2) KS-7
Summit Cem—*cemetery* (2) MI-6
Summit Cem—*cemetery* MN-6
Summit Cem—*cemetery* (2) NE-7
Summit Cem—*cemetery* OK-5
Summit Cem—*cemetery* OR-9
Summit Cem—*cemetery* (2) PA-2
Summit Cem—*cemetery* (2) SD-7
Summit Cem—*cemetery* TN-4
Summit Cem—*cemetery* (2) WI-6
Summit Center—*locale* WI-6
Summit Ch—*church* AL-4
Summit Ch—*church* AR-4
Summit Ch—*church* (2) IA-7
Summit Ch—*church* (2) KS-7
Summit Ch—*church* MI-6
Summit Ch—*church* MO-7
Summit Ch—*church* (3) PA-2
Summit Ch—*church* VA-3
Summit Chapel—*church* PA-2
**Summit Chapel**—*pop pl* IN-6
Summit Chief Lake—*lake* WA-9
Summit Chief Mtn—*summit* WA-9
Summit Christian Sch—*school* FL-3
Summit City—*locale* CA-9
**Summit City**—*pop pl* CA-9
**Summit City**—*pop pl* MI-6
**Summit City**—*pop pl* MO-7
Summit City Cem—*cemetery* UT-8
Summit City Creek—*stream* CA-9
**Summit Corners**—*pop pl* WI-6
Summit County—*civil* UT-8
**Summit (County)**—*pop pl* OH-6
Summit County Courthouse—*hist pl* UT-8
Summit County Courthouse and Annex—*hist pl* OH-6
Summit County Hospital Heliport—*airport* UT-8
**Summit Cove**—*pop pl* CO-8
*Summit Crater* WA-9
Summit Crater—*crater* WA-9
*Summit Creek* ID-8
Summit Creek—*stream* (6) AK-9
Summit Creek—*stream* (9) CA-9
Summit Creek—*stream* (3) CO-8
Summit Creek—*stream* (13) ID-8
Summit Creek—*stream* (3) MT-8
Summit Creek—*stream* (5) NV-8
Summit Creek—*stream* (11) OR-9
Summit Creek—*stream* (4) UT-8
Summit Creek—*stream* (5) WA-9
Summit Creek—*stream* WI-6
Summit Creek—*stream* WY-8
Summit Creek Campground—*locale* WA-9
Summit Creek Cavern—*cave* MT-8
Summit Creek Ditch—*canal* ID-8
Summit Creek Guard Station—*locale* CO-8
Summit Creek Number Two Dam—*dam* UT-8
Summit Creek Number Two Rsvr—*reservoir* UT-8
Summit Creek Trail—*trail* OR-9
Summit Crossing—*locale* NY-2
*Summit Cut* AL-4
Summit Cut—*gap* VA-3
Summit Dam—*dam* SD-7
Summit Diggings—*locale* CA-9
Summit District Sch (historical)—*school* IA-7
Summit Ditch—*canal* CO-8
Summit Ditch—*canal* WY-8
**Summit East**—*pop pl* NJ-2
Summit Elem Sch—*school* MS-4
Summit Elem Sch—*school* PA-2
Summit Elem Sch (historical)—*school* AL-4
**Summit Farm**—*pop pl* AL-4
**Summit Farms**—*pop pl* MD-2
Summit Flat—*flat* CA-9
Summit Flat—*flat* (5) ID-8
Summit Forest Service Station—*locale* CA-9
Summit Glacier—*glacier* AK-9
Summit Golf Course—*locale* PA-2
**Summit Grove**—*pop pl* IN-6
**Summit Grove**—*pop pl* MA-1
Summit Grove Camp—*locale* PA-2
Summit Grove Ch—*church* IL-6
*Summit Grove Station* IN-6
Summit Guard Station—*locale* ID-8
Summit Guard Station—*locale* (2) OR-9
Summit Guard Station—*locale* WA-9
Summit Gulch—*valley* CA-9
Summit Gulch—*valley* CO-8
Summit Gulch—*valley* ID-8
*Summit Hayfield* OR-9
**Summit Heights**—*pop pl* IL-6
**Summit Heights**—*pop pl* MI-6
Summit Heights—*uninc pl* TX-5
Summit Heights Ch—*church* KY-4
*Summit Hill* IN-6
*Summit Hill* OH-6
Summit Hill—*locale* GA-3
Summit Hill—*locale* PA-2
**Summit Hill**—*pop pl* NY-2
**Summithill**—*pop pl* OH-6
**Summit Hill**—*pop pl* PA-2
Summit Hill—*summit* (2) CA-9
Summit Hill—*summit* ME-1
Summit Hill—*summit* NV-8
Summit Hill—*summit* PA-2
Summit Hill Borough—*civil* PA-2
Summit Hill Cem—*cemetery* SD-7
Summit Hill Ch—*church* (2) PA-2
Summit Hill Landing—*locale* NC-3
Summit Hill Ranch—*locale* CA-9
Summit Hills—*other* NM-5
**Summit Hills**—*pop pl* PR-3
Summit Hill Sch—*school* KS-7
Summit Hill Sch (historical)—*school* TN-4
Summit Hills Country Club—*other* KY-4
**Summit Hills Heights**—*pop pl* KY-4
**Summit Hills (subdivision)**—*pop pl* NC-3
**Summit Hills (subdivision)**—*pop pl* TN-4
Summit (historical)—*locale* KS-7
Summit (historical)—*locale* (2) SD-7
**Summit (historical)**—*pop pl* IA-7
**Summit (historical)**—*pop pl* OR-9
Summit (historical P.O.)—*locale* IA-7
Summit House—*locale* CA-9
Summit House—*locale* CO-8
Summit HS—*school* NJ-2
Summit Inn—*locale* CA-9
Summit Interchange—*crossing* NV-8
Summit Island—*island* (2) AK-9
Summit King Mine—*mine* NV-8
Summit Knobs—*summit* TN-4
**Summit Knoll**—*pop pl* MD-2
*Summit Lake* CA-9
*Summit Lake* MI-6
*Summit Lake* PA-2
*Summit Lake* WY-8
Summit Lake—*lake* (6) AK-9
Summit Lake—*lake* (24) CA-9
Summit Lake—*lake* (2) CO-8
Summit Lake—*lake* (4) ID-8
Summit Lake—*lake* (2) IN-6
Summit Lake—*lake* (2) MI-6
Summit Lake—*lake* (3) MN-6
Summit Lake—*lake* (5) MT-8
Summit Lake—*lake* NV-8
Summit Lake—*lake* (5) NY-2
Summit Lake—*lake* (6) OR-9
Summit Lake—*lake* (2) SD-7
Summit Lake—*lake* UT-8
Summit Lake—*lake* (8) WA-9
Summit Lake—*lake* (5) WI-6
Summit Lake—*lake* (2) WY-8
**Summit Lake**—*pop pl* WI-6
Summit Lake—*reservoir* IA-7
Summit Lake—*reservoir* NJ-2
Summit Lake—*reservoir* NY-2
Summit Lake—*reservoir* NC-3
Summit Lake—*reservoir* OH-6
Summit Lake—*reservoir* (2) PA-2
Summit Lake—*reservoir* WV-2
Summit Lake—*reservoir* WY-8
Summit Lake Campground—*locale* ID-8
Summit Lake Cem—*cemetery* MN-6
Summit Lake Cem—*cemetery* NV-8
Summit Lake Creek—*stream* PA-2
Summit Lake Dam—*dam* (2) PA-2
Summit Lake Flats—*flat* CO-8
Summit Lake Guard Station—*locale* CO-8
**Summit Lake Ind Res**—*pop pl* NV-8
Summit Lake Mtn—*summit* NV-8
Summit Lake Ranger Station—*hist pl* CA-9
Summit Lake Rsvr—*reservoir* IN-6
Summit Lakes—*area* AK-9
Summit Lakes—*lake* AK-9
**Summit Lake (Township of)**—*pop pl* MN-6
Summit Lake Trail—*trail* OR-9
Summit Lake Trail—*trail* WA-9
Summit Lake Trail—*trail* (2) WY-8
Summit Lake Well—*well* NV-8
Summit Lane Sch—*school* NY-2
**Summit Lawn**—*pop pl* PA-2
Summit Lawn Cem—*cemetery* (4) IN-6
Summit Lawn Sch—*school* KS-7
Summit Level Cem—*cemetery* IL-6
Summit Level Ridge—*ridge* CA-9
Summit Lookout—*locale* ID-8
Summit Lookout Tower—*locale* MN-6
Summit Lookout Tower—*locale* MS-4
Summit Lookout Tower—*locale* WI-6
Summit Mall Shop Ctr—*locale* OH-6
Summit Marsh—*swamp* CA-9
Summit Meadow—*flat* (8) CA-9
Summit Meadow—*summit* OR-9
Summit Meadow Lake—*lake* (2) CA-9
Summit Meadows—*flat* CA-9
Summit Meadows—*flat* OR-9
Summit Meadows Cem—*cemetery* OR-9
**Summit Mills**—*pop pl* PA-2
*Summit Mine* SD-7
Summit Mine—*mine* (2) AZ-5
Summit Mine—*mine* CA-9
Summit Mine—*mine* CO-8
Summit Mine—*mine* ID-8
Summit Mine—*mine* NM-5
Summit Mine—*mine* OR-9
Summit Mine—*mine* SD-7
Summit Motorway—*trail* AZ-5
Summit Motorway 39A—*trail* AZ-5
*Summit Mountain* CA-9
*Summit Mountain* UT-8
Summit Mountains—*other* NM-5
Summit Mount Emily Trail (jeep)—*trail* OR-9
Summit Mtn—*summit* AK-9
Summit Mtn—*summit* AZ-5
Summit Mtn—*summit* ME-1
Summit Mtn—*summit* MI-6
Summit Mtn—*summit* (2) MT-8
Summit Mtn—*summit* NV-8
Summit Mtn—*summit* NY-2
Summit Mtn—*summit* OR-9
Summit Mtn—*summit* UT-8
Summit Mtn—*summit* WA-9
Summit Narrows—*gap* UT-8
*Summit Number 1 Mine* AL-4
Summit of the Original South Pass—*gap* WY-8
Summit Park—*flat* CO-8
Summit Park—*flat* (2) UT-8
Summit Park—*locale* WA-9
Summit Park—*park* IL-6
Summit Park—*park* ME-1
Summit Park—*park* MO-7
Summit Park—*park* NM-5
Summit Park—*park* PA-2
**Summit Park**—*pop pl* MD-2
**Summit Park**—*pop pl* NY-2
**Summit Park**—*pop pl* UT-8
**Summit Park**—*pop pl* WV-2
Summit Park Golf Course—*other* UT-8
Summit Park Sanatorium—*hospital* NY-2
*Summit Pass* CO-8
Summit Pass—*gap* CO-8
Summit Pass—*gap* NV-8
Summit Pass—*gap* SD-7
Summit Patrol Cabin—*locale* HI-9
*Summit Peak* AZ-5
Summit Peak—*summit* AZ-5
Summit Peak—*summit* CO-8
Summit Peak—*summit* NM-5
Summit Peak—*summit* SD-7
**Summit Place (subdivision)**—*pop pl* AL-4
Summit Plantation House—*hist pl* SC-3
Summit Playground—*park* MI-6
Summit Plaza—*locale* PA-2
Summit Plaza (Shop Ctr)—*locale* FL-3
Summit Point—*cliff* CO-8
Summit Point—*locale* UT-8
**Summit Point**—*pop pl* WV-2
Summit Point—*summit* OR-9
*Summit Pond* ME-1
*Summit Pond* MI-6
Summit Pond—*lake* FL-3
Summit Pond—*lake* ME-1
Summit Pond—*lake* (2) NY-2
Summit Pond—*reservoir* UT-8
Summit Post Office (historical)—*building* PA-2
Summit Prairie—*flat* (4) OR-9
Summit Prairie—*flat* WA-9
Summit Prairie Ch—*church* IL-6
Summit Prairie Creek—*stream* WA-9
Summit Prairie Truck Barns (historical)—*locale* OR-9
Summit Private Sch—*school* (2) FL-3
Summit Pyramid—*summit* WA-9
Summit Ranch—*locale* ID-8
Summit Ranch—*locale* NE-7
Summit Ranch—*locale* OR-9
Summit Range—*range* CA-9
Summit Range, The—*range* WA-9
Summit Ranger Station—*locale* OR-9
*Summit Ridge* UT-8
**Summit Ridge**—*pop pl* IN-6
Summit Ridge—*ridge* CA-9
Summit Ridge—*ridge* ME-1
Summit Ridge—*ridge* (2) OR-9
Summit Ridge—*ridge* SD-7
Summit Ridge—*ridge* WI-6
Summit Ridge Lookout—*locale* SD-7
Summit Ridge Sch (historical)—*school* PA-2
Summit Ridge Spring—*spring* OR-9
**Summit Ridge (subdivision)**—*pop pl* NC-3
Summit Rock—*pillar* (2) CA-9
Summit Rock—*pillar* ID-8
Summit Rock—*pillar* OR-9
Summit Rock—*summit* OR-9
Summit Rock Point—*cape* OR-9
Summit (RR name for Summit Station)—*other* OH-6
Summit Rsvr—*reservoir* AZ-5
Summit Rsvr—*reservoir* (2) CA-9
Summit Rsvr—*reservoir* CO-8
Summit Rsvr—*reservoir* (2) ID-8
Summit Rsvr—*reservoir* OR-9
Summit Rsvr—*reservoir* SD-7
Summit Rsvr—*reservoir* WY-8
Summit Rsvr No. 1—*reservoir* CO-8
Summit Rsvr No. 2—*reservoir* CO-8
*Summit Sch* PA-2
Summit Sch—*hist pl* WA-9
Summit Sch—*school* AL-4
Summit Sch—*school* (6) CA-9
Summit Sch—*school* (3) IL-6
Summit Sch—*school* MN-6
Summit Sch—*school* (2) MO-7
Summit Sch—*school* (2) NE-7
Summit Sch—*school* NJ-2
Summit Sch—*school* NC-3
Summit Sch—*school* (2) OH-6
Summit Sch—*school* PA-2
Summit Sch—*school* TN-4
Summit Sch—*school* (2) TX-5
Summit Sch—*school* UT-8
Summit Sch—*school* WI-6
Summit Sch (abandoned)—*school* MO-7
Summit Sch (abandoned)—*school* (2) PA-2
Summit Sch (historical)—*school* MO-7
Summit Sch (historical)—*school* (2) PA-2
Summit School Airp—*airport* NC-3
Summit Shop Ctr—*locale* MO-7
*Summit Siding* KS-7
Summit Siding—*locale* VT-1
Summit (Site)—*locale* CA-9
Summit Ski Club—*other* MI-6
Summit Soda Springs—*hist pl* CA-9
*Summit Spring* ID-8
Summit Spring—*locale* ME-1
Summit Spring—*spring* (4) AZ-5
Summit Spring—*spring* (7) CA-9
Summit Spring—*spring* CO-8
Summit Spring—*spring* (3) ID-8
Summit Spring—*spring* MT-8
Summit Spring—*spring* (26) NV-8
Summit Spring—*spring* NM-5
Summit Spring—*spring* (10) OR-9
Summit Spring—*spring* (2) SD-7
Summit Spring—*spring* (3) UT-8
Summit Spring—*spring* (2) WA-9
Summit Spring Canyon—*valley* NV-8
Summit Spring Forest Camp—*locale* OR-9
*Summit Spring Hill* ME-1
Summit Spring Number One—*spring* ID-8
Summit Spring Number Two—*spring* ID-8
Summit Spring Ridge—*ridge* OR-9
*Summit Springs* NV-8
Summit Springs—*spring* CA-9
Summit Springs—*spring* CO-8
Summit Springs—*spring* (2) ID-8
Summit Springs—*spring* (2) MT-8
Summit Springs—*spring* (4) NV-8
Summit Springs—*spring* (2) OR-9
Summit Springs—*spring* UT-8
Summit Springs Battlefield Historical Marker—*park* CO-8
Summit Springs Creek—*stream* ID-8
Summit Springs Guard Station—*locale* UT-8
Summit Springs Hill—*summit* CA-9
Summit Springs Pass—*gap* ID-8
Summit Springs Shop Ctr—*locale* MO-7
Summit Spring Wash—*valley* UT-8
*Summit Station* KS-7
*Summit Station* MA-1
*Summit Station* PA-2
*Summit Station* SD-7
Summit Station—*locale* NJ-2
Summit Station—*locale* PA-2
**Summit Station**—*pop pl* OH-6
**Summit Station**—*pop pl* PA-2
Summit Station Creek—*stream* ID-8
Summit Station (historical)—*locale* KS-7
Summit Station (Site)—*locale* NV-8
Summit Street Sch—*school* PA-2
**Summit (subdivision)**—*pop pl* MA-1
**Summit (subdivision)**—*pop pl* NC-3
**Summit (subdivision)**—*pop pl* TN-4
*Summitsville* IN-6
**Summit Switch**—*pop pl* CA-9
**Summitt**—*pop pl* KY-4
Summit Tank—*reservoir* (3) AZ-5
Summit Tank—*reservoir* NM-5
Summitt Ch—*church* AL-4
Summitt Lateral—*canal* ID-8
Summit Town Hall—*building* ND-7
**Summit (Town of)**—*pop pl* NY-2
**Summit (Town of)**—*pop pl* (4) WI-6
Summit Township—*civil* MO-7
Summit Township—*civil* SD-7
Summit Township—*fmr MCD* (4) IA-7
**Summit Township**—*pop pl* (4) KS-7
**Summit Township**—*pop pl* MO-7
**Summit Township**—*pop pl* (2) NE-7
**Summit Township**—*pop pl* ND-7
**Summit Township**—*pop pl* (2) SD-7
Summit (Township of)—*fmr MCD* (2) AR-4
**Summit (Township of)**—*pop pl* IL-6
**Summit (Township of)**—*pop pl* (2) MI-6
**Summit (Township of)**—*pop pl* (2) MN-6
**Summit (Township of)**—*pop pl* OH-6
**Summit (Township of)**—*pop pl* (5) PA-2
Summit (Township of)—*unorg* ME-1
Summit Trail—*trail* (5) CA-9
Summit Trail—*trail* HI-9
Summit Trail—*trail* MT-8
Summit Trail—*trail* NV-8
Summit Trail—*trail* NM-5
Summit Trail—*trail* OR-9
Summit Trail—*trail* (3) PA-2
Summit Trail—*trail* (2) UT-8
Summit Trail—*trail* WA-9
Summit Trail (Camp)—*locale* NY-2
Summit Troughs—*summit* CA-9
Summit United Methodist Ch—*church* MS-4
Summit (Unorganized Territory of)—*unorg* ME-1
Summit Valley—*basin* (2) CA-9
Summit Valley—*basin* WA-9
Summit Valley—*locale* MT-8
Summit Valley—*valley* AZ-5
Summit Valley—*valley* (3) CA-9
Summit Valley—*valley* MT-8
Summit Valley—*valley* WI-6
Summit Valley Cem—*cemetery* WA-9
Summit Valley Sch—*school* WA-9
Summit Valley Sch—*school* (2) WI-6
Summit Valley Trail—*trail* CA-9
**Summit View**—*pop pl* DE-2
**Summit View**—*pop pl* SC-3
Summit View Campground—*locale* ID-8
Summitview Cem—*cemetery* IL-6
Summit View Cem—*cemetery* NY-2
Summit View Cem—*cemetery* OK-5
Summitview Sch—*school* WA-9
**Summitville**—*pop pl* CO-8
**Summitville**—*pop pl* IN-6
**Summitville**—*pop pl* IA-7
**Summitville**—*pop pl* NY-2
**Summitville**—*pop pl* OH-6
**Summitville**—*pop pl* TN-4
Summitville Baptist Ch—*church* TN-4
Summitville (CCD)—*cens area* TN-4
Summitville Division—*civil* TN-4
Summitville Methodist Ch—*church* TN-4
Summitville Mtn—*summit* TN-4
Summitville Post Office—*building* TN-4
Summitville Sch—*school* PA-2
Summitville Sch (historical)—*school* TN-4
Summit Wash—*stream* CA-9
Summit Well—*well* (2) AZ-5
**Summit (Yellville (sta.))**—*pop pl* AR-4
**Summons (historical)**—*pop pl* OR-9
Summons Swamp—*stream* SC-3
**Summum**—*pop pl* IL-6
Sumner—*locale* FL-3
Sumner—*locale* IA-7
Sumner—*locale* ME-1
Sumner—*locale* OK-5
**Sumner**—*pop pl* GA-3
**Sumner**—*pop pl* IL-6
**Sumner**—*pop pl* IA-7
**Sumner**—*pop pl* MD-2
**Sumner**—*pop pl* MI-6
**Sumner**—*pop pl* MS-4
**Sumner**—*pop pl* MO-7
**Sumner**—*pop pl* MT-8
**Sumner**—*pop pl* NE-7
**Sumner**—*pop pl* NC-3
**Sumner**—*pop pl* OH-6
**Sumner**—*pop pl* OR-9
**Sumner**—*pop pl* TX-5
**Sumner**—*pop pl* WA-9
**Sumner**—*pop pl* WI-6
Sumner, Charles, House—*hist pl* MA-1
Sumner, Charles, HS—*hist pl* MO-7
Sumner, Charles, Sch—*hist pl* DC-2
Sumner, Gaylord, House—*hist pl* SD-7
Sumner, Mound—*summit* IL-6
Sumner Amphitheater—*basin* UT-8
Sumner and Gibbs Streets Hist Dist—*hist pl* MA-1
Sumner Ave Sch—*school* MA-1
Sumner Bridge—*bridge* MO-7
Sumner Bridge—*other* MO-7
Sumner Brook—*stream* CT-1
Sumner Brook—*stream* NY-2
Sumner Brook—*stream* VT-1
*Sumner Butte* AZ-5
Sumner Butte—*summit* AZ-5
Sumner (CCD)—*cens area* GA-3
Sumner (CCD)—*cens area* TX-5
Sumner Cem—*cemetery* IL-6
Sumner Cem—*cemetery* IN-6
Sumner Cem—*cemetery* KS-7
Sumner Cem—*cemetery* ME-1
Sumner Cem—*cemetery* MI-6
Sumner Cem—*cemetery* MN-6
Sumner Cem—*cemetery* MO-7
Sumner Cem—*cemetery* TX-5
Sumner Cem—*cemetery* WA-9
Sumner Center Ch—*church* MN-6
Sumner Ch—*church* AR-4
Sumner Ch—*church* NC-3
Sumner Ch of God—*church* MS-4
*Sumner City* KS-7
*Sumner County* MS-4
Sumner County—*civil* KS-7
**Sumner County**—*pop pl* TN-4
Sumner County Courthouse—*building* TN-4
Sumner County Fairgrounds—*locale* TN-4
Sumner County Health Center—*hospital* TN-4
Sumner County Home—*locale* TN-4
Sumner County Library—*building* TN-4
Sumner County Memorial Hosp—*hospital* TN-4
Sumner County Park—*park* TN-4
Sumner County Shop Ctr—*locale* TN-4
Sumner County Sportsman Club Lake Dam—*dam* TN-4
Sumner County Vocational Education Sch—*school* TN-4
*Sumner Creek* CT-1
Sumner Creek—*stream* IL-6
*Sumner Ditch* IN-6
Sumner Drain—*stream* MI-6
Sumnere Acad—*school* TN-4
Sumner Elem Sch—*hist pl* KS-7
Sumner Elem Sch—*school* KS-7
Sumner Elem Sch—*school* MS-4
Sumner Falls—*falls* NH-1
Sumner Falls—*falls* VT-1
*Sumner Female Acad* TN-4
*Sumner Female Institute* TN-4
Sumner Field—*park* MN-6
Sumner Grange—*locale* OR-9
Sumner Hill—*summit* KS-7
Sumner Hill—*summit* ME-1
Sumner Hill Cem—*cemetery* ME-1
Sumner Hill Hist Dist—*hist pl* MA-1
*Sumner Hill HS* MS-4
Sumner Hill Sch—*school* MS-4
Sumner (historical)—*locale* KS-7
Sumner (historical)—*locale* SD-7
Sumner HS—*school* ME-1
Sumner HS—*school* MO-7
Sumner Island—*island* AK-9
Sumner Island—*island* IL-6
Sumner Island—*island* NH-1
Sumner Knob—*summit* TN-4
*Sumner Lake* NY-2
Sumner Lake—*lake* (2) FL-3
Sumner Lake—*lake* MI-6
Sumner Memorial Gardens—*cemetery* KS-7
*Sumner Mine* AL-4
Sumner Mine—*mine* CO-8
Sumner Mine—*mine* ID-8
Sumner Mine—*mine* KY-4
Sumner Mountains—*summit* AK-9
Sumner No. 2 Township—*fmr MCD* IA-7
Sumner Oil Field—*other* MI-6
Sumner Park—*park* GA-3
Sumner Pioneer Cem—*cemetery* OR-9
Sumner Point—*summit* AZ-5
Sumner Ridge—*ridge* CA-9
Sumners Bend—*bend* TN-4
Sumners Bridge—*bridge* TN-4
Sumners Cem—*cemetery* GA-3
Sumner Sch—*school* CA-9
Sumner Sch—*school* (3) IL-6
Sumner Sch—*school* (2) MA-1
Sumner Sch—*school* (2) MN-6
Sumner Sch—*school* MS-4
Sumner Sch—*school* MT-8
Sumner Sch—*school* NJ-2
Sumner Sch—*school* NY-2
Sumner Sch—*school* NC-3
Sumner Sch—*school* UT-8
Sumner Sch—*school* WV-2
*Sumners Chapel* MS-4
Sumners Chapel Cem—*cemetery* MS-4
Sumner Sch Number 23—*school* IN-6
Sumner Slough—*gut* SD-7
Sumners Pond—*lake* NH-1
Sumner Sportsman Club Lake—*reservoir* TN-4
Sumner Spring—*spring* NV-8
Sumner Station Cem—*cemetery* MA-1
Sumner Strait—*channel* AK-9
Sumner Stream—*stream* NY-2
**Sumnersville (historical)**—*pop pl* NC-3
Sumner Townhall—*building* IA-7
**Sumner (Town of)**—*pop pl* ME-1
**Sumner (Town of)**—*pop pl* (2) WI-6
Sumner Township—*fmr MCD* (4) IA-7
**Sumner Township**—*pop pl* (4) KS-7
**Sumner Township**—*pop pl* SD-7
Sumner Township (historical)—*civil* SD-7
Sumner (Township of)—*fmr MCD* NC-3
**Sumner (Township of)**—*pop pl* (2) IL-6
**Sumner (Township of)**—*pop pl* MI-6
**Sumner (Township of)**—*pop pl* MN-6
Sumnerville—*locale* KS-7
**Sumnerville**—*pop pl* MI-6
**Sumneytown**—*pop pl* PA-2
*Sumond Pond* MA-1
Sumond Pond—*reservoir* MA-1
Sumonton Ch—*church* TN-4
Sump Drain—*stream* MI-6
Sumpet Lake—*lake* MN-6
Sump Hole Well—*well* WY-8
Sumpkins Branch—*stream* WV-2
Sump Lake—*lake* OR-9
Sump Lake—*lake* WI-6
Sumps Cave—*cave* AL-4
Sump Tank—*reservoir* NM-5
Sumpter—*locale* AR-4
Sumpter—*locale* KY-4
Sumpter—*locale* OK-5
**Sumpter**—*pop pl* MI-6
**Sumpter**—*pop pl* OR-9
Sumpter Branch—*stream* (2) KY-4
Sumpter Bridge—*other* IL-6
Sumpter Cabin Creek—*stream* NC-3
Sumpter Cem—*cemetery* IL-6
Sumpter Cem—*cemetery* TX-5
Sumpter Ch—*church* MI-6
Sumpter Community Ch—*church* MI-6
Sumpter Creek—*stream* OR-9
Sumpter Creek Camp—*locale* OR-9
Sumpter East Oil Field—*other* IL-6
Sumpter Hill Cem—*cemetery* WI-6
**Sumpter (historical)**—*pop pl* TN-4
Sumpter Hollow—*valley* KY-4
Sumpter Island—*island* MN-6
Sumpter North Oil Field—*other* IL-6
Sumpter Oil Field—*other* IL-6
Sumpter Post Office (historical)—*building* TN-4
Sumpter Rsvr—*reservoir* OR-9
Sumpters Canyon—*valley* NM-5
Sumpter Sch—*school* MI-6
Sumpter South Oil Field—*other* IL-6
Sumpter Spring—*spring* CO-8
**Sumpter (Town of)**—*pop pl* WI-6
Sumpter (Township of)—*fmr MCD* AR-4
**Sumpter (Township of)**—*pop pl* IL-6
**Sumpter (Township of)**—*pop pl* MI-6
Sumpter Valley—*valley* OR-9
SUMPTER VALLEY GOLD DREDGE (dredge)—*hist pl* OR-9
Sumpter Valley Railway, Middle Fork-John Day River—*hist pl* OR-9
Sumpter Valley Railway Hist Dist—*hist pl* OR-9
Sumpter Valley Railway Passenger Station—*hist pl* OR-9
Sumpter Windmill—*locale* CO-8
Sumption Prairie Cem—*cemetery* IN-6
Sumption Prairie Ch—*church* IN-6
Sumption Sch—*school* SD-7
*Sumpwams Brook* NY-2
*Sumpwam's Creek* NY-2
*Sumpwams River* NY-2
Sumrail Bayou—*stream* MS-4
**Sumrall**—*pop pl* (2) MS-4
Sumrall-Albritton House—*hist pl* MS-4
Sumrall Attendance Center—*school* MS-4
Sumrall Cem—*cemetery* (2) MS-4
Sumrall Elem Sch—*school* MS-4
Sumrall (historical)—*locale* MS-4
Sumrall Lake—*reservoir* MS-4
Sumrall Lake Dam—*dam* MS-4
Sumrall Methodist Ch—*church* MS-4
Sumrall Mill Creek—*stream* MS-4
Sumrall MS—*school* MS-4
Sumrall Sportsman Club Dam Number 3—*dam* MS-4
*Sumrun Creek* MT-8
Sumter—*locale* AL-4
Sumter—*locale* GA-3
Sumter—*locale* MN-6
Sumter—*locale* NE-7
**Sumter**—*pop pl* AL-4
**Sumter**—*pop pl* SC-3
Sumter Acad—*school* AL-4
Sumter Calvary Ch—*church* SC-3
Sumter (CCD)—*cens area* SC-3
Sumter Cem—*cemetery* MN-6
Sumter Cem—*cemetery* SC-3
Sumter Chapel—*church* SC-3
Sumter Correctional Institute—*building* FL-3
Sumter Country Club—*other* AL-4
**Sumter County**—*pop pl* AL-4
**Sumter County**—*pop pl* FL-3
**Sumter (County)**—*pop pl* GA-3
**Sumter (County)**—*pop pl* SC-3
Sumter County Area Vocational Sch—*school* AL-4
Sumter County Courthouse—*hist pl* AL-4
Sumter County HS—*school* AL-4
*Sumter County Park* AL-4
Sumter County Training Sch—*school* AL-4
Sumter Farm and Stock Company Dam—*dam* (3) AL-4
Sumter Farms & Stock Co Inc Airp—*airport* AL-4
Sumter Fire Tower—*tower* AL-4
**Sumter Hills**—*pop pl* TN-4
Sumter Hist Dist—*hist pl* SC-3
Sumter Junction—*locale* SC-3
Sumter Lake Number Four—*reservoir* AL-4
Sumter Lookout Tower—*locale* GA-3
Sumter Lookout Tower—*tower* FL-3
Sumter Memorial Gardens—*cemetery* AL-4
Sumter Mine (underground)—*mine* AL-4
Sumter Natl For—*forest* SC-3
Sumter North (CCD)—*cens area* SC-3
Sumter Northeast (CCD)—*cens area* SC-3
Sumter Pond—*lake* AL-4
*Sumter Pond Number One* AL-4
Sumter Rec Area—*park* AL-4
Sumter Riding Club—*locale* AL-4
Sumter Sch—*school* AL-4
Sumter Sch—*school* GA-3
Sumter South (CCD)—*cens area* FL-3
Sumter Southeast (CCD)—*cens area* SC-3
Sumter Southwest—*CDP* SC-3
Sumter Southwest (CCD)—*cens area* SC-3
Sumter State Park (historical)—*park* AL-4
Sumter Town Hall-Opera House—*hist pl* SC-3
**Sumter (Township of)**—*pop pl* MN-6
**Sumterville**—*pop pl* AL-4
**Sumterville**—*pop pl* FL-3
Sumterville Cem—*cemetery* FL-3
Sumterville Ch—*church* AL-4
Sumunit—*locale* VT-1
Sumurunifou—*bar* FM-9
*Sun* KS-7
*Sun* MS-4
Sun—*locale* NY-2
**Sun**—*pop pl* LA-4
**Sun**—*pop pl* MI-6
**Sun**—*pop pl* MS-4
**Sun**—*pop pl* TX-5
**Sun**—*pop pl* WV-2
Sun—*post sta* AZ-5
Sun—*uninc pl* TX-5
Sun, Mtn of the—*summit* UT-8
Sun, Tom, Ranch—*hist pl* WY-8
*Sun Academy* MS-4
Sunaghun Creek—*stream* AK-9
Sunago Rsvr—*reservoir* OR-9
Sunagun Creek—*stream* AK-9
**Sunaire**—*pop pl* OH-6
Sun Altar—*summit* AZ-5
Sun Angel Stadium (track and field arena)—*locale* AZ-5
**Sunapee**—*pop pl* NH-1

Sunapee Harbor—*bay* NH-1
*Sunapee Hill* MA-1
Sunapee Lake—*lake* NH-1
Sunapee Mtn—*summit* NH-1
Sunapee Station—*locale* NH-1
**Sunapee (Town of)**—*pop pl* NH-1
*Sunbarum* MH-9
Sun Bayou—*channel* LA-4
Sun Bayou—*gut* LA-4
Sunbeach—*locale* WA-9
Sunbeam—*locale* CO-8
Sunbeam—*locale* VA-3
Sunbeam—*mine* UT-8
**Sunbeam**—*pop pl* FL-3
**Sunbeam**—*pop pl* ID-8
**Sunbeam**—*pop pl* IL-6
**Sunbeam**—*pop pl* PA-2
**Sunbeam**—*pop pl* WV-2
Sunbeam Cem—*cemetery* SD-7
Sunbeam Ch—*church* IL-6
Sunbeam Ch—*church* SD-7
Sunbeam Ch—*church* VA-3
Sunbeam Chapel—*church* WV-2
Sunbeam Creek—*stream* ID-8
Sunbeam Creek—*stream* WA-9
Sunbeam Drain—*canal* CA-9
Sunbeam Falls—*falls* WA-9
Sunbeam Farm Lake Dam Number Two—*dam* NC-3
Sunbeam Farm Lake Number Two—*reservoir* NC-3
Sunbeam Gulch—*valley* CO-8
*Sunbeam Hot Spring* ID-8
Sunbeam Hot Springs—*spring* ID-8
Sunbeam Lake—*lake* CA-9
Sunbeam Lake Dam—*dam* MS-4
Sunbeam Mine—*hist pl* UT-8
Sunbeam Mine—*mine* CO-8
Sunbeam Mine—*mine* ID-8
Sunbeam Mine—*mine* SD-7
Sunbeam Peak—*summit* WY-8
Sunbeam Prairie—*flat* OH-6
Sunbeam Rec Area—*park* CA-9
Sunbeam Sch—*school* KS-7
Sunbeam Sch—*school* OH-6
Sunbean Mine—*mine* MT-8
Sunberry Ch—*church* GA-3
Sunbird Airp—*airport* UT-8
*Sunbird Heliport* UT-8
Sunbird Place (Shop Ctr)—*locale* FL-3
Sun Bldg—*hist pl* DC-2
Sunbonnet Rock—*pillar* UT-8
Sun Bowl Plaza Shop Ctr—*locale* AZ-5
Sun Bowl Stadium—*other* TX-5
Sun Branch—*stream* TN-4
Sun Bright—*hist pl* FL-3
Sunbright—*locale* VA-3
**Sunbright**—*pop pl* TN-4
Sunbright (CCD)—*cens area* TN-4
Sunbright Division—*civil* TN-4
Sunbright First Baptist Ch—*church* TN-4
*Sunbright High School* TN-4
Sunbright Oil Field—*oilfield* TN-4
Sunbright Post Office—*building* TN-4
Sunbright Sch—*school* TN-4
Sunbright Seminary (historical)—*school* TN-4
**Sunbrook**—*pop pl* PA-2
**Sunburg**—*pop pl* MN-6
Sunburg Ch—*church* MN-6
*Sunburn* NJ-2
Sunburnt Spring—*spring* CA-9
Sunburn Windmill—*well* AZ-5
**Sunburst**—*pop pl* MT-8
**Sunburst**—*pop pl* NC-3
**Sunburst Circle Subdivision**—*pop pl* UT-8
**Sunburst Homes (subdivision)**—*pop pl* (2) AZ-5
Sunburst Lake—*lake* MT-8
Sunburst Lake—*reservoir* ND-7
Sunburst Lake Dam—*dam* ND-7
Sunburst Lake Natl Wildlife Ref—*park* ND-7
**Sunburst Meadows**—*pop pl* UT-8
Sunburst Paradise Park—*park* AZ-5
Sunburst Park—*park* WA-9
Sunburst Plaza Shop Ctr—*locale* AZ-5
Sunburst Ranch Airp—*airport* MO-7
Sunburst Sch—*school* AZ-5
Sunburst Shelter—*hist pl* AR-4
Sunburst Tunnels—*mine* CO-8
*Sunbury* PA-2
Sunbury—*locale* GA-3
Sunbury—*locale* IL-6
**Sunbury**—*pop pl* IA-7
**Sunbury**—*pop pl* NJ-2
**Sunbury**—*pop pl* NC-3
**Sunbury**—*pop pl* (2) OH-6
**Sunbury**—*pop pl* PA-2
Sunbury Airp—*airport* PA-2
*Sunbury Airp and Seaplane Base* PA-2
Sunbury Almshouse—*building* PA-2
Sunbury Ch—*church* GA-3
Sunbury Channel—*channel* GA-3
Sunbury City—*civil* PA-2
Sunbury Creek—*stream* GA-3
Sunbury Elem Sch—*school* NC-3
Sunbury Fabridam—*dam* PA-2
Sunbury Hist Dist—*hist pl* PA-2
*Sunbury Landing* GA-3
*Sunbury MS* PA-2
Sunbury Sch—*school* IL-6
Sunbury Sch—*school* IA-7
Sunbury Tavern—*hist pl* OH-6
Sunbury Township Hall—*hist pl* OH-6
**Sunbury (Township of)**—*pop pl* IL-6
Sun Butte—*summit* MT-8
Sun Butte—*summit* TN-4
Sun Canyon Lodge—*locale* MT-8
**Sun City**—*pop pl* AZ-5
**Sun City**—*pop pl* CA-9
**Sun City**—*pop pl* FL-3
**Sun City**—*pop pl* KS-7
**Sun City Center**—*pop pl* FL-3
Sun City Center Plaza (Shop Ctr)—*locale* FL-3
Sun City Community Hall—*building* AZ-5
Sun City Country Club—*other* AZ-5
Sun City Oil Field—*oilfield* KS-7
Sun City Post Office—*building* AZ-5
Sun City Regional Med Ctr—*hospital* FL-3
**Sun City Township**—*pop pl* KS-7
**Sun City West**—*pop pl* AZ-5
Suncliff—*cliff* PA-2
**Suncliff**—*pop pl* PA-2
Suncoast Baptist Ch—*church* FL-3
Sun Coast Ch—*church* FL-3
Suncoast Ch—*church* FL-3
Suncoast Christian Center—*church* FL-3
Suncoast Christian Ch—*church* FL-3
Suncoast Christian Sch—*school* FL-3
Suncoast Elem Sch—*school* FL-3
Suncoast Estates—*CDP* FL-3
Sun Coast Hosp—*hospital* FL-3
Suncoast HS—*school* FL-3
Suncoast Keys, The—*island* FL-3
Suncoast MS—*school* FL-3
Sunco Brook—*stream* CT-1
Sun Colliery Station—*locale* PA-2
Sun Company-Radnor Airp—*airport* PA-2
**Suncook**—*pop pl* NH-1
*Suncook Mountains* NH-1
*Suncook Pond* NH-1
Suncook River—*stream* NH-1
Sun Coulee—*valley* MT-8
*Sun Creek* KS-7
*Sun Creek* TX-5
Sun Creek—*stream* AZ-5
Sun Creek—*stream* CO-8
Sun Creek—*stream* ID-8
Sun Creek—*stream* (2) MS-4
Sun Creek—*stream* (2) MT-8
Sun Creek—*stream* NV-8
Sun Creek—*stream* OR-9
Sun Creek—*stream* WA-9
Sun Creek Sch (historical)—*school* MS-4
Suncrest—*locale* WV-2
**Suncrest**—*pop pl* CA-9
**Suncrest**—*pop pl* WV-2
Suncrest Brook—*stream* IN-6
Suncrest Cem—*cemetery* NC-3
Suncrest Golf Course—*locale* PA-2
**Sun Crest Heights (subdivision)**—*pop pl* UT-8
Suncrest Hosp—*hospital* MI-6
Suncrest Memorial Gardens—*cemetery* GA-3
Suncrest Park—*park* WV-2
*Sun Crest Park Subdivision* UT-8
**Suncrest Park Subdivision**—*pop pl* (2) UT-8
Suncrest Point Lookout—*locale* OR-9
Suncrest Rest Wayside—*park* OR-9
Suncrest Sch—*school* KS-7
Suncrest Sch—*school* UT-8
Suncrest Sch—*school* WV-2
**Suncrest (subdivision)**—*pop pl* AL-4
**Suncrest Subdivision**—*pop pl* UT-8
Suncrest Truck Trail—*trail* CA-9
**Suncrest Villas Chandler (subdivision)**—*pop pl* (2) AZ-5
**Suncrest Villas East (subdivision)**—*pop pl* (2) AZ-5
**Suncrest Villas Mesa (subdivision)**—*pop pl* AZ-5
**Suncrest Villas Mesa (subdivsion)**—*pop pl* AZ-5
**Suncrest Villas West (subdivision)**—*pop pl* (2) AZ-5
**Sundad**—*pop pl* AZ-5
Sundahl—*other* MN-6
**Sundahl Trailer Court (subdivision)**—*pop pl* SD-7
Sundal—*locale* MN-6
Sundal Ch—*church* MN-6
Sundale—*locale* PA-2
**Sundale**—*pop pl* (2) OH-6
**Sundale**—*pop pl* WA-9
Sundale Sch—*school* CA-9
Sundall Dam—*dam* SD-7
**Sundal (Township of)**—*pop pl* MN-6
Sundance—*locale* MT-8
**Sundance**—*pop pl* UT-8
**Sundance**—*pop pl* WY-8
Sundance Creek—*stream* CO-8
Sundance Creek—*stream* MT-8
Sundance Creek—*stream* WY-8
Sundance Glacier—*glacier* MT-8
Sundance Ground—*area* CO-8
Sun Dance Ground—*locale* ID-8
*Sun Dance Lake* MI-6
Sun Dance Lake—*lake* MI-6
Sundance Lake—*lake* MT-8
Sundance Mine—*mine* AZ-5
Sundance Mine—*mine* NM-5
Sundance Mine—*mine* SD-7
Sundance Mtn—*summit* (2) CO-8
Sundance Mtn—*summit* ID-8
Sundance Mtn—*summit* MT-8
Sundance Mtn—*summit* WY-8
Sundance Pass—*gap* MT-8
Sundance Ranch—*locale* CO-8
Sundance Ridge—*ridge* MT-8
Sundance Sch—*hist pl* WY-8
Sundance Ski Area—*park* UT-8
Sundance State Bank—*hist pl* WY-8
*Sunday* OH-6
Sunday, Robert H., House—*hist pl* IA-7
Sunday Bay—*bay* FL-3
Sunday Bay—*bay* MN-6
Sunday Bay—*swamp* MN-6
Sunday Bluff—*cliff* FL-3
Sunday Branch—*stream* KY-4
Sunday Branch—*stream* (2) NC-3
Sunday Butte—*summit* MT-8
Sunday Canyon—*valley* CA-9
Sunday Canyon—*valley* (2) UT-8
Sunday Corners (historical)—*locale* PA-2
Sunday Cove—*bay* ME-1
*Sunday Creek* AL-4
*Sunday Creek* MT-8
*Sunday Creek* OH-6
Sunday Creek—*stream* (3) AK-9
Sunday Creek—*stream* CA-9
Sunday Creek—*stream* CO-8
Sunday Creek—*stream* (2) ID-8
Sunday Creek—*stream* (4) MT-8
Sunday Creek—*stream* NY-2
Sunday Creek—*stream* OH-6
Sunday Creek—*stream* OR-9
Sunday Creek—*stream* TX-5
Sunday Creek—*stream* (4) WA-9
Sunday Creek Coal Company Mine No. 6—*hist pl* OH-6
Sunday Creek Ditch—*canal* CO-8
Sunday Creek Rsvr—*reservoir* MT-8
Sunday Ditch—*canal* VA-3
Sunday Falls—*falls* WA-9
Sunday Flats—*flat* TX-5
Sunday Gulch—*valley* AK-9
Sunday Gulch—*valley* CA-9
Sunday Gulch—*valley* CO-8
Sunday Gulch—*valley* ID-8
Sunday Gulch—*valley* MT-8
Sunday Gulch—*valley* SD-7
Sunday Harbor—*bay* AK-9
Sunday Hill—*summit* OR-9
**Sunday (historical)**—*pop pl* MS-4
*Sunday Island* FM-9
Sunday Island (historical)—*island* ND-7
Sunday Lake—*lake* (2) MN-6
Sunday Lake—*lake* NY-2
Sunday Lake—*lake* ND-7
Sunday Lake—*lake* (2) WA-9
Sunday Lake—*lake* WI-6
Sunday Lake—*reservoir* MI-6
Sunday Lake Mine—*mine* MI-6
Sunday Lakes—*lake* MT-8
Sunday Lick—*stream* KY-4
Sunday Lick Run—*stream* WV-2
Sunday Mine—*mine* ID-8
Sunday Mine—*mine* UT-8
Sunday Morning Creek—*stream* WY-8
Sunday Morning Mine (active)—*mine* WY-8
Sunday Morning Windmill—*locale* TX-5
Sunday Mtn—*summit* (2) MT-8
Sunday Mtn—*summit* NH-1
Sunday No 2 Mine—*mine* CO-8
Sunday Pass—*gap* AZ-5
Sunday Peak—*summit* CA-9
Sunday Peak—*summit* WY-8
Sunday Pond—*lake* (3) ME-1
Sunday Pond (historical)—*lake* ME-1
Sunday Rapids—*rapids* AK-9
Sunday Reel Fishery—*locale* FL-3
Sunday Ridge—*ridge* MT-8
Sunday Ridge—*summit* CA-9
Sunday River—*stream* ME-1
Sunday River Bridge—*hist pl* ME-1
Sunday River Cem—*cemetery* ME-1
Sunday River Whitecap—*summit* ME-1
Sunday Road Ch—*church* WV-2
Sunday Rollaway Creek—*stream* FL-3
Sunday Sch—*school* IL-6
Sunday School Canyon—*valley* UT-8
Sunday School Flats—*flat* CA-9
Sunday School Rsvr—*reservoir* UT-8
Sundays Landing—*locale* NC-3
Sunday Spring—*spring* CO-8
Sunday Swamp—*swamp* NY-2
Sunday Tunnel—*mine* UT-8
Sundberg Cem—*cemetery* MN-6
Sundby Hill—*summit* MT-8
Sund Creek—*stream* WA-9
Sunde Creek—*stream* AK-9
Sundeen JHS—*school* TX-5
Sundell—*locale* MI-6
Sundell Creek—*stream* CO-8
Sundell Lateral—*canal* ID-8
Sundell Rsvr—*reservoir* CO-8
Sunderlan Ch—*church* AL-4
**Sunderland**—*pop pl* MD-2
**Sunderland**—*pop pl* MA-1
**Sunderland**—*pop pl* VT-1
Sunderland Branch—*stream* IN-6
Sunderland Bridge—*bridge* MA-1
Sunderland Brook—*stream* VT-1
Sunderland Canyon—*valley* OR-9
Sunderland Cem—*cemetery* IN-6
Sunderland Cem—*cemetery* PA-2
Sunderland Cem—*cemetery* VA-3
*Sunderland Cemetery* TN-4
*Sunderland Creek* IN-6
*Sunderland Pond* NY-2
**Sunderland (subdivision)**—*pop pl* MA-1
**Sunderland (Town of)**—*pop pl* MA-1
**Sunderland (Town of)**—*pop pl* VT-1
*Sunderland Village* MA-1
Sunderlinville—*locale* PA-2
Sundet Cem—*cemetery* MN-6
Sun Devil Stadium (football)—*locale* AZ-5
Sundew Lake—*lake* OR-9
Sundheim Park—*park* ND-7
Sundia Beach—*beach* OR-9
**Sundial**—*pop pl* WV-2
Sundial, The—*summit* UT-8
Sundial Lake—*lake* MN-6
Sundial Mobile Park—*locale* AZ-5
Sundial Mtn—*summit* NM-5
**Sundial Park Subdivision**—*pop pl* UT-8
Sundial Peak—*summit* UT-8
*Sundial Rock* UT-8
Sundi Lake—*lake* AK-9
Sundin Johnson Ranch—*locale* WY-8
Sundins Beach—*locale* WA-9
Sun Ditch—*canal* WY-8
Sundling Creek—*stream* MN-6
Sundoer Sch—*school* IL-6
Sundog Lake—*lake* MI-6
Sun Dome Shop Ctr—*locale* FL-3
**Sun Down**—*pop pl* IN-6
**Sundown**—*pop pl* MO-7
**Sundown**—*pop pl* NY-2
**Sundown**—*pop pl* TX-5
Sundown, Lake—*lake* WA-9
Sundown Bay—*bay* TX-5
Sundown Bowl—*basin* CO-8
Sundown (CCD)—*cens area* TX-5
Sundown Ch—*church* MN-6
**Sundown Condominiums at Powder Mountain**—*pop pl* UT-8
Sundown Creek—*stream* FL-3
Sundown Creek—*stream* NY-2
Sundown Creek—*stream* OR-9
**Sundowner Condominium**—*pop pl* UT-8
**Sundown Estates Subdivision**—*pop pl* UT-8
Sundown Gap—*gap* OR-9
Sundown Girls Ranch—*locale* AZ-5
Sundown Golf Course—*other* WI-6
Sundown Gulch—*valley* CA-9
Sundown Hill—*summit* OK-5
Sundown Island—*island* LA-4
Sundown Lake—*lake* AK-9
Sundown Lake—*lake* MN-6
**Sundown Manor**—*pop pl* IN-6
Sundown Meadows—*flat* IL-6
Sundown Mine—*mine* CA-9
Sundown Mtn—*summit* OR-9
Sundown Pass—*gap* WA-9
Sundown Ranch—*locale* WA-9
Sundown Rsvr—*reservoir* ID-8
Sundown Rsvr—*reservoir* NV-8
Sundown Sch—*school* MN-6
**Sundown Subdivision**—*pop pl* (2) UT-8
**Sundown Subdivision Five**—*pop pl* UT-8
**Sundown (Township of)**—*pop pl* MN-6
Sundquist Lake—*lake* MN-6
Sundquist Ranch—*locale* (2) WY-8
**Sundre Township**—*pop pl* ND-7
*Sundricks Creek* MD-2
Sundstrom Island—*island* AK-9
Sundstrom Place—*locale* OR-9
Sundstrum Island—*island* MI-6
Sundt, M. M., House—*hist pl* NM-5
**Sundy Place**—*pop pl* PA-2
Sundy Sch—*school* SD-7
*Suneluah Creek* MS-4
Sun Empire Sch—*school* CA-9
Sunetha Flats—*flat* CO-8
Suneva Lake—*lake* AK-9
**Sunfair**—*pop pl* CA-9
**Sunfair Heights**—*pop pl* CA-9
**Sunfield**—*pop pl* IL-6
**Sunfield**—*pop pl* MI-6
Sunfield Cem—*cemetery* MI-6
Sunfield (Election Precinct)—*fmr MCD* IL-6
**Sunfield (Township of)**—*pop pl* MI-6
**Sunfire**—*pop pl* KY-4
Sunfish—*locale* KY-4
Sunfish Bay—*bay* MS-4
Sunfish Bay Public Use Area—*park* MS-4
Sunfish (CCD)—*cens area* KY-4
Sunfish Cem—*cemetery* OH-6
Sunfish Cove—*bay* AZ-5
Sunfish Cove—*bay* (2) NY-2
Sunfish Cove—*valley* NC-3
Sunfish Creek—*stream* (2) KY-4
Sunfish Creek—*stream* (2) OH-6
Sunfish Creek—*stream* SC-3
Sunfish Flat—*flat* FL-3
*Sunfish Lake* MN-6
Sunfish Lake—*lake* (2) IA-7
Sunfish Lake—*lake* MI-6
Sunfish Lake—*lake* (8) MN-6
Sunfish Lake—*lake* NE-7
Sunfish Lake—*lake* (9) WI-6
**Sunfish Lake**—*pop pl* MN-6
Sunfish Mtn—*summit* SC-3
Sunfish Pond—*lake* NJ-2
Sunfish Pond—*lake* PA-2
Sunfish Pond—*reservoir* VA-3
Sunfish Run—*stream* NY-2
Sunfish Run—*stream* PA-2
Sunfish Run—*stream* WV-2
Sunfish Sch—*school* KY-4
Sunfish Slough—*stream* IL-6
**Sunfish (Township of)**—*pop pl* OH-6
*Sunflower* KS-7
Sunflower—*locale* AZ-5
Sunflower—*locale* KS-7
Sunflower—*locale* (2) PA-2
Sunflower—*locale* UT-8
Sunflower—*locale* WV-2
Sunflower—*obs name* KS-7
**Sunflower**—*pop pl* AL-4
**Sunflower**—*pop pl* (2) MS-4
**Sun Flower**—*pop pl* WV-2
Sunflower, Mount—*summit* KS-7
Sunflower Aerodrome—*airport* KS-7
*Sunflower Baptist Ch* MS-4
Sunflower Baptist Ch—*church* MS-4
Sunflower Basin—*basin* AK-9
Sunflower Bend—*bend* AL-4
Sunflower Bend—*bend* AR-4
*Sunflower Bend Cutoff* AL-4
Sunflower Butte—*summit* AZ-5
Sunflower Butte Wash—*valley* AZ-5
Sunflower Butte Well—*well* AZ-5
Sunflower Canal—*canal* AZ-5
Sunflower Canyon—*valley* (2) NM-5
Sunflower Cem—*cemetery* LA-4
Sunflower Cem—*cemetery* MS-4
Sunflower Ch—*church* (2) AL-4
Sunflower Ch—*church* AR-4
Sunflower Ch—*church* LA-4
Sunflower Ch—*church* (4) MS-4
Sunflower Ch—*church* (2) TX-5
Sunflower Ch—*church* VA-3
Sunflower Chapel—*church* MS-4
Sunflower Ch (historical)—*church* AL-4
*Sunflower City* KS-7
*Sunflower City* MS-4
**Sunflower County**—*pop pl* MS-4
*Sunflower County Agricultural High School* MS-4
Sunflower County Courthouse—*building* MS-4
Sunflower Creek—*stream* AK-9
Sunflower Creek—*stream* CA-9
Sunflower Creek—*stream* ID-8
Sunflower Creek—*stream* OR-9
Sunflower Creek—*stream* TX-5
*Sunflower Creek - in part* MS-4
Sunflower Cutoff Bar—*bar* AL-4
Sunflower Cut-Off (1942)—*bend* AR-4
Sunflower Ditch—*canal* CO-8
Sunflower Drain—*canal* NE-7
Sunflower Flat—*flat* (2) AZ-5
Sunflower Flat—*flat* (6) CA-9
Sunflower Flat—*flat* CO-8
Sunflower Flat—*flat* (2) ID-8
Sunflower Flat—*flat* NV-8
Sunflower Flat—*flat* NM-5
Sunflower Flat—*flat* (5) OR-9
Sunflower Flat—*flat* UT-8
Sunflower Flat—*flat* WA-9
Sunflower Flat Pond—*lake* OR-9
*Sunflower Flats* OR-9
Sunflower Flats—*flat* OR-9
Sunflower Flat Spring—*spring* OR-9
Sunflower Glade—*flat* CA-9
Sunflower Grange Hall—*building* KS-7
*Sunflower Greentree Rsvr* MS-4
Sunflower-Greentree Rsvr—*reservoir* MS-4
Sunflower Gulch—*valley* CA-9
Sunflower Hill—*summit* CA-9
Sunflower Hill—*summit* NV-8
Sunflower Hot Springs—*spring* ID-8
Sunflower Island—*island* NJ-2
Sunflower JHS (historical)—*school* AL-4
*Sunflower Junior College* MS-4
Sunflower Knob—*summit* CA-9
Sunflower Lagoon Dam—*dam* MS-4
*Sunflower Lake* LA-4
*Sunflower Lake* WI-6
Sunflower Lake—*lake* LA-4
Sunflower Lake—*lake* NE-7
Sunflower Lake—*lake* NM-5
Sunflower Landing—*locale* MS-4
Sunflower Landing (historical)—*locale* AL-4
*Sun Flower Mesa* AZ-5
Sunflower Mesa—*summit* (3) AZ-5
Sunflower Mesa—*summit* (2) NM-5
Sunflower Mesa Tank—*reservoir* AZ-5
Sunflower Methodist Ch—*church* MS-4
Sunflower Mine—*mine* AZ-5
Sunflower Mine—*mine* CO-8
Sunflower Mine—*mine* SD-7
Sunflower Mtn—*summit* MT-8
Sunflower Mtn—*summit* NV-8
Sunflower Ordnance Works—*military* KS-7
Sunflower Park—*park* KS-7
Sunflower Plantation (historical)—*locale* MS-4
Sunflower Point—*cape* LA-4
Sunflower Pond—*lake* IN-6
Sunflower Pond B Dam—*dam* KS-7
Sunflower Presbyterian Ch (historical)—*church* MS-4
Sunflower Ranger Station—*locale* AZ-5
Sunflower Revetment—*levee* MS-4
*Sunflower River* MS-4
Sunflower Rsvr—*reservoir* NV-8
Sunflower Saddle—*gap* AZ-5
Sunflower Sch—*school* CA-9
Sunflower Sch—*school* (2) KS-7
Sunflower Sch—*school* LA-4
Sunflower Sch—*school* MS-4
Sunflower Sch—*school* NE-7
Sunflower Sch—*school* SD-7
Sunflower Sch (historical)—*school* AL-4
Sunflower Sch (historical)—*school* (2) MS-4
Sunflower Shopping Plaza—*locale* FL-3
Sunflower Spring—*spring* AZ-5
Sunflower Spring—*spring* (2) CA-9
Sunflower Spring—*spring* OR-9
Sunflower Tank—*reservoir* AZ-5
Sunflower Tank—*reservoir* (3) NM-5
Sunflower Trail—*trail* CA-9
Sunflower Valley—*basin* CA-9
Sunflower Valley—*valley* AZ-5
Sunflower Wash—*stream* CA-9
Sunflower Waterfowl Project—*park* MS-4
Sunflower Work Center—*locale* AZ-5
Sungabi Creek—*stream* AZ-5
Sunganspaul, Infal—*stream* FM-9
Sun Garden—*locale* FL-3
**Sun Garden**—*pop pl* FL-3
**Sun Garden Village**—*pop pl* CA-9
**Sun Gate**—*pop pl* TX-5
Sungate Acad—*school* FL-3
Sungic Point—*cape* NY-2
*Sunglow* UT-8
Sunglow Forest Camp—*locale* UT-8
Sungold Mine—*mine* ID-8
**Sungopavi**—*pop pl* AZ-5
Sungovoak, Lake—*lake* AK-9
Sun Grove Ch—*church* TX-5
Sun Grove Mobile Home Park—*locale* AZ-5
**Sun Harbor**—*pop pl* WA-9
*Sunharon* MH-9
*Sunharon Roads* MH-9
**Sun Haven**—*pop pl* FL-3
**Sun Haven**—*pop pl* NY-2
Sunhigh Lake—*lake* MN-6
Sun Hill—*locale* GA-3
**Sun Hill**—*pop pl* GA-3
**Sun Hill**—*pop pl* WV-2
Sun Hill—*summit* OH-6
Sun Hill—*summit* PA-2
Sun Hill Cem—*cemetery* GA-3
Sun Hill Creek—*stream* GA-3
Sun House—*hist pl* CA-9
Sunhouse Peaks—*summit* NM-5
Sunia Lake—*lake* WI-6
Suniland Acad—*school* FL-3
Suniland Oil Field—*oilfield* TX-5
Suniland Park—*park* FL-3
Suniland Shop Ctr—*locale* FL-3
**Suniland (subdivision)**—*pop pl* FL-3
Sunior Drain—*canal* MI-6
Sunitsch Canyon—*valley* WA-9
**Sunizona**—*pop pl* AZ-5
Sunkauissia Creek—*stream* NY-2
Sunk Branch—*stream* NC-3
Sunk Brook—*stream* (2) MA-1
Sunk Cane Branch—*stream* TN-4
Sunk Canyon—*valley* CA-9
Sunk Creek—*stream* MT-8
Sunken Black Ledge—*bar* ME-1
Sunken Bog Brook—*stream* ME-1
Sunken Branch—*stream* NJ-2
Sunken Branch—*stream* PA-2
Sunken Branch Brook—*stream* ME-1
Sunken Bridge Drain—*stream* MI-6
*Sunken Brook* NJ-2
Sunken Brook—*stream* MA-1
Sunken Camp Lake—*lake* WI-6
Sunken Coral Heads—*bar* FL-3
Sunken Creek—*stream* IA-7
Sunken Duck Rock—*bar* ME-1
Sunken For—*woods* NY-2
Sunken Garden Park—*park* IA-7
Sunken Gardens—*hist pl* CO-8
Sunken Gardens—*park* IL-6
Sunken Gardens Park—*park* IL-6
*Sunken Grove* IA-7
Sunken Grove State Game Mngmt Area—*park* IA-7
Sunken Heath—*swamp* ME-1
Sunken Island—*island* FL-3
Sunken Island—*island* NH-1
Sunken Island—*island* NY-2
Sunken Island—*island* VT-1
Sunken Island—*island* VA-3
Sunken Island Lake—*lake* AK-9
Sunken Island Lake—*lake* IA-7
Sunken Island Marsh—*swamp* MD-2
*Sunken Lake* WI-6
Sunken Lake—*lake* AK-9
Sunken Lake—*lake* CO-8
Sunken Lake—*lake* IA-7
Sunken Lake—*lake* ME-1
Sunken Lake—*lake* (2) MI-6
Sunken Lake—*lake* MN-6
Sunken Ledge—*bar* ME-1
Sunken Ledge—*bar* (2) MA-1
Sunken Ledge—*rock* MA-1
Sunken Marsh—*swamp* VA-3
*Sunken Marsh Creek* VA-3
Sunken Meadow—*swamp* MA-1
Sunken Meadow—*swamp* NY-2
**Sunken Meadow Beach**—*pop pl* MA-1
Sunken Meadow Creek—*stream* NY-2
Sunken Meadow Creek—*stream* VA-3
Sunken Meadow Pond—*reservoir* VA-3
Sunken Meadows Marshes—*swamp* MA-1
Sunken Meadow State Park—*park* NY-2
Sunken Pond—*lake* ME-1
Sunken Pond Ledge—*bar* ME-1
Sunken Rock Lighthouse—*locale* NY-2
Sunken Stream—*stream* ME-1
Sunk Gulch—*valley* CA-9
Sunkhaze Meadows—*swamp* ME-1
Sunkhaze Stream—*stream* ME-1
Sunk Hill—*summit* LA-4
Sunkirk Mine—*mine* CO-8
Sunkissed Island—*island* NY-2
Sunkist—*locale* CA-9
Sunkist—*locale* NV-8
Sunkist—*locale* OK-5
Sunkist—*uninc pl* CA-9
**Sunkist Beach**—*pop pl* TN-4
Sunkist Estates Park—*park* FL-3
Sunkist Golf Course—*locale* MS-4
Sunkist Sch—*school* (2) CA-9
**Sunkist (subdivision)**—*pop pl* MS-4
Sunk Lake—*lake* LA-4
Sunk Lake—*lake* OK-5
Sunk Lake—*lake* TN-4
Sunk Lake Slough—*stream* OK-5
Sunkland, The—*basin* MO-7
Sunklands-Burr Oak State Wildlife Area—*park* MO-7
Sunk Meadow—*swamp* MA-1
Sunkota Ridge—*ridge* NC-3
Sunk Pond—*lake* FL-3
Sunk Pond—*lake* (2) MA-1
*Sunk Rock* RI-1
Sunk Rock—*rock* MA-1
Sunks Creek—*gut* NJ-2
Sunk Timber Lake—*flat* AR-4
Sun Lagoon—*lake* LA-4
*Sun Lake* MI-6
Sun Lake—*lake* AK-9
Sun Lake—*lake* IL-6
Sun Lake—*lake* MI-6
Sun Lake—*lake* MN-6
Sun Lake—*lake* MT-8
Sun Lake—*reservoir* FL-3
**Sun Lakes**—*pop pl* AZ-5
Sun Lakes Golf Course—*other* AZ-5
Sun Lakes State Park—*park* WA-9
Sunland—*locale* CA-9
Sunland—*locale* KS-7
**Sunland**—*pop pl* CA-9
Sunland Center State Park—*park* FL-3
**Sunland Estates**—*pop pl* FL-3
**Sunland Gardens**—*pop pl* FL-3
Sunland Gin Road Interchange—*crossing* AZ-5
**Sunland Hills**—*pop pl* MO-7
Sunland Hosp Unit—*hospital* FL-3
Sunland Mariana Cox Medical Services Center—*hospital* FL-3
*Sunland Memorial Park* AZ-5
Sun Land Memorial Park—*cemetery* AZ-5
Sunland Park—*park* CA-9
Sunland Park—*park* FL-3
**Sunland Park**—*pop pl* NM-5
Sunland Park Elem Sch—*school* FL-3
Sunland Park Racetrack—*other* NM-5
Sunland Ranch—*locale* CA-9
Sunland Sch—*school* AZ-5
Sunland Sch—*school* CA-9
**Sunland (Sunland Estates)**—*pop pl* FL-3
Sunland Training Center (State Hospital)—*hospital* FL-3
Sunland Village Golf Course—*other* AZ-5
Sun Lane Airp—*airport* KS-7
Sun Life Travel Trailer Park—*locale* AZ-5
Sunlight—*locale* MO-7
Sunlight—*locale* MT-8
Sunlight—*locale* WV-2
**Sunlight**—*pop pl* AL-4
**Sunlight**—*pop pl* VA-3
Sunlight Baptist Ch—*church* (2) AL-4
Sunlight Baptist Ch—*church* FL-3
Sun Light Baptist Ch—*church* MS-4
Sunlight Basin—*basin* MT-8
Sunlight Basin—*basin* WY-8
Sunlight Bay Rec Area—*park* AR-4
**Sunlight Beach**—*pop pl* WA-9
Sunlight Canal—*canal* WY-8
Sunlight Canyon—*valley* WY-8
Sunlight Cem—*cemetery* AR-4
Sunlight Cem—*cemetery* GA-3
Sunlight Ch—*church* (2) AL-4
Sunlight Ch—*church* (2) GA-3
Sunlight Ch—*church* (6) LA-4
Sunlight Ch—*church* (2) MS-4
Sunlight Ch—*church* NC-3
Sunlight Ch—*church* TX-5
Sunlight Creek—*stream* CO-8
Sunlight Creek—*stream* (2) MT-8
Sunlight Creek—*stream* WY-8
Sunlight Gulch—*valley* WY-8
Sunlight Lake—*lake* CO-8
Sunlight Lake—*lake* MT-8
Sunlight Mesa—*summit* WY-8
Sunlight Mine—*mine* CO-8
Sunlight Mining Region—*area* WY-8
Sunlight Mission—*locale* AZ-5
Sunlight Missionary Baptist Ch—*church* AL-4
**Sunlight Park**—*pop pl* GA-3
Sunlight Peak—*summit* (2) CO-8
Sunlight Peak—*summit* MT-8
Sunlight Peak—*summit* WY-8
Sunlight Picnic Ground—*locale* WY-8

Sun Oil Bldg—*hist pl* PA-2
**Sun Oil Camp**—*pop pl* TX-5
Sun Oil Company Canal—*canal* TX-5
Sun Oil Field—*oilfield* TX-5
Sunol—*locale* PA-2
**Sunol**—*pop pl* CA-9
**Sunol**—*pop pl* NE-7
Sunol Aqueduct—*canal* CA-9
Sunol Glen Sch—*school* CA-9
Sunol Ridge—*ridge* CA-9
Sunol Sch—*school* CA-9
Sunol Valley—*valley* CA-9
Sunol Valley Golf Course—*other* CA-9
Sunol Valley Regional Park—*park* CA-9
Sunowa Springs Camp—*locale* FL-3
*Sunower Spring* OR-9
Sun Park—*flat* CO-8
Sun Pass—*gap* OR-9
Sun Pass State For—*forest* OR-9
*Sun Peak* NV-8
Sun Pewee Mine (surface)—*mine* TN-4
Sun Plaza (Shop Ctr)—*locale* FL-3
Sun Point—*cape* FL-3
Sun Point—*cape* LA-4
Sun Point—*cape* TX-5
Sun Point—*cape* WA-9
Sun Point—*cliff* CO-8
Sunpoint and Office Center (Shop Ctr)—*locale* FL-3
Sun Point Pueblo—*locale* CO-8
Sun Pond—*lake* GA-3
Sun Post Office (historical)—*building* MS-4
Sun Prairie—*locale* MT-8
**Sun Prairie**—*pop pl* WI-6
Sun Prairie Baptist Cem—*cemetery* SD-7
Sun Prairie Ch—*church* SD-7
Sun Prairie Flats—*flat* MT-8
Sun Prairie Sch—*school* MT-8
**Sun Prairie (Town of)**—*pop pl* WI-6
**Sun Prairie Township**—*pop pl* SD-7
Sun Prairie Township Hall—*building* SD-7
Sunquam Sch—*school* NY-2
Sunquist Draw—*valley* WY-8
Sun Ranch—*locale* MT-8
Sun Ranch—*locale* (2) WY-8
Sunray—*locale* VA-3
**Sunray**—*pop pl* OK-5
**Sunray**—*pop pl* TX-5
Sunray Beach—*beach* NJ-2
**Sunray (Beckett)**—*pop pl* OK-5
Sunray (CCD)—*cens area* TX-5
**Sun Ray Homes**—*pop pl* FL-3
**Sunray Manor (subdivision)**—*pop pl* (2) AZ-5
Sun Ray Plaza Shop Ctr—*locale* AL-4
Sun Ray Shop Ctr—*locale* FL-3
**Sun Ray Subdivision**—*pop pl* UT-8
**Sunray Subdivision**—*pop pl* UT-8
*Sunray Village* OK-5
Sunray Village—*other* OK-5
*Sun Ridge* IL-6
**Sunridge Highlands Subdivision**—*pop pl* UT-8
**Sunridge IV (subdivision)**—*pop pl* (2) AZ-5
Sunrift Gorge—*valley* MT-8
Sunrift Hall—*building* MT-8
*Sunrise* AZ-5
*Sunrise* MP-9
Sunrise—*hist pl* WV-2
Sunrise—*locale* AK-9
Sunrise—*locale* AZ-5
Sunrise—*locale* CA-9
Sunrise—*locale* MS-4
Sunrise—*locale* OH-6
Sunrise—*locale* (2) OK-5
Sunrise—*locale* TN-4
Sunrise—*locale* WA-9
Sunrise—*mine* AZ-5
**Sunrise**—*pop pl* (3) FL-3
**Sunrise**—*pop pl* KY-4
**Sunrise**—*pop pl* LA-4
**Sunrise**—*pop pl* MD-2
**Sunrise**—*pop pl* MN-6
**Sunrise**—*pop pl* MS-4
**Sunrise**—*pop pl* MO-7
**Sunrise**—*pop pl* PA-2
**Sunrise**—*pop pl* (3) TN-4
**Sunrise**—*pop pl* (2) TX-5
**Sunrise**—*pop pl* WV-2
**Sunrise**—*pop pl* WY-8
Sunrise—*uninc pl* NC-3
Sunrise—*uninc pl* TX-5
Sunrise Acad—*school* FL-3
Sunrise Academy/Sunrise Sch—*school* FL-3
*Sun Rise Acres* NV-8
**Sunrise Acres**—*pop pl* TX-5
Sunrise Acres Ch—*church* LA-4
Sunrise Acres Sch—*school* NV-8
**Sunrise Acres (subdivision)**—*pop pl* (2) NC-3
Sunrise Airfield—*airport* AZ-5
Sunrise And Tuolumne Meadows Trail—*trail* CA-9
Sunrise Baptist Ch—*church* (2) MS-4
Sunrise Basin—*basin* NV-8
Sunrise Bay—*bay* FL-3
Sunrise Bay—*bay* ID-8
**Sunrise Bay**—*pop pl* WI-6
Sunrise Bay Center (Shop Ctr)—*locale* FL-3
Sunrise Bayou—*gut* MS-4
Sunrise Beach—*beach* (2) MA-1
Sunrise Beach—*locale* NJ-2
Sunrise Beach—*locale* WA-9
**Sunrise Beach**—*pop pl* IN-6
**Sunrise Beach**—*pop pl* MD-2
**Sunrise Beach**—*pop pl* MO-7
**Sunrise Beach**—*pop pl* NC-3
Sunrise Beach—*post sta* TX-5
**Sunrise Beach Village**—*pop pl* TX-5
Sunrise Branch—*stream* WV-2
Sunrise Bridge—*bridge* FL-3
**Sunrise (Br. P.O. name City of Sunrise)**—*pop pl* FL-3
Sunrise Burial Park—*cemetery* VA-3
Sunrise Butte—*summit* CA-9
Sunrise Butte—*summit* OR-9
Sunrise Camp—*locale* NV-8
Sunrise Camp—*locale* VT-1
Sunrise Campground—*locale* UT-8
Sunrise Canyon—*valley* CA-9
Sunrise Canyon—*valley* CO-8
Sunrise Canyon—*valley* UT-8
Sunrise Cem—*cemetery* AL-4
Sunrise Cem—*cemetery* AK-9
Sunrise Cem—*cemetery* AR-4
Sunrise Cem—*cemetery* GA-3
Sunrise Cem—*cemetery* MD-2
Sunrise Cem—*cemetery* MN-6
Sunrise Cem—*cemetery* MS-4
Sunrise Cem—*cemetery* MO-7
Sunrise Cem—*cemetery* (2) NE-7
Sunrise Cem—*cemetery* NC-3
Sunrise Cem—*cemetery* OH-6
Sunrise Cem—*cemetery* (2) OK-5
Sunrise Cem—*cemetery* OR-9
Sunrise Cem—*cemetery* (5) TN-4
Sunrise Cem—*cemetery* VA-3
Sunrise Ch—*church* (3) AR-4
Sunrise Ch—*church* (3) LA-4
Sunrise Ch—*church* (4) MS-4
Sunrise Ch—*church* (2) MO-7
Sunrise Ch—*church* NC-3
Sunrise Ch—*church* PA-2
Sunrise Ch—*church* (4) TN-4
Sunrise Ch—*church* TX-5
Sunrise Ch—*church* VA-3
Sunrise Ch—*church* WA-9
Sunrise Ch—*church* (3) WV-2
Sunrise Chapel—*church* IN-6
Sun Rise Chapel—*church* WV-2
Sunrise Chapel—*church* WV-2
Sunrise Ch (historical)—*church* MS-4
*Sunrise Church* KS-7
*Sunrise City* CA-9
Sunrise Club—*other* CA-9
Sunrise Country Club—*locale* FL-3
Sunrise Cove—*bay* WA-9
Sunrise Creek—*stream* (3) AK-9
Sunrise Creek—*stream* (3) CA-9
Sunrise Creek—*stream* MT-8
Sunrise Creek—*stream* NV-8
Sunrise Creek—*stream* OR-9
Sunrise Creek—*stream* (3) WA-9
Sunrise Dam—*dam* AZ-5
Sunrise Ditch—*canal* CO-8
Sunrise Drive Sch—*school* AZ-5
Sunrise Drive Sch—*school* NY-2
Sunrise Dugway—*trail* UT-8
*Sunrise Gap* NC-3
Sunrise Glacier—*glacier* AK-9
Sunrise Glacier—*glacier* MT-8
*Sunrise Golf Village* FL-3
Sunrise Golf Village—*other* FL-3
Sunrise Grange—*locale* WA-9
*Sunrise Gulch* MT-8
Sunrise Gulch—*valley* AK-9
Sunrise Gulch—*valley* MT-8
**Sunrise Harbor**—*pop pl* FL-3
**Sunrise Heights**—*pop pl* FL-3
Sunrise Heights Mobile Home Park—*locale* AZ-5
**Sunrise Heights (subdivision)**—*pop pl* MI-6
Sunrise Hill—*locale* WY-8
**Sunrise Hill**—*pop pl* CT-1
Sunrise Hill—*summit* MT-8
Sunrise Hill—*summit* SD-7
Sunrise Hill—*summit* TX-5
Sunrise Hill—*summit* UT-8
**Sunrise Hills Subdivision**—*pop pl* UT-8
Sunrise Hollow—*valley* AR-4
Sunrise Hosp—*hospital* FL-3
Sunrise Hosp—*hospital* KY-4
Sunrise Hosp—*hospital* NV-8
Sunrise Island Revetment—*levee* TN-4
Sunrise JHS—*school* FL-3
**Sunrise Key**—*pop pl* FL-3
Sunrise Lake—*lake* (2) AK-9
Sunrise Lake—*lake* FL-3
Sunrise Lake—*lake* IA-7
Sunrise Lake—*lake* MI-6
Sunrise Lake—*lake* (2) MN-6
Sunrise Lake—*lake* MT-8
Sunrise Lake—*lake* OH-6
Sunrise Lake—*lake* OR-9
Sunrise Lake—*lake* VT-1
Sunrise Lake—*lake* (2) WA-9
Sunrise Lake—*lake* WI-6
Sunrise Lake—*lake* WY-8
**Sunrise Lake**—*pop pl* PA-2
Sunrise Lake—*reservoir* AZ-5
Sunrise Lake—*reservoir* MS-4
Sunrise Lake—*reservoir* (2) MO-7
Sunrise Lake—*reservoir* NH-1
Sunrise Lake—*reservoir* NJ-2
Sunrise Lake—*reservoir* NY-2
Sunrise Lake—*reservoir* (2) PA-2
Sunrise Lake—*reservoir* SC-3
Sunrise Lake Dam—*dam* NJ-2
Sunrise Lake Dam—*dam* PA-2
Sunrise Lakes—*lake* CA-9
Sunrise Landing—*locale* LA-4
Sunrise Landing—*locale* MI-6
Sunrise Lode Mine—*mine* SD-7
Sunrise Manor—*CDP* NV-8
**Sunrise Meadows Subdivision**—*pop pl* UT-8
Sunrise Memorial Cem—*cemetery* CA-9
Sunrise Memorial Cem—*cemetery* MN-6
Sun Rise Memorial Gardens—*cemetery* GA-3
Sunrise Memorial Gardens—*cemetery* LA-4
Sunrise Memorial Gardens—*cemetery* MI-6
Sunrise Memorial Gardens—*cemetery* MO-7
Sunrise Mill—*hist pl* PA-2
Sunrise Mine—*mine* (2) AZ-5
Sunrise Mine—*mine* CO-8
*Sunrise Mountain* OR-9
Sunrise Mtn—*summit* (2) CA-9
Sunrise Mtn—*summit* (2) MT-8
Sunrise Mtn—*summit* NV-8
Sunrise Mtn—*summit* NJ-2
Sunrise Mtn—*summit* NY-2
Sunrise Mtn—*summit* WA-9
Sunrise Notch—*gap* NY-2
**Sunrise Oasis**—*pop pl* CA-9
Sunrise Oil and Gas Field—*oilfield* LA-4
Sunrise Park—*park* CO-8
Sunrise Park—*park* FL-3
Sunrise Park—*park* ID-8
Sunrise Park—*park* IL-6
Sunrise Park—*park* KS-7
Sunrise Park—*park* MI-6
Sunrise Park—*park* MN-6
Sunrise Park—*park* MT-8
Sunrise Park—*park* NC-3
**Sunrise Park**—*pop pl* NJ-2
Sunrise Park Sch—*school* MN-6
Sunrise Park Sch—*school* NY-2
**Sunrise Park (subdivision)**—*pop pl* NC-3
**Sunrise Park Subdivision**—*pop pl* UT-8
Sunrise Pass—*gap* NV-8
Sunrise Pass—*gap* WY-8
*Sunrise Peak* NV-8
Sunrise Peak—*summit* AK-9
Sunrise Peak—*summit* (2) AZ-5
Sunrise Peak—*summit* CA-9
Sunrise Peak—*summit* (2) MT-8
Sunrise Peak—*summit* UT-8
Sunrise Peak—*summit* (2) WA-9
Sunrise Peak Ski Area—*park* AZ-5
Sunrise Picnic Area—*locale* NV-8
Sunrise Plaza (Shop Ctr)—*locale* FL-3
Sunrise Point—*cape* AR-4
Sunrise Point—*cape* GA-3
Sunrise Point—*cape* LA-4
Sunrise Point—*cape* MN-6
Sun Rise Point—*cape* NJ-2
Sunrise Point—*cliff* UT-8
Sunrise Point—*cliff* WA-9
Sunrise Point—*locale* WA-9
Sunrise Point—*summit* MT-8
**Sunrise Point (subdivision)**—*pop pl* MS-4
**Sunrise Point (subdivision)**—*pop pl* NC-3
Sunrise Pond—*lake* ME-1
Sunrise Post Office (historical)—*building* TN-4
Sunrise Presbyterian Church Preschool—*school* FL-3
Sunrise Private Sch of Okeechobee—*school* FL-3
Sunrise Ranger Station—*locale* OR-9
Sunrise Relief Mine—*mine* AZ-5
*Sunrise Ridge* IL-6
**Sunrise Ridge**—*pop pl* IL-6
Sunrise Ridge—*ridge* (2) WA-9
*Sunrise Ridge (Honeytree)* IL-6
Sunrise River—*stream* MN-6
*Sunrise Sch* TN-4
Sunrise Sch—*school* FL-3
Sunrise Sch—*school* (2) IL-6
Sunrise Sch—*school* IA-7
Sunrise Sch—*school* (2) KS-7
Sunrise Sch—*school* (2) MS-4
Sunrise Sch—*school* (2) MO-7
Sunrise Sch—*school* NE-7
Sunrise Sch—*school* OR-9
Sunrise Sch—*school* PA-2
Sunrise Sch—*school* (2) SD-7
Sunrise Sch—*school* (2) TN-4
Sunrise Sch—*school* TX-5
Sunrise Sch—*school* UT-8
Sunrise Sch (abandoned)—*school* PA-2
Sun Rise Sch (historical)—*school* AL-4
Sunrise Sch (historical)—*school* MO-7
Sunrise Sch (historical)—*school* (2) TN-4
Sunrise School—*locale* (2) CO-8
Sunrise Shop Ctr—*locale* (3) FL-3
**Sunrise Shores (subdivision)**—*pop pl* AL-4
Sunrise Ski Lodge—*building* AZ-5
Sunrise Spring—*spring* (3) AZ-5
Sunrise Spring—*spring* MT-8
Sunrise Spring—*spring* OR-9
Sunrise Spring—*spring* TN-4
Sunrise Spring Creek—*stream* WY-8
Sunrise Springs—*locale* AZ-5
Sunrise Springs—*spring* OR-9
Sunrise Station Powerplant—*locale* NV-8
**Sunrise (subdivision)**—*pop pl* AL-4
**Sunrise Subdivision**—*pop pl* UT-8
Sunrise Temple—*church* WV-2
**Sunrise Terrace**—*pop pl* NY-2
Sunrise Terrace Ch—*church* WV-2
**Sunrise Terrace (subdivision)**—*pop pl* (2) AZ-5
**Sunrise Terrace Subdivision**—*pop pl* UT-8
Sunrise Towhead—*island* TN-4
Sunrise Towhead Chute—*channel* TN-4
**Sunrise (Township of)**—*pop pl* MN-6
*Sunrise Trading Post* AZ-5
Sunrise Trading Post—*locale* (2) AZ-5
**Sunrise (Trading Post)**—*pop pl* AZ-5
*Sunrise Valley* CA-9
*Sunrise Valley* UT-8
**Sunrise Valley**—*pop pl* TN-4
Sunrise Valley—*valley* OR-9
Sunrise View Ch—*church* TN-4
Sunrise Village Mobile Home Park—*locale* AZ-5
**Sunrise Vista**—*pop pl* CA-9
Sunrise Vista Mobile Home Park—*locale* AZ-5
Sunrise Waterhole—*spring* OR-9
Sunrise Well—*well* AZ-5
Sunrise Well—*well* CA-9
Sunriver—*CDP* OR-9
**Sun River**—*pop pl* MT-8
Sun River—*stream* MT-8
Sunriver Airp—*airport* OR-9
Sun River Bench—*bench* MT-8
Sun River Cem—*cemetery* MT-8
Sun River Game Preserve—*park* (2) MT-8
Sun River Game Range HQ—*locale* MT-8
Sun River Park (Wadsworth Park)—*park* MT-8
Sun River Pass—*gap* MT-8
Sun River Slope Canal—*canal* MT-8
**Sun River Terrace**—*pop pl* IL-6
Sun River Valley—*cens area* MT-8
Sun Rock—*summit* CA-9
Sun Rock Trail—*trail* CA-9
Sunrow Creek—*stream* TN-4
Sun Run—*stream* VA-3
**Sunsbury (Township of)**—*pop pl* OH-6
**Sunscape Homes (subdivision)**—*pop pl* (2) AZ-5
Sun Sch—*school* FL-3
Sunsela Saddle—*gap* AZ-5
*Sunset* MA-1
*Sunset* PA-2
*Sunset* MP-9
Sunset—*CDP* FL-3
Sunset—*locale* AK-9
Sunset—*locale* AZ-5
Sunset—*locale* AR-4
Sunset—*locale* CA-9
Sunset—*locale* CO-8
Sunset—*locale* KY-4
Sunset—*locale* MT-8
Sunset—*locale* NM-5
Sunset—*locale* OK-5
Sunset—*locale* OR-9
Sunset—*locale* TX-5
Sunset—*locale* (2) WA-9
Sunset—*locale* WI-6
**Sunset**—*pop pl* AR-4
**Sunset**—*pop pl* CA-9
**Sunset**—*pop pl* GA-3
**Sunset**—*pop pl* LA-4
**Sunset**—*pop pl* ME-1
**Sunset**—*pop pl* MS-4
**Sunset**—*pop pl* OR-9
**Sunset**—*pop pl* PA-2
**Sunset**—*pop pl* SC-3
**Sunset**—*pop pl* (2) TN-4
**Sunset**—*pop pl* TX-5
**Sunset**—*pop pl* UT-8
**Sunset**—*pop pl* WA-9
Sunset—*post sta* CO-8
Sunset—*uninc pl* CA-9
Sunset—*uninc pl* NY-2
Sunset—*uninc pl* TX-5
Sunset, Lake—*lake* NY-2
**Sunset Acres**—*pop pl* AL-4
**Sunset Acres**—*pop pl* AZ-5
**Sunset Acres**—*pop pl* IL-6
**Sunset Acres**—*pop pl* KS-7
**Sunset Acres**—*pop pl* MD-2
**Sunset Acres**—*pop pl* TN-4
**Sunset Acres**—*pop pl* TX-5
**Sunset Acres**—*pop pl* WV-2
Sunset Acres Sch—*school* LA-4
**Sunset Acres (subdivision)**—*pop pl* (3) NC-3
**Sunset Acres (subdivision)**—*pop pl* TN-4
Sunset Airp—*airport* WA-9
Sunset Air Strip—*airport* OR-9
Sunset Amphitheater—*basin* WA-9
Sunset and Highland Center (Shop Ctr)—*locale* FL-3
Sunset Ave Ch—*church* NC-3
Sunset Ave Lateral—*canal* CA-9
Sunset Ave Sch—*school* CA-9
*Sunset Bay* FL-3
Sunset Bay—*bay* MN-6
Sunset Bay—*bay* MO-7
Sunset Bay—*bay* MT-8
Sunset Bay—*bay* (5) NY-2
Sunset Bay—*bay* OR-9
Sunset Bay—*bay* WA-9
Sunset Bay—*bay* WI-6
**Sunset Bay**—*pop pl* (2) NY-2
Sunset Bay State Park—*park* OR-9
*Sunset Beach* NC-3
Sunset Beach—*beach* FL-3
Sunset Beach—*beach* HI-9
Sunset Beach—*beach* NJ-2
Sunset Beach—*beach* (2) OR-9
Sunset Beach—*beach* UT-8
Sunset Beach—*beach* WA-9
Sunset Beach—*locale* NJ-2
Sunset Beach—*locale* PA-2
Sunset Beach—*locale* (2) WA-9
**Sunset Beach**—*pop pl* (2) CA-9
**Sunset Beach**—*pop pl* (2) FL-3
**Sunset Beach**—*pop pl* HI-9
**Sunset Beach**—*pop pl* MD-2
**Sunset Beach**—*pop pl* (2) MI-6
**Sunset Beach**—*pop pl* NJ-2
**Sunset Beach**—*pop pl* (2) NY-2
**Sunset Beach**—*pop pl* NC-3
**Sunset Beach**—*pop pl* OH-6
**Sunset Beach**—*pop pl* OR-9
**Sunset Beach**—*pop pl* (3) WA-9
**Sunset Beach**—*pop pl* (2) WV-2
**Sunset Beach**—*pop pl* (2) WI-6
Sunset Beach (historical)—*beach* SD-7
Sunset Beach Hotel—*hist pl* MN-6
Sunset Beasley Cem—*cemetery* TX-5
Sunset Bench—*bench* MT-8
Sunset Blvd Bridge—*hist pl* WA-9
Sunset Blvd Ch—*church* SC-3
*Sunset Branch* DE-2
Sunset Branch—*stream* DE-2
Sunset Bridge—*other* MO-7
Sunset Brook—*stream* VT-1
Sunset Burial Park—*cemetery* MO-7
Sunset Butte—*summit* ND-7
Sunset Camp—*locale* CA-9
Sunset Camp—*locale* (2) OR-9
Sunset Campground—*locale* CA-9
Sunset Campground—*locale* (2) UT-8
Sunset Camps—*locale* ME-1
Sunset Campsite—*locale* ME-1
Sunset Canal—*canal* NM-5
Sunset Canal—*harbor* NJ-2
Sunset Canal Bridge—*bridge* FL-3
Sunset Canyon—*valley* (2) AZ-5
Sunset Canyon—*valley* CA-9
Sunset Canyon—*valley* UT-8
*Sunset Cem* OR-9
Sunset Cem—*cemetery* GA-3
Sunset Cem—*cemetery* IL-6
Sunset Cem—*cemetery* IN-6
Sunset Cem—*cemetery* (2) KS-7
Sunset Cem—*cemetery* ME-1
Sunset Cem—*cemetery* (2) MN-6
Sunset Cem—*cemetery* MS-4
Sunset Cem—*cemetery* NE-7
Sunset Cem—*cemetery* NJ-2
Sunset Cem—*cemetery* (3) NC-3
Sunset Cem—*cemetery* OH-6
Sunset Cem—*cemetery* OK-5
Sunset Cem—*cemetery* (2) OR-9
Sunset Cem—*cemetery* (2) TN-4
Sunset Cem—*cemetery* (3) TX-5
Sunset Cem—*cemetery* UT-8
Sunset Cem—*cemetery* VA-3
Sunset Cem—*cemetery* WV-2
Sunset Cem—*cemetery* WI-6
Sunset Ch—*church* FL-3
Sunset Ch—*church* MO-7
Sunset Ch—*church* NC-3
Sunset Ch—*church* OK-5
Sunset Ch—*church* (2) TN-4
Sunset Ch—*church* (6) TX-5
Sunset Chapel—*church* (2) FL-3
Sunset Chapel—*church* WV-2
Sunset Christian Acad—*school* FL-3
Sunset City—*locale* CO-8
Sunset City—*other* CA-9
Sunset City Gulch—*valley* CO-8
Sunset Cliffs—*cliff* CA-9
Sunset Cliffs—*cliff* UT-8
Sunset Cliffs—*park* CA-9
**Sunset Cliffs**—*pop pl* CA-9
Sunset Coal Mine—*mine* IL-6
Sunset Cone—*summit* ID-8
**Sunset Corner**—*pop pl* OK-5
Sunset Corners—*locale* NY-2
**Sunset Corners**—*pop pl* FL-3
Sunset Country Club—*other* GA-3
Sunset Country Club—*other* OK-5
Sunset Country Club—*other* SC-3
Sunset County Farm—*locale* MT-8
**Sunset Court**—*pop pl* WV-2
Sunset Cove—*basin* CA-9
Sunset Cove—*bay* AK-9
Sunset Cove—*bay* FL-3
Sunset Cove—*bay* OR-9
Sunset Cove—*cove* MA-1
**Sunset Cove**—*pop pl* AL-4
Sunset Cove Branch—*stream* AL-4
Sunset Cove Campground—*park* OR-9
Sunset Crags—*summit* MT-8
Sunset Crater—*crater* AZ-5
Sunset Crater Natl Monmt—*park* AZ-5
*Sunset Creek* VA-3
Sunset Creek—*stream* (4) AK-9
Sunset Creek—*stream* ID-8
Sunset Creek—*stream* (2) MI-6
Sunset Creek—*stream* MN-6
Sunset Creek—*stream* MT-8
Sunset Creek—*stream* OK-5
Sunset Creek—*stream* TN-4
Sunset Creek—*stream* VA-3
Sunset Creek—*stream* (2) WA-9
**Sunset Dale Subdivision**—*pop pl* (2) UT-8
Sunset Dam—*dam* AZ-5
**Sunset District**—*pop pl* CA-9
Sunset Dock—*locale* TN-4
**Sunset Downs Subdivision**—*pop pl* UT-8
Sunset Dugway—*trail* UT-8
Sunset Elem Sch—*school* (2) KS-7
*Sunset Estates* TN-4
**Sunset Estates (subdivision)**—*pop pl* NC-3
Sunset Falls—*falls* WA-9
**Sunset Falls (subdivision)**—*pop pl* NC-3
Sunset Farmers Co-op Colony—*locale* SD-7
Sunset Farms—*locale* CA-9
Sunset Field—*area* VA-3
Sunset Flat—*flat* UT-8
Sunset Gap—*gap* CA-9
Sunset Gap—*gap* TN-4
**Sunset Gap**—*pop pl* TN-4
Sunset Garden Memorial Cem—*cemetery* NC-3
Sunset Garden Park—*cemetery* MT-8
Sunset Gardens—*cemetery* FL-3
**Sunset Gardens**—*pop pl* FL-3
Sunset Gardens Cem—*cemetery* OK-5
Sunset Gardens (Cemetery)—*cemetery* ND-7
Sunset Glacier—*glacier* AK-9
Sunset Glade—*flat* AZ-5
Sunset Golf Course—*locale* PA-2
Sunset Grove Country Club—*other* TX-5
Sunset Guard Station—*locale* WA-9
Sunset Gulch—*valley* CA-9
Sunset Gulch—*valley* CO-8
Sunset Harbor—*locale* NC-3
**Sunset Harbor**—*pop pl* FL-3
**Sunset Harbor**—*pop pl* IL-6
**Sunset Harbor**—*pop pl* OH-6
Sunset Heights—*locale* GA-3
**Sunset Heights**—*pop pl* OH-6
**Sunset Heights**—*pop pl* TX-5
**Sunset Heights**—*pop pl* VA-3
Sunset Heights—*uninc pl* TX-5
Sunset Heights Baptist Ch—*church* AL-4
Sunset Heights Baptist Sch—*school* FL-3
Sunset Heights Hist Dist—*hist pl* TX-5
Sunset Heights Memorial Gardens—*cemetery* OR-9
Sunset Heights Park—*park* CA-9
Sunset Heights Sch—*school* IA-7
Sunset Heights Sch—*school* NH-1
**Sunset Heights Subdivision**—*pop pl* UT-8
*Sunset Highway Forest Wayside* OR-9
Sunset Highway Forest Wayside—*locale* OR-9
Sunset Highway State Park—*park* OR-9
**Sunset Hill**—*pop pl* NJ-2
**Sunset Hill**—*pop pl* TN-4
**Sunset Hill**—*pop pl* WA-9
Sunset Hill—*summit* AL-4
Sunset Hill—*summit* CA-9
Sunset Hill—*summit* (6) CT-1
Sunset Hill—*summit* IN-6
Sunset Hill—*summit* (2) ME-1
Sunset Hill—*summit* (5) MA-1
Sunset Hill—*summit* MN-6
Sunset Hill—*summit* (2) MT-8
Sunset Hill—*summit* (4) NH-1
Sunset Hill—*summit* (3) NY-2
Sunset Hill—*summit* RI-1
Sunset Hill—*summit* (2) VT-1
Sunset Hill—*summit* VA-3
Sunset Hill—*summit* WV-2
Sunset Hill—*summit* WY-8
Sunset Hill Brook—*stream* CT-1
Sunset Hill Cem—*cemetery* GA-3
Sunset Hill Cem—*cemetery* IN-6
Sunset Hill Cem—*cemetery* KS-7
Sunset Hill Cem—*cemetery* MI-6
Sunset Hill Cem—*cemetery* (4) MO-7
Sunset Hill Cem—*cemetery* (2) NY-2
Sunset Hill Cem—*cemetery* (2) NC-3
Sunset Hill Cem—*cemetery* SC-3
Sunset Hill Cem—*cemetery* VA-3
Sunset Hill Country Club—*other* MO-7
Sunset Hill Elem Sch—*school* KS-7
**Sunset Hill Garden**—*pop pl* NJ-2
*Sunset Hill Memorial Cemetery* PA-2
Sunset Hill Memorial Park—*cemetery* PA-2
Sunset Hills—*locale* VA-3
**Sunset Hills**—*pop pl* CA-9
**Sunset Hills**—*pop pl* IL-6
**Sunset Hills**—*pop pl* MD-2
**Sunset Hills**—*pop pl* MO-7
**Sunset Hills**—*pop pl* (3) NC-3
**Sunset Hills**—*pop pl* PA-2
**Sunset Hills**—*pop pl* (2) TN-4
Sunset Hills—*summit* FL-3
Sunset Hills Burial Park—*cemetery* OH-6
Sunset Hills Cem—*cemetery* IL-6
Sunset Hills Cem—*cemetery* MI-6
Sunset Hills Cem—*cemetery* MT-8
Sunset Hills Ch—*church* VA-3
Sunset Hill Sch—*school* IL-6
Sunset Hill Sch—*school* MN-6
Sunset Hills Country Club—*other* GA-3
Sunset Hills Evangelistic Ch—*church* AL-4
Sunset Hills Golf Club—*locale* NC-3
Sunset Hills Golf Course—*other* IL-6
Sunset Hills Memorial Gardens—*cemetery* OR-9
Sunset Hills Memorial Gardens Cem—*cemetery* GA-3
Sunset Hills Memorial Park (cemetery)—*cemetery* OR-9
Sunset Hills Park—*park* TX-5
Sunset Hills Sch—*school* FL-3
Sunset Hills Sch—*school* NE-7
Sunset Hills Sch—*school* TX-5
**Sunset Hills (subdivision)**—*pop pl* (2) AZ-5
**Sunset Hills (subdivision)**—*pop pl* NC-3
**Sunset Hills Subdivision**—*pop pl* (2) UT-8
Sunset (historical)—*locale* AL-4
Sunset (historical)—*locale* KS-7
**Sunset (historical)**—*pop pl* (2) OR-9
**Sunset Hollow Subdivision**—*pop pl* UT-8
Sunset Home—*building* TX-5
Sunset House—*locale* CO-8
Sunset HS—*school* CA-9
Sunset HS—*school* OR-9
Sunset HS—*school* TX-5
Sunset Island—*cape* MA-1
Sunset Island—*island* AK-9
Sunset Island—*island* FL-3
Sunset Island—*island* MN-6
Sunset Island—*island* VT-1
Sunset Island—*uninc pl* FL-3
Sunset Islands—*island* FL-3
Sunset JHS—*school* OR-9
Sunset JHS—*school* UT-8
*Sunset Knoll* IN-6
**Sunset Knoll**—*pop pl* MD-2
Sunset Knoll—*summit* AZ-5
Sunset Knoll Park—*park* IL-6
Sunset Lagoon—*gut* FL-3
*Sunset Lake* DE-2
*Sunset Lake* NH-1
*Sunset Lake* NJ-2
Sunset Lake—*lake* CA-9
Sunset Lake—*lake* (7) FL-3
Sunset Lake—*lake* ID-8
Sunset Lake—*lake* KY-4
Sunset Lake—*lake* (3) MA-1
Sunset Lake—*lake* (3) MI-6
Sunset Lake—*lake* (7) MN-6
Sunset Lake—*lake* (2) MT-8
Sunset Lake—*lake* (2) NH-1
Sunset Lake—*lake* (2) NJ-2
Sunset Lake—*lake* (3) NY-2
Sunset Lake—*lake* (3) OH-6
Sunset Lake—*lake* (3) OR-9
Sunset Lake—*lake* (2) PA-2
Sunset Lake—*lake* TX-5
Sunset Lake—*lake* (3) VT-1
Sunset Lake—*lake* (3) WA-9
Sunset Lake—*lake* (4) WI-6
Sunset Lake—*lake* WY-8
**Sunset Lake**—*pop pl* IL-6
Sunset Lake—*reservoir* (2) CO-8
Sunset Lake—*reservoir* (2) GA-3
Sunset Lake—*reservoir* IL-6
Sunset Lake—*reservoir* IN-6
Sunset Lake—*reservoir* KY-4
Sunset Lakes—*reservoir* MA-1
Sunset Lake—*reservoir* MS-4
Sunset Lake—*reservoir* (2) MO-7
Sunset Lake—*reservoir* (7) NJ-2
Sunset Lake—*reservoir* NY-2
Sunset Lake—*reservoir* (2) NC-3
Sunset Lake—*reservoir* (2) OH-6
Sunset Lake—*reservoir* (2) OK-5
Sunset Lake—*reservoir* PA-2
Sunset Lake—*reservoir* SC-3
Sunset Lake—*reservoir* TN-4
Sunset Lake—*reservoir* TX-5
Sunset Lake—*reservoir* VA-3
Sunset Lake Dam—*dam* DE-2
Sunset Lake Dam—*dam* IN-6
Sunset Lake Dam—*dam* MA-1
Sunset Lake Dam—*dam* (5) NJ-2
Sunset Lake Dam—*dam* NC-3
Sunset Lake Dam—*dam* TN-4
Sunset Lake Dam Number One—*dam* NC-3
Sunset Lake No. 2—*reservoir* CO-8
Sunset Lakes—*reservoir* KS-7
Sunset Lake Trail—*trail* OR-9
Sunset Landing—*locale* IL-6
Sunset Landing—*locale* ME-1
Sunset Landing—*locale* OR-9
Sunset Lane Cem—*cemetery* WA-9
Sunset Lawn Cem—*cemetery* CA-9
Sunset Lawn Cem—*cemetery* IL-6
Sunset Lawns Cem—*cemetery* KS-7
Sunset Lode Mine—*mine* SD-7
Sunset Log Pond—*reservoir* OR-9
Sunset Lookout Tower—*locale* LA-4
Sunset Loop—*trail* CA-9
**Sunset Manor**—*pop pl* NY-2
**Sunset Manor**—*pop pl* PA-2
**Sunset Manor**—*pop pl* VA-3
**Sunset Manor (subdivision)**—*pop pl* PA-2
Sunset Meadow—*flat* CA-9
**Sunset Meadows Village Subdivision**—*pop pl* UT-8
Sunset Memorial Cem—*cemetery* CO-8
Sunset Memorial Cem—*cemetery* IL-6
Sunset Memorial Cem—*cemetery* MN-6
Sunset Memorial Cem—*cemetery* MO-7
Sunset Memorial Cem—*cemetery* MT-8
Sunset Memorial Cem—*cemetery* SC-3
Sunset Memorial Cem—*cemetery* (2) WV-2
Sunset Memorial Cem—*cemetery* WI-6
*Sunset Memorial Cemetery* AL-4

Sunset Memorial Ch—church SC-3
Sunset Memorial Garden—cemetery AL-4
Sunset Memorial Garden—cemetery MS-4
Sunset Memorial Garden—cemetery ND-7
Sunset Memorial Garden Cem—cemetery OK-5
Sunset Memorial Gardens KS-7
Sunset Memorial Gardens—cemetery AL-4
Sunset Memorial Gardens—cemetery CO-8
Sunset Memorial Gardens—cemetery FL-3
Sunset Memorial Gardens—cemetery (2) GA-3
Sunset Memorial Gardens—cemetery (2) IA-7
Sunset Memorial Gardens—cemetery KY-4
Sunset Memorial Gardens—cemetery MI-6
Sunset Memorial Gardens—cemetery (6) MT-8
Sunset Memorial Gardens—cemetery NE-7
Sunset Memorial Gardens—cemetery NM-5
Sunset Memorial Gardens—cemetery ND-7
Sunset Memorial Gardens—cemetery (2) OK-5
Sunset Memorial Gardens—cemetery SC-3
Sunset Memorial Gardens—cemetery SD-7
Sunset Memorial Gardens—cemetery TN-4
Sunset Memorial Gardens—cemetery TX-5
Sunset Memorial Gardens—cemetery VA-3
Sunset Memorial Gardens—cemetery WA-9
Sunset Memorial Gardens Cem—cemetery AL-4
Sunset Memorial Gardens Cem—cemetery ID-8
Sunset Memorial Gardens Cem—cemetery IN-6
Sunset Memorial Gardens Cem—cemetery KS-7
Sunset Memorial Gardens Cem—cemetery ND-7
Sunset Memorial Gardens Cem—cemetery VA-3
Sunset Memorial Gardens (Cemetery)—cemetery (2) IL-6
Sunset Memorial Gardens (Cemetery)—cemetery ND-7
Sunset Memorial Park—cemetery AR-4
Sunset Memorial Park—cemetery FL-3
Sunset Memorial Park—cemetery IN-6
Sunset Memorial Park—cemetery MD-2
Sunset Memorial Park—cemetery NE-7
Sunset Memorial Park—cemetery NM-5
Sunset Memorial Park—cemetery (2) NC-3
Sunset Memorial Park—cemetery OR-9
Sunset Memorial Park—cemetery SC-3
Sunset Memorial Park—cemetery SD-7
Sunset Memorial Park—cemetery TX-5
Sunset Memorial Park—cemetery WA-9
Sunset Memorial Park—cemetery WV-2
Sunset Memorial Park—park IL-6
Sunset Memorial Park—park MT-8
Sunset Memorial Park—park NC-3
Sunset Memorial Park Cem—cemetery IL-6
Sunset Memorial Park Cem—cemetery MN-6
Sunset Memorial Park Cem—cemetery OH-6
Sunset Memorial Park Cem—cemetery VA-3
Sunset Memorial Park (Cemetery)—cemetery CA-9
Sunset Memorial Park (Cemetery)—cemetery PA-2
Sunset Memorial Park (Cemetery)—cemetery TX-5
Sunset Memorial Park (Cemetery)—cemetery WV-2
Sunset Memorial Tabernacle—church NY-2
Sunset Memory Gardens—cemetery GA-3
Sunset Memory Gardens—cemetery IN-6
Sunset Memory Gardens—cemetery KS-7
Sunset Memory Gardens—cemetery NC-3
Sunset Memory Gardens—cemetery SC-3
Sunset Memory Gardens—cemetery WV-2
Sunset Memory Gardens—cemetery WI-6
Sunset Mesa Subdivision Mini Park—park AZ-5
Sunset Mesa Subdivision Retention Basin—reservoir AZ-5
**Sunset Mill Village (subdivision)**—pop pl AL-4
Sunset Mine—mine AK-9
Sunset Mine—mine (3) AZ-5
Sunset Mine—mine (4) CA-9
Sunset Mine—mine (2) CO-8
Sunset Mine—mine ID-8
Sunset Mine—mine (2) NV-8
Sunset Mine—mine OR-9
Sunset Mine—mine WA-9
Sunset Mine—mine (2) WY-8
Sunset Montessori Sch—school FL-3
**Sunset Mountain**—pop pl AL-4
Sunset Mtn—summit AZ-5
Sunset Mtn—summit CA-9
Sunset Mtn—summit (2) ID-8
Sunset Mtn—summit MT-8
Sunset Mtn—summit NC-3
Sunset Mtn—summit OR-9
Sunset Mtn—summit TX-5
Sunset Natural Arch—arch UT-8
Sunset Natural Bridge—arch UT-8
**Sunset North (subdivision)**—pop pl (2) AZ-5
Sunset Number Two Mine—mine NV-8
Sunset Oaks Country Club—other CA-9
Sunset Oil Field—oilfield OK-5
Sunset Park ME-1
Sunset Park NC-3
Sunset Park—flat AZ-5
Sunset Park—locale ME-1
Sunset Park—park (2) AZ-5
Sunset Park—park (3) CA-9
Sunset Park—park (2) FL-3
Sunset Park—park (7) IL-6
Sunset Park—park (2) IN-6
Sunset Park—park (3) IA-7
Sunset Park—park KS-7
Sunset Park—park KY-4
Sunset Park—park (4) MI-6
Sunset Park—park (5) MO-7
Sunset Park—park NV-8
Sunset Park—park NY-2
Sunset Park—park (2) NC-3
Sunset Park—park (2) OH-6
Sunset Park—park (2) OK-5
Sunset Park—park TN-4
Sunset Park—park (3) TX-5
Sunset Park—park WA-9
**Sunset Park**—pop pl GA-3
**Sunset Park**—pop pl (2) KS-7
**Sunset Park**—pop pl ME-1
**Sunset Park**—pop pl NC-3
Sunset Park and Golf Course—park CO-8
Sunset Park Cem—cemetery FL-3
Sunset Park Elem Sch—school FL-3
Sunset Park Elem Sch—school NC-3
**Sunset Park Estates (subdivision)**—pop pl AL-4
Sunset Park Hist Dist—hist pl NY-2
Sunset Park JHS—school NC-3
Sunset Park Sch—school CO-8
Sunset Park Sch—school IL-6
**Sunset Park (subdivision)**—pop pl NC-3
Sunset Parkway IN-6
**Sunset Parkway**—pop pl IN-6
Sunset Pass—gap AK-9
Sunset Pass—gap (2) AZ-5
Sunset Pass—gap (2) UT-8
Sunset Pass Spring—spring AZ-5
Sunset Pass Tank—reservoir AZ-5
Sunset Peak AZ-5
Sunset Peak MT-8
Sunset Peak UT-8
Sunset Peak—summit (2) AK-9
Sunset Peak—summit (3) AZ-5
Sunset Peak—summit CA-9
Sunset Peak—summit (2) ID-8
Sunset Peak—summit (5) MT-8
Sunset Peak—summit NM-5
Sunset Peak—summit OK-5
Sunset Peak—summit (2) UT-8
**Sunset Pines**—pop pl PA-2
Sunset Playground—park AZ-5
Sunset Plaza—locale KS-7
Sunset Plaza—locale NC-3
Sunset Plaza (Shop Ctr)—locale FL-3
Sunset Plaza Shop Ctr—locale KS-7
Sunset Plaza (Shop Ctr)—locale MO-7
Sunset Point—cape AR-4
Sunset Point—cape (2) CA-9
Sunset Point—cape CO-8
Sunset Point—cape (2) FL-3
Sunset Point—cape (3) ME-1
Sunset Point—cape MA-1
Sunset Point—cape (2) MN-6
Sunset Point—cape NH-1
Sunset Point—cape NY-2
Sunset Point—cape (2) WI-6
Sunset Point—cliff AZ-5
Sunset Point—cliff CA-9
Sunset Point—cliff UT-8
Sunset Point—cliff WA-9
**Sunset Point**—pop pl FL-3
**Sunset Point**—pop pl OH-6
**Sunset Point**—pop pl WI-6
Sunset Point—summit AZ-5
Sunset Point—summit (2) CA-9
Sunset Point—summit CO-8
Sunset Point Baptist Sch—school FL-3
Sunset Point Campground—locale CA-9
Sunset Point Interchange—crossing AZ-5
Sunset Point Park—park WI-6
Sunset Point Rest Area—locale AZ-5
Sunset Point View Area—locale UT-8
Sunset Pond—lake CT-1
Sunset Pond—lake FL-3
Sunset Pond—lake ME-1
Sunset Pond—lake NY-2
Sun Set Pool—reservoir OK-5
Sunset Prairie—flat OR-9
Sunset Prairie Rsvr—reservoir OR-9
Sunset Preparatory Sch—school FL-3
Sunset Public Landing—locale FL-3
Sunset Pumping Station—locale CA-9
Sunset Quarry—mine CA-9
Sunset Ranch—locale TX-5
**Sunset Ranch (subdivision)**—pop pl AL-4
Sunset Rest Area—park OR-9
Sunset Rest Cem—cemetery IA-7
Sunset Rest Cem—cemetery MN-6
Sunset Rest Cem—cemetery MT-8
Sunset Rest Cem—cemetery ND-7
Sunset Ridge—ridge AR-4
Sunset Ridge—ridge CT-1
Sunset Ridge—ridge ID-8
Sunset Ridge—ridge MA-1
Sunset Ridge—ridge WA-9
**Sunset Ridge I (subdivision)**—pop pl (2) AZ-5
Sunset Ridge Memorial Park Cem—cemetery WI-6
Sunset Ridge Park—park FL-3
Sunset Ridge Public Use Area—park KS-7
Sunset Ridge Sch—school CO-8
Sunset Ridge Sch—school CT-1
Sunset Ridge Sch—school IL-6
Sunset Ridge Station—locale CA-9
**Sunset Ridge (subdivision)**—pop pl NC-3
Sunset Ridge Woods—woods IL-6
Sunset Road Ch—church NC-3
Sunset Rock AZ-5
Sunset Rock—cliff NC-3
Sunset Rock—pillar (2) AL-4
Sunset Rock—pillar AZ-5
Sunset Rock—pillar (2) TN-4
Sunset Rock—pillar WI-6
Sunset Rock—rock MA-1
Sunset Rock—summit CA-9
Sunset Rock—summit ME-1
Sunset Rock—summit NY-2
Sunset Rocks—cliff PA-2
Sunset Rocks—summit PA-2
Sunset Rock State Park—park CT-1
Sunset Rsvr—reservoir (2) CA-9
Sunset Rsvr—reservoir NV-8
Sunset Rsvr—reservoir WY-8
Sunset Sch—school AZ-5
Sunset Sch—school (8) CA-9
Sunset Sch—school CO-8
Sunset Sch—school (2) FL-3
Sunset Sch—school GA-3
Sunset Sch—school IA-7
Sunset Sch—school MI-6
Sunset Sch—school MT-8
Sunset Sch—school NY-2
Sunset Sch—school (4) OK-5
Sunset Sch—school (2) OR-9
Sunset Sch—school (3) TX-5
Sunset Sch—school (2) UT-8
Sunset Sch—school (3) WA-9
Sunset Sch—school WV-2
Sunset Sch—school WI-6
Sunset Shelter—locale OR-9
Sunset Shop Ctr—locale TN-4
Sunset Speedway—other TX-5
Sunset Spring—spring AZ-5
Sunset Spring—spring CA-9
Sunset Spring—spring (4) OR-9
**Sunset Square Subdivision**—pop pl UT-8
Sunset State Beach—park CA-9
Sunset Strait—channel NY-2
Sunset Strip—airport PA-2
**Sunset (subdivision)**—pop pl MS-4
**Sunset (subdivision)**—pop pl TN-4
**Sunset Subdivision**—pop pl UT-8
Sunset Tank—reservoir (2) AZ-5
Sunset Telephone & Telegraph Bldg—hist pl WA-9
Sunset Terrace OH-6
**Sunset Terrace**—pop pl CA-9
**Sunset Terrace**—pop pl GA-3
**Sunset Terrace**—pop pl MD-2
**Sunset Terrace**—pop pl PA-2
Sunset Terrace Park—park TX-5
**Sunset Terrace (subdivision)**—pop pl (2) NC-3
**Sunset Terrace (subdivision)**—pop pl TN-4
Sunsetter Sch—school MN-6
Sunset Towers—hist pl CA-9
**Sunset Tract**—pop pl CA-9
Sunset Trail—trail CO-8
Sunset Trail—trail MD-2
Sunset Trail—trail OR-9
Sunset Trailer Park IL-6
Sunset Trail Ranch (trailer park)—locale AZ-5
**Sunset Trail Ranch (trailer park)**—pop pl AZ-5
Sunset Tunnel—tunnel CA-9
Sunset Tunnel—tunnel OR-9
Sunset Valley—basin OR-9
**Sunset Valley**—pop pl (2) PA-2
**Sunset Valley**—pop pl TX-5
Sunset Valley—valley CA-9
Sunset Valley—valley FL-3
Sunset Valley Golf Club—other IL-6
Sunset Valley Ranch—locale AZ-5
Sunset Valley Sch—school OR-9
Sunset View—cliff CO-8
Sunset View—locale UT-8
**Sunset View**—pop pl CA-9
**Sunset View**—pop pl (2) MD-2
**Sunset View**—pop pl NY-2
Sunset View Cem—cemetery CA-9
Sunset View Cem—cemetery IA-7
Sunset View Cem—cemetery ME-1
Sunset View Cem—cemetery MI-6
Sunset View Cem—cemetery OH-6
Sunsetview Cem—cemetery PA-2
Sunset View Cem—cemetery PA-2
Sunset View Cem—cemetery VT-1
Sunset View Ch—church TN-4
**Sunset View Estates**—pop pl UT-8
Sunset View Memorial Gardens—cemetery VA-3
Sunset View Park—park PA-2
Sunset View Picnic Area—park OR-9
Sunset View Rsvr—reservoir CA-9
Sunset View Sch—school CA-9
Sunset View Sch—school UT-8
**Sunset View (subdivision)**—pop pl (2) TN-4
**Sunset Village**—pop pl GA-3
**Sunset Village**—pop pl IN-6
**Sunset Village**—pop pl VA-3
Sunset Village Ch—church TN-4
Sunset Village Shop Ctr—locale FL-3
**Sunset Village (subdivision)**—pop pl (2) AZ-5
**Sunset Vista (subdivision)**—pop pl (2) AZ-5
Sunset Wash—stream CA-9
Sunset Well—well ID-8
Sunset Well—well TX-5
Sunset West Shopping Plaza—locale FL-3
**Sunset-Whitney Ranch (Sunset City)**—pop pl CA-9
Sunset Woods Park—park IL-6
Sunset-19 Shop Ctr—locale FL-3
Suns Eye—summit AZ-5
Sunsey Square (Shop Ctr)—locale FL-3
Sunshine—locale AK-9
Sunshine—locale AZ-5
Sunshine—locale AR-4
Sunshine—locale CO-8
Sunshine—locale NM-5
Sunshine—locale OH-6
Sunshine—locale PA-2
Sunshine—locale TX-5
Sunshine—locale WA-9
Sunshine—locale WY-8
**Sunshine**—pop pl AL-4
**Sunshine**—pop pl AR-4
**Sunshine**—pop pl FL-3
**Sunshine**—pop pl IA-7
**Sunshine**—pop pl (2) KY-4
**Sunshine**—pop pl LA-4
**Sunshine**—pop pl ME-1
**Sunshine**—pop pl (2) MD-2
**Sunshine**—pop pl NM-5
**Sunshine**—pop pl NC-3
**Sunshine**—pop pl PA-2
**Sunshine**—pop pl TN-4
**Sunshine**—pop pl WV-2
Sunshine, Lake—lake FL-3
**Sunshine Acres**—pop pl AZ-5
Sunshine Acres Park—park NY-2
**Sunshine Acres (subdivision)**—pop pl AL-4
**Sunshine Acres (subdivision)**—pop pl NC-3
Sunshine and Light—school FL-3
Sunshine Assembly of God Ch—church FL-3
Sunshine Basin—basin MT-8
Sunshine Basin Ditch—canal WY-8
Sunshine Bay—bay AK-9
Sunshine Beach—locale WA-9
**Sunshine Beach**—pop pl FL-3
**Sunshine Beach**—pop pl MI-6
Sunshine Beach Camp—locale MO-7
Sunshine Bench—valley UT-8
Sunshine Bible Ch—church OK-5
Sunshine Blvd Interchange—crossing AZ-5
Sunshine Bottom—bend NE-7
Sunshine Camp—locale CA-9
Sunshine Camp—locale (2) MT-8
**Sunshine Camp**—pop pl CA-9
Sunshine Campground—locale CO-8
Sunshine Canal—canal NM-5
Sunshine Canyon—valley CO-8
Sunshine Canyon—valley NM-5
Sunshine Canyon—valley OR-9
Sunshine Canyon—valley UT-8
Sunshine Canyon—valley WA-9
Sunshine Canyon Spring—spring WA-9
Sunshine Cem—cemetery (2) AR-4
Sunshine Cem—cemetery OH-6
Sunshine Cem—cemetery TX-5
Sunshine Ch—church AL-4
Sunshine Ch—church (2) GA-3
Sunshine Ch—church (2) LA-4
Sunshine Ch—church MI-6
Sunshine Ch—church (2) MS-4
Sunshine Ch—church (2) MO-7
Sunshine Ch—church NC-3
Sunshine Ch—church OH-6
Sunshine Ch—church OK-5
Sunshine Ch—church SC-3
Sunshine Ch—church TX-5
Sunshine Ch (historical)—church AL-4
Sunshine Christian Private Sch—school FL-3
Sunshine Coal Company Number Sixteen Dam—dam PA-2
Sunshine Cooperative Preschool—school FL-3
Sunshine Cove—bay AK-9
Sunshine Creek—stream (4) AK-9
Sunshine Creek—stream CO-8
Sunshine Creek—stream (2) MT-8
Sunshine Creek—stream (5) OR-9
Sunshine Creek—stream (2) WA-9
Sunshine Creek—stream WY-8
Sunshine Dam—dam SD-7
Sunshine Day Care Center—school FL-3
Sunshine Ditch WY-8
Sunshine Draw—valley AZ-5
Sunshine Dump—flat NV-8
Sunshine Elem Sch—school FL-3
Sunshine Elem Sch—school NC-3
Sunshine Fines Pond—reservoir PA-2
Sunshine Flat—flat NV-8
Sunshine Flat—flat OR-9
Sunshine Flat Trail—trail OR-9
Sunshine Gardens IN-6
**Sunshine Gardens**—pop pl IN-6
Sunshine Gardens Sch—school CA-9
Sunshine Guard Station—locale OR-9
Sunshine Gulch CO-8
Sunshine Gulch—valley AZ-5
Sunshine High School AL-4
Sunshine Hill—summit PA-2
Sunshine Hill—summit SD-7
Sunshine Hill—summit TX-5
Sunshine Hill Oil Field—oilfield TX-5
Sunshine Hollow—valley OK-5
Sunshine Home—building TX-5
**Sunshine Homes**—pop pl CA-9
Sunshine Island—island AK-9
Sunshine Key FL-3
Sunshine Lake—lake (2) AK-9
Sunshine Lake—lake (3) FL-3
Sunshine Lake—lake MI-6
Sunshine Lake—lake MN-6
Sunshine Lake—lake OR-9
Sunshine Lake—lake SD-7
Sunshine Lake—reservoir CO-8
Sunshine Lake—reservoir MO-7
Sunshine Lake—reservoir TN-4
Sunshine Lake—reservoir TX-5
Sunshine Learning Center—school FL-3
Sunshine Locality—hist pl NV-8
Sunshine Mall—locale FL-3
Sunshine Mesa—summit (2) CO-8
Sunshine Mesa—summit NM-5
Sunshine Mica Prospect Mine—mine SD-7
Sunshine Microwave Relay Station—tower AZ-5
Sunshine Mine—mine AK-9
Sunshine Mine—mine (3) AZ-5
Sunshine Mine—mine (3) CO-8
Sunshine Mine—mine (2) ID-8
Sunshine Mine—mine MT-8
Sunshine Mine—mine NV-8
Sunshine Mine—mine OR-9
Sunshine Mine (Inactive)—mine ID-8
Sunshine Mountains—other AK-9
Sunshine Mtn—summit CA-9
Sunshine Mtn—summit (2) CO-8
Sunshine Mtn—summit TX-5
Sunshine Oil Field—oilfield KS-7
Sunshine Oil Field—oilfield LA-4
Sunshine Overpass—crossing AZ-5
Sunshine Park—park FL-3
Sunshine Park—park IL-6
Sunshine Park—park OH-6
Sunshine Park—park PA-2
**Sunshine Park**—pop pl FL-3
**Sunshine Park**—pop pl OH-6
Sunshine Park Lake—lake NJ-2
Sunshine Park RR Station—locale FL-3
**Sunshine Park (subdivision)**—pop pl NC-3
Sunshine Parkway (CCD)—cens area FL-3
Sunshine Peak UT-8
Sunshine Peak—summit CA-9
Sunshine Peak—summit CO-8
Sunshine Playground—park MN-6
Sunshine Plaza and Mall—locale FL-3
Sunshine Plaza (Shop Ctr)—locale (2) FL-3
Sunshine Point—cape MI-6
Sunshine Point—cape WA-9
Sunshine Point—summit AK-9
Sunshine Point—summit AZ-5
Sunshine Point—summit CO-8
Sunshine Point—summit MT-8
Sunshine Point Campground—locale WA-9
Sunshine Point Catchment—reservoir AZ-5
Sunshine Pond—lake NY-2
Sunshine Pond—reservoir AZ-5
Sunshine Post Office (historical)—building MS-4
Sunshine Private Sch—school FL-3
Sunshine Ranch—locale MT-8
Sunshine Ranch—locale SD-7
Sunshine Ranch Airp—airport KS-7
**Sunshine Ranches (subdivision)**—pop pl FL-3
Sunshine Ridge—ridge AZ-5
Sunshine RR Station—building AZ-5
Sunshine Rsvr—reservoir CO-8
Sunshine Rsvr—reservoir WY-8
Sunshine Saddle—gap CO-8
Sunshine Sch—school AL-4
Sunshine Sch—school (2) AR-4
Sunshine Sch—school (3) CA-9
Sunshine Sch—school (2) FL-3
Sunshine Sch—school (2) LA-4
Sunshine Sch—school MO-7
Sunshine Sch—school (2) NE-7
Sunshine Sch—school NM-5
Sunshine Sch—school OH-6
Sunshine Sch—school PA-2
Sunshine Sch—school (6) SD-7
Sunshine Sch—school WI-6
Sunshine Sch (historical)—school AL-4
Sunshine Sch (historical)—school (2) MS-4
Sunshine Sch (historical)—school SD-7
Sunshine Shop Ctr—locale FL-3
Sunshine (Site)—locale UT-8
Sunshine Skyway Channel—channel FL-3
Sunshine South Cooperative Preschool—school FL-3
Sunshine Spring—spring AZ-5
Sunshine Spring—spring (2) OR-9
Sunshine Springs—spring OR-9
Sunshine Springs—spring TX-5
Sunshine Springs—spring WI-6
Sunshine Square—locale UT-8
Sunshine Square (Shop Ctr)—locale FL-3
**Sunshine Subdivision**—pop pl UT-8
Sunshine Summit CA-9
Sunshine Summit—gap CA-9
Sunshine Supply Ditch—canal WY-8
Sunshine Tank—reservoir AZ-5
Sunshine Tank—reservoir NM-5
**Sunshine Township**—pop pl ND-7
Sunshine Trail—trail AZ-5
Sunshine Trail—trail CA-9
Sunshine Valley—basin CA-9
Sunshine Valley—basin OR-9
Sunshine Valley—valley AK-9
Sunshine Valley—valley ID-8
Sunshine Valley—valley NM-5
Sunshine Valley—valley WI-6
Sunshine Valley Cem—cemetery NM-5
Sunshine Valley Creek—stream ID-8
Sunshine Valley Mobile Home Park—locale AZ-5
Sunshine Valley Ranch—locale WY-8
**Sunshine Village (subdivision)**—pop pl AL-4
Sunshine Well—well NV-8
Sunshine Yard—locale TX-5
Sunshore Acad—school FL-3
Sunsi Bay—bay VI-3
**Sunside**—pop pl NY-2
**Sunside**—pop pl WY-8
Sunsi Point—cape VI-3
Sunsites AZ-5
Sun Sites AZ-5
Sunsites Community Center—building AZ-5
Sunsites Golf Course—other AZ-5
Sunsmith Drain—stream MI-6
Sunson Lake—lake MI-6
**Sunspot**—pop pl NM-5
Sun Springs—locale KS-7
Sun Springs—spring FL-3
**Sun Spur**—pop pl LA-4
Sunstone Area—area OR-9
Sunstone Knoll—summit UT-8
Sunstone Mine—mine OR-9
**Sunstone Subdivision**—pop pl UT-8
Sunstrip Forest Camp—locale OR-9
Sunstroke Creek—stream TX-5
Sun Studs Inc. Log Pond—reservoir OR-9
Sun Studs Log Pond—reservoir OR-9
**Sun Subdivision**—pop pl UT-8
Sunsweet—locale CA-9
Sunsweet—locale GA-3
Sunsweet—locale OK-5
**Sun Swept Isles**—pop pl FL-3
Suntaheen Creek—stream AK-9
Sun Tank—reservoir NM-5
Suntan Lake—reservoir NJ-2
**Sun-Tan Village**—pop pl FL-3
Suntaug Lake—lake MA-1
Suntaug Lake Dam—dam MA-1
Suntaug Lake Rsvr—reservoir MA-1
**Sun Tech (subdivision)**—pop pl (2) AZ-5
Sun Temple—locale CO-8
**Sun Terra Acres**—pop pl AZ-5
Sun Terrace—hist pl CT-1
Sun Terrace Sch—school CA-9
**Suntex**—pop pl OR-9
**Suntide**—pop pl TX-5
Sunton Park—park PA-2
Sun Top—summit WA-9
Suntop Lookout—hist pl WA-9
Sun Top Trail—trail WA-9
Sun Trailer Park—locale AZ-5
**Suntrails (subdivision)**—pop pl (2) AZ-5
**Suntrails Subdivision**—pop pl UT-8
**Suntrana**—pop pl AK-9
Suntranca Creek—stream AK-9
**Suntree**—pop pl FL-3
**Suntree (subdivision)**—pop pl (2) AZ-5
**Suntree Subdivision**—pop pl TN-4
Sunuitao Peak—summit AS-9
Sun Up Bay—bay ID-8
Sunup Bowl—basin CO-8
Sunup Knob—summit NC-3
Sunup Knob—summit TN-4
Sunup Lake—lake WA-9
Sun-Up Ranch—hist pl AZ-5
Sunvale—locale FL-3
Sun Valley PA-2
Sun Valley—locale AZ-5
Sun Valley—locale NM-5
**Sun Valley**—pop pl AL-4
**Sun Valley**—pop pl CA-9
**Sun Valley**—pop pl ID-8
**Sun Valley**—pop pl NV-8
**Sun Valley**—pop pl OH-6
**Sun Valley**—pop pl (2) PA-2
**Sun Valley**—pop pl TN-4
**Sun Valley**—pop pl TX-5
**Sun Valley**—pop pl (3) WV-2
Sun Valley—uninc pl TX-5
Sun Valley—valley CA-9
Sun Valley—valley NV-8
Sun Valley Airp—airport AZ-5
Sun Valley Ch—church KS-7
Sun Valley Ch—church TX-5
Sun Valley Ch of the Brethren—church AL-4
Sun Valley Christian Ch—church FL-3
Sun Valley Dam—dam PA-2
Sun Valley Estates OH-6
Sun Valley Estates Airp—airport UT-8
Sun Valley Golf Club—locale MA-1
Sun Valley Hosp—hospital CA-9
Sun Valley HS—school NC-3
Sun Valley HS—school PA-2
Sun Valley JHS—school CA-9
Sun Valley Lake—reservoir IA-7
Sun Valley Lake—reservoir OH-6
Sun Valley Lake—reservoir PA-2
Sun Valley Lake Dam—dam IA-7
Sun Valley Mobile Home Park—locale AZ-5
Sun Valley MS—school NC-3
Sun Valley Oil Field—oilfield TX-5
Sun Valley Park—park CA-9
Sun Valley Park—park MO-7
Sun Valley Plaza Shop Ctr—locale AZ-5
Sun Valley Ranch—locale CO-8
Sun Valley Ranch—locale NM-5
Sun Valley Sch—school CA-9
Sun Valley Sch—school NV-8
Sun Valley Sch—school WV-2
Sunvalley Square Shop Ctr—locale AZ-5
**Sun Valley (subdivision)**—pop pl NC-3
Sun Valley Trailer Park—locale AZ-5
**Sunview**—pop pl IN-6
**Sunview**—pop pl TX-5
**Sun View Additions 1-3 (subdivision)**—pop pl UT-8
Sunview Ch—church AR-4
Sunview Ch—church TX-5
Sun View Lake—reservoir SC-3
Sunview Park—park FL-3
Sunview Sch—school OH-6
**Sunview (subdivision)**—pop pl (2) AZ-5
**Sun Village**—pop pl CA-9
**Sun Village**—pop pl WA-9
Sun Village—uninc pl PA-2
**Sunville**—pop pl PA-2
Sunville Post Office (historical)—building PA-2
Sun Well—well NM-5
Sun Windmill—locale NM-5
Sun Windmill—locale (2) TX-5
**Sunyar**—pop pl MD-2
SUNY At Syracuse—school NY-2
SUNY Coll At Oswego—school NY-2
SUNY (State Univ of New York)—school NY-2
Suomi—locale MN-6
**Suomi**—pop pl GA-3
Suomi Cem—cemetery MN-6
Suomi Ch—church MN-6
Suomi Coll—school MI-6
Suomi Lake—lake MN-6
Supai—locale AZ-5
**Supai**—pop pl AZ-5
Supai Camp—locale AZ-5
Supai Falls AZ-5
Supai Mesa—summit AZ-5
Supai MS—school AZ-5
Supai Tank—reservoir AZ-5
Supan MH-9
Supan Gulch—valley CA-9
Supawna Meadows—swamp NJ-2
Supein MP-9
Supein-To MP-9
Supenau Coulee—valley MT-8
Super City Mall (Shop Ctr)—locale SD-7
Super City Shop Ctr—locale SD-7
Super Creek—stream CA-9
Super Creek Mine—mine CA-9
Superdome—building LA-4
Super Drive-in Speedway (Auto)—other GA-3
Super Hollow—valley KY-4
Superintendent Island NY-2
Superintendent of Lighthouses' Dwelling—hist pl PR-3
Superintendent's Cottage—hist pl MI-6
Superintendent's House—hist pl MT-8
Superintendent's House, Atlantic & Pacific RR—hist pl NM-5
Superintendent's Residence—hist pl (2) AZ-5
Superintendent's Residence—hist pl NM-5
Superintendent's Residence at the Utah State Hosp—hist pl UT-8
Superior KS-7
Superior—locale MI-6
Superior—locale OH-6
**Superior**—pop pl AL-4
**Superior**—pop pl AZ-5
**Superior**—pop pl CO-8
**Superior**—pop pl IN-6
**Superior**—pop pl IA-7
**Superior**—pop pl LA-4
**Superior**—pop pl MI-6
**Superior**—pop pl MT-8
**Superior**—pop pl NE-7
**Superior**—pop pl OH-6
**Superior**—pop pl (3) PA-2
**Superior**—pop pl WV-2
**Superior**—pop pl WI-6
**Superior**—pop pl WY-8
Superior, Lake—lake MI-6
Superior, Lake—lake MN-6
Superior, Lake—lake NY-2
Superior, Lake—lake WI-6
Superior Airport AZ-5
Superior Ave Viaduct—hist pl OH-6
Superior Bay—bay MN-6
Superior Bay—bay WI-6
**Superior Bottom**—pop pl WV-2
Superior Canal—canal (2) LA-4
Superior Canal—canal NE-7
Superior Cem—cemetery CO-8
Superior Center Park—park MI-6
Superior Courthouse and Bartlett Mall—hist pl MA-1
Superior-Courtland Dam—dam NE-7
Superior Creek—stream ID-8
Superior Ditch—canal WY-8
Superior Dump—locale AZ-5
Superior Entry—channel WI-6
Superior Entry Channel—channel MN-6

Superior Falls—falls MI-6
Superior Falls—falls WI-6
Superior Front Channel—channel WI-6
Superior Gun Club—locale MI-6
Superior Gun Club—other CA-9
Superior Harbor Basin—basin MN-6
Superior Harbor Basin—harbor WI-6
Superior (historical)—pop pl OR-9
Superior HS—school AZ-5
Superior HS—school MI-6
Superior Lake—flat CA-9
Superior Lake—lake CA-9
Superior Lake—lake UT-8
Superior Lake—lake WI-6
Superior Lake—reservoir IL-6
Superior Lake—reservoir UT-8
Superior Lake Dam—dam UT-8
Superior Mesa—summit NM-5
Superior Mill—locale CO-8
Superior Mine—mine (2) AZ-5
Superior Mine—mine CA-9
Superior Mine—mine (2) CO-8
Superior Mine—mine ID-8
Superior Mine—mine MT-8
Superior Mining Claim—mine NV-8
Superior Municipal Airp—airport AZ-5
Superior Natl For—forest MN-6
Superior Number One Drain—stream MI-6
Superior Ravine—valley CA-9
Superior Sch—school KS-7
Superior Sch—school (3) MT-8
Superior Sch—school OH-6
Superior School—locale ID-8
Superior School—locale KS-7
Superior Stadium—building AZ-5
Superior State Game Ref—park MN-6
Superior Station OH-6
Superior Station—building PA-2
Superior Stone Company Lake—reservoir NC-3
Superior Stone Company Lake Dam—dam NC-3
**Superior Subdivision**—pop pl UT-8
Superior Tank—reservoir AZ-5
Superior Townline Sch—school MI-6
**Superior (Town of)**—pop pl WI-6
Superior Township—fmr MCD IA-7
**Superior Township**—pop pl (2) KS-7
**Superior Township**—pop pl ND-7
Superior Township Cem—cemetery IA-7
**Superior (Township of)**—pop pl (2) MI-6
**Superior (Township of)**—pop pl OH-6
Superior Valley—valley CA-9
**Superior (village)**—pop pl WI-6
**Superior Village**—pop pl WI-6
Superior Water Tank—reservoir AZ-5
Super-Koll Park—park IL-6
Super Lateral—canal ID-8
Superoir Shaft—mine NV-8
Superstition Canyon—valley NV-8
Superstition Cave—cave AL-4
**Superstition Country Subdivision**—pop pl AZ-5
Superstition Creek—stream MN-6
**Superstition Estates**—pop pl AZ-5
Superstition Hills—range CA-9
Superstition Interchange AZ-5
Superstition Lake—lake MN-6
Superstition Mountain Monmt—park AZ-5
Superstition Mountains—summit AZ-5
Superstition Mountain Sch—school AZ-5
Superstition Mtn—summit AZ-5
Superstition Mtn—summit CA-9
Superstition Park AZ-5
Superstition Park East Number Two—park AZ-5
Superstition Park West Number One—park AZ-5
Superstition Peak AZ-5
Superstition Peak—summit AZ-5
Superstition Shadows Mobile Home Park—locale AZ-5
Superstition Substation—locale AZ-5
Supervisor Lake Dam—dam MS-4
Supervisor's House No. 1001—hist pl OR-9
Supervisor's Office HQ—hist pl MN-6
Sup Hor Spring—spring AZ-5
Supin Lick Mtn VA-3
Supin Lick Mtn—summit VA-3
Supin Lick Ridge—ridge VA-3
Supi Oidak—locale AZ-5
Supko Hill—summit PA-2
Suplee—locale OR-9
Suplee—locale PA-2
Supolvre Creek AZ-5
Supon Creek—stream ID-8
Suppah Windmill—locale OR-9
Supper Creek—stream ID-8
Supper Island—cape MA-1
Suppesville—locale KS-7
Supple Bridge—bridge IA-7
Supplee—locale WA-9
Supplejack Creek—stream TX-5
Supple Marsh—bay WI-6
Supples Cem—cemetery MS-4
Supple Sch—school KS-7
Supples Pond—lake CT-1
Supply OK-5
Supply—locale VA-3
Supply—other OK-5
**Supply**—pop pl AR-4
**Supply**—pop pl NC-3
Supply Basin Campground—locale CO-8
Supply Camp Spring—spring NV-8
Supply Canal—canal NE-7
Supply Canyon—valley UT-8
Supply Ch—church AR-4
Supply Creek—stream AK-9
Supply Creek—stream CA-9
Supply Creek—stream CO-8
Supply Creek—stream OR-9
Supply Creek Trail—trail CO-8
Supply Dam—dam PA-2
Supply Ditch—canal CO-8
Supply Ditch—canal MT-8
Supply Lake—lake AK-9
Supply Mine—mine CA-9
Supply Pond—lake ME-1
Supply Pond—reservoir NH-1
Supply Stream—stream ME-1
Support, Mount—summit NH-1
Supps Cem—cemetery TX-5
Suppulgaws River AL-4
**Supreme**—pop pl LA-4
**Supreme**—pop pl SC-3
Supreme Camp—locale TX-5
Supreme Council Of The House Of Jacob, The—church PA-2
Supreme Court Bldg—hist pl DC-2
Supreme Court Library Bldg—hist pl WV-2
Supreme Court of South Carolina Bldg—hist pl SC-3
Supreme Feeders Airp—airport KS-7
**Supreme (sta.)**—pop pl LA-4
Suprise Ch—church KY-4
Suprise Gulch—valley UT-8
Suprise Valley—valley UT-8
Supui Tank—reservoir AZ-5
**Supun**—pop pl FM-9
Supur FM-9
Supur, Unun En—cape FM-9
**Suqualena**—pop pl MS-4
Suqualena Cem—cemetery MS-4
Suqualena Creek—stream MS-4
Suqualena United Methodist Ch—church MS-4
**Suquamish**—pop pl WA-9
Suquamish Harbor WA-9
Sur, Cerro Del—summit CA-9
Suraci Pond—lake NJ-2
S U Ranch Tank—reservoir NM-5
Surat, Mount—summit MA-1
Surbaugh—locale WV-2
Surbaugh Creek—stream WV-2
Surber—locale VA-3
Surber Cem—cemetery KY-4
Surbon—locale UT-8
Sur Breakers—area CA-9
Surburban Country Club—other IL-6
Surcease Mine—mine CA-9
Sur Cree Creek—stream CA-9
Surdam Gulch—valley ID-8
Surebridge Brook—stream NY-2
Surebridge Mtn—summit NY-2
Surebridge Swamp—swamp NY-2
Sureganset River MA-1
Surenough Creek—stream MT-8
Sureshot Lake—lake MT-8
Sureshot Lake—lake WI-6
Sure Shot Mtn—summit WA-9
Sure Thing Mine—mine MT-8
Surette Creek—stream WI-6
Surety Bldg—hist pl OK-5
Surf NJ-2
Surf—locale FL-3
**Surf**—pop pl CA-9
**Surf**—pop pl FL-3
Surf, Lake—reservoir NC-3
Surface Creek CO-8
Surface Creek—stream CO-8
Surface Creek—stream WY-8
Surface Ditch—canal MO-7
Surface Hollow—valley WV-2
Surface Spring—spring OR-9
Surf Bay—bay AK-9
**Surf City**—pop pl NJ-2
**Surf City**—pop pl NC-3
Surf Oaks—locale TX-5
**Surf Pines**—pop pl OR-9
Surf Point—cape AK-9
Surf Rock—other AK-9
Surfside MA-1
Surfside OH-6
**Surfside**—pop pl CA-9
**Surfside**—pop pl FL-3
**Surfside**—pop pl ME-1
**Surfside**—pop pl (2) MA-1
**Surfside**—pop pl TX-5
Surfside Beach—beach MA-1
**Surfside Beach**—pop pl SC-3
**Surfside Beach**—pop pl TX-5
Surfside Elem Sch—school FL-3
Surfside Marina—locale AL-4
Surfside Station (historical)—locale MA-1
Surf 5 & 10—post sta FL-3
Surge Bay—bay AK-9
Surge Lake—lake AK-9
Surgener Cem—cemetery VA-3
**Surgeon**—pop pl IN-6
**Surgeon Hall**—pop pl PA-2
Surgeon Island—island MI-6
Surgeon Mtn—summit AK-9
Surgeres Isle MS-4
Surges Boat Dock—locale TN-4
Surge Tank Number Two—reservoir NV-8
Surget Cem—cemetery MS-4
**Surginer**—pop pl AL-4
Surgney Cem—cemetery LA-4
Surgoine Branch—stream MO-7
**Surgoinsville**—pop pl TN-4
Surgoinsville Baptist Ch—church TN-4
Surgoinsville (CCD)—cens area TN-4
Surgoinsville Creek—stream TN-4
Surgoinsville Division—civil TN-4
Surgoinsville Elem Sch—school TN-4
Surgoinsville HS (historical)—school TN-4
Surgoinsville MS—school TN-4
Surgoinsville Post Office—building TN-4
Suriappu FM-9
**Suring**—pop pl WI-6
**Surl**—pop pl NC-3
Surlaine Point—cape VI-3
Surl Ch—church NC-3
Surles Ch—church AL-4
Surline Branch—stream VA-3
Surlock Lake MS-4
Surnge Canyon—valley ID-8
Surok Point—cape AK-9
**Suromar**—pop pl PR-3
Surosa—locale WV-2
Surplus VA-3
Surplus Canal—canal UT-8
Surplus Mtn—summit ME-1
Surplus Pond—lake ME-1
Surprise—locale CA-9
Surprise—locale NY-2
Surprise—locale TN-4
**Surprise**—pop pl AZ-5
**Surprise**—pop pl IN-6
**Surprise**—pop pl NE-7
Surprise, Lake—lake AK-9
Surprise, Lake—lake FL-3
Surprise, Lake—lake TX-5
Surprise, Lake—lake WY-8
Surprise, Lake—reservoir NJ-2
Surprise, Lake—reservoir NY-2
Surprise, Mount—summit (2) NH-1
Surprise Arch—arch UT-8
Surprise Arroyo—stream CA-9
Surprise Basin—basin NV-8
Surprise Bay—bay AK-9
Surprise Beach—beach CO-8
Surprise Canyon AZ-5
Surprise Canyon—valley (4) AZ-5
Surprise Canyon—valley CA-9
Surprise Canyon—valley NV-8
Surprise Canyon Grove—woods CA-9
Surprise Cave—cave ID-8
Surprise Cem—cemetery NE-7
Surprise Ch—church SC-3
Surprise Cove—bay AK-9
Surprise Creek AZ-5
Surprise Creek ID-8
Surprise Creek OK-5
Surprise Creek—stream (8) AK-9
Surprise Creek—stream CA-9
Surprise Creek—stream (4) ID-8
Surprise Creek—stream (3) MT-8
Surprise Creek—stream (2) OR-9
Surprise Creek—stream (2) WA-9
Surprise Creek—stream WY-8
Surprise Creek Camp—locale ID-8
Surprise Creek Colony—locale MT-8
Surprise Ditch—canal CO-8
Surprise Draw—valley MT-8
Surprise Gap—gap WA-9
Surprise Glacier—glacier (2) AK-9
Surprise Gulch—valley AK-9
Surprise Gulch—valley MT-8
Surprise Gulch—valley WY-8
Surprise Gulch Spring—spring WY-8
Surprise Harbor—bay AK-9
Surprise Hill—locale VA-3
Surprise Hill—summit MT-8
Surprise (historical)—locale KS-7
Surprise Inlet—bay AK-9
Surprise Lake OR-9
Surprise Lake—lake AK-9
Surprise Lake—lake (2) CA-9
Surprise Lake—lake (2) CO-8
Surprise Lake—lake FL-3
Surprise Lake—lake ID-8
Surprise Lake—lake (2) MN-6
Surprise Lake—lake MT-8
Surprise Lake—lake NJ-2
Surprise Lake—lake (3) OR-9
Surprise Lake—lake PA-2
Surprise Lake—lake (5) WA-9
Surprise Lake—lake (3) WI-6
Surprise Lake—lake WY-8
Surprise Lake—reservoir NJ-2
Surprise Lake Dam—dam (2) NJ-2
Surprise Lakes—lake WA-9
Surprise Meadow—flat WA-9
Surprise Mica Mine—mine SD-7
Surprise Mine—mine AZ-5
Surprise Mine—mine MT-8
Surprise Mine—mine NV-8
Surprise Mtn—summit WA-9
Surprise Opera House—hist pl NE-7
Surprise Park—park AZ-5
Surprise Pass—gap MT-8
Surprise Pass Trail—trail MT-8
Surprise Peak—summit NV-8
Surprise Point—cape AK-9
Surprise Pond—lake NY-2
Surprise Pool—lake WY-8
Surprise Post Office—building AZ-5
Surprise Post Office (historical)—building TN-4
Surprise Rapids—rapids AZ-5
Surprise Reef—bar NV-8
Surprise Sch—school AZ-5
Surprise Sch—school MO-7
Surprise Sch—school TX-5
Surprise Sch (abandoned)—school (2) MO-7
Surprise Sch (historical)—school MO-7
Surprise School (historical)—locale MO-7
Surprise Spring—spring (2) AZ-5
Surprise Spring—spring CA-9
Surprise Spring—spring ID-8
Surprise Spring—spring MT-8
Surprise Spring—spring (3) OR-9
Surprise Springs—spring AZ-5
Surprise Springs—spring CA-9
Surprise Tank—reservoir (2) AZ-5
Surprise Tank—reservoir TX-5
Surprise Town Hall—building AZ-5
Surprise Truss Bridge—hist pl TN-4
Surprise Valley—basin (2) AZ-5
Surprise Valley—basin UT-8
Surprise Valley—locale WA-9
**Surprise Valley**—pop pl OR-9
Surprise Valley—valley (3) CA-9
Surprise Valley—valley ID-8
Surprise Valley—valley NV-8
Surprise Valley—valley UT-8
Surprise Valley (CCD)—cens area CA-9
Surprise Valley Mineral Wells—well CA-9
Surprise Valley Ranch—locale TX-5
Surprise Valley Sch—school SD-7
**Surprise Valley Township**—pop pl SD-7
Surprise Valley Union HS—school CA-9
Surprise Valley Youth Camp—locale WV-2
Surprise Wash—stream CA-9
Surprise Waterhole—lake ID-8
Surprise Waterway—gut FL-3
Surprise Well—well (2) AZ-5
Surprize Lake ID-8
Surpur Creek—stream CA-9
Surran (RR name for Tinsley)—other KY-4
Surrat Slough—stream AR-4
Surratsville MD-2
Surratt Branch—stream AR-4
Surratt Branch—stream OK-5
Surratt Creek—stream (2) MO-7
Surratt Hollow—valley MO-7
Surratt House—hist pl MD-2
Surratt Pond—reservoir MS-4
Surratt Sch (abandoned)—school MO-7
**Surratts Gardens**—pop pl MD-2
Surratt Spring—spring CO-8
Surrattsville MD-2
Surrattsville HS—school MD-2
Surrattsville JHS—school MD-2
Surrattsville Sch—school MD-2
Surrell Creek—stream WY-8
Surrena Sch (historical)—school PA-2
**Surrency**—pop pl GA-3
Surrency Cem—cemetery (2) GA-3
Surrency-Thornton (CCD)—cens area GA-3
Surrender Canyon—valley NM-5
Surrender Creek—stream CA-9
Surrender Ground—locale VA-3
Surrett Canyon—valley ID-8
Surrett Hill—summit KY-4
Surrett Spring—spring AL-4
Surrey PA-2
Surrey—locale IL-6
**Surrey**—pop pl IN-6
**Surrey**—pop pl ND-7
Surrey Cem—cemetery MI-6
Surrey Creek—stream WA-9
Surrey Downs Sch—school WA-9
**Surrey Downs Subdivision**—pop pl UT-8
Surrey Gulch—valley CO-8
**Surrey Hill**—pop pl OH-6
**Surrey Hills**—pop pl PA-2
Surrey Hills Golf Club—other OK-5
Surrey Hollow—valley KY-4
Surrey Meadows—CDP NY-2
Surrey Mtn—summit TX-5
**Surrey Park**—pop pl DE-2
**Surrey Place**—pop pl NJ-2
Surrey Ridge IL-6
**Surrey Ridge**—pop pl CO-8
Surrey Sch—school MD-2
**Surrey Square**—pop pl VA-3
Surrey Township—civil SD-7
**Surrey Township**—pop pl ND-7
**Surrey (Township of)**—pop pl MI-6
Surridge Sch—school AR-4
Sur River CA-9
Sur Rock—bar CA-9
Surrogate's Court—hist pl NY-2
Surrounded Hill—summit (2) AR-4
Surrounded Hill Cem—cemetery AR-4
Surrounded Hill Ch—church AR-4
Surrounded Ridges—summit AR-4
Surrounded Ridges Lake—lake AR-4
Surry NC-3
Surry—locale IA-7
**Surry**—pop pl ME-1
**Surry**—pop pl NH-1
**Surry**—pop pl VA-3
Surry Central HS—school NC-3
**Surry County**—pop pl NC-3
**Surry (County)**—pop pl VA-3
Surry County Community Coll—school NC-3
Surry County Courthouse—hist pl NC-3
Surry County Courthouse Complex—hist pl VA-3
Surry County Historical Farm Museum—building NC-3
Surry Fork—stream TN-4
Surry Lookout Tower—locale VA-3
Surry Martin Branch—stream VA-3
Surry Mountain Dam—dam NH-1
Surry Mtn—summit NH-1
**Surry (Town of)**—pop pl ME-1
**Surry (Town of)**—pop pl NH-1
Sur School (Abandoned)—locale CA-9
Sursuit Creek MA-1
Sursuit Harbor MA-1
**Survant**—pop pl IN-6
**Survey**—pop pl NE-7
Survey Butte—summit NV-8
Survey Cem—cemetery KS-7
Survey Cove—bay AK-9
Survey Creek WY-8
Survey Creek—stream (2) AK-9
Survey Creek—stream ID-8
Survey Creek—stream (2) WA-9
Survey Creek—stream WY-8
Survey Draw—valley ID-8
Survey (historical)—locale KS-7
Survey Lake—lake UT-8
Survey Mtn—summit MT-8
Surveyor—locale PA-2
**Surveyor**—pop pl WV-2
Surveyor Bay—bay AK-9
Surveyor Branch—stream WV-2
Surveyor Campground—locale CA-9
Surveyor Canyon—valley AZ-5
Surveyor Canyon—valley TX-5
Surveyor Creek—stream AK-9
Surveyor Creek—stream CO-8
Surveyor Creek—stream FL-3
Surveyor Creek—stream ID-8
Surveyor Creek—stream MT-8
Surveyor Creek—stream OR-9
Surveyor Creek—stream WA-9
Surveyor Creek—stream WV-2
Surveyor Creek—stream WI-6
Surveyor Gulch—valley CA-9
Surveyor Lake—lake MT-8
Surveyor Mountain Recreation Site—park OR-9
Surveyor Mtn—summit OR-9
Surveyor Park—flat (2) WY-8
Surveyor Park Trail—trail WY-8
Surveyor Passage—channel AK-9
Surveyor Peak—locale OR-9
Surveyor Pond—lake FL-3
Surveyor Run—stream PA-2
Surveyor's MI-6
Surveyors Bay—swamp FL-3
Surveyors Benches—bench OR-9
Surveyors Branch—stream AL-4
Surveyors Canyon—valley CA-9
Surveyors Canyon—valley NM-5
Surveyors Creek—stream AL-4
Surveyors Creek—stream FL-3
Surveyors Creek—stream GA-3
Surveyors Creek—stream MT-8
Surveyors Creek—stream WA-9
Surveyors Draw Rsvr—reservoir WY-8
Surveyors Flat—flat CA-9
Surveyors Glade—flat CA-9
Surveyors Gulch—valley MT-8
Surveyors Hill—summit SD-7
Surveyors Hole—basin UT-8
Surveyors Ice Cave—cave OR-9
Surveyors Island—island MI-6
Surveyors Island—island MN-6
Surveyors Lake UT-8
Surveyors Lake—lake FL-3
Surveyors Lake—lake OR-9
Surveyors Lake—lake UT-8
Surveyors Lake—lake WA-9
Surveyors Pass—gap CA-9
Surveyors Peak—summit ID-8
Surveyor Spring—spring (2) AZ-5
Surveyor Spring—spring CO-8
Surveyor Spring—spring (2) OR-9
Surveyors Reef—bar MI-6
Surveyors Ridge—ridge ID-8
Surveyors Ridge—ridge OR-9
Surveyors Run PA-2
Surveyors Spring—spring OR-9
Surveyors Tank—reservoir AZ-5
Surveyors Valley Rsvr—reservoir CA-9
Surveyors Waterhole OR-9
Survey Pass—gap AK-9
Survey Peak—summit WY-8
Survey Point—cape (3) AK-9
Survey Point—summit UT-8
Survey Point—summit WA-9
Survey Sch—school TX-5
Survey Spring—spring AZ-5
Survey Spring—spring OR-9
Survey Valley—basin NE-7
Survey 2429—civil AR-4
Survey 490—civil AR-4
Survorov MP-9
Sur war har na ha River SD-7
SUR 786—civil AK-9
SUR 948—civil AK-9
SUR 991—civil AK-9
Susan—locale VA-3
**Susan**—pop pl MT-8
Susan, Lake—lake CT-1
Susan, Lake—lake (3) FL-3
Susan, Lake—lake MN-6
Susan, Lake—lake NC-3
Susan, Lake—lake WI-6
Susan, Lake—lake WY-8
Susan, Lake—reservoir MO-7
Susan, Mount—summit CO-8
Susan, Mtn—summit TX-5
Susan, Port—bay WA-9
Susana Knolls—uninc pl CA-9
Susana Lake—lake MN-6
Susan B Anthony—building MA-1
Susan Bay—bay MN-6
Susan Beach Corner—locale DE-2
Susan Branch—stream IL-6
Susan Branch—stream (2) TN-4
Susan Branch 87-7 Dam—dam TN-4
Susan Brothers Creek—stream IN-6
Susan Branch Lake—reservoir TN-4
Susan Creek—stream KY-4
Susan Creek—stream MI-6
Susan Creek—stream (3) OR-9
Susan Creek Falls—falls OR-9
Susan Creek Indian Mounds Site—hist pl OR-9
Susan Creek State Park—park OR-9
Susan Hart Hollow—valley MO-7
Susan Hollow—valley ID-8
Susan Hollow—valley TN-4
Susan Island—island NY-2
Susan Jane, Lake—lake WA-9
**Susank**—pop pl KS-7
Susan Lake—lake MI-6
Susan Lake—lake (2) MN-6
Susan Lake—lake WA-9
Susan Lake—lake WI-6
SUSAN MAY—hist pl MD-2
Susan Moore AL-4
**Susan Moore**—pop pl AL-4
Susan Moore Cemetery TN-4
Susan Moore Sch—school AL-4
Susanna AL-4
Susanna WV-2
Susannaberg—locale VI-3
Susanna Canyon—valley CA-9
Susanna Farm—hist pl MD-2
Susannah, Lake—lake FL-3
Susannah Branch—stream SC-3
Susannah Ch—church WV-2
Susanna (RR name for Yukon)—other WV-2
Susanna Wesley Mission (historical)—church AL-4
Susanne Ch—church WV-2
Susan Park—uninc pl LA-4
Susan Peak—summit TX-5
Susan Peak Oil Field—oilfield TX-5
Susan Point—cape MA-1
Susan Pond—lake FL-3
Susan River—stream CA-9
Susan River Campground—locale CA-9
Susan Roll Leach Elem Sch—school IN-6
Susan Run—stream WV-2
Susans Bluff—cliff NV-8
Susans Branch—stream IN-6
Susans Branch—stream KY-4
Susans Island—island MN-6
Susan Smith Branch—stream GA-3
Susan Tank—reservoir AZ-5
Susan Thomas Shoals—rapids SC-3
Susan Union Ch—church SC-3
Susanville—locale OR-9
**Susanville**—pop pl CA-9
Susanville Canyon—valley CA-9
Susanville (CCD)—cens area CA-9
**Susanville Ind Res**—pop pl CA-9
Susanville Peak—summit CA-9
Susch Ranch—locale TX-5
Suscol—locale CA-9
Suscol Creek—stream CA-9
Suscol House—hist pl CA-9
**Suscon**—pop pl PA-2
Suscon Station—locale PA-2
Suses Branch—stream MO-7
Susett Cem—cemetery IN-6
Sushana River—stream AK-9
Sushana River Ranger Cabin No. 17—hist pl AK-9
Sushgitit Hills—other AK-9
Sushilna Island—island AK-9
Sushilnoi Island—island AK-9
Susian Ford Creek—stream GA-3
Susick Sch—school MI-6
Susie—locale KY-4
Susie—locale WA-9
**Susie**—pop pl MS-4
Susie, Lake—reservoir ND-7
Susie Bayou—gut LA-4
Susie B West Sch—school MS-4
Susie Chapel—church WV-2
Susie Creek—stream (3) AK-9
Susie Creek—stream MT-8
Susie Creek—stream NV-8
Susie Creek—stream OR-9
Susie Creek—stream WA-9
Susie E Allen Elem Sch—school AL-4
Susie Ebert Island—island SC-3
Susie Gap—gap NC-3
Susie Gibson HS—school VA-3
Susie Gulch—valley AZ-5
Susie Hole—bay AL-4
Susie Island—island MN-6
Susie Knob—summit NC-3
Susie Lake—lake CA-9
Susie Lake—lake MT-8
Susie Lake—lake ND-7
Susie Mine—mine WY-8
Susie Mtn—summit AK-9
Susie Oil Well—well AK-9
Susie Parker Stringfellow Memorial Hosp—hospital AL-4
Susie Peak—summit SD-7
Susie Perry Creek—stream MS-4
Susie Post Office (historical)—building MS-4
Susie P Trigg Elementary School MS-4
**Susie Ranch Subdivision**—pop pl UT-8
Susie Ridge—ridge UT-8
Susies Creek—stream NC-3
Susies Hill—summit NC-3
Susies Nipple—summit ID-8
Susie Spring—spring CA-9
Susies Ridge—ridge CO-8
Susina Plantation—hist pl GA-3
Susin Lake—lake MI-6
**Susitna**—pop pl AK-9
Susitna, Mount—summit AK-9
Susitna Flats—flat AK-9
Susitna Glacier—glacier AK-9
Susitna Lake—lake AK-9
Susitna Lodge—locale AK-9
Susitna River—stream AK-9
Susitna River Bridge—hist pl AK-9
Suskaralogh Point—cape AK-9
Suski Jima FM-9
Suslositna Creek—stream AK-9
Suslota—locale AK-9
Suslota Creek—stream AK-9
Suslota Lake—lake AK-9
Suslota Pass—gap AK-9
Susman Run—stream PA-2
Susong—locale TN-4
Susong Branch—stream VA-3
Susong Bridge—bridge TN-4
Susong Cem—cemetery (2) TN-4
Susong Cem—cemetery VA-3
Susong Island—island (2) TN-4
Susong Memorial Ch—church TN-4
Susong Post Office (historical)—building TN-4
Susong Spring—spring TN-4
Suson Park—park MO-7
Suspension—locale AL-4
Suspension Bridge (Bridge) NY-2
Suspension Bridge Campground—park AZ-5
Suspension Post Office (historical)—building AL-4
Sus Picnic Area—park AZ-5
Suspiro, Cape—cape AK-9
**Susquehanna**—pop pl PA-2
Susquehanna, Lake—reservoir NJ-2
Susquehanna Boy Scout Camp—locale PA-2
Susquehanna Bridge—locale PA-2
Susquehanna Ch—church (2) PA-2
Susquehanna Company Number 6 Colliery—building PA-2
Susquehanna Consolidated Sch—school PA-2
Susquehanna (corporate name Susquehanna Depot) PA-2
**Susquehanna County**—pop pl PA-2
Susquehanna Depot PA-2
Susquehanna Depot Borough—civil PA-2
**Susquehanna Depot (corporate name for Susquehanna)**—pop pl PA-2
**Susquehanna Heights**—pop pl PA-2
**Susquehanna Hills**—pop pl MD-2
Susquehannah River PA-2
Susquehannah Turnpike—hist pl NY-2
**Susquehanna Manor (subdivision)**—pop pl PA-2
Susquehanna Memorial Gardens—cemetery PA-2
Susquehanna Mine—mine MN-6
Susquehanna Natl Wildlife Ref—park MD-2
Susquehanna Neck MD-2
Susquehanna Neck—cape MD-2
Susquehanna Plains—flat CT-1
Susquehanna Point—cape MD-2
Susquehanna Post Office (historical)—building PA-2
Susquehanna River PA-2
Susquehanna River—stream MD-2
Susquehanna River—stream NY-2
Susquehanna River—stream PA-2
Susquehanna River Overlook—locale PA-2
Susquehanna Speedway—other PA-2
Susquehanna State For—forest PA-2
Susquehanna State Park—park PA-2
Susquehanna Township—CDP PA-2
Susquehanna Township—civil PA-2
**Susquehanna Township**—pop pl SD-7
Susquehanna Township HS—school PA-2
Susquehanna Township MS—school PA-2
**Susquehanna (Township of)**—pop pl (4) PA-2
Susquehanna Univ—school PA-2
Susquehanna Valley Country Club—other PA-2
Susquehanna Valley HS—school NY-2
Susquehanna Valley Mall—locale PA-2
Susquehanna Water Gaps—gap PA-2
Susquehannock Campground—locale PA-2
Susquehannock Overlook—locale PA-2
Susquehannock Sch—school PA-2
Susquehannock State For—area PA-2
Susquehannock State Park—park PA-2
Susquehecka Creek—stream PA-2

Susquetonscut Brook—*stream* CT-1
*Suss* MH-9
Sussaymin Lakes—*lake* AK-9
*Sussex* NJ-2
Sussex—*airport* NJ-2
Sussex—*locale* WY-8
**Sussex**—*pop pl* NJ-2
**Sussex**—*pop pl* NC-3
**Sussex**—*pop pl* (2) VA-3
**Sussex**—*pop pl* WI-6
**Sussex At Hampton**—*pop pl* VA-3
**Sussex at Norfolk**—*pop pl* VA-3
Sussex Central JHS—*school* DE-2
Sussex Central Senior HS—*school* DE-2
**Sussex County**—*pop pl* DE-2
**Sussex County**—*pop pl* NJ-2
**Sussex (County)**—*pop pl* VA-3
Sussex County Airp—*airport* DE-2
Sussex County Courthouse—*hist pl* NJ-2
Sussex County Courthouse and the Circle—*hist pl* DE-2
Sussex County Courthouse Hist Dist—*hist pl* VA-3
Sussex County Vo-Tech Center—*school* DE-2
*Sussex Court House* NJ-2
**Sussex Estates (subdivision)**—*pop pl* DE-2
Sussex Hilton—*uninc pl* VA-3
Sussex Irrigation Canal—*canal* WY-8
Sussex Mills—*locale* NJ-2
Sussex Natl Bank of Seaford—*hist pl* DE-2
Sussex Oil Field—*oilfield* WY-8
Sussex Repressuring Plant—*other* WY-8
Sussex Sch—*school* MD-2
Sussex Sch—*school* OH-6
Sussex Sch—*school* WY-8
**Sussex Shores**—*pop pl* DE-2
**Sussex Unit ( Continental Camp)**—*pop pl* WY-8
*Sussex Woods* IN-6
**Sussex Woods (subdivision)**—*pop pl* DE-2
Sussie Hill—*summit* ME-1
*Sussupe* MH-9
Sustacek Lake—*lake* MN-6
Sustacha Spring—*spring* NV-8
Sustacha Well—*well* NV-8
Susterka Lake—*lake* MI-6
**Susua**—*pop pl* (2) PR-3
Susua Alta (Barrio)—*fmr MCD* PR-3
Susua Baja (Barrio)—*fmr MCD* (2) PR-3
Susua (Barrio)—*fmr MCD* PR-3
*Susube* MH-9
*Susube Point* MH-9
*Susukijima* FM-9
*Susuki-Shima* FM-9
Susulatna Hills—*summit* AK-9
Susulatna River—*stream* AK-9
*Susupe Point* MH-9
Susupi—*flat* MH-9
**Susupi**—*pop pl* MH-9
Susupi, Puntan—*cape* MH-9
Susybole Creek—*stream* SC-3
*Sutabuco Creek* MS-4
*Sutalee* GA-3
**Sutalee**—*pop pl* GA-3
Sutallee—*locale* GA-3
Sutamachute Hill—*summit* RI-1
**Sutank**—*pop pl* CO-8
S U Tank—*reservoir* NM-5
Sutch Road Bridge in Marlborough Township—*hist pl* PA-2
**Sutcliffe**—*pop pl* NV-8
Sutcliffe Corners—*locale* WI-6
*Sutcliffe Creek* CA-9
Sutcliffe Creek—*stream* CA-9
Sutcliff Park—*park* PA-2
Suter Canyon—*valley* WY-8
Suter Creek—*stream* (2) AK-9
Suter Ditch—*canal* OH-6
Suter House—*hist pl* MS-4
Suter (RR name for Sutersville)—*other* PA-2
Suter Run—*stream* WV-2
Suter Sch—*school* FL-3
Suters Tavern—*locale* DC-2
**Sutersville**—*pop pl* PA-2
**Sutersville (RR name Suter)**—*pop pl* PA-2
*Suterville* (2) PA-2
Suterville—*locale* KY-4
Suterville Borough—*civil* PA-2
Sutfield-Thompson House—*hist pl* KY-4
*Sutherland* FL-3
Sutherland—*locale* MO-7
Sutherland—*locale* NC-3
Sutherland—*locale* TN-4
Sutherland—*locale* (2) VA-3
Sutherland—*locale* WI-6
**Sutherland**—*pop pl* IA-7
**Sutherland**—*pop pl* KY-4
**Sutherland**—*pop pl* NE-7
**Sutherland**—*pop pl* UT-8
**Sutherland**—*pop pl* VA-3
Sutherland, D. H., House—*hist pl* NM-5
Sutherland, Lake—*lake* WA-9
Sutherland, Lake—*reservoir* CA-9
Sutherland Bayou—*bay* FL-3
Sutherland Bluff—*cliff* GA-3
Sutherland Bridge—*hist pl* CO-8
Sutherland Cabin—*locale* OR-9
Sutherland Canal—*canal* NE-7
Sutherland Canyon—*valley* WA-9
Sutherland Cem—*cemetery* MS-4
Sutherland Cem—*cemetery* NE-7
Sutherland Cem—*cemetery* NY-2
Sutherland Cem—*cemetery* NC-3
Sutherland Cem—*cemetery* TN-4
Sutherland Cem—*cemetery* TX-5
Sutherland Cem—*cemetery* UT-8
Sutherland Cem—*cemetery* (5) VA-3
Sutherland Ch—*church* OH-6
Sutherland Consolidated Sch—*school* KY-4
Sutherland Creek—*stream* CO-8
Sutherland Creek—*stream* MT-8
Sutherland Creek—*stream* OR-9
Sutherland Creek—*stream* TX-5
Sutherland Creek—*stream* WA-9
Sutherland Crossroads—*locale* AR-4
Sutherland Ditch—*canal* CO-8
Sutherland Fruit Company—*hist pl* CA-9
Sutherland Gap—*gap* NC-3
Sutherland Hollow—*valley* TN-4
Sutherland Hollow—*valley* TX-5
Sutherland Lake—*lake* MI-6
Sutherland Mine (historical)—*mine* NV-8
Sutherland Mtn—*summit* NV-8
Sutherland Oemig Drain—*stream* MI-6
Sutherland Park—*park* MI-6
Sutherland Park—*park* NY-2
Sutherland Park Cem—*cemetery* IN-6
Sutherland Peak—*summit* AZ-5
Sutherland Pond—*lake* ME-1
Sutherland Pond—*lake* (2) NY-2
Sutherland Post Office (historical)—*building* TN-4
Sutherland Ranch—*locale* SD-7
Sutherland Ranch—*locale* WY-8
Sutherland Ranch (historical)—*locale* SD-7
*Sutherland Reservoir* CA-9
Sutherland Reservoir Park—*park* NE-7
Sutherland Reservoir State Park—*park* NE-7
Sutherland Ridge—*ridge* AZ-5
Sutherland Ridge—*ridge* TN-4
Sutherland Ridge—*ridge* VA-3
Sutherland Rsvr—*reservoir* NE-7
**Sutherlands**—*pop pl* NC-3
Sutherland Sch—*school* CA-9
Sutherland Sch—*school* IL-6
Sutherland Sch—*school* TN-4
*Sutherlands Creek* TX-5
Sutherland Spring—*spring* (2) SD-7
**Sutherland Springs**—*pop pl* TX-5
**Sutherlands Still**—*pop pl* FL-3
Sutherland Valley Ch—*church* NC-3
Sutherland Wash—*stream* AZ-5
Sutherland Wash Archeol District—*hist pl* AZ-5
Sutherlin—*locale* VA-3
**Sutherlin**—*pop pl* OR-9
**Sutherlin**—*pop pl* VA-3
Sutherlin, Lake—*reservoir* MT-8
Sutherlin Bank Bldg—*hist pl* OR-9
Sutherlin Branch—*stream* IN-6
Sutherlin Cabin—*hist pl* AR-4
Sutherlin Cem—*cemetery* IN-6
Sutherlin Cem—*cemetery* OR-9
Sutherlin Creek—*stream* (2) OR-9
Sutherlin Lake—*reservoir* KY-4
Sutherlin Log Dam—*dam* OR-9
Sutherlin Log Pond—*reservoir* OR-9
Sutherlin Log Pond Dam—*dam* OR-9
Sutherlin Millpond—*reservoir* VA-3
Sutherlin Municipal Airp—*airport* OR-9
*Sutherlin Valley* OR-9
Suthlawn Ch—*church* IN-6
Sutico—*locale* WA-9
**Sutiff**—*pop pl* IA-7
Sutiff Cem—*cemetery* IA-7
Sutil Island—*island* CA-9
*Sutleff* IA-7
Sutley Cem—*cemetery* (2) SD-7
Sutley Post Office (historical)—*building* SD-7
**Sutliff**—*pop pl* IA-7
Sutliff and Kenope Drain—*stream* MI-6
Sutliff Cem—*cemetery* IL-6
Sutliffe Brook—*stream* CT-1
Sutliff Private Airp—*airport* PA-2
Sut Mtn—*summit* VA-3
Sutorious Ditch—*canal* IN-6
Sutphen—*locale* KS-7
*Sutphens Mill* KS-7
Sutphens Run—*stream* IL-6
Sutphin—*locale* NC-3
Sutphin Cem—*cemetery* WV-2
*Sutre* UT-8
Sutro—*locale* NV-8
Sutro—*locale* UT-8
Sutro, Mount—*summit* CA-9
Sutro Creek—*stream* AK-9
*Sutro Crest* CA-9
Sutro For—*forest* CA-9
Sutro Heights Park—*park* CA-9
Sutro Rsvr—*reservoir* CA-9
Sutro Sch—*school* CA-9
Sutro Springs—*spring* NV-8
Sutro Tunnel—*tunnel* NV-8
Sutt Bayou—*gut* LA-4
Suttee Bridge—*other* MO-7
Suttell Ford—*locale* AL-4
Suttens Meadow—*area* WA-9
**Suttentown**—*pop pl* NC-3
Sutter—*CDP* CA-9
Sutter—*locale* IL-6
**Sutter**—*pop pl* IL-6
Sutter, Johann Agust, House—*hist pl* PA-2
Sutter and Eight Line Drain—*canal* MI-6
Sutter Basin—*basin* CA-9
Sutter Butte Canal—*canal* CA-9
Sutter Butte Outing Club—*other* CA-9
Sutter Buttes—*summit* CA-9
Sutter by-Pass—*canal* CA-9
Sutter By Pass—*canal* CA-9
Sutter By-Pass—*canal* CA-9
Sutter Bypass—*canal* CA-9
Sutter by-Pass—*canal* CA-9
Sutter By Pass—*canal* CA-9
Sutter Bypass—*canal* CA-9
Sutter Causeway—*bridge* CA-9
Sutter (CCD)—*cens area* CA-9
Sutter Cem—*cemetery* IL-6
Sutter Cem—*cemetery* MO-7
Sutter City Lateral—*canal* CA-9
**Sutter (County)**—*pop pl* CA-9
*Sutter County Buttes* CA-9
Sutter County Extension Canal—*canal* CA-9
Sutter County Hosp—*hospital* CA-9
*Sutter Creek* ID-8
*Sutter Creek* OR-9
**Sutter Creek**—*pop pl* CA-9
Sutter Creek—*stream* (2) AK-9
Sutter Creek—*stream* CA-9
Sutter Creek—*stream* WA-9
Sutter Creek Grammar Sch—*hist pl* CA-9
Sutter Creek-Plymouth (CCD)—*cens area* CA-9
Sutter Extension Canal—*canal* CA-9
Sutterfield Cem—*cemetery* MO-7
Sutterfield Hollow—*valley* MO-7
Sutter Hill—*locale* CA-9
Sutter Hosp—*hospital* CA-9
Sutter Island—*island* CA-9
**Sutter Island**—*pop pl* CA-9
Sutter JHS—*school* CA-9
Sutter Lake—*lake* AK-9
Sutter Lake—*lake* IL-6
Sutter Lake—*lake* MI-6
Sutter Memorial Hosp—*hospital* CA-9
Sutter-Meyer House—*hist pl* MO-7
Sutter Mtn—*summit* NY-2
Sutter Mtn—*summit* WA-9
Sutter Natl Wildlife Ref—*park* CA-9
Sutter Pond Dam—*dam* MS-4
*Sutters Buttes* CA-9
Sutter Sch—*school* (4) CA-9
Sutter's Fort—*hist pl* CA-9
Sutters Fort State Historical Monmt—*park* CA-9
Sutter Slough—*gut* CA-9
Sutter Slough—*stream* CA-9
Sutters Mill (Site)—*locale* CA-9
Sutter Street—*post sta* CA-9
Sutterville Sch—*school* CA-9
Sutterwhite Creek—*stream* NC-3
Suttle—*locale* AR-4
**Suttle**—*pop pl* AL-4
Suttle, Joseph, House—*hist pl* NC-3
Suttle Bldg—*hist pl* MS-4
Suttle Cem—*cemetery* AL-4
Suttle Cem—*cemetery* (2) GA-3
Suttle Creek—*stream* IA-7
Suttle Creek—*stream* OK-5
Suttle Ditch—*canal* CO-8
Suttle Lake—*lake* OR-9
Suttle Post Office—*building* AL-4
Suttler Creek—*stream* ID-8
Suttlers Canyon—*valley* NE-7
Suttles Basin—*basin* CO-8
Suttle Sch—*school* AL-4
Suttles Chapel—*church* TN-4
Suttles Ditch—*canal* NV-8
*Suttles Lake* OR-9
Suttles Mill—*locale* GA-3
Suttle Spring—*spring* NV-8
Suttles Rocks—*summit* MS-4
Suttles Sch (historical)—*school* TN-4
Suttle Tank—*reservoir* AZ-5
*Suttleton* AL-4
Suttner Rsvr—*reservoir* OR-9
*Sutton* FL-3
*Sutton* NC-3
Sutton—*locale* AR-4
Sutton—*locale* KS-7
Sutton—*locale* PA-2
Sutton—*locale* TX-5
Sutton—*locale* WA-9
**Sutton**—*pop pl* AK-9
**Sutton**—*pop pl* FL-3
**Sutton**—*pop pl* (2) IL-6
**Sutton**—*pop pl* (2) KY-4
**Sutton**—*pop pl* ME-1
**Sutton**—*pop pl* MA-1
**Sutton**—*pop pl* NE-7
**Sutton**—*pop pl* NH-1
**Sutton**—*pop pl* (2) NC-3
**Sutton**—*pop pl* ND-7
**Sutton**—*pop pl* OK-5
**Sutton**—*pop pl* VT-1
**Sutton**—*pop pl* WV-2
Sutton—*uninc pl* MD-2
Sutton, Ephraim D. and William D., House—*hist pl* UT-8
Sutton, John, Hall—*hist pl* PA-2
Sutton, John, House—*hist pl* ID-8
Sutton, Lake—*lake* SD-7
Sutton, Thomas, House—*hist pl* DE-2
**Sutton Acres**—*pop pl* MD-2
Sutton Airp—*airport* IN-6
Sutton Barn—*hist pl* WA-9
*Sutton Bay* MI-6
Sutton Bay—*bay* WA-9
Sutton Bay—*swamp* SC-3
Sutton Bayou—*gut* LA-4
Sutton Bayou—*stream* AR-4
Sutton Bay Rec Area—*park* SD-7
Sutton Block—*hist pl* MA-1
Sutton Bluff—*cliff* MO-7
Sutton Bluff Campground—*locale* MO-7
Sutton Branch—*stream* (2) GA-3
Sutton Branch—*stream* KS-7
Sutton Branch—*stream* (2) KY-4
Sutton Branch—*stream* (2) MO-7
Sutton Branch—*stream* (2) NC-3
Sutton Branch—*stream* SC-3
Sutton Branch—*stream* (2) TN-4
Sutton Bridge—*bridge* AL-4
Sutton Brook—*stream* (2) VT-1
Sutton Canyon—*valley* (2) CA-9
Sutton Canyon—*valley* ID-8
Sutton Cem—*cemetery* (2) AL-4
Sutton Cem—*cemetery* FL-3
Sutton Cem—*cemetery* ID-8
Sutton Cem—*cemetery* IN-6
Sutton Cem—*cemetery* IA-7
Sutton Cem—*cemetery* (4) KS-7
Sutton Cem—*cemetery* (3) KY-4
Sutton Cem—*cemetery* MS-4
Sutton Cem—*cemetery* (4) MO-7
Sutton Cem—*cemetery* NE-7
Sutton Cem—*cemetery* (5) NC-3
Sutton Cem—*cemetery* (4) TN-4
Sutton Cem—*cemetery* TX-5
Sutton Cem—*cemetery* VA-3
Sutton Cem—*cemetery* WV-2
Sutton Center Cem—*cemetery* MA-1
*Sutton Centre* MA-1
Sutton Ch—*church* GA-3
Sutton Ch—*church* MI-6
Sutton Ch—*church* OH-6
Sutton Ch—*church* SC-3
Sutton Chapel—*church* NC-3
Sutton Corners—*locale* PA-2
Sutton Coulee—*valley* MN-6
**Sutton (County)**—*pop pl* TX-5
Sutton County Courthouse—*hist pl* TX-5
*Sutton Creek* OR-9
Sutton Creek—*stream* AR-4
Sutton Creek—*stream* (2) CO-8
Sutton Creek—*stream* FL-3
Sutton Creek—*stream* IL-6
Sutton Creek—*stream* (2) KS-7
Sutton Creek—*stream* MI-6
Sutton Creek—*stream* MO-7
Sutton Creek—*stream* MT-8
Sutton Creek—*stream* (3) NC-3
Sutton Creek—*stream* (5) OR-9
Sutton Creek—*stream* PA-2
Sutton Creek—*stream* TN-4
Sutton Creek—*stream* (2) TX-5
Sutton Creek Campground—*park* OR-9
Sutton Downtown Hist Dist—*hist pl* WV-2
Sutton Drain—*stream* MI-6
Sutton Draw—*valley* CO-8
Sutton Elem Sch—*school* IN-6
**Sutton Estates Subdivision**—*pop pl* UT-8
Sutton Falls—*falls* MA-1
Sutton Falls Dam—*dam* (2) MA-1
Sutton Falls Rsvr—*reservoir* MA-1
Suttonfiled, Lake—*reservoir* CA-9
Sutton Ford Dam—*dam* TN-4
Sutton Gulch—*valley* OR-9
Sutton Gully—*valley* TX-5
Sutton Hill—*summit* AL-4
Sutton Hill—*summit* NV-8
Sutton Hill Sch (abandoned)—*school* PA-2
Sutton (historical)—*locale* KS-7
Sutton Hole Light—*locale* MA-1
Sutton Hollow—*valley* AR-4
Sutton Hollow—*valley* (2) MO-7
Sutton Hollow—*valley* NY-2
Sutton Hollow—*valley* (4) TN-4
Sutton Hollow Cem—*cemetery* NY-2
Sutton House—*hist pl* DE-2
Sutton House—*hist pl* OH-6
Sutton Island—*island* ME-1
**Sutton Island**—*pop pl* ME-1
Sutton Knob—*summit* AR-4
Sutton Knob—*summit* NC-3
Sutton Knob—*summit* WV-2
Sutton Lake—*lake* LA-4
Sutton Lake—*lake* MI-6
Sutton Lake—*lake* (2) MN-6
Sutton Lake—*lake* (2) MS-4
Sutton Lake—*lake* OR-9
Sutton Lake—*lake* WA-9
Sutton Lake—*reservoir* AL-4
Sutton Lake—*reservoir* TX-5
Sutton Lake—*reservoir* WV-2
Sutton Lake Campground—*park* OR-9
Sutton Lake Dam—*dam* AL-4
Sutton Lake Rec Area—*park* OR-9
Sutton Memorial Chapel—*church* NJ-2
Sutton Memorial Sch—*school* MA-1
Sutton-Metro Park—*airport* NJ-2
Sutton Mill—*locale* CO-8
**Sutton Mill**—*pop pl* PA-2
Sutton Mill Creek—*stream* GA-3
*Sutton Mills* NH-1
Sutton Mine—*mine* MO-7
Sutton Mission—*church* KY-4
Sutton Mountain—*ridge* OR-9
Sutton Mtn—*summit* MT-8
Sutton Mtn—*summit* NC-3
Sutton Neck—*cape* VA-3
Sutton-Newby House—*hist pl* NC-3
Sutton Park—*park* NC-3
**Sutton Park**—*pop pl* NJ-2
Sutton Park Ch—*church* NC-3
**Sutton Park (subdivision)**—*pop pl* NC-3
Sutton Place—*locale* MO-7
**Sutton Place**—*pop pl* VA-3
Sutton Place Hist Dist—*hist pl* NY-2
Sutton Place Shop Ctr—*locale* MO-7
**Sutton Place (subdivision)**—*pop pl* AL-4
*Sutton Point* IL-6
*Sutton Point* MI-6
Sutton Point—*cape* MD-2
Sutton Pond—*lake* MI-6
Sutton Pond—*lake* NY-2
Sutton Pond—*reservoir* GA-3
Sutton Pond—*reservoir* (2) MA-1
Sutton Post Office (historical)—*building* TN-4
Sutton Ranch—*locale* NE-7
Sutton Ranch—*locale* OR-9
*Sutton Ridge* NC-3
Sutton Ridge—*ridge* IN-6
Sutton Ridge—*ridge* LA-4
Sutton Ridge—*ridge* (2) TN-4
Sutton River—*stream* VT-1
Sutton Rocks—*bar* MA-1
Sutton RR Station—*locale* FL-3
*Sutton Rsvr* WV-2
Sutton Rsvr—*reservoir* CO-8
Sutton Run—*stream* (2) WV-2
*Suttons* MI-6
**Suttons**—*pop pl* SC-3
Suttons Bay—*bay* MI-6
**Suttons Bay**—*pop pl* MI-6
**Suttons Bay (Township of)**—*pop pl* MI-6
*Suttons Bluff* MO-7
Suttons Branch—*stream* KY-4
Suttons Branch—*stream* SC-3
Suttons Branch Ch—*church* SC-3
*Suttons Branch Creek* KS-7
Suttons Bridge—*bridge* NJ-2
Suttons Canyon—*valley* UT-8
Sutton Sch—*school* (2) AR-4
Sutton Sch—*school* CA-9
Sutton Sch—*school* IN-6
Sutton Sch—*school* MI-6
Sutton Sch—*school* WI-6
Sutton Sch—*school* (2) WY-8
Sutton Sch (historical)—*school* MS-4
Sutton Sch (historical)—*school* TN-4
Suttons Corner—*locale* GA-3
Suttons Corner—*locale* NC-3
**Suttons Corner**—*pop pl* NY-2
Suttons Creek—*locale* PA-2
Suttons Creek—*stream* UT-8
Suttons Ford—*crossing* TN-4
Suttons Gap—*gap* AL-4
*Suttons Island* ME-1
Sutton Slip—*channel* LA-4
Suttons Mill—*locale* TX-5
Suttons Mill—*other* KY-4
*Sutton's Mills* MA-1
**Suttons Mills**—*pop pl* MA-1
*Suttons Point* MI-6
Suttons Pond—*reservoir* IL-6
*Sutton Spring* MO-7
Sutton Spring—*spring* MT-8
Suttons Rsvr—*reservoir* UT-8
Suttons Store—*locale* NC-3
*Suttons Switch* MS-4
Sutton State For—*forest* MA-1
Sutton Station—*locale* PA-2
Sutton Station—*locale* VT-1
**Sutton Subdivision**—*pop pl* UT-8
Suttontown—*locale* NC-3
**Suttontown**—*pop pl* NC-3
Sutton Town Cem—*cemetery* MA-1
**Sutton (Town of)**—*pop pl* MA-1
**Sutton (Town of)**—*pop pl* NH-1
**Sutton (Town of)**—*pop pl* VT-1
**Sutton Township**—*pop pl* NE-7
**Sutton (Township of)**—*pop pl* OH-6
Sutton Valley Cem—*cemetery* KS-7
Sutton Well—*well* AZ-5
Sutton Windmill—*locale* CO-8
Sutwik Island—*island* AK-9
Sutzer Creek—*stream* KY-4
Sutzer Creek Ch—*church* KY-4
Suul, Toachel—*channel* PW-9
Suval—*locale* CA-9
Suvaloyuk Creek—*stream* AK-9
*Suvarov Atoll* MP-9
Suva Street Sch—*school* CA-9
Suver—*locale* OR-9
Suver Junction—*locale* OR-9
**Suver Junction**—*pop pl* OR-9
Suwanacoochee Spring—*spring* FL-3
Suwanee—*locale* KY-4
Suwanee—*locale* NM-5
**Suwanee**—*pop pl* GA-3
*Suwanee County* FL-3
Suwanee Creek—*stream* CA-9
Suwanee Creek—*stream* GA-3
Suwanee-Duluth (CCD)—*cens area* GA-3
Suwanee Grove—*woods* CA-9
*Suwanee Mountain* GA-3
**Suwanee Old Town (historical)**—*pop pl* FL-3
*Suwanee River* CA-9
*Suwanee River* FL-3
*Suwanee River* GA-3
Suwanee Spring—*spring* NM-5
**Suwanee Valley**—*pop pl* FL-3
*Suwaney River* FL-3
*Suwaney River* GA-3
*Suwannee* GA-3
Suwannee—*locale* FL-3
**Suwannee**—*pop pl* FL-3
Suwannee Canal—*canal* GA-3
Suwannee Ch—*church* GA-3
Suwannee County—*civil* FL-3
**Suwannee County**—*pop pl* FL-3
Suwannee County Hosp—*hospital* FL-3
Suwannee County Mall—*locale* FL-3
Suwannee Creek—*stream* GA-3
Suwannee Creek Islands—*island* GA-3
**Suwannee (Demory Hill)**—*pop pl* FL-3
Suwannee Elementary, East Sch—*school* FL-3
Suwannee Elementary, West Sch—*school* FL-3
Suwannee-Hamilton Area Vocational Technical Sch—*school* FL-3
Suwannee HS—*school* FL-3
Suwannee Lake—*lake* FL-3
Suwannee Lake—*lake* GA-3
Suwannee Lookout Tower—*tower* FL-3
Suwannee Mine—*mine* FL-3
Suwannee MS—*school* FL-3
Suwannee Reef—*bar* (2) FL-3
*Suwannee River* FL-3
Suwannee River—*other* FL-3
Suwannee River—*stream* FL-3
Suwannee River—*stream* GA-3
Suwannee River Ch—*church* FL-3
Suwannee River Research Educational Center—*school* FL-3
Suwannee River Sill—*canal* GA-3
Suwannee River State Park—*park* FL-3
Suwannee River Tabernacle—*church* FL-3
Suwannee Sound—*bay* FL-3
**Suwannee Springs**—*pop pl* FL-3
Suwannee Springs Ch—*church* FL-3
Suwannee Valley—*locale* FL-3
*Suwannochee River* GA-3
*Suwannoochee Creek* GA-3
Suwannoochee Creek—*stream* GA-3
*Suwanoochee Creek* GA-3
*Suwarow Atoll* MP-9
*Suwuki Vaya* AZ-5
Suwuk Tontk—*summit* AZ-5
Suyafe—*ridge* GU-9
Suyafe River—*stream* GU-9
Suydam Dam—*dam* PA-2
Suydam House—*hist pl* NY-2
Suydam Pond—*reservoir* PA-2
Suzanna Canyon—*valley* UT-8
Suzanne, Lake—*reservoir* IL-6
Suzanne Branch—*stream* TN-4
Suzanne Davis Mtn—*summit* AL-4
Suzanne Lake—*lake* OR-9
*Suzanne Mtn* AL-4
Suzanne Sch—*school* CA-9
Suz Anne Sch—*school* NJ-2
Suzar Bay—*bay* OH-6
Suzie Creek—*stream* ID-8
Suzie Creek—*stream* PA-2
*Suzuki Canyon* OR-9
*Suzuki Jima* FM-9
*Suzume Jima* FM-9
*Suzume-Shima* FM-9
Suzy Island—*island* OR-9
*Suzy Lake* CA-9
Suzy Q Creek—*stream* AK-9
Suzy Q Tank—*reservoir* AZ-5
Suzy's Cave—*cave* MI-6
*Suzzanne Mtn* AL-4
**Svahn Manor**—*pop pl* NY-2
Svatos, Frank, Rubblestone Barn—*hist pl* SD-7
Svatos Point—*cape* SD-7
SVC District French Lick Dam F-7—*dam* IN-6
S V Draw—*valley* WY-8
Svea—*locale* FL-3
**Svea**—*pop pl* MN-6
Svea Ch—*church* NE-7
Svea Ch—*church* WI-6
**Sveadahl**—*pop pl* MN-6
**Sveadal**—*pop pl* CA-9
Svea Dal Cem—*cemetery* NE-7
Svea Hill Cem—*cemetery* MN-6
Svea Hill Ch—*church* MN-6
Svea Land Company Office—*hist pl* AL-4
Svea Music Hall—*hist pl* IL-6
Svea Sch—*school* MN-6
Svea Town Hall—*building* ND-7
**Svea Township**—*pop pl* ND-7
**Svea (Township of)**—*pop pl* MN-6
Svedes Canyon—*valley* UT-8
Svee Creek—*stream* ID-8
**Svenite**—*pop pl* MO-7
Sven Lake—*lake* AK-9
**Svensen**—*pop pl* OR-9
Svensen Island—*island* OR-9
**Svensen Junction**—*pop pl* OR-9
Svensen Rock—*other* AK-9
Svensen Sch—*school* OR-9
Svensens Landing—*locale* WA-9
Svenska Mission Kyrka I Sodre Maple Ridge—*hist pl* MN-6
*Svenson* OR-9
Svenson Blacksmith Shop—*hist pl* OR-9
Svenson Coulee—*valley* WI-6
*Svenson Island* OR-9
Sverdrup Cem—*cemetery* MN-6
Sverdrup Cem—*cemetery* ND-7
Sverdrup Sch—*school* ND-7
Sverdrup Town Hall—*building* ND-7
**Sverdrup Township**—*pop pl* ND-7
**Sverdrup Township**—*pop pl* SD-7
**Sverdrup (Township of)**—*pop pl* MN-6
Svetcoff Ranch—*locale* SD-7
*S V Hill* UT-8
Sviechnikof Harbor—*bay* AK-9
Svihra Park—*park* CT-1
Svinth Creek—*stream* OR-9
Svitlak Island—*island* AK-9
*S V Marshall HS* MS-4
**Svoboda**—*pop pl* OK-5
Svoboda Ranch—*locale* WY-8
Svob Park—*park* AZ-5
Svoger Slough—*gut* AK-9
Svold—*locale* ND-7
S V Rsvr—*reservoir* OR-9
*S V Thompson HS* MS-4
S V White Colliery—*building* PA-2
Swaab Cem—*cemetery* OH-6
*Swab Creek* ID-8
*Swab Creek* WY-8
Swab Creek—*stream* ID-8
Swab Creek—*stream* IN-6
Swab Creek—*stream* OR-9
Swab Creek—*stream* WY-8
*Swaben Berg* PA-2
Swabia Creek—*stream* PA-2
*Swabian Creek* PA-2
Swab Mine—*mine* CO-8
Swab Run—*stream* IL-6
Swader Hollow—*valley* (2) TN-4
Swaderick Creek—*stream* MD-2
Swadkins, Thomas, House—*hist pl* MA-1
Swadley Cem—*cemetery* OH-6
Swadley Ditch—*canal* CO-8
Swadley Well—*well* AZ-5
*Swaenewyck* DE-2
Swafford Branch—*stream* IL-6
Swafford Branch—*stream* KY-4
Swafford Branch—*stream* MS-4
Swafford Branch—*stream* (2) TN-4
Swafford Canyon—*valley* AZ-5
Swafford Cem—*cemetery* AL-4
Swafford Cem—*cemetery* (3) TN-4
Swafford Ch—*church* KY-4
Swafford Chapel—*church* TN-4
Swafford Chapel Cem—*cemetery* TN-4
Swafford Cove—*valley* TN-4
Swafford Creek—*stream* LA-4
Swafford-David Cem—*cemetery* TN-4
Swafford Gap—*gap* NC-3
Swafford Hollow—*valley* AR-4
Swafford Knob—*summit* TN-4
Swafford Pond—*lake* TN-4
Swaffords Spring—*spring* MS-4
Swaford Creek—*stream* SC-3
Swag Ch—*church* TN-4
Swag Cove—*valley* NC-3
*Swager Creek* CA-9
Swager Creek—*stream* TX-5
Swager Ditch—*canal* CA-9
Swagerty Cove—*valley* TN-4
*Swagerty Cove Creek* TN-4
Swagerty Creek—*stream* TX-5
Swag Fork—*stream* WV-2
Swagg—*locale* AL-4
Swaggart Buttes—*summit* OR-9
Swaggart Spring—*spring* AZ-5
*Swagger Creek* CA-9
Swagger Creek—*stream* OR-9
Swagger Slough—*gut* AR-4
*Swaggerts Island* PA-2
Swaggerty Blockhouse—*hist pl* TN-4
Swaggerty Rsvr—*reservoir* OR-9
Swaggerty Spring—*spring* TN-4
*Swaggles Town* AL-4
Swag Gulch—*valley* CO-8
Swag Lake—*lake* IA-7
Swag Lake—*lake* MN-6
Swago Ch—*church* WV-2
Swago Creek—*stream* WV-2
Swago Mountain—*ridge* WV-2
Swago Pond—*lake* PA-2
*Swagzee Lake* LA-4
*Swahn Lake* WI-6
Swail Ditch—*canal* OH-6
Swails Cem—*cemetery* IN-6
*Swails Mountsin* NV-8
Swaim—*locale* AL-4
Swaim Branch—*stream* AR-4
Swaim Cave—*cave* AL-4
Swaim Cem—*cemetery* AL-4
Swaim Cove—*valley* GA-3
Swaim Creek—*stream* NC-3
Swaim Draw—*valley* WY-8
Swaim Gap—*gap* GA-3
Swaim House—*hist pl* TN-4
Swaim Knob—*summit* TN-4
Swaim Place—*locale* WY-8
Swaims Ch—*church* NC-3
Swaims Chapel—*church* AR-4
Swaim Spring—*spring* WY-8
**Swaimtown**—*pop pl* NC-3
Swain—*locale* NJ-2
Swain—*locale* OR-9
**Swain**—*pop pl* AR-4
**Swain**—*pop pl* KY-4

**Swain Acres**—pop pl DE-2
Swain and Truitt Ditch—canal DE-2
Swain Branch—stream IN-6
Swain Branch—stream NC-3
Swain Cem—cemetery VT-1
Swain Cem—cemetery WV-2
Swain Cemetery TN-4
Swain Channel—channel NJ-2
Swain Coulee—valley MT-8
**Swain County**—pop pl NC-3
Swain County Courthouse—hist pl NC-3
Swain County HS—school NC-3
Swain County Park—park NC-3
Swain Cove ME-1
Swain Creek—stream GA-3
Swain Creek—stream TN-4
Swain Ditch IL-6
Swain Ditch IN-6
Swain Drain IN-6
Swaine Point—cape AK-9
Swainey Brook—stream NH-1
Swain Gulch—valley ID-8
Swain-Harrison House—hist pl CT-1
Swain Hill—summit (2) CA-9
Swain Hill—summit MA-1
Swain Hill—summit NH-1
**Swain (historical)**—pop pl NC-3
Swain Hollow WI-6
Swain Hollow—valley MD-2
Swain Hollow—valley UT-8
Swain Johnson Brook—stream CT-1
Swain Meadow—flat CA-9
Swain Memorial Cem—cemetery NC-3
Swain Memorial For—forest IN-6
Swain Mountain Experimental Forest—park CA-9
Swain Mtn—summit AR-4
Swain Mtn—summit CA-9
Swain Mtn—summit GA-3
Swain Point—cape NJ-2
Swain Pond—lake FL-3
Swain Prairie Spring—spring OR-9
Swain Ravine—valley CA-9
Swain Ridge—ridge KY-4
Swain River GA-3
Swain River—gut LA-4
Swain River—stream GA-3
**Swain (RR name Swains)**—pop pl NY-2
Swains NJ-2
**Swains**—pop pl AS-9
**Swainsboro**—pop pl GA-3
Swainsboro (CCD)—cens area GA-3
Swainsboro Speedway—other GA-3
Swains Canyon—valley CA-9
Swain Sch—school NC-3
Swain Sch—school PA-2
Swain Sch (abandoned)—school MO-7
Swains Cove—bay ME-1
Swains Creek—gut NH-1
Swains Creek—stream UT-8
Swains Creek Airp—airport UT-8
Swains Flat—flat CA-9
Swains Hole—reservoir CA-9
Swains Island—fmr MCD AS-9
Swains Island—island AS-9
Swains Lake—lake MI-6
**Swains Lake**—pop pl MI-6
Swains Lake—reservoir NH-1
Swains Lock—other MD-2
Swain Slough—stream CA-9
Swain Slough—stream IL-6
Swains Mtn—summit VA-3
Swains Neck—cape MA-1
Swains Notch—gap ME-1
Swainson Island—island MD-2
Swains Pond—lake ME-1
Swains Pond—lake MA-1
Swains Pond—reservoir MA-1
Swains Pond Dam—dam MA-1
Swains (RR name for Swain)—other NY-2
Swainston Creek—stream MI-6
Swainston Hollow—valley ID-8
**Swainsville**—pop pl NC-3
Swainton—locale NJ-2
Swain (Township of)—fmr MCD AR-4
Swain Valley—valley CA-9
Swakane Creek—stream WA-9
Swakane Spring—spring WA-9
**Swaldale**—pop pl IA-7
Swale—locale WA-9
Swale, The—stream LA-4
Swale Brook—stream (2) PA-2
Swale Campground—locale CA-9
Swale Canyon—valley WA-9
Swale Cem—cemetery NY-2
Swale Creek—stream ID-8
Swale Creek—stream (3) OR-9
Swale Creek—stream WA-9
**Swaledale**—pop pl IA-7
Swale Meadow—flat VT-1
Swale Park—park OH-6
Swale Pond—lake OR-9
Swale Rsvr—reservoir OR-9
**Swales**—pop pl PA-2
Swales Cem—cemetery NY-2
Swale Sch—school VT-1
Swales Creek—stream NV-8
Swales Mtn—summit NV-8
Swale Spring—spring OR-9
Swale Springs—spring OR-9
Swale Tank—reservoir (2) AZ-5
Swall—locale CA-9
Swalley Canal—canal OR-9
Swalley Chapel—church IN-6
Swalley Ditch—canal OH-6
Swall Meadow—flat CA-9
Swallow Bay—bay NV-8
Swallow Bluff—cliff TN-4
Swallow Bluff Cave—cave TN-4
Swallow Bluff Hollow—valley MO-7
Swallow Bluff Island—island TN-4
Swallow Bluff Landing—locale TN-4
Swallow Bluff Post Office TN-4
Swallow Boathouse—hist pl NH-1
Swallow Branch—stream WV-2
Swallow Canyon—valley MT-8
Swallow Canyon—valley NV-8
Swallow Canyon—valley UT-8
Swallow Canyon Raft Ramp—locale UT-8
Swallow Cave—cave MA-1
Swallow Ch—church SD-7
Swallow Cliffs—cliff IL-6
Swallow Cliff Woods—woods IL-6
Swallow Cove NV-8
Swallow Creek—stream GA-3
Swallow Draw—valley SD-7
Swallow Falls Ch—church MD-2
Swallow Falls Sch—school MD-2
Swallow Falls State For—forest MD-2
**Swallowfield**—pop pl KY-4
Swallow Fork—stream NC-3
Swallow Fork Peak—summit NM-5
Swallow Head—cliff AK-9
**Swallow Hill**—pop pl DE-2
Swallow Hill—summit MA-1
Swallow Hill Hist Dist—hist pl CO-8
Swallow Lake MN-6
Swallow Lake OR-9
Swallow Lake—lake MN-6
Swallow Lake—lake OR-9
Swallow Lakes—lake WA-9
Swallow Lake Trail—trail OR-9
Swallow Mine—mine AZ-5
Swallow Mtn—summit AZ-5
Swallow Nest Canyon—valley NM-5
Swallow Nest Spring—spring MT-8
Swallow Park UT-8
Swallow Park Ranch—locale UT-8
Swallow Point—cape AK-9
Swallow Point—cape WI-6
Swallow Post Office (historical)—building TN-4
Swallow Ranch—locale NV-8
Swallow Ranch—locale WY-8
Swallow Rock WA-9
Swallow Rock—cape CA-9
Swallow Rock—pillar CA-9
Swallow Rock—summit CA-9
Swallow Rock—summit IL-6
Swallow Rock Campground—locale WV-2
Swallow Rock Run—stream WV-2
Swallow Rocks—pillar UT-8
Swallow Rock Trail—trail WV-2
Swallows—locale CO-8
Swallow Savanna—swamp SC-3
Swallow Savanna Cem—cemetery SC-3
Swallows Cave MA-1
Swallows Cem—cemetery (2) TN-4
Swallow Sch—school WI-6
Swallow Sch (abandoned)—school MO-7
Swallows Chapel—church TN-4
Swallows Hole—cave TN-4
Swallows Nest—cliff WA-9
Swallows Nest—locale CO-8
Swallows Nest Bend—bend AZ-5
Swallows Nest Golf Club—other WA-9
Swallows Nest Ruins—locale AZ-5
Swallow Spring—spring AZ-5
Swallow Spring Pond—lake KY-4
Swallows Sch—school TN-4
**Swallow Subdivision**—pop pl UT-8
Swallow Well—well NV-8
**Swalls**—pop pl IN-6
Swalls Cem—cemetery IN-6
Swall Sch—school MT-8
Swalwell Block and Adjoining Commercial Buildings—hist pl WA-9
Swalwell Cottage—hist pl WA-9
Swam Creek—stream WA-9
Swamill Hollow—valley VA-3
Swam Lake Oil Field—oilfield TX-5
Swamp PA-2
Swamp, Lake—lake FL-3
Swamp, The—flat NY-2
Swamp, The—swamp ND-7
Swamp, The—swamp OR-9
Swamp Angel—locale KS-7
Swamp Angel Lake—lake ID-8
Swamp Angel Mine—mine CA-9
Swamp Angel Sch—school IL-6
Swamp Bank Mines—mine TN-4
Swamp Basin—basin OR-9
Swamp Branch—locale KY-4
Swamp Branch—stream AL-4
Swamp Branch—stream (2) KY-4
Swamp Branch—stream PA-2
Swamp Branch—stream SC-3
Swamp Branch—stream TN-4
Swamp Branch—stream VA-3
Swamp Branch—stream WV-2
Swamp Branch Creek AL-4
Swamp Branch Trail—trail PA-2
Swamp Brook MA-1
Swamp Brook NJ-2
Swamp Brook RI-1
Swamp Brook—stream (2) CT-1
Swamp Brook—stream MA-1
Swamp Brook—stream PA-2
Swamp Brook—stream RI-1
Swampbuggy Lake—lake AK-9
Swamp Burying Ground—cemetery CT-1
Swamp Camp—locale ID-8
Swamp Canyon—valley CO-8
Swamp Canyon—valley UT-8
Swamp Canyon Butte—summit UT-8
Swamp Canyon Connecting Trail—trail UT-8
Swamp Ch—church (2) PA-2
**Swamp City**—pop pl TX-5
Swamp College Cem—cemetery OH-6
Swamp Coll Sch—school IL-6
Swamp Corners Drain—canal MI-6
Swamp Cove—cove MA-1
Swamp Creek IN-6
Swamp Creek MN-6
Swamp Creek OR-9
Swamp Creek PA-2
Swamp Creek RI-1
Swamp Creek SC-3
**Swamp Creek**—pop pl MT-8
Swamp Creek—stream AL-4
Swamp Creek—stream (3) AK-9
Swamp Creek—stream AZ-5
Swamp Creek—stream (6) CA-9
Swamp Creek—stream (2) CO-8
Swamp Creek—stream FL-3
Swamp Creek—stream (3) GA-3
Swamp Creek—stream (9) ID-8
Swamp Creek—stream (3) IN-6
Swamp Creek—stream MI-6
Swamp Creek—stream MN-6
Swamp Creek—stream MO-7
Swamp Creek—stream (20) MT-8
Swamp Creek—stream NC-3
Swamp Creek—stream ND-7
Swamp Creek—stream (2) OH-6
Swamp Creek—stream (32) OR-9
Swamp Creek—stream (5) PA-2
Swamp Creek—stream TN-4
Swamp Creek—stream TX-5
Swamp Creek—stream (11) WA-9
Swamp Creek—stream (5) WI-6
Swamp Creek—stream WY-8
Swamp Creek Buttes—summit OR-9
Swamp Creek Camp—locale WA-9
Swamp Creek Cem—cemetery AL-4
Swamp Creek Ch—church AL-4
Swamp Creek Ch—church GA-3
Swamp Creek Cow Camp—locale OR-9
Swamp Creek Cutoff Trail—trail CO-8
Swamp Creek Dam—dam OR-9
Swamp Creek Ditch—canal MT-8
Swamp Creek Hidden Meadows Trail—trail OR-9
Swamp Creek Hill—summit WY-8
Swamp Creek Mtn—summit AZ-5
Swamp Creek Ranch—locale OR-9
Swamp Creek Ridge—ridge CA-9
Swamp Creek Road Bridge—hist pl PA-2
Swamp Creek Rsvr—reservoir OR-9
Swamp Creek Sch—school MT-8
Swamp Creek Spring—spring MT-8
Swamp Ditch IN-6
Swamp Ditch—canal NV-8
Swamp Ditch—canal OH-6
Swamp Draft—valley PA-2
Swamp Drain—canal CO-8
Swamper Creek—stream MN-6
Swamper Lake—lake MN-6
**Swampers**—pop pl LA-4
Swamp Field—flat NC-3
Swamp Field Landing—locale FL-3
Swamp Fork—stream (2) KY-4
Swamp Fox Ranger Station—locale SC-3
Swamp Frog Mine—mine MT-8
Swamp Gulch—valley CA-9
Swamp Gulch—valley (2) MT-8
Swamp Gulch—valley OR-9
Swamp Gulch Creek—stream MT-8
Swamp Hollow—valley ID-8
Swamp Hollow—valley (2) MO-7
Swamp Hollow—valley OH-6
Swamp Hollow—valley TN-4
Swamp Lake MN-6
Swamp Lake WI-6
Swamp Lake—lake (4) CA-9
Swamp Lake—lake FL-3
Swamp Lake—lake (2) ID-8
Swamp Lake—lake (2) MI-6
Swamp Lake—lake (13) MN-6
Swamp Lake—lake (2) MT-8
Swamp Lake—lake (2) OR-9
Swamp Lake—lake (2) WA-9
Swamp Lake—lake (7) WI-6
Swamp Lake—lake WY-8
Swamp Lake—swamp MT-8
Swamp Lakes—lake CA-9
Swamp Lakes—lake CO-8
Swamp Lakes—lake MI-6
Swamp Lake State Wildlife Mngmt Area—park MN-6
Swamp Lake Trail—trail WA-9
Swamp Locks And Dam MA-1
Swamp Lodge Run PA-2
Swamp Meadow—flat CA-9
Swamp Mtn—summit MT-8
Swamp Mtn—summit OR-9
Swampoodle Creek—stream TX-5
Swamp Park—swamp CO-8
Swamp Peak—summit OR-9
Swamp Peak Trail—trail OR-9
Swamp Point—cliff AZ-5
Swamp Pond NY-2
Swamp Pond RI-1
Swamp Pond—lake NH-1
Swamp Pond—lake (2) NY-2
Swamp Pond—lake VT-1
Swamp Post Office (historical)—building AL-4
Swamp Raisin Creek—stream MI-6
Swamp Ridge—ridge AZ-5
Swamp Ridge—ridge ID-8
Swamp River MN-6
Swamp River—stream MN-6
Swamp River—stream NY-2
Swamproot PA-2
Swamproot (historical)—locale PA-2
Swamp Run PA-2
**Swamp Run**—pop pl WV-2
Swamp Run—stream MD-2
Swamp Run—stream OH-6
Swamp Run—stream (8) PA-2
Swamp Run—stream VA-3
Swamp Run—stream (5) WV-2
Swamp Run Sch—school WV-2
Swamps, The—lake IL-6
Swamps, The—swamp ID-8
Swamps, The—swamp TN-4
Swamp Saddle—gap AK-9
Swamp Sauger Creek WI-6
Swamp Sauger Lake WI-6
Swamp Sch—school (3) MI-6
Swamp Sch—school NY-2
Swamp Sch—school (2) PA-2
Swamp Sch—school VT-1
Swamp Sch (abandoned)—school PA-2
Swamp Sch (historical)—school PA-2
Swampscot MA-1
**Swampscott**—pop pl MA-1
Swampscott Cem—cemetery MA-1
Swampscott Fish House—hist pl MA-1
Swampscott Mall (Shop Ctr)—locale MA-1
Swampscott Townhall—building MA-1
**Swampscott (Town of)**—pop pl MA-1
Swamp Spring—spring ID-8
Swamp Spring—spring NV-8
Swamp Spring—spring NM-5
Swamp Spring—spring (2) OR-9
Swamp Spring—spring (2) UT-8
Swamp Springs Canyon—valley AZ-5
Swamp Tank—reservoir AZ-5
Swampton—locale KY-4
Swampton Ch—church KY-4
Swampton Sch—school KY-4
Swamp Trail—trail DC-2
Swamp Trail—trail PA-2
Swamp Way—trail OR-9
Swamp Wells—well OR-9
Swamp Wells Butte—summit OR-9
Swampwolf Bay—swamp GA-3
Swampy Branch—stream TN-4
Swampy Creek—stream CO-8
Swampy Creek—stream OR-9
Swampy Creek—stream WA-9
Swampy Draw—valley ID-8
Swampy Lake AZ-5
Swampy Lake—lake OR-9
Swampy Lakes—lake AK-9
Swampy Lakes—lake OR-9
Swampy Lakes Shelter—locale OR-9
Swampy Lakes Trail—trail OR-9
Swampy Meadows—flat WA-9
Swampy Park—flat MT-8
Swampy Park Spring—spring MT-8
Swampy Pass—gap CO-8
Swampy Point AZ-5
Swampy River—stream AK-9
Swamsauger Creek—stream WI-6
Swamsauger Lake—lake WI-6
Swamscot River NH-1
Swan AL-4
Swan—fmr MCD NE-7
Swan—locale CO-8
Swan—locale GA-3
Swan—locale WY-8
**Swan**—pop pl (2) IN-6
**Swan**—pop pl IA-7
**Swan**—pop pl MO-7
**Swan**—pop pl OR-9
**Swan**—pop pl TX-5
Swan, Asie, House—hist pl MA-1
Swan, Edward H., House—hist pl NY-2
Swan, George B., House—hist pl IA-7
Swan, Henry, House—hist pl MA-1
**Swan Acres**—pop pl PA-2
Swanagan Mtn—summit TN-4
**Swan Ave (subdivision)**—pop pl MA-1
**Swanay (historical)**—pop pl TN-4
Swanay Post Office (historical)—building TN-4
Swanback Clearing—flat ME-1
Swan Basin—basin CO-8
Swan Basin—basin ID-8
Swan Basin—bay TN-4
Swan Bay—bay NJ-2
Swan Bay—bay NY-2
Swan Bay—bay NC-3
Swan Bay—bay TN-4
Swan Bay—bay TX-5
Swan Bay—bay WA-9
Swan Bay Fish and Wildlife Mngmt Area—park NJ-2
Swan Bay Resort Dock—locale TN-4
Swanberger Rsvr—reservoir CA-9
Swan Bluff—locale TN-4
Swan Bluff-Haw Branch Mines—mine TN-4
Swan Bluff Post Office TN-4
Swanbluff Post Office (historical)—building TN-4
Swan Bluff Spring—spring TN-4
Swan Branch—stream (3) AL-4
Swan Branch—stream KY-4
Swan Branch—stream MO-7
Swan Branch—stream VA-3
Swan Brook—stream CT-1
Swan Brook—stream ME-1
Swan Buffalo Number 5 Dam—dam ND-7
Swan Buffalo Number 8 Dam—dam ND-7
Swan Buffalo 12 Dam—dam ND-7
**Swanburg**—pop pl MN-6
Swanburg Cem—cemetery MN-6
Swan Butte—summit WA-9
Swan Camp—locale WY-8
Swan Canyon—valley NM-5
Swan Cave—cave MO-7
Swan Cem—cemetery AL-4
Swan Cem—cemetery IL-6
Swan Cem—cemetery IN-6
Swan Cem—cemetery IA-7
Swan Cem—cemetery (2) KY-4
Swan Cem—cemetery (2) ME-1
Swan Cem—cemetery (2) MO-7
Swan Cem—cemetery NY-2
Swan Cem—cemetery (3) TN-4
Swan Center Sch—school NE-7
Swan Channel NJ-2
Swan Chapel—church TX-5
Swan Chapel (historical)—church MO-7
Swan Check—reservoir NV-8
**Swan Corner**—pop pl MA-1
Swancott—locale AL-4
**Swancott**—pop pl AL-4
Swancott Ch—church AL-4
Swancott Lookout Tower—locale NY-2
Swancott Mill—locale NY-2
Swancott Mill Cem—cemetery NY-2
Swancott Post Office (historical)—building AL-4
Swan Coulee—valley MT-8
Swan Cove—bay AK-9
Swan Cove—bay NC-3
Swan Creek AL-4
Swan Creek MD-2
Swan Creek MI-6
Swan Creek NE-7
Swan Creek NY-2
Swancreek NC-3
Swan Creek ND-7
Swan Creek OH-6
Swan Creek TN-4
Swan Creek VA-3
Swan Creek WA-9
Swan Creek WI-6
Swan Creek—fmr MCD NE-7
Swan Creek—locale MD-2
Swan Creek—locale MI-6
Swan Creek—locale OH-6
**Swan Creek**—pop pl IL-6
**Swan Creek**—pop pl NC-3
**Swancreek**—pop pl NC-3
**Swan Creek**—pop pl UT-8
Swan Creek—stream AL-4
Swan Creek—stream AK-9
Swan Creek—stream (2) DE-2
Swan Creek—stream GA-3
Swan Creek—stream (3) ID-8
Swan Creek—stream IL-6
Swan Creek—stream (4) MD-2
Swan Creek—stream (7) MI-6
Swan Creek—stream (2) MN-6
Swan Creek—stream (2) MO-7
Swan Creek—stream MT-8
Swan Creek—stream NE-7
Swan Creek—stream NV-8
Swan Creek—stream NJ-2
Swan Creek—stream NY-2
Swan Creek—stream (5) NC-3
Swan Creek—stream ND-7
Swan Creek—stream (2) OH-6
Swan Creek—stream OK-5
Swan Creek—stream (3) OR-9
Swan Creek—stream PA-2
Swan Creek—stream (2) SD-7
Swan Creek—stream (2) TN-4
Swan Creek—stream (2) UT-8
Swan Creek—stream (2) VA-3
Swan Creek—stream (2) WA-9
Swan Creek—stream (5) WI-6
Swan Creek Bridge—hist pl MO-7
Swan Creek Campground—locale MT-8
Swan Creek Ch—church (3) OH-6
Swan Creek Ch—church TN-4
Swan Creek Ch—church VA-3
Swan Creek Chapel—church TN-4
Swan Creek Cove—bay MD-2
**Swan Creek Estates**—pop pl UT-8
**Swan Creek Junction**—pop pl TN-4
Swan Creek Lake—lake NC-3
Swan Creek Marsh—swamp MI-6
Swan Creek Mines—mine TN-4
Swan Creek Park AL-4
Swan Creek Park—park OH-6
Swan Creek Park—park WI-6
Swan Creek Point—cape MD-2
Swan Creek Point—cape MI-6
Swan Creek Pond—lake MI-6
Swan Creek Rec Area—park SD-7
Swan Creek Sch—school OH-6
Swan Creek Spring—spring UT-8
Swan Creek Township—civil SD-7
**Swan Creek (Township of)**—pop pl MI-6
**Swan Creek (Township of)**—pop pl OH-6
Swan Creek Waterfowl Mngmt Area—park AL-4
Swan Creek Wildlife Mngmt Area AL-4
Swan Cut MD-2
Swan Cut VA-3
Swancy Hollow—valley AR-4
**Swandale**—pop pl WV-2
Swandale Cem—cemetery MA-1
Swandale Sch—school MN-6
Swan Dam—dam CO-8
Swandas Bluff—cliff WI-6
Swan Deer Brake—swamp AR-4
Swan Deer Lake—swamp AR-4
**Swander**—pop pl OH-6
Swander Ditch—canal IN-6
**Swanders**—pop pl OH-6
Swan Ditch—canal WY-8
Swan Drain—stream MI-6
Swan Draw—valley CO-8
Swan Draw—valley (2) SD-7
Swandyke—locale CO-8
**Swanee**—pop pl KY-4
Swanee Creek—stream CO-8
Swanee Hollow Country Club—other VA-3
Swanee Lake—lake WA-9
Swanee River FL-3
Swanee River GA-3
Swanegan Branch—stream TN-4
Swanendael DE-2
**Swanendael (subdivision)**—pop pl DE-2
**Swaners Place Addition Subdivision**—pop pl UT-8
Swanewick DE-2
Swaney, Mount—summit MT-8
Swaney Bean Sch—school VT-1
Swaney Cove—bay MD-2
Swaney Creek SC-3
Swaney Creek—stream MT-8
Swaney Elem Sch—school KS-7
Swaney Ridge—ridge MT-8
**Swan Falls**—pop pl ID-8
Swan Falls Dam and Power Plant—hist pl ID-8
Swanfelt Ditch—canal IN-6
Swan Flat—flat ID-8
Swan Flat—flat UT-8
Swan Fork—stream KY-4
Swan Fork—stream VA-3
Swange Chapel Cem—cemetery MS-4
Swanger Branch—stream TN-4
Swanger Hall—hist pl ID-8
Swan Glaciers—glacier MT-8
Swango Cem—cemetery IL-6
Swango Ch—church MS-4
Swango Fork—stream (2) KY-4
Swangs NC-3
Swangstown NC-3
Swan Gut MD-2
Swan Gut VA-3
Swan Gut—gut MD-2
Swan Gut Creek MD-2
Swan Gut Creek VA-3
Swan Hill—summit AL-4
Swan Hill—summit ME-1
Swan Hill—summit NM-5
Swan Hill—summit NY-2
Swan Hill—summit OR-9
Swan Hillman Sch—school IL-6
Swan Hills Country Club—other IL-6
Swanholm Creek—stream ID-8
Swanholm Peak—summit ID-8
Swan Hook DE-2
Swan House—hist pl GA-3
Swan House and Vita Spring Pavilion—hist pl WI-6
Swanigen Hollow—valley OH-6
**Swanington**—pop pl IN-6
Swan Island ME-1
Swan Island MI-6
Swan Island WA-9
Swan Island—cape OR-9
Swan Island—island (2) AK-9
Swan Island—island IN-6
Swan Island—island ME-1
Swan Island—island (2) MD-2
Swan Island—island MI-6
Swan Island—island MS-4
Swan Island—island NH-1
Swan Island—island NY-2
Swan Island—island (3) NC-3
Swan Island—island TN-4
Swan Island Basin—bay OR-9
Swan Island Ferry (historical)—locale TN-4
Swan Island Point—cape ME-1
Swan Island Post Office (historical)—building TN-4
Swan Island Site—hist pl IL-6
Swank, Jacob, House—hist pl MO-7
Swank Cabin—locale CO-8
Swank Cem—cemetery (2) IN-6
Swank Cem—cemetery OH-6
Swank Cem—cemetery TX-5
Swank Cem—cemetery WV-2
Swank Ch—church IA-7
Swank Chapel—church VA-3
Swank Creek—stream IL-6
Swank Creek—stream IN-6
Swankee Cem—cemetery NE-7
Swan Key—island FL-3
Swank Mtn—summit TX-5
Swank Springs—spring WA-9
Swanks Run—stream PA-2
**Swanktown**—pop pl OH-6
Swank Well—well MT-8
Swan Lagoon—uninc pl TX-5
Swan Lake AL-4
Swan Lake AR-4
Swan Lake IL-6
Swan Lake MS-4
Swan Lake WA-9
Swan Lake—bay TX-5
Swan Lake—fmr MCD NE-7
Swan Lake—lake (7) AK-9
Swan Lake—lake (10) AR-4
Swan Lake—lake (3) CA-9
Swan Lake—lake CT-1
Swan Lake—lake (2) FL-3
Swan Lake—lake (4) ID-8
Swan Lake—lake (6) IL-6
Swan Lake—lake (3) IA-7
Swan Lake—lake (4) LA-4
Swan Lake—lake ME-1
Swan Lake—lake (5) MI-6
Swan Lake—lake (17) MN-6
Swan Lake—lake (5) MS-4
Swan Lake—lake (3) MT-8
Swan Lake—lake (5) NE-7
Swan Lake—lake NV-8
Swan Lake—lake NM-5
Swan Lake—lake (3) NY-2
Swan Lake—lake (3) ND-7
Swan Lake—lake OH-6
Swan Lake—lake OK-5
Swan Lake—lake (4) OR-9
Swan Lake—lake (2) SD-7
Swan Lake—lake (2) TN-4
Swan Lake—lake (5) TX-5
Swan Lake—lake UT-8
Swan Lake—lake (2) WA-9
Swan Lake—lake (2) WI-6
Swan Lake—lake (2) WY-8
Swan Lake—locale ID-8
Swan Lake—locale IA-7
Swan Lake—locale KY-4
Swan Lake—locale NE-7
**Swan Lake**—pop pl AR-4
**Swan Lake**—pop pl GA-3
**Swanlake**—pop pl ID-8
**Swan Lake**—pop pl MS-4
**Swan Lake**—pop pl MT-8
**Swan Lake**—pop pl NY-2
**Swan Lake**—pop pl OK-5
Swan Lake—reservoir AL-4
Swan Lake—reservoir CT-1
Swan Lake—reservoir (2) GA-3
Swan Lake—reservoir (3) ID-8
Swan Lake—reservoir IA-7
Swan Lake—reservoir MS-4
Swan Lake—reservoir MO-7
Swan Lake—reservoir NV-8
Swan Lake—reservoir SC-3
Swan Lake—reservoir (2) SD-7
Swan Lake—reservoir (2) TX-5
Swan Lake—reservoir VA-3
Swan Lake—swamp AR-4
Swan Lake—swamp (3) MN-6
Swan Lake—swamp MS-4
Swan Lake and Christopherson Slough State Game Mngmt Area—park IA-7
Swan Lake Artesian Well—well OR-9
Swan Lake Bayou—gut TX-5
Swan Lake Branch—stream IA-7
Swan Lake Cem—cemetery IA-7
Swan Lake Cem—cemetery MA-1
Swan Lake Cem—cemetery MN-6
Swan Lake Ch—church (3) MN-6
Swan Lake Ch—church MS-4
Swan Lake Coll (historical)—school MS-4
Swan Lake Creek—stream ID-8
Swan Lake Creek—stream SD-7
Swan Lake Dam—dam MS-4
Swan Lake Ditch—canal IL-6
Swan Lake Drainage Ditch—canal AR-4
Swan Lake Ferry (historical)—locale MS-4
Swan Lake Flat—swamp WY-8
Swan Lake Gardens—park SC-3
Swan Lake Golf Course—park TN-4
Swan Lake Guard Station—locale MT-8
Swan Lake Gulch—valley ID-8
Swan Lake (historical)—lake AL-4
Swan Lake (historical)—lake (2) IA-7
Swan Lake (historical)—lake (2) MS-4
Swan Lake (historical)—locale SD-7
**Swan Lake (Hurd)**—pop pl NY-2
Swan Lake Junior—lake CA-9
Swan Lake Landing—locale MS-4
Swan Lake Meadow—flat OR-9
Swan Lake Memorial Gardens—cemetery IN-6
Swan Lake Memory Gardens Cem—cemetery IL-6
Swan Lake Mtn—summit OR-9
Swan Lake Natl Wildlife Ref—park MO-7

Swan Lake Natl Wildlife Refuge Habitat Trail—*trail* ... MO-7
Swan Lake Outlet—*stream* ... MN-6
Swan Lake Park—*park* ... LA-4
Swan Lake Point—*cape* ... OR-9
Swan Lake Post Office—*building* ... MS-4
Swan Lake Public Hunting Area—*area* ... IA-7
Swan Lake Rim—*cliff* (2) ... OR-9
Swan Lake Rock House Hist Dist—*hist pl* ... MT-8
Swan Lake Rsvr—*reservoir* ... NV-8
Swan Lakes—*lake* ... ID-8
Swan Lakes—*lake* ... OR-9
Swan Lake Salt Marsh—*lake* ... UT-8
Swan Lake Sch—*school* (3) ... IL-6
Swan Lake Sch—*school* ... MO-7
Swan Lake Sch (historical)—*school* ... MS-4
Swan Lake Slough—*stream* ... ID-8
Swan Lake Slough—*stream* ... MS-4
Swan Lake State Park—*park* ... IA-7
Swan Lake State Public Shooting Area—*park* (3) ... SD-7
Swan Lake Township—*civil* ... SD-7
Swan Lake Township—*fmr MCD* (2) ... IA-7
**Swan Lake Township**—*pop pl* ... SD-7
**Swan Lake (Township of)**—*pop pl* ... MN-6
Swan Lake Trail—*trail* ... WA-9
Swan Lake Valley—*valley* ... OR-9
**Swan Lake Village (subdivision)**—*pop pl* ... TN-4
Swan Land and Cattle Company HQ—*hist pl* ... WY-8
Swan Lookout—*locale* ... MO-7
Swan Marsh—*swamp* ... MI-6
Swan Marsh—*swamp* ... TX-5
Swan Meadows—*flat* ... NC-3
Swan Meadow Sch—*school* ... MD-2
Swan Mountain Rec Area—*locale* ... CO-8
Swan Mtn—*summit* ... AK-9
Swan Mtn—*summit* ... CO-8
Swan Mtn—*summit* ... NC-3
Swan Mtn—*summit* ... OR-9
Swann—*locale* ... WV-2
**Swann**—*pop pl* (3) ... NC-3
**Swann**—*pop pl* ... TN-4
Swann, Judge James Preston, House—*hist pl* ... TN-4
Swannann MS—*school* ... NC-3
*Swannanoa* (2) ... NJ-2
Swannanoa—*hist pl* ... VA-3
Swannanoa—*locale* ... VA-3
**Swannanoa**—*pop pl* ... NC-3
Swannanoa, Lake—*reservoir* ... NJ-2
Swannanoa Ch—*church* ... NC-3
Swannanoa Creek—*stream* ... NC-3
Swannanoa Gap—*gap* ... NC-3
Swannanoa Golf And Country Club—*other* ... VA-3
Swannanoa Heights Ch—*church* ... NC-3
**Swannanoa Hills**—*pop pl* ... NC-3
*Swannanoa Lake* ... NJ-2
Swannanoa Mountains—*range* ... NC-3
Swannanoa River—*stream* ... NC-3
Swannanoa Sch—*school* ... NC-3
Swannanoa (Township of)—*fmr MCD* ... NC-3
Swannanoa Tunnel—*tunnel* ... NC-3
*Swannanona* ... NC-3
Swann Bridge—*bridge* ... TN-4
Swann Brook—*stream* ... MA-1
Swann Cem—*cemetery* ... AL-4
Swann Cem—*cemetery* ... AR-4
Swann Cem—*cemetery* ... LA-4
Swann Cem—*cemetery* (3) ... TN-4
Swann Cem—*cemetery* ... WV-2
Swann Chapel—*church* ... TN-4
**Swann Chapel**—*pop pl* ... TN-4
Swann Chapel Cem—*cemetery* ... TN-4
Swann Covered Bridge—*bridge* ... AL-4
Swann Covered Bridge—*hist pl* ... AL-4
Swann Dock—*locale* ... TN-4
Swan Neck—*cape* ... MA-1
Swanneck Crossing—*other* ... AK-9
Swan Neck Point—*cape* ... MA-1
Swanneck Slough—*stream* ... AK-9
Swannell, Charles E., House—*hist pl* ... IL-6
Swanner Creek—*stream* ... ID-8
Swanner Creek—*stream* ... WY-8
Swanner Pass—*gap* ... TN-4
Swannigan Creek—*stream* ... KY-4
Swann Island (historical)—*island* ... TN-4
Swann Keys—*locale* ... DE-2
**Swann Keys (Trailer Park)**—*pop pl* ... DE-2
Swann Lakeside Airpark—*airport* ... TN-4
Swann Park—*park* ... FL-3
Swann Park—*park* ... MD-2
*Swann Point* ... VA-3
Swann Ridge—*ridge* ... TN-4
*Swanns* ... NC-3
Swanns—*other* ... NC-3
*Swanns Channel* ... NJ-2
*Swanns Island* ... TN-4
Swanns Island Shoals—*bar* ... TN-4
Swanns Point—*cape* ... VA-3
Swanns Point Ch—*church* ... VA-3
Swann's Point Plantation Site—*hist pl* ... VA-3
Swanns RR Station (historical)—*locale* ... FL-3
Swanns Shoals—*bar* ... TN-4
*Swann Station* ... NC-3
**Swannsylvania**—*pop pl* ... TN-4
Swannsylvania Cem—*cemetery* ... TN-4
Swannsylvania Ch—*church* ... TN-4
Swannsylvania Sch—*school* ... TN-4
Swan Park—*park* ... AZ-5
Swan Peak—*summit* (3) ... ID-8
Swan Peak—*summit* ... MT-8
Swan Peak—*summit* ... UT-8
Swan Peak Pond—*lake* ... UT-8
Swan Plateau—*plain* ... TX-5
*Swan Point* ... MD-2
*Swan Point* ... VA-3
Swan Point—*cape* (4) ... MD-2
Swan Point—*cape* ... NH-1
Swan Point—*cape* ... NJ-2
Swan Point—*cape* (3) ... NC-3
Swan Point—*cape* ... RI-1
Swan Point—*cape* ... TX-5
Swan Point—*cape* ... WI-6
**Swan Point**—*pop pl* ... MD-2
Swan Point—*summit* ... ID-8
Swan Point Bar—*bar* ... MD-2
Swan Point Cemetery—*hist pl* ... RI-1
Swan Point Cemetery and Trolley Shelter (Boundary Increase)—*hist pl* ... RI-1
Swan Point Creek—*stream* ... MD-2
Swan Point Neck—*cape* ... MD-2
Swan Point Shoal—*bar* ... NC-3
*Swan Pond* ... MA-1
Swan Pond—*hist pl* ... WV-2
Swan Pond—*lake* ... AL-4
Swan Pond—*lake* (2) ... AR-4
Swan Pond—*lake* (2) ... IN-6
Swan Pond—*lake* (2) ... KY-4
Swan Pond—*lake* (3) ... ME-1
Swan Pond—*lake* (2) ... MD-2
Swan Pond—*lake* (2) ... MA-1
Swan Pond—*lake* ... MO-7
Swan Pond—*lake* (2) ... NJ-2
Swan Pond—*lake* (2) ... NY-2
Swan Pond—*lake* ... NC-3
Swan Pond—*lake* ... SD-7
Swanpond—*locale* ... KY-4
Swan Pond—*locale* ... WV-2
Swan Pond—*swamp* ... MO-7
Swan Pond Bottom—*bend* ... KY-4
Swan Pond Branch—*stream* ... TN-4
Swan Pond Brook—*stream* (2) ... ME-1
Swan Pond Ch—*church* ... TN-4
Swan Pond Community Center—*building* ... TN-4
Swan Pond Creek—*stream* ... ME-1
Swan Pond Creek—*stream* ... MD-2
Swanpond Creek—*stream* ... TN-4
Swan Pond Creek—*stream* ... TN-4
*Swan Pond Ditch* ... IN-6
Swan Pond Ditch—*canal* (3) ... AR-4
Swan Pond Ditch—*canal* ... IN-6
Swan Pond Ditch—*canal* ... MO-7
Swan Pond Lateral—*canal* ... AR-4
Swan Pond Manor Hist Dist—*hist pl* ... WV-2
Swan Pond Marsh—*swamp* ... MD-2
Swan Pond Race—*stream* ... NJ-2
Swan Pond River—*stream* ... MA-1
Swan Pond River Marshes—*swamp* ... MA-1
Swan Ponds—*hist pl* ... NC-3
Swan Ponds—*lake* ... AR-4
Swan Pond Swamp (historical)—*swamp* ... TN-4
Swan Post Office (historical)—*building* ... AL-4
**Swanquarter**—*pop pl* ... NC-3
Swanquarter Bay—*bay* ... NC-3
Swanquarter Island—*island* ... NC-3
Swanquarter Natl Wildlife Ref—*park* ... NC-3
Swanquarter Sch—*school* ... NC-3
Swan Quarter (Township of)—*fmr MCD* ... NC-3
Swan Range—*range* ... MT-8
Swan Ridge—*ridge* ... UT-8
*Swan River* ... MT-8
**Swan River**—*pop pl* ... MN-6
Swan River—*stream* ... AK-9
Swan River—*stream* ... CO-8
Swan River—*stream* ... MI-6
Swan River—*stream* (2) ... MN-6
Swan River—*stream* ... MT-8
Swan River—*stream* ... NY-2
Swan River State For—*forest* ... MT-8
**Swan River (Township of)**—*pop pl* ... MN-6
Swan River Village Site—*hist pl* ... MN-6
Swan Rock—*pillar* ... CA-9
Swan Rsvr—*reservoir* ... WY-8
Swan Run—*stream* ... OH-6
Swan Run—*stream* ... WV-2
**Swans**—*pop pl* ... OH-6
**Swansboro**—*pop pl* ... NC-3
**Swansboro**—*pop pl* ... VA-3
Swansboro Elem Sch—*school* ... NC-3
Swansboro HS—*school* ... NC-3
Swansboro JHS—*school* ... NC-3
Swansboro MS—*school* ... NC-3
Swansboro Rescue Station—*building* ... NC-3
Swansboro (Township of)—*fmr MCD* ... NC-3
Swans Branch—*stream* ... NC-3
Swans Cem—*cemetery* ... IA-7
Swan Sch—*school* ... IL-6
Swan Sch—*school* ... MA-1
Swan Sch—*school* ... MO-7
Swan Sch—*school* ... NE-7
Swan Sch—*school* ... OH-6
Swans Chapel—*church* ... TX-5
Swans Corner—*locale* ... VA-3
*Swans Creek* ... WI-6
Swans Creek—*stream* ... NC-3
Swans Creek Ch—*church* ... NC-3
Swans Creek Sch—*school* ... NC-3
*Swanscut Creek* ... MD-2
*Swanscut Creek* ... VA-3
*Swanscutt Creek* ... MD-2
*Swanscutt Creek* ... VA-3
*Swansdak* ... DE-2
*Swansdale* ... DE-2
Swansea—*locale* ... AZ-5
Swansea—*locale* ... CA-9
**Swansea**—*pop pl* ... IL-6
**Swansea**—*pop pl* ... MA-1
**Swansea**—*pop pl* ... SC-3
Swansea (CCD)—*cens area* ... SC-3
**Swansea Center**—*pop pl* ... MA-1
*Swansea Centre* ... MA-1
*Swansea Factory* ... MA-1
Swansea Gulch—*valley* ... CO-8
Swansea (historical)—*locale* ... AL-4
Swansea II Shop Ctr—*locale* ... MA-1
Swansea JHS—*school* ... SC-3
Swansea Mall—*locale* ... MA-1
Swansea Manor—*uninc pl* ... VA-3
Swansea Mine—*mine* ... MT-8
Swansea Mine—*mine* ... UT-8
Swansea Park—*park* ... CO-8
Swansea Print Works Dam—*dam* ... MA-1
Swansea Pumping Station—*locale* ... AZ-5
*Swan Sea River* ... RI-1
Swansea Sch—*school* ... CO-8
**Swansea (Swansea Village)**—*pop pl* ... MA-1
**Swansea (Town of)**—*pop pl* ... MA-1
Swansea Village—*other* ... MA-1
*Swansecute Creek* ... MD-2
*Swansecute Creek* ... VA-3
Swansee Gap—*gap* ... NC-3
Swansee Knob—*summit* ... NC-3
Swanset Camp—*locale* ... PA-2
*Swansey* ... MA-1
*Swansey, Town of* ... MA-1
*Swansey Village* ... MA-1
Swans Falls—*falls* ... ME-1
Swans Gulch—*valley* ... CA-9
Swans Gut Creek—*stream* ... MD-2
Swans Gut Creek—*stream* ... VA-3
*Swan's Island* ... ME-1
Swans Island—*island* ... ME-1
**Swans Island**—*pop pl* ... ME-1
Swans Island Head—*cape* ... ME-1
**Swans Island (Town of)**—*pop pl* ... ME-1
Swanski Creek—*stream* ... WY-8
Swanski Rock—*summit* ... WY-8
Swan's Landing Archeol Site (12HR304)—*hist pl* ... IN-6
Swan Slough—*gut* ... MN-6
Swanson—*locale* ... MI-6
Swanson—*locale* ... OH-6
Swanson, Hans, House—*hist pl* ... WA-9
Swanson, John, House—*hist pl* ... MI-6
Swanson Airp—*airport* ... WA-9
Swanson Bay—*bay* ... AK-9
Swanson Bayou—*gut* ... LA-4
Swanson Bluff—*cliff* ... CA-9
Swanson Branch—*stream* ... KY-4
Swanson Branch—*stream* ... MO-7
Swanson Branch—*stream* ... VA-3
Swanson Cabin—*locale* ... MT-8
Swanson Camp—*locale* ... NE-7
Swanson Canyon—*valley* ... CA-9
Swanson Canyon—*valley* ... OR-9
Swanson Cem—*cemetery* ... KY-4
Swanson Cem—*cemetery* ... NE-7
Swanson Cem—*cemetery* ... TN-4
Swanson Cem—*cemetery* (2) ... TX-5
Swanson Ch—*church* ... NC-3
**Swanson Corners**—*pop pl* ... MA-1
Swanson Cottage Sch No 1—*school* ... CO-8
Swanson Coulee—*stream* ... MT-8
Swanson Cove—*bay* ... GA-3
*Swanson Creek* ... MD-2
*Swanson Creek* ... MT-8
Swanson Creek—*stream* ... AK-9
Swanson Creek—*stream* ... ID-8
Swanson Creek—*stream* ... MD-2
Swanson Creek—*stream* ... MI-6
Swanson Creek—*stream* ... MN-6
Swanson Creek—*stream* (2) ... MT-8
Swanson Creek—*stream* (4) ... OR-9
Swanson Creek—*stream* (2) ... WI-6
Swanson Dam—*dam* ... NY-2
Swanson Ditch—*canal* ... IA-7
Swanson Field—*park* ... FL-3
Swanson Grove Ch—*church* ... TX-5
Swanson Gulch—*valley* ... CA-9
Swanson Gulch—*valley* ... ID-8
Swanson Gulch—*valley* ... WA-9
Swanson Harbor—*bay* ... AK-9
Swanson Highlands Elem Sch—*school* ... IN-6
**Swanson Hill**—*pop pl* ... TX-5
Swanson Hill Ch—*church* ... TX-5
Swanson (historical)—*locale* ... AL-4
Swanson Hollow—*valley* ... TN-4
Swanson Homestead—*locale* ... MT-8
Swanson Island—*island* ... AK-9
Swanson Island—*island* (2) ... GA-3
Swanson JHS—*school* ... VA-3
Swanson Lagoon—*bay* ... AK-9
*Swanson Lake* ... MN-6
Swanson Lake—*lake* ... AK-9
Swanson Lake—*lake* ... CO-8
Swanson Lake—*lake* ... MI-6
Swanson Lake—*lake* (2) ... MN-6
Swanson Lake—*reservoir* ... AL-4
Swanson Lake—*reservoir* ... CO-8
Swanson Lake—*reservoir* ... NE-7
Swanson Lake—*reservoir* ... SD-7
Swanson Lake Dam—*dam* ... AL-4
Swanson Lakes—*area* ... AK-9
Swanson Lakes—*lake* ... WA-9
Swanson Lamporte Ditch—*canal* ... IN-6
Swanson Lateral—*canal* ... ID-8
Swanson Mill—*locale* ... GA-3
Swanson Mine—*mine* ... WY-8
Swanson Mtn—*summit* ... GA-3
Swanson Point—*cape* ... AK-9
Swanson Ranch—*locale* ... MT-8
Swanson Ranch—*locale* ... NE-7
Swanson Ranch 3 Airp—*airport* ... NV-8
*Swanson Reservoir* ... NE-7
Swanson River—*stream* ... AK-9
Swanson River Oil Field—*other* ... AK-9
Swanson Rsvr—*reservoir* ... OR-9
Swanson Saddle—*gap* ... ID-8
Swansons Bay—*bay* ... MN-6
Swanson Sch—*school* ... AK-9
Swanson Sch—*school* ... CO-8
Swanson Sch—*school* ... IL-6
Swanson Sch—*school* (2) ... SD-7
Swanson Sch—*school* ... WA-9
Swanson Sch (historical)—*school* ... AL-4
Swanson Sch Number 3 (historical)—*school* ... SD-7
Swansons Chute—*valley* ... ID-8
Swansons Landing—*locale* ... TX-5
Swanson Slough—*stream* ... AK-9
Swansons Mill—*locale* ... VA-3
Swanson Spring—*spring* ... UT-8
Swanson Swamp—*swamp* ... NE-7
Swansonville—*locale* ... VA-3
**Swansonville**—*pop pl* ... WA-9
Swansonville Ch—*church* ... VA-3
*Swans Point* ... VA-3
*Swans Pond* ... MA-1
Swans Pond—*reservoir* ... MA-1
Swans Pond Dam—*dam* ... MA-1
Swan Spring—*spring* ... NM-5
Swan Spring—*spring* ... UT-8
*Swan Station* ... NC-3
**Swan Station (Swanns)**—*pop pl* ... NC-3
Swanston—*locale* ... CA-9
Swans Trail Sch—*school* ... WA-9
Swansville Cem—*cemetery* ... MO-7
Swan Tank—*reservoir* ... NM-5
Swanton—*locale* ... IA-7
**Swanton**—*pop pl* ... CA-9
**Swanton**—*pop pl* ... MD-2
**Swanton**—*pop pl* ... NE-7
**Swanton**—*pop pl* ... OH-6
**Swanton**—*pop pl* ... VT-1
Swanton Covered RR Bridge—*hist pl* ... VT-1
Swanton (historical P.O.)—*locale* ... IA-7
Swanton House—*hist pl* ... GA-3
Swanton Junction—*locale* ... VT-1
Swanton Rsvr—*reservoir* ... OH-6
**Swanton (Town of)**—*pop pl* ... VT-1
**Swanton (Township of)**—*pop pl* ... OH-6
Swanton Ultralight—*airport* ... WA-9
Swantop Cem—*cemetery* ... NE-7
*Swan Town* ... MD-2
Swantown—*locale* ... WA-9
Swantown Creek—*stream* ... MD-2
Swantown Hill—*summit* ... CT-1
Swan Township—*civil* ... MO-7
**Swan Township**—*pop pl* ... KS-7
**Swan Township**—*pop pl* ... NE-7
**Swan (Township of)**—*pop pl* ... IL-6
**Swan (Township of)**—*pop pl* ... IN-6
**Swan (Township of)**—*pop pl* ... OH-6
**Swan Trail**—*pop pl* ... WA-9
Swan Trail Slough—*stream* ... WA-9
Swanty Creek—*stream* ... ID-8
Swanty Peak—*summit* ... ID-8
Swanty Spring—*spring* ... ID-8
*Swan Valley* ... ID-8
Swan Valley—*locale* ... ID-8
**Swan Valley**—*pop pl* ... ID-8
Swan Valley—*valley* ... ID-8
Swan Valley—*valley* ... OR-9
Swan Valley Cem—*cemetery* ... ID-8
Swan Valley Cem—*cemetery* ... MN-6
Swan Valley Ch—*church* ... MI-6
Swan Valley HS—*school* ... MI-6
Swan Valley Overlook—*locale* ... TN-4
Swan Valley Sch—*school* ... MT-8
Swan Valley Sch—*school* ... NE-7
**Swanville**—*pop pl* ... IN-6
**Swanville**—*pop pl* ... ME-1
**Swanville**—*pop pl* ... MN-6
**Swanville**—*pop pl* ... PA-2
Swanville Ch—*church* ... TX-5
Swanville Saint Peter Cem—*cemetery* ... MN-6
**Swanville (Town of)**—*pop pl* ... ME-1
**Swanville (Township of)**—*pop pl* ... MN-6
Swanwall Ch—*church* ... GA-3
Swanway Park—*park* ... AZ-5
Swan Well—*well* ... UT-8
*Swanwick* ... DE-2
Swanwick—*locale* ... MO-7
**Swanwick**—*pop pl* ... IL-6
Swanwick Creek—*stream* ... IL-6
Swanwick (Election Precinct)—*fmr MCD* ... IL-6
*Swanwike* ... DE-2
**Swanwood**—*pop pl* ... IA-7
Swanwyck—*hist pl* ... DE-2
**Swanwyck**—*pop pl* ... DE-2
**Swanwyck Estates (subdivision)**—*pop pl* ... DE-2
**Swanwyck Gardens (subdivision)**—*pop pl* ... DE-2
**Swanzey**—*pop pl* ... NH-1
*Swanzey, Town of* ... MA-1
**Swanzey Center**—*pop pl* ... NH-1
*Swanzey Factory* ... NH-1
**Swanzey Factory**—*pop pl* ... NH-1
Swanzey Lake—*lake* ... NH-1
**Swanzey Station**—*pop pl* ... NH-1
**Swanzey (Town of)**—*pop pl* ... NH-1
Swanzy—*locale* ... MI-6
Swanzy Beach Park—*park* ... HI-9
Swanzy Branch—*stream* ... TX-5
Swanzy (historical)—*locale* ... MS-4
*Swanzy Lake* ... CA-9
Swanzy Lake—*lake* ... MI-6
Swanzy Rsvr—*reservoir* ... CA-9
Swap Canyon—*valley* ... UT-8
*Swapecksiska* ... DE-2
Swap Mesa—*summit* ... UT-8
Swapp Canyon—*valley* (2) ... UT-8
Swapp Hollow—*valley* ... UT-8
Swapp Hollow Trough—*valley* ... UT-8
Swappingback Mission—*church* ... OK-5
Swapping Camp Creek—*stream* ... VA-3
Swapp Ranch—*locale* ... UT-8
Swapp Rsvr—*reservoir* ... AZ-5
*Swapps Ranch* ... UT-8
Swapp Tank—*reservoir* ... AZ-5
Swapp Well—*well* ... NM-5
Sward Sch—*school* ... IL-6
Swarey Spring—*spring* ... PA-2
Swaringen Ch—*church* ... IL-6
Swaringer Lake—*reservoir* ... NC-3
*Swar Pond Creek* ... TN-4
Swarr Run—*stream* ... PA-2
Swars Prairie—*area* ... MO-7
Swars Prairie Baptist Ch—*church* ... MO-7
Swars Prairie Ch of Christ—*church* ... MO-7
**Swart**—*pop pl* ... MO-7
**Swart**—*pop pl* ... PA-2
Swart Culver Cem—*cemetery* ... NY-2
Swarte Kill—*stream* ... NY-2
Swart Hill—*summit* ... NY-2
Swart Hill Sch—*school* ... NY-2
**Swart (historical)**—*pop pl* ... OR-9
**Swarthmore**—*pop pl* ... PA-2
*Swarthmore Boro* ... PA-2
Swarthmore Borough—*civil* ... PA-2
Swarthmore Coll—*school* ... PA-2
Swarthmore-Rutledge K-8—*school* ... PA-2
**Swarthmorwood**—*pop pl* ... PA-2
Swart Hollow—*valley* ... NY-2
*Swarthout Lake* ... MN-6
Swarthout Park—*park* ... WI-6
Swarthout Point—*cape* ... NY-2
Swarthout Valley—*valley* ... CA-9
Swart Island—*island* ... NY-2
*Swartmore College* ... PA-2
Swart Mtn—*summit* ... NY-2
Swartout—*locale* ... TX-5
Swartout Creek—*stream* ... MI-6
Swartout Lake—*lake* ... MN-6
**Swartoutville**—*pop pl* ... NY-2
Swarts—*locale* ... PA-2
*Swarts Kill* ... NY-2
**Swartswood**—*pop pl* ... NJ-2
**Swartswood Lake**—*pop pl* ... NJ-2
Swartswood Lake—*reservoir* ... NJ-2
Swartswood Lake Dam—*dam* ... NJ-2
Swartswood State Park—*park* ... NJ-2
Swartswood Station—*locale* ... NJ-2
*Swart Watts Lake* ... MN-6
Swartwont Lake—*lake* ... NY-2
**Swartwood**—*pop pl* ... NY-2
Swartwood Cem—*cemetery* ... KS-7
Swartwood Cem—*cemetery* ... NY-2
Swartwood Trail—*trail* ... PA-2
Swartwout Memorial Cem—*cemetery* ... NY-2
*Swartwout Post Office* ... MS-4
*Swartwouts Pond* ... NJ-2
**Swartz**—*pop pl* ... LA-4
Swartz Bar—*bar* ... ID-8
Swartz Canyon—*valley* (2) ... CA-9
Swartz Canyon—*valley* ... OR-9
Swartz-Carnahan Ditch—*canal* ... IN-6
Swartz Cem—*cemetery* ... KS-7
Swartz Corner—*locale* ... ID-8
Swartz Covered Bridge—*hist pl* ... OH-6
*Swartz Creek* ... ID-8
**Swartz Creek**—*pop pl* ... MI-6
Swartz Creek—*stream* ... CA-9
Swartz Creek—*stream* ... ID-8
Swartz Creek—*stream* ... MI-6
Swartz Creek—*stream* ... NE-7
Swartz Creek—*stream* (3) ... OR-9
Swartz Creek City Wells—*well* ... MI-6
Swartz Creek Valley Park—*park* ... MI-6
Swartz Ditch—*canal* (2) ... IN-6
Swartz Ditch—*canal* ... OH-6
Swartz Draw—*valley* ... WY-8
Swartzell Cem—*cemetery* ... IN-6
Swartz Hollow—*valley* ... PA-2
*Swartz Kill* ... NY-2
Swartz Lake—*lake* ... MT-8
Swartz Lake—*lake* ... WA-9
Swartz Lake—*lake* ... WI-6
Swartz Meadow Point—*summit* ... ID-8
Swartz Mill—*locale* ... OH-6
Swartz Pond—*reservoir* ... ID-8
Swartz Run—*stream* ... NE-7
Swartz Run—*stream* (2) ... PA-2
Swartz Run—*stream* ... WV-2
Swartz Sch—*school* ... PA-2
Swartz Spring—*spring* ... OR-9
Swartz Tunnel—*tunnel* ... PA-2
Swartz Union Chapel—*church* ... VA-3
*Swartz Valley* ... PA-2
Swartz Valley—*valley* ... PA-2
*Swartz Valley - in part* ... PA-2
Swartzville—*locale* ... PA-2
Swartzville Post Office (historical)—*building* ... PA-2
*Swarzs Ridge* ... PA-2
*Swasey Bottom* ... UT-8
Swasey Bottom—*basin* ... UT-8
Swasey Cabin—*locale* ... UT-8
Swasey Creek—*stream* ... UT-8
Swasey Hardpan Rsvr—*reservoir* ... UT-8
Swasey Hill—*summit* ... ME-1
Swasey Hole—*bend* ... UT-8
Swasey Knolls Wash—*valley* ... UT-8
Swasey Lakes—*lake* ... UT-8
Swasey Mtn—*summit* ... UT-8
Swasey Peak—*summit* ... UT-8
Swasey Point—*cliff* ... UT-8
Swasey Point Rsvr—*reservoir* ... UT-8
Swasey Ridge—*ridge* (2) ... UT-8
Swasey Rsvr No 2—*reservoir* ... UT-8
Swasey Rsvr No 3—*reservoir* ... UT-8
Swasey Rsvr No 4—*reservoir* ... UT-8
Swasey Sch—*school* ... NH-1
Swasey Spring—*spring* ... UT-8
Swasey Wash—*valley* ... UT-8
Swasey Wash Rsvr—*reservoir* ... UT-8
Swash, The—*bay* ... NC-3
Swash, The—*gut* ... VA-3
Swash, The—*stream* ... NC-3
Swash Bay—*bay* ... VA-3
Swash Channel—*channel* ... AL-4
Swash Channel—*channel* ... NJ-2
Swash Channel—*channel* ... NY-2
Swash Hole—*bay* ... VA-3
Swash Hole Island—*island* ... VA-3
Swash Inlet—*channel* ... NC-3
Swash Keys—*island* ... FL-3
Swash Lake—*lake* ... OR-9
Swastika—*locale* ... NY-2
**Swastika (historical)**—*pop pl* ... OR-9
Swastika Lake—*lake* ... WY-8
Swastika Mine—*mine* (2) ... AZ-5
Swastika Mine—*mine* ... ID-8
Swastika Mine—*mine* ... NV-8
Swastika Mountain Trail—*trail* ... OR-9
Swastika Mtn—*summit* ... OR-9
**Swatara**—*pop pl* ... MN-6
**Swatara**—*pop pl* ... PA-2
Swatara—*post sta* ... PA-2
Swatara, Lake—*lake* ... FL-3
Swatara Ch—*church* ... PA-2
*Swatara Creek* ... PA-2
Swatara Creek—*stream* ... PA-2
**Swatara Crest**—*pop pl* ... PA-2
Swatara Ferry House—*hist pl* ... PA-2
Swatara Gap—*gap* ... PA-2
Swatara Hill—*summit* ... PA-2
*Swatara Hill Church* ... PA-2
Swatara HS—*school* ... PA-2
Swatara Park—*park* ... PA-2
Swatara Path—*trail* ... PA-2
Swatara State Park—*park* ... PA-2
**Swatara Station (Swatara)**—*pop pl* ... PA-2
Swatara Township—*CDP* ... PA-2
**Swatara (Township of)**—*pop pl* (2) ... PA-2
Swatek Park—*park* ... OK-5
Swatek Ridge—*ridge* ... WI-6
Swathmore Mine—*mine* ... CO-8
Swathmore Station—*building* ... PA-2
Swatzell Springs—*spring* ... TN-4
Swauano Creek—*stream* ... TX-5
*Swauck Creek* ... WA-9
Swauger Creek—*stream* ... CA-9
*Swauger Ditch* ... ID-8
Swauger Ditch—*canal* ... ID-8
Swauger Gulch—*valley* ... ID-8
Swauger Lakes—*lake* ... ID-8
Swauger Ranch (historical)—*locale* ... ID-8
Swauger Slough—*stream* ... ID-8
Swauger Valley Run—*stream* ... OH-6
Swauger Valley Sch—*school* ... OH-6
Swauk Campground—*locale* ... WA-9
Swauk Creek—*stream* ... WA-9
Swauk Lodge—*locale* ... WA-9
Swauk Meadow—*flat* ... WA-9
Swauk Pass—*gap* ... WA-9
Swauk Prairie—*flat* ... WA-9
Swauk Prairie Cem—*cemetery* ... WA-9
Swauk Ridge—*ridge* ... WA-9
Swawilla Basin—*basin* ... WA-9
Sway Back—*basin* ... MT-8
Swayback Bridge—*bridge* ... AL-4
Swayback Creek—*stream* ... AK-9
Swayback Creek—*stream* ... TX-5
Swayback Knob—*summit* ... NC-3
Swayback Knoll—*summit* ... UT-8
Swayback Lakes—*lake* ... AK-9
Swayback Mtn—*summit* ... AK-9
Swayback Mtn—*summit* (2) ... TX-5
Swayback Ranch—*locale* ... CO-8
Swayback Ridge—*ridge* ... CA-9
Swayback Sch—*school* ... IL-6
Sway Hollow—*valley* ... UT-8
*Swayne Courthouse* ... AL-4
Swayne Creek—*stream* ... OR-9
Swayne Ditch—*canal* ... OR-9
Swayne Hall—*hist pl* ... AL-4
Swayne Hill—*summit* ... CA-9
Swayne Lookout Tower—*locale* ... WI-6
*Swayne Sch* ... AL-4
Swayne (Township of)—*fmr MCD* ... AR-4
**Swayney**—*pop pl* ... NC-3
Swayze, E. S., Drugstore/Otisville Mason Lodge No. 401—*hist pl* ... MI-6
Swayze Cem—*cemetery* ... NJ-2
Swayze Creek—*stream* ... OR-9
**Swayzee**—*pop pl* ... IN-6
Swayzee, Aaron, House—*hist pl* ... IN-6
Swayzee Elem Sch—*school* ... IN-6
Swayze Lake—*lake* ... LA-4
**Swayze Lake**—*pop pl* ... LA-4
Swayze Lake Dam—*dam* (2) ... MS-4
Swayze Pond Dam—*dam* ... MS-4
Swayze Sch—*school* ... LA-4
Swayze Sch—*school* ... MI-6
Swayzes Mills—*locale* ... NJ-2
*Swazee Lake* ... LA-4
Swazee Lake—*lake* ... LA-4
Swazey—*locale* ... OH-6
**Swazey Acres**—*pop pl* ... NY-2
Swazey Ledge—*bend* ... ME-1
Swazy Hole—*lake* ... UT-8
Swazy Seep—*spring* ... UT-8
Swazys Leap—*cliff* ... UT-8
*SW Branch of Manhan River* ... MA-1
S.W.B.T.S. (Southwestern Baptist Theological Sem.)—*facility* ... TX-5
**Swea City**—*pop pl* ... IA-7
**Swea (historical)**—*pop pl* ... IA-7
Swea (historical P.O.)—*locale* ... IA-7
Sweaney Sch (historical)—*school* ... TN-4
Sweany Creek—*stream* ... CA-9
Sweanys Well—*well* ... WA-9
Swear and Rogers Ford (historical)—*locale* ... MO-7
Swearengen Cem—*cemetery* ... MS-4
Swearengen Ditch—*canal* ... IN-6
Swearengen Lake—*reservoir* ... MS-4
Swearengin—*locale* ... AL-4
*Swearengin Cem* ... MS-4
Swearengin Cem—*cemetery* ... MS-4
Swearengin Cem—*cemetery* ... MO-7
Swearengin Ch—*church* ... AL-4
Swearing Creek—*stream* ... NC-3
Swearingen—*locale* ... TX-5
Swearingen, John J., House—*hist pl* ... FL-3
Swearingen Branch—*stream* ... KY-4
Swearingen Branch—*stream* ... TX-5
Swearingen Cem—*cemetery* ... TX-5
Swearingen Creek—*stream* ... TX-5
Swearingen Gulch—*valley* ... CA-9
Swearingen House—*hist pl* ... LA-4
Swearingen Oil Field—*oilfield* ... TX-5
Swearingen Rsvr—*reservoir* ... OR-9
Swearing Hill—*summit* ... VT-1
*Swearington Cem* ... MS-4
Swearngin Cave—*cave* ... AR-4
Swears Mtn—*summit* ... NY-2
Sweasey Creek—*stream* ... ID-8
Sweasey Lake—*lake* ... CA-9
Sweat Bog—*swamp* ... ME-1
Sweat Bog Brook—*stream* ... ME-1
Sweatbox, The—*area* ... GA-3
Sweat Branch—*stream* ... GA-3
Sweat Canyon—*valley* ... AZ-5
Sweat Cem—*cemetery* (2) ... GA-3
Sweat Cem—*cemetery* ... ME-1
Sweat Cem—*cemetery* ... OK-5
Sweat Cem—*cemetery* ... SC-3
Sweat Cem—*cemetery* (3) ... TN-4
Sweat Creek—*stream* ... OR-9
Sweat Creek—*stream* ... TX-5
Sweat Creek—*stream* ... UT-8
Sweat Creek—*stream* (2) ... WA-9
Sweater Bay—*bay* ... AK-9
*Sweater Creek* ... AZ-5
Sweater Creek—*stream* ... AZ-5
Sweater Tank—*reservoir* ... AZ-5
Sweat Heifer Creek—*stream* ... NC-3
Sweat Hill—*summit* ... MA-1
Sweat Hill—*summit* ... TN-4
Sweat Hollow—*valley* ... AR-4
Sweathouse Branch—*stream* ... MD-2
Sweathouse Creek—*stream* ... CA-9
Sweathouse Creek—*stream* ... MT-8
Sweathouse Creek—*stream* ... VA-3
Sweathouse Valley—*valley* ... AZ-5
**Sweatman**—*pop pl* ... MS-4
Sweatman Cem—*cemetery* ... TX-5
Sweatman Hollow—*valley* ... MO-7
Sweatmans Creek—*stream* ... MS-4
Sweatman Spring—*spring* ... AL-4
Sweat Meadows—*swamp* ... NH-1
Sweat Memorial Ch—*church* ... GA-3
Sweat Mtn—*summit* ... GA-3
Sweaton Bay—*bay* ... AK-9
Sweaton Island—*island* ... AK-9
Swea Township—*fmr MCD* ... IA-7
Sweat Peak—*summit* ... AZ-5
Sweat Point—*summit* ... OR-9
Sweat Pond—*lake* ... NH-1
Sweats Gulch—*valley* ... MT-8
*Sweat's Island* ... ME-1
Sweats Millpond—*lake* ... FL-3
Sweat Spring—*spring* ... AZ-5
Sweat Springs—*spring* ... ID-8

Sweet Ravine—*valley* ... MN-6
Sweet Rest Ch of Christ Holiness—*church* .. MS-4
Sweet Ridge—*ridge* ... CA-9
Sweet Ridge—*ridge* ... TN-4
*Sweet Rock Baptist Ch* ... AL-4
Sweet Rock Ch—*church* ... AL-4
*Sweet Rock Holiness Ch* ... AL-4
Sweet Rock Missionary Baptist Ch—*church* ... MS-4
Sweet Root Creek—*stream* ... PA-2
Sweet Root Gap—*gap* ... PA-2
Sweet Root Natural Area—*area* ... PA-2
Sweet Root Picnic Area—*area* ... PA-2
Sweet Root Run—*stream* ... PA-2
Sweet Rose Ch—*church* ... SC-3
Sweet Rsvr—*reservoir* ... OR-9
**Sweet Run**—*pop pl* ... WV-2
Sweet Run—*stream* ... OH-6
Sweet Run Sch—*school* ... IL-6
Sweets—*locale* ... NY-2
Sweet Sch—*school* ... MI-6
Sweet Sch—*school* ... WY-8
Sweets Chapel Cem—*cemetery* ... TX-5
**Sweets Corner**—*pop pl* ... MA-1
*Sweets Corners* ... MA-1
**Sweets Crossing**—*pop pl* (2) ... NY-2
**Sweetser**—*pop pl* ... IN-6
Sweetser Ditch—*canal* ... IN-6
Sweetser Elem Sch—*school* ... IN-6
Sweetser Improvement Ditch—*canal* ... IN-6
Sweetser Residence—*hist pl* ... CA-9
*Sweetsers* ... IN-6
Sweetser Sch—*school* ... ME-1
Sweetser Sch—*school* ... MA-1
Sweetser Spring—*spring* ... MT-8
Sweetsir Sch—*school* ... ME-1
Sweets Islands—*island* ... MI-6
Sweets Point—*cape* ... MI-6
*Sweet Spring* ... MO-7
Sweet Spring—*spring* ... GA-3
Sweet Spring—*spring* (2) ... NV-8
Sweet Spring—*spring* ... UT-8
Sweet Spring Creek—*stream* ... MO-7
Sweet Spring Creek—*stream* ... OR-9
Sweet Spring Creek—*stream* ... VA-3
Sweet Spring Hollow—*valley* (2) ... VA-3
Sweet Spring Mtn—*summit* ... OR-9
*Sweetsprings* ... WV-2
**Sweet Springs**—*pop pl* ... MO-7
**Sweet Springs**—*pop pl* ... WV-2
Sweet Springs—*spring* ... CA-9
Sweet Springs—*spring* ... MO-7
Sweet Springs—*spring* ... TX-5
Sweet Springs—*spring* ... UT-8
Sweet Springs Ch—*church* ... AL-4
Sweet Springs Ch—*church* ... AR-4
Sweet Springs Ch—*church* ... MO-7
Sweet Springs Ch—*church* ... NC-3
Sweet Springs Ch—*church* ... SC-3
Sweet Springs Ch—*church* ... WV-2
Sweet Spring Sch (historical)—*school* ... AL-4
Sweet Springs Creek—*stream* ... CA-9
Sweet Springs Creek—*stream* ... WV-2
Sweet Springs (historical)—*locale* ... AL-4
Sweet Springs (Magisterial District)—*fmr MCD* ... WV-2
Sweet Springs Valley—*valley* ... WV-2
Sweetster Brook—*stream* ... ME-1
Sweets Trail—*trail* ... ME-1
*Sweet Stream* ... MH-9
Sweet Suck Hollow—*valley* ... AR-4
**Sweet Township**—*pop pl* ... SD-7
**Sweet (Township of)**—*pop pl* ... MN-6
Sweet Union Ch—*church* ... LA-4
Sweet Union Ch—*church* ... TX-5
**Sweet Valley**—*pop pl* ... PA-2
Sweet Valley—*valley* ... ID-8
Sweet Valley Ch—*church* ... MS-4
Sweet Valley Golf Course—*locale* ... PA-2
Sweet Vengeance Mine—*mine* ... CA-9
Sweet View Ch—*church* ... LA-4
*Sweetwater* ... AL-4
*Sweetwater* ... AZ-5
*Sweetwater* ... MS-4
*Sweetwater* ... TN-4
*Sweetwater* ... WY-8
Sweetwater—*bay* ... FL-3
Sweetwater—*cens area* ... WY-8
Sweet Water—*lake* ... FL-3
Sweetwater—*locale* ... AZ-5
Sweetwater—*locale* (2) ... FL-3
Sweetwater—*locale* ... NE-7
Sweetwater—*locale* ... NC-3
**Sweetwater**—*pop pl* ... AL-4
**Sweet Water**—*pop pl* ... AL-4
**Sweetwater**—*pop pl* (2) ... AZ-5
**Sweetwater**—*pop pl* ... CO-8
**Sweetwater**—*pop pl* (3) ... FL-3
**Sweetwater**—*pop pl* ... ID-8
**Sweet Water**—*pop pl* ... IL-6
**Sweetwater**—*pop pl* (2) ... MO-7
**Sweetwater**—*pop pl* ... NJ-2
**Sweetwater**—*pop pl* ... NC-3
**Sweetwater**—*pop pl* ... ND-7
**Sweetwater**—*pop pl* ... OK-5
**Sweetwater**—*pop pl* ... PA-2
**Sweetwater**—*pop pl* ... SC-3
**Sweetwater**—*pop pl* (2) ... TN-4
**Sweetwater**—*pop pl* (2) ... TX-5
Sweetwater, Lake—*reservoir* ... TX-5
Sweetwater Archeol Site—*hist pl* ... NE-7
Sweetwater Baldy Saddle Trail 143—*trail* ... AZ-5
*Sweetwater Baptist Church* ... AL-4
Sweetwater Basin—*basin* ... MT-8
Sweetwater Basin—*basin* ... WY-8
Sweetwater Branch—*gut* (2) ... FL-3
Sweetwater Branch—*stream* (4) ... AL-4
Sweetwater Branch—*stream* (8) ... FL-3
Sweetwater Branch—*stream* (3) ... GA-3
Sweetwater Branch—*stream* (3) ... KY-4
Sweetwater Branch—*stream* ... MS-4
Sweetwater Branch—*stream* (2) ... MO-7
Sweetwater Branch—*stream* (2) ... NC-3
Sweet Water Branch—*stream* ... NC-3
Sweetwater Branch—*stream* (2) ... NC-3
Sweetwater Branch—*stream* ... SC-3
Sweetwater Branch—*stream* (6) ... TN-4
Sweetwater Branch—*stream* ... WV-2
Sweetwater Brewery—*hist pl* ... WY-8
Sweetwater Brook—*stream* ... MA-1
Sweetwater Camp—*locale* ... FL-3
Sweetwater Camp—*locale* ... MO-7
Sweet Water Campground—*locale* ... CA-9
Sweetwater Canal—*canal* ... ID-8
Sweetwater Canyon—*valley* (3) ... CA-9
Sweetwater Canyon—*valley* ... ID-8
Sweetwater Canyon—*valley* ... KS-7
Sweetwater Canyon—*valley* (2) ... NV-8
Sweetwater Canyon—*valley* (2) ... UT-8
Sweet Water Canyon—*valley* ... UT-8
Sweet Water (CCD)—*cens area* ... AL-4
Sweetwater (CCD)—*cens area* ... AZ-5
Sweetwater (CCD)—*cens area* ... TN-4
Sweetwater (CCD)—*cens area* ... TX-5
Sweetwater Cem—*cemetery* ... AL-4
Sweetwater Cem—*cemetery* ... GA-3
Sweetwater Cem—*cemetery* ... ID-8
Sweetwater Cem—*cemetery* (7) ... MS-4
Sweetwater Cem—*cemetery* ... MO-7
*Sweetwater Ch* ... AL-4
*Sweetwater Ch* ... MS-4
Sweetwater Ch—*church* (2) ... AL-4
Sweetwater Ch—*church* ... FL-3
Sweetwater Ch—*church* (6) ... GA-3
Sweetwater Ch—*church* ... LA-4
Sweetwater Ch—*church* (7) ... MS-4
Sweetwater Ch—*church* ... MO-7
Sweetwater Ch—*church* ... NC-3
Sweetwater Ch—*church* ... SC-3
Sweetwater Ch—*church* (2) ... TX-5
Sweetwater Ch (historical)—*church* ... MS-4
Sweetwater Ch of Christ—*church* ... TN-4
Sweetwater Ch of God—*church* ... TN-4
Sweetwater Ch of the Nazarene—*church* .. TN-4
Sweetwater City Hall—*building* ... TN-4
Sweetwater Club—*other* ... CA-9
Sweetwater Commercial Hist Dist—*hist pl* . TX-5
Sweetwater Cow Camp—*locale* ... NM-5
*Sweetwater Creek* ... AL-4
*Sweetwater Creek* ... FL-3
*Sweetwater Creek* ... GA-3
*Sweetwater Creek* ... ID-8
*Sweet Water Creek* ... MS-4
*Sweetwater Creek* ... TX-5
*Sweet Water Creek* ... UT-8
**Sweetwater Creek**—*pop pl* ... FL-3
Sweetwater Creek—*stream* (9) ... AL-4
Sweetwater Creek—*stream* (2) ... AR-4
Sweetwater Creek—*stream* (9) ... CA-9
Sweetwater Creek—*stream* (3) ... CO-8
Sweetwater Creek—*stream* (10) ... FL-3
Sweetwater Creek—*stream* (12) ... GA-3
Sweetwater Creek—*stream* (2) ... ID-8
Sweetwater Creek—*stream* ... IL-6
Sweetwater Creek—*stream* ... IN-6
Sweetwater Creek—*stream* (2) ... KS-7
Sweetwater Creek—*stream* (2) ... KY-4
Sweetwater Creek—*stream* (2) ... LA-4
Sweetwater Creek—*stream* ... MI-6
Sweetwater Creek—*stream* (9) ... MS-4
Sweetwater Creek—*stream* (3) ... MO-7
Sweetwater Creek—*stream* ... MT-8
Sweetwater Creek—*stream* ... NV-8
Sweetwater Creek—*stream* (2) ... NM-5
Sweetwater Creek—*stream* (3) ... NC-3
Sweetwater Creek—*stream* (4) ... OK-5
Sweetwater Creek—*stream* ... OR-9
Sweetwater Creek—*stream* (2) ... TN-4
Sweetwater Creek—*stream* (5) ... TX-5
Sweet Water Creek—*stream* ... TX-5
Sweetwater Creek—*stream* ... TX-5
Sweetwater Creek—*stream* ... UT-8
Sweet Water Creek—*stream* ... UT-8
Sweetwater Creek—*stream* (4) ... UT-8
Sweetwater Creek—*stream* (3) ... WY-8
Sweetwater Creek Falls—*falls* ... WY-8
Sweetwater Creek Project Lake—*reservoir* ... TN-4
Sweetwater Creek Watershed Dam Number Fifteen—*dam* ... TN-4
Sweetwater Creek Watershed Dam Number One—*dam* ... TN-4
Sweetwater Creek Watershed Dam Number Sixteen—*dam* ... TN-4
Sweetwater Creek Watershed Number One Rsvr—*reservoir* ... TN-4
Sweetwater Creek Watershed Number Sixteen Rsvr—*reservoir* ... TN-4
Sweetwater Crossing—*locale* ... WY-8
Sweet Water Dam—*dam* ... AL-4
*Sweetwater Divide* ... WY-8
Sweet Water Division—*civil* ... AL-4
Sweetwater Division—*civil* ... TN-4
Sweetwater Draw—*valley* ... SD-7
Sweetwater Elem Sch—*school* ... TN-4
Sweetwater Falls Dam—*dam* ... CA-9
*Sweetwater Falls Reservoir* ... CA-9
**Sweetwater Farms (subdivision)**—*pop pl* ... NC-3
Sweetwater Flat—*flat* ... NV-8
Sweetwater Gap—*gap* (2) ... NC-3
Sweetwater Gap—*gap* ... WY-8
Sweetwater Gap Ranch—*locale* ... WY-8
**Sweetwater Garden (subdivision)**—*pop pl* (2) ... AZ-5
Sweetwater Grove Ch—*church* ... SC-3
Sweetwater Guard Station—*locale* ... CO-8
Sweetwater Guard Station—*locale* ... WY-8
Sweetwater Guard Station (historical)—*locale* ... NV-8
Sweetwater Gulch—*valley* ... CA-9
Sweetwater Gulch—*valley* ... CO-8
Sweetwater Gulch—*valley* ... UT-8
Sweetwater Hollow—*valley* ... IN-6
Sweetwater Hollow—*valley* ... OK-5
Sweetwater Hollow—*valley* ... TN-4
Sweetwater Hosp—*hospital* ... TN-4
Sweet Water HS—*school* ... AL-4
Sweetwater HS—*school* ... OK-5
Sweetwater HS—*school* ... TN-4
Sweetwater Industrial Park—*locale* ... TN-4
Sweetwater Inn—*hist pl* ... GA-3
Sweetwater Island—*island* ... TN-4
Sweetwater JHS—*school* ... TN-4
Sweetwater Lake—*lake* ... AK-9
Sweetwater Lake—*lake* ... CO-8
Sweetwater Lake—*lake* ... FL-3
Sweet Water Lake—*lake* ... FL-3
Sweetwater Lake—*lake* (4) ... ND-7
Sweetwater Lake—*lake* ... SD-7
Sweetwater Lake—*lake* ... TX-5
**Sweetwater Lake**—*pop pl* ... IN-6
Sweetwater Lake—*reservoir* ... IN-6
Sweetwater Lake—*swamp* ... GA-3
Sweetwater Lake—*swamp* ... MN-6
Sweetwater Lake Campground—*locale* ... CO-8
Sweetwater Lake Dam—*dam* ... IN-6
Sweet Water Manufacturing Site—*hist pl* .. GA-3
Sweetwater Mesa—*summit* ... AZ-5
*Sweetwater Methodist Church* ... MS-4
Sweetwater Mine—*mine* ... CA-9
Sweetwater Mineral Springs—*locale* ... WY-8
Sweetwater Mine (underground)—*mine* ... AL-4
Sweetwater Missionary Baptist Ch—*church* ... AL-4
Sweetwater Missionary Baptist Ch—*church* ... MS-4
Sweetwater Missionary Ch—*church* ... AL-4
*Sweetwater Mountain* ... CA-9
*Sweetwater Mountains* ... WY-8
Sweetwater Mountains—*range* ... CA-9
Sweetwater Mtn—*summit* ... WY-8
Sweetwater Mtns—*range* ... NV-8
Sweetwater Needles—*summit* ... WY-8
*Sweetwater Oak Creek Lake* ... TX-5
**Sweetwater Oaks**—*pop pl* ... FL-3
Sweetwater Oil Field—*oilfield* ... TX-5
Sweetwater Park—*park* ... AZ-5
Sweetwater Park—*park* ... FL-3
Sweetwater Park—*park* ... TX-5
Sweetwater Pass—*gap* ... AZ-5
Sweetwater Plantation (historical)—*locale* .. AL-4
Sweetwater Point—*summit* ... CA-9
Sweetwater Pond—*lake* ... LA-4
Sweetwater Pony Express Station ( (ruins)—*locale* ... WY-8
*Sweetwater Post Office* ... TN-4
Sweetwater Post Office—*building* ... TN-4
Sweetwater Prairie—*flat* ... OK-5
Sweetwater Public Library—*building* ... TN-4
*Sweetwater Queally* ... WY-8
Sweetwater Ranch—*locale* ... AZ-5
Sweetwater Ranch—*locale* ... NV-8
**Sweetwater Ranch**—*pop pl* ... AZ-5
*Sweetwater Range* ... WY-8
Sweetwater Reef—*ridge* ... UT-8
Sweetwater Ridge—*ridge* ... CA-9
Sweetwater River—*stream* ... CA-9
Sweetwater River—*stream* ... WY-8
*Sweetwater Rocks* ... WY-8
Sweetwater Rocks—*summit* (2) ... WY-8
Sweetwater (RR name for Sweet Water)—*other* ... IL-6
Sweetwater Rsvr—*reservoir* ... CA-9
Sweetwater Sch—*school* ... AL-4
Sweetwater Sch—*school* ... FL-3
Sweetwater Sch—*school* ... NE-7
Sweetwater Sch—*school* ... NC-3
Sweetwater Sch—*school* ... TN-4
Sweetwater Sch (historical)—*school* ... AL-4
Sweetwater Sch (historical)—*school* (3) ... MS-4
Sweet Water Sch (historical)—*school* ... TN-4
Sweetwater Sch (historical)—*school* ... TN-4
*Sweet Water School* ... MS-4
Sweet Water Shoals—*bar* ... TN-4
Sweetwater Shop Ctr—*locale* ... TN-4
Sweetwater Spring—*spring* (4) ... AZ-5
Sweetwater Spring—*spring* (6) ... CA-9
Sweetwater Spring—*spring* ... NM-5
Sweetwater Spring—*spring* ... NC-3
Sweetwater Spring—*spring* (2) ... UT-8
Sweet Water Spring—*spring* ... UT-8
Sweetwater Spring—*spring* ... UT-8
Sweet Water Spring—*spring* ... UT-8
Sweetwater Spring—*spring* ... WY-8
Sweetwater Springs—*spring* ... FL-3
Sweetwater Square Center (Shop Ctr)—*locale* ... FL-3
Sweetwater State Wildlife Mngmt Area—*park* ... MN-6
**Sweetwater Station**—*pop pl* ... WY-8
Sweetwater Strand—*swamp* ... FL-3
Sweetwater Summit—*gap* ... NV-8
Sweetwater Swamp—*swamp* ... FL-3
Sweetwater Tank—*reservoir* ... AZ-5
Sweetwater Tank—*reservoir* ... TX-5
Sweetwater (Township of)—*fmr MCD* ... NC-3
**Sweetwater (Township of)**—*pop pl* ... MI-6
Sweetwater Trail—*trail* ... AZ-5
Sweetwater Trail—*trail* ... WY-8
Sweetwater Trail (Pack)—*trail* ... CA-9
Sweetwater Union HS—*school* ... CA-9
Sweetwater United Methodist Ch—*church* . TN-4
*Sweetwater Valley* ... NV-8
Sweetwater Valley—*basin* ... NE-7
Sweetwater Valley—*valley* ... CA-9
Sweetwater Valley—*valley* ... TN-4
Sweetwater Valley Memorial Park—*cemetery* ... TN-4
Sweetwater Wash—*stream* ... AZ-5
Sweetwater Wash—*stream* ... CA-9
Sweetwater Well—*well* ... AZ-5
Sweet Water Well—*well* (2) ... AZ-5
Sweetwater Well—*well* ... AZ-5
Sweetwater Well—*well* (2) ... NM-5
Sweetwater Well—*well* ... TX-5
Sweetwater Windmill—*locale* (2) ... NM-5
Sweetwater Windmill—*locale* ... TX-5
Sweet Well—*well* ... NM-5
Sweet William Spring—*spring* ... TN-4
Sweet William Well—*well* ... NM-5
Sweetwood Hollow—*valley* ... WV-2
Sweetwood Tank—*reservoir* ... AZ-5
Sweetzer Canyon—*valley* ... ID-8
Sweezer Creek—*stream* ... MO-7
Sweezer Ditch—*canal* ... IN-6
Sweezie Hollow—*valley* ... MO-7
*Sweezie Valley* ... MO-7
Sweezy Branch—*stream* ... MO-7
Sweezy Bridge (historical)—*locale* ... NC-3
Sweezy Cem—*cemetery* ... IA-7
Sweezy Creek—*stream* ... NY-2
Sweezy Island—*island* ... IA-7
Sweezy Pond—*lake* ... NY-2
*Sweganset* ... MA-1
*Sweganset River* ... MA-1
**Swegle**—*pop pl* ... OR-9
Swegle Creek—*stream* ... IL-6
Swegle Sch—*school* ... OR-9
Swegles Saint Sch—*school* ... MI-6
Sweigarts Island—*island* ... PA-2
Sweiger Creek—*stream* ... MI-6
Sweigert Cem—*cemetery* ... OH-6
Sweigert Creek—*stream* ... CA-9
Sweigert Run—*stream* ... OH-6
Sweigiler Creek—*stream* ... WA-9
Sweigoffer Creek—*stream* ... GA-3
*Sweitzer Creek* ... PA-2
Sweitzer Hills—*other* ... CA-9
Sweitzer Lake—*lake* ... MN-6
Sweitzer Ridge—*ridge* ... WA-9
*Sweitzer Run* ... PA-2
*Sweitzers Creek* ... MI-6
Sweitzers Run—*stream* ... PA-2
Swell, The—*summit* ... WV-2
Swell Brook—*stream* ... ME-1
Swelled Hickory Gap—*gap* ... WV-2
Swell Mtn—*summit* (2) ... WV-2
**Swelton Heights (subdivision)**—*pop pl* . NC-3
Swem—*locale* ... WA-9
*Swem Creek* ... WA-9
Swem Creek—*stream* ... WA-9
Swendener Ranch—*locale* ... NE-7
*Swendona Church* ... SD-7
*Swen Fork* ... UT-8
**Swengel**—*pop pl* ... PA-2
Swenk Knob—*summit* ... NC-3
Swenley Branch—*stream* ... LA-4
Swennes Archaeol District—*hist pl* ... WI-6
Swenney Swamp—*swamp* ... MI-6
Swenoda Lake—*lake* ... MN-6
**Swenoda (Township of)**—*pop pl* ... MN-6
Swens Canyon—*valley* ... UT-8
Swensen Basin—*basin* ... ID-8
Swensen Butte—*summit* ... ID-8
Swensen Gulch—*valley* ... MT-8
Swensens Slough—*lake* ... ND-7
Swens Fork—*stream* ... UT-8
**Swenson**—*pop pl* ... ND-7
**Swenson**—*pop pl* ... TX-5
Swenson, A. J., House—*hist pl* ... TX-5
Swenson, William and Shirley, House—*hist pl* ... TX-5
Swenson Airstrip—*airport* ... ND-7
Swenson Cem—*cemetery* ... ND-7
Swenson Cem—*cemetery* ... TX-5
Swenson Creek—*stream* ... KS-7
Swenson Creek—*stream* ... NE-7
**Swenson Drive**—*pop pl* ... NY-2
Swenson Field—*airport* ... ND-7
Swenson Lake—*lake* (3) ... MN-6
Swenson Lake—*lake* ... WA-9
Swenson Lake—*lake* ... WI-6
Swenson Lakebed—*flat* ... MN-6
Swenson Lateral—*canal* ... CA-9
Swenson Oil Field—*oilfield* ... TX-5
Swenson Park—*park* ... TX-5
Swenson Park Golf Course—*other* ... CA-9
Swenson Point—*cape* ... MN-6
Swenson Ranch—*locale* (2) ... ND-7
Swenson Ranch—*locale* (2) ... TX-5
Swensons Canyon—*valley* ... UT-8
Swenson Valley—*valley* ... ID-8
Swensrud Park—*park* ... IA-7
Swensson, Olof, Farmstead—*hist pl* ... MN-6
Swensson Cem—*cemetery* ... MN-6
Swens Spring—*spring* ... UT-8
*Swenter Hollow* ... MO-7
**Swepsonville**—*pop pl* ... NC-3
Swept Creek—*stream* ... AL-4
Sweringen Ditch—*canal* ... IN-6
*Seweseckechi* ... MA-1
*Seweseckechi Head* ... MA-1
Swesey Hollow—*valley* ... PA-2
Swesey Sch—*school* ... PA-2
Swet Creek—*stream* ... ID-8
Swet Lake—*lake* ... ID-8
Swet Lake Cabin—*locale* ... ID-8
Swet Lake Pond—*lake* ... ID-8
Swetland Homestead—*hist pl* ... PA-2
Swetland House—*hist pl* ... OH-6
Swetland-Pease House—*hist pl* ... MA-1
Swetman, Glenn, House—*hist pl* ... MS-4
Swetman House—*hist pl* ... AK-9
Swetmann Camp—*locale* ... AK-9
Swetmann Mine—*mine* ... AK-9
*Swetnam* ... VA-3
Swetnam Cem—*cemetery* ... KY-4
Swet Point—*summit* ... ID-8
**Swett**—*pop pl* ... SD-7
Swett Brook—*stream* ... ME-1
Swett Brook—*stream* ... NH-1
Swett Canyon—*valley* ... CA-9
Swett Creek—*stream* ... UT-8
Swett Ford (historical)—*crossing* ... TN-4
Swett Hill—*summit* ... ME-1
Swett Hills—*summit* ... UT-8
Swett Lake—*reservoir* ... MS-4
Swett Marsh—*swamp* ... ME-1
Swett Peak—*summit* ... UT-8
Swett Ranch—*hist pl* ... UT-8
Swett Ridge—*ridge* ... ME-1
Swetts Cem—*cemetery* ... NH-1
Swett Sch—*school* ... CA-9
Swett Sch—*school* ... NE-7
*Swett's Island* ... ME-1
Swetts Meadow—*swamp* ... ME-1
**Swetts Mills**—*pop pl* ... NH-1
Swetts Point—*cape* ... NH-1
Swetts Pond—*reservoir* ... ME-1
Swett Union HS—*school* ... CA-9
Swetz Branch—*stream* ... LA-4
Swetz Creek—*stream* ... LA-4
Sweutka Cem—*cemetery* ... OK-5
**Sweyze**—*pop pl* ... NY-2
Swezey Camp—*locale* ... VT-1
Swezzey Lake—*lake* ... MI-6
SW Gate Gulch Rsvr—*reservoir* ... ID-8
Swickard Cem—*cemetery* ... OH-6
Swickard Mines—*mine* ... NV-8
**Swickards Additions**—*pop pl* ... OH-6
Swick Cem—*cemetery* ... IL-6
Swick Creek—*stream* ... OR-9
Swicker Spring—*spring* ... AZ-5
Swickey Canyon—*valley* ... OR-9
Swickheimer Ranch—*locale* ... TX-5
Swick Sch—*school* ... IL-6
Swidinski Creek—*stream* ... CO-8
Swiekert Ranch—*locale* ... CA-9
Swiercz Drain—*canal* ... MI-6
Swiettendick Place Well—*well* ... AZ-5
Swift—*locale* ... MO-7
Swift—*locale* ... OH-6
Swift—*locale* ... TX-5
Swift—*locale* ... WA-9
**Swift**—*pop pl* ... AL-4
**Swift**—*pop pl* ... FL-3
**Swift**—*pop pl* ... IL-6
**Swift**—*pop pl* ... MN-6
**Swift**—*pop pl* ... TN-4
Swift, D. Wheeler, House—*hist pl* ... MA-1
Swift, Henry A., House—*hist pl* ... MN-6
Swift Bar—*bar* ... WA-9
Swift Bayou—*gut* ... AR-4
Swift Bayou—*gut* ... MS-4
Swift Bayou—*stream* ... LA-4
Swift Bayou—*stream* ... TX-5
Swift Bayou Canal—*canal* ... LA-4
Swift Bear Lake—*lake* ... SD-7
*Swift Birch Creek* ... SD-7
Swift Bird Bay—*bay* ... SD-7
Swift Bird Cem (historical)—*cemetery* ... SD-7
Swift Bird Ch (historical)—*church* ... SD-7
*Swiftbird Creek* ... SD-7
Swift Bird Creek—*stream* ... SD-7
Swift Bird Day Sch—*school* ... SD-7
Swift Bird Training Center—*building* ... SD-7
Swift Branch—*stream* ... FL-3
Swift Branch—*stream* ... NC-3
Swift Branch—*stream* ... TX-5
Swift Brook—*stream* ... ME-1
Swift Brook—*stream* ... VT-1
Swift Cambridge River—*stream* ... ME-1
Swift Camp Creek—*stream* ... KY-4
Swiftcamp Creek Trail—*trail* ... KY-4
Swift Canyon—*valley* ... AZ-5
Swift Canyon—*valley* ... CO-8
Swift Canyon Wash—*stream* ... AZ-5
Swift Cave—*cave* ... TN-4
Swift Cem—*cemetery* ... IN-6
Swift Cem—*cemetery* ... TN-4
Swift Ch—*church* ... AL-4
*Swift Consolidated Elementary School* ... AL-4
Swift Corner—*locale* ... NY-2
Swift Coulee—*valley* (2) ... MT-8
**Swift (County)**—*pop pl* ... MN-6
Swift County Courthouse—*hist pl* ... MN-6
*Swift Creek* ... NY-2
*Swift Creek* ... SD-7
*Swift Creek* ... WA-9
Swift Creek—*channel* (2) ... NY-2
Swift Creek—*gut* ... WI-6
Swift Creek—*stream* (2) ... AL-4
Swift Creek—*stream* (6) ... AK-9
Swift Creek—*stream* (4) ... CA-9
Swift Creek—*stream* (2) ... CO-8
Swift Creek—*stream* (3) ... FL-3
Swift Creek—*stream* (7) ... GA-3
Swift Creek—*stream* (2) ... ID-8
Swift Creek—*stream* ... MO-7
Swift Creek—*stream* (3) ... MT-8
Swift Creek—*stream* (3) ... NC-3
Swift Creek—*stream* ... OH-6
Swift Creek—*stream* (2) ... OR-9
Swift Creek—*stream* (3) ... SC-3
Swift Creek—*stream* (2) ... UT-8
Swift Creek—*stream* ... VA-3
Swift Creek—*stream* (6) ... WA-9
Swift Creek—*stream* (2) ... WI-6
Swift Creek—*stream* (2) ... WY-8
Swift Creek—*swamp* ... FL-3
Swift Creek—*uninc pl* ... VA-3
Swift Creek Bar—*bar* ... AL-4
Swift Creek Campground—*locale* ... UT-8
Swift Creek Campground—*locale* ... WY-8
Swift Creek (CCD)—*cens area* ... GA-3
Swift Creek Cem—*cemetery* ... FL-3
Swift Creek Ch—*church* ... FL-3
Swift Creek Ch—*church* ... NC-3
Swift Creek Ch—*church* ... SC-3
Swift Creek Dam—*dam* ... PA-2
Swift Creek Flow—*lava* ... WA-9
Swift Creek Hunting Club—*locale* ... AL-4
Swift Creek Lake—*lake* ... GA-3
Swift Creek Lake—*lake* ... WY-8
Swift Creek Lake—*reservoir* ... VA-3
Swift Creek Lake—*reservoir* ... WY-8
Swift Creek Mill—*hist pl* ... VA-3
Swift Creek Park—*park* ... AL-4
Swift Creek Pond—*lake* ... FL-3
*Swift Creek Reservoir* ... WA-9
Swift Creek Rsvr—*reservoir* ... VA-3
Swift Creek Sch—*school* ... GA-3
Swift Creek Sch—*school* ... NC-3
Swift Creek Swamp—*lake* ... FL-3
Swift Creek Swamp—*swamp* (2) ... FL-3
Swift Creek (Township of)—*fmr MCD* (2) .. NC-3
Swift Creek Trail—*trail* ... OR-9
**Swiftcurrent**—*pop pl* ... MT-8
Swiftcurrent Creek—*stream* ... MT-8
*Swiftcurrent Falls* ... MT-8
Swiftcurrent Falls—*falls* ... MT-8
Swiftcurrent Fire Lookout—*hist pl* ... MT-8
Swiftcurrent Glacier—*glacier* ... MT-8
Swiftcurrent Lake—*lake* ... MT-8
Swiftcurrent Mtn—*summit* ... MT-8
Swiftcurrent Pass—*gap* ... MT-8
Swiftcurrent Pass Trail—*trail* ... MT-8
Swiftcurrent Ranger Station Hist Dist—*hist pl* ... MT-8
Swiftcurrent Ridge—*ridge* ... MT-8
Swiftcurrent Ridge Lake—*lake* ... MT-8
Swift Dam—*dam* ... MT-8
Swift Diamond Farm—*locale* ... NH-1
Swift Diamond River—*stream* ... NH-1
Swift Ditch—*canal* ... IN-6
Swift Drain—*stream* ... MI-6
Swift Draw Tank—*reservoir* ... TX-5
**Swift Falls**—*pop pl* ... MN-6
*Swift Flow* ... WA-9
Swift Ford—*locale* ... AL-4
Swift Ford Branch—*stream* ... NC-3
Swift Fork—*stream* ... AK-9
Swift Glacier—*glacier* ... WA-9
Swift Gulch—*valley* ... CO-8
Swift Gulch—*valley* ... ID-8
Swift Gut—*stream* ... SC-3
*Swift Hill* ... MA-1
Swift Hill—*summit* ... NY-2
Swift Hill—*summit* ... WA-9
Swift Hollow—*valley* ... MO-7
Swift Hollow—*valley* ... TN-4
Swift House—*hist pl* ... IL-6
Swift Island—*island* ... VA-3
Swift Island (historical)—*locale* ... NC-3
Swift JHS—*school* ... CT-1
*Swift Kill Creek* ... NY-2
Swift-Kyle House—*hist pl* ... GA-3
*Swift Lake* ... CA-9
*Swift Lake* ... FL-3
Swift Lake—*lake* ... MI-6
Swift Lake—*lake* ... MN-6
Swift Lake—*lake* ... MT-8
Swift Lake—*lake* (2) ... TX-5
Swift Lake—*lake* ... WI-6
Swift Memorial Park—*park* ... DE-2
Swift Millpond—*reservoir* ... VA-3
*Swift Neck* ... MA-1
Swifton—*locale* ... KY-4
**Swifton**—*pop pl* ... AR-4
Swifton Cem—*cemetery* ... AR-4
Swifton Shop Ctr—*locale* ... OH-6
**Swiftown**—*pop pl* ... MS-4
Swiftown Ch of God in Christ—*church* ... MS-4
Swift Point—*cape* ... AK-9
Swift Point—*cape* ... MN-6
*Swift Pond* ... MA-1
Swift Pond—*lake* ... NY-2
Swift Prairie—*flat* ... TX-5
Swift Presbyterian Church—*hist pl* ... AL-4
Swift Ranch—*locale* ... TX-5
*Swift River* ... MA-1
**Swift River**—*pop pl* ... MA-1
Swift River—*stream* (2) ... AK-9
Swift River—*stream* ... ME-1
Swift River—*stream* (2) ... MA-1
Swift River—*stream* ... MN-6
Swift River—*stream* (2) ... NH-1
Swift River Pond—*lake* ... ME-1
Swift River Rsvr—*reservoir* ... MA-1
Swift River Trail—*trail* ... NH-1
Swift RR Station—*locale* ... FL-3
Swift Rsvr—*reservoir* ... MT-8
Swift Rsvr—*reservoir* ... WA-9
*Swiftrun* ... VA-3
Swiftrun—*other* ... VA-3
**Swift Run**—*pop pl* ... VA-3
Swift Run—*stream* ... IN-6
Swift Run—*stream* (3) ... PA-2
Swift Run—*stream* ... SC-3
Swift Run—*stream* (2) ... VA-3
Swift Run Ch—*church* ... VA-3
*Swift Run Creek* ... SC-3
Swift Run Gap—*gap* ... VA-3
Swift Run Lake—*reservoir* ... OH-6
Swift Run Overlook—*locale* ... VA-3
**Swift Run (Swiftrun)**—*pop pl* ... VA-3
Swift Run Trail—*trail* ... PA-2
Swifts Bay—*bay* ... WA-9
**Swifts Beach**—*pop pl* ... MA-1
Swifts Canyon—*valley* ... UT-8
Swift Sch—*school* ... AL-4
Swift Sch—*school* (2) ... IL-6
Swift Sch—*school* ... MA-1
Swift Sch—*school* ... MI-6
*Swifts Creek* ... TN-4
Swifts Creek Pond—*lake* ... FL-3
Swifts Hill—*summit* ... MA-1
Swiftshoal Branch—*stream* ... KY-4
Swift Shoal Creek—*stream* ... MO-7
Swift Shoals—*bar* ... VA-3
Swiftshore Mine—*mine* ... CA-9
Swift Siding—*locale* ... MI-6
Swifts Landing—*locale* ... AL-4
Swift Slough—*channel* ... FL-3
Swift Slough—*channel* ... IA-7
Swift Slough—*gut* ... AR-4
Swift Slough—*gut* ... FL-3
Swift Slough—*gut* ... IL-6
Swift Slough—*gut* ... IA-7
Swift Slough—*gut* ... TN-4
Swift Slough—*gut* ... UT-8
Swift Slough—*stream* ... WI-6
**Swifts Mills**—*pop pl* ... NY-2
Swifts Neck—*cape* ... MA-1
*Swifts Point* ... MN-6
*Swifts Pond* ... MA-1
Swift Spring—*spring* ... UT-8
Swift Spring Creek—*stream* ... UT-8
Swifts Slough—*gut* ... TN-4
Swifts Stone Corral—*locale* ... CA-9
Swiftsure Towhead—*island* ... IL-6
Swift Trail Junction—*locale* ... AZ-5
Swiftwater—*locale* ... MS-4
**Swiftwater**—*pop pl* ... NH-1
**Swiftwater**—*pop pl* ... PA-2
*Swiftwater Baptist Church* ... MS-4
Swiftwater Bayou—*stream* ... MS-4
Swiftwater Branch—*stream* ... VA-3
Swiftwater Ch—*church* ... MS-4
Swiftwater Covered Bridge—*hist pl* ... NH-1
Swiftwater Creek—*stream* ... ID-8
Swiftwater Creek—*stream* ... PA-2
Swiftwater Inn—*hist pl* ... PA-2
Swiftwater Lake—*reservoir* ... PA-2
Swift Water Picnic Area—*locale* ... WA-9
Swiftwater Point—*cape* ... NY-2
Swift Westside Baptist Ch—*church* ... AL-4
Swigart Coal Mine—*mine* ... WY-8
Swigart Pond—*lake* ... PA-2
Swigart's Mill—*hist pl* ... PA-2
Swiger Cem—*cemetery* ... WV-2
Swiger Knob—*summit* ... OH-6
Swigert Cow Camp—*locale* ... OR-9
Swigert Creek—*stream* ... WA-9
Swigert Sch—*school* ... IL-6
Swiggetts Pond—*reservoir* ... DE-2
Swiggetts Pond Dam—*dam* ... DE-2
*Swiggler Gulch* ... CO-8
Swigler Gulch—*valley* ... CO-8
Swigum Ridge—*ridge* ... WI-6
Swikert Meadow—*flat* ... OR-9
Swikshak—*locale* ... AK-9
Swikshak Lagoon—*bay* ... AK-9
Swikshak River—*stream* ... AK-9
Swilley Branch—*stream* ... MS-4
Swilley Hill Ch—*church* ... GA-3
Swilleys Bend—*bend* ... AL-4
Swilleys Landing (historical)—*locale* ... AL-4

Swillies Bend ... AL-4
Swilling Butte—summit ... AZ-5
Swilling Gulch—valley ... AZ-5
Swill Island—island ... NH-1
Swillup Creek—stream ... CA-9
Swim Bald—summit ... NC-3
Swim Branch—stream (2) ... KY-4
Swim Brook—stream ... IN-6
Swim Cem—cemetery ... VA-3
Swim Creek—stream ... WI-6
Swim Hollow—valley ... WV-2
Swim Lake—lake ... LA-4
Swim Lake—lake ... ND-7
Swimley—locale ... VA-3
Swimley Cem—cemetery ... PA-2
Swim Meadow—flat ... CA-9
Swimmer Branch—stream ... NC-3
Swimmer Ch—church ... OK-5
Swimmer Creek—stream ... SD-7
Swimmers Flat—flat ... NV-8
Swimming Bear Lake—lake ... ID-8
Swimming Bog—swamp ... ME-1
Swimming Creek—stream ... MD-2
Swimming Creek—stream ... NJ-2
Swimming Dam—reservoir ... PA-2
Swimming Deer Lake—lake ... WA-9
Swimming Hole—lake ... UT-8
Swimming Hole Creek—stream ... MI-6
Swimminghole Run—stream ... WV-2
Swimming Lake—lake ... MN-6
Swimming Lake—lake ... MT-8
Swimming Landing Run ... VA-3
Swimming Over Point—cape ... NJ-2
Swimming Pan Creek ... FL-3
Swimming Pen Creek—stream ... FL-3
Swimming Pen Slough—stream ... TX-5
Swimming Place Point ... MA-1
Swimming Place Point—cape ... MA-1
Swimming Point—cape ... NC-3
Swimming River—stream ... NJ-2
Swimming River Reservoir Dam—dam ... NJ-2
Swimming River Rsvr—reservoir ... NJ-2
Swimming Rock—island ... CT-1
Swimming Woman Creek ... MT-8
Swimming Woman Creek—stream ... MT-8
Swimm Lake—lake ... ID-8
Swimpkin Canyon ... WA-9
Swim Pond—lake ... FL-3
Swimptkin Creek—stream ... WA-9
Swim Ridge—ridge ... CA-9
Swim Run—stream ... WV-2
Swims Lake ... MN-6
Swims Under Sch—school ... MT-8
**Swin**—pop pl ... NY-2
Swinborne Spring—spring ... AZ-5
Swinborn Island ... NY-2
Swinburne Cem—cemetery ... NY-2
Swinburne Flat—flat ... AZ-5
Swinburne Island—island ... NY-2
Swinburne Spring—spring ... AZ-5
Swinburn Island ... NY-2
Swindall Dam—dam ... AL-4
Swindall Lake—reservoir ... AL-4
Swindall Sch (historical)—school ... TN-4
Swindel Cove ... WA-9
Swindell ... NC-3
Swindell—locale ... NC-3
Swindell, Albin B., House and Store—hist pl ... NC-3
Swindell Bay—bay ... NC-3
Swindell Cem—cemetery ... MO-7
Swindell Cem—cemetery ... TN-4
Swindell Creek—stream ... MS-4
Swindell Falls—falls ... AL-4
Swindell Fork—locale ... NC-3
Swindell Gap—locale ... AL-4
Swindells Canal—canal ... NC-3
Swindells Store—locale ... NC-3
Swindelly Cem—cemetery ... LA-4
Swindle Cem—cemetery ... AL-4
Swindle Creek—stream ... AR-4
Swindle Creek—stream ... TN-4
Swindle Hill Ch—church ... AL-4
Swindle Hollow—valley ... AL-4
Swindle Lake—lake (2) ... FL-3
Swindle Lake—lake ... OR-9
Swindle Mine (underground)—mine ... AL-4
Swindle Pond ... FL-3
Swindler Cem—cemetery ... OH-6
Swindler Creek—stream ... TX-5
Swindler House—hist pl ... KY-4
Swindler Pond—lake ... TX-5
Swindle Sch (historical)—school ... TN-4
Swindle Site—hist pl ... TX-5
Swindle Swamp—swamp ... FL-3
**Swindleville**—pop pl ... LA-4
Swindling Gap—gap ... KY-4
Swine Bend Hollow—valley ... ID-8
Swinebroad Cem—cemetery ... TN-4
Swine Cem—cemetery ... KY-4
Swine Creek—stream ... MN-6
Swine Creek—stream ... OH-6
Swine Creek—stream ... TX-5
Swinefield Bridge—bridge ... NJ-2
Swineford ... PA-2
Swineford—uninc pl ... PA-2
Swineford, Mount—summit ... AK-9
Swineford Lakes—lake ... AK-9
Swinehart Draw—valley ... SD-7
Swinehart Gulch—valley ... CO-8
Swinehart Hill—summit ... SD-7
Swinehart Ridge—ridge ... CO-8
Swinesburg—locale ... NJ-2
Swines Creek ... UT-8
Swineson Drain—canal ... MI-6
Swiney Branch—stream ... MO-7
Swiney Cem—cemetery ... MO-7
Swiney Hollow—valley ... MO-7
Swiney Spring—spring ... MO-7
Swinford Park—park ... IN-6
Swinford Sch (abandoned)—school ... MO-7
Swing Brook—stream ... IN-6
Swing Creek—stream ... ID-8
Swing Creek—stream ... KS-7
Swinge Camp Branch—stream ... KY-4
Swinger Ditch—canal ... OR-9
Swinger Slough—stream ... WI-6
Swing Field—swamp ... OR-9
Swing Grove Cem—cemetery ... IL-6
Swing Grove Sch—school ... IL-6
Swinging Bridge—bridge ... MO-7
Swinging Bridge—locale ... ID-8
Swinging Bridge Creek—stream ... UT-8
Swinging Bridge Lake—reservoir ... OH-6
Swinging Bridge Park—park ... TN-4
Swinging Bridge Rsvr—reservoir ... NY-2
Swinging Creek—stream ... IN-6
Swinging Cross Canyon—valley ... NM-5
Swinging Dome—summit ... AK-9
Swinging H Ranch—locale ... AZ-5
Swinging Lick Gap—gap ... NC-3
Swingington Cem—cemetery ... GA-3
Swing Lake—lake ... MN-6
Swingle—locale ... CA-9
**Swingle**—pop pl ... NE-7
Swingle Bench—bench ... NV-8
Swingle Canyon—valley ... NM-5
Swingle Cem—cemetery ... TN-4
Swingle Ditch—canal ... IN-6
Swingle Ranch—locale ... NV-8
Swingles Church ... TN-4
Swingle Spring—spring ... NM-5
Swingles School ... TN-4
Swingleville Post Office ... TN-4
Swingle Wash—stream ... AZ-5
Swingle Windmill—locale ... NM-5
Swingley Cem—cemetery ... IN-6
Swingley Farm Cem—cemetery ... OH-6
Swingley Ranch—locale ... MT-8
Swing Log Creek—stream ... OR-9
Swings Gap ... VA-3
Swings Lake—reservoir ... TN-4
Swink—locale ... AL-4
**Swink**—pop pl ... CO-8
**Swink**—pop pl ... OK-5
Swink Cem—cemetery ... OK-5
Swink Creek—stream ... SC-3
Swink Lateral—canal ... CO-8
Swink Rsvr No 1—reservoir ... CO-8
Swink Rsvr No 2—reservoir ... CO-8
Swink Rsvr No 5—reservoir ... CO-8
Swink Rsvr No 6—reservoir ... CO-8
Swink Sch—school ... CO-8
Swinks Mill—locale ... VA-3
Swinners Bend ... AL-4
Swinnerton Gulch—valley ... ID-8
Swinney, Thomas W., House—hist pl ... IN-6
Swinney Branch—stream ... GA-3
Swinney Branch—stream ... TN-4
Swinney Cem—cemetery ... IN-6
Swinney Cem—cemetery ... TX-5
Swinney Lake ... TX-5
Swinney Marsh—swamp ... TX-5
Swinney Park—park ... IN-6
Swinney Road Bay—bay ... TX-5
Swinney Sch—school ... MO-7
Swinney Sch—school ... OK-5
Swinney Switch—locale ... TX-5
Swinneytown Ch—church ... TX-5
Swinning Creek—stream ... OR-9
Swinning Spring—spring ... OR-9
Swinns Valley—valley ... WI-6
Swinomish ... WA-9
Swinomish Channel—channel ... WA-9
**Swinomish Ind Res**—pop pl ... WA-9
Swinomish Reservation (CCD)—cens area ... WA-9
Swinomish Slough ... WA-9
Swins Chapel—church ... MS-4
Swinson Park—park ... NC-3
Swins Ponds—lake ... NJ-2
Swint Creek—stream ... SD-7
Swint-Hammack Cem—cemetery ... AL-4
**Swinton**—pop pl ... MO-7
Swinton Cem—cemetery ... AR-4
Swinton Creek—stream ... MI-6
Swinton Creek—stream (2) ... SC-3
Swints Lake—reservoir ... SC-3
Swint Spring Ch—church ... GA-3
Swipkin Canyon—valley ... WA-9
Swirl Hole Bend—bend ... TN-4
Swirl Island—island ... WA-9
**Swisher**—pop pl ... IA-7
**Swisher**—pop pl ... TN-4
Swisher Branch—stream ... KS-7
Swisher Cem—cemetery ... IN-6
Swisher Cem—cemetery ... OH-6
Swisher Cem—cemetery ... TX-5
Swisher Cem—cemetery ... WV-2
**Swisher (County)**—pop pl ... TX-5
Swisher Creek—stream ... ID-8
Swisher Creek—stream ... IA-7
Swisher Hollow—valley ... WV-2
Swisher-Hurtz Cem—cemetery ... IN-6
Swisher Knob—summit ... WV-2
Swisher Lake—lake ... MT-8
Swisher Landing ... MS-4
Swisher Mine—mine ... UT-8
Swisher Mtn—summit ... ID-8
Swisher Ridge—ridge ... ID-8
Swisher Rsvr—reservoir ... CO-8
Swisher Rsvr—reservoir ... OR-9
Swisher Sch (abandoned)—school ... MO-7
Swishers Chapel—church ... TN-4
Swisher Spring—spring ... ID-8
Swisher Windmill—locale ... CO-8
Swishtall Bluff—cliff ... WI-6
**Swiss**—pop pl ... MO-7
**Swiss**—pop pl ... NC-3
**Swiss**—pop pl ... WV-2
Swiss Alp—locale ... TX-5
Swiss Alps ... TX-5
Swiss Ave Hist Dist—hist pl ... TX-5
Swiss Bar—bar ... CA-9
Swiss Bell Mine—mine ... AZ-5
Swiss Bob Canyon—valley ... NV-8
Swiss Bob Well—well ... NV-8
Swiss Canyon—valley ... AZ-5
Swiss Canyon—valley (2) ... CA-9
Swiss Cem—cemetery ... CT-1
Swiss Cem—cemetery ... IA-7
Swiss Cem—cemetery ... KS-7
Swiss Cem—cemetery ... TN-4
Swiss Cem—cemetery (2) ... WI-6
Swiss Ch—church ... OH-6
Swiss Colony Cem—cemetery ... TN-4
Swiss Creek—stream ... CA-9
Swiss Creek—stream ... ID-8
Swiss Creek—stream (2) ... NY-2
**Swissdale**—pop pl ... PA-2
Swissdale Sch (historical)—school ... PA-2
Swiss Elem Sch—school ... TN-4
Swiss Flat—flat ... OR-9
Swiss Gulch—valley ... CA-9
Swiss Heights Rec Area—park ... PA-2
Swisshelm Lodge—locale ... AZ-5
Swisshelm Mountains ... AZ-5
Swisshelm Mountains—ridge ... AZ-5
Swisshelm Mtn—summit ... AZ-5
Swiss Hill—summit ... NY-2
**Swisshome**—pop pl ... OR-9
Swiss Lake—lake ... WI-6
Swiss Legation Bldg—building ... DC-2
Swissmont—locale ... PA-2
Swiss Mtn—summit ... NV-8
Swiss Pine Lake—reservoir ... NC-3
Swiss Pine Lake Dam—dam ... NC-3
Swiss Ranch—locale ... CA-9
Swiss Spring—spring ... OR-9
Swiss Steam Laundry Bldg—hist pl ... MD-2
**Swiss (Town of)**—pop pl ... WI-6
Swissvale—locale ... CO-8
Swissvale—locale ... KS-7
**Swissvale**—pop pl ... PA-2
Swissvale Borough—civil ... PA-2
Swissvale HS—school ... PA-2
Swiss Valley ... IL-6
Swiss Valley—valley ... ID-8
Swiss Valley—valley ... IA-7
Swiss Valley—valley ... NE-7
Swiss Valley—valley ... WA-9
Swiss Valley Sch—school ... NE-7
Swissville ... IL-6
**Switch Back**—pop pl ... VA-3
**Switchback**—pop pl ... WV-2
Switchback Canyon—valley ... WA-9
Switchback Creek—stream (2) ... MT-8
Switchback Creek—stream ... OR-9
Switchback Falls—falls ... OR-9
Switchback Gulch—valley ... ID-8
Switchback Hollow—valley (2) ... WV-2
Switchback Lake—lake ... AR-4
Switchback Mtn—summit ... AK-9
Switchback Pass—gap ... MT-8
Switchback Peak—summit ... CA-9
**Switchback (RR name Lick Branch)**—pop pl ... WV-2
Switchbacks, The—slope ... UT-8
Switchback Spring—spring ... NV-8
Switchback Spring—spring ... UT-8
Switchback Spring—spring ... WA-9
Switchbacks Spring, The—spring ... AZ-5
Switchback Tank—reservoir (2) ... AZ-5
Switchback Trail—trail ... ID-8
Switchback Trail—trail (2) ... PA-2
Switchboard Hill—summit ... OR-9
Switch Branch—stream ... TN-4
Switch Creek—stream ... AK-9
Switch Creek—stream ... OR-9
Switcher No. 1670—hist pl ... PA-2
Switcher No. 94—hist pl ... PA-2
Switches Tank—reservoir ... TX-5
Switchgrass Slough—gut ... FL-3
Switch No 9—other ... MD-2
Switch Pond—lake ... WA-9
Switlick Dam ... NJ-2
Switlick Lake—reservoir ... NJ-2
Switlik Sch—school ... FL-3
Switlik Sch—school ... NJ-2
Swits City ... IN-6
**Switz City**—pop pl ... IN-6
Switz City Cem—cemetery ... IN-6
Switz City Central Sch—school ... IN-6
Switzer—locale ... PA-2
**Switzer**—pop pl ... KY-4
**Switzer**—pop pl ... OH-6
**Switzer**—pop pl ... SC-3
**Switzer**—pop pl ... WV-2
Switzer Camp—locale ... CA-9
Switzer Canyon—valley ... AZ-5
Switzer Cem—cemetery ... IA-7
Switzer Cem—cemetery ... KY-4
Switzer Cem—cemetery ... OH-6
Switzer Cem—cemetery ... WI-6
Switzer Ch—church ... SC-3
Switzer Chapel—church ... MO-7
Switzer Covered Bridge—hist pl ... KY-4
Switzer Creek ... KS-7
Switzer Creek—stream ... AK-9
Switzer Creek—stream ... OH-6
Switzer Creek—stream ... PA-2
**Switzer Crossroads**—pop pl ... IN-6
Switzer Hill Sch—school ... NY-2
Switzer Joe Gulch—valley ... MT-8
Switzer Lake—lake ... IL-6
Switzer Lake—lake ... MI-6
Switzerland—locale ... FL-3
**Switzerland**—pop pl ... OR-9
**Switzerland**—pop pl ... SC-3
Switzerland, Lake—reservoir ... NY-2
Switzerland Canal—canal ... SC-3
**Switzerland County**—pop pl ... IN-6
Switzerland County Elem Sch—school ... IN-6
Switzerland County Junior-Senior HS—school ... IN-6
Switzerland Lake—reservoir ... OH-6
**Switzerland Park**—pop pl ... CO-8
**Switzerland (Township of)**—pop pl ... OH-6
Switzerland Trail—trail ... MN-6
**Switzerland Village**—pop pl ... CO-8
Switzer Mesa ... AZ-5
Switzer Mesa—bench ... AZ-5
Switzer Mtn—summit ... VA-3
Switzer Park—park ... CA-9
Switzer Rock—island ... CA-9
Switzer Sch—school (2) ... IL-6
Switzer Sch—school ... MI-6
Switzer Sch (historical)—school ... MS-4
Switzers Gap Cem—cemetery ... KS-7
Switzers Gulch—valley ... CO-8
Switzer Station—locale ... CA-9
Switz Kill—stream ... NY-2
Switz Kills ... NY-2
Switzler—locale ... MO-7
Switzler Canyon—valley ... WA-9
Switzler Creek ... KS-7
Switzler Creek—stream ... KS-7
Switzler Island ... OR-9
Switzler Island (historical)—island ... OR-9
Swival Sch—school ... IL-6
Swizer Gulch—valley ... CO-8
S W N Henderson Ditch—canal ... IN-6
Swobe—locale ... CA-9
Swofford—locale ... WA-9
Swofford Cem—cemetery ... IL-6
Swoffords Creek—stream ... LA-4
Swofford Valley—valley ... WA-9
Swoope—locale ... VA-3
Swoope, Lake—lake ... FL-3
Swoope Bottom—flat ... AL-4
Swoope Branch—stream ... AL-4
Swoope Cem—cemetery (2) ... AL-4
Swoope Lake ... AL-4
Swoope Pond—lake ... AL-4
Swoope Quarters (historical)—locale ... MS-4
Swoope Run—stream ... VA-3
Swoopes Knob ... WV-2
Swoopes Knobs—ridge ... WV-2
Swop and Hurd Drain ... MI-6
Swope ... MS-4
Swope ... WV-2
Swope And Hurd Drain—stream ... MI-6
Swope Canyon—valley ... CA-9
Swope Cem—cemetery ... OH-6
Swope Cem—cemetery ... WV-2
Swope Creek ... PA-2
Swope Creek—stream ... MO-7
Swope Ditch—canal ... IN-6
Swope Drain—canal ... NV-8
Swope Draw—valley ... WY-8
Swope-Dudderar House and Mill Site—hist pl ... KY-4
Swope Gap—gap ... PA-2
Swope Hollow—valley ... PA-2
Swope Hollow—valley ... VA-3
Swope JHS—school ... NV-8
Swope Mtn—summit ... PA-2
Swope Park ... MO-7
Swope Park—park ... KS-7
Swope Park—park ... MO-7
Swope Parkway Shop Ctr—locale ... MO-7
Swope Rsvr—reservoir ... MT-8
Swope Sch—school ... PA-2
Swopes Knobs ... WV-2
Swopes Mill Hollow Cave—cave ... AL-4
Swopes Pond ... AL-4
Swopes Pond ... NY-2
Swope Tank—reservoir (2) ... NM-5
Swope Valley Run—stream ... PA-2
Swope Windmill—locale ... NM-5
Sword Bayou—stream ... LA-4
Sword Branch—stream ... KY-4
Sword Cem—cemetery ... KY-4
Sword Cem—cemetery (2) ... VA-3
Sword Creek—stream ... VA-3
Swordens Pond—lake ... NJ-2
Sword Fork—stream ... KY-4
Sword Gate Houses—hist pl ... SC-3
Sword Lake—lake ... CA-9
Sword Mtn—summit ... MD-2
Sword Point—cape (2) ... AK-9
Sword Point—cape ... FL-3
Sword Point—cape ... LA-4
Swords—locale ... GA-3
**Swords**—pop pl ... LA-4
Swords Branch—stream ... NC-3
**Swords Creek**—pop pl ... VA-3
Swords Pond—lake ... FL-3
Swore Lake ... MS-4
Swore Lake Dam—dam ... MS-4
Sworinger Rsvr—reservoir ... CA-9
**Swormville**—pop pl ... NY-2
Swortzets Camp—locale ... CA-9
Swouerville ... PA-2
Swoveberg—summit ... PA-2
Swovenberg ... PA-2
Swover Creek—stream ... VA-3
**Swoyersville**—pop pl ... PA-2
Swoyersville Borough—civil ... PA-2
**Swoyersville (corporate name for Swoyerville)**—pop pl ... PA-2
Swoyerville (corporate name Swoyersville) ... PA-2
S W Point ... RI-1
S W Seabrook Catfish Ponds Dam—dam (2) ... MS-4
S W Snowden Elem Sch—school ... NC-3
SWS Silicones—facility ... MI-6
S W Tank—reservoir ... AZ-5
Swygert—locale ... IL-6
Swygert Branch—stream ... SC-3
Swygert Creek—stream ... SC-3
Swygert Lake—reservoir ... GA-3
Swygert Sch—school ... IL-6
S X Ranch—locale ... AZ-5
Sybelia, Lake—lake ... FL-3
**Sybene**—pop pl ... OH-6
Sybert—locale ... GA-3
Sybert Hollow—valley ... PA-2
Syberton—locale ... PA-2
**Sybertsville**—pop pl ... PA-2
Sybial ... WV-2
Sybial—other ... WV-2
Sybil ... AL-4
Sybil Brand Institute For Women—other ... CA-9
Sybilla ... MP-9
Sybilla-Inseln Gaspar ... MP-9
Sybil Lake—lake ... MN-6
Sybil Lake Cem—cemetery ... MN-6
Sybille Creek ... WY-8
Sybille Creek—stream ... WY-8
Sybille Game And Fish Experimental Unit—park ... WY-8
Sybille Sch—school ... WY-8
Sybille Springs—spring ... WY-8
Syble Point—cape ... AK-9
Sybrant Community Cem—cemetery ... NE-7
Sybrant Community Ch—church ... NE-7
Sybylee Creek ... WY-8
Sybylle creek ... WY-8
Sycamore ... DE-2
Sycamore ... MS-4
Sycamore—locale ... AZ-5
Sycamore—locale (2) ... AR-4
Sycamore—locale ... DE-2
Sycamore—locale ... FL-3
Sycamore—locale ... MO-7
Sycamore—locale ... OK-5
Sycamore—locale ... TN-4
Sycamore—locale ... TX-5
Sycamore—locale ... VA-3
Sycamore—locale (2) ... WV-2
**Sycamore**—pop pl ... AL-4
**Sycamore**—pop pl ... CA-9
**Sycamore**—pop pl ... GA-3
**Sycamore**—pop pl ... IL-6
**Sycamore**—pop pl ... IN-6
**Sycamore**—pop pl ... KS-7
**Sycamore**—pop pl ... KY-4
**Sycamore**—pop pl (2) ... OH-6
**Sycamore**—pop pl ... OR-9
**Sycamore**—pop pl ... PA-2
**Sycamore**—pop pl ... SC-3
**Sycamore**—pop pl ... TN-4
**Sycamore**—pop pl ... TX-5
**Sycamore**—pop pl (2) ... WV-2
Sycamore—uninc pl ... CA-9
Sycamore—uninc pl ... TN-4
**Sycamore Acres**—pop pl ... MD-2
Sycamore Ave Sch—school ... NY-2
Sycamore Baptist Ch ... AL-4
Sycamore Baptist Ch—church ... AL-4
Sycamore Basin—basin (2) ... AZ-5
Sycamore Basin Tank—reservoir (2) ... AZ-5
Sycamore Basin Trail—trail ... AZ-5
Sycamore Bend—bend ... GA-3
Sycamore Bend—bend ... VA-3
**Sycamore Bend**—pop pl ... AR-4
**Sycamore Bend Farm**—pop pl ... AR-4
Sycamore Bend Park—locale ... TX-5
Sycamore Bottom—flat ... TN-4
Sycamore Bottom—valley ... TN-4
Sycamore Branch ... WV-2
Sycamore Branch—stream ... FL-3
Sycamore Branch—stream ... IL-6
Sycamore Branch—stream ... IN-6
Sycamore Branch—stream (6) ... KY-4
Sycamore Branch—stream (2) ... MO-7
Sycamore Branch—stream ... NC-3
Sycamore Branch—stream (2) ... TN-4
Sycamore Branch—stream (4) ... TX-5
Sycamore Branch—stream (8) ... WV-2
Sycamore Bridge—bridge ... KS-7
Sycamore Bridge—other ... MO-7
Sycamore Buttes—summit ... AZ-5
Sycamore Camp—locale ... AZ-5
Sycamore Camp—locale ... NM-5
Sycamore Campground—locale (2) ... CA-9
Sycamore Canyon ... CA-9
Sycamore Canyon—valley (25) ... AZ-5
Sycamore Canyon—valley (25) ... CA-9
Sycamore Canyon—valley (3) ... NM-5
Sycamore Canyon—valley (3) ... TX-5
Sycamore Canyon Creek ... CA-9
Sycamore Canyon Sch—school ... CA-9
Sycamore Canyon Wilderness—park ... AZ-5
Sycamore Cave—cave ... AL-4
Sycamore Cave—cave ... MO-7
Sycamore (CCD)—cens area ... GA-3
Sycamore (CCD)—cens area ... SC-3
Sycamore Cem—cemetery ... GA-3
Sycamore Cem—cemetery ... IN-6
Sycamore Cem—cemetery ... KY-4
Sycamore Cem—cemetery (2) ... MO-7
Sycamore Cem—cemetery ... WV-2
Sycamore Ch—church ... AL-4
Sycamore Ch—church ... FL-3
Sycamore Ch—church ... IN-6
Sycamore Ch—church (2) ... KY-4
Sycamore Ch—church ... MI-6
Sycamore Ch—church ... MS-4
Sycamore Ch—church ... MO-7
Sycamore Ch—church ... NC-3
Sycamore Ch—church ... OH-6
Sycamore Ch—church (2) ... TN-4
Sycamore Ch—church ... TX-5
Sycamore Ch—church (3) ... VA-3
Sycamore Ch—church (2) ... WV-2
Sycamore Chapel—church ... KY-4
Sycamore Chapel—church ... NC-3
Sycamore Chapel—church ... OK-5
Sycamore Chapel—church ... TN-4
Sycamore Chapel Baptist Ch ... NC-3
Sycamore Ch (historical)—church ... MO-7
Sycamore Ch of Christ—church ... TN-4
**Sycamore Corner**—pop pl ... IN-6
Sycamore Corner Sch (historical)—school ... TN-4
Sycamore Cottage—hist pl ... MD-2
Sycamore Cove—bay ... RI-1
Sycamore Cove—bay ... TX-5
Sycamore Cove—valley ... OK-5
Sycamore Cree—stream ... TN-4
Sycamore Creek ... AL-4
Sycamore Creek ... AZ-5
Sycamore Creek ... CA-9
Sycamore Creek ... TN-4
Sycamore Creek ... TX-5
**Sycamore Creek**—pop pl ... MD-2
Sycamore Creek—stream (2) ... AL-4
Sycamore Creek—stream (13) ... AZ-5
Sycamore Creek—stream (7) ... AR-4
Sycamore Creek—stream (15) ... CA-9
Sycamore Creek—stream (3) ... IL-6
Sycamore Creek—stream (4) ... IN-6
Sycamore Creek—stream (3) ... KS-7
Sycamore Creek—stream (8) ... KY-4
Sycamore Creek—stream ... MI-6
Sycamore Creek—stream ... MS-4
Sycamore Creek—stream (6) ... MO-7
Sycamore Creek—stream (3) ... NM-5
Sycamore Creek—stream (2) ... NC-3
Sycamore Creek—stream (7) ... OH-6
Sycamore Creek—stream (4) ... OK-5
Sycamore Creek—stream (5) ... TN-4
Sycamore Creek—stream (20) ... TX-5
Sycamore Creek—stream (4) ... VA-3
Sycamore Creek—stream (9) ... WV-2
Sycamore Creek Cave—cave ... TN-4
Sycamore Creek Country Club—other ... OH-6
Sycamore Crossroads—locale ... VA-3
Sycamore Dale—hist pl ... WV-2
Sycamore Dam—dam ... AZ-5
Sycamore Dam—dam ... TN-4
Sycamore Dell Sch (historical)—school ... TN-4
Sycamore Drain—stream ... MI-6
Sycamore Drainage Ditch—canal ... IL-6
Sycamore Draw—valley ... TX-5
Sycamore Drive Sch—school ... NJ-2
Sycamore Elementary School ... AL-4
**Sycamore Estates**—pop pl ... KY-4
Sycamore Falls—falls ... OK-5
Sycamore Flat—flat (2) ... CA-9
Sycamore Flat—locale ... KY-4
**Sycamore Flat**—pop pl ... CA-9
Sycamore Flat Campground—locale ... CA-9
Sycamore Flat One Campground—locale ... CA-9
Sycamore Flats—flat ... CA-9
Sycamore Flats Picnic Area ... NC-3
Sycamore Flats Rec Area—park ... NC-3
Sycamore Flat Two Campground—locale ... CA-9
**Sycamore Ford**—pop pl ... IN-6
Sycamore Ford (historical)—crossing ... TN-4
Sycamore Forest Camp—locale ... AZ-5
Sycamore Fork ... WV-2
Sycamore Fork—stream ... IN-6
Sycamore Fork—stream (3) ... KY-4
Sycamore Fork—stream ... OH-6
Sycamore Fork—stream ... TN-4
Sycamore Fork—stream ... VA-3
Sycamore Fork—stream (7) ... WV-2
Sycamore Fork Dam ... TN-4
Sycamore Fork Hollow ... OH-6
Sycamore Gap—gap ... CA-9
**Sycamore Gardens**—pop pl ... DE-2
**Sycamore Gardens Subdivision**—pop pl ... UT-8
Sycamore Golf Course—other ... TX-5
Sycamore Grove ... AL-4
Sycamore Grove Cem—cemetery ... MS-4
Sycamore Grove Ch ... MS-4
Sycamore Grove Ch—church (2) ... AR-4
Sycamore Grove Ch—church ... MS-4
Sycamore Grove Ch—church ... MO-7
Sycamore Grove Ch—church ... WV-2
Sycamore Grove Ch (historical)—church ... MS-4
Sycamore Grove Park—park ... CA-9
Sycamore Grove Sch (historical)—school ... MS-4
Sycamore Gulch ... AZ-5
Sycamore Gulch—valley (3) ... AZ-5
Sycamore Gulch—valley ... CA-9
Sycamore Hall—locale ... TN-4
Sycamore Hall Sch (historical)—school ... TN-4
**Sycamore Heights**—pop pl ... MD-2
Sycamore Hill—summit ... CA-9
Sycamore Hill Ch—church ... NC-3
**Sycamore Hills**—pop pl ... IN-6
**Sycamore Hills**—pop pl ... MO-7
Sycamore Hist Dist—hist pl ... IL-6
**Sycamore (historical)**—pop pl ... MS-4
**Sycamore (historical)**—pop pl ... TN-4
Sycamore Hole—lake ... TX-5
Sycamore Hollow ... MO-7
Sycamore Hollow ... OH-6
Sycamore Hollow—valley (4) ... AR-4
Sycamore Hollow—valley ... KY-4
Sycamore Hollow—valley (5) ... MO-7
Sycamore Hollow—valley (3) ... OH-6
Sycamore Hollow—valley ... OK-5
Sycamore Hollow—valley (2) ... TN-4
Sycamore Hollow—valley (3) ... TX-5
Sycamore HS—school ... OH-6
Sycamore Island—island ... KY-4
Sycamore Island—island (2) ... MD-2
Sycamore Island—island ... PA-2
Sycamore Island—island ... VA-3
Sycamore Island Club—locale ... MD-2
Sycamore Island (historical)—island (2) ... TN-4
Sycamore Island Pleasure Club ... MD-2
Sycamore JHS—school ... AL-4
Sycamore JHS—school ... CA-9
Sycamore Junction—uninc pl ... WV-2
Sycamore Knobs—ridge ... TN-4
**Sycamore Knolls**—pop pl ... IN-6
Sycamore Lake—lake ... IN-6
Sycamore Lake—lake ... KY-4
Sycamore Lake—lake ... OH-6
Sycamore Lake—reservoir ... IN-6
Sycamore Lake—reservoir ... KY-4
Sycamore Lake—reservoir ... NJ-2
Sycamore Lake—reservoir ... TN-4
Sycamore Landing—hist pl ... TN-4
Sycamore Landing—locale ... VA-3
Sycamore Landing (historical)—locale ... AL-4
Sycamore Landing Post Office (historical)—building ... TN-4
Sycamore Lane MS—school ... NC-3
Sycamore Lick—stream ... WV-2
Sycamore Log Ch—church ... MO-7
Sycamore Lookout Tower—locale ... OK-5
Sycamore Mall (Shop Ctr)—locale ... IA-7
Sycamore Mesa—summit (2) ... AZ-5
**Sycamore Mills**—pop pl ... PA-2
Sycamore Mills Post Office (historical)—building ... TN-4
Sycamore Mills Site—hist pl ... TN-4
Sycamore Mountain ... AL-4
Sycamore MS—school ... TN-4
Sycamore Mtn—summit ... TX-5
Sycamore Park—park ... AR-4
Sycamore Park—park ... CA-9
Sycamore Park—park ... IN-6
Sycamore Park—park ... IA-7
Sycamore Park—park ... MI-6
Sycamore Park—park ... TX-5
Sycamore Pass ... AZ-5
Sycamore Pass—gap ... AZ-5
Sycamore Pass Tank—reservoir ... AZ-5
Sycamore Patch Island—island ... TN-4
Sycamore Plain Cem—cemetery ... IL-6
Sycamore Plantation—locale ... MS-4
Sycamore Plaza—locale ... IN-6
Sycamore Point—cape ... AR-4
Sycamore Point—cape (2) ... MD-2
Sycamore Point—cape ... NY-2
Sycamore Point—cape ... VA-3
Sycamore Point—cliff ... AZ-5
Sycamore Pond—lake ... MO-7
Sycamore Pond—reservoir ... SC-3
Sycamore Post Office (historical)—building ... MS-4
Sycamore Post Office (historical)—building (2) ... TN-4
Sycamore Powder Mill Landing (historical)—locale ... TN-4
Sycamore Ranger Station—locale ... AZ-5
Sycamore Ridge ... WV-2
Sycamore Ridge—ridge ... CA-9
Sycamore Ridge Camp—locale ... TX-5
Sycamore Rim—cliff ... AZ-5
Sycamore RR Station—building ... AZ-5
Sycamore Rsvr—reservoir ... AZ-5
Sycamore Rsvr—reservoir ... CA-9

Sycamore Run—*stream* IN-6
Sycamore Run—*stream* KY-4
Sycamore Run—*stream* OH-6
Sycamore Run—*stream* VA-3
Sycamore Run—*stream* (7) WV-2
Sycamore Sch—*hist pl* OH-6
Sycamore Sch—*school* (5) CA-9
Sycamore Sch—*school* (2) IL-6
Sycamore Sch—*school* (2) KY-4
Sycamore Sch—*school* MO-7
Sycamore Sch—*school* (2) OH-6
Sycamore Sch—*school* (2) TN-4
Sycamore Sch—*school* (2) WV-2
Sycamore Sch (historical)—*school* (2) AL-4
Sycamore Sch (historical)—*school* (3) MS-4
Sycamore Sch (historical)—*school* MO-7
Sycamore Sch (historical)—*school* (2) TN-4
*Sycamore Shoals* TN-4
Sycamore Shoals—*bar* TN-4
Sycamore Shoals—*hist pl* TN-4
Sycamore Shoals—*rapids* TN-4
Sycamore Shoals Ford—*locale* TN-4
Sycamore Shoals Hosp—*hospital* TN-4
Sycamore Shoals Island—*island* TN-4
Sycamore Shoals Monmt—*park* TN-4
Sycamore Shoals State Historic Area—*park* TN-4
Sycamore Siding—*locale* CA-9
Sycamore Slough—*gut* (2) CA-9
Sycamore Slough—*stream* AR-4
Sycamore Slough—*stream* (2) CA-9
*Sycamore Spring* AZ-5
*Sycamore Spring* CA-9
**Sycamore Spring**—*pop pl* TN-4
Sycamore Spring—*spring* (27) AZ-5
Sycamore Spring—*spring* (2) AR-4
Sycamore Spring—*spring* (8) CA-9
Sycamore Spring—*spring* MO-7
Sycamore Spring—*spring* NM-5
Sycamore Spring—*spring* TN-4
Sycamore Spring—*spring* (2) TX-5
Sycamore Spring Hollow—*valley* MO-7
*Sycamore Spring Reservoir* AZ-5
Sycamore Springs—*locale* CA-9
Sycamore Springs—*spring* AZ-5
Sycamore Springs—*spring* CA-9
Sycamore Springs—*spring* (2) TX-5
Sycamore Springs Creek—*stream* CA-9
Sycamore Springs Creek—*stream* TX-5
Sycamore Springs (historical)—*locale* KS-7
Sycamore Square—*post sta* VA-3
Sycamore Station—*locale* CA-9
Sycamore Street Hist Dist—*hist pl* MS-4
**Sycamore (subdivision)**—*pop pl* AL-4
**Sycamore (subdivision)**—*pop pl* NC-3
**Sycamore Subdivision**—*pop pl* UT-8
Sycamore Substation—*locale* AZ-5
Sycamore Swamp—*locale* TN-4
Sycamore Tank—*reservoir* (6) AZ-5
Sycamore Tank—*reservoir* (2) NM-5
Sycamore Tank Number One—*reservoir* AZ-5
Sycamore Tank Number Two—*reservoir* AZ-5
Sycamore Tavern—*hist pl* VA-3
**Sycamore Township**—*pop pl* (2) KS-7
**Sycamore (Township of)**—*pop pl* IL-6
**Sycamore (Township of)**—*pop pl* (2) OH-6
Sycamore Trail (loop)—*trail* AZ-5
Sycamore Tunnel—*tunnel* TN-4
Sycamore Valley—*hist pl* NC-3
**Sycamore Valley**—*pop pl* OH-6
**Sycamore Valley**—*pop pl* TN-4
Sycamore Valley—*valley* CA-9
Sycamore Valley Camp—*park* IN-6
Sycamore Valley Ch—*church* KS-7
Sycamore Valley Ch—*church* TN-4
Sycamore Valley Ch—*church* VA-3
Sycamore Valley Sch (historical)—*school* (2) TN-4
Sycamore Wash—*stream* AZ-5
Sycamore Well—*well* (2) AZ-5
Sycamore Well—*well* NM-5
Sycamore-Winterboro (CCD)—*cens area* AL-4
Sycamore-Winterboro Division—*civil* AL-4
Sycamore-13th Street Grouping—*hist pl* OH-6
**Sycan**—*pop pl* OR-9
Sycan Butte—*summit* OR-9
*Sycan Fire Forest Service Station* OR-9
Sycan Fire Guard Station—*locale* OR-9
Sycan Flat—*flat* OR-9
*Sycan Guard Station* OR-9
Sycan Marsh—*swamp* OR-9
Sycan River—*stream* OR-9
Sycan Siding—*locale* OR-9
**Sycaway**—*pop pl* NY-2
**Sychar Road**—*pop pl* OH-6
*Syckamoore Creek* TN-4
*Syclon* VA-3
**Syclon**—*pop pl* VA-3
*Syco* AL-4
Sycolin—*locale* VA-3
Sycolin Creek—*stream* VA-3
*Sycoline Creek* VA-3
**Sycuan Ind Res**—*pop pl* CA-9
Syd Cabin Glade—*flat* CA-9
Syd Cabin Ridge—*ridge* CA-9
Sydenham (historical)—*locale* AL-4
Sydenham Hosp—*hospital* MD-2
Sydenham Hosp—*hospital* NY-2
Sydenham House—*hist pl* NJ-2
Sydenstricker Ch—*church* OH-6
Sydenstricker Ch—*church* VA-3
Sydenton (historical)—*locale* AL-4
Sydenton Slope Mine (underground)—*mine* AL-4
Sydna (historical)—*locale* ND-7
Sydna Town Hall—*building* ND-7
**Sydna Township**—*pop pl* ND-7
Sydnes Island—*island* TX-5
*Sydney* AZ-5
**Sydney**—*pop pl* FL-3
**Sydney**—*pop pl* ND-7
Sydney Butte—*summit* ID-8
*Sydney Gulch* CA-9
*Sydney Island* TX-5
Sydney Lake—*lake* LA-4
*Sydney Lanier High School* AL-4
Sydney O Chase Junior Bridge—*bridge* FL-3
Sydney Pier—*locale* MP-9
Sydney Sch—*school* CA-9
Sydneys Pond—*reservoir* MA-1
Sydneys Pond Dam—*dam* MA-1
Sydneyton Post Office (historical)—*building* TN-4
Sydney Town Hall—*building* ND-7
Sydney Township—*civil* SD-7
**Sydney Township**—*pop pl* ND-7
**Sydnor Addition**—*pop pl* WV-2
**Sydnor Addition (West End)**—*pop pl* WV-2
Sydnor Bayou—*gut* TX-5
Sydnor Cem—*cemetery* KY-4
Sydnor Jennings Sch—*school* VA-3
Sydnors Mill Creek—*stream* VA-3
Sydnors Millpond—*lake* VA-3
Sydnorsville—*locale* VA-3
*Syenan Ind Res* CA-9
*Syenan Peak* CA-9
**Syenite**—*pop pl* MO-7
Syers Creek—*stream* MI-6
Syers Lake—*lake* MI-6
*Syers Run* IN-6
Syes Lake—*lake* GA-3
Syfax Point—*cape* NC-3
Syftestad Creek—*stream* WI-6
**Sygan**—*pop pl* PA-2
**Sygan Hill**—*pop pl* PA-2
Sygan Hollow—*valley* PA-2
Sygitowicz Creek—*stream* WA-9
*Sykan River* OR-9
Syke Cem—*cemetery* AL-4
Syke Knob—*summit* AZ-5
Sykes—*locale* CA-9
Sykes—*locale* MS-4
Sykes—*locale* TN-4
Sykes, Mount—*summit* OR-9
Sykes, Point—*cape* AK-9
Sykes and Alford Ditch—*valley* CO-8
*Sykes Bluff* MS-4
Sykes Branch—*stream* NJ-2
Sykes Branch—*stream* (2) TN-4
Sykes Brook—*stream* (2) MA-1
Sykes Camp—*locale* CA-9
Sykes Cave—*cave* MT-8
Sykes Cem—*cemetery* AL-4
Sykes Cem—*cemetery* NE-7
Sykes Cem—*cemetery* NC-3
Sykes Cem—*cemetery* OH-6
Sykes Cem—*cemetery* (3) TN-4
Sykes Cem—*cemetery* VA-3
Sykes Ch—*church* (2) MS-4
Sykes Cove—*bay* AK-9
Sykes Creek—*gut* FL-3
Sykes Creek—*stream* MS-4
Sykes Creek—*stream* OR-9
Sykes Creek—*stream* VA-3
*Sykes Elementary School* MS-4
Sykes Ferry—*locale* LA-4
Sykes Gap—*gap* NJ-2
Sykes Gulch—*valley* CO-8
Sykes Hill—*summit* TX-5
**Sykes (historical)**—*pop pl* MS-4
*Sykes Hollow* TN-4
Sykes Hollow—*valley* (2) TN-4
Sykes Hollow—*valley* VT-1
Sykes House—*hist pl* MA-1
Sykes Knob Picnic Area—*park* AZ-5
Sykes Lake—*lake* AK-9
Sykes Lake—*reservoir* NC-3
Sykes Lake Dam—*dam* MS-4
Sykes Lake Dam—*dam* NC-3
Sykes Landing—*locale* FL-3
Sykes Landing—*locale* MS-4
Sykes Landing—*locale* NC-3
Sykes Lateral—*canal* NM-5
Sykes-Leigh House—*hist pl* MS-4
Sykes Mill (historical)—*locale* AL-4
Sykes Mill (historical)—*locale* MS-4
*Sykes Mills* AL-4
Sykes Mill Tunnel—*tunnel* VA-3
Sykes Mtn—*summit* AL-4
Sykes Mtn—*summit* MA-1
Sykes Mtn—*summit* WY-8
Sykes Park—*park* MS-4
Sykes Pond—*lake* AL-4
Sykes Post Office (historical)—*building* TN-4
Sykes Ranch—*locale* TX-5
Sykes Ridge—*ridge* OH-6
Sykes Sch—*school* MI-6
Sykes Sch—*school* MS-4
Sykes Sch (historical)—*school* TN-4
Sykes Spring—*spring* AZ-5
Sykes Spring—*spring* WY-8
Sykes Station (historical)—*locale* PA-2
Sykes Swamp—*stream* SC-3
**Sykeston**—*pop pl* ND-7
Sykeston Dam—*dam* ND-7
**Sykeston Township**—*pop pl* ND-7
*Sykestown* NJ-2
**Sykesville**—*pop pl* MD-2
**Sykesville**—*pop pl* NJ-2
**Sykesville**—*pop pl* PA-2
Sykesville Borough—*civil* PA-2
Sykesville Elem Sch—*school* PA-2
Sykesville Hist Dist—*hist pl* MD-2
Sykes Water Gap—*lake* GA-3
Sykes Woods—*woods* WA-9
**Sylacauga**—*pop pl* AL-4
Sylacauga (CCD)—*cens area* AL-4
Sylacauga Ch of Christ—*church* AL-4
Sylacauga City Hall—*building* AL-4
Sylacauga City Hosp—*hospital* AL-4
Sylacauga Division—*civil* AL-4
Sylacauga HS—*school* AL-4
Sylacauga Rsvr—*reservoir* AL-4
Sylacauga Shop Ctr—*locale* AL-4
*Sylacauga State Secondary Agricultural School* AL-4
Sy Lake—*lake* WI-6
**Sylamore**—*pop pl* AR-4
Sylamore Bottom—*bend* AR-4
Sylamore Cem—*cemetery* AR-4
Sylamore (Township of)—*fmr MCD* AR-4
Sylan Lake—*lake* WI-6
Sylar Cem—*cemetery* TN-4
Sylavon Baptist Ch—*church* AL-4
*Sylavon Elementary School* AL-4
Sylavon Sch—*school* AL-4
Sylburn Harbor—*bay* AK-9
Sylco—*locale* TN-4
Sylco Campground—*locale* TN-4
Sylco Creek—*stream* TN-4
Sylco Creek Trail—*trail* TN-4
Sylco Inlet—*bay* TN-4
Sylco Post Office (historical)—*building* TN-4
Sylco Ridge—*ridge* TN-4
Syler Cem—*cemetery* TN-4
Syler Flat—*flat* UT-8
Syler Spring—*spring* UT-8
Syler Tabernacle—*church* AL-4
Syll Branch—*stream* MS-4
Sylman Valley—*valley* OR-9
Sylmar—*locale* PA-2
**Sylmar**—*pop pl* CA-9
**Sylmar**—*pop pl* MD-2
Sylmar HS—*school* CA-9
Sylmar Park—*park* CA-9
Sylmar Post Office—*building* CA-9
Sylmar Sch—*school* CA-9
*Sylone Cemetery* AL-4
Sylopash Point—*cape* WA-9
Syls Fork—*stream* GA-3
Sylva—*locale* NY-2
**Sylva**—*pop pl* NC-3
Sylva-Bay Acad—*school* MS-4
*Sylvailles River* OR-9
Sylvain, Bayou—*stream* LA-4
Sylvain Park—*park* IL-6
*Sylvan* AL-4
*Sylvan* MI-6
*Sylvan* WA-9
Sylvan—*locale* IL-6
Sylvan—*locale* MN-6
Sylvan—*locale* TX-5
**Sylvan**—*pop pl* AL-4
**Sylvan**—*pop pl* CO-8
**Sylvan**—*pop pl* OR-9
**Sylvan**—*pop pl* PA-2
**Sylvan**—*pop pl* WA-9
**Sylvan**—*pop pl* WI-6
Sylvan, Lake—*lake* FL-3
Syl-van, Lake—*lake* IN-6
Sylvan, Lake—*lake* (2) MN-6
Sylvan, Lake—*lake* MT-8
Sylvan, Lake—*reservoir* OH-6
Sylvan Abbey Memorial Park Cem—*cemetery* FL-3
Sylvan Acad (historical)—*school* TN-4
Sylvan Ave Sch—*school* NY-2
Sylvan Bay—*bay* WY-8
Sylvan Beach—*beach* ID-8
Sylvan Beach—*locale* WA-9
**Sylvan Beach**—*pop pl* MI-6
**Sylvan Beach**—*pop pl* (2) NY-2
Sylvan Beach—*uninc pl* TX-5
Sylvan Beach Park—*park* TX-5
Sylvan Bldg—*hist pl* SC-3
Sylvan Cem—*cemetery* AL-4
Sylvan Cem—*cemetery* CA-9
Sylvan Cem—*cemetery* CO-8
Sylvan Cem—*cemetery* MI-6
Sylvan Cem—*cemetery* NY-2
Sylvan Cem—*cemetery* WA-9
**Sylvan Center**—*pop pl* MI-6
Sylvan Ch—*church* AL-4
Sylvan Ch—*church* MN-6
Sylvan Ch—*church* MO-7
Sylvan Corners—*locale* CA-9
Sylvan Cove—*bay* WA-9
Sylvan Cove—*cove* MA-1
Sylvan Creek—*stream* (2) ID-8
Sylvan Creek—*stream* MI-6
Sylvan Creek—*stream* WY-8
Sylvandale Cem—*cemetery* NY-2
Sylvandale Sch—*school* CA-9
Sylvan Dale Sch—*school* MO-7
Sylvandale Sch—*school* WA-9
Sylvan Dam—*dam* MN-6
Sylvandell—*locale* KY-4
**Sylvan Dell**—*pop pl* (2) PA-2
Sylvan Dell Valley—*valley* MD-2
Sylvan Falls—*falls* NY-2
**Sylvan Glen**—*pop pl* NJ-2
Sylvan Glen Golf Course—*other* MI-6
Sylvan Grove—*locale* AL-4
Sylvan Grove—*locale* MD-2
Sylvan Grove—*locale* PA-2
**Sylvan Grove**—*pop pl* IN-6
**Sylvan Grove**—*pop pl* KS-7
Sylvan Grove Cem—*cemetery* MS-4
Sylvan Grove Ch—*church* AL-4
Sylvan Grove Ch—*church* PA-2
Sylvan Grove Elem Sch—*school* KS-7
Sylvan Grove HS—*school* KS-7
Sylvan Grove Sch (abandoned)—*school* PA-2
Sylvan Grove Sch (historical)—*school* AL-4
*Sylvan Hart Bar* ID-8
*Sylvan Hart ranch Bar* ID-8
Sylvan Heights Cem—*cemetery* PA-2
Sylvan Heights Memorial Gardens—*cemetery* PA-2
Sylvan Heights Sch—*school* TN-4
**Sylvan Hill**—*pop pl* IL-6
**Sylvan Hills**—*pop pl* AR-4
**Sylvan Hills**—*pop pl* GA-3
**Sylvan Hills**—*pop pl* IN-6
**Sylvan Hills**—*pop pl* (2) PA-2
Sylvan Hills Camp—*locale* PA-2
Sylvan Hills Ch—*church* AR-4
Sylvan Hills HS—*school* GA-3
Sylvan Hills Park—*park* MN-6
Sylvan Hills Sch—*school* GA-3
Sylvan (historical)—*locale* PA-2
Sylvania—*hist pl* IN-6
Sylvania—*hist pl* SC-3
Sylvania—*locale* FL-3
Sylvania—*locale* WI-6
**Sylvania**—*pop pl* AL-4
**Sylvania**—*pop pl* AR-4
**Sylvania**—*pop pl* GA-3
**Sylvania**—*pop pl* IN-6
**Sylvania**—*pop pl* KY-4
**Sylvania**—*pop pl* MO-7
**Sylvania**—*pop pl* NV-8
**Sylvania**—*pop pl* OH-6
**Sylvania**—*pop pl* PA-2
Sylvania, Mount—*summit* OR-9
Sylvania Borough—*civil* PA-2
Sylvania Burnham Sch—*school* OH-6
Sylvania Canyon—*valley* CA-9
Sylvania Canyon—*valley* NV-8
Sylvania (CCD)—*cens area* GA-3
Sylvania Cem—*cemetery* PA-2
Sylvania Cem—*cemetery* WI-6
Sylvania Ch—*church* FL-3
Sylvania Ch—*church* GA-3
Sylvania Ch—*church* IN-6
Sylvania Country Club—*other* OH-6
*Sylvania Creek* VA-3
Sylvania Guyot (not verified)—*other* MP-9
**Sylvania Heights**—*pop pl* PA-2
**Sylvania Heights**—*pop pl* VA-3
Sylvania Heights Sch—*school* FL-3
Sylvania Hills Cem—*cemetery* PA-2
Sylvania Hills Ch—*church* PA-2
Sylvania Lake—*lake* MN-6
Sylvania Lake—*lake* PA-2
Sylvania Lake Dam—*dam* NC-3
Sylvania Mine—*mine* (2) NV-8
Sylvania Mountains—*area* CA-9
Sylvania Mtns—*range* NV-8
Sylvania of the Rockies—*locale* CO-8
Sylvania Park—*park* MN-6
Sylvania Park—*park* TX-5
*Sylvania (Riverside)* TX-5
Sylvania Sch—*school* AL-4
Sylvania Sch—*school* FL-3
Sylvania Sch—*school* MO-7
Sylvania Sylvan Sch—*school* OH-6
Sylvania Township—*civil* MO-7
**Sylvania (Township of)**—*pop pl* OH-6
**Sylvania (Township of)**—*pop pl* PA-2
Sylvan Iris Sch—*school* IL-6
Sylvan Island—*island* GA-3
Sylvan Island—*island* IL-6
Sylvan Island—*island* NY-2
**Sylvanite**—*pop pl* MT-8
Sylvanite (Abandoned)—*locale* NM-5
Sylvanite Creek—*stream* AK-9
Sylvanite Lode Mine—*mine* SD-7
Sylvan JHS—*school* MI-6
*Sylvan Lake* FL-3
*Sylvan Lake* MA-1
*Sylvan Lake* WI-6
*Sylvan Lake* WY-8
Sylvan Lake—*lake* CO-8
Sylvan Lake—*lake* CT-1
Sylvan Lake—*lake* FL-3
Sylvan Lake—*lake* GA-3
Sylvan Lake—*lake* IL-6
Sylvan Lake—*lake* IN-6
Sylvan Lake—*lake* MA-1
Sylvan Lake—*lake* (3) MI-6
Sylvan Lake—*lake* (4) MN-6
Sylvan Lake—*lake* MO-7
Sylvan Lake—*lake* (2) MT-8
Sylvan Lake—*lake* NY-2
Sylvan Lake—*lake* PA-2
Sylvan Lake—*lake* WA-9
Sylvan Lake—*lake* WI-6
Sylvan Lake—*lake* WY-8
Sylvan Lake—*locale* FL-3
**Sylvan Lake**—*pop pl* IL-6
**Sylvan Lake**—*pop pl* MI-6
**Sylvan Lake**—*pop pl* NJ-2
**Sylvan Lake**—*pop pl* NY-2
Sylvan Lake—*reservoir* (3) NJ-2
Sylvan Lake—*reservoir* OH-6
Sylvan Lake—*reservoir* SD-7
Sylvan Lake Dam—*dam* NJ-2
Sylvan Lake Dam—*dam* SD-7
Sylvan Lake (historical)—*lake* IA-7
**Sylvan Lake Resort**—*pop pl* SD-7
Sylvan Lake Rock Shelter—*hist pl* NY-2
Sylvan Lakes—*lake* CO-8
**Sylvan Lane**—*pop pl* PA-2
**Sylvan Lodge**—*pop pl* CA-9
**Sylvan Manor**—*pop pl* IN-6
*Sylvan Methodist Church* AL-4
**Sylvan Mounds**—*pop pl* WI-6
Sylvan Park—*park* (2) CA-9
Sylvan Park—*park* IN-6
Sylvan Park—*park* KS-7
Sylvan Park—*park* ME-1
Sylvan Park—*park* NJ-2
Sylvan Park Sch—*school* CA-9
Sylvan Park Sch—*school* TN-4
Sylvan Pass—*gap* WY-8
Sylvan Peak—*summit* MT-8
*Sylvan Point* OR-9
Sylvan Pond—*lake* MI-6
Sylvan Ponds—*lake* NY-2
Sylvan Public Use Area—*park* KS-7
Sylvan Retreat—*hist pl* LA-4
Sylvan Retreat—*locale* IA-7
Sylvan Ridge—*ridge* MO-7
Sylvan Ridge—*ridge* WI-6
Sylvan Road Bridge—*hist pl* IL-6
Sylvan Rsvr—*reservoir* CO-8
Sylvan Run—*stream* VA-3
Sylvan Run—*stream* WV-2
Sylvan Saddle—*gap* ID-8
Sylvan Saint Sch—*school* PA-2
Sylvan Sch—*school* (2) CA-9
Sylvan Sch—*school* (2) IL-6
Sylvan Sch—*school* (2) MI-6
Sylvan Sch—*school* NJ-2
Sylvan Sch—*school* NC-3
Sylvan Sch—*school* OR-9
Sylvan Sch (abandoned)—*school* (2) MO-7
Sylvan Sch (historical)—*school* AL-4
Sylvan Shores—*CDP* (2) FL-3
**Sylvan Shores**—*pop pl* MD-2
Sylvan Slough—*stream* IL-6
Sylvan Spring—*spring* WY-8
**Sylvan Springs**—*pop pl* AL-4
*Sylvan Springs Elementary School* AL-4
Sylvan Springs Park—*park* MO-7
Sylvan Springs Rsvr—*reservoir* NY-2
Sylvan Springs Sch (historical)—*school* AL-4
Sylvan Street Presbyterian Ch—*church* AL-4
**Sylvan (Sylvan Center)**—*pop pl* MI-6
Sylvan Theatre—*building* DC-2
**Sylvan (Town of)**—*pop pl* WI-6
**Sylvan (Township of)**—*pop pl* (2) MI-6
**Sylvan (Township of)**—*pop pl* MN-6
Sylvanus Sch (historical)—*school* TN-4
**Sylvan View**—*pop pl* MD-2
Sylvan View Sch—*school* NE-7
Sylvan Way Trail—*trail* NH-1
Sylva Plaza (Shop Ctr)—*locale* NC-3
**Sylvarena**—*pop pl* MS-4
Sylvarena Acad (historical)—*school* MS-4
Sylvarena Attendance Center—*school* MS-4
*Sylvarena Baptist Church* MS-4
Sylvarena Cem—*cemetery* MS-4
Sylva Rena Cem—*cemetery* MS-4
Sylvarena Ch—*church* (2) MS-4
Sylva Rena Ch—*church* MS-4
Sylvarena Post Office—*building* MS-4
Sylva Rena Sch (historical)—*school* MS-4
Sylva Rsvr—*reservoir* NC-3
Sylva (Township of)—*fmr MCD* NC-3
**Sylvatus**—*pop pl* VA-3
Sylva-Webster HS—*school* NC-3
*Sylverena Cemetery* MS-4
Sylverino Ch—*church* AR-4
Sylvest Cem—*cemetery* LA-4
Sylvest Creek—*stream* LA-4
Sylvester—*locale* MI-6
Sylvester—*locale* PA-2
**Sylvester**—*pop pl* GA-3
**Sylvester**—*pop pl* TX-5
**Sylvester**—*pop pl* WV-2
Sylvester, Lake—*lake* WA-9
Sylvester-Beasly Ditch—*canal* MT-8
Sylvester Branch—*stream* AR-4
Sylvester Branch—*stream* KY-4
Sylvester (CCD)—*cens area* GA-3
Sylvester Cem—*cemetery* AL-4
Sylvester Cem—*cemetery* GA-3
Sylvester Cem—*cemetery* (2) ME-1
Sylvester Cem—*cemetery* (2) MS-4
Sylvester Cem—*cemetery* TX-5
Sylvester Ch—*church* (2) AL-4
Sylvester Ch—*church* (2) GA-3
Sylvester Ch—*church* MS-4
Sylvester Commercial Hist Dist—*hist pl* GA-3
*Sylvester Cove* ME-1
Sylvester Cove—*bay* ME-1
Sylvester Creek—*stream* (2) MI-6
Sylvester Creek—*stream* (2) WA-9
Sylvester Creek—*stream* WI-6
Sylvester Dam—*dam* WY-8
Sylvester Drive—*uninc pl* GA-3
Sylvester Gulch—*valley* CO-8
Sylvester Hill—*summit* ME-1
Sylvester Hill—*summit* OH-6
Sylvester Hollow—*valley* MO-7
Sylvester Lake—*lake* MN-6
Sylvester Maroney Ditch—*canal* IN-6
Sylvester Park—*park* WA-9
Sylvester Place—*locale* OR-9
Sylvester Point—*cape* ME-1
*Sylvester Pond* MA-1
*Sylvester Pond* RI-1
Sylvester Ridge—*ridge* ME-1
Sylvester Rock—*rock* MA-1
Sylvester Run—*stream* OH-6
Sylvester Sch—*school* MA-1
Sylvester Sch—*school* MS-4
Sylvester Spring—*spring* AZ-5
Sylvester Spring—*spring* CA-9
**Sylvester (sta.)**—*pop pl* WV-2
**Sylvester (Town of)**—*pop pl* WI-6
Sylvest House—*hist pl* LA-4
*Sylvestra Cemetery* MS-4
Sylvestra Methodist Ch (historical)—*church* MS-4
Sylvestre Pond—*reservoir* RI-1
*Sylvestres Pond* RI-1
Sylvestria Cem—*cemetery* MS-4
Sylvestria (historical)—*locale* MS-4
Sylvestri Pond—*reservoir* MA-1
*Sylvia* IA-7
**Sylvia**—*pop pl* KS-7
**Sylvia**—*pop pl* TN-4
Sylvia, Lake—*lake* CA-9
Sylvia, Lake—*lake* (2) FL-3
Sylvia, Lake—*lake* MN-6
Sylvia, Lake—*reservoir* AR-4
Sylvia Branch—*stream* WV-2
Sylvia Cem—*cemetery* KS-7
Sylvia Chapel—*church* NC-3
Sylvia Creek—*stream* AK-9
Sylvia Creek—*stream* WA-9
Sylvia Elem Sch—*school* KS-7
Sylvia Falls—*falls* WA-9
Sylvia (historical)—*locale* SD-7
*Sylvia Lake* MN-6
Sylvia Lake—*lake* FL-3
Sylvia Lake—*lake* MT-8
Sylvia Lake—*lake* NY-2
Sylvia Lake—*reservoir* MN-6
Sylvia Lake—*reservoir* NJ-2
Sylvia Lake—*reservoir* WA-9
Sylvia Lake Dam—*dam* NJ-2
Sylvia Lake State Park—*park* WA-9
**Sylvia Lane**—*pop pl* SC-3
Sylvia Mine—*mine* MT-8
Sylvian—*locale* OK-5
Sylvian Branch—*stream* IN-6
Sylvian Oil Field—*oilfield* OK-5
**Sylvia Park**—*pop pl* CA-9
Sylvia Sch—*school* WV-2
Sylvia Township*—*civil* KS-7
**Sylvia Township**—*pop pl* KS-7
**Sylvia Township**—*pop pl* SD-7
*Sylvilles River* OR-9
Sylvina Wilson Ditch—*canal* OH-6
Sylvinia Lake—*reservoir* NC-3
*Sylvin Lake* MN-6
Sylvis—*locale* PA-2
Sylvis Creek—*stream* WA-9
*Symans Hill* MA-1
Symbol—*locale* KY-4
Symbol Bridge—*bridge* CA-9
Symbol Ridge—*ridge* OR-9
Symbol Rock—*pillar* OR-9
**Symco**—*pop pl* WI-6
Symentire Spring—*spring* OR-9
**Symerton**—*pop pl* IL-6
Symes And Deerlove Ditch—*canal* WY-8
*Symes Creek* OH-6
Symes JHS—*school* VA-3
Symington House—*hist pl* NJ-2
Symington Sch—*school* MO-7
*Symmes* OH-6
Symmes—*locale* OH-6
Symmes, Stephen, Jr., House—*hist pl* MA-1
Symmes Branch—*stream* WV-2
Symmes Chapel—*church* SC-3
*Symmes Corner* OH-6
Symmes Corner—*locale* OH-6
**Symmes Corner (subdivision)**—*pop pl* MA-1
Symmes Creek—*stream* CA-9
Symmes Creek—*stream* (2) OH-6
Symmes Creek Ch—*church* OH-6
Symmes Hosp—*hospital* MA-1
Symmes Mission Chapel—*hist pl* OH-6
Symmes Pond—*lake* ME-1
**Symmes (Township of)**—*pop pl* IL-6
**Symmes (Township of)**—*pop pl* (2) OH-6
Symmes Valley Ch—*church* OH-6
Symmes Valley HS—*school* OH-6
Symmetry Spire—*pillar* WY-8
Symmons Gulch—*valley* ID-8
Symms Gap—*gap* VA-3
Symms Gap—*gap* WV-2
Symns, J. A., Barn—*hist pl* KS-7
*Symond Creek* NC-3
**Symonds**—*pop pl* MS-4
Symonds, Thomas, House—*hist pl* MA-1
Symonds Bay—*bay* AK-9
**Symonds Creek**—*pop pl* NC-3
Symonds Creek—*stream* IN-6
Symonds Creek—*stream* NC-3
Symonds Creek Tabernacle—*church* NC-3
Symonds Hill—*summit* NY-2
Symonds Hill Sch—*school* NY-2
Symonds Point—*cape* AK-9
Symonds Pond—*lake* NH-1
Symonds Sch—*school* NH-1
*Symons Creek* IN-6
Symons Creek—*stream* IN-6
Symons Ditch—*canal* IN-6
Symons Drain—*canal* MI-6
*Symons Hill* MA-1
Symons House—*hist pl* MS-4
Symons Landing—*locale* GA-3
Symons Ranch—*locale* (2) CA-9
Symons Wood Camp—*locale* OR-9
Sympaug Brook—*stream* CT-1
Sympaug Pond—*lake* CT-1
Symphony and Horticultural Halls—*hist pl* MA-1
Symphony Hall—*building* MA-1
Symphony House—*hist pl* ME-1
Symphony Lake—*lake* AK-9
Sympson Lake—*reservoir* KY-4
Symrna Ch—*church* SC-3
**Symsonia**—*pop pl* KY-4
Symsonia (CCD)—*cens area* KY-4
Symsonia Cem—*cemetery* KY-4
Synacia Creek—*stream* GA-3
Synacia Creek—*stream* NC-3
**Synagogue**—*pop pl* MS-4
Synagogue-Dilworth Sch (historical)—*school* MS-4
Synagogue Gap—*gap* PA-2
*Synagogue Gap Run* PA-2
Synagogue Missionary Baptist Ch—*church* MS-4
*Synagouge* MS-4
Synaground Sch—*school* SD-7
Synama Grove Ch—*church* NC-3
Synarep—*locale* WA-9
*Syncline Canyon* UT-8
Syncline Divide—*gap* CA-9
Syncline Hill—*summit* CA-9
Syncline Hill—*summit* CO-8
Syncline Mtn—*summit* AK-9
Syncline Ridge—*ridge* NV-8
Syncline Valley—*valley* UT-8
Synder, John J., House—*hist pl* CA-9
Synder Access Rec Area—*park* IA-7
Synder Cem—*cemetery* IL-6
*Synder Lake* MI-6
Synder Pond—*reservoir* PA-2
Synder Swamp—*stream* VA-3
**Syndicate**—*pop pl* IN-6
Syndicate Gulch—*valley* SD-7
Syndicate Hills—*summit* TX-5
Syndicate Mill—*locale* CA-9
Syndicate Mine—*mine* UT-8
**Syndicate Place Subdivision**—*pop pl* UT-8
Syndicate Sch—*school* ND-7
Syndicate Wash—*stream* AZ-5
*Synepuxent* MD-2
*Synepuxent Bay* MD-2
Syner—*locale* PA-2
*Synider Lake* MI-6
**Synnes (Township of)**—*pop pl* MN-6
Synneva Creek—*stream* AK-9
*Synocia Creek* GA-3
*Synocia Creek* NC-3
Synod Cem—*cemetery* IA-7
Synod Cem—*cemetery* MN-6
Synope Plantation House—*hist pl* LA-4
Synopsis Mine—*mine* CO-8
Synsteby Site—*hist pl* MN-6
Synthianna Creek—*stream* MO-7
**Syosset**—*pop pl* NY-2
Syosset HS—*school* NY-2
Syosset Woodbury Park—*park* NY-2
Sypah Creek—*stream* ID-8
Sypert Branch—*stream* TX-5
Sypes Canyon—*valley* MT-8
Sypes Creek—*stream* MT-8
Syphax Sch—*school* DC-2
Sypher Brook—*stream* NH-1
*Sypher Draw* NM-5
Sypher Gulch—*valley* OR-9
Syphers Ranch—*locale* NM-5
Syphon Creek—*stream* MI-6
Syphon Lake—*lake* MI-6
Sypolt Run—*stream* WV-2
**Syracuse**—*pop pl* IN-6
**Syracuse**—*pop pl* KS-7
**Syracuse**—*pop pl* MO-7
**Syracuse**—*pop pl* NE-7
**Syracuse**—*pop pl* NY-2
**Syracuse**—*pop pl* OH-6
**Syracuse**—*pop pl* SC-3
**Syracuse**—*pop pl* UT-8
Syracuse Cem—*cemetery* KS-7
Syracuse Cem—*cemetery* UT-8
*Syracuse Church* TN-4
Syracuse City Hall—*hist pl* NY-2
Syracuse Country Club—*other* KS-7
Syracuse Creek—*stream* KS-7

# T

T ... AL-4
T ... AZ-5
T ... FL-3
T—reservoir ... TX-5
T, Mount—summit ... AK-9
T, Peak—summit ... AK-9
T, Rock—bar ... ME-1
T, The—lake ... AL-4
Taabab ... FM-9
Taabikku Suido ... MP-9
Taabikku To ... MP-9
Taabiywol—summit ... FM-9
Taabow—cape ... FM-9
Taacame ... MA-1
Taafean—summit ... FM-9
**Taafniith**—pop pl ... FM-9
**Ta'agan Point**—pop pl ... CT-1
Taagow—cape ... FM-9
Taah Iiti Wash—stream ... AZ-5
Taain Creek—stream ... AK-9
Taal, Lake—reservoir ... TN-4
Taala Bogue Creek ... MS-4
Taalah Creek ... MS-4
Taalay ... FM-9
Ta'aley ... FM-9
Taalgum—locale ... FM-9
Taalguw—summit ... FM-9
Taaneaqaaw—cape ... FM-9
Taangal—cape ... FM-9
Taanoonsogon—summit ... FM-9
Taapuw—cape ... FM-9
Taapuwoogachaal—summit ... FM-9
Taapuyappu—island ... FM-9
Taaquul—cape ... FM-9
Taaquum—summit ... FM-9
Taar ... MP-9
Taarin Island—island ... FM-9
Taaru To ... MP-9
Taasahdi Dzil—summit ... AZ-5
Taayer, Lake—lake ... ND-7
Tab—cape ... PW-9
**Tab**—pop pl ... IN-6
Tabagaten River ... PW-9
Tabaha Well—well ... AZ-5
Tabahinez Mesa—summit ... AZ-5
Tabal Island—island ... MP-9
Tabamapauge Pond ... RI-1
Tabanacle ... AL-4
Tabar To ... MP-9
Tabaru-to ... MP-9
Tabasco—locale ... NY-2
Tabasco Creek—stream ... AK-9
Tabasco Oil And Gas Field—oilfield ... TX-5
Tabaseca Tank—reservoir ... CA-9
Tabatiere Perdue—locale ... LA-4
**Tabb**—pop pl (2) ... VA-3
Tabb, Edward, House—hist pl ... WV-2
Tabb Cem—cemetery ... GA-3
Tabb Ch—church ... VA-3
Tabb (historical)—locale ... MS-4
Tabbie Mountain ... UT-8
Tabb Lake—reservoir ... AL-4
Tabb No 1 Mine—mine ... KY-4
Tabbot Narrows ... ME-1
Tabbott Ledge ... ME-1
Tabbott Narrows ... ME-1
Tabbott Rock ... ME-1
Tabbott's Rock ... ME-1
Tabbs Bay—bay ... TX-5
Tubbs Chapel Sch (historical) school ... MS-4
Tabbs Creek—stream ... NC-3
Tabbs Creek—stream (3) ... VA-3
Tabbs Creek Ch—church ... NC-3
Tabbs Creek Sch—school ... NC-3
Tabbs Hollow—valley ... KY-4
Tabbs Point—cape ... VA-3
Tabb Street Prebyterian Church—hist pl ... VA-3
Tabbville—locale ... MS-4
Tabbville Post Office (historical)—building ... MS-4
Tabby Canal—canal ... UT-8
Tabby Canyon—valley ... UT-8
Tabby Creek—stream ... GA-3
Tabby Creek—stream ... UT-8
Tabby House—hist pl ... FL-3
Tabby Manse—hist pl ... SC-3
Tabby Mtn—summit ... UT-8
Tabbys Canyon—valley ... UT-8
Tabbys Peak—summit ... UT-8
Tabbys Spring—spring ... UT-8
Tabby Swale—valley ... UT-8
Tabbyune Canyon—valley ... UT-8
Tabbyune Creek—stream ... UT-8
Tabcat Creek—stream ... TN-4
Tab Creek—stream ... GA-3
Tabeascot Lake—lake ... AK-9
Tabeaud, Lake—reservoir ... CA-9
Tabeaud Rsvr ... CA-9
Tabecheding—falls ... PW-9
Tabecheding—stream ... PW-9
Tabeelaeng—locale ... FM-9
Tabeguache Basin—basin ... CO-8
Tabeguache Creek—stream ... CO-8
Tabeguache Mountain ... CO-8
Tabeguache Peak—summit ... CO-8
Tabelang ... FM-9
Taber—locale ... ID-8
Taber—locale ... VA-3
Taber Cem—cemetery ... IN-6
Taber Cem—cemetery ... MO-7
Taber Creek—stream ... LA-4
Taber Duplex—hist pl ... FL-3
**Taberg**—pop pl ... NY-2
Taber Hill—summit ... ME-1
Taber Hill—summit ... VT-1
Taber Mine—mine ... CA-9
Taber Morey Canyon—valley ... NM-5
Tabernacle—locale ... GA-3
Tabernacle—locale ... KY-4
Tabernacle—locale ... MD-2
**Tabernacle**—pop pl (2) ... AL-4
**Tabernacle**—pop pl ... NJ-2
**Tabernacle**—pop pl (2) ... TN-4
**Tabernacle**—pop pl ... VA-3
Tabernacle, The—church ... FL-3
Tabernacle, The—church ... NC-3
Tabernacle, The—church (2) ... SC-3
Tabernacle, The—church ... TN-4
Tabernacle, The—summit ... AZ-5
Tabernacle, The—summit ... UT-8
Tabernacle AME Zion Ch—church ... AL-4
Tabernacle Baptist Ch—church (6) ... AL-4
Tabernacle Baptist Ch—church (4) ... FL-3
Tabernacle Baptist Ch—church ... KS-7
Tabernacle Baptist Ch—church ... MS-4
Tabernacle Baptist Ch—church ... NC-3
Tabernacle Baptist Ch—church (3) ... TN-4
Tabernacle Baptist Ch of Gautier—church ... MS-4
Tabernacle Baptist Church, The—church ... DE-2
Tabernacle Baptist Sch—school ... FL-3
Tabernacle Branch—stream ... AR-4
Tabernacle Branch—stream ... TX-5
Tabernacle Butte ... WY-8
Tabernacle Butte—summit ... WY-8
Tabernacle Campground—locale ... GA-3
Tabernacle (CCD)—cens area ... TN-4
Tabernacle Cem—cemetery (4) ... AL-4
Tabernacle Cem—cemetery (2) ... GA-3
Tabernacle Cem—cemetery ... MD-2
Tabernacle Cem—cemetery (4) ... MS-4
Tabernacle Cem—cemetery ... NC-3
Tabernacle Cem—cemetery ... SC-3
Tabernacle Cem—cemetery (2) ... TN-4
Tabernacle Cem—cemetery ... VA-3
Tabernacle Cem—cemetery ... WI-6
Tabernacle Ch ... AL-4
Tabernacle Ch—church (11) ... AL-4
Tabernacle Ch—church (3) ... AR-4
Tabernacle Ch—church ... FL-3
Tabernacle Ch—church (7) ... GA-3
Tabernacle Ch—church (2) ... KY-4
Tabernacle Ch—church ... MD-2
Tabernacle Ch—church ... MI-6
Tabernacle Ch—church (9) ... MS-4
Tabernacle Ch—church ... MO-7
Tabernacle Ch—church (17) ... NC-3
Tabernacle Ch—church ... OH-6
Tabernacle Ch—church (9) ... SC-3
Tabernacle Ch—church (5) ... TN-4
Tabernacle Ch—church (3) ... TX-5
Tabernacle Ch—church (11) ... VA-3
Tabernacle Ch (historical)—church ... AL-4
Tabernacle Ch (historical)—church ... MS-4
Tabernacle Ch of Deliverance—church ... FL-3
Tabernacle Ch of God in Christ—church ... KS-7
Tabernacle Christian Sch—school ... FL-3
Tabernacle Crater—crater ... UT-8
Tabernacle Division—civil ... TN-4
Tabernacle Dome—summit ... UT-8
Tabernacle Fellowship Ch—church ... FL-3
Tabernacle Hill—summit ... UT-8
Tabernacle (historical)—locale ... AL-4
**Tabernacle (historical)**—pop pl ... MS-4
Tabernacle Lookout—locale ... TX-5
Tabernacle Lookout Tower—locale ... TN-4
Tabernacle Methodist Ch ... AL-4
Tabernacle Methodist Ch ... MS-4
Tabernacle Methodist Ch—church ... AL-4
Tabernacle Methodist Ch—church ... MS-4
Tabernacle Missionary Baptist Ch—church (2) ... FL-3
Tabernacle Mountain ... TX-5
Tabernacle Mtn—summit ... AK-9
Tabernacle of Charity Ch—church ... MO-7
Tabernacle of Life Ch—church ... AL-4
Tabernacle of Prayer Ch—church ... MS-4
Tabernacle Park—park ... UT-8
Tabernacle Post Office (historical)—building ... TN-4
Tabernacle Presbyterian Ch—church ... IN-6
Tabernacle Ridge—ridge ... UT-8
Tabernacle Sch—school (2) ... NC-3
Tabernacle Sch—school (4) ... SC-3
Tabernacle Sch—school ... TN-4
Tabernacle Sch (historical)—school ... AL-4
Tabernacle Sch (historical)—school (2) ... MS-4
Tabernacle (Township of)—fmr MCD ... NC-3
**Tabernacle (Township of)**—pop pl ... NJ-2
Tabernacle United Methodist Church ... AL-4
Tabernacle Witness of Holy Deliverance Ch—church ... AL-4
**Tabernash**—pop pl ... CO-8
Tabernash Campground—locale ... CO-8
Taberncle Hill ... UT-8
Taber Point—cape ... MA-1
Tabert Lake—lake ... AK-9
Tabertown ... IN-6
**Tabertown**—pop pl ... IN-6
Taber Township—civil ... MO-7
**Taberville**—pop pl ... MO-7
Tabet Draw—valley ... NM-5
Tabguw ... FM-9
Tab Hollow—valley (2) ... TN-4
Tab Hollow—valley ... UT-8
Tabiigaaw—summit ... FM-9
Tabiilaeng—summit ... FM-9
Tabik—island ... MP-9
Tabik Channel—channel ... MP-9
Tabik Island ... MP-9
Tabikku-suido ... MP-9
Tabikku-to ... MP-9
Tabik Pass ... MP-9
Tabilaeg—summit ... FM-9
Tabilag ... FM-9
Tabilang ... FM-9
Tabinefi ... FM-9
Tabinif ... FM-9
Tabinifi ... FM-9
Tabinnifiy ... FM-9
**Tabiona**—pop pl ... UT-8
Tabiona Cemetery ... UT-8
Tabiona HS—school ... UT-8
Tabiona-Redcliff Cem—cemetery ... UT-8
Tabitekku ... MP-9
Tabitha Ch—church ... MN-6
Tabitha Home—locale ... NE-7
Tabitha Nelson Farm Site—locale ... MA-1
Tabitha Springs—spring ... UT-8
Tabithow—airport ... FM-9
Tabiygaw ... FM-9
Tablag ... FM-9
Tablas Tank—reservoir ... TX-5
Tabl'ay—bar ... FM-9
Tablazon Canyon—valley ... NM-5
Table—fmr MCD ... NE-7
Table—summit ... WY-8
Table, The—bench ... NV-8
Table, The—summit ... OR-9
Table Bay—bay ... AK-9
Table Bay—bay ... MT-8
Table Bench—bench ... UT-8
Table Bluff—cliff ... CA-9
Table Bluff—cliff (2) ... WI-6
Table Bluff—summit ... CA-9
Table Bluff Lighthouse—locale ... CA-9
**Table Bluff Rancheria**—pop pl ... CA-9
Table Branch—stream ... TX-5
Table Butte ... CA-9
Table Butte—summit (2) ... ID-8
Table Butte—summit ... MT-8
Table Butte—summit ... NV-8
Table Butte—summit ... NM-5
Table Butte—summit (2) ... ND-7
Table Butte—summit ... SD-7
Table Butte—summit ... UT-8
Table Butte Well—well ... ID-8
Table Camp—locale ... WA-9
Table Center Sch—school ... NE-7
Table Cliff—cliff ... UT-8
Table Cliff Creek ... UT-8
Table Cliff Plateau ... UT-8
Table Cliff Plateau—plateau ... UT-8
Table Creek ... NE-7
Table Creek—stream ... CA-9
Table Creek—stream ... MT-8
Table Creek—stream (4) ... OR-9
Table Creek—stream ... WA-9
Table Creek—stream ... WY-8
Table Gap—gap ... TX-5
Table Glade—flat ... OR-9
Table Grounds—flat ... UT-8
**Table Grove**—pop pl ... IL-6
Table Grove Community Church—hist pl ... IL-6
Table Hill ... CA-9
Table Hill ... OR-9
Table Hill—summit ... MS-4
Table Hill—summit ... MT-8
Table Hill—summit ... OK-5
Table Island—island (2) ... AK-9
Table Knoll—summit ... UT-8
Table Knoll Rsvr—reservoir ... UT-8
Table Lake—lake ... CA-9
Table Lake—lake ... MN-6
Table Lake—lake ... OR-9
Table Lake—lake ... WA-9
Table Lakes—lake ... NV-8
Tableland—area ... CA-9
Table Land—cens area ... CO-8
Table Land—cliff ... ME-1
Table Land—ridge ... OR-9
Tableland Ditch—canal ... WY-8
Tableland Rsvr—reservoir ... OR-9
Table Lands—ridge ... ID-8
Table Lands, The ... AZ-5
Tablelands, The—bench ... AZ-5
Tableland Sch—school ... NE-7
Table Legs Butte—summit ... ID-8
Tableman Cem—cemetery ... IN-6
Table Meadow—locale ... CA-9
Table Meadow Creek—stream ... CA-9
Table Meadows—flat ... CA-9
Table Meadows—flat ... ID-8
Table Mesa ... CO-8
Table Mesa ... WY-8
Table Mesa—summit ... KS-7
Table Mesa—summit ... NM-5
Table Mesa Interchange—crossing ... AZ-5
Table Mesa Oil Field—other ... NM-5
Table Mound—summit ... KS-7
Table Mound—summit ... UT-8
Table Mound Reservoir ... KS-7
Table Mounds—summit ... KS-7
Table Mound Sch—school ... IA-7
Table Mound Township—fmr MCD ... IA-7
Table Mountain ... CO-8
Table Mountain ... ID-8
Table Mountain ... NV-8
Table Mountain ... UT-8
Table Mountain ... WY-8
Table Mountain—ridge (2) ... CA-9
Table Mountain—ridge ... NV-8
Table Mountain Antenna Field Sites—area ... CO-8
Table Mountain Campground—locale ... CA-9
Table Mountain Canyon—valley ... AZ-5
Table Mountain Community Hall—locale ... WY-8
Table Mountain Creek—stream ... OR-9
Table Mountain Cutoff Trail (pack)—trail ... OR-9
Table Mountain District—hist pl ... CA-9
Table Mountain Ditch—canal ... CO-8
Table Mountain Ditch—canal (2) ... WY-8
Table Mountain Ditch Extension—canal ... WY-8
Table Mountain Draw—valley ... WY-8
Table Mountain Gulch—valley ... OR-9
Table Mountain Lateral—canal ... WY-8
Table Mountain Mine—mine ... AZ-5
Table Mountain Municipal Golf Course—other ... CA-9
Table Mountain Plateau—plain ... AZ-5
Table Mountain Ranch—locale ... WY-8
Table Mountain Spring—spring ... AZ-5
Table Mountain Spring—spring ... NV-8
Table Mountain Spring—spring (2) ... OR-9
Table Mountain Spring Number Two—spring ... OR-9
Table Mountain Tank—reservoir (4) ... AZ-5
Table Mountain Township—civil ... SD-7
Table Mountain Trail—trail ... AZ-5
Table Mountain Trail—trail ... ID-8
Table Mountain Trail—trail ... MT-8
Table Mountain Trail—trail (2) ... OR-9
Table Mountain Trail—trail ... WA-9
Table Mountain Trail—trail ... WY-8
Table Mountain Well—well ... OR-9
Table Mtn ... AZ-5
Table Mtn ... CA-9
Table Mtn ... OR-9
Table Mtn—summit (7) ... AK-9
Table Mtn—summit (15) ... AZ-5
Table Mtn—summit (22) ... CA-9
Table Mtn—summit (8) ... CO-8
Table Mtn—summit (6) ... ID-8
Table Mtn—summit (8) ... MT-8
Table Mtn—summit (15) ... NV-8
Table Mtn—summit ... NH-1
Table Mtn—summit (4) ... NM-5
Table Mtn—summit ... NY-2
Table Mtn—summit (15) ... OR-9
Table Mtn—summit ... SD-7
Table Mtn—summit ... TX-5
Table Mtn—summit (10) ... UT-8
Table Mtn—summit (5) ... WA-9
Table Mtn—summit (21) ... WY-8
Table Point—cape ... GA-3
Table Point Archeol District—hist pl ... GA-3
Tabler ... WV-2
Tabler—locale ... OK-5
Tabler Branch—stream ... TN-4
Tabler Cem—cemetery ... IN-6
Table Rock ... AZ-5
Table Rock ... NC-3
Table Rock—bar ... NY-2
Table Rock—island ... AK-9
Table Rock—island (2) ... OR-9
Table Rock—locale ... MD-2
Tablerock—locale ... NC-3
Table Rock—locale ... WV-2
Table Rock—pillar ... AZ-5
Table Rock—pillar ... CA-9
Table Rock—pillar ... ID-8
Table Rock—pillar ... NE-7
Table Rock—pillar ... NH-1
Table Rock—pillar (3) ... OR-9
**Table Rock**—pop pl ... MO-7
**Table Rock**—pop pl ... NE-7
**Table Rock**—pop pl ... OR-9
**Table Rock**—pop pl ... PA-2
**Tablerock**—pop pl ... WV-2
**Table Rock**—pop pl ... WY-8
Table Rock—ridge ... MN-6
Table Rock—summit (8) ... CA-9
Table Rock—summit (2) ... CO-8
Table Rock—summit (2) ... ID-8
Table Rock—summit ... ME-1
Table Rock—summit ... MO-7
Table Rock—summit ... NY-2
Table Rock—summit (8) ... OR-9
Table Rock—summit ... SC-3
Table Rock—summit ... VT-1
Table Rock—summit (2) ... WA-9
Table Rock—summit ... WY-8
Table Rock Airp—airport ... MO-7
Table Rock Archeol Site—hist pl ... NE-7
Table Rock Branch—stream ... NC-3
Table Rock Canyon—valley ... AZ-5
Table Rock Canyon—valley ... ID-8
Table Rock Ch—church ... AR-4
Tablerock Ch—church ... NC-3
Table Rock Ch—church ... WV-2
Table Rock Creek ... OR-9
Table Rock Creek—stream (2) ... KS-7
Table Rock Creek—stream ... OR-9
Table Rock Creek—stream ... TX-5
Table Rock Cross—rock ... ID-8
Table Rock Dam—dam ... MO-7
Table Rock Fish Hatchery Dam—dam ... NC-3
Table Rock Fish Hatchery Lake—reservoir ... NC-3
Table Rock Fork—stream ... OR-9
Table Rock Heliport—airport ... MO-7
Tablerock Hill—summit ... RI-1
Table Rock Knob—summit ... MO-7
Table Rock Lake—lake ... AR-4
Table Rock Lake—reservoir ... MO-7
Table Rock Mountain ... OR-9
Table Rock Mtn ... SC-3
Table Rock Mtn—summit ... NC-3
Tablerock Mtn—summit ... NC-3
Table Rock Mtn—summit ... TN-4
Table Rock Oil And Gas Field—oilfield ... WY-8
Table Rock Opera House—hist pl ... NE-7
Table Rock Reservoir ... AR-4
Table Rock Resident Office and Visitor Center—building ... MO-7
Table Rock Ridge—ridge ... NY-2
Table Rock Rsvr ... MO-7
Table Rock Rsvr—reservoir ... SC-3
Table Rock School (abandoned)—locale ... OR-9
Table Rock Spring—spring ... AZ-5
Table Rock Spring—spring ... UT-8
**Table Rock (sta)**—pop pl ... OR-9
Tablerock State Fish Hatchery—locale ... NC-3
Table Rock State Park—park ... MO-7
Table Rock State Park—park ... SC-3
Table Rock Station—locale ... PA-2
Table Rock Tank—reservoir ... AZ-5
**Table Rock Townsite**—pop pl ... MO-7
Tablers ... WV-2
**Tablers Station**—pop pl ... WV-2
**Tablers (Tablers Station)**—pop pl ... WV-2
Table Rsvr—reservoir ... ID-8
Table Rsvr—reservoir (2) ... OR-9
Tables of the Sun Hills—summit ... UT-8
Table Spring—spring ... AZ-5
Table Spring—spring ... ID-8
Table Spring—spring ... OR-9
Table Top ... AZ-5
Table Top—cape ... WA-9
Table Top—cemetery ... CA-9
Table Top—flat ... OR-9
Table Top—summit ... AK-9
Table Top—summit (3) ... AZ-5
Table Top—summit ... CO-8
Table Top—summit ... MT-8
Table Top—summit ... NM-5
Table Top—summit ... TX-5
Table Top—summit ... UT-8
Tabletop—summit ... WY-8
Table Top Butte—summit ... SD-7
Tabletop Cliff—cliff ... KY-4
Table Top Gulch—valley ... MT-8
Table Top Mesa—summit ... AZ-5
Table Top Mountains—summit ... AZ-5
Table Top Mtn ... AZ-5
Tabletop Mtn ... CA-9
Table Top Mtn ... TN-4
Table Top Mtn—summit (3) ... AK-9
Table Top Mtn—summit (2) ... AZ-5
Table Top Mtn—summit ... CA-9
Table Top Mtn—summit ... CO-8
Table Top Mtn—summit ... MT-8
Table Top Mtn—summit ... NV-8
Tabletop Mtn—summit ... NV-8
Table Top Mtn—summit ... NM-5
Table Top Mtn—summit ... NY-2
Tabletop Mtn—summit ... OK 5
Tabletop Mtn—summit (2) ... TX-5
Table Top Mtn—summit (2) ... TX-5
Table Top Number Two Tank—reservoir ... AZ-5
Table Top Peak ... AZ-5
Table Top Ranch—locale ... CO-8
Table Top Rsvr—reservoir ... OR-9
Table Top Summit—summit ... UT-8
Table Top Tank—reservoir (2) ... AZ-5
Table Top Valley—valley ... AZ-5
Tabletree Hollow—valley ... KY-4
Tablet Rock—rock ... MA-1
Table Wash—valley ... WY-8
**Tablonal**—pop pl ... PR-3
**Tablones**—pop pl ... PR-3
Tablow—locale ... KY-4
**Tabnifiy**—pop pl ... FM-9
Tabo Ch—church ... SC-3
Tabo Creek ... MD-2
Tabo Creek—stream ... MO-7
Tabola Cem—cemetery ... TX-5
Tabolt Corners—locale ... NY-2
**Tabonuco**—pop pl (2) ... PR-3
Tabonuco (Barrio)—fmr MCD ... PR-3
Tabook Point—cape ... WA-9
Taboose Creek—stream ... CA-9
Taboose Pass—gap ... CA-9
Taboose Ranch—locale ... CA-9
Tabor ... NE-7
Tabor—locale ... CO-8
Tabor—locale ... IL-6
Tabor—locale ... KS-7
Tabor—locale ... OK-5
Tabor—locale ... TX-5
**Tabor**—pop pl ... AL-4
**Tabor**—pop pl ... IA-7
**Tabor**—pop pl ... MN-6
**Tabor**—pop pl ... NJ-2
**Tabor**—pop pl ... OH-6
**Tabor**—pop pl ... PA-2
**Tabor**—pop pl ... SD-7
**Tabor**—pop pl ... TN-4
**Tabor**—pop pl ... WI-6
Tabor, Lake—reservoir ... NC-3
Tabor, Mount—summit ... CT-1
Tabor, Mount—summit ... MA-1
Tabor, Mount—summit ... OR-9
Tabor, Mount—summit ... VT-1
Tabor Branch—stream ... GA-3
Tabor Branch—stream ... KY-4
Tabor Branch—stream ... NC-3
Tabor Branch—stream ... VT-1
Tabor Cave—cave ... MO-7
Tabor Cem—cemetery ... CT-1
Tabor Cem—cemetery ... IN-6
Tabor Cem—cemetery ... KS-7
Tabor Cem—cemetery ... KY-4
Tabor Cem—cemetery ... MA-1
Tabor Cem—cemetery ... MN-6
Tabor Cem—cemetery ... MS-4
Tabor Cem—cemetery ... NE-7
Tabor Cem—cemetery (2) ... NC-3
Tabor Cem—cemetery ... ND-7
Tabor Cem—cemetery (2) ... SD-7
Tabor Cem—cemetery ... TN-4
Tabor Cem—cemetery ... VT-1
Tabor Cem—cemetery ... VA-3
Tabor Cem—cemetery (3) ... WV-2
Tabor Cem—cemetery (3) ... WI-6
Tabor Ch—church ... AL-4
Tabor Ch—church ... GA-3
Tabor Ch—church (3) ... IN-6
Tabor Ch—church ... IA-7
Tabor Ch—church ... MN-6
Tabor Ch—church (3) ... NC-3
Tabor Ch—church ... OH-6
Tabor Ch—church ... PA-2
Tabor Ch—church ... SC-3
Tabor Ch—church ... SD-7
Tabor Ch—church ... TX-5
Tabor Ch—church ... WV-2
Tabor Ch—church (2) ... WI-6
Tabor Chapel—church ... GA-3
Tabor Chapel—church ... KS-7
**Tabor City**—pop pl ... NC-3
Tabor City Elementary/HS—school ... NC-3
Tabor City West JHS—school ... NC-3
Tabor Community Center—building ... TX-5
Tabor Corners—locale ... NY-2
Tabor Creek ... MS-4
Tabor Creek—stream ... CO-8
Tabor Creek—stream (2) ... MO-7
Tabor Creek—stream ... NV-8
Tabor Creek—stream ... WV-2
Tabor Diggings—mine ... OR-9
Tabor Flats—flat ... NV-8
Tabor Grand Mine—mine ... WY-8
Tabor Gulch—valley ... WY-8
Tabor Hill—summit ... KS-7
Tabor (historical)—locale ... KS-7
**Tabor (historical)**—pop pl ... TN-4
Tabor Hollow—valley ... MO-7
Tabor Home—building ... PA-2
Tabor Home for Needy and Destitute Children—hist pl ... PA-2
Taborian Hall—hist pl ... AR-4
Tabor Lake—lake ... CO-8
Tabor Lake—lake ... OH-6
Tabor Lake—lake ... WI-6
**Tabor (local name Mount Tabor)**—pop pl ... NJ-2
Tabor Lutheran Ch—church ... SD-7
Tabor Missionary Baptist Ch ... AL-4
Tabor Mountain Cem—cemetery ... TX-5
Tabor Mtn—summit ... MT-8
Tabor Notch—gap ... NH-1
Tabor Ore Bank—mine ... TN-4
Tabor Pond—lake ... VT-1
Tabor Post Office (historical)—building ... TN-4
Tabor Rec Area—park ... SD-7
Tabor Reformed Church—hist pl ... PA-2
Tabor Reservoir ... MT-8
Tabor Run—stream ... IN-6
Tabors—locale ... VA-3
Tabor Sch—hist pl ... SD-7
Tabor Sch—school ... KS-7
Tabor Sch—school ... MO-7
Tabor Sch—school ... SC-3
Tabor Sch—school ... TN-4
Tabor Sch (historical)—school ... AL-4
Tabor Spring—spring ... MO-7
Tabor Spring—spring ... WY-8
**Taborton**—pop pl ... NY-2
Tabor Township—civil ... SD-7
Tabor Township (historical)—civil ... SD-7
**Tabor (Township of)**—pop pl ... MN-6
Tabor Valley—valley ... KS-7
**Taborville**—pop pl ... OH-6
Tabor-Wing House—hist pl ... NY-2
Tabour Ch—church ... KS-7
Tabox Sch—school ... MA-1
Tabregeyam Point ... PW-9
Tabrkeam—cape ... PW-9
Tabscott—locale ... VA-3
Tabscott Cem—cemetery ... KY-4
Tabs Creek ... VA-3
Tabta—island ... MP-9
Tabuguw—locale ... FM-9
Tabu Island—island ... MP-9
Tabunfiy ... FM-9
Tabuniff ... FM-9
Tabunifi ... FM-9

Taihonom...MH-9
Taijogan—area...GU-9
Tail-a-koom...WA-9
Tailawampa Ch—church...AL-4
Tail Creek—stream...WY-8
Tailes Creek—stream...TX-5
Tail Feather Coulee—valley...MT-8
Tailhold Mesa...AZ-5
Tailholt...IN-6
Tailholt...KS-7
Tail Holt...MS-4
**Tailholt**—pop pl...OK-5
Tailholt Creek—stream...ID-8
Tailholt Mesa—summit...AZ-5
Tail Holt Mine—mine...MT-8
Tailholt Mines—mine...CO-8
Tailholt Mtn—summit...NM-5
Tail Holt Spring—spring...CA-9
Tailing Pond—reservoir...PA-2
Tailings Creek—stream...NV-8
Tailings Dam...AZ-5
Tailings Gulch—valley...CA-9
Tailings Pond—lake...DE-2
Tailings Pond—lake...IN-6
Tailings Pond—lake...KY-4
Tailings Pond—reservoir...TN-4
Tailings Pond Number Eight—reservoir...TN-4
Tailings Pond Number Eight Dam—dam...TN-4
Tailings Pond Number Eleven—reservoir...TN-4
Tailings Pond Number Eleven Dam—dam...TN-4
Tailings Pond Number Five—reservoir...TN-4
Tailings Pond Number Nine—reservoir...TN-4
Tailings Pond Number One—reservoir...AZ-5
Tailings Pond Number Seven—reservoir...TN-4
Tailings Pond Number Seven Dam—dam...TN-4
Tailings Pond Number Ten—reservoir (2)...TN-4
Tailings Pond Number Three—reservoir...AZ-5
Tailings Pond Number Three—reservoir...TN-4
Tailings Pond Number Twelve—reservoir...TN-4
Tailings Pond Number Two—reservoir...AZ-5
Tailings Pond Number Two—reservoir...TN-4
Tailings Pond Number 12 Dike...TN-4
Tailings Pond Number 2—reservoir...AL-4
Tailings Pond Number 2 Dam...TN-4
Tailings Water Reclamation Dam—dam...AZ-5
Tailings Water Reclamation Rsvr—reservoir...AZ-5
Tail Lake—lake...MN-6
Tail Lake—lake...UT-8
Taille de Noyer—hist pl...MO-7
Tail Of The Square Handkerchief Shoal—bar...MS-4
Tail Race—canal...NY-2
Tailrace Canal—canal...CA-9
Tailrace Canal—canal...SC-3
Tailrace Canal—canal...UT-8
Tailrace Rec Area...SD-7
Tailrace Rec Area—park...SD-7
Tail Run—stream...IN-6
Tails Creek...TX-5
Tails Creek—locale...GA-3
Tails Creek—stream...GA-3
Tails Creek Ch—church...GA-3
Tailwaters Rec Area—park...SD-7
Tailwood Sch—school...VA-3
Taimama'—slope...MH-9
Tainamu Point—cape...AS-9
Tain Branch—stream...VA-3
Taine Mtn—summit...CT-1
Tainer Lake—lake...MI-6
Tainter, Louis Smith, House—hist pl...WI-6
Tainter, Mabel, Memorial Bldg—hist pl...WI-6
Tainter Ch—church...WI-6
Tainter Corner—locale...ME-1
Tainter Creek—stream (2)...WI-6
Tainter Lake—reservoir...WI-6
**Tainter (Town of)**—pop pl...WI-6
Taintor—locale...PA-2
**Taintor**—pop pl...IA-7
Taintor Creek...WI-6
Taintor Creek—stream...OK-5
Taintor Desert—plain...MT-8
Taintor Fork Canyon Creek—stream...MT-8
Taintor Hill—summit...CT-1
Taint Rsvr—reservoir...MT-8
Taintsuku...MH-9
Taipingon...MH-9
Taipingon Point...MH-9
Taipingot—summit...MH-9
Taipingot, Puntan—cape...MH-9
Taipinkoto...MH-9
Taira Jima...FM-9
Tairappu-to...MP-9
Taira-Shima...FM-9
Tairiti...HI-9
Taisani Island—island...AK-9
Tai's Landing Airp—airport...WA-9
Taisu-to...MP-9
Tait—locale...PA-2
Tait Bar—bar...AL-4
Tait Bridge—other...IL-6
Tait Brook—stream...NY-2
Tait Canyon—valley...UT-8
Tait Cem—cemetery...AL-4
Tait Corners—locale...NY-2
Tait Island—island...AL-4
Tait Lake—lake...MN-6
Tait Landing (historical)—locale...AL-4
Tait Memorial Park—park...MO-7
**Taiton**—pop pl...TX-5
Tait River—stream...MN-6
Taits Gap—gap...AL-4
Taits Gap—locale...AL-4
Taits Gap Ch—church...AL-4
Taits Gap Drift Mine (underground)—mine...AL-4
Taits Lake—lake...MN-6
Taits Landing...AL-4
Taits Middle Landing (historical)—locale...AL-4
**Taitsville**—pop pl...MO-7
Tait-Taylor House—hist pl...MS-4
Tait Well—well...NV-8
Taiwel—island...MP-9
Taixtsalda Hill—summit...AK-9
Taiya...AK-9
Taiya Inlet—bay...AK-9
Taiya Point—cape...AK-9
Taiya River—stream...AK-9
Taiyasanka Harbor—bay...AK-9
Tajanio Pinto Tank—reservoir...NM-5
Tajauta—civil...CA-9
Tajea Flat—flat...CA-9
Tajea Spring—spring...CA-9
Tajiguas—locale...CA-9
Tajiguas Creek—stream...CA-9
Tajiguas Ranch—locale...CA-9
**Tajique**—pop pl...NM-5
Tajique Cabin—locale...NM-5
Tajitos—lake...TX-5
Tajittro Creek—stream...AK-9
Tajones Creek...TX-5
Tajunga Canyon...CA-9
Taka...MP-9
Taka—island...MP-9
Taka Atoll—island (2)...MP-9
Takahula Lake—lake...AK-9
Takahula River—stream...AK-9
Takai...MP-9
Takai—island...FM-9
Takaiehu...FM-9
Takaieu—island...FM-9
Takaieu, Dolen—summit...FM-9
Takain...FM-9
Takain Ilol—summit...FM-9
Takain Mwas—summit...FM-9
Takain Ripkapehd—summit...FM-9
Taka Inseln...MP-9
Taka Island...MP-9
Taka Island—island...MP-9
Takai-to...MP-9
Takaiu...FM-9
Takai Uh...FM-9
Takaiuh—island...FM-9
Takaiu Island...FM-9
Takaiu Islands...FM-9
Takaiwa...MP-9
Takaiwa Byochi...MP-9
Takaiwa Hakuchi...MP-9
Takaiwa-suido...MP-9
Takaiwa-to...MP-9
Takaiyu...FM-9
Taka Lagoon—lake...MP-9
Takalai, Lake—reservoir...AZ-5
Takamushikan—bar...MP-9
Takamushikan-To...MP-9
Takanassee, Lake—reservoir...NJ-2
Takanis Bay—bay...AK-9
Takanis Creek—stream...AK-9
Takanis Lake—lake...AK-9
Takanis Peak—summit...AK-9
Takanis Peninsula—cape...AK-9
Taka Ocooloo River - in part...MS-4
Taka Passage—channel...MP-9
Takareppu...MP-9
Takareppuiisuto-to...MP-9
Takareppu Isoto To...MP-9
Takareppullsuto-To...MP-9
Takareppu-to...MP-9
Takareppu-tsuro...MP-9
Takassah Ridge—ridge...NC-3
Takasuna To...FM-9
Takateikku-To...FM-9
Takateikky-To...FM-9
Takatik...FM-9
Takatik Island...FM-9
Takatz Bay—bay...AK-9
Takatz Creek—stream...AK-9
Takatz Islands—area...AK-9
Takatz Lake—lake...AK-9
Takavo...MP-9
Takayofo Creek—stream...AK-9
Takeena Peninsula—cape...AK-9
Takee Tegi...MP-9
Take-In Creek—stream...WV-2
Take-In Ridge—ridge...WV-2
Take In Swamp—swamp...FL-3
Takeiu...FM-9
Take Jima...FM-9
Takemmy...MA-1
Takemmy (historical)—locale...MA-1
Takenaarun...MP-9
Takenaarun Island...MP-9
Takenaarun Island—island...MP-9
Takenaarun (not verified)—island...MP-9
Takena Park—park...OR-9
Takeoa...MP-9
Take Shima...FM-9
Takeshima Hakuchi...FM-9
Taket Creek...AK-9
Take-to...MP-9
Takhakhdona Hills—other...AK-9
Takhin Glacier—glacier...AK-9
Takhin Ridge—ridge...AK-9
Takhin River—stream...AK-9
Takhinsha Mountains—ridge...AK-9
Takhlakh Lake—lake...WA-9
Takhlakh Pond...WA-9
Takh Takh Meadow—flat...WA-9
Takiki...AL-4
**Takilma**—pop pl...OR-9
Takima, Lake—lake...AR-4
Takiol...FM-9
Takitezy—locale...PA-2
Takleb...MP-9
Taklebej...MP-9
Takleblol—island...MP-9
Tak-lib...MP-9
Tak-li b-ej...MP-9
Taklib Island...MP-9
Tak-lib-lol'...MP-9
Tak-lib Passage...MP-9
Takli Island—island...AK-9
Takli Island Archeol District—hist pl...AK-9
Tako Island—island...FM-9
Takoka Creek—stream...AK-9
Takoma Acad—school...MD-2
Takoma Bluff—cliff...AK-9
Takoma Cove—bay...AK-9
Takoma Creek—stream...AK-9
Takomahto Lake—lake...AK-9
**Takoma Park**—pop pl...MD-2
Takoma Park—uninc pl...DC-2
Takoma Park Hist Dist—hist pl...DC-2
Takoma Park Hist Dist—hist pl...MD-2
Takoma Park JHS—school...MD-2
Takoma Park Sch—school...DC-2
Takoma Sch—school...DC-2
Takonak Creek—stream...AK-9
Takonaki Island...PW-9
Takonran Island—island...FM-9
**Takotna**—pop pl...AK-9
Takotna ANV956—reserve...AK-9
Takotna Mtn—summit...AK-9
Takotna River—stream...AK-9
Takowa—island...MP-9
Takowa Anchorage—harbor...MP-9
Takowa Channel—channel...MP-9
Takowa Insel...MP-9
Takowa Island...MP-9
Takpochao—slope...MH-9
Takpochao, Laderon—cliff...MH-9
Takpochao, Okso'—summit...MH-9
Takpochau...MH-9
Takrak Lake—lake...AK-9
Taksakwivik Slough—gut...AK-9
**Takshak**—pop pl...AK-9
Takshanuk Mountains—ridge...AK-9
Takshilik Creek—stream...AK-9
Takslesluk Lake—lake...AK-9
Taksunok—slope...MH-9
Takta—slope...MH-9
Taktelak Creek—stream...AK-9
Taktusak Hill—summit...AK-9
Takuak Creek—stream...AK-9
Taku Channel—channel...AK-9
Takucho...MH-9
Takucmich Lake—lake...MN-6
Taku Creek—stream...AK-9
Taku Glacier—glacier...AK-9
Taku Harbor—bay...AK-9
Taku Harbor—locale...AK-9
Taku Inlet—bay...AK-9
Takukak Lake—lake...AK-9
Taku Lake—lake...AK-9
Taku Lodge—locale...AK-9
Taku Mtn—summit...AK-9
Taku Point—cape...AK-9
Takup Point...WA-9
Taku Range—other...AK-9
Taku River—stream...AK-9
Taku Towers—summit...AK-9
Takwaklanuk Slough—stream...AK-9
Talaalgi Tcapko Popka...FL-3
**Tala Apopka (historical)**—pop pl...FL-3
**Talache**—pop pl...ID-8
Talache Creek—stream...ID-8
Talache Landing—locale...ID-8
Talache Mine—mine...ID-8
Talachulitna Creek—stream...AK-9
Talachulitna Lake—lake...AK-9
Talachulitna River—stream...AK-9
Talac Lake—lake...MN-6
Taladega Post Office (historical)—building...MS-4
Talag Haya...MH-9
Talagu...FM-9
Talaguw...FM-9
Talahi Improvements—hist pl...TN-4
Talahi Island—island...GA-3
Talahi Park—park...MN-6
Talahogan...AZ-5
Talahogan Canyon—valley...AZ-5
Talahogan Spring...AZ-5
Talahogan Spring—spring...AZ-5
Tala Hogan Wash...AZ-5
Talahogan Wash—stream...AZ-5
Talaisina Stream—stream...AS-9
Talajasy...FL-3
Talakaya...MH-9
Talakayan...MH-9
Talakhatchee River...AL-4
Talakhatchee River...FL-3
Talakhaya—slope...MH-9
**Talala**—pop pl...OK-5
Talala Creek—stream...OK-5
Ta-lale, Lake—reservoir...AL-4
Talaloa Stream—stream...AS-9
Talamantes...CA-9
Talamantes Creek—stream...CO-8
Talamantoes Creek...CO-8
Talangith—locale...FM-9
Talangith—summit...FM-9
Talangiz...FM-9
Talante (Barrio)—fmr MCD...PR-3
Talap Island—island...FM-9
Tala Point—cape...WA-9
Talapoosa—locale...NV-8
Talapus, Mount—summit...OR-9
Talapus Butte—summit...OR-9
Talapus Creek—stream...ID-8
Talapus Creek—stream...WA-9
Talapus Lake—lake...WA-9
Talarhun River—stream...AK-9
Talasahatchie...AL-4
Talase...AL-4
Talasee Hatchee...AL-4
Talasha Creek...MS-4
Talasihatchie...AL-4
Talatekah...AL-4
Talatha...SC-3
**Talatha**—pop pl...SC-3
Talatha Ch—church...SC-3
Talatha-Hawthorne Sch—school...SC-3
Tala Town...MS-4
Talawa, Lake—lake...CA-9
Talawag Canyon—valley...UT-8
Talawanda Creek...OH-6
Talawanda No 1, Lake—reservoir...OK-5
Talawanda No 2, Lake—reservoir...OK-5
Talawanda Springs—locale...OH-6
Talawa Slough—stream...CA-9
Talaxe River...GA-3
Talaya Hill—ridge...NM-5
Talaya Hill Rsvr—reservoir...NM-5
Talber Cem—cemetery...OK-5
Talbert (2)...CA-9
Talbert—locale...KY-4
Talbert, Mount—summit...OR-9
Talbert Branch...SC-3
Talbert Branch—stream...AL-4
Talbert Branch—stream...MO-7
Talbert Branch—stream...SC-3
Talbert-Cassels House—hist pl...MS-4
Talbert Cem—cemetery (3)...MS-4
Talbert Cem—cemetery...VA-3
Talbert Channel—canal...CA-9
Talbert Creek...NV-8
Talbert Creek—stream...TX-5
Talbert Crossing—locale...TX-5
Talbert Dam—dam...AL-4
Talbert Ditch—canal...IN-6
Talbert Fire Tower (historical)—locale...MO-7
Talbert Gulch—valley...CO-8
Talbert Hosp—hospital...OH-6
Talbert Lake...AL-4
Talbert Lake—reservoir...AL-4
Talbert Landing—locale...AR-4
Talbert Pond Dam—dam...MS-4
Talbert Sch—school...KY-4
Talbert Spring—spring...MO-7
Talbiksok River—stream...AK-9
**Talbird**—pop pl...NC-3
Talbor Cem—cemetery...SC-3
Talbot...TN-4
Talbot...WV-2
Talbot—locale...MI-6
**Talbot**—pop pl...IN-6
**Talbot**—pop pl...OR-9
Talbot, James R., House—hist pl...ME-1
Talbot, Mount—summit...AK-9
Talbot Branch—stream...MD-2
Talbot Brook—stream...NH-1
Talbot Butte—summit...ND-7
Talbot Campground—locale...CA-9
Talbot Canal—canal...LA-4
Talbot Canyon—valley...WY-8
Talbot Cem—cemetery...MN-6
**Talbot (County)**—pop pl...GA-3
**Talbot (County)**—pop pl...MD-2
Talbot County Courthouse—hist pl...GA-3
Talbot Cove—bay...ME-1
Talbot Creek—stream...CA-9
Talbot Creek—stream...IL-6
Talbot Creek—stream...NV-8
Talbot Creek—stream...NY-2
Talbot Creek—stream...OR-9
Talbot Field—locale...MA-1
Talbot Grove Ch—church...GA-3
Talbot Gulch—valley...ID-8
Talbot Hill—summit...ME-1
Talbot Hollow...IL-6
Talbot Hollow—valley...VT-1
Talbot Island—island...FL-3
Talbot Island Cem—cemetery...FL-3
Talbot Lake—lake...AK-9
Talbot Lake—lake...TX-5
Talbot Landing—locale...LA-4
Talbot Lateral—canal...NM-5
Talbot Mills Dam...MA-1
**Talbot Park**—pop pl...VA-3
Talbot Pond...MA-1
Talbot Pond—lake...MI-6
Talbot Ridge—ridge...ME-1
Talbots Branch—stream...VA-3
Talbot Sch—school...IL-6
Talbot Sch—school (2)...MA-1
Talbot Sch (historical)—school...MS-4
Talbots Island...NY-2
Talbots Mill (historical)—locale...TN-4
Talbots Pond...MA-1
Talbot Spring—spring...WY-8
Talbot Swamp—swamp...NH-1
Talbott—dam...VA-3
Talbott—locale...WV-2
**Talbott**—pop pl...IL-6
**Talbott**—pop pl...TN-4
Talbott Cem—cemetery...IL-6
Talbott Cem—cemetery...IN-6
Talbott Creek...ID-8
Talbott Creek...OR-9
Talbott Hollow—valley...IL-6
**Talbotton**—pop pl...GA-3
Talbotton (CCD)—cens area...GA-3
Talbotton Sch—school...GA-3
**Talbot Township**—pop pl...ND-7
Talbott Post Office (historical)—building...TN-4
Talbott Quarry—mine...TN-4
Talbotts Branch—stream...NC-3
Talbott Sch—school...IL-6
Talbott Sch—school...TN-4
Talbott Slough—stream...OR-9
Talbotville...PA-2
Talby Creek—stream...WA-9
Talc—locale...MT-8
Talc Canyon—valley...CA-9
Talc City Hills—summit...CA-9
Talc Creek—stream...ID-8
Talc Mountain—locale...NC-3
Talc Mtn—summit...WA-9
**Talco**—pop pl...SC-3
**Talco**—pop pl...TX-5
Talco (CCD)—cens area...TX-5
Talco City Pumping Station—other...TX-5
Talco Oil Field—oilfield...TX-5
Talco Rodeo Ground—locale...TX-5
Talcose—locale...PA-2
Talcot Lake—lake...MN-6
Talcot Lake State Wildlife Mngmt Area—park...MN-6
**Talcott**—pop pl...SC-3
**Talcott**—pop pl...WV-2
Talcott, Joseph, House—hist pl...OH-6
Talcott Cem—cemetery...MA-1
Talcott Corners—locale...NY-2
Talcott Creek—stream...OH-6
Talcott Dam—dam...CT-1
Talcott Falls—falls...NY-2
Talcott Falls Site—hist pl...NY-2
Talcott JHS—school...CT-1
Talcott Lake...MN-6
Talcott Mtn—summit...CT-1
Talcott-Page Park—park...IL-6
Talcott Park—park...CT-1
Talcott Sch—school...IL-6
Talcott Sch—school...ME-1
**Talcott Village**—pop pl...CT-1
**Talcottville**—pop pl...CT-1
**Talcottville**—pop pl...NY-2
Talcpacana (historical)—locale...AL-4
Talcum—locale...KY-4
Talcut Draw—valley...SD-7
**Talcville**—pop pl...NY-2
**Talcville**—pop pl...VT-1
Taldaar—bay...FM-9
Talebenela Creek...MS-4
Talega Canyon—valley...CA-9
Talegu...FM-9
Taleman Gulch...CO-8
T A Lemaster Pond Dam—dam...MS-4
Tale Mountain Branch—stream...NC-3
**Talent**—pop pl...OR-9
Talent Branch—stream...KY-4
Talent Branch—stream...TN-4
Talent Cem—cemetery...KY-4
Talent Hollow—valley (2)...TN-4
Talent JHS—school...OR-9
Talent Knob—summit...GA-3
Talent Lateral—canal...OR-9
Talequah...WA-9
Taleyfac—area...GU-9
Taleyfac Bay—bay...GU-9
Taleyfac River—stream...GU-9
Taleyfac Spanish Bridge—hist pl...GU-9
Talford Brook—stream...NH-1
Talge Lake—lake...MN-6
Talguw...FM-9
Talhok, Lake—lake...AK-9
Talhonio...MA-1
Talhchoze Tohe Meadow—flat...AZ-5
Taliaferro, T. C., House—hist pl...FL-3
Taliaferro Bend—bend...TN-4
Taliaferro Branch—stream...TN-4
**Taliaferro (County)**—pop pl...GA-3
Taliaferro County Courthouse—hist pl...GA-3
Taliaferro Creek—stream...GA-3
Taliaferro Gap—gap...TN-4
Taliaferro Island (historical)—island...TN-4
Taliaferro Pond—lake...VA-3
Taliaferro Ridge—ridge...CA-9
Taliaferro Springs—spring...GA-3
Taliapakana...AL-4
Talica—uninc pl...CA-9
Talich—locale...CA-9
Taliesin...AZ-5
Taliesin—hist pl...WI-6
Taliesin West—hist pl...AZ-5
Taliesin West—locale...AZ-5
Taligai Cove—bay...AS-9
Tali Gap—gap...NC-3
Taliglig...FM-9
Tali Hata Creek...MS-4
**Talihina**—pop pl...OK-5
Talihina, Lake—reservoir...OK-5
Talihina (CCD)—cens area...OK-5
Talihina Cem—cemetery...OK-5
Tali Homma Creek...MS-4
Taliiw—cape...FM-9
Talikoot—locale...AK-9
Talik Ridge—ridge...AK-9
Talik River—gut...AK-9
Talimachusy (historical)—locale...AL-4
Talipohoga Rum Creek—stream...GA-3
Talisay River—stream...GU-9
Talishatchie...AL-4
**Talisheek**—pop pl...LA-4
Talisheek Bay—swamp...LA-4
Talisheek Creek—stream...LA-4
Talisheek Swamp—swamp...LA-4
Talisi (historical)—locale...AL-4
**Talisman**—pop pl...FL-3
**Talisman Drive Subdivision**—pop pl...UT-8
Talisman Lake...WA-9
Talisman Mine—mine...WA-9
Talitoelau Spring—spring...AS-9
Taliudek Island—island...AK-9
**Taliverde (subdivision)**—pop pl (2)...AZ-5
Taliw...FM-9
**Talkeetna**—pop pl...AK-9
Talkeetna Glacier—glacier...AK-9
Talkeetna Lakes—lake...AK-9
Talkeetna Mine—mine...AK-9
Talkeetna Mountains—range...AK-9
Talkeetna River—stream...AK-9
Talken Cem—cemetery...AR-4
Talking John Creek—stream...TX-5
Talking Mtn—summit...CA-9
**Talking Rock**—pop pl...GA-3
Talking Rock (CCD)—cens area...GA-3
Talking Rock Creek—stream...GA-3
Talking Rocks Cavern—cave...MO-7
Talkington Branch—stream...AL-4
Talkington Fork—stream...WV-2
Talkington Ranch—locale...ND-7
**Talkington (Township of)**—pop pl...IL-6
Talking Warrior Creek—stream...MS-4
Talking Warrior River...MS-4
Talking Water Creek—stream...MT-8
Talkire Lake—lake...WA-9
Talla...MS-4
Talla, Bayou—stream (2)...MS-4
**Talla Bena**—pop pl...LA-4
Talla Bena Bayou—gut...LA-4
Tallabinnela Creek—stream...MS-4
**Tallaboa**—pop pl...PR-3
**Tallaboa Alta**—pop pl...PR-3
Tallaboa Alta (Barrio)—fmr MCD...PR-3
**Tallaboa Poniente**—pop pl...PR-3
Tallaboa Poniente (Barrio)—fmr MCD...PR-3
Tallaboa Salient (Barrio)—fmr MCD...PR-3
Tallabogue—stream (2)...MS-4
Talla Bogue Creek...MS-4
Tallabogue Creek—stream...MS-4
Tallac, Mount—summit...CA-9
Tallac Creek—stream...CA-9
Tallachula Creek—stream...MS-4
Tallac Lake—lake...CA-9
Tallacoosa (historical)—locale...AL-4
Tallacoosa Sch (historical)—school...AL-4
Talla Creek...MS-4
Tallac Village...CA-9
**Tallac Village**—pop pl...CA-9
**Talladega**—pop pl...AL-4
Talladega Acad—school...AL-4
Talladega Area Vocational Sch—school...AL-4
Talladega Baptist Church...AL-4
Talladega Battleground—locale...AL-4
Talladega (CCD)—cens area...AL-4
Talladega Cheaha Lake...AL-4
Talladega Coll—school...AL-4
Talladega Country Club—locale...AL-4
**Talladega County**—pop pl...AL-4
Talladega County Courthouse—building...AL-4
Talladega County Elem Sch—school...AL-4
Talladega County HS...AL-4
Talladega County Industrial Park—locale...AL-4
Talladega County Training Sch—school...AL-4
Talladega Courthouse Square Hist Dist—hist pl...AL-4
Talladega Courthouse Square Hist Dist (Boundary Increase)—hist pl...AL-4
Talladega Creek—stream...AL-4
Talladega Creek Baptist Ch—church...AL-4
Talladega Division—civil...AL-4
Talladega Federal Correctional Institution—building...AL-4
Talladega Furnace...AL-4
Talladega Gap...AL-4
Talladega Hill—summit...AL-4
Talladega Hills...AL-4
Talladega HS—school...AL-4
Talladega Industrial Park—locale...AL-4
Talladega International Motor Speedway...AL-4
Talladega Lake—reservoir...AL-4
Talladega Lake Dam—dam...AL-4
Talladega Mountain...AL-4
Talladega MS—school...AL-4
Talladega Municipal Airp—airport...AL-4
Talladega Natl Forest—park...AL-4
Talladega Public Library—building...AL-4
Talladega Recreational Complex—park...AL-4
Talladega Shop Ctr—locale...AL-4
**Talladega Springs**—pop pl...AL-4
Talladega Springs Cem—cemetery...AL-4
Talladega Sulphur Springs—spring...AL-4
Talladega Sulphur Springs Valley...AL-4
Talladega (Township of)—fmr MCD...AR-4
Talladegee...AL-4
Talladigger...AL-4
Tallaferro Cem—cemetery...TN-4
Talloha, Lake—reservoir...MS-4
Talla Haga Creek...MS-4
Tallahaga Creek—stream...MS-4
Tallahaga Creek Structure 1 Dam—dam...MS-4
Tallahaga Creek Watershed Structure 12 Dam—dam...MS-4
Tallahaga Creek Watershed Structure 13 Dam—dam...MS-4
Tallahaga Creek 10 Dam—dam...MS-4
Tallahaga Creek 3 Dam—dam...MS-4
Tallahaga Watershed Structure 4 Dam—dam...MS-4
Tallahaga Watershed Structure 6 Dam—dam...MS-4
Tallahag Creek...MS-4
Tallahala...MS-4
Tallahala—locale...MS-4
Tallahala Baptist Church...MS-4
Tallahala Ch (historical)—church...MS-4
Tallahala Creek—stream...MS-4
Tallahala Creek Oil And Gas Field—oilfield...MS-4
Tallahala Game Mngmt Area...MS-4
Tallahala (historical)—locale (2)...MS-4
Tallahala Sch (historical)—school...MS-4
Tallahala State Wildlife Mngmt Area—park...MS-4
Tallahalla Creek—stream...MS-4
Tallahassee—locale...GA-3
**Tallahassee**—pop pl...FL-3
Tallahassee Baptist Ch—church...FL-3
Tallahassee (CCD)—cens area...FL-3
Tallahassee Center (Shop Ctr)—locale...FL-3
Tallahassee Ch—church (2)...OK-5
Tallahassee Christian Assembly—church...FL-3
Tallahassee Community Coll—school...FL-3
Tallahassee Community College Library—building...FL-3
Tallahassee Community Hosp—hospital...FL-3
Tallahassee Creek—stream...CO-8
Tallahassee Creek—stream...FL-3
Tallahassee Creek—stream...GA-3
Tallahassee Creek—stream...MI-6
Tallahassee Drain...MI-6
Tallahassee East (CCD)—cens area...FL-3
Tallahassee Heights Ch church...FL-3
Tallahassee Heights United Methodist Ch—church...FL-3
Tallahassee Hist Dist Zones I And II—hist pl...FL-3
Tallahassee Junior Acad—school...FL-3
Tallahassee Mall—locale...FL-3
Tallahassee Memorial Regional Med Ctr—hospital...FL-3
Tallahassee Memory Gardens—cemetery...FL-3
Tallahassee Municipal Airp—airport...FL-3
Tallahassee Northeast (CCD)—cens area...FL-3
Tallahassee Northwest (CCD)—cens area...FL-3
Tallahassee Sch—school...CO-8
Tallahassee Southeast (CCD)—cens area...FL-3
Tallahassee Southwest (CCD)—cens area...FL-3
**Tallahasse - Yuchi (historical)**—pop pl...FL-3
Tallahassihatchie...AL-4
Tallahata Methodist Ch—church...AL-4
Tallahatchee Creek...AL-4
Tallahatchie Bluff—cliff...MS-4
**Tallahatchie County**—pop pl...MS-4
Tallahatchie County Cem—cemetery...MS-4
Tallahatchie County Courthouse—building...MS-4
Tallahatchie General Hosp—hospital...MS-4
Tallahatchie (reduced Usage)—locale...MS-4
Tallahatchie River...MS-4
Tallahatchie River—stream...MS-4
Tallahatta AME Ch...AL-4
Tallahatta Cem for Blacks—cemetery...AL-4
Tallahatta Ch—church...AL-4
Tallahatta Creek...MS-4
Tallahatta Creek—stream...AL-4
Tallahatta Creek—stream...MS-4
Tallahattah Creek—stream...MS-4
**Tallahatta Springs**—pop pl...AL-4
Tallaher House—hist pl...WA-9
Tallahoga Creek...MS-4
Talla-Hogan...AZ-5
Talla-Hogran...AZ-5
Tallahoma...MS-4
Talla Homa Creek...MS-4
Tallahoma Creek—stream...MS-4
**Tallahoma (historical)**—pop pl...MS-4
**Tallahomo**—pop pl...MS-4
Tallahone Creek—stream...TX-5
Tallaloosa Cem—cemetery...MS-4
Tallaloosa (historical)—locale...MS-4
**Tallant**—pop pl...OK-5
Tallant Cem—cemetery...TN-4
Tallant Ch—church...TN-4
Tallant Creek—stream...WA-9
**Tallapoosa**—pop pl...GA-3
**Tallapoosa**—pop pl...MO-7
Tallapoosa, Bayou—gut...AL-4
Tallapoosa Acad—school...AL-4

Tallapoosa (CCD)—*cens area* GA-3
Tallapoosa Ch—*church* GA-3
**Tallapoosa City**—*pop pl* AL-4
**Tallapoosa County**—*pop pl* AL-4
Tallapoosa County HS (historical)—*school* AL-4
Tallapoosa County Memorial Gardens—*cemetery* AL-4
Tallapoosa East Ch—*church* GA-3
Tallapoosa Falls (historical)—*falls* AL-4
Tallapoosa River—*stream* AL-4
Tallapoosa River—*stream* GA-3
Tallapoosa River Hunting Club—*locale* AL-4
Tallapoosa Shoal—*bar* AK-9
*Tallasahatchee Creek* AL-4
*Tallasahatchie P.O.* AL-4
*Tallasahatchy Creek* AL-4
*Tallasee* AL-4
**Tallaseehatchee**—*pop pl* AL-4
Tallaseehatchee Ch—*church* AL-4
Tallaseehatchee Creek—*stream* AL-4
Tallaseehatchee Creek Watershed N—*reservoir* AL-4
Tallaseehatchee (historical)—*locale* AL-4
Tallaseehatchee Watershed Number Six Lake—*reservoir* AL-4
Tallaseehatchee Watershed Number 1—*reservoir* AL-4
*Tallasehatchee* AL-4
*Tallasher Creek* MS-4
Tallashua Creek—*stream* MS-4
*Tallashuah Creek* MS-4
Tallas Island—*island* MN-6
*Tallaspoosa River* AL-4
Tallassahatchie P.O. (historical)—*building* AL-4
Tallassarr Creek—*stream* AL-4
*Tallassee* TN-4
**Tallassee**—*pop pl* AL-4
**Tallassee**—*pop pl* TN-4
Tallassee Boat Launching Ramp—*locale* TN-4
Tallassee (CCD)—*cens area* (2) AL-4
Tallassee Ch—*church* AL-4
*Tallassee Creek* TN-4
Tallassee Creek—*stream* TN-4
*Tallassee Dam* AL-4
Tallassee Division—*civil* (2) AL-4
Tallassee Elem Sch—*school* AL-4
*Tallassee Experiment Station Plant Breeding Unit* AL-4
Tallassee Ford (historical)—*locale* TN-4
Tallasseehatchee Creek—*stream* AL-4
*Tallasseehatchee P.O.* AL-4
Tallassee HS—*school* AL-4
Tallassee Mtn—*summit* TN-4
Tallassee Municipal Airp—*airport* AL-4
*Tallassee Old Town* TN-4
Tallassee Post Office—*building* TN-4
Tallassee Rec Area—*park* TN-4
Tallassee Sch (historical)—*school* TN-4
Tallassee Sewage Disposal Pond—*reservoir* AL-4
Tallassee Sewage Disposal Pond Dam—*dam* AL-4
Tallatchee Ch—*church* AL-4
Tallatchee Creek—*stream* AL-4
*Tallau Guechapco* FL-3
*Tallauhatche River* MS-4
Tallavast (RR name for Tallevast)—*other* FL-3
*Tallawampa Baptist Church* AL-4
Tallawampa Ch—*church* AL-4
*Tallawampa Creek* AL-4
Tallawampa Creek—*stream* AL-4
Tallawampa Sch (historical)—*school* AL-4
*Tallawappa Creek* AL-4
Tallawassee Bar—*bar* AL-4
Tallawassee Creek—*stream* AL-4
Tallaweka—*uninc pl* AL-4
*Tallawessee Creek* AL-4
Tallawyah Creek—*stream* AL-4
Tall Bear Canyon—*valley* OK-5
Tall Cabin Creek—*stream* CA-9
Tall Chief Creek—*stream* OK-5
Tallclay Cem—*cemetery* WV-2
Tall Cone—*summit* AZ-5
Tall Corral Creek—*stream* NV-8
*Tall Creek* KS-7
Talleconocko Camp—*locale* AL-4
Tallega—*locale* KY-4
Tallega Mission Sch—*school* KY-4
Tallen Airp—*airport* MO-7
**Tallent**—*pop pl* MO-7
Tallent, Annie, House—*hist pl* SD-7
Tallent Post Office (historical)—*building* TN-4
Tallent Ranch—*locale* MT-8
Tallent Sch—*school* SD-7
Tallent Town—*locale* VA-3
*Tallequah* WA-9
Tallequah Landing (historical)—*locale* MS-4
*Taller Creek* AL-4
Taller Pinnacle—*pillar* AK-9
Tallery Mtn—*summit* WV-2
Tallette—*locale* NY-2
Tallette Creek—*stream* NY-2
**Tallevast**—*pop pl* FL-3
**Tallevast (RR name Tallavast)**—*pop pl* FL-3
Talley—*locale* AR-4
Talley—*locale* KY-4
Talley—*locale* TX-5
**Talley**—*pop pl* AL-4
**Talley**—*pop pl* TN-4
Talley, Hugh, House—*hist pl* AZ-5
Talley, William, House—*hist pl* AZ-5
Talley, William, House—*hist pl* DE-2
Talley-Beals House—*hist pl* TN-4
Talley Bend—*bend* MO-7
Talley Bend Cem—*cemetery* MO-7
Talley Bottom—*swamp* AL-4
Talley Branch—*stream* AL-4
Talley Branch—*stream* GA-3
Talley Branch—*stream* MO-7
Talley Branch—*stream* TN-4
Talley Branch—*stream* (2) TX-5
**Talley Brook (subdivision)**—*pop pl* DE-2
Talley Canyon—*valley* NM-5
Talley Cave—*cave* AL-4
**Talley Cavey**—*pop pl* PA-2
Talley Cem—*cemetery* AL-4
Talley Cem—*cemetery* (2) AR-4
Talley Cem—*cemetery* GA-3
Talley Cem—*cemetery* IN-6
Talley Cem—*cemetery* (11) TN-4
Talley Cem—*cemetery* TX-5
Talley Ch—*church* LA-4
Talley Chapel—*church* TN-4
Talley Ch (historical)—*church* TN-4
Talley Creek—*stream* SC-3
Talley Creek—*stream* TN-4
Talley Creek Cave—*cave* TN-4
Talley Crossing—*locale* TX-5
Talley Dam—*dam* SD-7
Talley Ditch—*canal* AL-4
Talley Ditch—*canal* IN-6
Talley Ditch Cave—*cave* AL-4
Talley Draw—*valley* TX-5
Talley Estates—*locale* PA-2
*Talley Gap* TN-4
Talley Hill—*summit* (3) TN-4
Talley (historical)—*locale* AL-4
Talley (historical P.O.)—*locale* MS-4
Talley Hollow—*valley* KY-4
Talley Hollow—*valley* (4) TN-4
Talley Island—*island* TX-5
Talley Island (historical)—*island* TN-4
Talley Lake—*lake* TX-5
Talley Memorial Sch (historical)—*school* TN-4
Talley Mill Creek—*stream* GA-3
Talley Mill Creek—*stream* NC-3
Talley Millpond—*reservoir* VA-3
Talley Mtn—*summit* TX-5
**Talley Place (subdivision)**—*pop pl* TN-4
Talley Post Office (historical)—*building* TN-4
Talley Ranch—*locale* TX-5
Talleyrand—*locale* IA-7
Talleyrand—*uninc pl* FL-3
Talleyrand Cem—*cemetery* IA-7
**Talleyrand Township**—*pop pl* KS-7
Talleys Branch—*stream* MO-7
Talley Sch (historical)—*school* (2) TN-4
**Talleys Corner**—*pop pl* DE-2
*Talleys Cove* TN-4
Talleys Creek—*stream* LA-4
**Talleys Crossing**—*pop pl* NC-3
Talleys Fork—*stream* TN-4
*Talleys Island* TN-4
Talleys Lake—*lake* LA-4
Talleys Lake—*reservoir* NC-3
Talley Spring—*spring* AZ-5
Talley Spring Branch—*stream* TN-4
Talleys Store (historical)—*locale* TN-4
*Talleysville* VA-3
Talley Tank—*reservoir* NM-5
Talley Top—*summit* TN-4
Talley Top Sch (historical)—*school* TN-4
**Talleyville**—*pop pl* DE-2
Talleyville Shop Ctr—*locale* DE-2
Talley Wash—*stream* AZ-5
**Talleywood (subdivision)**—*pop pl* NC-3
Tall Four Rsvr—*reservoir* UT-8
Tall Hill Cem—*cemetery* TN-4
*Talliaferro* MS-4
Talliaferros Crossing (historical)—*locale* MS-4
*Tallico Plains Post Office* TN-4
*Talliferro* TN-4
Tallin Ch—*church* NE-7
Tallin Sch—*school* NE-7
Tallin Table—*summit* NE-7
*Tallioferro* TN-4
Tallmadge—*locale* IL-6
**Tallmadge**—*pop pl* MI-6
**Tallmadge**—*pop pl* OH-6
Tallmadge and Boyer Block—*hist pl* CO-8
Tallmadge Drain—*stream* MI-6
Tallmadge Hill—*summit* NY-2
Tallmadge Hill Cem—*cemetery* NY-2
Tallmadge Memorial Park—*cemetery* OH-6
Tallmadge-Mithoff House—*hist pl* OH-6
Tallmadge Sch—*school* OH-6
**Tallmadge (Township of)**—*pop pl* MI-6
Tallmadge Town Square Hist Dist—*hist pl* OH-6
*Tallmage* MI-6
Tallman—*locale* OR-9
**Tallman**—*pop pl* MI-6
**Tallman**—*pop pl* NY-2
Tallman, Horace M., House—*hist pl* IL-6
Tallman Cem—*cemetery* (2) MO-7
Tallman Ditch—*canal* WY-8
Tallman Drain—*canal* MI-6
Tallman Gulch—*valley* CO-8
Tallman Hollow—*valley* AL-4
Tallman House—*hist pl* WI-6
Tallman Island—*island* MI-6
Tallman Island—*island* NY-2
Tallman Lake—*lake* MI-6
Tallman Lake—*lake* WI-6
Tallman Mine—*mine* ID-8
Tallman Mountain State Park—*park* NY-2
Tallman Mtn—*summit* NY-2
*Tallman Pond* NJ-2
Tall Man Reach—*channel* TX-5
Tallman Ridge—*ridge* WV-2
**Tallman (RR name Tallmans)**—*pop pl* NY-2
**Tallmans**—*pop pl* WV-2
Tallman Sch—*school* MI-6
Tallman Sch—*school* NY-2
Tallmans Pond—*lake* NJ-2
Tallmans (RR name for Tallman)—*other* NY-2
Tallman Supply Company Airp—*airport* PA-2
Tallmansville—*locale* WV-2
Tallmansville Ch—*church* WV-2
**Tallmansville (Strader)**—*pop pl* WV-2
Tallman-Vanderbeck House—*hist pl* NJ-2
Tallmanville—*locale* PA-2
Tall Mesa—*pillar* AZ-5
*Tallmoon* MN-6
Tall Mountain Well—*well* AZ-5
Tall Mtn—*summit* AZ-5
Tall Oaks—*hist pl* SC-3
**Tall Oaks**—*pop pl* VA-3
Tall Oak Sch—*school* MD-2
Tall Oaks Lake—*reservoir* IN-6
Tall Oaks Lake Dam—*dam* IN-6
Tall Oaks Park—*park* NJ-2
**Tall Oaks PUD Subdivision**—*pop pl* UT-8
Tall Oaks Roadside Park—*park* WV-2
*Tallobogue Creek* MS-4
Tallon Spring—*spring* WY-8
Tallos Lake—*reservoir* TX-5
*Tallow Bogue Creek* MS-4
Tallowbow Creek—*stream* OR-9
Tallowbox Mtn—*summit* OR-9
Tallow Branch—*stream* KY-4
Tallow Branch—*stream* TN-4
Tallow Butte—*summit* OR-9
Tallow Clay Hollow—*valley* AR-4
Tallow Creek—*stream* KY-4
Tallow Creek—*stream* (2) MT-8
Tallow Creek—*stream* OR-9
Tallow Creek Cem—*cemetery* KY-4
Tallow Creek Sch—*school* KY-4
Tallow Creek Sch—*school* MT-8
Tallow Face Mtn—*summit* TX-5
Tallow Flat—*flat* WA-9
Tallow Hill—*summit* MA-1
**Tallow (historical)**—*pop pl* MS-4
Tallow Knob—*summit* WV-2
Tallowpot Creek—*stream* AK-9
Tall Palm Landing—*locale* FL-3
Tall Peak—*summit* AR-4
Tall Pine Lake—*lake* AR-4
Tall Pine Lakes—*reservoir* SC-3
Tall Pines—*hist pl* MS-4
Tall Pines—*hist pl* NY-2
**Tall Pines**—*pop pl* TX-5
Tall Pines Country Day Sch—*school* FL-3
Tall Pines Golf Course—*other* NJ-2
**Tall Pines (subdivision)**—*pop pl* MS-4
Tall Prairie Chicken Creek—*stream* SD-7
Talls Tank—*reservoir* AZ-5
Tall Timber Camp—*locale* MI-6
**Tall Timber Camp**—*pop pl* CA-9
Tall Timber Dam—*dam* OR-9
Tall Timber Draw—*valley* WY-8
Tall Timber Natural Area—*area* PA-2
Tall Timber Ranch—*locale* WA-9
Tall Timber Rsvr—*reservoir* OR-9
**Tall Timbers**—*pop pl* IN-6
**Tall Timbers**—*pop pl* MD-2
Tall Timbers County Park—*park* AZ-5
Tall Timbers Cove—*bay* MD-2
Tall Tree—*locale* CA-9
Tall Tree Mesa—*summit* AZ-5
*Tall Trees* IL-6
Tall Trees Sch—*school* TN-4
*Tallula* AL-4
**Tallula**—*pop pl* IL-6
**Tallula**—*pop pl* MS-4
*Tallula Bend* MS-4
Tallula (Election Precinct)—*fmr MCD* IL-6
*Tallulah* MS-4
*Tallulah* NC-3
**Tallulah**—*pop pl* LA-4
Tallulah Creek—*stream* MT-8
**Tallulah Falls**—*pop pl* GA-3
Tallulah Falls Depot—*hist pl* GA-3
Tallulah Falls Lake—*reservoir* GA-3
Tallulah Falls Sch—*school* GA-3
**Tallulah Gap**—*pop pl* NC-3
Tallulah Gorge—*valley* GA-3
Tallulah Lake—*lake* CA-9
Tallulah Lodge—*locale* GA-3
Tallulah Massey Park—*park* GA-3
Tallulah Mtn—*summit* GA-3
Tallulah Park—*park* FL-3
Tallulah River—*stream* GA-3
Tallulah River—*stream* NC-3
Tallus Lake—*lake* MT-8
Tall Windmill—*locale* NM-5
Tallwood—*locale* ME-1
Tallwood Chapel—*church* IN-6
Tally Branch—*stream* (2) AL-4
Tally Branch—*stream* NC-3
Tally Branch—*stream* TN-4
Tally Branch—*stream* TX-5
Tally Cem—*cemetery* AL-4
Tally Cem—*cemetery* IN-6
Tally Creek—*stream* ID-8
Tally Creek—*stream* OR-9
Tally Gap—*gap* GA-3
Tallyhaly Creek—*stream* AL-4
Tally Hill—*summit* GA-3
*Tally Ho* PA-2
Tally Ho—*locale* LA-4
Tallyho—*locale* PA-2
Tallyho—*locale* WV-2
Tallyho Ch—*church* NC-3
Tally Hollow—*valley* TN-4
Tally-Ho Plantation House—*hist pl* LA-4
Tally Ho (Township of)—*fmr MCD* NC-3
*Tally Island* TX-5
Tally Lake—*lake* MT-8
Tally Lake Campground—*locale* MT-8
Tally Lake Ranger Station—*locale* MT-8
Tally Mtn—*summit* (2) GA-3
Tally Mtn—*summit* MT-8
Tally Pit Rsvr—*reservoir* WY-8
**Tallyrand**—*pop pl* FL-3
Tally's Bank—*hist pl* LA-4
Tally Sch—*school* KS-7
*Tallys Chapel School* TN-4
Tallys Creek—*stream* MS-4
Tally Slough—*stream* TX-5
*Tally's Point* MD-2
Tally Spring—*spring* AL-4
Tallysville—*locale* VA-3
Tally Taylor Tank—*reservoir* TX-5
Tally Valley Park—*park* GA-3
*Tallyville* DE-2
Tallywood—*uninc pl* NC-3
Tallywood Shop Ctr—*locale* NC-3
**Talma**—*pop pl* IN-6
*Talmadge* CA-9
*Talmadge* MI-6
Talmadge—*locale* GA-3
Talmadge, Lake—*reservoir* GA-3
Talmadge Canyon—*valley* CA-9
Talmadge Ch—*church* GA-3
Talmadge Creek—*stream* MI-6
Talmadge Drain—*canal* (2) MI-6
**Talmadge Hill**—*pop pl* CT-1
Talmadge Hill—*summit* CT-1
Talmadge Hill Chapel—*church* CT-1
Talmadge Hosp—*hospital* GA-3
Talmadge JHS—*school* OR-9
Talmadge Lake—*lake* MT-8
Talmadge River—*stream* MN-6
Talmadge Sch—*school* MA-1
Talmadge Spring—*spring* CA-9
**Talmadge (Town of)**—*pop pl* ME-1
*Talmage* AL-4
*Talmage* KS-7
*Talmage* MI-6
Talmage—*locale* ID-8
Talmage—*locale* IA-7
**Talmage**—*pop pl* CA-9
**Talmage**—*pop pl* KS-7
**Talmage**—*pop pl* KY-4
**Talmage**—*pop pl* NE-7
**Talmage**—*pop pl* PA-2
**Talmage**—*pop pl* UT-8
Talmage, James E. and Albert, House—*hist pl* UT-8
Talmage Cem—*cemetery* UT-8
Talmage Community Ch—*church* MO-7
Talmage Hollow—*valley* KY-4
Talmage Pond—*lake* CT-1
Talmage Post Office (historical)—*building* AL-4
*Talmage School* MO-7
Talmages Ice Pond—*lake* CT-1
Talmaks Campground—*locale* ID-8
Talman Cem—*cemetery* AR-4
Talman Creek—*stream* ID-8
**Talmar**—*pop pl* PA-2
Talmer—*locale* PA-2
**Talmo**—*pop pl* (2) GA-3
**Talmo**—*pop pl* KS-7
Talmo, Lake—*lake* FL-3
**Talmoon**—*pop pl* MN-6
Talmud Torah Sch—*school* MN-6
*Tal Ngith* FM-9
Talnik Point—*cape* AK-9
Talo'—*slope* MH-9
Taloah—*locale* OK-5
Taloelaey—*summit* FM-9
*Talofofo* MH-9
Talofofo—*area* GU-9
**Talofofo**—*pop pl* GU-9
Talofo'fo', Unai—*beach* MH-9
Talofofo Bay—*bay* GU-9
*Talofofo Beach* MH-9
Talofofo Caves—*cave* GU-9
Talofofo (Election District)—*fmr MCD* GU-9
Talofofo Falls—*falls* GU-9
*Talofofo Ridge* MH-9
Talofofo River—*stream* GU-9
Talofofo River Valley Site—*hist pl* GU-9
**Taloga**—*pop pl* OK-5
Taloga (historical)—*locale* KS-7
Taloga Oil and Gas Field—*oilfield* KS-7
Taloga Sch—*school* KS-7
Taloga Township—*civil* KS-7
*Talojen* MP-9
Taloka Creek—*stream* OK-5
*Talolay* FM-9
**Talome (historical)**—*pop pl* TN-4
Talome Post Office (historical)—*building* TN-4
Talona—*locale* GA-3
**Talona**—*pop pl* GU-9
Talona Ch—*church* GA-3
Talona Creek—*stream* GA-3
Talona Mtn—*summit* GA-3
*Talonega* GA-3
*Talooehajah* AL-4
Talow—*summit* FM-9
**Talowah**—*pop pl* MS-4
Talowah Cem—*cemetery* MS-4
**Talpa**—*pop pl* NM-5
**Talpa**—*pop pl* TX-5
Talpacate Creek—*stream* TX-5
Talpa (CCD)—*cens area* TX-5
Talpa Cem—*cemetery* NM-5
Talpa Cem—*cemetery* TX-5
Talpa City Lake—*reservoir* TX-5
Talpa Ridge—*ridge* NM-5
Talpa Rsvr—*reservoir* NM-5
Talpa Sch—*school* CA-9
Talp Hollow—*valley* KY-4
Talquin, Lake—*reservoir* FL-3
Talquin Wildlife Mngmt Area—*park* FL-3
Taltheadamund Lake—*lake* AK-9
Taltlinkho Creek—*stream* AK-9
Talto—*island* MP-9
*Talton Branch* MD-2
Talton Gap—*gap* TN-4
Talty—*locale* TX-5
*Talua Laka* AL-4
*Talua Lako* AL-4
Talucah—*locale* AL-4
Talucah Cave—*cave* AL-4
*Talucah Cemetery* AL-4
Talucah Ch—*church* AL-4
Talucah Ferry (historical)—*locale* AL-4
Talucah Post Office (historical)—*building* AL-4
*Talucan* AL-4
Talufo'fo'—*slope* MH-9
Talufo'fo, Okso'—*summit* MH-9
Talufo'fo', Sabanan—*slope* MH-9
Talufo'fo', Saddok—*stream* MH-9
*Taluga Branch* AL-4
Talum Glaciers—*glacier* WA-9
Talurarevuk Point—*cape* AK-9
Talus—*locale* CA-9
Talus Bay—*bay* AK-9
Talus Canyon—*valley* CA-9
Talus Creek—*stream* AK-9
Talus Glacier—*glacier* WA-9
Talus Gulch—*valley* ID-8
Talus Lake—*lake* CA-9
Talus Lake—*lake* MN-6
Talus Lake—*lake* MT-8
Talus Lake—*lake* WA-9
Talus Lake—*lake* WY-8
Talus Point—*cape* AK-9
Taluweed—*summit* FM-9
Taluyetlek Creek—*stream* AK-9
Tal Vez Oil Field—*oilfield* TX-5
*Talwed* FM-9
Tal-Wi-Wi Ranch—*locale* AZ-5
Tal-Wi-Wi Tank—*reservoir* AZ-5
Talyor Fork—*stream* UT-8
**Tama**—*pop pl* IA-7
**Tama**—*pop pl* LA-4
**Tama**—*pop pl* OH-6
*Tamaaf* FM-9
*Tamaalang* FM-9
*Tama City* IA-7
Tama County Courthouse—*hist pl* IA-7
Tama County Home—*building* IA-7
Tama County Jail—*hist pl* IA-7
Tama County Lake Dam—*dam* IA-7
Tama County Lake Park—*park* IA-7
Tama Creek—*stream* ID-8
*Tama El Paris* CA-9
Tamagel—*cape* FM-9
**Tamaha**—*pop pl* OK-5
Tamaha Cem—*cemetery* OK-5
Tamaha Jail and Ferry Landing—*hist pl* OK-5
Tama (historical)—*locale* SD-7
**Tama (historical)**—*pop pl* FL-3
Tama Ind Res—*reserve* GA-3
*Tamaire Mountain* PW-9
*Tamak* FM-9
Tamalaang—*summit* FM-9
**Tamalco**—*pop pl* IL-6
Tamalco Access Area—*locale* IL-6
**Tamalco (Township of)**—*pop pl* IL-6
Tamales Windmill—*locale* TX-5
Tamalpais, Mount—*ridge* CA-9
Tamalpais Convalescent Hosp—*hospital* CA-9
Tamalpais Creek—*stream* CA-9
Tamalpais-Homestead Valley—*CDP* CA-9
Tamalpais Sch For Boys—*school* CA-9
Tamalpais Union HS—*school* CA-9
**Tamalpais Valley**—*pop pl* CA-9
Tamalpais Valley—*valley* CA-9
**Tamalpais Valley Junction**—*pop pl* CA-9
Tamalpais Valley Sch—*school* CA-9
Tamal (San Quentin State Prison)—*building* CA-9
Tama Mud Creek—*stream* IA-7
*Taman* FM-9
Taman—*bar* FM-9
Taman, Laderan As—*cliff* MH-9
Tamanawas Falls—*falls* OR-9
*Tamanawaus Falls* OR-9
*Taman Cliffs* MH-9
Tamanend—*locale* PA-2
*Tamangaang'* FM-9
Tamangaang—*summit* FM-9
Tam Anne—*locale* TX-5
Tamanos Mtn—*summit* WA-9
Tamantaloi Hill—*summit* AK-9
Tamaqaf—*cape* FM-9
**Tamaqua**—*pop pl* PA-2
Tamaqua Area JHS—*school* PA-2
Tamaqua Area Senior HS—*school* PA-2
Tamaqua Borough—*civil* PA-2
*Tamaqua Borough Reservoirs* PA-2
Tamaqua Elem Sch—*school* PA-2
Tamaqua Reservoirs—*reservoir* PA-2
Tamaque Lake—*reservoir* PA-2
Tamaques Reservation—*park* NJ-2
*Tamarac* IL-6
**Tamarac**—*pop pl* (2) FL-3
Tamarac, Mount—*summit* NY-2
Tamarac Commercial Plaza (Shop Ctr)—*locale* FL-3
Tamarac Country Club—*locale* FL-3
*Tamarac Creek* WI-6
Tamarac Elem Sch—*school* FL-3
*Tamarack* IN-6
Tamarack—*locale* IL-6
Tamarack—*locale* MI-6
Tamarack—*locale* NY-2
Tamarack—*locale* WI-6
**Tamarack**—*pop pl* CA-9
**Tamarack**—*pop pl* ID-8
**Tamarack**—*pop pl* MI-6
**Tamarack**—*pop pl* MN-6
**Tamarack**—*pop pl* MT-8
**Tamarack**—*pop pl* NC-3
**Tamarack**—*pop pl* PA-2
**Tamarack**—*pop pl* TN-4
Tamarack, Lake—*lake* NY-2
Tamarack, Lake—*reservoir* GA-3
Tamarack, Lake—*reservoir* NJ-2
Tamarack Basin—*basin* OR-9
Tamarack Bay—*bay* MN-6
Tamarack Bluff—*cliff* AK-9
*Tamarack Branch* NY-2
Tamarack Branch—*stream* NY-2
Tamarack Brook—*stream* NY-2
Tamarack Brook—*stream* (3) VT-1
*Tamarack Butte* ID-8
Tamarack Butte—*summit* OR-9
Tamarack Butte—*summit* WA-9
Tamarack Butte Rsvr—*reservoir* OR-9
Tamarack Camp—*locale* OR-9
Tamarack Campground—*locale* MN-6
Tamarack Camp (historical)—*locale* OR-9
*Tamarack Canal* CA-9
Tamarack Canal—*canal* CA-9
Tamarack Canyon—*valley* (2) CA-9
Tamarack Canyon—*valley* (2) OR-9
Tamarack Canyon—*valley* (2) WA-9
Tamarack Cem—*cemetery* (3) IN-6
Tamarack Cem—*cemetery* OH-6
Tamarack Cem—*cemetery* WI-6
Tamarack Ch—*church* IN-6
Tamarack Ch—*church* MN-6
Tamarack Ch—*church* WI-6
Tamarack Coulee—*valley* WI-6
Tamarack Country Club—*other* CT-1
*Tamarack Creek* MN-6
*Tamarack Creek* WI-6
Tamarack Creek—*stream* (2) AK-9
Tamarack Creek—*stream* (7) CA-9
Tamarack Creek—*stream* (4) ID-8
Tamarack Creek—*stream* (3) MI-6
Tamarack Creek—*stream* MN-6
Tamarack Creek—*stream* (6) MT-8
Tamarack Creek—*stream* NY-2
Tamarack Creek—*stream* (15) OR-9
Tamarack Creek—*stream* PA-2
Tamarack Creek—*stream* (2) WA-9
Tamarack Creek—*stream* (3) WI-6
Tamarack Creek Spring—*spring* OR-9
Tamarack Creek State Wildlife Area—*park* WI-6
Tamarack Ditch—*canal* OH-6
Tamarack Drain—*canal* CA-9
Tamarack Drain—*canal* MI-6
*Tamarack Fire Tower* PA-2
Tamarack Flat—*flat* (5) CA-9
Tamarack Flat—*flat* (2) ID-8
Tamarack Flat—*flat* OR-9
Tamarack Flat—*flat* WA-9
*Tamarack Forest Camp* OR-9
**Tamarack Grange**—*pop pl* IN-6
Tamarack Gulch—*valley* ID-8
Tamarack Gulch—*valley* MT-8
Tamarack Gulch—*valley* (2) OR-9
Tamarack Gulch—*valley* SD-7
Tamarack Hill—*summit* MT-8
Tamarack Hill—*summit* NY-2
Tamarack Island—*island* PA-2
*Tamarack Lake* CA-9
*Tamarack Lake* MN-6
*Tamarack Lake* PA-2
*Tamarack Lake* WI-6
Tamarack Lake—*lake* (6) CA-9
Tamarack Lake—*lake* (4) IN-6
Tamarack Lake—*lake* (13) MI-6
Tamarack Lake—*lake* (32) MN-6
Tamarack Lake—*lake* (3) MT-8
Tamarack Lake—*lake* NV-8
Tamarack Lake—*lake* NY-2
Tamarack Lake—*lake* PA-2
Tamarack Lake—*lake* UT-8
Tamarack Lake—*lake* (9) WI-6
**Tamarack Lake**—*pop pl* MI-6
Tamarack Lake—*reservoir* NJ-2
Tamarack Lake—*reservoir* PA-2
Tamarack Lake—*reservoir* UT-8
Tamarack Lake Dam—*dam* UT-8
Tamarack Lake Dam A—*dam* PA-2
Tamarack Lake Dam B—*dam* PA-2
Tamarack Lakes—*lake* (2) CA-9
Tamarack Landing Field—*airport* KS-7
Tamarack Lodge Bungalow—*hist pl* CT-1
Tamarack Lookout Tower—*locale* PA-2
*Tamarack Meadow* CA-9
Tamarack Meadow—*flat* CA-9
Tamarack Mine—*mine* CA-9
Tamarack Mine—*mine* MT-8
*Tamarack Mtn* CA-9
Tamarack Mtn—*summit* (2) CA-9
Tamarack Mtn—*summit* ID-8
Tamarack Mtn—*summit* (2) OR-9
*Tamarack Peak* CA-9
Tamarack Peak—*summit* NV-8
Tamarack Peak—*summit* WA-9
*Tamarack Point* OR-9
Tamarack Point—*cape* (2) MN-6
*Tamarack Pond* NJ-2
Tamarack Pond—*lake* (2) NY-2
Tamarack Pond—*lake* PA-2
Tamarack Pond—*reservoir* NY-2
Tamarack Pool—*reservoir* MN-6
Tamarack Ranch—*locale* CA-9
Tamarack Ridge—*ridge* (3) ID-8
Tamarack Ridge—*ridge* VA-3
Tamarack Ridge—*ridge* WA-9
*Tamarack River* MN-6
*Tamarack River* WI-6
Tamarack River—*stream* MI-6
Tamarack River—*stream* MN-6
Tamarack Rsvr—*reservoir* OR-9
Tamarack Rsvr—*reservoir* UT-8
Tamarack Run—*stream* PA-2
Tamarack Saddle—*gap* ID-8
Tamarack Sch—*school* IN-6
Tamarack Sch—*school* KY-4
Tamarack Sch—*school* WI-6
Tamarack Spring—*spring* (2) CA-9
Tamarack Spring—*spring* (11) OR-9
Tamarack Spring—*spring* (3) WA-9
Tamarack Spring Campground—*park* OR-9
Tamarack State Wildlife Mngmt Area—*park* MN-6
**Tamarack Subdivision**—*pop pl* UT-8
Tamarack Substation—*other* CA-9
Tamarack Swale—*valley* CA-9
Tamarack Swale Trail—*trail* CA-9
Tamarack Swamp—*swamp* (2) CT-1
Tamarack Swamp—*swamp* MI-6
Tamarack Swamp—*swamp* (11) NY-2
Tamarack Swamp—*swamp* OR-9
Tamarack Swamp—*swamp* (6) PA-2
Tamarack Swamp—*swamp* WI-6
Tamarack Swamp Pond—*lake* PA-2
*Tamarack Swamps* OR-9
Tamarack Tank—*reservoir* AZ-5
Tamarack Valley—*valley* CA-9
Tamarack Valley—*valley* WI-6
Tamarack Vly—*swamp* (2) NY-2
Tamarack Waterworks—*locale* MI-6
Tamarac Lake—*lake* (3) MN-6
Tamarac Natl Wildlife Ref—*park* MN-6
Tamarac River—*stream* (2) MN-6
*Tamarac Swamp* PA-2
Tamarac Swamp—*swamp* CT-1
Tamarac Swamp—*swamp* WI-6
**Tamarac (Township of)**—*pop pl* MN-6
**Tamara Estates Subdivision**—*pop pl* UT-8
*Tamarak Lake* MN-6
Tamarancho Boy Scout Camp—*locale* CA-9
Tamarawa Cem—*cemetery* IL-6
Tamarawa Ridge—*ridge* IL-6
*Tamarck Mountain* ID-8
Tamarind Hammock—*island* FL-3
**Tamarindo**—*pop pl* PR-3
Tamarindo, Bahia—*bay* PR-3
*Tamarir* FM-9
Tamarisk Cem—*cemetery* TX-5
Tamarisk Country Club—*other* CA-9
Tamarisk Flat—*flat* NM-5
Tamarisk Grove Campground—*locale* CA-9
Tamarisk Park—*park* MI-6
**Tamaroa**—*pop pl* IL-6
Tamaroa (Election Precinct)—*fmr MCD* IL-6
Tamaroa Oil Field—*other* IL-6
Tamaroa South Oil Field—*other* IL-6
Tam-A-Roc Country Club—*other* OH-6
Tamarock Lake—*lake* MI-6
Tamarock Springs—*spring* OR-9
Tamaroo Bar—*bar* CA-9
**Tamarron**—*pop pl* CO-8
*Tamaryr Reef* FM-9
Tama Sch—*school* IA-7
*Tamasle* FL-3
**Tamassee**—*pop pl* SC-3
Tamassee Creek—*stream* SC-3
Tamassee DAR Sch—*school* SC-3
Tamassee Knob—*summit* SC-3
*Tamassee Park* TN-4
**Tamassee (subdivision)**—*pop pl* TN-4
Tamatam—*island* FM-9
*Tamatamansakir* FM-9
Tamatam (Municipality)—*civ div* FM-9
**Tamathli (historical)**—*pop pl* FL-3

Tama Township—fmr MCD (2) ... IA-7
Tama Township (historical)—civil ... SD-7
Tamatupu Point—cape ... AS-9
Tamaya—hist pl ... NM-5
Tamayariak River—stream ... AK-9
Tamayayak Channel—channel ... AK-9
Tamba Ranch—locale ... OR-9
Tambellini Ditch—canal ... CA-9
Tamberg—locale ... TX-5
Tamberlaine Canyon—valley ... NV-8
Tamberlaine Spring—spring ... NV-8
**Tambine**—pop pl ... PA-2
Tambling, Lucius T., House—hist pl ... OH-6
Tambling Lake—lake ... WI-6
Tamblyn Field—park ... NJ-2
Tambo—locale ... CA-9
Tambor Cem—cemetery ... KS-7
Tambour, Bayou—gut (2) ... LA-4
Tambour, Bayou—stream ... LA-4
Tambour, Lake—lake ... LA-4
Tambour Bay—bay ... LA-4
Tambour Cutoff—channel ... LA-4
**Tambs Station**—pop pl ... CA-9
**Tamburo (historical)**—pop pl ... MS-4
Tam Cem—cemetery ... OH-6
**Tamcliff**—pop pl ... WV-2
Tam Creek ... WA-9
Tame Buck Hill—summit ... CT-1
Tame Fish Lake—lake ... MN-6
Tamega ... TX-5
**Tamega**—pop pl ... TX-5
Tamel ... FM-9
Tamel ... MP-9
Tame Lake—lake ... MN-6
Tamel Pisc Mounta ... CA-9
Tamerix Lake—reservoir ... IN-6
Tamerix Lake Dam—dam ... IN-6
Tamer Win Country Club—other ... OH-6
Tames Creek—stream ... CO-8
Tamett Brook—stream ... MA-1
Tamgas Harbor—bay ... AK-9
Tamgas Lake—lake ... AK-9
Tamgas Mtn—summit ... AK-9
Tamgas Reef—bar ... AK-9
Tamiami—CDP ... FL-3
Tamiami Airp ... FL-3
Tamiami Airp—airport ... FL-3
Tamiami Baptist Ch—church ... FL-3
Tamiami Baptist Child Care—school ... FL-3
Tamiami Canal—canal ... FL-3
Tamiami Canal Number C-4—canal (2) ... FL-3
Tamiami Lakes Park—park (2) ... FL-3
Tamiami Park—park ... FL-3
Tamiami Pinelands Park—park ... FL-3
Tamiami Regional Park—park ... FL-3
Tamiami Shop Ctr—locale ... FL-3
Tamiami Trail—trail (2) ... FL-3
Tamiami Trail Park—park ... FL-3
Tamihi Lake ... WA-9
Tamihi Peak ... WA-9
Tamihy Cree ... WA-9
Tamil ... FM-9
Tamil ... MP-9
Tamil—civil ... FM-9
Tamilang Sch—school ... FM-9
Tamil District ... FM-9
Tamil Harbor—harbor ... FM-9
Tamiliyeeg—summit ... FM-9
Tamil Municipality ... FM-9
Tamilyeg ... FM-9
**Tamiment**—pop pl ... PA-2
Tamiment Resort Golf Course—locale ... PA-2
Tamiment (ski area)—locale ... PA-2
**Tamina**—pop pl ... TX-5
Tamina Arcenaut Oil Field—oilfield ... TX-5
Tamina Cem—cemetery ... TX-5
Tamina Ch—church ... TX-5
Taminah, Lake—lake ... WY-8
Taminent ... PA-2
Taminent Lake ... PA-2
Taminy Lake ... WA-9
Taminy Peak ... WA-9
Tam Lake—lake ... OR-9
Tamlang ... FM-9
**Tamlee Village Subdivision**—pop pl ... UT-8
Tamliyaq ... FM-9
Tammany—hist pl ... MD-2
Tammany, Mount—summit ... NJ-2
Tammany Cem—cemetery ... ID-8
Tammany Creek—stream ... ID-8
**Tammany Manor**—pop pl ... MD-2
Tammany Sch—school ... ID-8
Tamm Bend—bend ... AR-4
Tamm Bend—bend ... TN-4
Tamm Bend Revetment ... TN-4
Tam McArthur Rim—cliff ... OR-9
Tammett Brook ... MA-1
Tammin Ranch—locale ... TX-5
Tamm Landing—locale ... TN-4
**Tamms**—pop pl ... IL-6
Tamms (Election Precinct)—fmr MCD ... IL-6
Tammy Pit—basin ... WY-8
Tammy Pond—lake ... OR-9
Tamngang ... FM-9
**Tamo**—pop pl ... AR-4
Tamola—locale ... MS-4
Tamola Ch—church ... MS-4
Tamola Lookout Tower—locale ... MS-4
Tamola Sch (historical)—school ... MS-4
Tamola Station ... MS-4
Tamola Station Post Office (historical)—building ... MS-4
Tamol Island ... MP-9
Tamolitch Falls—falls ... OR-9
Tamolitsh Falls ... OR-9
Tamon ... FM-9
Tamoor—summit ... FM-9
Tamor ... FM-9
**Tamora**—pop pl ... NE-7
Tamora Cem—cemetery ... NE-7
Tamori ... MP-9
Tamori—island ... MP-9
Tamori-To ... MP-9
Tamoroi ... FM-9
Tamosee ... SC-3
Tam O'Shanter Country Club—other ... MI-6
Tam O'Shanter Country Club—other ... NY-2
Tam O'Shanter Peak—summit ... AZ-5
Tamossee ... SC-3
Tampa ... AL-4
Tampa—locale ... CO-8
**Tampa**—pop pl ... FL-3
**Tampa**—pop pl ... KS-7
Tampa Baptist Ch—church ... FL-3
Tampa Bay—bay ... FL-3
Tampa Bay Area Vocational Technical Center—school ... FL-3
Tampa Bay Baptist Ch—church ... FL-3
Tampa Bay Blvd Sch—school ... FL-3
Tampa Bay Channel—channel ... FL-3
Tampa Bay Community Hosp—hospital ... FL-3
Tampa Bay Hotel—hist pl ... FL-3
Tampa Branch—stream ... KY-4
Tampa Bypass Canal—canal ... FL-3
Tampa Canyon ... CA-9
Tampa Catholic HS—school ... FL-3
Tampa (CCD)—cens area ... FL-3
Tampa Cem—cemetery ... KS-7
Tampa Christian Acad—school ... FL-3
Tampa City Hall—hist pl ... FL-3
Tampa Creek—stream ... MS-4
Tampa Creek—stream ... SC-3
Tampa General Hosp—hospital ... FL-3
Tampa Heights Hosp—hospital ... FL-3
Tampa-Hillsborough County Public Library System—building ... FL-3
Tampa International Airp—airport ... FL-3
Tampa Junior Acad—school ... FL-3
Tampa Lake—lake ... FL-3
Tampa Marine Institute—school ... FL-3
Tampania House—hist pl ... FL-3
Tampa Northern Channel ... FL-3
Tampa Outlet Mall—locale ... FL-3
Tampa Post Office (historical)—building ... TN-4
Tampa Preparatory Sch—school ... FL-3
Tampa Reading Clinic and Day Sch—school ... FL-3
Tampa RR Station—locale ... FL-3
Tampashores ... FL-3
Tampa Theater and Office Bldg—hist pl ... FL-3
Tampa Water Works Lake—lake ... FL-3
Tamp Gilbert Flat—flat ... TN-4
Tamphery Creek—stream ... MT-8
Tampica—other ... VA-3
Tampico ... VA-3
Tampico—locale ... MT-8
Tampico—locale ... OH-6
Tampico—locale ... TN-4
Tampico—locale ... WA-9
**Tampico**—pop pl ... IL-6
**Tampico**—pop pl ... IN-6
**Tampico**—pop pl ... TX-5
Tampico Baptist Ch—church ... TN-4
Tampico Cem—cemetery ... TN-4
Tampico Draw—valley ... NM-5
Tampico (historical)—locale ... MS-4
Tampico Mounds—hist pl ... IL-6
Tampico Mounds—summit ... IL-6
Tampico Peak—summit ... NM-5
Tampico Post Office (historical)—building ... TN-4
Tampico Restaurant—hist pl ... UT-8
Tampico Sch—school ... VT-1
Tampico Siding—locale ... TX-5
Tampico Spring—spring ... NM-5
**Tampico (Township of)**—pop pl ... IL-6
Tampico Windmill—locale ... TX-5
Tampier Slough—reservoir ... IL-6
Tampke Cem—cemetery ... TX-5
Tamrock Well—well ... AZ-5
**Tams**—pop pl ... WV-2
Tamsin Park—park ... OH-6
Tam Tam Ridge—ridge ... WA-9
Ta (Municipality)—civ div ... FM-9
**Tamuning**—pop pl ... GU-9
Tamuning (Election District)—fmr MCD ... GU-9
Tamuning Sch—school ... GU-9
Tamura Sch—school ... CA-9
Tamureu ... FM-9
Tamuroi ... FM-9
Tamwahk—swamp ... FM-9
Tamwahs—unknown ... FM-9
Tamwarahlong ... FM-9
Tamwarohi—locale ... FM-9
Tamwatamw—summit ... FM-9
Tamwol—island ... MP-9
**Tamworohi**—pop pl ... FM-9
Tamworohi—ridge ... FM-9
Tamworth—locale ... VA-3
**Tamworth**—pop pl ... NH-1
Tamworth Sch—school ... NH-1
Tamworth Sch—school ... SD-7
**Tamworth (Town of)**—pop pl ... NH-1
**Tamworth Township**—pop pl ... SD-7
Tanaachau ... FM-9
Tanaak Cape—cape ... AK-9
Tanabaco ... MH-9
Tana Bight—bay ... AK-9
Tana Canyon—valley ... AK-9
**Tanacross**—pop pl ... AK-9
Tanacross ANV957—reserve ... AK-9
Tanada Creek—stream ... AK-9
Tanadak Island—island ... AK-9
Tanadak Pass—channel ... AK-9
Tanada Lake—lake ... AK-9
Tanada Lodge—locale ... AK-9
Tanada Peak—summit ... AK-9
Tanaga Bay—bay ... AK-9
Tanaga Island—island ... AK-9
Tanaga Pass—channel ... AK-9
Tanaga Volcano—summit ... AK-9
Tanager Branch—stream ... TN-4
Tanager Creek—stream ... MI-6
Tanager Lake—lake ... MN-6
Tanager Lake—lake ... WY-8
Tanager Point—cape ... AK-9
Tanager Wood Golf Club—other ... OH-6
Tana Glacier—glacier ... AK-9
Tanaher Pond—lake ... NY-2
Tan-a-hill Creek—stream ... AR-4
Tanaina Glacier—glacier ... AK-9
Tanaina Peak—summit ... AK-9
Tanaka (historical)—locale ... SD-7
Tanaklak Island—island ... AK-9
Tanalian Mtn—summit ... AK-9
Tanalian Point—cape ... AK-9
**Tanalian Point**—pop pl ... AK-9
Tanalian River—stream ... AK-9
Tana Lobe Bremner Glacier—glacier ... AK-9
Tanama (Barrio)—fmr MCD (2) ... PR-3
**Tanana**—pop pl ... AK-9
Tanana-Allakaket Winter Trail—trail ... AK-9
Tanana Island—island ... AK-9
Tanana Mission—hist pl ... AK-9
Tanana River—stream ... AK-9
**Tanani**—pop pl ... AK-9
Tanani Bay—bay ... AK-9
Tanani Point—cape ... AK-9
Tanapag—beach ... MH-9
**Tanapag**—pop pl ... MH-9
Tanapag, Lagunan—bay ... MH-9
Tanapag, Puetton—harbor ... MH-9
Tanapag, Unai—beach ... MH-9
Tanapag Beach ... MH-9
Tanapag Hafen ... MH-9
Tanapag Harbor ... MH-9
Tanapag Lagoon ... MH-9
Tanapag Port ... MH-9
Tanapagu ... MH-9
Tanapako ... MH-9
Tanapaku ... MH-9
Tana Point—cape ... AK-9
Tanaqen ... FM-9
Tana River—stream ... AK-9
Tanasee Bald—summit ... NC-3
Tanasee Creek—stream ... NC-3
Tanasee Creek Lake—reservoir ... NC-3
Tanasee Gap—gap ... NC-3
Tanasee Lake Dam—dam ... NC-3
Tanasee Ridge—ridge ... NC-3
Tanasi ... TN-4
Tanasia Lagoon—lake ... LA-4
Tanasi Council Girl Scout Camp—locale ... TN-4
Tanaskan Bay—bay ... AK-9
Tanassee ... TN-4
Tanatamsakir ... FM-9
Tanatee Creek ... GA-3
Tanawasher Spring—spring ... OR-9
Tanbark—locale ... KY-4
Tanbark Branch—stream ... KY-4
Tanbark Branch—stream ... NC-3
Tanbark Branch—stream ... TX-5
Tanbark Branch—stream ... VA-3
Tanbark Canyon ... NM-5
Tanbark Canyon—valley ... CA-9
Tanbark Canyon—valley ... NM-5
Tanbark Creek—stream ... CA-9
Tanbark Creek—stream ... NY-2
Tanbark Creek—stream ... TX-5
Tanbark Flat—summit ... VA-3
Tanbark Flats—flat ... CA-9
Tanbark Gap—gap ... NC-3
Tanbark Hill—summit ... KY-4
Tanbark Hill—summit ... TN-4
**Tanbark (historical)**—pop pl ... TN-4
Tanbark Hollow—valley ... MO-7
Tanbark Hollow—valley ... TN-4
Tanbark Knob—summit ... TN-4
Tanbark Point—cape ... OR-9
Tanbark Post Office (historical)—building ... TN-4
Tanbark Ridge—ridge ... NC-3
Tanbark Ridge—ridge ... VA-3
**Tanberg (Township of)**—pop pl ... MN-6
Tan Branch—stream ... FL-3
Tan Branch—stream ... KY-4
Tan Branch—stream ... MS-4
Tan Branch—stream ... VA-3
Tanby Ditch—canal ... OH-6
Tancaw Creek—stream ... SC-3
Tan Cem—cemetery ... MO-7
Tancha Bayou ... TX-5
T Anchor Ranch—locale ... AZ-5
Tanco RR Station—locale ... FL-3
Tancosa—area ... NM-5
Tancosa Wash—stream ... NM-5
Tancosa Windmill—locale ... NM-5
Tancred—locale ... CA-9
**Tancrede**—pop pl ... FL-3
Tan Creek—stream ... AL-4
Tan Creek—stream ... PA-2
Tancroft Hollow—valley ... VA-3
Tancum River ... WA-9
Tandakee Creek—stream ... TX-5
Tanda Lake—lake ... WI-6
Tandam Branch—stream ... NC-3
Tandem Spring—spring ... ID-8
T and L Windmill—locale ... TX-5
Tandon Lake—reservoir ... NC-3
Tandon Lake Dam—dam ... NC-3
T and P Hosp—hospital ... TX-5
T and P Lake—lake ... TX-5
T and P Well—well ... TX-5
Tandy—locale ... VA-3
**Tandy**—pop pl ... MS-4
Tandy, Lake—reservoir ... KY-4
Tandy Bay—bay ... OR-9
Tandy Bay Campground—park ... OR-9
Tandy Cem—cemetery ... KY-4
Tandy Center—post sta ... TX-5
Tandy Creek—stream ... OR-9
Tandy Knob—summit ... TN-4
Tandy Mesa—summit ... TX-5
Tandy Park—park ... MO-7
Tandy Ranch—locale ... MT-8
Tandy Sch—school ... IL-6
Tandy Sch—school ... TX-5
Tandy Tackett Branch—stream ... KY-4
Tandy Y Sch—school ... ND-7
Tandy 6 Coal Mine—mine ... MT-8
Taneaw ... FM-9
Tan en ... FM-9
Tanepei ... FM-9
Taneum Canyon—valley ... WA-9
Taneum Creek—stream ... WA-9
Taneum Ditch—canal ... WA-9
Taneum Forest Camp—locale ... WA-9
Taneum Lake—lake ... WA-9
Taneum Meadow—flat ... WA-9
Taneum Point—summit ... WA-9
Taneum Ridge—ridge ... WA-9
Taney Brook—stream ... RI-1
Taneycomo, Lake—reservoir ... MO-7
Taneycomo Country Club—other ... MO-7
Taney County—civil ... MO-7
**Taney (County)**—pop pl ... MO-7
Taney JHS—school ... MD-2
Taney Place—hist pl ... MD-2
**Taneytown**—pop pl ... MD-2
Taneytown Hist Dist—hist pl ... MD-2
Taneytown Sch—school ... MD-2
**Taneyville**—pop pl ... MO-7
Taneyville Sch—school ... MO-7
Taneyville Union Chapel—church ... MO-7
Tan Fat Hill—summit ... CT-1
Tanforan—uninc pl ... CA-9
Tanford Mine (underground)—mine ... AL-4
Tangahl ... FM-9
Tangair—locale ... CA-9
Tangal ... FM-9
Tangan Ranch (abandoned)—locale ... MT-8
Tanganyika, Lake—lake ... CA-9
Tangascootack Creek—stream ... PA-2
Tangedahl Lake—lake ... ND-7
Tangeel—summit ... FM-9
Tangel ... FM-9
Tangelo Baptist Ch—church ... FL-3
**Tangelo Park**—pop pl ... FL-3
Tangelo Park Elem Sch—school ... FL-3
Tangeman—locale ... NE-7
Tangeman, John, House—hist pl ... OH-6
Tangen Cem—cemetery ... IL-6
Tangen Draw—valley ... MT-8
Tangen Mtn—summit ... MT-8
Tangen Rsvr—reservoir ... OR-9
**Tangent**—pop pl ... OR-9
Tangent Peak—summit ... AK-9
Tangent Peak—summit ... UT-8
Tangent Point—cape (2) ... AK-9
Tangent Sch—school ... OR-9
Tanger Cem—cemetery ... OH-6
**Tangerine**—pop pl ... FL-3
Tangerine Bowl—locale ... FL-3
Tangerine Cem—cemetery ... FL-3
Tangerine Interchange—crossing ... AZ-5
Tangerine Lake—lake ... FL-3
Tangerman Creek—stream ... OR-9
Tangerra Lake—lake ... AK-9
Tanger Sch—school ... MI-6
Tanget Ra Medu ... PW-9
Tangier—locale ... OK-5
**Tangier**—pop pl ... IN-6
**Tangier**—pop pl (2) ... VA-3
Tangier Creek ... VA-3
Tangier Island—island ... VA-3
Tangier North Channel—channel ... VA-3
Tangier Sound—bay ... MD-2
Tangier Sound—bay ... VA-3
Tangik Island—island ... AK-9
Tanginak Anchorage—bay ... AK-9
Tanginak Island—island ... AK-9
**Tangipahoa**—pop pl ... LA-4
**Tangipahoa**—pop pl ... MS-4
Tangipahoa, Lake—reservoir ... MS-4
Tangipahoa Baptist Church ... MS-4
Tangipahoa Cem—cemetery ... MS-4
Tangipahoa Ch—church (3) ... MS-4
**Tangipahoa Parish**—pop pl ... LA-4
Tangipahoa Parish Training Sch Dormitory—hist pl ... LA-4
Tangipahoa River—stream ... LA-4
Tangipahoa River—stream ... MS-4
Tangke—slope ... MH-9
Tangke, Laderan—cliff ... MH-9
Tangke, Puntan—cape ... MH-9
Tangle ... MP-9
Tangleblue Creek—stream ... AK-9
Tangle Blue Creek—stream ... CA-9
Tangle Blue Lake—lake ... CA-9
Tangle Brook—stream ... ME-1
Tangle Creek—stream ... AZ-5
Tangle Creek—stream ... ID-8
Tangle Creek Cabin—locale ... AZ-5
Tangled Creek—stream ... WY-8
Tanglefoot Bay—bay ... AK-9
Tanglefoot Canyon—valley ... CA-9
Tanglefoot Creek—stream ... MT-8
Tanglefoot Hollow—valley ... PA-2
Tanglefoot Island—island ... WA-9
Tanglefoot Lake—lake ... MI-6
Tanglefoot Point—summit ... ID-8
Tanglefoot Run—stream ... PA-2
Tangle Gulch—valley ... CO-8
Tangle Lakes—lake ... AK-9
Tangle Lakes Archeol District—hist pl ... AK-9
Tanglenook Sch—school ... MO-7
Tanglen Sch—school ... MN-6
Tangle Peak—summit ... AZ-5
Tangle Peak Tank—reservoir ... AZ-5
Tangle River—stream ... AK-9
**Tanglewild**—pop pl ... WA-9
Tanglewilde-Thompson Place—CDP ... WA-9
Tanglewood ... IL-6
Tanglewood ... IN-6
Tanglewood ... MS-4
Tanglewood ... NC-3
Tanglewood—CDP ... FL-3
Tanglewood—hist pl ... AL-4
Tanglewood—hist pl ... OH-6
Tanglewood—locale ... MS-4
**Tanglewood**—pop pl ... CA-9
**Tanglewood**—pop pl ... IN-6
**Tanglewood**—pop pl (2) ... LA-4
**Tanglewood**—pop pl ... MD-2
**Tanglewood**—pop pl ... MA-1
**Tanglewood**—pop pl (2) ... PA-2
**Tanglewood**—pop pl ... SC-3
**Tanglewood**—pop pl ... TN-4
**Tanglewood**—pop pl ... TX-5
**Tanglewood**—pop pl ... VA-3
Tanglewood—uninc pl ... KY-4
Tanglewood, Lake—reservoir ... TX-5
**Tanglewood Acres**—pop pl ... CO-8
**Tanglewood Acres Subdivision**—pop pl ... UT-8
Tanglewood Airp—airport ... PA-2
Tanglewood Auditorium—building ... MA-1
Tanglewood Cem—cemetery ... MS-4
Tanglewood Cem—cemetery ... NC-3
Tanglewood Ch—church ... IN-6
Tanglewood Ch—church ... OK-5
Tanglewood Creek—stream ... CO-8
Tanglewood Dam Number Two—dam ... NC-3
Tanglewood Dam Upper—dam ... NC-3
Tanglewood Elem Sch—school ... FL-3
**Tanglewood Estates**—pop pl ... TN-4
**Tanglewood Estates (subdivision)**—pop pl ... NC-3
Tanglewood Golf Course—locale (2) ... PA-2
Tanglewood Golf Course Airp—airport ... PA-2
Tanglewood (historical P.O.)—locale ... IN-6
Tanglewood Island—island ... MI-6
Tanglewood Island—island ... WA-9
Tanglewood Lake—lake ... MN-6
Tanglewood Lake—lake ... OH-6
Tanglewood Lake—reservoir ... IN-6
Tanglewood Lake—reservoir ... KS-7
Tanglewood Lake—reservoir ... NY-2
Tanglewood Lake Number Two—reservoir ... NC-3
Tanglewood Lake Upper—reservoir ... NC-3
Tanglewood Manor Golf Course—locale ... PA-2
Tanglewood Park—park (2) ... NC-3
Tanglewood Park—park ... TX-5
Tanglewood Park and Golf Course ... NC-3
**Tanglewood (Pilgrim Gardens)**—pop pl ... DE-2
Tanglewood Plantation—hist pl ... SC-3
Tanglewood Plantation—locale ... LA-4
Tanglewood Plantation (historical)—locale (2) ... MS-4
Tanglewood Playground—park ... MS-4
Tanglewood Preserve—park ... NY-2
Tanglewood Sch—school ... MD-2
Tanglewood Sch—school ... NC-3
Tanglewood Sch—school ... OK-5
Tanglewood School ... TN-4
Tanglewood (ski area)—locale ... PA-2
Tanglewoods Sch (historical)—school ... TN-4
**Tanglewood (subdivision)**—pop pl (2) ... AL-4
**Tanglewood (subdivision)**—pop pl (2) ... MS-4
**Tanglewood (subdivision)**—pop pl (3) ... NC-3
**Tanglewood (subdivision)**—pop pl (2) ... TN-4
**Tanglewood Subdivision**—pop pl ... UT-8
**Tanglewood Subdivision #3**—pop pl ... UT-8
Tanglewood University of Alabama Biological Station—locale ... AL-4
Tanglwood Ski Area Airp—airport ... PA-2
Tangnes Trail—trail ... MN-6
Tango—locale ... WV-2
Tango Bay—bay ... MN-6
Tango Bayou—stream ... MS-4
Tango Branch—stream ... WV-2
Tango Creek—stream ... AK-9
Tango Creek—stream (3) ... ID-8
Tango Creek—stream ... MT-8
**Tang-O-Mar Beach**—pop pl ... FL-3
Tango Mine—mine ... ID-8
Tangon Rock—island ... GU-9
Tango Point—summit ... MT-8
Tango Ranch Airp—airport ... WA-9
Tang Post Office (historical)—building ... TN-4
Tangs Creek—stream ... MD-2
Tangue Allegre Cem—cemetery ... TX-5
Tanguisson Point—summit ... GU-9
Tanguy—locale ... PA-2
Tan House Creek ... AZ-5
Tanhouse Creek—stream ... MD-2
Tan House Run—stream ... OH-6
Tani—bar ... FM-9
Tanian ... MH-9
Tanignak Lake—lake ... AK-9
Tanima Peak—summit ... CO-8
Tanion—bar ... FM-9
Tanion—island ... FM-9
Tanion Island ... FM-9
Tanislado Canyon—valley ... TX-5
Tanis Lake—lake ... AK-9
Tanis River—stream ... AK-9
Tanjoga Lake—lake ... AK-9
Tank ... AZ-5
Tank—locale ... PA-2
Tank, Arroyo—reservoir ... TX-5
Tank, Lake—lake ... AZ-5
Tank, Lake—lake (2) ... NM-5
Tank, The—flat ... NV-8
Tank, The—reservoir ... UT-8
Tanka Grande Windmill—locale ... NM-5
Tank Ahupu Gulch—valley ... HI-9
Tankard Creek—stream ... NC-3
**Tankards Beach**—pop pl ... VA-3
Tank Branch—stream ... NC-3
Tank Branch—stream ... WV-2
Tank Brook—stream ... NY-2
Tank Butte ... AZ-5
Tank Canyon ... AZ-5
Tank Canyon ... NV-8
Tank Canyon—valley (4) ... AZ-5
Tank Canyon—valley ... CA-9
Tank Canyon—valley ... NV-8
Tank Canyon—valley (2) ... NM-5
Tank Canyon—valley (7) ... UT-8
Tank Cem—cemetery ... MD-2
Tank Ch—church ... AL-4
Tank Cottage—hist pl ... WI-6
Tank Coulee—valley (2) ... MT-8
Tank Creek ... MI-6
Tank Creek ... TX-5
Tank Creek—stream (3) ... AZ-5
Tank Creek—stream ... CA-9
Tank Creek—stream ... CO-8
Tank Creek—stream ... ID-8
Tank Creek—stream (2) ... MI-6
Tank Creek—stream ... MN-6
Tank Creek—stream (2) ... MT-8
Tank Creek—stream (2) ... NC-3
Tank Creek—stream (2) ... OR-9
Tank Creek—stream ... PA-2
Tank Creek—stream ... VA-3
Tank Creek—stream (2) ... WI-6
Tank Creek Mesa—summit ... AZ-5
Tank Creek Tank—reservoir ... AZ-5
Tank Dam—dam ... AZ-5
Tank Drain—stream ... MI-6
Tank Draw—valley (2) ... NM-5
Tanke ... MH-9
Tanke Chalie Well—well ... TX-5
Tanke Cliffs ... MH-9
Tanke Hal Well—well ... TX-5
Tank Eighteen—reservoir ... NM-5
Tanke Point ... MH-9
Tanker Branch—stream ... SC-3
Tanker Creek—stream ... VA-3
Tankerhoosen Lake—lake ... CT-1
Tankerhoosen Lakes ... CT-1
Tankerhoosen River—stream ... CT-1
Tanker Island—island ... AK-9
Tankersley Branch—stream ... SC-3
Tankersley Branch—stream ... TN-4
Tankersley Cem—cemetery (2) ... TN-4
Tankersley Creek—stream ... TX-5
Tankersley Lake—lake ... TX-5
Tankersley Lake—reservoir ... SC-3
Tankersley Lake—reservoir ... TN-4
Tankersley Lake—reservoir ... TX-5
Tankersley Lake Dam—dam ... TN-4
Tankersley Ridge—ridge ... TN-4
Tankersley Sch—school ... AL-4
Tankersley Tavern—hist pl ... VA-3
Tankersley-Twin Mountain Sch—school ... TX-5
Tankersly ... TX-5
**Tankersly**—pop pl ... TX-5
Tankersly Park—park ... IA-7
Tank Flat—flat ... MT-8
Tank Four Gulch—valley ... CA-9
Tank Gulch—valley ... AZ-5
Tank Gulch—valley (2) ... CA-9
Tank Gulch—valley ... CO-8
Tank Gulch—valley ... MT-8
Tank Gulch Tank—reservoir ... AZ-5
Tank Hill—ridge ... AZ-5
Tank Hill—summit ... ID-8
Tank Hill—summit ... NV-8
Tank Hollow—valley ... AL-4
Tank Hollow—valley (2) ... PA-2
Tank Hollow—valley (3) ... TN-4
Tank Hollow—valley ... TX-5
Tank Hollow—valley (2) ... UT-8
Tank Hollow—valley (2) ... VA-3
Tank Hollow—valley ... WV-2
Tank Hollow Falls—falls ... VA-3
Tank Hollow Spring—spring ... UT-8
Tankiln Run—stream ... WV-2
Tank in the Flat—reservoir ... NM-5
Tank in the Road—reservoir ... AZ-5
Tank Island—island (2) ... FL-3
Tank Island—island ... NY-2
Tank Lake ... MN-6
Tank Lake ... WI-6
Tank Lake—lake ... AR-4
Tank Lake—lake (3) ... FL-3
Tank Lake—lake ... LA-4
Tank Lake—lake ... MI-6
Tank Lake—lake (4) ... MN-6
Tank Lake—lake ... SC-3
Tank Lake—lake ... TX-5
Tank Lake—lake (4) ... WI-6
Tank Lake—reservoir ... OK-5
Tank Lakes—lake ... WA-9
Tank Mesa—summit ... CO-8
Tank Mesa—summit ... UT-8
Tank Mountains—ridge ... AZ-5
Tank Mtn—summit (2) ... NM-5
Tank Nineteen—reservoir ... NM-5
Tan Knob—summit ... KY-4
Tank No 1—reservoir (2) ... NM-5
Tank No 1 South—reservoir ... NM-5
Tank No 10 South—reservoir ... NM-5
Tank No 11—reservoir ... NM-5
Tank No 2—reservoir (2) ... NM-5
Tank No 2 South—reservoir ... NM-5
Tank No 3—reservoir (2) ... NM-5
Tank No 4—reservoir (2) ... NM-5
Tank No 4 North—reservoir ... NM-5
Tank No 5 North—reservoir ... NM-5
Tank No 5 South—reservoir ... NM-5
Tank No 6 North—reservoir ... NM-5
Tank No 6 South—reservoir ... NM-5
Tank No 7—reservoir ... NM-5
Tank No 7 North—reservoir ... NM-5
Tank No 7 South—reservoir ... NM-5
Tank No 8 North—reservoir ... NM-5
Tank No 8 South—reservoir ... NM-5
Tank No 9 South—reservoir ... NM-5
Tank Number Two—reservoir ... NM-5
Tank On The Hill—reservoir ... TX-5
Tank Pass—gap ... AZ-5
Tank Peak ... CO-8
Tank Point Well—well ... UT-8
Tank Pond—lake (2) ... FL-3
Tank Pond—lake ... MO-7
Tank Pond—lake ... NY-2
Tank Pond—reservoir ... KY-4
Tank Pond Creek—stream ... IA-7
Tank Pond Hollow—valley ... KY-4
Tank Ridge—ridge ... CA-9
Tank Ridge—ridge ... UT-8
Tanks, The—locale ... CA-9
Tanks, The—locale ... UT-8
Tanks, The—reservoir ... NV-8
Tanks Canyon—valley ... AZ-5
Tanks Canyon—valley ... NV-8
Tanks Canyon Tank—reservoir ... AZ-5
Tank Sch—school ... PA-2
Tank Sch—school ... WI-6
Tank Seven Creek—stream ... CO-8
**Tanks (historical)**—pop pl ... OR-9
Tanksley—locale ... KY-4
Tanksley Bridge—bridge ... TN-4
Tanksley Cem—cemetery ... IN-6
Tanksley Cem—cemetery ... MS-4
Tanks Peak—summit ... CO-8
Tank Spring—spring ... ID-8
Tank Spring—spring ... IN-6
Tank Spring—spring ... MO-7
Tank Spring—spring (2) ... NV-8
Tank Spring—spring (2) ... OR-9
Tank Summit—summit ... NV-8
Tank Thirty-one—reservoir ... NM-5
Tankville—locale ... IL-6
Tank Wash—stream (2) ... AZ-5
Tank Wash—valley (3) ... UT-8
Tank Water Creek—stream ... TX-5
Tank Water Tank—reservoir ... AZ-5
Tank Windmill—locale ... NM-5
Tank 13—reservoir ... NM-5
Tank 16—reservoir ... NM-5
Tank 16 East—reservoir ... NM-5
Tan Lake—lake ... MI-6
Tan Lake (historical)—lake ... MO-7
Tanlund Lake—lake ... MI-6
**Tannahill Estates (subdivision)**—pop pl ... AL-4
Tannawasha Pasture—flat ... WA-9
Tann Cem—cemetery ... IL-6
Tannehill—locale ... LA-4
**Tannehill**—pop pl ... AL-4
Tannehill, Capt. James Boggs, House—hist pl ... OH-6
Tannehill Branch—stream ... TX-5
Tannehill Cem—cemetery ... IN-6
Tannehill Cem—cemetery ... KS-7
Tannehill Cem—cemetery ... OK-5

Tannehill Ch—*church* ... AL-4
Tannehill Covered Bridge—*bridge* ... IN-6
Tannehill Creek—*stream* ... LA-4
Tannehill Furnace—*hist pl* ... AL-4
Tannehill Furnace (historical)—*locale* ... AL-4
Tannehill (historical)—*locale* ... KS-7
*Tannehill Historical State Park* ... AL-4
*Tannehill Mill Creek* ... AL-4
Tannehill Mill (historical)—*locale* ... AL-4
Tannehill Prairie—*flat* ... OK-5
Tannehill Ranch—*locale* ... CA-9
Tannehill Sch—*school* ... NE-7
Tannehill Sch—*school* ... OK-5
Tannehill State Park—*park* ... AL-4
**Tannehill Valley Estates (subdivision)**—*pop pl* ... AL-4
Tannehill Valley Lake—*reservoir* ... AL-4
Tannehill Valley Lake Dam—*dam* ... AL-4
Tannen Creek—*stream* ... OR-9
Tannenhauf Golf Course—*other* ... OH-6
Tannen Lake—*lake* ... OR-9
Tannen Mtn—*summit* ... OR-9
Tanner—*locale* ... GA-3
Tanner—*locale* ... KY-4
**Tanner**—*pop pl* ... AL-4
**Tanner**—*pop pl* ... IN-6
**Tanner**—*pop pl* ... MO-7
**Tanner**—*pop pl* ... WA-9
**Tanner**—*pop pl* ... WV-2
Tanner, Albert H., House—*hist pl* ... OR-9
Tanner, A. N., House—*hist pl* ... UT-8
Tanner, Henry M., House—*hist pl* ... UT-8
Tanner, Henry O., House—*hist pl* ... PA-2
Tanner, Jake, House—*hist pl* ... UT-8
Tanner, John, House—*hist pl* ... KY-4
Tanner, Lake—*lake* ... FL-3
Tanner, Lake—*reservoir* ... AL-4
Tanner, Sidney, House—*hist pl* ... UT-8
Tanner, William A., House—*hist pl* ... IL-6
Tanner, William C., House—*hist pl* ... OH-6
Tanner Bayou—*stream* ... TX-5
Tanner Branch—*stream* ... MS-4
Tanner Branch—*stream* ... MO-7
Tanner Branch—*stream* ... TN-4
Tanner Branch—*stream* ... VA-3
Tanner Bridge—*bridge* ... AL-4
*Tanner Brook* ... MA-1
Tanner Brook—*stream* (2) ... CT-1
Tanner Brook—*stream* ... VT-1
Tanner Butte—*summit* ... OR-9
Tanner Butte Trail—*trail* ... OR-9
Tanner Canal—*canal* ... ID-8
*Tanner Canyon* ... AZ-5
Tanner Canyon—*valley* ... AZ-5
Tanner Canyon—*valley* ... CO-8
Tanner Canyon—*valley* ... NM-5
Tanner Canyon Rapids—*rapids* ... AZ-5
Tanner Cem—*cemetery* (2) ... AL-4
Tanner Cem—*cemetery* ... IL-6
Tanner Cem—*cemetery* ... MI-6
Tanner Cem—*cemetery* ... MS-4
Tanner Cem—*cemetery* ... NE-7
Tanner Cem—*cemetery* (3) ... NY-2
Tanner Cem—*cemetery* (2) ... TN-4
Tanner Cem—*cemetery* ... TX-5
Tanner Cem—*cemetery* ... WV-2
Tanner Ch—*church* ... AL-4
Tanner Ch—*church* ... GA-3
Tanner Ch of Christ—*church* ... AL-4
Tanner Cove—*bay* ... GA-3
*Tanner Creek* ... NY-2
*Tanner Creek* ... OR-9
*Tanner Creek* ... VA-3
Tanner Creek—*bay* ... MD-2
Tanner Creek—*stream* ... AR-4
Tanner Creek—*stream* ... LA-4
Tanner Creek—*stream* ... MI-6
Tanner Creek—*stream* (3) ... MT-8
Tanner Creek—*stream* ... NY-2
Tanner Creek—*stream* ... OK-5
Tanner Creek—*stream* (4) ... OR-9
Tanner Creek—*stream* ... UT-8
Tanner Creek—*stream* ... WV-2
*Tanner Creek Butte* ... OR-9
Tanner Creek Falls—*falls* ... OR-9
Tanner Creek Narrows—*gap* ... UT-8
*Tanner Crossing* ... AZ-5
**Tanner Crossroads**—*pop pl* ... AL-4
**Tanner Crossroads (Stewards Store)**—*pop pl* ... AL-4
Tanner Cutoff Trail—*trail* ... OR-9
Tanner Draw—*valley* ... TX-5
Tanner Elem Sch—*school* ... AL-4
Tanner First United Pentecostal Ch—*church* ... AL-4
Tanner Flat—*flat* ... TX-5
Tanner Flowage—*reservoir* ... WI-6
*Tanner Fork* ... WV-2
Tanner Fork—*stream* (3) ... WV-2
Tanner Gulch—*valley* (2) ... CA-9
Tanner Gulch—*valley* ... CO-8
Tanner Gulch—*valley* ... OR-9
Tanner Gulch—*valley* ... UT-8
Tanner Head—*summit* ... AK-9
**Tanner Heights**—*pop pl* ... AL-4
Tanner Heights Plaza Shop Ctr—*locale* ... AL-4
*Tanner Hill* ... RI-1
Tanner Hill—*summit* ... CT-1
Tanner Hill—*summit* ... NY-2
Tanner Hill Cem—*cemetery* ... NY-2
Tanner Hollow—*valley* ... AR-4
Tanner Hollow—*valley* (2) ... TN-4
Tanner Hollow—*valley* ... UT-8
Tanner Homestead—*locale* ... CO-8
Tanner HS—*school* ... AL-4
Tanner Hunt Garrett—*canal* ... WY-8
**Tannerie Woods**—*pop pl* ... PA-2
Tanner Industrial Park—*locale* ... AL-4
Tanner Knob—*summit* ... WV-2
Tanner Knoll—*summit* ... UT-8
Tanner Lake—*lake* ... FL-3
Tanner Lake—*lake* ... LA-4
Tanner Lake—*lake* ... MI-6
Tanner Lake—*lake* ... MN-6
Tanner Lake—*lake* ... WA-9
Tanner Lake—*reservoir* (2) ... NM-5
Tanner Lake Dam—*dam* ... MS-4
**Tanner Lane Condo**—*pop pl* ... UT-8
Tanner Mesa—*summit* ... CO-8
Tanner Methodist Ch—*church* ... AL-4
Tanner Mill—*locale* ... GA-3
*Tanner Mountain* ... MA-1
*Tanner Mountain* ... OR-9
Tanner Mtn—*summit* ... UT-8
Tanner Neck—*cape* ... NY-2
Tanner Park—*park* ... NY-2
Tanner Peak—*summit* ... AZ-5
Tanner Peak—*summit* ... CO-8
Tanner Point—*cape* ... VA-3
Tanner Pond—*lake* ... PA-2
Tanner Post Office—*building* ... AL-4
Tanner Ranch—*locale* ... AZ-5
Tanner Ranch—*locale* ... NM-5
Tanner Ranch—*locale* (2) ... SD-7
*Tanner Rapids* ... AZ-5
Tanner Ridge—*ridge* (2) ... UT-8
Tanner Rsvr—*reservoir* ... CA-9
Tanner Rsvr—*reservoir* (2) ... CO-8
Tanner Rsvr—*reservoir* ... UT-8
Tanner Run—*stream* ... OH-6
Tanner Run—*stream* (2) ... WV-2
*Tanner's* ... OH-6
Tanners—*locale* ... VA-3
Tanners Bluff—*cliff* ... TX-5
*Tanners Branch* ... DE-2
Tanners Branch—*stream* ... VA-3
Tanners Brook—*stream* ... NJ-2
Tanners Cem—*cemetery* ... MS-4
Tanners Ch—*church* ... GA-3
Tanner Sch—*school* (2) ... IL-6
Tanner Sch—*school* (2) ... MI-6
Tanner Sch—*school* ... MN-6
Tanner Sch—*school* ... TN-4
Tanners Chapel—*church* ... MS-4
**Tanners Corner**—*pop pl* ... NJ-2
Tanners Corners—*locale* ... NY-2
**Tanners Corners**—*pop pl* ... NJ-2
*Tanners Creek* ... IN-6
*Tanner's Creek* ... VA-3
Tanners Creek—*stream* ... IN-6
Tanners Creek—*stream* ... KY-4
Tanners Creek—*stream* ... LA-4
Tanners Creek—*stream* ... MD-2
Tanners Crossing—*locale* ... AZ-5
**Tanners Cross Roads (historical)**—*pop pl* ... VA-3
Tanner Settlement—*locale* ... TX-5
Tanners Falls—*locale* ... PA-2
Tanners Ferry (historical)—*locale* ... MS-4
Tanners Flat Campground—*park* ... UT-8
Tanners Grove Ch—*church* ... NC-3
Tanner's Hosp—*hist pl* ... MN-6
Tanners Lake—*lake* ... MI-6
Tanners Lake—*lake* ... MN-6
Tanner Slough—*stream* ... CA-9
Tanner's Mill—*hist pl* ... GA-3
Tanners Mill (historical)—*locale* ... AL-4
Tanners Pass—*gap* ... OR-9
Tanners Peak—*summit* ... CA-9
Tanners Peak Trail—*trail* ... CA-9
Tanners Point—*cape* ... MD-2
Tanners Point—*summit* ... CA-9
Tanners Point Trail—*trail* ... CA-9
Tanner Spring—*spring* ... AL-4
Tanner Spring—*spring* ... OR-9
Tanner Springs—*locale* ... AZ-5
Tanner Springs—*spring* ... FL-3
Tanner's Ranch—*locale* ... MT-8
Tanners Ridge—*ridge* ... VA-3
Tanners Ridge Cem—*cemetery* ... VA-3
Tanners Ridge Overlook—*locale* ... VA-3
Tanners Rock—*summit* ... CA-9
**Tanner Subdivision**—*pop pl* ... UT-8
*Tannersville* ... PA-2
Tannersville—*locale* ... VA-3
**Tannersville**—*pop pl* ... IN-6
**Tannersville**—*pop pl* ... NY-2
**Tannersville**—*pop pl* ... PA-2
Tannersville Ch—*church* ... VA-3
*Tannersville Cranberry Bog* ... PA-2
Tannersville Learning Center—*school* ... PA-2
Tannersville Reservoirs—*reservoir* ... NY-2
Tannersville Station (historical)—*locale* ... PA-2
Tanner Tank—*reservoir* ... AZ-5
Tanner Tank—*reservoir* ... NM-5
**Tannertown**—*pop pl* ... PA-2
**Tanner Township**—*pop pl* ... ND-7
Tanner Trail—*trail* ... CO-8
*Tanner Wash* ... AZ-5
Tanner Wash—*arroyo* ... AZ-5
Tanner Wash—*stream* (2) ... AZ-5
Tanner Well—*well* ... AZ-5
**Tanner Williams**—*pop pl* ... AL-4
Tanner-Williams (CCD)—*cens area* ... AL-4
*Tanner Williams Church* ... AL-4
Tanner-Williams Division—*civil* ... AL-4
Tanner Williams Sch—*school* ... AL-4
*Tannery* (2) ... MD-2
Tannery—*locale* ... KY-4
Tannery—*locale* ... MD-2
**Tannery**—*pop pl* ... KY-4
**Tannery**—*pop pl* ... PA-2
**Tannery**—*pop pl* ... WV-2
Tannery—*uninc pl* ... WI-6
Tannery, The—*hist pl* ... PA-2
Tannery Branch—*stream* ... IN-6
Tannery Branch—*stream* ... TN-4
*Tannery Brook* ... MA-1
Tannery Brook—*stream* ... CT-1
Tannery Brook—*stream* (4) ... ME-1
Tannery Brook—*stream* (3) ... MA-1
Tannery Brook—*stream* ... NH-1
Tannery Brook—*stream* (4) ... NY-2
Tannery Brook—*stream* (2) ... VT-1
Tannery Cem—*cemetery* ... VA-3
Tannery Cem—*cemetery* ... WI-6
Tannery Corners—*locale* ... NY-2
Tannery Creek—*stream* ... CA-9
Tannery Creek—*stream* (3) ... MI-6
Tannery Creek—*stream* (4) ... NY-2
Tannery Creek—*stream* ... PA-2
Tannery Falls—*falls* ... MA-1
Tannery Flats—*flat* ... TN-4
Tannery Gulch—*valley* (2) ... CA-9
Tannery Gulf—*valley* ... GA-3
Tannery Gully—*stream* ... MI-6
Tannery Hill—*summit* ... ME-1
Tannery Hill—*summit* ... PA-2
Tannery Hill Trail—*trail* ... PA-2
Tannery Hole—*cave* ... PA-2
Tannery Hollow—*valley* ... PA-2
Tannery Hollow Run—*stream* ... PA-2
Tannery Island—*island* ... TN-4
Tannery Knobs—*ridge* ... TN-4
**Tannery (Lehigh Tannery)**—*pop pl* ... PA-2
*Tannery Pond* ... MA-1
Tannery Pond—*lake* ... ME-1
Tannery Pond—*lake* (2) ... MA-1
Tannery Pond—*lake* ... NH-1
Tannery Pond—*reservoir* ... MA-1
Tannery Pond Dam—*dam* ... MA-1
Tannery Ridge—*ridge* ... CA-9
Tannery Sch—*school* ... KY-4
Tannery Sch—*school* ... MI-6
Tannery Sch—*school* ... NY-2
Tannery Sch (historical)—*school* ... TN-4
Tannery Spring—*spring* ... GA-3
Tannessee Flat—*flat* ... WA-9
Tanney Draw—*valley* ... WY-8
Tanning Brook—*stream* ... ME-1
Tannings Point—*cape* ... WI-6
*Tannum Lake* ... WA-9
Tannybill Windmill—*locale* ... TX-5
Tanny Hill—*summit* ... OK-5
**Tanoak**—*pop pl* ... CA-9
Tan Oak Camp—*locale* ... CA-9
Tan Oak Creek—*stream* ... CA-9
**Tan Oak Park**—*pop pl* ... CA-9
Tan Oak Ridge—*ridge* ... CA-9
**Tanoma**—*pop pl* ... PA-2
*Tanonsogon* ... FM-9
Tanquary Cem—*cemetery* ... IL-6
Tanquary Cem—*cemetery* ... OH-6
Tanquary Windmill—*locale* ... TX-5
Tanque—*locale* ... AZ-5
Tanque Alegre Windmill—*locale* ... TX-5
**Tanque Aloma**—*pop pl* ... AZ-5
Tanque Aloma—*reservoir* ... AZ-5
Tanque del Burro—*reservoir* ... TX-5
Tanque Escondido—*reservoir* ... TX-5
Tanque Grande—*reservoir* ... NM-5
Tanque Grava—*reservoir* ... TX-5
Tanque Las Tres Puertas—*reservoir* ... TX-5
Tanque La Trampa Los Chivos—*reservoir* ... TX-5
Tanque Llano—*reservoir* (2) ... TX-5
Tanque los Cuates—*reservoir* ... TX-5
Tanque Mula—*reservoir* ... TX-5
Tanque Noche Triste—*reservoir* ... TX-5
Tanque Pendejo—*lake* ... NM-5
Tanque Piedra—*reservoir* ... AZ-5
Tanque Porfido—*reservoir* ... TX-5
Tanques de Luis Well (Windmill)—*locale* ... TX-5
Tanquesitos Cem—*cemetery* ... TX-5
Tanque Trampa—*reservoir* ... TX-5
**Tanque Verde**—*pop pl* ... AZ-5
Tanque Verde Canyon—*valley* ... AZ-5
Tanque Verde Creek—*stream* ... AZ-5
Tanque Verde Falls—*falls* ... AZ-5
*Tanque Verde Mountains* ... AZ-5
Tanque Verde Peak—*summit* ... AZ-5
Tanque Verde Ranch—*locale* ... AZ-5
Tanque Verde Ridge—*ridge* ... AZ-5
Tanque Verde Sch—*school* ... AZ-5
Tanque Verde Shop Ctr—*locale* ... AZ-5
Tanque Verde Trail—*trail* ... AZ-5
Tanque Verde Wash—*stream* ... AZ-5
Tan Rara Airp—*airport* ... TN-4
**Tan Rara Oesta**—*pop pl* ... TN-4
Tans Bay—*swamp* ... SC-3
Tans Bay HS—*school* ... SC-3
Tans Bay Sch—*school* ... SC-3
**Tansboro**—*pop pl* ... NJ-2
Tansboro Sch—*school* ... NJ-2
*Tansborough* ... NJ-2
Tan Seep—*spring* ... UT-8
Tansel Branch—*stream* ... IN-6
Tansem—*locale* ... MN-6
Tansem Lake—*lake* ... MN-6
**Tansem (Township of)**—*pop pl* ... MN-6
*Tanset Ra Medu* ... PW-9
Tansey—*locale* ... LA-4
Tansey Island—*island* ... MS-4
Tansey Sch—*school* ... MA-1
Tansi, Lake—*reservoir* ... TN-4
Tansi Lake—*reservoir* ... TN-4
Tansi Lake Dam—*dam* ... TN-4
Tansil Cem—*cemetery* ... TN-4
Tansill—*locale* ... IL-6
Tansill Dam—*dam* ... NM-5
Tansi Resort—*locale* ... TN-4
Tan Swamp—*stream* ... NC-3
Tansy Creek—*stream* ... OR-9
Tansy Point—*cape* ... OR-9
Tansy Point Range Channel—*channel* ... OR-9
Tansy Point Turn—*channel* ... OR-9
Tansy Rsvr—*reservoir* ... OR-9
Tantabogue Creek—*stream* ... TX-5
Tantallon—*locale* ... TN-4
**Tantallon**—*pop pl* ... MD-2
Tantallon Country Club—*other* ... MD-2
Tantallon Park—*park* ... MD-2
Tantallon Point—*cape* ... AK-9
**Tantalus**—*pop pl* ... HI-9
Tantalus—*summit* ... HI-9
Tantalus Creek—*stream* ... UT-8
Tantalus Creek—*stream* ... WY-8
Tantalus Flats—*flat* ... UT-8
*Tantalus Hill* ... HI-9
*Tantalus Peak* ... HI-9
Tantapalo Point—*cape* ... GU-9
Tan Tar A Resort Seaplane Base—*airport* ... MO-7
Tantasqua Regional HS—*school* ... MA-1
Tantau Park—*park* ... CA-9
**Tanterra (Lakewood At Tanterra)**—*pop pl* ... MD-2
*Tantic* ... FL-3
Tantiusques Reservation—*hist pl* ... MA-1
Tanton Cem—*cemetery* ... MO-7
*Tantousque Lake* ... MA-1
Tantrattle Mtn—*summit* ... ME-1
Tantraugh Branch—*stream* ... NC-3
Tan Troff Branch—*stream* ... AL-4
Tantroft Branch—*stream* ... AL-4
Tantroft Branch—*stream* ... KY-4
Tantrott Branch—*stream* ... AL-4
Tan Trough—*valley* ... WV-2
Tantrough Branch—*stream* ... AL-4
Tantrough Branch—*stream* ... DE-2
Tantrough Branch—*stream* (3) ... KY-4
Tantrough Branch—*stream* (2) ... NC-3
Tan Trough Branch—*stream* ... SC-3
Tantrough Branch—*stream* ... TX-5
Tantrough Branch—*stream* ... WV-2
Tan Trough Branch—*stream* ... WV-2
Tantrough Branch—*stream* ... WV-2
Tantrough Cove—*bay* ... GA-3
Tan Trough Creek—*stream* ... AL-4
Tan Trough Creek—*stream* ... AR-4
Tan Trough Creek—*stream* ... GA-3
Tan Trough Creek—*stream* ... LA-4
Tan Trough Creek—*stream* ... MS-4
Tantrough Creek—*stream* ... TN-4
Tantrough Creek—*stream* ... TX-5
*Tantrough Ditch* ... DE-2
Tantrough Fork—*stream* ... KY-4
Tantrough Hollow—*valley* ... MO-7
Tantrough Hollow—*valley* ... TN-4
Tan Trough Run—*stream* ... WV-2
**Tants Crossroads**—*pop pl* ... NC-3
*Tantuesque* ... MA-1
*Tanum Creek* ... WA-9
*Tanum Lake* ... WA-9
*Tanum River* ... WA-9
Tanunak Bay—*bay* ... AK-9
Tanunak River—*stream* ... AK-9
Tanunak (Tununak)—*other* ... AK-9
**Tanunak (Tununak Post Office)**—*pop pl* ... AK-9
Tanuth—*summit* ... FM-9
Tan Vat Branch—*stream* ... FL-3
Tan Vat Hole—*channel* ... MO-7
Tanwax—*locale* ... WA-9
Tanwax Creek—*stream* ... WA-9
Tanwax Lake—*lake* ... WA-9
Tanya Lake—*lake* ... TN-4
Tanyard—*locale* ... MD-2
Tanyard—*locale* ... TX-5
Tan Yard—*locale* ... TX-5
**Tanyard**—*pop pl* (2) ... AL-4
**Tanyard**—*pop pl* ... MO-7
*Tanyard Bayou* ... TX-5
Tan Yard Bend—*bend* ... TN-4
*Tanyard Branch* ... DE-2
*Tanyard Branch* ... IN-6
*Tanyard Branch* ... VA-3
Tanyard Branch—*stream* (19) ... AL-4
Tan Yard Branch—*stream* ... AR-4
Tanyard Branch—*stream* ... AR-4
Tanyard Branch—*stream* ... DE-2
Tanyard Branch—*stream* ... FL-3
Tanyard Branch—*stream* (7) ... GA-3
Tanyard Branch—*stream* (2) ... IN-6
Tanyard Branch—*stream* (4) ... KY-4
Tanyard Branch—*stream* (2) ... LA-4
Tanyard Branch—*stream* (2) ... MD-2
Tanyard Branch—*stream* (4) ... MS-4
Tan Yard Branch—*stream* ... MS-4
Tanyard Branch—*stream* (3) ... MS-4
Tanyard Branch—*stream* (4) ... MO-7
Tanyard Branch—*stream* ... NC-3
Tanyard Branch—*stream* ... OK-5
Tanyard Branch—*stream* (4) ... SC-3
Tanyard Branch—*stream* (11) ... TN-4
Tanyard Branch—*stream* ... TX-5
Tan Yard Branch—*stream* ... TX-5
Tanyard Branch—*stream* (3) ... TX-5
Tan Yard Branch—*stream* ... TX-5
Tanyard Branch—*stream* (2) ... TX-5
Tanyard Branch—*stream* (13) ... VA-3
Tanyard Branch—*stream* ... WV-2
Tanyard Branch Furnace (40HR121)—*hist pl* ... TN-4
Tanyard Bridge—*bridge* ... SC-3
*Tanyard Brook* ... RI-1
Tanyard Brook—*stream* ... RI-1
Tanyard Cem—*cemetery* ... AR-4
Tanyard Cem—*cemetery* ... LA-4
Tan Yard Cem—*cemetery* ... TX-5
Tanyard Cove—*bay* ... MD-2
*Tanyard Creek* ... TX-5
Tanyard Creek—*stream* (5) ... AL-4
Tanyard Creek—*stream* (2) ... AR-4
Tan Yard Creek—*stream* ... FL-3
Tanyard Creek—*stream* (3) ... GA-3
Tanyard Creek—*stream* (2) ... LA-4
Tanyard Creek—*stream* (3) ... MS-4
Tanyard Creek—*stream* ... MO-7
Tanyard Creek—*stream* (3) ... NC-3
Tanyard Creek—*stream* ... OK-5
Tanyard Creek—*stream* (5) ... TX-5
Tanyard Creek—*stream* (2) ... VA-3
*Tanyard Crossing* ... TX-5
Tanyard Gap—*gap* ... AL-4
Tanyard Gap—*gap* ... NC-3
Tanyard Gap—*gap* ... WV-2
Tanyard Hill—*summit* ... AL-4
Tan Yard Hill—*summit* ... KY-4
Tanyard Hill Gap—*gap* ... AL-4
**Tanyard (historical)**—*pop pl* ... TN-4
Tanyard Hollow—*valley* (3) ... AL-4
Tanyard Hollow—*valley* ... AR-4
Tanyard Hollow—*valley* ... KY-4
Tanyard Hollow—*valley* ... MO-7
Tanyard Hollow—*valley* (9) ... TN-4
Tanyard Lake—*lake* ... LA-4
Tanyard Landing—*locale* ... VA-3
Tanyard Park—*park* ... TN-4
Tanyard Point—*cape* ... TN-4
**Tanyard Point**—*pop pl* ... MD-2
Tanyard Pond—*lake* ... FL-3
Tanyard Ridge—*ridge* ... VA-3
Tanyard Run—*stream* ... VA-3
Tanyard Run—*stream* (2) ... WV-2
Tanyard Sch—*school* ... KY-4
Tanyard Shoal Sluice—*hist pl* ... NC-3
Tanyard Spring—*spring* (3) ... AL-4
Tanyard Spring—*spring* ... AR-4
Tanyard Spring—*spring* (2) ... TN-4
Tan Yard Spring—*spring* ... TX-5
Tanyard Springs Dam—*dam* ... TN-4
Tanyard Springs Lake—*reservoir* ... TN-4
Tanyard Swamp—*stream* ... VA-3
Tanzy Hollow—*valley* ... VA-3
*Taoch Ra Iwekei* ... PW-9
*Taoch Ra Klai* ... PW-9
*Taoch Ra Medorm* ... PW-9
Taogam—*other* ... GU-9
Taogam Archeol Settlement—*hist pl* ... GU-9
Taogam Point—*summit* ... GU-9
*Taogil Mid Passage* ... PW-9
*Taog Ra Klai* ... PW-9
Taoist Temple—*hist pl* ... CA-9
Taongi Atoll—*island* (2) ... MP-9
*Taongi Island* ... MP-9
Taongi Island—*island* ... MP-9
*Taongi Island Passage* ... MP-9
Taongi Island Passage—*channel* ... MP-9
Taongi Lagoon (not verified)—*lake* ... MP-9
*Taopi* ... TX-5
**Taopi**—*pop pl* ... MN-6
Taopi Cem—*cemetery* ... SD-7
Taopi (historical)—*locale* ... SD-7
**Taopi Township**—*pop pl* ... SD-7
Taormina, Lake—*lake* ... NE-7
**Taos**—*pop pl* (2) ... MO-7
**Taos**—*pop pl* ... NM-5
Taos (CCD)—*cens area* ... NM-5
Taos Cone—*summit* ... NM-5
**Taos (County)**—*pop pl* ... NM-5
Taos Creek—*stream* ... WA-9
Taos Downtown Hist Dist—*hist pl* ... NM-5
Taos Golf Course—*other* ... NM-5
Taos Inn—*hist pl* ... NM-5
Taos Junction—*locale* ... NM-5
Taos Mountains—*range* (2) ... NM-5
Taos Peak—*summit* ... NM-5
Taos Pueblo—*civil* ... NM-5
Taos Pueblo—*hist pl* ... NM-5
**Taos Pueblo**—*pop pl* ... NM-5
Taos Pueblo (CCD)—*cens area* ... NM-5
**Taos Pueblo (Indian Reservation)**—*pop pl* ... NM-5
**Taos Pueblo (Place)**—*pop pl* ... NM-5
**Taos Ski Valley**—*pop pl* ... NM-5
Taos Valley Canal—*canal* ... CO-8
Taos Valley Ditch No 1—*canal* ... CO-8
Taos Valley Ditch No 1—*canal* ... NM-5
Taos Valley Ditch No 2—*canal* ... CO-8
Taos Valley Ditch No 3—*canal* ... CO-8
*Tap* ... MH-9
*Tapaan Creek* ... NJ-2
*Tapaan Creek* ... NY-2
Tapado Canyon—*valley* ... TX-5
Tapaghtalghee Bay—*bay* ... AK-9
Tapaha Well—*well* ... AZ-5
*Tapak* ... FM-9
*Tapak Island* ... FM-9
*Tapakku-to* ... FM-9
Tapalcat Bayou—*gut* ... LA-4
Tapalcomes—*hist pl* ... TX-5
*Tapashaw Creek* ... MS-4
Tapatuli (historical)—*locale* ... AL-4
**Tapawingo, Lake**—*pop pl* ... MO-7
Tapawingo, Lake—*reservoir* ... MO-7
Tapawingo Boy Scout Camp—*locale* ... VA-3
Tapawingo Camp—*locale* ... ME-1
Tapawingo Lake—*reservoir* ... IN-6
Tapblan Kattan, Kannat—*stream* ... MH-9
Tapblan Lichan, Kannat—*stream* ... MH-9
Tapco—*locale* ... AZ-5
Tapco Cliff Dwellings—*locale* ... AZ-5
Tapco Power Plant and Substation—*locale* ... AZ-5
Tapco RR Station—*building* ... AZ-5
Tapeats Amphitheater—*basin* ... AZ-5
Tapeats Cave—*cave* ... AZ-5
*Tapeats Creek* ... AZ-5
Tapeats Creek—*stream* ... AZ-5
Tapeats Rapids—*rapids* ... AZ-5
Tapeats Spring—*spring* ... AZ-5
Tapeats Terrace—*bench* ... AZ-5
Tape Creek—*stream* ... TX-5
Tape Lake—*lake* ... WA-9
*Tapelau Island* ... FM-9
Tapepe Ridge—*ridge* ... AS-9
Taper Ave Sch—*school* ... CA-9
Tapers Ranch—*locale* ... WY-8
*Tapes Branch* ... VA-3
Tapestry Arch—*arch* ... UT-8
Tapestry Slab—*ridge* ... UT-8
Tapestry Wall—*cliff* ... UT-8
Tap-Gove Drain—*canal* ... MI-6
Taphook Mtn—*summit* ... AK-9
Taphook Point—*cape* ... AK-9
Tap Horn Canyon—*valley* ... OR-9
Tap Horn Gap—*gap* ... OR-9
Tapia Canyon—*valley* ... CA-9
Tapia Canyon—*valley* ... NM-5
Tapia Cem—*cemetery* ... CO-8
Tapia Cem—*cemetery* ... NM-5
Tapiado, Arroyo—*stream* ... CA-9
*Tapia Oil Field* ... CA-9
Tapia Park—*park* ... CA-9
Tapia Ranch—*locale* (2) ... NM-5
Tapia Tank—*reservoir* ... NM-5
Tapia Tank No 1—*reservoir* ... NM-5
Tapia Tank No 2—*reservoir* ... NM-5
Tapia Well—*well* ... NM-5
Tapicito Creek—*stream* ... NM-5
Tapicitoes—*locale* ... NM-5
Tapicito Ridge—*ridge* ... NM-5
Tapicito Ruin (LA 2298)—*hist pl* ... NM-5
Tapie Canyon—*valley* ... CA-9
Tapie Lake—*lake* ... CA-9
*Tapimoor Island* ... MP-9
*Tapimoor Pass* ... MP-9
*Tapingot* ... MH-9
Tapioca Creek—*stream* ... AK-9
**Tapiola**—*pop pl* ... MI-6
Tapisaghak River—*stream* ... AK-9
Tapisi Point—*cape* ... AS-9
Tapkaluk Islands—*area* ... AK-9
Tapkaurak Entrance—*channel* ... AK-9
Tapkaurak Lagoon—*bay* ... AK-9
Tapkaurak Point—*cape* ... AK-9
Tapkaurak Spit—*bar* ... AK-9
Tapler Point—*cape* ... MD-2
*Tapler's Bar* ... MD-2
*Tapley* ... KS-7
Tapley Bldg—*hist pl* ... MA-1
Tapley Brook—*stream* ... MA-1
Tapley Cem—*cemetery* ... MO-7
Tapley Cove—*bay* ... ME-1
Tapley Ridge—*ridge* ... ME-1
*Tapleys Brook* ... MA-1
Tapley Sch—*school* ... MA-1
Tapley Street Annex—*uninc pl* ... MA-1
**Tapleyville**—*pop pl* ... MA-1
*Tapleyville Station* ... MA-1
Tapleyville Station (historical)—*locale* ... MA-1
**Taplin**—*pop pl* ... WV-2
Taplin Bourn—*stream* ... NY-2
Taplin Ch—*church* ... WV-2
Taplin Gorge Dam—*dam* ... MN-6
Taplin Hill—*summit* ... VT-1
Taplin Pond—*lake* ... NY-2
Taploe Cave—*cave* ... AL-4
Tapman Creek—*stream* ... OR-9
Tapo Canyon—*valley* (2) ... CA-9
*Tapochiyo* ... MH-9
*Tapocho* ... MH-9
*Tapocho Hill* ... MH-9
*Tapocho Mountain* ... MH-9
*Tapocho San* ... MH-9
**Tapoco**—*pop pl* ... NC-3
Tapo Gillibrand Mine—*mine* ... CA-9
*Tapolis Bar* ... MD-2
Tapon Tank—*reservoir* ... AZ-5
Tapon Tank—*reservoir* ... TX-5
Tapo Point—*summit* ... NM-5
Tapo Ranch—*locale* ... CA-9
*Tapo Ridge Oil Field* ... CA-9
*Tapotchau* ... MH-9
*Tappaans* ... NJ-2
Tappahanna Ditch—*stream* ... DE-2
*Tappahannak Creek* ... DE-2
**Tappahannock**—*pop pl* ... VA-3
Tappahannock Hist Dist—*hist pl* ... VA-3
*Tappahunnah Creek* ... DE-2
*Tappaku To* ... FM-9
*Tappan* ... NJ-2
Tappan—*locale* ... MI-6
Tappan—*locale* ... OH-6
Tappan—*locale* ... WV-2
**Tappan**—*pop pl* ... NY-2
Tappan, James C., House—*hist pl* ... AR-4
Tappan, Judge Abraham, House—*hist pl* ... OH-6
Tappan, Lake—*reservoir* ... NJ-2
Tappan, Maj. James Alexander, House—*hist pl* ... AR-4
*Tappan Bay* ... NY-2
**Tappan Corners**—*pop pl* ... NH-1
Tappan Creek—*stream* ... CO-8
Tappan Creek—*stream* ... WY-8
Tappan Gulch—*valley* ... CO-8
Tappan Hill Sch—*school* ... NY-2
Tappan (historical)—*locale* ... AL-4
Tappan House—*hist pl* ... OH-6
*Tappan Island* ... ME-1
Tappan JHS—*school* ... MI-6
*Tappan Lake* ... WY-8
Tappan Lake—*reservoir* ... OH-6
Tappan Lake Park—*park* ... OH-6
Tappan Mtn—*summit* ... CO-8
*Tappan Rsvr* ... OH-6
Tappan Rsvr—*reservoir* ... OH-6
*Tappan Run* ... NJ-2
*Tappan Run* ... NY-2
Tappan Sch—*school* (2) ... MI-6
Tappan Sch—*school* ... OH-6
*Tappan Sea* ... NY-2
Tappan Spring—*spring* ... AZ-5
Tappan Spring Canyon—*valley* ... AZ-5
Tappan (Township of)—*fmr MCD* ... AR-4
Tappan Valley—*valley* ... NE-7
Tappan Valley Sch—*school* ... NE-7
Tappan-Viles House—*hist pl* ... ME-1
Tappan Wash—*stream* ... AZ-5
Tappan Zee—*lake* ... NY-2
Tappan Zee Bridge—*bridge* ... NY-2
Tappan Zee HS—*school* ... NY-2
Tappan Zee Playhouse—*hist pl* ... NY-2
Tapp Cem—*cemetery* (3) ... KY-4
Tapp Cem—*cemetery* ... MO-7
Tapp Creek—*stream* ... OR-9
Tapp Creek—*stream* ... WA-9
**Tappen**—*pop pl* ... ND-7
Tappen Coulee—*valley* ... WI-6
Tappen Gulch—*valley* ... ID-8
Tappen Ranch—*locale* ... ID-8
Tappen Slough—*lake* ... ND-7
Tappen Spring—*spring* ... AZ-5
**Tappen Township**—*pop pl* ... ND-7
Tappers Corner—*locale* ... MD-2
*Tappin Creek* ... ID-8
*Tappin Creek* ... OR-9
Tappin Ditch—*canal* ... IN-6
Tapping Hill—*summit* ... NC-3
T-Apple Ranch—*locale* ... OK-5
Tappleridge Shop Ctr—*locale* ... MS-4
Tappley Branch—*stream* ... KY-4
Tappley Branch—*stream* ... MS-4
Tapplin Gulch—*valley* ... CA-9
*Tappocho* ... MH-9
*Tap Point* ... PW-9
Tapps, Lake—*lake* ... WA-9
Tapps Ridge—*ridge* ... IN-6
*Taprass Bar* ... MD-2
Taprengesang—*cape* ... PW-9
*Taprkeam* ... PW-9
Taps Ch—*church* ... AR-4
Tapscott—*locale* ... VA-3
Tapscott Cem—*cemetery* ... AL-4
Tapscott Ch—*church* ... OH-6
Taps Lake—*lake* ... MI-6
Tapsville Cem—*cemetery* ... AL-4
Tap Tank—*reservoir* ... AZ-5
Tapto Creek—*stream* ... WA-9
Tapto Lakes—*lake* ... WA-9
Tapto Shelter—*locale* ... WA-9
Tapua Stream—*stream* ... AS-9
*Tapudgechal* ... FM-9
Taputapu, Cape—*cape* ... AS-9
Taputapu Island—*island* ... AS-9
**Taputimu**—*pop pl* ... AS-9
*Tapuw* ... FM-9
*Tapuwogachal* ... FM-9
Taqabaab—*summit* ... FM-9
Taqaley—*summit* ... FM-9
Taquache Creek—*stream* ... TX-5
Taquache Tank—*reservoir* ... TX-5
*Taquamenon* ... MI-6
*Taquamenon Bay* ... MI-6
*Taquamenon Island* ... MI-6
Taques Creek—*stream* ... PA-2
Tar—*bay* ... FM-9
Tara—*locale* ... IA-7
**Tara**—*pop pl* ... MO-7
**Tara**—*pop pl* ... VA-3
Tara—*spring* ... FM-9

Tara, Lake—*reservoir* GA-3
**Tara Acres (subdivision)**—*pop pl* NC-3
Taraang—*island* FM-9
Tarabusi Creek—*stream* MI-6
**Tara Condominium**—*pop pl* UT-8
**Tara Estates**—*pop pl* (3) TN-4
**Tara Estates (subdivision)**—*pop pl* MS-4
**Tara Estates Subdivision**—*pop pl* UT-8
Tara Field—*airport* NC-3
*Taragaja* MH-9
**Tara Gardens Condominium**—*pop pl* UT-8
**Taragate Farms (subdivision)**—*pop pl* NC-3
Tarage—*beach* MH-9
Taragen—*summit* FM-9
Tarague Beach—*beach* GU-9
Tarague Cave—*cave* GU-9
Tarague Channel—*channel* GU-9
Tarague Point—*cape* GU-9
Tara Hills—*uninc pl* CA-9
Tara Hills-Montalvin Manor—*CDP* CA-9
Tara Hills Sch—*school* CA-9
Tara (historical P.O.)—*locale* IA-7
*Tarahoho* MH-9
Tara Island—*island* VT-1
Taral—*locale* AK-9
Taral Creek—*stream* AK-9
Taramat—*island* FM-9
*Taran* FM-9
Taranai—*bar* FM-9
*Taranap* FM-9
Tarancahuas Creek—*stream* TX-5
T A Ranch—*locale* WY-8
*Tarang* FM-9
*Tarang Islands* FM-9
*Tarangu-To* FM-9
Taranovokchovik Pass—*gut* AK-9
Tarantula Canyon—*valley* NV-8
Tarantula Gulch—*valley* CA-9
Tarantula Mesa—*summit* UT-8
Tarantula Mine—*mine* CA-9
Tarantula Rsvr—*reservoir* CO-8
Tarantula Spring—*spring* (2) NV-8
Tarantula Tank—*reservoir* AZ-5
Tarantula Wash—*stream* CA-9
*Tarapin Creek* MS-4
Tara Plaza—*locale* MA-1
*Taraqen* FM-9
Taraque Well No 4—*well* GU-9
Tarascon—*locale* KY-4
Tarasof Point—*cape* AK-9
**Tara (subdivision)**—*pop pl* AL-4
**Tara (Township of)**—*pop pl* (2) MN-6
*Tar'aw* FM-9
Tarawa Plantation (historical)—*locale* MS-4
**Tarawa Terrace**—*pop pl* NC-3
Tarawa Terrace Elem Sch—*school* NC-3
*Tarawa Terrace II Quarters* NC-3
**Tarawa Terrace II (subdivision)**—*pop pl* NC-3
*Tarawa Terrace I Quarters* NC-3
**Tarawa Terrace I (subdivision)**—*pop pl* NC-3
Tarawa Terrance #1 Elem Sch—*school* NC-3
**Tarawoods (subdivision)**—*pop pl* NC-3
Tarbaby Mine—*mine* UT-8
Tar Barrel—*ridge* NC-3
Tar Bay—*bay* MD-2
Tar Bay—*bay* (2) VA-3
Tarbell and Alexander Ditch—*canal* CO-8
Tarbell Brook—*stream* MA-1
Tarbell Brook—*stream* NH-1
Tarbell Brook—*stream* NY-2
Tarbell Creek—*stream* NE-7
Tarbell Hill—*summit* MA-1
Tarbell Hill—*summit* NY-2
Tarbell Pocket—*basin* CA-9
Tarbell Post Office (historical)—*building* ND-7
Tarbell Sch—*school* MA-1
**Tarbellville**—*pop pl* VT-1
Tarbert Plantation (historical)—*locale* MS-4
Tarberts Landing—*locale* MS-4
Tarbet Cem—*cemetery* TN-4
*Tarbetts Pond* PA-2
Tarbill Cem—*cemetery* OH-6
Tar Blanket Lodge (historical)—*locale* MO-7
*Tarble Pond* PA-2
Tarblue Lakebed—*flat* AR-4
Tar Blue Spring—*spring* MO-7
Tar Bluff—*cliff* SC-3
Tarbone Mtn—*summit* OK-5
*Tarboo* WA-9
Tarboo Bay—*bay* WA-9
Tarboo Creek—*stream* WA-9
Tarboo Lake—*lake* WA-9
*Tarbore* MS-4
Tarboro—*locale* SC-3
**Tarboro**—*pop pl* GA-3
**Tarboro**—*pop pl* NC-3
Tarboro Edgecombe Acad—*school* NC-3
Tarboro Hist Dist—*hist pl* NC-3
Tarboro HS—*school* NC-3
Tarboro Post Office—*building* NC-3
Tarboro Town Common—*hist pl* NC-3
Tarboro Town Hall—*building* NC-3
Tarbottom Well—*well* TX-5
Tarbox Arroyo—*stream* CO-8
Tarbox Brook—*stream* PA-2
Tar Box Canyon—*valley* AZ-5
Tarbox Cem—*cemetery* ME-1
Tarbox Corner—*locale* RI-1
Tarbox Cove—*bay* ME-1
Tar Box Creek—*stream* TX-5
Tarbox Hill—*summit* MT-8
Tar Box Hollow—*valley* NE-7
Tarbox Island—*island* ME-1
Tarbox Mine—*mine* MT-8
Tarbox Pond—*lake* ME-1
Tarbox Pond—*reservoir* RI-1
Tarbox Pond Dam—*dam* RI-1
Tarboz Lake—*lake* NE-7
*Tar Branch* AL-4
Tar Branch—*stream* (2) KY-4
Tar Branch—*stream* NC-3
Tar Branch—*stream* OK-5
Tar Branch—*stream* (2) TX-5
*TAR Bridge* RI-1
Tar Bucket—*spring* UT-8
Tar Bully—*ridge* CA-9
Tarbung—*summit* FM-9
Tarburner Ridge—*ridge* PA-2
Tarburner Run—*stream* OH-6
Tarburner Spring—*spring* PA-2
Tarbutton Creek—*stream* MO-7
Tarby Sch—*school* OK-5
Tar Camp Creek—*stream* AR-4
Tar Camp Hollow—*valley* KY-4
Tar Camp Public Use Area—*park* AR-4
Tarcamp Run—*stream* OH-6
Tar Cem—*cemetery* ME-1
Tar City Ch—*church* GA-3
Tar Cliff—*cliff* UT-8
*Tar Coal* MD-2
*Tarcoat* MD-2
*Tar Coat Creek* WV-2
Tar Corner—*locale* NC-3
Tar Cove—*bay* (2) MD-2
Tar Cove Marsh—*swamp* NC-3
Tar Creek—*bay* MD-2
Tar Creek—*stream* CA-9
Tar Creek—*stream* (2) GA-3
Tar Creek—*stream* IL-6
Tar Creek—*stream* (2) KS-7
Tar Creek—*stream* MI-6
Tar Creek—*stream* MS-4
Tar Creek—*stream* NV-8
Tar Creek—*stream* (3) NC-3
Tar Creek—*stream* OH-6
Tar Creek—*stream* OK-5
Tar Creek—*stream* OR-9
Tar Creek—*stream* TN-4
*Tardieu* FM-9
Tardy Branch—*stream* NC-3
Tardy Branch—*stream* VA-3
Tardy Canyon—*valley* TX-5
Tardy Spring—*spring* TX-5
Tarebreeches Creek—*stream* MS-4
Tarecoat Creek—*stream* IA-7
Tare Creek—*stream* OH-6
Tareeb—*island* MP-9
**Tarentum**—*pop pl* AL-4
**Tarentum**—*pop pl* PA-2
Tarentum Borough—*civil* PA-2
Tarentum Sch—*school* AL-4
*Tare-over Bridge* NC-3
Tareover Bridge—*bridge* NC-3
*Tarep* MP-9
Tarey Hill—*summit* PA-2
Tar Fall Run—*stream* WV-2
Tar Ferry—*locale* NC-3
*Tar Flat* CA-9
Tar Flat—*flat* CA-9
Tar Fork—*locale* KY-4
Tar Fork—*stream* (2) KY-4
Tar Fork Ch—*church* KY-4
Tar Fork Sch—*school* KY-4
Tar Gap—*gap* CA-9
Target Bluff—*cliff* CO-8
Target Ch—*church* SC-3
Target Creek—*stream* (2) OK-5
Target Flat (historical)—*flat* SD-7
Target Hill—*summit* NV-8
Target Hill—*summit* (2) TX-5
Target Hill—*summit* VA-3
Target Island—*island* AK-9
Target Lake—*lake* MN-6
Target Meadows—*flat* OR-9
Target Meadows Campground—*park* OR-9
Target Point—*cape* NY-2
Target Range Sch—*school* MT-8
Target Rock—*pillar* VI-3
Target Rock—*summit* MT-8
Target Rsvr—*reservoir* NM-5
Target Swamp—*stream* SC-3
Target Windmill—*locale* NM-5
Target 95—*other* CA-9
Targhee Cem—*cemetery* ID-8
Targhee Creek—*stream* ID-8
Targhee Pass—*gap* ID-8
Targhee Pass—*gap* MT-8
*Targhee Peak* ID-8
Targhee Peak—*summit* ID-8
Tar Gulch—*valley* CO-8
Tar Head Creek—*stream* MT-8
*Tarheel* NC-3
Tarheel—*locale* NC-3
**Tar Heel**—*pop pl* NC-3
Tarheel Arm—*bay* OR-9
Tarheel Army Missile Plant—*military* NC-3
Tar Heel Ch—*church* NC-3
**Tarheel Courts (subdivision)**—*pop pl* NC-3
Tarheel Creek—*stream* OR-9
Tarheel Creek Dam—*dam* OR-9
Tar Heel Farm Pond—*reservoir* NC-3
Tar Heel Farm Pond Dam—*dam* NC-3
Tarheel Flat—*flat* WA-9
*Tarheel Hill* WA-9
Tarheel Lagoon—*lake* AK-9
Tar Heel Lake—*reservoir* NC-3
Tarheel Lake Dam—*dam* NC-3
Tar Heel Landing—*locale* NC-3
Tarheel Rsvr—*reservoir* OR-9
Tarheel Trail—*trail* NC-3
Tarhe Run—*stream* OH-6
Tar Hill—*locale* KY-4
Tar Hill—*summit* WV-2
Tarhole Canyon—*valley* NM-5
Tar Hole Inlet—*bay* NC-3
*Tar Hole Plain* NC-3
Tar Hole Plains—*flat* NC-3
Tarhole Tank—*reservoir* NM-5
Tarhole Well—*well* NM-5
Tar Hollow—*valley* IL-6
Tar Hollow—*valley* NY-2
Tar Hollow—*valley* OH-6
Tar Hollow—*valley* VA-3
Tar Hollow—*valley* WI-6
Tar Hollow State For—*forest* OH-6
**Tarico Heights**—*pop pl* WV-2
Tariff—*locale* WV-2
Tariff Commission Bldg—*building* DC-2
Tariff Oil Field—*other* WV-2
Tariffville—*locale* TN-4
**Tariffville**—*pop pl* CT-1
Tariffville Post Office (historical)—*building* TN-4
*Tarik Island* FM-9
*Tarima Key* FL-3
Taring—*bar* FM-9
Tar Island—*island* LA-4
Tar Island—*island* MP-9
Tar Island Slough—*gut* LA-4
Tar Island Slough—*gut* TX-5
Ta River—*stream* VA-3
Tar Jacket Ridge—*ridge* VA-3
Tarke—*locale* CA-9
**Tarkeo Corner**—*pop pl* IN-6
**Tarkey Tail (historical)**—*pop pl* NC-3
Tarkhill Branch—*stream* KY-4
Tark Hill Run—*stream* PA-2
*Tarkill Branch* NC-3
*Tarkill Branch* SC-3
Tar Kill Branch—*stream* KY-4
Tarkill Branch—*stream* NC-3
Tarkill Brook—*stream* MA-1
Tarkill Cove—*bay* MD-2
*Tarkill Creek* VA-3
Tarkill Creek—*stream* PA-2
Tarkill Creek—*stream* VA-3
Tarkill Demonstration Area—*area* PA-2
*Tarkill Hollow* WV-2
Tar Kill Hollow—*valley* PA-2
Tarkill Lake—*lake* LA-4
Tarkill Lake—*lake* TX-5
Tarkill Point—*cape* MD-2
Tarkill Pond—*lake* ME-1
Tarkill Pond—*lake* NY-2
Tarkiln—*locale* RI-1
**Tarkiln**—*pop pl* KY-4
**Tarkiln**—*pop pl* MA-1
Tarkiln Bay—*bay* FL-3
Tarkiln Bay—*swamp* NC-3
Tarkiln Bayou—*bay* FL-3
Tarkiln Branch—*stream* (3) AL-4
Tar Kiln Branch—*stream* AR-4
Tarkiln Branch—*stream* (2) KY-4
Tar Kiln Branch—*stream* KY-4
Tarkiln Branch—*stream* (2) KY-4
Tar Kiln Branch—*stream* LA-4
Tarkiln Branch—*stream* (3) NJ-2
Tarkiln Branch—*stream* (3) NC-3
Tar Kiln Branch—*stream* (2) NC-3
Tarkiln Branch—*stream* PA-2
Tar Kiln Branch—*stream* SC-3
Tarkiln Branch—*stream* (2) TN-4
Tar Kiln Branch—*stream* TN-4
Tar Kiln Branch—*stream* TX-5
*Tar Kiln Brook* MA-1
*Tar Kiln Brook* NJ-2
Tarkiln Brook—*stream* (2) NJ-2
Tarkiln Brook—*stream* RI-1
Tarkiln Cave—*cave* KY-4
Tarkiln Ch—*church* KY-4
*Tarkiln Creek* PA-2
*Tar Kiln Creek* VA-3
Tar Kiln Creek—*stream* AR-4
Tarkiln Creek—*stream* KY-4
Tarkiln Creek—*stream* (2) NC-3
Tarkiln Creek—*stream* SC-3
Tarkiln Creek Bay—*bay* NC-3
Tarkiln Draft—*valley* PA-2
Tarkiln Ford—*locale* TN-4
Tarkiln Gap—*gap* GA-3
Tar Kiln Gap—*gap* KY-4
Tarkiln Gap—*gap* (2) NC-3
Tarkiln Gap—*gap* (2) TN-4
Tarkiln Head Hollow—*valley* FL-3
Tarkiln Hill—*summit* ME-1
Tarkiln Hill—*summit* (2) MA-1
*Tar Kiln Hollow* PA-2
Tarkiln Hollow—*valley* AR-4
Tar Kiln Hollow—*valley* (2) MO-7
Tarkiln Hollow—*valley* OH-6
Tarkiln Hollow—*valley* (2) TN-4
Tar Kiln Hollow—*valley* UT-8
Tarkiln Hollow—*valley* WV-2
Tarkiln Knob—*summit* GA-3
Tar Kiln Lookout Tower—*locale* AR-4
Tarkiln Mtn—*summit* AL-4
Tar Kiln Mtn—*summit* AR-4
Tarkiln Mtn—*summit* (2) NC-3
Tar Kiln Mtn—*summit* VA-3
Tarkiln Neck—*cape* NC-3
Tarkiln Point—*cape* FL-3
Tar Kiln Point—*cape* TN-4
Tarkiln Pond—*reservoir* RI-1
Tarkiln Pond Dam—*dam* RI-1
Tarkiln Ridge—*ridge* GA-3
Tarkiln Ridge—*ridge* (2) NC-3
Tarkiln Ridge—*ridge* PA-2
Tarkiln Ridge—*ridge* TN-4
Tar Kiln Ridge—*ridge* TN-4
Tarkiln Ridge—*ridge* TN-4
Tarkiln Ridge—*ridge* VA-3
*Tarkiln River* RI-1
Tarkiln Run—*stream* MD-2
Tarkiln Run—*stream* (5) PA-2
Tar Kiln Run—*stream* WV-2
Tarkiln Run—*stream* (2) WV-2
Tar Kiln Sch (historical)—*school* MS-4
Tarkiln Trail—*trail* PA-2
Tarkiln Valley—*valley* TN-4
Tarkin Branch—*stream* KY-4
Tarkington Bayou—*stream* TX-5
Tarkington Cave—*cave* AL-4
*Tarkington Creek* TX-5
Tarkington Farm Cave—*cave* AL-4
Tarkington Park—*park* IN-6
Tarkington Prairie—*flat* TX-5
**Tarkington Prairie**—*pop pl* TX-5
Tarkington Prairie Sch—*school* TX-5
Tarkington Prairie School (historical ruins)—*locale* TX-5
Tarkington Sch—*school* IL-6
*Tarkington School* IN-6
Tarkington Windmill—*locale* NM-5
Tarkin Hollow—*valley* WV-2
*Tarkin Run* WV-2
Tarkio—*locale* MT-8
**Tarkio**—*pop pl* MO-7
**Tarkio City (historical)**—*pop pl* IA-7
Tarkio Coll—*school* MO-7
*Tarkio Creek* IA-7
*Tarkio Creek* MO-7
*Tarkio Ditch* MO-7
Tarkio (historical P.O.)—*locale* IA-7
*Tarkio River* MO-7
Tarkio River—*stream* IA-7
Tarkio River—*stream* MO-7
Tarkio Township—*civil* MO-7
Tarkio Township—*fmr MCD* IA-7
*Tarklin Bay* FL-3
*Tarklin Bayou* FL-3
Tarklin Cem—*cemetery* OH-6
Tarklin Cove—*bay* GA-3
Tarklin Creek—*stream* NC-3
*Tarklin Point* FL-3
*Tarklin Ridge* GA-3
Tarklin Ridge—*ridge* NC-3
*Tarklin Run* PA-2
Tar Klin Run—*stream* OH-6
Tarklin Valley Ch—*church* TN-4
Tar Knob—*summit* PA-2
Tarky Sch—*school* MA-1
Tarlac Creek—*stream* ID-8
Tar Lake—*lake* GA-3
Tar Lake—*lake* MI-6
Tar Lake—*lake* SC-3
*Tar Landing* NC-3
Tar Landing—*locale* (4) NC-3
**Tar Landing**—*pop pl* NC-3
Tar Landing Bay—*bay* NC-3
Tar Landing Gut—*stream* NC-3
Tarlatt Slough—*stream* WA-9
Tarlechia Creek—*stream* MS-4
**Tarleton**—*pop pl* DE-2
Tarleton, Lake—*lake* NH-1
Tarleton Bayou—*stream* LA-4
Tarleton Branch—*stream* MD-2
Tarleton Creek—*stream* AR-4
Tarleton Ditch—*canal* AR-4
Tarleton State Coll Farm—*school* TX-5
Tarleton (Tarleton State College)—*uninc pl* TX-5
Tar Lick Hollow—*valley* KY-4
*Tarlinga* TX-5
*Tarlit Creek* WA-9
Tarlow Creek—*stream* MS-4
Tarlton—*locale* TN-4
**Tarlton**—*pop pl* OH-6
Tarlton Bldg—*hist pl* TX-5
Tarlton Branch—*stream* NC-3
Tarlton Cross Mound—*hist pl* OH-6
Tarlton Flats—*flat* AR-4
Tarlton Post Office (historical)—*building* TN-4
Tarlton Sch (historical)—*school* TN-4
Tarlton State Park—*park* OH-6
Tarma—*other* KY-4
Tarman Run Access Area—*area* PA-2
*Tarmans Branch* MD-2
*Tarmans Creek* IN-6
Tar Mine—*mine* AZ-5
*Tarmon Branch* WV-2
Tarn, The—*lake* CA-9
Tarn, The—*lake* ME-1
Tarn, The—*lake* NJ-2
Tarnans Branch—*stream* MD-2
Tarney Run—*stream* WV-2
Tarn Mtn—*summit* AK-9
**Tarnov**—*pop pl* NE-7
Tarn Valley—*valley* AK-9
Tarnwood Lake—*lake* MI-6
Taro—*locale* VA-3
Taroa Anchorage—*harbor* (2) MP-9
*Taroa Island* MP-9
Taroa Island—*island* MP-9
*Taroa-to* MP-9
*Taro Creek* CA-9
*Taroda Creek* WA-9
Taroga, Lake—*reservoir* NC-3
*Tarogqua Peak* NV-8
*Tarohoho* MH-9
Taroka Arm—*bay* AK-9
*Tarota Creek* WA-9
Tarover—*hist pl* VA-3
*Tarowatt Island* MP-9
Tarpan Lake—*lake* FL-3
Tarpaulin Cove—*cove* MA-1
Tarpaulin Cove Light—*hist pl* MA-1
Tarpaulin Cove Light—*locale* MA-1
*Tarp Brake* MS-4
Tar Peak—*summit* CA-9
Tarpen Ridge—*ridge* WV-2
Tarpey—*locale* CA-9
Tarpey, Mount—*summit* UT-8
Tarpey Sch—*school* CA-9
**Tarpey (Tarpey Village)**—*pop pl* CA-9
**Tarpey Village**—*pop pl* CA-9
Tarpine Valley—*valley* TN-4
Tarpine Valley Branch—*stream* TN-4
Tarpine Valley Ch—*church* TN-4
Tarpin Hollow—*valley* AR-4
Tarpin Lick Branch—*stream* KY-4
Tarpin Valley Sch (historical)—*school* TN-4
Tarpiscan Creek—*stream* WA-9
Tarpit Hollow—*valley* MO-7
Tar Pit Trail—*trail* PA-2
**Tarpley**—*pop pl* AL-4
**Tarpley**—*pop pl* TN-4
**Tarpley**—*pop pl* TX-5
Tarpley Bluff—*cliff* TN-4
Tarpley Branch—*stream* GA-3
Tarpley Cem—*cemetery* KY-4
Tarpley Cem—*cemetery* MS-4
Tarpley Cem—*cemetery* (3) TN-4
Tarpley Cem—*cemetery* TX-5
Tarpley Cutoff—*channel* MS-4
Tarpley Neck—*cape* MS-4
Tarpley Pass—*gap* TX-5
Tarpley Point—*cape* VA-3
Tarpley Post Office (historical)—*building* TN-4
Tarpley Sch—*school* MO-7
Tarpleys Chapel—*church* VA-3
Tarpleys Pond—*reservoir* NC-3
Tarpleys Store (historical)—*locale* TN-4
Tarpley Well—*well* (2) NM-5
Tar Point—*cape* MN-6
Tarpon—*locale* FL-3
Tarpon—*locale* VA-3
Tarpon, Lake—*lake* FL-3
Tarpon, Port—*harbor* FL-3
Tarpon Basin—*basin* FL-3
Tarpon Bay—*bay* (4) FL-3
Tarpon Bayou—*gut* FL-3
Tarpon Belly Keys—*island* FL-3
Tarpon Bend—*bend* FL-3
Tarpon Bend—*bend* TX-5
Tarpon Branch—*stream* VA-3
Tarpon Cove—*bay* NJ-2
Tarpon Creek—*gut* (2) FL-3
Tarpon Creek—*stream* FL-3
Tarpon Gut—*gut* NJ-2
Tarpon Inn—*hist pl* TX-5
Tarpon Island—*island* FL-3
Tarpon Junction (railroad junction)—*locale* FL-3
Tarpon Key—*island* FL-3
*Tarpon Lake* FL-3
Tarpon Mall—*locale* FL-3
Tarpon Plaza (Shop Ctr)—*locale* FL-3
*Tarpon Point* FL-3
**Tarpon Point**—*pop pl* FL-3
Tarpon River—*stream* FL-3
**Tarpon Springs**—*pop pl* FL-3
Tarpon Springs (CCD)—*cens area* FL-3
Tarpon Springs Elem Sch—*school* FL-3
Tarpon Springs Fundamental Sch—*school* FL-3
Tarpon Springs General Hosp—*hospital* FL-3
Tarpon Springs MS—*school* FL-3
Tarpon Springs Senior HS—*school* FL-3
Tarpon Square (Shop Ctr)—*locale* FL-3
Tar Pouch—*rock* MA-1
Tarqaaw—*locale* FM-9
Tarr, John, House—*hist pl* ME-1
Tarr, Lucy, Mansion—*hist pl* WV-2
Tarr, Peter, Furnace Site—*hist pl* WV-2
Tarradiddle—*summit* CT-1
**Tarrallton**—*pop pl* VA-3
*Tarrant* AL-4
Tarrant—*locale* WI-6
**Tarrant**—*pop pl* AL-4
**Tarrant**—*pop pl* TX-5
Tarrant Cem—*cemetery* TN-4
Tarrant Cem—*cemetery* TX-5
Tarrant Ch of Christ—*church* AL-4
Tarrant Ch of the Nazarene—*church* AL-4
**Tarrant City**—*pop pl* AL-4
Tarrant City Ch of God—*church* AL-4
Tarrant City Elem Sch—*school* AL-4
Tarrant City Hall—*building* AL-4
Tarrant City HS—*school* AL-4
Tarrant City MS—*school* AL-4
Tarrant City Public Library—*building* AL-4
**Tarrant (County)**—*pop pl* TX-5
Tarrant County Courthouse—*hist pl* TX-5
Tarrant First United Methodist Ch—*church* AL-4
Tarrant Gap—*gap* AL-4
**Tarrant Heights**—*pop pl* AL-4
Tarrant Heights Cave—*cave* AL-4
Tarrant Lake—*lake* WI-6
Tarrant Park—*park* TX-5
Tarrant Road Ch—*church* TX-5
Tarrant Rock Methodist Ch—*church* AL-4
**Tarrants**—*pop pl* MO-7
Tarrant Sewage Disposal—*other* TX-5
Tarrants Millpond—*reservoir* SC-3
Tarrant Spring—*spring* AL-4
Tarrant Spring Branch—*stream* AL-4
Tarrara Creek—*stream* VA-3
Tarratine—*locale* ME-1
Tarraville Canyon—*valley* CA-9
Tarraville Creek—*stream* CA-9
Tarr Branch—*stream* MD-2
Tarr Canyon—*valley* UT-8
Tarr Creek—*stream* WI-6
Tarr Ditch—*canal* CA-9
Tarred Rat Creek—*stream* VA-3
*Tarrell creek* MT-8
*Tarrelton* VA-3
Tarrence Round Barn—*hist pl* IA-7
Tarrey Creek—*stream* MS-4
Tar Ridge—*ridge* KY-4
Tar Ridge—*ridge* ME-1
Tar Ridge—*ridge* (2) NC-3
Tar Ridge Sch—*school* ME-1
Tarr Inlet—*bay* AK-9
Tarrino Canyon—*valley* CO-8
Tarr Island (historical)—*island* TN-4
**Tar River**—*pop pl* NC-3
Tar River—*stream* GA-3
Tar River—*stream* (2) NC-3
Tar River Ch—*church* NC-3
Tar River Dam—*dam* NC-3
Tar River Rsvr—*reservoir* NC-3
Tar River Sch—*school* NC-3
*Tarr Kill* PA-2
Tarr Lake—*lake* MN-6
Tar Road Ch—*church* VA-3
*Tarroda Creek* WA-9
Tarrot Hill—*summit* MA-1
Tarrowatt Island—*island* MP-9
Tarr Ridge—*ridge* (2) KY-4
Tarr Ridge Sch—*school* KY-4
Tarr (RR name for Tarrs)—*other* PA-2
**Tarrs**—*pop pl* PA-2
Tarrs Mtn—*summit* ME-1
**Tarrs (RR name Tarr)**—*pop pl* PA-2
Tarrs Run—*stream* OH-6
**Tarrtown**—*pop pl* PA-2
Tar Run—*stream* OH-6
Tar Run—*stream* PA-2
Tar Run—*stream* WV-2
Tar Run Dam—*dam* PA-2
Tar Run Rsvr—*reservoir* PA-2
Tarr Valley Sch—*school* WI-6
**Tarry**—*pop pl* AR-4
**Tarryall**—*pop pl* CO-8
Tarryall Campground—*locale* CO-8
*Tarryall Creek* CO-8
Tarryall Creek—*stream* CO-8
Tarryall Mtns—*range* CO-8
*Tarryall Peak* CO-8
Tarryall Rsvr—*reservoir* CO-8
Tarryall Sch—*hist pl* CO-8
Tarry Creek—*stream* OR-9
Tarry Lake—*lake* MN-6
**Tarry Park**—*pop pl* IN-6
*Tarryton* MI-6
**Tarrytown**—*pop pl* FL-3
**Tarrytown**—*pop pl* GA-3
**Tarrytown**—*pop pl* MO-7
**Tarrytown**—*pop pl* (2) NY-2
Tarrytown (CCD)—*cens area* GA-3
Tarrytown Cem—*cemetery* NY-2
Tarrytown Heights—*uninc pl* NY-2
Tarrytown Lighthouse—*hist pl* NY-2
Tarrytown Mall (Shop Ctr)—*locale* NC-3
Tarrytown Rsvr—*reservoir* NY-2
Tarrywile—*hist pl* CT-1
Tarrywile Lake—*lake* CT-1
Tarsaville Sch—*school* WV-2
Tars Creek—*stream* WI-6
**Tarsney**—*pop pl* MO-7
Tarsney Lake—*reservoir* MO-7
**Tarsney Lakes**—*pop pl* MO-7
Tars Pond—*lake* WI-6
Tar Spring—*spring* WY-8
*Tar Spring Branch* AL-4
Tar Spring Creek—*stream* (2) CA-9
Tar Spring Hollow—*valley* AL-4
Tar Spring Ranch—*locale* CA-9
Tar Spring Ridge—*ridge* CA-9
Tar Springs—*spring* KY-4
**Tarsus**—*pop pl* AL-4
**Tarsus**—*pop pl* AR-4
**Tarsus**—*pop pl* TN-4
Tarsus Ch—*church* TN-4
Tarsus (historical)—*locale* AL-4
**Tartan**—*pop pl* KY-4
*Tartar* OR-9
Tartar Cem—*cemetery* TN-4
Tartar Cem—*cemetery* TX-5
Tartar Creek—*stream* CA-9
Tartar Gulch—*valley* (2) ID-8
Tartar's Ferry Bridge—*hist pl* IL-6
Tartellon, Bayou—*gut* LA-4
Tarter—*locale* OR-9
Tarter Branch—*stream* KY-4
Tarter Branch—*stream* TN-4
Tarter Cem—*cemetery* KY-4
Tarter Cem—*cemetery* TN-4
Tarter Ditch—*canal* WY-8
Tarter Gulch—*stream* OR-9
Tarter Gulch—*valley* OR-9
Tarter Gulch—*valley* WY-8
Tarter Knob—*summit* KY-4
Tarter Ranch—*locale* SD-7
Tarters Cem—*cemetery* KY-4
Tarters Island—*island* WY-8
**Tarters Store**—*pop pl* VA-3
*Tart Hill Hollow* WV-2
Tartia Cem—*cemetery* CT-1
*Tartlatt Slough* WA-9
Tart Millpond—*reservoir* NC-3
**Tarton**—*pop pl* AZ-5
Tartown—*other* PA-2
**Tartown**—*pop pl* PA-2
Tartron—*locale* AZ-5
Tartron Well—*well* AZ-5
Tarts Store—*locale* NC-3
Tartuguan Point—*cape* GU-9
*Taruga* MH-9
Tarums Dam—*dam* MT-8
Tarup Creek—*stream* CA-9
Tarus Cem—*cemetery* ND-7
*Taru-to* MP-9
Tarva Cem—*cemetery* GA-3
Tar Valley—*basin* NE-7
Tarver—*locale* GA-3
**Tarver**—*pop pl* TX-5
Tarver Bar—*bar* AL-4
Tarver Bay—*swamp* GA-3
Tarver Branch—*stream* GA-3
Tarver Branch—*stream* TN-4
Tarver Cem—*cemetery* GA-3
Tarver Cem—*cemetery* TX-5
Tarver Creek—*stream* AL-4
Tarver Creek—*stream* LA-4
*Tarvers Branch* LA-4
Tarvers Branch—*stream* GA-3
Tarver Sch—*school* TX-5
Tarvers Creek—*stream* MS-4
Tarvers Landing (historical)—*locale* AL-4
*Tarvers Mill Creek* AL-4
Tarvers Mill (historical)—*locale* AL-4
Tarversville—*locale* GA-3
Tarvid Cem—*cemetery* MO-7
Tar Wash—*stream* AZ-5
Tar Water Branch—*stream* AL-4
Tarwater Creek—*stream* CA-9
Tar Water Creek—*stream* PA-2
Tarwater Hollow—*valley* TN-4
Tarwater Pond—*lake* ME-1
Tarwater Spring—*spring* AR-4
**Tarwater (subdivision)**—*pop pl* AL-4
*Tarwij* MP-9
*Tarwojirok* MP-9
*Tarwoj Island* MP-9
Tarwood Flat—*flat* UT-8
Tary Hollow—*valley* KY-4
**Tarzan**—*pop pl* FL-3
**Tarzan**—*pop pl* TX-5
**Tarzana**—*pop pl* CA-9
Tarzana Siding—*locale* CA-9
Tarzan Falls—*falls* GU-9
Tarzan-Lenorah (CCD)—*cens area* TX-5
Tarzan River—*stream* GU-9
Tarzan RR Station—*locale* FL-3
Tarzan Springs—*spring* OR-9
Tarzian, Lake—*reservoir* IN-6
*Tasa Airfield* PA-2
*Tasajala Lake* TX-5
Tasajal Lake—*lake* TX-5
Tasajal Windmill—*locale* TX-5
Tasakili River—*stream* AK-9
*Tasa Lingo* TX-5
Tasal Windmill—*locale* TX-5
Tasa Tank—*reservoir* TX-5
Tasa Windmill—*locale* TX-5
Tasaychek Lagoon—*lake* AK-9
Tascala Canyon—*valley* AZ-5
Tascala Tank—*reservoir* AZ-5
*Tascaloussa River* AL-4
Tascal Ravine—*valley* AZ-5
Tascal Tank—*reservoir* AZ-5
Tasco—*locale* ND-7
**Tasco**—*pop pl* KS-7
Tasco Cem—*cemetery* ND-7
Tascohoma Cem—*cemetery* MS-4
Tascosa—*locale* TX-5
Tascosa Cem—*cemetery* TX-5
Tascosa Country Club—*other* TX-5
Tascosa Creek—*stream* TX-5
Tascosa HS—*school* TX-5
Tascotal Mesa—*summit* TX-5
Tascuela Canyon—*valley* AZ-5
Tascuela Wash—*stream* AZ-5
Tase Golman—*locale* NM-5
Taseohoma Ch—*church* MS-4
Taseohoma Sch—*school* MS-4
Tasha Creek—*stream* UT-8

Tashalich River—*stream* AK-9
Tasha Spring—*spring* UT-8
Tash Cem—*cemetery* IN-6
Tash Creek—*stream* CA-9
Tash Drain Ditch—*canal* MT-8
Tasher Islands—*island* MN-6
*Tashi* FM-9
Tashmoo, Lake—*lake* MA-1
Tashmoo Hill—*summit* MA-1
*Tashmoo Pond* MA-1
*Tashmoo Spirngs* MA-1
Tashmoo Spring—*spring* MA-1
*Tashmu Spring* MA-1
Tashnke-Ko-Ki-Pa-Pi Cem—*cemetery* SD-7
*Tashnuc Spring* MA-1
Tash Peak—*summit* MT-8
Tashua Burial Ground—*cemetery* CT-1
Tashua Hill—*summit* CT-1
*Tasi* MH-9
Tasighoovik Bay—*bay* AK-9
Tasikpak Creek—*stream* AK-9
Tasikpak Lagoon—*lake* AK-9
Tasin House—*hist pl* TX-5
Tasiswane Lake—*lake* AK-9
Tasita Tank—*reservoir* TX-5
Taska—*locale* MS-4
*Taska Picnic Area* AL-4
Taska Recreation Site—*locale* AL-4
Taskee Ch—*church* MO-7
*Taskeles Canyon* AZ-5
*Taskeles Tank* AZ-5
Tasker—*locale* WA-9
**Tasker**—*pop pl* DE-2
Tasker Corners—*locale* MD-2
Tasker Coulee—*valley* ND-7
Tasker Hill—*summit (2)* NH-1
Tasker JHS—*school* MD-2
Taskers Coulee—*valley* ND-7
Taskers Gap—*gap* VA-3
Taskigi (historical)—*locale* AL-4
Taskinas Creek—*stream* VA-3
Taskmakers Creek—*bay* VA-3
*Taskmer Creek* VA-3
*Taskmers Creek* VA-3
**Tasley**—*pop pl* VA-3
Taslina (Tazlina)—*other* AK-9
**Tasmas Corners**—*pop pl* MI-6
Tasnuna Glacier—*glacier* AK-9
Tasnuna River—*stream* AK-9
Taso Cove—*flat* TX-5
*Tasolingo* TX-5
*Tason Cove* TX-5
Tasqui (historical)—*locale* AL-4
*Tasquiki* AL-4
*Tassahaw Creek* GA-3
**Tassajara**—*pop pl* CA-9
Tassajara (CCD)—*cens area* CA-9
Tassajara Creek—*stream (2)* CA-9
**Tassajara Hot Springs**—*pop pl* CA-9
Tassajara Park—*park* CA-9
Tassajara School (Abandoned)—*locale* CA-9
*Tassajera Creek* CA-9
Tassajera Creek—*stream* CA-9
*Tassajero* CA-9
*Tassaka Creek* GA-3
*Tassawassa Creek* NY-2
*Tassawassa Lake* NY-2
Tassel Creek—*stream* WA-9
Tassel Hill—*summit* NY-2
Tassel Spring—*spring* AR-4
**Tasseltop**—*pop pl* MA-1
Tassi Ranch—*locale* AZ-5
Tassi Spring—*spring* AZ-5
Tassi Wash—*valley* AZ-5
**Tasso**—*pop pl* AL-4
**Tasso**—*pop pl* TN-4
**Tasso**—*pop pl* VA-3
Tasso Cem—*cemetery* TN-4
Tasso Christian Ch—*church* TN-4
**Tasso Heights**—*pop pl* TN-4
Tasso Methodist Ch—*church* TN-4
Tasso Mine—*mine* UT-8
Tasso Post Office (historical)—*building* TN-4
Tasso Sch (historical)—*school* TN-4
*Tastekis* AL-4
Tastine Swamp—*stream* VA-3
Tastykake Airp—*airport* PA-2
*Taswaijeeskil* DE-2
**Taswell**—*pop pl* IN-6
*Tata* AZ-5
*Tataacho* MH-9
*Tataacho Point* MH-9
*Tataach Point* MH-9
*Tatacho* MH-9
*Tatachog* MH-9
Tatachok—*slope* MH-9
*Tataesset Hill* MA-1
Tataga-Matau Fortified Quarry Complex (AS-34-10)—*hist pl* AS-9
Tatahatso Point—*cliff* AZ-5
Tatahatso Wash—*stream* AZ-5
Tatahoysa Wash—*stream* AZ-5
Tatai Toak—*locale* AZ-5
Tatalina Air Force Station—*locale* AK-9
Tatalina (Air Force) Station—*military* AK-9
Tatalina River—*stream* AK-9
*Tatam* PA-2
*Tatamis Gap* PA-2
*Tatamumera* AZ-5
**Tatamy**—*pop pl* PA-2
Tatamy Borough—*civil* PA-2
*Tatamys Gap* PA-2
*Tatamys Gap Tatamis Gap* PA-2
Tatanka Lake—*reservoir* SD-7
*Tatatallahoatska* FL-3
Tata Vique—*stream* NM-5
Tatchers Ford (historical)—*crossing* TN-4
Tatches Bayou—*gut* MI-6
Tate—*locale* AR-4
Tate—*locale* WV-2
**Tate**—*pop pl* GA-3
**Tate**—*pop pl* TN-4
Tate, Franklin Pierce, House—*hist pl* NC-3
Tate, J. C., General Merchandise Store—*hist pl* TN-4
Tate, Lake—*reservoir* AL-4
Tate, Netherland, House—*hist pl* TN-4
Tate Airp—*airport* MS-4
Tate Arroyo—*valley* TX-5
Tate Bar Landing (historical)—*locale* AL-4
Tate Bend—*bend* TN-4
Tate Branch—*stream (2)* AL-4
Tate Branch—*stream* GA-3
Tate Branch—*stream* NC-3
Tate Branch—*stream (2)* TN-4
Tate Branch Creek—*stream* KS-7
*Tate Brook* NY-2
Tate Brook—*stream* ME-1
Tate Brook—*stream* VT-1
Tate Cave—*cave* AL-4
Tate Cave Spring—*spring* TN-4
Tate (CCD)—*cens area* GA-3
Tate Cem—*cemetery (3)* AL-4
Tate Cem—*cemetery (6)* AR-4
Tate Cem—*cemetery* GA-3
Tate Cem—*cemetery (2)* IL-6
Tate Cem—*cemetery* LA-4
Tate Cem—*cemetery (5)* MS-4
Tate Cem—*cemetery* MO-7
Tate Cem—*cemetery (7)* TN-4
Tate Cem—*cemetery* TX-5
Tate Cem—*cemetery (3)* VA-3
Tate Ch—*church* AL-4
Tate Chapel—*church* AL-4
Tate Chapel—*church* IL-6
Tate Chapel—*church* VA-3
Tate City—*locale* GA-3
Tate City Sch—*school* GA-3
**Tate County**—*pop pl* MS-4
*Tate County Agricultural High School* MS-4
Tate County Courthouse—*building* MS-4
*Tate Cove* AL-4
**Tate Cove**—*pop pl* LA-4
Tate Cove—*valley* AL-4
Tate Cove—*valley* TN-4
Tate Cove Creek—*stream* TN-4
*Tate Creek* KS-7
Tate Creek—*stream* CA-9
Tate Creek—*stream* CO-8
Tate Creek—*stream (2)* GA-3
Tate Creek—*stream* KY-4
Tate Creek—*stream* OK-5
Tate Creek—*stream* OR-9
Tate Creek—*stream* WA-9
Tate Creek—*stream* WV-2
*Tate Creek Ch* AL-4
Tate Creek Ch—*church* AL-4
*Tate Creek Rapid* OR-9
Tate Dam—*dam* AL-4
Tate Fire Tower—*tower* FL-3
Tate Gap—*gap (2)* NC-3
Tate Gap—*gap* TN-4
Tategnak Point—*cape* AK-9
*Tate Grave* LA-4
Tate Hill—*summit* FL-3
Tate Hill—*summit* ME-1
**Tate (historical)**—*pop pl* TN-4
Tate Hollow—*valley* AL-4
Tate Hollow—*valley* PA-2
Tate Hollow—*valley (5)* TN-4
Tate House—*hist pl* GA-3
Tate House—*hist pl* ME-1
Tate House—*hist pl* NC-3
Tate JHS—*school* AL-4
Tate JHS (Abandoned)—*school* AL-4
Tate Lake—*lake* AR-4
Tate Lake—*lake* NE-7
Tate Lake Dam—*dam (2)* MS-4
*Tate Landing* AL-4
Tate Lodge—*locale* AR-4
Tate Lookout Tower—*locale* GA-3
Tate Magnolia Ch—*church* MS-4
Tate Memorial Mission—*church* SC-3
Tatem Hollow—*valley* TN-4
Tate Mill (historical)—*locale* TN-4
Tate Mine—*mine* TN-4
Tate Mine (underground)—*mine* AL-4
Tate Mountain Cem—*cemetery* OK-5
Tatem Sch—*school* NJ-2
Tate Mtn—*summit* NC-3
Tate Mtn—*summit* OK-5
Tate Mtn—*summit* VT-1
*Tatenka* SD-7
Tate Number 5 Mine (Underground)—*mine* TN-4
Tate Number 6 Mine (underground)—*mine* TN-4
*Tatenville* AL-4
Tate Parris Branch—*stream* OK-5
Tate Place—*locale* ID-8
Tate Place—*locale* MT-8
*Tater* NC-3
Tater Branch—*stream* TN-4
Tater Canyon—*valley* AZ-5
Tater Canyon—*valley* UT-8
Tater Canyon Springs—*spring* AZ-5
Tater Cave—*cave* MO-7
Tater Cave—*cave (2)* TN-4
Tater Cave Mtn—*summit* MO-7
*Tater Creek* GA-3
Tater Creek—*stream (2)* AL-4
Tater Creek—*stream* ID-8
Tater Creek—*stream* IL-6
Tater Creek—*stream* MS-4
Tater Heap—*summit* CO-8
Tater Hill—*summit* AL-4
Tater Hill—*summit (13)* AR-4
Tater Hill—*summit* CA-9
Tater Hill—*summit* CO-8
Tater Hill—*summit* IL-6
Tater Hill—*summit* KY-4
Tater Hill—*summit (4)* MO-7
Tater Hill—*summit* NC-3
Tater Hill—*summit* OK-5
Tater Hill—*summit (4)* OR-9
Tater Hill—*summit* SC-3
Tater Hill—*summit (2)* TN-4
Tater Hill—*summit (6)* TX-5
Tater Hill Cem—*cemetery* CT-1
Tater Hill Creek—*stream* AL-4
Tater Hill Creek—*stream* MO-7
*Tater Hill Mtn* AL-4
*Tater Hill Mtn* OR-9
Tater Hill Mtn—*summit* AL-4
Taterhill Mtn—*summit* TX-5
Tater Hill Mtn—*summit* TX-5
Tater Hills—*summit* TX-5
Tater Hill Sch—*school* IA-7
Tater Hole Hollow—*valley* KY-4
Tater Hollow—*valley* MO-7
Tater Hollow Cave—*cave* MO-7
Tater Island—*island* FL-3
Tater Knob—*summit (2)* AL-4
Tater Knob—*summit (2)* AR-4
Tater Knob—*summit (2)* KY-4
Tater Knob—*summit* NC-3
Tater Knob—*summit (3)* TN-4
Tater Knob—*summit* VA-3
Tater Knob—*summit* WV-2
Tater Knoll—*summit* CA-9
Tater Lick Branch—*stream* KY-4
Tater Miller Field—*park* AL-4
Tater Nob—*summit* TX-5
Tater Patch Gulch—*valley* OR-9
**Tater Peeler (historical)**—*pop pl* TN-4
Tater Point—*cliff* AZ-5
Tater Ridge—*ridge* AZ-5
Tater Ridge—*ridge* OH-6
Tater Ridge—*ridge* TN-4
Tater Run—*stream* KY-4
Tater Run—*stream* WV-2
Taters Creek—*stream* ID-8
Tate Rsvr—*reservoir* MT-8
Tater Top Mtn—*summit* NC-3
Tatertown (historical)—*locale* AL-4
Tate Run—*stream* VA-3
Tate Run—*stream* WV-2
Tate-Russell Cem—*cemetery* AL-4
Taterville—*locale* LA-4
Tate's Barn—*hist pl* AR-4
Tates Bluff—*cliff* AR-4
Tates Bluff—*locale* AR-4
Tates Bluff Ch—*church* AR-4
Tates Branch—*stream* VA-3
Tates Brook—*stream* NH-1
Tates Cem—*cemetery* AL-4
Tates Cem—*cemetery* MS-4
*Tate Sch* AL-4
Tate Sch—*school* AL-4
Tate Sch—*school* AR-4
Tate Sch—*school* FL-3
Tate Sch—*school* KY-4
Tate Sch—*school* NM-5
Tate Sch (abandoned)—*school* MO-7
Tates Chapel—*church (2)* AL-4
*Tates Chapel Baptist Ch* AL-4
Tates Chapel Cem—*cemetery* AL-4
*Tates Chapel Elementary School* AL-4
Tate Sch (historical)—*school (2)* TN-4
*Tates Cove* AL-4
Tates Creek—*stream* GA-3
Tates Creek Ch—*church* GA-3
Tates Creek Country Club—*other* KY-4
Tates Creek HS—*school* KY-4
Tates Creek JHS—*school* KY-4
Tates Fish Camp—*locale* AL-4
Tates Grove Ch—*church* GA-3
Tates Gulch—*valley* CO-8
Tates Hell Swamp—*swamp* FL-3
Tates Hollow—*valley* IN-6
Tates Island—*island* TN-4
*Tates Lake* MI-6
Tate Slough—*gut* AL-4
*Tates Magnolia Church* MS-4
Tates Mill—*locale* AR-4
Tates Mills (historical)—*locale* AL-4
Tate Spring—*spring* AL-4
Tate Spring—*spring* AR-4
Tate Spring—*spring* GA-3
Tate Spring—*spring* ID-8
Tate Spring—*spring* OR-9
Tate Spring Number Two—*spring* OR-9
Tate Springs—*locale* AL-4
**Tate Springs**—*pop pl* TN-4
**Tate Springs**—*pop pl* TX-5
Tate Springs—*spring* AL-4
*Tate Springs Branch* AL-4
Tate Springs Post Office (historical)—*building* TN-4
Tate Springs Springhouse—*hist pl* TN-4
**Tate Springs (Tate Spring)**—*pop pl* TN-4
*Tate Spring Station* TN-4
Tates Run—*stream* PA-2
Tates Sch—*school* TN-4
Tates Swamp—*stream* VA-3
*Tates Switch* MS-4
Tate Street—*uninc pl* NC-3
Tate Street Baptist Ch—*church* MS-4
**Tatesville**—*pop pl* PA-2
**Tatesville**—*pop pl* TN-4
Tatesville (historical)—*locale* MS-4
Tatesville Post Office (historical)—*building* TN-4
Tatesville Sch—*school* TN-4
Tates Wash—*stream* NV-8
Tate Town Ch—*church* AR-4
Tate (Township of)—*fmr MCD* AR-4
**Tate (Township of)**—*pop pl* IL-6
**Tate (Township of)**—*pop pl* OH-6
Tatetuck Brook—*stream* CT-1
**Tateville**—*pop pl* KY-4
Tate Well—*well* MT-8
Tate Windmill—*locale* TX-5
Tate Woods Sch—*school* IL-6
Tatezaka Tank—*reservoir* AZ-5
*Tatgua*—*slope* MH-9
**Tatham**—*pop pl* MA-1
Tatham Cabin Branch—*stream* NC-3
Tatham Creek—*stream (2)* NC-3
Tatham Gap—*gap* NC-3
Tatham Ridge—*ridge* CA-9
Tatham Springs—*locale* KY-4
Tatheethaey—*summit* FM-9
*Tathethay* FM-9
Tathiil—*cape* FM-9
Tathul—*summit* FM-9
*Tatia Toak* AZ-5
Tatie Peak—*summit* WA-9
Tatigirok Creek—*stream* AK-9
Tatik Point—*cape* AK-9
*Tatillaba Creek* AL-4
Tatina Glacier—*glacier* AK-9
Tatina River—*stream* AK-9
*Tating Hill* ME-1
**Tatitlek**—*pop pl* AK-9
Tatitlek ANV960—*reserve* AK-9
Tatitlek Narrows—*channel* AK-9
Tatk Kam Vo—*locale* AZ-5
Tatlalingik Pass—*gut* AK-9
Tatlanika Creek—*stream* AK-9
Tatlawiksuk River—*stream* AK-9
Tatley Lake—*lake* MN-6
Tatlignagpeke Mtn—*summit* AK-9
Tatlock Lake—*reservoir* TN-4
Tatlock Lake Dam—*dam* TN-4
**Tatman**—*pop pl* ND-7
*Tatman Access* PA-2
Tatman Canal—*canal* WY-8
Tatman Gulch—*valley* WA-9
Tatman Mtn—*summit* WA-9
Tatman Mtn—*summit* WY-8
Tatman Ranch—*locale* WY-8
Tatman Run—*stream* PA-2
Tatman Run Access Area—*area* PA-2
*Tatman Run Boat Launch* PA-2
**Tatmans**—*pop pl* OH-6
Tatman Tank—*reservoir* NM-5
**Tatman Township**—*pop pl* ND-7
Tat Momoli—*locale* AZ-5
Tat Momolikot Dam—*dam* AZ-5
Tat Momoli Mountains—*summit* AZ-5
Tat Momoli Pass—*gap* AZ-5
Tat Momoli Valley—*valley* AZ-5
Tat Momoli Wash—*stream* AZ-5
*Tatnall School* DE-2
Tatnall School, The—*school* DE-2
**Tatnic**—*pop pl* ME-1
Tatnic Brook—*stream* CT-1
Tatnic Hill—*summit* CT-1
Tatnic Hill—*summit* ME-1
Tatnic Hills—*summit* ME-1
*Tatnick* MA-1
Tatnick—*locale* AZ-5
*Tatnick Brook* MA-1
*Tatnick Hills* MA-1
Tatnuck Brook—*stream (2)* MA-1
Tatnuck Country Club—*locale* MA-1
Tatnuck Hill—*summit* MA-1
**Tatnuck (subdivision)**—*pop pl* MA-1
Tato Falls—*falls* WA-9
Tatondan Lake—*lake* AK-9
Tatonduk River—*stream* AK-9
*Tatonville* AL-4
Tatoosh Buttes—*summit* WA-9
Tatoosh Creek—*stream* WA-9
Tatoosh Hills—*summit* WA-9
Tatoosh Island—*hist pl* WA-9
Tatoosh Island—*island* WA-9
Tatoosh Islands—*area* AK-9
Tatoosh Lakes—*lake* WA-9
Tatoosh Lookout—*locale* WA-9
Tatoosh Point—*cape* AK-9
Tatoosh Range—*range* WA-9
Tatoosh Rocks—*area* AK-9
Tatoosh Trail—*trail* WA-9
Tator Hills—*summit* AZ-5
Tator Hole—*basin* UT-8
Tatouche Peak—*summit* OR-9
Tatow Knob—*summit* UT-8
*Tatria Toak* AZ-5
**Tatria Toak**—*pop pl* AZ-5
Tatro Brook—*stream* MA-1
*Tatroe Brook* MA-1
Tatro Sch—*school* IL-6
*Tats Gap* PA-2
Tatsie—*locale* TX-5
Tatsie Crossing—*locale* TX-5
Tatsolo Point—*cape* WA-9
Tats Spring—*spring* OR-9
*Tatsu* FM-9
*Tatsumi* MP-9
Tatsumi Reef—*bar* MH-9
*Tatsumi Riff* MH-9
*Tatsumi-Sho* MH-9
*Tatsu Shima* FM-9
Tatter Knob—*summit* MO-7
Tattersall, Joseph, House—*hist pl* UT-8
Tatterson Creek—*stream* UT-8
Tattilaba Creek—*stream* AL-4
Tattilaba (historical)—*locale* AL-4
Tattitgak Bluff—*cliff* AK-9
Tattle Branch—*stream* TN-4
Tattle Branch—*stream (2)* VA-3
**Tattle Corner**—*pop pl* ME-1
*Tattle Creek* OH-6
Tattle Creek—*stream (2)* AR-4
Tattle Creek—*stream* MO-7
Tattle Creek—*stream* OH-6
Tattle Creek—*stream* AK-9
Tattlers Hollow—*valley* KY-4
**Tattlersville**—*pop pl* KY-4
Tattles Grove Ch—*church* NC-3
*Tattle Square* ME-1
Tattnall—*locale* MT-8
Tattnall Campground—*locale* GA-3
**Tattnall (County)**—*pop pl* GA-3
Tattnall Square—*locale* GA-3
Tattnall Square Acad—*school* GA-3
Tattys Creek—*stream* MO-7
*Tatu* FM-9
Tatu—*locale* CA-9
Tatu Creek—*stream* CA-9
*Tatum* MA-1
Tatum—*locale* VA-3
**Tatum**—*pop pl* FL-3
**Tatum**—*pop pl* MS-4
**Tatum**—*pop pl* NM-5
**Tatum**—*pop pl* SC-3
**Tatum**—*pop pl* TX-5
Tatum, Mount—*summit* AK-9
*Tatum and Ewing Mill* AL-4
*Tatumasket* MA-1
Tatum Baca—*lake* AZ-5
Tatum Branch—*stream (2)* AR-4
Tatum Branch—*stream (2)* TN-4
Tatum Branch—*stream* TX-5
Tatum (CCD)—*cens area* NM-5
Tatum (CCD)—*cens area* TX-5
Tatum Cem—*cemetery (2)* AL-4
Tatum Cem—*cemetery* GA-3
Tatum Cem—*cemetery* KY-4
Tatum Cem—*cemetery* MS-4
Tatum Cem—*cemetery* TX-5
Tatum Ch—*church* TN-4
Tatum Chapel—*church (2)* MO-7
*Tatum Creek* AL-4
Tatum Creek—*stream* AL-4
Tatum Creek—*stream* GA-3
Tatum Creek—*stream* MS-4
Tatum Creek—*stream* TN-4
Tatum Creek—*stream* TX-5
Tatum Draw—*valley* CO-8
Tatum Gas Field—*oilfield* TX-5
Tatum Gulch—*valley* CO-8
Tatum Gulf—*bay* GA-3
Tatum Gulf—*valley (2)* GA-3
Tatum Gully—*stream* FL-3
Tatum Hill—*summit* MO-7
Tatum Hollow—*valley* TN-4
*Tatumi Reef* MH-9
Tatum Lake—*reservoir* GA-3
Tatum Macedonia Ch—*church* VA-3
Tatum Millpond Bay—*swamp* NC-3
Tatum Mtn—*summit (3)* GA-3
Tatum Park—*flat* CO-8
Tatum Park—*park (2)* FL-3
Tatum Pond Dam—*dam (2)* MS-4
Tatum Ridge—*ridge* CO-8
Tatum Ridge Baptist Ch—*church* FL-3
**Tatum Ridge (subdivision)**—*pop pl* FL-3
Tatum Rsvr—*reservoir* CO-8
**Tatums**—*pop pl* OK-5
Tatum Sawgrass—*swamp* FL-3
Tatums Camps—*locale* MS-4
Tatum Sch—*school* GA-3
Tatum Sch—*school* MS-4
Tatum Sch—*school (2)* TX-5
Tatum Sch (historical)—*school* TN-4
Tatums Landing—*locale* MS-4
*Tatums Mill* AL-4
Tatum Spring—*spring* AR-4
*Tatum Station* SC-3
Tatums (Township of)—*fmr MCD* NC-3
**Tatumsville**—*pop pl* GA-3
**Tatumsville**—*pop pl* KY-4
Tatumsville (historical)—*locale* MS-4
Tatum Tank—*reservoir* AZ-5
Tatumville—*locale* IL-6
**Tatumville**—*pop pl* TN-4
Tatumville Bottom—*basin* TN-4
Tatumville Ch (historical)—*church* TN-4
Tatumville Gully—*valley* AL-4
Tatumville Post Office (historical)—*building* TN-4
Tatumville Sch (historical)—*school* TN-4
Tatum Waterway—*channel* FL-3
Tatus Cem—*cemetery* OK-5
**Tau**—*pop pl* AS-9
**Ta'u**—*pop pl* AS-9
*Tauabit* AZ-5
*Tauache* FM-9
*Tauadsche* FM-9
*Tauai* HI-9
*Tauak* FM-9
*Tauak Einfahrt* FM-9
*Tauak-Hafen* FM-9
Tauak Island—*island* FM-9
Tauak Passage—*channel* FM-9
*Tauaku Suido* FM-9
*Tauaku To* FM-9
*Taualap Pass* FM-9
Tauanap, Mochun—*channel* FM-9
*Tauanap Pass* FM-9
Tauaninny Branch—*stream* MO-7
Tau Beta Camp—*locale* MI-6
Taub Park—*park* TX-5
*Tauche* FM-9
Tauckett Creek—*stream* KS-7
*Tauconnuck Mountain Plantation* MA-1
*Tauconnuck Mountains Plantation* MA-1
Ta'u (County of)—*civ div* AS-9
Tauenai Channel—*channel* FM-9
Tauenpalang—*channel* FM-9
*Tauenpalang-Hafen* FM-9
Tauese Ridge—*ridge* AS-9
Tauese Stream—*stream* AS-9
Taufanua Ridge—*ridge* AS-9
Taufer Park—*park* UT-8
Taufusi Marsh—*swamp* AS-9
Taufusitele Marsh—*swamp* AS-9
Taugamalama Point—*cape* AS-9
Tauga Point—*cape* AS-9
Tauga Ridge—*ridge* AS-9
Tauga Rock (pyramid rock)—*island* AS-9
Taugasega Ridge—*ridge* AS-9
Taughannock Creek—*stream* NY-2
Taughannock Falls—*falls* NY-2
Taughannock Falls—*locale* NY-2
Taughannock Falls State Park—*park* NY-2
Taughannock Point—*cape* NY-2
*Taughanuc Mountain* MA-1
Taugh Creek—*stream* NJ-2
Taughenbaugh Mesa—*summit* CO-8
Taughn Hollow—*valley* TN-4
Taugh Point—*cape* NJ-2
Tauher Park—*park* IA-7
Tau Island—*island* AS-9
*Taukemy* MA-1
Taukomas Sch—*school* NY-2
*Taul* FM-9
**Taulaga**—*pop pl* AS-9
Taulaotoga Rock—*island* AS-9
*Taular Creek* AL-4
Taulbee—*locale* KY-4
Taulbee (CCD)—*cens area* KY-4
Taulbee Fork—*stream* KY-4
Taul Cem—*cemetery* KY-4
*Taul Creek* AZ-5
Tauler Creek—*stream* AL-4
*Taulmans Hill* NY-2
*Taulonica* GA-3
*Taul Peaks* AZ-5
*Taul Spring* AZ-5
*Tau'ma* FM-9
Ta'u Manu'a—*post sta* AS-9
Taumata Mtn—*summit* AS-9
Taumata Stream—*stream* AS-9
Taum Sauk Cem—*cemetery* MO-7
Taum Sauk Creek—*stream* MO-7
Taum Sauk Mtn—*summit* MO-7
Taum Sauk Nature Museum—*other* MO-7
Taum Sauk Pumped-Storage Hydroelectric Powe—*other* MO-7
Taum Sauk Trail—*trail* MO-7
Tau Mtn—*summit* AS-9
Taumulimolo Stream—*stream* AS-9
**Taunton**—*pop pl* MA-1
**Taunton**—*pop pl* MN-6
**Taunton**—*pop pl* NY-2
**Taunton**—*pop pl* WA-9
Taunton Alms House—*hist pl* MA-1
Taunton Bay—*bay* ME-1
Taunton Cem—*cemetery* CT-1
Taunton Cem—*cemetery* NY-2
Taunton City Hall—*building* MA-1
Taunton-Coleman Cem—*cemetery* LA-4
Taunton Common—*park* MA-1
Taunton Dam—*dam* AL-4
*Taunton Furnace* NJ-2
*Taunton Green* MA-1
Taunton Green Hist Dist—*hist pl* MA-1
Taunton Gully—*valley* NY-2
Taunton Hill—*summit* CT-1
Taunton Hill—*summit* NH-1
Taunton HS—*school* MA-1
Taunton HS East—*school* MA-1
Taunton Lake—*locale* NJ-2
Taunton Lake—*reservoir* AL-4
Taunton Lake—*reservoir* NJ-2
*Taunton Lake Dam* NJ-2
*Taunton Lakes* NJ-2
**Taunton Lakes**—*pop pl* NJ-2
*Taunton North Purchase* MA-1
Taunton Pond—*lake* CT-1
Taunton Public Library—*hist pl* MA-1
Taunton & Raynham Academy Grant—*unorg* ME-1
*Taunton River* ME-1
Taunton River—*stream* MA-1
Taunton Rock—*island* CT-1
Taunton State Hosp—*hospital* MA-1
Taunton State Hosp (Borden Colony)—*hospital* MA-1
Taunton (Town of)—*civil* MA-1
Taupa—*locale* OK-5
Taupawshas Swamp—*swamp* MA-1
Taureau, Bayou—*stream (2)* LA-4
Taureau, Bayou—*woods* LA-4
**Tauria**—*pop pl* MO-7
Tauroma (historical)—*locale* KS-7
*Tauromee* KS-7
Taurus—*uninc pl* NJ-2
Taurusa—*locale* CA-9
Taurusa Sch—*school* CA-9
**Taus**—*pop pl* WI-6
Tausch Creek—*stream* TX-5
Tauscher Pond—*reservoir* PA-2
Taussig—*locale* KS-7
Taussig Ranch—*locale* CO-8
Taussig Rsvr No 1—*reservoir* CO-8
*Tautabit* AZ-5
*Taut Creek* AZ-5
*Tautemco Pond* MA-1
Tautog Cove—*bay* RI-1
Tautphaus Park—*park* ID-8
Tauuneacie Cem—*cemetery* OK-5
**Tauxemont**—*pop pl* VA-3
Tauy Ch—*church* KS-7
Tauy Creek—*stream* KS-7
Tauy Jones Hall—*hist pl* KS-7
*Tav* FM-9
Tava Cove—*valley* NC-3
Tava Island—*island* AK-9
Tavalagi Ridge—*ridge* AS-9
Tavan Elem Sch—*school* AZ-5
**Tavares**—*pop pl* FL-3
Tavares, Frank, House—*hist pl* HI-9
Tavares, Lake—*lake* FL-3
Tavares (CCD)—*cens area* FL-3
Tavares Cem—*cemetery* FL-3
Tavares Christian Sch—*school* FL-3
Tavares Elem Sch—*school* FL-3
Tavares HS—*school* FL-3
Tavares Lake—*lake* WA-9
Tavares MS—*school* FL-3
Tavasci Mine—*mine* AZ-5
Tavasel Marsh—*swamp* AZ-5
Taveau Church—*hist pl* SC-3
Taveeluk Point—*cape* AK-9
Tavegia Sch—*school* WY-8
Tavener—*locale* TX-5
Tavener-Sears Tavern—*hist pl* OH-6
Tavenner House—*hist pl* WV-2
Tavenner Run—*stream* VA-3
**Tavennersville**—*pop pl* WV-2
Tavera—*locale* WI-6
Tavera Cem—*cemetery* WI-6
Taveres Center (Shop Ctr)—*locale* FL-3
Tavern—*locale* MO-7
Tavern, The—*hist pl* AL-4
Tavern, The—*hist pl* AR-4
Tavern Bay—*bay* CA-9
Tavern Branch—*stream* SC-3
Tavern Branch—*stream* TN-4
Tavern Cave—*hist pl* MO-7
Tavern Club—*hist pl* OH-6
*Tavern Creek* AL-4
Tavern Creek—*stream* ID-8
Tavern Creek—*stream* MD-2
Tavern Creek—*stream (3)* MO-7
Tavern Creek—*stream* SC-3
Taverner, George, House—*hist pl* OR-9
*Tavern Gap* TN-4
Tavern Hill—*summit* NH-1
**Tavern Hill (subdivision)**—*pop pl* MS-4
**Tavernier**—*pop pl* FL-3
Tavernier Creek—*gut* FL-3
Tavernier Harbor—*bay* FL-3
Tavernier Key—*island* FL-3
Tavernier Towne II (Shop Ctr)—*locale* FL-3
Tavern Island—*island* CT-1
Tavern Island—*island* NY-2
Tavern Millpond—*reservoir* VA-3
Tavern on Mutton Hill—*hist pl* VT-1
Tavern Post Office (historical)—*building* TN-4
Tavern Rock—*summit* MO-7
Tavern Rock Cave—*cave* MO-7
Tavern Rock Quarry—*mine* MO-7
Tavern Run—*stream* VA-3
Tavern Sch—*school* AZ-5
Tavern School (historical)—*locale* MO-7
Tavern Spring—*spring* KY-4
Tavern Spring Hollow—*valley* KY-4
Tavern Township—*civil* MO-7
**Tavern Village**—*pop pl* NH-1
*Tavinifi* FM-9
Tavis Canyon—*valley* WA-9
Tavis Creek—*stream* ND-7
Tavis Sch Number 1—*school* ND-7

Tavis Sch Number 6—school ... ND-7
Tavis Sch Number 8—school ... ND-7
Tavistock—pop pl ... DE-2
Tavistock—pop pl ... NJ-2
Tavistock Country Club—other ... NJ-2
Tavnton—locale ... WA-9
Ta-vo-num ... AZ-5
Tawoar—cape ... FM-9
Tawah ... OK-5
Tawah Creek—stream ... AK-9
Tawakani Camp—locale ... ID-8
Tawakoni, Lake—reservoir ... TX-5
Tawakoni Causeway—bridge ... TX-5
Tawakoni Golf Club—other ... TX-5
Tawak Passage—channel ... AK-9
Tawalitch River ... WA-9
Tawananau—bar ... FM-9
Tawanap ... FM-9
Tawanap—bar ... FM-9
Tawanap, Mochun—channel ... FM-9
Tawanap, Namun—channel ... FM-9
Tawanka Sch—school ... PA-2
Tawanta—locale ... MS-4
Tawanta Sch (historical)—school ... MS-4
Tawa Park—park ... AZ-5
Tawapa Spring—spring ... AZ-5
Tawa Point—cliff ... AZ-5
Tawa Run—stream ... OH-6
Tawasa Creek ... AL-4
Tawasa (historical)—locale ... AL-4
Tawas Bay—bay ... MI-6
Tawas Centre—pop pl ... MI-6
Tawas City—pop pl ... MI-6
Tawasentha Hill—summit ... MA-1
Tawasha Creek ... AL-4
Tawas Lake—lake ... MI-6
Tawas Point—cape ... MI-6
Tawas Point Light Station—hist pl ... MI-6
Tawas Point State Park—park ... MI-6
Tawa Spring—spring ... NM-5
Tawas River ... MI-6
Tawas River—stream ... MI-6
Tawas (Township of)—pop pl ... MI-6
Tawawa—pop pl ... OH-6
Tawawa Creek ... OH-6
Tawawa Lake—lake ... OH-6
Tawawe Lake—lake ... AK-9
Taw Branch—stream ... AR-4
Tawcaw Ch—church ... SC-3
Tawene—bar ... FM-9
Tawenjokola River ... FM-9
Tawes Creek—stream ... VA-3
Tawes Point ... VA-3
Taw (historical)—locale ... KS-7
Tawney—locale ... MN-6
Tawney—pop pl ... OR-9
Tawney Cem—cemetery ... WV-2
Tawney Run—stream ... PA-2
Tawney Sch—school ... NE-7
Tawny Point—summit ... CA-9
Tawoowaay—locale ... FM-9
Tawormeal—summit ... FM-9
Tawpaw, Bayou—stream (2) ... LA-4
Tawtemco Pond ... MA-1
Tawtemeo Pond ... MA-1
Tawwassa ... AL-4
Tax ... GA-3
Tax—pop pl ... GA-3
Taxahaw—pop pl ... SC-3
Tax Crossroads—locale ... GA-3
Tax Post Office ... MS-4
Taxville—locale ... PA-2
Taxville Ch—church ... PA-2
Taxville Quarry Caves—cave ... PA-2
Tay, Jesse, House—hist pl ... MA-1
Tayac Sch—school ... MD-2
Tay-Cal-Mar Sch—school ... WI-6
Taycheedah—pop pl ... WI-6
Taycheedah Cem—cemetery ... WI-6
Taycheedah Creek—stream ... WI-6
Taycheedah (Town of)—pop pl ... WI-6
Tayco Street Bridge—hist pl ... WI-6
Tay Creek ... KS-7
Tayes Hollow—valley ... TN-4
Tayey—locale ... FM-9
T'ayin—bar ... FM-9
Tayler Ditch ... IN-6
Taylers Creek—stream ... PA-2
Taylers Ferry ... NC-3
Tayles Hidden Acres—area ... CA-9
Tayloe—locale ... AL-4
Tayloe Bend—bend ... KY-4
Tayloe Branch—stream ... AL-4
Tayloe-Cameron House ... DC-2
Tayloe Creek—stream ... AL-4
Tayloe House (historical)—building ... DC-2
Tayloe Neck—cape ... MD-2
Tayloes Neck ... MD-2
Taylor ... KS-7
Taylor ... KY-4
Taylor ... MD-2
Taylor ... NC-3
Taylor ... OH-6
Taylor ... OR-9
Taylor ... TX-5
Taylor—locale ... AL-4
Taylor—locale ... CA-9
Taylor—locale ... FL-3
Taylor—locale ... IL-6
Taylor—locale ... IA-7
Taylor—locale ... MD-2
Taylor—locale ... MO-7
Taylor—locale ... NY-2
Taylor—locale (2) ... OK-5
Taylor—locale (2) ... PA-2
Taylor—locale ... UT-8
Taylor—locale ... VA-3
Taylor—locale ... WV-2
Taylor—pop pl ... AL-4
Taylor—pop pl ... AK-9
Taylor—pop pl ... AZ-5
Taylor—pop pl ... AR-4
Taylor—pop pl ... ID-8
Taylor—pop pl (2) ... IN-6
Taylor—pop pl ... LA-4
Taylor—pop pl ... MI-6
Taylor—pop pl ... MS-4
Taylor—pop pl ... NE-7
Taylor—pop pl ... NY-2
Taylor—pop pl ... ND-7
Taylor—pop pl (2) ... PA-2
Taylor—pop pl ... TN-4
Taylor—pop pl ... TX-5
Taylor—pop pl ... WI-6
Taylor—pop pl ... WY-8
Taylor, A. E., House—hist pl ... WI-6
Taylor, Archibald, House—hist pl ... NC-3
Taylor, Arthur, House—hist pl ... ID-8
Taylor, Arthur, House—hist pl ... UT-8
Taylor, Bayard, Sch—hist pl ... PA-2
Taylor, Benjamin, Homestead—hist pl ... PA-2
Taylor, Campbell and Greenlief Fisk, House—hist pl ... TX-5
Taylor, Capt. Samuel, House—hist pl ... KY-4
Taylor, Chauncey S., House—hist pl ... NE-7
Taylor, Christopher, House—hist pl ... TN-4
Taylor, Col. Richard P., House—hist pl ... NC-3
Taylor, Col. Robert Z., House—hist pl ... TN-4
Taylor, David, House—hist pl ... WI-6
Taylor, David W., Model Basin—hist pl ... MD-2
Taylor, Dr. Henry Genet, House and Office—hist pl ... NJ-2
Taylor, Duckworth and Company Foundry Bldg—hist pl ... CA-9
Taylor, Edward T., House—hist pl ... CO-8
Taylor, Elisha, House—hist pl ... MI-6
Taylor, F., Mill—hist pl ... KY-4
Taylor, Fernando G., House—hist pl ... IN-6
Taylor, George, House—hist pl ... OR-9
Taylor, George, House—hist pl ... PA-2
Taylor, George, Jr., House—hist pl ... UT-8
Taylor, George W., House—hist pl ... MN-6
Taylor, Isaac, House—hist pl ... NC-3
Taylor, J. B., and Son Feed Store—hist pl ... KY-4
Taylor, J. H., House—hist pl ... TX-5
Taylor, Judson L., House—hist pl ... TX-5
Taylor, Lake—lake ... FL-3
Taylor, Lake—lake ... ND-7
Taylor, Lake—lake ... OH-6
Taylor, Lake—reservoir ... VA-3
Taylor, Lake—swamp ... LA-4
Taylor, Lucy Hobbs, Bldg—hist pl ... KS-7
Taylor, Mount—summit ... NV-8
Taylor, Mount—summit ... NM-5
Taylor, Oscar, House—hist pl ... IL-6
Taylor, Patty Person, House—hist pl ... NC-3
Taylor, Peter, House and Haehlen, Gotlieb, House—hist pl ... OR-9
Taylor, Phillip, House—hist pl ... PA-2
Taylor, Phillip R., House—hist pl ... KY-4
Taylor, Ridge, Farm—hist pl ... KY-4
Taylor, Thomas N., House—hist pl ... UT-8
Taylor, Wenzil, Bldg—hist pl ... IA-7
Taylor, William, House—hist pl ... KY-4
Taylor, Zachary, House—hist pl ... KY-4
Taylor, Zachary, Natl Cemetery—hist pl ... KY-4
Taylor Acres—pop pl ... TN-4
Taylor Addition (subdivision)—pop pl ... UT-8
Taylor Airp—airport ... AZ-5
Taylor Airp—airport ... NC-3
Taylor Alderdice HS—school ... PA-2
Taylor Arroyo—stream ... CO-8
Taylor Ashley Ditch—canal ... CO-8
Taylor Assembly of God Church ... AL-4
Taylor Ave Reservoir ... FL-3
Taylor Aviation Air Field—airport ... PA-2
Taylor Baptist Ch—church ... MS-4
Taylor Bar—bar ... ID-8
Taylor Basin—basin ... AZ-5
Taylor Basin—basin ... WY-8
Taylor Basin Tank—reservoir ... AZ-5
Taylor Bay—bay (2) ... AK-9
Taylor Bay—bay ... MT-8
Taylor Bay—bay ... NC-3
Taylor Bay—bay ... WA-9
Taylor Bay—stream ... AR-4
Taylor Bay—swamp ... FL-3
Taylor Bay (Carolina Bay)—swamp ... NC-3
Taylor Bayou ... LA-4
Taylor Bayou—stream ... LA-4
Taylor Bayou—stream (2) ... TX-5
Taylor Bayou Ch—church ... LA-4
Taylor Bench—bench ... AR-4
Taylor Bend—bend ... TN-4
Taylor Bend—bend ... TX-5
Taylor Bldg—hist pl ... AR-4
Taylor Bluff—cliff ... KY-4
Taylor Bluff—cliff ... OK-5
Taylor Bluff—cliff ... TN-4
Taylor Bluff—summit ... IL-6
Taylor Bluffs—cliff ... CA-9
Taylor Borough—civil ... PA-2
Taylor Box Draw—valley ... TX-5
Taylor Branch ... FL-3
Taylor Branch ... TX-5
Taylor Branch—canal ... MI-6
Taylor Branch—stream (4) ... AL-4
Taylor Branch—stream (3) ... AR-4
Taylor Branch—stream ... DE-2
Taylor Branch—stream (2) ... FL-3
Taylor Branch—stream (5) ... GA-3
Taylor Branch—stream (2) ... IL-6
Taylor Branch—stream (2) ... IN-6
Taylor Branch—stream ... KS-7
Taylor Branch—stream (11) ... KY-4
Taylor Branch—stream (3) ... LA-4
Taylor Branch—stream ... ME-1
Taylor Branch—stream ... MD-2
Taylor Branch—stream (2) ... MS-4
Taylor Branch—stream (4) ... MO-7
Taylor Branch—stream ... NE-7
Taylor Branch—stream (8) ... NC-3
Taylor Branch—stream (3) ... SC-3
Taylor Branch—stream (14) ... TN-4
Taylor Branch—stream (9) ... TX-5
Taylor Branch—stream (5) ... VA-3
Taylor Branch—stream (3) ... WV-2
Taylor Bridge—bridge ... OR-9
Taylor Bridge—bridge ... PA-2
Taylor Bridge—other ... MO-7
Taylor Bridge—pop pl ... VT-1
Taylor Brook ... MA-1
Taylor Brook—stream (2) ... CT-1
Taylor Brook—stream (5) ... ME-1
Taylor Brook—stream (6) ... MA-1
Taylor Brook—stream (2) ... NH-1
Taylor Brook—stream ... NJ-2
Taylor Brook—stream (4) ... NY-2
Taylor Brook—stream ... PA-2
Taylor Brook—stream (5) ... VT-1
Taylor Brook Pond—lake ... ME-1
Taylor Brothers Dam—dam ... SD-7
Taylor Brothers Ranch—locale ... WY-8
Taylor Brothers Sheep Camp—locale ... WY-8
Taylor (Br. P.O. name Taylor-Old Forge)—pop pl ... PA-2
Taylor Burn Guard Station—locale ... OR-9
Taylor Butte—summit ... AZ-5
Taylor Butte—summit (2) ... MT-8
Taylor Butte—summit ... ND-7
Taylor Butte—summit (6) ... OR-9
Taylor Buttes—ridge ... OR-9
Taylor Butte Sch—school ... ND-7
Taylor Butte Township—pop pl ... ND-7
Taylor Cabin—locale ... AZ-5
Taylor Cabin—locale ... CA-9
Taylor Cabin Line Camp—hist pl ... AZ-5
Taylor Cabin Trail—trail ... AZ-5
Taylor Camp—locale ... CO-8
Taylor Camp—locale ... TX-5
Taylor Canal—canal ... CA-9
Taylor Canal—canal ... ID-8
Taylor Canal—canal ... NV-8
Taylor Canal—canal ... SC-3
Taylor Canal—canal ... WY-8
Taylor Canyon ... AZ-5
Taylor Canyon ... ID-8
Taylor Canyon ... NV-8
Taylor Canyon ... UT-8
Taylor Canyon—valley (6) ... CA-9
Taylor Canyon—valley (4) ... CO-8
Taylor Canyon—valley (5) ... ID-8
Taylor Canyon—valley ... MT-8
Taylor Canyon—valley (4) ... NV-8
Taylor Canyon—valley (7) ... NM-5
Taylor Canyon—valley ... TX-5
Taylor Canyon—valley (5) ... UT-8
Taylor Canyon—valley ... WA-9
Taylor Canyon Oil Field ... CA-9
Taylor Carpet Company Bldg—hist pl ... IN-6
Taylor Castle—summit ... OR-9
Taylor Cave—cave ... AL-4
Taylor (CCD)—cens area ... TX-5
Taylor Cem ... AL-4
Taylor Cem ... MS-4
Taylor Cem—cemetery (14) ... AL-4
Taylor Cem—cemetery ... AZ-5
Taylor Cem—cemetery (10) ... AR-4
Taylor Cem—cemetery ... FL-3
Taylor Cem—cemetery (7) ... GA-3
Taylor Cem—cemetery ... ID-8
Taylor Cem—cemetery (5) ... IL-6
Taylor Cem—cemetery (7) ... IN-6
Taylor Cem—cemetery ... IA-7
Taylor Cem—cemetery ... KS-7
Taylor Cem—cemetery (15) ... KY-4
Taylor Cem—cemetery (8) ... LA-4
Taylor Cem—cemetery (2) ... ME-1
Taylor Cem—cemetery ... MA-1
Taylor Cem—cemetery (2) ... MI-6
Taylor Cem—cemetery ... MN-6
Taylor Cem—cemetery (11) ... MS-4
Taylor Cem—cemetery (6) ... MO-7
Taylor Cem—cemetery ... MT-8
Taylor Cem—cemetery (2) ... NE-7
Taylor Cem—cemetery (3) ... NY-2
Taylor Cem—cemetery (7) ... NC-3
Taylor Cem—cemetery (5) ... OH-6
Taylor Cem—cemetery ... OK-5
Taylor Cem—cemetery ... OR-9
Taylor Cem—cemetery (3) ... PA-2
Taylor Cem—cemetery (2) ... SC-3
Taylor Cem—cemetery ... SD-7
Taylor Cem—cemetery (35) ... TN-4
Taylor Cem—cemetery (6) ... TX-5
Taylor Cem—cemetery (9) ... VA-3
Taylor Cem—cemetery (10) ... WV-2
Taylor Center ... MI-6
Taylor Center—pop pl ... NY-2
Taylor Center HS—school ... MI-6
Taylor Center Sch—school ... MI-6
Taylor Center (subdivision)—pop pl ... MI-6
Taylor Ch—church (2) ... AL-4
Taylor Ch—church ... GA-3
Taylor Ch—church ... IL-6
Taylor Ch—church ... KY-4
Taylor Ch—church ... MN-6
Taylor Ch—church (2) ... MS-4
Taylor Ch—church ... MO-7
Taylor Ch—church ... OH-6
Taylor Ch—church ... PA-2
Taylor Chapel ... TN-4
Taylor Chapel—church (3) ... AL-4
Taylor Chapel—church (2) ... AR-4
Taylor Chapel—church (2) ... GA-3
Taylor Chapel—church ... IN-6
Taylor Chapel—church ... KY-4
Taylor Chapel—church ... MS-4
Taylor Chapel—church ... MO-7
Taylor Chapel—church ... NC-3
Taylor Chapel—church ... SC-3
Taylor Chapel—church (5) ... TN-4
Taylor Chapel—church ... WV-2
Taylor Chapel—locale ... TN-4
Taylor Chapel Baptist Ch ... MS-4
Taylor Chapel Cem—cemetery ... AL-4
Taylor Chapel Cem—cemetery ... LA-4
Taylor Chapel Cem—cemetery ... TN-4
Taylor Chapel Cem—cemetery ... TX-5
Taylor Chapel (historical)—church ... MS-4
Taylor Chapel Sch—school ... TN-4
Taylor Chapel Sch (historical)—school ... TN-4
Taylor Ch (historical)—church ... TN-4
Taylor Circle (subdivision)—pop pl ... AL-4
Taylor Coates Hollow—valley ... KY-4
Taylor-Condrey House—hist pl ... WV-2
Taylor-Cooper House—hist pl ... TX-5
Taylor-Cope Hist Dist—hist pl ... PA-2
Taylor Corner—pop pl (2) ... IN-6
Taylor Corner Gin—locale ... OK-5
Taylor Corners—locale ... NY-2
Taylor Corners—pop pl ... CT-1
Taylor Corners—pop pl ... OH-6
Taylor Coulee—valley (4) ... MT-8
Taylor County—pop pl ... FL-3
Taylor (County)—pop pl ... GA-3
Taylor (County)—pop pl ... KY-4
Taylor (County)—pop pl ... TX-5
Taylor (County)—pop pl ... WV-2
Taylor (County)—pop pl ... WI-6
Taylor County Area Education Center—school ... FL-3
Taylor County Clerk's Office—hist pl ... KY-4
Taylor County Courthouse—hist pl ... IA-7
Taylor County Courthouse—hist pl ... WI-6
Taylor County HS—school ... FL-3
Taylor County HS—school ... KY-4
Taylor County JHS—school ... FL-3
Taylor County Park—park ... KY-4
Taylor County Public Library—building ... FL-3
Taylor County Sch—school ... KY-4
Taylor Cove—bay (2) ... MD-2
Taylor Cow Camp—locale (2) ... WY-8
Taylor Creek ... CA-9
Taylor Creek ... CO-8
Taylor Creek ... GA-3
Taylor Creek ... MS-4
Taylor Creek ... MT-8
Taylor Creek ... SC-3
Taylor Creek ... TN-4
Taylor Creek ... UT-8
Taylor Creek ... WA-9
Taylor Creek—CDP ... FL-3
Taylor Creek—channel ... NC-3
Taylor Creek—gut ... NC-3
Taylor Creek—pop pl ... AK-9
Taylor Creek—stream (7) ... AL-4
Taylor Creek—stream (6) ... AK-9
Taylor Creek—stream (5) ... AR-4
Taylor Creek—stream (11) ... CA-9
Taylor Creek—stream (5) ... CO-8
Taylor Creek—stream (4) ... FL-3
Taylor Creek—stream (3) ... GA-3
Taylor Creek—stream (9) ... ID-8
Taylor Creek—stream ... IL-6
Taylor Creek—stream (3) ... IN-6
Taylor Creek—stream (2) ... KS-7
Taylor Creek—stream (4) ... KY-4
Taylor Creek—stream (2) ... LA-4
Taylor Creek—stream (8) ... MI-6
Taylor Creek—stream ... MN-6
Taylor Creek—stream (6) ... MS-4
Taylor Creek—stream (11) ... MT-8
Taylor Creek—stream (2) ... NE-7
Taylor Creek—stream (3) ... NV-8
Taylor Creek—stream ... NJ-2
Taylor Creek—stream (2) ... NM-5
Taylor Creek—stream (3) ... NY-2
Taylor Creek—stream (5) ... NC-3
Taylor Creek—stream (2) ... OH-6
Taylor Creek—stream (4) ... OK-5
Taylor Creek—stream (13) ... OR-9
Taylor Creek—stream (2) ... PA-2
Taylor Creek—stream (3) ... SC-3
Taylor Creek—stream (8) ... TN-4
Taylor Creek—stream (5) ... TX-5
Taylor Creek—stream (3) ... UT-8
Taylor Creek—stream (4) ... VA-3
Taylor Creek—stream (2) ... WA-9
Taylor Creek—stream ... WV-2
Taylor Creek—stream (4) ... WI-6
Taylor Creek—stream (5) ... WY-8
Taylor Creek Bar—bar ... OR-9
Taylor Creek Causeway—bridge ... TN-4
Taylor Creek East Subdivision—pop pl ... TN-4
Taylor Creek Falls—falls ... OR-9
Taylor Creek Gorge—valley ... OR-9
Taylor Creek Pass—gap ... CO-8
Taylor Creek Rsvr Number One—reservoir ... MT-8
Taylor Creek Rsvr Number Two—reservoir ... MT-8
Taylor Creek Sawmill Spring—spring ... MT-8
Taylor Creek State For—forest ... NY-2
Taylor Creek (Township of)—civ div ... OH-6
Taylor Creek Trail—trail ... ID-8
Taylor Creek West Subdivision—pop pl ... TN-4
Taylor Crossing—locale ... CA-9
Taylor Cross Roads ... NC-3
Taylor Crossroads—locale (2) ... NC-3
Taylor Crossroads—locale (2) ... TN-4
Taylor Cross Roads—pop pl ... NC-3
Taylor Crossroads—pop pl ... NC-3
Taylor Cross Roads—pop pl ... TN-4
Taylor Crossroads Ch—church ... AL-4
Taylor Cut ... DC-2
Taylor Cut—channel ... TX-5
Taylor-Dallin House—hist pl ... MA-1
Taylor Dam ... AL-4
Taylor Dam—dam ... NE-7
Taylor Dam—dam (2) ... NC-3
Taylor Dam—dam ... TN-4
Taylor Dam—dam ... VA-3
Taylor Dental Clinic—hospital ... TN-4
Taylor Ditch ... IN-6
Taylor Ditch—canal ... ID-8
Taylor Ditch—canal ... IL-6
Taylor Ditch—canal (5) ... IN-6
Taylor Ditch—canal ... MT-8
Taylor Ditch—canal ... OH-6
Taylor Ditch—canal (2) ... OR-9
Taylor Ditch—canal ... UT-8
Taylor Ditch—canal (3) ... WY-8
Taylor Ditch Extension—canal ... WY-8
Taylor Divide—gap ... MT-8
Taylor Divide—ridge ... CA-9
Taylor Divide—ridge ... WY-8
Taylor Drain—canal (4) ... MI-6
Taylor Drain—stream (2) ... WV-2
Taylor Drain Cem—cemetery ... WV-2
Taylor Draw ... NM-5
Taylor Draw—valley (3) ... CO-8
Taylor Draw—valley (2) ... NM-5
Taylor Draw—valley ... SD-7
Taylor Draw—valley ... TX-5
Taylor Draw—valley (6) ... WY-8
Taylor Elem Sch—school ... IN-6
Taylor Elem Sch—school ... PA-2
Taylor Elza Run—stream ... WV-2
Taylor Estates—pop pl ... DE-2
Taylor Estates (subdivision)—pop pl ... TN-4
Taylor Estates Subdivision—pop pl (2) ... UT-8
Taylor Falls—falls ... MT-8
Taylor Falls Bridge—bridge ... NH-1
Taylor-Falls House—hist pl ... MS-4
Taylor Family Cem—cemetery ... MS-4
Taylor Farm Acres—pop pl ... OH-6
Taylor Ferry—pop pl ... OK-5
Taylor Ferry Camp—locale ... AL-4
Taylor Ferry (historical)—locale ... AL-4
Taylor Ferry North Rec Area—park ... OK-5
Taylor Ferry South Rec Area—park ... OK-5
Taylor Field—airport ... ND-7
Taylor Field—flat ... NV-8
Taylor Field—other ... MO-7
Taylor Field—park ... AL-4
Taylor Field—park ... AZ-5
Taylor Field—park ... OH-6
Taylor Field Branch—stream ... PA-2
Taylor-Fipps Sch—school ... CA-9
Taylor Flat—flat ... CA-9
Taylor Flat—flat ... MT-8
Taylor Flat—flat (2) ... NV-8
Taylor Flat—flat ... OR-9
Taylor Flat—flat (4) ... UT-8
Taylor Flat—flat (2) ... WA-9
Taylor Flat—flat ... WY-8
Taylor Flats—flat ... WY-8
Taylor Ford—locale ... AL-4
Taylor Fork—stream (3) ... KY-4
Taylor Fork—stream ... OH-6
Taylor Fork—stream ... PA-2
Taylor Fork—stream ... UT-8
Taylor Fork—stream ... WV-2
Taylor Fork Lake—reservoir ... KY-4
Taylor Foster Branch—stream ... AR-4
Taylor-Frohman House—hist pl ... OH-6
Taylor Gap ... AL-4
Taylor Gap—gap ... GA-3
Taylor Gap—gap ... TN-4
Taylor Gate Ch—church ... MD-2
Taylor Glacier—glacier ... AK-9
Taylor Glacier—glacier ... CO-8
Taylor Green—flat ... OR-9
Taylor Grove—woods ... OR-9
Taylor Grove Ch—church ... AL-4
Taylor Grove Ch—church ... GA-3
Taylor Grove Ch—church ... KY-4
Taylor Grove Ch—church ... MS-4
Taylor Grove Ch—church ... NC-3
Taylor Grove Ch—church ... TN-4
Taylor Gulch—valley ... AL-4
Taylor Gulch—valley ... AZ-5
Taylor Gulch—valley (4) ... CA-9
Taylor Gulch—valley (4) ... CO-8
Taylor Gulch—valley ... ID-8
Taylor Gulch—valley (3) ... OR-9
Taylor Gully—valley ... TX-5
Taylor Gut—stream ... NC-3
Taylor Hall—hist pl ... GA-3
Taylor Heights (subdivision)—pop pl ... NC-3
Taylor Highland—pop pl ... PA-2
Taylor Highlands—uninc pl ... PA-2
Taylor Hill—locale ... IA-7
Taylor Hill—pop pl ... IL-6
Taylor Hill—pop pl ... LA-4
Taylor Hill—pop pl ... TN-4
Taylor Hill—summit ... CA-9
Taylor Hill—summit ... CO-8
Taylor Hill—summit ... CT-1
Taylor Hill—summit ... FL-3
Taylor Hill—summit (2) ... IN-6
Taylor Hill—summit ... KY-4
Taylor Hill—summit ... ME-1
Taylor Hill—summit ... MA-1
Taylor Hill—summit ... MI-6
Taylor Hill—summit ... MS-4
Taylor Hill—summit ... NV-8
Taylor Hill—summit ... NH-1
Taylor Hill—summit ... NY-2
Taylor Hill—summit ... OH-6
Taylor Hill—summit (2) ... PA-2
Taylor Hill—summit ... TN-4
Taylor Hill Cem—cemetery (2) ... NY-2
Taylor Hill Ch—church ... AL-4
Taylor Hill Ch—church (2) ... MS-4
Taylor Hill Pond—lake ... ME-1
Taylor Hills—range ... TX-5
Taylor Hills—summit ... MT-8
Taylor Hills—summit ... NM-5
Taylor Hole—bay ... KY-4
Taylor Hole—lake ... MO-7
Taylor- Holeman Ranch—locale ... NM-5
Taylor Hollow ... IN-6
Taylor Hollow—locale ... NY-2
Taylor Hollow—stream ... IN-6
Taylor Hollow—valley ... AL-4
Taylor Hollow—valley ... AR-4
Taylor Hollow—valley ... IN-6
Taylor Hollow—valley ... KY-4
Taylor Hollow—valley (3) ... MO-7
Taylor Hollow—valley (2) ... NY-2
Taylor Hollow—valley ... OH-6
Taylor Hollow—valley (9) ... TN-4
Taylor Hollow—valley ... UT-8
Taylor Hollow—valley (4) ... VA-3
Taylor Hollow—valley (2) ... WV-2
Taylor Hollow—valley ... WI-6
Taylor Hollow Gap—gap ... NC-3
Taylor Homestead—locale ... CO-8
Taylor Hosp—hospital ... ME-1
Taylor Hosp—hospital (2) ... PA-2
Taylor Hosp—hospital ... TX-5
Taylor House—hist pl ... KY-4
Taylor House—hist pl ... MS-4
Taylor House—hist pl ... PA-2
Taylor House—hist pl ... SC-3
Taylor House—hist pl ... WV-2
Taylor HS—school ... FL-3
Taylor HS—school ... VA-3
Taylor HS (historical)—school ... MS-4
Taylor Hunt Branch—stream ... KY-4
Tayloria—pop pl ... PA-2
Taylor-Ina Oil Field—oilfield ... TX-5
Taylor Island ... AL-4
Taylor Island ... ME-1
Taylor Island ... MD-2
Taylor Island—island ... AK-9
Taylor Island—island ... AR-4
Taylor Island—island (2) ... IL-6
Taylor Island—island ... ME-1
Taylor Island—island ... MD-2
Taylor Island—island ... MI-6
Taylor Island—island ... MN-6
Taylor Island—island ... MT-8
Taylor Island—island ... TX-5
Taylor Island—island (2) ... WI-6
Taylor Island Point—cape ... MD-2
Taylor JHS—school ... MI-6
Taylor JHS—school ... NM-5
Taylor Junction—locale ... CA-9
Taylor Junior-Senior HS—school ... IN-6
Taylor Junior Senior HS—school ... PA-2
Taylor Knob—summit ... CA-9
Taylor Knob—summit ... NC-3
Taylor Knob—summit (3) ... TN-4
Taylor Knob—summit ... VA-3
Taylor Knob—summit ... WV-2
Taylor Knoll—summit ... AZ-5
Taylor Lagoon—lake ... AK-9
Taylor Lake ... IL-6
Taylor Lake ... MI-6
Taylor Lake ... ND-7
Taylor Lake ... WI-6
Taylor Lake—lake ... AK-9
Taylor Lake—lake (2) ... AR-4
Taylor Lake—lake (3) ... CA-9
Taylor Lake—lake (2) ... CO-8
Taylor Lake—lake (2) ... IN-6
Taylor Lake—lake ... KY-4
Taylor Lake—lake (6) ... MI-6
Taylor Lake—lake (9) ... MN-6
Taylor Lake—lake (3) ... MS-4
Taylor Lake—lake (2) ... NE-7
Taylor Lake—lake ... NY-2
Taylor Lake—lake ... OK-5
Taylor Lake—lake (4) ... OR-9
Taylor Lake—lake (4) ... TX-5
Taylor Lake—lake ... UT-8
Taylor Lake—lake ... WA-9
Taylor Lake—lake (8) ... WI-6
Taylor Lake—reservoir ... AL-4
Taylor Lake—reservoir ... FL-3
Taylor Lake—reservoir ... IN-6
Taylor Lake—reservoir ... NJ-2
Taylor Lake—reservoir ... NC-3
Taylor Lake—reservoir ... OK-5
Taylor Lake—reservoir (2) ... TN-4
Taylor Lake—reservoir ... TX-5
Taylor Lake—reservoir ... VA-3
Taylor Lake—swamp ... MN-6
Taylor Lake Branch ... FL-3
Taylor Lake (Carnahan Lake)—lake ... OR-9
Taylor Lake Dam—dam ... IN-6
Taylor Lake Dam—dam (3) ... MS-4
Taylor Lake Dam—dam ... NC-3
Taylor Lake Dam—dam ... TN-4
Taylor Lake (historical)—lake ... MO-7
Taylor Lakes—lake ... TX-5
Taylor Lake Village—pop pl ... TX-5
Taylor Land Company Lake Dam—dam ... MS-4
Taylor Landing—area ... NC-3
Taylor Landing—locale ... GA-3
Taylor Landing—locale ... MD-2
Taylor-Lane Cem—cemetery ... OR-9
Taylor Lane Subdivision—pop pl ... UT-8
Taylor Lateral—canal ... NM-5
Taylor Line Sch (historical)—school ... MS-4
Taylor-Link Oil And Gas Field—oilfield ... TX-5
Taylor Lodge—locale ... VT-1
Taylor (Magisterial District)—fmr MCD (3) ... VA-3
Taylor Manor Nursing Home—hospital ... KY-4
Taylor Mansion-Lakehurst—hist pl ... OH-6
Taylor-Mansker House—hist pl ... MS-4
Taylor-Mayo House—hist pl ... VA-3
Taylor Meadow—flat ... CA-9
Taylor Meadow—locale ... ID-8
Taylor Memorial Baptist Day Sch—school ... FL-3
Taylor Memorial Cem—cemetery ... FL-3
Taylor Memorial Ch—church ... NM-5
Taylor Memorial Ch—church ... NC-3
Taylor Memorial Library—hist pl ... CT-1
Taylor Memorial Park—park ... KY-4
Taylor Memorial Park—park ... NV-8
Taylor Memorial Stadium—other ... GA-3
Taylor Mesa—summit ... CO-8
Taylor Mesa Lake—lake ... CO-8
Taylor Meso Rsvr—reservoir ... CO-8
Taylor Methodist Ch—church ... AL-4
Taylor Mill—locale ... TN-4
Taylor Mill—pop pl ... KY-4
Taylor Mill Creek—stream ... AL-4
Taylor Mill (historical)—locale ... AL-4
Taylor Mill Lake—reservoir ... GA-3
Taylor Millpond—reservoir ... NC-3
Taylor Millpond—reservoir ... SC-3
Taylor Mills—pop pl ... NJ-2
Taylor Mill Sch—school ... KY-4
Taylor Mills Sch (historical)—school ... MO-7
Taylor Mine ... AL-4
Taylor Mine ... TN-4
Taylor Mine—mine (2) ... CA-9
Taylor Mine—mine ... CO-8
Taylor Mine—mine ... MT-8
Taylor Mine—mine ... NV-8
Taylor Mine—mine ... WY-8
Taylor Mine Canyon—valley ... NV-8
Taylor Mines—locale ... KY-4
Taylor Mines Ch—church ... KY-4
Taylor Mine Spring—spring ... NV-8
Taylor Monmt—pillar ... CA-9
Taylor-Moore Sch (historical)—school ... AL-4
Taylor Mound And Village Site—hist pl ... OH-6
Taylor Mountain Plateau—plain ... UT-8
Taylor Mountains—other ... AK-9
Taylor Mountains Mine—mine ... AK-9
Taylor Mountain Trail—trail ... WY-8
Taylor Mtn—summit ... AL-4
Taylor Mtn—summit ... AK-9
Taylor Mtn—summit ... AR-4
Taylor Mtn—summit (3) ... CA-9
Taylor Mtn—summit (2) ... CO-8
Taylor Mtn—summit (4) ... ID-8
Taylor Mtn—summit (2) ... KY-4
Taylor Mtn—summit ... MA-1
Taylor Mtn—summit (2) ... MT-8
Taylor Mtn—summit ... NM-5
Taylor Mtn—summit (3) ... NY-2
Taylor Mtn—summit ... OK-5
Taylor Mtn—summit ... OR-9
Taylor Mtn—summit (3) ... TX-5
Taylor Mtn—summit ... UT-8
Taylor Mtn—summit ... WA-9
Taylor Mtn—summit (2) ... WY-8
Taylor Natl Bank—hist pl ... TX-5
Taylor-Newbold House—hist pl ... NJ-2
Taylor Notch—gap ... MA-1

Taylor-Old Forge (Br. P.O. name for Taylor)—other PA-2
Taylor Old River—lake AR-4
Taylor-Ord Canal—canal NE-7
Taylor Ore Bank Mine—mine TN-4
Taylor Park MI-6
Taylor Park—flat CO-8
Taylor Park—park AL-4
Taylor Park—park CO-8
Taylor Park—park FL-3
Taylor Park—park IL-6
Taylor Park—park KY-4
Taylor Park—park NE-7
Taylor Park—park NJ-2
Taylor Park—park NM-5
Taylor Park—park (2) OK-5
Taylor Park—park TX-5
Taylor Park—park (2) WI-6
Taylor Park—pop pl CO-8
Taylor Park—pop pl MI-6
Taylor Park Ranger Station—locale CO-8
Taylor Park Rsvr—reservoir CO-8
Taylor Park Sch—school IL-6
Taylor Park Sch—school MI-6
Taylor Pass—channel LA-4
Taylor Pass—gap AZ-5
Taylor Pass—gap CO-8
Taylor Peak MT-8
Taylor Peak—summit CA-9
Taylor Peak—summit (2) CO-8
Taylor Peak—summit ID-8
Taylor Peak—summit (2) MT-8
Taylor Peak—summit NV-8
Taylor Peak—summit (2) NM-5
Taylor Peaks—spring MT-8
Taylor Place—locale AZ-5
Taylor Place (site)—locale OR-9
Taylor Plantation—locale MS-4
Taylor Point MA-1
Taylor Point—cape FL-3
Taylor Point—cape LA-4
Taylor Point—cape ME-1
Taylor Point—cape (2) MD-2
Taylor Point—cape MA-1
Taylor Point—cape OR-9
Taylor Point—cape RI-1
Taylor Point—cape WA-9
Taylor Point—cliff AR-4
Taylor Point—summit KS-7
Taylor Point—summit UT-8
Taylor Pond MA-1
Taylor Pond—lake CT-1
Taylor Pond—lake KY-4
Taylor Pond—lake ME-1
Taylor Pond—lake (2) MA-1
Taylor Pond—lake (2) NH-1
Taylor Pond—lake (4) NY-2
Taylor Pond—lake (2) TX-5
Taylor Pond—lake UT-8
Taylor Pond—reservoir AL-4
Taylor Pond—reservoir AR-4
Taylor Pond—reservoir CT-1
Taylor Pond—reservoir ME-1
Taylor Pond—reservoir NY-2
Taylor Pond—reservoir PA-2
Taylor Pond—reservoir (2) SC-3
Taylor Pond—reservoir VA-3
Taylor Pond Dam—dam MS-4
Taylor Pond Dam—dam PA-2
Taylor Pond Outlet—stream NY-2
Taylor Post Office (historical)—building AL-4
Taylor Prospect—mine TN-4
Taylor Providence Ch—church TN-4
Taylor Ranch—locale (2) AZ-5
Taylor Ranch—locale (2) CA-9
Taylor Ranch—locale CO-8
Taylor Ranch—locale NE-7
Taylor Ranch—locale (4) NM-5
Taylor Ranch—locale (3) OR-9
Taylor Ranch—locale (2) SD-7
Taylor Ranch—locale (7) TX-5
Taylor Ranch—locale WA-9
Taylor Ranch—locale (6) WY-8
Taylor Ranch (reduced usage)—locale TX-5
Taylor Rapids—range WI-6
Taylor Rapids (historical)—locale KS-7
Taylor Ray Hollow—valley TX-5
Taylor Reef—bar ME-1
Taylor Reef—bar MI-6
Taylor Reservoir CO-8
Taylor Reservoir Dam—dam AZ-5
Taylor Ridge—pop pl IL-6
Taylor Ridge—ridge AL-4
Taylor Ridge—ridge AR-4
Taylor Ridge—ridge (2) CA-9
Taylor Ridge—ridge (2) GA-3
Taylor Ridge—ridge (2) IN-6
Taylor Ridge—ridge (2) KY-4
Taylor Ridge—ridge MO-7
Taylor Ridge—ridge OH-6
Taylor Ridge—ridge OR-9
Taylor Ridge—ridge (4) TN-4
Taylor Ridge—ridge TX-5
Taylor Ridge—ridge WA-9
Taylor Ridge—ridge WV-2
Taylor Ridge Cem—cemetery IN-6
Taylor Ridge Cem—cemetery OH-6
Taylor Ridge Ch—church KY-4
Taylor Ridge Ch—church OH-6
Taylor Ridge Mine—mine TN-4
Taylor Ridges—ridge UT-8
Taylor River—stream CO-8
Taylor River—stream FL-3
Taylor River—stream NH-1
Taylor River—stream WA-9
Taylor River Forest Camp—locale WA-9
Taylor Road Ch—church VA-3
Taylor Rock—summit CA-9
Taylor Ross Ranch—locale NM-5
Taylor (RR name for South Shore)—other KY-4
Taylor (RR name Nelson)—pop pl LA-4
Taylor Rsvr—reservoir CA-9
Taylor Rsvr—reservoir MT-8
Taylor Rsvr—reservoir (2) OR-9
Taylor Run OH-6
Taylor Run PA-2
Taylor Run—stream IN-6
Taylor Run—stream (2) OH-6
Taylor Run—stream (6) PA-2
Taylor Run—stream VA-3
Taylor Run—stream (4) WV-2
Taylor Run Sch—school KY-4
Taylors MS-4
Taylors TN-4
Taylors—locale TN-4
Taylors—pop pl IN-6
Taylors—pop pl SC-3
Taylors—pop pl TN-4
Taylors Addition (subdivision)—pop pl UT-8
Taylor Saddle—gap ID-8
Taylor Sands—bar OR-9
Taylors Bar—bar AL-4
Taylors Bayou—gut LA-4
Taylors Beach—pop pl NC-3
Taylors Branch TN-4
Taylors Branch—stream NC-3
Taylors Branch—stream TN-4
Taylors Branch—stream VA-3
Taylors Branch Landing—locale TN-4
Taylors Bridge—bridge DE-2
Taylors Bridge—bridge NC-3
Taylors Bridge—locale DE-2
Taylors Bridge—pop pl NC-3
Taylors Bridge (Township of)—fmr MCD NC-3
Taylors Brook MA-1
Taylorsburg OH-6
Taylorsburg TN-4
Taylorsburg—pop pl OH-6
Taylorsburgh TN-4
Taylorsburg (historical)—locale AL-4
Taylorsburgh Post Office TN-4
Taylors Camp AL-4
Taylors Camp—locale AL-4
Taylor's Candy Factory—hist pl ID-8
Taylors Cave—cave AL-4
Taylors (CCD)—cens area SC-3
Taylors Cem—cemetery GA-3
Taylors Cem—cemetery KY-4
Taylor Sch AL-4
Taylors Ch AL-4
Taylor Sch PA-2
Taylors Ch—church AL-4
Taylors Ch—church NC-3
Taylor Sch—hist pl IA-7
Taylor Sch—hist pl MS-4
Taylor Sch—school AL-4
Taylor Sch—school AR-4
Taylor Sch—school (3) CA-9
Taylor Sch—school (2) CO-8
Taylor Sch—school DC-2
Taylor Sch—school FL-3
Taylor Sch—school ID-8
Taylor Sch—school (5) IL-6
Taylor Sch—school IN-6
Taylor Sch—school IA-7
Taylor Sch—school (2) KY-4
Taylor Sch—school MD-2
Taylor Sch—school MA-1
Taylor Sch—school (3) MI-6
Taylor Sch—school (2) MN-6
Taylor Sch—school (3) MO-7
Taylor Sch—school (2) NE-7
Taylor Sch—school NV-8
Taylor Sch—school NM-5
Taylor Sch—school (3) OH-6
Taylor Sch—school OK-5
Taylor Sch—school (3) PA-2
Taylor Sch—school SD-7
Taylor Sch—school (3) TN-4
Taylor Sch—school (2) TX-5
Taylor Sch—school (3) UT-8
Taylor Sch—school (2) VA-3
Taylor Sch—school WV-2
Taylor Sch—school WI-6
Taylor Sch—school (2) WY-8
Taylor Sch (abandoned)—school MO-7
Taylor Sch (abandoned)—school PA-2
Taylors Chapel—church AL-4
Taylors Chapel—church (2) GA-3
Taylors Chapel—church (2) KY-4
Taylors Chapel—church MD-2
Taylors Chapel—church MS-4
Taylors Chapel—church (3) NC-3
Taylors Chapel—church OH-6
Taylors Chapel—church (2) TN-4
Taylors Chapel—church (2) TX-5
Taylors Chapel—church VA-3
Taylor's Chapel—hist pl MD-2
Taylors Chapel—pop pl TN-4
Taylors Chapel Cem—cemetery AL-4
Taylors Chapel Cem—cemetery OH-6
Taylors Chapel Cem—cemetery (2) TN-4
Taylors Chapel Post Office (historical)—building TN-4
Taylors Chapel Sch—school KY-4
Taylors Chapel Sch (historical)—school TN-4
Taylor Sch (historical)—school AL-4
Taylor Sch (historical)—school (2) MO-7
Taylor Sch (historical)—school PA-2
Taylor Sch (historical)—school (3) TN-4
Taylors Corner—locale DE-2
Taylors Corner—locale NY-2
Taylors Corner—locale (2) VA-3
Taylors Corner—pop pl NC-3
Taylors Corners—pop pl NC-3
Taylors Creek FL-3
Taylors Creek MD-2
Taylors Creek NJ-2
Taylors Creek SC-3
Taylors Creek TN-4
Taylors creek UT-8
Taylors Creek—locale OH-6
Taylors Creek—stream AL-4
Taylors Creek—stream CA-9
Taylors Creek—stream (3) GA-3
Taylors Creek—stream KY-4
Taylors Creek—stream (2) MS-4
Taylors Creek—stream (4) NC-3
Taylors Creek—stream (4) VA-3
Taylors Creek Bridge—bridge GA-3
Taylors Creek Cem—cemetery GA-3
Taylors Creek Ch—church IN-6
Taylors Crossing—pop pl TN-4
Taylors Crossroads NC-3
Taylors Crossroads—locale AL-4
Taylors Crossroads—locale NC-3
Taylors Crossroads—locale SC-3
Taylors Crossroads—pop pl TN-4
Taylors Cross Roads—pop pl TN-4
Taylors Crossroads Methodist Ch—church TN-4
Taylors Dam—dam AL-4
Taylor's Daughters Hist Dist—hist pl KY-4
Taylors Depot MS-4
Taylors Ditch—canal AR-4
Taylor Settlement—locale NY-2
Taylors Falls—pop pl MN-6
Taylors Falls Public Library—hist pl MN-6
Taylors Ferry AL-4
Taylors Ferry Site—locale NC-3
Taylors Flat—flat UT-8
Taylors Flat Wildlife Mngmt Area—park UT-8
Taylors Fork—stream KY-4
Taylors Fork Campground—park UT-8
Taylors Gap DE-2
Taylors Gap—gap AL-4
Taylors Gap—gap VA-3
Taylors Grove—locale IA-7
Taylors Grove Ch—church SC-3
Taylors Grove Ch (historical)—church TN-4
Taylors Gulch OR-9
Taylors Gut—gut (2) DE-2
Taylors Gut Landing—locale DE-2
Taylor Shaft—mine NV-8
Taylor Shaft—mine PA-2
Taylors Hill—summit VA-3
Taylors Hill (historical)—locale AL-4
Taylorshire—pop pl NY-2
Taylors (historical)—pop pl MS-4
Taylor Shoals—bar TN-4
Taylors Inn (historical)—locale MS-4
Taylor's Island MD-2
Taylors Island—island MD-2
Taylors Island—island MN-6
Taylors Island—island TN-4
Taylors Island—pop pl MD-2
Taylor Site—hist pl SC-3
Taylor (Site)—locale NV-8
Taylor(Site)—locale WA-9
Taylor Site 16.65—hist pl ME-1
Taylors Lake—lake GA-3
Taylors Lake—reservoir (2) NC-3
Taylors Lake—reservoir TX-5
Taylors Lake Dam—dam MS-4
Taylors Lake Dam—dam NC-3
Taylors Landing—locale GA-3
Taylors Landing—locale MD-2
Taylors Landing—locale TN-4
Taylors Landing (historical)—locale MS-4
Taylor Slope—flat WY-8
Taylor Slough—gut AR-4
Taylor Slough—gut (2) CA-9
Taylor Slough—gut FL-3
Taylor Slough—gut ID-8
Taylor Slough—gut IL-6
Taylor Slough—stream TX-5
Taylor Slough Archeol Site—hist pl TX-5
Taylor's Mill—hist pl NC-3
Taylors Mill—locale GA-3
Taylors Mill—pop pl AL-4
Taylors Mill (historical)—locale NC-3
Taylors Mill (historical)—locale TN-4
Taylors Millpond—reservoir (2) NC-3
Taylors Millpond—reservoir VA-3
Taylors Mill Pond Dam—dam NC-3
Taylors Millpond Dam—dam NC-3
Taylors Mills—locale NJ-2
Taylors Mountain—ridge AL-4
Taylors Mountain Overlook—locale VA-3
Taylors Mtn—summit NJ-2
Taylors Mtn—summit (2) VA-3
Taylors Narrows—gut VA-3
Taylor Soda Spring—spring CO-8
Taylor Sound—bay NJ-2
Taylors Peak MT-8
Taylors Pinnacle—summit VT-1
Taylors Point MA-1
Taylors Point RI-1
Taylors Point—cape NY-2
Taylors Point—cape VA-3
Taylors Pond MA-1
Taylors Pond—lake CT-1
Taylors Pond—lake GA-3
Taylors Pond—lake MA-1
Taylors Pond—lake TN-4
Taylors Pond—reservoir AL-4
Taylorsport—pop pl KY-4
Taylors Post Office (historical)—building TN-4
Taylor Spring—spring AL-4
Taylor Spring—spring AZ-5
Taylor Spring—spring (6) CA-9
Taylor Spring—spring GA-3
Taylor Spring—spring (3) ID-8
Taylor Spring—spring MO-7
Taylor Spring—spring (2) MT-8
Taylor Spring—spring (3) NV-8
Taylor Spring—spring (2) NM-5
Taylor Spring—spring (2) OR-9
Taylor Spring—spring SD-7
Taylor Spring—spring (2) TN-4
Taylor Spring—spring (2) UT-8
Taylor Spring—spring WA-9
Taylor Spring—spring (3) WY-8
Taylor Spring Branch—stream TN-4
Taylor Spring Number Five—spring NV-8
Taylor Spring Number Four—spring NV-8
Taylor Spring Number Three—spring NV-8
Taylor Springs AL-4
Taylor Springs—locale NM-5
Taylor Springs—pop pl IL-6
Taylor Springs—spring OR-9
Taylor Springs Branch—stream TX-5
Taylor Springs Cem—cemetery AL-4
Taylor Springs Ch—church AL-4
Taylor Springs Ch—church NC-3
Taylor Springs Freewill Baptist Ch AL-4
Taylor Springs Numbers One and Two—spring NV-8
Taylor Spur—cape AK-9
Taylor Spur—pop pl WA-9
Taylor Square Firehouse—hist pl MA-1
Taylor Square Shop Ctr—locale FL-3
Taylors Quarry AL-4
Taylor's Ranch—locale MT-8
Taylors Ridge—ridge WV-2
Taylors Ridge Ch—church WV-2
Taylors Rsvr—reservoir NH-1
Taylors Rsvr—reservoir OR-9
Taylors Run PA-2
Taylors Run—stream PA-2
Taylors Seminary—church TN-4
Taylors Shoals TN-4
Taylors Sound NJ-2
Taylors Spring—spring AL-4
Taylors Station AL-4
Taylors Station Post Office AL-4
Taylors Store—locale AR-4
Taylors Store—locale KY-4
Taylors Store—pop pl (2) NC-3
Taylors Store—pop pl VA-3
Taylors Store (historical)—locale (2) TN-4
Taylors Subdivision—pop pl UT-8
Taylors Swamp—swamp GA-3
Taylors Switch MS-4
Taylor State For—forest NH-1
Taylor Station—pop pl OH-6
Taylor Station Ch—church OH-6
Taylor Station (historical)—locale AL-4
Taylor Station (historical P.O.)—locale IA-7
Taylor-Stokes House—hist pl AR-4
Taylor Store (historical)—locale MS-4
Taylorstown—locale VA-3
Taylorstown—pop pl PA-2
Taylorstown Hist Dist—hist pl PA-2
Taylorstown Hist Dist—hist pl VA-3
Taylorstown Station (Crothers)—pop pl PA-2
Taylor Strand Sch (abandoned)—school PA-2
Taylor Street Sch PA-2
Taylor Street Sch—school CA-9
Taylor Street School TN-4
Taylor Summers Run—stream WV-2
Taylors Valley—bend TX-5
Taylors Valley—locale VA-3
Taylors Valley—pop pl VA-3
Taylors Valley Ch—church TX-5
Taylorsville AL-4
Taylorsville IN-6
Taylorsville MD-2
Taylorsville OH-6
Taylorsville TN-4
Taylorsville VA-3
Taylorsville—locale IA-7
Taylorsville—locale (2) OH-6
Taylorsville—locale PA-2
Taylorsville—locale TN-4
Taylorsville—locale TX-5
Taylorsville—locale VA-3
Taylorsville—other AL-4
Taylorsville—other OH-6
Taylorsville—pop pl CA-9
Taylorsville—pop pl GA-3
Taylorsville—pop pl IN-6
Taylorsville—pop pl KY-4
Taylorsville—pop pl MD-2
Taylorsville—pop pl (2) MS-4
Taylorsville—pop pl NC-3
Taylorsville—pop pl PA-2
Taylorsville—pop pl TN-4
Taylorsville—pop pl UT-8
Taylorsville Acad (historical)—school TN-4
Taylorsville Airp—airport NC-3
Taylorsville Beach—pop pl NC-3
Taylorsville Canal Inn—hist pl OH-6
Taylorsville (CCD)—cens area KY-4
Taylorsville Ch—church MS-4
Taylorsville Consolidated School MS-4
Taylorsville Cove Subdivision—pop pl UT-8
Taylorsville Dam—dam OH-6
Taylorsville Elem Sch—school IN-6
Taylorsville Elem Sch—school MS-4
Taylorsville Elem Sch—school NC-3
Taylorsville Gardens Subdivision—pop pl UT-8
Taylorsville HS—school MS-4
Taylorsville HS—school UT-8
Taylorsville Lookout Tower—locale MS-4
Taylorsville Memorial Park Cem—cemetery UT-8
Taylorsville Post Office AL-4
Taylorsville Post Office TN-4
Taylorsville Rancheria—locale CA-9
Taylorsville Reserve—reservoir OH-6
Taylorsville Rsvr—reservoir OH-6
Taylorsville Sch—school GA-3
Taylorsville Sch—school UT-8
Taylorsville Sewage Lagoon Dam—dam MS-4
Taylorsville Signal Office and Watkins General Store—hist pl MS-4
Taylorsville (Township of)—fmr MCD NC-3
Taylor Swamp NC-3
Taylor Swamp—stream NC-3
Taylor Swamp—swamp VT-1
Taylor Tank—reservoir (2) AZ-5
Taylor Tank—reservoir (5) NM-5
Taylor Tank—reservoir (2) TX-5
Taylor Tower—pillar LA-4
Taylortown PA-2
Taylortown—locale NY-2
Taylortown—locale (2) NC-3
Taylor Town—locale TX-5
Taylortown—other PA-2
Taylortown—pop pl DE-2
Taylortown—pop pl KY-4
Taylortown—pop pl (2) LA-4
Taylortown—pop pl NJ-2
Taylortown—pop pl NC-3
Taylortown—pop pl (2) OH-6
Taylortown—pop pl TN-4
Taylortown Branch—stream VA-3
Taylortown Ch—church (2) KY-4
Taylortown Ch—church TN-4
Taylortown Creek—stream PA-2
Taylor Town Hall—building AL-4
Taylor (Town of)—pop pl NY-2
Taylortown Rsvr—reservoir NJ-2
Taylor Township—civil (2) MO-7
Taylor Township—fmr MCD (6) IA-7
Taylor Township—pop pl (2) MO-7
Taylor Township—pop pl ND-7
Taylor Township—pop pl (2) SD-7
Taylor (Township of)—civ div MI-6
Taylor (Township of)—fmr MCD (3) AR-4
Taylor (Township of)—fmr MCD NC-3
Taylor (Township of)—pop pl IL-6
Taylor (Township of)—pop pl (4) IN-6
Taylor (Township of)—pop pl (2) MN-6
Taylor (Township of)—pop pl OH-6
Taylor (Township of)—pop pl (4) PA-2
Taylor Tubs Windmill—locale TX-5
Taylor Univ—school IN-6
Taylor-Utley House—hist pl NC-3
Taylor Valley—basin CA-9
Taylor Valley—basin NV-8
Taylor Valley—locale NY-2
Taylor Valley—valley NY-2
Taylor Valley Mine—mine TN-4
Taylor-Van Note—hist pl IA-7
Taylorville LA-4
Taylorville MS-4
Taylorville PA-2
Taylorville—locale MD-2
Taylorville—pop pl AL-4
Taylorville—pop pl ID-8
Taylorville—pop pl IL-6
Taylorville—pop pl IN-6
Taylorville—pop pl LA-4
Taylorville—pop pl (2) OR-9
Taylorville—pop pl (2) PA-2
Taylorville—pop pl TX-5
Taylorville—pop pl VT-1
Taylorville—pop pl WV-2
Taylorville, Lake—reservoir IL-6
Taylorville Baptist Ch—church AL-4
Taylorville Cem—cemetery AL-4
Taylorville Chautauqua Auditorium—hist pl IL-6
Taylorville Courthouse Square Hist Dist—hist pl IL-6
Taylorville Creek—stream MD-2
Taylorville Heights (subdivision)—pop pl AL-4
Taylorville Methodist Ch—church AL-4
Taylorville Pond—reservoir NY-2
Taylorville (Township of)—pop pl IL-6
Taylor Vly—swamp NY-2
Taylor-Wall-Yancy House—hist pl MS-4
Taylor Weir—dam CA-9
Taylor Well—locale ID-8
Taylor Well—locale NM-5
Taylor Well—well CA-9
Taylor Well—well (6) NM-5
Taylor Well—well TX-5
Taylor Well—well WA-9
Taylor Wharf—locale VA-3
Taylor Wharf (historical)—locale NC-3
Taylor-Whittle House—hist pl VA-3
Taylor Wholesale Grocers and Cotton Factors Warehouse-Lee Hardware Bldg—hist pl LA-4
Taylor Williams Cem—cemetery MS-4
Taylor Windmill—locale (2) NM-5
Taylor Windmill—locale TX-5
Taylor Windmills—other NM-5
Taylorwood Estates—pop pl VA-3
Taylorwood Estates (subdivision)—pop pl AL-4
Taylor-Zent House—hist pl IN-6
Tayman Park—park CA-9
Taymouth—locale MI-6
Taymouth Cem—cemetery MI-6
Taymouth Ch—church MI-6
Taymouth Sch—school MI-6
Taymouth (Township of)—pop pl MI-6
Taynard Branch—stream AL-4
Taynore—building MS-4
Taynter Brook—stream NY-2
Tayo Creek—stream WY-8
Tayo Park—park WY-8
Tays Bog—swamp MA-1
Tays Branch—stream KY-4
Taywa Creek—stream NC-3
Taza Tank—reservoir TX-5
Taza Windmill—locale TX-5
Taz Basin—bay AK-9
Tazewell—locale IL-6
Tazewell—locale TX-5
Tazewell—pop pl GA-3
Tazewell—pop pl TN-4
Tazewell—pop pl VA-3
Tazewell Acad (historical)—school TN-4
Tazewell (CCD)—cens area TN-4
Tazewell (County)—pop pl IL-6
Tazewell (County)—pop pl VA-3
Tazewell County Courthouse—hist pl IL-6
Tazewell County Sportsmen Club Lake—reservoir VA-3
Tazewell Division—civil TN-4
Tazewell-New Tazewell Elem Sch—school TN-4
Tazewell Post Office—building TN-4
Tazewell Rsvr—reservoir VA-3
Tazewell Saltpeter Cave—cave TN-4
Tazewells-Claiborne County Airp—airport TN-4
Tazewell Square Shop Ctr—locale TN-4
Tazewell (sta.) (RR name for New Tazewell)—other TN-4
Tazimina River—stream AK-9
Tazlina—locale AK-9
Tazlina ANV961—reserve AK-9
Tazlina Glacier—glacier AK-9
Tazlina Lake—lake AK-9
Tazlina River—stream AK-9
TB MD-2
T B—pop pl MD-2
T Baker Ranch—locale TX-5
T Bar Canyon—valley NM-5
T Bar Canyon—valley TX-5
T Bar P Lake Dam—dam MS-4
T-Bar Ranch—locale AZ-5
T Bar Ranch—locale TX-5
T Bar Ridge—ridge NM-5
T-Bar Tank—reservoir AZ-5
T Bar Tank—reservoir NM-5
T-bar Tank Number One—reservoir AZ-5
T-bar Tank Number Two—reservoir AZ-5
T Bar T Camp—locale NM-5
T Bar Y Tank—reservoir AZ-5
T Bayou—gut LA-4
T B Creek—stream WY-8
TB Crossroads—pop pl VA-3
Tbekuulii—cave PW-9
T Bells Ferry NC-3
T-Bench-Bar Ranch—locale AZ-5
T B Flat—flat WY-8
T B Flats—flat WY-8
T B Hosp—hospital LA-4
T B L Canyon—valley NM-5
T-Bone Creek—stream ID-8
T-Bone Creek Rapids—rapids ID-8
T-Bone Hill—summit UT-8
T-Bone Mine—mine NV-8
T Bone Ranch—locale CO-8
T Bone Spring Campground—locale CO-8
T-Bone Tank—reservoir AZ-5
T Bone Tank—reservoir AZ-5
T B Ranch—locale WY-8
T Bridge Corner—locale WA-9
T Briggs Lake—lake NE-7
TB Spring—spring AZ-5
Tcacca AZ-5
T Caffey Robertson Lake Dam—dam MS-4
T Caffey Robertson Pond Dam—dam MS-4
T Canal—canal NV-8
T Canal—canal (2) OR-9
T Cave—cave AL-4
T C Bower School TN-4
Tchackehou Bayou—stream LA-4
Tchanke River MS-4
Tchefuncta Country Club—other LA-4
Tchefuncta River—stream LA-4
Tchefuncte River Range Rear Light—hist pl LA-4
Tchikachae MS-4
Tchikachas AL-4
Tchil-ae-cum WA-9
Tchopahk Mountain WA-9
Tcho-park Mountain WA-9
Tchotee TN-4
Tchoutacabouffa River—stream MS-4
Tchouticabouffa River MS-4
Tchukolaho, Lake—reservoir GA-3
Tchula—pop pl MS-4
Tchula Attendance Center—school MS-4
Tchulacabawfa MS-4
Tchula City Landing (historical)—locale MS-4
Tchula Junction (historical)—locale MS-4
Tchula Lake—lake MS-4
Tchula River MS-4
Tchula Sewage Lagoon Dam—dam MS-4
Tchulkade Lake—lake AK-9
T C I Lake Dam—dam AL-4
T C Morris Ranch—locale MT-8
T C Null Dam—dam AL-4
T C Null Lake—reservoir AL-4
T Coleman—locale TX-5
T Cook Pond Dam—dam MS-4
T C Ranch—locale FL-3
TC Ranch—locale TX-5
T Creek—stream MT-8
T Creek—stream NV-8
TC Roberson HS—school NC-3
T Cross K Ranch—locale CA-9
T-Cross Ranch—locale CO-8
T Cross Ranch—locale CO-8
T Cross Ranch—locale WY-8
T Cross T Ranch—locale WY-8
T C Steele JHS—school IN-6
TC Steele State Memorial—park IN-6
TCU Tank—reservoir TX-5
T.C.U. (Texas Christian University)—school TX-5
T C Williams HS—school VA-3
T Dam 7—dam TX-5
T D Buford Pond Dam—dam MS-4
Tde-yak-yah HI-9
T D Holden Stadium—park MS-4
T Diamond Ranch—locale TX-5
T Doland Ranch (historical)—locale SD-7
T-Down Park—park CO-8
T Drain—canal CA-9
T Draw—valley CO-8
T D Southwest Draw—valley WY-8
T D Tank—reservoir AZ-5
Tea—pop pl MO-7
Tea—pop pl SD-7
Teab—pop pl FM-9
Teabeau Lake—lake WI-6
Teaberry—pop pl KY-4
Teaberry—pop pl WV-2
Teaberry Flats VA-3
Teaberry Flats—other VA-3
Teaberry Hill—summit WV-2
Teaberry Hollow—valley PA-2
Teaberry Ridge—ridge NC-3
Teaberry Sch—school KY-4
Teaberry Sch (abandoned)—school PA-2
Teaberry Woods (subdivision)—pop pl DE-2
Teabo—pop pl NJ-2
Teabone Ridge WA-9
Tea Branch—stream VA-3
Tea Branch—stream WV-2
Tea Brook—stream ME-1
Tea Brush Flat—flat UT-8
Tea Canyon—valley CA-9
Tea Cave—cave AL-4
Tea Cem—cemetery OK-5
Tea Cem—cemetery SD-7
Teachers Bay—bay ID-8
Teachers Beach—beach CA-9
Teachers Coll—school MO-7
Teachers Coll—school WI-6
Teachers College—uninc pl TN-4
Teachers Driver Training Sch PA-2
Teachers Driving Sch—school PA-2
Teaches Hole Channel—channel NC-3
Teaches Hole Channel Light—tower NC-3
Teachey—pop pl NC-3
Teachey (corporate name for Teacheys)—pop pl NC-3
Teacheys NC-3
Teachey Sch—school NC-3
Teacheys (corporate name Teachey) NC-3
Teacheys Store—locale NC-3
Teachout Cem—cemetery KS-7
Teachout Creek—stream CO-8
Teachout Ditch—canal CO-8
Teachout Valley—valley WI-6
Teach Sch—school CA-9
Teachs Gut—stream NC-3
Teackle Mansion—hist pl MD-2
Tea Cracker Lake—lake MN-6
Tea Creek CA-9
Tea Creek—bay FL-3
Tea Creek—stream AK-9
Tea Creek—stream AR-4
Tea Creek—stream (2) IN-6
Tea Creek—stream MI-6
Tea Creek—stream OR-9
Tea Creek—stream PA-2
Tea Creek—stream WV-2
Tea Creek Ch—church IN-6
Tea Creek Cutoff—channel FL-3

Teepee Mountains ... WY-8
Teepeeota Point—cape ... MN-6
Teepee Peak—summit ... NM-5
Teepee Pole Flats—flat ... WY-8
Teepee Pole Prong ... WY-8
Teepee Ridge—ridge ... OR-9
Teepee Spring—spring (2) ... OR-9
Teepee Glacier—glacier ... WY-8
Teepe Pillar—pillar ... WY-8
Teeple Barn—hist pl ... IL-6
Teeple Cem—cemetery ... MO-7
Teeple Creek—stream ... IA-7
Teeple Hill—summit ... MI-6
Teeple Lake—lake ... MI-6
Teeple Rsvr—reservoir ... CO-8
Teeples Canyon ... UT-8
Teeples Canyon—valley ... UT-8
Teeples Ridge—ridge ... UT-8
Teeples Spring—spring ... MT-8
Teeples Spring—spring (2) ... UT-8
Teeples Wash—valley ... UT-8
**Teepleville**—pop pl ... PA-2
Teeple Well—well ... CO-8
Tee Quee Canon ... CO-8
Tee Quee Canyon—valley ... NM-5
Teer—locale ... NC-3
Tee Ranch—locale ... AZ-5
**Teer Siding**—pop pl ... NC-3
Teesdale Lake—lake ... MI-6
Teeseteska Ridge—ridge ... NC-3
Teesquatnee Hollow—valley ... OK-5
Tees Spa Spring—spring ... AZ-5
Tees To ... AZ-5
Tees Toh—locale ... AZ-5
Tees Toh Spring—spring ... AZ-5
Tees Toh Wash—stream ... AZ-5
**Tees To (Trading Post)**—pop pl ... AZ-5
Teeter Branch—stream ... TX-5
Teeter Camp Run—stream ... WV-2
Teeter Canyon—valley ... WY-8
Teeter Cem—cemetery ... IN-6
Teeter Cem—cemetery ... MS-4
Teeter Cem—cemetery ... VA-3
Teeter Creek ... OR-9
Teeter Creek—stream ... MO-7
Teeter Creek—stream ... NY-2
Teeter Creek—stream ... OK-5
Teeter Creek—stream ... OR-9
Teeter Creek—stream ... SD-7
Teeter Creek Loop—trail ... OR-9
Teeter Creek Rec Area—area ... OR-9
Teeters Branch—stream ... KS-7
Teeters Cem—cemetery ... IN-6
Teeters Lake—reservoir ... IN-6
Teeters Lake Dam—dam ... IN-6
Teeters Landing (site)—locale ... OR-9
Teeters Peak—summit ... MT-8
Teeters Peak Trail—trail ... MT-8
Teeters Post Office (historical)—building ... TN-4
Teeters Ranch—locale ... WY-8
**Teetersville**—pop pl ... KY-4
Teeterville—locale ... GA-3
Teeterville—locale ... MI-6
Teethcanoe Lake—lake ... AK-9
Teeth Creek—stream ... MT-8
Teeth Lake ... OR-9
Teetiu ... FM-9
Teetiw ... FM-9
Teetors Gulch—valley ... ID-8
Teets Cem—cemetery ... WV-2
Teets Drain—canal ... MI-6
Teets Sch—school ... MI-6
Teets Sch—school ... PA-2
Teetum Ridge—ridge ... CO-8
Tee Wees Butte—summit ... OR-9
Teewinot Mtn—summit ... WY-8
**Tefft**—pop pl ... IN-6
Tefft Hill—summit (2) ... RI-1
Tefft Pond—lake ... NY-2
Teffts Hill ... RI-1
**Teft**—pop pl ... CO-8
Teft Brook—stream ... CT-1
Teft Sch—school ... MO-7
Tefts Pond ... RI-1
**Tega Cay**—pop pl ... SC-3
Tegakwitha Indian Mission and School ... AZ-5
Tegakwithan Mission—school ... AZ-5
Tegarden—locale ... OK-5
Tegart Bluff—cliff ... OR-9
Tegeler Pond—lake ... IA-7
Tegener Creek—stream ... TX-5
Tegerman Hollow—valley ... PA-2
Teges—locale ... KY-4
Tegesta ... FL-3
**Tegner (Township of)**—pop pl ... MN-6
Tego Brothers Drugstore-State Natl Bank of Louisville—hist pl ... CO-8
Tegulero Windmill—locale ... TX-5
Tegure ... MP-9
Tegure Island ... MP-9
Tegure (not verified)—island ... MP-9
Tegure-to ... MP-9
Tehachapai ... CA-9
Tehachapai Pass ... CA-9
**Tehachapi**—pop pl ... CA-9
Tehachapi Afterbay—bay ... CA-9
Tehachapi (CCD)—cens area ... CA-9
Tehachapi Creek—stream ... CA-9
Tehachapi Mountain Park—park ... CA-9
Tehachapi Mountains—range ... CA-9
Tehachapi Mtn—summit ... CA-9
Tehachapi Pass—gap ... CA-9
Tehachapi Valley—valley ... CA-9
Teh-Aith Cheed Wash ... AZ-5
**Tehama**—pop pl ... CA-9
Tehama Canyon—valley ... NV-8
Tehama Cem—cemetery ... CA-9
Tehama Colusa Canal—canal ... CA-9
**Tehama (County)**—pop pl ... CA-9
Tehama Creek—stream ... NV-8
Tehama (historical)—locale ... KS-7
Tehama Mine—mine ... NV-8
Tehama Ravine—valley ... CA-9
Tehan Canyon—valley ... CA-9
Tehan Falls—falls ... CA-9
Tehan Sch—school ... IL-6
Tehelengerael ... PW-9
Teheran—locale ... IL-6
Tehichipi Mountains ... CA-9
Tehipite Dome—summit ... CA-9
Tehipite Valley—basin ... CA-9
Teh LaPa Low Cem—cemetery ... ID-8
**Tehuacana**—pop pl ... TX-5
Tehuacana Cem—cemetery ... TX-5
Tehuacana Creek ... TX-5
Tehuacana Creek—stream (3) ... TX-5
Tehuacana Grove Ch—church ... TX-5
Tehuacana Hills—summit ... TX-5
Tehuacana Oil Field—oilfield ... TX-5
Tehuacano Creek ... TX-5
Tehua Hills—range ... AZ-5
Teibel-Sykora Rubblestone Barn—hist pl ... SD-7
Teichert Homestead—locale ... MT-8
Teichert Ranch—locale ... MT-8
Teichgraber Oil Field—oilfield ... KS-7
Teichman Point—cape ... TX-5
Teichmans Point ... TX-5
Teien Ch—church ... MN-6
**Teien (Township of)**—pop pl ... MN-6
**Teigen**—pop pl ... MT-8
Teightaquid ... MA-1
Teiken-Dalve State Wildlife Mngmt Area—park ... MN-6
Teilers Chapel ... AL-4
Teilman Ditch—canal ... CA-9
Teilman Sch—school ... CA-9
Teircos Mill (historical)—locale ... AL-4
Teiteiripucchi ... MP-9
Teiteiripucchi Island ... MP-9
Teiteiripucchi-To ... MP-9
Teiteiriputchi-to ... MP-9
Tejana Arroyo ... CO-8
Tejana Arroyo—stream ... CO-8
Tejana Draw—valley ... NM-5
Tejana Mesa—summit ... NM-5
Tejana Windmill—locale ... NM-5
Tejano Canyon—valley ... NM-5
Tejano Spring—spring ... AZ-5
Tejano Spring—spring ... NM-5
Tejanos Spring—spring ... AZ-5
Tejares ... CO-8
Tejas, Lake—reservoir ... TX-5
Tejas (Barrio)—fmr MCD (3) ... PR-3
Tejas Golf Course—other ... TX-5
Tejay—locale ... KY-4
Tejay (CCD)—cens area ... KY-4
Tejera ... CO-8
Tejon—locale ... NM-5
Tejon Canyon—valley ... CA-9
Tejon Cem—cemetery ... NM-5
Tejon Creek—stream ... CA-9
Tejones Artesian Well—well ... TX-5
Tejones Creek—stream (2) ... TX-5
Tejones Tank—reservoir ... TX-5
Tejon (ghost Town)—locale ... NM-5
Tejon Hills—range ... CA-9
Tejon Hills Oil Field ... CA-9
Tejon Lookout—locale ... CA-9
Tejon Oil Field ... CA-9
Tejon Pass—gap ... CA-9
Tejon Ranch—locale ... CA-9
Tejon Rsvr Number One—reservoir ... CA-9
Tejon Rsvr Number Two—reservoir ... CA-9
Tejon Windmill—locale ... NM-5
Tejon Windmill—locale (2) ... TX-5
Tejua Hills ... AZ-5
**Tekakwitha**—pop pl ... SD-7
Tekakwitha, Lake—reservoir ... MO-7
Tekakwitha Dam—dam ... SD-7
Tekakwitha Friary—church ... NY-2
Tekakwitha Lake—lake ... WI-6
**Tekamah**—pop pl ... NE-7
Tekamah Cem—cemetery ... NE-7
Tekamah Ch—church ... NE-7
Tekamah Creek—stream ... NE-7
Tekamah Ditch—canal ... NE-7
Tekapo—locale ... NM-5
Tekapo Reservoir—reservoir ... NM-5
Tekawitha Dam—dam ... AL-4
Tekawitha Lake—reservoir ... AL-4
Tekeaksakrak Lake—lake ... AK-9
Tekegakrok Point—cape ... AK-9
Tek-E-Nink Lake—lake ... MI-6
Tekerlip Island—island ... MP-9
Tekeruppu To ... MP-9
Tekerurippu-to ... MP-9
Teketanoah Creek ... AL-4
Teke-To ... MP-9
Tekison Cave—hist pl ... WA-9
Tekison Creek—stream ... WA-9
Tekiu Point—cape ... WA-9
Tek Lake—lake ... MI-6
Teklanika Archeol District—hist pl ... AK-9
Teklanika Campground—locale ... AK-9
Teklanika Channel Lake—lake ... AK-9
Teklanika River—stream ... AK-9
**Tekoa**—pop pl ... TN-4
**Tekoa**—pop pl ... WA-9
Tekoa (CCD)—cens area ... WA-9
Tekoa Ch—church ... TN-4
Tekoa Country Club—locale ... MA-1
Tekoa Dam—dam ... MA-1
Tekoa Grain Company Elevator & Flathouse—hist pl ... WA-9
Tekoa Gulch—valley ... MT-8
Tekoa Mtn—summit ... MA-1
Tekoa Mtn—summit ... WA-9
Tekoa Rsvr—reservoir ... MA-1
Tekol—island ... MP-9
**Tekonsha**—pop pl ... MI-6
Tekonsha Creek—stream ... MI-6
Tekonsha Sch—school ... MI-6
**Tekonsha (Township of)**—pop pl ... MI-6
Tekoppel Elementary and JHS—school ... IN-6
Tekoppel Sch—school ... IN-6
**Tekram (Belo)**—pop pl ... WV-2
Telab ... MP-9
Telac Bayou—stream ... LA-4
Telael—channel ... PW-9
Telamay Hollow—valley ... OK-5
Te'lang—slope ... MH-9
Telaquana Lake—lake ... AK-9
Telaquana Mtn—summit ... AK-9
Telaquana Pass—gap ... AK-9
Telaquana River—stream ... AK-9
Telavirak Hills—range ... AK-9
**Telbasta**—pop pl ... NE-7
Telbasta Sch—school ... NE-7
Telcher Creek—stream (2) ... ID-8
Teldow ... FM-9
Teledega ... AL-4
Telefone Artesian Well—well ... TX-5
Telefon Trail—trail ... VT-1
Teleford ... MI-6
Telegraph—locale ... TX-5
Telegraph Bay—bay ... WA-9
Telegraph Bight—bay ... WA-9
Telegraph Canyon ... NV-8
Telegraph Canyon—valley ... AZ-5
Telegraph Canyon—valley (3) ... CA-9
Telegraph Canyon—valley (3) ... NV-8
Telegraph Canyon—valley ... TX-5
Telegraph Ch—church ... MO-7
Telegraph City—locale ... CA-9
Telegraph Creek—stream ... AK-9
Telegraph Creek—stream (2) ... CA-9
Telegraph Creek—stream ... FL-3
Telegraph Creek—stream (4) ... MT-8
Telegraph Creek—stream ... NV-8
Telegraph Draw—valley ... SD-7
Telegraph Draw—valley ... UT-8
Telegraph Estates—locale ... FL-3
Telegraph Flat—flat ... CA-9
Telegraph Flat—flat ... ID-8
Telegraph Flat—flat ... NV-8
Telegraph Flat—flat ... UT-8
Telegraph Flat (historical)—flat ... SD-7
Telegraph Gulch—valley ... MT-8
Telegraph Gulch—valley ... SD-7
Telegraph Hill ... MA-1
Telegraph Hill ... MH-9
Telegraph Hill—hist pl ... MA-1
Telegraph Hill—locale ... ID-8
Telegraph Hill—locale ... OR-9
Telegraph Hill—summit ... AK-9
Telegraph Hill—summit (5) ... CA-9
Telegraph Hill—summit ... ME-1
Telegraph Hill—summit (8) ... MA-1
Telegraph Hill—summit ... NV-8
Telegraph Hill—summit ... NJ-2
Telegraph Hill Lookout Tower—locale ... OH-6
Telegraph Hill Park—park ... NJ-2
Telegraph Hollow—valley ... ID-8
Telegraph Island—island ... WA-9
Telegraph Island Petroglyphs—hist pl ... WA-9
Telegraph Mine—mine (3) ... CA-9
Telegraph Mine—mine ... NM-5
Telegraph Mtn—summit ... MT-8
Telegraph Mtn—summit ... NM-5
Telegraph Pass—gap (2) ... AZ-5
Telegraph Peak—summit ... CA-9
Telegraph Peak—summit ... NV-8
Telegraph Point ... ME-1
Telegraph Point—cape ... LA-4
Telegraph Point—cape ... UT-8
Telegraph Ridge—ridge (3) ... CA-9
Telegraph Rock—pillar ... CA-9
Telegraph Sch (abandoned)—school ... MO-7
Telegraph Shearing Corrals—locale ... NV-8
Telegraph Slough—gut ... WA-9
Telegraph Spring—locale ... VA-3
Telegraph Spring Windmill—locale ... AZ-5
Telegraph Swamp—swamp ... FL-3
Telegraph Wash—stream (2) ... AZ-5
Telegraph Wash—stream ... CA-9
Telegraph Wash—valley ... UT-8
Telemark, Lake—reservoir ... NJ-2
Telemark, Mount—summit ... WI-6
Telemarken Ch—church ... MN-6
Telemarken Ch—church ... SD-7
Telemitz Island—island ... AK-9
Telepedelel Ngkesol ... PW-9
Telepedele Ngerael ... PW-9
**Telephone**—pop pl ... TX-5
Telephone Artesian Well—well ... TX-5
Telephone Basin—basin ... MT-8
Telephone Bench—bench ... UT-8
Telephone Booth Hill—summit ... ID-8
Telephone Brook—stream ... VT-1
Telephone Building, Old—hist pl ... OH-6
Telephone Butte—summit ... MT-8
Telephone Butte—summit ... OR-9
Telephone Camp—locale ... CA-9
Telephone Camp—locale ... ID-8
Telephone Camp—locale ... WA-9
Telephone Campground—locale ... CA-9
Telephone Canyon—valley (2) ... AZ-5
Telephone Canyon—valley (3) ... CA-9
Telephone Canyon—valley ... ID-8
Telephone Canyon—valley (4) ... NV-8
Telephone Canyon—valley (7) ... NM-5
Telephone Canyon—valley ... OR-9
Telephone Canyon—valley (2) ... TX-5
Telephone Canyon—valley ... UT-8
Telephone Canyon—valley ... WA-9
Telephone Canyon—valley (3) ... WY-8
Telephone Canyon Spring—spring ... CA-9
Telephone Canyon Trail—trail ... TX-5
Telephone Co. Bldg—hist pl ... ND-7
Telephone Company Bungalow—hist pl ... ID-8
Telephone Creek ... WA-9
Telephone Creek—stream ... AK-9
Telephone Creek—stream (6) ... ID-8
Telephone Creek—stream (2) ... MT-8
Telephone Creek—stream ... NV-8
Telephone Creek—stream ... OK-5
Telephone Creek—stream (2) ... OR-9
Telephone Creek—stream ... WY-8
Telephone Cut—canal ... CA-9
Telephone Dam—dam ... AZ-5
Telephone Dam—dam ... CO-8
Telephone Draw—valley ... CO-8
Telephone Draw—valley (4) ... ID-8
Telephone Draw—valley ... MT-8
Telephone Draw—valley ... OR-9
Telephone Draw—valley ... TX-5
Telephone Draw—valley (5) ... WY-8
Telephone Draw Tank—reservoir ... AZ-5
Telephone Draw Trail—trail ... CO-8
Telephone Exchange Bldg—hist pl ... CT-1
Telephone Flat—flat ... CA-9
Telephone Flat—flat (2) ... OR-9
Telephone Flat Rsvr—reservoir ... CA-9
Telephone Gap—gap ... NM-5
Telephone Gap—gap ... VT-1
Telephone Gulch—valley (3) ... CA-9
Telephone Gulch—valley ... ID-8
Telephone Gulch—valley ... MT-8
Telephone Gulch—valley (2) ... OR-9
Telephone Hill—summit ... AZ-5
Telephone Hill—summit ... ME-1
Telephone Hills—other ... CA-9
Telephone Hill Windmill—locale ... TX-5
Telephone Hole Riffle—rapids ... OR-9
Telephone Hollow—valley (3) ... UT-8
Telephone Hollow—valley ... WY-8
Telephone Island ... WA-9
Telephone Island—island ... WY-8
Telephone Lake—lake ... AK-9
Telephone Lake—lake ... MN-6
Telephone Lake—reservoir ... GA-3
Telephone Lakes—lake ... WY-8
Telephone Lake (sewage disposal)—lake ... AZ-5
Telephone Line Ridge—ridge ... AZ-5
Telephone Line Ridge—ridge ... WY-8
Telephone Line Trail—trail (2) ... CA-9
Telephone Mesa—summit ... AZ-5
Telephone Mtn—summit ... MT-8
Telephone Pass—gap ... WY-8
Telephone Point—cape (2) ... AK-9
Telephone Pole Canyon—valley ... NV-8
Telephone Pole Spring—spring ... ID-8
Telephone Ridge—ridge (6) ... AZ-5
Telephone Ridge—ridge (5) ... CA-9
Telephone Ridge—ridge ... ID-8
Telephone Ridge—ridge (2) ... MT-8
Telephone Ridge—ridge ... NM-5
Telephone Ridge—ridge (2) ... OR-9
Telephone Ridge—ridge ... WY-8
Telephone Ridge Trail—trail ... ID-8
Telephone Slough—gut ... AK-9
Telephone Spring—spring (2) ... AZ-5
Telephone Spring—spring ... CA-9
Telephone Spring—spring ... ID-8
Telephone Spring—spring ... NM-5
Telephone Spring—spring (5) ... OR-9
Telephone Spring Picnic Area—locale ... WY-8
Telephone Tank—reservoir (6) ... AZ-5
Telephone Tank—reservoir (3) ... NM-5
Telephone Tank—reservoir (6) ... TX-5
Telephone Trail—trail (2) ... CO-8
Telephone Trail—trail ... ID-8
Telephone Trail—trail (2) ... ME-1
Telephone Trail—trail (3) ... PA-2
Telephone Utilities/tiw/ Heliport—airport ... WA-9
Telephone Well—well ... NV-8
Telephone Well (Windmill)—locale ... TX-5
Telephone Windmill—locale (2) ... TX-5
Telesco Creek—stream ... TX-5
Telescope—locale ... PA-2
Telescope Coulee—valley ... MT-8
Telescope Mtn—summit ... CO-8
Telescope Peak—summit (2) ... CA-9
Telesfors Tank—reservoir ... NM-5
Televoi Stream—stream ... AS-9
Television City (CBS)—other ... CA-9
Television Tank—reservoir ... NM-5
Telfair Acad—hist pl ... GA-3
Telfair Ave Sch—school ... CA-9
Telfair Bay—bay ... GA-3
**Telfair (County)**—pop pl ... GA-3
Telfair Hosp—hospital ... GA-3
Telfair House—hist pl ... TX-5
Telfair Junction—locale ... GA-3
Telfair Lookout Tower—locale ... GA-3
Telfair Memorial Gardens—cemetery ... GA-3
Telfairs Creek ... NC-3
Telfairs Creek—stream ... NC-3
Telfairville ... GA-3
Telfair Woods—locale ... GA-3
Telfener (RR name for Telferner)—other ... TX-5
Telfer, Lake—lake ... FL-3
Telfer Butte—summit ... OR-9
**Telferner**—pop pl ... TX-5
**Telferner (RR name Telfener)**—pop pl ... TX-5
Telfer Sch—school ... ND-7
**Telfer Township**—pop pl ... ND-7
Telford—locale ... WA-9
**Telford**—pop pl ... PA-2
**Telford**—pop pl ... TN-4
Telford, Thomas, House—hist pl ... TN-4
Telford Baptist Ch—church ... TN-4
Telford Borough—civil (2) ... PA-2
Telford (CCD)—cens area ... TN-4
Telford Cem—cemetery ... TN-4
Telford Division—civil ... TN-4
Telford Elementary School ... PA-2
Telford Hill—summit ... NH-1
Telford Hollow—valley ... NY-2
Telford Industrial Park—locale ... PA-2
Telford Pipe—other ... ID-8
Telford Post Office—building ... TN-4
Telford Sch—school ... IL-6
Telford Sch—school ... PA-2
Telford Sch (historical)—school ... TN-4
Telford Spring—spring ... FL-3
**Telford Subdivision**—pop pl ... UT-8
Telgmann Valley—valley ... TX-5
Tel-Hai Camp—locale ... PA-2
Teliamina Lake—lake ... AK-9
Telick Run—stream ... PA-2
Telico—locale ... TX-5
Telico Branch—stream ... AL-4
Telico Ch—church ... AR-4
Telico Ch—church ... TX-5
Telico (Township of)—fmr MCD ... AR-4
Telida—locale ... AK-9
Telida ANV963—reserve ... AK-9
Telida Mountains—other ... AK-9
Telidaside Creek—stream ... AK-9
Telkakl—island ... PW-9
Tell—locale ... GA-3
Tell—locale ... WI-6
**Tell**—pop pl ... TX-5
**Tellassee (historical)**—pop pl ... TN-4
Tellaugue Hatche River ... AL-4
Tell Cem—cemetery ... ND-7
Tell Ch—church ... WI-6
**Tell City**—pop pl ... IN-6
Tell City HS—school ... IN-6
Tell City JHS—school ... IN-6
Telleck Branch—stream ... MO-7
Tellefson Lake—lake ... WI-6
**Teller**—pop pl ... AK-9
Teller Butte—summit ... OR-9
Teller Cem—cemetery ... OK-5
Teller Cigar Factory—hist pl ... PA-2
Teller City Campground—locale ... CO-8
Teller Creek—stream ... AK-9
Teller Creek—stream ... OR-9
Teller Ditch—canal ... CO-8
Teller Flat—flat ... OR-9
Teller Hill—summit ... NY-2
Teller House—hist pl ... CO-8
Teller HS ... NC-3
Teller HS—school ... NC-3
Teller Lake—reservoir (2) ... CO-8
Teller Lake No. 5—reservoir ... CO-8
Teller Mission (Brevig Mission)—other ... AK-9
Teller Mtn—summit ... CO-8
Teller Mtn—summit ... OK-5
Teller Point—cape ... TX-5
Teller Pond—reservoir ... OK-5
Teller Rsvr—reservoir ... CO-8
Teller Sch—school ... CO-8
Tellers Point—cape ... NY-2
Tellesburg Siding—locale ... OH-6
Telles Ranch—locale ... AZ-5
Tellico—locale ... NC-3
Tellico Bald—summit ... NC-3
Tellico Beach—locale ... TN-4
Tellico Blockhouse State Historic Site—hist pl ... TN-4
Tellico Bloomary Forge ... TN-4
Tellico Branch—stream ... TN-4
Tellico Camp—locale ... TN-4
Tellico Cem—cemetery ... TN-4
Tellico Ch—church ... NC-3
Tellico Ch—church ... TN-4
Tellico Creek—stream ... NC-3
Tellico Dam—dam ... TN-4
Tellico Gap—gap ... NC-3
**Tellico Hills**—pop pl ... TN-4
Tellico Iron Works (historical)—locale ... TN-4
Tellico Junction ... TN-4
Tellico Junction Post Office ... TN-4
Tellico Lake—reservoir (2) ... TN-4
Tellico Lake Dam—dam ... TN-4
Tellico Mtn—summit ... TN-4
Tellico Plains—flat ... TN-4
**Tellico Plains**—pop pl ... TN-4
Tellico Plains (CCD)—cens area ... TN-4
Tellico Plains Cem—cemetery ... TN-4
Tellico Plains Division—civil ... TN-4
Tellico Plains Elem Sch—school ... TN-4
Tellico Plains Furance ... TN-4
Tellico Plains HS—school ... TN-4
Tellico Plains JHS—school ... TN-4
Tellico Plains Post Office—building ... TN-4
Tellico Ranger Station—locale ... TN-4
Tellico Ridge ... NC-3
Tellico River—stream ... NC-3
Tellico River—stream ... TN-4
Tellico River Lodge—locale ... TN-4
Tellier Island—island ... AR-4
Telling, William E., House—hist pl ... OH-6
Tellin Rsvr—reservoir ... OR-9
Tellott Windmill—locale ... NM-5
Tells Creek—stream ... CA-9
Tells Peak—summit ... CA-9
Tell Street Ch—church ... IN-6
Telltale Bluffs—cliff ... NM-5
**Tell Township**—pop pl ... ND-7
**Tell (Township of)**—pop pl ... PA-2
**Telluride**—pop pl ... CO-8
**Telluride**—pop pl ... ID-8
Telluride Cabin—building ... UT-8
Telluride Hist Dist—hist pl ... CO-8
Telluride Mine—mine ... NV-8
Telluride Mines—mine ... UT-8
Telluride Mtn—summit ... CO-8
Telluride Peak—summit ... CO-8
Telluride School ... ID-8
Telluride Sch (reduced usage)—school ... ID-8
Tellurium Creek—stream ... CO-8
Tellurium Gulch—valley ... CO-8
Tellurium Lake—lake (2) ... CO-8
Tellurium Park—flat ... CO-8
Tellurium Peak—summit ... OR-9
**Telma**—pop pl ... WA-9
**Telmar Subdivision (subdivision)**—pop pl ... AL-4
Telmo ... GA-3
Telmore ... GA-3
Telmore Ch—church ... GA-3
**Telocaset**—pop pl ... OR-9
Telocaset Hill—summit ... OR-9
Telocvicna Jednota Sokol—hist pl ... NE-7
Telogo—locale ... GA-3
Teloga Creek—stream ... GA-3
Teloga Sch—school ... GA-3
**Telogia**—pop pl ... FL-3
Telogia Creek—stream ... FL-3
Telonalis Chevallis ... AL-4
Telong—summit ... PW-9
Telos Brook—stream ... ME-1
Telos Dam—dam ... ME-1
Telos Lake—reservoir ... ME-1
Telos Landing—locale ... ME-1
Telos Landing Campsite—locale ... ME-1
Telos Mtn—summit ... ME-1
Telos Stream—stream ... ME-1
Telos Tote Road—trail ... ME-1
Telphic Creek (historical)—gut ... NC-3
Telreka ... MI-6
Telrod Cove—bay ... AK-9
**Tels**—pop pl ... FL-3
Telshaw Pond—reservoir ... PA-2
Telshaw Pond ... PA-2
Telsitna Ridge—ridge ... AK-9
Telsitna River—stream ... AK-9
Telstad Pumping Station—other ... MT-8
Telstar Lake—lake ... WI-6
Telstar Landing Field—airport ... SD-7
Telstar Regional HS—school ... ME-1
Telstar Sch—school ... OK-5
Telukhti Creek—stream ... AK-9
Telulah Park—park ... WI-6
Telutkarungutes ... PW-9
Tem, Lake—lake ... FL-3
Tema Cem—cemetery ... FL-3
Temagami Island ... NY-2
Temagami Islands—island ... NY-2
Temalo, Lake—lake ... NY-2
Te Mamou Cem—cemetery ... LA-4
**Teman**—pop pl ... VA-3
Temascal—civil ... CA-9
Temblodero Slough—stream ... CA-9
Temble Hill Ch—church ... MS-4
Temblor Creek ... CA-9
Temblor Creek—stream ... CA-9
Temblor Pumping Station—other ... CA-9
Temblor Ranch—locale ... CA-9
Temblor Ranch Oil Field ... CA-9
Temblor Range—range ... CA-9
Temblor Valley—valley ... CA-9
Temco—locale ... TX-5
Temecha Creek ... AZ-5
Temecula—civil ... CA-9
**Temecula**—pop pl ... CA-9
Temecula Canyon—valley ... CA-9
Temecula Creek—stream ... CA-9
Temecula Hot Springs—locale ... CA-9
Temecula Valley—valley ... CA-9
**Temescal**—pop pl ... CA-9
Temescal, Lake—reservoir ... CA-9
Temescal Canyon—valley (2) ... CA-9
Temescal Creek—stream (3) ... CA-9
Temescal Peak ... CA-9
Temescal Station—locale ... CA-9
Temescal Valley—valley (2) ... CA-9
Temescal Wash—stream ... CA-9
Temettate Creek—stream ... CA-9
Temettate Ridge—ridge ... CA-9
Temett Brook ... MA-1
Temmes Pond—lake ... IL-6
Temming Sch (historical)—school ... MS-4
Temnac Bay—bay ... AK-9
Temnac P-38G Lightning—hist pl ... AK-9
Temnac River—stream ... AK-9
Temo ... MP-9
Te-Moak Ind Res ... NV-8
Te-Moak Ind Res—reserve ... NV-8
Te-Moak Well—well ... NV-8
Temo Insel ... MP-9
Temo Island ... MP-9
Temolime Canyon—valley ... NM-5
Temora—hist pl ... MD-2
**Temora Lake Estates (subdivision)**—pop pl ... NC-3
Tempa—locale ... WV-2
Tempa Mine—mine ... NV-8
Tempa Mtn—summit ... NC-3
**Tempe**—pop pl ... AZ-5
Tempe Beach Park—park ... AZ-5
Tempe Beach Stadium—hist pl ... AZ-5
Tempe Bridge—hist pl ... AZ-5
Tempe Butte—summit ... AZ-5
Tempe Camp—locale ... AZ-5
Tempe Canal—canal ... AZ-5
Tempe Cascade—falls ... WY-8
Tempe Cascade (trailer park)—locale ... AZ-5
**Tempe Cascade (trailer park)**—pop pl ... AZ-5
Tempe Cem—cemetery ... AZ-5
Tempe Community Center—building ... AZ-5
Tempe Community Hospital ... AZ-5
Tempe Concrete Arch Highway Bridge—hist pl ... AZ-5
Tempe Costa Ch—church ... NM-5
Tempe Cotton Exchange Cotton Gin Seed Storage Bldg—hist pl ... AZ-5
Tempe Creek—stream ... NJ-2
Tempe Creek—stream ... TX-5
Tempe Cross Cut Canal—canal ... AZ-5
Tempe Drainage District Number Two Ditch—canal ... AZ-5
Tempe Gut—stream ... NC-3
Tempe Hardware Bldg—hist pl ... AZ-5
Tempe High School Tennis and Racquetball Courts—locale ... AZ-5
Tempe Historical Museum—building ... AZ-5
Tempe HS—school ... AZ-5
Tempe Junction—locale ... AZ-5
Tempe Junction RR Station (historical)—building ... AZ-5
Tempe Knob ... MA-1
Tempel Emanu-el—church ... AL-4
Tempelton Elem Sch—school ... PA-2
Tempe Municipal Golf Course—other ... AZ-5
Tempe Municipal Stadium—building ... AZ-5
Tempe Park ... AZ-5
Tempe Park—park ... AZ-5
Tempe Public Library—building ... AZ-5
Temperance—locale ... GA-3
Temperance—locale ... KY-4
**Temperance**—pop pl ... MI-6
**Temperance**—pop pl ... SC-3
Temperance Arm—bay ... CA-9
Temperance Bell—locale ... GA-3
Temperance Ch—church (2) ... GA-3
Temperance Chapel—church ... WV-2
Temperance Creek—stream (2) ... CA-9
Temperance Creek—stream ... OR-9
Temperance Ditch—canal ... CA-9
Temperance Flat—flat ... CA-9
Temperance Hall—church ... NC-3
**Temperance Hall**—pop pl ... TN-4
Temperance Hall African Methodist Episcopal Ch (historical)—church ... TN-4
Temperance Hall Ch ... TN-4
Temperance Hall Colored Sch (historical)—school ... TN-4
Temperance Hall (historical)—locale ... MS-4
Temperance Hall Post Office (historical)—building ... TN-4
Temperance Hall Sch—school ... TN-4
Temperance Hill ... TN-4
**Temperance Hill**—pop pl ... SC-3
Temperance Hill—summit ... NY-2
Temperance Hill Cem—cemetery ... AR-4
Temperance Hill Cem—cemetery ... MS-4
Temperance Hill Ch—church ... AR-4
Temperance Hill Ch—church ... MS-4
Temperance Hills Baptist Ch ... MS-4
Temperance Hill Sch—school ... AL-4
Temperance Hill Sch—school ... IL-6
Temperance Hollow—valley ... OH-6
Temperance Island—island ... MI-6
Temperance Island—island ... MN-6
Temperance-Kutner Sch—school ... CA-9
Temperance Lake ... MN-6
Temperance Lake—lake ... MN-6
Temperance (Magisterial District)—fmr MCD ... VA-3
Temperance Oak Cem—cemetery ... AL-4
Temperance Oak Ch—church ... AL-4
Temperance Oak Sch (historical)—school ... AL-4
Temperance River—stream ... MN-6
Temperance River Lake—lake ... MN-6
Temperance Road Sch—school ... MI-6

Tenino Junction—pop pl WA-9
Tenino Lateral—canal CA-9
Tenino Stone Company Quarry—hist pl WA-9
Tenion Island FM-9
Tenisee TN-4
Ten Island—flat MS-4
Ten Island Cem—cemetery AL-4
Ten Island Ch—church AL-4
Ten Island Missionary Baptist Ch AL-4
Ten Islands—pop pl AL-4
Ten Islands (historical)—island AL-4
Ten Islands (historical)—island TN-4
Ten Island Shoals—bar TN-4
Ten Islands P.O. AL-4
Tenis Post Office (historical)—building AL-4
Tenjo, Mount—summit GU-9
Tenjo River—stream GU-9
Tenkiller Ferry Dam—dam OK-5
Tenkiller Ferry Lake—reservoir OK-5
Tenkiller Ferry Rsvr OK-5
Tenkiller Sch—school OK-5
Ten Kilns Brook—stream VT-1
Ten Lake—lake (3) MN-6
Ten Lake—lake WA-9
Tenlake Basin—basin ID-8
Tenlake Creek—stream ID-8
Ten Lake Park—flat CO-8
Ten Lakes—lake CA-9
Ten Lakes Basin—basin MT-8
Ten Lakes Trail—trail CA-9
Ten Lake (Township of)—pop pl MN-6
Tenland Homestead—locale MT-8
Ten Landing Lake—lake MS-4
Tenley Circle—other DC-2
Tenley House—building DC-2
Tenleytown—pop pl DC-2
Ten Lots Chapel—church ME-1
Tenmil Canyon—valley OR-9
Tenmile CA-9
Ten Mile KS-7
Tenmile MS-4
Tenmile PA-2
Ten Mile WV-2
Ten Mile—locale MO-7
Tenmile—locale NV-8
Tenmile—locale TX-5
Tenmile—locale WA-9
Tenmile—locale WY-8
Ten Mile—pop pl ID-8
Tenmile—pop pl IA-7
Ten Mile—pop pl IA-7
Ten Mile—pop pl MS-4
Tenmile—pop pl MO-7
Tenmile—pop pl (2) OR-9
Ten Mile—pop pl PA-2
Ten Mile—pop pl SC-3
Tenmile—pop pl SC-3
Ten Mile—pop pl SC-3
Ten Mile—pop pl (2) TN-4
Ten Mile—pop pl WV-2
Tenmile—pop pl WV-2
Tenmile Bay—bay MI-6
Tenmile Bay—swamp GA-3
Tenmile Bay—swamp SC-3
Tenmile Bayou—stream (2) AR-4
Tenmile Bayou—stream LA-4
Ten Mile Bayou—stream MS-4
Tenmile Bayou Diversion Ditch—canal AR-4
Tenmile Bottom PA-2
Tenmile Bottom—bend UT-8
Tenmile Bottom—pop pl PA-2
Tenmile Branch—stream (2) AL-4
Tenmile Branch—stream FL-3
Tenmile Branch—stream LA-4
Tenmile Branch—stream NC-3
Tenmile Branch—stream WV-2
Tenmile Bridge—bridge TX-5
Ten Mile Brook RI-1
Tenmile Brook—stream (3) ME-1
Tenmile Brook—stream NH-1
Ten Mile Butte UT-8
Tenmile Butte—summit (2) OR-9
Tenmile Butte—summit UT-8
Tenmile Camp—locale WA-9
Tenmile Campground—locale ID-8
Tenmile Canal—canal FL-3
Ten Mile Canyon UT-8
Tenmile Canyon—valley ID-8
Tenmile Canyon—valley NM-5
Tenmile Canyon—valley (2) UT-8
Tenmile (CCD)—cens area OR-9
Ten Mile (CCD)—cens area TN-4
Tenmile Cedars—woods AZ-5
Tenmile Cem—cemetery LA-4
Tenmile Cem—cemetery OR-9
Tenmile Cem—cemetery TX-5
Tenmile Cem—cemetery WV-2
Tenmile Center Ch—church NC-3
Tenmile Ch—church AR-4
Tenmile Ch—church GA-3
Tenmile Ch—church IL-6
Tenmile Ch—church KY-4
Ten Mile Ch—church MS-4
Ten Mile Ch—church (2) MO-7
Tenmile Ch—church NC-3
Tenmile Ch—church PA-2
Tenmile Ch—church (3) WV-2
Tenmile Community Center—building WV-2
Tenmile Community Ch—church ID-8
Tenmile Corner—locale FL-3
Tenmile Corner—locale MN-6
Tenmile County Park—park OR-9
Ten Mile Creek CA-9
Tenmile Creek FL-3
Tenmile Creek KY-4
Tenmile Creek MI-6
Tenmile Creek NV-8
Ten Mile Creek OH-6
Tenmile Creek OR-9
Ten Mile Creek PA-2
Ten Mile Creek WA-9
Tenmile Creek WY-8
Tenmile Creek—gut FL-3
Tenmile Creek—stream AL-4
Tenmile Creek—stream (2) AK-9
Tenmile Creek—stream (8) AR-4
Tenmile Creek—stream (5) CA-9
Tenmile Creek—stream (4) CO-8
Tenmile Creek—stream (8) FL-3
Tenmile Creek—stream (6) GA-3
Tenmile Creek—stream (8) ID-8
Tenmile Creek—stream (3) IL-6
Tenmile Creek—stream IN-6
Ten Mile Creek—stream IA-7
Ten Mile Creek—stream KS-7
Tenmile Creek—stream (2) KY-4
Ten Mile Creek—stream KY-4
Tenmile Creek—stream KY-4
Tenmile Creek—stream (4) LA-4
Tenmile Creek—stream MD-2
Tenmile Creek—stream (4) MI-6
Tenmile Creek—stream MN-6
Tenmile Creek—stream (2) MS-4
Tenmile Creek—stream MO-7
Ten Mile Creek—stream MO-7
Tenmile Creek—stream (9) MT-8
Tenmile Creek—stream NV-8
Tenmile Creek—stream (3) NY-2
Ten Mile Creek—stream NC-3
Tenmile Creek—stream (2) OH-6
Tenmile Creek—stream OK-5
Tenmile Creek—stream (6) OR-9
Tenmile Creek—stream PA-2
Ten Mile Creek—stream (2) TN-4
Tenmile Creek—stream TN-4
Tenmile Creek—stream (4) TX-5
Tenmile Creek—stream (2) UT-8
Tenmile Creek—stream (7) WA-9
Tenmile Creek—stream (5) WV-2
Tenmile Creek—stream (4) WI-6
Tenmile Creek—stream WY-8
Ten Mile Creek Cave—cave TN-4
Tenmile Creek Ch—church GA-3
Tenmile Creek Forest Camp—locale OR-9
Tenmile Crossing—locale (2) TX-5
Tenmile Cut—gut TX-5
Tenmile Ditch—canal MT-8
Ten Mile Division—civil TN-4
Tenmile Draw—valley AZ-5
Tenmile Draw—valley TX-5
Tenmile Draw—valley WY-8
Tenmile Feeder Canal—canal ID-8
Tenmile Flat—flat ID-8
Ten Mile Flat—flat OK-5
Tenmile Flat—flat UT-8
Tenmile Flat—flat WY-8
Ten Mile Fork NC-3
Tenmile Fork—locale NC-3
Tenmile Fork—stream WV-2
Tenmile Grange—locale WA-9
Tenmile Grove—woods CA-9
Tenmile Gulch—valley CO-8
Tenmile Gully—valley TX-5
Tenmile Hill—summit AK-9
Tenmile Hill—summit CT-1
Tenmile Hill—summit ID-8
Tenmile Hill—summit NM-5
Tenmile Hill—summit OK-5
Tenmile Hill—summit UT-8
Tenmile Hill—summit WY-8
Tenmile Hills—range NV-8
Ten Mile (historical)—locale KS-7
Tenmile Hollow—valley CA-9
Tenmile Hollow—valley FL-3
Ten Mile House—hist pl AR-4
Tenmile House—locale CA-9
Tenmile House—locale MT-8
Tenmile Island—island AK-9
Ten Mile Island—island MO-7
Tenmile Island—island WA-9
Ten Mile Knob—summit TN-4
Tenmile Knoll—summit UT-8
Tenmile Lake—lake AK-9
Tenmile Lake—lake FL-3
Tenmile Lake—lake ME-1
Ten Mile Lake—lake MI-6
Tenmile Lake—lake (3) MN-6
Tenmile Lake—lake MT-8
Tenmile Lake—lake OK-5
Tenmile Lake—lake OR-9
Tenmile Lake—lake WI-6
Tenmile Lake—swamp MN-6
Ten Mile Lake Cem—cemetery MN-6
Tenmile Lake Ch—church MN-6
Tenmile Lakes—lake MT-8
Ten Mile Lake (Township of)—civ div MN-6
Tenmile Lookout Tower—locale GA-3
Tenmile Meadows—flat ID-8
Ten Mile Methodist Ch—church TN-4
Tenmile Mine—mine NV-8
Ten Mile Mountain CO-8
Tenmile Mtn—summit MT-8
Tenmile Park—flat CO-8
Ten Mile Pass WA-9
Tenmile Pass—gap ID-8
Tenmile Pass—gap UT-8
Tenmile Pass—gap WA-9
Tenmile Peak—summit CO-8
Ten Mile Pit—cave TN-4
Tenmile Place, The—locale UT-8
Tenmile Point—cape MI-6
Tenmile Point—cape NY-2
Ten Mile Point—cape PA-2
Tenmile Point—cliff CO-8
Tenmile Point—ridge UT-8
Tenmile Pond—lake (2) FL-3
Tenmile Pond—lake ME-1
Tenmile Pond—lake MO-7
Tenmile Post—locale AK-9
Ten Mile Post Office—building TN-4
Tenmile Post Office (historical)—building MS-4
Tenmile Prairie—flat FL-3
Tenmile Ranch—locale FL-3
Tenmile Ranch—locale NV-8
Tenmile Range—range CO-8
Tenmile Range Peak 1—summit CO-8
Tenmile Range Peak 10—summit CO-8
Tenmile Range Peak 3—summit CO-8
Tenmile Range Peak 4—summit CO-8
Tenmile Range Peak 5—summit CO-8
Tenmile Range Peak 6—summit CO-8
Tenmile Range Peak 7—summit CO-8
Tenmile Range Peak 8—summit CO-8
Tenmile Range Peak 9—summit CO-8
Tenmile Rapids—rapids ID-8
Tenmile Rapids—rapids MI-6
Tenmile Rapids—rapids WA-9
Ten Mile Reservation Dam—dam RI-1
Tenmile Ridge—ridge (2) ID-8
Tenmile Ridge—ridge OR-9
Ten Mile Ridge—ridge TN-4
Tenmile Rim—cliff WY-8
Tenmile River CA-9
Ten Mile River CT-1
Tenmile River MA-1
Tenmile River RI-1
Tenmile River—stream AK-9
Ten Mile River—stream CA-9
Tenmile River—stream (3) CT-1
Tenmile River—stream ME-1
Ten Mile River—stream MA-1
Tenmile River—stream (2) NY-2
Ten Mile River—stream RI-1
Ten Mile River Bluff—cape CA-9
Tenmile River Camps—locale NY-2
Ten Mile River Dam—dam MA-1
Ten Mile River Reservation—reservoir RI-1
Ten Mile River Rsvr—reservoir MA-1
Ten Mile River (Scout Camp)—pop pl NY-2
Tenmile Rodeo Grounds—locale ID-8
Tenmile Rsvr No 3—reservoir WY-8
Tenmile Rsvr No 4—reservoir WY-8
Ten Mile Run—pop pl NJ-2
Tenmile Run—stream NJ-2
Tenmile Run—stream (3) PA-2
Tenmile Run—stream (2) WV-2
Ten Mile Run Cem—cemetery NJ-2
Tenmile Sch—school ID-8
Tenmile Sch—school IL-6
Tenmile Sch—school KS-7
Ten Mile Sch—school MI-6
Ten Mile Sch—school MO-7
Ten Mile Sch—school TN-4
Tenmile Sch—school WV-2
Tenmile Shelter—locale OR-9
Tenmile Shelter—locale (3) WA-9
Tenmile Slough—gut CA-9
Tenmile Spring—spring CA-9
Tenmile Spring—spring MT-8
Tenmile Spring—spring NV-8
Tenmile Spring—spring UT-8
Tenmile Spring—spring WY-8
Tenmile Springs—spring CO-8
Tenmile Stand Post Office TN-4
Ten Mile Still Landing—locale GA-3
Tenmile Swamp—stream GA-3
Tenmile Swamp—stream (2) NC-3
Tenmile Swamp—swamp FL-3
Tenmile Swing—locale ME-1
Tenmile Tailings Pond—other CO-8
Tenmile Tank—reservoir AZ-5
Ten Mile Township—civil MO-7
Ten Mile Township—pop pl KS-7
Tenmile Trail—trail WA-9
Tenmile Trail Lake—lake GA-3
Ten Mile Village PA-2
Tenmile Wash—stream AZ-5
Tenmile Wash—stream UT-8
Tenmile Wash Rsvr—reservoir UT-8
Tenmile Waterhole—lake (2) TX-5
Tenmile Well—well AZ-5
Tenmile Well—well MT-8
Tenmile Well—well (2) NV-8
Tenmile Well—well TX-5
Tennala—pop pl AL-4
Tennala Ch—church AL-4
Tenna Lake MI-6
Tennanah—pop pl NY-2
Tennanah Lake—lake NY-2
Tennanah Lake—pop pl NY-2
Tennant—locale AL-4
Tennant—pop pl CA-9
Tennant—pop pl IA-7
Tennant, J. D., House—hist pl WA-9
Tennant Branch—stream TX-5
Tennant Brook—stream CT-1
Tennant Cem—cemetery OH-6
Tennant Cem—cemetery (4) WV-2
Tennant Creek—stream WY-8
Tennant Ditch—canal IN-6
Tennant Gulch—valley CO-8
Tennant Lake—lake IN-6
Tennant Lake—lake WA-9
Tennant Memorial Cem—cemetery WV-2
Tennant Ranch—locale WY-8
Tennant Ranch Landing Strip—airport SD-7
Tennants Branch—stream SC-3
Tennant's Harbor ME-1
Tennant Spring—spring WY-8
Tennassillihi Island OR-9
Tenn Bald NC-3
Tenn Beard Cem—cemetery IN-6
Tennear Pumping Station Pond CT-1
Tenneboe Slough—gut SD-7
Tenneco Heliport—airport PA-2
Tenneco Well—well AZ-5
Tennelina—pop pl NC-3
Tennell Chapel—church AL-4
Tennell Chapel Cem—cemetery AL-4
Tennell Creek—stream ID-8
Tennell Creek—stream NV-8
Tennelle Chapel—church GA-3
Tennelle Creek—stream GA-3
Tennelue Cem—cemetery MS-4
Tennemo—locale TN-4
Tennemo Bar—bar TN-4
Tennemo Landing—locale TN-4
Tennemo Post Office (historical)—building TN-4
Tennent—locale NJ-2
Tennent, Josiah Smith, House—hist pl SC-3
Tennent Brook—stream NJ-2
Tennent Brook Dam—dam NJ-2
Tennent HS—school PA-2
Tennent Mtn—summit NC-3
Tennent Pond—reservoir NJ-2
Tennents Brook NJ-2
Tennerton—pop pl WV-2
Tennerton Sch—school WV-2
Tennerville TX-5
Tenneryville TX-5
Tenneryville—pop pl TX-5
Tenneson Creek—stream MD-2
Tennessee—pop pl AR-4
Tennessee—pop pl IL-6
Tennessee, Lake—lake (2) FL-3
Tennessee Acad (historical)—school TN-4
Tennessee Acres—pop pl NC-3
Tennessee Agricultural And Industrial State—school TN-4
Tennessee Air Natl Guard—building TN-4
Tennessee Ave Baptist Ch—church TN-4
Tennessee Bald NC-3
Tennessee Bar—ridge MS-4
Tennessee Bluff—summit NC-3
Tennessee Bluff—summit TN-4
Tennessee Branch—stream AR-4
Tennessee Branch—stream GA-3
Tennessee Branch—stream NC-3
Tennessee Brewery—hist pl TN-4
Tennessee Camp (historical)—locale TN-4
Tennessee Cem—cemetery IL-6
Tennessee Cem—cemetery IA-7
Tennessee Cem—cemetery MO-7
Tennessee Cem—cemetery TX-5
Tennessee Ch—church AR-4
Tennessee Ch—church TN-4
Tennessee Chapel—church TN-4
Tennessee City—pop pl TN-4
Tennessee City (CCD)—cens area TN-4
Tennessee City Division—civil TN-4
Tennessee Club-Overall Goodbar Bldg—hist pl TN-4
Tennessee Coal and Iron Dam—dam AL-4
Tennessee Colony—pop pl TX-5
Tennessee Cove—bay CA-9
Tennessee Creek NC-3
Tennessee Creek—stream AR-4
Tennessee Creek—stream (3) CA-9
Tennessee Creek—stream (2) CO-8
Tennessee Creek—stream KS-7
Tennessee Creek—stream MS-4
Tennessee Creek—stream MO-7
Tennessee Creek—stream NM-5
Tennessee Creek—stream OR-9
Tennessee Creek Campground—locale ID-8
Tennessee Farms—pop pl AL-4
Tennessee Fork CO-8
Tennessee Furnace (historical)—locale TN-4
Tennessee Furnace (40MT383)—hist pl TN-4
Tennessee Gap NC-3
Tennessee Gas Lake Dam—dam MS-4
Tennessee-Georgia Memorial Park Cem—cemetery GA-3
Tennessee Gulch—valley (3) CA-9
Tennessee Gulch—valley CO-8
Tennessee Gulch—valley ID-8
Tennessee Gulch—valley NV-8
Tennessee Gulch—valley (3) OR-9
Tennessee Highway Department—building TN-4
Tennessee Hill—locale TN-4
Tennessee Hills—pop pl TN-4
Tennessee (historical)—pop pl TN-4
Tennessee Hollow—valley TN-4
Tennessee Hollow Ch—church TN-4
Tennessee HS—school TN-4
Tennessee Industrial School Camp—locale TN-4
Tennessee Knob—summit CA-9
Tennessee Lake—lake MS-4
Tennessee Lake—reservoir TX-5
Tennessee Landing—locale MS-4
Tennessee Military Institute—school TN-4
Tennessee Mine—mine AZ-5
Tennessee Mine—mine CA-9
Tennessee Mine (underground)—mine AL-4
Tennessee Mtn—summit CA-9
Tennessee Mtn—summit CO-8
Tennessee Mtn—summit ID-8
Tennessee Mtn—summit NV-8
Tennessee Mtn—summit OR-9
Tennessee Natl Guard Armory—military TN-4
Tennessee Natl Migratory Wildlife Refuge TN-4
Tennessee Natl Wildlife Ref—park TN-4
Tennessee Orphans Home—locale TN-4
Tennessee Park—flat CO-8
Tennessee Pass—gap CO-8
Tennessee Pass—gap OR-9
Tennessee Pass—locale CO-8
Tennessee Point—cape CA-9
Tennessee Point—summit CA-9
Tennessee Polytechnic Institute—school TN-4
Tennessee Pond—reservoir CO-8
Tennessee Ravine—valley CA-9
Tennessee Rebel—mine UT-8
Tennessee Reef—bar FL-3
Tennessee Ridge NC-3
Tennessee Ridge—pop pl TN-4
Tennessee Ridge—ridge CA-9
Tennessee Ridge—ridge (2) KY-4
Tennessee Ridge—ridge TN-4
Tennessee Ridge (CCD)—cens area TN-4
Tennessee Ridge Division—civil TN-4
Tennessee Ridge Elem Sch—school TN-4
Tennessee Ridge Post Office—building TN-4
Tennessee River—stream AL-4
Tennessee River—stream KY-4
Tennessee River—stream MS-4
Tennessee River—stream TN-4
Tennessee River Basin MS-4
Tennessee River Institute (historical)—school AL-4
Tennessee River Pulp And Paper Company East Dam—dam TN-4
Tennessee River Pulp And Paper Company West Dam—dam TN-4
Tennessee River Pulp And Paper East Lake—reservoir TN-4
Tennessee River Pulp And Paper West Lake—reservoir TN-4
Tennessee Sch—school CA-9
Tennessee Sch—school IL-6
Tennessee Sch—school OR-9
Tennessee Sch (historical)—school TN-4
Tennessee Spring—spring CA-9
Tennessee Spring—spring NV-8
Tennessee State Capitol—hist pl TN-4
Tennessee State Capitol Complex—building TN-4
Tennessee Tech—school TN-4
Tennessee Temple Coll—school TN-4
Tennessee-Tombigbee Waterway—channel AL-4
Tennessee (Township of)—fmr MCD AR-4
Tennessee (Township of)—pop pl IL-6
Tennessee Trust Bldg—hist pl TN-4
Tennessee Tuberculosis Hosp—hospital TN-4
Tennessee Valley—basin NE-7
Tennessee Valley—valley AL-4
Tennessee Valley—valley CA-9
Tennessee Valley—valley MS-4
Tennessee Valley Agriculture Experiment Station AL-4
Tennessee Valley Authority Steam Plant—building KY-4
Tennessee Valley Authority Steam Plant(Browns Ferry)—facility AL-4
Tennessee Valley Boy Scouts Camp AL-4
Tennessee Valley Cem—cemetery TX-5
Tennessee Valley Ch—church IN-6
Tennessee Valley Community Ch—church AL-4
Tennessee Valley Country Club and Golf Course—other AL-4
Tennessee Valley Divide—ridge AL-4
Tennessee Valley Divide—ridge GA-3
Tennessee Valley Divide—ridge KY-4
Tennessee Valley Divide—ridge MS-4
Tennessee Valley Divide—ridge NC-3
Tennessee Valley Divide—ridge SC-3
Tennessee Valley Divide—ridge TN-4
Tennessee Valley Divide—ridge VA-3
Tennessee Valley JHS—school AL-4
Tennessee Valley Memory Gardens—cemetery TN-4
Tennessee Valley Mine (underground)—mine AL-4
Tennessee Valley RR Museum—building TN-4
Tennessee Valley RR Museum Rolling Stock—hist pl TN-4
Tennessee Valley State Vocational Technical School AL-4
Tennessee Valley Unitarian Ch—church TN-4
Tennessee Vocational Sch—school TN-4
Tennessee Vocational Sch for Girls—school TN-4
Tennessee Walking Horse Natl Showgrounds—locale TN-4
Tennessee Wash—stream AZ-5
Tennessee Wesleyan Coll—school TN-4
Tennessee Wildlife Ref—park TN-4
Tennessee Williams Canal—canal LA-4
Tennessee Yards—locale TN-4
Tenney—pop pl HI-9
Tenney—pop pl MN-6
Tenney, Levi, House—hist pl TX-5
Tenney, Samuel, House—hist pl NH-1
Tenney Brook—stream ME-1
Tenney Brook—stream VT-1
Tenney Canyon UT-8
Tenney Center—building HI-9
Tenney Circle—pop pl NC-3
Tenney Cove—bay ME-1
Tenney Crags—pillar CO-8
Tenney Creek UT-8
Tenney Creek—stream TX-5
Tenney Creek Ch—church TX-5
Tenney Creek Oil Field—oilfield TX-5
Tenney Fire Hall—hist pl MN-6
Tenney Hill—ridge NH-1
Tenney HS—school MA-1
Tenney Mtn—summit AZ-5
Tenney Mtn—summit NH-1
Tenney Park—park WI-6
Tenney Peak—summit CA-9
Tenney Pond—lake NH-1
Tenney Pond—reservoir VT-1
Tenneys Camp AZ-5
Tenney Tank—reservoir AZ-5
Tenney Village—pop pl HI-9
Tenneyville—pop pl MA-1
Tennga—pop pl GA-3
Tennga—pop pl TN-4
Tenn Gap NC-3
Tennie Lou Ch (historical)—church MS-4
Tennille—locale FL-3
Tennille—pop pl AL-4
Tennille—pop pl GA-3
Tennille (CCD)—cens area GA-3
Tennille Ch—church AL-4
Tennis—locale KS-7
Tennis Gap—gap PA-2
Tennis (historical)—locale SD-7
TENNISON, WM. B. (Chesapeake Bay Bugeye)—hist pl MD-2
Tennison Bay—bay WI-6
Tennison Canyon—valley CA-9
Tennison Cem—cemetery MO-7
Tennison Creek—stream ID-8
Tennison Ridge—ridge ID-8
Tennison Sch (abandoned)—school MO-7
Tennison Spring—spring CA-9
Tennis Run—stream PA-2
Tenn Sheriffs Youthtown Dam—dam TN-4
Tenn Sheriffs Youthtown Lake—reservoir TN-4
Tenn-Wood Club—other TX-5
Tenny, Dr. J. T., House—hist pl WI-6
Tenny Brook ME-1
Tenny Castle Gatehouse—hist pl MA-1
Tenny Creek—stream AR-4
Tenny Creek—stream UT-8
Tenny Flat—flat AZ-5
Tenny Hill—summit (2) ME-1
Tenny Lewis Branch—stream TX-5
Tenny River—stream ME-1
Tennys Creek—stream OR-9
Tennyson—locale OH-6
Tennyson—pop pl IN-6
Tennyson—pop pl TX-5
Tennyson—pop pl WI-6
Tennyson Cem—cemetery TX-5
Tennyson Creek KS-7
Tennyson Creek—stream KS-7
Tennyson Creek—stream LA-4
Tenny Son Dam SD-7
Tennyson Dam—dam SD-7
Tennyson Heights CO-8
Tennyson Hollow—valley MO-7
Tennyson HS—school CA-9
Tennyson Lake—lake MN-6
Tennyson Point—cape MD-2
Tennyson Sch—school CA-9
Tennyson Sch—school IL-6
Tennyson Sch—school OH-6
Tenny Spring Creek—stream WI-6
Tennyville MA-1
Tennyville—pop pl MA-1
Ten Oaks Lake—reservoir GA-3
Ten O'Clock Creek—stream WA-9
Ten of Diamonds Creek—stream AZ-5
Ten of Diamonds Ranch—locale AZ-5
Teno Hollow—valley TN-4
Tenold—locale IA-7
Tenor Chapel AL-4
Tenorio Ditch—canal NM-5
Tenorio Ranch—locale NM-5
Tenorio Tract Taos Pueblo—civil NM-5
Tenor Lake—lake MN-6
Tenoroc—pop pl FL-3
Tenoroc Mine—mine FL-3
Tenos Brothers Airp—airport PA-2
Tenpeak Mtn—summit WA-9
Tenpenny Cave—cave TN-4
Tenpenny Hollow—valley TN-4
Ten Petticoat Lane—locale MO-7
Tenpin Gulch—valley ID-8
Ten P.M. Island FM-9
Ten Pool—reservoir WI-6
Ten Post Oak Ch—church IL-6
Ten-pound Island MA-1
Tenpound Island—island (2) ME-1
Tenpound Island—island MA-1
Tenpound Island Ledge—rock MA-1
Ten Pound Island Light—hist pl MA-1
Tenpound Island Light—locale MA-1
Tenpound Island Lighthouse—locale MA-1
Ten Pup—stream AK-9
Ten Ranch—locale AZ-5
Tenroc RR Station—locale FL-3
Ten Rsvr—reservoir MT-8
Tensa River AL-4
Tensas Basin—basin LA-4
Tensas Bay—bay LA-4
Tensas Bayou—stream (2) LA-4
Tensas Bluff—locale LA-4
Tensas Bluff Landing—locale LA-4
Tensas Cem—cemetery LA-4
Tensas Ch—church LA-4
Tensas Ditch—canal (2) LA-4
Tensas Lake—lake LA-4
Tensas Parish—pop pl LA-4
Tensas Parish Courthouse—hist pl LA-4
Tensas Point—cape LA-4
Tensas River AL-4
Tensas River—stream LA-4
Tensaw—locale AL-4
Tensaw Bayou LA-4
Tensaw Ch—church AL-4
Tensaw Creek—stream AL-4
Tensaw Creek—stream MT-8
Tensaw Lake—lake AL-4
Tensaw Land And Timber Co Dam—dam AL-4
Tensaw Land And Timber Co Pond—reservoir AL-4
Tensaw Memorial Cem—cemetery AL-4
Tensaw River LA-4
Tensaw River—stream AL-4
Ten Section Lake—lake MN-6
Ten Section Oil Field CA-9
Ten Section Refinery—other CA-9
Tensed—pop pl ID-8
Tensee TN-4
Tensey Drain MI-6
Tenskwatawa Falls—falls WV-2
Tensleep WY-8
Ten Sleep—pop pl WY-8
Tensleep Campground—locale WY-8
Tensleep Canyon—valley (2) WY-8
Tensleep Creek—stream WY-8
Tensleep Fish Hatchery—locale WY-8
Tensleep Lake WY-8
Ten Sleep Mercantile—hist pl WY-8
Tensmuir Sch (Abandoned)—school CA-9
Tenso—locale VA-3
Ten Spot—pop pl KY-4
Tenstrike—pop pl MN-6
Tenstrike Mine—mine AZ-5
Tensulate—uninc pl FL-3
Ten Sycamore Flat—flat CA-9
Tent—locale DE-2
Tent, Bayou—stream LA-4
T-en-ta AZ-5
Tentan—well FM-9
Ten Tank—reservoir AZ-5
Ten Tank—reservoir NM-5
Ten Tapo Trail—trail CA-9
Tent Branch—stream WV-2
Tent Brook—stream IN-6
Tent Camp (Site)—locale CA-9
Tent Canyon—valley CO-8
Tent Canyon—valley NM-5
Tent Canyon—valley UT-8
Tent Canyon—valley WY-8
Tent Ch—church PA-2
Tent Ch—church WV-2
Tent Church Cem—cemetery OH-6
Tent City—locale MI-6
Tent City—uninc pl CA-9
Tent Creek—stream CO-8
Tent Creek—stream (3) ID-8
Tent Creek—stream MT-8
Tent Creek—stream OR-9
Tent Creek—stream WY-8
Tent Creek Point—cliff ID-8
Tent Creek Rsvr—reservoir ID-8
Tenter Lake—lake (2) MN-6
Tenth and Green Streets Elem Sch—school PA-2
Tenth Ave—uninc pl PA-2
Tenth Ave Park—park AL-4
Tenth Ave Park—park IL-6
Tenth Cavalry Creek—stream TX-5
Tenth Crow Wing Lake—lake MN-6
Tenth District Sch—school KY-4
Tenth Field Artillery Bluff—cliff WA-9
Tent Hills—ridge CA-9
Tenth Legion—pop pl VA-3
Tent Hollow—valley MO-7
Tent Hollow—valley UT-8
Ten Thousand Acre Pond—lake ME-1
Ten Thousand Foot Ridge—ridge CA-9
Ten Thousand Islands—island FL-3
Tenthouse Creek—bay MD-2
Tenth Precinct Station House—hist pl DC-2
Tenth Siding ND-7
Tenth Street Baptist Ch—church MS-4
Tenth Street Bridge—bridge (2) PA-2
Tenth Street Dam PA-2
Tenth Street Ditch—canal CA-9
Tenth Street Elem Sch—school IN-6
Tenth Street Elem Sch—school PA-2
Tenth Street Methodist Church TN-4

Tenth Street Missionary Baptist Ch—*church* AL-4
Tenth Street Park—*park* AZ-5
Tenth Street Sch—*school* AL-4
Tenth Street Sch—*school* CA-9
Tenth Street Sch—*school* (2) GA-3
Tenth Street Sch—*school* NY-2
Tenth Ward Square—*hist pl* UT-8
Tent Lake—*lake* MN-6
Tent Lake—*lake* MS-4
Tent Lake—*lake* MT-8
*Tent Mountain* OR-9
Tent Mtn—*summit* (2) MT-8
Tent Mtn—*summit* NV-8
Tento Creek—*stream* ID-8
*Tentop* TX-5
Tent Point—*cape* (2) AK-9
Tent Prairie—*flat* OR-9
Ientree Island—*island* AK-9
Ten Trees Creek—*stream* MT-8
Tentrock Canyon—*valley* CA-9
Tent Rock Ranch—*locale* NM-5
Tent Rocks—*other* NM-5
Tent Rocks—*ridge* NM-5
*Tents, The* CA-9
*Tents Creek* CO-8
Tents Creek—*stream* CO-8
Tent Spring—*spring* ID-8
Tenville—*locale* IA-7
**Tenville Junction**—*pop pl* IA-7
Ten Voord Spring—*spring* NV-8
Tenwak—*locale* FM-9
Ten-Well State Wildlife Mngmt Area—*park* MN-6
Tenweneno—*bar* FM-9
Tenwen Men—*summit* FM-9
Ten X Campground—*park* AZ-5
Ten X Tank—*reservoir* AZ-5
*Ten Yard Branch* TN-4
Ten Year Rsvr—*reservoir* OR-9
**Tenysville (historical)**—*pop pl* OR-9
Teo', As—*slope* MH-9
Teo', Bo'bo'As—*spring* MH-9
Teoc—*locale* MS-4
Teocalli Mountains—*range* AK-9
Teocalli Mtn—*summit* CO-8
Teocalli Ridge—*ridge* CO-8
*Teo Cave* MH-9
Teoc Cem—*cemetery* MS-4
Teoc Ch—*church* MS-4
Teoc Creek—*stream* AL-4
Teoc Creek—*stream* MS-4
Teoc Creek Site—*hist pl* MS-4
Teock Creek—*stream* MS-4
Teodoro Windmill—*locale* TX-5
*Teoe Creek* AL-4
Teongel—*bay* PW-9
Teongel—*channel* PW-9
*Teongel Bay* PW-9
*Teo Place* MH-9
*Teouachis* AL-4
**Tepat**—*pop pl* FM-9
Tepatasi Mtn—*summit* AS-9
**Tepco**—*pop pl* TN-4
Tepecate Creek—*stream* TX-5
*Tepee* SD-7
Tepee, The—*summit* NM-5
Tepee Basin—*basin* (2) MT-8
*Tepee Butte* SD-7
Tepee Butte—*summit* AZ-5
Tepee Butte—*summit* (3) MT-8
Tepee Butte—*summit* ND-7
Tepee Butte—*summit* TX-5
Tepee Butte Cem—*cemetery* ND-7
Tepee Butte Rsvr—*reservoir* MT-8
Tepee Buttes—*range* (2) ND-7
Tepee Buttes—*range* SD-7
Tepee Buttes Cem—*cemetery* ND-7
**Tepee Butte Township**—*pop pl* ND-7
Tepee Campground—*locale* WA-9
Tepee Canyon—*valley* NM-5
Tepee Canyon—*valley* SD-7
Tepee Canyon—*valley* UT-8
*Tepee Canyon Creek* SD-7
Tepee Canyon Creek—*stream* SD-7
Tepee Canyon Spring—*spring* SD-7
Tepee Canyon Well—*well* SD-7
Tepee Circles—*locale* ID-8
Tepee Coulee—*valley* MT-8
*Tepee Creek* WY-8
Tepee Creek—*stream* CA-9
Tepee Creek—*stream* (3) CO-8
Tepee Creek—*stream* (7) ID-8
Tepee Creek—*stream* MI-6
Tepee Creek—*stream* (16) MT-8
Tepee Creek—*stream* NV-8
Tepee Creek—*stream* ND-7
Tepee Creek—*stream* (2) OK-5
Tepee Creek—*stream* OR-9
Tepee Creek—*stream* (3) SD-7
Tepee Creek—*stream* TX-5
Tepee Creek—*stream* (2) WA-9
Tepee Creek—*stream* (10) WY-8
Tepee Creek Ridge—*ridge* WY-8
Tepee Creek Trail—*trail* CO-8
Tepee Creek Trail—*trail* WY-8
Tepee Draw—*valley* CO-8
Tepee Draw—*valley* OR-9
Tepee Draw—*valley* TX-5
Tepee Flat—*flat* MT-8
Tepee Flats—*flat* ID-8
*Tepee Gulch* CO-8
*Tepee Gulch* WY-8
Tepee Gulch—*stream* ID-8
Tepee Gulch—*valley* CO-8
Tepee Gulch—*valley* ID-8
Tepee Gulch—*valley* SD-7
Tepee Gulch Camp—*locale* CA-9
Tepee Hill—*summit* MT-8
Tepee (historical)—*locale* SD-7
Tepee Hole—*bend* CO-8
Tepee Lake—*lake* MI-6
Tepee Lake—*lake* (3) MN-6
Tepee Lake—*lake* (3) MT-8
Tepee Lake—*lake* WI-6
Tepee Lakes—*lake* MN-6
Tepee Lakes—*lake* UT-8
Tepee Lodge—*locale* WY-8
Tepee Lookout Tower—*locale* MI-6
Tepee Mtn—*summit* CO-8
Tepee Mtn—*summit* (5) MT-8
Tepee Mtn—*summit* (2) OK-5
Tepee Mtn—*summit* SD-7
Tepee Mtns—*range* UT-8
Tepee Mtns—*range* WY-8
Tepee Number One Spring—*spring* SD-7
Tepee Park—*flat* (2) CO-8
Tepee Pass—*gap* WY-8
*Tepee Peak* ID-8
Tepee Peak—*summit* ID-8
Tepee Peak—*summit* SD-7
Tepee Point—*summit* MT-8
Tepee Point—*summit* UT-8
Tepee Pole Canyon—*valley* TX-5
*Tepee Pole Creek* WY-8
Tepee Pole Draw—*stream* WY-8
*Tepee Pole Fork* WY-8
Tepee Pole Ridge—*ridge* MT-8
Tepee Pole Spring—*spring* MT-8
Tepee Pond—*lake* RI-1
Tepee Ranch—*locale* CO-8
Tepee Ranger Station—*locale* SD-7
Tepee Ridge Trail—*trail* MT-8
Tepee Ring Creek—*stream* WY-8
Tepee Rock—*summit* NV-8
Tepee Rock (historical)—*summit* NV-8
Tepee Rocks—*summit* NV-8
Tepees, The—*pillar* AZ-5
Tepee Spring—*spring* MT-8
Tepee Spring—*spring* (2) OR-9
Tepee Spring—*spring* SD-7
Tepee Springs—*spring* ID-8
Tepee Springs—*spring* SD-7
Tepee Springs—*spring* WA-9
Tepee Summit—*summit* ID-8
Tepee Tank—*reservoir* TX-5
Tepee Windmill—*locale* TX-5
Tepeguaje Ranch—*locale* TX-5
*Tepehemus Branch* NJ-2
Tepehemus Brook—*stream* NJ-2
Tepeh Towers—*ridge* WA-9
**Tepetate**—*pop pl* LA-4
Tepetate Oil and Gas Field—*oilfield* LA-4
*Teplan Branch* LA-4
*Teplan Creek* LA-4
Tepona Point—*cape* CA-9
Tepo Ridge—*ridge* CA-9
*Tepper Elementary School* MS-4
Tepper Sch—*school* MS-4
Teppim Cem—*cemetery* TX-5
**Tepungan**—*pop pl* GU-9
Tepungan Channel—*channel* GU-9
Tepusquet—*civil* CA-9
Tepusquet Canyon—*valley* CA-9
Tepusquet Creek—*stream* CA-9
Tepusquet Peak—*summit* CA-9
Tequa—*locale* AZ-5
Tequa Creek—*stream* KS-7
*Tequamenau* MI-6
*Tequamenon Bay* MI-6
*Tequamenon Island* MI-6
*Tequamenon River* MI-6
Tequa Spring—*spring* AZ-5
Tequepis—*civil* CA-9
Tequepis Canyon—*valley* CA-9
Tequepis Point—*cape* CA-9
Tequepis Trail—*trail* CA-9
Tequesquite Arroyo—*stream* CA-9
Tequesquite Canyon—*valley* NM-5
Tequesquite Creek—*stream* NM-5
Tequesquite Creek—*stream* TX-5
Tequesquite Spring—*spring* TX-5
Tequesquito Arroyo—*stream* CA-9
**Tequesta**—*pop pl* FL-3
Tequesta Plaza (Shop Ctr)—*locale* FL-3
Tequila Tank—*reservoir* (2) AZ-5
Tequileras Windmill—*locale* TX-5
Tequios, Loma de los—*summit* TX-5
Tequisquita Slough—*stream* CA-9
Teran Basin—*basin* AZ-5
TE Ranch—*locale* WY-8
T E Ranch—*locale* WY-8
T E Ranch HQ—*hist pl* WY-8
**Tera North**—*pop pl* IN-6
Teran Wash—*stream* AZ-5
**Tera Rosa**—*pop pl* WV-2
Terbilon Island—*island* AK-9
Tercero (Barrio)—*fmr MCD* PR-3
Tercett Lake—*lake* NE-7
Tercia Pond—*lake* NY-2
Tercio—*locale* CO-8
Tercio Cem—*cemetery* CO-8
Tercio Mine—*mine* CO-8
*Terebebai* PW-9
*Terebebai To* PW-9
Tereherst Hollow—*valley* AR-4
Terell Branch—*stream* MO-7
Terence Lake—*lake* WA-9
Terentiev Lake—*lake* AK-9
**Tererro**—*pop pl* NM-5
**Teresa**—*pop pl* (3) PR-3
*Teresa Branch* LA-4
Teresa Branch—*stream* LA-4
Teresa Creek—*stream* AK-9
Teresa Lake—*lake* NV-8
Teresa Tank—*reservoir* AZ-5
**Terese**—*pop pl* AL-4
*Teresea Bay* FL-3
Teresita—*locale* KY-4
Teresita—*locale* MO-7
Teresita—*locale* NC-3
Teresita—*locale* OK-5
Teresita Cem—*cemetery* OK-5
Terge Creek—*stream* MT-8
Tergeson Flats—*flat* UT-8
**Terhune**—*pop pl* IN-6
Terhune (abandoned)—*locale* WY-8
Terhune Cem—*cemetery* IN-6
Terhune-Gardner-Lindenmeyr House—*hist pl* NJ-2
Terhune-Hopper House—*hist pl* NJ-2
Terhune House—*hist pl* NJ-2
Terhune Park—*park* NJ-2
Terhune-Ranlett House—*hist pl* NJ-2
Terhune Run—*stream* NJ-2
Terhune Spring—*spring* KY-4
Teri Lake—*lake* WY-8
Terimate Tank—*reservoir* AZ-5
*teris Cove* NY-2
*Terles River* NJ-2
*Terlinga* TX-5
*Terlingo* TX-5
Terlingua—*locale* TX-5
Terlingua Abaja—*locale* TX-5
Terlingua Creek—*stream* TX-5
Terlingua Ranch Lodge—*locale* TX-5
Terlingua Sinkhole—*basin* TX-5
Terlingua Trail—*trail* TX-5
**Terlton**—*pop pl* OK-5
Terlton Cem—*cemetery* OK-5
Terman JHS—*school* CA-9
Terman Ridge—*ridge* TN-4
*Terminal* CT-1
**Terminal**—*pop pl* AK-9
**Terminal**—*pop pl* PA-2
**Terminal**—*pop pl* UT-8
Terminal—*uninc pl* NY-2
*Terminal Annex* CO-8
**Terminal Annex**—*pop pl* MT-8
**Terminal Annex**—*pop pl* TX-5
Terminal Annex—*post sta* WA-9
Terminal Annex—*uninc pl* CA-9
Terminal Arcade—*hist pl* IN-6
Terminal Bldg—*hist pl* KS-7
Terminal Bldg—*hist pl* NE-7
Terminal Bridge—*other* MO-7
Terminal Channel—*channel* FL-3
Terminal Channel—*channel* NJ-2
*Terminal City* OR-9
**Terminal City (historical)**—*pop pl* OR-9
**Terminal City (subdivision)**—*pop pl* OR-9
Terminal Geyser—*geyser* CA-9
Terminal Hotel—*hist pl* AR-4
Terminal Island—*island* CA-9
Terminal Island—*post sta* CA-9
Terminal Island Coast Guard Base—*military* CA-9
*Terminal Junction* IL-6
*Terminal Junction* OH-6
**Terminal Junction**—*pop pl* WV-2
Terminal Junction—*uninc pl* AL-4
Terminal Monument Creek—*stream* MT-8
Terminal Monument Creek—*stream* WY-8
Terminal Newark One Helistop—*airport* NJ-2
Terminal No 1—*locale* OR-9
Terminal Ocean County—*airport* NJ-2
Terminal Park—*park* IL-6
Terminal Park Sch—*school* WA-9
Terminal RR Association—*other* MO-7
Terminal Rsvr—*reservoir* CA-9
Terminal Rsvr—*reservoir* UT-8
Terminal Station—*hist pl* KS-7
Terminal Station—*hist pl* TN-4
Terminal Warehouse—*hist pl* MD-2
Terminal Warehouse Bldg—*hist pl* AR-4
Termination Point—*cape* (2) AK-9
Termination Point—*cape* WA-9
Termination Point—*summit* WA-9
**Terminous**—*pop pl* CA-9
Terminous Culling Chute—*hist pl* CA-9
**Terminous Junction**—*pop pl* CA-9
Terminous Tract—*civil* CA-9
*Termintin Creek* CO-8
Terminus—*locale* CA-9
Terminus Dam—*dam* CA-9
*Terminus Reservoir* CA-9
**Termo**—*pop pl* CA-9
Termo Buttes—*summit* CA-9
Ternell Sch—*school* LA-4
Terneros Creek—*stream* TX-5
Terneur-Hutton House—*hist pl* NY-2
Terney Cem—*cemetery* IA-7
Tern Island—*island* MA-1
Tern Island Sanctuary—*park* MA-1
Tern Keys—*island* FL-3
Tern Lake—*lake* AK-9
Tern Lake—*lake* MN-6
Tern Lake—*lake* WY-8
Tern Lake Trail—*trail* WY-8
Tern Mtn—*summit* AK-9
*Teroa* MP-9
*Teroda Creek* WA-9
*Teroken, Mount* FM-9
*Teroken-Berg* FM-9
Teroy Cem—*cemetery* MO-7
Terpena Hill—*summit* ND-7
**Terpening Corners**—*pop pl* NY-2
Terpinning Drain—*canal* MI-6
**Terra**—*pop pl* UT-8
Terra Agua Lakes—*lake* OH-6
**Terra Alta**—*pop pl* WV-2
Terra Alta Dam—*dam* TN-4
Terra Alta Lake—*reservoir* TN-4
Terra Alta Lake—*reservoir* WV-2
**Terra Bella**—*pop pl* CA-9
Terra Bella (CCD)—*cens area* CA-9
*Terra Buena* CA-9
**Terrace**—*pop pl* MN-6
**Terrace**—*pop pl* PA-2
**Terrace**—*pop pl* TX-5
*Terrace, The* IL-6
Terrace, The—*cliff* UT-8
Terrace, The—*hist pl* CO-8
Terrace, The—*locale* PA-2
**Terrace, The**—*pop pl* NY-2
**Terrace Acres**—*pop pl* PA-2
**Terrace Acres (subdivision)**—*pop pl* AL-4
Terrace Ave Playground—*park* CA-9
Terrace Bay—*bay* IN-6
**Terrace Bay**—*pop pl* IN-6
Terrace Beach—*beach* WI-6
*Terrace Brook* NJ-2
Terrace Campground—*locale* UT-8
Terrace Canyon—*valley* ID-8
Terrace Cem—*cemetery* TX-5
Terrace Cem—*cemetery* UT-8
**Terrace Circle Subdivision**—*pop pl* UT-8
Terrace Country Club—*other* MN-6
Terrace Creek—*stream* (2) AK-9
Terrace Creek—*stream* CA-9
Terrace Creek—*stream* ID-8
Terrace Creek—*stream* WY-8
Terrace Creek Camp—*locale* CA-9
Terraced Falls—*falls* WY-8
Terraced Hills—*summit* NV-8
Terrace Falls—*falls* MT-8
**Terrace Falls Condominium**—*pop pl* UT-8
*Terrace Garden* NC-3
**Terrace Gardens**—*pop pl* MD-2
**Terrace Gardens**—*pop pl* NC-3
Terrace Gardens Nursing Home—*hospital* TX-5
Terrace Grove Cem—*cemetery* NM-5
Terrace Guard Station—*locale* NV-8
Terrace Heights—*locale* WA-9
**Terrace Heights**—*pop pl* NY-2
Terrace Hill—*hist pl* IA-7
Terrace Hill—*summit* CA-9
Terrace Hill Cem—*cemetery* TN-4
Terrace Hill Cem—*cemetery* UT-8
Terrace Hills Sch—*school* CA-9
Terrace Hist Dist—*hist pl* MN-6
**Terra Ceia**—*pop pl* FL-3
**Terra Ceia**—*pop pl* NC-3
*Terraceia Bay* FL-3
Terra Ceia Bay—*bay* FL-3
*Terraceia cutoff* FL-3
*Terraceia Island* FL-3
Terra Ceia Island—*island* FL-3
Terra Ceia Junction (railroad junction)—*locale* FL-3
*Terraceia Point* FL-3
Terra Ceia Point—*cape* FL-3
*Terra Ceia River* FL-3
Terra Ceia River—*gut* FL-3
Terrace Island—*island* AK-9
*Terrace Lake* IN-6
Terrace Lake—*lake* (2) CA-9
Terrace Lake—*lake* (2) MT-8
Terrace Lake—*reservoir* IN-6
Terrace Lake—*reservoir* NJ-2
Terrace Lake Dam—*dam* IN-6
Terrace Lake Dam—*dam* NJ-2
*Terrace Lake Gardens* MO-7
Terrace Lake Park—*park* OH-6
Terrace Lakes—*lake* ID-8
Terrace Lakes—*lake* MT-8
Terrace Lakes—*lake* WA-9
Terrace Lawn Cem—*cemetery* MN-6
Terrace Main Canal—*canal* CO-8
Terrace Meadows—*flat* WY-8
Terrace Mill Hist Dist—*hist pl* MN-6
*Terrace Mountains* UT-8
Terrace Mtn—*summit* AK-9
Terrace Mtn—*summit* NH-1
Terrace Mtn—*summit* (2) NY-2
Terrace Mtn—*summit* PA-2
Terrace Mtn—*summit* UT-8
Terrace Mtn—*summit* WA-9
Terrace Mtn—*summit* (2) WY-8
Terrace Park—*park* CA-9
Terrace Park—*park* FL-3
Terrace Park—*park* (3) MN-6
Terrace Park—*park* SD-7
Terrace Park—*park* WI-6
**Terrace Park**—*pop pl* NY-2
**Terrace Park**—*pop pl* OH-6
Terrace Park Cem—*cemetery* CA-9
Terrace Park Country Club—*other* OH-6
**Terrace Park (subdivision)**—*pop pl* MS-4
*Terrace Pass* WY-8
Terrace Plaza (Shop Ctr)—*locale* FL-3
Terrace Point—*cape* (2) CA-9
Terrace Point—*cape* MN-6
Terrace Point—*cape* WY-8
Terrace Point—*cliff* WY-8
Terrace Point—*summit* AK-9
Terrace Pond—*lake* NJ-2
Terrace Rsvr—*reservoir* CO-8
Terraces at Highland Oaks (Shop Ctr), The—*locale* NC-3
Terrace Sch—*school* CA-9
Terrace Sch—*school* NY-2
**Terraces Condominium, The**—*pop pl* UT-8
Terrace Shop Ctr—*locale* MA-1
Terrace (Site)—*locale* UT-8
**Terraces Mount Olympus Condominium**—*pop pl* UT-8
*Terraces of Rose Park Condominium* UT-8
**Terraces of Rose Park Condominium, The**—*pop pl* UT-8
*Terrace Spit* UT-8
Terrace Spring—*spring* WY-8
Terrace Springs—*spring* CA-9
Terraces Recreation Site—*locale* NV-8
**Terrace Subdivision**—*pop pl* UT-8
Terrace View—*locale* TN-4
Terrace View Ch—*church* VA-3
Terrace View Park—*park* IL-6
Terrace View Park—*park* WA-9
Terrace View Resort—*locale* TN-4
Terrace View Sch—*school* CA-9
**Terrace View (subdivision)**—*pop pl* AL-4
**Terrace View Subdivision**—*pop pl* UT-8
Terrace Well—*well* UT-8
Terracina—*hist pl* PA-2
Terra Cotta—*locale* CA-9
Terra Cotta—*locale* IL-6
Terra Cotta—*locale* KS-7
**Terra Cotta**—*pop pl* DC-2
**Terra Cotta**—*pop pl* GA-3
**Terra Cotta**—*pop pl* NC-3
Terra Cotta Bldg—*hist pl* NY-2
Terra Cotta Cem—*cemetery* IL-6
Terra Cotta Cem—*cemetery* KS-7
Terra Cotta Mountains—*range* AK-9
Terra Cotta Sch—*school* IL-6
**Terra Heights**—*pop pl* KS-7
Terra Heights Baptist Ch—*church* KS-7
**Terral**—*pop pl* OK-5
Terral Cem—*cemetery* OK-5
**Terra Linda**—*pop pl* CA-9
Terra Linda HS—*school* CA-9
Terra Linda (P.O.)—*uninc pl* CA-9
Terra Linda Sch—*school* CA-9
Terra Linda Sch—*school* UT-8
**Terra Linda Subdivision**—*pop pl* UT-8
**Terra Loma**—*pop pl* CA-9
**Terra Mana**—*pop pl* FL-3
**Terra Mar**—*pop pl* FL-3
Terramuggus, Lake—*lake* CT-1
Terrangel—*bay* PW-9
*Terranova* MP-9
Terranova (Barrio)—*fmr MCD* PR-3
Terra Nova HS—*school* CA-9
*Terrapen Creek* VA-3
Terrapin—*locale* KY-4
Terrapin Bay—*bay* FL-3
Terrapin Branch—*stream* AR-4
Terrapin Branch—*stream* (3) KY-4
Terrapin Branch—*stream* MD-2
Terrapin Branch—*stream* NC-3
Terrapin Branch—*stream* TN-4
Terrapin Branch—*stream* TX-5
Terrapin Cave—*cave* AL-4
Terrapin Cove—*valley* AR-4
*Terrapin Creek* KY-4
*Terrapin Creek* NC-3
*Terrapin Creek* TN-4
Terrapin Creek—*channel* MD-2
Terrapin Creek—*stream* AL-4
Terrapin Creek—*stream* (3) AR-4
Terrapin Creek—*stream* FL-3
Terrapin Creek—*stream* GA-3
Terrapin Creek—*stream* KS-7
Terrapin Creek—*stream* (2) KY-4
Terrapin Creek—*stream* (2) MS-4
Terrapin Creek—*stream* MO-7
Terrapin Creek—*stream* (3) NC-3
Terrapin Creek—*stream* (3) OK-5
Terrapin Creek—*stream* SC-3
Terrapin Creek—*stream* (3) TN-4
Terrapin Creek—*stream* (2) TX-5
Terrapin Creek—*stream* (2) VA-3
Terrapin Creek Bay—*bay* NC-3
*Terrapin Creek Lake Number 14* AL-4
Terrapin Creek Lake Number 15—*reservoir* AL-4
Terrapin Creek Lake Number 17—*reservoir* AL-4
Terrapin Creek Lake Number 21—*reservoir* AL-4
Terrapin Creek Lake Number 22—*reservoir* AL-4
Terrapin Creek Lake Number 31—*reservoir* AL-4
Terrapin Creek Lake Number 33—*reservoir* AL-4
Terrapin Creek Lake Number 8—*reservoir* AL-4
Terrapin Creek Point—*cape* NC-3
Terrapin Creek Watershed Dam Number 14—*dam* AL-4
Terrapin Creek Watershed Dam Number 15—*dam* AL-4
Terrapin Creek Watershed Dam Number 17—*dam* AL-4
Terrapin Creek Watershed Dam Number 21—*dam* AL-4
Terrapin Creek Watershed Dam Number 22—*dam* AL-4
Terrapin Creek Watershed Dam Number 31—*dam* AL-4
Terrapin Creek Watershed Dam Number 33—*dam* AL-4
Terrapin Creek Watershed Dam Number 6—*dam* AL-4
Terrapin Creek Watershed Dam Number 8—*dam* AL-4
Terrapin Creek Watershed Dam Number 9—*dam* AL-4
Terrapin Gut—*gut* DE-2
Terrapin Gut—*gut* NJ-2
Terrapin Hill—*summit* AL-4
Terrapin Hill—*summit* DE-2
Terrapin Hill—*summit* TX-5
Terrapin Hill Overlook—*locale* VA-3
Terrapin Hills Golf Estates—*other* AL-4
**Terrapin Hill (subdivision)**—*pop pl* MS-4
Terrapin Hollow—*valley* AR-4
Terrapin Hollow—*valley* MO-7
Terrapin Hollow—*valley* OH-6
Terrapin Hollow—*valley* TN-4
Terrapin Island—*island* AL-4
Terrapin Key—*island* FL-3
*Terrapin Lake* MN-6
Terrapin Lake—*lake* KS-7
Terrapin Lake—*lake* MN-6
Terrapin Landing—*locale* NC-3
*Terrapin Mountain* AL-4
Terrapin Mountain Overlook—*locale* VA-3
Terrapin Mountain Trail—*trail* VA-3
Terrapin Mtn—*summit* MS-4
Terrapin Mtn—*summit* NC-3
Terrapin Mtn—*summit* VA-3
Terrapin Neck—*cape* WV-2
Terrapin Pass—*gap* AZ-5
Terrapin Point—*cape* FL-3
Terrapin Point—*cape* GA-3
Terrapin Point—*cape* NY-2
Terrapin Point—*cape* (2) NC-3
Terrapin Point—*cape* VA-3
Terrapin Pond—*stream* DE-2
Terrapin Reef—*bar* LA-4
Terrapin Ridge—*ridge* IL-6
Terrapin Ridge Cem—*cemetery* IL-6
Terrapin Run—*stream* MD-2
Terrapin Run—*stream* TN-4
Terrapin Sand Cove—*bay* MD-2
Terrapin Sand Point—*cape* MD-2
Terrapin Sch (historical)—*school* TN-4
Terrapin Skin Creek—*stream* MS-4
Terrapin Spring—*spring* MO-7
Terrapin Swamp—*stream* VA-3
Terrapin Thorofare—*channel* NJ-2
*Terrarin Branch* MO-7
Terra Rubra—*hist pl* MD-2
Terrasas Well—*well* NM-5
*Terrasilla Bay* FL-3
**Terra Subdivision**—*pop pl* UT-8
Terra Tomah Mtn—*summit* CO-8
**Terraville**—*pop pl* SD-7
*Terra Vista* IN-6
Terra Vista Archeol District—*hist pl* OH-6
Terra Vista Ch—*church* TN-4
Terrazo Switch—*locale* NC-3
Terre Aux Boeufs, Bayou—*stream* LA-4
Terre-Beau Bayou—*gut* LA-4
Terre Blanc, Bayou—*stream* LA-4
Terre Bleue Creek—*stream* MO-7
**Terrebonne**—*pop pl* MN-6
**Terrebonne**—*pop pl* OR-9
Terrebonne, Bayou—*stream* LA-4
Terrebonne Bay—*bay* LA-4
Terrebonne Cem—*cemetery* OR-9
Terrebonne Creek—*stream* MN-6
Terrebonne HS—*school* LA-4
Terrebonne Island—*island* LA-4
Terrebonne Lafourche Drainage Canal—*canal* LA-4
**Terrebonne Parish**—*pop pl* LA-4
Terrebonne Sch—*school* OR-9
**Terrebonne (Township of)**—*pop pl* MN-6
Terre Chene Blanc—*ridge* LA-4
**Terre Coupee**—*pop pl* IN-6
**Terre DuLac**—*pop pl* MO-7
**Terre Du Lac**—*pop pl* MO-7
*Terre Hall* IN-6
Terre Haute—*locale* MO-7
**Terre Haute**—*pop pl* IL-6
**Terre Haute**—*pop pl* IN-6
**Terre Haute**—*pop pl* IA-7
**Terre Haute**—*pop pl* OH-6
Terre Haute Boys Club Lake—*reservoir* IN-6
Terre Haute Boys Club Lake Dam—*dam* IN-6
Terre Haute Federal Penitentiary—*other* IN-6
Terre Haute Plantation—*locale* LA-4
Terre Haute Post Office and Federal Bldg—*hist pl* IN-6
Terre Haute Saddle Club—*other* IN-6
**Terre Haute (Township of)**—*pop pl* IL-6
**Terre Hill**—*pop pl* PA-2
Terre Hill—*summit* NY-2
Terre Hill Borough—*civil* PA-2
*Terrel* TX-5
Terrel Canyon—*valley* CO-8
Terrel Ch—*church* LA-4
Terrel Ditch—*canal* CO-8
*Terrel Gap* NC-3
Terrell—*locale* GA-3
Terrell—*locale* MS-4
Terrell—*locale* MO-7
**Terrell**—*pop pl* FL-3
**Terrell**—*pop pl* NC-3
**Terrell**—*pop pl* TN-4
**Terrell**—*pop pl* TX-5
Terrell, Lake—*lake* WA-9
Terrell, Mary Church, House—*hist pl* DC-2
Terrell, William, Homeplace—*hist pl* GA-3
Terrell Acad—*school* (2) GA-3
Terrell and Ford Ditch—*canal* CO-8
Terrell Bay—*basin* SC-3
*Terrell Branch* TN-4
Terrell Branch—*stream* (4) TN-4
Terrell Branch—*stream* TX-5
Terrell (CCD)—*cens area* TX-5
Terrell Cem—*cemetery* (2) AL-4
Terrell Cem—*cemetery* AR-4
Terrell Cem—*cemetery* (3) KY-4
Terrell Cem—*cemetery* (5) MS-4
Terrell Cem—*cemetery* MO-7
Terrell Cem—*cemetery* (2) TN-4
Terrell Cem—*cemetery* (3) TX-5
**Terrell (County)**—*pop pl* GA-3
**Terrell (County)**—*pop pl* TX-5
Terrell County Courthouse—*hist pl* GA-3
Terrell Cove—*valley* NC-3
Terrell Cove—*valley* TN-4
*Terrell Creek* NC-3
Terrell Creek—*stream* CO-8
Terrell Creek—*stream* KY-4
Terrell Creek—*stream* (2) MS-4
Terrell Creek—*stream* MO-7
Terrell Creek—*stream* WA-9
Terrell Creek Sch—*school* KY-4
Terrell Creek Tabernacle—*church* KY-4
**Terrell Crossroad**—*pop pl* SC-3
Terrell Ditch—*canal* NM-5
*Terrell-Farrell Cemetery* MS-4
Terrell Fork—*stream* KY-4
Terrell Gap—*gap* NC-3
**Terrell Hills**—*pop pl* TX-5
Terrell Hist Dist—*hist pl* NC-3
Terrell Hole—*reservoir* NV-8
Terrell Hollow—*valley* AR-4
Terrell Hollow—*valley* (2) TN-4
Terrell HS—*school* TX-5
Terrell Island—*island* WI-6
Terrell JHS—*school* DC-2
Terrell JHS—*school* TX-5
Terrell Lake—*lake* OK-5
Terrell Lake—*lake* TX-5
Terrell Mine—*mine* NV-8
Terrell Plaza—*locale* TX-5
Terrell Point Oil Field—*oilfield* TX-5
Terrell Post Office (historical)—*building* TN-4
Terrell Ranch—*locale* TX-5
Terrell-Reuss Streets Hist Dist—*hist pl* TX-5
Terrell Ridge—*ridge* WV-2
Terrell River—*stream* NY-2
Terrells—*locale* NC-3
Terrell Sch—*school* CA-9
Terrell Sch—*school* IL-6
Terrell Sch—*school* KY-4
Terrell Sch—*school* TX-5
Terrells Chapel—*church* NC-3
Terrell Sch (historical)—*school* TN-4
Terrells Corral Creek—*stream* ID-8
Terrells Creek—*stream* NC-3
Terrells Creek Ch—*church* NC-3
**Terrells Crossroads**—*pop pl* SC-3
**Terrells (historical)**—*pop pl* MS-4
Terrells Millpond (Ways Millpond)—*swamp* GA-3
Terrells Mtn—*summit* NC-3
Terrell South (CCD)—*cens area* TX-5
Terrells Spring—*spring* ID-8
Terrell Station—*locale* TX-5
**Terrell Store**—*pop pl* VA-3
**Terrell Subdivision**—*pop pl* UT-8
Terrell Times Star Bldg—*hist pl* TX-5
**Terrell Wells**—*pop pl* TX-5
Terrell Wells (RR name San Jose)—*uninc pl* TX-5
Terrels Gun Club—*other* CA-9
Terrel Wells JHS—*school* TX-5
*Terrence Place* MS-4
Terrene Landing—*locale* MS-4
Terre Noire Creek—*stream* AR-4
Terre Noire (Township of)—*fmr MCD* AR-4
Terrero—*park* NM-5
Terrero Draw—*valley* NM-5
Terre Rouge Creek—*stream* AR-4
Terresa, Lake—*reservoir* GA-3
**Terrestria**—*pop pl* NJ-2
**Terreton**—*pop pl* ID-8
*Terre Town* IN-6
**Terre Town**—*pop pl* IN-6
Terre Town Elem Sch—*school* IN-6
Terrett Butte—*summit* MT-8
Terrett Draw—*valley* TX-5
*Terrible Creek* CO-8

Terrible Creek—*stream* CO-8
Terrible Creek—*stream* MS-4
Terrible Creek—*stream* MO-7
Terrible Creek—*stream* NC-3
Terrible Creek—*stream* SC-3
Terrible Creek—*stream* VA-3
Terrible Mine—*mine* CO-8
Terrible Mtn—*summit* AK-9
Terrible Mtn—*summit* CO-8
Terrible Mtn—*summit* VT-1
**Terril**—*pop pl* IA-7
*Terril Cemetery* IN-6
**Terrill**—*pop pl* KY-4
**Terrill**—*pop pl* WI-6
Terrill, Mount—*summit* UT-8
Terrill Beach—*beach* WA-9
*Terrill Branch* TN-4
Terrill Branch—*stream* IN-6
Terrill Branch—*stream* KY-4
Terrill Cem—*cemetery* IN-6
Terrill Clay Pit—*mine* MO-7
Terrill Creek—*stream* TN-4
Terrill Draw—*valley* ID-8
Terrill Gorge—*valley* VT-1
Terrill Hill—*summit* VT-1
Terrill Hollow—*valley* (2) MO-7
Terrill Lake—*lake* MS-4
Terrill Mtns—*summit* NV-8
Terrill Ridge—*ridge* IN-6
Terrill Ridge Road—*reservoir* IN-6
Terrill Sch—*school* MO-7
Terrill Well—*locale* NM-5
*Terril Ridge* IN-6
*Terril Ridge Pond* IN-6
Territorial Capitol of Former Indiana Territory—*hist pl* IN-6
Territorial Commercial District—*hist pl* OK-5
Territorial Government Formation Site Historical Monmt—*park* AZ-5
Territorial Sch—*school* MI-6
*Territorial Statehouse* UT-8
*Territorial Statehouses State Park* UT-8
*Territorial Statehouse State Historical Monument* UT-8
Territorial-State Prison—*hist pl* MN-6
Territory of Cimarron (historical)—*civil* OK-5
*Territory of the Pacific Islands* MP-9
Territory Prairie—*swamp* GA-3
**Terri Wood (subdivision)**—*pop pl* AL-4
Terror, Mount—*summit* WA-9
Terror Bay—*bay* AK-9
Terror Creek—*stream* CO-8
Terror Creek—*stream* WA-9
Terror Creek Rsvr—*reservoir* CO-8
Terror Glacier—*glacier* WA-9
Terror Gulch—*valley* ID-8
Terror Lake—*lake* AK-9
Terror Lake—*lake* NY-2
Terror River—*stream* AK-9
Terror Trail—*trail* CO-8
*Terruno Canyon* AZ-5
Terry—*locale* SD-7
Terry—*locale* TX-5
Terry—*other* GA-3
**Terry**—*pop pl* IN-6
**Terry**—*pop pl* LA-4
**Terry**—*pop pl* MS-4
**Terry**—*pop pl* MO-7
**Terry**—*pop pl* MT-8
**Terry**—*pop pl* TN-4
**Terry**—*pop pl* WV-2
Terry, A. P., House—*hist pl* NC-3
Terry, Bayou—*stream* LA-4
Terry, Lake—*lake* FL-3
Terry, Lake—*lake* WY-8
Terry, William L., House—*hist pl* AR-4
Terry Acad—*school* MS-4
**Terry Acres**—*pop pl* OH-6
Terry Allen Drain—*canal* MI-6
Terry Andrae State Park—*park* WI-6
Terry and Terry Number 1 Claims Mine—*mine* SD-7
Terryann Sch—*school* MT-8
Terry Anticline—*summit* WY-8
Terry Benches—*bench* NV-8
Terry Block Bldg—*hist pl* AR-4
*Terry Branch* OK-5
*Terry Branch* TN-4
Terry Branch—*stream* (5) KY-4
Terry Branch—*stream* MD-2
Terry Branch—*stream* NC-3
Terry Branch—*stream* TN-4
Terry Branch—*stream* TX-5
Terry Branch—*stream* VA-3
Terry Branch—*stream* (2) WV-2
Terry Brook—*stream* CT-1
Terry Brook—*stream* VT-1
Terry Brook Pond—*reservoir* MA-1
Terry Brook Pond Dam—*dam* MA-1
Terry Canyon—*valley* CA-9
Terry Canyon—*valley* NM-5
Terry Cave—*cave* AL-4
Terry Cave—*cave* TN-4
Terry Cem—*cemetery* (2) AL-4
Terry Cem—*cemetery* AR-4
Terry Cem—*cemetery* IN-6
Terry Cem—*cemetery* (2) KY-4
Terry Cem—*cemetery* (4) MS-4
Terry Cem—*cemetery* (2) MO-7
Terry Cem—*cemetery* NY-2
Terry Cem—*cemetery* (5) TN-4
Terry Cem—*cemetery* TX-5
Terry Cem—*cemetery* WV-2
Terry Chapel—*church* KY-4
Terry Chapel—*locale* TX-5
Terry Clove—*valley* NY-2
**Terry (County)**—*pop pl* TX-5
Terry Cove—*bay* AL-4
*Terry Creek* AR-4
*Terry Creek* LA-4
*Terry Creek* UT-8
Terry Creek—*channel* GA-3
**Terry Creek**—*pop pl* SC-3
**Terry Creek**—*pop pl* TN-4
Terry Creek—*stream* IL-6
Terry Creek—*stream* (2) MS-4
Terry Creek—*stream* NC-3
Terry Creek—*stream* OK-5
Terry Creek—*stream* PA-2
Terry Creek—*stream* SC-3
Terry Creek—*stream* TN-4
Terry Creek—*stream* TX-5
Terry Creek Baptist Ch—*church* MS-4
Terry Creek Cem—*cemetery* MS-4
Terry Creek Ch—*church* SC-3
Terry Creek Sch—*school* TN-4
Terry Crossroads—*locale* AL-4
**Terry Dale Subdivision**—*pop pl* UT-8
Terrydiddle, Mount—*summit* MA-1
Terry Ditch—*canal* UT-8
Terry Drain—*canal* MI-6
Terry Draw—*valley* NM-5
Terry Draw—*valley* (2) WY-8
**Terry Estates**—*pop pl* TN-4
**Terry Estates Subdivision**—*pop pl* UT-8
Terry Flat—*flat* AZ-5
Terry Flat—*flat* UT-8
**Terry Fork**—*pop pl* NC-3
Terry Fork—*stream* (3) KY-4
Terry Fork—*stream* NC-3
Terry Gap—*gap* (2) NC-3
Terry Grove Baptist Ch—*church* MS-4
Terry-Hayden House—*hist pl* CT-1
**Terry Heights**—*pop pl* (2) AL-4
Terry Heights Elem Sch—*school* AL-4
Terry Hill—*summit* OK-5
Terry Hill Cem—*cemetery* NY-2
Terry Hill Cem—*cemetery* OH-6
Terry Hollow—*valley* MO-7
Terry Hollow—*valley* TN-4
Terry Hollow—*valley* TX-5
Terry House—*hist pl* OK-5
Terry HS—*school* MS-4
Terry Junction—*locale* WV-2
Terry Knob—*summit* TN-4
Terry Lake—*lake* CA-9
Terry Lake—*lake* IN-6
Terry Lake—*lake* (2) MI-6
Terry Lake—*lake* MN-6
Terry Lake—*lake* TX-5
Terry Lake—*reservoir* (2) CO-8
Terry Lake Inlet—*canal* CO-8
Terry Lake Park—*park* MI-6
Terry Lateral—*canal* CO-8
Terry Main Canal—*canal* MT-8
**Terry Manor**—*pop pl* KY-4
Terry Methodist Ch—*church* MS-4
Terry Mill Creek—*stream* AL-4
Terry Mtn—*summit* NY-2
Terry-Mulford House—*hist pl* NY-2
Terry North—*cens area* MT-8
Terry Number One Tank—*reservoir* AZ-5
Terry Number Three Tank—*reservoir* AZ-5
Terry Number Two Tank—*reservoir* AZ-5
Terry Park—*park* FL-3
Terry Peak—*summit* SD-7
Terry Peak—*summit* WY-8
Terry Peak Camp—*locale* WY-8
Terry Point—*cape* NY-2
Terry Point Boat Dock—*locale* TN-4
Terry Point Campground—*locale* TN-4
Terry Pond—*lake* SC-3
Terry Pond—*reservoir* (2) NC-3
Terry Post Office—*building* MS-4
Terry Post Office (historical)—*building* TN-4
Terry Ranch—*locale* AZ-5
Terry Ranch—*locale* CA-9
Terry Ranch—*locale* NM-5
Terry Ranch—*locale* OR-9
Terry Ranch—*locale* WY-8
Terry Ridge—*ridge* UT-8
Terry Rsvr—*reservoir* OR-9
Terry Rsvr—*reservoir* WY-8
Terry Sanctified Ch—*church* MS-4
Terry Sanford HS—*school* NC-3
Terrys Bridge—*bridge* VA-3
Terry Scenic View—*locale* MT-8
Terry Sch—*school* AR-4
Terry Sch—*school* CO-8
Terry Sch—*school* KS-7
Terry Sch—*school* KY-4
Terry Sch—*school* SC-3
Terry Sch—*school* TX-5
Terry Sch—*school* WV-2
Terry Sch (abandoned)—*school* MO-7
Terrys Chapel—*church* MS-4
**Terrys Chapel**—*pop pl* TX-5
*Terrys Chapel Congregational Methodist Ch* MS-4
Terry Sch (historical)—*school* AL-4
Terry Sch (historical)—*school* MO-7
*Terrys Corner* NY-2
Terrys Corner—*locale* WA-9
**Terrys Corners**—*pop pl* NY-2
*Terry's Creek* NY-2
Terrys Creek—*locale* MS-4
Terrys Creek—*stream* LA-4
Terrys Creek—*stream* MS-4
Terrys Creek—*stream* NY-2
Terrys Creek—*stream* (2) VA-3
Terrys Creek Cem—*cemetery* MS-4
*Terrys Creek Ch* MS-4
Terrys Creek Ch—*church* MS-4
Terrys Day Nursery—*school* FL-3
**Terrys Fork**—*pop pl* VA-3
Terry Sheep Camp—*locale* MT-8
Terrys Landing (historical)—*locale* MS-4
*Terrys Mill* AL-4
Terry South—*cens area* MT-8
*Terrys Peak* SD-7
Terrys Plain—*flat* CT-1
*Terry's Point* NY-2
Terry Spring—*spring* IL-6
Terry Spring—*spring* MS-4
Terry Spring—*spring* OR-9
Terry Spring—*spring* TX-5
Terry Spring—*spring* UT-8
Terry Square—*locale* CT-1
Terrys Run—*stream* VA-3
Terrys Stand (historical)—*locale* TN-4
Terry Station—*locale* SD-7
**Terry Subdivision**—*pop pl* TN-4
Terrysville Cem—*cemetery* TX-5
Terry Tank—*reservoir* (2) NM-5
Terry Thompson Ranch—*locale* TX-5
Terryton (historical)—*locale* KS-7
*Terrytown* KS-7
*Terry Town* PA-2
Terrytown—*locale* FL-3
Terrytown—*locale* PA-2
**Terrytown**—*pop pl* AL-4
**Terrytown**—*pop pl* AR-4
**Terrytown**—*pop pl* LA-4
**Terrytown**—*pop pl* NE-7
Terrytown (census name for Terry Town)—*CDP* LA-4
Terry Town (census name Terrytown)—*other* LA-4
Terrytown Sch—*school* LA-4
**Terry Township**—*pop pl* KS-7
**Terry (Township of)**—*pop pl* PA-2
Terry Trail—*trail* WA-9
Terry Union Sch—*school* CA-9
Terryville—*locale* KY-4
Terryville—*locale* TX-5
Terryville—*locale* VA-3
**Terryville**—*pop pl* CT-1
**Terryville**—*pop pl* NY-2
Terryville Cem—*cemetery* TX-5
Terryville Rsvr No 2—*reservoir* CT-1
Terryville Sch—*school* LA-4
**Terryville (sta.) (Pequabuck)**—*pop pl* CT-1
Terryville Station—*locale* CT-1
Terryville Tunnel—*tunnel* CT-1
Terry Walker Country Club—*locale* AL-4
Terry Wash—*valley* UT-8
Terry Windmill—*locale* NM-5
Terry Windmill—*locale* TX-5
Terteling, Joseph A., House—*hist pl* ID-8
*Teruno Canyon* AZ-5
*Terunom* MH-9
*Terunon* MH-9
*Teruno Tank* AZ-5
*Teruson* MH-9
Tervin Mill Creek—*stream* AL-4
*Terwah Creek* CA-9
Terway Lake—*lake* MN-6
*Terwer Creek* CA-9
Terwiliger Creek—*stream* PA-2
Terwilleger Creek—*stream* NY-2
Terwilliger House—*hist pl* IL-6
Terwilliger House—*hist pl* NY-2
*Terwilliger Lake* NJ-2
Terwilliger Peak—*summit* CA-9
Terwilliger Sch—*school* FL-3
Terwilliger Sch—*school* OR-9
*Terwilliger Valley* CA-9
Terwilliger Valley—*valley* CA-9
**Terwood**—*pop pl* (2) PA-2
Terwood Run—*stream* PA-2
**Terza**—*pop pl* MS-4
Terza Flat—*flat* UT-8
*Terza P.O.* MS-4
Terzia HS—*school* LA-4
Tesaker Lake—*lake* MN-6
*Tesbito Wash* AZ-5
Tesca Ch—*church* OK-5
**Tesch**—*pop pl* MI-6
Tesch Draw—*valley* OR-9
T Eschenko Ranch—*locale* ND-7
Tesch Strip—*airport* ND-7
Tesco—*locale* TX-5
*Tescot* KS-7
**Tescott**—*pop pl* KS-7
*Tesener* AL-4
Tesesquite Creek—*stream* NM-5
Tesesquite Creek—*stream* OK-5
*Teshbi* AZ-5
*Tesheeah* MS-4
*Tesheevah* MS-4
Teshekpak Lake—*lake* AK-9
Teshekpuk Lake—*lake* AK-9
Tesheva Creek—*stream* MS-4
*Teshevah Creek* MS-4
Tesihim Butte—*summit* AZ-5
*Tesi Point* WA-9
Tesk Drain—*stream* MI-6
Teske—*locale* WA-9
Tesky Creek—*stream* MT-8
**Tesla**—*pop pl* WV-2
Tesla (site)—*locale* CA-9
**Tesley**—*pop pl* KY-4
*Tesnatee Creek* GA-3
Tesnatee Creek—*stream* GA-3
Tesnatee Gap—*gap* GA-3
Tesnattee Ch—*church* GA-3
Tes Nez Iah—*locale* AZ-5
*Tes Nos Pas* AZ-5
*Tes Nos Pas Trading Post* AZ-5
*Tes Nos Pes* (2) AZ-5
Tesnus—*locale* TX-5
*Tesoker Lake* MN-6
Tesora—*mine* UT-8
Tesoro, Paso de—*gap* AZ-5
*Tesota* AZ-5
*Tessantee Creek* GA-3
*Tessantee Gap* GA-3
**Tess Corners**—*pop pl* WI-6
Tess Corners—*uninc pl* WI-6
Tessentee Ch—*church* NC-3
Tessentee Creek—*stream* NC-3
Tessiehall Ch—*church* GA-3
**Tessie-Maringola Estates (subdivision)**—*pop pl* DE-2
Tessier Buildings—*hist pl* LA-4
Tessiers Bend—*bay* LA-4
Tess Lake—*lake* MN-6
Tessmer Cem—*cemetery* WI-6
**Tessner**—*pop pl* AL-4
**Tesson**—*pop pl* MO-7
Tesson, Bayou—*stream* LA-4
Tesson Cem—*cemetery* KS-7
*Tessville* IL-6
*Tesswijreskijl* DE-2
Testament Baptist Ch—*church* TN-4
Testament Creek—*stream* OR-9
Test Bldg—*hist pl* IN-6
Test Bridge—*other* IL-6
Test Creek—*stream* ID-8
Test Creek—*stream* WA-9
Tester and Polin General Merchandise Store—*hist pl* WI-6
Testerina Primitive Baptist Ch—*church* FL-3
Testerman Branch—*stream* KY-4
Testerman Cem—*cemetery* TN-4
Testerman Hollow—*valley* TN-4
Testerman Knob—*summit* KY-4
Tester Mtn—*summit* NC-3
Tester Sch—*school* IL-6
Tester Sch—*school* ND-7
Test Hole Tank—*reservoir* AZ-5
*T E Stickler Ranch* OR-9
Testing and Remediation Center/Rivendell Acad—*school* FL-3
Testman—*locale* VI-3
Testo—*locale* SC-3
T E Stogner Cem—*cemetery* MS-4
Teston Cem—*cemetery* GA-3
Teston Lake—*lake* GA-3
Testreana Ch—*church* FL-3
*Test Sch* IN-6
Test Well Tank—*reservoir* NM-5
*Tesuker Lake* MN-6
**Tesuque**—*pop pl* NM-5
Tesuque Creek—*stream* NM-5
Tesuque Pueblo Day Sch—*school* NM-5
Tesuque Pueblo Grant—*civil* NM-5
**Tesuque Pueblo (Indian Reservation)**—*pop pl* NM-5
**Tesuque Pueblo (Place)**—*pop pl* NM-5
Tesuque Pueblo Reservoirs—*reservoir* NM-5
Tetabar Creek—*stream* FL-3
Tetagouche Lake—*lake* MN-6
*Tetanka Dam* SD-7
T E Tanner Pond Dam—*dam* MS-4
Tete Bayou—*stream* (2) LA-4
Tete Butte Reef—*bar* LA-4
*Tete de Mort River* IA-7
Tete De Ours, Bayou—*gut* LA-4
Tete des Morts Creek—*stream* IA-7
Tete Des Morts Township—*fmr MCD* IA-7
*Tetehquet Swamp* MA-1
Tete L'Ours, Bayou—*stream* LA-4
*Tete Mots* IA-7
Teter—*locale* WV-2
Teterboro—*airport* NJ-2
**Teterboro**—*pop pl* NJ-2
Teter Branch—*stream* IN-6
Teter Cem—*cemetery* IN-6
Teter Cem—*cemetery* IA-7
Teter Creek—*stream* IA-7
Teter Creek—*stream* WV-2
Teter Creek Lake—*reservoir* WV-2
Teter Gap—*gap* WV-2
Teter Meadow Brook—*stream* NH-1
Teter Oil Field—*oilfield* KS-7
Teter Ranch—*locale* CO-8
Teter Run—*stream* WV-2
**Tetersburg**—*pop pl* IN-6
Teterton—*locale* WV-2
Teterville—*locale* KS-7
Teteseau Lake—*lake* MO-7
Tete'to—*slope* MH-9
Tetfair Pond—*reservoir* GA-3
Tether Lake—*lake* CA-9
Tetherow Butte—*ridge* OR-9
Teti Canyon—*valley* CO-8
Tetilesook Creek—*stream* AK-9
Tetilla Canyon—*valley* NM-5
Tetilla Peak—*summit* (2) NM-5
Tetillas Peak—*summit* NM-5
*Tetiquet* MA-1
Tetley Hill—*summit* MO-7
Tetley Spring—*spring* WY-8
*Tetlich Range* WY-8
Tetlin—*locale* AK-9
Tetlin ANV965—*reserve* AK-9
Tetlin Hills—*other* AK-9
Tetlin Junction—*locale* AK-9
Tetlin Lake—*lake* AK-9
Tetlin River—*stream* AK-9
Tetlow—*locale* GA-3
*Tetlow Ridge* ME-1
Tetogue Lake—*lake* LA-4
Tetohge—*slope* MH-9
Teto Lake—*lake* OR-9
*Teton* WY-8
Teton—*locale* SD-7
**Teton**—*pop pl* ID-8
Teton Basin—*basin* ID-8
Teton Butte—*summit* MT-8
Teton Buttes—*spring* MT-8
Teton Camp—*locale* WY-8
Teton Campground—*locale* WY-8
Teton Canal—*canal* ID-8
Teton Canyon—*valley* WY-8
Teton Cem—*cemetery* CO-8
Teton Cem—*cemetery* ID-8
Teton County Courthouse—*hist pl* ID-8
*Teton Creek* WY-8
Teton Creek—*stream* AK-9
Teton Creek—*stream* ID-8
Teton Creek—*stream* WY-8
Teton Crest Trail—*trail* WY-8
Teton Ditch—*canal* MT-8
Teton Game Mngmt Area—*park* WY-8
Teton Glacier—*glacier* WY-8
Teton Gulch—*valley* MT-8
Teton HS—*school* ID-8
**Tetonia**—*pop pl* ID-8
Teton Island Canal—*canal* ID-8
Teton JHS—*school* ID-8
Tetonkaha, Lake—*lake* SD-7
Tetonka Lake—*reservoir* MN-6
**Tetonka Township**—*pop pl* SD-7
*Teton Lake* WY-8
Teton Natl For—*forest* (2) WY-8
Teton-Newdale—*cens area* ID-8
Teton Pass—*gap* MT-8
Teton Pass—*gap* WY-8
Teton Peak—*summit* MT-8
Teton Point Turnout—*locale* WY-8
Teton Ridge—*ridge* MT-8
*Teton River* ID-8
*Teton River* MT-8
*Teton River* SD-7
*Teton River* WY-8
Teton River—*stream* ID-8
Teton River—*stream* MT-8
Tetons—*summit* OR-9
Tetons, The—*summit* UT-8
Teton-Spring Creek Bird Res—*park* MT-8
Teton Station—*locale* MT-8
*Teton Valley* ID-8
*Teton Valley* WY-8
Teton Valley Ranch—*locale* WY-8
Tetonview Sch—*school* MT-8
**Teton Village**—*pop pl* WY-8
Teton Wilderness—*park* WY-8
Tetotum—*locale* VA-3
Tetotum Flats—*flat* VA-3
Tetouka (historical)—*locale* SD-7
Tetram Pond—*lake* CT-1
Tetrault Lake—*lake* MT-8
Tetravun Lakes—*area* AK-9
Tetreault Pond—*lake* CT-1
Tetro Creek—*stream* SD-7
Tetrokof Point—*cape* AK-9
Tetro Rock—*summit* SD-7
Tetro Shaft—*mine* UT-8
Tetro Tunnel—*mine* UT-8
Tetsc Ranch—*locale* WY-8
Tetsyeh Lake—*lake* AK-9
Tetsyeh Mtn—*summit* AK-9
Tett Cove—*valley* NC-3
Tetter Lake Dam—*dam* MS-4
Tetterman Spring—*spring* AZ-5
Tettertiller Hill—*summit* TX-5
Tetterton Gut—*stream* NC-3
Tetterton Lodge—*locale* NC-3
Tetthajik Creek—*stream* AK-9
Tettington—*locale* VA-3
**Tetuan**—*pop pl* PR-3
Tetuan (Barrio)—*fmr MCD* PR-3
Tetzlaff Lateral—*canal* CA-9
Tetzlaff Peak—*summit* UT-8
*Teuajo Alta* AZ-5
Teubner Cem—*cemetery* ND-7
Teuchet Creek—*stream* AK-9
Teufels Farm Strip—*airport* OR-9
*Teunis Lake* NY-2
*Teuson* AZ-5
Teuton Branch—*stream* TN-4
Teutonia—*uninc pl* WI-6
Teutonia Mine—*mine* CA-9
Teutonia Peak—*summit* CA-9
Teutonic Ridge—*ridge* UT-8
**Teutopolis**—*pop pl* IL-6
**Teutopolis (Township of)**—*pop pl* IL-6
Teutsch Ditch—*canal* IN-6
**Teva**—*pop pl* KY-4
Tevealt Cem—*cemetery* IL-6
Tevebaugh Chapel—*church* WV-2
Tevebaugh Creek—*stream* WV-2
Tevebau Run—*stream* PA-2
*Tevibaugh Run* PA-2
Teviotdale—*hist pl* NY-2
**Tevis**—*pop pl* TN-4
Tevis Block—*hist pl* CA-9
*Tevis Bluff* TX-5
Tevis Cottage—*hist pl* KY-4
Tevis Creek—*stream* MT-8
Tevis Spring—*spring* TN-4
Tevis Spring Ch—*church* TN-4
Tevoet, Lambert, House—*hist pl* IA-7
Tevs Rocks—*pillar* AZ-5
Tevyaraq Lake—*lake* AK-9
*Tewa* AZ-5
**Tewa**—*pop pl* AZ-5
Tewalt Ridge—*ridge* WI-6
*Tewa Spring* AZ-5
Tewaukon, Lake—*reservoir* ND-7
Tewaukon (historical)—*locale* ND-7
Tewaukon Natl Wildlife Ref—*park* ND-7
**Tewaukon Township**—*pop pl* ND-7
Tewaukon WS-T-1-A Dam—*dam* ND-7
Tewaukon WS-T-2 Dam—*dam* ND-7
Tewaukon WS-T-7 Dam—*dam* ND-7
Tew Branch—*stream* AL-4
Tew Cem—*cemetery* AL-4
Tew Cem—*cemetery* OH-6
Tewell Creek—*stream* KY-4
Tewell House—*hist pl* LA-4
Teweneche—*bar* FM-9
Tewenier—*bar* FM-9
Tewenier, Ununen—*bar* FM-9
*Teweniik* FM-9
Tewenik—*island* FM-9
Tewfel Gulch—*valley* MT-8
Tewhitt JHS—*school* TN-4
Tewinipa—*bay* FM-9
Te Winkle Park—*park* CA-9
Te Winkle Sch—*school* CA-9
*Tewinot* WY-8
Tewksberry Brook—*stream* NH-1
Tewksberry Creek—*stream* CO-8
**Tewksbury**—*pop pl* MA-1
*Tewksbury Center* MA-1
**Tewksbury Center**—*pop pl* MA-1
Tewksbury Center Sch—*school* MA-1
*Tewksbury Centre* MA-1
*Tewksbury Creek* CO-8
**Tewksbury Heights**—*pop pl* CA-9
Tewksbury HS—*school* MA-1
Tewksbury JHS—*school* MA-1
**Tewksbury Junction**—*pop pl* MA-1
Tewksbury Pond—*lake* NH-1
Tewksbury Pond—*lake* PA-2
Tewksbury Rock—*rock* MA-1
Tewksbury Rsvr—*reservoir* CA-9
Tewksbury Shop Ctr—*locale* MA-1
Tewksbury Spring—*spring* AZ-5
Tewksbury State Hosp—*hospital* MA-1
Tewksbury State Hospital Cem—*cemetery* MA-1
**Tewksbury (Town of)**—*pop pl* MA-1
**Tewksbury (Township of)**—*pop pl* NJ-2
*Tewksbury Village* MA-1
Tew Lake—*lake* LA-4
Tew Lake—*lake* SC-3
Tew Lake Oil Field—*oilfield* LA-4
Tew Recreation Center—*building* AL-4
*Tewsley Lake* IN-6
Tews Ponds—*reservoir* AL-4
Tewsville—*locale* NE-7
**Texaco**—*pop pl* SC-3
Texaco Basin—*basin* OR-9
*Texaco Beach* NC-3
**Texaco Beach**—*pop pl* NC-3
Texaco Country Club—*other* TX-5
Texaco Hill—*summit* KS-7
Texaco Number One Windmill—*locale* TX-5
Texaco Number Two Windmill—*locale* TX-5
**Texaco Town**—*pop pl* NY-2
Texaco Windmill—*locale* TX-5
Texada Cem—*cemetery* LA-4
Texada Tavern—*hist pl* MS-4
**Texana**—*pop pl* NC-3
Texana (historical)—*locale* SD-7
Texana Oil Field—*oilfield* TX-5
Texana Presbyterian Church—*hist pl* TX-5
Texan Mtn—*summit* TX-5
Texanna—*locale* OK-5
Texanna Branch—*stream* OK-5
Texanna Mtn—*summit* OK-5
Texano, Lake—*reservoir* TX-5
**Texans**—*pop pl* NC-3
Texan Tunnel—*mine* UT-8
**Texarkana**—*pop pl* AR-4
**Texarkana**—*pop pl* TX-5
Texarkana (CCD)—*cens area* TX-5
Texarkana Country Club—*other* AR-4
Texarkana Dam—*dam* TX-5
Texarkana Junior Coll—*school* TX-5
Texarkana Municipal Airp (Webb Field)—*airport* AR-4
Texarkana Phase Archeol District—*hist pl* TX-5
Texarkana Union Station—*hist pl* AR-4
Texarkana Union Station—*hist pl* TX-5
*Texas* IN-6
*Texas* PA-2
Texas—*locale* GA-3
Texas—*locale* MS-4
Texas—*locale* (2) NJ-2
Texas—*locale* NY-2
Texas—*locale* NC-3
Texas—*locale* (2) PA-2
Texas—*locale* VT-1
**Texas**—*pop pl* AL-4
**Texas**—*pop pl* IL-6
**Texas**—*pop pl* IN-6
**Texas**—*pop pl* KY-4
**Texas**—*pop pl* LA-4
**Texas**—*pop pl* MD-2
**Texas**—*pop pl* MA-1
**Texas**—*pop pl* NY-2
**Texas**—*pop pl* OH-6
Texas, The—*hist pl* AL-4
Texas, The—*hist pl* GA-3
Texas A and I Univ—*school* TX-5
Texas A and M Coll Experimental Station—*school* (2) TX-5
Texas A and M Coll Experimental Station Number 6—*school* TX-5
Texas A and M Experimental Station—*school* (2) TX-5
Texas A and M Research Center—*locale* TX-5
Texas A and M Univ—*school* TX-5
Texas A and M Univ Agricultural Research Station—*school* TX-5
Texas A And M Univ Research Annex—*school* TX-5
Texas A and M Univ Research Center—*school* TX-5
Texas Agricultural Experimental Station—*other* TX-5
Texas Agricultural Experiment Station—*other* (3) TX-5
Texas and Pacific RR Depot—*hist pl* LA-4
Texas and Pacific Terminal Complex—*hist pl* TX-5
Texas Ave Buildings—*hist pl* LA-4
Texas Bar—*bar* CA-9
Texas Bar Creek—*stream* OR-9
Texas Basin—*basin* ID-8
Texas Basin—*basin* NV-8
Texas Basin Spring—*spring* ID-8
Texas Basin Spring—*spring* NV-8
Texas Bayou—*gut* TX-5
Texas Bend—*bend* TX-5
Texas Bend Cem—*cemetery* MO-7
Texas Bldg—*hist pl* TX-5
Texas Blind- Deaf and Orphan Sch—*school* TX-5
Texas Bottoms—*bend* TN-4
Texas Branch—*stream* AL-4
Texas Branch—*stream* FL-3
Texas Brook—*stream* VT-1
Texas Butte—*summit* OR-9
Texas Camp—*locale* CO-8
Texas Canyon—*valley* AZ-5
Texas Canyon—*valley* (2) CA-9
Texas Canyon—*valley* NM-5
Texas Canyon—*valley* UT-8
Texas Canyon Fire Control Station—*locale* CA-9
Texas Canyon Spring—*spring* NM-5
*Texas Canyon Summit* AZ-5
Texas (CCD)—*cens area* GA-3
Texas Cem—*cemetery* OH-6
Texas Centennial Exposition Buildings (1936–1937)—*hist pl* TX-5
Texas Ch—*church* GA-3
Texas Ch—*church* IL-6
Texas Ch—*church* OK-5
Texas Ch—*church* WV-2
Texas Charley Gulch—*valley* CA-9
Texas Chief Mine—*mine* CO-8
Texas Chiropractic Coll—*school* TX-5
Texas Chow Creek—*stream* CA-9
Texas Christian Univ—*school* TX-5
*Texas Christian University* TX-5
Texas Chute—*channel* IL-6
**Texas City**—*pop pl* IL-6
**Texas City**—*pop pl* TX-5
Texas City Dike—*dam* TX-5
Texas City Junction—*locale* TX-5
Texas City Junction (Texas City Terminal Junction)—*uninc pl* TX-5
Texas City-League City (CCD)—*cens area* TX-5
Texas City Ship Channel—*channel* TX-5
Texas City Terminal Junction—*locale* TX-5
Texas Coll—*school* TX-5
Texas Coll of Arts and Industries—*school* TX-5
Texas Company Filling Station—*hist pl* TX-5
Texas Confederate Home—*building* TX-5
Texas Corner—*locale* PA-2
**Texas Corners**—*pop pl* MI-6
Texas County—*civil* MO-7
**Texas (County)**—*pop pl* MO-7
**Texas (County)**—*pop pl* OK-5
Texas County Courthouse—*hist pl* OK-5
Texas County Memorial Hospital Heliport—*airport* MO-7
Texas Cowboy Reunion Grounds—*locale* TX-5
*Texas Creek* CA-9
Texas Creek—*locale* CO-8
Texas Creek—*stream* AL-4
Texas Creek—*stream* (5) AK-9
Texas Creek—*stream* (2) CA-9
Texas Creek—*stream* (7) CO-8

Theodore Basin—*basin* ... NV-8
Theodore (CCD)—*cens area* ... AL-4
Theodore Cem—*cemetery* ... SD-7
Theodore Creek—*stream* ... AK-9
Theodore Creek—*stream* (2) ... MT-8
Theodore Division—*civil* ... AL-4
Theodore Francis Green State Airp—*airport* ... RI-1
Theodore Gordon Brook—*stream* ... NY-2
Theodore Gordon Cove—*bay* ... NY-2
Theodore Granville Barcus Wildlife Area—*park* ... KS-7
Theodore (historical)—*locale* ... SD-7
Theodore HS—*school* ... AL-4
Theodore Industrial Park—*locale* ... AL-4
Theodore Island—*island* ... AK-9
Theodore Johnston Creek—*stream* ... OR-9
Theodore Kjerstad Dam—*dam* ... SD-7
Theodore MS—*school* ... AL-4
Theodore Point—*cape* ... AK-9
Theodore Post Office (historical)—*building* ... TN-4
Theodore Potter Elem Sch—*school* ... IN-6
Theodore Ridge—*ridge* ... AK-9
Theodore River—*stream* ... AK-9
Theodore Roosevelt, Mount—*summit* ... SD-7
Theodore Roosevelt Birthplace Natl Historic Site—*park* ... NY-2
Theodore Roosevelt Bridge—*bridge* ... DC-2
Theodore Roosevelt Dam—*dam* ... AZ-5
Theodore Roosevelt Grave—*cemetery* ... NY-2
Theodore Roosevelt House—*building* ... DC-2
Theodore Roosevelt HS—*school* ... CA-9
Theodore Roosevelt HS—*school* (2) ... IN-6
Theodore Roosevelt HS—*school* (2) ... NY-2
Theodore Roosevelt HS—*school* ... TX-5
Theodore Roosevelt Inaugural Natl Historic Site—*park* ... NY-2
Theodore Roosevelt Indian Sch—*school* ... AZ-5
Theodore Roosevelt Island—*park* ... DC-2
Theodore Roosevelt Island Natl Memorial—*hist pl* ... DC-2
*Theodore Roosevelt JHS* ... PA-2
Theodore Roosevelt JHS—*school* ... FL-3
Theodore Roosevelt JHS—*school* ... NY-2
Theodore Roosevelt JHS—*school* ... OR-9
Theodore Roosevelt JHS—*school* ... PA-2
Theodore Roosevelt Lake—*reservoir* ... AZ-5
Theodore Roosevelt Memorial Park—*park* . NY-2
Theodore Roosevelt Natl Memorial Park—*park* ... ND-7
Theodore Roosevelt Natl Park—*park* (2) ... ND-7
Theodore Roosevelt Pass—*gap* ... MT-8
*Theodore Roosevelt Peak* ... SD-7
Theodore Roosevelt Sch—*school* (5) ... CA-9
Theodore Roosevelt Sch—*school* (2) ... NJ-2
Theodore Roosevelt Sch—*school* ... NY-2
Theodore Roosevelt Sch—*school* ... OH-6
Theodore Roosevelt Sch—*school* ... TX-5
Theodore Roosevelt Sch—*school* ... WI-6
Theodore Sch—*school* ... IL-6
Theodore Ship Channel—*canal* ... AL-4
Theodore Shop Ctr—*locale* ... AL-4
Theodore Township—*civil* ... SD-7
**Theodosia**—*pop pl* ... MO-7
Theoff Point—*cape* ... NC-3
Theo League Lake—*reservoir* ... AL-4
Theo League Lake Dam—*dam* ... AL-4
Theological Building-A.M.E. Zion Theological Institute—*hist pl* ... AL-4
Theological Coll—*school* ... DC-2
Theological Seminary—*facility* ... VA-3
**Theon**—*pop pl* ... TX-5
Theon Cem—*cemetery* ... WA-9
Theoni Sch—*school* ... KS-7
Theony—*locale* ... MT-8
Theophilus Ch—*church* ... NE-7
Theopold Mercantile Co. Wholesale Grocery Bldg—*hist pl* ... MN-6
Theo Roosevelt Sch—*school* ... OH-6
Thera—*locale* ... WA-9
T Herd Lake Dam—*dam* ... MS-4
**Theresa**—*pop pl* ... NY-2
**Theresa**—*pop pl* ... WI-6
Theresa, Lake—*lake* ... FL-3
Theresa, Lake—*lake* ... MI-6
Theresa Ch—*church* ... NC-3
Theresa Creek—*stream* ... AK-9
**Theresa Heights**—*pop pl* ... TN-4
Theresa (historical)—*locale* ... MS-4
Theresa Lake—*lake* ... FL-3
Theresa Marsh State Wildlife Area—*park* .. WI-6
Theresa Rodriquez Grant—*civil* ... FL-3
**Theresa Station**—*pop pl* ... WI-6
**Theresa (Town of)**—*pop pl* ... NY-2
**Theresa (Town of)**—*pop pl* ... WI-6
**Theresa Township**—*pop pl* ... SD-7
Thereses Sch—*school* ... MA-1
Theressa—*locale* ... FL-3
Theriault Creek—*stream* ... ID-8
Theriault Lake—*lake* ... ID-8
Theriaults Ice Pond—*lake* ... CT-1
"The Rim" and Site of Fort Foster—*hist pl* ... ME-1
Theriot—*locale* ... LA-4
**Theriot**—*pop pl* ... LA-4
Theriot, Lake—*lake* ... LA-4
Theriot Canal—*canal* ... LA-4
Therkelsen Heliport—*airport* ... WA-9
*Therma* ... NM-5
**Thermal**—*pop pl* ... CA-9
**Thermal**—*pop pl* ... KY-4
**Thermal**—*pop pl* ... NC-3
Thermalands—*area* ... CA-9
Thermal Canyon—*valley* ... CA-9
Thermal City—*locale* ... NC-3
Thermal G Ranch Airp—*airport* ... PA-2
*Thermal G Ranch Gliderport* ... PA-2
Thermal (historical)—*locale* ... AL-4
**Thermalito**—*pop pl* ... CA-9
Thermalito Afterbay—*reservoir* ... CA-9
Thermalito Diversion Dam—*dam* ... CA-9
Thermalito Diversion Pool—*reservoir* ... CA-9
Thermalito Forebay—*reservoir* ... CA-9
Thermalito Forebay North Picnic Area—*park* ... CA-9
Thermalito Forebay South Boat Ramp—*locale* ... CA-9
Thermalito Power Canal—*canal* ... CA-9
Thermal Lake—*lake* ... MN-6
Thermal Mine—*mine* ... IL-6
Thermal Number 1 Mine (underground)—*mine* ... AL-4
**Thermal Valley (subdivision)**—*pop pl* ... NC-3
Therman Bend—*bend* ... TX-5
Thermans Bridge (historical)—*bridge* ... TN-4
Thermo—*locale* ... TX-5
Thermo—*locale* ... UT-8
Thermo Branch—*stream* ... NC-3
Thermo Hot Springs—*spring* ... UT-8
Thermokarst Creek—*stream* ... AK-9
Thermo Knob—*summit* ... NC-3
**Thermopolis**—*pop pl* ... WY-8
Thermopolis East—*cens area* ... WY-8
Thermopolis West—*cens area* ... WY-8
Thermopylae—*gap* ... MA-1
**Thermopylae**—*pop pl* ... MA-1
Theron Jones Sch—*school* ... TX-5
Theron Wood Mine (underground)—*mine* ... AL-4
Therp Cem—*cemetery* ... IA-7
*Therriault Creek* ... ID-8
Therriault Creek—*stream* ... MT-8
Therriault Gulch—*valley* ... MT-8
*Therriault Lake* ... ID-8
Therriault Pass—*gap* ... MT-8
*Therriaults Creek* ... MT-8
Theseus Creek—*stream* ... WA-9
Theseus Lake—*lake* ... WA-9
Thesing Bar—*bar* ... OR-9
Thespian Mine—*mine* ... CO-8
Thessalia—*locale* ... VA-3
Thessalonia Missionary Ch—*church* ... FL-3
Thessalonian Ch—*church* (2) ... VA-3
Thessalonto Ch—*church* ... TX-5
**Thessing**—*pop pl* ... AR-4
**Theta**—*pop pl* ... NC-3
**Theta**—*pop pl* ... TN-4
**Theta**—*pop pl* ... VA-3
Theta Cave—*cave* ... AL-4
*Thetford* ... TN-4
*Thetford* ... VT-1
Thetford and Arbela Drain—*canal* ... MI-6
**Thetford Center**—*pop pl* ... MI-6
**Thetford Center**—*pop pl* ... VT-1
Thetford Center Covered Bridge—*hist pl* ... VT-1
**Thetford Hill**—*pop pl* ... VT-1
Thetford Hill Hist Dist—*hist pl* ... VT-1
Thetford (sta.) (RR name for East Thetford)—*other* ... VT-1
**Thetford (Thetford Hill)**—*pop pl* ... VT-1
**Thetford (Town of)**—*pop pl* ... VT-1
**Thetford (Township of)**—*pop pl* ... MI-6
Thetis Bay—*bay* ... AK-9
Thetis Creek—*stream* ... AK-9
Thetis Creek—*stream* ... WA-9
Thetis Island—*island* ... AK-9
Thetis Mound—*summit* ... AK-9
Thetis Ridge—*ridge* ... AK-9
Theuerhauf Sch—*school* ... CA-9
Theurer Hollow—*valley* ... UT-8
Theurer-Wrigley House—*hist pl* ... IL-6
Theus Cem—*cemetery* ... LA-4
Theuvenins Creek—*stream* ... TX-5
Theuvenins Oil Field—*oilfield* ... TX-5
*Theuvinins Creek* ... TX-5
Thevenet Hall—*locale* ... NY-2
Thewarley Ch—*church* ... OK-5
Thewatle Ch—*church* ... OK-5
Thew Cem—*cemetery* ... OH-6
Thexton Ranch—*locale* ... MT-8
*Thi* ... IA-7
Thiard—*locale* ... ID-8
Thias, Henry C., House—*hist pl* ... MO-7
*Thib* ... FM-9
Thibadeau, Lake—*lake* ... MT-8
Thibadeau Brook—*stream* ... ME-1
Thibadeau Coulee—*valley* ... MT-8
Thibau Creek—*stream* ... CA-9
Thibaut Creek—*stream* (2) ... CA-9
Thibaut Point Public Use Area—*park* ... MO-7
Thibideau Brook—*stream* ... ME-1
Thibideau Rapids—*rapids* ... MT-8
**Thibodaux**—*pop pl* ... LA-4
Thibodaux, Jean Baptiste, House—*hist pl* .. LA-4
Thibodaux Cem—*cemetery* ... LA-4
Thibodaux Coll—*school* ... LA-4
Thibodaux Gas and Oil Field—*oilfield* ... LA-4
Thibodaux Junction—*locale* ... LA-4
Thibodeau Brook—*stream* ... ME-1
Thibodeau Island—*island* ... ME-1
*Thibodeaux* ... LA-4
Thibodeaux Mtn—*summit* ... AK-9
**Thick**—*pop pl* ... TN-4
Thick Branch—*stream* ... NC-3
Thick Branch Bay—*swamp* ... NC-3
Thick Creek—*stream* (2) ... GA-3
Thick Creek—*stream* ... TN-4
Thicket—*locale* ... TX-5
**Thicket (Bracken Store)**—*pop pl* ... TX-5
Thicket Branch—*stream* ... KY-4
Thicket Branch—*stream* ... NC-3
Thicket Creek—*stream* ... AK-9
Thicket Creek—*stream* ... ID-8
Thicket Creek—*stream* ... MT-8
Thicket Creek—*stream* ... VA-3
Thicket Point—*cape* (2) ... VA-3
Thicket Point Bay—*bay* ... VA-3
Thicket Rsvr—*reservoir* ... OR-9
Thickets Creek—*stream* ... TX-5
Thicket Siding—*locale* ... TX-5
Thicket Spring—*spring* (2) ... AZ-5
Thicket Spring—*spring* ... OR-9
Thicket Spring, The—*spring* ... NM-5
*Thicket Springs* ... OR-9
Thicket Tank—*reservoir* (2) ... AZ-5
Thickett Branch—*stream* ... TX-5
**Thicketty**—*pop pl* ... SC-3
Thicketty Creek—*stream* ... SC-3
Thicketty Mountain Creek—*stream* ... SC-3
Thicketty Mountain Lake—*reservoir* ... SC-3
Thicketty Mountain Ore Pits (38CK74)—*hist pl* ... SC-3
Thicketty Mtn—*summit* ... SC-3
Thickety Ch—*church* ... NC-3
Thickety Creek—*stream* (2) ... NC-3
Thickety Creek—*stream* ... TX-5
Thickhead Mtn—*summit* ... PA-2
Thickhead State Wildlife Area—*area* ... PA-2
*Thickhead Wild Area* ... PA-2
*Thick Mountain* ... PA-2
Thick Mountain Trail—*trail* ... PA-2
*Thick Neck Point* ... MD-2
Thick Sch (historical)—*school* ... TN-4
**Thida**—*pop pl* ... AR-4
Thiebault Lake—*lake* ... MN-6
Thiebeau Point—*cape* ... WI-6
Thief Bay Pool—*reservoir* ... MN-6
*Thief Creek* ... OR-9
Thief Creek—*stream* ... AK-9
Thief Creek—*stream* ... MT-8
Thief Creek—*stream* ... UT-8
Thief Creek—*stream* (2) ... WY-8
Thief Hollow—*valley* ... MO-7
Thief Hollow—*valley* ... TX-5
Thief Hollow Windmill—*locale* ... TX-5
Thief Island—*island* ... ME-1
Thief Lake—*lake* ... MN-6
Thief Lake—*lake* ... WI-6
Thief Lakes—*reservoir* ... TX-5
Thief Lake State Wildlife Mngmt Area—*park* ... MN-6
**Thief Lake (Township of)**—*pop pl* ... MN-6
Thief Neck Bend—*bend* ... TN-4
Thief Neck Island—*island* ... TN-4
Thief River—*stream* ... MN-6
**Thief River Falls**—*pop pl* ... MN-6
Thief River Falls Public Library—*hist pl* ... MN-6
Thief River Falls Regional Airp—*airport* ... MN-6
*Thief Rock* ... AZ-5
Thief Slough—*gut* ... WI-6
Thief Valley—*valley* ... OR-9
Thief Valley County Park—*park* ... OR-9
Thief Valley Dam—*dam* ... OR-9
Thief Valley Rsvr—*reservoir* ... OR-9
Thiel—*locale* ... AR-4
Thiel—*locale* ... WA-9
Thiel Coll—*school* ... PA-2
Thiel Creek—*stream* ... MT-8
Thiel Creek—*stream* ... OR-9
Thiele, J., Bldg—*hist pl* ... TX-5
Thiele Cem—*cemetery* ... TX-5
Thiele Ditch—*canal* ... IN-6
Thiele House and Thiele Cottage—*hist pl* ... TX-5
Thielen Airp—*airport* ... KS-7
Thielen Draw—*valley* ... WY-8
Thielen Park—*park* ... MN-6
Thiel Glacier—*glacier* ... AK-9
Thielke Lake—*lake* ... MN-6
Thiel Lake—*lake* ... MT-8
**Thiells**—*pop pl* ... NY-2
**Thielman Crossroads**—*pop pl* ... PA-2
Thielman-Stoddard House—*hist pl* ... SD-7
Thiel Mine—*mine* ... MT-8
Thiel Pass—*gap* ... AK-9
**Thiel's Corner**—*pop pl* ... WI-6
Thielsen, Mount—*summit* ... OR-9
Thielsen Creek—*stream* ... OR-9
Thielsen Creek Trail—*trail* ... OR-9
Thielsen Forest Camp—*locale* ... OR-9
Thielsen View Campground—*park* ... OR-9
Thielson—*locale* ... OR-9
*Thielson Creek Camp* ... OR-9
Thieltge Ranch—*locale* ... MT-8
Thieman Hill—*summit* ... WI-6
Thienes Sch—*school* ... CT-1
**Thiensville**—*pop pl* ... WI-6
Thierer Branch—*stream* ... KS-7
Thiering Sch—*school* ... NE-7
Thierman Apartments—*hist pl* ... KY-4
Thiese Creek—*stream* ... WA-9
Thiesen Bldg—*hist pl* ... FL-3
Thiesen Creek—*stream* ... ID-8
Thies Lake—*lake* ... MN-6
Thiessen Canyon—*valley* ... ID-8
Thiessen Gulch—*valley* ... ID-8
Thieves Ledge—*bar* ... MA-1
Thieying Rock—*summit* ... NM-5
Thift Cem—*cemetery* ... GA-3
Thighman Lake—*lake* ... MS-4
Thigpen, Dr. C. A., House—*hist pl* ... AL-4
Thigpen Branch—*stream* ... GA-3
Thigpen Cem—*cemetery* ... MS-4
Thigpen Chapel—*church* ... GA-3
Thigpen Creek—*stream* ... GA-3
Thigpen Creek—*stream* ... LA-4
Thigpen Field (airport)—*airport* ... MS-4
Thigpen Lake (historical)—*lake* ... MS-4
Thigpen Mill Creek—*stream* ... GA-3
Thigpen Sch—*school* ... TX-5
Thigpen Sch (historical)—*school* ... MS-4
Thigpens Pond—*reservoir* ... AL-4
Thiib—*bay* ... FM-9
Thileer—*summit* ... FM-9
Thilenius, Col, George C., House—*hist pl* . MO-7
*Thiler* ... FM-9
*Thilimad Island* ... FM-9
*Thilimal* ... FM-9
T Hill—*summit* ... WY-8
Thill Branch—*stream* ... MO-7
Thimble, The—*summit* ... CA-9
Thimbleberry Bay—*bay* ... AK-9
Thimbleberry Canyon—*valley* ... UT-8
Thimbleberry Creek—*stream* ... CA-9
Thimbleberry Creek—*stream* ... UT-8
Thimbleberry Lake—*lake* ... AK-9
Thimbleberry Mtn—*summit* ... OR-9
Thimbleberry Ridge—*ridge* ... CA-9
Thimbleberry Spring—*spring* ... ID-8
Thimbleberry Spring—*spring* ... OR-9
Thimble Canyon—*valley* ... NM-5
Thimble Cove—*bay* ... AK-9
Thimble Creek—*stream* ... ID-8
Thimble Island—*island* ... MA-1
Thimble Lake—*lake* ... MN-6
Thimble Mountain Trail—*trail* ... OR-9
Thimble Mtn—*summit* ... AZ-5
Thimble Mtn—*summit* ... OR-9
Thimble Mtn—*summit* ... WA-9
Thimble Peak—*summit* ... AZ-5
Thimble Peak—*summit* (2) ... CA-9
Thimble Peak—*summit* ... WI-6
Thimble Rock—*pillar* ... CO-8
Thimble Rock—*summit* ... UT-8
Thimble Rock Point—*cliff* ... CO-8
Thimbles, The—*island* ... CT-1
Thimble Shoal Channel—*channel* ... VA-3
Thimble Shoal Channel Tunnel—*tunnel* ... VA-3
Thing Ranch—*locale* ... CA-9
Thingvalla Town Hall—*building* ... ND-7
**Thingvalla Township**—*pop pl* ... ND-7
Thingvalla Township (historical)—*civil* ... ND-7
Thing Valley—*valley* ... CA-9
Thin Mtn—*summit* ... AZ-5
Thin Point—*cape* ... AK-9
Thinpoint Cove—*bay* ... AK-9
Thinpoint Lake—*lake* ... AK-9
Thin Rock Mesa—*summit* ... AZ-5
Thin Run—*stream* ... IN-6
T Hinton Ranch—*locale* ... AZ-5
Thiokol Airp—*airport* ... UT-8
Third Addition to Rockville and Old St. Mary's Church & Cemetery—*hist pl* ... MD-2
Third and Jefferson Streets Hist Dist—*hist pl* ... KY-4
Third and Market Streets Hist Dist—*hist pl* ... KY-4
**Third and M Townhouse Condominium**—*pop pl* ... UT-8
Third Apache Canyon—*valley* ... NM-5
Third Ave Hist Dist—*hist pl* (2) ... WI-6
Third Ave Holiness Ch—*church* ... AL-4
Third Ave Sch—*school* ... IN-6
Third Ave Sch—*school* ... KS-7
Third Baptist Ch—*church* (3) ... AL-4
Third Baptist Church—*hist pl* ... TN-4
Third Basin—*lake* ... IN-6
Third Bay—*bay* ... CT-1
Third Bay—*bay* ... FL-3
Third Bay—*lake* ... LA-4
Third Bayou—*gut* ... MS-4
Third Beach—*beach* ... WA-9
Third Beach—*locale* ... RI-1
Third Bench—*bench* ... MT-8
Third Bethel Ch—*church* ... FL-3
Third Black Lake—*lake* ... WI-6
Third Boulder—*stream* ... NV-8
*Third Branch* ... PA-2
Third Branch—*stream* ... GA-3
Third Branch—*stream* ... TN-4
Third Branch—*stream* ... VA-3
Third Branch Lake—*reservoir* ... VA-3
Third Branch McGraw Creek—*stream* ... TX-5
Third Branch White River—*stream* ... VT-1
Third Bridge Lake—*lake* ... MS-4
Third Brook—*stream* ... MA-1
Third Brook—*stream* ... NY-2
Third Brother—*summit* ... NY-2
Third Brother Island—*island* ... NY-2
Third Brushy Canyon—*valley* ... CA-9
Third Burnt Hill—*summit* ... NY-2
Third Butte—*summit* ... CA-9
Third Butte—*summit* ... NV-8
Third Caney Creek—*stream* ... TX-5
*Third Canon* ... MT-8
Third Canyon—*valley* ... CO-8
Third Canyon—*valley* ... NM-5
Third Canyon—*valley* ... TX-5
Third Canyon—*valley* (2) ... UT-8
Third Canyon Mesa—*summit* ... NM-5
Third Cape—*cape* ... AK-9
Third Ch—*church* ... VA-3
Third Chain Lake—*lake* ... ME-1
Third Chain of Islands—*island* ... TX-5
Third Chapel Ch—*church* ... GA-3
Third Christian Ch—*church* ... VA-3
Third Church of Christ Scientist—*hist pl* ... OH-6
Third Cliff—*cliff* ... MA-1
**Third Cliff**—*pop pl* ... MA-1
Third Connecticut Lake—*lake* ... NH-1
*Third Coulee* ... WA-9
Third Coulee—*valley* ... MT-8
Third Cove—*bay* ... MD-2
*Third Creek* ... NC-3
*Third Creek* ... ND-7
*Third Creek* ... TX-5
Third Creek—*channel* ... MA-1
**Third Creek**—*pop pl* ... TN-4
Third Creek—*stream* (2) ... AL-4
Third Creek—*stream* ... AK-9
Third Creek—*stream* ... CA-9
Third Creek—*stream* ... CO-8
Third Creek—*stream* (5) ... ID-8
Third Creek—*stream* ... IL-6
Third Creek—*stream* ... IA-7
Third Creek—*stream* (2) ... KS-7
Third Creek—*stream* (2) ... MI-6
Third Creek—*stream* ... MS-4
Third Creek—*stream* ... MO-7
Third Creek—*stream* (5) ... MT-8
Third Creek—*stream* (2) ... NV-8
Third Creek—*stream* (3) ... NY-2
Third Creek—*stream* ... NC-3
Third Creek—*stream* ... ND-7
Third Creek—*stream* (5) ... OR-9
Third Creek—*stream* ... SC-3
Third Creek—*stream* ... SD-7
Third Creek—*stream* ... TN-4
Third Creek—*stream* (2) ... TX-5
Third Creek—*stream* (4) ... WA-9
Third Creek—*stream* (5) ... WY-8
Third Creek Baptist Ch—*church* ... TN-4
Third Creek Cem—*cemetery* ... MO-7
Third Creek Ch—*church* (2) ... NC-3
Third Creek Pond—*lake* ... MI-6
Third Creek Presbyterian Church and Cemetery—*hist pl* ... NC-3
Third Creek Rsvr—*reservoir* ... OR-9
*Third Creek School* ... TN-4
Third Creek Spring—*spring* ... OR-9
*Third Creek Station* ... NC-3
Third Creek Township—*civil* ... MO-7
Third Creek Watershed Dam Number Nine—*dam* ... NC-3
Third Creek Watershed Dam Ten—*dam* ... NC-3
*Third Creek Watershed Dam 74* ... NC-3
*Third Creek W/S Dam Number 11* ... NC-3
*Third Creek W/S Dam Number 12c* ... NC-3
*Third Creek W/S Dam Number 18* ... NC-3
*Third Creek W/S Dam Number 19* ... NC-3
*Third Creek W/S Dam Number 20* ... NC-3
*Third Creek W/S Dam Number 21* ... NC-3
*Third Creek W/S Dam Number 34a* ... NC-3
*Third Creek W/S Dam Number 37* ... NC-3
Third Crossing—*locale* (2) ... TX-5
Third Crow Wing Lake—*lake* ... MN-6
**Third Crow Wing Lake**—*pop pl* ... MN-6
Third Currier Pond—*lake* ... ME-1
Third Dam—*dam* ... UT-8
Third Davis Pond—*lake* ... ME-1
Third Debsconeag Lake—*lake* ... ME-1
Third District Sch—*school* ... PA-2
Third Divide—*gap* ... CA-9
Third East Branch Magalloway River—*stream* ... ME-1
Third Fitzwilliam Meetinghouse—*hist pl* ... NH-1
*Third Forest* ... AZ-5
Third Fork—*stream* ... MO-7
Third Fork—*stream* ... UT-8
Third Fork Big Creek—*stream* ... KY-4
Third Fork Creek—*stream* ... NC-3
Third Fork Guard Station—*locale* ... ID-8
*Third Fork Platte River* ... MO-7
Third Fork Project Camp—*locale* ... ID-8
Third Fork Ridge—*ridge* ... ID-8
Third Fork Rock Creek—*stream* ... ID-8
Third Fork Squaw Creek—*stream* ... ID-8
Third Gap—*gap* ... PA-2
Third Gap Trail—*trail* ... PA-2
Third Greely Pond—*lake* ... ME-1
Third Green Knob—*summit* ... PA-2
Third Guide Lake—*lake* ... MN-6
Third Gulch—*valley* ... CO-8
Third Gulch—*valley* ... ID-8
Third Gulch—*valley* ... MT-8
Third Gulch Spring—*spring* ... CO-8
*Third Hanson Lake* ... MN-6
Third Hay Creek—*stream* ... MT-8
Third Herring Brook—*stream* ... MA-1
Third Hill—*summit* (2) ... ME-1
Third Hill—*summit* (2) ... VA-3
Third Hill Mtn—*summit* ... WV-2
Third Hole—*basin* ... UT-8
Third Hollow—*valley* ... AZ-5
Third Hollow—*valley* (2) ... ID-8
Third Hollow—*valley* ... KY-4
Third Hollow—*valley* ... PA-2
Third House Flat—*flat* ... UT-8
Third Island—*island* ... LA-4
Third Island—*island* ... MA-1
Third Island—*island* ... MI-6
Third Island—*island* ... MN-6
Third Island—*island* ... PA-2
Third Judicial District Courthouse—*hist pl* .. NY-2
Third Kekur—*island* ... AK-9
*Third Kimball Lake* ... MN-6
Third Knob—*summit* ... NC-3
*Third Kokadjo Lake* ... ME-1
Third Kyger Ch—*church* ... OH-6
*Third Lake* ... IN-6
*Third Lake* ... ME-1
Third Lake—*lake* (2) ... AK-9
Third Lake—*lake* ... CA-9
Third Lake—*lake* ... IL-6
Third Lake—*lake* (5) ... ME-1
Third Lake—*lake* (8) ... MI-6
Third Lake—*lake* (8) ... MN-6
Third Lake—*lake* (6) ... NY-2
Third Lake—*lake* ... OR-9
Third Lake—*lake* ... WA-9
Third Lake—*lake* (3) ... WI-6
**Third Lake**—*pop pl* ... IL-6
*Third Lake Brook* ... ME-1
Third Lake Creek—*stream* ... NY-2
Third Lake Ridge—*ridge* ... ME-1
Third Lake Swamp—*swamp* ... NY-2
Third Lefthand Fork—*stream* ... UT-8
Third Level Canal—*canal* ... MA-1
Third Lift Canal—*canal* ... CA-9
*Third Little River* ... NC-3
Third Louisiana Redan (historical)—*locale* ... MS-4
Third Machias Lake—*lake* ... ME-1
Third Meetinghouse—*hist pl* ... MA-1
*Third Mesa* ... AZ-5
Third Mesa—*summit* (2) ... AZ-5
Third Mine Branch—*stream* ... MD-2
Third Missionary Baptist Ch (historical)—*church* ... MS-4
Third Mound—*summit* ... TX-5
Third Mount Olive Baptist Ch—*church* ... MS-4
Third Mount Zion Ch—*church* ... VA-3
Third Mtn—*summit* ... ME-1
Third Mtn—*summit* ... PA-2
Third Mtn—*summit* ... VA-3
Third Musquacook Lake—*reservoir* ... ME-1
Third Musquash Pond—*lake* ... ME-1
Third Napa Slough—*gut* ... CA-9
Third Natl Bank—*hist pl* ... KY-4
Third Natl Bank—*hist pl* ... NY-2
Third Natl Bank—*hist pl* ... OH-6
Third Natl Bank Bldg—*hist pl* ... NC-3
*Third Negro Brook Lake* ... ME-1
Third Neshanic River—*stream* ... NJ-2
Third Newlin Creek—*stream* ... CO-8
*Third Nigger Brook Lake* ... ME-1
Third Order Villa—*locale* ... NY-2
Third Park—*flat* ... CO-8
Third Peak—*summit* ... VA-3
Third Pelletier Brook—*stream* ... ME-1
Third Pelletier Brook Lake—*lake* ... ME-1
Third Perch Lake—*lake* ... MN-6
Third Point—*cape* ... FL-3
Third Point—*cape* ... MA-1
Third Point—*cliff* ... VA-3
*Third Pond* ... PA-2
Third Pond—*lake* ... ME-1
Third Pond—*lake* (2) ... NY-2
Third Pond—*lake* ... PA-2
*Third Pond Tomar Pond* ... NY-2
*Third Precinct* ... MA-1
Third Precinct Police Station—*hist pl* ... MI-6
Third Presbyterian Ch—*church* ... AL-4
Third Presbyterian Church—*hist pl* ... OH-6
Third Price Pond—*lake* ... OH-6
Third Puncheon Branch—*swamp* ... FL-3
Third Pup—*stream* ... AK-9
Third Range—*range* ... AK-9
Third Rapids—*rapids* ... WI-6
Third Recess—*valley* ... CA-9
Third Recess Lake—*lake* ... CA-9
Third Red Knoll—*summit* ... UT-8
Third Reformed Church—*hist pl* ... MI-6
Third Reformed Church of Holland—*hist pl* ... MI-6
Third Ridge—*ridge* ... MT-8
Third River—*stream* ... MN-6
Third River—*stream* ... NJ-2
Third River Flowage—*channel* ... MN-6
Third River Rec Area—*park* ... MN-6
**Third River (Township of)**—*pop pl* ... MN-6
Third Roach Pond—*lake* ... ME-1
Third RR Station—*hist pl* ... MA-1
Third Rsvr—*reservoir* ... NY-2
Third Run—*stream* (2) ... WV-2
Third Saint John Pond—*lake* ... ME-1
Third Salt Creek—*stream* ... UT-8
Third Sand Creek—*stream* ... WY-8
Third Set Spring—*spring* ... CO-8
*Third Siding* ... ND-7
Third Silver Lake—*lake* ... MN-6
Third Slough—*stream* ... MT-8
Third Slough—*stream* ... OR-9
Third South Fork East Fork Clear Creek—*stream* ... CA-9
*Third Spring* ... ID-8
Third Spring—*spring* ... ID-8
Third Spring—*spring* ... UT-8
*Third Spring Creek* ... ID-8
Third Spring Creek—*stream* ... ID-8
Third Spring Hollow—*valley* ... UT-8
Third St. Joseph County Courthouse—*hist pl* ... IN-6
Third Street Bethel A.M.E. Church—*hist pl* ... VA-3
Third Street Bridge—*hist pl* ... OH-6
Third Street Bridge—*hist pl* ... WI-6
Third Street Ch of God—*church* ... TN-4
*Third Street Elem Sch* ... NC-3
Third Street Elem Sch—*school* ... IN-6
Third Street Hist Dist—*hist pl* (2) ... KY-4
Third Street Sch—*school* ... CA-9
Third Street Sch—*school* ... NC-3
Third Street Sch—*school* ... OH-6
Third Street Sch—*school* ... PA-2
Third Sucker Lake—*lake* ... MN-6
Third Temple Ch—*church* ... MS-4
Third Term Mine—*mine* ... MT-8
Third Term Mine—*mine* ... UT-8
Third Tributary—*stream* ... NC-3
Third Union Cem—*cemetery* ... MS-4
Third Union Ch—*church* ... MS-4
Third Union Ch—*church* ... VA-3
*Third Union Missionary Baptist Ch* ... MS-4
*Third Upper Saint John Pond* ... ME-1
Third Ward Elem Sch—*school* (3) ... PA-2
Third Ward Grade Sch (historical)—*school* .. PA-2
Third Ward Hist Dist—*hist pl* ... NY-2
Third Ward Hist Dist—*hist pl* ... WI-6
Third Ward Park—*park* ... OH-6
Third Ward Sch—*hist pl* ... WI-6
Third Ward Sch—*school* ... GA-3
Third Ward Sch—*school* ... LA-4
Third Ward Sch—*school* (6) ... PA-2
Third Ward Sch (abandoned)—*school* (3) ... PA-2
**Third Ward (subdivision)**—*pop pl* ... NC-3
Third Wash—*stream* ... CA-9
Third Washburn Tunnel—*tunnel* ... NC-3
Third Water Creek—*stream* ... CA-9
Third Water Creek—*stream* ... UT-8
Third Water Gulch—*valley* ... CO-8
Third Water Ridge—*ridge* ... UT-8
Third Water Spring—*spring* ... CO-8
Third West Branch Pond—*lake* ... ME-1
*Third Wolverine Creek* ... MT-8
*Third Yegua Creek* ... TX-5
Third Yellow Mule Creek—*stream* ... MT-8
Third Zion Cem—*cemetery* ... LA-4
Third Zion Ch—*church* ... AR-4
Third Zion Ch—*church* ... LA-4
Thirkell Sch—*school* ... MI-6
Thirlwell Sch—*school* ... IL-6
Thirst Branch—*stream* ... TN-4
Thirst Creek—*stream* ... ID-8
Thirsting Lake—*lake* ... FL-3
Thirsty Camp Trail—*trail* ... OR-9
Thirsty Canyon—*valley* ... NV-8
Thirsty Creek—*stream* ... ID-8
Thirsty Creek—*stream* ... OR-9
Thirsty Creek—*stream* ... WA-9
Thirsty Gulch—*valley* ... OR-9
Thirsty Gulch Spring—*spring* ... OR-9
Thirsty Lake—*lake* ... CT-1
Thirsty Lake—*lake* ... MT-8
Thirsty Mesa—*summit* ... AZ-5
Thirsty Mtn—*summit* ... MT-8
Thirsty Mtn—*summit* ... NV-8
Thirsty Peak—*summit* ... CO-8
Thirsty Point—*cape* ... OR-9
Thirsty Pond—*lake* ... NY-2
Thirteen, Canal (historical)—*canal* ... AZ-5
Thirteen, Lake—*lake* (3) ... MI-6
Thirteen, Lake—*lake* (3) ... MN-6
Thirteen, Lake No—*reservoir* ... AR-4
*Thirteen Creek* ... MI-6
Thirteen Creek—*stream* ... ID-8
Thirteen Creek—*stream* ... WA-9
Thirteen Creek, Lake—*stream* ... MI-6
Thirteen Faces—*pillar* ... UT-8
Thirteen Forks—*locale* ... GA-3
Thirteen Gulch—*valley* ... AK-9
Thirteen Gulch—*valley* (2) ... MT-8
Thirteen Lake—*lake* (2) ... MN-6
Thirteen Lakes—*lake* ... ID-8
Thirteen Mile—*locale* ... FL-3
*Thirteenmile Creek* ... CO-8
*Thirteenmile Creek* ... FL-3
Thirteenmile Creek—*stream* ... AK-9
Thirteenmile Creek—*stream* ... CA-9
Thirteenmile Creek—*stream* ... CO-8
Thirteenmile Creek—*stream* ... MI-6
Thirteenmile Creek—*stream* ... MT-8
Thirteenmile Creek—*stream* ... OR-9
Thirteenmile Creek—*stream* (2) ... WA-9
Thirteenmile Creek—*stream* ... WV-2
Thirteenmile Draw—*valley* (2) ... NM-5
Thirteenmile Lake—*lake* ... MI-6
Thirteenmile Mtn—*summit* ... WA-9
Thirteenmile Rock Butte—*summit* ... AZ-5
*Thirteenmile Run* ... FL-3
Thirteenmile Run—*stream* ... FL-3
Thirteen Mile Spring—*spring* ... AZ-5
Thirteenmile Spring—*spring* ... OR-9
Thirteen Mile Tank—*reservoir* ... AZ-5
Thirteenmile Tank—*reservoir* ... AZ-5
*Thirteen Mile Wash* ... AZ-5
Thirteenmile Wash—*stream* ... AZ-5
Thirteen Mile Woods—*woods* ... NH-1
Thirteen Mtn—*summit* ... ID-8
Thirteen North Lake Well—*well* ... NM-5
Thirteen Points Landing—*locale* ... LA-4

Thirteen Pup—*stream* AK-9
Thirteen Ranch—*locale* AZ-5
Thirteen Tank—*reservoir* AZ-5
Thirteenth and Green Streets Elem Sch—*school* PA-2
**Thirteenth Ave Subdivision**—*pop pl* UT-8
Thirteenth Division Prairie—*flat* WA-9
Thirteenth Lake—*lake* NY-2
Thirteenth Sch (hsitorical)—*school* MS-4
*Thirteenth Siding* ND-7
**Thirteenth South Subdivision**—*pop pl* UT-8
Thirteenth Street Center—*locale* KS-7
Thirteenth Street Ch of God—*church* FL-3
Thirteenth Street Sch—*school* NY-2
Thirtieth and Lorraine Shop Ctr—*locale* KS-7
Thirtieth Infantry Bluff—*cliff* WA-9
Thirtieth Street Station—*hist pl* PA-2
Thirtieth Street Station—*locale* PA-2
**Thirty**—*pop pl* IA-7
Thirty, Lake—*lake* (2) WI-6
Thirty Acre Island—*island* TN-4
Thirty Acre Pond—*lake* RI-1
Thirtyacre Pond—*reservoir* MA-1
Thirty Cent Creek—*stream* WA-9
*Thirty Corner* IA-7
Thirty Day Creek—*stream* ID-8
Thirty Day Tank—*reservoir* AZ-5
Thirty-eight Creek—*stream* ID-8
Thirty Eighth Baptist Ch—*church* MS-4
Thirtyeight Hill—*summit* TX-5
Thirty Eighth Street County Park—*park* CA-9
Thirty Eighth Street Sch—*school* WI-6
Thirty-eight Infantry Bluff—*cliff* WA-9
Thirtyeight Mile Lake—*lake* AK-9
Thirtyeight Tank—*reservoir* TX-5
Thirtyeight Windmill—*locale* TX-5
Thirty-Fifth Parallel Route—*hist pl* AZ-5
Thirty Fifth Street Sch—*school* WI-6
Thirtyfirst Ave Baptist Ch—*church* MS-4
Thirty First Street Sch—*school* WI-6
Thirtyfive Brook—*stream* ME-1
Thirtyfive Canyon—*valley* CA-9
Thirtyfive Canyon—*valley* UT-8
Thirtyfive Lakes—*lake* WI-6
Thirtyfive Mile Point—*cape* LA-4
Thirtyfive Outlet—*stream* NY-2
Thirtyfive Pond—*lake* NY-2
Thirtyfive Ridge—*ridge* ME-1
Thirtyfive Spring—*spring* CA-9
Thirtyfive Tank—*reservoir* AZ-5
Thirty-Foot Canal—*canal* NC-3
Thirtyfoot Falls—*falls* ME-1
Thirtyfour, Lake—*lake* MN-6
Thirtyfour Corner—*locale* MO-7
Thirtyfour Corner Blue Hole—*lake* MO-7
**Thirty Four Corner (Corner)**—*pop pl* MO-7
Thirty Four Corner Sch (historical)—*school* MO-7
Thirtyfourth Ave Sch—*school* AR-4
Thirtyfourth Street—*post sta* OK-5
Thirtyfourth Street Baptist Ch—*church* TN-4
Thirty Lake—*lake* MN-6
Thirtymile—*locale* OR-9
**Thirty-mile**—*pop pl* OR-9
Thirtymile Campground—*locale* CO-8
Thirtymile Campground—*locale* WA-9
Thirtymile Canal—*canal* NE-7
Thirtymile Canyon—*valley* NV-8
Thirtymile Creek—*stream* FL-3
Thirtymile Creek—*stream* MT-8
Thirtymile Creek—*stream* ND-7
Thirtymile Creek—*stream* OR-9
Thirtymile Creek—*stream* (2) WA-9
Thirtymile Lake—*lake* AK-9
Thirtymile Meadows—*flat* WA-9
Thirtymile Peak—*summit* WA-9
Thirtymile Point—*cape* NY-2
Thirty Mile Point Light—*hist pl* NY-2
Thirtymile Ranch—*locale* MT-8
Thirtymile Ranch—*locale* NV-8
Thirtymile Rsvr—*reservoir* MT-8
Thirtymile Shoals—*bar* TN-4
Thirtymile Slough—*stream* AK-9
Thirtymile Trail—*trail* WA-9
Thirtymile Wash—*stream* NV-8
Thirtynine Creek—*stream* MI-6
Thirtynine (historical)—*locale* AL-4
Thirtynine Mile Mtn—*summit* CO-8
Thirtynine Spring—*spring* AZ-5
Thirty-Nine Tannery—*locale* ME-1
Thirty-ninth and Noland Center (Shop Ctr)—*locale* MO-7
Thirtyninth Ave Ch of Christ—*church* MS-4
Thirty-ninth Street—*uninc pl* OK-5
Thirtyninth Street Sch—*school* CA-9
Thirtyninth Street Sch—*school* NY-2
Thirty-one Draw—*valley* NM-5
Thirtyone Hollow—*valley* MO-7
Thirtyone Hollow—*valley* WV-2
Thirtyone Lake—*lake* MN-6
Thirty-One Lake—*lake* MN-6
Thirty-One Lake—*lake* NE-7
Thirty One Mile Bluff—*cliff* AL-4
Thirtyone Mile Creek—*stream* CO-8
Thirtyone Mile Mtn—*summit* CO-8
Thirty One Rsvr—*reservoir* CO-8
Thirty One Swamp—*swamp* FL-3
Thirtyone Tank—*reservoir* AZ-5
Thirty-second Ave Sch—*school* AL-4
Thirty Seven Mile Bluff—*cliff* AL-4
Thirtyseventh Street Sch—*school* CA-9
Thirty Seventh Street Sch—*school* WI-6
Thirtysix, Lake—*lake* (2) MI-6
Thirtysix Canyon—*valley* NM-5
Thirtysix Draw—*valley* TX-5
Thirtysix Island—*island* MN-6
Thirtysix Lake—*lake* (2) MN-6
Thirty-Six Lake—*lake* NE-7
Thirtysix Mile Cabin—*locale* AK-9
*Thirty-six Mile Siding* SD-7
Thirty Six Mine—*mine* OR-9
Thirtysix Spring—*spring* UT-8
Thirtysix Tank—*reservoir* (3) AZ-5
Thirtysixth Street Sch—*school* CA-9
Thirty-third Street Bridge in Philadelphia—*hist pl* PA-2
Thirtythird Street Sch—*school* CA-9
Thirty-Thirty Spring—*spring* (2) OR-9
Thirty-three, Island—*island* FL-3
Thirtythree, Tank—*reservoir* AZ-5
*Thirty Three Creek* MI-6
Thirtythree Creek—*stream* MI-6
Thirtythree Creek—*stream* WI-6
Thirtythree Hollow—*valley* MO-7
Thirtythree Lake—*lake* ID-8
Thirtythree Lake—*lake* MN-6
Thirtythree Mile Ranch—*locale* WY-8
Thirtythree Mile Rsvr—*reservoir* WY-8
Thirtythree Pond—*reservoir* WY-8
Thirtythree Tank—*reservoir* AZ-5
Thirtythree Tank—*reservoir* NM-5
Thirty Two, Lake—*lake* MI-6
Thirty Two, Lake—*lake* WA-9
Thirty-Two, Lake—*lake* WA-9
Thirtytwo, Tank—*reservoir* AZ-5
Thirtytwo Canyon—*valley* WY-8
Thirty-two Creek—*stream* ID-8
Thirtytwo Creek—*stream* WY-8
Thirtytwo Kazyga Slough—*gut* AK-9
Thirtytwo Mile Cabin—*locale* AK-9
Thirtytwo Mile Creek—*stream* AK-9
Thirtytwo Mile Creek—*stream* NE-7
Thirty Two Mile Gulch—*valley* CO-8
Thirty-Two Mile Station Site—*hist pl* NE-7
Thirtytwo Point Creek—*stream* OR-9
Thirtytwo Tank—*reservoir* NM-5
Thirtytwo Well—*well* AZ-5
**Thiry Daems**—*pop pl* WI-6
Thisbe—*locale* NV-8
This Gospel Tabernacle—*church* MO-7
This is the Place Monmt—*park* UT-8
Thissell Bog—*lake* ME-1
Thissell Brook—*stream* ME-1
Thissell Pond—*lake* ME-1
Thisted, Lake—*lake* SD-7
Thistle—*locale* UT-8
**Thistle**—*pop pl* MD-2
Thistle Brook—*stream* NH-1
Thistleburn Creek—*stream* OR-9
Thistleburn Ridge—*ridge* OR-9
Thistle Canal—*canal* CA-9
Thistle Cem—*cemetery* NY-2
Thistle Cove—*bay* AK-9
Thistle Creek—*stream* (2) AK-9
Thistle Creek—*stream* (2) OR-9
Thistle Creek—*stream* UT-8
Thistle Creek—*stream* WY-8
Thistledew Campground—*locale* MN-6
Thistledew Lake—*lake* MN-6
Thistledew Lookout Tower—*locale* MN-6
Thistledew Ranger Station—*locale* MN-6
Thistledew Spring—*spring* OR-9
Thistledown—*locale* CO-8
Thistledown Creek—*stream* CO-8
Thistledown Racetrack—*other* OH-6
Thistle Drain—*canal* CA-9
Thistle Five Drain—*canal* CA-9
Thistle Flat—*flat* UT-8
Thistle Flat Pond—*reservoir* AZ-5
Thistle Four Drain—*canal* CA-9
Thistle Glade Campground—*locale* CA-9
Thistle Glade Creek—*stream* CA-9
Thistle Glenn Camp—*locale* CA-9
*Thistle Hill* MA-1
Thistle Hill—*summit* VT-1
Thistle Hollow—*valley* AZ-5
Thistle Hollow—*valley* TN-4
Thistle Hollow—*valley* WY-8
Thistle Island—*island* CT-1
Thistle Island—*island* NY-2
Thistle Lateral Eight—*canal* CA-9
Thistle Lateral Five—*canal* CA-9
Thistle Lateral Four—*canal* CA-9
Thistle Lateral One—*canal* CA-9
Thistle Lateral Seven—*canal* CA-9
Thistle Ledge—*other* AK-9
Thistle Mine—*mine* TN-4
Thistle Pond—*lake* ME-1
Thistle Ridge Cem—*cemetery* LA-4
Thistle Ridge Plantation—*locale* LA-4
Thistle Rock—*island* AK-9
Thistle Rock—*other* AK-9
Thistle Seven Drain—*canal* CA-9
Thistle Shaft (Site)—*locale* CA-9
Thistle Spring—*spring* CA-9
Thistle Spring—*spring* ID-8
Thistle Substation—*flat* UT-8
Thistle Tank—*reservoir* (5) AZ-5
Thistlethwaite State Wildlife Mngmt Area—*park* LA-4
Thistleton Subdivision—*uninc pl* KY-4
**Thistlewaite**—*pop pl* LA-4
*Thistlewaite Ditch* IN-6
Thistle Well—*well* AZ-5
Thivener—*locale* OH-6
**Thixton**—*pop pl* KY-4
Thixton Creek—*stream* NY-2
Thixton Lane Ch—*church* KY-4
Thlakalchka Cholockominne (historical)—*locale* AL-4
*Thlomar* FM-9
Thlopthlocco Ch—*church* OK-5
Thluichohnjik Creek—*stream* AK-9
Thobolocco Branch—*stream* AL-4
**Thoburn**—*pop pl* WV-2
Thode Cabin—*locale* AZ-5
Thode Creek—*stream* WY-8
Thody Drain—*stream* MI-6
Thody Pond—*lake* CT-1
Thoelaeb—*bay* FM-9
Thoel Drain—*stream* MI-6
Thoelecke Valley—*valley* NE-7
Thoelke Cem—*cemetery* WI-6
Thoeming Draw—*valley* WY-8
Thoeming Lake—*lake* WI-6
*Thoen Lake* MN-6
Thoen Lake—*lake* MN-6
Thoit Coulee—*valley* MT-8
Thoits Branch—*stream* ME-1
*Thol* FM-9
Thola—*locale* AR-4
*Tholab* FM-9
Thole Lake—*lake* MN-6
Tholocco, Lake—*reservoir* AL-4
Tholomar—*summit* FM-9
T Holt Haywood Dam—*dam* NC-3
T Holzwarth Dam—*dam* SD-7
Thom, Mount—*summit* WI-6
Thoma Butte—*summit* AZ-5
Thoma Creek—*stream* MT-8
Thomae Ranch—*locale* MT-8
Thoma Lookout—*locale* MT-8
**Thomann**—*pop pl* CA-9
Thoman Sch—*school* WY-8
*Thomas* KS-7
*Thomas* ND-7
Thomas—*locale* IA-7
Thomas—*locale* KY-4
Thomas—*locale* NH-1
Thomas—*locale* NM-5
Thomas—*locale* PA-2
Thomas—*locale* TN-4
Thomas—*locale* TX-5
Thomas—*locale* VA-3
**Thomas**—*pop pl* AL-4
**Thomas**—*pop pl* ID-8
**Thomas**—*pop pl* IL-6
**Thomas**—*pop pl* IN-6
**Thomas**—*pop pl* KY-4
**Thomas**—*pop pl* LA-4
**Thomas**—*pop pl* MD-2
**Thomas**—*pop pl* (2) MI-6
**Thomas**—*pop pl* OK-5
**Thomas**—*pop pl* PA-2
**Thomas**—*pop pl* SD-7
**Thomas**—*pop pl* TX-5
**Thomas**—*pop pl* WA-9
**Thomas**—*pop pl* WV-2
Thomas, Abijah, House—*hist pl* VA-3
Thomas, Alma, House—*hist pl* DC-2
Thomas, Andrew, House—*hist pl* IN-6
Thomas, Bayou—*gut* LA-4
Thomas, Benjamin F., House—*hist pl* TN-4
Thomas, Charles, House—*hist pl* PA-2
Thomas, Charles A., House—*hist pl* SD-7
Thomas, Dr. A. O., House—*hist pl* NE-7
Thomas, Dr. Nathan M., House—*hist pl* MI-6
Thomas, F. D., House—*hist pl* IL-6
Thomas, Frank, House—*hist pl* IL-6
Thomas, George C., JHS—*hist pl* PA-2
Thomas, George C., Memorial Library—*hist pl* AK-9
Thomas, H. H., House—*hist pl* CO-8
Thomas, H.P., House—*hist pl* MA-1
Thomas, I. C., Drug Store—*hist pl* WI-6
Thomas, Jack, House—*hist pl* KY-4
Thomas, James A., Farm—*hist pl* NC-3
Thomas, Kings, III, House—*hist pl* KY-4
Thomas, Lake—*lake* CO-8
Thomas, Lake—*lake* (2) FL-3
Thomas, Lake—*lake* ND-7
Thomas, Lake—*lake* PA-2
Thomas, Lake—*lake* WA-9
Thomas, Lake—*lake* WV-2
Thomas, Lake—*reservoir* CO-8
Thomas, Lake—*reservoir* MS-4
Thomas, Lewis H., House—*hist pl* IL-6
Thomas, Milton and Minerva, House—*hist pl* UT-8
Thomas, Mount—*summit* AK-9
Thomas, Mount—*summit* (2) AZ-5
Thomas, Mount—*summit* (2) CO-8
Thomas, Samuel B., House—*hist pl* KY-4
Thomas, Solomon, House—*hist pl* KY-4
Thomas, William, House—*hist pl* PA-2
Thomas, William J., House—*hist pl* KY-4
**Thomas Acres**—*pop pl* AL-4
**Thomas Addition**—*pop pl* TN-4
Thomas A Edison, Lake—*reservoir* CA-9
Thomas A Edison Elem Sch—*school* IN-6
Thomas A Edison JHS—*school* (2) IN-6
Thomas A Edison JHS—*school* TX-5
*Thomas A. Edison Lake* CA-9
Thomas A Edison MS—*school* IN-6
Thomas A Edison Sch—*school* IL-6
Thomas A Edison Senior HS—*school* IN-6
Thomas A Gemignani Lake—*reservoir* TN-4
Thomas A Hendricks Elem Sch—*school* IN-6
Thomas Airp—*airport* MO-7
Thomas Allen Point—*cape* AR-4
Thomas A. Mathis Bridge—*bridge* NJ-2
Thomas Arroyo—*stream* NM-5
Thomas Ave Sch—*school* MD-2
Thomas Basin—*bay* AK-9
Thomas Basin—*bay* MA-1
Thomas Bass Dam—*dam* NC-3
Thomas Bay—*bay* AK-9
Thomas Bay—*bay* FL-3
Thomas Bay—*bay* (2) ME-1
Thomas Bay—*swamp* FL-3
Thomas Bay—*swamp* NC-3
Thomas Bay Branch—*stream* MS-4
Thomas Bay Rec Area—*park* SD-7
Thomas B Collier Cem—*cemetery* AL-4
Thomas Bed Mine (underground)—*mine* AL-4
Thomas Bend—*bend* (2) KY-4
Thomasboro—*locale* GA-3
**Thomasboro**—*pop pl* IL-6
**Thomasboro**—*pop pl* NC-3
*Thomasboro Crossroads* NC-3
**Thomasboro Crossroads**—*pop pl* NC-3
*Thomasboro High School* NC-3
Thomasboro Sch—*school* NC-3
**Thomasboro (subdivision)**—*pop pl* NC-3
*Thomasboro X-roads* NC-3
Thomas Bottom—*basin* TN-4
Thomas Brake—*swamp* LA-4
*Thomas Branch* TN-4
Thomas Branch—*stream* (4) AL-4
Thomas Branch—*stream* AR-4
Thomas Branch—*stream* FL-3
Thomas Branch—*stream* (2) GA-3
Thomas Branch—*stream* IN-6
Thomas Branch—*stream* (8) KY-4
Thomas Branch—*stream* (2) LA-4
Thomas Branch—*stream* (3) MD-2
Thomas Branch—*stream* MS-4
Thomas Branch—*stream* (2) MO-7
Thomas Branch—*stream* (3) NC-3
Thomas Branch—*stream* (2) SC-3
Thomas Branch—*stream* (9) TN-4
Thomas Branch—*stream* TX-5
Thomas Branch—*stream* VA-3
Thomas Branch—*stream* (2) WV-2
Thomas Bridge—*bridge* NC-3
Thomas Bridge—*bridge* PA-2
Thomas Bridge—*bridge* VA-3
Thomas Bridge—*locale* TN-4
**Thomas Bridge**—*pop pl* VA-3
Thomas Bridge (historical)—*bridge* AL-4
Thomas Brook—*stream* (2) ME-1
Thomas Brook—*stream* MA-1
Thomas Brook—*stream* (2) NY-2
Thomas Bros Mine—*mine* CA-9
Thomas Brothers Landing Strip—*airport* SD-7
Thomasburg Sch (abandoned)—*school* PA-2
Thomas Burke Dam Number 1—*dam* SD-7
Thomas Butte—*summit* MT-8
Thomas Cairn—*locale* OR-9
Thomas Canal—*canal* NC-3
Thomas Canyon—*valley* (2) AZ-5
Thomas Canyon—*valley* CO-8
Thomas Canyon—*valley* (3) NV-8
Thomas Canyon—*valley* NM-5
Thomas Canyon—*valley* (3) UT-8
Thomas Canyon—*valley* WY-8
Thomas Canyon Forest Camp—*locale* NV-8
*Thomas Canyon Recreation Site* NV-8
Thomas Canyon Wash—*stream* AZ-5
Thomas-Carithers House—*hist pl* GA-3
Thomas Carr Howe HS—*school* IN-6
*Thomas Cave* TN-4
Thomas Cave—*cave* AL-4
Thomas Cave Branch—*stream* KY-4
Thomas C Bower Elem Sch—*school* TN-4
Thomas (CCD)—*cens area* OK-5
*Thomas Cem* MS-4
Thomas Cem—*cemetery* (4) AL-4
Thomas Cem—*cemetery* (6) AR-4
Thomas Cem—*cemetery* (5) GA-3
Thomas Cem—*cemetery* IL-6
Thomas Cem—*cemetery* (3) IN-6
Thomas Cem—*cemetery* IA-7
Thomas Cem—*cemetery* KS-7
Thomas Cem—*cemetery* (9) KY-4
Thomas Cem—*cemetery* (4) LA-4
Thomas Cem—*cemetery* (2) ME-1
Thomas Cem—*cemetery* MD-2
Thomas Cem—*cemetery* (2) MA-1
Thomas Cem—*cemetery* (5) MS-4
Thomas Cem—*cemetery* (8) MO-7
Thomas Cem—*cemetery* NM-5
Thomas Cem—*cemetery* (3) NY-2
Thomas Cem—*cemetery* (8) NC-3
Thomas Cem—*cemetery* (7) OH-6
Thomas Cem—*cemetery* OK-5
Thomas Cem—*cemetery* (5) PA-2
Thomas Cem—*cemetery* SC-3
Thomas Cem—*cemetery* (18) TN-4
Thomas Cem—*cemetery* (5) TX-5
Thomas Cem—*cemetery* (5) VA-3
Thomas Cem—*cemetery* (6) WV-2
Thomas Cem—*cemetery* (2) WI-6
Thomas Cem (historical)—*cemetery* MO-7
Thomas Ch—*church* AR-4
Thomas Ch—*church* LA-4
Thomas Ch—*church* OK-5
Thomas Ch—*church* PA-2
Thomas Ch—*church* TN-4
Thomas Chapel—*church* (3) AL-4
Thomas Chapel—*church* AR-4
Thomas Chapel—*church* DE-2
Thomas Chapel—*church* (4) GA-3
Thomas Chapel—*church* (2) LA-4
Thomas Chapel—*church* MS-4
Thomas Chapel—*church* (2) MO-7
Thomas Chapel—*church* (4) NC-3
Thomas Chapel—*church* OK-5
Thomas Chapel—*church* (2) TN-4
Thomas Chapel—*church* (3) VA-3
Thomas Chapel—*church* WV-2
Thomas Chapel Cem—*cemetery* OK-5
Thomas Chapel Cem—*cemetery* TN-4
Thomas Chapel C.M.E. Church—*hist pl* KY-4
Thomas Chapel Methodist Ch—*church* AL-4
Thomas Chapel Sch—*school* OK-5
Thomas Chapel Sch (historical)—*school* TN-4
Thomas Chappel Malone Cem—*cemetery* AL-4
Thomas C Head Sch—*school* AL-4
Thomas Cheatham Cem—*cemetery* MS-4
Thomas Cherry Dam—*dam* AL-4
Thomas Ch (historical)—*church* (2) TN-4
**Thomas Choice**—*pop pl* MD-2
Thomas Chute—*stream* MO-7
Thomas Circle—*locale* DC-2
Thomas City—*locale* FL-3
Thomas Clark Grant—*civil* FL-3
Thomas Coal Bed Mine (underground)—*mine* AL-4
Thomas Cole Mtn—*summit* NY-2
Thomas Conley Branch—*stream* KY-4
Thomas Copley Ch—*church* WV-2
Thomas Corner—*locale* SC-3
Thomas Corner—*locale* VA-3
Thomas Corners—*locale* (2) DE-2
Thomas Corners—*locale* (2) NY-2
Thomas Corners Cem—*cemetery* NY-2
Thomas Coulee Rsvr—*reservoir* WY-8
Thomas County—*civil* KS-7
**Thomas (County)**—*pop pl* GA-3
Thomas County Courthouse—*hist pl* GA-3
Thomas County Courthouse—*hist pl* KS-7
Thomas County Fairgrounds—*locale* KS-7
Thomas Cove—*valley* AL-4
Thomas Cove—*valley* NC-3
Thomas Cove Branch—*stream* NC-3
Thomas Covered Bridge—*hist pl* PA-2
*Thomas Creek* CA-9
*Thomas Creek* ID-8
*Thomas Creek* MD-2
*Thomas Creek* TN-4
*Thomas Creek* UT-8
Thomas Creek—*stream* (2) AL-4
Thomas Creek—*stream* (2) AK-9
Thomas Creek—*stream* (3) AZ-5
Thomas Creek—*stream* (3) AR-4
Thomas Creek—*stream* (2) CA-9
Thomas Creek—*stream* (2) CO-8
Thomas Creek—*stream* (2) FL-3
Thomas Creek—*stream* (4) GA-3
Thomas Creek—*stream* (5) ID-8
Thomas Creek—*stream* (2) KS-7
Thomas Creek—*stream* KY-4
Thomas Creek—*stream* (3) LA-4
Thomas Creek—*stream* MD-2
Thomas Creek—*stream* (3) MS-4
Thomas Creek—*stream* (2) MO-7
Thomas Creek—*stream* (2) MT-8
Thomas Creek—*stream* (2) NE-7
Thomas Creek—*stream* (4) NV-8
Thomas Creek—*stream* (2) NY-2
Thomas Creek—*stream* (3) NC-3
Thomas Creek—*stream* OK-5
Thomas Creek—*stream* (9) OR-9
Thomas Creek—*stream* PA-2
Thomas Creek—*stream* TN-4
Thomas Creek—*stream* (6) TX-5
Thomas Creek—*stream* (5) VA-3
Thomas Creek—*stream* (3) WA-9
Thomas Creek—*stream* WV-2
Thomas Creek—*stream* (2) WY-8
Thomas Creek Archeol District—*hist pl* FL-3
Thomas Creek Basin—*basin* OR-9
Thomas Creek Campground—*park* OR-9
Thomas Creek-Gilkey Covered Bridge—*hist pl* OR-9
Thomas Creek Rest Area—*locale* OR-9
Thomas Creek Ridge—*ridge* OR-9
Thomas Creek-Shimanek Covered Bridge—*hist pl* OR-9
Thomas Creek Spring—*spring* AZ-5
Thomas Creek Spring—*spring* ID-8
Thomas Creek Weir—*dam* AZ-5
Thomas Creek Work Center—*locale* OR-9
Thomas Crossing—*locale* TX-5
**Thomas Crossroad**—*pop pl* AL-4
Thomas Crossroads—*locale* GA-3
Thomas Crossroads—*locale* PA-2
**Thomas Crossroads**—*pop pl* NC-3
Thomas C Russell Field (airport)—*airport* AL-4
**Thomasdale**—*pop pl* PA-2
Thomasdale Sch (abandoned)—*school* PA-2
*Thomas Dam* AL-4
Thomas Davis Canyon—*valley* ID-8
Thomas Davis Springs—*spring* ID-8
*Thomas Dee Memorial Hospital* UT-8
Thomas D Gregg Elem Sch—*school* IN-6
*Thomas Ditch* IN-6
Thomas Ditch—*canal* (2) IN-6
Thomas Ditch—*canal* OH-6
Thomas Ditch—*stream* IA-7
Thomas Divide Overlook—*locale* NC-3
Thomas Dooley Sch—*school* MI-6
Thomas Drain—*canal* MI-6
Thomas Draw—*valley* AZ-5
Thomas Draw—*valley* CO-8
Thomas Draw—*valley* ID-8
Thomas Draw—*valley* MT-8
Thomas Draw—*valley* TX-5
Thomas Draw Well—*well* MT-8
Thomas Dugan Dam—*dam* SD-7
Thomas East Shop Ctr—*locale* AZ-5
Thomas E Barret Elem Sch—*school* PA-2
Thomas E Huckabee Lake—*reservoir* AL-4
Thomas E Huckabee Lake Dam—*dam* AL-4
Thomas English Grant—*civil* FL-3
*Thomases Creek* VA-3
**Thomas Estates (subdivision)**—*pop pl* UT-8
Thomas Ewing Sch—*school* OH-6
Thomas Farm Brook—*stream* ME-1
Thomas Field—*flat* GA-3
Thomas Field—*island* FL-3
*Thomas Fitzwater Elem Sch* PA-2
Thomas Flats—*flat* ID-8
Thomas Forbes Grant—*civil* (2) FL-3
Thomas Forbes (Heirs) Grant—*civil* FL-3
Thomas Foreman Park—*park* NC-3
**Thomas Forest (subdivision)**—*pop pl* NC-3
*Thomas Fork* OH-6
*Thomas Fork* WY-8
Thomas Fork—*stream* ID-8
Thomas Fork—*stream* OH-6
Thomas Fork—*stream* OR-9
Thomas Fork—*stream* WV-2
*Thomas Fork Canyon* WY-8
*Thomas Fork Creek* OH-6
*Thomas Fork Creek* WY-8
Thomas Fork Valley—*valley* ID-8
Thomas Fort (historical)—*locale* TN-4
Thomas Fowler Sch—*school* OR-9
*Thomas Francis School* AL-4
Thomas G. Alcorn Elem Sch—*school* CT-1
*Thomas Gap* GA-3
*Thomas Gap* PA-2
Thomas Gap—*gap* AL-4
**Thomas Gardens Subdivision**—*pop pl* UT-8
Thomas Great Toe—*island* ME-1
Thomas Grove Ch—*church* (2) GA-3
Thomas Grove Ch—*church* MS-4
Thomas Grove Ch—*church* SC-3
Thomas Grove Ch—*church* VA-3
Thomas Grove Sch—*school* KS-7
Thomas Grove Sch—*school* TN-4
Thomas Gulch—*valley* ID-8
Thomas Hall—*hist pl* FL-3
Thomas Hammock—*island* FL-3
Thomas Hariot Nature Trail—*trail* NC-3
Thomas H Dummett Grant—*civil* FL-3
**Thomas Heights**—*pop pl* TN-4
Thomas H Ford Sch—*school* PA-2
**Thomas Hill**—*pop pl* MO-7
Thomas Hill—*ridge* OR-9
Thomas Hill—*summit* CA-9
Thomas Hill—*summit* CO-8
Thomas Hill—*summit* ID-8
Thomas Hill—*summit* (2) ME-1
Thomas Hill—*summit* (2) NY-2
Thomas Hill—*summit* OR-9
Thomas Hill—*summit* (2) PA-2
Thomas Hill—*summit* VA-3
Thomas Hill Cem—*cemetery* GA-3
Thomas Hill Cem—*cemetery* IL-6
Thomas Hill Ch—*church* GA-3
Thomas Hill Park—*park* TX-5
Thomas Hill Rsvr—*reservoir* MO-7
**Thomas Hill (subdivision)**—*pop pl* AL-4
Thomas (historical)—*locale* KS-7
**Thomas (historical)**—*pop pl* OR-9
Thomas Hollow—*valley* (2) AL-4
Thomas Hollow—*valley* AR-4
Thomas Hollow—*valley* KY-4
Thomas Hollow—*valley* (2) MO-7
Thomas Hollow—*valley* OK-5
Thomas Hollow—*valley* (4) TN-4
Thomas Hollow—*valley* TX-5
Thomas Hollow—*valley* UT-8
Thomas Hollow—*valley* WV-2
Thomas Homestead—*hist pl* AR-4
Thomas Hosp—*hospital* AL-4
Thomas Hosp—*hospital* MA-1
Thomas Hosp—*hospital* OH-6
Thomas House—*hist pl* CO-8
Thomas House—*hist pl* KY-4
Thomas House—*hist pl* MD-2
Thomas House—*locale* CO-8
Thomas HS—*school* NY-2
Thomas HS—*school* TX-5
Thomas Hughes Public Library—*building* TN-4
Thomas Hunting Grounds—*area* CA-9
*Thomasin Bayou* LA-4
Thomasin Bayou—*gut* LA-4
Thomas Indian Sch—*hist pl* NY-2
Thomasin Lumps—*island* LA-4
*Thomas Island* LA-4
Thomas Island—*cape* MA-1
Thomas Island—*island* AK-9
Thomas Island—*island* GA-3
Thomas Island—*island* KY-4
Thomas Island—*island* ME-1
Thomas Island—*island* PA-2
Thomas Island—*island* SC-3
Thomas Island—*island* TN-4
Thomas Island Gut—*gut* MD-2
Thomas Jarnagin Cem—*cemetery* TN-4
Thomas Jay Regional Park—*park* AZ-5
Thomas Jefferson Bldg—*building* DC-2
Thomas Jefferson Elem Sch—*school* FL-3
Thomas Jefferson Elem Sch—*school* (5) IN-6
Thomas Jefferson Elem Sch—*school* PA-2
Thomas Jefferson Home—*other* VA-3
Thomas Jefferson HS—*hist pl* TX-5
Thomas Jefferson HS—*school* CO-8
Thomas Jefferson HS—*school* IL-6
Thomas Jefferson HS—*school* KY-4
Thomas Jefferson HS—*school* PA-2
Thomas Jefferson JHS—*school* (2) FL-3
Thomas Jefferson JHS—*school* IL-6
Thomas Jefferson JHS—*school* IN-6
Thomas Jefferson JHS—*school* NJ-2
Thomas Jefferson JHS—*school* TX-5
Thomas Jefferson JHS—*school* UT-8
Thomas Jefferson JHS—*school* VA-3
Thomas Jefferson Memorial—*hist pl* DC-2
Thomas Jefferson Payne Home—*park* TX-5
Thomas Jefferson Playground—*park* FL-3
Thomas Jefferson Sch—*school* AR-4
Thomas Jefferson Sch—*school* CA-9
Thomas Jefferson Sch—*school* GA-3
Thomas Jefferson Sch—*school* HI-9
Thomas Jefferson Sch—*school* IL-6
Thomas Jefferson Sch—*school* MD-2
Thomas Jefferson Sch—*school* MI-6
Thomas Jefferson Sch—*school* MO-7
Thomas Jefferson Sch—*school* NJ-2
Thomas Jefferson Sch—*school* PA-2
Thomas Jefferson Sch—*school* TN-4
Thomas Jefferson Sch—*school* TX-5
Thomas Jefferson Sch—*school* (3) VA-3
Thomas Jefferson University Hospital Airp—*airport* PA-2
Thomas JHS—*school* AL-4
Thomas JHS—*school* FL-3
Thomas JHS—*school* IL-6
Thomas JHS—*school* PA-2
Thomas JHS—*school* VA-3
Thomas J Miller Lake—*reservoir* IN-6
Thomas J Miller Lake Dam—*dam* IN-6
Thomas J O'Brien Lock and Dam—*dam* IL-6
Thomas Joe Canyon—*valley* NV-8
Thomas Jones Reservation—*park* AL-4
Thomas J Shave, Junior Bridge—*bridge* FL-3
**Thomas Junction**—*pop pl* ID-8
Thomas Junction—*uninc pl* AL-4
Thomas Junior Cave—*cave* AL-4
Thomas Knob—*summit* NC-3
Thomas Knob—*summit* TN-4
*Thomas Lake* MI-6
*Thomas Lake* MN-6
Thomas Lake—*lake* AZ-5
Thomas Lake—*lake* (3) FL-3
Thomas Lake—*lake* (2) IN-6
Thomas Lake—*lake* IA-7
Thomas Lake—*lake* (4) MI-6
Thomas Lake—*lake* (5) MN-6
Thomas Lake—*lake* OK-5
Thomas Lake—*lake* SC-3
Thomas Lake—*lake* SD-7
Thomas Lake—*lake* (3) TX-5
Thomas Lake—*lake* (2) WA-9
Thomas Lake—*lake* (3) WI-6
**Thomas Lake**—*pop pl* IN-6
Thomas Lake—*reservoir* (4) AL-4
Thomas Lake—*reservoir* GA-3
Thomas Lake—*reservoir* (3) IN-6
Thomas Lake—*reservoir* MS-4
Thomas Lake—*reservoir* (2) NC-3
Thomas Lake—*reservoir* TN-4
Thomas Lake—*swamp* FL-3
Thomas Lake Dam—*dam* (2) IN-6
Thomas Lake Dam—*dam* (3) MS-4
Thomas Lake Dam—*dam* (3) NC-3
Thomas Lake Rsvr—*reservoir* CO-8
Thomas Lakes—*lake* ID-8
Thomas Lakes—*reservoir* CO-8
Thomas Landing—*locale* DE-2
Thomas Landing—*locale* GA-3
Thomas Landing—*locale* NC-3
Thomas Landing (historical)—*locale* AL-4
Thomas Landing (historical)—*locale* TN-4
Thomas Landing (inundated)—*locale* AL-4
**Thomas Lane**—*pop pl* CA-9
Thomas Lateral—*canal* NM-5
**Thomas L Williams Estates Subdivision**—*pop pl* UT-8
Thomas Mall—*locale* AZ-5
Thomas Manor—*uninc pl* TX-5
Thomas Marble Quarry Houses—*hist pl* PA-2
Thomas Marsh—*swamp* NC-3
Thomas Marshall Elem Sch—*school* IN-6
Thomas Massacre Graves Historical—*cemetery* MT-8
Thomas Mauvel Bridge—*bridge* FL-3
Thomas McCarthy Memorial Sch—*school* CA-9
Thomas-McJunkin-Love House—*hist pl* WV-2
Thomas Mckean HS—*school* DE-2
Thomas McRae Tuberculosis Home—*hospital* AR-4
Thomas Meadows—*flat* NV-8
Thomas Memorial Ch—*church* SC-3
Thomas Memorial Ch—*church* VA-3

*Thomas Mill* ... NC-3
*Thomas Mill* ... TN-4
Thomas Mill—*locale* ... GA-3
**Thomas Mill**—*pop pl* ... AL-4
**Thomas Mill**—*pop pl* ... PA-2
Thomas Mill and Miller's House—*hist pl* ... PA-2
Thomas Mill Branch—*stream* ... AL-4
*Thomas Mill Church* ... AL-4
Thomas Mill Covered Bridge—*hist pl* ... PA-2
Thomas Mill Creek—*stream* ... AL-4
Thomas Mill Creek—*stream* ... FL-3
Thomas Mill Creek—*stream* ... VA-3
Thomas Mill Creek Park—*park* ... AL-4
Thomas Mill Hammock—*island* ... FL-3
Thomas Mill (historical)—*locale* ... TN-4
Thomas Mill Island—*island* ... FL-3
Thomas Millpond—*reservoir* ... GA-3
Thomas Mill Pond Dam—*dam* ... MS-4
Thomas Mill Run—*channel* ... FL-3
*Thomas Mills* ... PA-2
Thomas Mills—*locale* ... PA-2
**Thomas Mills**—*pop pl* ... PA-2
Thomas Mills Post Office
(historical)—*building* ... TN-4
Thomas Mine—*mine* ... CO-8
Thomas Mine—*mine* ... NM-5
Thomas Mine (underground)—*mine* ... AL-4
Thomas Mitchell County Park—*park* ... IA-7
Thomas Moore Cem—*cemetery* ... MS-4
**Thomas Mountain**—*pop pl* ... CA-9
*Thomas Mtn* ... GA-3
Thomas Mtn—*summit* ... AL-4
Thomas Mtn—*summit* ... CA-9
Thomas Mtn—*summit* ... CO-8
Thomas Mtn—*summit* ... CT-1
Thomas Mtn—*summit* ... GA-3
Thomas Mtn—*summit* (2) ... NY-2
Thomas Mtn—*summit* ... OR-9
Thomas Mtn—*summit* (3) ... VA-3
Thomas Mtn—*summit* (2) ... WA-9
Thomas Mtn—*summit* ... WV-2
Thomas Napier Grant—*civil* (2) ... FL-3
Thomas Neck—*cape* ... VA-3
Thomas Norris Dam—*dam* ... AL-4
Thomas Norris Pond—*reservoir* ... AL-4
Thomas-Norwood Cem—*cemetery* ... TX-5
Thomas Number 1 Dam—*dam* ... SD-7
Thomas Number 2 Dam—*dam* ... SD-7
Thomas Number 3 Dam—*dam* ... SD-7
Thomas Oil Field—*oilfield* ... OK-5
Thomas Oliver Sch—*school* ... GA-3
Thomason, John W., House—*hist pl* ... TX-5
Thomason Branch—*stream* ... NC-3
Thomason Cave—*cave* ... AL-4
Thomason Cem—*cemetery* ... AL-4
Thomason Cem—*cemetery* ... AR-4
Thomason Cem—*cemetery* ... IL-6
Thomason Cem—*cemetery* ... IN-6
Thomason Cem—*cemetery* (2) ... KY-4
Thomason Cem—*cemetery* ... LA-4
Thomason Cem—*cemetery* ... NC-3
Thomason Cem—*cemetery* (2) ... TN-4
Thomason Cem—*cemetery* ... TX-5
Thomason Cem—*cemetery* ... WV-2
*Thomason Creek* ... GA-3
Thomason Creek—*stream* ... OR-9
Thomason Creek—*stream* ... WA-9
Thomason Meadow—*flat* ... OR-9
Thomason Meadow Guard
Station—*locale* ... OR-9
Thomason Meadow Rsvr—*reservoir* ... OR-9
*Thomason Mine* ... AL-4
Thomason Mine—*mine* ... OR-9
Thomason Park—*park* ... TX-5
**Thomason Park**—*pop pl* ... VA-3
Thomason Post Office
(historical)—*building* ... TN-4
Thomason Rice Barn—*hist pl* ... ID-8
Thomason Sch—*school* ... NM-5
Thomason-Scott House—*hist pl* ... TX-5
Thomason Slough—*gut* ... LA-4
*Thomasons Mill* ... AL-4
Thomason Spring Hill Ch—*church* ... GA-3
*Thomason Village* ... VA-3
Thomas O. Smith Sch—*school* ... UT-8
Thomas Paine Sch—*school* ... CA-9
Thomas Paine Sch—*school* ... IL-6
Thomas Park—*cemetery* ... TX-5
Thomas Park—*park* (2) ... IN-6
Thomas Park—*park* ... IA-7
Thomas Park—*park* ... KS-7
Thomas Park—*park* ... ME-1
Thomas Park—*park* ... MA-1
*Thomas Peak* ... AZ-5
Thomas Peak—*summit* ... NC-3
Thomas Place—*locale* ... AL-4
Thomas Place—*locale* ... NE-7
Thomas Place—*locale* (2) ... NV-8
Thomas Place Sch—*school* ... TX-5
Thomas Point—*cape* ... LA-4
Thomas Point—*cape* (2) ... ME-1
Thomas Point—*cape* (4) ... MD-2
Thomas Point—*cape* (2) ... NH-1
Thomas Point—*cape* ... RI-1
Thomas Point—*cliff* ... OR-9
Thomas Point Park—*park* ... MD-2
Thomas Point Shoal—*bar* ... MD-2
Thomas Point Shoal Lighthouse—*locale* ... MD-2
Thomas Point Shoals Light
Station—*hist pl* ... MD-2
Thomas Point Tank—*reservoir* ... AZ-5
Thomas Pond—*lake* ... AL-4
Thomas Pond—*lake* ... ME-1
Thomas Pond—*lake* ... MA-1
Thomas Pond—*lake* ... NY-2
Thomas Pond—*lake* ... PA-2
Thomas Pond—*lake* ... TN-4
Thomas Pond—*reservoir* (2) ... AL-4
Thomas Pond—*reservoir* ... GA-3
Thomas Pond—*reservoir* ... NC-3
Thomas Pond—*reservoir* ... PA-2
Thomas Post Office—*locale* ... KY-4
*Thomas Prairie* ... IL-6
Thomas Prairie—*flat* ... FL-3
Thomas Prairie—*other* ... IL-6
Thomas Price Branch—*stream* ... WV-2
Thomas Ranch—*locale* ... CA-9
Thomas Ranch—*locale* (2) ... CO-8
Thomas Ranch—*locale* ... MT-8
Thomas Ranch—*locale* (3) ... TX-5
Thomas Ranch—*locale* ... WY-8
*Thomas Range* ... UT-8
Thomas Range—*range* ... UT-8
Thomas Rehabilitization Hosp—*hospital* ... NC-3
*Thomas Reservoir* ... CA-9
Thomas Rich Dam—*dam* ... NJ-2
Thomas Rich Lake—*reservoir* ... NJ-2
Thomas Ridge—*ridge* ... KY-4
Thomas Ridge—*ridge* ... MD-2
Thomas Ridge—*ridge* ... NC-3
Thomas Ridge—*ridge* ... PA-2
Thomas Ridge—*ridge* ... SC-3
Thomas Ridge—*ridge* ... TN-4
Thomas Ridge—*ridge* ... UT-8
Thomas Ridge—*ridge* (3) ... WV-2
Thomas Ridge Ch—*church* ... KY-4
Thomas Riverside Cem—*cemetery* ... ID-8
Thomas Road Ch—*church* ... VA-3
Thomas Road Rest Stop—*park* ... AZ-5
Thomas Rock—*bar* ... AK-9
Thomas Rock—*bar* ... NH-1
Thomas Rodger Cem—*cemetery* ... CO-8
Thomas Rsvr—*reservoir* (3) ... CO-8
Thomas Rsvr—*reservoir* ... MT-8
Thomas Rsvr—*reservoir* ... NV-8
Thomas Rsvr—*reservoir* (2) ... WY-8
Thomas Rsvr No 1—*reservoir* ... WY-8
Thomas Rsvr No 2—*reservoir* ... WY-8
*Thomas Run* ... VA-3
Thomas Run—*locale* ... MD-2
Thomas Run—*stream* ... MD-2
Thomas Run—*stream* (4) ... PA-2
Thomas Run—*stream* (3) ... WV-2
Thomas Run Church—*hist pl* ... MD-2
*Thomas Sch* ... TN-4
Thomas Sch—*school* (2) ... AL-4
Thomas Sch—*school* ... CA-9
Thomas Sch—*school* ... DC-2
Thomas Sch—*school* ... GA-3
Thomas Sch—*school* (2) ... IL-6
Thomas Sch—*school* ... IN-6
Thomas Sch—*school* ... KS-7
Thomas Sch—*school* (3) ... KY-4
Thomas Sch—*school* ... MA-1
Thomas Sch—*school* (2) ... MI-6
Thomas Sch—*school* ... MT-8
Thomas Sch—*school* ... NE-7
Thomas Sch—*school* ... NV-8
Thomas Sch—*school* ... OH-6
Thomas Sch—*school* (2) ... OK-5
Thomas Sch—*school* ... PA-2
Thomas Sch—*school* ... SC-3
Thomas Sch—*school* (2) ... TN-4
Thomas Sch—*school* ... WA-9
Thomas Sch—*school* ... WV-2
Thomas Sch (abandoned)—*school* ... MO-7
Thomas Sch (abandoned)—*school* (2) ... PA-2
Thomas Sch (historical)—*school* ... PA-2
Thomas Sch (historical)—*school* (3) ... TN-4
Thomas School—*locale* ... MS-4
Thomas Select Sch—*hist pl* ... OH-6
Thomas Settlement—*locale* ... NY-2
Thomas Shoal—*bar* ... FL-3
Thomas Shoals—*bar* ... TN-4
Thomassin Pond—*bay* ... LA-4
Thomas Slough—*stream* ... WI-6
Thomasson—*locale* ... CA-9
Thomasson Bayou—*stream* ... MS-4
Thomasson Creek—*stream* ... GA-3
*Thomasson Park* ... VA-3
Thomasson Park (Military
Housing)—*uninc pl* ... VA-3
*Thomas's Point* ... MD-2
*Thomas Spragues Reservoir* ... RI-1
Thomas Spring—*spring* (3) ... AZ-5
Thomas Spring—*spring* ... FL-3
Thomas Spring—*spring* (2) ... ID-8
Thomas Spring—*spring* ... MT-8
Thomas Spring—*spring* ... OR-9
Thomas Spring—*spring* (3) ... TN-4
Thomas Spring—*spring* ... VA-3
Thomas Spring—*spring* ... WV-2
Thomas Spring Hill Sch—*school* ... GA-3
Thomas Springs—*locale* ... TN-4
Thomas Springs—*spring* ... TX-5
Thomas Springs—*spring* ... UT-8
Thomas Springs Branch—*stream* ... TX-5
Thomas Springs Cem—*cemetery* ... TN-4
Thomas Springs Sch (historical)—*school* ... TN-4
Thomas Square—*hist pl* ... HI-9
Thomas.Starr Cem—*cemetery* ... TX-5
Thomas State Wildlife Ref—*park* ... AL-4
*Thomas Station* ... AL-4
Thomas Statue—*park* ... DC-2
Thomas Stone Natl Historic Site—*park* ... MD-2
Thomas Store (historical)—*locale* ... AL-4
Thomas Store (historical)—*locale* ... MS-4
Thomas Store (historical)—*locale* ... TN-4
Thomas Street Baptist Ch—*church* ... MS-4
*Thomas Street Elementary School* ... MS-4
Thomas Street Sch—*school* ... MS-4
**Thomas Subdivision**—*pop pl* ... UT-8
Thomas Swamp—*swamp* ... SC-3
Thomas Tank—*reservoir* (4) ... AZ-5
Thomas Tank—*reservoir* ... TX-5
**Thomas Terrace**—*pop pl* ... VA-3
Thomas Thrifts Grant—*civil* ... FL-3
*Thomas Tolen Ditch* ... IN-6
**Thomaston**—*pop pl* ... AL-4
**Thomaston**—*pop pl* ... CT-1
**Thomaston**—*pop pl* ... GA-3
**Thomaston**—*pop pl* ... IN-6
**Thomaston**—*pop pl* ... ME-1
**Thomaston**—*pop pl* ... MI-6
**Thomaston**—*pop pl* ... NY-2
**Thomaston**—*pop pl* ... TX-5
Thomaston Athletic Field—*park* ... ME-1
Thomaston (CCD)—*cens area* ... AL-4
Thomaston (CCD)—*cens area* ... GA-3
Thomaston Center (census name
Thomaston)—*other* ... ME-1
Thomaston Community Cem—*cemetery* ... TX-5
Thomaston Compressor Station—*other* ... TX-5
Thomaston Dam—*dam* ... CT-1
Thomaston Division—*civil* ... AL-4
Thomaston Gas Field—*oilfield* ... TX-5
Thomaston Hist Dist—*hist pl* ... ME-1
Thomaston Hollow—*valley* ... TN-4
Thomaston Oil Field—*oilfield* ... TX-5
Thomaston Opera House—*hist pl* ... CT-1
Thomaston Road Ch—*church* ... GA-3
**Thomaston (Town of)**—*pop pl* ... CT-1
**Thomaston (Town of)**—*pop pl* ... ME-1
Thomas Tots Kindergarten—*school* ... FL-3
*Thomastown* ... OH-6
Thomas Town—*locale* ... MD-2
**Thomastown**—*pop pl* ... LA-4
**Thomastown**—*pop pl* ... MA-1
**Thomastown**—*pop pl* ... MS-4
**Thomastown**—*pop pl* ... OH-6
**Thomastown**—*pop pl* ... VA-3
Thomastown Attendance Center—*school* ... MS-4
Thomastown Baptist Cem—*cemetery* ... MS-4
Thomastown Baptist Ch—*church* ... MS-4
Thomastown Cem—*cemetery* ... KY-4
Thomastown Cem—*cemetery* ... LA-4
Thomastown Cem—*cemetery* ... MA-1
Thomas Town Cem—*cemetery* ... OK-5
Thomastown Ch—*church* ... MS-4
Thomas Town Ch—*church* ... OK-5
Thomastown Christian Cem—*cemetery* ... MS-4
**Thomas Town (historical)**—*pop pl* ... TN-4
Thomastown Methodist Episcopal
Ch—*church* ... MS-4
Thomastown Sch—*school* ... GA-3
Thomas Township—*civil* ... MO-7
**Thomas Township**—*pop pl* ... KS-7
**Thomas (Township of)**—*pop pl* ... MI-6
**Thomastown (Township of)**—*pop pl* ... MN-6
Thomastown United Methodist
Ch—*church* ... MS-4
Thomas Trail—*trail* ... OR-9
Thomas Trail—*trail* ... PA-2
Thomas Trailer Court—*locale* ... AZ-5
Thomas Tunnel—*tunnel* ... PA-2
Thomas Turner Lake Dam—*dam* ... MS-4
Thomas Union Ch—*church* ... MO-7
**Thomas Valley**—*pop pl* ... NC-3
Thomas Valley—*valley* ... NC-3
Thomas Viaduct—*other* ... MD-2
Thomas Viaduct, Baltimore & Ohio
RR—*hist pl* ... MD-2
*Thomas Village* ... NC-3
Thomasville—*locale* ... AR-4
Thomasville—*locale* ... GA-3
Thomasville—*locale* ... IL-6
Thomasville—*locale* ... IA-7
Thomasville—*locale* ... NY-2
**Thomasville**—*pop pl* ... AL-4
**Thomasville**—*pop pl* ... CO-8
**Thomasville**—*pop pl* ... GA-3
**Thomasville**—*pop pl* ... MS-4
**Thomasville**—*pop pl* ... MO-7
**Thomasville**—*pop pl* ... NC-3
**Thomasville**—*pop pl* ... PA-2
**Thomasville**—*pop pl* ... TN-4
Thomasville Acad—*school* ... AL-4
Thomasville (CCD)—*cens area* ... AL-4
Thomasville (CCD)—*cens area* ... GA-3
Thomasville Ch—*church* ... NC-3
Thomasville Commercial Hist
Dist—*hist pl* ... GA-3
Thomasville Depot—*hist pl* ... GA-3
Thomasville Division—*civil* ... AL-4
Thomasville Elem Sch—*school* ... AL-4
Thomasville Hollow—*valley* ... MO-7
Thomasville Hospital—*building* ... AL-4
Thomasville HS—*school* ... AL-4
Thomasville Oil and Gas Field—*oilfield* ... MS-4
Thomasville Post Office
(historical)—*building* ... MS-4
Thomasville Post Office
(historical)—*building* ... TN-4
*Thomasville Public School* ... AL-4
Thomasville Quarry Cave—*cave* ... PA-2
Thomasville Road Baptist Ch—*church* ... FL-3
Thomasville Road Ch—*church* ... FL-3
Thomasville RR Passenger Depot—*hist pl* ... NC-3
Thomasville Sch—*school* ... GA-3
Thomasville Sch—*school* ... LA-4
Thomasville Senior HS—*school* ... NC-3
Thomasville Sewer Lagoon—*reservoir* ... AL-4
Thomasville Sewer Lagoon Dam—*dam* ... AL-4
Thomasville Tower Site—*locale* ... MO-7
Thomasville (Township of)—*fmr MCD* ... NC-3
Thomas Warehousing Subdivision—*locale* ... UT-8
Thomas W. Bacchus Sch—*school* ... UT-8
Thomas W. Butcher Sch—*school* ... KS-7
THOMAS W. CLYDE—*hist pl* ... MD-2
Thomas Well—*well* ... AZ-5
*Thomas Wharton Elementary School* ... PA-2
*Thomas Wildlife Mngmt Area* ... AL-4
Thomas Williamson Ditch—*canal* ... MT-8
*Thomas Williams Park* ... PA-2
Thomas Windmill—*locale* ... AZ-5
Thomas Windmill—*locale* (3) ... TX-5
Thomas W Kelly Sch—*school* ... MO-7
Thomas W Koon Dam—*dam* ... PA-2
*Thomas W. Koon Lake* ... PA-2
**Thomas Woods (subdivision)**—*pop pl* ... NC-3
Thomas-Wright Battle Site—*hist pl* ... CA-9
Thomas W Shaft—*mine* ... NV-8
Thomas Zoo—*park* ... AL-4
Thom Block—*hist pl* ... MA-1
*Thom Carroll Property Mine* ... SD-7
Thom Creek—*stream* ... LA-4
Thome And Wieber Drain—*canal* ... MI-6
Thomerson Cem—*cemetery* ... KY-4
Thomes Brook—*stream* ... ME-1
Thome Sch—*school* ... NE-7
Thomes Creek—*stream* ... CA-9
Thomes Pocket Ridge—*ridge* ... CA-9
**Thom (historical)**—*pop pl* ... TN-4
Thomilson Cem—*cemetery* ... MS-4
*Thom Island* ... FL-3
Thomison Cem—*cemetery* ... TN-4
Thomkins Arroyo—*stream* ... CO-8
Thomkins Arroyo—*valley* ... CO-8
Thomkins Knob—*summit* ... NC-3
Thomkins Knob Overlook—*locale* ... NC-3
Thomley Mill Creek—*stream* ... AL-4
*Thomlinson* ... VT-1
*Thomoston* ... ME-1
Thompkin Cem—*cemetery* ... TN-4
Thompkin Chapel African Methodist Episcopal
Zion Ch—*church* ... TN-4
*Thompkins Cove* ... NY-2
Thompkins Elementary and JHS—*school* ... IN-6
*Thompkins Knob* ... NC-3
Thompkinsville AME Zion Ch—*church* ... AL-4
Thompkinville P. O. (historical)—*locale* ... AL-4
Thompsom Windmill—*locale* ... NM-5
*Thompson* ... KS-7
*Thompson* ... MN-6
*Thompson* ... TN-4
*Thompson* ... UT-8
Thompson—*cens area* ... UT-8
Thompson—*fmr MCD* ... NE-7
Thompson—*locale* ... AR-4
Thompson—*locale* ... CA-9
Thompson—*locale* ... IA-7
Thompson—*locale* ... ME-1
Thompson—*locale* ... MD-2
Thompson—*locale* (2) ... MS-4
Thompson—*locale* ... NY-2
**Thompson**—*pop pl* ... AL-4
**Thompson**—*pop pl* ... AR-4
**Thompson**—*pop pl* ... CT-1
**Thompson**—*pop pl* ... DE-2
**Thompson**—*pop pl* (2) ... FL-3
**Thompson**—*pop pl* ... IA-7
**Thompson**—*pop pl* ... KY-4
**Thompson**—*pop pl* ... MI-6
**Thompson**—*pop pl* ... MO-7
**Thompson**—*pop pl* (2) ... NE-7
**Thompson**—*pop pl* ... ND-7
**Thompson**—*pop pl* ... OH-6
**Thompson**—*pop pl* (2) ... PA-2
**Thompson**—*pop pl* ... TX-5
**Thompson**—*pop pl* ... WI-6
Thompson—*uninc pl* ... KY-4
Thompson, Absalom, House—*hist pl* ... TN-4
Thompson, Ada, Memorial Home—*hist pl* ... AR-4
Thompson, Albert W., Hall—*hist pl* ... WA-9
Thompson, Boyce, Southwestern
Arboretum—*hist pl* ... AZ-5
Thompson,-Builder House—*hist pl* ... OH-6
Thompson, Cassius Clark, House—*hist pl* ... OH-6
Thompson, Charles J., House—*hist pl* ... IA-7
Thompson, Daniel, and Ryle, John,
Houses—*hist pl* ... NJ-2
Thompson, David, House—*hist pl* ... NJ-2
Thompson, D. H., House—*hist pl* ... TX-5
Thompson, Dr. George W., House—*hist pl* ... IN-6
Thompson, Enoch, House—*hist pl* ... OH-6
Thompson, Erick J., House—*hist pl* ... WI-6
Thompson, Gamaliel, House—*hist pl* ... MI-6
Thompson, Gen. John, House—*hist pl* ... PA-2
Thompson, George Oscar, House—*hist pl* ... VA-3
Thompson, Henry Dwight, House—*hist pl* ... NY-2
Thompson, James, House—*hist pl* ... KY-4
Thompson, John, House—*hist pl* ... PA-2
Thompson, John Henry, House—*hist pl* ... KY-4
Thompson, John L., House—*hist pl* ... OR-9
Thompson, Lake—*lake* ... SD-7
Thompson, Lake—*lake* ... WI-6
Thompson, Mary I., House—*hist pl* ... UT-8
Thompson, Mount—*summit* ... CA-9
Thompson, Mount—*summit* (2) ... MT-8
Thompson, Mount—*summit* ... WA-9
Thompson, Mount—*summit* ... WY-8
Thompson, P. J., House—*hist pl* ... AZ-5
Thompson, Point—*cape* ... WA-9
Thompson, Smith, Log House—*hist pl* ... KY-4
Thompson, S. R., House—*hist pl* ... PA-2
Thompson, Thomas Henry, House—*hist pl* ... WI-6
Thompson, Walter, House and Carriage
House—*hist pl* ... NY-2
Thompson, W. B., Mansion—*hist pl* ... NY-2
Thompson, Will H., House—*hist pl* ... WA-9
Thompson, William, House—*hist pl* ... KY-4
Thompson, William, House—*hist pl* ... TN-4
Thompson, William, House—*hist pl* ... UT-8
Thompson, William, Jr., House—*hist pl* ... UT-8
Thompson, William N., House—*hist pl* ... IN-6
Thompson, W. O., House—*hist pl* ... UT-8
**Thompson Acres Subdivision**—*pop pl* ... UT-8
Thompson African Methodist Episcopal Zion
Ch—*church* ... AL-4
Thompson Airstrip—*airport* ... CO-8
**Thompson and Dieters
Subdivision**—*pop pl* ... UT-8
Thompson And Kirby Ditch—*canal* ... WY-8
Thompson And Mathews Ditch No
35—*canal* ... WY-8
Thompson And Meserves Purchase—*civil* ... NH-1
Thompson and Platte Ditch—*canal* ... CO-8
Thompson Arboretum—*park* ... AZ-5
Thompson Arroyo—*stream* ... CO-8
Thompson Arroyo—*stream* ... NM-5
Thompson Arroyo—*valley* ... CO-8
Thompson-Arthur Lake—*reservoir* ... NC-3
Thompson-Arthur Lake Dam—*dam* ... NC-3
Thompson Baptist Ch—*church* ... MS-4
Thompson Bay—*bay* ... AZ-5
Thompson Bay—*bay* ... NY-2
Thompson Bay—*bay* ... PA-2
Thompson Bay—*swamp* ... FL-3
Thompson Bayou—*stream* ... FL-3
Thompson Bayou—*stream* (2) ... LA-4
*Thompson Beach* ... NJ-2
**Thompson Beach**—*pop pl* ... NJ-2
Thompson Bend—*bend* ... AL-4
Thompson Bend—*bend* ... OK-5
Thompson Bend Sch (historical)—*school* ... MO-7
Thompson Block—*hist pl* ... ME-1
Thompson Bluff—*cliff* ... CA-9
Thompson Bluff—*cliff* ... MO-7
Thompson Borough—*civil* ... PA-2
Thompson Brake—*swamp* ... AR-4
*Thompson Branch* ... IN-6
*Thompson Branch* ... OK-5
*Thompson Branch* ... TX-5
Thompson Branch—*stream* (7) ... AL-4
Thompson Branch—*stream* (3) ... AR-4
Thompson Branch—*stream* ... DE-2
Thompson Branch—*stream* ... FL-3
Thompson Branch—*stream* (2) ... GA-3
Thompson Branch—*stream* (2) ... IN-6
Thompson Branch—*stream* ... KS-7
Thompson Branch—*stream* (8) ... KY-4
Thompson Branch—*stream* (3) ... LA-4
Thompson Branch—*stream* (5) ... MS-4
Thompson Branch—*stream* (3) ... MO-7
Thompson Branch—*stream* (3) ... NC-3
Thompson Branch—*stream* (2) ... SC-3
Thompson Branch—*stream* (10) ... TN-4
Thompson Branch—*stream* (5) ... TX-5
Thompson Branch—*stream* (2) ... VA-3
Thompson Branch—*stream* (2) ... WV-2
*Thompson Branch Ditch* ... DE-2
Thompson Branch Sch—*school* ... WV-2
Thompson Bridge—*bridge* (2) ... AL-4
Thompson Bridge—*bridge* ... DE-2
Thompson Bridge—*bridge* (3) ... GA-3
Thompson Bridge—*bridge* ... NC-3
Thompson Bridge—*bridge* ... TN-4
Thompson Bridge Access Point—*bridge* ... GA-3
Thompson Bridge Ch—*church* ... GA-3
*Thompson Brook* ... NH-1
Thompson Brook—*stream* (3) ... CT-1
Thompson Brook—*stream* (8) ... ME-1
Thompson Brook—*stream* (2) ... MA-1
Thompson Brook—*stream* (4) ... NH-1
Thompson Brook—*stream* ... NY-2
Thompson-Brown House—*hist pl* ... TN-4
Thompson-Brown-Sandusky
House—*hist pl* ... MO-7
Thompson-Bullock House—*hist pl* ... OH-6
**Thompsonburg**—*pop pl* ... VT-1
*Thompson Butte* ... OR-9
Thompson Butte—*summit* ... AZ-5
Thompson Butte—*summit* ... ID-8
Thompson Butte—*summit* ... OR-9
Thompson Butte—*summit* ... SD-7
Thompson Cabin—*locale* ... AK-9
Thompson Cabin—*locale* ... CA-9
Thompson Cabin—*locale* ... OR-9
Thompson Camp—*locale* (2) ... CA-9
Thompson Camp—*locale* ... ME-1
Thompson Camp Spring—*spring* ... CA-9
Thompson Canal—*canal* ... CA-9
Thompson (canal)—*canal* ... FL-3
*Thompson Canyon* ... OR-9
Thompson Canyon—*valley* ... AZ-5
Thompson Canyon—*valley* (5) ... CA-9
Thompson Canyon—*valley* ... NE-7
Thompson Canyon—*valley* ... NV-8
Thompson Canyon—*valley* (6) ... NM-5
Thompson Canyon—*valley* (2) ... OR-9
Thompson Canyon—*valley* ... SD-7
Thompson Canyon—*valley* (2) ... UT-8
Thompson Canyon—*valley* ... WY-8
Thompson Cave—*cave* (2) ... AL-4
Thompson Cave—*cave* ... TN-4
*Thompson Cem* ... MS-4
Thompson Cem—*cemetery* (14) ... AL-4
Thompson Cem—*cemetery* (9) ... AR-4
Thompson Cem—*cemetery* (7) ... GA-3
Thompson Cem—*cemetery* (7) ... IL-6
Thompson Cem—*cemetery* (8) ... IN-6
Thompson Cem—*cemetery* (3) ... IA-7
Thompson Cem—*cemetery* (10) ... KY-4
Thompson Cem—*cemetery* ... LA-4
Thompson Cem—*cemetery* (3) ... MI-6
Thompson Cem—*cemetery* ... MN-6
Thompson Cem—*cemetery* (14) ... MS-4
Thompson Cem—*cemetery* (9) ... MO-7
Thompson Cem—*cemetery* ... NE-7
Thompson Cem—*cemetery* ... NY-2
Thompson Cem—*cemetery* (4) ... NC-3
Thompson Cem—*cemetery* (2) ... ND-7
Thompson Cem—*cemetery* (4) ... OH-6
Thompson Cem—*cemetery* (3) ... OK-5
Thompson Cem—*cemetery* (4) ... PA-2
Thompson Cem—*cemetery* (2) ... SC-3
Thompson Cem—*cemetery* ... SD-7
Thompson Cem—*cemetery* (26) ... TN-4
Thompson Cem—*cemetery* (8) ... TX-5
Thompson Cem—*cemetery* ... UT-8
Thompson Cem—*cemetery* (12) ... VA-3
Thompson Cem—*cemetery* (6) ... WV-2
Thompson Cemeteries—*cemetery* ... VA-3
Thompson Center Cem—*cemetery* ... OH-6
Thompson Ch—*church* ... GA-3
Thompson Ch—*church* ... NC-3
Thompson Ch—*church* ... OH-6
Thompson Ch—*church* ... SC-3
Thompson Ch—*church* ... TX-5
Thompson Chapel—*church* (2) ... AL-4
Thompson Chapel—*church* (3) ... AR-4
Thompson Chapel—*church* ... GA-3
Thompson Chapel—*church* ... IN-6
Thompson Chapel—*church* ... KY-4
Thompson Chapel—*church* (2) ... MS-4
Thompson Chapel—*church* (2) ... NC-3
Thompson Chapel—*church* ... OH-6
Thompson Chapel—*church* (2) ... SC-3
Thompson Chapel—*church* (2) ... TN-4
Thompson Chapel—*church* (3) ... WV-2
Thompson Chapel—*locale* ... TX-5
Thompson Chapel Cem—*cemetery* (2) ... MS-4
Thompson Chapel (historical)—*church* ... MS-4
Thompson Chapel (historical)—*church* ... MO-7
Thompson Chapel (historical)—*church* ... TN-4
Thompson Cone—*summit* ... NM-5
Thompson Consolidated Sch
(historical)—*school* ... MS-4
Thompson Corner—*locale* ... HI-9
Thompson Corner—*locale* ... IA-7
Thompson Corner—*locale* ... ME-1
Thompson Corner—*locale* ... MD-2
Thompson Corner—*locale* ... NH-1
Thompson Corner—*locale* ... OK-5
Thompson Corner—*locale* ... SC-3
Thompson Corners—*locale* ... ME-1
Thompson Corners—*locale* ... NY-2
Thompson Corral—*locale* (2) ... OR-9
Thompson Cottage—*hist pl* ... PA-2
Thompson Coulee—*valley* ... MT-8
Thompson Coulee—*valley* ... WI-6
Thompson County Park—*locale* ... MI-6
*Thompson Cove* ... ME-1
Thompson Cove—*bay* ... ME-1
Thompson Cove—*bay* ... RI-1
Thompson Cove—*bay* ... WA-9
Thompson Cove—*slope* ... GA-3
Thompson Cove—*valley* ... AL-4
Thompson Cove—*valley* ... NC-3
*Thompson Creek* ... CA-9
*Thompson Creek* ... CO-8
*Thompson Creek* ... GA-3
*Thompson Creek* ... MS-4
*Thompson Creek* ... NC-3
*Thompson Creek* ... OR-9
*Thompson Creek* ... UT-8
*Thompson Creek* ... WA-9
Thompson Creek—*stream* (6) ... AL-4
Thompson Creek—*stream* (3) ... AK-9
Thompson Creek—*stream* (2) ... AZ-5
Thompson Creek—*stream* (7) ... AR-4
Thompson Creek—*stream* (14) ... CA-9
Thompson Creek—*stream* (5) ... CO-8
Thompson Creek—*stream* (3) ... GA-3
Thompson Creek—*stream* (9) ... ID-8
Thompson Creek—*stream* (2) ... IN-6
Thompson Creek—*stream* (2) ... IA-7
Thompson Creek—*stream* (2) ... KS-7
Thompson Creek—*stream* (5) ... KY-4
Thompson Creek—*stream* (3) ... LA-4
Thompson Creek—*stream* (2) ... MD-2
Thompson Creek—*stream* (3) ... MI-6
Thompson Creek—*stream* (4) ... MN-6
Thompson Creek—*stream* (10) ... MS-4
Thompson Creek—*stream* (3) ... MO-7
Thompson Creek—*stream* (13) ... MT-8
Thompson Creek—*stream* ... NE-7
Thompson Creek—*stream* (3) ... NV-8
Thompson Creek—*stream* ... NJ-2
Thompson Creek—*stream* ... NY-2
Thompson Creek—*stream* (3) ... NC-3
Thompson Creek—*stream* ... OH-6
Thompson Creek—*stream* (4) ... OK-5
Thompson Creek—*stream* (15) ... OR-9
Thompson Creek—*stream* ... PA-2
Thompson Creek—*stream* (4) ... SC-3
Thompson Creek—*stream* ... SD-7
Thompson Creek—*stream* (10) ... TN-4
Thompson Creek—*stream* (4) ... TX-5
Thompson Creek—*stream* (4) ... UT-8
Thompson Creek—*stream* (4) ... VA-3
Thompson Creek—*stream* (6) ... WA-9
Thompson Creek—*stream* (4) ... WI-6
Thompson Creek—*stream* (4) ... WY-8
Thompson Creek Access Point—*locale* ... GA-3
Thompson Creek Branch—*stream* ... TN-4
Thompson Creek Ch—*church* ... MS-4
Thompson Creek Ch—*church* ... SC-3
Thompson Creek Ch—*church* ... TN-4
Thompson Creek Ch (historical)—*church* ... MS-4
Thompson Creek Ch (historical)—*church* ... PA-2
Thompson Creek Dam—*dam* ... CA-9
Thompson Creek Dam Four—*dam* ... TN-4
*Thompson Creek Ditch* ... AR-4
Thompson Creek Ditch—*canal* ... AR-4
Thompson Creek Ditch—*canal* ... CO-8
Thompson Creek Forest Camp—*locale* ... OR-9
Thompson Creek Guard Station—*locale* ... CO-8
Thompson Creek Guard Station—*locale* ... OR-9
Thompson Creek Landing Public Use
Area—*park* ... MS-4
Thompson Creek Lodge—*locale* ... MS-4
Thompson Creek Mine—*mine* ... CO-8
Thompson Creek Number Eight
Dam—*dam* ... TN-4
Thompson Creek Number Eight
Lake—*reservoir* ... TN-4
Thompson Creek Number Five
Dam—*dam* ... TN-4
Thompson Creek Number Five
Dam—*reservoir* ... TN-4
Thompson Creek Number Three
Dam—*dam* ... TN-4
Thompson Creek Number Three
Lake—*reservoir* ... TN-4
Thompson Creek Number Two Dam—*dam* ... TN-4
Thompson Creek Number Two
Lake—*reservoir* ... TN-4
Thompson Creek Oil Field—*oilfield* (2) ... MS-4
Thompson Creek Park—*park* ... MS-4
Thompson Creek Sch—*school* ... WY-8
*Thompson Crossroad* ... VA-3
Thompson Crossroad—*locale* ... GA-3
Thompson Crossroads—*locale* ... TN-4
Thompson Cutoff—*channel* ... FL-3
Thompson Cutoff—*gut* ... FL-3
*Thompson Dam* ... SD-7
Thompson Dam—*dam* ... AL-4
Thompson Dam—*dam* ... CA-9
Thompson Dam—*dam* ... NC-3
Thompson Dam—*dam* (2) ... OR-9
Thompson Deadwater—*swamp* ... ME-1
*Thompson Ditch* ... IL-6
*Thompson Ditch* ... IN-6
Thompson Ditch—*canal* (2) ... CO-8
Thompson Ditch—*canal* (14) ... IN-6
Thompson Ditch—*canal* (2) ... MT-8
Thompson Ditch—*canal* ... OH-6
Thompson Ditch—*canal* ... OR-9
Thompson Ditch—*canal* ... SD-7
Thompson Ditch—*canal* ... WY-8
Thompson Ditch Draw—*valley* ... CO-8
Thompson Ditch No 2—*canal* ... CO-8
Thompson Division—*civil* ... UT-8
Thompson Drain—*canal* ... CA-9
Thompson Drain—*canal* (5) ... MI-6
Thompson Drain—*stream* ... MI-6
Thompson Draw—*valley* (3) ... AZ-5
Thompson Draw—*valley* ... CO-8
Thompson Draw—*valley* ... MT-8
Thompson Draw—*valley* (2) ... NM-5
Thompson Draw—*valley* ... SD-7
Thompson Draw—*valley* (3) ... WY-8
Thompson Elem Sch—*school* (2) ... AL-4
Thompson Elem Sch—*school* ... FL-3
Thompson Epperson Ditch—*canal* ... CO-8
Thompson Extension Canal—*canal* ... CA-9
Thompson Falls—*falls* ... AL-4
Thompson Falls—*falls* ... NH-1
Thompson Falls—*falls* ... OR-9
**Thompson Falls**—*pop pl* ... MT-8
Thompson Falls Dam—*dam* ... MT-8
Thompson Falls Gap—*gap* ... AL-4
Thompson Falls Hydroelectric Dam Hist
Dist—*hist pl* ... MT-8
*Thompson Falls Recreation Site* ... MT-8
Thompson Falls Rsvr—*reservoir* ... MT-8
Thompson Falls Spring—*spring* ... OR-9
Thompson Falls State Rec Area—*park* ... MT-8
Thompson Falls-West End—*cens area* ... MT-8
Thompson Farm—*hist pl* ... OH-6
Thompson Farm—*hist pl* ... PA-2
Thompson-Fasbender House—*hist pl* ... MN-6
Thompson Ferry—*locale* ... LA-4
Thompson Field—*flat* ... CA-9
Thompson Flat—*flat* (3) ... CA-9
Thompson Flat—*flat* ... CO-8
Thompson Flat—*flat* ... ID-8
Thompson Flat—*flat* ... OR-9
Thompson Flat—*flat* ... TN-4

Thompson Flat Campground—locale ID-8
Thompson Flat Cem—cemetery CA-9
Thompson Flats—flat MT-8
Thompson Flat Well—well OR-9
Thompson Ford—locale MO-7
Thompson Ford—locale VA-3
Thompson Ford (historical)—locale AL-4
Thompson Fork AR-4
Thompson Fork OH-6
Thompson Fork—stream (2) KY-4
Thompson Fork—stream WY-8
Thompson Gap AL-4
Thompson Gap—gap AL-4
Thompson Gap—gap VA-3
**Thompson Gardens Subdivision**—pop pl UT-8
Thompson Gin—locale TX-5
Thompson Grass Pond—swamp TX-5
Thompson Grove MN-6
Thompson Grove—locale TX-5
Thompson Grove Ch—church (3) GA-3
Thompson Grove Ch—church VA-3
Thompson Grove Sch—school MO-7
Thompson Grove Sch—school TN-4
Thompson Grove Sch (historical)—school TN-4
Thompson Gulch MT-8
Thompson Gulch—valley (4) CA-9
Thompson Gulch—valley (4) CO-8
Thompson Gulch—valley (3) ID-8
Thompson Gulch—valley (2) MT-8
Thompson Gulch—valley NV-8
Thompson Gulch—valley (3) OR-9
Thompson Gulch—valley (2) WY-8
Thompson Gulch Guard Station—locale MT-8
Thompson Gully—stream (2) LA-4
Thompson Gut—gut NC-3
Thompson Hall Sch—school TN-4
Thompson Heights MN-6
**Thompson Heights**—pop pl MN-6
Thompson Heliport—airport WA-9
Thompson Hill MA-1
Thompson Hill—ridge AL-4
Thompson Hill—summit CA-9
Thompson Hill—summit CO-8
Thompson Hill—summit CT-1
Thompson Hill—summit GA-3
Thompson Hill—summit (5) ME-1
Thompson Hill—summit MI-6
Thompson Hill—summit MS-4
Thompson Hill—summit MO-7
Thompson Hill—summit (4) NH-1
Thompson Hill—summit OK-5
Thompson Hill—summit (3) PA-2
Thompson Hill—summit RI-1
Thompson Hill—summit TN-4
Thompson Hill—summit VA-3
Thompson Hill Cem—cemetery MA-1
Thompson Hill Creek—stream MO-7
Thompson Hill Hist Dist—hist pl CT-1
Thompson Hills—summit TN-4
Thompson Hills Ch—church TX-5
Thompson Hill Sch—school MO-7
Thompson Hills Shop Ctr—locale MO-7
**Thompson (historical)**—pop pl MS-4
**Thompson (historical)**—pop pl OR-9
Thompson Hole—reservoir ID-8
Thompson Hollow—valley (2) AL-4
Thompson Hollow—valley AR-4
Thompson Hollow—valley GA-3
Thompson Hollow—valley IL-6
Thompson Hollow—valley (6) KY-4
Thompson Hollow—valley (5) MO-7
Thompson Hollow—valley NY-2
Thompson Hollow—valley (2) OH-6
Thompson Hollow—valley (2) PA-2
Thompson Hollow—valley (12) TN-4
Thompson Hollow—valley TX-5
Thompson Hollow—valley (2) UT-8
Thompson Hollow—valley VA-3
Thompson Hollow—valley WI-6
Thompson Hollow Run—stream PA-2
Thompson Hollow Sch—school NY-2
Thompson Home—hist pl MI-6
Thompson House—building NY-2
Thompson House—hist pl KY-4
Thompson House—hist pl LA-4
Thompson House—hist pl NJ-2
Thompson House—hist pl (2) NY-2
Thompson House—hist pl TX-5
Thompson HS—school AL-4
Thompson HS—school MO-7
Thompson HS—school TX-5
Thompson Icehouse—hist pl ME-1
Thompson Institute—school NY-2
Thompson Iron Mine—mine WA-9
Thompson Island PA-2
Thompson Island—island DE-2
Thompson Island—island FL-3
Thompson Island—island (2) ME-1
Thompson Island—island MA-1
Thompson Island—island MI-6
Thompson Island—island (2) NY-2
Thompson Island Shoals—bar TN-4
Thompson Island Village MA-1
Thompson JHS—school CA-9
Thompson JHS—school MI-6
Thompson JHS—school NY-2
Thompson JHS—school NC-3
Thompson JHS—school TX-5
Thompson-Kinney Divide—ridge SD-7
Thompson Knob—summit AR-4
Thompson Knob—summit NC-3
Thompson Knoll—summit UT-8
Thompson Ladder—trail AZ-5
Thompson Lake FL-3
Thompson Lake IL-6
Thompson Lake MI-6
Thompson Lake MN-6
Thompson Lake ND-7
Thompson Lake—flat OR-9
Thompson Lake—lake AK-9
Thompson Lake—lake AR-4
Thompson Lake—lake (3) CA-9
Thompson Lake—lake CO-8
Thompson Lake—lake (2) FL-3
Thompson Lake—lake ID-8
Thompson Lake—lake ME-1
Thompson Lake—lake (6) MI-6
Thompson Lake—lake (8) MN-6
Thompson Lake—lake MS-4
Thompson Lake—lake (3) MT-8
Thompson Lake—lake (2) NE-7
Thompson Lake—lake ND-7
Thompson Lake—lake (2) TX-5
Thompson Lake—lake UT-8
Thompson Lake—lake (3) WA-9
Thompson Lake—lake (5) WI-6
Thompson Lake—reservoir (2) AL-4
Thompson Lake—reservoir CO-8
Thompson Lake—reservoir (3) GA-3
Thompson Lake—reservoir (2) IN-6
Thompson Lake—reservoir MA-1
Thompson Lake—reservoir NM-5
Thompson Lake—reservoir NC-3
Thompson Lake—reservoir OK-5
Thompson Lake—reservoir OR-9
Thompson Lake—reservoir TN-4
Thompson Lake—swamp MN-6
Thompson Lake Dam—dam IN-6
Thompson Lake Dam—dam MA-1
Thompson Lake Dam—dam (5) MS-4
Thompson Lake Dam—dam NC-3
Thompson Lake Dam—dam TN-4
Thompson Lake Pumping Station—other IL-6
Thompson Lake Rsvr—reservoir MA-1
Thompson Lakes—lake MT-8
Thompson Lakes—lake WY-8
Thompson Landing—airport NJ-2
Thompson Landing—locale MO-7
Thompson Landing—locale VA-3
Thompson Landing Field—airport SD-7
Thompson Landing (historical)—locale AL-4
Thompson Landing (historical)—locale MS-4
Thompson Lateral—canal CA-9
Thompson Lateral—canal WY-8
Thompson Ledge—bench UT-8
Thompson Ledges—bar ME-1
Thompson Ledge Township Park—park OH-6
Thompson Long Round—bend GA-3
Thompson Marsh—swamp LA-4
Thompson Meadow—flat (2) CA-9
Thompson Meadows—flat CA-9
Thompson Meadows—swamp CT-1
Thompson Memorial Bridge—bridge SC-3
Thompson Memorial Cem—cemetery PA-2
Thompson Memorial Ch—church NC-3
Thompson Memorial Methodist Ch (historical)—church MS-4
Thompson Memorial Sch—school ME-1
Thompson Mesa—summit AZ-5
Thompson Mesa—summit NM-5
Thompson Mesa—summit UT-8
Thompson Middle School MS-4
Thompson Mill AL-4
Thompson Mill—locale TN-4
Thompson Mill Bridge—other IL-6
Thompson Mill Covered Bridge—hist pl IL-6
Thompson Mill Creek—stream GA-3
Thompson Mill Creek—stream MS-4
Thompson Mill (historical)—locale NC-3
Thompson Mill Hollow—valley AL-4
Thompson Millpond—reservoir VA-3
Thompson Mine—mine AZ-5
Thompson Mine—mine (2) NV-8
Thompson Mine (underground)—mine (3) AL-4
Thompson Mine (underground)—mine TN-4
Thompson Mortuary Chapel—hist pl ID-8
Thompson Mound—summit IN-6
Thompson Mountain CA-9
Thompson MS—school AL-4
Thompson Mtn—summit AL-4
Thompson Mtn—summit (2) AR-4
Thompson Mtn—summit CO-8
Thompson Mtn—summit ME-1
Thompson Mtn—summit MA-1
Thompson Mtn—summit NY-2
Thompson Mtn—summit NC-3
Thompson Mtn—summit OK-5
Thompson Mtn—summit OR-9
Thompson Mtn—summit TN-4
Thompson Mtn—summit TX-5
Thompson Mtn—summit VA-3
**Thompson No. 1**—pop pl PA-2
**Thompson No 1**—pop pl PA-2
**Thompson No 2**—pop pl PA-2
**Thompson No. 2**—pop pl PA-2
Thompson Number 1 Mine (surface)—mine TN-4
Thompson Number 2 Mine (surface)—mine TN-4
Thompson Orphanage—school NC-3
Thompson Park MN-6
Thompson Park—flat AZ-5
Thompson Park—flat (2) CO-8
Thompson Park—park FL-3
Thompson Park—park IL-6
Thompson Park—park (2) MT-8
Thompson Park—park NY-2
Thompson Park—park (2) OH-6
Thompson Park—park OK-5
Thompson Park—park OR-9
Thompson Park—park TX-5
Thompson Park—park WI-6
Thompson Park Cem—cemetery CO-8
Thompson Park Sch—school CO-8
Thompson Pass—gap AK-9
Thompson Pass—gap ID-8
Thompson Pass—gap MT-8
Thompson Pass—gap (2) UT-8
Thompson Pass—gap WY-8
Thompson Passage—channel AK-9
Thompson Peak—summit (2) AZ-5
Thompson Peak—summit (6) CA-9
Thompson Peak—summit (2) ID-8
Thompson Peak—summit (3) MT-8
Thompson Peak—summit NM-5
Thompson Peak—summit OR-9
Thompson Peak—summit UT-8
Thompson Peak Trail—trail NM-5
Thompson Pine Island—island FL-3
Thompson Place OH-6
Thompson Place—locale CA-9
Thompson Place—locale ID-8
Thompson Place—locale NM-5
**Thompson Place**—pop pl WA-9
Thompson Plantation—locale AR-4
**Thompson Plantation (subdivision)**—pop pl NC-3
Thompson Point ID-8
Thompson Point VT-1
Thompson Point—cape (3) ME-1
Thompson Point—cape MT-8
Thompson Point—cape NJ-2
Thompson Point—cape UT-8
Thompson Point—cape WA-9
Thompson Point—cliff AZ-5
Thompson Point—cliff CO-8
Thompson Point—summit AR-4
Thompson Point—summit ID-8
Thompson Point—summit OR-9
Thompson Pond ME-1
Thompson Pond—basin FL-3
Thompson Pond—lake CT-1
Thompson Pond—lake FL-3
Thompson Pond—lake GA-3
Thompson Pond—lake ME-1
Thompson Pond—lake MA-1
Thompson Pond—lake MI-6
Thompson Pond—lake NY-2
Thompson Pond—reservoir AL-4
Thompson Pond—reservoir GA-3
Thompson Pond—swamp FL-3
Thompson Pond Ditch—stream FL-3
Thompson Ponds CT-1
Thompson Prairie—area CA-9
Thompson Prong—stream NC-3
Thompson Pup—stream AK-9
Thompson Raceway—other CT-1
Thompson Ranch—hist pl AZ-5
Thompson Ranch—locale AZ-5
Thompson Ranch—locale (2) CA-9
Thompson Ranch—locale (2) CO-8
Thompson Ranch—locale (4) MT-8
Thompson Ranch—locale (2) NE-7
Thompson Ranch—locale (2) NV-8
Thompson Ranch—locale (5) NM-5
Thompson Ranch—locale ND-7
Thompson Ranch—locale SD-7
Thompson Ranch—locale TX-5
Thompson Ranch—locale (4) WY-8
Thompson Ravine—valley MN-6
Thompson Reef—bar NY-2
Thompson Reservation—reserve AL-4
**Thompson Ridge**—pop pl NY-2
Thompson Ridge—ridge AK-9
Thompson Ridge—ridge (5) CA-9
Thompson Ridge—ridge MO-7
Thompson Ridge—ridge NC-3
Thompson Ridge—ridge OR-9
Thompson Ridge—ridge (2) TN-4
Thompson Ridge—ridge UT-8
Thompson Ridge—ridge VA-3
Thompson Ridge—ridge (2) WA-9
Thompson Ridge—ridge WV-2
Thompson Ridge Trail—trail NC-3
Thompson River CO-8
Thompson River—stream IA-7
Thompson River—stream MO-7
Thompson River—stream MT-8
Thompson River—stream NC-3
Thompson River—stream SC-3
Thompson River Mount Headley Trail—trail MT-8
Thompson River Sch—school MT-8
**Thompson River Spur**—pop pl MT-8
Thompson River State For—forest MT-8
Thompson Riverview Terrace MN-6
**Thompson Riverview Terrace**—pop pl MN-6
Thompson Road Ch—church NY-2
Thompson Road Independent Baptist Ch—church IN-6
Thompson Rock—bar ME-1
Thompson Rsvr OR-9
Thompson Rsvr—reservoir CA-9
Thompson Rsvr—reservoir MT-8
Thompson Rsvr—reservoir (3) OR-9
Thompson Rsvr—reservoir WY-8
Thompson Rsvr Campground—locale OR-9
Thompson Rsvr Forest Camp—locale OR-9
Thompson Rsvr No. 1—reservoir CO-8
Thompson Rsvr No 1—reservoir WY-8
Thompson Rsvr No. 2—reservoir CO-8
Thompson Rsvr No 2—reservoir WY-8
Thompson Rsvr No. 3—reservoir CO-8
Thompson Run PA-2
Thompson Run—stream IN-6
Thompson Run—stream (5) OH-6
Thompson Run—stream (6) PA-2
Thompson Run Mines—mine PA-2
Thompsons ME-1
Thompsons UT-8
Thompsons—locale VA-3
**Thompsons**—pop pl OH-6
**Thompsons**—pop pl TX-5
Thompsons Beach—beach NJ-2
Thompson's Block—hist pl WI-6
Thompsons Bluff—cliff MS-4
Thompsons Branch KS-7
Thompsons Branch—stream NY-2
Thompsons Branch—stream TX-5
Thompson's Bromine and Arsenic Springs—hist pl NC-3
Thompsons Brook MA-1
Thompsons Camp—locale CA-9
Thompsons Cem—cemetery AR-4
Thompson Sch—school AL-4
Thompson Sch—school AR-4
Thompson Sch—school (3) CA-9
Thompson Sch—school CT-1
Thompson Sch—school (3) IL-6
Thompson Sch—school (2) IN-6
Thompson Sch—school (3) KY-4
Thompson Sch—school ME-1
Thompson Sch—school (5) MI-6
Thompson Sch—school MN-6
Thompson Sch—school (2) MS-4
Thompson Sch—school (2) MO-7
Thompson Sch—school (2) NY-2
Thompson Sch—school (2) NC-3
Thompson Sch—school OK-5
Thompson Sch—school (2) OR-9
Thompson Sch—school (3) PA-2
Thompson Sch—school (2) SC-3
Thompson Sch—school (2) SD-7
Thompson Sch—school (2) TN-4
Thompson Sch—school TX-5
Thompson Sch—school WA-9
Thompson Sch—school WV-2
Thompson Sch—school (2) WI-6
Thompson Sch (abandoned)—school PA-2
Thompsons Chapel—church (2) NC-3
Thompsons Chapel—church TN-4
Thompsons Chapel—church WV-2
Thompsons Chapel AME Zion Ch—church AL-4
Thompsons Chapel Cem—cemetery TN-4
Thompson Sch (historical)—school AL-4
Thompson Sch (historical)—school MS-4
Thompson Sch (historical)—school MO-7
Thompson Sch (historical)—school (2) TN-4
Thompsons Corner MO-7
Thompsons Corner—locale MD-2
Thompsons Corner—locale NY-2
**Thompsons Corner**—pop pl MO-7
Thompson's Cove ME-1
Thompsons Cove NY-2
Thompsons Creek MS-4
Thompsons Creek TN-4
Thompsons Creek TX-5
Thompson's Creek—stream MS-4
Thompsons Creek—stream NY-2
Thompsons Creek—stream SC-3
Thompsons Creek—stream TX-5
Thompsons Crossing—locale NY-2
Thompsons Crossroads—locale TN-4
Thompsons Cut Point—cape SC-3
Thompson Seep—spring UT-8
Thompson-Seton, Mount—summit MT-8
Thompson Settlement Ch—church VA-3
Thompsons Ferry (historical)—locale (2) MS-4
Thompsons Fork OH-6
Thompsons Fork—stream NC-3
Thompsons Grove—woods CA-9
Thompsons Harbor—bay MI-6
Thompson-Shelton Cem—cemetery TN-4
Thompsons Hill MA-1
Thompsons Hole—valley UT-8
Thompsons Island MA-1
Thompsons Island NH-1
Thompsons Island NY-2
Thompsons Island—island PA-2
Thompsons Island (historical)—island AL-4
Thompsons Island Shoals TN-4
Thompsons Island Site—hist pl DE-2
Thompsons Ladder Fourteen—trail AZ-5
Thompsons Lake MI-6
Thompsons Lake MS-4
Thompsons Lake SD-7
Thompsons Lake—lake NY-2
**Thompsons Lake**—pop pl NY-2
Thompsons Lake—reservoir IN-6
Thompsons Landing MO-7
Thompsons Landing TN-4
Thompson's Loss and Gain Site—hist pl DE-2
Thompson Slough—gut OR-9
Thompson Slough—gut SD-7
Thompson Slough—gut TX-5
Thompson Slough—stream IN-6
Thompson Slough—stream TN-4
Thompson Slough—stream WI-6
Thompsons Meadow—swamp MA-1
Thompson Smelter (Site)—locale NV-8
Thompsons Mill KS-7
Thompsons Mill—locale GA-3
Thompsons Mill (historical)—locale AL-4
Thompsons Mill (historical)—locale (2) MS-4
Thompsons Mill (historical)—locale TN-4
Thompsons Mill Pond MA-1
**Thompsons Mills**—pop pl GA-3
**Thompsons Mills**—pop pl PA-2
Thompsons Mount MA-1
Thompsons Oil Field—oilfield TX-5
Thompsons Old Ferry (historical)—locale AL-4
Thompsons Peak CA-9
Thompson Spit—bar WA-9
Thompson Split—bar WA-9
Thompsons Point ME-1
Thompsons Point NJ-2
Thompson's Point VT-1
Thompsons Point—cape VT-1
Thompsons Point—cliff AZ-5
**Thompson's Point**—pop pl ME-1
**Thompson's Point**—pop pl VT-1
Thompsons Point Landing—locale TN-4
Thompsons Pond SC-3
Thompsons Pond—lake VT-1
Thompsons Pond—reservoir GA-3
Thompsons Pond—reservoir MA-1
Thompsons Pond Dam—dam MA-1
Thompson Spring—spring AL-4
Thompson Spring—spring (4) AZ-5
Thompson Spring—spring (4) CA-9
Thompson Spring—spring (2) CO-8
Thompson Spring—spring ID-8
Thompson Spring—spring MO-7
Thompson Spring—spring MT-8
Thompson Spring—spring (2) NM-5
Thompson Spring—spring (7) OR-9
Thompson Spring—spring PA-2
Thompson Spring—spring SD-7
Thompson Spring—spring (2) UT-8
Thompson Spring—spring WY-8
Thompson Spring Branch—stream AL-4
Thompson Spring Branch—stream FL-3
Thompson Spring Branch—stream GA-3
**Thompson Springs**—pop pl UT-8
Thompson Springs—spring CO-8
Thompson Springs—spring NV-8
Thompson Springs—spring TN-4
Thompson Springs—spring WY-8
Thompson Springs Cem—cemetery TN-4
Thompson Springs Ch—church TN-4
Thompson Square—park MA-1
Thompsons (RR name for Thompsons Station)—other TN-4
Thompsons Run PA-2
Thompsons Sch (historical)—school AL-4
Thompsons Sch (historical)—school TN-4
Thompsons Shoal—bar AL-4
Thompsons Shop TN-4
Thompsons Shop (historical)—locale TN-4
Thompsons Slough—gut MN-6
Thompsons Station AL-4
**Thompsons Station**—pop pl TN-4
Thompsons Station (historical)—locale PA-2
Thompsons Station Post Office—building TN-4
**Thompsons Station (RR name Thompsons)**—pop pl TN-4
**Thompsons Store**—pop pl TN-4
Thompsons Store (historical)—building MS-4
Thompsons Store (historical)—locale AL-4
**Thompsons Subdivision**—pop pl UT-8
Thompson Station MS-4
Thompson Station Bank—hist pl TN-4
Thompson Store—hist pl TN-4
Thompsons Valley AZ-5
Thompson Swamp—stream NC-3
Thompson Swamp—stream SC-3
Thompson Tank—reservoir (6) AZ-5
Thompson Tank—reservoir (4) NM-5
Thompson Towhead—other MO-7
Thompsontown—locale NJ-2
**Thompsontown**—pop pl MD-2
**Thompsontown**—pop pl (2) PA-2
**Thompson Town**—pop pl WV-2
Thompsontown Borough—civil PA-2
**Thompson (Town of)**—pop pl CT-1
**Thompson (Town of)**—pop pl NY-2
Thompson Township—civil SD-7
Thompson Township—fmr MCD IA-7
Thompson (Township of)—fmr MCD AR-4
Thompson (Township of)—fmr MCD NC-3
**Thompson (Township of)**—pop pl IL-6
**Thompson (Township of)**—pop pl MI-6
**Thompson (Township of)**—pop pl MN-6
**Thompson (Township of)**—pop pl (3) OH-6
**Thompson (Township of)**—pop pl (2) PA-2
**Thompsontown Station**—pop pl PA-2
Thompson Valley—flat CA-9
**Thompson Valley**—pop pl VA-3
Thompson Valley—valley AK-9
Thompson Valley—valley AZ-5
Thompson Valley—valley (2) CA-9
Thompson Valley—valley OR-9
Thompson Valley—valley VA-3
Thompson Valley—valley (2) WI-6
Thompson Valley Cem—cemetery WI-6
Thompson Valley Ch—church FL-3
Thompson Valley Ch—church VA-3
Thompson Valley Ch—church WI-6
Thompson Valley Creek—stream WI-6
Thompson Valley Dam—dam OR-9
Thompson Valley Dam Rsvr—reservoir OR-9
Thompson Valley Rsvr OR-9
Thompson Valley Sch—school AZ-5
Thompson Village MA-1
Thompson Village—other MA-1
Thompsonville NC-3
Thompsonville—locale DE-2
Thompsonville—locale GA-3
Thompsonville—locale KY-4
Thompsonville—locale MS-4
Thompsonville—locale (2) TX-5
Thompsonville—locale UT-8
Thompsonville—other NC-3
**Thompsonville**—pop pl CT-1
**Thompsonville**—pop pl IL-6
**Thompsonville**—pop pl KS-7
**Thompsonville**—pop pl MA-1
**Thompsonville**—pop pl MI-6
**Thompsonville**—pop pl (2) NY-2
**Thompsonville**—pop pl PA-2
**Thompsonville**—pop pl WI-6
Thompsonville Ch—church KY-4
Thompsonville Ch—church MS-4
Thompsonville Lake—reservoir IL-6
Thompsonville Post Office (historical)—building MS-4
Thompsonville Public Use Area—park KS-7
Thompsonville (RR name for Oak Grove)—other KY-4
Thompson Wash AZ-5
Thompson Wash UT-8
Thompson Wash—stream CA-9
Thompson Wash—stream UT-8
Thompson Wash Rock Art District—hist pl UT-8
Thompson Well—well AZ-5
Thompson Well—well (2) NM-5
Thompson Well—well (2) OR-9
Thompson Windmill—locale NE-7
Thompson Windmill—locale (2) NM-5
Thompson Windmill—locale TX-5
Thompson-Wohlschlegel Round Barn—hist pl KS-7
**Thoms**—pop pl MO-7
Thoms Cove—bay MD-2
Thoms Creek CA-9
Thoms Creek UT-8
Thoms Creek—gut VA-3
Thoms Creek—stream AK-9
Thoms Creek—stream CA-9
Thomsen Boat Harbor AK-9
Thomsen Harbor—bay AK-9
Thomsen Round Barn—hist pl IA-7
Thoms Island—island FL-3
Thoms Lake—lake AK-9
Thomson PA-2
Thomson—locale KY-4
**Thomson**—pop pl GA-3
**Thomson**—pop pl IL-6
**Thomson**—pop pl MN-6
**Thomson**—pop pl NY-2
Thomson, C.R., House and Barn—hist pl MA-1
Thomson, Elihu, House—hist pl MA-1
Thomson, Gen. David, House—hist pl MO-7
Thomson, James S., House—hist pl SD-7
Thomson, Mount—summit WA-9
Thomson, Peter G., House—hist pl OH-6
Thomson, W. F., House—hist pl TX-5
Thomson Airp—airport PA-2
Thomson (CCD)—cens area GA-3
Thomson Cem—cemetery IA-7
Thomson Country Club—other GA-3
Thomson Country Club, The—locale MA-1
Thomson Creek CO-8
Thomson Creek OR-9
Thomson Creek TX-5
Thomson Creek—stream PA-2
Thomson Creek—stream (2) WA-9
**Thomson Estates**—pop pl MD-2
Thomson Ford Branch—stream GA-3
Thomson Gap—gap AK-9
Thomson Hollow UT-8
Thomsonite Beach—beach MI-6
Thomson Lake CA-9
Thomson Lateral—canal ID-8
Thomson Point NJ-2
Thomson Ranch—locale ID-8
Thomson Ranch—locale OR-9
Thomson Rsvr—reservoir MN-6
Thomson Sch—school CA-9
Thomson Sch—school (2) MA-1
Thomson Seep UT-8
Thomsons Island MA-1
Thomsons Mill Warehouse—hist pl KY-4
Thomson State Wildlife Mngmt Area—park MN-6
Thomson Township—civil MO-7
**Thomson (Township of)**—pop pl MN-6
Thomsonville DE-2
Thomsonville TX-5
Thoms Place—bay AK-9
Thoms Point MD-2
Thoms Point—cape AK-9
Thoms Run—stream PA-2
Thomure—locale MO-7
Thom Windmill—locale TX-5
Thone Cem—cemetery NE-7
Thoney Point MI-6
Thoneys Point—cape MI-6
Thong Run—stream IN-6
**Thonotosassa**—pop pl FL-3
Thonotosassa, Lake—lake FL-3
Thonotosassa (CCD)—cens area FL-3
Thonotosassa Ch—church FL-3
Thonotosassa Ch of God—church FL-3
Thonotosassa Elem Sch—school FL-3
**Thool**—pop pl FM-9
**Thor**—pop pl IA-7
**Thor**—pop pl MN-6
**Thor**—pop pl SC-3
Thor, Mount—summit AK-9
Thoracic Hosp—hospital NY-2
Thoralson Lake—lake MN-6
Thorbiskope—hist pl NC-3
Thor Creek—stream ID-8
Thor Creek—stream WA-9
Thordarson Estate Hist Dist—hist pl WI-6
**Thordenskjold Township**—pop pl ND-7
**Thoreau**—pop pl NM-5
Thoreau-Alcott House—hist pl MA-1
Thoreau Campsite—locale ME-1
Thoreau Falls—falls NH-1
Thoreau Falls Trail—trail NH-1
Thoreau Intermediate Sch—school VA-3
Thoreau Lyceum—building MA-1
Thoreau Park Sch—school OH-6
Thoreau Bog—swamp MA-1
Thoreaus Cabin, Site of—locale MA-1
Thoreau Sch—school MA-1
Thoreau's Peak ME-1
Thoreau Spring—spring ME-1
Thore Cem—cemetery NC-3
Thoren Hall—hist pl IA-7
**Thorensen**—pop pl ID-8
Thoreson, Andreus, Farmhouse—hist pl MN-6
Thoreson-Monson Dam—dam ND-7
Thorfare, The—bay MD-2
Thorguson Canal—canal LA-4
Thorhult—locale MN-6
Thorhult Waskish Trail—trail MN-6
Thorin AL-4
**Thorin**—pop pl AL-4
Thorington Lake—lake MI-6
Thorland Lake—lake MI-6
Thorley Point—cape UT-8
Thorley Sch—school MI-6
Thor Mine—mine NV-8
Thormodson Barn—hist pl MN-6
Thormpson Pond—lake FL-3
Thor Mtn—summit ID-8
Thorn (2) CA-9
Thorn WV-2
Thorn—locale (2) CA-9
**Thorn**—pop pl MS-4
**Thornapple**—pop pl WI-6
Thornapple and Extension Drain MI-6
Thornapple and Old Maid Drain—canal MI-6
Thornapple Creek—stream MI-6
Thornapple Creek—stream WI-6
Thornapple Dam—dam WI-6
Thornapple Drain—canal MI-6
Thornapple Extension Drain MI-6
Thornapple Lake—lake MI-6
Thornapple River—stream MI-6
Thornapple River—stream WI-6
Thornapple Sch—school MI-6
Thornapple Spring—spring WI-6
**Thornapple (Township of)**—pop pl MI-6
Thornber Cem—cemetery IL-6
Thornberg Lake—lake MT-8
Thornberg State Wildlife Mngmt Area—park MN-6
Thornberry—locale OR-9
Thornberry—locale TX-5
Thornberry Branch—stream KY-4
Thornberry Drift Mine (underground)—mine AL-4
Thornberry Mtn—summit CA-9
Thornberry Oil Field—oilfield TX-5
Thornberry Ranch—locale TX-5
Thornbottom Creek—stream PA-2
Thorn Branch—stream AL-4
Thorn Branch—stream VA-3
Thorn Bridge—bridge AL-4
Thorn Brook—stream ME-1
Thorn Brook—stream PA-2
Thornbrough Air Force Base—military AK-9
Thornburg CO-8
Thornburg TN-4
Thornburg—fmr MCD NE-7
Thornburg—locale KS-7
**Thornburg**—pop pl AR-4
**Thornburg**—pop pl IA-7
**Thornburg**—pop pl PA-2
**Thornburg**—pop pl VA-3
Thornburg Borough—civil PA-2
Thornburg Branch—stream TN-4
Thornburg Canyon—valley CA-9
Thornburg Cem—cemetery IN-6
Thornburg Creek—stream TX-5
Thornburg Draw—valley CO-8
Thornburgh—locale CO-8
Thornburgh Gas Field—oilfield CO-8
Thornburgh Gulch—valley CO-8
Thornburgh House—hist pl KY-4
Thornburgh Hist Dist—hist pl PA-2
Thornburgh Mtn—summit CO-8
Thornburgh Sch (abandoned)—school MO-7
Thornburgh Spring—spring CO-8
Thornburg Lake—lake MS-4

*Thornburg Mountain* CO-8
Thornburg Park—*park* CA-9
Thornburg Placer Mine—*mine* OR-9
Thornburg Ridge—*ridge* TN-4
Thornburg Spring—*spring* OR-9
Thornburg Trail—*trail* CO-8
Thornburn Sch—*school* IL-6
Thornbury Ch—*church* PA-2
*Thornbury Mountain* CA-9
**Thornbury (Township of)**—*pop pl* (2) PA-2
Thorn Canal—*canal* CA-9
Thorn Canal—*canal* NY-2
Thorn Cem—*cemetery* IN-6
Thorn Cem—*cemetery* MS-4
Thorn Cem—*cemetery* WV-2
Thorn Ch—*church* AL-4
Thorn Ch—*church* MS-4
Thorn Ch—*church* WV-2
Thorn Ch of God—*church* MS-4
Thorncliff—*locale* VA-3
Thorncrag Hill—*summit* ME-1
*Thorn Creek* OR-9
Thorn Creek—*stream* (11) ID-8
Thorn Creek—*stream* IL-6
Thorn Creek—*stream* IN-6
Thorn Creek—*stream* MI-6
Thorn Creek—*stream* (12) OR-9
Thorn Creek—*stream* (2) PA-2
Thorn Creek—*stream* UT-8
Thorn Creek—*stream* VA-3
Thorn Creek—*stream* (3) WA-9
Thorn Creek—*stream* WV-2
Thorn Creek—*stream* WY-8
Thorn Creek Butte—*locale* OR-9
Thorn Creek Butte—*summit* ID-8
Thorncreek Center Sch—*school* IN-6
Thorn Creek Ch—*church* (2) IN-6
Thorn Creek Ch—*church* PA-2
Thorn Creek Fire Camp—*locale* ID-8
Thorn Creek Ranch—*locale* ID-8
Thorn Creek Rsvr—*reservoir* ID-8
Thorn Creek Sch—*school* ID-8
**Thorncreek (Township of)**—*pop pl* IN-6
Thorn Crossing—*locale* PA-2
Thorndale—*hist pl* NC-3
Thorndale—*locale* PA-2
**Thorndale**—*pop pl* PA-2
**Thorndale**—*pop pl* TX-5
**Thorndale Acres**—*pop pl* WY-8
Thorndale Ave Park—*park* IL-6
Thorndale (CCD)—*cens area* TX-5
Thorndale Cem—*cemetery* TX-5
Thorndale Country Club—*locale* NC-3
**Thorndale Heights**—*pop pl* PA-2
Thornden Park—*park* NY-2
**Thorndike**—*pop pl* ME-1
**Thorndike**—*pop pl* MA-1
Thorndike, George, House—*hist pl* ME-1
Thorndike Camp—*locale* CA-9
**Thorndike Center**—*pop pl* ME-1
Thorndike Center Sch—*school* ME-1
Thorndike Mine—*mine* CA-9
Thorndike Point—*cape* ME-1
Thorndike Pond—*lake* NH-1
Thorndike Sch—*school* MA-1
**Thorndike (Town of)**—*pop pl* ME-1
Thorndike (Township of)—*unorg* ME-1
*Thorndike Village* MA-1
Thorn Divide—*ridge* WY-8
Thorn Divide Sch—*school* WY-8
Thorndyk Branch—*stream* DE-2
*Thorndyke* OH-6
Thorndyke Bay—*bay* WA-9
Thorndyke Canyon—*valley* CA-9
Thorndyke Cem—*cemetery* OH-6
Thorndyke Creek—*stream* WA-9
Thorndyke Lake—*lake* WA-9
Thorndyke Mine—*mine* CA-9
Thorndyke Street Sch—*school* MA-1
Thorne—*locale* TX-5
**Thorne**—*pop pl* NV-8
**Thorne**—*pop pl* ND-7
Thorne, Parson, Mansion—*hist pl* DE-2
Thorne, W. T., Bldg—*hist pl* NE-7
Thorne and Eddy Estates—*hist pl* NJ-2
Thorne and Wisdom Lake—*lake* OR-9
Thorne Arm—*bay* AK-9
Thorne Bay—*bay* AK-9
**Thorne Bay**—*pop pl* AK-9
Thorne Bridge—*bridge* OR-9
Thorne Brook—*stream* CT-1
Thorne Brook—*stream* MA-1
Thorne Brook—*stream* VT-1
Thorne Cem—*cemetery* SC-3
Thorne Ch—*church* AL-4
Thorne Creek—*stream* (2) MT-8
Thorne Grove Sch (abandoned)—*school* PA-2
Thorne Gulch—*valley* CA-9
Thorne Gut—*stream* MD-2
Thorne Gut Marsh—*swamp* MD-2
Thorne Hay Draw Tank—*reservoir* NM-5
*Thorne Head* ME-1
Thorne Head—*cape* AK-9
Thorne Head—*cape* ME-1
Thorne Hollow—*valley* TN-4
Thorne Island—*island* AK-9
Thorne Island Ledge—*bar* ME-1
*Thorne Lake* OR-9
Thorne Lake—*lake* AK-9
Thorne Lake—*lake* CO-8
Thornell Road Sch—*school* NY-2
Thorne Mine—*mine* CA-9
Thorne Mtn—*summit* ME-1
Thorne Museum and Studio—*building* UT-8
Thorne Park—*park* KY-4
Thorne Ranch—*locale* NM-5
Thorne Ridge Stadium—*locale* WY-8
Thorne River—*stream* AK-9
Thornes Ch—*church* NC-3
Thorne Sch—*school* (2) MI-6
*Thorne School* AL-4
*Thornes head* ME-1
Thorne Spring—*spring* AZ-5
Thorne Spring—*spring* (2) ID-8
Thorne Spring Ch—*church* VA-3
Thorne Springs Branch—*stream* VA-3
Thorne Store—*locale* TN-4
Thornewood—*hist pl* WA-9
Thorney—*locale* AR-4
Thorney Branch—*stream* AR-4
*Thorney Creek* AR-4
Thorney Point—*cape* VA-3
**Thornfield**—*pop pl* MO-7
Thornfield Township—*civil* MO-7
Thorn Fire Control Station—*locale* CA-9
Thorn Flat—*flat* OR-9
*Thorn Fork* WV-2
Thorn Gap—*gap* TN-4
Thorngate Country Club—*other* IL-6
**Thorngrove**—*pop pl* TN-4
**Thorn Grove**—*pop pl* TN-4
Thorngrove Baptist Ch—*church* TN-4
Thorn Grove Ch—*church* AR-4
Thorn Grove Christian Ch—*church* TN-4
*Thorn Grove Post Office* TN-4
Thorngrove Post Office (historical)—*building* TN-4
Thorn Grove Sch—*school* IL-6
Thorn Grove Sch (historical)—*school* MO-7
*Thorn Gulch* OR-9
Thorn Gulch—*valley* ID-8
Thorn Gulch—*valley* OR-9
*Thorn Hill* AL-4
*Thorn Hill* PA-2
Thornhill—*hist pl* AL-4
Thornhill—*hist pl* MO-7
Thorn Hill—*hist pl* VA-3
Thornhill—*locale* AL-4
Thorn Hill—*locale* TN-4
Thornhill—*locale* VA-3
**Thorn Hill**—*pop pl* AL-4
**Thornhill**—*pop pl* (2) AL-4
**Thornhill**—*pop pl* KY-4
**Thorn Hill**—*pop pl* NY-2
**Thorn Hill**—*pop pl* TX-5
**Thornhill**—*pop pl* WV-2
Thorn Hill—*summit* AL-4
Thorn Hill—*summit* AR-4
Thorn Hill—*summit* NH-1
Thorn Hill—*summit* NY-2
Thorn Hill—*summit* PA-2
Thorn Hill—*summit* VA-3
Thorn Hill—*uninc pl* KY-4
Thornhill and Schulz State Wildlife Area—*park* MO-7
*Thornhill Baptist Ch* MS-4
Thornhill Bay—*swamp* GA-3
Thornhill Butte—*summit* MT-8
Thorn Hill (CCD)—*cens area* TN-4
Thornhill Cem—*cemetery* (3) AL-4
Thornhill Cem—*cemetery* GA-3
Thornhill Cem—*cemetery* (2) MS-4
Thornhill Cem—*cemetery* MO-7
Thornhill Cem—*cemetery* TN-4
Thorn Hill Cem—*cemetery* TN-4
Thorn Hill Ch—*church* AL-4
Thorn Hill Ch—*church* MS-4
Thorn Hill Ch—*church* SC-3
Thorn Hill Ch—*church* TN-4
*Thornhill Ch of Christ* AL-4
Thorn Hill Division—*civil* TN-4
Thorn Hill Gap—*gap* TN-4
Thorn Hill Heights—*uninc pl* KY-4
Thorn Hill Industrial Sch—*school* PA-2
Thornhill Lake—*lake* FL-3
Thorn Hill Lake—*reservoir* KY-4
*Thornhill Plantation* AL-4
Thorn Hill Post Office—*building* TN-4
Thornhill Sch—*school* CA-9
Thorn Hill Sch—*school* KY-4
Thornhill Sch—*school* SC-3
Thorn Hill Sch—*school* TN-4
Thornhill Sch (historical)—*school* MO-7
Thornhill Station—*locale* AL-4
**Thorn Hollow**—*pop pl* OR-9
Thorn Hollow—*valley* NY-2
Thorn Hollow—*valley* (3) OR-9
Thorn Hollow—*valley* UT-8
Thorn Hollow—*valley* WA-9
Thorn Hollow Creek—*stream* OR-9
**Thornhope**—*pop pl* IN-6
Thorn House—*hist pl* CA-9
Thorn Howard Acad—*school* FL-3
**Thornhurst**—*pop pl* PA-2
Thornhurst Picnic Area—*area* PA-2
Thorn Junction—*locale* CA-9
Thorn Lake—*lake* CO-8
Thorn Lake—*lake* MI-6
Thorn Lake—*lake* MS-4
Thorn Lake—*lake* ND-7
Thorn Lake—*lake* (2) OR-9
Thorn Lake—*lake* (2) WI-6
**Thornleigh**—*pop pl* MD-2
Thornley Memorial Cem—*cemetery* SC-3
**Thornleys Subdivision**—*pop pl* UT-8
Thorn Lookout Tower—*locale* WA-9
Thorn Meadows—*flat* CA-9
Thorn Meadows Guard Station—*locale* CA-9
Thorn Mountain—*ridge* WV-2
Thorn Mtn—*summit* NH-1
Thorn Mtn—*summit* NC-3
Thorn Mtn—*summit* OR-9
Thorn No 1 Canal—*canal* CA-9
Thorn Park—*park* MN-6
Thorn Patch Spring—*spring* OR-9
Thorn Peak—*summit* AZ-5
Thorn Peak Tank—*reservoir* AZ-5
Thorn Plum Point—*cape* ME-1
Thorn Point—*summit* CA-9
**Thornport**—*pop pl* OH-6
Thorn Post Office (historical)—*building* MS-4
Thorn Prairie—*flat* OR-9
Thorn Prospect—*mine* TN-4
Thornquist Gulch—*valley* MT-8
Thorn Ranch—*locale* CO-8
Thorn Ranch—*locale* TX-5
Thorn Reservation—*park* AL-4
Thorn Rider Camp—*locale* WY-8
*Thorn Ridge* WY-8
**Thornridge**—*pop pl* PA-2
Thorn Ridge—*ridge* IN-6
Thorn Ridge—*ridge* WV-2
Thornridge HS—*school* IL-6
Thorn Rsvr—*reservoir* PA-2
Thorn Run—*stream* IN-6
Thorn Run—*stream* (2) OH-6
Thorn Run—*stream* PA-2
Thorn Run—*stream* WV-2
Thorn Run Dam—*dam* PA-2
Thorn Run Rsvr—*reservoir* PA-2
Thorn Run Sch—*school* PA-2
Thornsberry Cem—*cemetery* MO-7
Thornsberry Ch—*church* AR-4
Thornsberry Point—*cape* MO-7
Thornsburg Bend—*bend* KY-4
Thornsbury Branch—*stream* KY-4
Thorn Sch—*school* AR-4
Thorn Sch—*school* IA-7
Thorn Sch—*school* WV-2
Thorn Sch (historical)—*school* AL-4
Thorns Creek—*stream* NJ-2
Thorns Creek Guard Station—*locale* OR-9
Thorn Spring—*spring* ID-8
Thorn Spring—*spring* NV-8
Thorn Spring—*spring* (7) OR-9
Thorn Spring—*spring* WA-9
Thorn Spring Butte—*summit* OR-9
Thorn Spring Creek—*stream* ID-8
Thorn Spring Creek—*stream* OR-9
Thorn Springs—*spring* OR-9
Thorn Springs Creek—*stream* ID-8
Thorns Run—*stream* WV-2
Thorn Station (historical)—*locale* PA-2
**Thorn Subdivision**—*pop pl* UT-8
Thorn Thicket Creek—*stream* WA-9
*Thornton* NC-3
Thornton—*locale* PA-2
Thornton—*locale* WY-8
**Thornton**—*pop pl* (2) AL-4
**Thornton**—*pop pl* AR-4
**Thornton**—*pop pl* CA-9
**Thornton**—*pop pl* CO-8
**Thornton**—*pop pl* ID-8
**Thornton**—*pop pl* IL-6
**Thornton**—*pop pl* IN-6
**Thornton**—*pop pl* IA-7
**Thornton**—*pop pl* KY-4
**Thornton**—*pop pl* MI-6
**Thornton**—*pop pl* MS-4
**Thornton**—*pop pl* NH-1
**Thornton**—*pop pl* NY-2
**Thornton**—*pop pl* RI-1
**Thornton**—*pop pl* TN-4
**Thornton**—*pop pl* TX-5
**Thornton**—*pop pl* WA-9
**Thornton**—*pop pl* WV-2
**Thornton**—*pop pl* WI-6
Thornton, Albert E., House—*hist pl* GA-3
Thornton, Bayou—*stream* LA-4
Thornton, Charles Irving, Tombstone—*hist pl* VA-3
Thornton, Dr. Penn B., House—*hist pl* TX-5
Thornton, Mansfield, House—*hist pl* NC-3
Thornton, Matthew, House—*hist pl* NH-1
Thornton Acad—*school* ME-1
Thornton Airp—*airport* TN-4
Thornton Beach State Park—*park* CA-9
Thornton Branch—*stream* (4) AL-4
Thornton Branch—*stream* FL-3
Thornton Branch—*stream* MD-2
Thornton Bridge—*bridge* AL-4
Thornton Brook—*stream* CT-1
Thornton Brook—*stream* MA-1
Thornton Canyon—*valley* TX-5
Thornton (CCD)—*cens area* CA-9
Thornton (CCD)—*cens area* TX-5
Thornton Cem—*cemetery* (5) AL-4
Thornton Cem—*cemetery* GA-3
Thornton Cem—*cemetery* IL-6
Thornton Cem—*cemetery* IN-6
Thornton Cem—*cemetery* IA-7
Thornton Cem—*cemetery* (4) MS-4
Thornton Cem—*cemetery* (3) MO-7
Thornton Cem—*cemetery* OH-6
Thornton Cem—*cemetery* (4) TN-4
Thornton Cem—*cemetery* VA-3
Thornton Cem—*cemetery* WI-6
Thornton Center Sch—*school* NH-1
Thornton Ch—*church* MS-4
Thornton Ch—*church* TX-5
Thornton Ch—*church* VA-3
Thornton Chapel—*church* MS-4
*Thornton Creek* TX-5
Thornton Creek—*stream* (3) AL-4
Thornton Creek—*stream* (2) GA-3
Thornton Creek—*stream* KY-4
Thornton Creek—*stream* MI-6
Thornton Creek—*stream* MS-4
Thornton Creek—*stream* MT-8
Thornton Creek—*stream* (2) OR-9
Thornton Creek—*stream* (3) WA-9
Thornton Ditch—*canal* (2) WY-8
Thornton Gap—*gap* NH-1
Thornton Gap—*gap* VA-3
Thornton Gap Ch—*church* VA-3
Thornton Gap Sch—*school* KY-4
**Thornton Grove**—*pop pl* NY-2
Thornton-Guise Kitchen And House—*hist pl* OH-6
Thornton Gulch—*valley* OR-9
*Thornton Heights* ME-1
**Thornton Heights**—*pop pl* ME-1
**Thornton Heights**—*pop pl* NY-2
**Thornton Heights**—*pop pl* TN-4
*Thornton Hill* AL-4
Thornton Hill—*summit* AL-4
*Thornton Hill Baptist Church* MS-4
Thornton Hollow—*valley* AR-4
Thornton Hollow—*valley* MO-7
Thornton Hollow—*valley* (2) TN-4
Thornton Hollow—*valley* UT-8
Thornton Hollow—*valley* VA-3
Thornton Hollow Overlook—*locale* VA-3
Thornton HS—*school* IL-6
Thornton JHS—*school* CA-9
Thornton JHS—*school* OH-6
*Thornton Junction* IL-6
**Thornton Junction**—*pop pl* IL-6
**Thornton Junction**—*pop pl* PA-2
Thornton Lake—*lake* MI-6
Thornton Lake—*lake* MN-6
Thornton Lake—*lake* MT-8
Thornton Lake—*lake* OR-9
Thornton Lake—*lake* WA-9
Thornton Lake—*lake* WY-8
Thornton Lake—*reservoir* AL-4
Thornton Lake—*reservoir* TX-5
Thornton Lake Dam—*dam* AL-4
Thornton Lake Dam—*dam* MS-4
Thornton Lakes—*lake* WA-9
Thornton Lateral—*canal* CA-9
Thornton Lookout Tower—*tower* AZ-5
Thornton Meadow—*flat* CA-9
Thornton Mtn—*summit* AK-9
Thornton Mtn—*summit* VA-3
Thornton Number 1 Lake—*reservoir* AL-4
Thornton Number 2 Lake—*reservoir* AL-4
Thornton Number 3 Lake—*reservoir* AL-4
Thornton Number 4 Lake—*reservoir* AL-4
Thornton Number 5 Lake—*reservoir* AL-4
Thornton Number 6 Lake—*reservoir* AL-4
Thornton Park—*park* IL-6
Thornton Park—*park* IN-6
Thornton Park—*park* OH-6
Thornton Place Landing (historical)—*locale* MS-4
*Thornton Plantation* AL-4
Thornton Point—*cape* ME-1
Thornton Point—*cape* NY-2
Thornton Point Ledge—*bar* ME-1
Thornton Ranch—*locale* CO-8
Thornton Ranch—*locale* NM-5
Thornton Ridge—*ridge* MT-8
Thornton River—*stream* VA-3
Thornton River Camp—*locale* VA-3
**Thornton (RR name Bastin)**—*pop pl* KY-4
Thornton Rsvr—*reservoir* WY-8
Thornton Run—*stream* PA-2
Thorntons Bluff P.O. (historical)—*building* AL-4
Thornton Sch—*school* CA-9
Thornton Sch—*school* IL-6
Thornton Sch—*school* IN-6
Thornton Sch—*school* MI-6
Thornton Sch—*school* NH-1
Thornton Sch—*school* NC-3
Thornton Sch—*school* PA-2
Thornton Sch—*school* (2) TX-5
Thornton Sch (historical)—*school* MO-7
Thorntons Corner—*locale* NY-2
Thorntons Creek—*stream* NC-3
Thorntons Creek—*stream* VA-3
**Thorntons Ferry**—*pop pl* NH-1
Thorntons Ferry Sch—*school* NH-1
Thorntons Landing (historical)—*locale* AL-4
Thornton Slough—*lake* ND-7
*Thorntons Lower Landing* AL-4
Thornton Spring—*spring* OR-9
Thornton Spring—*spring* TN-4
Thornton Springs—*locale* AL-4
**Thornton Spur**—*pop pl* WA-9
Thornton Station (historical)—*locale* MA-1
Thornton Store—*locale* NC-3
Thornton Swamp—*swamp* MI-6
Thornton Tank—*reservoir* AZ-5
**Thorntontown**—*pop pl* AL-4
**Thornton (Town of)**—*pop pl* NH-1
**Thornton Township**—*pop pl* NE-7
**Thornton (Township of)**—*pop pl* IL-6
*Thorntonville* PA-2
**Thorntonville**—*pop pl* TX-5
Thornton Wash—*stream* AZ-5
**Thorntown**—*pop pl* IN-6
Thorntown Public Library—*hist pl* IN-6
**Thorn (Township of)**—*pop pl* OH-6
Thorntree—*hist pl* SC-3
Thorn Tree Acad (historical)—*school* MS-4
Thorn Tree Bayou—*gut* LA-4
Thorntree Creek—*stream* SC-3
Thorntree Swamp—*stream* SC-3
*Thorn United Methodist Church* MS-4
Thorn Valley—*valley* AZ-5
**Thornville**—*pop pl* MI-6
**Thornville**—*pop pl* OH-6
**Thornville (sta.) (Thornport)**—*pop pl* OH-6
**Thornwell**—*pop pl* LA-4
Thorn Well—*well* NM-5
Thornwell Drainage Canal—*canal* LA-4
Thornwell-Presbyterian College Hist Dist—*hist pl* SC-3
Thornwell Sch—*school* SC-3
*Thornwilde* IL-6
Thornwood—*hist pl* KY-4
Thornwood—*locale* WA-9
**Thornwood**—*pop pl* NY-2
**Thornwood**—*pop pl* PA-2
**Thornwood**—*pop pl* WV-2
Thornwood Ch—*church* MI-6
Thornwood Park—*park* IL-6
Thornwood Park—*park* MD-2
**Thorny Acres**—*pop pl* OH-6
Thorny Bottom—*valley* WV-2
Thorny Bottom Ch—*church* VA-3
Thorny Bottom Ridge—*ridge* WV-2
Thorny Brake—*swamp* LA-4
*Thorny Branch* VA-3
Thorny Branch—*stream* LA-4
Thorny Branch—*stream* TN-4
Thorny Branch—*stream* (2) VA-3
Thorny Branch—*stream* WV-2
Thorny Creek—*locale* WV-2
Thorny Creek—*stream* MO-7
Thorny Creek—*stream* OR-9
Thorny Creek—*stream* WV-2
Thorny Creek Mtn—*summit* WV-2
Thornydale Sch—*school* AZ-5
Thorny Flat—*flat* WV-2
Thorny Gap—*gap* MO-7
Thorny Head Branch—*stream* FL-3
*Thorny Hollow* MO-7
Thorny Hollow—*valley* (2) MO-7
Thorny Hollow—*valley* WV-2
Thorny Knob—*summit* WV-2
Thorny Lake—*lake* LA-4
Thorny Lea Golf Club—*locale* MA-1
Thorny Mtn—*summit* MO-7
Thorny Mtn—*summit* TN-4
Thorny Run—*stream* WV-2
*Thorny Wood River* MN-6
Thorn 1 Canal—*canal* CA-9
**Thorobred Acres**—*pop pl* KY-4
*Thorobred Creek* ID-8
*Thorobred Pond Spring* ID-8
*Thorobred Spring* ID-8
*Thorodin Mountain* CO-8
Thorodin Mtn—*summit* CO-8
*Thorofare* DE-2
*Thorofare* MD-2
*Thorofare* VA-3
Thorofare—*channel* ME-1
Thorofare—*channel* (2) NC-3
Thorofare—*channel* (3) VA-3
Thorofare—*gut* NC-3
Thorofare—*locale* VA-3
**Thorofare**—*pop pl* NJ-2
*Thorofare, The* DE-2
*Thorofare, The* NC-3
Thorofare, The—*channel* ID-8
Thorofare, The—*channel* (3) ME-1
Thorofare, The—*channel* MD-2
Thorofare, The—*channel* MA-1
Thorofare, The—*channel* (4) VA-3
Thorofare Bay—*bay* NC-3
Thorofare Branch—*stream* KY-4
Thorofare Bridge—*bridge* NC-3
Thorofare Buttes—*summit* WY-8
Thorofare Canal—*canal* MI-6
Thorofare Community Chapel—*church* VA-3
Thorofare Cove—*bay* (2) MD-2
Thorofare Creek—*gut* VA-3
Thorofare Creek—*stream* MD-2
Thorofare Creek—*stream* SC-3
Thorofare Creek—*stream* WY-8
*Thorofare Gap* VA-3
Thorofare Gap—*gap* VA-3
Thorofare Hill—*island* VA-3
Thorofare (historical)—*gut* DE-2
Thorofare Island—*island* ME-1
Thorofare Island—*island* (2) NJ-2
Thorofare Island—*island* (3) NC-3
Thorofare Island—*island* SC-3
Thorofare Island—*island* (2) VA-3
Thorofare Marsh—*swamp* (2) MD-2
Thorofare Mountain Overlook—*locale* VA-3
Thorofare Mtn—*summit* (2) VA-3
Thorofare Mtn—*summit* WY-8
Thorofare Pass—*gap* AK-9
Thorofare Plateau—*area* WY-8
Thorofare Point—*cape* (2) MD-2
Thorofare Point—*cape* NJ-2
Thorofare Point—*cape* NC-3
Thorofare Point—*cape* VA-3
Thorofare Ranger Station—*locale* WY-8
Thorofare Ridge—*ridge* VA-3
Thorofare River—*stream* AK-9
Thorofare Run—*stream* WV-2
Thorofare Swamp—*stream* NC-3
Thorofare Swamp—*swamp* NC-3
**Thorofare (Thoroughfare)**—*pop pl* NJ-2
Thorofare Trail—*trail* (2) WY-8
Thorofare West Day Beacon—*tower* NC-3
Thorofare West Light—*tower* NC-3
Thorotare Island—*island* ME-1
Thorougfare Island—*island* NC-3
**Thoroughbred Acres**—*pop pl* (2) KY-4
Thoroughbred Creek—*stream* ID-8
Thoroughbred Flat—*flat* ID-8
Thoroughbred Pasture Tank—*reservoir* AZ-5
Thoroughbred Pond Spring—*spring* ID-8
Thoroughbred Spring—*spring* (2) ID-8
Thoroughbred Spring No 1—*spring* ID-8
Thoroughbred Spring No 2—*spring* ID-8
*Thoroughfare* MD-2
Thoroughfare—*channel* ME-1
Thoroughfare—*locale* VA-3
*Thoroughfare, The* VA-3
Thoroughfare, The—*channel* (3) ME-1
Thoroughfare, The—*gut* WI-6
Thoroughfare, The—*stream* WV-2
Thoroughfare Bay—*swamp* NC-3
Thoroughfare Bay—*swamp* SC-3
Thoroughfare Branch—*stream* SC-3
Thoroughfare Brook—*stream* (3) ME-1
Thoroughfare Creek—*stream* AK-9
Thoroughfare Creek—*stream* SC-3
Thoroughfare Creek—*stream* WI-6
Thoroughfare Gap—*gap* (3) VA-3
Thoroughfare Island—*island* MD-2
Thoroughfare Mtn—*summit* AK-9
Thoroughfare Neck—*cape* DE-2
Thoroughfare Stream—*stream* KY-4
Thoroughfare Swamp—*stream* NC-3
*Thoroughfare (Thorofare)* NJ-2
**Thoroughgood**—*pop pl* VA-3
Thoroughgood Canyon—*valley* (2) NM-5
Thoroughgood Cove—*bay* VA-3
Thoroughgood House—*hist pl* VA-3
Thoroughgood Sch—*school* VA-3
Thoroughman Branch—*stream* KY-4
Thoroughman Canyon—*valley* CO-8
*Thorp* OH-6
**Thorp**—*pop pl* WA-9
**Thorp**—*pop pl* WI-6
Thorp, Manville, Residence—*hist pl* OH-6
Thorp, W. A., House—*hist pl* OH-6
Thorp Branch—*stream* MO-7
Thorp Branch—*stream* TX-5
Thorp Brook—*stream* MA-1
Thorp Brook—*stream* NY-2
Thorp Brook—*stream* VT-1
Thorp Cem—*cemetery* CO-8
Thorp Cem—*cemetery* IL-6
Thorp Cem—*cemetery* KY-4
Thorp Cem—*cemetery* MO-7
Thorp Cem—*cemetery* WA-9
Thorp Creek—*stream* MO-7
Thorp Creek—*stream* NY-2
Thorp Creek—*stream* OR-9
Thorp Creek—*stream* (2) WA-9
**Thorpe**—*pop pl* IA-7
**Thorpe**—*pop pl* MO-7
**Thorpe**—*pop pl* WV-2
Thorpe, Jim, House—*hist pl* OK-5
Thor Peak—*summit* CA-9
Thor Peak—*summit* WY-8
Thorpe Branch—*stream* KY-4
Thorpe Branch—*stream* VA-3
*Thorpe Brook* VT-1
Thorpe Canyon—*valley* CA-9
Thorpe Canyon—*valley* NV-8
Thorpe Cem—*cemetery* KY-4
Thorpe Cem—*cemetery* MO-7
Thorpe Cem—*cemetery* OH-6
Thorpe Creek—*stream* IN-6
Thorpe Creek—*stream* MT-8
Thorpe Creek—*stream* NV-8
Thorpe Creek—*stream* OR-9
Thorpe Dam Number Two—*dam* NC-3
Thorpe Ford Bridge—*hist pl* IN-6
Thorpe Ford Covered Bridge—*bridge* IN-6
Thorpe Gulch—*valley* CO-8
Thorpe Hills—*summit* UT-8
Thorpe Hollow—*valley* NY-2
*Thorpe Island* ME-1
Thorpe JHS—*school* VA-3
Thorpe Lake—*lake* FL-3
Thorpe Lake—*reservoir* NC-3
Thorpe Lookout Tower—*locale* MN-6
Thorpe Mine—*mine* AK-9
Thorpe Mtn—*summit* AR-4
Thorpe Mtn—*summit* CO-8
Thorpe Mtn—*summit* CT-1
Thorpe Number One Dam—*dam* NC-3
Thorpe Park—*park* AZ-5
Thorpe Sch—*school* SD-7
*Thorpe's Island* ME-1
Thorpe's Opera House—*hist pl* NE-7
Thorpe Spring—*spring* NV-8
Thorpe Tank—*reservoir* AZ-5
Thorpe (Thorp Station)—*locale* MN-6
**Thorpe (Township of)**—*pop pl* MN-6
Thorpe Union Cem—*cemetery* IA-7
Thorp Hill—*summit* WI-6
Thorp HS—*school* IL-6
*Thorp Lake* MI-6
Thorp Lake—*lake* WA-9
Thorp Mill—*hist pl* WA-9
Thorp Mtn—*summit* WA-9
Thorp Prairie—*flat* WA-9
**Thorps**—*pop pl* OH-6
*Thorps Bay* VT-1
*Thorps Brook* VT-1
Thorp Sch—*school* IL-6
Thorps Chapel—*church* TN-4
Thorps Ch (historical)—*church* TN-4
Thorps Creek—*stream* CA-9
Thorps Creek—*stream* NC-3
Thorps Entrance Cave—*cave* AL-4
**Thorpshire Farm (subdivision)**—*pop pl* NC-3
*Thorps Peak* CA-9
**Thorp Spring**—*pop pl* TX-5
Thorp Spring Cem—*cemetery* TX-5
Thorps Sch (historical)—*school* TN-4
**Thorp (Town of)**—*pop pl* WI-6
**Thorp Township**—*pop pl* SD-7
Thorp Vly—*swamp* NY-2
Thor Run—*stream* IN-6
**Thorsby**—*pop pl* AL-4
Thorsby HS—*school* AL-4
Thorsby Institute (historical)—*school* AL-4
Thorsen, William R., House—*hist pl* CA-9
Thorsen Creek—*stream* ND-7
Thorsen Mtn—*summit* AK-9
Thorsens Pond—*lake* MT-8
Thorsen Spring—*spring* UT-8
*Thors Hammer* AZ-5
Thors Hammer—*pillar* UT-8
Thors Hammer—*summit* OR-9
Thorson Airfield—*airport* SD-7
Thorson Gully—*valley* TX-5
Thorson Lake—*lake* (2) MN-6
Thorson Meadow—*flat* WA-9
Thorson Sch—*school* MN-6
Thorson Sch—*school* SD-7
Thorsons Lake—*lake* ND-7
**Thorson Township**—*pop pl* ND-7
Thorstad, Lake—*lake* MN-6
*Thorstad Creek* WI-6
Thorstad Lake—*lake* MN-6
Thorstensen 1 Dam—*dam* SD-7
Thorstensen 2 Dam—*dam* SD-7
Thorstensen 3 Dam—*dam* SD-7
Thorstrand—*hist pl* WI-6
Thor Temple—*summit* AZ-5
Thorton—*locale* MI-6
Thorton Bldg—*hist pl* GA-3
Thorton Cem—*cemetery* NY-2
*Thorton Creek* MS-4
*Thorton Creek* OR-9
Thorton Creek—*stream* NJ-2
Thorton Hill Sch (historical)—*school* MS-4
Thorton Key—*island* FL-3
Thorton Lakes—*reservoir* AL-4
Thorton Number 1 Dam—*dam* AL-4
Thorton Number 2 Dam—*dam* AL-4
Thorton Number 3 Dam—*dam* AL-4
Thorton Number 4 Dam—*dam* AL-4
Thorton Number 5 Dam—*dam* AL-4
Thorton Number 6 Dam—*dam* AL-4
Thorton Road Interchange—*crossing* AZ-5
Thorton Valley Drain—*canal* MI-6
**Thorup Estates Subdivision**—*pop pl* UT-8
Thorval Dam—*dam* AL-4
Thorval Jensen Ranch—*locale* WY-8
Thorval Lake—*reservoir* AL-4
**Thorwood Park**—*pop pl* MD-2
**Thoten**—*pop pl* IA-7
*Thotis Brook* ME-1
*Thouching Creek* TX-5
Thouching Creek—*stream* TX-5
*Thourguson Canal* LA-4
Thousand Acre Bog—*swamp* (2) ME-1
Thousand Acre Brook—*stream* MA-1
Thousand Acre Brook—*stream* NY-2
Thousand Acre Flats—*flat* CO-8
Thousand Acre Hill—*summit* VT-1
Thousand Acre Lake—*reservoir* OK-5
*Thousand Acre Meadow* MA-1
Thousand Acre Meadow—*flat* WA-9
*Thousand Acre Meadow Brook* MA-1
Thousand Acre Pasture—*flat* OR-9
Thousand Acre Pond—*lake* CT-1
Thousand Acre Rsvr—*reservoir* MA-1
Thousand Acres Bay (Carolina Bay)—*swamp* NC-3
Thousand Acre Site Number 1 Dam—*dam* MA-1
Thousand Acre Swamp—*swamp* ME-1
Thousand Acre Swamp—*swamp* (2) MA-1
Thousand Acre Swamp—*swamp* (2) NY-2
Thousand Acre Swamp—*swamp* PA-2
Thousand Acre Swamp Rsvr—*reservoir* MA-1
Thousand Acre Well—*well* TX-5
Thousand Acre Woods—*forest* IN-6
Thousand Creek—*stream* NV-8
Thousand Creek Gorge—*valley* NV-8
Thousand Creek Ranch—*locale* NV-8
Thousand Creek Spring—*spring* NV-8
Thousand Dollar Dam—*dam* TX-5
Thousand Dollar Gulch—*valley* UT-8

Thousand Dollar Ridge—*ridge* ... UT-8
Thousand Dollar Tank—*reservoir* ... TX-5
Thousand Falls—*falls* ... CO-8
Thousand Hills State Park—*park* ... MO-7
Thousand Hills State Park Petroglyphs Archeol Site—*hist pl* ... MO-7
Thousand Island Lake—*lake* ... CA-9
Thousand Island Lake—*lake* ... MI-6
**Thousand Island Park**—*pop pl* ... NY-2
Thousand Island Park Hist Dist—*hist pl* ... NY-2
Thousand Islands—*island* ... FL-3
Thousand Islands—*island* ... NY-2
Thousand Islands Bridge—*bridge* ... NY-2
Thousand Islands Country Club—*other* ... NY-2
Thousand Island State Conservancy Area—*park* ... WI-6
Thousand Lake Mtn—*summit* ... UT-8
Thousand Lakes Valley—*basin* ... CA-9
Thousand Lakes Valley Wild Area—*locale* .. CA-9
Thousandmile Canyon—*valley* ... NM-5
Thousandmile Creek—*stream* ... FL-3
**Thousand Oaks**—*pop pl* ... CA-9
**Thousand Oaks**—*pop pl* ... MO-7
Thousand Oaks (CCD)—*cens area* ... CA-9
Thousand Oaks HS—*school* ... CA-9
Thousand Oaks Park—*park* ... CA-9
Thousand Oaks Sch—*school* ... CA-9
Thousand Palm Canyon Wash—*stream* ... CA-9
**Thousand Palms**—*pop pl* ... CA-9
*Thousand Palms Canyon* ... CA-9
Thousand Palms Canyon—*valley* ... CA-9
Thousand Palms Dry Camp Siding—*locale*. CA-9
Thousand Palms Oasis—*locale* ... CA-9
Thousand Peaks Ranch—*locale* ... UT-8
Thousand Pines Camp—*locale* ... CA-9
Thousand Pockets—*basin* ... AZ-5
Thousand Spring—*spring* ... AZ-5
Thousand Spring Canyon—*valley* ... CA-9
*Thousand Spring Creek* ... NV-8
*Thousand Spring Creek* ... UT-8
Thousand Spring Creek—*stream* ... OR-9
Thousand Spring Ranch—*locale* ... OR-9
*Thousand Springs* ... NV-8
Thousand Springs—*locale* ... CA-9
**Thousand Springs**—*pop pl* ... NV-8
Thousand Springs—*spring* ... ID-8
Thousand Springs—*spring* ... NV-8
Thousand Springs—*spring* (2) ... OR-9
Thousand Springs—*spring* ... UT-8
Thousand Springs—*swamp* ... ID-8
Thousand Springs Creek—*stream* (2) ... ID-8
Thousand Springs Creek—*stream* ... NV-8
Thousand Springs Creek—*stream* ... UT-8
*Thousand Springs Trading Post* ... NV-8
Thousand Springs Trail—*trail* ... OR-9
Thousand Springs Valley—*valley* (2) ... ID-8
Thousand Springs Valley—*valley* ... NV-8
Thousandsticks—*locale* ... KY-4
Thousandsticks Branch—*stream* ... KY-4
*Thousand Wells* ... AZ-5
Thousand Yard Bay—*swamp* ... FL-3
Thousand Yard Bayou—*stream* ... MS-4
*Thowaenifeeng* ... FM-9
*Thowanifeng* ... FM-9
*Thowenifeng* ... FM-9
Thowrntown—*locale* ... DE-2
Thox Rock—*island* ... MO-7
Thox Rock—*locale* ... MO-7
*Thox Rock Camp* ... MO-7
Thrace Cem—*cemetery* ... OK-5
Thraikill Cem—*cemetery* ... IN-6
Thraikill Cem—*cemetery* ... SC-3
Thrailkill Branch—*stream* ... MO-7
Thrailkill (historical)—*locale* ... MS-4
Thrailkill Spring—*spring* ... CO-8
Thrailkill Windmill—*locale* ... TX-5
**Thrali**—*pop pl* ... WA-9
Thrall—*locale* ... IA-7
Thrall—*locale* ... WA-9
**Thrall**—*pop pl* ... KS-7
**Thrall**—*pop pl* ... TX-5
Thrall-Aagard Oil Field—*oilfield* ... KS-7
Thrall Dam Park—*park* ... NY-2
Thrall Lake—*lake* ... MI-6
Thrall Mtn—*summit* ... SD-7
Thrall Oil Field—*oilfield* ... TX-5
Thrall Run—*stream* ... IN-6
**Thralls Prairie (historical)**—*pop pl* ... MO-7
Thralltown—*locale* ... CT-1
T-H Ranch—*locale* ... AZ-5
Thrapp Mtn—*summit* ... WA-9
Thrash Branch—*stream* ... NC-3
Thrash Cem—*cemetery* ... AL-4
Thrash Cem—*cemetery* (2) ... GA-3
Thrash Creek—*stream* ... NC-3
Thrash Creek—*stream* ... WA-9
Thrash Dam—*dam* ... NC-3
**Thrasher**—*pop pl* ... MS-4
**Thrasher**—*pop pl* ... TX-5
Thrasher Attendance Center—*school* ... MS-4
Thrasher Baptist Ch—*church* ... MS-4
Thrasher Bluff—*cliff* ... AL-4
Thrasher Branch—*stream* (2) ... SC-3
Thrasher Brook—*stream* ... CT-1
Thrasher Brook—*stream* ... MA-1
Thrasher Cave—*cave* ... AL-4
Thrasher Cem—*cemetery* (4) ... AL-4
Thrasher Cem—*cemetery* ... MO-7
Thrasher Chapel Cem—*cemetery* ... MO-7
Thrasher Coal Bed Mine (underground)—*mine* ... AL-4
Thrasher Creek—*stream* ... ID-8
Thrasher Creek—*stream* ... MI-6
Thrasher Crossroads—*locale* ... AL-4
Thrasher Dam—*dam* ... AL-4
*Thrasher High School* ... MS-4
Thrasher Hill—*summit* ... NH-1
Thrasher House—*hist pl* ... LA-4
Thrasher Knob—*summit* ... WV-2
Thrasher Lake—*lake* ... MN-6
Thrasher Lake—*reservoir* ... AL-4
Thrasher Methodist Ch—*church* ... MS-4
Thrasher Nest Pond—*lake* ... FL-3
Thrasher Park—*park* ... CA-9
Thrasher Peaks—*summit* ... ME-1
Thrasher Ridges—*ridge* ... FL-3
**Thrashers**—*pop pl* ... MS-4
Thrashers Cem—*cemetery* ... KY-4
Thrasher Sch (historical)—*school* ... AL-4
**Thrashers Corner**—*pop pl* ... WA-9
Thrashers Creek—*stream* ... VA-3
Thrashers Crossroads—*locale* ... AL-4
Thrashers Quarry—*mine* ... TN-4
Thrashhouse Run—*stream* ... WV-2
Thrashing Branch—*stream* ... TN-4
*Thrashing Creek* ... TN-4
Thrash Lake—*reservoir* ... NC-3
Thrash Ranch—*locale* ... CA-9
Thrawl Cem—*cemetery* ... OK-5
Thread Cem—*cemetery* ... IL-6
Thread Creek—*stream* ... MI-6
Threadgill Canyon—*valley* ... NM-5
Threadgill Cem—*cemetery* ... AR-4
Threadgill Creek—*stream* ... TX-5
*Threadgill Elementary School* ... MS-4
Threadgill Elem Sch—*school* ... AL-4
Threadgill Mill Creek—*stream* ... AL-4
Threadgill Sch—*school* ... MS-4
Threadgill Tank—*reservoir* ... NM-5
Thread Lake—*lake* ... MI-6
Threadmill Brook—*stream* ... RI-1
Threadneedle Point—*cape* ... VI-3
Thread of Life Ledges—*bar* ... ME-1
**Threadville**—*pop pl* ... MS-4
Threadville Post Office (historical)—*building* ... MS-4
Threat Branch—*stream* ... MS-4
Threats Grove Ch—*church* ... GA-3
Three, Bayou—*stream* ... LA-4
Three, Canal (historical)—*canal* ... AZ-5
Three, Canyon—*valley* ... CA-9
Three, Hill—*summit* ... AZ-5
Three, Lake—*lake* ... AZ-5
Three, Lake—*lake* (3) ... MN-6
Three, Lake—*lake* (3) ... WI-6
Three, Lake—*reservoir* ... NJ-2
Three, Lake No—*reservoir* (2) ... AR-4
Three, Lake on—*lake* ... MN-6
Three, Well—*well* ... NV-8
Three Aces Oil Field—*oilfield* ... TX-5
Three Acre Lake—*lake* ... GA-3
Three A M Mtn—*summit* ... WA-9
Three and One-half Fathom Ledge—*bar* .. MA-1
Three and Twenty Creek—*stream* ... SC-3
Three And Twentymile Branch—*stream* ... VA-3
Three Apostles, The—*summit* ... CO-8
**Three Arch Bay**—*pop pl* ... CA-9
Three Arch Rocks—*island* ... OR-9
Three Arch Rocks Natl Wildlife Ref—*park* .. OR-9
Three Arm Bay—*bay* ... AK-9
Three Bar Cabin—*locale* ... AZ-5
Three Bar C Ranch—*locale* ... WY-8
Three Bar Creek—*stream* ... MT-8
Three Bar Creek—*stream* ... WY-8
Three Bar Oil Field—*oilfield* ... TX-5
Three Bar Ranch—*locale* ... MT-8
Three Bar Ranch—*locale* ... NV-8
Three Bar Ranch—*locale* ... TX-5
Three Bar Ranch—*locale* ... WY-8
Three Bar Watershed Research Area—*area* ... AZ-5
Three Bar Wildlife Area—*park* ... AZ-5
Three Bayou—*stream* (3) ... LA-4
Three Bayou Bay—*lake* ... LA-4
Three Bayou Bay Oil and Gas Field—*oilfield* ... LA-4
Three Bayous—*gut* ... LA-4
Three Bear Camp—*locale* ... ID-8
Three Bear Creek—*stream* ... ID-8
Three Bear Gulch—*valley* ... WY-8
*Three Bears Creek* ... ID-8
Three Bears Lake—*lake* ... MT-8
Three Bear Spring—*spring* ... OR-9
Three Beech Prairie—*flat* ... AR-4
Three Beech Prairie—*flat* ... LA-4
Three Biscuit Gulch—*valley* ... CA-9
Three Black Rocks—*pillar* ... AZ-5
Three Blaze Meadow—*flat* ... ID-8
Three Blaze Trail—*trail* ... ID-8
Three Bluff Draw—*valley* ... TX-5
Three Branches Creek—*stream* ... LA-4
**Three Branches Estates (subdivision)**—*pop pl* ... AL-4
Three Bridge Run—*stream* ... PA-2
Three Bridges—*locale* ... CO-8
Three Bridges—*locale* ... TX-5
Three Bridges—*locale* ... WY-8
**Three Bridges**—*pop pl* ... NJ-2
Three Bridges Branch—*stream* ... MD-2
Three Bridges Sch—*school* ... IL-6
Three Brooks—*bay* ... ME-1
Three Brooks—*stream* ... ME-1
Three Brooks Cove—*bay* ... ME-1
Three Brooks Fire Tower—*locale* ... ME-1
Three Brothers—*island* ... CA-9
**Three Brothers**—*pop pl* ... AR-4
Three Brothers—*spring* ... MT-8
Three Brothers—*summit* ... AR-4
Three Brothers—*summit* ... CA-9
Three Brothers—*summit* ... NY-2
Three Brothers—*summit* ... WA-9
Three Brothers Cem—*cemetery* ... AR-4
Three Brothers Ch—*church* ... AR-4
Three Brothers Creek—*gut* ... FL-3
Three Brothers Creek—*stream* ... OH-6
Three Brothers Hills, The—*summit* ... AZ-5
Three Brothers Islands—*island* ... NY-2
Three Brothers Light—*locale* ... AK-9
Three Brothers Mtn—*summit* ... NY-2
Three Brothers Mtns—*range* ... WY-8
Three Brothers Trail—*trail* ... WA-9
Three Buck Bayou—*gut* ... LA-4
Threebuck Creek—*stream* ... OR-9
Three Bucket Spring—*spring* ... OR-9
Three Bucks Lakes—*lake* ... WI-6
Three Burnt Mtn—*summit* ... ME-1
Three Bush Island—*island* ... ME-1
Three Buttes—*other* ... NM-5
Three Buttes—*range* ... ND-7
Three Buttes—*spring* (3) ... MT-8
Three Buttes—*summit* ... AZ-5
Three Buttes—*summit* ... CA-9
Three Buttes—*summit* ... MT-8
Three Buttes—*summit* ... OR-9
Three Buttes—*summit* ... WA-9
Three Buttes—*summit* (2) ... WY-8
Three Buttes Creek—*stream* ... WY-8
Three Buttes Drain—*canal* ... ID-8
Three Buttes Rsvr—*reservoir* ... WY-8
Three Cabbage Island—*island* ... FL-3
Three Cabbages—*lake* ... FL-3
Three Cabin Creek—*stream* ... OR-9
Three Cabin Ridge—*ridge* ... OR-9
Three Cabins—*locale* ... CA-9
Three Cabins Creek—*stream* ... ID-8
Three Cabins Creek—*stream* ... MT-8
Three Cabin Spring—*spring* ... OR-9
*Three Camp Mtn* ... AZ-5
Three Canyon—*valley* ... AZ-5
Three Canyon—*valley* ... NM-5
Three Canyon—*valley* ... OR-9
Three Canyon—*valley* (2) ... UT-8
Three Canyon Rapids—*rapids* ... UT-8
Three Castle Mtn—*summit* ... AK-9
*Three Castles* ... AZ-5
*Three Castles, The* ... AZ-5
Three Cent Gulch—*valley* (2) ... OR-9
Three Cent Spring—*spring* ... OR-9
Three Chimneys—*pillar* ... WI-6
Three Chimneys, The—*summit* ... CA-9
Three Chop Ridge—*ridge* ... CA-9
Three Chopt Community Center—*locale* ... VA-3
Three Chopt (Magisterial District)—*fmr MCD* ... VA-3
Three Churches—*locale* ... TN-4
**Three Churches**—*pop pl* ... WV-2
**Three Churches Corner**—*pop pl* ... MI-6
Three Churches Run—*stream* ... WV-2
*Three Church Hill* ... PA-2
Three Chutes Bar—*bar* ... AL-4
Three Circle Canyon—*valley* ... NM-5
Three Circle Ranch—*locale* ... MT-8
Three C Mine—*mine* ... CA-9
*Three Concerened Pond* ... PA-2
Three Cornered Cem—*cemetery* ... MA-1
Three Cornered Hassock—*island* ... NY-2
*Three Cornered Pond* ... NJ-2
*Three Cornered Pond* ... PA-2
Threecornered Pond—*lake* ... ME-1
Three Cornered Pond—*lake* ... MA-1
Three Corner Hole—*bay* ... NV-8
Three Corner Lake—*lake* ... MI-6
Three Corner Lake—*lake* ... WA-9
Three Corner Pond—*lake* ... CT-1
Three Corner Pond—*lake* ... ME-1
Three Corner Pond—*lake* ... SC-3
Three Corner Rock—*pillar* ... WA-9
Three Corners—*gap* ... CA-9
Three Corners—*locale* ... CA-9
Three Corners—*locale* ... MD-2
Three Corner Sch—*school* ... OK-5
Three Corners Creek—*stream* ... CA-9
Three Corners Dam—*dam* ... CA-9
Three Corners Lake—*lake* ... NE-7
Three Corner Slough—*stream* ... CA-9
Three Corner Spring—*spring* ... MT-8
Three Corners Sch—*school* ... KS-7
Three Corners Tank—*reservoir* ... TX-5
Three Corners Windmill—*locale* ... TX-5
Three Corner Well—*well* ... AZ-5
Three Corner Well—*well* ... NM-5
Three Corner Windmill—*locale* ... TX-5
Three Corn Ruin (LA 1871)—*hist pl* ... NM-5
Three Corrals Creek—*stream* ... TX-5
Three Coves Rsvr—*reservoir* ... UT-8
Three C Ranch—*locale* ... AZ-5
*Three Creek* ... AR-4
*Three Creek* ... LA-4
*Three Creek* ... UT-8
**Three Creek**—*pop pl* ... ID-8
Three Creek—*stream* (2) ... ID-8
Three Creek—*stream* ... NV-8
Three Creek—*stream* (3) ... OR-9
Three Creek—*stream* ... VA-3
Three Creek—*stream* ... WA-9
Three Creek Butte—*summit* ... OR-9
Three Creek Guard Station—*locale* ... OR-9
Three Creek Lake—*lake* ... OR-9
Three Creek Lake Campground—*park* ... OR-9
Three Creek Lake Trail—*trail* ... OR-9
Three Creek Meadow—*area* ... OR-9
*Three Creek Reservoir* ... UT-8
Three Creek Ridge—*ridge* ... OR-9
Three Creek Ridge Camp—*locale* ... WA-9
*Three Creeks* ... AR-4
Three Creeks—*locale* ... AR-4
Three Creeks—*locale* ... UT-8
Three Creeks—*stream* ... AR-4
Three Creeks—*stream* (2) ... CA-9
Three Creeks—*stream* ... LA-4
Three Creeks—*stream* ... MT-8
Three Creeks—*stream* ... SC-3
Three Creeks—*stream* (2) ... UT-8
Three Creeks—*stream* ... WA-9
Three Creeks Cem—*cemetery* ... AR-4
Three Creeks Ch—*church* ... AR-4
Three Creeks Dam—*dam* (2) ... UT-8
Three Creeks Flat—*flat* ... UT-8
Three Creeks Rsvr—*reservoir* (2) ... UT-8
Three Creeks Spring—*spring* ... UT-8
Three Creeks Summit—*summit* ... CA-9
Three Creek Trail—*trail* ... OR-9
Three Cripples Creek—*stream* ... WY-8
Three Crossing—*locale* ... CA-9
Three Cs Nursery—*school* ... FL-3
Three C Spring—*spring* ... OR-9
Three C Spring—*spring* ... WA-9
Three C Tank—*reservoir* ... AZ-5
Three C Tank—*reservoir* ... NM-5
Three Curve Park—*park* ... MI-6
Three C Wash—*valley* ... CO-8
Three C Well—*well* ... NV-8
Three-C Windmill—*locale* ... NV-8
Three Day Creek—*stream* ... NV-8
Three Day Creek Trailhead—*locale* ... NV-8
Three Day Slough—*gut* ... AK-9
Three D Beach—*beach* ... WA-9
Threed Cedar Rapids—*rapids* ... WI-6
Three Deer Creek—*stream* ... WA-9
Three Devils—*valley* ... WA-9
Three Devils Creek—*stream* ... ID-8
Three Devils Picnic Area—*park* ... ID-8
Three Divide Lakes—*lake* ... UT-8
Three Dog Site, RI-151—*hist pl* ... RI-1
Three Dollar Bar—*bar* ... CA-9
Threed Porcupine Rapids—*rapids* ... WI-6
Three Drag Road Canyon—*valley* ... UT-8
Three D Street Sch—*school* ... AZ-5
Three Dunes Campgrounds—*park* ... AZ-5
Threed Wannigan Rapids—*rapids* ... WI-6
Three Eagles Lakes—*lake* ... MT-8
Three Eagles Mtn—*summit* ... MT-8
Three Elk Creek—*stream* ... CO-8
Three Elk Lake—*lake* ... WY-8
Three Elms County Park—*park* ... IA-7
Three Entrance Bay—*bay* ... AK-9
Three Entrance Cave Archeol District—*hist pl* ... OK-5
Three E Spring—*spring* ... OR-9
Threefall Run—*stream* ... PA-2
Three Falls Boy Scout Camp—*locale* ... CA-9
Three Falls Cave—*cave* ... AL-4
Three Falls Glen—*valley* ... PA-2
Three Falls Harbor—*bay* ... ME-1
Three Falls Point—*cape* ... ME-1
Three Fathom Ledge—*bar* ... ME-1
Three Feathers Tank—*reservoir* ... AZ-5
Three Finger Cove—*bay* ... AR-4
Three Finger Cove—*bay* ... OK-5
Three Fingered Jack—*summit* ... OR-9
Three Fingered Lake—*reservoir* ... GA-3
Three Finger Lake—*lake* ... CA-9
Three Finger Lake—*lake* ... MN-6
Three Fingers—*summit* ... WA-9
Three Fingers Bay Public Use Area—*park* .. OK-5
Three Fingers Gulch—*valley* ... OR-9
Three Fingers Lookout—*hist pl* ... WA-9
*Three Fingers Mountain* ... WA-9
Three Fingers Rock—*summit* ... OR-9
Three Fingers Spring—*spring* ... OR-9
Three Fires, Lake of—*lake* ... IA-7
Three Fools Creek—*stream* ... WA-9
Three Fools Pass—*gap* ... WA-9
Three Fools Peak—*summit* ... WA-9
Threefoot Bldg—*hist pl* ... MS-4
Threefoot Rock—*island* ... CT-1
*Three Foot Shoal* ... MI-6
*Three Ford Canyon* ... UT-8
Three Fords Benches—*bench* ... UT-8
Three Fords Canyon—*valley* (2) ... UT-8
Three Fords Rapids—*rapids* ... UT-8
Three Fork—*stream* ... TN-4
Three Fork Branch—*stream* ... VA-3
Three Fork Branch—*stream* ... WV-2
Threefork Branch—*stream* ... WV-2
**Threefork Bridge**—*pop pl* ... WV-2
Three Fork Ch—*church* ... AL-4
Three Fork Creek—*stream* ... WV-2
Three Fork Gap—*gap* ... NC-3
Threefork Hollow—*valley* ... TN-4
*Three Forks* ... WV-2
Three Forks—*area* ... CO-8
Three Forks—*bend* ... NV-8
Three Forks—*locale* (2) ... AL-4
Three Forks—*locale* ... AK-9
Three Forks—*locale* ... AZ-5
Three Forks—*locale* ... AR-4
Three Forks—*locale* ... CA-9
Three Forks—*locale* ... CO-8
Three Forks—*locale* (2) ... GA-3
Three Forks—*locale* (3) ... ID-8
Three Forks—*locale* ... KY-4
Threeforks—*locale* ... KY-4
Three Forks—*locale* ... KY-4
Three Forks—*locale* (2) ... MT-8
Three Forks—*locale* ... NM-5
Three Forks—*locale* ... NC-3
Three Forks—*locale* ... OR-9
Three Forks—*locale* (2) ... TN-4
Three Forks—*locale* (3) ... UT-8
Three Forks—*locale* (4) ... VA-3
Three Forks—*locale* ... WA-9
Three Forks—*locale* ... WY-8
Three Forks—*other* ... WV-2
**Three Forks**—*pop pl* ... AL-4
**Three Forks**—*pop pl* ... MT-8
**Three Forks**—*pop pl* ... OH-6
**Three Forks**—*pop pl* ... WY-8
Three Forks—*stream* ... ID-8
Three Forks—*stream* ... UT-8
Three Forks—*stream* ... VA-3
Three Forks—*stream* ... WA-9
Three Forks—*stream* ... WV-2
*Three Forks Baptist Church* ... AL-4
Three Forks Branch—*stream* ... KY-4
Three Forks Branch—*stream* (2) ... TN-4
Three Forks Bridge—*bridge* ... TN-4
Three Forks Cabin—*locale* ... WA-9
Three Forks Campground—*locale* ... CO-8
Three Forks Campground—*locale* ... UT-8
Three Forks Cave—*cave* ... TN-4
Three Forks (CCD)—*cens area* ... KY-4
Three Forks Cem—*cemetery* ... TN-4
Three Forks Cem—*cemetery* ... VA-3
Three Forks Ch—*church* (3) ... NC-3
Three Forks Ch—*church* ... TN-4
Three Forks Ch (historical)—*church* ... TN-4
*Three Forks Church* ... AL-4
Three Forks Cow Camp—*locale* ... MT-8
Three Forks Crawley—*locale* ... WV-2
Three Forks Creek—*stream* ... CO-8
Three Forks Creek—*stream* ... ID-8
Three Forks Creek—*stream* ... KY-4
Three Forks Creek—*stream* (2) ... WA-9
Three Forks Greasy Sch—*school* ... KY-4
Three Forks (historical)—*locale* ... SD-7
*Three Forks Holiness Church* ... AL-4
Three Forks Hollow—*valley* ... TN-4
Three Forks Junction—*locale* ... MT-8
Three Forks Lake—*lake* ... ID-8
Three Forks Meadow—*flat* ... ID-8
*Three Forks Meeting House* ... TN-4
Three Forks Mill (historical)—*locale* ... TN-4
Three Forks Mtn—*summit* ... CO-8
Three Forks Mtn—*summit* ... GA-3
Three Forks Mtn—*summit* ... NC-3
Three Forks of Beaver Overlook—*locale* ... KY-4
Three Forks of Gauley—*locale* ... WV-2
Three Forks of the Missouri—*hist pl* ... MT-8
Three Forks of Williams River—*locale* ... WV-2
Three Forks Park—*flat* (2) ... WY-8
*Three forks Post Office* ... TN-4
*Three Forks Prong* ... NC-3
Three Forks Ranch—*locale* ... CO-8
Three Forks Rim—*cliff* ... OR-9
Three Forks Rsvr—*reservoir* ... WY-8
Three Forks Run—*stream* ... MD-2
Three Forks Run—*stream* ... WV-2
Threeforks Sch—*school* ... KY-4
Three Forks Sch—*school* ... WV-2
*Three Forks School* ... AL-4
Three Forks Shelter—*locale* ... WA-9
Three Forks Spring—*spring* ... NV-8
Three Forks Summit Springs—*spring* ... ID-8
Three Forks Tank—*reservoir* ... NM-5
**Threeforks (Three Forks)**—*pop pl* ... KY-4
Three Forks Trail—*trail* ... GA-3
Three Forks Wash—*stream* ... NV-8
**Three Fountains Bountiful Condominium**—*pop pl* ... UT-8
**Three Fountains East Condominium**—*pop pl* ... UT-8
**Three Fountains Manor House Condominium**—*pop pl* ... UT-8
**Three Fountains North Ogden Condominium**—*pop pl* ... UT-8
Three Fountains Professional Building Condominium—*locale* ... UT-8
**Three Fountains Townhomes and Manor Houses**—*pop pl* ... UT-8
Three Fountains (trailer park)—*locale* ... AZ-5
**Three Fountains (trailer park)**—*pop pl* ... AZ-5
**Three Fountains Young American Family Condominium**—*pop pl* ... UT-8
*Three-G Gas Plant* ... CA-9
Three Golden Stairs—*summit* ... UT-8
Three Gossips—*pillar* ... UT-8
*Three Gossips, The* ... UT-8
Three Gothic Villas—*hist pl* ... KY-4
*Three Graces, The* ... UT-8
*Three Grass Lakes* ... WI-6
Three Gray Hills—*summit* ... UT-8
Three Groves Ch—*church* ... MO-7
Three Gun Spring—*spring* ... NM-5
Three Hat Mtn—*summit* ... NC-3
Three High Heads—*cliff* ... VA-3
Three Hill—*summit* ... UT-8
Three Hill Creek—*stream* ... MO-7
Three Hill Island—*island* ... AK-9
Three Hill Mine—*mine* ... NV-8
Three Hills—*other* ... AK-9
Three Hills Trail—*trail* ... PA-2
Three Hole Bay—*bay* ... AK-9
Three Hole Cave—*cave* ... TN-4
Three Hole Point—*cape* ... AK-9
Three Hole Swamp—*stream* ... SC-3
Three Hollow Creek—*stream* ... FL-3
Three Hollow Head—*stream* ... FL-3
Threehorn Mtn—*summit* ... OR-9
Three Horse Lake—*lake* ... WA-9
Three Hundred and Twenty Ranch—*locale* ... MT-8
*Three Hundred Eleven Canyon* ... NV-8
Three Hundred North Radioactive Waste Dump—*other* ... WA-9
Three Hundred Springs—*spring* ... KY-4
Three Hundred Thirty Spring Pinic Ground—*locale* ... ID-8
Three Inch Windmill—*locale* ... TX-5
Three In One Ditch—*canal* ... ID-8
Three In One Mine—*mine* ... CA-9
Three Island—*island* ... MN-6
Three Island Bay—*bay* ... AK-9
Three Island Cove—*cove* ... FL-3
Three Island Crossing—*locale* ... ID-8
Three Island Lake—*lake* ... CA-9
Three Island Lake—*lake* ... CO-8
Three Island Lake—*lake* ... ID-8
Three Island Lake—*lake* (4) ... MN-6
Three Island Lake County Park—*park* ... MN-6
Three Island Lakes—*lake* ... FL-3
Three Island Lake Trail—*trail* ... CO-8
Three Island Pass—*channel* ... LA-4
Three Island Ponds—*lake* ... TX-5
*Three Islands* ... AL-4
*Three Islands* ... TX-5
Three Islands—*area* ... AK-9
Three Islands—*island* ... ME-1
Three Islands—*island* ... MT-8
Three Islands—*island* ... NH-1
Three Islands—*island* ... TX-5
Three Island Shoals (historical)—*bar* ... AL-4
Three Islands Park—*park* ... FL-3
Three Jim Ditch—*canal* ... MT-8
Three-Jim Tank—*reservoir* ... AZ-5
Three Johns Lake—*lake* ... WI-6
Three J Spring—*spring* ... OR-9
Three Kids Mine—*mine* ... NV-8
Three Kiln Knob—*summit* ... KY-4
Three Kilns Spring—*spring* ... UT-8
Three Kings—*mine* ... UT-8
Three Kiva Pueblo—*locale* ... UT-8
Three Knob Mtn—*summit* ... AR-4
Three Knobs—*summit* ... AR-4
Three Knobs—*summit* ... CO-8
Three Knobs—*summit* (2) ... NC-3
Three Knolls—*summit* ... ID-8
Three Knolls—*summit* ... UT-8
*Three Knolls Ridge* ... ID-8
Three Knolls Summit—*summit* ... UT-8
Three Knot Bayou—*stream* ... LA-4
*Three Lake* ... MN-6
*Three Lake* ... WI-6
Three Lake—*lake* ... ID-8
Three Lake—*lake* (2) ... MI-6
Three Lake Creek—*stream* ... MI-6
*Three Lakes* ... MI-6
*Three Lakes* ... MN-6
*Three Lakes* ... UT-8
*Three Lakes* ... WA-9
*Three Lakes* ... WI-6
Three Lakes—*lake* ... AK-9
Three Lakes—*lake* ... AZ-5
Three Lakes—*lake* ... CO-8
Three Lakes—*lake* (5) ... MI-6
Three Lakes—*lake* ... NE-7
Three Lakes—*lake* (2) ... OR-9
Three Lakes—*lake* (3) ... UT-8
Three Lakes—*lake* (3) ... WA-9
Three Lakes—*lake* (2) ... WI-6
Three Lakes—*locale* ... MI-6
Three Lakes—*locale* ... WA-9
**Three Lakes**—*pop pl* ... WI-6
Three Lakes—*reservoir* ... CA-9
Three Lakes—*reservoir* ... OK-5
Three Lakes—*swamp* ... SC-3
Three Lakes Camp—*park* ... OR-9
Three Lakes Canyon—*valley* ... UT-8
Three Lakes Corral—*locale* ... AZ-5
Three Lakes Country—*area* ... OR-9
Three Lakes Creek—*stream* ... CO-8
Three Lakes Creek—*stream* (2) ... ID-8
Three Lakes Creek—*stream* ... MT-8
Three Lakes Lakebed—*flat* ... MN-6
Three Lakes Lookout Tower—*locale* ... MI-6
Three Lakes Peak—*summit* ... MT-8
*Three Lakes Reservoir* ... WA-9
**Three Lakes (Town of)**—*pop pl* ... WI-6
**Three Lakes (Township of)**—*pop pl* ... MN-6
Three Lakes Trail—*trail* ... OR-9
Three Lakes Valley—*valley* ... NV-8
Three Lakes Valley Rsvr—*reservoir* ... NV-8
Three Lakes Waterhole—*lake* ... OR-9
Three Lakes Wildlife Mngmt Area—*park* ... FL-3
*Three Lanes End* ... PA-2
Three League Bayou—*gut* ... LA-4
**Three Leagues**—*pop pl* ... TX-5
Three Ledges Shoal Sluice—*hist pl* ... NC-3
Three Legged Lake—*lake* ... MI-6
Three Legged Windmill—*locale* ... NM-5
Three Legs Creek—*stream* ... SD-7
Three Leg Windmill—*locale* ... TX-5
Three Lick Branch—*stream* ... KY-4
*Three Lick Creek* ... PA-2
Three Lick Creek—*stream* ... KY-4
Threelick Fork—*stream* ... KY-4
Three Lick Hollow—*valley* ... PA-2
Three Lick Run—*stream* ... PA-2
Three Lick Run—*stream* ... WV-2
Threelick Run—*stream* (2) ... WV-2
Three Licks Creek—*stream* ... CO-8
*Three Links* ... OR-9
Threelinks—*locale* ... KY-4
*Three Links Creek* ... OR-9
Three Links Creek—*stream* ... ID-8
Three Links Meadows—*flat* ... ID-8
Three Links Point—*cliff* ... ID-8
Three Little Hills—*summit* ... NM-5
Three Little Lakes—*lake* (2) ... WI-6
Three Locks—*locale* ... OH-6
Three Locks Cem—*cemetery* ... OH-6
Three Locks Ch—*church* ... OH-6
Three Log Bridge—*bridge* ... SC-3
Three Log Spring Canyon—*valley* ... NM-5
Three Log Well—*well* ... NM-5
**Three Lynx**—*pop pl* ... OR-9
Three Lynx Creek—*stream* ... OR-9
Three Lynx Sch—*school* ... OR-9
Three Maples Sch (abandoned)—*school* ... PA-2
Three Marys—*rock* ... UT-8
Three Meadows—*flat* ... CA-9
Three Meadows Ranch—*locale* ... CO-8
**Three Meadows (subdivision)**—*pop pl* .. NC-3
Three Mediterranean Cottages on Pajarito Street—*hist pl* ... AZ-5
*Three Mellon Bank Center Airport* ... PA-2
Three Men Swamp—*swamp* ... GA-3
*Three Mice Creek* ... CO-8
*Three Mile* ... PA-2
Threemile—*locale* ... PA-2
**Three Mile**—*pop pl* ... NC-3
**Three Mile**—*pop pl* ... WV-2
Threemile Arm—*bay* ... AK-9
Three Mile Bay—*bay* ... AK-9
Three Mile Bay—*bay* ... LA-4
Three Mile Bay—*bay* ... NY-2
Threemile Bay—*bay* ... NY-2
**Three Mile Bay**—*pop pl* ... NY-2
*Three Mile Bayou* ... LA-4
Threemile Bayou—*stream* (3) ... LA-4
Threemile Bay State Game Mngmt Area—*park* ... NY-2
*Three Mile Branch* ... FL-3
*Three Mile Branch* ... NC-3
*Threemile Branch* ... TN-4
Threemile Branch—*stream* (2) ... AL-4
Threemile Branch—*stream* (2) ... FL-3
Threemile Branch—*stream* (2) ... IL-6
Threemile Branch—*stream* (2) ... KY-4
Threemile Branch—*stream* (2) ... MS-4
Threemile Branch—*stream* ... NC-3
Threemile Branch—*stream* (3) ... SC-3
Threemile Branch—*stream* ... TN-4
Threemile Branch—*stream* (2) ... TX-5
Threemile Branch—*stream* ... WV-2
Threemile Bridge—*bridge* ... VT-1
*Three Mile Brook* ... MA-1
Threemile Brook—*stream* (3) ... ME-1
Threemile Brook—*stream* ... MA-1
Threemile Butte—*summit* ... WY-8
Threemile Buttes—*summit* ... MT-8
Threemile Campground—*locale* ... MI-6
Threemile Campground—*locale* ... WY-8
Threemile Campsite—*locale* ... MT-8
*Threemile Canyon* ... TX-5
Threemile Canyon—*valley* ... AK-9
Threemile Canyon—*valley* ... CA-9
Threemile Canyon—*valley* (3) ... NV-8
Threemile Canyon—*valley* (2) ... NM-5
Threemile Canyon—*valley* ... OK-5
Threemile Canyon—*valley* (2) ... OR-9
Threemile Canyon—*valley* ... TX-5
Threemile Canyon—*valley* (5) ... UT-8
Threemile Canyon Well—*well* ... NV-8
Threemile Cem—*cemetery* ... MI-6
Threemile Ch—*church* ... KY-4
*Three Mile Coleto Creek* ... TX-5
Threemile Corner—*locale* ... ID-8
Threemile Corner—*locale* ... VA-3
Threemile Coulee—*valley* (3) ... MT-8
*Three Mile Creek* ... AL-4
*Three Mile Creek* ... AR-4
*Three Mile Creek* ... CO-8
*Three Mile Creek* ... GA-3
*Threemile Creek* ... IN-6
*Three Mile Creek* ... IA-7
*Three Mile Creek* ... KS-7
*Three Mile Creek* ... MI-6
*Threemile Creek* ... OH-6
*Threemile Creek* ... OR-9
*Three Mile Creek* ... TX-5
*Threemile Creek* ... UT-8
*Three Mile Creek* ... VA-3
*Three Mile Creek* ... WI-6
Threemile Creek—*stream* (3) ... AL-4
Three Mile Creek—*stream* ... AL-4
Threemile Creek—*stream* (3) ... AL-4
Threemile Creek—*stream* (5) ... AK-9
Threemile Creek—*stream* (2) ... AR-4

Threemile Creek—*stream* (5) CO-8
Threemile Creek—*stream* (2) GA-3
Threemile Creek—*stream* (13) ID-8
Threemile Creek—*stream* IL-6
Threemile Creek—*stream* (2) IN-6
Threemile Creek—*stream* (3) IA-7
Threemile Creek—*stream* (4) KS-7
Threemile Creek—*stream* (2) KY-4
Threemile Creek—*stream* LA-4
Threemile Creek—*stream* (4) MI-6
Threemile Creek—*stream* (3) MN-6
Threemile Creek—*stream* MO-7
Threemile Creek—*stream* (10) MT-8
Threemile Creek—*stream* NE-7
Threemile Creek—*stream* (2) NV-8
Three Mile Creek—*stream* NY-2
Threemile Creek—*stream* (2) NY-2
Threemile Creek—*stream* NC-3
Three Mile Creek—*stream* NC-3
Threemile Creek—*stream* (5) OH-6
Threemile Creek—*stream* OK-5
Threemile Creek—*stream* (9) OR-9
Threemile Creek—*stream* SC-3
Threemile Creek—*stream* SD-7
Threemile Creek—*stream* (2) TN-4
Threemile Creek—*stream* (9) TX-5
Threemile Creek—*stream* (6) UT-8
Threemile Creek—*stream* (6) WA-9
Threemile Creek—*stream* (4) WV-2
Threemile Creek—*stream* (4) WI-6
Threemile Creek—*stream* (5) WY-8
*Three Mile Creek Rsvr* OR-9
Threemile Creek Rsvr—*reservoir* WY-8
Threemile Crossing—*locale* ID-8
Threemile Cut—*channel* GA-3
Threemile Dam—*dam* (2) OR-9
Threemile Ditch—*canal* AL-4
Threemile Ditch—*canal* CO-8
Threemile Ditch—*canal* OR-9
Threemile Ditch—*canal* WY-8
*Threemile Drain* MI-6
Threemile Draw—*valley* NM-5
Threemile Draw—*valley* (4) TX-5
Threemile Drive Park—*park* MI-6
Threemile Enlargement and Extension—*canal* CO-8
*Threemile Falls Dam* OR-9
Threemile Falls Diversion Works—*dam* OR-9
Three Mile Falls Pool—*reservoir* OR-9
Threemile Fork—*stream* WV-2
Threemile Gulch—*valley* (2) CO-8
*Three Mile Harbor* NY-2
Threemile Harbor—*bay* NY-2
Threemile Hill—*summit* CT-1
Three Mile Hill—*summit* MA-1
Threemile Hill—*summit* OR-9
Three Mile Hill—*summit* TX-5
Threemile Hills—*summit* NM-5
Threemile Hollow—*valley* MO-7
Threemile Hollow—*valley* TN-4
Threemile Hollow—*valley* TX-5
Threemile Hollow—*valley* UT-8
Threemile Island—*island* FL-3
Threemile Island—*island* KY-4
Three Mile Island—*island* ME-1
Threemile Island—*island* MN-6
Threemile Island—*island* NH-1
Threemile Island—*island* NY-2
Threemile Island—*island* PA-2
Three Mile Island Nuclear Power Plant—*building* PA-2
Three Mile Island Number Two Airp—*airport* PA-2
Threemile Knoll—*summit* (2) ID-8
*Three Mile Lake* MA-1
*Three Mile Lake* MS-4
Threemile Lake—*lake* (2) AK-9
Threemile Lake—*lake* (2) AZ-5
Threemile Lake—*lake* FL-3
Threemile Lake—*lake* MI-6
Threemile Lake—*lake* MN-6
Threemile Lake—*lake* MS-4
Threemile Lake—*lake* NE-7
Threemile Lake—*lake* OR-9
Threemile Lake—*lake* SD-7
Threemile Lake—*lake* TX-5
**Three Mile Lake**—*pop pl* MI-6
Three Mile Lake Drain—*stream* MI-6
*Three Mile Lakes* NE-7
Three Mile Landing (historical)—*locale* AL-4
Threemile Lateral—*canal* ID-8
Threemile Meadow—*flat* WY-8
*Threemile Mesa* TX-5
Threemile Mesa—*summit* NM-5
*Threemile Mountain* TX-5
Threemile Mtn—*summit* NY-2
Threemile Mtn—*summit* VA-3
Threemile Oak Corner—*locale* MD-2
Threemile Park—*flat* CO-8
Three Mile Pass—*channel* LA-4
Threemile Peak—*summit* ID-8
Threemile Peak—*summit* TX-5
*Threemile Point* FL-3
Threemile Point—*cape* ID-8
Three Mile Point—*cape* NY-2
Threemile Point—*cape* (2) NY-2
Threemile Point—*summit* MT-8
Threemile Point—*summit* WA-9
Threemile Pond—*lake* (2) ME-1
Threemile Pond—*lake* MA-1
Threemile Pond—*reservoir* MA-1
Threemile Pond Dam—*dam* MA-1
Three Mile Prairie—*area* OR-9
Threemile Prairie—*flat* IL-6
Threemile Ranch—*locale* NV-8
Threemile Ranch—*locale* NM-5
Threemile Ranch—*locale* OR-9
Threemile Rapids (historical)—*rapids* OR-9
Threemile Rapids Light—*locale* WA-9
Threemile Reach—*channel* VA-3
Threemile Ridge—*ridge* KY-4
Threemile Ridge—*ridge* ME-1
Threemile Ridge—*ridge* MT-8
*Three Mile River* MA-1
Three Mile River—*reservoir* MA-1
Threemile River—*stream* CT-1
Threemile River—*stream* MA-1
Three Mile River Dam—*dam* MA-1
Threemile Rock—*summit* CA-9
Threemile Rsvr—*reservoir* CA-9
Threemile Rsvr—*reservoir* CO-8
Threemile Rsvr—*reservoir* ID-8
Threemile Rsvr—*reservoir* MT-8
Threemile Rsvr—*reservoir* (2) OR-9
*Three Mile Run* PA-2
Threemile Run—*stream* KY-4
Threemile Run—*stream* (4) PA-2
Threemile Run—*stream* WV-2
Threemile Sch—*school* CO-8
Threemile Sch—*school* KY-4
Threemile Sch—*school* MO-7
Threemile Sch—*school* MT-8
Threemile Sch—*school* OR-9
Three Mile Sch (historical)—*school* MS-4
Threemile Sch (historical)—*school* MS-4
Threemile Shelter—*locale* OR-9
Three Mile Slough—*gut* AR-4
Threemile Slough—*gut* CA-9
Three Mile Slough—*stream* LA-4
Threemile Slough—*stream* TN-4
Threemile Slough (historical)—*gut* TN-4
Threemile Spring—*reservoir* WY-8
Threemile Spring—*spring* ID-8
Threemile Spring—*spring* NM-5
Threemile Spring—*spring* OR-9
Threemile Spring—*spring* WY-8
Threemile Spring (Sulphur)—*spring* NV-8
Threemile Table—*bench* MT-8
Threemile Tank—*reservoir* (2) TX-5
Threemile Trail—*trail* OR-9
Threemile Valley—*valley* CA-9
Threemile Vly—*lake* NY-2
Threemile Well—*well* MT-8
Threemile Well—*well* TX-5
Threemile Well—*well* UT-8
Three Mills Tank—*reservoir* NM-5
Three Mills Well—*well* NM-5
Three Moccasin Park—*park* SD-7
Three Mounds—*summit* KS-7
Three Mounds—*summit* TX-5
**Three Mountains**—*pop pl* TN-4
Three Mountains—*summit* TX-5
Three Mountains Sch—*school* TN-4
Three Mouths, The—*lake* NJ-2
Three Needles—*summit* CO-8
*Three Needles Peak* CO-8
Threenob Rock—*other* AK-9
**Three Notch**—*pop pl* AL-4
Three Notch Baptist Ch—*church* AL-4
Three Notch Cem—*cemetery* AL-4
*Three Notches* AL-4
Three Notches—*gap* CT-1
**Three Notches**—*pop pl* AL-4
Three Notch Museum—*building* AL-4
Three Notch Sch—*school* AL-4
Three Notch Shop Ctr—*locale* AL-4
Three Oak Ch—*church* MS-4
Three Oak Gap—*gap* AR-4
Three Oaks—*locale* TN-4
Three Oaks—*locale* TX-5
**Three Oaks**—*pop pl* LA-4
**Three Oaks**—*pop pl* MI-6
**Three Oaks**—*pop pl* TN-4
Three Oaks Bayou—*stream* MS-4
Three Oaks Ch—*church* TX-5
Three Oaks (historical)—*locale* TN-4
Three Oaks Sch—*school* FL-3
Three Oaks Sch—*school* TX-5
**Three Oaks (Township of)**—*pop pl* MI-6
Three O'Clock Ridge—*ridge* WA-9
Three O'Clock Spring (historical)—*spring* PA-2
Three-On Lake—*lake* MI-6
Three Otter Creek—*stream* FL-3
Three Otters—*hist pl* VA-3
Three Palms (not verified)—*other* MP-9
Three Patches Picnic Area—*park* WY-8
Three Patriarchs—*summit* UT-8
*Three Peaks* MT-8
Three Peaks—*summit* AZ-5
Three Peaks—*summit* (6) CA-9
Three Peaks—*summit* NY-2
Three Peaks—*summit* UT-8
Three Peaks—*summit* (2) WA-9
Three Peaks, The—*summit* UT-8
Three Peaks Trail—*trail* WA-9
Three Penguins—*summit* UT-8
Three Pillar Point—*cape* AK-9
Three Pine Butte—*summit* OR-9
Three Pine Creek—*stream* UT-8
Three Pine Island—*island* ME-1
Three Pines—*locale* UT-8
**Three Pines**—*pop pl* OR-9
Three Pines Baptist Ch—*church* AL-4
Three Pines Canyon—*valley* CA-9
Three Pines Ch—*church* LA-4
Three Pinnacles—*pillar* WA-9
*Three Point* CA-9
*Three Point* DE-2
*Three Point* TX-5
Three Point—*locale* TN-4
**Three Point**—*pop pl* CA-9
**Three Point**—*pop pl* KY-4
**Three Point**—*pop pl* TX-5
Three Point Airp—*airport* AZ-5
Three Point Bend—*bend* AZ-5
Three Point Camp—*locale* PA-2
Three Point Ch—*church* TN-4
Threepoint Hollow—*valley* PA-2
Threepoint Hollow Trail—*trail* PA-2
Three Point Lake—*reservoir* IN-6
Three Point Lake Dam—*dam* IN-6
*Three Point Mountain* CO-8
Three Point Mtn—*summit* ID-8
Three Point Rsvr—*reservoir* ID-8
Three Points—*cape* DE-2
Three Points—*locale* AZ-5
Three Points—*locale* CA-9
Three Points—*locale* GA-3
Three Points—*locale* TX-5
**Three Points**—*pop pl* CA-9
**Three Points**—*pop pl* GA-3
**Three Points**—*pop pl* (2) TN-4
**Three Points**—*pop pl* TX-5
Three Points—*summit* TX-5
Three Points Baptist Ch—*church* TN-4
Three Points Mtn—*summit* CO-8
**Three Points (Robles Junction)**—*pop pl* AZ-5
Three Points Rsvr—*reservoir* NV-8
Three Points Sch—*school* WA-9
Three Points Sch (historical)—*school* AL-4
Three Pond—*lake* FL-3
Three Pond Branch—*stream* NJ-2
Three Ponds—*lake* KY-4
Three Ponds—*lake* NH-1
Three Ponds—*lake* NY-2
Three Ponds—*lake* RI-1
Three Ponds, The—*lake* NY-2
Three Ponds Bluff—*cliff* KY-4
Three Ponds Brook—*stream* RI-1
Three Ponds Mtn—*summit* NY-2
Three Ponds Trail—*trail* NH-1
Three Poplars Ch—*church* WV-2
Three Post Windmill—*locale* TX-5
Three P Plant—*other* CA-9
Three Prong Branch—*stream* KY-4
Three Prong Campground—*locale* CA-9
Three Prong Creek—*stream* ID-8
Three Prong Creek—*stream* WA-9
*Three Prong Lake* LA-4
Three Prong Lake—*lake* AR-4
Three Prong Mtn—*summit* ID-8
*Three Prong Ridge* ID-8
Three Prong Ridge—*ridge* ID-8
Three Prong Valley—*basin* CA-9
Three Prune Creek—*stream* WA-9
Three Prune Shelter—*locale* WA-9
Three P Trap Windmill—*locale* NM-5
Three Pyramids—*summit* OR-9
Three Quarter Circles Ranch—*locale* CO-8
Three Quarters Creek—*stream* NC-3
Three-Quarter Tank—*reservoir* TX-5
Three Queens—*summit* WA-9
Three Queens Lake—*lake* WA-9
Three Queens Mine—*mine* CA-9
Three Ridges—*ridge* VA-3
Three Ridges Overlook—*locale* VA-3
Three Ridge Trail—*trail* PA-2
Three River Junction—*locale* WY-8
*Three River Lake* AL-4
Three River Mtn—*summit* AK-9
*Three River Peak* WY-8
Three River Reach—*channel* CA-9
Three Rivers—*bay* AL-4
Three Rivers—*locale* AL-4
**Three Rivers**—*pop pl* CA-9
**Three Rivers**—*pop pl* MA-1
**Three Rivers**—*pop pl* MI-6
**Three Rivers**—*pop pl* MS-4
**Three Rivers**—*pop pl* NM-5
**Three Rivers**—*pop pl* NY-2
**Three Rivers**—*pop pl* TX-5
Three Rivers—*stream* NM-5
Three Rivers—*stream* OR-9
Three Rivers Canyon—*valley* NM-5
Three Rivers (CCD)—*cens area* TX-5
Three Rivers Cem—*cemetery* MS-4
Three Rivers Cem—*cemetery* MO-7
Three Rivers Cem—*cemetery* OK-5
Three Rivers Ch—*church* MO-7
Three Rivers Ch—*church* PA-2
*Three Rivers Community Hospital* TN-4
Three Rivers Creek—*stream* MO-7
Three Rivers Golf Course—*other* CA-9
Three Rivers Highway—*channel* MI-6
Three Rivers Lake—*lake* AL-4
Three Rivers Mill Pond—*lake* WA-9
Three Rivers Peak—*summit* WY-8
Three Rivers Post Office (historical)—*building* MS-4
Three Rivers Quarry—*mine* KY-4
Three Rivers Ranch—*locale* CO-8
Three Rivers Ranch—*locale* WY-8
Three Rivers Stadium—*park* PA-2
Three Rivers State Game Mngmt Area—*park* NY-2
Three Rivers State Park—*park* FL-3
**Three Rivers Township**—*pop pl* SD-7
*Threerock Creek* OR-9
Three Rock Creek—*stream* OR-9
Three Rock Run—*stream* PA-2
Three Rocks—*island* CA-9
Three Rocks—*island* OR-9
Three Rocks—*locale* OR-9
Three Rocks—*pillar* OR-9
**Three Rocks**—*pop pl* CA-9
**Three Rocks**—*pop pl* OR-9
Three Rocks—*range* WA-9
Three Rocks—*summit* CA-9
Three Rocks—*summit* WA-9
Three Rooker Bar—*bar* FL-3
Three-Room House—*hist pl* ID-8
Three R Ranch—*locale* CO-8
Three R Tank—*reservoir* AZ-5
Three Run—*stream* WV-2
Three Run Creek—*stream* AL-4
Three Runs—*locale* GA-3
*Three Runs Creek* SC-3
*Three Runs Fire Tower* PA-2
Three Runs Lookout Tower—*locale* PA-2
Three Saints Bay—*bay* AK-9
Three Saints Lateral—*canal* NM-5
Three Saints Lateral—*canal* TX-5
Three Saints Point—*cape* AK-9
Three Saints Site—*hist pl* AK-9
Three Saints West Lateral—*canal* NM-5
Three Sands Oil Field—*oilfield* OK-5
**Three Seasons (trailer park)**—*pop pl* DE-2
Three Section Tank—*reservoir* TX-5
Three Section Well—*well* TX-5
Three Section Windmill—*locale* NM-5
Three Section Windmill—*locale* (2) TX-5
Three-Seven Spring—*spring* OR-9
Three Shanties Brook—*stream* VT-1
Three Shoot Ford—*locale* AR-4
Three Sirens, The—*summit* CA-9
Three Sirens Island—*island* NY-2
Three Sisiters—*summit* CA-9
*Three Sisters* CA-9
*Three Sisters* KS-7
Three Sisters—*island* CA-9
Three Sisters—*island* NY-2
Three Sisters—*pillar* RI-1
Three Sisters—*range* (3) CA-9
Three Sisters—*ridge* ID-8
Three Sisters—*ridge* NH-1
Three Sisters—*ridge* NM-5
Three Sisters—*ridge* WY-8
Three Sisters—*summit* (3) AZ-5
Three Sisters—*summit* (4) CA-9
Three Sisters—*summit* MT-8
Three Sisters—*summit* NM-5
Three Sisters—*summit* NY-2
Three Sisters—*summit* OR-9
Three Sisters—*summit* UT-8
Three Sisters—*summit* VA-3
*Three Sisters, The* DC-2
Three Sisters, The—*island* AK-9
Three Sisters, The—*summit* CA-9
Three Sisters, The—*summit* NY-2
Three Sisters, The—*summit* WA-9
Three Sisters Buttes—*summit* AZ-5
*Three Sisters Creek* SD-7
Three Sisters Creek—*stream* ID-8
Three Sisters Creek—*stream* MT-8
Three Sisters Creek—*stream* NC-3
Three Sisters Gulch—*valley* CA-9
Three Sisters Hill—*summit* ND-7
Three Sisters Hollow—*valley* KY-4
Three Sisters Island—*island* FL-3
Three Sisters Island—*island* KY-4
Three Sisters Island—*island* MI-6
Three Sisters Island—*island* NH-1
Three Sisters Islands—*island* DC-2
Three Sisters Islands—*island* FL-3
Three Sisters Islands—*island* MN-6
Three Sisters Islands—*island* (2) NY-2
Three Sisters Islands (historical)—*island* SD-7
Three Sisters Knobs—*summit* VA-3
Three Sisters Lake—*lake* AR-4
Three Sisters Lakes—*lake* MD-2
Three Sisters Landing—*locale* AR-4
Three Sisters Mountains (CCD)—*cens area* GA-3
Three Sisters Mtn—*summit* AK-9
Three Sisters Mtn—*summit* AZ-5
Three Sisters Mtn—*summit* GA-3
Three Sisters Mtn—*summit* NY-2
Three Sisters of Nauset (Twin Lights)—*hist pl* MA-1
Three Sisters Peaks—*summit* CA-9
Three Sisters Peaks—*summit* CO-8
Three Sisters Peaks—*summit* ID-8
Three Sisters Point—*cape* NM-5
Three Sisters Pond—*swamp* FL-3
Three Sisters Range—*summit* MI-6
*Three Sisters Ridge* NH-1
Three Sisters Rock—*island* AK-9
Three Sisters Rocks—*island* AK-9
Three Sisters Shell Midden (22-Ha-596)—*hist pl* MS-4
Three Sisters Tank—*reservoir* (2) AZ-5
Three Sisters Wilderness Area—*reserve* OR-9
Three Sleep Point—*cape* AK-9
Three Slide Mtn—*summit* ME-1
Threesome Mtn—*summit* AK-9
**Three Spring**—*pop pl* VA-3
Three Spring—*spring* NV-8
Three Spring Brook—*stream* PA-2
Three Spring Ranch—*locale* OR-9
Three Spring Run—*stream* WV-2
Three Springs—*flat* CO-8
Three Springs—*locale* KY-4
**Three Springs**—*pop pl* KY-4
**Three Springs**—*pop pl* PA-2
**Three Springs**—*pop pl* TN-4
**Three Springs**—*pop pl* VA-3
Three Springs—*spring* (4) CA-9
Three Springs—*spring* (2) ID-8
Three Springs—*spring* KY-4
Three Springs—*spring* MT-8
Three Springs—*spring* NV-8
Three Springs—*spring* OK-5
Three Springs—*spring* (2) OR-9
Three Springs—*spring* UT-8
Three Springs—*spring* WY-8
Three Springs Bar—*bar* WA-9
Three Springs Borough—*civil* PA-2
*Three Springs Branch* WV-2
Three Springs Branch—*stream* NC-3
*Three Springs Brook* PA-2
Three Springs Canyon—*valley* AZ-5
Three Springs Canyon—*valley* NV-8
*Three Springs Cave* TN-4
Three Springs Cem—*cemetery* MO-7
Three Springs Cem—*cemetery* WV-2
Three Springs Ch—*church* PA-2
Three Springs Ch—*church* TN-4
Three Springs Ch—*church* VA-3
Three Springs Creek—*stream* CA-9
Three Springs Creek—*stream* PA-2
Three Springs Creek—*stream* VA-3
Three Springs Creek—*stream* WY-8
Three Springs Dock—*locale* TN-4
Three Springs Draw—*valley* CO-8
Three Springs Farm Sch (abandoned)—*school* PA-2
Three Springs Gap—*gap* NC-3
**Three Springs (historical)**—*pop pl* OR-9
Three Springs Hollow—*valley* IL-6
Three Springs Hollow—*valley* MO-7
Three Springs Knob—*summit* KY-4
Three Springs Pumphouse—*other* KY-4
**Three Springs Run**—*pop pl* PA-2
Three Springs Run—*stream* (3) PA-2
Three Springs Run—*stream* WV-2
Three Springs Sch (historical)—*school* TN-4
Three Springs Trail—*trail* MT-8
Three Square—*locale* (2) VA-3
Three Square Creek—*stream* VA-3
Three Square Hollow—*valley* PA-2
Three Square Hollow Run—*stream* PA-2
Three Square Knob—*summit* WV-2
Three Squares Hist Dist—*hist pl* NY-2
Three Star Mall Shop Ctr—*locale* TN-4
Three Star Point—*cape* AK-9
**Three States**—*pop pl* LA-4
**Three States**—*pop pl* TX-5
Three States Ch—*church* LA-4
Three States Landing—*locale* MO-7
Three States Towhead—*area* MO-7
Three Step Hill—*summit* UT-8
Three Step Mtn—*summit* AK-9
Three Stepping Stones Lakes—*lake* WI-6
Three Story Rim—*cliff* OR-9
Three Streams—*locale* ME-1
Three Summit Peak—*summit* MT-8
Threesuns Mtn—*summit* MT-8
Three Swamp Brook—*stream* MA-1
Threet—*locale* AL-4
Three Tabernacle Ch—*church* NC-3
Three Tanks Lakes—*lake* NE-7
Threet Creek—*stream* AL-4
Threet Creek—*stream* TN-4
*Three Tetons* CO-8
*Three Tetons, The* CO-8
Three Thousand Acre Pond—*lake* NH-1
Threetime Mtn—*summit* AK-9
Threet Mtn—*summit* TN-4
*Threetons* PA-2
Three Top Ch—*church* NC-3
Three Top Creek—*stream* NC-3
*Threetop Mtn* TN-4
Three Top Mtn—*summit* NC-3
Three Top Mtn—*summit* TN-4
Three Top Mtn—*summit* VA-3
*Three Topped Mtn* VA-3
*Three Tops* NC-3
Threetops Mtn—*summit* MT-8
Threetops Trail—*trail* MT-8
Three Town Bridge—*locale* NY-2
Three Trails Sch—*school* MO-7
Three Trappers—*ridge* OR-9
Three Tree Butte—*summit* ID-8
Three Tree Camp (historical)—*park* OR-9
Three Tree Creek—*stream* TX-5
Three Tree Draw—*valley* SD-7
Three Tree Island—*island* AK-9
Threetree Ledge—*bar* ME-1
Three Tree Lookout (historical)—*locale* OR-9
Three Tree Point—*cape* (2) WA-9
Three Tree Ridge—*ridge* NC-3
**Three Trees**—*pop pl* SC-3
Three Tree Spring—*spring* WY-8
Three Trees Rsvr—*reservoir* MT-8
Three Trough Creek—*stream* OR-9
Three Troughs—*spring* CA-9
Three Troughs Canyon—*valley* CA-9
Three Trough Spring—*spring* OR-9
Three Trough Spring—*spring* UT-8
Three Troughs Spring—*spring* NM-5
Three T Rsvr—*reservoir* WY-8
Threet Sch (historical)—*school* AL-4
Threets Park—*park* AL-4
Three Tubs—*summit* WY-8
*Three Tuns* (2) NJ-2
**Three Tuns**—*pop pl* PA-2
Three Turkey Canyon—*valley* AZ-5
Three Turkey Ruins—*locale* AZ-5
Three Turkey Ruins Navajo Tribal Park—*park* AZ-5
Threety Two Lake—*lake* WI-6
Three V Crossing—*locale* ND-7
Three V Ranch—*locale* ND-7
Three VS Well—*well* TX-5
Three V Tank—*reservoir* AZ-5
Three Wall Tank—*reservoir* AZ-5
Three Waters Mountain—*ridge* WY-8
Three Way—*locale* AZ-5
Three Way—*locale* TX-5
Threeway—*locale* VA-3
**Three Way**—*pop pl* AR-4
**Three Way**—*pop pl* TN-4
Three Way Cem—*cemetery* AR-4
Three Way Ch—*church* AR-4
Threeway Ch—*church* TN-4
Three-Way Corner—*locale* OK-5
Threeway Gulch—*valley* AZ-5
Three Way Passage—*channel* AK-9
Three Way Sch—*school* TX-5
Threeway Tank—*reservoir* AZ-5
Three Way Tank—*reservoir* (2) AZ-5
Three Way Tank—*reservoir* NM-5
Threeway Wash—*stream* AZ-5
Three Way Watershed Marker—*other* MN-6
Threeway Well—*well* TX-5
Threeway Windmill—*locale* TX-5
Three-Way Windmill—*locale* TX-5
Three Way Windmill—*locale* TX-5
Three Wells—*well* NM-5
Three Wells—*well* TX-5
Three Well Windmill—*locale* NM-5
Three West Hollow—*valley* KY-4
Three Willow Spring—*spring* WY-8
Three Wiseman—*pillar* UT-8
Three Wise Men—*arch* AZ-5
Threewit Mtn—*summit* TN-4
Three Wolf Creek—*stream* MT-8
Three X Bar Rsvr—*reservoir* MT-8
Three X Bar Rsvr Number Two—*reservoir* MT-8
Threlkel Cem—*cemetery* (2) KY-4
Threlkeld, Thomas, House—*hist pl* KY-4
Threlkeld Cem—*cemetery* IN-6
Threlkeld Creek—*stream* KY-4
Threlkeld Pass—*gap* WY-8
Threlkeld Sch—*school* KY-4
Thresher Branch—*stream* LA-4
Thresher Hill—*summit* VT-1
Thresher Park—*park* VA-3
Threshing Bee Airp—*airport* KS-7
Threshing Mill Brook—*stream* NH-1
Threshold, The—*flat* UT-8
Threwer Point—*cape* AL-4
Thrid Creek—*stream* MT-8
Thrift—*locale* GA-3
Thrift—*locale* MD-2
Thrift—*locale* NC-3
Thrift—*locale* TX-5
Thrift—*locale* WA-9
Thrift Chapel—*church* VA-3
Thrift Cove—*valley* NC-3
Thrift Dam—*dam* AL-4
Thrift Hill Sch (historical)—*school* NC-3
Thrifton—*locale* OH-6
Thrift Pond—*reservoir* AL-4
Thrift Road Ch—*church* NC-3
Thrift (RR name for Paw Creek)—*other* NC-3
Thrift Sch—*school* WI-6
Thrifty—*locale* TX-5
Thrilkeld Branch—*stream* KY-4
Thrity-First Street Bridge—*bridge* PA-2
Thritynine Mile Creek—*stream* WA-9
Throat River—*stream* AK-9
**Throckmorton**—*pop pl* TN-4
**Throckmorton**—*pop pl* TX-5
Throckmorton, Lake—*reservoir* TX-5
Throckmorton Branch—*stream* AL-4
Throckmorton (CCD)—*cens area* TX-5
Throckmorton Cem—*cemetery* OH-6
**Throckmorton (County)**—*pop pl* TX-5
Throckmorton County Courthouse and Jail—*hist pl* TX-5
*Throckmorton Creek* TX-5
Throckmorton Creek—*stream* TX-5
Throckmorton Hill—*summit* AR-4
*Throckmorton Reservoir* TX-5
Throckmorton Run—*stream* PA-2
Throckmorton Sch (historical)—*school* TN-4
*Throggs Neck* NY-2
Throgg's Neck—*uninc pl* NY-2
Throgmartin Hollow—*valley* TN-4
*Throgmorton* TN-4
*Throgmorton Cem* TN-4
Throgmorton Cem—*cemetery* TN-4
*Throg's Neck* NY-2
Throgs Neck—*cape* NY-2
**Throgs Neck**—*pop pl* NY-2
Throgs Neck Bridge—*bridge* NY-2
Throgs Point—*cape* NY-2
*Throley Point* UT-8
*Thromartin* TN-4
*Thromartin School* TN-4
Thronateeska—*hist pl* GA-3
Throne, The—*summit* MA-1
*Throne Church* AL-4
Throne Oil Field—*oilfield* WY-8
Throng Creek—*stream* ID-8
Thron Gulch—*valley* ID-8
Thronson, J. A., House—*hist pl* WA-9
Thronson Creek—*stream* OR-9
Throns Pond—*lake* NY-2
Thronton Cem—*cemetery* TN-4
**Thronwell**—*pop pl* LA-4
Throop—*locale* NY-2
**Throop**—*pop pl* PA-2
Throop Borough—*civil* PA-2
Throop Cem—*cemetery* AR-4
Throop Ditch—*canal* OR-9
Throop Elem Sch Number 1—*school* IN-6
Throop Lake—*lake* MT-8
*Throop Memorial Sch* IN-6
Throop Number One Drain—*stream* MI-6
Throop Number Two Drain—*stream* MI-6
Throop Playground—*park* IL-6
**Throopsville**—*pop pl* NY-2
Throopsville Rural Cem—*cemetery* NY-2
**Throop (Town of)**—*pop pl* NY-2
*Throp* OH-6
Thrope Creek—*stream* AK-9
*Throp Springs* TX-5
Throttle Dam—*dam* NM-5
*Throufare Creek* NC-3
*Throufare Island* NC-3
*Through Canyon* UT-8
Through Canyon—*valley* CA-9
Through Channel—*channel* NJ-2
Through Creek—*channel* NJ-2
Through Creek—*stream* AK-9
Through Creek—*stream* MA-1
Through Creek—*stream* NJ-2
*Throughfare* VA-3
Throughfare Campsite—*locale* ME-1
Through Glacier—*glacier* AK-9
Through Hollow—*valley* TX-5
Through Line Trail—*trail* CO-8
Throwaenifeeng—*cape* FM-9
Throwaenifeeng—*summit* FM-9
Thrower Brook—*stream* MA-1
Throwout Knee Spring—*spring* NV-8
T H Rsvr—*reservoir* WY-8
Thru Creek—*channel* MD-2
Thru Creek—*stream* AK-9
*Thrumb Cap* DE-2
*Thrumbcap* ME-1
*Thrumbcap, The* ME-1
*Thrumb Caps* DE-2
Thrumcap—*cape* DE-2
Thrumcap—*island* (2) ME-1
*Thrumcap, The* DE-2
Thrumcap, The—*island* ME-1
Thrumcap Cape—*cape* ME-1
*Thrumcap Island* ME-1
Thrumcap Island—*island* (3) ME-1
Thrumcap Ledge—*bar* (2) ME-1
*Thrumcap Monument* ME-1
*Thrump Cape* DE-2
Thrums Sch Number 1—*school* ND-7
Thrums Sch Number 4—*school* ND-7
**Thrush**—*pop pl* MO-7
Thrush Cem—*cemetery* OR-9
Thrush Creek—*stream* ID-8
Thrush Lake—*lake* MI-6
Thrush Lake—*lake* MN-6
Thrush Pond—*lake* OR-9
Thrush Rsvr—*reservoir* ID-8
Thruston—*locale* KY-4
Thruston Lake—*lake* NE-7
Thruston Park—*park* KY-4
Thruway Shop Ctr—*locale* NC-3
Thsohotso Wash—*valley* AZ-5
T H Spree Eight Feet Dam—*dam* AL-4
T H Spree Fourteen Feet Dam—*dam* AL-4
*T H Stone State Park* FL-3
Thudium Sch—*school* MO-7
Thuermer Hollow—*valley* IN-6
Thuesen-Petersen House—*hist pl* UT-8
Thula—*locale* TN-4
Thula Post Office (historical)—*building* TN-4
Thule Cove—*bay* RI-1
Thulemeyer Park—*park* TX-5
Thumann Log House—*hist pl* OH-6
*Thumb* WY-8
Thumb—*summit* AZ-5
Thumb, Lake—*lake* MI-6
Thumb, The—*cape* NH-1
Thumb, The—*pillar* CA-9
Thumb, The—*pillar* NM-5
Thumb, The—*summit* CA-9
Thumb, Tom, House—*hist pl* CT-1
Thumb Bay—*bay* AK-9
Thumb Butte—*summit* (5) AZ-5
Thumb Butte—*summit* SD-7
Thumb Butte Campground—*park* AZ-5
Thumb Butte Mine—*mine* AZ-5
Thumb Butte Park—*park* AZ-5
Thumb Butte Tank—*reservoir* AZ-5
*Thumbcap* ME-1
Thumb Cove—*bay* AK-9
Thumb Cove—*cove* MA-1
Thumb Creek—*stream* AK-9

Thumb Flat—flat ... AZ-5
Thumb Glacier—glacier ... AK-9
Thumb Junction ... WY-8
Thumb Knob—summit ... NV-8
Thumb Lake—lake ... AK-9
Thumb Lake—lake ... MN-6
Thumb Mtn—summit ... AK-9
Thumb Mtn—summit ... NH-1
Thumb Paintpots—spring ... WY-8
Thumb Peak—summit ... AZ-5
Thumb Point—cape (3) ... AK-9
Thumb Point—cape ... FL-3
Thumb Point—cape ... SC-3
Thumb Pond—lake ... NY-2
Thumb Pour Off, The—falls ... UT-8
Thumb Ridge—ridge ... NM-5
Thumb River—stream ... AK-9
Thumb Rock ... UT-8
Thumb Rock—pillar ... CA-9
Thumb Rock—pillar ... UT-8
Thumb Rock Picnic Area—park ... AZ-5
Thumb Rock Well—well ... AZ-5
Thumb Run—stream ... VA-3
Thumb Run Ch—church ... VA-3
Thumb Run Mtn—summit ... VA-3
Thumb Swamp—swamp ... NC-3
Thumb Swamp (Carolina Bay)—swamp ... NC-3
Thumb Tank—reservoir ... NM-5
Thumb Tank Canyon—valley ... NM-5
Thumb Tank Peak—summit ... NM-5
Thumb Well—well ... UT-8
Thume Drain—stream ... MI-6
Thumma Ditch—canal (2) ... IN-6
Thumper, The—bar ... ME-1
Thumper Branch—stream ... NC-3
**Thumpertown Beach**—pop pl ... MA-1
Thumping Branch ... NC-3
Thumping Creek—stream ... NC-3
Thump Peak—summit ... CA-9
**Thumptown**—pop pl ... PA-2
Thum Sch—school ... IL-6
Thumuth ... FM-9
Thum'uuth—cape ... FM-9
Thunbaliy ... FM-9
Thunbiliy ... FM-9
Thunborg, Jacob and Cristina, House—hist pl ... ID-8
**Thunder**—pop pl ... GA-3
Thunder and Lightning Lake—lake ... CA-9
Thunder Arm—bay ... WA-9
Thunder Basin—basin ... WA-9
Thunder Basin Natl Grassland—park ... WY-8
Thunder Bay—bay ... AK-9
Thunder Bay—bay ... MI-6
Thunder Bay Island—island ... MI-6
Thunder Bay Island Light Station—hist pl . MI-6
Thunder Bay River—stream ... MI-6
Thunder Bay River Mill Pond ... MI-6
Thunder Bay River State For—forest ... MI-6
**Thunderbird**—pop pl ... KY-4
Thunderbird, Lake—reservoir ... AR-4
Thunderbird, Lake—reservoir ... IL-6
Thunderbird, Lake—reservoir ... OK-5
Thunderbird Acad—school ... AZ-5
Thunderbird Acres Park Campground—park ... UT-8
Thunderbird Archeol District—hist pl ... VA-3
Thunderbird Camp—locale ... CO-8
Thunderbird Camp—locale ... NY-2
Thunderbird Country Club—other ... AZ-5
Thunderbird Country Club—other ... CA-9
Thunder Bird Creek—stream ... AK-9
Thunderbird Creek—stream ... MT-8
Thunderbird Dry lake ... NV-8
Thunderbird Falls—falls ... MT-8
Thunder Bird Falls Campground—locale ... AK-9
Thunderbird Glacier—glacier ... MT-8
Thunderbird Golf Course—locale ... PA-2
Thunderbird Golf Course—other ... AZ-5
**Thunderbird Graduate School**—pop pl . AZ-5
**Thunderbird Hills**—pop pl ... TX-5
**Thunderbird Homes Addition (subdivision)**—pop pl ... SD-7
Thunderbird HS—school ... AZ-5
Thunderbird Island—island ... MT-8
Thunderbird Lake—lake ... CO-8
Thunderbird Lake—lake ... IL-6
Thunderbird Lake—lake (2) ... MN-6
Thunderbird Lake—lake ... OR-9
Thunderbird Lake—reservoir ... MS-4
Thunderbird Mesa—summit ... AZ-5
Thunderbird Mine—mine ... AZ-5
Thunderbird Mine Dam ... IN-6
Thunderbird Mtn—summit ... MT-8
**Thunderbird North**—pop pl ... MN-6
**Thunderbird Palms II (subdivision)**—pop pl (2) ... AZ-5
Thunderbird Park—park ... AZ-5
Thunder Bird Peak—summit ... AK-9
Thunderbird Plaza Shop Ctr—locale ... AZ-5
Thunderbird Pond—reservoir ... IN-6
Thunderbird Racetrack—other ... TX-5
Thunderbird Ranch—locale ... AZ-5
Thunderbird Rec Area—park ... AZ-5
Thunderbird Regional Park ... AZ-5
Thunderbird Sch—school ... OK-5
Thunderbird Sch—school ... TX-5
Thunderbird Semi-regional Park ... AZ-5
Thunderbird Shopping Village—locale ... AZ-5
**Thunderbird South**—pop pl ... MN-6
Thunderbird Square Shop Ctr—locale (2) .. AZ-5
**Thunderbird (Trailer Park)**—pop pl ... FL-3
**Thunderbird Valley Number Two (subdivision)**—pop pl (2) ... AZ-5
**Thunderbolt**—pop pl ... GA-3
Thunderbolt Bay—bay ... NV-8
Thunderbolt Canyon—valley ... NV-8
Thunderbolt Cave—cave ... AL-4
Thunderbolt C C C Camp—locale ... MO-7
Thunderbolt Creek—stream ... CO-8
Thunderbolt Creek—stream (2) ... KS-7
Thunderbolt Creek—stream ... MT-8
Thunderbolt Creek—stream ... OK-5
Thunderbolt Hill—summit ... IL-6
Thunderbolt Lake—lake ... MT-8
Thunderbolt Landing—locale ... NC-3
Thunderbolt Mine—mine ... AZ-5
Thunderbolt Mine—mine ... CA-9
Thunderbolt Mine—mine ... CO-8
Thunderbolt Mtn—summit ... ID-8
Thunderbolt Mtn—summit (2) ... MT-8
Thunderbolt Mtn—summit ... NY-2
Thunderbolt Mtn—summit ... WY-8
Thunderbolt Peak—summit ... CA-9
Thunderbolt Peak—summit ... CO-8
Thunderbolt Shaft—mine ... NM-5
Thunderbolt Ski Trail—trail ... MA-1
Thunder Branch—stream ... AR-4
Thunder Branch—stream ... WI-6
Thunder Bridge—bridge ... MA-1
Thunder Brook—stream ... MA-1
Thunderburg Hollow—valley ... TX-5
Thunder Butte ... SD-7
Thunder Butte—locale ... SD-7
Thunder Butte—summit ... CO-8
Thunder Butte—summit ... SD-7
Thunder Butte Creek—stream ... SD-7
Thunder Camp—locale ... CA-9
Thunder Canyon—valley ... NV-8
Thunder Canyon Camp—locale ... AL-4
Thunder Cave—cave ... AZ-5
Thunder City (Site)—locale ... ID-8
Thunder Cliff—cliff ... CA-9
Thunder Creek ... SD-7
Thunder Creek ... WA-9
Thunder Creek ... WY-8
Thunder Creek—stream (3) ... AK-9
Thunder Creek—stream (2) ... ID-8
Thunder Creek—stream ... IL-6
Thunder Creek—stream ... IA-7
Thunder Creek—stream ... MN-6
Thunder Creek—stream (2) ... MT-8
Thunder Creek—stream (3) ... OR-9
Thunder Creek—stream ... SD-7
Thunder Creek—stream (9) ... WA-9
Thunder Creek—stream (2) ... WI-6
Thunder Egg Lake—lake ... OR-9
Thunderer, The—summit ... WY-8
Thunderer Cutoff Trail—trail ... WY-8
Thunder Falls—falls ... CO-8
Thunder Glacier—glacier (2) ... WA-9
Thunder Gulch—valley ... ID-8
Thunder Gulch—valley ... OR-9
Thundergust Brook—stream ... NJ-2
Thundergust Lake—reservoir ... NJ-2
Thundergust Pond Dam—dam ... NJ-2
Thundergut Pond—reservoir ... NJ-2
Thundergut Pond Dam—dam ... NJ-2
**Thunder Hawk**—pop pl ... SD-7
Thunder Hawk Butte—summit ... SD-7
Thunder Hawk Creek—stream ... SD-7
Thunder Hawk Township—civ div ... SD-7
Thunder Head—summit ... VT-1
Thunderhead, Lake—reservoir ... MO-7
Thunderhead Airp—airport ... AZ-5
Thunderhead Falls Tunnel—tunnel ... SD-7
Thunderhead Mtn—summit ... MT-8
Thunderhead Mtn—summit ... NC-3
Thunderhead Mtn—summit ... SD-7
Thunderhead Mtn—summit ... TN-4
Thunderhead Pit Rsvr—reservoir ... MT-8
Thunderhead Prong—stream ... TN-4
Thunderhead Tank—reservoir ... NM-5
Thunder Hill—summit ... CA-9
Thunder Hill—summit ... ID-8
Thunder Hill—summit ... NH-1
Thunder Hill—summit ... NY-2
Thunder Hill—summit ... NC-3
Thunder Hill—summit ... VA-3
Thunderhill Run—stream ... WV-2
Thunder Hole—bay ... ME-1
Thunderhole—cave ... TN-4
Thunderhole Cave—cave ... AL-4
Thunderhole Creek—stream ... NC-3
Thunder Hollow Dam—dam ... TN-4
Thunder Hollow Lake—reservoir ... TN-4
Thundering Herd Ranch—locale ... CA-9
Thundering Spring—spring ... FL-3
Thundering Spring—spring ... GA-3
Thundering Springs Branch—stream ... TX-5
Thundering Springs Cem—cemetery ... GA-3
Thundering Springs Ch—church ... GA-3
Thunder Island—cape ... ME-1
Thunder Island—island ... OR-9
Thunder Lake ... MN-6
Thunder Lake ... MT-8
Thunder Lake ... WA-9
Thunder Lake—lake ... CO-8
Thunder Lake—lake (3) ... MI-6
Thunder Lake—lake (3) ... MN-6
Thunder Lake—lake ... MT-8
Thunder Lake—lake (3) ... WA-9
Thunder Lake—lake (3) ... WI-6
Thunder Lake—reservoir ... MN-6
Thunder Lake—reservoir ... NC-3
Thunder Lake Dam—dam ... NC-3
Thunder Lake Inlet—stream ... WI-6
Thunder Lake Outlet—stream ... WI-6
Thunder Lake Patrol Cabin—hist pl ... CO-8
Thunder Lakes—lake ... WA-9
Thunder Lake State Wildlife Area—park ... WI-6
Thunder Lake (Township of)—civ div ... MN-6
Thunder Lake Trail—trail ... CO-8
Thunder Meadow—flat ... MN-6
Thunder Mine—mine ... AZ-5
Thunder Mine—mine ... CO-8
Thunder Mine Road—trail ... AZ-5
Thunder Mountain Cavern—cave ... NV-8
Thunder Mountain Ranch—locale ... WI-6
Thunder Mountain Trail—trail (2) ... OR-9
Thunder Mtn ... NY-2
Thunder Mtn—summit (4) ... AK-9
Thunder Mtn—summit ... AZ-5
Thunder Mtn—summit (3) ... CA-9
Thunder Mtn—summit (2) ... CO-8
Thunder Mtn—summit (3) ... ID-8
Thunder Mtn—summit (2) ... MI-6
Thunder Mtn—summit (4) ... MT-8
Thunder Mtn—summit (3) ... NV-8
Thunder Mtn—summit (2) ... OR-9
Thunder Mtn—summit ... UT-8
Thunder Mtn—summit (4) ... WA-9
Thunder Mtn—summit ... WI-6
Thunder Mtn—summit ... WY-8
Thunder Pass—gap ... CO-8
Thunder Pass Trail—trail ... CO-8
Thunder Point—cape (2) ... AK-9
Thunder Point—cape ... TX-5
Thunder Rapids—rapids ... MT-8
Thunder Ridge—ridge ... VA-3
Thunder Ridge Campground—park ... UT-8
Thunder Ridge Country Club—other ... NY-2
Thunder Ridge Overlook—locale ... VA-3
Thunder River ... AZ-5
Thunder River ... WI-6
Thunder River—stream ... AZ-5
Thunder River—stream ... WI-6
Thunder River State Rearing Station—other ... WI-6
Thunder Rock—summit ... OR-9
Thunder Rock Rec Area—park ... TN-4
Thunder Rocks—pillar ... NY-2
Thunder Run—stream ... PA-2
Thundershower ... PA-2
Thundershower Run—stream ... PA-2
Thunders Lake ... MN-6
Thunder Spring—spring ... AZ-5
Thunder Spring—spring ... ID-8
Thunder Spring Creek—stream ... AL-4
Thunderstruck Branch—stream ... NC-3
Thunder Struck Knob—summit ... KY-4
Thunderstruck Knob—summit (2) ... NC-3
Thunderstruck Knob—summit ... TN-4
Thunder-Struck Mtn—summit ... GA-3
Thunderstruck Ridge—ridge ... NC-3
Thunderstruck Ridge Overlook—locale ... NC-3
Thunderstruck Rock—rock ... WV-2
Thunderstruck Run—stream ... WV-2
Thunderstruck Shoals—bar ... KY-4
Thunder Swamp—swamp ... NC-3
Thunder Swamp Ch—church ... NC-3
Thunder Valley—valley ... CA-9
Thunder Valley Drag Strip—locale ... SD-7
Thunder Von Tranc, Bayou—gut ... LA-4
Thunder Woman County Park—park ... IA-7
Thundery Peak ... ID-8
Thune Mtn—summit ... OR-9
Thurber—locale ... IL-6
Thurber—locale ... TX-5
Thurber, James, House—hist pl ... OH-6
Thurber Brook—stream ... NY-2
Thurber Canyon—valley ... UT-8
Thurber Cem—cemetery ... TX-5
Thurber Fork—stream ... UT-8
Thurber Hist Dist—hist pl ... TX-5
Thurber Lake—reservoir ... TX-5
Thurber Pond—lake (2) ... NY-2
Thurber Ranch—locale ... AZ-5
Thurber Ridge—ridge ... UT-8
Thurber Sch—school ... UT-8
Thurber Strait ... NH-1
Thurburn Creek ... ID-8
Thurburn Ridge ... ID-8
Thurf Marsh Islands—island ... VA-3
Thurford ... KS-7
Thurgood Canyon—valley (2) ... NM-5
**Thurgood Estates Subdivision**—pop pl .. UT-8
Thurley Mtn—summit ... NH-1
Thurlo Tank—reservoir ... AZ-5
Thurlow—locale ... KY-4
Thurlow—locale ... MT-8
Thurlow Brook—stream (3) ... ME-1
Thurlow Ch—church ... KY-4
Thurlow Dam ... AL-4
Thurlow Dam—dam ... AL-4
Thurlow Head—cape ... ME-1
Thurlow Hill—summit ... ME-1
Thurlo Wildlife Tanks—reservoir ... AZ-5
Thurlow Island ... ME-1
Thurlow Knob ... ME-1
Thurlow Lake—lake ... WA-9
Thurlow Rsvr—reservoir ... AL-4
Thurlows Lake—reservoir ... NC-3
Thurlows Lake Dam—dam ... NC-3
Thurlow Station—building ... PA-2
Thurlow Tile Drain—canal ... MI-6
Thurman ... GA-3
Thurman—fmr MCD ... NE-7
Thurman—locale ... MO-7
Thurman—locale ... NY-2
Thurman—locale ... TN-4
**Thurman**—pop pl ... CO-8
**Thurman**—pop pl ... IN-6
**Thurman**—pop pl ... IA-7
**Thurman**—pop pl ... NC-3
**Thurman**—pop pl ... OH-6
**Thurman Addition**—pop pl ... TN-4
Thurman Branch—stream ... KY-4
Thurman Cem—cemetery ... GA-3
Thurman Cem—cemetery ... IL-6
Thurman Cem—cemetery ... MS-4
Thurman Cem—cemetery ... NE-7
Thurman Cem—cemetery ... OH-6
Thurman Cem—cemetery (2) ... TN-4
Thurman Chapel (historical)—church ... TN-4
Thurman Creek ... KS-7
Thurman Creek—stream ... AK-9
Thurman Creek—stream ... CA-9
Thurman Creek—stream ... IL-6
Thurman Creek—stream ... KS-7
Thurman Creek—stream ... MO-7
Thurman Creek—stream (2) ... TN-4
Thurmand Cem—cemetery ... TN-4
Thurman Draw—valley ... NM-5
Thurman Flats Picnic Area—park ... CA-9
Thurman Gulch—valley ... CO-8
Thurman (historical)—locale ... KS-7
Thurman Hollow—valley (2) ... TN-4
Thurman Hollow—valley ... TX-5
Thurman Homestead (abandoned)—locale ... MT-8
Thurman Lateral—canal ... AZ-5
Thurman L Willett Fieldhouse—building ... MO-7
Thurman Mill Canal—canal ... ID-8
Thurman Point—cape ... TN-4
Thurman Point Public Use Area—locale ... MO-7
Thurman Pond—lake ... NY-2
Thurman Rock—summit ... CA-9
Thurman Sch—school ... AR-4
Thurman Sch—school ... MO-7
Thurman Sch—school ... NE-7
Thurman Sch—school ... TN-4
Thurmans Dock—locale ... TN-4
Thurman Spring Branch—stream ... TN-4
Thurman Station—locale ... NY-2
Thurman Tanks—reservoir ... NM-5
**Thurman (Town of)**—pop pl ... NY-2
Thurman W Dix Rsvr—reservoir ... VT-1
Thurmon Creek ... ID-8
Thurmon Creek—stream ... ID-8
**Thurmond**—pop pl (2) ... NC-3
**Thurmond**—pop pl ... WV-2
Thurmond Cem—cemetery ... IL-6
Thurmond Cem—cemetery ... MS-4
Thurmond Cem—cemetery ... SC-3
Thurmond Chatham Game Land ... NC-3
Thurmond Chatham Wildlife Mngmt Area—park ... NC-3
Thurmond Coulee—valley ... MT-8
Thurmond Creek—stream ... GA-3
Thurmond Glenn Field (airport)—airport ... TN-4
Thurmond Hist Dist—hist pl ... WV-2
Thurmond (historical)—locale ... MS-4
Thurmond House—hist pl ... AR-4
Thurmond House—hist pl ... LA-4
Thurmond HS—school ... SC-3
Thurmond Lake—lake ... TX-5
Thurmond Pond—lake ... AL-4
Thurmond Pond—reservoir ... GA-3
Thurmon Ridge—ridge ... ID-8
**Thurmont**—pop pl ... MD-2
Thurnau State Wildlife Area—park ... MO-7
Thurnberry Isle Country Club—locale ... FL-3
Thurn Creek ... OR-9
Thurso—locale ... SC-3
Thursby Cem—cemetery ... GA-3
Thursday—locale ... WV-2
Thursday Bay—bay ... MN-6
Thursday Creek ... OR-9
Thursday Creek—stream ... AK-9
Thursday Creek—stream ... OR-9
Thursday Friday Mine—mine ... MT-8
Thursday Island ... FM-9
Thursday Mine—mine ... UT-8
Thursday Point—cape ... FL-3
Thurso ... AZ-5
Thurso ... NY-2
Thurso Bay—bay ... NY-2
Thurso Butte ... AZ-5
Thurso Cem—cemetery ... NY-2
Thurston ... AL-4
Thurston ... KY-4
Thurston—locale ... AL-4
Thurston—locale ... MD-2
Thurston—locale ... PA-2
**Thurston**—pop pl ... GA-3
**Thurston**—pop pl ... NE-7
**Thurston**—pop pl ... NY-2
**Thurston**—pop pl ... OH-6
**Thurston**—pop pl ... OR-9
Thurston Adams Dam—dam ... AL-4
Thurston Adams Pond—reservoir ... AL-4
Thurston Basin—bay ... NY-2
Thurston Bldg—hist pl ... OH-6
Thurston Branch—stream ... VA-3
Thurston Brook—stream (2) ... ME-1
Thurston Brook—stream ... MA-1
Thurston Canyon ... TX-5
Thurston Canyon—valley ... AK-9
Thurston Canyon—valley ... TX-5
Thurston (CCD)—cens area ... GA-3
Thurston Ch—church ... PA-2
**Thurston County**—pop pl ... WA-9
Thurston County Courthouse—hist pl ... WA-9
Thurston Cove—bay ... NH-1
Thurston Creek—stream ... AK-9
Thurston Creek—stream (2) ... CA-9
Thurston Creek—stream ... IN-6
Thurston Creek—stream (3) ... WA-9
Thurston Ditch—canal ... IN-6
Thurston Draft—valley ... PA-2
Thurston Gulch—valley ... CA-9
Thurston Hill—summit ... ME-1
Thurston Hill Cem—cemetery ... NY-2
Thurston Hill Cem—cemetery ... WI-6
Thurston Hill Sch—school ... NY-2
Thurston Hollow—valley ... PA-2
Thurston Hollow—valley ... UT-8
Thurston House—hist pl ... AR-4
Thurston HS—school ... MI-6
Thurston HS—school ... OR-9
Thurston Lake—lake ... CA-9
Thurston Lake—lake ... MI-6
Thurston Lava Tube—crater ... HI-9
Thurston Mtn—summit ... ME-1
Thurston Park—park ... NY-2
Thurston Peaks—summit ... CA-9
Thurston Point—cape ... MA-1
Thurston Pond—lake ... ME-1
Thurston Pond—lake ... NY-2
Thurston Pond—reservoir ... NH-1
Thurston Road—uninc pl ... NY-2
Thurston Rsvr—reservoir ... CO-8
Thurston Sch—school ... CA-9
Thurston Sch—school ... GA-3
Thurston Sch—school (2) ... MI-6
Thurston Sch—school ... NY-2
Thurston Sch—school ... OR-9
**Thurstons Corner**—pop pl ... ME-1
Thurston South (CCD)—cens area ... WA-9
Thurston Spring—spring ... NV-8
Thurston State Park—park ... OH-6
Thurston Tank—reservoir ... AZ-5
**Thurston (Town of)**—pop pl ... NY-2
Thury Sch (historical)—school ... SD-7
Thurz Knob—summit ... NC-3
Thut Creek—stream ... TX-5
Thuunbil'iy ... FM-9
Thuvgood Well—well ... NM-5
Thwattles Landing—locale ... TN-4
Thweatt Branch—stream ... VA-3
Thweatt Chute—gut ... TN-4
**Thweatt (historical)**—pop pl ... MS-4
Thweatt Post Office (historical)—building . MS-4
**Thyatira**—locale ... GA-3
**Thyatira**—pop pl ... MS-4
Thyatira Cem—cemetery ... TN-4
Thyatira Ch—church ... MS-4
Thyatira Ch—church ... NC-3
Thyatira Ch—church ... TN-4
Thyatira Ch of Christ—church ... MS-4
Thyatira Elem Sch (historical)—school ... MS-4
**Thyatira (historical)**—pop pl ... TN-4
Thyatira Post Office (historical)—building . MS-4
Thyatira Presbyterian Church, Cemetery, and Manse—hist pl ... NC-3
Thyatria ... MS-4
Thybo Pond Dam—dam ... SD-7
Thybo Ranch—locale ... SD-7
Thybo Spring—spring ... SD-7
Thybo Well—well ... SD-7
Thydean Lake—lake ... MN-6
Thyden Lake ... MN-6
Thygerson Ranch—locale ... NM-5
Thyle—locale ... CA-9
Thyne Sch—school ... VA-3
Ti ... MH-9
Ti—locale ... OK-5
Tiadaghton—locale ... PA-2
Tiadaghton State For ... PA-2
Tiadaghton State For—forest ... PA-2
Tiadaghton Trail—trail ... PA-2
Tiadaghton Valley Mall—locale ... PA-2
Tiafou Point—cape ... AS-9
Tiago (historical)—locale ... KS-7
Tiago Lake—lake ... CO-8
Tiah Cove—cove ... MA-1
Tiahs Cove ... MA-1
Tiaiu Fall—falls ... AS-9
Tia Juana ... CA-9
**Tia Juana**—pop pl ... OK-5
Tia Juana Bottom—bend ... UT-8
Tiajuana Mine—mine ... AZ-5
Tia Juana Ridge—ridge ... AZ-5
Tiajuana River ... CA-9
Tiak Dam—dam ... MS-4
Tia Khata, Lake—reservoir ... TN-4
Tiak Lake—reservoir ... MS-4
Tiak-O' Khata, Lake—reservoir ... MS-4
Tialeogaumu Ridge—ridge ... AS-9
Tialiufau Ridge—ridge ... AS-9
Tial Spring ... PW-9
Tialu Stream—stream ... AS-9
Tian ... MP-9
**Tiana**—pop pl ... NY-2
Tiana Bay—bay ... NY-2
Tiana Beach—beach ... NY-2
Tiana Creek—stream ... NY-2
**Tiana Shores**—pop pl ... NY-2
Tiancaco Creek ... NC-3
Tianderah—hist pl ... NY-2
Tia Nena Windmill—locale ... TX-5
Tian-kakeek ... IN-6
Tianna Country Club—other ... MN-6
Tiaoolii Rock—island ... AS-9
Tiapea Point (Bat Point)—cape ... AS-9
Tia Ramona Windmill—locale ... TX-5
Tiara Park—park ... LA-4
Tia Ridge—ridge ... AS-9
Tia Rosa Windmill—locale ... TX-5
Tiaseu Ridge—ridge ... AS-9
Tiasquam River—stream ... MA-1
Tiasquin River ... MA-1
Tiatauala Ridge—ridge ... AS-9
Tiatele Ridge—ridge ... AS-9
Tiati ... FM-9
Tiati-en-Reu ... FM-9
Tiati-en-Roi ... FM-9
Tia Tules, Loma—summit ... TX-5
Tiawah—locale ... OK-5
Tiawah Hills—range ... OK-5
Tiawaka Mine—mine ... ID-8
Tiawasee Creek—stream ... AL-4
Tiawichi Creek—stream ... TX-5
Tibab—island ... MP-9
Tiba Dah Silahi—area ... AZ-5
Tibadore Canyon—valley ... UT-8
Tibajong—island ... MP-9
Ti Bar—bar ... CA-9
Ti Bar Sch—school ... CA-9
Ti Bayou—stream ... LA-4
Tibbals Hill—summit ... CT-1
Tibbals Lake—lake ... WA-9
Tibbals Rsvr—reservoir ... WY-8
Tibb Creek—stream ... AL-4
**Tibbee**—pop pl ... MS-4
Tibbee Bridge—hist pl ... MS-4
Tibbee Cem—cemetery ... MS-4
Tibbee Creek—stream ... MS-4
Tibbee Lake—lake ... MS-4
Tibbee River ... MS-4
Tibbee Station ... MS-4
Tibbehoy Creek—stream ... MS-4
Tibbet ... WI-6
Tibbet Bench—bench ... UT-8
Tibbet Canyon—valley ... UT-8
Tibbet Creek ... MN-6
Tibbet Creek—stream ... WI-6
Tibbet Island—island ... ME-1
Tibbet Knob—summit ... VA-3
Tibbet Knob—summit ... WV-2
Tibbet Knob Trail—trail ... VA-3
Tibbet Knob Trail—trail ... WV-2
Tibbet Point—cape ... ME-1
**Tibbets**—pop pl ... WI-6
Tibbets Cem—cemetery ... KS-7
Tibbets Cem—cemetery ... ME-1
Tibbets Cem—cemetery ... MN-6
Tibbets Creek ... MN-6
Tibbets Creek—stream ... CA-9
Tibbets Creek—stream ... RI-1
Tibbets Drain—canal ... WY-8
Tibbets Falls—falls ... MI-6
Tibbets Gulch—valley ... WY-8
Tibbet's Island ... ME-1
Tibbets Lake—lake (2) ... MI-6
Tibbets Point ... NY-2
Tibbet Spring—spring ... UT-8
Tibbets Ridge—ridge ... ME-1
Tibbets Sch—school ... WI-6
Tibbett Arch ... UT-8
Tibbett Island—island ... ME-1
Tibbett Ledge—bar ... ME-1
Tibbett Narrows—channel ... ME-1
Tibbett Rock—bar ... ME-1
Tibbetts Brook—stream ... MN-6
Tibbetts Brook Park—park ... NY-2
**Tibbetts Corners**—pop pl ... OH-6
Tibbetts Creek ... MN-6
Tibbetts Creek—stream ... IA-7
Tibbetts Creek—stream ... MI-6
Tibbetts Creek—stream ... WA-9
Tibbetts Drain—canal ... MI-6
Tibbetts Draw—valley ... TX-5
Tibbetts Hill—summit ... ME-1
Tibbetts Hill—summit ... NH-1
Tibbetts JHS—school ... NM-5
Tibbetts Ledge ... ME-1
Tibbetts Mtn—summit (2) ... ME-1
Tibbetts Mtn—summit ... WA-9
Tibbetts Point—cape ... NY-2
Tibbetts Point Light—hist pl ... NY-2
Tibbetts Pond—lake ... ME-1
Tibbett Spring—spring ... OR-9
Tibbetts Ridge—ridge ... CO-8
**Tibbettstown**—pop pl ... ME-1
**Tibbie**—pop pl ... AL-4
Tibbie Baptist Ch—church ... AL-4
Tibbie Methodist Ch ... AL-4
Tibbie Peak—summit ... NV-8
Tibbit Creek ... NY-2
Tibbits ... WI-6
Tibbits Brook—stream ... MN-6
Tibbits Creek—stream ... NY-2
Tibbits House—hist pl ... NY-2
Tibbits Lake—lake ... CO-8
Tibbits Ledge—bar ... ME-1
**Tibbits Park Palms**—pop pl ... FL-3
Tibbitts Hollow—valley ... PA-2
Tibbitts Lake—lake ... IN-6
**Tibbitts Subdivision**—pop pl ... UT-8
Tibble Fork—stream ... UT-8
Tibble Fork Dam—dam ... UT-8
Tibble Fork Rsvr—reservoir ... UT-8
Tibble Fork Summer Home Area—locale ... UT-8
Tibble Peak ... NV-8
Tibb Ridge—ridge ... NC-3
Tibbs—locale ... TN-4
**Tibbs**—pop pl ... MS-4
Tibbs Bend—bend ... KY-4
Tibbs Branch—stream ... NJ-2
Tibbs Butte—summit ... WY-8
Tibbs Cem—cemetery ... AL-4
Tibbs Cem—cemetery ... KY-4
Tibbs Creek—stream ... AK-9
Tibbs Hollow—valley ... MT-8
Tibbs Hollow—valley ... TN-4
Tibbs Meadow Brook ... MA-1
Tibbs Post Office (historical)—building ... TN-4
Tibbs Run—stream (2) ... WV-2
Tibbs Run Rsvr—reservoir ... WV-2
Tibbs Sch—school ... TN-4
Tibbstown—locale ... VA-3
Tibby Creek—stream (2) ... MS-4
Tibby Sch—school ... CA-9
Tibeb ... MP-9
Tibedul—summit ... PW-9
Tiber—locale ... CA-9
Tiber—locale ... MT-8
Tiber Canyon—valley ... CA-9
Tiber Coulee—valley ... MT-8
Tiber Creek—stream (2) ... IL-6
Tiber Creek—stream ... KY-4
Tiber Dam—dam ... MT-8
**Tiber Dam Camp**—pop pl ... MT-8
Tiberias, Lake—lake ... TX-5
Tiber Reservoir ... MT-8
Tiber Town Hall—building ... ND-7
**Tiber Township**—pop pl ... ND-7
Tibes (Barrio)—fmr MCD ... PR-3
Tibet, Lake—lake ... FL-3
Tibet, Lake—lake ... NY-2
Tibetts Creek—stream ... IA-7
**Tibitha**—pop pl ... VA-3
Tible River ... GA-3
Tiblis Ranch (historical)—locale ... SD-7
Tiblow ... KS-7
Tiburcio Artesian Well—well ... TX-5
**Tiburon**—pop pl ... CA-9
**Tiburones**—pop pl (2) ... PR-3
Tiburon Naval Net Depot—military ... CA-9
Tiburon Peninsula—cape ... CA-9
**Tiburon (subdivision)**—pop pl (2) ... AZ-5
**Tibwin**—pop pl ... SC-3
Tibwin Creek—stream ... SC-3
Tibwin Plantation—locale ... SC-3
Ticabo Creek ... UT-8
**Ticaboo**—pop pl (2) ... UT-8
Ticaboo Creek—stream ... UT-8
Ticaboo HS—school ... UT-8
Ticaboo Mesa—summit ... UT-8
Ticaboo No 1 Rapids—rapids ... UT-8
Ticaboo No 2 Rapids—rapids ... UT-8
Ticaboo Rsvr—reservoir ... UT-8
Ticaboo Sch—school ... UT-8
Ticaboo Shelf Spring—spring ... UT-8
Ticanotloo ... GA-3
Ticanetlee Creek ... GA-3
Tice ... KS-7
Tice—locale ... IL-6
Tice—locale ... KS-7
**Tice**—pop pl ... FL-3
**Tice**—pop pl ... VT-1
Tice Cem—cemetery ... WI-6
Tice Creek ... CA-9
Tice Creek—stream ... CA-9
Tice Lake—lake ... FL-3
Ticer Branch—stream ... NC-3
Tice Run—stream ... OH-6
Tice Sch—school ... FL-3
Tice School (Abandoned)—locale ... WI-6
Tices Community Cem—cemetery ... NC-3
Tices Ferry (historical)—locale ... IA-7
Ticeska—locale ... ID-8
**Ticeska**—pop pl ... ID-8
Tices Shoal—bar ... NJ-2
Ticetonyk Mtn—summit ... NY-2
Tice Valley—valley ... CA-9
Ticey Hollow—valley ... TN-4
**Tichenal**—pop pl ... WV-2
Tichenor, William, House—hist pl ... KY-4
Tichenor Cem—cemetery ... OR-9
Tichenor Cove—bay ... OR-9
Tichenor Gully—valley ... NY-2
Tichenor Point—cape ... NY-2
Tichenor Rock—island ... OR-9
**Tichigan**—pop pl ... WI-6
Tichigan Lake—CDP ... WI-6
Tichigan Lake—reservoir ... WI-6
Tichnel Ch—church ... WV-2
Tichnell Cem—cemetery ... MD-2
Tichner Creek ... CA-9
Tichner Draw—valley ... CO-8
**Tichnor**—pop pl ... AR-4
Tichnor Cem—cemetery ... KY-4
Tichora Cem—cemetery ... WI-6
Tichy Creek ... AL-4
Tickahoe—area ... NC-3
Tickanetley—locale ... GA-3
Tickanetley Bald—summit ... GA-3

Tighner Mine (Inactive)—*mine* CA-9
Tig Hollow—*valley* VA-3
Tigh Park—*park* NV-8
Tightbark Hollow—*valley* TN-4
Tight Cut Branch—*stream* VA-3
Tight Entrance Pit—*cave* AL-4
Tight Eye Bar—*bar* AL-4
Tight Eye Creek—*stream* AL-4
Tighteye Creek—*stream* LA-4
Tight Hollow—*valley* KY-4
Tight Island—*island* LA-4
Tight Pit—*cave* AL-4
Tight Pond—*lake* NH-1
Tights, The—*gap* CO-8
*Tightsqueeze* VA-3
Tight Squeeze—*locale* VA-3
Tightsqueeze, Lake—*reservoir* GA-3
Tightsqueeze Field Airp—*airport* MO-7
Tightsqueeze Gap—*gap* GA-3
Tightsqueeze Hollow—*valley* WV-2
Tight Squeeze Hollow—*valley* WV-2
**Tightwad**—*pop pl* MO-7
Tigiwon Community House—*locale* CO-8
Tiglukpuk Creek—*stream* AK-9
Tignagvik Point—*cape* AK-9
**Tignall**—*pop pl* GA-3
Tignall (CCD)—*cens area* GA-3
Tigner Canyon—*valley* TX-5
Tigner-Farrer Rsvr—*reservoir* TX-5
Tigner Ranch—*locale* (2) NM-5
Tigners Ford—*locale* TN-4
Tignor—*locale* VA-3
Tignor Cem—*cemetery* VA-3
**Tigo**—*pop pl* KY-4
Tigrak Hill—*summit* AK-9
Tigre, Arroyo del—*stream* TX-5
Tigre, Bayou—*stream* (2) LA-4
Tigre Arroyo—*stream* NM-5
Tigre Bay—*bay* AR-4
Tigre Chiquita, Arroyo del—*valley* TX-5
Tigre Creek—*stream* AR-4
Tigre Grande, Arroyo del—*valley* TX-5
Tigre Lagoon—*lake* LA-4
Tigre Lagoon Oil and Gas Field—*oilfield* (2) LA-4
Tigre Mine, El—*mine* (2) AZ-5
Tigre Point—*cape* LA-4
**Tigrett**—*pop pl* TN-4
Tigrett JHS—*school* TN-4
Tigrett Post Office—*building* TN-4
Tigrett Wildlife Mngmt Area—*park* TN-4
Tigre Windmill—*locale* TX-5
**Tigris**—*pop pl* MO-7
Tigs Cove—*bay* MD-2
Tigs Point—*cape* MD-2
**Tigua**—*pop pl* TX-5
Tigua Ind Res—*reserve* TX-5
Tigue Branch—*stream* GA-3
Tigue Branch—*stream* TN-4
Tigue Gap—*gap* GA-3
Tigues Creek—*stream* TN-4
Tigus Creek—*stream* CA-9
Tigvariak Island—*island* AK-9
Tigyukauivet Mtn—*summit* AK-9
*Tihart Lake* MI-6
**Tihonet**—*pop pl* MA-1
Tihonet Cranberry Bogs—*swamp* MA-1
Tihonet Pond—*reservoir* MA-1
Tihonet Pond Number 1 Dam—*dam* MA-1
Tihonet Pond Number 2 Dam—*dam* MA-1
*Tihonet Village* MA-1
Tiinkdhul Lake—*lake* AK-9
Tiis Holoni—*locale* AZ-5
Tiis Ndiitsooi Wash—*stream* AZ-5
Tijera—*locale* GU-9
**Tijeras**—*pop pl* CO-8
**Tijeras**—*pop pl* NM-5
Tijeras Arroyo—*stream* NM-5
Tijeras Arroyo—*valley* TX-5
Tijeras (Barrio)—*fmr MCD* PR-3
Tijeras Canyon—*valley* CA-9
Tijeras Canyon—*valley* NM-5
Tijeras Cem—*cemetery* CO-8
Tijeras Club Gardens—*locale* NM-5
Tijeras Ranch—*locale* NM-5
Tijeras Rincon—*other* NM-5
Tijeras Spring—*spring* TX-5
*Tijeras* CO 8
Tijerina-Canales-Blucher Oil Field—*oilfield* TX-5
Tijerina Oil Field—*oilfield* TX-5
Tijerina Ranch—*locale* TX-5
*Tijuana Cove* MA-1
Tijuana John Peak—*summit* NV-8
Tijuana River—*stream* CA-9
Tikaboo Valley—*valley* NV-8
Tikaghapuk Point—*cape* AK-9
Tikan Creek—*stream* AK-9
Tikander Lake—*lake* MN-6
Tikchik Lake—*lake* AK-9
Tikchik Lakes—*lake* AK-9
Tikchik Mtn—*summit* AK-9
Tikchik River—*stream* AK-9
Tikhaia Islands—*area* AK-9
Tik Hill—*summit* AK-9
**Tiki Island**—*pop pl* TX-5
*Tikikluk* AK-9
Tikikluk Creek—*stream* AK-9
*Tikilook* AK-9
*Tikiluk* AK-9
Tiki Tai Village (trailer park)—*locale* AZ-5
**Tiki Tai Village (trailer park)**—*pop pl* AZ-5
Tikizat—*locale* AK-9
Tikka Rsvr—*reservoir* CO-8
Tikkinen Ranch—*locale* WY-8
Tikmiakpalik Creek—*stream* AK-9
Tikugha Point—*cape* AK-9
Tikura—*locale* ID-8
Tikyitsal Mtn—*summit* AK-9
*Tilahanchee Creek* WV-2
Tilard Canal—*canal* WY-8
Tilberg County Park—*park* MN-6
Tilberry Run—*stream* OH-6
*Tilby Creek* MS-4
*Tilchancos Creek* WV-2
Tilch Drain—*stream* MI-6
Tilch Ranch—*locale* NM-5
*Tilda* MP-9
Tilda Anderson Branch—*stream* VA-3
Tilda Bogue—*hist pl* MS-4
Tilda Bogue—*stream* MS-4
Tilda Branch—*stream* LA-4
Tilda Fork—*stream* WV-2
Tilda High Top—*summit* TN-4
Tilda Hole—*spring* TN-4
Tilda Ridge—*ridge* TN-4
Tilda Spring—*spring* UT-8
Tilday Mtn—*summit* KY-4
Tilde Creek—*stream* TX-5
Tilde Lake—*lake* MN-6
*Tilden* KS-7
*Tilden* NC-3
Tilden—*locale* PA-2
Tilden—*locale* WV-2
**Tilden**—*pop pl* AL-4
**Tilden**—*pop pl* IL-6
**Tilden**—*pop pl* IN-6
**Tilden**—*pop pl* KY-4
**Tilden**—*pop pl* MS-4
**Tilden**—*pop pl* NE-7
**Tilden**—*pop pl* ND-7
**Tilden**—*pop pl* PA-2
**Tilden**—*pop pl* TX-5
**Tilden**—*pop pl* WI-6
Tilden, Daniel, House—*hist pl* OH-6
Tilden, Lake—*lake* FL-3
Tilden, Samuel J., House—*hist pl* NY-2
Tilden, William J., JHS—*hist pl* PA-2
Tilden Bluffs—*cliff* OR-9
Tilden Bridge—*bridge* ID-8
Tilden Canyon—*valley* CA-9
Tilden Canyon Creek—*stream* CA-9
Tilden (CCD)—*cens area* TX-5
Tilden Cem—*cemetery* IN-6
Tilden Cem—*cemetery* MS-4
Tilden Cem—*cemetery* WI-6
Tilden Ch of Christ—*church* MS-4
Tilden Creek—*stream* CA-9
Tilden Creek—*stream* MT-8
Tilden Creek—*stream* (2) OR-9
Tilden Ditch—*canal* IN-6
Tilden (Election Precinct)—*fmr MCD* IL-6
Tilden-Hogge Sch—*school* KY-4
Tilden HS—*school* IL-6
Tilden HS—*school* NY-2
Tilden Island—*island* MA-1
Tilden JHS—*school* PA-2
Tilden Junction—*locale* MN-6
Tilden Lake—*lake* CA-9
Tilden Lake—*lake* LA-4
Tilden Lake—*lake* MI-6
Tilden Metcalf Creek—*stream* NC-3
Tilden Millpond—*reservoir* WI-6
Tilden Mine—*mine* MI-6
*Tilden Park* CA-9
Tilden Park—*park* MD-2
Tilden Pond—*lake* (2) ME-1
Tilden Sch—*school* AL-4
Tilden Sch—*school* MN-6
Tilden State Wildlife Mngmt Area—*park* MN-6
Tilden Swamp—*swamp* MA-1
**Tilden (Town of)**—*pop pl* WI-6
Tilden Township—*fmr MCD* IA-7
**Tilden Township**—*pop pl* KS-7
**Tilden (Township of)**—*pop pl* MI-6
**Tilden (Township of)**—*pop pl* MN-6
**Tilden (Township of)**—*pop pl* PA-2
**Tildenville**—*pop pl* FL-3
Tildenville Elem Sch—*school* FL-3
Tildenville Missionary Baptist Ch—*church* FL-3
**Tilden Woods**—*pop pl* MD-2
Tildon Hill—*summit* NY-2
*Tildys Pond* VT-1
*Tile* FM-9
Tile Canyon—*valley* CA-9
Tile Creek—*stream* IN-6
**Tiledale**—*pop pl* OH-6
*Tilehance Creek* WV-2
**Tile Plant**—*pop pl* KY-4
Tiler Cem—*cemetery* MO-7
*Tiler Ditch* IN-6
**Tile Siding**—*pop pl* IN-6
Tile Spring—*spring* AL-4
Tileston, Mount—*summit* CO-8
Tileston Sch—*school* NC-3
*Tilette Bayou* FL-3
**Tileville**—*pop pl* IA-7
*Tilewa Crater* HI-9
**Tilo Works** *pop pl* IA 7
**Tilf**—*pop pl* KY-4
**Tilford**—*pop pl* (2) KY-4
**Tilford**—*pop pl* SD-7
Tilford—*uninc pl* GA-3
Tilford Cem—*cemetery* IA-7
Tilford Creek—*stream* KY-4
Tilford Gulch—*valley* SD-7
Tilford Knob—*summit* KY-4
Tilford Mine—*mine* NV-8
Tilford Spring—*spring* NV-8
*Tilghman* MD-2
Tilghman—*locale* TN-4
**Tilghman**—*pop pl* MD-2
Tilghman, Marshal William M., Homestead—*hist pl* OK-5
*Tilghman Branch* TN-4
Tilghman Branch—*stream* MD-2
Tilghman Cove—*bay* MD-2
Tilghman Creek—*bay* MD-2
Tilghman Creek—*stream* MD-2
Tilghman Island—*island* MD-2
Tilghman Island Landing—*locale* MD-2
Tilghman Mill Branch—*stream* MD-2
Tilghman Neck—*cape* MD-2
Tilghman Point—*cape* MD-2
Tilghman Race—*stream* MD-2
Tilghman Sch—*school* MD-2
**Tilghmans Corner**—*pop pl* NJ-2
Tilghmans Sch (historical)—*school* TN-4
Tilghman Street Station—*locale* PA-2
**Tilghmanton**—*pop pl* MD-2
Tilhance Creek—*stream* WV-2
Tilicum Park—*park* WA-9
Tilifie Pond—*bay* LA-4
Tiligliig—*summit* FM-9
**Tiline**—*pop pl* KY-4
Tiline Cem—*cemetery* KY-4
Til Jones Spring—*spring* CA-9
Tilk Hollow—*valley* MO-7
**Till**—*pop pl* AL-4
**Tillamook**—*pop pl* OR-9
Tillamook Airp—*airport* OR-9
Tillamook Bay—*bay* OR-9
Tillamook (CCD)—*cens area* OR-9
**Tillamook County**—*pop pl* OR-9
Tillamook County General Hospital Heliport—*airport* OR-9
Tillamook Cove—*bay* AK-9
Tillamook Head—*cape* OR-9
Tillamook River—*stream* OR-9
Tillamook River Rest Area—*park* OR-9
Tillamook Rock—*bar* OR-9
Tillamook Rock Lighthouse—*hist pl* OR-9
Tillamook Rsvr—*reservoir* OR-9
Tillamook State For—*forest* OR-9
Tillandsia—*hist pl* LA-4
Tillangora Creek—*stream* OR-9
Tillans Chapel—*church* NC-3
**Tillar**—*pop pl* AR-4
Tillar Brake—*swamp* AR-4
Tillar Cem—*cemetery* AR-4
Tillar Cem—*cemetery* TX-5
Tillard Ranch—*locale* WY-8
*Tillasana Creek* OR-9
*Tillasana River* OR-9
Tillas Island—*island* CA-9
*Tillasqua Creek* OR-9
Tillas Slough—*gut* CA-9
**Tillatoba**—*pop pl* MS-4
Tillatoba, Lake—*reservoir* MS-4
Tillatoba Acad (historical)—*school* MS-4
Tillatoba Creek—*stream* MS-4
Tillatoba Creek Watershed Y-17b-8 Dam—*dam* MS-4
Tillatoba Creek Y-17b-17 Dam—*dam* MS-4
Tillatoba Creek Y-17b-7 Dam—*dam* MS-4
Tillatoba Creek Y-17b-9 Dam—*dam* MS-4
Tillatoba Cut-Off—*bend* MS-4
Till Bay—*swamp* NC-3
Till Cem—*cemetery* TX-5
Till Cove—*valley* NC-3
Till Creek—*stream* AK-9
*Till Crib Hollow* AL-4
Till Drain—*stream* IN-6
**Tilleda**—*pop pl* WI-6
*Tillehances Creek* WV-2
Tille Lake—*lake* ID-8
**Tiller**—*pop pl* OR-9
Tiller, F. M., House—*hist pl* KY-4
Tiller Bay—*bay* FL-3
Tiller Branch—*stream* FL-3
Tiller Cem—*cemetery* AL-4
Tiller Cem—*cemetery* FL-3
Tiller Cem—*cemetery* MO-7
Tiller Cem—*cemetery* (2) VA-3
Tiller Cem—*cemetery* (2) WV-2
Tiller Creek—*stream* OR-9
Tiller Creek—*stream* WI-6
Tiller Crossroads—*locale* AL-4
Tiller-Ford Cem—*cemetery* TN-4
Tiller Fork—*stream* VA-3
Tiller Mill Lake—*swamp* FL-3
*Tiller Mill Pond* FL-3
Tiller Pond—*lake* FL-3
*Tillers Cross Roads* AL-4
**Tillery**—*pop pl* NC-3
Tillery, George W., House—*hist pl* TN-4
Tillery, Lake—*reservoir* NC-3
Tillery, Virginia, Round Barn—*hist pl* IL-6
Tillery Branch—*stream* NC-3
Tillery Cem—*cemetery* AL-4
Tillery Cem—*cemetery* MO-7
Tillery Cem—*cemetery* NC-3
Tillery Chapel—*church* NC-3
Tillery Chapel Sch—*school* NC-3
Tillery Chapel Sch (historical)—*school* TN-4
Tillery Cove—*bay* AL-4
Tillery Creek Sch (historical)—*school* AL-4
Tillery Crossroad—*locale* AL-4
*Tillery Crossroads* AL-4
**Tillery Crossroads**—*pop pl* AL-4
Tillery Flat—*flat* TN-4
Tillery Hill—*summit* IN-6
Tillery Hill State Rec Area—*park* IN-6
Tillery Lake—*lake* WY-8
Tillery Post Office (historical)—*building* AL-4
Tillery Post Office (historical)—*building* TN-4
Tillery Spring—*spring* TN-4
Tilles Park—*park* AR-4
Tilles Park—*park* (2) MO-7
Tilles Sch—*school* AR-4
Tillet Mtn—*summit* SC-3
Tillets Cove—*bay* NC-3
Tillets Hole—*stream* WY-8
Tillett Branch—*stream* TN-4
Tillette Bayou—*bay* FL-3
Tillett Ranch—*locale* MT-8
Tilley, John, House—*hist pl* AR-4
*Tilley Bend* GA-3
Tilley Bend—*bend* GA-3
Tilley Branch—*stream* TN-4
Tilley Branch—*stream* VA-3
Tilley Canyon—*valley* OR-9
Tilley Cem—*cemetery* GA-3
Tilley Cem—*cemetery* NC-3
Tilley Cem—*cemetery* TX-5
Tilley Ch—*church* GA-3
Tilley Creek—*stream* IL-6
Tilley Creek—*stream* NC-3
Tilley Ditch—*canal* IN-6
Tilley Ditch—*canal* MO-7
Tilley Lake—*lake* NE-7
Tilley Mine—*mine* ID-8
Till Hollow—*valley* AL-4
**Tillicum**—*pop pl* WA-9
Tillicum Beach—*locale* WA-9
**Tillicum Beach**—*pop pl* OR-9
Tillicum Beach Campground—*park* OR-9
Tillicum Campground—*locale* WA-9
*Tillicum Creek* OR-9
*Tillicum Creek* WA-9
Tillicum Creek—*stream* (2) OR-9
Tillicum Creek—*stream* (3) WA-9
Tillicum Mine—*mine* OR-9
Tillicum Peak—*summit* WA-9
Tillicum Point—*summit* WA-9
Tillicum Siding—*locale* WA-9
Tillie—*locale* KY-4
Tillie Creek—*stream* CA-9
Tillie Creek—*stream* UT-8
Tillie Creek Campground—*locale* CA-9
Tillie Hall Canyon—*valley* AZ-5
Tillie Hall Canyon—*valley* NM-5
Tillie Hall Peak—*summit* NM-5
*Tillie Lake* WI-6
Tillie Lake—*lake* MI-6
Tillie Lake—*reservoir* TX-5
Tillie Miller Bridge—*bridge* FL-3
Tillie Spring—*spring* OR-9
Tillinghast, Charles, House—*hist pl* RI-1
Tillinghast, John, House—*hist pl* RI-1
Tillinghast Cem—*cemetery* WI-6
Tillinghast Creek—*stream* MT-8
Tillinghast Mill Site—*hist pl* RI-1
Tillinghast Pond—*lake* RI-1
Tillinghast Road Hist Dist—*hist pl* RI-1
Tillinghouse Cem—*cemetery* TX-5
Tillinghurst Elem Sch—*school* GA-3
Tillis HS—*school* AR-4
Tillison Branch—*stream* TN-4
*Tillison Brook* MA-1
Tillison Cem—*cemetery* AL-4
Tillison Creek—*stream* OR-9
Tillisons Bend—*bend* AL-4
Tillisons Mine—*mine* SD-7
Tillis Pond—*reservoir* AL-4
Tillis Prairie Cem—*cemetery* TX-5
Tillman—*locale* GA-3
Tillman—*locale* IL-6
Tillman—*locale* MS-4
**Tillman**—*pop pl* IN-6
**Tillman**—*pop pl* MS-4
**Tillman**—*pop pl* MO-7
**Tillman**—*pop pl* SC-3
Tillman Bayou—*stream* MS-4
Tillman Brook—*stream* NJ-2
Tillman Cem—*cemetery* (2) GA-3
Tillman Cem—*cemetery* IL-6
Tillman Cem—*cemetery* OK-5
Tillman Cem—*cemetery* TN-4
Tillman Cem—*cemetery* TX-5
*Tillman Cemetery* MS-4
Tillman Ch—*church* LA-4
Tillman Chapel—*church* MS-4
Tillman Chapel—*church* TN-4
Tillman Corner Ch of God—*church* AL-4
**Tillman (County)**—*pop pl* OK-5
Tillman County Courthouse—*hist pl* OK-5
Tillman Creek—*stream* IN-6
Tillman Creek—*stream* WA-9
Tillman Draw—*valley* AZ-5
Tillman Falls—*falls* NJ-2
Tillman Hall—*hist pl* SC-3
Tillman Hollow—*valley* TN-4
Tillman House—*hist pl* MS-4
Tillman Island—*island* GA-3
*Tillman Lake* AL-4
Tillman Lake Dam—*dam* AL-4
Tillman Lookout Tower—*locale* MS-4
Tillman Mill Creek—*stream* GA-3
Tillman Mtn—*summit* WA-9
*Tillmann* IN-6
Tillman Park—*park* SC-3
Tillman Pond—*reservoir* GA-3
Tillman Ranch—*locale* AZ-5
Tillman Ranch—*locale* WY-8
*Tillmans* IN-6
Tillmans—*other* VA-3
Tillmans Bay—*swamp* SC-3
Tillmans Branch—*stream* SC-3
Tillman Sch—*school* MO-7
Tillman Sch—*school* SC-3
**Tillmans Corner**—*pop pl* AL-4
Tillmans Corner Assembly of God Ch—*church* AL-4
Tillmans Mill (historical)—*locale* AL-4
Tillmans Pond—*lake* FL-3
Tillmans Pond—*reservoir* AL-4
Tillman Spring—*spring* AZ-5
Tillmans Wash—*stream* AZ-5
Tillman Tank—*reservoir* (2) AZ-5
Tillman Water Catchment—*reservoir* AZ-5
Tillman Well—*well* AZ-5
Tillmon Cem—*cemetery* TN-4
Tillotson—*locale* PA-2
Tillotson Brook—*stream* MA-1
Tillotson Camp—*locale* VT-1
Tillotson Cem—*cemetery* FL-3
Tillotson Cem—*cemetery* (2) NY-2
Tillotson Cem—*cemetery* NC-3
Tillotson Cem—*cemetery* OR-9
*Tillotson Corners* PA-2
Tillotson Creek—*stream* NY-2
Tillotson Creek—*stream* OR-9
Tillotson Hill—*summit* MA-1
Tillotson Lake—*lake* MI-6
Tillotson Lateral—*canal* ID-8
Tillotson Mill—*locale* VT-1
Tillotson Peak—*locale* VT-1
Tillotson Peak—*summit* AZ-5
Tillou Ch—*church* LA-4
Till Rock—*summit* MA-1
Tills Cove—*bay* ME-1
**Tillson**—*pop pl* NY-2
Tillson, Gen. Davis, House—*hist pl* ME-1
*Tillson Brook* MA-1
Tillson Cem—*cemetery* MS-4
Tillson Coulee—*valley* MT-8
Tillson Creek—*stream* SD-7
Tillson Lake—*lake* NY-2
Tillson Peak—*summit* MT-8
*Tillsons Brook* MA-1
*Tillsons Hill* MA-1
Tills Point—*cape* ME-1
Tills Pond—*reservoir* AL-4
*Tilltill Valley* CA-9
*Tillusqua Creek* OR-9
Tillusqua Fish Hatchery—*other* OR-9
Till Valley—*valley* AK-9
**Tilly**—*pop pl* AR-4
Tilly Branch—*stream* AL-4
Tilly Branch—*stream* MO-7
Tilly Branch—*stream* SC-3
*Tilly Brook* MA-1
**Tilly Foster**—*pop pl* NY-2
Tilly Homestead—*locale* WY-8
Tilly Island—*island* SC-3
Tilly Jane Creek—*stream* OR-9
Tilly Jane Guard Station—*locale* OR-9
Tilly Jane Trail—*trail* OR-9
Tilly Lake—*lake* SC-3
Tilly Lake—*lake* WI-6
Tilly Park—*park* NY-2
Tilly Pond—*lake* ME-1
Tillys Branch—*stream* LA-4
Tilly Starbuck Mine—*mine* AZ-5
Tilly Swamp—*stream* SC-3
*Tilman* MO-7
Tilman Chapel—*church* MS-4
Tilman Hill—*summit* NY-2
Tilmans Wharf—*locale* VA-3
Tilmon—*locale* TX-5
*Tilnguy* FM-9
Tilotson Canyon—*valley* NM-5
Tilsey Brook—*stream* NH-1
Tilseys Creek—*stream* MS-4
**Tilsit**—*pop pl* MO-7
Tilson Bay—*bay* MN-6
Tilson Branch—*stream* TN-4
Tilson Brook—*stream* MA-1
Tilson Cem—*cemetery* TN-4
Tilson Cem—*cemetery* VA-3
Tilson Cove—*bay* RI-1
Tilson Creek—*stream* MN-6
Tilson Gap—*gap* VA-3
Tilson Hollow—*valley* TN-4
Tilson Mounds-Summerhill Lake Place (41BW14)—*hist pl* TX-5
Tilson Mtn—*summit* TN-4
Tilted Hills—*other* AK-9
Tilted Mesa—*summit* AZ-5
Tilthammer Shoals—*bar* TN-4
Tiltill Creek—*stream* CA-9
Tiltill Mtn—*summit* CA-9
Tiltill Valley—*basin* CA-9
*Tiltil Valley* CA-9
*Tilton* NH-1
Tilton—*locale* FL-3
Tilton—*locale* GA-3
Tilton—*locale* MS-4
**Tilton**—*pop pl* AR-4
**Tilton**—*pop pl* IL-6
**Tilton**—*pop pl* IA-7
**Tilton**—*pop pl* KY-4
**Tilton**—*pop pl* NH-1
Tilton, Charles E., Mansion—*hist pl* NH-1
Tilton, Mount—*summit* CO-8
Tilton Bridge—*bridge* GA-3
Tilton Brook—*stream* MA-1
Tilton Brook—*stream* (2) NH-1
Tilton Cem—*cemetery* GA-3
Tilton Cem—*cemetery* NY-2
Tilton Cem—*cemetery* TX-5
Tilton Ch—*church* AR-4
Tilton Corner—*locale* ME-1
Tilton Creek—*stream* IL-6
Tilton Creek—*stream* MS-4
Tilton Creek—*stream* OR-9
Tilton Crossroads—*locale* OH-6
Tilton Downtown Hist Dist—*hist pl* NH-1
*Tilton Hill* MA-1
Tilton Hill—*summit* MA-1
Tilton Hill—*summit* NH-1
Tilton Island Park Bridge—*hist pl* NH-1
Tilton Lookout Tower—*locale* MS-4
Tilton Park—*park* (2) IL-6
Tilton Point—*cape* NJ-2
Tilton Pond—*lake* ME-1
Tilton Pond—*lake* NH-1
Tilton River—*stream* WA-9
Tilton Sch—*school* AR-4
Tilton Sch—*school* IL-6
Tilton Sch—*school* MA-1
*Tiltons Hill* MA-1
*Tiltons Point* MA-1
Tilton Spring Creek—*stream* MT-8
Tilton Springs—*spring* AZ-5
Tiltons Run—*stream* OH-6
Tiltons Tower (historical)—*building* MA-1
**Tiltonsville**—*pop pl* OH-6
**Tilton (Town of)**—*pop pl* NH-1
*Tiltonville* MA-1
*Tiltonville* OH-6
Tiltonville Cem—*cemetery* OH-6
Tiltonville (RR name for Tiltonsville)—*other* OH-6
Tilts Windmill—*locale* NM-5
Tily—*locale* AR-4
Timan Lake—*lake* WI-6
Tim Artesian Well—*well* TX-5
Timba—*locale* CA-9
Timbalier Bay—*bay* LA-4
Timbalier Bay Oil Field—*oilfield* LA-4
Timbalier Island—*island* LA-4
*Timbalier Islands* LA-4
**Timbar**—*pop pl* WV-2
Timber—*locale* AK-9
Timber—*locale* MO-7
Timber—*locale* OR-9
Timber—*locale* TX-5
Timber and Beaver Swamp—*swamp* NJ-2
Timber-Antelope Well—*well* AZ-5
Timber Basin—*basin* CO-8
Timber Basin—*basin* OR-9
Timber Bayou—*gut* LA-4
Timber Bench Tank—*reservoir* AZ-5
Timber Branch—*stream* FL-3
Timber Branch—*stream* LA-4
Timber Branch—*stream* MO-7
Timber Branch—*stream* (2) TX-5
Timber Branch—*stream* VA-3
Timber Branch Swamp—*stream* VA-3
Timber Brook—*stream* ME-1
Timber Brook—*stream* NJ-2
Timber Butte—*summit* (2) ID-8
Timber Butte—*summit* (6) MT-8
Timber Butte—*summit* (3) OR-9
Timber Buttes—*summit* MT-8
Timber Cabin—*locale* OR-9
Timber Camp—*locale* AZ-5
*Timber Camp Mountains* AZ-5
*Timber Camp Mtn* AZ-5
Timber Camp Mtn—*summit* AZ-5
Timber Camp Tank—*reservoir* AZ-5
Timber Canal—*canal* LA-4
*Timber Canyon* OR-9
Timber Canyon—*valley* CA-9
Timber Canyon—*valley* (2) CO-8
Timber Canyon—*valley* (2) ID-8
Timber Canyon—*valley* KS-7
Timber Canyon—*valley* (3) MT-8
Timber Canyon—*valley* (2) NV-8
Timber Canyon—*valley* NM-5
Timber Canyon—*valley* (3) OR-9
Timber Canyon—*valley* SD-7
Timber Canyon—*valley* (3) UT-8
Timber Canyon—*valley* (2) WY-8
Timber Canyon Spring—*spring* OR-9
Timber Canyon Waterhole—*reservoir* OR-9
Timber Claim Gulch—*valley* CO-8
Timber Coulee—*valley* (3) MT-8
Timber Coulee—*valley* ND-7
Timber Coulee—*valley* WI-6
Timber Cove—*bay* CA-9
Timber Cove—*bay* (3) ME-1
**Timber Cove**—*pop pl* TX-5
Timber Cove Creek—*stream* CA-9
**Timbercove (subdivision)**—*pop pl* MS-4
Timber Crater—*crater* OR-9
*Timber Creek* CO-8
*Timber Creek* ID-8
*Timber Creek* KS-7
*Timber Creek* MO-7
*Timber Creek* MT-8
*Timber Creek* NJ-2
*Timber Creek* SD-7
*Timber Creek* TX-5
*Timber Creek* WY-8
**Timber Creek**—*pop pl* NE-7
Timber Creek—*stream* (6) AK-9
Timber Creek—*stream* (3) CA-9
Timber Creek—*stream* (3) CO-8
Timber Creek—*stream* (10) ID-8
Timber Creek—*stream* (2) IL-6
Timber Creek—*stream* (2) IA-7
Timber Creek—*stream* (3) KS-7
Timber Creek—*stream* (2) KY-4
Timber Creek—*stream* (2) MN-6
Timber Creek—*stream* (16) MT-8
Timber Creek*—*stream* NE-7
Timber Creek—*stream* NE-7
Timber Creek—*stream* (4) NV-8
Timber Creek—*stream* NC-3
Timber Creek—*stream* (3) ND-7
Timber Creek—*stream* (3) OK-5
Timber Creek—*stream* (5) OR-9
Timber Creek—*stream* SC-3
Timber Creek—*stream* (5) SD-7
Timber Creek—*stream* (8) TX-5
Timber Creek—*stream* UT-8
Timber Creek—*stream* (4) WA-9
Timber Creek—*stream* WI-6
Timber Creek—*stream* (7) WY-8
Timber Creek—*unorg reg* ND-7
Timber Creek Basin Rsvr—*reservoir* MT-8
Timber Creek Basin Spring—*spring* MT-8
Timber Creek Campground—*locale* CO-8
Timber Creek Campground—*locale* NV-8
Timber Creek Campground Comfort Station No. 245—*hist pl* CO-8
Timber Creek Campground Comfort Station No. 246—*hist pl* CO-8
Timber Creek Campground Comfort Station No. 247—*hist pl* CO-8
**Timbercreek Canyon**—*pop pl* TX-5
Timber Creek Cem—*cemetery* IA-7
Timber Creek Cem—*cemetery* (2) KS-7
Timber Creek Ch—*church* KS-7
Timber Creek Ch—*church* ND-7
*Timber Creek Forest Service Recreation Site* NV-8
Timber Creek (historical P.O.)—*locale* IA-7
Timber Creek Lake—*reservoir* KS-7
Timber Creek Pass—*gap* ID-8
Timber Creek Ranger Station—*locale* WY-8
*Timber Creek Reservoir* ID-8
Timber Creek Road Camp Barn—*hist pl* CO-8
Timber Creek Road Camp Storage Bldg—*hist pl* CO-8
Timber Creek Rsvr—*reservoir* MT-8
Timber Creek Sch—*school* NE-7
Timber Creek Sch—*school* SD-7
Timber Creek Spring—*spring* MT-8
Timber Creek Spring Number One—*spring* MT-8
**Timbercreek (subdivision)**—*pop pl* NC-3
**Timber Creek (subdivision)**—*pop pl* NC-3
**Timbercreek (subdivision)**—*pop pl* NC-3
*Timber Creek Township* KS-7
Timber Creek Township—*fmr MCD* IA-7
**Timber Creek Township**—*pop pl* NE-7
Timber Creek Trail—*trail* CO-8
Timber Creek Trail—*trail* WY-8
*Timbercrest* IL-6
**Timbercrest**—*pop pl* (2) IN-6
**Timbercrest**—*pop pl* (2) TN-4
Timbercrest Ch—*church* TX-5
**Timbercrest (subdivision)**—*pop pl* AL-4
**Timbercrest (subdivision)**—*pop pl* NC-3
Timber Culture Gulch—*valley* OR-9
Timber Ditch—*canal* CO-8
Timberdock Lodge—*locale* SC-3
Timber Draw—*valley* AZ-5
Timber Draw—*valley* (2) ID-8
Timber Draw—*valley* SD-7
Timber Draw—*valley* UT-8
Timber Draw—*valley* (4) WY-8
Timber Draw Rsvr—*reservoir* ID-8
Timbered Branch—*stream* NC-3
Timbered Crater—*crater* CA-9
Timbered Dome—*summit* ID-8
Timbered Dome Creek—*stream* ID-8
*Timbered Dome Peak* ID-8
Timber Edge Sch—*school* IL-6
Timbered Hill—*summit* CO-8
Timbered Hill Ch—*church* OK-5
Timbered Hollow—*valley* AR-4
Timbered Island—*island* AK-9
Timbered Island—*ridge* WY-8
Timbered Knob—*summit* MO-7
Timbered Knoll—*summit* OR-9
Timbered Knoll—*summit* UT-8
Timbered Mountain Tank—*reservoir* CA-9
Timbered Mtn—*summit* CA-9
Timbered Peak—*summit* WA-9
*Timbered Ridge* CA-9
Timbered Ridge—*ridge* (2) CA-9
Timbered Ridge—*ridge* NC-3
Timbered Ridge—*ridge* TN-4
Timbered Ridge Ch—*church* NC-3
Timbered Ridge Rsvr—*reservoir* CA-9
Timbered Rock—*pillar* OR-9
*Timber Fall Butte* OR-9

Timber Fall Butte—summit OR-9
Timber Flat Creek—stream ID-8
Timber Fork—stream MT-8
Timber Fork Hollow—valley AR-4
Timber Gap—gap CA-9
Timber Gap Creek—stream CA-9
**Timber Grove**—pop pl MD-2
**Timber Grove**—pop pl OR-9
Timber Grove Ch—church OK-5
Timber Gulch MT-8
Timber Gulch OR-9
Timber Gulch—valley (4) CA-9
Timber Gulch—valley (2) CO-8
Timber Gulch—valley (7) ID-8
Timber Gulch—valley (4) MT-8
Timber Gulch—valley (2) NV-8
Timber Gulch—valley (4) OR-9
Timber Gulch—valley SD-7
Timber Gulch Spring Number 3—spring CO-8
Timber Gut Creek AL-4
Timbergut Creek—stream AL-4
Timberhead Mtn—summit WA-9
Timber Hill—summit CO-8
Timber Hill—summit KS-7
Timber Hill—summit MA-1
Timber Hill—summit MO-7
Timber Hill—summit (2) MT-8
Timber Hill—summit NV-8
Timber Hill—summit (3) OK-5
Timber Hill—summit PA-2
Timber Hill—summit WA-9
Timber Hill Ch—church MO-7
Timber Hill Ch—church (2) OK-5
Timberhill Park—park OR-9
Timber Hill Rsvr—reservoir OR-9
**Timber Hills**—pop pl TN-4
Timber Hill Sch—school MO-7
Timber Hill Township KS-7
**Timberhill Township**—pop pl KS-7
Timber Hollow—valley TX-5
Timber Hollow—valley (2) VA-3
Timber Hollow Overlook—locale VA-3
Timber Hollow Trail—trail VA-3
Timberhouse—hist pl SC-3
Timber House Airp—airport IN-6
**Timberhurst**—pop pl IN-6
Timberidge Ch—church GA-3
Timber Island WY-8
Timber Island—island FL-3
Timber Island—island LA-4
Timber Island—island (2) ME-1
Timber Island—island MN-6
Timber Island—island NH-1
Timber Knob—summit AK-9
Timber Knob—summit CA-9
Timber Knob—summit MO-7
Timber Knob Mtn—summit AL-4
Timber Knoll—summit AZ-5
Timber Knot CA-9
Timber Lake CO-8
Timber Lake VA-3
Timber Lake—lake (2) AK-9
Timber Lake—lake AR-4
Timber Lake—lake (2) CA-9
Timber Lake—lake (3) CO-8
Timber Lake—lake CT-1
Timber Lake—lake FL-3
Timber Lake—lake IL-6
Timber Lake—lake LA-4
Timber Lake—lake (4) MI-6
Timber Lake—lake (2) MN-6
Timber Lake—lake MO-7
Timber Lake—lake MT-8
Timber Lake—lake NV-8
Timber Lake—lake (2) OR-9
Timber Lake—lake SC-3
Timber Lake—lake SD-7
Timber Lake—lake (3) TX-5
Timber Lake—lake (2) WI-6
**Timber Lake**—pop pl (2) IL-6
**Timberlake**—pop pl NC-3
**Timberlake**—pop pl OH-6
**Timber Lake**—pop pl SD-7
**Timberlake**—pop pl (2) TN-4
**Timberlake**—pop pl TX-5
**Timberlake**—pop pl VA-3
Timber Lake—reservoir AR-4
Timber Lake—reservoir (2) IN-6
Timber Lake—reservoir (2) KS-7
Timber Lake—reservoir MO-7
Timber Lake—reservoir NJ-2
Timber Lake—reservoir NM-5
Timber Lake—reservoir NY-2
Timber Lake—reservoir PA-2
Timber Lake—reservoir TN-4
Timber Lake—reservoir TX-5
Timber Lake—reservoir (2) VA-3
Timber Lake—swamp MN-6
Timber Lakebed—flat (2) MN-6
Timberlake-Branham House—hist pl VA-3
Timber Lake Camp—locale TX-5
Timber Lake Cattle Company Number 3 Dam—dam SD-7
Timberlake Cem—cemetery IA-7
Timber Lake Ch—church OK-5
Timber Lake Country Club—locale SD-7
Timber Lake Creek AR-4
Timberlake Creek—stream CO-8
Timberlake Creek—stream OK-5
Timber Lake Dam—dam (2) IN-6
Timber Lake Dam—dam KS-7
Timber Lake Dam—dam NJ-2
Timber Lake Dam—dam PA-2
Timber Lake Dam—dam TN-4
**Timberlake Estates**—pop pl IL-6
**Timber Lake Estates**—pop pl TX-5
Timberlake Hollow—valley IN-6
Timberlake Hollow—valley TN-4
Timberlake Lower Dam—dam NC-3
Timberlake Lower Lake—reservoir NC-3
Timber Lake Municipal Airp—airport SD-7
Timber Lake Plantation (historical)—locale MS-4
Timberlake Pond—reservoir IN-6
**Timberlake (RR name Helena)**—pop pl NC-3
Timber Lakes—lake TX-5
**Timber Lakes**—pop pl NJ-2
Timber Lakes—reservoir NJ-2
Timber Lakes—reservoir TX-5
Timberlake Sch—school TN-4
Timber Lakes Dam—dam NJ-2
**Timber Lakes (subdivision)**—pop pl MS-4
**Timberlake (subdivision)**—pop pl NC-3
**Timber Lake (subdivision)**—pop pl NC-3
**Timberlake (subdivision)**—pop pl NC-3
**Timberlake (subdivision)**—pop pl TN-4
Timber Lake Trail—trail CO-8
Timberlake Village IL-6
Timberlake Windmill—locale TX-5
Timber Lake Windmill—locale TX-5
Timberland—locale WI-6
**Timberland**—pop pl NC-3
Timberland Ch—church WI-6
Timberland Creek—stream MI-6
**Timberland Estates**—pop pl TN-4
Timberland Heights IA-7
Timberland Park—park WV-2
Timber Lands Lake—reservoir SC-3
**Timberland (subdivision)**—pop pl NC-3
Timberlane—CDP LA-4
**Timberlane**—pop pl OK-5
**Timberlane Acres**—pop pl TX-5
Timberlane Country Club—other LA-4
Timberlane Regional HS—school NH-1
Timberlane Sch—school OH-6
Timber Lane Sch—school VA-3
Timberlane Shops on the Square—locale FL-3
**Timberlane (subdivision)**—pop pl (2) AL-4
**Timberlane (subdivision)**—pop pl MS-4
Timberlawn Baptist Ch—church MS-4
Timberlawn Elementary School MS-4
Timberlawn Sch—school MS-4
Timberlee Chapel—church MN-6
**Timberline**—pop pl IL-6
Timberline, Lake—lake PA-2
Timberline, Lake—reservoir (2) MO-7
Timber Line Airpark Airp—airport MO-7
Timberline Cabin—hist pl CO-8
Timberline Camp—locale CA-9
Timberline Campground—locale (2) WA-9
Timberline Creek—stream (2) AK-9
Timberline Creek—stream (2) MT-8
Timberline Creek—stream OR-9
**Timber Line Estates**—pop pl TN-4
Timberline Estates Dam—dam TN-4
Timberline Estates Lake—reservoir TN-4
Timberline Falls—falls CO-8
Timberline Lake—lake (2) CO-8
Timberline Lake—lake (2) MT-8
Timberline Lake—lake WY-8
Timber Line Lake—reservoir MO-7
Timberline Lodge—hist pl OR-9
Timberline Lodge—locale OR-9
Timberline Mtn—summit MI-6
Timberline Mtn—summit MT-8
Timberline Pass—gap CO-8
Timberline Quarter Horse Farm Airp—airport WA-9
Timberline Ranch—locale WY-8
Timberline Spring—spring CO-8
Timberline Tarns—lake CA-9
Timberline Trail—trail CO-8
Timberline Trail—trail OR-9
**Timberlinks**—pop pl TN-4
Timberlinks Golf Course—locale PA-2
Timber-Linn Lake—lake OR-9
Timber-Linn Memorial Park—cemetery OR-9
Timber Lodge—locale CA-9
Timber Lodge Lake—lake NE-7
Timberloft Camp—locale CA-9
**Timberlost**—pop pl MI-6
Timberlost Lake—lake AK-9
Timberly Creek—stream OK-5
**Timberly Heights**—pop pl PA-2
**Timberly Heights**—pop pl VA-3
**Timberlyne (subdivision)**—pop pl NC-3
Timberman Homestead—locale MT-8
Timberman Ridge—ridge WV-2
Timber Marsh—swamp NY-2
Timber Mesa—summit AZ-5
Timber Mesa—summit NM-5
Timber Mesa—summit TX-5
Timber Mount NV-8
Timber Mountain ID-8
Timber Mountain Pass—gap NV-8
Timber Mountain Ranch—locale CA-9
Timber Mountain Trail—trail ID-8
Timber Mtn WA-9
Timber Mtn—summit AZ-5
Timber Mtn—summit (2) CA-9
Timber Mtn—summit (2) CO-8
Timber Mtn—summit ID-8
Timber Mtn—summit (3) NV-8
Timber Mtn—summit (2) OR-9
Timber Mtn—summit TX-5
Timber Mtn—summit (4) UT-8
Timber Mtn—summit (2) WA-9
Timber Mtn—summit WV-2
Timber Neck—cape (2) VA-3
Timberneck—hist pl VA-3
Timberneck Creek—stream VA-3
Timber Neck Creek—stream VA-3
Timber Neck Farm—hist pl MD-2
**Timberon**—pop pl NM-5
Timber Peak NV-8
Timber Peak—summit CA-9
Timber Peak—summit ID-8
Timber Peak—summit NM-5
Timber Pit Rsvr—reservoir MT-8
Timber Point—cape AK-9
Timber Point—cape CA-9
Timber Point—cape ID-8
Timber Point—cape (2) ME-1
Timber Point—cape MD-2
Timber Point—cape NV-8
Timber Point—cape NY-2
Timber Point—cliff UT-8
Timber Point Country Club—other NY-2
Timber Point Sch—school NY-2
Timber Products Company Dam—dam OR-9
Timber Prong Creek—stream ND-7
Timber Ranger Station—locale AZ-5
Timber Ridge CA-9
Timber Ridge IL-6
Timber Ridge TN-4
Timber Ridge—locale (2) VA-3
**Timber Ridge**—pop pl IL-6
**Timber Ridge**—pop pl (2) MD-2
**Timber Ridge**—pop pl (2) TN-4
Timber Ridge—ridge (3) CA-9
Timber Ridge—ridge ID-8
Timber Ridge—ridge MD-2
Timber Ridge—ridge MT-8
Timber Ridge—ridge (5) NC-3
Timber Ridge—ridge OK-5
Timber Ridge—ridge OR-9
Timber Ridge—ridge (2) PA-2
Timber Ridge—ridge (2) TN-4
Timber Ridge—ridge (8) VA-3
Timber Ridge—ridge WA-9
Timber Ridge—ridge (4) WV-2
Timber Ridge—summit CO-8
Timber Ridge, Lake—reservoir MO-7
Timber Ridge Baptist Church TN-4
Timber Ridge Branch—stream SC-3
Timber Ridge Cem—cemetery OK-5
Timber Ridge Ch—church GA-3
Timber Ridge Ch—church MO-7
Timber Ridge Ch—church (2) OK-5
Timber Ridge Ch—church TN-4
Timber Ridge Ch—church (3) VA-3
Timber Ridge Lake—lake NC-3
Timber Ridge Lake—reservoir IN-6
Timber Ridge Lake—reservoir NC-3
Timber Ridge Lake Dam—dam IN-6
Timber Ridge Lake Dam—dam NC-3
Timber Ridge (Magisterial District)—fmr MCD WV-2
Timber Ridge Park—park IL-6
Timberridge Post Office (historical)—building TN-4
Timber Ridge Presbyterian Church—hist pl VA-3
Timber Ridge Sch—school IL-6
Timber Ridge Sch—school KS-7
Timber Ridge Sch (abandoned)—school MO-7
**Timber Ridge (subdivision)**—pop pl DE-2
**Timber Ridge (subdivision)**—pop pl MS-4
**Timber Ridge (subdivision)**—pop pl NC-3
**Timber Ridge (subdivision)**—pop pl PA-2
Timber Ridge Trail—trail VA-3
Timber Run—stream MD-2
Timber Run—stream NJ-2
Timber Run—stream OH-6
Timber Run Ch—church OH-6
Timbers CO-8
**Timbers, The**—pop pl DE-2
**Timbers, The**—pop pl VA-3
Timber Sch—school CA-9
Timber Sch—school MO-7
Timber Sink—cave TN-4
Timber Spring—spring ID-8
Timber Spring—spring NV-8
**Timbers (subdivision)**—pop pl (2) AL-4
Timber Substation—locale OR-9
Timber Swamp—stream (2) VA-3
Timber Swamp Brook—stream NJ-2
Timber Top—summit CA-9
Timber Top—summit WY-8
Timber Top Mtn—summit UT-8
Timber Town—post sta HI-9
**Timber (Township of)**—pop pl IL-6
Timbertrail Camp—locale VT-1
Timber Trails IL-6
Timber Trails—uninc pl LA-4
Timber Trails Golf Club—other IL-6
**Timber Trails (subdivision)**—pop pl NC-3
Timber Tree Branch—stream KY-4
Timbertree Branch—stream TN-4
Timbertree Branch—stream VA-3
**Timberview**—pop pl MD-2
Timberville MS-4
**Timberville**—pop pl VA-3
Timber Wash—stream AZ-5
Timber Well—well AZ-5
Timberwheel Lakes—lake LA-4
**Timberwick (subdivision)**—pop pl TN-4
Timber Wolf Creek—stream WA-9
Timberwolf Mtn—summit WA-9
**Timberwyck**—pop pl PA-2
**Timblin**—pop pl PA-2
Timblin Borough—civil PA-2
Timblin Creek—arroyo NV-8
**Timbo**—pop pl AR-4
Timbo Creek—stream AR-4
Timbo (Township of)—fmr MCD AR-4
Tim Bowers Creek—stream MI-6
Tim Bowers Pond—lake MI-6
Tim Branch—stream KY-4
Tim Branch Swamp VA-3
Tim Brook—stream ME-1
Tim Brown Spring—spring OR-9
Timbuck—locale PA-2
Timbuctoo—locale CA-9
**Timbuctoo**—pop pl NJ-2
Timbuctoo Bend—bend CA-9
Timbuktu—locale OR-9
Tim Butte—summit WY-8
Tim Carroll Brook—stream VT-1
Tim Corners—locale OH-6
Tim Creek—stream NC-3
Tim Creek—stream OR-9
Tim Creek—stream SC-3
Time—locale PA-2
**Time**—pop pl IL-6
Time and a Half Spring—spring OR-9
Time Lake—lake MN-6
Timely Gull Ridge—ridge UT-8
Timene Canyon—valley OR-9
Timentwa Flat—flat WA-9
Time-O-Day Spring—spring OK-5
Times and Olympia Buildings—hist pl MA-1
**Times Beach**—pop pl MO-7
Times Bldg—hist pl AL-4
Times Bldg—hist pl WA-9
Times Building Rock—summit OR-9
Times Corner—post sta IN-6
Times Gulch—valley AZ-5
Times Plaza—locale NY-2
Time Spring—spring ID-8
Times Square IL-6
Times Square—locale NY-2
Times Square—uninc pl WA-9
Times Square Plaza (Shop Ctr)—locale FL-3
Times Square (Shop Ctr)—locale FL-3
Times-Star Bldg—hist pl OH-6
Timesville—locale TX-5
**Timesville**—pop pl TN-4
Timesville Ave Baptist Ch—church TN-4
Timewell (corporate name Mound Station) IL-6
Tim Garrard Reservoir MT-8
Tim Holt Summit—gap NV-8
Timia—summit NM-5
Timico Lake—lake WY-8
Timico Lake Trail—trail WY-8
Timicula PA-2
Tim Ives Run PA-2
**Timken**—pop pl KS-7
Timken, Henry H., Estate Barn—hist pl OH-6
Timken Vocation Sch—school OH-6
Timkham Hill VT-1
Timkin KS-7
Tim Long Creek OR-9
Tim Long Creek—stream OR-9
Tim Lynn Lake—lake WI-6
Timma Drain—stream MI-6
Timm Creek—stream ID-8
Timme WI-6
Timme—other WI-6
**Timmer**—pop pl ND-7
Timmerhuset—hist pl ME-1
Timmer kill NJ-2
Timmerman Bay—bay GA-3
Timmerman Bridge—bridge SC-3
Timmerman Cem—cemetery ID-8
Timmerman Cem—cemetery SC-3
Timmerman Creek—stream NY-2
Timmerman Hill—summit NY-2
Timmerman Hills—range ID-8
Timmerman Lake—lake MI-6
Timmerman Law Office—hist pl SC-3
Timmerman Pond—reservoir NC-3
Timmerman Pond Dam—dam NC-3
Timmerman Sch—school SC-3
Timmerman Spring—spring ID-8
Timmer Mine—mine NM-5
Timm Lake WI-6
Timm Lake—swamp MN-6
Timm Mine—mine UT-8
Timmoco Creek—stream WY-8
Timmons Branch—stream AL-4
Timmons Cem—cemetery AL-4
Timmons Cem—cemetery GA-3
Timmons Cem—cemetery IN-6
Timmons Cem—cemetery MS-4
Timmons Cem—cemetery NC-3
Timmons Cem—cemetery (2) OH-6
Timmons Cem—cemetery TN-4
Timmons Cove—bay DE-2
Timmons Creek—stream NE-7
Timmons Creek—stream NC-3
Timmons Creek—stream TX-5
Timmons Dam—dam AL-4
Timmons Ditch—canal (3) IN-6
Timmons Field Spring—spring ID-8
Timmons Grove Ch—church NC-3
Timmons Grove County Park—park IA-7
Timmons Hill NJ-2
Timmons Hill—summit OH-6
Timmons Lake—reservoir AL-4
Timmons Mtn—summit PA-2
Timmons Pond—reservoir GA-3
Timmons River—channel GA-3
Timmons Sch—school KS-7
Timmons Springs (historical)—locale AL-4
Timmons Tank—reservoir TX-5
Timmonstown—locale MD-2
Timmonstown Branch—stream MD-2
**Timmonsville**—pop pl SC-3
Timmonsville (CCD)—cens area SC-3
Timmonsville Ch—church SC-3
Timmous Sch—school IL-6
Timms Chapel—church GA-3
Timms Creek—stream CA-9
Timms Creek—stream GA-3
Timms Creek—stream MN-6
Timms Hill—summit WI-6
Timms Lake—lake (2) WI-6
Tim Mtn—summit ME-1
Timmy Branch—stream KY-4
Timmy Knob—summit KY-4
Timmy Lake—lake OR-9
Timmy Point—cape ME-1
Timmy Point—cape MA-1
Timmy Point Shoal—bar MA-1
**Timnath**—pop pl CO-8
Timnath Cem—cemetery CO-8
Timnath Reservoir Outlet—canal CO-8
Timnath Rsvr—reservoir CO-8
Timnath-Wellington—cens area CO-8
Timo MP-9
Timolea Ridge—ridge AS-9
Tim O'Leary Canyon—valley CA-9
Timon—locale LA-4
Timon Campground—park SD-7
Timon Creek—stream TX-5
Timoney—locale ME-1
Timoney Lake—lake ME-1
Timoney Mtn—summit ME-1
**Timonium**—pop pl MD-2
Timonium Creek—stream WA-9
Timosea Peak—summit CA-9
Timoteo Artesian Well—well TX-5
Timothy—locale IL-6
**Timothy**—pop pl GA-3
**Timothy**—pop pl NC-3
**Timothy**—pop pl TN-4
**Timothy**—pop pl TX-5
Timothy Ball Elem Sch—school IN-6
Timothy Branch—stream KY-4
Timothy Branch—stream MD-2
Timothy Branch—stream TN-4
Timothy Branch—stream WV-2
Timothy Butte—summit OR-9
Timothy Canyon—valley UT-8
Timothy Cem—cemetery LA-4
Timothy Cem—cemetery TX-5
Timothy Ch—church AR-4
Timothy Ch—church GA-3
Timothy Ch—church OH-6
Timothy Ch—church OK-5
Timothy Ch—church VA-3
Timothy Chapel—church NC-3
Timothy Christian Sch—school IA-7
Timothy Creek—stream ID-8
Timothy Creek—stream MT-8
Timothy Creek—stream (2) OR-9
Timothy Creek—stream (2) SC-3
Timothy Creek—stream TN-4
Timothy Creek—stream UT-8
Timothy Creek—stream WA-9
Timothy Creek—stream WY-8
Timothy Creek Rsvr—reservoir UT-8
Timothy Ditch—canal CO-8
Timothy Drain—canal CA-9
Timothy Flats—flat ID-8
Timothy Guard Station—locale OR-9
Timothy Gulch—valley CA-9
**Timothy Heights**—pop pl NY-2
Timothy Hill Ditch—canal CO-8
Timothy Hollow—valley TN-4
Timothy HS—school IL-6
Timothy Knob—summit NC-3
Timothy Lake—lake OR-9
Timothy Lake—reservoir OR-9
Timothy Lake Dam—dam OR-9
Timothy Lake Rsvr OR-9
Timothy Lakes—lake UT-8
Timothy Lateral—canal CA-9
Timothy Meadow—flat MT-8
Timothy Meadow—flat (2) WA-9
Timothy Meadow—swamp OR-9
Timothy Meadows (historical)—flat OR-9
Timothy One Drain—canal CA-9
**Timothy Park**—pop pl VA-3
Timothy Patch—flat OR-9
Timothy Post Office (historical)—building TN-4
Timothy Ridge—ridge OH-6
Timothy Ridge—ridge OR-9
Timothy Ridge—ridge WA-9
Timothy Rsvr OR-9
Timothy Sch—school IL-6
Timothy Spring—spring (2) OR-9
**Timothy (Township of)**—pop pl MN-6
Timothy Two Drain—canal CA-9
Timothy Wash—valley UT-8
Timothy Well (dry)—well OR-9
Timothy 1 Drain—canal CA-9
Timp, The—summit NY-2
Timpa Creek—stream ID-8
Timpahute Range NV-8
Timpahute Range—range NV-8
Timpa Lake—lake ID-8
Timpanogas Lake—lake OR-9
Timpanogas Way—trail OR-9
Timpanogos, Mount—summit UT-8
Timpanogos Basin—basin UT-8
Timpanogos Campground UT-8
Timpanogos Canal—canal UT-8
Timpanogos Cave—cave UT-8
Timpanogos Cave Hist Dist—hist pl UT-8
Timpanogos Cave Natl Monmt—park UT-8
Timpanogos Cave Ntional Monument—park UT-8
Timpanogos Cave Visitor Center—locale UT-8
Timpanogos Glacier—glacier UT-8
Timpanogos Memorial Gardens—cemetery UT-8
Tim-pan-o-gos River UT-8
Timpanogos Scenic Area—area UT-8
Timpanogos Sch—school UT-8
**Timpas**—pop pl CO-8
Timpas Creek—stream CO-8
Timp Brook, The—stream NY-2
Timp Canyon—valley AZ-5
Timp Haven Ski Area UT-8
Timpi Canyon—valley NV-8
Timpie—locale UT-8
Timpie Springs State Waterfowl Mngmt Area UT-8
Timpie Springs Waterfowl Mngmt Area—park UT-8
Timpie Valley—valley UT-8
Timpi Wash—arroyo NV-8
Timpkin Station KS-7
Tim Plate Mine—mine SD-7
Tim Pond—lake MA-1
Tim Pond—reservoir ME-1
Tim Pond Camp—locale ME-1
Tim Ponds—lake WA-9
Tim Pond (Township of)—unorg ME-1
Timpooneke Campground—park UT-8
Timpooneke Guard Station—locale UT-8
Timp Point—cliff AZ-5
**Timpson**—pop pl TX-5
Timpson, Lake—reservoir TX-5
Timpson (CCD)—cens area TX-5
Timpson Cem—cemetery NC-3
Timpson Chapel—church OK-5
Timpson Cove—bay GA-3
Timpson Creek—stream GA-3
Timpson Falls—falls GA-3
Timpson Lookout—locale TX-5
Timpson Mtn—summit GA-3
Timp Spring—spring AZ-5
Timpview HS—school UT-8
**Timp View Plat A,B,C,D**—pop pl UT-8
Timranogos Canal—canal UT-8
Tim Rod Ch—church SC-3
Timsbury Creek—stream VA-3
Tims Canyon—valley CA-9
Tims Cem—cemetery AL-4
Tims Cove—bay ME-1
Tims Cove—cove MA-1
Tims Creek—stream CA-9
Tims Creek—stream MD-2
Tims Creek—stream NY-2
Tims Creek—stream NC-3
Tims Creek—stream OR-9
Tims Draft—valley VA-3
Tims Draft Right Prong VA-3
Tims Ford Bridges—bridge TN-4
Tims Ford Dam—dam TN-4
Tims Ford Lake—reservoir TN-4
Tims Ford Rsvr TN-4
Tims Ford State Rustic Park—park TN-4
Tims Fork—stream WV-2
Tims Hole—basin UT-8
Tims Island—cape MI-6
Tims Knob—summit (2) VA-3
Tims Lake WI-6
Tims Lake—lake MI-6
Timsley—locale KY-4
Tims Memorial Ch—church FL-3
Tims Memorial Presbyterian Ch—church FL-3
Tims Mtn—summit MO-7
Timson Creek GA-3
Tims Peak—summit CA-9
Tims Peak—summit ID-8
Tims Peak—summit OR-9
Tims Peak Rsvr—reservoir OR-9
Tims Peak Spring—spring OR-9
Tims Point—cape MA-1
Tims Point—cape VA-3
Tims Pond—lake MA-1
Tim Spring—spring NV-8
Tim Spring—spring OR-9
Tim Springs Petroglyphs—hist pl NV-8
Tims Saddle—gap AZ-5
Tims Swamp—swamp PA-2
**Timtony**—pop pl WV-2
Timucuan Elem Sch—school FL-3
Timuquana Country Club—locale FL-3
Timwe—cape FM-9
Timwenleu—cape FM-9
Timwen Men—summit FM-9
Timwenpwel—cape FM-9
Timwensong—swamp FM-9
Tina WV-2
Tina—locale KY-4
**Tina**—pop pl MO-7
**Tina**—pop pl SC-3
Tina, Lake—reservoir AL-4
Tinago River—stream GU-9
Tinaja—locale (2) NM-5
Tinaja—locale TX-5
**Tinaja**—pop pl TX-5
Tinajaa AZ-5
Tinaja Arroyo—stream NM-5
Tinaja Blanca—reservoir TX-5
Tinaja Blanca, Arroyo—valley TX-5
Tinaja Canyon—valley (2) AZ-5
Tinaja Canyon—valley CO-8
Tinaja Cem—cemetery NM-5
Tinaja Creek—stream NM-5
Tinaja Dam—dam AZ-5
Tinaja de las Palmas Battle Site—hist pl TX-5
Tinaja Escondido, Arroyo—valley TX-5
Tinaja Grande—reservoir TX-5
Tinaja Hills—summit AZ-5
Tinaja Lake—lake NM-5
Tinaja Lujan—lake TX-5
Tinaja Mesa—summit NM-5
Tinaja Mountains—summit TX-5
Tinaja Mtn—summit NM-5
Tinaja Peak—summit AZ-5
Tinaja Pinta, Sierra—summit TX-5
Tinaja Prieta, Canon —valley TX-5
Tinaja Rana—reservoir TX-5
Tinaja Ranch—locale AZ-5
Tinajas, Arroyo—stream TX-5
Tinajas Altas—falls AZ-5
Tinajas Altas Mountains—range AZ-5
Tinajas Altas Pass—gap AZ-5
Tinajas Atlaa AZ-5
Tinajas Atlas Mountains AZ-5
Tinajas Atlas Spring AZ-5
Tinaja Sega—spring AZ-5
Tinajas Mountains AZ-5
Tinajas Pass AZ-5
Tinaja Spring—spring (2) AZ-5
Tinaja Spring—spring TX-5
Tinajas Tank—reservoir TX-5
Tinaja Tank—reservoir (2) AZ-5
Tinaja Wash—stream AZ-5
Tinaja Well—well AZ-5
Tinajo Draw—valley TX-5
Tinajos Windmill—locale TX-5
Tinajota Mountains AZ-5
Tinajualto AZ-5
Tinak MP-9
Ti-na-ka Spring AZ-5
Tina Lake—lake AK-9
Tina Larga Tank—reservoir AZ-5
Tinaquaic—civil CA-9
Tinayguk River—stream AK-9
Tin Barn Well—well AZ-5
Tin Boom Mine—mine SD-7
Tin Branch—stream WV-2
Tin Bridge Pond CT-1
Tin Brook—stream NY-2
Tin Cabin Creek—stream CA-9
Tin Camp Ranch—locale NE-7
Tin Can Alley—gap CA-9
Tin Can Alley—valley WY-8
Tin Can Basin—basin CO-8
Tin Can Branch—stream KY-4
Tin Can Cabin Campground—locale CA-9
Tin Can Canyon CA-9
Tin Can Canyon—valley CA-9
Tin Can Coulee—valley MT-8
Tincan Creek—stream AK-9
Tin Can Creek—stream CA-9
Tin Can Creek—stream ID-8
Tin Can Draw—valley AZ-5
Tin Can Draw—valley OR-9
Tin Can Draw—valley (2) WY-8
Tin Can Draw Rsvr—reservoir OR-9
Tincanebitts Canyon—valley AZ-5
Tincanebitts Point—summit AZ-5
Tincanebitts Spring—spring AZ-5
Tincanebitts Tank—reservoir AZ-5
Tin Can Flat—flat CA-9
Tin Can Flat Campground—locale ID-8
Tin Can Gap—gap WA-9
Tin Can Gulch—valley MT-8
Tin Can Hill—summit ID-8
Tincan Hill—summit WY-8
Tin Can Hollow—valley (2) PA-2
Tin Can Hollow—valley TN-4
Tincan Lake—lake AK-9
Tin Can Lake—lake NE-7
Tin Can Lake—lake WY-8
Tin Can Mike Lake—lake MN-6
Tin Can Park—flat WY-8
Tincan Peak—summit AK-9
Tin Can Point—cape AK-9
Tin Can Ridge—ridge OR-9
Tin Can Rsvr—reservoir OR-9
Tincan Spring—spring ID-8
Tin Can Spring—spring (2) OR-9
Tin Can Tank—reservoir (3) AZ-5
Tincan Tank—reservoir NM-5
Tin Can Wash—valley AZ-5
Tin Can Well—well NM-5
Tin Canyon—valley NV-8
Tin Canyon Gulch—valley OR-9
Tin Canyon Spring—spring OR-9
Tin Center Mine—mine SD-7
Tin Chance Mine—mine SD-7

**Tipperary**—*pop pl* IA-7
Tipperary Bench—*bench* WY-8
Tipperary Camp—*locale* WA-9
Tipperary Corner—*locale* ID-8
Tipperary Creek—*stream* CO-8
Tipperary Creek—*stream* MT-8
Tipperary Hill—*summit* KS-7
Tipperary Lake—*lake* CO-8
Tipperary Mine—*mine* AZ-5
Tipperary Mine—*mine* NV-8
Tipperary Point—*cape* WI-6
Tipperary Ranch—*locale* WY-8
Tipperary Tank—*reservoir* AZ-5
Tipperary Wash—*stream* AZ-5
Tipperary Well—*well* AZ-5
**Tipperton Place**—*pop pl* VA-3
**Tippery**—*pop pl* PA-2
Tippery Sch—*school* PA-2
Tippet Branch—*stream* NC-3
Tippet Cem—*cemetery* NC-3
Tippet Creek—*stream* NC-3
Tippet Place—*locale* MT-8
Tippets Mountain—*ridge* VA-3
Tippets Valley—*valley* UT-8
**Tippett**—*pop pl* MD-2
**Tippett**—*pop pl* NV-8
Tippett Branch—*stream* MO-7
Tippett Canyon—*valley* NV-8
Tippett Cem—*cemetery* IL-6
Tippett Gas Plant—*oilfield* TX-5
Tippett Hollow—*valley* IL-6
Tippett Lake—*flat* NV-8
Tippett Oil Field—*oilfield* TX-5
Tippett Pass—*gap* NV-8
Tippett Ranch—*locale* TX-5
**Tippetts**—*pop pl* GA-3
Tippetts Chapel—*church* NC-3
Tippetts Lake—*lake* WI-6
*Tippetts Millpond* NC-3
Tippett Springs—*spring* NV-8
Tippettville—*locale* GA-3
**Tippetville**—*pop pl* GA-3
*Tippex Ditch* IN-6
Tippey Ditch—*canal* IN-6
Tippie Branch—*stream* GA-3
Tippie Canoe—*locale* PA-2
Tippie Creek—*stream* KS-7
Tipping Point—*cape* AK-9
*Tipping Spring* AZ-5
Tippins Cem—*cemetery* GA-3
Tippins Eddy—*rapids* AL-4
Tippins Lake—*reservoir* GA-3
*Tippinville* KS-7
Tippipah Point—*summit* NV-8
Tippipah Spring—*spring* NV-8
Tippit Sch—*school* LA-4
Tippitt Cem—*cemetery* TN-4
Tippitt Pond—*lake* MD-2
Tippity Wichity Island—*island* MD-2
*Tipple* WV-2
Tipple—*locale* CO-8
Tipple Branch—*stream* KY-4
Tipplersville Baptist Ch—*church* MS-4
Tipplersville Cem—*cemetery* MS-4
Tipplersville Ch of Christ—*church* MS-4
**Tippletown**—*pop pl* PA-2
Tippling Rock—*summit* MA-1
**Tippo**—*pop pl* MS-4
Tippo Bayou—*gut* MS-4
Tippo Bayou—*stream* MS-4
Tippo Elem Sch (historical)—*school* MS-4
Tip Post Office (historical)—*building* TN-4
Tipps Cem—*cemetery* (2) TN-4
Tipps Creek—*stream* NE-7
Tipps Point—*cape* OK-5
*Tippy Backwater* MI-6
Tippy Dam Pond—*reservoir* MI-6
*Tippy Rsvr* MI-6
Tip Ray Lake Dam—*dam* MS-4
**Tiprell**—*pop pl* TN-4
Tiprell Sch (historical)—*school* TN-4
Tipsaw Lake—*reservoir* IN-6
Tipsico Lake—*lake* MI-6
Tipson Branch—*stream* TN-4
Tipsoo Butte—*summit* OR-9
Tipsoo Creek—*stream* (2) OR-9
Tipsoo Lake—*lake* WA-9
Tipsoo Peak—*summit* OR-9
Tipsoo Trail—*trail* (2) OR-9
Tips Park—*park* TX-5
Tipsy Branch—*stream* AR-4
Tipsy Cem—*cemetery* AR-4
Tip Tank—*reservoir* (2) AZ-5
Tiptoe Mtn—*summit* ME-1
Tiptoe Ridge—*ridge* CA-9
*Tipton* TN-4
Tipton—*fmr MCD* NE-7
Tipton—*locale* CA-9
Tipton—*locale* (2) IL-6
Tipton—*mine* UT-8
**Tipton**—*pop pl* IN-6
**Tipton**—*pop pl* IA-7
**Tipton**—*pop pl* KS-7
**Tipton**—*pop pl* MI-6
**Tipton**—*pop pl* MO-7
**Tipton**—*pop pl* OH-6
**Tipton**—*pop pl* OK-5
**Tipton**—*pop pl* PA-2
**Tipton**—*pop pl* (2) TN-4
**Tipton**—*pop pl* WV-2
**Tipton**—*pop pl* WY-8
Tipton, Mount—*summit* AZ-5
Tipton, Samuel J., House—*hist pl* KS-7
Tipton Airfield—*airport* KS-7
Tipton Bar—*bar* AL-4
Tipton Bayou—*stream* MS-4
Tipton Brake—*swamp* MS-4
*Tipton Branch* GA-3
Tipton Branch—*stream* KY-4
Tipton Branch—*stream* NC-3
Tipton Branch—*stream* TN-4
Tipton Canyon—*valley* AZ-5
Tipton Canyon—*valley* KS-7
Tipton Canyon—*valley* NE-7
Tipton Canyon—*valley* NV-8
Tipton Canyon—*valley* NM-5
Tipton Cave—*cave* TN-4
Tipton (CCD)—*cens area* CA-9
Tipton (CCD)—*cens area* OK-5
Tipton Cem—*cemetery* (2) AL-4
Tipton Cem—*cemetery* CA-9
Tipton Cem—*cemetery* IN-6
Tipton Cem—*cemetery* KY-4
Tipton Cem—*cemetery* OK-5
Tipton Cem—*cemetery* (4) TN-4
Tipton Ch—*church* TN-4
Tipton Chapel—*church* TX-5
Tipton Community Ch—*church* SD-7
Tipton Community Hall—*locale* OK-5
**Tipton County**—*pop pl* IN-6
**Tipton County**—*pop pl* TN-4
Tipton County Courthouse—*building* TN-4
Tipton County Courthouse—*hist pl* IN-6
Tipton County Jail and Sheriff's
Home—*hist pl* IN-6
Tipton County Public Library—*building* TN-4
Tipton Creek—*stream* ID-8
Tipton Creek—*stream* IN-6
Tipton Creek—*stream* IA-7
Tipton Creek—*stream* MT-8
Tipton Creek—*stream* NM-5
Tipton Creek—*stream* NC-3
Tipton Creek—*stream* TN-4
Tipton Dam—*dam* PA-2
Tipton Ditch—*canal* CO-8
Tipton Ditch—*canal* NM-5
Tipton Elem Sch—*school* IN-6
Tipton Elem Sch—*school* KS-7
*Tipton Ferry* TN-4
Tipton-Fillauer House—*hist pl* TN-4
Tipton Flat Campground—*locale* ID-8
Tipton Ford—*locale* MO-7
Tipton Gap—*gap* GA-3
Tipton Gap—*gap* NC-3
Tipton Grove Cem—*cemetery* IA-7
Tipton Grove (historical P.O.)—*locale* IA-7
Tipton-Haynes Cem—*cemetery* TN-4
Tipton-Haynes Farm—*locale* TN-4
Tipton-Haynes House—*hist pl* TN-4
**Tipton Hill**—*pop pl* NC-3
Tipton Hill—*ridge* CA-9
Tipton Hill Elem Sch—*school* NC-3
Tipton Hollow—*valley* (3) TN-4
Tipton HS—*school* AL-4
Tipton HS—*school* KS-7
*Tiptonia* IN-6
*Tipton JHS* AL-4
Tipton Knob—*summit* NC-3
Tipton Knob—*summit* OH-6
Tipton Memorial Gardens—*cemetery* TN-4
Tipton Mtn—*summit* GA-3
Tipton Norwegian Cem—*cemetery* IA-7
Tipton Oliver Place—*locale* TN-4
Tipton Orchard Hollow—*valley* TN-4
*Tipton Park* IN-6
Tipton Post Office—*building* TN-4
Tipton Prospect—*mine* (2) TN-4
Tipton Ranch—*locale* NV-8
Tipton Ranch—*locale* NM-5
Tipton Ridge—*ridge* KY-4
Tipton Ridge Sch—*hist pl* OK-5
Tipton Ridge Sch—*school* KY-4
Tipton Rsvr—*reservoir* PA-2
Tipton Run—*stream* PA-2
Tipton Saint Sch—*school* MS-4
Tipton Sch—*school* KY-4
Tipton Sch (historical)—*school* MO-7
Tipton Sch (historical)—*school* TN-4
*Tiptons Ferry* TN-4
Tiptons Forge (historical)—*locale* TN-4
Tipton (site)—*locale* OR-9
Tipton Spring—*spring* NM-5
Tipton Spring—*spring* OR-9
Tipton Spring—*spring* TN-4
Tipton Spring Branch—*stream* TN-4
Tiptons Sugar Cove—*valley* TN-4
Tiptons Sugar Cove Branch—*stream* TN-4
Tipton Station—*locale* TN-4
Tipton Station Ch—*church* TN-4
Tipton Township—*fmr MCD* IA-7
**Tipton (Township of)**—*pop pl* IN-6
**Tiptonville**—*pop pl* NM-5
**Tiptonville**—*pop pl* TN-4
Tiptonville (CCD)—*cens area* TN-4
Tiptonville Cem—*cemetery* NM-5
Tiptonville Chute—*gut* TN-4
Tiptonville City Hall—*building* TN-4
Tiptonville Division—*civil* TN-4
Tiptonville Ferry—*crossing* TN-4
Tiptonville First Baptist Ch—*church* TN-4
Tiptonville Post Office—*building* TN-4
Tiptonville Public Library—*building* TN-4
Tiptonville Towhead—*bar* TN-4
Tipton Well—*well* (2) NM-5
*Tiptop* TN-4
Tip Top—*locale* KY-4
Tip Top—*locale* MO-7
Tip Top—*locale* NY-2
Tiptop—*locale* TN-4
**Tiptop**—*pop pl* KY-4
**Tip Top**—*pop pl* (2) KY-4
**Tip Top**—*pop pl* (2) TN-4
**Tiptop**—*pop pl* VA-3
Tip Top—*summit* GA-3
Tip Top—*summit* PA-2
Tip Top—*summit* TN-4
Tip Top—*summit* UT-8
Tiptop—*summit* WA-9
Tiptop Canal—*canal* (2) LA-4
Tiptop Ch—*church* TN-4
Tip Top Gap—*gap* VA-3
Tiptop Hill—*summit* WA-9
Tip-Top House—*hist pl* NH-1
Tiptop Knob—*summit* IL-6
Tip Top Lake—*lake* ID-8
Tiptop Meadows—*flat* OR-9
Tip Top Mine—*mine* AZ-5
Tiptop Mine—*mine* AZ-5
Tip Top Mine—*mine* (3) CA-9
Tiptop Mine—*mine* CO-8
Tip Top Mine—*mine* CO-8
Tip Top Mine—*mine* (3) ID-8
Tiptop Mine—*mine* NV-8
Tip Top Mine—*mine* NV-8
Tip Top Mine—*mine* OR-9
Tiptop Mine—*mine* SD-7
Tip Top Mine—*mine* UT-8
Tiptop Mount Lillian Trail—*trail* WA-9
Tip Top Mtn—*summit* CA-9
Tip Top Mtn—*summit* MO-7
Tip Top Peak—*summit* CA-9
Tiptop Peak—*summit* CO-8
Tip Top Picnic Area—*locale* MO-7
Tiptop Playground—*park* PA-2
Tiptop Post Office (historical)—*building* TN-4
Tiptop Prospect—*summit* CA-9
Tip Top Ranch—*locale* CA-9
Tip Top Ridge—*ridge* (2) CA-9
Tip Top (RR name for Tiptop)—*other* VA-3
**Tiptop (RR name Tip Top)**—*pop pl* VA-3
Tip Top Sch—*school* MT-8
Tiptop Sch (abandoned)—*school* (2) MO-7
*Tip Top School* TN-4
Tip Top Spring—*spring* OR-9
Tip Top Spring—*spring* WY-8
Tip Top Station—*locale* KY-4
Tiptop Tank—*reservoir* AZ-5
Tip Top Tank—*reservoir* NM-5
Tiptop Trail—*trail* AZ-5
Tip Top Well—*well* NV-8
Tip Top Wells—*well* NM-5
Tipwen Deleur—*unknown* FM-9
Tipwen Dongalap—*unknown* FM-9
Tipwen Palapal—*bar* FM-9
Tipweson—*bar* FM-9
**Tira**—*pop pl* TX-5
Tiradores Windmill—*locale* (2) TX-5
Tirbircio Creek—*stream* CO-8
Tire Creek—*stream* OR-9
Tired Creek—*stream* GA-3
Tired Creek—*stream* WA-9
Tired Creek Ch—*church* (2) GA-3
Tired Horse Rsvr—*reservoir* OR-9
Tired Mtn—*summit* AK-9
Tired Pup Creek—*stream* AK-9
Tired Pup Glacier—*glacier* AK-9
Tired Wolf Creek—*stream* ID-8
**Tire Hill**—*pop pl* PA-2
Tire Junction—*locale* WA-9
Tire'm, Mount—*summit* ME-1
Tire Mountain Trail—*trail* OR-9
Tire Mtn—*summit* OR-9
Tire Tank—*reservoir* AZ-5
Tiretown—*uninc pl* NC-3
Tire Tube Cave—*cave* OR-9
*Tire Wash* AZ-5
Tirey Lake Dam—*dam* MS-4
**Tiro**—*pop pl* OH-6
Tirol—*locale* PA-2
Tiro Pit, El—*basin* AZ-5
Tiro Wash, El—*stream* AZ-5
Tirrell Mtn—*summit* NY-2
Tirrell Playground—*locale* MA-1
Tirrell Pond—*lake* NH-1
Tirrel Pond—*lake* NY-2
Tirrill Park—*park* IA-7
*Tiryah* SC-3
Tiry Sch—*school* SD-7
Tirza Ch—*church* KY-4
Tirzah—*locale* PA-2
**Tirzah**—*pop pl* SC-3
Tirzah Ch—*church* NC-3
Tirzah Ch—*church* SC-3
Tirzah Peak—*summit* WA-9
Tirzah Turf Airp—*airport* NC-3
Tisawee Lake—*lake* FL-3
*Tisbury, Town of* MA-1
Tisbury Great Pond—*lake* MA-1
Tisbury Sch—*school* MA-1
**Tisbury (Town of)**—*pop pl* MA-1
Tischel Bay—*bay* TN-4
Tischel Creek—*stream* TN-4
Tischer Creek—*stream* MN-6
*Tischigan* WI-6
Tisch Lake—*lake* MI-6
**Tisch Mills**—*pop pl* WI-6
Tisch Mills Creek—*stream* WI-6
*Tischner Phillips Condominium* UT-8
Tischudy Gulch—*valley* SD-7
Tiscornia Park—*park* MI-6
Tisdale—*locale* CA-9
Tisdale—*locale* KS-7
Tisdale—*locale* SC-3
Tisdale Brake—*swamp* LA-4
*Tisdale Branch* VA-3
Tisdale Branch—*stream* MS-4
Tisdale Brook—*stream* CT-1
Tisdale By-Pass—*canal* CA-9
Tisdale Cem—*cemetery* IL-6
Tisdale Cem—*cemetery* KS-7
Tisdale Cem—*cemetery* MA-1
Tisdale Cem—*cemetery* MS-4
Tisdale Cem—*cemetery* PA-2
Tisdale Creek—*stream* TN-4
Tisdale Creek—*stream* WY-8
Tisdale Ditch—*canal* WY-8
Tisdale Divide—*ridge* WY-8
Tisdale Ford—*locale* AR-4
Tisdale-Jones House—*hist pl* NC-3
Tisdale Lake—*reservoir* SD-7
Tisdale Lake Dam—*dam* MS-4
Tisdale Lake Dam—*dam* SD-7
Tisdale-Morse House—*hist pl* MA-1
Tisdale Mtn—*summit* WY-8
Tisdale Sch—*school* NJ-2
Tisdale Sch (historical)—*school* AL-4
*Tisdales Creek* MS-4
Tisdale Spring—*spring* NH-1
Tisdale Stock Rsvr—*reservoir* WY-8
Tisdale Swamp—*swamp* PA-2
**Tisdale Township**—*pop pl* KS-7
Tisdale Weir—*dam* CA-9
Tisdell Landing—*locale* MS-4
Tisdell Ranch—*locale* CO-8
Tisdell Spring—*spring* OK-5
Tisdels Place—*locale* CO-8
Tisdel Towhead—*island* IL-6
Tiseras Peak—*summit* CO-8
Tise Ridge—*ridge* OH-6
Tiser Spring—*spring* NV-8
Tishabee—*locale* AL-4
*Tishagan* WI-6
*Tishchigan* WI-6
*Tish Creek* OR-9
Tish Creek—*stream* OR-9
Tishdogatumina Lake—*lake* AK-9
Tishel Landing (historical)—*locale* TN-4
*Ti-Shena-Ze Creek* SD-7
Tishepi Spring—*spring* AZ-5
*Tisher Pond* FL-3
Tisher Ridge—*ridge* OH-6
*Tishigan* WI-6
Tishimna Lake—*lake* AK-9
Tishkill Creek—*stream* MS-4
Tishlarka Creek—*stream* AL-4
Tishler Pond—*lake* FL-3
*Tishner Pond* IN-6
**Tishomingo**—*pop pl* MS-4
**Tishomingo**—*pop pl* OK-5
Tishomingo, Lake—*reservoir* MO-7
Tishomingo Attendance Center—*school* MS-4
Tishomingo Baptist Ch—*church* MS-4
Tishomingo (CCD)—*cens area* OK-5
Tishomingo Cem—*cemetery* MS-4
Tishomingo Chapel—*church* MS-4
*Tishomingo Chapel Baptist Ch* MS-4
Tishomingo Ch of Christ—*church* MS-4
Tishomingo City Hall—*hist pl* OK-5
**Tishomingo County**—*pop pl* MS-4
Tishomingo County Airp—*airport* MS-4
Tishomingo County Courthouse—*building* MS-4
Tishomingo County Game Ref—*park* MS-4
Tishomingo County Hosp—*hospital* MS-4
*Tishomingo County Refuge* MS-4
Tishomingo Creek—*stream* MS-4
Tishomingo Natl Fish Hatchery—*locale* OK-5
Tishomingo Natl Wildlife Ref—*park* OK-5
Tishomingo Pentecostal Ch—*church* MS-4
Tishomingo State Park—*park* MS-4
Tishomingo State Park Lake Dam—*dam* MS-4
Tishomingo United Methodist Ch—*church* MS-4
Tishomingo Vocational Technical
Center—*school* MS-4
*Tish-shar-gan* WI-6
Tish Tang a Tang Creek—*stream* CA-9
Tish Tang a Tang Ridge—*ridge* CA-9
Tish Tang Campground—*locale* CA-9
Tish Tang Point—*cape* CA-9
Tishtony Creek—*stream* MS-4
Tisinger Sch—*school* TX-5
*Tisissas Pond* MA-1
Tiskeet Lake—*lake* AK-9
**Tiskilwa**—*pop pl* IL-6
T Island—*island* CA-9
Tislo Post Office (historical)—*building* SD-7
Tismyr Lake—*lake* SC-3
*Tisnasbas* AZ-5
*Tisnasbas Canyon* AZ-5
Tison—*locale* GA-3
Tison—*locale* IL-6
Tison Cem—*cemetery* GA-3
Tison Cem—*cemetery* LA-4
Tison Gulch—*valley* OR-9
Tisonia—*locale* FL-3
Tisonia Lookout Tower—*tower* FL-3
Tison Sch—*school* OR-9
Tison Trail—*trail* OR-9
Tispaquin Pond—*lake* MA-1
*Tisquaquin Pond* MA-1
Tissdell Brook—*stream* MA-1
Tissel Hollow—*valley* IA-7
**Tississa**—*pop pl* MA-1
Tississa Pond—*lake* MA-1
*Tistah Wash* AZ-5
*Tistah Wash* UT-8
Tisuk River—*stream* AK-9
*Tiswalds Creek* MS-4
*Tiswals Creek* MS-4
Tis Ya Toh Spring—*spring* AZ-5
*Titabawassee* MI-6
Titakoclos Waterfall—*falls* WA-9
Titaluk River—*stream* AK-9
Titaluk Test Well—*well* AK-9
Titan Gulch—*valley* MT-8
Titanic—*locale* OK-5
Titanic Creek—*stream* OR-9
Titanium Mine And Plant—*other* NY-2
Titanium Reach—*channel* NJ-2
Titan Mine—*mine* WY-8
Titanothere Canyon—*valley* CA-9
Titan Post Office (historical)—*building* TN-4
**Titan Siding**—*pop pl* KY-4
Titans Piazza—*cliff* MA-1
Titantic Ditch—*canal* CO-8
Titan Tower—*summit* UT-8
Titan Trail—*trail* AK-9
Titchenal Canyon—*valley* WA-9
Titcliff Island—*island* AK-9
Titcomb Basin Trail—*trail* WY-8
Titcomb Brook—*stream* ME-1
Titcomb Flat—*flat* CA-9
Titcomb Gulch—*valley* CA-9
Titcomb Hill—*summit* ME-1
Titcomb Hill—*summit* MA-1
Titcomb Hill—*summit* NH-1
Titcomb Lakes—*lake* WY-8
Titcomb Pond—*lake* ME-1
Tithe Creek—*stream* AK-9
Tithelo Lake—*reservoir* MS-4
Tithelo Lake Dam—*dam* MS-4
Tither—*cape* FM-9
*Tithethay* FM-9
*Tithiir* FM-9
Tithing Mtn—*summit* UT-8
*Tithir* FM-9
Tithumiji Point—*cliff* AZ-5
Titi Artesian Well—*well* TX-5
Titi Branch—*gut* FL-3
TiTi Branch—*gut* FL-3
Titi Branch—*stream* AL-4
Titi Branch—*stream* FL-3
TiTi Branch—*stream* FL-3
Titi Branch—*stream* GA-3
Titicaca, Lake—*lake* WA-9
Titicaca Creek—*stream* WA-9
Titicaed Creek—*stream* WA-9
Titicaed Lake—*lake* WA-9
*Titi Creek* AL-4
Titi Creek—*stream* FL-3
Titicus—*locale* CT-1
Titicus Mtn—*summit* CT-1
Titicus Mtn—*summit* NY-2
Titicus River—*stream* CT-1
Titicus River—*stream* NY-2
Titicus Rsvr—*reservoir* NY-2
Titicut—*locale* MA-1
Titicut Station (historical)—*locale* MA-1
Titicut Swamp—*swamp* MA-1
*Titicut Village* MA-1
*Titiquit River* MA-1
Titi Swamp—*swamp* (2) AL-4
Titi Swamp—*swamp* FL-3
Title and Trust Bldg—*hist pl* AZ-5
Title Guarantee and Trust Company
Bldg—*hist pl* CA-9
Titler Cem—*cemetery* IA-7
**Titley**—*pop pl* TX-5
Titley Creek—*stream* ID-8
*Titloe Lake* MN-6
**Titlow**—*pop pl* WA-9
Titlow Beach Park—*park* WA-9
*Titlow Creek* VA-3
Titlow Creek—*stream* VA-3
Titlow Hill—*summit* CA-9
Titlow Lagoon—*lake* WA-9
Titlow Lake—*lake* MN-6
**Titlows Corner**—*pop pl* PA-2
Titlum-Tatlum Bayou—*channel* TX-5
*Titlum-Tatlum Island* TX-5
*Titmore Bend* AL-4
Titmouse Branch—*stream* TN-4
Titmouse Creek—*stream* MI-6
Titmouse Creek—*stream* NJ-2
Titmouse Gulch—*valley* CA-9
Titna River—*stream* AK-9
Titnuk Creek—*stream* AK-9
Tito—*locale* VA-3
**Tito**—*pop pl* AL-4
**Titonka**—*pop pl* IA-7
*Titon River* SD-7
Titon Sch—*school* IL-6
Tito Tank—*reservoir* NM-5
Titrud Round Barn—*hist pl* MN-6
Titsworth, Lake—*lake* TX-5
Titsworth Ditch—*canal* CO-8
Titsworth Gap—*gap* WY-8
Titsworth Spring—*spring* WY-8
Titsworth (Township of)—*fmr MCD* AR-4
Tittabawassee River—*stream* MI-6
Tittabawassee River State For—*forest* MI-6
Tittabawassee (Township of)—*civ div* MI-6
*Tittabawassink* MI-6
*Tittibawassee* MI-6
Tittie Butte—*summit* OR-9
Tittle Branch—*stream* AL-4
Tittle Bridge—*bridge* OK-5
Tittle Cabin—*locale* CO-8
Tittle Cem—*cemetery* AL-4
Tittle Cem—*cemetery* OH-6
Tittle Cem—*cemetery* TN-4
Tittle Cove—*valley* TN-4
*Tittle Creek* AL-4
Tittle Creek—*stream* OK-5
Tittle Lake—*lake* MN-6
Tittle Mtn—*summit* AL-4
Tittle Rsvr—*reservoir* CO-8
Tittmann, Mount—*summit* AK-9
Tittmann Glacier—*glacier* AK-9
*Tittoin* MP-9
Titt Run—*stream* WV-2
Tittsworth Cem—*cemetery* KY-4
Tittsworth Cem—*cemetery* TN-4
**Titu**—*pop pl* IA-7
Titus—*locale* CA-9
Titus—*locale* GA-3
Titus—*locale* IL-6
Titus—*locale* MI-6
Titus—*locale* TN-4
**Titus**—*pop pl* AL-4
**Titus**—*pop pl* IN-6
**Titus**—*pop pl* IA-7
Titus, Frank, House—*hist pl* AZ-5
Titus, Lake—*lake* NY-2
Titus, Willet, House—*hist pl* NY-2
Titus Bog—*swamp* PA-2
Titus Bridge—*bridge* VA-3
Titus Brook—*stream* CT-1
Titus Brook—*stream* NH-1
Titus-Bunce House—*hist pl* NY-2
Titus Canyon—*valley* CA-9
Titus Canyon—*valley* NV-8
Titus Canyon—*valley* UT-8
Titus (CCD)—*cens area* AL-4
Titus Cem—*cemetery* (3) OH-6
Titus Ch—*church* AL-4
**Titus (County)**—*pop pl* TX-5
Titus Creek—*stream* AK-9
Titus Creek—*stream* CA-9
Titus Creek—*stream* ID-8
Titus Creek—*stream* MO-7
Titus Creek—*stream* MT-8
Titus Creek—*stream* TN-4
Titus Creek—*stream* (2) VA-3
Titus Creek—*stream* WA-9
Titus Ditch—*canal* IN-6
Titus Division—*civil* AL-4
Titus Gap—*gap* CA-9
Titus Hill—*summit* (2) NY-2
Titus Hill Cem—*cemetery* NY-2
Titus (historical)—*locale* AZ-5
Titus Hollow—*valley* AR-4
Titus Island—*island* AK-9
Titus Lake—*lake* ID-8
Titus Lake—*lake* MI-6
Titus Lake—*lake* NY-2
Titus Lakes—*lake* AK-9
Titus Lateral—*canal* CA-9
Titus Millpond—*lake* NY-2
Titus Mtn—*summit* AK-9
Titus Mtn—*summit* CT-1
Titus Paul Hill—*summit* AK-9
Titus Pond—*reservoir* OR-9
Titus Ranch—*locale* CO-8
Titus Ranch—*locale* UT-8
Titus Ridge—*ridge* (2) CA-9
Titus Ridge Trail—*trail* CA-9
Titus Run—*stream* NY-2
Titus Run—*stream* WV-2
Titus Sch—*school* (2) IL-6
Titus Sch—*school* MI-6
Titus Sch—*school* SD-7
Titus Sch—*school* TX-5
Titus Sch—*school* VA-3
**Titustown**—*pop pl* VA-3
Titustown Sch—*school* VA-3
*Titusville* NY-2
**Titusville**—*pop pl* FL-3
**Titusville**—*pop pl* NJ-2
**Titusville**—*pop pl* NY-2
**Titusville**—*pop pl* PA-2
Titusville Airp—*airport* PA-2
Titusville Astronaut HS—*school* FL-3
Titusville Beach—*beach* FL-3
**Titusville Beach**—*pop pl* FL-3
Titusville (CCD)—*cens area* FL-3
Titusville City—*civil* PA-2
Titusville City Hall—*hist pl* PA-2
Titusville Country Club—*other* PA-2
Titusville Gulch—*valley* CO-8
Titusville Hist Dist—*hist pl* NJ-2
Titusville Hist Dist—*hist pl* PA-2
Titusville (historical P.O.)—*locale* IN-6
Titusville HS—*school* FL-3
Titusville JHS—*school* PA-2
Titusville Mine—*mine* CO-8
Titusville Mtn—*summit* NY-2
Titusville Senior HS—*school* PA-2
Tiurpa Island—*island* AK-9
Tiva Canyon—*valley* NV-8
Tivali—*locale* IA-7
Ti Valley—*valley* OK-5
Tivate Canyon—*valley* OR-9
Tivehvun Lake—*lake* AK-9
*Tivelaugh Run* PA-2
*Tivepaugh Run* PA-2
*Tiverton* OH-6
**Tiverton**—*pop pl* OH-6
**Tiverton**—*pop pl* RI-1
Tiverton Airp—*airport* RI-1
Tiverton Cem—*cemetery* OH-6
**Tiverton Center**—*pop pl* OH-6
Tiverton Ch—*church* OH-6
Tiverton Ch—*church* SC-3
**Tiverton Four Corners**—*pop pl* RI-1
Tiverton Four Corners—*summit* RI-1
Tiverton Four Corners Hist Dist—*hist pl* RI-1
**Tiverton (Town of)**—*pop pl* RI-1
**Tiverton (Township of)**—*pop pl* OH-6
*Tivetaugh Run* PA-2
**Tivett**—*pop pl* TX-5
Tivis—*locale* VA-3
Tivis Branch—*stream* VA-3
Tivis Flynn Hollow—*valley* AR-4
Tivis Hollow—*valley* KY-4
Tivis Sch—*school* VA-3
*Tivola* GA-3
Tivoli—*hist pl* MD-2
Tivoli—*locale* PA-2
**Tivoli**—*pop pl* NY-2
**Tivoli**—*pop pl* TX-5
Tivoli Brewery Company—*hist pl* CO-8
Tivoli Cem—*cemetery* MN-6
Tivoli Island—*island* WA-9
Tivoli Lake—*lake* FL-3
Tivoli Lake—*lake* NY-2
*Tivoli Pond* NY-2
Tivoli River—*stream* GA-3
Tivoli School—*locale* IA-7
Tivoli Theater—*hist pl* DC-2
Tivoli Theater—*hist pl* TN-4
Tivyagak Creek—*stream* AK-9
Tivydale—*locale* TX-5
Tivy HS—*school* TX-5
Tivy Mountain Cem—*cemetery* TX-5
Tivy Mtn—*summit* CA-9
Tivy Mtn—*summit* TX-5
Tivy Valley—*flat* CA-9
**Tivy Valley**—*pop pl* CA-9
*Tiwashy Creek* AL-4
Tiyaktalik Mtn—*summit* AK-9
Tiyo Point—*cliff* AZ-5
Tiyo Point Trail—*trail* AZ-5
*Tizer Creek* MT-8
Tizer Lakes—*lake* MT-8
Tizer Ranger Station—*locale* MT-8
Tizzard Island—*island* MD-2
Tizzle Branch—*stream* VA-3
Tizzle Flats—*flat* VA-3
Tjan island—*island* MP-9
T J Barrier Lake Dam—*dam* MS-4
*Tjeavolitak* AZ-5
T Jennings Dam—*dam* SD-7
T J F Draw—*valley* TX-5
*Tjiuvak* AZ-5
T J Lake—*lake* CA-9
*Tjool* FM-9
Tjossem Ditch—*canal* WA-9
Tjossem Pond—*lake* WA-9
T J Ruins—*locale* NM-5
T J Spring—*spring* OR-9
T J Stewart Lake—*reservoir* AL-4
TJ Tank—*reservoir* (2) NM-5
*Tjuitjo* AZ-5
*Tjukutko* AZ-5
T Junction Cave—*cave* TN-4
*Tjuulik* AZ-5
T J Wilson Lake—*reservoir* NC-3
T J Windmill—*locale* TX-5
TJW Rsvr—*reservoir* OR-9
T K Armstrong Catfish Ponds Dam—*dam* MS-4
T K Bar Ranch—*locale* AZ-5
TK Cem—*cemetery* TX-5
T Kellogg Ranch—*locale* ND-7
Tketau, Bkul A—*bar* PW-9
*T'kope* WA-9
*T'kopt* WA-9
TK Tank—*reservoir* AZ-5
T K Tank—*reservoir* AZ-5
Tlacuache Windmill—*locale* TX-5
*T Lake* MI-6
*T Lake* MN-6
T Lake—*lake* (2) AK-9
T Lake—*lake* AR-4
T Lake—*lake* (2) IN-6
T Lake—*lake* MI-6
T Lake—*lake* MN-6
T Lake—*lake* NY-2
T Lake—*lake* WA-9
T Lake—*lake* WI-6
T Lake—*lake* WY-8
T Lake Falls—*falls* NY-2
T Lake Mtn—*summit* NY-2
T'lam Cem—*cemetery* IA-7
T Latham Ranch—*locale* NM-5
Tlatl Hills—*other* AK-9
Tlatskokat Slough—*stream* AK-9
T Lazy S Farm—*locale* NV-8
T L Cow Camp—*locale* WY-8
T L Creek—*stream* MT-8
TL Creek—*stream* WY-8

Tlechegn Lake—*lake* AK-9
Tlevak Narrows—*channel* AK-9
Tlevak Strait—*channel* AK-9
T L Faulkner Trade Sch—*school* AL-4
T L Gap—*gap* MT-8
T L Harris Lake Dam—*dam* MS-4
*Tliglig* FM-9
Tlikakila River—*stream* AK-9
Tlingit Peak—*summit* AK-9
Tlingit Point—*cape* AK-9
Tlocogn Lake—*lake* AK-9
Tloi Eechii Cliffs—*cliff* AZ-5
T Louis Bayou—*stream* MO-7
Tlozhavun Lake—*lake* AK-9
T L Ranch—*locale* WY-8
T L Spring—*spring* ID-8
Tluna Icefall—*falls* AK-9
Tlutkaraguis—*island* PW-9
*Tlutkarnguis* PW-9
*T L Weston Junior High School* MS-4
T Mahaffey Dam—*dam* SD-7
*Tmasch* PW-9
T Mason Dam—*dam* SD-7
T-M Draw—*valley* SD-7
Tmederial, Bkul A—*bar* PW-9
Tmetoi—*cape* PW-9
*Tmier* MP-9
*Tmier Island* MP-9
Tmiet Island—*island* MP-9
TM Mine—*mine* CO-8
T M Moore Pond Dam—*dam* MS-4
Tmong—*bend* PW-9
*T M Rogers HS* AL-4
Tngabard—*island* PW-9
Tngebard—*channel* PW-9
**Tngeronger**—*pop pl* PW-9
Tngerulachang—*bar* PW-9
TNT Creek—*stream* OR-9
TNT Gulch—*valley* OR-9
T N T Mine—*mine* CA-9
TNT No 1 Mine—*mine* CO-8
TNT No 2 Mine—*mine* CO-8
TNT No 3 Mine—*mine* CO-8
T N Ward Airp—*airport* PA-2
T N Y Spring—*spring* CO-8
*To* PW-9
To—*island* FM-9
**Toa**—*pop pl* GU-9
**Toa Alta**—*pop pl* PR-3
Toa Alta (Municipio)—*civil* PR-3
Toa Alta (Pueblo)—*fmr MCD* PR-3
**Toa Baja**—*pop pl* PR-3
Toa Baja (Municipio)—*civil* PR-3
Toa Baja (Pueblo)—*fmr MCD* PR-3
Toa Cove—*bay* AS-9
Toad, The—*summit* UT-8
*Toad Coulee Creek* WA-9
Toad Creek—*stream* AR-4
Toad Creek—*stream* (2) MI-6
Toad Creek—*stream* MT-8
Toad Creek—*stream* NJ-2
Toad Creek—*stream* OR-9
Toad Creek—*stream* PA-2
Toad Creek—*stream* (2) WI-6
**Toad Harbor**—*pop pl* NY-2
Toad Harbor Swamp—*swamp* NY-2
Toad Head—*summit* UT-8
Toad Hole—*bay* NY-2
Toad Hollow—*valley* CT-1
Toad Hollow—*valley* KS-7
Toad Hollow—*valley* MO-7
Toad Hollow—*valley* (2) NY-2
Toad Hollow—*valley* (3) OH-6
Toad Hollow—*valley* (3) PA-2
Toad Hollow—*valley* TN-4
Toad Hollow Camp—*locale* NY-2
**Toad Hop**—*pop pl* IN-6
*Toadinda-aska Mesa* AZ-5
Toadindaaska Mesa—*summit* AZ-5
Toad Island—*island* PA-2
*Toad Lake* OR-9
Toad Lake—*lake* (2) CA-9
Toad Lake—*lake* MI-6
Toad Lake—*lake* MN-6
Toad Lake—*lake* MT-8
Toad Lake—*lake* OR-9
Toad Lake—*lake* WA-9
**Toad Lake**—*pop pl* MN-6
**Toad Lake (Township of)**—*pop pl* MN-6
**Toadlena**—*pop pl* NM-5
Toadlena Lake—*lake* NM-5
Toad Mine—*mine* CA-9
Toad Mtn—*summit* CA-9
Toad Mtn—*summit* MN-6
Toad Point—*cliff* UT-8
Toad Point Sch—*school* NY-2
Toad Pond—*lake* (2) NY-2
Toad Pond—*lake* (2) VT-1
Toad River—*stream* MN-6
Toad Rock—*pillar* ID-8
Toad Run—*stream* VA-3
*Toads Coula creek* WA-9
Toadstool Park—*park* NE-7
*Toadstools* UT-8
Toadstools, The—*other* AK-9
Toadstool Waterhole—*spring* TX-5
Toad Suck—*locale* AR-4
Toad Suck Ferry—*locale* AR-4
Toad Tank—*reservoir* AZ-5
Toadtown—*locale* CA-9
Toad Valley Sch (historical)—*school* MO-7
**Toadvine**—*pop pl* AL-4
Toadvine Branch—*stream* KY-4
Toadvine Cem—*cemetery* AL-4
Toadvine Ch—*church* AL-4
*Toad Vines* AL-4
Toad Well—*well* CA-9
Toady Hollow—*valley* MO-7
Toaga—*locale* AS-9
*Toagel Geikadlukes* PW-9
*Toagel Liou* PW-9
*Toagel Mid* PW-9
*Toagel Mlungui* PW-9
*Toagel Mlungui Channel* PW-9
*Toagel Mlungui Einlass* PW-9
*Toagel Mlungui Passage* PW-9
*Toagel Ngel* PW-9
*Toagel Pelau* PW-9
*Toagel Sar* PW-9
*Toagil Mid Passage* PW-9
*Toaje* MP-9
*Toakl Denges* PW-9
*Toakl Pelau* PW-9
*Toal* FM-9
Toan—*bar* FM-9
*Toana Range* NV-8
Toandos Peninsula—*cape* WA-9
**Toano**—*pop pl* VA-3
*Toano Crossing* ID-8
Toano Draw—*valley* NV-8
*Toano Mountains* NV-8
Toano Range—*range* NV-8
Toano (Site)—*locale* NV-8
Toano Well Number One—*well* NV-8
Toano Well Number Two—*well* NV-8
*Toapit* AZ-5
Toa Point—*cape* AS-9
Toa Ridge—*ridge* AS-9
Toasa Rock—*island* AS-9
Toas Island—*island* FM-9
Toasperns Pond—*lake* NY-2
**Toast**—*pop pl* NC-3
Toast Brook—*stream* IN-6
Toast Camp—*locale* OR-9
Toatai Rock—*island* AS-9
*To atin da haska* AZ-5
*To atin da haska Mesa* AZ-5
*Toatipk* AZ-5
Toats Campground—*locale* UT-8
*Toats Coula Creek* WA-9
*Toats Coulee* WA-9
*Toats Coulee Creek* WA-9
Toats Coulee Creek—*stream* WA-9
Toats Spring—*spring* UT-8
Toauta Rock—*island* AS-9
Toawlevic Point—*cape* AK-9
Toaz JHS—*school* NY-2
Tobacco—*locale* MT-8
Tobacco—*other* KY-4
Tobacco, Bayou—*gut* LA-4
Tobacco Barn Field—*gap* NC-3
Tobacco Barn Hollow—*valley* OH-6
Tobacco Bed Pond—*lake* FL-3
Tobacco Bottom—*flat* SD-7
Tobacco Bowl—*park* TN-4
Tobacco Branch—*stream* KY-4
Tobacco Branch—*stream* NC-3
Tobacco Can Creek—*stream* ID-8
*Tobacco Creek* MI-6
*Tobacco Creek* ND-7
*Tobacco Creek* VA-3
Tobacco Creek—*stream* (2) CA-9
Tobacco Creek—*stream* NE-7
Tobacco Creek—*stream* SD-7
Tobacco Creek—*stream* TX-5
Tobacco Flat—*flat* CA-9
*Tobacco Flats* CA-9
Tobacco Garden Bay—*bay* ND-7
Tobacco Garden Creek—*stream* (2) ND-7
Tobacco Garden Creek Rec Area—*park* ND-7
Tobacco Garden Creek State Game Mngmt Area—*park* ND-7
Tobacco Garden (historical)—*locale* ND-7
Tobacco House Hollow—*valley* VA-3
Tobacco House Pond—*lake* FL-3
Tobacco House Ridge Trail—*trail* VA-3
Tobacco Island—*island* NE-7
Tobacco Island—*island* VA-3
Tobacco Juice Creek—*stream* MS-4
Tobacco Knob—*summit* VA-3
Tobacco Lake—*lake* CA-9
Tobacco Lake—*lake* CO-8
Tobacco Lake—*lake* MN-6
Tobacco Landing—*locale* IN-6
Tobacco Leaf Lake—*reservoir* KY-4
Tobaccolot Bay—*bay* NY-2
Tobaccolot Pond—*lake* NY-2
Tobacco Meadow—*flat* ID-8
Tobacco Patch Hollow—*valley* TN-4
Tobacco Patch Landing—*locale* FL-3
Tobacco Patch Mtn—*summit* PA-2
Tobacco Plains—*flat* MT-8
Tobaccoport—*locale* TN-4
Tobaccoport Ferry (historical)—*locale* TN-4
*Tobacco Port Post Office* TN-4
Tobaccoport Post Office (historical)—*building* TN-4
Tobaccoport Public Use Area—*park* TN-4
Tobaccoport Saltpeter Cave—*cave* TN-4
Tobacco Pouch Branch—*stream* GA-3
Tobacco Realty Company—*hist pl* KY-4
Tobacco River—*stream* (2) MI-6
Tobacco River—*stream* MT-8
Tobacco Root Mtns—*range* MT-8
Tobacco Row Mtn—*summit* VA-3
Tobacco Run—*stream* MD-2
*Tobacco Stick* MD-2
Tobacco Tank—*reservoir* TX-5
**Tobacco (Township of)**—*pop pl* MI-6
Tobacco Valley—*valley* MT-8
Tobaccoville—*locale* VA-3
**Tobaccoville**—*pop pl* NC-3
Tobac Oil Field—*other* NM-5
*Tobagnding River* PW-9
*Tobago Bay* VA-3
*Tobanao Canyon* CA-9
*Toban Bench* UT-8
*Tobanca Canyon* CA-9
Tobannee Creek—*stream* GA-3
Tobar—*locale* NV-8
T O Bar Ranch—*locale* MT-8
Tobar Terrace—*bench* AZ-5
**Tobasco**—*pop pl* OH-6
Tobasco Creek—*stream* WA-9
*Tobas Ridge* MS-4
Tobatokh Creek—*stream* AK-9
Tobay Beach—*beach* NY-2
Tobay Beach Bird And Game Sanctuary—*park* NY-2
Tobay Beach Park—*park* NY-2
Tobay Heading—*bay* NY-2
*Tobbs Creek* NC-3
Tobe—*locale* CO-8
Tobe, Mount—*summit* CT-1
*Tobe Arroyo* CO-8
Tobe Branch—*stream* AR-4
Tobe Branch—*stream* TX-5
Tobe Canyon—*valley* CO-8
Tobeco Creek—*stream* MI-6
Tobe Creek—*stream* CO-8
Tobe Creek—*stream* OR-9
Tobe Creek—*stream* TN-4
Tobe Gap—*gap* TX-5
Tobe Hahn—*uninc pl* TX-5
Tobehanna Creek—*stream* NY-2
Tobe Hollow—*valley* PA-2
Tobe Lake—*lake* AR-4
Tobe Lake—*lake* (2) FL-3
Tobe Lake—*lake* GA-3
Tobe Lake—*lake* MS-4
**Tobemory**—*pop pl* NC-3
Tobenayoli Pond—*lake* AZ-5
Toben Valley Sch (abandoned)—*school* MO-7
Tober Cave—*cave* AR-4
Tober Hollow—*valley* AR-4
Toberman, C. E., Estate—*hist pl* CA-9
**Tobermory**—*pop pl* NC-3
Toberts (historical)—*locale* MS-4
Tobe Run—*stream* PA-2
Tobes Creek—*stream* TN-4
Tobes Hill—*summit* NY-2
Tobesofkee, Lake—*reservoir* GA-3
Tobesofkee Creek—*stream* GA-3
Tobe Spring—*spring* (2) NV-8
Tobe Spring—*spring* (2) TX-5
Tobes Run—*stream* WV-2
Tobey Brook—*stream* (2) ME-1
Tobey Brook—*stream* VT-1
Tobey Cem—*cemetery* IL-6
Tobey Cem—*cemetery* MA-1
Tobey Cem—*cemetery* MI-6
Tobey Cem—*cemetery* TX-5
Tobey Hollow—*valley* TN-4
Tobey Homestead—*hist pl* MA-1
*Tobey Island* MA-1
Tobey - Jones Reservoir Dam—*dam* MA-1
Tobey - Jones Rsvr—*reservoir* MA-1
Tobey Lake—*lake* MI-6
Tobey Neck—*summit* RI-1
Tobey Pond—*lake* ME-1
Tobey Pond—*reservoir* CT-1
Tobey Pond Brook—*stream* CT-1
Tobey Ponds—*lake* ME-1
Tobey Sch—*school* MI-6
**Tobeys Corner**—*pop pl* ME-1
**Tobeys Island**—*pop pl* MA-1
Tob Hammock—*island* GA-3
Tob Hill—*summit* MA-1
Tobian Ch—*church* MS-4
Tobias—*locale* OH-6
**Tobias**—*pop pl* NE-7
**Tobias**—*pop pl* OR-9
Tobias, Mount—*summit* NY-2
Tobias Cem—*cemetery* MS-4
Tobias Cem—*cemetery* NE-7
Tobias Creek—*stream* CA-9
Tobias Creek—*stream* ID-8
Tobias Creek Trail—*trail* CA-9
*Tobias Ledge* MA-1
Tobias Ledge—*rock* MA-1
Tobias Meadow—*flat* CA-9
Tobias Northwest Oil Field—*oilfield* KS-7
Tobias Oil Field—*oilfield* KS-7
Tobiason, Lake—*lake* ND-7
Tobias Peak—*summit* CA-9
Tobias Pond—*lake* ME-1
*Tobias Rock* MA-1
Tobias Sch (historical)—*school* MS-4
Tobiassen Draw—*valley* NE-7
Tobias Spring—*spring* NM-5
Tobias-Thompson Complex—*hist pl* KS-7
Tobias Trail—*trail* CA-9
Tobias Windmill—*locale* NM-5
**Tobico Beach**—*pop pl* MI-6
*Tobico Lagoon* MI-6
Tobico Lagoon—*lake* MI-6
Tobico Marsh—*swamp* MI-6
Tobico Marsh State Game Area—*park* MI-6
Tobi (County-equivalent)—*civil* PW-9
Tobie Creek—*stream* MT-8
Tobikle—*locale* MP-9
To-bil-hask-idi Wash—*stream* NM-5
Tobin—*locale* CA-9
Tobin—*locale* CO-8
Tobin—*locale* MT-8
**Tobin**—*pop pl* AR-4
**Tobin**—*pop pl* TX-5
**Tobin**—*pop pl* WI-6
Tobin, Mount—*summit* NV-8
Tobin Bench—*bench* UT-8
Tobin Brook—*stream* ME-1
Tobin Cabin—*locale* OR-9
Tobin Cem—*cemetery* MO-7
Tobin Creek—*stream* AK-9
Tobin Creek—*stream* CO-8
Tobin Creek—*stream* MI-6
Tobin Creek—*stream* MO-7
Tobin Creek—*stream* MT-8
Tobin Creek Dam—*reservoir* CO-8
Tobin Creek Well—*well* CO-8
Tobin Ditch—*canal* IN-6
Tobin Ditch—*canal* OR-9
Tobin Draw—*valley* SD-7
Tobin Harbor—*bay* MI-6
Tobin Harbor Trail—*trail* MI-6
*Tobin Lake* MI-6
Tobin Lake—*lake* MI-6
**Tobin Location**—*pop pl* MI-6
Tobin Mtn—*summit* AK-9
Tobin Park—*park* TX-5
Tobin Pass—*gap* AK-9
Tobin Ranch—*locale* TX-5
Tobin Range—*range* NV-8
Tobin Reef—*bar* MI-6
Tobin Ridge—*ridge* CA-9
*Tobin Road* WI-6
Tobin-Rock Harbor Campground—*locale* MI-6
Tobin Rsvr—*reservoir* MT-8
Tobin Sch—*school* IL-6
Tobin Sch—*school* PA-2
Tobins Gulch—*valley* MT-8
*Tobins Harbor* MI-6
**Tobins Harbor**—*pop pl* MI-6
Tobin Snyder Drain—*canal* MI-6
*Tobins Port* IN-6
**Tobinsport**—*pop pl* IN-6
Tobin Spring—*spring* OR-9
Tobin Township—*civil* MO-7
**Tobin Township**—*pop pl* SD-7
**Tobin (Township of)**—*pop pl* IN-6
Tobin Wash—*valley* UT-8
Tobin Well—*well* NV-8
Tobique—*locale* MN-6
Tobique Lake—*lake* MN-6
Tobit Creek—*stream* AK-9
*Tobi Tubby Creek* MS-4
*Tobler Creek* GA-3
*Tobler Creek* SC-3
Tobler Creek—*stream* (3) GA-3
Tobler Creek—*stream* SC-3
*Tobler's Creek* GA-3
Toblers Creek—*stream* GA-3
Tobogan Canyon—*valley* NM-5
Toboggan Creek—*stream* (2) ID-8
Toboggan Creek—*stream* (2) MT-8
Toboggan Creek—*stream* WA-9
Toboggan Glacier—*glacier* AK-9
Toboggan Hill—*summit* ID-8
Toboggan Lake—*lake* WY-8
Toboggan Lakes—*lake* WY-8
Toboggan Ridge—*ridge* ID-8
Tobolton Creek—*stream* WA-9
Tobona (Ruins)—*locale* AK-9
Toborg Oil Field—*oilfield* TX-5
Tobosa Flats—*flat* NM-5
*Tobosco* OH-6
**Toboso**—*pop pl* (2) OH-6
Toboso Flats—*flat* NM-5
**Toboyne (Township of)**—*pop pl* PA-2
Tobuk Creek—*stream* AK-9
*Tobwaal* MP-9
Toby—*locale* PA-2
**Toby**—*pop pl* PA-2
Toby, Mount—*summit* MA-1
Toby Branch—*stream* TN-4
Toby Canyon—*valley* CO-8
Toby Cem—*cemetery* TX-5
*Toby Creek* PA-2
Toby Creek—*stream* AK-9
Toby Creek—*stream* NC-3
Toby Creek—*stream* OH-6
Toby Creek—*stream* (2) PA-2
Toby Creek—*stream* (2) SC-3
Toby Creek—*stream* WI-6
Toby Farms—*uninc pl* PA-2
Toby Farms Sch—*school* PA-2
*Tobyhanna* NY-2
**Tobyhanna**—*pop pl* PA-2
Tobyhanna Army Depot—*military* PA-2
Tobyhanna Army Depot Airp—*airport* PA-2
Tobyhanna Creek—*stream* PA-2
*Tobyhanna Dam* PA-2
Tobyhanna Falls—*falls* PA-2
Tobyhanna Lake—*lake* PA-2
Tobyhanna Number Two Dam—*dam* PA-2
Tobyhanna State Park—*park* PA-2
*Tobyhanna Storage and Supply Company Dam Number 2* PA-2
**Tobyhanna (Township of)**—*pop pl* PA-2
Toby Hill—*summit* CT-1
Toby Hill—*summit* MA-1
Toby Hill—*summit* NH-1
Toby Hollow—*valley* MA-1
Toby Hollow—*valley* MO-7
Toby Hollow—*valley* TX-5
Toby Island Bay—*bay* VA-3
Toby Islands—*island* VA-3
Toby Knob—*summit* VA-3
Toby Lake—*lake* (2) MI-6
Toby Mine—*mine* PA-2
*Toby Mines* PA-2
Toby Mines—*other* PA-2
Tobyne Hill—*summit* KS-7
Toby Park—*park* TN-4
Toby Point—*cape* RI-1
*Toby Pond* CT-1
Toby Pond—*lake* ME-1
Toby Run—*stream* OH-6
Toby Run—*stream* PA-2
Tobys Bluff—*locale* SC-3
Tobys Bluff Ch—*church* SC-3
Tobys Cabin—*locale* AK-9
*Tobys Hill* MA-1
Tobys Island—*island* MA-1
*Tobys Mountain* MA-1
*Tobys Point* RI-1
Tobys Point—*cape* VA-3
Toby Spring—*spring* MO-7
Toby Spring—*spring* WI-6
Toby Springs Sch (abandoned)—*school* PA-2
Tobys Rock Mtn—*summit* CT-1
Toby Stone Branch—*stream* TN-4
**Tobytown**—*pop pl* MD-2
**Toby (Township of)**—*pop pl* PA-2
Toby Tubby Cem—*cemetery* MS-4
Toby Tubby Ch—*church* MS-4
Toby Tubby Creek—*stream* MS-4
Toby Tubby Ferry (historical)—*locale* MS-4
Toby Tubby Sch (historical)—*school* MS-4
**Toca**—*pop pl* LA-4
To Cai—*spring* AZ-5
Tocaland—*hist pl* SC-3
Tocaloma—*locale* CA-9
*Tocassee* SC-3
*Tocawa Springs* MS-4
**Toccoa**—*pop pl* GA-3
Toccoa, Lake—*reservoir* GA-3
Toccoa (CCD)—*cens area* GA-3
Toccoa Cem—*cemetery* GA-3
Toccoa Ch—*church* GA-3
Toccoa Cove—*bay* GA-3
Toccoa Creek—*stream* GA-3
Toccoa Creek Ch—*church* GA-3
Toccoa Falls—*falls* GA-3
**Toccoa Falls**—*pop pl* GA-3
Toccoa Falls Institute—*school* GA-3
*Toccoa Lake* GA-3
*Toccoa River* GA-3
Toccoa River—*stream* GA-3
Toccoa Rsvr—*reservoir* GA-3
*Toccoa Water Works Reservoir* GA-3
**Toccopola**—*pop pl* MS-4
*Toccopola Academy* MS-4
Toccopola Baptist Ch—*church* MS-4
Toccopola Coll (historical)—*school* MS-4
Toccopola Creek—*stream* MS-4
Toccopola HS (historical)—*school* MS-4
Toccopola Post Office—*building* MS-4
Toccopola United Methodist Ch—*church* MS-4
Tocha Park—*park* AZ-5
Tocher Lake—*lake* CA-9
Tochobei—*summit* PW-9
Tocito—*locale* NM-5
Tocito Dome—*summit* NM-5
Tocito Dome Oil Field—*other* NM-5
Tocito Lake—*lake* NM-5
Tocito Wash—*stream* (2) NM-5
*Tockapullo* MS-4
*Tockhockonetcunk* NJ-2
*Tockshish Ch* MS-4
Tockshish (historical)—*locale* MS-4
Tockshish Mission (historical)—*church* MS-4
Tocks Island—*island* NJ-2
**Tocktoethla (historical)**—*pop pl* FL-3
*Tockwogh River* DE-2
*Tockwotten* RI-1
Tockwotton-Love Place Hist Dist—*hist pl* GA-3
**Toco**—*pop pl* TX-5
**Toco Hills**—*pop pl* GA-3
Tocoi—*locale* FL-3
Tocoi Creek—*stream* FL-3
Tocoi Junction—*locale* FL-3
Tocoi Point—*cape* FL-3
Toc-O-Leen, Lake—*reservoir* MS-4
*Tocolete Creek* TX-5
Tocoma, The—*hist pl* MO-7
Toconee Sch—*school* TN-4
*Tocopola* MS-4
**Tocowa**—*pop pl* MS-4
Tocowa Ch—*church* MS-4
*Tocquan Creek* PA-2
T-O Creek—*stream* TX-5
*Tocshish Ch* MS-4
**Tocsin**—*pop pl* IN-6
Tod—*uninc pl* TX-5
Tod, Lake—*reservoir* PA-2
Todacheene Lake—*lake* NM-5
Todahaidekani Preschool—*school* UT-8
*Todastoni Wash* AZ-5
*Todastoni Wash* UT-8
Todatonten, Lake—*lake* AK-9
Tod Ave Sch—*school* OH-6
Tod Creek—*stream* OR-9
Tod Creek—*stream* TX-5
Todd—*locale* NE-7
Todd—*locale* OK-5
Todd—*locale* TX-5
**Todd**—*pop pl* AK-9
**Todd**—*pop pl* CA-9
**Todd**—*pop pl* NC-3
**Todd**—*pop pl* ND-7
**Todd**—*pop pl* PA-2
Todd, Charles and Letitia Shelby, House—*hist pl* KY-4
Todd, Dr. John W., House—*hist pl* LA-4
Todd, Edwin, House—*hist pl* MI-6
Todd, Hiram Charles, House—*hist pl* NY-2
Todd, John, House—*hist pl* PA-2
Todd, Lake—*lake* MN-6
Todd, Lake—*lake* SD-7
Todd, Lake—*reservoir* OK-5
Todd, Robert, Summer Home—*hist pl* KY-4
Todd, William Lytle, House—*hist pl* KY-4
**Todd Acres (subdivision)**—*pop pl* AL-4
Todd Airp—*airport* CO-8
Todd Barranca—*valley* CA-9
Todd Basin—*basin* AZ-5
Todd Bay—*bay* ME-1
Todd Bay—*swamp* SC-3
Todd Block—*hist pl* NH-1
Todd Branch—*stream* AL-4
Todd Branch—*stream* FL-3
Todd Branch—*stream* IA-7
Todd Branch—*stream* KY-4
Todd Branch—*stream* (2) MS-4
Todd Branch—*stream* (2) SC-3
Todd Branch—*stream* (7) TN-4
Todd Branch—*stream* TX-5
Todd Brook—*stream* MA-1
Todd Brook—*stream* NY-2
Todd Browning Spring—*spring* NM-5
Todd Cabin—*locale* CA-9
Todd Canyon—*valley* OR-9
Todd Cave—*cave* TN-4
Todd Cem—*cemetery* AL-4
Todd Cem—*cemetery* (3) IN-6
Todd Cem—*cemetery* KS-7
Todd Cem—*cemetery* KY-4
Todd Cem—*cemetery* (3) MO-7
Todd Cem—*cemetery* NY-2
Todd Cem—*cemetery* NC-3
Todd Cem—*cemetery* (7) TN-4
Todd City—*locale* TX-5
Todd Congregational Ch—*church* AL-4
*Todd Corners* ME-1
Todd Coulee—*valley* (2) MT-8
Todd County—*civil* SD-7
**Todd (County)**—*pop pl* KY-4
**Todd (County)**—*pop pl* MN-6
Todd County Courthouse—*hist pl* KY-4
Todd County Courthouse, Sheriff's House and Jail—*hist pl* MN-6
*Todd Cove* MI-6
Todd Cove—*bay* MD-2
Todd Creek—*fmr MCD* NE-7
Todd Creek—*stream* AK-9
Todd Creek—*stream* (2) CA-9
Todd Creek—*stream* (2) CO-8
Todd Creek—*stream* (2) GA-3
Todd Creek—*stream* ID-8
Todd Creek—*stream* MI-6
Todd Creek—*stream* MO-7
Todd Creek—*stream* MT-8
Todd Creek—*stream* NE-7
Todd Creek—*stream* (2) OR-9
Todd Creek—*stream* SC-3
Todd Creek—*stream* (2) TN-4
Todd Creek—*stream* WA-9
Todd Creek Camp—*locale* OR-9
Todd Creek School (historical)—*locale* MO-7
*Todd Dam* AL-4
Todd Deep Oil Field—*oilfield* TX-5
Todd Ditch—*canal* IN-6
Todd Ditch—*canal* WY-8
Todd Drain—*canal* (3) MI-6
Todd Draw—*valley* AZ-5
Todd Draw Tank—*reservoir* AZ-5
**Todd (Elkland)**—*pop pl* NC-3
**Todd Estates**—*pop pl* DE-2
Todd Farm—*hist pl* RI-1
Todd Farm—*locale* ME-1
Todd Farmhouse—*hist pl* MD-2
Todd Ferry—*locale* TX-5
Todd Field—*park* OH-6
Todd Fork—*stream* OH-6
Todd Gulch—*valley* CO-8
Todd Harbor—*bay* MI-6
Todd Harbor Campground—*locale* MI-6
*Todd Harbour* MI-6
Todd Head—*cliff* ME-1
Todd Hill—*summit* CT-1
Todd Hill—*summit* NH-1
Todd Hill—*summit* UT-8
Todd Hill—*summit* VT-1
Todd (historical)—*locale* MS-4
Todd Hollow—*valley* AL-4
Todd Hollow—*valley* KY-4
Todd Hollow—*valley* (4) MO-7
Todd Hollow—*valley* (5) TN-4
Todd Hollow—*valley* UT-8
Todd Hollow Brook—*stream* CT-1
Todd House —*building* PA-2
Todd House—*hist pl* AL-4
Todd House—*hist pl* IA-7
Todd House—*hist pl* ME-1
Todd HS—*school* AL-4
Todd Industrial Park—*locale* AL-4
Toddish Sch—*school* MI-6
Todd Island—*island* CA-9
Todd Island—*island* ME-1
Todd Knob—*summit* TN-4
*Todd Lake* CT-1
Todd Lake—*lake* AK-9
Todd Lake—*lake* MI-6
Todd Lake—*lake* NH-1
Todd Lake—*lake* OK-5
Todd Lake—*lake* OR-9
Todd Lake—*lake* PA-2
Todd Lake—*lake* WA-9
Todd Lake—*reservoir* AL-4
Todd Lake—*reservoir* MS-4
Todd Lake—*reservoir* NJ-2
Todd Lake—*reservoir* TN-4
Todd Lake Campground—*park* OR-9
Todd Lake Dam—*dam* TN-4
Todd Lake Picnic Ground—*park* OR-9
Todd Lake Rec Area—*locale* VA-3
Todd Lakes—*lake* MT-8
Todd Landing—*locale* NC-3
Todd Memorial HS—*school* MS-4
Todd Memorial Park—*park* CA-9
Todd Mill Branch—*stream* SC-3
*Todd Mill Creek* MS-4
Todd Mine—*mine* CO-8
Todd Mine—*mine* TN-4
**Todd Mission**—*pop pl* TX-5
Todd-Montgomery Houses—*hist pl* KY-4
Todd Mtn—*summit* MA-1
Todd Mtn—*summit* NY-2
Todd Mtn—*summit* TN-4
Todd Mtn—*summit* TX-5
Todd Oil Field—*oilfield* TX-5
Todd Oil Field—*oilfield* WY-8
Todd Oil Field—*other* NM-5
Todd Oval—*park* NY-2
Todd Park—*park* CA-9
Todd Park—*park* MN-6
Todd Place—*locale* CA-9
*Todd Point* MD-2
Todd Point—*cape* CT-1
Todd Point—*cape* ME-1
Todd Point—*cape* MD-2
Todd Point—*cliff* CO-8
Todd Pond—*lake* FL-3
Todd Pond—*lake* MA-1
Todd Pond—*reservoir* NC-3
Todd Pond Dam—*dam* NC-3
Todd Ranch—*locale* CA-9
Todd Ranch—*locale* (2) WY-8
Todd-Ray Cem—*cemetery* GA-3
Todd Ridge—*ridge* AL-4
*Todd River* WI-6
Todd River—*stream* GA-3
Todd Rsvr—*reservoir* CO-8
Todd Run—*stream* OH-6
Todd Run—*stream* WV-2
Todds—*locale* OH-6
*Todds Brook* ME-1
Toddsbury—*hist pl* VA-3
Toddsbury Creek—*stream* VA-3
Todds Cem—*cemetery* MI-6
Todds Ch—*church* DE-2
Todd Sch—*school* (2) IL-6
Todd Sch—*school* (2) KY-4
Todd Sch—*school* MO-7
Todd Sch—*school* NY-2
Todd Sch—*school* SC-3
Todd Sch—*school* (3) SD-7
Todd Sch—*school* UT-8
Todd Sch—*school* WI-6
*Todds Chapel* DE-2
Todds Chapel—*church* MD-2
Todds Chapel—*church* MO-7
**Todds Corner**—*pop pl* ME-1
Todds Creek—*stream* IA-7
**Todds Crossroads**—*pop pl* NC-3
Todds Farm—*locale* ME-1
*Todds Fork* OH-6
*Todds Harbor* MI-6
*Todds Hill* AL-4
Todds Hill—*ridge* CA-9
Todd Siding—*locale* TN-4
Todds Island—*island* DE-2
*Todds Lake* NH-1
Todds Lake—*reservoir* TN-4
Todds Lake Dam—*dam* TN-4
Todds Lake Number Two—*reservoir* TN-4
Todds Lake Number Two Dam—*dam* TN-4
Todds Landing (historical)—*locale* TN-4
Todd Slough—*stream* TN-4
Todds Mill—*locale* IL-6
*Todds Mountain* MA-1
*Toddspoint* KY-4
*Todd's Point* MD-2
Todds Point—*cape* ME-1
Todds Point—*cape* MD-2
Todds Point—*cape* VA-3
Todds Point—*locale* KY-4
**Todds Point**—*pop pl* IL-6
**Toddspoint**—*pop pl* KY-4

**Todds Point (Township of)**—*pop pl* IL-6
Todds Pond—*lake* MA-1
Todds Pond—*reservoir* RI-1
Todd Spring—*spring* MO-7
Todd Spring—*spring* MT-8
Todd Spring Ch—*church* TX-5
Todd Spring Dam—*dam* PA-2
Todd Spring Rsvr—*reservoir* PA-2
Todd Springs Ch—*church* TX-5
Todds Spring—*spring* AL-4
Todds Spring—*spring* CA-9
Todds Spring Canyon—*valley* CA-9
Todds Tavern—*locale* VA-3
**Todds Tavern (Finchville)**—*pop pl* VA-3
**Toddsville**—*pop pl* NY-2
Todd Swamp—*stream* SC-3
Todd Tabernacle—*church* PA-2
Todd Tank—*reservoir* AZ-5
Todd Tank—*reservoir* NM-5
**Todd (Tod)**—*pop pl* PA-2
Todd Town—*locale* TN-4
**Toddtown**—*pop pl* AL-4
**Todd (Township of)**—*pop pl* MN-6
**Todd (Township of)**—*pop pl* (2) PA-2
Todd Trail—*trail* PA-2
Todd Valley—*locale* CA-9
**Todd Villa Subdivision**—*pop pl* UT-8
Toddville—*locale* KY-4
Toddville—*locale* NC-3
**Toddville**—*pop pl* IA-7
**Toddville**—*pop pl* MD-2
**Toddville**—*pop pl* NY-2
**Toddville**—*pop pl* SC-3
Toddville (historical P.O.)—*locale* IA-7
Todd Wharf—*locale* MD-2
**Toddy**—*pop pl* NC-3
Toddy Brook—*stream* ME-1
Toddy Brook—*stream* VT-1
Toddy Draw—*valley* WY-8
Toddy Mtn—*summit* TN-4
Toddy Pond—*lake* (2) ME-1
Toddy Rocks—*bar* MA-1
Toddys Branch—*stream* IN-6
Toddy Spring—*spring* WY-8
*Toddy Station* NC-3
Toddy Station—*locale* NC-3
Tode Baho Tsiquini—*spring* AZ-5
Tod Homestead Cem—*cemetery* OH-6
Tod Homestead Cemetery Gate—*hist pl* OH-6
Tod Hunter Rsvr—*reservoir* NM-5
Todicheenie Bench—*bench* AZ-5
Todie Canyon—*valley* UT-8
Todie Flat—*flat* UT-8
Todie Spring—*spring* UT-8
To-dil-hil Wash—*stream* NM-5
Todilto Park—*area* NM-5
*Todlan* MH-9
*Todmorden* PA-2
Todmorden Mills—*locale* PA-2
**Todmorron**—*pop pl* PA-2
Tod Mtn—*summit* TX-5
*Todokozh Spring* AZ-5
Todosio Canyon—*valley* NM-5
Todos Santos—*uninc pl* CA-9
Todos Santos Creek—*stream* TX-5
Todos Santos Windmill—*locale* TX-5
Todos Santos Y San Antonio—*civil* CA-9
Tod Park—*locale* UT-8
Tod Park—*park* IN-6
T-O Draw—*valley* TX-5
Tod Reese Tank—*reservoir* AZ-5
Todrik Pass—*channel* MP-9
Tod Sch—*school* (2) OH-6
Todt Hill—*summit* NY-2
Todt Hill—*uninc pl* NY-2
**Tod (Township of)**—*pop pl* OH-6
Todville—*locale* TX-5
Tody Lake—*lake* MI-6
*Toe* NC-3
Toe, The—*summit* UT-8
**Toecane**—*pop pl* NC-3
*Toecane Creek* GA-3
Toeclout Branch—*stream* VA-3
Toedgar Windmill—*locale* TX-5
Toe Drain—*canal* CA-9
Toedtli Rsvr—*reservoir* CO-8
Toe Gulch—*valley* SD-7
*Toehead Lake* CA-9
Toe Ink Swamp—*stream* VA-3
Toe Ink Wayside—*locale* VA-3
Toe Island—*island* OR-9
Toe Jam Canyon—*valley* ID-8
Toe Jam Creek—*stream* NV-8
Toejam Lake—*lake* CA-9
Toe Jam Mtn—*summit* NV-8
Toe Jam Spring—*spring* CO-8
Toe Jam Spring—*spring* ID-8
Toe Lake—*lake* CA-9
Toe Lake—*lake* (2) MN-6
Toeley—*bay* FM-9
*Toelle Peak* UT-8
*Toelle Valley* UT-8
Toem Lake—*lake* CA-9
Toenail Cem—*cemetery* MS-4
Toenail Hollow—*valley* KY-4
Toenail Oil Field—*oilfield* TX-5
Toenail Ridge—*ridge* ME-1
Toenleshushe Canyon—*valley* AZ-5
Toensing Cem—*cemetery* IL-6
Toe of the Boot—*cape* ME-1
Toe Point—*cape* AK-9
Toe Point—*cape* WA-9
Toe River—*stream* AL-4
Toe River Sch—*school* NC-3
Toe River (Township of)—*fmr MCD* NC-3
**Toeruw**—*pop pl* FM-9
*Toes Point* VA-3
Toestring Branch—*stream* TN-4
Toestring Cove Resort—*locale* TN-4
Toestring Valley—*valley* TN-4
*Toeter* IA-7
Toeter Cem—*cemetery* IA-7
**Toeterville**—*pop pl* IA-7
Toetown Branch—*stream* TN-4
*Toey* FM-9
*Toe-yah-yah* HI-9
Toeyniim'—*cape* FM-9
Tofa—*bar* FM-9
**Tofol**—*pop pl* FM-9
Tofol, Infal—*stream* FM-9
**Tofte**—*pop pl* MN-6
Tofte Lake—*lake* MN-6
**Tofte (Township of)**—*pop pl* MN-6
Toft Lake—*lake* MI-6
Toft Lake Village Site—*hist pl* MI-6
**Toftrees**—*pop pl* PA-2
Toftrees Golf Course—*locale* PA-2
Tofty—*locale* AK-9
Tofty Gulch—*valley* AK-9
Tofu Stream—*stream* AS-9
Toga—*locale* VA-3
**Toga**—*pop pl* MO-7
*Togai Spring* AZ-5
Togari Mtn—*summit* MH-9
Togari Rock—*island* MH-9
*Togari-Sho* MH-9
*Togatatic River* WI-6
*Togatic Lake* WI-6
*Togay Spring* AZ-5
Togcha—*area* GU-9
Togcha Bay—*bay* GU-9
Togcha Beach—*other* GU-9
Togcha Cem—*cemetery* GU-9
Togcha Point—*cape* GU-9
Togcha River—*stream* GU-9
*Togey* MS-4
Togeye Canyon—*valley* NM-5
Togeye Flats—*flat* NM-5
Togeye Lake—*lake* NM-5
*Toggapluw* FM-9
Toggie Canyon—*valley* AZ-5
Toggle Meadows—*flat* OR-9
Toggletown—*locale* NY-2
**Togiak**—*pop pl* AK-9
Togiak Bay—*bay* AK-9
Togiak Lake—*lake* AK-9
Togiak River—*stream* AK-9
Togie Well—*well* NM-5
Togleson Cem—*cemetery* MO-7
Tognini Mtns—*range* NV-8
Tognini Spring—*spring* NV-8
Tognoni Springs—*spring* NV-8
Togo—*locale* KS-7
Togo—*locale* OK-5
Togo—*locale* TX-5
**Togo**—*pop pl* AR-4
**Togo**—*pop pl* MN-6
**Togo**—*pop pl* MS-4
Togo Cem—*cemetery* MS-4
Togo Ch—*church* AR-4
Togo Chapel—*church* MN-6
Togo Creek—*stream* WA-9
Togo Gulch—*valley* ID-8
**Togo (historical)**—*pop pl* IA-7
*Togoholtase Spring* AZ-5
*To-go-hol-tso-e* AZ-5
Togoholtsoe Spring—*spring* AZ-5
Togo Island—*island* LA-4
Togo Mine—*mine* WA-9
Togo Mtn—*summit* WA-9
Togo Post Office (historical)—*building* MS-4
*Togopuluw* FM-9
Togotogo Ridge—*ridge* AS-9
Togoyuk Creek—*stream* AK-9
Togpaola—*area* GU-9
Togstad Post Office (historical)—*building* SD-7
Toguan—*area* GU-9
Toguan Bay—*bay* GU-9
Toguan River—*stream* GU-9
*Toguczou* FM-9
Togue Brook—*stream* ME-1
Togue Ledge—*bench* ME-1
Togue Point—*cape* ME-1
Togue Pond—*lake* ME-1
Togue Pond Camp—*locale* ME-1
Togue Stream—*stream* (2) ME-1
Togus—*locale* ME-1
Togus Creek—*stream* WY-8
Togus Pond—*lake* ME-1
Togus Stream—*stream* ME-1
Togwotee Lodge—*locale* WY-8
Togwotee Pass—*gap* WY-8
Togy Mound—*summit* WY-8
Tohache Rec Area—*park* AZ-5
*Tohache Wash* AZ-5
*Tohache Wash* UT-8
Tohache Wash—*stream* AZ-5
Tohache Wash—*stream* NM-5
Tohachi Wash—*stream* AZ-5
*To hahaltsoi Spring* AZ-5
Toh Ah Chi—*spring* AZ-5
Toh Ah Glau—*lake* AZ-5
Toh Ah Honnie Betoh—*spring* AZ-5
*Toh-ahtnda* AZ-5
Tohakum Peak—*summit* NV-8
*Toh Alth Wash* AZ-5
*Tohal ushi* AZ-5
*To Hanadli Spring* UT-8
Tohanadli Spring—*spring* UT-8
**Tohatchi**—*pop pl* NM-5
Tohatchi Flats—*flat* (2) NM-5
Tohatchi Lookout—*locale* NM-5
Tohatchi Spring—*spring* AZ-5
*Toh-Atin Mesa* AZ-5
Toh Atin Mesa—*summit* AZ-5
*To-haul-hace* AZ-5
Toh Bih Nosteny—*spring* AZ-5
Toh Cathlie Cod—*spring* AZ-5
*Toh-Chin-Lini Canyon* AZ-5
Toh Chin Lini Canyon—*valley* AZ-5
Toh Chin Lini Mesa—*summit* AZ-5
Toh Dah Hee Dat Conii—*spring* AZ-5
Toh Dahstini Spring—*spring* AZ-5
Toh Dahstini Wash—*stream* AZ-5
Toh Dahstini Wash—*valley* UT-8
Toh De Coz—*spring* AZ-5
Toh De Kaish—*spring* AZ-5
Toh Del Toshi Hydrant—*reservoir* AZ-5
Toh Del Toshi Spring—*spring* AZ-5
Tohdenasshai Trading Post—*locale* AZ-5
Toh De Niihe—*lake* AZ-5
Tohdildonih Wash—*stream* NM-5
Tohe Thlany Begay Mine—*mine* AZ-5
Tohet Spring—*spring* OR-9
Toh Ha Ha Clah—*lake* AZ-5
Toh Ha Hao Cheen—*spring* AZ-5
Toh Ha Tsil Dize—*spring* AZ-5
*Tohhoku Suido* MP-9
Toh Honi Ni Toh—*spring* AZ-5
Tohicken Hill Sch—*school* PA-2
Tohickon Cem—*cemetery* PA-2
Tohickon Creek—*stream* PA-2
Tohickon Quarry—*mine* PA-2
Tohickon Valley Elem Sch—*school* PA-2
*Tohickon Valley Sch* PA-2
Tohill Cem—*cemetery* IL-6
Tohitkah Mtn—*summit* AK-9
**Tohlakai Trading Post**—*pop pl* NM-5
Tohnalchai Spring—*spring* AZ-5
*Toh-na-lea Mesa* AZ-5
Toh Nalen—*well* AZ-5
Tohnali—*spring* AZ-5
Tohnali Mesa—*summit* AZ-5
Toh Nee Di Kishi—*spring* AZ-5
Toh Ne Zhonnie Spring—*spring* AZ-5
Toh Ne Zhonnie Valley—*valley* AZ-5
Toh Ne Zhonnie Wash—*valley* AZ-5
Toh-Ni-Tsa Lookout—*locale* NM-5
Toh-Noz-Bosa Well—*well* NM-5
Tohobit Peak—*summit* ID-8
Tohonadla Oil Field—*oilfield* UT-8
*Tohonadla Spring* UT-8
**Tohopeka**—*pop pl* AL-4
*Tohopekalica* FL-3
Tohopekaliga, Lake—*lake* FL-3
**Tohopikaliga (historical)**—*pop pl* FL-3
Tohopkee—*locale* FL-3
Tohotso Creek—*stream* AZ-5
Tohrner and Cannon Spring—*spring* TN-4
Toik Hill—*summit* AK-9
Toikiming (historical)—*locale* MA-1
Toikka Lake—*lake* MN-6
*Toi Klemadaol* PW-9
Toilet Paper Tank—*reservoir* AZ-5
Toilet Well Number One—*well* NV-8
Toilet Well Number Two—*well* NV-8
Toiloto Ridge—*ridge* AS-9
**Toilsome Hill**—*pop pl* CT-1
Toimi—*locale* MN-6
**Toimi**—*pop pl* MN-6
Toimi Cem—*cemetery* MN-6
Toimi Creek—*stream* MN-6
Toinen Gulch—*valley* OR-9
Toinette—*locale* AL-4
Toinom—*island* FM-9
Toirachuil—*island* PW-9
*Toira Klemadaol* PW-9
Toirius—*island* PW-9
Toir Rois—*summit* PW-9
Toisnot Cem—*cemetery* NC-3
Toisnot Park—*park* NC-3
Toisnot Rsvr—*reservoir* NC-3
Toisnot Swamp—*stream* NC-3
Toisnot (Township of)—*fmr MCD* NC-3
*Toison* AZ-5
**Toita**—*pop pl* PR-3
Toita (Barrio)—*fmr MCD* (2) PR-3
**Toivola**—*pop pl* MI-6
**Toivola**—*pop pl* (2) MN-6
Toivola Cem—*cemetery* MI-6
Toivola Cem—*cemetery* MN-6
Toivola Lake—*lake* MI-6
Toivola Lakes—*lake* MI-6
Toivola (Station)—*locale* MN-6
Toivola Swamp—*swamp* MN-6
**Toivola (Township of)**—*pop pl* MN-6
*Toiyabe* KS-7
Toiyabe Campground—*locale* CA-9
*Toiyabe Come Southeast Summit* NV-8
Toiyabe Crest Trail—*trail* NV-8
*Toiyabe Dome* NV-8
Toiyabe Dome—*summit* NV-8
Toiyabe Dome Southeast Summit—*summit* NV-8
Toiyabe Natl For—*forest* NV-8
*Toiyabe NF, subdivision of* NV-8
*Toiyabe Peak* NV-8
Toiyabe Range—*range* NV-8
*Toiyabe Range Peak* NV-8
Toiyabe Range Peak—*summit* NV-8
*Toiyabe Summit Trail* NV-8
Tojan Island—*island* LA-4
**Tok**—*pop pl* AK-9
Toka—*island* MP-9
Tokaen Island—*island* MP-9
*Tokaen-to* MP-9
TOKAI MARU—*hist pl* GU-9
Tokaine Creek—*stream* AK-9
*Toka Island* MP-9
*Tokaji To* FM-9
**Tokalon**—*pop pl* AR-4
Tokalon Cem—*cemetery* AR-4
Tokaloo Rock—*summit* WA-9
Tokaloo Spire—*summit* WA-9
*Tokar* UT-8
Tokatee Dam—*dam* OR-9
Tokatee Lakes—*lake* OR-9
Tokatjikh Creek—*stream* AK-9
Tokatjikh Hill—*summit* AK-9
Tokay—*locale* CA-9
Tokay—*locale* NM-5
Tokay Canal—*canal* CA-9
Tokay Colony Sch—*school* CA-9
Tokay Drain—*canal* CA-9
Tokay Drain One—*canal* CA-9
Tokay Drain Two—*canal* CA-9
Tokay Heights—*uninc pl* NC-3
Tokay Hill—*summit* CA-9
Tokay Lateral One—*canal* CA-9
**Tokay (subdivision)**—*pop pl* NC-3
*Toke* MP-9
Toke—*unknown* FM-9
Tokeba Bayou—*stream* MS-4
Tokeba Bayou Landing—*locale* MS-4
Toke (County-equivalent)—*civil* MP-9
Tokeen—*locale* AK-9
**Tokeena Crossroads**—*pop pl* SC-3
Tokeen Bay—*bay* AK-9
Tokeen (Content)—*locale* TX-5
Tokeen Peak—*summit* AK-9
*Tokeeostee River* TN-4
**Tokeland**—*pop pl* WA-9
Tokeland Hotel—*hist pl* WA-9
Tokel Bend—*bend* FL-3
Tokembamy Ranch—*locale* ID-8
**Token Creek**—*pop pl* WI-6
Token Creek—*stream* WI-6
Token Creek Pond—*reservoir* WI-6
Token Creek Sch—*school* WI-6
Tokeneke—*locale* CT-1
*Tokeneke Park* CT-1
Tokeneke Sch—*school* CT-1
Tokenraito Island—*island* MP-9
**Token (Token Creek)**—*pop pl* WI-6
*Tokeostee River* TN-4
Toke Point—*cape* WA-9
*Toker* UT-8
*Tokerville* UT-8
Toketa Creek—*stream* OR-9
Toketee Airfield USFS—*airport* OR-9
Toketee Falls—*falls* OR-9
**Toketee Falls**—*pop pl* OR-9
Toketee Lake—*reservoir* OR-9
Toketee Lake Campground—*park* OR-9
*Toketee Rsvr* OR-9
Toketie, Lake—*lake* WA-9
Toke Tie, Lake—*lake* WA-9
Toketie Creek—*stream* WA-9
*Toketie Falls* OR-9
*Toke-Tie Lake* WA-9
Toketie Lake—*lake* WA-9
*Tokewa* MP-9
Tokewanna Peak—*summit* UT-8
Tokezje Spring—*spring* AZ-5
Tok Glacier—*glacier* AK-9
Tokhakklanten, Lake—*lake* AK-9
Tokhini Creek—*stream* AK-9
Tokiahok Head—*bench* MI-6
Tokio—*locale* TX-5
Tokio—*locale* WA-9
Tokio—*other* OH-6
**Tokio**—*pop pl* AR-4
**Tokio**—*pop pl* MS-4
**Tokio**—*pop pl* ND-7
Tokio Ch—*church* (2) AR-4
Tokio Ch—*church* TX-5
Tokio Post Office (historical)—*building* MS-4
Toki Point—*ridge* MP-9
Tok Junction—*other* AK-9
To Kla Daa Aakee Pond—*lake* AZ-5
Toklat—*locale* AK-9
Toklat Lodge—*locale* CO-8
Toklat Ranger Station-Pearson Cabin No. 4—*hist pl* AK-9
Toklat River—*stream* AK-9
Toklik—*locale* AK-9
Tokoberu—*bar* FM-9
To-ko-chi Canyon—*valley* UT-8
Tokodakaaka—*bar* FM-9
*Tokoeoa* MP-9
Tokomarik Mtn—*summit* AK-9
Tokoma Wildlife Mngmt Area—*park* FL-3
Tokona Hosp—*hospital* TN-4
Tokop—*locale* NV-8
Tokopah Falls—*falls* CA-9
Tokopah Valley—*flat* CA-9
Tokop Well—*well* NV-8
Tokoraara—*bar* FM-9
Tokoruo—*bar* FM-9
Tokosha Mountains—*other* AK-9
Tokositna Glacier—*glacier* AK-9
Tokositna River—*stream* AK-9
*Tokowa* MP-9
*Tokowa Anchorage* MP-9
*Tokowa Channel* MP-9
Tokowa Channel—*channel* MP-9
*Tokowa Island* MP-9
Tokowa Island—*island* MP-9
Tok River—*stream* AK-9
*Tokshish Church* MS-4
*Tokshish Creek* MS-4
**Toksook Bay**—*pop pl* AK-9
Toksook River—*stream* AK-9
Toksook (Toksook Bay)—*other* AK-9
**Tokul**—*pop pl* WA-9
Tokul Creek—*stream* WA-9
Tokul (Siding)—*locale* WA-9
Tokun, Lake—*lake* AK-9
Tokun Creek—*stream* AK-9
Tokun Ridge—*ridge* AK-9
Tokusatatquaten Lake—*lake* AK-9
Tokyo Artesian Well—*well* TX-5
Tokyo Hill—*summit* TX-5
*Tol* FM-9
Tol—*island* FM-9
*Tola* MP-9
Tola—*locale* IA-7
**Tola**—*pop pl* VA-3
Tola, Bayou—*gut* AL-4
*Tolab* MP-9
Tolache Mine—*mine* ID-8
*Tolacon* AZ-5
**Tolacon**—*pop pl* AZ-5
Tola Creek—*stream* ID-8
Tola Creek—*stream* WA-9
*Toladjau* FM-9
Tolaeyuus River—*stream* GU-9
Tolageak (Abandoned)—*locale* AK-9
Tolah Nascin—*reservoir* AZ-5
Tolah Nascin—*spring* AZ-5
Tolaktovut Point—*cape* AK-9
Tolan Creek—*stream* KY-4
Tolan Creek—*stream* (2) MT-8
Toland—*locale* TX-5
**Toland**—*pop pl* PA-2
Toland Cem—*cemetery* OH-6
Toland Creek—*stream* AL-4
Toland Creek—*stream* MT-8
Toland Drain—*canal* CA-9
Toland Hill—*summit* WA-9
Toland Hollow—*valley* TN-4
*Tolan Ditch* IN-6
Toland Landing—*locale* CA-9
Toland Mtn—*summit* GA-3
Toland Ridge—*ridge* CA-9
Toland Way Sch—*school* CA-9
*Tolaneville* MI-6
Tolange—*area* GU-9
Tolani—*lake* AZ-5
**Tolani**—*pop pl* AZ-5
To-lani, Lake—*reservoir* GA-3
*Tolani Lake* (2) AZ-5
Tolani Lake Day Sch—*school* AZ-5
Tolani Lakes—*lake* AZ-5
**Tolani (Tolani Lake)**—*pop pl* AZ-5
*Tolan Lake* LA-4
Tolan Lake—*lake* LA-4
Tolan Park—*park* MI-6
Tolan Park—*park* OK-5
Tolan Place—*locale* CO-8
Tolan Ridge—*ridge* MT-8
Tolans Branch—*stream* IL-6
*Tolap* FM-9
Tolapai Draw—*valley* AZ-5
Tolapai Spring—*spring* AZ-5
Tola Point—*summit* ID-8
*Tolap Pass* MP-9
Tolap Pass—*channel* MP-9
*Tolap Peak* FM-9
Tolar—*locale* NM-5
**Tolar**—*pop pl* TX-5
Tolar Cem—*cemetery* (3) MS-4
Tolar Cem—*cemetery* NM-5
Tolar Cem—*cemetery* TX-5
Tolar Farms—*locale* AL-4
Tolar Lake—*lake* AR-4
Tolar Landing—*locale* NC-3
Tolar Ponds Dam—*dam* MS-4
**Tolar Subdivision**—*pop pl* MS-4
*Tolarsville* MS-4
Tolarsville—*locale* NC-3
Tolarville—*locale* MS-4
Tolarville Post Office (historical)—*building* MS-4
Tolar Well—*well* NM-5
Tolay Creek—*stream* CA-9
Tolbert—*locale* TX-5
*Tolbert Baptist Church* AL-4
Tolbert Branch—*stream* SC-3
Tolbert Cabin—*locale* AZ-5
Tolbert Canyon—*valley* NV-8
Tolbert Cem—*cemetery* AL-4
Tolbert Cem—*cemetery* NC-3
Tolbert Cem—*cemetery* ND-7
Tolbert Cem—*cemetery* (2) TN-4
Tolbert Ch—*church* AL-4
Tolbert Chapel—*church* AL-4
Tolbert Ditch—*canal* UT-8
Tolbert Hollow—*valley* TN-4
Tolbert-Jones Creek—*stream* MS-4
Tolbert Park—*park* TX-5
*Tolberts Branch* SC-3
Tolbert Sch—*school* FL-3
Tolberts Chapel Cem—*cemetery* IN-6
*Tolbert Spring* AL-4
Tolbert Springs—*spring* AL-4
**Tolbertsville (historical)**—*pop pl* TN-4
Tolbertsville Post Office (historical)—*building* TN-4
Tolby Branch—*stream* KY-4
Tolby Creek—*stream* NM-5
Tolby Peak—*summit* NM-5
Tolcats Canyon—*valley* UT-8
*Tol-Chac* AZ-5
*Tolchaco* AZ-5
Tolchaco Gap—*gap* AZ-5
**Tolchester Beach**—*pop pl* MD-2
Tolchico—*locale* AZ-5
*Tolchiko* AZ-5
Tolch Rock—*other* AK-9
*Tolcok Point* WA-9
*Toldar* FM-9
**Toldeo**—*pop pl* MO-7
Tol-Dohn Spring—*spring* NM-5
Toleak Point—*cape* WA-9
Tolean Lake—*lake* MT-8
Tole Cem—*cemetery* TN-4
Toledano-Philbrick-Tullis House—*hist pl* MS-4
*Toledo* IN-6
Toledo—*locale* AR-4
Toledo—*locale* GA-3
Toledo—*locale* (2) MO-7
Toledo—*locale* NC-3
Toledo—*locale* TX-5
**Toledo**—*pop pl* IL-6
**Toledo**—*pop pl* IN-6
**Toledo**—*pop pl* IA-7
**Toledo**—*pop pl* KS-7
**Toledo**—*pop pl* OH-6
**Toledo**—*pop pl* OR-9
**Toledo**—*pop pl* WA-9
Toledo and Ohio Central Depot—*hist pl* OH-6
Toledo and Ohio Central RR Station—*hist pl* OH-6
Toledo Arroyo—*stream* NM-5
Toledo Beach—*locale* MI-6
Toledo Bend Rsvr—*reservoir* LA-4
Toledo Bend Rsvr—*reservoir* TX-5
Toledo (CCD)—*cens area* OR-9
Toledo Cem—*cemetery* OR-9
Toledo Cem—*cemetery* TX-5
Toledo Ch—*church* IL-6
Toledo Club—*hist pl* OH-6
Toledo Country Club—*other* OH-6
Toledo Creek—*stream* MI-6
Toledo Ditch—*canal* CO-8
*Toledo Dock (Presque Isle)* OH-6
Toledo Express Airp—*airport* OH-6
Toledo Gulch—*valley* CA-9
Toledo Harbor—*bay* AK-9
Toledo Harbor Light—*hist pl* OH-6
Toledo Heights—*uninc pl* CO-8
Toledo (historical)—*locale* SD-7
Toledo Hosp—*hospital* OH-6
Toledo HS—*school* OR-9
**Toledo Junction**—*pop pl* OH-6
Toledo Lookout Tower—*locale* GA-3
Toledo Memorial Park—*cemetery* OH-6
Toledo Mine—*mine* CA-9
Toledo Mine—*mine* MT-8
Toledo Pond—*lake* CA-9
Toledo (Site)—*locale* CA-9
Toledo State Airp—*airport* OR-9
Toledo State Hosp—*hospital* OH-6
Toledo Township—*fmr MCD* IA-7
**Toledo Township**—*pop pl* KS-7
Toledo Township (historical)—*civil* ND-7
Toledo Univ—*school* OH-6
Toledo-Winlock Ed Carlson Memorial Field Airp—*airport* WA-9
Toledo Yacht Club—*hist pl* OH-6
Toleej—*island* MP-9
*Tolej* MP-9
*Tolemuan* FM-9
Tolena Point—*cape* MN-6
Tolenas—*civil* CA-9
Tolenas—*locale* CA-9
Tolenas Springs—*spring* CA-9
*Tolenawak* FM-9
*Tolen Awak Peak* FM-9
Tolen Cem—*cemetery* GA-3
Tolen Creek—*stream* KS-7
*Tolen Ditch* IN-6
Tolen Ditch—*canal* IN-6
*Tolenot Peak* FM-9
*Tolen Palikir* FM-9
*Tolent* OR-9
*Tolen Talikir* FM-9
Tolentine Coll—*school* IL-6
**Toler**—*pop pl* KY-4
Toler Bridge—*bridge* VA-3
Toler Cem—*cemetery* IL-6
Toler Cem—*cemetery* MO-7
Toler Cem—*cemetery* WV-2
Toler Ch—*church* WV-2
Toler Creek—*stream* CA-9
Toler Creek—*stream* KY-4
Toler Creek—*stream* NV-8
Toler Fork—*stream* WV-2
Toler Gap—*gap* KY-4
Toler Heights Sch—*school* CA-9
Toler Hollow—*valley* WV-2
Toler Mtn—*summit* KY-4
Toler-Oak Hill Sch—*school* NC-3
Toler Ridge—*ridge* KY-4
Tolers Bay—*bay* NC-3
Toler Sch—*school* CA-9
Toler Sch (historical)—*school* MS-4
Tolers (historical)—*locale* MS-4
**Toler Spur**—*pop pl* WV-2
Tolerton Post Office (historical)—*building* MS-4
Tolerville—*locale* KS-7
Toles Branch—*stream* MS-4
Toles Cem—*cemetery* SD-7
*Toles Creek* ID-8
Toles Creek—*stream* ID-8
Toles Creek—*stream* (2) MI-6
Toles Hollow—*valley* PA-2
Toles Mesa Windmill—*locale* TX-5
*Toleston* IN-6
*Toletik* FM-9
*Toletik Island* FM-9
*Toletik Peak* FM-9
*Toletik Point* FM-9
*Toley* KY-4
Tolfee Hill—*summit* MI-6
Tolfrey Creek—*stream* MI-6
Tolgen Ch—*church* MN-6
**Tolgen Township**—*pop pl* ND-7
*Tol Hafen* FM-9
**Tolham Estates (subdivision)**—*pop pl* DE-2
*Tol Harbor* FM-9
Tolicha Peak—*summit* NV-8
Tolicha Wash—*stream* NV-8
Tolieson Branch—*stream* GA-3
Tolishden Slough—*stream* AK-9
Tolisi Point—*cape* AS-9
*Tol Island* FM-9
Toliva Shoal—*bar* WA-9
Toliver—*locale* KY-4
**Toliver**—*pop pl* NC-3
Toliver Basin Canyon—*valley* TX-5
Toliver Branch—*stream* TX-5
Toliver Cem—*cemetery* IL-6
Toliver Cem—*cemetery* MS-4
Toliver Cem—*cemetery* TN-4
Toliver Cem—*cemetery* TX-5
Toliver Hollow—*valley* IN-6
Toliver Island—*island* TN-4
Toliver Lake—*reservoir* TN-4
Toliver Lake Dam—*dam* TN-4
Toliver Ridge—*ridge* IN-6
Toliver Run—*stream* MD-2
Tolivers Canyon—*valley* UT-8
Tolivers Creek—*stream* UT-8
*To'liy* FM-9
Tolkan Campground—*locale* CA-9
Tolke Canyon—*valley* OR-9
Toll, Alfred, House—*hist pl* MO-7
Toll, Mount—*summit* CO-8
Tolladay Peak—*summit* CA-9
Tollage Creek—*stream* KY-4
*Tollamatoxa* MS-4
*Tolland* MA-1
**Tolland**—*pop pl* CO-8
**Tolland**—*pop pl* CT-1
**Tolland**—*pop pl* MA-1
Tolland Cem—*cemetery* CT-1
Tolland Cem—*cemetery* MA-1
**Tolland Center**—*pop pl* MA-1
*Tolland Centre* MA-1
**Tolland County**—*pop pl* CT-1
Tolland Hill—*summit* CT-1
*Tolland Marsh* CT-1
Tolland Marsh Pond—*lake* CT-1
*Tolland Reservoir Brook* CT-1
Tolland State For—*forest* MA-1
**Tolland (Town of)**—*pop pl* CT-1
**Tolland (Town of)**—*pop pl* MA-1
Tollar Branch—*stream* MO-7
Toll Branch—*stream* (2) TN-4
*Toll Bridge Brook* CT-1
Toll Bridge County Park—*park* OR-9
Tollbridge Park—*park* OR-9
Toll Canyon—*valley* (2) CA-9
Toll Canyon—*valley* CO-8
Toll Canyon—*valley* MT-8
Toll Canyon—*valley* NV-8
Toll Canyon—*valley* UT-8
Toll Chapel Sch—*school* TN-4
Toll Corner—*locale* NY-2
Toll Creek—*stream* MT-8
Toll Creek—*stream* TN-4
Toll Creek—*stream* WA-9
Toll Dam—*locale* ME-1
*Tolle* KS-7
Tollebu Cem—*cemetery* WI-6
*Tolle Cemetery* TN-4
Tolle Ditch—*canal* IN-6
Tollefson Coulee—*valley* WI-6
*Tollefson Lake* MN-6
Tolle Hill—*summit* OH-6
*Toller Bogue* AL-4
Toller Branch—*stream* KY-4
Tollerburg Flats—*flat* CO-8
Toller Cem—*cemetery* NC-3
Tollers Spring—*spring* CO-8
*Tollerville* KS-7
Tolles—*locale* CT-1
**Tollesboro**—*pop pl* KY-4

Tom Gooding Spring—*spring* ID-8
Tom Graham Oil Field—*oilfield* TX-5
Tom Graham Pass—*gap* MT-8
Tom Gray Creek—*stream* AK-9
Tom Gray Ford—*locale* KY-4
Tom Gray Gulch—*valley* CA-9
**Tom Green (County)**—*pop pl* TX-5
Tom Green County Courthouse—*hist pl* TX-5
Tom Green County Jail—*hist pl* TX-5
Tom Green Mine—*mine* CA-9
Tom Green Mtn—*summit* TX-5
Tom Gulch—*valley* CA-9
Tom Hahn Creek—*stream* FL-3
Tom Hale Gulf—*valley* TN-4
Tom Hall Branch—*stream* NC-3
Tom Hallett Cem—*cemetery* NY-2
Tom Handle Creek—*stream* TX-5
Tom Haney Windmill—*locale* NM-5
**Tomhannock**—*pop pl* NY-2
Tomhannock Creek—*stream* NY-2
Tomhannock Rsvr—*reservoir* NY-2
Tom Harris Branch—*stream* TN-4
Tom Harris Branch—*stream* TX-5
Tom Harris Hollow—*valley* UT-8
Tom Hauk Number 1 Dam—*dam* SD-7
Tom Head Creek—*stream* CA-9
Tomhead Gulch—*valley* CA-9
Tomhead Mine—*mine* CA-9
Tomhead Mtn—*summit* CA-9
Tomhead Spring—*spring* CA-9
Tom Heath Ridge—*ridge* KY-4
Tomhegan Cove—*bay* ME-1
Tomhegan Game Sanctuary—*park* ME-1
Tomhegan Point—*cape* ME-1
Tomhegan Pond—*lake* ME-1
Tomhegan Stream—*stream* (2) ME-1
Tomhegan (Township of)—*unorg* ME-1
Tom Henry Branch—*stream* TN-4
Tomhicken Creek—*stream* PA-2
Tomhicken Falls—*falls* PA-2
Tomhicken (RR name for Sugarloaf)—*other* PA-2
Tomhicken Shaft Number Four—*mine* PA-2
**Tomhicken (Sugarloaf Post Office)**—*pop pl* PA-2
*Tomhickon* PA-2
Tomhickon Colliery—*building* PA-2
*Tomhickon Creek* PA-2
Tom Hill—*summit* (2) MA-1
Tom Hill—*summit* NY-2
Tom Hill Creek—*stream* SD-7
Tom Hill Hollow—*valley* MO-7
Tom Hollow—*valley* AR-4
Tom Hollow—*valley* CO-8
Tom Hollow—*valley* (2) MO-7
Tom Hollow—*valley* (3) TN-4
Tom Hollow—*valley* TX-5
Tom Hollow Branch—*stream* TN-4
Tom Hollow Ford (historical)—*locale* MO-7
Tom Hunters Well—*well* AZ-5
Tomichi Cem—*cemetery* CO-8
Tomichi Creek—*stream* CO-8
Tomichi Dome—*summit* CO-8
Tomichi Pass—*gap* CO-8
Tomico, Lake—*reservoir* PA-2
Tomike Creek—*stream* OK-5
*Tomil* FM-9
*Tomil-Gamil* FM-9
*Tomil-Hafen* FM-9
*Tomil Harbor* FM-9
*Tomil Harbor Entrance* FM-9
*Tomil Island* FM-9
Tomil (Municipality)—*civ div* FM-9
Tominson Sch—*school* MI-6
*Tomiru* FM-9
*Tom Jack Creek* PA-2
Tom Jack Creek—*stream* NC-3
Tomjack Creek—*stream* PA-2
Tom Jack Hollow—*valley* AR-4
Tom Jackson Park—*park* AL-4
Tom Jenkins Dam—*dam* OH-6
*Tom Jenkins Flood Control Reservoir* OH-6
Tom Joe Spring—*spring* AZ-5
Tom John Pond—*lake* FL-3
Tom Johns Crossing—*locale* KY-4
Tom Johnson Hollow—*valley* TN-4
Tom Jones Branch—*stream* GA-3
Tom Jones Branch—*stream* KY-4
Tom Jones Mtn—*summit* NY-2
Tom Jones Point—*cape* VA-3
Tom Jones Rsvr—*reservoir* CA-9
Tom Ketchum Canyon—*valley* AZ-5
Tom Ketchum Tank—*reservoir* AZ-5
Tom Kettle Lake—*lake* NY-2
Tomki Creek—*stream* CA-9
Tom King Bayou—*stream* FL-3
Tom King Ditch—*canal* IA-7
Tom King Hollow—*valley* IA-7
Tom Kings Creek—*stream* MI-6
**Tomkins**—*pop pl* WA-9
**Tomkins Cove**—*pop pl* NY-2
Tomkins Lake—*lake* NY-2
*Tomkins School* IN-6
Tomkins Tank—*reservoir* AZ-5
*Tom Knob* NC-3
Tom Knob—*summit* KY-4
*Tom Lake* MN-6
Tom Lake—*lake* AK-9
Tom Lake—*lake* MN-6
Tom Lamb Rsvr—*reservoir* AZ-5
Tom Lang Gulch—*valley* CA-9
Tom Large Flat—*flat* CA-9
Tom Lavin Creek—*stream* ID-8
Tom Lay Prairie—*flat* MT-8
Tom Lee Draft—*valley* VA-3
Tom Lee Meadows—*flat* CA-9
Tom Leighton Point—*cape* ME-1
Tomley Creek—*stream* AL-4
Tom Lick Run—*stream* (2) WV-2
Tomlike Mtn—*summit* OR-9
Tomlin—*locale* NJ-2
Tomlin, Lake—*lake* TN-4
Tomlin Branch—*stream* TX-5
Tomlin Cem—*cemetery* KY-4
Tomlin Cem—*cemetery* TX-5
Tomlin Ditch—*canal* IL-6
Tomlin JHS—*school* FL-3
Tomlin Lake—*reservoir* TX-5
Tomlin Mill Creek—*stream* AL-4
Tomlin Sch—*school* NJ-2
Tomlins Chapel—*church* TN-4
*Tomlins Lake* MA-1
*Tomlinson* VT-1
Tomlinson—*locale* IL-6
**Tomlinson**—*pop pl* IL-6
**Tomlinson**—*pop pl* WV-2
Tomlinson, Samuel J., House—*hist pl* MI-6
Tomlinson Cem—*cemetery* AR-4
Tomlinson Cem—*cemetery* IL-6
Tomlinson Cem—*cemetery* IN-6
Tomlinson Cem—*cemetery* LA-4
Tomlinson Cem—*cemetery* OH-6
Tomlinson Cem—*cemetery* (3) TN-4
Tomlinson Cem—*cemetery* VA-3
Tomlinson Ch—*church* GA-3
Tomlinson Chair Manufacturing Company Complex—*hist pl* NC-3
Tomlinson Coll—*school* TN-4
**Tomlinson Corners**—*pop pl* NY-2
Tomlinson Creek—*stream* MN-6
Tomlinson Creek—*stream* OR-9
Tomlinson Field (airport)—*airport* ND-7
Tomlinson Fire Tower—*locale* SC-3
**Tomlinson Hill**—*pop pl* TX-5
Tomlinson House—*hist pl* NY-2
Tomlinson-Huddleston House—*hist pl* PA-2
Tomlinson Inn and the Little Meadows—*hist pl* MD-2
Tomlinson JHS—*school* OK-5
Tomlinson Lake—*lake* (2) MN-6
Tomlinson Mansion—*hist pl* WV-2
Tomlinson Park—*park* MI-6
Tomlinson Pond—*lake* CT-1
Tomlinson Prairie—*flat* FL-3
Tomlinson Ranch—*locale* UT-8
Tomlinson Run—*stream* WV-2
Tomlinson Run Ch—*church* PA-2
Tomlinson Run Lake—*lake* WV-2
Tomlinson Run State Park—*park* WV-2
Tomlinson Sch—*school* NC-3
Tomlinson Slough—*stream* OR-9
Tomlinsons Mill—*locale* NJ-2
Tomlinsons Mill Dam—*dam* NJ-2
Tomlinson (Township of)—*fmr MCD* (2) AR-4
Tomlins Swamp—*swamp* MA-1
*Tomlin Swamp* MA-1
*Tomlintons Mill* NJ-2
**Tomlison Addition**—*pop pl* OH-6
Tom Little Draw—*valley* CO-8
Tom Loar Pass—*channel* LA-4
Tom Lockett Draw—*valley* AZ-5
Tom Lockett Tank—*reservoir* AZ-5
Tom Lock Hollow—*valley* MO-7
Tom Long Creek—*stream* CA-9
Tom Lucas Campground—*locale* CA-9
Tom Lykes Park (county park)—*park* FL-3
Tom Man Branch—*stream* AL-4
Tom Mann Creek—*bay* NC-3
Tom Mann Swamp—*swamp* FL-3
*Tommany Hill* RI-1
*Tommaquay Brook* RI-1
Tom Martin Creek—*stream* CA-9
Tom Martin Peak—*summit* CA-9
Tom Mason Dam—*dam* SD-7
Tom McBee Dam—*dam* TN-4
Tom McBee Lake—*reservoir* TN-4
Tom McDonald Creek—*stream* CA-9
Tommeheton Creek—*stream* VA-3
Tommeheton Lake—*reservoir* VA-3
Tommelson Creek—*stream* TX-5
Tommie Bayou—*stream* MS-4
Tommie Creek—*stream* MO-7
Tommies Homestead—*locale* OR-9
Tommie Spring—*spring* AZ-5
Tommies Tank—*reservoir* AZ-5
Tommie Tank—*reservoir* AZ-5
Tom Milan Pond Dam—*dam* MS-4
Tom Miller Dam—*dam* TX-5
*Tom Mills Cemetery* MS-4
Tom Miner Basin—*basin* MT-8
Tom Miner Creek—*stream* MT-8
*Tom Miner Pass* MT-8
Tom Mix Monmt—*park* AZ-5
Tom Mix Wash—*stream* AZ-5
*Tommoeweague Brook* RI-1
Tom Moore Branch—*stream* AR-4
Tom Moore Canyon—*valley* NM-5
Tom Moore Hollow—*valley* KY-4
Tom Moore Mesa—*summit* NM-5
Tom Moore Mine—*mine* CA-9
Tom Moore Rock—*rock* MA-1
Tom Moore Slough—*stream* WA-9
*Tommoquag Brook* RI-1
Tom Moss Branch—*stream* AR-4
**Tommotley (historical)**—*pop pl* TN-4
Tom Mount—*summit* OR-9
*Tom Mountain* ID-8
*Tom Mountain* ME-1
Tom Mtn—*summit* VA-3
Tom Mtn—*summit* WI-6
Tom Muir Spring—*spring* UT-8
Tom Murray—*uninc pl* TN-4
Tommy, Bayou—*stream* (2) LA-4
Tommy Bluff—*cliff* MO-7
Tommy Bond Branch—*stream* OK-5
Tommy Cain Ravine—*valley* CA-9
*Tommy Canyon* UT-8
Tommy Canyon—*valley* UT-8
Tommy Clark Pond Dam—*dam* MS-4
Tommy Cork Spring—*spring* OR-9
Tommy Cove—*valley* NC-3
*Tommy Creek* UT-8
Tommy Creek—*stream* AK-9
Tommy Creek—*stream* CO-8
Tommy Creek—*stream* NY-2
Tommy Creek—*stream* OR-9
Tommy Creek—*stream* TN-4
Tommy Creek—*stream* UT-8
Tommy Creek—*stream* WA-9
Tommy Creek—*stream* WV-2
Tommy Dantz Bayou—*gut* LA-4
Tommy Dean Cem—*cemetery* OR-9
Tommy Dodson Canyon—*valley* CO-8
Tommy Dowell Spring—*spring* CO-8
Tommy Ege Dam—*dam* AL-4
Tommy Ellis Lake Dam—*dam* MS-4
Tommy Ellis Pond Dam—*dam* MS-4
Tommy Glacier—*glacier* AK-9
Tommy Graham Pond Dam—*dam* MS-4
Tommy Hammock—*island* NC-3
*Tommy Hill* RI-1
Tommy Hill—*summit* PA-2
Tommy Hill Canyon—*valley* NM-5
Tommy Hill Tank—*reservoir* NM-5
Tommy Hollow—*valley* PA-2
Tommy Hollow—*valley* (2) UT-8
Tommy Island—*island* AK-9
Tommy Island—*island* (2) ME-1
Tommy Island—*island* MA-1
Tommy Island—*island* RI-1
Tommy James Basin—*basin* WY-8
Tommy James Creek—*stream* WY-8
Tommy Jones Flat Tank—*reservoir* NM-5
Tommy Knob—*summit* NC-3
Tommy Lake—*lake* AK-9
Tommy Lake—*lake* WY-8
Tommy Long Gulch—*valley* CO-8
Tommy Mine—*mine* CO-8
Tommy Point—*cape* AK-9
Tommy Pond—*lake* IN-6
Tommy Pond Spring—*spring* CO-8
Tommy Reed Creek—*stream* NC-3
Tommy Ridge—*ridge* WV-2
Tommy Roaring Creek—*stream* NY-2
Tommy Run—*stream* OH-6
Tommys Branch—*stream* NJ-2
Tommys Cave—*cave* AL-4
Tommys Ditch—*canal* VA-3
*Tommys Draw* CO-8
Tommys Draw—*valley* CO-8
Tommys Fishing Lake Dam—*dam* NC-3
Tommys Gulch—*valley* CO-8
*Tommys Hammock* NC-3
Tommys Knob—*summit* SC-3
Tommys Lake—*lake* MI-6
Tommy Smith Creek—*stream* UT-8
Tommy Smith Lake Dam—*dam* MS-4
**Tommys Point**—*pop pl* NC-3
Tommy Spring—*spring* CO-8
Tommys Pup—*stream* AK-9
Tommys Rock—*summit* NY-2
Tommys Spring—*spring* OR-9
Tommy Tigers Camp—*locale* FL-3
**Tommytown**—*pop pl* FL-3
Tommy Tucker Rsvr—*reservoir* WY-8
Tommy Water—*spring* UT-8
Tommy Well—*well* NM-5
Tommy White Park—*park* TX-5
Tommy Wright Branch—*stream* MD-2
Tomname Lagoon—*lake* AK-9
Tomname Mtn—*summit* AK-9
Tomname Point—*cape* AK-9
Tom Nations Cem—*cemetery* NC-3
Tom Nat Stogner Cem—*cemetery* MS-4
Tom Neal Creek—*stream* CA-9
Tom Neck Point—*cape* MA-1
Tom Ned Tank—*reservoir* NM-5
*Tom Neil Creek* CA-9
*Tom Never's Head* MA-1
Tom Nevers Head—*cliff* MA-1
*Tom Never's Pond* MA-1
Tom Nevers Pond—*lake* MA-1
Tom Nevers Swamp—*swamp* MA-1
Tom Niece Spring—*spring* AZ-5
**Tomnolen**—*pop pl* (2) MS-4
Tomnolen Baptist Ch—*church* MS-4
Tomnolen Methodist Ch (historical)—*church* MS-4
Tomnolen Sch (historical)—*school* MS-4
Tom Nunn Hill—*summit* TX-5
Tom O'Connor Oil Field—*oilfield* TX-5
*Tomocquoague Brook* RI-1
Tomoe Lake—*lake* WI-6
Tomoka Basin—*bay* FL-3
*Tomoka Creek* FL-3
Tomoka Elem Sch—*school* FL-3
**Tomoka Estates**—*pop pl* FL-3
Tomoka Lookout Tower—*tower* FL-3
Tomoka Marsh Aquatic Preserve—*park* FL-3
Tomoka River—*stream* FL-3
Tomoka State Park—*park* FL-3
Tomoka United Methodist Ch—*church* FL-3
*Tomoka Wildlife Mngmt Area* FL-3
Tomoka Wildlife Mngmt Area Union-Camp Tract—*park* FL-3
Tomoka Wildlife Mngmt Area Volusia Recharge Tract—*park* FL-3
*Tomoko Basin* FL-3
*Tomomacori* AZ-5
Tom O'Neal Hollow—*valley* KY-4
Tomonpa (historical)—*locale* AL-4
*Tomopa* AL-4
*Tomora* FM-9
*Tomorolong* FM-9
*Tomororon* FM-9
Tomorrow River—*stream* WI-6
*Tomorrowway* IL-6
Tomorur—*bar* FM-9
Tomotla—*locale* NC-3
Tomotla Ford—*locale* TN-4
**Tomotley**—*pop pl* SC-3
Tomotley Site—*hist pl* TN-4
Tomotli Shoals—*bar* TN-4
*Tomototon* FM-9
Tom Pack Hollow—*valley* TN-4
Tom Paine Creek—*stream* AK-9
Tom Paine Slough—*stream* CA-9
Tom Patterson Canyon—*valley* UT-8
Tom Patterson Point—*summit* UT-8
Tom Patterson Ridge—*ridge* UT-8
Tom Patterson Spring—*spring* UT-8
Tom Payne Creek—*stream* CA-9
Tom Payne Gulch—*valley* NM-5
Tom Payne Hill—*locale* CO-8
Tom Payne Peak—*summit* CA-9
Tompeat Creek—*stream* MS-4
Tom Peck Pond—*lake* NY-2
*Tom Peek Pond* NY-2
Tom Perry Canyon—*valley* ID-8
Tom Phelps Well—*well* NM-5
Tompkin Branch—*stream* NC-3
Tompkins—*locale* GA-3
Tompkins—*locale* PA-2
Tompkins—*locale* SC-3
Tompkins—*locale* WA-9
**Tompkins**—*pop pl* MI-6
Tompkins, Henry B., House—*hist pl* GA-3
Tompkins, James, House—*hist pl* WI-6
Tompkins Bar—*bar* OR-9
Tompkins Bend Rec Area—*park* AR-4
Tompkins Bluff—*cliff* AL-4
Tompkins Branch—*stream* VA-3
Tompkins-Buchanan House—*hist pl* KY-4
Tompkins Butte—*summit* OR-9
Tompkins Canyon—*valley* (2) AZ-5
Tompkins Cem—*cemetery* AL-4
Tompkins Cem—*cemetery* FL-3
Tompkins Cem—*cemetery* GA-3
Tompkins Cem—*cemetery* TN-4
*Tompkins Center* MI-6
Tompkins Center—*other* MI-6
*Tompkins Centre* MI-6
Tompkins Ch—*church* AL-4
Tompkins Ch—*church* AR-4
Tompkins Ch—*church* PA-2
Tompkins Community House—*locale* SC-3
Tompkins Corners—*locale* PA-2
**Tompkins Corners**—*pop pl* (3) NY-2
Tompkins Corners Cem—*cemetery* NY-2
Tompkins Corners United Methodist Church—*hist pl* NY-2
Tompkins Corners Vista—*summit* PA-2
**Tompkins (County)**—*pop pl* NY-2
Tompkins County Airp—*airport* NY-2
Tompkins Cove—*valley* TN-4
Tompkins Creek—*stream* (2) CA-9
Tompkins Creek—*stream* MN-6
Tompkins Creek—*stream* PA-2
Tompkins Dam—*dam* AL-4
Tompkins Ditch—*canal* CO-8
Tompkins Falls—*falls* NY-2
Tompkins Hill—*summit* CA-9
Tompkins Hollow—*valley* NY-2
Tompkins Inn—*hist pl* GA-3
*Tompkins Knob* NC-3
Tompkins Lake—*lake* TN-4
Tompkins Lake—*reservoir* AL-4
Tompkins Lake—*reservoir* TN-4
Tompkins Lake Dam—*dam* TN-4
Tompkins Landing—*locale* OR-9
Tompkins Memorial Park—*cemetery* AZ-5
Tompkins Mill Creek—*stream* TX-5
Tompkins Park—*park* NY-2
Tompkins Pass—*gap* OR-9
Tompkins Point—*cape* NY-2
Tompkins Sch—*school* CA-9
Tompkins Sch—*school* MI-6
Tompkins Sch—*school* (2) NY-2
Tompkins Sch (historical)—*school* MO-7
Tompkins Shaft (historical)—*mine* PA-2
Tompkins Square—*park* NY-2
Tompkins Street Hist Dist—*hist pl* NY-2
Tompkins Street/Main Street Hist Dist (Boundary Increase)—*hist pl* NY-2
**Tompkins (Town of)**—*pop pl* NY-2
**Tompkins (Township of)**—*pop pl* IL-6
**Tompkins (Township of)**—*pop pl* MI-6
Tompkinsville—*locale* MD-2
**Tompkinsville**—*pop pl* AL-4
**Tompkinsville**—*pop pl* KY-4
**Tompkinsville**—*pop pl* NY-2
**Tompkinsville**—*pop pl* PA-2
Tompkinsville (CCD)—*cens area* KY-4
Tom Plain Spring—*spring* NV-8
*Tom Point* MD-2
*Tom Point* NC-3
Tom Point—*cape* MD-2
Tom Point Creek—*stream* SC-3
Tom Pond—*lake* NH-1
Tom Pond—*swamp* FL-3
Tom Poole Lake—*lake* MT-8
Tom Porter Springs—*spring* UT-8
Tom Post Office (historical)—*building* MS-4
Tom Post Office (historical)—*building* TN-4
Tom Powell Cove—*valley* AL-4
Tom Price Mtn—*summit* NC-3
*Tompson Bridge* AL-4
*Tompson Lake* CA-9
Tompson Rsvr—*reservoir* (2) NM-5
*Tompsons Island* MA-1
*Tompsons Mountain* MA-1
*Tompsonville* PA-2
Tom Ranch—*locale* NM-5
Tom Ranch—*locale* TX-5
*Tom Ray Cemetery* TN-4
Tom Ray Phillips Lake Dam—*dam* MS-4
Tom Redford Ridge—*ridge* TN-4
Tom Reed Mine—*mine* AZ-5
Tom Reed Mine—*mine* CA-9
Tom Reese Creek—*stream* MT-8
Tom Rice Hill—*summit* IN-6
*Tom Rice Hills* IN-6
Tom Richardson Cem—*cemetery* TX-5
Tom Ridge—*ridge* MD-2
Tom Ritter Hollow—*valley* AR-4
Tom Roark Slough—*bay* TN-4
Tom Robinette Dam—*dam* AL-4
Tom Robinette Lake—*reservoir* AL-4
Tom Rock—*bar* ME-1
Tom Rock—*pillar* OR-9
Tom Rsvr—*reservoir* OR-9
Tom Run—*stream* PA-2
Tom Run—*stream* WV-2
Toms, Lake—*lake* LA-4
*Tom Sauk Creek* MO-7
*Tom Sauk Mountain* MO-7
Tom Sawyer, Lake—*lake* MO-7
Tom Sawyer Lake—*lake* CA-9
Toms Bar—*bar* AL-4
*Toms Bayou* FL-3
Toms Bayou—*bay* FL-3
Toms Bayou—*stream* LA-4
Toms Bight—*bay* FL-3
**Toms Bottom**—*pop pl* VA-3
*Tom's Branch* AR-4
Toms Branch—*stream* AL-4
Toms Branch—*stream* AR-4
Toms Branch—*stream* (10) KY-4
Toms Branch—*stream* MS-4
Toms Branch—*stream* NJ-2
Toms Branch—*stream* (5) NC-3
Toms Branch—*stream* (3) SC-3
Toms Branch—*stream* (2) TN-4
Toms Branch—*stream* TX-5
Toms Branch—*stream* (3) VA-3
Toms Branch—*stream* (6) WV-2
Toms Branch Ch—*church* KY-4
Toms Branch Sch—*school* KY-4
Toms Bridge—*bridge* NJ-2
*Toms Brook* AR-4
**Toms Brook**—*pop pl* VA-3
Toms Brook—*stream* NY-2
Toms Brook—*stream* VA-3
*Tomsburg* WV-2
Toms Butte—*summit* ND-7
Toms Cabin—*locale* WY-8
Toms Cabin Creek—*stream* UT-8
Toms Cabin Gulch—*valley* CA-9
Toms Cabin Spring—*spring* CA-9
Toms Cabin Spring—*spring* UT-8
Toms Camp Branch—*stream* MS-4
Toms Canyon—*basin* CA-9
Toms Canyon—*valley* CA-9
Toms Canyon—*valley* CO-8
Toms Canyon—*valley* (2) ID-8
Toms Canyon—*valley* NV-8
Toms Canyon—*valley* NM-5
Toms Canyon—*valley* TX-5
Toms Canyon—*valley* UT-8
Toms Canyon Spring—*spring* CO-8
Toms Canyon Spring—*spring* ID-8
Toms Coulee—*valley* MT-8
Toms Cove—*bay* VA-3
*Toms Creek* CA-9
*Toms Creek* NJ-2
*Toms Creek* NC-3
Toms Creek—*channel* GA-3
Toms Creek—*locale* GA-3
**Toms Creek**—*pop pl* NC-3
**Toms Creek**—*pop pl* VA-3
Toms Creek—*stream* (2) AL-4
Toms Creek—*stream* AK-9
Toms Creek—*stream* AZ-5
Toms Creek—*stream* AR-4
Toms Creek—*stream* (2) CA-9
Toms Creek—*stream* CT-1
Toms Creek—*stream* (2) FL-3
Toms Creek—*stream* (3) GA-3
Toms Creek—*stream* (2) ID-8
Toms Creek—*stream* IL-6
Toms Creek—*stream* (2) KY-4
Toms Creek—*stream* MD-2
Toms Creek—*stream* MI-6
Toms Creek—*stream* MS-4
Toms Creek—*stream* MO-7
Toms Creek—*stream* MT-8
Toms Creek—*stream* (9) NC-3
Toms Creek—*stream* OR-9
Toms Creek—*stream* (2) PA-2
Toms Creek—*stream* SC-3
Toms Creek—*stream* (3) TN-4
Toms Creek—*stream* TX-5
Toms Creek—*stream* UT-8
Toms Creek—*stream* (3) VA-3
Toms Creek—*stream* (2) WV-2
Toms Creek—*stream* WY-8
Toms Creek Canyon—*valley* WY-8
Toms Creek Ch—*church* KY-4
Toms Creek Ch—*church* MD-2
Toms Creek Ch—*church* (2) NC-3
Toms Creek Ch—*church* WV-2
Toms Creek Dock—*locale* TN-4
Toms Creek Ford—*locale* TN-4
**Toms Creek (historical)**—*pop pl* TN-4
Toms Creek Post Office (historical)—*building* TN-4
Toms Dam Branch—*stream* DE-2
Toms Den Branch—*stream* AL-4
Toms Draw—*valley* WY-8
Tom Seay Cem—*cemetery* SC-3
Tom Self Lake—*lake* LA-4
Tom Sellers Branch—*stream* KY-4
Toms Falls—*falls* NC-3
Toms Field—*flat* LA-4
Toms Fork—*stream* (2) NC-3
Toms Fork—*stream* SC-3
Toms Fork—*stream* VA-3
Toms Fork—*stream* (3) WV-2
Toms Fork Ch—*church* WV-2
Toms Gap—*gap* TN-4
Toms Gulch—*valley* CA-9
Toms Gulch—*valley* (2) ID-8
Toms Gulch—*valley* (2) MT-8
Toms Gut—*gut* (2) VA-3
Toms Gut—*stream* MD-2
Toms Harbor—*bay* FL-3
Toms Harbor Channel—*channel* FL-3
*Toms Harbor Cut* FL-3
Toms Harbor Cut—*channel* FL-3
Toms Harbor Keys—*island* FL-3
Tom Sherry Creek—*stream* UT-8
*Toms Hill* MA-1
Toms Hill—*summit* CA-9
Toms Hill—*summit* CT-1
Toms Hill—*summit* IN-6
Toms Hill—*summit* MD-2
Toms Hill—*summit* NY-2
Tom Shoal—*bar* MA-1
Toms Hole—*valley* UT-8
Toms Hollow—*valley* MD-2
Toms Hollow—*valley* OH-6
Toms Hollow—*valley* WV-2
Tomsich Butte—*summit* UT-8
Tomsick Ranch—*locale* CO-8
Tomsik Well (Dry)—*well* UT-8
Toms Island—*island* (2) ME-1
Toms Island—*island* NJ-2
Tom Skillman Ranch—*locale* MT-8
Toms Knob—*summit* NC-3
Toms Knob—*summit* (3) VA-3
Toms Knoll—*summit* UT-8
Toms Knoll Pass—*gap* UT-8
Toms Lake—*lake* (2) CA-9
Toms Lake—*lake* IN-6
Toms Lake—*lake* MI-6
Toms Lake—*lake* MN-6
Toms Lake—*lake* NJ-2
Toms Lake—*lake* OR-9
Toms Lake—*lake* TX-5
Toms Lake—*lake* UT-8
Toms Lake—*swamp* MN-6
Toms Landing—*locale* NY-2
Toms Landing Strip—*airport* PA-2
Toms Mine—*mine* NV-8
Tom Smith Branch—*channel* FL-3
Tom Smith Cabin—*locale* CA-9
Tom Smith Hollow—*valley* TN-4
Toms Mountain—*ridge* AR-4
*Toms Mtn* CT-1
Toms Mtn—*summit* NC-3
Toms Neck—*cape* (2) MA-1
*Tom's Neck Point* MA-1
Toms Neck Point—*cape* MA-1
**Tomson**—*pop pl* PA-2
*Tomsons Island* MA-1
Tomson Station—*locale* PA-2
Toms Peak—*summit* MT-8
**Toms Place**—*pop pl* CA-9
Toms Point—*cape* CA-9
Toms Point—*cape* MA-1
Toms Point—*cape* (2) NY-2
Toms Point—*cape* RI-1
Toms Point—*summit* NJ-2
**Toms Prairie**—*pop pl* IL-6
Tom Spring—*spring* AZ-5
Tom Spring—*spring* (3) NV-8
Tom Spring—*spring* OR-9
Tom Spring—*spring* SD-7
Tom Spring—*spring* (2) UT-8
Tomspur—*locale* CA-9
Toms Ridge—*ridge* ID-8
Toms Ridge—*ridge* UT-8
**Toms River**—*pop pl* NJ-2
Toms River—*stream* NJ-2
*Toms River Bay* NJ-2
Toms River Cem—*cemetery* NJ-2
Toms River HS—*school* NJ-2
Toms Rock—*summit* NM-5
Toms Rock Well—*well* NM-5
*Toms Run* WV-2
Toms Run—*stream* (2) MD-2
Toms Run—*stream* (2) OH-6
Toms Run—*stream* (7) PA-2
Toms Run—*stream* (8) WV-2
Toms Spring—*spring* CO-8
Toms Spring—*spring* UT-8
Toms Spring Run—*stream* MD-2
Toms Spur—*ridge* KY-4
Toms Tank—*reservoir* (2) AZ-5
Tom Station—*locale* TN-4
Tom Steed Rsvr—*reservoir* OK-5
Tom Stein, Mount—*summit* NY-2
Tom Still Hammock—*island* FL-3
Tom Stith Gulch—*valley* CO-8
Toms Top—*summit* NC-3
*Toms Town* PA-2
**Tomstown**—*pop pl* PA-2
Tomstown Dolomite Quarry—*mine* PA-2
*Tom Suck Creek* MO-7
Tom Sullivan Cem—*cemetery* MS-4
Toms Valley Creek—*stream* CA-9
Tom Swamp—*swamp* MA-1
Tom Swamp Run—*stream* MD-2
*Toms Wash* ND-7
Toms Wash—*stream* ND-7
Toms Waterhole—*spring* OR-9
Toms Well—*well* WY-8
Tom Taha Creek—*stream* ID-8
Tom Tank—*reservoir* (3) AZ-5
Tom Tank—*reservoir* NM-5
Tom Tanks—*reservoir* AZ-5
Tom Taylor Branch—*stream* NC-3
Tom Taylor Cabin—*locale* CA-9
Tom Taylor Canyon—*valley* OR-9
Tomter Coulee—*valley* WI-6
Tom Thumb—*summit* AZ-5
Tom Thumb Bay—*swamp* GA-3
Tom Thumb Cem—*cemetery* AR-4
Tom Thumb Creek—*stream* GA-3
Tom Thumb Creek—*stream* NC-3
Tom Thumb Mine—*mine* CO-8
Tom Thumb Mine—*mine* WA-9
Tom Thumb Spring—*spring* AR-4
Tom Thumb Tunnel—*tunnel* ID-8
Tomtit Branch—*stream* VA-3
Tomtit Lake—*lake* WA-9
*Tom Tit Run* PA-2
Tomtit Run—*stream* PA-2
Tom Tom Lake—*lake* MT-8
Tom Tom Mtn—*summit* MT-8
Tom Town—*locale* TN-4
Tom Township—*civil* MO-7
Tomty Coulee—*valley* MT-8
Tomu—*bar* FM-9
*Tomuch Lake* MN-6
*Tomun* FM-9
Tom Valley—*valley* CA-9
Tom Vawn Creek—*stream* OR-9
Tom Virden Lake Dam—*dam* MS-4
Tom Walder Memorial Park—*cemetery* AZ-5
Tom Walker Coulee—*valley* MT-8
Tom Wallace Lake—*reservoir* KY-4
Tom Walls Branch—*stream* MD-2
Tom Wanlass Ditch—*canal* CO-8
Tomwara—*civil* FM-9
Tomwara—*locale* FM-9
Tomwara, Dawen—*gut* FM-9
Tomwarahlong—*civil* FM-9
Tom Waters Creek—*bay* NC-3
Tom Watkins Park—*park* MO-7
Tom Watts Lake Dam—*dam* MS-4
Tom Way Branch—*stream* MS-4
Tom Weeks Head—*swamp* FL-3
Tomwena Island—*island* FM-9
Tom Westcott Spring—*spring* CO-8
Tom White, Mount—*summit* AK-9
Tom White Branch—*stream* GA-3
Tom White Hollow—*valley* TX-5
Tom Williams Bay—*swamp* FL-3
Tom Williams Ditch—*canal* MT-8
Tom Williams Hollow—*valley* WV-2
Tom Willis Camp—*locale* AZ-5
Tom Wright Hollow—*valley* TN-4
Tom Wright Mill—*locale* NM-5
*Tomyhawk Creek* ID-8
Tomyhoi Creek—*stream* WA-9
Tomyhoi Lake—*lake* WA-9
Tomyhoi Peak—*summit* WA-9
*Tomyhoy Creek* WA-9
Tomy Kill—*stream* NY-2
Tom Young Creek—*stream* OR-9
Tom Young Flat—*flat* CA-9
Tom Young Hollow—*valley* AR-4
Tom Young Pond—*lake* ME-1
Tom Young Spring—*spring* AR-4
Tom Young Well—*well* NM-5
*Ton* FM-9
Tona—*summit* FM-9
*Tonaachau* FM-9
Tonacana Creek—*stream* MS-4

Toothacher Creek—*stream* OR-9
*Toothacher Hill* VT-1
Toothacher Ledge—*bar* ME-1
Toothacker Bay—*bay* ME-1
Toothacre Sch—*school* MI-6
*Toothaker Brook* ME-1
Toothaker Brook—*stream* ME-1
Toothaker Brook Number One—*stream* ME-1
Toothaker Brook Number Two—*stream* ME-1
Toothaker Bros Ditch—*canal* WY-8
Toothaker Cem—*cemetery* IL-6
Toothaker Cem—*cemetery* ME-1
Toothaker Creek—*stream* NY-2
Toothaker Ditch No 1 And 2—*canal* WY-8
Toothaker Ditch No 2—*canal* WY-8
Toothaker Hill—*summit* VT-1
Toothaker Island—*island* ME-1
*Toothaker Place* AZ-5
Toothaker Pond—*lake* ME-1
Toothaker Pond—*lake* NY-2
Tooth Cove—*bay* AK-9
Toot Hill—*summit* VT-1
Tooth Lake—*lake* AK-9
Tooth Lake—*lake* CA-9
Tooth Lake—*lake* MN-6
Toothman Cem—*cemetery* WV-2
Toothman Run—*stream* WV-2
Tooth Mtn—*summit* AK-9
Tooth of Time—*pillar* NM-5
Tooth of Time Ridge—*ridge* NM-5
Toot Hollow Branch—*stream* NC-3
Toothpick Canyon—*valley* AZ-5
Toothpick Island—*island* NY-2
Toothpick Lake—*lake* WI-6
Toothpick Ridge—*ridge* AZ-5
Toothpick Ridge—*ridge* MO-7
*Toothpick Rock* MA-1
Tooth Rock—*pillar* AZ-5
Tooth Rock Tunnel—*tunnel* OR-9
Tooth Spring—*spring* UT-8
Tootin Hill Sch—*school* CT-1
Tootle Bay—*swamp* MS-4
*Tootoosa Hatchee Creek* FL-3
Tootoosahatchee Creek—*stream* FL-3
*Tootoosahatchie Creek* FL-3
*Toot Pond* RI-1
Toots Creek—*stream* VA-3
**Toots Crossroads**—*pop pl* OH-6
Tootsie Creek—*stream* (2) MT-8
Toots Lake—*lake* MI-6
*Toots Pond* RI-1
*Toovai* FM-9
Toowa Range—*ridge* CA-9
Tooze Creek—*stream* OR-9
Top—*locale* OR-9
Top—*locale* PA-2
Top, The—*summit* GA-3
Topache Peak—*summit* UT-8
Topacoba Gorge—*valley* AZ-5
*Topage* KS-7
Topagoruk River—*stream* AK-9
Topagoruk Test Well No 1—*well* AK-9
*Topahua* AZ-5
*Topahua Well* AZ-5
Topanemus, Lake—*reservoir* NJ-2
**Topanga**—*pop pl* CA-9
**Topanga Beach**—*pop pl* CA-9
*Topanga Canyon* CA-9
Topanga Canyon—*valley* CA-9
Topanga Lookout—*locale* CA-9
Topanga Malibu Sequit—*civil* CA-9
*Topanga Malibu Sequit Point* CA-9
**Topanga Oaks**—*pop pl* CA-9
**Topanga Park**—*pop pl* CA-9
Topanga Sch—*school* CA-9
*Topango Canyon* CA-9
*Topans Creek* ID-8
*Topasaw Creek* MS-4
Topashaw Creek—*stream* MS-4
Topashaw Creek Canal—*canal* MS-4
**Topa Topa**—*pop pl* CA-9
Topatopa Bluff—*cliff* CA-9
Topatopa Mountains—*range* CA-9
Topatopa Peak—*summit* CA-9
Topatopa Trail—*trail* CA-9
**Topawa**—*pop pl* AZ-5
Topawa Hills—*summit* AZ-5
Topawa Wash—*stream* AZ-5
Topawa Well—*well* AZ-5
*Topawo* AZ-5
Topaz—*locale* MO-7
**Topaz**—*pop pl* (2) AR-4
**Topaz**—*pop pl* ID-8
**Topaz**—*pop pl* MI-6
Topaz Basin—*basin* AZ-5
Topaz Camp—*locale* UT-8
Topaz Canyon—*valley* AZ-5
Topaz Lake—*lake* CA-9
Topaz Lake—*lake* MN-6
Topaz Lake—*lake* NV-8
**Topaz Lake**—*pop pl* NV-8
Topaz Marsh Waterfowl Mngmt Area—*park* UT-8
Topaz Mtn—*summit* CO-8
Topaz Mtn—*summit* UT-8
Topaz Mtn—*summit* WA-9
**Topaz PO**—*pop pl* CA-9
**Topaz Ranch Estates**—*pop pl* NV-8
Topaz RR Station—*building* AZ-5
Topaz (site)—*locale* CA-9
Topaz Slough—*gut* UT-8
Topaz Slough Conservation Area—*area* UT-8
Topaz Spring—*spring* MO-7
*Topaz State Waterfowl Mngmt Area* UT-8
Topaz Tank—*reservoir* AZ-5
Topaz Valley—*valley* UT-8
Topaz War Relocation Center Site—*hist pl* UT-8
Topbar Township (historical)—*civil* SD-7
Top Bay—*swamp* FL-3
Top Creek—*stream* OR-9
Topea Stream—*stream* AS-9
Top East Windmill—*locale* TX-5
*Topeca* KS-7
Topeco Ch—*church* VA-3
Tope Creek—*stream* OR-9
*To-pe-ka* KS-7
**Topeka**—*pop pl* IL-6
**Topeka**—*pop pl* IN-6
**Topeka**—*pop pl* KS-7
**Topeka**—*pop pl* MN-6
**Topeka**—*pop pl* MS-4
Topeka Ave Bridge—*bridge* KS-7
Topeka Bible Ch—*church* KS-7
Topeka Cem—*cemetery* KS-7
Topeka Ch of the Brethren—*church* KS-7
Topeka Country Club—*other* KS-7
Topeka Creek—*stream* PA-2
Topeka Elem Sch—*school* IN-6
Topeka Glacier—*glacier* AK-9
Topeka Golf Course—*other* KS-7
Topeka Gulch—*valley* CO-8
Topeka HS—*school* KS-7
Topeka Islands—*island* MN-6
Topeka Junction—*locale* GA-3
Topeka Peak—*summit* NE-7
Topeka Post Office (historical)—*building* MS-4
Topeka Reformed Latter Day Saints Central Ch—*church* KS-7
Topeka Service Area—*locale* KS-7
Topeka Tank—*reservoir* AZ-5
Topeka- Tilton Sch—*school* MS-4
**Topeka Township**—*pop pl* KS-7
*Tope Kobe Gorge* AZ-5
Topelius Cem—*cemetery* MN-6
Tope Ranch—*locale* WY-8
Toper Cem—*cemetery* KS-7
Toper Ridge—*ridge* TN-4
*Toper Spring* ID-8
Tope Sch—*school* CO-8
*Tope's Mill* OH-6
Tope Spring—*spring* OR-9
*Topham Hill* RI-1
Top Hat Ranch—*locale* (2) MT-8
Top Hat Rsvr—*reservoir* OR-9
*Tophenemus Brook* NJ-2
*Tophet* WV-2
**Tophet**—*pop pl* WV-2
Tophet Brook—*stream* MA-1
Tophet Sch—*school* NY-2
Tophet Swamp—*swamp* (4) MA-1
Tophet Swamp—*swamp* NH-1
Tophill—*locale* OR-9
*Tophulga* FL-3
Topia—*locale* NC-3
Topia Creek—*stream* NV-8
Topia Spring—*spring* NV-8
Topier Canyon—*valley* NV-8
**Topinabee**—*pop pl* MI-6
*Topinish* WA-9
*Topinish Creek* WA-9
Topins Grove—*locale* WV-2
Topis—*bar* FM-9
Topisaw—*locale* MS-4
*Topisaw Baptist Church* MS-4
Topisaw Ch—*church* MS-4
*Topisaw Creek* MS-4
Topisaw Creek—*stream* (2) MS-4
*Topisaw River* MS-4
Topisaw Watershed Structure Y-27-15 Dam—*dam* MS-4
Topisaw Watershed Structure Y-27-3 Dam—*dam* MS-4
**Topkegaiga (historical)**—*pop pl* FL-3
*Topkelake* FL-3
Topknot Hill—*summit* NM-5
Topknot Mtn—*summit* NY-2
Topkok—*locale* AK-9
Topkok Head—*cliff* AK-9
Top Lake—*lake* AK-9
Top Lake—*lake* CA-9
Top Lake—*lake* (3) OR-9
Top Lake—*lake* (2) WA-9
Top Lake—*lake* WY-8
*Topler Canyon* NV-8
*Toplico Creek* AL-4
Topliff—*locale* UT-8
Topliff Drain—*canal* MI-6
Topliff Hill—*summit* UT-8
Top Line Helipad—*airport* OR-9
Top Mine—*mine* CO-8
Topmost—*locale* KY-4
Top Mountain Trail—*trail* PA-2
Topnot—*locale* NC-3
**Topnot**—*pop pl* VA-3
Top Notch—*summit* NY-2
Topnotch Creek—*stream* AK-9
Topnotch Creek—*stream* ID-8
Top Notch Mine—*mine* AZ-5
Top Notch Peak—*summit* WY-8
Topnotch Ridge—*ridge* CA-9
Top Notch Sch—*school* NY-2
Topo Artesian Well—*well* TX-5
**Topocapa (historical)**—*pop pl* FL-3
Topock—*locale* AZ-5
Topock Bay—*bay* AZ-5
Topock Gorge—*valley* AZ-5
Topock Gorge—*valley* CA-9
Topock Marsh—*swamp* AZ-5
Topock Maze Archeol Site—*hist pl* CA-9
*Topock Swamp* AZ-5
Topocoba Hilltop—*locale* AZ-5
*To-po-co-bah Spring* AZ-5
Topocoba Spring—*spring* AZ-5
Topocoba Trail—*trail* AZ-5
*Topocobya Spring* AZ-5
Topo Creek—*stream* CA-9
*Topoc Slough* AZ-5
Top O'Deep—*locale* MT-8
Top of Allegheny—*locale* WV-2
Top of Pines—*summit* AZ-5
Top of the Hill Waterhole—*lake* OR-9
Top of the Mesa Well—*well* NM-5
*Top of the Mountain* TN-4
Top of the Mountain Canyon—*valley* AZ-5
Top of the Mountain Tank—*reservoir* (2) AZ-5
**Top-of-the-Ridge**—*pop pl* OH-6
**Top of the Wedge**—*pop pl* DE-2
Top of the World—*other* NM-5
**Top of the World**—*pop pl* CA-9
Top of the World—*ridge* NM-5
Top of the World—*summit* NH-1
Top Of The World—*summit* WY-8
Top of the World Estates—*locale* TN-4
Top of the World Mine—*mine* WY-8
Top of the World Picnic Area—*locale* CO-8
Top of the World Picnic Ground—*locale* CO-8
**Top Of The World Subdivision**—*pop pl* UT-8
Topog Peak—*summit* NV-8
Topographers Peak—*summit* AK-9
Topolovec Farmstead—*hist pl* UT-8
**Toponanaulka (historical)**—*pop pl* FL-3
**Toponas**—*pop pl* CO-8
Toponas Creek—*stream* CO-8
Toponas Creek Campground—*locale* CO-8
Toponas Rock—*pillar* CO-8
Toponce and Chesterfield Land Co Ditch—*canal* ID-8
Toponce Canyon—*valley* UT-8
Toponce Creek—*stream* ID-8
Toponou—*cape* FM-9
*Topons Creek* ID-8
Topony River—*stream* GU-9
*To-poo-ka* KS-7
Topopah Spring—*spring* NV-8
Topopah Wash—*stream* NV-8
Topopkin Creek—*stream* AL-4
Top O' Scott Golf Course—*other* OR-9
*Toposhaw Creek* MS-4
Topout Divide—*ridge* AZ-5
Topout Peak—*summit* AZ-5
Topo Valley—*valley* CA-9
*Topowa* AZ-5
Toppan Lake—*lake* WY-8
Topp Creek—*stream* IN-6
Toppen Coulee—*valley* WI-6
**Toppenish**—*pop pl* WA-9
Toppenish Creek—*stream* WA-9
Toppenish Drain—*canal* WA-9
Toppenish Mtn—*summit* WA-9
Toppenish Natl Wildlife Ref—*park* WA-9
Toppenish Ridge—*ridge* WA-9
Toppenish-Wapato (CCD)—*cens area* WA-9
Topper Lake—*lake* MN-6
**Toppers**—*pop pl* OK-5
**Toppertown**—*pop pl* MO-7
Toppin Creek—*stream* ID-8
Toppin Creek—*stream* (2) OR-9
Toppin Creek Butte—*summit* OR-9
Toppin Creek Canyon—*valley* OR-9
Toppin Creek Rsvr—*reservoir* OR-9
**Topping**—*pop pl* VA-3
Topping, J. R., House—*hist pl* OH-6
Topping Cem—*cemetery* IL-6
Topping Cem—*cemetery* MI-6
Topping Creek—*stream* VA-3
Topping Drain—*canal* MI-6
Topping Hill—*summit* TN-4
Topping Park—*park* OK-5
Topping Pond—*reservoir* CT-1
Toppings Lakes—*lake* WY-8
Top Point—*cape* MD-2
Topps Shop Ctr—*locale* MA-1
Toppys Cave—*cave* AZ-5
Toppys Spring—*spring* AZ-5
Top Rsvr—*reservoir* OR-9
**Topsail**—*pop pl* NC-3
**Topsail Beach**—*pop pl* NC-3
Topsail Bluff—*cliff* FL-3
Topsail Hill—*summit* FL-3
Topsail HS—*school* (2) NC-3
Topsail Primary Sch—*school* NC-3
*Topsail Sound* NC-3
Topsail Sound—*bay* NC-3
Topsail (Township of)—*fmr MCD* NC-3
Tops Airstrip—*airport* ND-7
*Topsaw River* MS-4
Top Sch (historical)—*school* TN-4
Top School—*locale* OR-9
**Topsey**—*pop pl* TX-5
Topsey Sch (historical)—*school* TN-4
**Topsfield**—*pop pl* ME-1
**Topsfield**—*pop pl* MA-1
Topsfield Station—*locale* MA-1
**Topsfield (Town of)**—*pop pl* ME-1
**Topsfield (Town of)**—*pop pl* MA-1
**Topsham**—*pop pl* ME-1
Topsham Cem—*cemetery* ME-1
Topsham Center (census name Topsham)—*other* ME-1
**Topsham (East Topsham)**—*pop pl* VT-1
**Topsham Four Corners**—*pop pl* VT-1
Topsham Hist Dist—*hist pl* ME-1
**Topsham (Town of)**—*pop pl* ME-1
**Topsham (Town of)**—*pop pl* VT-1
Topside—*hist pl* ME-1
Topside—*hist pl* TN-4
Topside—*locale* TN-4
Topside—*locale* WI-6
Topside Canyon—*valley* NM-5
Topside Lake—*lake* WI-6
Topside Pond—*lake* NH-1
Topside Rsvr—*reservoir* AZ-5
**Top Siding**—*pop pl* WV-2
Topso Butte—*summit* OR-9
Top Spring—*spring* CA-9
Top Spring—*spring* (2) NV-8
Top Spring No 1—*spring* CO-8
Top Spring No 2—*spring* CO-8
Topstone—*locale* CT-1
Topstone Mtn—*summit* CT-1
Top Strip Windmill—*locale* NM-5
Tops Windmill—*locale* NM-5
*Topsy* OK-5
Topsy—*locale* NC-3
**Topsy**—*pop pl* LA-4
**Topsy**—*pop pl* OK-5
**Topsy**—*pop pl* TN-4
Topsy Ch—*church* MO-7
Topsy Creek—*stream* AK-9
Topsy (historical)—*locale* KS-7
**Topsy (historical)**—*pop pl* OR-9
Topsy Key—*island* FL-3
Topsy Recreation Site—*park* OR-9
Topsy Turvy Lake—*lake* CA-9
Top Tank—*reservoir* AZ-5
Top Tank—*reservoir* NM-5
Top Tank—*reservoir* TX-5
Topton—*locale* AL-4
Topton—*locale* MS-4
**Topton**—*pop pl* KY-4
**Topton**—*pop pl* NC-3
**Topton**—*pop pl* PA-2
Topton Borough—*civil* PA-2
Topton Mtn—*summit* PA-2
Topton Post Office (historical)—*building* MS-4
Toptree Hammock Key—*island* FL-3
Topwe—*bar* FM-9
Top Well—*well* NM-5
Top West Posture Well—*well* TX-5
Top Windmill—*locale* CO-8
Topy Creek—*stream* LA-4
Topy Creek Oil Field—*oilfield* LA-4
Toqayong—*lake* FM-9
Toqiliy—*cape* FM-9
**Toqua**—*pop pl* TN-4
Toqua Boat Launching Ramp—*locale* TN-4
Toqua Cem—*cemetery* TN-4
Toqua Ch—*church* TN-4
Toqua Community Center—*building* TN-4
Toqua Creek—*stream* TN-4
**Toqua (historical)**—*pop pl* TN-4
Toqua Lakes Park—*park* MN-6
Toqua Rec Area—*park* TN-4
Toqua Sch—*school* TN-4
Toqua Site—*hist pl* TN-4
**Toqua (Township of)**—*pop pl* MN-6
*Toquema Range* NV-8
Toquer Catchment—*reservoir* AZ-5
Toquer Lake—*lake* UT-8
Toquer Tank—*reservoir* AZ-5
**Toquerville**—*pop pl* UT-8
Toquerville Cem—*cemetery* UT-8
Toquerville Post Office—*building* UT-8
Toquerville Springs—*spring* UT-8
Toquima Cave—*cave* NV-8
Toquima Range—*range* NV-8
**Toquin**—*pop pl* MI-6
*Toquo* TN-4
Toquop Gap—*gap* NV-8
Toquop Gap Rsvr—*reservoir* NV-8
Toquop Wash—*stream* NV-8
*Toquruuf* FM-9
*Toqus Creek* WY-8
Toqus Spring—*spring* WY-8
*Tora'* FM-9
*Toraa* FM-9
*Torag* FM-9
*Tora Island* FM-9
*Tora Island Pass* FM-9
*Torakku* FM-9
*Torakku-Ko* FM-9
*Torakku Shoto* FM-9
T O Ranch—*locale* NM-5
**T-o Ranch**—*pop pl* NM-5
*Torappenjokaji* FM-9
*Torappennotto* FM-9
*Torappu Channel* MP-9
Torappu Channel—*channel* MP-9
*Torappu-suido* MP-9
Toras Emes Acad of Miami (1st Campus)—*school* FL-3
*Tora Shima* FM-9
*Torashima Pass* FM-9
Torath Chaim Cem—*cemetery* PA-2
*Tora To* FM-9
*Toray Peak* TX-5
Torbert—*locale* PA-2
**Torbert**—*pop pl* LA-4
Torbert, Mount—*summit* AK-9
Torbert Lake—*reservoir* AL-4
Torbert Park—*park* OK-5
Torbert Post Office—*locale* LA-4
Torberts Lake Dam—*dam* AL-4
**Torbert (Sta.)**—*pop pl* LA-4
Torbert Trail—*trail* PA-2
**Torbet**—*pop pl* TN-4
*Torbet Lake Dam* PA-2
Torbett Hollow Trail—*trail* PA-2
**Torbit**—*pop pl* GA-3
Torboy—*locale* WA-9
**Torch**—*pop pl* MO-7
**Torch**—*pop pl* OH-6
Torch Bay—*bay* AK-9
Torch Bay—*bay* MI-6
Torch Channel—*channel* FL-3
Torch Hill (RR name for Torch)—*other* OH-6
Torch JHS—*school* CA-9
**Torch Key**—*pop pl* FL-3
Torch Key Mangroves—*island* FL-3
*Torch Lake* MI-6
Torch Lake—*lake* (2) MI-6
Torch Lake—*lake* WI-6
**Torch Lake**—*pop pl* MI-6
**Torch Lake (Township of)**—*pop pl* (2) MI-6
**Torch Lake Village**—*pop pl* MI-6
Torchlight—*locale* KY-4
Torchlight Dome Oil Field—*oilfield* WY-8
Torchlight Gulch—*valley* OR-9
Torchlight Hollow—*valley* KY-4
Torchlight Lake—*lake* MN-6
Torchlight Spring—*spring* OR-9
Torch Ramrod Channel—*channel* FL-3
**Torch River**—*pop pl* MI-6
Torch River—*stream* MI-6
Torch River—*stream* WI-6
*Torch Sar har na Creek, The* ND-7
Torch Speedway—*other* OH-6
Torcido, Arroyo—*stream* CA-9
Torcido, Arroyo—*valley* TX-5
Torcido Canyon—*valley* NM-5
Torcido Tank—*reservoir* NM-5
Torcindo Creek—*stream* CO-8
*Tordan Lake* MN-6
Tord Creek—*stream* MN-6
Tordenskjold Ch—*church* MN-6
Tordenskjold (Township of)—*civ div* MN-6
Tordillas Windmill—*locale* TX-5
Tordillo Cem—*cemetery* TX-5
Tordillo Creek—*stream* (2) TX-5
Tordillo Hill—*summit* TX-5
Tordillo Hills—*other* TX-5
Tordillo Mtn—*summit* AZ-5
Tordillo Tank—*reservoir* TX-5
Tordillo Windmill—*locale* TX-5
Tord Lake—*lake* MN-6
*Torechi Island* MP-9
Torechi Island—*island* MP-9
*Torechikku To* FM-9
*Toreechi Island* MP-9
*Toreechi-To* MP-9
*Toreson Reservoir* CA-9
*Toretekku* FM-9
**Toreva**—*pop pl* AZ-5
Toreva Spring—*spring* AZ-5
Torey Drain—*canal* MI-6
*Torey Lake Township* SD-7
Torfin—*locale* MN-6
Torgenson Creek—*stream* MN-6
Torgerson Flat—*flat* UT-8
Torgerson Hollow—*valley* (2) WI-6
Torgerson Lake—*lake* (2) MN-6
Torgerson Lake—*lake* UT-8
Torgerson Spring—*spring* UT-8
**Torgerson Township**—*pop pl* ND-7
*Torgeson Canal* LA-4
Torhorst Sch—*school* WI-6
Toria—*locale* KY-4
Torian—*locale* TX-5
Torian Cem—*cemetery* AR-4
Torian Cem—*cemetery* KY-4
Torian Creek—*stream* KY-4
Torian Springs—*spring* KY-4
Torido Tank—*reservoir* TX-5
Toriette Lakes—*reservoir* (2) NM-5
*Tori Jima* FM-9
Toril—*locale* NM-5
Torino—*locale* IL-6
Torino Creek—*stream* MT-8
Torino Peak—*summit* MT-8
*Tori Sh* FM-9
Torkelson Creek—*stream* MN-6
Torkiln Branch—*stream* SC-3
*Torliyag* FM-9
Torliyog—*locale* FM-9
Tormay Mine (Inactive)—*mine* ID-8
Torment Creek—*stream* AK-9
Torment Hill—*summit* NY-2
Tormentor, Lake—*reservoir* VA-3
Tormentor Creek—*stream* VA-3
**Tormey**—*pop pl* CA-9
Tornada Experimental Range HQ—*locale* NM-5
*Tornada Reserve HQ* NM-5
Tornado Canyon—*valley* AZ-5
Tornado Creek—*stream* CA-9
Tornado Lake—*lake* MN-6
Tornado Meadow—*flat* CA-9
Tornado Mine—*mine* SD-7
Tornado Peak—*summit* AZ-5
**Tornado (RR name Upper Falls)**—*pop pl* WV-2
Tornado Sch—*school* WI-6
Torne, The—*summit* NY-2
Torne Brook—*stream* NY-2
Torne Brook Farm—*hist pl* NY-2
Torne Mount Ivy Trail—*trail* NY-2
Torne Mtn—*summit* NJ-2
Tornero—*locale* NM-5
*Torneros Creek* TX-5
Torngren Library—*building* MI-6
Tornilla Creek—*stream* MT-8
**Tornillo**—*pop pl* TX-5
Tornillo Canal—*canal* TX-5
Tornillo Creek—*stream* TX-5
Tornillo Drain—*canal* TX-5
Tornillo Flat—*flat* TX-5
Tornillo Intercepting Drain Number One—*canal* TX-5
Tornillo Intercepting Drain Number Two—*canal* TX-5
Tornillo Spur—*ridge* TX-5
**Torning Township**—*pop pl* ND-7
**Torning (Township of)**—*pop pl* MN-6
Tornow Number 1 Dam—*dam* SD-7
*Toro* MH-9
Toro—*locale* LA-4
Toro, Arroyo Del—*stream* CA-9
Toro, Bayou—*stream* LA-4
Toro, Canada del —*valley* AZ-5
Toro, Fernando Luis, Casa—*hist pl* PR-3
Toro, Laguna del—*reservoir* TX-5
*Toroa Creek* WA-9
Toro Blanco Hill—*summit* NV-8
Toro Canyon—*valley* (2) CA-9
Toro Canyon—*valley* CO-8
Toro Canyon—*valley* NV-8
Toro Canyon—*valley* NM-5
Toro Canyon Creek—*stream* CA-9
Toro Canyon Reservoir—*reserve* CA-9
Toro (CCD)—*cens area* CA-9
Toro Cem—*cemetery* CA-9
Toro Cem—*cemetery* LA-4
Toro Ch—*church* LA-4
Toro Creek—*stream* (2) CA-9
Toro Creek—*stream* LA-4
Toro Creek—*stream* (2) TX-5
*Toroda* WA-9
Toroda—*locale* WA-9
*Toroda City* WA-9
Toroda Creek—*stream* WA-9
Toroda Mtn—*summit* WA-9
Torode Pit—*cave* AL-4
Toro Gas Field—*oilfield* TX-5
Toroges Creek—*stream* CA-9
*Torohoho* MH-9
*Toro Island* TX-5
Torok Creek—*stream* AK-9
*Toro Magpi* MH-9
Toro Melon Windmill—*locale* TX-5
*Toro Misake* MH-9
*Toro Misaki* MH-9
*Toro Mistake* MH-9
Toro Negro (Barrio)—*fmr MCD* PR-3
Toro Negro Central Hidroelectrica Numero 2—*other* PR-3
Toronto—*locale* IL-6
Toronto—*locale* MO-7
**Toronto**—*pop pl* FL-3
**Toronto**—*pop pl* IN-6
**Toronto**—*pop pl* IA-7
**Toronto**—*pop pl* KS-7
**Toronto**—*pop pl* OH-6
**Toronto**—*pop pl* SD-7
**Toronto**—*pop pl* TX-5
*Toronto Brook Lake* NY-2
Toronto Cem—*cemetery* KS-7
Toronto Cem—*cemetery* SD-7
*Toronto Creek* TX-5
Toronto Dam—*dam* KS-7
Toronto Elem Sch—*school* KS-7
Toronto Lake—*lake* NY-2
Toronto Lake—*reservoir* KS-7
Toronto Point Public Use Area—*park* KS-7
*Toronto Reservoir* KS-7
Toronto RR Station—*locale* FL-3
Toronto Rsvr—*reservoir* NY-2
Toronto State Park—*park* KS-7
**Toronto Township**—*pop pl* KS-7
Toronto Wildlife Area—*park* KS-7
Toropah Mine—*mine* ID-8
Toro Peak—*summit* CA-9
*ToroPoint* MH-9
Toro Prieto, Laguna Del—*lake* TX-5
Toror—*well* FM-9
Toro Santos Tank—*reservoir* TX-5
Toro Spring—*spring* AZ-5
Toro Spring—*spring* NV-8
Toro Spring—*spring* NM-5
*Toros Ranch* AZ-5
Toros Ranch (historical)—*locale* AZ-5
Toros Spring—*spring* AZ-5
Toros Wash—*stream* AZ-5
Toro Tank—*reservoir* NM-5
Toro Tank—*reservoir* TX-5
Torote Canyon—*valley* CA-9
*To-ro-weap Cliffs* AZ-5
Toroweap Cliffs—*cliff* AZ-5
Toroweap Lake—*flat* AZ-5
Toroweap Landing Strip—*airport* AZ-5
Toroweap Point—*cliff* AZ-5
Toroweap Ranger Station—*locale* AZ-5
*To-ro-weap Valley* AZ-5
Toroweap Valley—*valley* AZ-5
Toro Windmill—*locale* (4) TX-5
Tor Peak—*summit* NV-8
Torpedo—*locale* OK-5
Torpedo—*locale* PA-2
**Torpedo**—*pop pl* TX-5
Torpedo Eclipse Mine—*mine* CO-8
Torpedo Lake—*lake* AK-9
Torpee Creek—*stream* WI-6
Torpee Springs—*lake* WI-6
Torpid Creek—*stream* ID-8
Torpy Gulch—*valley* MT-8
Torpy Hill—*summit* NY-2
Torpy Lake—*lake* WI-6
Torpy Pond—*lake* NY-2
Torqua Spring—*spring* CA-9
Torquemada, Mount—*summit* CA-9
**Torrance**—*pop pl* CA-9
**Torrance**—*pop pl* PA-2
Torrance Annex—*uninc pl* CA-9
Torrance Cave—*cave* PA-2
Torrance (CCD)—*cens area* CA-9
Torrance Chapel—*church* GA-3
**Torrance (County)**—*pop pl* NM-5
Torrance County Beach—*beach* CA-9
Torrance (historical)—*locale* KS-7
Torrance (historical)—*locale* MS-4
**Torrance (historical)**—*pop pl* NC-3
Torrance House—*hist pl* IA-7
Torrance Post Office (historical)—*building* MS-4
Torrance Post Office (historical)—*building* PA-2
Torrance Sch—*hist pl* CA-9
Torrance Sch—*school* CA-9
Torrance State Hosp—*hospital* PA-2
Torrance Well—*well* AZ-5
**Torras**—*pop pl* LA-4
Torras Landing—*locale* LA-4
Torr Cem—*cemetery* NH-1
*Torrea Flats* TX-5
*Torrea Peak* TX-5
*Torrea Tank* TX-5
Torre (Barrio)—*fmr MCD* PR-3
Torre Canyon—*valley* CA-9
Torrecilla Alta (Barrio)—*fmr MCD* (2) PR-3
Torrecilla Baja (Barrio)—*fmr MCD* PR-3
**Torrecillas**—*pop pl* PR-3
Torrecillas (Barrio)—*fmr MCD* PR-3
Torre Creek—*stream* NV-8
Torre Flat—*flat* NV-8
Torrelle Falls—*falls* ID-8
Torrell Hill—*summit* GA-3
Torrence—*locale* NM-5
Torrence Ave Interchange—*other* IL-6
Torrence Branch—*stream* NC-3
Torrence Branch—*stream* SC-3
Torrence Bridge—*bridge* WA-9
Torrence Cem—*cemetery* VA-3
Torrence Chapel—*church* NC-3
Torrence Creek—*stream* NC-3
Torrence Grove Ch—*church* NC-3
Torrence Hill—*summit* AL-4
Torrence Park—*park* IL-6
Torrence Sch—*school* IA-7
*Torrence School Number 83* IN-6
Torrens Sch—*school* MN-6
Torrent—*locale* KY-4
Torrent Creek—*stream* ID-8
Torrent Creek—*stream* WA-9
Torrent Creek—*stream* WY-8
Torrent Spring—*spring* OR-9
**Torreon**—*pop pl* NM-5
Torreon Arroyo—*stream* NM-5
Torreon Cem—*cemetery* NM-5
Torreon Day Sch—*school* NM-5
Torreon Draw—*stream* (2) NM-5
Torreon Indian Shop—*locale* NM-5
Torreon Navajo Mission—*locale* NM-5
Torreon Springs—*spring* NM-5
Torreon Trading Post—*locale* NM-5
**Torreon (Trading Post)**—*pop pl* NM-5
Torreon Wash—*stream* NM-5
*Torres* FM-9
Torres—*locale* (2) CO-8
**Torres**—*pop pl* PR-3
Torres, Antonio, House—*hist pl* NM-5
Torres Canyon—*valley* CO-8
Torres Cave Archeol Site—*hist pl* CO-8
Torres Creek—*stream* TX-5
**Torresdale**—*pop pl* PA-2
Torresdale-Frankford Country Club—*other* PA-2
**Torresdale Manor**—*pop pl* PA-2
Torresdale Range—*channel* NJ-2
Torresdale Range—*channel* PA-2
Torres Ditch—*canal* CO-8
*Torres Island* FM-9
**Torres-Martinez Ind Res**—*pop pl* CA-9
Torres Ranch—*locale* NM-5
Torres Sch—*school* GU-9
Torres (Site)—*locale* CA-9
Torres Tank—*reservoir* (2) NM-5
Torres Well—*well* NM-5
Torreuil Ranch, A—*locale* NV-8
Torrey—*locale* FL-3
Torrey—*locale* PA-2
**Torrey**—*pop pl* UT-8
Torrey Airp—*airport* UT-8
Torreya State Park—*hist pl* FL-3

Torreya State Park—*park* FL-3
Torrey Brook—*stream* MA-1
Torrey Canal—*canal* UT-8
Torrey Canyon—*valley* CA-9
Torrey Canyon—*valley* TX-5
Torrey Canyon Windmill—*locale* TX-5
Torrey Castle—*island* ME-1
Torrey Cem—*cemetery* MA-1
Torrey Cem—*cemetery* MO-7
Torrey Cem—*cemetery* UT-8
Torrey Cem—*cemetery* VT-1
Torrey Corrals—*locale* CA-9
*Torrey Creek* WY-8
Torrey Creek—*stream* MA-1
Torrey Creek—*stream* WY-8
Torrey Crossing—*locale* CA-9
Torrey Drain—*canal* MI-6
Torrey Flats—*area* TX-5
Torrey Hill—*summit* ME-1
Torrey Hill—*summit* NH-1
Torrey Hill—*summit* NY-2
Torrey Hill Cem—*cemetery* NY-2
Torrey House (Ruins)—*locale* TX-5
*Torrey Island* ME-1
Torrey Lake—*lake* MT-8
Torrey Lake—*lake* OR-9
Torrey Lake—*lake* WI-6
Torrey Lake—*lake* WY-8
Torrey Lake—*swamp* SD-7
Torrey Lake Ranch—*locale* WY-8
Torrey Lake Sch—*school* SD-7
**Torrey Lake Township**—*pop pl* SD-7
Torrey Ledge—*bar* ME-1
Torrey Mtn—*summit* MT-8
*Torrey Municipal Airport* UT-8
Torrey Peak—*summit* TX-5
Torrey Peak—*summit* WY-8
Torrey Peak Camp—*locale* TX-5
Torrey Pines Homes—*uninc pl* CA-9
*Torrey Pines Mesa* CA-9
Torrey Pines Park—*park* CA-9
Torrey Pines Sch—*school* CA-9
Torrey Pines State Res—*reserve* CA-9
Torrey Pond—*lake* ME-1
Torrey Pond—*lake* MA-1
Torrey Pond—*reservoir* MA-1
Torrey Pond Dam—*dam* MA-1
Torrey Ridge—*ridge* CA-9
Torrey Rim—*ridge* WY-8
*Torrey River* OR-9
Torreys—*locale* ID-8
Torrey Sch—*school* MA-1
*Torreys Creek* MS-4
Torreys Landing—*locale* GA-3
Torreys Peak—*summit* CO-8
*Torreys Pond* MA-1
Torrey's Trading House No. 2
Site—*hist pl* TX-5
Torrey Tank—*reservoir* TX-5
**Torrey (Town of)**—*pop pl* NY-2
**Torrey (Township of)**—*pop pl* MN-6
Torrez Ranch—*locale* NM-5
Torrie Brook—*stream* ME-1
**Torrimar**—*pop pl* PR-3
*Torringford* CT-1
**Torringford**—*pop pl* CT-1
Torringford Brook—*stream* CT-1
Torringford Ch—*church* CT-1
Torringford Sch—*school* CT-1
**Torrington**—*pop pl* CT-1
**Torrington**—*pop pl* WY-8
Torrington Country Club—*other* CT-1
Torrington Ditch—*canal* WY-8
Torrington Fire Department HQ—*hist pl* CT-1
Torrington Point—*cape* ME-1
Torrington (Town of)—*civ div* CT-1
Torrivio Mesa—*summit* (2) NM-5
*Torroda Creek* WA-9
Torro Well—*well* AZ-5
Torrutj—*island* MP-9
*Torrutj Island* MP-9
Torry Bay—*bay* NC-3
Torry Brook—*stream* CT-1
*Torry Castle* ME-1
*Torry Creek* WY-8
Torry Drain—*stream* MI-6
Torry Gulch—*valley* WY-8
Torry Hill—*summit* CT-1
Torry Hill—*summit* ME-1
Torry Hill—*summit* NY-2
Torry (historical)—*locale* KS-7
Torry Island—*island* FL-3
Torry Island—*island* ME-1
*Torry Keys* FL-3
Torry Mtn—*summit* VA-3
**Torry Pines Subdivision**—*pop pl* UT-8
*Torry Pond* ME-1
Torry Ridge—*ridge* VA-3
Torry Rock—*bar* ME-1
Torry Run—*stream* PA-2
Torry Sch—*school* MI-6
Torry Sch (abandoned)—*school* PA-2
Torsar Island—*island* AK-9
Torsey Lake—*lake* ME-1
Torsido Creek—*stream* CO-8
Torsney Playground—*park* NY-2
Torso Creek—*stream* CO-8
Torso Lake—*lake* OR-9
Torstenson Lake—*lake* MN-6
*Tortilla Campground* AZ-5
Tortilla Camp Trail—*trail* AZ-5
Tortilla Creek—*stream* AZ-5
Tortilla Flat—*flat* AZ-5
Tortilla Flat—*locale* AZ-5
*Tortilla Flat Campground* AZ-5
Tortilla Flat Recreation Site Number Two
Hundred Fifty Six—*park* AZ-5
*Tortilla Mountains* AZ-5
Tortilla Mountains—*range* AZ-5
Tortilla Mtn—*summit* AZ-5
Tortilla Pass—*gap* AZ-5
Tortilla Ranch—*locale* AZ-5
*Tortillata Mountains* AZ-5
Tortilla Well—*well* AZ-5
*Tortillita Flat* AZ-5
*Tortillita Mountains* AZ-5
Tortillon, Bayou—*gut* (2) LA-4
**Tortoise and Hare Trailer**
**Court**—*pop pl* UT-8
Tortoise Island—*island* FL-3

Tortola, Arroyo—*valley* TX-5
Tortola Spring—*spring* (2) NM-5
Tortolita Canyon—*valley* (2) NM-5
Tortolita Creek—*stream* NM-5
Tortolita Mountains—*range* AZ-5
*Tortolitas Flat* AZ-5
*Tortolitas Mountains* AZ-5
*Tortollita Flat* AZ-5
*Tortollita Mountains* AZ-5
Tortolo Creek—*stream* TX-5
Tortue—*locale* LA-4
Tortue, Bayou—*stream* LA-4
Tortuga—*locale* CA-9
Tortuga, Canada —*valley* CA-9
Tortuga Banco Number 65—*levee* TX-5
Tortuga Butte, La—*summit* AZ-5
Tortuga Creek—*stream* TX-5
Tortuga Mtn—*summit* TX-5
**Tortugas**—*pop pl* NM-5
Tortugas Arroyo—*stream* NM-5
Tortugas Bank—*bar* FL-3
Tortugas Cem—*cemetery* NM-5
Tortugas Mtn—*summit* NM-5
Tortuga Tank—*reservoir* (4) TX-5
Tortuga Well, La—*well* AZ-5
Tortuga Windmill—*locale* TX-5
Tortugo (Barrio)—*fmr MCD* PR-3
Tortuguero, Campo—*military* PR-3
Tortuous Creek—*stream* AK-9
Torture Cave—*cave* AL-4
*Toru* FM-9
*Torua* MP-9
*Torua To* MP-9
*To'ruf* FM-9
Torun—*locale* WI-6
Toruno Canyon—*valley* AZ-5
Toruno Spring—*spring* NM-5
Toruno Tank—*reservoir* AZ-5
*Toruw* FM-9
**Torvik Subdivision**—*pop pl* SD-7
*Torwa* MP-9
*Tory Branch* VA-3
Tory Camp Run—*stream* WV-2
Tory Cem—*cemetery* MO-7
Tory Creek—*stream* MO-7
Tory Creek—*stream* VA-3
Tory Creek Ch—*church* VA-3
Tory Fork—*stream* TN-4
**Tory Hill**—*pop pl* ME-1
Tory Hill—*summit* ME-1
Tory Hill—*summit* (2) NH-1
Tory Hill—*summit* NY-2
Tory Hill Pond—*lake* ME-1
Tory Hollow—*valley* VA-3
Tory Island—*island* NC-3
Tory Knob—*summit* VA-3
*Tory Lake Township* SD-7
Torys Den—*cave* NC-3
Torytown Run—*stream* WV-2
Toscano Ditch—*canal* CA-9
*Toschi River* LA-4
Tosh Bridge—*bridge* TN-4
Tosh Cem—*cemetery* KY-4
Tosher Creek State Wildlife Mngmt
Area—*park* MN-6
Toshes—*locale* VA-3
*Tosh Ferry* TN-4
Tosh Mill (historical)—*locale* TN-4
Tosich—*bar* FM-9
Tosi Creek—*stream* WY-8
Tosi Creek Basin—*basin* WY-8
Tosi Peak—*summit* WY-8
*Tosi Point* WA-9
Tosis—*bar* FM-9
Tosity Creek—*stream* SC-3
*Toskegee* TN-4
*Tosnata Creek* GA-3
*Tosnata Gap* GA-3
*Tosohatchee Creek* FL-3
Tosohatchee Wildlife Mngmt Area—*park* FL-3
**Tosquero**—*pop pl* PR-3
Toss Gulch—*valley* OR-9
Toss-up Creek—*stream* CA-9
Tostaskwinu Site (FS-579, LA-
479)—*hist pl* NM-5
Tostin Creek—*stream* CA-9
**Toston**—*pop pl* MT-8
Toston Canal—*canal* MT-8
*Toston Canal East Fork* MT-8
*Toston Canal West Fork* MT-8
Toston Dam—*dam* MT-8
Toston Tunnel—*tunnel* MT-8
*Totabit* AZ-5
*Totacaticonce river* WI-6
Totache Windmill—*locale* TX-5
Totacon—*locale* AZ-5
*Totagatic Flowage* WI-6
Totagatic Flowage—*reservoir* WI-6
Totagatic Lake—*lake* WI-6
Totagatic Lake State Wildlife Managament
Area—*park* WI-6
Totagatic Park—*park* WI-6
Totagatic River—*stream* WI-6
Totagatic River State Wildlife Managemnet
Area—*park* WI-6
Total Wreck Mine—*mine* AZ-5
*Totant* MA-1
Totaro—*locale* VA-3
Totaro Creek—*stream* VA-3
Totaro (Magisterial District)—*fmr MCD* VA-3
Totatlanika River—*stream* AK-9
Totavi—*locale* NM-5
*Totawa* NJ-2
Totchaket Slough—*stream* AK-9
Tote Creek—*stream* MI-6
Totek Hills—*other* AK-9
Tote Lake—*lake* MN-6
Totem Bay—*bay* AK-9
Totem Bight—*bay* AK-9
Totem Bight State Historic Site—*hist pl* AK-9
Totem Canyon—*valley* AZ-5
Totem Gulch—*valley* WA-9
Totem Lake—*lake* MN-6
Totem Lake—*lake* WA-9
Totem Lake—*post sta* WA-9
Totem Lake—*reservoir* PA-2
Totem Lake Dam—*dam* PA-2
Totem Lodge—*locale* AK-9
Totem Lodge—*locale* NY-2
Totem Park—*park* PA-2

**Totem Park**—*pop pl* AK-9
Totem Pass—*gap* WA-9
Totem Peak—*summit* MT-8
Totem Peak Lake—*lake* MT-8
Totem Point—*cape* AK-9
Totem Pole—*pillar* AZ-5
Totem Pole—*pillar* UT-8
Totem Pole, The—*pillar* UT-8
Totem Pole Point—*cape* CA-9
Totem Town Sch—*school* MN-6
Toten Creek—*stream* AL-4
*Toten Lake* CO-8
Toteover Creek—*stream* (2) GA-3
*Totepache* AL-4
Tote Road Lake—*lake* MI-6
Tote Road Lake—*lake* MT-8
Tote Road Pond—*lake* ME-1
*Tot Gap* PA-2
Totheroh Cem—*cemetery* IN-6
Totherow Branch—*stream* GA-3
Totherow Branch—*stream* NC-3
Tothill Cem—*cemetery* NE-7
*To thlani Lakes* AZ-5
Totiakton Site—*hist pl* NY-2
Toti Creek—*stream* OH-6
Totier Creek—*stream* VA-3
Toti Island—*island* AK-9
Tot Island—*island* NY-2
Totiu—*island* FM-9
Totiwen Tomu—*bar* FM-9
*Totket Mtn* CT-1
*Totlacon* AZ-5
Totman Gulf—*valley* NY-2
Totman Hill—*summit* VT-1
Totman Ranch—*locale* TX-5
Tot Mtn—*summit* OR-9
Totness—*locale* SC-3
**Toto**—*pop pl* IN-6
**Toto**—*pop pl* TX-5
**Toto**—*pop pl* GU-9
*Totoawathla* FL-3
*Totobit* AZ-5
*Toto-Bitk* AZ-5
*Totobit Tanks* AZ-5
*Totocong Spring* AZ-5
Toto Creek—*stream* GA-3
Toto Creek Access Point—*cape* GA-3
Toto Creek Bridge—*bridge* GA-3
Toto Gas Field—*oilfield* TX-5
*Totogaticanse River* WI-6
*Totogatic Flowage* WI-6
*Totogatic River* WI-6
**Totoket**—*pop pl* CT-1
Totoket Mtn—*summit* CT-1
*Totolom* FM-9
*To-to-lose Hatchee Creek* FL-3
Totomoi—*hist pl* VA-3
*Toton* MP-9
Toton—*island* MP-9
*Toton Channel* MP-9
*Toton Island* MP-9
*Toton-suido* MP-9
Totonteac Mtn—*summit* AZ-5
*Toton-to* MP-9
*Totoon* MP-9
Totopitk—*locale* AZ-5
Totopotomoy Creek—*stream* VA-3
*Totoran-mine* FM-9
*Totoromu* FM-9
*Totoron Ho* FM-9
*Totosahatchee Creek* FL-3
*Totowa* NJ-2
**Totowa**—*pop pl* NJ-2
*Totowa Falls* NJ-2
*Totoweap Valley* AZ-5
*Tots* PA-2
Tots Brook—*stream* ME-1
Totschunda Creek—*stream* AK-9
Tots for Christ Sch—*school* FL-3
Totson Mtn—*summit* AK-9
*Totstakahoeetska* FL-3
**Totstalahoeetska (historical)**—*pop pl* FL-3
Tots Town Univ Child Care Center—*school* FL-3
*Totsu Zan* MH-9
*Totten* ND-7
**Totten**—*pop pl* VA-3
Totten Bend—*bend* IL-6
Totten Branch—*stream* VA-3
Totten-Butterfield House—*hist pl* WI-6
Totten Camp—*locale* CA-9
Totten Campground—*locale* CA-9
Totten Cem—*cemetery* IN-6
Totten Cem—*cemetery* VA-3
Totten Cem—*cemetery* WV-2
Totten Chapel—*church* WV-2
Totten Creek—*stream* (2) OR-9
Totten Ford Bridge—*bridge* IN-6
Totten Hollow—*valley* PA-2
Totten Hollow—*valley* VA-3
Totten Inlet—*bay* WA-9
Totten Key—*island* FL-3
Totten Lake—*lake* MI-6
Totten Lake—*reservoir* CO-8
Totten Ranch—*locale* CO-8
*Totten Reservoir* CO-8
Totten Ridge—*ridge* WV-2
Tottens Battery—*locale* MO-7
Totten Sch—*school* MO-7
*Totten's Landing* NY-2
Tottens Pond—*lake* MA-1
Totten (Township of)—*fmr MCD* AR-4
Totten Trail Park—*park* ND-7
**Tottenville**—*pop pl* NY-2
Tottery Pole Creek—*stream* GA-3
Tottman Cove—*bay* ME-1
Totton Coulee—*valley* MT-8
**Totts Corners**—*pop pl* OH-6
Totts Gap—*gap* PA-2
Totts Gap Sch (abandoned)—*school* PA-2
Totty Branch—*stream* TN-4
Totty Cem—*cemetery* TN-4
Totty Hollow—*valley* TN-4
Totty Hollow Mines—*mine* TN-4
**Tottys**—*pop pl* TN-4
Tottys Bend—*bend* TN-4
**Tottys Bend**—*pop pl* TN-4
Tottys Bend Bridge—*bridge* TN-4
Tottys Bend Ch—*church* TN-4
Tottys Bend Mines (surface)—*mine* TN-4
*Tottys Bend Post Office* TN-4

*Tottys Branch* TN-4
Tottys Post Office (historical)—*building* TN-4
Totuck Lake—*lake* AK-9
Totuskey—*locale* VA-3
Totuskey Bridge—*bridge* VA-3
Totuskey Ch—*church* VA-3
Totuskey Creek—*stream* VA-3
*Totusky Creek* VA-3
Totzitigi Portage (Kobuk Portage)—*gap* AK-9
**Totz (Pine Mountain Station)**—*pop pl* KY-4
Tou—*bar* FM-9
Tou, Unun En—*bar* FM-9
*Touacha* AL-4
Touby Run—*stream* OH-6
Touchee Spring—*spring* UT-8
**Touchet**—*pop pl* WA-9
Touchet (CCD)—*cens area* WA-9
Touchet East Side Ditch—*canal* WA-9
*Touchet River* WA-9
Touchet River—*stream* WA-9
Touchets Canal—*canal* LA-4
Touchet Valley—*valley* WA-9
Touchet Valley Airp—*airport* WA-9
Touchet West Side Ditch—*canal* WA-9
Touchit Cove—*bay* AK-9
Touchmenot Hollow—*valley* TN-4
Touch-Me-Not Mtn—*summit* NM-5
Touchmenot Mtn—*summit* NY-2
Touchstone—*locale* MS-4
Touchstone Branch—*stream* TX-5
*Touchstone Creek* TX-5
Touchstone Post Office
(historical)—*building* MS-4
Touchstone Prairie—*flat* AR-4
Touchy Park—*park* IL-6
*Toudes Coule* WA-9
Touey Pond—*lake* NY-2
**Tougaloo**—*pop pl* MS-4
Tougaloo Coll—*school* MS-4
Tougaloo Garden Memorial
Park—*cemetery* MS-4
*Tougaloo Southern Christian College* MS-4
*Tougaloo University* MS-4
Tough Branch—*stream* KY-4
Tough Branch—*stream* MO-7
Tough Creek—*stream* IN-6
Tough Creek—*stream* MT-8
Tough Creek—*stream* (2) WY-8
Tough Drain—*canal* MI-6
Tough Hill—*summit* NC-3
Tough Hill Branch—*stream* NC-3
Tough Hollow—*valley* ID-8
**Toughkenamon**—*pop pl* PA-2
Tough Luck Creek—*stream* AK-9
*Tough Mire Creek* MI-6
Tough Nut Shafts—*mine* AZ-5
Tough Nut Spring—*spring* CA-9
Tough Ridge—*ridge* NC-3
Tough Run—*stream* IN-6
Toughy Tank—*reservoir* AZ-5
Touglaalek Bay—*bay* AK-9
Touhey—*locale* WA-9
**Touhy**—*pop pl* NE-7
Touhy Park—*park* IL-6
*Touisett* MA-1
*Touisset* RI-1
Touisset—*cape* MA-1
**Touisset**—*pop pl* MA-1
**Touisset**—*pop pl* RI-1
Touisset Country Club—*locale* MA-1
**Touisset Highlands**—*pop pl* RI-1
*Touisset Neck* RI-1
*Touissett* MA-1
*Touissett Neck* MA-1
Toulish Lake—*lake* WI-6
Toulmins Spring Branch—*stream* AL-4
**Toulminville**—*pop pl* AL-4
Toulminville Branch Mobile Public
Library—*building* AL-4
*Toulminville High School* AL-4
Toulon—*locale* KS-7
**Toulon**—*pop pl* IL-6
**Toulon**—*pop pl* NV-8
**Toulon**—*pop pl* TN-4
Toulon Bayou—*stream* (2) LA-4
Toulon Drain—*canal* NV-8
Toulon Lake—*lake* NV-8
Toulon Peak—*summit* NV-8
Toulon Post Office (historical)—*building* TN-4
Toulon Spring—*spring* NV-8
**Toulon (Township of)**—*pop pl* IL-6
Toulou Creek—*stream* WA-9
Toulou Mtn—*summit* WA-9
**Toulouse**—*pop pl* KY-4
Toulouse, Bayou—*stream* LA-4
Toulouse Corner—*locale* ME-1
Toulouse Shop Ctr—*locale* AL-4
Toumer Mill Pond—*lake* LA-4
Toumey Hosp—*hospital* SC-3
*Touvuay* FM-9
*Toupchue* MA-1
*Toupchue Pond* MA-1
Toupin Sch Number 1—*school* ND-7
Toupin Sch Number 4—*school* ND-7
Touraine, The—*hist pl* PA-2
Tourcotte Lake—*lake* MI-6
Tour Creek—*stream* OR-9
*Tourish Lake* WI-6
**Tourison**—*pop pl* WV-2
Tourist Creek—*stream* (2) ID-8
Tourist Creek—*stream* WY-8
Tourist Hotel—*hist pl* MT-8
Tourist Park—*park* WI-6
Tourist Run—*stream* CO-8
Touristville—*locale* KY-4
Tourmaline Gorge—*valley* CO-8
Tourmaline King Mine—*mine* CA-9
Tourmaline Lake—*lake* CO-8
Tourmaline Park—*park* LA-4
Tourmaline Queen Mine—*mine* CA-9
Tourmaline Queen Mtn—*summit* CA-9
Tourmaline Surfing Park—*park* CA-9
Tour Mtn—*summit* MT-8
Tournament Creek—*stream* AZ-5
Tournament Flat—*flat* AZ-5
Tournament Park—*park* CA-9
**Tournapull**—*pop pl* GA-3
Tournear Creek—*stream* IL-6
Tourney Park—*park* AZ-5
Tournquist Spring—*spring* CA-9

Touro Infirmary—*hospital* LA-4
Touro Synagogue Natl Historic
Site—*hist pl* RI-1
**Tours**—*pop pl* MS-4
**Tours**—*pop pl* TX-5
Tourtellotte, John, Bldg—*hist pl* ID-8
Tourtellotte Hill—*summit* RI-1
Tourtellotte Park—*flat* CO-8
Tourtellotte Sch—*school* CT-1
Tourtelotte Park—*park* MN-6
Tourtelotte Ridge—*ridge* ME-1
Tourtillotte Creek—*stream* WI-6
*Tousers Branch* MD-2
Tousey—*locale* KY-4
Tousey Cem—*cemetery* KY-4
Tousley Lake—*reservoir* IN-6
Touson Lake—*lake* AL-4
Toussaint, Winand, House—*hist pl* MA-1
*Toussaint Creek* OH-6
Toussaint Creek—*stream* OH-6
Toussaint Creek Wildlife Area—*park* OH-6
Toussaint Island—*island* AK-9
Toussaint Reef—*bar* OH-6
Toussaint River—*stream* OH-6
Tout Ditch—*canal* CA-9
*Toutena Mary Creek* OR-9
Toutle—*locale* WA-9
*Toutle Glacier* WA-9
Toutle Glacier—*glacier* WA-9
Toutle Lake Sch—*school* WA-9
Toutle Mtn—*summit* WA-9
Toutle Mtn Range—*range* WA-9
Toutle River—*stream* WA-9
Toutle River Trail—*trail* WA-9
*Toutney Mary Creek* OR-9
Tou Velle State Park—*park* OR-9
*Touway* FM-9
Touzalin—*locale* OK-5
Tovakwa Site—*hist pl* NM-5
Tovakwa Site (FS-7, LA 483)—*hist pl* NM-5
*Tovalon* FM-9
Tovar Creek—*stream* TX-5
Tovar Mesa—*summit* AZ-5
Tovar Ranch—*locale* TX-5
Tovera Tank—*reservoir* AZ-5
Toverii Tuppa—*hist pl* CA-9
Toves House—*hist pl* GU-9
**Tovey**—*pop pl* IL-6
**Tovey Humphrey Station**—*pop pl* IL-6
Tovrea—*locale* AZ-5
Tovrea Ranch—*locale* TX-5
Tovrea Tank—*reservoir* AZ-5
Tovson Lake—*lake* MN-6
*Tow* NC-3
**Tow**—*pop pl* TX-5
Towachi Channel—*channel* FM-9
Towackhow Mtn—*summit* NJ-2
**Towaco**—*pop pl* NJ-2
Towaelbug—*summit* FM-9
*Towaelbuq* FM-9
Towago Point—*cliff* AZ-5
Towahmina Lake—*lake* AK-9
*Towai* FM-9
*Towaihae* HI-9
*Towaihae Bay* HI-9
Towak Creek—*stream* AK-9
*Towakhow Mountain* NJ-2
Towak Mtn—*summit* AK-9
Towal—*locale* WA-9
Towalaga—*locale* GA-3
*Towalgee River* GA-3
Towali Ch—*church* OK-5
Towaliga (CCD)—*cens area* GA-3
Towaliga Ch—*church* GA-3
Towaliga River—*stream* GA-3
Towamencin Ch—*church* PA-2
Towamencin Creek—*stream* PA-2
**Towamencin (Township of)**—*pop pl* PA-2
Towamensing Cem—*cemetery* PA-2
Towamensing Elem Sch—*school* PA-2
*Towamensing Sch* PA-2
**Towamensing (Township of)**—*pop pl* PA-2
**Towamensing Trails**—*pop pl* PA-2
Towamensing Trails Dam—*dam* PA-2
Towamudo Channel—*channel* FM-9
*To Wan-aho-che Creek* AZ-5
*Towan aho choo Creek* AZ-5
**Towanda**—*pop pl* IL-6
**Towanda**—*pop pl* KS-7
**Towanda**—*pop pl* PA-2
Towanda Airp—*airport* PA-2
Towanda Area MS—*school* PA-2
Towanda Area Senior HS—*school* PA-2
Towanda Borough—*civil* PA-2
Towanda Creek—*stream* PA-2
Towanda Elem Sch—*school* KS-7
Towanda Flats—*flat* PA-2
Towanda Golf Course—*locale* PA-2
Towanda Gun Club—*locale* PA-2
Towanda Lake—*lake* WI-6
Towanda Playground—*park* MD-2
Towanda Service Area—*locale* KS-7
**Towanda Township**—*pop pl* (2) KS-7
Towanda Township Elem Sch—*school* PA-2
**Towanda (Township of)**—*pop pl* IL-6
**Towanda (Township of)**—*pop pl* PA-2
*Towansett Neck* MA-1
Towanta Flat—*flat* UT-8
Towantic Brook—*stream* CT-1
Towantic Hill—*summit* CT-1
Towantic Pond—*lake* CT-1
**Towaoc**—*pop pl* CO-8
*Towar* FM-9
Towash Ch—*church* TX-5
Towash Creek—*stream* TX-5
Towash Reach—*channel* TX-5
Towassa Water Pollution Control
Plant—*building* AL-4
Towave Dam—*dam* UT-8
Towave Rsvr—*reservoir* UT-8
Tow Cem—*cemetery* TX-5
Tow Creek—*stream* CO-8
Tow Creek Oil Field—*oilfield* CO-8
Tow Dam—*dam* MT-8
Towd Point—*cape* NY-2
Toweatmy Cem—*cemetery* WA-9
Towe Cem—*cemetery* NY-2
Towe Chapel—*church* GA-3
**Towee**—*pop pl* TN-4
Towee Ch—*church* TN-4

Towee Creek—*stream* TN-4
Towee Falls Ch—*church* TN-4
**Towee Falls (historical)**—*pop pl* TN-4
Towee Falls Post Office
(historical)—*building* TN-4
Towee Mtn—*summit* TN-4
Towee Rec Area—*park* TN-4
Towee Ridge—*ridge* TN-4
Toweinuk—*bar* FM-9
*Toweje Pass* MP-9
*Towelaggee River* GA-3
Towe Lake—*lake* MN-6
Towel Creek—*stream* AZ-5
Towel Creek Trail—*trail* AZ-5
Towel Creek Trail Sixty Six - Sixty Seven
Loop—*trail* AZ-5
Towel Grove Cem—*cemetery* IL-6
T O Well—*well* TX-5
Towell Ave Sch—*school* IA-7
Towell Ford—*locale* VA-3
Towel Peaks—*ridge* AZ-5
Towel Peaks Tank—*reservoir* AZ-5
Towel Spring—*spring* AZ-5
Towel Tank—*reservoir* AZ-5
Tower—*locale* IA-7
Tower—*locale* MT-8
Tower—*locale* WA-9
**Tower**—*pop pl* IN-6
**Tower**—*pop pl* MI-6
**Tower**—*pop pl* MN-6
Tower—*uninc pl* CA-9
Tower, Horatio, House—*hist pl* MA-1
Tower, Lewis, House—*hist pl* RI-1
Tower, Maj. Morton, House—*hist pl* OR-9
Tower, The—*locale* UT-8
**Tower Acres**—*pop pl* MD-2
Tower and Shoppes at the
Sanctuary—*tower* FL-3
Tower Arch—*arch* UT-8
Tower Basin—*basin* WA-9
Tower Bay—*bay* GA-3
Tower Bay Slip—*harbor* WI-6
Tower Blackwell Lake—*reservoir* IN-6
Tower Bldg—*hist pl* IN-6
Tower Bluff Rapids—*rapids* AK-9
Tower Bluffs—*cliff* AK-9
Tower Branch—*stream* PA-2
Tower Branch—*stream* VA-3
Tower Bridge—*bridge* CA-9
Tower Bridge—*hist pl* CA-9
Tower Bridge—*other* UT-8
Tower Brook—*stream* (5) MA-1
Tower Butte—*summit* (2) AZ-5
Tower Butte—*summit* ND-7
Tower Canyon—*valley* CA-9
Tower Canyon—*valley* WY-8
Tower Cem—*cemetery* MO-7
Tower Cem—*cemetery* WA-9
Tower Ch—*church* TX-5
**Tower City**—*pop pl* ND-7
**Tower City**—*pop pl* PA-2
Tower City Borough—*civil* PA-2
Tower City Interchange—*crossing* ND-7
Tower Creek—*stream* CO-8
Tower Creek—*stream* ID-8
Tower Creek—*stream* IL-6
Tower Creek—*stream* (2) MN-6
Tower Creek—*stream* (2) WA-9
Tower Creek—*stream* WY-8
Tower Dam—*dam* SD-7
Tower Ditch—*canal* IN-6
Tower Divide—*ridge* WY-8
Tower Divide Sch—*school* WY-8
Tower Fall—*falls* WY-8
Tower Fall Campground—*locale* WY-8
*Tower Falls* WY-8
Tower Fire Hall—*hist pl* MN-6
Tower-Flanagan House—*hist pl* OR-9
Tower Four Ridge—*ridge* OK-5
**Tower Garden on the Bay**—*pop pl* MD-2
*Tower Gardens* MI-6
**Tower Gate (subdivision)**—*pop pl* NC-3
*Tower Grove* MO-7
**Tower Grove**—*pop pl* MO-7
Tower Grove—*uninc pl* KS-7
Tower Grove Park—*hist pl* MO-7
Tower Grove Park—*park* MO-7
Tower Grove Sch—*school* MO-7
Tower Height Cem—*cemetery* IL-6
Tower Heights MS—*school* OH-6
**Tower Heights (subdivision)**—*pop pl* NC-3
Tower Hill—*locale* IA-7
Tower Hill—*locale* VA-3
Tower Hill—*pillar* NE-7
**Tower Hill**—*pop pl* IL-6
**Tower Hill**—*pop pl* MA-1
**Tower Hill**—*pop pl* MI-6
Tower Hill—*summit* (3) CT-1
Tower Hill—*summit* (7) MA-1
Tower Hill—*summit* MI-6
Tower Hill—*summit* MN-6
Tower Hill—*summit* MO-7
Tower Hill—*summit* (2) NH-1
Tower Hill—*summit* NM-5
Tower Hill—*summit* (3) NY-2
Tower Hill—*summit* OK-5
Tower Hill—*summit* (2) PA-2
Tower Hill—*summit* RI-1
Tower Hill—*summit* TX-5
Tower Hill—*summit* VA-3
Tower Hill—*summit* WI-6
Tower Hill—*uninc pl* NY-2
Tower Hill Cem—*cemetery* MO-7
Tower Hill Cem—*cemetery* PA-2
**Tower Hill Condominium**—*pop pl* UT-8
Tower Hill Lake—*lake* CT-1
Tower Hill Mountain Trail—*trail* VA-3
Tower Hill Mtn—*summit* VA-3
**Tower Hill Number One**—*pop pl* PA-2
**Tower Hill Number Two**—*pop pl* PA-2
*Tower Hill Pond* CT-1
Tower Hill Pond—*lake* NH-1
Tower Hills—*range* NV-8
Tower Hill Sch—*school* DE-2
Tower Hill Sch—*school* MA-1
**Tower Hill Shorelands**—*pop pl* MI-6
Tower Hill State Park—*park* WI-6
**Tower Hill (Township of)**—*pop pl* IL-6
Tower Hill Woods—*locale* PA-2

Tower Homestead and Masonic Temple—*hist pl* NY-2
Tower House—*locale* CA-9
Tower House District—*hist pl* CA-9
Tower House-Soo-Yeh-Choo-Pus—*hist pl* CA-9
**Towering Heights**—*pop pl* TN-4
Tower Island—*island* IL-6
Tower Island Chute—*gut* IL-6
Tower Island Chute—*stream* MO-7
*Tower Junction* MN-6
Tower Junction—*locale* MN-6
Tower Junction—*locale* WY-8
Tower Knob—*summit* MO-7
*Tower Lake* WI-6
Tower Lake—*lake* CA-9
Tower Lake—*lake* FL-3
Tower Lake—*lake* IL-6
Tower Lake—*lake* (3) MI-6
Tower Lake—*lake* (3) WI-6
**Tower Lake**—*pop pl* IL-6
Tower Lake—*reservoir* SD-7
**Tower Lakes**—*pop pl* IL-6
Tower Lateral—*canal* CA-9
Tower Lodge Sch—*school* MI-6
Tower Mine—*mine* CA-9
Tower Mtn—*summit* AR-4
Tower Mtn—*summit* CO-8
Tower Mtn—*summit* GA-3
Tower Mtn—*summit* MA-1
Tower Mtn—*summit* MT-8
Tower Mtn—*summit* (2) NY-2
Tower Mtn—*summit* OR-9
Tower Mtn—*summit* WA-9
*Tower of Babel* AZ-5
Tower of Babylon—*summit* AZ-5
Tower of Light Ch—*church* MO-7
Tower of Memories—*hist pl* CO-8
Tower of the Americas—*building* TX-5
Tower of the Standing God (LA 55839)—*hist pl* NM-5
*Tower Park* MN-6
Tower Park—*park* (2) IN-6
Tower Park—*park* MI-6
Tower Park—*park* (2) MN-6
Tower Park—*park* MO-7
Tower Park—*park* OK-5
Tower Park—*uninc pl* LA-4
Tower Peak—*summit* AZ-5
Tower Peak—*summit* MT-8
Tower Peak—*summit* WY-8
Tower Place Festival Shop Ctr—*locale* NC-3
Tower Plaza—*locale* KS-7
Tower Plaza Shop Ctr—*locale* AZ-5
Tower Point—*cape* AK-9
Tower Point—*summit* OR-9
Tower Pond—*reservoir* MI-6
Tower Ranch—*locale* (2) CA-9
Tower Ranger Station—*locale* WY-8
Tower Reach (historical)—*bend* SD-7
Tower Ridge—*ridge* AL-4
Tower Ridge—*ridge* UT-8
Tower Ridge Yacht Club—*other* NY-2
Tower Road Dam—*dam* IL-6
Tower Road Park—*park* IL-6
*Tower Rock* ID-8
Tower Rock—*cliff* IA-7
Tower Rock—*hist pl* MO-7
Tower Rock—*island* MO-7
Tower Rock—*island* OR-9
Tower Rock—*pillar* WA-9
Tower Rock—*pillar* WI-6
Tower Rock—*summit* (2) CA-9
Tower Rock—*summit* KY-4
Tower Rock—*summit* WA-9
Tower Rock Campground—*locale* WA-9
Tower Rock Sch—*school* WI-6
Tower Ruin—*locale* UT-8
*Towers* NY-2
Towers—*locale* NE-7
Towers—*locale* VA-3
Towers—*locale* VI-3
Towers—*uninc pl* FL-3
Towers, Lake—*reservoir* AZ-5
Towers, The—*hist pl* RI-1
Towers, The—*summit* VA-3
Towers, The—*summit* WY-8
Towers Arm—*bay* AK-9
*Towers Brook* MA-1
Towers Brook—*stream* ME-1
Towers Brook—*stream* NY-2
Towers Chapel—*church* KY-4
**Towers Chapel**—*pop pl* KY-4
**Towers Corners**—*pop pl* NY-2
Towers Creek—*stream* AZ-5
*Towers Forge* NY-2
Towers Fork—*stream* NC-3
Towers Hall, Otterbein College—*hist pl* OH-6
Towers Hist Dist—*hist pl* RI-1
**Tower Shores (subdivision)**—*pop pl* DE-2
Tower Site—*hist pl* OH-6
Towers Lake—*lake* AK-9
Towers Lake—*lake* MN-6
Tower Slough—*lake* ND-7
Towers Mtn—*summit* AZ-5
*Towers of Cibola* AZ-5
Towers Of The Virgin—*pillar* UT-8
Tower-Soudan State Park—*park* MN-6
Towers Overlook, The—*locale* VA-3
Towers Plaza (Shop Ctr)—*locale* MA-1
*Tower Spring* KS-7
Tower Spring—*spring* NV-8
Tower Spring—*spring* OR-9
Towerspring (historical)—*locale* KS-7
Towers Sch—*school* CA-9
Towers Sch—*school* VT-1
Towers Shop Ctr—*locale* VA-3
*Towers Station* NE-7
Tower State Wildlife Mngmt Area—*park* MN-6
Tower Station—*building* PA-2
**Tower Station (historical)**—*pop pl* IA-7
Tower Stream—*stream* ME-1
Towers Tunnel—*tunnel* VA-3
Tower Swamp—*swamp* GA-3
Tower Tank—*reservoir* AZ-5
**Tower Township**—*pop pl* ND-7
Tower Trail—*trail* (4) PA-2
**Tower Trailer Park**—*pop pl* DE-2
Tower View—*hist pl* MN-6
**Towerville**—*pop pl* NY-2
**Towerville**—*pop pl* PA-2
**Towerville**—*pop pl* WI-6
**Towerville Corners**—*pop pl* NY-2
Towervue Golf Course—*other* PA-2
Tower Windmill—*locale* TX-5
Tower Yards—*locale* NY-2
Towery Branch—*stream* KY-4
Towery Bridge—*bridge* KY-4
Towery Cem—*cemetery* KY-4
*Towesa* MP-9
Towes Creek—*stream* MI-6
*Toweset* RI-1
*Toweset Neck* MA-1
Toweset Point—*cape* RI-1
Towesick Neck—*cape* ME-1
Towgith—*summit* FM-9
Tow Gray Hill—*summit* UT-8
Tow Gray Spring—*spring* UT-8
*Tow Head* WA-9
Towhead—*summit* UT-8
Towhead Basin—*basin* ID-8
Towhead Bayou—*gut* LA-4
Towhead Bayou—*stream* LA-4
Towhead Branch—*stream* TN-4
Towhead Creek—*stream* KS-7
Towhead Creek—*stream* TX-5
Towhead Flat—*flat* CA-9
Towhead Gap—*gap* WA-9
Towhead Gulch—*valley* MT-8
Towhead Island—*island* AR-4
Towhead Island—*island* FL-3
Towhead Island—*island* IA-7
Towhead Island—*island* (4) KY-4
Towhead Island—*island* MO-7
Towhead Island—*island* (2) WA-9
Towhead Island (historical)—*island* SD-7
Towhead Island (historical)—*island* TN-4
Towhead Lake—*lake* CA-9
Towhead Lake—*lake* IL-6
Towhead Lake—*lake* IA-7
Towhead Lake—*lake* LA-4
Towhead Lake State Game Mngmt Area—*park* IA-7
Towhead Mtn—*summit* AK-9
Towhead Of Island No 34—*island* AR-4
Towhead of Island Number Eighteen—*flat* TN-4
Towhead of Island Number Thirty-five—*island* TN-4
Towhead Sch—*school* KS-7
Towhee, Lake—*reservoir* PA-2
Towhee Creek—*stream* MI-6
Towhee Tank—*reservoir* AZ-5
*Towhey Creek* MN-6
*Towhey Lake* MN-6
Tow Hill—*summit* MA-1
*Towhy Lake* MI-6
*Towigith* FM-9
Tow Island—*island* NJ-2
Towle—*locale* CA-9
Towle Cem—*cemetery* IA-7
Towle Gulf—*valley* NY-2
Towle Hill—*summit* NH-1
Towle Mill Site—*locale* CA-9
Towle Mtn—*summit* ME-1
Towler Sch—*school* NV-8
Towles Camp—*locale* WV-2
Towles Cem—*cemetery* (2) MO-7
*Towles Cemetery* SD-7
**Towles Corner**—*pop pl* NH-1
Towles Creek—*stream* VA-3
Towles Hill—*summit* ME-1
Towles Point—*cape* VA-3
Towles Pond—*reservoir* VA-3
Towles Sch (historical)—*school* MO-7
**Towlesville**—*pop pl* NY-2
*Towline Lake* MN-6
Towmile Gulch—*valley* MT-8
Towmile Run—*stream* PA-2
Tow Motor Corporation—*facility* OH-6
Town—*post sta* NY-2
Town—*post sta* UT-8
**Town Acres**—*pop pl* TN-4
**Town and Country**—*pop pl* LA-4
**Town and Country**—*pop pl* MO-7
Town And Country—*post sta* CA-9
**Town and Country Acres**—*pop pl* GA-3
Town and Country Center (Shop Ctr)—*locale* FL-3
Town and Country Ch—*church* MO-7
Town and Country Ch of God—*church* FL-3
Town and Country Christian Ch—*church* (2) KS-7
Town And Country Club—*other* GA-3
Town and Country Club—*other* MN-6
Town and Country Elem Sch—*school* FL-3
**Town and Country Estates**—*pop pl* OH-6
**Town and Country Estates**—*pop pl* VA-3
**Town and Country Estates (subdivision)**—*pop pl* TN-4
**Town and Country Estates Subdivision**—*pop pl* UT-8
Town and Country Golf Course—*other* AZ-5
Town and Country Hosp—*hospital* FL-3
Town and Country Lake—*reservoir* MO-7
Town and Country (Linwood)—*CDP* WA-9
Town and Country Mall—*locale* MO-7
Town and Country Plaza—*locale* MO-7
Town and Country Plaza—*locale* UT-8
Town and Country Plaza—*post sta* FL-3
Town and Country Plaza Shop Ctr—*locale* (2) AL-4
Town and Country Plaza (Shop Ctr)—*locale* FL-3
Town and Country Plaza (Shop Ctr)—*locale* IA-7
Town and Country Sch—*school* (2) CA-9
Town and Country Shop Ctr—*locale* AZ-5
Town and Country Shop Ctr—*locale* AR-4
Town and Country Shop Ctr—*locale* (3) FL-3
Town and Country Shop Ctr—*locale* MS-4
Town and Country Shop Ctr—*locale* (2) NC-3
Town and Country Shop Ctr—*locale* ND-7
Town and Country Shop Ctr—*locale* TN-4
Town And Country Shop Ctr—*locale* TX-5
Town and Country Shop Ctr—*locale* VA-3
**Town and Country (subdivision)**—*pop pl* AL-4
**Town and Country Trailer Park**—*pop pl* CA-9
Town and Country Valley Mall—*locale* AZ-5
**Town and Country Village**—*pop pl* CA-9
**Town Bank**—*pop pl* NJ-2
*Town Bar Point* MD-2
Town Beach—*beach* MA-1
Town Beach—*beach* NY-2
Town Bluff—*locale* TX-5
Town Bluff Dam—*dam* TX-5
*Town Bluff Lake* TX-5
Town Bluff Landing—*locale* GA-3
Town Boundary Marker—*hist pl* MA-1
*Town Branch* AR-4
*Town Branch* MS-4
*Town Branch* VA-3
*Town Branch* WV-2
Town Branch—*stream* (2) AL-4
Town Branch—*stream* (9) AR-4
Town Branch—*stream* FL-3
Town Branch—*stream* (8) GA-3
Town Branch—*stream* (3) IL-6
Town Branch—*stream* IN-6
Town Branch—*stream* IA-7
Town Branch—*stream* (14) KY-4
Town Branch—*stream* (3) MD-2
Town Branch—*stream* (6) MO-7
Town Branch—*stream* NE-7
Town Branch—*stream* (4) NC-3
Town Branch—*stream* OH-6
Town Branch—*stream* OK-5
Town Branch—*stream* (7) TN-4
Town Branch—*stream* (11) TX-5
Town Branch—*stream* (6) VA-3
**Town Branch Estates (subdivision)**—*pop pl* TN-4
Town Branch Sch—*school* KY-4
Town Bridge Pond—*reservoir* VA-3
Town Bridge Swamp—*stream* VA-3
*Town Brook* CT-1
*Town Brook* MA-1
Town Brook—*locale* NJ-2
Town Brook—*stream* (3) MA-1
Town Brook—*stream* (2) NH-1
Town Brook—*stream* NJ-2
Town Brook—*stream* NY-2
Town Brook Rsvr—*reservoir* MA-1
Town Camp Run—*stream* WV-2
Town Canal—*canal* WA-9
Town Canyon—*valley* NV-8
Town Cave Number One—*cave* TN-4
Town Cave Number Two—*cave* TN-4
Town Cem—*cemetery* GA-3
Town Cem—*cemetery* MA-1
Town Cem—*cemetery* (2) NH-1
Town Cem—*cemetery* (3) WI-6
Town Center—*locale* NC-3
**Town Center**—*pop pl* NJ-2
Town Center—*post sta* OR-9
Town Center—*uninc pl* CA-9
Town Center at Boca Raton (Shop Ctr)—*locale* FL-3
Town Center District—*hist pl* OH-6
Town Center Hist Dist—*hist pl* NH-1
*Town Center Lake* MN-6
Town Center Plaza (Shop Ctr)—*locale* FL-3
Town Clock Church—*hist pl* MD-2
Town Clock Plaza—*locale* IA-7
Town Club, The—*hist pl* OR-9
Town Common—*park* NC-3
*Town Common Park* NC-3
Town Concrete Pipe Airstrip—*airport* OR-9
Town Consolidated Sch—*school* MA-1
Town Corner Creek—*stream* WI-6
Town Corner Lake—*lake* MI-6
Town Corner Lake—*lake* WI-6
Town Corners—*locale* MI-6
Town Corners—*locale* NY-2
Town Corner State Wildlife Mngmt Area—*park* WI-6
Town Corral (Shop Ctr)—*locale* FL-3
Town & Country Plaza—*locale* MA-1
*Town Cove* MA-1
Town Cove—*bay* MA-1
Town Cove—*cove* MA-1
*Town Creek* AL-4
*Town Creek* AR-4
*Town Creek* MS-4
*Town Creek* NC-3
*Town Creek* OH-6
*Town Creek* SC-3
*Town Creek* TN-4
*Town Creek* TX-5
Town Creek—*arroyo* TX-5
Town Creek—*bay* (2) MD-2
Town Creek—*bay* NY-2
Town Creek—*channel* SC-3
Town Creek—*gut* (2) SC-3
Town Creek—*locale* GA-3
Town Creek—*locale* MD-2
Town Creek—*locale* NV-8
Town Creek—*locale* NC-3
**Town Creek**—*pop pl* AL-4
**Town Creek**—*pop pl* MD-2
**Town Creek**—*pop pl* NC-3
**Town Creek**—*pop pl* TN-4
Town Creek—*stream* (17) AL-4
Town Creek—*stream* (4) AR-4
Town Creek—*stream* (3) CA-9
Town Creek—*stream* (22) GA-3
Town Creek—*stream* (2) ID-8
Town Creek—*stream* (2) IL-6
Town Creek—*stream* (2) IN-6
Town Creek—*stream* KS-7
Town Creek—*stream* (6) KY-4
Town Creek—*stream* MD-2
Town Creek—*stream* MA-1
Town Creek—*stream* (16) MS-4
Town Creek—*stream* (4) MO-7
Town Creek—*stream* NE-7
Town Creek—*stream* NV-8
Town Creek—*stream* (8) NC-3
Town Creek—*stream* (2) OH-6
Town Creek—*stream* (2) OK-5
Town Creek—*stream* OR-9
Town Creek—*stream* PA-2
Town Creek—*stream* (5) SC-3
Town Creek—*stream* (15) TN-4
Town Creek—*stream* (9) TX-5
Town Creek—*stream* (5) VA-3
Town Creek—*stream* WV-2
Town Creek—*stream* (2) WI-6
Town Creek Archeol Site—*hist pl* CA-9
Town Creek Bar (historical)—*bar* AL-4
Town Creek Bridge—*bridge* AL-4
Town Creek Canal—*canal* MS-4
Town Creek Cave—*cave* AL-4
Town Creek (CCD)—*cens area* AL-4
Town Creek Cem—*cemetery* AL-4
*Town Creek Ch* AL-4
Town Creek Ch—*church* (3) AL-4
Town Creek Ch—*church* (2) GA-3
Town Creek Ch—*church* MS-4
Town Creek Ch—*church* SC-3
Town Creek Ch—*church* TN-4
Town Creek Ch—*church* VA-3
Town Creek-Courtland (CCD)—*cens area* AL-4
Town Creek-Courtland Division—*civil* AL-4
Town Creek Cutoff—*channel* MS-4
Town Creek Division—*civil* AL-4
*Town Creek Drift Mine* AL-4
Town Creek Flat—*flat* NV-8
Town Creek Indian Mound—*hist pl* NC-3
Town Creek Indian Mound—*locale* NC-3
Town Creek Knob—*summit* WV-2
**Town Creek Manor**—*pop pl* MD-2
Town Creek Marina—*locale* AL-4
Town Creek Marshes—*swamp* MA-1
*Town Creek Missionary Baptist Church* MS-4
Town Creek Missionary Ch—*church* AL-4
Town Creek Post Office—*building* AL-4
Town Creek Rec Area—*park* MS-4
Town Creek Sch (historical)—*school* AL-4
Town Creek Sch (historical)—*school* GA-3
Town Creek Spring—*spring* (2) NV-8
Town Creek Structure 15b Dam—*dam* MS-4
Town Creek Structure 16 Dam—*dam* MS-4
Town Creek Structure 19 Dam—*dam* MS-4
Town Creek Structure 20 Dam—*dam* MS-4
Town Creek Structure 22 Dam—*dam* MS-4
Town Creek Structure 23 Dam—*dam* MS-4
Town Creek Structure 24 Dam—*dam* MS-4
Town Creek Structure 28 Dam—*dam* MS-4
Town Creek Structure 29 Dam—*dam* MS-4
Town Creek Structure 46a Dam—*dam* MS-4
Town Creek Structure 6 Dam—*dam* MS-4
Town Creek Structure 9 Dam—*dam* MS-4
Town Creek (Township of)—*fmr MCD* NC-3
Town Creek Watershed Dam Number Thirteen—*dam* NC-3
Town Creek Watershed Dam Number 11—*dam* AL-4
Town Creek Watershed Dam Number 12—*dam* AL-4
Town Creek Watershed Number 14 Dam—*dam* AL-4
Town Creek Watershed Number 22 Dam—*dam* AL-4
Town Creek Watershed Number 3—*dam* AL-4
Towncreek Watershed 17 Dam—*dam* MS-4
Towncreek Watershed 18 Dam—*dam* MS-4
Town Creek Well—*well* NV-8
Towncrest JHS—*school* IN-6
Towncrest Shop Ctr—*locale* FL-3
**Towncrest Terrace Subdivision**—*pop pl* UT-8
**Town Crest Village**—*pop pl* MA-1
*Town Dam* SD-7
Town Ditch—*canal* CO-8
Town Ditch—*canal* ID-8
Town Ditch—*canal* MO-7
Town Ditch—*canal* MT-8
Town Ditch—*canal* (2) UT-8
Town Drain—*stream* WI-6
Town Draw—*valley* AZ-5
Town Draw—*valley* TX-5
Town Draw—*valley* WY-8
Towndrow Peak—*summit* NM-5
Towne Acres Elem Sch—*school* TN-4
**Towne Acres (subdivision)**—*pop pl* TN-4
Towne-Akenson House—*hist pl* MN-6
Towne and Country Shop Ctr—*locale* FL-3
**Towne and Country Village Subdivision**—*pop pl* UT-8
Town East Christian Sch—*school* FL-3
Towne Ave Sch—*school* CA-9
Towne Brook—*stream* MA-1
Towne Brook—*stream* NH-1
Towne Center Square (Shop Ctr)—*locale* FL-3
Towne Cove—*bay* ME-1
*Towne Creek* ID-8
Towne Creek—*stream* CA-9
Towne Creek—*stream* ID-8
Towne East Baptist Ch—*church* FL-3
Towne East Lateral—*canal* CA-9
Towne East Square—*locale* KS-7
*Towne Forest* NC-3
Towne Gulch—*valley* MT-8
Towne Gulch—*valley* OR-9
Towne Hill—*summit* (2) NH-1
**Towne Hills**—*pop pl* TN-4
*Town Elementary School* PA-2
Towne Mall—*locale* NC-3
Towne Mall—*post sta* FL-3
Towne Mine—*mine* AZ-5
Towne Oaks—*locale* IL-6
Towne Pass—*gap* CA-9
Towne Plaza—*locale* PA-2
Towne Plaza Shop Ctr—*locale* TN-4
Towne Point—*cape* MT-8
**Towne Point**—*pop pl* DE-2
Towne Point Elem Sch—*school* DE-2
Towne Pond—*lake* ME-1
Towne Pond—*lake* MA-1
Towne Pond Dam—*dam* MA-1
Towner—*locale* PA-2
**Towner**—*pop pl* CO-8
**Towner**—*pop pl* ND-7
Towne Ranch—*locale* SD-7
Towner Cem—*cemetery* CO-8
Towner County—*civil* ND-7
Towner County Courthouse—*hist pl* ND-7
Towner Cove—*bay* MD-2
Towner Hill—*summit* CT-1
Towner Lake—*lake* WY-8
Towner Municipal Airp—*airport* ND-7
Towner Ranch—*locale* NM-5
Towner Run—*stream* PA-2
Towners—*locale* NY-2
Towner Sch—*school* NY-2
Towners Pond—*lake* MA-1
Towner Swamp—*swamp* CT-1
Towner Well—*well* NM-5
Townes, Clayton, House—*hist pl* OH-6
Townes Cem—*cemetery* MS-4
Towne Sch—*school* MO-7
Townes Creek—*stream* SC-3
Townes Dam—*dam* VA-3
Townes Hollow—*valley* MO-7
Towne Shop Ctr—*locale* MA-1
Towne South Plaza (Shop Ctr)—*locale* FL-3
Towne South Shop Ctr—*locale* FL-3
Towne Square Shop Ctr—*locale* TN-4
Townes Reef—*bar* VT-1
Townes Switch (historical)—*locale* MS-4
**Town Estates**—*pop pl* NJ-2
Towne Station Post Office—*building* UT-8
Townes Tunnel—*tunnel* VA-3
*Townesville* NC-3
Towne West Square—*locale* KS-7
Towne-Williams House—*hist pl* ND-7
Town Farm—*locale* VT-1
Town Farm Bay—*bay* VT-1
Town Farm Brook—*stream* CT-1
Town Farm Brook—*stream* (2) ME-1
Town Farm Brook—*stream* MA-1
Town Farm Brook—*stream* NH-1
Town Farm Cem—*cemetery* MA-1
Town Farm Creek—*stream* VA-3
**Town Farm Hill**—*pop pl* ME-1
Town Farm Hill—*summit* (3) ME-1
Town Farm Hill—*summit* MA-1
Town Farm Hill—*summit* (2) VT-1
Town Farms Inn—*hist pl* CT-1
**Town Forest**—*pop pl* NC-3
*Town Fork* NC-3
Town Fork—*stream* IL-6
Town Fork—*stream* (2) KY-4
Town Fork—*stream* MO-7
Town Fork—*stream* (3) OH-6
Town Fork Creek—*stream* NC-3
Town Fork Creek Watershed Dam Number Fifteen—*dam* NC-3
Town Fork Creek Watershed Dam Number Five—*dam* NC-3
Town Fork Creek Watershed Dam Number Fourteen—*dam* NC-3
Town Fork Creek Watershed Dam Number Six—*dam* NC-3
Town Fork Creek Watershed Dam Number Sixteen—*dam* NC-3
Town Fork Creek Watershed Dam Number Ten—*dam* NC-3
Town Fork Creek Watershed Dam Number Thirteen—*dam* NC-3
Town Fork Creek Watershed Dam Number Two—*dam* NC-3
Town Fork Creek Watershed Lake Fifteen—*reservoir* NC-3
Town Fork Creek Watershed Lake Five—*reservoir* NC-3
Town Fork Creek Watershed Lake Fourteen—*reservoir* NC-3
Town Fork Creek Watershed Lake Six—*reservoir* NC-3
Town Fork Creek Watershed Lake Sixteen—*reservoir* NC-3
Town Fork Creek Watershed Lake Ten—*reservoir* NC-3
Town Fork Creek Watershed Lake Thirteen—*reservoir* (2) NC-3
Town Fork Creek Watershed Lake Two—*reservoir* NC-3
Towngil—*summit* FM-9
Town Gulch—*valley* (2) OR-9
*Town Hall* NC-3
Town Hall—*hist pl* CT-1
Town Hall—*hist pl* MA-1
Town Hall—*hist pl* NH-1
Town Hall—*hist pl* NJ-2
Town Hall—*hist pl* NY-2
Town Hall—*hist pl* OH-6
Townhall—*locale* NE-7
Town Hall—*locale* NJ-2
**Town Hall**—*pop pl* MA-1
**Town Hall**—*pop pl* TX-5
Town Hall and Courthouse—*hist pl* NH-1
Town Hall and District Sch No. 6—*hist pl* CT-1
Town Hall (Castle Hall)—*hist pl* IN-6
Town Hall Cem—*cemetery* NH-1
**Town Hall Corner**—*pop pl* NH-1
Townhall Hill—*summit* WI-6
Townhall Lake—*lake* MN-6
Townhall Sch—*school* IL-6
Townhall Sch—*school* MI-6
Town Hall Sch—*school* NJ-2
Town Hall Sch—*school* WI-6
Town Hall Square Hist Dist—*hist pl* MA-1
*Town Harbor* MA-1
Town Head—*cliff* MA-1
Townhead Lake State Game Mgt Area—*park* IA-7
*Town Hill* MA-1
*Town Hill* PA-2
Town Hill—*locale* CT-1
**Town Hill**—*pop pl* IN-6
**Town Hill**—*pop pl* ME-1
**Town Hill**—*pop pl* PA-2
**Town Hill**—*pop pl* WV-2
Town Hill—*range* MD-2
Town Hill—*range* PA-2
Town Hill—*ridge* WV-2
Town Hill—*summit* (5) CT-1
Town Hill—*summit* (4) MA-1
Town Hill—*summit* NH-1
Town Hill—*summit* (3) VT-1
Town Hill Burying Ground—*cemetery* MA-1
Town Hill Creek—*stream* VA-3
Town Hill District—*hist pl* MA-1
Townhill Lateral—*canal* CA-9
Town Hill Lookout Tower—*locale* AL-4
Town Hill Sch—*school* VT-1
**Town Hills (subdivision)**—*pop pl* TN-4
Town Hollow—*valley* KY-4
Town Hollow—*valley* (3) MO-7
Town Hollow—*valley* PA-2
Town Hollow—*valley* VA-3
Town Hollow—*valley* WV-2
*Town House* MA-1
Town House—*hist pl* NH-1
Town House—*locale* IL-6
Town House—*locale* ME-1
**Town House**—*pop pl* NH-1
Townhouse Branch—*stream* NC-3
Townhouse Brook—*stream* ME-1
Town House Cem—*cemetery* VT-1
Townhouse Ch—*church* OH-6
**Townhouse Condominium**—*pop pl* UT-8
Townhouse Corner—*locale* ME-1
Town House Corners—*locale* ME-1
**Town House Corners**—*pop pl* ME-1
Townhouse Creek—*stream* NC-3
Town House Hill—*summit* (2) ME-1
Townhouse Hill—*summit* MA-1
Town House Mine—*mine* CO-8
Town House Pond—*lake* NH-1
Townhouse Ridge—*ridge* NC-3
Townhouse Row—*hist pl* PA-2
Townhouse Sch—*school* OH-6
Town Island—*island* MA-1
Town Knob—*summit* KY-4
Town Knobs—*ridge* TN-4
*Town Lake* MS-4
*Town Lake* OR-9
Town Lake—*lake* AK-9
Town Lake—*lake* IN-6
Town Lake—*lake* IA-7
Town Lake—*lake* KY-4
Town Lake—*lake* LA-4
Town Lake—*lake* MI-6
Town Lake—*lake* (2) MN-6
Town Lake—*reservoir* OR-9
Town Lake—*reservoir* TX-5
Town Lake Dam—*dam* TX-5
Town Lakes—*reservoir* CO-8
Town Landing—*locale* CT-1
Town Landing—*locale* ME-1
Town Lateral—*canal* CO-8
Town Lateral—*canal* ID-8
Town Lateral—*canal* WY-8
**Townley**—*pop pl* AL-4
**Townley**—*pop pl* IN-6
**Townley**—*pop pl* MO-7
**Townley**—*pop pl* NJ-2
**Townley**—*pop pl* TX-5
Townley, James, House—*hist pl* NJ-2
Townley, W. J., House—*hist pl* OR-9
Townley (CCD)—*cens area* AL-4
Townley Cem—*cemetery* MO-7
Townley Cem—*cemetery* PA-2
Townley Ch—*church* AL-4
Townley Ch—*church* NJ-2
Townley Creek—*stream* VA-3
Townley Division—*civil* AL-4
Townley Field—*park* IL-6
Townley Hill—*summit* AL-4
Townley Hill—*summit* NY-2
Townley Hollow—*valley* OK-5
Townley JHS—*school* AL-4
Townley Mine (underground)—*mine* AL-4
Townley Ranch—*locale* SD-7
Townley Run—*stream* PA-2
Townley Spring—*spring* SD-7
*Town Line* MI-6
Town Line—*locale* PA-2
**Town Line**—*pop pl* NY-2
Townline Bluff—*cliff* WI-6
Town Line Boundary Marker—*hist pl* MA-1
Townline Brook—*stream* (2) ME-1
Townline Brook—*stream* NH-1
Town Line Brook—*stream* NH-1
Townline Brook—*stream* NY-2
Town Line Cem—*cemetery* IN-6
Town Line Cem—*cemetery* NY-2
Town Line Cem—*cemetery* OH-6
Town Line Cem—*cemetery* VT-1
Townline Cem—*cemetery* (3) WI-6
Town Line Ch—*church* IN-6
Town Line Ch—*church* (2) MI-6
Town Line Ch—*church* NY-2
Town Line Ch—*church* PA-2
Town Line Creek—*stream* MI-6
Townline Creek—*stream* MI-6
Town Line Creek—*stream* (2) MI-6
Townline Creek—*stream* (2) MI-6
Town Line Creek—*stream* WI-6
Townline Creek—*stream* WI-6
Town Line Day Camp—*locale* NY-2
Townline Drain—*canal* MI-6
Town Line Drain—*canal* MI-6
Townline Drain—*canal* MI-6
Townline Drain—*stream* (2) MI-6
Town Line Flowage—*reservoir* WI-6
Townline Flowage—*reservoir* WI-6
Town Line Hill—*summit* MA-1
*Town Line Lake* MI-6
*Town Line Lake* MN-6
*Town Line Lake* WI-6
Townline Lake—*lake* MI-6
Town Line Lake—*lake* MI-6
Townline Lake—*lake* (5) MI-6
Town Line Lake—*lake* MI-6
Townline Lake—*lake* MI-6
Town Line Lake—*lake* MN-6
Townline Lake—*lake* (2) MN-6
Town Line Lake—*lake* MN-6
Townline Lake—*lake* MN-6
Town Line Lake—*lake* WI-6
Townline Lake—*lake* (4) WI-6
Town Line Lake—*lake* WI-6
Townline Lake—*lake* WI-6
*Town Line Lakes* MI-6
Town Line Lakes—*lake* MI-6
Townline Marsh—*swamp* MI-6
Town Line Pond—*lake* NY-2
Townline Rsvr—*reservoir* WI-6
Town Line Run—*stream* (2) PA-2
Town Line Sch—*school* IL-6
Townline Sch—*school* IL-6
Townline Sch—*school* MI-6
Townline Sch—*school* NY-2
Town Line Sch—*school* NY-2
Townline Sch—*school* (3) WI-6
Townline Sch (abandoned)—*school* (2) PA-2
Townline Sch (historical)—*school* PA-2
**Town Line Station**—*pop pl* NY-2
Town Line Swamp—*swamp* RI-1
Town Lot Brook—*stream* MA-1
*Townly* AL-4
Town Marsh—*swamp* NC-3
Town Meadow Brook—*stream* MA-1
Town Millpond—*lake* CT-1
Town Mountain—*ridge* GA-3

Town Mountain Gap—gap NC-3
Town Mountain Sch—school KY-4
Townmount Ch—church IL-6
Town Mtn—summit CA-9
Town Mtn—summit (2) KY-4
Town Mtn—summit NM-5
Town Mtn—summit NC-3
Town Mtn—summit TX-5
Town Mtn—summit WV-2
Town 'n' Country—CDP FL-3
Town 'N Country Plaza (Shop Ctr)—locale (2) FL-3
Town 'N' Country Shop Ctr—locale NC-3
Town Neck—cape MA-1
Town Neck Creek—gut NJ-2
Town Neck Hill—summit MA-1
Town Neck Sch—school MD-2
**Town N Four Village**—pop pl MO-7
Town North—post sta TX-5
Town Oaks—post sta TX-5
Town Of Abiquiu Grant—civil NM-5
Town Of Alameda—civil NM-5
Town Of Albuquerque—civil NM-5
Town of Atrisco Grant—civil NM-5
Town of Boonton Reservoir NJ-2
Town of Crested Butte—hist pl CO-8
Town of East Windsor CT-1
Town of Enfield CT-1
Town Of Manzano Grant—civil NM-5
Town of Milwaukee Town Hall—hist pl WI-6
Town of Palo Alto—hist pl MS-4
**Town of Pines**—pop pl IN-6
Town of Socorro—civil NM-5
Town of Suffield CT-1
Town Of Tajique Grant—civil NM-5
Town Of Tejon Grant—civil NM-5
**Town of Tonawanda**—pop pl NY-2
Town Of Torreon Grant—civil NM-5
Town of Windsor CT-1
Town of Windsor Farms CT-1
Town on Matecomack Creek NC-3
Town on Queen Annes Creek NC-3
Town Orchard Country Club—other IL-6
Townotonkemig Pond RI-1
Town Park—park (2) CT-1
**Town Park**—pop pl PR-3
**Town Park Estates**—pop pl FL-3
Town Park South—park NY-2
**Town Park (subdivision)**—pop pl NC-3
**Town Pasture**—pop pl MA-1
Town Peak—summit TX-5
Town Plaza—locale MO-7
Town Plaza Shop Ctr—locale AL-4
Town Plaza (Shop Ctr)—locale (3) FL-3
Town Plot Hill CT-1
**Town Plot Hill**—pop pl CT-1
Town Point FL-3
Town Point MD-2
Town Point VA-3
Town Point—cape (2) FL-3
Town Point—cape (4) MD-2
Town Point—cape NC-3
Town Point—cape UT-8
Town Point—cape (2) VA-3
Town Point—cliff UT-8
Town Point—hist pl DE-2
Town Point—park DE-2
**Town Point**—pop pl MD-2
Town Point Landing—locale VA-3
Town Point Neck—cape (2) MD-2
Town Point Reach—channel VA-3
Town Pond—lake MA-1
Town Pond—lake NY-2
Town Pond—lake RI-1
Town Pool—lake CT-1
**Town Pump**—pop pl NY-2
**Town Ranch Heights (subdivision)**—pop pl NC-3
Town Resaca—lake TX-5
Town Reservoir Dam—dam UT-8
Town River MA-1
Town River—bay MA-1
Town River—stream MA-1
Town River Bay—bay MA-1
Town River Dam—dam MA-1
Town River Marshes—swamp MA-1
Town River Rsvr—reservoir (2) MA-1
Town Rsvr—reservoir CO-8
Town Rsvr—reservoir UT-8
Town Run VA-3
Town Run—stream (3) IN-6
Town Run—stream MD-2
Town Run—stream (5) OH-6
Town Run—stream (3) PA-2
Town Run—stream (3) VA-3
Town Run—stream (3) WV-2
**Towns**—pop pl GA-3
Towns, George W. B., House—hist pl GA-3
Townsand Lucas Ditch—canal IN-6
Towns Branch—stream GA-3
Townsbury—locale NJ-2
Town Sch—school CA-9
Town Sch—school CT-1
Town Sch—school NH-1
Town Sch Number 2—school VT-1
Town Sch Number 3—school NY-2
Town Sch Number 9—school NY-2
Towns Corner Sch—school VT-1
**Towns (County)**—pop pl GA-3
Towns County HS—school GA-3
Towns County Jail—hist pl GA-3
Towns County Park (historical)—park GA-3
Towns Creek—stream AL-4
Townsel Cem—cemetery MS-4
Townsel Hill—summit TN-4
Townsen Cem—cemetery TX-5
Townsen Creek—stream MO-7
Townsend KS-7
Towns End ME-1
Townsend—locale FL-3
Townsend—locale MS-4
Townsend—locale UT-8
**Townsend**—pop pl DE-2
**Townsend**—pop pl GA-3
**Townsend**—pop pl MA-1
**Townsend**—pop pl MT-8
**Townsend**—pop pl NY-2
**Townsend**—pop pl TN-4
**Townsend**—pop pl VA-3
**Townsend**—pop pl WI-6

Townsend, Henry, Bldg—hist pl DE-2
Townsend, Henry, House—hist pl WY-8
Townsend, Jabez, House—hist pl NH-1
Townsend, James W., House—hist pl FL-3
Townsend, Lake—reservoir NC-3
Townsend, Mount—summit WA-9
Townsend, Port—bay WA-9
Townsend, Thomas B., House—hist pl CO-8
Townsend, William S., House—hist pl NJ-2
Townsend, William T., House—hist pl OH-6
Townsend Airp—airport IN-6
Townsend Basin—basin CO-8
Townsend Bayou—stream TX-5
Townsend Branch—stream (2) AL-4
Townsend Branch—stream FL-3
Townsend Branch—stream GA-3
Townsend Branch—stream (2) KY-4
Townsend Branch—stream MS-4
Townsend Branch—stream NC-3
Townsend Branch—stream (2) TN-4
Townsend Bridge—bridge DE-2
Townsend Brook—stream ME-1
Townsend Brook—stream NH-1
Townsend Brook—stream VT-1
Townsend Butte—summit AZ-5
Townsend Camp Hollow—valley TX-5
Townsend Canal—canal FL-3
Townsend (CCD)—cens area GA-3
Townsend (CCD)—cens area TN-4
Townsend Cem—cemetery (2) AL-4
Townsend Cem—cemetery (2) AR-4
Townsend Cem—cemetery CT-1
Townsend Cem—cemetery DE-2
Townsend Cem—cemetery FL-3
Townsend Cem—cemetery (2) KY-4
Townsend Cem—cemetery ME-1
Townsend Cem—cemetery MI-6
Townsend Cem—cemetery MS-4
Townsend Cem—cemetery MO-7
Townsend Cem—cemetery NY-2
Townsend Cem—cemetery NC-3
Townsend Cem—cemetery PA-2
Townsend Cem—cemetery SC-3
Townsend Cem—cemetery TN-4
Townsend Cem—cemetery (3) TX-5
Townsend (census name for Townsend Center)—CDP MA-1
Townsend Center MA-1
Townsend Center Cem—cemetery MA-1
Townsend Center (census name Townsend)—other MA-1
Townsend Ch—church IN-6
Townsend Ch—church NC-3
Townsend Channel—channel NJ-2
Townsend Chapel AL-4
Townsend Church AL-4
Townsend Coover Cem—cemetery AL-4
Townsend Corners—locale NY-2
Townsend Corners—locale VT-1
Townsend Creek TN-4
Townsend Creek—stream (2) AL-4
Townsend Creek—stream FL-3
Townsend Creek—stream ID-8
Townsend Creek—stream KY-4
Townsend Creek—stream MT-8
Townsend Creek—stream NV-8
Townsend Creek—stream NY-2
Townsend Creek—stream OR-9
Townsend Creek—stream (2) TX-5
Townsend Creek—stream WA-9
Townsend Creek—stream WI-6
Townsend Creek—stream WY-8
**Townsend Crossroads**—pop pl AL-4
Townsend Dam—dam NC-3
Townsend Ditch—canal CO-8
Townsend Division—civil TN-4
Townsend Draft—valley VA-3
Townsend Drain—canal CA-9
Townsend Drain—canal MI-6
Townsend East—cens area MT-8
Townsend Elem Sch—school DE-2
Townsend Elem Sch—school TN-4
Townsend Farm—hist pl NH-1
Townsend Field—park OH-6
Townsend Flowage—lake WI-6
Townsend Fork—stream KY-4
Townsend Gap—gap NC-3
Townsend Grove Ch—church KY-4
Townsend Gulch MT-8
Townsend Gulch NV-8
Townsend Gulch—valley (2) CA-9
Townsend Gulch—valley ID-8
Townsend Gulch—valley MT-8
Townsend Gut—gut ME-1
**Townsend Harbor**—pop pl MA-1
Townsend Harbor Dam—dam MA-1
Townsend Hill—summit (2) MA-1
Townsend Hill—summit NY-2
Townsend Hill—summit RI-1
Townsend Hist Dist—hist pl DE-2
Townsend (historical)—locale AL-4
**Townsend (historical)**—pop pl OR-9
Townsend Hollow—valley (2) NY-2
Townsend Hollow—valley OH-6
Townsend Hotel—hist pl WY-8
Townsend House—hist pl LA-4
Townsend House—hist pl MA-1
Townsend House—hist pl PA-2
Townsend House Cem—cemetery FL-3
Townsend HS—school TN-4
Townsend HS (historical)—school MS-4
Townsend Inlet NJ-2
Townsend Island DE-2
Townsend Island—island NY-2
Townsend JHS—school AZ-5
Townsend Lake NE-7
Townsend Lake—lake IL-6
Townsend Lake—lake (2) MI-6
Townsend Lake—lake NE-7
Townsend Lake—reservoir LA-4
Townsend Lake—swamp AR-4
Townsend Lake Number 1 TN-4
Townsend Lateral—canal AR-4
Townsend Lateral—canal ID-8
Townsend Mill DE-2
Townsend Mill—locale GA-3
Townsend Monmt—park MD-2
Townsend MS—school NC-3
Townsend Mtn—summit WA-9
Townsend Oil Field—other NM-5

Townsend-Palmer House—hist pl UT-8
Townsend Park—flat WY-8
Townsend Park—park AZ-5
Townsend Park—park AR-4
Townsend Peak—summit AK-9
Townsend Peak—summit CA-9
Townsend Photography Studio—hist pl NE-7
Townsend Point—cape ME-1
Townsend Point—cape NJ-2
Townsend Point—summit TX-5
Townsend Pond—lake FL-3
Townsend Pond—lake NH-1
Townsend Pond—lake NY-2
Townsend Post Office—building TN-4
Townsend Post Office (historical)—building MS-4
Townsend Post Office (historical)—building TN-4
Townsend Ranch—locale WY-8
Townsend Reservoir MA-1
Townsend Ridge—ridge ME-1
Townsend River SC-3
Townsend River—stream SC-3
Townsend Rsvr—reservoir MT-8
Townsend's, Hephzibah Jenkins, Tabby Oven Ruins—hist pl SC-3
Townsends Cem—cemetery FL-3
Townsend Sch—school AR-4
Townsend Sch—school KY-4
Townsend Sch—school NE-7
Townsend Sch—school OK-5
Townsend Sch—school TN-4
Townsends Channel NJ-2
Townsends Creek TN-4
Townsend's Draft VA-3
Townsends Ferry TN-4
Townsend Shop Ctr—locale MA-1
Townsends Inlet—bay NJ-2
**Townsends Inlet**—pop pl NJ-2
Townsends Island TN-4
Townsend Site—hist pl DE-2
Townsend Slough—stream MO-7
Townsends Mission Sch (historical)—school (2) AL-4
Townsend Sound—bay NJ-2
Townsend Spring—spring NV-8
Townsends River SC-3
Townsend Street Sch—school WI-6
Townsend Swamp—swamp PA-2
Townsend-Taylor Cem—cemetery AL-4
**Townsend (Town of)**—pop pl MA-1
**Townsend (Town of)**—pop pl WI-6
**Townsend (Township of)**—pop pl (2) OH-6
Townsend Valley—valley MT-8
**Townsendville**—pop pl NY-2
Townsend Well—well AZ-5
Townsend Well—well NV-8
Townsend West—cens area MT-8
Townsend-Wilkins House—hist pl TX-5
Townsen Lake—lake FL-3
Townsers Neck MA-1
Townset Lake MN-6
Townshend—locale MD-2
**Townshend**—pop pl VT-1
Townshend State For—forest VT-1
**Townshend (Town of)**—pop pl VT-1
Towns Hill—summit PA-2
**Township**—pop pl MI-6
Township—post sta MI-6
Township Butte—summit AZ-5
Township Butte—summit ID-8
Township C—unorg ME-1
Township Campground—locale MI-6
Township Cem—cemetery (9) KS-7
Township Cem—cemetery (2) MI-6
Township Cem—cemetery (7) OH-6
Township Cemetery SD-7
Township Central Sch—school IN-6
Township Central Sch—school NJ-2
Township Central Sch—school PA-2
Township Corners State Wildlife Mngmt Area—park WI-6
Township Corner Tank—reservoir AZ-5
Township D—unorg ME-1
Township Ditch—canal IN-6
Township Drain—canal (2) CA-9
Township Drainage Ditch IL-6
Township E—unorg ME-1
Township Gulch—valley CA-9
Township HS—school ME-1
Township HS—school (2) OH-6
Township HS North—school IL-6
Township HS South—school (2) IL-6
Township HS West—school IL-6
Township Lake—reservoir ND-7
Township Lateral—canal CA-9
Township Lateral—canal ID-8
Township Line Bridge—hist pl KS-7
Township Line Cem—cemetery OH-6
Township Line Ch—church (2) MO-7
Township Line Dam—dam (2) PA-2
Township Line Rsvr—reservoir PA-2
Township Line Run—stream PA-2
Township Line Sch (abandoned)—school MO-7
Township Meadow—flat OR-9
Township Meadows OR-9
Township Number Seven—civil KS-7
Township Number 1—civil (3) KS-7
Township Number 10—civil (2) KS-7
Township Number 11—civil (2) KS-7
Township Number 12—civil (2) KS-7
Township Number 2—civil (3) KS-7
Township Number 3—civil (3) KS-7
Township Number 4—civil (3) KS-7
Township Number 5 MA-1
Township Number 5—civil (3) KS-7
Township Number 6—civil (4) KS-7
Township Number 7—civil (2) KS-7
Township Number 8—civil (3) KS-7
Township Number 9—civil (3) KS-7
Township of Abington Game Preserve—locale PA-2
Township of Madison NJ-2
Township of Matawan NJ-2
Township of Union NJ-2
Township of Upper Penns Neck NJ-2
Township of Wannamoisett MA-1
Township Park—park MI-6
Township Park—park (2) OH-6
Township Rock—island ME-1

Township Run—stream (2) PA-2
Township Sch—school CA-9
Township Sch—school IN-6
Township Sch—school ME-1
Township Sch—school MO-7
Township Sch—school (3) NC-3
Township Sch—school OH-6
Township Sch Number 1 IN-6
Township Sch Number 1 PA-2
Township Sch Number 1—school OH-6
Township Sch Number 1—school PA-2
Township Sch Number 2—school OH-6
**Township School Scotch Ridge**—pop pl OH-6
Township Tank—reservoir AZ-5
Township Trail—trail PA-2
Township Valley—valley NY-2
Township 1—civil (2) NC-3
**Township 1**—pop pl NE-7
Township 1, Carthage—civil NC-3
Township 1, Charlotte—civil NC-3
Township 1, Dunn—civil NC-3
Township 1, Edenton—civil NC-3
Township 1, Greenwood—civil NC-3
Township 1, Harrisburg—civil NC-3
Township 1, Marshall—civil NC-3
Township 1, Patterson—civil NC-3
Township 1, River—civil NC-3
Township 1, Tarboro—civil NC-3
Township 1, White Oak—civil NC-3
Township 10, Knob Creek—civil NC-3
Township 10, Lemley—civil NC-3
Township 10, Little River—civil NC-3
Township 10, Louisburg—civil NC-3
Township 10, Lower Town Creek—civil NC-3
Township 10, Melville—civil NC-3
Township 10, Midland—civil NC-3
Township 11, Casar—civil NC-3
Township 11, Central Cabarrus—civil NC-3
Township 11, Long Creek—civil NC-3
Township 11, Pleasant Grove—civil NC-3
Township 11, Walnut Creek—civil NC-3
Township 12, Burlington—civil NC-3
Township 12, Concord—civil NC-3
Township 12, Paw Creek—civil NC-3
Township 12, Rocky Mount—civil NC-3
Township 13, Cokey—civil NC-3
Township 13, Haw River—civil NC-3
Township 13, Morning Star—civil NC-3
Township 14, Pineville—civil NC-3
Township 14, Upper Town Creek—civil NC-3
Township 15, Huntersville—civil NC-3
Township 2—civil (2) NC-3
**Township 2**—pop pl NE-7
Township 2, Bensalem—civil NC-3
Township 2, Berryhill—civil NC-3
Township 2, Boiling Springs—civil NC-3
Township 2, Coble—civil NC-3
Township 2, Harris—civil NC-3
Township 2, Jonesboro—civil NC-3
Township 2, Laurel—civil NC-3
Township 2, Lower Conetoe—civil NC-3
Township 2, Middle—civil NC-3
Township 2, Pollocksville—civil NC-3
Township 2, Poplar Tent—civil NC-3
Township 3—civ div NE-7
Township 3—civil (2) NC-3
Township 3, Boone Station—civil NC-3
Township 3, Cape Fear—civil NC-3
Township 3, Mars Hill—civil NC-3
Township 3, Odell—civil NC-3
Township 3, Rippys—civil NC-3
Township 3, Sheffields—civil NC-3
Township 3, Steel Creek—civil NC-3
Township 3, Trenton—civil NC-3
Township 3, Upper—civil NC-3
Township 3, Upper Conetoe—civil NC-3
Township 3, Youngsville—civil NC-3
Township 4—civ div NE-7
Township 4—civil NC-3
Township 4, Beech Glenn—civil NC-3
Township 4, Cypress Creek—civil NC-3
Township 4, Deep Creek—civil NC-3
Township 4, Deep River—civil NC-3
Township 4, Franklinton—civil NC-3
Township 4, Kannapolis—civil NC-3
Township 4, Kings Mountain—civil NC-3
Township 4, Morton—civil NC-3
Township 4, Ritters—civil NC-3
Township 4, Sharon—civil NC-3
Township 4, Yeopim—civil NC-3
Township 5—civil (2) NC-3
**Township 5**—pop pl NE-7
Township 5, Deep River—civil NC-3
Township 5, East Sanford—civil NC-3
Township 5, Faucette—civil NC-3
Township 5, Hayesville—civil NC-3
Township 5, Lower Fishing Creek—civil NC-3
Township 5, New Gilead—civil NC-3
Township 5, Providence—civil NC-3
Township 5, Tuckahoe—civil NC-3
Township 5, Walnut—civil NC-3
Township 5, Warlick—civil NC-3
Township 6—civil NC-3
**Township 6**—pop pl NE-7
Township 6—unorg ME-1
Township 6, Chinquapin—civil NC-3
Township 6, Clear Creek—civil NC-3
Township 6, Graham—civil NC-3
Township 6, Greenwood—civil NC-3
Township 6, Hot Springs—civil NC-3
Township 6, Rimertown—civil NC-3
Township 6, Sandy Creek—civil NC-3
Township 6, Shelby—civil NC-3
Township 6, Upper Fishing Creek—civil NC-3
Township 6, West Sanford—civil NC-3
Township 7—civil NC-3
**Township 7**—pop pl NE-7
Township 7, Albright—civil NC-3
Township 7, Beaver Creek—civil NC-3
Township 7, Crab Orchard—civil NC-3
Township 7, Ebbs Chapel—civil NC-3
Township 7, Gold Hill—civil NC-3
Township 7, Gold Mine—civil NC-3
Township 7, McNeills—civil NC-3
Township 7, Pocket—civil NC-3
Township 7, Sandy Run—civil NC-3
Township 7, Swift Creek—civil NC-3
Township 8—civil NC-3
Township 8, Cedar Rock—civil NC-3

Township 8, Mallard Creek—civil NC-3
Township 8, Mount Pleasant—civil NC-3
Township 8, Newlin—civil NC-3
Township 8, Polkville—civil NC-3
Township 8, Sand Hill—civil NC-3
Township 8, Sparta—civil NC-3
Township 8, Spring Creek—civil NC-3
Township 9—civil NC-3
Township 9, Cypress Creek—civil NC-3
Township 9, Deweese—civil NC-3
Township 9, Double Shoals—civil NC-3
Township 9, Georgeville—civil NC-3
Township 9, Mineral Springs—civil NC-3
Township 9, Otter Creek—civil NC-3
Township 9, Thompson—civil NC-3
Townshire Shop Ctr—locale TX-5
**Townside Park Subdivision**—pop pl UT-8
Townsite Ditch—canal OR-9
Townsite Gulch—valley CO-8
Townsite Lateral—canal ID-8
Town Site Lateral—canal SD-7
Town Site Lateral A—canal SD-7
Town Site Lateral B—canal SD-7
Town Site Lateral C—canal SD-7
Townsite Mine—mine SD-7
Townsite Point—cape TX-5
Townsite Prospect—mine CA-9
Townsite Spring—spring NV-8
Towns Lake MS-4
Towns Landing (historical)—locale AL-4
Townsley Cem—cemetery IN-6
Townsley Lake—lake CA-9
Townsley Spring—spring ID-8
Town Slough—lake MN-6
Townsman Draft VA-3
Towns Mtn—summit GA-3
Towns Mtn—summit NH-1
Towson Lake—lake MS-4
Towns Pond MA-1
Towns Prairie—flat FL-3
Town Spring AL-4
Town Spring—spring CA-9
Town Springs—spring TN-4
Townsprings Cave—cave TN-4
Town Square—hist pl WA-9
Town Square Center (Shop Ctr)—locale FL-3
Town Square Shopping Center TN-4
**Town Square (subdivision), The**—pop pl (2) AZ-5
Town Stable—hist pl MA-1
Townstead of Writestown PA-2
Town Street Cem—cemetery CT-1
Townsville SC-3
**Townsville**—pop pl NC-3
Townsville Landing—locale NC-3
Townsville (Township of)—fmr MCD NC-3
Town Swamp MA-1
Town Swamp—swamp NC-3
**Town Talk**—pop pl CA-9
Town Tank—reservoir AZ-5
Town Thatch Bed—swamp ME-1
Town Theatre—hist pl SC-3
Town Tract of Saluria TX-5
Townview Sch—school OH-6
Townview Sch—school WI-6
**Townville**—pop pl PA-2
**Townville**—pop pl SC-3
Townville Borough—civil PA-2
Townwanda Lake—reservoir VA-3
Town Wash—arroyo UT-8
Town Wash—stream NV-8
Town Wash—valley UT-8
Town Well—well AZ-5
Town Well—well TX-5
Town West—post sta OK-5
Town West Baptist Ch—church KS-7
Town West Shop Ctr—locale MS-4
Town Wharf—locale ME-1
**Townwood**—pop pl OH-6
Town Woods—woods ME-1
Town Woods Brook—stream ME-1
Town Woods Hill—summit CT-1
Tow of Charlestown RI-1
Towolbu' FM-9
TO Woody Windmill—locale TX-5
Towormeal FM-9
Towosahgy State Park—park MO-7
Towoway FM-9
Towpath Mtn—summit NY-2
Tow Point—cape AR-4
Tow Rock Charcoal Kilns—locale UT-8
Towry Post Office (historical)—building TN-4
Towser Branch—stream VA-3
Towser Ranch—locale AZ-5
Towsers Branch—stream MD-2
Towsers Neck—swamp MA-1
Towsers Swamp—swamp MA-1
Towser Tank—reservoir AZ-5
Towslee Sch—school OH-6
Towsley Canyon—valley CA-9
Towsley Creek MT-8
Towsley Gulch MT-8
Towsley Gulch—valley MT-8
**Towson**—pop pl MD-2
Towson Acad—hist pl MD-2
Towson Cem—cemetery TN-4
**Towson Estates**—pop pl MD-2
**Towson Park**—pop pl MD-2
Towson Run—stream MD-2
Towson State Teachers Coll—school MD-2
Tow Stake Point—cape VA-3
Tow String Ch—church NC-3
Towstring Creek—stream MO-7
Tow String Creek—stream NC-3
Towtaid MA-1
Towtaid, Town of MA-1
Towyard Branch—stream MS-4
**Toxaway**—pop pl SC-3
Toxaway, Lake—reservoir (2) NC-3
Toxaway Ch—church SC-3
Toxaway Creek—stream NC-3
Toxaway Creek—stream SC-3
Toxaway Falls—falls NC-3
**Toxaway Falls (subdivision)**—pop pl NC-3
Toxaway Lake—lake ID-8
Toxaway Lower Dam—dam NC-3
Toxaway Mtn—summit NC-3
Toxaway River—stream NC-3
Toxaway River—stream SC-3
**Toxey**—pop pl AL-4

Toxey Bend AL-4
Toxey Ch—church AL-4
Toxey Oil Field—oilfield AL-4
Toxeys Spring Branch—stream AL-4
Tox Hill—summit MT-8
Toxish MS-4
Toxish Baptist Church MS-4
Toxish Ch—church MS-4
Toxy Bend—bend AL-4
Toy FM-9
**Toy**—pop pl NV-8
Toyabe Dome NV-8
Toyabe Range NV-8
Toyack Future Farmers of America Chapter House—hist pl UT-8
**Toyah**—pop pl TX-5
Toyah Creek—stream TX-5
Toyah Lake—lake TX-5
Toyah New Cem—cemetery TX-5
Toyah Old Cem—cemetery TX-5
**Toyahvale**—pop pl TX-5
To'yang FM-9
Toyatte Glacier—glacier AK-9
Toy Canyon WY-8
Toy Canyon—valley WY-8
Toyee—church NM-5
Toyee Spring—spring NM-5
**Toyei**—pop pl AZ-5
Toyei Sch—school AZ-5
Toyei School Airp—airport AZ-5
Toy Flat—flat ID-8
Toy Harbor—bay AK-9
Toy Hill—summit GA-3
Toy Hill—summit VA-3
Toy Lake—lake WI-6
Toy Mtn—summit ID-8
Toyn Creek—stream NV-8
Toyne Windmill—locale CO-8
Toynim FM-9
Toyon—locale CA-9
**Toyon**—pop pl CA-9
Toyon Bay—bay CA-9
Toyon Camp—locale CA-9
To'yong FM-9
Toyon Mine—mine CA-9
Toyon Sch—school (2) CA-9
Toy Pass—gap ID-8
Toy Point—cape WA-9
Toy Seep—spring ID-8
Toy Springs—spring TX-5
Toy Spring Sch—school KY-4
Toza Island—island AK-9
Tozer Canyon—valley CO-8
Tozer Creek—stream AK-9
Tozer Lake—lake WI-6
Tozer Springs—spring WI-6
Tozi, Mount—summit AK-9
Tozier Cem—cemetery ME-1
**Tozier Corner**—pop pl MA-1
Tozier Creek—stream WA-9
**Toziers Corner**—pop pl NY-2
Tozimoran Creek—stream AK-9
Tozitna Island—island AK-9
Tozitna River—stream AK-9
Tozitna Slough—stream AK-9
Tozo, Arroyo—stream CA-9
T Patram Ditch IN-6
T P Creek—stream ID-8
T Pendleton Ranch—locale NM-5
T P Lake TX-5
T P Lake—reservoir (4) TX-5
T Pool—reservoir MI-6
T P Spring—spring OR-9
T P Tank—reservoir TX-5
T P Well—well TX-5
T P Windmill—locale TX-5
Trabajo Creek—stream NM-5
Traband, John H., House—hist pl MD-2
Traber—locale SC-3
Trabing—locale WY-8
Trabing Creek—stream WY-8
Trabing Draw—valley WY-8
Trabing Dry Creek—stream WY-8
Trabucco Creek—stream CA-9
Trabucco Flat—flat CA-9
Trabucco Gardens—locale CA-9
Trabuco CA-9
Trabuco—civil CA-9
Trabuco, Arroyo—stream CA-9
Trabuco Campground—locale CA-9
**Trabuco Canyon**—pop pl CA-9
Trabuco Canyon—valley CA-9
Trabuco Canyon Trail—trail CA-9
Trabuco (CCD)—cens area CA-9
Trabuco Creek CA-9
Trabuco Creek—stream CA-9
Trabuco Guard Station—locale CA-9
Trabuco Mtn—summit CA-9
Trabuco Oaks (2) CA-9
Trabuco Peak CA-9
Trabuco Peak—summit CA-9
Trabuco Sch—school CA-9
Trabue, Daniel, House—hist pl KY-4
Trabue Airp—airport KS-7
Trabur Cem—cemetery VA-3
Trace—locale AR-4
Trace—locale WV-2
**Trace**—pop pl KY-4
Trace, Lake—reservoir NC-3
Trace Branch TN-4
Trace Branch WV-2
Trace Branch—stream (3) AL-4
Trace Branch—stream IN-6
Trace Branch—stream (26) KY-4
Trace Branch—stream MS-4
Trace Branch—stream NC-3
Trace Branch—stream VA-3
Trace Branch—stream (11) WV-2
Trace Branch Boat Ramp—locale KY-4
Trace Branch Ch—church KY-4
Trace Branch Sch—school KY-4
Trace Ch—church WV-2
Trace City Baptist Ch—church MS-4
Trace Coulee—valley MT-8
Trace Creek TN-4
Trace Creek—stream (8) AR-4
Trace Creek—stream (7) KY-4
Trace Creek—stream (4) MO-7
Trace Creek—stream (2) OH-6
Trace Creek—stream (9) TN-4

Trace Creek—*stream* (5) WV-2
Trace Creek Baptist Ch—*church* TN-4
Trace Creek Cave—*cave* TN-4
Trace Creek Cem—*cemetery* TN-4
Trace Creek Ch—*church* KY-4
Trace Creek Ch—*church* MO-7
Trace Creek Country Club—*other* AR-4
Trace Creek Industrial Site—*locale* TN-4
*Trace Creek Post Office* TN-4
Trace Creek Sch (historical)—*school* MO-7
Trace Creek Trail—*trail* MO-7
**Trace End Estates**—*pop pl* TN-4
Trace Ford—*locale* AL-4
*Trace Fork* WV-2
**Trace Fork**—*pop pl* WV-2
Trace Fork—*stream* (21) KY-4
Trace Fork—*stream* (5) VA-3
Trace Fork—*stream* (29) WV-2
Trace Fork Cem—*cemetery* KY-4
Trace Fork Ch—*church* KY-4
Trace Fork Ch—*church* (5) WV-2
Trace Fork Sch—*school* VA-3
Trace Fork Sch—*school* (2) WV-2
Trace Gap—*gap* KY-4
Trace Gap—*gap* VA-3
Trace Hollow—*valley* MO-7
Trace Hollow—*valley* VA-3
**Trace Junction**—*pop pl* WV-2
Trace Lake—*lake* MN-6
**Traceland North (subdivision)**—*pop pl* MS-4
**Traceland (subdivision)**—*pop pl* MS-4
Tracer Brook—*stream* VT-1
Trace Ridge—*ridge* AR-4
Trace Ridge—*ridge* (2) KY-4
Trace Ridge—*ridge* NC-3
Trace Ridge—*ridge* VA-3
Trace Ridge—*ridge* WV-2
Trace Ridge Baptist Ch—*church* MS-4
Trace Ridge Ch—*church* AR-4
Trace Road Ch—*church* MS-4
*Trace Road Independent Baptist Ch* MS-4
Trace Run—*stream* (2) KY-4
Trace Run—*stream* (3) OH-6
Trace Run—*stream* (2) WV-2
Trace Sch—*school* CA-9
Trace Sch—*school* KY-4
Trace Sch—*school* PA-2
Traces Creek—*stream* KY-4
Tracetown—*post sta* MS-4
Trace Town Shop Ctr—*locale* MS-4
**Traceview**—*pop pl* TN-4
Traceway Park—*park* MS-4
*Tracewell* IN-6
Tracewell Cem—*cemetery* WV-2
**Tracewood (subdivision)**—*pop pl* MS-4
Trace Work Center—*locale* MS-4
Tracey Cem—*cemetery* KY-4
Tracey Ch—*church* IA-7
Tracey Creek—*stream* IA-7
Tracey Creek—*stream* MO-7
Tracey Hollow—*valley* TN-4
Tracey Run—*stream* MI-6
Tracey Run—*stream* OH-6
*Traceys* NC-3
Tracey Sch—*school* NE-7
Traceys Landing—*locale* AR-4
Tracey Slough—*gut* MN-6
Tracey Swamp—*stream* NC-3
Tracey Woodframe Grain Elevator—*hist pl* OK-5
**Trachsville**—*pop pl* PA-2
Trachyte Creek—*stream* UT-8
Trachyte Knob—*summit* CO-8
Trachyte Point—*ridge* UT-8
Trachyte Ranch—*locale* UT-8
*Track* MS-4
Track Bus No. 19—*hist pl* CA-9
*Track Fork Peak Creek* VA-3
Track Lake—*lake* MN-6
Trackle Pond—*lake* MA-1
Trackler Mtn—*summit* MO-7
Track Mine Number 16 (underground)—*mine* AL-4
Track Rock—*other* AK-9
Trackrock Branch—*stream* GA-3
Track Rock Ch—*church* GA-3
Trackrock Ch—*church* GA-3
Trackrock Gap—*gap* GA-3
Tracks Draw—*valley* MT-8
Track Tank—*reservoir* AZ-5
Tracktowne—*uninc pl* PA-2
Tracktowne Station—*locale* PA-2
Track Well—*locale* NM-5
Tract A Taos Pueblo—*civil* NM-5
Tract Between San Jacinto and San Gorgonio—*civil* CA-9
Tract B Taos Pueblo—*civil* NM-5
Tract C Taos Pueblo—*civil* NM-5
Tract Fork—*stream* VA-3
Tract Hill—*summit* WV-2
Traction Gulch—*valley* ID-8
Traction Ranch—*locale* CA-9
Tract Mtn—*summit* VA-3
Tract Of Land In Monterey County (Castro)—*civil* CA-9
Tract Of Land In Monterey County (Cocks)—*civil* CA-9
Tract Of Land Near San Gabriel (Sexton)—*civil* CA-9
Tract Of Land Near San Gabriel (White)—*civil* CA-9
Tract Of Land Near San Juan Bautista—*civil* CA-9
Tract Of Land Near San Juan Bautista (Breen)—*civil* CA-9
Tract of Land 1000 Varas Square (Sexton)—*civil* CA-9
Tractor—*locale* KS-7
Tractor Creek—*stream* AK-9
Tractor Flat—*flat* ID-8
Tractor Lake—*lake* AK-9
Tracts Of Land Near San Gabriel (Aguilar)—*civil* CA-9
Tracts Of Land Near San Gabriel (Domingo)—*civil* CA-9
Tracts Of Land Near San Gabriel (Saint Meon)—*civil* CA-9
Tracts Of Land Near San Gabriel (Sales)—*civil* CA-9
Tracy—*locale* KY-4
Tracy—*locale* MO-7
Tracy—*locale* NJ-2
Tracy—*locale* PA-2
Tracy—*locale* TX-5
Tracy—*locale* WA-9
Tracy—*locale* WY-8
Tracy—*other* OH-6
Tracy—*other* OK-5
**Tracy**—*pop pl* CA-9
**Tracy**—*pop pl* CT-1
**Tracy**—*pop pl* IN-6
**Tracy**—*pop pl* IA-7
**Tracy**—*pop pl* MN-6
**Tracy**—*pop pl* MO-7
**Tracy**—*pop pl* MT-8
**Tracy**—*pop pl* NC-3
**Tracy**—*pop pl* OK-5
**Tracy**—*pop pl* OR-9
**Tracy**—*pop pl* PA-2
Tracy, Lake—*lake* FL-3
Tracy, Lake—*swamp* FL-3
Tracy, Lee, House—*hist pl* VT-1
Tracy Arm—*channel* AK-9
*Tracy Branch* MD-2
*Tracy Branch* WV-2
Tracy Branch—*stream* FL-3
Tracy Branch—*stream* KY-4
Tracy Branch—*stream* TN-4
Tracy Branch Ch—*church* KY-4
Tracy Brook—*stream* (6) ME-1
Tracy Brook—*stream* (2) MA-1
Tracy Brook—*stream* (3) NH-1
Tracy Brook—*stream* (3) NY-2
Tracy Brook—*stream* VT-1
Tracy Canal—*canal* FL-3
Tracy Canyon—*valley* (2) CO-8
Tracy (CCD)—*cens area* CA-9
Tracy (CCD)—*cens area* KY-4
Tracy Cem—*cemetery* CA-9
Tracy Cem—*cemetery* IA-7
Tracy Cem—*cemetery* KY-4
Tracy Cem—*cemetery* MN-6
Tracy Ch—*church* IN-6
Tracy Ch—*church* KY-4
**Tracy City**—*pop pl* TN-4
Tracy City (CCD)—*cens area* TN-4
Tracy City Cem—*cemetery* TN-4
Tracy City Coke Ovens—*hist pl* TN-4
Tracy City Division—*civil* TN-4
Tracy City First Baptist Ch—*church* TN-4
Tracy City Hall and Jail—*hist pl* CA-9
Tracy City Post Office—*building* TN-4
Tracy City United Methodist Ch—*church* TN-4
**Tracy-Clark**—*pop pl* NV-8
**Tracy Corner**—*pop pl* MA-1
Tracy Corners—*locale* ME-1
Tracy Corners—*locale* WI-6
Tracy Country Club—*other* MN-6
*Tracy Creek* MD-2
*Tracy Creek* NE-7
*Tracy Creek* OR-9
**Tracy Creek**—*pop pl* NY-2
Tracy Creek—*stream* CA-9
Tracy Creek—*stream* MI-6
Tracy Creek—*stream* NE-7
Tracy Creek—*stream* (2) NY-2
Tracy Creek—*stream* OR-9
Tracy Creek—*stream* (2) TX-5
Tracy Creek—*stream* (2) WI-6
Tracy Creek Cem—*cemetery* NY-2
Tracy Creek Ch—*church* NY-2
Tracy Creek State For—*forest* NY-2
Tracy Ditch—*canal* CA-9
Tracy Ditch—*canal* IN-6
Tracy Drain—*canal* MI-6
*Tracy Elementary School* PA-2
Tracy Elem Sch—*school* TN-4
Tracy Fork—*stream* WV-2
Tracy Grove Ch—*church* NC-3
Tracy Grove Community Center—*building* NC-3
Tracy Gulch—*valley* OR-9
Tracy Hill—*summit* CO-8
Tracy Hill—*summit* RI-1
Tracy Hill—*summit* (2) WA-9
Tracy (historical)—*locale* MS-4
Tracy Hollow—*valley* (2) MO-7
Tracy Inn—*hist pl* CA-9
Tracy Lake—*lake* CA-9
Tracy Lake—*lake* NY-2
Tracy Lake—*lake* WI-6
Tracy Lake—*lake* WY-8
Tracy Landing Field—*airport* KS-7
Tracy Loan and Trust Company Bldg—*hist pl* UT-8
Tracy Maintenance Camp—*locale* AZ-5
Tracy Mine—*mine* MI-6
Tracy Mtn—*summit* CO-8
Tracy Mtn—*summit* ME-1
Tracy Mtn—*summit* ND-7
Tracy Mtn—*summit* OR-9
Tracy Park—*park* OK-5
Tracy Park Hist Dist—*hist pl* OK-5
*Tracy Pond* CT-1
Tracy Pond—*lake* (2) ME-1
Tracy Pond—*lake* (2) MA-1
Tracy Pond—*lake* (2) NY-2
Tracy Pumping Station—*other* CA-9
Tracy Ranch—*locale* NE-7
Tracy Rock—*pillar* WA-9
Tracy Run—*stream* PA-2
Tracys Cave—*cave* WA-9
Tracy Sch—*school* CA-9
Tracy Sch—*school* (2) CT-1
Tracy Sch—*school* MA-1
Tracy Sch—*school* MI-6
Tracy Sch—*school* PA-2
Tracy Sch Number 4 (historical)—*school* SD-7
Tracys Creek—*stream* MD-2
Tracys Landing—*locale* MD-2
Tracy's Landing Tobacco House No. 2—*hist pl* MD-2
Tracys Pond—*reservoir* CT-1
*Tracy Spring* OR-9
*Tracys Trading Post* AZ-5
Tracy Substa—*other* CA-9
**Tracyton**—*pop pl* WA-9
Tracyton Cem—*cemetery* WA-9
**Tracy Township**—*pop pl* SD-7
Tracy Valley Cem—*cemetery* NE-7
*Tracyville* PA-2
Tracy Well—*well* NM-5
Tracy Wigwam—*locale* UT-8
Trade—*locale* AL-4
**Trade**—*pop pl* TN-4
Trade and Commerce Bldg—*hist pl* WI-6
Trade Branch—*stream* TN-4
**Trade City**—*pop pl* PA-2
Trade City Station—*locale* PA-2
Tradedollar Creek—*stream* WA-9
Tradedollar Lake—*lake* WA-9
Trade Dollar Mine—*mine* ID-8
*Tradedollars Lake* WA-9
Trade Elem Sch—*school* TN-4
Trade (historical)—*locale* MS-4
Trade HS—*school* (2) MA-1
*Trade Lake* WI-6
**Trade Lake**—*pop pl* WI-6
Trade Lake Sch—*school* WI-6
**Trade Lake (Town of)**—*pop pl* WI-6
Trade Mart Bldg—*hist pl* KY-4
Trade Post Office—*building* TN-4
Trade Post Office (historical)—*building* AL-4
Trader Commercial Center—*locale* NC-3
Trader Fork—*stream* WV-2
Trader Hill—*summit* MI-6
**Trade River**—*pop pl* WI-6
Trade River—*stream* WI-6
Trade River Sch—*school* WI-6
*Trader Lake* MN-6
Trader Lake—*lake* MN-6
Trader Mine—*mine* MI-6
Trader Mtn—*summit* AK-9
Traders Bay—*bay* MN-6
Traders Bayou—*gut* WI-6
Traders Cove—*bay* AK-9
Traders Creek—*stream* OK-5
Traders Falls—*falls* MI-6
Traders Head—*cliff* AK-9
Traders Hill—*locale* GA-3
Traders Hollow—*valley* IN-6
Traders Island—*island* AK-9
*Traders Mill* GA-3
Traders Mtn—*summit* AK-9
*Traders Point* IN-6
**Traders Point**—*pop pl* IN-6
Traders Point (historical)—*locale* IA-7
Traders Point Lake—*reservoir* IN-6
Traders Point Lake Dam—*dam* IN-6
**Tradersville**—*pop pl* OH-6
*Traders Wharf* VA-3
Trade Sch—*school* MA-1
Trade Sch—*school* TX-5
Tradesman's Natl Bank Bldg—*hist pl* OK-5
Tradesville—*locale* PA-2
**Tradesville**—*pop pl* SC-3
Tradesville (CCD)—*cens area* SC-3
Trade Tech Junior Coll—*school* CA-9
Tradewater River—*stream* KY-4
Tradewater Valley Ch—*church* KY-4
Tradewinds North Shop Ctr—*locale* TN-4
Trade Winds Park North—*park* FL-3
Trade Winds Park South—*park* FL-3
Tradewinds Shop Ctr—*locale* MS-4
Tradewinds Shop Ctr, The—*locale* FL-3
Tradewinds South Shop Ctr—*locale* TN-4
Trading Bay—*bay* AK-9
Trading Cove—*bay* CT-1
Trading Cove Brook—*stream* CT-1
Trading Cove Dike—*levee* CT-1
Trading Creek—*stream* VA-3
**Tradingford**—*pop pl* NC-3
**Trading Ford**—*pop pl* NC-3
Trading Ford Ch—*church* NC-3
Tradinghouse Creek—*stream* TX-5
Tradinghouse Creek Rsvr—*reservoir* TX-5
Trading House Sch—*school* IL-6
Trading Point—*cape* AS-9
Trading Post—*locale* CO-8
Trading Post—*locale* NM-5
**Trading Post**—*pop pl* KS-7
**Trading Post**—*pop pl* TX-5
Trading Post Cem—*cemetery* KS-7
Trading Post Lake—*lake* MN-6
Trading Post Lake—*reservoir* NC-3
Trading Post Lake Dam—*dam* NC-3
Trading Post Shop Ctr—*locale* MA-1
Trading Post Wash—*valley* AZ-5
Trading Run—*stream* MD-2
Traditional Catholic Ch—*church* FL-3
Tradition Creek—*stream* MI-6
Tradition Lake—*lake* MN-6
Tradition Lake—*lake* WA-9
Traekabas Mill Dam—*dam* IN-6
**Traer**—*pop pl* IA-7
**Traer**—*pop pl* KS-7
Traer Agua Canyon—*valley* CA-9
Traer Cem—*cemetery* KS-7
Traer Creek—*stream* CO-8
Trafalgar—*locale* AR-4
**Trafalgar**—*pop pl* IN-6
Trafalgar Site, RI-639—*hist pl* RI-1
*Traffic* MN-6
Traffic—*locale* VA-3
Traffic Bridge—*bridge* VA-3
Traffic Safety Center—*school* FL-3
**Trafford**—*pop pl* AL-4
**Trafford**—*pop pl* PA-2
Trafford, Lake—*lake* FL-3
Trafford Borough—*civil* (2) PA-2
*Trafford City* PA-2
*Trafford Creek* KY-4
Trafford Elem Sch—*school* AL-4
Trafford Elem Sch (historical)—*school* PA-2
Trafford HS (historical)—*school* PA-2
Trafford Station—*building* PA-2
Traffton Meadow—*swamp* ME-1
Trafton—*locale* WA-9
**Trafton**—*pop pl* ME-1
Trafton Brook—*stream* (2) ME-1
Trafton Halftide Beacon—*locale* ME-1
Trafton Halftide Ledge—*bar* ME-1
Trafton Island—*island* ME-1
Trafton Island Ledge—*bar* ME-1
Trafton Lake—*lake* WA-9
Trafton Park—*park* MA-1
Trafton Pond—*lake* (2) ME-1
Trafton Rock—*island* ME-1
Trafton Siding—*locale* ME-1
Traft Ridge—*ridge* CA-9
*Tragedy Creek* CA-9
Tragedy Creek—*stream* CA-9
Tragedy Spring—*spring* CA-9
Trager Dam—*dam* ND-7
Tragesser Airp—*airport* IN-6
**Trago Lake**—*pop pl* IL-6
Trago Lake—*reservoir* IL-6
Trahan Canyon—*valley* OR-9
Trahan Cem—*cemetery* LA-4
*Trahans Creek* MS-4
Trahern's Station—*hist pl* OK-5
Trahin Sch—*school* TX-5
Trahlyta, Lake—*reservoir* GA-3
*Trahlytas Cairn Gap* GA-3
Trahon Creek—*stream* MS-4
*Trail* NC-3
Trail—*locale* MO-7
Trail—*locale* OK-5
**Trail**—*pop pl* MN-6
**Trail**—*pop pl* OH-6
**Trail**—*pop pl* OR-9
Trail—*trail* AK-9
Trail—*trail* AZ-5
Trail Branch—*stream* AL-4
Trail Branch—*stream* NC-3
Trail Branch—*stream* OK-5
Trail Branch—*stream* SC-3
Trail Branch—*stream* TN-4
Trail Branch—*stream* WV-2
Trail Branch Ch—*church* GA-3
Trail Bridge Dam—*dam* OR-9
Trail Bridge Forest Camp—*locale* OR-9
Trail Bridge Rsvr—*reservoir* OR-9
Trail Brook—*stream* ME-1
Trail Butte—*summit* OR-9
Trail Camp—*locale* OR-9
*Trail Canon* UT-8
*Trail Canyon* UT-8
Trail Canyon—*stream* CO-8
Trail Canyon—*valley* (7) AZ-5
Trail Canyon—*valley* (4) CA-9
Trail Canyon—*valley* (6) CO-8
Trail Canyon—*valley* (7) ID-8
Trail Canyon—*valley* KS-7
Trail Canyon—*valley* (2) NE-7
Trail Canyon—*valley* (18) NV-8
Trail Canyon—*valley* (16) NM-5
Trail Canyon—*valley* (4) OR-9
Trail Canyon—*valley* (2) TX-5
Trail Canyon—*valley* (31) UT-8
Trail Canyon—*valley* (2) WY-8
Trail Canyon Creek—*stream* NV-8
Trail Canyon Lodge—*locale* CO-8
Trail Canyon Rapids—*rapids* UT-8
Trail Canyon Saddle—*gap* NV-8
Trail Canyon Spring—*spring* (2) ID-8
Trail Canyon Spring—*spring* UT-8
Trail Canyon Wash—*stream* CO-8
Trail Canyon Well—*well* NM-5
Trail Cem—*cemetery* (2) MO-7
Trail Cem—*cemetery* OK-5
Trail Cem—*cemetery* SC-3
Trail Cem—*cemetery* TN-4
Trail Cem—*cemetery* WV-2
**Trail Center**—*pop pl* FL-3
**Trail City**—*pop pl* FL-3
**Trail City**—*pop pl* (2) SD-7
Trail City Cem—*cemetery* SD-7
*Trail City Lake Dam* SD-7
Trail City RR Lake—*reservoir* SD-7
Trail Cliff—*cliff* UT-8
*Trail Coulee* MT-8
Trail Coulee—*valley* MT-8
*Trail Creek* CO-8
*Trail Creek* ID-8
*Trail Creek* IN-6
*Trail Creek* MT-8
*Trail Creek* UT-8
*Trail Creek* WY-8
Trailcreek—*locale* MT-8
**Trail Creek**—*pop pl* IN-6
Trail Creek—*stream* (10) AK-9
Trail Creek—*stream* (2) CA-9
Trail Creek—*stream* (12) CO-8
Trail Creek—*stream* GA-3
Trail Creek—*stream* (52) ID-8
Trail Creek—*stream* IL-6
Trail Creek—*stream* (2) IN-6
Trail Creek—*stream* KS-7
Trail Creek—*stream* (2) MI-6
Trail Creek—*stream* (2) MO-7
Trail Creek—*stream* (32) MT-8
Trail Creek—*stream* (3) NV-8
Trail Creek—*stream* (3) NM-5
Trail Creek—*stream* (4) OK-5
Trail Creek—*stream* (17) OR-9
Trail Creek—*stream* (2) SD-7
Trail Creek—*stream* (2) TX-5
Trail Creek—*stream* (6) UT-8
Trail Creek—*stream* (6) WA-9
Trail Creek—*stream* (32) WY-8
Trail Creek Camp—*locale* WY-8
Trail Creek Campground—*locale* CO-8
Trail Creek Campground—*locale* ID-8
Trail Creek Campground—*locale* WY-8
Trail Creek Cem—*cemetery* KS-7
Trail Creek (historical)—*stream* OR-9
Trail Creek Lakes—*lake* ID-8
Trail Creek Park—*flat* WY-8
Trail Creek Patrol Cabin—*locale* WY-8
Trail Creek Ranch—*locale* CO-8
Trail Creek Ranch—*locale* UT-8
Trail Creek Ranch—*locale* (2) WY-8
Trail Creek Rsvr—*reservoir* MT-8
Trail Creek Sch—*school* (2) MT-8
Trail Creek Spring—*spring* (2) ID-8
Trail Creek Spring—*spring* (2) OR-9
Trail Creek Summit—*summit* (2) ID-8
**Trail Creek Township**—*pop pl* MO-7
Trail Creek Trail—*trail* OR-9
Trail Creek Trail—*trail* (2) WY-8
Trail Creek Work Center—*locale* ID-8
Trail Crest—*gap* CA-9
Trail Cross Trail—*trail* CO-8
Trail Dam—*dam* CO-8
Trail Draw—*valley* (2) CO-8
Trail Draw—*valley* MT-8
Trail Draw—*valley* (2) UT-8
Trail Draw—*valley* WY-8
Trail End—*hist pl* WY-8
Trail End Ranch—*locale* NM-5
Trailer Canyon—*valley* CA-9
Trailer Cem—*cemetery* KY-4
**Trailer City**—*pop pl* FL-3
Trailer Corral (trailer park)—*locale* AZ-5
**Trailer Corral (trailer park)**—*pop pl* AZ-5
Trailer Creek—*stream* AR-4
Trailer Creek—*stream* WY-8
*Trailer Draw* CO-8
**Trailer Estates**—*pop pl* FL-3
Trailer Haven—*uninc pl* FL-3
Trailer Hill—*summit* CA-9
Trailer House Gulch—*valley* NE-7
Trailer House Spring—*spring* AZ-5
Trailer Lake—*lake* AR-4
Trailer Lakes—*lake* ID-8
Trailer Park Campground—*locale* CA-9
Trailer Pass—*gap* NV-8
Trailer Tank—*reservoir* NM-5
*Trailer Wash* UT-8
Trailfinders Camp—*locale* CA-9
Trail Flat—*flat* OR-9
*Trail Fork* UT-8
Trail Fork—*stream* CA-9
Trail Fork—*stream* MT-8
Trail Fork—*stream* TN-4
Trail Fork—*stream* (2) WV-2
Trail Fork—*stream* WY-8
Trail Fork Canyon—*valley* OR-9
*Trail Fork Creek* UT-8
Trail Fork Sch—*school* OR-9
Trail Fork Springs—*spring* CA-9
Trail Glacier—*glacier* AK-9
Trail Glades Range—*locale* FL-3
Trail Glade Tower—*tower* FL-3
Trail Gospel Center—*locale* FL-3
Trail Guard Station—*locale* ID-8
Trail Gulch—*valley* (7) CA-9
Trail Gulch—*valley* (8) CO-8
Trail Gulch—*valley* (3) ID-8
Trail Gulch—*valley* (3) MT-8
Trail Gulch—*valley* (3) NV-8
Trail Gulch—*valley* (3) OR-9
Trail Gulch—*valley* UT-8
Trail Gulch—*valley* WA-9
Trail Gulch Cow Camp—*locale* CO-8
*Trail Gulch Lake* CA-9
Trail Gulch Lake—*lake* CA-9
Trail Gulch Spring—*spring* CO-8
Trail Head Campground—*locale* UT-8
*Trail Head Hill* CA-9
Trail Head Picnic Area—*park* MA-1
Trail Hill—*summit* ID-8
Trail Hill—*summit* NV-8
*Trail Hollow* CO-8
*Trail Hollow* MO-7
*Trail Hollow* UT-8
Trail Hollow—*valley* (2) ID-8
Trail Hollow—*valley* MT-8
Trail Hollow—*valley* OR-9
Trail Hollow—*valley* PA-2
Trail Hollow—*valley* TN-4
Trail Hollow—*valley* (11) UT-8
Trail Hollow Branch—*stream* TN-4
Trail Hollow Creek—*stream* OR-9
Trail Hollow Spring—*spring* UT-8
Trailing R Mobile Park—*locale* AZ-5
Trail Inn Lodge (trailer park)—*locale* AZ-5
**Trail Inn Lodge (trailer park)**—*pop pl* AZ-5
Trail Junction Picnic Grounds—*locale* CO-8
*Trail Lake* ID-8
*Trail Lake* MS-4
Trail Lake—*lake* (2) AK-9
Trail Lake—*lake* CA-9
Trail Lake—*lake* CO-8
Trail Lake—*lake* ID-8
Trail Lake—*lake* MN-6
Trail Lake—*lake* MT-8
Trail Lake—*lake* NM-5
Trail Lake—*lake* UT-8
Trail Lake—*lake* WI-6
Trail Lake—*lake* (5) WY-8
Trail Lake—*reservoir* WA-9
Trail Lake Coulee—*valley* WA-9
Trail Lake Ranch—*locale* WY-8
Trail Lakes—*lake* CA-9
Traill County—*civil* ND-7
Traill County Courthouse—*hist pl* ND-7
Trail Meadow—*flat* CA-9
Trail Meadow—*flat* OR-9
Trail Mountain Hollow—*valley* UT-8
Trail Mountain Mine—*mine* UT-8
Trail Mtn—*summit* CA-9
Trail Mtn—*summit* CO-8
Trail Mtn—*summit* (2) UT-8
Trail Of Tears State Park—*park* MO-7
Trail of Tears State Park Archeol Site—*hist pl* MO-7
Trail of the Ancients—*trail* UT-8
Trail Of The Lonesome Pine—*trail* VA-3
*Trailor Draw* CO-8
Trailover Creek—*stream* (2) OR-9
Trail Park—*flat* CO-8
**Trailpark Gardens**—*pop pl* IL-6
Trail Pass—*gap* CA-9
Trail Pass—*gap* UT-8
Trail Pass Rsvr—*reservoir* UT-8
Trail Peak—*summit* CA-9
Trail Peak—*summit* ID-8
Trail Peak—*summit* NM-5
Trail Peak—*summit* UT-8
Trail Peak—*summit* WA-9
Trail Plaza (Shop Ctr)—*locale* (2) FL-3
Trail Point—*cape* (2) UT-8
Trail Point—*locale* ID-8
Trail Point Rsvr—*reservoir* CO-8
Trail Pond—*reservoir* AZ-5
Trail Pond—*swamp* GA-3
Trail Race, The—*gut* LA-4
Trailrace Park—*park* MS-4
Trail Rapids Bay—*bay* AZ-5
Trail Rapids Wash—*stream* AZ-5
Trail-R-Dale Mobile Home Park—*locale* AZ-5
Trail Rider Pass—*gap* CO-8
Trail Rider Pass—*gap* UT-8
Trail Riders Holiday Park (trailer park)—*locale* AZ-5
**Trail Riders Holiday Park (trailer park)**—*pop pl* AZ-5
Trailriders Wall—*ridge* NM-5
Trail Ridge—*ridge* AK-9
Trail Ridge—*ridge* AZ-5
Trail Ridge—*ridge* (4) CO-8
Trail Ridge—*ridge* FL-3
Trail Ridge—*ridge* (3) GA-3
Trail Ridge—*ridge* NV-8
Trail Ridge—*ridge* (7) NC-3
Trail Ridge—*ridge* (2) OR-9
Trail Ridge—*ridge* TN-4
Trail Ridge—*ridge* (2) UT-8
Trail Ridge—*ridge* VA-3
Trail Ridge—*ridge* (3) WY-8
Trailridge JHS—*school* KS-7
Trail Ridge Mine—*mine* FL-3
Trail Ridge Road—*hist pl* CO-8
Trail Ridge Rsvr—*reservoir* CO-8
Trailridge Shop Ctr—*locale* KS-7
Trail Ridge Spring—*spring* UT-8
Trail River—*stream* (2) AK-9
Trail Rsvr—*reservoir* (2) CO-8
Trail Rsvr—*reservoir* (3) OR-9
Trail Rsvr—*reservoir* (2) UT-8
**Trail Run**—*pop pl* OH-6
Trail Run—*stream* IN-6
Trail Run—*stream* (4) OH-6
Trail Run—*stream* PA-2
Trail Sch—*school* OK-5
Trail Sch—*school* PA-2
Trails Corner—*locale* CT-1
Trailsend—*hist pl* OH-6
Trails End—*locale* CO-8
Trails End—*locale* MN-6
**Trails End**—*pop pl* IN-6
**Trails End**—*pop pl* TN-4
Trails End Airstrip—*airport* AZ-5
Trails End Bay—*bay* MI-6
Trails End Camp—*locale* OK-5
Trails End Ch—*church* LA-4
Trails End Dock—*locale* TN-4
Trails End Lake—*lake* WA-9
Trails End Mine—*mine* AZ-5
Trails End Pond—*lake* CT-1
Trails End Ranch—*locale* (2) CO-8
Trails End Ranch—*locale* (2) TX-5
**Trails End (subdivision)**—*pop pl* NC-3
Trail Side—*locale* WY-8
Trailside—*post sta* FL-3
Trailside Rsvr—*reservoir* WY-8
**Trails III (subdivision), The**—*pop pl* (2) AZ-5
Trails Pond—*lake* CT-1
Trail Spring—*spring* AZ-5
Trail Spring—*spring* CA-9
Trail Spring—*spring* ID-8
Trail Spring—*spring* (2) MT-8
Trail Spring—*spring* (3) NV-8
Trail Spring—*spring* (5) OR-9
Trail Spring—*spring* SD-7
Trail Spring—*spring* (6) UT-8
Trail Spring Bench—*bench* UT-8
Trail Spring Camp—*locale* CA-9
Trail Spring Canyon—*valley* UT-8
*Trail Spring Fork* UT-8
Trail Springs—*spring* AZ-5
Trail Springs—*spring* NV-8
Trails Shop Ctr—*locale* FL-3
**Trails West**—*pop pl* TN-4
Trails West Mobile Home Park—*locale* AZ-5
Trail Tank—*reservoir* (16) AZ-5
Trail Tank—*reservoir* (4) NM-5
Trail to the World Day Care Nursery—*school* FL-3
Trailtown—*locale* FL-3
**Trail Township**—*pop pl* SD-7
Trailwaters Rec Area—*park* SD-7
Trail Well—*well* AZ-5
Trail West Shop Ctr—*locale* KS-7
**Trailwood**—*pop pl* PA-2
Trailwood Elem Sch—*school* KS-7
*Trailwood Lake* PA-2
Trailwood Shop Ctr—*locale* KS-7
**Trailwood (subdivision)**—*pop pl* MS-4
*Train* MI-6
Train, Samuel, House—*hist pl* MA-1
Train Brook—*stream* VT-1
Train Canyon—*valley* NM-5
*Train Creek* MA-1
Traine, Bayou—*stream* LA-4
Trainer—*locale* WV-2
**Trainer**—*pop pl* PA-2
Trainer Borough—*civil* PA-2
Trainer Cem—*cemetery* TN-4
Trainer Creek—*stream* TN-4
Trainer Dam—*dam* AZ-5
Trainer Gulch—*valley* MT-8
Trainer Hills—*other* CA-9
Trainer Homestead—*locale* MT-8
Trainers Shop Ctr—*locale* PA-2
Trainer Station—*building* PA-2
Trainer Tank—*reservoir* AZ-5
Traingle Peak—*summit* AK-9
Train Hill—*summit* MA-1
Training Lake Spring—*spring* AL-4
Training School Cem—*cemetery* MD-2
Train Lake—*lake* OR-9
*Traino Landing* LA-4
Trainor Corner—*locale* ME-1
Trainor Hill—*summit* NY-2
Trainor Sch—*school* IL-6
Train Pond—*lake* NY-2
Trainrobber Cave—*cave* AL-4
Train Rock—*pillar* ID-8
Train Rock—*summit* UT-8
Train Rock Wash—*valley* UT-8
Train Sch—*school* NE-7
Trains Creek—*stream* MA-1
*Trains Hill* MA-1
Trainsmeadow—*uninc pl* NY-2
Traisville—*locale* GA-3
*Traitor Ridge* PA-2
Traitors Cove—*bay* AK-9
Traitors Creek—*stream* AK-9
Trajer Bridge—*bridge* LA-4
**Tralake**—*pop pl* MS-4
Tralee—*locale* WV-2
Traleika Col—*gap* AK-9
Traleika Glacier—*glacier* AK-9
Traleika Icefall—*falls* AK-9
*Tralton* OH-6
Tram—*locale* KY-4
*Tram Branch* PA-2

Tram Creek—stream ID-8
Tramell Cem—cemetery GA-3
Tram Gulch—valley WY-8
Tram Hill—summit CO-8
Tram Hollow—valley (3) MO-7
Tram Hollow Run—stream PA-2
Tram Lake—lake WI-6
Tramline Tank—reservoir AZ-5
Tram Lookout—locale MO-7
Trammel—locale KY-4
**Trammel**—pop pl VA-3
Trammel Branch—stream GA-3
Trammel Branch—stream (3) TN-4
Trammel Branch—stream VA-3
Trammel Cem—cemetery TN-4
Trammel Creek KY-4
Trammel Creek—stream AR-4
Trammel Creek—stream FL-3
Trammel Creek—stream KY-4
Trammel Creek—stream NY-2
Trammel Creek—stream TN-4
Trammel Crossroads—locale AL-4
Trammel Fork KY-4
Trammel Fork—stream KY-4
Trammel Fork Ch—church KY-4
Trammel Fork Creek KY-4
Trammel Gap—gap NC-3
Trammel Gap—gap SC-3
Trammel Gap—gap VA-3
Trammell, Lake—reservoir TX-5
Trammel Lake—lake AR-4
Trammell Cem—cemetery AR-4
Trammell Creek—stream KY-4
Trammell Lake—reservoir SC-3
Trammells TX-5
**Trammells**—pop pl AL-4
**Trammells**—pop pl TX-5
Trammells Sch—school AL-4
Trammells Station AL-4
**Trammellville**—pop pl AR-4
Trammel Memorial Cem—cemetery TN-4
Trammel Mtn—summit AR-4
Trammel Mtn—summit GA-3
Trammel Ridge—ridge TN-4
Trammels—locale TX-5
Tramontane Trail—trail WV-2
Trampa Canyon—valley CA-9
Trampa Colorado Windmill—locale TX-5
**Trampas**—pop pl NM-5
Trampas Canyon—valley CA-9
Trampas Lakes—lake NM-5
**Trampas (Las Trampas)**—pop pl NM-5
Trampas Peak—summit NM-5
Trampa Spring—spring AZ-5
Trampas Seca Well—well TX-5
Trampas Trail—trail NM-5
Trampas Wash—stream CA-9
Trampa Verde Windmill—locale TX-5
Tramp Ch—church AL-4
Tramp Creek—stream CA-9
Tramperos Canyon—valley NM-5
Tramperos Creek—stream NM-5
Tramp Harbor—bay WA-9
Tramp Hollow Pond NJ-2
Trampled Water Canyon—valley AZ-5
Trampmill Run—stream PA-2
Tramp Mine—mine NV-8
Tramp No 2 Mine—mine CO-8
Tram Pond—reservoir MO-7
Tramp Point—cape AK-9
Tramp Ridge—ridge NV-8
Tramp Spring—spring CA-9
Tram Ridge—ridge NV-8
Tram Ridge—ridge OK-5
Tram Road Branch—stream TN-4
Tram Road Hollow—valley KY-4
Tramrood Hollow—valley PA-2
Tram Rood Hollow—valley TN-4
Tramrood Hollow—valley TN-4
Tramrood Hollow—valley VA-3
Tram Road Sch (historical)—school MS-4
Tramrod Hollow—valley WV-2
Tram Trail—trail OK-5
Tramway—locale ID-8
Tramway—locale ME-1
**Tramway**—pop pl NC-3
Tramway Bar—locale AK-9
Tramway Bldg—hist pl CO-8
Tramway Cem—cemetery WI-6
Tramway Creek—stream CO-8
Tramway Gulch—valley (2) CA-9
Tramway Gulch—valley MT-8
Tramway Hist Dist—hist pl ME-1
Tramway Spur—locale OR-9
Tramway Tank—reservoir AZ-5
Tranbarger Hollow—valley TN-4
**Trancas**—pop pl CA-9
Trancas, Arroyo Las—stream CA-9
Trancas Beach—beach CA-9
Trancas Canyon—valley CA-9
Trancept, The AZ-5
Traner JHS—school NV-8
Trane Udden DE-2
Trang Island FM-9
Tranham Creek—stream SC-3
**Tranquil**—pop pl MS-4
Tranquil, Lake—reservoir MO-7
**Tranquil Acres**—pop pl CO-8
**Tranquil Acres**—pop pl SC-3
**Tranquil Acres (subdivision)**—pop pl NC-3
Tranquil Basin—basin ID-8
Tranquil Basin—basin MT-8
Tranquil Cem—cemetery AR-4
Tranquil Cem—cemetery GA-3
Tranquil Cem—cemetery TX-5
Tranquil Ch—church (2) MS-4
Tranquil Ch—church (3) SC-3
Tranquil Cove—bay OR-9
Tranquil Cove Campground—park OR-9
Tranquilechee Lake—reservoir TN-4
Tranquilichee Lake—reservoir TN-4
Tranquilichee Lake Dam—dam TN-4
Tranquilino Windmill—locale NM-5
Tranquility NJ-2
Tranquility TN-4
**Tranquility**—pop pl NJ-2
**Tranquility**—pop pl OH-6
Tranquility, Lake—reservoir NJ-2
Tranquility Ch—church NJ-2
Tranquility Cove—bay SC-3
Tranquility Dam—dam NJ-2
Tranquility Farm—hist pl CT-1
Tranquility Lake—lake AK-9
**Tranquility Park**—pop pl FL-3
Tranquility State Wildlife Area—park OH-6
**Tranquility (subdivision)**—pop pl NC-3
Tranquility (Tranquillity) CA-9
Tranquil Lake—lake OR-9
Tranquil Lake—lake WA-9
Tranquillity—locale IA-7
**Tranquillity**—pop pl CA-9
**Tranquillity**—pop pl TN-4
Tranquillity, Lake—lake MI-6
Tranquillity Sch (historical)—school TN-4
**Tranquillity (Tranquility)**—pop pl CA-9
Tranquillon Mtn—summit CA-9
Tranquillon Ridge—ridge CA-9
Tranquillo Pine—locale NM-5
Tranquil Mtn—summit MT-8
Tranquil Point—cape AK-9
Tranquil Sch (historical)—school MS-4
Tranquil United Methodist Church MS-4
Tranquitas Creek—stream TX-5
Tranquitas Lake—reservoir TX-5
**Trans**—pop pl GA-3
Trans-Alaska Pipeline, The (Under Construction)—other AK-9
Transalpine Cem—cemetery ME-1
Trans-Canyon Telephone Line, Grand Canyon Natl Park—hist pl AZ-5
Transcendent Mine—mine AZ-5
Transco Dam—dam AL-4
Transcontinental Gas Pipe Line Compressor Station—facility LA-4
Transcontinental Oil Field—oilfield TX-5
Transco Village—locale VA-3
Transeau Sch—school PA-2
Transept, The—valley AZ-5
Transept Trail—trail AZ-5
Transept Trail Campgrounds—park AZ-5
Transfer—locale CA-9
Transfer—locale ID-8
**Transfer**—pop pl PA-2
Transfer Cabin—locale ID-8
Transfer Camp—locale NV-8
Transfer Campground—locale CO-8
Transfer Campground—locale ID-8
Transfer Creek—stream WY-8
Transfer Ditch—canal CO-8
Transfer Gulch—valley ID-8
Transfer Hollow—valley MS-4
Transfer Hollow—valley PA-2
Transfer Park Campground—locale CO-8
Transfer Ridge—ridge CA-9
Transfer Spring—spring UT-8
Transfer Trail—trail CO-8
Transfiguration Cem—cemetery IL-6
Transfiguration Cem—cemetery PA-2
Transfiguration Ch—church MI-6
Transfiguration of Our Lord Chapel—hist pl AK-9
Transfiguration Parish Sch—school FL-3
Transfiguration Sch—school CA-9
Transfiguration Sch—school MI-6
Transfiguration Sch—school MN-6
Transfiguration Sch—school (2) NY-2
Trans Fisheries Incorporated Pond Dam—dam MS-4
Transient Spring—spring NV-8
Transier Cem—cemetery IN-6
Transit Bridge—bridge NY-2
Transit Bridge Ch—church NY-2
Transit Cem—cemetery NY-2
Transit Ch—church NY-2
Transitown—post sta NY-2
Transitown Shop Ctr—locale NY-2
Transit Plaza Shop Ctr—locale IA-7
Transit (RR name for East Amherst)—other NY-2
Transit Rural Cem—cemetery NY-2
**Transit (Township of)**—pop pl MN-6
Transitville IN-6
Transmission Line and Blue River Pipe Line—other CO-8
Transmontania Acad (historical)—school TN-4
Transoceanic Telephone Receiving Station—other ME-1
Transom Windmill—locale TX-5
Transon NC-3
**Transou**—pop pl NC-3
Transou Ch—church NC-3
Trans-Pecos Ranch—locale TX-5
Transportation Administration Center—locale DE-2
Transport Ch—church LA-4
Transport Rock—bar NY-2
Transquaking River—stream MD-2
Trans River Canal—canal UT-8
Trans Run Ch—church PA-2
Trans-State Waterway FL-3
Transtrum Hollow—valley ID-8
Transue—locale PA-2
Transue Cem—cemetery MO-7
Transue Creek—stream PA-2
Transue Run—stream PA-2
Transvaal Mines—mine OR-9
Transview Mtn—summit UT-8
Transwestern Pipeline Number Four Airstrip—airport AZ-5
Transwestern Pipeline Number One Airp—airport AZ-5
Transwestern Pipeline Number Three Airp—airport AZ-5
Transwestern Well—well NM-5
**Transwest Estates Subdivision**—pop pl UT-8
**Transwest Hollow Subdivision**—pop pl UT-8
**Transwest Village Subdivision**—pop pl UT-8
**Transylvania**—pop pl LA-4
**Transylvania Beach**—pop pl KY-4
Transylvania Bible Sch—school PA-2
Transylvania Brook—stream CT-1
Transylvania Chute—gut LA-4
Transylvania Community Hosp—hospital NC-3
**Transylvania County**—pop pl NC-3
Transylvania County Courthouse—hist pl NC-3
Transylvania Pond—reservoir CT-1
Transylvania School Camp—locale NC-3
Transylvania Univ—school KY-4
Tran Tank—reservoir AZ-5
Tranters Creek—stream NC-3
Tranters Creek Ch—church NC-3
Trantham Cave—cave MO-7
Trantham Cem—cemetery AL-4
Trantham Creek—stream NC-3
Trantham Creek—stream TN-4
Trantham Hollow—valley MO-7
Trantham Hollow—valley (2) TN-4
Tranthem Post Office (historical)—building TN-4
Trants Point—cape VA-3
Trants School TN-4
Trantus Creek NC-3
Trantwood Sch—school VA-3
**Trantwood Shores**—pop pl VA-3
Tranus Creek—stream WI-6
Tranus Lake—lake WI-6
Tranwick Gas Field—oilfield TX-5
Trap DE-2
Trap MD-2
Trap—locale NC-3
Trap, The DE-2
Trap, The NC-3
Trap, The—bend WY-8
Trap, The—channel PA-2
Trap Bay—bay AK-9
Trap Branch—stream (2) KY-4
Trap Branch—stream MO-7
Trap Branch—stream (2) NC-3
Trap Branch—stream WV-2
Trap Brook—stream NY-2
Trap Butte—summit NV-8
Trap Camp—locale FL-3
Trap Canyon—valley (2) AZ-5
Trap Canyon—valley CA-9
Trap Canyon—valley OR-9
Trap Canyon—valley (2) UT-8
Trap Canyon Spring—spring AZ-5
Trap Canyon Spring—spring OR-9
Trap Canyon Wash—valley UT-8
Trap Cave—cave AL-4
Trap Chute—stream AR-4
Trap Cliff—cliff NY-2
**Trap Corner**—pop pl ME-1
Trap Corral Canyon—valley AZ-5
Trap Corral Canyon—valley NM-5
Trap Corral Spring—spring AZ-5
Trap Corral Spring—spring NV-8
Trap Creek—stream AK-9
Trap Creek—stream CA-9
Trap Creek—stream CO-8
Trap Creek—stream (5) ID-8
Trap Creek—stream KS-7
Trap Creek—stream (3) OR-9
Trap Creek—stream (2) WA-9
Trap Creek Lookout—locale WA-9
Trap Creek Narrows—gap ID-8
Trap Draw—valley CO-8
Trape Springs—spring OR-9
Trap Fall Brook MA-1
Trapfall Brook—stream MA-1
Trap Falls—falls MI-6
Trap Falls Brook MA-1
Trap Falls Rsvr—reservoir CT-1
Trap Fork—stream KY-4
Trap Fork—stream WV-2
Trap Fork Cem—cemetery WV-2
Trap Gulch—valley CO-8
Traphagen, Oliver G., House—hist pl MN-6
Traphagen Lake MI-6
Traphall Brook MA-1
Trap Hill NC-3
**Traphill**—pop pl NC-3
**Traphill**—pop pl WV-2
**Trap Hill**—pop pl WV-2
Traphill Hist Dist—hist pl NC-3
Trap Hill HS—school WV-2
Trap Hill (Township of)—fmr MCD NC-3
Trap Hole—lake OR-9
Traphole Brook—stream MA-1
Trap House Hills—other AK-9
Trap Lake MN-6
Trap Lake—lake AK-9
Trap Lake—lake CO-8
Trap Lake—lake ID-8
Trap Lake—lake LA-4
Trap Lake—lake MI-6
Trap Lake—lake MN-6
Trap Lake—lake NM-5
Trap Lake—lake WA-9
Trap Line Ditch—canal CA-9
Trap Line Mine—mine CA-9
Traplog Hollow—valley PA-2
Trap Mesa Spring—spring AZ-5
Trap Mountain—ridge AR-4
Trap Mtn—summit AR-4
Trap Mtn—summit MT-8
Trap Mtn—summit OR-9
Trap Mtn—summit TX-5
Trapnall Hall—hist pl AR-4
Trapnell—locale FL-3
Trapnell Point—summit TX-5
Trapnell Sch—school FL-3
Trap Number One Spring—spring AZ-5
Trap Number Two Spring—spring AZ-5
Trapp—locale KY-4
Trapp—locale MS-4
Trapp—locale VA-3
Trapp and Chandler Pottery Site (38GN169)—hist pl SC-3
Trap Park—flat CO-8
Trapp Branch—stream KY-4
Trapp Branch—stream VA-3
Trapp Creek—stream OR-9
Trapp Ditch No 1—canal WY-8
Trapp Ditch No 2—canal WY-8
Trappe MD-2
Trappe—locale MD-2
**Trappe**—pop pl (2) MD-2
**Trappe**—pop pl PA-2
Trap Peak—summit AZ-5
Trap Peak—summit NM-5
Trappe Borough—civil PA-2
Trappe Cem—cemetery MD-2
Trappe Creek—stream MD-2
Trapped Rock Draw—valley NM-5
Trappe Landing—locale MD-2
Trappe Pond Forestry Site DE-2
Trapper—locale CO-8
Trapper Brook—stream ME-1
Trapper Butte OR-9
Trapper Cabin—locale ID-8
Trapper Cabin Creek—stream MT-8
Trapper Canyon—valley UT-8
Trapper Canyon—valley WY-8
Trapper Creek ID-8
Trapper Creek WY-8
Trapper Creek—post sta AK-9
Trapper Creek—stream (2) AK-9
Trapper Creek—stream CA-9
Trapper Creek—stream CO-8
Trapper Creek—stream (14) ID-8
Trapper Creek—stream (11) MT-8
Trapper Creek—stream (7) OR-9
Trapper Creek—stream (5) WA-9
Trapper Creek—stream (3) WY-8
Trapper Creek Forest Camp—locale OR-9
Trapper Creek Rural Conservation Center—locale MT-8
Trapper Flat—flat (2) ID-8
Trapper Gulch—valley (3) ID-8
Trapper Gulch—valley MT-8
Trapper Gulch—valley OR-9
Trappe River MD-2
Trappe River—stream WI-6
Trapper Joe Lake—lake AK-9
Trapper John Shelter—locale NH-1
Trapper Lake—lake AK-9
Trapper Lake—lake MI-6
Trapper Lake—lake (3) MT-8
Trapper Lake—lake OR-9
Trapper Lake—lake WA-9
Trapper Lake—lake WI-6
Trapper Lake—lake (2) WY-8
Trapper Lake Stock Trail—trail WY-8
Trapper Lodge Ranch—locale WY-8
Trapper Meadow Camp—locale OR-9
Trapper Mine—mine MT-8
Trapper Mtn—summit ID-8
Trapper Mtn—summit MT-8
Trapper Mtn—summit WA-9
Trapper Peak—summit (2) ID-8
Trapper Peak—summit (2) MT-8
Trapper Peak Trail—trail MT-8
Trapper Point—cape CA-9
Trapper Ridge—ridge ID-8
Trapper Ridge—ridge OR-9
Trappers Bay—bay IA-7
Trappers Bay State Park—park IA-7
Trappers Butte—summit OR-9
Trappers Cabin Spring—spring MT-8
Trappers Camp—locale OR-9
Trappers Coulee—valley ND-7
Trappers Cove—bay AK-9
Trappers Creek MN-6
Trappers Creek WY-8
Trappers Creek—stream CA-9
Trappers Creek—stream ID-8
Trappers Creek—stream (2) MN-6
Trappers Creek—stream UT-8
Trappers Creek—stream WA-9
Trappers Creek—stream WI-6
Trappers Creek—stream (2) WY-8
Trappers Den—locale AK-9
Trappers Falls—falls MI-6
Trappers Flat—flat ID-8
Trappers Gulch—valley (2) CO-8
Trapper Shelter—locale OR-9
Trappers Lake—lake CO-8
Trappers Lake—lake MI-6
Trappers Lake—lake MN-6
Trappers Lake Campground—locale CO-8
Trappers Lodge—locale VA-3
Trappers Slough—gut CA-9
Trappers Peak—summit CO-8
Trappers Peak—summit WA-9
Trappers Point Historical Monument—locale WY-8
Trapper Spring—spring CA-9
Trapper Spring—spring MT-8
Trapper Spring—spring OR-9
Trapper Spring—spring WY-8
Trapper Spring Meadow—flat OR-9
Trapper Spring Rsvr—reservoir WY-8
Trappers Run—stream MN-6
**Trappers Run (subdivision)**—pop pl NC-3
Trappers Trail—trail CA-9
Trappers Zoo—locale FL-3
Trappe Station—locale MD-2
Trapp Filling Station—hist pl WI-6
Trapping Brook—stream NY-2
Trapping Hollow—valley PA-2
Trapping Hollow Trail—trail PA-2
**Trappist (Abbey of Gethsemani)**—pop pl KY-4
Trappist Abbey of Our Lady of Guadalupe—church OR-9
Trapp Lake WI-6
Trapp Lake—lake MI-6
Trappman Hills—summit NV-8
Trappman Ranch—locale AZ-5
Trap Point—cape (3) AK-9
Trap Point—summit ID-8
Trap Pond—reservoir DE-2
Trap Pond Dam—dam DE-2
Trap Pond State Park—park DE-2
Trapp Pond MA-1
Trap Post Office (historical)—building MS-4
Trapp River WI-6
Trapps Bridge—bridge NY-2
Trapp Sch—school CA-9
Trapp Sch—school KS-7
Trapp Sch (historical)—school AL-4
Trapps Pond—lake MA-1
**Trapptown**—pop pl AL-4
Trapptown Sch—school AL-4
Trap River WI-6
Traprock PA-2
Trap Rock—island ME-1
Trap Rock—other AK-9
**Trap Rock**—pop pl PA-2
Trap Rock—summit PA-2
Traprock Hill—summit TX-5
Trap Rock Ledge—summit MA-1
Trap Rock River—stream MI-6
Traprock Sch—school MI-6
Trap Rock Sch—school WI-6
Trap Run—stream MD-2
Trap Run—stream (2) PA-2
Trap Run—stream (4) WV-2
Traps PA-2
Traps Bay—bay NC-3
Traps Creek—stream ID-8
Traps Creek—stream NC-3
**Trapshire**—pop pl NH-1
Trap Spring—spring (7) AZ-5
Trap Spring—spring NV-8
Trap Spring—spring NM-5
Trap Spring—spring TX-5
Trap Spring—spring UT-8
Trap Swamp Brook—stream MA-1
Trap Tank TX-5
Trap Tank—reservoir (7) AZ-5
Trap Tank—reservoir (3) TX-5
Trap Well—well (2) TX-5
Trap Windmill—locale NM-5
Trap Windmill—locale (5) TX-5
Trasero Island—island AK-9
Trash Branch—stream AL-4
Trash Cem—cemetery ME-1
Trash Dam—dam AZ-5
Trash Gulch—valley CO-8
Trask—locale MT-8
**Trask**—pop pl MO-7
**Trask**—pop pl OR-9
**Trask**—pop pl SC-3
Trask, Lake—lake FL-3
Trask Bridge—other IL-6
Trask Brook—stream ME-1
Trask Brook—stream MA-1
Trask Cem—cemetery ME-1
Trask Creek—stream OR-9
Trask Creek—stream WI-6
Trask Guard Station—locale OR-9
Trask Gulch MT-8
Trask Gulch—valley MT-8
Trask Hall—hist pl MT-8
Trask Hill—summit NH-1
Trask House—locale OR-9
Trask House Museum—building MA-1
Trask Lake—lake MI-6
Trask Lake—lake WA-9
Trask Lakes—lake MT-8
Trask Lawn Cem—cemetery ME-1
Trask Ledge—summit ME-1
Trask Mtn—summit ME-1
Trask Mtn—summit OR-9
Trask Park—park OR-9
Trask Pond—lake MA-1
Trask Pond—lake NY-2
Trask Pond—lake WA-9
Trask Ranch—locale AZ-5
Trask Ranch—locale WY-8
Trask River—stream OR-9
Trask River Dam—dam OR-9
Trask Sch—school CT-1
Trask Summit—summit OR-9
Trask Well—well AZ-5
**Traskwood**—pop pl AR-4
Traskwood (Township of)—fmr MCD AR-4
Trasquila Tank—reservoir NM-5
Trasta Cem—cemetery SD-7
**Tras Talleres**—pop pl PR-3
**Tratebas Mill**—pop pl IN-6
Traub Knob—summit OH-6
Traub Sch—school OK-5
Trauchsville PA-2
Trauchville PA-2
**Trauger**—pop pl PA-2
Trauger Sch (abandoned)—school PA-2
Traugers Park—park PA-2
Traughber Cem TN-4
Traughber Cem—cemetery IL-6
Traughber Cem—cemetery KY-4
Traughber Cem—cemetery TN-4
Traugh Fork—stream WV-2
Traugoots Siding—locale WI-6
Traums Sch—school NE-7
Traung Club—other CA-9
**Traunik**—pop pl MI-6
Trautman OH-6
Trautman Hill—summit OH-6
Trautman Slough—lake ND-7
Traut Run PA-2
Trautwein Sch—school WI-6
Travail Creek—stream OR-9
Trava Point—cape AK-9
Travare (historical)—locale SD-7
**Travel Air**—pop pl KS-7
Travelair Creek—stream AK-9
Travel Brook—stream ME-1
Traveler, The—summit ME-1
Traveler Brook—stream ME-1
Traveler Gap—gap ME-1
Traveler Mtn—summit ME-1
Traveler Pond—lake ME-1
Travelers Canal CO-8
Travelers Ch—church GA-3
Travelers Home—hist pl OR-9
Travelers Home—other CA-9
Travelers' Hotel—hist pl CA-9
Travelers Hotel—hist pl OH-6
Travelers Repose WV-2
Traveler's Rest—hist pl GA-3
Traveler's Rest—hist pl KY-4
Traveler's Rest—hist pl MT-8
Travelers Rest—locale AL-4
**Travelers Rest**—pop pl SC-3
Travelers Rest Baptist Ch—church IN-6
Travelers Rest (CCD)—cens area SC-3
Travelers Rest Cem—cemetery (2) AL-4
Travelers Rest Cem—cemetery AR-4
Travelers Rest Cem—cemetery GA-3
Travelers Rest Cem—cemetery WI-6
Travelers Rest Ch MS-4
Travelers Rest Ch—church (2) AL-4
Travelers Rest Ch—church AR-4
Travelers Rest Ch—church (2) FL-3
Travelers Rest Ch—church (2) GA-3
Travelers Rest Ch—church (4) MS-4
Travelers Rest Ch—church NC-3
Travelers Rest Ch—church (2) SC-3
Travelers Rest Ch—church TN-4
Travelers Rest Ch—church VA-3
Travelers Rest Church—locale FL-3
Traveler's Rest Creek ID-8
Travelers Rest Missionary Baptist Ch MS-4
Travelers Rest Sch—school (2) TN-4
Travelers Spring—spring PA-2
Travel Home Ch—church GA-3
Traveling Creek—stream ID-8
Travellers Repose WV-2
Travellers Rest AL-4
Travellers Rest SC-3
Traveller's Rest—hist pl MS-4
Travellers' Rest—hist pl TN-4
Traveller's Rest—hist pl WV-2
**Travellers Rest**—pop pl KY-4
Travellers' Rest Inn—hist pl OH-6
Travell Sch—school NJ-2
Travel Pond—lake ME-1
Travel Rest Cem—cemetery MS-4
Travel Rest Ch MS-4
Travel Rest Ch—church GA-3
Travel Rest Ch—church MS-4
Travelute Rsvr—reservoir WY-8
Travena Sch—school TN-4
Travenol Laboratories—facility IL-6
Travenol Laboratories—facility NC-3
Travenrse Lake Dam—dam OR-9
**Traver**—pop pl CA-9
Traver, J. E., Farm—hist pl NY-2
Traver, John H., Farm—hist pl NY-2
Travera WI-6
Traver Basin—basin CO-8
Traver Canal—canal CA-9
Traver Cem—cemetery MN-6
Traver Cem—cemetery NY-2
Traver Cem—cemetery TX-5
Traver Creek—stream AK-9
Traver Creek—stream CO-8
Traver Hill—summit NY-2
Traver Hollow—valley NY-2
Traver House—hist pl NY-2
Traver Mesa—summit CO-8
Traver Peak—summit CO-8
Travers MD-2
Travers—locale ID-8
**Travers Corners**—pop pl NY-2
Travers Cove MD-2
Travers Creek—stream AK-9
Travers Creek—stream CA-9
Travers Ditch—canal IN-6
Traverse MN-6
Traverse—locale MI-6
Traverse—locale MN-6
Traverse, Bayou—stream (2) LA-4
Traverse, Lake—reservoir MN-6
Traverse, Lake—reservoir SD-7
**Traverse Bay**—pop pl MI-6
Traverse Cem—cemetery IL-6
**Traverse City**—pop pl MI-6
Traverse City Coast Guard Air Station—military MI-6
Traverse City State Park—park MI-6
**Traverse (County)**—pop pl MN-6
Traverse Creek WI-6
Traverse Creek—stream AK-9
Traverse Creek—stream (2) CA-9
Traverse Creek—stream KY-4
Traverse Creek—stream (2) OR-9
Traverse Creek—stream PA-2
Traverse Creek Dam—dam PA-2
Traverse des Sioux—hist pl MN-6
Traverse Des Sioux Wayside Park—park MN-6
Traverse Gulch CO-8
Traverse Heights Sch—school MI-6
Traverse Island—island MI-6
Traverse Lake—lake OR-9
Traverse Lakes—lake MI-6
Traverse Mtns—range UT-8
Traverse Peak WY-8
Traverse Peak—summit AK-9
Traverse Peak—summit WY-8
Traverse Point—cape (2) MI-6
Traverse Range UT-8
Traverse Ridge—ridge OR-9
Traverse River—stream MI-6
**Traverse (Township of)**—pop pl MN-6
Traverse Valley—valley WI-6
Traverse Valley Creek—stream WI-6
Traversey Islands MP-9
Travers Island—island NY-2
Travers Lake WA-9
Travers Lake—lake WI-6
Travers Point MD-2
Travers Pond—reservoir MA-1
Travers Spring—spring SD-7
Travers Spring Number One—spring SD-7
Travers Wharf—locale MD-2
Travertine Canyon—valley (2) AZ-5
Travertine Creek—stream OK-5
Travertine Falls—falls AZ-5
Travertine Falls—falls OK-5
Travertine Hot Spring—spring CA-9
Travertine Palms Wash—stream CA-9
Travertine Point—cliff CA-9
Travertine Rapids—rapids AZ-5
Travertine Rock—summit CA-9
Travertine Springs—spring CA-9
Traver Trail—trail CO-8
Travesser Creek—stream NM-5
Travesser Park—flat NM-5
Travilah—locale MD-2
Travilah Sch—school MD-2
**Travilla**—pop pl AL-4
Travilla Wharf—locale MD-2
Travillion Cem—cemetery TN-4
Travillion HS—school MS-4
Travillion-Koester Ditch—canal OR-9
**Travis**—pop pl NY-2
**Travis**—pop pl (2) NC-3
**Travis**—pop pl TX-5
Travis, Lake—lake TX-5
Travis Acad—school SC-3
Travis AFB—military CA-9
Travis Airp—airport PA-2
Travis Branch—stream (3) KY-4
Travis Branch—stream TX-5
**Travis Bridge**—pop pl AL-4
Travis Brook—stream NY-2
Travis Cabin—locale AK-9
Travis Cem AL-4
Travis Cem—cemetery (2) AL-4
Travis Cem—cemetery IL-6
Travis Cem—cemetery (3) KY-4
Travis Cem—cemetery (2) MS-4
Travis Cem—cemetery (2) MO-7
Travis Cem—cemetery PA-2
Travis Cem—cemetery (4) TN-4

Trinity United Church of Christ Cem—cemetery ... PA-2
Trinity United Methodist Ch ... AL-4
Trinity United Methodist Ch—church (3) ... AL-4
Trinity United Methodist Ch—church (2) ... DE-2
Trinity United Methodist Ch—church (4) ... FL-3
Trinity United Methodist Ch—church (2) ... MS-4
Trinity United Methodist Ch—church ... MT-8
Trinity United Methodist Ch—church (4) ... TN-4
Trinity United Methodist Ch—church ... UT-8
Trinity United Methodist Church—hist pl ... CO-8
Trinity United Methodist Church—hist pl ... MI-6
Trinity United Methodist Curch—hist pl ... TN-4
Trinity United Methodist Kindergarden—school ... FL-3
Trinity United Presbyterian Ch—church ... DE-2
Trinity United Presbyterian Ch—church ... FL-3
Trinity United Presbyterian Ch—church ... MS-4
Trinity Univ—school ... TX-5
Trinity Valley Sch—school ... CA-9
**Trinity Village**—pop pl ... CA-9
Trinity Wesleyan Ch—church ... IN-6
Trinity Woodmore Ch—church ... TN-4
**Trinity Woods (subdivision)**—pop pl ... NC-3
Trinket ... PA-2
Trinkle Canyon—valley ... WA-9
Trinkle Creek—stream ... IA-7
Trinkle Flat ... NE-7
Trinklein Drain—canal ... MI-6
Trinkus Lake—lake ... MT-8
Trinton Hollow—valley ... WV-2
Trinty Ch—church ... MA-1
Trinty Islands—island ... AK-9
**Trinway**—pop pl ... OH-6
Trio—locale ... AL-4
Trio—locale ... TX-5
**Trio**—pop pl ... SC-3
**Tri Oaks Subdivision**—pop pl ... UT-8
Trio (CCD)—cens area ... SC-3
Trio Cem—cemetery ... LA-4
Trio Creek—stream ... WA-9
Trio Falls—falls ... CO-8
Trio Lake Number 1—lake ... OR-9
Trio Lake Number 2—lake ... OR-9
Trio Lake Number 3—lake ... OR-9
Trio Lakes—lake ... MT-8
Trio Mtn—summit ... MT-8
Trion ... AL-4
Trion ... TN-4
**Trion**—pop pl ... GA-3
Trion (CCD)—cens area ... GA-3
**Trionda**—pop pl ... NY-2
Trion Heights Ch—church ... GA-3
Trion Post Office (historical)—building ... TN-4
Trio Ponds—lake ... NH-1
Trio Rsvr—reservoir ... CO-8
Trip ... GA-3
Tri Par Estates—CDP ... FL-3
Tripas Canyon—valley ... CA-9
Trip Cove—bay ... AK-9
Triphammer Falls—falls ... NY-2
Triphammer Pond—reservoir ... MA-1
Triphammer Pond Dam—dam ... MA-1
Trip Hill—summit ... VT-1
Trip Hollow—valley ... AR-4
Tripie Horn Well—well ... TX-5
Trip Lake ... PA-2
Trip Lake—lake ... MN-6
Triple A Golf Club—other ... MO-7
Triple Alcoves—basin ... AZ-5
Triple Arch—arch ... UT-8
Triple Arches—arch ... MT-8
Triple Brook ... MA-1
Triple Butte—summit ... TX-5
Triple Creek ... WA-9
Triple Creek—stream ... AK-9
Triple Creek—stream ... GA-3
Triple Creek—stream (2) ... ID-8
Triple Creek—stream ... OR-9
Triple Creek—stream ... WA-9
Triple Crossing Rsvr—reservoir ... MT-8
**Triple Divide**—pop pl ... MT-8
Triple Divide—ridge ... MT-8
Triple Divide—summit ... PA-2
Triple Divide Pass—gap ... CA-9
Triple Divide Pass—gap ... MT-8
Triple Divide Peak ... WY-8
Triple Divide Peak—summit ... AK-9
Triple Divide Peak—summit (2) ... CA-9
Triple Divide Peak—summit ... MT-8
Triple Divide Trail—trail ... MT-8
Triple Draw—valley ... WY-8
Triple E Mine—mine ... NM-5
Triple Engle Pit—basin ... NM-5
Triple Eye—arch ... AZ-5
Triple Eye Catchment—basin ... AZ-5
Triple Falls—falls ... CA-9
Triple Falls—falls ... NH-1
Triple Falls—falls ... NC-3
Triple Glaciers—glacier ... WY-8
Triple Hill—summit ... TX-5
Triple H Mine—mine ... WA-9
Triple H Ranch—locale ... NM-5
Triple H Ranch—locale ... TX-5
Triple K Ranch—locale ... MI-6
Triple Lakes—lake ... AK-9
Triple Lakes—lake ... FL-3
Triple Lakes—lake ... ID-8
Triple Lakes—lake ... IL-6
Triple Lakes—lake ... IN-6
Triple Lakes—lake ... MI-6
Triple Lakes—lake ... MT-8
Triple Lakes—lake ... NJ-2
Triple Lakes—lake ... WI-6
**Triple Lakes**—pop pl ... MD-2
Triple Lakes—reservoir ... CO-8
Triple Lakes—reservoir ... MO-7
Triple Lakes—reservoir ... SC-3
Triple Lakes Creek—stream ... MI-6
**Triple Lance Heights**—pop pl ... IL-6
Triple Mountain ... TX-5
Triple M Ranch—locale ... OK-5
Triple Oaks Camp—locale ... PA-2
Triple Pass—channel ... LA-4
Triple Peak—summit ... WY-8
Triple Peak Fork—stream ... CA-9
Triple Pocket Mine—mine ... CA-9
Triple Point Bunker—locale ... NV-8
Tripler Army Med Ctr—military ... HI-9
**Triple R Estates**—pop pl ... CA-9
Triple Ridge—ridge ... WA-9
Triple Seven Number 1 Dam—dam ... SD-7
Triple Seven Number 2 Dam—dam ... SD-7
Triple S Lake—reservoir ... GA-3
Triple S Mine—mine ... CO-8
Triple Spring—spring ... ID-8
Triple Spring—spring ... OR-9
**Triple Springs**—pop pl ... NC-3
Triplet—island ... AK-9
Triplet—locale ... VA-3
Triplet, Mount—summit ... AZ-5
Triple Tank—reservoir ... NM-5
Triple Tank—reservoir ... TX-5
Triple Tanks—reservoir (2) ... TX-5
Triple Tanks Windmill—locale ... TX-5
Triplet Butte—summit ... CA-9
Triplet Butte—summit ... ID-8
Triplet Canyon—valley ... ID-8
Triplet Creek—stream ... ID-8
Triplet Falls—falls ... CO-8
Triplet Gulch—valley ... NV-8
Triplet Hill—summit ... NY-2
Triplet Islands—area ... AK-9
Triplet Islands—island ... NY-2
Triplet Keys—island ... FL-3
Triplet Lake—lake ... FL-3
Triplet Lakes—lake (2) ... MN-6
Triplet Lakes—lake ... WA-9
Triple T Mobilcity—locale ... AZ-5
Triplet Rocks—area ... AK-9
Triplets, The—area ... AK-9
Triplets, The—island ... AK-9
Triplets, The—summit ... WA-9
**Triplets Corners**—pop pl ... MS-4
Triplet Spring—spring ... ID-8
Triplet Spring—spring ... OR-9
Triplets Run—stream ... WV-2
Triplets Tank—reservoir ... AZ-5
Triplett—locale ... KY-4
Triplett—locale (2) ... WV-2
**Triplett**—pop pl ... MO-7
**Triplett**—pop pl ... NC-3
Triplett Branch—stream ... KY-4
Triplett Cem—cemetery ... KY-4
Triplett Cem—cemetery (2) ... MS-4
Triplett Cem—cemetery ... MO-7
Triplett Cem—cemetery ... OK-5
Triplett Cem—cemetery (2) ... TN-4
Triplett Cem—cemetery (2) ... WV-2
Triplett Ch—church ... NC-3
Triplett Ch—church ... WV-2
Triplett Creek—stream ... AL-4
Triplett Creek—stream ... KY-4
Triplett Creek—stream ... MI-6
Triplett Creek—stream ... NC-3
Triplett Fork—stream ... WV-2
Triplett Gulch—valley ... CA-9
Triplett Hollow—valley (2) ... TN-4
Triplett Institute—school ... VA-3
Triplett Lake Dam—dam (2) ... MS-4
Triplett Mtn—summit ... AL-4
Tripletts Run—stream ... WV-2
Tripletts Bluff—cliff ... AR-4
Triplett Sch—school ... VA-3
Triplett Spring—spring ... TN-4
Triplett Town ... MS-4
**Triplett Township**—pop pl ... MO-7
Triplet Wash ... AZ-5
Triplet Wash—stream (2) ... AZ-5
Triple U Enterprise Dam ... SD-7
Triple W Air Park Airp—airport ... NC-3
Trip Mtn—summit ... AZ-5
Tripoa Bayou—stream ... LA-4
Tripod, Lake—lake ... LA-4
Tripod Banks—bar ... FL-3
Tripod Camp—locale ... OR-9
Tripod Creek—stream (2) ... FL-3
Tripod Creek—stream (2) ... ID-8
Tripod Creek—stream ... WY-8
Tripod Flat—flat ... WA-9
Tripod Hill—summit ... AK-9
Tripod Hill—summit ... WY-8
Tripod Key—island (2) ... FL-3
Tripod Meadow—flat ... ID-8
Tripod Mine—mine ... CO-8
Tripod Mtn—summit ... NM-5
Tripod Mtn—summit ... NY-2
Tripod Peak—summit ... ID-8
Tripod Peak—summit ... WA-9
Tripod Peak—summit ... WY-8
Tripod Point ... HI-9
Tripod Point—cape ... FL-3
Tripod Point—cape ... ID-8
Tripod Rsvr—reservoir ... ID-8
Tripod Well—well ... MT-8
Tripole ... PA-2
Tripoli—locale ... NY-2
**Tripoli**—pop pl ... IA-7
**Tripoli**—pop pl ... NY-2
**Tripoli**—pop pl ... PA-2
**Tripoli**—pop pl (2) ... WI-6
Tripoli Cave ... AL-4
Tripoli Golf Club—other ... WI-6
Tripoli Mill—locale ... NH-1
Tripoli Mine—mine ... NV-8
Tripolis Ch—church ... MN-6
Tripoli Sch—school ... WI-6
Tripoli Temple—hist pl ... WI-6
Tripon Pass—gap ... NV-8
Tripp—locale ... TX-5
**Tripp**—pop pl ... SD-7
**Tripp**—pop pl ... WV-2
Tripp, Lake—reservoir ... SD-7
Tripp and Extension Drain—stream ... MI-6
Tripp and Underwood Wash—stream ... AZ-5
Tripp-Bauer Bldg—hist pl ... OH-6
Tripp Bay ... MD-2
Tripp Branch—stream ... GA-3
Tripp Canyon ... AZ-5
Tripp Canyon—valley ... AZ-5
Tripp Canyon—valley ... OR-9
Tripp Canyon—valley ... WA-9
**Tripp (Cassie)**—pop pl ... WV-2
Tripp Cem—cemetery ... IL-6
Tripp Cem—cemetery ... OH-6
Tripp Cem—cemetery ... TN-4
Tripp Cem—cemetery ... TX-5
Tripp Cem—cemetery ... WI-6
Tripp Coulee—valley ... MT-8
Tripp County—civil ... SD-7
Tripp Creek—stream ... CA-9
Tripp Dam—dam ... SD-7
Tripp Divide—ridge ... MT-8
**Trippe**—pop pl ... AR-4
Trippe Bay—bay ... MD-2
Trippe Cem—cemetery ... GA-3
Trippe Creek—stream ... MD-2
Trippe Gulch—valley ... UT-8
Trippe Junction—locale ... AR-4
Trippe's Creek ... MD-2
Trippet Cem—cemetery ... IN-6
Trippet Ditch—canal ... IN-6
Trippet Ranch—locale ... CA-9
Trippet-Shive House—hist pl ... TX-5
Trippett Run—stream ... WV-2
Trippetts Branch—stream ... OH-6
Tripp Family Homestead—hist pl ... PA-2
Tripp Ferry (historical)—locale ... AL-4
Tripp Flats—flat ... CA-9
Tripp Gap—gap ... GA-3
Tripp Gulch—valley ... CA-9
Tripp Gulch—valley ... CO-8
Tripp Hill—summit ... TX-5
Tripp Hollow—valley ... TN-4
Tripp Hollow Brook—stream ... CT-1
Trippier Point—cape ... OR-9
Trippiloo Creek—stream ... NC-3
Trippiloo Creek—stream ... SC-3
Tripp Lake—lake ... MI-6
Tripp Lake—lake (2) ... MN-6
Tripp Lake—lake ... PA-2
Tripp Lake—lake ... WI-6
Tripp Lake—reservoir ... SD-7
Tripp Lake—reservoir ... WI-6
Tripple Brook—stream ... MA-1
Tripple Creek—stream ... AK-9
Tripp Ledge—rock ... MA-1
Tripple Lye Cave—cave ... AL-4
Tripp Meadow—flat ... CA-9
Tripp Memorial Library and Hall—hist pl ... WI-6
Tripp Mtn—summit ... NY-2
Tripp Park—park ... SD-7
Tripp Pinnacle—summit ... NY-2
Tripp Pit—mine ... NV-8
Tripp Point—cape ... CA-9
Tripp Point—cape ... NC-3
Tripp Pond ... PA-2
Tripp Pond—lake ... ME-1
Tripp Pond—lake ... NY-2
Tripp Pond—reservoir ... MA-1
Tripp Run—stream ... OH-6
Tripps Bay ... MD-2
Tripp Sch—school ... CA-9
Tripp Sch—school ... IL-6
Tripp Sch—school ... KS-7
Tripp Sch—school ... MA-1
Tripp Sch—school ... MO-7
Tripps Corner—locale ... RI-1
Tripps Cove—bay ... VA-3
Tripps Creek ... MD-2
Tripp Shaft—mine ... PA-2
Tripps Knob—summit ... WA-9
Tripps Neck—cape ... MD-2
Tripps Pond—lake ... NY-2
Tripps Run—stream ... VA-3
Tripp Tank—reservoir ... TX-5
Tripp Town Branch—stream ... TN-4
**Tripp (Town of)**—pop pl ... WI-6
Tripp Township (historical)—civil ... SD-7
Trippville—locale ... WI-6
Trippville Valley—valley ... WI-6
Trip Rapids—rapids ... WI-6
**Trips Subdivision**—pop pl ... MI-6
Triptown ... RI-1
Trip Up Branch—stream ... GA-3
Tripup Run—stream ... PA-2
Tripyramid, Mount—summit ... NH-1
Tri Run—stream ... IN-6
Tri Sauvages ... MA-1
Trischman Knob—summit ... WY-8
Trisglaff Lake ... MN-6
Trish-American Dam—dam ... MN-6
Trisko Lake—lake ... MN-6
Trisky Creek—stream ... MT-8
Trisky Point—summit ... MT-8
**Trisler**—pop pl ... KY-4
Trisler Cem—cemetery ... LA-4
Trissel Cem—cemetery ... OH-6
Trissel Ch—church ... VA-3
Triss Lake—reservoir ... PA-2
Trist—locale ... MI-6
Tristan—locale ... WV-2
**Tristan Village (subdivision)**—pop pl ... FL-3
Tri-State—uninc pl ... KY-4
Tri State Airp—airport ... IN-6
Tri-State Airp (Walker-Long Field)—airport ... WV-2
Tri-State Bank—hist pl ... TN-4
Tri-State Brick and Tile Lake Dam—dam ... MS-4
Tri-State Canal ... NE-7
Tri-State Canal—canal ... NE-7
Tri-state Ch—church ... WV-2
Tri-State College ... IN-6
Tri-State Fair and Exposition—locale ... AL-4
Tri State Fairground—locale ... TX-5
Tri-State Fairgrounds—locale ... IA-7
Tri State Mall ... DE-2
Tri-State Mall—locale ... DE-2
**Tri-State Mobile Home Park (trailer park)**—pop pl ... DE-2
Tri-State Peak—summit ... KY-4
Tri-State Peak—summit ... VA-3
**Tristates**—pop pl ... NY-2
Tri State Speedway—locale ... ND-7
Tri-State Steuben County—airport ... IN-6
Tri-State Strip Mine—mine ... MT-8
Tri-State Temple—church ... OH-6
Tri-State Univ—school ... IN-6
Tri-State Viewpoint—locale ... AZ-5
Tristate Village—other ... IL-6
**Tri-state Village (Tristate Village)**—pop pl ... IL-6
Triste Draw Oil Field—other ... NM-5
Tristle Island—island ... AK-9
Tristle Point—cape ... AK-9
Trist Millpond—lake ... MI-6
Tri Story Canyon—valley ... UT-8
Tristram Creek—stream ... UT-8
Trist Sch—school ... LA-4
Trisvan Cem—cemetery ... VA-3
Tri S Village Estates ... UT-8
**Tri-S Village Estates (subdivision)**—pop pl ... UT-8
Tri-Taylor Hist Dist—hist pl ... IL-6
Tri-Taylor Hist Dist (Boundary Increase)—hist pl ... IL-6
Trites Lake—lake ... CO-8
Trit Knob—summit ... NC-3
Tritle, Mount—summit ... AZ-5
Tritle Peak—summit ... AZ-5
Triton—locale ... WA-9
Triton Beach—beach ... MD-2
Triton Central HS—school ... IN-6
Triton Cove—bay ... WA-9
Triton Head—summit ... WA-9
Triton HS ... IN-6
Triton HS—school ... NC-3
Triton Regional HS—school ... NJ-2
Triton Valley—valley ... AK-9
Tri-Towhead—island ... TN-4
Tri-Township Tabernacle—church ... OH-6
Tri-Town Shop Ctr—locale ... MA-1
Tritt Cem—cemetery ... AR-4
Tritt Cem—cemetery ... TN-4
Tritt Creek—stream ... AK-9
Tritt Gap—gap ... GA-3
Trittipo Ditch—canal ... IN-6
Tritt Knob—summit ... NC-3
Tritts Millpond—lake ... OH-6
Triump Ch—church ... WV-2
Triumph (2) ... MN-6
Triumph—locale ... OH-6
Triumph—locale ... PA-2
**Triumph**—pop pl ... ID-8
**Triumph**—pop pl ... IL-6
**Triumph**—pop pl ... LA-4
**Triumph**—pop pl ... PA-2
Triumph, Mount—summit ... WA-9
Triumphal Arch Rapids—rapids ... AZ-5
Triumphant Ch of God—church ... PA-2
Triumph Apostolic Faith Ch—church ... FL-3
Triumph Baptist Ch—church ... MS-4
Triumph Cem—cemetery ... OK-5
Triumph Ch ... MS-4
Triumph Ch—church (8) ... AL-4
Triumph Ch—church ... FL-3
Triumph Ch—church ... IN-6
Triumph Ch—church ... KS-7
Triumph Ch—church ... KY-4
Triumph Ch—church ... MS-4
Triumph Ch—church (2) ... NC-3
Triumph Ch—church ... TX-5
Triumph Ch—church (2) ... VA-3
Triumph Ch (historical)—church ... AL-4
Triumph Ch of God—church ... AL-4
Triumph Ch of God—church ... FL-3
Triumph Creek—stream ... MN-6
Triumph Creek—stream ... WA-9
Triumph Gulch—valley ... ID-8
Triumph Holiness Ch—church ... IN-6
Triumph Lake—lake ... MN-6
Triumph Mine—mine ... ID-8
Triumph Mine—mine ... NV-8
Triumph Mine (Inactive)—mine ... CA-9
Triumph Pass—gap ... WA-9
Triumph Sch—school ... IL-6
Triumph Sch—school ... IA-7
Triumph Sch—school (2) ... MO-7
Triumph Sch—school ... NE-7
Triumph Sch (abandoned)—school ... PA-2
Triumph the Ch and Kingdom of God Church—church ... AL-4
Triumph the Ch and Kingdom of God in Christ (historical)—church ... AL-4
**Triumph Township**—pop pl ... NE-7
**Triumph Township**—pop pl ... ND-7
**Triumph (Township of)**—pop pl ... PA-2
**Triumvera**—pop pl ... IL-6
Triumvirate Glacier—glacier ... AK-9
**Triune**—pop pl ... TN-4
**Triune**—pop pl ... WV-2
Triune Cem—cemetery ... TN-4
Triune Ch—church ... MS-4
Triune Masonic Temple—hist pl ... MN-6
Triune Mine—mine ... WA-9
Triune Missionary Baptist Ch—church ... AL-4
Triune Post Office (historical)—building ... TN-4
Triune Sch—school ... SC-3
Triune Sch (historical)—school ... TN-4
Triune United Methodist Ch—church ... TN-4
Triunfo Canyon—valley ... CA-9
Triunfo Corner—locale ... CA-9
Triunfo Lookout—locale ... CA-9
Triunfo Pass—gap ... CA-9
Triunfo Pass-Coastal (CCD)—cens area ... CA-9
Triunion Ch—church ... MS-4
Tri Valley HS—school ... PA-2
Tri Valley Sch—school ... NY-2
Trivett Branch—stream (2) ... NC-3
Trivett Branch—stream ... TN-4
Trivett Cem—cemetery ... NC-3
Trivett Cem—cemetery ... TN-4
Trivett Gap—gap ... NC-3
Tri-Village ... OH-6
Trivitt Cem—cemetery ... VA-3
Trivole ... KS-7
**Trivoli**—pop pl ... IL-6
Trivoli Cem—cemetery ... IL-6
Trivoli (historical)—locale ... KS-7
Trivoli River ... GA-3
**Trivoli Township**—pop pl ... KS-7
**Trivoli (Township of)**—pop pl ... IL-6
Tri-West HS—school ... IN-6
Tri-West JHS—school ... IN-6
Trixie—locale ... KY-4
Trixie—mine ... UT-8
Trixie Creek—stream ... MT-8
Trixie Falls—falls ... WA-9
Trixie Pass—gap ... MT-8
Trix-Liz Oil Field—oilfield ... TX-5
Trix Sch—school ... MI-6
Trobough Branch—stream ... AR-4
Trobraught Cem—cemetery ... IL-6
Trocadero Bay—bay ... AK-9
Trocha—locale ... CA-9
Troedel Spring—spring ... CA-9
Troemper Cem—cemetery ... KS-7
Troendle, Lucas, House—hist pl ... MN-6
Troesser Creek—stream ... MO-7
Troff Canyon—valley ... OR-9
Troffer Canyon—valley ... NM-5
Trofton Hollow—valley ... WV-2
Trogden Hollow—valley ... TN-4
Trogdons Ford—crossing ... TN-4
Trogshak—locale ... AK-9
Trohs Memorial Airpark—airport ... OR-9
Troiscent Piquets Bay—bay ... LA-4
Troiscent Piquette Bay ... LA-4
Trois Chenes, Bayou—gut ... LA-4
Trojan—locale ... OR-9
Trojan—locale ... SD-7
Trojan Airstrip—airport ... OR-9
Trojanek Cem—cemetery ... MI-6
Trojan Lake—lake ... CO-8
Trojan Lake—lake ... NY-2
Trojan Peak—summit ... CA-9
Trojan Ranch—locale ... CO-8
Trojan (Site)—locale ... CA-9
Trojillo Ranch—locale ... NM-5
Trolinger Cem—cemetery ... MO-7
Troll Brook Gulf Club—locale ... MA-1
Troller Islands—area ... AK-9
Troller Point—cape ... AK-9
Troller Run—stream ... WA-9
Trollers Cove—bay ... AK-9
Trollers Creek—stream ... AK-9
Trolley—post sta ... MI-6
Trolley Museum—building ... CA-9
Trolley Museum—building ... ME-1
Trolley Square—locale ... UT-8
Trollinger Cem—cemetery ... MS-4
Trollin Lake—lake ... MN-6
Trollop Creek—stream ... CO-8
Trolls Lake—reservoir ... PA-2
Trolls Lake Dam ... PA-2
Troly Lake—lake ... OK-5
Trombka Drain—canal ... MI-6
Tromble House—hist pl ... MI-6
**Trombley**—pop pl ... OH-6
Trombley Bay—bay ... NY-2
Trombley Bay Cem—cemetery ... NY-2
Trombley Drain ... MI-6
Trombley Drain—canal ... MI-6
Trombley Landing—locale ... NY-2
Trombley Point ... NY-2
Trombley Sch—school ... MI-6
Trombly—locale ... MI-6
Trombly, Charles, House—hist pl ... MI-6
Trombly Drain ... MI-6
Trombly Park—park ... MI-6
Trombly Sch—school ... MI-6
Trombly's Point ... NY-2
Trombone Creek ... MT-8
Trombone Creek—stream ... MT-8
Trombone Spring—spring ... MT-8
Tromley, George, Jr., House—hist pl ... IA-7
Tromley, George, Sr., House—hist pl ... IA-7
Tromley Gulch—valley ... WY-8
Tromley Hill—summit ... NH-1
**Trommald**—pop pl ... MN-6
Tromp Point—cape ... VT-1
Tromp Spring—spring ... WY-8
Trom Rsvr—reservoir ... OR-9
Tromso Cem—cemetery ... MN-6
**Trona**—pop pl ... CA-9
Trona Water Pipeline—other ... CA-9
Trondhjem Cem—cemetery ... SD-7
Trondhjem Ch—church ... MN-6
Trondhjem Ch—church (3) ... SD-7
**Trondhjem (Township of)**—pop pl ... MN-6
Trondjem—locale ... MN-6
Trondjem Ch—church ... MN-6
**Trone**—pop pl ... VA-3
Trone Gulch—valley ... WY-8
Troneys Point ... MI-6
Tronrud Ditch—canal ... MT-8
Tronsel Lake—lake ... LA-4
Tronsen Creek—stream ... WA-9
Tronsen Creek Trail—trail ... WA-9
Tronsen Meadow—flat ... WA-9
Tronsen Meadow Campground—locale ... WA-9
Tronsen Ridge—ridge ... WA-9
Tronson Island—island ... OR-9
Trooks Flat—flat ... CA-9
Troon Mtn—summit ... AZ-5
Troop Cem—cemetery ... TN-4
**Trooper**—pop pl ... PA-2
Trooper Island—island ... KY-4
Trooper Island—island ... TN-4
Troope Station ... TX-5
Troop Grove—cemetery ... GA-3
Troop Point Cave—cave ... AL-4
Troop's Creek ... NY-2
Troop's Creek ... PA-2
T. Roosevelt Elem Sch—school ... KS-7
T Roosevelt HS—school ... HI-9
Troost Sch—school ... MO-7
Troot Hills ... MA-1
Troots Swamp ... MA-1
Troot Swamp ... MA-1
Tropaco Point—cape ... VI-3
Trop Farm—hist pl ... OH-6
Troph Cem—cemetery ... MO-7
**Trophy Club**—pop pl ... TX-5
Trophy Lake—lake ... AK-9
Trophy Lake—reservoir ... AZ-5
Trophy Lake Dam—dam ... AZ-5
Tropic—locale ... FL-3
**Tropic**—pop pl ... OH-6
**Tropic**—pop pl ... UT-8
Tropic—post sta ... FL-3
**Tropical Acres**—pop pl ... TX-5
**Tropical Bend**—pop pl ... LA-4
Tropical Christian Sch—school ... FL-3
Tropical Elem Sch—school (2) ... FL-3
Tropical Estates Park—park ... FL-3
Tropical Fish Farm—locale ... CA-9
**Tropical Gulf Acres**—pop pl ... FL-3
Tropical Island—island ... FL-3
Tropical Park—locale ... FL-3
Tropical Park RR Station—locale ... FL-3
**Tropical Park (subdivision)**—pop pl ... FL-3
Tropical Sands Christian Ch—church ... FL-3
Tropical Sch—school ... FL-3
**Tropical Shores Manor**—pop pl ... FL-3
Tropicana, Lake—reservoir ... TX-5
Tropicana Country Club—locale ... NV-8
Tropicana Wash—stream ... NV-8
**Tropicanna Mobile Manor**—pop pl ... FL-3
Tropic Canyon—valley ... UT-8
Tropic Cem—cemetery ... UT-8
Tropic Division—civil ... UT-8
**Tropic Heights**—pop pl ... FL-3
**Tropic Isle**—pop pl ... FL-3
Tropic Isle Harbor—harbor ... FL-3
Tropic Isles Baptist Ch—church ... FL-3
Tropic Isles Elem Sch—school ... FL-3
Tropic Isles Shop Ctr—locale ... FL-3
Tropic Junction ... UT-8
Tropico—uninc pl ... CA-9
Tropico Hill—summit ... CA-9
Tropico Sch—school ... CA-9
Tropico Shaft—mine ... CA-9
**Tropico Village**—pop pl ... CA-9
Tropic Reservoir Dam—dam ... UT-8
Tropic Rsvr—reservoir (2) ... UT-8
Tropic Spring Ditch—canal ... UT-8
Tropic Valley—basin ... UT-8
Tropic Vista (subdivision)—locale ... FL-3
Troque Island—island ... MI-6
Trosada Well—well ... TX-5
Trosado Tank—reservoir ... TX-5
Trosclair Cem—cemetery ... LA-4
Trosdahl, Erick, House—hist pl ... MT-8
Trosi Canyon—valley (2) ... CA-9
Trosi Canyon Ranch—locale ... CA-9
Trosi Spring—spring ... CA-9
**Trosky**—pop pl ... MN-6
Trosky Cem—cemetery ... MN-6
Trospar Dam—dam ... NC-3
Trospar Lake—reservoir ... NC-3
Trosper—locale ... KY-4
**Trosper (Bennettsville)**—pop pl ... KY-4
Trosper (CCD)—cens area ... KY-4
Trosper Creek ... WY-8
Trosper House—hist pl ... LA-4
Trosper Lake—lake ... WA-9
Trosper Park—park ... OK-5
Trost, Henry C., House—hist pl ... TX-5
Trostel Lake—lake ... WI-6
Troste Lookout Tower—locale ... WI-6
Troster—locale ... IL-6
Trostle Pond—lake ... PA-2
Trostle Ridge—ridge ... PA-2
Trostletown Bridge—hist pl ... PA-2
Trotachaud Lake ... MN-6
Trot and Holler Canyon—valley ... AZ-5
Trot and Holler Well—well ... AZ-5
Trot Hollow—valley ... OK-5
Troth Saint Sch—school ... CA-9
Troth's Fortune—hist pl ... MD-2
Trotman Bay ... LA-4
Trotman Creek—stream ... NC-3
Trotman Wharf—locale ... VA-3
Trotochaud Lake ... MN-6
**Trots Hills**—pop pl ... MA-1
Trots Hills—summit ... MA-1
Trots Swamp—swamp ... MA-1
Trott Brook—stream ... MN-6
Trott Brook Cem—cemetery ... MN-6
Trott Brook Ch—church ... MN-6
Trotten Plantation (historical)—locale ... MS-4
**Trotter**—pop pl ... OR-9
**Trotter**—pop pl ... PA-2
Trotter, Lake—reservoir ... WV-2
Trotter, William Monroe, House—hist pl ... MA-1
Trotter Bluff—cliff ... TN-4
Trotter Branch—stream ... AR-4
Trotter Branch—stream ... WV-2
Trotter Branch—stream ... WI-6
Trotter-Byrd House—hist pl ... MS-4
Trotter Cabin—locale ... NM-5
Trotter Camp—locale ... TN-4
Trotter Cem—cemetery ... AL-4
Trotter Cem—cemetery ... IL-6
Trotter Cem—cemetery ... KS-7
Trotter Cem—cemetery ... MO-7
Trotter Cem—cemetery ... OH-6
Trotter Cem—cemetery (2) ... TN-4
Trotter Ch—church ... MO-7
Trotterchaud Lake—lake ... MN-6
Trotter Cove—bay ... AL-4
Trotter Creek—stream ... IN-6
Trotter Creek—stream ... KY-4
**Trotter Crossing**—pop pl ... IN-6
Trotter Hollow—valley ... AR-4
Trotter Hollow—valley ... TN-4
Trotter Landing—locale ... MS-4
Trotter Landing Revetment—levee ... MS-4
Trotter Lateral—canal ... CO-8
Trotter-McMahan House—hist pl ... TN-4
Trotter Pond—reservoir ... AL-4
Trotter Ranch Dam—dam ... SD-7
Trotters ... MS-4
**Trotters**—pop pl ... ND-7
Trotters Brake—swamp ... AR-4
Trotters Branch—stream (2) ... TN-4
Trotters Bridge (historical)—bridge ... MS-4
Trotters Cem—cemetery ... AR-4
Trotter Sch (abandoned)—school ... MO-7
Trotters Creek—stream ... NC-3
Trotters Creek—stream ... OH-6
Trotters Creek—stream ... VA-3
Trotters Ferry (historical)—crossing ... TN-4
Trotters Lake Dam—dam ... MS-4
Trotters Landing—locale ... TN-4
Trotters Point—cape ... MS-4
Trotters Shoal Lake ... GA-3
Trotters Shoal Reservoir ... GA-3
Trotters Shoals—bar ... GA-3
Trotters Shoals—bar ... SC-3
Trotters Station—locale ... WY-8
Trotter's Warehouse—hist pl ... KY-4
**Trotter Township**—pop pl ... MO-7
Trotter Trail—trail ... NM-5
Trotter Woods—woods ... WA-9
Trotti Cem—cemetery ... TX-5
Trotti Creek—stream ... TX-5
Trotting Pond—lake ... FL-3
Trotting Ridge—ridge ... KY-4
Trott Island—island ... ME-1
Trott Ledge—bar ... ME-1
Trottman ... MS-4
Trotts Branch—stream ... MD-2
Trotts Hills ... MA-1
Trotts Point—cape ... ME-1
Trotts Point—cape ... VA-3
Trotts Rock—bar (2) ... ME-1
Trott Vocational Sch—school ... NY-2
**Trotville**—pop pl ... NC-3

**Trotwood**—*pop pl* OH-6
**Trotwood**—*pop pl* PA-2
Trotwood, Lake—*reservoir* SC-3
**Trotwood Park**—*pop pl* AL-4
Trotwood RR Station and Depot—*hist pl* OH-6
Trouant Island—*island* MA-1
*Trouants Island* MA-1
Trouble Bayou—*gut* LA-4
Trouble Canyon—*valley* ID-8
*Trouble Creek* FL-3
*Trouble Creek* WY-8
Trouble Creek—*gut* FL-3
Trouble Creek—*stream* AL-4
Trouble Creek—*stream* AK-9
Trouble Creek—*stream* ID-8
Trouble Creek—*stream* OH-6
Trouble Creek—*stream* OR-9
Trouble Creek—*stream* TN-4
Trouble Creek—*stream* WA-9
Trouble Creek—*stream* WY-8
Trouble Creek Mall—*locale* FL-3
Trouble Creek Shop Ctr—*locale* FL-3
Trouble Field Creek—*stream* NC-3
Trouble Hill—*summit* CO-8
Trouble Island—*island* AK-9
Trouble Rsvr—*reservoir* WY-8
Troublesome—*locale* CO-8
Troublesome Branch—*stream* AL-4
Troublesome Branch—*stream* AR-4
Troublesome Brook—*stream* NY-2
Troublesome Canyon—*valley* TX-5
*Troublesome Creek* CO-8
Troublesome Creek—*stream* AL-4
Troublesome Creek—*stream* (4) AK-9
Troublesome Creek—*stream* (2) CO-8
Troublesome Creek—*stream* FL-3
Troublesome Creek—*stream* (3) GA-3
Troublesome Creek—*stream* IL-6
Troublesome Creek—*stream* (3) IA-7
Troublesome Creek—*stream* (4) KS-7
Troublesome Creek—*stream* (4) KY-4
Troublesome Creek—*stream* MO-7
Troublesome Creek—*stream* NC-3
Troublesome Creek—*stream* (3) TX-5
Troublesome Creek—*stream* (3) VA-3
Troublesome Creek—*stream* WA-9
Troublesome Creek—*stream* (2) WY-8
Troublesome Creek Campground—*locale* WA-9
Troublesome Creek Ironworks—*hist pl* NC-3
Troublesome Creek Lake—*reservoir* NC-3
Troublesome Creek Trail—*trail* CO-8
Troublesome Ditch—*canal* CO-8
Troublesome Gap—*gap* NC-3
Troublesome (historical)—*locale* KS-7
*Troublesome Hollow* AL-4
Troublesome Hollow—*valley* MO-7
Troublesome Hollow—*valley* (2) TN-4
Troublesome Hollow Branch—*stream* AL-4
Troublesome Mtn—*summit* WA-9
Troublesome Pass—*gap* CO-8
Troublesome Point—*cape* NC-3
Troublesome Ridge—*ridge* TN-4
Troublesome Ridge—*ridge* WY-8
Troublesome Valley—*valley* WV-2
Trouble Valley—*flat* GA-3
Trouble Well—*well* NM-5
Trouble Well Canyon—*valley* NM-5
Trouble Windmill—*locale* NM-5
*Trough* SC-3
Trough, The—*valley* CO-8
Trough, The—*valley* WV-2
Trough Branch—*stream* NC-3
Trough Camp Creek—*stream* KY-4
*Trough Canyon* ID-8
Trough Canyon—*valley* (4) CA-9
Trough Canyon—*valley* CO-8
Trough Canyon—*valley* (2) TX-5
Trough Canyon—*valley* (2) UT-8
Trough Canyon Spring—*spring* NV-8
Trough Canyon Spring—*spring* TX-5
*Trough Creek* PA-2
*Trough Creek* WV-2
**Trough Creek**—*pop pl* PA-2
Trough Creek—*stream* CA-9
Trough Creek—*stream* CO-8
Trough Creek—*stream* ID-8
Trough Creek—*stream* (2) MT-8
Trough Creek—*stream* OR-9
Trough Creek Campground—*park* OR-9
Trough Creek Ch—*church* PA-2
Trough Creek State Park—*park* PA-2
Trough Creek Trail—*trail* OR-9
Trough Creek Valley—*valley* PA-2
Trough Creek Valley Sch—*school* PA-2
Trough Creek Wild Area—*area* PA-2
Trough Draw—*valley* UT-8
Trough Draw—*valley* (2) WY-8
Trough Fork—*stream* (3) WV-2
Trough Fork Sch—*school* WV-2
Trough Gulch—*valley* CO-8
Trough Gulch—*valley* OR-9
Trough Hollow—*valley* NY-2
Trough Hollow—*valley* (4) UT-8
Trough Hollow—*valley* WY-8
Trough Hollow Creek—*stream* UT-8
Trough Lick—*stream* KY-4
Trough Lick Branch—*stream* KY-4
Trough Mountain Spring—*spring* NV-8
Trough Mtn—*summit* NV-8
Trough Ridge—*ridge* (2) CA-9
Trough Rock Hollow—*valley* OK-5
Trough Run—*stream* OH-6
Trough Run—*stream* PA-2
Trough Run—*stream* VA-3
Trough Run—*stream* WV-2
*Troughs, The* CA-9
Troughs, The—*locale* NV-8
Troughs, The—*spring* OR-9
Troughs, The—*valley* UT-8
*Trough Spring* OR-9
Trough Spring—*spring* (2) AZ-5
Trough Spring—*spring* (2) CA-9
Trough Spring—*spring* (7) NV-8
Trough Spring—*spring* NM-5
Trough Spring—*spring* (3) OR-9
Trough Spring—*spring* (4) TX-5
Trough Spring—*spring* (8) UT-8
Trough Spring—*spring* (2) WY-8
Trough Spring Branch—*stream* PA-2
Trough Spring Canyon—*valley* NV-8
Trough Spring Creek—*stream* TX-5
Trough Spring Draw—*valley* AZ-5
Trough Spring Draw—*valley* WY-8
Trough Spring Hollow—*valley* UT-8
Trough Spring Ridge—*ridge* (2) CA-9
Trough Spring Ridge—*ridge* UT-8
Trough Springs—*spring* AZ-5
Trough Springs—*spring* TX-5
Trough Springs Canyon—*valley* UT-8
Trough Springs Ridge—*ridge* UT-8
Troughs Spring, The—*spring* AZ-5
**Troup**—*pop pl* MS-4
**Troup**—*pop pl* TX-5
Troup-Arp (CCD)—*cens area* TX-5
Troup Branch—*stream* TN-4
Troup Cem—*cemetery* (2) AL-4
Troup Cem—*cemetery* GA-3
Troup Cem—*cemetery* TN-4
*Troup Club Lake* TX-5
**Troup (County)**—*pop pl* GA-3
Troup Creek—*stream* GA-3
*Troupe* TX-5
Troupe Cem—*cemetery* AL-4
Troupe Run—*stream* MD-2
Troupe Springs—*locale* MD-2
Troup Hill—*summit* TN-4
Troup JHS—*school* CT-1
Troup Lake—*lake* GA-3
Troup Point—*cape* AL-4
**Troupsburg**—*pop pl* NY-2
**Troupsburg (Town of)**—*pop pl* NY-2
Troup Sch—*school* PA-2
Troups Creek—*stream* NY-2
Troups Creek—*stream* PA-2
Troup Spring Landing—*locale* GA-3
**Troupville**—*pop pl* GA-3
Trousdale—*locale* OK-5
Trousdale—*locale* TN-4
**Trousdale**—*pop pl* KS-7
**Trousdale**—*pop pl* (2) TN-4
**Trousdale County**—*pop pl* TN-4
Trousdale County Courthouse—*building* TN-4
Trousdale County Elem Sch—*school* TN-4
Trousdale County HS—*school* TN-4
Trousdale Hollow—*valley* AL-4
Trousdale Hollow—*valley* TN-4
Trousdale Place—*hist pl* TN-4
Trousdale Post Office
(historical)—*building* TN-4
Trousdales Ferry (historical)—*crossing* TN-4
*Trout* MI-6
*Trout* TX-5
Trout—*locale* ID-8
Trout—*locale* KY-4
Trout—*locale* NE-7
**Trout**—*pop pl* LA-4
**Trout**—*pop pl* MD-2
**Trout**—*pop pl* NC-3
**Trout**—*pop pl* WV-2
Trout—*stream* KS-7
Trout, Thomas and Katherine,
House—*hist pl* TX-5
Trout, Walter C.-White House—*hist pl* TX-5
Trout Bay—*bay* MI-6
Trout Bayou—*channel* TX-5
Trout Bayou—*gut* LA-4
Trout Bayou—*stream* FL-3
Trout Bayou—*stream* TX-5
*Trout Branch* TN-4
Trout Branch—*stream* AR-4
Trout Branch—*stream* KY-4
Trout Branch—*stream* PA-2
Trout Branch—*stream* TN-4
Trout Branch—*stream* (3) VA-3
Trout Branch—*stream* WV-2
*Trout Brook* MA-1
*Trout Brook* (2) MN-6
*Trout Brook* NH-1
*Troutbrook* NY-2
*Trout Brook* WI-6
Trout Brook—*stream* (4) CT-1
Trout Brook—*stream* (18) ME-1
Trout Brook—*stream* (11) MA-1
Trout Brook—*stream* (2) MI-6
Trout Brook—*stream* (6) MN-6
Trout Brook—*stream* (2) NH-1
Trout Brook—*stream* (7) NJ-2
Trout Brook—*stream* (20) NY-2
Trout Brook—*stream* (2) PA-2
Trout Brook—*stream* RI-1
Trout Brook—*stream* (6) VT-1
Trout Brook—*stream* (2) WI-6
Trout Brook Cem—*cemetery* ME-1
Trout Brook Farm—*locale* ME-1
*Trout Brook Junction* MN-6
Trout Brook Mtn—*summit* ME-1
Trout Brook Mtn—*summit* NY-2
Trout Brook No 1—*stream* CT-1
Trout Brook Pond—*reservoir* MI-6
Trout Brook Pond—*reservoir* RI-1
Trout Brook Ridge—*ridge* (2) ME-1
Trout Brook (Township of)—*unorg* ME-1
**Troutburg**—*pop pl* NY-2
Trout Camp—*locale* CA-9
Trout Canyon—*valley* NV-8
Trout Canyon—*valley* WY-8
Trout Cem—*cemetery* IL-6
Trout Cem—*cemetery* IN-6
Trout Cem—*cemetery* KY-4
Trout Cem—*cemetery* MO-7
Trout Cem—*cemetery* TN-4
Trout Ch—*church* LA-4
Trout Channel—*channel* VA-3
*Trout Corners* PA-2
**Trout Corners**—*pop pl* PA-2
Trout Cove—*bay* FL-3
Trout Cove—*valley* NC-3
Trout Cove Branch—*stream* NC-3
*Trout Creek* AL-4
*Trout Creek* AZ-5
*Trout Creek* CA-9
*Trout Creek* CO-8
*Trout Creek* ID-8
*Trout Creek* MN-6
*Trout Creek* MT-8
*Trout Creek* NV-8
*Trout Creek* OR-9
*Trout Creek* TX-5
*Trout Creek* WA-9
*Trout Creek* WY-8
Trout Creek—*canal* OR-9
Trout Creek—*channel* FL-3
Trout Creek—*gut* FL-3
Trout Creek—*locale* OR-9
Trout Creek—*locale* UT-8
**Trout Creek**—*pop pl* MI-6
**Trout Creek**—*pop pl* MT-8
**Trout Creek**—*pop pl* NY-2
**Trout Creek**—*pop pl* (2) OR-9
**Trout Creek**—*pop pl* PA-2
**Trout Creek**—*pop pl* TX-5
Trout Creek—*stream* AL-4
Trout Creek—*stream* (7) AK-9
Trout Creek—*stream* (2) AZ-5
Trout Creek—*stream* (18) CA-9
Trout Creek—*stream* (9) CO-8
Trout Creek—*stream* (10) FL-3
Trout Creek—*stream* (15) ID-8
Trout Creek—*stream* IN-6
Trout Creek—*stream* (2) IA-7
Trout Creek—*stream* (2) LA-4
Trout Creek—*stream* (6) MI-6
Trout Creek—*stream* (3) MN-6
Trout Creek—*stream* (16) MT-8
Trout Creek—*stream* (9) NV-8
Trout Creek—*stream* (2) NM-5
Trout Creek—*stream* (5) NY-2
Trout Creek—*stream* (2) NC-3
Trout Creek—*stream* (27) OR-9
Trout Creek—*stream* (6) PA-2
Trout Creek—*stream* (2) TX-5
Trout Creek—*stream* (3) UT-8
Trout Creek—*stream* (2) VA-3
Trout Creek—*stream* (12) WA-9
Trout Creek—*stream* (11) WI-6
Trout Creek—*stream* (8) WY-8
Trout Creek Bridge—*bridge* NY-2
Trout Creek Butte—*summit* CA-9
Trout Creek Butte—*summit* OR-9
Trout Creek Camp—*locale* OR-9
Trout Creek Campground—*locale* ID-8
Trout Creek Campground—*locale* (2) MT-8
Trout Creek Canyon—*valley* ID-8
Trout Creek Canyon—*valley* MT-8
Trout Creek Cem—*cemetery* IN-6
Trout Creek Cem—*cemetery* MI-6
Trout Creek Ch—*church* LA-4
Trout Creek Cow Camp—*locale* OR-9
Trout Creek Ditch—*canal* CO-8
Trout Creek Ditch No. 4—*canal* CO-8
Trout Creek Forest Camp—*locale* OR-9
Trout Creek Forest Camp—*locale* WA-9
Trout Creek Guard Station—*locale* UT-8
Trout Creek Gulch—*valley* CA-9
Trout Creek Hill—*summit* WA-9
**Trout Creek (historical)**—*pop pl* OR-9
Trout Creek Lake—*lake* WY-8
Trout Creek Lookout Tower—*locale* MI-6
Trout Creek Mine—*mine* CA-9
Trout Creek Mine View No 2 Mine—*mine* CO-8
*Trout Creek Mountains* NV-8
*Trout Creek Mountains* OR-9
Trout Creek Mountains—*range* OR-9
Trout Creek Mtn—*summit* ID-8
Trout Creek Mtns—*range* NV-8
Trout Creek Oil Field—*oilfield* LA-4
Trout Creek Park—*flat* (2) UT-8
Trout Creek Park—*park* PA-2
Trout Creek Pass—*gap* CO-8
Trout Creek Pass—*gap* ID-8
Trout Creek Pass Spring—*spring* ID-8
Trout Creek Peak—*summit* UT-8
Trout Creek Ranch—*locale* CO-8
Trout Creek Ranch—*locale* (3) NV-8
Trout Creek Ranch—*locale* OR-9
Trout Creek Ranch—*locale* WY-8
Trout Creek Ranger Station—*locale* MT-8
Trout Creek Ridge—*ridge* CA-9
Trout Creek Ridge—*ridge* ID-8
Trout Creek Ridge—*ridge* OR-9
Trout Creek Ridge—*ridge* UT-8
Trout Creek Rsvr—*reservoir* OR-9
Trout Creek Sch—*school* CO-8
Trout Creek Spring—*spring* CO-8
Trout Creek Spring—*spring* ID-8
Trout Creek Stock Driveway—*trail* MT-8
Trout Creek Swamp—*swamp* OR-9
Trout Creek Trail—*trail* ID-8
*Trout Creek Valley* WI-6
Trout Creek Valley—*valley* OR-9
*Troutdale* VA-3
Troutdale—*locale* ME-1
**Troutdale**—*pop pl* CO-8
**Troutdale**—*pop pl* OR-9
**Trout Dale**—*pop pl* VA-3
Troutdale Campground—*locale* ID-8
Trout Dale Cem—*cemetery* VA-3
**Troutdale (corporate name for Trout
Dale)**—*pop pl* VA-3
*Trout Dale (corporate name Troutdale)* VA-3
Troutdale Creek—*stream* CA-9
Troutdale Guard Station—*locale* ID-8
Troutdale Sch—*school* OR-9
Troutdale Substation—*locale* OR-9
Trout Dam—*dam* SD-7
Trout Draw—*valley* WY-8
*Troute Lake* AK-9
Trout Falls Creek—*stream* MI-6
Trout Farm Camp—*locale* OR-9
Trout Farm Spring—*spring* OR-9
Trout Glen Pool—*lake* MO-7
Trout-Good Pine—*CDP* LA-4
Trout Hall—*hist pl* PA-2
**Trout Haven**—*pop pl* CO-8
*Trout Hill* WA-9
Trout Hill—*summit* AK-9
Trout Hill Trail—*trail* PA-2
Trout Hole Run—*stream* PA-2
*Trout Hole Trail* PA-2
Trout Hollow—*valley* IL-6
Trout Hollow—*valley* PA-2
Trout Hollow Cave—*cave* PA-2
Trout House—*hist pl* KY-4
*Trout Island* ID-8
Trout Island—*island* MI-6
Trout Lagoon—*lake* AK-9
*Trout Lake* MI-6
*Trout Lake* MN-6
*Trout Lake* MS-4
*Trout Lake* NY-2
*Trout Lake* PA-2
*Trout Lake* WA-9
*Trout Lake* WY-8
Trout Lake—*lake* (4) AK-9
Trout Lake—*lake* CO-8
Trout Lake—*lake* (13) FL-3
Trout Lake—*lake* (3) GA-3
Trout Lake—*lake* ID-8
Trout Lake—*lake* (2) ME-1
Trout Lake—*lake* (13) MI-6
Trout Lake—*lake* (5) MN-6
Trout Lake—*lake* (2) MS-4
Trout Lake—*lake* (3) MT-8
Trout Lake—*lake* NE-7
Trout Lake—*lake* (6) NY-2
Trout Lake—*lake* OR-9
Trout Lake—*lake* SC-3
Trout Lake—*lake* TX-5
Trout Lake—*lake* (8) WA-9
Trout Lake—*lake* (7) WI-6
Trout Lake—*lake* WY-8
**Trout Lake**—*pop pl* CO-8
**Trout Lake**—*pop pl* MI-6
**Trout Lake**—*pop pl* WA-9
Trout Lake—*reservoir* (2) CO-8
Trout Lake—*reservoir* FL-3
Trout Lake—*reservoir* (4) NC-3
Trout Lake—*reservoir* (2) PA-2
Trout Lake—*reservoir* (2) WI-6
Trout Lake Airp—*airport* WA-9
Trout Lake Big Tree—*locale* WA-9
Trout Lake Cem—*cemetery* MN-6
Trout Lake Cem—*cemetery* WA-9
Trout Lake Ch—*church* MN-6
Trout Lake Creek—*stream* NY-2
Trout Lake Creek—*stream* WA-9
Trout Lake Creek Campground—*locale* WA-9
Trout Lake Dam—*dam* (4) NC-3
Trout Lake Dam—*dam* PA-2
Trout Lake Lookout Tower—*locale* MI-6
Trout Lake Mtn—*summit* NY-2
Trout Lake Park—*park* MI-6
Trout Lake Prairie—*swamp* GA-3
Trout Lake Ridge—*ridge* ME-1
Trout Lakes—*lake* NM-5
Trout Lake State For—*forest* NY-2
Trout Lake Stream—*stream* ME-1
**Trout Lake (Township of)**—*pop pl* MI-6
**Trout Lake (Township of)**—*pop pl* MN-6
Troutman—*locale* GA-3
Troutman—*locale* PA-2
**Troutman**—*pop pl* NC-3
Troutman Airp—*airport* MO-7
Troutman Bend—*bend* GA-3
Troutman Branch—*stream* IN-6
Troutman Cem—*cemetery* IL-6
Troutman Cem—*cemetery* KY-4
Troutman Cem—*cemetery* MO-7
Troutman Cem—*cemetery* NC-3
Troutman Chapel—*church* AR-4
*Troutman Creek* IN-6
Troutman Draw—*valley* CO-8
Troutman Elem Sch—*school* NC-3
Troutman Grove Cem—*cemetery* IL-6
Troutman Gulch—*valley* OR-9
Troutman Hogan Ditch—*canal* IN-6
Troutman Homestead—*locale* MT-8
Troutman Knob—*summit* KY-4
Troutman Lake—*lake* AK-9
Troutman Lateral—*canal* NM-5
Troutman Mtn—*summit* CA-9
Troutman Ranch—*locale* NM-5
Troutman Run—*stream* PA-2
*Troutmans* NC-3
Troutmans Creek—*stream* NJ-2
*Troutmans Run* PA-2
Troutman Station (historical)—*locale* PA-2
Trout Meadow—*flat* OR-9
Trout Meadows—*flat* CA-9
Trout Meadows—*flat* OR-9
Trout Meadows Butte—*summit* OR-9
Trout Meadows Guard Station—*locale* CA-9
Trout Meadows Trail—*trail* OR-9
*Troutmens* NC-3
Troutmere Creek—*stream* WI-6
*Trout Mountain* ID-8
*Trout Mountain* OR-9
Trout Mtn—*summit* CO-8
Trout Mtn—*summit* (2) ME-1
Trout Mtn—*summit* MI-6
Trout Park—*park* IL-6
*Trout Pass* CO-8
*Trout Peak* UT-8
Trout Peak—*summit* (2) ID-8
Trout Peak—*summit* WY-8
Trout Point—*cape* FL-3
Trout Point—*cape* MI-6
Trout Point—*cape* TX-5
Trout Point—*cape* WI-6
Trout Point—*summit* ID-8
Trout Point Logging Camp—*hist pl* WI-6
*Trout Pond* ME-1
*Trout Pond* NY-2
*Trout Pond* RI-1
*Trout Pond* VT-1
Trout Pond—*lake* (2) CT-1
Trout Pond—*lake* FL-3
Trout Pond—*lake* (13) ME-1
Trout Pond—*lake* (4) MA-1
Trout Pond—*lake* MS-4
Trout Pond—*lake* (5) NH-1
Trout Pond—*lake* (10) NY-2
Trout Pond—*lake* TN-4
Trout Pond—*lake* WV-2
Trout Pond—*reservoir* GA-3
Trout Pond—*reservoir* MT-8
Trout Pond—*reservoir* NY-2
Trout Pond Brook—*stream* NY-2
Trout Pond Dam—*dam* (3) MA-1
Trout Pond Hill—*summit* NY-2
Trout Pond Mtn—*summit* (2) ME-1
Trout Pond Ridge—*ridge* WV-2
Trout Pond Run—*stream* WV-2
Trout Pond Trail—*trail* WV-2
*Trout River* MI-6
**Trout River**—*pop pl* NY-2
Trout River—*stream* FL-3
Trout River—*stream* IA-7
Trout River—*stream* MI-6
Trout River—*stream* NY-2
Trout River—*stream* VT-1
Trout River—*stream* WI-6
Trout River Cut—*channel* FL-3
Trout Rock—*cape* MN-6
*Trout Run* PA-2
**Trout Run**—*pop pl* PA-2
**Trout Run**—*pop pl* WI-6
Trout Run—*stream* (2) IA-7
Trout Run—*stream* (2) MD-2
Trout Run—*stream* (2) MN-6
Trout Run—*stream* NJ-2
Trout Run—*stream* NY-2
Trout Run—*stream* (38) PA-2
Trout Run—*stream* (2) VA-3
Trout Run—*stream* (6) WV-2
Trout Run—*stream* WI-6
Trout Run Ch—*church* WI-6
Trout Run Creek Valley—*valley* WI-6
*Trout Run Dam* PA-2
Trout Run Dam—*dam* PA-2
Trout Run Dam Number Four—*dam* PA-2
Trout Run Mtn—*summit* PA-2
Trout Run Ridge Trail—*trail* PA-2
Trout Run Rsvr—*reservoir* PA-2
Trout Run Sch (historical)—*school* (2) PA-2
Trout Run Station—*locale* NJ-2
Trout Run Valley—*valley* WV-2
Trout Sch—*school* (2) IL-6
Trout Sch—*school* OK-5
Trout Sch (abandoned)—*school* PA-2
**Trouts Corners**—*pop pl* PA-2
**Trouts Crossing**—*pop pl* PA-2
*Trout Siding* ID-8
Trout Spring—*spring* (2) ID-8
Trout Spring—*spring* UT-8
Trout Springs—*locale* NM-5
Trout Springs—*spring* NV-8
Trout Springs—*spring* UT-8
Trout Springs—*spring* (2) WI-6
Trout Springs Canyon—*valley* NM-5
*Trout Spur* TX-5
Trout Stream—*stream* ME-1
Trout Stream—*stream* PA-2
*Troutt* TN-4
Troutt—*locale* MO-7
*Troutts* TN-4
*Troutvale Lakes* CO-8
*Trout Valley* WV-2
**Trout Valley**—*pop pl* IL-6
Trout Valley—*valley* PA-2
Troutville—*locale* MD-2
**Troutville**—*pop pl* PA-2
**Troutville**—*pop pl* VA-3
Troutville Borough—*civil* PA-2
Trout Water Canyon—*valley* UT-8
Trout Water Canyon Spring—*spring* UT-8
**Troutwell**—*pop pl* PA-2
Troutwine Cem—*cemetery* OH-6
Troutwine Run—*stream* WV-2
Trouve, Bayou—*gut* LA-4
*Troux Creek* OR-9
Trovener (historical)—*locale* AL-4
Trover Boys Ranch—*school* FL-3
Trovillon Cem—*cemetery* AR-4
Trovinger Mill—*hist pl* MD-2
*Trowbridge* MI-6
Trowbridge—*locale* MI-6
Trowbridge—*locale* PA-2
**Trowbridge**—*pop pl* CA-9
**Trowbridge**—*pop pl* IL-6
**Trowbridge**—*pop pl* OH-6
Trowbridge, Charles, House—*hist pl* MI-6
Trowbridge Archeol Site—*hist pl* KS-7
Trowbridge Cem—*cemetery* OK-5
Trow Bridge Ch—*church* MI-6
Trowbridge Creek—*stream* NY-2
Trowbridge Creek—*stream* OR-9
Trowbridge Creek—*stream* PA-2
Trowbridge Dairy—*hist pl* MT-8
Trowbridge Dam—*locale* MI-6
Trowbridge Gulch—*valley* ID-8
Trowbridge Hill—*summit* CT-1
Trowbridge Lake—*lake* MN-6
Trowbridge Mtn—*summit* NJ-2
**Trowbridge Park**—*pop pl* MI-6
Trowbridge Ranch—*locale* MT-8
Trowbridge Ranch—*locale* WY-8
Trowbridge Sch—*school* NY-2
Trowbridge Sch—*school* WI-6
Trowbridge Square Hist Dist—*hist pl* CT-1
Trowbridges Resort—*locale* MI-6
**Trowbridge (Township of)**—*pop pl* MI-6
*Trowbridgeville Pond* MA-1
Trow Brook—*stream* NH-1
Trowed, Lake—*lake* FL-3
Trowe Drain—*stream* WI-6
Troweek—*locale* AZ-5
Trowel Ditch—*canal* CO-8
Trowel Gulch—*valley* ID-8
*Trowells Branch* SC-3
*Trowells Landing* GA-3
Trowells Mill Branch—*stream* SC-3
Trowel Ranch—*locale* CO-8
Trowel Shop Pond—*reservoir* MA-1
Trowel Shop Pond Dam—*dam* MA-1
Trowe Marsh—*swamp* WI-6
*Trower* VA-3
Trower—*locale* VA-3
Trower Hollow—*valley* MO-7
Trower Sch (abandoned)—*school* MO-7
**Trow Hill**—*pop pl* VT-1
Trow Hill—*summit* NH-1
Trow Hill—*summit* VT-1
Trow Lake—*reservoir* WI-6
*Trow Mound* WI-6
Trow Mounds—*summit* WI-6
Trownsell Ranch—*locale* CO-8
**Troxel**—*pop pl* IL-6
**Troxel**—*pop pl* NE-7
Troxel Cem—*cemetery* KY-4
Troxel Cem—*cemetery* MO-7
Troxel Hill—*summit* WA-9
Troxell JHS—*school* PA-2
Troxell-Steckel House—*hist pl* PA-2
Troxel Point—*cape* CA-9
**Troxelville**—*pop pl* PA-2
Troxler Cem—*cemetery* TN-4
Troxlers Mill—*locale* NC-3
Troxtel Gap—*gap* AL-4
*Troy* IL-6
*Troy* MS-4
*Troy* NJ-2
*Troy* ND-7
Troy—*hist pl* MD-2
Troy—*locale* AZ-5
Troy—*locale* AR-4
Troy—*locale* CA-9
Troy—*locale* LA-4
Troy—*locale* ME-1
Troy—*locale* MI-6
Troy—*locale* MN-6
Troy—*locale* VA-3
**Troy**—*pop pl* AL-4
**Troy**—*pop pl* CO-8
**Troy**—*pop pl* ID-8
**Troy**—*pop pl* IL-6
**Troy**—*pop pl* IN-6
**Troy**—*pop pl* IA-7
**Troy**—*pop pl* KS-7
**Troy**—*pop pl* KY-4
**Troy**—*pop pl* LA-4
**Troy**—*pop pl* MI-6
**Troy**—*pop pl* MS-4
**Troy**—*pop pl* MO-7
**Troy**—*pop pl* MT-8
**Troy**—*pop pl* NH-1
**Troy**—*pop pl* NY-2
**Troy**—*pop pl* NC-3
**Troy**—*pop pl* OH-6
**Troy**—*pop pl* OK-5
**Troy**—*pop pl* OR-9
**Troy**—*pop pl* (3) PA-2
**Troy**—*pop pl* SC-3
**Troy**—*pop pl* SD-7
**Troy**—*pop pl* TN-4
**Troy**—*pop pl* TX-5
**Troy**—*pop pl* VT-1
**Troy**—*pop pl* WV-2
**Troy**—*pop pl* WI-6
Troy, Mount—*summit* AK-9
*Troy, Town of* MA-1
Troy Acad—*hist pl* IA-7
Troy Airp—*airport* KS-7
Troy Baptist Ch—*church* MS-4
Troy Borough—*civil* PA-2
Troy Brand Lake Dam—*dam* MS-4
Troy Brook—*stream* CT-1
Troy Brook—*stream* NJ-2
Troyburg Mesa—*summit* NM-5
Troy Canyon—*valley* CA-9
Troy Canyon—*valley* (2) NV-8
Troy (CCD)—*cens area* AL-4
Troy (CCD)—*cens area* SC-3
Troy Cedar Lake—*lake* IN-6
Troy Cem—*cemetery* AR-4
Troy Cem—*cemetery* (2) IA-7
Troy Cem—*cemetery* MN-6
Troy Cem—*cemetery* (2) OH-6
Troy Cem—*cemetery* PA-2
Troy Cem—*cemetery* SD-7
Troy Center—*locale* ME-1
Troy Center—*locale* PA-2
**Troy Center**—*pop pl* WI-6
**Troy Center (Township name
Troy)**—*pop pl* PA-2
Troy Central Sch—*school* ME-1
Troy Ch—*church* (2) AR-4
Troy Ch—*church* IN-6
Troy Ch—*church* ND-7
Troy Ch—*church* (2) OH-6
Troy Chapel—*church* AL-4
Troy Chapel—*church* OH-6
Troy Chapel Cem—*cemetery* AL-4
Troy Church Sch—*school* OH-6
Troy City Hall—*building* NC-3
Troy City Rsvr—*reservoir* MT-8
*Troy College* AL-4
**Troy Compact (census name
Troy)**—*pop pl* NH-1
*Troy Corners* MI-6
Troy Country Club—*other* AL-4
*Troy Creek* MT-8
Troy Creek—*stream* IA-7
Troy Creek—*stream* MN-6
Troy Creek—*stream* (2) MT-8
Troy Creek—*stream* NE-7
Troy Creek—*stream* NV-8
Troy Creek—*stream* TN-4
Troy Creek—*stream* VA-3
**Troy Crossing**—*pop pl* IL-6
Troy Division—*civil* AL-4
*Troy Dry Lake* CA-9
Troy Elem Sch—*school* AL-4
Troy Elem Sch—*school* KS-7
Troy Elem Sch—*school* NC-3
Troyer—*locale* MD-2
Troyer Cem—*cemetery* IL-6
Troyer Dam—*dam* PA-2
Troyer Hollow—*valley* OH-6
Troyer Sch—*school* OH-6
Troyer Spring—*spring* CO-8
Troyer Valley Creek—*stream* OH-6
*Troy Farm Siding* ND-7
Troy Female Coll (historical)—*school* AL-4
Troy Ferry (historical)—*locale* MS-4
Troy Ferry Post Office
(historical)—*building* TN-4
Troy Flat—*flat* CA-9
Troy Gas Light Company—*hist pl* NY-2
Troy Gilmore Hollow—*valley* KY-4
Troy Gravel Pit—*mine* TN-4
**Troy Grove**—*pop pl* IL-6
**Troy Grove (Township of)**—*pop pl* IL-6
**Troy Hill**—*pop pl* (2) PA-2
Troy Hill—*summit* PA-2
Troy Hill Playground—*park* PA-2
**Troy Hills**—*pop pl* NJ-2
Troy Hill Sch—*school* PA-2
Troy Hills Golf Course—*other* MI-6
Troy (historical)—*locale* AL-4
Troy (historical)—*locale* MS-4
**Troy (historical)**—*pop pl* IA-7
Troy Hollow—*valley* KY-4
Troy HS—*hist pl* AL-4
Troy HS—*school* KS-7
Troy HS—*school* MI-6
Troy Island—*island* MD-2
Troy JHS—*school* AL-4
Troy JHS—*school* NC-3
Troy-Juliaetta-Kendrick—*cens area* ID-8

Troy Junction—locale ... IL-6
Troy Junction (historical)—locale ... KS-7
Troy Lake—flat ... CA-9
Troy Lake—reservoir ... SD-7
Troy Lakes Cem—cemetery ... WI-6
Troy Lake State Public Shooting Area—park ... SD-7
Troy Laundry—hist pl ... CA-9
Troy Lee Hunt Dam—dam ... SD-7
Troy Lock—other ... NY-2
Troy Lookout Tower—locale ... MS-4
Troy Lumber Company Dam—dam ... NC-3
Troy (Magisterial District)—fmr MCD ... WV-2
Troy Meadows—flat ... CA-9
Troy Meadows—swamp ... NJ-2
Troy Mill Branch—stream ... NC-3
**Troy Mills**—pop pl ... IA-7
Troy Mills Cem—cemetery ... IA-7
Troy Mills Sch (historical)—school ... MO-7
Troy Mills State Fish And Game Area—park ... IA-7
Troy Mills Wapsie County Park—park ... IA-7
Troy Mine—mine ... NV-8
Troy Mountain ... AL-4
Troy Mtn—summit ... AZ-5
Troy Municipal Airp—airport ... AL-4
Troy Normal Coll (historical)—school ... MS-4
Troy Normal School ... AL-4
Troyo Ch—church ... MS-4
Troy Oil Field—oilfield ... AR-4
Troy Park—park ... IA-7
Troy Park—park ... WI-6
Troy Peak—summit ... NV-8
Troy Post Office—building ... TN-4
Troy Post Office (historical)—building ... SD-7
Troy Presbyterian Church ... AL-4
Troy Prison Camp—other ... AL-4
Troy Public Library—hist pl ... NY-2
Troy Public Square—hist pl ... OH-6
Troy Ranch—locale ... AZ-5
Troy Ranger Station—locale (2) ... MT-8
Troy Reservoirs—reservoir ... NC-3
Troy Reservoirs Dam—dam ... NC-3
Troy Rod And Gun Club—dam ... AL-4
Troy Rsvr—reservoir ... NY-2
Troy Rsvr—reservoir ... PA-2
Troy Sch—school ... IL-6
Troy Sch—school (2) ... OH-6
Troy Sch—school ... SD-7
Troy Sch—school ... TN-4
Troy Sch (historical)—school ... MS-4
Troys Creek ... IN-6
Troy Spring—spring ... FL-3
Troy Spring—spring ... NV-8
Troy State College ... AL-4
Troy State Normal College ... AL-4
Troy State Teachers College ... AL-4
Troy State Univ—school ... AL-4
Troy State Wildlife Mngmt Area—park ... MN-6
Troy Station ... TN-4
Troy Tank—reservoir ... AZ-5
Troyton—locale ... OH-6
**Troytown**—pop pl ... PA-2
**Troy Town**—pop pl ... WV-2
**Troy (Town of)**—pop pl ... ME-1
**Troy (Town of)**—pop pl ... NH-1
**Troy (Town of)**—pop pl ... VT-1
**Troy (Town of)**—pop pl (3) ... WI-6
Troy Township—civil ... SD-7
Troy Township—fmr MCD (4) ... IA-7
**Troy Township**—pop pl ... KS-7
**Troy Township**—pop pl ... ND-7
**Troy Township**—pop pl (2) ... SD-7
Troy (Township of)—fmr MCD ... AR-4
Troy (Township of)—fmr MCD ... NC-3
**Troy (Township of)**—pop pl ... IL-6
**Troy (Township of)**—pop pl (3) ... IN-6
**Troy (Township of)**—pop pl ... MI-6
**Troy (Township of)**—pop pl (2) ... MN-6
**Troy (Township of)**—pop pl (7) ... OH-6
**Troy (Township of)**—pop pl (2) ... PA-2
Troy Union Cem—cemetery ... MI-6
Troy Valley Sch—school ... NE-7
Troyview Ch—church ... OH-6
Troywood Learning Environment—school ... FL-3
T R Simmons Elem Sch—school ... AL-4
T Rsvr—reservoir ... OR-9
Truant Island ... MA-1
**Truax**—pop pl ... IA-7
**Truax**—pop pl ... ND-7
**Truax**—pop pl ... WI-6
Truax Canyon—valley ... AZ-5
Truax Canyon—valley ... WA-9
Truax Ch—church ... WI-6
Truax Creek—stream ... MI-6
Truax Creek—stream ... MT-8
Truax Creek—stream ... OR-9
Truax Ditch—canal ... IN-6
Truax Group Mine ... SD-7
Truax Hill—summit ... IN-6
Truax Island—island ... OR-9
Truax Lake—lake (3) ... MI-6
Truax Lake—lake ... TX-5
Truax Mtn—summit ... OR-9
Truax (RR name for Dorothy)—other ... WV-2
**Truax Township**—pop pl ... ND-7
**Trubada**—pop pl ... WV-2
Trubie Run—stream ... WV-2
Trubitsin Point—cape ... AK-9
Tru-Blue Ch—church ... NY-2
Truby—locale ... TX-5
Truby Cem—cemetery ... TX-5
Truby Creek—stream ... CO-8
Truby Oil Field—oilfield ... TX-5
Truby Ranch—locale ... NM-5
Truby Run—stream ... PA-2
Truby's Tower (LA 2434)—hist pl ... NM-5
Trucchi Shopping Plaza—locale ... MA-1
Truce—locale ... TX-5
**Truce**—pop pl ... PA-2
Truceangle Post Office (historical)—building ... TN-4
**Truchas**—pop pl ... NM-5
Truchas Creek—stream ... NM-5
Truchas Lakes—lake ... NM-5
Truchas Peak—summit ... NM-5
Truchot Hill—locale ... MT-8
Truck Corner—locale ... FL-3
Truckdrivers Creek—stream ... WY-8
Truckee ... CA-9
**Truckee**—pop pl ... CA-9
Truckee Canal—canal ... NV-8
Truckee Canyon—valley ... CA-9
Truckee Canyon—valley ... NV-8
Truckee Creek—stream ... CA-9
Truckee Marsh—swamp ... CA-9
Truckee Meadows—flat ... NV-8
Truckee Range—range ... NV-8
Truckee River—stream ... CA-9
Truckee River—stream ... NV-8
Truckee Spring—spring ... NV-8
Truckees River ... CA-9
Truckees River ... NV-8
Trucker Run—stream ... PA-2
Truckers ... VA-3
Truckers—locale ... GA-3
Truckers Creek ... PA-2
Truckers Family Camp—park ... UT-8
Truckers Run ... PA-2
Truckey Lake—lake ... MI-6
Truckhaven—locale ... CA-9
Truckhaven Trail—trail ... CA-9
**Truckland**—pop pl ... FL-3
Truck Mine Number 5 (underground)—mine ... AL-4
Truck Mine (underground)—mine ... AL-4
Truck Ravine—valley ... CA-9
Trucks Dam—dam ... AL-4
Trucks Lake—lake ... NE-7
Trucks Lake—reservoir ... AL-4
**Trucksville**—pop pl ... PA-2
**Trucksville Gardens**—pop pl ... PA-2
Trucks Woodyard Landing—locale ... MS-4
Truckton—locale ... CO-8
Truck Wheel Branch—stream ... AR-4
Truckwheel Mtn—summit ... NC-3
Trudau Lake—lake ... MT-8
Trude—locale ... ID-8
Trude—locale ... WA-9
**Trudeau**—pop pl ... NY-2
Trudeau Landing—hist pl ... LA-4
Trudeaus 1794 Camp (historical)—locale ... SD-7
Trude Lake—lake ... WI-6
Trudell Bridge—bridge ... ND-7
Truder Park—hist pl ... NM-5
Trude Siding ... WA-9
Trudgen Well—well ... NV-8
Trudgeon Ranch—locale ... WA-9
Trudie—locale ... GA-3
Trudo Creek—stream ... LA-4
Trudy Lake—reservoir ... AL-4
True—locale ... TX-5
True—locale ... WV-2
Truebada—locale ... WV-2
True Belief Baptist Ch—church ... IN-6
Trueblood Creek—stream ... NE-7
Trueblood Gulch—valley ... CA-9
Truebloods Point—cape ... NC-3
Trueblue ... VA-3
True Blue—locale ... VA-3
**Trueblue**—pop pl ... VA-3
True Blue Creek—stream (2) ... SC-3
True Blue Gulch—valley ... OR-9
True Blue Lake—lake ... SC-3
True Blue Mine—mine ... AZ-5
True Blue Mine—mine ... CA-9
True Blue Rsvr—reservoir ... OR-9
True Blue Tunnel—mine ... NV-8
True Born Miracle Restoration Temple—church ... AL-4
True Brook—stream ... NY-2
True Canal—canal ... LA-4
True Cem—cemetery ... KY-4
True Cem—cemetery ... MA-1
True Cem—cemetery ... OH-6
True Cem—cemetery ... TN-4
True Ch of God—church ... FL-3
True Cove—bay ... ME-1
True Cove—bay ... NH-1
True Creek—stream ... CO-8
Trued—locale ... NE-7
Truedale Lake—lake ... WI-6
True Draw—valley ... SD-7
True Faith Ch—church ... AL-4
True Fissure Mine—mine ... MT-8
True Gospel Ch—church ... GA-3
True Gospel Ch—church ... MI-6
True Gospel Ch—church ... MO-7
True Gospel Ch—church (2) ... NC-3
True Grit Mine (Site)—mine ... CA-9
True Gulch—stream ... CO-8
Trueheart-Adriance Bldg—hist pl ... TX-5
True Hill—summit ... ME-1
True Holiness Campground ... AL-4
True Holiness Ch of God—church ... AL-4
True Holiness Ch of Jesus Christ—church ... AL-4
True Hollow—valley ... OH-6
True Honor Ch—church ... TX-5
True Hope Ch—church ... MO-7
True Lee Ch—church ... TX-5
True Light Baptist Ch ... AL-4
True Light Baptist Ch—church ... AL-4
True Light Baptist Ch—church ... IN-6
True Light Baptist Ch—church ... MS-4
True Light Cem—cemetery ... LA-4
True Light Cem—cemetery (3) ... MS-4
Truelight Ch ... AL-4
True Light Ch ... MS-4
True Light Ch—church (2) ... AL-4
True Light Ch—church ... AR-4
True Light Ch—church ... IL-6
True Light Ch—church (2) ... LA-4
Truelight Ch—church ... LA-4
True Light Ch—church (2) ... LA-4
True Light Ch—church (2) ... MS-4
Truelight Ch—church ... MS-4
True Light Ch—church (4) ... MS-4
Truelight Ch—church ... MS-4
True Light Ch—church (2) ... NC-3
True Light Ch—church ... TX-5
True Light Ch—church ... VA-3
True Light Holiness Ch ... AL-4
True Light Holy Tabernacle—church ... NC-3
True Light Missionary Baptist Ch ... MS-4
Truelight Sch—school ... MS-4
Truelight Sch (historical)—school ... MS-4
True Love Bar—bar ... AR-4
True Love Cem—cemetery ... LA-4
True Love Cem—cemetery ... MO-7
Truelove Ch—church ... AL-4
Truelove Ch—church ... IN-6
Truelove Knob—summit ... GA-3
Truelson Ranch—locale ... CO-8
Truelson Sch—school ... ND-7
Trueman Lake—lake ... MI-6
Trueman Point ... MD-2
Trueman Point—cape ... MD-2
Truemans—locale ... PA-2
True Meadow—flat ... CA-9
True Mtn—summit ... CO-8
True Mtn—summit ... ME-1
True Ranch—locale ... TX-5
True Sch—school ... FL-3
True Sch—school ... NH-1
Trues Creek—stream ... NY-2
**Truesdail (corporate name for Truesdale)**—pop pl ... MO-7
Truesdale ... KS-7
**Truesdale**—pop pl ... IA-7
**Truesdale**—pop pl ... MO-7
Truesdale (corporate and RR name Truesdail) ... MO-7
Truesdale Ditch—canal ... IN-6
Truesdale Hosp—hist pl ... MA-1
Truesdale Hosp—hospital ... MA-1
Truesdale Lake—lake ... NY-2
**Truesdale Lake**—pop pl ... NY-2
Truesdale Mtn—summit ... ME-1
Truesdale Pond—lake ... ME-1
Truesdale Sch—school ... SC-3
**Truesdale Terrace**—pop pl ... PA-2
Truesdell—locale ... WI-6
Truesdell Creek—stream ... CO-8
Truesdell Creek—stream ... SD-7
Truesdell Drain—stream ... MI-6
Truesdell JHS—school ... KS-7
Truesdell Park—park ... FL-3
Truesdell Sch—school ... DC-2
Truesdell Sch—school ... MI-6
Trues Island—island ... MA-1
Trues Lake—lake ... FL-3
True Spiritual Ch—church ... IN-6
Trues Pond—reservoir ... ME-1
True Tabernacle—church ... TN-4
True Temple Ch—church ... NC-3
True Temple of Faith—church ... FL-3
Truetown—locale ... OH-6
**True (Town of)**—pop pl ... WI-6
Truett—locale ... AL-4
Truett, Alpheus, House—hist pl ... TN-4
Truett Branch—stream ... FL-3
Truett Branch—stream (2) ... NC-3
Truett Creek—stream ... AR-4
Truett McConnell Coll—school ... GA-3
Truett Memorial Ch—church ... NC-3
Truett Mine—mine ... TN-4
Truett Ranch—locale ... NV-8
Truett Sch—school ... TX-5
Truett Spring—spring ... NV-8
Truevine—locale ... VA-3
Truevine Baptist Ch—church (2) ... AL-4
True Vine Baptist Ch—church (2) ... MS-4
True Vine Baptist Ch—church ... TN-4
Truevine Cem—cemetery ... AR-4
Truevine Cem—cemetery ... LA-4
True Vine Cem—cemetery ... LA-4
True Vine Cem—cemetery (2) ... MS-4
Truevine Cem—cemetery ... MO-7
Truevine Ch ... AL-4
True Vine Ch—church ... AL-4
Truevine Ch—church (2) ... AL-4
Truevine Ch—church ... AR-4
True Vine Ch—church ... AR-4
True Vine Ch—church ... LA-4
Truevine Ch—church ... LA-4
True Vine Ch—church (2) ... LA-4
True Vine Ch—church (2) ... MS-4
Truevine Ch—church (2) ... MS-4
True Vine Ch—church ... TX-5
True-Vine Ch—church ... TX-5
Truevine Missionary Baptist Ch—church ... KS-7
Truevine Primitive Baptist Ch—church ... AL-4
Truevine Sch—school ... MS-4
Truevine Sch—school ... VA-3
Trueway Ch—church ... MS-4
Trueway Ch—church ... NC-3
True Way Ch—church ... NC-3
True Way Church, The—church ... AL-4
Trueway Holiness Ch—church ... MS-4
Trueworthy Brook—stream ... ME-1
Trueworthy Cem—cemetery ... ME-1
Trueworthy Pond—lake ... ME-1
True Zion Ch—church ... MS-4
**Trufant**—pop pl ... MI-6
Trufant Cem—cemetery ... MI-6
Trufant Ledge—bar ... ME-1
Trugg Rsvr—reservoir ... OR-9
Truhart—locale ... VA-3
Truitt—locale ... KY-4
Truitt—locale ... MD-2
Truitt—locale ... MS-4
Truitt, Gov. George, House—hist pl ... DE-2
Truitt Branch—stream ... MD-2
Truitt Cem—cemetery ... AL-4
Truitt Cem—cemetery ... IN-6
Truitt Cem—cemetery ... MI-6
Truitt Cem—cemetery ... MO-7
Truitt Cem—cemetery (2) ... NC-3
Truitt Cem—cemetery ... TX-5
Truitt Ch—church ... MS-4
Truitt Chapel—church ... TX-5
Truitt Creek—stream ... CA-9
Truitt Creek—stream ... MO-7
Truitt Ditch—stream ... IN-6
Truitt Hill—summit ... AL-4
Truitt Hollow—valley ... OH-6
Truitt JHS—school ... VA-3
Truitt Landing ... MD-2
Truitt Pond—lake ... NY-2
Truitt Post Office (historical)—building ... MS-4
Truitt Ranch—locale ... NM-5
**Truittsburg**—pop pl ... PA-2
**Truitts Midway Development (subdivision)**—pop pl ... DE-2
**Truitts Park**—pop pl ... DE-2
Truitt Tank—reservoir ... TX-5
Truitt Well—well ... NM-5
Trujilla Spring—spring ... CO-8
Trujillo—locale ... CO-8
Trujillo—locale ... NM-5
Trujillo, Manuelita, House—hist pl ... NM-5
Trujillo, Maria J. and Juan, House—hist pl ... NM-5
Trujillo, Sr., Fernando, House—hist pl ... NM-5
**Trujillo Alto**—pop pl ... PR-3
Trujillo Alto (Municipio)—civil ... PR-3
Trujillo Alto (Pueblo)—fmr MCD ... PR-3
**Trujillo Bajo**—pop pl ... PR-3
Trujillo Bajo (Barrio)—fmr MCD ... PR-3
Trujillo Camp—locale ... NM-5
Trujillo Camp—locale ... TX-5
Trujillo Canon—valley ... NM-5
Trujillo Canyon—valley ... AZ-5
Trujillo Canyon—valley (3) ... CO-8
Trujillo Canyon—valley (2) ... NM-5
Trujillo Cem—cemetery ... NM-5
Trujillo Creek—stream (2) ... CA-9
Trujillo Creek—stream (2) ... CO-8
Trujillo Creek—stream ... NM-5
Trujillo Creek—stream ... TX-5
Trujillo Creek Cem—cemetery ... CO-8
Trujillo Draw—valley ... NM-5
Trujillo-Gonzales House—hist pl ... NM-5
Trujillo Lateral—canal ... NM-5
Trujillo Meadows—flat ... CO-8
Trujillo Meadows Campground—locale ... CO-8
Trujillo Meadows Rsvr—reservoir ... CO-8
Trujillo Mesa—summit ... NM-5
Trujillo Park—flat ... NM-5
Trujillo Park Canyon—valley ... NM-5
Trujillo Ranch—locale (3) ... NM-5
Trujillo Rsvr—reservoir ... NM-5
Trujillo School (Abandoned)—locale ... NM-5
Trujillo Spring—spring ... NM-5
Trujillo Tank—reservoir (4) ... NM-5
Trujillo Tank—reservoir ... TX-5
Trujillo Well—well ... TX-5
Trujillo Windmill—locale ... NM-5
Trujillo Windmill—locale (2) ... TX-5
**Truk (County-equivalent)**—pop pl ... FM-9
Truk Draw—valley ... WY-8
Truk Harbor ... FM-9
Truk Islands—island ... FM-9
Truk Lagoon—bay ... FM-9
Truk Lagoon Underwater Fleet, Truk Atoll—hist pl ... FM-9
Trukule, Mount ... FM-9
Truland Brook—stream ... VT-1
Trulite Ch—church ... NC-3
Trull—locale ... CA-9
Trull Brook ... MA-1
Trull Cem—cemetery ... NC-3
Trull Cove—valley ... NC-3
Trull Creek—stream ... CO-8
Trull Creek Rsvr No. 1—reservoir ... CO-8
Trull Hollow—valley ... TN-4
Trull Hosp—hospital ... ME-1
Trullinger Cem—cemetery ... IA-7
Trullys Lake Dam—dam ... MS-4
Trulner Creek—stream ... IA-7
**Tru Lock Acres**—pop pl ... IL-6
Trulock Cem—cemetery ... SD-7
Trulock-Cook House—hist pl ... AR-4
Trulock-Gould-Mullis House—hist pl ... AR-4
Trulock Lake—reservoir ... IL-6
Trulock Public Use Area—park ... AR-4
Truloix Bayou—gut ... LA-4
Truloix Point—cape ... LA-4
Trulse Lake—lake ... MN-6
Trulson Field—airport ... ND-7
Trulson Lake—lake ... MN-6
Truly—locale ... MT-8
Truly Bench—bench ... MT-8
Truly Cem—cemetery ... MS-4
Truly Sch—school ... MT-8
Trulys Lake ... MS-4
Truman—locale ... WI-6
**Truman**—pop pl ... MN-6
**Truman**—pop pl ... PA-2
**Truman**—pop pl ... PR-3
Truman, Harry, Birthplace Memorial—hist pl ... MO-7
Truman, Harry S, Hist Dist—hist pl ... MO-7
Truman Beach—beach ... NY-2
Truman Bench—bench ... UT-8
Truman Cabin—locale ... MT-8
Truman Canyon—valley ... CA-9
Truman Canyon—valley ... NV-8
**Truman Corners**—pop pl ... MO-7
Truman Creek ... CO-8
Truman Creek—stream ... AK-9
Truman Creek—stream ... KY-4
Truman Creek—stream ... MT-8
Truman Creek—stream ... OR-9
Truman Dam—dam ... SD-7
Truman Draw—valley ... WY-8
Truman Gulch—valley ... MT-8
Truman Hill—summit ... NY-2
Truman Home—building ... MO-7
Truman HS—school ... MO-7
Truman JHS—school ... WA-9
Truman Lake ... MI-6
Truman Library—building ... MO-7
Truman Meadows—flat ... NV-8
**Trumann**—pop pl ... AR-4
Truman Point ... MD-2
Truman Pond—reservoir ... PA-2
Truman-Randall House—hist pl ... AZ-5
Truman Roberts Lake Dam—dam ... MS-4
Truman Root Run ... PA-2
Truman Run ... PA-2
Truman Run—stream ... PA-2
**Trumansburg**—pop pl ... NY-2
Trumansburg Creek—stream ... NY-2
Truman Sch—school ... CT-1
Truman Sch—school ... IA-7
Truman Sch—school (2) ... MO-7
Truman Sch—school ... WI-6
Truman's Place—hist pl ... MD-2
Trumans Point ... MD-2
Truman Spring—spring ... NV-8
Trumans Ridge ... WA-9
**Truman Township**—pop pl ... ND-7
Truman Trail—trail ... PA-2
Truman Windmill—locale ... TX-5
Truman Wood Creek—stream ... WA-9
**Trumbauersville**—pop pl ... PA-2
Trumbauersville Borough—civil ... PA-2
**Trumbauersville (Cressman)**—pop pl ... PA-2
Trumbell Canyon—valley ... NM-5
Trumble Brook—stream ... MA-1
Trumble Cem—cemetery ... TX-5
Trumble Draw—valley ... CO-8
Trumble Mtn—summit ... WV-2
Trumble Ranch—locale ... CA-9
Trumble Sch—school ... NE-7
Trumbles Rock—island ... ME-1
Trumbo, A. C., House—hist pl ... OK-5
Trumbo, Andrew, Log House—hist pl ... KY-4
Trumbo Bottom—bend ... KY-4
Trumbo Cem—cemetery ... IL-6
Trumbo Cem—cemetery ... KY-4
Trumbo Cem—cemetery ... OH-6
Trumbo Draw—valley ... SD-7
Trumbo Hollow—valley ... VA-3
Trumbolt Picnic Area—locale ... UT-8
Trumbo Point—cape ... FL-3
Trumbo Ranch—locale ... MT-8
Trumbo Sch—school ... SD-7
Trumbull—CDP ... CT-1
Trumbull—park ... IL-6
**Trumbull**—pop pl ... CO-8
**Trumbull**—pop pl ... CT-1
**Trumbull**—pop pl ... IL-6
**Trumbull**—pop pl ... NE-7
**Trumbull**—pop pl ... OH-6
**Trumbull**—pop pl ... TX-5
Trumbull, John, Birthplace—hist pl ... CT-1
Trumbull, John, House—hist pl ... WA-9
Trumbull, Lyman, House—hist pl ... IL-6
Trumbull, Mount—summit ... AZ-5
Trumbull Cem—cemetery ... CT-1
Trumbull Cem—cemetery ... ME-1
Trumbull Cem—cemetery ... OH-6
Trumbull Corners—locale ... MI-6
**Trumbull Corners**—pop pl ... NY-2
**Trumbull (County)**—pop pl ... OH-6
Trumbull County Courthouse—hist pl ... OH-6
Trumbull Creek—stream ... MT-8
Trumbull Creek—stream ... OH-6
Trumbull Island—island ... WI-6
Trumbull Lake—lake ... CA-9
Trumbull Lake—lake ... IA-7
Trumbull Lake—lake ... MI-6
Trumbull Lake—lake ... NE-7
Trumbull Lake State Game Mngmt Area—park ... IA-7
Trumbull Mtn—summit ... NY-2
Trumbull Mtn—summit ... VT-1
Trumbull Oil Field—other ... IL-6
Trumbull Peak—summit ... CA-9
Trumbull Pond—lake ... NH-1
Trumbull Ranch—locale ... NE-7
Trumbull Sch—school ... CT-1
Trumbull Sch—school ... IL-6
Trumbull Sch—school ... MI-6
**Trumbulls Corners**—pop pl ... NY-2
**Trumbull (Township of)**—pop pl ... OH-6
Trum Field—locale ... MA-1
Trummonds Hill—summit ... NY-2
Trump—locale ... CO-8
Trump, Edwin, House—hist pl ... MI-6
Trumpbour Homestead Farm—hist pl ... NY-2
Trump Cem—cemetery (2) ... WV-2
Trump Coulee—valley ... WI-6
Trump Coulee Cem—cemetery ... WI-6
Trump Coulee Creek—stream ... WI-6
Trumpet Branch—stream ... VA-3
Trumpeter Lake—lake (3) ... AK-9
Trumpeter Swamp—stream ... NC-3
Trumpet Island—island ... ME-1
Trump Harbor ... WA-9
Trump Hollow—valley ... PA-2
Trumpington—hist pl ... MD-2
Trump Island—island ... WA-9
Trump Lake—lake ... MN-6
Trump Lake—lake ... WI-6
Trump Post Office (historical)—building ... TN-4
Trump Run—stream ... WV-2
Trump Sch—school ... OH-6
Trumps Ferry (historical)—locale ... NC-3
Trump Shaft—mine ... UT-8
Trumptown ... PA-2
Trumstock Branch—stream ... KY-4
T-Run Branch—stream ... KY-4
**Trundle Crossroad**—pop pl ... TN-4
Trundy Point—cape ... ME-1
Trundy Point Lookout Tower—locale ... ME-1
Trundy Reef—bar ... ME-1
Trune Lake—lake ... MI-6
Trunk Bay—bay ... VI-3
Trunk Bay Sugar Factory—hist pl ... VI-3
Trunk Branch—stream ... TN-4
Trunk Butte—ridge ... MT-8
Trunk Butte—summit ... NE-7
Trunk Butte Creek—stream ... NE-7
Trunk Butte Sch—school ... NE-7
Trunk Canyon—valley ... AZ-5
Trunk Canyon—valley ... UT-8
Trunk Canyon Tank—reservoir ... AZ-5
Trunk Cay—island ... VI-3
Trunk Creek ... NE-7
Trunk Creek—stream ... OK-5
Trunk Creek—stream ... SD-7
Trunk Creek—stream ... WY-8
Trunk Ditch—canal ... UT-8
Trunk Ditch—gut ... DE-2
**Trunkeyville**—pop pl ... PA-2
Trunk Gut—stream ... MD-2
Trunk Hill—summit ... TX-5
Trunk Island—island ... AK-9
Trunk Lake—lake ... TX-5
Trunk Point—cape ... AK-9
Trunnell Sch—school ... KY-4
Truog, George, House—hist pl ... MD-2
Truro—locale ... IL-6
Truro—locale ... ND-7
Truro—locale ... OH-6
**Truro**—pop pl ... IA-7
**Truro**—pop pl ... MA-1
Truro Cem—cemetery (2) ... OH-6
Truro Creek—stream ... CO-8
Truro Lake—lake ... CO-8
Truro Peak—summit ... CO-8
**Truro Station**—pop pl ... MA-1
Truro Town Hall—building ... MA-1
**Truro (Town of)**—pop pl ... MA-1
**Truro Township**—pop pl ... SD-7
**Truro (Township of)**—pop pl ... IL-6
**Truro (Township of)**—pop pl ... OH-6
Truro Village ... MA-1
Trusal Bridge—bridge ... PA-2
Trusal Covered Bridge—hist pl ... PA-2
**Truscott**—pop pl ... TX-5
Truscott Cem—cemetery ... TX-5
Truscott JHS—school ... CO-8
Truscot Waterhole—reservoir ... OR-9
Trus Creek ... MT-8
Trusdale Canyon—valley ... NM-5
Trusler Lake—lake ... LA-4
Truslow Ch—church ... MS-4
Truslow Methodist Ch ... MS-4
Truss ... AL-4
Truss Creek—stream ... CA-9
Trussel Cem—cemetery ... MS-4
Trussel Cem—cemetery ... NE-7
Trussel Cem—cemetery ... PA-2
Trussell Cave—cave ... TN-4
Trussell Cem—cemetery ... IA-7
Trussell Cem—cemetery ... LA-4
Trussell Cem—cemetery ... MS-4
Trussell Cem—cemetery ... TN-4
Trussell Cove—valley ... TN-4
Trussell Creek—stream ... TN-4
Trussell Point—cape ... TN-4
Trussells Bar ... AL-4
Trussells Creek—stream ... AL-4
Trussells Ferry (historical)—locale ... AL-4
Trussells Mills (historical)—locale ... AL-4
Trussel Run—stream ... WV-2
Trussels Bar ... AL-4
Trussel Shoals—bar ... AL-4
Trussels Landing—locale ... AL-4
Trussem Pond ... DE-2
Truss Ferry (historical)—locale ... AL-4
Trussler Branch—stream ... SC-3
Trussler Creek—stream ... WY-8
Trussman Draw—valley ... SD-7
Truss Mill (historical)—locale (2) ... AL-4
Truss Sch (historical)—school ... AL-4
Trussum Pond—reservoir ... DE-2
Trussum Pond Dam—dam ... DE-2
**Trussville**—pop pl ... AL-4
Trussville Cave—cave ... AL-4
Trussville (CCD)—cens area ... AL-4
Trussville Division—civil ... AL-4
Trussville Elem Sch (historical)—school ... AL-4
**Trussville Manor (subdivision)**—pop pl ... AL-4
Trust—locale ... NC-3
**Trust**—pop pl ... PA-2
Trust Buster Mine—mine ... CA-9
Trust Lake—lake ... MN-6
Trustom Pond—lake ... RI-1
Trust Territory of the Pacific Islands United States Trust Territ ... MP-9
Trust-to-Luck Gulch—valley ... MT-8
Trusty, William H., House—hist pl ... VA-3
Trusty Gulch—valley ... MT-8
Trusty Gulch Spring One—spring ... MT-8
Trusty Gulch Spring Two—spring ... MT-8
Trusty (historical)—locale ... MS-4
Trusty Lake—lake ... MT-8
Trusty Mtn—summit ... NY-2
Truth Branch ... SC-3
Truth Ch—church ... AL-4
Truth Ch—church ... NJ-2
**Truth Or Consequences**—pop pl ... NM-5
Truth or Consequences East (CCD)—cens area ... NM-5
**Truth or Consequences (Hot Springs)**—pop pl ... NM-5
Truth or Consequences West (CCD)—cens area ... NM-5
Truth Post Office (historical)—building ... TN-4
Truth River—stream ... AK-9
**Truthville**—pop pl ... NY-2
Trutschell House—hist pl ... KY-4
Trutsch Lake—reservoir ... MO-7
Trutt Sch (historical)—school ... AL-4
Truuli Creek—stream ... AK-9
Truuli Peak—summit ... AK-9
**Tru Vale Acres (subdivision)**—pop pl ... DE-2
Truvine Cem—cemetery ... FL-3
Truvine Ch—church ... FL-3
Truvine Ch—church ... TX-5
**Truxall**—pop pl ... PA-2
Truxaw-Gervais House—hist pl ... CA-9
Truxillo—locale ... VA-3
**Truxno**—pop pl ... LA-4
Truxno Oil Field—oilfield ... LA-4
**Truxton**—pop pl ... AZ-5
**Truxton**—pop pl ... MO-7
**Truxton**—pop pl ... NY-2
Truxton Canyon—valley ... AZ-5
**Truxton Heights**—pop pl ... MD-2
Truxton Hill—summit ... NY-2
Truxton Park—park ... MD-2
Truxton RR Station—building ... AZ-5
Truxton (siding)—locale ... AZ-5
Truxton Spring—spring ... AZ-5
**Truxton (Town of)**—pop pl ... NY-2
Truxton Wash—stream ... AZ-5
Truxtun Hist Dist—hist pl ... VA-3
Truxtun Sch—school ... VA-3
Tryall Creek—stream ... VA-3
Tryan Hollow—valley ... UT-8
Tryanis Creek ... ID-8
Tryannis Creek ... ID-8
Tryannus Gulch ... ID-8
Trygg Lake—lake ... MN-6
**Trygg Township**—pop pl ... ND-7
Trygstad Law and Commerce Bldg—hist pl ... SD-7
Trygveson—hist pl ... GA-3
Tryme—locale ... VA-3
Tryon ... AL-4
**Tryon**—pop pl ... FL-3
**Tryon**—pop pl ... NE-7
**Tryon**—pop pl (2) ... NC-3
**Tryon**—pop pl ... OK-5
**Tryon**—pop pl ... TN-4
Tryon Canyon—valley ... CO-8
Tryon Cem—cemetery ... TN-4
Tryon Corner—locale ... CA-9
Tryon County Courthouse Historical Site—park ... NC-3
Tryon Creek—stream ... CA-9
Tryon Creek—stream (2) ... OR-9
Tryon Creek Ranch—locale ... OR-9
Tryon Draw—valley ... WY-8

Tryon Elem Sch—*school* ... NC-3
Tryon Hill—*summit* ... CT-1
Tryon Hill Sch—*school* ... NC-3
**Tryon Hills (subdivision)**—*pop pl* ... NC-3
Tryon Mall—*locale* ... NC-3
Tryon Meadow—*flat* ... CA-9
*Tryon Mountain* ... NC-3
*Tryon Mountains* ... NC-3
Tryon Mtn—*summit* ... ME-1
Tryon Park—*park* ... NJ-2
Tryon Peak—*summit* ... CA-9
Tryon Peak—*summit* ... NC-3
Tryon Rsvr—*reservoir* ... WY-8
Tryon Saddle—*gap* ... OR-9
Tryon Sch—*school* ... FL-3
Tryon Sch (historical)—*school* ... AL-4
Tryons Corners—*locale* ... NY-2
*Tryons County* ... NC-3
Tryon State Sch For Boys—*school* ... NY-2
Tryon (Township of)—*fmr MCD* ... NC-3
**Tryonville**—*pop pl* ... PA-2
Tryonville Station—*locale* ... PA-2
Tryphosa—*other* ... NC-3
Trypoli Creek—*stream* ... NY-2
Try Run—*stream* ... IN-6
Trysil Cem—*cemetery* ... MN-6
Trysil (historical)—*locale* ... ND-7
Tryson Cem—*cemetery* ... TX-5
Try Spring—*spring* ... OR-9
Tryst Post Office (historical)—*building* ... AL-4
Trythall—*locale* ... PA-2
Trytten, J. M., House—*hist pl* ... MT-8
Tryus—*locale* ... MS-4
Tryus Ch—*church* ... IN-6
Tryus Post Office (historical)—*building* ... MS-4
Trywood Camp—*locale* ... NY-2
Try Yard Creek—*gut* ... NC-3
Try Yard Creek—*stream* ... NC-3
Tsaadidosi Spring—*spring* ... AZ-5
Tsa Cove—*bay* ... AK-9
Tsadaka Canyon—*valley* ... AK-9
Tsagieto Canyon—*valley* ... AZ-5
Tsagieto Canyon—*valley* ... UT-8
Tsahpek—*hist pl* ... CA-9
Tsah Tah Trading Post—*locale* ... NM-5
*Tsail* ... AZ-5
**Tsaile**—*pop pl* ... AZ-5
Tsaile Creek—*stream* ... AZ-5
Tsaile Dam—*dam* ... AZ-5
Tsaile Elem Sch—*school* ... AZ-5
Tsaile Lake—*reservoir* ... AZ-5
Tsaile Lake Campground—*park* ... AZ-5
Tsaile Peak—*summit* ... AZ-5
*Tsaiskizzia Rock* ... AZ-5
*Tsai Skizzie Rock* ... AZ-5
Tsai Skizzi Rock—*pillar* ... AZ-5
Tsala Apopka Lake—*lake* ... FL-3
Tsa La Gi Indian Village—*locale* ... OK-5
*Tsa-lee Creek* ... AZ-5
Tsama Pueblo—*hist pl* ... NM-5
Tsankawi Ruins—*locale* ... NM-5
*Tsaputik* ... FM-9
Tsaritsa Rock—*other* ... AK-9
*Tsatsa* ... MH-9
*Tsatsawassa Creek* ... NY-2
*Tsatsawassa lake* ... NY-2
*Tsa-tsil-too Springs* ... AZ-5
Tsaya—*locale* ... NM-5
Tsaya Canyon—*valley* ... NM-5
Tsayagtulek Creek—*stream* ... AK-9
Tsa Yah Das lahi Spring—*spring* ... AZ-5
Tsaya Trading Post—*locale* ... NM-5
*Tsay-nun-na-ah* ... UT-8
Tsay O Ah Butte—*summit* ... AZ-5
Tsay-se-zhin Butte—*summit* ... AZ-5
Tsbantotloden Lake—*lake* ... AK-9
Tschaekofske Cem—*cemetery* ... ND-7
Tschetter Cem—*cemetery* ... SD-7
Tschetter Colony—*locale* ... SD-7
Tschetter Lake—*lake* ... ND-7
Tschetter Slough—*lake* ... SD-7
Tschetter Slough State Public Shooting Area—*park* ... SD-7
Tschida, Lake—*reservoir* ... ND-7
*Tschida Reservoir* ... ND-7
Tschiener House—*hist pl* ... AL-4
Tschirgi Ditch No 1—*canal* ... WY-8
*Tschischmareffstrasse* ... MP-9
*Tschiulikam* ... AZ-5
*t'Schnichte Wacki* ... PA-2
T Scholzen-Glen Schillingstad Dam—*dam* ... SD-7
Tschuddi Gulch—*valley* ... CO-8
T S Cooper Elem Sch—*school* ... NC-3
T-S Ditch—*canal* ... NV-8
*Tse Aa le Creek* ... AZ-5
Tse Abe I—*pillar* ... AZ-5
*Tse-a-lee* ... AZ-5
Tse Ba Ni Zi Ni Wash—*valley* ... AZ-5
*Tse-Ba-Zi-Ni Wash* ... AZ-5
Tse Biyi—*basin* ... AZ-5
**Tse Bonita**—*pop pl* ... AZ-5
Tse Bonita Sch—*school* ... NM-5
Tse Bonita Trading Post—*locale* ... NM-5
Tse Bonita Tribal Park—*park* ... AZ-5
*Tse Bonita Valley* ... NM-5
*Tse Bonita Wash* ... AZ-5
*Tse Bonita Wash* ... NM-5
Tse Bonito—*locale* ... NM-5
**Tse Bonito**—*pop pl* ... NM-5
Tse Bonito Campground—*park* ... AZ-5
*Tse Bonito Museum* ... AZ-5
Tse Bonito Valley—*valley* ... NM-5
Tse Bonito Wash—*stream* ... NM-5
Tse Bonito Wash—*valley* ... AZ-5
Tse Chizzi Spring—*spring* ... AZ-5
Tse Chizzi Wash—*stream* ... AZ-5
Tse-clani-to Wash—*stream* ... NM-5
Tse Da Ahoodzo Canyon—*valley* ... AZ-5
Tse Da Ahoodzo Peak—*summit* ... AZ-5
Tsedadahotsosi—*summit* ... AZ-5
Tse-dahascani—*ridge* ... UT-8
Tse-dahascani—*summit* ... UT-8
Tsedatoh Canyon—*valley* ... AZ-5
Tse Deeshzhaai Wash—*stream* ... AZ-5
Tse De Tha Well—*well* ... NM-5
Tsedolalindin Lake—*lake* ... AK-9
Tsegi—*locale* ... AZ-5
*Tsegi Branch of Laguna Canyon* ... AZ-5
Tsegi Canyon—*valley* ... AZ-5
Tsegi Canyon Campground—*park* ... AZ-5
*Tsegihatsosi Canyon* ... AZ-5
*Tsegi Mesas* ... AZ-5
Tsegi Overlook—*locale* ... AZ-5
Tsegi Point—*cliff* ... AZ-5
Tsegi Point Overlook—*locale* ... AZ-5
Tse Gis Toh—*spring* ... AZ-5
Tsegitoe Spring—*spring* ... AZ-5
Tsegito Spring—*spring* ... AZ-5
Tsegi Trading Post—*locale* ... AZ-5
**Tsegi (Trading Post)**—*pop pl* ... AZ-5
Tseh Any—*summit* ... AZ-5
*Tsehili* ... AZ-5
*Tsehili Creek* ... AZ-5
*Tseh Ligi* ... AZ-5
*Tsehotsoibizazhe Canyon* ... AZ-5
Tseh-Ya-Kin Canyon—*valley* ... AZ-5
Tsekadebehgon—*cliff* ... AZ-5
*Tseklagai-deza Canyon* ... AZ-5
*Tse Lagai* ... AZ-5
*Tselani* ... AZ-5
*Tse layai dez-a Canyon* ... AZ-5
Tselayazhe—*summit* ... AZ-5
Tselayazhe Wash—*valley* ... AZ-5
Tse Lichii Dah Azka—*summit* ... AZ-5
Tse Lichii Point—*cliff* ... AZ-5
Tse Ligai—*basin* ... AZ-5
Tseligaideeza Canyon—*valley* ... AZ-5
Tse It gai Sinil Well—*well* ... AZ-5
Tsena Commoko Ch—*church* ... VA-3
*Tsenakaahn* ... AZ-5
*Tsenakahn* ... AZ-5
*Tsenakahn Butte* ... AZ-5
*Tse nakani* ... AZ-5
Tse-nas-chii Wash—*stream* ... NM-5
Tse-ni-cha—*pillar* ... NM-5
Tse No Dozz—*spring* ... AZ-5
Tse Notahs Pond—*reservoir* ... AZ-5
Tse Taa Ruins—*locale* ... AZ-5
Tse Tai De Linne Well—*well* ... AZ-5
Tse To Baah Naali Spring—*spring* ... AZ-5
Tse To Baah Naali Wash—*stream* ... AZ-5
Tse Tonte—*summit* ... AZ-5
*Tsetsiltso* ... AZ-5
Tse-yaa-tohi Wash—*stream* ... NM-5
Tseyah—*summit* ... AZ-5
Tseya-Kinsikadi Spring—*spring* ... AZ-5
Tseya Neechee Canyon—*valley* ... AZ-5
Tse Ya Toe Spring—*spring* ... AZ-5
*Tseye-ha-tsazi Canon* ... AZ-5
*Tseyi Hatsosi Canyon* ... AZ-5
*Tseyi To-e Spring* ... AZ-5
*Tsezhini* ... AZ-5
Tshachaling-Atachtoli Lake—*lake* ... AK-9
*Tshapetank* ... DE-2
Tshimakain Creek—*stream* ... WA-9
*Tshiuliseik* ... AZ-5
Tshletshy Creek—*stream* ... WA-9
Tshletshy Ridge—*ridge* ... WA-9
Tsidu-Weza—*summit* ... NM-5
Tsilchin Lake—*lake* ... AK-9
*Tsiltcoos* ... OR-9
*Tsiltcoos Lake* ... OR-9
Tsimpshian Point—*cape* ... AK-9
Tsina Glacier—*glacier* ... AK-9
Tsi Na Jinnie Spring—*spring* ... AZ-5
Tsina River—*stream* ... AK-9
Tsinat Mesa—*bench* ... NM-5
Tsinat Ruins—*locale* ... NM-5
Tsin Beskunt Well—*well* ... AZ-5
Tsingigkalik Lake—*lake* ... AK-9
Tsinia Wildlife Viewing Area—*park* ... AL-4
Tsin Kletzin Ruins—*locale* ... NM-5
Tsin Naan Tee—*ridge* ... AZ-5
Tsin-nas-kid—*summit* ... NM-5
Tsinnie Well—*well* ... AZ-5
**Tsintaa Yiti li**—*pop pl* ... AZ-5
Tsin Yatoh—*spring* ... AZ-5
Tsiping—*hist pl* ... NM-5
Tsirku Glacier—*glacier* ... AK-9
Tsirku River—*stream* ... AK-9
Tsisi Creek—*stream* ... AK-9
*Tsis Island* ... FM-9
*Tsis Islet* ... FM-9
Tsis (Municipality)—*civ div* ... FM-9
Tsis Sch—*school* ... FM-9
*Tsistugi* ... TN-4
Tsitah Valley—*basin* ... UT-8
Tsitah Wash—*arroyo* ... UT-8
Tsitah Wash—*stream* ... AZ-5
*Tsi Tsi Aie Creek* ... WA-9
Tsiu River—*stream* ... AK-9
Tsivat River—*stream* ... AK-9
T-Six Canyon—*valley* ... AZ-5
T-Six Mtn—*summit* ... AZ-5
T-Six Point—*summit* ... AZ-5
T-Six Spring—*spring* ... AZ-5
T-Six Tank—*reservoir* ... AZ-5
Tsiyeehuun Lake—*lake* ... AK-9
Tskawahyah Island—*island* ... WA-9
Tskutsko Point—*cape* ... WA-9
*Tsokes* ... FM-9
*Tsokes Hafen* ... FM-9
Tsolmund Lake—*lake* ... AK-9
*Tsoo-e-ez River* ... WA-9
Tsosie Well—*well* ... AZ-5
Tsos Trading Post—*locale* ... AZ-5
Tso Tsosic Wash—*valley* ... AZ-5
T Spring—*spring* ... OR-9
T-Square Tank—*reservoir* ... AZ-5
T-S Ranch—*locale* ... NV-8
T S Rowland Lake Dam—*dam* ... MS-4
T S Stewart Dam—*dam* ... NC-3
T Sternard Dam—*dam* ... SD-7
T Street—*post sta* ... DC-2
T S Turnipseed Dam—*dam* ... AL-4
T S Turnipseed Lake—*reservoir* ... AL-4
*Tsubaki Shima* ... FM-9
*Tsubaki-To* ... FM-9
*Tsubeppu Island* ... MP-9
Tsubeppu Island—*island* ... MP-9
Tsuga Creek—*stream* ... ID-8
Tsuga Lake—*lake* ... OR-9
Tsuga Lakes—*lake* ... WA-9
Tsugenoban Island—*island* ... MP-9
*Tsugenoban-To* ... MP-9
*Tsuinsu To* ... MP-9
*Tsuirimado To* ... FM-9
*Tsu Kimi Island* ... MH-9
*Tsukimishima Bay* ... MH-9
Tsukon—*locale* ... AK-9
Tsum Creek—*stream* ... ID-8
Tsun-Je-Zhin—*area* ... NM-5
Tsunsu, Mount—*summit* ... PW-9
*Tsunsu Mtn* ... PW-9
*Tsunsu San* ... PW-9
*Tsuragan Island* ... MP-9
*Tsuragan-To* ... MP-9
Tsurotlurna Slough—*stream* ... AK-9
Tsusena Butte—*summit* ... AK-9
Tsusena Creek—*stream* ... AK-9
*Tsutsuman* ... MH-9
*Tsutsuram* ... MH-9
*Tsutsuran* ... MH-9
*Tsutsuuran* ... MH-9
Tsyooktuihvun Lake—*lake* ... AK-9
T Tarnavsky Ranch—*locale* ... ND-7
TT Canyon—*valley* ... OR-9
*T Town* ... DE-2
TT Ranch—*locale* ... AZ-5
TT Ranch—*locale* ... NV-8
T Trent Number 1 Dam—*dam* ... SD-7
T T Tank Number One—*reservoir* ... AZ-5
T T Tank Number Three—*reservoir* ... AZ-5
T T Tank Number Two—*reservoir* ... AZ-5
TTT Camp—*locale* ... MN-6
Ttt Ranch—*locale* ... WY-8
T T Well—*well* ... AZ-5
Tuafanua—*locale* ... AS-9
Tuakay Hot Springs—*spring* ... AZ-5
*Tuakay Springs* ... AZ-5
Tualatai (County of)—*civ div* ... AS-9
**Tualatin**—*pop pl* ... OR-9
Tualatin Acad—*hist pl* ... OR-9
Tualatin Country Club—*other* ... OR-9
Tualatin Grange Hall—*locale* ... OR-9
*Tualatin Hospital* ... OR-9
Tualatin Mountains—*ridge* ... OR-9
Tualatin Plains Cem—*cemetery* ... OR-9
Tualatin River—*stream* ... OR-9
Tualatin Rsvr—*reservoir* ... OR-9
Tualatin Sch—*school* ... OR-9
*Tualatin Valley Junior Acad* ... OR-9
Tualatin View Sch—*school* ... OR-9
Tualaty Hosp—*hospital* ... OR-9
Tualauta (County of)—*civ div* ... AS-9
Tualco Valley—*basin* ... WA-9
Tualiliu Point—*cape* ... AS-9
*Tualitin* ... OR-9
*Tualitin River* ... OR-9
*Tualtin* ... OR-9
*Tualtin River* ... OR-9
Tuana Gulch—*valley* ... ID-8
Tuana Spring—*spring* ... ID-8
Tuanna Butte—*summit* ... ID-8
Tuanna Crossing—*locale* ... ID-8
Tuaolo—*locale* ... AS-9
Tuapaktushak Creek—*stream* ... AK-9
Tuasaine, Point—*cape* ... MS-4
Tuasina Ridge—*ridge* ... AS-9
Tuasivitasi Ridge—*ridge* ... AS-9
Tuatafa Ridge—*ridge* ... AS-9
Tuavaa Stream—*stream* ... AS-9
*Tub* ... PA-2
Tub, The—*well* ... NM-5
*Tuba* ... AZ-5
Tub A—*reservoir* ... AZ-5
Tubaal—*bar* ... FM-9
Tuba Butte—*summit* ... AZ-5
**Tubac**—*pop pl* ... AZ-5
Tubac Creek—*stream* ... AZ-5
Tubac Interchange—*crossing* ... AZ-5
**Tuba City**—*pop pl* ... AZ-5
Tuba City Airp—*airport* ... AZ-5
Tuba City (CCD)—*cens area* ... AZ-5
Tuba City Elem Sch—*school* ... AZ-5
Tuba City Hosp—*hospital* ... AZ-5
Tuba City HS—*school* ... AZ-5
Tuba City JHS—*school* ... AZ-5
Tuba City Road Tank—*reservoir* ... AZ-5
Tuba City Substation—*locale* ... AZ-5
Tubac Presidio—*hist pl* ... AZ-5
Tubac Presidio State Historical Park—*park* ... AZ-5
*Tubadore Canyon* ... UT-8
Tubal Cain Mine—*mine* ... WA-9
Tubal Cain Mine Trail—*trail* ... WA-9
Tubal Furnace Archeol Site—*hist pl* ... VA-3
Tubal (Township of)—*fmr MCD* ... AR-4
Tub B—*reservoir* ... AZ-5
Tubbalubba Creek—*stream* ... MS-4
Tubb Canyon—*valley* ... CA-9
Tubb Canyon Spring—*spring* ... CA-9
Tubb Cem—*cemetery* ... MS-4
Tubb Cem—*cemetery* ... TN-4
*Tubb Creek* ... AL-4
Tubb Creek—*stream* ... OR-9
Tubb Lake—*lake* ... TX-5
Tubb Run—*stream* ... PA-2
Tubbs, Poker Alice, House—*hist pl* ... SD-7
Tubbs Bar—*bar* ... AL-4
Tubbs Branch—*stream* (2) ... AL-4
Tubbs Branch—*stream* ... DE-2
Tubbs Branch—*stream* ... KY-4
Tubbs Bridge—*bridge* ... AL-4
Tubbs Canal—*canal* ... SD-7
Tubbs Cem—*cemetery* ... AL-4
Tubbs Cem—*cemetery* ... LA-4
Tubbs Cem—*cemetery* ... TN-4
Tubbs Cem—*cemetery* ... TX-5
Tubbs Ch—*church* ... AL-4
*Tubbs Ch of Christ* ... AL-4
Tubbs Cordage Company Office Bldg—*hist pl* ... CA-9
Tubbs Corner—*locale* ... TX-5
Tubbs Cove—*bay* ... DE-2
Tubbs Creek—*stream* (2) ... AL-4
Tubbs Creek—*stream* (2) ... AR-4
Tubbs Creek—*stream* ... MI-6
Tubbs Creek—*stream* ... TX-5
*Tubbs Cross Roads* ... MS-4
Tubbs Dam—*dam* ... SD-7
*Tubbs Ferry* ... AL-4
Tubbs Ford Bridge—*bridge* ... TN-4
*Tubbs Hill* ... AL-4
Tubbs Hill—*summit* ... AL-4
Tubbs Hill—*summit* ... GA-3
Tubbs Hill—*summit* ... ID-8
Tubbs Hill—*summit* ... PA-2
Tubbs Hollow—*valley* ... ID-8
Tubbs Hollow—*valley* (2) ... PA-2
Tubbs Hollow—*valley* ... TN-4
Tubbs Inlet—*channel* ... NC-3
Tubbs Island—*island* ... CA-9
Tubbs Lake—*lake* (2) ... MI-6
Tubbs Meadow Brook—*stream* ... MA-1
Tubbs Moss Agate Dam—*dam* ... SD-7
Tubb Spring—*spring* ... AZ-5
Tubb Spring—*spring* ... NM-5
Tubb Spring—*spring* ... OR-9
Tubb Springs—*spring* ... OR-9
Tubbs Run—*stream* ... PA-2
Tubbs Sch—*school* ... IL-6
Tubbs Sch—*school* ... KS-7
Tubbs Sch—*school* ... MI-6
Tubbs Sch (historical)—*school* ... AL-4
Tubbs Sch (historical)—*school* ... PA-2
Tubbs Spring—*spring* ... NV-8
Tubbs Spring—*spring* ... TN-4
Tubbs Spring Branch—*stream* ... TN-4
**Tubbs Subdivision**—*pop pl* ... UT-8
Tub Butte—*summit* ... ND-7
Tub Butte—*summit* ... OR-9
Tubbville Post Office (historical)—*building* ... TN-4
Tubb Wells—*well* ... TX-5
Tubby Cove—*bay* ... MD-2
Tubby Creek—*stream* ... AL-4
Tubby Creek—*stream* ... MS-4
Tubby Creek—*stream* ... MT-8
Tubby Hook—*cape* ... NY-2
Tubby Lake—*lake* ... MN-6
*Tubbys Cove* ... MD-2
*Tubbys Creek* ... MI-6
Tubbys Creek—*gut* ... FL-3
Tubbyville (historical)—*locale* ... MS-4
Tub Canyon—*valley* ... NM-5
Tub Canyon—*valley* ... UT-8
Tub Creek—*stream* ... CA-9
Tub Creek—*stream* ... IN-6
Tub Creek—*stream* ... MO-7
Tub Ditch—*canal* ... UT-8
Tub Draw—*valley* ... AZ-5
Tube Branch—*stream* ... MO-7
Tube Cave—*cave* ... AL-4
T U Bench—*bench* ... MT-8
Tuber—*locale* ... CA-9
Tuber—*locale* ... CO-8
Tuber Canyon—*valley* ... CA-9
Tuberculosis Hosp—*hospital* ... MO-7
Tuberculosis Sanitorium—*hospital* ... AR-4
Tuber Lake—*lake* ... MN-6
Tuberose Canal—*canal* ... CA-9
Tuber Spring—*spring* ... CA-9
Tubes Creek—*stream* ... LA-4
Tubessing Creek—*stream* ... OR-9
Tub Flat—*flat* ... UT-8
Tubfull Creek—*stream* ... MN-6
Tub Gulch—*valley* ... CO-8
Tub Gulch—*valley* ... MT-8
*Tubguw* ... FM-9
Tub Hollow—*valley* (2) ... PA-2
Tub Lake—*lake* ... FL-3
Tub Lake—*lake* ... MI-6
Tub Lake—*lake* ... MN-6
Tub Lake—*lake* ... MT-8
Tub Lake—*lake* ... OR-9
Tub Lake—*lake* (2) ... TX-5
Tub Lake—*lake* ... WA-9
Tub Lake—*lake* ... WI-6
Tub Lakes—*lake* ... NM-5
*Tub Lewis Cemetery* ... MS-4
Tublick Run—*stream* ... PA-2
Tubman HS—*school* ... MD-2
Tubman JHS—*school* ... GA-3
Tubman-King Community Ch—*church* ... FL-3
Tubmill Branch—*stream* ... DE-2
Tubmill Branch—*stream* ... MD-2
Tub Mill Branch—*stream* ... NJ-2
Tub Mill Brook—*stream* ... NY-2
*Tub Mill Creek* ... PA-2
Tub Mill Creek—*stream* (2) ... NC-3
Tubmill Creek—*stream* ... PA-2
Tubmill Dam—*dam* ... PA-2
Tub Mill Pond—*lake* ... NY-2
Tubmill Pond—*reservoir* ... DE-2
Tubmill Pond Dam—*dam* ... DE-2
Tubmill Rsvr—*reservoir* ... PA-2
*Tub Mill Run* ... PA-2
Tub Mill Run—*stream* (3) ... PA-2
Tubmill Sch—*school* ... PA-2
Tub Mtn—*summit* ... NY-2
Tub Mtn—*summit* ... OR-9
Tub Number One—*reservoir* (2) ... AZ-5
Tub Number Three—*reservoir* (2) ... AZ-5
Tub Number Two—*reservoir* (2) ... AZ-5
*Tubon* ... AZ-5
Tub Peak—*summit* ... NV-8
Tub Pond—*lake* ... AZ-5
Tub Pond—*reservoir* ... AZ-5
Tub Ranch—*locale* ... AZ-5
Tub Ridge—*ridge* ... UT-8
Tub Run—*stream* ... KY-4
Tub Run—*stream* ... OR-9
Tub Run—*stream* ... PA-2
Tub Run—*stream* ... VA-3
Tub Run—*stream* (2) ... WV-2
Tub Run Cave—*cave* ... PA-2
Tubs—*locale* ... AZ-5
Tub S Creek—*stream* ... MT-8
Tubs Lake—*lake* ... MI-6
*Tubson* ... AZ-5
Tub Spring—*spring* (3) ... AZ-5
Tub Spring—*spring* ... CA-9
Tub Spring—*spring* ... CO-8
Tub Spring—*spring* (5) ... ID-8
Tub Spring—*spring* ... MT-8
Tub Spring—*spring* (3) ... NV-8
Tub Spring—*spring* (4) ... NM-5
Tub Spring—*spring* (9) ... OR-9
Tub Spring—*spring* ... TN-4
Tub Spring—*spring* (2) ... UT-8
Tub Spring Gulch—*valley* ... NV-8
Tub Spring Rsvr—*reservoir* ... NV-8
Tub Springs—*spring* ... CA-9
Tub Springs—*spring* ... NE-7
Tub Springs—*spring* (3) ... OR-9
Tub Springs Canyon—*valley* ... OR-9
Tub Springs Drain—*canal* ... NE-7
Tub Springs Draw—*valley* ... TX-5
Tub Springs Lake—*lake* ... WA-9
Tub Springs Rsvr—*reservoir* ... OR-9
Tub Spring Wash—*stream* ... AZ-5
Tubs Run—*stream* ... PA-2
Tubs Spring—*spring* ... AZ-5
Tubs Springs—*spring* ... CO-8
Tubs Windmill, The—*locale* ... TX-5
Tub Tank—*reservoir* (2) ... TX-5
Tub Trail—*trail* ... PA-2
Tubungaluk Creek—*stream* ... AK-9
Tubutana Mine—*mine* ... AZ-5
Tubutulik River—*stream* ... AK-9
*Tubville* ... TN-4
Tubwreck Brook—*stream* ... MA-1
*Tubwuj* ... MP-9
Tucalota Creek—*stream* ... CA-9
Tucalota Hills—*range* ... CA-9
Tucalota Valley—*valley* ... CA-9
Tucannon—*locale* (2) ... WA-9
Tucannon Campground—*locale* ... WA-9
Tucannon Guard Station—*locale* ... WA-9
Tucannon River—*stream* ... WA-9
Tucannon Spring—*spring* ... WA-9
*Tucanon River* ... WA-9
*Tucanyon River* ... WA-9
*Tucapau* ... SC-3
Tuc-a-way Lake—*reservoir* ... NC-3
Tucca Creek—*stream* ... OR-9
Tucca Park—*park* ... CA-9
*Tucceluba Creek* ... MS-4
Tuccori Coulee—*valley* ... MT-8
*Tuchaleeche* ... TN-4
Tuchuck Campground—*locale* ... MT-8
Tuchuck Creek—*stream* ... MT-8
Tuchuck Mtn—*summit* ... MT-8
Tuck—*locale* ... KY-4
Tuck—*uninc pl* ... AR-4
Tuck, Mount—*summit* ... ME-1
*Tuckabatchee* ... AL-4
Tuckabatchee Ch—*church* ... OK-5
*Tuckabatchee Harjos Town* ... AL-4
Tuckabatchie (historical)—*locale* ... AL-4
Tuckabatchie Monmt—*park* ... AL-4
Tuckabum Creek—*stream* ... AL-4
Tuckabum Creek—*stream* ... MS-4
*Tuckaburne Creek* ... AL-4
Tuckahatchee (historical)—*locale* ... AL-4
*Tuckahoe* ... NJ-2
Tuckahoe—*hist pl* ... VA-3
Tuckahoe—*locale* ... NC-3
Tuckahoe—*locale* ... WV-2
**Tuckahoe**—*pop pl* ... MO-7
**Tuckahoe**—*pop pl* ... NJ-2
**Tuckahoe**—*pop pl* (2) ... NY-2
**Tuckahoe**—*pop pl* ... TN-4
**Tuckahoe**—*pop pl* ... VA-3
Tuckahoe Bay—*swamp* ... SC-3
Tuckahoe Branch—*stream* ... AL-4
Tuckahoe Branch—*stream* (2) ... NC-3
Tuckahoe Ch—*church* ... NC-3
Tuckahoe Ch—*church* ... VA-3
*Tuckahoe Church* ... TN-4
Tuckahoe Chute—*channel* ... TN-4
Tuckahoe-Corbin City Fish and Wildlife Mngmt Area—*park* ... NJ-2
*Tuckahoe Creek* ... AL-4
*Tuckahoe Creek* ... NC-3
Tuckahoe Creek—*stream* ... MD-2
Tuckahoe Creek—*stream* (2) ... NC-3
Tuckahoe Creek—*stream* ... TN-4
Tuckahoe Creek—*stream* ... VA-3
Tuckahoe Dam—*dam* ... NJ-2
Tuckahoe Golf Course—*other* ... AL-4
**Tuckahoe Heights**—*pop pl* ... AL-4
Tuckahoe HS—*school* ... NY-2
Tuckahoe HS—*school* ... VA-3
Tuckahoe Island—*island* ... VA-3
Tuckahoe Lake—*reservoir* ... NJ-2
Tuckahoe (Magisterial District)—*fmr MCD* ... VA-3
Tuckahoe Neck—*cape* ... MD-2
Tuckahoe Park—*park* ... PA-2
**Tuckahoe Park**—*pop pl* ... VA-3
Tuckahoe Point—*cape* ... NC-3
Tuckahoe Post Office (historical)—*building* ... TN-4
Tuckahoe River—*stream* ... NJ-2
Tuckahoe River Island—*island* ... NJ-2
Tuckahoe Run—*stream* ... WV-2
Tuckahoe Sch—*school* ... NY-2
Tuckahoe Sch—*school* (2) ... VA-3
Tuckahoe Shoals—*bar* ... TN-4
Tuckahoe Shop Ctr—*locale* ... VA-3
Tuckahoe Station—*hist pl* ... NJ-2
**Tuckahoe (subdivision)**—*pop pl* (2) ... NC-3
*Tuckahoe Swamp* ... NC-3
Tuckahoe Swamp—*stream* ... NC-3
**Tuckahoe Village**—*pop pl* ... VA-3
**Tuckaleecha (historical)**—*pop pl* ... TN-4
*Tuckaleeche* ... TN-4
**Tuckaleechee**—*pop pl* ... TN-4
Tuckaleechee Campground Cem—*cemetery* ... TN-4
Tuckaleechee Caverns—*cave* ... TN-4
Tuckaleechee Cem—*cemetery* ... TN-4
Tuckaleechee Chapel—*church* ... TN-4
Tuckaleechee Chapel Cem—*cemetery* ... TN-4
Tuckaleechee Cove—*valley* ... TN-4
Tuckaleechee Cove Post Office (historical)—*building* ... TN-4
*Tuckaleechee Post Office* ... TN-4
*Tuckaleechy* ... TN-4
*Tuckalubba Creek* ... MS-4
Tuckaluge Creek—*stream* ... GA-3
*Tuckanuckett Island* ... MA-1
Tuckanuck Ledge—*bar* ... ME-1
Tuckapahwox Point—*cape* ... WA-9
Tuckaseegee Elem Sch—*school* ... NC-3
*Tuckaseegee River* ... NC-3
*Tuckaseeking* ... GA-3
Tuckasee King Landing—*locale* ... GA-3
*Tuckasegee* ... NC-3
**Tuckasegee**—*pop pl* ... NC-3
Tuckasegee Dock—*locale* ... NC-3
Tuckasegee Lake—*reservoir* ... NC-3
Tuckasegee Lake Dam—*dam* ... NC-3
Tuckasegee River—*stream* ... NC-3
*Tuckaseigee River* ... NC-3
*Tuckassee King* ... GA-3
Tuckaway—*post sta* ... WI-6
Tuckaway, Lake—*reservoir* ... MS-4
Tuckaway Country Club—*other* ... WI-6
Tuckaway Lake—*lake* ... WA-9
Tuckaway Lake Dam—*dam* ... MS-4
**Tuckaway Park**—*pop pl* ... NC-3
Tuckayou Wash—*stream* ... AZ-5
Tuck Branch—*stream* ... TX-5
Tuck Canyon—*valley* ... NM-5
Tuck Cem—*cemetery* ... AL-4
Tuck Cem—*cemetery* ... GA-3
Tuck Cem—*cemetery* ... TN-4
Tuck Cem—*cemetery* ... TX-5
Tuck Creek—*stream* ... AK-9
Tuck Creek—*stream* ... WA-9
Tuck-Crockett Ditch—*canal* ... MT-8
Tuckedaway Branch—*stream* ... VA-3
Tucke Flat—*flat* ... OR-9
Tucke Lake—*flat* ... OR-9
Tucke Monmt—*park* ... NH-1
Tucken Gulch—*valley* ... MT-8
Tucke Place—*locale* ... OR-9
*Tucker* ... FL-3
*Tucker* ... IL-6
*Tucker* ... KY-4
*Tucker* ... MS-4
Tucker—*locale* ... AZ-5
Tucker—*locale* ... MO-7
Tucker—*locale* ... MT-8
Tucker—*locale* ... UT-8
**Tucker**—*pop pl* (2) ... AL-4
**Tucker**—*pop pl* ... AZ-5
**Tucker**—*pop pl* ... AR-4
**Tucker**—*pop pl* ... GA-3
**Tucker**—*pop pl* ... KY-4
**Tucker**—*pop pl* ... MS-4
**Tucker**—*pop pl* ... OK-5
**Tucker**—*pop pl* ... TX-5
Tucker, Hazael, Farm (Boundary Increase)—*hist pl* ... KY-4
Tucker, Hazael, House—*hist pl* ... KY-4
Tucker, Henry Crawford, Log House and Farmstead—*hist pl* ... GA-3
Tucker, Horace, House—*hist pl* ... WA-9
Tucker, John A., House—*hist pl* ... GA-3
Tucker, John W., House—*hist pl* ... NC-3
Tucker, Lee, House—*hist pl* ... MO-7
Tucker, Mount—*summit* ... NH-1
Tucker Bay—*bay* ... AR-4
Tucker Bayou—*stream* ... FL-3
Tucker Bayou—*stream* ... LA-4
Tucker Bayou—*stream* ... MS-4
Tucker Bayou—*stream* ... TX-5
Tucker Bay Sch (historical)—*school* ... MS-4
Tucker Bend—*bend* (2) ... TN-4
Tucker Bend (inundated)—*bend* ... AL-4
Tucker Bluff—*cliff* ... AR-4
Tucker Bluff—*cliff* ... FL-3
Tucker Bluff—*cliff* ... MS-4
Tucker Bottom—*flat* ... OK-5
Tucker Bottoms—*bend* ... KY-4
Tucker Box—*basin* ... AZ-5
Tucker Branch—*stream* (6) ... AL-4
Tucker Branch—*stream* (2) ... AR-4
Tucker Branch—*stream* (2) ... GA-3
Tucker Branch—*stream* ... KS-7
Tucker Branch—*stream* (3) ... KY-4
Tucker Branch—*stream* (2) ... MS-4
Tucker Branch—*stream* ... MO-7
Tucker Branch—*stream* (5) ... TN-4
Tucker Branch—*stream* (2) ... TX-5
Tucker Branch—*stream* ... WV-2
Tucker Branch Lake—*reservoir* ... GA-3
Tucker Branch Mtn—*summit* ... ME-1
Tucker Bridge—*bridge* ... MN-6
Tucker Bridge—*bridge* ... OR-9
Tucker Brook—*stream* (3) ... ME-1
Tucker Brook—*stream* ... MA-1
Tucker Brook—*stream* (2) ... NH-1
Tucker Brook—*stream* ... NY-2
Tucker Brook—*stream* ... RI-1
Tucker Brook—*stream* (2) ... VT-1
Tucker Butte—*summit* (2) ... CA-9
Tucker Camp—*locale* ... CA-9
*Tucker Canyon* ... CO-8
Tucker Canyon—*valley* ... AZ-5
Tucker Canyon—*valley* ... CA-9
Tucker Canyon—*valley* ... ID-8
Tucker Canyon—*valley* ... NM-5
Tucker Canyon—*valley* ... OR-9
Tucker Canyon—*valley* ... UT-8
Tucker-Capps Sch—*school* ... VA-3
Tucker Carriage House—*hist pl* ... NC-3
*Tucker Catholic Mission School* ... MS-4
Tucker (CCD)—*cens area* ... GA-3
Tucker Cem—*cemetery* (4) ... AL-4
Tucker Cem—*cemetery* (3) ... AR-4
Tucker Cem—*cemetery* ... FL-3
Tucker Cem—*cemetery* (3) ... GA-3
Tucker Cem—*cemetery* (2) ... IN-6
Tucker Cem—*cemetery* ... IA-7
Tucker Cem—*cemetery* (5) ... KY-4
Tucker Cem—*cemetery* ... LA-4
Tucker Cem—*cemetery* (2) ... MI-6
Tucker Cem—*cemetery* (4) ... MS-4
Tucker Cem—*cemetery* ... MO-7
Tucker Cem—*cemetery* ... NY-2
Tucker Cem—*cemetery* (2) ... NC-3
Tucker Cem—*cemetery* (12) ... TN-4
Tucker Cem—*cemetery* (3) ... TX-5
Tucker Cem—*cemetery* (4) ... VA-3
Tucker Cem—*cemetery* ... WV-2
Tucker Cem—*cemetery* ... WI-6
Tucker Ch—*church* ... MS-4
Tucker Ch—*church* ... MO-7
Tucker Ch—*church* ... PA-2
Tucker Coal Mine—*mine* ... UT-8
**Tucker (County)**—*pop pl* ... WV-2
Tucker County Courthouse and Jail—*hist pl* ... WV-2
Tucker Cove—*bay* ... AL-4
Tucker Cove—*bay* ... FL-3
Tucker Cove—*bay* ... OK-5
Tucker Cove—*valley* ... AL-4
Tucker Cove—*valley* ... AR-4
*Tucker Creek* ... GA-3
*Tucker Creek* ... MT-8
*Tucker Creek* ... OR-9
Tucker Creek—*stream* (2) ... AL-4
Tucker Creek—*stream* (2) ... AR-4
Tucker Creek—*stream* ... CA-9
Tucker Creek—*stream* ... FL-3
Tucker Creek—*stream* ... IN-6
Tucker Creek—*stream* (2) ... KY-4

Tucker Creek—*stream* (2) LA-4
Tucker Creek—*stream* ME-1
Tucker Creek—*stream* (2) MO-7
Tucker Creek—*stream* (4) MT-8
Tucker Creek—*stream* NE-7
Tucker Creek—*stream* (2) NC-3
Tucker Creek—*stream* (2) OK-5
Tucker Creek—*stream* (5) OR-9
Tucker Creek—*stream* (2) TN-4
Tucker Creek—*stream* TX-5
Tucker Creek—*stream* (2) WA-9
Tucker Creek—*stream* WV-2
Tucker Creek—*stream* WI-6
**Tucker Crossroads**—*pop pl* AL-4
**Tuckerdale**—*pop pl* NC-3
*Tucker Ditch* IN-6
Tucker Ditch—*canal* CO-8
Tucker Ditch—*canal* IL-6
Tucker Ditch—*canal* (2) IN-6
Tucker Drain—*stream* MI-6
Tucker Draw—*valley* CO-8
Tucker Draw—*valley* NM-5
Tucker Draw—*valley* (2) TX-5
**Tucker Estates**—*pop pl* NC-3
Tucker Farm—*locale* (2) WA-9
Tucker Farm Hist Dist—*hist pl* MA-1
**Tucker Farms (subdivision)**—*pop pl* NC-3
Tucker Ferry (historical)—*locale* TN-4
Tucker Flat—*flat* AZ-5
Tucker Flat—*flat* CA-9
Tucker Flat—*flat* OR-9
Tucker Flat Camp—*locale* OR-9
Tucker Flat Wash—*valley* AZ-5
Tucker Ford—*locale* TN-4
Tucker Fork—*stream* (3) WV-2
Tucker Gap—*gap* AL-4
Tucker Gap—*gap* KY-4
Tucker Gap—*gap* NM-5
Tucker Gap—*gap* NC-3
Tucker Gap—*gap* OR-9
Tucker Gap—*gap* TN-4
Tucker Gap—*gap* VA-3
Tucker-Garrett Cem—*cemetery* TN-4
Tucker Grove Ch—*church* AR-4
Tucker Grove Ch—*church* GA-3
Tucker Grove Society Hall—*other* GA-3
Tucker Gulch—*valley* CA-9
Tucker Gulch—*valley* (2) CO-8
Tucker Gulch—*valley* ID-8
Tucker Gulch—*valley* (5) MT-8
Tucker Hall—*building* NC-3
Tucker Hall—*school* OR-9
**Tucker Heights**—*pop pl* NY-2
Tucker Hill—*locale* PA-2
Tucker Hill—*locale* VA-3
Tucker Hill—*summit* FL-3
Tucker Hill—*summit* IL-6
Tucker Hill—*summit* MA-1
Tucker Hill—*summit* NH-1
Tucker Hill—*summit* OR-9
Tucker Hill—*summit* TX-5
Tucker Hill Cem—*cemetery* FL-3
Tucker Hill Ch—*church* KY-4
*Tucker Hill Mine* TN-4
Tucker Hill Tower—*tower* FL-3
Tucker (historical)—*locale* AL-4
**Tucker (historical)**—*pop pl* (2) OR-9
Tucker Hole Creek—*stream* NC-3
Tucker Hollow—*valley* (3) AL-4
Tucker Hollow—*valley* (2) AR-4
Tucker Hollow—*valley* IL-6
Tucker Hollow—*valley* KY-4
Tucker Hollow—*valley* MO-7
Tucker Hollow—*valley* NC-3
Tucker Hollow—*valley* OK-5
Tucker Hollow—*valley* TN-4
Tucker Hollow—*valley* TX-5
Tucker Hollow—*valley* UT-8
Tucker Hollow—*valley* (2) VA-3
Tucker Hollow—*valley* WV-2
Tucker Hollow—*valley* WI-6
Tucker Hollow Rec Area—*park* AR-4
Tucker House and Myers House—*hist pl* DC-2
Tucker HS—*school* VA-3
Tucker Indian Sch—*school* MS-4
Tucker Island—*cape* NJ-2
Tucker Jones Drain—*stream* MI-6
Tucker Knob—*summit* IL-6
Tucker Knob—*summit* OK-5
Tucker Knob—*summit* (2) TN-4
Tucker Knob—*summit* TX-5
*Tucker Lake* MO-7
Tucker Lake—*lake* (2) FL-3
Tucker Lake—*lake* KY-4
Tucker Lake—*lake* (5) MI-6
Tucker Lake—*lake* (2) MN-6
Tucker Lake—*lake* (2) MS-4
Tucker Lake—*lake* OK-5
Tucker Lake—*lake* WA-9
Tucker Lake—*lake* (3) WI-6
Tucker Lake—*reservoir* CO-8
Tucker Lake—*reservoir* IN-6
Tucker Lake—*reservoir* OK-5
Tucker Lake—*reservoir* TX-5
Tucker (Magisterial District)—*fmr MCD* WV-2
**Tuckerman**—*pop pl* AR-4
Tuckerman, William F., House—*hist pl* MA-1
Tuckerman Ditch—*canal* AR-4
Tuckerman Ravine—*valley* NH-1
Tucker Mesa—*summit* AZ-5
Tucker Mill Bridge—*bridge* VA-3
*Tucker Mine* TN-4
Tucker Mine—*mine* TN-4
Tucker Mine (underground)—*mine* (2) AL-4
Tucker Mtn—*summit* (2) AR-4
Tucker Mtn—*summit* (2) CA-9
Tucker Mtn—*summit* CO-8
Tucker Mtn—*summit* ME-1
Tucker Mtn—*summit* NH-1
Tucker Mtn—*summit* VT-1
*Tuckernuc Island* MA-1
Tuckernuck Bank—*bar* MA-1
Tuckernuck Island—*island* MA-1
Tuckernuck Island South East Light—*locale* MA-1
Tuckernuck Shoal—*bar* MA-1
Tucker Oil Field—*oilfield* TX-5
Tucker Park—*flat* CO-8
Tucker Park—*park* IA-7
Tucker Park—*park* MI-6
Tucker Pasture—*flat* KS-7
Tucker Peak—*summit* UT-8
**Tucker Place (subdivision)**—*pop pl* MS-4
Tucker Plantation—*locale* AR-4
Tucker Point—*cape* MI-6
Tucker Point—*cape* UT-8
Tucker Pond—*lake* CT-1
Tucker Pond—*lake* (2) FL-3
Tucker Pond—*lake* MA-1
Tucker Pond—*lake* NH-1
Tucker Pond—*lake* RI-1
Tucker Pond—*reservoir* MA-1
Tucker Pond (historical)—*lake* TN-4
Tucker Prairie—*flat* WA-9
Tucker Prison Farm—*other* AR-4
Tucker Ranch—*locale* NV-8
Tucker Ranch—*locale* (2) NM-5
Tucker Ranch (Abandoned)—*locale* NM-5
*Tucker Ridge* AL-4
*Tucker Ridge* GA-3
Tucker Ridge—*ridge* AL-4
Tucker Ridge—*ridge* (2) AR-4
Tucker Ridge—*ridge* CA-9
Tucker Ridge—*ridge* (3) KY-4
Tucker Ridge—*ridge* ME-1
Tucker Ridge—*ridge* MS-4
Tucker Ridge—*ridge* TN-4
Tucker Ridge—*ridge* WV-2
Tucker Ridge Ch—*church* TN-4
*Tucker River* MT-8
Tucker River—*stream* MN-6
Tucker RR Station—*building* AZ-5
Tucker Rsvr—*reservoir* CO-8
*Tucker Run* PA-2
Tucker Run—*stream* IN-6
Tucker Run—*stream* (2) OH-6
Tucker Run—*stream* PA-2
Tucker Run—*stream* (2) WV-2
*Tuckers* MS-4
Tuckers—*locale* AK-9
**Tuckers**—*pop pl* MS-4
*Tuckers Beach* MA-1
Tuckers Branch—*stream* KY-4
Tuckers Branch—*stream* MD-2
Tuckers Branch—*stream* TX-5
Tuckersburg—*locale* AL-4
Tucker Sch—*hist pl* OK-5
Tucker Sch—*school* CA-9
Tucker Sch—*school* GA-3
Tucker Sch—*school* LA-4
Tucker Sch—*school* MA-1
Tucker Sch—*school* (2) NE-7
Tucker Sch—*school* VA-3
Tucker Sch—*school* WI-6
Tucker Sch (abandoned)—*school* MO-7
*Tuckers Chapel* TN-4
Tuckers Chapel—*church* AL-4
Tuckers Chapel Cem—*cemetery* AL-4
Tuckers Chapel Methodist Ch (historical)—*church* TN-4
Tuckers Chapel Sch (historical)—*school* TN-4
Tucker Sch (historical)—*school* AL-4
Tucker Sch (historical)—*school* MO-7
Tucker Sch (historical)—*school* TN-4
Tuckers Corner—*locale* FL-3
Tuckers Corner—*locale* TX-5
**Tuckers Corner**—*pop pl* MO-7
**Tuckers Corner**—*pop pl* NY-2
**Tuckers Corner**—*pop pl* TN-4
Tuckers Corners—*locale* IL-6
Tuckers Creek—*stream* NC-3
Tuckers Crossing—*locale* MS-4
**Tuckers Crossing**—*pop pl* MS-4
Tuckers Crossing Baptist Ch—*church* MS-4
Tuckers Crossroad—*locale* GA-3
**Tuckers Crossroads**—*pop pl* TN-4
Tuckers Crossroads Elem Sch—*school* TN-4
Tuckers Cross Roads Post Office (historical)—*building* TN-4
Tuckers Fish Camp—*locale* AK-9
Tuckers Flat—*flat* GA-3
**Tuckers Gap (historical)**—*pop pl* TN-4
Tuckers Gap Post Office (historical)—*building* TN-4
Tuckers Grove Campground—*locale* NC-3
Tucker's Grove Camp Meeting Ground—*hist pl* NC-3
Tuckers Grove Ch—*church* NC-3
Tuckers Grove County Park—*park* CA-9
Tucker Siding—*locale* AZ-5
*Tuckers Island* NJ-2
Tucker Site (41NU46)—*hist pl* TX-5
Tuckers Lake—*lake* TX-5
Tucker Slough—*stream* OR-9
Tuckers Mill (historical)—*locale* MS-4
*Tuckers Mill Point* VA-3
Tucker Smith Township (historical)—*civil* SD-7
Tuckers Pocosin—*swamp* VA-3
*Tuckers Pond* RI-1
Tuckers Pond—*reservoir* AL-4
Tuckers Pond—*reservoir* MA-1
*Tucker Spring* OR-9
Tucker Spring—*spring* (2) AZ-5
Tucker Spring—*spring* MT-8
Tucker Spring—*spring* (3) OR-9
Tucker Spring—*spring* UT-8
Tucker Spring Hollow—*valley* AL-4
**Tucker Springs**—*pop pl* TN-4
Tucker Springs Post Office (historical)—*building* TN-4
Tuckers Ridge—*ridge* KY-4
Tuckers Ridge—*ridge* NM-5
Tuckers Run—*stream* PA-2
*Tuckers School* TN-4
Tuckers Slough—*gut* AK-9
Tuckers Store—*locale* TN-4
Tucker State Prison—*other* AR-4
Tucker Station—*locale* KY-4
Tuckers Temple Ch—*church* KY-4
Tucker Store (historical)—*locale* TN-4
Tuckersville Cem—*cemetery* MS-4
Tuckersville Ch—*church* MS-4
Tuckersville Post Office (historical)—*building* TN-4
Tucker Swamp—*stream* VA-3
Tucker Swamp Ch—*church* VA-3
Tucker Tank—*reservoir* AZ-5
Tucker Tank—*reservoir* NM-5
Tucker Temple—*church* TN-4
**Tucker Terrace**—*pop pl* NY-2
*Tuckerton* FL-3
Tuckerton—*locale* PA-2
**Tuckerton**—*pop pl* NJ-2
Tuckerton Bay—*bay* NJ-2
Tuckerton Cove—*bay* NJ-2
*Tuckerton Creek* NJ-2
Tuckerton Creek—*stream* NJ-2
Tucker Tower—*pillar* OK-5
*Tucker Town* SC-3
Tuckertown—*locale* KY-4
Tuckertown—*locale* NC-3
**Tuckertown**—*pop pl* AR-4
**Tuckertown**—*pop pl* NC-3
**Tuckertown**—*pop pl* PA-2
**Tuckertown**—*pop pl* RI-1
**Tuckertown**—*pop pl* SC-3
Tuckertown Dam—*dam* NC-3
**Tuckertown Four Corners**—*pop pl* RI-1
Tuckertown Lake—*reservoir* NC-3
Tuckertown Lake Dam—*dam* NC-3
Tuckertown Rsvr—*reservoir* NC-3
Tuckertown Sch—*school* WI-6
Tucker Valley Brook—*stream* ME-1
Tuckerville—*locale* CO-8
Tuckerway Ranch—*locale* CA-9
Tucker Well—*well* TX-5
Tucker Windmill—*locale* TX-5
*Tucket Canyon* AZ-5
Tuckett Lake—*lake* MI-6
Tucke Windmill—*locale* NM-5
Tuckey Drain—*canal* MI-6
Tuckey Sch—*school* MA-1
Tuck Fork—*locale* VA-3
Tucki Mtn—*summit* CA-9
Tucki Wash—*stream* CA-9
*Tucklahoma* MS-4
Tuck Lake—*lake* WA-9
Tuck Lateral—*canal* CO-8
Tuckleberry Branch—*stream* NC-3
Tuckler Creek—*stream* IA-7
Tuck Point—*cape* MA-1
Tuck Point—*cape* RI-1
Tuck Rsvr—*reservoir* OR-9
Tucks Chapel—*church* AR-4
Tucksel Point—*cape* WA-9
*Tucks Island* CT-1
*Tucks Point* MA-1
Tucks Point—*cape* MA-1
*Tuck's Pond* CT-1
Tucks Pot—*lake* WA-9
Tuck Spring—*spring* OR-9
Tuckston Ch—*church* GA-3
Tuckta Trail—*trail* OR-9
**Tucktown**—*pop pl* AL-4
Tuckup Canyon—*valley* AZ-5
Tuckup Point—*cliff* AZ-5
Tuckup Rocky Point—*cliff* AZ-5
Tuckup Trail—*trail* AZ-5
Tuckway Lake—*lake* WA-9
Tuckwiller Tavern—*hist pl* WV-2
Tucky Hammock—*island* LA-4
*Tucky Lake* OR-9
Tucky Run—*stream* OH-6
**Tuco**—*pop pl* TX-5
Tucquala Lake—*lake* WA-9
Tucquan Creek—*stream* PA-2
Tucson—*locale* OH-6
**Tucson**—*pop pl* AZ-5
Tucson Botanical Garden—*park* AZ-5
Tucson (CCD)—*cens area* AZ-5
Tucson Community Center—*park* AZ-5
Tucson Community Sch—*school* AZ-5
Tucson Compressor Station—*locale* AZ-5
**Tucson Country Club Estates**—*pop pl* AZ-5
Tucson Country Day Sch—*school* AZ-5
**Tucson Estates**—*pop pl* AZ-5
Tucson Estates Shop Ctr—*locale* AZ-5
Tucson General Hosp—*hospital* AZ-5
*Tucson Hill* AZ-5
Tucson Hollow—*valley* UT-8
Tucson HS—*school* AZ-5
*Tucsonimon* AZ-5
Tucson International Airp—*airport* AZ-5
Tucson Mall—*locale* AZ-5
Tucson Med Ctr—*hospital* AZ-5
Tucson Med Ctr Heliport—*airport* AZ-5
Tucson Mine—*mine* CO-8
Tucson Mountain County Park—*park* AZ-5
Tucson Mountains—*range* AZ-5
Tucson Mountain Trail (Pack)—*trail* NM-5
Tucson Mountain Wildlife Area—*park* AZ-5
**Tucson Natl Estates**—*pop pl* AZ-5
Tucson Natl Golf Course—*other* AZ-5
Tucson Sports Center—*building* AZ-5
Tucson Trap and Skeet Club—*other* AZ-5
Tucson Veterans Hosp—*hospital* AZ-5
Tucson Wash—*stream* AZ-5
*Tucsson* AZ-5
*Tucubits Mountains* NV-8
**Tucumcari**—*pop pl* NM-5
Tucumcari (CCD)—*cens area* NM-5
Tucumcari Lake—*lake* NM-5
Tucumcari Lateral—*canal* NM-5
Tucumcari Memorial Park (Cemetery)—*cemetery* NM-5
Tucumcari Metropolitan Park—*park* NM-5
Tucumcari Mtn—*summit* NM-5
Tucupit Point—*cape* UT-8
*Tuczon* AZ-5
Tudecoz Spring—*spring* AZ-5
Tudek Site—*hist pl* PA-2
Tudor—*locale* CA-9
**Tudor**—*pop pl* IN-6
Tudor—*uninc pl* NY-2
Tudor Bluff—*cliff* KY-4
Tudor Branch—*stream* GA-3
Tudor Canyon—*valley* (2) OR-9
Tudor Cem—*cemetery* TN-4
Tudor Cem—*cemetery* TX-5
Tudor City Hist Dist—*hist pl* NY-2
Tudor Ditch—*canal* OH-6
Tudor Ditch—*canal* OR-9
Tudor Draw—*valley* WY-8
Tudor Hall—*hist pl* (3) MD-2
Tudor Hall (Boundary Decrease)—*hist pl* MD-2
*Tudor Hall School* IN-6
*Tudor Haven* MA-1
Tudor Hill—*summit* CT-1
Tudor Hollow—*valley* TN-4
Tudor House—*hist pl* VT-1
Tudor Lake—*lake* OR-9
Tudor Manor—*hist pl* IL-6
Tudor Place—*hist pl* DC-2
Tudor Warm Springs—*spring* OR-9
Tudy Creek—*stream* NC-3
Tudy Hollow—*valley* KY-4
Tuecke Hollow—*valley* IA-7
Tueeulala Falls—*falls* CA-9
Tuefer Lake—*lake* MN-6
Tuell Cem—*cemetery* ME-1
Tueller, Jacob, Jr., House—*hist pl* ID-8
Tueller, Jacob, Sr., House—*hist pl* ID-8
Tue Marshes Lighthouse—*locale* VA-3
Tu-Endie-Wei State Park—*park* WV-2
Tue Point—*cape* VA-3
Tuers Park—*park* NJ-2
Tuerto Canyon—*valley* UT-8
Tuerto Spring—*spring* NM-5
Tuerto Windmill—*locale* TX-5
Tuesday Gulch—*valley* OR-9
*Tuesday Island* FM-9
Tuesday Lake—*lake* MI-6
Tuesday Rsvr—*reservoir* OR-9
Tueverson Coulee—*valley* MT-8
Tuey Lake—*swamp* MN-6
*Tufa* MP-9
Tufa Falls—*falls* CA-9
Tufa Island—*island* MP-9
Tufa Stone Dam—*dam* AZ-5
Tufa Stone Tank—*reservoir* AZ-5
Tuff—*locale* TX-5
Tuff Canyon—*valley* TX-5
Tuff Coulee—*valley* WI-6
Tuff Draw—*valley* MT-8
*Tuffed Creek* WY-8
Tuffet Tank—*reservoir* AZ-5
Tuffield Creek—*stream* WY-8
Tuffield Willey Brook—*stream* VT-1
Tuffly Park—*park* TX-5
Tufford Sch—*school* NE-7
Tuffs Island—*island* NY-2
Tuff Tank—*reservoir* AZ-5
*Tuffts Brook* MA-1
Tuffy Creek—*stream* (2) OR-9
Tuffys Lake—*lake* MT-8
Tuffy Springs—*spring* NV-8
*Tuft Brook* MA-1
Tuft Creek—*stream* CA-9
Tuft Draw—*valley* UT-8
Tufte Dam—*dam* SD-7
**Tuft (historical)**—*pop pl* OR-9
Tufti Creek—*stream* OR-9
Tufti Mtn—*summit* OR-9
**Tuftonboro**—*pop pl* NH-1
*Tuftonboro Bay* NH-1
Tuftonboro Neck—*cape* NH-1
**Tuftonboro (Town of)**—*pop pl* NH-1
*Tufton Branch* VA-3
Tuft Rock—*island* AK-9
Tuft Rsvr—*reservoir* UT-8
Tufts, Joshua B., House—*hist pl* CA-9
Tufts, Peter, House—*hist pl* MA-1
Tufts Branch—*stream* CT-1
Tufts Branch—*stream* MA-1
*Tufts Brook* MA-1
Tufts Brook—*stream* MA-1
Tufts Brook—*stream* NH-1
Tufts College (RR name for Tufts University)—*other* MA-1
*Tufts Creek* UT-8
Tufts Creek—*stream* UT-8
*Tuft'S Hill* MA-1
Tufts Hill—*summit* MA-1
Tufts House—*hist pl* ME-1
Tufts Mtn—*summit* NH-1
Tufts Park—*park* MA-1
Tufts Point—*cape* NJ-2
Tufts Pond—*lake* ME-1
Tufts Pond—*lake* NH-1
Tufts Pond Brook—*stream* ME-1
Tufts Sch—*school* MA-1
Tufts Univ—*school* MA-1
Tufts University (RR name Tufts College)—*uninc pl* MA-1
**Tufts Village (historical)**—*pop pl* MA-1
Tufu Point—*cape* AS-9
Tufu Stream—*stream* AS-9
Tufveson House—*hist pl* ND-7
Tug, Mount—*summit* (4) NH-1
Tug, Mount—*summit* VT-1
Tugak Lagoon—*lake* AK-9
Tugak Peak—*summit* AK-9
*Tugalo* GA-3
**Tugalo**—*pop pl* GA-3
Tugalo Ch—*church* GA-3
*Tugalo Lake* GA-3
*Tugaloo* MS-4
Tugaloo—*locale* GA-3
Tugaloo Ch—*church* (2) SC-3
Tugaloo Creek—*stream* SC-3
Tugaloo Lake—*reservoir* GA-3
Tugaloo Lake—*reservoir* SC-3
Tugaloo River—*stream* GA-3
Tugaloo River—*stream* SC-3
*Tugalo River* GA-3
Tugamak Range—*other* AK-9
Tug Branch—*stream* KY-4
Tug Creek—*stream* KY-4
Tug Creek—*stream* WV-2
*Tugels Branch* AL-4
*Tugers Creek* VA-3
Tug Fork—*stream* KY-4
Tug Fork—*stream* NC-3
Tug Fork—*stream* VA-3
Tug Fork—*stream* (4) WV-2
Tug Fork Big Indian Creek—*stream* (2) IA-7
*Tug Fork River* KY-4
*Tug Fork River* VA-3
*Tug Fork River* WV-2
Tuggle—*locale* VA-3
Tuggle Bend—*bend* AL-4
Tuggle Branch—*stream* GA-3
Tuggle Branch—*stream* KS-7
Tuggle Branch—*stream* TX-5
Tuggle Cem—*cemetery* (3) KY-4
Tuggle Cem—*cemetery* TN-4
Tuggle Cem—*cemetery* VA-3
Tuggle Creek—*stream* (2) GA-3
Tuggle Creek—*stream* KY-4
Tuggle Creek—*stream* VA-3
Tuggle Fork—*stream* KY-4
Tuggle Gap—*gap* VA-3
Tuggle Hollow—*valley* KY-4
Tuggle Hollow—*valley* TN-4
Tuggle Hollow—*valley* WV-2
*Tuggles Bend* AL-4
Tuggle Sch—*school* AL-4
Tuggle Spring—*spring* TN-4
Tuggle Springs Cem—*cemetery* TX-5
Tuggles Sink—*basin* GA-3
Tuggleville—*locale* KY-4
Tug Hill—*summit* (4) NY-2
Tug Hill Cem—*cemetery* NY-2
*Tug Hill Plateau* NY-2
Tug Hollow—*locale* RI-1
Tug Hollow—*valley* WI-6
Tug Hollow Sch—*school* WI-6
*Tugibaxtchi* AL-4
Tugidak Island—*island* AK-9
Tugidak Passage—*channel* AK-9
Tug Lake—*lake* WI-6
Tugler Creek—*stream* KY-4
*Tuglup* FM-9
Tugman Mtn—*summit* NC-3
Tugman State Park—*park* OR-9
Tug Mtn—*summit* ME-1
Tug Mtn—*summit* NH-1
Tug Mtn—*summit* VT-1
Tug-Of-War Historical Marker—*park* AZ-5
Tug River (Magisterial District)—*fmr MCD* WV-2
*Tugson* AZ-5
**Tugtown**—*pop pl* SC-3
*Tugua Creek* KS-7
*Tuguczap* FM-9
Tugue Creek—*stream* MO-7
*Tuguison* AZ-5
Tugwell—*locale* NC-3
**Tugwell**—*pop pl* AR-4
**Tugwell (historical)**—*pop pl* NC-3
Tuhare Lakes—*lake* CO-8
Tuhavi Park—*park* AZ-5
Tuhey Park—*park* IN-6
Tuhkapw—*unknown* FM-9
Tuholke Cem—*cemetery* ND-7
Tuigaava Ridge—*ridge* AS-9
Tuila Island—*island* FM-9
*Tuilla* UT-8
*Tuison* AZ-5
*Tuity Brook* MA-1
Tujunga—*civil* CA-9
**Tujunga**—*pop pl* CA-9
*Tujunga Canyon* CA-9
*Tujunga Creek* CA-9
Tujunga Valley—*valley* CA-9
Tujunga Wash—*stream* CA-9
Tukabatchee Camp—*locale* AL-4
*Tukabatchi* AL-4
Tukallah Lake—*lake* AK-9
*Tukanon River* WA-9
**Tuke**—*pop pl* WA-9
T U Kelly Number 1 Dam—*dam* AL-4
T U Kelly Number 2 Dam—*dam* AL-4
Tuker—*summit* PW-9
**Tukertown**—*pop pl* AR-4
Tukesbury Branch—*stream* MD-2
Tukes Mtn—*summit* WA-9
**Tukey**—*pop pl* WA-9
Tukey Bridge—*bridge* ME-1
**Tukeys**—*pop pl* WA-9
Tukgahgo Mtn—*summit* AK-9
Tukingarok Creek—*stream* AK-9
*Tukipahtchi* AL-4
*Tukipaxtchi* AL-4
Tuklo Creek—*stream* OK-5
Tuklomarak Lake—*lake* AK-9
Tuklung—*locale* AK-9
Tuklung River—*stream* AK-9
Tukmakna Creek—*stream* AK-9
*Tukomat-Durchfahrt* FM-9
*Tukomat Pass* FM-9
*Tukonick* MA-1
Tukpahlearik Creek—*stream* AK-9
Tukrok River—*stream* AK-9
Tuksuk Channel—*stream* AK-9
Tuktu Bluff—*cliff* AK-9
Tukuhnikivatz, Mount—*summit* UT-8
Tukukapak—*locale* AK-9
Tukunsru—*locale* FM-9
Tukunsru, Molsron—*harbor* FM-9
Tukuto Creek—*stream* AK-9
Tukuto Lake—*lake* AK-9
**Tukwila**—*pop pl* WA-9
Tukwila Operations Center Heliport—*airport* WA-9
Tukwila Sch—*hist pl* WA-9
Tula—*locale* MI-6
**Tula**—*pop pl* MI-6
**Tula**—*pop pl* MS-4
**Tula**—*pop pl* AS-9
Tulaby Creek—*stream* MN-6
Tulaby Lake—*lake* MN-6
Tulaby Lookout Tower—*locale* MN-6
Tula Cem—*cemetery* MS-4
Tula Creek—*stream* MI-6
Tulagalla Sch (historical)—*school* TN-4
Tulagamatuu Rock—*island* AS-9
Tulageak Point—*cape* AK-9
Tulahteka—*hist pl* TX-5
Tulainyo Lake—*lake* CA-9
Tula Lake—*lake* MS-4
Tula Lake—*lake* WI-6
**Tulalip**—*pop pl* WA-9
Tulalip Bay—*bay* WA-9
Tulalip (CCD)—*cens area* WA-9
Tulalip Creek—*stream* WA-9
Tulalip Indian Agency Office—*hist pl* WA-9
**Tulalip Ind Res**—*pop pl* WA-9
Tulalip Shores—*beach* WA-9
**Tulalip Shores**—*pop pl* WA-9
**Tulalip (sta.)**—*pop pl* WA-9
Tulalip Storage Depot (Military Reservation)—*military* WA-9
Tulana Farms—*locale* OR-9
*Tulandic Stream* ME-1
Tulane—*locale* TX-5
**Tulane**—*pop pl* FL-3
Tulane, Lake—*lake* FL-3
Tulane Bldg—*hist pl* AL-4
*Tulane Ferry* AL-4
Tulane Stadium (Sugar Bowl)—*building* LA-4
*Tulanesville* AL-4
Tulane Univ—*school* LA-4
Tulane Univ of Louisiana—*hist pl* LA-4
Tulane Univ Research Center—*school* LA-4
Tulane Univ Research Laboratories—*school* LA-4
Tula Normal Coll (historical)—*school* MS-4
*Tulapai Creek* AZ-5
Tulapai Creek—*stream* AZ-5
Tularcitos Creek—*stream* (2) CA-9
Tularcitos Guard Station—*locale* CA-9
Tularcitos (Higuera)—*civil* CA-9
Tularcitos Ranch—*locale* CA-9
Tularcitos Ridge—*ridge* CA-9
Tularcitos Sch—*school* CA-9
**Tulare**—*pop pl* CA-9
**Tulare**—*pop pl* SD-7
**Tulare Beach**—*pop pl* WA-9
Tulare Canal—*canal* (2) CA-9
Tulare (CCD)—*cens area* CA-9
Tulare Cem—*cemetery* CA-9
Tulare Cem—*cemetery* SD-7
Tulare Colony Ditch—*canal* CA-9
**Tulare (County)**—*pop pl* CA-9
Tulare County Farm Labor Supply Center—*other* CA-9
Tulare Dolomite Quarry—*mine* WA-9
Tulare Duck Club—*other* CA-9
Tulare East—*CDP* CA-9
Tulare Gun Club—*other* CA-9
Tulare Hill—*summit* CA-9
Tulare Irrigation Canal—*canal* CA-9
Tulare Irrigation District Canal—*canal* CA-9
*Tulare Lake* CA-9
Tulare Lake Bed—*flat* CA-9
Tulare Lake Canal—*canal* CA-9
Tulare Northwest—*CDP* CA-9
Tulare Peak—*summit* CA-9
**Tulare Township**—*pop pl* SD-7
Tulare Western HS—*school* CA-9
**Tularosa**—*pop pl* NM-5
Tularosa Canyon—*valley* (2) NM-5
Tularosa (CCD)—*cens area* NM-5
Tularosa Cem—*cemetery* MS-4
Tula Rosa Ch—*church* MS-4
Tularosa Creek—*stream* NM-5
Tularosa Mountains—*other* NM-5
Tularosa Mtn—*summit* NM-5
Tularosa Original Townsite District—*hist pl* NM-5
Tularosa Peak—*summit* NM-5
Tularosa Range Camp—*locale* NM-5
*Tularosa River* NM-5
Tularosa River—*stream* NM-5
Tularosa Spring—*spring* NM-5
Tularosa Tank—*reservoir* NM-5
Tularosa Valley—*area* NM-5
*Tula Rose Ch* MS-4
Tulasco—*locale* NV-8
*Tula Tulia* CA-9
*Tula Tulia* NV-8
Tula Windmill—*locale* TX-5
Tulcan Slough—*bay* AK-9
*Tulclier Creek* UT-8
Tule—*locale* NV-8
Tule, Mount—*summit* CA-9
Tulebagh Lake—*lake* AK-9
Tule Basin—*basin* AZ-5
Tule Bay—*bay* ID-8
Tule Belle Club—*other* CA-9
Tule Bend—*bend* TX-5
Tule Butte—*summit* AZ-5
Tule Butte—*summit* WY-8
Tule Canal—*canal* (3) CA-9
*Tule Canyon* AZ-5
*Tule Canyon* WA-9
Tule Canyon—*valley* (6) AZ-5
Tule Canyon—*valley* (4) CA-9
Tule Canyon—*valley* (2) NV-8
Tule Canyon—*valley* WA-9
Tule Canyon Tank—*reservoir* AZ-5
*Tule Creek* CA-9
*Tule Creek* NV-8
*Tule Creek* NM-5
Tule Creek—*stream* (2) AZ-5
Tule Creek—*stream* (4) CA-9
Tule Creek—*stream* MT-8
Tule Creek—*stream* TX-5
Tule Creek—*stream* WA-9
Tuledad Canyon—*valley* CA-9
Tuledad Creek—*stream* NV-8
Tuledad Valley—*valley* CA-9
Tule Dam Spring—*spring* NV-8
Tule Desert—*flat* NV-8
Tule Desert—*plain* AZ-5
Tule Desert Rsvr—*reservoir* NV-8
Tule Desert Well—*well* NV-8
Tule Divide Trail—*trail* CA-9
Tule Elk Res State Park—*park* CA-9
Tule Field Rsvr—*reservoir* NV-8
Tule Glade—*flat* CA-9
Tule Goose Gun Club—*other* CA-9
Tule Gulch—*valley* CA-9
Tule Gulch—*valley* MT-8
**Tule (historical)**—*pop pl* OR-9
Tule Island—*island* (2) CA-9
Tule Island—*island* ID-8
*Tule Lake* WA-9
Tule Lake—*lake* AZ-5
Tule Lake—*lake* (7) CA-9
Tule Lake—*lake* (2) ID-8
Tule Lake—*lake* (2) NM-5
Tule Lake—*lake* (3) OR-9
Tule Lake—*lake* (2) TX-5
Tule Lake—*lake* (5) WA-9
**Tulelake**—*pop pl* CA-9
Tule Lake—*reservoir* (2) CA-9
Tule Lake—*reservoir* ID-8
Tule Lake—*reservoir* MT-8
Tule Lake—*reservoir* NV-8
Tule Lake—*reservoir* NM-5
Tule Lake—*reservoir* TX-5
Tule Lake Bed—*flat* TX-5
Tule Lake (CCD)—*cens area* (2) CA-9
Tule Lake Channel—*channel* TX-5
Tule Lake Landing—*locale* NV-8
Tule Lake Natl Wildlife Ref—*park* CA-9
Tule Lakes—*lake* UT-8
*Tule Lake Sump* CA-9

*Tule Lake (Tulelake)* CA-9
**Tulelake (Tule Lake)**—*pop pl* CA-9
Tulelake Tunnel—*tunnel* CA-9
Tule Lake Turning Basin—*harbor* TX-5
Tule Lake Valley—*valley* OR-9
Tule Marsh—*swamp* NV-8
Tule Meadow—*flat* (2) CA-9
Tule Mesa—*summit* AZ-5
*Tule Mountains* AZ-5
Tule Mountains—*range* AZ-5
Tule Mountain Tank—*reservoir* AZ-5
Tule Mtn—*summit* CA-9
Tule Mtn—*summit* TX-5
Tule Patch Spring—*spring* CA-9
Tule Peak—*summit* CA-9
Tule Peak—*summit* NV-8
*Tulepehauken Creek* NJ-2
Tule Pens—*locale* TX-5
Tule Pond—*lake* CA-9
Tule Pond—*lake* OR-9
Tule Pond—*lake* WA-9
Tule Pond—*reservoir* CA-9
Tule Prong—*valley* WA-9
Tule Ranch—*locale* (2) NV-8
Tule Ranch—*locale* TX-5
Tule Ridge—*ridge* CA-9
Tule Ridge—*ridge* NV-8
Tule River—*stream* (2) CA-9
**Tule River Ind Res**—*pop pl* CA-9
Tules, The—*summit* ID-8
Tules Creek—*stream* KY-4
Tule Slough—*stream* CA-9
*Tule Spring* CA-9
Tule Spring—*spring* (6) AZ-5
Tule Spring—*spring* (6) CA-9
Tule Spring—*spring* (4) NV-8
Tule Spring—*spring* (2) OR-9
Tule Spring—*spring* TX-5
Tule Spring—*spring* UT-8
Tule Springs—*spring* (3) AZ-5
Tule Springs—*spring* CA-9
Tule Springs Archeol Site—*hist pl* NV-8
Tule Springs Hills—*summit* NV-8
Tule Springs Park—*park* NV-8
Tule Springs Ranch—*hist pl* NV-8
Tule Springs Ranch—*locale* AZ-5
Tule Springs Rims—*cliff* OR-9
Tules Run—*stream* PA-2
Tule Summit—*gap* NV-8
Tule Swamp—*swamp* OR-9
**Tuleta**—*pop pl* TX-5
**Tuleta Hills**—*pop pl* WI-6
*Tule Tank* AZ-5
Tule Tank—*reservoir* (10) AZ-5
Tule Tank Wash—*stream* AZ-5
*Tule Tub* AZ-5
Tule Tubs—*locale* AZ-5
Tule Valley—*valley* CA-9
Tule Valley—*valley* MT-8
Tule Valley—*valley* NV-8
Tule Valley—*valley* UT-8
Tule Vista Sch—*school* CA-9
Tule Wash—*arroyo* AZ-5
Tule Wash—*stream* AZ-5
Tule Wash—*stream* CA-9
*Tule Well* AZ-5
Tule Well—*well* AZ-5
Tule Wells—*well* AZ-5
Tule Wells Canyon—*valley* AZ-5
Tule Wells Draw—*valley* AZ-5
Tule Windmill—*locale* (3) TX-5
Tuley Canyon—*valley* CA-9
Tuley Cem—*cemetery* TN-4
Tuley Hill—*summit* TN-4
Tuley Hollow—*valley* MO-7
Tuley HS—*school* IL-6
Tuley Park—*park* IL-6
Tuleyries, The—*hist pl* VA-3
**Tulia**—*pop pl* TX-5
Tulia (CCD)—*cens area* TX-5
*Tulifinny River* SC-3
Tulifiny River—*stream* SC-3
Tulik Volcano—*summit* AK-9
Tulilik, Lake—*lake* AK-9
Tulimanik Island—*island* AK-9
**Tulin (historical)**—*pop pl* NC-3
Tulip—*locale* AR-4
Tulip—*locale* LA-4
Tulip—*locale* MO-7
Tulip—*locale* OH-6
Tulip—*locale* TX-5
**Tulip**—*pop pl* IN-6
**Tulip**—*pop pl* VA-3
Tulip Branch—*stream* TN-4
Tulip Cem—*cemetery* LA-4
Tulip Cemetery—*hist pl* AR-4
Tulip Ch—*church* IN-6
*Tulip Creek* AR-4
*Tulip Creek* OK-5
Tulip Creek—*stream* (2) AR-4
Tulip Creek—*stream* MS-4
*Tulipehaukin Creek* NJ-2
Tulip Grove—*hist pl* TN-4
Tulip Grove Sch—*school* MD-2
Tulip Hill—*hist pl* MD-2
**Tulip Hill**—*pop pl* (2) MD-2
Tulip Methodist Church—*hist pl* LA-4
*Tulip Point* AZ-5
Tulips—*locale* WA-9
*Tulip Sch* TN-4
Tulissus Branch—*stream* WV-2
Tulita Sch—*school* CA-9
Tulitos Windmill—*locale* TX-5
Tuliumnit Point—*cape* AK-9
Tulker—*locale* WA-9
Tulk Oil Field—*other* NM-5
**Tull**—*pop pl* AR-4
Tulla—*locale* LA-4
**Tullahassee**—*pop pl* OK-5
Tullahassee Loop Rec Area—*park* OK-5
Tullahassee Mission Site—*hist pl* OK-5
*Tullahoma* MS-4
**Tullahoma**—*pop pl* TN-4
Tullahoma, Lake—*reservoir* TN-4
Tullahoma (CCD)—*cens area* TN-4
Tullahoma City Hall—*building* TN-4
Tullahoma Coll (historical)—*school* TN-4
Tullahoma Division—*civil* TN-4
Tullahoma First Baptist Ch—*church* TN-4
Tullahoma First United Methodist Ch—*church* TN-4
Tullahoma First United Presbyterian Ch—*church* TN-4
Tullahoma Golf And Country Club—*locale* TN-4
Tullahoma HS—*school* TN-4
Tullahoma Municipal Airport; Soesbe-Martin Field—*airport* TN-4
Tullahoma Plaza Shop Ctr—*locale* TN-4
Tullahoma Post Office—*building* TN-4
Tullahoma Public Sch (historical)—*school* TN-4
*Tullahoma United Lutheran Church* TN-4
*Tullamore* IL-6
Tullamore Lake—*swamp* MI-6
Tullamore Playground—*park* NY-2
*Tullapa Creek* MS-4
Tull Bay—*bay* NC-3
Tull Branch—*stream* MD-2
Tull Brook—*stream* MA-1
Tull Cem—*cemetery* IL-6
Tull Creek—*stream* KY-4
Tull Creek—*stream* NC-3
Tull Creek—*stream* TN-4
Tull Crest Lake—*reservoir* OK-5
Tulle Creek—*stream* NV-8
*Tuller College* AZ-5
Tuller Creek—*stream* OR-9
Tuller Hill—*summit* NY-2
Tuller Pre Sch—*school* AZ-5
Tuller Sch—*school* CT-1
Tullers Lake—*lake* MI-6
Tuller Town Hall—*building* ND-7
**Tuller Township**—*pop pl* ND-7
Tulles Cem—*cemetery* OK-5
Tulley Branch—*stream* KY-4
*Tulley Canyon* CA-9
Tulley Creek—*stream* AR-4
Tulley Creek—*stream* OR-9
Tulley Creek Ranch—*locale* OR-9
Tulley Ditch—*canal* MT-8
Tulley Lake—*lake* AR-4
Tulleys, Lysander, House—*hist pl* IA-7
Tulley Spring—*spring* MT-8
Tulleys Real Estate Lake Dam—*dam* AL-4
*Tullick's Fork* ID-8
*Tullifinny River* SC-3
Tullis—*locale* AL-4
Tullis—*locale* LA-4
Tullis—*locale* WY-8
**Tullis Addition**—*pop pl* UT-8
Tullis Chapel Cem—*cemetery* IN-6
Tullis Sch—*school* IL-6
Tullis Sch (historical)—*school* AL-4
Tulliver Cem—*cemetery* WV-2
Tull Lake—*lake* AR-4
Tull Lake—*lake* MI-6
*Tull Mill* NC-3
**Tull Mill**—*pop pl* NC-3
Tull Millpond—*reservoir* NC-3
Tull Millpond Dam—*dam* NC-3
Tulloch Dam—*dam* CA-9
Tulloch Gulch—*valley* CA-9
*Tulloch Lake* CA-9
Tulloch Lake—*lake* NM-5
Tulloch Lateral—*canal* CA-9
Tulloch Mine—*mine* CA-9
Tulloch Mtn—*summit* CA-9
Tulloch Peak—*summit* NM-5
Tulloch Rsvr—*reservoir* CA-9
Tullock Cem—*cemetery* MO-7
Tullock Creek—*stream* MT-8
Tullock Creek Sch—*school* MT-8
*Tullock Gulch* CA-9
*Tullock Mountain* CA-9
*Tullock Peak* NM-5
*Tullocks Fork* ID-8
**Tullos**—*pop pl* LA-4
Tullos Cem—*cemetery* LA-4
Tullos Cem—*cemetery* TX-5
Tullos Field (airport)—*airport* MS-4
Tullos Ranch—*locale* TX-5
Tulloss Cem—*cemetery* TN-4
Tullos Urania Oil Field—*oilfield* LA-4
Tullous Creek—*stream* NM-5
Tullous Ranch—*locale* NM-5
Tullous Tank—*reservoir* NM-5
Tullous Upper Ranch—*locale* NM-5
Tull Park—*park* OK-5
Tull Ranch—*locale* CA-9
Tull Rsvr—*reservoir* OR-9
Tulls—*locale* NC-3
Tulls Branch—*stream* MD-2
Tull Sch (abandoned)—*school* MO-7
Tulls Corner—*locale* MD-2
**Tulls Creek**—*pop pl* NC-3
Tulls Island—*island* MD-2
Tulls Lake—*reservoir* TX-5
Tulls Mill—*locale* NC-3
Tulls Point—*cape* MD-2
Tulls Sch (abandoned)—*school* PA-2
Tulls School—*locale* DE-2
Tulls Swamp—*swamp* MD-2
*Tullulah Gorge* GA-3
Tully—*locale* AZ-5
**Tully**—*pop pl* AR-4
**Tully**—*pop pl* MA-1
**Tully**—*pop pl* NY-2
Tully, Pinckney R., House—*hist pl* NM-5
Tully, William, House—*hist pl* CT-1
Tully, William J., House—*hist pl* MI-6
Tully Brook—*stream* (2) MA-1
Tully Brook—*stream* NH-1
Tully Canyon—*valley* CA-9
**Tully Center**—*pop pl* NY-2
Tully Creek—*stream* (2) CA-9
Tully Dam—*dam* MA-1
Tully Ditch—*canal* IN-6
Tully For (New York State College Of Forestry)—*forest* NY-2
Tully Hall—*locale* CA-9
Tully Hill—*summit* OK-5
Tully Hole—*basin* CA-9
Tully Hollow—*valley* OK-5
Tully Island—*island* IL-6
Tully Lake—*lake* CA-9
Tully Lake—*lake* MI-6
Tully Lake—*lake* NY-2
Tully Lake—*reservoir* MA-1
**Tully Lake Park**—*pop pl* NY-2
Tully Meadow—*flat* MA-1
*Tully Meadows* MA-1
*Tully Mill* MA-1
Tully Mtn—*summit* CA-9
Tully Mtn—*summit* (2) MA-1
Tully Park—*park* IL-6
Tully Pond—*reservoir* MA-1
Tully Pond Dam—*dam* MA-1
*Tully Reservoir* MA-1
Tully Ridge—*ridge* WV-2
Tully River—*stream* MA-1
Tully River Dam—*dam* MA-1
Tully RR Station—*building* AZ-5
*Tullys Brook* MA-1
Tully Sch—*school* AZ-5
Tully Seale Lake Dam—*dam* MS-4
**Tullytown**—*pop pl* PA-2
Tullytown Borough—*civil* PA-2
**Tully (Town of)**—*pop pl* NY-2
**Tully (Township of)**—*pop pl* (2) OH-6
**Tully (Tullyville)**—*pop pl* MA-1
Tully Valley—*locale* NY-2
Tully Valley—*valley* NY-2
*Tullyville* MA-1
Tullyville—*other* MA-1
Tully Well—*well* AZ-5
Tulmochusse Ch—*church* OK-5
*Tulnguy* FM-9
Tulno Mine—*mine* KY-4
Tulocay Cem—*cemetery* CA-9
*Tulon* TN-4
*Tulon Lake* NV-8
Tulosa—*uninc pl* TX-5
Tulosa Creek—*stream* NM-5
Tulosa Draw—*valley* NM-5
Tulosa Lake—*reservoir* TX-5
Tulosa Tank—*reservoir* NM-5
Tulosa Windmill—*locale* NM-5
Tulosa Windmill—*locale* TX-5
Tuloso Cem—*cemetery* NM-5
Tuloso-Midway HS—*school* TX-5
Tuloso-Midway Sch—*school* TX-5
**Tulot**—*pop pl* AR-4
Tulot Ch—*church* AR-4
Tulot Sch—*school* AR-4
Tulpehocken—*other* PA-2
Tulpehocken—*uninc pl* PA-2
Tulpehocken Ch—*church* PA-2
Tulpehocken Creek—*stream* NJ-2
Tulpehocken Creek—*stream* PA-2
Tulpehocken Creek Hist Dist—*hist pl* PA-2
Tulpehocken Creek Valley Park—*park* PA-2
Tulpehocken Manor Plantation—*hist pl* PA-2
Tulpehocken Station Hist Dist—*hist pl* PA-2
**Tulpehocken (Township of)**—*pop pl* PA-2
*Tulpenhocken* PA-2
**Tulpohocken**—*pop pl* PA-2
*Tulquson* AZ-5
*Tulsa* FL-3
Tulsa—*locale* OR-9
**Tulsa**—*pop pl* OK-5
Tulsa (CCD)—*cens area* OK-5
Tulsa Country Club—*other* OK-5
**Tulsa (County)**—*pop pl* OK-5
Tulsa International Airp—*airport* OK-5
Tulsa Municipal Bldg—*hist pl* OK-5
*Tulsa Ridge* WY-8
Tulsa State Fairground—*locale* OK-5
Tulsa Street Sch—*school* CA-9
**Tulse**—*pop pl* AL-4
**Tulsita**—*pop pl* TX-5
Tulsita Oil Field—*oilfield* TX-5
Tulsona Creek—*stream* AK-9
*Tulu* NC-3
**Tulu**—*pop pl* TN-4
Tulucay—*civil* CA-9
Tulucay Creek—*stream* CA-9
Tulu Cem—*cemetery* TN-4
Tulugak Creek—*stream* AK-9
Tulugak Lake—*lake* (2) AK-9
Tuluga River—*stream* AK-9
Tulukak Creek—*stream* AK-9
Tuluk Creek—*stream* AK-9
**Tuluksak**—*pop pl* AK-9
Tuluksak River—*stream* AK-9
**Tulula**—*pop pl* NC-3
Tulula Creek—*stream* NC-3
*Tu-lu-la-wi-ak* CA-9
*Tu-lu-la-wi-ak Creek* CA-9
*Tululowehack* CA-9
Tulunguy—*summit* FM-9
Tulu Post Office (historical)—*building* TN-4
*Tuluq Creek* AK-9
*Tuluski* TN-4
Tulutulu Point—*cape* AS-9
Tuluvak Bluffs—*cliff* AK-9
Tuly Canyon—*valley* TX-5
Tuly Spring—*spring* TX-5
**Tumacacori**—*pop pl* AZ-5
Tumacacori Carmen Interchange—*crossing* AZ-5
*Tumacacori Mountains* AZ-5
Tumacacori Mountains—*range* AZ-5
Tumacacori Museum—*hist pl* AZ-5
Tumacacori Natl Monmt—*hist pl* AZ-5
Tumacacori Natl Monmt—*park* AZ-5
Tumacacori Peak—*summit* AZ-5
Tumacacori Private Land Grant—*civil* AZ-5
Tumac Mtn—*summit* WA-9
Tumag—*area* GU-9
Tumakof Lake—*lake* AK-9
**Tumalaglago**—*pop pl* GU-9
Tuma Lake—*lake* IL-6
Tuma Lake—*lake* WI-6
**Tumalo**—*pop pl* OR-9
Tumalo Butte—*summit* OR-9
Tumalo Canal—*canal* OR-9
Tumalo (CCD)—*cens area* OR-9
Tumalo Cem—*cemetery* OR-9
Tumalo Creek—*stream* OR-9
Tumalo Dam—*dam* OR-9
Tumalo Falls—*falls* OR-9
Tumalo Falls Camp—*locale* OR-9
Tumalo Falls Shelter—*locale* OR-9
Tumalo Feed Canal—*canal* OR-9
Tumalo Lake—*lake* OR-9
Tumalo Mtn—*summit* OR-9
Tumalo State Park—*park* OR-9
Tumalt Creek—*stream* OR-9
Tumalum Creek—*stream* WA-9
Tumalum Sch—*school* OR-9
Tumamoc Hill—*summit* AZ-5
Tuman Head—*cliff* AK-9
Tuman Mill (site)—*locale* CA-9
Tuman Point—*cape* AK-9
*Tuman Sawmill* CA-9
Tumarion Peak—*summit* AZ-5
Tuma Run—*stream* OH-6
*Tumas Lake* WI-6
Tumas Park—*park* AZ-5
Tumatolu Point—*cape* AS-9
Tumbaloo Creek—*stream* MS-4
Tumbez—*locale* VA-3
Tumble Brook—*stream* CT-1
Tumble Brook—*stream* PA-2
Tumblebug Creek—*stream* IN-6
Tumblebug Creek—*stream* NC-3
Tumblebug Creek—*stream* OR-9
Tumblebug Way—*trail* OR-9
Tumble Buttes—*summit* CA-9
*Tumble Creek* CO-8
Tumble Creek—*stream* AK-9
Tumble Creek—*stream* (2) CO-8
Tumble Creek—*stream* (3) ID-8
Tumble Creek—*stream* (3) MT-8
Tumble Creek—*stream* (5) OR-9
Tumble Creek—*stream* (6) WA-9
Tumble Dick Mtn—*summit* NH-1
Tumbledown Bridge—*locale* ID-8
Tumbledown Brook—*stream* ME-1
Tumbledown Creek—*stream* (2) ID-8
Tumbledown Creek—*stream* MT-8
Tumbledown Creek—*stream* (3) OR-9
Tumbledown Dick Head—*summit* ME-1
Tumbledown Dick Mtn—*summit* (2) ME-1
Tumbledown Dick Mtn—*summit* NH-1
Tumbledown Dick Pond—*lake* ME-1
Tumbledown Dick Stream—*stream* ME-1
Tumbledown Hill—*ridge* MA-1
*Tumbledown Hollow* PA-2
Tumbledown Mtn—*summit* (2) ME-1
Tumbledown Mtn—*summit* TX-5
Tumbledown Pond—*lake* ME-1
Tumbledown Spring—*spring* OR-9
Tumble Falls—*locale* NJ-2
Tumble Inn—*locale* CA-9
Tumble Inn Campground—*locale* CA-9
Tumble Lake—*lake* OR-9
Tumble Mtn—*summit* CO-8
Tumble Mtn—*summit* MT-8
Tumbler Canyon—*valley* CA-9
Tumbler Creek—*stream* MT-8
Tumbler Creek—*stream* OK-5
Tumbler Island—*island* ME-1
Tumble Rock—*pillar* OR-9
Tumblerville—*locale* NC-3
Tumblesom Lake—*lake* CO-8
Tumble Spring—*spring* OR-9
**Tumbleton**—*pop pl* AL-4
Tumbleton Ch—*church* AL-4
Tumbleweed Draw—*valley* NM-5
Tumbleweed Flat—*flat* NV-8
Tumble Weed Park—*park* AZ-5
Tumbleweed Rsvr—*reservoir* ID-8
Tumbleweed Sch—*school* AZ-5
Tumbleweed Spring—*spring* AZ-5
Tumbleweed Spring—*spring* OR-9
Tumbleweed Tank—*reservoir* AZ-5
Tumbling—*locale* TN-4
Tumbling Branch—*stream* KY-4
Tumbling Branch—*stream* TN-4
Tumbling Brook—*stream* MA-1
Tumbling Cem—*cemetery* WV-2
Tumbling Cove—*valley* VA-3
Tumbling Creek—*locale* VA-3
Tumbling Creek—*stream* CO-8
Tumbling Creek—*stream* GA-3
Tumbling Creek—*stream* MO-7
Tumbling Creek—*stream* OR-9
Tumbling Creek—*stream* (4) TN-4
Tumbling Creek—*stream* VA-3
Tumbling Creek—*stream* WA-9
Tumbling Creek Baptist Ch—*church* TN-4
Tumbling Creek Cave—*cave* MO-7
Tumbling Creek Cem—*cemetery* TN-4
Tumbling Creek Rec Area—*park* TN-4
Tumbling Creek Sch (historical)—*school* TN-4
Tumbling Lead—*ridge* GA-3
Tumbling Post Office (historical)—*building* TN-4
Tumbling Rapids Rec Area—*park* WA-9
Tumbling Rock Camping Shelter—*locale* WV-2
Tumbling Rock Run—*stream* WV-2
Tumbling Rock Trail—*trail* WV-2
Tumbling Run—*stream* NC-3
Tumbling Run—*stream* (6) PA-2
Tumbling Run—*stream* TN-4
Tumbling Run—*stream* VA-3
Tumbling Run—*stream* WV-2
Tumbling Run Game Preserve—*park* PA-2
Tumbling Run Trail—*trail* PA-2
Tumbling Sch (historical)—*school* TN-4
*Tumbling Shoal Hollow* MO-7
Tumbling Shoal Hollow—*valley* MO-7
Tumbling Shoals—*bar* TN-4
Tumbling Shoals—*locale* SC-3
**Tumbling Shoals**—*pop pl* AR-4
*Tumbling Shoals Cave* TN-4
Tumbling Shoals Creek—*stream* NC-3
Tumbling T Spring—*spring* NV-8
Tumbling Waters Camp—*locale* GA-3
Tumblins Lake—*reservoir* GA-3
Tumco Mine—*mine* CA-9
Tumco Wash—*stream* CA-9
Tumey Gulch—*valley* CA-9
Tumey Hills—*other* CA-9
**Tumia (historical)**—*pop pl* OR-9
Tumi Creek—*stream* AK-9
Tuminson Cem—*cemetery* TX-5
*Tumintal, Mount* FM-9
*Tumitche* CO-8
*Tumitche Dome* CO-8
Tumit Creek—*stream* (2) AK-9
Tumkeehatchee Creek—*stream* AL-4
*Tumkeehathee Creek* AL-4
Tum Lake—*lake* OR-9
Tumlame Branch—*stream* AL-4
Tumleys Tanyards (historical)—*locale* AL-4
*Tumlin Creek* TN-4
Tumlin Creek—*stream* AL-4
Tumlin Creek—*stream* (2) GA-3
Tumlin Gap—*gap* AL-4
**Tumlin Gap**—*pop pl* AL-4
Tumlin Gap Station (historical)—*locale* AL-4
Tumlinson Cem—*cemetery* TX-5
Tumlum Mine—*mine* WY-8
*Tummeahai Creek* WA-9
*Tummeahai Lake* WA-9
*Tummeahai Peak* WA-9
*Tummeahia Creek* WA-9
*Tummeahia Lake* WA-9
*Tummeahia peak* WA-9
Tummings Branch—*stream* TN-4
Tummy Grove—*woods* CA-9
**Tumon**—*pop pl* GU-9
Tumon Bay—*bay* GU-9
**Tumon Chama**—*pop pl* GU-9
Tumon Maui Well—*well* GU-9
*Tumpaloo Creek* MS-4
Tump Gut—*bay* NC-3
Tump Island—*island* NC-3
Tump Point—*cape* NC-3
*Tump Range* WY-8
Tumsden Bridge—*bridge* CA-9
Tumtum—*locale* WA-9
Tum Tum, Mount—*summit* AK-9
Tumtum Cem—*cemetery* WA-9
Tumtum Lake (salt)—*lake* OR-9
Tumtum Mtn—*summit* WA-9
Tumtum Peak—*summit* WA-9
Tumtum River—*stream* OR-9
*Tumuital, Mount* FM-9
**Tumuli (Township of)**—*pop pl* MN-6
Tumu Mtn—*summit* AS-9
*Tu'-Mu-Ur-Ru-Gwait'Si-Gaip Tu-Weap'* UT-8
Tumwata Creek—*stream* WA-9
**Tumwater**—*pop pl* WA-9
Tumwater Basin—*basin* WA-9
Tumwater Bridge—*bridge* WA-9
Tumwater Butte—*summit* WA-9
Tumwater Campground—*locale* (2) WA-9
Tumwater Canyon—*valley* WA-9
Tumwater Creek—*stream* (3) WA-9
*Tumwater Falls* WA-9
Tumwater Hist Dist—*hist pl* WA-9
Tumwater Lake—*lake* WA-9
Tumwater Methodist Church—*hist pl* WA-9
Tumwater Mountian—*summit* WA-9
Tumwater Mtn—*summit* (2) WA-9
**Tuna**—*pop pl* PA-2
Tuna (Barrio)—*fmr MCD* PR-3
Tuna Bunch Hollow—*valley* OK-5
Tuna Canyon—*valley* CA-9
*Tuna Creek* PA-2
Tuna Creek—*stream* AZ-5
Tuna Creek—*stream* CA-9
*Tuna Creek Dam* PA-2
Tunalik River—*stream* AK-9
Tunalkten Lake—*lake* AK-9
*Tunangwant Creek* NY-2
*Tunangwant Creek* PA-2
**Tunas**—*pop pl* MO-7
Tunas Branch—*stream* MO-7
*Tunas Creek* TX-5
Tunas Creek—*stream* (2) TX-5
*Tunasee* TN-4
Tuna Siding—*locale* TX-5
Tunawee Canyon—*valley* CA-9
Tunawee Ranch—*locale* CA-9
Tunbridge—*locale* IL-6
**Tunbridge**—*pop pl* ND-7
**Tunbridge**—*pop pl* VT-1
Tunbridge Cem—*cemetery* IL-6
Tunbridge Ch—*church* ND-7
Tunbridge Hill—*summit* VT-1
**Tunbridge (subdivision)**—*pop pl* TN-4
**Tunbridge (Town of)**—*pop pl* VT-1
**Tunbridge (Township of)**—*pop pl* IL-6
Tunbridge Trout Pond—*lake* VT-1
Tundle Cem—*cemetery* TN-4
Tundra—*locale* TX-5
Tundra Creek—*stream* (2) AK-9
Tundra Curves—*locale* CO-8
Tundra George—*locale* AK-9
Tundra Lake—*lake* (2) AK-9
Tune Branch—*stream* TN-4
Tune Cem—*cemetery* MO-7
Tune Cem—*cemetery* (4) TN-4
*Tunegawant Creek* NY-2
*Tunegawant Creek* PA-2
Tune Hollow—*valley* TN-4
*Tunell Church* AL-4
Tunemah Lake—*lake* CA-9
Tunemah Pass—*gap* CA-9
Tunemah Peak—*summit* CA-9
*Tuners Lake* MN-6
Tunerville—*locale* SD-7
Tunes Branch—*stream* NJ-2
Tungaich Point—*cape* AK-9
Tunga Inlet—*bay* AK-9
Tungak Creek—*stream* (2) AK-9
Tungaluk Slough—*gut* AK-9
*Tungd* PW-9
Tungnak Creek—*stream* AK-9
Tungnak Hill—*summit* AK-9
Tungo—*cape* PW-9
Tungo Tank—*reservoir* AZ-5
Tungpuk River—*stream* AK-9
**Tungroc**—*pop pl* FL-3
Tungroc RR Station—*locale* FL-3
Tungstar Mine—*mine* CA-9
Tungsten—*locale* CO-8
Tungsten—*locale* NV-8
**Tungsten**—*pop pl* NC-3
Tungsten Blue Mine—*mine* CA-9
Tungsten Canyon—*valley* (2) NV-8
Tungsten Chief Mine—*mine* CA-9
Tungsten Creek—*stream* WA-9
Tungsten Flat—*flat* CA-9
Tungsten Gulch—*valley* AK-9
Tungsten Hill—*summit* AK-9
Tungsten Hill Mine—*mine* ID-8
Tungsten Hills—*flat* CA-9
Tungsten Hollow—*valley* UT-8
Tungsten King Mine—*mine* AZ-5
*Tungsten Lake* UT-8
Tungsten Lake—*lake* UT-8
Tungsten Lake—*lake* WA-9
Tungsten Lode Mine—*mine* SD-7
Tungsten Mill—*locale* (2) MT-8
Tungsten Mine—*mine* MT-8
Tungsten Mine (Inactive), The—*mine* NM-5
Tungsten Mine Park—*park* CT-1
*Tungsten Mountain* ID-8
Tungsten Mountain Mine—*mine* NV-8
Tungsten Mtn—*summit* CO-8
Tungsten Mtn—*summit* ID-8
Tungsten Mtn—*summit* NV-8
Tungsten Pass—*gap* UT-8
Tungsten Peak Mine—*mine* CA-9
Tungsten Queen Mine—*mine* NV-8
Tungsten Shaft—*mine* CO-8
*Tungston Hollow* UT-8
Tungstonia—*locale* NV-8
Tungstonia Wash—*valley* UT-8
Tungulara Mtn—*summit* AK-9
Tungunbinaew—*channel* FM-9
*Tungunbinaw* FM-9
*Tungunebinaw* FM-9
Tuniakpuk (Site)—*locale* AK-9
**Tunica**—*pop pl* LA-4
**Tunica**—*pop pl* MS-4
Tunica Airp—*airport* MS-4
Tunica Bayou—*stream* LA-4
Tunica Bayou—*stream* MS-4
**Tunica-Biloxi Ind Res**—*pop pl* LA-4
Tunica Ch—*church* LA-4
**Tunica County**—*pop pl* MS-4
Tunica County Hosp—*hospital* MS-4
Tunica Hills Ch—*church* LA-4
Tunica Island—*island* LA-4
Tunica JHS—*school* MS-4
Tunica Lake—*lake* MS-4
Tunica Landing—*locale* LA-4
**Tunica North**—*pop pl* MS-4
Tunica North (census name North Tunica)—*other* MS-4
Tunica-Rosa Fort HS—*school* MS-4
Tunica Sch—*school* LA-4
Tunica Swamp—*swamp* LA-4
*Tunicha Creek* AZ-5
Tuni Creek—*stream* AR-4
Tuni Gap—*gap* NC-3
Tunilkhanten, Lake—*lake* AK-9
*Tunington* NC-3
**Tunipus**—*pop pl* RI-1
*Tunipus Beach* RI-1
Tunipus Pond—*lake* RI-1
Tunis—*locale* AR-4
Tunis—*locale* MI-6
Tunis—*locale* MT-8
Tunis—*locale* NM-5
Tunis—*locale* VA-3
**Tunis**—*pop pl* GA-3
**Tunis**—*pop pl* NC-3
**Tunis**—*pop pl* TX-5
Tunis Brook—*stream* NH-1
*Tunis Creek* TX-5
Tunis Creek—*stream* CA-9
Tunis Lake—*reservoir* NY-2
**Tunis Mills**—*pop pl* MD-2
Tunis Mtn—*summit* AK-9
Tunis Pond—*lake* NY-2
Tunis Run—*stream* PA-2
Tunis Sch—*school* MT-8
Tunis Sch—*school* NH-1
*Tunitas* CA-9
**Tunitas**—*pop pl* CA-9
Tunitas Beach—*beach* CA-9
Tunitas Creek—*stream* CA-9
Tunitas Sch—*school* CA-9
*Tunitcha Creek* AZ-5
Tunitcha Mountains—*other* NM-5
Tunitcha Mountains—*range* AZ-5
*Tunka* FM-9
Tunkaleshna Creek—*stream* AK-9
Tunk Creek—*stream* WA-9
**Tunk Creek Spur**—*pop pl* WA-9
**Tunker**—*pop pl* IN-6
Tunker House—*hist pl* VA-3
Tunkethandle Hill—*summit* NY-2
Tunket Hole—*bend* PA-2
*Tunkhanna Creek* PA-2
**Tunkhannock**—*pop pl* PA-2
Tunkhannock Borough—*civil* PA-2
Tunkhannock Creek—*stream* (2) PA-2
Tunkhannock HS—*school* PA-2
*Tunkhannock Lake* PA-2
Tunkhannock MS—*school* PA-2
**Tunkhannock (Township of)**—*pop pl* (2) PA-2
Tunkhannock Viaduct—*hist pl* PA-2
Tunk Hill—*summit* RI-1
*Tunkis* CT-1
Tunk Lake—*lake* ME-1
**Tunk Lake**—*pop pl* ME-1
Tunk Mtn—*summit* ME-1
Tunk Mtn—*summit* WA-9
*Tunk Pond* ME-1
Tunk Stream—*stream* ME-1
Tunk Valley—*valley* WA-9
Tunmore Lake—*lake* MN-6
Tunnabora Peak—*summit* CA-9
Tunnel—*locale* AK-9
Tunnel—*locale* CA-9
Tunnel—*locale* CO-8
Tunnel—*locale* MO-7
Tunnel—*locale* OH-6
Tunnel—*locale* PA-2
Tunnel—*locale* WI-6
**Tunnel**—*pop pl* NY-2
**Tunnel**—*pop pl* (2) WV-2
Tunnel, The—*channel* NY-2
Tunnel, The—*gap* MN-6
Tunnel, The—*tunnel* AZ-5
Tunnel, The—*valley* NY-2
Tunnel Air Camp—*locale* CA-9
Tunnel Arch—*arch* UT-8
Tunnel Bluff—*cliff* MO-7
Tunnel Branch—*stream* AL-4
Tunnel Branch—*stream* AR-4
Tunnel Branch—*stream* (4) KY-4
Tunnel Branch—*stream* NC-3
Tunnel Branch—*stream* TN-4
Tunnel Branch—*stream* (2) VA-3
Tunnel Brook—*stream* MA-1
Tunnel Brook—*stream* NH-1
Tunnel Brook—*stream* VT-1
Tunnel Brook Trail—*trail* NH-1
Tunnel Cabin—*locale* ID-8
Tunnel Camp—*locale* NV-8
Tunnel Campground—*locale* CO-8

Turkey Creek Watershed Y-20-63 Dam—*dam* MS-4
Turkey Creek Watershed Y-20-66 Dam—*dam* MS-4
Turkey Creek Watershed Y-20-72 Dam—*dam* MS-4
Turkey Creek Watershed Y-20-73 Dam—*dam* MS-4
Turkey Creek Well—*well* AZ-5
Turkey Creek Windmill—*locale* TX-5
Turkey Crossing—*locale* AZ-5
Turkey Dam—*dam* CO-8
Turkey Draw—*valley* (2) AZ-5
Turkey Draw—*valley* NM-5
Turkey Draw—*valley* (3) TX-5
Turkey Draw Spring—*spring* AZ-5
Turkey Draw Tank—*reservoir* AZ-5
*Turkeye* AL-4
Turkey Egg Creek—*stream* (2) VA-3
Turkeyfeather Creek—*stream* NM-5
Turkeyfeather Mtn—*summit* NM-5
Turkeyfeather Spring—*spring* NM-5
Turkey Flat—*flat* (2) AZ-5
Turkey Flat—*flat* (2) CA-9
Turkey Flat—*flat* OK-5
**Turkey Flat**—*pop pl* AZ-5
Turkey Flat Hollow—*valley* MO-7
Turkey Flats—*flat* WV-2
Turkey Flyup—*summit* NC-3
Turkey Foot—*locale* FL-3
Turkey Foot—*locale* KY-4
Turkeyfoot—*locale* (2) PA-2
**Turkeyfoot**—*pop pl* PA-2
**Turkeyfoot**—*pop pl* TN-4
Turkeyfoot Bayou—*stream* MS-4
Turkey Foot Bend—*bend* WV-2
Turkeyfoot Brake—*stream* MS-4
Turkeyfoot Branch—*stream* MS-4
Turkeyfoot Branch—*stream* VA-3
Turkey Foot Cave—*cave* MO-7
Turkey Foot Ch—*church* KY-4
Turkey Foot Corner—*locale* OH-6
*Turkeyfoot Creek* OH-6
Turkeyfoot Creek—*stream* KY-4
Turkeyfoot Creek—*stream* OH-6
Turkeyfoot Creek—*stream* TN-4
Turkey Foot Fork Ch—*church* MS-4
Turkeyfoot Gap—*gap* KY-4
Turkeyfoot Island—*island* OH-6
Turkey Foot Island—*island* OH-6
Turkeyfoot Knob—*summit* KY-4
Turkeyfoot Lake—*lake* OH-6
Turkey Foot Lake—*reservoir* WV-2
Turkey Foot Mtn—*summit* MO-7
Turkeyfoot Point—*cape* OH-6
Turkeyfoot Rock—*summit* OH-6
Turkeyfoot Run—*stream* MD-2
Turkeyfoot Run—*stream* (3) OH-6
Turkeyfoot Run—*stream* WV-2
Turkey Foot Run—*stream* WV-2
Turkeyfoot Run—*stream* WV-2
Turkey Foot Sch—*school* NE-7
Turkeyfoot Sch—*school* OH-6
Turkey Foot Station Forest Camp—*locale* AL-4
Turkeyfoot Valley Sch—*school* PA-2
Turkey Ford—*locale* AL-4
Turkey Ford—*locale* OK-5
**Turkey Ford**—*pop pl* NC-3
**Turkey Ford**—*pop pl* OK-5
Turkey Ford Bar—*bar* AL-4
Turkey Ford Lake—*lake* FL-3
Turkey Ford Sch—*school* OK-5
Turkey Fork—*locale* VA-3
**Turkey Fork**—*pop pl* VA-3
Turkey Fork—*stream* (2) IN-6
Turkey Fork—*stream* (3) KY-4
Turkey Fork—*stream* MS-4
Turkey Fork—*stream* OH-6
Turkey Fork—*stream* VA-3
Turkey Fork—*stream* (5) WV-2
*Turkey Fork Creek* MS-4
Turkey Fork Recreation Site—*park* MS-4
Turkey Fork Rsvr—*reservoir* MS-4
Turkey Fork Sch—*school* KY-4
Turkey Gap—*gap* GA-3
Turkey Gap—*gap* KY-4
Turkey Gap—*gap* NC-3
Turkey Gap—*gap* TN-4
Turkey Gap—*gap* (3) VA-3
Turkey Gap—*gap* WV-2
**Turkey Gap**—*pop pl* WV-2
Turkey Gap Branch—*stream* KY-4
Turkey Gap Branch—*stream* WV-2
Turkey Gobbler Creek—*stream* FL-3
Turkey Grove Sch (historical)—*school* MO-7
*Turkey Gulch* CO-8
Turkey Gulch—*valley* (2) CO-8
Turkey Gulch—*valley* KS-7
Turkey Hammock—*island* (3) FL-3
*Turkey Head* CO-8
Turkey Head—*summit* NM-5
Turkey Head Butte—*summit* ID-8
*Turkey Head Rock* AZ-5
Turkey Heaven Mountain Lookout Tower—*tower* AL-4
Turkey Heaven Mtn—*summit* AL-4
Turkey Heaven Ridge—*ridge* KY-4
Turkey Hen Branch—*stream* SC-3
Turkey Hen Creek—*stream* FL-3
Turkey Hen Mtn—*summit* NC-3
Turkeyhen Run—*stream* OH-6
*Turkey Hill* MA-1
*Turkey Hill* TX-5
Turkey Hill—*cape* TX-5
Turkey Hill—*hist pl* MD-2
Turkey Hill—*summit* AL-4
Turkey Hill—*summit* AZ-5
Turkey Hill—*summit* AR-4
Turkey Hill—*summit* (7) CT-1
Turkey Hill—*summit* IL-6
Turkey Hill—*summit* (2) IN-6
Turkey Hill—*summit* (2) KY-4
Turkey Hill—*summit* (9) MA-1
Turkey Hill—*summit* (2) NH-1
Turkey Hill—*summit* (7) NY-2
Turkey Hill—*summit* (2) OR-9
Turkey Hill—*summit* (6) PA-2
Turkey Hill—*summit* RI-1
Turkey Hill—*summit* SC-3
Turkey Hill—*summit* SD-7
Turkey Hill—*summit* (2) TX-5
Turkey Hill—*summit* (2) VT-1
Turkey Hill—*summit* (2) VA-3
Turkey Hill Branch—*stream* SC-3
*Turkey Hill Brook* CT-1
Turkey Hill Brook—*stream* (3) CT-1
Turkey Hill Brook—*stream* (2) MA-1
Turkey Hill Cem—*cemetery* CT-1
Turkey Hill Cem—*cemetery* NH-1
*Turkey Hill Cemetery* OR-9
Turkey Hill Creek—*stream* NC-3
Turkey Hill Mine—*mine* CA-9
Turkey Hill Park—*park* MA-1
*Turkey-hill Pond* MA-1
Turkey Hill Pond—*lake* (2) MA-1
Turkey Hill Pond—*lake* NY-2
*Turkey Hill Ridge* MA-1
Turkey Hill Rsvr—*reservoir* CT-1
Turkey Hill Run—*stream* MA-1
Turkey Hills—*summit* AZ-5
Turkey Hill Sch—*school* CT-1
Turkey Hill Sch—*school* PA-2
**Turkey Hill Shores**—*pop pl* MA-1
Turkey Hills Pueblo—*locale* AZ-5
Turkey Hole—*basin* AZ-5
Turkey Hole Run—*stream* OH-6
Turkey Hollow—*basin* KY-4
Turkey Hollow—*locale* TX-5
Turkey Hollow—*valley* AR-4
Turkey Hollow—*valley* KY-4
Turkey Hollow—*valley* (5) MO-7
Turkey Hollow—*valley* NY-2
Turkey Hollow—*valley* OH-6
Turkey Hollow—*valley* OK-5
Turkey Hollow—*valley* PA-2
Turkey Hollow—*valley* (5) TN-4
Turkey Hollow—*valley* (8) TX-5
Turkey Hollow—*valley* VT-1
Turkey Hollow—*valley* (2) VA-3
Turkey Hollow—*valley* WV-2
Turkey Hollow Creek—*stream* IL-6
Turkey Hollow Creek—*stream* LA-4
Turkey Hollow Ranch—*locale* TX-5
Turkey Hop Branch—*stream* AL-4
Turkey Hop Ch—*church* AL-4
*Turkey Island* TN-4
Turkey Island—*flat* AR-4
Turkey Island—*island* (4) FL-3
Turkey Island—*island* (2) GA-3
Turkey Island—*island* (3) IL-6
Turkey Island—*island* (2) IA-7
Turkey Island—*island* MD-2
Turkey Island—*island* (2) MA-1
Turkey Island—*island* (2) MO-7
Turkey Island—*island* OK-5
Turkey Island—*island* (2) PA-2
Turkey Island—*island* SC-3
Turkey Island—*island* (2) TX-5
Turkey Island—*island* (2) VA-3
Turkey Island—*swamp* LA-4
*Turkey Island Bend* VA-3
Turkey Island Creek—*stream* VA-3
Turkey Island Cutoff—*bend* VA-3
Turkey Island Slough—*gut* AR-4
Turkey Island Slough—*stream* TX-5
Turkey Joe Boat Ramp—*locale* MT-8
Turkey Key—*island* FL-3
*Turkey Knob* AR-4
**Turkey Knob**—*pop pl* WV-2
Turkey Knob—*summit* (6) AR-4
Turkey Knob—*summit* (4) GA-3
Turkey Knob—*summit* IL-6
Turkey Knob—*summit* (4) KY-4
Turkey Knob—*summit* (3) MO-7
Turkey Knob—*summit* NM-5
Turkey Knob—*summit* (8) NC-3
Turkey Knob—*summit* OK-5
Turkey Knob—*summit* (2) PA-2
Turkey Knob—*summit* (5) TN-4
Turkey Knob—*summit* TX-5
Turkey Knob—*summit* UT-8
Turkey Knob—*summit* (3) VA-3
Turkey Knob—*summit* (4) WV-2
Turkey Knob Ridge—*ridge* KY-4
Turkey Knobs—*ridge* TN-4
Turkey Knob Windmill—*locale* NM-5
Turkey Knoll—*summit* PA-2
*Turkey Lake* IN-6
Turkey Lake—*lake* AZ-5
Turkey Lake—*lake* (3) FL-3
Turkey Lake—*lake* IL-6
Turkey Lake—*lake* (4) LA-4
Turkey Lake—*lake* MI-6
Turkey Lake—*lake* MN-6
Turkey Lake—*lake* MO-7
Turkey Lake—*lake* NM-5
Turkey Lake—*reservoir* ID-8
Turkey Lake—*reservoir* KY-4
Turkey Lake—*reservoir* TX-5
Turkey Lake Branch—*stream* TX-5
Turkey Lake Tank—*reservoir* AZ-5
Turkey Lake Trail—*trail* CO-8
Turkey Lake Village Center (Shop Ctr)—*locale* FL-3
Turkeyland Cove—*bay* MA-1
Turkey Landing—*locale* FL-3
Turkey Landing (historical)—*locale* TN-4
*Turkey Lee Branch* AL-4
Turkey Lick—*stream* KY-4
Turkeylick Branch—*stream* VA-3
Turkeylick Run—*stream* WV-2
Turkey Lodge Ridge—*ridge* MD-2
*Turkey Meadow Brook* RI-1
Turkey Meadow Brook—*stream* RI-1
Turkey Mountain—*ridge* WV-2
Turkey Mountain Brook—*stream* VT-1
Turkey Mountain Cave—*cave* AL-4
Turkey Mountain Estates Airp—*airport* MO-7
Turkey Mountain Lake—*reservoir* GA-3
Turkey Mountain Park—*park* OK-5
Turkey Mountains—*range* NM-5
Turkey Mountain Tank—*reservoir* AZ-5
*Turkey Mtn* AZ-5
*Turkey Mtn* VA-3
Turkey Mtn—*summit* AL-4
Turkey Mtn—*summit* (3) AZ-5
Turkey Mtn—*summit* AR-4
Turkey Mtn—*summit* CO-8
Turkey Mtn—*summit* (3) GA-3
Turkey Mtn—*summit* MO-7
Turkey Mtn—*summit* NJ-2
Turkey Mtn—*summit* (2) NM-5
Turkey Mtn—*summit* (2) NY-2
Turkey Mtn—*summit* (3) NC-3
Turkey Mtn—*summit* (3) OK-5
Turkey Mtn—*summit* TN-4
Turkey Mtn—*summit* TX-5
Turkey Mtn—*summit* VT-1
Turkey Mtn—*summit* (3) VA-3
Turkey Mtn—*summit* WV-2
Turkey Mullen Gulch—*valley* CA-9
Turkey Neck—*cape* (2) MD-2
Turkey Neck Bend—*bend* KY-4
Turkey Neck Creek—*stream* MD-2
Turkey Neck Point—*cape* MD-2
Turkey Neck Trail—*trail* VA-3
Turkey Nest Head—*area* GA-3
Turkey Nest Knob—*summit* VA-3
Turkey Number Three Tank—*reservoir* AZ-5
Turkey Number Two Tank—*reservoir* AZ-5
Turkey Oak Cem—*cemetery* MO-7
Turkey Paint Creek—*stream* TX-5
Turkey Park—*flat* (2) AZ-5
Turkey Park—*flat* (4) NM-5
Turkey Park Canyon—*valley* NM-5
Turkey Park Spring—*spring* CO-8
Turkey Park Spring—*spring* NM-5
Turkey Park Tank—*reservoir* NM-5
Turkey Pass—*gap* OK-5
Turkey Paw Branch—*stream* AL-4
Turkey Peak—*summit* AZ-5
Turkey Peak—*summit* NM-5
Turkey Peak—*summit* (3) TX-5
Turkey Peak Mtn—*summit* TX-5
Turkeypen Bay—*swamp* FL-3
Turkeypen Bay—*swamp* NC-3
Turkey Pen Bayou—*gut* MS-4
Turkeypen Bluff—*cliff* TN-4
Turkey Pen Branch—*stream* (2) AL-4
Turkeypen Branch—*stream* AL-4
Turkeypen Branch—*stream* GA-3
Turkey Pen Branch—*stream* KY-4
Turkeypen Branch—*stream* (2) KY-4
Turkeypen Branch—*stream* NC-3
Turkey Pen Branch—*stream* NC-3
Turkeypen Branch—*stream* (2) NC-3
Turkeypen Branch—*stream* (7) TN-4
Turkey Pen Branch—*stream* TX-5
Turkey Pen Branch—*stream* VA-3
Turkeypen Branch—*stream* VA-3
Turkeypen Branch—*stream* (2) WV-2
Turkey Pen Canyon—*valley* AZ-5
Turkey Pen Canyon—*valley* NM-5
Turkey Pen Canyon Trail Two Hundred Sixtytwo—*trail* AZ-5
Turkey Pen Cave—*cave* TX-5
Turkey Pen Cem—*cemetery* GA-3
Turkeypen Cem—*cemetery* TN-4
Turkeypen Checking Station—*locale* NC-3
Turkey Pen Cove—*valley* NC-3
Turkeypen Cove—*valley* (2) TN-4
*Turkey Pen Creek* AL-4
Turkeypen Creek—*stream* (2) AL-4
Turkey Pen Creek—*stream* AL-4
Turkey Pen Creek—*stream* AR-4
Turkey Pen Creek—*stream* IN-6
Turkeypen Creek—*stream* KY-4
Turkey Pen Creek—*stream* MS-4
Turkeypen Creek—*stream* TN-4
Turkeypen Creek—*stream* WV-2
Turkey Pen Draw—*valley* TX-5
Turkeypen Flats—*flat* GA-3
Turkeypen Fork—*stream* (2) KY-4
Turkeypen Gap—*gap* (2) GA-3
Turkeypen Gap—*gap* KY-4
Turkeypen Gap—*gap* (3) NC-3
Turkeypen Gap—*gap* (2) TN-4
Turkeypen Gap—*gap* VA-3
**Turkey Pen Gap (subdivision)**—*pop pl* NC-3
*Turkeypen Hollow* AR-4
*Turkeypen Hollow* VA-3
Turkey Pen Hollow—*valley* (2) AR-4
Turkeypen Hollow—*valley* KY-4
Turkey Pen Hollow—*valley* (3) KY-4
Turkey Pen Hollow—*valley* (2) MO-7
Turkeypen Hollow—*valley* (3) MO-7
Turkey Pen Hollow—*valley* NC-3
Turkeypen Hollow—*valley* TN-4
Turkeypen Hollow—*valley* (2) VA-3
Turkeypen Island—*island* SC-3
Turkey Pen Knob—*summit* KY-4
Turkeypen Knob—*summit* NC-3
Turkeypen Lake—*reservoir* TN-4
Turkeypen Lake Dam—*dam* TN-4
Turkey Pen Mtn—*summit* AR-4
Turkeypen Mtn—*summit* (2) GA-3
Turkeypen Mtn—*summit* TN-4
Turkey Pen Peak—*summit* MT-8
Turkey Pen Point—*summit* KY-4
Turkey Pen Pond—*lake* FL-3
Turkey Pen Ridge—*ridge* AL-4
Turkey Pen Ridge—*ridge* AZ-5
Turkeypen Ridge—*ridge* GA-3
Turkeypen Ridge—*ridge* (2) MO-7
Turkeypen Ridge—*ridge* NC-3
Turkeypen Ridge—*ridge* (3) TN-4
Turkey Pen Ridge—*ridge* TN-4
Turkey Pen Ridge—*ridge* (2) VA-3
Turkey Pen Ridge Trail—*trail* VA-3
Turkey Pen Ruin—*locale* UT-8
Turkeypen Run—*stream* (3) WV-2
Turkeypen Sch (historical)—*school* TN-4
*Turkey Pen School* TN-4
Turkey Pen Spring—*spring* NM-5
Turkey Pens Trail—*trail* PA-2
Turkey Pen Swamp—*swamp* SC-3
Turkeypen Top—*summit* GA-3
Turkey Plot Rsvr—*reservoir* CO-8
Turkey Plot Spring—*spring* CO-8
Turkey Point—*cape* AL-4
Turkey Point—*cape* (4) FL-3
Turkey Point—*cape* ME-1
Turkey Point—*cape* (4) MD-2
Turkey Point—*cape* MO-7
Turkey Point—*cape* (2) NJ-2
Turkey Point—*cape* NY-2
Turkey Point—*cape* (2) NC-3
**Turkey Point**—*pop pl* FL-3
**Turkey Point**—*pop pl* MD-2
Turkey Point—*summit* ID-8
Turkey Point—*summit* IL-6
**Turkey Point Corner**—*pop pl* NJ-2
Turkey Point Nuclear Power Plant—*building* FL-3
Turkey Point Ridge—*ridge* IN-6
Turkey Point Spring—*spring* CO-8
Turkey Pond—*lake* FL-3
Turkey Pond—*lake* (2) GA-3
Turkey Pond—*lake* LA-4
Turkey Pond—*lake* MS-4
Turkey Pond—*lake* NH-1
Turkey Pond—*lake* TN-4
Turkey Pond—*lake* TX-5
Turkey Pond—*locale* SC-3
Turkey Pond—*swamp* AR-4
Turkey Pond—*swamp* NC-3
Turkey Pond—*swamp* SC-3
Turkey Pond (historical)—*lake* PA-2
Turkey Pond Sch—*school* SC-3
Turkey Post Office (historical)—*building* MS-4
Turkey Prairie—*flat* (2) FL-3
Turkey Prairie—*swamp* FL-3
Turkey Quarter Creek—*stream* NC-3
Turkey Quarter Creek—*stream* SC-3
*Turkey Ridge* AZ-5
*Turkey Ridge* VA-3
Turkey Ridge—*locale* SD-7
**Turkey Ridge**—*pop pl* MO-7
Turkey Ridge—*ridge* AZ-5
Turkey Ridge—*ridge* CO-8
Turkey Ridge—*ridge* (2) KY-4
Turkey Ridge—*ridge* MS-4
Turkey Ridge—*ridge* (2) MO-7
Turkey Ridge—*ridge* (3) NM-5
Turkey Ridge—*ridge* (2) NC-3
Turkey Ridge—*ridge* (2) OH-6
Turkey Ridge—*ridge* PA-2
Turkey Ridge—*ridge* (2) TN-4
Turkey Ridge—*ridge* (4) VA-3
Turkey Ridge—*ridge* WV-2
Turkey Ridge—*summit* IL-6
Turkey Ridge Ch—*church* WV-2
Turkey Ridge Creek—*stream* SD-7
Turkey Ridge Park—*park* OH-6
Turkey Ridge Sch—*school* CO-8
Turkey Ridge School (abandoned)—*locale* MO-7
Turkey Ridge Tank—*reservoir* AZ-5
**Turkey River**—*pop pl* IA-7
Turkey River—*stream* IA-7
Turkey River—*stream* NH-1
*Turkey River Access Public Hunting Area* IA-7
Turkey River Access State Wildlife Area—*area* IA-7
Turkey River Area—*park* IA-7
Turkey River Mounds State Monmt—*park* IA-7
Turkey Rock—*bar* NY-2
Turkey Rock—*pillar* KY-4
Turkey Rock—*pillar* TN-4
Turkey Rock—*rock* WV-2
Turkey Rock—*summit* CO-8
Turkey Rock Hollow—*valley* KY-4
Turkey Rock Ranch—*locale* CO-8
Turkey Roost—*summit* CO-8
Turkey Roost Creek—*stream* (2) TX-5
Turkey Roost Drain—*stream* AR-4
Turkey Roost Draw—*valley* TX-5
Turkey Roost Hammock—*island* FL-3
Turkey Roost (historical)—*locale* AL-4
Turkey Roost Hollow—*valley* (2) MO-7
Turkeyroost Mtn—*summit* TX-5
Turkey Roost Petroglyph Site—*hist pl* TX-5
Turkey Roost Sch—*school* NE-7
Turkey Roost Slough—*gut* FL-3
Turkey Roost Tank—*reservoir* (2) AZ-5
Turkey (RR name for Turkey City)—*other* PA-2
Turkey Rsvr—*reservoir* AZ-5
Turkey Rsvr—*reservoir* CO-8
Turkey Ruins Tank—*reservoir* NM-5
*Turkey Run* PA-2
**Turkey Run**—*pop pl* PA-2
Turkey Run—*stream* DE-2
Turkey Run—*stream* (2) IL-6
Turkey Run—*stream* (7) IN-6
Turkey Run—*stream* (3) IA-7
Turkey Run—*stream* (7) KY-4
Turkey Run—*stream* MO-7
Turkey Run—*stream* NM-5
Turkey Run—*stream* (19) OH-6
Turkey Run—*stream* OK-5
Turkey Run—*stream* OR-9
Turkey Run—*stream* (5) PA-2
Turkey Run—*stream* TX-5
Turkey Run—*stream* (8) VA-3
Turkey Run—*stream* (16) WV-2
Turkey Run Canyon—*valley* NM-5
Turkey Run Ch—*church* OH-6
Turkey Run Creek—*stream* KY-4
Turkey Run Creek—*stream* VA-3
Turkey Run Elem Sch—*school* IN-6
Turkey Run HS—*school* IN-6
Turkey Run Mine—*mine* CA-9
Turkey Run Rec Area—*park* VA-3
Turkey Run Ridge Campground—*locale* VA-3
*Turkey Run Sch* IN-6
Turkey Run Sch (abandoned)—*school* PA-2
Turkey Run State Park—*park* IN-6
Turkey Run Trail—*trail* WV-2
Turkey Saddle—*gap* NM-5
Turkeysag Creek—*stream* VA-3
Turkeysag Gap—*gap* VA-3
Turkey Sandy Creek—*stream* OK-5
**Turkey Scratch**—*pop pl* AR-4
Turkeyscratch Cave—*cave* TN-4
Turkey Scratch Ch—*church* FL-3
Turkey Scratch Knob—*summit* KY-4
Turkey Scratch Lake—*lake* GA-3
Turkeyscratch Mtn—*summit* TN-4
*Turkeys Creek Landing* AL-4
Turkey Seep—*spring* AZ-5
Turkey Shoals—*bar* (3) AL-4
Turkeyshoot Canyon—*valley* AZ-5
Turkey Slough—*stream* AR-4
Turkey Slough—*stream* (2) FL-3
Turkey Slough—*stream* TX-5
Turkey Snout Creek—*stream* OK-5
Turkey Snout Ridge—*ridge* OK-5
Turkey Spring—*spring* (13) AZ-5
Turkey Spring—*spring* (2) CO-8
Turkey Spring—*spring* MS-4
Turkey Spring—*spring* MO-7
Turkey Spring—*spring* NV-8
Turkey Spring—*spring* (7) NM-5
Turkey Spring Canyon—*valley* CO-8
Turkey Spring Canyon—*valley* (3) NM-5
Turkey Spring Corral—*locale* AZ-5
Turkey Spring Gap—*gap* NC-3
Turkey Spring No 2—*spring* NM-5
Turkey Springs—*spring* AZ-5
Turkey Springs—*spring* (2) NM-5
Turkey Springs—*spring* WY-8
Turkey Springs Campground—*locale* CO-8
Turkey Springs Creek—*stream* WY-8
Turkey Springs Guard Station—*locale* CO-8
Turkey Springs Rsvr—*reservoir* CO-8
Turkey Spur Rock—*summit* WV-2
Turkey Stamp—*summit* GA-3
Turkey Stand Lead—*ridge* GA-3
Turkey Swamp—*stream* NC-3
Turkey Swamp—*swamp* AR-4
Turkey Swamp—*swamp* GA-3
Turkey Swamp—*swamp* (2) MA-1
Turkey Swamp Fish and Wildlife Mngmt Area—*park* NJ-2
Turkey Tail Islands—*island* ME-1
Turkey Tail Lake—*lake* ME-1
Turkey Tank—*reservoir* (15) AZ-5
Turkey Tank—*reservoir* CO-8
Turkey Tank—*reservoir* (5) NM-5
Turkey Tank—*reservoir* (2) TX-5
Turkey Tanks—*dam* AZ-5
Turkey Tank Spring—*spring* AZ-5
Turkey Top Creek—*stream* NC-3
Turkeytoter Spring—*spring* GA-3
*Turkey Town* AL-4
*Turkeytown* TN-4
Turkeytown—*locale* KY-4
Turkeytown—*other* TN-4
**Turkeytown**—*pop pl* AL-4
**Turkeytown**—*pop pl* PA-2
*Turkeytown Baptist Church* AL-4
Turkeytown (CCD)—*cens area* AL-4
Turkeytown Cem—*cemetery* TN-4
Turkeytown Creek—*stream* AL-4
Turkeytown Diggings—*mine* CA-9
Turkeytown Division—*civil* AL-4
*Turkeytown Elementary School* AL-4
Turkeytown Gap—*gap* AL-4
Turkey Town (historical)—*locale* AL-4
**Turkeytown (historical)**—*pop pl* TN-4
Turkeytown Methodist Ch—*church* AL-4
Turkeytown Mine—*mine* TN-4
Turkeytown Post Office (historical)—*building* TN-4
Turkeytown Ridge—*ridge* TN-4
Turkeytown Sch—*school* AL-4
Turkey (Township of)—*fmr MCD* NC-3
Turkey Track—*area* CA-9
Turkey Track—*locale* TN-4
**Turkey Track**—*pop pl* IN-6
Turkey Track Butte—*summit* AZ-5
Turkey Track Canyon—*valley* TX-5
Turkey Track Ch—*church* TN-4
Turkey Track Corners—*locale* PA-2
Turkey Track Creek—*stream* VA-3
Turkey Track Ditch—*canal* WY-8
Turkey Track Flat Tank—*reservoir* AZ-5
Turkey Track Flat Tank Dam—*dam* AZ-5
Turkey Track Mine—*mine* AZ-5
Turkey Track Pit—*basin* MT-8
Turkeytrack Ranch—*locale* AZ-5
Turkey Track Ranch—*locale* CO-8
Turkey Track Ranch—*locale* TX-5
Turkey Track Ranch—*locale* WY-8
Turkey Track Sch (historical)—*school* TN-4
Turkey Trail—*trail* AR-4
Turkey Trail—*trail* (2) PA-2
Turkey Trail Branch—*stream* TN-4
*Turkey Trail Creek* IL-6
Turkey Trail Creek—*stream* IL-6
Turkey Trap Ridge—*ridge* CA-9
Turkey Trap Tank—*reservoir* AZ-5
Turkey Tree Tank—*reservoir* AZ-5
Turkey Trot Creek—*stream* MO-7
*Turkeytrot Point* OH-6
Turkey Valley—*basin* TX-5
Turkey Valley—*flat* PA-2
Turkey Valley—*valley* PA-2
Turkey Valley Cem—*cemetery* SD-7
Turkey Valley Ch—*church* SD-7
Turkey Valley Community Sch—*school* IA-7
**Turkey Valley Township**—*pop pl* SD-7
Turkey Walk Trail—*trail* SC-3
Turkeywallow Branch—*stream* WV-2
Turkey Wash—*valley* UT-8
Turkey Water Catchment—*basin* AZ-5
Turkey Water Tank—*reservoir* AZ-5
Turkey Well—*locale* NM-5
Turkey Well—*well* (2) NM-5
Turkey Windmill—*locale* (6) TX-5
Turkey Wing Ridge—*ridge* AR-4
Turkeywing Run—*stream* WV-2
Turkeywoman Gulch—*valley* MT-8
Turk Gap—*gap* VA-3
Turk Group Mine—*mine* SD-7
Turk Hill—*summit* (2) NY-2
*Turk Hollow* NY-2
Turk Hollow—*valley* NY-2
Turkish Embassy Bldg—*building* DC-2
Turk Island—*summit* CA-9
Turk Lake—*lake* CA-9
Turk Lake—*lake* MI-6
Turk Lake—*lake* WI-6
**Turk Lake**—*pop pl* MI-6
Turk Lake Ch—*church* MI-6
Turk Lake Sch—*school* MI-6
Turkland (historical)—*locale* MS-4
Turkle Pond—*lake* DE-2
Turkloin Brook—*stream* ME-1
Turk Mine—*mine* CA-9
Turk Mine—*mine* WA-9
Turk Mountain Overlook—*locale* VA-3
Turk Mountain Trail—*trail* VA-3
*Turk Mtn* VA-3
Turk Mtn—*summit* VA-3
Turknett Well—*well* NM-5
Turk Point—*cape* CA-9
Turk Ranch—*locale* WY-8
*Turks Gap* VA-3
*Turks Head* CO-8
Turks Head—*summit* TX-5
Turks Head—*summit* UT-8
Turkshead Peak—*summit* CO-8
*Turk's Island* CT-1
Turk Site (15CE6)—*hist pl* KY-4
Turk Slashings—*swamp* NY-2
Turks Mtn—*summit* VA-3
*Turk's Pond* CT-1
Turks Pond—*reservoir* CO-8
Turk Spring—*spring* WI-6
Turk Springs—*spring* WY-8
Turks Ranch—*locale* NV-8
Turkville—*locale* KS-7
**Turley**—*pop pl* MO-7
**Turley**—*pop pl* NM-5
**Turley**—*pop pl* OK-5
**Turley**—*pop pl* TN-4
Turley, Benjamin F., House—*hist pl* KY-4
Turley Branch—*stream* MO-7
Turley Branch—*stream* TN-4
Turley Branch—*stream* WV-2
Turley Bridge (historical)—*bridge* TN-4
Turley Cem—*cemetery* AL-4
Turley Cem—*cemetery* IL-6
Turley Cem—*cemetery* (2) MO-7
Turley Cem—*cemetery* TN-4
Turley Creek—*stream* VA-3
Turley Ditch—*canal* IN-6
Turley Falls—*falls* NC-3
Turley Ferry (historical)—*crossing* TN-4
Turley Hollow—*valley* KY-4
Turley Hollow—*valley* MO-7
Turley Island (historical)—*island* TN-4
Turley Mill and Distillery Site—*hist pl* NM-5
**Turley Mills (historical)**—*pop pl* TN-4
Turley Mine—*mine* TN-4
Turley Mtn—*summit* TN-4
Turley Petree Mine (underground)—*mine* TN-4
Turley Post Office (historical)—*building* TN-4
**Turleys**—*pop pl* IN-6
Turley Sch (historical)—*school* TN-4
*Turleys Mill* TN-4
Turleys Mill (historical)—*locale* TN-4
Turleys Mill Post Office (historical)—*building* TN-4
Turley Spring—*spring* TN-4
**Turley Subdivision**—*pop pl* UT-8
Turley Tank—*reservoir* AZ-5
Turleytown—*locale* VA-3
Turley Well—*well* NM-5
Turlington—*locale* TX-5
**Turlington**—*pop pl* NC-3
*Turlington Crossroads* NC-3
Turlington Grove Ch—*church* NC-3
*Turlington Millpond* NC-3
**Turlock**—*pop pl* CA-9
Turlock (CCD)—*cens area* CA-9
Turlock Country Club—*other* CA-9
Turlock Lake—*reservoir* CA-9
Turlock Lake State Park—*park* CA-9
Turlock Main Canal—*canal* CA-9
Turlo Creek—*stream* WA-9
Turman—*locale* GA-3
Turman Branch—*stream* TX-5
Turman Creek—*stream* IN-6
Turman Creek—*stream* MT-8
Turman Prairie—*area* IN-6
*Turmans Creek* IN-6
Turman Spring—*spring* CA-9
**Turman (Township of)**—*pop pl* IN-6
Turmath Creek—*stream* AK-9
*Turme'* FM-9
Turmeaq—*cape* FM-9
Turmina Basin—*basin* TX-5
Turmoil Creek—*stream* MT-8
**Turn**—*pop pl* NM-5
Turn, John, Farm—*hist pl* PA-2
Turnabout Island—*island* AK-9
Turnagain—*locale* AK-9
Turnagain Arm—*bay* AK-9
Turnagain Bay—*bay* NC-3
Turnagain Bay Spit—*bar* NC-3
Turnagain-By-The-Sea—*uninc pl* AK-9
Turnagain Childrens Home—*building* AK-9
**Turnagain Heights**—*pop pl* AK-9
Turnagain Pass—*gap* AK-9
Turnage—*locale* NC-3
Turnage Cem—*cemetery* MS-4
Turnage Chapel—*church* MS-4
Turnage Chapel Cem—*cemetery* MS-4
Turnage Millpond—*reservoir* NC-3
Turnage Millpond Dam—*dam* NC-3
Turnage Sch (historical)—*school* TN-4
Turnage Trails Camp—*locale* MS-4
Turnalay Creek—*stream* TN-4
Turn Around Bay—*swamp* FL-3
Turnaround Creek—*stream* AK-9
Turnaround Lake—*lake* CA-9
Turnaround Tank—*reservoir* AZ-5
Turnaround Wash—*stream* CA-9
Turnback Branch—*stream* TN-4
Turnback Creek—*stream* AL-4
Turnback Creek—*stream* CA-9
Turnback Creek—*stream* MO-7
Turnback Hollow—*valley* MO-7
Turnback Prairie—*flat* FL-3
Turn Back Ridge—*ridge* MO-7
Turnback Township—*civil* MO-7
Turn Basin—*basin* NC-3
Turnbaugh Corner—*locale* TX-5
Turn Bayou—*stream* MS-4
**Turnberry**—*pop pl* IL-6
**Turnberry Vistas (subdivision)**—*pop pl* TN-4
Turnblad, Swan, House—*hist pl* MN-6
Turnbo Canyon—*valley* NM-5
Turnbo Cem—*cemetery* TN-4
Turnbo Creek—*stream* MO-7
Turnbo Creek—*stream* TN-4
Turnbo Hollow—*valley* (2) TN-4
Turnbolm Point—*cape* MI-6
Turnbough Cem—*cemetery* MO-7
Turnbough Town—*locale* AL-4
Turnbow Cabin—*locale* UT-8
Turnbow Cem—*cemetery* TN-4
Turnbow Cem—*cemetery* TX-5
Turnbow Creek—*stream* OR-9
Turnbow Flat—*flat* WA-9
Turnbow Gulch—*valley* ID-8
Turnbow Hollow—*valley* (2) TN-4

Turnbow Lake—swamp TX-5
Turnbow Mtn—summit TX-5
Turnbow Point—summit ID-8
Turnbow Spring—spring AL-4
Turnbreeches Creek—stream NC-3
Turnbridge Landing—locale SC-3
Turn Bridge Trail—trail VA-3
Turnbull—locale AL-4
Turnbull—locale FL-3
Turnbull—locale LA-4
Turnbull—locale MS-4
**Turnbull**—pop pl TN-4
**Turnbull**—pop pl VA-3
Turnbull, Mount—summit AZ-5
Turnbull, R.P., House—hist pl MA-1
Turnbull Bar—bar AR-4
Turnbull Bay—bay FL-3
Turnbull Branch—stream AL-4
Turnbull Butte—summit ID-8
Turnbull Canyon—valley CA-9
Turnbull Cave—cave MO-7
Turnbull (CCD)—cens area WA-9
Turnbull Cem—cemetery AL-4
Turnbull Cem—cemetery LA-4
Turnbull Cem—cemetery MO-7
Turnbull Cem—cemetery OK-5
Turnbull Cem—cemetery VA-3
Turnbull Ch—church TN-4
Turnbull Corner—locale NY-2
Turn Bull Creek OR-9
Turnbull Creek—stream (3) FL-3
Turnbull Creek—stream ID-8
Turnbull Creek—stream MS-4
Turnbull Creek—stream NC-3
Turnbull Creek—stream OK-5
Turnbull Creek—stream OR-9
Turnbull Creek—stream TN-4
Turnbull Ditch—canal WY-8
Turnbull Drop—canal MT-8
Turnbull Forge (historical)—locale TN-4
Turnbull Forge (40CH97)—hist pl TN-4
Turnbull Gulch—valley WY-8
Turnbull Hollow—valley AR-4
Turnbull Hollow—valley (2) MO-7
Turnbull Hollow—valley UT-8
Turnbull Island—island LA-4
Turnbull Lake—lake (2) MI-6
Turnbull Lakebed—flat OR-9
Turnbull Lunguen Ditch—canal CO-8
Turnbull Mountains AZ-5
Turnbull Mtn AZ-5
Turnbull Mtn—summit OR-9
Turnbull Natl Wildlife Ref—park WA-9
Turnbull Peak—summit OR-9
Turnbull Pines Rock Shelter—hist pl WA-9
Turnbull Point—cape MN-6
Turnbull Post Office (historical)—building MS-4
Turnbull-Ritter House—hist pl FL-3
Turnbull Sch—school CA-9
Turnbull Sch—school IL-6
Turnbulls Island LA-4
Turnbull Slough—gut WA-9
Turnbull Springs—spring OK-5
Turnbull Swamp—swamp FL-3
Turnbull Swamp—swamp NC-3
Turnbull (Township of)—fmr MCD NC-3
Turnbull Well—well OR-9
Turnbull Woods—woods IL-6
Turn Canyon—valley NV-8
Turner—locale AL-4
Turner—locale CA-9
Turner—locale ID-8
Turner—locale MD-2
Turner—locale MI-6
Turner—locale PA-2
Turner—locale WV-2
Turner—other WV-2
**Turner**—pop pl (2) AL-4
**Turner**—pop pl (2) AR-4
**Turner**—pop pl CA-9
**Turner**—pop pl IN-6
**Turner**—pop pl KS-7
**Turner**—pop pl KY-4
**Turner**—pop pl ME-1
**Turner**—pop pl MI-6
**Turner**—pop pl MS-4
**Turner**—pop pl MT-8
**Turner**—pop pl OK-5
**Turner**—pop pl OR-9
**Turner**—pop pl PA-2
**Turner**—pop pl WA-9
Turner—unisc pl KS-7
Turner, Charles E., House—hist pl GA-3
Turner, Dr. Philip, House—hist pl CT-1
Turner, Frank and Clara, House—hist pl SD-7
Turner, Fred and Juliette, House—hist pl TX-5
Turner, Fred G., House—hist pl IA-7
Turner, Henry, House and Caldwell-Turner Mill Site—hist pl NC-3
Turner, Henry Gray, House and Grounds—hist pl GA-3
Turner, James, House—hist pl TX-5
Turner, Joe E., House—hist pl TX-5
Turner, John E., House—hist pl OK-5
Turner, John G., House—hist pl ID-8
Turner, Kate, House—hist pl AR-4
Turner, Mount—summit AK-9
Turner, Mount—summit WA-9
Turner, Point—cape WA-9
Turner, Stephen, House—hist pl MA-1
Turner Acad (historical)—school TN-4
Turner Arant Pond Dam—dam MS-4
Turner Ashby HS—school VA-3
Turner Bar—bar TN-4
Turner Basin—basin OR-9
Turner Bay—bay AK-9
Turner Bay—bay ID-8
Turner Bay—bay LA-4
Turner Bay—bay VI-3
**Turner Bay**—pop pl ID-8
Turner Bay—swamp FL-3
Turner Bay—swamp SC-3
Turner Bend—bend GA-3
Turner Bend—bend TX-5
Turner Bluff—cliff IL-6
Turner Bluff—cliff MO-7
Turner Bobo Branch—stream AL-4
Turner Bottom—bend MT-8
Turner Bottoms—bend MT-8
Turner Branch—stream (3) AL-4
Turner Branch—stream AR-4
Turner Branch—stream (2) GA-3
Turner Branch—stream IL-6
Turner Branch—stream (7) KY-4
Turner Branch—stream ME-1
Turner Branch—stream MS-4
Turner Branch—stream NC-3
Turner Branch—stream SC-3
Turner Branch—stream (5) TN-4
Turner Branch—stream (3) TX-5
Turner Bridge—bridge KS-7
Turner Bridge—bridge ME-1
Turner Brook—stream (2) CT-1
Turner Brook—stream (4) ME-1
Turner Brook—stream NY-2
Turner Brook—stream VT-1
Turner Brook Campsite—locale ME-1
Turner Butte—summit ID-8
Turner Butte—summit MT-8
Turner Butte—summit OR-9
Turner Butte Dam—dam ID-8
Turner Cabin—locale OR-9
**Turner Camp**—pop pl IL-6
Turner Canal—canal CA-9
Turner Canal—canal LA-4
Turner Canyon—valley (4) CA-9
Turner Canyon—valley OR-9
Turner Canyon—valley UT-8
Turner Cave—cave AL-4
Turner Cave—cave MO-7
Turner Cem MS-4
Turner Cem—cemetery (9) AL-4
Turner Cem—cemetery (5) AR-4
Turner Cem—cemetery CT-1
Turner Cem—cemetery FL-3
Turner Cem—cemetery GA-3
Turner Cem—cemetery (2) IL-6
Turner Cem—cemetery (3) IN-6
Turner Cem—cemetery (2) IA-7
Turner Cem—cemetery (2) KS-7
Turner Cem—cemetery (12) KY-4
Turner Cem—cemetery LA-4
Turner Cem—cemetery (4) ME-1
Turner Cem—cemetery (8) MS-4
Turner Cem—cemetery (10) MO-7
Turner Cem—cemetery MT-8
Turner Cem—cemetery NE-7
Turner Cem—cemetery NJ-2
Turner Cem—cemetery NY-2
Turner Cem—cemetery NC-3
Turner Cem—cemetery (2) OH-6
Turner Cem—cemetery (3) SC-3
Turner Cem—cemetery (17) TN-4
Turner Cem—cemetery (6) TX-5
Turner Cem—cemetery (7) VA-3
Turner Cem—cemetery WA-9
Turner Cem—cemetery (3) WV-2
Turner Cemetary—cemetery TN-4
Turner Cem Number One—cemetery TN-4
Turner Cem Number Three—cemetery TN-4
Turner Cem Number Two—cemetery TN-4
**Turner Center**—pop pl ME-1
Turner Ch—church (2) AR-4
Turner Ch—church (3) GA-3
Turner Ch—church KY-4
Turner Ch—church LA-4
Turner Ch—church NC-3
Turner Ch—church TX-5
Turner Chapel MS-4
Turner Chapel NC-3
Turner Chapel—church (2) AL-4
Turner Chapel—church AR-4
Turner Chapel—church (3) GA-3
Turner Chapel—church MS-4
Turner Chapel—church NC-3
Turner Chapel—church TN-4
**Turner Chapel**—pop pl AL-4
Turner Chapel AME Ch—church AL-4
Turner Chapel AME Ch—church MS-4
Turner Chapel Elem Sch—school MS-4
Turner Chapel (historical)—church TN-4
Turner Chapel HS MS-4
Turner Chapel Sch—school AL-4
Turner Chapel Sch—school MS-4
Turner-Chew-Carhart Farm—hist pl NJ-2
Turner Christian Church AL-4
**Turner City**—pop pl GA-3
**Turner Corner**—pop pl WA-9
Turner Coulee—valley MT-8
Turner County—civil SD-7
**Turner (County)**—pop pl GA-3
Turner County Courthouse—hist pl GA-3
Turner County Jail—hist pl GA-3
Turner Cove—bay MD-2
Turner Cove—bay RI-1
Turner Creek GA-3
Turner Creek WY-8
Turner Creek—channel GA-3
Turner Creek—stream (2) AL-4
Turner Creek—stream (2) AK-9
Turner Creek—stream AR-4
Turner Creek—stream (4) CA-9
Turner Creek—stream (3) CO-8
Turner Creek—stream FL-3
Turner Creek—stream (5) GA-3
Turner Creek—stream (2) ID-8
Turner Creek—stream (3) IL-6
Turner Creek—stream (2) IA-7
Turner Creek—stream (2) KS-7
Turner Creek—stream KY-4
Turner Creek—stream LA-4
Turner Creek—stream MD-2
Turner Creek—stream (2) MI-6
Turner Creek—stream (2) MS-4
Turner Creek—stream (2) MO-7
Turner Creek—stream MT-8
Turner Creek—stream NM-5
Turner Creek—stream NY-2
Turner Creek—stream (2) NC-3
Turner Creek—stream (7) OR-9
Turner Creek—stream PA-2
Turner Creek—stream TN-4
Turner Creek—stream (5) TX-5
Turner Creek—stream VA-3
Turner Creek—stream (5) WA-9
Turner Creek—stream (2) WI-6
Turner Creek—stream (2) WY-8
Turner Creek Camp—locale CA-9
Turner Creek Camp—locale OR-9
Turner Creek Ch—church NC-3
Turner Creek Dam—dam OR-9
Turner Creek Rsvr—reservoir OR-9
Turner Creek Trail—trail CA-9
Turner Creek Wharf—locale MD-2
Turnercrest—locale WY-8
Turner Crossroads NC-3
Turner Crossroads—locale AL-4
Turner Cut—canal CA-9
Turner Cut-Off—trail WY-8
Turner Dam—dam MA-1
Turner Deadwater—lake ME-1
Turner Ditch—canal CA-9
Turner Ditch—canal CO-8
Turner Ditch—canal IN-6
Turner Divide—ridge WY-8
Turner Douglas WV-2
**Turner Douglass**—pop pl WV-2
Turner Drain—canal MI-6
Turner Drain—stream MI-6
Turner Draw—valley KS-7
Turner Draw—valley NM-5
Turner Draw—valley SD-7
Turner Draw—valley (2) WY-8
Turner Elem Sch—school PA-2
Turner Falls—falls OK-5
Turner Falls Hist Dist—hist pl MA-1
Turner Falls Park—park OK-5
Turner Farm II—hist pl ME-1
Turner Farm Site—hist pl ME-1
Turner Ferry (historical)—locale MS-4
Turner Field—airport ND-7
Turner Field—airport PA-2
Turner Field (airport)—airport MS-4
Turner Field Cem—cemetery AL-4
Turner Flat—flat (2) CA-9
Turner Flat Campground—locale ID-8
Turner Flats—flat WY-8
Turner Flats—gut FL-3
Turner Ford—locale TN-4
Turner Ford Camp—locale OK-5
Turner Ford (historical)—locale MO-7
Turner Fork—stream MO-7
Turner Fork—stream NJ-2
Turner Fork—stream WV-2
Turner Fork—stream WY-8
Turner Gap—gap GA-3
Turner Glacier—glacier AK-9
Turner Golf Course—other MO-7
Turner Gulch—valley CA-9
Turner Gulch—valley (2) CO-8
Turner Gulch—valley (2) ID-8
Turner Gulch—valley OR-9
Turner Hall—hist pl IA-7
Turner Hall—hist pl MN-6
Turner Hall—hist pl WI-6
Turner Hill MA-1
Turner Hill—hist pl MA-1
Turner Hill—summit CO-8
Turner Hill—summit GA-3
Turner Hill—summit (2) ME-1
Turner Hill—summit MA-1
Turner Hill—summit MO-7
Turner Hill—summit PA-2
Turner Hill—summit SC-3
Turner Hill Ch—church GA-3
Turner Hill Park—park OK-5
Turner Hills Cem—cemetery AR-4
Turner Hill Sch (historical)—school AL-4
Turner (historical)—locale SD-7
**Turner (historical)**—pop pl IA-7
Turner Hole—bay VI-3
Turner Hollow—valley AR-4
Turner Hollow—valley KY-4
Turner Hollow—valley (3) MO-7
Turner Hollow—valley NY-2
Turner Hollow—valley (5) TN-4
Turner Hollow—valley UT-8
Turner Hollow—valley VA-3
Turner Hotel—hist pl ID-8
Turner House—hist pl AR-4
Turner House—hist pl MI-6
Turner HS—school GA-3
Turner HS—school KS-7
Turner HS—school NY-2
Turner HS—school TN-4
Turner HS—school (2) TX-5
Turner HS—school WI-6
Turner Island—island AK-9
Turner Island—island CA-9
Turner Island—island IL-6
Turner Island—island LA-4
Turner Island—island ME-1
Turner JHS—school OH-6
Turner Junction SD-7
Turner Key—island FL-3
Turner-Koepf House—hist pl WA-9
Turner Lake MN-6
Turner Lake—lake (2) AK-9
Turner Lake—lake AR-4
Turner Lake—lake (2) CA-9
Turner Lake—lake FL-3
Turner Lake—lake (2) GA-3
Turner Lake—lake (2) IL-6
Turner Lake—lake KY-4
Turner Lake—lake (2) MI-6
Turner Lake—lake (2) MN-6
Turner Lake—lake TX-5
Turner Lake—lake WA-9
Turner Lake—lake WI-6
Turner Lake—locale TX-5
Turner Lake—reservoir AR-4
Turner Lake—reservoir GA-3
Turner Lake—reservoir (2) TN-4
Turner Lake—reservoir TX-5
Turner Lake Dam—dam (2) MS-4
Turner Lake Dam—dam TN-4
Turner Lake Ford—locale GA-3
Turner Lakes—lake GA-3
Turner Landing—locale IL-6
Turner Landing—locale KY-4
Turner Landing—locale TN-4
Turner Landing (historical)—locale MS-4
Turner Landing (historical)—locale TN-4
Turner-LaRowe House—hist pl VA-3
Turner Lateral—canal ID-8
Turner Lateral—canal WY-8
Turner-Ledbetter House—hist pl AR-4
Turner Lodge—building OK-5
Turner Logan—swamp ME-1
Turner Lookout Tower—locale LA-4
Turner Marina—locale AL-4
Turner Meadows—flat CA-9
Turner Meadows—flat UT-8
Turner Memorial Bridge—bridge KS-7
Turner Memorial Ch—church NC-3
Turner Mine—mine CO-8
Turner M Lawrence Coll (historical)—school TN-4
Turner Mountain Ski Area—other MT-8
Turner Mountain Trail—trail CA-9
Turner Mtn—summit (2) CA-9
Turner Mtn—summit CT-1
Turner Mtn—summit ME-1
Turner Mtn—summit MT-8
Turner Mtn—summit NY-2
Turner Mtn—summit NC-3
Turner Mtn—summit OR-9
Turner Mtn—summit (3) VA-3
Turner Natural Bridge—other MO-7
Turner Neck—cape VA-3
Turner North Oil Field—oilfield KS-7
Turner Opening—area CA-9
Turner-Pardue Cem—cemetery TN-4
Turner Park IL-6
Turner Park—park MA-1
Turner Park—park OK-5
Turner Park—park TN-4
Turner Park—park TX-5
Turner Park Dam—dam MA-1
Turner Peak—summit CA-9
Turner Peak—summit (2) ID-8
Turner Peak—summit NE-7
Turner Peak—summit NM-5
Turner Point ID-8
Turner Point—cape (2) ME-1
Turner Point—cape MI-6
Turner Point—cape VI-3
Turner Pond AL-4
Turner Pond ME-1
Turner Pond—lake FL-3
Turner Pond—lake (4) ME-1
Turner Pond—lake (2) MA-1
Turner Pond—reservoir (2) MA-1
Turner Pond—reservoir NC-3
Turner Pond Dam—dam (3) MA-1
Turner Pond On High Hill Road Dam—dam MA-1
Turner Ponds—lake FL-3
Turner Ranch—locale AZ-5
Turner Ranch—locale CA-9
Turner Ranch—locale CO-8
Turner Ranch—locale MT-8
Turner Ranch—locale NE-7
Turner Ranch—locale (2) NM-5
Turner Ranch—locale OR-9
Turner Ranch—locale TX-5
Turner Ranch HQ—locale TX-5
Turner Ridge—ridge CA-9
Turner Ridge—ridge CT-1
Turner Ridge—ridge KY-4
Turner Ridge—ridge (2) OH-6
Turner Ridge—ridge TN-4
Turner Ridge—ridge VA-3
Turner Ridge Cem—cemetery KY-4
Turner Ridge Ch—church KY-4
Turner River—stream AK-9
Turner River—stream FL-3
Turner River Canal—canal FL-3
Turner River (Indian Reservation)—reserve FL-3
Turner River Site—hist pl FL-3
Turner Rsvr—reservoir (2) CO-8
Turner Rsvr—reservoir ID-8
Turner Rsvr—reservoir (2) OR-9
Turner Run WV-2
Turner Run—stream PA-2
Turner Run—stream (3) VA-3
Turners IN-6
Turners Bar TN-4
Turners Bay—bay WA-9
Turners Bayou—stream LA-4
Turners Bayou Canal—canal LA-4
Turners Bend—bend TN-4
Turners Bend—locale AR-4
Turners Bend Cem—cemetery AR-4
Turners Bluff—cliff UT-8
Turners Branch—stream SC-3
Turners Bridge—bridge NY-2
Turnersburg—locale NC-3
Turnersburgh NC-3
Turnersburgh VT-1
Turnersburg (Township of)—fmr MCD NC-3
Turners Campground Ch—church AR-4
Turners Cem—cemetery AL-4
Turner Sch—school AR-4
Turner Sch—school (3) CA-9
Turner Sch—school DC-2
Turner Sch—school GA-3
Turner Sch—school (3) IL-6
Turner Sch—school IA-7
Turner Sch—school KY-4
Turner Sch—school (2) MI-6
Turner Sch—school (8) MO-7
Turner Sch—school NY-2
Turner Sch—school OR-9
Turner Sch—school SD-7
Turner Sch—school TN-4
Turner Sch—school (3) TX-5
Turner Sch—school VA-3
Turner Sch—school WV-2
Turner Sch (abandoned)—school MO-7
Turners Chapel—church GA-3
Turners Chapel—church (2) MS-4
Turners Chapel—church NC-3
Turners Chapel Baptist Ch MS-4
Turners Chapel Cem—cemetery (2) MS-4
Turner Sch (historical)—school AL-4
Turner Sch (historical)—school MS-4
Turner School PA-2
Turner School (abandoned)—locale MO-7
**Turners Corner**—pop pl GA-3
**Turners Corner**—pop pl ME-1
**Turners Corner**—pop pl MI-6
Turners Cove—bay FL-3
Turners Creek GA-3
Turners Creek MS-4
Turners Creek PA-2
Turners Creek—stream AR-4
Turners Creek—stream CO-8
Turners Creek—stream FL-3
Turners Creek—stream KY-4
Turners Creek—stream MI-6
Turners Creek—stream (2) VA-3
Turners Crossroads—locale NC-3
Turners Crossroads—locale VA-3
Turners Cut—canal NC-3
Turners Falls—falls MA-1
**Turners Falls**—pop pl MA-1
Turners Falls Canal Headgates—dam MA-1
Turners Falls Dam—dam MA-1
Turners Falls HS—school MA-1
Turners Falls JHS—school MA-1
Turners Falls Number 1 Dam—dam MA-1
Turners Falls Rsvr—reservoir MA-1
Turners Ferry (historical)—locale AL-4
**Turners Flat**—pop pl MS-4
Turners Fork MO-7
Turners Gap—gap MD-2
Turner's Hall—hist pl LA-4
Turners Hill MA-1
Turners Hill—summit MA-1
Turners (historical)—locale AL-4
Turners (historical)—locale MS-4
Turner Shoals—bar AL-4
Turner Shoals Dam—dam NC-3
**Turner Shores**—pop pl MI-6
Turner's Island IL-6
Turners Kindergarten—school FL-3
Turners Knob—summit VA-3
Turners Lake—lake MO-7
Turners Lake—reservoir GA-3
Turners Lake—swamp LA-4
Turners Landing—locale MS-4
Turners Landing (historical)—locale AL-4
Turners Mill AL-4
Turners Mill—locale MO-7
Turners Mill (historical)—locale AL-4
Turners Mill (historical)—locale TN-4
Turners Mill Pond MA-1
Turners Mtn—summit VA-3
Turners Point—cape CT-1
Turners Pond MA-1
Turners Pond—lake CT-1
Turners Pond—lake MA-1
Turners Pond—reservoir GA-3
Turners Pond—reservoir NC-3
Turners Pond—reservoir UT-8
Turners Pond Dam—dam NC-3
Turner Spring—spring CA-9
Turner Spring—spring (2) ID-8
Turner Spring—spring KY-4
Turner Spring—spring (2) OR-9
Turner Springs WA-9
Turner Springs—spring CA-9
Turner Springs—spring WA-9
Turner Spur—ridge KY-4
Turners Ranch (historical)—locale AZ-5
**Turners Rock**—pop pl GA-3
Turners (RR name for Turners Station)—other KY-4
Turners Run—stream WV-2
Turners Shoal AL-4
Turners Shoal Landing AL-4
**Turners Siding**—pop pl VA-3
Turners Spring—spring CA-9
Turners Spring—spring MO-7
**Turners Station**—pop pl KY-4
**Turners Station**—pop pl TN-4
**Turners Station**—pop pl VA-3
**Turners Station (RR name Turners)**—pop pl KY-4
Turners Stations KS-7
Turners Station Sch (historical)—school TN-4
Turners Store—locale MS-4
Turners Store (historical)—locale MS-4
Turner Stork Grant—civil FL-3
Turner Station—building MO-7
**Turner Station**—pop pl CA-9
**Turner Store**—pop pl VA-3
Turner Store (historical)—locale AL-4
**Turners (Turners Station)**—pop pl MO-7
Turnersville MS-4
Turnersville—locale TX-5
**Turnersville**—pop pl KY-4
**Turnersville**—pop pl NJ-2
**Turnersville**—pop pl (2) PA-2
**Turnersville**—pop pl TN-4
**Turnersville**—pop pl TX-5
Turnersville (CCD)—cens area TX-5
Turnersville Cem—cemetery TX-5
Turnersville Post Office (historical)—building TN-4
Turner Swamp—stream NC-3
Turner Swamp—swamp (2) PA-2
Turner Swamp Ch—church NC-3
Turner Table—summit ID-8
Turner Tank—reservoir AZ-5
Turner Tank—reservoir (2) NM-5
Turner Tank—reservoir TX-5
Turner Timber Spring—spring UT-8
Turner Top—summit NC-3
Turnertown AL-4
Turnertown MS-4
Turnertown—locale KY-4
**Turnertown**—pop pl WV-2
Turnertown (Berrys Lick P O)—locale KY-4
Turner Town House—hist pl ME-1
**Turner (Town of)**—pop pl ME-1
**Turnertown (Selman City Post Office)**—pop pl TX-5
**Turner Township**—pop pl SD-7
**Turner (Township of)**—pop pl MI-6
**Turner (Township of)**—pop pl MN-6
**Turnertown (Turner)**—pop pl WV-2
Turner Trail—trail MA-1
Turner Valley—valley NE-7
Turner Valley—valley WA-9
Turner Valley Sch—school NE-7
Turnerville—locale MS-4
**Turnerville**—pop pl AL-4
**Turnerville**—pop pl GA-3
**Turnerville**—pop pl LA-4
**Turnerville**—pop pl MO-7
**Turnerville**—pop pl NM-5
**Turnerville**—pop pl WY-8
Turnerville Acad (historical)—school MS-4
Turnerville (CCD)—cens area GA-3
Turnerville Ch—church AL-4
Turnerville Community—locale WY-8
Turnerville (historical)—locale KS-7
Turnerville Post Office (historical)—building MS-4
Turnerville Sch—school AL-4
Turner Ward Knob—summit AR-4
Turner-Ward Sch (historical)—school TN-4
Turner Wash—valley UT-8
Turner Water Canyon—valley UT-8
Turner Well—well (3) NM-5
Turner Well—well TX-5
Turner-White-McGee House—hist pl TX-5
Turner Windmill—locale AZ-5
Turner Windmill—locale (2) NM-5
Turner Windmill—locale TX-5
**Turnetta**—pop pl MS-4
Turnetta P. O. MS-4
Turney AR-4
Turney—locale TX-5
**Turney**—pop pl MO-7
**Turney**—pop pl TN-4
Turney, Canal (historical)—canal AZ-5
Turney Branch—stream TN-4
Turney Cave—cave TX-5
Turney Cem—cemetery (2) AL-4
Turney Cem—cemetery PA-2
Turney Cem—cemetery TN-4
Turney Center for Youthful Offenders—locale TN-4
Turney Corners—locale NY-2
Turney Crossroads—locale AL-4
Turney Draw—valley TX-5
Turney Gulch Campground—park AZ-5
Turney Hill—summit WI-6
Turney Hill Cem—cemetery WI-6
Turney Knob—summit TN-4
Turney Peak—summit TX-5
Turney Ranch Trail—trail OK-5
Turney Ridge AR-4
Turney Sch—school IL-6
Turney Spring—spring (2) AL-4
Turney Spring—spring AZ-5
Turney Spring—spring CA-9
Turney Township (historical)—civil SD-7
Turnham McCowan Cem—cemetery TX-5
Turnham Mtn—summit OK-5
Turn Hole LA-4
Turn Hole—bend AL-4
Turn Hole—lake GA-3
Turn Hole—lake SC-3
Turn Hole—lake TN-4
Turnhole Bend—bend KY-4
Turnhole Branch—stream KY-4
Turnhole Branch—stream WV-2
Turnhole Knob—summit VA-3
Turning Basin—basin FL-3
Turning Basin—basin OH-6
Turning Basin—bay FL-3
Turning Basin—channel LA-4
Turning Basin—harbor MI-6
Turning Basin No 1—other IL-6
Turning Basin No 3—other IL-6
Turning Basin No 5—other IL-6
Turning Hill—summit AZ-5
Turning Island—island AK-9
Turninglathe Branch—stream GA-3
Turning Point Mine—mine AZ-5
Turnip Branch—stream KY-4
Turnip Canal—canal CA-9
Turnip Creek—stream VA-3
Turnip Hill—summit KY-4
**Turnip Hole**—pop pl PA-2
Turniphole Mtn—summit WV-2
Turnip Island—island (4) ME-1
Turnip Island Ledge—bar ME-1
Turnip Knob—summit MO-7
Turnip Lake—lake MN-6
Turnip Meadow (Historical)—swamp CT-1
Turnip Mountain—ridge GA-3
Turnippatch Hollow—valley KY-4
Turnip Patch Point—cape DE-2
Turnip Patch Ridge—ridge VA-3
Turnip Patch Run—stream PA-2
Turnippatch Trail—trail PA-2
Turnip Pond—lake FL-3
Turnip Run PA-2
Turnip Run—stream PA-2
Turnipseed Cem—cemetery (3) MS-4
Turnipseed Creek—stream ID-8
Turnipseed Creek—stream TN-4
Turnipseed (historical)—locale AL-4
Turnipseed Lake—reservoir AL-4
Turnipseed Lake—reservoir GA-3
Turnipseed Lake Dam—dam AL-4
Turnipseed Shoals—bar AL-4
Turnipseeds Store (historical)—locale AL-4
Turnip Top—summit SC-3
Turnip Top Hollow—valley MO-7
Turniptown Ch—church GA-3
Turniptown Creek—stream GA-3
Turniptown Mtn GA-3
Turniptown Mtn—summit GA-3
Turnip Yard—bar ME-1
Turnip Yard—bay ME-1
Turn Island—island (2) AK-9
Turn Island—island WA-9
Turn Island State Park—park WA-9
**Turnkey**—pop pl DE-2
Turnley Canyon—valley NV-8
Turnley Cem—cemetery LA-4
Turnley Creek—stream MT-8
Turnley Spring—spring NV-8
Turnmill Run—stream WV-2
Turn Mtn—summit AK-9
Turn of Bullfrog—summit UT-8
Turn off the Wash—bend AZ-5
Turn Of River CT-1
**Turn of River**—pop pl CT-1
Turn-of-River Bridge—hist pl CT-1
Turn of the Road Well—well NV-8
Turn Of The Swamp—area GA-3
Turnout—locale NC-3
Turnout Spring—spring AZ-5
Turnover Cem—cemetery AL-4
Turnover Creek—stream IN-6
Turnover Creek—stream TX-5
Turnover Hill—summit TN-4
Turnow Cem—cemetery WA-9
Turnpike MA-1
Turnpike—locale ID-8
Turnpike—locale TN-4
**Turnpike**—pop pl MS-4

**Turnpike**—pop pl ... NC-3
Turnpike—post sta ... CT-1
Turnpike—post sta ... VA-3
*Turnpike Baptist Church* ... MS-4
Turnpike Bluff—cliff ... MO-7
Turnpike Branch—stream ... AL-4
Turnpike Branch—stream ... FL-3
Turnpike Branch—stream ... GA-3
Turnpike Branch—stream ... KY-4
Turnpike Branch—stream ... NC-3
Turnpike Bridge—bridge ... MS-4
Turnpike Cem—cemetery (2) ... PA-2
Turnpike Cem—cemetery ... TN-4
Turnpike Ch—church ... GA-3
Turnpike Ch—church ... MS-4
Turnpike Creek—stream (2) ... GA-3
Turnpike Creek—stream ... NY-2
Turnpike Creek—stream (2) ... NC-3
Turnpike Creek—stream ... TX-5
Turnpike Creek—stream ... VA-3
Turnpike Creek—stream ... WA-9
**Turnpike (Fairlawn)**—pop pl ... MA-1
*Turnpike Hill* ... MA-1
Turnpike Hill—summit ... MS-4
*Turnpike Hollow* ... TN-4
Turnpike Hollow—valley ... AR-4
Turnpike Hollow—valley ... KY-4
Turnpike House—hist pl ... MA-1
Turnpike (Hungerford)—uninc pl ... PA-2
Turnpike Lake—lake ... MA-1
Turnpike Mtn—summit ... TX-5
Turnpike Number One Airp—airport ... PA-2
Turnpike Point—cape ... TN-4
Turnpike Pond—lake ... NY-2
*Turnpike Ponds* ... MA-1
Turnpike Sch—school ... MS-4
Turnpike Sch—school ... NH-1
Turnpike Sch—school (2) ... VT-1
Turnpike Sch (historical)—school ... TN-4
Turnpike Spring—spring ... TN-4
Turnpike Station—locale ... PA-2
Turnpike Station (historical)—locale ... MA-1
Turnpike Swamp, The—swamp ... AL-4
Turn Point—cape (2) ... AK-9
Turn Point—cape ... LA-4
Turn Point—cape ... WA-9
Turn Point Cem—cemetery ... AK-9
Turnridge Creek—stream ... OR-9
Turn Rock—pillar ... AK-9
Turn Rock Light—locale ... WA-9
Turn Round—locale ... AL-4
Turnstake Island—island ... TX-5
Turn Store and the Tinsmith's Shop—hist pl ... PA-2
Turn Table—summit ... CA-9
Turntable Creek—stream ... WI-6
Turntable Hollow—valley ... PA-2
Turntable Mtn—summit ... ID-8
Turntime Branch—stream ... GA-3
Turntime Crossroads—locale ... GA-3
Turntine Hollow—valley ... AL-4
*Turnup* ... PA-2
Turnup Run—stream ... PA-2
Turn Villa—locale ... PA-2
Turn Wash Tank—reservoir ... AZ-5
Turnwold—hist pl ... GA-3
Turnwood—locale ... NY-2
Turo Brake—swamp ... MS-4
*Turo Creek* ... TX-5
Turo (historical)—locale ... MS-4
Turo Mine—mine ... NV-8
**Turon**—pop pl ... KS-7
**Turon**—pop pl ... MS-4
Turon Cem—cemetery ... KS-7
Turon Elem Sch—school ... KS-7
*Turpee Brook* ... NY-2
Turpeinen Creek—stream ... MI-6
Turpela Lake—lake ... MN-6
Turpen Ranch—locale ... CO-8
*Turpentine* ... NJ-2
Turpentine Branch—stream ... GA-3
Turpentine Branch—stream ... KY-4
Turpentine Branch—stream ... LA-4
Turpentine Camp—locale (2) ... AL-4
Turpentine Creek—stream (2) ... OR-9
Turpentine Creek—stream ... TX-5
Turpentine Dam—dam ... SC-3
Turpentine Hollow—valley ... AR-4
Turpentine Hollow—valley ... WA-9
Turpentine Lake—lake ... OR-9
Turpentine Peak—summit ... OR-9
Turpentine Peak Trail—trail ... OR-9
Turpentine Run—stream ... VI-3
Turpentine Spring—spring ... LA-4
Turpentine Spring—spring ... TX-5
Turpentine Still Branch—stream ... AL-4
Turper Park—flat ... UT-8
Turpin—locale ... AL-4
Turpin—locale ... IL-6
Turpin—locale ... VA-3
**Turpin**—pop pl ... IN-6
**Turpin**—pop pl ... OK-5
Turpin Branch—stream ... KY-4
Turpin Branch—stream ... MO-7
Turpin Branch—stream ... NC-3
Turpin Branch—stream ... SC-3
Turpin Canyon—valley ... OR-9
Turpin Cem—cemetery ... AL-4
Turpin Cem—cemetery (2) ... KY-4
Turpin Cem—cemetery ... MS-4
Turpin Cem—cemetery ... MO-7
Turpin Cem—cemetery ... OK-5
Turpin Cem—cemetery ... TN-4
Turpin Ch—church ... OK-5
Turpin Cove—bay ... MD-2
Turpin Creek—stream ... MS-4
Turpin Creek—stream ... VA-3
Turpin Creek—stream (2) ... WY-8
Turpine Lake—reservoir ... TN-4
Turpin Grain Elevator—hist pl ... OK-5
**Turpin Hill**—pop pl ... IN-6
Turpin Hill—summit ... AR-4
Turpin Hill—uninc pl ... GA-3
**Turpin Hills**—pop pl ... OH-6
Turpin Hollow—valley ... AL-4
Turpin Hollow—valley ... KY-4
Turpin Hollow—valley ... TN-4
Turpin House—hist pl ... KY-4
Turpin-Kofler-Buja House—hist pl ... LA-4
Turpin Lake—lake (2) ... NE-7
Turpin Lake—lake ... OR-9
Turpin Meadow—flat ... WY-8
Turpin Meadow Campground—locale ... WY-8
Turpin Meadow Lodge—locale ... WY-8
*Turpin Mill* ... IN-6
Turpin Ridge—ridge ... OR-9
Turpin Rsvr—reservoir ... WY-8
Turpin Sch—school ... KY-4
Turpin Sch—school ... MO-7
Turpin Site—hist pl ... OH-6
Turpin Slough—lake ... AL-4
Turpin Spring—spring ... OR-9
Turpin Spring—spring ... TN-4
Turpin Switch (historical)—locale ... MS-4
Turpin Tank—reservoir ... NM-5
*Turpin Vill* ... IN-6
Turps—locale ... LA-4
Turpy Creek—stream ... OR-9
Turquaise Lake—lake ... WA-9
**Turquillo**—pop pl ... NM-5
Turquoise—locale ... NM-5
**Turquoise Beach**—pop pl ... FL-3
Turquoise Butte—summit ... AZ-5
Turquoise Butte—summit ... NM-5
Turquoise Canyon—valley ... AZ-5
Turquoise Gulch—valley ... CO-8
Turquoise Hill—summit ... NM-5
Turquoise Lake—lake ... AK-9
Turquoise Lake—lake ... CA-9
Turquoise Lake—lake ... ID-8
Turquoise Lake—lake ... MT-8
Turquoise Lake—lake (2) ... WY-8
Turquoise Lake—reservoir ... CO-8
Turquoise Mine—mine (2) ... NV-8
Turquoise Mine—mine ... NM-5
Turquoise Mining Area—mine ... CA-9
Turquoise Mtn—summit (2) ... AZ-5
Turquoise Mtn—summit ... CA-9
Turquoise Mtn—summit ... NM-5
Turquoise Park—park ... AZ-5
Turquoise Peak—summit ... AZ-5
Turquoise RV Park—park ... UT-8
Turquoise Spring—spring ... NV-8
Turquoise Trading Post—locale ... NM-5
Turquois Lakes—lake ... PA-2
Turquois Spring—spring ... NM-5
**Turramurra Lodge Condominiums**—pop pl ... UT-8
*Turrel Hill* ... NY-2
**Turrell**—pop pl ... AR-4
Turrell Canyon—valley ... OR-9
Turrell Corners—locale ... PA-2
*Turrenteins Store* ... AL-4
Turrentine Cem—cemetery ... AR-4
**Turrentine Estates (subdivision)**—pop pl ... NC-3
Turrentine JHS—school ... NC-3
Turret—locale ... CO-8
Turret Arch—arch ... UT-8
*Turret Butte* ... AZ-5
Turret Creek—stream ... CA-9
Turret Creek—stream ... CO-8
Turret Creek—stream ... WY-8
Turret Creek Meadows—flat ... CO-8
Turret Field—park ... KY-4
*Turret Mountain* ... MT-8
Turret Mtn—summit ... WY-8
Turret Needles—pillar ... CO-8
Turret Peak—summit ... AZ-5
Turret Peak—summit ... CA-9
Turret Peak—summit (3) ... CO-8
Turret Peak—summit ... WY-8
Turret Point—cape ... AK-9
Turrets, The—hist pl ... ME-1
Turrill Brook—stream ... CT-1
Turrill Sch—school ... MI-6
**Turro**—pop pl ... IA-7
T U Rsvr—reservoir ... MT-8
Turtle—locale ... MI-6
Turtle—pillar ... UT-8
**Turtle**—pop pl ... MO-7
Turtle Back Arch—arch ... KY-4
*Turtle Back Dome* ... CA-9
Turtleback Dome—summit ... CA-9
Turtleback Island—island ... AL-4
*Turtleback Mtn* ... AZ-5
Turtleback Mtn—summit ... AZ-5
Turtleback Mtn—summit ... WA-9
*Turtle Back Range* ... WA-9
Turtleback Rock—island ... VI-3
Turtleback Wash—stream ... AZ-5
*Turtle Bay* ... TX-5
Turtle Bay—bay (2) ... FL-3
Turtle Bay—bay ... LA-4
Turtle Bay—bay ... MN-6
Turtle Bay—bay ... TX-5
Turtle Bay—bay ... WI-6
Turtle Bay—bay ... VI-3
Turtle Bay—swamp ... FL-3
Turtle Bay Gardens Hist Dist—hist pl ... NY-2
Turtle Bay Oil Field—oilfield ... TX-5
Turtle Bayou—channel ... TX-5
Turtle Bayou—gut (5) ... LA-4
**Turtle Bayou**—pop pl ... TX-5
Turtle Bayou—stream (2) ... LA-4
Turtle Bayou—stream (2) ... TX-5
Turtle Bayou Gas Field—oilfield ... LA-4
Turtle Bend—bend ... MA-1
Turtle Bend Mtn—summit ... MA-1
Turtle Branch—stream ... AL-4
Turtle Branch—stream ... DE-2
Turtle Branch—stream (2) ... KY-4
Turtle Branch—stream ... MD-2
Turtle Branch—stream ... NC-3
Turtle Brook—stream (2) ... ME-1
Turtle Brook—stream (2) ... NJ-2
Turtle Brook Trail—trail ... NH-1
*Turtle Butte* ... SD-7
Turtle Butte—summit ... MT-8
Turtle Butte—summit ... SD-7
Turtle Buttes—summit ... CO-8
Turtle Canyon—valley ... CA-9
Turtle Canyon—valley ... UT-8
Turtle Cauldron—cave ... TN-4
Turtle Cave—cave ... AL-4
Turtle Cave—cave ... HI-9
Turtle Cem—cemetery ... WI-6
*Turtle Cove* ... RI-1
Turtle Cove—basin ... OR-9
Turtle Cove—bay ... ME-1
Turtle Cove—bay (2) ... NJ-2
Turtle Cove—bay (2) ... NY-2
Turtle Cove—bay ... TX-5
Turtle Cove Lake—lake ... FL-3
Turtlecrawl Bank—bar ... FL-3
Turtlecrawl Point—cape ... FL-3
*Turtle Creek* ... DE-2
*Turtle Creek* ... IN-6
*Turtle Creek* ... KS-7
*Turtle Creek* ... OH-6
*Turtle Creek* ... TX-5
Turtle Creek—gut ... NJ-2
Turtle Creek—locale ... WV-2
**Turtle Creek**—pop pl ... PA-2
Turtle Creek—stream ... AR-4
Turtle Creek—stream (3) ... CA-9
Turtle Creek—stream ... CO-8
Turtle Creek—stream (3) ... FL-3
Turtle Creek—stream (2) ... IL-6
Turtle Creek—stream (2) ... IN-6
Turtle Creek—stream (2) ... IA-7
Turtle Creek—stream (2) ... KS-7
Turtle Creek—stream (2) ... KY-4
Turtle Creek—stream (4) ... MI-6
Turtle Creek—stream (3) ... MN-6
Turtle Creek—stream (5) ... NE-7
Turtle Creek—stream ... NJ-2
Turtle Creek—stream (2) ... ND-7
Turtle Creek—stream (3) ... OH-6
Turtle Creek—stream (2) ... OK-5
Turtle Creek—stream (3) ... PA-2
Turtle Creek—stream ... SC-3
Turtle Creek—stream (3) ... SD-7
Turtle Creek—stream (5) ... TX-5
Turtle Creek—stream ... WV-2
Turtle Creek—stream (3) ... WI-6
Turtle Creek Bay—bay ... FL-3
Turtle Creek Bay—bay ... OH-6
Turtle Creek Borough—civil ... PA-2
Turtle Creek Cem—cemetery ... OH-6
Turtle Creek Cem—cemetery ... TX-5
Turtle Creek Dam—dam ... SD-7
Turtle Creek (historical)—stream ... ND-7
Turtle Creek HS—school ... PA-2
Turtle Creek Lake—reservoir ... IN-6
Turtle Creek Lake Area—park ... OH-6
Turtle Creek Lake Dam—dam ... IN-6
Turtle Creek Point—cape ... FL-3
Turtle Creek Rec Area—park ... IA-7
*Turtle Creek River* ... SD-7
Turtle Creek Sch—school ... IL-6
Turtle Creek Site (15BK13)—hist pl ... KY-4
Turtle Creek State Wildlife Mngmt Area—park ... MN-6
**Turtle Creek (subdivision)**—pop pl (2) ... AZ-5
**Turtle Creek (subdivision)**—pop pl ... MS-4
Turtle Creek Township (historical)—civil ... SD-7
Turtle Creek (Township of)—civ div ... MN-6
Turtle Creek (Township of)—civ div (2) ... OH-6
**Turtle Creek (Westinghouse)**—pop pl ... PA-2
Turtle Dam—dam ... WI-6
*Turtle Dome* ... CA-9
Turtledove Cay—island ... VI-3
*Turtledove Ridge* ... VA-3
Turtle Draw—valley ... MT-8
Turtle Flambeau Flowage—reservoir ... WI-6
Turtlefoot Lake—lake ... SD-7
Turtle Graveyard Cave—cave ... TN-4
Turtle Ground Creek—stream ... NJ-2
Turtle Gut—gut (2) ... NJ-2
Turtle Gut—gut ... NC-3
*Turtle Gut Inlet* ... NJ-2
Turtle Gut Shoals—bar ... NJ-2
*Turtle Gutt* ... NJ-2
Turtle Harbor—harbor ... FL-3
Turtle Harbor—lake ... FL-3
*Turtle Harbor Channel* ... FL-3
Turtle Head—cape ... ME-1
Turtle Head Cove—bay ... ME-1
Turtle Head Lake—lake ... IL-6
Turtlehead Mtn—summit ... MT-8
Turtlehead Mtn—summit ... NV-8
Turtle Hill—summit ... AK-9
Turtle Hill—summit ... WY-8
Turtle Hole, The—basin ... CA-9
Turtle Hole Camp—locale ... TX-5
Turtle Hole Creek—stream (2) ... TX-5
Turtle Hook JHS—school ... NY-2
Turtle Island—island (2) ... AK-9
Turtle Island—island ... FL-3
Turtle Island—island ... IL-6
Turtle Island—island ... IA-7
Turtle Island—island (3) ... ME-1
Turtle Island—island ... MA-1
Turtle Island—island ... MI-6
Turtle Island—island ... MN-6
Turtle Island—island ... NH-1
Turtle Island—island ... NJ-2
Turtle Island—island (2) ... NY-2
Turtle Island—island ... OH-6
Turtle Island—island ... SC-3
Turtle Island Hollow—valley ... MO-7
Turtle Island Ledge—bar ... ME-1
Turtle Island Spring—spring ... MO-7
Turtle Key—island (2) ... FL-3
*Turtle lake* ... IA-7
*Turtle Lake* ... ME-1
*Turtle Lake* ... MI-6
*Turtle Lake* ... MN-6
*Turtle Lake* ... OH-6
*Turtle Lake* ... WI-6
Turtle Lake—lake ... AR-4
Turtle Lake—lake (4) ... CA-9
Turtle Lake—lake ... ID-8
Turtle Lake—lake ... IL-6
Turtle Lake—lake (2) ... LA-4
Turtle Lake—lake (8) ... MI-6
Turtle Lake—lake (16) ... MN-6
Turtle Lake—lake ... MO-7
Turtle Lake—lake ... MT-8
Turtle Lake—lake ... ND-7
Turtle Lake—lake ... SD-7
Turtle Lake—lake (5) ... WA-9
Turtle Lake—lake (14) ... WI-6
**Turtle Lake**—pop pl ... LA-4
**Turtle Lake**—pop pl ... ND-7
**Turtle Lake**—pop pl ... WI-6
Turtle Lake—swamp ... WI-6
Turtle Lake Branch—stream ... FL-3
Turtle Lake Cem—cemetery ... MN-6
Turtle Lake Cem—cemetery ... ND-7
Turtle Lake Hill—summit ... MI-6
Turtle Lake Island—island ... LA-4
Turtle Lake Lookout Tower—locale ... MI-6
Turtle Lake Park—park ... MN-6
Turtle Lake Sch—school ... MN-6
**Turtle Lake (Town of)**—pop pl ... WI-6
**Turtle Lake Township**—pop pl ... ND-7
**Turtle Lake (Township of)**—pop pl (2) ... MN-6
Turtlelick Hollow—valley ... WV-2
Turtle Lot Brook—stream ... NY-2
Turtle Marsh State Wildlife Mngmt Area—park ... MN-6
Turtle Mill Brook—stream ... NJ-2
Turtle Mine—mine ... ID-8
Turtle Mound—hist pl ... FL-3
Turtle Mound—summit ... FL-3
*Turtle Mountain* ... ND-7
Turtle Mountain—ridge ... CA-9
Turtle Mountain Ch—church ... ND-7
**Turtle Mountain Ind Res**—pop pl ... ND-7
Turtle Mountains—range ... CA-9
Turtle Mountains—range ... ND-7
Turtle Mountains—unorg reg ... ND-7
Turtle Mountain Trail Two Hundred Nineteen—trail ... AZ-5
*Turtle Mtn* ... AZ-5
Turtle Mtn—summit (2) ... AZ-5
Turtle Mtn—summit ... CA-9
Turtle Mtn—summit ... CO-8
Turtle Mtn—summit ... NM-5
Turtle Neck Creek—stream ... TX-5
Turtle Neck Point—cape ... VA-3
Turtle Oracle Mound—hist pl ... MN-6
Turtlepen Point—cape ... FL-3
Turtle Pen Point—cape ... TX-5
Turtle Pen Slough—gut ... FL-3
*Turtle Point* ... PA-2
*Turtle Point* ... TX-5
Turtle Point—cape ... FL-3
Turtle Point—cape ... TX-5
Turtle Point—cape ... VA-3
**Turtlepoint**—pop pl ... PA-2
Turtle Point—summit ... PA-2
Turtle Point Hollow—valley ... PA-2
Turtle Point (RR name for Turtlepoint)—other ... PA-2
**Turtlepoint (RR name Turtle Point)**—pop pl ... PA-2
Turtle Point Station—locale ... PA-2
Turtle Point Yacht and Country Club—other ... AL-4
*Turtle Pond* ... DE-2
*Turtle Pond* ... FL-3
*Turtle Pond* ... MA-1
Turtle Pond—lake (3) ... CT-1
Turtle Pond—lake ... IL-6
Turtle Pond—lake (2) ... ME-1
Turtle Pond—lake (5) ... MA-1
Turtle Pond—lake (2) ... NH-1
Turtle Pond—lake (2) ... NJ-2
Turtle Pond—lake (3) ... NY-2
Turtle Pond—lake ... RI-1
Turtle Pond—lake ... VT-1
Turtle Pond Creek—stream ... NC-3
Turtle Rapids—rapids ... WI-6
Turtle Reef—bar ... AK-9
Turtle Reef—bar ... FL-3
Turtle Ridge—ridge ... ME-1
*Turtle River* ... SD-7
**Turtle River**—pop pl ... MN-6
Turtle River—stream ... GA-3
Turtle River—stream (2) ... MN-6
Turtle River—stream ... ND-7
Turtle River—stream ... WI-6
Turtle River (historical)—locale ... ND-7
*Turtle River Lake* ... MN-6
Turtle River Lake—lake ... MN-6
Turtle River State Park—park ... ND-7
*Turtle River Station* ... ND-7
Turtle River Swamp—swamp ... GA-3
**Turtle River Township**—pop pl ... ND-7
Turtle River (Township of)—civ div ... MN-6
Turtle Rock—bar ... NC-3
Turtle Rock—cape ... NH-1
Turtle Rock—cliff ... AZ-5
Turtle Rock—island ... CA-9
Turtle Rock—pillar ... CA-9
Turtle Rock—pillar ... ID-8
Turtle Rock—pillar ... OR-9
Turtle Rock—summit ... CT-1
Turtle Rock—summit ... WA-9
Turtle Rock—summit ... WY-8
Turtle Rock County Park—park ... CA-9
Turtle Rocks—island ... NY-2
Turtle Rocks—other ... PA-2
Turtle Rocks—rock ... FL-3
Turtle Rock Spring—spring ... NV-8
Turtle Rsvr—reservoir ... MT-8
*Turtle Run* ... OH-6
*Turtle Run* ... PA-2
Turtle Run—stream ... WV-2
Turtle Shell Island—island ... OH-6
Turtle Shell Pond—lake ... GA-3
Turtleskin Cem—cemetery ... MS-4
*Turtleskin Church* ... MS-4
Turtleskin Creek—stream ... MS-4
Turtle Spring—spring (2) ... AZ-5
Turtle Spring Branch—stream ... MO-7
Turtle Springs—spring ... OK-5
*Turtle Stuck* ... AZ-5
*Turtle Tail* ... AZ-5
Turtle Tank—reservoir ... AZ-5
Turtle Tank—reservoir ... TX-5
*Turtle Thorofare* ... NJ-2
**Turtletown**—pop pl ... TN-4
Turtletown Baptist Ch—church ... TN-4
Turtletown (CCD)—cens area ... TN-4
Turtletown Creek—stream ... TN-4
Turtletown Division—civil ... TN-4
Turtletown Elem Sch—school ... TN-4
**Turtle (Town of)**—pop pl ... WI-6
Turtletown Post Office—building ... TN-4
Turtletree Fork—stream ... WV-2
Turtle Valley—valley ... CA-9
**Turtleville**—pop pl ... PA-2
Turtleville Iron Bridge—hist pl ... WI-6
Turtle Windmill—locale ... NM-5
**Turton**—pop pl ... SD-7
Turton Creek—stream ... WI-6
**Turton Township**—pop pl ... SD-7
Turuno Canyon—valley ... AZ-5
*Turupah Flat* ... NV-8
*Turvals Creek* ... MD-2
Turvey Creek—stream ... WA-9
*Turvile Creek* ... MD-2
*Turvill Creek* ... MD-2
Turville Creek—stream ... MD-2
Turville Neck—cape ... MD-2
Turvin Creek—stream ... GA-3
Turvoid Woods County Park—park ... IA-7
*Turwah Creek* ... CA-9
Turwar Creek—stream ... CA-9
*Turwur Creek* ... CA-9
Tusas Box—valley ... NM-5
Tusas Cem—cemetery ... NM-5
Tusas Corral—locale ... NM-5
Tusas Mountains—range ... NM-5
Tusas Mtn—summit ... NM-5
Tusas Ridge—ridge ... NM-5
Tusayan—area ... AZ-5
**Tusayan**—pop pl ... AZ-5
Tusayan Airp—airport ... AZ-5
*Tusayan Province* ... AZ-5
Tusayan Ranger Station—locale ... AZ-5
Tusayan Ruins—hist pl ... AZ-5
Tusayan Ruins—locale ... AZ-5
*Tuscahoma* ... AL-4
Tuscahoma Acad (historical)—school ... MS-4
Tuscahoma Ch (historical)—church ... MS-4
Tuscahoma Ferry (historical)—locale ... MS-4
Tuscahoma (historical)—locale ... MS-4
Tuscahoma Landing—locale ... AL-4
*Tuscalameta* ... MS-4
*Tuscalamita Creek* ... MS-4
**Tuscaloosa**—pop pl ... AL-4
Tuscaloosa, Lake—reservoir ... AL-4
Tuscaloosa Acad—school ... AL-4
Tuscaloosa Area Vocational Sch—school ... AL-4
*Tuscaloosa Baptist Tuscaloosa Baptist Church* ... AL-4
Tuscaloosa Bible Institute—school ... AL-4
Tuscaloosa (CCD)—cens area ... AL-4
Tuscaloosa Ch of God—church ... AL-4
Tuscaloosa Christian Sch—school ... AL-4
*Tuscaloosa City-County Park* ... AL-4
Tuscaloosa Community Center—building ... AL-4
Tuscaloosa Country Club—locale ... AL-4
**Tuscaloosa County**—pop pl ... AL-4
Tuscaloosa County Health Center—hospital ... AL-4
Tuscaloosa County HS—school ... AL-4
Tuscaloosa County Industrial Park—locale ... AL-4
*Tuscaloosa County Lake* ... AL-4
*Tuscaloosa County Training School* ... AL-4
*Tuscaloosa District High School* ... AL-4
Tuscaloosa Division—civil ... AL-4
*Tuscaloosa Female College* ... AL-4
*Tuscaloosa High School* ... AL-4
*Tuscaloosa Institute* ... AL-4
Tuscaloosa Jaycees Fairground—park ... AL-4
*Tuscaloosa Junior High School* ... AL-4
*Tuscaloosa Lock and Dam* ... AL-4
Tuscaloosa Memorial Park (Cemetery)—cemetery ... AL-4
Tuscaloosa Mine (underground)—mine (2) ... AL-4
Tuscaloosa MS—school ... AL-4
Tuscaloosa Municipal Airp—airport ... AL-4
Tuscaloosa Number 1 Mine (surface)—mine ... AL-4
Tuscaloosa Primitive Baptist Ch—church ... AL-4
Tuscaloosa Public Library—building ... AL-4
Tuscaloosa Public Sch (historical)—school ... AL-4
Tuscaloosa Sailing Club—locale ... AL-4
Tuscaloosa Shoals (historical)—bar ... AL-4
Tuscaloosa Surgical Center—hospital ... AL-4
Tuscaloosa Univ HS (historical)—school ... AL-4
Tuscaloosa Water Works—building ... AL-4
*Tuscalum* ... OH-6
Tuscan—locale ... MS-4
**Tuscan**—pop pl ... NY-2
Tuscan Buttes—summit ... CA-9
Tuscania Sch—school ... MT-8
**Tuscanooga**—pop pl ... FL-3
Tuscanooga Ch—church ... FL-3
Tuscan Sch—school ... NJ-2
Tuscan Springs—spring ... CA-9
Tusca Plaza—locale ... PA-2
**Tuscarawas**—pop pl ... OH-6
Tuscarawas Ave Sch—school ... OH-6
**Tuscarawas (County)**—pop pl ... OH-6
Tuscarawas County Courthouse—hist pl ... OH-6
Tuscarawas River—stream ... OH-6
Tuscarawas River Diversion Dam—dam ... OH-6
**Tuscarawas (Township of)**—pop pl (2) ... OH-6
Tuscarawas Valley HS—school ... OH-6
Tuscarora—locale ... IL-6
**Tuscarora**—pop pl ... MD-2
**Tuscarora**—pop pl ... NV-8
**Tuscarora**—pop pl ... NY-2
**Tuscarora**—pop pl ... NC-3
**Tuscarora**—pop pl (2) ... PA-2
Tuscarora, Mount—summit ... NY-2
Tuscarora, Mount—summit ... UT-8
Tuscarora Acad—hist pl ... PA-2
Tuscarora Academy Historic Site—locale ... PA-2
Tuscarora Bay—bay ... NY-2
**Tuscarora Beach**—pop pl ... NC-3
Tuscarora Camp—locale ... NC-3
Tuscarora Ch—church ... PA-2
Tuscarora Ch—church ... WV-2
Tuscarora Country Club—other ... VA-3
*Tuscarora Creek* ... PA-2
Tuscarora Creek—stream (2) ... MD-2
Tuscarora Creek—stream ... MT-8
Tuscarora Creek—stream (3) ... NY-2
Tuscarora Creek—stream (3) ... PA-2
Tuscarora Creek—stream (2) ... VA-3
Tuscarora Creek—stream ... WV-2
Tuscarora Creek Hist Dist—hist pl ... WV-2
Tuscarora Falls—falls ... PA-2
Tuscarora Gulch—valley ... CO-8
Tuscarora Hill—summit ... NY-2
Tuscarora Ind Res—873 (1980) ... NY-2
Tuscarora Lake—lake ... MN-6
Tuscarora Lake—lake ... NY-2
Tuscarora Lake—lake ... PA-2
Tuscarora Lake—reservoir ... PA-2
Tuscarora Lake Dam—dam ... PA-2
Tuscarora Mine—mine ... MT-8
*Tuscarora Mountains* ... PA-2
*Tuscarora Mtn* ... PA-2
Tuscarora Mtn—range ... PA-2
Tuscarora Mtns—range ... NV-8
*Tuscarora Narrows* ... PA-2
Tuscarora Park—locale ... NY-2
Tuscarora Sch—school (2) ... NY-2
Tuscarora State For—forest ... PA-2
Tuscarora State Park—park ... PA-2
*Tuscarora State Park Dam* ... PA-2
Tuscarora Station—locale ... MD-2
**Tuscarora Summit**—pop pl ... PA-2
Tuscarora Summit—reservoir ... PA-2
**Tuscarora (Town of)**—pop pl ... NY-2
**Tuscarora Township**—pop pl ... ND-7
**Tuscarora (Township of)**—pop pl ... MI-6
**Tuscarora (Township of)**—pop pl (3) ... PA-2
Tuscarora Trail—trail ... PA-2
Tuscarora Tunnel—tunnel ... PA-2
Tuscarora Valley Sch—school ... PA-2
Tuscarora Wild Area—area ... PA-2
Tuscatucket Brook—stream ... RI-1
Tuscawilla—hist pl ... WV-2
Tuscawilla Assembly of God—church ... FL-3
Tuscawilla Lake—lake ... FL-3
Tuscawilla Park Hist Dist—hist pl ... FL-3
T U Sch—school ... MT-8
Tuschen Slough—lake ... SD-7
*Tuscher Wash* ... UT-8
*Tuscklum* ... TN-4
*Tuscoba* ... AL-4
**Tuscobia**—pop pl ... WI-6
Tuscobia Lake—lake ... WI-6
Tuscobia Park Falls State Trail—trail ... WI-6
Tuscocoillo Canyon—valley ... NM-5
Tuscohatchie Creek—stream ... WA-9
Tuscohatchie Lake—lake ... WA-9
**Tuscola**—pop pl ... IL-6
**Tuscola**—pop pl (2) ... MI-6
**Tuscola**—pop pl ... MS-4
**Tuscola**—pop pl ... TX-5
Tuscola Cem—cemetery ... MI-6
**Tuscola (County)**—pop pl ... MI-6
Tuscola HS—school ... NC-3
Tuscola Landing (historical)—locale ... MS-4
Tuscolameta Creek—stream ... MS-4
*Tuscola Methodist Church* ... MS-4
Tuscola Missionary Baptist Ch—church ... MS-4
**Tuscola Park**—pop pl ... NC-3
Tuscola Post Office (historical)—building ... MS-4
Tuscola Sch (historical)—school ... MS-4
Tuscola State Game Area—park ... MI-6
Tuscola Station—locale ... MI-6
**Tuscola (Township of)**—pop pl ... IL-6
**Tuscola (Township of)**—pop pl ... MI-6
**Tusconita (Littletown)**—pop pl ... AZ-5
*Tusconola* ... MS-4
Tuscor—locale ... MT-8
Tuscora Park—park (2) ... OH-6
Tuscor Creek—stream ... MT-8
Tuscor Hill—summit ... MT-8
*Tuscosso Creek* ... TX-5
**Tusculam**—pop pl ... PA-2
Tusculum—hist pl ... NJ-2
Tusculum—hist pl ... NC-3
Tusculum—locale ... GA-3
Tusculum—locale ... OH-6
**Tusculum**—pop pl ... PA-2
**Tusculum**—pop pl (2) ... TN-4
Tusculum Baptist Ch—church ... TN-4
Tusculum Ch—church ... GA-3
Tusculum Chapel—church ... TN-4
Tusculum Coll—school ... TN-4
*Tusculum College (corporate name Tusculum)* ... TN-4
Tusculum College Hist Dist—hist pl ... TN-4
Tusculum College Post Office—building ... TN-4
**Tusculum (corporate name for Tusculum College)**—pop pl ... TN-4
**Tusculum Heights**—pop pl ... TN-4
**Tusculum Place**—pop pl ... TN-4
*Tusculum Post Office* ... TN-4
Tusculum Town Hall—building ... TN-4
*Tusculum View Elementary School* ... TN-4
Tusculum View Sch—school ... TN-4
**Tuscumbia**—pop pl ... AL-4
**Tuscumbia**—pop pl ... MO-7
*Tuscumbia Baptist Church* ... AL-4
*Tuscumbia Baptist Church* ... MS-4
Tuscumbia Bar (inundated)—bar ... AL-4
Tuscumbia Bend—bend ... MS-4
Tuscumbia Cem—cemetery ... MS-4
Tuscumbia Ch—church (2) ... MS-4
Tuscumbia Creek—stream ... AZ-5
*Tuscumbia Grade and High School* ... AL-4
*Tuscumbia Graded School* ... AL-4
Tuscumbia Hist Dist—hist pl ... AL-4
Tuscumbia Landing (historical)—locale ... AL-4
Tuscumbia Landing Site—hist pl ... AL-4
Tuscumbia Mine—mine ... AZ-5
Tuscumbia Mtn—summit ... AZ-5
*Tuscumbia Public Sch* ... AL-4
*Tuscumbia River* ... MS-4
*Tuscumbia River* ... TN-4
Tuscumbia River—stream ... TN-4
Tuscumbia River Canal—canal ... MS-4
Tuscumbia River Canal—canal ... TN-4
Tuscumbia Sch (historical)—school (2) ... MS-4
Tuscumbias Grave—cemetery ... MS-4
*Tuscumbia Spring* ... AL-4
Tuscumbia Structure 38 Dam—dam ... MS-4
Tuscumbia Structure 39 Dam—dam ... MS-4
Tuscumbia Valley—valley ... AL-4
Tuscumbia Valley Ch—church ... AL-4
*Tuscumbia Valley Missionary Baptist Ch* ... AL-4
Tuscumbia Watershed Structure 24 Dam—dam ... MS-4
Tuscumbia Watershed Structure 8 Dam—dam ... MS-4
*Tuseral Mountains* ... AZ-5
Tuseral Tank—reservoir ... AZ-5
Tusero Windmill—locale ... NM-5
Tushaday Lake—lake ... AK-9
*Tushalamita* ... MS-4
Tushar Mtns—range ... UT-8
Tushar Ridge—ridge ... UT-8
Tushar Trail—trail ... UT-8
Tushaus Slough—gut ... MN-6
Tusher Canyon—valley (2) ... UT-8
*Tusher Pond* ... FL-3

Twin Falls Campground—*locale* PA-2
Twin Falls City-County Airport—*airport* ID-8
Twin Falls City Park Hist Dist—*hist pl* ID-8
Twin Falls Creek—*stream* AK-9
Twin Falls Creek—*stream* MI-6
Twin Falls Creek—*stream* (2) WA-9
Twin Falls Dam—*dam* MI-6
Twin Falls Dam—*dam* WI-6
Twin Falls Flowage—*channel* WI-6
Twin Falls Flowage—*reservoir* MI-6
Twin Falls (historical)—*locale* KS-7
Twin Falls Main Canal—*canal* ID-8
Twin Falls Military Reservation—*area* ID-8
Twin Falls State Park—*park* WA-9
Twin Falls State Park—*park* WV-2
Twin Fir Spring—*spring* CO-8
Twin Flats—*flat* CA-9
Twinflower—*locale* PA-2
Twin Fork—*stream* KY-4
Twin Fork Ch—*church* KY-4
Twin Fork Creek—*stream* ID-8
Twin Fork Draw—*valley* WY-8
Twin Fork Lake—*reservoir* AL-4
Twin Fork Rsvr—*reservoir* WY-8
*Twin Forks* MS-4
Twin Forks—*locale* CO-8
Twin Forks—*locale* ID-8
Twin Forks Ditch—*canal* CO-8
**Twin Forks Estates**—*pop pl* NM-5
Twin Forks Rsvr—*reservoir* (2) MT-8
Twing, Joshua, Gristmill—*hist pl* VT-1
Twin Gates Carriage House—*hist pl* KY-4
**Twin Gates Estates (subdivision)**—*pop pl* AL-4
Twin Gates Park—*park* AL-4
*Twinging Pond North* MA-1
*Twinging Pond North Dam* MA-1
Twin Glacier—*glacier* AK-9
Twin Glacier Camp—*hist pl* AK-9
Twin Glacier Lake—*lake* AK-9
Twin Glacier Peak—*summit* AK-9
*Twin Glaciers* WY-8
Twin Glens—*valley* NY-2
Twing Point—*cape* ME-1
Twin Grove—*locale* IL-6
Twin Grove—*locale* MN-6
Twin Grove—*locale* TX-5
**Twin Grove**—*pop pl* WI-6
Twin Grove Branch Richland Creek—*stream* WI-6
Twin Grove Cem—*cemetery* IL-6
Twin Grove Cem—*cemetery* KS-7
Twin Grove Cem—*cemetery* MO-7
Twin Grove Creek—*stream* IA-7
Twin Grove Park—*locale* PA-2
Twin Groves—*locale* ID-8
Twin Groves—*locale* WY-8
Twin Groves Canal—*canal* ID-8
Twin Grove Sch—*school* WI-6
Twin Groves Township—*civil* MO-7
**Twin Grove Township**—*pop pl* KS-7
Twin Gulch—*valley* (2) CA-9
Twin Gulch—*valley* CO-8
Twin Gulch—*valley* WA-9
Twin Gulch—*valley* WY-8
Twin Gulch Fire Tank—*reservoir* CA-9
Twin Halls Plantation (historical)—*locale* MS-4
Twin Hammocks—*island* FL-3
Twin Harbor—*bay* WA-9
Twin Harbor Creek—*stream* WA-9
Twin Harbor Loop Spring—*spring* OR-9
Twin Harbors—*bay* CA-9
Twin Harbors Beach State Park—*park* WA-9
*Twin Harbors State Park* WA-9
**Twin Harbor (subdivision)**—*pop pl* MS-4
*Twin Hill* WY-8
Twin Hill—*summit* NY-2
Twin Hill Creek—*stream* MI-6
Twin Hill Creek—*stream* WI-6
Twin Hill Lake—*lake* WI-6
**Twin Hill Park**—*pop pl* NJ-2
Twin Hills—*other* NM-5
**Twin Hills**—*pop pl* AK-9
**Twin Hills**—*pop pl* OK-5
Twin Hills—*range* TX-5
Twin Hills—*range* WY-8
Twin Hills—*summit* AK 9
Twin Hills—*summit* (2) AZ-5
Twin Hills—*summit* CO-8
Twin Hills—*summit* IN-6
Twin Hills—*summit* KS-7
Twin Hills—*summit* NM-5
Twin Hills—*summit* (3) OK-5
Twin Hills—*summit* OR-9
Twin Hills—*summit* TX-5
Twin Hills—*summit* (2) UT-8
Twin Hills ANV975—*reserve* AK-9
Twin Hills Cem—*cemetery* KS-7
Twinhill Sch—*school* CA-9
Twin Hills Country Club—*other* MO-7
Twin Hills Country Club—*other* OK-5
Twin Hills Memorial Park (Cemetery)—*cemetery* PA-2
Twin Hills Park—*park* FL-3
Twin Hills Point—*cape* TX-5
Twin Hills Sch—*school* CA-9
Twin Hills Sch—*school* OK-5
Twin Hills Tank—*reservoir* NM-5
**Twin Hill Township**—*pop pl* ND-7
*Twin Hollow* UT-8
Twin Hollow—*valley* PA-2
Twin Hollow—*valley* TX-5
Twin Hollow—*valley* (5) UT-8
Twin Hollow—*valley* VA-3
Twin Hollow—*valley* WY-8
Twin Hollows—*locale* PA-2
Twin Hollows—*valley* (2) KY-4
Twin Hollows—*valley* UT-8
**Twin Hollows Subdivision**—*pop pl* UT-8
Twin Honeycutt Windmills—*locale* NM-5
Twin Houses—*hist pl* NC-3
Twining—*locale* NM-5
**Twining**—*pop pl* DC-2
**Twining**—*pop pl* MI-6
Twining Blue Lake Trail—*trail* NM-5
Twining Brook Pond—*lake* MA-1
Twining Cem—*cemetery* IL-6
Twining Cem—*cemetery* ME-1
*Twining City* DC-2
Twining Farm—*hist pl* PA-2
Twining Ford Covered Bridge—*hist pl* PA-2
Twining Golf Course—*locale* PA-2
Twining Hollow—*valley* MA-1
Twining Park—*park* WI-6
Twining Pond—*lake* MA-1
*Twining Pond Main Dam* MA-1
Twining Sch—*school* ND-7
Twinings Pond—*lake* MA-1
Twining Valley Golf Course—*locale* PA-2
*Twin Island* NH-1
Twin Island—*island* (2) AK-9
Twin Island—*island* FL-3
Twin Island—*island* IN-6
Twin Island—*island* LA-4
Twin Island—*island* MI-6
Twin Island—*island* (2) MN-6
Twin Island—*island* (2) NY-2
Twin Island—*island* TX-5
Twin Island—*island* WI-6
Twin Island Creek—*stream* AK-9
Twin Island Lake—*lake* (3) AK-9
Twin Island Lake—*lake* (3) MN-6
Twin Island Lake—*lake* NY-2
Twin Island Lake—*lake* WI-6
Twin Island Lakes—*lake* CA-9
Twin Island Pond—*lake* ME-1
*Twin Islands* NY-2
*Twin Islands* TN-4
Twin Islands—*area* AK-9
Twin Islands—*island* AK-9
Twin Islands—*island* CT-1
Twin Islands—*island* FL-3
Twin Islands—*island* ID-8
Twin Islands—*island* IL-6
Twin Islands—*island* LA-4
Twin Islands—*island* (3) ME-1
Twin Islands—*island* MD-2
Twin Islands—*island* MN-6
Twin Islands—*island* MS-4
Twin Islands—*island* MO-7
Twin Islands—*island* NH-1
Twin Islands—*island* RI-1
Twin Islands—*island* WI-6
Twin Isle—*island* MN-6
Twin Joe Tank—*reservoir* AZ-5
Twin Key Bank—*bar* FL-3
Twin Keys—*island* FL-3
Twinkle Lake—*lake* MN-6
**Twinkling Acres**—*pop pl* MD-2
*Twin Knob* AR-4
*Twin Knobs* AR-4
Twin Knobs—*summit* AR-4
Twin Knobs—*summit* CA-9
Twin Knobs—*summit* CO-8
Twin Knobs—*summit* ID-8
Twin Knobs—*summit* (2) KY-4
Twin Knobs—*summit* MO-7
Twin Knobs—*summit* NC-3
Twin Knobs—*summit* (2) OH-6
Twin Knobs—*summit* OR-9
Twin Knobs—*summit* TX-5
Twin Knobs Ch—*church* MO-7
Twin Knoll Buttes—*summit* NM-5
*Twin Knolls* CO-8
Twin Knolls—*summit* (2) AZ-5
Twin Knolls—*summit* OR-9
Twin Knolls—*summit* (6) UT-8
**Twin Knolls (Desert Sage)**—*pop pl* AZ-5
Twin Knolls Spring—*spring* OR-9
Twin Knolls (trailer park)—*locale* AZ-5
Twinky Spring—*spring* CA-9
*Twin Lake* ID-8
*Twin Lake* MI-6
*Twin Lake* MN-6
*Twin Lake* NE-7
*Twin Lake* ND-7
*Twin Lake* WI-6
Twin Lake—*lake* AK-9
Twin Lake—*lake* CA-9
Twin Lake—*lake* CO-8
Twin Lake—*lake* (4) FL-3
Twin Lake—*lake* (2) IN-6
Twin Lake—*lake* IA-7
Twin Lake—*lake* KY-4
Twin Lake—*lake* LA-4
Twin Lake—*lake* ME-1
Twin Lako lako (13) MI 6
Twin Lake—*lake* (11) MN-6
Twin Lake—*lake* (2) MS-4
Twin Lake—*lake* NE-7
Twin Lake—*lake* NM-5
Twin Lake—*lake* ND-7
Twin Lake—*lake* (2) OK-5
Twin Lake—*lake* OR-9
Twin Lake—*lake* TN-4
Twin Lake—*lake* (2) TX-5
Twin Lake—*lake* UT-8
Twin Lake—*lake* WA-9
Twin Lake—*lake* (7) WI-6
Twin Lake—*locale* MS-4
**Twin Lake**—*pop pl* MI-6
**Twin Lake**—*pop pl* NC-3
Twin Lake—*reservoir* CA-9
Twin Lake—*reservoir* (2) CO-8
Twin Lake—*reservoir* MO-7
Twin Lake—*reservoir* OH-6
Twin Lake—*reservoir* TN-4
Twin Lake—*reservoir* TX-5
Twin Lake—*reservoir* UT-8
Twin Lake—*swamp* MN-6
Twin Lake—*uninc pl* FL-3
Twin Lake Bed—*flat* MN-6
Twin Lake Campground—*locale* CO-8
Twin Lake Creek—*stream* AK-9
Twin Lake Creek—*stream* MI-6
Twin Lake Creek—*stream* OR-9
Twin Lake Dam—*dam* TN-4
Twin Lake Dam—*dam* UT-8
**Twin Lake Estates**—*pop pl* AL-4
**Twin Lake Hill**—*pop pl* SC-3
Twin Lake (historical)—*locale* SD-7
Twin Lake No. 1—*reservoir* CO-8
Twin Lake No. 2—*reservoir* CO-8
Twin Lake Number One—*reservoir* NC-3
Twin Lake Number One Dam—*dam* NC-3
Twin Lake Number Two—*reservoir* NC-3
Twin Lake Number Two Dam—*dam* NC-3
Twin Lake Par 3 Golf Course—*locale* PA-2
*Twin Lake Reservoir* UT-8
Twin Lake Rsvr—*reservoir* CO-8
Twin Lake Rsvr—*reservoir* OH-6
*Twin Lakes* CA-9
*Twin Lakes* FL-3
*Twin Lakes* IL-6
*Twin Lakes* IN-6
*Twin Lakes* MI-6
*Twin Lakes* MN-6
*Twin Lakes* NE-7
*Twin Lakes* NV-8
*Twin Lakes* NH-1
*Twin Lakes* NY-2
*Twin Lakes* PA-2
*Twin Lakes* SD-7
*Twin Lakes* TX-5
*Twin Lakes* UT-8
*Twin Lakes* WA-9
*Twin Lakes* WI-6
Twin Lakes—*bay* TX-5
Twin Lakes—*flat* OR-9
Twin Lakes—*lake* (6) AK-9
Twin Lakes—*lake* (4) AZ-5
Twin Lakes—*lake* (4) AR-4
Twin Lakes—*lake* (24) CA-9
Twin Lakes—*lake* (10) CO-8
Twin Lakes—*lake* CT-1
Twin Lakes—*lake* (12) FL-3
Twin Lakes—*lake* (5) GA-3
Twin Lakes—*lake* (12) ID-8
Twin Lakes—*lake* (5) IL-6
Twin Lakes—*lake* (6) IN-6
Twin Lakes—*lake* IA-7
Twin Lakes—*lake* (2) LA-4
Twin Lakes—*lake* (31) MI-6
Twin Lakes—*lake* (46) MN-6
Twin Lakes—*lake* (2) MS-4
Twin Lakes—*lake* (3) MO-7
Twin Lakes—*lake* (26) MT-8
Twin Lakes—*lake* (4) NE-7
Twin Lakes—*lake* (3) NV-8
Twin Lakes—*lake* NJ-2
Twin Lakes—*lake* (5) NM-5
Twin Lakes—*lake* (9) NY-2
Twin Lakes—*lake* (10) ND-7
Twin Lakes—*lake* OK-5
Twin Lakes—*lake* (9) OR-9
Twin Lakes—*lake* (3) PA-2
Twin Lakes—*lake* (6) SD-7
Twin Lakes—*lake* (2) TN-4
Twin Lakes—*lake* (8) TX-5
Twin Lakes—*lake* (8) UT-8
Twin Lakes—*lake* VA-3
Twin Lakes—*lake* (18) WA-9
Twin Lakes—*lake* (28) WI-6
Twin Lakes—*lake* (11) WY-8
Twin Lakes—*lakes* CO-8
Twin Lakes—*locale* KY-4
**Twin Lakes**—*pop pl* (3) CA-9
**Twin Lakes**—*pop pl* CO-8
**Twin Lakes**—*pop pl* CT-1
**Twin Lakes**—*pop pl* GA-3
**Twin Lakes**—*pop pl* ID-8
**Twin Lakes**—*pop pl* IL-6
**Twin Lakes**—*pop pl* (2) IN-6
**Twin Lakes**—*pop pl* (2) MI-6
**Twin Lakes**—*pop pl* MN-6
**Twin Lakes**—*pop pl* MS-4
**Twin Lakes**—*pop pl* NM-5
**Twin Lakes**—*pop pl* NC-3
**Twin Lakes**—*pop pl* (2) OH-6
**Twin Lakes**—*pop pl* OK-5
**Twin Lakes**—*pop pl* PA-2
**Twin Lakes**—*pop pl* WI-6
Twin Lakes—*reservoir* (2) AL-4
Twin Lakes—*reservoir* CA-9
Twin Lakes—*reservoir* (9) GA-3
Twin Lakes—*reservoir* (2) ID-8
Twin Lakes—*reservoir* IL-6
Twin Lakes—*reservoir* (2) KY-4
Twin Lakes—*reservoir* MS-4
Twin Lakes—*reservoir* (2) NE-7
Twin Lakes—*reservoir* NJ-2
Twin Lakes—*reservoir* (2) NM-5
Twin Lakes—*reservoir* NC-3
Twin Lakes—*reservoir* (2) OH-6
Twin Lakes—*reservoir* (2) OK-5
Twin Lakes—*reservoir* OR-9
Twin Lakes—*reservoir* (3) SC-3
Twin Lakes—*reservoir* (2) TN-4
Twin Lakes—*reservoir* (7) TX-5
Twin Lakes—*reservoir* VA-3
Twin Lakes—*reservoir* WV-2
Twin Lakes—*swamp* MS-4
Twin Lakes—*uninc pl* AR-4
Twin Lakes Airp—*airport* NC-3
Twin Lakes Bayou—*stream* MS-4
Twin Lakes Beach—*beach* CA-9
Twin Lakes Campground—*locale* CA-9
Twin Lakes Campground—*locale* MI-6
Twin Lakes Campground—*locale* WY-8
Twin Lakes Canal—*canal* FL-3
Twin Lakes Canal—*canal* ID-8
Twin Lakes Canal East Lateral—*canal* ID-8
Twin Lakes Canal West Lateral—*canal* ID-8
Twin Lakes Cem—*cemetery* FL-3
Twin Lakes Cem—*cemetery* IA-7
Twin Lakes Cem—*cemetery* WI-6
Twin Lakes Center—*locale* KS-7
Twin Lakes Ch—*church* MI-6
Twin Lakes Ch—*church* WI-6
Twin Lake Sch—*school* FL-3
Twin Lakes Country Club—*locale* AL-4
Twin Lakes Country Club—*locale* PA-2
Twin Lakes Country Club—*other* MI-6
Twin Lakes Country Club—*other* OK-5
Twin Lakes Country Club and Golf Course—*other* AZ-5
Twin Lake Scout Camp—*locale* WI-6
Twin Lakes Cow Camp—*locale* MT-8
Twin Lakes Creek—*stream* AK-9
Twin Lakes Creek—*stream* (2) CA-9
Twin Lakes Creek—*stream* (2) ID-8
Twin Lakes Creek—*stream* (2) MI-6
Twin Lakes Creek—*stream* (2) MT-8
Twin Lakes Creek—*stream* PA-2
Twin Lakes Creek—*stream* WA-9
Twin Lakes Creek—*stream* WI-6
Twin Lakes Cut -Off—*bend* MS-4
*Twin Lakes Dam* TN-4
*Twin Lakes Dam* UT-8
Twin Lakes Dam—*dam* MS-4
Twin Lakes Dam—*dam* PA-2
Twin Lakes Dam—*dam* UT-8
Twin Lakes District—*hist pl* CO-8
Twin Lakes Ditch—*canal* WA-9
Twin Lakes Ditch—*stream* WA-9
Twin Lakes Drain—*canal* MI-6
Twin Lakes Elem Sch—*school* FL-3
**Twin Lakes Estates**—*pop pl* NC-3
Twin Lakes Fishing Lodge—*building* AL-4
Twin Lakes Golf Course—*locale* AL-4
Twin Lakes Golf Course—*locale* PA-2
Twin Lakes Golf Course—*other* CA-9
Twin Lakes HS—*school* FL-3
Twin Lakes Inlet—*stream* NY-2
Twin Lakes Lower Dam—*dam* NJ-2
Twin Lakes Marsh—*swamp* NY-2
Twin Lakes Mtn—*summit* NY-2
Twin Lakes Mtn—*summit* OR-9
Twin Lakes Natl Wildlife Ref—*park* ND-7
Twin Lakes Number One Dam—*dam* PA-2
Twin Lakes Number One Dam—*dam* TN-4
Twin Lakes Number One Lake—*reservoir* TN-4
Twin Lakes Number One Rsvr—*reservoir* PA-2
Twin Lakes Number Three Dam—*dam* TN-4
Twin Lakes Number Three Lake—*reservoir* TN-4
Twin Lakes Number Two Dam—*dam* TN-4
Twin Lakes Number Two Lake—*reservoir* TN-4
Twin Lakes Number Two Rsvr—*reservoir* PA-2
*Twin Lakes Number 2 Dam* PA-2
Twin Lakes Outlet—*stream* MI-6
Twin Lakes Outlet—*stream* NY-2
*Twin Lakes Park* CA-9
Twin Lakes Park—*park* MI-6
Twin Lakes Park—*park* ND-7
**Twin Lakes Park (subdivision)**—*pop pl* PA-2
Twin Lakes Picnic Area—*locale* ID-8
Twin Lakes Plaza Shop Ctr—*locale* TN-4
Twin Lakes Rec Area—*park* PA-2
*Twin Lakes Reservoir* CA-9
Twin Lakes Reservoir and Canal Company Tunnel no. 1—*tunnel* CO-8
Twin Lakes Reservoir Tunnel No. 2—*tunnel* CO-8
Twin Lakes Ridge—*ridge* ID-8
Twin Lakes RR Station—*locale* FL-3
Twin Lakes Rsvr—*reservoir* CO-8
Twin Lakes Rsvr—*reservoir* (2) ID-8
Twin Lakes Rsvr—*reservoir* UT-8
Twin Lakes RV Park—*park* UT-8
Twin Lakes Sch—*school* AR-4
Twin Lakes Sch—*school* CA-9
Twin Lakes Sch—*school* (2) MN-6
Twin Lakes Sch—*school* NV-8
Twin Lakes Sch—*school* ND-7
Twin Lakes State Access Point—*locale* WI-6
Twin Lakes State Beach—*park* CA-9
Twin Lakes State Park—*park* IA-7
Twin Lakes State Park West—*park* IA-7
Twin Lakes State Public Shooting Area—*park* SD-7
Twin Lakes State Rec Area—*park* SD-7
Twin Lakes Station—*locale* ID-8
Twin Lakes Stream—*stream* NY-2
**Twin Lakes (subdivision)**—*pop pl* FL-3
**Twin Lakes (subdivision)**—*pop pl* PA-2
**Twin Lakes Subdivision**—*pop pl* UT-8
Twin Lakes Subdivision Lake Dam—*dam* MS-4
Twin Lakes Township—*fmr MCD* IA-7
**Twin Lakes (Township of)**—*pop pl* (2) MN-6
**Twin Lakes (Trading Post)**—*pop pl* NM-5
Twin Lakes Trail—*trail* NY-2
Twin Lakes Trail—*trail* (3) OR-9
Twin Lake Stream—*stream* NY-2
**Twin Lakes Village**—*pop pl* NH-1
**Twin Lakes Village**—*pop pl* NY-2
Twin Lake Township—*fmr MCD* IA-7
**Twin Lake Township**—*pop pl* ND-7
**Twin Lake Township**—*pop pl* SD-7
Twin Lake Trail—*trail* CO-8
Twinlava Point—*cape* AK-9
Twin Ledge Spring—*spring* NV-8
Twin Lick—*spring* OR-9
Twin Lick—*stream* KY-4
Twin Lick Branch—*stream* KY-4
Twin Lick Fork—*stream* KY-4
Twin Lick Run—*stream* PA-2
Twin Licks Branch—*stream* KY-4
Twin Lights—*hist pl* NJ-2
Twin Lights Hist Dist—*hist pl* MA-1
Twin Lode Mine—*mine* CA-9
**Twinlow**—*pop pl* ID-8
Twin Mandall Lakes—*lake* CO-8
**Twin Manor (subdivision)**—*pop pl* AL-4
Twin Meadows—*flat* (4) CA-9
Twin Meadows—*flat* CO-8
Twin Meadows—*flat* (2) OR-9
**Twin Meadows**—*pop pl* MT-8
Twin Meadows—*swamp* MT-8
Twin Meadows—*swamp* OR-9
Twin Meadows Creek—*stream* MT-8
Twin Meadows Guard Station—*locale* MT-8
Twin Meadows Lake—*lake* CA-9
Twin Meadows Ranch—*locale* NV-8
Twin Meadows Trail—*trail* OR-9
Twin Mesa—*summit* NM-5
*Twin Mesas* AZ-5
Twin Mill—*locale* TX-5
Twin Mill Branch—*stream* TX-5
Twin Mills—*locale* CO-8
Twin Mills—*locale* TX-5
Twin Mills—*summit* AZ-5
Twin Mott Lake—*lake* TX-5
Twin Mound—*summit* KS-7
Twin Mound Cem—*cemetery* KS-7
Twin Mound (historical)—*locale* KS-7
*Twin Mounds* KS-7
Twin Mounds—*summit* AR-4
Twin Mounds—*summit* (2) CO-8
Twin Mounds—*summit* (6) KS-7
Twin Mounds—*summit* KY-4
Twin Mounds—*summit* NM-5
Twin Mounds—*summit* (6) OK-5
Twin Mounds Cem—*cemetery* KS-7
Twin Mounds Cem—*cemetery* OK-5
Twin Mounds Ch—*church* (2) KS-7
Twin Mounds Sch—*school* CO-8
Twin Mounds Sch—*school* KS-7
*Twin Mound Township* KS-7
*Twin Mountain* CO-8
*Twin Mountain* NV-8
*Twin Mountain* WY-8
Twin Mountain—*locale* WV-2
**Twin Mountain**—*pop pl* NH-1
**Twin Mountain**—*pop pl* NM-5
Twin Mountain Creek—*stream* AK-9
Twin Mountain Creek—*stream* OR-9
Twin Mountain Fire Station—*locale* WA-9
Twin Mountain Lakes—*reservoir* GA-3
Twin Mountain Rsvr—*reservoir* NH-1
*Twin Mountains* OK-5
**Twin Mountains**—*pop pl* TX-5
Twin Mountains—*range* TX-5
Twin Mountains—*range* WA-9
Twin Mountains—*summit* AL-4
Twin Mountains—*summit* AR-4
Twin Mountains—*summit* ME-1
Twin Mountains—*summit* NY-2
Twin Mountains—*summit* OK-5
Twin Mountains—*summit* (5) TX-5
Twin Mountains Lake—*lake* WY-8
*Twin Mtn* NY-2
Twin Mtn—*summit* (4) AK-9
Twin Mtn—*summit* AR-4
Twin Mtn—*summit* (2) CO-8
Twin Mtn—*summit* ME-1
Twin Mtn—*summit* MO-7
Twin Mtn—*summit* MT-8
Twin Mtn—*summit* NM-5
Twin Mtn—*summit* (3) NY-2
Twin Mtn—*summit* OR-9
Twin Mtn—*summit* (4) TX-5
Twin Mtn—*summit* WY-8
Twin Mtns—*range* WY-8
Twin Mtns—*summit* CO-8
Twin Needles—*pillar* WA-9
Twinnies, The—*island* ME-1
Twin Oak—*locale* IA-7
**Twin Oak**—*pop pl* NC-3
**Twin Oak**—*pop pl* TN-4
**Twin Oak**—*pop pl* TX-5
Twin Oak Canyon—*valley* AZ-5
Twin Oak Cem—*cemetery* TX-5
Twin Oak Center (Shop Ctr)—*locale* (2) FL-3
Twin Oak Ch—*church* GA-3
Twin Oak Ch—*church* (2) LA-4
Twin Oak Ch—*church* MO-7
Twin Oak Ch—*church* (2) OK-5
Twin Oak Ch—*church* TN-4
Twin Oak Ch—*church* TX-5
**Twin Oak Estates**—*pop pl* TN-4
Twin Oak (historical P.O.)—*locale* IA-7
Twin Oak Lake—*lake* FL-3
*Twin Oaks* WI-6
Twin Oaks—*building* TN-4
Twin Oaks—*hist pl* DC-2
Twin Oaks—*hist pl* GA-3
Twin Oaks—*hist pl* MD-2
Twin Oaks—*hist pl* OH-6
Twin Oaks—*locale* CA-9
Twin Oaks—*locale* PA-2
Twin Oaks—*locale* TN-4
**Twin Oaks**—*pop pl* CA-9
**Twin Oaks**—*pop pl* DE-2
**Twin Oaks**—*pop pl* (2) IL-6
**Twin Oaks**—*pop pl* KY-4
**Twin Oaks**—*pop pl* LA-4
**Twin Oaks**—*pop pl* MO-7
**Twin Oaks**—*pop pl* NC-3
**Twin Oaks**—*pop pl* OK-5
**Twin Oaks**—*pop pl* (3) PA-2
**Twin Oaks**—*pop pl* (2) TN-4
Twin Oaks Cave—*cave* TN-4
Twin Oaks Cem—*cemetery* OR-9
Twin Oaks Ch—*church* GA-3
Twin Oak Sch—*school* TN-4
Twin Oaks Country Club—*other* IL-6
Twin Oaks Country Club—*other* MO-7
Twin Oaks Farm Lake—*reservoir* NC-3
Twin Oaks Farm Lake Dam—*dam* NC-3
**Twin Oaks Farms**—*pop pl* PA-2
Twin Oaks Golf Course—*locale* PA-2
Twin Oaks Lake—*lake* MN-6
**Twin Oaks Lake**—*pop pl* IN-6
Twin Oaks Lake—*reservoir* IN-6
Twin Oaks Lake Dam—*dam* IN-6
Twin Oaks Memorial Gardens—*cemetery* OR-9
Twin Oaks Park—*park* CA-9
Twin Oaks Park—*park* MN-6
Twin Oak Spring—*spring* TN-4
Twin Oaks Ranch—*locale* TX-5
Twin Oaks Rsvr—*reservoir* ID-8
Twin Oaks Sch—*school* OR-9
Twin Oaks Sch—*school* PA-2
Twin Oaks Shop Ctr—*locale* MO-7
**Twin Oaks (subdivision)**—*pop pl* AL-4
**Twin Oaks (subdivision)**—*pop pl* NC-3
**Twin Oaks (subdivision)**—*pop pl* TN-4
Twin Oaks Valley—*valley* CA-9
Twin Oaks Village Shop Ctr—*locale* AL-4
**Twin Orchard**—*pop pl* NY-2
**Twin Orchards**—*pop pl* NY-2
**Twin Orchards**—*pop pl* VT-1
Twin Owls, The—*pillar* CO-8
**Twin Palms**—*pop pl* FL-3
Twin Palms Island—*island* FL-3
Twin Parks—*area* UT-8
Twin Parks Creek—*stream* WY-8
*Twin Peak* CA-9
*Twin Peak* MT-8
Twin Peak—*summit* (2) CA-9
Twin Peak—*summit* ID-8
*Twin Peak Branch* CA-9
*Twin Peaks* CA-9
*Twin Peaks* NV-8
*Twin Peaks* TX-5
*Twin Peaks* UT-8
Twin Peaks—*gap* WA-9
Twin Peaks—*pillar* NM-5
**Twin Peaks**—*pop pl* AK-9
**Twin Peaks**—*pop pl* CA-9
Twin Peaks—*spring* MT-8
Twin Peaks—*summit* (4) AK-9
Twin Peaks—*summit* (11) AZ-5
Twin Peaks—*summit* (17) CA-9
Twin Peaks—*summit* (7) CO-8
Twin Peaks—*summit* (9) ID-8
Twin Peaks—*summit* KS-7
Twin Peaks—*summit* ME-1
Twin Peaks—*summit* (4) MT-8
Twin Peaks—*summit* (8) NV-8
Twin Peaks—*summit* (3) NM-5
Twin Peaks—*summit* OK-5
Twin Peaks—*summit* (3) OR-9
Twin Peaks—*summit* SD-7
Twin Peaks—*summit* (3) TX-5
Twin Peaks—*summit* (17) UT-8
Twin Peaks—*summit* (5) WA-9
Twin Peaks—*summit* WI-6
Twin Peaks—*summit* (3) WY-8
Twin Peaks Bible and Missionary Camp—*locale* CO-8
Twin Peaks Camp—*locale* WA-9
Twin Peaks Campground—*locale* CO-8
Twin Peaks Canyon—*valley* UT-8
**Twin Peaks Circle Subdivision**—*pop pl* UT-8
**Twin Peaks Condominium**—*pop pl* UT-8
Twin Peaks Cove—*bay* NV-8
Twin Peaks Creek—*stream* CO-8
Twin Peaks Creek—*stream* MT-8
Twin Peaks Flat—*flat* UT-8
Twin Peaks Lookout—*locale* ID-8
Twin Peaks Mine—*mine* CA-9
Twin Peaks Mine—*mine* ID-8
Twin Peaks Mine—*mine* MT-8
Twin Peaks Mine—*mine* NM-5
Twin Peaks Ranch—*locale* ID-8
Twin Peaks Sch—*school* CA-9
Twin Peaks Sch—*school* UT-8
Twin Peaks Sports—*hist pl* ID-8
Twin Peaks Spring—*spring* NV-8
Twin Peaks Spring—*spring* (2) UT-8
**Twin Peaks Subdivision**—*pop pl* UT-8
Twin Peaks Tank—*reservoir* NM-5
Twin Peaks Trail—*trail* AZ-5
Twin Peaks Trail—*trail* OR-9
Twin Peaks Tunnel—*tunnel* CA-9
Twin Peaks Wash—*valley* UT-8
Twin Pike Shop Ctr—*locale* MO-7
*Twin Pillars* WA-9
Twin Pillars—*pillar* OR-9
Twin Pine—*airport* NJ-2
*Twin Pine Conference Lake Dam* AL-4
Twin Pine Hill—*summit* MA-1
Twin Pine Lake—*reservoir* AL-4
**Twin Pines**—*pop pl* CA-9
**Twin Pines**—*pop pl* VA-3
Twin Pines Camp—*locale* CA-9
Twin Pines Camp—*locale* PA-2
Twin Pines Creek—*stream* CA-9
Twin Pines Golf Course—*other* AL-4
Twin Pines Golf Course—*other* IA-7
Twin Pines Mine—*mine* CA-9
Twin Pines Mine—*mine* CO-8
Twin Pines Point—*cape* CO-8
Twin Pines Ranch—*locale* CA-9
Twin Pines Ranch—*locale* CO-8
Twin Pines Ranch—*locale* MT-8
Twin Pines Sch—*school* NY-2
Twin Pines Trail—*trail* PA-2
Twin Pinon Gulch —*valley* NV-8
Twin Platte Sch—*school* WI-6
Twin Point—*cape* (2) AK-9
Twin Point—*cliff* AZ-5
Twin Points—*cape* CA-9
Twin Points—*cape* OR-9
Twin Points Beach—*beach* TX-5
Twin Pole—*locale* FL-3
*Twin Pond* ME-1
Twin Pond—*lake* FL-3
Twin Pond—*lake* KY-4
Twin Pond—*lake* ME-1
Twin Pond—*lake* MA-1
Twin Pond—*lake* (2) NY-2
Twin Pond—*lake* UT-8
Twin Pond Brook—*stream* ME-1
Twin Pond Creek—*stream* TX-5
Twin Pond Marsh—*swamp* MD-2
Twin Pond Mtn—*summit* NY-2
Twin Pond Park—*park* IA-7
*Twin Ponds* NY-2
*Twin Ponds* TN-4
Twin Ponds—*lake* DE-2
Twin Ponds—*lake* FL-3
Twin Ponds—*lake* IL-6
Twin Ponds—*lake* KY-4
Twin Ponds—*lake* (3) ME-1
Twin Ponds—*lake* MD-2
Twin Ponds—*lake* (3) MO-7
Twin Ponds—*lake* (13) NY-2
Twin Ponds—*lake* OR-9
Twin Ponds—*lake* TX-5
Twin Ponds—*lake* (2) UT-8
Twin Ponds—*lake* VT-1
Twin Ponds—*reservoir* AZ-5
Twin Ponds—*reservoir* CA-9
Twin Ponds—*reservoir* OR-9
Twin Ponds—*reservoir* (2) UT-8
Twin Ponds—*swamp* AR-4
Twin Ponds Camp—*locale* OR-9
Twin Ponds Golf Club—*other* NY-2
Twin Ponds Golf Course—*locale* PA-2
Twin Ponds Outlet—*stream* NY-2
*Twin Ponds Rsvr* CA-9
Twin Ponds Sch—*school* MN-6
Twin Ponds Trail—*trail* OR-9
Twin Poplars—*locale* VA-3
Twin Pots Dam—*dam* UT-8
Twin Pots Rsvr—*reservoir* UT-8
*Twin Potts Reservoir* UT-8
Twin Prairie Buttes—*summit* OR-9
Twin Pups Lakes—*lake* MI-6
Twin Red Hills—*summit* AZ-5
*Twin Reservoir* UT-8
*Twin Reservoirs* NE-7
Twin Reservoirs—*reservoir* HI-9
Twin Reservoirs—*reservoir* ID-8
Twin Reservoirs—*reservoir* WY-8
*Twin Ridge* UT-8
Twinridge Hill—*summit* NV-8
Twin Ridge Marina—*locale* VA-3
Twin Ridges—*ridge* UT-8
*Twin Ridges Lake* NY-2
Twin Rift—*summit* AK-9
Twin River—*stream* WI-6
**Twin River Beach**—*pop pl* MD-2
Twin River Park—*park* MO-7
**Twin Rivers**—*pop pl* NJ-2
Twin Rivers Ch—*church* GA-3
Twin River Sch—*school* NY-2

Twin Rivers Dam ... RI-1
Twin Rivers Ferry (historical)—locale ... TN-4
Twin Rivers Mall—locale ... NC-3
Twin Rivers Regional Med Ctr Heliport—airport ... MO-7
Twin Road Waterhole—lake ... OR-9
Twin Rock—pillar ... TX-5
**Twin Rock**—pop pl ... CO-8
Twin Rock Ditch—canal ... CO-8
Twin Rock Mtn—summit ... OK-5
Twin Rock Ridge—ridge ... CA-9
Twin Rocks—area ... AK-9
Twin Rocks—bar ... AK-9
Twin Rocks—bar ... OR-9
Twin Rocks—cliff ... MO-7
Twin Rocks—island (2) ... AK-9
Twin Rocks—island (2) ... CA-9
Twin Rocks—island ... CT-1
Twin Rocks—island ... HI-9
Twin Rocks—island ... MN-6
Twin Rocks—island ... OR-9
Twin Rocks—island ... WA-9
Twin Rocks—other ... MO-7
Twin Rocks—pillar ... CA-9
Twin Rocks—pillar ... WY-8
**Twin Rocks**—pop pl ... OR-9
**Twin Rocks**—pop pl ... PA-2
Twin Rocks—summit (2) ... CA-9
Twin Rocks—summit ... CO-8
Twin Rocks—summit ... OR-9
Twin Rocks—summit ... UT-8
Twin Rocks—summit ... WA-9
Twin Rocks Camp—locale ... KY-4
Twin Rocks Canyon ... WY-8
Twin Rocks Creek—stream (2) ... CA-9
Twin Rocks Ridge—ridge ... CA-9
Twin Rocks Shelter—locale ... WA-9
Twin Rocks Trail (Jeep)—trail ... CA-9
Twin Rose School—locale ... KS-7
Twin Rsvr ... OR-9
Twin Rsvr—reservoir ... ID-8
Twin Rsvr—reservoir ... MT-8
Twin Rsvr—reservoir (2) ... OR-9
Twin Rsvr—reservoir ... WY-8
Twin Run ... PA-2
Twin Run—stream ... OH-6
Twin Run—stream (2) ... PA-2
Twin Run—stream (2) ... WV-2
Twins—island ... AK-9
Twins, The ... NY-2
Twins, The ... OK-5
Twins, The—area (2) ... AK-9
Twins, The—bar ... MA-1
Twins, The—island ... AK-9
Twins, The—island ... WA-9
Twins, The—island ... MP-9
Twins, The—summit ... AK-9
Twins, The—summit ... NH-1
**Twins at Little Willow Subdivision**—pop pl ... UT-8
**Twinsburg**—pop pl ... OH-6
Twinsburg Congregational Church—hist pl ... OH-6
**Twinsburg Heights**—pop pl ... OH-6
Twinsburg Institute—hist pl ... OH-6
**Twinsburg (Township of)**—pop pl ... OH-6
Twins Crane Prairie Trail—trail ... OR-9
Twin Seeps—spring ... UT-8
**Twins Estates (subdivision)**—pop pl ... NC-3
Twins Glacier—glacier ... WY-8
Twin Shaft (historical)—mine ... PA-2
Twins Hollow—valley ... UT-8
Twins Islands ... KY-4
Twin Sister—summit ... CA-9
Twin Sister Creek ... OR-9
Twin Sister Creek—stream ... NY-2
Twin Sister Hills Park—park ... IL-6
Twin Sister Island—island ... MI-6
Twin Sister Island Number Two—island ... IN-6
Twin Sister Keys ... FL-3
Twin Sister Knobs—summit ... OH-6
Twin Sister Lake—lake ... NY-2
Twin Sister Lights ... MA-1
Twin Sister Peaks—summit ... TX-5
Twin Sisters—cliff ... OR-9
Twin Sisters—locale ... TX-5
Twin Sisters—pillar ... NE-7
Twin Sisters—spring ... MT-8
Twin Sisters—summit ... AK-9
Twin Sisters—summit (3) ... CA-9
Twin Sisters—summit (2) ... CO-8
Twin Sisters—summit (2) ... ID-8
Twin Sisters—summit ... NM-5
Twin Sisters—summit ... OR-9
Twin Sisters—summit (2) ... SD-7
Twin Sisters—summit (3) ... TX-5
Twin Sisters—summit (3) ... WA-9
Twin Sisters, The—spring ... MT-8
Twin Sisters Cem—cemetery ... TX-5
Twin Sisters Creek—stream ... NM-5
Twin Sisters Creek Camp—locale ... OR-9
Twin Sisters Guard Station—locale ... OR-9
Twin Sisters Gulch—valley ... ID-8
Twin Sisters Gun Club—other ... CA-9
Twin Sisters Hollows—valley ... PA-2
Twin Sisters Lake—lake ... MS-4
Twin Sisters Lakes—lake ... ID-8
Twin Sisters Lakes—lake ... WA-9
Twin Sisters Mine—mine ... ID-8
Twin Sisters Mtn—summit ... CA-9
Twin Sisters Mtn—summit ... CO-8
Twin Sisters Mtn—summit ... WA-9
Twin Sisters Peak—summit ... AK-9
Twin Sisters Peak—summit ... CO-8
Twin Sisters Peaks ... TX-5
Twin Sisters Peaks—summit ... CO-8
Twin Sisters Range—range ... SD-7
Twin Sisters Tanks—reservoir ... TX-5
Twin Sisters Trail—trail ... OR-9
Twin Sisters Trail—trail ... PA-2
Twin Sisters Trail—trail ... WA-9
Twin Sister Tank Number One—reservoir ... NM-5
Twin Sister Tank Number Two—reservoir ... NM-5
Twin Sister Trail—trail ... CO-8
Twin Slough—stream ... AL-4
Twin Slough—stream ... AK-9
Twin Slough—stream ... AR-4
Twin Sloughs—gut ... AR-4
Twin Sloughs—lake ... CA-9
Twin Sloughs—lake ... SD-7
Twins Mine—mine ... AZ-5
Twins Mine—mine ... CO-8
Twin Snag Rsvr—reservoir ... MT-8
**Twins of Arden Subdivision**—pop pl ... UT-8
Twin Spires ... WA-9
Twin Spires—summit ... AZ-5
Twin Spires Canyon—valley ... AZ-5
Twin Spring ... NV-8
Twin Spring ... OR-9
Twin Spring ... UT-8
Twin Spring—spring ... AL-4
Twin Spring—spring ... AZ-5
Twin Spring—spring ... CO-8
Twin Spring—spring ... ID-8
Twin Spring—spring ... MO-7
Twin Spring—spring ... NM-5
Twin Spring—spring (6) ... OR-9
Twin Spring—spring ... TX-5
Twin Spring—spring (2) ... UT-8
Twin Spring—spring (2) ... WA-9
Twin Spring Canyon—valley ... AZ-5
Twin Spring Cem—cemetery ... IN-6
Twin Spring Creek ... NV-8
Twin Spring Creek—stream (2) ... ID-8
Twin Spring Creek—stream ... OK-5
Twin Spring Creek—stream ... UT-8
Twin Spring Hills—summit ... NV-8
Twin Spring Rsvr—reservoir ... NV-8
Twin Spring Rsvr—reservoir ... OR-9
Twinsprings ... AL-4
Twin Springs—locale ... AL-4
Twin Springs—locale ... ID-8
Twin Springs—locale (2) ... IA-7
Twin Springs—locale ... VA-3
**Twinsprings**—pop pl ... AL-4
**Twin Springs**—pop pl ... AR-4
**Twin Springs**—pop pl ... IA-7
**Twin Springs**—pop pl ... MO-7
**Twin Springs**—pop pl ... TN-4
Twin Springs—spring (5) ... AZ-5
Twin Springs—spring ... AR-4
Twin Springs—spring (9) ... CA-9
Twin Springs—spring (3) ... CO-8
Twin Springs—spring (8) ... ID-8
Twin Springs—spring (5) ... MO-7
Twin Springs—spring ... MT-8
Twin Springs—spring (20) ... NV-8
Twin Springs—spring ... NM-5
Twin Springs—spring ... NC-3
Twin Springs—spring ... OK-5
Twin Springs—spring (10) ... OR-9
Twin Springs—spring (2) ... SD-7
Twin Springs—spring (3) ... TN-4
Twin Springs—spring ... TX-5
Twin Springs—spring (4) ... UT-8
Twin Springs—spring (2) ... WA-9
Twin Springs—spring (3) ... WY-8
Twin Springs Canyon ... AZ-5
Twin Springs Canyon—valley ... CA-9
Twin Springs Canyon—valley ... NV-8
Twin Springs Canyon—valley ... WA-9
Twin Springs Cave—cave ... AL-4
Twin Springs Ch—church ... KS-7
Twin Springs Ch—church (2) ... MO-7
Twin Springs Cove—bay ... NV-8
Twin Springs Creek ... ID-8
Twin Springs Creek ... OR-9
Twin Springs Creek—stream ... ID-8
Twin Springs Creek—stream ... KS-7
Twin Springs Creek—stream (2) ... NV-8
Twin Springs Creek—stream ... OR-9
Twin Springs Creek—stream ... WY-8
Twin Springs Dam—dam ... TN-4
Twin Springs Draw—valley ... UT-8
Twin Springs Forest Camp—locale ... OR-9
Twin Springs Hollow—valley (2) ... MO-7
Twin Springs Lake—reservoir ... TN-4
Twin Springs Park—park ... IA-7
Twin Springs Park—park ... MI-6
Twin Springs Ranch—locale ... NV-8
Twin Springs Ridge—ridge ... ID-8
Twin Springs Rsvr—reservoir ... OR-9
Twin Springs Slough—stream ... NV-8
Twin Springs Trail—trail ... OR-9
Twin Springs Trail—trail ... PA-2
Twin Springs Wash—stream ... NV-8
**Twin Spruce**—pop pl ... CO-8
Twin Spruce Lodge—locale ... AK-9
Twin Spruces ... CO-8
Twins Springs Canyon ... NV-8
Twin State Regional Shop Ctr—locale ... MA-1
Twin States Fairgrounds (historical)—locale ... TN-4
Twin Stone Lakes—lake ... MI-6
Twin Stoves Creek—stream ... OR-9
Twin Sugars—summit ... WV-2
Twin Summit—summit ... NV-8
Twin Summit Ridge—ridge ... AK-9
Twin Sump Canyon—valley ... UT-8
Twin Sun Lakes—lake ... MI-6
Twin Tank—reservoir (6) ... AZ-5
Twin Tank—reservoir (3) ... NM-5
Twin Tank—reservoir (2) ... TX-5
Twin Tank Draw—valley ... AZ-5
Twin Tanks—reservoir (20) ... AZ-5
Twin Tanks—reservoir ... CA-9
Twin Tanks—reservoir (10) ... NM-5
Twin Tanks—reservoir (8) ... TX-5
Twin Tanks Dam—dam ... AZ-5
Twin Tank Spring—spring (2) ... OR-9
Twin Tanks Wash—stream ... AZ-5
Twin Tanks Well—well ... CA-9
Twin Tanks Windmill—locale ... NM-5
Twin Tank Windmill—locale ... TX-5
Twin Technical Sch—school ... AL-4
Twin Thumbs—summit ... CO-8
Twin Tomahawk Lake ... MI-6
Twin Tomahawk Lakes—lake ... MI-6
**Twinton**—pop pl ... TN-4
Twinton Post Office (historical)—building ... TN-4
Twinton Sch (historical)—school ... TN-4
Twin Tops—summit ... MT-8
Twin Tower Sanctuary—hist pl ... IL-6
Twin Towers (ruins)—locale ... UT-8
Twin Town—locale ... WI-6
Twin Township—civil ... SD-7
**Twin (Township of)**—pop pl (3) ... OH-6
Twin Trail Canyon—valley ... AZ-5
Twin Trail Shop Ctr—locale ... KS-7
Twin Tree Canyon—valley ... AZ-5
Twin Tree Dam ... ND-7
Twin Trees—area ... UT-8
Twin Trees—locale ... KY-4
Twin Trees Campground—locale ... UT-8
Twin Trees Farm—hist pl ... PA-2
**Twin Tree Township**—pop pl ... ND-7
Twin Trough Spring—spring ... OR-9
Twin Tubs Windmill—locale ... TX-5
Twin Tunnels—tunnel ... NC-3
Twin Tunnels—tunnel ... VA-3
Twin Tunnel Spring—spring ... AZ-5
Twintyone Creek—stream ... WY-8
**Twin Valley**—pop pl ... MN-6
**Twin Valley**—pop pl ... OH-6
Twin Valley—stream ... CA-9
Twin Valley—valley ... CA-9
Twin Valley—valley ... WI-6
Twin Valley Camp—locale ... CA-9
Twin Valley Cem—cemetery ... OH-6
Twin Valley Ch—church ... VA-3
Twin Valley Country Club—locale ... NC-3
Twin Valley Creek—stream (3) ... CA-9
Twin Valley HS—school ... PA-2
Twin Valley Memorial Park Cem—cemetery ... PA-2
Twin Valley Rsvr—reservoir ... ID-8
Twin Valleys ... CA-9
Twin Valleys—area ... UT-8
Twin Valleys—basin ... UT-8
Twin Valleys—locale ... NV-8
Twin Valley Sch—school ... CA-9
Twin Valleys Creek ... CA-9
Twin Valley Springs—spring ... NV-8
Twin Valley State Wildlife Mngmt Area—park ... MN-6
**Twin Valley (subdivision)**—pop pl ... TN-4
**Twin Valley Township**—pop pl ... ND-7
**Twin View Heights**—pop pl ... IA-7
Twin Village (RR name Hebronville)—uninc pl ... MA-1
**Twinville**—pop pl ... TN-4
Twinville Ch—church ... TN-4
Twinville Post Office (historical)—building ... TN-4
Twinville Sch—school ... KS-7
Twin Vlys—swamp ... NY-2
Twin Wash—stream ... AZ-5
Twin Wash—stream (2) ... CO-8
Twin Washes—stream ... UT-8
Twinway Trail—trail ... NH-1
Twin Well—well ... NM-5
Twin Well—well ... TX-5
Twin Wells—well (4) ... NM-5
Twin Wells—well ... OR-9
Twin Wells—well (2) ... TX-5
Twin Wells Ranch—locale ... NM-5
Twin Wells Stock Pens—other ... NM-5
Twin West, Lake—lake ... OH-6
Twin Willows Lake—reservoir ... OH-6
Twin Willows Sch—school ... WI-6
**Twin Willows Subdivision**—pop pl ... UT-8
Twin Windmill—locale (2) ... NM-5
Twin Windmill—locale (4) ... TX-5
Twin Windmills—locale ... CO-8
Twin Windmills—locale (9) ... NM-5
Twin Windmills—locale (5) ... TX-5
Twinwood Lake—lake ... MI-6
Twin Woods Golf Course—locale ... PA-2
**Twisp**—pop pl ... WA-9
Twisp Lake ... WA-9
Twisp Lake—lake ... WA-9
Twisp Mtn—summit ... WA-9
Twisp Muni Airp—airport ... WA-9
Twisp Pass—gap ... WA-9
Twisp River—stream ... WA-9
Twiss Creek—stream ... KS-7
Twisselmann Lake—lake ... CA-9
Twisselmann Ranch—locale ... CA-9
Twisselmann Well—well ... CA-9
Twiss Hollow—valley ... WY-8
**Twist**—pop pl ... AR-4
Twist, The—bend ... UT-8
Twist, The—summit ... UT-8
Twistabout Creek—stream ... WV-2
Twistal Swamp—swamp ... MN-6
Twistback Hill—summit ... NH-1
Twist Canyon—valley ... UT-8
Twist Creek—stream ... AK-9
Twist Creek—stream ... ID-8
Twist Drill Dam ... MA-1
Twisted Creek—stream ... TX-5
Twisted Doughnut Arch—arch ... UT-8
Twisted Draw—valley ... ID-8
Twisted Gun Gap—gap ... WV-2
Twisted Tree Well Cave—cave ... AL-4
Twistem Creek—stream ... AK-9
Twister Creek—stream ... AK-9
Twister Falls—falls ... WY-8
Twist Hills—ridge ... AZ-5
Twist Hollow—valley ... UT-8
Twisting Chute Creek—stream ... WV-2
Twisting Falls—falls ... TN-4
Twisting Pine Mtn—summit ... SC-3
Twisting Wood Creek ... MS-4
Twist Lake ... MN-6
Twist Lake—lake ... MI-6
Twist Mtn—summit ... NY-2
Twist Ridge—ridge ... UT-8
Twist Run—stream ... OH-6
Twist Sch—school ... KS-7
Twist (Township of)—fmr MCD ... AR-4
Twist Trail—valley ... UT-8
**Twistville**—pop pl ... WV-2
Twist Vly—swamp ... NY-2
Twistwood ... MS-4
Twistwood Creek—stream ... MS-4
Twistwood Sch—school ... MS-4
Twisty Bayou—stream ... LA-4
Twisty Creek—stream ... OR-9
Twisty Park—swamp ... CO-8
Twitch Cove—bay ... MD-2
Twitchel Cem—cemetery ... MN-6
Twitchel Cem—cemetery ... NY-2
**Twitchell**—pop pl ... TX-5
Twitchell, Ancil, House—hist pl ... UT-8
Twitchell, Ginery, House—hist pl ... MA-1
Twitchell, Joseph, House—hist pl ... MA-1
Twitchell Brook—stream (5) ... ME-1
Twitchell Canyon—valley ... ID-8
Twitchell Canyon—valley (2) ... UT-8
Twitchell Cem—cemetery ... IL-6
Twitchell Corner—locale ... ME-1
Twitchell Creek—stream ... NY-2
Twitchell Creek—stream ... UT-8
Twitchell Dam—dam ... CA-9
Twitchell Hill—summit ... ME-1
Twitchell Island—island ... CA-9
Twitchell Lake—lake ... NY-2
Twitchell Mtn—summit ... NY-2
Twitchell Pass—gap ... MT-8
Twitchell Pond—reservoir ... ME-1
Twitchell Ranch—locale ... MT-8
Twitchell Rsvr—reservoir ... CA-9
Twitchells Knoll—summit ... ID-8
Twite Rapids—rapids ... MN-6
Twitley Branch—stream ... MS-4
Twitley Branch Park—park ... MS-4
Twitter Creek—stream ... AK-9
Twitters Branch—stream ... KY-4
**Twitty**—pop pl ... TX-5
Twitty, Lake—reservoir ... NC-3
Twitty Bridge—bridge ... NC-3
Twitty Cem—cemetery ... AL-4
Twitty City-Music Village USA—park ... TN-4
Twitty Creek—stream ... MS-4
Twitty Dam—dam ... NC-3
Twitty Hollow—valley ... TN-4
Twitty Knob—summit ... TN-4
Twitty Park—park ... GA-3
Twitty Prong—stream ... SC-3
Twittys Creek—stream ... VA-3
Twitty Spring—spring ... TN-4
Twlight Canyon—valley ... UT-8
T W Lyman Dam—dam ... SD-7
TW Mountain ... MT-8
Two, Canyon—valley ... CA-9
Two, Hill—summit ... AZ-5
Two, Lake—lake ... AK-9
Two, Lake—lake ... AZ-5
Two, Lake—lake ... MI-6
Two, Lake—lake ... MN-6
Two, Lake—lake (3) ... WI-6
Two, Lake—reservoir ... MN-6
Two, Lake No—reservoir (2) ... AR-4
Two-A, Lateral—canal ... NV-8
Two Acre Flat—flat ... TX-5
Two and a Half Mile Creek—stream ... ID-8
Two and One Half Creek—stream ... CO-8
Two and Three Quarter Mile Creek—stream ... WV-2
Two Arches—arch ... OR-9
Two Arm Bay—bay ... AK-9
Two Axe Lake—lake ... WI-6
Two-B, Lateral—canal ... NV-8
Two Baby Creek—stream ... OK-5
Two Bar Camp—locale ... WY-8
Two Bar Canyon—valley ... AZ-5
Two Bar Creek—stream ... CA-9
Two Bar Creek—stream ... WY-8
Two Bar Ditch—canal ... WY-8
Two Bar Draw—valley ... CO-8
Two Bar Mtn—summit ... AZ-5
Two-Bar Ranch—hist pl ... CO-8
Two Bar Ranch—locale ... AZ-5
Two Bar Ranch—locale ... CO-8
Two Bar Ranch—locale ... WY-8
Two Barrel Branch—stream ... FL-3
Two Barrell Branch ... FL-3
Two-Barrel Spring—spring ... CA-9
Two-Bar Ridge ... AZ-5
Two Bar Ridge—ridge ... AZ-5
Two Bars—bar ... OR-9
Two Bar Spring—spring ... WY-8
Two Bar Springs—spring ... CO-8
Two Bayou ... AR-4
Two Bayou—stream ... AR-4
Two Bayou Ch—church ... AR-4
Two Bayou Creek ... AR-4
Two Bear Camp—locale ... WI-6
Two Bear Creek—stream ... MT-8
Two Bear Creek—stream ... OR-9
Two Bear Lake—lake ... WI-6
Two Bear Meadows—flat ... MT-8
Two Bear Ridge—ridge ... MT-8
Two-bit Creek—stream ... AK-9
Two-bit Creek—stream ... ID-8
Two Bit Creek—stream ... ID-8
Two-bit Creek—stream ... ID-8
Two-Bit Creek—stream ... MT-8
Two-Bit Creek—stream ... OR-9
Two Bit Creek—stream ... SD-7
Two Bit Creek—stream ... WA-9
Two Bit Fork—stream ... OR-9
Two Bit Gulch—valley ... CA-9
Twobit Gulch—valley ... CA-9
Twobit Gulch—valley ... CO-8
Two Bit Gulch—valley ... OR-9
Twobit (historical)—locale ... SD-7
Two Bit Lake—lake ... AK-9
Two Bit Mine (historical)—locale ... SD-7
Two Bit Mine (historical)—mine ... SD-7
Two Bit Ranch—locale ... WY-8
Two-Bit Spring—spring ... OR-9
Two Bit Tank—reservoir ... AZ-5
Two Bottom Lake—lake ... ID-8
Two Boys Lake—lake ... WI-6
Two B Ranch—locale ... TX-5
Two Branch Ferry (historical)—locale ... AL-4
Two Branch Hollow—valley ... IL-6
Two Branch Island—island ... MO-7
Twobridge Brook—stream ... NY-2
Two Bridge Run—stream ... NY-2
Two Bridges ... NJ-2
Two Bridges—arch ... UT-8
**Two Bridges**—pop pl ... NJ-2
Two Bridge Swamp—swamp ... SC-3
Two Brooks—locale ... NY-2
Two Brooks—stream ... NY-2
Two Brothers—island ... VI-3
**Two Brothers**—pop pl ... VI-3
Two Brothers Islands—island ... FL-3
Two BS Mine—mine ... AZ-5
Twobuck Creek—stream (2) ... OR-9
Two Buck Gulch—valley ... CO-8
Two Buck Ring—ridge ... CT-1
Two Buck Rsvr—reservoir ... MT-8
Two Buck Spring—spring ... ID-8
Two Bunch Palms—locale ... CA-9
Two Bush Branch—stream ... TX-5
Two Bush Channel—channel ... ME-1
Two Bush Island ... ME-1
Two Bush Island—island (5) ... ME-1
Twobush Island—island ... ME-1
Two Bush Knob—summit (2) ... TX-5
Two Bush Ledge—bar (2) ... ME-1
Two Bush Reef—bar ... ME-1
Two Butte—summit ... NM-5
Two Butte—summit ... OR-9
Two Butte Creek—cens area ... CO-8
Two Butte Creek—stream ... CO-8
Two Butte Rsvr—reservoir ... MT-8
**Two Buttes**—pop pl ... CO-8
Two Buttes—summit ... CA-9
Two Buttes—summit ... CO-8
Two Buttes—summit ... MT-8
Two Buttes—summit ... WY-8
Two Buttes Canal—canal ... CO-8
Two Buttes Cem—cemetery ... CO-8
Two Buttes Creek ... CO-8
Two Buttes Creek—stream ... WA-9
Two Buttes Lake ... CO-8
Two Buttes Pond—reservoir ... CO-8
Two Butte Springs—spring ... CO-8
Two Buttes Rsvr—reservoir ... CO-8
Two Buttes Rsvr—reservoir ... WY-8
Two By Four Creek—stream ... AK-9
Two By Four Creek—stream ... CO-8
Two Cabin Creek—stream ... OR-9
Two Cabin Creek—stream ... WY-8
Two Cabin Draw—valley ... WY-8
Two Calf Creek—stream ... MT-8
Two Canal, An—canal ... MT-8
Twocanyon River ... WA-9
Two Capitans ... WA-9
Two Cent Bridge—hist pl ... ME-1
**Two Chestnut**—pop pl ... TN-4
Two Children Island ... FM-9
Two Churches Sch—school ... PA-2
Two Color Campground—park ... OR-9
Two Color Creek—stream ... OR-9
Two Color Guard Station—locale ... OR-9
Two Color Lake—lake ... OR-9
Twocone Point—cape ... AK-9
Two Connection Lake ... MN-6
Two Corral Creek—stream ... OR-9
Twocrack Island—island ... AK-9
Two Creek ... WY-8
Two Creek—stream (2) ... CO-8
Two Creek—stream ... ID-8
Two Creek—stream (3) ... MT-8
Two Creek—stream ... WY-8
Two Creek Ranch—locale ... MT-8
**Two Creeks**—pop pl ... WI-6
Two Creeks Buried State Forest—park ... WI-6
Two Creeks County Park—park ... WI-6
**Two Creeks (Town of)**—pop pl ... WI-6
Two Cross Arroyo—stream ... NM-5
Two Cross Ranch—locale ... NM-5
Two-D, Lateral—canal ... NV-8
Twoday Mtn—summit ... AK-9
Two Day Rsvr—reservoir ... OR-9
Two Deer Coulee—valley ... MT-8
Two Deer Lake—lake ... MN-6
Two Deer Lake—lake ... WI-6
Two Dog Creek—stream ... MT-8
Two Dog Flats—flat ... MT-8
Two Dog Pass—gap ... CA-9
Two Dollar Gulch—valley ... CA-9
**Twodot**—pop pl ... MT-8
Twodot Canal—canal ... MT-8
Two Dot Flats—flat ... WY-8
Twodot Peak—summit ... ID-8
Two Dot Ranch—locale ... WY-8
Two Dot Spring—spring ... OR-9
Two Dot Windmill—locale ... TX-5
Two Draw Lake—reservoir ... TX-5
Two Draw Rsvr—reservoir ... WY-8
Two Drink Springs—spring ... MT-8
Two Duck Site—hist pl ... KS-7
Two Duck Tank—reservoir ... TX-5
Two-E, Lateral—canal ... NV-8
Two Echo Park—flat ... WY-8
Two Egg—locale ... FL-3
Two Elk Creek—stream ... CO-8
Two Elk Pass—gap ... CO-8
Two Elk Trail—trail ... CO-8
Two E Spring—spring ... AZ-5
Two E Wash—stream ... AZ-5
Two Fault Butte—summit ... NM-5
Two F Crossing—locale ... TX-5
Two Feathers Hill—summit ... NM-5
Two Fork Rsvr—reservoir ... CO-8
Two Forks—locale ... ID-8
Two Forks Check Dam—dam ... OR-9
Two Forks Creek—stream ... ID-8
Two Forks Rsvr ... OR-9
Two Forks Rsvr—reservoir ... MT-8
Two-Forty Mine—mine ... CO-8
Two Freds Oil Field—oilfield ... TX-5
Two Friends—locale ... VI-3
Two Girls—summit ... OR-9
Two Girls Creek—stream ... OR-9
Twogood Flat—flat ... ID-8
**Two Gray Hills (Trading Post)**—pop pl ... NM-5
Two Grey Hills—locale ... NM-5
Two Grey Hills—summit (2) ... NM-5
Two Guns—locale ... AZ-5
Two Guns Interchange—crossing ... AZ-5
Two Gun Town ... AZ-5
Two Guys Shop Ctr—locale ... PA-2
Two G Windmill—locale ... TX-5
Two-Gwo-Tee-e Pass ... WY-8
Twogwotee Pass ... WY-8
Two Hands Cave—cave ... MT-8
**Two Harbors**—pop pl ... MN-6
Two Harbors Carnegie Library—hist pl ... MN-6
**Two Harbors Junction**—pop pl ... MN-6
Two Harbors Light Station—hist pl ... MN-6
Two Harbors (Unorganized Territory of)—unorg ... MN-6
Two Hatchet Creek—stream ... OK-5
Two-Headed Island—island ... AK-9
Two Heart Creek—stream ... MT-8
Two Hearted Lakes—lake ... MI-6
Two Hearted River ... MI-6
Two Hearted River—stream ... MI-6
Two Hearted River Campground—locale ... MI-6
Twohey Creek ... MN-6
Twohey Lake ... MN-6
Two- High Tanks- —reservoir ... NM-5
Two Hill Canyon—valley ... NV-8
Two Hole Branch—stream ... FL-3
Two Hole Ruin—locale ... AZ-5
Two Holes Pond—lake ... NY-2
Two Hole Spring—spring ... CA-9
Two Holes Tank—reservoir ... AZ-5
Two Horse Butte—summit ... UT-8
Two Hour Rock—island ... ME-1
Two Hundred and Fifteenmile Creek—stream ... AZ-5
Two Hundred and Fivemile Creek—stream ... AZ-5
Two Hundred and Fivemile Rapids—falls ... AZ-5
Two Hundred and Fortymile Rapids—rapids ... AZ-5
Two Hundred and Fortyone Mile Rapids—rapids ... AZ-5
Two Hundred and Fourteenmile Creek—stream ... AZ-5
Two Hundred and Ninemile Canyon—valley ... AZ-5
Two Hundred And One Spur—locale ... CA-9
Two Hundred and Seventeenmile Canyon—valley ... AZ-5
Two Hundred And Seventeenmile Canyon Rapids ... AZ-5
Two Hundred And Seventeenmile Rapids ... AZ-5
Two Hundred and Seventeen Mile Rapids—rapids ... AZ-5
Two Hundred and Thirtyfour Mile Rapids—rapids ... AZ-5
Two Hundred and Thirtyone Mile Rapids—rapids ... AZ-5
Two Hundred and Thirtyseven Mile Rapids—rapids ... AZ-5
Two Hundred and Thirtytwo Mile Rapids—rapids ... AZ-5
Two Hundred and Twentyeightmile Canyon—valley ... AZ-5
Two Hundred and Twentyfour Mile Canyon—valley ... AZ-5
Two Hundred and Twentyfour Mile Rapids—rapids ... AZ-5
Two Hundred and Twentymile Canyon—valley ... AZ-5
Two Hundred and Twentytwo Mile Creek—stream ... AZ-5
Two Hundred Block West Franklin Street Hist Dist—hist pl ... VA-3
Two Hundred Eleventh Street—other ... IL-6
Two Hundred Thirty-Second Place Sch—school ... CA-9
Two Hundred Twenty-Third Street Sch—school ... CA-9
Twohy Creek ... MN-6
Twohy Lake ... MN-6
Two Inch Gap—gap ... NC-3
**Two Inlets**—pop pl ... MN-6
Two Inlets Lake—lake ... MN-6
Two Inlets State For—forest ... MN-6
**Two Inlets (Township of)**—pop pl ... MN-6
Two Iron Tank ... AZ-5
Two Island Bay—bay ... FL-3
Two Island Lake—lake ... AK-9
Two Island Lake—lake (2) ... MN-6
Two Island Lake—lake ... SD-7
Two Island Lake—lake (2) ... WI-6
Two Island River—stream ... MN-6
Two Isle Lake ... MI-6
Two Jim Tank—reservoir ... AZ-5
Two Johns—locale ... MD-2
Two Johns Mine—mine ... SD-7
Two Jump Canyon—valley ... UT-8
Two Lake ... MN-6
Two Lakes—lake ... AK-9
Two Lakes—lake ... ID-8
Two Lakes—lake ... MI-6
Two Lakes—lake ... MT-8
Two Lakes—lake (2) ... WA-9
Two Lakes Campground—locale ... WI-6
Two Ledge Rsvr—reservoir ... CO-8
Two-legged Windmill—locale ... NM-5
Two Leggin Creek ... MT-8
Two Leggins Canal—canal ... MT-8
Two Leggins Creek ... MT-8
Two Leggins Creek—stream ... MT-8
Two Leggins Tunnel—tunnel ... MT-8
**Two Lick**—pop pl ... PA-2
**Two Lick**—pop pl ... WV-2
Twolick Branch—stream ... KY-4
Two Lick Branch—stream ... WV-2
Twolick Creek ... PA-2
Two Lick Creek—stream ... IN-6
Twolick Creek—stream ... KY-4
Two Lick Creek—stream ... KY-4
Two Lick Creek—stream ... PA-2
Two Lick Creek—stream ... WV-2
Two Lick Creek Dam—dam ... PA-2
Two Lick Creek Rsvr—reservoir ... PA-2
Two Lick Hollow—valley ... KY-4
Twolick Run—stream ... WV-2
Two Lick Run—stream ... WV-2
Twolick Run—stream ... WV-2
Two Lick Run—stream ... WV-2
Twolick Run—stream (2) ... WV-2
Two Licks ... PA-2
Two-Licks Creek ... PA-2
Two Lights—hist pl ... ME-1
**Two Lights**—pop pl ... ME-1
Two Line Well—well ... TX-5
Two Lion Tank—reservoir ... AZ-5
Two Little Lakes—lake ... WA-9
Two Locks—locale ... MD-2
Two Log Creek—stream ... CA-9
Two Log Run—stream ... PA-2
Two Lovers Leap—cliff ... GU-9
Two Man Rock—summit ... WA-9
Twombly Brook—stream ... NH-1
Twombly Creek—stream ... OR-9
Twombly Landing—locale ... NJ-2
Twombly Mtn—summit ... ME-1
Twombly Mtn—summit ... MI-6
Twombly Ridge—ridge ... ME-1
Twomblys Landing ... NJ-2
Twombly (Unorganized Territory of)—unorg ... ME-1
Two Meadows—flat ... MT-8
Two Meadows Creek—stream ... MT-8
Two Medicine Campground—locale ... MT-8
Two Medicine Community Center—building ... MT-8

Two Medicine Creek—stream MT-8
Two Medicine Falls—falls MT-8
Two Medicine Fight Site—hist pl MT-8
Two Medicine General Store—hist pl MT-8
Two Medicine Lake—lake MT-8
Two Medicine Main Canal—canal MT-8
Two Medicine Pass—gap MT-8
Two Medicine Pass Trail—trail MT-8
Two Medicine Ridge—ridge (2) MT-8
Two Medicine River—stream MT-8
Two Mesas—summit AZ-5
Twomey—pop pl TN-4
Twomey Cem—cemetery WV-2
Twomey Hole—basin TN-4
Twomey Hole Branch—stream TN-4
Twomey Post Office (historical)—building TN-4
Twomey Spring—spring TN-4
Two Mile—locale AZ-5
Twomile—locale OR-9
Twomile—locale PA-2
Two Mile—pop pl FL-3
Twomile—pop pl WV-2
Two Mile—uninc pl WV-2
Twomile Arroyo—stream CO-8
Two Mile Baptist Church MS-4
Twomile Bayou—stream (2) LA-4
Two Mile Beach—beach NJ-2
Twomile Branch—stream AR-4
Twomile Branch—stream FL-3
Twomile Branch—stream (2) GA-3
Twomile Branch—stream IL-6
Twomile Branch—stream KY-4
Twomile Branch—stream LA-4
Twomile Branch—stream MO-7
Twomile Branch—stream (2) NC-3
Two Mile Branch—stream SC-3
Twomile Branch—stream SC-3
Twomile Branch—stream (2) TN-4
Two Mile Branch—stream TN-4
Two Mile Branch—stream (2) TX-5
Twomile Branch—stream TX-5
Twomile Branch—stream (4) WV-2
Two Mile Bridge (historical)—bridge MS-4
Two Mile Brook ME-1
Twomile Brook—stream CT-1
Twomile Brook—stream (2) ME-1
Twomile Brook—stream NY-2
Twomile Camp—locale WA-9
Two Mile Canyon UT-8
Twomile Canyon—valley CO-8
Twomile Canyon—valley ID-8
Twomile Canyon—valley (2) NM-5
Twomile Canyon—valley OR-9
Twomile Canyon—valley TX-5
Twomile Canyon—valley (3) UT-8
Twomile Cem—cemetery MA-1
Twomile Ch—church AR-4
Two Mile Ch—church MS-4
Twomile Ch—church SC-3
Twomile Ch—church TX-5
Twomile Ch—church WV-2
Two Mile Channel—channel FL-3
Twomile Corner—summit RI-1
Twomile Corrals—locale AZ-5
Twomile Coulee—valley MT-8
Two Mile Creek AL-4
Two Mile Creek ID-8
Two Mile Creek KS-7
Two Mile Creek MS-4
Twomile Creek NC-3
Two Mile Creek PA-2
Twomile Creek WV-2
Twomile Creek—stream (2) AL-4
Two Mile Creek—stream AL-4
Twomile Creek—stream (2) AK-9
Two Mile Creek—stream AR-4
Twomile Creek—stream (5) AR-4
Twomile Creek—stream (3) CA-9
Twomile Creek—stream CO-8
Twomile Creek—stream FL-3
Twomile Creek—stream (2) GA-3
Twomile Creek—stream (5) ID-8
Twomile Creek—stream (2) IL-6
Twomile Creek—stream IN-6
Twomile Creek—stream (2) IA-7
Twomile Creek—stream KS-7
Twomile Creek—stream (5) KY-4
Twomile Creek—stream (2) MI-6
Twomile Creek—stream (2) MN-6
Twomile Creek—stream (3) MS-4
Twomile Creek—stream (4) MO-7
Twomile Creek—stream (3) MT-8
Twomile Creek—stream NV-8
Twomile Creek—stream (5) NY-2
Twomile Creek—stream NC-3
Twomile Creek—stream (4) OH-6
Twomile Creek—stream (2) OK-5
Twomile Creek—stream (6) OR-9
Twomile Creek—stream (2) PA-2
Twomile Creek—stream (2) SC-3
Twomile Creek—stream (5) TX-5
Twomile Creek—stream (2) UT-8
Twomile Creek—stream (8) WV-2
Twomile Creek—stream WI-6
Twomile Creek—stream WY-8
Twomile Creek Access Point—locale GA-3
Twomile Creek Bridge—bridge GA-3
Two Mile Curve—locale ME-1
Twomile Ditch—canal IN-6
Twomile Ditch—canal MI-6
Twomile Draw—valley (3) TX-5
Twomile Draw—valley (2) WY-8
Twomile Fork—stream KY-4
Twomile Fork—stream (2) WV-2
Twomile Gap—gap GA-3
Twomile Gap—gap OR-9
Twomile Grove Cem—cemetery IL-6
Twomile Gulch—valley MT-8
Twomile Hill—summit CT-1
Twomile Hill—summit MT-8
Twomile Hill—summit TX-5
Twomile Hollow—valley AL-4
Twomile Hollow—valley WY-8
Twomile Island—island AK-9
Twomile Island—island CT-1
Twomile Island—island IL-6
Twomile Island—island ME-1
Two Mile Island—island MO-7
Twomile Island—island NH-1
Twomile Lake WI-6
Twomile Lake—lake AK-9
Twomile Lake—lake (2) FL-3
Twomile Lake—lake LA-4
Twomile Lake—lake MI-6
Twomile Lake—lake MN-6
Two Mile Lake—lake MS-4
Twomile Lake—lake MS-4
Twomile Lake—lake NE-7
Twomile Lake—lake SD-7
Two Mile Lake—lake WI-6
Twomile Lead—ridge TN-4
Twomile Ledge—bar MA-1
Two Mile Limit Rsvr—reservoir ID-8
Twomile Mesa—summit NM-5
Twomile Point—cape CA-9
Twomile Point—cape MI-6
Twomile Pond—lake FL-3
Twomile Pond—lake MT-8
Two Mile Prairie—area MO-7
Twomile Prairie Lake—lake FL-3
Twomile Prairie Sch—school MO-7
Twomile Rapids—rapids OR-9
Twomile Ridge—ridge MT-8
Twomile Ridge—ridge OR-9
Twomile Ridge Trail—trail VA-3
Twomile Reef—rock MA-1
Two Mile Rsvr—reservoir AZ-5
Twomile Rsvr—reservoir NM-5
Twomile Rsvr—reservoir WY-8
Two Mile Run PA-2
Twomile Run—stream MD-2
Twomile Run—stream (4) OH-6
Twomile Run—stream (6) PA-2
Two Mile Run—stream PA-2
Twomile Run—stream (3) PA-2
Twomile Run—stream VA-3
Twomile Run—stream (2) WV-2
Twomile Run County Park—park PA-2
Two Mile Run Dam—dam PA-2
Twomile Run Overlook—locale VA-3
Two Mile Run Rsvr—reservoir PA-2
Two Miles Beach NJ-2
Twomile Sch—school IL-6
Twomile Sch—school PA-2
Twomile Sch—school WV-2
Twomile Sch—school WI-6
Twomile Sch (abandoned)—school MO-7
Two Mile Seep AZ-5
Twomile Seep—spring AZ-5
Twomile Slough—stream IL-6
Twomile Spring—spring AZ-5
Twomile Spring—spring OR-9
Twomile Spring Tank—reservoir AZ-5
Twomile Swamp—stream NC-3
Twomile Tank—reservoir (2) TX-5
Twomile Tanks—reservoir NM-5
Twomile Trail—trail PA-2
Twomile Valley—basin OR-9
Twomile Wash—stream AZ-5
Twomile Waterhole—bay TX-5
Twomile Well—well AZ-5
Twomile Windmill—locale (3) TX-5
Two Mill Draw—valley TX-5
Two Mill Tank—reservoir AZ-5
Two Moon Bay—bay AK-9
Two Moon Creek—stream MT-8
Two Moon Rsvr—reservoir MT-8
Two Mouth Bayou—stream LA-4
Two Mouth Creek—stream ID-8
Two Mouth Guard Station—locale ID-8
Two Mouth Lakes—lake ID-8
Two Mouths Creek—stream VA-3
Two Mule Camp Hollow—valley MO-7
Two Notch Branch—stream KY-4
Twons—island OR-9
Two Ocean Glacier—glacier MT-8
Two Ocean Lake—lake WY-8
Two Ocean Lake Trail—trail WY-8
Two Ocean Mtn—summit WY-8
Two Ocean North Buffalo Trail—trail WY-8
Two Ocean Pass—gap WY-8
Two Ocean Plateau—area WY-8
Two Ocean Plateau Trail—trail WY-8
Two O'Clock—summit UT-8
Two O'Clock Bayou—stream LA-4
Two O'Clock Point—cape LA-4
Two Peak—summit CO-8
Two Peaks—summit AZ-5
Two Peaks—summit CA-9
Two Pecan Waterhole—lake TX-5
Twopenny Loaf—cape MA-1
Twopenny Loaf—summit MA-1
Two Penny Run—stream NJ-2
Two Pigs—bar NY-2
Two Pine—flat CA-9
Two Pine Island—island ME-1
Two Pine Rsvr—reservoir CO-8
Two Pine Sch—school MT-8
Two Pines Condominium—pop pl UT-8
Two Pines Tank—reservoir NM-5
Two Pipe Spring UT-8
Two Pipe Springs—spring UT-8
Two Pipes Springs—spring OR-9
Two Plate Creek—stream AK-9
Two P.M. Island FM-9
Two Point—cape MT-8
Two Point Butte—summit ID-8
Two Point Creek—stream ID-8
Two Point Lake—lake MT-8
Two Point Mtn—summit ID-8
Two Point Mtn—summit WA-9
Two Point Peak—summit ID-8
Two Points—cape MN-6
Two Point Spring—spring WA-9
Two Pole Branch—stream NC-3
Two Pond Bay—swamp NC-3
Two Ponds—lake MA-1
Two Prairie, Bayou—stream AR-4
Two Prairie Bayou—stream AR-4
Twoprong Mtn—summit AK-9
Two Queens Mine—mine AZ-5
Two Red Mesas—summit AZ-5
Two Red Peaks Valley—valley AZ-5
Two Red Rocks—pillar AZ-5
Two Ridges Cem—cemetery OH-6
Two Ridges Ch—church OH-6
Two Ripple Run—stream WV-2
Two Ripple Run Ch—church WV-2
Two Ripple Run Sch—school WV-2
Two River MN-6
Two River—stream MN-6
Two River Lake—lake MN-6
Two Rivers MN-6
Two Rivers TX-5
Two Rivers—CDP AK-9
Two Rivers—hist pl TN-4
Two Rivers—locale AK-9
Two Rivers—locale MI-6
Two Rivers—locale WA-9
Two Rivers—pop pl CA-9
Two Rivers—pop pl WI-6
Two Rivers—stream MN-6
Two Rivers Ch—church MN-6
Two Rivers Ch—church NE-7
Two Rivers Ch—church TN-4
Two Rivers Farm—locale NE-7
Two Rivers Forest Camp—locale OR-9
Two Rivers HS—school TN-4
Two Rivers Islands—island WA-9
Two Rivers Lake MN-6
Two Rivers Lake—lake CO-8
Two Rivers Lake—reservoir TN-4
Two Rivers Lake Dam—dam TN-4
Two Rivers Mall Shop Ctr—locale TN-4
Two Rivers Marina—other IL-6
Two Rivers Park—park TN-4
Two Rivers Ranch—locale SD-7
Two Rivers River MN-6
Two Rivers River Access—locale MO-7
Two Rivers River South Branch MN-6
Two Rivers Sch—school AK-9
Two Rivers State Rec Area—park NE-7
Two Rivers (Town of)—pop pl WI-6
Two Rivers (Township of)—pop pl MN-6
Two Rock—pillar CA-9
Two Rock—pop pl CA-9
Two Rock—summit CA-9
Two Rock Charcoal Kilns (historical)—locale UT-8
Two Rock Coast Guard Station—post sta CA-9
Two Rock Creek CA-9
Two Rock Mtn—summit AZ-5
Two Rock Point—cape CA-9
Two Rock Ranch Station—other CA-9
Two Rock Ranch Station Milit Reservation—military CA-9
Two Rock Ridge—ridge CA-9
Two Rock Run—stream PA-2
Two Rocks—island AZ-5
Two Rock Sch—school CA-9
Two Rock Union Sch—school CA-9
Tworoose Lake—lake UT-8
Tworoose Pass—gap UT-8
Two Root Creek OH-6
Two Routes Lake MN-6
Two-R Sch—school NE-7
Two Run—pop pl WV-2
Two Run—stream (6) WV-2
Two Run Branch—stream MD-2
Two Run Creek—stream (2) GA-3
Two Runs PA-2
Two Runs Ch—church WV-2
Two Section Canyon—valley TX-5
Two Section Draw—valley TX-5
Two Section Presley Windmill—locale NM-5
Two Sections Windmill—locale TX-5
Two Section Tank—reservoir (2) AZ-5
Two Section Tank—reservoir (4) TX-5
Two Section Tank Number Two—reservoir AZ-5
Two Section Windmill—locale NM-5
Two Section Windmill—locale (10) TX-5
Two Shacks Flat—flat MT-8
Two Shay Ranch—locale CA-9
Two Sheep Waterhole—reservoir OR-9
Two Sisters WA-9
Two Sisters—spring MT-8
Two Sisters Archeol Site—hist pl OK-5
Two Sisters Bar—bar OR-9
Two Sisters Bayou—gut LA-4
Two Sisters Creek—stream SC-3
Two Sisters Islands KY-4
Two Sisters Lake—lake WI-6
Two Sisters Lakes WI-6
Two Sisters Lakes—lake WI-6
Two Sloughs State Wildlife Mngmt Area—park MN-6
Two Spjirngs spring—spring TN-4
Two Spot Mtn—summit AK-9
Two Spring—spring CA-9
Two Springs—spring OR-9
Two Spring—spring (2) UT-8
Two Spring—spring WA-9
Two Spring Creek—stream OR-9
Two Spring Run—stream WV-2
Two Springs CA-9
Two Springs—spring AR-4
Two Springs—spring (2) CA-9
Two Springs—spring ID-8
Two Springs—spring MT-8
Two Springs—spring (2) OR-9
Two Springs—spring WA-9
Two Springs Campground—locale CA-9
Two Springs Gulch—valley MT-8
Two Springs Ranch—locale OR-9
Two Springs Ridge—ridge AZ-5
Two Stone Brook—stream CT-1
Two Story Hill—summit IL-6
Two Story (Trading Post)—pop pl AZ-5
Two Story Well—well NM-5
Two Story Well—well TX-5
Two Strike Bridge—bridge SD-7
Two Suertes—civil CA-9
Two Tail Peak—summit ID-8
Two Tank—reservoir NM-5
Two Tanks—reservoir AZ-5
Two Tanks Spring—spring NV-8
Two Taverns—pop pl PA-2
Two Teats—summit CA-9
Two-thirteen Well—well AZ-5
Two Times Four Prairie—flat WA-9
Two Tips—summit NV-8
Two Tom Hill—summit UT-8
Two Top—summit WY-8
Two Top, Mount—summit ID-8
Two Top Butte SD-7
Two Top Butte—summit SD-7
Two Top Lake WY-8
Two Top Lakes—lake WY-8
Two-Top Mesa ND-7
Two Top Mtn—summit NY-2
Two Top Mtn—summit PA-2
Two Top Mtn—summit TX-5
Two Top Peak SD-7
Two Top Peak—summit SD-7
Two Tops—summit NY-2
Two Trails—pop pl ME-1
Two Tree Butte—summit MT-8
Two Tree Creek—stream MT-8
Two Tree Gulch—valley ID-8
Two Tree Island CT-1
Two Tree Island—island AK-9
Twotree Island—island CT-1
Two Tree Island—island MI-6
Two Tree Island—island OK-5
Twotree Island Channel—channel CT-1
Two Tree Mine—mine MT-8
Two Tree Rsvr—reservoir WY-8
Two Trees Point—summit MT-8
Two Troughs Canyon—valley AZ-5
Two Trough Spring—spring MT-8
Two Troughs Spring—spring AZ-5
Two Troughs Spring Tank—reservoir AZ-5
Two Two Mesa—summit AZ-5
Two U D Rest Area—park AZ-5
Two V Basin—basin CO-8
Two VF Tank—reservoir AZ-5
Two V Ranch—locale CO-8
Two V Ranch—locale FL-3
Two Wash Dam—other WY-8
Two Water Creek—stream WY-8
Two Waters Creek UT-8
Two Way Cave—cave AL-4
Two-way Pond—lake ID-8
Two Way Rsvr—reservoir OR-9
Twoweeks Spring Canyon—valley AZ-5
Two Wells—locale NM-5
Two White Rocks Wash—valley AZ-5
Two Woods Lake SD-7
Two Year Old Creek—stream TX-5
Two Y Junction—gap MT-8
Two Y Saddle MT-8
Twp Park—park OH-6
T.W.U. (Texas Womans University)—uninc pl TX-5
T Wyche—locale TX-5
Twyford Point—cape KY-4
Twyman Park—hist pl OK-5
Twyman Park—park OK-5
Twymans Mill—locale VA-3
TX Canyon—valley NM-5
T X L Oil Field—oilfield TX-5
T X Ranch—locale (2) NM-5
TX Tank—reservoir NM-5
Tyan Pond CT-1
Tyas Bend—bend OK-5
Tyas Bend—bend TX-5
Tyaskin—pop pl MD-2
Tyaskin Creek—stream MD-2
Tyasquam River MA-1
Tyasquan River MA-1
Tyasquin River MA-1
Tybee Creek GA-3
Tybee Creek—stream GA-3
Tybee Cut—channel GA-3
Tybee Island GA-3
Tybee Island—island GA-3
Tybee Island—pop pl GA-3
Tybee Island-Wilmington (CCD)—cens area GA-3
Tybee Knoll Spit—bar GA-3
Tybee Lighthouse—locale GA-3
Tybee River GA-3
Tyber Creek DC-2
Tybo—locale NV-8
Tybo Charcoal Kilns—hist pl NV-8
Tybo Creek—stream NV-8
Tybo Peak—summit WY-8
Tybo Spring—spring NV-8
Tybouts Corner—locale DE-2
Tybow Canyon—valley OR-9
Tybo Well—well NV-8
Tybrook—pop pl DE-2
Tycer Cem—cemetery LA-4
Tycer Creek—stream OR-9
Tycoon Lake—reservoir OH-6
Tycoon Lake State Wildlife Area—park OH-6
Tydings On The Bay—pop pl MD-2
Tydol Lake—reservoir OK-5
Tye—pop pl (2) TX-5
Tye Canyon—valley OR-9
Tyecraft Canyon NV-8
Tye Draw—valley WY-8
Tyee WA-9
Tyee—locale OR-9
Tyee—pop pl AK-9
Tyee—pop pl WA-9
Tyee Lake—lake WA-9
Tyee, Mount—summit AK-9
Tyee Beach—pop pl WA-9
Tyee Butte—summit OR-9
Tyee Camp—pop pl OR-9
Tyee Campground—park OR-9
Tyee City—pop pl CA-9
Tyee Creek—stream AK-9
Tyee Creek—stream ID-8
Tyee Creek—stream (2) OR-9
Tyee Creek—stream WA-9
Tyee Hill—summit WA-9
Tyee Hills, The WA-9
Tyee JHS—school WA-9
Tyee Lake—lake AK-9
Tyee Lakes—lake CA-9
Tyee Mine—mine WA-9
Tyee Mtn—summit ID-8
Tyee Mtn—summit OR-9
Tyee Mtn—summit WA-9
Tyeen Glacier—glacier AK-9
Tyee Peak—summit WA-9
Tyee Pool Camp—locale WA-9
Tyee Prairie—flat WA-9
Tyee Rapids—rapids OR-9
Tyee Ridge—ridge WA-9
Tyee Ridge Spring No 1—spring WA-9
Tyee Ridge Spring No 2—spring WA-9
Tyee Ridge Spring No 3—spring WA-9
Tyee Ridge Spring No 6—spring WA-9
Tyee Ridge Spring No 7—spring WA-9
Tyee Ridge Spring No 8—spring WA-9
Tyee Springs—spring WA-9
Tye Fork KY-4
Tye Fork—stream KY-4
Tye House—hist pl MS-4
Tye Lake—lake MN-6
Tyende Creek AZ-5
Tyende Creek—stream AZ-5
Tyende Mesa—summit AZ-5
Tyende Wa AZ-5
Tye Point NY-2
Tyer Branch—stream TX-5
Tyer Cem—cemetery TX-5
Tyer Cemetery TX-5
Tye River—pop pl VA-3
Tye River—stream VA-3
Tye River—stream WA-9
Tye River Gap—gap VA-3
Tyer Ridge—ridge AR-4
Tyers Cove MA-1
Tyers Pond—reservoir NC-3
Tyers Pond Dam—dam NC-3
Tyer Water Wheel (historical)—building TX-5
Tyes Branch—stream TN-4
Tyes Fork—stream KY-4
Tye To MP-9
Tye Town Sch—school KY-4
Tye Walter Ch—church MS-4
Tyewhoppety—locale KY-4
T Y Fleming Elementary School MS-4
Tygard Reservoir WV-2
Tygard Sch—school MO-7
Tygars Valley WV-2
Tygart—uninc pl WV-2
Tygart Cem—cemetery GA-3
Tygart Creek—stream WV-2
Tygart Junction—locale WV-2
Tygart Lake—reservoir WV-2
Tygart Lake State Park—park WV-2
Tygart (Magisterial District)—fmr MCD WV-2
Tygart Reservoir WV-2
Tygart River WV-2
Tygart River Reservoir WV-2
Tygart River Valley WV-2
Tygarts (CCD)—cens area KY-4
Tygart Sch—school WV-2
Tygarts Creek—stream KY-4
Tygarts State For—forest KY-4
Tygarts Valley WV-2
Tygarts Valley—locale KY-4
Tygarts Valley Church—hist pl WV-2
Tygarts Valley River WV-2
Tygart Valley—valley WV-2
Tygart Valley Ch—church WV-2
Tygart Valley HS—school WV-2
Tygart Valley River—stream WV-2
Tygee Creek—stream (2) ID-8
Tygee Creek Basin—basin ID-8
Tygee Ridge—ridge ID-8
Tygee Ridge—ridge WY-8
Tyger—pop pl SC-3
Tyger Ch—church SC-3
Tyger River—stream SC-3
Tygers Creek—stream VA-3
Tygers Valley WV-2
Tygerts Valley River WV-2
Tygert Swamp—swamp NY-2
Tygerville SC-3
Tygharts Valley River WV-2
Tygh Creek—stream OR-9
Tygh Creek Trail—trail OR-9
Tygh Ridge—ridge OR-9
Tygh Ridge Summit—gap OR-9
Tygh Valley—pop pl OR-9
Tygh Valley—valley OR-9
Tygh Valley Cem—cemetery OR-9
Tygh Valley Fairgrounds—locale OR-9
Tygh Valley State Wayside—park OR-9
Tygh Valley Storage Pond—reservoir OR-9
Ty Hatch Bench—bench UT-8
Ty Hatch Creek UT-8
Ty Hatch Creek—stream UT-8
Tyhee—pop pl ID-8
Tyhee Lateral—canal ID-8
Tyhee Wasteway—canal ID-8
Tykel Gulch OR-9
Ty Lake—lake WA-9
Tyler—locale FL-3
Tyler—locale KS-7
Tyler—locale KY-4
Tyler—locale MS-4
Tyler—locale NH-1
Tyler—locale ND-7
Tyler—locale OK-5
Tyler—locale PA-2
Tyler—pop pl AL-4
Tyler—pop pl KY-4
Tyler—pop pl MD-2
Tyler—pop pl MN-6
Tyler—pop pl MO-7
Tyler—pop pl PA-2
Tyler—pop pl TX-5
Tyler—pop pl VA-3
Tyler—pop pl WA-9
Tyler—pop pl WV-2
Tyler—uninc pl KS-7
Tyler, Daniel, House—hist pl UT-8
Tyler, George F., Mansion—hist pl PA-2
Tyler, John, House—hist pl CT-1
Tyler, John, House—hist pl VA-3
Tyler, Lake—lake FL-3
Tyler, Lake—reservoir TX-5
Tyler, Moses, House—hist pl KY-4
Tyler, Solomon, House—hist pl CT-1
Tyler, William H., House—hist pl NE-7
Tyler Arboretum—park PA-2
Tyler Bay CA-9
Tyler Bayou—gut MI-6
Tyler Bend—bend AR-4
Tyler Bend—bend VA-3
Tyler Bight—bay CA-9
Tyler Block—hist pl KY-4
Tyler Bluff—cliff TX-5
Tyler Bog—lake NH-1
Tyler Branch—stream AL-4
Tyler Branch—stream MO-7
Tyler Branch—stream NC-3
Tyler Branch—stream SC-3
Tyler Branch—stream (3) TN-4
Tyler Branch—stream VT-1
Tyler Brook—stream CT-1
Tyler Brook—stream (2) ME-1
Tyler Brook—stream (2) MA-1
Tyler Brook—stream NH-1
Tyler Brook—stream NY-2
Tyler Brook—stream PA-2
Tyler Canyon—valley CA-9
Tyler Canyon—valley ID-8
Tyler (CCD)—cens area TX-5
Tyler Cem—cemetery IL-6
Tyler Cem—cemetery LA-4
Tyler Cem—cemetery MI-6
Tyler Cem—cemetery MO-7
Tyler Cem—cemetery NY-2
Tyler Cem—cemetery NC-3
Tyler Cem—cemetery OH-6
Tyler Cem—cemetery (2) TN-4
Tyler Cem—cemetery VT-1
Tyler Cem—cemetery VA-3
Tyler Cem—cemetery WI-6
Tyler Community Club—building AL-4
Tyler Corner—locale ME-1
Tyler Corners—locale PA-2
Tyler (County)—pop pl TX-5
Tyler (County)—pop pl WV-2
Tyler County Courthouse and Jail—hist pl WV-2
Tyler Cove—bay ME-1
Tyler Cove—bay MD-2
Tyler Creek MI-6
Tyler Creek OR-9
Tyler Creek—stream (2) CA-9
Tyler Creek—stream ID-8
Tyler Creek—stream IL-6
Tyler Creek—stream (2) MD-2
Tyler Creek—stream (2) MT-8
Tyler Creek—stream OR-9
Tyler Creek—stream SC-3
Tyler Creek—stream UT-8
Tyler Creek—stream (2) VA-3
Tyler Creek—stream (2) WA-9
Tyler Creek—stream (2) WV-2
Tyler Creek Fire Control Station—locale CA-9
Tyler Creek For Preserve—forest IL-6
Tyler Crossroads—locale AL-4
Tyler Crossroads—locale SC-3
Tylerdale—pop pl PA-2
Tylerdale Junction—pop pl PA-2
Tyler Ditch—canal (2) IN-6
Tyler Ditch—canal MD-2
Tyler Drain—stream MI-6
Tyler Draw—valley OR-9
Tyler Draw—valley WY-8
Tyler East, Lake—reservoir TX-5
Tyler East (CCD)—cens area TX-5
Tyler Falls—falls NE-7
Tyler Ferry Lake—lake TX-5
Tyler Ford—locale AL-4
Tyler Forks—locale WI-6
Tyler Forks—stream WI-6
Tyler Forks River WI-6
Tyler Gardens—pop pl VA-3
Tyler Glacier WA-9
Tyler-Goodwin Bridge—bridge AL-4
Tyler Gulch—valley (2) CA-9
Tyler Heights—pop pl MD-2
Tyler Heights—pop pl WV-2
Tyler Heights (Mount Tyler)—pop pl WV-2
Tyler Hill—pop pl PA-2
Tyler Hill—summit CO-8
Tyler Hill—summit ME-1
Tyler Hill—summit (2) PA-2
Tyler Hill Cem—cemetery PA-2
Tyler Hill Residential Hist Dist—hist pl AL-4
Tyler Hollow—valley (2) NY-2
Tyler Hollow—valley (2) PA-2
Tyler Holmes Memorial Hosp—hospital MS-4
Tyler Homestead—locale WY-8
Tylerhorse Canyon—valley CA-9
Tyler Hotel—hist pl KY-4
Tyler House—hist pl TX-5
Tyler HS—school TX-5
Tyler HS—school VA-3
Tyler Hydraulic-Fill Dam—hist pl TX-5
Tyler Intake Tower—locale TX-5
Tyler Island—island CA-9
Tyler Island—island GA-3
Tyler Island—island WV-2
Tyler Islands—island ME-1
Tyler Junior Coll—school TX-5
Tyler Knob—summit VA-3
Tyler Lake AR-4
Tyler Lake—lake AR-4
Tyler Lake—lake CA-9
Tyler Lake—lake FL-3
Tyler Lake—lake MN-6
Tyler Lake—lake PA-2
Tyler Lake—lake WI-6
Tyler Lake—reservoir CT-1
Tyler Lake Drain*—stream IA-7
Tyler Lake Heights—pop pl CT-1
Tyler (Magisterial District)—fmr MCD (2) VA-3
Tyler Meadow—flat CA-9
Tyler Meadows—flat CA-9
Tyler Memorial Cem—cemetery TX-5
Tyler Mine—mine CO-8
Tyler Mine—mine NV-8
Tyler Mountain—pop pl WV-2
Tyler Mountain Memory Gardens (Cemetery)—cemetery WV-2
Tyler Mtn—summit CO-8
Tyler Mtn—summit ME-1
Tyler Mtn—summit PA-2
Tyler Mtn—summit (2) TN-4
Tyler Mtn—summit VT-1
Tyler Mtn—summit WV-2
Tyler-Muldoon House—hist pl KY-4
Tyler Notch—gap ME-1
Tyler Park—park AL-4
Tyler Park—park IA-7
Tyler Park—park KY-4
Tyler Park—park MA-1
Tyler Park—park NC-3
Tyler Park—pop pl NJ-2
Tyler Park—pop pl VA-3
Tyler Peak—summit CA-9
Tyler Peak—summit ID-8
Tyler Peak—summit WA-9
Tyler Plains—flat MI-6
Tyler Point—cape NH-1
Tyler Point—cape NY-2
Tyler Point—cape PA-2
Tyler Point—cape RI-1

Tyler Point—*summit* MT-8
*Tyler Pond* CT-1
Tyler Pond—*lake* ME-1
Tyler Pond—*lake* MA-1
Tyler Pond—*swamp* MA-1
*Tyler Pond Brook* CT-1
Tyler Ponds—*lake* SC-3
Tyler Public Sch—*hist pl* MN-6
Tyler Ridge—*ridge* TN-4
Tyler Rips—*rapids* ME-1
*Tyler River* MD-2
*Tyler River* VA-3
Tyler Road Baptist Ch—*church* KS-7
Tyler Rose Park—*park* TX-5
Tyler Rsvr—*reservoir* NH-1
Tyler Rsvr—*reservoir* PA-2
Tyler Run—*stream* PA-2
Tyler Run—*stream* WV-2
**Tylers**—*pop pl* VA-3
**Tylers Bluff**—*pop pl* TX-5
Tylers Branch—*stream* VA-3
**Tylersburg**—*pop pl* PA-2
Tylersburg Station (RR name for Leeper)—*locale* PA-2
Tyler Sch—*school* CA-9
Tyler Sch—*school* DC-2
Tyler Sch—*school* IL-6
Tyler Sch—*school* (4) MI-6
Tyler Sch—*school* OK-5
Tyler Sch—*school* PA-2
Tyler Sch—*school* SD-7
Tyler Sch—*school* TX-5
Tyler Sch—*school* (2) VA-3
Tyler Sch—*school* (2) WI-6
Tyler Sch (historical)—*school* AL-4
Tylers Corner—*locale* ME-1
Tylers Corner—*locale* NY-2
**Tylers Corner**—*pop pl* CA-9
Tylers Corners—*locale* NY-2
**Tylers Corners**—*pop pl* OH-6
Tylers Cove—*bay* CT-1
*Tylers Creek* MD-2
*Tylers Creek* VA-3
*Tylers Ditch* MD-2
Tyler Settlement Rural Hist Dist—*hist pl* KY-4
*Tylers Fork* WI-6
*Tylers Fork River* WI-6
Tylers Landing (historical)—*locale* MS-4
Tyler Slough—*swamp* AR-4
*Tylers Mill* AL-4
*Tylers Mill* MS-4
Tylers Mill Pond—*reservoir* NJ-2
*Tylers Point* RI-1
*Tyler's Pond* CT-1
Tylers Pond—*reservoir* SC-3
*Tylers Port* PA-2
**Tylersport**—*pop pl* PA-2
Tyler Spring—*spring* AL-4
Tyler Spring—*spring* NV-8
Tyler Spring—*spring* OK-5
Tyler Spring Cem—*cemetery* OK-5
Tylers Ridge—*ridge* ID-8
*Tylers River* MD-2
*Tylers River* VA-3
Tylers Run—*stream* OH-6
Tylers Switch—*locale* NY-2
Tyler State Park—*park* PA-2
Tyler State Park—*park* TX-5
**Tyler Subdivision**—*pop pl* UT-8
Tylersville—*locale* PA-2
Tylersville—*locale* SC-3
**Tylersville**—*pop pl* NY-2
**Tylersville**—*pop pl* OH-6
**Tylersville**—*pop pl* PA-2
**Tylersville**—*pop pl* TN-4
Tylersville Spring—*spring* PA-2
**Tyler's Western Village**—*pop pl* ND-7
**Tylerton**—*pop pl* MD-2
**Tylerton**—*pop pl* VA-3
Tylertown—*locale* NJ-2
Tylertown—*locale* NY-2
**Tylertown**—*pop pl* MS-4
Tylertown Airp—*airport* MS-4
Tylertown Baptist Ch—*church* MS-4
Tylertown Cem—*cemetery* MS-4
Tylertown City Hall—*building* MS-4
Tylertown Elem Sch—*school* MS-4
Tylertown First Baptist Ch—*church* MS-4
*Tylertown High School* MS-4
Tylertown Post Office—*building* MS-4
Tylertown Sewage Lagoon Dam—*dam* MS-4
Tyler Township—*civil* MO-7
Tyler (Township of)—*fmr MCD* (2) AR-4
Tylertown United Methodist Ch—*church* MS-4
Tyler Tunnel—*tunnel* KY-4
Tyler Union Sch—*school* AL-4
Tyler Valley—*valley* (2) CA-9
*Tylerville* IL-6
*Tylerville* MA-1
*Tylerville* SC-3
Tylerville (local name for South Rutland)—*other* NY-2
Tylerville Sch—*school* IL-6
Tyler Weisjahn Ditch—*canal* IN-6
Tyler Wood Sch (historical)—*school* PA-2
Tylo, Mount—*summit* AL-4
Tylor, Robert, Place—*hist pl* KY-4
Tyman Branch—*stream* MI-6
Tyman Place—*locale* MT-8
*Tymase* SC-3
*Tymochee Creek* OH-6
**Tymochtee**—*pop pl* OH-6
Tymochtee Creek—*stream* OH-6
**Tymochtee (Township of)**—*pop pl* OH-6
**Tynan**—*pop pl* TX-5
Tynan, Lake—*lake* CA-9
Tynan Sch—*school* TX-5
**Tyndall**—*pop pl* OH-6
**Tyndall**—*pop pl* SD-7
Tyndall, Mount—*summit* CA-9
Tyndall, Mount—*summit* CO-8
Tyndall AFB—*military* FL-3
Tyndall and James Ditch—*canal* DE-2
*Tyndall Branch* DE-2
Tyndall Branch—*stream* DE-2
Tyndall Cem—*cemetery* AR-4
Tyndall Cem—*cemetery* SC-3
Tyndall Cem—*cemetery* SD-7
Tyndall Cove—*bay* AK-9
Tyndall Creek—*stream* CA-9
Tyndall Creek—*stream* (2) ID-8
Tyndall Creek Patrol Cabin—*locale* CA-9
Tyndall Creek Trail—*trail* ID-8
Tyndall Dome—*summit* AZ-5
Tyndall Glacier—*glacier* AK-9
Tyndall Glacier—*glacier* CO-8
Tyndall Gorge—*valley* CO-8
Tyndall Grove Ch—*church* NC-3
Tyndall Gulch—*valley* CO-8
Tyndall Landing—*locale* CA-9
Tyndall Landing Field—*airport* SD-7
Tyndall Meadows—*flat* ID-8
Tyndall Mound—*summit* CA-9
*Tyndall Mountain* CO-8
Tyndall Park—*park* AR-4
**Tyndall Park (subdivision)**—*pop pl* NC-3
Tyndall Point—*cape* NC-3
Tyndall Ridge—*ridge* ID-8
Tyndall Ridge Trail—*trail* ID-8
*Tyndalls Bar* AL-4
Tyndall Sch—*school* FL-3
Tyndall Sch—*school* (2) MI-6
Tyndall Sch—*school* NC-3
Tyndall Slough—*stream* AR-4
**Tyndall Village**—*pop pl* NJ-2
Tyndal Point—*cape* NY-2
Tyne Brook—*stream* MA-1
*Tyner* NC-3
Tyner—*locale* OK-5
**Tyner**—*pop pl* IN-6
**Tyner**—*pop pl* KY-4
**Tyner**—*pop pl* NY-2
**Tyner**—*pop pl* NC-3
**Tyner**—*pop pl* TN-4
Tyner Baptist Ch—*church* TN-4
Tyner Bay—*swamp* FL-3
Tyner Branch—*stream* FL-3
Tyner Cem—*cemetery* MS-4
Tyner Cem—*cemetery* ND-7
Tyner Cem—*cemetery* OK-5
**Tyner (Centre Hill)**—*pop pl* NC-3
Tyner Chapel—*church* KY-4
Tyner Ch of Christ—*church* TN-4
Tyner Creek—*stream* LA-4
Tyner Creek—*stream* (3) OK-5
**Tyner Crossing**—*pop pl* IN-6
Tyner Ditch—*canal* IN-6
Tyner Hill—*summit* AR-4
**Tyner Hills**—*pop pl* TN-4
Tyner (historical)—*locale* AL-4
Tyner (historical)—*locale* KS-7
Tyner (historical)—*locale* ND-7
Tyner HS—*school* KY-4
Tyner HS—*school* TN-4
Tyner JHS—*school* TN-4
Tyner Lake—*lake* WI-6
Tyner Post Office—*building* TN-4
Tyner Sch (historical)—*school* MS-4
Tyner United Methodist Ch—*church* TN-4
Tynes and Ferguson Cem—*cemetery* VA-3
Tynes Branch—*stream* MS-4
Tynes Cem—*cemetery* LA-4
Tynes Cem—*cemetery* MS-4
Tynes Chapel—*church* VA-3
Tynes House—*hist pl* MS-4
Tynes Post Office (historical)—*building* MS-4
Tyne Swamp—*swamp* MA-1
Tyng, Col. Jonathan, House—*hist pl* MA-1
**Tyngsboro**—*pop pl* MA-1
Tyngsboro Bridge—*bridge* MA-1
Tyngsboro Country Club—*locale* MA-1
Tyngsboro Sportsmens Club—*locale* MA-1
**Tyngsboro (Town name Tyngsborough)**—*pop pl* MA-1
*Tyngsborough* MA-1
*Tyngsborough Centre* MA-1
**Tyngsborough (Town of)**—*pop pl* MA-1
Tyng Sch—*school* IL-6
Tyngs Island—*island* MA-1
*Tyngs Pond* MA-1
Tyngs Swamp—*swamp* MA-1
Tyngston—*other* ME-1
Tyn Head Court—*hist pl* DE-2
Tyn Head Court—*park* DE-2
Tyni Bldg—*hist pl* WA-9
Tynjala Creek—*stream* MN-6
Tynon Bluffs—*cliff* OK-5
Tyn Rhos Ch—*church* OH-6
**Tynsid (Township of)**—*pop pl* MN-6
Tyone Creek—*stream* (2) AK-9
**Tyonek**—*pop pl* AK-9
Tyonek ANV976—*reserve* AK-9
Tyonek Creek—*stream* AK-9
Tyone Lake—*lake* AK-9
Tyone River—*stream* AK-9
Tyone Village—*locale* AK-9
**Type**—*pop pl* (2) TX-5
Type Ch—*church* TX-5
Typhoid Spring—*spring* UT-8
Typhoon Peak—*summit* AK-9
Typhoon Ridge—*ridge* CA-9
Typh Valley Log Pond—*reservoir* OR-9
Typh Valley Sch—*school* OR-9
Typical Cave—*cave* AL-4
Typnahda Mtn—*summit* NY-2
*Typner Lake* WI-6
Typner Lake—*lake* WI-6
Typo—*locale* KY-4
Typo Lake—*lake* MN-6
Typo Tunnel—*tunnel* KY-4
Tyra Branch—*stream* KY-4
Tyra Cem—*cemetery* TX-5
Tyra Lake—*lake* WI-6
Tyran—*locale* WI-6
Tyrannis Creek—*stream* ID-8
Tyrannis Mine—*mine* ID-8
Tyrant Branch—*stream* TN-4
Tyranza, Lake—*lake* MS-4
Tyrconnell—*hist pl* MD-2
**Tyre**—*pop pl* MI-6
**Tyre**—*pop pl* NY-2
Tyre Branch—*stream* KY-4
Tyre Cem—*cemetery* AR-4
Tyre Cem—*cemetery* GA-3
Tyre Cem—*cemetery* MI-6
Tyre Ch—*church* NY-2
Tyre Creek—*stream* FL-3
Tyre Drain—*canal* MI-6
Tyre Drain—*stream* MI-6
*Tyree* OR-9
Tyree—*uninc pl* VA-3
**Tyreeanna**—*pop pl* VA-3
Tyreeanna Ch—*church* VA-3
Tyree Basin—*basin* SD-7
Tyree Bldg—*hist pl* GA-3
Tyree Branch—*stream* (2) KY-4
Tyree Cem—*cemetery* KY-4
Tyree Cem—*cemetery* (3) WV-2
Tyree Ch—*church* MD-2
Tyree Chapel—*church* KY-4
Tyree Cove—*valley* TN-4
Tyree Lake—*reservoir* TN-4
Tyrees Mills Post Office (historical)—*building* TN-4
Tyree Springs—*spring* TN-4
**Tyree Springs (historical)**—*pop pl* TN-4
Tyree Springs Post Office (historical)—*building* TN-4
Tyree Stone Tavern—*hist pl* WV-2
Tyre Knob—*summit* NC-3
Tyrell Camp—*locale* MT-8
*Tyrell Creek* MT-8
Tyrell Creek—*stream* MT-8
Tyrell House—*hist pl* AZ-5
Tyrell Spring—*spring* OR-9
Tyre Mill Creek—*stream* AL-4
Tyre Mill Pond—*lake* AL-4
Tyrena Creek—*stream* AK-9
**Tyre (Santiago)**—*pop pl* PA-2
*Tyres Cove* MA-1
**Tyre (Town of)**—*pop pl* NY-2
Tyrey Creek—*stream* MO-7
Tyrie Branch—*stream* KY-4
Tyrie Ch—*church* KY-4
Tyrie Mine—*mine* KY-4
**Tyringham**—*pop pl* MA-1
Tyringham Cobble Park—*park* MA-1
Tyringham Shaker Settlement Hist Dist—*hist pl* MA-1
**Tyringham (Town of)**—*pop pl* MA-1
Tyringham Valley—*valley* MA-1
*Tyro* AL-4
Tyro—*locale* AR-4
Tyro—*locale* VA-3
**Tyro**—*pop pl* KS-7
**Tyro**—*pop pl* MS-4
**Tyro**—*pop pl* NC-3
Tyro Baptist Ch—*church* MS-4
Tyro Camp—*locale* PA-2
Tyro Cem—*cemetery* MS-4
Tyro Ch—*church* MS-4
Tyro Creek—*stream* AL-4
Tyro Creek Hill—*summit* AL-4
Tyro (historical P.O.)—*locale* IA-7
Tyro JHS—*school* NC-3
Tyrol—*locale* NV-8
Tyrola—*locale* OK-5
**Tyrol Township**—*pop pl* ND-7
Tyro Mine—*mine* AZ-5
*Tyrone* MS-4
*Tyrone* PA-2
Tyrone—*fmr MCD* NE-7
Tyrone—*locale* CA-9
Tyrone—*locale* CO-8
Tyrone—*locale* GA-3
Tyrone—*locale* LA-4
Tyrone—*locale* OH-6
**Tyrone**—*pop pl* FL-3
**Tyrone**—*pop pl* GA-3
**Tyrone**—*pop pl* IA-7
**Tyrone**—*pop pl* KY-4
**Tyrone**—*pop pl* MD-2
**Tyrone**—*pop pl* MO-7
**Tyrone**—*pop pl* NM-5
**Tyrone**—*pop pl* NY-2
**Tyrone**—*pop pl* OK-5
**Tyrone**—*pop pl* PA-2
**Tyrone**—*pop pl* (2) WV-2
Tyrone, Lake—*reservoir* GA-3
Tyrone Area Junior Senior HS—*school* PA-2
Tyrone Borough—*civil* PA-2
Tyrone (CCD)—*cens area* GA-3
Tyrone (CCD)—*cens area* NM-5
Tyrone Cem—*cemetery* IA-7
Tyrone Cem—*cemetery* LA-4
Tyrone Cem—*cemetery* MS-4
Tyrone Cem—*cemetery* NE-7
Tyrone Cem—*cemetery* OK-5
Tyrone Center—*locale* MI-6
Tyrone Ch—*church* PA-2
Tyrone Creek—*stream* AL-4
Tyrone Creek—*stream* NV-8
Tyrone Dam Number One—*dam* PA-2
Tyrone Elem Sch—*school* FL-3
Tyrone Flats—*flat* CO-8
**Tyrone Forge**—*pop pl* PA-2
Tyrone Gap—*gap* NV-8
Tyrone Gardens Shop Ctr—*locale* FL-3
Tyrone Gulch—*valley* CA-9
Tyrone Hills Golf Club—*other* MI-6
Tyrone JHS—*school* FL-3
Tyrone Lake—*lake* MI-6
**Tyrone Lake**—*pop pl* MI-6
Tyrone Prairie—*flat* MN-6
Tyrone RR Station—*locale* FL-3
Tyrone Rsvr—*reservoir* PA-2
Tyrone Rsvr Number One—*reservoir* PA-2
Tyrone Rsvr Number Two—*reservoir* PA-2
Tyrone Sch—*school* MI-6
Tyrone Sch—*school* MN-6
Tyrone Sch (historical)—*school* PA-2
Tyrone Square (Shop Ctr)—*locale* FL-3
Tyrone Tank—*reservoir* NM-5
**Tyrone (Town of)**—*pop pl* NY-2
**Tyrone Township**—*pop pl* ND-7
**Tyrone (Township of)**—*pop pl* IL-6
**Tyrone (Township of)**—*pop pl* (2) MI-6
**Tyrone (Township of)**—*pop pl* MN-6
**Tyrone (Township of)**—*pop pl* (3) PA-2
Tyrone Union Cem—*cemetery* NY-2
*Tyronville* PA-2
**Tyronza**—*pop pl* AR-4
Tyronza Bayou—*stream* AR-4
**Tyronza Junction**—*pop pl* AR-4
Tyronza River—*stream* AR-4
Tyronza River Cutoff—*bend* AR-4
Tyronza Sunk Lands—*flat* AR-4
Tyronza (Township of)—*fmr MCD* (3) AR-4
Tyro Post Office (historical)—*building* AL-4
Tyro Post Office (historical)—*building* MS-4
Tyro Sch (historical)—*school* MS-4
Tyro State Wildlife Mngmt Area—*park* MN-6
Tyro Tavern—*hist pl* NC-3
Tyro (Township of)—*fmr MCD* NC-3
**Tyro (Township of)**—*pop pl* MN-6
Tyrouge Bayou—*stream* LA-4
*Tyro United Methodist Church* MS-4
Tyro Wash—*stream* AZ-5
Tyrrel Farm Corners—*locale* PA-2
Tyrrel Island—*island* ID-8
Tyrrell—*locale* OH-6
Tyrrell—*locale* PA-2
Tyrrel Lake—*lake* NY-2
Tyrrell County—*civil* NC-3
Tyrrell County Courthouse—*hist pl* NC-3
Tyrrell County Schools Administration Office—*building* NC-3
Tyrrell Elem Sch—*school* NC-3
Tyrrell Hill—*summit* NY-2
*Tyrrell Lake* NY-2
Tyrrell Park—*park* TX-5
Tyrrell Park Ch—*church* TX-5
Tyrrell Ranger Station—*locale* WY-8
Tyrrell Sch—*school* CA-9
Tyrrell Sch—*school* CT-1
Tyrrell Sch—*school* TX-5
*Tyrrells Creek* NC-3
Tyrrel Sch (historical)—*school* PA-2
Tysdal Ranch—*locale* SD-7
Tysdal Sch (historical)—*school* SD-7
*Tyson* AZ-5
Tyson—*locale* AL-4
Tyson—*locale* AZ-5
Tyson—*locale* MS-4
Tyson—*locale* TX-5
**Tyson**—*pop pl* MO-7
**Tyson**—*pop pl* TN-4
**Tyson**—*pop pl* VT-1
Tyson Branch—*stream* KY-4
Tyson Branch—*stream* LA-4
Tyson Cem—*cemetery* MS-4
Tyson Cem—*cemetery* NC-3
Tyson Cem—*cemetery* ND-7
Tyson Cem—*cemetery* PA-2
Tyson Cem—*cemetery* TX-5
*Tyson Chapel* AL-4
*Tyson Chapel* NC-3
Tyson Chrome Mine—*mine* CA-9
**Tyson Creek**—*pop pl* ID-8
Tyson Creek—*stream* CA-9
Tyson Creek—*stream* FL-3
Tyson Creek—*stream* ID-8
Tyson Creek—*stream* IL-6
Tyson Creek—*stream* NE-7
Tyson Creek—*stream* NC-3
Tyson Creek—*stream* TX-5
Tyson Hollow—*valley* MO-7
Tyson House—*hist pl* NV-8
Tyson Island—*cape* OR-9
Tyson Island State Wildlife Mngmt Area—*park* IA-7
Tyson JHS—*school* TN-4
Tyson Lake—*lake* FL-3
Tyson Lake—*reservoir* CA-9
Tyson Lake—*reservoir* TN-4
Tyson Lake—*swamp* MN-6
Tyson Lake Dam—*dam* TN-4
Tyson-Maner House—*hist pl* AL-4
Tyson Marsh—*stream* NC-3
Tyson Memorial Ch—*church* GA-3
**Tyson (Morganville)**—*pop pl* AL-4
Tyson Park—*park* TN-4
Tyson Peak—*summit* ID-8
Tyson Point—*cape* NC-3
Tyson Post Office (historical)—*building* TN-4
Tyson Run—*stream* OH-6
Tysons Bend—*bend* IA-7
Tysons Bend—*bend* NE-7
Tysons Ch—*church* NC-3
Tysons Chapel—*church* NC-3
Tyson Schoener Elem Sch—*school* PA-2
Tysons Corner—*locale* VA-3
Tysons Creek—*stream* NC-3
Tysons Creek Ch—*church* NC-3
*Tysons Crossroads* VA-3
**Tysons Green**—*pop pl* VA-3
Tysons Hill—*summit* PA-2
Tysons Lake—*reservoir* AL-4
**Tyson Store**—*pop pl* TN-4
**Tyson Store**—*pop pl* WV-2
Tyson (Township of)—*fmr MCD* NC-3
**Tysonville**—*pop pl* AL-4
**Tysonville**—*pop pl* NC-3
Tysonville Cem—*cemetery* AL-4
Tysonville Ferry (historical)—*locale* AL-4
**Tysonville (historical)**—*pop pl* TN-4
Tyson Wash—*valley* AZ-5
Tysver Ranch—*locale* ND-7
Tytus, John B., House—*hist pl* OH-6
**Ty Ty**—*pop pl* GA-3
Ty Ty Branch—*stream* GA-3
Ty Ty (CCD)—*cens area* GA-3
Ty Ty Creek—*stream* (2) GA-3
Ty Ty Lookout Tower—*locale* GA-3
**Tyus**—*pop pl* GA-3
Tyus Cem—*cemetery* TX-5
Tyvola Mall—*locale* NC-3
Tywappity, Lake—*reservoir* MO-7
Tywappity Township—*civil* (2) MO-7
Tywhappity Sch (abandoned)—*school* MO-7
Tywhiskey Creek—*stream* MS-4
*Tyya* AK-9
Tzabaco—*civil* CA-9
Tzelena Canyon—*valley* AZ-5
Tze-Midi—*summit* NM-5
*Tzues River* WA-9
Tzuse Shoal—*bar* AK-9
*T 1 S* MT-8
*T16N* NV-8
*T-2 Dam* ND-7
*T2-4 Dam* ND-7
T3 Indian Purchase—*unorg* ME-1
*T3-6 Dam* ND-7
T4 Indian Purchase—*unorg* ME-1
T 4 Ranch—*locale* AZ-5
T4 Springs—*spring* AZ-5
T-6 Spring—*spring* OR-9
T-7 Prong—*stream* WY-8
T 7 Ranch—*locale* WY-8
*T7-1 Dam* ND-7
*T8S* AL-4
*T8-1 Dam* ND-7

# U

*U* ... FM-9
*U, Cape* ... FM-9
U, The—*cape* ... CA-9
*Uahia Hill* ... HI-9
*Uahra River* ... NC-3
*Uala* ... HI-9
*Ualakaa* ... HI-9
**Ualapue**—*pop pl* ... HI-9
Ualapue Fishpond—*lake* ... HI-9
Ualik Lake—*lake* ... AK-9
*U All Creek* ... MT-8
Uall Creek—*stream* ... MT-8
*Ualtis Creek* ... CA-9
Uamacutah, Lake—*reservoir* ... GA-3
*Uana Church* ... MS-4
*Uanajan* ... FM-9
*Uanayan* ... FM-9
U and I Landing—*locale* ... LA-4
*Uanedai Einfahrt* ... FM-9
Uaoa Bay—*bay* ... HI-9
Uaoa Stream—*stream* ... HI-9
*Uap* ... FM-9
Uapa—*summit* ... HI-9
*Uaree River* ... NC-3
Uataluk Island—*island* ... FM-9
U A Tank—*reservoir* ... AZ-5
*Uataruku* ... FM-9
*Uato* ... FM-9
Uatschaluk—*island* ... FM-9
*Uau* ... HI-9
*Uau Mtn* ... HI-9
Uban Creek—*stream* ... PA-2
Ubank Place—*locale* ... AZ-5
Ubanks Creek—*stream* ... TX-5
U Bar Camp—*locale* ... TX-5
U-Bar Ranch—*locale* ... UT-8
U Bar Tank—*reservoir* ... AZ-5
U Bar Wells—*other* ... NM-5
Ubehebe Crater—*crater* ... CA-9
Ubehebe Mine—*mine* ... CA-9
Ubehebe Peak—*summit* ... CA-9
Ubehebe Talc Mine—*mine* ... CA-9
*Uben, Mount* ... FM-9
Ubet—*locale* ... WI-6
U Bet Mine—*mine* ... NV-8
U Bet Post Office (historical)—*building* ... TN-4
Ubi Island—*island* ... AK-9
Ublutuoch River—*stream* ... AK-9
**Ubly**—*pop pl* ... MI-6
*Uboen* ... FM-9
U B Rangeline Cabin—*locale* ... AZ-5
*Ubut* ... FM-9
U-Butte—*summit* ... NM-5
U Canal—*canal* ... ID-8
U Canal—*canal* ... NV-8
Ucchuwanen Island—*island* ... MP-9
U C Cow Camp—*locale* ... CO-8
U C Creek—*stream* ... CO-8
**Uceba**—*pop pl* ... TN-4
*Uceba Creek* ... TN-4
Uceba Post Office (historical)—*building* ... TN-4
Ucelly Gulch—*valley* ... ID-8
*Uceta (Uceta Yard)* ... FL-3
Uceta Yard—*locale* ... FL-3
**Uceta Yard (Utceta)**—*pop pl* ... FL-3
U C Gulch—*valley* ... ID-8
Uchee—*locale* ... AL-4
*Uchee Bridge* ... AL-4
Uchee Cem—*cemetery* ... AL-4
Uchee Ch—*church* ... AL-4
Uchee Chapel—*church* (2) ... AL-4
Uchee Creek—*stream* ... AL-4
Uchee Creek—*stream* ... GA-3
Uchee Hill Ch—*church* ... AL-4
*Uchee Methodist Ch* ... AL-4
Uchee Sch—*school* ... AL-4
Uchee Shoals P.O. (historical)—*locale* ... AL-4
Uchee Shooting Range—*park* ... AL-4
Uchee Valley Sch—*school* ... AL-4
Uchelbeluu—*bar* ... PW-9
Ucheliungs—*island* ... PW-9
**Ucherael**—*pop pl* ... PW-9
Uchias—*bar* ... FM-9
Uchi (historical)—*locale* ... AL-4
Uchugrak Hills—*summit* ... AK-9
Uchul A Kerekar, Elechol Ra—*beach* ... PW-9
Uchulalei—*cape* ... PW-9
Uchulameradel—*island* ... PW-9
Uchulangas—*island* ... PW-9
Uchularriu—*harbor* ... PW-9
Uchulayas—*cape* ... PW-9
Uchuson, Ununen—*cape* ... FM-9
Uchuu—*bar* ... PW-9
Ucil Lake—*lake* ... WI-6
Ucker Road Cem—*cemetery* ... WI-6
*Ucloj* ... FM-9
**Ucolo**—*pop pl* ... UT-8
**Ucon**—*pop pl* ... ID-8
Ucon Basin—*basin* ... ID-8
Ucon Creek—*stream* ... ID-8
UC Ranch—*locale* ... NV-8
U C Ranch—*locale* ... WY-8
Ucross—*locale* ... WY-8
**Ucross**—*pop pl* ... WY-8
U-Cross Ranch—*locale* ... AZ-5
U-Cross Ranch—*locale* ... NE-7
U C Spring—*spring* ... ID-8
Udagak Bay—*bay* ... AK-9
Udagak Strait—*channel* ... AK-9
Udager Dam—*dam* ... SD-7
**Udall**—*pop pl* ... KS-7
**Udall**—*pop pl* ... MO-7
Udall Cem—*cemetery* ... KS-7
Udall Draw—*valley* ... AZ-5
Udall Draw Springs—*spring* ... AZ-5
Udall Elem Sch—*school* ... KS-7
Udall HS—*school* ... KS-7
Udall Landing—*locale* ... MO-7
Udall Park—*flat* ... AZ-5
Udall Park Tank—*reservoir* ... AZ-5
Udalls Millpond—*reservoir* ... NY-2
Udamak Cove—*bay* ... AK-9
Udamat Bay—*bay* ... AK-9
Uddy Hot Springs—*spring* ... UT-8
**Ude**—*pop pl* ... WV-2
Udee Creek—*stream* ... MT-8
**Udell**—*pop pl* ... IA-7
**Udell**—*pop pl* ... MI-6
Udell Hills—*summit* ... MI-6
Udell Lookout Tower—*locale* ... MI-6
Udell Township—*fmr MCD* ... IA-7
*Uden Creek* ... WA-9
Uden Drain—*stream* ... MI-6
*Udio-Mikai* ... MP-9
U-Diamond Ranch—*locale* ... AZ-5
*Udidan Pass* ... FM-9
**Udina**—*pop pl* ... IL-6
Uditj Island—*island* ... MP-9
*Udjae* ... MP-9
UDLH Flood Control Dam—*dam* ... SD-7
Udo Bend—*bend* ... MO-7
**Udolpho (Township of)**—*pop pl* ... MN-6
Udot—*island* ... FM-9
*Udot Island* ... FM-9
Udot (Municipality)—*civ div* ... FM-9
Udot Sch—*school* ... FM-9
U Drain—*canal* ... CA-9
Udrivik, Lake—*lake* ... AK-9
U D Spring—*spring* ... MT-8
*Ueada Tank* ... TX-5
Uea Point—*cape* ... AS-9
Uebel House—*hist pl* ... KY-4
Ueckers Lake—*lake* ... NE-7
Ueckert Cem—*cemetery* ... TX-5
Ueding Airp—*airport* ... IN-6
Ueeck Lake—*lake* ... WI-6
**Uehling**—*pop pl* ... NE-7
Uehling, Frank, Barn—*hist pl* ... NE-7
Uehling Cem—*cemetery* ... NE-7
Uekert Dam—*dam* ... ND-7
Ueland Dam—*dam* ... ND-7
Ueland Place (Site)—*locale* ... CA-9
*Uelei* ... FM-9
*Ueloi* ... FM-9
*Ueloj* ... FM-9
*Ueloy* ... FM-9
Ueltsch Run—*stream* ... OH-6
*Uenfra* ... FM-9
*Uenfura* ... FM-9
*Ueno Island* ... PW-9
*Ueroi* ... FM-9
Ueru Island—*island* ... FM-9
*Ueruniyaato To* ... FM-9
Uesper Country Club—*locale* ... MA-1
*Uetouerakke To* ... MP-9
*Ufa Cliffs* ... MH-9
*Ufalla Creek* ... AL-4
*Ufallah* ... FL-3
*Ufaupee Creek* ... AL-4
Uffelman Elem Sch—*school* ... TN-4
Ufferman Site—*hist pl* ... OH-6
Uffert Park—*park* ... CA-9
Uffington—*locale* ... WV-2
Ufford Corners—*locale* ... NY-2
U-Fish Creek—*stream* ... CA-9
U F Plaza (Shop Ctr)—*locale* ... FL-3
*Ufuno, Mount* ... FM-9
Ugadaga Bay—*bay* ... AK-9
Ugaiushak Island—*island* ... AK-9
Ugak Bay—*bay* ... AK-9
Ugak Island—*island* ... AK-9
Ugaklik River—*stream* ... AK-9
Ugalak Creek—*stream* ... AK-9
Ugamak Bay—*bay* ... AK-9
Ugamak Island—*island* ... AK-9
Ugamak Strait—*channel* ... AK-9
**Uganik**—*pop pl* ... AK-9
Uganik Bay—*bay* ... AK-9
Uganik Island—*island* ... AK-9
Uganik Lake—*lake* ... AK-9
Uganik Passage—*channel* ... AK-9
Uganik River—*stream* ... AK-9
Ugarte Tank—*reservoir* ... TX-5
**Ugashik**—*pop pl* ... AK-9
Ugashik, Mount—*summit* ... AK-9
Ugashik ANV978—*reserve* ... AK-9
Ugashik Bay—*bay* ... AK-9
Ugashik Creek—*stream* ... AK-9
Ugashik River—*stream* ... AK-9
Ugchirnak Mtn—*summit* ... AK-9
*Ugeliungs* ... PW-9
*Ugem* ... FM-9
Ugh Lake—*lake* ... ME-1
Ugidak Island—*island* ... AK-9
Ugis—*slope* ... MH-9
*Ugly* ... NC-3
Ugly Branch—*stream* ... NC-3
Ugly Branch—*stream* (2) ... WV-2
Ugly Creek—*stream* ... GA-3
Ugly Creek—*stream* ... KY-4
Ugly Creek—*stream* (2) ... NC-3
Ugly Creek—*stream* ... TN-4
Ugly Creek Mines—*mine* ... TN-4
Ugly Hollow—*valley* ... TN-4
Ugly Mtn—*summit* ... WV-2
Ugly Run—*stream* ... PA-2
Ugnuravik River—*stream* ... AK-9
*Ugula Kerregar* ... PW-9
*Ugula Kerregar A Ilagiai* ... PW-9
*Ugula Maradel* ... PW-9
*Ugula Maradel Island* ... PW-9
Ugum River—*stream* ... GU-9
Uh, Dolen—*summit* ... FM-9
Uhalde Spring—*spring* ... NV-8
Uhalde Well—*well* ... NV-8
Uhaldi Well—*well* ... NV-8
*Uhaoiole Stream* ... HI-9
*Uharie Mountains* ... NC-3
*Uharie River* ... NC-3
Uhau Iole Falls—*falls* ... HI-9
Uhau Iole Stream—*stream* ... HI-9
Uhd, Dolen—*summit* ... FM-9
Uhdey—*locale* ... PA-2
Uhi Pocket—*basin* ... CA-9
Uhi Station—*locale* ... CA-9
Uhk Ahlek—*unknown* ... FM-9
Uhlan Bay—*gut* ... LA-4
Uhlan Coulee—*valley* ... MT-8
Uhland—*locale* ... AL-4
**Uhland**—*pop pl* ... TX-5
Uhland Ch (historical)—*church* ... AL-4
Uhl Basin—*basin* ... CA-9
Uhl Cabin—*locale* ... CO-8
Uhl Cem—*cemetery* ... WV-2
Uhl Creek—*stream* ... CA-9
Uhl Creek—*stream* ... CO-8
Uhl Creek—*stream* ... KY-4
Uhl Ditch—*canal* ... IN-6
Uhl Draw—*valley* ... NM-5
Uhl Draw—*valley* ... WY-8
*Uhlen* ... MN-6
Uhlenkolts Lake—*lake* ... MN-6
Uhlens Run—*stream* ... KY-4
Uhlen Valley—*valley* ... CA-9
Uhler Creek—*stream* ... AK-9
Uhler Creek—*stream* ... MT-8
Uhler Ranch—*locale* ... CO-8
*Uhlers* ... PA-2
**Uhlers Crossing**—*pop pl* ... PA-2
Uhlers Station—*building* ... PA-2
Uhlerstown—*locale* ... PA-2
Uhlerstown Covered Bridge—*bridge* ... PA-2
*Uhlersville* ... PA-2
**Uhlersville (historical)**—*pop pl* ... PA-2
*Uhlersville Post Office* ... PA-2
Uhl Hill—*summit* ... CA-9
Uhl Hill—*summit* ... WY-8
Uhl (historical)—*locale* ... KS-7
Uh Likin Pein Awak—*school* ... FM-9
Uhl Lake—*lake* ... MN-6
Uhlman Creek—*stream* ... ID-8
Uhlman Creek—*stream* ... IN-6
Uhlman Drain—*stream* ... MI-6
Uhlmeyer—*spring* ... CA-9
Uhl Peak—*summit* ... CA-9
Uhl Rsvr—*reservoir* ... CO-8
Uhl Run—*stream* ... OH-6
Uhl Spring—*spring* ... CA-9
Uhl Tank—*reservoir* ... NM-5
Uhl Well—*well* ... NM-5
Uh (Municipality)—*civ div* ... FM-9
*Uhmwehmwe* ... FM-9
Uhra—*bar* ... FM-9
U-H Ranch—*locale* ... MT-8
Uhrenholdt Memorial State For—*forest* ... WI-6
**Uhrichsville**—*pop pl* ... OH-6
Uhrig Mine—*mine* ... ID-8
Uhsapw—*island* ... FM-9
*Uhs Kug* ... AZ-5
Uhs Kug—*locale* ... AZ-5
UHS - University Hospital Heliport—*airport* ... MO-7
*Uichukula* ... FM-9
Uihlein, Herman, House—*hist pl* ... WI-6
Uihlein Creek—*stream* ... WY-8
Uihlein Mercy Center—*hospital* ... NY-2
*Uijas* ... FM-9
*Uijec* ... FM-9
*Uijec Island* ... FM-9
*Uikku-San* ... FM-9
*Uilec* ... FM-9
*Uilek* ... FM-9
Uilmerton Pointe Plaza (Shop Ctr)—*locale* ... FL-3
Uinkaret Mountains—*range* ... AZ-5
Uinkaret Plateau—*area* ... AZ-5
Uinkaret Plateau—*plain* ... UT-8
*Uinku, Mount* ... FM-9
*Uinta* ... UT-8
Uinta Basin—*basin* ... UT-8
Uinta Basin Seismological Observatory—*other* ... UT-8
Uinta Bottoms—*basin* ... UT-8
*Uinta Canal* ... UT-8
Uinta Canyon Campground—*locale* ... UT-8
Uinta Canyon Forest Service Station—*locale* ... UT-8
Uinta Canyon Summer Homes—*locale* ... UT-8
Uinta County Courthouse—*hist pl* ... WY-8
Uinta Flat—*flat* ... UT-8
Uinta Gulch—*valley* ... UT-8
**Uintah**—*pop pl* ... UT-8
Uintah and Ouray—*cens area* (3) ... UT-8
Uintah and Ouray Division—*civil* ... UT-8
Uintah and Ouray Indian Cem—*cemetery* ... UT-8
**Uintah and Ouray Indian Reservation**—*pop pl* ... UT-8
*Uintah Basin* ... UT-8
*Uintah Basin Seismological Observatory* ... UT-8
Uintah Canal—*canal* ... UT-8
Uintah Canyon Youth Camp—*locale* ... UT-8
Uintah Cem—*cemetery* ... UT-8
Uintah Central Canal—*canal* ... UT-8
Uintah County—*civil* ... UT-8
*Uintah Highlands Subdivision* ... UT-8
**Uintah-Highlands Subdivision**—*pop pl* ... UT-8
*Uintah Highline Trail* ... UT-8
Uintah HS—*school* ... UT-8
Uinta Highline Trail—*trail* ... UT-8
Uintah Independent Canal—*canal* ... UT-8
Uintah Junction—*locale* ... UT-8
Uintah Lake—*lake* ... UT-8
Uintah Mer—*other* ... UT-8
Uintah Mine—*mine* ... CO-8
*Uintah Mountains* ... UT-8
Uintah No 1 Canal—*canal* ... UT-8
Uintah Powerplant—*other* ... UT-8
*Uintah River* ... UT-8
Uintah Sch—*school* (2) ... UT-8
*Uintah Special Mer* ... UT-8
**Uintah Village Subdivision**—*pop pl* ... UT-8
Uinta Mtn—*summit* ... UT-8
Uinta Mtns—*range* ... CO-8
Uinta Mtns—*range* ... UT-8
Uinta Natl For—*forest* ... UT-8
Uinta Park Guard Station—*locale* ... UT-8
Uinta Picnic Area—*locale* ... UT-8
Uinta River—*stream* ... UT-8
*Uinta Special Mer* ... UT-8
Uinta Spring—*spring* ... UT-8
*Uinta Valley* ... UT-8
Uinta Valley—*valley* ... UT-8
Uinta Well—*well* ... UT-8
Uirion—*island* ... MP-9
*Uirion-to* ... MP-9
*Uisas* ... FM-9
Uisco—*locale* ... UT-8
*U Island* ... FM-9
*Uitjap, Mount* ... FM-9
*Uitonap* ... FM-9
*Uitonnap* ... FM-9
*Uitrukula, Mount* ... FM-9
Uivaksak Creek—*stream* ... AK-9
Uivanta Post Office (historical)—*building* ... AL-4
Uiyabi Canyon—*valley* ... UT-8
Ujae Atoll—*island* ... MP-9
**Ujae (County-equivalent)**—*pop pl* ... MP-9
*Ujae Island* ... MP-9
Ujae Island—*island* ... MP-9
*Ujae Island Ujae Islands* ... MP-9
*Ujae-to* ... MP-9
*Ujaijii Su* ... MP-9
Ujajii—*island* ... MP-9
*Ujajiirikku Passage* ... MP-9
*Ujajiirukku Island* ... MP-9
*Ujajiirukku Passage* ... MP-9
*Ujajiirukku-To* ... MP-9
Ujajiivan—*island* ... MP-9
*Ujajiivan Island* ... MP-9
*Ujajiiyan* ... MP-9
*Ujajiiyan Island* ... MP-9
*Ujaziirukku Island* ... MP-9
*Ujaziirukku-To* ... MP-9
*Ujelang* ... MH-9
Ujelang—*island* ... MP-9
Ujelang Atoll—*island* (2) ... MP-9
Ujelang (County-equivalent)—*civil* ... MP-9
*Ujelang Island* ... MP-9
Ujelang Lagoon—*lake* ... MP-9
*Uji* ... FM-9
*Ujiej Island* ... MP-9
*Ujilong Islands* ... MP-9
*Ujiran-to* ... MP-9
*Uji-Shima* ... FM-9
*Uji To* ... FM-9
**Ukak**—*pop pl* ... AK-9
Ukak River—*stream* ... AK-9
Ukalikchik—*locale* ... AK-9
Ukalikchik River—*stream* ... AK-9
Ukanipo Heiau—*hist pl* ... HI-9
*Ukaopua Mountain* ... HI-9
Ukawutni Creek—*stream* ... AK-9
Ukfigag Creek—*stream* ... AK-9
**Ukiah**—*pop pl* ... CA-9
**Ukiah**—*pop pl* ... OR-9
Ukiah (CCD)—*cens area* ... CA-9
Ukiah Cem—*cemetery* ... OR-9
Ukiah-Dale Wayside—*park* ... OR-9
Ukiah Elementary and HS—*school* ... OR-9
Ukiah Sewage Disposal—*other* ... CA-9
Ukiah Sewage Lagoon—*reservoir* ... OR-9
Ukiah Sewage Lagoon Dam—*dam* ... OR-9
*Ukiesa Pond* ... MA-1
Ukim—*swamp* ... FM-9
Ukinrek Craters—*crater* ... AK-9
Ukinyak Creek—*stream* ... AK-9
Ukivok—*locale* ... AK-9
Ukivok ANV979—*reserve* ... AK-9
Uknavik—*locale* ... AK-9
*U Know* ... IN-6
Ukoa Pond—*lake* ... HI-9
Ukolnoi Island—*island* ... AK-9
Ukolnoi Rocks—*island* ... AK-9
*Ukon Island* ... MP-9
Ukon Island—*island* ... MP-9
Ukonom Creek—*stream* ... CA-9
Ukonom Lake—*reservoir* ... CA-9
Ukonom Mtn—*summit* ... CA-9
Ukonom Ranger Station—*locale* ... CA-9
Ukoon—*island* ... MP-9
Ukrainian Catholic Ch Assumption of the Blessed Virgin Mary—*church* ... FL-3
Ukrainian Cem—*cemetery* (2) ... PA-2
Ukrainian Cemeterys—*cemetery* ... NJ-2
Ukrainian Orthodox Ch—*church* ... WI-6
**Ukrainian Village**—*pop pl* ... NJ-2
Ukrainia Sch—*school* ... ND-7
Ukranian Cem—*cemetery* ... CT-1
Ukranian Cem—*cemetery* ... PA-2
Ukranian Ch—*church* ... NJ-2
Ukranian Greek Catholic Cem—*cemetery* ... PA-2
Ukudu—*area* ... GU-9
Ukulele Camp—*locale* ... HI-9
Ukumehame—*civil* ... HI-9
Ukumehame Gulch—*valley* ... HI-9
Ukumehame Reservoirs—*reservoir* ... HI-9
Ukumehame Shaft (Well)—*well* ... HI-9
*Ukumehame Stream* ... HI-9
*Ukwalla Point* ... AZ-5
*Ul* ... FM-9
Ula—*locale* ... KY-4
Ula Cem—*cemetery* ... CO-8
Ula Cem—*cemetery* ... WI-6
Ulach—*channel* ... PW-9
Ula Ditch—*canal* ... CO-8
Ulafala Stream—*stream* ... AS-9
**Ulah**—*pop pl* ... IL-6
**Ulah**—*pop pl* ... NC-3
Ulah Brown Spring—*spring* ... CO-8
Ula (historical)—*locale* ... SD-7
Ulaino—*civil* ... HI-9
Ulaino—*locale* ... HI-9
Ulakaia Hill—*summit* ... AK-9
U Lake—*lake* ... AK-9
U Lake—*lake* ... WA-9
Ulak Island—*island* ... AK-9
Ulak Pass—*channel* ... AK-9
Ulakta Head—*cliff* ... AK-9
*Ulala Islands* ... FM-9
Ulalena—*summit* ... HI-9
*Ulalu Island* ... FM-9
Ulan—*locale* ... OK-5
Ulan Cem—*cemetery* ... OK-5
Ulaneak Creek—*stream* ... AK-9
Ulao—*locale* ... WI-6
Ulao Sch—*school* ... WI-6
Ulape Island—*island* ... FM-9
Ula Prairie—*area* ... CO-8
U Lateral—*canal* ... CA-9
U Lateral—*canal* ... CO-8
Ulatis Creek—*stream* ... CA-9
*Ulaula* ... HI-9
Ulaula—*summit* ... HI-9
U Lazy S Ranch—*locale* ... TX-5
U L Bend—*bend* (2) ... MT-8
UL Bend Natl Wildlife Ref—*park* ... MT-8
*Ulcanush Baptist Church* ... AL-4
Ulcanush Cem—*cemetery* ... AL-4
Ulcanush Creek—*stream* ... AL-4
*Ulcer Gulch* ... AZ-5
Ulch Ditch—*canal* ... IN-6
*Ulcofauhachee* ... GA-3
*Ulcofauhachee Mountain* ... GA-3
*Ulcofauhachee River* ... GA-3
*Ulcohatchee Creek* ... GA-3
Ulcohatchee Creek—*stream* ... GA-3
Ule, Lae o ka—*cape* ... HI-9
*Uleai* ... MH-9
Uleanush Ch—*church* ... AL-4
Uleberg Sch—*school* ... MT-8
Ulebsechel—*island* ... PW-9
Uleda Creek—*stream* ... ID-8
Uleda Point—*cliff* ... ID-8
**Uledi**—*pop pl* ... PA-2
**Uledi (Revere)**—*pop pl* ... PA-2
U-Lee Bend—*bend* ... FL-3
Uleejen—*island* ... MP-9
Ulehawa Beach Park—*park* ... HI-9
Ulehawa Stream—*stream* ... HI-9
Ulekuwale—*cape* ... HI-9
*Ulen* ... MP-9
**Ulen**—*pop pl* ... IN-6
**Ulen**—*pop pl* ... MN-6
Ulen Park—*park* ... SD-7
Ulen State Wildlife Mngmt Area—*park* ... MN-6
**Ulen (Township of)**—*pop pl* ... MN-6
*Ule Point* ... HI-9
Uler—*locale* ... WV-2
Ulerich Ditch—*canal* ... IN-6
Ulery, Eli, House—*hist pl* ... IL-6
Ulery Hill—*summit* ... PA-2
Ulery Mill—*hist pl* ... PA-2
Ulery Sch (abandoned)—*school* ... PA-2
Ulerys Lakes—*lake* ... MT-8
**Uleta**—*pop pl* ... FL-3
Uleta Park—*park* ... FL-3
Ulett Hollow—*valley* ... KY-4
U L Gordy Elem Sch—*school* ... PA-2
**Ulhers (Uhlers Crossing)**—*pop pl* ... PA-2
Uliaga Island—*island* ... AK-9
Uliaga Pass—*channel* ... AK-9
*Ulibahali* ... AL-4
Ulibarri Canyon—*valley* (2) ... NM-5
Ulibarri Place—*locale* ... NM-5
*Uliberu Island* ... FM-9
*Ulibis* ... FM-9
Ulida Flat—*flat* ... CA-9
Ulida Mine—*mine* ... CA-9
Ulidei—*island* ... FM-9
*Ulien* ... MP-9
*Ulifauro Durchfahrt* ... FM-9
*Ulifauro Pass* ... FM-9
Uliga—*island* ... MP-9
*Uliga Island* ... MP-9
*Uligar Pass* ... FM-9
*Ulika* ... MP-9
Ulika—*island* ... MP-9
*Ulika Island* ... MP-9
Ulimakoli—*summit* ... HI-9
*Uliman* ... PW-9
**Ulimang**—*pop pl* ... PW-9
Ulinoi Island—*island* ... AK-9
*Ulion* ... FM-9
*Uliperu* ... FM-9
Ulistac—*civil* ... CA-9
Ulithi Atoll—*island* ... FM-9
Ulithi (Municipality)—*civ div* ... FM-9
*Ulitja Reef* ... FM-9
*Ulitju Riff* ... FM-9
Ulitka, Cape—*cape* ... AK-9
Ulitka Bay—*bay* ... AK-9
*Ulityu Reef* ... FM-9
*Ulka* ... MP-9
*Ulkanush Creek* ... AL-4
*Ulkinask Creek* ... AL-4
*Ull* ... FM-9
Ullathorne Creek—*stream* ... CA-9
Ullemetamel—*island* ... PW-9
Ullery Ranch—*locale* ... WY-8
Ullery Sch—*school* ... IN-6
*Ulliga* ... MP-9
Ullin—*locale* ... NV-8
**Ullin**—*pop pl* ... IL-6
Ullin (Election Precinct)—*fmr MCD* ... IL-6
Ullius, Fred W., Jr., House—*hist pl* ... WI-6
Ullman Cem—*cemetery* ... OH-6
Ullman Park—*flat* ... WY-8
Ullman Sch—*school* ... AL-4
Ullmore Cove—*bay* ... FL-3
Ulloa Channel—*channel* ... AK-9
Ulloa Island—*island* ... AK-9
Ulloa Sch—*school* ... CA-9
Ullom Sch—*school* ... WI-6
Ullrich—*locale* ... IL-6
Ullrich Ranch—*locale* ... AZ-5
Ullrich Sch—*school* ... IL-6
Ullyses Lee Pond Dam—*dam* ... MS-4
Ulm—*locale* ... IA-7
Ulm—*locale* ... WY-8
**Ulm**—*pop pl* ... AR-4
**Ulm**—*pop pl* ... MT-8
**Ulman**—*pop pl* ... MO-7
Ulman State Tower Site—*locale* ... MO-7
Ulmar—*locale* ... CA-9
Ulm Creek—*stream* ... ID-8
Ulmer—*locale* ... MT-8
**Ulmer**—*pop pl* ... IA-7
**Ulmer**—*pop pl* ... SC-3
Ulmer, J. W., House—*hist pl* ... SD-7
Ulmer Brook—*stream* ... ME-1
Ulmer Cave—*cave* ... PA-2
Ulmer Cem—*cemetery* ... SD-7
*Ulmer Chapel* ... MS-4
**Ulmer (corporate name for Ulmers)**—*pop pl* ... SC-3
Ulmer Creek—*stream* ... AL-4
Ulmer Lake—*lake* ... SD-7
Ulmer Mtn—*summit* ... OR-9
Ulmer Park—*park* ... FL-3
Ulmer Park—*park* ... TX-5
Ulmer Ridge—*ridge* ... IN-6
*Ulmers* ... SC-3
Ulmer Sch—*school* ... SD-7
*Ulmers (corporate name Ulmer)* ... SC-3
Ulmers Landing (historical)—*locale* ... AL-4
Ulmers Pond—*lake* ... GA-3
Ulmers Pond—*reservoir* ... SC-3
Ulmer-Summers House—*hist pl* ... SC-3
**Ulmerton**—*pop pl* ... FL-3
Ulm Flats—*flat* ... MT-8
Ulmoris—*locale* ... NM-5
Ulm Peak—*summit* ... ID-8
Ulm Peak—*summit* ... MT-8
Ulm Pishkun—*hist pl* ... MT-8
Ulmsteads Point—*cape* ... MD-2
Ulness (historical)—*locale* ... ND-7
Ulokat Hills—*other* ... AK-9
Ulomnia Beach—*beach* ... GU-9
Ulong—*island* ... PW-9
*Ulo Po Heiau* ... HI-9
Ulor Island—*island* ... FM-9
*Ulrey Ditch* ... IN-6
Ulrey Run—*stream* ... OH-6
Ulrich, Robert, House—*hist pl* ... KS-7
Ulrich Cem—*cemetery* ... IN-6
Ulrich Cem—*cemetery* ... OH-6
Ulrich Creek—*stream* ... ID-8
Ulrich Creek—*stream* ... IN-6
*Ulrich Ditch* ... IN-6
Ulrich Ditch—*canal* ... CO-8
Ulrich Lake—*reservoir* ... IN-6
Ulrich Lake Dam—*dam* ... IN-6
Ulrich Ranch—*locale* ... OR-9
Ulrichs Bridge—*bridge* ... PA-2
Ulrich Sch—*school* ... CA-9
**Ulrich Subdivision**—*pop pl* ... UT-8
Ulsch Ditch—*canal* ... IN-6

Ulsh Creek PA-2
Ulsh Gap—gap PA-2
Ulsh Gap Creek PA-2
Ulsh Gap Run—stream PA-2
Ulsh Gap Trail—trail PA-2
Ulster—locale IA-7
**Ulster**—pop pl PA-2
**Ulster (County)**—pop pl NY-2
**Ulster Gardens (subdivision)**—pop pl NC-3
**Ulster Heights**—pop pl NY-2
Ulster Heights Lake—lake NY-2
Ulster Lake NY-2
**Ulster Landing**—pop pl NY-2
Ulster Mine—mine SD-7
**Ulster Park**—pop pl NY-2
**Ulster (Town of)**—pop pl NY-2
Ulster Township—fmr MCD IA-7
**Ulster (Township of)**—pop pl PA-2
**Ulsterville**—pop pl NY-2
Ulteh Chubby Pothan Creek MS-4
Ultima Island TX-5
Ultima Thule—locale OK-5
Ultimo, Canal (historical)—canal AZ-5
Ultimo, Cerro—summit CA-9
Ultimo Island—island TX-5
Ultimo Mine—mine AZ-5
Ultonia Ledge—bar MA-1
**Ultra**—pop pl CA-9
Ultramarine Glacier—glacier AK-9
Ultramont Mall—locale FL-3
ULT Rsvr—reservoir MT-8
Ulu FM-9
Uluang—bar PW-9
Uluang—summit PW-9
Uluawaa—summit HI-9
Uluboson PW-9
Uluchel—cape PW-9
Ulufala Point—cape AS-9
Ulugol PW-9
Uluhi—summit HI-9
Uluhlen Dakehlap—unknown FM-9
Uluhlen Doaroapap—ridge FM-9
Uluhlen Doll Katar—gap FM-9
Uluhlen Dollokole—unknown FM-9
Uluhlen Koanokoapwot—ridge FM-9
Uluhlen Pahnpar—ridge FM-9
Uluhlen Pwoaipwoai—ridge FM-9
Uluhlen Saladenre—unknown FM-9
Uluhllen Lou Rahn—ridge FM-9
Uluhllen Pehsarep—ridge FM-9
Uluhul PW-9
Uluhulu Gulch—valley HI-9
Uluini Stream—stream HI-9
Ulukluk Creek—stream AK-9
Uluksian Creek—stream AK-9
Uluksrak Bluff—cliff AK-9
Ululani Rsvr (Site)—reservoir HI-9
Ululen Pukuou FM-9
Ulul Island—island FM-9
Ulul (Municipality)—civ div FM-9
Ulumalu—bay HI-9
Ulumalu—civil HI-9
**Ulumalu**—pop pl HI-9
Ulumawao—summit HI-9
Ulunalu HI-9
Ulunno FM-9
Uluong—ridge PW-9
**Ulupalakua**—pop pl HI-9
Ulupalakua Sch—school HI-9
Ulupau Crater—crater HI-9
Ulupau Head—summit HI-9
Ulupehupehu—summit HI-9
Ulu Po Heiau—hist pl HI-9
Ulupo Heiau—locale HI-9
Uluruk Point—cape AK-9
Uluwini Gulch—valley HI-9
Ulva Cove—bay AK-9
Ulvah—locale KY-4
**Ulvilla**—pop pl WV-2
Ulvin Hill—summit WI-6
**Ulvstad (historical)**—pop pl OR-9
Ulyatt, Abraham, House—hist pl OH-6
Ulymeyer Spring CA-9
**Ulysse**—pop pl LA-4
Ulyssee—locale LA-4
Ulysses KS-7
Ulysses—locale ID-8
Ulysses—locale KY-4
**Ulysses**—pop pl KS-7
**Ulysses**—pop pl NE-7
**Ulysses**—pop pl PA-2
Ulysses Airp—airport KS-7
Ulysses Airp—airport PA-2
Ulysses Borough—civil PA-2
Ulysses Cem—cemetery KS-7
Ulysses Cem—cemetery NE-7
Ulysses City Dam—dam KS-7
Ulysses City Lake—reservoir KS-7
Ulysses Creek—stream KY-4
Ulysses Creek Sch—school KY-4
Ulysses Mine—mine ID-8
Ulysses Mtn—summit ID-8
Ulysses Post Office (historical)—building PA-2
Ulysses S Grant Memorial—park DC-2
Ulysses S Grant Park—park OR-9
Ulysses S. Grant Peak—summit CO-8
**Ulysses (Town of)**—pop pl NY-2
**Ulysses Township**—pop pl NE-7
**Ulysses (Township of)**—pop pl PA-2
Uma FM-9
Uma—summit HI-9
Umafit—area GU-9
Umagatsaiak Mtn—summit AK-9
Umagatsiak Creek—stream AK-9
Umak Bight—bay AK-9
Umak Island—island AK-9
Umak Pass—channel AK-9
Umalei HI-9
Umalei Point—cape HI-9
Uman—island FM-9
Umanangula Bluffs—cliff AK-9
Umanangula Lake—lake AK-9
Umang FM-9
Umang—area GU-9
Umang Island FM-9
Uman Island FM-9
Uman (Municipality)—civ div FM-9
Uman Sch—school FM-9
Umap—island FM-9
**Umapine**—pop pl OR-9
Umapine (CCD)—cens area OR-9
Umapine Creek—stream OR-9
U Mara FM-9
Umarachek Creek—stream AK-9
Umarachek Peak—summit AK-9
Uma Shima FM-9
**Umatac**—pop pl GU-9
Umatac Bay—bay GU-9
Umatac (Election District)—fmr MCD GU-9
Umatac River—stream GU-9
Umatallow River OR-9
Umatella River OR-9
**Umatilla**—pop pl FL-3
**Umatilla**—pop pl OR-9
Umatilla, Lake—lake FL-3
Umatilla, Lake—reservoir OR-9
Umatilla, Lake—reservoir WA-9
Umatilla Army Air Field—military OR-9
Umatilla Army Depot—military OR-9
Umatilla Brakes Viewpoint—locale OR-9
Umatilla Breaks Viewpoint OR-9
Umatilla Butte—summit OR-9
Umatilla (CCD)—cens area FL-3
Umatilla Cem—cemetery FL-3
Umatilla Cem—cemetery OR-9
**Umatilla County**—pop pl OR-9
Umatilla Creek—stream ID-8
Umatilla Creek—stream OR-9
Umatilla Drain—canal OR-9
Umatilla Elem Sch—school FL-3
Umatilla Forks Campground—park OR-9
Umatilla HS—school FL-3
**Umatilla Ind Res**—pop pl OR-9
Umatilla Meadows—flat OR-9
Umatilla Mine—mine CA-9
Umatilla Mine—mine ID-8
Umatilla MS—school FL-3
Umatilla Natl For—forest OR-9
Umatilla Natl Wildlife Ref—park OR-9
Umatilla Reef—bar WA-9
Umatilla River—stream OR-9
Umatilla Rock—summit WA-9
Umatilla Site (35 UM 1)—hist pl OR-9
Umatilla Toll Bridge—bridge OR-9
Umauma—civil HI-9
Umauma Creek HI-9
Umauma Stream—stream HI-9
Umbagog Lake—lake ME-1
Umbagog Lake—lake NH-1
**Umbarger**—pop pl (2) TX-5
Umbarger Ch—church FL-3
Umbarger Sch—school WA-9
Umbar Run—stream SC-3
Umbazooksis Lake ME-1
Umbazooksus Lake—lake ME-1
Umbazooksus Stream—stream ME-1
Umbenhour Ditch—canal IN-6
**Umber**—pop pl MO-7
Umberci Mine—mine CA-9
Umberger Sch—school PA-2
Umbergers Sch PA-2
Umber Hill—summit PA-2
**Umber View Heights**—pop pl MO-7
Umbles Run—stream PA-2
Umbrella Bay—bay LA-4
Umbrella Bay—bay WA-9
Umbrella Bayou—stream MS-4
Umbrella Butte CA-9
Umbrella Butte—summit CA-9
Umbrella Butte—summit ID-8
Umbrella Butte—summit NM-5
Umbrella Canyon—valley CO-8
Umbrella Creek—stream CA-9
Umbrella Creek—stream GA-3
Umbrella Creek—stream WA-9
Umbrella Cut—channel GA-3
Umbrella Falls—falls OR-9
Umbrella Falls Trail—trail OR-9
Umbrella Flat—flat AZ-5
Umbrella Glacier—glacier AK-9
Umbrella Hill—summit CA-9
Umbrella Hill—summit VT-1
Umbrella Island—island CT-1
Umbrella Island—island FL-3
Umbrella Key—island FL-3
Umbrella Mesa—summit NM-5
Umbrella Point—bay NH-1
Umbrella Point—cape LA-4
Umbrella Point—cape (2) NY-2
Umbrella Point—cape TX-5
Umbrella Point—cape WA-9
Umbrella Point Oil Field—oilfield TX-5
Umbrella Reef—bar AK-9
Umbrella Rock—pillar OH-6
Umbrella Rock—pillar OK-5
Umbrella Rock—summit NM-5
Umbrights Hill—summit MT-8
Umbrite Lake—lake OR-9
UM/Canterbury Child Care Center—school FL-3
Umcolcus Brook ME-1
Umcolcus Deadwater—lake ME-1
Umcolcus Lake—lake ME-1
Umcolcus Stream ME-1
Um Creek UT-8
U M Creek—stream UT-8
Umculcus Lake ME-1
Umculcus Stream ME-1
Umeinu—gut FM-9
Um Eten Ankerplatz FM-9
Umeumelehelehe Point HI-9
Umga Island—island AK-9
Umi—summit HI-9
Umi, Mauna o—summit HI-9
Umiahu—summit HI-9
**Umiat**—pop pl AK-9
Umiat Lake—lake AK-9
Umiat Mtn—summit AK-9
Umi Caverns—cave HI-9
**Umikoa (Kukaiau Ranch)**—pop pl (2) HI-9
Umilehi Point—cape HI-9
Umin FM-9
Umipaa—locale HI-9
Umi Peak HI-9
Umipoho Gulch—valley HI-9
Umi Rsvr—reservoir HI-9
Umis Well—well HI-9
Umiumilehilehi Point HI-9
Umiversity of Florida—school FL-3
Umiwai Bay—bay HI-9
**Umkumiut**—pop pl AK-9
**Umkumiut (Variant: Umkumute)**—pop pl AK-9
Umla Island—island AK-9
Umli—locale OR-9
Umm En Sopu FM-9
Umm En Uninefou FM-9
Umnak Island—island AK-9
Umnak Lake—lake AK-9
Umnak Pass—channel AK-9
Umol FM-9
Umong—island FM-9
Umpachene Brook MA-1
Umpachenee Brook MA-1
Umpachene Falls—falls MA-1
Umpachene River—stream MA-1
Umpah Mine—mine CA-9
Umpa Lake—lake CA-9
Um Pan UT-8
Umpaqua River Light House—hist pl OR-9
U M Pass—gap UT-8
Umpawaug Cem—cemetery CT-1
Umpawaug District Sch—hist pl CT-1
Umpawaug Hill—summit CT-1
Umpawaug Pond—lake CT-1
Umpawaug Pond Brook—stream CT-1
Umpcoos Ridge—ridge OR-9
Umphers Knob—summit AR-4
Umphress-Taylor House—hist pl TX-5
**Umpire**—pop pl AR-4
Umpire Brook—stream VT-1
Umpire Mtn—summit VT-1
Umpire Perlite Mine—mine NV-8
Umpire Ranch—locale AZ-5
Umpire (Township of)—fmr MCD AR-4
UM Plateau UT-8
U M Plateau—plateau UT-8
Umpleby Ranch Airstrip—airport OR-9
Umpqua—locale OR-9
Umpqua Gulch—valley OR-9
Umpqua Hot Springs—spring OR-9
Umpquah River OR-9
Umpqua Log Pond—reservoir OR-9
Umpqua Mine—mine OR-9
Umpqua Natl For—forest OR-9
Umpqua River—stream OR-9
Umpqua River Safety Rest Area—locale OR-9
Umpqua Rogue Trail—trail OR-9
Umpqua Wayside State Park—park OR-9
Umpsted Ridge—ridge WV-2
Umptanum Creek WA-9
Umptanum Ridge WA-9
**Umqua City**—pop pl OR-9
Umquemenkeag Lakes ME-1
Umsaskis Lake—lake ME-1
Umsquasquospem ME-1
Umstead Branch—stream TN-4
Umstead Park Lake Lower Dam—dam NC-3
Umstead Park Lake Upper—reservoir NC-3
Umstead Park Lake Upper Dam—dam NC-3
Umstead Park Lower Lake—reservoir NC-3
Umsted Farm—hist pl OH-6
Umtalah WA-9
Um-ta-lah River WA-9
Umtanum—locale WA-9
Umtanum Creek—stream WA-9
Umtanum Ridge—ridge WA-9
**Umtanum (Umptanum)**—pop pl WA-9
Umtux, Lake—lake WA-9
Umun FM-9
Umung FM-9
Umungu FM-9
Umunhum, Mount—summit CA-9
Umurbogol Mountain PW-9
Umurbrogel Mountain PW-9
Umurbrogol Mountain PW-9
Umwen—locale MP-9
U M Yogo Saddle—gap UT-8
Una—locale CA-9
Una—locale CO-8
Una—locale SC-3
**Una**—pop pl MS-4
**Una**—pop pl SC-3
**Una**—pop pl TN-4
Una, Lake—lake AK-9
**Una Bella (Trailer Park)**—pop pl VT-1
Unachiech—bar FM-9
Una Creek—stream MT-8
Una Creek—stream NC-3
Una de Gato Cem —cemetery TX-5
Una de Gato Creek—stream NM-5
Una de Gato Creek —stream TX-5
Una de Gato (site)—locale NM-5
Una de Gato Windmill—locale TX-5
**Unadilla**—pop pl GA-3
**Unadilla**—pop pl MI-6
**Unadilla**—pop pl NE-7
**Unadilla**—pop pl NY-2
Unadilla Brook MA-1
Unadilla (CCD)—cens area GA-3
Unadilla Cem—cemetery MI-6
Unadilla Cem—cemetery NE-7
Unadilla Center—locale NY-2
**Unadilla Forks**—pop pl NY-2
Unadilla Lake—lake NY-2
Unadilla River—stream NY-2
Unadilla State Wildlife Area—park MI-6
Unadilla Stockbridge Drain—stream MI-6
**Unadilla (Town of)**—pop pl NY-2
**Unadilla (Township of)**—pop pl MI-6
Una Gap—gap NC-3
Unahala—locale NC-3
U-Nah-Li-Ya Camp—locale WI-6
Unai Achugau MH-9
Unai Bapot MH-9
Unai Chiguet MH-9
Unai Dangkulo MH-9
Unai Dangkulo Agingan MH-9
Unai Dikiki MH-9
Unai Dikiki Agingan MH-9
Unai Dikiki Matuis MH-9
Unai Fahang MH-9
Unai Fanunchuluyan MH-9
Unai Hagman MH-9
Unai Lagua MH-9
Unai Lagua Japanese Defense Pillbox—hist pl MH-9
Unai Laulau MH-9
Unai Laulau Katan MH-9
Unai Magpi MH-9
Unai Matuis MH-9
Unai Obyan MH-9
Unai Obyan Latte Site—hist pl MH-9
Unai Papau MH-9
Unai Papua MH-9
Unai Paupau MH-9
Unairikiki—bay MH-9
Unai Sa MH-9
Unai Talofofo MH-9
Unai Tuturan MH-9
Unai Tuturon MH-9
Unaka TN-4
**Unaka**—pop pl NC-3
Unaka Acad (historical)—school TN-4
Unaka Baptist Ch—church (2) TN-4
Unaka Cem—cemetery NC-3
Unaka Ch—church TN-4
Unaka Elem Sch—school NC-3
Unaka HS—school TN-4
Unaka Mountains—range NC-3
Unaka Mountains—ridge TN-4
Unaka Mountain Scenic Trail—trail TN-4
Unaka Mtn—summit NC-3
Unaka Mtn—summit TN-4
Unaka Muntain Rec Area—park TN-4
Unaka Natl Forest TN-4
Unaka Post Office (historical)—building TN-4
Unaka Range NC-3
Unaka Range TN-4
Unaka Sch—school TN-4
Unaka Sch (historical)—school TN-4
**Unaka Springs**—pop pl TN-4
Unaka Springs—spring TN-4
Unaka Springs Post Office (historical)—building TN-4
Unaka Springs Prospect—mine TN-4
**Unaka Station (historical)**—pop pl TN-4
Unaka Station Post Office (historical)—building TN-4
Unaka View—locale TN-4
Unaka View Sch (historical)—school TN-4
Unakserak River—stream AK-9
Unakwik Inlet—bay AK-9
Unakwik Peak—summit AK-9
Unakwik Point—cape (2) AK-9
Una Lake—reservoir CA-9
**Unalakleet**—pop pl AK-9
Unalakleet Airp—airport AK-9
Unalakleet Native Reservation—reserve AK-9
Unalakleet River—stream AK-9
**Unalaska**—pop pl AK-9
Unalaska Airp—airport AK-9
Unalaska Island—island AK-9
Unalaska Lake—lake AK-9
Unalga Island—island AK-9
Unalga Pass—channel AK-9
Unaluk River—stream AK-9
Unami Creek—stream PA-2
Una Mine—mine ID-8
Unami Park—park NJ-2
**Unamis**—pop pl PA-2
Una Mtn—summit MT-8
Una Mtn—summit NC-3
Unana, Mount—summit AK-9
Unanatti Creek GA-3
Unangashak River—stream AK-9
Unanimous Creek—stream AK-9
Unap—cape FM-9
Unap Mtn—summit OK-5
Una Post Office (historical)—building MS-4
Unatex—locale LA-4
Unatilla OR-9
Una Vida Ruins—locale NM-5
Unavikshak Island—island AK-9
Unawah Creek—stream MT-8
Unawah Mtn—summit MT-8
Unawatti Creek—stream GA-3
Unawb FM-9
Unawe—spring FM-9
**Unaweep**—pop pl CO-8
Unaweep Canyon—valley CO-8
Unaweep Divide—ridge CO-8
Unbanar Island—island KY-4
Uncachewalunk Pond MA-1
Uncanodnuck Mountains NH-1
Uncanoonuck Mountains NH-1
Uncanoonuc Lake—lake NH-1
Uncanoonuc Mountains—summit NH-1
Unca-pah-gre CO-8
Un-cap-i-cun-ump UT-8
Uncas—locale WA-9
**Uncas**—pop pl OK-5
Uncas, Lake—lake NY-2
Uncas Brook—stream MA-1
Uncas Gulch—valley WA-9
Uncas Hill—summit CT-1
Uncas Island—island NY-2
Uncas Point CT-1
Uncas Pond—lake CT-1
Uncas Pond—lake MA-1
Uncas Sch—hist pl WA-9
Uncas Sch—school WA-9
**Uncasville**—pop pl CT-1
Uncataquisset MA-1
Uncataquisset Brook MA-1
Uncataquissett MA-1
Uncataquissett, Town of MA-1
Uncataquissit Brook MA-1
Uncatena Island—island MA-1
UNCC (University Of North Carolina-Charlotte)—hospital NC-3
**Uncertain**—pop pl TX-5
Unchachogue—stream NY-2
Unchachogue Creek—summit NY-2
Unchaula (historical)—locale AL-4
Unchechehaton Lake MA-1
Unchechewalom Pond MA-1
Unchechewalunk Pond MA-1
Unchechewhalon Pond MA-1
Unchechewhaton Pond MA-1
Unchechewhton Pond MA-1
Uncle Aarons Creek—stream NJ-2
Uncle Abe Mine—mine AZ-5
Uncle Ben Gulch—valley MT-8
Uncle Benneys Orchard—woods UT-8
Uncle Billys Cabin—locale CA-9
Uncle Billys Flats—flat WY-8
Uncle Bob Mtn—summit CO-8
Uncle Bob Spring—spring CO-8
Uncle Bud Creek—stream AR-4
Uncle Charlie Slough—stream TX-5
Uncle Charlie Spring—spring CO-8
Uncle Creek OR-9
Uncle Creek—stream OR-9
Uncle Daniels Point—cape NY-2
Uncle Dan Mine—mine OR-9
Uncle Dick Hill—summit ME-1
Uncle Frank Creek—stream TX-5
Uncle George Creek—stream MT-8
Uncle George McLean Point—cape AL-4
Uncle Georges Cove—bay MA-1
Uncle Georges Pit—cave AL-4
Uncle George Well—well TX-5
Uncle Harvey Pond—lake MA-1
Uncle Ike Creek—stream ID-8
Uncle Ikes Post Office (historical)—building MO-7
Uncle Israels Pond—lake MA-1
Uncle Jimmys Landing—locale NC-3
Uncle Jim Point—cliff AZ-5
Uncle Joes Chapel—church OH-6
Uncle Joe Warren Mtn—summit AR-4
Uncle John Coulee—valley SD-7
Uncle John Creek OK-5
Uncle John Creek—stream CA-9
Uncle John Creek—stream WA-9
Uncle John Island ME-1
Uncle John Point ME-1
Uncle Johns Creek WA-9
Uncle Johns Creek—stream OK-5
Uncle Johns Gulch—valley ID-8
Uncle John Windmill—locale TX-5
Uncle Judas Creek—stream MN-6
Uncle Ned Spring—spring SD-7
Uncle Olivers Brook MA-1
Uncle Remus District HQ—other GA-3
Uncle Robert Creek—stream MD-2
Uncle Roberts Cove—cove MA-1
Uncle Sam—mine AZ-5
**Uncle Sam**—pop pl LA-4
Uncle Sam Canyon—valley CA-9
Uncle Sam Cove—bay ME-1
Uncle Sam Creek—stream (3) AK-9
Uncle Sam Creek—stream NV-8
Uncle Sam Gulch—valley AZ-5
Uncle Sam Gulch—valley MT-8
Uncle Sam Hill—summit AZ-5
Uncle Sam Mine SD-7
Uncle Sam Mine—mine AK-9
Uncle Sam Mine—mine AZ-5
Uncle Sam Mine—mine (3) CA-9
Uncle Sam Mine—mine CO-8
Uncle Sam Mine—mine NM-5
Uncle Sam Mine—mine (2) OR-9
Uncle Sam Mtn CA-9
Uncle Sam Mtn—summit AK-9
Uncle Sam Mtn—summit CA-9
Uncle Sam Mtn—summit WA-9
Uncle Sammys Spring—spring MO-7
Uncle Sammy Tank—reservoir TX-5
Uncle Sam Plantation—locale LA-4
Uncle Sams Pond MA-1
Uncle Sam Spring—spring NV-8
Uncle Sam Well—well NM-5
Uncles Branch—stream NC-3
Uncles Branch—stream WV-2
Uncles Canyon—valley CA-9
Uncles Creek—stream CA-9
Uncles Creek—stream NC-3
Uncle Seths Pond MA-1
Uncle Seths Pond—lake MA-1
Uncles Lake—lake CA-9
Uncles Neck Creek—stream VA-3
Uncle Stephans Pond—lake MA-1
Uncle Tom Creek—stream MI-6
Uncle Tom Lake—lake MI-6
Uncle Tom Mtn—summit ME-1
Uncle Tommy—summit CA-9
Uncle Toms Brook—stream NY-2
Uncle Toms Cabin—locale CA-9
Uncle Tom Slough—canal OR-9
Uncle Tom Spring—spring WY-8
Uncle Zeke Island—island ME-1
Unco—locale AR-4
Uncommons Shop Ctr, The—locale IN-6
Uncompahgre—locale CO-8
Uncompahgre Butte—summit CO-8
Uncompahgre Creek—stream AK-9
Uncompahgre Gorge—valley CO-8
Uncompahgre Memorial Gardens—cemetery CO-8
Uncompahgre Mountain CO-8
Uncompahgre Natl For—forest CO-8
Uncompahgre Peak—summit CO-8
Uncompahgre River—stream CO-8
Uncuetnassette Brook MA-1
Uncuettnasseette Brook MA-1
Undecided Rock UT-8
Underberg Lake—lake MN-6
Under Calabasas Dam AZ-5
Undercliff NJ-2
Undercliff—locale NJ-2
**Undercliff**—pop pl NY-2
**Undercliff**—pop pl PA-2
Undercliff Community Center CO-8
Under Cliff Dock NJ-2
Undercliffe Community Center—locale CO-8
Undercliff (historical)—locale CO-8
Undercliff Junction—locale NJ-2
Undercliff Santorium—hospital CT-1
Under Cloud Mtn—summit AK-9
Underdal Ranch—locale MT-8
Underdown Canyon—valley NV-8
Underdown Cem—cemetery KY-4
Underdown JHS—school AZ-5
Underdown Lake—lake MS-4
Underground Atlanta Hist Dist—hist pl GA-3
Underground Branch—stream SC-3
Underground Creek—stream CA-9
Underground Passage—locale WA-9
**Underhill**—pop pl VT-1
**Underhill**—pop pl WI-6
Underhill, Lake—lake FL-3
Underhill Ave Sch—school NY-2
Underhill Branch—stream FL-3
Underhill Branch—stream VA-3
Underhill Brook—stream MA-1
Underhill Brook—stream NH-1
Underhill (CCD)—cens area TN-4
Underhill Cem—cemetery IN-6
Underhill Cem—cemetery MS-4
Underhill Cem—cemetery NY-2
Underhill Cem—cemetery WI-6
**Underhill Center**—pop pl VT-1
Underhill Creek—gut FL-3
Underhill Creek—stream AK-9
Underhill Creek—stream VA-3
Underhill Division—civil TN-4
Underhill Field—park NJ-2
Underhill Flats—other VT-1
Underhill Playground—park WA-9
Underhill Point—cape FL-3
Underhill Pond—reservoir NY-2
Underhill Sawgrass Pond—swamp FL-3
Underhill Sch—school NH-1
Underhill Sch—school WI-6
Underhill Slough—gut FL-3
Underhill Swamp—swamp PA-2
**Underhill (Town of)**—pop pl VT-1
**Underhill (Town of)**—pop pl WI-6
Underkoflers Corner—locale ID-8
Undermine Branch—stream NC-3
Undermine Creek—stream AL-4
Under Mountain Cem—cemetery CT-1
Underpass Pond—lake VT-1
Under Rock Spring—spring AZ-5
Undertakers Camp—locale CA-9
Undertaker Tank—reservoir NM-5
Under-The-Arm Canyon UT-8
Under The Hill Tank—reservoir NM-5
Under The Mesa Well—well NM-5
Under the Rainbow Montessori Learning Center—school FL-3
Under the Rim Trail—trail UT-8
Under the Road Cave—cave AL-4
Underwood AL-4
Underwood KS-7
Underwood SD-7
Underwood—locale GA-3
Underwood—locale TN-4
Underwood—locale TX-5
**Underwood**—pop pl (2) AL-4
**Underwood**—pop pl IN-6
**Underwood**—pop pl IA-7
**Underwood**—pop pl MI-6
**Underwood**—pop pl MN-6
**Underwood**—pop pl NY-2
**Underwood**—pop pl ND-7
**Underwood**—pop pl WA-9
Underwood, Ammon, House—hist pl TX-5
Underwood, John, House—hist pl GA-3
Underwood, Oscar W., House—hist pl DC-2
Underwood Baptist Ch—church AL-4
Underwood Bay—swamp FL-3
Underwood Bend—bend TN-4
Underwood Branch—stream AR-4
Underwood Branch—stream MS-4
Underwood Branch—stream NC-3
Underwood Branch—stream SC-3
Underwood Branch—stream (4) TN-4
Underwood Branch—stream TX-5
Underwood Bridge—bridge AL-4
Underwood Brook—stream MA-1
Underwood Brook—stream NH-1
Underwood Canyon—valley AZ-5
Underwood Canyon—valley NV-8
Underwood Canyon—valley WA-9
Underwood Canyon—valley WY-8
Underwood Cem—cemetery (4) AL-4
Underwood Cem—cemetery (2) AR-4
Underwood Cem—cemetery (2) GA-3
Underwood Cem—cemetery IL-6
Underwood Cem—cemetery KS-7
Underwood Cem—cemetery KY-4
Underwood Cem—cemetery MI-6
Underwood Cem—cemetery (5) MO-7
Underwood Cem—cemetery (2) NY-2
Underwood Cem—cemetery ND-7
Underwood Cem—cemetery (2) OH-6
Underwood Cem—cemetery OK-5
Underwood Cem—cemetery (6) TN-4
Underwood Cem—cemetery TX-5
Underwood Cem—cemetery (3) WV-2
Underwood Ch—church SD-7
Underwood Ch—church TN-4
**Underwood Club**—pop pl NY-2
Underwood Corner—locale DE-2
Underwood Corner—locale NY-2
Underwood Creek WI-6
Underwood Creek—stream AL-4
Underwood Creek—stream (2) CA-9
Underwood Creek—stream GA-3
Underwood Creek—stream MI-6
Underwood Creek—stream (2) MS-4
Underwood Creek—stream MT-8
Underwood Creek—stream NC-3
Underwood Creek—stream TX-5
Underwood Creek—stream WI-6
Underwood Crossing—locale FL-3
Underwood Crossing—locale WY-8
**Underwood Crossroads**—pop pl AL-4
**Underwood (Dogwood)**—pop pl AL-4
Underwood Drain—stream IN-6
Underwood Draw—valley CO-8
Underwood Draw—valley WY-8
Underwood Elem Sch—school AL-4
**Underwood Estates (subdivision)**—pop pl AL-4
Underwood Ferry (historical)—locale AL-4
Underwood Grove Ch—church TN-4
Underwood Gun Club—other CA-9
**Underwood Heights**—pop pl AL-4
**Underwood Heights**—pop pl WA-9
Underwood Heights Ch of Christ—church AL-4
Underwood Heights Elem Sch—school AL-4
Underwood Heights JHS—school AL-4
Underwood Hill—summit FL-3
Underwood Hill—summit MA-1
Underwood Hill—summit MO-7
Underwood Hill—summit (2) NY-2
Underwood Hills NE-7
Underwood Hollow—valley AR-4
Underwood Hollow—valley IN-6
Underwood Hollow—valley KY-4
Underwood Hosp—hospital NJ-2
Underwood Hotel—hist pl ID-8
Underwood-Jones House—hist pl KY-4
Underwood Lake AL-4
Underwood Lake TX-5
Underwood Lake—lake MI-6
Underwood Lake—lake NM-5

Underwood Lake—lake PA-2
Underwood Lake—lake WI-6
Underwood Lake—reservoir AL-4
Underwood Lake Dam—dam AL-4
Underwood Lake Number One—reservoir AL-4
Underwood Lakes—reservoir NM-5
Underwood Ledge—bar ME-1
Underwood Lookout Tower—locale AL-4
Underwood Lookout Tower—locale MI-6
**Underwood Meadows**—pop pl IN-6
Underwood Mill—locale AL-4
Underwood Mill (historical)—locale AL-4
Underwood Millpond—reservoir GA-3
Underwood Mtn—summit AL-4
Underwood Mtn—summit CA-9
Underwood Mtn—summit TX-5
Underwood Mtn—summit WA-9
Underwood Municipal Airp—airport ND-7
Underwood Neck—cape TN-4
Underwood Number 1 Dam—dam AL-4
Underwood Number 2 Dam—dam AL-4
Underwood Oil Field—oilfield TX-5
Underwood Park—park AL-4
Underwood Park—park WA-9
**Underwood Park**—pop pl CA-9
Underwood Park Dam—dam TN-4
Underwood Park Lake—reservoir TN-4
Underwood-Petersville—CDP AL-4
Underwood Pond—reservoir AL-4
Underwood Ranch—locale (2) ND-7
Underwood Ray Oil Field—oilfield TX-5
Underwood Rsvr No 2—reservoir WY-8
Underwood Run—stream IN-6
Underwood Sch—school ME-1
Underwood Sch—school MA-1
Underwood Sch—school MI-6
Underwood Sch—school (2) MO-7
Underwood Sch—school NE-7
Underwood Sch—school NY-2
Underwood Sch—school NC-3
Underwood Sch—school SC-3
Underwood Sch—school TN-4
Underwood Sch—school TX-5
Underwood Sch—school WI-6
Underwood Sch (historical)—school SD-7
Underwood Sch (historical)—school TN-4
Underwoods Corner DE-2
Underwoods Ferry AL-4
Underwoods Mill—locale NC-3
Underwood Spring—spring MO-7
Underwood Spring—spring NV-8
Underwood Spring—spring TN-4
Underwood Spring—spring TX-5
Underwood Spring Branch—stream TN-4
**Underwood Springs (historical)**—pop pl TN-4
Underwoods Store (historical)—locale TN-4
Underwood State Wildwood Area—park WI-6
Underwood Station SD-7
Underwood Store (historical)—locale TN-4
Underwood Swamp—swamp PA-2
Underwood Tank—reservoir AZ-5
Underwood Township—civil SD-7
**Underwood (Township of)**—pop pl MN-6
Underwood Trail—trail PA-2
Underwood Valley PA-2
Underwood Valley—basin CA-9
Underwood Wash AZ-5
Underwood Wash—stream AZ-5
Underwriters Salvage Corps—hist pl OH-6
Undine—locale GA-3
Undine—mine UT-8
Undine, Mount—summit MA-1
Undine Bay—bay ME-1
Undine Brook MA-1
Undine Cem—cemetery MI-6
Undine Falls—falls WY-8
Undine Park—flat WY-8
Undine Pond MA-1
Undulata—hist pl KY-4
Uneche—bar FM-9
Unechep—bar FM-9
Uned FM-9
**Uneeda**—pop pl WV-2
**Uneeda Beach**—pop pl NY-2
Uneedus—locale LA-4
Uneior FM 9
Uneiro—cape FM-9
Unen—bar FM-9
Unen, Mochun—channel FM-9
Unenen Meirop FM-9
Uneniwa, Unun En—bar FM-9
Uneva Lake—reservoir CO-8
Uneva Pass—gap CO-8
Uneva Peak—summit CO-8
Unexpected Sch—school WV-2
Unexplored Cave—cave AL-4
Unfried Gulch—valley WA-9
Unfried Ridge WA-9
Unfried Ridge—ridge WA-9
Unfug Ridge—ridge CO-8
Unga FM-9
**Unga**—pop pl AK-9
Unga ANV983—reserve AK-9
Unga Cape—cape AK-9
Ungacta House—hist pl GU-9
**Ungaguan**—pop pl GU-9
Unga Island—island AK-9
Ungalak Mtn—summit AK-9
**Ungalik**—pop pl AK-9
Ungalik River—stream AK-9
Ungalikthluk—locale AK-9
Ungalikthluk Bay—bay AK-9
Ungalikthluk River—stream AK-9
Un Gallo Flat—flat CA-9
Unga Reef—bar AK-9
Unga Spit—bar AK-9
Unga Strait—channel AK-9
Ungellel—cape PW-9
**Unger**—pop pl OK-5
**Unger**—pop pl WV-2
Unger, George B., House—hist pl OH-6
Unger Coulee—valley MT-8
Unger Dam—dam OR-9
Unger Dam—dam PA-2
Unger Ditch—canal IN-6
Unger Ditch—canal MS-4
Unger Hollow—valley OH-6
Unger Lake—reservoir PA-2
Ungerman Field—park NJ-2
Unger Oil Field—oilfield KS-7
Unger Rsvr—reservoir OR-9
Unger Run—stream PA-2
Ungers Lake—reservoir PA-2
Ungers Store WV-2
Ungina Wongo—summit NV-8
Ungluayagat Mtn—summit AK-9
Ungulungwak Hill—summit AK-9
Unibon (Barrio)—fmr MCD PR-3
Unibor—island MP-9
Unico, Lake—reservoir AR-4
**Unicoi**—pop pl TN-4
Unicoi Baptist Ch—church TN-4
Unicoi (CCD)—cens area TN-4
Unicoi Cem—cemetery TN-4
Unicoi Ch—church TN-4
Unicoi Ch (historical)—church TN-4
**Unicoi County**—pop pl TN-4
Unicoi County HS—school TN-4
Unicoi County Memorial Hosp—hospital TN-4
Unicoi Dam—dam TN-4
Unicoi Division—civil TN-4
Unicoi Elem Sch—school TN-4
Unicoi Gap—gap GA-3
Unicoi Gap—gap NC-3
Unicoi Gap—gap TN-4
Unicoi Lake—reservoir GA-3
Unicoi Lake—reservoir TN-4
Unicoi Mine—mine TN-4
Unicoi Mountains—range NC-3
Unicoi Mountains—ridge TN-4
Unicoi Mountain Trail—trail TN-4
Unicoi Post Office—building TN-4
Unicoi Prospect—mine TN-4
Unicoi Sch—school TN-4
Unicoi State Park—park GA-3
Unicoi Trail—trail TN-4
Unicol Wildlife Mngmt Area—park TN-4
Unicorn—locale PA-2
**Unicorn**—pop pl MD-2
Unicorn Branch—stream MD-2
Unicorn Creek—stream CA-9
Unicorn Creek—stream WA-9
Unicorn Glacier—glacier WA-9
Unicorn Lake—reservoir TX-5
Unicorn Mill Pond—reservoir MD-2
Unicorn Peak—summit CA-9
Unicorn Peak—summit (2) WA-9
Unicorn Point—cape UT-8
Unicoy Gap GA-3
Unida IL-6
Unife FM-9
Unifei FM-9
Unification Ch—church IN-6
Unified Sch District—school CA-9
Uniform—locale AL-4
Unifoucho—summit FM-9
Unika TN-4
Unikapi FM-9
Unikappi—cape FM-9
Unikar, Mochun—channel FM-9
Unikopos—summit FM-9
Unikos FM-9
Unikos, Mount FM-9
Uniktali Bay—bay AK-9
**Unimak**—pop pl AK-9
Unimak Bight—bay AK-9
Unimak Cove—bay AK-9
Unimak Island—island AK-9
Unimak Pass—channel AK-9
Unimakur FM-9
Unimas FM-9
Unimas—summit FM-9
Unimeito—bar FM-9
Unimoch—bar FM-9
Unimock FM-9
Unimokur—summit FM-9
Unimongemong—summit FM-9
Unimor, Mount FM-9
Unimoso—bar FM-9
Uninc KS-7
Uninor, Ununen—bar FM-9
Union CA-9
Union DE-2
Union IL-6
Union IN-6
Union MS-4
Union OH-6
Union PA-2
Union VA-3
Union—fmr MCD (5) NE-7
Union—locale AZ-5
Union—locale (3) AR-4
Union—locale CO-8
Union—locale (8) GA-3
Union—locale (3) IL-6
Union—locale MN-6
Union—locale (2) MS-4
Union—locale NJ-2
Union—locale NY-2
Union—locale (2) NC-3
Union—locale OK-5
Union—locale PA-2
Union—locale SC-3
Union—locale (2) TN-4
Union—locale (6) TX-5
Union—locale (2) VA-3
Union—locale WI-6
Union—locale PR-3
Union—other OH-6
**Union**—pop pl (10) AL-4
**Union**—pop pl (2) AR-4
**Union**—pop pl CA-9
**Union**—pop pl CT-1
**Union**—pop pl FL-3
**Union**—pop pl IL-6
**Union**—pop pl IN-6
**Union**—pop pl IA-7
**Union**—pop pl KY-4
**Union**—pop pl LA-4
**Union**—pop pl ME-1
**Union**—pop pl MI-6
**Union**—pop pl (5) MS-4
**Union**—pop pl (2) MO-7
**Union**—pop pl NE-7
**Union**—pop pl NV-8
**Union**—pop pl NH-1
**Union**—pop pl NJ-2
**Union**—pop pl (3) NC-3
**Union**—pop pl ND-7
**Union**—pop pl OH-6
**Union**—pop pl OK-5
**Union**—pop pl OR-9
**Union**—pop pl (2) PA-2
**Union**—pop pl (3) SC-3
**Union**—pop pl (4) TN-4
**Union**—pop pl TX-5
**Union**—pop pl UT-8
**Union**—pop pl (2) WA-9
**Union**—pop pl WV-2
**Union**—pop pl WI-6
**Union**—pop pl PR-3
Union—uninc pl NY-2
Union, Lake—lake MN-6
Union, Lake—lake WA-9
**Union, Mount**—pop pl PA-2
Union, Mount—summit AZ-5
Union, The—summit FL-3
Union Acad AL-4
Union Acad—school (2) AL-4
Union Acad—school (3) CA-9
Union Acad—school FL-3
Union Acad—school MS-4
Union Acad—school (2) SC-3
Union Acad—school TX-5
Union Academy Ch—church AL-4
Union Academy Ch—church TN-4
Union Acad (historical)—school (3) AL-4
Union Acad (historical)—school PA-2
Union Acad (historical)—school (4) TN-4
**Union Addition (Union Mines)**—pop pl WV-2
Union African Methodist Episcopal Ch—church DE-2
Union Agency—hist pl OK-5
Union-Amity Ch—church PA-2
Union and East Jordan Ditch—canal UT-8
Union and Mount Washington—locale VI-3
Union Aqueduct—canal UT-8
Union Arbor Ch—church GA-3
Union Area HS—school PA-2
Union Area MS—school PA-2
Union Ark Ch—church AR-4
Union Attendance Center—school MS-4
Union Ave Ch—church GA-3
Union Ave Hist Dist—hist pl NY-2
Union Ave Historic Commerical District—hist pl CO-8
Union Ave Methodist Episcopal Church, South—hist pl TN-4
Union Ave Missionary Baptist Ch—church AL-4
Union Ave Sch—school (2) CA-9
Union Ave Sch—school (2) NJ-2
Union Ave Sch—school NY-2
Union Baker Ch—church MO-7
Union Band Ch—church TX-5
Union Bank—hist pl FL-3
Union Banking Company Bldg—hist pl GA-3
Union Baptist Cem—cemetery OR-9
Union Baptist Ch AL-4
Union Baptist Ch MS-4
Union Baptist Ch TN-4
Union Baptist Ch—church AL-4
Union Baptist Ch—church FL-3
Union Baptist Ch—church (3) MS-4
Union Baptist Ch—church TN-4
Union Baptist Ch (historical)—church AL-4
Union Baptist Church—hist pl CT-1
Union Battery F, Battle of Corinth—hist pl MS-4
Union Bay MI-6
Union Bay—bay AK-9
Union Bay—bay MI-6
Union Bay—bay WA-9
**Union Beach**—pop pl NJ-2
Union Belle Ch—church VA-3
Union Bend Sch—school KS-7
Union Bethel African Methodist Episcopal Ch—church AL-4
Union Bethel Cem—cemetery IN-6
Union Bethel Ch—church GA-3
Union Bethel Ch—church IN-6
Union Bethel Ch—church LA-4
Union Bethel Ch—church (2) MD-2
Union Bethel Ch—church NC-3
Union Bethel Ch—church (3) VA-3
**Union Bleachery**—pop pl SC-3
Union Block—hist pl (2) KS-7
Union Block—hist pl ME-1
Union Block—hist pl MI-6
Union Block—hist pl ND-7
Union Block—hist pl OH-6
Union Block and Montandon Buildings—hist pl ID-8
Union Bluff—cliff MS-4
Union Bluff (Abandoned)—locale TX-5
Union Bluff Landing (historical)—locale MS-4
Union Bower—uninc pl TX-5
Union Bower Sch—school TX-5
Union Branch NJ-2
Union Branch—stream AR-4
Union Branch—stream IN-6
Union Branch—stream KY-4
Union Branch—stream MD-2
Union Branch—stream MS-4
Union Branch—stream NJ-2
Union Branch—stream OH-6
Union Branch—stream TN-4
Union Branch Ch—church (2) FL-3
Union Branch Ch—church (2) NC-3
Union Branch Ch—church SC-3
Union Branch Ch—church (4) VA-3
Union Branch Sch—school AL-4
Union Branch Sch—school VA-3
Union Brewery—hist pl IA-7
Union Brick Cem—cemetery NJ-2
Union Brick Sch—school IL-6
Union Bridge—bridge NC-3
Union Bridge—other MO-7
**Union Bridge**—pop pl MD-2
Union Bridge (historical)—bridge TN-4
Union Bridge Station—hist pl MD-2
Union Brook—stream VT-1
Union Bryarly's Mill—hist pl WV-2
Union B Sch—school TN-4
Union B Sch (historical)—school TN-4
Unionburg—locale NJ-2
**Unionburg**—pop pl GA-3
**Union Burg (historical)**—pop pl IA-7
Unionbury (Union) NJ-2
Union Camp—locale HI-9
Union Camp—locale TN-4
Union Camp Corporation—facility VA-3
Union Camp Ground Branch—stream TN-4
Union Camp Post Office (historical)—building TN-4
Union Camp Waste Treatment Pond AL-4
Union Canal—canal AZ-5
Union Canal—canal CA-9
Union Canal—canal NE-7
Union Canal—canal NV-8
Union Canal—canal NY-2
Union Canal—canal PA-2
Union Canal—canal TX-5
Union Canal—canal WA-9
Union Canal Tunnel—hist pl PA-2
Union Canyon—valley CA-9
Union Canyon—valley CO-8
Union Carbide Corporation—facility SC-3
Union Carbide Mine—mine CO-8
Union Carbide Plant—facility GA-3
Union Carbide Pond—reservoir NC-3
Union Carbide Pond Dam—dam NC-3
Union (CCD)—cens area OR-9
Union (CCD)—cens area SC-3
Union Cem AL-4
Union Cem MS-4
Union Cem—cemetery (19) AL-4
Union Cem—cemetery (6) AR-4
Union Cem—cemetery (3) CA-9
Union Cem—cemetery (11) CT-1
Union Cem—cemetery (2) DE-2
Union Cem—cemetery (3) FL-3
Union Cem—cemetery (6) GA-3
Union Cem—cemetery (25) IL-6
Union Cem—cemetery (20) IN-6
Union Cem—cemetery (21) IA-7
Union Cem—cemetery (12) KS-7
Union Cem—cemetery (3) KY-4
Union Cem—cemetery (3) LA-4
Union Cem—cemetery (6) ME-1
Union Cem—cemetery (2) MD-2
Union Cem—cemetery (9) MA-1
Union Cem—cemetery (4) MI-6
Union Cem—cemetery (13) MN-6
Union Cem—cemetery (25) MS-4
Union Cem—cemetery (12) MO-7
Union Cem—cemetery (9) NE-7
Union Cem—cemetery (5) NH-1
Union Cem—cemetery (7) NJ-2
Union Cem—cemetery (43) NY-2
Union Cem—cemetery NC-3
Union Cem—cemetery (9) ND-7
Union Cem—cemetery (35) OH-6
Union Cem—cemetery (4) OK-5
Union Cem—cemetery (2) OR-9
Union Cem—cemetery (34) PA-2
Union Cem—cemetery (3) SC-3
Union Cem—cemetery (6) SD-7
Union Cem—cemetery (15) TN-4
Union Cem—cemetery (9) TX-5
Union Cem—cemetery UT-8
Union Cem—cemetery (2) VT-1
Union Cem—cemetery (4) VA-3
Union Cem—cemetery (5) WV-2
Union Cem—cemetery (40) WI-6
Union Cemeteries—cemetery OK-5
Union Cemetery—hist pl CA-9
Union Cemetery-Beatty Park—hist pl OH-6
Union Cem Number Two—cemetery MS-4
Union Center KS-7
Union Center—locale SD-7
Union Center—locale TX-5
Union Center—locale WA-9
**Union Center**—pop pl IL-6
**Union Center**—pop pl IN-6
**Union Center**—pop pl IA-7
**Union Center**—pop pl NJ-2
**Union Center**—pop pl (2) NY-2
**Union Center**—pop pl PA-2
**Union Center**—pop pl SD-7
**Union Center**—pop pl WI-6
Union Center Cem—cemetery (2) KS-7
Union Center Cem—cemetery OK-5
Union Center Ch—church (2) IN-6
Union Center Ch—church (2) OK-5
Union Center Elementary School MS-4
Union Center Elem Sch—school (2) IN-6
Union Center JHS IN-6
Union Center Sch—school KS-7
Union Center Sch—school MS-4
Union Center Sch—school SD-7
Union Center Sch—school TX-5
**Union Center Township**—pop pl KS-7
**Union Central**—pop pl TN-4
Union Central HS—school LA-4
Union Central Sch—hist pl TN-4
Union Central Sch—school IL-6
Union Central Sch (historical)—school TN-4
Union Centre PA-2
Union Centre—locale IA-7
Union Centre (historical)—locale KS-7
Union Ch DE-2
Union Ch FL-3
Union Ch PA-2
Union Ch TN-4
Union Ch—church (61) AL-4
Union Ch—church (23) AR-4
Union Ch—church CO-8
Union Ch—church (3) DE-2
Union Ch—church (10) FL-3
Union Ch—church (42) GA-3
Union Ch—church (21) IL-6
Union Ch—church (25) IN-6
Union Ch—church (6) IA-7
Union Ch—church (2) KS-7
Union Ch—church (19) KY-4
Union Ch—church (16) LA-4
Union Ch—church (7) ME-1
Union Ch—church (11) MD-2
Union Ch—church (4) MA-1
Union Ch—church (5) MI-6
Union Ch—church MN-6
Union Ch—church (36) MS-4
Union Ch—church (28) MO-7
Union Ch—church (2) NE-7
Union Ch—church NH-1
Union Ch—church (6) NJ-2
Union Ch—church (4) NY-2
Union Ch—church (32) NC-3
Union Ch—church ND-7
Union Ch—church (17) OH-6
Union Ch—church (3) OK-5
Union Ch—church (26) PA-2
Union Ch—church (25) SC-3
Union Ch—church SD-7
Union Ch—church (28) TN-4
Union Ch—church (17) TX-5
Union Ch—church VT-1
Union Ch—church (40) VA-3
Union Ch—church (7) WV-2
Union Ch—church WI-6
Union Ch—church WY-8
Union Ch (abandoned)—church (2) MO-7
Union Chapel AL-4
Union Chapel IN-6
Union Chapel MO-7
Union Chapel TN-4
Union Chapel—church (9) AL-4
Union Chapel—church (3) AR-4
Union Chapel—church CA-9
Union Chapel—church CT-1
Union Chapel—church FL-3
Union Chapel—church (6) GA-3
Union Chapel—church (6) IL-6
Union Chapel—church (18) IN-6
Union Chapel—church (5) IA-7
Union Chapel—church (3) KS-7
Union Chapel—church (6) KY-4
Union Chapel—church (2) LA-4
Union Chapel—church MD-2
Union Chapel—church MA-1
Union Chapel—church MI-6
Union Chapel—church MN-6
Union Chapel—church (8) MS-4
Union Chapel—church (15) MO-7
Union Chapel—church (2) NY-2
Union Chapel—church (25) NC-3
Union Chapel—church (14) OH-6
Union Chapel—church (4) OK-5
Union Chapel—church (6) PA-2
Union Chapel—church (2) SC-3
Union Chapel—church (8) TN-4
Union Chapel—church (10) TX-5
Union Chapel—church VT-1
Union Chapel—church (9) VA-3
Union Chapel—church (8) WV-2
Union Chapel—hist pl MD-2
Union Chapel—hist pl NY-2
Union Chapel—locale TN-4
**Union Chapel**—pop pl AL-4
**Union Chapel**—pop pl MA-1
Union Chapel AME Zion Ch—church AL-4
Union Chapel Baptist Ch AL-4
Union Chapel Baptist Ch MS-4
Union Chapel Baptist Ch—church TX-5
Union Chapel Cem—cemetery (3) AL-4
Union Chapel Cem—cemetery IL-6
Union Chapel Cem—cemetery (2) IN-6
Union Chapel Cem—cemetery (2) IA-7
Union Chapel Cem—cemetery KS-7
Union Chapel Cem—cemetery LA-4
Union Chapel Cem—cemetery MS-4
Union Chapel Cem—cemetery (2) MO-7
Union Chapel Cem—cemetery OH-6
Union Chapel Cem—cemetery OK-5
Union Chapel Cem—cemetery TN-4
Union Chapel Cem—cemetery (2) TX-5
Union Chapel Ch AL-4
Union Chapel Ch—church (3) AL-4
Union Chapel Ch—church GA-3
Union Chapel Ch—church MD-2
Union Chapel Ch—church (2) MS-4
Union Chapel Ch—church NC-3
Union Chapel Community Center—building AL-4
Union Chapel Freewill Baptist Church AL-4
Union Chapel (historical)—church (4) AL-4
Union Chapel (historical)—church (3) MO-7
Union Chapel (historical)—church (2) TN-4
Union Chapel House of Prayer MS-4
Union Chapel JHS—school AL-4
Union Chapel Methodist Church AL-4
Union Chapel Missionary Baptist Ch—church AL-4
Union Chapel Sch—school AR-4
Union Chapel Sch—school KS-7
Union Chapel Sch—school (2) KY-4
Union Chapel Sch—school NC-3
Union Chapel Sch—school SC-3
Union Chapel Sch—school TN-4
Union Chapel Sch (historical)—school TN-4
Union Chapel School AL-4
Union Chapel School (abandoned)—locale MO-7
Union Ch (historical)—church (3) AL-4
Union Ch (historical)—church LA-4
Union Ch (historical)—church (5) MS-4
Union Ch (historical)—church (2) MO-7
Union Ch (historical)—church (2) PA-2
Union Ch (historical)—church (4) TN-4
Union Ch of Christ MS-4
Union Christian Cemetery AL-4
Union Christian Ch AL-4
Union Christian College—hist pl IN-6
Union Church AL-4
Union Church MS-4
Union Church MO-7
Union Church—hist pl IA-7
Union Church—hist pl (2) ME-1
Union Church—hist pl NH-1
Union Church—hist pl OH-6
Union Church—hist pl RI-1
**Union Church**—pop pl AL-4
**Union Church**—pop pl LA-4
**Union Church**—pop pl MS-4
**Union Church**—pop pl WI-6
Union Church—school MO-7
Union Church and Burial Ground—hist pl PA-2
Union Church Bridge—bridge VA-3
Union Church Cem—cemetery IN-6
Union Church Cem—cemetery NJ-2
Union Church Cem—cemetery PA-2
Union Church Hollow—valley TN-4
Union Church HS (historical)—school MS-4
Union Church of Vinalhaven—hist pl ME-1
Union Church Post Office—building MS-4
Union Church Post Office (historical)—building TN-4
Union Church Presbyterian Church—hist pl MS-4
Union Church/St. Paul's Church—hist pl CT-1
Union City AL-4
Union City AR-4
Union City CT-1
Union City MO-7
Union City WA-9
Union City—locale FL-3
Union City—locale KY-4
**Union City**—pop pl CT-1
**Union City**—pop pl GA-3
**Union City**—pop pl IN-6
**Union City**—pop pl KY-4
**Union City**—pop pl MI-6
**Union City**—pop pl MO-7
**Union City**—pop pl NJ-2
**Union City**—pop pl OH-6
**Union City**—pop pl OK-5
**Union City**—pop pl PA-2
**Union City**—pop pl TN-4
**Union City**—pop pl WV-2
**Union City (Alvarado)**—pop pl CA-9
Union City Borough—civil PA-2
Union City (CCD)—cens area TN-4
Union City Cem—cemetery IN-6
Union City Cem—cemetery OK-5
Union City Community HS—school IN-6
**Union City (corporate and RR name for Union)**—pop pl OK-5
Union City Country Club—other PA-2
Union City Dam—dam MI-6
Union City Dam—dam PA-2
**Union City (Decoto)**—pop pl CA-9
Union City Division—civil TN-4
Union City Golf Course—locale PA-2
Union City HS—school TN-4
Union City Junior-Senior HS—school PA-2
Union City Lake—reservoir PA-2
Union City MS—school TN-4
Union City Passenger Depot—hist pl IN-6
Union City Post Office—building TN-4
Union City Reservoir Dam—dam PA-2
Union City Rsvr—reservoir PA-2
Union City Township—fmr MCD IA-7
Union Civil Cem—cemetery IN-6
Union Civil War Fortification—hist pl WV-2
Union Club—hist pl OH-6
Union Coll—school KY-4
Union Coll—school NE-7
Union Coll—school NJ-2
Union Coll—school NY-2
Union Coll Environmental Education Center—school KY-4
Union Coll (historical)—school TN-4
Union Community Center—locale IL-6
Union Congregational Ch AL-4
Union Congregational Ch—church FL-3
Union Congregational Church—hist pl (2) MA-1
Union Congregational Church and Parsonage—hist pl WY-8
Union Consolidated Sch MS-4
Union Corner—locale PA-2
Union Corner—locale WV-2
**Union Corner**—pop pl MD-2
Union Corner Cem—cemetery IL-6
Union Corner Ch—church IL-6
Union Corner Ch—church MN-6
Union Corners PA-2
Union Corners—locale ME-1
Union Corners—locale MI-6
Union Corners—locale (2) NY-2
Union Corners—locale OH-6
**Union Corners**—pop pl (3) NY-2
**Union Corners**—pop pl OH-6
Union (corporate and RR name Union City) OK-5
Union Corral Creek KS-7
Union Country Club—other SC-3
Union County—airport NJ-2
Union County—civil NC-3
Union County—civil SD-7
**Union (County)**—pop pl AR-4
**Union County**—pop pl FL-3
**Union (County)**—pop pl GA-3
**Union (County)**—pop pl IL-6
**Union County**—pop pl IN-6
**Union (County)**—pop pl KY-4
**Union County**—pop pl MS-4
**Union County**—pop pl NJ-2
**Union (County)**—pop pl NM-5
**Union (County)**—pop pl OH-6
**Union County**—pop pl OR-9
**Union County**—pop pl PA-2
**Union (County)**—pop pl SC-3
**Union County**—pop pl TN-4
Union County Adult HS—school FL-3
Union County Career Center—school NC-3
Union County Cem—cemetery SD-7
Union County Courthouse—building MS-4
Union County Courthouse—hist pl AR-4
Union County Courthouse—hist pl IN-6
Union County Courthouse—hist pl KY-4
Union County Courthouse—hist pl NM-5
Union County Courthouse—hist pl NC-3
Union County Elem Sch—school GA-3
Union County General Hosp—hospital MS-4
Union County HS—school GA-3
Union County HS—school IN-6
Union County Jail—hist pl GA-3
Union County Jail—hist pl SC-3
Union County Lake MS-4
Union County Lake Dam—dam MS-4
Union County Park Commission Administration Buildings—hist pl NJ-2
Union County State For—forest IL-6
Union County State Park—park SD-7
Union Covered Bridge—hist pl MO-7
Union Creek CO-8
Union Creek NE-7
Union Creek TX-5
Union Creek—fmr MCD NE-7
Union Creek—locale (2) OR-9
Union Creek—stream (3) AK-9
Union Creek—stream (5) CA-9
Union Creek—stream CO-8
Union Creek—stream GA-3
Union Creek—stream ID-8
Union Creek—stream (4) IN-6
Union Creek—stream IA-7
Union Creek—stream KS-7

Union Rodgers Canal—*canal* NV-8
Union Rosenwald Sch—*school* AL-4
Union RR Station—*hist pl* FL-3
Union Rsvr—*reservoir* (3) CA-9
*Union Run* PA-2
Union Run—*stream* OH-6
Union Run—*stream* PA-2
Union Run Ch—*church* VA-3
Union Salem Ch—*church* PA-2
Union Savings Bank and Trust—*hist pl* IA-7
*Union Sch* AL-4
*Union Sch* MS-4
*Union Sch* MO-7
*Union Sch* PA-2
*Union Sch* TN-4
Union Sch—*hist pl* CT-1
Union Sch—*hist pl* MI-6
Union Sch—*hist pl* PA-2
Union Sch—*school* (3) AL-4
Union Sch—*school* AZ-5
Union Sch—*school* (6) AR-4
Union Sch—*school* (20) CA-9
Union Sch—*school* CO-8
Union Sch—*school* (5) CT-1
Union Sch—*school* DE-2
Union Sch—*school* (2) FL-3
Union Sch—*school* (2) GA-3
Union Sch—*school* ID-8
Union Sch—*school* (47) IL-6
Union Sch—*school* (7) IA-7
Union Sch—*school* (8) KS-7
Union Sch—*school* (7) KY-4
Union Sch—*school* (2) LA-4
Union Sch—*school* MA-1
Union Sch—*school* (3) MI-6
Union Sch—*school* MN-6
Union Sch—*school* (6) MS-4
Union Sch—*school* (12) MO-7
Union Sch—*school* MT-8
Union Sch—*school* (2) NE-7
Union Sch—*school* (2) NV-8
Union Sch—*school* (2) NH-1
Union Sch—*school* (2) NJ-2
Union Sch—*school* (7) NY-2
Union Sch—*school* (3) NC-3
Union Sch—*school* (6) OH-6
Union Sch—*school* (2) OK-5
Union Sch—*school* OR-9
Union Sch—*school* (5) PA-2
Union Sch—*school* (5) SC-3
Union Sch—*school* (3) SD-7
Union Sch—*school* (9) TN-4
Union Sch—*school* (4) TX-5
Union Sch—*school* VA-3
Union Sch—*school* (2) WA-9
Union Sch—*school* (5) WV-2
Union Sch—*school* (2) WI-6
Union Sch (abandoned)—*school* (5) MO-7
Union Sch (abandoned)—*school* (12) PA-2
Union Sch (historical)—*school* (11) AL-4
Union Sch (historical)—*school* (10) MS-4
Union Sch (historical)—*school* (3) MO-7
Union Sch (historical)—*school* PA-2
Union Sch (historical)—*school* (4) TN-4
Union Sch No 1—*school* IL-6
Union Sch No 1—*school* IA-7
*Union School* IN-6
Union School—*locale* CO-8
Union School—*locale* IL-6
Union School—*locale* OH-6
Union School (Abandoned)—*locale* IA-7
Union School (abandoned)—*locale* (3) MO-7
Union School (Abandoned)—*locale* (2) MO-7
Union School (Abandoned)—*locale* OK-5
Union Schoolhouse—*hist pl* NJ-2
Union School Slough—*stream* CA-9
Union-Scioto HS—*school* OH-6
Union Seminary—*hist pl* VA-3
Union Seminary Cem—*cemetery* MS-4
Union Seminary Ch—*church* MS-4
*Union Seminary Missionary Baptist Ch* MS-4
Union Senior Ch—*church* MS-4
**Union Settlement**—*pop pl* NY-2
Union Shaft—*mine* NV-8
Union Shiloh Ch—*church* VA-3
Union Slough—*stream* WA-9
Union Slough Ditch—*canal* IA-7
Union Slough Natl Wildlife Ref—*park* IA-7
Union Sportsman Club Lake Dam—*dam* MS-4
Union Spring—*spring* NV-8
Union Spring—*spring* OR-9
Union Spring—*spring* TN-4
Union Spring Cem—*cemetery* GA-3
Union Spring Ch—*church* AL-4
Union Spring Ch—*church* GA-3
Union Spring Number Eight—*spring* NV-8
*Union Springs* AL-4
Union Springs—*locale* GA-3
Union Springs—*locale* LA-4
**Union Springs**—*pop pl* AL-4
**Union Springs**—*pop pl* NY-2
**Union Springs**—*pop pl* TX-5
Union Springs Acad—*school* NY-2
*Union Springs Baptist Church* AL-4
Union Springs Branch—*stream* TX-5
Union Springs (CCD)—*cens area* AL-4
Union Springs Cem—*cemetery* AL-4
Union Springs Central Sch—*school* NY-2
*Union Springs Ch* AL-4
Union Springs Ch—*church* (6) AL-4
Union Springs Ch—*church* (5) GA-3
Union Springs Ch—*church* IL-6
Union Springs Ch—*church* LA-4
Union Springs Ch—*church* NC-3
Union Springs Ch—*church* TN-4
Union Springs Ch—*church* (2) TX-5
Union Springs Country Club—*other* AL-4
Union Springs Dam—*dam* VA-3
Union Springs Division—*civil* AL-4
Union Springs Elem Sch—*school* AL-4
*Union Springs Female Coll* AL-4
*Union Springs Freewill Baptist Church* AL-4
**Union Springs (Hatcher)**—*pop pl* LA-4
*Union Springs Missionary Baptist Church* AL-4
*Union Springs Primitive Baptist Church* AL-4
Union Springs Public Sch (historical)—*school* AL-4
Union Springs Run—*stream* VA-3
Union Spring Three—*spring* NV-8
Union Spring Two—*spring* NV-8
Union Square—*locale* (2) MA-1
Union Square—*locale* (2) PA-2
Union Square—*locale* UT-8
Union Square—*park* CA-9
Union Square—*park* MD-2
**Union Square**—*pop pl* NJ-2
**Union Square**—*pop pl* PA-2
Union Square-Hollins Market Hist Dist—*hist pl* MD-2
Union Square Park—*park* CA-9
Union Square Park—*park* NY-2
Union Square Shop Ctr—*locale* AL-4
**Union Square Subdivision**—*pop pl* UT-8
**Union (sta.)**—*pop pl* LA-4
Union Staff Ch—*church* MS-4
**Union Star**—*pop pl* KY-4
**Union Star**—*pop pl* MO-7
Union Star Cem—*cemetery* AR-4
Union Star Cem—*cemetery* NE-7
Union Star Cem—*cemetery* TN-4
Union Star Ch—*church* IL-6
Union Star Ch—*church* MS-4
Union Star Ch (historical)—*church* MO-7
*Union Star Missionary Baptist Ch* MS-4
Union Star Sch—*school* AR-4
Union State Line Cem—*cemetery* IA-7
Union State Wildlife Mngmt Area—*park* LA-4
Union Station—*building* KY-4
Union Station—*building* MA-1
Union Station—*building* (2) OH-6
Union Station—*hist pl* AZ-5
Union Station—*hist pl* AR-4
Union Station—*hist pl* CO-8
Union Station—*hist pl* CT-1
Union Station—*hist pl* DC-2
Union Station—*hist pl* (2) IL-6
Union Station—*hist pl* (2) KY-4
Union Station—*hist pl* (2) MA-1
Union Station—*hist pl* MS-4
Union Station—*hist pl* MO-7
Union Station—*hist pl* (3) NY-2
Union Station—*hist pl* NC-3
Union Station—*hist pl* RI-1
Union Station—*hist pl* SC-3
Union Station—*hist pl* TN-4
Union Station—*hist pl* TX-5
Union Station—*hist pl* VT-1
Union Station—*hist pl* WA-9
Union Station—*locale* (2) AL-4
Union Station—*locale* CA-9
Union Station—*locale* CO-8
Union Station—*locale* (2) FL-3
Union Station—*locale* (2) GA-3
Union Station—*locale* (2) IL-6
Union Station—*locale* LA-4
Union Station—*locale* MI-6
Union Station—*locale* (2) MO-7
Union Station—*locale* NY-2
Union Station—*locale* OK-5
Union Station—*locale* PA-2
Union Station—*locale* TN-4
Union Station—*locale* (4) TX-5
Union Station—*locale* VT-1
Union Station—*locale* VA-3
Union Station—*locale* WA-9
Union Station—*locale* WI-6
Union Station—*other* KY-4
Union Station—*other* NE-7
Union Station—*other* OH-6
**Union Station**—*pop pl* OH-6
Union Station and Burlington Freight House—*hist pl* IA-7
Union Station Plaza and Columbus Fountain—*hist pl* DC-2
Union Station Plaza Fountain—*park* DC-2
Union Station Post Office Annex—*hist pl* MO-7
Union Station (railroad station)—*building* AZ-5
Union Station Sch—*school* KY-4
Union Stock Yard—*locale* NY-2
Union Stock Yards—*locale* TX-5
Union Stock Yards (RR name for Stock Yards)—*other* IL-6
Union Street—*uninc pl* DE-2
Union Street-Academy Hill Hist Dist—*hist pl* NY-2
Union Street Baptist Ch—*church* AL-4
Union Street Cem—*cemetery* MA-1
Union Street Hist Dist—*hist pl* MA-1
Union Street Hist Dist—*hist pl* (2) NY-2
Union Street JHS—*school* LA-4
Union Street JHS—*school* ME-1
Union Street Private Hosp (historical)—*hospital* AL-4
Union Street Railway Carbarn, Repair Shop—*hist pl* MA-1
Union Street Sch—*school* (2) MA-1
Union Street Sch—*school* MI-6
Union Street Sch—*school* NJ-2
Union Street Sch—*school* VT-1
Union Street Sch (abandoned)—*school* PA-2
*Union Street Vocational Center* AL-4
Union Summit—*summit* NV-8
Union Sunday Sch—*hist pl* IA-7
Union Sunday Sch (abandoned)—*school* PA-2
Union Swamp—*stream* VA-3
Union Tabernacle—*church* AL-4
Union Tabernacle—*church* MI-6
Union Tabernacle—*church* TN-4
Union Tarheel Cem—*cemetery* NC-3
Union Tar Spring (historical)—*spring* IN-6
Union Tavern—*hist pl* NC-3
Union Temple—*church* MS-4
Union Temple—*church* MO-7
Union Temple—*church* TN-4
**Union Temple**—*pop pl* TN-4
Union Temple Cem—*cemetery* KY-4
Union Temple Cem—*cemetery* MS-4
Union Temple Cem—*cemetery* TN-4
Union Temple Ch—*church* KY-4
Union Temple Ch—*church* TN-4
Union Temple Creek—*stream* TN-4
Union Temple (historical)—*church* MS-4
Union Temple Sch (historical)—*school* TN-4
Union Terminal—*locale* OH-6
Union Terminal Group—*hist pl* OH-6
Union Terrace Elem Sch—*school* PA-2
*Union Terrace Sch* PA-2
**Union Terrace (subdivision)**—*pop pl* NC-3
Union Theological Seminary—*hist pl* NY-2
Union Theological Seminary—*school* VA-3
*Union Town* IN-6
*Uniontown* KS-7
*Uniontown* OH-6
*Union Town* PA-2
Uniontown—*locale* IL-6
Union Town—*locale* IL-6
Uniontown—*locale* IA-7
Uniontown—*locale* VA-3
Uniontown—*locale* WV-2
Uniontown—*other* PA-2
**Uniontown**—*pop pl* AL-4
**Uniontown**—*pop pl* AR-4
**Uniontown**—*pop pl* (2) IN-6
**Uniontown**—*pop pl* KS-7
**Uniontown**—*pop pl* KY-4
**Uniontown**—*pop pl* MD-2
**Uniontown**—*pop pl* (2) MO-7
**Uniontown**—*pop pl* NJ-2
**Uniontown**—*pop pl* (2) OH-6
**Uniontown**—*pop pl* (5) PA-2
**Uniontown**—*pop pl* WA-9
Uniontown Acad—*hist pl* MD-2
Uniontown-Alameda Hist Dist—*hist pl* OR-9
Uniontown Baptist Ch—*church* AL-4
Uniontown (CCD)—*cens area* AL-4
Uniontown (CCD)—*cens area* KY-4
Uniontown (CCD)—*cens area* WA-9
Uniontown Cem—*cemetery* CA-9
Uniontown Cem—*cemetery* IL-6
Uniontown Cem—*cemetery* KY-4
Uniontown Cem—*cemetery* OH-6
Uniontown Ch—*church* IN-6
Union Town Ch—*church* NC-3
Uniontown Ch of God—*church* AL-4
Uniontown City—*civil* PA-2
*Uniontown (corporate name Fultonham)* OH-6
Uniontown District Acad (historical)—*school* AL-4
Uniontown Division—*civil* AL-4
Uniontown Elem Sch—*school* AL-4
Uniontown Female Acad (historical)—*school* AL-4
*Uniontown Female Institute* AL-4
Union Townhall—*building* IA-7
Union Town Hall—*building* IA-7
Union Town Hall—*building* ND-7
**Uniontown Heights**—*pop pl* PA-2
Uniontown Hist Dist—*hist pl* MD-2
Union Town (historical)—*locale* KS-7
**Uniontown (historical)**—*pop pl* MS-4
*Uniontown HS* AL-4
Uniontown HS—*school* KS-7
Uniontown Male Acad (historical)—*school* AL-4
Uniontown Mall—*locale* PA-2
Uniontown MS—*school* AL-4
Uniontown Municipal Airp—*airport* AL-4
**Uniontown North**—*pop pl* PA-2
**Union (Town of)**—*pop pl* CT-1
**Union (Town of)**—*pop pl* ME-1
**Union (Town of)**—*pop pl* NY-2
**Union (Town of)**—*pop pl* (7) WI-6
*Uniontown Reservoirs* PA-2
Uniontown Sch—*school* MO-7
Union Township—*civ div* NE-7
Union Township—*civil* KS-7
Union Township—*civil* (25) MO-7
Union Township—*civil* PA-2
Union Township—*civil* (2) SD-7
Union Township—*fmr MCD* (43) IA-7
Union Township—*inact MCD* NV-8
**Union Township**—*pop pl* (18) KS-7
**Union Township**—*pop pl* (8) MO-7
**Union Township**—*pop pl* (5) NE-7
**Union Township**—*pop pl* ND-7
**Union Township**—*pop pl* (13) SD-7
Union Township—*unorg reg* KS-7
Union Township Cem—*cemetery* (2) IA-7
*Union (Township of)* AR-4
Union (Township of)—*fmr MCD* (22) AR-4
Union (Township of)—*fmr MCD* (5) NC-3
Union (Township of)—*other* OH-6
**Union (Township of)**—*pop pl* (4) IL-6
**Union (Township of)**—*pop pl* (35) IN-6
**Union (Township of)**—*pop pl* (3) MI-6
**Union (Township of)**—*pop pl* MN-6
**Union (Township of)**—*pop pl* (2) NJ-2
**Union (Township of)**—*pop pl* (28) OH-6
**Union (Township of)**—*pop pl* (19) PA-2
Union Township Sch—*school* IN-6
Union Township Sch—*school* NC-3
Union Township Works II—*hist pl* OH-6
Uniontown Shop Ctr—*locale* PA-2
Union Trust—*uninc pl* PA-2
Union Trust Bldg—*hist pl* DC-2
Union Trust Bldg—*hist pl* PA-2
Union Trust Company Bldg—*hist pl* MA-1
Union Trust Company Bldg—*hist pl* MO-7
Union Trust Company Bldg—*hist pl* RI-1
Union Trust & Deposit Co./Union Trust Natl Bank—*hist pl* WV-2
Union Tunnel—*tunnel* CA-9
Union-Turnbow-Mays Cem—*cemetery* OR-9
Union-Udell Cem—*cemetery* MI-6
Union (Unionbury)—*CDP* NJ-2
Union United Ch—*church* PA-2
Union United Methodist Ch—*church* (2) DE-2
Union United Methodist Ch—*church* (2) MS-4
Union Univ—*school* TN-4
**Unionvale**—*pop pl* OH-6
**Unionvale**—*pop pl* OR-9
**Union Vale (Town of)**—*pop pl* NY-2
*Union Valley* IN-6
Union Valley—*basin* VA-3
Union Valley—*fmr MCD* NE-7
Union Valley—*locale* NJ-2
Union Valley—*locale* NY-2
Union Valley—*locale* TN-4
Union Valley—*locale* (2) TX-5
**Union Valley**—*pop pl* AR-4
**Union Valley**—*pop pl* NY-2
**Union Valley**—*pop pl* OK-5
**Union Valley**—*pop pl* PA-2
**Union Valley**—*pop pl* TX-5
Union Valley—*valley* CA-9
Union Valley—*valley* NE-7
Union Valley—*valley* NJ-2
Union Valley—*valley* (2) NY-2
Union Valley—*valley* (2) TN-4
Union Valley—*valley* WA-9
Union Valley Cem—*cemetery* AR-4
Union Valley Cem—*cemetery* CO-8
Union Valley Cem—*cemetery* KS-7
Union Valley Ch—*church* AL-4
Union Valley Ch—*church* (3) AR-4
Union Valley Ch—*church* (3) IN-6
Union Valley Ch—*church* (2) LA-4
Union Valley Ch—*church* MS-4
Union Valley Ch—*church* (2) NY-2
Union Valley Ch—*church* (2) NC-3
Union Valley Ch—*church* OH-6
Union Valley Ch—*church* OK-5
Union Valley Ch—*church* (2) PA-2
Union Valley Ch—*church* (3) TN-4
Union Valley Ch—*church* TX-5
Union Valley Ch—*church* VA-3
Union Valley Ch—*church* (3) WV-2
Union Valley Creek—*stream* IA-7
Union Valley Elem Sch—*school* KS-7
Union Valley (historical)—*locale* KS-7
Union Valley (historical)—*locale* MS-4
Union Valley Rsvr—*reservoir* CA-9
Union Valley Sch—*school* AR-4
Union Valley Sch—*school* (2) KS-7
Union Valley Sch—*school* (2) NE-7
Union Valley Sch—*school* OH-6
Union Valley Sch (abandoned)—*school* MO-7
Union Valley Sch (historical)—*school* MS-4
Union Valley Sch (historical)—*school* (2) TN-4
Union Valley (Township of)—*fmr MCD* AR-4
Union Victory Sch (historical)—*school* MO-7
Union View Ch—*church* MS-4
Union View Ch—*church* NC-3
Union View Ch—*church* VA-3
Union View Sch (historical)—*school* MS-4
**Union View Subdivision**—*pop pl* UT-8
*Union Village* IN-6
Union Village—*locale* RI-1
**Union Village**—*pop pl* NJ-2
**Union Village**—*pop pl* OH-6
**Union Village**—*pop pl* VT-1
Union Village Ch—*church* NJ-2
Union Village Covered Bridge—*hist pl* VT-1
Union Village Hist Dist—*hist pl* RI-1
Union Village Rural Cem—*cemetery* NY-2
Union Village Shop Ctr—*locale* NC-3
*Unionville* IN-6
*Unionville* MA-1
*Unionville* NJ-2
*Unionville* NY-2
*Unionville* OH-6
*Unionville* PA-2
*Unionville* VA-3
Unionville—*locale* GA-3
Unionville—*locale* (2) NJ-2
Unionville—*locale* OH-6
Unionville—*locale* PA-2
Unionville—*locale* VA-3
**Unionville**—*pop pl* CT-1
**Unionville**—*pop pl* GA-3
**Unionville**—*pop pl* (3) IL-6
**Unionville**—*pop pl* (2) IN-6
**Unionville**—*pop pl* IA-7
**Unionville**—*pop pl* LA-4
**Unionville**—*pop pl* ME-1
**Unionville**—*pop pl* (4) MD-2
**Unionville**—*pop pl* (2) MA-1
**Unionville**—*pop pl* MI-6
**Unionville**—*pop pl* MO-7
**Unionville**—*pop pl* MT-8
**Unionville**—*pop pl* NV-8
**Unionville**—*pop pl* NJ-2
**Unionville**—*pop pl* (6) NY-2
**Unionville**—*pop pl* NC-3
**Unionville**—*pop pl* (3) OH-6
**Unionville**—*pop pl* (7) PA-2
**Unionville**—*pop pl* (2) TN-4
Unionville—*uninc pl* GA-3
Unionville Acad (historical)—*school* TN-4
Unionville Airp—*airport* MO-7
Unionville Borough—*civil* PA-2
Unionville Brook—*stream* CT-1
Unionville (CCD)—*cens area* TN-4
Unionville Cem—*cemetery* NJ-2
Unionville Cem—*cemetery* TN-4
**Unionville Center**—*pop pl* OH-6
Unionville Ch—*church* NC-3
Unionville Ch—*church* SC-3
Unionville Ch—*church* TX-5
**Unionville (corporate and RR name for Fleming)**—*pop pl* PA-2
Unionville District Sch—*hist pl* OH-6
Unionville Division—*civil* TN-4
Unionville Elem Sch—*school* IN-6
Unionville Elem Sch—*school* PA-2
Unionville First Baptist Ch—*church* TN-4
Unionville Gas Field—*oilfield* LA-4
Unionville Hist Dist—*hist pl* PA-2
Unionville HS—*school* PA-2
Unionville Methodist Ch—*church* TN-4
Unionville MS—*school* IN-6
Unionville Pond—*reservoir* MA-1
Unionville Post Office—*building* TN-4
Unionville (RR name for Unionville Center)—*other* OH-6
Unionville Rsvr—*reservoir* CT-1
Unionville Rsvr—*reservoir* MO-7
Unionville Sch—*school* GA-3
Unionville Sch—*school* MA-1
Unionville Sch—*school* NC-3
Unionville Sch—*school* PA-2
Unionville Sch—*school* TN-4
Unionville Sch—*school* VA-3
Unionville Sch—*school* WI-6
Unionville Tavern—*hist pl* OH-6
Unionville Village Hist Dist—*hist pl* PA-2
Union Vine Ch—*church* LA-4
Union Warehouse—*hist pl* CO-8
**Union Water Works**—*pop pl* PA-2
Union Well Creek—*stream* TX-5
Union Wesley United Methodist Ch—*church* DE-2
Union West Ch—*church* MS-4
Union West Sch—*school* MS-4
Union Wharf—*hist pl* MA-1
Union Wharf—*locale* MA-1
**Union Wharf**—*pop pl* NH-1
Union Whitely Ch—*church* GA-3
**Unionwood Place Subdivision**—*pop pl* UT-8
Union Worship Ch—*church* KY-4
Union Zion Ch—*church* NC-3
Union Zion Ch—*church* PA-2
Union Zion Ch—*church* VA-3
Union Zion Ch (historical)—*church* TN-4
Union Zion Sch—*school* KY-4
**Uniopolis**—*pop pl* OH-6
*Unipat* FM-9
*Unipis* FM-9
Unipisung—*swamp* FM-9
*Unipot* FM-9
Unique—*locale* IA-7
**Unique**—*pop pl* IA-7
Unique Sch—*school* IL-6
**Uniroyal**—*pop pl* OK-5
Uniroyal Tire Company—*facility* GA-3
Unishka Island—*island* AK-9
Unison—*locale* VA-3
Unitaa—*island* MP-9
*Unitaa Island* MP-9
*Unitaa-To* MP-9
*Unitah and Ouray Indian Reservation* UT-8
Unitah Sch—*school* UT-8
Unitarian Ch in Fort Lauderdale—*church* FL-3
Unitarian Church—*hist pl* NH-1
Unitarian Church—*hist pl* SC-3
Unitarian Church of Houlton—*hist pl* ME-1
Unitarian Church of the Messiah—*hist pl* MO-7
Unitarian Fellowship Ch—*church* AL-4
Unitarian Meetinghouse—*hist pl* CT-1
Unitarian Society, The—*hist pl* MA-1
Unitarian Universalist Ch Indian River—*church* FL-3
Unitarian Universalist Ch of Clearwater—*church* FL-3
Unitarian Universalist Ch of Fort Myers—*church* FL-3
Unitarian Universalist Ch of Saint Petersburg—*church* FL-3
Unitarian Universalist Ch of Tallahassee—*church* FL-3
Unitarian-Universalist Church—*hist pl* CT-1
Unitarian Universalist Church—*hist pl* MI-6
Unitarian Universalist Church and Parsonage—*hist pl* MA-1
Unitarian Universalist Congregation Ch—*church* FL-3
Unitarian Universalist Fellowship—*church* FL-3
Unitarian Universalist Fellowship—*church* KS-7
Unitarian Universalist Fellowship Ch—*church* (2) FL-3
Unitarian Universalist Fellowship of Marion—*church* FL-3
Unitarian University Ch of Huntsville—*church* AL-4
Unitary Plan Wind Tunnel—*hist pl* CA-9
Unit A Sch—*school* IL-6
United—*locale* FL-3
**United**—*pop pl* LA-4
**United**—*pop pl* PA-2
**United**—*pop pl* WV-2
United American Freewill Baptist Ch—*church* FL-3
United Amo Ch—*church* MN-6
United Arizona Mine (abandoned)—*mine* AZ-5
United Bank Bldg—*hist pl* CT-1
United Baptist Ch—*church* MS-4
*United Baptist Ch of Christ at Mount Pleasant* TN-4
*United Baptist Ch of Jesus Christ at Harmony* AL-4
United Baptist Church of Lakeport—*hist pl* NH-1
United Beaver Camperland—*park* UT-8
United Brethren Camp—*locale* ID-8
United Brethren Camp—*park* IN-6
United Brethren Cem—*cemetery* (2) IN-6
United Brethren Cem—*cemetery* (2) MN-6
United Brethren Cem—*cemetery* MO-7
United Brethren Cem—*cemetery* ND-7
United Brethren Cem—*cemetery* WI-6
United Brethren Ch—*church* IL-6
United Brethren Ch—*church* (2) KS-7
United Brethren Ch—*church* KY-4
United Brethren Ch—*church* (4) MI-6
United Brethren Ch—*church* (5) NE-7
United Brethren Ch—*church* (2) OH-6
United Brethren Ch—*church* OK-5
United Brethren Ch—*church* (3) WI-6
United Brethren Church Camp—*locale* MI-6
United Brethren Church (historical)—*locale* MO-7
United Brethren in Christ—*hist pl* OH-6
United Brick Corporation Brick Complex—*hist pl* DC-2
United Brotherhood Cem—*cemetery* NJ-2
United Cape Cod Cranberry Company Dam Number 2—*dam* MA-1
United Cape Cod Cranberry Company Number 1—*dam* MA-1
United Catholic Cem—*cemetery* NY-2
United Cem—*cemetery* ID-8
United Cem—*cemetery* IA-7
United Cem—*cemetery* KS-7
United Cem—*cemetery* (2) MN-6
United Cem—*cemetery* NE-7
United Cem—*cemetery* (2) ND-7
United Cem—*cemetery* OH-6
United Cem—*cemetery* (2) PA-2
United Cem—*cemetery* (4) SD-7
United Center Sch—*school* KS-7
United Cerebral Palsy Sch of Panama City—*school* FL-3
*United Ch* MS-4
United Ch—*church* (4) AL-4
United Ch—*church* (5) AR-4
United Ch—*church* (3) FL-3
United Ch—*church* (2) GA-3
United Ch—*church* IL-6
United Ch—*church* (2) IA-7
United Ch—*church* (8) LA-4
United Ch—*church* (2) ME-1
United Ch—*church* MA-1
United Ch—*church* MI-6
United Ch—*church* MN-6
United Ch—*church* (4) MS-4
United Ch—*church* (2) MO-7
United Ch—*church* NJ-2
United Ch—*church* NY-2
United Ch—*church* NC-3
United Ch—*church* (2) OH-6
United Ch—*church* (2) OK-5
United Ch—*church* (5) PA-2
United Ch—*church* (2) SD-7
United Ch—*church* (2) TN-4
United Ch—*church* (4) TX-5
United Ch—*church* VA-3
United Ch—*church* (5) WI-6
United Charities Bldg Complex—*hist pl* NY-2
United Ch in Tallahassee—*church* FL-3
United Ch of Christ—*church* FL-3
United Ch of Christ Congregation—*church* UT-8
United Ch of God by Faith—*church* FL-3
*United Ch of Huntsville* AL-4
United Ch of Practical Christianity—*church* MS-4
United Ch of Religious Science—*church* FL-3
United Christian Ch—*church* MS-4
United Christian Sch—*school* FL-3
United Church, The—*church* AL-4
United Church of Canastota—*hist pl* NY-2
*United Church of Christ* SD-7
United Church of Christ—*hist pl* SD-7
United Church of Christ, Congregational—*hist pl* SD-7
United Church of Christ in Keene—*hist pl* NH-1
United Church of Huntington—*hist pl* OH-6
United Church Seminary—*hist pl* MN-6
United Community Ch—*church* OH-6
United Community Pentecostal Ch—*church* MS-4
United Congregational Church—*hist pl* CT-1
United Congregational Church—*hist pl* RI-1
United Consol Sch—*school* TX-5
United Copper No 1 Mine—*mine* WA-9
United Copper No 2 Mine—*mine* WA-9
United Day Sch—*school* TX-5
United Eastern Mine—*mine* AZ-5
United Electric Co. Bldg—*hist pl* MA-1
United Electronics Institute—*school* FL-3
United Elem Sch—*school* PA-2
United Emanuel Ch—*church* NM-5
United First Parish Church (Unitarian) of Quincy—*hist pl* MA-1
United Freewill Baptist Ch—*church* AL-4
United Hebrew Cem—*cemetery* MD-2
United Hebrew Cem—*cemetery* MN-6
United Hebrew Cem—*cemetery* NY-2
United Hebrew Sch—*school* MI-6
United Hebrew Sch—*school* NJ-2
United Holiness Ch—*church* AL-4
United Holiness Ch—*church* OH-6
United House of Prayer—*church* NC-3
United House of Prayer Ch—*church* AL-4
United Illuminating Company Bldg—*hist pl* CT-1
**United Industrial Park**—*pop pl* NC-3
United Jewish Cem—*cemetery* OH-6
United Jewish Center Cem—*cemetery* CT-1
United Joint HS—*school* PA-2
United Junction—*locale* OR-9
*United Junior Senior HS* PA-2
United Laymen Bible Student Tabernacle—*hist pl* WI-6
United Lutheran Cem—*cemetery* MN-6
United Lutheran Ch—*church* ND-7
United Memorial Gardens—*cemetery* MI-6
United Methodist Camp—*locale* FL-3
*United Methodist Campground Tabernacle* AL-4
United Methodist Ch—*church* AR-4
United Methodist Ch—*church* FL-3
United Methodist Ch—*church* GA-3
United Methodist Ch—*church* (2) MI-6
United Methodist Ch—*church* MO-7
United Methodist Ch—*church* MT-8
United Methodist Ch—*church* PA-2
United Methodist Ch—*church* TN-4
United Methodist Ch of the Savior—*church* IN-6
United Methodist Ch (Price)—*church* UT-8
United Methodist Christian Science Society Park City Community Ch—*church* UT-8
United Methodist Church—*hist pl* FL-3
United Methodist Church—*hist pl* (2) NY-2
United Methodist Church—*hist pl* (3) OH-6
United Methodist Church, The—*church* DE-2
United Methodist Church and Parsonage—*hist pl* NY-2
United Methodist Church of Batavia—*hist pl* IL-6
United Mine—*mine* NM-5
United Mission—*church* NY-2
United Missionary Ch—*church* MI-6
United Missions Sch—*school* MI-6
United Motor Service Bldg—*hist pl* OH-6
United Nations HQ—*building* NY-2
United Nations New York (United Nations)—*building* NY-2
United Nations Park—*park* CO-8
United Nations Tablet—*summit* UT-8
United Norwegian Ch—*church* SD-7
United Oaks Sch—*school* MI-6
United Oatman Mine—*mine* AZ-5
United Orthodox Hebrew Congregation—*church* IN-6
United Pentecostal Center Ch—*church* AL-4
*United Pentecostal Ch* AL-4
United Pentecostal Ch—*church* AL-4
United Pentecostal Ch—*church* AR-4
United Pentecostal Ch—*church* (5) FL-3
United Pentecostal Ch—*church* (2) LA-4
United Pentecostal Ch—*church* MI-6
United Pentecostal Ch—*church* OK-5
United Pentecostal Ch (Midvale)—*church* UT-8
United Pentecostal Ch of Gautier—*church* MS-4
United Pentecostal Ch of Hollywood—*church* FL-3
United Pentecostal Ch of Orlando—*church* FL-3
United Pentecostal Ch of West Palm Beach—*church* FL-3
United Pentecostal Ch (Roy)—*church* UT-8
United Pilgrim Ch—*church* OH-6
United Presbyterian Cem—*cemetery* PA-2
United Presbyterian Church—*hist pl* ID-8
United Presbyterian Church, Summerset—*hist pl* IA-7
United Presbyterian Church and Rectory—*hist pl* OR-9
United Presbyterian Church of Canehill—*hist pl* AR-4
United Presbyterian Homes—*building* TX-5

University Mine (underground)—mine ... AL-4
University Mobile Home Park—locale ... AZ-5
University MS—school ... IN-6
University Mtn—summit ... MT-8
University Museum—hist pl ... MA-1
University Of Akron—school ... OH-6
University Of Akron Memorial Stadium—other ... OH-6
University of Alabama—school ... AL-4
University of Alabama Birmingham—school ... AL-4
University of Alabama Birmingham Airp—airport ... AL-4
*University of Alabama Extension* ... AL-4
University of Alabama Golf Course—locale ... AL-4
University of Alabama Huntsville Center—school ... AL-4
University of Alabama Med Ctr—hospital ... AL-4
University Of Alabama (Northington Campus)—school ... AL-4
University of Alabama Research Institute—school ... AL-4
University of Alaska—school ... AK-9
University of Arizona—school ... AZ-5
University of Arizona Agricultural Experimen—other ... AZ-5
University of Arizona Agricultural Experiment Station—other (2) ... AZ-5
University of Arizona Campus Hist Dist—hist pl ... AZ-5
University of Arizona Cotton Research Center—other ... AZ-5
University of Arizona Experimental Farm—other (2) ... AZ-5
University of Arizona Experiment Farm—other ... AZ-5
University of Arizona Farm—other ... AZ-5
University of Arizona Geochronology Laboratories—other ... AZ-5
University of Arizona Hosp and Med Ctr—hospital ... AZ-5
University of Arizona Observatory—other ... AZ-5
University of Arkansas—school (2) ... AR-4
University Of Arkansas Agricultural Experimental StaTION—other ... AR-4
University of Arkansas Cammack Campus—school ... AR-4
University Of Arkansas Experimental Farm—other (2) ... AR-4
University of Arkansas Experimental Farm—park ... AR-4
University of Arkansas Experimental Farm—school ... AR-4
University Of Arkansas Experiment Station—school ... AR-4
University Of Arkansas Institute Of Technology—school ... AR-4
University Of Arkansas Med Ctr—school ... AR-4
University of Baltimore—school ... MD-2
University Of Bridgeport—school ... CT-1
University of California—school ... CA-9
University of California Agricultural Field—school ... CA-9
University of California At Los Angeles—school ... CA-9
University of California At Santa Barbara—school ... CA-9
University of California Cow Camp—locale ... CA-9
**University of California-Davis Campus**—pop pl ... CA-9
University of California Engineering Field Sch—school ... CA-9
University of California Experiment Station—school ... CA-9
University of California Extension—school ... CA-9
University of California Forestry Camp—locale ... CA-9
University of California Imperial Valley—school ... CA-9
University of California Irvine—school ... CA-9
University of California Marine Laboratory—school ... CA-9
University of California Med Ctr—hospital ... CA-9
University of California Riverside—school ... CA-9
University of California San Diego—school ... CA-9
University of California Santa Cruz—school ... CA-9
University of Central Florida—school ... FL-3
University of Central Florida Library—building ... FL-3
University Of Chicago—school ... IL-6
University Of Cincinnati—school ... OH-6
University Of Cincinnati Observatory—building ... OH-6
University of Colorado—school ... CO-8
University of Colorado Camp—locale ... CO-8
University of Colorado Observatory—other ... CO-8
University Of Connecticut—school ... CT-1
University of Connecticut—school ... CT-1
University of Connecticut Experiment Farm—school ... CT-1
University of Connecticut Sch of Law—school ... CT-1
University of Conn Sch of Law—school ... CT-1
University Of Corpus Christi—school ... TX-5
University of Dallas—school ... TX-5
University of Dayton—school ... OH-6
University of Delaware—school ... DE-2
University of Delaware Experiment Station—school ... DE-2
University of Delaware Stadium—building ... DE-2
University of Denver—school ... CO-8
University of Detroit—school (2) ... MI-6
University of Detroit HS—school ... MI-6
University Of Dubuque—school ... IA-7
University of Evansville—school ... IN-6
University of Florida Agricultural Experimental Farm—school ... FL-3
University of Florida Agricultural Experimental Station—school ... FL-3
University of Florida Agricultural Research Center—school ... FL-3
University of Florida Beef Research Unit—school ... FL-3
University of Florida Experimental Farm—school ... FL-3
University of Florida Experimental Station—school (2) ... FL-3
University of Florida Field Laboratory—school ... FL-3
University of Florida Library—building ... FL-3
University of Florida Lighted Data Tower—tower ... FL-3
University of Florida State Experimental Farm—school ... FL-3
University of Florida Suwannee Valley Experiment Station—locale ... FL-3
University Of Georgia—school ... GA-3
University Of Georgia Experimental Farm—school ... GA-3
University Of Georgia Medical Coll—school ... GA-3
University Of Georgia (Off Campus Center)—school ... GA-3
University of Georgia Poultry Research Center—school ... GA-3
University Of Georgia Research Labs—school ... GA-3
University of Georgia Sch of Forestry—school ... GA-3
University of Georgia (Whitehall Farm)—school ... GA-3
University of Guam—school ... GU-9
University of Hartford—school ... CT-1
University Of Hawaii—school ... HI-9
University of Hawaii Agricultural Experiment Station—other ... HI-9
University of Hawaii Agricultural Experiment Station—school ... HI-9
University of Hawaii Experimental Station—school (3) ... HI-9
University of Hawaii (Hilo Campus)—school ... HI-9
University of Hawaii Marine Laboratory—school ... HI-9
University of Hawaii Solar Observatory—building ... HI-9
University of Holly Springs (historical)—school ... MS-4
University Of Houston—school ... TX-5
University of Idaho—school ... ID-8
University of Idaho Clark Fork Field Campus—school ... ID-8
University of Idaho Gymnasium and Armory—hist pl ... ID-8
University Of Illinois—school ... IL-6
University of Illinois—school ... IL-6
University of Illinois Astronomical Observatory—hist pl ... IL-6
University of Illinois- Willard Airp—airport ... IL-6
University Of Iowa—school ... IA-7
University of Iowa Med Ctr—school ... IA-7
University of Kansas—school ... KS-7
University of Kansas Geology Summer Camp—locale ... CO-8
University of Kansas Med Ctr—hospital ... KS-7
University Of Kentucky—school ... KY-4
University Of Kentucky Agricultural Experimental Station—school (3) ... KY-4
University of Kentucky Community Coll—school (2) ... KY-4
University Of Kentucky Experimental Farm—other ... KY-4
University Of Kentucky Extension Center—school ... KY-4
University Of Kentucky 4-H Camp—locale ... KY-4
University Of Louisville—school ... KY-4
University of Louisville Belknap Campus—hist pl ... KY-4
University Of Louisville Potomological Institution—school ... KY-4
University of Louisville Sch of Medicine—hist pl ... KY-4
University of Louisville Sch of Music—school ... KY-4
University of Maine—school ... ME-1
University of Maine Agriculture Station—other ... ME-1
University of Maine at Orono Hist Dist—hist pl ... ME-1
University of Maine Forest—school ... ME-1
University of Maine Forestry Camp—school ... ME-1
University of Maine ( Portland)—school ... ME-1
University Of Maryland—school ... MD-2
University of Maryland Eastern Shore—school ... MD-2
University Of Maryland Plant Research Farm—school ... MD-2
University of Maryland Sch of Medicine—school ... MD-2
University of Maryland Tobacco Experiment Farm—school ... MD-2
University of Massachusetts—school (2) ... MA-1
University of Massachusetts Coll of Agriculture—school ... MA-1
University of Massachusetts Marine Station—building ... MA-1
University of Massachusetts Research Center—building ... MA-1
University of Massachussetts Medical Sch—school ... MA-1
University of Miami—building ... FL-3
University of Miami—school ... FL-3
University of Miami Hosp and Clinics—hospital ... FL-3
University of Miami-Jackson Memorial Med Ctr—school ... FL-3
University of Miami (Marine Laboratory)—school ... FL-3
University of Miami (Miami University)—uninc pl ... FL-3
University of Miami (South Campus)—school ... FL-3
University of Michigan—school (2) ... MI-6
University of Michigan Biological Station—school ... MI-6
University of Michigan Botanical Gardens—other ... MI-6
University Of Michigan Central Campus Hist Dist—hist pl ... MI-6
University of Michigan Forestry Camp—locale ... MI-6
University of Michigan Institute of Science—school ... MI-6
University of Michigan Med Ctr—hospital ... MI-6
University of Michigan Stadium—other ... MI-6
University Of Minnesota—school ... MN-6
University of Minnesota at Morris—school ... MN-6
University of Minnesota Duluth Branch—school ... MN-6
University of Minnesota Experimental Station—other ... MN-6
University of Minnesota Experimental Station—school ... MN-6
University of Minnesota Experiment Station—school ... MN-6
University of Minnesota Forestry Sch—school ... MN-6
University of Minnesota Golf Course—other ... MN-6
University of Minnesota Old Campus Hist Dist—hist pl ... MN-6
University Of Minnesota Rosemount Research Center—other ... MN-6
University Of Minnesota (Saint Paul Campus)—school ... MN-6
University of Minnesota (Southern Sch—school ... MN-6
University Of Mississippi—school ... MS-4
University of Mississippi Med Ctr—hospital ... MS-4
University Of Mississippi Med Ctr Airp—airport ... MS-4
University of Mississippi Seismic Station—locale ... MS-4
University Of Missouri—school ... MO-7
University Of Missouri Ashland Wildlife Reserve—park ... MO-7
University of Missouri at Kansas City—school ... MO-7
University Of Missouri Environmental Health—other ... MO-7
University of Missouri Experimental Farm—other ... MO-7
University Of Missouri Forestry Camp—locale ... MO-7
University of Missouri Geology Camp—locale ... WY-8
University Of Missouri-Rolla—school ... MO-7
University Of Missouri Saint Louis Campus—school ... MO-7
University Of Missouri Weldon Spring Experimental Station—school ... MO-7
University of Montana—school ... MT-8
University of Montevallo—school ... AL-4
University Of Montevallo Dam—dam ... AL-4
*University of Montevallo Lake* ... AL-4
University Of Montevallo Lake—reservoir ... AL-4
University Of Montevallo Lake Dam—dam ... AL-4
University Of N C—post sta ... NC-3
University Of Nebraska—school ... NE-7
University of Nebraska Coll of Agri—school ... NE-7
University Of Nebraska Coll Of Med—school ... NE-7
University Of Nebraska Experimenta Farm—school ... NE-7
University of Nebraska Experimental Station—school ... NE-7
University Of Nebraska Field Lab—school ... NE-7
*University of Nevada Experimental Station* ... NV-8
University of Nevada Farm—school ... NV-8
University of Nevada Reno Hist Dist—hist pl ... NV-8
University of New Hampshire—school ... NH-1
University Of New Mexico—school ... NM-5
University of New Mexico Experimental Farm—school ... NM-5
University of New Mexico (Lawrence Ranch)—school ... NM-5
University of New Mexico Lodge, Bldg 219 Albuquerque Indian School—hist pl ... NM-5
University of North Alabama—school ... AL-4
University Of North Carolina—school ... NC-3
University of North Carolina - Asheville—school ... NC-3
University of North Carolina at Charlotte—school ... NC-3
University Of North Carolina At Wilmington—school ... NC-3
University of North Carolina - Botanical Gardens—school ... NC-3
*University Of North Dakota* ... ND-7
University of North Dakota—school ... ND-7
University of Northern Colorado—school ... CO-8
University Of Northern Iowa—school ... IA-7
University of North Florida—school ... FL-3
University of Notre Dame—school ... IN-6
University of Notre Dame: Main and South Quadrangles—hist pl ... IN-6
University Of Oklahoma—school ... OK-5
University Of Oklahoma Research Park—school ... OK-5
University Of Oklahoma South Campus—school ... OK-5
University of Oklahoma Summer Geology Camp—locale ... CO-8
University Of Omaha—school ... NE-7
University of Oregon—school ... OR-9
University of Oregon Dental Sch—school ... OR-9
University of Oregon Health Sciences Center Heliport—airport ... OR-9
University of Oregon Housing—school ... OR-9
University of Oregon Medical Sch—school ... OR-9
University of Oregon Museum of Art—hist pl ... OR-9
University of Pacific Marine Station of Biology—school ... CA-9
University of Palm Beach Library—building ... FL-3
University Of Pennsylvania—school ... PA-2
University of Pennsylvania Campus Hist Dist—hist pl ... PA-2
University Of Pennsylvania Graduate Sch—school ... PA-2
University of Pittsburgh—school ... PA-2
University of Pittsburgh, Bradford Campus—school ... PA-2
University Of Pittsburgh At Titusville—school ... PA-2
University of Pittsburgh - Johnstown Campus—school ... PA-2
University of Portland—school ... OR-9
University of Puerto Rico (Aguadilla)—school ... PR-3
University of Puerto Rico (Arecibo)—school ... PR-3
University of Puerto Rico (Cayey)—school ... PR-3
University of Puerto Rico (Mayaguez)—school ... PR-3
University of Puerto Rico (Rio Piedras)—school ... PR-3
University of Puerto Rico (San Juan)—school ... PR-3
University of Puerto Rico Tower and Quadrangle—hist pl ... PR-3
University of Puget Sound—school ... WA-9
University of Redlands—school ... CA-9
University Of Richmond—school ... VA-3
University Of Rochester—school ... NY-2
University of Saint Thomas—school ... TX-5
University of San Diego—school ... CA-9
University of San Francisco—school ... CA-9
University of Santa Clara—school ... CA-9
University of Sarasota—school ... FL-3
University of Science Arts—post sta ... OK-5
University of Scranton—school ... PA-2
University of South Alabama—school ... AL-4
University of South Alabama Brookley Complex—school ... AL-4
University of South Alabama Med Ctr—hospital ... AL-4
University Of South Carolina—school ... SC-3
University Of South Carolina (Aiken Branch)—school ... SC-3
University Of South Carolina Extension College—school ... SC-3
University of South Carolina Regional Campus—school (2) ... SC-3
University of South Dakota—school ... SD-7
University of South Dakota at Springfield—school ... SD-7
University of Southern California—school ... CA-9
University of Southern Colorado—school ... CO-8
University of Southern Florida—school ... FL-3
*University of Southern Mississipp-Gulf Park Campus* ... MS-4
University of Southern Mississippi—school ... MS-4
University of Southern Mississippi Golf Course Lake Dam—dam ... MS-4
University of South Florida—school ... FL-3
University of South Florida, University Library—building ... FL-3
University of South Florida (Saint Petersburg Campus)—school ... FL-3
University of South Florida (Sarasota Campus)—school ... FL-3
University Of Southwestern Louisiana—school ... LA-4
University of Tampa—school ... FL-3
University of Tampa, Merl Kelce Library—building ... FL-3
University of Tampa Stadium—locale ... FL-3
University of Tennessee Agriculture Extension—school ... TN-4
University Of Tennessee—school ... TN-4
University of Tennessee—school ... TN-4
University of Tennessee Agricultural Experimental Farm—locale ... TN-4
University of Tennessee Agricultural Experiment Station—locale ... TN-4
University of Tennessee Agricultural Extension Service—locale ... TN-4
University of Tennessee Agriculture Experiment Station—school ... TN-4
University of Tennessee Agriculture Research Laboratory—school ... TN-4
University of Tennessee Animal Science Field Laboratory—locale ... TN-4
University of Tennessee Arboretum—locale ... TN-4
University of Tennessee Chattanooga—school ... TN-4
University of Tennessee Fxperimental Farm—locale ... TN-4
University of Tennessee Experimental Farm Lake—reservoir ... TN-4
University of Tennessee Experimental Farm Lake Dam—dam ... TN-4
University of Tennessee Hospital Airp—airport ... TN-4
University of Tennessee Med Ctr—hospital ... TN-4
University of Tennessee Space Institute—school ... TN-4
University Of Texas—school ... TX-5
University of Texas at El Paso—uninc pl ... TX-5
University of Texas at San Antonio—school ... TX-5
University Of Texas Balcones Research Center—school ... TX-5
University of Texas El Paso—school ... TX-5
University of Texas Marine Science Institute—school ... TX-5
University of Texas Medical Coll—school ... TX-5
University of Texas Sch of Dentistry—school ... TX-5
University of Texas Tumor Institute—school ... TX-5
University of the District of Columbia—school ... DC-2
University of The Pacific—school ... CA-9
University of the South—school ... TN-4
University Of The South—uninc pl ... TN-4
University Of Tulsa—school ... OK-5
University Of Utah—school ... UT-8
University of Utah Circle—hist pl ... UT-8
University of Utah Hosp—hospital ... UT-8
University of Utah Med Ctr Heliport—airport ... UT-8
University of Vermont—school ... VT-1
University of Vermont Morgan Horse Farm—hist pl ... VT-1
University Of Virginia—school ... VA-3
University Of Virginia Biological Station—school ... VA-3
University Of Virginia Eastern Shore Branch—school ... VA-3
University Of Virginia Hist Dist—hist pl ... VA-3
University of Virginia (Patrick Henry Branch)—school ... VA-3
University of Virginia (Roanoke Center)—school ... VA-3
University Of Washington—school ... WA-9
University Of Washington Arboretum—park ... WA-9
University of West Florida—school ... FL-3
University of Wisconsin—school (2) ... WI-6
University of Wisconsin Arboretum—school ... WI-6
University of Wisconsin At Green Bay—school ... WI-6
University of Wisconsin at Milwaukee—school ... WI-6
University Of Wisconsin (Baraboo-Sauk Co Center)—school ... WI-6
University of Wisconsin (Barron County Center)—school ... WI-6
University of Wisconsin Eau Claire—school ... WI-6
University of Wisconsin Experimental Farm—school ... WI-6
University of Wisconsin Experiment Station—school ... WI-6
University of Wisconsin (Extension)—school ... WI-6
University of Wisconsin Farm—other ... WI-6
University of Wisconsin (La Crosse Campus)—school ... WI-6
University of Wisconsin (Medford Campus)—school ... WI-6
University of Wisconsin River Falls—school ... WI-6
University of Wisconsin Rock Co Campus—school ... WI-6
University of Wisconsin Surveying Camp—locale ... WI-6
University Of Wyoming—school ... WY-8
University Of Wyoming Agronomy Farm—locale ... WY-8
University Of Wyoming Camp—locale ... WY-8
University Of Wyoming Dairy Farm—locale ... WY-8
University Of Wyoming Experimental Station—school ... WY-8
University Of Wyoming Experiment Station—locale ... WY-8
University Of Wyoming Science Camp—locale ... WY-8
University (Ohio State University)—school ... OH-6
University Oil Field—oilfield ... LA-4
University (Oklahoma Baptist University)—uninc pl ... OK-5
University-Oxford Airp—airport ... MS-4
*University Park* ... CO-8
University Park—CDP ... NM-5
University Park—park ... AL-4
University Park—park ... AZ-5
University Park—park ... FL-3
University Park—park ... KS-7
University Park—park ... ND-7
University Park—park ... OR-9
University Park—park ... TN-4
University Park—park ... WI-6
**University Park**—pop pl (2) ... FL-3
**University Park**—pop pl (2) ... IL-6
**University Park**—pop pl ... IA-7
**University Park**—pop pl ... MD-2
**University Park**—pop pl ... MO-7
**University Park**—pop pl ... OR-9
**University Park**—pop pl ... PA-2
**University Park**—pop pl ... TX-5
University Park—post sta ... NC-3
University Park—uninc pl ... CA-9
University Park—uninc pl ... FL-3
University Park—uninc pl (2) ... TX-5
*University Park Airp* ... PA-2
University Park Airp—airport ... PA-2
University Park Christian Ch—church ... IN-6
University Park Elem Sch—school ... FL-3
University Park Mall—locale ... IN-6
University Park (Penn State College)—uninc pl ... PA-2
University Park Plaza—locale ... PA-2
University Park Sch—school ... AK-9
University Park Sch—school ... CO-8
University Park Sch—school ... MD-2
University Park Sch—school ... NC-3
University Park Sch—school ... PA-2
University Park Sch—school ... TX-5
University Park Shop Ctr—other ... PA-2
**University Park (subdivision)**—pop pl ... AL-4
**University Park (subdivision)**—pop pl ... MA-1
**University Park (subdivision)**—pop pl ... TX-5
**University Park Subdivision**—pop pl ... UT-8
University Peak—summit ... AK-9
University Peak—summit ... CA-9
University (Phillips University)—uninc pl ... OK-5
*University Place* ... TN-4
**University Place**—pop pl ... LA-4
**University Place**—pop pl ... NE-7
**University Place**—pop pl ... NC-3
**University Place**—pop pl ... WA-9
University Place—post sta ... IA-7
University Place—post sta ... TX-5
**University Place Addition (subdivision)**—pop pl ... UT-8
*University Place Elementary School* ... AL-4
University Place Park—park ... NE-7
University Place Sch—school (2) ... AL-4
University Place Sta.—post sta ... WA-9
**University Place (subdivision)**—pop pl ... AL-4
**University Place Subdivision**—pop pl ... UT-8
University Plaza—locale ... IN-6
University Plaza Shop Ctr—locale ... AL-4
University Plaza (Shop Ctr)—locale (4) ... FL-3
University Plaza Shop Ctr—locale ... NC-3
*University Point* ... MN-6
University Point—cape ... WA-9
University Point Campground—locale ... IL-6
University Pond—lake ... OH-6
University Post Office—building ... AZ-5
University Post Office (historical)—building ... AL-4
University Presbyterian Ch—church ... AL-4
University Quarry—other ... WY-8
University Range—range ... AK-9
University Research Park—locale ... NC-3
University Sch—school ... CA-9
University Sch—school ... GA-3
University Sch—school ... IL-6
University Sch—school ... LA-4
University Sch—school ... OH-6
University Sch—school ... TN-4
University Sch—school ... WA-9
University Sch (historical)—school ... TN-4
University Sch of Nova Univ—school ... FL-3
*University School* ... AL-4
University Settlement House—hist pl ... NY-2
University Shoal (historical)—bar ... AL-4
University Shop Ctr—locale ... AL-4
University Shop Ctr—locale ... FL-3
University Square—locale ... NC-3
University Square Shop Ctr—locale ... AZ-5
University Square (Shop Ctr)—locale (2) ... FL-3
**University (subdivision)**—pop pl ... MS-4
**University Subdivision**—pop pl ... UT-8
University Tank—reservoir ... NM-5
University Terrace Sch—school ... LA-4
University Training Sch (historical)—school ... AL-4
University United Congregational Ch—church ... FL-3
University United Methodist Ch—church ... IN-6
University United Methodist Ch—church ... KS-7
*University United Methodist Church* ... AL-4
University (University of Alabama)—uninc pl ... AL-4
University (University of Arizona)—uninc pl ... AZ-5
University (University of Florida)—uninc pl ... FL-3
**University (University of Hawaii)**—pop pl ... HI-9
University (University of Kansas)—uninc pl ... KS-7
University (University of Oregon)—uninc pl ... OR-9
University (University of Syracuse)—uninc pl ... NY-2
University (University of Texas)—uninc pl ... TX-5
University (University of Virginia)—uninc pl ... VA-3
University View—locale ... TN-4
**University View**—pop pl ... OH-6
**University Village**—pop pl ... UT-8
University Village—uninc pl ... WA-9
University Village Mall—locale ... KS-7
University Village (Shop Ctr)—locale ... FL-3
University Watershed Rsvr Project—reservoir ... PA-2
University Woodlands Park—park ... FL-3
University Yacht Club—other ... GA-3
**Univeter**—pop pl ... GA-3
Univ. of AR at Monticello (State School)—school ... AR-4
Univ Of Connecticut (Waterbury Branch)—school ... CT-1
Univ Of Idaho Agr Experimental Station—locale ... ID-8
Univ Of Idaho Agr Experiment Station—school ... ID-8
Univ of Idaho Agriculture Experiment Station—school ... ID-8
*Unjoined Rock* ... UT-8
Unkamet Brook—stream ... MA-1
*Unkappi* ... FM-9
Unkar Creek—stream ... AZ-5
Unkar Creek Rapids—rapids ... AZ-5
*Unkaseri* ... PW-9
*Unkateme Island* ... MA-1
*Unka-timpe-wa-wince-pooh-ich* ... UT-8
*Unkerseri Island* ... PW-9
Unkety Brook—stream ... MA-1
Unknown Bay—bay ... FL-3
Unknown Bottom—bend ... UT-8
Unknown Branch—stream ... WV-2
Unknown Creek—stream ... MT-8
Unknown Glacier—glacier ... AK-9
Unknown Gulch—valley ... ID-8
*Unknown Mountains* ... UT-8
Unknown Pass—channel ... LA-4
Unknown Pond—lake (3) ... ME-1
Unknown Pond—lake (2) ... NH-1
Unknown Pond—lake ... NY-2
Unknown Pond—lake (2) ... VT-1
*Unknown River* ... NV-8
Unknown Soldier Monmt—pillar ... NY-2
Unknown Stream—stream ... ME-1
Unknown Tank—reservoir ... AZ-5
*Unkonoonuc Mountains* ... NH-1
Unkpapa Peak—summit ... SD-7
Unks Dam—dam ... ND-7
Unks Windmill—locale ... NM-5
Unky, Lake—lake ... MI-6
Unload Lake—lake ... MN-6
Unlucky Island—island ... AK-9
Unmanokuk Creek—stream ... AK-9
Unmans Cutoff Lake—lake ... OK-5
Unnamed Battery—hist pl ... SC-3
Unnamed Battery No. 1—hist pl ... SC-3
Unnamed Creek—stream ... MT-8
Unnamed Creek—stream ... WY-8
Unnamed Lake—lake ... MT-8
Unnamed Spring Creek—stream ... MT-8
Unnamed Wash—stream ... CA-9
Unnene—bar ... FM-9
*Unnugot Pass* ... FM-9
*Unnun En Sopuram* ... FM-9
Unnuno—well ... FM-9
Uno—locale ... AR-4
Uno—locale ... KY-4
Uno—locale ... PA-2
Uno—locale ... VA-3
**U-No**—pop pl ... NC-3
**Uno**—pop pl ... WV-2
Uno Basin—basin ... AK-9
Unochop, Unun En—cape ... FM-9
Uno Creek—stream ... AK-9
*Uno Lake* ... MI-6
*Unon En Nameis* ... FM-9
*Unon Grove Church of God* ... MS-4
Unoni—bar ... FM-9
Unon Island—island ... FM-9
Uno Peak—summit ... WA-9

*Unora Park Lake* ... MI-6
Uno Run—*stream* ... IN-6
Unos—*ridge* ... FM-9
Unoso—*spring* ... FM-9
*Unoso, Cape* ... FM-9
Unqua Point—*cape* ... NY-2
Unqua Sch—*school* ... NY-2
*Unquetenarsett Brook* ... MA-1
*Unquetenassett Brook* ... MA-1
*Unquetenorset Brook* ... MA-1
*Unquety* ... MA-1
*Unquety Brook* ... MA-1
*Unquetynasset Brook* ... MA-1
*Unquity Brook* ... MA-1
Unquity Brook—*stream* ... MA-1
*Unquity-Quisset Brook* ... MA-1
Unquomonk Brook—*stream* ... MA-1
Unquomonk Hill—*summit* ... MA-1
Unquomonk Rsvr—*reservoir* ... MA-1
Unquowa Sch—*school* ... CT-1
Unrah Ditch—*canal* ... IN-6
Unreachable Rockshelter (LA 55841)—*hist pl* ... NM-5
Unr Gund Ranch Airp—*airport* ... NV-8
Unroojithok Lake—*lake* ... AK-9
U N Rsvr—*reservoir* ... MT-8
Unruh Cem—*cemetery* ... ND-7
*Unsal Point* ... WA-9
*Unsel Wuap* ... FM-9
Unshagi Site (FS-337, LA-123)—*hist pl* ... NM-5
Unsicker-Craig Ditch—*canal* ... IN-6
Unsworth Sch—*school* ... CA-9
Untermann, Mount—*summit* ... UT-8
Untermeyer Dam—*dam* ... NJ-2
Untermeyer Lake—*reservoir* ... NJ-2
Untermyer Park—*hist pl* ... NY-2
Untermyer Park—*park* ... NY-2
Unthank Ditch—*canal* ... IN-6
**Unthanks**—*pop pl* ... VA-3
Untiedt, Claus, House—*hist pl* ... IA-7
*Untsville* ... IN-6
Unu—*bar* ... FM-9
Unualoha Point—*cape* ... HI-9
*Unubis, Cape* ... FM-9
Unuf, Unun En—*bar* ... FM-9
Unufa, Unun En—*bar* ... FM-9
Unufeisu, Unumen—*cape* ... FM-9
Unufouach—*summit* ... FM-9
*Unufoucho* ... FM-9
Unukanau—*spring* ... FM-9
Unuko—*bar* ... FM-9
Unukop, Unun En—*bar* ... FM-9
Unuk River—*stream* ... AK-9
Unukuchu—*cape* ... FM-9
Unukunkutu, Unun En—*bar* ... FM-9
Unulau—*bay* ... HI-9
*Unulou* ... FM-9
Unum, Unun En—*bar* ... FM-9
Unumenei—*spring* ... FM-9
*Unumou* ... FM-9
Unumun—*spring* ... FM-9
*Unun* ... FM-9
Ununata—*bar* ... FM-9
Ununda Cem—*cemetery* ... KS-7
*Unun En* ... FM-9
*Unun En Amachang* ... FM-9
*Unun En Choisialfa* ... FM-9
*Unun En Choisinlfa* ... FM-9
*Unun En Chosinifa* ... FM-9
*Unun En Elin* ... FM-9
*Unun En Ennin* ... FM-9
*Unun En Epin* ... FM-9
*Unun En Fanikop* ... FM-9
*Unun En Fankop* ... FM-9
*Unun En Faut* ... FM-9
*Unun En Foucho* ... FM-9
*Unun En Ian* ... FM-9
*Unun En Kucha* ... FM-9
*Unun En Kuchua* ... FM-9
*Unun En Michikei* ... FM-9
*Unun En Nafouoch* ... FM-9
*Unun En Nameis* ... FM-9
*Unun En Neauwo* ... FM-9
*Unun En Neawachang* ... FM-9
*Ununen Nekuk* ... FM-9
*Unun En Nemeis* ... FM-9
*Unun En Nenimokut* ... FM-9
*Unun En Nepenas* ... FM-9
*Unun En Nepon* ... FM-9
*Unun En Nepor* ... FM-9
*Unun En Nikanap* ... FM-9
*Unun En Nukanap* ... FM-9
*Unun En Nukunachaw* ... FM-9
*Unun En Nukunau* ... FM-9
*Unun En Onoet* ... FM-9
*Unun En Onoit* ... FM-9
*Unun En Penianok* ... FM-9
*Unun En Penianuk* ... FM-9
*Unun En Piesich* ... FM-9
*Unun En Sapotiu* ... FM-9
*Unun En Sapou* ... FM-9
*Unun En Sapu* ... FM-9
*Unun En Saton* ... FM-9
*Unun En Sopu* ... FM-9
*Unun En Taweneon* ... FM-9
*UnunEn Tenio* ... FM-9
*Unun En Tenion* ... FM-9
*Unun En Tomu* ... FM-9
*Unun En Unap* ... FM-9
*Unun En Unifei* ... FM-9
*Unun En Unikei* ... FM-9
*Unun En Unikopi* ... FM-9
*Unun En Winifeisu* ... FM-9
*Unun En Winikai* ... FM-9
Ungungoung—*summit* ... FM-9
Ununiowu—*bar* ... FM-9
*Ununo* ... FM-9
**Ununo**—*pop pl* ... FM-9
Ununo, Oror En—*locale* ... FM-9
*Unun Och* ... FM-9
*Unun Och Win* ... FM-9
Ununomoch—*bar* ... FM-9
Ununonona—*bar* ... FM-9
Ununou—*beach* ... FM-9
**Ununu, Oror En**—*pop pl* ... FM-9
*Unun Uninefou* ... FM-9
Unup—*bay* ... FM-9
Unupeias—*bar* ... FM-9
Unupennechonkis—*bar* ... FM-9
Unupennechonnap—*bar* ... FM-9
Unupi—*bar* ... FM-9
Unupuker, Oror En—*locale* ... FM-9
Unupuker Ch—*church* ... FM-9
Unupun—*bar* ... FM-9
Unus—*bay* ... FM-9
Unus—*locale* ... WV-2
Unus Ch—*church* ... WV-2
Unuso—*beach* ... FM-9
Unutiu—*bar* ... FM-9
Unuwo—*locale* ... FM-9
Unversity Of Iowa Observatory—*school* ... IA-7
Unzicker-Cook House—*hist pl* ... OH-6
*Uo Cone* ... HI-9
*Uoharee River* ... NC-3
*Uola* ... FM-9
*Uola Insel* ... FM-9
*Uonean* ... FM-9
*Uoon Piyepi* ... FM-9
*Uoraa-to* ... MP-9
*Uoraru* ... MP-9
Uorikku—*island* ... MP-9
*Uorikku-To* ... MP-9
Uoruchiyakoaru—*bar* ... MP-9
*Uorumetchi-to* ... MP-9
*Uoruuoru* ... FM-9
*Uosech* ... PW-9
*Uossha To* ... MP-9
*Uosshiya-to* ... MP-9
*Uotcha-to* ... MP-9
*Uotchie* ... MP-9
*Uoten* ... FM-9
*Uoten Island* ... FM-9
*Uotjaa* ... MP-9
*Uotsusha To* ... MP-9
*Uotto-to* ... MP-9
**Upalco**—*pop pl* ... UT-8
Upalco Cem—*cemetery* ... UT-8
Upaliko—*locale* ... MO-7
Upaliko Pond—*locale* ... MO-7
Upaliko Pond—*reservoir* ... MO-7
Up and Down Lake—*lake* ... FL-3
Upapak Point—*cape* ... AK-9
**Upatoi**—*pop pl* ... GA-3
Upatoi Ch—*church* ... GA-3
Upatoi Creek—*stream* ... GA-3
*Upatoie* ... GA-3
*Upatoie Creek* ... GA-3
U P Canyon—*valley* ... UT-8
Up Cem—*cemetery* ... OH-6
Upchurch—*locale* ... KY-4
Upchurch—*locale* ... NC-3
Upchurch—*locale* ... TN-4
Upchurch Boy Scout Camp—*locale* ... NC-3
Upchurch Branch—*stream* ... KY-4
Upchurch Branch—*stream* ... TN-4
Upchurch Cem—*cemetery* ... AR-4
Upchurch Cem—*cemetery* ... KS-7
Upchurch Cem—*cemetery* (4) ... TN-4
Upchurch Cem—*cemetery* ... TX-5
Upchurch Ch—*church* ... TN-4
Upchurches Pond—*reservoir* ... NC-3
Upchurches Pond Dam—*dam* ... NC-3
Upchurch Hollow—*valley* ... KY-4
Upchurch House—*hist pl* ... TX-5
Upchurch Lake Dam—*dam* ... AL-4
Upchurch Pond—*lake* ... FL-3
Upchurch Post Office (historical)—*building* ... TN-4
Upchurch Sch—*school* ... NC-3
Upco—*locale* ... LA-4
**Upco**—*pop pl* ... WA-9
**Upcounty (trailer park)**—*pop pl* ... DE-2
**Updegraff**—*pop pl* ... IA-7
Updegraff Ridge—*ridge* ... CA-9
Updegrave Rsvr—*reservoir* ... OR-9
*Updike* ... VA-3
Updike—*locale* ... MS-4
Updike, Robert L., House—*hist pl* ... VA-3
Updike Mine—*mine* ... NV-8
Updike Run—*stream* ... PA-2
Updike Sch—*school* ... SD-7
*Updikes Harbor* ... RI-1
Updraft Arch—*arch* ... UT-8
Updyke—*locale* ... MI-6
Upeart Park—*park* ... AZ-5
*Upeen, Mount* ... FM-9
*Upel* ... FM-9
*Upen* ... FM-9
*Upham* ... WA-9
Upham—*locale* ... NM-5
**Upham**—*pop pl* ... ND-7
Upham, Gov. William H., House—*hist pl* ... WI-6
*Upham Branch* ... VA-3
Upham Brook—*stream* ... VA-3
Upham Cem—*cemetery* ... CA-9
Upham Cem—*cemetery* ... CT-1
Upham Creek—*stream* (2) ... MT-8
Upham Gulch—*valley* ... CO-8
Upham Sch—*school* ... MA-1
**Uphams Corner (subdivision)**—*pop pl* ... MA-1
**Upham (Town of)**—*pop pl* ... WI-6
Upham-Walker House—*hist pl* ... NH-1
Upham-Wright House—*hist pl* ... OH-6
Uphans Rsvr—*reservoir* ... MT-8
*Uphapee Creek* ... AL-4
Uphapee Creek—*stream* ... AL-4
Uphaus Ditch—*canal* ... IN-6
Uphaus Ranch—*locale* ... MT-8
Upheaval Bottom—*bend* ... UT-8
Upheaval Canyon—*valley* ... UT-8
Upheaval Dome—*summit* ... UT-8
Upheaval Dome Trail—*trail* ... UT-8
Uphill Creek—*stream* (2) ... MT-8
Uphill Creek—*stream* ... OK-5
Uphill Falls Brook—*stream* ... NY-2
Uphill Run—*stream* ... IN-6
Uphill Water Hole—*spring* ... ID-8
Uphilly Bowers Trail—*trail* ... OK-5
*Upjohn* ... MI-6
Upjohn Playground—*park* ... MI-6
Upjohn Pond—*lake* ... MI-6
Upjohn Sch—*school* ... MI-6
Upkuarok Creek—*stream* ... AK-9
U P Lake—*lake* ... ID-8
Upland—*locale* ... AR-4
Upland—*locale* ... KS-7
Upland—*locale* ... LA-4
Upland—*locale* ... PA-2
Upland—*locale* ... TX-5
Upland—*locale* ... WV-2
**Upland**—*pop pl* ... CA-9
**Upland**—*pop pl* ... IN-6
**Upland**—*pop pl* ... KS-7
**Upland**—*pop pl* ... NE-7
**Upland**—*pop pl* ... PA-2
**Upland**—*pop pl* ... WV-2
Upland and Home Ditch No. 1—*canal* ... CO-8
Upland Borough—*civil* ... PA-2
Upland Branch—*stream* ... TN-4
Upland Canal—*canal* ... CA-9
Upland Cem—*cemetery* ... IA-7
Upland Cem—*cemetery* ... NE-7
Upland Ch—*church* ... AR-4
Upland Ch—*church* ... KY-4
Upland Ch—*church* ... WV-2
Upland Coll—*school* ... CA-9
Upland Ditch—*canal* ... MT-8
Upland Drain—*stream* ... IN-6
Upland Elementary and MS—*school* ... IN-6
Upland Farm—*hist pl* ... OH-6
**Upland Heights**—*pop pl* ... OH-6
Upland (historical)—*locale* ... KS-7
Upland HS—*school* ... CA-9
Upland Lake—*lake* ... MN-6
Upland Lake—*reservoir* ... TN-4
Upland Memorial Park—*cemetery* ... CA-9
Upland Park—*park* ... NE-7
**Upland Park**—*pop pl* ... PA-2
Uplands—*building* ... DC-2
*Upland Sanitarium* ... TN-4
Upland Sch—*school* ... NE-7
Uplands General Hosp (historical)—*hospital* ... TN-4
**Uplands Park**—*pop pl* ... MO-7
Uplands Sch—*school* ... OR-9
Upland State Game Bird Habitat—*park* ... WA-9
Upland State Game Ref—*park* ... ND-7
Upland Station—*building* ... PA-2
**Upland Subdivision**—*pop pl* ... UT-8
**Upland Terrace**—*pop pl* ... PA-2
Upland Terrace Sch—*school* ... UT-8
Upland Thorofare—*channel* ... NJ-2
**Upland Township**—*pop pl* ... ND-7
Upnuk Lake—*lake* ... AK-9
Upola—*locale* ... KS-7
Upola Cem—*cemetery* ... KS-7
*Upola Station* ... KS-7
Upole Cem—*cemetery* ... MD-2
*Upolu* ... HI-9
Upolu—*civil* ... HI-9
Upolu Point—*cape* ... HI-9
*Up-pa Mountain* ... CA-9
Upp Creek—*stream* ... CA-9
Upper Abbot—*locale* ... ME-1
Upper Abner Branch Sch—*school* ... KY-4
Upper Addison Bay—*bay* ... FL-3
**Upper Addis Run**—*pop pl* ... WV-2
Upper Adobe Spring—*spring* ... NV-8
Upper Aero Lake—*lake* ... MT-8
Upper Aetna Lake—*reservoir* ... NJ-2
Upper Aetna Lake Dam—*dam* ... NJ-2
Upper Aimer Lake—*lake* ... WI-6
Upper Alamo Tank—*reservoir* ... AZ-5
Upper Albany Hist Dist—*hist pl* ... CT-1
Upper Albert Lake—*lake* ... CA-9
Upper Alder Creek Spring—*spring* ... AZ-5
Upper Alford Pond—*lake* ... PA-2
*Upper Alkali Lake* ... CA-9
Upper Allen Branch—*stream* ... KY-4
Upper Allen Elem Sch—*school* ... PA-2
Upper Allen Pond—*lake* ... ME-1
**Upper Allen (Township of)**—*pop pl* ... PA-2
Upper Alpha Branch—*stream* ... KY-4
*Upper Alton* ... IL-6
Upper Alton Hist Dist—*hist pl* ... IL-6
Upper American Legion Lake Dam—*dam* ... MS-4
Upper Ammonoosuc River—*stream* ... NH-1
Upper Ammonoosuc Trail—*trail* ... NH-1
Upper Anahola Ditch—*canal* ... HI-9
Upper Anderson Branch—*stream* ... TN-4
Upper Anderson Meadows—*swamp* ... MT-8
Upper And Lower Dams—*dam* ... PA-2
Upper Angel Lake—*reservoir* ... NC-3
Upper Angel Lake Dam—*dam* ... NC-3
Upper Antelope—*summit* ... AZ-5
Upper Antelope Rsvr—*reservoir* ... ID-8
Upper Anton Chico—*locale* ... NM-5
**Upper Anton Chico (Los Ranchitos)**—*pop pl* ... NM-5
Upper Aquetong Valley Hist Dist—*hist pl* ... PA-2
Upper Araujo Spring—*spring* ... CA-9
Upper Arcadia Rsvr—*reservoir* ... ID-8
*Upper Arlington* ... OH-6
**Upper Arlington**—*pop pl* (2) ... OH-6
Upper Arlington Hist Dist—*hist pl* ... OH-6
Upper Arlington (Township of)—*other* ... OH-6
Upper Arm Cabin Cove—*bay* ... AK-9
Upper Arm Camp—*locale* ... OR-9
Upper Armstrong Bridge—*bridge* ... NC-3
Upper Arnold Fork Sch—*school* ... KY-4
Upper Arsnicker Keys—*island* ... FL-3
Upper Artichoke Rsvr—*reservoir* ... MA-1
Upper Ash Creek Tank—*reservoir* ... AZ-5
Upper Ash Spring—*spring* ... AZ-5
Upper Ash Spring—*spring* ... NV-8
Upper Asuable Lake—*lake* ... NY-2
Upper Aubrey Lake—*reservoir* ... GA-3
**Upper Augusta (Township of)**—*pop pl* ... PA-2
Upper Ave A Hist Dist—*hist pl* ... GA-3
Upper Avilas Tank—*reservoir* ... NM-5
Upper Backwater—*bay* ... WI-6
Upper Bad Creek—*stream* (2) ... KY-4
Upper Badger Creek—*stream* ... MN-6
*Upper Badger Draw Rsvr* ... OR-9
Upper Baer Lake—*lake* ... WY-8
Upper Bailey Dam—*dam* ... UT-8
Upper Bailey Rsvr—*reservoir* ... UT-8
Upper Bailey Spring—*spring* ... UT-8
Upper Baisley-Elkhorn Mine—*mine* ... OR-9
Upper Baker Pond—*lake* ... NH-1
*Upper Baker Reservoir* ... WA-9
*Upper Baker River* ... WA-9
Upper Bald Hills—*ridge* ... MA-1
Upper Bald Mountain Tank—*reservoir* ... AZ-5
Upper Baldy Lake—*lake* ... MT-8
Upper Balsam Rsvr—*reservoir* ... UT-8
Upper Bamberry Cem—*cemetery* ... MD-2
Upper Banjo Pond Dam—*dam* ... MA-1
Upper Bankhead Dam—*dam* ... UT-8
Upper Bankhead Rsvr—*reservoir* ... UT-8
Upper Bannock Shoals Run—*stream* ... WV-2
Upper Bar—*bar* (3) ... AL-4
Upper Bar—*bar* ... TN-4
Upper Baraga Lake—*lake* ... MI-6
Upper Barbero Tank Sch—*school* ... NM-5
Upper Barbourville—*locale* ... NY-2
Upper Bar Neck Point—*cape* ... MD-2
Upper Barnes Creek Dam—*dam* ... TX-5
Upper Barnhart Lake—*lake* ... MI-6
Upper Baron Lake—*lake* ... ID-8
Upper Barton Camp—*locale* ... CO-8
Upper Barton Creek—*stream* ... NC-3
*Upper Barton Lake* ... OR-9
*Upper Basin* ... NV-8
Upper Basin—*basin* ... AK-9
Upper Basin—*basin* ... AZ-5
Upper Basin—*basin* ... CA-9
Upper Basin—*basin* ... ID-8
Upper Basin—*basin* ... UT-8
Upper Basin—*lake* ... IN-6
Upper Basin Spring—*spring* ... AZ-5
Upper Basin Tank—*reservoir* ... AZ-5
Upper Basket Ledge—*bar* ... ME-1
Upper Bassett Landing—*locale* ... AL-4
Upper Bassie Canyon Spring—*spring* ... NV-8
Upper Bassi Ranch—*locale* ... CA-9
Upper Bass Lake—*lake* ... MN-6
Upper Bass Landing (historical)—*locale* ... AL-4
Upper Bastian Spring—*spring* ... NV-8
Upper Battle Creek Crossing—*locale* ... ID-8
Upper Bay—*bay* ... ME-1
Upper Bay—*bay* ... NJ-2
Upper Bay—*bay* ... NY-2
Upper Bay—*lake* ... ME-1
Upper Bay District Sch—*school* ... ME-1
Upper Beach—*beach* ... NY-2
Upper Bean Creek Sch—*school* ... MO-7
Upper Bear Butte Tank—*reservoir* ... AZ-5
Upper Bear Canyon—*valley* ... UT-8
*Upper Bear Creek* ... MT-8
Upper Bear Creek—*stream* ... KY-4
Upper Bear Creek Dam (Proposed)—*dam* ... AL-4
Upper Bear Creek Ditch—*canal* ... CO-8
Upper Bear Creek Rsvr—*reservoir* ... AL-4
Upper Bear Creek Sch—*school* ... KY-4
Upper Bear Gulch Meadows—*flat* ... MT-8
Upper Bear Island—*island* ... PA-2
Upper Bear Lake—*lake* ... ID-8
Upper Bearpen Branch—*stream* ... KY-4
Upper Bear Spring—*spring* (2) ... AZ-5
Upper Bear Spring—*spring* ... UT-8
Upper Bear Springs—*spring* ... UT-8
Upper Bear Swamp—*swamp* ... NJ-2
Upper Bear Valley—*basin* ... UT-8
Upper Beaver Cem—*cemetery* ... CO-8
Upper Beaver Creek Ch—*church* ... WI-6
*Upper Beaver Creek Dam* ... UT-8
*Upper Beaver Creek Reservoir* ... UT-8
Upper Beaver Creek Sch—*school* ... WY-8
Upper Beaverdam Branch—*stream* ... KY-4
Upper Beaverdam Creek—*stream* ... NC-3
Upper Beaver Meadow—*flat* ... CO-8
Upper Beaver Rsvr—*reservoir* ... CO-8
Upper Beaver Sch—*school* ... CO-8
Upper Beaver Sch—*school* ... KY-4
Upper Beck Spring—*spring* ... CA-9
Upper Beech Creek Sch—*school* ... KY-4
Upper Beecher Well—*well* ... AZ-5
Upper Beech Hill Brook—*stream* ... NY-2
Upper Beech Pond—*lake* ... NH-1
Upper Beechwood—*locale* ... NY-2
Upper Beef Pasture Windmill—*locale* ... TX-5
Upper Belcher Branch—*stream* ... WV-2
Upper Belen Riverside Drain—*canal* ... NM-5
Upper Bell Ch—*church* ... GA-3
Upper Bell Creek—*stream* ... GA-3
Upper Bell Creek—*stream* ... NC-3
Upper Bells Canyon Rsvr—*reservoir* ... UT-8
Upper Bell Tank—*reservoir* ... AZ-5
Upper Belmont Well—*well* ... AZ-5
Upper Bemis Pond Dam—*dam* ... MA-1
Upper Bench—*ridge* ... OR-9
Upper Bench Trail—*trail* ... CO-8
Upper Bend—*bend* ... NC-3
Upper Bennett Spring—*spring* ... OR-9
Upper Benson—*locale* ... NY-2
Upper Bent Branch—*stream* ... KY-4
**Upper Berkshire Valley**—*pop pl* ... NJ-2
Upper Berley Lake—*lake* ... OR-9
Upper Bernard Island—*island* ... VA-3
**Upper Bern (Township of)**—*pop pl* ... PA-2
**Upper Bethlehem**—*pop pl* ... VI-3
Upper Big Bay—*bay* ... NY-2
Upper Big Bigby (CCD)—*cens area* ... TN-4
Upper Big Bigby Division—*civil* ... TN-4
Upper Big Blue River Structure Number 15—*dam* ... IN-6
Upper Big Blue Structure Number 14—*dam* ... IN-6
Upper Big Bottom—*bend* ... TN-4
*Upper Big Branch* ... WV-2
Upper Big Branch—*stream* ... WV-2
Upper Big Creek—*stream* ... WI-6
Upper Big Creek Campground—*locale* ... MT-8
Upper Big Creek Sch—*school* ... WI-6
Upper Big Dey Tank—*reservoir* ... AZ-5
Upper Big Flat Windmill—*locale* ... NM-5
Upper Big Gulch—*valley* ... WY-8
*Upper Big Nemaha River* ... NE-7
Upper Big Pine Sch—*school* ... NC-3
Upper Big Run—*stream* (4) ... WV-2
*Upper Big Stone Lake* ... MI-6
Upper Big Timber Falls—*falls* ... MT-8
Upper Big Tom Hollow Spring—*spring* ... UT-8
Upper Big Tujunga Canyon—*valley* ... CA-9
Upper Birch Creek Bar—*bar* ... MT-8
Upper Birch Island—*island* ... ME-1
Upper Birch Lake—*lake* ... MN-6
Upper Birch Spring—*spring* ... ID-8
Upper Bitney Gulch—*valley* (2) ... MT-8
Upper Bitter Creek Well—*well* ... AZ-5
Upper Black Bar Falls—*falls* ... OR-9
Upper Black Bayou—*gut* ... LA-4
Upper Black Canyon Spring—*spring* ... NV-8
Upper Black Creek—*stream* ... GA-3
Upper Black Creek—*stream* ... MI-6
Upper Black Creek Ch—*church* ... GA-3
Upper Black Creek Ch—*church* ... NC-3
**Upper Black Eddy**—*pop pl* (2) ... PA-2
Upper Black Lake—*lake* ... MI-6
Upper Black Pond—*lake* ... ME-1
*Upper Black River* ... MI-6
Upper Black Top Mesa Pass—*gap* ... AZ-5
Upper Blackwater Ch—*church* ... KY-4
Upper Blaine Trace Sch—*school* ... KY-4
Upper Blakey Windmill—*locale* ... TX-5
Upper Blauvelt Lake—*reservoir* ... NJ-2
Upper Blaylock Canyon Spring—*spring* ... OR-9
Upper Blind Spring—*spring* ... NV-8
Upper Blue Basin—*lake* ... TN-4
Upper Blue Campground—*park* ... AZ-5
Upper Blue Creek Tabernacle—*church* ... OH-6
Upper Blue Hills—*summit* ... UT-8
Upper Blue Hole Sch—*school* ... KY-4
*Upper Bluejohn Spring* ... UT-8
Upper Blue Lake—*reservoir* ... CA-9
Upper Blue Licks—*locale* ... KY-4
Upper Blue Mountain Lake—*reservoir* ... NJ-2
Upper Blue Mountain Lake Dam—*dam* ... NJ-2
Upper Blue Point Cem—*cemetery* ... IA-7
Upper Blue River Island—*island* ... KY-4
Upper Blue Spring—*spring* ... AZ-5
Upper Bluffer Pond—*lake* ... ME-1
Upper Bluff Lake—*lake* ... IL-6
Upper Bluff Spring—*spring* ... OR-9
Upper Boardman Canal—*canal* ... CA-9
Upper Bogue—*stream* ... MS-4
Upper Bohn Lake—*reservoir* ... CA-9
Upper Bostwick Park—*flat* ... CO-8
Upper Bottle Lake—*lake* ... MN-6
Upper Bottom Canyon—*valley* ... UT-8
Upper Boulder Basin—*basin* ... WY-8
Upper Boulder Creek—*stream* ... AK-9
Upper Boulder Lake—*lake* ... MT-8
*Upper Bouse Wash* ... AZ-5
Upper Bouse Wash—*stream* ... AZ-5
Upper Bowens Creek Sch—*school* ... KY-4
Upper Bowman Canal—*canal* ... CA-9
Upper Bowman Run—*stream* ... WV-2
Upper Box Canyon Lake—*lake* ... ID-8
Upper Box Creek Dam—*dam* ... UT-8
Upper Box Creek Rsvr—*reservoir* ... UT-8
Upper Box Elder Sch—*school* ... NE-7
*Upper Box Reservoir* ... UT-8
Upper Boy Scout Lake—*lake* ... CA-9
Upper Brace Lake—*lake* ... MI-6
Upper Bradford Windmill—*locale* ... TX-5
**Upper Bradley Place**—*pop pl* ... GA-3
Upper Brady Tank—*reservoir* ... AZ-5
Upper Bramlet Lake—*lake* ... MT-8
Upper Branch—*gut* ... MI-6
Upper Branch—*stream* ... KS-7
Upper Branch—*stream* ... KY-4
Upper Branch Canyon Spring—*spring* ... CA-9
Upper Branch Clesson Brook—*stream* ... MA-1
Upper Branch North Fork Little River—*stream* ... KY-4
Upper Branch Sch—*school* ... VT-1
Upper Branch Yellow Creek—*stream* ... IA-7
Upper Brandon—*locale* ... VA-3
Upper Branigan Lake—*lake* ... CA-9
Upper Break—*gut* ... DE-2
Upper Brehedo Windmill—*locale* ... NM-5
Upper Brennan Lake—*lake* ... MI-6
Upper Brentwood Lake—*lake* ... AK-9
Upper Brian Spring—*spring* ... MT-8
Upper Bridge—*bridge* ... KY-4
Upper Bridge Creek Draw Rsvr—*reservoir* ... OR-9
Upper Bridgeport Dam—*dam* ... PA-2
Upper Bridgeport Rsvr—*reservoir* ... PA-2
Upper Bridger Sch—*school* ... MT-8
Upper Bridle Tunnel—*tunnel* ... NC-3
Upper Brier Ridge—*church* ... KY-4
Upper Broad Creek—*stream* ... NC-3
Upper Brooks Lakes—*lake* ... WY-8
**Upper Brookville**—*pop pl* ... NY-2
Upper Brother Bar—*bar* ... AL-4
Upper Brothers Creek—*stream* (2) ... NJ-2
Upper Brown Canyon—*valley* ... ID-8
Upper Brown Lake—*lake* ... IA-7
Upper Browns Gulch Spring—*spring* ... MT-8
**Upper Brownville**—*pop pl* ... PA-2
*Upper Brunet Flowage* ... WI-6
Upper Bruno Tank—*reservoir* ... AZ-5
Upper Brush Creek—*stream* ... KY-4
Upper Brush Creek—*stream* ... WI-6
Upper Brush Creek Sch—*school* ... TN-4
Upper Brushy Gap—*gap* ... VA-3
Upper Brushy Windmill—*locale* (2) ... TX-5
Upper Bryant Canyon Tank—*reservoir* ... AZ-5
Upper Bucheit Sch (historical)—*school* ... PA-2
*Upper Buckatabon Lake* ... WI-6
Upper Buckatabon Lake—*lake* ... WI-6
Upper Buckbrush Rsvr—*reservoir* ... OR-9
Upper Buckeye Sch—*school* ... WV-2
Upper Buckhorn Gap—*gap* ... TN-4
Upper Buck Landing—*locale* ... NC-3
Upper Buck Mtn—*summit* ... ME-1
Upper Bucks Christian Sch—*school* ... PA-2
*Upper Bucks County Airport* ... PA-2
Upper Bucks County Area Vocational Technical Sch—*school* ... PA-2
Upper Buck Spring—*spring* ... AZ-5
Upper Buffalo Corral Rsvr—*reservoir* ... CA-9
Upper Bug Lake—*lake* ... MN-6
Upper Bulge—*swamp* ... GA-3
Upper Bull Canyon Tank—*reservoir* ... AZ-5
Upper Bull Creek Flat—*flat* ... CA-9
Upper Bull Creek Ranger Station—*locale* ... CA-9
Upper Bull Pond—*lake* ... AZ-5
Upper Burke Windmill—*locale* ... CO-8
Upper Burning Creek—*stream* ... WV-2
Upper Burns Sch—*school* ... WI-6
Upper Burns Valley—*valley* ... WI-6
Upper Burnt Canyon Spring—*spring* ... NV-8
Upper Burnt Creek Rsvr—*reservoir* ... ID-8
**Upper Burrell (Township of)**—*pop pl* ... PA-2
Upper Burrell Township Sch—*school* ... PA-2
Upper Burro Canyon—*valley* ... CO-8
Upper Burro Canyon Pond—*reservoir* ... NM-5
Upper Burro Canyon Sch—*school* ... CO-8
Upper Burro Canyon Well—*well* ... NM-5
Upper Bushman Lake—*lake* ... MI-6
Upper Bushnell Draw—*valley* ... WY-8
Upper Bushnell Rsvr—*reservoir* ... WY-8
Upper Buss Tank—*reservoir* ... AZ-5
Upper Butcher Bar—*bar* ... ID-8
Upper Butler Rsvr—*reservoir* ... OR-9
Upper Butte Spring—*spring* ... UT-8
Upper Buzzard Sch—*school* ... KY-4
Upper Buzzard Windmill—*locale* ... TX-5
Upper Cabeza Tank—*reservoir* ... NM-5
Upper Cabin—*locale* ... AK-9
Upper Cabin Creek—*stream* ... WY-8
Upper Cabin Run—*stream* ... WV-2
Upper Cabin Spring—*spring* ... MT-8
Upper Cabin Tank—*reservoir* ... AZ-5
Upper Cache Creek Rapids—*rapids* ... ID-8
Upper Cache Creek Rapids—*rapids* ... OR-9
Upper Cactus Flat—*flat* ... CA-9
Upper Cahoe Lake—*lake* ... AK-9
Upper Cains Creek Sch—*school* ... KY-4
Upper Calabasas Dam—*dam* ... AZ-5
Upper Calf Creek Falls—*falls* ... UT-8
Upper Calf Creek Tank—*reservoir* ... AZ-5
Upper California Landing (historical)—*locale* ... AL-4
Upper Camel Lake—*lake* ... MN-6
Upper Cameron Lake—*lake* ... MS-4
*Upper Camp* ... CO-8
Upper Campaign Spring—*spring* ... AZ-5
Upper Campbell Lake—*lake* ... OR-9
*Upper Campbellton* ... NC-3
Upper Camp Bird—*locale* ... CO-8
Upper Camp Branch—*stream* ... KY-4
Upper Camp Branch—*stream* ... VA-3
Upper Camp Creek Cem—*cemetery* ... OK-5
Upper Camp Creek Sch—*school* ... KY-4
Upper Campground—*locale* ... CA-9
Upper Campground—*park* ... OR-9
Upper Campground Cem—*cemetery* ... AR-4
Upper Camp Lake—*lake* (2) ... CO-8
Upper Camp Lake—*lake* ... MN-6
*Upper Camp Three* ... HI-9
Upper Canada Lake—*lake* ... AR-4
*Upper Canada Pond* ... RI-1
*Upper Canadian River* ... CO-8
*Upper Canadian River* ... OK-5
*Upper Canadian River* ... TX-5
Upper Canal—*canal* ... ID-8
Upper Canal—*canal* ... UT-8
Upper Cane Branch—*stream* ... VA-3
Upper Cane Creek Ch—*church* ... AL-4
Upper Cane Island Cem—*cemetery* ... AR-4
Upper Caney Sch—*school* ... KY-4
Upper Cannon Lake—*lake* ... ID-8
Upper Canton Bar (historical)—*bar* ... AL-4
Upper Canyon—*valley* ... AK-9
*Upper Canyon Creek* ... WY-8
Upper Canyon Creek Meadows—*flat* ... CA-9
Upper Canyon Creek Tank—*reservoir* ... AZ-5
Upper Capuchin Sch—*school* ... TN-4
Upper Card Creek Sch—*school* ... KY-4
Upper Cardelli Ditch—*canal* ... NV-8
Upper Carmen River—*stream* ... AK-9
Upper Carpp Lake—*lake* ... MT-8
Upper Carrizo Well—*well* ... AZ-5
Upper Carroll Lake—*lake* ... UT-8
Upper Carter Bloomary Forge (historical)—*locale* ... TN-4
Upper Carter Lake—*lake* ... MS-4
Upper Cart Hollow Springs—*spring* ... UT-8
Upper Cascade Falls—*falls* ... NC-3
Upper Cascade Lake—*lake* ... NY-2
Upper Castanea Reservoir Dam—*dam* ... PA-2
Upper Castanea Rsvr—*reservoir* ... PA-2
Upper Castle Creek—*stream* ... CA-9
Upper Cataract Falls—*falls* ... IN-6
Upper Cataract Lake—*lake* ... CO-8
*Upper Catasauqua* ... PA-2
*Upper Cataula* ... AL-4
Upper Cathedral Lake—*lake* ... WA-9
Upper Cathedral Lake—*lake* ... WY-8
Upper Cat Pond—*lake* ... NY-2
Upper Cattle Gulch Spring—*spring* ... MT-8
Upper Cause Bar—*bar* ... AL-4
Upper Cave Ridge—*ridge* ... VA-3
Upper CCC Pool—*reservoir* ... MN-6
Upper Cedar Creek—*stream* ... ID-8
Upper Cedar Creek Cem—*cemetery* ... TX-5
Upper Cedar Hollow—*valley* ... TX-5
*Upper Cedar Island* ... DE-2
Upper Cedar Lake—*lake* ... MT-8
Upper Cedar Point—*cape* ... MD-2
Upper Cem—*cemetery* ... AL-4
Upper Cem—*cemetery* ... AR-4
Upper Cem—*cemetery* ... CT-1
Upper Cem—*cemetery* ... ME-1
Upper Cem—*cemetery* ... NY-2
Upper Centennial Control Dam—*dam* ... AZ-5
Upper Centennial Flat—*flat* ... CA-9
Upper Centennial Spring—*spring* ... CA-9
Upper Center Hill Sch—*school* ... SC-3
Upper Center Point Canal—*canal* ... ID-8
Upper Chadwick Creek—*stream* ... KY-4
Upper Chain Lake—*lake* ... ME-1
Upper Chain Lake—*lake* ... UT-8
Upper Chain Lake—*reservoir* ... UT-8
Upper Chain Lake Dam—*dam* ... UT-8
Upper Chandler Pond—*reservoir* ... MA-1
Upper Chandler Pond Dam—*dam* ... MA-1
Upper Charcoal Tank—*reservoir* ... AZ-5
Upper Charette Lake—*lake* ... NM-5
Upper Charlebois Ditch—*canal* ... NV-8
Upper Charleston Canal—*canal* ... UT-8
Upper Chatauqua Mine—*mine* ... CO-8
Upper Chateaugay Lake—*lake* ... NY-2
Upper Chavez Tank—*reservoir* ... AZ-5
Upper Checats Lake—*lake* ... AK-9
Upper Cherry Creek Ditch—*canal* ... MT-8
Upper Cherry Creek Ranch—*locale* ... OR-9
Upper Cherry Creek Sch (historical)—*school* ... TN-4
Upper Cherry Log Cem—*cemetery* ... GA-3
Upper Cherry Spring—*spring* ... AZ-5
Upper Cherry Spring—*spring* ... NV-8
Upper Cherum Spring—*spring* ... AZ-5
Upper Chestnut Flats—*flat* ... TN-4
Upper Chetco Sch—*school* ... OR-9
Upper Chetco Trail—*trail* ... OR-9
Upper Chewaucan Marsh—*flat* ... OR-9
Upper Chical Acequia—*canal* ... NM-5
Upper Chical Lateral—*canal* ... NM-5
Upper Chical Windmill—*locale* ... NM-5
Upper Chichester Township—*CDP* ... PA-2
**Upper Chichester (Township of)**—*pop pl* ... PA-2
Upper Chicken Cock Bar—*bar* ... AL-4
Upper Chicosa Rsvr—*reservoir* ... CO-8
Upper Chimney Ditch—*canal* ... UT-8
Upper Chimney Spring—*spring* ... NV-8

Upper Howard Camp—*locale* ... OR-9
Upper Howard Creek—*stream* ... KY-4
Upper Hudson Meadow—*flat* ... WY-8
Upper Hudson Pond—*lake* ... ME-1
Upper Hull Spring—*spring* ... AZ-5
Upper Humboldt Cem—*cemetery* ... KS-7
Upper Huntington Canyon—*valley* ... UT-8
Upper Huntington Creek—*stream* ... UT-8
Upper Hunt Lake—*lake* ... MN-6
Upper Hurrican Creek Sch (historical)—*school* ... TN-4
Upper Hurricane Rsvr—*reservoir* ... VT-1
Upper Hurricane Valley—*valley* ... AZ-5
Upper Hyde Spring—*spring* ... AZ-5
Upper Ice Cave—*cave* ... CA-9
Upper Idaho Ranch—*locale* ... ID-8
Upper Indiana Ch—*church* ... IN-6
*Upper Indian Bayou* ... MS-4
Upper Indian Creek—*stream* ... IN-6
Upper Indian Creek Rsvr—*reservoir* ... MT-8
Upper Indian Creek Sch—*school* ... KY-4
Upper Indian Lake—*lake* ... CA-9
Upper Indian Sch—*school* ... KY-4
Upper Indian Spring—*spring* ... AZ-5
Upper Indian Spring—*spring* (2) ... NV-8
Upper Indian Spring—*spring* ... UT-8
Upper Indian Springs—*spring* ... NV-8
Upper Indian Tank—*reservoir* ... NM-5
Upper Indian Well—*locale* ... NM-5
Upper Ingram Sch—*school* ... TN-4
Upper Inlet—*stream* ... WI-6
Upper Iowa River—*stream* ... IA-7
Upper Iowa River—*stream* ... MN-6
Upper Iowa Univ—*school* ... IA-7
Upper Island—*island* ... LA-4
Upper Island—*island* ... NJ-2
Upper Island Lake—*lake* ... CO-8
Upper Island Lake—*lake* ... OR-9
Upper Island Lake—*lake* ... WI-6
Upper Island Point—*cape* ... NC-3
Upper Island Pond—*lake* ... ME-1
Upper Jack Creek Rsvr—*reservoir* ... OR-9
Upper Jacks Creek—*stream* ... KY-4
Upper Jacks Creek Sch—*school* (2) ... KY-4
Upper Jack Springs Camp—*locale* ... CO-8
Upper Jade Lake—*lake* ... WY-8
Upper Jarvis Range Channel—*channel* (2) . OR-9
**Upper Jay**—*pop pl* ... NY-2
Upper Jb Williams Pond—*reservoir* ... NC-3
Upper Jb Williams Pond Dam—*dam* ... NC-3
Upper Jean Lake—*lake* ... AK-9
Upper Jean Lake—*lake* ... WY-8
Upper Jellico Ch—*church* ... TN-4
Upper Jeptha Lake—*lake* ... MI-6
Upper Jerry Lake—*lake* ... MS-4
Upper Jerry Run—*stream* ... PA-2
Upper J H D Camp—*locale* ... WY-8
Upper Jim River Tank—*reservoir* ... AZ-5
Upper Jocko Lake—*lake* ... MT-8
Upper Joe Fork—*stream* ... KY-4
Upper Joe Green Cabin—*locale* ... CA-9
Upper Joes Valley—*valley* ... UT-8
Upper Joes Valley Guard Station—*locale* ... UT-8
Upper John G Rsvr—*reservoir* ... ID-8
Upper Johnson Creek—*stream* ... OR-9
Upper Johnson Lake—*lake* ... WA-9
Upper Johnson Mine—*mine* ... TN-4
Upper Johnson Valley—*valley* ... CA-9
Upper Jo-Mary Lake—*reservoir* ... ME-1
Upper Jo-Mary Stream—*stream* ... ME-1
Upper Jonathan Run—*stream* ... WV-2
Upper Jones Canyon Rsvr—*reservoir* ... OR-9
Upper Jones Fork—*stream* ... KY-4
Upper Jones Fork Sch—*school* ... KY-4
Upper Jones Lake—*spring* ... WI-6
Upper Jones Tract—*civil* ... CA-9
Upper Jones Valley—*basin* ... NE-7
Upper Jones Valley—*valley* ... CA-9
Upper Jones Windmill—*locale* ... TX-5
*Upper Jordan Creek* ... MO-7
Upper Jordan Lake—*lake* ... WA-9
*Upper Josie* ... AL-4
Upper Juan Miller Campground—*park* ... AZ-5
Upper Juan Miller Picnic Area—*park* ... AZ-5
Upper Jug Creek Rsvr—*reservoir* ... ID-8
Upper July Run—*stream* ... WV-2
Upper Jump—*falls* ... UT-8
Upper Jump Canyon—*valley* ... AZ-5
Upper Jump Springs—*spring* ... AZ-5
Upper Junction Tank—*reservoir* ... AZ-5
Upper Juniper Rsvr—*reservoir* ... OR-9
Upper Juniper Spring—*spring* ... TX-5
Upper Kaimu Homesteads—*civil* ... HI-9
**Upper Kalskag (native name: Kalskag)**—*pop pl* ... AK-9
*Upper Kanab* ... UT-8
Upper Kanab Creek—*stream* ... UT-8
Upper Kane Spring Rsvr—*reservoir* ... OR-9
Upper Kaubashine Lake—*lake* ... WI-6
Upper Keechi Creek—*stream* ... TX-5
*Upper Keechie Creek* ... TX-5
Upper Keene Broad—*channel* ... MD-2
Upper Keener Lick—*stream* ... WV-2
Upper Keeney Spring—*spring* ... OR-9
Upper Kelly Lake—*lake* ... WI-6
Upper Kelly Spring—*spring* ... AZ-5
Upper Kents Lake—*lake* ... UT-8
Upper Kepple Rockshelters (45SP7)—*hist pl* ... WA-9
Upper Kesick Dam—*dam* ... NJ-2
Upper Ketchikan Lake—*lake* ... AK-9
**Upper Key Largo**—*pop pl* ... FL-3
Upper Keys (CCD)—*cens area* ... FL-3
Upper Kickapoo Creek—*stream* ... TX-5
Upper Kidderville—*locale* ... NH-1
Upper Kilgore Pond—*lake* ... ME-1
Upper Killey Lake—*lake* ... AK-9
Upper Kilns—*locale* ... NY-2
Upper Kimbaberly Mine—*mine* ... UT-8
*Upper Kimball Lake* ... NH-1
Upper Kimball Lake—*lake* ... WI-6
Upper Kimball Pond—*lake* ... NH-1
Upper Kimball Seep—*spring* ... UT-8
Upper Kimberly—*locale* ... UT-8
Upper King And Queen Ch—*church* ... VA-3
**Upper Kings Addition**—*pop pl* ... KY-4
Upper Kings Creek Sch—*school* ... KY-4
Upper King Shoals Run—*stream* ... WV-2
Upper Kings Pond—*reservoir* ... GA-3
**Upper Kingston (subdivision)**—*pop pl* ... AL-4
Upper Kin Klizhin Archeol Site—*hist pl* ... NM-5
Upper Kinney Lake—*lake* ... CA-9
Upper Kintla Lake—*lake* ... MT-8
Upper Kintla Lake Patrol Cabin—*hist pl* ... MT-8
Upper Kirby Rapids—*rapids* ... ID-8
Upper Kirby Rapids—*rapids* ... OR-9
Upper Kittanning Dam—*dam* ... PA-2
Upper Klamath Lake—*lake* ... OR-9
Upper Klamath Natl Wildlife Ref—*park* ... OR-9
Upper Klondike Pond—*reservoir* ... PA-2
Upper Knob Lake—*lake* ... ID-8
Upper Kobuk Canyon—*area* ... AK-9
*Upper Kohala Ditch* ... HI-9
Upper Kohanza Lake—*reservoir* ... CT-1
Upper Kolob Plateau—*plain* ... UT-8
Upper LaBarge Box Canyon—*valley* ... AZ-5
Upper LaBarge Spring—*spring* ... AZ-5
Upper Labell Rsvr—*reservoir* ... MT-8
Upper La Cinta Windmill—*locale* ... NM-5
*Upper Lagoon* ... CT-1
Upper Lagoon—*lake* ... CT-1
Upper Lagoon Pond—*reservoir* ... MA-1
Upper Lagrange Landing (historical)—*locale* ... TN-4
Upper La Jara—*locale* ... NM-5
Upper La Junta Campground—*locale* ... NM-5
*Upper Lake* ... NV-8
*Upper Lake* ... NJ-2
*Upper Lake* ... RI-1
*Upper Lake* ... WI-6
Upper Lake—*lake* ... AK-9
Upper Lake—*lake* (2) ... CA-9
Upper Lake—*lake* ... CO-8
Upper Lake—*lake* (2) ... MI-6
Upper Lake—*lake* ... MN-6
Upper Lake—*lake* ... MT-8
Upper Lake—*lake* ... NV-8
Upper Lake—*lake* ... NJ-2
Upper Lake—*lake* (2) ... NY-2
Upper Lake—*lake* (2) ... OR-9
Upper Lake—*lake* ... PA-2
Upper Lake—*lake* ... TX-5
Upper Lake—*lake* ... WI-6
**Upper Lake**—*pop pl* ... CA-9
Upper Lake—*reservoir* ... AL-4
Upper Lake—*reservoir* ... MS-4
Upper Lake—*reservoir* ... NY-2
Upper Lake—*reservoir* ... NC-3
Upper Lake Blethen—*lake* ... WA-9
Upper Lake Campground—*locale* ... MT-8
Upper Lake-Clearlake Oaks (CCD)—*cens area* ... CA-9
Upper Lake Cohasset—*reservoir* ... NY-2
Upper Lake Creek—*stream* ... WA-9
*Upper Lake Dam* ... AL-4
*Upper Lake Erskine* ... NJ-2
Upper Lake George—*lake* ... AK-9
Upper Lake Goldwater Dam—*dam* ... AZ-5
Upper Lake Gulch—*valley* ... CO-8
Upper Lake Louise—*lake* ... FL-3
Upper Lake Mary—*reservoir* ... AZ-5
Upper Lake Mary Dam—*dam* ... AZ-5
Upper Lake McDonald Ranger Station Hist Dist—*hist pl* ... MT-8
Upper Lake Mohawk—*lake* ... NJ-2
*Upper Lake Nemahbin* ... WI-6
**Upper Lake Rancheria**—*pop pl* ... CA-9
Upper Lake Substation—*other* ... CA-9
Upper Lake Toxaway—*reservoir* ... NC-3
Upper Lake Toxaway Dam—*dam* ... NC-3
Upper Lake Traverse State Wildlife Mngmt Area—*park* ... SD-7
Upper Lakeville Lake—*lake* ... MI-6
Upper Lake (Woodlot)—*area* ... CA-9
Upper La Manga Windmill—*locale* ... NM-5
Upper Lamarck Lake—*lake* ... CA-9
Upper Lamar River Patrol Station—*locale* ... WY-8
Upper Lambert Bar—*bar* ... OR-9
Upper Land Creek—*stream* ... OR-9
Upper Landers Trail—*trail* ... MT-8
*Upper Landing* ... DE-2
Upper Landing—*locale* ... ME-1
Upper Landing Creek—*stream* ... VA-3
Upper Langston Landing—*locale* ... FL-3
**Upper La Posada**—*pop pl* ... NM-5
*Upper LaSalle Lake* ... MN-6
Upper Last Chance Spring—*spring* ... AZ-5
Upper Lateral—*canal* ... MT-8
Upper Lateral No Two And One Half—*canal* ... CA-9
Upper Lateral Number Four—*canal* ... CA-9
Upper Lateral Number Three—*canal* ... CA-9
Upper Lateral Number Two ... CA-9
Upper Lateral Number Two And One Half—*civil* ... CA-9
Upper Laurel Branch—*stream* ... KY-4
Upper Laurel Ch—*church* ... NC-3
Upper Laurel Creek—*stream* ... KY-4
Upper Laurel Fork—*stream* ... NC-3
Upper Laurel Fork—*stream* ... WV-2
Upper Laurel Run—*stream* ... WV-2
Upper Laurel Sch—*school* ... KY-4
Upper Laurel Sch—*school* (2) ... WV-2
**Upper Lawn**—*pop pl* ... PA-2
**Upper Leacock (Township of)**—*pop pl* ... PA-2
Upper Lead King Lake—*lake* ... WA-9
Upper Lead Mountain Pond—*lake* ... ME-1
Upper Leaf River Number 9 Dam—*dam* ... MS-4
Upper Leatherwood—*locale* ... WV-2
Upper Leavry Pond—*lake* ... NM-5
Upper Ledge—*bar* ... ME-1
Upper Lee Trail—*locale* ... AZ-5
*Upper Left Foot Creek* ... WI-6
Upper Left Hand Needle Creek—*stream* ... CO-8
Upper Legion Lake—*reservoir* ... SC-3
**Upper Lehigh**—*pop pl* ... PA-2
Upper Lehigh Junction—*uninc pl* ... PA-2
Upper Letts Lake—*reservoir* ... CA-9
Upper Level Run—*stream* ... WV-2
Upper Lewis Run—*stream* ... VA-3
Upper Lick—*stream* ... OH-6
Upper Lick Branch—*stream* ... KY-4
Upper Lick Branch—*stream* ... WV-2
*Upper Lick Fork* ... KY-4
Upper Lick Fork—*stream* (2) ... KY-4
Upper Lick Fork Sch—*school* ... KY-4
Upper Lightning Lake—*lake* ... MN-6
Upper Lihue Ditch—*canal* ... HI-9
Upper Lillies Spring—*spring* ... NM-5
Upper Lime Mountain Well—*well* ... NV-8
Upper Limestone Creek—*stream* ... IN-6
Upper Limestone Creek—*stream* ... SC-3
*Upper Limestone Dam* ... AZ-5
Upper Limestone Sch—*school* ... SC-3
Upper Limestone Tank—*reservoir* ... AZ-5
Upper Limestone Tank Dam—*dam* ... AZ-5
Upper Limestone Valley Creek—*stream* ... CA-9
Upper Lindgren Lake—*lake* ... MN-6
**Upper Lisle**—*pop pl* ... NY-2
Upper Little Beaver Rsvr—*reservoir* ... CO-8
Upper Little Bighorn Canal Number Two—*canal* ... MT-8
Upper Little Creek—*stream* ... MS-4
*Upper Little Fish Lake* ... NV-8
Upper Little Joe Pond—*reservoir* ... AZ-5
Upper Little Park—*flat* ... AZ-5
Upper Little Pine Sch—*school* ... NC-3
*Upper Little River* ... MS-4
*Upper Little River* ... NC-3
Upper Little River—*stream* (2) ... NC-3
Upper Little River (Township of)—*fmr MCD* ... NC-3
Upper Little Swatara Creek—*stream* ... PA-2
Upper Little Willow Sch—*school* ... WI-6
Upper Little Windmill—*locale* ... TX-5
Upper Little York Lake—*lake* ... NY-2
Upper Live Water Spring—*spring* ... AZ-5
Upper Loch Katrine—*lake* ... WA-9
Upper Lockwood Tank—*reservoir* ... AZ-5
Upper Loco Well—*well* ... NM-5
Upper Lodgepole Meadow—*flat* ... ID-8
Upper Logging Lake Snowshoe Cabin—*hist pl* ... MT-8
Upper Logue Hollow—*valley* ... PA-2
Upper Logue Run—*stream* ... PA-2
Upper Lola Montez Lake—*lake* ... CA-9
Upper Loman Well—*locale* ... NM-5
Upper Long Branch—*stream* (2) ... KY-4
Upper Long Cane Cem—*cemetery* ... SC-3
Upper Long Cane Ch—*church* ... SC-3
Upper Long Canyon Windmill—*locale* ... TX-5
Upper Long Creek—*stream* ... NC-3
Upper Long Creek Sch (historical)—*school* . TN-4
Upper Long Hollow Tank—*reservoir* ... AZ-5
*Upper Long Lake* ... MN-6
Upper Long Lake—*lake* ... CA-9
Upper Long Lake—*lake* ... IN-6
Upper Long Lake—*lake* ... MI-6
Upper Long Lake—*lake* ... WY-8
**Upper Long Lake**—*pop pl* ... IN-6
Upper Long Lake—*reservoir* ... CO-8
Upper Long Meadow—*flat* ... OR-9
Upper Long Pond—*reservoir* ... MA-1
Upper Long Pond Dam—*dam* ... MA-1
Upper Long Valley—*valley* ... CA-9
Upper Long Valley Tank—*reservoir* ... AZ-5
Upper Longwood—*locale* ... NJ-2
Upper Loon Lake—*lake* ... MN-6
*Upper Loop* ... WV-2
*Upper Loop Creek* ... WV-2
Upper Lopez Campground—*locale* ... CA-9
Upper Lord Brook—*stream* ... ME-1
Upper Lost Camp Spring—*spring* ... NV-8
Upper Lost Parks—*flat* ... UT-8
Upper Lost Valley Spring—*spring* ... ID-8
Upper Lostwood Lake—*lake* ... ND-7
Upper Louisville Bend—*bend* ... NE-7
Upper Loutre Township—*civil* ... MO-7
Upper Love—*locale* ... VI-3
Upper Lovett Place—*locale* ... NM-5
**Upper Lowell**—*pop pl* ... OH-6
Upper Lucky Canyon Spring—*spring* ... AZ-5
Upper Lyman Ditch—*canal* ... AZ-5
Upper Lynde Basin Dam—*dam* ... MA-1
Upper Lynde Basin Rsvr—*reservoir* ... MA-1
Upper Lytle Creek Ridge—*ridge* ... CA-9
Upper Lytle Spring—*spring* ... AZ-5
Upper Machodoc Creek—*stream* ... VA-3
Upper MacIntosh Sch—*school* ... KY-4
Upper Macopin—*locale* ... NJ-2
**Upper Macungie (Township of)**—*pop pl* ... PA-2
Upper Madera Windmill—*locale* ... TX-5
Upper Madison Ch—*church* ... WV-2
Upper Madison Lodge—*locale* ... AL-4
Upper Madison Sch—*hist pl* ... MT-8
Upper Madison Sch—*school* ... MT-8
*Upper Madison Valley* ... MT-8
*Upper Madison Valley* ... WY-8
Upper Magazine Street Hist Dist—*hist pl* . MA-1
Upper Maggie Spring—*spring* ... NV-8
Upper Magill Prospect—*mine* ... TN-4
Upper Magpie Rsvr—*reservoir* ... MT-8
Upper Magpie Spring—*spring* ... MT-8
**Upper Mahanoy (Township of)**—*pop pl* ... PA-2
**Upper Mahantongo (Township of)**—*pop pl* ... PA-2
Upper Mahoney Lake—*lake* ... AK-9
Upper Mailbox Park—*flat* ... CO-8
Upper Main Canal—*canal* ... CA-9
Upper Main Street Hist Dist—*hist pl* ... CT-1
Upper Main Street Hist Dist—*hist pl* ... WI-6
**Upper Makefield (Township of)**—*pop pl* ... PA-2
Upper Malina Lake—*lake* ... AK-9
*Upper Manchester* ... IN-6
Upper Manhattan Spring—*spring* ... OR-9
Upperman HS—*school* ... TN-4
*Uppermans* ... PA-2
Upper Maple Spring—*spring* ... CA-9
Upper Marais—*swamp* ... WI-6
Upper Marilyn Lake—*lake* ... OR-9
Upper Marion HS—*school* ... PA-2
Upper Marion MS—*school* ... PA-2
Upper Mark Island—*island* ... ME-1
**Upper Marlboro (Marlboro)**—*pop pl* ... MD-2
Upper Marlton Lake—*reservoir* ... NJ-2
Upper Marr Tank—*reservoir* ... NM-5
Upper Marsh Creek—*stream* ... WY-8
Upper Marsh Creek Ch—*church* ... KY-4
Upper Marsh Creek Sch—*school* ... KY-4
Upper Martine Bar—*bar* ... OR-9
Upper Martinez Tank—*reservoir* ... AZ-5
Upper Mason Lake—*lake* ... MT-8
Upper Mason Pond—*reservoir* ... ME-1
Upper Massapoag Pond—*reservoir* ... MA-1
*Upper Matecumbe Key* ... FL-3
Upper Matecumbe Key—*island* ... FL-3
Upper Mattawamkeag Lake—*lake* ... ME-1
Upper Mattole Sch—*school* ... CA-9
Upper McBride Spring—*spring* ... AZ-5
Upper McBride Spring—*spring* ... CA-9
Upper McCabe Lake—*lake* ... CA-9
Upper McCain Springs—*spring* ... OR-9
Upper McCammon Island—*island* ... TN-4
Upper McCarley Cem—*cemetery* ... OH-6
Upper McCauley Tank—*reservoir* ... AZ-5
Upper McCotter Bay—*bay* ... NC-3
Upper McDermit Spring—*spring* ... AZ-5
Upper McDougal Ranch—*locale* ... WY-8
Upper McKay Sch—*school* ... OR-9
Upper McKellars Pond—*reservoir* ... NC-3
Upper McKinley Crossing—*other* ... AK-9
Upper McKinney Tank—*reservoir* ... AZ-5
Upper McNally Pond—*lake* ... ME-1
Upper McNulty Rsvr—*reservoir* ... OR-9
*Upper Meadow* ... OR-9
Upper Meadow—*flat* (2) ... CA-9
Upper Meadow—*flat* ... UT-8
Upper Meadow—*flat* ... VT-1
Upper Meadow Cem—*cemetery* ... MA-1
Upper Meadow Rsvr—*reservoir* ... OR-9
*Upper Meadows Campground* ... UT-8
Upper Meadow Trail—*trail* ... WV-2
Upper Medicine Lodge Lake—*lake* ... WY-8
Upper Medio Windmill—*locale* ... NM-5
Upper Meeker Canal—*canal* ... NE-7
Upper Melakwa Lake—*lake* ... WA-9
Upper Meloy Summit—*gap* ... NV-8
Upper Melton Landing (historical)—*locale* . TN-4
Upper Memorial Lake—*reservoir* ... FL-3
Upper Mendenhall Valley—*uninc pl* ... AK-9
Upper Menton Lake—*lake* ... MN-6
Upper Merced Pass Lake—*lake* ... CA-9
Upper Merchants Lake—*reservoir* ... NC-3
Upper Merchants Lake Dam—*dam* ... NC-3
Upper Merion—*other* ... PA-2
Upper Merion ( CDP name: Upper Merion Township )—*CDP* ... PA-2
**Upper Merion (Township of)**—*pop pl* ... PA-2
**Upper Merryall**—*pop pl* ... CT-1
Upper Merryall Cem—*cemetery* ... CT-1
Upper Mesa Falls—*falls* ... ID-8
Upper Mesa Tank—*reservoir* ... AZ-5
Upper Mesquite Canyon Spring—*spring* ... AZ-5
Upper Meyersville—*locale* ... TX-5
*Upper Miakka Lake* ... FL-3
Upper Michigan Ditch—*canal* ... CO-8
Upper Midas Spring—*spring* ... NV-8
Upper Middle—*bar* ... NC-3
Upper Middle Branch Pond—*lake* ... ME-1
Upper Middle Inlet—*stream* ... WI-6
Upper Middle Tank—*reservoir* ... AZ-5
**Upper Middletown**—*pop pl* ... PA-2
Upper Midway Dam—*dam* ... OR-9
Upper Midway Rsvr—*reservoir* ... OR-9
**Upper Mifflin (Township of)**—*pop pl* ... PA-2
Upper Milford Ch—*church* ... PA-2
Upper Milford School—*locale* ... WY-8
**Upper Milford (Township of)**—*pop pl* ... PA-2
*Upper Mill* ... TN-4
Upper Mill—*locale* ... WA-9
**Upper Mill**—*pop pl* ... NJ-2
**Upper Mill**—*pop pl* ... PA-2
Upper Mill Branch—*stream* ... VA-3
*Upper Mill Brook Reservoir* ... MA-1
*Uppermill Canyon* ... ID-8
Upper Mill Cem—*cemetery* ... GA-3
Upper Mill Creek—*stream* ... WV-2
Upper Mill Creek Sch—*school* (2) ... KY-4
Upper Mill Creek Sch—*school* ... MO-7
Upper Mill Creek Sch—*school* ... WY-8
Upper Mill Dam—*dam* ... PA-2
*Upper Millecoquin River* ... MI-6
Upper Miller Creek Patrol Station—*locale* ... WY-8
*Upper Mill Pond* ... MA-1
Upper Millpond—*lake* ... MA-1
Upper Millpond—*reservoir* (2) ... CT-1
Upper Millpond—*reservoir* ... MA-1
Upper Millpond Dam—*dam* ... MA-1
Upper Mill Run—*stream* ... WV-2
Upper Mills Creek Lake—*lake* ... CA-9
Upper Millstone Sch—*school* ... KY-4
Upper-Mill Street Hist Dist—*hist pl* ... NY-2
Upper Milton Lake—*lake* ... MN-6
Upper Miner Lakes—*lake* ... MT-8
**Upper Mingo**—*pop pl* ... WV-2
Upper Mint Spring—*spring* ... TN-4
Upper Miocene Canal—*canal* ... CA-9
Upper Misery Pond—*lake* ... ME-1
Upper Mission Lake—*lake* ... MN-6
Upper Mission Lake—*lake* ... MT-8
Upper Mississippi River State Wildlife Management Area—*park* ... MO-7
Upper Mississippi River Wild Life And Fish Refuge—*park* (2) ... IL-6
Upper Mississippi River Wildlife & Fish Rfg—*park* ... IA-7
Upper Mississippi Wild Life And Fish Ref—*park* ... MN-6
Upper Missouri Bible Camp—*locale* ... ND-7
Upper Missouri Lake—*lake* ... WY-8
Upper Moccasin Springs—*spring* ... AZ-5
Upper Mockeson—*locale* ... TN-4
Upper Mohave Tank—*reservoir* ... AZ-5
**Upper Mohawk**—*pop pl* ... NJ-2
*Upper Mohawk Lake* ... NJ-2
Upper Mohawk Lake—*reservoir* ... NJ-2
Upper Mohawk Lake Dam—*dam* ... NJ-2
Upper Molunkus (Township of)—*unorg* ... ME-1
Upper Monegaw Sch—*school* ... MO-7
**Upper Mongaup**—*pop pl* ... NY-2
Upper Monk Tank—*reservoir* ... AZ-5
Upper Mono Trail—*trail* ... CA-9
Upper Montana Ridge Cem—*cemetery* ... WI-6
**Upper Montclair**—*pop pl* ... NJ-2
Upper Montclair Country Club—*other* ... NJ-2
Upper Montclair Station—*hist pl* ... NJ-2
Upper Montclair Station—*locale* ... NJ-2
Upper Montosa Well—*well* ... NM-5
Upper Montvale—*locale* ... NJ-2
Upper Moore Lake—*reservoir* ... AR-4
*Upper Moose Creek* ... PA-2
*Upper Moose Creek - in part* ... PA-2
Upper Moose Pond—*lake* ... ME-1
Upper Moose Pond—*lake* ... NY-2
Upper Moreland MS—*school* ... PA-2
Upper Moreland Sch—*school* ... NY-2
Upper Moreland Sch—*school* ... PA-2
*Upper Moreland Senior HS* ... PA-2
Upper Moreland Township—*CDP* ... PA-2
**Upper Moreland (Township of)**—*pop pl* ... PA-2
Upper Morgan Lake—*lake* ... CA-9
Upper Morgan Run—*stream* ... PA-2
Upper Morganton Shoals—*bar* ... TN-4
*Upper Morgantown Shoals* ... TN-4
Upper Mormon Pocket Tank—*reservoir* ... AZ-5
Upper Mormon Spring—*spring* ... WY-8
Upper Morse Lake—*reservoir* ... NJ-2
Upper Moss Spring—*spring* ... AZ-5
Upper Mound Cem—*cemetery* ... IN-6
Upper Mountain Lick—*stream* ... VA-3
Upper Mountain Meadows—*flat* ... OR-9
Upper Mountain Pond—*lake* ... NH-1
**Upper Mount Bethel (Township of)**—*pop pl* ... PA-2
Upper Mount Glen Lake—*reservoir* ... NJ-2
Upper Mount Glen Lake Dam—*dam* ... NJ-2
Upper Mount Holly Dam—*dam* ... PA-2
Upper Mount Hope Spring—*spring* ... AZ-5
Upper Mount Landing—*locale* ... VA-3
Upper Mount Moriah Cem—*cemetery* ... LA-4
Upper Mount Pleasant Dam—*dam* ... PA-2
Upper Mouth—*locale* ... NY-2
Upper Mouth Birch Creek—*stream* ... AK-9
Upper Mouth Porcupine River—*stream* ... AK-9
Upper Mtn—*summit* ... NC-3
Upper Mtn—*summit* ... WV-2
*Upper Mudabock* ... NJ-2
*Upper Mud Lake* ... WI-6
Upper Mud Lake—*lake* (2) ... CA-9
Upper Mud Lake—*lake* ... LA-4
Upper Mud Lake—*lake* ... ME-1
Upper Mud Lake—*lake* ... MN-6
Upper Mudlick Run—*stream* ... WV-2
*Upper Mud Spring* ... OR-9
Upper Mud Spring—*spring* ... AZ-5
Upper Mud Spring—*spring* ... CA-9
Upper Mud Spring—*spring* ... NV-8
Upper Mud Spring—*spring* (4) ... OR-9
Upper Mulberry Branch—*stream* ... KY-4
Upper Muldoon Tank—*reservoir* ... CA-9
*Upper Mule Tank* ... NM-5
Upper Mumbo Lake—*lake* ... CA-9
*Upper Mungers pond* ... CT-1
*Upper Musco Creek* ... MO-7
*Upper Myakka Lake* ... FL-3
Upper Mystic Lake—*reservoir* ... MA-1
Upper Mystic Lake Dam—*dam* ... MA-1
Upper Naches Valley—*valley* ... WA-9
Upper Naneum Meadow—*flat* ... WA-9
Upper Napier Cem—*cemetery* ... WV-2
*Upper Narrows* ... NY-2
Upper Narrows—*channel* ... ME-1
Upper Narrows—*channel* (2) ... NH-1
Upper Narrows—*channel* ... VT-1
Upper Narrows—*gap* ... CA-9
Upper Narrows—*gap* ... ME-1
Upper Narrows—*gap* (2) ... UT-8
Upper Narrows—*gap* ... WI-6
**Upper Narrows**—*pop pl* ... VT-1
Upper Narrows—*ridge* ... MO-7
Upper Narrows Campground—*park* ... UT-8
Upper Narrows Pond—*lake* ... ME-1
*Upper Narrows Reservoir* ... CA-9
Upper Narrows Spring—*spring* ... UT-8
Upper Naselle Ranger Station—*locale* ... WA-9
Upper Nash Fork Campground—*locale* ... WY-8
Upper Nash Mine—*mine* ... CA-9
Upper Nashotah Lake—*lake* ... WI-6
*Upper Nashota Lake* ... WI-6
Upper Natural Bridge Cave—*cave* ... AL-4
Upper Naukeag Lake—*reservoir* ... MA-1
Upper Naukeag Lake Dam—*dam* ... MA-1
*Upper Naukeag Pond* ... MA-1
Upper Navajo Canyon Trail—*trail* ... CO-8
**Upper Nazareth (Township of)**—*pop pl* ... PA-2
Upper Neck—*cape* ... MA-1
Upper Neck Cove—*cove* ... MA-1
Upper Neely Branch—*stream* ... MO-7
Upper Neely Sch (historical)—*school* ... MO-7
Upper Neenah Creek State Fishery Area—*park* ... WI-6
Upper Negro Island—*island* ... ME-1
**Upper Nehalem**—*pop pl* ... OR-9
*Upper Nehmabin Lake* ... WI-6
Upper Nemahbin Lake—*lake* ... WI-6
Upper Newhouse Coulee—*valley* ... MT-8
Upper Newport Bay—*bay* ... CA-9
Upper Newsome Spring—*spring* ... CA-9
Upper New Tank—*reservoir* ... AZ-5
Upper New Virginia Canal—*canal* ... NV-8
*Upper New York Bay* ... NJ-2
Upper Nickeyville—*uninc pl* ... AK-9
*Upper Nicollet* ... MN-6
Upper Nidifer Branch—*stream* ... TN-4
Upper Niklaremut Creek—*stream* ... AK-9
Upper Ninemile Creek—*stream* ... WV-2
Upper Nodine Spring—*spring* ... OR-9
Upper Noland Cem—*cemetery* ... NC-3
Upper North Canyon—*valley* ... AZ-5
Upper North Crow Rsvr—*reservoir* ... WY-8
Upper North Eden Rsvr—*reservoir* ... UT-8
Upper North Falls—*falls* ... OR-9
*Upper North Fork* ... OR-9
Upper North Fork—*stream* ... OH-6
Upper North Fork—*stream* ... OR-9
Upper North Fork Grouse Creek Trail—*trail* ... ID-8
Upper North Fork Honeydew Creek—*stream* ... CA-9
Upper North Fork Matilija Creek—*stream* . CA-9
Upper North Fork Mattole River—*stream* ... CA-9
*Upper North Fork of the Wilson River* ... OR-9
Upper North Fork Skookumchuck Creek—*stream* ... WA-9
*Upper north Fork Wilson River* ... OR-9
Upper North (Township of)—*fmr MCD* ... AR-4
Upper Notton Spring Cave—*cave* ... TN-4
Upper Nowlin Meadow—*flat* ... WY-8
Upper Nowood Sch—*school* ... WY-8
Upper No 5 Rsvr—*reservoir* ... WY-8
Upper Number Two Gulch—*valley* ... MT-8
Upper Nunemille Lake—*lake* ... WI-6
**Upper Nutria**—*pop pl* ... NM-5
**Upper Nyack**—*pop pl* ... NY-2
Upper Nyack Firehouse—*hist pl* ... NY-2
Upper Nyack Snowshoe Cabin—*hist pl* ... MT-8
Upper Oak Creek Windmill—*locale* ... AZ-5
Upper O'brien Campground—*locale* ... ID-8
Upper Ochoco—*locale* ... OR-9
Upper Oconomowoc Lake—*reservoir* ... WI-6
Upper Octoraro—*locale* ... PA-2
Upper Odell Sch (abandoned)—*school* ... MO-7
Upper Ogden Bowl—*basin* ... UT-8
Upper Ohmer Lake—*lake* ... AK-9
Upper Ojai Valley—*valley* ... CA-9
Upper Olaa For Res—*forest* ... HI-9
Upper Olalla Sch—*school* ... OR-9
Upper Old Brake—*lake* ... AR-4
Upper Old River—*lake* ... AR-4
Upper Old River—*stream* ... LA-4
Upper Old River Lake—*lake* ... AR-4
Upper Old River Lake—*lake* ... MS-4
Upper Old Soldier—*swamp* ... GA-3
*Upper Old Soldier Creek* ... GA-3
Upper Omaha Mission Bend—*bend* ... IA-7
Upper Omaha Mission Bend—*bend* ... NE-7
Upper O'Neil Creek—*stream* ... WA-9
Upper One Tank—*reservoir* ... AZ-5
Upper Open Brook Sch (historical)—*school* ... PA-2
Upper Ophelia Landing—*locale* ... AL-4
*Upper Orange Reservoir* ... VT-1
**Upper Orchard**—*pop pl* ... PA-2
Upper Oso Campground—*locale* ... CA-9
Upper Otay Lake—*reservoir* ... CA-9
*Upper Otay Rsvr* ... CA-9
Upper Otter Creek Overlook—*locale* ... VA-3
Upper Otter Sch—*school* ... KY-4
Upper Ottoson Lake—*lake* ... UT-8
Upper Ottoway Lake—*lake* ... CA-9
Upper Ouachita Natl Wildlife Ref—*park* (2) ... LA-4
Upper Owl Creek Dam—*dam* ... PA-2
Upper Owl Creek Rsvr—*reservoir* ... PA-2
Upper Oxbrook Lake—*lake* ... ME-1
Upper Ox Creek—*stream* ... WI-6
**Upper Oxford (Township of)**—*pop pl* ... PA-2
Upper Oxhead Pond—*lake* ... ME-1
Upper Ox Lake—*lake* ... WI-6
Upper Paauhau—*civil* ... HI-9
Upper Pacheta Cienega—*swamp* ... AZ-5
Upper Pacifico Campground—*locale* ... CA-9
Upper Page Brook Cem—*cemetery* ... NY-2
Upper Paget Well—*well* ... MT-8
Upper Pahranagat Lake—*reservoir* ... NV-8
Upper Paint Creek Sch (historical)—*school* ... TN-4
Upper Painted Grotto—*cave* ... NM-5
Upper Paint Rock Lake—*lake* ... WY-8
Upper Paiute Drain—*canal* ... NV-8
Upper Paiute Number Two—*canal* ... NV-8
*Upper Palisade Lake* ... ID-8
Upper Palisades Lake—*lake* ... ID-8
Upper Palisades Lake—*lake* ... WA-9
Upper Panaca Lake—*lake* ... MN-6
Upper Panther Island—*island* ... AR-4
Upper Paradise Lake—*lake* ... AK-9
Upper Paradise Lake—*lake* ... WY-8
Upper Paradise Lake—*reservoir* ... IN-6
Upper Paradise Lake Dam—*dam* ... IN-6
Upper Pardoes Camp—*locale* ... CA-9
Upper Park—*flat* ... CO-8
Upper Park—*flat* ... MT-8
Upper Park Creek Patrol Cabin—*hist pl* ... MT-8
Upper Parker Ch—*church* ... MO-7
Upper Parker Meadow—*flat* ... CA-9
Upper Parker Sch—*school* ... MO-7
*Upper Park of Flat River* ... RI-1
*Upper Park Reservoir* ... CO-8
Upper Park Sch—*school* ... NE-7
Upper Park Tank—*reservoir* ... NM-5
Upper Parson Well—*well* ... AZ-5
*Upper Partridge Lake* ... MN-6
Upper Partridge Pond—*lake* ... ME-1
Upper Pass—*channel* ... LA-4
Upper Pass—*gap* ... UT-8
Upper Pass—*gap* ... WI-6
Upper Passage—*channel* ... AK-9
Upper Pasture—*flat* (2) ... UT-8
Upper Pasture Spring—*spring* ... AZ-5
Upper Path Valley Ch—*church* ... PA-2
Upper Paul Creek Spring—*spring* ... OR-9
Upper Pauls Lake—*reservoir* ... TX-5
*Upper Pauness Lake* ... MN-6
Upper Pauness Lake—*lake* ... MN-6
Upper Pawn Lake—*lake* ... WA-9
Upper Pawtucket Canal Dam—*dam* ... MA-1
Upper Pawtucket Canal Rsvr—*reservoir* ... MA-1
**Upper Paxton (Township of)**—*pop pl* ... PA-2
Upper Payette Campground—*locale* ... ID-8
Upper Payette Lake—*lake* ... ID-8
*Upper Peach Spring* ... AZ-5
Upper Peachtree—*locale* ... NC-3
Upper Peachtree Ch—*church* ... NC-3
**Upper Peachtree (Frog Pond)**—*pop pl* .. NC-3
Upper Peaked Prairie—*flat* ... CA-9
**Upper Peanut**—*pop pl* ... PA-2
Upper Pease Spring—*spring* ... CO-8
Upper Peavine Creek—*stream* ... MO-7
Upper Peavine Flat—*flat* ... OR-9
Upper Peavine Ranch—*locale* ... NV-8
Upper Pechahallee Lake—*reservoir* ... MS-4
Upper Peck Mines—*mine* ... TN-4
Upper Peck Spring—*spring* ... AZ-5
Upper Pecks Run Sch—*school* ... WV-2
Upper Peedee Mine—*mine* ... TN-4
Upper Peeler Lakes—*lake* ... CO-8
Upper Pendleton Canyon—*valley* ... NM-5
Upper Peninsula Brewing Company Bldg—*hist pl* ... MI-6
Upper Peninsula Lake—*lake* ... CA-9
Upper Penitencia Creek—*stream* ... CA-9
Upper Pennridge HS—*school* ... PA-2
*Upper Penns Neck (Township of)* ... NJ-2
*Upper Pensotau* ... AL-4
Upper Penstemon Campground—*locale* ... ID-8
Upper Peoria Lake—*lake* ... IL-6
Upper Pequawket Pond—*lake* ... NH-1
Upper Peralta Riverside Drain—*canal* ... NM-5
Upper Perish Spring—*spring* ... NV-8
*Upper Perk Golf Course* ... PA-2
Upper Perkiomen Golf Course—*locale* ... PA-2
Upper Perkiomen HS—*school* ... PA-2
Upper Perkiomen MS—*school* ... PA-2

Upper Perkiomen Park—*park* PA-2
Upper Perkiomen Valley County Park—*park* PA-2
Upper Perra Windmill—*locale* NM-5
*Upper Perry* OR-9
Upper Pesqueira Tank—*reservoir* AZ-5
*Upper Pesquiera Tank* AZ-5
Upper Pete Branch—*stream* WV-2
Upper Peterson Bay—*swamp* FL-3
Upper Petrified Spring—*spring* NV-8
Upper Pettibone Lake—*lake* MI-6
*Upper Phantom Lake* WI-6
Upper Phil Kearny Ditch—*canal* WY-8
Upper Phillips Lake—*lake* WY-8
Upper Phoenix Ditch—*canal* NM-5
*Upper Pickensville Cemetery* AL-4
*Upper Pickerel* MI-6
Upper Pickerel Lake—*lake* MI-6
Upper Piedra Campground—*locale* CO-8
Upper Pierce Pond—*lake* ME-1
Upper Pierce Ranch—*locale* CA-9
Upper Pigeon Branch—*stream* KY-4
Upper Pigeon Creek Ch—*church* WI-6
Upper Pigeon Hill Dam—*dam* PA-2
Upper Pigeon Hill Lake—*reservoir* PA-2
Upper Pigeon Lake—*lake* MN-6
Upper Pigeonroost—*locale* NC-3
Upper Pigeon Spring—*spring* AZ-5
Upper Piletas Canyon—*valley* CA-9
Upper Pilot Knob—*summit* MO-7
Upper Pinal Rec Area—*park* AZ-5
Upper Pinch Sch—*school* WV-2
*Upper Pinebottom Run* PA-2
Upper Pine Bottom Run—*stream* PA-2
Upper Pine Bottom State Park—*park* PA-2
Upper Pine Branch—*stream* TN-4
Upper Pine Branch Mines—*mine* TN-4
Upper Pine Creek—*stream* WI-6
Upper Pine Creek Sch—*school* WV-2
Upper Pine Draft—*valley* PA-2
Upper Pine Grove—*woods* UT-8
Upper Pine Grove Cem—*cemetery* SC-3
Upper Pine Hollow—*valley* PA-2
*Upper Pine Lake* MI-6
Upper Pine Lake—*lake* CA-9
Upper Pine Lake—*lake* MN-6
Upper Pine Lake—*reservoir* IA-7
Upper Pine Lake—*reservoir* OR-9
Upper Pine Lake Dam—*dam* IA-7
Upper Pine Lake Dam—*dam* OR-9
Upper Pine Lakes—*lake* NY-2
Upper Pine Mtn—*summit* NY-2
Upper Pine Ridge—*ridge* WY-8
Upper Pine Ridge Spring—*spring* OR-9
*Upper Pine River* WI-6
Upper Pine Run Sch (historical)—*school* (2) PA-2
Upper Pinery Canyon Campground—*park* AZ-5
Upper Pines Campground—*park* UT-8
Upper Pine Spring—*spring* AZ-5
Upper Pine Spring—*spring* NM-5
Upper Pine Spring—*spring* TX-5
Upper Pine Spring—*spring* UT-8
Upper Pine Tunnel—*tunnel* (2) NC-3
Upper Pine Well—*well* NM-5
Upper Piney Falls—*falls* TN-4
Upper Piney Lake—*lake* CO-8
Upper Piney Reach—*channel* FL-3
Upper Pinto Spring—*spring* AZ-5
*Upper Pipestone Falls* MN-6
Upper Pistol Lake—*lake* ME-1
Upper Pittsboro Water Supply Pond—*reservoir* NC-3
Upper Pittsburg Landing—*locale* ID-8
Upper Pittsburg Rapids—*rapids* OR-9
Upper Pittsgrove Sch—*school* NJ-2
Upper Pittsgrove (Township of)—*civ div* NJ-2
**Upper Pittston**—*pop pl* PA-2
Upper Pitt-Taylor Rsvr—*reservoir* NV-8
Upper Piute Creek Rsvr—*reservoir* ID-8
Upper Piute Meadows—*flat* CA-9
Upper Pizona Spring—*spring* CA-9
Upper Platte and Beaver Canal—*canal* CO-8
Upper Pleasant Pond—*lake* ME-1
Upper Pleasant Valley Canal—*canal* UT-8
Upper Pleasant Valley Rapids—*rapids* ID-8
Upper Pleasant Valley Rapids—*rapids* OR-9
Upper Pleasant Valley Sch—*school* SD-7
Upper Pleasantview Rsvr—*reservoir* ID-8
Upper Plug—*dam* AL-4
Upper Pocosin—*locale* VA-3
Upper Pohatcong Mtn—*summit* NJ-2
Upper Point—*cape* UT-8
Upper Polecat—*summit* GA-3
Upper Pole Rsvr—*reservoir* CO-8
Upper Polls Creek Sch—*school* KY-4
Upper Pomeroy Lake—*lake* CO-8
Upper Pompelli Lake—*reservoir* NC-3
Upper Pompelli Lake Dam—*dam* NC-3
Upper Pompey Branch—*stream* KY-4
*Upper Pond* MA-1
Upper Pond—*lake* (3) CT-1
Upper Pond—*lake* (4) ME-1
Upper Pond—*lake* (2) MA-1
Upper Pond—*lake* NH-1
Upper Pond—*lake* (3) NY-2
Upper Pond—*lake* RI-1
Upper Pond—*lake* UT-8
Upper Pond—*reservoir* (2) CT-1
Upper Pond—*reservoir* (2) MA-1
Upper Pond—*reservoir* SC-3
Upper Pond Lick—*stream* WV-2
Upper Pond Sch—*school* KY-4
Upper Pony Creek Dam—*dam* OR-9
Upper Pony Creek Rsvr—*reservoir* OR-9
Upper Poplar—*locale* NC-3
Upper Popple Creek Cem—*cemetery* WI-6
Upper Portage Pond—*lake* ME-1
Upper Porter Canyon Spring—*spring* NV-8
Upper Porter Pond—*lake* MA-1
Upper Porter Pond—*reservoir* MA-1
Upper Porter Pond Dam—*dam* MA-1
Upper Portland Bar—*bar* AL-4
Upper Post Corral Spring—*spring* NV-8
Upper Post Lake—*lake* WI-6
*Upper Potato Valley* UT-8
*Upper Potter* PA-2
Upper Potter Mesa Tank—*reservoir* AZ-5
Upper Potter Rsvr—*reservoir* OR-9
**Upper Pottsgrove (Township of)**—*pop pl* PA-2
Upper Pound Swamp—*swamp* NY-2
*Upper Pouness Lake* MN-6
Upper Powder Spring—*spring* WY-8
Upper Powell Canyon*—*valley* NE-7
Upper Powerhouse—*other* HI-9
Upper Prairie Creek—*stream* OH-6
*Upper Prairie Creek Missionary Baptist Church* MS-4
**Upper Preston**—*pop pl* WA-9
Upper Price Lake—*lake* WI-6
Upper Price Lake—*reservoir* NV-8
*Upper Prichard Point* FL-3
Upper Priest Falls—*falls* ID-8
Upper Priest Lake—*lake* ID-8
Upper Priest River—*stream* ID-8
Upper Prior Lake—*lake* MN-6
Upper Pritchard Long Point—*cape* FL-3
Upper Prong Sinkhole Creek—*stream* TN-4
Upper Protection Levee—*levee* LA-4
**Upper Providence**—*pop pl* PA-2
Upper Providence Industrial Park—*locale* PA-2
Upper Providence Sch—*school* PA-2
Upper Providence Township—*CDP* PA-2
**Upper Providence (Township of)**—*pop pl* (2) PA-2
Upper Providence Township Park—*park* PA-2
Upper Provo Bridge Picnic Area—*locale* UT-8
*Upper Provo Falls* UT-8
*Upper Provo River* UT-8
*Upper Provo River Campground* UT-8
**Upper Pueblo**—*pop pl* NM-5
*Upper Pueblo Tank* AZ-5
Upper Puerto Tank—*reservoir* AZ-5
Upper Pug Lake—*lake* ME-1
Upper Pug Stream—*stream* ME-1
Upper Pungo Sch—*school* NC-3
Upper Purchase Brook—*stream* CT-1
Upper Quaking Asp Canyon—*valley* UT-8
Upper Quartz Creek—*stream* AK-9
Upper Quicksand Sch—*school* KY-4
Upper Quinn Lake—*lake* OR-9
Upper Quiver River—*stream* MS-4
Upper Racetrack Mesa—*summit* AZ-5
Upper Rader Sch—*school* KY-4
Upper Radical Mine—*mine* CO-8
Upper Raft River Valley—*basin* UT-8
Upper Raft River Valley—*valley* ID-8
Upper Rainbow Cave—*cave* AL-4
Upper Rakes Branch—*stream* VA-3
Upper Ramey Meadows—*flat* ID-8
Upper Ramparts—*valley* AK-9
Upper Ramsey Lake—*lake* MS-4
Upper Ranch—*slope* UT-8
Upper Ranch Opening—*flat* CA-9
Upper Ranch (site)—*locale* NM-5
Upper Range Lake—*lake* WI-6
Upper Range Pond—*lake* ME-1
Upper Rapid Sch—*school* SD-7
Upper Rattlesnake Mtn—*summit* NH-1
Upper Rattlesnake Ranch Number One Rsvr—*reservoir* UT-8
Upper Rattlesnake Rsvr—*reservoir* ID-8
Upper Rattlesnake Spring—*spring* AZ-5
Upper Rattlesnake Tank—*reservoir* AZ-5
Upper Rattlesnake Tank—*reservoir* NM-5
Upper Rattlesnake Tank—*reservoir* TX-5
Upper Rattlesnake Windmill—*locale* NM-5
Upper Rattling Springs Lake—*lake* MN-6
Upper Ray Spring—*spring* OR-9
Upper Razor Creek Park—*flat* CO-8
Upper Reach—*channel* VA-3
Upper Red Castle Lake—*lake* UT-8
Upper Red Cut Mine—*mine* TN-4
*Upper Redfish Lake* ID-8
Upper Redfish Lakes—*lake* ID-8
**Upper Red Hook**—*pop pl* NY-2
Upper Red Lake—*flat* UT-8
Upper Red Lake—*lake* MN-6
Upper Red Lake (Unorganized Territory of)—*unorg* MN-6
Upper Red Mud Sch—*school* TX-5
**Upper Red Owl Township**—*pop pl* SD-7
Upper Red Rock Lake—*lake* MT-8
*Upper Red Top Meadow* ID-8
Upper Red Top Meadows—*flat* ID-8
Upper Reedy Branch Lake—*lake* GA-3
**Upper Reese**—*pop pl* PA-2
Upper Reiley Tank—*reservoir* AZ-5
Upper Relief Valley—*basin* CA-9
Upper Reserve—*reservoir* SC-3
*Upper Reservoir* CO-8
*Upper Reservoir* MT-8
*Upper Reservoir* RI-1
*Upper Reservoir* WA-9
*Upper Reservoir Dam* MA-1
Upper Reservoir Dam—*dam* (2) MA-1
Upper Reservoir Dam—*dam* NJ-2
Upper Reynolds Creek Spring No 1—*spring* CO-8
Upper Reynolds Creek Spring No 2—*spring* CO-8
Upper Reynolds Creek Spring No 3—*spring* CO-8
Upper Reynolds Creek Spring No 4—*spring* CO-8
Upper Reynolds Creek Spring No 5—*spring* CO-8
Upper Reynolds Creek Spring No 6—*spring* CO-8
Upper Reynolds Creek Spring No 7—*spring* CO-8
Upper Reynolds Creek Springs—*spring* CO-8
*Upper Rhoda Lake* NY-2
Upper Rhoda Pond—*lake* NY-2
Upper Rice Lake—*lake* (2) MN-6
Upper Rice Lake Site—*hist pl* MN-6
Upper Rice Lake State Wildlife Mngmt Area—*park* MN-6
Upper Richardson Lake—*lake* ME-1
Upper Richbar Picnic Area—*park* CA-9
Upper Richwoods Cem—*cemetery* IA-7
Upper Riddell Lake—*lake* MT-8
Upper Ridge—*ridge* ME-1
Upper Ridge Cem—*cemetery* IL-6
Upper Ridge Cem—*cemetery* VA-3
Upper Ridge Road Sch—*school* NY-2
Upper Ridge School—*locale* IL-6
Upper Rifle Creek Sch—*school* CO-8
Upper Rigdon Lake—*lake* OR-9
Upper Riggs Spring—*spring* NV-8
Upper Rim Campgrounds—*park* AZ-5
Upper Rim Tank—*reservoir* AZ-5
Upper Rines Lake—*lake* MS-4
Upper Ringtail Tank—*reservoir* AZ-5
Upper Ripshin Branch—*stream* NC-3
Upper Riser Spring—*spring* NV-8
Upper Risue Canyon Spring—*spring* NV-8
Upper River Cave—*cave* AL-4
Upper River Deshee—*stream* IN-6
Upper River Rouge—*stream* MI-6
Upper River Windmill—*locale* TX-5
*Upper Roach Pond* ME-1
Upper Road Branch—*stream* (2) WV-2
Upper Road Spring—*spring* OR-9
Upper Roberts Rsvr—*reservoir* CA-9
Upper Rociada—*locale* NM-5
Upper Rock Canyon Spring—*spring* MT-8
Upper Rock Creek—*stream* AK-9
Upper Rock Creek—*stream* ID-8
Upper Rock Creek—*stream* OR-9
Upper Rock Creek Sch—*school* KY-4
Upper Rock Fork Sch—*school* KY-4
Upper Rockhouse Branch—*stream* VA-3
Upper Rock Lake—*lake* OR-9
Upper Rock Lake—*lake* UT-8
Upper Rock Quarry Canyon Rsvr—*reservoir* OR-9
Upper Rock Spring—*spring* NV-8
Upper Rock Tank—*reservoir* NM-5
Upper Rocky Fork Ch—*church* OH-6
Upper Rocky Honcut Creek—*stream* CA-9
Upper Rocky Point—*cape* NJ-2
Upper Rogers Dam—*dam* NC-3
Upper Rogers Lake—*reservoir* NC-3
Upper Rolling Springs Rsvr—*reservoir* WY-8
Upper Romero Windmill—*locale* NM-5
Upper Room Assembly of God—*church* FL-3
Upper Room Ch—*church* FL-3
Upper Room Temple of Apostolic Faith, The—*church* AL-4
Upper Rosebud Spring—*spring* NM-5
Upper Ross Lake—*lake* WY-8
Upper Ross Mine—*mine* MT-8
Upper Rotten Draw—*valley* TX-5
Upper Rough And Ready Ditch—*canal* CA-9
Upper Rough Run—*stream* WV-2
Upper Roundabout—*bend* GA-3
Upper Round Lake—*lake* MN-6
Upper Round Rock Sch—*school* TN-4
Upper Roxborough Rsvr—*reservoir* PA-2
Upper RR Spring—*spring* WA-9
Upper RR Tank—*reservoir* AZ-5
*Upper Rsvr* MA-1
Upper Rsvr—*reservoir* (2) CO-8
Upper Rsvr—*reservoir* (5) MA-1
Upper Rsvr—*reservoir* MO-7
Upper Rsvr—*reservoir* MT-8
Upper Rsvr—*reservoir* NV-8
Upper Rsvr—*reservoir* (2) NY-2
Upper Rsvr—*reservoir* OH-6
Upper Rsvr—*reservoir* (2) OR-9
Upper Rsvr—*reservoir* PA-2
Upper Rsvr—*reservoir* (2) WY-8
Upper Rsvr Bear Swamp—*reservoir* MA-1
Upper Ruby Cem—*cemetery* MT-8
Upper Ruby Sch—*school* MT-8
Upper Rugg Spring—*spring* OR-9
*Upper Ruin* AZ-5
Upper Run—*stream* NC-3
Upper Run—*stream* (2) WV-2
Upper Running Water Ch—*church* MS-4
Upper Rush Creek Campground—*locale* CA-9
Upper Russell Pond—*lake* ME-1
Upper Russian Lake—*lake* AK-9
Upper Rustler Spring—*spring* AZ-5
Upper Ruth Lake—*lake* CA-9
*Upper Sabao Lake* ME-1
Upper Sabao Lake—*lake* ME-1
Upper Sabinal Riverside Drain—*canal* NM-5
*Upper Sackett* MA-1
Upper Sackett Rsvr—*reservoir* MA-1
Upper Saddle Butte Rsvr—*reservoir* OR-9
Upper Saddle Horse Tank—*reservoir* AZ-5
**Upper Saddle River**—*pop pl* NJ-2
Upper Sagar Dam—*dam* NC-3
Upper Sage Creek—*stream* MT-8
Upper Sage Creek Spring—*spring* UT-8
Upper Sag Harbor Cove—*bay* NY-2
Upper Saginaw Rsvr—*reservoir* AZ-5
**Upper Sagon**—*pop pl* PA-2
Upper Saguache Guard Station—*locale* CO-8
Upper Sahuarita Dam—*dam* AZ-5
**Upper Saint Clair (Township of)**—*pop pl* PA-2
Upper Saint Croix Lake—*lake* WI-6
**Upper Sainte Clair**—*pop pl* PA-2
Upper Sainte Clair HS—*school* PA-2
**Upper Saint Regis**—*pop pl* NY-2
Upper Saint Regis Lake—*lake* MT-8
Upper Saint Regis Lake—*lake* NY-2
Upper Saint Vrain—*cens area* CO-8
*Upper Sakatah Lake* MN-6
Upper Salem Ch—*church* IL-6
**Upper Salford (Township of)**—*pop pl* PA-2
Upper Salida Tank—*reservoir* AZ-5
Upper Salmon Falls—*falls* ID-8
Upper Salmon Junction—*locale* WA-9
Upper Salmon Lake—*lake* CA-9
Upper Salmon Lake—*lake* OR-9
*Upper Salt Creek* OR-9
Upper Salt Creek Resort—*locale* CA-9
Upper Salt Fork Drainage Ditch—*canal* IL-6
Upper Salt Ground Tank—*reservoir* AZ-5
Upper Salt House Tank—*reservoir* AZ-5
Upper Salt Lick Ch—*church* KY-4
Upper Salt Lick Spring—*spring* CA-9
Upper Salt River Archeol District—*hist pl* VI-3
Upper Salty Spring—*spring* NM-5
Upper Sam Canyon Tank—*reservoir* AZ-5
Upper Sampson Tank—*reservoir* AZ-5
Upper San Antonio Valley—*valley* CA-9
Upper Sandbar Lake—*lake* CO-8
Upper Sand Brook—*stream* ME-1
Upper Sand Cove Dam—*dam* UT-8
Upper Sand Cove Rsvr—*reservoir* UT-8
Upper Sand Creek Lake—*reservoir* CO-8
Upper Sand Hill Sch—*school* PA-2
*Upper Sand Lake* MN-6
Upper Sandlick Branch—*stream* WV-2
Upper Sandlick Creek—*stream* KY-4
Upper Sand Ridge Sch—*school* IL-6
Upper Sand Run—*stream* OH-6
Upper Sand Slide—*slope* UT-8
Upper Sand Spring—*spring* OR-9
Upper Sandtown Bottom—*bend* OK-5
**Upper Sandusky**—*pop pl* OH-6
Upper Sandy Bayou—*stream* AR-4
Upper Sandy Creek—*stream* MO-7
Upper Sandy Guard Station—*locale* OR-9
Upper Sandy Slough—*stream* IL-6
Upper Sanford Springs—*spring* NV-8
Upper San Gabriel Valley (CCD)—*cens area* CA-9
*Upper San Gernando Reservoir* CA-9
Upper San Jacinto Bay—*bay* TX-5
Upper San Juan Campground—*locale* CA-9
Upper San Juan Riverside Drain—*canal* NM-5
Upper San Leandro Filtration Plant—*other* CA-9
Upper San Leandro Rsvr—*reservoir* CA-9
Upper San Luis Well—*well* AZ-5
Upper Sansavilla Landing—*locale* GA-3
Upper Santa Clara Bench Canal—*canal* UT-8
Upper Santa Ynez Camp Ground—*locale* CA-9
*Upper Saranac* NY-2
Upper Saranac Lake—*lake* NY-2
Upper Sardine Lake—*lake* CA-9
Upper Sardine Lake—*reservoir* CA-9
Upper Sardis Ch—*church* GA-3
Upper Sassafras Gap—*gap* NC-3
Upper Saucon Sch (abandoned)—*school* PA-2
**Upper Saucon (Township of)**—*pop pl* PA-2
*Upper Saugatuck River* CT-1
*Upper Sault Island* NY-2
Upper Sawmill Tank—*reservoir* NM-5
*Upper Scenic Lake* WA-9
Upper Sch—*school* GA-3
Upper Sch—*school* NH-1
**Upper Scheelite**—*pop pl* CA-9
Upper Schodack Island—*flat* NY-2
Upper Schooner Creek—*stream* IN-6
Upper Scott Brook—*stream* ME-1
Upper Scott Lake—*lake* MI-6
Upper Scott Ranch—*locale* NV-8
Upper Scott Spring—*spring* NV-8
Upper Second Creek—*stream* KY-4
*Upper Section Ferry* AL-4
Upper Seep Tank—*reservoir* AZ-5
Upper Seibert Lake—*lake* AR-4
*Upper Semoneaston Thorofare* VA-3
Upper Settlement Rural Hist Dist—*hist pl* TX-5
Upper Seven Lake—*lake* CA-9
Upper Sevenmile Creek—*stream* MT-8
Upper Sevenmile Tank—*reservoir* AZ-5
Upper Sevenmile Well—*well* AZ-5
Upper Seymour Lake—*lake* MT-8
Upper Shady—*locale* TN-4
Upper Shady Grove Ch—*church* MS-4
Upper Shake Campground—*locale* CA-9
Upper Shaker Lake—*reservoir* OH-6
**Upper Shaker Village**—*pop pl* NH-1
Upper Shannon Branch—*stream* WV-2
Upper Sharp Tank—*reservoir* AZ-5
Upper Shaw Hollow—*valley* OH-6
Upper Shawme Lake—*lake* MA-1
Upper Sheep Canyon Well—*well* NV-8
Upper Sheep Cave—*cave* TN-4
Upper Sheep Creek Rsvr—*reservoir* OR-9
Upper Sheep Creek Spring—*spring* AZ-5
Upper Sheephorn Sch—*school* CO-8
Upper Sheets Run—*stream* WV-2
**Upper Shell Creek**—*pop pl* TN-4
Upper Shell Creek Sch (historical)—*school* TN-4
Upper Shepaug Rsvr—*reservoir* CT-1
Upper Sheriff Run—*stream* PA-2
Upper Sherman Ranch—*locale* OR-9
*Upper Sherriff Run* PA-2
Upper Sherwin Bar—*bar* ID-8
*Upper Shields Pond* NH-1
Upper Shin Pond—*lake* ME-1
Upper Shirley—*hist pl* VA-3
Upper Shirley Corner—*locale* ME-1
Upper Shoals—*other* MO-7
Upper Shoe Lake—*lake* MI-6
Upper Short Creek—*stream* CO-8
Upper Sibley Pond—*reservoir* MA-1
Upper Signor Rsvr—*reservoir* WY-8
Upper Silas Lake—*lake* WY-8
Upper Silver Creek Ranch—*locale* OR-9
Upper Silver Creek Sch—*school* KY-4
*Upper Silver Lake* WY-8
Upper Silver Lake—*lake* MI-6
Upper Silver Lakes—*lake* WY-8
Upper Silver Run Lake—*lake* WY-8
Upper Silvis Lake—*lake* AK-9
Upper Simmons Well—*well* AZ-5
Upper Simon Bar—*bar* OR-9
Upper Simoneaston Thorofare—*channel* VA-3
Upper Sinepuxent Neck—*cape* MD-2
Upper Sinking—*locale* TN-4
Upper Sinking Ch—*church* TN-4
Upper Sinking Creek—*stream* KY-4
Upper Sinking Creek—*stream* TN-4
Upper Sinking Sch (historical)—*school* TN-4
Upper Sioux Agency—*hist pl* MN-6
Upper Sioux Agency State Park—*park* MN-6
Upper Sioux City Bend—*bend* IA-7
Upper Sioux City Bend—*bend* NE-7
Upper Sioux Community (Indian Reservation)—*reserve* MN-6
Upper Sioux Indian Community—*reserve* MN-6
Upper Sioux Ind Res—*reserve* MN-6
Upper Sister Bar—*bar* AL-4
Upper Sister Creek—*stream* FL-3
Upper Sister Creek—*stream* OH-6
Upper Sister Island—*island* ME-1
Upper Sister Lake—*lake* NY-2
Upper Siuslaw (CCD)—*cens area* OR-9
Upper Sizemore Spring—*spring* OR-9
Upper Skagit (CCD)—*cens area* WA-9
**Upper Skagit Ind Res**—*pop pl* WA-9
Upper Skegg Fork—*stream* VA-3
Upper Skippack Ch—*church* PA-2
Upper Skolai Lake—*lake* AK-9
Upper Sky High Lake—*lake* CA-9
Upper Slate Creek—*locale* AK-9
Upper Slate Creek Trail—*trail* ID-8
Upper Slate Lake—*lake* CO-8
Upper Slate Lake—*lake* ID-8
Upper Slavonia Mine—*mine* CO-8
Upper Sleith Ch—*church* WV-2
Upper Sleith Fork—*stream* WV-2
Upper Slickrock—*summit* UT-8
Upper Slide—*flat* WY-8
Upper Slide Lake—*lake* CO-8
Upper Slide Lake—*lake* WY-8
Upper Slim and Fatty Rsvr—*reservoir* OR-9
Upper Slope Rsvr—*reservoir* ID-8
Upper Smith Branch Sch—*school* KY-4
Upper Smith Ditch—*canal* CO-8
Upper Smith River Trail—*trail* CA-9
Upper Smyrna Ch—*church* AR-4
Upper Snake River Trail—*trail* OR-9
Upper Snively Spring—*spring* WA-9
Upper Snoqualmie Valley (CCD)—*cens area* WA-9
Upper Snowshoe Lake—*lake* OR-9
Upper Snowy Lake—*lake* WA-9
Upper Snyder Lake—*lake* MT-8
Upper Soda—*locale* OR-9
Upper Soda Falls—*falls* OR-9
*Upper Soda Springs* OR-9
**Upper Soda Springs**—*pop pl* CA-9
Upper Soper Pond—*lake* ME-1
Upper Sound Point—*cape* FL-3
Upper South Amana—*locale* IA-7
Upper Southampton Township—*CDP* PA-2
**Upper Southampton (Township of)**—*pop pl* PA-2
Upper South Branch Pond—*lake* ME-1
Upper South Branch Thunder Bay River—*stream* (2) MI-6
Upper South Fork Campground—*locale* CO-8
Upper South Fork Forest Camp—*locale* OR-9
Upper South Fork Little River—*stream* CA-9
*Upper South Fork of Little River* CA-9
Upper South Long Lake—*lake* MN-6
Upper South Pond—*lake* NY-2
Upper Sow Hole Spring—*spring* UT-8
Upper Spang Creek—*stream* MT-8
Upper Spanish Mine (Inactive)—*mine* CA-9
*Upper Spavinaw Lake* OK-5
Upper Spavinaw Rec Area—*park* OK-5
Upper Spear Ditch—*canal* MT-8
Upper Spectacle Island—*island* MA-1
Upper Spectacle Pond—*reservoir* MA-1
Upper Spectacle Pond Dam—*dam* MA-1
*Upper Spednik Lake* ME-1
**Upper Spencer**—*pop pl* KY-4
Upper Spirit Lake—*lake* WI-6
Upper Sprague Reservoir Dam—*dam* RI-1
Upper Sprague Rsvr—*reservoir* RI-1
Upper Spring—*spring* (3) AZ-5
Upper Spring—*spring* (2) ID-8
Upper Spring—*spring* TX-5
Upper Spring—*spring* (2) UT-8
Upper Spring—*spring* WA-9
Upper Spring Creek—*stream* NC-3
Upper Spring Creek Ch—*church* AR-4
Upper Spring Creek Sch—*school* MT-8
Upper Spring Creek Sch—*school* NE-7
Upper Springdale Estates Dam—*dam* NC-3
Upper Springdale Estates Lake—*reservoir* NC-3
Upper Springfield Meetinghouse—*hist pl* NJ-2
Upper Spring Grove Cem—*cemetery* IA-7
Upper Springhill Campground—*locale* CA-9
Upper Spring Lake—*lake* MN-6
Upper Spring Lake—*reservoir* IN-6
Upper Spring Lake—*reservoir* WI-6
Upper Spring Lake Dam—*dam* IN-6
Upper Springstead Lake—*lake* WI-6
Upper Spring Tank—*reservoir* NM-5
Upper Spring Water Windmill—*well* AZ-5
Upper Springy Pond—*lake* ME-1
Upper Spruce Creek—*stream* KY-4
Upper Spunk Lake—*lake* MN-6
*Upper Squankum* NJ-2
Upper Squaw Brook—*stream* ME-1
Upper Squaw Creek Spring—*spring* ID-8
Upper Squaw Tank—*reservoir* AZ-5
Upper Stafford Marsh—*lake* NY-2
Upper Stairs Brook—*stream* NH-1
Upper Standard Canal—*canal* CA-9
*Upper Stasburg* PA-2
Upper State Game Sanctuary—*park* AL-4
Upper State Lake—*reservoir* AL-4
Upper State Lake Dam—*dam* AL-4
Upper State Park—*flat* CO-8
Upper State Spring—*spring* WY-8
Upper State Street Hist Dist—*hist pl* CT-1
Upper St. Clair—*CDP* PA-2
Upper Steer Run Ch—*church* WV-2
Upper Stephens Meadows—*swamp* CA-9
**Upper Stepney**—*pop pl* CT-1
Upper Steve Creek Flowage—*reservoir* WI-6
Upper Stevens Lake—*lake* ID-8
Upper Stillwater Campground—*locale* UT-8
Upper Stillwater Lake—*lake* MT-8
*Upper Stillwater Lakes* MT-8
Upper Stillwater Rsvr—*reservoir* CO-8
Upper Stimpson Run—*stream* PA-2
Upper Stinnett Sch—*school* KY-4
Upper Stinson Creek—*stream* KY-4
Upper Stokes Dam—*dam* NJ-2
Upper Stokes Pond—*reservoir* NJ-2
Upper Stone Branch—*stream* WV-2
Upper Stone Canyon Rsvr—*reservoir* CA-9
Upper Stone Schoolhouse—*hist pl* IA-7
Upper Stoneville Reservoir Dam—*dam* MA-1
Upper Stony Brook—*stream* ME-1
Upper Storm Lake—*lake* CO-8
*Upper Story Lake* IN-6
Upper Story Lake—*lake* IN-6
Upper Straight Canyon—*valley* UT-8
Upper Straight Creek Sch (historical)—*school* TN-4
Upper Straits Lake—*lake* MI-6
**Upper Strasburg**—*pop pl* PA-2
Upper Stratton Spring—*spring* AZ-5
Upper Street Cem—*cemetery* ME-1
Upper Stringtown Branch—*stream* KY-4
Upper Stump Canyon Rsvr—*reservoir* ID-8
Upper Stump Lake—*lake* IL-6
Upper Sturgeon Branch—*stream* WV-2
Upper Sucker Creek—*stream* AK-9
Upper Sugarbush Lake—*lake* WI-6
Upper Sugar Creek—*stream* IN-6
*Upper Sugarloaf Mountain* OR-9
Upper Sugarloaf Mtn—*summit* CO-8
Upper Sugarloaf Sound—*bay* FL-3
Upper Sulphur Creek—*stream* IN-6
Upper Sulphur Creek—*stream* TX-5
Upper Sulphur Spring—*spring* NV-8
Upper Sulphur Springs Ch—*church* AL-4
Upper Summerhouse Pond—*reservoir* SC-3
Upper Summers Meadows—*flat* CA-9
Upper Summit Lake—*lake* IN-6
Upper Summit Spring—*spring* NV-8
Upper Suncook Lake—*lake* NH-1
Upper Sunk Lake—*lake* LA-4
**Upper Sunnyside**—*pop pl* UT-8
Upper Sunset Lake—*lake* CA-9
Upper Sunset Lake—*reservoir* NJ-2
**Upper Sunset Park**—*pop pl* IN-6
Upper Sunshine Basin—*basin* WY-8
Upper Sureshot Lake—*lake* MT-8
Upper Surrounded Hill (Township of)—*fmr MCD* AR-4
Upper Swale—*valley* ID-8
Upper Swan Lake—*lake* AR-4
Upper Swan Lake—*lake* IL-6
Upper Sweater Tank—*reservoir* AZ-5
Upper Sweeney Lake—*lake* WY-8
Upper Sweetheart Lake—*lake* AK-9
Upper Sweetwater Creek—*stream* FL-3
Upper Switzer Campground—*locale* CA-9
Upper Swope Tank—*reservoir* NM-5
Upper Sycamore Spring—*spring* (2) AZ-5
Upper Sycamore Tank—*reservoir* AZ-5
Upper Sylvan Lake—*lake* WY-8
*Upper Symes Pond* VT-1
Upper Syrup Spring—*spring* OR-9
Upper Sysladobsis Lake—*lake* ME-1
Upper Sysladobsis Stream—*stream* ME-1
Upper Table—*summit* WY-8
Upper Table Rock—*pillar* OR-9
Upper Tailholt Spring—*spring* AZ-5
Upper Talarik Creek—*stream* AK-9
Upper Tamarack River—*stream* MN-6
Upper Tamarack River—*stream* WI-6
Upper Tampa Bay Archeol District—*hist pl* FL-3
Upper Tangle Lake—*lake* AK-9
Upper Tank—*reservoir* (16) AZ-5
Upper Tank—*reservoir* (2) NM-5
Upper Tank—*reservoir* TX-5
Upper Tank Draw—*valley* AZ-5
Upper Tater Canyon—*valley* AZ-5
Upper Taylor Brook—*stream* ME-1
Upper Taylor Lake—*lake* AR-4
Upper Taylor Rsvr—*reservoir* MT-8
Upper Tazimina Lake—*lake* AK-9
Upper Tebay Lake—*lake* AK-9
Upper Teges Creek—*stream* KY-4
Upper Telida Lake—*lake* AK-9
Upper Tenmile Ch—*church* PA-2
Upper Tenmile Ch—*church* WV-2
Upper Tennessee Sch (abandoned)—*school* MO-7
Upper Tent Meadow—*flat* CA-9
Upper Ten X Tank—*reservoir* AZ-5
Upper Tepee Basin—*basin* MT-8
Upper Terrace—*flat* NV-8
Upper Texas—*locale* LA-4
Upper Tex Tank—*reservoir* AZ-5
Upper Third Street—*uninc pl* WI-6
Upper Thirteen Tank—*reservoir* AZ-5
Upper Thirty-six Bay—*bay* FL-3
Upper Thompson Lake—*lake* MT-8
Upper Thompson Lake—*lake* ND-7
Upper Thompson Mesa Tank—*reservoir* AZ-5
Upper Thompson Spring—*spring* AZ-5
Upper Thorofare—*channel* MD-2
Upper Thorofare—*channel* NJ-2
Upper Thousandsticks Sch—*school* KY-4
Upper Three Meadow—*flat* CA-9
Upper Threemile Fork—*stream* WV-2
Upper Three Prong Sch—*school* KY-4
*Upper Three Run* PA-2
Upper Three Runs—*stream* PA-2
Upper Three Runs—*stream* SC-3
Upper Thunder Lake—*lake* MI-6
Upper Tiger Creek Ch—*church* TN-4
Upper Tillicum Creek—*stream* WA-9
*Upper Timber Canyon* OR-9
Upper Timber Canyon—*valley* OR-9
Upper Tincup Spring—*spring* AZ-5
Upper Tinicum Union Ch—*church* PA-2
Upper Tippah Watershed LT-6-1 Dam—*dam* MS-4
Upper Tippah Watershed LT-6-17 Dam—*dam* MS-4
Upper Tippah Watershed LT-6-2 Dam—*dam* MS-4
Upper Tippah Watershed LT-6-4 Dam—*dam* MS-4
*Upper Tippecanoe Lake* IN-6
Upper Togiak Lake—*lake* AK-9
Upper Togue Pond—*lake* ME-1
Upper Toklat River Cabin No. 24—*hist pl* AK-9
Upper Tomahawk Lake—*lake* MI-6
Upper Tom Brown Well—*well* AZ-5
Upper Toposhaw Structure Y-27-1 Dam—*dam* MS-4
Upper Topsaw Landing—*locale* SC-3
Upper Tornillo Drain—*canal* TX-5
Upper Torrey Island—*island* ME-1
Upper Town—*locale* CA-9
Upper Town Creek Ch—*church* NC-3
Upper Town Creek Rural Hist Dist—*hist pl* NC-3
*Upper Town Dock* NY-2
Uppertown (historical)—*locale* NV-8
Upper Town Landing—*locale* NY-2
Upper (Township of)—*fmr MCD* (2) AR-4
**Upper (Township of)**—*pop pl* NJ-2
**Upper (Township of)**—*pop pl* OH-6
Upper Trace Branch—*stream* KY-4
Upper Trace Branch Sch—*school* KY-4
Upper Trace Fork—*stream* WV-2
Upper Trace Fork Sch—*school* KY-4
Upper Trace Sch—*school* WV-2
**Upper Tract**—*pop pl* WV-2
Upper Trail—*trail* UT-8
Upper Trail Canyon—*valley* UT-8
Upper Trail Lake—*lake* AK-9
Upper Trail Ridge—*ridge* NC-3
Upper Trapper Flat—*flat* ID-8
Upper Trelipe Lake—*lake* MN-6

Urumangnak River—stream AK-9
Uruno Beach—beach GU-9
Uruno Beach Site—hist pl GU-9
Uruno Point—summit GU-9
Uruno Site—hist pl GU-9
Urur—island FM-9
Ururion FM-9
Uruuro FM-9
Uruuro, Cape FM-9
Urururu—gap FM-9
Urushi Anchorage—harbor FM-9
Urusline HS—school OH-6
Urutoi-To PW-9
Uruwadowan—island MP-9
Uruwadowan Island MP-9
Uruwadowan-To MP-9
Urvi Creek—stream MT-8
Urvi Gulch—valley MT-8
Ury—locale OK-5
**Ury**—pop pl WV-2
U S A A—post sta TX-5
USA Canal OR-9
USAEC Pantex Plant—other TX-5
USAF Bombing Range No 4—locale WY-8
USAF Hospital—post sta FL-3
US Air Force—post sta MN-6
U S Air Force Gunnery Range—military LA-4
Usai-Saki MH-9
U-saki FM-9
Usal—locale CA-9
Usal Creek—stream CA-9
Usal Rock—island CA-9
U.S. Animal Quarantine Station—hist pl NJ-2
**USAR Center**—pop pl NC-3
U.S. Army Corps of Engineers Superintendent's House and Workmen's Office—hist pl KY-4
U.S. Army Fort Thomas Mess Hall—hist pl KY-4
U.S. Army Military Ocean Terminal—hist pl NY-2
U.S. Army Reserve Center—locale FL-3
U.S. Army Reserve Center—military GA-3
U.S. Arsenal (Arsenal Technical HS)—hist pl IN-6
U.S. Arsenal Bldg—hist pl AR-4
U.S. Arsenal-Officers Quarters—hist pl FL-3
Usas—cape PW-9
Usas, Bkul A—cape PW-9
U S Atomic Energy Commission (Oak Ridge A—locale TN-4
U-Save Shop Ctr—locale FL-3
Usave Spring—spring NV-8
U S Basin—basin CO-8
U S B Line Canal—canal OR-9
USBR Pumping Plant E—other OR-9
USBR Pumping Plant F—other OR-9
US Bullion Depository, Fort Knox, Kentucky—hist pl KY-4
US Bullion Depository, West Point, New York—hist pl NY-2
U S Camp—locale AK-9
U S Capitol—other DC-2
U.S. Capitol Gatehouses And Gateposts—hist pl DC-2
**Uscarco**—pop pl LA-4
U.S. Car. No. 1—hist pl FL-3
U S C C—post sta NY-2
USCE HQ—other CA-9
U S Census Bureau—building MD-2
Usce Test Laboratory—building OH-6
USCGC TANEY (WHEC-37)—hist pl MD-2
U. S. Chemical—facility IL-6
US Coast Guard and Geodetic Survey Seismological and Geomagnetic House—hist pl AK-9
U.S. Coast Guard Bldg—hist pl OH-6
U.S. Coast Guard Diamond Head Lighthouse—hist pl HI-9
U.S. Coast Guard Headquarters, Key West Station—hist pl FL-3
U.S. Coast Guard Hist Dist—hist pl SC-3
U.S. Coast Guard Makapuu Point Light—hist pl HI-9
U.S. Coast Guard Molokai Light—hist pl HI-9
U.S. Coast Guard Station—hist pl VA-3
US Coast Guard Station—locale NC-3
U S Coast Guard Station Lighthouse—locale OH-6
U.S. Coast Guard Yard Curtis Bay—hist pl MD-2
U.S. Courthouse—hist pl CA-9
U.S. Courthouse—hist pl ME-1
U.S. Courthouse—hist pl NM-5
US Courthouse—hist pl NY-2
U.S. Courthouse—hist pl OR-9
US Courthouse—hist pl SC-3
U.S. Courthouse—hist pl WA-9
U.S. Courthouse, Post Office and Customs House—hist pl VT-1
U.S. Courthouse and Post Office—hist pl AL-4
U.S. Courthouse and Post Office—hist pl IN-6
U.S. Courthouse and Post Office—hist pl MS-4
U.S. Court of Appeals-Fifth Circuit—hist pl LA-4
U.S. Court Of Military Appeals—hist pl DC-2
U S Creek—stream AK-9
U S Creek—stream ID-8
U S Creek—stream WA-9
US Custom House—hist pl AZ-5
U.S. Customhouse—hist pl (2) CA-9
U.S. Customhouse—hist pl CO-8
U.S. Customhouse—hist pl GA-3
U.S. Customhouse—hist pl LA-4
U.S. Customhouse—hist pl (2) ME-1
U.S. Custom House—hist pl MD-2
U.S. Customhouse—hist pl MA-1
US Customhouse—hist pl MA-1
U.S. Customhouse—hist pl (3) NY-2
U.S. Customhouse—hist pl OR-9
U.S. Customhouse—hist pl SC-3
U.S. Customhouse—hist pl TX-5
U.S. Customhouse—hist pl VA-3
US Custom House—hist pl (4) PR-3
U.S. Customhouse and Post Office—hist pl (2) ME-1
U.S. Customhouse and Post Office—hist pl (2) MO-7
U.S. Customhouse (Old Customhouse) and Post Office—hist pl ME-1
U.S. Customshouse—hist pl MA-1
U.S. Customshouse—hist pl NY-2
U.S. Customshouse—hist pl RI-1
U S Dam Number Four—dam IN-6
USDA Plant Materials Center—building CA-9
USDA Rice Experimental Station—locale CA-9
U S Dept Of Agriculture Research Center—building PA-2
U S Dept of the Interior Biological Laboratory—locale FL-3
U.S. District Courthouse—hist pl MS-4
U S Ditch—canal ID-8
Usechees AL-4
Useful—locale MO-7
U.S. Electronics Proving Ground AZ-5
Useless Bay—bay WA-9
Useless Bay—swamp GA-3
Useless Cove—bay AK-9
Useppa Island—island FL-3
**Useppa Island**—pop pl FL-3
Useppa Oyster Bar—bar FL-3
**Usera**—pop pl PR-3
Usery Cem—cemetery TN-4
Usery Mountain Rec Area—park AZ-5
Usery Mountains—summit AZ-5
Usery Mtn AZ-5
Usery Mtn—summit AZ-5
Usery Pass—gap AZ-5
Usevia Gulch—valley CO-8
U.S. Feed Canal OR-9
U.S. Fish Control Laboratory—hist pl WI-6
U S Forest Service Aerial Fire Depot—other MT-8
U S Forest Service Airp—airport UT-8
U.S. Forest Service Clinic—hospital UT-8
U.S. Forest Service Clinic Heliport—airport UT-8
U.S. Forest Service Remount Depot—hist pl MT-8
USFS Center—other CA-9
USFS Fire Station—locale MT-8
U.S.F.S. Guard Station—locale OR-9
USFS HQ—building CA-9
USFS Lyon Work Camp—locale MT-8
U S F S Station—locale CA-9
USFS Trail Creek Station—locale MT-8
USFS West Fork Camp—locale MT-8
U.S. General Post Office—hist pl NY-2
U S Geological Survey Camp Oil and Gas CA-9
Usg Number One Tank—reservoir TX-5
US Government Tuberculosis Hosp (historical)—hospital AL-4
US Grant Mines—mine MT-8
USGSA Depot—locale AZ-5
USGS Camp—locale HI-9
USGS Center—locale MO-7
USGS Natl Center—building VA-3
U S Gulch—valley CO-8
Ushagat Island—island AK-9
**Usher**—pop pl FL-3
Usher, John Palmer, House—hist pl KS-7
Usher Cem—cemetery GA-3
Usher Cem—cemetery IN-6
Usher Cove—bay RI-1
Usher Gulch—valley CA-9
Usher House—hist pl GA-3
Usher Inlet—stream ME-1
Usher Lake—reservoir MS-4
Usher Point—cape RI-1
Usher Pond—lake GA-3
Usher Pond—reservoir SC-3
Usher Rock—other AK-9
**Ushers**—pop pl NY-2
Ushers Cove RI-1
Ushers Millpond—reservoir GA-3
Ushers Point RI-1
Ushers Temple—church GA-3
Usher Valley Ch—church MS-4
Ushi FM-9
U S Highway Canal Number C-109—canal FL-3
Ushi Island FM-9
Ushi Island Pass—channel FM-9
U S Hill—gap NM-5
Ushima FM-9
Ushi Point MH-9
Ushi Saki MH-9
Ushishima Pass FM-9
Ushishima Suido FM-9
Ushi To FM-9
Ushkabwahka RiA VAR Ushkabwakka River MN-6
Ushkabwahka River MN-6
Ushkabwakka River MN-6
Ushkabwakke River MN-6
Ushk Bay—bay AK-9
Ushk Point—cape AK-9
U S Hydrologic Experiment Station—other OH-6
**Usibelli**—pop pl AK-9
Usibelli Mine—COP AK-9
Usibelli Mine—mine AK-9
Usibelli Peak—summit AK-9
Usick NC-3
U.S. Immigrant Station and Assay Office—hist pl WA-9
US Immigration Bldg—hist pl WA-9
U.S. Immigration Office—hist pl HI-9
Usinas Beach—locale FL-3
U.S. Indian Industrial Sch—hist pl NE-7
U S Indian Industrial School SD-7
U.S. Inspection Station/U.S. Custom House—hist pl CA-9
Usi Point—cape AS-9
Usi Saki MH-9
Usi-Saki-Si MH-9
Usi Si MH-9
**Usk**—pop pl WA-9
Uskabwanka River MN-6
Us-Kab-Wan-Ka River—stream MN-6
Uski Island—island AK-9
U.S. Life Saving Station Station No. 14—hist pl NJ-2
USLM—other (4) AZ-5
USLM No 1—other (2) NM-5
U S L M No 1—other NM-5
USLM No 113—other CA-9
USLM No 15—other AK-9
USLM No 18—other AK-9
USLM No 2—other UT-8
USLM No 3—other AK-9
Uslm No 3—other NM-5
USLM No 3—other UT-8
U S L M No 4—other NM-5
USLM No 4790—other MT-8
USLM No 5740—other MT-8
USLM No 5789—other MT-8
USLM No 6582—other CA-9
USLM No 6939—other MT-8
USLM No 9—other UT-8
USLM Number 1—other AZ-5
USLM Number 2650—other AZ-5
USLM Number 2652—other AZ-5
USLM 1—other AK-9
USLM 1—other (4) AZ-5
USLM 1—other (3) UT-8
USLM 1075—other AZ-5
USLM 1085—other AZ-5
USLM 1101—other AZ-5
USLM 1112—other AZ-5
USLM 1124—other AZ-5
USLM 1132—other AZ-5
USLM 1179—other AZ-5
USLM 1181—other AZ-5
USLM 1184—other AZ-5
USLM 1204—other AZ-5
USLM 1220—other AZ-5
USLM 1224—other AZ-5
USLM 123—other CA-9
USLM 1240—other UT-8
USLM 1248—other AZ-5
USLM 1256—other AZ-5
USLM 1257—other AZ-5
USLM 1258—other AZ-5
USLM 1259—other AZ-5
USLM 1260—other AZ-5
USLM 127—other CA-9
USLM 1273—other AZ-5
USLM 1274—other AZ-5
USLM 1275—other AZ-5
USLM 1277—other AZ-5
USLM 1286—other AZ-5
USLM 1307—other AZ-5
USLM 1319—other AZ-5
USLM 132—other CA-9
USLM 1345—other AZ-5
USLM 1368—other AZ-5
USLM 1390—other AZ-5
USLM 1396—other AZ-5
USLM 1446—other AZ-5
USLM 1450—other AZ-5
USLM 1453—other AZ-5
USLM 1477—other AZ-5
USLM 1481—other AZ-5
USLM 1486—other AK-9
USLM 1488—other AZ-5
USLM 1494—other AZ-5
USLM 15—other AK-9
USLM 150—other CA-9
USLM 1528—other AZ-5
USLM 153—other AZ-5
USLM 1542—other AZ-5
USLM 1550—other AZ-5
USLM 1555—other AZ-5
USLM 1576—other AZ-5
USLM 1577—other AZ-5
USLM 1579—other AZ-5
USLM 1591—other AZ-5
USLM 160—other AZ-5
USLM 1602—other AZ-5
USLM 1623—other AZ-5
USLM 166—other CA-9
USLM 1671—other AZ-5
USLM 1677—other AZ-5
USLM 1679—other AZ-5
USLM 1683A—other AZ-5
USLM 1691—other AZ-5
USLM 1699A—other AZ-5
USLM 1699B—other AZ-5
USLM 1706—other AZ-5
USLM 1738—other AZ-5
USLM 1746—other AZ-5
USLM 1754—other AZ-5
USLM 179—other AZ-5
USLM 1804—other AZ-5
USLM 1860—other AZ-5
USLM 1913—other AZ-5
USLM 1971—other AZ-5
USLM 1992—other AZ-5
USLM 2—other AK-9
USLM 2—other AZ-5
USLM 2—other (4) UT-8
USLM 2099—other AZ-5
USLM 2123—other AZ-5
USLM 2171—other AZ-5
USLM 2180—other AZ-5
USLM 226—other AZ-5
USLM 227—other AZ-5
USLM 2338—other AZ-5
USLM 2340—other AZ-5
USLM 2344—other AZ-5
USLM 235—other UT-8
USLM 2359—other AZ-5
USLM 2393—other AZ-5
USLM 2395—other AZ-5
USLM 2397—other AZ-5
USLM 24—other UT-8
USLM 2419—other AZ-5
USLM 2483 A—other AZ-5
USLM 2483 B—other AZ-5
USLM 2489—other AZ-5
USLM 2518—other AZ-5
USLM 2541—other AZ-5
U S L M 255—other UT-8
USLM 2551—other AZ-5
USLM 2579—other AZ-5
U S L M 258—other UT-8
USLM 2584—other AZ-5
USLM 2602—other AZ-5
USLM 263—other UT-8
USLM 2630—other AZ-5
USLM 2670—other AZ-5
USLM 2675—other AZ-5
USLM 2695—other AZ-5
USLM 2698—other AZ-5
U S L M 270—other UT-8
USLM 2748—other (2) AZ-5
USLM 2785—other AZ-5
USLM 2797—other AZ-5
USLM 2801—other AZ-5
USLM 2878—other AZ-5
USLM 290—other AZ-5
USLM 2928—other AZ-5
USLM 3—other AK-9
USLM 3—other NM-5
USLM 30—other AK-9
USLM 300—other AZ-5
USLM 30068—other AZ-5
USLM 3160 B—other AZ-5
USLM 319—other AZ-5
USLM 320—other AZ-5
USLM 321—other AZ-5
USLM 3212—other AZ-5
USLM 3238—other AZ-5
USLM 328—other AZ-5
USLM 3286—other AZ-5
USLM 3328—other AZ-5
USLM 333—other AZ-5
USLM 334—other AZ-5
USLM 337—other AZ-5
USLM 3380—other AZ-5
USLM 3578—other AZ-5
USLM 3634—other AZ-5
USLM 3673—other AZ-5
USLM 3708—other AZ-5
USLM 3747—other AZ-5
USLM 38—other AZ-5
USLM 4—mine UT-8
USLM 4—other AK-9
USLM 4—other AZ-5
USLM 4015—other AZ-5
USLM 4016—other AZ-5
USLM 4027—other AZ-5
USLM 4063—other AZ-5
USLM 4066—other AZ-5
USLM 4110—other AZ-5
USLM 4-1245—other AZ-5
USLM 414—other AZ-5
USLM 415—other AZ-5
USLM 416—other AZ-5
USLM 4315—other AZ-5
USLM 44—other AZ-5
USLM 448—other AZ-5
USLM 6—other UT-8
USLM 632—other AZ-5
USLM 70—other CA-9
USLM 78—other CA-9
USLM 84—other CA-9
USLM 90—other AZ-5
USLM 95—other CA-9
USLM 97—other CA-9
U.S. Marine Corps Barracks and Commandant's House—hist pl DC-2
U.S. Marine Hosp—hist pl AL-4
U.S. Marine Hosp—hist pl KY-4
U.S. Marine Hosp—hist pl WA-9
U S Marine Hosp—hospital WA-9
U.S. Marine Hosp Executive Bldg and Laundry-Kitchen—hist pl TN-4
USMC Mountain Warfare Sch—school CA-9
U.S. Military Acad—hist pl NY-2
U S Milit Reservation Indiana Arsenal—military IN-6
U S Milit Reservation Ravenna Arsenal—military OH-6
U S Mine—mine AZ-5
US Mine—mine ID-8
U S Mint—building PA-2
US Mint—hist pl CA-9
U.S. Mint—hist pl NV-8
U.S. Mint, New Orleans Branch—hist pl LA-4
USMM—other (3) AZ-5
USMM—other (2) CA-9
USMMI—other AZ-5
USMM M2—other AZ-5
USMM No 1—other NM-5
USMM No 182—other CA-9
USMM No 2—other NM-5
USMM No 3—other NM-5
USMM No 32—other CA-9
USMM No 45—other CA-9
USMM Number 2—other AZ-5
USMM Number 3—other AZ-5
USMM Number 5—other AZ-5
USMM Wingate—other CA-9
USMM 1—other (17) AZ-5
USMM 1—other CA-9
USMM 1—other (8) UT-8
USMM 108—other CA-9
USMM 10915—other MT-8
USMM 12—other (2) CA-9
USMM 122—other CA-9
USMM 13—other CA-9
USMM 131—other CA-9
Usmm 135—other CA-9
USMM 155—other CA-9
USMM 1597—other AZ-5
USMM 1631—other AZ-5
USMM 17—other CA-9
USMM 1707—other AZ-5
USMM 18—other CA-9
USMM 1810—other AZ-5
USMM 1886—other AZ-5
USMM 2—other (11) AZ-5
USMM 2—other (3) UT-8
USMM 206—other CA-9
USMM 22—other CA-9
USMM 227—other AZ-5
USMM 23—other CA-9
USMM 239—other UT-8
USMM 25—other CA-9
USMM 2522—other AZ-5
USMM 277—other UT-8
USMM 2817—other AZ-5
USMM 2825—other AZ-5
USMM 2871—other AZ-5
USMM 2927—other AZ-5
USMM 2948—other AZ-5
USMM 2948B—other AZ-5
USMM 3—other (6) AZ-5
USMM 3—other (2) UT-8
USMM 30—other CA-9
USMM 3030—other AZ-5
USMM 3184—other AZ-5
USMM 3256—other AZ-5
USMM 3275—other AZ-5
USMM 3290 A—other AZ-5
USMM 3445—other AZ-5
USMM 35—other CA-9
USMM 3770—other AZ-5
USMM 3777—other AZ-5
USMM 38—other CA-9
USMM 3933—other AZ-5
USMM 3934—other AZ-5
USMM 4—other (3) AZ-5
USMM 4—other UT-8
USMM 4032—other AZ-5
USMM 4142—other AZ-5
USMM 4143—other AZ-5
USMM 4233—other AZ-5
USMM 44—other CA-9
USMM 46—other CA-9
USMM 47—other CA-9
USMM 48—other CA-9
USMM 5—other (2) AZ-5
USMM 5—other CA-9
USMM 5—other UT-8
USMM 6—other (2) AZ-5
USMM 6—other CA-9
USMM 6507—other MT-8
USMM 6716—other CA-9
USMM 7—other AZ-5
USMM 7—other CA-9
USMM 7—other UT-8
USMM 76—other CA-9
USMM 8—other UT-8
USMM 8893—other AZ-5
USMM 9—other UT-8
USMM 948—other UT-8
US MONTGOMERY (Snagboat)—hist pl FL-3
U S Mtn—summit NY-2
U S Mtn—summit WA-9
US-M101/1975 UT-8
US-M116/Utah/1986 UT-8
US-M9062/Bright Angel 62) AZ-5
US-M9062/LEESBURG/50 ID-8
U.S. Natl Bank—hist pl TX-5
US Natl Bank Bldg—hist pl OR-9
U.S. Natl Bank Bldg—hist pl WA-9
U S Natl Cem—cemetery DC-2
U.S. Naval Acad—hist pl MD-2
U S Naval Air Station (Cecil Field)—military FL-3
US Naval Air Station (Whitehouse Field)—military FL-3
U S Naval Air Station (Willow Grove)—military PA-2
US Naval Base—post sta PA-2
U.S. Naval Const. Batt.—post sta MS-4
U. S. Naval Home—hist pl PA-2
U S Naval Hosp—hospital PA-2
U S Naval Observatory—military DC-2
U.S. Naval Reservation—military FL-3
U S Naval Reservation (Mechanicsburg Supply Depot)—military PA-2
U S Naval Reservation Weapons Support Center—military IN-6
U.S. Naval Reserve Center—military FL-3
US Naval Station—hist pl FL-3
US Naval War College—hist pl RI-1
U S Navy Oceanographic Office—building MD-2
U S Navy Photo Interpretation Center—building MD-2
Usof Bay—bay AK-9
Usona P.O. (historical)—building AL-4
U S Park Service Campgrounds—locale NC-3
U S Park Service Docks—locale NC-3
Usphoe Creek MS-4
U S Plant Introduction Station—building FL-3
Uspoha Creek—stream MS-4
U.S. Pollution Control Heliport—airport UT-8
US Post Main Office-San Mateo—hist pl CA-9
US Post Office—hist pl AL-4
U.S. Post Office—hist pl (5) AL-4
US Post Office—hist pl AL-4
U.S. Post Office—hist pl AZ-5
US Post Office—hist pl AZ-5
U.S. Post Office—hist pl (5) CA-9
U.S. Post Office—hist pl (2) CO-8
U.S. Post Office—hist pl CT-1
U.S. Post Office—hist pl FL-3
US Post Office—hist pl FL-3
U.S. Post Office—hist pl FL-3
US Post Office—hist pl FL-3
US Post Office—hist pl GA-3
U.S. Post Office—hist pl GA-3
U.S. Post Office—hist pl ID-8
U.S. Post Office—hist pl IL-6
U. S. Post Office—hist pl IL-6
U.S. Post Office—hist pl IL-6
U.S. Post Office—hist pl IA-7
U. S. Post Office—hist pl IA-7
U.S. Post Office—hist pl (2) IA-7
U.S. Post Office—hist pl KY-4
US Post Office—hist pl LA-4
U. S. Post Office—hist pl LA-4
U.S. Post Office—hist pl LA-4
US Post Office—hist pl LA-4
U.S. Post Office—hist pl ME-1
US Post Office—hist pl MA-1
U.S. Post Office—hist pl MI-6
U.S. Post Office—hist pl (3) MS-4
US Post Office—hist pl MS-4
U.S. Post Office—hist pl (5) MS-4
U.S. Post Office—hist pl MO-7
US Post Office—hist pl MT-8
U. S. Post Office—hist pl MT-8
U.S. Post Office—hist pl MT-8
U.S. Post Office—hist pl (2) NE-7
US Post Office—hist pl NM-5
U.S. Post Office—hist pl (2) NY-2
US Post Office—hist pl (2) NC-3
U.S. Post Office—hist pl NC-3
US Post Office—hist pl NC-3
U.S. Post Office—hist pl ND-7
U.S. Post Office—hist pl (5) OH-6
U.S. Post Office—hist pl OR-9
US Post Office—hist pl (2) OR-9
U.S. Post Office—hist pl OR-9
US Post Office—hist pl OR-9
U.S. Post Office—hist pl (3) PA-2
US Post Office—hist pl RI-1
U.S. Post Office—hist pl RI-1
U.S. Post Office—hist pl SC-3
U.S. Post Office—hist pl TN-4
US Post Office—hist pl (2) TN-4
U. S. Post Office—hist pl TN-4
US Post Office—hist pl TN-4
U.S. Post Office—hist pl (2) TN-4
U.S. Post Office—hist pl (2) TN-4
US Post Office—hist pl TX-5
U.S. Post Office—hist pl TX-5
US Post Office—hist pl TX-5
U.S. Post Office—hist pl TX-5
U.S. Post Office—hist pl (2) WA-9
U.S. Post Office, Courthouse, and Customhouse—hist pl DE-2
U.S. Post Office, Courthouse, and Customhouse—hist pl MS-4
US Post Office, Courthouse, and Custom House—hist pl WA-9
U.S. Post Office, Courthouse and Federal Bldg—hist pl CA-9
U.S. Post Office, Customhouse, and Courthouse—hist pl HI-9
US Post Office, Federal Bldg, and Federal Courthouse-Sterling Main—hist pl CO-8
US Post Office-Akron—hist pl NY-2
US Post Office-Albion—hist pl NY-2
U.S. Post Office-Alexandria—hist pl MN-6
US Post Office-Amory—hist pl MS-4
US Post Office-Amsterdam—hist pl NY-2
US Post Office-Anaconda Main—hist pl MT-8
US Post Office and Annex—hist pl WA-9
U.S. Post Office and County Courthouse—hist pl NC-3
U.S. Post Office and Courthouse—hist pl AZ-5
U.S. Post Office and Courthouse—hist pl (2) CA-9
US Post Office and Courthouse—hist pl FL-3
U.S. Post Office and Courthouse—hist pl (5) GA-3
U.S. Post Office and Courthouse—hist pl IL-6
U.S. Post Office and Courthouse—hist pl IA-7
U.S. Post Office and Courthouse—hist pl LA-4
U.S. Post Office and Courthouse—hist pl MD-2
US Post Office and Courthouse—hist pl MS-4
U.S. Post Office and Courthouse—hist pl NE-7
U.S. Post Office and Courthouse—hist pl NV-8
U.S. Post Office and Courthouse—hist pl (3) ND-7
U.S. Post Office and Courthouse—hist pl OH-6
U.S. Post Office and Courthouse—hist pl OR-9
US Post Office and Courthouse—hist pl OR-9
U.S. Post Office and Courthouse—hist pl SC-3
US Post Office and Courthouse—hist pl SC-3
U.S. Post Office and Courthouse—hist pl UT-8
U.S. Post Office and Courthouse—hist pl VA-3
U.S. Post Office and Courthouse—hist pl VA-3
U.S. Post Office and Courthouse—hist pl WA-9
U. S. Post Office and Courthouse—hist pl WA-9
U.S. Post Office and Courthouse—hist pl WV-2
US Post Office and Courthouse—hist pl (2) PR-3
US Post Office and Courthouse-Billings—hist pl MT-8
US Post Office and Courthouse-Glasgow Main—hist pl MT-8
US Post Office and Courthouse-Globe Main—hist pl AZ-5
US Post Office and Courthouse-Great Falls—hist pl MT-8
US Post Office and Courthouse-Havre Main—hist pl MT-8
US Post Office and Courthouse-Lander Main—hist pl WY-8
US Post Office and Courthouse-Littleton Main—hist pl NH-1
US Post Office and Courthouse-Prescott Main—hist pl AZ-5
US Post Office and Customhouse—hist pl MS-4
US Post Office and Custom House—hist pl OR-9
U.S. Post Office and Customhouse—hist pl VT-1
U.S. Post Office and Customhouse—hist pl VA-3
U.S. Post Office and Customshouse—hist pl WA-9
US Post Office and Customs House-Douglas Main—hist pl AZ-5
U.S. Post Office and Federal Bldg—hist pl CO-8
U.S. Post Office and Federal Bldg—hist pl CT-1
U. S. Post Office and Federal Bldg—hist pl NC-3
U.S. Post Office and Federal Bldg—hist pl OR-9
US Post Office and Federal Bldg—hist pl TX-5
U.S. Post Office and Federal Bldg—hist pl TX-5
US Post Office and Federal Building-Canon City Main—hist pl CO-8
US Post Office and Federal Building-Delta Main—hist pl CO-8
US Post Office and Federal Building-Lewistown—hist pl MT-8
US Post Office and Federal Building-Monte Vista Main—hist pl CO-8
US Post Office and Federal Building-Zanesville—hist pl OH-6
US Post Office and Federal Courthouse-Colorado Springs Main—hist pl CO-8
US Post Office and Immigration Station-Nogales Main—hist pl AZ-5
U.S. Post Office and Mine Rescue Station—hist pl TN-4
U.S. Post Office and Office Bldg—hist pl HI-9
US Post Office-Angola—hist pl NY-2
US Post Office-Ansonia Main—hist pl CT-1
US Post Office-Arlington—hist pl VA-3
US Post Office-Arlington Main—hist pl MA-1
US Post Office-Ashland—hist pl KY-4
US Post Office-Attica—hist pl NY-2
US Post Office-Attleboro Main—hist pl MA-1
US Post Office-Ballston Spa—hist pl NY-2
US Post Office-Bar Harbor Main—hist pl ME-1
US Post Office-Basin Main—hist pl WY-8
US Post Office-Bath—hist pl NY-2
US Post Office-Bay Shore—hist pl NY-2
US Post Office-Beacon—hist pl NY-2
US Post Office-Beverly Hills Main—hist pl CA-9
US Post Office-Beverly Main—hist pl MA-1
U.S. Post Office Bldg—hist pl AL-4
U.S. Post Office/Board of Education Bldg—hist pl KY-4

# V

V, The—*area* UT-8
V, The—*basin* UT-8
V, The—*cape* WY-8
Vaage Cem—*cemetery* ND-7
Vaaogeoge Cove—*bay* AS-9
Vaara Creek—*stream* MN-6
Vaaui Stream—*stream* AS-9
Vaca, Mount—*summit* CA-9
Vaca Canyon—*valley* CA-9
Vaca Dixon Substation—*other* CA-9
Vaca Flat—*flat* CA-9
Vacahanyande Mtn—*summit* AK-9
Vaca Hills—*summit* AZ-5
Vaca Key—*island* FL-3
Vaca Key Bight—*bay* FL-3
Vaca Key Rock—*island* FL-3
Vaca Mountains—*range* CA-9
Vacant Hollow—*valley* MO-7
*Vaca Peak* CA-9
Vaca Pond—*lake* NM-5
Vaca Ranch—*locale* AZ-5
Vacas, Loma de las—*summit* TX-5
Vacas (Barrio)—*fmr MCD* PR-3
Vacas Well—*well* TX-5
**Vacation**—*pop pl* CA-9
**Vacation Beach**—*pop pl* CA-9
Vacation Camp for the Blind—*locale* NY-2
Vacation Canyon—*valley* ID-8
Vacation Isle—*island* CA-9
Vacation Pass—*gap* CA-9
Vacation Pass—*gap* MT-8
Vacation Tank—*reservoir* TX-5
Vacation Valley Camp—*locale* MI-6
**Vaca Valley**—*pop pl* CA-9
Vaca Valley—*valley* CA-9
Vaca Valley Raceway—*other* CA-9
**Vacaville**—*pop pl* CA-9
Vacaville (CCD)—*cens area* CA-9
Vacaville Elmira Cem—*cemetery* CA-9
Vacaville Junction—*locale* CA-9
Vacaville Town Hall—*hist pl* CA-9
Vacchiou Gulch—*valley* MT-8
**Vacco**—*pop pl* TN-4
*V. A. Center* TX-5
Vache Branch—*stream* MO-7
Vache Grasse Creek—*stream* AR-4
Vache Grasse Public Use Area—*locale* AR-4
Vacheire, Bayou—*gut* LA-4
**Vacherie**—*pop pl* LA-4
Vacherie, Bayou—*stream* LA-4
Vacherie Canal—*canal* (2) LA-4
Vacherie Oil and Gas Field—*oilfield* LA-4
Vacher Rsvr—*reservoir* WY-8
*Vachicha Canyon* CO-8
*Vachicha Creek* CO-8
*Vachiche Canyon* CO-8
*Vachiche Creek* CO-8
*Vachichi Canyon* CO-8
*Vachichi Creek* CO-8
Vachina Apartments-California Apartments—*hist pl* NV-8
*Vachita Canyon* CO-8
*Vachita Creek* CO-8
Vacho Island—*island* AK-9
**Vaco Junction**—*pop pl* WV-2
Vacoma Cem—*cemetery* NE-7
Vacuum Oil Field—*other* NM-5
Vada—*locale* KY-4
Vada—*locale* MO-7
**Vada**—*pop pl* (2) GA-3
Vada Lookout (historical)—*locale* MO-7
Vada Oil Field—*other* (2) NM-5
**Vade**—*pop pl* CA-9
**Vade Mecum**—*pop pl* NC-3
Vade Mecum Creek—*stream* NC-3
Vaden—*locale* AR-4
**Vaden**—*pop pl* TN-4
Vaden, W. C. and Kate, House—*hist pl* TX-5
Vaden Branch—*stream* TN-4
Vaden Cem—*cemetery* AR-4
Vaden Cem—*cemetery* NC-3
Vaden Cem—*cemetery* TN-4
Vaden Ch—*church* AR-4
Vaden Chapel—*church* TN-4
Vaden Creek—*stream* TX-5
Vaden Hill—*summit* TN-4
Vaden Hollow—*valley* TN-4
Vaden Sch (historical)—*school* TN-4
Vadens Mill—*locale* VA-3
**Vader**—*pop pl* WA-9
Vader Creek—*stream* ID-8
Vader Drain—*canal* MI-6
Vadia Ancha—*lake* TX-5
Vadine Creek—*stream* AK-9
Vadis—*locale* OR-9
**Vadis**—*pop pl* OH-6
**Vadis**—*pop pl* WV-2
**Vadito**—*pop pl* NM-5
**Vadnais Heights**—*pop pl* MN-6
Vadnais Heights Sch—*school* MN-6
Vadnais Lake—*lake* MN-6
Vadner Cave—*cave* AL-4
**Vado**—*pop pl* NM-5
Vado Arroyo—*stream* NM-5
Vado Crossing—*locale* TX-5
Vado Hill—*summit* NM-5
Vador Bridge—*bridge* IA-7
Vadoso, Arroyo—*stream* CA-9
Vaea Hill—*summit* AS-9
*Vaeger Valley* WI-6
Vaenita Cem—*cemetery* AR-4
*Vae View Elementary School* UT-8
Vae View Sch—*school* UT-8
**Vae View Subdivision**—*pop pl* UT-8
Vaga (Barrio)—*fmr MCD* PR-3
Vagabond Lake—*reservoir* AR-4
**Vagabond Trailer Park**—*pop pl* DE-2
*Vagner Lake* WY-8
Vagner Lake—*lake* WY-8
**Vago**—*pop pl* WV-2
Vagthus Point—*cape* VI-3
Vagt Lake—*lake* AK-9
*Vaheja* AZ-5
**Vahki**—*pop pl* AZ-5
Vahlsing—*locale* TX-5
Vahlsing Lake—*reservoir* TX-5
V.a. Hosp—*hospital* KS-7
*VA Hospital* UT-8
V.A. Hospital—*uninc pl* NJ-2
**Vaiala**—*pop pl* AS-9
Vaialae Stream—*stream* AS-9
Vaiala Ridge—*ridge* AS-9
Vaialili Stream—*stream* AS-9
Vaialufai Stream—*stream* AS-9
Vaiava Strait—*channel* AS-9
Vai Cove—*bay* AS-9
Vaiden—*locale* AL-4
**Vaiden**—*pop pl* MS-4
Vaiden Attendance Center—*school* MS-4
Vaiden Field (airport)—*airport* AL-4
Vaiden Hill Ch—*church* MS-4
*Vaiden HS* MS-4
Vaiden Institute (historical)—*school* MS-4
Vaiden Post Office (historical)—*building* AL-4
Vaiden Sch (historical)—*school* AL-4
Vaifanua (County of)—*civ div* AS-9
Vaifoa Cove—*bay* AS-9
Vaifusi Stream—*stream* AS-9
Vail—*locale* MI-6
Vail—*locale* WA-9
**Vail**—*pop pl* AZ-5
**Vail**—*pop pl* AR-4
**Vail**—*pop pl* CO-8
**Vail**—*pop pl* IA-7
**Vail**—*pop pl* KY-4
**Vail**—*pop pl* NJ-2
**Vail**—*pop pl* PA-2
Vail, A. M., House—*hist pl* DE-2
Vail, Mrs. Marion D.-Prof. Charles Noyes Kinney House—*hist pl* IA-7
Vail Ave Sch—*school* CA-9
Vail Brook—*stream* VT-1
Vail Canal—*canal* CA-9
Vail Canyon—*valley* NV-8
Vail Cem—*cemetery* IA-7
Vail Creek—*stream* MT-8
Vail Creek—*stream* OR-9
Vail Cut Off Drain—*canal* CA-9
Vail Dean Sch—*school* NJ-2
Vail Drain—*canal* CA-9
Vail Drain Spur—*canal* CA-9
Vaile, Harvey M., Mansion—*hist pl* MO-7
Vaile Elem Sch—*school* IN-6
Vailega Spring—*spring* AS-9
Vail Elem Sch—*school* AZ-5
Vaile Rsvr—*reservoir* CO-8
*Vailes Lake* MN-6
Vail Five Drain—*canal* CA-9
Vail Four-A Drain—*canal* CA-9
Vail Four Drain—*canal* CA-9
*Vail Gate* NY-2
Vail Hill—*summit* NY-2
Vail Hill—*summit* VT-1
**Vail Homes**—*pop pl* NJ-2
Vail Hotel—*hist pl* CO-8
Vail JHS—*school* AZ-5
Vail Lake—*lake* AZ-5
Vail Lake—*reservoir* CA-9
Vail Lake Dam—*dam* MS-4
Vail Lateral—*canal* CA-9
Vail Lateral Five—*canal* CA-9
Vail Lateral Five-A—*canal* CA-9
Vail Lateral Four—*canal* CA-9
Vail Lateral Four-A—*canal* CA-9
Vail Lateral Seven—*canal* CA-9
Vail Lateral Six—*canal* CA-9
Vail Lateral Three—*canal* CA-9
Vail Lateral Three-A—*canal* CA-9
Vail Lateral Two—*canal* CA-9
Vail Lateral Two-A—*canal* CA-9
Vail-Leavitt Music Hall—*hist pl* NY-2
Vaill Island—*island* ME-1
Vail Memorial Cem—*cemetery* NJ-2
**Vail Mills**—*pop pl* NY-2
Vail Mine—*mine* WY-8
Vail Mtn—*summit* CO-8
Vail Mtn—*summit* MO-7
Vailoa Stream—*stream* AS-9
**Vailoatai**—*pop pl* AS-9
Vailoatai Crater—*crater* AS-9
Vailoloaitiiti Cove—*bay* AS-9
Vailolootele Cove—*bay* AS-9
Vailolo Stream—*stream* AS-9
Vail One Drain—*canal* CA-9
Vail Overpass—*crossing* AZ-5
Vail Park—*park* NM-5
*Vail Pass* CO-8
Vail Pass—*gap* CO-8
Vail Placer—*mine* NV-8
Vail Pond—*lake* NY-2
Vail Pond—*lake* VT-1
Vail Ranch—*locale* CA-9
*Vails* NJ-2
Vailsburg—*uninc pl* NJ-2
Vailsburg HS—*school* NJ-2
Vailsburg Park—*park* NJ-2
Vail Sch—*school* (2) NJ-2
Vail Sch—*school* SD-7
**Vails Corners**—*pop pl* OH-6
Vail Seven Drain—*canal* CA-9
*Vailsgate* NY-2
**Vails Gate**—*pop pl* NY-2
**Vails Gate Junction**—*pop pl* NY-2
**Vail's Grove**—*pop pl* NY-2
Vails Island—*island* IL-6
Vail Site—*hist pl* ME-1
Vail Site 81.1 (Boundary Increase)—*hist pl* ME-1
Vail Six-A Drain—*canal* CA-9
Vail Six Drain—*canal* CA-9
Vail Ski Area—*other* CO-8
Vails Lake—*lake* MN-6
Vails Mill—*locale* VA-3
Vail Supply Canal—*canal* CA-9
**Vails (Vail)**—*pop pl* NJ-2
Vail Tank—*reservoir* NM-5
Vail Three-A Drain—*canal* CA-9
Vail Three Drain—*canal* CA-9
**Vail Township**—*pop pl* SD-7
**Vail (Township of)**—*pop pl* MN-6
*Vail Trap Spring* AZ-5
Vail Two-A Drain—*canal* CA-9
Vail Two Drain—*canal* CA-9
Vaima Stream—*stream* AS-9
Vaimumu Stream—*stream* AS-9
Vainom Kug—*locale* AZ-5
*Vainomkux* AZ-5
Vainuulua Stream—*stream* AS-9
Vainuu Mtn—*summit* AS-9
Vainuu Point—*cape* AS-9
**Vainville**—*pop pl* WV-2
Vaiola Point—*cape* AS-9
Vaiola Stream—*stream* AS-9
Vaiolefuga Stream—*stream* AS-9
Vaipito Stream—*stream* AS-9
Vaipito Valley—*valley* AS-9
Vaipuna Stream—*stream* AS-9
Voir—*locale* TX-5
*Va Trench* NC-3
Vaisaili Point—*cape* AS-9
Vaisa Point—*cape* AS-9
Vaisa Stream—*stream* AS-9
Vaisigano Point—*cape* AS-9
Vaisina Stream—*stream* AS-9
*Vais Spring* OR-9
Vaitai Stream—*stream* AS-9
Vaitanoa Pool—*lake* AS-9
Vaita Point—*cape* AS-9
Vaitele Point—*cape* AS-9
Vaitele Stream—*stream* AS-9
**Vaitogi**—*pop pl* AS-9
Vaitolu Stream—*stream* AS-9
Vaiva Hills—*summit* AZ-5
*Vaivavo* AZ-5
**Vaiva Vo**—*pop pl* AZ-5
Vakamok—*locale* AZ-5
Vakeekalik Creek—*stream* AK-9
*Valabat* FM-9
Valadeces Banco Number 130—*levee* TX-5
Valadez Cem—*cemetery* TX-5
**Valaho**—*pop pl* VA-3
**Valaire Subdivision**—*pop pl* UT-8
Valaite Lake—*lake* WY-8
Valambrosia Canal—*canal* GA-3
Valandra Bridge—*bridge* SD-7
Valaparaiso (historical)—*locale* KS-7
**Valatie**—*pop pl* NY-2
Valatie Colony—*locale* NY-2
Valatie Kill—*stream* NY-2
Valatier Wash—*stream* NV-8
*Valavat* FM-9
Valberg-Lamb State Public Shooting Area—*park* SD-7
Valburg Ranch Landing Strip—*airport* SD-7
Valby—*locale* OR-9
Valby Cem—*cemetery* OR-9
Valcalda Spring—*spring* NV-8
**Valcam**—*pop pl* UT-8
Valcan Ditch—*canal* CO-8
Val Cave—*cave* AL-4
Valcour—*locale* NY-2
Valcour Bay—*hist pl* NY-2
Valcour Chapel—*church* NY-2
Valcour Island—*island* NY-2
Valcour Lighthouse Light—*locale* NY-2
Valcourt—*locale* PA-2
Valcourt Coulee—*stream* LA-4
Valdasta—*locale* TX-5
**Valdawood (subdivision)**—*pop pl* AL-4
Val Day Creek—*stream* WY-8
Val Day Spring—*spring* WY-8
Valdea Cem—*cemetery* CO-8
**Valdeau**—*pop pl* TN-4
Valdeau Post Office (historical)—*building* TN-4
*Val de Chino* AZ-5
**Val De Neige Subdivision**—*pop pl* UT-8
Valder Creek—*stream* NV-8
*Valderas Creek* TX-5
**Valde Rouge**—*pop pl* LA-4
**Valders**—*pop pl* WI-6
Valders Cem—*cemetery* WI-6
Valders Tank—*reservoir* TX-5
*Valdes* AK-9
**Valdes, Desvio**—*pop pl* PR-3
**Valdese**—*pop pl* NC-3
Valdese Elem Sch—*hist pl* NC-3
Valdese Elem Sch—*school* NC-3
Valdese Hosp—*hospital* NC-3
Valdese JHS—*school* NC-3
Valdese Lake Dam—*dam* NC-3
Valdeses Cem—*cemetery* CO-8
*Valdez* AK-9
Valdez—*locale* CA-9
**Valdez**—*pop pl* AK-9
**Valdez**—*pop pl* CO-8
**Valdez**—*pop pl* FL-3
**Valdez**—*pop pl* NM-5
Valdez, Miguel, Barn—*hist pl* NM-5
Valdez, Narciso, House—*hist pl* NM-5
Valdez Arm—*bay* AK-9
Valdez Canyon—*valley* CO-8
Valdez Canyon—*valley* NM-5
Valdez Cem—*cemetery* (2) CO-8
**Valdez-Cordova (Census Area)**—*pop pl* AK-9
Valdez Creek—*stream* AK-9
Valdez Creek—*stream* CO-8
Valdez Ditch—*canal* CO-8
Valdez Ditch No 5—*canal* CO-8
Valdez Draw—*valley* NM-5
Valdez Glacier—*glacier* AK-9
Valdez Goat Camp—*locale* TX-5
Valdez Lake—*lake* CO-8
Valdez Narrows—*channel* AK-9
Valdez Place—*locale* NM-5
Valdez Spring—*spring* CO-8
Valdez Spring—*spring* NM-5
Valdie Tank—*reservoir* AZ-5
**Valdina Farms**—*pop pl* TX-5
Valdine State Wildlife Mngmt Area—*park* MN-6
Val-do-mar, Lake—*lake* GA-3
Val-Don Day Care Center—*school* FL-3
**Valdora (historical)**—*pop pl* IA-7
**Valdosta**—*pop pl* AL-4
**Valdosta**—*pop pl* GA-3
Valdosta Baptist Ch—*church* AL-4
Valdosta (CCD)—*cens area* GA-3
Valdosta Ch of Christ—*church* AL-4
Valdosta Commercial Hist Dist—*hist pl* GA-3
Valdosta Country Club—*other* GA-3
*Valdosta Elementary School* AL-4
Valdosta Municipal Airp—*airport* GA-3
Valdosta State Coll—*school* GA-3
*Vale* MO-7
Vale—*locale* CA-9
Vale—*locale* MO-7
Vale—*locale* VA-3
Vale—*locale* WV-2
**Vale**—*pop pl* MD-2
**Vale**—*pop pl* (2) NC-3
**Vale**—*pop pl* OR-9
**Vale**—*pop pl* SD-7
**Vale**—*pop pl* TN-4
Vale, The—*hist pl* MA-1
*Valeau Lake* MI-6
Vale Butte—*summit* OR-9
Vale (CCD)—*cens area* OR-9
Vale Cem—*cemetery* MO-7
Vale Cem—*cemetery* NY-2
Vale Cem—*cemetery* OH-6
Vale Cem—*cemetery* SD-7
*Vale Creek* TX-5
Vale Creek—*stream* MT-8
Vale Creek—*stream* NC-3
Vale Creek—*stream* UT-8
Vale Creek—*stream* WY-8
Vale Creek Ranch—*locale* MT-8
Vale Cut Off Belle Fourche River Bridge—*hist pl* SD-7
**Valeda**—*pop pl* KS-7
Vale District Sch—*school* AZ-5
Valedon—*locale* NM-5
Vale Drain—*canal* MI-6
**Valee**—*pop pl* VA-3
Vale End Cem—*cemetery* NH-1
**Valeene**—*pop pl* IN-6
Vale Gulch—*valley* CA-9
Vale Hotel and Grand Opera House—*hist pl* OR-9
*Vale Lake* WA-9
Vale Lake—*lake* MN-6
Vale Lateral—*canal* SD-7
*Vale Main Canal* OR-9
*Vale Mills* TN-4
*Vale Mills Post Office* TN-4
**Valemont Heights**—*pop pl* PA-2
**Valena (historical)**—*pop pl* MS-4
Valena Post Office (historical)—*building* MS-4
Valencia—*hist pl* SC-3
Valencia—*locale* KS-7
Valencia—*locale* UT-8
**Valencia**—*pop pl* AZ-5
**Valencia**—*pop pl* CA-9
**Valencia**—*pop pl* MT-8
**Valencia**—*pop pl* NM-5
**Valencia**—*pop pl* PA-2
**Valencia**—*pop pl* (3) PR-3
Valencia, Jesus, House—*hist pl* NM-5
Valencia, Ojo de—*spring* PR-3
Valencia, Ysabel, House—*hist pl* NM-5
Valencia Borough—*civil* PA-2
Valencia Canyon—*valley* CO-8
Valencia Canyon—*valley* NM-5
Valencia Cem—*cemetery* KS-7
Valencia Ch—*church* NM-5
Valencia Community Coll (East Campus)—*school* FL-3
Valencia Community Coll (West Campus)—*school* FL-3
**Valencia (County)**—*pop pl* NM-5
*Valencia Creek* CA-9
Valencia Creek—*stream* CA-9
Valencia Ditch—*canal* NM-5
Valencia Drain—*canal* NM-5
*Valencia (East Irvine)* CA-9
Valencia Hall—*hist pl* CA-9
Valencia Heights—*CDP* SC-3
Valencia Lagoon—*swamp* CA-9
Valencia Mine—*mine* CA-9
Valencia Mtn—*summit* AZ-5
Valenciano Abajo (Barrio)—*fmr MCD* PR-3
Valenciano Arriba (Barrio)—*fmr MCD* PR-3
Valencia Park Sch—*school* (2) CA-9
Valencia Peak—*summit* CA-9
Valencia Playground—*park* SC-3
Valencia Ranch Historic Archaeol District—*hist pl* NM-5
Valencia Road Interchange—*crossing* AZ-5
Valencia Sch—*school* AZ-5
Valencia Sch—*school* (3) CA-9
Valencia Sch—*school* NM-5
Valencia Siding—*locale* MT-8
Valencia Site (BB:13:15;BB:13:74)—*hist pl* AZ-5
Valencia Spring—*spring* (2) NM-5
Valencia Tank—*reservoir* AZ-5
Valencia Wash—*stream* AZ-5
Valenda HS—*school* CA-9
Valen Lake—*lake* OR-9
Valent Canyon—*valley* CO-8
Valentia—*hist pl* MD-2
Valentiers Pond—*bay* LA-4
Valentime Tank—*reservoir* NM-5
*Valentine* KS-7
Valentine—*locale* MT-8
Valentine—*locale* SC-3
**Valentine**—*pop pl* AZ-5
**Valentine**—*pop pl* AR-4
**Valentine**—*pop pl* IN-6
**Valentine**—*pop pl* LA-4
**Valentine**—*pop pl* NE-7
**Valentine**—*pop pl* NJ-2
**Valentine**—*pop pl* TX-5
Valentine, John, House—*hist pl* IN-6
Valentine Bayou—*gut* LA-4
Valentine Bldg—*hist pl* AK-9
Valentine Bottom—*bend* UT-8
Valentine Branch—*stream* KY-4
Valentine Branch—*stream* (2) TN-4
Valentine Branch—*stream* TX-5
Valentine Brook—*stream* NJ-2
Valentine Canyon—*valley* AZ-5
Valentine Canyon—*valley* MT-8
Valentine Canyon—*valley* NM-5
Valentine Cave—*cave* CA-9
Valentine (CCD)—*cens area* TX-5
Valentine Cem—*cemetery* AR-4
Valentine Cem—*cemetery* IA-7
Valentine Cem—*cemetery* LA-4
Valentine Cem—*cemetery* MS-4
Valentine Cem—*cemetery* (3) TN-4
Valentine Corners—*locale* NY-2
*Valentine Creek* MT-8
*Valentine Creek* OR-9
*Valentine Creek* TX-5
Valentine Creek—*gut* GA-3
Valentine Creek—*stream* CA-9
Valentine Creek—*stream* LA-4
Valentine Creek—*stream* MD-2
Valentine Creek—*stream* MI-6
Valentine Creek—*stream* (3) MT-8
Valentine Creek—*stream* OR-9
Valentine Creek—*stream* VA-3
Valentine Creek—*stream* WA-9
Valentine Creek—*stream* WI-6
Valentine Ditch—*canal* IN-6
Valentine Ditch—*canal* LA-4
Valentine Elem Sch—*school* AZ-5
Valentine Elem Sch—*school* KS-7
Valentine Flat—*flat* MT-8
Valentine Ford—*locale* MO-7
Valentine-French House—*hist pl* MA-1
Valentine Gulch—*valley* CA-9
Valentine Gulch—*valley* MT-8
Valentine Hill—*summit* PA-2
**Valentine Hills**—*pop pl* VA-3
**Valentine (Hulapai Agency)**—*pop pl* AZ-5
Valentine Island—*island* MN-6
*Valentine Lake* LA-4
Valentine Lake—*lake* CA-9
Valentine Lake—*lake* MI-6
Valentine Lake—*lake* MN-6
Valentine Lake—*lake* WY-8
Valentine Lake—*reservoir* LA-4
Valentine Mine—*mine* MT-8
Valentine Mine—*mine* NV-8
Valentine Mtn—*summit* WY-8
Valentine Museum—*hist pl* VA-3
Valentine Natl Wildlife Ref—*park* NE-7
Valentine Oil Field—*oilfield* LA-4
Valentine Peak—*summit* UT-8
*Valentine Plantation* MS-4
Valentine Point—*cape* MI-6
Valentine Pond—*lake* NJ-2
Valentine Pond—*lake* NY-2
Valentine Post Office—*building* AZ-5
Valentine Public Sch—*hist pl* NE-7
Valentine Rec Area—*park* LA-4
Valentine Ridge—*ridge* AZ-5
Valentine Ridge—*ridge* CA-9
Valentine Ridge—*ridge* ME-1
Valentine Ridge—*ridge* WA-9
Valentine RR Station—*building* AZ-5
Valentine Run—*stream* PA-2
Valentines—*locale* VA-3
**Valentines**—*pop pl* NJ-2
**Valentines Beach**—*pop pl* NY-2
Valentine Sch—*hist pl* MA-1
Valentine Sch—*school* CA-9
Valentine Sch—*school* CO-8
Valentine Sch—*school* ME-1
Valentine Sch—*school* MI-6
Valentines Day Cave—*cave* PA-2
Valentines Gulch—*valley* UT-8
Valentines (siding)—*locale* AZ-5
*Valentines Landing* MS-4
Valentine Soap Workers Cottage—*hist pl* MA-1
Valentine Spring—*spring* CA-9
Valentine Square—*hist pl* TN-4
Valentine Tank—*reservoir* AZ-5
Valentine Tank—*reservoir* TX-5
Valentine Theater Bldg—*hist pl* OH-6
Valentine-Varian House—*hist pl* NY-2
Valentine Well—*well* AZ-5
Valenzuela Mine—*mine* AZ-5
Valenzuela Ranch HQ—*hist pl* TX-5
Vale of Rest Cem—*cemetery* NY-2
Vale of Tears—*valley* CO-8
*Vale of West Boylston* MA-1
Valeo Mine—*mine* UT-8
*Vale Oregon Canal* OR-9
Vale Oregon Main Canal—*canal* OR-9
Vale Pond—*swamp* TN-4
Vale Post Office (historical)—*building* MS-4
Vale Post Office (historical)—*building* TN-4
**Valera**—*pop pl* TX-5
Valera Cem—*cemetery* TX-5
Valer Canal—*canal* LA-4
Vale Reservation—*reserve* MA-1
Valeria—*locale* KY-4
**Valeria**—*pop pl* IA-7
Valeria Home—*locale* NY-2
Valeriano, Arroyo—*valley* TX-5
**Valerie**—*pop pl* CA-9
Valerie, Lac—*lake* LA-4
Valerie, Lake—*lake* LA-4
Valerie Glacier—*glacier* AK-9
Valerie Mine—*mine* NV-8
**Valerie Subdivision**—*pop pl* UT-8
Valerio Street Sch—*school* CA-9
Valermosos Cem—*cemetery* AL-4
Vale Run—*stream* IN-6
Vale Run—*stream* MD-2
Valery (site)—*locale* NV-8
Vales Canyon—*valley* NV-8
Vales Ch—*church* TX-5
Vale Sch—*hist pl* SD-7
Vale Sch—*school* WA-9
Vale Sch (historical)—*school* TN-4
Vales Lake—*lake* MI-6
Vales Mills—*locale* OH-6
**Vale Summit**—*pop pl* MD-2
Vale Summit Ch—*church* MD-2
Vale Summit Sch (historical)—*school* TN-4
**Vale Township**—*pop pl* ND-7
**Vale Township**—*pop pl* SD-7
Valet Spring—*spring* OR-9
**Valewood**—*pop pl* MS-4
Valhalla Point—*cape* ID-8
Valhalla Substation—*other* WA-9
*Valhalla* ND-7
Valhalla—*area* CA-9
Valhalla—*hist pl* MD-2
**Valhalla**—*pop pl* AL-4
**Valhalla**—*pop pl* FL-3
**Valhalla**—*pop pl* NY-2
**Valhalla**—*pop pl* (2) NC-3
Valhalla—*uninc pl* WA-9
Valhalla, Lake—*lake* NY-2
Valhalla, Lake—*lake* WA-9
Valhalla, Lake—*reservoir* NJ-2
Valhalla, Mount—*summit* AK-9
Valhalla, Mount—*summit* WI-6
Valhalla Airp—*airport* IN-6
Valhalla Canyon—*valley* WY-8
Valhalla Cove—*cave* AL-4
Valhalla Cem—*cemetery* AL-4
Valhalla Cem—*cemetery* (2) IL-6
Valhalla Cem—*cemetery* MO-7
Valhalla Cem—*cemetery* WI-6
Valhalla Dome—*summit* NC-3
**Valhalla Estates Subdivision**—*pop pl* UT-8
*Valhalla Glades* AZ-5
Valhalla HS—*school* NY-2
Valhalla Mausoleum—*cemetery* TX-5
Valhalla Memorial Gardens—*cemetery* AL-4
Valhalla Memorial Park—*cemetery* CO-8
Valhalla Memorial Park (cemetery)—*cemetery* CA-9
Valhalla Memory Gardens—*cemetery* IN-6
Valhalla Mtn—*summit* WA-9
*Valhalla Plateau* AZ-5
Valhalla P O—*locale* MO-7
Valhalla Store—*locale* MO-7
**Valhalla Township**—*pop pl* ND-7

*Valhermoso Mountain* ... AL-4
Valhermoso Spring Cave—*cave* ... AL-4
Valhermoso Spring Ch—*church* ... AL-4
**Valhermoso Springs**—*pop pl* ... AL-4
Valhermoso Springs—*spring* ... AL-4
Valhermoso Springs Cem—*cemetery* ... AL-4
Valhermoso Springs Ch (historical)—*church* ... AL-4
Valhermoso Springs Creek—*stream* ... AL-4
Valhermoso Springs Post Office—*building* ... AL-4
*Valiant Spring* ... ID-8
Valieaux Spring—*spring* ... ID-8
Valient Cem—*cemetery* ... LA-4
Valiente Peak—*summit* ... NM-5
Valiente Well—*well* ... NM-5
*Valient Spring* ... ID-8
**Valier**—*pop pl* ... IL-6
**Valier**—*pop pl* ... MT-8
**Valier**—*pop pl* ... PA-2
Valier-Dupuyer—*cens area* ... MT-8
**Valier Junction**—*pop pl* ... MT-8
Valier Mine Pond—*reservoir* ... IL-6
**Valier Patch**—*pop pl* ... IL-6
Valier Public Sch—*hist pl* ... MT-8
**Valinda**—*pop pl* ... CA-9
Valinda Sch—*school* ... CA-9
Valines Lake—*lake* ... MN-6
Valino Island—*island* ... OR-9
Valiton Ditch—*canal* ... MT-8
Valitons Creek—*stream* ... ID-8
Valjean—*locale* ... CA-9
Valjean Dunes—*summit* ... CA-9
Valjean Hills—*other* ... CA-9
Valjean Valley—*valley* ... CA-9
**Val-Jo Subdivision**—*pop pl* ... UT-8
**Valkaria**—*pop pl* ... FL-3
Valkaria Missile Tracking Annex—*locale* ... FL-3
Valla—*locale* ... CA-9
Valla Cem—*cemetery* ... ND-7
**Vallamont Hills**—*pop pl* ... PA-2
Vallance Sch (abandoned)—*school* ... PA-2
Vall Branch—*stream* ... SC-3
Vall Creek—*stream* ... WV-2
*Valle* ... AZ-5
Valle—*locale* ... AZ-5
**Valle**—*pop pl* ... AZ-5
Valle, Arroyo—*stream* ... CA-9
Valle, Lake Del—*reservoir* ... CA-9
Valle Airp—*airport* ... AZ-5
**Valle Arriba Heights**—*pop pl* ... PR-3
Valleau Cem—*cemetery* ... NJ-2
*Valleau Lake* ... MI-6
Valle Ch—*church* ... MN-6
Valle Chimal—*valley* ... NM-5
Vallecitas (CCD)—*cens area* ... NM-5
**Vallecito**—*pop pl* ... CA-9
**Vallecito**—*pop pl* ... CO-8
**Vallecito**—*pop pl* ... NM-5
Vallecito Basin—*basin* ... CO-8
Vallecito Campground—*locale* ... CO-8
*Vallecito Creek* ... CA-9
Vallecito Creek—*stream* ... CA-9
Vallecito Creek—*stream* ... CO-8
Vallecito Creek—*stream* ... NM-5
Vallecito Damian—*basin* ... NM-5
Vallecito de los Caballos—*valley* ... NM-5
Vallecito de los Pinos—*other* ... NM-5
Vallecito del Rio Puerco—*locale* ... NM-5
Vallecito Guard Station—*locale* ... CO-8
Vallecito Lake—*lake* ... CO-8
*Vallecito Mountains* ... CA-9
Vallecito Mountains—*range* ... CA-9
Vallecito Mtn—*summit* ... CO-8
Vallecito Mtn—*summit* ... NM-5
Vallecito Rsvr—*reservoir* ... CO-8
Vallecitos—*area* (2) ... CA-9
Vallecitos—*area* ... NM-5
Vallecitos—*locale* (3) ... NM-5
**Vallecitos**—*pop pl* ... NM-5
Vallecitos—*valley* ... CA-9
Vallecitos Atomic Laboratory—*building* ... CA-9
Vallecitos Canyon—*valley* ... NM-5
Vallecito Sch—*school* ... CA-9
Vallecitos Corrales—*locale* ... NM-5
Vallecitos Creek—*stream* (2) ... CA-9
Vallecitos Creek—*stream* ... NM-5
Vallecitos de Abajo—*valley* ... NM-5
Vallecitos de Arriba—*valley* ... NM-5
Vallecitos de en Medio—*valley* ... NM-5
Vallecitos De Los Chamisos—*valley* ... NM-5
Vallecitos de los Chamisos Tank—*reservoir* ... NM-5
**Vallecitos de los Indios**—*pop pl* ... NM-5
Vallecitos de los Indios—*valley* ... NM-5
Vallecitos Oil Field—*oilfield* ... CA-9
Vallecitos Sch—*school* (2) ... CA-9
Vallecito Stage Station County Park—*park* ... CA-9
Vallecitos Valley—*valley* ... CA-9
*Vallecitos Wash* ... CA-9
Vallecito Valley—*valley* ... CA-9
*Vallecito Wash* ... CA-9
Vallecito Wash—*stream* ... CA-9
Vallecito Western Mine—*mine* ... CA-9
**Valle Crucis**—*pop pl* ... NC-3
Valle Crucis Elem Sch—*school* ... NC-3
Valle Crucis Mission—*school* ... NC-3
Valle de Adrian Tank—*reservoir* ... NM-5
*Vallo do Agua Prieta* ... AZ-5
*Valle de la Agua Prieta* ... AZ-5
Valle de la Cabra—*valley* ... NM-5
Valle de la Grulla—*valley* ... NM-5
Valle De Lajas—*valley* ... PR-3
Valle de la Osha—*area* ... NM-5
Valle de la Piedra—*area* ... NM-5
Valle De Las Animas—*valley* ... NM-5
Valle de las Cotorras—*valley* ... PR-3
Valle Del Ojo De La Parida—*area* ... NM-5
Valle de los Caballos—*valley* ... NM-5
Valle de los Cerritos Canyon—*valley* ... NM-5
Valle de los Posos—*valley* (2) ... NM-5
Valle del Toro—*area* ... NM-5
Valle De Oro—*post sta* ... TX-5
Valle De Pamo Or Santa Maria—*civil* ... CA-9
*Valle De San Bernardo* ... CA-9
Valle De San Felipe—*civil* ... CA-9
Valle De San Jose (Portilla)—*civil* ... CA-9
Valle de San Jose (Sunol and Bernal)—*civil* ... CA-9
Valle de Yabucoa—*valley* ... PR-3
Valle Diablo Tank—*reservoir* ... NM-5
Valle Diamante—*basin* ... NM-5
Vallee Family House—*hist pl* ... ME-1
Valle Escondido—*area* ... NM-5
**Valle Escondido**—*pop pl* ... NM-5
**Vallee Villa Subdivision**—*pop pl* ... UT-8
Valle Frutosa—*area* ... NM-5
Valle Grande—*area* ... NM-5
Valle Grande—*basin* ... NM-5
**Vallegrande**—*pop pl* ... AL-4
Valle Grande—*summit* ... NM-5
Valle Grande—*valley* ... NM-5
**Valle Grande Condominium**—*pop pl* ... UT-8
**Valle Grande East Condominium**—*pop pl* ... UT-8
Valle Grande Pumice Mine—*locale* ... NM-5
Valle Grande Traill—*trail* ... NM-5
Valle Grande Truck Trail—*trail* ... NM-5
Valle Hollow—*valley* (2) ... MO-7
Valle Jaramillo—*valley* (2) ... NM-5
**Vallejo**—*pop pl* ... CA-9
Vallejo Beach—*beach* ... CA-9
Vallejo (CCD)—*cens area* ... CA-9
Vallejo City Hall and County Bldg Branch—*hist pl* ... CA-9
Vallejo Estate—*hist pl* ... CA-9
Vallejo Gulch—*valley* ... CA-9
Vallejo Gulch—*valley* ... CO-8
Vallejo Heights—*summit* ... CA-9
Vallejo Home State Historical Monmt—*park* ... CA-9
Vallejo Mill Ruins—*locale* ... CA-9
Vallejo Mill Sch—*school* ... CA-9
Vallejo Municipal Golf Course—*other* ... CA-9
Vallejo Old City Hist Dist—*hist pl* ... CA-9
*Vallejo Reservoir* ... CA-9
*Vallejos Creek* ... CO-8
Vallejos Creek—*stream* ... CO-8
Vallejos Windmill—*locale* ... TX-5
Valle Lake—*reservoir* ... MO-7
Valle Largo—*area* ... NM-5
Valle Largo—*flat* ... NM-5
Valle Largo—*valley* ... NM-5
Valle Lindo Sch—*school* ... CA-9
*Vallemar* ... CA-9
**Vallemar**—*pop pl* ... CA-9
Vallemar Sch—*school* ... CA-9
Valle Medio—*area* ... NM-5
Valle Mtn—*summit* ... NC-3
*Vallena* ... VA-3
Vallenar Bay—*bay* ... AK-9
Vallenar Creek—*stream* ... AK-9
Vallenar Point—*cape* ... AK-9
Vallenar Rock—*other* ... AK-9
Valle Redondo—*other* ... NM-5
Valle Romero—*area* ... NM-5
Vallerreno Cem —*cemetery* ... TX-5
Valle RR Station—*building* ... AZ-5
Vallers State Wildlife Mngmt Area—*park* ... MN-6
**Vallers (Township of)**—*pop pl* ... MN-6
**Vallersville**—*pop pl* ... MA-1
**Vallery**—*pop pl* ... CO-8
Vallery Bay—*bay* ... UT-8
Vallery Ditch—*canal* ... OH-6
Valle San Antonio—*valley* ... NM-5
Valle Santa Rosa—*valley* ... NM-5
Valles Canyon—*valley* ... NM-5
Valle Seco—*valley* ... CO-8
Valle Seco—*valley* ... NM-5
Valle Siding—*locale* ... AZ-5
**Valles Mines**—*pop pl* ... MO-7
Valles Mines Creek—*stream* ... MO-7
Valle Spring—*spring* ... MO-7
Valle Spring Branch—*stream* ... MO-7
Valle Spring Ch—*church* ... MO-7
Valles Tank—*reservoir* ... NM-5
Valles Trailer Park—*park* ... UT-8
Valle Tank—*reservoir* ... AZ-5
Valle Tank—*reservoir* ... NM-5
Vallet-Danuser House—*hist pl* ... MO-7
Valle Toledo—*valley* (2) ... NM-5
**Valleton**—*pop pl* ... CA-9
Valle Township—*civil* ... MO-7
Valle Trading Post (historical)—*locale* ... SD-7
Valle Vidal—*valley* ... NM-5
Valle Vista—*locale* ... CA-9
**Valle Vista**—*pop pl* ... CA-9
**Valle Vista**—*pop pl* ... OR-9
Valle Vista—*uninc pl* ... CA-9
Valle Vista JHS—*school* ... CA-9
Valle Vista Sch—*school* ... CA-9
Valle Vista Sch—*school* ... NM-5
Valle Vista Shop Ctr—*locale* ... MO-7
*Valley* ... AL-4
*Valley* ... AR-4
*Valley* ... KS-7
Valley—*civ div* ... SD-7
Valley—*fmr MCD* (5) ... NE-7
Valley—*locale* ... AR-4
Valley—*locale* ... CO-8
Valley—*locale* ... IA-7
Valley—*locale* ... NV-8
Valley—*locale* ... OH-6
Valley—*locale* ... SD-7
Valley—*locale* ... WY-8
**Valley**—*pop pl* ... AL-4
**Valley**—*pop pl* ... IL-6
**Valley**—*pop pl* ... KY-4
**Valley**—*pop pl* ... ME-1
**Valley**—*pop pl* (2) ... MS-4
**Valley**—*pop pl* ... NE-7
**Valley**—*pop pl* (3) ... NJ-2
**Valley**—*pop pl* ... NY-2
**Valley**—*pop pl* ... NC-3
**Valley**—*pop pl* ... WA-9
**Valley**—*pop pl* ... WI-6
Valley, Lake Of The—*lake* ... MN-6
Valley, The—*basin* ... UT-8
**Valley Acres**—*pop pl* ... CA-9
**Valley Acres**—*pop pl* ... IN-6
Valley Acres Rsvr—*reservoir* ... TX-5
Valley Airp—*airport* ... AL-4
Valley Airpark—*airport* ... CO-8
Valley Anchorage—*bay* ... CA-9
Valley Annex Sch—*school* ... IA-7
Valley Arco Mine—*mine* ... ID-8
Valley Assembly of God Ch—*church* ... UT-8
*Valley Attendance Center* ... MS-4
Valley Baptist Ch—*church* ... AL-4
Valley Baptist Hosp—*hospital* ... TX-5
Valley Belle Sch—*school* ... WV-2
Valley Bend—*bend* ... WV-2
**Valley Bend**—*pop pl* (2) ... WV-2
Valley Bend Ch—*church* ... WV-2
Valley Bend (Magisterial District)—*fmr MCD* ... WV-2
Valley Bethel Ch—*church* ... IN-6
Valley Bethel Ch—*church* ... VA-3
Valley Bible Ch—*church* ... IN-6
Valley Bible Ch—*church* ... UT-8
*Valley Bonito* ... AZ-5
Valley Brake—*swamp* ... AR-4
Valley Branch—*stream* ... AL-4
Valley Branch—*stream* ... AR-4
Valley Branch—*stream* ... IN-6
Valley Branch—*stream* ... IA-7
Valley Branch—*stream* ... KY-4
Valley Branch—*stream* ... MN-6
Valley Branch—*stream* (2) ... TN-4
Valley Branch—*stream* (4) ... TX-5
Valley Branch—*stream* (3) ... VA-3
*Valley Brook* ... CT-1
*Valley Brook* ... IN-6
*Valley Brook* ... MA-1
*Valley Brook* ... NH-1
**Valley Brook**—*pop pl* ... IN-6
**Valley Brook**—*pop pl* ... NY-2
**Valley Brook**—*pop pl* ... OK-5
**Valleybrook**—*pop pl* ... TN-4
**Valley Brook**—*pop pl* ... VA-3
Valley Brook—*stream* (2) ... CT-1
Valley Brook—*stream* ... KS-7
Valley Brook—*stream* (2) ... ME-1
Valley Brook—*stream* ... MA-1
Valley Brook Cem—*cemetery* ... CO-8
Valley Brook Cem—*cemetery* ... KS-7
Valley Brook Cem—*cemetery* ... NY-2
Valleybrook Golf and Country Club—*locale* ... TN-4
Valleybrook Golf Course—*locale* ... PA-2
Valley Brook (historical)—*locale* ... KS-7
Valley Brook Park—*park* ... TN-4
**Valley Brook Township**—*pop pl* ... KS-7
**Valley Camp**—*pop pl* ... PA-2
**Valley Camp**—*pop pl* ... WV-2
Valley Campground—*locale* ... PA-2
Valley Canal—*canal* ... NM-5
Valley Canyon—*valley* ... UT-8
Valley Cave—*cave* ... TN-4
Valley (CCD)—*cens area* ... GA-3
Valley Cem—*cemetery* ... AR-4
Valley Cem—*cemetery* ... CA-9
Valley Cem—*cemetery* (3) ... IN-6
Valley Cem—*cemetery* ... IA-7
Valley Cem—*cemetery* (2) ... KS-7
Valley Cem—*cemetery* (2) ... KY-4
Valley Cem—*cemetery* ... ME-1
Valley Cem—*cemetery* ... MA-1
Valley Cem—*cemetery* ... MI-6
Valley Cem—*cemetery* (2) ... MN-6
Valley Cem—*cemetery* ... MT-8
Valley Cem—*cemetery* ... NE-7
Valley Cem—*cemetery* (3) ... NH-1
Valley Cem—*cemetery* ... ND-7
Valley Cem—*cemetery* (2) ... OH-6
Valley Cem—*cemetery* (2) ... OK-5
Valley Cem—*cemetery* (3) ... PA-2
Valley Cem—*cemetery* (2) ... TX-5
Valley Cem—*cemetery* ... WY-8
Valley Center—*locale* ... MI-6
Valley Center—*locale* ... VA-3
**Valley Center**—*pop pl* ... CA-9
**Valley Center**—*pop pl* ... KS-7
Valley Center (CCD)—*cens area* ... CA-9
Valley Center Cem—*cemetery* ... CA-9
Valley Center Cem—*cemetery* ... MI-6
Valley Center Cem—*cemetery* ... MO-7
Valley Center Cem—*cemetery* ... OK-5
Valley Center Ch—*church* ... IL-6
Valley Center Ch—*church* ... MO-7
Valley Center Drain—*canal* ... MI-6
Valley Center HS—*school* ... KS-7
Valley Center Sch—*school* ... CA-9
Valley Center Sch—*school* ... CO-8
Valley Center Sch—*school* ... IL-6
Valley Center Sch—*school* ... MI-6
Valley Center Sch—*school* ... MO-7
Valley Center Sch—*school* ... MT-8
Valley Center School (Abandoned)—*locale* ... NE-7
**Valley Center Subdivision**—*pop pl* ... UT-8
**Valley Center Subdivision - Number 2**—*pop pl* ... UT-8
**Valley Center Township**—*pop pl* (2) ... KS-7
Valley Central Ch—*church* ... VA-3
*Valley Ch* ... TN-4
Valley Ch—*church* ... AZ-5
Valley Ch—*church* ... AR-4
Valley Ch—*church* ... GA-3
Valley Ch—*church* ... IN-6
Valley Ch—*church* (2) ... KY-4
Valley Ch—*church* ... MO-7
Valley Ch—*church* (2) ... NE-7
Valley Ch—*church* ... NC-3
Valley Ch—*church* (3) ... OH-6
Valley Ch—*church* (4) ... PA-2
Valley Ch—*church* (2) ... VA-3
Valley Ch—*church* (2) ... WV-2
Valley Chapel—*church* ... AR-4
Valley Chapel—*church* ... MS-4
Valley Chapel—*church* ... MO-7
Valley Chapel—*church* (2) ... OH-6
Valley Chapel—*church* ... PA-2
Valley Chapel—*church* ... TN-4
Valley Chapel—*church* ... TX-5
Valley Chapel—*church* ... VA-3
Valley Chapel—*church* (5) ... WV-2
**Valley Chapel**—*pop pl* ... WV-2
Valley Chapel Cem—*cemetery* ... WA-9
Valley Chapel Ch—*church* ... PA-2
Valley Ch (historical)—*church* ... MS-4
Valley Christian Ch—*church* ... UT-8
Valley Christian HS—*school* ... CA-9
*Valley Church* ... AL-4
Valley Church—*locale* ... OH-6
**Valley Church**—*pop pl* ... FL-3
Valley Church, The—*church* ... OH-6
**Valley City**—*pop pl* ... IL-6
**Valley City**—*pop pl* ... IN-6
**Valley City**—*pop pl* ... MO-7
**Valley City**—*pop pl* ... ND-7
**Valley City**—*pop pl* ... OH-6
Valley City Carnegie Library—*hist pl* ... ND-7
Valley City Cem—*cemetery* ... KS-7
Valley City Interchange—*crossing* ... ND-7
Valley City Mill Dam—*dam* ... ND-7
Valley City Natl Fish Hatchery—*locale* ... ND-7
Valley City Park Dam—*dam* ... ND-7
Valley City Pumping Station—*other* ... IL-6
Valley City Rsvr—*reservoir* ... UT-8
Valley City (Site)—*locale* ... UT-8
**Valley City Station**—*pop pl* ... OH-6
Valley Club—*other* ... CA-9
Valley Community Ch—*church* ... OH-6
Valley Community Presbyterian Ch—*church* ... UT-8
Valley Convalescent Hosp—*hospital* ... CA-9
**Valley Corners**—*pop pl* ... PA-2
Valley Cottage—*hist pl* ... MD-2
**Valley Cottage**—*pop pl* ... NY-2
Valley Country Club—*locale* ... CO-8
Valley Cove—*bay* ... ME-1
*Valley Creek* ... AL-4
*Valley Creek* ... AR-4
*Valley Creek* ... ID-8
*Valley Creek* ... IA-7
*Valley Creek* ... MT-8
*Valley Creek* ... NY-2
*Valley Creek* ... TN-4
*Valley Creek* ... TX-5
*Valley Creek* ... UT-8
**Valley Creek**—*pop pl* ... AL-4
**Valley Creek**—*pop pl* ... TN-4
**Valleycreek**—*pop pl* ... TX-5
**Valley Creek**—*pop pl* ... VA-3
Valley Creek—*stream* (4) ... AL-4
Valley Creek—*stream* ... AK-9
Valley Creek—*stream* ... AR-4
Valley Creek—*stream* ... CA-9
Valley Creek—*stream* (2) ... ID-8
Valley Creek—*stream* ... KS-7
Valley Creek—*stream* ... KY-4
Valley Creek—*stream* ... MS-4
Valley Creek—*stream* (2) ... MT-8
Valley Creek—*stream* ... NC-3
Valley Creek—*stream* ... OK-5
Valley Creek—*stream* ... OR-9
Valley Creek—*stream* (3) ... PA-2
Valley Creek—*stream* ... SD-7
Valley Creek—*stream* (3) ... TN-4
Valley Creek—*stream* (3) ... TX-5
Valley Creek—*stream* (4) ... VA-3
Valley Creek—*stream* (2) ... WA-9
Valley Creek Bar—*bar* ... AL-4
Valley Creek Cem—*cemetery* (2) ... AL-4
Valley Creek Ch—*church* (2) ... AL-4
Valley Creek Ch—*church* ... KY-4
Valley Creek Ch—*church* ... TX-5
Valley Creek Ch—*church* ... VA-3
Valley Creek Chapel—*church* ... VA-3
Valley Creek Community Center—*locale* ... TX-5
Valley Creek Gorge—*valley* ... PA-2
*Valley Creek Junction* ... AL-4
**Valley Creek Junction**—*pop pl* ... AL-4
Valley Creek Lake—*lake* ... ID-8
Valley Creek Lake—*reservoir* ... AL-4
Valley Creek Missionary Baptist Ch—*church* ... TN-4
Valley Creek Park Lake Dam—*dam* ... AL-4
*Valley Creek Presbyterian Church* ... AL-4
Valley Creek Presbyterian Church—*hist pl* ... AL-4
Valley Creek Ranger Station—*locale* ... ID-8
Valley Creek Sch (historical)—*school* ... TN-4
*Valley Creek State Park* ... AL-4
Valley Creek Structure No 4—*dam* ... KY-4
**Valley Crest**—*pop pl* ... MD-2
**Valley Crest Estates**—*pop pl* ... UT-8
Valley Crest Sch—*school* ... CT-1
Valley Crest Sch—*school* ... UT-8
*Valley Crossing* ... OH-6
Valley Crossing—*locale* ... CA-9
**Valley Crossing**—*pop pl* ... OH-6
Valley Dairy Spring—*spring* ... PA-2
**Valleydale**—*pop pl* ... CA-9
**Valleydale**—*pop pl* ... OH-6
Valley Dale Ballroom—*hist pl* ... OH-6
**Valleydale Estates (subdivision)**—*pop pl* ... NC-3
Valleydale Sch—*school* ... CA-9
*Valley de Chino* ... AZ-5
Valley Dell Sch—*school* ... WV-2
Valley Ditch—*canal* ... CO-8
Valley Ditch—*canal* ... MT-8
Valley Ditch—*canal* (2) ... WY-8
Valley Doctors Hosp—*hospital* ... CA-9
**Valley Downs**—*pop pl* ... KY-4
**Valley Down Subdivision**—*pop pl* ... UT-8
**Valley Down Subdivision Two**—*pop pl* ... UT-8
Valley Drainage Ditch—*canal* ... IL-6
Valley Draw—*valley* ... WY-8
Valley Drift Mine (surface)—*mine* ... AL-4
**Valley Drive**—*pop pl* ... OK-5
Valley East Plaza Shop Ctr—*locale* ... AZ-5
Valley Elem Sch—*school* ... AL-4
**Valley Estates (subdivision)**—*pop pl* ... NC-3
**Valley Estates Subdivision**—*pop pl* ... UT-8
Valley Fair—*post sta* ... CA-9
Valley Fair—*post sta* ... WI-6
**Valley Fair Estates Subdivision**—*pop pl* ... UT-8
Valley Fair Mall—*locale* ... UT-8
Valley Fair Shop Ctr—*locale* (2) ... AZ-5
Valley Falls—*locale* ... PA-2
Valley Falls—*locale* ... WV-2
**Valley Falls**—*pop pl* ... KS-7
**Valley Falls**—*pop pl* ... NY-2
**Valley Falls**—*pop pl* ... OR-9
**Valley Falls**—*pop pl* ... RI-1
**Valley Falls**—*pop pl* ... SC-3
Valley Falls Elem Sch—*school* ... KS-7
**Valley Falls (historical)**—*pop pl* ... MA-1
Valley Falls HS—*school* ... KS-7
Valley Falls Mill—*hist pl* ... RI-1
Valley Falls Mill, Office and Bath House—*hist pl* ... RI-1
Valley Falls Park—*park* ... CT-1
Valley Falls Pond—*reservoir* ... RI-1
Valley Falls Pond Dam—*dam* ... RI-1
Valley Falls Station—*building* ... PA-2
Valley Farm—*hist pl* ... TN-4
Valley Farm—*locale* ... AR-4
Valley Farm—*locale* ... IA-7
Valley Farm—*locale* ... TX-5
Valley Farm Ch—*church* ... MS-4
Valley Farm Ruins—*hist pl* ... KY-4
*Valley Farms* ... MI-6
Valley Farms—*locale* ... TX-5
**Valley Farms**—*pop pl* ... AZ-5
**Valley Farms**—*pop pl* ... MI-6
Valley Farms Airp—*airport* ... AZ-5
Valley Field—*park* ... MI-6
Valley Flying Service Airp—*airport* ... MS-4
**Valley Ford**—*pop pl* ... CA-9
**Valley Ford**—*pop pl* ... OH-6
**Valleyford**—*pop pl* ... WA-9
Valleyford (CCD)—*cens area* ... WA-9
Valley Ford Cem—*cemetery* ... TX-5
Valleyford County Park—*park* ... WA-9
**Valley Forge**—*pop pl* (2) ... PA-2
**Valley Forge**—*pop pl* ... TN-4
**Valley Forge Acres**—*pop pl* ... PA-2
Valley Forge Army Hospital—*other* ... PA-2
Valley Forge Bicentennial Heliport—*airport* ... PA-2
Valley Forge Canyon—*valley* ... CA-9
Valley Forge Caves—*cave* ... PA-2
Valley Forge Center—*locale* ... PA-2
Valley Forge Ch—*church* ... TN-4
Valley Forge Christian Coll—*school* ... PA-2
Valley Forge Corporate Center—*locale* ... PA-2
Valley Forge Country Club—*other* ... PA-2
Valley Forge Elem Sch—*school* ... TN-4
**Valley Forge Estates**—*pop pl* ... PA-2
Valley Forge Furnace (historical)—*locale* ... TN-4
Valley Forge General Hospital—*other* ... PA-2
*Valley Forge Golf Course* ... PA-2
Valley Forge Heart Institute—*hospital* ... PA-2
*Valley Forge High School* ... PA-2
**Valley Forge Homes**—*pop pl* ... PA-2
Valley Forge HS—*school* ... OH-6
*Valley Forge Interchange* ... PA-2
*Valley Forge Intermediate School* ... PA-2
Valley Forge JHS—*school* ... PA-2
Valley Forge Lake—*reservoir* ... IN-6
Valley Forge Lake Dam—*dam* ... IN-6
Valley Forge Landing (historical)—*locale* ... MS-4
Valley Forge Mall—*locale* ... PA-2
**Valley Forge Manor**—*pop pl* ... PA-2
Valley Forge Memorial Gardens—*cemetery* ... PA-2
Valley Forge Military Acad—*school* ... PA-2
*Valley Forge Military Acad Junior Coll* ... PA-2
*Valley Forge Military Junior Coll* ... PA-2
Valley Forge Mine—*mine* ... TN-4
Valley Forge Natl Historical Park—*hist pl* ... PA-2
Valley Forge Natl Historical Park—*park* ... PA-2
Valley Forge Sch—*school* ... OH-6
Valley Forge Sch—*school* ... PA-2
Valley Forge Sch—*school* ... SC-3
*Valley Forge State Park* ... PA-2
**Valley Forge (subdivision)**—*pop pl* ... AL-4
Valley Forge Trail—*trail* ... CA-9
**Valley Forge Trailer Park**—*pop pl* ... PA-2
Valley Forge (40DS28)—*hist pl* ... TN-4
*Valleyfork* ... WV-2
Valley Fork—*locale* ... WV-2
Valleyfork—*other* ... WV-2
Valley Fork—*stream* (4) ... WV-2
Valley Fork—*stream* ... WY-8
Valley Fork Run—*stream* ... PA-2
**Valley Fork (Valleyfork)**—*pop pl* ... WV-2
Valley Furnace—*locale* ... WV-2
**Valley Furnace**—*pop pl* ... PA-2
Valley Garden Park—*park* ... DE-2
Valley Garden Ranch—*locale* ... MT-8
Valley Garden Recreation Site—*locale* ... MT-8
**Valley Gardens**—*pop pl* ... KY-4
Valley Gardens Trailer Park—*locale* ... AZ-5
Valley Gate Lateral—*canal* ... TX-5
Valley Gin—*locale* ... AR-4
Valley Gin—*locale* ... OK-5
**Valley Glen**—*pop pl* ... OH-6
Valley Glenn—*locale* ... PA-2
Valley Golf Course—*other* ... OH-6
Valley Golf Course—*other* ... WI-6
Valley Gospel Mission—*church* ... VA-3
**Valley Grande**—*pop pl* ... AL-4
Valley Grande Acad—*school* ... TX-5
Valley Grange—*fmr MCD* ... NE-7
**Valley Green**—*pop pl* (2) ... PA-2
**Valley Green Estates (subdivision)**—*pop pl* ... PA-2
**Valley Green Estates (subdivision)**—*pop pl* ... TN-4
**Valley Green Estates Subdivision**—*pop pl* ... UT-8
Valley Green Golf Course—*locale* ... PA-2
Valley Green Mall—*locale* ... PA-2
Valley Grove—*hist pl* ... MN-6
Valley Grove—*locale* ... AL-4
Valley Grove—*locale* ... TX-5
Valley Grove—*locale* ... WA-9
**Valley Grove**—*pop pl* ... TN-4
**Valley Grove**—*pop pl* (2) ... WV-2
*Valley Grove Baptist Church* ... AL-4
*Valley Grove Baptist Church* ... MS-4
Valley Grove Branch—*stream* ... WV-2
Valley Grove Cem—*cemetery* ... AL-4
Valley Grove Cem—*cemetery* (2) ... AR-4
Valley Grove Cem—*cemetery* (2) ... MS-4
Valley Grove Cem—*cemetery* ... ND-7
Valley Grove Cem—*cemetery* ... OK-5
Valley Grove Cem—*cemetery* ... TX-5
Valley Grove Cem—*cemetery* ... WV-2
Valley Grove Ch—*church* (9) ... AL-4
Valley Grove Ch—*church* ... AR-4
Valley Grove Ch—*church* ... FL-3
Valley Grove Ch—*church* (2) ... GA-3
Valley Grove Ch—*church* ... IN-6
Valley Grove Ch—*church* ... KY-4
Valley Grove Ch—*church* ... MN-6
Valley Grove Ch—*church* ... MS-4
Valley Grove Ch—*church* ... NE-7
Valley Grove Ch—*church* ... NM-5
Valley Grove Ch—*church* ... NC-3
Valley Grove Ch—*church* (4) ... TN-4
Valley Grove Ch—*church* ... TX-5
Valley Grove Ch (historical)—*church* (2) ... AL-4
Valley Grove Elem Sch—*school* ... IN-6
Valley Grove Farm—*locale* ... TN-4
*Valley Grove Mine* ... AL-4
Valley Grove Sch—*school* ... AL-4
Valley Grove Sch—*school* ... IL-6
Valley Grove Sch—*school* ... IA-7
Valley Grove Sch—*school* ... MO-7
Valley Grove Sch—*school* ... PA-2
Valley Grove Sch—*school* (2) ... WV-2
Valley Grove Sch (historical)—*school* ... PA-2
Valley Grove Sch (historical)—*school* ... TN-4
*Valley Grove School* ... TN-4
**Valleyhall (subdivision)**—*pop pl* ... NC-3
**Valleyhaven**—*pop pl* ... AL-4
Valley Haven Ch—*church* ... NC-3
Valley Haven Sch—*school* ... AL-4
**Valley Head**—*pop pl* ... AL-4
**Valley Head**—*pop pl* ... WV-2
Valley Head Cem—*cemetery* ... AL-4
Valley Head Ch—*church* ... GA-3
Valley Head Ch—*church* ... TN-4
Valleyhead Hosp—*hospital* ... MA-1
Valley Head-Mentone (CCD)—*cens area* ... AL-4
Valley Head-Mentone Division—*civil* ... AL-4
Valley Head Sch (historical)—*school* ... TN-4
**Valley Heights**—*pop pl* ... WV-2
Valley Heights Elem Sch—*school* ... KS-7
Valley Heights Golf Course—*other* ... PA-2
**Valley Heights Twin Home Condo**—*pop pl* ... UT-8
**Valley Hi**—*pop pl* ... OH-6
**Valley-Hi**—*pop pl* ... PA-2
**Valley Hi**—*pop pl* ... TX-5
Valley-hi—*uninc pl* ... TX-5
Valley Hi Country Club—*other* ... CA-9
Valley-Hi Eagle Lake—*reservoir* ... PA-2
*Valley-Hi Eagle Lake Dam* ... PA-2
Valley High Country Club—*other* ... MN-6
**Valley High Subdivision**—*pop pl* ... UT-8
Valley Hill—*locale* ... KY-4
**Valley Hill**—*pop pl* ... AR-4
**Valley Hill**—*pop pl* ... MS-4
**Valley Hill**—*pop pl* ... NC-3
Valley Hill Cem—*cemetery* ... AL-4
Valley Hill Cem—*cemetery* ... MS-4
Valley Hill Ch—*church* ... AL-4
Valley Hill Ch—*church* ... MS-4
Valley Hill Golf and Country Club—*other* ... AL-4
Valley Hill Post Office (historical)—*building* ... MS-4
Valley Hill Sch—*school* ... KY-4
Valley Hills Mall—*locale* ... NC-3
**Valley Hills (subdivision)**—*pop pl* ... TN-4
**Valley Hi Mountain Estates**—*pop pl* ... CO-8
Valley Hi Sch—*school* ... TX-5
Valley (historical)—*locale* ... MS-4
**Valley (historical)**—*pop pl* ... OR-9
Valley (historical P.O.)—*locale* ... IA-7
**Valley Hi Subdivision**—*pop pl* ... UT-8
Valley Home—*locale* ... TN-4
**Valley Home**—*pop pl* ... CA-9
**Valleyhome**—*pop pl* ... TN-4
**Valley Home**—*pop pl* ... TN-4
Valley Home Cem—*cemetery* ... CA-9
Valley Home Cem—*cemetery* ... MS-4
Valley Home Ch—*church* ... AR-4
*Valley Home Church* ... TN-4
Valley Home Plantation (historical)—*locale* ... MS-4
Valley Home Post Office (historical)—*building* ... TN-4
Valley Home Sch—*school* ... KS-7
Valley Home Sch—*school* ... TN-4
Valley Home Sch (historical)—*school* ... MO-7
Valley Home United Methodist Ch—*church* ... TN-4
**Valley Home View Subdivision**—*pop pl* ... UT-8
Valley Hosp—*hist pl* ... OR-9
Valley Hosp—*hospital* ... CA-9
Valley Hosp—*hospital* ... GA-3
Valley Hospital, The—*hospital* ... NJ-2
Valley Hospital Med Ctr Heliport—*airport* ... NV-8
Valley HS—*school* ... AL-4
Valley HS—*school* ... AZ-5
Valley HS—*school* ... CA-9
Valley HS—*school* ... ID-8
Valley HS—*school* (3) ... IA-7
Valley HS—*school* ... KY-4
Valley HS—*school* ... MO-7
Valley HS—*school* ... NV-8
Valley HS—*school* ... NM-5
Valley HS—*school* (2) ... UT-8
Valley HS—*school* ... VA-3
Valley Indoor Market Place—*locale* ... UT-8
Valley Inn—*locale* ... PA-2
Valley Inn Sch—*school* ... PA-2
Valley Institute—*school* ... VA-3
**Valley Island**—*pop pl* ... MI-6
*Valley Isle* ... HI-9
Valley JHS—*school* ... CA-9
Valley JHS—*school* ... MN-6
Valley JHS—*school* ... ND-7
Valley JHS—*school* ... UT-8
Valley Juction—*locale* ... OH-6
*Valley Junction* ... IA-7
Valley Junction—*locale* ... AR-4
Valley Junction—*locale* ... OH-6
Valley Junction—*locale* ... PA-2
Valley Junction—*locale* ... TX-5
**Valley Junction**—*pop pl* ... AL-4
**Valley Junction**—*pop pl* ... IL-6
**Valley Junction**—*pop pl* ... IA-7
**Valley Junction**—*pop pl* ... OH-6
**Valley Junction**—*pop pl* ... OR-9
**Valley Junction**—*pop pl* ... WI-6
Valley Junction-West Des Moines City Hall and Engine House—*hist pl* ... IA-7
Valley Lake—*lake* ... AL-4
Valley Lake—*lake* ... IL-6
Valley Lake—*lake* (2) ... MI-6
Valley Lake—*lake* ... MN-6
Valley Lake—*lake* ... NY-2
Valley Lake—*lake* (2) ... OH-6
Valley Lake—*lake* ... VT-1
Valley Lake—*lake* (2) ... WI-6
Valley Lake—*lake* ... WY-8
Valley Lake—*reservoir* ... NJ-2
Valley Lake—*reservoir* ... SC-3
Valley Lake—*reservoir* ... VA-3
**Valley Lake Estates (subdivision)**—*pop pl* ... UT-8

Valley Lakes—*reservoir* GA-3
Valley Lakes—*reservoir* KS-7
Valley Lane Hosp—*hospital* OR-9
**Valley Lee**—*pop pl* MD-2
*Valley Lo* IL-6
Valley Local HS—*school* OH-6
Valley Lodge—*hist pl* ME-1
**Valley Lodge**—*pop pl* TX-5
Valley Lodge Clubhouse—*building* TX-5
Valley Long Pond—*lake* FL-3
Valley (Magisterial District)—*fmr MCD* VA-3
Valley (Magisterial District)—*fmr MCD* (2) WV-2
Valley Mall—*post sta* PA-2
Valley Med Ctr Heliport—*airport* WA-9
**Valley Mede**—*pop pl* MD-2
Valley Meetinghouse—*building* PA-2
Valley Memorial Gardens—*cemetery* TX-5
Valley Memorial Park—*cemetery* IL-6
Valley Memorial Park—*park* WA-9
Valley Memorial Park Cem—*cemetery* AZ-5
Valley Methodist Ch—*church* AL-4
Valley Mill—*locale* MD-2
Valley Mill—*locale* PA-2
Valley Mill—*locale* VA-3
Valley Mills—*hist pl* IA-7
**Valley Mills**—*pop pl* IN-6
**Valley Mills**—*pop pl* MS-4
**Valley Mills**—*pop pl* NY-2
**Valley Mills**—*pop pl* TX-5
**Valley Mills**—*pop pl* VA-3
**Valley Mills**—*pop pl* WV-2
Valley Mills (CCD)—*cens area* TX-5
Valley Mills Cem—*cemetery* TX-5
Valley Mills Society of Friends—*church* IN-6
Valley Mine—*mine* CO-8
Valley Mine—*mine* NM-5
**Valley Mission**—*pop pl* IL-6
Valley Mission Ch—*church* IN-6
Valley Mission Park—*park* WA-9
Valley Mobile Homes Estate—*locale* AZ-5
*Valley Mountain* UT-8
Valley MS—*school* PA-2
Valley Mtn—*summit* CA-9
Valley Mtn—*summit* NV-8
Valley Mtn—*summit* VT-1
Valley Mtn—*summit* (2) WV-2
Valley Mtns—*range* UT-8
Valley North Mall (Shop Ctr)—*locale* ND-7
Valley Oak—*locale* KY-4
Valley Oak Golf Club—*other* TX-5
Valley Oaks Farm—*locale* CA-9
Valley Oaks Sch—*school* CA-9
Valley Oaks Sch—*school* TX-5
**Valley Oaks (subdivision)**—*pop pl* NC-3
**Valley Oak (Valleyoak)**—*pop pl* KY-4
**Valley of Enchantment**—*pop pl* CA-9
Valley of Fire State Park—*park* NV-8
Valley of Fire Wash—*stream* NV-8
*Valley of Los Alisos* CA-9
*Valley of Mystery* AZ-5
*Valley of Nuanu* HI-9
Valley of Ollas—*valley* CA-9
Valley of Peace Cem—*cemetery* IL-6
Valley of Precipices—*valley* AK-9
Valley Of Retreat—*valley* VA-3
**Valley of Shiloh**—*pop pl* AL-4
Valley of Ten Thousand Smokes—*valley* AK-9
*Valley of the Bears* CA-9
Valley of the Falls—*falls* CA-9
*Valley of the Moon* CA-9
Valley of the Moon—*basin* NV-8
Valley of the Moon—*locale* CA-9
Valley of the Moon—*valley* CA-9
Valley of the Springs—*valley* CA-9
Valley of the Sun Memorial Park—*cemetery* (2) AZ-5
Valley of the Sun Sch—*school* AZ-5
Valley of the Temples (Cemetery)—*cemetery* HI-9
Valley of the Thousand Springs—*valley* CA-9
Valley of the Willows—*area* AK-9
Valley Oil Field—*oilfield* CO-8
Valley Palms Mobile Home Park—*locale* AZ-5
Valley Park—*park* AL-4
Valley Park—*park* CA-9
Valley Park—*park* IL-6
Valley Park—*park* LA-4
Valley Park—*park* OH-6
Valley Park—*park* PA-2
Valley Park—*park* (2) WI-6
**Valley Park**—*pop pl* MS-4
**Valley Park**—*pop pl* MO-7
**Valley Park**—*pop pl* OK-5
**Valley Park**—*pop pl* TN-4
Valley Park Baptist Ch—*church* AL-4
Valley Park Estates—*locale* PA-2
**Valley Park Estates Subdivision**—*pop pl* UT-8
Valley Park Lake—*lake* MS-4
Valley Park Post Office—*building* MS-4
Valley Park Ranch—*locale* CO-8
Valley Park Sch—*school* CA-9
Valley Park Sch—*school* IA-7
Valley Park Sch—*school* LA-4
Valley Park Sch—*school* PA-2
**Valley Park (subdivision)**—*pop pl* AL-4
**Valley Park Subdivision**—*pop pl* UT-8
**Valley Park (Valley Industrial Park)**—*pop pl* MN-6
Valley Pass—*locale* NV-8
Valley Peak—*summit* ME-1
Valley Pike Ch—*church* VA-3
Valley Pike Covered Bridge—*hist pl* KY-4
Valley Pike Sch—*school* TN-4
Valley Plains Cem—*cemetery* TX-5
*Valley Plantation* MS-4
Valley Plaza—*post sta* CA-9
Valley Plaza (Shop Ctr)—*locale* AZ-5
Valley Plumbing & Sheet Metal—*hist pl* AZ-5
Valley Point—*locale* PA-2
**Valley Point**—*pop pl* WV-2
Valley Point—*summit* NV-8
Valley Point Ch—*church* PA-2
Valley Point Sch—*school* GA-3
Valley Pond—*lake* CT-1
Valley Pond—*reservoir* MA-1
**Valley Pond Estates**—*pop pl* NY-2
Valley Prairie—*flat* WA-9
Valley Preparatory Sch—*school* CA-9
Valley Psychiatric Hosp—*hospital* TN-4
Valley Pumping Station—*other* IL-6
Valley Queen Cem—*cemetery* OK-5
Valley Queen Ch—*church* VA-3
Valley Queen Mill—*hist pl* RI-1
Valley Queen Missionary Baptist Ch—*church* MS-4
Valley Railway Hist Dist—*hist pl* OH-6
Valley Ranch—*locale* AZ-5
Valley Ranch—*locale* TX-5
Valley Ranch (historical)—*locale* SD-7
Valley Ranch Spring—*spring* AZ-5
Valley Rang Sch—*school* NE-7
Valley Regional HS—*school* CT-1
Valley Reservoir, Lake—*reservoir* CA-9
Valley Rest Cem—*cemetery* KY-4
*Valley Ridge* MN-6
*Valley Ridge* VA-3
Valley Ridge—*CDP* WA-9
**Valley Ridge**—*pop pl* MO-7
**Valley Ridge**—*pop pl* TX-5
**Valley Ridge**—*pop pl* VA-3
Valley Ridge—*ridge* NY-2
Valley Ridge—*ridge* TN-4
Valley Ridge—*ridge* UT-8
Valley Ridge—*ridge* WV-2
Valley Ridge Ch—*church* (2) WV-2
Valley Ridge Lookout Tower—*locale* VA-3
**Valley Ridge Subdivision**—*pop pl* UT-8
Valley Rim Trail—*trail* PA-2
*Valley River* WV-2
Valley River—*stream* MN-6
Valley River—*stream* NC-3
Valley River Cem—*cemetery* NC-3
Valley River Ch—*church* NC-3
Valley River Mountains—*ridge* NC-3
Valley River Trail—*trail* MN-6
Valley Road Ch—*church* TN-4
Valley Road Chapel—*church* VA-3
Valley Road Hist Dist—*hist pl* NY-2
Valley Road Sch—*school* MA-1
Valley (RR name for Valley Station)—*other* KY-4
Valley RR Stone Bridge—*hist pl* VA-3
Valley Rsvr—*reservoir* MT-8
Valley Rsvr—*reservoir* UT-8
Valley Rsvr—*reservoir* WY-8
Valley Rsvr No 1—*reservoir* CO-8
Valley Rsvr No 2—*reservoir* CO-8
*Valley Run* PA-2
Valley Run—*stream* IL-6
Valley Run—*stream* OH-6
Valley Run—*stream* (3) PA-2
Valley Run—*stream* (2) WV-2
**Valley Run (subdivision)**—*pop pl* DE-2
Valleys, The—*basin* UT-8
Valley Sch—*hist pl* UT-8
Valley Sch—*school* AR-4
Valley Sch—*school* (3) CA-9
Valley Sch—*school* IL-6
Valley Sch—*school* IA-7
Valley Sch—*school* KS-7
Valley Sch—*school* KY-4
Valley Sch—*school* MD-2
Valley Sch—*school* MI-6
Valley Sch—*school* MN-6
Valley Sch—*school* MS-4
Valley Sch—*school* (3) MO-7
Valley Sch—*school* (2) NE-7
Valley Sch—*school* NY-2
Valley Sch—*school* OH-6
Valley Sch—*school* (5) PA-2
Valley Sch—*school* (2) SD-7
Valley Sch—*school* UT-8
Valley Sch—*school* (2) VT-1
Valley Sch—*school* VA-3
Valley Sch—*school* WA-9
Valley Sch—*school* (2) WI-6
Valley Sch—*school* WY-8
Valley Sch (abandoned)—*school* MO-7
Valley Sch (abandoned)—*school* PA-2
Valley Sch for Girls—*school* AZ-5
Valley Sch (historical)—*school* (2) AL-4
Valley Sch (historical)—*school* (2) MS-4
Valley Sch (historical)—*school* (3) PA-2
Valley Sch (historical)—*school* SD-7
Valley Sch (historical)—*school* TN-4
Valleys End Ranch—*locale* CA-9
Valley Senior HS—*school* PA-2
Valley Shop Ctr—*locale* AL-4
Valley Shop Ctr—*locale* (2) UT-8
**Valley Side Circle (subdivision)**—*pop pl* UT-8
Valleyside Sch—*school* NE-7
Valley Side Sch (abandoned)—*school* MO-7
**Valley Side Subdivision**—*pop pl* (2) UT-8
Valley Sink—*basin* UT-8
*Valley Spring* CA-9
Valley Spring—*locale* TX-5
Valley Spring—*spring* AL-4
Valley Spring—*spring* NV-8
Valley Spring—*spring* UT-8
Valley Spring Branch—*stream* KY-4
Valley Spring Cem—*cemetery* TX-5
Valley Spring Ch—*church* TX-5
Valley Spring Lake—*reservoir* NJ-2
*Valley Springs* AL-4
**Valley Springs**—*pop pl* AR-4
**Valley Springs**—*pop pl* CA-9
**Valley Springs**—*pop pl* NC-3
**Valley Springs**—*pop pl* SD-7
Valley Springs Cem—*cemetery* AR-4
Valley Springs Cem—*cemetery* MO-7
Valley Springs Ch—*cburch* AL-4
Valley Spring Sch (abandoned)—*school* MO-7
Valley Springs Hosp—*hospital* FL-3
Valley Springs Lakes—*reservoir* TX-5
Valley Springs (Magisterial District)—*fmr MCD* VA-3
Valley Springs Minnow Farm—*locale* TN-4
Valley Springs Peak—*summit* CA-9
*Valley Springs Reservoir* CA-9
Valley Springs Sch—*school* LA-4
Valley Springs Sch—*school* NC-3
**Valley Springs Township**—*pop pl* SD-7
**Valley Springs (Valley Spring)**—*pop pl* CA-9
**Valley Spring Township**—*pop pl* ND-7
*Valley Spring (Valley Springs)* CA-9
Valley Spur Creek—*stream* MI-6
Valley Star Sch (abandoned)—*school* MO-7
Valley Station—*locale* PA-2
**Valley Station**—*pop pl* KY-4
**Valley Station**—*pop pl* WY-8
Valley Station (RR name Valley)—*CDP* KY-4
**Valley Station (subdivision)**—*pop pl* AL-4
Valley Stone—*locale* AR-4
Valley Store—*locale* PA-2
Valley Store Spring—*spring* AZ-5
**Valley Stream**—*pop pl* MD-2
**Valley Stream**—*pop pl* NY-2
Valley Stream—*stream* NY-2
Valley Stream—*uninc pl* VA-3
**Valley Stream Estates**—*pop pl* MD-2
**Valley Stream Estates (subdivision)**—*pop pl* PA-2
Valley Stream State Park—*park* NY-2
**Valley Stream (subdivision)**—*pop pl* NC-3
Valley Swamp—*swamp* MA-1
Valley Tabernacle—*church* NY-2
Valley Tank—*reservoir* (4) AZ-5
Valley Tank—*reservoir* NM-5
**Valley Terrace Condominium**—*pop pl* UT-8
Valleytown—*locale* MT-8
**Valleytown**—*pop pl* NC-3
Valleytown Cem—*cemetery* NC-3
Valley Town Hall—*building* ND-7
*Valley Township* SD-7
Valley Township—*civ div* SD-7
Valley Township—*civil* KS-7
Valley Township—*civil* MO-7
Valley Township—*civil* (2) SD-7
Valley Township—*fmr MCD* (4) IA-7
**Valley Township**—*pop pl* (13) KS-7
**Valley Township**—*pop pl* (2) NE-7
**Valley Township**—*pop pl* (3) ND-7
**Valley Township**—*pop pl* (6) SD-7
Valley Township—*unorg reg* KS-7
Valley Township (historical)—*civil* ND-7
Valley (Township of)—*fmr MCD* (7) AR-4
**Valley (Township of)**—*pop pl* IL-6
**Valley (Township of)**—*pop pl* MI-6
**Valley (Township of)**—*pop pl* MN-6
**Valley (Township of)**—*pop pl* (2) OH-6
**Valley (Township of)**—*pop pl* (3) PA-2
Valley Town (Township of)—*fmr MCD* NC-3
Valley Trail—*trail* DC-2
Valley Trail—*trail* (2) WY-8
Valley Union HS—*school* AZ-5
Valley Union Sch—*school* NE-7
Valley United Methodist Ch—*church* AL-4
*Valley View* IL-6
*Valley View* SD-7
Valley View—*hist pl* GA-3
Valley View—*locale* CA-9
Valley View—*locale* NV-8
Valley View—*locale* NY-2
Valleyview—*locale* SD-7
Valleyview—*locale* TN-4
Valley View—*locale* (5) TX-5
Valley View—*park* PA-2
**Valley View**—*pop pl* AL-4
**Valley View**—*pop pl* AZ-5
**Valley View**—*pop pl* AR-4
**Valley View**—*pop pl* CO-8
**Valley View**—*pop pl* DE-2
**Valley View**—*pop pl* GA-3
**Valley View**—*pop pl* (2) IL-6
**Valley View**—*pop pl* KY-4
**Valley View**—*pop pl* (2) MD-2
**Valley View**—*pop pl* MA-1
**Valley View**—*pop pl* (3) MO-7
**Valley View**—*pop pl* NC-3
**Valley View**—*pop pl* (3) OH-6
**Valleyview**—*pop pl* OH-6
**Valley View**—*pop pl* (2) OH-6
**Valley View**—*pop pl* (5) PA-2
**Valley View**—*pop pl* SD-7
**Valley View**—*pop pl* (2) TN-4
**Valley View**—*pop pl* (7) TX-5
**Valley View**—*pop pl* (2) VA-3
**Valley View Acres**—*pop pl* PA-2
**Valley View Acres (subdivision)**—*pop pl* PA-2
**Valley View Acres Subdivision**—*pop pl* UT-8
**Valley View Addition (subdivision)**—*pop pl* UT-8
Valley View and Foothill Mine—*mine* NV-8
Valley View Baptist Ch—*church* (2) TN-4
Valley View Baptist Ch—*church* UT-8
Valley View Cabin—*locale* OR-9
Valley View Canal—*canal* CA-9
Valley View Canyon—*valley* AZ-5
Valleyview Canyon—*valley* UT-8
Valley View Cave—*cave* TN-4
Valley View (CCD)—*cens area* TX-5
Valley View Cem—*cemetery* (2) AL-4
Valley View Cem—*cemetery* AZ-5
Valley View Cem—*cemetery* AR-4
Valley View Cem—*cemetery* (2) CO-8
Valley View Cem—*cemetery* IL-6
Valley View Cem—*cemetery* (4) IA-7
Valley View Cem—*cemetery* (2) KS-7
Valley View Cem—*cemetery* MN-6
Valley View Cem—*cemetery* MS-4
Valley View Cem—*cemetery* MT-8
Valley View Cem—*cemetery* (3) NE-7
Valley View Cem—*cemetery* (5) NY-2
Valley View Cem—*cemetery* (2) OH-6
Valley View Cem—*cemetery* (2) OK-5
Valley View Cem—*cemetery* (2) OR-9
Valley View Cem—*cemetery* (4) PA-2
Valley View Cem—*cemetery* (3) TN-4
Valley View Cem—*cemetery* (3) TX-5
Valleyview Cem—*cemetery* UT-8
Valley View Cem—*cemetery* UT-8
Valley View Cem—*cemetery* VA-3
Valley View Cem—*cemetery* WA-9
Valley View Cem—*cemetery* WV-2
Valley View Cem—*cemetery* (2) WY-8
*Valley View Cemetery* UT-8
Valley View Ch—*church* (5) AL-4
Valley View Ch—*church* (4) AR-4
Valley View Ch—*church* GA-3
Valley View Ch—*church* (2) KY-4
Valley View Ch—*church* MI-6
Valley View Ch—*church* (2) MS-4
Valley View Ch—*church* (3) MO-7
Valley View Ch—*church* NM-5
Valley View Ch—*church* NY-2
Valley View Ch—*church* OH-6
Valley View Ch—*church* (3) OK-5
Valley View Ch—*church* (2) PA-2
Valley View Ch—*church* (11) TN-4
Valley View Ch—*church* (4) TX-5
Valley View Ch—*church* (6) VA-3
Valley View Ch—*church* WV-2
Valley View Chapel—*church* IN-6
Valley View Ch (historical)—*church* TN-4
Valley View Community Center—*building* MT-8
Valley View Community Hosp—*hospital* AZ-5
Valley View Community Hosp—*hospital* CO-8
Valley View Convalescent Home—*hospital* KS-7
Valleyview Corner—*locale* VA-3
*Valley View Creek* TX-5
Valley View Dam—*dam* PA-2
Valley View Elem Sch—*school* KS-7
Valley View Elem Sch (abandoned)—*school* PA-2
**Valley View Estates (subdivision)**—*pop pl* AL-4
**Valley View Estates (subdivision)**—*pop pl* SD-7
Valleyview Farm—*locale* TX-5
**Valley View Farms**—*pop pl* (2) PA-2
Valley View Golf—*other* NY-2
Valley View Golf Club—*other* MT-8
Valley View Golf Club—*other* NJ-2
Valley View Golf Course—*other* AL-4
Valley View Golf Course—*other* WA-9
Valley View Heights—*locale* ID-8
Valley View Heights—*locale* OH-6
**Valley View Heights**—*pop pl* PA-2
**Valley View Heights**—*pop pl* TN-4
**Valley View Heights Subdivision**—*pop pl* UT-8
**Valley View Hills**—*pop pl* IN-6
Valley View Hills—*spring* MT-8
Valley View (historical)—*locale* MO-7
Valleyview (historical)—*locale* SD-7
Valley View Hollow—*valley* TN-4
Valley View Hosp—*hospital* CO-8
Valley View Hosp—*hospital* WA-9
Valley View Hot Springs—*locale* CO-8
Valley View JHS—*school* CA-9
Valley View JHS—*school* MN-6
Valley View Lake—*lake* AL-4
Valley View Lake—*lake* OH-6
Valley View Lake—*reservoir* (2) PA-2
Valley View Lake Dam—*dam* AL-4
Valley View Lake Dam—*dam* PA-2
Valley View Lookout Tower—*locale* CA-9
Valley View Med Ctr—*hospital* UT-8
Valley View Memorial Cem—*cemetery* KS-7
Valley View Memorial Park (Cemetery)—*cemetery* UT-8
*Valley View Memory Gardens* AL-4
Valley View Mine—*mine* (3) CA-9
Valley View Mine—*mine* ID-8
Valley View Mine—*mine* NV-8
Valley View Mine—*mine* OR-9
*Valley View Missionary Baptist Church* AL-4
Valley View Mobile Home Park—*locale* PA-2
Valley View Mtn—*summit* CA-9
Valley View Orchard—*locale* (2) CA-9
Valley View Park—*locale* PA-2
Valley View Park—*park* MN-6
Valley View Park—*park* NV-8
Valley View Park—*park* TX-5
**Valley View Park**—*pop pl* CA-9
**Valley View Park Subdivision - Numbers 1-6**—*pop pl* UT-8
**Valley View Park Subdivision - Plats A, B**—*pop pl* UT-8
Valley View Picnic Area—*park* AZ-5
Valley View Playfield—*park* MN-6
Valley View Point—*summit* AZ-5
Valley View Ranch—*locale* AZ-5
Valley View Ranch—*locale* CA-9
Valley View Ranch—*locale* CO-8
Valley View Roadside Park—*locale* MO-7
Valley View Rsvr—*reservoir* CA-9
Valley View Rsvr—*reservoir* OR-9
Valley View Sanatorium—*hospital* NJ-2
Valley View Sch—*school* AZ-5
Valley View Sch—*school* AR-4
Valley View Sch—*school* (10) CA-9
Valley View Sch—*school* (3) CO-8
Valley View Sch—*school* CT-1
Valley View Sch—*school* ID-8
Valley View Sch—*school* (3) IL-6
Valley View Sch—*school* KS-7
Valley View Sch—*school* KY-4
Valley View Sch—*school* (2) MI-6
Valley View Sch—*school* (2) MN-6
Valley View Sch—*school* MO-7
Valley View Sch—*school* MT-8
Valley View Sch—*school* (11) NE-7
Valley View Sch—*school* (2) NM-5
Valley View Sch—*school* (2) OH-6
Valley View Sch—*school* OR-9
Valley View Sch—*school* (2) SD-7
Valley View Sch—*school* (4) TN-4
Valley View Sch—*school* (5) TX-5
Valley View Sch—*school* (3) UT-8
Valley View Sch—*school* VA-3
Valley View Sch—*school* (2) WV-2
Valley View Sch—*school* (3) WI-6
Valley View Sch (abandoned)—*school* MO-7
Valley View Sch (historical)—*school* TN-4
*Valley View School* AL-4
*Valley View School* PA-2
Valley View School (Abandoned)—*locale* ID-8
Valley View School (Abandoned)—*locale* MN-6
Valley View School (abandoned)—*locale* OR-9
Valley View Shop Ctr—*locale* KS-7
Valley View Shop Ctr—*locale* MS-4
Valley View Site—*hist pl* WI-6
Valley View Spring—*spring* CA-9
Valley View Spring—*spring* CO-8
*Valley View Springs* CO-8
Valley View Store—*locale* WY-8
**Valley View (subdivision)**—*pop pl* (2) AL-4
**Valley View (subdivision)**—*pop pl* (2) AZ-5
**Valley View (subdivision)**—*pop pl* MS-4
**Valleyview Subdivision**—*pop pl* TN-4
**Valley View (subdivision)**—*pop pl* TN-4
**Valleyview Subdivision**—*pop pl* TN-4
**Valley View Subdivision**—*pop pl* (2) UT-8
Valley View Tank—*reservoir* AZ-5
Valley View Trailer Park—*locale* PA-2
**Valley View Trailer Park**—*pop pl* UT-8
Valleyview Truck Trail—*trail* CA-9
**Valley View Village**—*pop pl* OH-6
Valley View Vista—*locale* PA-2
**Valley View Vistas (subdivision)**—*pop pl* NC-3
**Valley Village**—*pop pl* KY-4
**Valley Village**—*pop pl* TN-4
Valley Village—*uninc pl* CA-9
Valley Village Shop Ctr—*locale* NC-3
Valley Vista Cem—*cemetery* VA-3
Valley Vista Sch—*school* (3) CA-9
Valley Vista Sch—*school* OH-6
Valley Vocational Center—*school* CA-9
Valley Vocational Sch—*school* VA-3
**Valley Water Mills**—*pop pl* MO-7
Valley Way—*trail* NH-1
Valley Well—*well* NV-8
Valley Well—*well* (2) TX-5
*Valley Wells* CA-9
Valley Wells—*locale* (2) CA-9
Valley Wells—*locale* TX-5
*Valley Wells Ranch* CA-9
**Valley Wells Station**—*pop pl* CA-9
Valley West Baptist Ch—*church* UT-8
**Valley West Estates Subdivision**—*pop pl* UT-8
**Valley West Estates Subdivision Number Two**—*pop pl* UT-8
*Valley West Hospital* UT-8
Valley West Mall—*locale* AZ-5
**Valley West Ranches Subdivision**—*pop pl* UT-8
**Valley West Subdivision**—*pop pl* UT-8
**Valleywest Subdivision**—*pop pl* UT-8
**Valley Whispers (subdivision)**—*pop pl* AL-4
**Valleywood**—*pop pl* MD-2
**Valleywood**—*pop pl* OH-6
**Valleywood**—*pop pl* VA-3
Valley Wood Golf Club—*locale* OH-6
Valleywood JHS—*school* MI-6
Valley Woods Sch—*school* MI-6
**Valliant**—*pop pl* OK-5
Valliant (CCD)—*cens area* OK-5
Valliant Cem—*cemetery* OK-5
Valliant Point—*cape* MD-2
Valliant Ranch—*locale* TX-5
Valliant Sch Gymnasium-Auditorium—*hist pl* OK-5
*Vallicita* CA-9
*Vallicitos Desert Area* CA-9
Vallie—*locale* CO-8
Vallier—*locale* AR-4
Vallier—*locale* LA-4
*Valliet Spring* ID-8
Vallis Ditch—*canal* MT-8
Vallito Peak—*summit* NM-5
*Vallmer Creek* OR-9
Vallonia—*locale* OH-6
**Vallonia**—*pop pl* IN-6
Vallonia Cem—*cemetery* KS-7
Vallonia Ch—*church* IN-6
Vallonia (historical)—*locale* KS-7
Vallonia Springs—*locale* NY-2
Vallorso—*locale* CO-8
Vallo Spring—*spring* NM-5
**Vallscreek**—*pop pl* WV-2
**Vallscreek (RR name Hartwell)**—*pop pl* WV-2
**Vallyd Acres**—*pop pl* IN-6
**Valmar**—*pop pl* LA-4
**Val Mar Subdivision**—*pop pl* UT-8
**Valmead**—*pop pl* NC-3
Valmead Sch—*school* NC-3
*Val me China* AZ-5
**Valmeyer**—*pop pl* IL-6
Valmont—*locale* CO-8
Valmont—*locale* NM-5
Valmont Butte—*summit* CO-8
Valmont Cem—*cemetery* CO-8
Val Monte Country Club—*other* AL-4
Val Monte Marina—*locale* AL-4
Valmonte Sch—*school* CA-9
Valmont Memorial Ch—*church* AL-4
Valmont Rsvr—*reservoir* CO-8
Valmont Village Park—*park* NY-2
**Valmora**—*pop pl* NM-5
**Valmy**—*pop pl* NV-8
**Valmy**—*pop pl* WI-6
**Valois**—*pop pl* NY-2
Valois, Mount—*summit* CO-8
Valois Cem—*cemetery* NY-2
Valois Point—*cape* NY-2
**Valona**—*pop pl* CA-9
**Valona**—*pop pl* GA-3
Valon Tuote Raittiusseura—*hist pl* MN-6
Valor Lake—*lake* CA-9
Valpa Creek—*stream* AK-9
*Valparaiso* KS-7
**Valparaiso**—*pop pl* (2) FL-3
**Valparaiso**—*pop pl* IN-6
**Valparaiso**—*pop pl* NE-7
*Valparaiso Bay* FL-3
Valparaiso Cem—*cemetery* NE-7
Valparaiso Country Club—*other* IN-6
Valparaiso Elem Sch—*school* FL-3
Valparaiso HS—*school* IN-6
Valparaiso Mine—*mine* CA-9
Valparaiso Technical Institute—*school* IN-6
Valparaiso Univ—*school* IN-6
*Valpariso* FL-3
Valpe Creek—*stream* CA-9
*Valpee* AZ-5
*Valpe Ridge* CA-9
Valpe Ridge—*ridge* CA-9
Valpey Butte—*summit* OR-9
**Valpico**—*pop pl* CA-9
Val Point—*cape* ME-1
**Valrico**—*pop pl* FL-3
Valrico Lake—*lake* FL-3
Valrico Lookout Tower—*tower* FL-3
Valrico Square (Shop Ctr)—*locale* FL-3
**Valroy**—*pop pl* FL-3
Vals Camp—*locale* NV-8
Valsetz—*locale* OR-9
Valsetz Falls—*falls* OR-9
Valsetz Guard Station—*locale* OR-9
Valsetz Lake—*reservoir* OR-9
Valsetz Lake Dam—*dam* OR-9
Valsetz Rsvr—*reservoir* OR-9
*Val-shima Wash* AZ-5
*Valshnia Wash* AZ-5
*Valshni Wash* AZ-5
*Valshuni Wash* AZ-5
Vals Tank—*reservoir* AZ-5
**Valton**—*pop pl* WI-6
**Value**—*pop pl* MS-4
Value Creek—*stream* AK-9
Value Post Office (historical)—*building* MS-4
Value Run—*stream* IN-6
Valu Plaza (Shop Ctr)—*locale* FL-3
Valve House—*locale* AZ-5
Valve House Draw—*valley* ID-8
Valve House Spring—*spring* ID-8
**Valverda**—*pop pl* LA-4
**Val Verda**—*pop pl* UT-8
**Val Verda Condominium**—*pop pl* UT-8
**Val Verda Heights Subdivision**—*pop pl* UT-8
Valverda Sch—*school* LA-4
**Val Verda Subdivision**—*pop pl* UT-8
*Val Verde* AZ-5
Val Verde—*locale* CA-9
Val Verde—*locale* NM-5
Val Verde—*locale* TX-5
**Val Verde**—*pop pl* CA-9
**Val Verde**—*pop pl* TX-5
Val Verde Camp—*locale* TX-5
Val Verde Ch—*church* TX-5
**Val Verde (County)**—*pop pl* TX-5
Val Verde County Courthouse And Jail—*hist pl* TX-5
Val Verde Hotel—*hist pl* NM-5
Val Verde Memorial Hosp—*hospital* TX-5
*Val Verde Park* CA-9
Valverde Park—*park* CO-8
Val Verde Park (LA County)—*park* CA-9
Val Verde Sch—*school* CA-9
Valverde Sch—*school* CO-8
**Val Verde (Ski Area)**—*pop pl* NM-5
**Valverde Township**—*pop pl* KS-7
Val Verde Tunnel—*tunnel* CA-9
*Valverde Valley* TX-5
**Val Vista Subdivision**—*pop pl* UT-8
Val Vista Trailer Park—*locale* AZ-5
Val Vista Village Trailer Park Mini Park—*park* AZ-5
Val Vista Village Trailer Park Water Retention Basin—*reservoir* AZ-5
Val Wash—*valley* UT-8
Valwood Sch—*school* TX-5
Valyermo—*locale* CA-9
Valyermo Ranch—*locale* CA-9
Va Med Ctr Heliport—*airport* MO-7
**Vamo**—*pop pl* FL-3
**Vamoosa**—*pop pl* OK-5
Vamoosa Cem—*cemetery* OK-5
**Vamori**—*pop pl* AZ-5
Vamori Valley—*valley* AZ-5
Vamori Wash—*stream* AZ-5
Vamp Bldg—*hist pl* MA-1
Vampire Mine—*mine* AZ-5
*Van* IN-6
Van—*locale* AR-4
Van—*locale* KY-4
Van—*locale* OH-6
Van—*locale* OR-9
Van—*locale* UT-8
**Van**—*pop pl* IA-7
**Van**—*pop pl* MI-6
**Van**—*pop pl* MO-7
**Van**—*pop pl* PA-2
**Van**—*pop pl* TX-5
**Van**—*pop pl* VA-3
**Van**—*pop pl* WV-2
Van, Lake—*lake* FL-3
**Vanada**—*pop pl* IN-6
*Vanada Camps* IN-6
**Vanada Camps**—*pop pl* IN-6
Vanada Cem—*cemetery* KY-4
Vanadate Mine—*mine* CO-8
**Vanada Woods**—*pop pl* NJ-2
**Vanadis**—*pop pl* OH-6
Vanadium—*locale* CO-8
**Vanadium**—*pop pl* NM 5
**Vanadium (Hanover Junction)**—*pop pl* NM-5
Vanadium Mine—*mine* AZ-5
Vanadium Queen Mine—*mine* UT-8
Vanadium Ranch—*locale* CA-9
Vanadium Shaft—*mine* AZ-5
Vanadium Springs—*spring* AZ-5
Vanaimes Hill—*summit* PA-2
Vanaking No 1 Mine—*mine* CO-8
Vanalden Ave Sch—*school* CA-9
Van Alderstien Gulch—*valley* CO-8
Van Alen, Johannis L., Farm—*hist pl* NY-2
Van Alen, Luycas, House—*hist pl* NY-2
**Van Allen**—*pop pl* CA-9
Van Allen Cem—*cemetery* (2) NY-2
Van Allen House—*hist pl* NJ-2
**Van Allen Park**—*pop pl* NY-2
Van Allen Ridge—*ridge* CA-9
Van Allen Store—*hist pl* IA-7
Van Alstin Lake—*lake* MI-6
**Van Alstyne**—*pop pl* TX-5
Van Alstyne House—*hist pl* NY-2
Van Alstyne Sewage Disposal—*other* TX-5
Van Altena, William, House—*hist pl* WI-6
Van Amringe Millpond—*reservoir* NY-2
**Vananda**—*pop pl* MT-8
Van Anda Mine—*mine* OR-9
Van Anda Park—*park* NE-7
Vanango Cem—*cemetery* NE-7
*Vananken Creek* CA-9
Van Antwerp Creek—*stream* NY-2
Van Antwerp Sch—*school* NY-2
Vanar—*locale* AZ-5
Vanare, Lake—*lake* NY-2
*Van Arken Creek* CA-9
*Vanarkin Creek* CA-9
Vanar RR Station—*building* AZ-5
Van Arsdale—*locale* KS-7
Van Arsdale Rsvr—*reservoir* CA-9
Vanarsdale Run—*stream* PA-2
Van Arsdel, William C., House—*hist pl* IN-6
Vanarsdell—*locale* KY-4
Van Arsdol, C. C., House—*hist pl* WA-9

Van Arthur Lead—*ridge* GA-3
Vanar Wash—*stream* AZ-5
Van Asch, William, House-Huibert Debooy Commercial Room—*hist pl* IA-7
Van Aspen Creek—*stream* OR-9
Van Asselt—*uninc pl* WA-9
Vanasse Mine—*mine* WA-9
*Van Asshan Creek* OR-9
*Van Asshon Creek* OR-9
Vanata Basin—*basin* OR-9
Vanata Creek—*stream* OR-9
**Vanatta**—*pop pl* OH-6
Vanatta Ditch—*canal* IN-6
Vanatta House—*hist pl* KY-4
Vanatta Lateral—*canal* IN-6
Vanauken Brook—*stream* NY-2
Van Auken Cem—*cemetery* MI-6
*Vanauken Creek* PA-2
Vanauken Creek—*stream* CA-9
Van Auken Creek—*stream* PA-2
Van Auken Lake—*lake* MI-6
Van Auken Sch—*school* CA-9
Van Auken Sch—*school* MI-6
*Van Austin Lake* MI-6
*Van Bebber Spring* TN-4
**Vanbebber Spring**—*pop pl* TN-4
Vanbebber Spring—*spring* TN-4
Van Beek State Wildlife Mngmt Area—*park* MN-6
*Van Benber Springs* TN-4
**Van Benber Springs**—*pop pl* TN-4
Van Benschoten Cem—*cemetery* NY-2
Van Benthuysen Brook—*stream* NY-2
Van Bibber—*locale* MD-2
Van Bibber Creek—*stream* CO-8
Vanbibber Hollow—*valley* TN-4
Van Bibber Lake—*reservoir* IN-6
Van Bibber Lake Dam—*dam* IN-6
**Van Bibber Lake (Mobile Home Park)**—*pop pl* IN-6
**Van Bibber Manor**—*pop pl* MD-2
Van Blarcom—*uninc pl* TN-4
Van Blarcom, Albert, House—*hist pl* NJ-2
Van Blarcom House—*hist pl* NJ-2
Van Blarcom - Jardine House—*hist pl* NJ-2
*Van Blarcum Creek* WI-6
Van Boddie, Nathan, House—*hist pl* GA-3
Van Boxel Creek—*stream* CO-8
Van Boxel Lakes—*lake* CO-8
Van Brogt Park—*park* MI-6
Van Branch—*stream* KY-4
Van Bremer Arroyo—*stream* CO-8
*Van Bremmel Arroyo* CO-8
Van Bremmer Canyon—*valley* NM-5
Van Bremmer Creek—*stream* NM-5
Van Bremmer Park—*park* NM-5
Van Bremmer Well—*well* NM-5
Van Brimmer Canal—*canal* CA-9
Van Brimmer Canal—*canal* OR-9
Van Brocklin Cem—*cemetery* IL-6
Van Brocklin Sch—*school* IL-6
Van Bruggen Canyon—*valley* NM-5
Van Brunt—*uninc pl* NY-2
Van Brunt, Daniel C., House—*hist pl* WI-6
Van Brunt Arm—*bay* FL-3
Van Brunt Cem—*cemetery* AR-4
Van Brunt Cem—*cemetery* FL-3
Van Brunt Creek—*stream* PA-2
Van Brunt Hollow—*valley* AR-4
Van Brunt Mtn—*summit* WA-9
Van Buggenem Ranch—*locale* WY-8
Van Bunschooten, Elias, House—*hist pl* NJ-2
*Van Buren* AL-4
*Vanburen* KY-4
*Vanburen* OH-6
Van Buren—*locale* IA-7
Van Buren—*locale* PA-2
**Van Buren**—*pop pl* AR-4
**Van Buren**—*pop pl* IN-6
**Van Buren**—*pop pl* KY-4
**Van Buren**—*pop pl* ME-1
**Van Buren**—*pop pl* MS-4
**Van Buren**—*pop pl* MO-7
**Van Buren**—*pop pl* NY-2
**Vanburen**—*pop pl* OH-6
**Van Buren**—*pop pl* OH-6
**Van Buren**—*pop pl* PA-2
**Van Buren**—*pop pl* TN-4
**Van Buren**—*pop pl* WA-9
Van Buren, David, House—*hist pl* NY-2
Van Buren, John, Tavern—*hist pl* NY-2
Van Buren, Martin, Natl Historic Site—*hist pl* NY-2
Van Buren, Sarah Belle, House—*hist pl* WI-6
Van Buren, Volkert, House—*hist pl* NY-2
Van Buren Acad (historical)—*school* TN-4
Van Buren Bay—*bay* (2) NY-2
**Van Buren Bay**—*pop pl* NY-2
Van Buren Bayou—*gut* LA-4
Van Buren Cem—*cemetery* MO-7
Van Buren Cem—*cemetery* NY-2
Van Buren Cem—*cemetery* WI-6
Van Buren Center (census name Van Buren)—*other* ME-1
Van Buren Ch—*church* (2) MO-7
**Van Buren (County)**—*pop pl* AR-4
**Van Buren (County)**—*pop pl* MI-6
**Van Buren County**—*pop pl* TN-4
Van Buren County Courthouse—*building* TN-4
Van Buren County Courthouse—*hist pl* IA-7
Van Buren County Courthouse Complex—*hist pl* MI-6
Van Buren County Home—*building* IA-7
Van Buren County HS—*school* TN-4
Van Buren Creek—*stream* CA-9
Van Buren Creek—*stream* ID-8
Van Buren Creek—*stream* IN-6
VanBuren Creek—*stream* KY-4
Van Buren Elementary and MS—*school* IN-6
*Van Buren Elementary School* AL-4
Van Buren Elem Sch—*school* (2) IN-6
Van Buren Furnace—*locale* VA-3
Van Buren Furnace (historical)—*locale* TN-4
Van Buren Hist Dist—*hist pl* AR-4
Van Buren Hollow—*valley* MO-7
Van Buren HS—*school* AR-4
Van Buren HS—*school* IN-6
Van Buren JHS—*school* AR-4
Van Buren JHS—*school* FL-3
Van Buren JHS—*school* OH-6
Van Buren Lake State Res—*park* OH-6
Van Buren Lodge—*locale* KY-4
Van Buren Memorial Hosp—*hospital* AR-4
Van Buren MS—*school* AR-4
Van Buren Municipal Park—*park* AR-4
Van Buren Park—*park* IA-7
**Van Buren Park**—*pop pl* IN-6
Van Buren Point—*cape* NY-2
**Van Buren Point**—*pop pl* NY-2
Van Buren Post Office (historical)—*building* PA-2
Van Buren Post Office (historical)—*building* TN-4
Van Buren Rec Area—*park* AR-4
**Van Burensbrug**—*pop pl* IL-6
**Van Burensburg**—*pop pl* IL-6
Van Buren Sch—*school* AL-4
Van Buren Sch—*school* AR-4
Van Buren Sch—*school* (2) CA-9
Van Buren Sch—*school* ID-8
Van Buren Sch—*school* IA-7
Van Buren Sch—*school* MI-6
Van Buren Sch—*school* MN-6
Van Buren Sch—*school* (2) NY-2
Van Buren Sch—*school* OH-6
Van Buren Sch—*school* OK-5
Van Buren Sch—*school* TN-4
Van Buren Sch—*school* (2) WI-6
Van Buren Sch No 43—*school* AR-4
Van Buren School (Abandoned)—*locale* WI-6
Van Buren State Park—*locale* MI-6
*Van Buren Street* IL-6
**Van Buren (Town of)**—*pop pl* ME-1
**Van Buren (Town of)**—*pop pl* NY-2
Van Buren Township—*civil* (2) MO-7
Van Buren Township—*fmr MCD* (4) IA-7
**Van Buren Township**—*pop pl* MO-7
**Van Buren Township**—*pop pl* ND-7
Van Buren (Township of)—*fmr MCD* (3) AR-4
Van Buren (Township of)—*other* OH-6
**Van Buren (Township of)**—*pop pl* (11) IN-6
**Van Buren (Township of)**—*pop pl* MI-6
**Van Buren (Township of)**—*pop pl* MN-6
**Van Buren (Township of)**—*pop pl* (4) OH-6
**Van Buren (Vanburen)**—*pop pl* KY-4
**Van Burenville**—*pop pl* NY-2
Van Buren Water Hole—*lake* TX-5
Van Buren Water Rsvr—*reservoir* AR-4
Vanburg Cem—*cemetery* LA-4
Van Burton Creek—*stream* MT-8
**Van Buskirk**—*pop pl* WI-6
Van Buskirk, Andries Thomas, House—*hist pl* NJ-2
Van Buskirk, John, Farm House—*hist pl* MI-6
Van Buskirk, Laurance Thomas, House—*hist pl* NJ-2
Van Buskirk Cem—*cemetery* (2) IN-6
*Vanbuskirk Gorge* NY-2
VanBuskirk Gulf—*valley* NY-2
Van Buskirk Municipal Park—*park* CA-9
Van Buskirk-Oakley House—*hist pl* NJ-2
Van Buskirk Park—*park* CA-9
Van Buskirk Sch—*school* AZ-5
Van Camp—*locale* PA-2
**Van Camp**—*pop pl* WV-2
Van Camp Canyon—*valley* MT-8
Van Camp Cem—*cemetery* AR-4
Van Camp Cem—*cemetery* WV-2
Van Camp Creek—*stream* ID-8
Van Camp Ditch—*canal* MT-8
Van Campen Creek—*stream* NY-2
*Vancampen Mill Brook* NJ-2
Vancampens Brook—*stream* NJ-2
Van Campen Sch—*school* IL-6
*Van Camps Brook* NJ-2
Van Camp Slough—*stream* MT-8
Van Carr Canal—*canal* TX-5
Van Cave—*cave* AL-4
Van (CCD)—*cens area* TX-5
Vance—*locale* AR-4
Vance—*locale* KS-7
Vance—*locale* MO-7
Vance—*locale* NE-7
Vance—*locale* NC-3
Vance—*locale* ND-7
Vance—*locale* VA-3
Vance—*locale* WV-2
**Vance**—*pop pl* AL-4
**Vance**—*pop pl* CA-9
**Vance**—*pop pl* KS-7
**Vance**—*pop pl* KY-4
**Vance**—*pop pl* MS-4
**Vance**—*pop pl* PA-2
**Vance**—*pop pl* SC-3
**Vance**—*pop pl* TN-4
**Vance**—*pop pl* TX-5
Vance, Lake—*reservoir* NC-3
Vance Acad—*school* NC-3
Vance Air Force Base—*military* OK-5
Vance Baptist Ch—*church* AL-4
**Vanceboro**—*pop pl* ME-1
**Vanceboro**—*pop pl* NC-3
Vanceboro Landing—*locale* NC-3
**Vanceboro (Town of)**—*pop pl* ME-1
Vance Branch—*stream* (2) AR-4
Vance Branch—*stream* KY-4
Vance Branch—*stream* MO-7
Vance Branch—*stream* VA-3
Vance Branch—*stream* WV-2
**Vanceburg**—*pop pl* KY-4
Vanceburg (CCD)—*cens area* KY-4
Vanceburg Cem—*cemetery* WI-6
Vance Canyon—*valley* CA-9
Vance Canyon—*valley* CO-8
Vance Canyon—*valley* ID-8
Vance (CCD)—*cens area* SC-3
Vance Cem—*cemetery* IL-6
Vance Cem—*cemetery* KS-7
Vance Cem—*cemetery* (3) KY-4
Vance Cem—*cemetery* MS-4
Vance Cem—*cemetery* MO-7
Vance Cem—*cemetery* (2) OH-6
Vance Cem—*cemetery* (5) TN-4
Vance Cem—*cemetery* (7) WV-2
Vance Chapel—*church* MI-6
**Vance County**—*pop pl* NC-3
Vance County Courthouse—*hist pl* NC-3
*Vance Creek* TX-5
Vance Creek—*stream* (3) CO-8
Vance Creek—*stream* (2) ID-8
Vance Creek—*stream* KY-4
Vance Creek—*stream* (2) MT-8
Vance Creek—*stream* OH-6
Vance Creek—*stream* OR-9
Vance Creek—*stream* (2) WA-9
Vance Creek—*stream* WI-6
Vance Creek Bridge—*hist pl* WA-9
Vance Creek Saddle—*gap* ID-8
Vance Creek Safety Rest Area—*locale* OR-9
**Vance Creek (Town of)**—*pop pl* WI-6
Vance Ditch—*canal* KY-4
Vance Draw—*valley* (2) OR-9
Vance Elem Sch—*school* AL-4
Vance Elem Sch—*school* KS-7
Vance Fork—*stream* KY-4
Vance Fork—*stream* VA-3
Vance Fork—*stream* WV-2
Vance Gap—*gap* TN-4
Vance-Granville Institute Pond—*reservoir* NC-3
Vance-Granville Technical Institute Pond Dam—*dam* NC-3
Vance Grove Sch—*school* NC-3
*Vance Gulch* OR-9
Vance Gulch—*valley* CA-9
Vance Gulch—*valley* ID-8
Vance Hill—*summit* MT-8
Vance (historical)—*locale* MS-4
Vance Hollow—*valley* MO-7
Vance Hollow—*valley* VA-3
Vance Hollow—*valley* WV-2
Vance Homestead—*locale* NC-3
Vance House Museum—*building* NC-3
Vance HS—*school* NC-3
*Vance Island* TN-4
Vance Island—*island* KY-4
Vance Junction—*locale* CO-8
*Vance Junior High School* TN-4
Vance Knob—*summit* NC-3
Vance Lake—*lake* AR-4
Vance Lake—*lake* MI-6
Vance Lake—*lake* MN-6
Vance Lake—*lake* WI-6
Vance Lake—*reservoir* GA-3
Vance Lake—*reservoir* IN-6
Vance Lake Dam—*dam* MS-4
Vancel Creek—*stream* AR-4
Vance Lick Hollow—*valley* VA-3
Vancel Mill—*locale* TN-4
Van Cem—*cemetery* OK-5
Van Cem—*cemetery* (2) SC-3
Vance-Maxwell House—*hist pl* SC-3
Vance Memorial Ch—*church* NC-3
*Vance Mill* PA-2
Vance Mill (historical)—*locale* MS-4
**Vance Mill Junction**—*pop pl* PA-2
Vance Mtn—*summit* ID-8
Vance Mtn—*summit* ME-1
Vance Mtn—*summit* MO-7
Vance Mtn—*summit* (2) NC-3
Vance Mtn—*summit* SC-3
Vance Mtn—*summit* TN-4
Vance Neck—*cape* DE-2
Vance Payne Canal—*canal* ID-8
Vance Payne Lake—*reservoir* AL-4
Vance Peak—*summit* CO-8
Vance Place—*locale* CO-8
Vance Point—*summit* ID-8
Vance Pond Dam Number One—*dam* NC-3
Vance Pond Dam Number Two—*dam* NC-3
Vance Pond Number One—*reservoir* NC-3
Vance Pond Number Two—*reservoir* NC-3
Vance Post Office (historical)—*building* TN-4
Vance Ranch—*locale* OR-9
Vance Rsvr—*reservoir* UT-8
Vance Run—*stream* WV-2
*Vances Canyon* UT-8
Vance Sch—*school* AL-4
Vance Sch—*school* GA-3
Vance Sch—*school* IL-6
Vance Sch—*school* IA-7
Vance Sch—*school* ME-1
Vance Sch—*school* MO-7
Vance Sch—*school* (3) NC-3
Vance Sch (abandoned)—*school* PA-2
Vance Sch (historical)—*school* TN-4
Vances Cove—*bay* VA-3
*Vances Crossing* MS-4
Vance-Seaman Cem—*cemetery* MO-7
Vances Lake—*lake* WA-9
**Vances Mill**—*pop pl* PA-2
**Vances Mills**—*pop pl* PA-2
Vance Spring—*spring* UT-8
*Vances Tank Post Office* TN-4
*Vance Station* AL-4
Vance Store (historical)—*locale* MS-4
Vances Twin Lakes—*reservoir* NC-3
Vance (Township of)—*fmr MCD* (2) NC-3
**Vance (Township of)**—*pop pl* IL-6
Vance Tunnel—*tunnel* NC-3
*Vanceville* KS-7
Vanceville—*locale* LA-4
**Vanceville**—*pop pl* GA-3
**Vanceville**—*pop pl* PA-2
Vancey Sch—*school* NC-3
Van Ch—*church* PA-2
Van Chapel—*church* WV-2
Van Choick Ridge—*ridge* CA-9
Vancil Cem—*cemetery* IL-6
Vancill Towhead—*island* IL-6
Vancil Union Ch—*church* IL-6
Van Cleave—*locale* KY-4
**Vancleave**—*pop pl* MS-4
*Van Cleave Bar* AL-4
Vancleave Bar—*bar* AL-4
Vancleave Cottage—*hist pl* MS-4
Van Cleave Flats—*hist pl* IN-6
Vancleave HS—*school* MS-4
Van Cleave Mound—*summit* TX-5
Vancleaves Landing (historical)—*locale* AL-4
*Vancleaves Shoals* AL-4
Van Cleef Lake—*reservoir* NY-2
*Van Cleve* KY-4
Vancleve—*locale* KY-4
**Van Cleve**—*pop pl* IA-7
**Vancleve**—*pop pl* MO-7
**Van Cleve**—*pop pl* MO-7
Van Cleve, Col. John, Homestead—*hist pl* NJ-2
Van Cleve, Horatio P., House—*hist pl* MN-6
**Vancleve (Calla)**—*pop pl* KY-4
Vancleve Cem—*cemetery* MO-7
VanCleve Cem—*cemetery* OH-6
Vancleve Ch—*church* KY-4
Van Cleve County Park—*park* IA-7
Van Cleve Creek—*stream* OR-9
Van Cleve Ditch—*canal* OH-6
Van Cleve Glacier—*glacier* AK-9
Van Cleve Lake—*lake* AK-9
Van Cleve Park—*park* MI-6
Van Cleve Park—*park* MN-6
Van Cleve Ranch—*locale* NM-5
Vancleve Sch—*school* KY-4
Van Cleve Sch—*school* (2) OH-6
**Vanclevesville**—*pop pl* WV-2
**Van Clevesville**—*pop pl* WV-2
**Van Cleve (Van Cleave)**—*pop pl* KY-4
Van Cliff Canyon—*valley* CA-9
Van Collins Number 2 Dam—*dam* SD-7
**Vancoram (Vanadium Corporation)**—*pop pl* OH-6
Van Corlaer JHS—*school* NY-2
Van Cortlandt—*uninc pl* NY-2
Van Cortlandt, Frederick, House—*hist pl* NY-2
Van Cortlandt Lake—*lake* NY-2
*Van Cortlandt Manor* NY-2
Van Cortlandt Manor—*hist pl* NY-2
Van Cortlandt Park—*park* NY-2
Van Cortlandt Sch—*school* NY-2
Van Cortlandt Upper Manor House—*hist pl* NY-2
**Van Cortlandtville**—*pop pl* NY-2
*Van Cortlandville* NY-2
**Vancorum**—*pop pl* CO-8
Van Cott—*uninc pl* NY-2
Van Cott, Mount—*summit* UT-8
Van Coulten Coulee—*valley* MT-8
Vancourt—*locale* TX-5
Van Court Air Force Auxiliary Airfield No 6—*military* TX-5
Van Court Town House—*hist pl* MS-4
**Vancouver**—*pop pl* WA-9
Vancouver, Mount—*summit* AK-9
Vancouver, Point—*cape* WA-9
Vancouver Boys Acad—*school* WA-9
Vancouver (CCD)—*cens area* WA-9
*Vancouver City* WA-9
**Vancouver (historical)**—*pop pl* TN-4
*Vancouver Island* OR-9
*Vancouver Island* WA-9
Vancouver Island—*island* AK-9
**Vancouver Junction**—*pop pl* WA-9
Vancouver Lake—*lake* WA-9
Vancouver Lower Range—*channel* OR-9
Vancouver Lower Range—*channel* WA-9
*Vancouver Point* WA-9
Vancouver-Portland Bridge—*hist pl* OR-9
Vancouver-Portland Bridge—*hist pl* WA-9
Vancouver Post Office (historical)—*building* TN-4
Vancouver Public Library—*hist pl* WA-9
Vancouver Range—*channel* OR-9
Vancouver Range—*channel* WA-9
Vancouvers Shoals—*bar* TN-4
Vancouver Telephone Bldg—*hist pl* WA-9
Van Creek—*stream* GA-3
Van Creek—*stream* (2) ID-8
Van Creek—*stream* MI-6
Van Creek—*stream* WA-9
Van Creek Ch—*church* GA-3
Vancroft—*hist pl* WV-2
Van Curan Gulch—*valley* MT-8
Van Curen Creek—*stream* OR-9
*Van Cycle Canyon* OR-9
*Van Cycle Canyon* WA-9
Van Daele Ranch—*locale* ND-7
Vandagriff Cem—*cemetery* TN-4
Vandahl Airp—*airport* MO-7
Vandale Fork—*stream* WV-2
Vandale Sch—*school* WV-2
*Vandal Fork* WV-2
Vandalia—*locale* MT-8
Vandalia—*locale* TX-5
Vandalia—*locale* WV-2
**Vandalia**—*pop pl* IL-6
**Vandalia**—*pop pl* IN-6
**Vandalia**—*pop pl* IA-7
**Vandalia**—*pop pl* MI-6
**Vandalia**—*pop pl* (2) MO-7
**Vandalia**—*pop pl* NY-2
**Vandalia**—*pop pl* NC-3
**Vandalia**—*pop pl* OH-6
**Vandalia**—*pop pl* (2) WV-2
Vandalia Airpark Airp—*airport* MO-7
Vandalia Cem—*cemetery* IA-7
Vandalia Cem—*cemetery* MO-7
Vandalia Community Lake—*park* MO-7
Vandalia Correctional Center—*other* IL-6
Vandalia Country Club—*other* MO-7
Vandalia Dam—*dam* MT-8
Vandalia Ditch—*canal* IL-6
Vandalia Elem Sch—*school* NC-3
**Vandalia Junction**—*pop pl* IN-6
Vandalia Lake—*reservoir* IL-6
Vandalia Lake—*reservoir* MO-7
Vandalia Mine—*mine* CA-9
Vandalia Rsvr—*reservoir* MO-7
Vandalia South Canal—*canal* MT-8
Vandalia Sportsman Club Lakes—*lake* MO-7
**Vandalia (sta.)**—*pop pl* OH-6
Vandalia Statehouse—*hist pl* IL-6
Vandalia (Township of)—*other* OH-6
**Vandalia (Township of)**—*pop pl* IL-6
Van Dal Lake—*reservoir* NJ-2
Van Damme Beach—*bay* CA-9
Van Damme Beach State Park—*park* CA-9
Vandamore Draw—*valley* CO-8
Van Dam Peak—*summit* CA-9
Van Darvall Sch—*school* VA-3
Vandatta Cem—*cemetery* TN-4
Vandber Hollow—*valley* TN-4
Vandeburgh Cem—*cemetery* IL-6
Vandeburg Lake—*lake* CA-9
Vandecar Drain—*stream* MI-6
Van Deemen Mine—*mine* AZ-5
Van Deene Ave Sch—*school* CA-9
Vandegriff Creek—*stream* GA-3
Vandegrift, J., House—*hist pl* DE-2
Vandegrift Pond—*reservoir* AL-4
Vandegrift Pond Dam—*dam* AL-4
Van Del—*uninc pl* NY-2
*Vandel Brook* MN-6
Van Del HS—*school* OH-6
Vandelinda, Adam, House—*hist pl* NJ-2
Vandelinda, James, House—*hist pl* NJ-2
Vandelinde Cem—*cemetery* WV-2
Van Delinder Cem—*cemetery* NY-2
*Vandell Brook* MN-6
Van Dellen Sch—*school* CO-8
Van Deman, Henry, House—*hist pl* OH-6
Van De Mark, Charles W., House—*hist pl* KS-7
Vandemark Cem—*cemetery* NY-2
**Vandemere**—*pop pl* NC-3
Vandemere Creek—*stream* NC-3
**Vanden**—*pop pl* CA-9
Vandenbark Lake—*reservoir* IN-6
Vandenbark Lake Dam—*dam* IN-6
**Vandenberg**—*pop pl* CA-9
Vandenberg AFB—*military* CA-9
Vandenberge, J. V., House—*hist pl* TX-5
Van Denbergh-Simmons House—*hist pl* NY-2
Vandenberg Sch—*school* (4) MI-6
Vandenberg Village—*CDP* CA-9
**Vandenberg Village**—*pop pl* AZ-5
**Vandenbroek (Town of)**—*pop pl* WI-6
*Vandenburg* NJ-2
**Vandenburg**—*pop pl* TX-5
Vandenburg Cem—*cemetery* MO-7
Vandenburgh Hill—*summit* NY-2
*Van Denburg Hill* NY-2
Vandenburgh Point—*cape* NY-2
Vandenburgh Pond—*lake* NY-2
Vandenburg Park—*park* MI-6
*Vandenburg Pond* NY-2
Vandenburg Ridge—*ridge* CA-9
Vandenburg Sch—*school* MO-7
**Vandenburg Village**—*pop pl* AZ-5
Vandenbush Ditch—*canal* OH-6
Vanden Hoek Sch (historical)—*school* SD-7
Vanden HS—*school* CA-9
V Anderson Ranch—*locale* ND-7
Van De Plasch Airp—*airport* WA-9
Vandeput, Point—*cape* AK-9
**Vander**—*pop pl* NC-3
Vanderbeck, Jacob, Jr., House—*hist pl* NJ-2
Vanderbeck House—*hist pl* NJ-2
Vanderbeck House—*hist pl* NY-2
Vanderbeek House—*hist pl* NJ-2
*Vanderberg Cove* NY-2
Vanderbie Park—*park* MN-6
*Vanderbilt* TN-4
Vanderbilt—*locale* CA-9
**Vanderbilt**—*pop pl* AL-4
**Vanderbilt**—*pop pl* MI-6
**Vanderbilt**—*pop pl* PA-2
**Vanderbilt**—*pop pl* TX-5
Vanderbilt, Mrs. Graham Fair, House—*hist pl* NY-2
Vanderbilt, William K., Estate-Eagles Nest—*hist pl* NY-2
*Vanderbilt Beach* FL-3
Vanderbilt Beach—*locale* FL-3
**Vanderbilt Beach Estates (subdivision)**—*pop pl* FL-3
**Vanderbilt Beach (Vanderbilt)**—*pop pl* FL-3
Vanderbilt Borough—*civil* PA-2
Vanderbilt (CCD)—*cens area* TX-5
Vanderbilt Cem—*cemetery* MI-6
Vanderbilt Cem—*cemetery* NY-2
Vanderbilt Ch—*church* AL-4
Vanderbilt Channel—*channel* FL-3
Vanderbilt Gap—*gap* WA-9
Vanderbilt Gulch—*valley* ID-8
**Vanderbilt Hill**—*pop pl* AK-9
Vanderbilt Hill—*summit* ID-8
Vanderbilt (historical)—*locale* SD-7
Vanderbilt Island—*island* NY-2
Vanderbilt Mansion Natl Historic Site—*park* NY-2
Vanderbilt Mine—*mine* NV-8
Vanderbilt Mine—*mine* UT-8
Vanderbilt Museum—*building* NY-2
Vanderbilt Oil Field—*oilfield* TX-5
Vanderbilt Park—*park* MI-6
**Vanderbilt Park**—*pop pl* FL-3
Vanderbilt Peak—*summit* NM-5
Vanderbilt Post Office (historical)—*building* SD-7
Vanderbilt Presbyterian Ch—*church* FL-3
Vanderbilt Reef—*bar* AK-9
Vanderbilt Sch—*school* NY-2
Vanderbilt Univ—*school* TN-4
*Vanderbilt (Vanderbilt Beach)* FL-3
Vanderbilt Peak—*summit* NV-8
Vanderburg—*locale* KY-4
**Vanderburg**—*pop pl* NJ-2
Vanderburg Ch—*church* NC-3
Vanderburg Creek—*stream* MT-8
**Vanderburgh County**—*pop pl* IN-6
Vanderburg Cove—*bay* NY-2
Vanderburg Mtn—*summit* NY-2
Vanderburg Pond—*lake* NY-2
Vanderbush Lake—*reservoir* NJ-2
*Vandercook* IL-6
Vandercook—*other* MI-6
Vandercook Creek—*stream* MI-6
Vandercook Lake—*lake* MI-6
Vandercook Lake—*lake* WI-6
**Vandercook Lake**—*pop pl* MI-6
Vandercook Park—*park* WA-9
Vandercook Sch—*school* IL-6
*Vandercook Lake* WI-6
Vanderdasson Sch—*school* ID-8
Vander Ende-Onderdonk House Site—*hist pl* NY-2
Van Deren Spring—*spring* AZ-5
Vanderfoot Canyon—*valley* OR-9
Vanderford Branch—*stream* SC-3
Vandergriff Cem—*cemetery* TN-4
Vandergriff Corners—*locale* PA-2
Vandergriff Creek—*stream* AR-4
Vandergriff Hollow—*valley* TN-4
Vandergriff Keys Gas Field—*other* NM-5
**Vandergrift**—*pop pl* PA-2
Vandergrift Borough—*civil* PA-2
Vandergrift Cem—*cemetery* (2) PA-2
Vandergrift Golf Course—*other* PA-2
**Vandergrift Heights**—*pop pl* PA-2
Vandergrift Lake—*lake* CA-9
Vandergrift Park—*park* PA-2
Vandergrift Spring—*spring* TN-4
Vandergrift Tank—*reservoir* NM-5
Vanderheiden Mtn—*summit* OK-5
Vanderhoef Cem—*cemetery* OH-6
**Vanderhoof**—*pop pl* OH-6
Vanderhoof Coulee—*valley* ND-7
Vanderhoof Hill—*summit* MT-8
Vanderhoof Ranch—*locale* CA-9
Vanderhoof Sch—*school* CO-8
Vanderhoof Sch—*school* IL-6
Vanderhoof Sch—*school* VT-1
Vander Horst, Arnoldus, House—*hist pl* SC-3
*Vander Horst Creek* SC-3
Vanderhorst Creek—*stream* SC-3
Vanderipe RR Station—*locale* FL-3
Vanderipe Slough—*gut* FL-3
Vanderkamp Lake—*lake* NY-2
*Vanderkamp Pond* NY-2
Vanderlaan Bay—*bay* SD-7
Vanderlaan Sch—*school* MI-6
Vanderlehr Creek—*stream* SD-7
Vanderlehrs Ranch (historical)—*locale* SD-7
Van Der Linden Field—*park* CA-9
Van Der Linden Pond—*lake* NY-2
Van Derlin Lake—*lake* MI-6
**Vanderlip (RR name West Romney)**—*pop pl* WV-2
Vanderman Branch—*stream* MO-7
Vandermark Corners—*locale* PA-2
Vandermark Creek—*stream* NY-2
Vandermark Creek—*stream* PA-2
Vanderplat Ranch (historical)—*locale* SD-7
Vanderplew Playground—*park* MI-6
Vanderpoel Sch—*school* IL-6
Vanderpool—*locale* TX-5
Vanderpool—*locale* VA-3
Vanderpool Branch—*stream* KY-4
Vanderpool Cem—*cemetery* NY-2
Vanderpool Cem—*cemetery* VA-3
Vanderpool Ch—*church* NC-3
Vanderpool Creek—*stream* NC-3
Vanderpool Crossing—*locale* WA-9
Vanderpool Farm Complex—*hist pl* NY-2
Vanderpool Gap—*gap* VA-3
Vanderpool Mtn—*summit* KY-4
Vanderpool Ridge—*ridge* TN-4
Vanderpool Sch—*school* MO-7
Vanderporten Sch—*school* IL-6
V Anders Dam—*dam* SD-7
Vandersnick Cem—*cemetery* NE-7
Vanderstucken Ranch—*locale* TX-5
Vanderveer—*post sta* NY-2
Vanderveer Dam—*dam* OR-9
Vanderveer Island—*island* TX-5
Vander Veer Park—*park* IA-7
Vander Veer Park Hist Dist—*hist pl* IA-7
Vanderveer Ranch—*locale* SD-7
Van Derveer Rsvr—*reservoir* OR-9
Vanderveer Sch—*school* PA-2
**Vanderveer Sta.**—*pop pl* NY-2
Vanderventer Cem—*cemetery* VA-3
Vandervere Mtn—*summit* CA-9
**Vandervert Ranch**—*pop pl* OR-9
Vanderville—*locale* IL-6
*Van Der Voight Lake* MI-6
Vandervoight Lake—*lake* MI-6
**Vandervoort**—*pop pl* AR-4
Vandervort Cem—*cemetery* PA-2
Vandervort Hill—*summit* NY-2
**Vandervorts Corners**—*pop pl* OH-6
Vanderwagen—*locale* NM-5
Vanderwagen Draw—*valley* NM-5
Vander Wagen Reservior No 1—*reservoir* NM-5
Vander Wagen Rsvr No 2—*reservoir* NM-5
**Vanderwagen (Whitewater)**—*pop pl* NM-5
*Vanderwalker Coulee* ND-7
Vanderwat Swamp—*swamp* MI-6
*Vander Whacken Mtn* NY-2
Vanderwhacker Brook—*stream* NY-2
Vanderwhacker Mtn—*summit* NY-2
Vanderwhacker Pond—*lake* NY-2
**Vandetta**—*pop pl* KY-4
*Van Deusen* MA-1
Van Deusen, H. M., Whip Company—*hist pl* MA-1
Van Deusen Ranch—*locale* CO-8
Vandeusen Sch—*school* NE-7
*Vandeusenville* MA-1
**Van Deusenville**—*pop pl* MA-1
**Van Deusenville**—*pop pl* NY-2
Van Devan, G. B., House—*hist pl* WI-6
*Van Devanter Island* MD-2
Vandeveers (historical)—*locale* DE-2
Van Devender Cem—*cemetery* MS-4
Van Devender Ditch—*canal* IN-6
*Van Devender Island* MD-2
VanDevender JHS—*school* WV-2
Vandevender Lake Dam—*dam* MS-4
*Vandevener Island* MD-2
Vandeventer Bay—*bay* WI-6
Vandeventer Branch—*stream* TN-4
Vandeventer Cem—*cemetery* IN-6
Vandeventer Flat—*flat* CA-9
Van Deventer Island—*island* MD-2
Vandeventer Mtn—*summit* AR-4
Vandeventer Sch—*school* IL-6
Vandever—*locale* TN-4
Vandever Baptist Ch—*church* TN-4
Vandever Mtn—*summit* CA-9
Vandever Post Office (historical)—*building* TN-4
Vandever Sch (historical)—*school* TN-4
Vandevert Ranch—*locale* OR-9
Vandevort Sch—*school* WV-2
Van de Walle Park—*park* TX-5
Van Dien, Harmon, House—*hist pl* NJ-2
Van Dien House—*hist pl* NJ-2
Vandier Cem—*cemetery* OK-5
Van Diest Peak—*summit* NM-5
Vandil Cem—*cemetery* IL-6
Van Dillon Dam—*dam* NC-3
Vandine Cem—*cemetery* WV-2
Van Dine Ch—*church* PA-2
Van Dine Creek—*stream* OR-9
Van Ditch—*canal* WY-8
Vandiver—*locale* GA-3
**Vandiver**—*pop pl* AL-4
**Vandiver**—*pop pl* MO-7
Vandiver Arroyo—*stream* CO-8
Vandiver Branch—*stream* GA-3
Vandiver Brothers Lake—*reservoir* AL-4
Vandiver Brothers Lake Dam—*dam* AL-4

Vandiver Causeway—*other* GA-3
Vandiver Cem—*cemetery* (2) AL-4
*Vandiver Church* AL-4
Vandiver Ditch—*canal* WY-8
Vandiver Elem Sch (historical)—*school* AL-4
**Vandiver Heights**—*pop pl* GA-3
Vandiver Hollow—*valley* AL-4
Vandiver Hollow Ch—*church* AL-4
Vandiver House—*hist pl* GA-3
Vandiver Low Gap—*gap* AL-4
Vandiver Negro Cem—*cemetery* AL-4
Vandiver Sch—*school* TX-5
Vandivers Lake—*reservoir* GA-3
Vandiver-Trout-Clause House—*hist pl* WV-2
Vandivier Ditch—*canal* IN-6
**Vandling**—*pop pl* PA-2
Vandling Borough—*civil* PA-2
Van Doele Ranch—*locale* ND-7
Vandola—*locale* VA-3
Vandola Ch—*church* VA-3
Vandolah—*locale* FL-3
Van Donne Canal—*canal* LA-4
Van Dorans Mill Dam—*dam* NJ-2
Van Dorans Mill Pond—*reservoir* NJ-2
Van Dorans Mills—*locale* NJ-2
*Vandora Springs Elementary School* NC-3
Vandore Bay—*swamp* SC-3
VanDoren, Jacob, House—*hist pl* WV-2
*Van Dorn* AL-4
Van Dorn Canyon—*valley* ID-8
Van Dorn Corner—*locale* NY-2
Vandorn Ditch—*canal* IN-6
Van Dorn House—*hist pl* MS-4
Van Dorn Park—*park* NE-7
Van Dorrien Mtn—*summit* NY-2
Van Dorsen Creek—*stream* MO-7
Vandover Sch—*school* MO-7
Van Drain—*canal* (2) MI-6
Vandra Ranch—*locale* WY-8
Vandriver Cave—*cave* AL-4
Vandruff Cem—*cemetery* IL-6
Vandruff Creek—*stream* OK-5
Vandruff Island—*island* IL-6
Vand Sch—*school* MI-6
Van Duesan Ranch—*locale* ID-8
Van Duesen Ridge—*ridge* UT-8
Vanduse Lake—*lake* MN-6
Van Dusen Canyon—*valley* CA-9
Van Dusen Cem—*cemetery* NY-2
Van Dusen Ranch—*locale* NE-7
Van Dusen Spring—*spring* MT-8
*Vanduser* AR-4
**Vanduser**—*pop pl* MO-7
Van Duyne, James, Farm House—*hist pl* NJ-2
Van Duyn Hosp—*hospital* NY-2
Van Duyn Sch—*school* IN-6
Van Duyn Sch—*school* NY-2
**Van Duzen**—*pop pl* CA-9
Van Duzen County Park—*park* CA-9
*Van Duzen Fork of Eel River* CA-9
Van Duzen River—*stream* CA-9
Van Duzen Sch—*school* CA-9
*Van Duzer* AR-4
Vanduzer—*locale* AR-4
Van Duzer, Samuel D., House—*hist pl* MI-6
Van Duzer Cem—*cemetery* NY-2
Van Duzer Creek—*stream* NV-8
Van Duzer Forest Corridor State Wayside—*park* OR-9
Van Duzer Lateral—*canal* ID-8
Vandy Cem—*cemetery* AR-4
Van Dyck Mtn—*summit* NH-1
*Vandy Creek* OR-9
*Vandy Creek Church* MS-4
*Van Dyke* DE-2
*Van Dyke* MI-6
*Van Dyke* PA-2
Vandyke—*locale* DE-2
Van Dyke—*locale* TN-4
Vandyke—*locale* TX-5
Vandyke—*locale* VA-3
**Vandyke**—*pop pl* PA-2
Vandyke, Jeremiah, House—*hist pl* NJ-2
Van Dyke, Peter, House—*hist pl* MI-6
**Van Dyke and Willey Condominium**—*pop pl* UT-8
Van Dyke Branch—*stream* VA-3
Vandyke Creek—*stream* GA-3
Van Dyke Grove Cem—*cemetery* TN-4
Van Dyke Grove Ch (historical)—*church* TN-4
Van Dyke Gulch—*valley* MT-8
*Van Dyke Hill* VT-1
Van Dyke House—*hist pl* KY-4
Van Dyke Lake—*lake* FL-3
Van Dyke Lake—*lake* NC-3
VanDyke-Libby House—*hist pl* MN-6
Van Dyke Mtn—*summit* ME-1
Van Dyke Mtn—*summit* VT-1
Van Dyke Park—*park* IN-6
Van Dyke Ranch—*locale* CA-9
Vandyke Run—*stream* IN-6
**Van Dykes**—*pop pl* PA-2
Van Dyke Sch (historical)—*school* PA-2
Van Dyke Sch (historical)—*school* TN-4
Van Dyke Shaft—*mine* AZ-5
Van Dyke Spring—*spring* AZ-5
VanDyke Spring—*spring* PA-2
*Vandyke Station* PA-2
Van Dyke Village—*uninc pl* DE-2
Van Dyk Park—*park* MN-6
**Vandyne**—*pop pl* WI-6
Van Dyne Cem—*cemetery* NY-2
Van Dyne Civic Bldg—*hist pl* PA-2
Van Dyne Creek—*stream* WI-6
Van Dyne (RR name for Vandyne)—*other* WI-6
Vandys Pond—*lake* MA-1
Vandyver Slough—*gut* AL-4
*Vandzant Cemetery* MO-7
Van Earl Tank—*reservoir* TX-5
Van East Mtn—*summit* MO-7
Van Eaton Creek—*stream* NV-8
Van Eaton Draw—*valley* NM-5
Van Eaton Ranch—*locale* (2) NM-5
Van Eaton Spring—*spring* ID-8
Van Eck State Wildlife Mngmt Area—*park* MN-6
**Van Eden**—*pop pl* NC-3
Van Emman—*locale* PA-2
Van Emmans Ponds—*lake* PA-2
Van Epps, William H., House—*hist pl* IL-6
Van Epps Creek—*stream* WA-9
Van Epps Mine—*mine* WA-9
Van Epps Pass—*gap* WA-9
Van Eps Cem—*cemetery* NY-2
Van Eps Park—*park* SD-7
Vane Ranch Dam—*dam* OR-9
Vane Ranch Rsvr—*reservoir* OR-9
*Vane Rsvr* OR-9
Vanervorsite Bay Rec Area—*park* SD-7
**Vanetia**—*pop pl* TX-5
Vanetta—*locale* WV-2
*Van Ettan Creek* MI-6
*Van Ettan Lake* MI-6
*Vanetten* NY-2
**Van Etten**—*pop pl* NY-2
Van Etten Cem—*cemetery* NY-2
Van Etten Creek—*stream* (3) MI-6
Vanetten House—*hist pl* AR-4
**Van Etten Junction**—*pop pl* NY-2
Van Etten Lake—*lake* MI-6
**Van Etten Lake**—*pop pl* MI-6
**Van Etten (Town of)**—*pop pl* NY-2
*Van Ettenville* NY-2
Vanettes Rsvr—*reservoir* MT-8
Van Every Cove—*bay* NJ-2
Vaney Bayou—*gut* MS-4
Van-Far HS—*school* MO-7
Van Felt Ditch—*canal* IN-6
*Van Fleet* NY-2
**Van Fleet**—*pop pl* NY-2
Van Fleet Creek—*stream* UT-8
Van Fleet Ditch—*canal* OH-6
Van Fleet Draw—*valley* WY-8
Van Fleet Hollow—*valley* UT-8
Van Frank Cottages—*hist pl* AR-4
**Vang**—*pop pl* ND-7
**Vangale**—*pop pl* AL-4
Vang Cem—*cemetery* MN-6
Vang Ch—*church* (3) ND-7
Vang Ch—*church* WI-6
Van Gelder, Abraham, House—*hist pl* NJ-2
Van Gelder, David, House—*hist pl* NJ-2
Van Gelder House—*hist pl* NJ-2
Van Gelder Sch—*school* NJ-2
Van Gelders Pond—*lake* NJ-2
Vangen Ch—*church* SD-7
Vangen Church—*hist pl* SD-7
Vang Hill—*summit* ND-7
Van Giesen Dam—*dam* CA-9
Van Gilder Cem—*cemetery* IL-6
Vangilder Cem—*cemetery* MO-7
Van Gilder Hotel—*hist pl* AK-9
Van Gilder Ranch—*locale* MT-8
Vangilder Sch—*school* MI-6
Van Gilder Spring—*spring* WY-8
**Vang Junction**—*pop pl* PA-2
Vang Junction Station—*locale* PA-2
Van Gordan Ranch—*locale* WY-8
**Vangordon**—*pop pl* AL-4
Van Gordon Creek—*stream* (2) CA-9
Vangsness State Wildlife Mngmt Area—*park* MN-6
**Vang Township**—*pop pl* ND-7
Vang Tunnel—*tunnel* PA-2
**Vanguard**—*pop pl* CA-9
Vanguard HS—*school* FL-3
Vanguard JHS—*school* CA-9
Vanguard Mine No 1—*mine* WY-8
Vanguard Sch—*school* FL-3
Vanguard Sch of Coconut Grove—*school* FL-3
Vanguard Voc And Technical Center—*locale* OH-6
Van Gulch—*valley* ID-8
Van Gulch—*valley* OR-9
Van Gulch Spring—*spring* OR-9
Vanham Creek—*stream* TX-5
Van Hatcher Lake Dam—*dam* MS-4
Van Hatten Creek—*stream* AK-9
Van Hetton Creek—*stream* MI-6
Van Hill—*locale* TN-4
*Van Hill Post Office* TN-4
Vanhill Post Office (historical)—*building* TN-4
Van Hill Sch (historical)—*school* TN-4
Van Hise Rock—*pillar* WI-6
Van Hise Sch—*school* WI-6
**Van Hiseville**—*pop pl* NJ-2
Vanhock Cem—*cemetery* KY-4
Van Hoesen, Jan, House—*hist pl* NY-2
Van Hoesen Station—*locale* NY-2
Van Hoevenberg, Henry, Jr., House—*hist pl* OR-9
Van Hoevenberg, Mount—*summit* NY-2
Van Hoevenberg Trail—*trail* NY-2
Van Hollow—*valley* AR-4
Van Hollow—*valley* OK-5
Van Holten Company (Plant)—*facility* WI-6
Vanhook—*locale* KY-4
Van Hook, Jay, Potato Cellar—*hist pl* ID-8
Van Hook Arm—*bay* ND-7
Vanhook Branch—*stream* (2) KY-4
Van Hook Branch—*stream* VA-3
*Vanhook Camp Ground* NC-3
Van Hook Cem—*cemetery* KY-4
Van Hook Cem—*cemetery* TN-4
Vanhook Cem—*cemetery* (2) TN-4
Vanhook Hollow—*valley* TN-4
Van Hook Ridge—*ridge* MT-8
Vanhook Spring—*spring* TN-4
Van Hook State Game Mngmt Area—*park* ND-7
**Van Hook Township**—*pop pl* ND-7
Vanhook Wayside Park—*park* NC-3
Vanhooser Cem—*cemetery* KY-4
*Van Hoose Shaft Mine* AL-4
Van Hoosier Creek—*stream* ID-8
Vanhoosier Hollow—*valley* TN-4
*Vanhorn* IA-7
Van Horn—*locale* OR-9
Van Horn—*locale* WA-9
**Van Horn**—*pop pl* TX-5
Van Horn, David & Cornelius, House—*hist pl* NJ-2
Van Horn-Ackerman House—*hist pl* NJ-2
Van Horn Bay—*swamp* FL-3
Van Horn Bldg—*hist pl* OH-6
Van Horn Branch—*stream* KS-7
Van Horn (CCD)—*cens area* TX-5
Van Horn Cem—*cemetery* IA-7
Van Horn Cem—*cemetery* (2) OH-6
Vanhorn Cem—*cemetery* WV-2
Van Horn Ch—*church* MO-7
*Van Horn Creek* PA-2
Van Horn Creek—*stream* (3) CA-9
Van Horn Creek—*stream* ID-8
Van Horn Creek—*stream* KS-7
Van Horn Creek—*stream* OH-6
Van Horn Creek—*stream* OR-9
Vanhorn Creek—*stream* TN-4
Van Horn Creek—*stream* TX-5
Van Horn Creek—*stream* WA-9
Vanhorn Drain—*canal* MI-6
Van Horn Drain—*canal* MI-6
*Van Horne* WA-9
**Van Horne**—*pop pl* IA-7
Van Horne Cem—*cemetery* MO-7
Van Horne Creek—*stream* PA-2
*Van Horner Creek* KS-7
*Van Horner Creek* OK-5
*Van Hornes* WA-9
Van Horne Sch—*school* AZ-5
**Van Hornesville**—*pop pl* NY-2
Van Horne Woods Forest Preserve—*park* IL-6
Van Horn Falls—*falls* WA-9
Van Horn Flats—*flat* CA-9
Van Horn Glen—*valley* PA-2
Van Horn Gulch—*valley* CA-9
Van Horn Gulch—*valley* ID-8
Van Horn Hotel—*hist pl* ND-7
Van Horn HS—*school* MO-7
Van Horn Landing—*locale* FL-3
Van Horn Lateral—*canal* SD-7
Van Horn Mountains—*range* TX-5
Van Horn-Newcomb House—*hist pl* NJ-2
Van Horn Park—*flat* CO-8
Van Horn Park—*park* MA-1
Van Horn Park Lower Dam—*dam* MA-1
Van Horn Park Lower Pond—*reservoir* MA-1
Van Horn Park Upper Dam—*dam* MA-1
Van Horn Park Upper Pond—*reservoir* MA-1
Van Horn Peak—*summit* CA-9
Van Horn Peak—*summit* ID-8
Van Horn Ridge—*ridge* AK-9
Van Horn Ridge—*ridge* CA-9
Van Horn Rsvr—*reservoir* MA-1
Van Horn Rural (CCD)—*cens area* TX-5
Van Horn Sch—*school* PA-2
Van Horn Slough—*gut* FL-3
*Van Horns Run* PA-2
*Van Horns Spur* WA-9
*Vanhorns Tavern* PA-2
**Van Horn Township**—*pop pl* MO-7
Van Horn Wells (Historical Monument)—*well* TX-5
*Van Houghten Draw* WY-8
Vanhoughton Cem—*cemetery* MS-4
*Van Houken Draw* WY-8
Van Hountin Drain—*stream* MI-6
Vanhouse Cem—*cemetery* KY-4
Van House Corners—*locale* NY-2
Van Houten—*locale* NM-5
Van Houten-Ackerman House—*hist pl* NJ-2
Van Houten Camp—*locale* NM-5
Van Houten Canyon—*valley* NM-5
Van Houten Cem—*cemetery* NJ-2
Van Houten Draw—*valley* WY-8
Van Houten-Hillman House—*hist pl* NJ-2
Van Houten House—*hist pl* NJ-2
Van Houten Lake—*lake* MT-8
Van Houten Mtn—*summit* GA-3
Van Hoy Cem—*cemetery* TN-4
Van Huss Cem—*cemetery* TN-4
Vanhuss Grove Ch—*church* VA-3
Van Hyning Creek—*stream* OH-6
Van Hyning Run—*stream* OH-6
Van Iderstine, Charles, Mansion—*hist pl* NY-2
Vanier Well—*well* NM-5
**Vanilla**—*pop pl* PA-2
Vanilla Bay—*swamp* SC-3
Vanilla Sch (historical)—*school* AL-4
Vanio Lake—*lake* MI-6
Vanishing Falls—*falls* OR-9
Vanity Ballroom Bldg—*hist pl* MI-6
*Vanity Corner* AR-4
**Vanity Corner**—*pop pl* AR-4
Vanity Creek—*stream* ID-8
Vanity Fair Lake—*reservoir* AL-4
Vanity Fair Lake Dam—*dam* AL-4
*Vanity Lake* ID-8
Vanity Lakes—*lake* ID-8
Vanity Summit—*summit* ID-8
**Van Junction**—*pop pl* WV-2
Vankara Sch—*school* FL-3
Van Keuren Cem—*cemetery* MI-6
Van Keuren Cem—*cemetery* NY-2
Van Keuren Lake—*lake* NY-2
Van Keurens—*locale* (2) NY-2
*Van Kirk* PA-2
Vankirk—*locale* PA-2
**Vankirk**—*pop pl* PA-2
Van Kirk Cem—*cemetery* OH-6
Van Kirk Ch—*church* PA-2
Van Kirk Farm—*hist pl* PA-2
Vank Island—*island* AK-9
**Vank Island**—*pop pl* AK-9
Van Kleeck Cem—*cemetery* NY-2
Van Kleef Drain—*stream* MI-6
Van Koert-Winters House—*hist pl* NJ-2
Van Korlaar Sch—*school* MI-6
Van Kuren Hill—*summit* WA-9
Van Lake—*lake* MI-6
Van Lake—*lake* MN-6
Van Lake—*lake* MT-8
Van Lake—*lake* TX-5
Van Lake—*lake* WA-9
Van Lake—*reservoir* MO-7
VanLandingham Estate—*hist pl* NC-3
Vanlandingham Mill—*locale* AL-4
Van Land Landing—*locale* MS-4
Van-Laningham Wildlife Area—*park* IA-7
**Van Lear**—*pop pl* (2) KY-4
**Vanlear**—*pop pl* VA-3
*Van Lear Junction* KY-4
Van Lear Junction (RR name for West Van Lear)—*other* KY-4
**Van Lear Manor**—*pop pl* MD-2
**Vanleer**—*pop pl* TN-4
Vanleer (CCD)—*cens area* TN-4
Vanleer Cem—*cemetery* TN-4
Vanleer Division—*civil* TN-4
Van Leer Furnace (historical)—*locale* TN-4
Van Leer Mine—*mine* TN-4
Van Leuvans Sch—*school* NY-2
Vanlieu Corners—*locale* NJ-2
Van Liew Cem—*cemetery* NJ-2
Van Lindley Sch—*school* NC-3
Van Lint Mine—*mine* NM-5
Van Loan Creek—*stream* CA-9
Van Loan Hill—*summit* NY-2
Van Loan Rsvr—*reservoir* CA-9
Van Lone Draw—*valley* SD-7
VanLone Hill—*summit* NY-2
**Van Loon**—*pop pl* IN-6
Van Loon, Albertus, House—*hist pl* NY-2
Van Loon, Dirk, House—*hist pl* IA-7
Van Loon Cem—*cemetery* MN-6
Van Loon Cem—*cemetery* TN-4
Van Loon Lake—*lake* NE-7
Van Loon Lake—*lake* WI-6
Van Loon State Public Hunting Grounds—*park* WI-6
**Vanlue**—*pop pl* OH-6
Van Luik State Wildlife Mngmt Area—*park* MN-6
Van Luven Lake—*lake* NY-2
Van Marter Bldg—*hist pl* AZ-5
**Van Marters Corner**—*pop pl* NJ-2
Van Mater Shaft—*mine* VA-3
Van Matre Creek—*stream* CA-9
Van Matre Meadows—*flat* CA-9
**Van Meer**—*pop pl* MI-6
**Van Meter**—*pop pl* IA-7
**Van Meter**—*pop pl* OH-6
**Van Meter**—*pop pl* PA-2
Van Meter, Jacob, House—*hist pl* KY-4
Van Meter Bridge (historical)—*other* MO-7
Van Meter Cem—*cemetery* IA-7
Vanmeter Church Street House—*hist pl* OH-6
Van Meter Distillery—*hist pl* KY-4
Van Meter Ditch—*canal* IN-6
Van Meter Ditch—*canal* MO-7
Van Meter Flat—*flat* OR-9
Van Meter Gulch—*valley* MT-8
Van Meter Hall—*hist pl* KY-4
Van Meter Hill—*summit* ID-8
**Vanmeter Park**—*pop pl* IN-6
Van Meter Ranch—*locale* NM-5
Van Meter Run—*stream* OH-6
Van Meter Sch—*school* (2) MO-7
Van Meter Sch—*school* WI-6
Van Meter Site—*hist pl* KY-4
Van Meter State Park—*park* MO-7
Van Meter State Park Combination Bldg—*hist pl* MO-7
Van Meter State Park Shelter Bldg—*hist pl* MO-7
Vanmeter Stone House and Outbuildings—*hist pl* OH-6
Van Meter Tank—*reservoir* TX-5
*Van Meter Township* SD-7
Van Meter Township—*fmr MCD* IA-7
**Van Meter Township**—*pop pl* ND-7
**Van Metre**—*pop pl* SD-7
Van Metre Ford Stone Bridge—*hist pl* WV-2
Van Metre Township—*civil* SD-7
Van Milligan Creek—*stream* AK-9
Van Mine Station—*locale* PA-2
Van Mtn—*summit* CO-8
Vann—*locale* CA-9
Vann, Lake—*reservoir* AL-4
**Vanna**—*pop pl* (2) GA-3
Vann Acad—*school* (2) FL-3
Vanna Chapel—*church* GA-3
*Vannatta* NJ-2
Vannatta—*locale* TN-4
Van Natta Ditch—*canal* IN-6
Vannatta Post Office (historical)—*building* TN-4
Van Nattas Dam—*dam* NY-2
Van Natter Lake—*lake* MI-6
Vannatti Ditch—*canal* IN-6
Vann Branch—*stream* TX-5
Vann Cabin—*locale* CA-9
Vann Camp—*locale* TX-5
Vann Cave—*cave* AL-4
Vann Cem—*cemetery* AL-4
Vann Cem—*cemetery* NC-3
Vann Cem—*cemetery* (2) OK-5
Vann Cliff—*cliff* NC-3
Vann Coulee—*valley* MT-8
Vann Creek—*stream* CA-9
**Vann Crossroads**—*pop pl* NC-3
**Vanndale**—*pop pl* AR-4
Vanndy Hollow—*valley* TN-4
Vannerson Cem—*cemetery* OK-5
**Van Ness**—*pop pl* CA-9
Van Ness Ave Sch—*school* CA-9
Vanness Cem—*cemetery* TX-5
Van Ness Creek—*stream* (2) CA-9
Van Ness Creek—*stream* MT-8
Vanness Crossing—*locale* AR-4
Vanness Ditch—*canal* IN-6
Van Ness Hill Cem—*cemetery* PA-2
Van Ness House—*hist pl* NJ-2
Van Ness Mausoleum—*hist pl* DC-2
Van Ness Mine—*mine* NV-8
Van Ness Playground—*park* CA-9
Van Ness Point—*summit* MT-8
Van Ness Sch—*school* DC-2
Van Ness Sch—*school* MI-6
Van Ness Slough—*stream* CA-9
Van Ness Tot Lot Park—*park* UT-8
*Van Ness Town* IN-6
Van Ness/VDC Metro Station—*locale* DC-2
**Van Nest**—*pop pl* NY-2
Van Nest Burying Ground—*cemetery* NJ-2
Van Neste Sch—*school* IL-6
Van Nest Ref Fish and Wildlife Mngmt Area—*park* NJ-2
Van Nest Sch—*school* MI-6
Van Nest Yard—*locale* NY-2
Vann House—*building* GA-3
Vann House—*hist pl* GA-3
Vannice Sch—*school* NE-7
**Vann (La Barge)**—*pop pl* OK-5
Vann Mill Creek—*stream* AL-4
Vannoort Lake—*reservoir* TN-4
Vannoort Lake Dam—*dam* TN-4
Van Norden, Lake—*reservoir* CA-9
**Van Norman**—*pop pl* MT-8
*Van Norman Lake* CA-9
Van Norman Lake—*lake* MI-6
*Van Norman Lakes* CA-9
Van Norman Sch—*school* MT-8
Van Norman Springs—*spring* NV-8
Van Nortwick Valley—*basin* NE-7
Van Nostrand Lake—*lake* NJ-2
Van Note Sch (abandoned)—*school* MO-7
Van (not verified)—*island* MP-9
Vannoy—*locale* NC-3
Van Noy, Ira C. and Charles S., Houses—*hist pl* MO-7
**Vannoy Acres**—*pop pl* VA-3
Van Noy Branch—*stream* NC-3
Van Noy Canyon—*valley* ID-8
Vannoy Cem—*cemetery* NC-3
Vannoy Cem—*cemetery* TN-4
Vannoy Cem—*cemetery* TX-5
Vannoy Creek—*stream* OR-9
Van Noy Ditch—*canal* CA-9
Vannoy Hollow—*valley* TN-4
Vannoy Hollow—*valley* VA-3
**Vannoy Park**—*pop pl* VA-3
Vannoy Sch—*school* CA-9
Vannoy Sch (abandoned)—*school* MO-7
Vannoys Mill—*locale* WV-2
Van Noy Valley—*valley* CO-8
Vann Park—*park* IN-6
Vann Ranch—*locale* TX-5
**Vanns**—*pop pl* AL-4
Vanns Branch—*stream* AL-4
Vanns Branch—*stream* GA-3
Vann Sch—*school* NC-3
Vann Sch—*school* OK-5
Vann Sch—*school* TN-4
Vann Sch (historical)—*school* AL-4
Vanns Creek—*stream* GA-3
Vanns Island—*island* FL-3
Vanns Slough—*gut* FL-3
Vanns Tavern Access Point—*locale* GA-3
**Vann (subdivision)**—*pop pl* AL-4
**Vanntown**—*pop pl* TN-4
**Van Nuys**—*pop pl* CA-9
**Van Nuys**—*pop pl* IN-6
Van Nuys Branch—*hist pl* CA-9
Van Nuys Farm—*hist pl* IN-6
Van Nuys Golf Course—*other* CA-9
Van Nuys HS—*school* CA-9
Van Nuys JHS—*school* CA-9
Van Nuys Rec Area—*park* CA-9
Van Nuys Sch—*school* CA-9
Van Nuys-Sherman Oaks War Memorial Park—*park* CA-9
Vann Valley—*valley* AL-4
Vann Valley Ch—*church* AL-4
Vanny Branch—*stream* NC-3
*Vannyning Creek* OH-6
Van Oak Hollow—*valley* PA-2
Vanocker Creek—*stream* SD-7
Vano Ditch—*canal* CO-8
Van Offern Butte—*summit* SD-7
Van Oil Field—*oilfield* TX-5
Van Oosting Ranch—*locale* ND-7
Vanora—*locale* KS-7
Vanora (site)—*locale* OR-9
**Van Orden Heights Subdivision**—*pop pl* UT-8
VanOrder Pond—*reservoir* WI-6
Van Order Township—*civil* SD-7
**Van Orin**—*pop pl* IL-6
*Vanori Wash* AZ-5
**Van Ormer**—*pop pl* PA-2
Vanormer Pumping Station—*other* CA-9
Van Ornam & Murdock Block—*hist pl* NY-2
Van Ornum Creek—*stream* WA-9
Van Ornum Ranch—*locale* MT-8
Van Ornum's Addition Hist Dist—*hist pl* MI-6
Vanorsdale Cem—*cemetery* LA-4
Van Orsdall Cem—*cemetery* IA-7
Van Ortwick Hill—*summit* WY-8
Van Osdel House—*hist pl* SD-7
Vanose Lake—*lake* MN-6
Vanose State Wildlife Mngmt Area—*park* MN-6
**Vanoss**—*pop pl* OK-5
*Vanoss Lake* MN-6
Vanosting Dam—*dam* ND-7
Van Ostrand Corners—*locale* NY-2
Vanover Branch—*stream* KY-4
Van Over Branch—*stream* MO-7
Vanover Cem—*cemetery* KY-4
Van Over Cem—*cemetery* TN-4
Vanover Cem—*cemetery* (2) VA-3
Vanover Hollow—*valley* KY-4
Van Over Hollow—*valley* TN-4
Vanover Spring—*spring* NV-8
Vanowen—*uninc pl* CA-9
*Van-Pak Landing Strip* KS-7
Van Pak Landing Strip—*airport* KS-7
Van Patten Barn Complex—*hist pl* NY-2
Van Patten Butte—*summit* OR-9
Van Patten Ditch—*canal* CO-8
Van Patten House—*hist pl* IA-7
Van Patten Lake—*lake* OR-9
Van Patten Lake Dam—*dam* OR-9
Van Patten Ridge—*ridge* OR-9
Van Patter Lake—*lake* MN-6
Van Patton Shoals—*rapids* SC-3
Van Patton Slough—*swamp* ND-7
Van Peak—*summit* MT-8
Van Peak—*summit* WA-9
*Van Pelham* MI-6
**Van Pelt**—*pop pl* TX-5
Vanpelt Cem—*cemetery* IN-6
Van Pelt Cem—*cemetery* TN-4
Van Pelt Ditch—*canal* IN-6
Van Pelt Hollow—*valley* TX-5
Van Pelt House—*hist pl* TX-5
Van Pelt Manor House—*building* NY-2
Van Pelt Ranch—*locale* TX-5
Van Pelt Rsvr—*reservoir* CO-8
Van Petten—*locale* IL-6
Van Platen-Fox Lumber Camp Historic Complex—*hist pl* MI-6
Van Point—*summit* ID-8
Van Poland Sch—*school* ME-1
Van Pool Branch—*stream* MO-7
Van Pool Cem—*cemetery* MO-7
Van Pool School (historical)—*locale* MO-7
*Vanport* OR-9
**Vanport**—*pop pl* PA-2
Vanport City (site)—*locale* OR-9
**Vanport (Township of)**—*pop pl* PA-2
Van Pugh Park—*park* GA-3
Vanquard Sch—*school* PA-2
Van Raalte Sch—*school* MI-6
Van Raden Dam—*dam* OR-9
Van Raden Rsvr—*reservoir* OR-9
Van Rankin Landing Strip—*airport* KS-7
Van Raub—*locale* TX-5
Van Reed Cem—*cemetery* IN-6
Van Reeds Mill—*locale* PA-2
*Van Rensalaer* OH-6
Van Rensselaer, Jacob Rutsen, House and Mill Complex—*hist pl* NY-2
Van Rensselaer Creek—*stream* NY-2
Van Rensselaer Elem Sch—*school* IN-6
Van Rensselaer House—*building* PA-2
Van Rensselar, Stephen, House—*hist pl* NY-2
Van Reyper-Bond House—*hist pl* NJ-2
*Van Ridge* ID-8
Van Ridge—*ridge* CA-9
Van Ridge—*ridge* ID-8
Van Riper Coulee—*valley* WI-6
Van Riper-Hopper House—*hist pl* NJ-2
Van Riper Lakes—*lake* MI-6
Van Riper Park—*park* MI-6
Van Riper Place—*locale* NV-8
Van Riper Spring—*spring* CA-9
Van Ripper Trail—*trail* PA-2
*Van Ross Creek* SC-3
**Van Ross Estates**—*pop pl* UT-8
Van Run—*stream* IN-6
Vansandt Cem—*cemetery* MO-7
**Vansant**—*pop pl* VA-3
Van Sant, Samuel, House—*hist pl* IA-7
*Van Sant Airp* PA-2
Vansant Airp—*airport* PA-2
Van Sant Cove—*bay* AK-9
Van Sant Covered Bridge—*hist pl* PA-2
Vansant Farmhouse—*hist pl* PA-2
*Van Saun Creek* NJ-2
Van Saun Mill Brook—*stream* NJ-2
*Vansaun Mill Creek* NJ-2
Van Saun Park—*park* NJ-2
*Van Sawn Creek* NJ-2
Vansburg Cem—*cemetery* KS-7
*Vansburgh* KS-7
Vans Camp—*locale* MI-6
Vans Canyon—*valley* UT-8
Van Schaick House—*hist pl* NY-2
Van Schaick Island—*island* NY-2
*Van Schoaick Ridge* CA-9
Vanschoiack Cem—*cemetery* MO-7
Van Sciver Lake—*reservoir* PA-2
Van Sciver Lake Dam—*dam* PA-2
Van Sciver Sch—*school* NJ-2
Vans Corner (Priest Lake PO)—*locale* ID-8
**Van Scoy**—*pop pl* PR-3
Van Scoyk Ranch—*locale* NM-5
Vanscoyoc Run—*stream* PA-2
Vans Creek—*stream* TN-4
Vans Harbor—*bay* MI-6
Vans Heliport—*airport* MO-7
Van Shoick Sch—*school* MI-6
Vansickland Drain—*canal* MI-6
Van Sickle Brook—*stream* MN-6
Vansickle Cem—*cemetery* OH-6
Van Sickle Cem—*cemetery* PA-2
Van Sickle Cem—*cemetery* TX-5
Van Sickle Cem—*cemetery* WV-2
Van Sickle Community Center—*locale* TX-5
Van Sickle Hollow—*valley* PA-2
Van Sickle Island—*island* CA-9
Van Sickle Lake—*lake* CA-9
Van Sicklen Grove—*woods* CA-9
*Van Sickles* NJ-2
*Van Sickles Island* CA-9
Van Sicklin Butte—*summit* CA-9
**Van Siding**—*pop pl* IL-6
Van Skinner Island (historical)—*island* OR-9
Vans Lake—*lake* OK-5
Vans Lake Ch—*church* OK-5
Van Slyck Cem—*cemetery* NY-2
*Van Slyck Island* NY-2
Van Slyke Cem—*cemetery* KS-7
Van Slyke Sch—*school* MI-6
Vanson Lake—*lake* WA-9
Vanson Moadow—*flat* WA 9
Vanson Peak—*summit* WA-9
Van Spring—*spring* CA-9
Van Spring Gulch—*valley* CA-9
Van Springs Rsvr—*reservoir* CO-8
Vanstel Cem—*cemetery* MT-8
Vanstel (Site)—*locale* MT-8
Van Stone Mine—*mine* WA-9
Vanstory Hills Elem Sch—*school* NC-3
**Van Story Hills (subdivision)**—*pop pl* NC-3
**Vanstory Hills (subdivision)**—*pop pl* NC-3
Vans Valley—*locale* GA-3
Vans Valley—*valley* GA-3
Vans Valley Cem—*cemetery* OH-6
Vans Valley Ch—*church* OH-6
**Vansville**—*pop pl* MD-2
Van Swamp—*swamp* NC-3
Van Swamp Bridge—*bridge* NC-3
Van Swearingen Creek—*gut* FL-3
Van Swearingens Fault—*cave* AL-4
Van Swearingen-Shepherd House—*hist pl* WV-2
*Van Sycde Canyon* OR-9
*Van Sycde Canyon* WA-9
Van Syckel—*locale* NJ-2
Van Syckel Corner District—*hist pl* NJ-2
*Van Syckles* NJ-2
Van Syckles—*locale* NJ-2
Vansycle—*locale* OR-9
Vansycle Canyon—*valley* OR-9
Vansycle Canyon—*valley* WA-9
Van Syke Cem—*cemetery* TX-5
Vantage—*locale* WA-9
Vantage Airp—*airport* WA-9
**Vantage Park Subdivision**—*pop pl* UT-8
Vantage Peak—*summit* AK-9
Vantage Rock—*island* AK-9
Vantage Substation—*other* WA-9
**Vantage View (subdivision)**—*pop pl* TN-4
Van Tassel, Ernest Shelton, House—*hist pl* HI-9
Van Tassel Canyon—*valley* CA-9
Van Tassel Creek—*stream* UT-8
Van Tassel Creek—*stream* WY-8

Van Tassel Gulch—*valley* CO-8
**Van Tassell**—*pop pl* WY-8
Van Tassel Lake—*lake* WY-8
Van Tassell Carriage Barn—*hist pl* WY-8
Van Tassell Creek—*stream* WY-8
Van Tassells Corners—*locale* NY-2
Van Tassells Point—*cape* WI-6
Van Tassel Ridge—*ridge* CA-9
Van Tassle Island—*island* WI-6
Vanticlese Creek—*stream* AK-9
**Vantine**—*pop pl* NC-3
Vantine Brook—*stream* PA-2
**Vantown**—*pop pl* MI-6
Van Trap Spring—*spring* AZ-5
Vantreace Post Office (historical)—*building* TN-4
Van Treese Ch—*church* IL-6
Vantress Lateral—*canal* ID-8
Van Trojen House—*hist pl* WA-9
Van Trump Falls Creek—*stream* WA-9
Van Trump Glacier—*glacier* WA-9
Van Trump Park—*flat* WA-9
Van Tuyl Homeplace—*hist pl* OK-5
Van Tyle Tank—*reservoir* TX-5
Van Tyle Windmill—*locale* TX-5
Van Vac Lake—*lake* MN-6
Van Valer Canyon—*valley* AZ-5
Van Valer Spring—*spring* AZ-5
Van Valkenburgh Pond—*lake* NY-2
Van Valkenburg Ranch—*locale* CO-8
Van Valkenburg Rsvr—*reservoir* CO-8
Van Valter Tank—*reservoir* AZ-5
**Vanva Settlement**—*pop pl* TX-5
Van Vechten Cem—*cemetery* NY-2
Van Vechten Park—*park* IA-7
Van Veghten House—*hist pl* NJ-2
Vanvig Ranch—*locale* ND-7
**Vanville**—*pop pl* WV-2
Vanville Cem—*cemetery* ND-7
Vanville Sch—*school* ND-7
**Vanville Township**—*pop pl* ND-7
Van Vleck—*CDP* TX-5
Van Vleck—*locale* CA-9
**Van Vleck**—*pop pl* TX-5
Van Vleck House—*hist pl* NY-2
Van Vleck HS—*school* TX-5
Van Vleck Ranch—*locale* CA-9
*Vanvleet* MS-4
**Van Vleet**—*pop pl* MS-4
**Van Vleet**—*pop pl* NY-2
Van Vleet Consolidated HS (historical)—*school* MS-4
Van Vleet Post Office—*building* MS-4
Van Vleet Road Sch—*school* MI-6
Van Vleet United Methodist Ch—*church* MS-4
Van Vlett Baptist Ch—*church* MS-4
Van Vliet Lake—*lake* WI-6
Van Vlissingen Sch—*school* IL-6
Van Voorhees-Quackenbush House—*hist pl* NJ-2
Van Voorhies House—*hist pl* CA-9
Van Voorhies Lake Dam—*dam* IN-6
Vanvoorhis—*other* WV-2
**Van Voorhis**—*pop pl* PA-2
**Van Voorhis**—*pop pl* WV-2
**Van Voorhis Hill**—*pop pl* PA-2
**Van Voorhis Manor**—*pop pl* KY-4
Van Voorhis-Quackenbush House—*hist pl* NJ-2
*Van Voorst Ditch* IN-6
**Van Vorhis (Vanvoorhis)**—*pop pl* WV-2
Vanvoris Hill—*summit* GA-3
Van Vorst Park Hist Dist—*hist pl* NJ-2
Van Vorst Park Hist Dist (Boundary Increase)—*hist pl* NJ-2
Van Vredenburg Farm—*hist pl* NY-2
Van Vuren Sch (historical)—*school* SD-7
Van Wagenen, Mount—*summit* AK-9
Van Wagenen Cem—*cemetery* NY-2
Van Wagener, Jacob B., Barn—*hist pl* ID-8
Van Wagener, Jacob B., Caretaker's House—*hist pl* ID-8
Van Wagner, Harvey, House—*hist pl* MI-6
Van Wagoner Canyon—*valley* UT-8
Van Wagoner Mine—*mine* UT-8
Van Wagoner Ridge—*ridge* AR-4
*Van Walden Branch* MS-4
Van Warmer Bay—*bay* NY-2
Van Wart Well—*well* NM-5
**Van Wert**—*pop pl* GA-3
**Van Wert**—*pop pl* IA-7
**Van Wert**—*pop pl* OH-6
**Van Wert**—*pop pl* PA-2
Van Wert Bandstand—*hist pl* OH-6
**Van Wert (County)**—*pop pl* OH-6
Van Wert County Courthouse—*hist pl* OH-6
Van Wickle Sch—*school* MI-6
Van Wie Creek—*stream* NY-2
Van Wies Point—*cape* NY-2
*Van Wies's Point* NY-2
Van Wig Sch—*school* CA-9
**Van Winkle**—*pop pl* MS-4
Van Winkle, E., Gin and Machine Works—*hist pl* GA-3
Van Winkle, Peter G., House—*hist pl* WV-2
Van Winkle Baptist Ch—*church* MS-4
Vanwinkle Branch—*stream* IL-6
Van Winkle Canyon—*valley* AZ-5
Van Winkle Cem—*cemetery* OH-6
Van Winkle Cem—*cemetery* TN-4
Van Winkle Cem—*cemetery* TX-5
Vanwinkle Coulee—*valley* MT-8
Van Winkle Creek—*stream* WA-9
Van Winkle Elem Sch—*school* MS-4
Van Winkle-Fox House—*hist pl* NJ-2
Van Winkle Gulch—*valley* TX-5
Van Winkle Hollow—*valley* MO-7
Van Winkle House—*hist pl* NJ-2
Van Winkle Lake—*lake* MI-6
Van Winkle Lake—*lake* NM-5
Van Winkle Lake—*reservoir* IL-6
Van Winkle Lodge—*locale* AR-4
Van Winkle Mtn—*summit* CA-9
Vanwinkle Post Office (historical)—*building* MS-4
Van Winkle Ranch—*locale* AZ-5
Van Winkler Cem—*cemetery* KS-7
Van Winkle Shop Ctr—*locale* MS-4
Van Winkles Pond—*reservoir* NJ-2
Van Winkle Spring—*spring* AZ-5
Van Winkle Spring—*spring* CA-9
Van Winkle United Methodist Ch—*church* MS-4
Van Winkle Wash—*stream* CA-9
Van Winkleys Canyon—*valley* CA-9
Van Wirt Mtn—*summit* CO-8
*Vanwood* WV-2
Van Wood—*locale* IL-6
Van Wormer Creek—*stream* WY-8
Van Wyck—*locale* WA-9
**Van Wyck**—*pop pl* SC-3
Van Wyck, Cornelius, House—*hist pl* NY-2
Van Wyck Brooks Hist Dist—*hist pl* NJ-2
Van Wyck Camp—*locale* CA-9
Van Wyck (CCD)—*cens area* SC-3
Van Wyck Cem—*cemetery* NY-2
Van Wyck Creek—*stream* CA-9
Van Wyck-Lefferts Tide Mill—*hist pl* NY-2
Van Wyck Mtn—*summit* NY-2
Van Wyck Ridge—*ridge* NY-2
Van Wyck Sheep Trail—*trail* ID-8
Van Wyck-Wharton House—*hist pl* NY-2
Van Wyper Spring—*spring* NV-8
Van Y Sch—*school* MI-6
**Van Zandt**—*pop pl* WA-9
Van Zandt Cem—*cemetery* GA-3
Vanzandt Cem—*cemetery* MO-7
Vanzandt Cem—*cemetery* TN-4
Van Zandt Cem—*cemetery* WA-9
**Van Zandt (County)**—*pop pl* TX-5
Van Zandt County Park—*park* TX-5
Van Zandt Dike—*ridge* WA-9
Van Zandt Hill—*summit* GA-3
Van Zandt Hollow—*valley* AL-4
Van Zandt Hollow—*valley* NY-2
Van Zandt Meadows—*flat* OR-9
Van Zandt Sch—*school* MO-7
Van Zandt Tanks—*reservoir* TX-5
Van Zanot Sch—*school* TX-5
Vanzant—*locale* KY-4
**Vanzant**—*pop pl* MO-7
Vanzant Bend—*bend* TN-4
Van Zant Branch—*stream* TX-5
Vanzant Cem—*cemetery* MO-7
Vanzant Cem—*cemetery* TN-4
*Vanzant Cemetery* GA-3
Vanzant Ch—*church* MO-7
Vanzant Ch—*church* OK-5
Vanzant Creek—*stream* MS-4
Van Zant Creek—*stream* MO-7
Van Zante Creek—*stream* IA-7
Van Zant Peak—*summit* NV-8
Vanzant Spring—*spring* TN-4
*Vanzant's Store* GA-3
Van Zeeland Park—*park* WI-6
Van Zee Sch—*school* SD-7
Van Zee Sch (historical)—*school* SD-7
Van Zile House—*hist pl* NJ-2
Van Zile Lake—*lake* WI-6
Van Zile Sch—*school* MI-6
VanZolenburg, Jacob, House—*hist pl* MI-6
Vanzora Ch—*church* KY-4
Vaoaga Point—*cape* AS-9
Vaotamu Rocks—*island* AS-9
Vaoto Marsh—*swamp* AS-9
**Vapo**—*pop pl* VA-3
Vapor—*locale* PR-3
Vapor Creek—*stream* MT-8
*Vapot* MH-9
Vaquero Camp—*locale* CA-9
Vaquero Campsite—*locale* CA-9
Vaquero Flat—*flat* CA-9
*Vaquero Mesa* AZ-5
Vaqueros Cabin—*other* NM-5
Vaqueros Canyon—*valley* NM-5
Vaqueros Creek—*stream* CA-9
Vaquero Spring—*spring* CA-9
Vaqueteria Banco Number 118—*levee* TX-5
Vaquias Windmill—*locale* TX-5
**Vaquinas**—*pop pl* PR-3
Varal, Arroyo—*valley* TX-5
Varbrough Cem—*cemetery* TN-4
Varco—*locale* MN-6
Varco Well—*well* OR-9
Varda Lake—*reservoir* NC-3
**Vardaman**—*pop pl* MS-4
Vardaman Cem—*cemetery* MS-4
Vardaman Ch—*church* MS-4
Vardaman Elem Sch—*school* MS-4
Vardaman HS—*school* MS-4
Vardaman Sch (historical)—*school* MS-4
Vardaman United Methodist Ch—*church* MS-4
Vardell Hall—*school* NC-3
Vardeman Branch—*stream* TX-5
**Varden**—*pop pl* PA-2
Varden Branch—*stream* AL-4
Varden Creek—*stream* WA-9
Varden Lake—*lake* WA-9
Varder Bridge—*other* IL-6
Vardo—*locale* MD-2
Vardry McBee Rock—*pillar* NC-3
**Vardy**—*pop pl* TN-4
Vardy Community Sch—*school* TN-4
Vardy Sch Community Hist Dist—*hist pl* TN-4
Vare, Abigail, Sch—*hist pl* PA-2
Vare, Edwin H., JHS—*hist pl* PA-2
Vare JHS—*school* PA-2
**Varela**—*pop pl* PR-3
Varel Oil Field—*oilfield* TX-5
Varennes Ch—*church* SC-3
Vareno Tank—*reservoir* TX-5
Vare Playground—*park* PA-2
Vare Sch—*school* PA-2
Varey Creek—*stream* CA-9
Varga Pond—*lake* CT-1
Vargas Creek—*stream* TX-5
Vargas Pasture—*flat* TX-5
Vargas Windmill—*locale* (2) TX-5
Vargo Hill—*summit* IN-6
Vargo Hill—*summit* PA-2
Vargy Chapel Cem—*cemetery* TX-5
Variable Density Tunnel—*hist pl* VA-3
Variable Marsh—*swamp* MD-2
**Variadero (Garita Po)**—*pop pl* NM-5
Variadero Mesa—*summit* NM-5
Varian, B. S., House—*hist pl* ID-8
Varian Lake—*reservoir* VA-3
Varick Memorial Ch—*church* NJ-2
Varicks Chapel—*church* VA-3
**Varick (Town of)**—*pop pl* NY-2
Variegated Glacier—*glacier* AK-9
**Varien**—*pop pl* OR-9
Varien Canyon—*valley* OR-9
Variety Club Boys Ranch—*locale* TX-5
Variety Lake—*lake* MN-6
Variety Mills—*locale* VA-3
Variety Park—*locale* MI-6
Variety Sch—*school* NV-8
Variety Store Bldg and Theatre—*hist pl* OH-6
Varilek Fishpond Number One—*reservoir* SD-7
Varilek Fishpond Number Two—*reservoir* SD-7
Varilek Fishpond Number 1 Dam—*dam* SD-7
Varilek Fishpond Number 2 Dam—*dam* SD-7
**Varilla**—*pop pl* KY-4
*Varina* NC-3
**Varina**—*pop pl* IA-7
**Varina**—*pop pl* VA-3
Varina—*uninc pl* NC-3
**Varina Grove**—*pop pl* VA-3
Varina HS—*school* VA-3
Varina (Magisterial District)—*fmr MCD* VA-3
Varina Plantation—*hist pl* VA-3
Varina Sch—*school* VA-3
*Various Creek* NC-3
Varisco—*locale* TX-5
Varity Creek—*stream* MI-6
*Varkens Kill* NJ-2
*Varkins Kill* NJ-2
**Varlano**—*pop pl* DE-2
*Varmah Creek* ME-1
Varmint Creek—*stream* (2) OR-9
Varmit Camp—*locale* OR-9
Varna—*locale* WA-9
**Varna**—*pop pl* IL-6
**Varna**—*pop pl* NY-2
Varnado—*locale* MS-4
**Varnado**—*pop pl* LA-4
Varnado Cem—*cemetery* (4) LA-4
Varnado Cem—*cemetery* MS-4
Varnadore Pond—*reservoir* SC-3
Varnah Brook—*stream* ME-1
Varnals Creek—*stream* NC-3
**Varnamtown**—*pop pl* NC-3
Varnedoe Cave—*cave* AL-4
*Varnel* MS-4
**Varnell**—*pop pl* GA-3
Varnell Cem—*cemetery* AR-4
Varnell Cem—*cemetery* (2) TN-4
Varnell Cem—*cemetery* TX-5
Varnell Creek—*stream* AR-4
Varnell Creek—*stream* MS-4
Varnell Creek—*stream* NC-3
Varnell Creek—*stream* TN-4
**Varnell Estates**—*pop pl* TN-4
Varnell Spring—*spring* GA-3
Varnell Springs—*spring* TN-4
Varner—*locale* AR-4
Varner—*locale* KS-7
Varner—*locale* WV-2
**Varner**—*pop pl* NE-7
Varner Cem—*cemetery* KS-7
Varner Cem—*cemetery* MO-7
Varner Cem—*cemetery* (2) OH-6
Varner Cem—*cemetery* (3) TN-4
Varner Cem—*cemetery* WV-2
Varner Creek—*stream* TX-5
Varner Dam—*dam* AL-4
Varner Ditch—*canal* IN-6
Varner Gap—*gap* PA-2
Varner Hill—*summit* VA-3
Varner-Hogg Plantation—*hist pl* TX-5
Varner Hollow—*valley* WV-2
Varner Lake—*lake* MN-6
Varner Lake—*reservoir* AL-4
Varner Lake Dam—*dam* MS-4
Varner Sch—*school* MN-6
Varner Sch—*school* SC-3
Varner Sch (historical)—*school* TN-4
Varners Landing (historical)—*locale* TN-4
Varners Store (historical)—*locale* AL-4
Varner Township—*civil* MO-7
Varnes Cem—*cemetery* FL-3
Varnes Ch—*church* MN-6
Varnes Lake—*lake* FL-3
*Varnes Road* OR-9
Varney—*locale* KY-4
Varney—*locale* MT-8
Varney—*locale* NM-5
**Varney**—*pop pl* WV-2
Varney Branch—*stream* KY-4
Varney Branch—*stream* WV-2
Varney Branch Ch—*church* KY-4
Varney Branch Ch—*church* WV-2
Varney Bridge—*bridge* MT-8
Varney Bridge Recreation Site—*locale* MT-8
Varney Brook—*stream* (2) NH-1
Varney Camp—*locale* (2) NH-1
Varney Cem—*cemetery* (2) KY-4
Varney Cem—*cemetery* ME-1
Varney Cem—*cemetery* VT-1
Varney Cem—*cemetery* (2) WV-2
Varney Corner—*locale* ME-1
Varney Creek—*stream* OR-9
**Varney Crossing**—*pop pl* ME-1
Varney Drain—*canal* MI-6
Varney Hill—*summit* (4) ME-1
Varney Hill—*summit* MI-6
Varney Hill—*summit* NY-2
Varney Islands—*island* NH-1
Varney Park—*park* AZ-5
Varney Point—*cape* NH-1
Varney River—*gut* MO-7
Varney River Canal—*canal* MO-7
Varney River Ch—*church* MO-7
Varney River Ditch—*canal* MO-7
Varney Sch—*hist pl* NH-1
Varney Sch—*school* NH-1
Varney Sch—*school* VT-1
Varneys Memorial Camp—*locale* WY-8
**Varneytown**—*pop pl* WV-2
Varnhagan Creek—*stream* TX-5
Varnie Cem—*cemetery* WV-2
Varnon Branch—*stream* MO-7
Varnon Cem—*cemetery* TX-5
**Varnons**—*pop pl* AL-4
Varnon Sch (abandoned)—*school* MO-7
Varnon Slough—*gut* MO-7
Varn RR Station (historical)—*locale* FL-3
**Varnum**—*pop pl* NC-3
Varnum, Gen. James Mitchell, House—*hist pl* RI-1
Varnum Bayou—*gut* TX-5
Varnum Bldg—*hist pl* MA-1
Varnum Brook—*stream* MA-1
Varnum Cem—*cemetery* MA-1
Varnum Ch—*church* OK-5
Varnum Creek—*stream* ID-8
Varnum Mtn—*summit* ME-1
Varnum Pond—*lake* ME-1
*Varnums Brook* MA-1
Varnum Sch—*school* MA-1
Varnum Sch—*school* OK-5
Varnum Stream—*stream* ME-1
*Varnum Town* NC-3
**Varnumtown**—*pop pl* MA-1
**Varnum Town**—*pop pl* NC-3
Varnuna, Lake—*reservoir* MD-2
**Varnville**—*pop pl* SC-3
**Varona Village**—*pop pl* HI-9
Varrier Playground—*park* MI-6
Varsh Ford—*locale* MO-7
Varsity Lake—*lake* CO-8
**Varsity Park**—*pop pl* VA-3
Varsity Shop Ctr—*locale* FL-3
Varvel Creek—*stream* KS-7
Varvel Sch (abandoned)—*school* MO-7
**Varysburg**—*pop pl* NY-2
Varyville (Site)—*locale* NV-8
**Vasa**—*pop pl* MN-6
**Vasaaiga**—*pop pl* AS-9
Vasa Country Club—*other* MI-6
Vasa Hist Dist—*hist pl* MN-6
**Vasa Home**—*pop pl* NJ-2
Vasa Park—*park* IL-6
Vasa Ranch—*locale* NE-7
**Vasa (Township of)**—*pop pl* MN-6
Vasco—*locale* TX-5
Vascocu Cem—*cemetery* LA-4
Vase Ch—*church* ND-7
Vaseux Lake—*lake* MN-6
Vaseux Portage—*trail* MN-6
Vaseys Paradise—*area* AZ-5
Vasher Prairie—*flat* LA-4
**Vashon**—*pop pl* WA-9
Vashon, Point—*cape* WA-9
Vashon Center—*locale* WA-9
Vashon Heights—*locale* WA-9
Vashon HS—*school* MO-7
Vashon Island—*island* WA-9
Vashon Island (CCD)—*cens area* WA-9
Vashon Muni Airp—*airport* WA-9
Vashon Sch—*school* WA-9
Vashti—*locale* AL-4
Vashti—*locale* VA-3
**Vashti**—*pop pl* NC-3
**Vashti**—*pop pl* ND-7
**Vashti**—*pop pl* TX-5
Vashti HS—*school* GA-3
Vashti Landing (historical)—*locale* AL-4
Vasilief Bank—*bar* AK-9
Vasilief Bay—*bay* AK-9
Vasilief Islands—*island* AK-9
Vasilief Rock—*bar* AK-9
Vasilief Rock—*other* AK-9
Vasiliki Ridge—*ridge* WA-9
*Vasilky Ridge* WA-9
Vaso Island—*island* MD-2
Vasold Cem—*cemetery* MI-6
Vasold Lateral—*canal* ID-8
Vasona—*uninc pl* CA-9
*Vasona Creek* CA-9
Vasona Creek—*stream* CA-9
Vasona Dam—*dam* CA-9
**Vasona Junction**—*pop pl* CA-9
Vasona Rsvr—*reservoir* CA-9
**Vasper**—*pop pl* TN-4
Vasper Baptist Ch—*church* TN-4
Vasper Cem—*cemetery* TN-4
Vasper Hollow—*valley* TN-4
Vasper Post Office (historical)—*building* TN-4
Vasper Sch (historical)—*school* TN-4
*Vasques Creek* CA-9
**Vasquez**—*pop pl* CO-8
Vasquez Camp—*locale* NM-5
Vasquez Canyon—*valley* CA-9
Vasquez Cem—*cemetery* TX-5
*Vasquez Creek* CO-8
Vasquez Creek—*stream* (3) CA-9
Vasquez Creek—*stream* CO-8
Vasquez Crossing—*locale* CA-9
Vasquez House—*hist pl* AZ-5
Vasquez Knob—*summit* CA-9
Vasquez Lake—*lake* CO-8
Vasquez Lateral—*canal* NM-5
Vasquez Pass—*gap* CO-8
Vasquez Peak—*summit* CA-9
Vasquez Peak—*summit* CO-8
Vasquez Rock—*summit* CA-9
Vasquez Rocks—*hist pl* CA-9
Vasquez Rocks—*summit* CA-9
Vasquez Tree Historical Marker—*park* CA-9
Vasquez Tunnel—*tunnel* CO-8
Vasquez Well—*well* AZ-5
**Vass**—*pop pl* NC-3
**Vassalboro**—*pop pl* ME-1
Vassalborough (Town of)—*civ div* ME-1
Vassar—*locale* ID-8
**Vassar**—*pop pl* KS-7
**Vassar**—*pop pl* MI-6
**Vassar**—*pop pl* WA-9
Vassar, Matthew, Estate—*hist pl* NY-2
Vassar and Fremont Drain—*canal* MI-6
Vassar Brothers Hosp—*hospital* NY-2
Vassar Canyon—*valley* CA-9
Vassar Cem—*cemetery* KS-7
Vassar Cem—*cemetery* OK-5
Vassar Ch—*church* MI-6
Vassar Ch—*church* OK-5
Vassar Coll—*school* NY-2
Vassar Creek—*stream* KS-7
Vassar Glacier—*glacier* AK-9
**Vassar (historical)**—*pop pl* MS-4
Vassar Hollow—*valley* TN-4
Vassar Home for Aged Men—*hist pl* NY-2
Vassar Institute—*hist pl* NY-2
Vassar Lake—*lake* NY-2
Vassar Meadows—*flat* ID-8
Vassar Park Ch—*church* MI-6
Vassar State Game Area—*park* MI-6
*Vassar State Park* KS-7
Vassar Temple—*church* NY-2
**Vassar (Township of)**—*pop pl* MI-6
Vassar-Warner Row—*hist pl* NY-2
Vass Creek—*stream* WY-8
Vasser Creek—*stream* CA-9
Vasser Ford Bridge—*other* MO-7
Vasser-Pettus Cem—*cemetery* AL-4
**Vasser (subdivision)**—*pop pl* MS-4
Vassey Creek—*stream* FL-3
Vass-Lakeview Sch—*school* NC-3
Vasterling Cem—*cemetery* TX-5
Vasterling Creek—*stream* TX-5
Vaster Sch—*school* AR-4
Vastine—*locale* CO-8
Vastine Run—*stream* OH-6
Vastines Island—*island* PA-2
**Vastus**—*pop pl* MO-7
VA Tank—*reservoir* AZ-5
Vat Camp—*locale* TX-5
Vat Creek—*stream* ID-8
Vat Creek—*stream* UT-8
Vat Creek Ridge—*ridge* UT-8
Vater Cem—*cemetery* TX-5
**Vater (historical)**—*pop pl* TN-4
Vat Hollow—*valley* TX-5
**Vatia**—*pop pl* AS-9
Vatia Bay—*bay* AS-9
**Vatican**—*pop pl* LA-4
Vatican Oil Field—*oilfield* LA-4
Vat Lake—*lake* MN-6
Vat Line Camp—*locale* TX-5
Vatman Park—*park* IL-6
Vatoss Gully—*valley* TX-5
Vat Tank—*reservoir* TX-5
Vatters Pond—*lake* VT-1
Vattman Cem—*cemetery* TX-5
*Vattman Creek* TX-5
**Vattmannville**—*pop pl* TX-5
Vat Windmill—*locale* (2) TX-5
Vauces—*locale* OH-6
Vaucluse—*hist pl* VA-3
Vaucluse—*locale* AR-4
Vaucluse—*locale* VA-3
Vaucluse—*locale* WV-2
**Vaucluse**—*pop pl* SC-3
Vaucluse Bar—*bar* AR-4
Vaucluse Point—*cape* VA-3
Vaucluse Pond—*reservoir* SC-3
Vaucluse Spring—*spring* VA-3
**Vaudreuil**—*pop pl* WI-6
Vaughan—*locale* IA-7
Vaughan—*locale* MS-4
Vaughan—*locale* TX-5
**Vaughan**—*pop pl* IN-6
**Vaughan**—*pop pl* MS-4
**Vaughan**—*pop pl* NC-3
**Vaughan**—*pop pl* WV-2
Vaughan, Iredell P., House—*hist pl* AL-4
Vaughan, John, House—*hist pl* OH-6
Vaughan, Rev. Joshua, House—*hist pl* PA-2
Vaughan Bend—*bend* TN-4
Vaughan Branch—*stream* KY-4
Vaughan Bridge—*bridge* TN-4
Vaughan Cem—*cemetery* AL-4
Vaughan Cem—*cemetery* AR-4
Vaughan Cem—*cemetery* NC-3
Vaughan Cem—*cemetery* OH-6
Vaughan Cem—*cemetery* SC-3
Vaughan Cem—*cemetery* TN-4
Vaughan Cem—*cemetery* TX-5
Vaughan Cem—*cemetery* (2) VA-3
*Vaughan Creek* LA-4
Vaughan Creek—*stream* MS-4
Vaughan Dam—*dam* OR-9
Vaughan Elem Sch—*school* NC-3
Vaughan Gulch—*valley* ID-8
*Vaughan Hill* MA-1
Vaughan Hollow—*valley* TN-4
Vaughan Homestead—*hist pl* ME-1
*Vaughan Lake* CO-8
Vaughan Lewis Glacier—*glacier* AK-9
**Vaughan Meadows (subdivision)**—*pop pl* AL-4
Vaughan Mtn—*summit* AR-4
Vaughan Neck—*cape* ME-1
*Vaughan Pond* MA-1
*Vaughans* MS-4
Vaughans Ch—*church* NC-3
Vaughan Sch—*school* (2) VA-3
Vaughans Creek—*stream* (2) VA-3
Vaughans Crossroad—*locale* AL-4
Vaughans Crossroads—*locale* SC-3
*Vaughans Hill* MA-1
Vaughans Lake—*lake* AL-4
Vaughans Mill Pond—*reservoir* AL-4
Vaughans Millpond—*reservoir* SC-3
Vaughans Mill Pond Dam—*dam* AL-4
*Vaughans Pond* MA-1
Vaughan Spring—*spring* TN-4
Vaughans Ranch Airp—*airport* WA-9
*Vaughan Switch* MS-4
Vaughanville—*locale* AL-4
Vaughanville—*locale* SC-3
Vaughanville Ch—*church* AL-4
Vaugh Cem—*cemetery* TN-4
*Vaughen Hill* MA-1
*Vaughen Hills* MA-1
Vaughin Chapel—*church* TN-4
*Vaugh Lake* CO-8
Vaugh-McClaren Cem—*cemetery* TN-4
*Vaughn* MS-4
*Vaughn* NC-3
Vaughn—*locale* FL-3
Vaughn—*locale* KS-7
Vaughn—*locale* LA-4
Vaughn—*locale* VA-3
**Vaughn**—*pop pl* AL-4
**Vaughn**—*pop pl* AR-4
**Vaughn**—*pop pl* GA-3
**Vaughn**—*pop pl* IN-6
**Vaughn**—*pop pl* MS-4
**Vaughn**—*pop pl* MT-8
**Vaughn**—*pop pl* NM-5
**Vaughn**—*pop pl* OR-9
**Vaughn**—*pop pl* WA-9
Vaughn, Andrew C., House—*hist pl* TN-4
Vaughn, Daniel, Homestead—*hist pl* OH-6
Vaughn, H. G., House—*hist pl* MA-1
Vaughn, Lake—*lake* AR-4
Vaughn, Robert, Homestead—*hist pl* MT-8
Vaughn Airp—*airport* IN-6
Vaughn Bay—*bay* WA-9
Vaughn Bayou—*gut* MS-4
Vaughn Branch—*stream* GA-3
Vaughn Branch—*stream* (2) KY-4
Vaughn Branch—*stream* NC-3
Vaughn Branch—*stream* TN-4
Vaughn Branch—*stream* (2) TX-5
Vaughn Branch—*stream* (2) VA-3
**Vaughn (Brand)**—*pop pl* VA-3
Vaughn Bridge (historical)—*bridge* AL-4
Vaughn Brook—*stream* CT-1
Vaughn Brook—*stream* ME-1
Vaughn Brook—*stream* NY-2
Vaughn Brook—*stream* VT-1
Vaughn Cabin—*locale* CA-9
Vaughn Canyon—*valley* AZ-5
Vaughn Canyon—*valley* CA-9
Vaughn Canyon—*valley* OR-9
Vaughn (CCD)—*cens area* GA-3
Vaughn (CCD)—*cens area* NM-5
*Vaughn Cem* MS-4
Vaughn Cem—*cemetery* (4) AL-4
Vaughn Cem—*cemetery* FL-3
Vaughn Cem—*cemetery* GA-3
Vaughn Cem—*cemetery* (3) IL-6
Vaughn Cem—*cemetery* (3) KY-4
Vaughn Cem—*cemetery* (2) MS-4
Vaughn Cem—*cemetery* (3) MO-7
Vaughn Cem—*cemetery* NJ-2
Vaughn Cem—*cemetery* OH-6
Vaughn Cem—*cemetery* (8) TN-4
Vaughn Cem—*cemetery* (2) TX-5
Vaughn Cem—*cemetery* VA-3
Vaughn Ch—*church* IL-6
Vaughn Ch—*church* NC-3
Vaughn Chapel—*church* KY-4
*Vaughn Corners* AL-4
**Vaughn Corners**—*pop pl* AL-4
*Vaughn Creek* ID-8
Vaughn Creek—*stream* AL-4
Vaughn Creek—*stream* AR-4
Vaughn Creek—*stream* CO-8
Vaughn Creek—*stream* ID-8
Vaughn Creek—*stream* KY-4
Vaughn Creek—*stream* LA-4
Vaughn Creek—*stream* (2) MI-6
Vaughn Creek—*stream* MS-4
Vaughn Creek—*stream* MT-8
Vaughn Creek—*stream* NC-3
Vaughn Creek—*stream* (3) OR-9
Vaughn Creek—*stream* SC-3
Vaughn Creek—*stream* WA-9
Vaughn Creek—*stream* WI-6
Vaughn Dam—*dam* OR-9
Vaughn Ditch—*canal* KY-4
Vaughn Ditch—*canal* MT-8
Vaughn Draw—*valley* CO-8
Vaughn Evergreen Cem—*cemetery* NM-5
Vaughn Family Graves—*cemetery* TX-5
Vaughn Grove Ch—*church* KY-4
Vaughn Gulch—*valley* CA-9
*Vaughn Hill* MA-1
Vaughn Hill—*summit* MA-1
Vaughn Hill—*summit* NC-3
Vaughn Hills—*summit* MA-1
Vaughn (historical P.O.)—*locale* IA-7
Vaughn Hollow—*locale* RI-1
Vaughn Hollow—*valley* (2) AL-4
Vaughn Hollow—*valley* AR-4
Vaughn Hollow—*valley* IN-6
Vaughn Hollow—*valley* (2) MO-7
Vaughn Hollow—*valley* OK-5
Vaughn Hollow—*valley* TN-4
Vaughn House—*hist pl* AR-4
Vaughn Island—*island* ME-1
Vaughn JHS—*school* AL-4
Vaughn-King Cem—*cemetery* TN-4
Vaughn Knob—*summit* KY-4
Vaughn Lake—*lake* AL-4
Vaughn Lake—*lake* CO-8
Vaughn Lake—*lake* (2) MI-6
Vaughn Lake—*lake* NE-7
Vaughn Lake—*lake* NV-8
Vaughn Lake Dam—*dam* (3) MS-4
Vaughn Landing—*locale* DE-2
Vaughn Landing—*locale* FL-3
Vaughn Lateral—*canal* CA-9
Vaughn Log Dam—*dam* OR-9
Vaughn Memorial Hosp—*hospital* AL-4
Vaughn Mill (historical)—*locale* (2) AL-4
*Vaughn Mill Pond* SC-3
Vaughn Mine—*mine* KY-4
Vaughn Oil Field—*oilfield* TX-5
Vaughn Plaza Shop Ctr—*locale* AL-4
Vaughn Point—*cape* OR-9
*Vaughn Pond* SC-3
Vaughn Pond—*lake* MA-1
Vaughn Pond—*lake* TN-4
Vaughn Ranch—*locale* CA-9
Vaughn Ranch—*locale* NV-8
Vaughn Ranch—*locale* (2) NM-5
Vaughn Road Park—*park* AL-4
Vaughn Road Sch—*school* AL-4
Vaughn Rsvr—*reservoir* (2) OR-9
Vaughn Run—*stream* PA-2
*Vaughns* NY-2
Vaughns Branch—*stream* KY-4
Vaughns Bridge—*bridge* AL-4
Vaughns Cem—*cemetery* VA-3
Vaughns Ch—*church* GA-3
Vaughn Sch—*school* CO-8
Vaughn Sch—*school* KY-4
Vaughn Sch—*school* MI-6
Vaughn Sch—*school* MS-4
Vaughn Sch—*school* MO-7
Vaughn Sch—*school* NV-8
Vaughn Sch (abandoned)—*school* (2) MO-7
*Vaughns Chapel* TN-4
Vaughns Chapel—*church* MS-4
Vaughns Chapel—*church* VA-3
Vaughns Chapel Cem—*cemetery* OH-6
Vaughn Sch (historical)—*school* AL-4
Vaughn Sch (historical)—*school* TN-4
*Vaughns Church* MS-4
**Vaughns Corners**—*pop pl* NY-2
*Vaughns Creek* MS-4
Vaughns Creek—*stream* MS-4
Vaughns Creek—*stream* OR-9
Vaughns Creek—*stream* VA-3
*Vaughns Gap* TN-4
Vaughns Gap—*gap* SC-3

Vaughn's Gap—*uninc pl* TN-4
Vaughns Gap Branch—*stream* TN-4
Vaughns Grove—*locale* TN-4
Vaughns Grove Cem—*cemetery* TN-4
Vaughns Grove Ch of Christ—*church* TN-4
Vaughns Grove Sch (historical)—*school* AL-4
*Vaughns Hill* MA-1
Vaughn Site (33CU65)—*hist pl* OH-6
Vaughns Landing (historical)—*locale* AL-4
Vaughn Slough—*stream* NV-8
Vaughns Mill—*locale* KY-4
Vaughns Mill Cem—*cemetery* AL-4
Vaughns Mill Ch—*church* KY-4
Vaughns Neck—*cape* CT-1
*Vaughns Pond* MA-1
Vaughn Spring—*spring* AZ-5
Vaughn Spring—*spring* (2) CA-9
Vaughn Spring—*spring* MO-7
*Vaughns Run* PA-2
Vaughns Sch (historical)—*school* TN-4
Vaughn's Stage Coach Stop—*hist pl* SC-3
Vaughns Store (historical)—*locale* AL-4
Vaughn State Wildlife Mngmt Area—*park* MD-2
**Vaughn Station**—*pop pl* OR-9
Vaughn Stream—*stream* ME-1
Vaughn Stree Sch—*school* CA-9
**Vaughn (subdivision)**—*pop pl* PA-2
Vaughn Summit Ch—*church* VA-3
*Vaughnsville* SC-3
**Vaughnsville**—*pop pl* OH-6
Vaughn Tabernacle—*church* GA-3
*Vaughn (Township of)* AR-4
*Vaughnville* SC-3
Vaughn Well—*well* NM-5
Vaught, Mount—*summit* MT-8
Vaught Branch—*stream* KY-4
Vaught Branch—*stream* TN-4
Vaught Branch—*stream* VA-3
Vaught Cem—*cemetery* AL-4
Vaught Cem—*cemetery* (3) KY-4
Vaught Cem—*cemetery* OK-5
Vaught Chapel—*church* WV-2
Vaught Cove—*valley* AL-4
Vaught Creek—*stream* TN-4
Vaughter Cem—*cemetery* IL-6
Vaughters Cem—*cemetery* OH-6
Vaughters Knob—*summit* TN-4
Vaughters Run—*stream* OH-6
Vaught Gap—*gap* NC-3
Vaught Gap—*gap* TN-4
Vaught-Hemingway Stadium—*park* MS-4
Vaught House—*hist pl* AL-4
Vaught Lake—*lake* SC-3
Vaught Memorial Ch—*church* WV-2
Vaught Ridge—*ridge* KY-4
Vaughtrin Well—*well* NM-5
Vaughts—*locale* MS-4
Vaught Sch—*school* (2) KY-4
Vaught Sch—*school* TN-4
*Vaughts Mill* MS-4
Vaughts Rsvr—*reservoir* AR-4
Vaughts Run—*stream* WV-2
**Vaughtsville (historical)**—*pop pl* TN-4
Vaughtsville Post Office (historical)—*building* TN-4
Vaugine (Township of)—*fmr MCD* AR-4
*Vaugn Creek* MI-6
Vault (Abandoned)—*locale* AK-9
Vault Creek—*stream* AK-9
Vault Mine Trail One Hundred Forty—*trail* AZ-5
Vault Point—*cliff* IN-6
Vault Spring—*spring* MO-7
*Vaurenhoek* DE-2
Vaur Run—*stream* PA-2
Vause Branch Ochlockonee River—*stream* FL-3
Vause Cem—*cemetery* NC-3
Vause Landing—*locale* FL-3
Vauters Ch—*church* VA-3
Vauter's Church—*hist pl* VA-3
Vautrin, Claude, House—*hist pl* NY-2
Vauvilliers, Point—*cape* FM-9
Vaux, Roberts, JHS—*hist pl* PA-2
Vaux Creek—*stream* SC-3
**Vauxhall**—*pop pl* NJ-2
Vaux Island—*island* SC-3
Vaux JHS—*school* PA-2
Vaux Rsvr Number One—*reservoir* MT-8
Vaux Rsvr Number Two—*reservoir* MT-8
Vaux Town—*uninc pl* PA-2
Vava Cove—*bay* AS-9
Vavak Cem—*cemetery* MO-7
**Vavas**—*pop pl* PR-3
Vaver Rsvr—*reservoir* MT-8
Vawter—*locale* MN-6
Vawter—*locale* PA-2
Vawter, J. G. and Elizabeth S., House—*hist pl* IA-7
Vawter Canyon—*valley* OR-9
Vawter Corner—*locale* VA-3
Vawter Hall and Old President's House—*hist pl* VA-3
**Vawter Park**—*pop pl* IN-6
Vawter Sch—*school* IA-7
Vawter Sch—*school* MO-7
Vawter Spring—*spring* OR-9
**Vawters Shore**—*pop pl* VA-3
Vay—*locale* ID-8
**Vaya Chin**—*pop pl* AZ-5
**Vayas**—*pop pl* PR-3
Vayas (Barrio)—*fmr MCD* PR-3
Vaya Windmill—*locale* CO-8
**Vayden**—*pop pl* NE-7
**Vayland**—*pop pl* SD-7
Vazquez—*CDP* PR-3
**Vazquez**—*pop pl* PR-3
V Bar Tank—*reservoir* AZ-5
VCA Mine—*mine* UT-8
V Canal—*canal* NV-8
V Canal—*canal* OR-9
V Canyon—*valley* NV-8
V Canyon—*valley* OR-9
V Canyon—*valley* UT-8
V C Bar Ranch—*locale* CO-8
V Cross Ranch—*locale* NM-5
V-Cross-T Lake—*lake* NM-5
V-Day Mine—*mine* IL-6
VD Tank—*reservoir* AZ-5
V D Tank—*reservoir* AZ-5

Veach Canyon—*valley* AZ-5
Veach Cem—*cemetery* KY-4
Veach Gap—*gap* VA-3
Veach Gap Trail—*trail* VA-3
Veach Knob—*summit* KY-4
**Veachland**—*pop pl* KY-4
Veach-May-Wilson Industrial Park—*locale* TN-4
Veach Ridge—*ridge* AZ-5
Veach (Site)—*locale* TX-5
Veahna Creek—*stream* AK-9
Veal—*locale* GA-3
Veal, Thomas J., Ranch—*hist pl* SD-7
*Veal Branch* TX-5
Veal Cem—*cemetery* (2) GA-3
Veale Creek—*stream* IN-6
Veale Creek—*stream* TX-5
Veale Creek Cem—*cemetery* TX-5
Veale Creek Ch—*church* IN-6
*Veale Island* SD-7
*Veales Creek* IN-6
**Veale (Township of)**—*pop pl* IN-6
Veale Tract—*civil* CA-9
Veale Well—*well* TX-5
**Vealmoor**—*pop pl* TX-5
Vealmoor Cem—*cemetery* TX-5
Vealmoor Oil Field—*oilfield* TX-5
Veal Pond—*reservoir* GA-3
**Veals**—*pop pl* TX-5
Vealsburg—*locale* KY-4
*Veals Creek* IN-6
Veals Gulch—*valley* MT-8
*Veals Pond* MA-1
Veal Springs Branch—*stream* TX-5
*Veals Station* TX-5
Veal Station—*locale* TX-5
Veal Tank—*reservoir* TX-5
*Vealtown* NJ-2
Vealy Drain—*stream* MI-6
**Veasey**—*pop pl* WV-2
Veasey Chapel—*church* AL-4
Veasey Creek—*stream* AL-4
Veasey Creek—*stream* GA-3
*Veasey Creek Access* AL-4
Veasey Creek Rec Area—*park* AL-4
Veasey Hollow—*valley* WV-2
Veasey (Township of)—*fmr MCD* AR-4
Veatch—*locale* OR-9
Veatch Canyon—*valley* NV-8
Veatch Creek—*stream* OR-9
Veatch Ditch—*canal* IN-6
Veatch Gulch—*valley* CO-8
Veatch Sch—*school* IL-6
Veater Ranch—*locale* CA-9
*Veater Spring* UT-8
Veats Draw—*arroyo* OR-9
*Veaver Creek* ID-8
*Veaver Creek* WA-9
*Veavitts Canyon* UT-8
Veazey—*locale* GA-3
Veazey—*locale* KY-4
Veazey—*locale* WA-9
Veazey Cem—*cemetery* KY-4
Veazey Cem—*cemetery* MD-2
Veazey Cove—*bay* MD-2
Veazey Neck—*cape* MD-2
**Veazey (Veazie)**—*pop pl* WA-9
Veazie—*CDP* ME-1
Veazie—*locale* LA-4
Veazie—*other* WA-9
**Veazie**—*pop pl* LA-4
Veazie, Jones P., House—*hist pl* ME-1
Veazie, William T. and Clara H., House—*hist pl* ID-8
**Veazie Center**—*pop pl* ME-1
Veazie Creek—*stream* OR-9
Veazie Gore—*unorg* ME-1
Veazie Rocks—*bar* MA-1
Veazie Springs—*spring* WI-6
**Veazie (Town of)**—*pop pl* ME-1
Veazsys Lake—*reservoir* NC-3
Veazsys Lake Dam—*dam* (2) NC-3
*Veazy* GA-3
Veazy Ridge—*ridge* ME-1
Vebber Corners—*locale* NY-2
**Veblen**—*pop pl* SD-7
Veblen Farmstead—*hist pl* MN-6
**Veblen Junction**—*pop pl* ND-7
**Veblen Township**—*pop pl* SD-7
Vecino—*uninc pl* CA-9
Veckatimest Island—*island* MA-1
Veda Butte—*summit* OR-9
Veda Grand Sch—*school* IL-6
Veda Lake—*lake* OR-9
Vedauwoo Glen—*locale* WY-8
Vedder, Lake—*lake* MI-6
Vedder Cem—*cemetery* NY-2
*Vedder Corners* NY-2
*Vedder Hill* NY-2
Vedder Mtn—*summit* NY-2
Vedder Mtn—*summit* WA-9
Vedin Corner—*locale* SD-7
**Vedra**—*pop pl* WV-2
Vedra, Lake—*lake* FL-3
**Vee**—*pop pl* OH-6
*Vee, The* UT-8
Vee Bar Ranch Lodge—*hist pl* WY-8
Veech—*locale* KY-4
**Veechdale**—*pop pl* KY-4
Veech Haven Ch—*church* KY-4
Vee Creek—*stream* WA-9
Vee Dam—*dam* NM-5
Veeder, Mount—*summit* CA-9
Veeder Ch—*church* ND-7
Veeder Farmhouse #1—*hist pl* NY-2
Veeder Farmhouse #2—*hist pl* NY-2
Veeder Memorial Ch—*church* NY-2
**Veedersburg**—*pop pl* IN-6
Veeder Sch Number 2—*school* ND-7
**Veedum**—*pop pl* WI-6
Veefkind—*locale* WI-6
Veefkind Cem—*cemetery* WI-6
Vee Hollow—*valley* TN-4
Veeh Rsvr—*reservoir* CA-9
Vee Lake—*lake* CA-9
Vee Lake—*lake* MN-6
Vee Lake—*lake* OR-9
Veenker Memorial Golf Course—*other* IA-7
Vee Pond—*lake* NY-2
Veercamp Sch—*school* MO-7
Vees, The—*range* WY-8

Vee Seven Tank—*reservoir* AZ-5
Vee Springs—*spring* OR-9
Veeta Mine—*mine* CA-9
Veezey Hill—*summit* NH-1
Vega—*civ div* MN-6
Vega—*locale* CA-9
Vega—*locale* GA-3
Vega—*locale* MI-6
**Vega**—*pop pl* NY-2
**Vega**—*pop pl* OH-6
**Vega**—*pop pl* TX-5
Vega, The—*area* NM-5
Vega, The—*flat* CO-8
**Vega Alta**—*pop pl* PR-3
Vega Alta (Municipio)—*civil* PR-3
Vega Alta (Pueblo)—*fmr MCD* PR-3
**Vega Baja**—*pop pl* PR-3
Vega Baja (Municipio)—*civil* PR-3
Vega Baja (Pueblo)—*fmr MCD* PR-3
Vega Bay—*bay* AK-9
Vega Canyon—*valley* CO-8
Vega Cem—*cemetery* MN-6
Vega Cem—*cemetery* NY-2
Vega Cem—*cemetery* SD-7
Vega Ch—*church* OH-6
Vega Cochina—*valley* NM-5
Vega Corral—*locale* CO-8
*Vega Creek* UT-8
Vega Creek—*stream* (2) CO-8
Vega Creek—*stream* MI-6
Vega Creek—*stream* (2) UT-8
Vega del Estillero—*area* NM-5
Vega del Oso—*area* NM-5
Vega Del Rio Del Pajaro—*civil* CA-9
Vega Draw—*valley* TX-5
Vega East (CCD)—*cens area* TX-5
**Vega Grande**—*pop pl* PR-3
Vega (historical)—*locale* SD-7
Vega (historical P.O.)—*locale* IA-7
Vega la Juana Creek—*stream* CO-8
Vega Larga—*flat* CO-8
Vega Lateral—*canal* NM-5
Vega Mine—*mine* CO-8
Vegan—*locale* WV-2
**Vega Park Subdivision**—*pop pl* UT-8
Vega Paz Tank—*reservoir* NM-5
Vega Point—*cape* AK-9
Vega Ranch—*locale* NV-8
Vega Redonda—*swamp* NM-5
Vega Redonda (Barrio)—*fmr MCD* PR-3
Vegars Cem—*cemetery* IA-7
**Vegas**—*pop pl* PR-3
Vegas Abajo (Barrio)—*fmr MCD* PR-3
Vegas Arriba (Barrio)—*fmr MCD* PR-3
Vegas (Barrio)—*fmr MCD* (2) PR-3
*Vegas Bay* NV-8
Vegas Bonita—*area* NM-5
Vega Sch—*school* SD-7
**Vegas Creek**—*pop pl* NV-8
*Vegas Heights* NV-8
Vegas Island—*area* AK-9
Vega Sixtysix—*area* NM-5
Vegas Junction—*locale* NM-5
**Vegas Subdivision**—*pop pl* UT-8
Vegas Verde Sch—*school* NV-8
*Vegas View* NV-8
Vegas Village Shop Ctr—*locale* NV-8
Vega Tank—*reservoir* NM-5
Vega Tank—*reservoir* TX-5
*Vega Wash* UT-8
Vega Well—*well* (2) NM-5
Vega West (CCD)—*cens area* TX-5
Vegch Plantation—*locale* AR-4
Vegetable RR Station—*locale* FL-3
Vegetarian Creek—*stream* KS-7
*Vegosa Creek* NM-5
Vegoso, Arroyo—*stream* NM-5
Vegoso, Arroyo—*valley* NM-5
Vegoso, Rito—*stream* NM-5
**Veguita**—*pop pl* NM-5
Veguitas (Barrio)—*fmr MCD* PR-3
Vehrs Spring—*spring* OR-9
Vehtenjerlo Lakes—*lake* AK-9
Veh-Tenjerlow Lakes—*lake* AK-9
V Eighteen Wash—*stream* AZ-5
Veiled Lady Cave—*cave* PA-2
Veiled Peak—*summit* WY-8
*Veil Lake* WI-6
Veillard House—*hist pl* FL-3
Veillon, Bayou—*stream* LA-4
Veillon Cem—*cemetery* LA-4
**Veilstown**—*pop pl* PA-2
Vein Creek—*stream* ID-8
Vein Lake—*lake* MN-6
Vein Mountain—*locale* NC-3
Vein Mountain Ch—*church* NC-3
Vein Mtn—*summit* AK-9
Vein Mtn—*summit* NC-3
*Vein Peak* ID-8
Vein Point—*cape* AK-9
Veira Park—*park* MA-1
Veit Airp—*airport* PA-2
Veith Bldg—*hist pl* NE-7
Veitsburg (historical)—*locale* KS-7
Vejar Sch—*school* CA-9
Vejo Lake—*lake* WI-6
Vekol Interchange—*crossing* AZ-5
Vekol Mine—*mine* AZ-5
*Vekol Mountain* AZ-5
Vekol Mountains—*range* AZ-5
*Vekol Range* AZ-5
Vekol Valley—*valley* AZ-5
Vekol Wash—*stream* AZ-5
*Velabat* FM-9
Vela Cem—*cemetery* TX-5
Veladeras Windmill—*locale* TX-5
**Velarde**—*pop pl* NM-5
Velarde Cem—*cemetery* NM-5
Velarde Dams—*dam* NM-5
Velarde Sch—*school* NM-5
Vela Rsvr—*reservoir* CO-8
Velas Cem—*cemetery* TX-5
Velasco—*uninc pl* TX-5
Velasco Cem—*cemetery* TX-5
**Velasco Heights**—*pop pl* TX-5
Velasco House—*hist pl* AZ-5
Velasco Pit—*mine* AZ-5
Velasco Reef—*bar* PW-9
Velasco Sch—*school* TX-5
Velasquez Butte—*summit* AZ-5

Velasquez Butte Tank Number Two—*reservoir* AZ-5
**Velasquez Plaza**—*pop pl* CO-8
Velasquez Spring—*spring* NM-5
**Velasquez Subdivision**—*pop pl* UT-8
Velasquez Tank—*reservoir* AZ-5
Vela Tank—*reservoir* TX-5
**Velazquez**—*pop pl* (2) PR-3
**Velbar Subdivision**—*pop pl* UT-8
Velburton Lake—*lake* FL-3
**Velda**—*pop pl* MO-7
**Velda Rose Estates**—*pop pl* AZ-5
Velda Rose Gardens (trailer park)—*locale* AZ-5
**Velda Rose Gardens (Trailer Park)**—*pop pl* AZ-5
Velda Rose Shop Ctr—*locale* AZ-5
**Velda Village**—*pop pl* MO-7
**Velda Village Hills**—*pop pl* MO-7
**Veldt (Township of)**—*pop pl* MN-6
*Velederos* TX-5
*Velederos Creek* TX-5
Veleno, Arroyo—*valley* TX-5
Velenzuela Creek—*stream* TX-5
Velenzuela Ranch—*locale* TX-5
Veleska Lake—*lake* AK-9
Veley Fork—*stream* PA-2
Velian Wash—*stream* CA-9
Velie—*locale* AR-4
Velie Ch—*church* AR-4
Velie Chute—*stream* IL-6
Velie Park—*park* IL-6
*Velilis* FM-9
Vellieur Pond—*lake* ME-1
Velma—*locale* IL-6
Velma—*locale* NE-7
Velma—*locale* VA-3
**Velma**—*pop pl* LA-4
**Velma**—*pop pl* MS-4
**Velma**—*pop pl* OK-5
Velma-Alma (CCD)—*cens area* OK-5
Velma Farm (historical)—*locale* AL-4
Velma Jackson HS—*school* MS-4
Velox—*locale* WA-9
**Velpen**—*pop pl* IN-6
**Veltin**—*pop pl* LA-4
Veltin Oil and Gas Field—*oilfield* LA-4
**Velva**—*pop pl* ND-7
Velva Sportsman Dam—*dam* ND-7
**Velva Township**—*pop pl* ND-7
Velvet—*locale* WA-9
Velvet Branch—*stream* SC-3
Velvet Creek—*stream* AK-9
Velvet Creek—*stream* ID-8
Velvet Creek—*stream* (2) OR-9
Velvet Hill—*summit* MI-6
Velvet Knob—*summit* WV-2
*Velvet Lake* MI-6
Velvet Lake—*lake* MN-6
Velvet Lake—*lake* WI-6
Velvet Lake—*swamp* UT-8
Velvet Mine—*mine* (2) NV-8
Velvet Peak—*summit* NV-8
**Velvet Ridge**—*pop pl* AR-4
Velvet Ridge—*ridge* UT-8
Velvet Ridge Cem—*cemetery* AR-4
Velvet Ridge (Township of)—*fmr MCD* AR-4
Velvet Rocks—*pillar* NH-1
Velvet Silver Mine—*mine* UT-8
V E Lynch Camp—*locale* ME-1
Velzer, N., House and Caretaker's Cottage—*hist pl* NY-2
Vemo—*locale* TX-5
Vena Ave Sch—*school* CA-9
*Venable* NC-3
Venable—*locale* TX-5
Venable—*other* NC-3
**Venable**—*pop pl* NC-3
Venable Branch—*stream* TX-5
Venable Cave—*cave* MO-7
Venable Cem—*cemetery* NC-3
Venable Cem—*cemetery* OK-5
Venable Cem—*cemetery* VA-3
Venable Ch—*church* LA-4
Venable-Chase House—*hist pl* KY-4
Venable-Comanche Trail—*trail* CO-8
**Venable Community (subdivision)**—*pop pl* NC-3
Venable Creek—*stream* AL-4
Venable Creek—*stream* CO-8
Venable Creek—*stream* VA-3
Venable Elem Sch—*school* NC-3
Venable Falls—*falls* CO-8
Venable Hollow—*valley* TN-4
Venable Hollow—*valley* VA-3
Venable Lake—*reservoir* AL-4
*Venable Lakes* CO-8
Venable Lakes—*lake* CO-8
Venable Mine—*mine* ID-8
Venable Pass—*gap* CO-8
Venable Peak—*summit* CO-8
Venables Bridge—*bridge* VA-3
Venable Sch—*school* MO-7
Venable Sch—*school* VA-3
**Venable Spring**—*pop pl* TN-4
Venable Spring Branch—*stream* MO-7
Venable Street Sch—*school* VA-3
Venable Tobacco Company Warehouse—*hist pl* NC-3
Venable-Todhunter Houses—*hist pl* KY-4
Venada Brazil Windmill—*locale* TX-5
Venada Ranch—*locale* TX-5
Venada Windmill—*locale* (5) TX-5
Venadito—*locale* TX-5
Venadito, Canada Del —*valley* CA-9
Venadito Draw—*valley* AZ-5
Venadito Draw—*valley* NM-5
Venadito Windmill—*locale* NM-5
Venadito Windmill—*locale* TX-5
*Venado* CA-9
Venado—*locale* CA-9
**Venado**—*pop pl* NV-8
Venado, Arroyo—*stream* CA-9
Venado, Arroyo—*valley* TX-5
Venado, Laguna—*lake* CO-8
Venado Canyon—*valley* NM-5
Venado Creek—*stream* (3) TX-5
Venado Lakes—*lake* TX-5
Venado Peak—*summit* NM-5
Venado Section House—*building* NV-8
Venados Ranch—*locale* CA-9

Venados Tank—*reservoir* TX-5
Venado Tank—*reservoir* NM-5
Venado Tank—*reservoir* (3) TX-5
Venado Well—*well* NM-5
Venado Well—*well* TX-5
Venado Windmill—*locale* (2) TX-5
Vena Gains Branch—*stream* DE-2
Venancio Tank—*reservoir* TX-5
Venango—*locale* PA-2
**Venango**—*pop pl* KS-7
**Venango**—*pop pl* NE-7
**Venango**—*pop pl* PA-2
Venango Borough—*civil* PA-2
Venango Campus—*school* PA-2
Venango Cem—*cemetery* PA-2
*Venango Christian High School* PA-2
**Venango County**—*pop pl* PA-2
Venango HS—*school* PA-2
Venango Public Use Area—*park* KS-7
**Venango (Township of)**—*pop pl* (3) PA-2
Venango Trail Golf Course—*locale* PA-2
Venango Valley Golf Course—*locale* PA-2
Venard Cem—*cemetery* IN-6
Venard Coll—*school* PA-2
Vena Stuart Sch—*school* TN-4
*Venatchee Creek* WA-9
Venator—*locale* OR-9
Venator Creek—*stream* (2) OR-9
Venator Ranch—*locale* OR-9
Venator Rsvr—*reservoir* OR-9
Venator Rsvr Five—*reservoir* OR-9
Vence Williams Cem—*cemetery* MS-4
Venchoner Creek—*stream* TX-5
Venchy Branch—*stream* LA-4
Vencia Mine—*mine* CA-9
Vencill Cem—*cemetery* VA-3
Vencill Drain—*canal* NV-8
*Venderburgh* NJ-2
Vendetta Gulch—*valley* ID-8
Vendome—*locale* MT-8
**Vendor**—*pop pl* AR-4
Vendovi Island—*island* WA-9
**Vendy Station**—*pop pl* IL-6
Venedito Camp—*locale* NM-5
Venedo Canyon—*valley* CA-9
**Venedocia**—*pop pl* OH-6
**Venedy**—*pop pl* IL-6
**Venedy (sta.)**—*pop pl* IL-6
Venedy Station—*locale* IL-6
**Venedy (Township of)**—*pop pl* IL-6
Venegas Prospects—*mine* AZ-5
Venell Airfield—*airport* OR-9
Venema Creek—*stream* WA-9
Veneman Cem—*cemetery* IN-6
Venerable Sch (abandoned)—*school* MO-7
*Venersbord* WA-9
**Venersborg**—*pop pl* WA-9
Veness Brook—*stream* NY-2
**Veneta**—*pop pl* OR-9
Venetia—*locale* TX-5
**Venetia**—*pop pl* FL-3
**Venetia**—*pop pl* PA-2
Venetia Creek—*stream* AK-9
Venetia Elem Sch—*school* FL-3
Venetia Lookout Tower—*tower* FL-3
Venetian Bay—*lake* FL-3
Venetian Bayou—*bay* NJ-2
Venetian Court Apartments—*hist pl* CA-9
Venetian Garden—*park* FL-3
**Venetian Gardens**—*pop pl* FL-3
Venetian Harbor—*harbor* CT-1
Venetian Islands—*island* FL-3
Venetian Islands—*uninc pl* FL-3
**Venetian Isles**—*pop pl* LA-4
Venetian Isle Shop Ctr—*locale* FL-3
Venetian Lake—*lake* TX-5
Venetian Park—*park* FL-3
Venetian Pool—*hist pl* FL-3
Venetian Pool—*reservoir* FL-3
Venetian Sch—*school* GA-3
**Venetian Village**—*pop pl* IL-6
Venetian Village—*uninc pl* CO-8
Venetia Plaza (Shop Ctr)—*locale* FL-3
**Venetia (RR name Anderson)**—*pop pl* PA-2
**Venetia Terrace**—*pop pl* FL-3
Venetia Terrace Ch—*church* FL-3
Venetia Village (Shop Ctr)—*locale* FL-3
**Venetie**—*pop pl* AK-9
Venetie ANV987—*reserve* AK-9
Venetie Lake—*lake* AK-9
Venetie Landing—*locale* AK-9
Venewitz Creek—*stream* MN-6
Veneys Millpond—*reservoir* GA-3
Venezia—*locale* AZ-5
Venezuela—*post sta* PR-3
Venezuelan Embassy Bldg—*building* DC-2
Vengeance Creek—*stream* NC-3
Vengeance Creek Ch—*church* NC-3
Venia—*locale* VA-3
Veniaminof, Mount—*summit* AK-9
*Venice* (2) OH-6
Venice—*locale* AR-4
Venice—*locale* MO-7
Venice—*other* OH-6
**Venice**—*pop pl* CA-9
**Venice**—*pop pl* FL-3
**Venice**—*pop pl* IL-6
**Venice**—*pop pl* LA-4
**Venice**—*pop pl* NE-7
**Venice**—*pop pl* NY-2
**Venice**—*pop pl* OH-6
**Venice**—*pop pl* PA-2
**Venice**—*pop pl* UT-8
**Venice**—*pop pl* WA-9
Venice Area MS—*school* FL-3
Venice Beach—*beach* (2) CA-9
**Venice Beach**—*pop pl* FL-3
**Venice Beach Park**—*pop pl* FL-3
Venice Branch—*hist pl* CA-9
Venice Canal—*canal* LA-4
Venice Canal—*canal* UT-8
Venice Canal Hist Dist—*hist pl* CA-9
Venice (CCD)—*cens area* FL-3
Venice Cem—*cemetery* OH-6
Venice Cem—*cemetery* UT-8
**Venice Center**—*pop pl* NY-2
Venice Center Cem—*cemetery* NY-2
Venice Cove—*valley* CA-9
*Venice Crossing* IL-6
Venice Cut—*canal* CA-9

**Venice East**—*pop pl* FL-3
Venice Elem Sch—*school* FL-3
Venice Farms—*locale* FL-3
Venice Ferry—*locale* CA-9
Venice Fishing Pier Obstruction Lights—*locale* FL-3
**Venice Gardens**—*pop pl* FL-3
**Venice Groves**—*pop pl* FL-3
**Venice Heights**—*pop pl* OH-6
Venice Hills—*other* CA-9
Venice (historical)—*locale* KS-7
Venice Hosp—*hospital* FL-3
Venice HS—*school* CA-9
Venice Inlet—*channel* FL-3
Venice Island—*island* CA-9
Venice King Sch—*school* CA-9
Venice Lagoon—*gut* NJ-2
Venice Memorial Gardens—*cemetery* FL-3
Venice Mine—*mine* NM-5
Venice-Nokomis Ch—*church* FL-3
Venice Oil Field—*oilfield* LA-4
**Venice on the Bay**—*pop pl* MD-2
**Venice Park**—*pop pl* NJ-2
Venice Plaza (Shop Ctr)—*locale* FL-3
Venice Reach—*channel* CA-9
Venice Sch—*school* CA-9
Venice Senior HS—*school* FL-3
Venice Shop Ctr—*locale* FL-3
**Venice South**—*pop pl* FL-3
**Venice (Town of)**—*pop pl* NY-2
**Venice (Township of)**—*pop pl* IL-6
**Venice (Township of)**—*pop pl* MI-6
**Venice (Township of)**—*pop pl* OH-6
Venida—*locale* CA-9
**Venier Subdivision**—*pop pl* UT-8
*Venik* FM-9
Venisa Point—*cape* AK-9
Venison Branch—*stream* AL-4
Venison Creek—*stream* MI-6
Venison Creek—*stream* WI-6
Venison Fork—*stream* WV-2
Venisonham Creek—*stream* OH-6
Venison Lake—*lake* WI-6
Venison Mtn—*summit* NY-2
Venison Spring—*spring* WI-6
Venita, Lake—*reservoir* MO-7
*Venita Township* KS-7
**Venlo**—*pop pl* ND-7
Vennacher Needle—*summit* CA-9
Vennard Coll—*school* IA-7
Vennard Drain—*canal* MI-6
Venner—*locale* WA-9
Venner Creek—*stream* OR-9
**Vennie Park (subdivision)**—*pop pl* MS-4
Vennie Tank—*reservoir* AZ-5
Venning Cem—*cemetery* SC-3
Venning Creek—*stream* CA-9
Venning Creek—*stream* MN-6
Venning Creek—*stream* SC-3
Vennink Club—*other* CA-9
Venn Ranch—*locale* MT-8
Vennum Cem—*cemetery* IL-6
Venoah Lake—*lake* MN-6
*Venobles Creek* VA-3
Venola—*locale* CA-9
Venrick Run—*stream* VA-3
Vens Run—*stream* WV-2
Venstrom Lake—*lake* MN-6
**Venta**—*pop pl* CA-9
Venta Mine—*mine* CO-8
*Ventana* AZ-5
**Ventana**—*pop pl* AZ-5
Ventana, La—*arch* CO-8
Ventana Camp—*locale* CA-9
Ventana Canyon—*valley* AZ-5
Ventana Canyon Wash—*stream* AZ-5
Ventana Cave—*cave* AZ-5
Ventana Cave—*hist pl* AZ-5
Ventana Cone—*summit* CA-9
*Ventana Creek* CA-9
Ventana Creek—*stream* CA-9
Ventana Double Cone—*summit* CA-9
*Ventana Double Summit* CA-9
Ventana Mesa—*summit* AZ-5
Ventana Mesa Creek—*stream* CA-9
Ventana Pass—*gap* AZ-5
*Ventana Ranch* AZ-5
Ventanas Creek—*stream* NM-5
Ventana Tank—*reservoir* AZ-5
Ventana Trail—*trail* CA-9
Ventana Well—*well* NM-5
Ventana Windmill—*locale* AZ-5
*Ventano Canyon* AZ-5
Venta Spring—*spring* OR-9
Venter—*locale* VA-3
Venter Bluff—*cliff* MO-7
Ventero—*locale* NM-5
Ventero Creek—*stream* CO-8
Ventero Creek—*stream* NM-5
**Venters**—*pop pl* KY-4
**Venters**—*pop pl* NC-3
**Venters**—*pop pl* SC-3
Venters Branch—*stream* KY-4
Venters Branch—*stream* TN-4
Venters Branch Sch—*school* KY-4
Venters Farm Hist Dist—*hist pl* NC-3
Vent Fork—*stream* WV-2
Ventland PO (historical)—*building* PA-2
Ventlers Chapel (historical)—*church* MS-4
Ventling Cem—*cemetery* MT-8
Ventling Ranch—*locale* (2) SD-7
Ventling Rsvr—*reservoir* SD-7
Vent Mtn—*summit* AK-9
*Ventnor* NJ-2
**Ventnor City**—*pop pl* NJ-2
**Ventnor City (Ventor)**—*pop pl* NJ-2
**Ventnor Heights**—*pop pl* NJ-2
*Ventnor Manor* MI-6
Vento—*locale* KY-4
Vento—*uninc pl* KY-4
**Venton**—*pop pl* MD-2
Ventor Lake—*lake* WI-6
Ventosa—*locale* NV-8
**Ventosa**—*pop pl* VA-3
Ventosa Plantation Airp—*airport* NC-3
*Ventous Branch* TN-4
Vent Pass—*gap* NV-8
Vent Pumping Station—*other* TX-5
Vent Ranch—*locale* ID-8
*Ventrees* KY-4

*Ventrees Creek* ... KY-4
**Ventress**—*pop pl* ... LA-4
Ventress Ch—*church* ... MS-4
Ventress Ditch—*canal* ... IN-6
Ventress Mill (historical)—*locale* ... AL-4
Ventress Pond—*reservoir* ... AL-4
Ventris Hollow—*valley* ... AR-4
Ventris Public Use Area—*park* ... AR-4
Ventucopa—*locale* ... CA-9
Ven-Tu Park—*park* ... CA-9
Ventura—*locale* ... TX-5
Ventura—*locale* ... PR-3
**Ventura**—*pop pl* ... CA-9
**Ventura**—*pop pl* ... IA-7
Ventura Canyon Canal—*canal* ... CA-9
Ventura (CCD)—*cens area* ... CA-9
Ventura Cem—*cemetery* ... MI-6
Ventura Ch—*church* ... MI-6
Ventura Coll—*school* ... CA-9
*Ventura (corporate name San Buenaventura)* ... CA-9
**Ventura (County)**—*pop pl* ... CA-9
Ventura County Courthouse—*hist pl* ... CA-9
*Ventura County Small Craft Harbor* ... CA-9
Ventura Cove—*cape* ... CA-9
Ventura Creek—*stream* ... AK-9
Ventura Esperero Trail Twenty-five—*trail* ... AZ-5
Ventura Gulch—*valley* ... MT-8
Ventura Harbor—*harbor* ... CA-9
**Ventura Heights**—*pop pl* ... IA-7
Ventura Junction—*uninc pl* ... CA-9
Ventura Junior Coll—*school* ... CA-9
Ventura Keys—*harbor* ... CA-9
*Ventura Marina* ... CA-9
Ventura Marsh State Game Mngmt Area—*park* ... IA-7
Ventura Municipal Golf Course—*other* ... CA-9
Ventura Park Sch—*school* ... OR-9
Ventura Point—*cape* ... CA-9
Ventura River—*stream* ... CA-9
Ventura Rocks—*island* ... CA-9
**Ventura (San Buenaventura)**—*pop pl* ... CA-9
Ventura Sch—*school* ... CA-9
Ventura Sch for Girls—*school* ... CA-9
Ventura Street Sch—*school* ... CA-9
Ventura Tank—*reservoir* ... TX-5
Ventura Theatre—*hist pl* ... CA-9
Ventura Well—*well* ... TX-5
Venture Brook—*stream* ... ME-1
Venture Grove Ch—*church* ... VA-3
Venture Out (trailer park)—*locale* ... AZ-5
**Venture Out (Trailer Park)**—*pop pl* ... AZ-5
Venture Pond—*lake* ... MA-1
*Venturers Pond* ... MA-1
Venture Shaft—*mine* ... CO-8
**Venturetown**—*pop pl* ... PA-2
**Venturia**—*pop pl* ... ND-7
Venturi Lake—*lake* ... AK-9
*Venturo Creek* ... CO-8
Venturoso Park—*park* ... AZ-5
*Venus* ... TN-4
Venus—*locale* ... AR-4
Venus—*locale* ... FL-3
Venus—*locale* ... KY-4
Venus—*locale* ... MO-7
Venus—*locale* ... NE-7
**Venus**—*pop pl* ... NE-7
**Venus**—*pop pl* ... PA-2
**Venus**—*pop pl* ... TX-5
**Venus**—*pop pl* ... WV-2
Venus—*summit* ... OR-9
Venus, Lake—*lake* ... FL-3
Venus, Lake—*lake* ... MN-6
Venus, Mount—*summit* ... WA-9
Venus Basin Trail—*trail* ... WY-8
Venus Branch—*stream* ... KY-4
Venus Branch—*stream* (2) ... VA-3
Venus Cem—*cemetery* ... AR-4
Venus Cem—*cemetery* ... LA-4
Venus Cem—*cemetery* ... PA-2
Venus Ch—*church* ... AR-4
Venus Creek—*stream* ... ID-8
Venus Creek—*stream* ... WY-8
Venus Creek Cabin—*locale* ... WY-8
Venus Gap—*gap* ... NC-3
Venus Hill—*hist pl* ... VI-3
Venus Hill—*summit* ... VA-3
Venus Lake—*lake* ... MN-6
Venus Lake—*lake* (2) ... WA-9
Venus Lake—*lake* ... WI-6
Venus Mine—*mine* ... ID-8
Venus Mtn—*summit* ... AR-4
Venus Needle—*pillar* ... NM-5
*Venus Peak* ... OR-9
Venus Post Office (historical)—*building* ... MS-4
Venus Post Office (historical)—*building* ... TN-4
Venus Sch—*school* ... NE-7
Venus Temple—*summit* ... AZ-5
Venus (Township of)—*fmr MCD* ... AR-4
*Venzant Creek* ... MS-4
**Veo**—*pop pl* ... IA-7
Veo Creek—*stream* ... CO-8
Veo Creek—*stream* ... SD-7
Veo Ditch—*canal* ... CO-8
*Vera* ... SD-7
*Vera* ... WA-9
*Vera* ... MP-9
Vera—*locale* ... KS-7
Vera—*locale* ... MO-7
Vera—*locale* ... WA-9
**Vera**—*pop pl* ... IL-6
**Vera**—*pop pl* ... OK-5
**Vera**—*pop pl* ... TX-5
**Vera**—*pop pl* ... VA-3
Vera, Lake—*lake* ... WY-8
Vera, Lake—*reservoir* ... CA-9
Vera and the Olga—*hist pl* ... IN-6
Vera Bay—*bay* ... AK-9
Vera Ch—*church* ... OK-5
Vera Creek—*stream* ... OR-9
Vera Cruz—*locale* ... PA-2
Vera Cruz—*locale* ... TX-5
**Vera Cruz**—*pop pl* ... IN-6
**Vera Cruz**—*pop pl* ... MO-7
**Vera Cruz**—*pop pl* ... OH-6
**Vera Cruz**—*pop pl* ... PA-2
Vera Cruz Branch—*stream* ... KY-4
Vera Cruz Cem—*cemetery* ... OH-6
Vera Cruz Cem—*cemetery* ... TX-5
Vera Cruz Ch—*church* ... AL-4
Vera Cruz Elem Sch—*school* ... PA-2
Vera Cruz Jasper Pits—*mine* ... PA-2
Vera Cruz Mountains—*other* ... NM-5
Vera Cruz Mtn—*summit* ... NM-5
Vera Cruz Shoal—*bar* ... NC-3
Vera Cruz Spring—*spring* ... NM-5
**Vera Cruz Station**—*pop pl* ... PA-2
**Veradale**—*pop pl* ... WA-9
Veradale (RR name Vera)—*CDP* ... WA-9
Verada Piedra Blanca—*trail* ... PR-3
Veraestau—*hist pl* ... IN-6
Vera (historical)—*locale* ... SD-7
Vera Lake—*lake* ... MN-6
Vera Lake—*lake* ... MT-8
Vera Lake—*lake* ... OR-9
Veraldi JHS—*school* ... NY-2
**Vera Lee Subdivision**—*pop pl* ... UT-8
Veranda House—*hist pl* ... MS-4
**Verano**—*pop pl* ... CA-9
Vera (RR name for Veradale)—*other* ... WA-9
*Vera Slough* ... OR-9
Vera Strawn Oil Field—*oilfield* ... TX-5
**Verba**—*pop pl* ... MS-4
Verba Buena Ranch—*locale* ... AZ-5
Verbank—*locale* ... NY-2
**Verbank Village**—*pop pl* ... NY-2
Verba Post Office (historical)—*building* ... MS-4
Verbeck (historical)—*locale* ... KS-7
Verbeck House—*hist pl* ... NY-2
Verbeck Island—*island* ... PA-2
Verbena—*hist pl* ... AL-4
Verbena—*locale* ... TX-5
Verbena—*locale* ... VA-3
**Verbena**—*pop pl* ... AL-4
Verbena (CCD)—*cens area* ... AL-4
Verbena Ch—*church* (2) ... AL-4
Verbena Division—*civil* ... AL-4
Verbena HS—*school* ... AL-4
Verbena JHS—*school* ... AL-4
*VerBerkmoes Island* ... MI-6
Verbies Branch—*stream* ... AL-4
**Verble**—*pop pl* ... TN-4
Verble Branch—*stream* ... TN-4
Verble Ch—*church* ... TN-4
Verble Hollow—*valley* (2) ... TN-4
Verble Knobs—*summit* ... TN-4
Verble Mtn—*summit* ... TN-4
**Verboort**—*pop pl* ... OR-9
Verbum Dei HS—*school* ... CA-9
Vercher Lake—*swamp* ... LA-4
Verchot Cem—*cemetery* ... AL-4
**Verda**—*pop pl* ... KY-4
**Verda**—*pop pl* ... LA-4
Verda Lookout Tower—*locale* ... LA-4
Verda (New Verda)—*uninc pl* ... LA-4
Verdant—*locale* ... CA-9
Verdant Creek—*stream* ... AK-9
Verdant Island—*island* (2) ... AK-9
Verdant Lake—*lake* ... MI-6
**Verda (P.O.)**—*pop pl* ... LA-4
*Verde* ... AZ-5
Verde—*locale* ... CA-9
Verde—*locale* ... UT-8
**Verde, Canada**—*pop pl* ... TX-5
Verde, Canada —*valley* (5) ... CA-9
Verde, Canon—*valley* ... CO-8
Verde, Mesa—*area* ... CO-8
Verde, Mount—*summit* ... TX-5
Verde, Point—*cape* ... AK-9
Verde Canyon—*valley* ... CA-9
Verde (CCD)—*cens area* ... AZ-5
Verde Cem—*cemetery* ... CO-8
Verde Central Shaft—*mine* ... AZ-5
Verde Combination Shaft—*mine* ... AZ-5
Verde Creek—*stream* ... CO-8
Verde Creek—*stream* ... MT-8
Verde Creek—*stream* (2) ... TX-5
Verde Drain—*canal* ... CA-9
Verde Drain Four—*canal* ... CA-9
Verde Drain One—*canal* ... CA-9
Verde Drain Three—*canal* ... CA-9
Verde Drain Two—*canal* ... CA-9
Verde Drain Two A—*canal* ... CA-9
Verde Drain Two B—*canal* ... CA-9
Verde Drain Two C—*canal* ... CA-9
Verde Drain Two D—*canal* ... CA-9
Verde Elem Sch—*school* ... FL-3
Verde Hot Springs—*spring* ... AZ-5
*Verde Indian Hot Springs* ... AZ-5
**Verdel**—*pop pl* ... NE-7
Verde Lake—*lake* ... CO-8
Verde Lake—*lake* ... OR-9
**Verdella**—*pop pl* ... MO-7
Verdella Ch—*church* ... MO-7
Verdel Sch—*school* ... NE-7
Verde Meadows Park—*park* ... AZ-5
Verde Mine—*mine* ... WY-8
**Verdemont**—*pop pl* ... CA-9
*Verdemonte* ... CA-9
Verdemont Ranch—*locale* ... CA-9
**Verdemont (Verdemont Boys' Ranch)**—*pop pl* ... CA-9
**Verden**—*pop pl* ... OK-5
Verde Oil Field—*other* ... NM-5
Verde Park—*park* ... AZ-5
Verde Pass—*gap* ... TX-5
Verderas Windmill—*locale* ... TX-5
Verde Ravine—*valley* ... CA-9
**Verde Real (subdivision)**—*pop pl* (2) ... AZ-5
Verde Rim—*cliff* ... AZ-5
Verde Rim Trail—*trail* ... AZ-5
*Verde River* ... WY-8
Verde River—*stream* ... AZ-5
Verde River Bridge—*hist pl* ... AZ-5
**Verde River Meadows One (subdivision)**—*pop pl* (2) ... AZ-5
Verde River Sheep Bridge—*hist pl* ... AZ-5
Verde River Trail Number Eleven—*trail* ... AZ-5
**Verdery**—*pop pl* ... SC-3
Verdery Pond—*reservoir* ... NC-3
Verdery Pond Dam—*dam* ... NC-3
Verderys Pond—*reservoir* ... GA-3
Verde Saddle Tank—*reservoir* ... AZ-5
Verde Sch—*school* (2) ... CA-9
Verde School—*locale* ... CO-8
Verde Spring—*spring* ... AZ-5
Verde Tank—*reservoir* ... AZ-5
Verde Vale Sch—*school* ... CA-9
Verde Valley Country Club—*other* ... AZ-5
Verde Valley Lookout—*locale* ... AZ-5
Verde Valley Sch—*school* ... AZ-5
Verde Wash—*stream* ... CA-9
Verdi—*locale* ... MN-6
Verdi—*locale* ... TX-5
Verdi—*locale* ... VA-3
**Verdi**—*pop pl* ... KS-7
**Verdi**—*pop pl* ... NV-8
Verdi Bridge—*bridge* ... KS-7
Verdie—*locale* ... FL-3
Verdier, John Mark, House—*hist pl* ... SC-3
Verdiere Point—*cape* ... FL-3
Verdiersville—*locale* ... VA-3
**Verdigre**—*pop pl* ... NE-7
*Verdigrease River* ... KS-7
Verdigre Creek—*stream* ... NE-7
**Verdigre Township**—*pop pl* ... NE-7
*Verdigris* ... NE-7
Verdigris—*locale* ... OK-5
Verdigris Ch—*church* ... KS-7
Verdigris Ch—*church* ... OK-5
Verdigris Creek—*stream* ... MT-8
Verdigris (historical)—*locale* ... KS-7
*Verdigris River* ... KS-7
Verdigris River—*stream* ... KS-7
Verdigris River—*stream* ... OK-5
Verdigris River Bridge—*hist pl* ... KS-7
**Verdigris Township**—*pop pl* ... KS-7
**Verdigris Township**—*pop pl* (2) ... NE-7
Verdi Lake—*lake* ... NV-8
Verdilla—*locale* ... PA-2
*Verdilla Run* ... PA-2
Verdi Lumber Company Bldg—*hist pl* ... NV-8
Verdin Chapel—*church* ... AL-4
Verdin Creek—*stream* ... AL-4
Verdine, Bayou—*stream* ... LA-4
Verdi Peak—*summit* ... CA-9
Verdi Peak—*summit* ... NV-8
Verdi Range—*range* ... CA-9
Verdi Sch—*school* ... NV-8
**Verdi Sierra Pines**—*pop pl* ... CA-9
Verdi Township—*inact MCD* ... NV-8
**Verdi (Township of)**—*pop pl* ... MN-6
Verdolaga Lake—*lake* ... TX-5
Verdon—*locale* ... VA-3
**Verdon**—*pop pl* ... NE-7
**Verdon**—*pop pl* ... SD-7
Verdon Cem—*cemetery* ... NE-7
Verdon Cem—*cemetery* ... SD-7
Verdon State Rec Area—*park* ... NE-7
**Verdon (Township of)**—*pop pl* ... MN-6
Verdot Cem—*cemetery* ... MO-7
**Verdoy**—*pop pl* ... NY-2
Verdoy Sch—*hist pl* ... NY-2
*Verdrey* ... SC-3
Verdrick Ditch—*canal* ... IN-6
Verdrietege Hook—*cape* ... NY-2
Verdugo Canyon—*valley* (2) ... CA-9
**Verdugo City**—*pop pl* ... CA-9
Verdugo Hills Cem—*cemetery* ... CA-9
Verdugo Hills HS—*school* ... CA-9
Verdugo Mountains—*range* ... CA-9
Verdugo Park—*park* ... AZ-5
Verdugo Park—*park* ... CA-9
Verdugo Potrero—*flat* ... CA-9
Verdugo Recreation Center—*park* (2) ... CA-9
Verdugo Truck Trail—*trail* ... CA-9
Verdugo Viejo—*uninc pl* ... CA-9
Verdugo Wash—*stream* ... CA-9
Verdugo Woodlands—*uninc pl* ... CA-9
Verdugo Woodlands Sch—*school* ... CA-9
**Verdun**—*pop pl* ... LA-4
**Verdun**—*pop pl* ... TN-4
Verdun Creek—*stream* ... MT-8
Verdun Hill—*summit* ... VT-1
Verdun Rock—*pillar* ... OR-9
Verdun (RR Name For Verdunville)—*other* ... WV-2
Verdun Sch—*school* ... IL-6
**Verdunville**—*pop pl* ... LA-4
**Verdunville**—*pop pl* ... WV-2
Verdunville Canal—*canal* ... LA-4
**Verdunville (RR name Verdun)**—*pop pl* ... WV-2
Verdun Way—*trail* ... OR-9
Verdure—*locale* ... OR-9
Verdure—*locale* ... UT-8
Verdure Creek—*stream* ... UT-8
Verdure Point—*cape* ... AK-9
Verdurette Cem—*cemetery* ... NE-7
Verdy Gulch—*valley* ... MT-8
**Vere Cruz**—*pop pl* ... PA-2
Vereda Alcantarilla—*trail* ... PR-3
Vereda Caracol—*trail* ... PR-3
Vereda de las Cotorras—*trail* ... PR-3
Vereda Descanso—*trail* ... PR-3
Vereda Helechal—*trail* ... PR-3
Vereen—*locale* ... FL-3
Vereen Memorial Hosp—*hospital* ... GA-3
Vereen Sch—*school* ... GA-3
**Vereeville**—*pop pl* ... PA-2
**Veremos**—*pop pl* ... PR-3
Verendo Windmill—*locale* ... TX-5
**Verendrye**—*pop pl* ... ND-7
Verendrye Cem—*cemetery* ... ND-7
Verendrye Hill—*summit* ... SD-7
*Veret* ... LA-4
*Verette* ... LA-4
Verf Kill—*stream* ... NY-2
**Verga**—*pop pl* ... NJ-2
Verga Pond—*lake* ... PA-2
**Vergas**—*pop pl* ... MN-6
Vergas Cem—*cemetery* ... MN-6
Verga Sch—*school* ... NJ-2
Vergas Park—*park* ... MN-6
**Vergennes**—*pop pl* ... IL-6
**Vergennes**—*pop pl* ... VT-1
Vergennes Ch—*church* ... MI-6
Vergennes Hist Dist—*hist pl* ... VT-1
**Vergennes (Township of)**—*pop pl* ... IL-6
**Vergennes (Township of)**—*pop pl* ... MI-6
Vergennes Watershed—*lake* ... VT-1
Verges Park—*park* ... NE-7
Verges Ranch—*locale* ... OR-9
Vergil Mound—*summit* ... MO-7
Vergin Arm—*canal* ... IN-6
Verhagen Park—*park* ... WI-6
Verhalen—*locale* ... TX-5
Verhalen Lake—*reservoir* ... TX-5
Verhelle—*locale* ... TX-5
Verhelle Oil Field—*oilfield* ... TX-5
Verhoeff Catchment Dam—*dam* ... CO-8
Verhoeff Dam—*dam* ... CO-8
Verhoeff Ditch—*canal* ... CO-8
Verhoeff Rsvr—*reservoir* ... CO-8
Verhoeffs Big Dam—*dam* ... CO-8
Verhoeffs Little Dam—*dam* ... CO-8
Verhoeff Spring—*spring* ... CO-8
Verhoff Sch (abandoned)—*school* ... MO-7
Verhulst Spring—*spring* ... SD-7
Veribest—*locale* ... GA-3
**Veribest**—*pop pl* ... TX-5
Veritas Sch—*school* ... CA-9
Verkamp Shelter—*hist pl* ... MO-7
Verkeerder Kill—*stream* ... NY-2
Verkeerder Kill Falls—*falls* ... NY-2
Verl Fuller Catfish Ponds Dam—*dam* ... MS-4
**Verlie**—*pop pl* ... AL-4
Verlie Barton Lake One—*reservoir* ... AL-4
Verlie Barton Lake Two—*reservoir* ... AL-4
Verlie Lake—*lake* ... UT-8
Verlinden Ave Sch—*school* ... MI-6
Verlin Phillips Mine (underground)—*mine* ... TN-4
Verlot—*locale* ... WA-9
Verlot Ranger Station-Public Service Center—*hist pl* ... WA-9
Vermejo Creek—*stream* ... NM-5
Vermejo Ditch—*canal* ... NM-5
Vermejo Park—*flat* ... NM-5
Vermejo Park—*locale* ... NM-5
Vermejo Peak—*summit* ... CO-8
Vermejo Peak—*summit* ... NM-5
*Vermejo River* ... CO-8
Vermejo River—*stream* ... NM-5
Vermer Channel—*channel* ... MI-6
Vermetti Pond—*lake* ... NH-1
Vermiculite Mine—*mine* ... NV-8
Vermiculite Mtn—*summit* ... MT-8
Vermilac—*locale* ... MI-6
Vermilac River—*stream* ... MI-6
*Vermilion* ... MN-6
*Vermilion* ... SD-7
**Vermilion**—*pop pl* ... IL-6
**Vermilion**—*pop pl* ... MI-6
**Vermilion**—*pop pl* ... NY-2
**Vermilion**—*pop pl* ... OH-6
Vermilion, Lake—*reservoir* ... IL-6
Vermilion Bay—*bay* ... LA-4
Vermilion Bay Oil and Gas Field—*oilfield* ... LA-4
*Vermilion Bayou* ... LA-4
*Vermilion Bluffs* ... CO-8
Vermilion Cem—*cemetery* ... IL-6
Vermilion Cem—*cemetery* ... NY-2
Vermilion Chapel—*church* ... IL-6
Vermilion Chasm—*valley* ... ID-8
Vermilion Chasm Flow—*lava* ... ID-8
Vermilion Cliffs—*cliff* ... CA-9
Vermilion Cliffs—*cliff* ... UT-8
Vermilion Cliffs Lodge—*locale* ... AZ-5
**Vermilion (County)**—*pop pl* ... IL-6
*Vermilion Creek* ... CO-8
*Vermilion Creek* ... WY-8
Vermilion Creek—*stream* ... ID-8
Vermilion Creek—*stream* (2) ... IL-6
Vermilion Creek—*stream* ... MI-6
Vermilion Dam—*dam* ... MN-6
Vermilion Dam Club—*building* ... MN-6
Vermilion Dam Lookout Tower—*locale* ... MN-6
Vermilion Estate—*hist pl* ... IA-7
Vermilion Forest Camp—*locale* ... OR-9
Vermilion Gorge—*valley* ... MN-6
**Vermilion Grove**—*pop pl* ... IL-6
Vermilion Heights—*CDP* ... IL-6
**Vermilion Heights**—*pop pl* ... IL-6
**Vermilion Hill**—*pop pl* ... PA-2
Vermilion Inn—*hist pl* ... LA-4
Vermilion Institute—*hist pl* ... OH-6
*Vermilion Lake* ... CA-9
*Vermilion Lake* ... MN-6
Vermilion Lake—*lake* ... CA-9
Vermilion Lake—*lake* ... MN-6
Vermilion Lake Cem—*cemetery* ... MN-6
Vermilion Lake (Township of)—*civ div* ... MN-6
*Vermilion Lock* ... LA-4
Vermilion Mine—*mine* ... MT-8
*Vermilion-on-the-Lake* ... OH-6
**Vermilion-on-the-Lake**—*pop pl* ... OH-6
**Vermilion Parish**—*pop pl* ... LA-4
Vermilion Pass—*gap* ... MT-8
Vermilion Peak—*summit* ... CO-8
Vermilion Peak—*summit* ... ID-8
Vermilion Peak—*summit* ... MT-8
Vermilion Ranch—*locale* ... MT-8
*Vermilion Rapids* ... IL-6
*Vermilion River* ... IL-6
*Vermilion River* ... MN-6
*Vermilion River* ... SD-7
Vermilion River—*stream* (2) ... IL-6
Vermilion River—*stream* ... IN-6
Vermilion River—*stream* ... LA-4
Vermilion River—*stream* ... MN-6
Vermilion River—*stream* ... MT-8
Vermilion River—*stream* ... OH-6
*Vermilion River Cutoff* ... LA-4
*Vermilion River Cutoff Channel* ... LA-4
Vermilion Springs—*spring* ... WY-8
Vermilion Town Hall—*hist pl* ... OH-6
Vermilion Township—*fmr MCD* ... IA-7
Vermilion (Township of)—*other* ... IL-6
**Vermilion (Township of)**—*pop pl* ... OH-6
**Vermilionville**—*pop pl* ... IL-6
*Vermillion* ... IL-6
*Vermillion* ... OH-6
**Vermillion**—*pop pl* ... KS-7
**Vermillion**—*pop pl* ... MN-6
**Vermillion**—*pop pl* ... SD-7
**Vermillion**—*pop pl* ... UT-8
**Vermillion Acres (Moble Home Park)**—*pop pl* ... IN-6
Vermillion-Andrew Carnegie Library—*hist pl* ... SD-7
*Vermillion Bay* ... LA-4
Vermillion Bluffs—*cliff* ... CO-8
Vermillion Branch—*stream* ... IN-6
Vermillion Canal—*canal* ... UT-8
Vermillion Canyon—*valley* ... CA-9
Vermillion Castle—*pillar* ... UT-8
Vermillion Castle Campground—*locale* ... UT-8
Vermillion Castle Guard Station—*locale* ... UT-8
Vermillion Cem—*cemetery* ... KS-7
Vermillion Cem—*cemetery* ... OH-6
Vermillion Cem—*cemetery* ... UT-8
Vermillion Ch—*church* ... IN-6
Vermillion Ch—*church* ... OH-6
*Vermillion City* ... KS-7
*Vermillion Cliffs* ... AZ-5
*Vermillion Cliffs* ... CA-9
Vermillion Cliffs—*cliff* ... AZ-5
**Vermillion County**—*pop pl* ... IN-6
*Vermillion Creek* ... KS-7
Vermillion Creek—*stream* (2) ... CO-8
Vermillion Creek—*stream* ... IN-6
Vermillion Creek—*stream* ... KS-7
Vermillion Creek—*stream* ... WY-8
Vermillion Creek Archeol District—*hist pl* ... KS-7
Vermillion Creek Crossing, Oregon Trail—*hist pl* ... KS-7
Vermillion Creek Tributary Stone Arch Bridge—*hist pl* ... KS-7
**Vermillion Dam**—*pop pl* ... MN-6
Vermillion Ditch—*canal* ... WY-8
**Vermillion Estates (Trailer Park)**—*pop pl* ... IL-6
Vermillion Falls—*falls* ... IN-6
Vermillion Flats—*flat* ... SD-7
Vermillion Hist Dist—*hist pl* ... SD-7
Vermillion Hollow—*valley* ... MO-7
*Vermillion Lake* ... MN-6
*Vermillion Lake* ... WI-6
Vermillion Lake—*lake* ... MN-6
Vermillion Lake Ind Res—*reserve* ... MN-6
Vermillion Meetinghouse—*building* ... IN-6
Vermillion Mesa—*summit* ... CO-8
Vermillion Mine—*mine* ... UT-8
*Vermillion River* ... CO-8
*Vermillion River* ... IL-6
*Vermillion River* ... IN-6
*Vermillion River* ... KS-7
*Vermillion River* ... LA-4
*Vermillion River* ... OH-6
*Vermillion River* ... WY-8
Vermillion River—*stream* (2) ... MN-6
Vermillion River—*stream* ... SD-7
Vermillion River—*stream* ... WI-6
Vermillion Slough—*stream* ... MN-6
**Vermillion Township**—*pop pl* ... KS-7
**Vermillion Township**—*pop pl* (2) ... SD-7
Vermillion Township (historical)—*civil* ... SD-7
**Vermillion (Township of)**—*pop pl* ... IL-6
**Vermillion (Township of)**—*pop pl* ... IN-6
**Vermillion (Township of)**—*pop pl* ... MN-6
**Vermillion (Township of)**—*pop pl* ... OH-6
Vermillion Valley Sch—*school* ... KS-7
Vermilon, Lake—*lake* ... MS-4
Vermilyea Ranch—*locale* ... WY-8
*Vermition Peak* ... ID-8
**Vermona**—*pop pl* ... OH-6
*Vermont* ... FL-3
**Vermont**—*pop pl* ... IL-6
**Vermont**—*pop pl* ... IN-6
**Vermont Ave**—*pop pl* ... CA-9
Vermont Ave Sch—*school* ... CA-9
Vermont Ave Sch—*school* ... OH-6
Vermont Bldg—*hist pl* ... MA-1
Vermont Bridge—*bridge* ... VT-1
Vermont Canyon—*valley* ... CA-9
Vermont Cem—*cemetery* ... IL-6
Vermont Cem—*cemetery* ... MI-6
Vermont Ch—*church* ... AL-4
Vermont Ch—*church* ... TN-4
Vermont Ch—*church* ... WV-2
Vermont Ch—*church* ... WI-6
Vermont Coll—*school* ... VT-1
Vermont Creek—*stream* ... AK-9
Vermont Creek—*stream* ... MT-8
Vermont Creek—*stream* ... WI-6
Vermont Dome—*summit* ... AK-9
**Vermont Heights**—*pop pl* ... FL-3
Vermont Hill—*summit* ... NY-2
**Vermont Hills**—*pop pl* ... OR-9
Vermont House and Fenton Grain Elevator—*hist pl* ... MI-6
Vermont Lake—*lake* ... MN-6
Vermont Masonic Hall—*hist pl* ... IL-6
Vermont Park—*park* ... MO-7
Vermont Pass—*gap* ... AK-9
Vermont Research Forest Agriculture Experiment Station—*park* ... VT-1
Vermont Sanatorium—*hospital* ... VT-1
Vermont Sch—*school* ... AL-4
Vermont Sch—*school* ... CA-9
Vermont Square—*park* ... CA-9
Vermont Square Branch—*hist pl* ... CA-9
Vermont State Capitol—*building* ... VT-1
Vermont Statehouse—*hist pl* ... VT-1
Vermont Street Park—*park* ... MS-4
Vermont Thorpe Camp—*locale* ... VT-1
**Vermont (Town of)**—*pop pl* ... WI-6
**Vermont Township**—*pop pl* ... SD-7
**Vermont (Township of)**—*pop pl* ... IL-6
**Vermontville**—*pop pl* ... MI-6
**Vermontville**—*pop pl* ... NY-2
Vermontville Chapel and Acad—*hist pl* ... MI-6
Vermontville (Township of)—*civ div* ... MI-6
Vermont Windmill—*locale* ... TX-5
**Vern**—*pop pl* ... MN-6
**Vern**—*pop pl* ... OK-5
Verna—*locale* ... FL-3
Verna—*locale* ... MS-4
Verna, Lake—*lake* ... CO-8
Verna-Anacacho Oil Field—*oilfield* ... TX-5
Vernacular Frame House—*hist pl* ... DE-2
Vernado Canyon—*valley* ... NM-5
Vernal—*locale* ... CO-8
Vernal—*locale* ... IL-6
Vernal—*locale* ... MS-4
**Vernal**—*pop pl* ... NY-2
**Vernal**—*pop pl* ... UT-8
Vernal Airport—*airport* ... UT-8
Vernal Ch—*church* ... MS-4
*Vernal Chapel Church* ... AL-4
Vernal Christian Ch—*church* ... UT-8
Vernal Corners—*locale* ... NY-2
Vernal Division—*civil* ... UT-8
*Vernal Fall* ... CA-9
Vernal Fall—*falls* ... CA-9
Vernal Golf Course—*other* ... UT-8
Vernal Grove Ch—*church* ... KY-4
Vernalia Plantation (historical)—*locale* ... MS-4
Vernalis—*locale* ... CA-9
*Vernalis Gas Field* ... CA-9
Vernal JHS—*school* ... UT-8
Vernal Lake—*lake* ... WY-8
Vernal Landmark Missionary Baptist Ch—*church* ... UT-8
Vernal Memorial Park (Cemetery)—*cemetery* ... UT-8
*Vernal Mesa* ... CO-8
Vernal Mesa—*summit* ... CO-8
Vernal Mesa Ditch—*canal* ... CO-8
Vernal MS—*school* ... UT-8
Vernal Park—*flat* ... WA-9
Vernal Post Office—*building* ... UT-8
Vernal Sch—*school* ... UT-8
Vernal Sch (historical)—*school* ... MS-4
Vernal Substation—*other* ... UT-8
Vernal Tithing Office—*hist pl* ... UT-8
Vernam Basin—*bay* ... NY-2
Vern Anders Dam—*dam* ... SD-7
Vernant Park Ch—*church* ... AL-4
Verna Pentecostal Ch—*church* ... MS-4
Verna Second Baptist Ch—*church* ... MS-4
Vernatter Branch—*stream* ... WV-2
Vernatter Cem—*cemetery* ... WV-2
Vernay Lake—*reservoir* ... NY-2
*Vern Creek* ... ID-8
**Verndale**—*pop pl* ... MN-6
Vern Dam—*dam* ... WY-8
*Verne* ... KY-4
Verne—*locale* ... KY-4
**Verne**—*pop pl* ... IN-6
**Verne**—*pop pl* ... WY-8
Verne, Lake—*lake* ... GA-3
**Verner**—*pop pl* ... WV-2
Verner Cem—*cemetery* ... IL-6
Verner Cem—*cemetery* ... TX-5
*Verner Elem Sch* ... AL-4
Verner Elem Sch—*school* ... AL-4
Verner Elem Sch—*school* ... PA-2
Verner Ridge—*ridge* ... AR-4
*Verners Branch* ... TN-4
Verner Sch—*school* ... AL-4
**Verner Township**—*pop pl* ... ND-7
Vernes Ch—*church* ... MN-6
Vernetta Hotel—*hist pl* ... AZ-5
*Verney Lake* ... NY-2
Vernezobre Creek—*stream* ... SC-3
Vernfield—*locale* ... PA-2
**Vern G Taylor Subdivision**—*pop pl* ... UT-8
*Vernier* ... KS-7
Vernigor Ditch—*canal* ... IN-6
Verning Cem—*cemetery* ... KS-7
Vern Lake—*lake* ... MN-6
Vernledge—*locale* ... AL-4
Vernledge Baptist Ch—*church* ... AL-4
Vernledge Cem—*cemetery* ... AL-4
Vern Long Dam—*dam* ... SD-7
Vern McKinney Sch—*school* ... OR-9
*Vernon* ... AL-4
*Vernon* ... MD-2
*Vernon* ... OH-6
*Vernon* ... RI-1
Vernon—*hist pl* ... NC-3
Vernon—*locale* ... DE-2
Vernon—*locale* ... GA-3
Vernon—*locale* ... ID-8
Vernon—*locale* ... KS-7
Vernon—*locale* ... KY-4
Vernon—*locale* ... LA-4
Vernon—*locale* ... MD-2
Vernon—*locale* ... MN-6
Vernon—*locale* ... MS-4
Vernon—*locale* ... NV-8
Vernon—*locale* ... OH-6
Vernon—*locale* ... TN-4
Vernon—*locale* (2) ... WV-2
**Vernon**—*pop pl* ... AL-4
**Vernon**—*pop pl* ... AZ-5
**Vernon**—*pop pl* ... CA-9
**Vernon**—*pop pl* ... CO-8
**Vernon**—*pop pl* (2) ... CT-1
**Vernon**—*pop pl* ... FL-3
**Vernon**—*pop pl* ... IL-6
**Vernon**—*pop pl* ... IN-6
**Vernon**—*pop pl* (2) ... IA-7
**Vernon**—*pop pl* ... MI-6
**Vernon**—*pop pl* (2) ... MS-4
**Vernon**—*pop pl* (2) ... NJ-2
**Vernon**—*pop pl* ... NY-2
**Vernon**—*pop pl* ... OH-6
**Vernon**—*pop pl* ... OK-5
**Vernon**—*pop pl* ... PA-2
**Vernon**—*pop pl* ... RI-1
**Vernon**—*pop pl* ... TX-5
**Vernon**—*pop pl* ... UT-8
**Vernon**—*pop pl* ... VT-1
**Vernon**—*pop pl* ... WI-6
Vernon, Edgar, House—*hist pl* ... SD-7
Vernon, Lake—*lake* ... CA-9
**Vernon, Mount**—*pop pl* ... NE-7
Vernon, Mount—*summit* ... AZ-5
Vernon, Mount—*summit* ... CA-9
Vernon, Mount—*summit* ... MT-8
Vernon, Mount—*summit* ... NE-7
Vernon, Mount—*summit* ... OR-9
Vernon Airstrip—*airport* ... UT-8
Vernon Assembly of God Ch—*church* ... MS-4
Vernon Ave Playground—*park* ... WI-6
Vernon Bailey Peak—*summit* ... TX-5
*Vernon Baptist Ch* ... MS-4
Vernon Bottom—*bend* ... KY-4
Vernon Branch—*stream* ... MS-4
Vernon Branch—*stream* ... MO-7
Vernon Branch—*stream* ... NC-3
Vernon Brook—*stream* ... IN-6
**Vernonburg**—*pop pl* ... GA-3
Vernon (CCD)—*cens area* ... AL-4
Vernon (CCD)—*cens area* ... FL-3
Vernon (CCD)—*cens area* ... TX-5
*Vernon Cem* ... TN-4
Vernon Cem—*cemetery* (2) ... AL-4
Vernon Cem—*cemetery* ... AZ-5
Vernon Cem—*cemetery* ... GA-3
Vernon Cem—*cemetery* (2) ... IL-6
Vernon Cem—*cemetery* ... IN-6
Vernon Cem—*cemetery* ... KY-4
Vernon Cem—*cemetery* ... LA-4
Vernon Cem—*cemetery* (2) ... MS-4
Vernon Cem—*cemetery* ... MO-7
Vernon Cem—*cemetery* ... NE-7
Vernon Cem—*cemetery* (4) ... OH-6

Vernon Cem—*cemetery* (2) ... OK-5
Vernon Cem—*cemetery* (4) ... TN-4
Vernon Cem—*cemetery* ... UT-8
Vernon Cem—*cemetery* ... WI-6
**Vernon Center**—*pop pl* ... CT-1
**Vernon Center**—*pop pl* ... MN-6
**Vernon Center**—*pop pl* ... NY-2
Vernon Center Cem—*cemetery* ... MN-6
Vernon Center Green Hist Dist—*hist pl* ... NY-2
Vernon Center JHS—*school* ... CT-1
Vernon Center (Township of)—*civ div* ... MN-6
Vernon Ch—*church* ... AL-4
Vernon Ch—*church* ... GA-3
Vernon Ch—*church* ... IA-7
Vernon Ch—*church* ... KY-4
Vernon Ch—*church* ... MS-4
Vernon Ch—*church* ... NC-3
Vernon Ch—*church* ... WV-2
Vernon Ch—*church* (2) ... WI-6
Vernon Chapel—*church* ... AL-4
Vernon Chapel—*church* ... AR-4
Vernon Chapel—*church* ... TN-4
Vernon Ch (historical)—*church* ... MO-7
*Vernon Ch of the Brethern* ... TN-4
**Vernon City**—*pop pl* ... MI-6
Vernon City Sch—*school* ... CA-9
Vernon Consolidated Sch—*school* ... AL-4
Vernon Corner Sch—*school* ... TN-4
*Vernon County* ... TN-4
Vernon County—*civil* ... MO-7
**Vernon (County)**—*pop pl* ... MO-7
**Vernon (County)**—*pop pl* ... WI-6
Vernon County Courthouse—*hist pl* ... WI-6
Vernon County Jail, Sheriff's House and Office—*hist pl* ... MO-7
Vernon Cove—*valley* ... AL-4
*Vernon Creek* ... TN-4
Vernon Creek—*stream* ... AZ-5
Vernon Creek—*stream* ... NC-3
Vernon Creek—*stream* ... TN-4
Vernon Creek—*stream* ... UT-8
Vernon Cumberland Presbyterian Ch (historical)—*church* ... MS-4
**Vernondale**—*pop pl* ... PA-2
Vernondale Elem Sch—*school* ... PA-2
Vernon Dam—*dam* ... NH-1
Vernon Dam—*dam* ... UT-8
Vernon Dam—*dam* ... VT-1
Vernon Division—*civil* ... AL-4
Vernon Downs—*other* ... NY-2
*Vernon Elementary School* ... IN-6
Vernon Fork—*stream* ... IN-6
Vernon Furnace (historical)—*locale* ... TN-4
Vernon Furnace Post Office (historical)—*building* ... TN-4
**Vernon (Gemmills)**—*pop pl* ... MD-2
Vernon Grove Cem—*cemetery* ... MA-1
Vernon Grove Ch—*church* ... GA-3
*Vernon Heights* ... OH-6
**Vernon Heights**—*pop pl* ... TN-4
Vernon Hill—*locale* ... VA-3
Vernon Hill Ch—*church* ... NC-3
**Vernon Hills**—*pop pl* ... IL-6
Vernon Hills—*range* ... UT-8
Vernon Hills Country Club—*other* ... NY-2
**Vernon Hill (subdivision)**—*pop pl* ... MA-1
Vernon Hist Dist—*hist pl* ... IN-6
Vernon (historical)—*locale* ... SD-7
**Vernon (historical)**—*pop pl* ... OR-9
Vernon House—*hist pl* ... RI-1
Vernon Howell Lake Dam—*dam* ... MS-4
**Vernonia**—*pop pl* ... OR-9
Vernonia Airfield—*airport* ... OR-9
Vernonia (CCD)—*cens area* ... OR-9
Vernonia Cem—*cemetery* ... OR-9
Vernonia Grange—*locale* ... OR-9
Vernonia Lake—*reservoir* ... OR-9
Vernonia Log Pond Dike—*dam* ... OR-9
*Vernonia Pond* ... OR-9
Vernon JHS—*school* ... CA-9
Vernon JHS—*school* ... IA-7
*Vernon Junction* ... WI-6
**Vernon Junction**—*pop pl* ... OH-6
Vernon Lake—*lake* ... ID-8
Vernon Lake—*lake* ... MN-6
Vernon Lake—*lake* ... MT-8
Vernon Lake—*lake* ... TX-5
Vernon Lake—*reservoir* ... LA-4
Vernon Lookout Tower—*locale* ... AL-4
Vernon Lookout Tower—*locale* (2) ... LA-4
Vernon McDonnell Pond Dam—*dam* ... MS-4
Vernon Methodist Ch—*church* ... MS-4
Vernon Mill Pond—*lake* ... MS-4
Vernon Mills—*locale* ... VA-3
Vernon Mine—*mine* ... CO-8
**Vernon (Mount Vernon)**—*pop pl* ... IN-6
*Vernon Municipal Airport* ... UT-8
Vernon Oil Field—*oilfield* ... KS-7
Vernon Oil Field—*oilfield* ... MS-4
**Vernon Parish**—*pop pl* ... LA-4
Vernon Parish Courthouse—*hist pl* ... LA-4
Vernon Park—*park* ... IL-6
Vernon Park—*park* ... PA-2
Vernon Park—*park* ... WA-9
**Vernon Park**—*pop pl* ... NY-2
Vernon Payne Lake—*reservoir* ... IN-6
Vernon Payne Lake Dam—*dam* ... IN-6
Vernon Place—*hist pl* ... NC-3
Vernon Post Office—*building* ... AL-4
Vernon Post Office, Mount—*building* ... TN-4
Vernon Post Office (historical)—*building* ... MS-4
Vernon Post Office (historical)—*building* ... TN-4
Vernon Prairie Cem—*cemetery* ... IA-7
Vernon Ridge—*ridge* ... IN-6
Vernon Ridge—*ridge* ... KY-4
Vernon River—*stream* ... GA-3
Vernon Road Hist Dist—*hist pl* ... GA-3
Vernon Rock, Mount—*bar* ... NC-3
Vernon-Rockville—*post sta* ... CT-1
Vernon Rsvr—*reservoir* ... UT-8
Vernon Run—*stream* ... PA-2
Vernon Sch—*school* ... CT-1
Vernon Sch—*school* ... FL-3
Vernon Sch—*school* ... IL-6
Vernon Sch—*school* ... IN-6
Vernon Sch—*school* ... IA-7
Vernon Sch—*school* ... KS-7
Vernon Sch—*school* ... LA-4
Vernon Sch—*school* ... MO-7
Vernon Sch—*school* ... NY-2
Vernon Sch—*school* ... OH-6
Vernon Sch—*school* ... OK-5
Vernon Sch—*school* (2) ... OR-9
Vernon Sch—*school* ... PA-2
Vernon Sch—*school* ... TX-5
Vernon Sch—*school* ... UT-8
Vernon Sch (historical)—*school* ... MO-7
Vernon School (Abandoned)—*locale* ... OK-5
Vernons Lake—*lake* ... IL-6
Vernon Spring—*spring* ... OR-9
Vernon Springs—*locale* ... IA-7
Vernon Springs Township—*fmr MCD* ... IA-7
**Vernon Square**—*pop pl* ... VA-3
Vernon Square-Columbus Square Hist Dist—*hist pl* ... GA-3
Vernon State Hosp—*hospital* ... TX-5
Vernon Station—*locale* ... WI-6
Vernon Street Sch—*school* ... MA-1
Vernon Tank—*reservoir* ... AZ-5
Vernon Thomas Ranch—*locale* ... CA-9
Vernontown—*locale* ... AL-4
*Vernontown Cemetery* ... AL-4
Vernon Town Hall—*building* ... ND-7
**Vernon (Town of)**—*pop pl* ... NY-2
**Vernon (Town of)**—*pop pl* ... VT-1
**Vernon (Town of)**—*pop pl* ... WI-6
Vernontown Sch (historical)—*school* ... AL-4
Vernon Township—*civil* ... MO-7
Vernon Township—*fmr MCD* (5) ... IA-7
**Vernon Township**—*pop pl* ... KS-7
**Vernon Township**—*pop pl* (2) ... ND-7
**Vernon Township**—*pop pl* (2) ... SD-7
Vernon Township Cem—*cemetery* ... IA-7
Vernon Township Hall—*building* ... SD-7
**Vernon (Township of)**—*pop pl* ... IL-6
**Vernon (Township of)**—*pop pl* (4) ... IN-6
**Vernon (Township of)**—*pop pl* (2) ... MI-6
**Vernon (Township of)**—*pop pl* ... MN-6
**Vernon (Township of)**—*pop pl* ... NJ-2
**Vernon (Township of)**—*pop pl* (4) ... OH-6
**Vernon (Township of)**—*pop pl* ... PA-2
**Vernon Valley**—*pop pl* ... NY-2
Vernon Valley—*valley* ... NJ-2
Vernon Valley Lake—*CDP* ... NJ-2
Vernon Valley Lake—*reservoir* ... NJ-2
**Vernon (Vernon Junction)**—*pop pl* ... OH-6
Vernon View—*locale* ... GA-3
**Vernon View**—*pop pl* ... IA-7
Vernooy Falls—*falls* ... NY-2
Vernooy Falls Trail—*trail* ... NY-2
Vernooy Kill—*stream* ... NY-2
Vernor Lake—*reservoir* ... IL-6
Vernor Playground—*park* ... MI-6
Vernor Sch—*school* ... MI-6
**Vernoy**—*pop pl* ... NJ-2
*Vern Peak* ... ID-8
Vernridge Elem Sch—*school* ... PA-2
*Vern Ridge Sch* ... PA-2
Vern River—*stream* ... MN-6
Vern Steeds Ranch—*locale* ... UT-8
*Vern Steeds Ranch US-M62/Kelton Pass* ... UT-8
Vernum Hollow—*valley* ... MO-7
**Vero Beach**—*pop pl* ... FL-3
Vero Beach Alliance Ch—*church* ... FL-3
Vero Beach (CCD)—*cens area* ... FL-3
Vero Beach Central Plaza (Shop Ctr)—*locale* ... FL-3
Vero Beach Elem Sch—*school* ... FL-3
**Vero Beach Highlands**—*pop pl* ... FL-3
Vero Beach JHS—*school* ... FL-3
Vero Beach SDA Elem Sch—*school* ... FL-3
Vero Beach Senior HS—*school* ... FL-3
Vero Beach South—*CDP* ... FL-3
Vero Christian Ch—*church* ... FL-3
*Vero Creek* ... AL-4
Vero Lake Estates—*locale* ... FL-3
Vero Mall—*locale* ... FL-3
*Verona* (2) ... MI-6
Verona—*hist pl* ... NC-3
Verona—*locale* ... AR-4
Verona—*locale* ... CA-9
Verona—*locale* ... IA-7
Verona—*locale* ... MT-8
Verona—*locale* ... PA-2
Verona—*locale* ... TX-5
Verona—*locale* ... WY-8
**Verona**—*pop pl* ... IL-6
**Verona**—*pop pl* ... IN-6
**Verona**—*pop pl* ... KY-4
**Verona**—*pop pl* ... ME-1
**Verona**—*pop pl* ... MD-2
**Verona**—*pop pl* (3) ... MI-6
**Verona**—*pop pl* ... MS-4
**Verona**—*pop pl* ... MO-7
**Verona**—*pop pl* ... NE-7
**Verona**—*pop pl* ... NJ-2
**Verona**—*pop pl* ... NY-2
**Verona**—*pop pl* ... NC-3
**Verona**—*pop pl* ... ND-7
**Verona**—*pop pl* ... OH-6
**Verona**—*pop pl* ... PA-2
**Verona**—*pop pl* ... TN-4
**Verona**—*pop pl* ... VA-3
**Verona**—*pop pl* ... WI-6
Verona, Lake—*lake* ... FL-3
Verona Apartments—*hist pl* ... MI-6
Verona Baptist Cem—*cemetery* ... NE-7
**Verona Beach**—*pop pl* ... NY-2
Verona Beach State Park—*park* ... NY-2
Verona Borough—*civil* ... PA-2
**Verona Borough (Township of)**—*pop pl* ... NJ-2
Verona Branch—*stream* ... KY-4
Verona Cem—*cemetery* ... MI-6
Verona Cem—*cemetery* ... MN-6
Verona Cem—*cemetery* ... MS-4
Verona Cem—*cemetery* ... NE-7
Verona Cem—*cemetery* ... OH-6
Verona Cem—*cemetery* ... TX-5
Verona Ch—*church* ... MS-4
Verona Ch—*church* ... TX-5
Verona Ch of Christ—*church* ... MS-4
*Verona Christian Church* ... MS-4
Verona Fathers Seminary—*school* ... MI-6
**Verona Heights (subdivision)**—*pop pl* ... MS-4
*Verona Hills* ... MO-7
**Verona Hills**—*pop pl* ... PA-2
Verona Hills Golf Club—*other* ... MI-6
Verona Island—*island* ... ME-1
Verona Lake—*reservoir* ... NJ-2
Verona Lake Dam—*dam* ... NJ-2
**Verona Landing**—*pop pl* ... CA-9
Verona Lookout Tower—*locale* ... MI-6
Verona Methodist Episcopal Church, South—*hist pl* ... TN-4
*Verona Mills* ... MI-6
**Verona Mills**—*pop pl* ... NY-2
Verona Park—*CDP* ... MI-6
Verona Park—*park* ... NJ-2
**Verona Park**—*pop pl* ... ME-1
Verona Post Office (historical)—*building* ... TN-4
Verona Sch—*hist pl* ... VA-3
Verona Sch—*school* ... MS-4
Verona Sch (historical)—*school* ... TN-4
*Verona Siding* ... WY-8
*Verona Station* ... VA-3
**Verona Station**—*pop pl* ... NY-2
Verona Swamp—*swamp* ... NY-2
**Verona (Town of)**—*pop pl* ... ME-1
**Verona (Town of)**—*pop pl* ... NY-2
**Verona (Town of)**—*pop pl* ... WI-6
**Verona Township**—*pop pl* ... NE-7
**Verona (Township of)**—*pop pl* ... MI-6
**Verona (Township of)**—*pop pl* ... MN-6
Verona United Methodist Ch—*church* ... MS-4
Verona United Methodist Ch—*church* ... TN-4
Veronica Springs—*spring* ... CA-9
Vero RR Station—*hist pl* ... FL-3
**Vero Shores**—*pop pl* ... FL-3
**Verplanck**—*pop pl* ... NY-2
Ver Plancke Rsvr—*reservoir* ... WY-8
Ver Plancke Snow Water Ditch—*canal* ... WY-8
Verplanck Point—*cape* ... NY-2
Verplanck Ridge—*ridge* ... NY-2
Verplanck Sch—*school* ... CT-1
Verplanck Sch—*school* ... MI-6
*Verplanck's Point* ... NY-2
Verplank Creek—*stream* ... CA-9
Verplank Ridge—*ridge* ... CA-9
Verplank Saddle—*gap* ... CA-9
*Verracca Creek* ... CO-8
Verrando Windmill—*locale* ... TX-5
Verrazano-Narrows Bridge—*bridge* ... NY-2
Verrendos Artesian Well—*well* ... TX-5
**Verret**—*pop pl* (2) ... LA-4
Verret, Bayou—*gut* ... LA-4
Verret, Bayou—*stream* ... LA-4
Verret, Lake—*lake* ... LA-4
Verret Canal—*canal* ... LA-4
Verret Cem—*cemetery* ... LA-4
*Verret Lake* ... LA-4
Verrill Lake—*lake* ... UT-8
Verrills Ledges—*bench* ... ME-1
Verruga, Canada —*stream* ... CA-9
Versailles—*locale* ... CT-1
Versailles—*locale* ... TN-4
**Versailles**—*pop pl* ... IL-6
**Versailles**—*pop pl* ... IN-6
**Versailles**—*pop pl* ... KY-4
**Versailles**—*pop pl* ... MO-7
**Versailles**—*pop pl* ... NY-2
**Versailles**—*pop pl* ... OH-6
**Versailles**—*pop pl* ... PA-2
Versailles Airp—*airport* ... IN-6
Versailles Borough—*civil* ... PA-2
Versailles (CCD)—*cens area* ... KY-4
Versailles Elem Sch—*school* ... IN-6
Versailles Hollow—*valley* ... MO-7
Versailles Knob—*summit* ... TN-4
Versailles Municipal Airp (historical)—*airport* ... MO-7
*Versailles-on-the-Lake* ... IL-6
Versailles Pond—*lake* ... CT-1
Versailles Sch—*school* ... PA-2
Versailles State Park—*park* ... IN-6
Versailles State Park Dam—*dam* ... IN-6
Versailles Station—*locale* ... CT-1
Versailles Town Hall and Wayne Township House—*hist pl* ... OH-6
**Versailles (Township of)**—*pop pl* ... IL-6
*Versche River* ... MA-1
Verse—*locale* ... WY-8
Versely Number 1 Dam—*dam* ... SD-7
Versely Number 2 Dam—*dam* ... SD-7
Verser Cem—*cemetery* ... AR-4
**Vershire**—*pop pl* ... VT-1
Vershire Center—*locale* ... VT-1
Vershire Heights—*locale* ... VT-1
**Vershire (Town of)**—*pop pl* ... VT-1
Versippi Sch—*school* ... ND-7
Versluis Park—*park* ... MI-6
Versteeg, Mount—*summit* ... CA-9
Verstovia, Mount—*summit* ... AK-9
**Vertagreen**—*pop pl* ... AL-4
**Vertagreen**—*pop pl* ... FL-3
**Vertagreen**—*pop pl* ... MO-7
Vertagreen RR Station—*locale* ... FL-3
Vertain Park—*locale* ... VA-3
**Vertedero**—*pop pl* (2) ... PR-3
Verterans Memorial Sch—*school* ... MA-1
Vertiflite Airp—*airport* ... TN-4
Vert Island—*island* ... AK-9
**Vertland**—*pop pl* ... IN-6
Vertrees—*locale* ... KY-4
Vertrees, Eliza, House—*hist pl* ... KY-4
Vertrees Ch—*church* ... KY-4
Vertrees Creek—*stream* ... KY-4
Vertrees Ditch—*canal* ... IN-6
Vertrees Rsvr—*reservoir* ... CO-8
Vervalen House—*hist pl* ... NJ-2
Vervilla—*locale* ... TN-4
Vervilla Post Office (historical)—*building* ... TN-4
Verville—*hist pl* ... VA-3
Very Inlet—*bay* ... AK-9
Veryl Schroeder 1 Dam—*dam* ... SD-7
Veryl Schroeder 2 Dam—*dam* ... SD-7
*Very Pond* ... MA-1
Very Sudden Pond—*lake* ... MI-6
Verza Canyon—*valley* ... NV-8
Verzuh Ditch—*canal* ... CO-8
Verzuh Young Bafand Ditch—*canal* ... CO-8
Vesa Bluffs—*cliff* ... CA-9
Vesa Creek—*stream* ... CA-9
Vesa Creek Trail—*trail* ... CA-9
**Veseleyville**—*pop pl* ... ND-7
**Veseli**—*pop pl* ... MN-6
Veselik, John Ludwig, House—*hist pl* ... KS-7
Veseth Flat—*flat* ... MT-8
Veseth Ranch—*locale* ... MT-8
Veseth Rsvr—*reservoir* ... MT-8
Vesey, Denmark, House—*hist pl* ... SC-3
Vesey Cem—*cemetery* (2) ... OH-6
Vesey Lake—*lake* ... WI-6
*Vesey Paradise* ... AZ-5
Vesey Park—*park* ... IN-6
Vesey Sch—*school* ... AZ-5
Vesi Cem—*cemetery* ... PA-2
Vesitau Ridge—*ridge* ... AS-9
Vesle Run—*stream* ... PA-2
Vesley Cem—*cemetery* ... TX-5
Vesley Mine—*mine* ... NM-5
**Vesper**—*pop pl* ... KS-7
**Vesper**—*pop pl* ... NY-2
**Vesper**—*pop pl* ... WI-6
Vesper-Buick Auto Company Bldg—*hist pl* ... MO-7
Vesper Cem—*cemetery* ... KS-7
Vesper Cem—*cemetery* (2) ... OH-6
Vesper Creek—*stream* ... MI-6
Vesper Creek—*stream* ... WA-9
Vesper Hill—*summit* ... NY-2
Vesper Hill—*summit* ... VA-3
Vesper Knoll—*summit* ... WV-2
Vesper Lake—*lake* ... MN-6
Vesper Peak—*summit* ... AK-9
Vesper Peak—*summit* ... WA-9
Vesper School (abandoned)—*locale* ... OR-9
Vesper Song Chapel—*church* ... MN-6
Vespers Pond—*lake* ... MA-1
**Vesper Township**—*pop pl* ... KS-7
Vespie Branch—*stream* ... TN-4
Vesrue—*locale* ... TX-5
*Vessel Church* ... AL-4
Vessel Point—*cape* ... AL-4
Vessel Point—*cape* ... MI-6
Vessels Ford—*locale* ... GA-3
Vesser Creek—*stream* ... IA-7
Vessey—*locale* ... TX-5
Vessey, Robert S., House—*hist pl* ... SD-7
Vessey Dam—*dam* ... SD-7
Vessey Lake—*reservoir* ... SD-7
Vessey Sch—*hist pl* ... SD-7
Vessey Springs—*spring* ... WA-9
Vessey Township—*civil* ... SD-7
Vessup Bay—*bay* ... VI-3
Vest—*locale* ... KY-4
Vest, John S., House—*hist pl* ... AR-4
Vesta—*locale* ... GA-3
Vesta—*locale* ... WA-9
**Vesta**—*pop pl* ... AR-4
**Vesta**—*pop pl* ... IN-6
**Vesta**—*pop pl* ... MN-6
**Vesta**—*pop pl* ... NE-7
**Vesta**—*pop pl* ... TN-4
**Vesta**—*pop pl* ... VA-3
Vesta Bay—*bay* ... AK-9
**Vestaburg**—*pop pl* ... MI-6
**Vestaburg**—*pop pl* ... PA-2
Vestaburg Sch—*school* ... MI-6
Vesta Cem—*cemetery* ... NE-7
*Vesta Creek* ... WA-9
Vesta Creek—*stream* ... MN-6
Vesta Creek—*stream* ... WA-9
Vesta Dam—*dam* ... SD-7
Vesta-Enterprise (CCD)—*cens area* ... GA-3
**Vesta Heights**—*pop pl* ... PA-2
Vesta (historical)—*locale* ... ND-7
**Vestal**—*pop pl* ... AR-4
**Vestal**—*pop pl* ... CA-9
**Vestal**—*pop pl* ... NY-2
**Vestal**—*pop pl* ... TN-4
Vestal Branch—*stream* ... AR-4
Vestal Branch—*stream* ... IN-6
Vestal Branch—*stream* ... TX-5
Vestal Butte—*summit* ... OR-9
Vestal Cem—*cemetery* ... IN-6
Vestal Cem—*cemetery* ... TN-4
**Vestal Center**—*pop pl* ... NY-2
Vestal Central Schools—*school* ... NY-2
**Vestal Corner**—*pop pl* ... NY-2
Vestal Creek—*stream* ... NC-3
Vestal Ditch—*canal* ... IN-6
Vestal Flat—*flat* ... CA-9
**Vestal Gardens**—*pop pl* ... NY-2
Vestal Hill—*summit* ... TN-4
Vestal Hill Cem—*cemetery* ... NY-2
Vestal Hills Golf Club—*other* ... NY-2
Vestal Hills Sch—*school* ... NY-2
Vestal Lake—*lake* ... CO-8
Vestal Park—*park* ... AR-4
Vestal Peak—*summit* ... CO-8
Vestal Sch—*school* ... OR-9
Vestal Sch—*school* ... TN-4
Vestal Sch—*school* ... TX-5
*Vestal's Gap* ... VA-3
*Vestals Gap* ... WV-2
Vestal Shoal—*bar* ... FL-3
Vestal Springs—*locale* ... SD-7
Vestals Swamp—*swamp* ... CA-9
**Vestal (Town of)**—*pop pl* ... NY-2
**Vestal-Twin Orchards**—*pop pl* ... NY-2
Vestal United Methodist Ch—*church* ... TN-4
Vesta No 6—*uninc pl* ... PA-2
**Vesta Number Six**—*pop pl* ... PA-2
Vesta Point—*cape* ... AK-9
Vesta Post Office (historical)—*building* ... TN-4
*Vesta Switch* ... TX-5
Vesta Temple—*summit* ... AZ-5
Vesta Town Hall—*building* ... ND-7
Vesta Township—*civ div* ... KS-7
**Vesta Township**—*pop pl* ... ND-7
**Vesta (Township of)**—*pop pl* ... MN-6
Vesta Truck Trail—*trail* ... WA-9
*Vestavia* ... AL-4
Vestavia Country Club—*other* ... AL-4
**Vestavia East (subdivision)**—*pop pl* ... AL-4
*Vestavia Elem Sch* ... AL-4
Vestavia Elem Sch—*school* ... AL-4
**Vestavia Estates (subdivision)**—*pop pl* (2) ... AL-4
**Vestavia Gardens (subdivision)**—*pop pl* ... AL-4
**Vestavia Hills**—*pop pl* ... AL-4
Vestavia Hills HS—*school* ... AL-4
Vestavia Hills Sch—*school* ... AL-4
**Vestavia Hills (subdivision)**—*pop pl* ... AL-4
Vestavia Hills United Methodist Ch—*church* ... AL-4
Vestavia Lake—*reservoir* ... AL-4
Vestavia Lake Dam—*dam* ... AL-4
Vestavia Sch (historical)—*school* ... AL-4
**Vestavia (subdivision)**—*pop pl* ... NC-3
Vest Branch—*stream* ... KY-4
Vest Camp—*locale* ... NM-5
Vest Camp Oil Field—*other* ... NM-5
Vest Cem—*cemetery* ... AR-4
Vest Creek—*stream* ... AL-4
Vest Draw—*valley* ... WY-8
Vester—*locale* ... KY-4
Vester Bridge—*bridge* ... LA-4
Vester Cem—*cemetery* ... IN-6
*Vester Creek* ... KS-7
Vester Creek—*stream* ... OR-9
Vester Creek Meadows—*flat* ... OR-9
Vesthaven—*uninc pl* ... AL-4
Vest Hollow—*valley* ... MO-7
Vestibule Ch—*church* ... NC-3
**Vesticor Subdivision**—*pop pl* ... UT-8
Vest Knob—*summit* ... TN-4
Vest Lake—*lake* ... NM-5
Vest Ranch—*locale* ... WY-8
**Vestry**—*pop pl* ... MS-4
Vestry Post Office (historical)—*building* ... MS-4
Vests—*locale* ... NC-3
Vest Spring Branch—*stream* ... AR-4
**Vests Store**—*pop pl* ... VA-3
Vest Township—*civil* ... MO-7
Vest Wells—*locale* ... NM-5
Vest Windmill—*locale* ... TX-5
*Vesuvious Furnace* ... NC-3
**Vesuvius**—*pop pl* ... OH-6
**Vesuvius**—*pop pl* ... VA-3
Vesuvius, Lake—*reservoir* ... OH-6
Vesuvius, Mount—*summit* ... MT-8
Vesuvius Cem—*cemetery* ... OH-6
Vesuvius Ch—*church* ... VA-3
Vesuvius Furnace—*hist pl* ... NC-3
Vesuvius Furnace—*locale* ... OH-6
Vesuvius (historical)—*locale* ... AL-4
Vesuvius Mine—*mine* ... CO-8
Vesuvius Mine—*mine* ... ID-8
*Vesuvius Point* ... NY-2
Vesuvius Rec Area—*park* ... OH-6
Vesuvius Valley—*valley* ... AK-9
Veta, Mount—*summit* ... AK-9
Veta Bay—*bay* ... AK-9
*Veta Creek* ... CO-8
Veta Creek—*stream* ... AK-9
Veta Creek—*stream* ... WA-9
Veta Grande Mine—*mine* ... NV-8
**Vetal**—*pop pl* ... SD-7
Vetal Sch—*school* ... MI-6
Veta Mad Mine—*mine* ... CO-8
*Veta Mountain* ... CO-8
*Veta Pass* ... CO-8
Veta Pass—*gap* ... CO-8
*veta Peak* ... CO-8
Veta Point—*cape* ... AK-9
Vetch Creek—*stream* ... WA-9
Veteado Camp—*locale* ... NM-5
Veteado Draw—*valley* ... NM-5
Veteado Mtn—*summit* ... NM-5
Vetera—*locale* ... PA-2
*Vetera Dam* ... PA-2
*Veteran* ... KS-7
**Veteran**—*pop pl* ... NY-2
**Veteran**—*pop pl* ... WY-8
**Veteran Heights**—*pop pl* ... CA-9
Veteran Lookout Tower—*tower* ... SD-7
Veteran Memorial Park—*park* ... WI-6
Veteran Pit—*mine* ... NV-8
Veterans Acres Park—*park* ... IL-6
Veterans Administration—*other* ... TN-4
Veterans Administration—*post sta* ... NY-2
Veterans Administration Bldg—*building* ... DC-2
*Veterans Administration Center* ... AZ-5
Veterans Administration Center—*building* ... TN-4
Veterans Administration Center—*hospital* ... MS-4
Veterans Administration Facility—*hospital* ... AR-4
Veterans Administration Facility (V.A. Hospital)—*hospital* ... NY-2
Veterans Administration Facility (Veterans Hospital)—*hospital* ... AL-4
*Veterans Administration Home* ... KS-7
Veterans Administration Hosp—*hospital* ... AZ-5
Veterans Administration Hosp—*hospital* ... CA-9
Veterans Administration Hosp—*hospital* ... FL-3
Veterans Administration Hosp—*hospital* ... KY-4
Veterans Administration Hosp—*hospital* ... LA-4
Veterans Administration Hosp—*hospital* ... MA-1
Veterans Administration Hosp—*hospital* (2) ... MI-6
Veterans' Administration Hosp—*hospital* ... NE-7
Veterans Administration Hosp—*hospital* ... NY-2
Veterans Administration Hosp—*hospital* ... NC-3
Veterans Administration Hosp—*hospital* ... PA-2
Veterans Administration Hosp—*hospital* ... UT-8
Veterans Administration Hosp—*hospital* ... VA-3
Veterans Administration Hosp—*hospital* (2) ... WA-9
Veterans Administration Hosp—*hospital* ... WI-6
*Veterans Administration Hospital* ... NJ-2
*Veterans Administration Hospital* ... TX-5
*Veterans Administration Hospital* ... WY-8
Veterans Administration Hospital—*hospital* ... CO-8
Veterans Administration Hospital—*hospital* ... WA-9
Veterans Administration Hospital—*other* ... LA-4
Veterans Administration Hospital—*uninc pl* ... CA-9
Veterans Administration Hospital (Deshon Gen. Hosp.)—*hospital* ... PA-2
Veterans Administration Hospital Heliport—*airport* ... UT-8
*Veterans Administration Med Ctr* ... PA-2
Veterans Administration Med Ctr—*hist pl* ... LA-4
Veterans Administration Med Ctr Heliport—*airport* ... MO-7
Veterans Administration (RR name Nat. Military Home)—*28hospital* ... OH-6
Veterans Administration (V.A. Center)—*hospital* ... CA-9
Veterans Administration (V.A. Center)—*hospital* ... TX-5
Veterans Administration (V.A. Center Hospital)—*hospital* ... NY-2
Veterans Administration (V.A. Hospital)—*hospital* ... TN-4
Veterans Administration (VA Hospital)—*hospital* ... TX-5
Veterans Annex—*post sta* ... VI-3
Veterans Bureau Hospital—*post sta* ... CA-9
Veterans Camp (historical)—*locale* ... TN-4
Veterans Cem—*cemetery* ... CT-1
Veterans Cem—*cemetery* ... IL-6
Veterans Cem—*cemetery* ... IN-6
Veterans Cem—*cemetery* ... MI-6
Veterans Cem—*cemetery* ... NM-5
Veterans Cem—*cemetery* ... OR-9
Veterans Cottages Hist Dist—*hist pl* ... WI-6
Veterans Creek—*stream* ... OR-9
Veterans Dam—*dam* ... OR-9
Veterans Field—*locale* ... MA-1
Veterans Field—*park* ... MA-1
Veterans Home Cem—*cemetery* ... WA-9
Veterans Home Chapel—*hist pl* ... WI-6
Veterans Home of California Chapel—*hist pl* ... CA-9
Veterans Home (Veterans Home of California)—*uninc pl* ... CA-9
Veterans Hosp—*hospital* ... CA-9
Veterans Hosp—*hospital* ... CO-8
Veterans Hosp—*hospital* ... GA-3
Veterans Hosp—*hospital* ... MO-7
Veterans Hosp—*hospital* ... NE-7
Veterans Hosp—*hospital* ... NM-5
Veterans Hosp—*hospital* ... NY-2
Veterans Hosp—*hospital* ... NC-3
Veterans Hosp—*hospital* ... OH-6
*Veterans Hospital* ... UT-8
Veterans Hospital—*post sta* ... CA-9
Veterans Hospital (Veterans Administration Hospital)—*uninc pl* (2) ... PA-2
Veterans Hosp (V.A. Hospital)—*hospital* ... AL-4
Veterans Hosp (V.A. Hospital)—*hospital* ... PA-2
*Veterans Lake* ... MS-4
Veterans Lake—*reservoir* ... OK-5
Veterans Memorial Auditorium—*building* ... CA-9
*Veterans Memorial Bridge* ... AL-4
*Veterans Memorial Bridge* ... TN-4
Veterans Memorial Bridge—*bridge* ... ME-1
Veterans Memorial Cem—*cemetery* ... CT-1
Veterans Memorial Cem—*cemetery* ... OH-6
Veterans Memorial County Park—*park* ... WI-6
Veterans Memorial County Park Camp—*locale* ... WI-6
Veterans' Memorial Hall—*hist pl* ... NH-1
Veterans Memorial Lake Dam—*dam* ... NJ-2
Veterans Memorial Park—*cemetery* (2) ... CA-9
Veterans Memorial Park—*cemetery* ... CT-1
Veterans Memorial Park—*cemetery* ... MI-6
Veterans Memorial Park—*cemetery* (2) ... NY-2
Veterans Memorial Park—*cemetery* ... PA-2
Veterans Memorial Park—*park* ... AL-4
Veterans Memorial Park—*park* (2) ... CA-9
Veterans Memorial Park—*park* ... CO-8
Veterans Memorial Park—*park* ... CT-1
Veterans Memorial Park—*park* (2) ... FL-3
Veterans Memorial Park—*park* (2) ... IL-6
Veterans Memorial Park—*park* ... IN-6
Veterans Memorial Park—*park* ... IA-7
Veterans Memorial Park—*park* ... KS-7
Veterans Memorial Park—*park* ... MA-1
Veterans Memorial Park—*park* (3) ... MI-6
Veterans Memorial Park—*park* ... MS-4
Veterans Memorial Park—*park* (4) ... NY-2
Veterans Memorial Park—*park* ... NC-3
Veterans Memorial Park—*park* (2) ... PA-2
Veterans Memorial Park—*park* ... WV-2
Veterans Memorial Park—*park* ... WI-6
Veterans Memorial Park And Golf Course—*other* ... WA-9
Veterans Memorial Sch—*school* (2) ... MA-1
Veterans Memorial Sch—*school* ... NV-8
Veterans Memorial Stadium—*locale* ... CA-9
Veterans Of Foreign Wars Lake—*reservoir* ... KS-7
Veterans of Foreign Wars of the United States Bldg—*building* ... DC-2
*Veterans Park* ... NC-3
Veterans Park—*park* (2) ... CA-9
Veterans Park—*park* ... CT-1
Veterans Park—*park* ... FL-3
Veterans Park—*park* (2) ... IL-6
Veterans Park—*park* ... KS-7
Veterans Park—*park* ... LA-4
Veterans Park—*park* ... NY-2
Veterans Park—*park* ... RI-1
Veterans Park—*park* ... TX-5
Veterans Park—*park* ... WV-2
Veterans Park Sch—*school* ... MA-1
Veterans Peak—*summit* ... CA-9
Veteran Square—*locale* ... PA-2
Veterans Rsvr—*reservoir* ... OR-9
Veterans Stadium—*other* ... PA-2
Veterans Trade Sch—*school* ... MD-2
Veterans Village (Oklahoma State University Housing)—*school* ... OK-5
Veterans Vocational Sch—*school* ... AL-4
Veterans Vocational Sch—*school* ... MI-6
Veterans War Memorial Bldg—*building* ... CA-9
**Veteran (Town of)**—*pop pl* ... NY-2
*Veto* ... AL-4
Veto—*locale* ... OH-6
Veto—*locale* ... WV-2
**Veto**—*pop pl* ... AL-4
**Veto**—*pop pl* ... MS-4
Veto, Mount—*summit* ... ME-1
Veto Lake—*reservoir* ... OH-6
Veto Post Office (historical)—*building* ... AL-4
Veto Post Office (historical)—*building* ... MS-4
Vetrans Administration Hosp—*hospital* ... MA-1
Vets Field—*other* ... MN-6
**Vets Row**—*pop pl* ... IL-6
Vettatrin Lake—*lake* ... AK-9
Vettekwi Lake—*lake* ... AK-9
Vetter, George, House—*hist pl* ... SD-7
Vetter Creek—*stream* ... ID-8
Vetter-Kauffman Cem—*cemetery* ... AR-4
Vetter Mtn—*summit* ... CA-9
Vetter Sch—*school* ... NJ-2
Vetters Hill—*summit* ... MO-7
Vetter Slough—*gut* ... IL-6
Vetting Lake—*lake* ... WI-6
Veva Blunt Sch—*school* ... CA-9
Vevay—*locale* ... NM-5
**Vevay**—*pop pl* ... IN-6
Vevay Island—*island* ... KY-4
Vevay Park—*locale* ... IL-6

**Vevay (Township of)**—*pop pl* MI-6
V Everit Macy Park—*park* NY-2
Vexation Hill—*summit* CT-1
Vexation Point—*cape* AK-9
Vex Cave—*cave* PA-2
**Vexit Junction**—*pop pl* PA-2
Vex Post Office (historical)—*building* MS-4
*Vex Station* MS-4
Vey, Joseph, House—*hist pl* OR-9
**Veyo**—*pop pl* UT-8
Veyo Cem—*cemetery* UT-8
Veyo Volcano—*summit* UT-8
Vey Ranch—*locale* OR-9
Vey Ranch—*range* OR-9
Vey Sheep Ranch Airstrip—*airport* OR-9
Vey Spring—*spring* OR-9
V Foreman Ranch—*locale* ND-7
V Fortytwo Spring—*spring* AZ-5
V-F Spring—*spring* AZ-5
VF Tank—*reservoir* AZ-5
VFW Campground—*locale* MO-7
VFW Cem—*cemetery* MT-8
VFW Club—*hist pl* MT-8
VFW Country Club—*other* PA-2
VFW Golf Course—*locale* PA-2
VFW Lake—*lake* TN-4
VFW Lake—*reservoir* TN-4
VFW Lake Dam—*dam* TN-4
VFW Memorial Park—*park* WI-6
V F W Park—*park* IL-6
V F W Park—*park* KY-4
V F W Park—*park* MI-6
VFW Park—*park* MO-7
V Garrett Dam—*dam* SD-7
V Gulch—*valley* CO-8
Vhay Lake—*lake* MI-6
V H Camp—*locale* CO-8
V H Lassen JHS—*school* AZ-5
Vhoins Branch—*stream* TN-4
V H Pasture Rsvr—*reservoir* CO-8
*Vi* FM-9
Via Coeli Monastery—*church* NM-5
**Viacova**—*pop pl* WV-2
Viaduct—*locale* PA-2
**Viaduct**—*pop pl* MD-2
Viaduct Creek—*stream* OR-9
Viaduct Park—*park* CA-9
*Viaduct Station* PA-2
Via Gap—*gap* VA-3
Vial Canal—*canal* LA-4
Vial Knob—*summit* KY-4
**Viall**—*pop pl* KY-4
Viall, Samuel, House—*hist pl* MA-1
Viall Hill—*locale* PA-2
Viall Sch—*school* MT-8
*Vialls Creek Cove* RI-1
Vialpondo Windmill—*locale* NM-5
**Vian**—*pop pl* OK-5
Viana Canyon—*valley* CO-8
Vian (CCD)—*cens area* OK-5
Vian Creek—*stream* MT-8
Vian Creek—*stream* OK-5
Vian Creek Ch—*church* OK-5
Vian Garden of Memories
(Cemetery)—*cemetery* OK-5
Vian Lake—*reservoir* OK-5
Vianna—*locale* KY-4
Vian Ranch—*locale* NE-7
Vians Valley—*valley* NC-3
Vians Valley Ch—*church* NC-3
Viapan Lake—*lake* AK-9
**Viar**—*pop pl* TN-4
Viar Cem—*cemetery* TN-4
Viar Sch (historical)—*school* TN-4
*Via Santee* AZ-5
Via Sch—*school* MO-7
*Viasoh Chin* AZ-5
Viason Chin—*locale* AZ-5
Vias Ranch (historical)—*locale* NV-8
Viatorian Seminary—*school* DC-2
**Vibbard**—*pop pl* MO-7
Viberg Chapel—*church* IN-6
Viberg Lake—*lake* IN-6
Vibika Creek—*stream* ID-8
Vible Cem—*cemetery* WY-8
Vible Rsvr—*reservoir* WY-8
Vibo Lake—*lake* MN-6
Viboras—*locale* TX-5
Viboras, Arroyo De Las—*stream* CA-9
Viboras Oil Field—*oilfield* TX-5
Viboras Pasture—*flat* TX-5
Viboras Well—*well* (2) TX-5
Viboras Windmill—*locale* TX-5
Vibora Windmill—*locale* TX-5
**Viborg**—*pop pl* SD-7
Viborg Interchange—*crossing* SD-7
Viboro, Cerro del—*summit* NM-5
**Viburnum**—*pop pl* MO-7
Viburnum Airp—*airport* MO-7
Viburnum Mine—*mine* MO-7
Vicar Hollow—*valley* VA-3
**Vicario**—*pop pl* PR-3
Vicars—*locale* WV-2
Vicars Cem—*cemetery* VA-3
Vicars Chapel—*church* VA-3
Vicars Island—*island* NY-2
Vicary, Capt. William, House—*hist pl* PA-2
Vicary House—*hist pl* OH-6
Vic Branch—*stream* KY-4
Vicco—*locale* VA-3
**Vicco**—*pop pl* KY-4
Vicee Canyon—*valley* NV-8
Vice Grove Ch—*church* AL-4
Vicente, Lake—*lake* WA-9
Vicente Arroyo—*stream* NM-5
Vicente Baca Windmill—*locale* NM-5
*Vicente Camp* CA-9
Vicente Canyon—*valley* CO-8
Vicente Creek—*stream* CA-9
Vicente Flat—*locale* CA-9
Vicente Park—*park* CA-9
Vicentia Sch—*school* CA-9
*Vicenti Canyon* NV-8
Vicenti Site—*hist pl* NM-5
Vicenti Spring—*spring* NM-5
Vice Pocket—*basin* WY-8
Vice Presidents Island Number Forty-
six—*flat* TN-4
Viceroy Mine—*mine* AZ-5
Vicey—*locale* VA-3
Vichnefski Rock—*island* AK-9
**Vichy**—*pop pl* MO-7
*Vichy Airport* MO-7
Vichy Campground Ch—*church* MO-7
Vichy Lookout Tower—*tower* MO-7
**Vichy Springs**—*pop pl* (2) CA-9
**Vici**—*pop pl* OK-5
*Vicic* IL-6
Vici (CCD)—*cens area* OK-5
Vicie Branch—*stream* AL-4
Vicinity Cem—*cemetery* TX-5
Vick—*locale* AR-4
Vick—*locale* LA-4
Vick—*locale* MI-6
**Vick**—*pop pl* AL-4
**Vick**—*pop pl* TX-5
Vick Branch—*stream* TN-4
Vick Cem—*cemetery* NC-3
Vick Cem—*cemetery* TX-5
Vick Ch—*church* LA-4
Vick Creek—*stream* ID-8
Vick Creek—*stream* WY-8
Vick Creek Cutoff Trail—*trail* WY-8
**Vicker**—*pop pl* VA-3
Vicker Bridge—*bridge* KY-4
**Vicker Heights**—*pop pl* VA-3
Vickerman Hill—*summit* NY-2
Vickerman Sch—*school* WI-6
*Vickers* OH-6
Vickers and Schumacher
Buildings—*hist pl* AL-4
Vickers Bay—*bay* KY-4
Vickers Branch—*stream* GA-3
Vickers Branch—*stream* WV-2
Vickers Canyon—*valley* NM-5
Vickers Cem—*cemetery* FL-3
Vickers Cem—*cemetery* GA-3
Vickers Cem—*cemetery* IL-6
Vickers Cem—*cemetery* LA-4
Vickers Cem—*cemetery* MO-7
Vickers Cem—*cemetery* TX-5
Vickers Cem—*cemetery* VA-3
Vickers Cem—*cemetery* (4) WV-2
*Vickers Cemetery* AL-4
Vickers Ch—*church* GA-3
Vickers Chapel—*church* GA-3
*Vickers Creek* KY-4
Vickers Creek—*stream* AL-4
Vickers Creek—*stream* AR-4
Vickers Creek—*stream* KY-4
Vickers Crossing—*locale* GA-3
Vickers Hill—*summit* AL-4
Vickers Hill Ch—*church* GA-3
Vickers Hollow—*valley* TN-4
Vickers Hollow—*valley* VA-3
Vickers House—*hist pl* LA-4
Vickers Lake Dam—*dam* MS-4
Vicker Springs—*spring* CA-9
Vickers Ranch—*locale* CO-8
Vickers Ridge—*ridge* TN-4
Vickers Sch—*school* KS-7
Vickers Sch—*school* WI-6
Vickers Store (historical)—*locale* AL-4
**Vickers Township**—*pop pl* SD-7
**Vickery**—*pop pl* OH-6
Vickery—*uninc pl* TX-5
Vickery, Capt. David, House—*hist pl* MA-1
Vickery, Mount—*summit* MA-1
Vickery, Richard, House—*hist pl* TX-5
Vickery-Baylies House—*hist pl* MA-1
Vickery Bldg—*hist pl* ME-1
Vickery Brook—*stream* ME-1
Vickery Cem—*cemetery* GA-3
*Vickery Hill* MA-1
Vickery Hollow—*valley* AR-4
Vickery House—*hist pl* GA-3
**Vickery Landing**—*pop pl* MI-6
Vickery Mtn—*summit* MO-7
Vickery Pond—*lake* NH-1
Vickery Sch—*school* IL-6
Vickery Sch—*school* (2) TX-5
Vickerys Corner—*locale* ME-1
Vickery Street Hist Dist—*hist pl* GA-3
**Vickeryville**—*pop pl* MI-6
Vickeryville Cem—*cemetery* MI-6
Vickey Post Office (historical)—*building* AL-4
Vickham Lake—*lake* WI-6
Vick Hill—*summit* IL-6
Vick Hill—*summit* KY-4
Vick Hollow—*valley* TN-4
**Vicki**—*pop pl* KY-4
Vickie Lynn Oil Field—*oilfield* TX-5
**Vickland**—*pop pl* MS-4
Vickland Cem—*cemetery* MS-4
Vickle Ch—*church* TX-5
Vicknair, Bayou—*stream* LA-4
Vickory Canyon—*valley* UT-8
Vickory Creek—*stream* AR-4
Vickory Lake—*reservoir* TX-5
Vickory Mtn—*summit* UT-8
Vick Pond—*swamp* TX-5
Vickrey Ch—*church* NC-3
Vickrey House—*hist pl* TX-5
Vickrey Mtn—*summit* PA-2
Vickrey Spring—*spring* TN-4
Vickroy Hollow—*valley* OH-6
Vickroy Park—*park* CA-9
Vicks Bluffs—*cliff* KY-4
**Vicksboro**—*pop pl* NC-3
Vicks Branch—*stream* KY-4
Vicksburg—*locale* FL-3
Vicksburg—*locale* KY-4
**Vicksburg**—*pop pl* (2) AZ-5
**Vicksburg**—*pop pl* CO-8
**Vicksburg**—*pop pl* IN-6
**Vicksburg**—*pop pl* MI-6
**Vicksburg**—*pop pl* MS-4
**Vicksburg**—*pop pl* (2) PA-2
Vicksburg, Shreveport, and Pacific RR
Depot—*hist pl* LA-4
Vicksburg Canyon—*valley* NV-8
Vicksburg Ch—*church* MO-7
Vicksburg Ch—*church* OK-5
Vicksburg Ch of God in Christ—*church* MS-4
Vicksburg City Hall—*building* MS-4
Vicksburg City Library—*building* MS-4
Vicksburg City Park—*park* MS-4
Vicksburg Country Club—*locale* MS-4
Vicksburg Fire Tower—*tower* FL-3
*Vicksburgh* KS-7
*Vicksburgh* MS-4
Vicksburg Harbor Project—*other* MS-4
*Vicksburg High School* MS-4
*Vicksburg Junction* AZ-5
Vicksburg Junction—*locale* AZ-5
Vicksburg Memorial Stadium—*park* MS-4
*Vicksburg Middle School* MS-4
Vicksburg Mine—*mine* UT-8
Vicksburg Mining Camp—*hist pl* CO-8
Vicksburg Municipal Airp—*airport* MS-4
Vicksburg Municipal
Auditorium—*building* MS-4
Vicksburg Natl Cem—*cemetery* MS-4
Vicksburg Natl Military Park—*hist pl* MS-4
Vicksburg RR Station—*building* AZ-5
Vicksburg Siege Cave—*hist pl* MS-4
Vicksburg (Site)—*locale* NV-8
**Vicksburg Township**—*pop pl* KS-7
Vicks Canyon—*valley* UT-8
Vicks Cem—*cemetery* MS-4
Vick Sch—*school* NC-3
Vicks Chapel—*church* NC-3
Vicks Ditch—*canal* WI-6
Vicks Island—*island* FL-3
Vicks Island—*island* VA-3
Vicks Lake—*lake* WI-6
*Vicks Landing* MS-4
Vicks Peak—*summit* NM-5
Vick Spring—*spring* CO-8
Vick Spring—*spring* TX-5
Vicksville—*locale* OH-6
Vicksville—*locale* VA-3
Vick Township—*civil* SD-7
Vic Lake—*lake* WI-6
Vic Meadow—*flat* WA-9
Vicory Creek—*stream* ID-8
Vi Creek—*stream* AK-9
Vic Rsvr—*reservoir* MT-8
Vics Lake—*lake* ID-8
Vic Swaim Hill—*summit* IN-6
*Vic Swain Hill* IN-6
Victim Island—*island* WA-9
Victim Island State Park—*park* WA-9
*Victor* OH-6
Victor—*fmr MCD* NE-7
Victor—*locale* AR-4
Victor—*locale* FL-3
Victor—*locale* KS-7
Victor—*locale* MS-4
Victor—*locale* MO-7
Victor—*locale* OK-5
Victor—*locale* OR-9
Victor—*locale* (2) TX-5
Victor—*locale* UT-8
Victor—*locale* (2) WA-9
Victor—*locale* WV-2
**Victor**—*pop pl* CA-9
**Victor**—*pop pl* CO-8
**Victor**—*pop pl* ID-8
**Victor**—*pop pl* IL-6
**Victor**—*pop pl* IN-6
**Victor**—*pop pl* IA-7
**Victor**—*pop pl* MT-8
**Victor**—*pop pl* NY-2
**Victor**—*pop pl* PA-2
**Victor**—*pop pl* SD-7
**Victor**—*pop pl* WV-2
Victor, Charles A., House—*hist pl* MN-6
Victor, Lake—*lake* FL-3
Victor, Lake—*lake* WY-8
Victor, Lake—*reservoir* GA-3
Victor, Mount—*summit* WY-8
Victor, Point—*cape* WA-9
Vic-to-Rae Camp—*locale* WI-6
Victora Springs State Park—*park* NE-7
Victor Bend—*bend* CA-9
Victor Canal—*canal* LA-4
Victor Cem—*cemetery* ID-8
Victor Cem—*cemetery* IL-6
Victor Cem—*cemetery* KS-7
Victor Cem—*cemetery* (2) OK-5
Victor Ch—*church* (2) MO-7
Victor Ch—*church* SD-7
Victor Chapel—*church* WV-2
Victor Chapel Cem—*cemetery* IN-6
Victor Cons Mine—*mine* CA-9
Victor Cotton Oil Company
Complex—*hist pl* SC-3
Victor Creek—*stream* AK-9
Victor Creek—*stream* CA-9
Victor Creek—*stream* (2) ID-8
Victor Creek—*stream* MD-2
Victor Crossing—*locale* (2) MT-8
*Victor Crowell Park Lake Dam* NJ-2
Victor Cullen State Hosp—*hospital* MD-2
*Victor Cullen State School* MD-2
Victor Cutoff—*channel* MS-4
Victor Ditch—*canal* CO-8
Victor Downtown Hist Dist—*hist pl* CO-8
**Victor E Hurley Estates
(subdivision)**—*pop pl* DE-2
Victor Falls—*falls* WA-9
Victor Gulch—*valley* AK-9
Victor Gulch—*valley* OR-9
**Victor Haven**—*pop pl* MD-2
Victor Head—*summit* NH-1
Victor Hill Cem—*cemetery* MN-6
Victor Hill Ch—*church* NC-3
Victor (historical)—*locale* NV-8
Victor Hollow—*valley* PA-2
Victor Hotel—*hist pl* CO-8
Victor HS—*school* NY-2
*Victoria* NC-3
*Victoria* OH-6
Victoria—*hist pl* NC-3
Victoria—*locale* KY-4
Victoria—*locale* PA-2
Victoria—*locale* SD-7
Victoria—*locale* TX-5
Victoria—*other* OH-6
**Victoria**—*pop pl* AL-4
**Victoria**—*pop pl* (2) AR-4
**Victoria**—*pop pl* GA-3
**Victoria**—*pop pl* IL-6
**Victoria**—*pop pl* IN-6
**Victoria**—*pop pl* KS-7
**Victoria**—*pop pl* KY-4
**Victoria**—*pop pl* LA-4
**Victoria**—*pop pl* MI-6
**Victoria**—*pop pl* MN-6
**Victoria**—*pop pl* MS-4
**Victoria**—*pop pl* MO-7
**Victoria**—*pop pl* NJ-2
**Victoria**—*pop pl* NY-2
**Victoria**—*pop pl* TN-4
**Victoria**—*pop pl* TX-5
**Victoria**—*pop pl* VA-3
**Victoria**—*pop pl* WV-2
**Victoria**—*pop pl* PR-3
Victoria, Lake—*lake* AL-4
Victoria, Lake—*lake* FL-3
Victoria, Lake—*lake* MN-6
Victoria, Lake—*lake* WA-9
Victoria, Lake—*reservoir* MI-6
Victoria Ave Sch—*school* CA-9
Victoria Ball Park—*park* AL-4
Victoria Barge Canal—*canal* TX-5
Victoria (Barrio)—*fmr MCD* PR-3
Victoria Beach—*beach* CA-9
Victoria Bluffs—*cliff* AR-4
Victoria Blvd Hist Dist—*hist pl* VA-3
Victoria Bryant State Park—*park* GA-3
Victoria Canal—*canal* (2) CA-9
Victoria Canyon—*valley* NM-5
Victoria (CCD)—*cens area* AL-4
Victoria (CCD)—*cens area* TX-5
Victoria Cem—*cemetery* AL-4
Victoria Cem—*cemetery* IL-6
Victoria Cem—*cemetery* IA-7
Victoria Cem—*cemetery* MO-7
*Victoria Ch* AL-4
Victoria Ch—*church* AL-4
Victoria Ch—*church* (2) LA-4
Victoria Ch—*church* PA-2
*Victoria Channel* TX-5
Victoria City Wells—*well* KS-7
Victoria Coll—*school* TX-5
Victoria Colored Sch—*hist pl* TX-5
*Victoria Copper Mines* NV-8
Victoria Country Club—*other* TX-5
**Victoria (County)**—*pop pl* TX-5
Victoria Court—*post sta* CA-9
*Victoria Creek* TX-5
Victoria Creek—*stream* (5) AK-9
Victoria Creek—*stream* MI-6
Victoria Creek—*stream* NE-7
Victoria Creek—*stream* OH-6
Victoria Creek—*stream* SD-7
Victoria Creek—*stream* TX-5
Victoria Creek—*stream* WA-9
Victoria Crossroads—*locale* KY-4
Victoria Dam—*dam* MI-6
Victoria Dam—*dam* SD-7
Victoria Ditch—*canal* (2) WY-8
Victoria Division—*civil* AL-4
Victoria Elem Sch—*school* KS-7
Victoria Furnace—*locale* PA-2
Victoria Golf Course—*other* CA-9
Victoria Grist Windmill—*hist pl* TX-5
Victoria Gulch—*valley* CA-9
Victoria Gulch—*valley* CO-8
Victoria Gulch—*valley* SD-7
Victoria Heights Baptist Ch—*church* MS-4
Victoria Heights Sch—*school* TX-5
Victoria Hill—*summit* CA-9
**Victoria Hills**—*pop pl* VA-3
Victoria (historical)—*locale* MS-4
Victoria (historical)—*locale* NV-8
Victoria (historical)—*locale* SD-7
Victoria Hosp—*hospital* FL-3
Victoria HS—*school* KS-7
Victoria Island—*island* CA-9
Victoria Island—*island* MI-6
Victoria Lake—*lake* (2) CO-8
Victoria Lake—*lake* IL-6
Victoria Lake—*reservoir* VA-3
*Victoria Landing* MS-4
Victoria Landing—*locale* GA-3
**Victoria Meadow Condo**—*pop pl* UT-8
Victoria Mine—*hist pl* AZ-5
Victoria Mine—*mine* (2) AZ-5
Victoria Mine—*mine* (2) CO-8
Victoria Mine—*mine* MT-8
Victoria Mine—*mine* NV-8
Victoria Mine—*mine* NM-5
Victoria Mine (underground)—*mine* TN-4
Victoria Mtn—*summit* AK-9
Victoria Mtn—*summit* MO-7
Victorian Commercial Block—*hist pl* KY-4
**Victorian Condominium**—*pop pl* UT-8
Victorian Corn Cribs—*hist pl* MD-2
Victorian Dover Hist Dist—*hist pl* DE-2
**Victorian Oaks Subdivision**—*pop pl* UT-8
Victoria Northwest Mine—*mine* UT-8
Victorian Village District—*hist pl* TN-4
Victoria Oil Field—*oilfield* TX-5
Victoria Park—*flat* NM-5
Victoria Park—*park* (2) CA-9
Victoria Park—*park* TN-4
Victoria Park—*park* TX-5
Victoria Park Canyon—*valley* NM-5
Victoria Park Mtn—*summit* NM-5
Victoria Park Shop Ctr—*locale* UT-8
*Victoria Peak* CA-9
*Victoria Peak* TX-5
Victoria Peak—*summit* AZ-5
Victoria Peak—*summit* CA-9
Victoria Place Hist Dist—*hist pl* AZ-5
**Victoria Place Subdivision**—*pop pl* UT-8
Victoria Pond—*reservoir* GA-3
Victoria Post Office (historical)—*building* TN-4
Victoria Pratt Airp—*airport* KS-7
Victoria Quarry—*mine* TN-4
Victoria Rsvr—*reservoir* MI-6
Victoria Sch—*school* (2) CA-9
Victoria Sch—*school* MN-6
Victoria Sch—*school* (2) TN-4
Victoria Sch (historical)—*school* MO-7
Victoria Shaft—*mine* UT-8
Victoria South (CCD)—*cens area* TX-5
*Victorias Point* SD-7
Victoria Springs Cem—*cemetery* NE-7
Victoria Springs State Park—*park* NE-7
Victoria Street—*post sta* PR-3
Victoria Tank—*reservoir* NM-5
Victoria Theatre—*hist pl* PA-2
Victoria Township—*fmr MCD* IA-7
**Victoria Township**—*pop pl* (2) KS-7
**Victoria Township**—*pop pl* NE-7
**Victoria Township**—*pop pl* ND-7
Victoria (Township of)—*fmr MCD* AR-4
**Victoria (Township of)**—*pop pl* IL-6
Victoria Trail—*trail* PA-2
Victoria West (CCD)—*cens area* TX-5
Victoria Winsor Ditch—*canal* WY-8
**Victoria Woods (subdivision)**—*pop pl* DE-2
Victorine Canyon—*valley* NV-8
Victorine Crossing—*locale* AZ-5
Victorine Mine—*mine* NV-8
Victorine Tank—*reservoir* AZ-5
Victorino Mesa—*summit* NM-5
Victorino Ranch—*locale* NM-5
Victorino Spring—*spring* NM-5
Victorino Well—*well* NM-5
Victorio Canyon—*valley* NM-5
Victorio Canyon—*valley* TX-5
Victorio Cem—*cemetery* NM-5
Victorio Draw—*valley* NM-5
Victorio Mountains—*other* NM-5
Victorio Peak—*summit* AZ-5
Victorio Peak—*summit* TX-5
Victorio Ranch—*locale* NM-5
Victorious Cross Ch of God in
Christ—*church* KS-7
Victorio Well—*well* NM-5
Victorio Well—*well* TX-5
*Victorio Wells* TX-5
Victor Island—*island* AK-9
Victor Island—*swamp* LA-4
Victor Lake—*lake* AK-9
Victor Lake—*lake* ID-8
Victor Lake—*lake* MN-6
Victor Lake—*lake* OK-5
Victor Lutheran Cem—*cemetery* SD-7
*Victor Lutheran Church* SD-7
*Victor Lutheran Church Cemetery* SD-7
**Victor Mills**—*pop pl* SC-3
Victor Millsaps Hollow—*valley* AR-4
Victor Mills Village—*uninc pl* SC-3
Victor Mine—*mine* (2) AZ-5
Victor Mine—*mine* (2) CA-9
Victor Mine—*mine* (2) OR-9
Victor Mine (underground)—*mine* AL-4
Victor Neck—*cape* MD-2
Victor Park—*park* CA-9
Victor Pasture—*flat* AZ-5
Victor Peak—*summit* ID-8
Victor Point—*cape* MD-2
Victor Point Sch—*school* OR-9
*Victor Rock* OR-9
Victor Rock—*pillar* OR-9
Victor Rsvr—*reservoir* CO-8
*Victor Run* PA-2
*Victors* SD-7
Victors Bayou—*stream* LA-4
Victor Sch—*school* CA-9
Victor Sch—*school* (3) IL-6
Victor Sch—*school* IA-7
Victor Sch—*school* KS-7
Victor Sch—*school* MO-7
Victor Sch—*school* NY-2
Victor Sch (abandoned)—*school* (2) MO-7
Victor Sch (historical)—*school* MO-7
Victor Siding—*locale* MT-8
Victor Slough—*stream* AK-9
Victors Pit—*lake* NM-5
*Victor Spring* AZ-5
Victor Spring—*spring* UT-8
Victor State Wildlife Mngmt Area—*park* MN-6
Victor State Wildlife Mngmt Area—*park* SD-7
Victor Temple—*church* AR-4
**Victor (Town of)**—*pop pl* NY-2
**Victor Township**—*pop pl* KS-7
**Victor Township**—*pop pl* ND-7
**Victor Township**—*pop pl* (2) SD-7
**Victor (Township of)**—*pop pl* IL-6
**Victor (Township of)**—*pop pl* MI-6
**Victor (Township of)**—*pop pl* MN-6
Victor Valley Country Club—*other* CA-9
Victor Valley HS—*school* CA-9
Victor Valley Memorial Park—*park* CA-9
Victor View—*cliff* OR-9
**Victorville**—*pop pl* CA-9
Victorville City Dump—*other* CA-9
*Victory* NY-2
*Victory* PA-2
Victory—*locale* GA-3
Victory—*locale* KY-4
Victory—*locale* OK-5
Victory—*locale* TN-4
Victory—*locale* TX-5
Victory—*locale* VT-1
**Victory**—*pop pl* NY-2
**Victory**—*pop pl* PA-2
**Victory**—*pop pl* WI-6
Victory—*uninc pl* (2) NC-3
Victory, Lake—*lake* IL-6
Victory Assembly of God Ch—*church* MS-4
*Victory Baptist Ch* MS-4
*Victory Baptist Ch* TN-4
Victory Baptist Ch—*church* (2) AL-4
Victory Baptist Ch—*church* (3) FL-3
Victory Baptist Ch—*church* (2) MS-4
Victory Baptist Ch—*church* (2) TN-4
Victory Baptist Christian Sch—*school* FL-3
Victory Bible Baptist Ch—*church* FL-3
Victory Bldg—*hist pl* NE-7
Victory Blvd Sch—*school* CA-9
Victory Branch—*stream* TN-4
Victory Branch—*stream* TX-5
Victory Bridge—*bridge* FL-3
Victory Bridge—*bridge* NJ-2
**Victory Camp**—*pop pl* OH-6
Victory Cem—*cemetery* FL-3
Victory Cem—*cemetery* KS-7
Victory Cem—*cemetery* MI-6
Victory Cem—*cemetery* MS-4
Victory Cem—*cemetery* OK-5
Victory Cem—*cemetery* TN-4
**Victory Center**—*pop pl* WI-6
Victory Center—*post sta* CA-9
**Victory Center Annex**—*pop pl* CA-9
Victory Ch—*church* (2) AL-4
Victory Ch—*church* AR-4
Victory Ch—*church* (6) GA-3
Victory Ch—*church* IL-6
Victory Ch—*church* (2) KY-4
Victory Ch—*church* (2) MI-6
Victory Ch—*church* (6) MS-4
Victory Ch—*church* (6) MO-7
Victory Ch—*church* (8) NC-3
Victory Ch—*church* (2) OH-6
Victory Ch—*church* (2) PA-2
Victory Ch—*church* SC-3
Victory Ch—*church* (5) TN-4
Victory Ch—*church* (4) TX-5
Victory Ch—*church* (2) VA-3
Victory Ch—*church* (6) WV-2
Victory Chapel—*church* AL-4
Victory Chapel—*church* DE-2
Victory Chapel—*church* IN-6
Victory Chapel—*church* KY-4
Victory Chapel—*church* NC-3
Victory Chapel—*church* (2) OH-6
Victory Chapel—*church* VA-3
*Victory Chapel Ch* AL-4
Victory Ch of the Lord Jesus
Christ—*church* MS-4
Victory Christian Acad—*school* AL-4
Victory Christian Acad—*school* FL-3
Victory Christian Acad—*school* MS-4
Victory Christian Fellowship—*church* UT-8
Victory Christian Sch—*school* CA-9
**Victory City**—*pop pl* TX-5
Victory Community Center—*locale* MO-7
Victory Community Hall—*locale* OK-5
**Victory (corporate name for Victory
Mills)**—*pop pl* NY-2
Victory Ditch—*canal* MT-8
Victory Dude Ranch—*locale* CA-9
Victory Elem Sch—*school* IN-6
Victory Field—*locale* (2) MA-1
Victory Field—*park* IN-6
Victory Field—*park* NY-2
*Victory Freewill Baptist Ch* MS-4
**Victory Gardens**—*pop pl* FL-3
**Victory Gardens**—*pop pl* NJ-2
**Victory Gardens**—*pop pl* TX-5
Victory Grange—*locale* CO-8
Victory Grove Camp—*locale* NY-2
Victory Grove Ch—*church* AL-4
Victory Grove Ch—*church* NC-3
**Victory Heights**—*pop pl* GA-3
**Victory Heights**—*pop pl* NY-2
**Victory Heights**—*pop pl* PA-2
**Victory Heights**—*pop pl* WI-6
Victory Heights—*uninc pl* TN-4
Victory Heights Ch—*church* GA-3
Victory Heights Ch—*church* TN-4
Victory Heights Chapel—*church* WI-6
Victory Heights Sch—*school* KY-4
*Victory Hill* PA-2
**Victory Hill**—*pop pl* MA-1
Victory Hill—*summit* OH-6
Victory Hill Cem—*cemetery* VT-1
Victory Hill Ch—*church* TN-4
Victory Hill Oil Field—*oilfield* OK-5
**Victory Hills**—*pop pl* PA-2
Victory 'Hill Sch—*school* (2) NE-7
Victory Hills Country Club—*other* (2) KS-7
**Victory (historical)**—*pop pl* TN-4
Victory Holiness Ch—*church* AL-4
Victory Homes Rec Area—*park* FL-3
Victory HS—*school* WV-2
*Victory Independent Baptist Ch* MS-4
Victory in God Chapel—*church* MO-7
Victory in Jesus Fellowship Ch—*church* FL-3
Victory in Jesus Ministries—*church* FL-3
Victory Joint Sch—*school* PA-2
**Victory Junction**—*pop pl* KS-7
Victory Lake—*lake* AZ-5
Victory Lake—*lake* AR-4
Victory Lake—*lake* NY-2
Victory Lake—*reservoir* GA-3
Victory Lake—*reservoir* MA-1
Victory Lake Dam—*dam* MA-1
**Victory Lakes**—*pop pl* NJ-2
Victory Lakes—*reservoir* NJ-2
Victory Lakes Dam Number One—*dam* NJ-2
Victory Lakes Dam Number Two—*dam* NJ-2
Victory Lodge—*building* GA-3
**Victory Manor**—*pop pl* VA-3
Victory Memorial Hosp—*hospital* IL-6
Victory Memorial Hosp—*hospital* NY-2
Victory Memorial Park—*park* MI-6
Victory Memorial United Methodist
Ch—*church* IN-6
**Victory Mills**—*pop pl* NY-2
*Victory Mills (corporate name Victory)* NY-2
Victory Mine—*mine* CO-8
Victory Mine—*mine* IL-6
Victory Mine—*mine* MT-8
Victory Mine—*mine* NV-8
Victory Mine—*mine* OR-9
Victory Mine—*mine* SD-7
Victory Mine (Inactive)—*mine* CA-9
Victory Mission—*church* NC-3
*Victory Missionary Baptist Ch* MS-4
Victory Missionary Baptist Ch—*church* AL-4
Victory Missionary Baptist Ch—*church* MS-4
Victory Missionary Ch—*church* LA-4
Victory Mission Ch—*church* MO-7
Victory Mission Ch—*church* VA-3
*Victory Mountain* UT-8
Victory Northgate Plaza—*locale* MA-1
Victory Number 1 Prospect Mine—*mine* SD-7
Victory Oil and Gas Field—*oilfield* KS-7
Victory Palms—*locale* CA-9
Victory Park—*park* (3) CA-9
Victory Park—*park* FL-3
Victory Park—*park* IL-6
Victory Park—*park* (2) IA-7
Victory Park—*park* KY-4
Victory Park—*park* LA-4
Victory Park—*park* MA-1
Victory Park—*park* NY-2
Victory Park—*park* OH-6
Victory Park—*park* (2) PA-2
**Victory Park**—*pop pl* NY-2
**Victory Park**—*pop pl* VA-3
Victory Park Sch—*school* CA-9
Victory Park Sch—*school* OH-6
**Victory Park Subdivision**—*pop pl* UT-8
Victory Pass—*gap* CA-9
**Victory Plams**—*pop pl* CA-9
Victory Plaza—*locale* (2) MA-1
Victory Post Office (historical)—*building* TN-4
Victory Ridge—*ridge* WA-9
Victory Ridge—*ridge* WV-2
Victory Ridge—*ridge* WI-6

Village Park—park CA-9
Village Park—park FL-3
Village Park—park (3) NY-2
Village Park—park (2) OH-6
Village Park—park WI-6
Village Park, The—park OK-5
Village Park Bandstand—hist pl WI-6
Village Park Elem Sch—school PA-2
Village Park Hist Dist—hist pl NY-2
Village Park Hist Dist (Boundary Increase)—hist pl NY-2
**Village Park (subdivision)**—pop pl (2) AZ-5
Village Pharmacy—uninc pl LA-4
Village Pines Sch—school FL-3
**Village Pines (subdivision)**—pop pl AL-4
Village Plaza—locale (2) KS-7
Village Plaza, The (Shop Ctr)—locale FL-3
Village Plaza (Shop Ctr)—locale FL-3
Village Plaza Shop Ctr—locale TN-4
Village Point NC-3
Village Point—cape AL-4
Village Point—cape (2) AK-9
Village Point—cape CA-9
Village Point—cape WA-9
Village Pond—lake MA-1
Village Pond—reservoir NH-1
Village Professional Building Condominium—locale UT-8
Villager—post sta FL-3
Village Reefs—bar AK-9
Village Rock—other AK-9
Villager Peak—summit CA-9
Village Run—stream VA-3
Village Sch—school (5) CA-9
Village Sch—school MA-1
Village Sch—school MI-6
Village Sch—school NH-1
Village Sch—school NJ-2
Village Sch—school NY-2
Village Sch—school WV-2
Village School, The—school IN-6
Village Shoal—bar AK-9
Village Shop Ctr—locale AR-4
Village Shop Ctr—locale (2) FL-3
Village Shop Ctr—locale IN-6
Village Shop Ctr—locale MS-4
Village Shop Ctr—locale NC-3
Village Shop Ctr—locale TN-4
Village Shop Ctr, The—locale NC-3
Village Shoppes—locale FL-3
Village Shoppes, The—locale FL-3
Village Shopping Plaza—locale FL-3
Village Shops—locale FL-3
**Village Six**—pop pl HI-9
Village Slough—stream (2) TX-5
Village Spit—bar AK-9
**Village Springs**—pop pl AL-4
Village Springs Cem—cemetery AL-4
Village Springs Ch—church AL-4
Village Square NC-3
Village Square—locale ND-7
Village Square—locale SD-7
Village Square—locale UT-8
**Village Square**—pop pl IL-6
Village Square—school MA-1
Village Square, The—locale KS-7
Village Square at Belleaireast (Shop Ctr)—locale FL-3
Village Square Mall—locale PA-2
**Village Square North (Village North)**—pop pl MD-2
Village Square Plaza (Shop Ctr)—locale FL-3
Village Square Shop Ctr—locale AL-4
Village Square Shop Ctr—locale AZ-5
Village Square (Shop Ctr)—locale (4) FL-3
Village Square Shop Ctr—locale (2) MS-4
Village Square (Shop Ctr)—locale MO-7
Village Square Shop Ctr—locale (2) TN-4
**Village Square (subdivision)**—pop pl MS-4
**Village St. George**—pop pl LA-4
Village Store—hist pl FL-3
Village Stores Shop Ctr—locale MA-1
Village Street Sch—school CT-1
**Village (subdivision), The**—pop pl AL-4
Villa Gesu Convent—church MO-7
**Village Ten**—pop pl HI-9
**Village Thirteen**—pop pl HI-9
**Village Three Condominium**—pop pl UT-8
Village Township—fmr MCD IA-7
Village (Township of)—fmr MCD (2) AR-4
**Village Two**—pop pl HI-9
**Village Two Condo**—pop pl UT-8
Village Two Dam—dam PA-2
Village Two Pond—reservoir PA-2
Village United Methodist Ch of North Lauderdale—church FL-3
Village View—hist pl VA-3
Village View Methodist Episcopal Ch (historical)—church AL-4
Village View Sch—school CA-9
**Village West (subdivision)**—pop pl AL-4
Village Woods JHS—school IN-6
**Village 10**—pop pl HI-9
**Village 2**—pop pl HI-9
**Village 3**—pop pl HI-9
**Village 7**—pop pl HI-9
**Villa Graciela**—pop pl PR-3
Villa Granada Condominium UT-8
**Villa Granade Condominium, The**—pop pl UT-8
**Villa Grande**—pop pl CA-9
**Villa Green**—pop pl PA-2
**Villa Grillasca**—pop pl PR-3
**Villa Grove**—pop pl CO-8
**Villa Grove**—pop pl IL-6
**Villa Grove**—pop pl PA-2
Villa Grove Cem—cemetery CO-8
Villa Grove Junction IL-6
Villa Grove Mine—mine CO-8
Villa Grove Sch—school PA-2
Villa Heights MO-7
Villa Heights—CDP VA-3
**Villa Heights**—pop pl MD-2
**Villa Heights**—pop pl TN-4
**Villa Heights**—pop pl VA-3
Villa Heights Sch—school NC-3
**Villa Heights (subdivision)**—pop pl NC-3
Villa High Park—park KS-7
**Villa Hills**—pop pl IL-6
**Villa Hills**—pop pl KY-4

Villa Hist Dist—hist pl IL-6
Villa Hist Dist (Boundary Increase)—hist pl IL-6
Villa Immaculate—church NY-2
Villa Joseph Marie HS—school PA-2
Villa Julie Junior Coll—school MD-2
Villa Julita—hist pl PR-3
Villa Katherine Park—park IL-6
Villa La Font CO-8
Villa Lamar—hist pl GA-3
Villa Laun—hist pl WI-6
**Villalba**—pop pl PR-3
Villalba Abajo (Barrio)—fmr MCD PR-3
Villalba Arriba (Barrio)—fmr MCD PR-3
Villalba (Municipio)—civil PR-3
Villalba (Pueblo)—fmr MCD PR-3
Villa Lewaro—hist pl NY-2
Villa Loretto Rest Home—building WI-6
Villa Loretto Sch—school NY-2
**Villa Loring**—pop pl VA-3
Villa Louis—hist pl WI-6
Villa Madonna—locale NJ-2
Villa Madonna—locale NM-5
Villa Madonna—school FL-3
Villa Madonna Acad—school KY-4
Villa Madonna School, The—school OH-6
**Villa Mar**—pop pl PR-3
Villa Maria—hist pl MI-6
**Villa Maria**—pop pl MD-2
**Villa Maria**—pop pl PA-2
Villa Maria Acad—school (2) NY-2
Villa Maria Acad—school PA-2
Villa Maria Acad—school VA-3
Villa Maria Academey—school MN-6
Villa Maria Coll—school PA-2
Villa Maria HS—school TX-5
**Villa Maria Infirmary**—pop pl PA-2
Villa Maria Sch—school MI-6
**Villa Marie**—pop pl IL-6
Villa Marie Acad—school PA-2
Villa Marie Claire—locale NJ-2
**Villa Marie Subdivision**—pop pl UT-8
Villa Marillac Hosp—hospital MI-6
**Villamay**—pop pl VA-3
Villa Mercy Hosp—hospital AL-4
**Villa Milagros**—pop pl PR-3
Villa Mira Monte—hist pl CA-9
**Villamont**—pop pl VA-3
**Villa Montaige Condominium**—pop pl UT-8
Villa Montalvo—hist pl CA-9
Villa Montalvo—locale CA-9
**Villa Monterey**—pop pl DE-2
Villa Monterey Golf Course—other AZ-5
**Villa Monte Vista (subdivision)**—pop pl (2) AZ-5
Villa Montezuma—hist pl CA-9
**Villa Monticello**—pop pl MD-2
**Villa Moritz Subdivision**—pop pl UT-8
**Villa Nevares**—pop pl PR-3
Villa North IN-6
Villa North Hist Dist—hist pl IN-6
Villa Nova MS-4
Villanova WV-2
Villa Nova—hist pl NC-3
Villanova—locale IA-7
**Villa Nova**—pop pl MD-2
**Villanova**—pop pl MS-4
**Villa Nova**—pop pl OH-6
**Villanova**—pop pl PA-2
**Villa Nova Condominium**—pop pl UT-8
Villanova Ridge—ridge WV-2
Villa Nova (RR name for Duck)—other WV-2
Villanova Sch—school CA-9
Villanova Station—building PA-2
Villanova Univ—school PA-2
**Villa Novena (subdivision)**—pop pl (2) AZ-5
Villanow—locale GA-3
Villanow (CCD)—cens area GA-3
**Villanueva**—pop pl NM-5
**Villa Nueva**—pop pl TX-5
Villa Nueva—school TX-5
Villanueva (CCD)—cens area NM-5
Villanueva Dam—dam NM-5
Villanueva Northside Ditch—canal NM-5
Villanueva Southside Ditch—canal NM-5
Villanueva State Park—park NM-5
Villa Olivia Country Club—other IL-6
**Villa Palmeras**—pop pl PR-3
Villa Panorama—hist pl MO-7
Villapark NJ-2
Villa Park—park CA-9
**Villa Park**—pop pl CA-9
**Villa Park**—pop pl IL-6
**Villa Park**—pop pl NJ-2
Villa Park Dam—dam CA-9
Villa Park HS—school CA-9
Villa Park JHS—school IL-6
Villa Park Sch—school CA-9
Villa Park Shop Ctr—locale NC-3
**Villa Park Subdivision**—pop pl UT-8
**Villa Perez**—pop pl (2) PR-3
**Villa Prades**—pop pl PR-3
Villa Queen of Peace—church TX-5
Villara Lake WI-6
Villa Ranchaero—CDP SD-7
Villa Ranchero Shop Ctr—locale SD-7
**Villard**—pop pl MN-6
Villard—uninc pl WI-6
Villard, Mount—summit AK-9
Villard, Mount—summit MT-8
Villard Flats Rsvr—reservoir CO-8
Villard Glacier—glacier OR-9
Villard Hall—hist pl OR-9
Villard Houses—hist pl NY-2
Villard Junction—locale WA-9
Villard Lake—lake MN-6
Villard Lake—lake WI-6
Villard Pond—lake WA-9
Villard Ranch—locale (2) CA-9
**Villard Township**—pop pl ND-7
**Villard (Township of)**—pop pl MN-6
Villareal Canyon—valley CO-8
Villareal Cem—cemetery TX-5
**Villareales**—pop pl TX-5
Villa Redeemer Monastery—church IL-6
**Villa Rica**—pop pl GA-3
**Villa Rica**—pop pl PR-3
Villa Rica—uninc pl FL-3
Villa Rica (CCD)—cens area GA-3
Villa Rica HS—school GA-3

Villa Rica RR Station—locale FL-3
Villa Ridge MS-4
**Villa Ridge**—pop pl (2) IL-6
**Villa Ridge**—pop pl MS-4
**Villa Ridge**—pop pl MO-7
**Villa Ridge**—pop pl OR-9
Villa Ridge (Election Precinct)—fmr MCD IL-6
Villa Rivas AZ-5
Villaronga House—hist pl PR-3
Villa Rosa Preschool—school FL-3
Villarreal Artesian Well—well TX-5
Villarreales Banco Number 136—levee TX-5
Villarreo Ranch—locale TX-5
Villars, Bayou—channel LA-4
Villars, Lake—lake LA-4
Villars Chapel—church OH-6
Villars Creek—stream MT-8
Villa Run—stream (2) IN-6
Villas NC-3
Villas—CDP FL-3
Villas—locale IL-6
**Villas**—pop pl NJ-2
**Villas, The**—pop pl VA-3
**Villa Sabine**—pop pl FL-3
Villa Saint Anthony Convent—church MI-6
Villa San Pio X—church NM-5
Villa Santini Plaza (Shop Ctr)—locale FL-3
Villa Sch—school AZ-5
Villase Ch—church NC-3
Villas Elem Sch—school FL-3
Villa Serena Park—park AZ-5
Villa Siesta Retirement Village—locale TX-5
**Villas La Montagne PUB Subdivision**—pop pl UT-8
**Villas of Country Lane Subdivision**—pop pl UT-8
Villas Plaza (Shop Ctr)—locale FL-3
**Villas Plaza (subdivision)**—pop pl (2) AZ-5
Villas Salceda IL-6
Villas Sch—school TX-5
Villas South (Shop Ctr)—locale FL-3
**Villa Subdivision**—pop pl UT-8
Villa Tank—reservoir TX-5
**Villa Tasso**—pop pl FL-3
Villa Teresa Sch—school OK-5
**Villa Trailer Court**—pop pl SD-7
Villa Vaughn—locale ME-1
Villa Verde IL-6
Villa Verde—hist pl CA-9
**Villa Verona**—pop pl CA-9
Villa Victoria Sch—school NJ-2
Villa View Hosp—hospital CA-9
Villa Virginia—hist pl MA-1
**Villa Vista Subdivision**—pop pl UT-8
Villa Vista (trailer park)—locale AZ-5
**Villa Vista (trailer park)**—pop pl AZ-5
Villa Von Baumbach—hist pl WI-6
Villa Walsh—building NJ-2
**Villa West**—pop pl IL-6
Villa Westbrook IL-6
Villa West Shop Ctr—locale KS-7
**Villboro**—pop pl VA-3
Ville, The VT-1
Villegas Park—park CA-9
Villegreen—locale CO-8
Villemont (Township of)—fmr MCD AR-4
Villenova Cem—cemetery NY-2
**Villenova (Town of)**—pop pl NY-2
**Ville Platte**—pop pl LA-4
Ville Platte Oil and Gas Field—oilfield LA-4
Villere, Bayou—gut LA-4
Villers Cem—cemetery WV-2
Ville Run—stream IN-6
**Villiage Meadows (subdivision)**—pop pl AZ-5
Villines Cem—cemetery TN-4
Villines Mill—hist pl AR-4
Villines Swamp—stream VA-3
Villinger—locale CA-9
**Villisca**—pop pl IA-7
Villisca Cem—cemetery IA-7
Villiska IA-7
Villitas Banco Number 24—levee TX-5
Villnave Airp—airport MO-7
Villneauve Lake—lake ND-7
**Villodas**—pop pl PR-3
Villstad Ch—church MN-6
**Villula**—pop pl AL-4
Villum Branch—stream AR-4
Villwock Rsvr—reservoir OR-9
**Vilonia**—pop pl AR-4
Vilonia Cem—cemetery AR-4
Vilonia Ch—church AR-4
Viloxy River MS-4
Vils Ranch—locale CO-8
**Vilula**—pop pl AL-4
Vilula Ch—church GA-3
Vilulah Ch—church (2) GA-3
Vilula Post Office (historical)—building AL-4
Vilula Sch (historical)—school AL-4
Vily TN-4
Vimalkirti Spring OR-9
Vim Sch—school CO-8
Vimville—locale MS-4
Vimville Post Office (historical)—building MS-4
**Vimy**—pop pl WV-2
Vimy Lake—lake MT-8
**Vimy Ridge**—pop pl AR-4
Vimy Ridge—ridge (2) MT-8
Vimy Ridge—ridge WA-9
Vimy Ridge Sch—school OK-5
**Vina**—pop pl AL-4
**Vina**—pop pl CA-9
Vina, Canada De La —valley CA-9
Vina (CCD)—cens area AL-4
Vina Division—civil AL-4
Vina First Baptist Ch—church AL-4
Vina Flat—flat UT-8
Vinagre Wash—stream CA-9
Vina HS—school AL-4
Vinal, Albert, House—hist pl MA-1
Vinal Cove—bay ME-1
Vinal Creek—stream MT-8
**Vinalhaven**—pop pl ME-1
Vinalhaven Galamander, The—hist pl ME-1
**Vinalhaven (Town of)**—pop pl ME-1
Vinal Hill—summit MA-1
Vinal Lake—lake MT-8
Vina Lookout Tower—locale AL-4
Vinal Regional Technical Sch—school CT-1

Vinal Sch—school MA-1
Vinasale—locale AK-9
Vinasale Mtn—summit AK-9
Vinateria Tank—reservoir TX-5
Vinatero Well—well TX-5
Vinau FM-9
Vina United Methodist Ch—church AL-4
**Vina Vista**—pop pl CA-9
**Vina Vista**—pop pl NC-3
Vina Windmill—locale TX-5
Vince Bayou—stream TX-5
Vince Bluff—cliff AR-4
Vince Cem—cemetery MO-7
Vince Island—island MI-6
Vince Knob—summit MO-7
**Vincennes**—pop pl IN-6
**Vincennes**—pop pl IA-7
Vincennes, Mount—summit AK-9
Vincennes City Ditch IN-6
Vincennes Common—park IN-6
Vincennes Creek CO-8
Vincennes Executive Inn Airp—airport IN-6
Vincennes Hist Dist—hist pl IN-6
Vincennes Prairie—flat IN-6
Vincennes Run—stream IN-6
**Vincennes (Township of)**—pop pl IN-6
Vincennes Trail—trail IN-6
Vincennes Univ—school IN-6
Vincent AL-4
Vincent—locale AL-4
Vincent—locale CA-9
Vincent—locale GA-3
Vincent—locale KS-7
Vincent—locale KY-4
Vincent—locale MT-8
Vincent—locale OR-9
**Vincent**—pop pl AL-4
**Vincent**—pop pl AR-4
**Vincent**—pop pl IA-7
**Vincent**—pop pl LA-4
**Vincent**—pop pl NY-2
**Vincent**—pop pl (2) OH-6
**Vincent**—pop pl OR-9
**Vincent**—pop pl TX-5
Vincent, Bayou—stream LA-4
Vincent, James, House—hist pl WI-6
Vincent, Lake—lake NJ-2
Vincent, Point—cape AK-9
Vincent Branch—stream (2) WV-2
Vincent Brook—stream MA-1
Vincent Brook—stream NY-2
Vincent Cabin—locale WY-8
Vincent Canal—canal LA-4
Vincent (CCD)—cens area AL-4
Vincent Cem—cemetery (2) AL-4
Vincent Cem—cemetery KS-7
Vincent Cem—cemetery KY-4
Vincent Cem—cemetery (2) MO-7
Vincent Cem—cemetery NJ-2
Vincent Cem—cemetery (4) TN-4
Vincent Cem—cemetery (3) TX-5
Vincent Cem—cemetery VA-3
Vincent Cem—cemetery (2) WV-2
Vincent Ch—church GA-3
Vincent Ch—church IN-6
Vincent Ch—church KS-7
Vincent Ch—church KY-4
Vincent Ch—church NJ-2
Vincent Ch—church (2) PA-2
Vincent Ch—church TN-4
Vincent Chapel—church AL-4
Vincent Community Club—building WA-9
Vincent Corner—locale VA-3
Vincent Corners—locale NY-2
Vincent Creek—stream CA-9
Vincent Creek—stream LA-4
Vincent Creek—stream (2) MI-6
Vincent Creek—stream (3) OR-9
Vincent Creek—stream TX-5
Vincent Creek—stream WA-9
Vincent Creek Guard Station—locale OR-9
Vincent Dam—dam PA-2
Vincent Ditch—canal MT-8
Vincent Division—civil AL-4
Vincent Draw—valley WY-8
Vincente Flat CA-9
Vincent Elementary School PA-2
Vincent Elem Sch—school AL-4
Vincent Fire Station—locale CA-9
Vincent Forge Mansion—hist pl PA-2
Vincent Gap—gap CA-9
Vincent Grove Cem—cemetery TN-4
Vincent Grove Ch—church TN-4
Vincent Grove Ch—church VA-3
Vincent Grove Sch—school TN-4
Vincent Gulch—valley CA-9
**Vincent (Heistand)**—pop pl PA-2
Vincent (historical)—locale SD-7
Vincent House—hist pl IA-7
Vincent HS—school AL-4
Vincent HS—school PA-2
Vincentian HS—school PA-2
Vincentian Institute—school NY-2
Vincenti Canyon—valley NV-8
Vincent Island AL-4
Vincent Island—island CT-1
Vincent Island—island LA-4
Vincent Lake—lake (2) MI-6
Vincent Lake—lake (2) WI-6
Vincent Landing—locale CA-9
Vincent Landing—locale LA-4
Vincent Meadow—flat CA-9
Vincent Memorial Chapel—church PA-2
Vincent MS—school AL-4
**Vincentown**—pop pl NJ-2
Vincentown Hist Dist—hist pl NJ-2
Vincentown Mill Dam—dam NJ-2
Vincentown Millpond—reservoir NJ-2
Vincent Pallotti Hosp—hospital WV-2
**Vincent Park**—pop pl LA-4
Vincent Point—cape WI-6
Vincent Pond—reservoir CT-1
Vincent Post Office (historical)—building PA-2
Vincent Ranch—locale AZ-5
Vincent Ranch—locale (2) CA-9
Vincent Ranch—locale OR-9
Vincent Reef—bar AK-9
Vincent Rsvr No. 1—reservoir CO-8
Vincent Rsvr No. 2—reservoir CO-8
Vincent Run—stream IL-6

Vincent Run—stream WV-2
Vincents Camp—locale AK-9
Vincents Causeway DE-2
Vincent Sch—school AL-4
Vincent Sch—school (3) CA-9
Vincent Sch—school CT-1
Vincent Sch—school KS-7
Vincent Sch—school KY-4
Vincent Sch—school MI-6
Vincent Sch—school PA-2
Vincent Sch—school WI-6
Vincents Crossroads AL-4
Vincents Island AL-4
Vincents Landing (historical)—locale TN-4
Vincent Spring—spring AL-4
Vincent State For—forest NH-1
Vincents Town NJ-2
Vincent Street Hist Dist—hist pl SC-3
Vincent Street Park—park TX-5
Vincent Thomas Bridge (Toll)—bridge CA-9
Vincenttown NJ-2
Vincent Townships Consolidated Sch—school PA-2
Vincent Tram Trail—trail PA-2
Vincent United Methodist Ch—church MS-4
Vincent Valley—basin NE-7
Vince Ridge—ridge VA-3
Vince Tank—reservoir NM-5
Vince-Tynes Cem—cemetery MS-4
Vincey Branch—stream GA-3
Vincit—locale MO-7
**Vinco**—pop pl OK-5
**Vinco**—pop pl PA-2
Vinco PO (historical)—building PA-2
Vindex MD-2
Vindicator Canyon—valley UT-8
Vindicator Mine—mine CO-8
Vindicator Mine—mine NV-8
Vindicator Mine—mine NM-5
Vindicator Mtn—summit NV-8
Vindon FM-9
Vine KS-7
Vine—locale KY-4
Vine—locale VA-3
**Vine**—pop pl IN-6
**Vine**—pop pl MI-6
**Vine**—pop pl TN-4
Vine Area Hist Dist—hist pl MI-6
Vine Bluff Cem—cemetery UT-8
Vine Branch—stream TN-4
Vine Brook MA-1
Vine Brook—stream (3) MA-1
**Vineburg**—pop pl CA-9
Vine Cem—cemetery GA-3
Vine Cem—cemetery WV-2
Vine Creek ND-7
Vine Creek—locale KS-7
Vine Creek—stream CA-9
Vine Creek—stream ID-8
Vine Creek—stream KS-7
Vine Creek—stream MI-6
Vine Creek—stream OR-9
Vine Creek Cem—cemetery KS-7
Vinedale—hist pl NC-3
Vinedale Sch—school CA-9
Vine Fountain Ch—church AL-4
**Vinegar Bend**—pop pl AL-4
Vinegar Branch—stream MO-7
Vinegar Branch—stream WI-6
Vinegar Creek—stream AK-9
Vinegar Creek—stream ID-8
Vinegar Creek—stream (2) MT-8
Vinegar Creek—stream OK-5
Vinegar Creek—stream OR-9
Vinegar Creek Boat Ramp—other ID-8
Vinegar Creek Rapids—rapids ID-8
Vinegar Gulch—valley WA-9
Vinegar Hill—locale PA-2
**Vinegar Hill**—pop pl NC-3
**Vinegar Hill**—pop pl TN-4
Vinegar Hill—ridge MN-6
Vinegar Hill—summit CT-1
Vinegar Hill—summit ID-8
Vinegar Hill—summit IN-6
Vinegar Hill—summit (2) ME-1
Vinegar Hill—summit MA-1
Vinegar Hill—summit MO-7
Vinegar Hill—summit MT-8
Vinegar Hill—summit NY-2
Vinegar Hill—summit OK-5
Vinegar Hill—summit OR-9
Vinegar Hill—summit PA-2
Vinegar Hill—summit TN-4
Vinegar Hill—summit TX-5
Vinegar Hill—summit WY-8
Vinegar Hill—uninc pl VA-3
Vinegar Hill Mine—mine IL-6
Vinegar Hill Sch—school (2) IL-6
Vinegar Hill (Township of)—civ div IL-6
Vinegar Hollow—valley OH-6
Vinegar Jack Hill—summit IL-6
Vinegar Lake—lake MN-6
Vinegar Lake—lake WA-9
Vinegar Mtn—summit MT-8
Vinegarone—locale TX-5
Vinegarone Draw—valley TX-5
Vinegaron Well—well AZ-5
Vinegar Peak—summit CA-9
Vinegar Peak—summit NV-8
Vinegar Ridge—ridge WI-6
Vinegarroon Wash—stream AZ-5
Vinegar Run—stream OH-6
Vinegar Run—stream VA-3
Vinegar Valley—valley TN-4
**Vine Grove**—pop pl KY-4
Vine Grove Cemetery UT-8
Vine Grove Ch—church TX-5
Vine Grove Hist Dist—hist pl KY-4
**Vine Grove Junction**—pop pl KY-4
Vine Grove Sch—school TX-5
Vinehill AL-4
Vine Hill MA-1
Vine Hill—hist pl NC-3
Vine Hill—hist pl TN-4
**Vine Hill**—pop pl AL-4
**Vine Hill**—pop pl CA-9
Vine Hill—summit CA-9
Vine Hill—summit PA-2
Vine Hill Cem—cemetery PA-2
Vine Hill Ch—church AL-4

Vine Hill Ch—church KY-4
Vine Hill Ch—church MO-7
Vine Hill-Pacheco—CDP CA-9
Vine Hill Sch MO-7
Vine Hill Sch—school CA-9
Vine Hill Sch—school (2) MO-7
Vine Hill Sch (abandoned)—school (2) MO-7
Vine Hill Sch (historical)—school TN-4
Vine Hill Station (historical)—locale AL-4
Vine Hollow—valley KY-4
Vine Island LA-4
Vine JHS—school TN-4
Vine Lake Cem—cemetery MA-1
Vineland NC-3
Vineland WA-9
Vineland—locale FL-3
**Vineland**—pop pl AL-4
**Vineland**—pop pl CO-8
**Vineland**—pop pl MI-6
**Vineland**—pop pl MN-6
**Vineland**—pop pl MO-7
**Vineland**—pop pl NJ-2
Vineland Bay—bay MN-6
Vineland Bay Site—hist pl MN-6
Vineland Cem—cemetery WA-9
Vineland Ch—church AL-4
Vineland Ch—church CO-8
Vineland Circle—locale NJ-2
Vineland-Downstown—airport NJ-2
Vineland Elem Sch—school FL-3
Vineland HS—school NJ-2
**Vineland Park**—pop pl AL-4
**Vineland Park (subdivision)**—pop pl NC-3
Vineland Sch—school (4) CA-9
Vineland Sch—school MN-6
Vineland Sch—school MO-7
Vineland Sch—school SC-3
Vineland State Sch—school NJ-2
**Vineland (Township of)**—pop pl MN-6
Vineland Training Sch—school NJ-2
Vineman Cem—cemetery KS-7
**Vinemaple**—pop pl OR-9
Vine Maple Creek—stream OR-9
Vine Maple Creek—stream WA-9
Vinemont—locale PA-2
Vinemont—other AL-4
**Vinemont**—pop pl AL-4
Vinemont (CCD)—cens area AL-4
Vinemont Division—civil AL-4
Vinemont First Baptist Ch (historical)—church AL-4
Vinemont HS—school AL-4
Vinemont Post Office—building AL-4
Vine Mount PA-2
Vine Oak Cem—cemetery NC-3
Vine-Oakwood-Green Bay Road Hist Dist—hist pl IL-6
Vinepis FM-9
Vine Post Office (historical)—building TN-4
**Vine Prairie**—pop pl AR-4
Vine Prairie Creek—stream AR-4
Vine Prairie Public Use Area—park AR-4
Vine Prairie (Township of)—fmr MCD AR-4
Viner IL-6
Vine-Reservoir Hist Dist—hist pl WI-6
**Vine Ridge**—pop pl TN-4
Vine Ridge Baptist Ch—church TN-4
Vine Ridge Sch (historical)—school TN-4
Vine Run Ch—church KY-4
Vines Bay—swamp NC-3
Vines Branch DE-2
Vines Branch—stream OK-5
Vines Camp—locale AL-4
Vines Cem—cemetery TN-4
Vines Ch—church LA-4
Vine Sch—school CA-9
Vine Sch—school MI-6
Vines Creek—stream DE-2
Vines Creek—stream SC-3
Vines Ditch—canal OR-9
Vines Hill—summit OR-9
Vines Hollow—valley TN-4
Vines Mill—locale AL-4
Vines Oil Field—oilfield OK-5
Vines Old River Lake—lake LA-4
Vine Spring—spring CA-9
Vine Spring Mine—mine CA-9
Vine Springs (historical P.O.)—locale IN-6
Vine Street OH-6
Vine Street Ch of God—church TN-4
**Vine Street East Condominium**—pop pl UT-8
Vine Street Elem Sch—school MS-4
Vine Street Hill Cem—cemetery OH-6
Vine Street Houses—hist pl CO-8
Vine Street Presbyterian Ch—church AL-4
Vine Street Sch—school CA-9
Vine Street Sch—school CT-1
Vine Street Sch—school ME-1
Vine Street Sch—school OH-6
Vine Street Station—building PA-2
Vinesville—uninc pl AL-4
Vine Swamp—stream NC-3
Vine Swamp Ch—church NC-3
**Vinet**—pop pl (2) PR-3
Vineta Hotel—hist pl FL-3
Vinette AL-4
Vine Valley—locale NY-2
Vineville—uninc pl GA-3
Vineville Branch—stream GA-3
Vineville Hist Dist—hist pl GA-3
Vineville (historical)—locale AL-4
Vinewood—hist pl KY-4
Vinewood—locale KS-7
Vinewood Cem—cemetery MI-6
Vinewood Park—park CA-9
Vinewood Sch—school CA-9
Vineyard VT-1
Vineyard—locale AR-4
Vineyard—locale KY-4
Vineyard—locale PA-2
Vineyard—locale TX-5
**Vineyard**—pop pl KY-4
**Vineyard**—pop pl NY-2
**Vineyard**—pop pl UT-8
Vineyard, Charles C., House—hist pl ID-8
Vineyard, The IN-6
Vineyard, The—area CA-9
Vineyard Bend—bend TN-4
Vineyard Branch—stream AL-4

Vineyard Branch—*stream* AR-4
Vineyard Canyon—*valley* AZ-5
Vineyard Canyon—*valley* (2) CA-9
Vineyard Cem—*cemetery* (2) MO-7
Vineyard Cem—*cemetery* (7) TN-4
Vineyard Cem—*cemetery* (2) VA-3
Vineyard Cem—*cemetery* WV-2
Vineyard Ch—*church* AR-4
**Vineyard Condominium**—*pop pl* UT-8
Vineyard Coulee—*valley* WI-6
Vineyard Creek—*stream* AR-4
Vineyard Creek—*stream* CA-9
Vineyard Creek—*stream* GA-3
Vineyard Creek—*stream* NC-3
Vineyard Creek—*stream* PA-2
Vineyard Creek Ch—*church* GA-3
Vineyard Crossroads—*locale* GA-3
Vineyard Gap—*gap* NC-3
Vineyard Gap—*gap* WV-2
**Vineyard Glen Subdivision**—*pop pl* UT-8
*Vineyard Grove* MA-1
Vineyard Grove Cem—*cemetery* TX-5
Vineyard Gulch—*valley* ID-8
**Vineyard Haven**—*pop pl* MA-1
Vineyard Haven Breakwater
Light—*locale* MA-1
Vineyard Haven Ferry Slip Light—*locale* MA-1
Vineyard Haven Harbor—*harbor* MA-1
Vineyard Haven (Town name
Tisbury)—*CDP* MA-1
**Vineyard Highlands**—*pop pl* MA-1
*Vineyard Hill* OR-9
Vineyard Hill—*summit* MA-1
Vineyard (historical P.O.)—*locale* IA-7
**Vineyard Homes**—*pop pl* NJ-2
Vineyard Knob—*summit* KY-4
Vineyard Knob—*summit* WV-2
Vineyard Lake—*lake* MI-6
Vineyard Lake—*reservoir* ID-8
Vineyard Landing—*locale* TN-4
Vineyard Mtn—*summit* AL-4
Vineyard Mtn—*summit* AZ-5
Vineyard Mtn—*summit* GA-3
Vineyard Mtn—*summit* NC-3
Vineyard Mtn—*summit* OR-9
Vineyard of Mission Soledad—*locale* CA-9
Vineyard Park—*park* MI-6
Vineyard Park—*park* MN-6
Vineyard Plaza Shop Ctr—*locale* NC-3
Vineyard Point—*cape* CT-1
Vineyard Point—*cape* TN-4
Vineyard Point—*cliff* PA-2
Vineyard Point Marina—*locale* NC-3
Vineyard Ranch—*locale* CA-9
Vineyard Ranch—*locale* NV-8
Vineyard Recreation Center—*park* CA-9
Vineyard Road Dam—*dam* AZ-5
Vineyard Run—*stream* (2) PA-2
Vineyard Run—*stream* WV-2
Vineyard Sch—*school* (3) CA-9
Vineyard Sch—*school* GA-3
Vineyard Sch—*school* KY-4
Vineyard Sch—*school* UT-8
Vineyard Shoal—*bar* VA-3
Vineyard Sound—*gut* MA-1
Vineyard Spring—*spring* AZ-5
**Vineyards (subdivision), The**—*pop pl* AL-4
**Vineyard Subdivision**—*pop pl* UT-8
Vineyard Swamp—*swamp* NC-3
Vineyard Tank—*reservoir* AZ-5
Vineyard Township—*civil* MO-7
Vineyard (Township of)—*fmr MCD* AR-4
Viney Bend—*bend* TX-5
Viney Bottom—*bend* KY-4
Viney Brake—*lake* AR-4
Viney Branch—*stream* FL-3
Viney Cem—*cemetery* MO-7
Viney Cem—*cemetery* OH-6
Viney Creek—*stream* MS-4
Viney Creek—*stream* MO-7
Viney Creek Ch—*church* MS-4
*Viney Creek Missionary Baptist Ch* MS-4
Viney Creek Public Use Area—*locale* MO-7
**Viney Grove**—*pop pl* AR-4
**Vineygrove**—*pop pl* AR-4
Viney Grove Cem—*cemetery* AR-4
Viney Hill—*summit* CT-1
Viney Hill Brook—*stream* CT-1
Viney Hollow—*valley* MO-7
Viney Lake—*lake* LA-4
Viney Mtn—*summit* WV-2
Viney Pond—*swamp* TX-5
Viney Ridge—*ridge* IL-6
Viney Rough—*flat* MS-4
Viney School (historical)—*locale* MO-7
Viney Slough Ditch—*canal* AR-4
Vinge Lake—*lake* MN-6
Vinger Cem—*cemetery* MN-6
*Vingetun Islands* TX-5
Vingie Creek—*stream* OR-9
*Vingt and Un Islands* TX-5
*Vingtan Islands* TX-5
*Vingtetun Islands* TX-5
Vingt-et-un Islands—*island* TX-5
*Vingt'Une Islands* TX-5
*Vini* FM-9
Viniard Field—*locale* GA-3
*Vinibau* FM-9
*Viniboat* FM-9
Vinica Brook—*stream* MA-1
Vinica Pond—*reservoir* MA-1
Vinica Pond Dam—*dam* MA-1
*Vinice Island* CA-9
*Vinien* FM-9
Vinie Slough—*gut* TX-5
*Vinifaula* FM-9
*Vinifaup* FM-9
*Vinifauren Ridge* FM-9
*Vinifei* FM-9
*Vinifei, Mount* FM-9
*Vinifoula* FM-9
*Vinigero Durchfahrt* FM-9
*Vinikero Pass* FM-9
*Vinimas Berg* FM-9
*Vinimer, Mount* FM-9
*Vinimorr Krater* FM-9
Vining—*locale* OK-5
**Vining**—*pop pl* IA-7
**Vining**—*pop pl* KS-7
**Vining**—*pop pl* MN-6
Vining, Gorham, P., House—*hist pl* WI-6
Vining Airp—*airport* ND-7
Vining Cem—*cemetery* GA-3
Vining Cem—*cemetery* KS-7
Vining Cem—*cemetery* ME-1
Vining Cem—*cemetery* MN-6
*Vining Creek* CA-9
Vining Drain—*canal* MI-6
**Vining Hill**—*pop pl* MA-1
Vining Lake—*lake* ME-1
*Vining Peak* CA-9
Vining Pond—*lake* AL-4
Vining Pond Dam—*dam* AL-4
Vinings—*locale* GA-3
Vinings (CCD)—*cens area* GA-3
Vining Sch—*school* MA-1
Vinini Creek—*stream* NV-8
Vinita—*locale* VA-3
**Vinita**—*pop pl* OK-5
Vinita Cem—*cemetery* KS-7
Vinita County Park—*other* MO-7
Vinita East (CCD)—*cens area* OK-5
Vinita Interchange—*other* OK-5
**Vinita Park**—*pop pl* MO-7
**Vinita Terrace**—*pop pl* MO-7
**Vinita Township**—*pop pl* KS-7
Vinita Waterworks—*other* OK-5
Vinita West (CCD)—*cens area* OK-5
Vinity Corner—*locale* AR-4
Vinje—*locale* IA-7
Vinje Ch—*church* ND-7
Vinje Sch—*school* ND-7
Vinland—*locale* CA-9
**Vinland**—*pop pl* KS-7
**Vinland**—*pop pl* WA-9
Vinland Cem—*cemetery* KS-7
Vinland Ch—*church* WA-9
Vinland Park—*park* CA-9
Vinland Sch—*school* CA-9
Vinland Sch—*school* IA-7
**Vinland (Town of)**—*pop pl* WI-6
Vinland Valley Aerodrome—*airport* KS-7
*Vinland Valley Landing Field* KS-7
**Vinnette**—*pop pl* AL-4
Vinnie—*locale* KY-4
**Vinnie Ha Ha**—*pop pl* WI-6
Vinning Creek—*stream* NE-7
Vinning Lake—*lake* LA-4
Vinnin Hill—*summit* MA-1
Vino (historical P.O.)—*locale* IA-7
Vinola—*locale* PA-2
Vinoy Park Hotel—*hist pl* FL-3
Vinsant Cem—*cemetery* TN-4
Vinsant Hollow—*valley* AL-4
**Vinson**—*pop pl* MO-7
**Vinson**—*pop pl* OK-5
**Vinson**—*pop pl* OR-9
**Vinson**—*pop pl* TN-4
**Vinson**—*pop pl* TX-5
Vinson, Fred M., Birthplace—*hist pl* KY-4
Vinson Branch—*stream* AL-4
Vinson Branch—*stream* AR-4
Vinson Branch—*stream* KY-4
Vinson Branch—*stream* MO-7
Vinson Branch—*stream* TN-4
Vinson Branch—*stream* (2) WV-2
Vinson-Bynum Sch—*school* NC-3
Vinson Canyon—*valley* OR-9
Vinson Cave—*cave* (2) AL-4
Vinson Cem—*cemetery* AL-4
Vinson Cem—*cemetery* GA-3
Vinson Cem—*cemetery* IN-6
Vinson Cem—*cemetery* KY-4
Vinson Cem—*cemetery* NC-3
Vinson Cem—*cemetery* OR-9
Vinson Cem—*cemetery* (3) TN-4
Vinson Cem—*cemetery* TX-5
Vinson Ch—*church* MO-7
Vinson Chapel—*church* AR-4
Vinson Chapel—*church* WV-2
Vinson Creek—*stream* MT-8
Vinson Cross Roads—*locale* TN-4
Vinson Drain—*stream* IN-6
Vinson Hollow—*valley* AL-4
Vinson Hollow—*valley* MO-7
Vinson House—*hist pl* (2) AR-4
Vinson House—*hist pl* TN-4
Vinson HS—*school* WV-2
Vinson Island—*island* TN-4
Vinson Lake—*lake* AL-4
**Vinson Manor (subdivision)**—*pop pl* NC-3
Vinson Mtn—*summit* GA-3
Vinson-Owen Sch—*school* MA-1
Vinson Pond—*lake* MO-7
Vinson Pond—*lake* NC-3
Vinson Pond—*lake* OR-9
Vinson Pond (historical)—*lake* TN-4
Vinson Ponds—*reservoir* AL-4
Vinson Ranch—*locale* OR-9
Vinsons Chapel Ch (historical)—*church* MS-4
Vinsons Chapel Sch (historical)—*school* MS-4
Vinson Sch (historical)—*school* TN-4
Vinson School (abandoned)—*locale* MO-7
Vinsons Lake—*lake* GA-3
Vinsons Lake—*reservoir* NC-3
Vinson Slough—*gut* TX-5
Vinsons Mill (historical)—*locale* NC-3
Vinsons Mill Springs—*spring* TN-4
Vinson Village—*uninc pl* GA-3
Vinson Wash—*valley* ID-8
**Vintage**—*pop pl* PA-2
**Vintage Station**—*pop pl* PA-2
Vintage Street—*school* CA-9
**Vintage Village**—*pop pl* DE-2
**Vintage (Williamstown)**—*pop pl* PA-2
Vinta Mill—*locale* TN-4
Vinther and Nelson Cabin—*hist pl* ID-8
Vint Hill Farms—*post sta* VA-3
Vint Hill Farms Station—*military* VA-3
Vint Hill Farms Station Milit
Reservation—*military* VA-3
*Vintin Gulch* CA-9
Vinton—*locale* KS-7
Vinton—*locale* OH-6
**Vinton**—*pop pl* CA-9
**Vinton**—*pop pl* IA-7
**Vinton**—*pop pl* LA-4
**Vinton**—*pop pl* MS-4
**Vinton**—*pop pl* OH-6
**Vinton**—*pop pl* TX-5
**Vinton**—*pop pl* VA-3
Vinton Bldg—*hist pl* MI-6
Vinton Canyon—*valley* TX-5
Vinton Cem—*cemetery* CA-9
Vinton Cem—*cemetery* KS-7
Vinton Cem—*cemetery* MS-4
Vinton Chapel—*church* OH-6
Vinton Country Club—*other* IA-7
**Vinton (County)**—*pop pl* OH-6
Vinton Cutoff—*channel* MS-4
**Vintondale**—*pop pl* PA-2
Vintondale Borough—*civil* PA-2
Vintondale Ch—*church* WV-2
Vinton Drain—*canal* NM-5
Vinton Drain—*canal* TX-5
Vinton Drainage Canal—*canal* LA-4
Vinton Elem Sch—*school* IN-6
Vinton Ferry (historical)—*locale* MS-4
Vinton Gulch—*valley* CA-9
Vinton Hill—*summit* CT-1
Vinton (historical)—*locale* KS-7
Vinton Lake—*lake* CA-9
Vinton Lateral—*canal* NM-5
Vinton Lateral—*canal* TX-5
Vinton (Magisterial District)—*fmr MCD* VA-3
Vinton Memorial Cem—*cemetery* OH-6
Vinton Oil Field—*oilfield* LA-4
*Vinton-Orange Canal* LA-4
Vinton Pond—*lake* MA-1
Vinton Post Office (historical)—*building* MS-4
Vinton Public Library—*hist pl* IA-7
Vinton River Drain—*canal* TX-5
Vinton Sch—*school* CT-1
Vinton Sch—*school* (2) NE-7
*Vinton's Mill Pond* CT-1
Vintons Millpond—*lake* CT-1
**Vintonton**—*pop pl* NY-2
Vinton Township—*civ div* NE-7
**Vinton (Township of)**—*pop pl* OH-6
Vinton Valley—*basin* NE-7
**Vinton Woods**—*pop pl* NC-3
Vinum Park—*park* CA-9
**Vinvale**—*pop pl* CA-9
Vinyard Cabin—*locale* OR-9
Vinyard Mine—*mine* IL-6
Vinyard Sch—*school* LA-4
Vinyard Well—*well* NM-5
Viny Fork—*stream* KY-4
Vinzant Landing—*locale* FL-3
Vinzant Sch—*school* KS-7
Vinzant Swamp—*swamp* GA-3
*Viola* AL-4
Viola—*locale* CA-9
Viola—*locale* GA-3
Viola—*locale* TX-5
Viola—*locale* WV-2
Viola—*other* MI-6
**Viola**—*pop pl* AR-4
**Viola**—*pop pl* CO-8
**Viola**—*pop pl* DE-2
**Viola**—*pop pl* ID-8
**Viola**—*pop pl* IL-6
**Viola**—*pop pl* IA-7
**Viola**—*pop pl* KS-7
**Viola**—*pop pl* KY-4
**Viola**—*pop pl* MN-6
**Viola**—*pop pl* MO-7
**Viola**—*pop pl* NY-2
**Viola**—*pop pl* OR-9
**Viola**—*pop pl* PA-2
**Viola**—*pop pl* TN-4
**Viola**—*pop pl* WV-2
**Viola**—*pop pl* WI-6
**Viola**—*pop pl* WY-8
Viola, Lake—*lake* FL-3
Viola Bend—*bend* GA-3
Viola Canyon—*valley* OR-9
Viola Cem—*cemetery* IL-6
Viola Cem—*cemetery* MO-7
Viola Cem—*cemetery* OR-9
*Viola Cemetery* TN-4
**Viola Center**—*pop pl* IA-7
Viola Center Cem—*cemetery* IA-7
Viola Ch—*church* SD-7
Viola Ch—*church* TN-4
Viola Channel—*channel* TX-5
Viola Courts Apartments—*hist pl* TX-5
Viola Creek—*stream* (2) WA-9
Viola Gulch—*valley* ID-8
Viola (historical)—*locale* AL-4
Viola Lake—*lake* (2) WI-6
Viola Lake Cem—*cemetery* WI-6
Viola Lake Ch—*church* WI-6
Viola Mine—*mine* CO-8
*Viola P.O.* AL-4
Viola Post Office—*building* TN-4
Viola Public Use Area—*locale* MO-7
Viola Ridge—*ridge* ID-8
Viola Rockshelter (47 Ve 640)—*hist pl* WI-6
Viola Sch—*school* DE-2
Viola Sch—*school* TN-4
Viola Sch (historical)—*school* TX-5
Viola Sch Number 1—*school* ND-7
Violas Helistop—*airport* NJ-2
Violas Peak—*summit* AZ-5
Viola Spring—*spring* OK-5
*Violas Tit* AZ-5
Violation Lake—*lake* MN-6
Viola Township—*fmr MCD* (3) IA-7
**Viola Township**—*pop pl* KS-7
**Viola Township**—*pop pl* SD-7
**Viola (Township of)**—*pop pl* IL-6
**Viola (Township of)**—*pop pl* MN-6
Viola Turning Basin—*harbor* TX-5
Viola Valley Cem—*cemetery* SD-7
Viola Valley Sch—*school* SD-7
Viola Verellen Sch—*school* MI-6
Violenta (historical)—*locale* KS-7
*Violet* KS-7
*Violet* MP-9
Violet—*locale* MS-4
Violet—*locale* WV-2
**Violet**—*pop pl* LA-4
**Violet**—*pop pl* MO-7
**Violet**—*pop pl* NC-3
**Violet**—*pop pl* TX-5
Violet, Lake—*reservoir* GA-3
Violet Ave Sch—*school* NY-2
Violet Bank—*hist pl* VA-3
Violet Bank—*levee* VA-3
Violet Canal—*canal* LA-4
Violet Cem—*cemetery* AR-4
Violet Cem—*cemetery* MN-6
Violet Cem—*cemetery* TN-4
Violet City Entrance—*cave* KY-4
Violet Creek—*stream* AK-9
Violet Creek—*stream* MT-8
Violet Creek—*stream* TX-5
Violet Creek—*stream* WY-8
Violet Gulch—*valley* ID-8
**Violet Hill**—*pop pl* AR-4
**Violet Hill**—*pop pl* PA-2
Violet Hill—*summit* OR-9
Violet Hill Cem—*cemetery* IA-7
Violet Hill Cem—*cemetery* NC-3
Violet Hill Ch—*church* AL-4
Violet Hill Sch—*school* PA-2
Violet Hill Sch (historical)—*school* AL-4
Violet Hill Sch (historical)—*school* MS-4
Violet Hill (Township of)—*fmr MCD* AR-4
Violet Lake—*lake* FL-3
Violet Lake—*lake* HI-9
Violet Lake—*lake* MI-6
Violet Lake—*lake* MT-8
Violet Point—*cape* WA-9
Violet Point—*cliff* AZ-5
Violet Point—*cliff* OH-6
Violet Prairie—*flat* WA-9
Violet Sch—*school* LA-4
Violet Sch—*school* MI-6
Violets Creek—*stream* TX-5
Violets Hollow—*valley* ID-8
Violet Spring—*spring* CA-9
Violet Springs—*spring* WY-8
Violett, William N., House—*hist pl* IN-6
Violetta Farm Pond—*lake* FL-3
Violett Cem—*cemetery* IN-6
*Violette* ME-1
**Violette**—*pop pl* ME-1
Violette, Merritt, House—*hist pl* MO-7
Violette Brook—*stream* (2) ME-1
Violette House—*hist pl* ME-1
Violette Pond—*lake* (2) ME-1
Violette Sch—*school* CA-9
**Violette Settlement**—*pop pl* ME-1
Violette Stream—*stream* ME-1
**Violet (Township of)**—*pop pl* OH-6
**Violetville**—*pop pl* MD-2
**Violet Wood**—*pop pl* PA-2
*Violin Bay* LA-4
Violin Bayou—*stream* LA-4
Violin Canyon—*valley* CA-9
*Violin Lake* LA-4
Violin Summit—*gap* CA-9
Violott Ch—*church* TX-5
*Viols River Cove* RI-1
Viona (historical P.O.)—*locale* IA-7
*Viopoli* AZ-5
*Viopuli* AZ-5
Viopuli Wash—*stream* AZ-5
**Vipco**—*pop pl* IL-6
**Viper**—*pop pl* KY-4
Viper (CCD)—*cens area* KY-4
Viper Sch—*school* KY-4
Vipham, Thomas, House—*hist pl* ID-8
*Vipoint Creek* NV-8
*Vipond Creek* MT-8
Vipond Creek—*stream* MI-6
Vipond Creek—*stream* MT-8
Vipond Park—*flat* MT-8
*Vipont Creek* NV-8
Vipont Creek—*stream* NV-8
Vipont Mine—*mine* UT-8
*Vira* MP-9
**Vira**—*pop pl* PA-2
Vira Branch—*stream* NC-3
Virden—*locale* KY-4
Virden—*locale* MT-8
Virden—*locale* WA-9
**Virden**—*pop pl* IL-6
**Virden**—*pop pl* NM-5
Virden Cem—*cemetery* OH-6
Virden Creek—*stream* IA-7
Virden Creek—*stream* WY-8
Virden Grove Baptist Ch—*church* MS-4
Virden Lake—*lake* MT-8
Virden Pass—*gap* WY-8
Virden-Patton House—*hist pl* MS-4
**Virden (Township of)**—*pop pl* IL-6
*Virdie* AL-4
**Virelco**—*pop pl* VA-3
Vireo Lake—*lake* MN-6
Vires Fork—*stream* KY-4
Virey Oil Field—*oilfield* TX-5
Virga Hollow—*valley* KY-4
Virge Cove—*valley* NC-3
Virgelle—*locale* MT-8
Virgelle Ferry—*locale* MT-8
*Virgen* AZ-5
*Virgen Canyon* AZ-5
*Virgen Canyon* NV-8
*Virgenes Canyon* CA-9
*Virgen Mountains* NV-8
*Virgen Valley* NV-8
*Virgenville* PA-2
*Virgess Creek* LA-4
**Virgie**—*pop pl* IN-6
**Virgie**—*pop pl* KY-4
Virgil—*locale* OK-5
**Virgil**—*pop pl* IL-6
**Virgil**—*pop pl* KS-7
**Virgil**—*pop pl* NY-2
**Virgil**—*pop pl* SD-7
Virgil Cauthorn Ranch—*locale* TX-5
Virgil Cem—*cemetery* IL-6
Virgil Cem—*cemetery* KS-7
Virgil Chapel—*church* GA-3
**Virgil City**—*pop pl* MO-7
Virgil Connell Spring—*spring* CA-9
Virgil Creek—*stream* AL-4
Virgil Creek—*stream* NY-2
Virgil Ditch No 1—*canal* IL-6
Virgil Ditch No 2—*canal* IL-6
Virgil Ditch No 3—*canal* IL-6
Virgilee Park—*park* GA-3
Virgil Grissom HS—*school* AL-4
Virgil Gulch—*valley* ID-8
Virgil Hill Ch—*church* NC-3
Virgil Horton 1 Dam—*dam* SD-7
Virgil Horton 2 Dam—*dam* SD-7
Virgil Horton 4 Dam—*dam* SD-7
Virgil Hunter Gap—*gap* GA-3
**Virgilia**—*pop pl* CA-9
Virgil I Bailey Elem Sch—*school* IN-6
Virgil I Grissom Municipal Airp—*airport* IN-6
**Virgilina**—*pop pl* NC-3
**Virgilina**—*pop pl* VA-3
Virgilio Trujillo Cem—*cemetery* NM-5
Virgil JHS—*school* CA-9
**Virgil Location**—*pop pl* MI-6
Virgil Mtn—*summit* NY-2
**Virgilna**—*pop pl* VA-3
Virgil North Oil Field—*oilfield* KS-7
Virgil Oil Field—*oilfield* KS-7
Virgil O McWhorter Spring—*spring* WA-9
Virgil Rott Private Landing Strip—*airport* ND-7
Virgil Rural Cem—*cemetery* NY-2
Virgils Windmill—*locale* NM-5
**Virgil (Town of)**—*pop pl* NY-2
**Virgil Township**—*pop pl* MO-7
**Virgil Township**—*pop pl* SD-7
**Virgil (Township of)**—*pop pl* IL-6
Virgil Well—*well* NM-5
Virgin—*locale* NV-8
**Virgin**—*pop pl* UT-8
Virgin Basin—*basin* (2) AZ-5
Virgin Basin—*basin* NV-8
Virgin Bay—*bay* AK-9
Virgin Bluff—*cliff* MO-7
*Virgin Buttes* CA-9
Virgin Canal—*canal* UT-8
Virgin Canyon—*valley* AZ-5
Virgin Canyon—*valley* NV-8
Virgin Canyon—*valley* (2) NM-5
Virgin Cave—*cave* AL-4
Virgin Cem—*cemetery* UT-8
*Virgin City* UT-8
Virgin Creek—*stream* AK-9
Virgin Creek—*stream* (2) CA-9
Virgin Creek—*stream* MO-7
Virgin Creek—*stream* MT-8
Virgin Creek—*stream* (2) NV-8
Virgin Creek—*stream* SD-7
Virgin Creek—*stream* WA-9
Virgin Creek—*stream* (2) WI-6
Virgin Creek Buttes—*summit* CA-9
Virgin Falls—*falls* TN-4
Virgin Falls Cave—*cave* TN-4
Virgin Falls Pit—*cave* TN-4
Virgin Falls State Natural Area—*park* TN-4
Virgin Flats—*flat* UT-8
Virgin Gulch—*valley* MT-8
*Virginia* IN-6
*Virginia* PA-2
Virginia—*locale* KY-4
Virginia—*locale* SD-7
**Virginia**—*pop pl* AL-4
**Virginia**—*pop pl* ID-8
**Virginia**—*pop pl* IL-6
**Virginia**—*pop pl* ME-1
**Virginia**—*pop pl* MN-6
**Virginia**—*pop pl* MO-7
**Virginia**—*pop pl* NE-7
**Virginia**—*pop pl* WA-9
Virginia—*uninc pl* PA-2
Virginia, Lake—*lake* CA-9
Virginia, Lake—*lake* (3) FL-3
Virginia, Lake—*lake* MN-6
Virginia, Lake—*lake* WI-6
Virginia, Lake—*reservoir* AL-4
Virginia, Lake—*reservoir* MO-7
Virginia, The—*hist pl* VA-3
Virginia and Truckee RR. Engines No. 18, The
Dayton; and No. 22,—*hist pl* NV-8
Virginia and Truckee RR Shops—*hist pl* NV-8
Virginia Ann Mine—*mine* CA-9
Virginia Ave—*uninc pl* MD-2
Virginia Ave District—*hist pl* IN-6
Virginia Ave Sch—*school* KY-4
Virginia Ave Sch—*school* VA-3
Virginia Ave Shop Ctr—*locale* TN-4
Virginia Ave United Methodist
Ch—*church* TN-4
Virginia Bank and Trust Bldg—*hist pl* VA-3
Virginia Basin—*basin* CO-8
Virginia Beach—*beach* FL-3
Virginia Beach City—*civil* VA-3
Virginia Beach City Hall—*building* VA-3
Virginia Beach County Park—*park* FL-3
**Virginia Beach (ind. city)**—*pop pl* VA-3
Virginia Blvd Ch of God—*church* AL-4
Virginia Brewery—*hist pl* MN-6
Virginia Brook—*stream* NY-2
Virginia Butte—*summit* AK-9
Virginia Canyon—*valley* CA-9
Virginia Canyon—*valley* CO-8
Virginia Cascade—*falls* WY-8
*Virginia Cascades* WY-8
Virginia Cem—*cemetery* MO-7
Virginia Cem—*cemetery* NE-7
Virginia Ch—*church* AR-4
Virginia Ch—*church* LA-4
Virginia Ch—*church* VA-3
*Virginia City* MS-4
Virginia City—*locale* VA-3
**Virginia City**—*pop pl* MT-8
**Virginia City**—*pop pl* NV-8
Virginia City (Abandoned)—*locale* NM-5
Virginia City Hist Dist—*hist pl* MT-8
Virginia City Hist Dist—*hist pl* NV-8
Virginia City (site)—*locale* AZ-5
**Virginia Colony**—*pop pl* CA-9
Virginia Commonwealth Univ—*school* VA-3
Virginia Court Sch—*school* CO-8
Virginia Creek—*stream* (5) AK-9
Virginia Creek—*stream* (2) CA-9
Virginia Creek—*stream* CO-8
Virginia Creek—*stream* (4) MT-8
Virginia Creek—*stream* NC-3
Virginia Creek—*stream* OH-6
Virginia Creek—*stream* OR-9
Virginia Creek—*stream* VA-3
Virginia Creek—*stream* WY-8
Virginia Cut—*stream* FL-3
Virginia Dale—*locale* CO-8
Virginia Dale Ch—*church* CO-8
Virginia Dale Mine—*mine* CA-9
Virginia Dale Sch—*school* CO-8
Virginia Dale Spring—*spring* NV-8
Virginia Dale Stage Station—*hist pl* CO-8
Virginia Depot—*hist pl* MN-6
Virginia Ditch—*canal* CO-8
Virginia Draw—*valley* TX-5
**Virginia Estates**—*pop pl* VA-3
**Virginia Estates (subdivision)**—*pop pl* AL-4
Virginia Falls—*falls* MT-8
Virginia Field Park—*park* TX-5
**Virginia Forest**—*pop pl* VA-3
Virginia Fork—*stream* PA-2
**Virginia Gardens**—*pop pl* FL-3
**Virginia Gardens**—*pop pl* VA-3
Virginia Group—*mine* CA-9
Virginia Grove Park—*park* IA-7
Virginia Gulch—*valley* AK-9
Virginia Gulch—*valley* CO-8
Virginia Gulch—*valley* (2) ID-8
Virginia Hall—*hist pl* TX-5
**Virginia Heights**—*pop pl* (3) VA-3
**Virginia Heights**—*pop pl* WV-2
Virginia Heights Ch—*church* VA-3
Virginia Heights Sch—*school* VA-3
**Virginia Heights Subdivision**—*pop pl* UT-8
**Virginia Highlands**—*pop pl* VA-3
Virginia Hill—*summit* AZ-5
Virginia Hill—*summit* MT-8
Virginia Hill Ch—*church* TX-5
**Virginia Hills**—*pop pl* (2) VA-3
Virginia Hills Ch—*church* VA-3
Virginia Hills Sch—*school* VA-3
**Virginia (historical)**—*pop pl* SD-7
Virginia HS—*school* VA-3
Virginia Institute of Research—*school* VA-3
*Virginia Intermont Camp* TN-4
Virginia Intermont Coll—*school* VA-3
Virginia Intermont College—*hist pl* VA-3
Virginia International Racetrack—*other* VA-3
Virginia JHS—*school* VA-3
Virginia Kendall Park—*park* OH-6
Virginia Key—*island* FL-3
Virginia Key Park—*park* (2) FL-3
Virginia Lake—*lake* (2) AK-9
Virginia Lake—*lake* (3) CA-9
Virginia Lake—*lake* CO-8
Virginia Lake—*lake* ID-8
Virginia Lake—*lake* ME-1
Virginia Lake—*lake* MI-6
Virginia Lake—*lake* MN-6
Virginia Lake—*lake* NJ-2
Virginia Lake—*lake* WA-9
Virginia Lake—*reservoir* NV-8
Virginia Lake—*swamp* OR-9
Virginia Lake Dam—*dam* AL-4
Virginia Lakes—*lake* CA-9
Virginia Lakes—*reservoir* TX-5
Virginia Manor—*hist pl* VA-3
**Virginia Manor (subdivision)**—*pop pl* NC-3
Virginia May Mine—*mine* CA-9
Virginia Meadows—*flat* WY-8
Virginia Memorial Park—*cemetery* VA-3
Virginia Military Institute—*school* VA-3
Virginia Military Institute Hist
Dist—*hist pl* VA-3
**Virginia Mills**—*pop pl* PA-2
Virginia Mine—*mine* CA-9
Virginia Mine—*mine* (2) MN-6
Virginia Mine (Abandoned)—*locale* CA-9
**Virginia Mineral Springs**—*pop pl* VA-3
*Virginia Mines* AL-4
Virginia Mines (abandoned)—*mine* MO-7
Virginia Mines Cem—*cemetery* AL-4
Virginia Mines Ch—*church* MO-7
Virginia Mines Elem Sch
(historical)—*school* AL-4
Virginia Mines (historical)—*mine* MO-7
Virginia Mine (underground)—*mine* AL-4
*Virginia Mountains* NV-8
Virginia Mtns—*range* NV-8
Virginia Museum—*building* VA-3
Virginia Mutual Bldg—*hist pl* VA-3
Virginian Hotel—*hist pl* WY-8
Virginia-North Carolina Sch—*school* NC-3
Virginia-NorthCarolina Sch—*school* VA-3
Virginian Ridge—*ridge* WA-9
Virginia Park—*flat* UT-8
Virginia Park—*park* AZ-5
Virginia Park—*park* MI-6
**Virginia Park**—*pop pl* MI-6
Virginia Park Hist Dist—*hist pl* MI-6
Virginia Pass—*gap* CA-9
Virginia Peak—*summit* AK-9
Virginia Peak—*summit* CA-9
Virginia Peak—*summit* CO-8
Virginia Peak—*summit* MT-8
Virginia Peak—*summit* NV-8
Virginia Peak—*summit* WA-9
Virginia Peak—*summit* WY-8
Virginia Pina Well—*well* NM-5
**Virginia Place**—*pop pl* VA-3
Virginia Point—*cape* WV-2
**Virginia Point**—*pop pl* TX-5
Virginia Point—*summit* CA-9
Virginia Point Ch—*church* TX-5
Virginia Polytechnic Institute—*school* VA-3
Virginia Polytechnic Institute Tobacco Research
Center—*school* VA-3
Virginia-Rainy Lake Lumber Company
Manager's Residence—*hist pl* MN-6
Virginia-Rainy Lake Lumber Company
Office—*hist pl* MN-6
Virginia Ranch Rsvr—*reservoir* CA-9
Virginia Range—*range* NV-8
Virginia Recreation Bldg—*hist pl* MN-6
Virginia Reginae Sch—*school* NY-2
Virginia Ridge—*ridge* OH-6
Virginia Ridge Cem—*cemetery* OH-6
Virginia Ridge Sch (abandoned)—*school* MO-7
Virginia Rill—*stream* IN-6
Virginia Road Sch—*school* CA-9
Virginia Road Sch—*school* NY-2
Virginia Rock—*summit* PA-2
Virginia (RR name for Virginville)—*other* WV-2
Virginia Sch—*school* CA-9
Virginia Sch—*school* KS-7
Virginia Sch—*school* (2) MO-7
Virginia Sch—*school* NE-7
Virginia Sch for the Deaf and
Blind—*hist pl* VA-3
Virginia Sch For The Deaf And
Blind—*school* VA-3
Virginia School—*locale* IA-7

Vols Island—*island* NH-1
Vol Spring—*spring* OR-9
Volstead, Andrew John, House—*hist pl* MN-6
Volstead Creek—*stream* WA-9
Volstead Rsvr—*reservoir* OR-9
**Volt**—*pop pl* MT-8
**Volta**—*pop pl* CA-9
Volta Bureau—*hist pl* DC-2
Voltage—*locale* OR-9
Voltage—*locale* WA-9
*Voltage Siding* WA-9
Voltage Well—*well* OR-9
**Voltaire**—*pop pl* ND-7
Voltaire Canyon—*valley* NV-8
Voltaire (historical)—*locale* KS-7
**Voltaire Township**—*pop pl* KS-7
**Voltaire Township**—*pop pl* ND-7
Volta Powerhouse—*other* CA-9
*Voltz* IN-6
**Voltz**—*pop pl* WI-6
Voltz Lake—*lake* WI-6
Voluntee Park—*park* MS-4
Volunteer—*locale* SD-7
**Volunteer**—*pop pl* NC-3
Volunteer Army Ammunition Plant (US Military Reservation)—*military* TN-4
**Volunteer Bay**—*pop pl* OH-6
Volunteer Canyon—*valley* AZ-5
Volunteer Cem—*cemetery* WI-6
Volunteer Creek—*stream* AK-9
**Volunteer Estates (subdivision)**—*pop pl* TN-4
Volunteer Gap—*gap* VA-3
Volunteer General Hosp—*hospital* TN-4
Volunteer Gulch—*valley* CA-9
**Volunteer Heights**—*pop pl* TN-4
Volunteer HS—*school* TN-4
Volunteer Lookout Cabin—*hist pl* AZ-5
Volunteer Mine—*mine* CA-9
Volunteer Mtn—*summit* AZ-5
Volunteer Park—*hist pl* WA-9
Volunteer Park—*park* TN-4
Volunteer Park—*park* WA-9
*Volunteer Peak* CA-9
Volunteer Peak—*summit* CA-9
Volunteer Plaza Shop Ctr—*locale* TN-4
Volunteer Rock—*rock* MA-1
Volunteer Sch—*school* (2) SD-7
Volunteer State Community Coll—*school* TN-4
Volunteer Tank—*reservoir* AZ-5
**Volunteertown**—*pop pl* PA-2
Volunteer Wash—*stream* (2) AZ-5
**Voluntown**—*pop pl* CT-1
**Voluntown (Town of)**—*pop pl* CT-1
**Volusia**—*pop pl* FL-3
**Volusia**—*pop pl* NY-2
Volusia Ave Sch—*school* FL-3
Volusia Bar—*bar* FL-3
Volusia Bar Wharf—*locale* FL-3
Volusia Bear Hole—*lake* FL-3
Volusia Centre (Shop Ctr)—*locale* FL-3
**Volusia County**—*pop pl* FL-3
Volusia County Kennel Club—*locale* FL-3
Volusia County Law Library—*building* FL-3
Volusia Cove—*bay* FL-3
Volusia Mall—*locale* FL-3
Volusia Memory Park—*cemetery* FL-3
Volusia Nursing Home—*building* FL-3
Volusia Plaza (Shop Ctr)—*locale* FL-3
Volusia Point (Shop Ctr)—*locale* FL-3
Volvee Camp—*locale* NC-3
Volz Drain—*canal* MI-6
Volz Gulch—*valley* CO-8
Volz Homestead—*locale* CO-8
Volz Sch—*school* NJ-2
Vomburg Well—*well* WY-8
V O Mine—*mine* AZ-5
**Vona**—*pop pl* CO-8
Vona Cem—*cemetery* CO-8
Von Ach, Frank J., House—*hist pl* IA-7
**Vonachen Knolls**—*pop pl* IL-6
Vonada Gap—*gap* PA-2
Vonada Landing Field—*airport* KS-7
Vonaventure State Memorial Forest And—*park* MO-7
Vonberge Gulch—*valley* ID-8
Von Braun Civic Center—*building* AL-4
Von Burg Draw—*valley* WY-8
Von Burg Spring—*spring* WY-8
Von Canon Lake—*reservoir* NC-3
Von Canyon—*valley* ID-8
Vonda, Lake—*reservoir* TN-4
*Vondel Brook* MN-6
Vondell Brook—*stream* MN-6
Vondell Reservoir—*lake* VT-1
Vonder Ahe, Fred, House and Summer Kitchen—*hist pl* OR-9
Vondergreen Hill—*summit* OR-9
Voneida Run—*stream* PA-2
Voneida State Forest Park (historical)—*park* PA-2
Voneye Slough—*reservoir* SD-7
Von Fange Ditch—*canal* IN-6
Von Frank Creek—*stream* AK-9
Von Frank Mtn—*summit* AK-9
Von Geldern Cove—*bay* WA-9
Vongol Lake Number One—*reservoir* AL-4
Vongol Lake Number Two—*reservoir* AL-4
Vongol Number 1 Dam—*dam* AL-4
Vongol Number 2 Dam—*dam* AL-4
Von Hellum Creek—*stream* CA-9
Von Helm Rock—*bar* CA-9
Von (historical)—*locale* KS-7
Von (historical P.O.)—*locale* IA-7
Von Hoffman House—*hist pl* ND-7
Von Hoffman Lake—*lake* MO-7
Von Hoffman Lake (historical)—*locale* MO-7
Von Hollen Creek—*stream* SC-3
Von Holt Memorial Park—*cemetery* HI-9
Von Humboldt Mine—*mine* CA-9
Von Humboldt Sch—*school* IL-6
Vonich Gulch—*valley* CA-9
Vonich Mine—*mine* CA-9
von KleinSmid Mansion—*hist pl* IL-6
Von Krosigh Lake—*lake* NE-7
Vonnegut Sch Number 9—*school* IN-6
Von Nieda Park—*park* NJ-2
**Vonore**—*pop pl* TN-4
Vonore Baptist Ch—*church* TN-4
Vonore Boat Dock—*locale* TN-4
Vonore Boat Launching Ramp—*locale* TN-4
Vonore (CCD)—*cens area* TN-4
Vonore Cem—*cemetery* TN-4
Vonore Division—*civil* TN-4
Vonore Elem Sch—*school* TN-4
Vonore HS—*school* TN-4
*Vonore Methodist Episcopal Church South* TN-4
Vonore-Niles Ferry Industrial Park—*locale* TN-4
Vonore Post Office—*building* TN-4
Vonore United Methodist Ch—*church* TN-4
**Von Ormy**—*pop pl* TX-5
Von Ormy Oil Field—*oilfield* TX-5
Von Rsvr—*reservoir* OR-9
Von Ruden Memorial Park—*cemetery* WI-6
Von Ruden Sch—*school* WI-6
Vons Airstrip—*airport* OR-9
Von Schmid House—*hist pl* NJ-2
Vonschriltz Cem—*cemetery* OH-6
Von Schulenburg, Ernst, House—*hist pl* OH-6
Von Sloughs Airp—*airport* IN-6
Von Solbrig Hosp—*hospital* IL-6
Von Steuben, Gen. Frederick, HQ—*hist pl* PA-2
Von Steuben HS—*school* IL-6
Von Steuben Sch—*school* IL-6
Von Steuben Sch—*school* MI-6
Von Steuben Statue—*park* DC-2
Von Storch Breaker—*building* PA-2
Von Storch Colliery—*building* PA-2
Von Storch Shaft—*mine* PA-2
Vonstraten Creek—*stream* MI-6
Von Syckle Lake—*lake* MI-6
Vontay—*locale* VA-3
Von Tobel JHS—*school* NV-8
Vonton Cem—*cemetery* OK-5
Vontrigger Hills—*range* CA-9
Vontrigger Spring—*spring* CA-9
Von Wald Sch—*school* SD-7
Von Wedel-Gardiner Sch—*school* FL-3
Von Wedel Montessori Sch—*school* FL-3
Von Woehrmann Bldg—*hist pl* SD-7
*Vooland Gulch* ID-8
Voorde Park—*park* IN-6
**Voorhees**—*pop pl* NJ-2
Voorhees—*post sta* NJ-2
Voorhees, John K., House—*hist pl* IA-7
Voorhees Brook—*stream* NY-2
Voorhees Cem—*cemetery* IL-6
Voorhees Cem—*cemetery* OH-6
Voorhees Chapel—*hist pl* ND-7
Voorhees College Hist Dist—*hist pl* SC-3
**Voorhees Corner**—*pop pl* NJ-2
*Voorhees Creek* NE-7
Voorhees Creek—*gut* NJ-2
Voorhees Park—*park* OH-6
Voorhees Sch—*school* NY-2
Voorhees Sch Number 2 (historical)—*school* SD-7
Voorhees State Park—*park* NJ-2
Voorhees Township—*civil* KS-7
**Voorhees (Township of)**—*pop pl* NJ-2
**Voorheesville**—*pop pl* NY-2
Voorheis Lake—*lake* MI-6
Voorhess Coll—*school* SC-3
**Voorhies**—*pop pl* IL-6
**Voorhies**—*pop pl* IA-7
**Voorhies**—*pop pl* LA-4
**Voorhies**—*pop pl* OR-9
**Voorhies**—*pop pl* TN-4
Voorhies Bend—*bend* TN-4
Voorhies Branch—*stream* TN-4
Voorhies Castle—*hist pl* IL-6
Voorhies Cem—*cemetery* TN-4
Voorhies Hollow—*valley* TN-4
Voorhies Post Office (historical)—*building* TN-4
*Voories* TN-4
Voorlezer's House—*hist pl* NY-2
Vopats Canyon—*valley* WY-8
*Vopelohavooka* AZ-5
Vopoki Ridge—*ridge* AZ-5
Vopolo Havoka—*locale* AZ-5
Vopolo Havoka—*park* AZ-5
Voquelin Gulch—*valley* ID-8
Vorberg Gulch—*valley* ID-8
Vorce Creek—*stream* NY-2
Vorden—*locale* CA-9
V Ordosgoity Grant—*civil* FL-3
Vorea—*locale* NY-2
Vore Buffalo Jump—*hist pl* WY-8
Vore Cem—*cemetery* OH-6
Vore Cem—*cemetery* OK-5
Vore Creek—*stream* IA-7
Vore Draw—*valley* WY-8
Vore Ridge—*ridge* OH-6
Vore Ridge Ch—*church* OH-6
Vor Frelsers Cem—*cemetery* WI-6
Vorhees Corners—*locale* NY-2
Vorhees Creek—*stream* NE-7
Vorhees Hill—*summit* NY-2
Vorhees (historical)—*locale* KS-7
Vorhes Drain—*canal* MI-6
Vorhies Creek—*stream* CO-8
Vories Canyon—*valley* CO-8
*Vorile* FM-9
Voris Sch—*school* OH-6
Vorota Island—*island* AK-9
*Vorovo* FM-9
Vorrhees Park—*park* IN-6
Vorse Lake—*lake* MN-6
V O Rsvr—*reservoir* MT-8
Vortex—*locale* KY-4
Vortex Spring—*spring* FL-3
Vortog Radio Navigation Station—*other* CA-9
*Vorvor* FM-9
Vorwerk Canyon—*valley* NM-5
Vorzui Mtn—*summit* AK-9
*Vosberg Mountain* AZ-5
*Vosburg* MS-4
Vosburg—*locale* NY-2
Vosburg—*locale* PA-2
Vosburgh Airp—*airport* PA-2
*Vosburgh Hill* MA-1
Vosburgh (historical)—*locale* KS-7
*Vosburg Hill* MA-1
Vosburgh Swamp—*swamp* NY-2
Vosburg Mesa—*summit* AZ-5
Vosburg Mine—*mine* MT-8
*Vosburg Mtn* AZ-5
Vosburg Pike—*summit* CO-8
Vosburg Place—*locale* ID-8
Vosburg Pond—*lake* NY-2
*Vosburg Post Office* MS-4
Vosburg Sch—*school* IA-7
Vosburg Tank—*reservoir* AZ-5
Vosburg Trick Tank—*reservoir* AZ-5
Vosburg Tunnel—*tunnel* PA-2
Voscha Mine (historical)—*mine* ID-8
**Vose**—*pop pl* MA-1
**Vose**—*pop pl* TN-4
Vose Brook—*stream* VT-1
Vose Canyon—*valley* CO-8
Vose Cem—*cemetery* ME-1
Vose Hill—*summit* MA-1
Vose Mtn—*summit* ME-1
*Vosen Kill* NY-2
Vose Pond—*lake* ME-1
Vose Pond—*lake* MA-1
Vose Sch—*school* OR-9
Vose Sch (historical)—*school* TN-4
*Voses Fish Pond* MA-1
Vose Spur—*ridge* NH-1
Vosges Ridge—*ridge* MI-6
Voshell, John M., House—*hist pl* DE-2
**Voshell Cove**—*pop pl* DE-2
**Voshell Mill**—*pop pl* DE-2
Voshell Mill Pond Dam—*dam* DE-2
Voshell Oil Field—*oilfield* KS-7
Voshell Pond—*reservoir* DE-2
Vos Lake—*lake* MN-6
Voss—*locale* CA-9
Voss—*locale* TX-5
**Voss**—*pop pl* ND-7
Voss, Alfred R., Farmstead—*hist pl* MN-6
**Vossburg**—*pop pl* MS-4
Vossburg Cem—*cemetery* MS-4
Vossburg Hill—*summit* MA-1
Vossburg Post Office—*building* MS-4
Voss Canal—*canal* LA-4
Voss Cem—*cemetery* KS-7
Voss Cem—*cemetery* TX-5
Vos Sch—*school* MI-6
Voss Creek—*stream* AK-9
Voss Creek—*stream* MO-7
Voss Creek—*stream* NC-3
Vosse Coulee—*valley* WI-6
Vosseller's-Castner's-Allen's Tavern—*hist pl* NJ-2
Vossenkemper Sch—*school* MO-7
Voss Hill—*summit* OR-9
Voss Hollow—*valley* TN-4
Vossinbury Creek—*stream* FL-3
*Voss Lake* MN-6
Voss Lake—*lake* AR-4
Voss Lake—*lake* WI-6
Voss Mohr Cem—*cemetery* NE-7
Voss Park—*park* MN-6
Voss Ranch—*locale* NE-7
**Voss Resort**—*pop pl* WA-9
*Voss School* SD-7
Voss State Wildlife Mngmt Area—*park* MN-6
Voss Valley—*basin* NE-7
Vosteen-Hauck House—*hist pl* MO-7
Votaw—*locale* OR-9
**Votaw**—*pop pl* TX-5
Votaw Camp—*locale* CA-9
*Votaw Ditch* IN-6
Votaw Ditch—*canal* IN-6
Vote Creek—*stream* FL-3
Voter Hill—*summit* ME-1
Voters Brook—*stream* VT-1
Vote Run—*stream* IN-6
**Voth**—*pop pl* TX-5
Voth Cem—*cemetery* MN-6
**Vothees**—*pop pl* NE-7
*Vothees Creek* NE-7
Voth Oil Field—*oilfield* TX-5
Voth-Rosedale Sch—*school* TX-5
Voting House Hollow—*valley* KY-4
Votler Creek—*stream* ID-8
Voto Hollow—*valley* MO-7
Votrobeck Playground—*park* MI-6
Voucherie Mounds—*summit* MS-4
Vouga Rsvr—*reservoir* CO-8
Vought Corners—*locale* PA-2
Vought Creek—*stream* PA-2
Vought Rock—*summit* PA-2
*Vought Rocks* PA-2
*Vought Run* PA-2
Vought Run—*stream* PA-2
Vouters Landing—*locale* AL-4
Vouvia Bayou—*gut* LA-4
Vowell—*locale* MS-4
Vowell Branch—*stream* TN-4
Vowell Cem—*cemetery* MS-4
Vowell Cem—*cemetery* TN-4
Vowell Mtn—*summit* TN-4
Vowell Sch (historical)—*school* MS-4
Vowell Sch (historical)—*school* TN-4
Vowells Mill—*locale* LA-4
Vowell Tank—*reservoir* TX-5
*Vowell Town* MS-4
*Vowels Mill* LA-4
**Vowinckel**—*pop pl* PA-2
Vowles Cem—*cemetery* KY-4
Vowles Sch—*school* MI-6
Vox—*locale* KY-4
Vox Sch—*school* SC-3
Voyageur Lake—*lake* WI-6
Voyageurs Natl Park—*park* MN-6
Voyageur Vistor Center—*building* MN-6
*Voyer Creek* MI-6
Voyer Lake—*lake* MI-6
Voy (historical)—*locale* MS-4
Voyles Cem—*cemetery* IN-6
Voyles Cem—*cemetery* KY-4
Voyles Lazy V Ranch—*locale* TX-5
Voyles Pond—*lake* UT-8
V P Mine—*mine* CA-9
**V Point**—*pop pl* NC-3
**Vraman**—*pop pl* CO-8
V Ranch—*locale* (2) TX-5
V R Camp—*locale* AZ-5
V R Camp—*locale* WY-8
V R Ditch—*canal* WY-8
*Vredenburg* AL-4
**Vredenburgh**—*pop pl* AL-4
Vredenburgh (CCD)—*cens area* AL-4
Vredenburgh Division—*civil* AL-4
Vredenburgh Junction—*locale* AL-4
Vreeland, John and Anna, House—*hist pl* NJ-2
Vreeland, Lake—*reservoir* NJ-2
Vreeland Ave Station—*locale* NJ-2
Vreeland Cem—*cemetery* NJ-2
Vreeland Creek—*stream* AK-9
Vreeland Ditch—*stream* NJ-2
Vreeland House—*hist pl* NJ-2
Vreeland Park—*park* MI-6
*Vreeland Pond* NJ-2
Vreeland Pond—*lake* NJ-2
Vrender Swamp—*swamp* NE-7
V Ridge—*ridge* WY-8
**Vriesland**—*pop pl* MI-6
Vriesland Cem—*cemetery* MI-6
Vriner's Confectionery—*hist pl* IL-6
V Rock—*cliff* CO-8
V Rock—*pillar* CO-8
V Rock Trail—*trail* CO-8
Vroman—*locale* NE-7
**Vroman**—*pop pl* CO-8
Vroman Corners—*locale* NY-2
Vroman Hill—*locale* PA-2
Vroman Hill Ch (historical)—*church* PA-2
Vroman Ranch—*locale* SD-7
Vromans Nose—*cliff* NY-2
Vrooman—*locale* PA-2
Vrooman Ave Sch—*hist pl* NY-2
Vrooman Ave Sch—*school* NY-2
Vrooman Creek—*stream* NY-2
Vrooman Gulf—*valley* NY-2
*Vrooman Ridge* NY-2
Vrooman Ridge—*ridge* NY-2
**Vrooman Township**—*pop pl* SD-7
**Vrue (historical)**—*pop pl* MS-4
Vrue Post Office (historical)—*building* MS-4
Vruwink Ditch—*canal* WY-8
VR-105 Rsvr—*reservoir* MT-8
VR 33 Rsvr—*reservoir* MT-8
VR 44 Rsvr—*reservoir* MT-8
VR 78 Rsvr—*reservoir* MT-8
VR-80 Rsvr—*reservoir* MT-8
Vsetin—*locale* TX-5
Vsevidof, Mount—*summit* AK-9
Vsevidof Island—*island* AK-9
**V & S Junction**—*pop pl* OR-9
V S Pintado Grant—*civil* FL-3
V Spring—*spring* AZ-5
V Spring—*spring* UT-8
V Strom Ranch—*locale* ND-7
V Swanson Ranch—*locale* WY-8
V-Tail Draw—*valley* SD-7
V T Hill—*summit* AZ-5
V Thirtyseven Spring—*spring* AZ-5
V T Lake—*lake* AZ-5
*V T Park* AZ-5
V T Park Landing Strip—*airport* AZ-5
*V T Park Tourist Ranch* AZ-5
*VT Ridge Number One Tank* AZ-5
V T Ridge Number One Tank—*reservoir* AZ-5
V T Ridge Number Two Tank—*reservoir* AZ-5
*Vturituc* AZ-5
V-two Tank—*reservoir* AZ-5
**Vue de l'eau**—*pop pl* RI-1
Vukku Ch—*church* MN-6
**Vukote**—*pop pl* NY-2
Vukpalik Creek—*stream* AK-9
*Vulcan* IL-6
*Vulcan* OH-6
Vulcan—*hist pl* AL-4
Vulcan—*locale* AL-4
Vulcan—*locale* CO-8
Vulcan—*locale* PA-2
Vulcan—*locale* TN-4
Vulcan—*locale* VA-3
**Vulcan**—*pop pl* GA-3
**Vulcan**—*pop pl* IL-6
**Vulcan**—*pop pl* MI-6
**Vulcan**—*pop pl* MO-7
**Vulcan**—*pop pl* OH-6
**Vulcan**—*pop pl* WV-2
Vulcan Archeol Site (40HA140)—*hist pl* TN-4
**Vulcan City**—*pop pl* AL-4
Vulcan Creek—*stream* AK-9
Vulcan Creek—*stream* CO-8
Vulcan Creek—*stream* MI-6
*Vulcan Forge* AL-4
Vulcan Gulch—*valley* ID-8
Vulcan Gulf—*valley* TN-4
**Vulcan (historical)**—*pop pl* IA-7
Vulcan Hot Springs—*spring* ID-8
Vulcan Island—*island* CA-9
Vulcanite—*uninc pl* NJ-2
Vulcan Lake—*lake* OR-9
Vulcan Lookout—*locale* WA-9
Vulcan Lookout Tower—*locale* MI-6
Vulcan Lookout Tower—*locale* MO-7
Vulcan Mine—*mine* AZ-5
Vulcan Mine—*mine* CA-9
Vulcan Mine—*mine* ID-8
Vulcan Mine—*mine* NV-8
Vulcan Mine—*mine* UT-8
Vulcan Mtn—*summit* CO-8
Vulcan Mtn—*summit* WA-9
Vulcan Mtn—*summit* WY-8
Vulcano Mine—*mine* NV-8
Vulcan Park—*park* AL-4
Vulcan Peak—*summit* OR-9
Vulcan Point—*cape* AK-9
*Vulcan Rapid* AZ-5
*Vulcan Rapids* AZ-5
Vulcans Castle—*summit* CA-9
Vulcans Throne—*summit* AZ-5
*Vuleka* MP-9
**Vultare**—*pop pl* NC-3
Vultee Arch—*arch* AZ-5
Vultee Arch Twenty Two—*trail* AZ-5
Vulton Creek—*stream* KY-4
*Vulture* NC-3
Vulture—*locale* AZ-5
*Vulture City* AZ-5
Vulture Crags—*cliff* CA-9
Vulture Glacier—*glacier* MT-8
Vulture Gold Mine Landing Strip—*airport* AZ-5
Vulture Hammock—*island* FL-3
Vulture Mine—*mine* AZ-5
Vulture Mountains—*range* AZ-5
Vulture Mtn—*summit* VT-1
Vulture Peak—*summit* AZ-5
Vulture Peak—*summit* MT-8
*Vulture Range* AZ-5
Vulture Ridge—*ridge* CA-9
Vulture Rock—*summit* CA-9
*Vulture Siding* AZ-5
Vulture Spring—*spring* CA-9
*Vuluol* FM-9
Vundik Lake—*lake* AK-9
*Vunigeigei* FM-9
Vunikth Lakes—*lake* AK-9
Vunittsieh Lakes—*lake* AK-9
Vunle Lakes—*lake* AK-9
Vunlui Lake—*lake* AK-9
Vunte Lakes—*lake* AK-9
*Vunuknuk* FM-9
Vunvekottlui Lake—*lake* AK-9
Vunzik Lake—*lake* AK-9
Vurl Rsvr—*reservoir* CO-8
V V N Ranch—*locale* CO-8
*vVrken Island* NY-2
VVS Central Sch—*school* NY-2
VVV Ranch—*locale* WY-8
V Wall Dam—*dam* SD-7
V W Burkhead Dam Number One—*dam* NC-3
V W Burkhead Dam Number Two—*dam* NC-3
V W Landen Pond Dam—*dam* MS-4
V W McCormack Area—*park* OR-9
V W Rsvr—*reservoir* WY-8
**Vya**—*pop pl* NV-8
Vyre Lake—*lake* MN-6
Vysehrad Sch—*school* TX-5
VZ Rogers Sch—*school* TX-5

# W

Wadels Hill—*summit* WI-6
Wadel Spring—*spring* NV-8
**Wadely Landing**—*pop pl* LA-4
Wade Martin Lake Dam—*dam* AL-4
Wade Memorial Ch—*church* SC-3
Wade Memorial Chapel—*hist pl* OH-6
**Wade Mills**—*pop pl* NC-3
Wade Mtn—*summit* AL-4
Wade Mtn—*summit* OK-5
Wadena—*locale* OK-5
**Wadena**—*pop pl* IN-6
**Wadena**—*pop pl* IA-7
**Wadena**—*pop pl* MN-6
Wadena Cem—*cemetery* MN-6
Wadena Country Club—*other* MN-6
**Wadena (County)**—*pop pl* MN-6
Wadena Lake—*lake* MN-6
**Wadena (Township of)**—*pop pl* MN-6
Wade Park—*flat* OH-6
Wade Park—*park* MN-6
Wade Park District—*hist pl* OH-6
Wade Park Sch—*school* OH-6
**Wade Park Subdivision**—*pop pl* UT-8
Wade Peak—*summit* MT-8
Wade Pit—*cave* TN-4
Wade Place—*locale* CA-9
*Wade Point* MD-2
*Wade Point* NC-3
Wade Point—*cape* NC-3
Wade Point—*summit* AL-4
Wade Pond—*lake* ME-1
Wade Pond—*lake* OR-9
Wade Pond—*reservoir* MA-1
Wade Pond Dam—*dam* MA-1
Wade Post Office (historical)—*building* MS-4
Wade Prairie—*lake* FL-3
Wade Ranch—*locale* CO-8
Wade Ranch—*locale* NM-5
Wade Ranch—*locale* (2) TX-5
Wade Reeves Hollow—*valley* TX-5
Wade-Reynolds Prospect—*mine* TN-4
**Wade Road**—*pop pl* ME-1
Wade Rsvr—*reservoir* OR-9
Wade Run—*stream* PA-2
Wades—*locale* GA-3
Wades Bay—*bay* MD-2
Wades Bayou—*stream* MS-4
Wades Bluff—*locale* NC-3
Wadesboro—*locale* FL-3
Wadesboro—*locale* KY-4
**Wadesboro**—*pop pl* LA-4
**Wadesboro**—*pop pl* NC-3
Wadesboro Air Natl Guard
Station—*building* NC-3
Wadesboro Airp—*airport* NC-3
Wadesboro Cem—*cemetery* KY-4
Wadesboro Cem—*cemetery* LA-4
**Wadesboro Junction**—*pop pl* NC-3
Wadesboro Municipal Lake—*reservoir* NC-3
Wadesboro Post Office
(historical)—*building* MS-4
Wadesboro Sch—*school* NC-3
Wadesboro Springs—*spring* FL-3
Wadesboro (Township of)—*fmr MCD* NC-3
*Wadesborough* NC-3
Wades Branch—*stream* (2) TN-4
Wades Butte—*summit* AZ-5
Wades Canyon—*valley* UT-8
Wades Cem—*cemetery* GA-3
Wades Ch—*church* GA-3
Wade Sch—*school* (3) IL-6
Wade Sch—*school* (2) MI-6
Wade Sch—*school* MS-4
Wade Sch—*school* (2) MO-7
Wade Sch—*school* NJ-2
Wade Sch—*school* TN-4
Wade Sch—*school* (2) WV-2
Wade Sch (abandoned)—*school* PA-2
Wades Chapel—*church* GA-3
Wades Chapel—*church* TN-4
Wades Chapel—*church* TX-5
Wades Chapel (historical)—*church* MS-4
Wade Sch (historical)—*school* MS-4
Wade Sch (historical)—*school* MO-7
**Wades Corner**—*pop pl* MA-1
Wades Corners—*locale* PA-2
Wades Cove—*cove* MA-1
Wades Creek—*stream* KY-4
Wades Creek—*stream* WV-2
*Wades Draft* WV-2
Wades Flat—*flat* OR-9
Wades Flat Gulch—*valley* CA-9
Wades Gap—*gap* VA-3
Wades Gap Ch—*church* VA-3
Wades Island—*island* MD-2
Wades Lake—*lake* CA-9
Wades Mill—*locale* KY-4
Wades Mill—*locale* VA-3
Wades Mill (historical)—*locale* MS-4
*Wades Mountain* CA-9
*Wades Point* NC-3
Wades Point—*cape* MD-2
Wades Point—*cape* NC-3
Wades Point—*cliff* OR-9
**Wades Point**—*pop pl* NC-3
Wades Point Ch—*church* NC-3
Wades Pond—*lake* VA-3
Wade Spring—*spring* AZ-5
Wade Spring—*spring* OR-9
Wades Run—*stream* WV-2
*Wades Station* AL-4
Wade State Wildlife Mngmt Area—*park* MN-6
**Wadestown**—*pop pl* WV-2
Wadesville—*locale* PA-2
Wadesville—*locale* VA-3
**Wadesville**—*pop pl* IN-6
Wadesville Ch—*church* OK-5
Wade Tank—*reservoir* TX-5
Wade Tank—*well* TX-5
Wade Town (historical)—*locale* MS-4
**Wade (Town of)**—*pop pl* ME-1
**Wade (Township of)**—*pop pl* (2) IL-6
Wade Trail—*trail* CO-8
Wade Valley—*valley* CA-9
Wadeview Park—*park* FL-3
**Wadeville**—*pop pl* NC-3
**Wadeville**—*pop pl* WV-2
Wadeville Ch—*church* NC-3
Wadeville Sch—*school* WV-2
Wade Well—*well* NM-5
Wade Williams Spring—*spring* CA-9
Wadewitz Sch—*school* WI-6
Wadford Sch (historical)—*school* AL-4
Wadham Creek—*stream* PA-2
Wadham Creek Dam—*dam* PA-2
**Wadhams**—*pop pl* MI-6
**Wadhams**—*pop pl* NY-2
Wadhams Hall Seminary—*school* NY-2
**Wadhams Park**—*pop pl* NY-2
Wad Hardin Hollow—*valley* TN-4
Wadi Creek—*stream* ID-8
Wadie Branch—*stream* AL-4
Wading Branch Ridge—*ridge* NC-3
Wading Cave—*cave* AL-4
Wading Creek—*bay* NC-3
Wading Creek—*stream* NC-3
Wadinger Creek—*stream* VA-3
Wading Place Creek—*stream* NC-3
Wading Point—*cape* NC-3
*Wading River* MA-1
Wading River—*locale* NJ-2
**Wading River**—*pop pl* NY-2
Wading River—*stream* MA-1
Wading River—*stream* NJ-2
Wading River—*stream* NY-2
Wading River Cem—*cemetery* NY-2
Wading River Dam—*dam* MA-1
Wading River Landing—*locale* NY-2
Wading River Rsvr—*reservoir* MA-1
Wading Thorofare—*channel* NJ-2
WADJ-AM (Somerset)—*tower* PA-2
WADK-AM (Newport)—*tower* RI-1
Wadkin Hill—*summit* MA-1
Wadkins Cem—*cemetery* TN-4
**Wadleigh**—*pop pl* IA-7
Wadleigh Bog—*swamp* (2) ME-1
Wadleigh Branch—*stream* AR-4
Wadleigh Brook—*stream* (4) ME-1
Wadleigh Cem—*cemetery* NH-1
Wadleigh Deadwater—*lake* ME-1
Wadleigh Hill—*summit* NH-1
Wadleigh Island—*island* AK-9
Wadleigh Mtn—*summit* (3) ME-1
Wadleigh Point—*cape* NH-1
*Wadleigh Pond* ME-1
Wadleigh Pond—*lake* (3) ME-1
Wadleigh Rock—*other* AK-9
Wadleigh Sch—*school* IL-6
Wadleighs Head—*cape* ME-1
Wadleigh State Park—*park* NH-1
Wadleigh Stream—*stream* ME-1
Wadleigh Valley—*valley* ME-1
**Wadley**—*pop pl* AL-4
**Wadley**—*pop pl* GA-3
**Wadley**—*pop pl* TX-5
Wadley, Edward, House—*hist pl* UT-8
Wadley Barron Park—*park* TX-5
Wadley (CCD)—*cens area* AL-4
Wadley (CCD)—*cens area* GA-3
Wadley Cem—*cemetery* GA-3
Wadley Division—*civil* AL-4
**Wadley Falls**—*pop pl* NH-1
Wadley HS—*school* AL-4
Wadley Lake—*lake* WI-6
Wadley Lake—*reservoir* AR-4
Wadley Mine—*mine* NV-8
Wadley Pass—*channel* FL-3
Wadley Pond—*lake* ME-1
Wadley Rsvr No 1—*reservoir* CO-8
Wadley Rsvr No 2—*reservoir* CO-8
Wadley Rsvr No 3—*reservoir* CO-8
Wadley Well—*well* NM-5
Wadlington Cem—*cemetery* KY-4
Wadlington Lateral—*canal* TX-5
Wadlow Gap—*gap* TN-4
Wadlow Gap—*gap* VA-3
Wadmacon Creek—*stream* SC-3
Wadmacon Island—*island* SC-3
Wadmalaw Island—*island* SC-3
**Wadmalaw Island**—*pop pl* SC-3
Wadmalaw Island (CCD)—*cens area* SC-3
Wadmalaw Island Post Office—*locale* SC-3
Wadmalaw Point—*cape* SC-3
Wadmalaw River—*stream* SC-3
Wadmalaw Sch—*school* SC-3
Wadmalaw Sound—*bay* SC-3
WADM-AM (Decatur)—*tower* IN-6
*Wadmelaw Island* SC-3
*Wadmelaw Point* SC-3
*Wadmelaw River* SC-3
*Wadmelaw Sound* SC-3
WADM-FM (Decatur)—*tower* IN-6
*Wadoerukku* MP-9
Wadop Lake—*lake* MN-6
Wadr Ford—*locale* TN-4
Wads Creek—*stream* NC-3
Wadstrom—*locale* CA-9
Wadsworth Cem—*cemetery* NY-2
Wadsworth—*locale* KS-7
Wadsworth—*locale* SC-3
**Wadsworth**—*pop pl* (3) AL-4
**Wadsworth**—*pop pl* IL-6
**Wadsworth**—*pop pl* MA-1
**Wadsworth**—*pop pl* NV-8
**Wadsworth**—*pop pl* NY-2
**Wadsworth**—*pop pl* OH-6
**Wadsworth**—*pop pl* PA-2
**Wadsworth**—*pop pl* TX-5
Wadsworth—*uninc pl* PA-2
Wadsworth, Benjamin, House—*hist pl* OH-6
Wadsworth, Frederick, House—*hist pl* OH-6
Wadsworth, James, House—*hist pl* OH-6
Wadsworth, Lake—*reservoir* AL-4
Wadsworth Atheneum—*hist pl* CT-1
Wadsworth Ave Sch—*school* CA-9
Wadsworth Boy Scout Camp—*locale* NY-2
Wadsworth Brook—*stream* CT-1
Wadsworth Brook—*stream* ME-1
Wadsworth Brook—*stream* MA-1
**Wadsworth (Camp Wadsworth
Village)**—*pop pl* SC-3
Wadsworth Canal—*canal* CA-9
Wadsworth Canyon—*valley* UT-8
Wadsworth Cem—*cemetery* IL-6
Wadsworth Cem—*cemetery* ME-1
Wadsworth Cem—*cemetery* MA-1
Wadsworth Ch—*church* AL-4
Wadsworth Cove—*bay* (2) ME-1
**Wadsworth Cove**—*pop pl* NY-2
Wadsworth Creek—*stream* NV-8
Wadsworth Creek—*stream* TX-5
Wadsworth Ditch—*canal* IN-6
Wadsworth Falls—*falls* CT-1
Wadsworth Falls State Park—*park* CT-1
Wadsworth Flat—*flat* CA-9
Wadsworth Fort Site—*hist pl* NY-2
Wadsworth Hall—*hist pl* ME-1
Wadsworth Hill—*summit* GA-3
Wadsworth Hill—*summit* MA-1
Wadsworth Hill—*summit* NH-1
Wadsworth Hollow—*valley* IN-6
Wadsworth Lake—*reservoir* AL-4
Wadsworth Lake—*reservoir* IN-6
Wadsworth Lake Dam—*dam* (2) AL-4
Wadsworth Lake Dam—*dam* IN-6
Wadsworth-Longfellow House—*hist pl* ME-1
Wadsworth Monmt—*pillar* VA-3
Wadsworth Mtn—*summit* NY-2
*Wadsworth Peak* UT-8
Wadsworth Ponds—*reservoir* AL-4
Wadsworth Ranch—*locale* NV-8
**Wadsworth (RR name Greigsville
(sta.))**—*pop pl* NY-2
Wadsworth Sch—*school* (2) IL-6
Wadsworth Sch—*school* MA-1
*Wadsworth School* IN-6
Wadsworths (historical)—*locale* AZ-5
*Wadsworth Slope Mine* AL-4
Wadsworth Slough—*stream* TX-5
Wadsworths Old Ferry (historical)—*locale* AL-4
*Wadsworth Station* MA-1
Wadsworth Township—*inact MCD* NV-8
**Wadsworth Township**—*pop pl* ND-7
**Wadsworth (Township of)**—*pop pl* OH-6
Wadus Lake—*lake* SC-3
WADV-AM (Vincennes)—*tower* IN-6
Wadworth Ch—*church* NC-3
*Waeanae* HI-9
WAEB-AM (Allentown)—*tower* (2) PA-2
Waechter Canyon—*valley* WY-8
Waechter Gulch—*valley* CO-8
WAED-FM (Huntsville)—*tower* AL-4
Waegle Draw—*valley* WY-8
**Waelder**—*pop pl* TX-5
Waelder (CCD)—*cens area* TX-5
Waernicke-Hille House And Store—*hist pl* OH-6
*Waertown* NJ-2
Waespe Point—*ridge* OR-9
*Waeuntug* MA-1
WAEW-AM (Crossville)—*tower* TN-4
Wafco Mills—*hist pl* NC-3
Wafer Creek—*stream* LA-4
Wafer Creek—*stream* TX-5
Waffelow Creek—*stream* TX-5
Waffle Lake—*lake* MN-6
*Wafford Creek* GA-3
WAFF-TV (Huntsville)—*tower* AL-4
WAFL-FM (Milford)—*tower* DE-2
WAFM-FM (Amory)—*tower* MS-4
Waford Mtn—*summit* OK-5
Waford Spring—*spring* CA-9
WAFR-FM (Durham)—*tower* NC-3
WAFV-TV (Evansville)—*tower* IN-6
WAFX-AM (Fort Wayne)—*tower* IN-6
Wagaathiy—*summit* FM-9
*Wagamons Lake* DE-2
Wagamons Pond—*reservoir* DE-2
Wagamons Pond Dam—*dam* DE-2
*Waganerville* KS-7
*Waganon Ferry* AL-4
**Wagar**—*pop pl* AL-4
Wagar Dam—*dam* MI-6
Wagar Park—*park* OH-6
**Wagar Township**—*pop pl* ND-7
**Wagarville**—*pop pl* AL-4
**Wagarville**—*pop pl* MI-6
*Wagarville Baptist Church* AL-4
Wagarville (CCD)—*cens area* AL-4
Wagarville Ch—*church* AL-4
Wagarville Division—*civil* AL-4
Wagarville Sch—*school* AL-4
*Wagash Lake* MN-6
WAGC-AM (Centre)—*tower* AL-4
Wag Cem—*cemetery* ME-1
Wag Creek—*stream* ID-8
Wagejo, Lake—*lake* MI-6
Wagenblast Sch—*school* IL-6
**Wagendorf Township**—*pop pl* ND-7
**Wagener**—*pop pl* SC-3
Wagener (CCD)—*cens area* SC-3
Wagener County Park—*locale* MI-6
Wagener Fire Tower—*locale* SC-3
Wagener Glen—*valley* NY-2
Wagenschein Ranch—*locale* TX-5
Wager Airstrip—*airport* OR-9
Wager Cem—*cemetery* MI-6
Wager Creek—*stream* AK-9
Wager Drain—*canal* MI-6
Wager Drain—*stream* MI-6
Wager Gulch—*valley* CO-8
Wager Lake—*lake* MN-6
Wager Pond—*reservoir* NY-2
Wagers Cem—*cemetery* KY-4
Wager Sch—*school* MI-6
Wagers Hollow—*valley* KY-4
Wagers Sch—*school* KY-4
Wagersville—*locale* KY-4
Wagersville Cem—*cemetery* KY-4
Wagersville Ch—*church* KY-4
Wager (Township of)—*fmr MCD* AR-4
Wages Ch—*church* CO-8
Wages Creek—*stream* CA-9
Wages Pond—*lake* FL-3
WAGF-AM (Dothan)—*tower* AL-4
Wagga Coulee—*valley* MT-8
Waggamam Canal—*canal* LA-4
**Waggaman**—*pop pl* LA-4
**Waggaman Heights**—*pop pl* MD-2
Waggaman Pond—*swamp* LA-4
Waggaman Sch (abandoned)—*school* PA-2
*Waggamons Pond* DE-2
Waggart Hollow—*valley* TN-4
Waggener, B. P., House—*hist pl* KS-7
Waggener Ch—*church* KY-4
Waggener (Magisterial
District)—*fmr MCD* WV-2
Waggener Sch—*school* KY-4
*Waggie Creek* OR-9
Waggit Spring—*spring* CA-9
Waggle Creek—*stream* AR-4
Waggle Tail—*stream* CA-9
Waggley Hollow—*valley* AR-4
Waggner Cem—*cemetery* IN-6
Waggners Lake—*reservoir* KY-4
**Waggoner**—*pop pl* IL-6
Waggoner, Daniel, Log House and
Barn—*hist pl* PA-2
Waggoner, W. T. Bldg—*hist pl* TX-5
Waggoner Branch—*stream* TX-5
Waggoner-Buckeye Cem—*cemetery* TN-4
Waggoner Cem—*cemetery* IL-6
Waggoner Cem—*cemetery* (3) IN-6
Waggoner Cem—*cemetery* MS-4
Waggoner Cem—*cemetery* OH-6
Waggoner Cem—*cemetery* (4) TN-4
Waggoner Cem—*cemetery* TX-5
Waggoner Ch—*church* PA-2
Waggoner Chapel—*church* IN-6
Waggoner Covered Bridge—*hist pl* PA-2
Waggoner Creek—*stream* IL-6
Waggoner Creek—*stream* MS-4
Waggoner Creek—*stream* OR-9
Waggoner Dam—*dam* SD-7
Waggoner Draw—*valley* CO-8
Waggoner Gap—*gap* TX-5
Waggoner Graveyard—*hist pl* NC-3
Waggoner Knobs—*ridge* IN-6
Waggoner Lake—*lake* NC-3
Waggoner Lake—*reservoir* SD-7
Waggoner Mansion—*hist pl* TX-5
Waggoner Memorial Park—*park* TN-4
**Waggoner Place**—*pop pl* OH-6
Waggoner Ranch—*locale* NM-5
Waggoner Ripple Ch—*church* OH-6
Waggoner Run—*stream* OH-6
Waggoner Sch—*school* AZ-5
*Waggoners Creek* MS-4
Waggoners Gap—*gap* PA-2
Waggoner Tank—*reservoir* AZ-5
Waggoner Tank—*reservoir* TX-5
W A Gideon Lake Dam—*dam* MS-4
Wagler Cem—*cemetery* IN-6
*Wagles Lake* MI-6
Wagley Cem—*cemetery* AR-4
Wagleys Creek—*stream* WA-9
Wagman Chapel—*church* IL-6
Wag Meadows—*flat* ID-8
Wagmech—*summit* FM-9
Wagnalls Memorial, The—*park* OH-6
*Wagner* (2) IN-6
*Wagner* OR-9
Wagner—*locale* CA-9
Wagner—*locale* FL-3
Wagner—*locale* TX-5
Wagner—*locale* WI-6
**Wagner**—*pop pl* CA-9
**Wagner**—*pop pl* KY-4
**Wagner**—*pop pl* MT-8
**Wagner**—*pop pl* PA-2
**Wagner**—*pop pl* SD-7
**Wagner**—*pop pl* WA-9
Wagner—*stream* IA-7
Wagner—*uninc pl* CA-9
Wagner, Anton, Duplex—*hist pl* CA-9
Wagner, Gen. Louis, JHS—*hist pl* PA-2
Wagner, J. H., House—*hist pl* OK-5
Wagner, Lake—*reservoir* SD-7
Wagner, Mount—*summit* WY-8
Wagner, Webster, House—*hist pl* NY-2
Wagner And Bayer Rsvr—*reservoir* WY-8
Wagner and Pink Drain—*stream* MI-6
Wagner Basin—*basin* MT-8
**Wagner Beach**—*pop pl* MI-6
Wagner Bend—*bend* TN-4
Wagner Branch—*stream* MO-7
Wagner Branch—*stream* NC-3
Wagner Branch—*stream* OH-6
Wagner Branch—*stream* TN-4
Wagner Bridge—*bridge* LA-4
Wagner Brothers Bottling Works—*hist pl* OH-6
Wagner Butte—*summit* OR-9
*Wagner Canyon* OR-9
Wagner Canyon—*valley* CA-9
Wagner Canyon—*valley* NM-5
Wagner Canyon—*valley* OR-9
Wagner Canyon—*valley* WA-9
Wagner Cem—*cemetery* AR-4
Wagner Cem—*cemetery* IL-6
Wagner Cem—*cemetery* (2) IN-6
Wagner Cem—*cemetery* IA-7
Wagner Cem—*cemetery* LA-4
Wagner Cem—*cemetery* (3) MO-7
Wagner Cem—*cemetery* SD-7
Wagner Cem—*cemetery* (2) TN-4
Wagner Cem—*cemetery* (3) VA-3
Wagner Cem—*cemetery* WI-6
Wagner Ch—*church* MO-7
Wagner Ch—*church* OH-6
Wagner Ch—*church* PA-2
Wagner Coulee—*valley* MT-8
Wagner County (historical)—*civil* SD-7
Wagner Covered Bridge No. 19—*hist pl* PA-2
*Wagner Creek* MS-4
*Wagner Creek* TN-4
Wagner Creek—*stream* AR-4
Wagner Creek—*stream* (3) CA-9
Wagner Creek—*stream* FL-3
Wagner Creek—*stream* IA-7
Wagner Creek—*stream* (2) MI-6
Wagner Creek—*stream* MN-6
Wagner Creek—*stream* MS-4
Wagner Creek—*stream* (2) MT-8
Wagner Creek—*stream* NE-7
Wagner Creek—*stream* NJ-2
Wagner Creek—*stream* (2) OR-9
Wagner Creek—*stream* SC-3
Wagner Creek—*stream* (2) TN-4
Wagner Creek—*stream* TX-5
Wagner Creek—*stream* WI-6
Wagner Creek—*stream* WY-8
Wagner Ditch—*canal* IN-6
Wagner Drain—*canal* (2) MI-6
Wagner Drain—*stream* MI-6
Wagner Draw—*valley* SD-7
Wagner Draw—*valley* WY-8
Wagner Electric Corporation—*facility* MO-7
Wagner Falls—*falls* MI-6
Wagner Field—*flat* ID-8
Wagner Fork—*stream* KY-4
Wagner Gap—*gap* OR-9
Wagner Gap—*gap* (2) PA-2
Wagner Glade Gap—*gap* OR-9
Wagner Grove Ch—*church* GA-3
Wagner Gulch—*valley* AK-9
Wagner Gulch—*valley* CA-9
Wagner Gulch—*valley* ID-8
Wagner Gulch—*valley* (2) MT-8
Wagner Gulch—*valley* (2) OR-9
Wagner Gulch Trail—*trail* OR-9
Wagner Hill—*summit* AZ-5
Wagner Hill—*summit* MD-2
Wagner Hill—*summit* (2) NY-2
Wagner Hill—*summit* WV-2
Wagner Hill Cem—*cemetery* TX-5
**Wagner (historical)**—*pop pl* OR-9
Wagner Historical Monument—*locale* SD-7
Wagner Hollow—*valley* AL-4
Wagner Hollow—*valley* NY-2
Wagner Hollow—*valley* TN-4
Wagner Homestead (abandoned)—*locale* MT-8
Wagner Houseboat—*hist pl* WA-9
Wagner HS—*school* NY-2
*Wagner Island* VT-1
Wagner Island (historical)—*island* TN-4
Wagner JHS—*school* PA-2
Wagner Knob—*summit* (2) WV-2
*Wagner Lake* SD-7
Wagner Lake—*lake* (5) MI-6
Wagner Lake—*lake* (4) MN-6
Wagner Lake—*lake* (3) WA-9
Wagner Lake—*lake* (2) WI-6
Wagner Lake—*lake* WY-8
Wagner Lake—*reservoir* IN-6
Wagner Lake—*reservoir* MS-4
Wagner Lake Dam—*dam* SD-7
Wagner Lake Lookout Tower—*locale* MN-6
Wagner Landing—*locale* MD-2
Wagner Lookout Tower—*locale* PA-2
**Wagner Manor**—*pop pl* CO-8
Wagner Memorial Coll—*school* NY-2
Wagner Mine—*mine* AK-9
Wagner Mine—*mine* ID-8
Wagner-Mozart Music Hall—*hist pl* IA-7
Wagner Mtn—*summit* OR-9
Wagner Municipal Airp—*airport* SD-7
Wagner Number One Ditch—*canal* IN-6
Wagner Oak Grove Cem—*cemetery* PA-2
Wagner Palace—*hist pl* OH-6
Wagner Park—*park* IA-7
Wagner Park—*park* KS-7
Wagner Park—*park* MI-6
Wagner Park—*park* MS-4
Wagner Park—*park* NH-1
Wagner Park—*park* SD-7
Wagner Park—*park* TN-4
Wagner Park—*park* TX-5
**Wagner Park**—*pop pl* MD-2
Wagner Pass—*gap* WY-8
Wagner Point—*cape* SC-3
Wagner Point—*cape* VT-1
Wagner Point—*summit* KS-7
Wagner Pond—*lake* CT-1
Wagner Pond—*swamp* TX-5
*Wagner Prong* WY-8
*Wagner Prong Dutch Creek* WY-8
Wagner Prong Dutch Creek—*stream* WY-8
Wagner Prospect—*mine* TN-4
Wagner Ranch—*locale* AZ-5
Wagner Ranch—*locale* CA-9
Wagner Ranch—*locale* MT-8
Wagner Ranch—*locale* OR-9
Wagner Ranch—*locale* SD-7
Wagner Ridge—*ridge* CA-9
*Wagner River* ID-8
Wagner Rsvr—*reservoir* MT-8
Wagner Rsvr—*reservoir* WY-8
Wagner Run—*stream* OH-6
Wagner Run—*stream* (4) PA-2
Wagner Run—*stream* WV-2
**Wagners**—*pop pl* PA-2
Wagner's, Charlie, Cafe—*hist pl* PA-2
Wagner's Block—*hist pl* MI-6
Wagners Branch—*stream* NC-3
Wagnersburg—*locale* WA-9
Wagner Sch—*school* AL-4
Wagner Sch—*school* (2) CA-9
Wagner Sch—*school* (3) IL-6
Wagner Sch—*school* MN-6
Wagner Sch—*school* NE-7
Wagner Sch—*school* OH-6
Wagner Sch—*school* (2) PA-2
Wagner Sch—*school* SD-7
Wagner Sch—*school* WA-9
Wagner Sch (abandoned)—*school* PA-2
Wagner Sch (historical)—*school* MO-7
Wagner Sch (historical)—*school* PA-2
Wagner Sch (historical)—*school* TN-4
Wagners Cliff—*cliff* WI-6
Wagners Corners—*locale* NY-2
*Wagners Creek* TN-4
**Wagners Crossroads**—*pop pl* MD-2
*Wagners Ferry* AL-4
**Wagners Forest Park**—*pop pl* PA-2
Wagners Forge (historical)—*locale* TN-4
Wagners Island—*island* TN-4
**Wagners Lake**—*pop pl* NE-7
Wagners Landing (historical)—*locale* (2) TN-4
Wagners Mill—*locale* MD-2
Wagners Point—*cape* MD-2
Wagners Point—*uninc pl* MD-2
Wagner Spring—*spring* MT-8
Wagner Spring—*spring* TX-5
Wagner Spring—*spring* UT-8
Wagner Springs—*spring* NV-8
Wagner Springs—*spring* OR-9
**Wagner Springs (historical)**—*pop pl* OR-9
**Wagner Spur**—*pop pl* MO-7
Wagners Sch—*school* PA-2
Wagners Sch (historical)—*school* TN-4
Wagners Store (historical)—*locale* AL-4
Wagner State Public Shooting
Area—*park* SD-7
Wagner Station—*locale* KY-4
Wagners Valley—*basin* CA-9
*Wagnersville* PA-2
**Wagnersville**—*pop pl* PA-2
Wagner Swamp—*swamp* PA-2
Wagner Tank—*reservoir* (6) AZ-5
*Wagnertown* PA-2
**Wagner (Town of)**—*pop pl* WI-6
Wagner Township—*fmr MCD* IA-7
**Wagner (Township of)**—*pop pl* MN-6
Wagner Trace Branch—*stream* VA-3
Wagner Trail—*trail* PA-2
Wagner Union Ch—*church* OH-6
Wagner Valley—*valley* CA-9
Wagnerville—*locale* PA-2
Wagnerville (historical)—*locale* KS-7
Wagner Wash—*stream* AZ-5
Wagner Wash Well—*well* AZ-5
Wagner Well—*locale* NM-5
Wagner Well—*well* WY-8
Wagner Windmill—*locale* NM-5
**Wagne Station**—*pop pl* IN-6
Wagnon—*locale* AR-4
Wagnon Cem—*cemetery* GA-3
*Wagnon Creek* IN-6
Wagnon Ferry—*locale* AL-4
Wagnon Mountain Ch—*church* AL-4
Wagnon Mtn—*summit* AL-4
*Wagnons Ferry* AL-4
Wago—*locale* KY-4
Wago Junction—*locale* PA-2
Wagon Bay Creek—*stream* ID-8
*Wagon Bayou* AR-4
Wagon Bayou—*gut* AR-4
Wagon Bayou—*stream* AR-4
Wagonbed Canyon—*valley* NM-5
Wagon Bed Draw—*valley* TX-5
Wagonbed Knob—*summit* KY-4
Wagon Bed Knob—*summit* KY-4
Wagon Bed Spring—*spring* KS-7
Wagonbed Spring—*spring* NM-5
Wagon Bed Spring—*spring* WY-8
*Wagon Bed Springs* KS-7
Wagon Bed Springs—*hist pl* KS-7
Wagonblast Canyon—*valley* OR-9
Wagon Body Branch—*stream* AL-4
Wagon Boss Canyon—*valley* UT-8
Wagon Bow Ranch—*locale* AZ-5
Wagon Box—*valley* UT-8
Wagon Box Basin—*basin* ID-8
Wagon Box Battle Monmt—*park* WY-8
Wagon Box Canal—*canal* MT-8
Wagon Box Canyon—*valley* UT-8
Wagon Box Coulee—*valley* (2) MT-8
Wagon Box Creek—*stream* AK-9
Wagon Box Creek—*stream* ID-8
Wagon Box Creek—*stream* WY-8
Wagon Box Draw—*valley* AZ-5
Wagon Box Gulch—*valley* CO-8
Wagon Box Mesa—*summit* UT-8
Wagon Box Pass—*gap* NV-8
Wagon Box ( Site)—*locale* WY-8
Wagonbox Spring—*spring* ID-8
Wagon Box Spring—*spring* (2) MT-8
Wagon Box Spring—*spring* NV-8
Wagon Box Trail—*trail* PA-2
Wagon Branch—*stream* AR-4
Wagon Branch—*stream* MS-4
Wagon Branch—*stream* SC-3
Wagon Branch—*stream* TX-5
Wagon Butte—*summit* ID-8
Wagon Camp—*locale* CA-9
Wagon Camp—*locale* WA-9
Wagon Canyon—*valley* (2) AZ-5
Wagon Canyon—*valley* CO-8
Wagon Canyon—*valley* NV-8
Wagon Canyon—*valley* NM-5
Wagon Canyon—*valley* SD-7
Wagon Canyon—*valley* TX-5
Wagon Canyon—*valley* WY-8
Wagon Canyon Spring—*spring* AZ-5
Wagon Canyon Spring—*spring* SD-7
Wagon Caves—*cave* CA-9
Wagon Coulee—*valley* MT-8
*Wagon Creek* IN-6
Wagon Creek—*stream* CA-9
Wagon Creek—*stream* CO-8
Wagon Creek—*stream* IL-6
Wagon Creek—*stream* MT-8
Wagon Creek—*stream* (2) OK-5
Wagon Creek—*stream* SD-7
Wagon Creek—*stream* (3) TX-5
Wagon Creek—*stream* WY-8
*Wagon Creek Pass* CO-8
**Wagonda Hills**—*pop pl* TN-4
Wagon Draw—*valley* AZ-5
Wagon Draw Tank—*reservoir* AZ-5
Wagoneer Creek—*stream* SD-7
Wagoner—*locale* AZ-5
Wagoner—*locale* WV-2
**Wagoner**—*pop pl* IN-6
**Wagoner**—*pop pl* MO-7
**Wagoner**—*pop pl* (2) NC-3
**Wagoner**—*pop pl* OK-5
Wagoner Airfield—*airport* OR-9
Wagoner Branch—*stream* MS-4
Wagoner Bridge—*other* IL-6
Wagoner Brook—*stream* NY-2
Wagoner Canyon—*valley* CA-9
Wagoner (CCD)—*cens area* OK-5
Wagoner Cem—*cemetery* IL-6
Wagoner Cem—*cemetery* IN-6
Wagoner Cem—*cemetery* MO-7
Wagoner Cem—*cemetery* NE-7
**Wagoner (County)**—*pop pl* OK-5
*Wagoner Creek* MS-4
Wagoner Creek—*stream* KS-7
Wagoner Ditch—*canal* IN-6
Wagoner Ditch—*canal* WY-8
*Wagoner Hill* PA-2
Wagoner Hill—*summit* TN-4
Wagoner Hollow—*valley* KY-4
Wagoner Hollow—*valley* TN-4
Wagoner Plaza Shop Ctr—*locale* AZ-5
Wagoner Sch—*school* AR-4
Wagoner Sch—*school* IL-6
Wagoners Chapel—*church* KY-4
*Wagoners Creek* KS-7
Wagoner Trail Number Two Hundred
Thirteen—*trail* AZ-5
Wagonfeur Creek—*stream* WY-8
Wagon Flat Campground—*locale* CA-9
Wagon Ford Branch—*stream* TN-4
Wagonga Lake—*lake* MN-6
Wagon Gap—*gap* CO-8
Wagon Gap—*gap* NV-8
Wagon Gulch—*valley* (2) CO-8
Wagon Gulch—*valley* WY-8

Wagonhammer Butte—summit WY-8
Wagonhammer Creek—stream ID-8
Wagonhammer Ranch—locale WY-8
Wagonhammer Spring—spring ID-8
Wagon Hollow—valley TN-4
Wagon Hollow—valley UT-8
Wagon Hound Bedground—flat WY-8
Wagonhound Bench—bench WY-8
Wagon Hound Canyon—valley UT-8
Wagonhound Creek WY-8
Wagonhound Creek—stream (3) WY-8
Wagon Hound Creek—stream WY-8
Wagonhound Creek—stream WY-8
Wagon Hound Ditch No 3—canal WY-8
Wagon Hound Falls—falls WY-8
Wagon Hound Gorge—valley WY-8
Wagonhound Spring—spring WY-8
Wagon Johnnies Ranch—locale NV-8
Wagon Lake—swamp IL-6
Wagon Lake Tank—reservoir AZ-5
Wagon Landing Cem—cemetery WI-6
Wagon Landing Springs State Public Fishing Area—park WI-6
Wagon Mesa—summit CO-8
Wagon Mine (underground)—mine (2) AL-4
Wagon Mound—hist pl NM-5
**Wagon Mound**—pop pl NM-5
Wagon Mound, The—summit NM-5
Wagon Mound (CCD)—cens area NM-5
Wagon Mtn—summit MT-8
Wagonner Ch—church IL-6
Wagon Park—flat CO-8
Wagon Prong WY-8
Wagon Prong—stream WY-8
Wagon Prong Rsvr—reservoir WY-8
Wagon Road Bench—bench UT-8
Wagon Road Branch—stream KY-4
Wagon Road Canyon—valley CA-9
Wagonroad Coulee—valley WA-9
Wagonroad Fork—stream KY-4
Wagon Road Gap—gap (2) NC-3
Wagon Road Gulch—valley CA-9
Wagonroad Gulch—valley CO-8
Wagon Road Gulch—valley ID-8
Wagon Road Gulch—valley OR-9
Wagonroad Ridge—ridge CO-8
Wagon Road Ridge—ridge GA-3
Wagon Road Ridge—ridge NC-3
Wagon Road Ridge—ridge (4) UT-8
Wagon Road Run PA-2
Wagonroad Run—stream PA-2
Wagon Road Spring—spring OR-9
Wagon Road Tank—reservoir AZ-5
Wagonroad Tunnel—tunnel KY-4
Wagonroad Tunnel—tunnel VA-3
Wagon Rock—pillar TN-4
Wagon Rsvr—reservoir OR-9
Wagon Run—stream WV-2
Wagonshed Creek—stream CA-9
Wagon Shed Hollow—valley AR-4
Wagonslide—other OR-9
Wagon Spring ID-8
Wagon Spring—spring AZ-5
Wagon Spring—spring ID-8
Wagon Spring—spring NV-8
Wagon Springs—spring NV-8
Wagons West RV Campground—park UT-8
Wagon Timber Branch—stream NC-3
Wagon Timber Creek—stream TX-5
Wagontire—locale OR-9
Wagontire Creek—stream CA-9
Wagon Tire Creek—stream NV-8
Wagon Tire Creek—stream TX-5
Wagontire Draw—valley NM-5
Wagon Tire Flat—flat AZ-5
Wagontire Flat—flat CA-9
Wagontire Mountains OR-9
Wagontire Mountains—summit OR-9
Wagon Tire Mtn—summit NV-8
Wagontire Mtn—summit OR-9
Wagon Tire Pass—gap NV-8
Wagontire Rsvr—reservoir CA-9
Wagontire Spring—spring CA-9
Wagontire Spring—spring NV-8
Wagon Tire Spring—spring NV-8
Wagon Tire Spring—spring WY-8
Wagon Tire Tank—reservoir AZ-5
Wagon Tire Wash—stream AZ-5
Wagon Tongue Campground—locale CO-8
Wagontongue Creek—stream AL-4
Wagon Tongue Creek—stream CO-8
Wagon Tongue Creek—stream NE-7
Wagon Tongue Gulch—valley CO-8
Wagontongue Mtn—summit NM-5
Wagon Tongue Tank—reservoir AZ-5
Wagon Top—summit TX-5
Wagon Top Rsvr—reservoir MT-8
**Wagontown**—pop pl PA-2
Wagontown Creek—stream ID-8
Wagontown Dam—dam PA-2
Wagon Town (Site)—locale ID-8
Wagon Trace—trail MO-7
Wagon Track Branch—stream MS-4
Wagon Trail Ranch—locale OR-9
Wagon Trail Wash—stream NM-5
Wagon Train Lake—reservoir NE-7
Wagontree Branch—stream NC-3
Wagon Truck Ridge—ridge CO-8
Wagon Wheel—locale FL-3
**Wagon Wheel**—pop pl GA-3
Wagon Wheel Bay—bay ID-8
Wagonwheel Campground—locale MA-1
Wagon Wheel Campground—park AZ-5
Wagon Wheel Canyon—valley AZ-5
Wagon Wheel Canyon—valley CA-9
Wagon Wheel Creek—stream AK-9
Wagon Wheel Creek—stream AR-4
Wagonwheel Creek—stream CO-8
Wagon Wheel Creek—stream NV-8
Wagon Wheel Creek—stream OR-9
Wagon Wheel Ditch—canal CO-8
Wagon Wheel Draw—valley CA-9
Wagon Wheel Flat—flat OR-9
Wagonwheel Gap CO-8
Wagon Wheel Gap—gap CO-8
Wagon Wheel Gap—gap MO-7
Wagon Wheel Gap—gap TX-5
Wagon Wheel Gap—locale CO-8
Wagon Wheel Gap RR Station—hist pl CO-8
Wagon Wheel Hill TX-5
Wagon Wheel Hill—summit MI-6
Wagon Wheel Hill—summit ND-7
Wagonwheel Hole—bay OR-9
Wagon Wheel Island—island FL-3
Wagon Wheel Island—island WI-6
Wagon Wheel Lake—lake AZ-5
Wagon Wheel Lake—lake CA-9
Wagon Wheel Lake—lake IN-6
Wagon Wheel Lake—lake MN-6
Wagonwheel Lake—lake WA-9
Wagon Wheel Lake—reservoir AL-4
Wagon Wheel Lake Dam—dam AL-4
Wagon Wheel Landing—locale NY-2
Wagon Wheel Mobile Ranch—locale AZ-5
Wagon Wheel Mtn—summit CA-9
Wagonwheel Park—park OR-9
Wagon Wheel Point—cliff CO-8
Wagon Wheel Ranch—locale CA-9
Wagonwheel Ranch—locale CA-9
Wagon Wheel Ranch—locale CO-8
Wagon Wheel Ranch—locale MT-8
Wagon Wheel Ranch—locale TX-5
Wagonwheel Ranch—locale TX-5
**Wagon Wheel Ranch**—pop pl KS-7
Wagon Wheel Rest Area—park AZ-5
Wagon Wheel Sch—school OK-5
Wagon Wheel Shop Ctr—locale AZ-5
Wagon Wheel Spring ID-8
Wagonwheel Spring—spring ID-8
Wagon Wheel Spring—spring NV-8
Wagon Wheel Spring—spring WY-8
Wagon Wheel Tank—reservoir TX-5
Wagon Wheel Trading Post—locale AZ-5
Wagon Wheel Trail—trail MT-8
**Wagon Wheel Trailer Park**—pop pl UT-8
Wagon Wheel Wash—stream AZ-5
Wagon Wheel Well—well (2) AZ-5
Wagon Works OH-6
Wagosh Lake—lake MN-6
Wagram KS-7
**Wagram**—pop pl NC-3
**Wagram**—pop pl OH-6
Wagram Cem—cemetery TX-5
Wagram Creek VA-3
Wagram Creek—stream MD-2
WAGR-AM (Lumberton)—tower NC-3
Wagram Sch—school NC-3
Wagram Swamp Branch—stream MD-2
Wagsam KS-7
Wags Pinnacle—pillar WY-8
**Wagstaff**—pop pl KS-7
**Wagstaff Acres Subdivision**—pop pl UT-8
Wagstaff Corner—locale NY-2
Wagstaff Draw UT-8
Wagstaff Hollow—valley UT-8
Wagstaff Lake—reservoir KS-7
Wagstaff Pond—reservoir NC-3
Wagstaff Pond Dam—dam NC-3
Wagstaff Ranch—locale WY-8
WAGY-AM (Forest City)—tower NC-3
Wagy Flat—flat CA-9
**Wagy Flats**—pop pl CA-9
Wagyoel—cape FM-9
Wagy Sch—school IL-6
Waha—locale ID-8
Waha, Lake—lake ID-8
Wahaboncey, Lake (historical)—lake IA-7
Wahachee Creek—stream GA-3
Wahackick NJ-2
Wahagbonsy—locale IA-7
Wahajhamka (FS-573)—hist pl NM-5
Wahak Hotontk AZ-5
**Wahak Hotrontk**—pop pl AZ-5
Wahalak—locale MS-4
Wahalak Baptist Church AL-4
Wahalak Ch—church AL-4
Wahalak Ch—church MS-4
Wahalak Creek—stream AL-4
Wahalak Creek—stream MS-4
Wahalak First Baptist Church MS-4
Wahalak Landing (historical)—locale AL-4
Wahalak Post Office (historical)—building MS-4
Wahalee Canyon—valley NM-5
Wahalla Hollow—valley OH-6
Wahama HS—school WV-2
Wahane Gulch—valley HI-9
Wahane Valley—valley HI-9
Wahanna Creek OR-9
Wahanna Lake—lake OR-9
Waha Oil Field—oilfield TX-5
Wahapa Lake AL-4
Waha Pele—crater HI-9
Waha Pele Crater HI-9
Wahapuu Point HI-9
W A Harral Ranch—locale TX-5
Wahatawangang Lake MN-6
Wahathako FL-3
Wahatis Peak—summit WA-9
Wahatoya Camp—locale CO-8
Wahatoya Creek—stream CO-8
Wahatoya Lake Rsvr—reservoir CO-8
Wahatoya Sch—school CO-8
Wahatoye Creek CO-8
Wahaula Heiau—locale HI-9
Wahbay SD-7
Wahbay Post Office (historical)—building SD-7
Wahbay Township (historical)—civil SD-7
Wahbegon Island—island WI-6
Wahb Springs (sulphur)—spring WY-8
Wahcheechee Mtn—summit MT-8
Wahclella Natural Park—flat WA-9
Wahcohah Park—park MA-1
Wahconah County Club—locale MA-1
Wahconah Falls—falls MA-1
Wahconah Falls Brook—stream MA-1
Wahconah Falls Dam MA-1
Wahconah Regional HS—school MA-1
Wahcoutah Island—island WI-6
Wahee Cem—cemetery SC-3
Wahee Neck—cape SC-3
Wahe Falls—falls OR-9
**Wahehe Township**—pop pl SD-7
Wahelo, Lake—lake IL-6
Waherak Maiher—hist pl MH-9
Wahguyhe Peak—summit NV-8
Wahhi Falls—falls WY-8
Wah Hoo Lake—lake CA-9
Wahi, Puu—summit HI-9
Wahiawa—area HI-9
Wahiawa—civil (2) HI-9
**Wahiawa**—pop pl HI-9
Wahiawa Bay—bay HI-9
Wahiawa (CCD)—cens area HI-9
Wahiawa Harbor HI-9
Wahiawa Homesteads—civil HI-9
Wahiawa Intermediate Sch—school HI-9
Wahiawa Naval Communications Station—military HI-9
Wahiawa Reservoir Ditch—canal HI-9
Wahiawa Rsvr—reservoir HI-9
Wahiawa Sch—school HI-9
Wahiawa Stream—stream HI-9
Wahi Cem—cemetery ND-7
Wahie, Lae—cape HI-9
Wahie Point HI-9
Wahikuli HI-9
Wahikuli—civil HI-9
Wahikuli Gulch—valley HI-9
Wahikuli Pump Ditch—canal HI-9
Wahikuli Rsvr—reservoir HI-9
Wahilauhue—locale HI-9
Wahilauhue Gulch—valley HI-9
Wahiloa Falls—falls HI-9
Wahine Maka Nui—island HI-9
Wahinepee Stream—stream HI-9
Wahiola Falls HI-9
Wahir, Dolen—summit FM-9
Wahi Serek—cape FM-9
Wahiuli HI-9
Wahjamega—locale MI-6
Wahjamega Cem—cemetery MI-6
Wahjamegal MI-6
Wahkeena Creek—stream OR-9
Wahkeena Falls—falls OR-9
Wahkeena Rearing Lake—reservoir OR-9
**Wah Keeney Park**—pop pl CO-8
**Wahketa Village**—pop pl CO-8
**Wahkiacus**—pop pl WA-9
Wahkiacus Canyon—valley WA-9
**Wahkiacus (RR name Wahkiakus)**—pop pl WA-9
**Wahkiakum County**—pop pl WA-9
Wahkiakus WA-9
Wahkiakus Canyon WA-9
Wahkiakus (CCD)—cens area WA-9
Wahkiakus (RR name for Wahkiacus)—other WA-9
**Wahkon**—pop pl MN-6
Wahkon Bay—bay MN-6
Wahl—locale AL-4
Wahl—locale WA-9
Wah-Lal-La-Kite Cem—cemetery WA-9
Wahlamath River OR-9
Wahl Branch—stream AR-4
Wahl Brook—stream NY-2
Wahl Ditch—canal OH-6
Wahl Knoll—summit AZ-5
Wahl Lake—lake MI-6
Wahl Lake—lake ND-7
Wahl Mine (historical)—mine ID-8
Wahloh Creek AL-4
Wahlok Creek AL-4
Wahl Park—park WI-6
Wahlquist Creek—stream MT-8
Wahlquist JHS—school UT-8
Wahl Ranch—locale CO-8
**Wahlsburg**—pop pl OH-6
Wahlsten—locale MN-6
Wahlstrom Hollow—valley ID-8
Wahlstrom Lake—lake MI-6
Wahluke—locale WA-9
Wahluke Branch Canal—canal WA-9
Wahluke Siphon—other WA-9
Wahluke Slope—slope WA-9
**Wahlville**—pop pl PA-2
**Wahmeda**—pop pl NY-2
Wahmonie Flat—flat NV-8
Wahmonie (Site)—locale NV-8
**Wahnena (Township of)**—pop pl MN-6
Wahneshin Lake—lake MN-6
Wahneta—locale PA-2
**Wahneta**—pop pl FL-3
Wahneta Elem Sch—school FL-3
Wahneta Farms Drainage Canal—canal FL-3
Wahnetah (East Mauch Chunk)—uninc pl PA-2
Wahnoosnook Hills MA-1
Waho Gulch—valley MT-8
**Wahoma**—pop pl GA-3
Wahoo—locale FL-3
**Wahoo**—pop pl GA-3
**Wahoo**—pop pl NE-7
**Wahoo**—pop pl WV-2
Wahoo Bay Public Use Area—park OK-5
Wahoo Burlington Depot—hist pl NE-7
Wahoo Canyon—valley NM-5
Wahoo Ch—church GA-3
Wahoo Creek—stream (2) GA-3
Wahoo Creek—stream (2) ID-8
Wahoo Creek—stream MT-8
Wahoo Creek—stream NE-7
Wahoo Creek Access Point—cape GA-3
Wahoo Creek Bridge—bridge GA-3
Wahoo Ditch—canal OH-6
Wahoo Gulch—valley OR-9
**Wahoo (historical)**—pop pl TN-4
Wahoo Island—island GA-3
Wahoo Lake—lake AK-9
Wahoo Lake—lake CA-9
Wahoo Lake—lake TX-5
Wahoo Lake—reservoir MO-7
Wahoo Pass—gap ID-8
Wahoo Pass—gap MT-8
Wahoo Peak—summit ID-8
Wahoo Post Office (historical)—building TN-4
Wahoo Prairie Drain—stream MI-6
Wahoo Ranch—locale NM-5
Wahoo River—stream GA-3
Wahoo (Site)—locale CA-9
**Wahoo Subdivision**—pop pl UT-8
**Wahoo Township**—pop pl NE-7
Wahoo Valley—valley TN-4
Wahoo Waters, Lake—reservoir MO-7
Wahorlock MS-4
Wahorlock Creek MS-4
**Wahouma**—pop pl AL-4
Wahouma Park—park AL-4
**Wahpco**—pop pl NE-7
Wahpenayo Peak—summit WA-9
**Wahpeton**—pop pl IA-7
**Wahpeton**—pop pl ND-7
Wahpeton Hosp—hist pl ND-7
Wahpeton Indian Sch—school ND-7
**Wahpeton Junction**—pop pl ND-7
Wahpeton Sch Number 5—school ND-7
Wahpoo Creek—stream AK-9
Wahpugaissee WI-6
Wahrani Swamp—stream VA-3
Wahrenberger House—hist pl TX-5
WAHR-FM (Huntsville)—tower AL-4
Wahrikidam FM-9
Wahsatch—locale UT-8
Wahsatch Range UT-8
Wahseeja Lake—lake MT-8
Wah-Shah-She Girl Scout Camp—locale OK-5
Wah-Sha-She Prairie State Wildlife Area—park MO-7
Wah-shing Wash AZ-5
WAHT-AM (Annville-Cleona)—tower PA-2
Wah-toh-sah Lake WI-6
Wahtoke—locale CA-9
Wahtoke Creek—stream CA-9
Wahtoke Ditch—canal CA-9
Wahtoke Lake—lake CA-9
Wahtom Pocosin—swamp NC-3
Wahtom Swamp—stream NC-3
Wahtonka HS—school OR-9
Wahtonsa Sch—school IA-7
Wahtum Campground OR-9
Wahtum Creek—stream WA-9
Wahtum Lake—lake OR-9
Wahtum Lake Campground—park OR-9
Wahtum Lake Guard Station—locale OR-9
Wahuaalapai—summit HI-9
W A Hughes Lake—reservoir AL-4
W A Hughes Lake Dam—dam AL-4
Wah Wah Cove—valley UT-8
Wah Wah Mtns—range UT-8
Wah Wah Ranch—locale UT-8
Wah Wah Range UT-8
Wah Wah Rsvr—reservoir UT-8
Wah Wah Spring UT-8
Wah Wah Springs—spring UT-8
Wah Wah Summit—summit UT-8
Wah-wah-tay WI-6
Wah Wah Valley—valley UT-8
Wah Wah Valley Hardpan—flat UT-8
Wah Wah Wash—valley UT-8
Wah Wah Well—well UT-8
**Wahweap**—pop pl AZ-5
Wahweap Airp—airport AZ-5
Wahweap Bay—bay AZ-5
Wahweap Bay—bay UT-8
Wahweap Creek—stream AZ-5
Wahweap Creek—stream UT-8
Wahweap Lodge and Marina—locale AZ-5
Wahweap Wash UT-8
Wahweap Window—arch UT-8
Wah Weep Creek UT-8
Wahyah Creek NC-3
Wahyah Island WA-9
Waiaaka Stream—stream HI-9
Waiaalala Stream—stream HI-9
Waiaama Bay—bay HI-9
Waiaama Gulch—valley HI-9
Waiaama Stream—stream HI-9
Waiaele Gulch—valley HI-9
Waiaelepi—lake HI-9
Waiaha—bay HI-9
Waiaha—civil HI-9
Waiaha Springs For Res—forest HI-9
Waiaha Stream HI-9
Waiaha Stream—stream HI-9
Waiahewahewa Gulch—valley HI-9
Waiahi-Aqueduct—canal HI-9
Waiahi Iliiliula Ditch—canal HI-9
Waiahi Stream—stream HI-9
Waiahole—civil HI-9
**Waiahole**—pop pl HI-9
Waiahole Camp—locale HI-9
Waiahole Ditch—canal HI-9
Waiahole Ditch Company Tunnel HI-9
Waiahole Ditch Tunnel—tunnel HI-9
Waiahole For Res—forest HI-9
Waiahole Homesteads—civil HI-9
Waiahole Stream—stream HI-9
Waiahookalo Gulch—valley HI-9
Waiahuakua—summit HI-9
Waiahuakua Stream—stream HI-9
Waiahukini—locale HI-9
Waiahuli—lake HI-9
Waiahulu Stream—stream HI-9
Waiaka—civil HI-9
**Waiaka**—pop pl HI-9
Waiakaa HI-9
Waiaka Gulch—valley HI-9
Waiaka Heiau—locale HI-9
Waiakahiula One—civil HI-9
Waiakahiula Two—civil HI-9
Waiakailio—spring HI-9
Waiakailio Bay—bay HI-9
Waiakaiole Gulch—valley HI-9
Waiakalae Gulch—valley (2) HI-9
Waiakaloa Gulch—valley HI-9
Waiakalua Rsvr—reservoir HI-9
Waiakamali Gulch—valley HI-9
Waiakamoi HI-9
Waiakamoi Stream HI-9
Waiakamoo Valley—valley HI-9
Waiakanapo—cape HI-9
Waiakane Gulch—valley HI-9
Waiakane Spring—spring HI-9
Waiakanonula—summit HI-9
Waiaka Pond—lake HI-9
Waiakapuaa—area HI-9
Waiakapuhi—island HI-9
Waiaka Ridge—ridge HI-9
Waiaka Stream—stream HI-9
Waiakauaua Gulch—valley HI-9
Waiaka Valley—valley HI-9
Waiakea—civil HI-9
**Waiakea**—pop pl HI-9
**Waiakea Camps**—pop pl HI-9
Waiakea Camp (Site)—locale HI-9
Waiakea Creek HI-9
Waiakea For Res—forest HI-9
Waiakea Homesteads—civil HI-9
**Waiakea Houselots**—pop pl HI-9
Waiakea-Kai Sch—school HI-9
Waiakeakua—area HI-9
Waiakeakua—spring HI-9
Waiakeakua Stream—stream (2) HI-9
Waiakea Pond—lake HI-9
Waiakea Rsvr—reservoir HI-9
Waiakea Stream HI-9
Waiakea Stream—stream HI-9
Waiakea-Uka Sch—school HI-9
Waiakea-Uka Springs—spring HI-9
Waiakea-Waena Sch—school HI-9
Waiakoa—civil HI-9
**Waiakoa**—pop pl HI-9
**Waiakoa (census name Kula)**—pop pl HI-9
Waiakoa Gulch—valley HI-9
Waiakoa Homesteads—civil HI-9
Waiakoali Stream—stream HI-9
Waiakolea Pond—lake HI-9
Waiakuhi—lake HI-9
Waiakuilani Gulch—valley HI-9
Waiakumalae Point—cape HI-9
Waiakuna Pond—lake HI-9
**Waialae**—pop pl HI-9
Waialae Beach Park—park HI-9
Waialae Cabin—locale HI-9
Waialae Falls—falls (2) HI-9
Waialae Golf Course—other HI-9
Waialae Iki—civil HI-9
**Waialae-kahala**—pop pl HI-9
Waialae Nui—civil HI-9
Waialaenui Gulch—valley HI-9
Waialae River HI-9
Waialae Sch—school HI-9
Waialae Stream—stream HI-9
Waialala Gulch—valley HI-9
Waialama Canal HI-9
Waialana Gulch—valley HI-9
Waialapai Gulch—valley HI-9
Waialea Bay—bay HI-9
Waialeale—area HI-9
Waialeale Gulch—valley HI-9
Waialeale Mountain HI-9
Waialeale One—civil HI-9
Waialeale Peak HI-9
Waialeale Two—civil HI-9
Waialee—civil HI-9
**Waialee**—pop pl HI-9
Waialee Bay HI-9
Waialee Gulch—valley HI-9
Waialee Station HI-9
Waiale Falls—falls HI-9
Waiale Gulch—valley HI-9
Waialeia HI-9
Waialeia Stream—stream HI-9
Waiale Reservoirs—reservoir HI-9
Waialohe Point—cape HI-9
Waialua—civil HI-9
Waialua—lake HI-9
**Waialua**—pop pl (2) HI-9
Waialua Agricultural Company Engine No. 6—hist pl HI-9
Waialua Bay HI-9
Waialua Bay—bay HI-9
Waialua (CCD)—cens area HI-9
Waialua Fire Station—hist pl HI-9
Waialua Gakuen Sch—school HI-9
Waialua Mill HI-9
**Waialua Mill**—pop pl HI-9
Waialua Sch—hist pl HI-9
Waialua Sch—school HI-9
Waialua Stream—stream HI-9
Waiamoa Falls—falls HI-9
**Waianae**—pop pl HI-9
Waianae (CCD)—cens area HI-9
Waianae District—hist pl HI-9
Waianae Homesteads—civil HI-9
Waianae HS—school HI-9
Waianae Kai—civil HI-9
Waianae Kai For Res—forest HI-9
Waianae Pililaau Field—park HI-9
Waianae Range—range HI-9
Waianae Uka—civil HI-9
Waianae Valley—valley HI-9
Waianai HI-9
Waianapanapa Cave—cave HI-9
Waianu—cape HI-9
Waianuenue Falls—falls HI-9
Waianuenue Stream—stream HI-9
Waianui Gulch—valley HI-9
Waianukole—beach HI-9
Waianu Stream—stream HI-9
Waiaooli Gulch—valley HI-9
Waiaopae HI-9
Waiapaa Gulch—valley HI-9
Waiapele Bay—bay HI-9
Waiapuaa Valley—valley HI-9
Waiapuka—civil HI-9
Waiapuka—lake HI-9
Waiapuka Gulch—valley HI-9
Waiapuka Stream—stream HI-9
Waiarua HI-9
Waiau—civil HI-9
**Waiau**—pop pl HI-9
Waiau, Lake—lake HI-9
Waiau Flume—canal HI-9
Waiauia—civil HI-9
Waiau Lake HI-9
Waiau Pond HI-9
Waiau Sch—school HI-9
Waiau Spring—spring HI-9
Waiau Station HI-9
Waiau Stream—stream (2) HI-9
Waiawa—civil HI-9
Waiawaawa Rsvr—reservoir HI-9
Waiawa Gulch HI-9
Waiawa Rsvr—reservoir HI-9
Waiawa Shaft—reservoir HI-9
Waiawa Spring—spring HI-9
Waiawa Stream—stream HI-9
WAID-FM (Clarksdale)—tower MS-4
Waid Gap—gap AL-4
Waidler Lake—reservoir PA-2
Waidman Coal Mine—mine MT-8
Waidozen MP-9
Waidozen-To MP-9
Waid Run—stream PA-2
Waids Bluff OR-9
Waidsboro—locale VA-3
Waid Sch—school VA-3
Waids Draft—valley WV-2
Waiea—civil HI-9
Waiehu—area HI-9
Waiehu—civil HI-9
**Waiehu**—pop pl HI-9
Waiehu Falls HI-9
Waiehu Golf Course—other HI-9
Waiehu Point—cape (2) HI-9
Waiehu Stream—stream HI-9
**Waiehu Village**—pop pl HI-9
Waiele HI-9
Waieli—summit HI-9
Waieli Draw—stream HI-9
Waieli Gulch—valley HI-9
Waieli Hill HI-9
Waiemi Falls—falls HI-9
Waiene Falls HI-9
Waiers Mill NJ-2
Waif Mine—mine AZ-5
Waight Spring—spring OR-9
Waihaiu Pond HI-9
Waihaka Gulch—valley HI-9
Waihale Stream HI-9
Waihali Gulch—valley HI-9
Waihanau Stream—stream HI-9
Waihanu Pond HI-9
Waihee—civil (2) HI-9
**Waihee**—pop pl HI-9
Waihee Ditch—canal HI-9
Waihee Falls HI-9
Waihee Farm—locale HI-9
Waihee Point—cape HI-9
Waihee Reef—bar HI-9
Waihee River—stream HI-9
Waihee Stream HI-9
Waihee Stream—stream (2) HI-9
Waihee Tunnel—cave HI-9
Waihee Valley—valley HI-9
Waihee-Waikapu (CCD)—cens area HI-9
Waihii—spring HI-9
Waihii Gulch—valley HI-9
Waihilahila Fishpond—lake HI-9
Waihilau Stream—stream HI-9
Waihi Spring—spring HI-9
Waihi Stream—stream HI-9
Waihiumalu Falls—falls HI-9
Waihohonu Hill HI-9
Waihohonu Stream—stream HI-9
Waihoi Springs—spring HI-9
Waihoi Valley—valley HI-9
Waihole Gulch—valley HI-9
Waiholoa Falls—falls HI-9
Waihonu Pond—bay HI-9
Waihoolana—area HI-9
**Waihou**—pop pl HI-9
Waihou Spring—spring HI-9
Waihou Spring Reserve—other HI-9
Waihuna—summit HI-9
Waihuna Hill HI-9
Waihunahuna—area HI-9
Waihunehune Falls—falls HI-9
Waihu Spring—spring HI-9
Waiias—unknown FM-9
Waiilikahi Falls—falls HI-9
Waiilikahi Stream—stream HI-9
Waiio Kipuka—area HI-9
Waika—civil HI-9
Waikaalulu—civil HI-9
Waikaalulu Gulch—valley HI-9
Waikaea Canal—canal HI-9
Waikahalulu Bay—bay HI-9
Waikahalulu Gulch—valley HI-9
Waikahekahe—civil HI-9
Waikahekahe Iki—civil HI-9
Waikahekahe Nui—civil HI-9
Waikaia Rsvr—reservoir HI-9
Waikai Rsvr—reservoir HI-9
Waikai Valley—valley HI-9
Waikaka Falls—falls HI-9
Waikakalaua Ditch—canal HI-9
Waikakalaua Gulch HI-9
Waikakalaua Stream—stream HI-9
Waikakalauna HI-9
Waikakulu—summit HI-9
Waikakuu—civil HI-9
Waikalae Gulch HI-9
Waikaloa Stream—stream HI-9
Waikama Gulch—valley HI-9
Waikamakapo (site)—locale HI-9
Waikamoi Creek HI-9
Waikamoi Stream—stream HI-9
Waikamo Stream HI-9
Waikanaloa Wet Cave—cave HI-9
Waikane—civil HI-9
**Waikane**—pop pl HI-9
Waikane Camp—locale HI-9
Waikane Stream—stream HI-9
Waikane Taro Flats—hist pl HI-9
Waikani Falls—falls HI-9
Waikani Gulch—valley HI-9
Waikapalae Wet Cave—cave HI-9
Waikapu—civil (2) HI-9
**Waikapu**—pop pl HI-9
Waikapuna—locale HI-9
Waikapuna Bay—bay HI-9
Waikapuna Pali—cliff HI-9
**Waikapu Reservoir Village**—pop pl HI-9
Waikapu South Side Ditch HI-9
Waikapu Stream—stream HI-9
Waikapu Valley—valley HI-9
Waikau Cabin—locale HI-9
Waikaulapala Gulch—valley HI-9
Waikaumalo—civil HI-9
Waikaumalo-Mauaua Homesteads—civil HI-9
Waikaumalo Park—park HI-9
Waikaumalo Stream—stream HI-9
Waikeakua Gulch—valley HI-9
Waikeekee Stream—stream HI-9
Waikekeehia—area HI-9
Waikele—civil HI-9
Waikele Stream—stream HI-9
**Waikii**—pop pl HI-9
Waikii Gulch—valley HI-9
Waikii Paddock Game Mngmt Area—park HI-9
Waikii Pump Station—other HI-9
**Waikiki**—pop pl HI-9
Waikiki Beach—beach HI-9
Waikiki Sch—school HI-9
Waikiki Shell—other HI-9
Waikiki Springs—spring WA-9
Waikoana Stream—stream HI-9
Waikoekoe—civil HI-9
Waikoekoe Gulch—valley HI-9

Waikoko—*civil* HI-9
Waikoko Stream—*stream* HI-9
*Waikola* HI-9
*Waikola Stream* HI-9
Waikoloa—*civil* (2) HI-9
Waikoloa Gulch—*valley* HI-9
Waikoloaiki—*civil* HI-9
Waikoloa Ponds—*lake* HI-9
Waikoloa Stream—*stream* (2) HI-9
Waikoloa Village—*post sta* HI-9
*Waikolo Gulch* HI-9
Waikoloi Gulch—*valley* HI-9
Waikoloi Rsvr—*reservoir* HI-9
Waikolu—*civil* HI-9
Waikolu Stream—*stream* (2) HI-9
Waikomo Stream—*stream* HI-9
**Waikui**—*pop pl* HI-9
Waikui Beach—*beach* HI-9
Waikulukulu—*crater* HI-9
Waikumono—*area* HI-9
Waikupanaha Pond—*lake* HI-9
*Wailacks Point* CT-1
Wailaki Campground—*locale* CA-9
Wailapa Stream—*stream* HI-9
*Wailau* HI-9
Wailau—*civil* (2) HI-9
Wailau—*locale* HI-9
Wailaulau—*civil* HI-9
Wailaulau Gulch—*valley* HI-9
Wailau Stream—*stream* HI-9
Wailau Trail—*trail* (2) HI-9
Wailau Valley—*valley* HI-9
*Wailda River* HI-9
Wailea—*cape* (2) HI-9
Wailea—*CDP* HI-9
Wailea—*civil* HI-9
**Wailea**—*pop pl* HI-9
Wailea Bay—*bay* HI-9
Wailea Point—*cape* HI-9
Wailele Falls—*falls* HI-9
Wailele Gulch—*valley* HI-9
Wailele Spring—*spring* HI-9
Wailena Gulch—*valley* HI-9
Wailepua Spring—*spring* HI-9
Wail Lake—*lake* MN-6
Wailoa Ditch—*canal* HI-9
Wailoa Falls—*falls* HI-9
*Wailoa River* HI-9
Wailoa River—*stream* HI-9
Wailoa River Park—*park* HI-9
Wailoa Stream—*stream* HI-9
Wailohi—*area* HI-9
Wailoku Gulch—*valley* HI-9
Wailua—*civil* (3) HI-9
Wailua—*locale* HI-9
**Wailua**—*pop pl* (2) HI-9
Wailua-Anahola (CCD)—*cens area* HI-9
Wailua Bay—*bay* HI-9
Wailua Complex of Heiaus—*hist pl* HI-9
Wailua Cove—*bay* HI-9
Wailua Falls—*falls* (2) HI-9
Wailua Homesteads—*civil* HI-9
Wailua Homesteads—*other* HI-9
**Wailua House Lots**—*pop pl* HI-9
Wailuaiki—*civil* HI-9
Wailuaiki Bay—*bay* HI-9
Wailuaiki Stream—*stream* HI-9
Wailuanui—*civil* HI-9
Wailuanui Bay—*bay* HI-9
Wailuanui Stream—*stream* HI-9
Wailua River—*stream* HI-9
Wailua River State Park—*park* HI-9
Wailua Rsvr—*reservoir* HI-9
Wailua Stream—*stream* HI-9
**Wailua (Wailua Homesteads)**—*pop pl* HI-9
Wailua (Wailua Houselots)—*CDP* HI-9
Wailuku—*civil* HI-9
**Wailuku**—*pop pl* HI-9
Wailuku (CCD)—*cens area* HI-9
Wailuku Civic Center Hist Dist—*hist pl* HI-9
**Wailuku Heights**—*pop pl* HI-9
*Wailuku River* HI-9
Wailuku River—*stream* HI-9
*Wailupe* HI-9
Wailupe—*civil* HI-9
**Wailupe**—*pop pl* HI-9
Wailupe Beach Park—*park* HI-9
Wailupe Gulch—*valley* HI-9
Wailupe Peninsula—*cape* HI-9
*Wailupe Stream* HI-9
Wailupe Valley Sch—*school* HI-9
Waimaauou Stream—*stream* HI-9
Waimahaihai—*beach* HI-9
Waimaile Stream—*stream* HI-9
Waimalu—*civil* HI-9
Waimalu Stream—*stream* HI-9
Waimana—*area* HI-9
*Waimanalo* HI-9
Waimanalo—*civil* HI-9
**Waimanalo**—*pop pl* HI-9
*Waimanalo Anchorage* HI-9
Waimanalo Bay—*bay* HI-9
**Waimanalo Beach**—*pop pl* HI-9
Waimanalo Beach Park—*park* HI-9
Waimanalo For Res—*forest* HI-9
Waimanalo Gulch—*valley* HI-9
Waimanalo Stream—*stream* HI-9
*Waimanalo Village* HI-9
**Waimane Home (Farm Colony)**—*pop pl* HI-9
Waimano—*civil* HI-9
*Waimano Gulch* HI-9
Waimano Stream—*stream* HI-9
Waimano Trail—*trail* HI-9
Waimanu—*civil* HI-9
Waimanu Bay—*bay* HI-9
Waimanu Falls—*falls* HI-9
Waimanu Gap—*gap* HI-9
Waimanu Stream—*stream* HI-9
Waimanu Trail—*trail* HI-9
Waimanu Valley—*valley* HI-9
Waima Point—*cape* HI-9
Waima Stream—*stream* HI-9
Waimea—*civil* (2) HI-9
**Waimea**—*pop pl* (2) HI-9
Waimea Bay—*bay* (2) HI-9
Waimea Bay Beach Park—*park* HI-9
Waimea Canyon—*valley* HI-9
Waimea Canyon Lookout—*locale* HI-9
Waimea Canyon State Park—*park* HI-9
Waimea (census name for Kamuela)—*CDP* HI-9
Waimea Ditch—*canal* HI-9
Waimea Falls—*falls* HI-9
Waimea Homesteads—*civil* HI-9
**Waimea (Kamuela Post Office)**—*pop pl* HI-9
Waimea-Kohala Airp—*airport* HI-9
Waimea River—*stream* (2) HI-9
*Waimea Roadstead* HI-9
Waimea Rsvr—*reservoir* HI-9
*Waimea Station* HI-9
*Waimea Stream* HI-9
Waimoku Falls—*falls* HI-9
*Waimuki Fall* HI-9
Waimuku—*civil* HI-9
*Wainae* HI-9
*Wainae Uku* HI-9
Wainaia Cem—*cemetery* HI-9
Wainaia Gulch—*valley* HI-9
Wainaku—*civil* HI-9
**Wainaku**—*pop pl* HI-9
Wainaku Camp—*locale* HI-9
*Wainaku Landing* HI-9
*Wainaku Mill* HI-9
Wainee—*civil* HI-9
**Wainee**—*pop pl* HI-9
Waineke Swamp—*stream* HI-9
Waineku Rsvr—*reservoir* HI-9
Wainene—*cape* HI-9
*Wainiha* HI-9
Wainiha—*civil* HI-9
Wainiha—*locale* HI-9
Wainiha Bay—*bay* HI-9
Wainiha Pali—*cliff* HI-9
Wainiha River—*stream* HI-9
*Wainike* HI-9
**Waino**—*pop pl* WI-6
Wainola—*locale* MI-6
Wainola Ch—*church* MI-6
Wainonoia Stream—*stream* HI-9
*Wainooset Hills* MA-1
Wainright Landing—*locale* FL-3
**Wainscott**—*pop pl* NY-2
Wainscott Beach—*beach* NY-2
Wainscott Cem—*cemetery* NY-2
Wainscott Pond—*lake* NY-2
Wainscott Windmill—*hist pl* NY-2
Wainville—*locale* WV-2
*Wainwright* KS-7
Wainwright—*locale* AL-4
**Wainwright**—*pop pl* AK-9
**Wainwright**—*pop pl* MO-7
**Wainwright**—*pop pl* (2) OH-6
**Wainwright**—*pop pl* OK-5
Wainwright—*uninc pl* TX-5
Wainwright Bldg—*hist pl* MO-7
Wainwright Cem—*cemetery* LA-4
Wainwright Draw—*valley* CO-8
Wainwright Hill—*summit* VT-1
Wainwright Inlet—*bay* AK-9
Wainwright Island—*island* NC-3
Wainwright Mtn—*summit* NY-2
Wainwright Park—*park* FL-3
Wainwright Pond—*reservoir* NC-3
Wainwright Pond Dam—*dam* NC-3
Wainwright Run—*stream* PA-2
Wainwrights Airp—*airport* PA-2
Wainwright Sch—*school* MI-6
Wainwright Sch—*school* (2) TX-5
Wainwright Sch—*school* WA-9
Wainwright Sch (abandoned)—*school* PA-2
Wainwright Slue—*gut* NC-3
Wainwright Spring—*spring* CO-8
Wainwright Tomb—*hist pl* MO-7
Waioala Spring—*spring* HI-9
*Waioa Stream* HI-9
Waiohinu—*civil* HI-9
**Waiohinu**—*pop pl* HI-9
*Waiohinu Area* HI-9
Waiohinu Park—*park* HI-9
Waiohiwi Falls—*falls* HI-9
Waiohiwi Gulch—*valley* HI-9
Waiohonu—*civil* HI-9
Waiohonu—*summit* HI-9
*Waiohonu Gulch* HI-9
Waiohonu Kakio Homesteads—*civil* HI-9
Waiohonu Stream—*stream* HI-9
Waiohookalo Stream—*stream* HI-9
*Waiohue* HI-9
Waiohue—*civil* HI-9
Waiohue Bay—*bay* HI-9
Waiohue Gulch—*valley* HI-9
*Waiohue Stream* HI-9
*Waiohukini* HI-9
Waiohuli—*civil* HI-9
Waiohuli—*summit* HI-9
Waiohuli Gulch—*valley* HI-9
Waiohuli Keokea—*civil* HI-9
Waiohuli Keokea Beach Homesteads—*civil* HI-9
Waiohuli-Keokea Homesteads—*civil* HI-9
Waioka—*bay* HI-9
Waiokala—*cape* HI-9
*Wai o Kamilo* HI-9
Waiokamilo Stream—*stream* HI-9
Waiokanalopaka Falls—*falls* HI-9
*Waiokane Falls* HI-9
Waiokawa—*crater* HI-9
Waiokeela Stream—*stream* HI-9
Waiokihi—*summit* HI-9
Waiokila Gulch—*valley* HI-9
*Wai o Kilo* HI-9
Waiokilo Falls—*falls* HI-9
*Waiokilo Stream* HI-9
Wai o Kuna Falls—*falls* HI-9
Waiola Cem—*cemetery* HI-9
Waiolai Gulch—*valley* HI-9
Waiolama Canal—*canal* HI-9
Waiola Park—*park* IL-6
Waioli—*civil* HI-9
Waioli Beach Park—*park* HI-9
Waioli Mission District—*hist pl* HI-9
Waioli Park—*park* HI-9
*Waioli River* HI-9
Waioli Stream—*stream* HI-9
Waiolue Falls—*falls* HI-9
Waiomao—*civil* HI-9
Waiomao Stream—*stream* HI-9
*Waioming* PA-2
Waioni Gulch—*valley* HI-9
Waiono—*civil* HI-9
Waiopa—*area* HI-9
Waiopae—*beach* HI-9
Waiopae—*lake* HI-9
Waiopa Gulch—*valley* HI-9
Waiopai Gulch—*valley* HI-9
Waiopai Island—*island* HI-9
Waiopili Heiau—*locale* HI-9
Waiopipi—*summit* HI-9
Waipa—*civil* HI-9
*Waipaa Stream* HI-9
Waipahee Slide—*other* HI-9
Waipahi Point—*cape* HI-9
Waipahi Stream—*stream* HI-9
Waipahoehoe—*locale* HI-9
Waipahoehoe Gulch—*valley* (2) HI-9
*Waipahoehoe Stream* HI-9
Waipahoehoe Stream—*stream* (2) HI-9
**Waipahu**—*pop pl* HI-9
Waipahu Field—*park* HI-9
Waipahu HS—*school* HI-9
Waipahu Intermediate Sch—*school* HI-9
Waipahu Sch—*school* HI-9
Waipake—*civil* HI-9
*Waipake River* HI-9
Waipake Stream—*stream* HI-9
Waipao—*civil* HI-9
*Waipao Gulch* HI-9
Waipaoiki Valley—*valley* HI-9
Waipao Valley—*valley* (2) HI-9
Waipa Stream—*stream* HI-9
*Waipau* HI-9
Waipauma Point—*cape* HI-9
Waipiele Gulch—*valley* HI-9
Waipili Gulch—*valley* HI-9
Waipilopilo Gulch—*valley* HI-9
*Waipio* HI-9
Waipio—*civil* (2) HI-9
**Waipio**—*pop pl* HI-9
**Waipio Acres**—*pop pl* HI-9
Waipio Acres (Libby-Waipio)—*CDP* HI-9
Waipio Bay—*bay* (2) HI-9
*Waipio Camp A* HI-9
*Waipio Gulch* HI-9
Waipioiki—*civil* HI-9
Waipionui—*civil* HI-9
Waipio Pali—*cliff* HI-9
Waipio Peninsula—*cape* HI-9
Waipio Point—*cape* HI-9
*Waipio River* HI-9
*Waipio Stream* HI-9
Waipio Stream—*stream* (2) HI-9
Waipio Valley—*valley* HI-9
Waipoo Falls—*falls* HI-9
Waipouli—*bay* HI-9
Waipouli—*civil* HI-9
Waipouli—*lake* HI-9
**Waipouli**—*pop pl* HI-9
Waipu—*beach* (2) HI-9
Waipuhia Falls—*falls* HI-9
Waipuhi Fishpond—*lake* HI-9
Waipuhi Gulch—*valley* HI-9
Waipuilani Gulch—*valley* HI-9
Waipuku Point—*cape* HI-9
Waipuloku Spring—*spring* HI-9
Waipunaea Stream—*stream* HI-9
Waipunahina Gulch—*valley* HI-9
Waipunahoe Gulch—*valley* HI-9
Waipunalau Gulch—*valley* (2) HI-9
Waipunalei—*civil* HI-9
Waipunalei Homesteads—*civil* HI-9
Waipunalei Stream—*stream* HI-9
Waipunalei Trail—*trail* HI-9
Waipunaula—*civil* HI-9
Waipuni—*summit* HI-9
WAIQ-TV (Montgomery)—*tower* AL-4
WAIR-AM (Winston-Salem)—*tower* NC-3
Wair Chapel—*church* MO-7
Wair Sch (abandoned)—*school* MO-7
Waiska Bay—*bay* MI-6
Waiska River—*stream* MI-6
Waisley Airp—*airport* PA-2
Waisnan Ranch—*locale* SD-7
Waisner Draw—*valley* WY-8
*Wait* AL-4
**Wait**—*pop pl* KY-4
Wait, F. W., House—*hist pl* NY-2
Wait, Walton, House—*hist pl* WV-2
Wait-A-Bit Lake—*lake* AK-9
Waita Rsvr—*reservoir* HI-9
Wait Bay—*bay* VT-1
*Wait Canyon* TX-5
Wait Cem—*cemetery* KS-7
Wait Cem—*cemetery* VT-1
Wait Corners—*locale* NY-2
Wait Creek—*stream* AK-9
Wait Drain—*canal* (2) MI-6
*Waite* AL-4
**Waite**—*pop pl* KY-4
**Waite**—*pop pl* ME-1
Waite, Davis, House—*hist pl* CO-8
Waite And Debolt Drain—*canal* MI-6
*Waite Bay* VT-1
Waite Brook—*stream* VT-1
Waite Cem—*cemetery* CT-1
Waite Cem—*cemetery* IL-6
Waite Cem—*cemetery* TN-4
Waite Cem—*cemetery* TX-5
Waite Cem—*cemetery* VT-1
Waite Creek—*stream* MT-8
Waite Creek—*stream* (2) OR-9
Waite Ditch—*canal* IN-6
Waite Ditch—*canal* (2) MT-8
Waite Ford (historical)—*locale* TN-4
Waite-Friendship Cem—*cemetery* TN-4
Waite Gulch—*valley* SD-7
**Waite Hill**—*pop pl* OH-6
Waite Hill—*summit* ME-1
Waite Hill—*summit* OH-6
Waite Hill (Township of)—*other* OH-6
Waite Hollow—*valley* NY-2
Waite Island—*island* AK-9
Waite Lake—*lake* WI-6
Waite Lake—*reservoir* CO-8
Waite Mtn—*summit* NY-2
Waite Park—*park* MN-6
**Waite Park**—*pop pl* MN-6
Waite Park Sch—*school* MN-6
Waite Pond—*reservoir* (2) MA-1
Waite Pond Dam—*dam* (2) MA-1
*Waitepond Reservoir* MA-1
Waite Ranch—*locale* SD-7
*Waiter Creek* NV-8
Waiter Island—*island* SC-3
Waites—*locale* MS-4
*Waites Bridge* AL-4
Waites Bridge (historical)—*bridge* AL-4
Waites Cem—*cemetery* AL-4
Waite Sch—*school* CA-9
Waite Sch—*school* IL-6
Waite Sch—*school* MO-7
Waite Sch—*school* (2) OH-6
Waite Sch (historical)—*school* PA-2
**Waites Corner**—*pop pl* MA-1
Waites Dam—*dam* AL-4
*Waites Hollow* WV-2
Waites Lake—*reservoir* AL-4
*Waites Landing* AL-4
Waites Landing—*locale* AL-4
Waites Landing—*locale* ME-1
Waites Run—*stream* WV-2
*Waites Siding* MS-4
**Waite (Town of)**—*pop pl* ME-1
Waiteville—*locale* WV-2
Wait Ferry (historical)—*locale* AL-4
Waiting Hill—*summit* MA-1
*Wait Island* CT-1
*Waititi* HI-9
*Waititi Be* HI-9
Wait Knob—*summit* KY-4
Waitman—*locale* KY-4
Waitman-Barbe JHS—*school* WV-2
Waitman Cem—*cemetery* IL-6
Waitojaiing—*island* MP-9
Waitojairik—*island* MP-9
*Waits* MS-4
Waits—*locale* NY-2
**Waitsburg**—*pop pl* WA-9
Waitsburg (CCD)—*cens area* WA-9
Waitsburg Hist Dist—*hist pl* WA-9
**Waitsburg Junction**—*pop pl* WA-9
Waits Cem—*cemetery* KY-4
Waits Ch—*church* OH-6
Wait Sch—*school* MA-1
**Waitsfield**—*pop pl* VT-1
Waitsfield, Mount—*summit* VT-1
**Waitsfield Common**—*pop pl* VT-1
Waitsfield Gap—*gap* VT-1
**Waitsfield (Town of)**—*pop pl* VT-1
Waitsfield Village Hist Dist—*hist pl* VT-1
Waits Hill—*summit* AR-4
*Waits' Island* CT-1
Waits Junction—*locale* FL-3
*Waits Lake* AL-4
*Waits Lake* WA-9
Waits Mtn—*summit* VA-3
Waits Post Office (historical)—*building* MS-4
Waits Ranch—*locale* NE-7
Waits Ranch—*locale* NM-5
**Waits River**—*pop pl* VT-1
Waits River—*stream* VT-1
Waits River Schoolhouse—*hist pl* VT-1
Waits Station—*locale* CA-9
Waitt Brick Block—*hist pl* MA-1
*Waitts Creek* AL-4
Waitts Creek—*stream* WA-9
Waitts Lake—*lake* WA-9
Waitts Mtn—*summit* MA-1
Waiu—*summit* HI-9
Waiu Bay—*bay* HI-9
Waiuha Bay—*bay* HI-9
Waiulaula Gulch—*valley* HI-9
Waiulaula Point—*cape* HI-9
Waiulili Stream—*stream* HI-9
Waiulua Bay—*bay* HI-9
*Waiumakua Peak* HI-9
Waiu Spring—*spring* HI-9
Waiwelawela Point—*cape* HI-9
WAJC-FM (Indianapolis)—*tower* IN-6
WAJE-AM (Ebensburg)—*tower* PA-2
WAJF-AM (Decatur)—*tower* AL-4
WAJN-AM (Ashland City)—*tower* TN-4
**Waka**—*pop pl* TX-5
*Wakahoota School* MS-4
Wakaina—*area* HI-9
*Wakakoi River* AL-4
*Wa-kal-la* CA-9
Wakamiya Inari Shrine—*hist pl* HI-9
Wakanda Park—*park* WI-6
Wakapp—*summit* FM-9
*Wa-ka-ri-chits* UT-8
**Wakarusa**—*pop pl* IN-6
**Wakarusa**—*pop pl* KS-7
*Wakarusa Creek* KS-7
Wakarusa Crossing—*locale* KS-7
Wakarusa Elementary and MS—*school* IN-6
Wakarusa Hotel—*hist pl* KS-7
Wakarusa Presbyterian Ch—*church* KS-7
Wakarusa River—*stream* KS-7
Wakarusa Station (historical)—*locale* KS-7
**Wakarusa Township**—*pop pl* KS-7
**Wakasassa (historical)**—*pop pl* FL-3
**Wakatomika**—*pop pl* OH-6
Wakatomika Creek—*stream* OH-6
*Wake* TX-5
Wake—*locale* VA-3
**Wake**—*pop pl* TX-5
Wake, Wake Island—*post sta* HI-9
Wake Acad—*school* NC-3
WAKE-AM (Valparaiso)—*tower* IN-6
Wakeawasis Creek—*stream* WA-9
Wake Butte—*ridge* OR-9
**Wakeby**—*pop pl* MA-1
Wakeby Pond—*lake* MA-1
*Wake Chapel* MS-4
Wake Chapel—*church* (2) NC-3
Wake County—*civil* NC-3
Wake Creek—*stream* AR-4
Wake Creek—*stream* OR-9
**Wake Crossroads**—*pop pl* NC-3
Wake Crossroads Lake—*reservoir* NC-3
Wake Crossroads Lake Dam—*dam* NC-3
**Wa Keeney**—*pop pl* KS-7
Wa Keeney Township—*civ div* KS-7
Wakeeny Cem—*cemetery* KS-7
*Wakefast School* TN-4
*Wakefield* (2) RI-1
Wakefield—*hist pl* LA-4
Wakefield—*locale* KY-4
Wakefield—*locale* LA-4
Wakefield—*locale* MD-2
Wakefield—*locale* MS-4
Wakefield—*locale* OR-9
Wakefield—*locale* TX-5
Wakefield—*locale* VA-3
Wakefield—*locale* WA-9
Wakefield—*other* VA-3
**Wakefield**—*pop pl* IL-6
**Wakefield**—*pop pl* IN-6
**Wakefield**—*pop pl* KS-7
**Wakefield**—*pop pl* MD-2
**Wakefield**—*pop pl* MA-1
**Wakefield**—*pop pl* MI-6
**Wakefield**—*pop pl* NE-7
**Wakefield**—*pop pl* NH-1
**Wakefield**—*pop pl* NY-2
**Wakefield**—*pop pl* NC-3
**Wakefield**—*pop pl* (2) OH-6
**Wakefield**—*pop pl* RI-1
**Wakefield**—*pop pl* (3) VA-3
Wakefield—*uninc pl* AZ-5
Wakefield, James B., House—*hist pl* MN-6
Wakefield Bend—*bend* TN-4
Wakefield Brook—*stream* MN-6
Wakefield Cabin—*locale* OR-9
Wakefield Camp—*locale* AZ-5
Wakefield Canyon—*valley* AZ-5
Wakefield Cem—*cemetery* AL-4
Wakefield Cem—*cemetery* NC-3
Wakefield Cem—*cemetery* (2) TN-4
Wakefield Cem—*cemetery* TX-5
*Wakefield Center* MA-1
**Wakefield Center**—*pop pl* MA-1
Wakefield Ch—*church* AR-4
Wakefield Ch—*church* TX-5
Wakefield Chapel—*church* TN-4
**Wakefield Chapel**—*pop pl* VA-3
Wakefield Chapel (historical)—*church* TN-4
Wakefield Chapel Sch—*school* VA-3
**Wakefield Chapel Woods**—*pop pl* VA-3
Wakefield Community Center—*building* AL-4
Wakefield Community Hunt Club—*other* VA-3
Wakefield Corner—*locale* VA-3
Wakefield Creek—*stream* (2) MT-8
Wakefield Creek—*stream* OR-9
Wakefield Creek—*stream* WI-6
Wakefield Ditch—*canal* CO-8
Wakefield Elem Sch—*school* KS-7
Wakefield Flat—*flat* CA-9
**Wakefield Forest**—*pop pl* VA-3
Wakefield Forest Sch—*school* VA-3
Wakefield Gulch—*valley* ID-8
Wakefield Hill—*summit* CO-8
**Wakefield (historical)**—*pop pl* (2) OR-9
Wakefield Hollow—*valley* MO-7
Wakefield Hollow—*valley* TN-4
Wakefield House—*hist pl* NH-1
Wakefield HS—*school* KS-7
Wakefield HS—*school* MA-1
Wakefield HS—*school* VA-3
Wakefield JHS—*school* AZ-5
Wakefield JHS—*school* MA-1
**Wakefield Junction**—*pop pl* MA-1
*Wakefield Lake* TX-5
Wakefield Lake—*lake* (3) MN-6
Wakefield Lake—*lake* TX-5
Wakefield Lake—*lake* WI-6
Wakefield Lakes—*area* AK-9
Wakefield Lateral—*canal* CA-9
Wakefield Lookout Tower—*locale* TX-5
Wakefield (Magisterial District)—*fmr MCD* (2) VA-3
Wakefield Manor—*locale* VA-3
Wakefield Mansion—*building* VA-3
**Wakefield Meadows**—*pop pl* MD-2
Wakefield Mesa—*summit* CO-8
Wakefield Mill—*locale* MD-2
Wakefield Mine—*mine* AZ-5
Wakefield Mtn—*summit* AR-4
Wakefield Municipal Airstrip—*airport* KS-7
Wakefield Park—*park* MN-6
**Wakefield (Peach Botton Po)**—*pop pl* PA-2
Wakefield Peak—*summit* NV-8
Wakefield Pond—*lake* CT-1
Wakefield Pond—*reservoir* RI-1
Wakefield Pond—*reservoir* SC-3
Wakefield Pond Number One—*reservoir* NC-3
Wakefield Pond Number One Dam—*dam* NC-3
Wakefield Pond Number Two—*reservoir* NC-3
Wakefield Pond Number Two Dam—*dam* NC-3
Wakefield Post Office (historical)—*building* MS-4
Wakefield Post Office (historical)—*building* PA-2
Wakefield Public Library—*hist pl* NH-1
*Wakefield Reservoir* CO-8
Wakefield Rsvr—*reservoir* OR-9
Wakefield Run—*stream* PA-2
Wakefields—*hist pl* NC-3
Wakefield Sch—*school* AR-4
Wakefield Sch—*school* CA-9
Wakefield Sch—*school* (2) IL-6
Wakefield Sch—*school* TX-5
Wakefield Spring—*spring* AZ-5
Wakefield Spring—*spring* MT-8
Wakefield Spring—*spring* SD-7
Wakefield Station—*locale* MD-2
**Wakefield Subdivision**—*pop pl* UT-8
Wakefield Town Forest Park—*park* MA-1
Wakefield Townhall—*building* MA-1
**Wakefield (Town of)**—*pop pl* MA-1
**Wakefield (Town of)**—*pop pl* NH-1
**Wakefield Township**—*pop pl* NE-7
**Wakefield (Township of)**—*pop pl* MI-6
**Wakefield (Township of)**—*pop pl* MN-6
Wakefield Valley—*valley* MD-2
**Wakefield Village**—*pop pl* AR-4
**Wakefield Village**—*pop pl* IN-6
Wakefield Village Hist Dist—*hist pl* NH-1
Wakefield Vocational Sch—*school* MA-1
Wakefield Waterhole—*reservoir* (2) OR-9
*Wake Forest* WV-2
**Wake Forest**—*pop pl* NC-3
**Wake Forest**—*pop pl* VA-3
*Wake Forest Baptist Church* MS-4
Wake Forest Cem—*cemetery* (3) MS-4
Wake Forest Cem—*cemetery* VA-3
Wake Forest Ch—*church* (3) MS-4
Wake Forest Ch—*church* VA-3
Wake Forest Elem Sch—*school* NC-3
Wake Forest Municipal Dam—*dam* NC-3
Wake Forest-Rolesville MS—*school* NC-3
Wake Forest-Rolesville Senior HS—*school* NC-3
Wake Forest Rsvr—*reservoir* NC-3
Wake Forest Sch—*school* TN-4
Wake Forest Sch—*school* VA-3
Wake Forest Sch—*school* WV-2
Wakeforest Sch (historical)—*school* TN-4
Wake Forest (Township of)—*fmr MCD* NC-3
Wake Forest Univ—*school* NC-3
Wakeham Sch—*school* CA-9
**Wakeland**—*pop pl* IN-6
**Wakeland**—*pop pl* MS-4
**Wakelee**—*pop pl* MI-6
Wakelee Field—*park* NJ-2
Wakelee Sch—*school* CT-1
Wakeley—*locale* WY-8
Wakeley Creek—*stream* MI-6
*Wakeley Dam* NY-2
Wakeley-Giles Commercial Bldg—*hist pl* WI-6
Wakeley Lake—*lake* MI-6
*Wakeley Pond* NY-2
Wakeley Sch—*school* WY-8
Wakeley's Tavern—*hist pl* WI-6
Wakelon—*locale* NC-3
Wakelon Ch—*church* NC-3
Wakelon HS—*school* NC-3
Wakelon Sch—*hist pl* NC-3
Wakely Brook—*stream* (2) NY-2
*Wakely Cove* SC-3
Wakely Dam—*dam* NY-2
Wakely Mtn—*summit* NY-2
*Wakely Peak* ID-8
Wakely Pond—*lake* NY-2
Wakema—*locale* VA-3
**Wakeman**—*pop pl* OH-6
Wakeman Bay—*bay* MN-6
Wakeman Beach—*beach* OR-9
Wakeman Brook—*stream* NY-2
Wakeman (historical)—*locale* KS-7
Wakeman Island—*island* CT-1
Wakemans Grove—*locale* VA-3
Wakemans Grove Ch—*church* VA-3
**Wakeman (Township of)**—*pop pl* OH-6
Wake Memorial Hosp—*hospital* NC-3
Wake Minster Ch—*church* NC-3
**Wakemup**—*pop pl* MN-6
Wakemup Bay—*bay* MN-6
Wakemup Bay Campground—*locale* MN-6
Wakemup Narrows—*channel* MN-6
**Wakena**—*pop pl* PA-2
**Wakenda**—*pop pl* MO-7
Wakenda Ch—*church* (2) MO-7
Wakenda Chute—*stream* MO-7
Wakenda Creek—*stream* MO-7
**Wakenda Township**—*pop pl* MO-7
Wakenva—*locale* VA-3
Wakenva Branch—*stream* VA-3
Wakenva Sch—*school* VA-3
Wakepish Creek—*stream* WA-9
Waker Cem—*cemetery* IN-6
**Wake Robin Fields**—*pop pl* IN-6
Wakeshma Ch—*church* MI-6
Wakeshma Tabernacle—*church* MI-6
**Wakeshma (Township of)**—*pop pl* MI-6
Wake Spring—*spring* VA-3
Wakes Valley Landing (historical)—*locale* MS-4
*Waketagnay Pond* MA-1
*Waketicha Creek* WA-9
*Waketichie Creek* WA-9
Waketickeh Creek—*stream* WA-9
*Waketicky Creek* WA-9
**Waketon**—*pop pl* TX-5
Wake Union Ch—*church* NC-3
Wakeup Creek—*stream* AK-9
*Wakeup Rilea Creek* OR-9
Wake Up Rilea Creek—*stream* OR-9
**Wakeview (subdivision)**—*pop pl* (2) NC-3
**Wake Village**—*pop pl* TX-5
**Wakeville Village**—*pop pl* IN-6
Wakey Sch—*school* IL-6
*Wakfield* MS-4
WAKH-FM (Mccomb)—*tower* MS-4
*Wakia* MS-4
WAKI-AM (McMinnville)—*tower* TN-4
Waking Spring—*spring* NV-8
**Wakita**—*pop pl* OK-5
Wakita (CCD)—*cens area* OK-5
Wakita Cem—*cemetery* OK-5
Wakita Trend Gas Field—*oilfield* OK-5
Wakiu—*civil* HI-9
*Wakiwa River* FL-3
WAKK-AM (Mccomb)—*tower* MS-4
*Wakka Pilatka* FL-3
Waklarok—*locale* AK-9
*Wakle Peak* ID-8
Wakley Peak—*summit* ID-8
Wako Kayi (historical)—*locale* AL-4
Wakole Cem—*cemetery* OK-5
**Wakonda**—*pop pl* SD-7
Wakonda, Lake—*lake* SD-7
**Wakonda Beach**—*pop pl* OR-9
Wakonda Beach State Airp—*airport* OR-9
Wakonda Country Club—*other* IA-7
Wakondah Pond—*lake* NH-1
*Wa-ko-ne-kin Creek* UT-8
Wakopa Creek—*stream* ND-7
Wakopa Dam—*dam* ND-7
Wakopa State Game Mngmt Area—*park* ND-7
*Wakoquet* MA-1
*Wak-p* SD-7
**Wakpala**—*pop pl* SD-7
**Wakpala Township**—*pop pl* SD-7
Wakpamani Lake—*lake* SD-7
WAKS-AM (Fuquay-Varina)—*tower* NC-3
WAKS-FM (Fuquay-Varina)—*tower* NC-3
**Wakulia**—*pop pl* NC-3
**Wakulla**—*pop pl* FL-3
**Wakulla**—*pop pl* NC-3
Wakulla Beach—*locale* FL-3
**Wakulla County**—*pop pl* FL-3
Wakulla County Adult Sch—*school* FL-3
**Wakulla Gardens**—*pop pl* FL-3
Wakulla HS—*school* FL-3
Wakulla MS—*school* FL-3
Wakulla River—*stream* FL-3
Wakulla Springs—*locale* FL-3
*Walaces Channel* NC-3
Walahleng—*bar* FM-9

**Walair**—pop pl WA-9
Walaka FL-3
Walakpa Bay—bay AK-9
Walakpa River—stream AK-9
Walamantague Brook ME-1
walamatogue Stream ME-1
Walamontage Stream ME-1
Walamontogo Stream ME-1
Walamp Pond MA-1
Walan Point—cape WA-9
Walaohia Gulch—valley HI-9
Walapai—locale AZ-5
Walapai Lateral—canal CA-9
Walapai Point AZ-5
Walapai Point—cliff AZ-5
Walapai RR Station—building AZ-5
Walasi-Yi Inn—hist pl GA-3
W A Lateral—canal OR-9
WALA-TV (Mobile)—tower AL-4
Walavia HI-9
W Albemarle Sch—school NC-3
Walberg Creek MN-6
Walberg Creek—stream MN-6
**Walbert**—pop pl PA-2
Walberta Park Sch—school NY-2
Walberts PA-2
Walbert Station PA-2
Walbo—locale MN-6
Walborn Sch—school PA-2
Wal'brach FM-9
Walbridge—locale KY-4
**Walbridge**—pop pl OH-6
Walbridge Creek—stream IL-6
Walbridge Grove (historical)—locale IA-7
Walbridge Gulch—valley CA-9
Walbridge Park—park OH-6
Walbridge Ridge—ridge CA-9
Walbridge Sch—school MO-7
Walbridge Sch—school OH-6
Walbridge Tanks TX-5
Walbridge Yard—locale OH-6
Walbright Creek—stream WY-8
**Walbrook**—pop pl MD-2
Walbrook Park—park LA-4
**Walburg**—pop pl TX-5
Walburg Creek—channel GA-3
Walburg Island—island GA-3
**Walburg Township**—pop pl ND-7
Walburn Run—stream PA-2
Walby Creek—stream AK-9
Walby Lake—lake AK-9
**Walcan**—pop pl FL-3
Walch Creek—stream OR-9
Walche Cut—locale KY-4
Walchli Dam—dam OR-9
Walchli Rsvr—reservoir OR-9
Walch Ranch—locale NV-8
Walck Ditch—canal WY-8
Walck Ranch—locale WY-8
**Walcksville**—pop pl PA-2
Walco Park—park CT-1
**Walco (subdivision)**—pop pl AL-4
Walcot Basin—basin ID-8
Walcot Basin Rsvr—reservoir ID-8
Walcott CO-8
Walcott—locale TX-5
**Walcott**—pop pl AR-4
**Walcott**—pop pl IA-7
**Walcott**—pop pl ND-7
**Walcott**—pop pl WY-8
Walcott, F. M., House—hist pl NE-7
Walcott, Lake—reservoir ID-8
Walcott Brook—stream PA-2
Walcott Cem—cemetery IA-7
Walcott Covered Bridge—hist pl KY-4
Walcott Ditch WY-8
Walcott Draw—valley WY-8
Walcott Hill—summit MA-1
Walcott Island—island NH-1
Walcott JHS—school MI-6
Walcott Junction—locale WY-8
Walcott Lake—lake UT-8
Walcott Number 1 Dam—dam SD-7
Walcott Sch—school KS-7
Walcott Sch—school MI-6
Walcott Sch—school SD-7
Walcotts Run MA-1
Walcotts Run RI-1
**Walcott Township**—pop pl ND-7
**Walcott (Township of)**—pop pl MN-6
Walcott Tunnel—tunnel OR-9
Walcott Windmill—locale TX-5
Walcourt Bldg—hist pl OK-5
Walczak Creek—stream WI-6
Wald—locale AL-4
Wald—locale IA-7
Walda—locale TX-5
Waldameer Park—park PA-2
Waldamere Park PA-2
Waldberggaard—locale VI-3
Waldbillig Mtn—summit MT-8
Wald Ch—church AL-4
Waldeck—locale (2) KS-7
Waldeck—locale MN-6
**Waldeck**—pop pl LA-4
**Waldeck**—pop pl PA-2
**Waldeck**—pop pl TX-5
**Waldeck**—pop pl WV-2
Waldeck Cem—cemetery TX-5
Waldeck Ch—church TX-5
Waldeck Ch—church WV-2
Walde Creek—stream ID-8
Walde Lake—lake MN-6
Waldemer Flying W Ranch Airp—airport MO-7
Walde Mtn—summit ID-8
Walden IA-7
Walden—locale GA-3
Walden—locale IA-7
Walden—locale KY-4
Walden—locale ND-7
**Walden**—pop pl CO-8
**Walden**—pop pl IN-6
**Walden**—pop pl (2) NY-2
**Walden**—pop pl OR-9
**Walden**—pop pl TN-4
**Walden**—pop pl TX-5
**Walden**—pop pl VT-1
**Walden**—pop pl VA-3
Walden, Lake—lake MI-6
Walden, Nicholas O., House—hist pl OR-9

Waldena Lake—lake FL-3
Walden Bayou—stream LA-4
Walden Branch—stream AL-4
Walden Branch—stream (2) GA-3
Walden Branch—stream SC-3
Walden Branch—stream (2) TN-4
Walden Bridge—bridge NC-3
**Waldenburg**—pop pl AR-4
**Waldenburg**—pop pl MI-6
Walden Cem AL-4
Walden Cem—cemetery (3) AL-4
Walden Cem—cemetery AR-4
Walden Cem—cemetery (2) GA-3
Walden Cem—cemetery (2) MS-4
Walden Cem—cemetery (3) TN-4
Walden Cem—cemetery VA-3
Walden Chapel—church AL-4
Walden Chapel Cave—cave AL-4
**Walden Cliffs**—pop pl NY-2
Walden Correctional Institution—locale SC-3
Walden Creek NC-3
**Walden Creek**—pop pl TN-4
Walden Creek—stream GA-3
Walden Creek—stream NC-3
Walden Creek—stream TN-4
Walden Ditch—canal CO-8
Walden Farms—locale MD-2
Walden Four Corners Sch—school VT-1
**Walden Glen Subdivision**—pop pl UT-8
Walden Grove Cem—cemetery MO-7
**Walden Heights**—pop pl VT-1
Waldenheim Park PA-2
Waldenheim Park—uninc pl PA-2
Walden Hill MA-1
**Walden Hills Subdivision**—pop pl UT-8
**Walden (historical)**—pop pl MS-4
Walden (historical P.O.)—locale IA-7
Walden Hollow—valley CO-8
Walden Hollow—valley GA-3
Walden Hollow—valley TN-4
Walden Island—island CT-1
Walden - Jackson County Airp—airport CO-8
Walden Lake MA-1
Walden Lake—lake MI-6
Walden Lake—reservoir MS-4
Walden Lake—uninc pl FL-3
Walden Mtn—summit VA-3
**Walden Park Subdivision**—pop pl UT-8
Walden Place—hist pl KY-4
Walden Point—cape AK-9
Walden Pond WI-6
Walden Pond—hist pl MA-1
Walden Pond—lake IA-7
Walden Pond—lake ME-1
Walden Pond—lake MA-1
Walden Pond—lake PA-2
Walden Pond—reservoir MA-1
Walden Pond East End Dam—dam MA-1
**Walden Pond Estates (subdivision)**—pop pl AL-4
Walden Pond Outlet Dam—dam MA-1
Walden Quarters—locale AL-4
Walden Ranch—locale OK-5
Walden Ridge—locale (2) TN-4
Walden Ridge—ridge (2) TN-4
Walden Ridge (CCD)—cens area (2) TN-4
Walden Ridge Ch—church TN-4
Walden Ridge Division—civil (2) TN-4
Walden Ridge Sch (historical)—school MS-4
**Walden Ridge Subdivision**—pop pl UT-8
Walden Rocks—area AK-9
Walden Rsvr—reservoir CO-8
Walden Rsvr—reservoir MT-8
Walden Run—stream OH-6
Walden Sch—school IL-6
Waldens Hill—summit MA-1
Waldensia—locale TN-4
Waldensia, Lake—reservoir TN-4
Waldensian Ch—church MO-7
Waldensian Church and Cemetery of Stone Prairie—hist pl MO-7
Waldensian Presbyterian Church—hist pl NC-3
Waldensia Post Office (historical)—building TN-4
Walden Spring—spring AL-4
Walden Springs—spring OR-9
Waldens Ridge TN-4
**Waldens Ridge**—pop pl TN-4
Waldens Ridge Ch (historical)—church TN-4
Waldens Ridge Elem Sch—school TN-4
**Walden (sta.)**—pop pl VT-1
Walden Station—locale VT-1
**Walden (subdivision)**—pop pl NC-3
Walden Swamp—swamp NJ-2
Walden Town Hall—building TN-4
**Walden (Town of)**—pop pl VT-1
**Walden (Township of)**—pop pl (2) MN-6
Walden Trail—trail NH-1
Walden-Turner House—hist pl GA-3
Walden Univ—school FL-3
Walden View Ch—church TN-4
Walden Woods—locale TX-5
**Walden Woods (subdivision)**—pop pl NC-3
Walderman Run—stream WV-2
Waldern Hill Cem—cemetery OH-6
Walder Spring Sch (historical)—school MS-4
Wald Gap Mine (underground)—mine AL-4
**Waldheim**—pop pl LA-4
**Waldheim**—pop pl PA-2
Waldheim Cem—cemetery IL-6
Waldheim Cem—cemetery IN-6
Waldheim Cem—cemetery TX-5
Waldheim Ch—church LA-4
Waldheim Lookout Tower—locale LA-4
**Waldheim Park (subdivision)**—pop pl PA-2
Waldhiem Ch—church ND-7
Waldhill Church of Christ MS-4
Wald Hollow—valley AL-4
**Walding**—pop pl LA-4
Walding Cem—cemetery AL-4
Waldmeier Ditch—canal IL-6
Waldmeister Farm Airp—airport MO-7
Waldner Creek—stream CO-8
Waldness Hill WI-6
Waldness Hill—summit WI-6
Waldo MO-7
Waldo—locale CA-9
Waldo—locale KY-4
Waldo—locale ME-1
Waldo—locale MN-6

Waldo—locale MS-4
Waldo—locale MO-7
Waldo—locale NM-5
**Waldo**—pop pl AL-4
**Waldo**—pop pl AR-4
**Waldo**—pop pl FL-3
**Waldo**—pop pl KS-7
**Waldo**—pop pl MO-7
**Waldo**—pop pl OH-6
**Waldo**—pop pl WI-6
Waldo—uninc pl NJ-2
Waldo, Edward, House—hist pl CT-1
Waldo, George A., House—hist pl MA-1
Waldo, Gertrude Rhinelander, Mansion—hist pl NY-2
Waldo, Homer, Farm—hist pl VT-1
Waldo, Mount—summit ME-1
Waldo Bar—bar ID-8
Waldo Block—hist pl OR-9
**Waldoboro**—pop pl ME-1
**Waldoboro (Town of)**—pop pl ME-1
Waldoborough Town Pound—hist pl ME-1
Waldo Brook—stream CT-1
Waldo Canyon—valley CO-8
Waldo (CCD)—cens area FL-3
Waldo Cem—cemetery AR-4
Waldo Ch—church (2) IL-6
Waldo Chapel (historical)—church AL-4
Waldo Community Sch—school FL-3
**Waldo (County)**—pop pl ME-1
Waldo Covered Bridge—bridge AL-4
Waldo Creek—stream NY-2
Waldo Drain—stream MI-6
Waldo Glacier—glacier OR-9
Waldo Gulch—valley NM-5
Waldo Gulch—valley OR-9
Waldo-Hancock Bridge—hist pl ME-1
Waldo Hill—summit MI-6
Waldo Hill—summit NY-2
Waldo Hill—summit OR-9
Waldo Hills—summit OR-9
Waldo Hills Grange Hall—locale OR-9
Waldo JHS—school IL-6
Waldo JHS—school OR-9
Waldo Junction—locale CA-9
**Waldo Junction**—pop pl MN-6
Waldo J Wood Memorial HS—school IN-6
Waldo Lake—lake MA-1
Waldo Lake—lake (2) OR-9
Waldo Lake Dam—dam MA-1
Waldo Lake Rsvr Dam—dam OR-9
Waldo Lake Trail—trail OR-9
Waldo Meadows Guard Station—locale OR-9
Waldo Mill Pond—reservoir WI-6
Waldo Mine—mine NM-5
Waldomore—hist pl WV-2
Waldo Mtn—summit AR-4
Waldo Mtn—summit OR-9
Waldon Branch—stream LA-4
Waldon Bridge—bridge MS-4
Waldon Cem—cemetery (2) MS-4
Waldon Cem—cemetery SC-3
Waldon Cem—cemetery TN-4
Waldon Ch—church GA-3
Waldon Creek NC-3
Waldon Hills—ridge NE-7
Waldon Hollow—valley MO-7
Waldon Lake—lake FL-3
Waldon Mine (underground)—mine AL-4
Waldon Mtn—summit AR-4
Waldon Place Windmill—locale TX-5
Waldon Ridge Ch (historical)—church TN-4
**Waldon Woods**—pop pl MD-2
**Waldon Woods**—pop pl VA-3
Waldo Park—park MI-6
Waldo Point—cape ME-1
Waldo Post Office (historical)—building MS-4
Waldo Powell Roadside Park—locale MO-7
Waldorf—locale CA-9
**Waldorf**—pop pl MD-2
**Waldorf**—pop pl MN-6
Waldorf Cem—cemetery MD-2
Waldorf Crossing—locale CA-9
Waldorff Flat—flat CA-9
Waldorf Hotel—hist pl SD-7
Waldorf Lake—lake FL-3
Waldorf Mine—mine CO-8
Waldorf Plaza (Shop Ctr)—locale FL-3
Waldorf Sch—school NY-2
Waldorr CA-9
Waldo Run—stream WV-2
Waldo Sch (abandoned)—school MO-7
Waldo Sch (abandoned)—school PA-2
Waldos Corners—locale NY-2
Waldo (site)—locale OR-9
Waldo Spring—spring FL-3
Waldo Spring—spring OR-9
Waldo Street Police Station—hist pl MA-1
Waldo Theatre—hist pl ME-1
**Waldo (Town of)**—pop pl ME-1
**Waldo Township**—pop pl KS-7
**Waldo Township**—pop pl ND-7
Waldo (Township of)—fmr MCD AR-4
**Waldo (Township of)**—pop pl IL-6
**Waldo (Township of)**—pop pl OH-6
Waldo Tunnel—mine NM-5
Waldo Water Tower—hist pl MO-7
Waldo Wayside Ch—church KY-4
Waldo Windmill—locale TX-5
Wald Park—park KY-4
**Waldport**—pop pl OR-9
Waldport (CCD)—cens area OR-9
Waldport Ranger Station—locale OR-9
**Waldrep**—pop pl AL-4
Waldrep Cem—cemetery AR-4
Waldrep Creek—stream AR-4
Waldridge Butte OR-9
Waldrip—locale TX-5
Waldrip Airstrip—airport AZ-5
Waldrip Branch—stream AR-4
Waldrip Cem—cemetery MS-4
Waldrip Church AL-4
Waldrip Lake—lake TX-5
Waldrom Branch—stream TX-5
Waldron—locale OK-5
Waldron—locale OR-9
Waldron—locale WA-9
**Waldron**—pop pl AR-4
**Waldron**—pop pl IN-6
**Waldron**—pop pl KS-7

**Waldron**—pop pl MI-6
**Waldron**—pop pl MO-7
Waldron Acad—school PA-2
Waldronaire Airp—airport WA-9
Waldron-Beck House and Carriage House—hist pl IN-6
Waldron Bottom—valley MA-1
Waldron Branch—stream AR-4
Waldron-Brandon Cem—cemetery NY-2
Waldron Canyon—valley NM-5
Waldron Cem—cemetery GA-3
Waldron Cem—cemetery KS-7
Waldron Cem—cemetery (2) NY-2
Waldron Cem—cemetery TN-4
Waldron Cem—cemetery VA-3
Waldron Cem—cemetery WV-2
Waldron Corners—locale NY-2
**Waldron Corners**—pop pl RI-1
Waldron Creek—stream AK-9
Waldron Creek—stream AR-4
Waldron Creek—stream CA-9
Waldron Creek—stream MT-8
Waldron Creek—stream OR-9
Waldron Ditch—canal WY-8
Waldron Elem Sch—school IN-6
Waldron Field—park TX-5
Waldron Hill—summit NH-1
Waldron Island—island WA-9
Waldron Junior-Senior HS—school IN-6
Waldron Lake IN-6
Waldron Lake MI-6
Waldron Lake—lake IN-6
**Waldron Lake**—pop pl IN-6
Waldron Ledge—bench HI-9
Waldron Millpond—swamp FL-3
Waldron Pass—gap CA-9
Waldron Pond—lake NY-2
Waldron Post Office (historical)—building AL-4
Waldron Ranch—locale CO-8
Waldron Ridge—ridge AR-4
Waldron Sch—school OR-9
Waldron Street Christian Ch—church MS-4
Waldron Township—civil MO-7
Waldroop Hollow—valley TX-5
**Waldrop**—pop pl VA-3
Waldrop Branch—stream TX-5
Waldrop Cem—cemetery AR-4
Waldrop Ch—church VA-3
Waldrop Church AL-4
Waldrop Creek—stream MS-4
Waldrop Creek—stream TN-4
Waldrope Cem—cemetery KY-4
Waldrop Lake Dam—dam MS-4
Waldrop Mtn—summit AR-4
Waldrops Lake—reservoir SC-3
Waldrops Mill (historical)—locale AL-4
Waldrop Store—locale TN-4
Waldrop Tabernacle—church TX-5
Waldro Sch—school SD-7
**Waldro Township**—pop pl SD-7
Waldroup Place Tank—reservoir AZ-5
Waldroup Tank—reservoir (2) AZ-5
**Waldrue Heights**—pop pl CA-9
Waldruhe Park—park OH-6
Waldrup—locale MS-4
Waldrup Bridge—bridge GA-3
Waldrup Church AL-4
Waldrup Post Office (historical)—building MS-4
Waldschmidt-Camp Dennison District—hist pl OH-6
Waldum Cem—cemetery MN-6
**Wald View**—pop pl IN-6
Waldvogel Canal—canal ID-8
Waldvogel Canal Wasteway—canal ID-8
**Waldwick**—pop pl NJ-2
**Waldwick**—pop pl WI-6
Waldwick RR Station—hist pl NJ-2
**Waldwick (Town of)**—pop pl WI-6
Waldy Pond—lake NV-8
Waldy Run—stream PA-2
Walea Cem—cemetery GA-3
Wale Cem—cemetery NC-3
Walek Knob—summit WI-6
Walenburg Landing Field—airport CO-8
Walen Creek—stream OR-9
Walerga—locale CA-9
Wales MI-6
Wales OH-6
Wales PA-2
Wales—hist pl VA-3
Wales—locale KY-4
**Wales**—pop pl AK-9
**Wales**—pop pl IA-7
**Wales**—pop pl MA-1
**Wales**—pop pl MN-6
**Wales**—pop pl ND-7
**Wales**—pop pl TN-4
**Wales**—pop pl UT-8
**Wales**—pop pl WI-6
Wales, Lake—lake FL-3
Wales, Mary Anne, House—hist pl NH-1
Wales, The—locale CT-1
Wales Beach—beach ME-1
**Walesboro**—pop pl IN-6
Wales Brook—stream MA-1
Walesca GA-3
Wales Canyon—valley CA-9
Wales Canyon—valley CO-8
Wales Canyon—valley (2) UT-8
Wales Cem—cemetery LA-4
Wales Cem—cemetery UT-8
Wales Center—locale MI-6
**Wales Center**—pop pl ME-1
**Wales Center**—pop pl NY-2
Wales Central Sch—school ME-1
Wales Corner—locale ME-1
**Wales Corners**—pop pl OH-6
Wales Coulee—valley MT-8
Wales Creek—stream MI-6
Wales Creek—stream WI-6
Wales Creek Rsvr—reservoir MT-8
Wales Dam—dam UT-8
Wales Ditch—canal CO-8
Wales Ditch—canal IA-7
Walesheba Creek—stream MS-4
**Wales Hollow**—pop pl NY-2
Wales Ind Res—reserve AK-9
Wales Junction—other PA-2
**Waleska**—pop pl GA-3
Waleska (CCD)—cens area GA-3

Waleska Ch—church GA-3
Wales Lake—lake CA-9
Wales Mine—mine NV-8
Wales Plateau UT-8
Wales Pond MA-1
Wales Pond—lake ME-1
Wales Pond—lake MA-1
Wales Post Office (historical)—building TN-4
Wales Ranch—locale WY-8
Wales Rsvr—reservoir UT-8
Wales Rsvr—reservoir WY-8
Wales Sch—school NY-2
Wales Sch (historical)—school TN-4
Wales Shellabarger Ditch No 1—canal CO-8
Wales Siding—locale MO-7
Wales Sites—hist pl AK-9
Wales Station Post Office TN-4
**Wales (Town of)**—pop pl ME-1
**Wales (Town of)**—pop pl MA-1
**Wales (Town of)**—pop pl NY-2
**Wales (Township of)**—pop pl MI-6
Wales Travis Ditch—canal CO-8
Wales Union Ch—church ME-1
Wales Village MA-1
**Walesville**—pop pl NY-2
**Walet**—pop pl LA-4
**Walford**—pop pl IA-7
Walford Bay—swamp FL-3
Walford Cem—cemetery IL-6
Walford Creek—stream OK-5
Walford Johnson Creek—stream OR-9
**Walford Manor**—pop pl IN-6
Walford (RR name for Bessemer)—other PA-2
Walford Sch—school OH-6
Walgamuth Ch—church PA-2
Walgamuth Sch—school SD-7
Walgreen Ranch—locale WY-8
Walgren Lake—lake NE-7
Walgren State Rec Area—park NE-7
Walgrove—locale WV-2
Walgrove Ave Sch—school CA-9
**Walhain**—pop pl WI-6
Walhalla—locale TX-5
**Walhalla**—pop pl MI-6
**Walhalla**—pop pl ND-7
**Walhalla**—pop pl SC-3
Walhalla (CCD)—cens area SC-3
Walhalla Cem—cemetery ND-7
Walhalla Country Club—locale ND-7
Walhalla Filtration Point—other SC-3
Walhalla Fish Hatchery—other SC-3
Walhalla Glades—flat AZ-5
Walhalla Municipal Airp—airport ND-7
Walhalla Plateau—plain AZ-5
Walhalla Rocks—summit NY-2
Walhalla Rsvr—reservoir SC-3
Walhalla Slough—gut AK-9
**Walhalla Township**—pop pl ND-7
**Walhaven**—pop pl VA-3
Walhill Ch—church MS-4
Walhill Lake—lake NC-3
Walhonde Roadside Park—park WV-2
**Walhonding**—pop pl (2) OH-6
Walhonding Canal—canal OH-6
Walhonding River—stream OH-6
Walhounding Canal Lock No. 9—hist pl OH-6
Walik Creek—stream AK-9
Waliser Ranch—locale WY-8
Walis Run PA-2
Walka Mountain Ch—church GA-3
Walkaround Creek—stream AK-9
Walk Bottom—bend IN-6
**Walkchalk**—pop pl PA-2
Walk Drain—stream MI-6
Walke Point—cape VA-3
Walker DE-2
Walker LA-4
Walker MS-4
Walker PA-2
Walker VA-3
Walker—locale (2) AR-4
Walker—locale CO-8
Walker—locale DE-2
Walker—locale GA-3
Walker—locale ID-8
Walker—locale IL-6
Walker—locale KY-4
Walker—locale ME-1
Walker—locale MD-2
Walker—locale SC-3
Walker—locale SD-7
Walker—locale WA-9
**Walker**—pop pl AZ-5
**Walker**—pop pl (2) CA-9
**Walker**—pop pl IL-6
**Walker**—pop pl IA-7
**Walker**—pop pl KS-7
**Walker**—pop pl (2) LA-4
**Walker**—pop pl (2) MI-6
**Walker**—pop pl MN-6
**Walker**—pop pl MS-4
**Walker**—pop pl MO-7
**Walker**—pop pl (2) NY-2
**Walker**—pop pl OR-9
**Walker**—pop pl PA-2
**Walker**—pop pl WV-2
Walker—uninc pl CA-9
Walker—uninc pl NM-5
Walker—uninc pl OK-5
Walker—uninc pl TN-4
Walker, Albion, Chalkrock House—hist pl SD-7
Walker, Cristopher C., House and Farm—hist pl OH-6
Walker, David S., Library—hist pl FL-3
Walker, E. W., House—hist pl KY-4
Walker, Franklin H., House—hist pl MI-6
Walker, H. Alexander, Residence—hist pl HI-9
Walker, Harry, House—hist pl AZ-5
Walker, Harry B., House—hist pl WI-6
Walker, Howard, House—hist pl TX-5
Walker, J. A., House and Rogers, R. B., House—hist pl TX-5
Walker, James, House—hist pl KY-4
Walker, John P., House—hist pl OR-9
Walker, Joseph, House—hist pl PA-2
Walker, J. W., Building-Central Arizona Light & Power—hist pl AZ-5
Walker, Lake—lake FL-3
Walker, Madame C. J., Bldg—hist pl IN-6
Walker, Maggie Lena, House—hist pl VA-3

Walker, Morgan, House—hist pl LA-4
Walker, Mount—summit WA-9
Walker, O. E., House—hist pl AZ-5
Walker, Peter, House—hist pl MA-1
Walker, Phillip, House—hist pl RI-1
Walker, R., Barn—hist pl DE-2
Walker, Samuel D., House—hist pl UT-8
Walker, T. J., Hist Dist—hist pl ND-7
Walker, William, Jr., House—hist pl OH-6
Walker Air Base Auxiliary Landing Field No 1—other NM-5
Walker Air Base Auxiliary Landing Field No 3—other NM-5
Walker Air Base Emergency Landing Field—other NM-5
Walker Airfield—airport OR-9
Walker Air Force Base—military NM-5
Walker Air Force Base—other NM-5
Walker and Leonard Mine (underground)—mine AL-4
Walker and Riddles Store AL-4
Walker and Valentine House—hist pl MN-6
Walker and Webster Gulch—valley UT-8
Walker and Webster Mine—mine UT-8
Walker and Weeks Office Bldg—hist pl OH-6
Walker Area Vocational Center—school AL-4
Walker Arena—building MI-6
Walker Ave Sch—school TN-4
Walker Baccus Family Cem—cemetery AL-4
Walker Bald—summit NC-3
Walker Bar—bar OR-9
Walker Basin—basin (2) AZ-5
Walker Basin—basin (2) CA-9
Walker Basin Canal—canal OR-9
Walker Basin Creek—stream CA-9
Walker Basin Tank—reservoir AZ-5
Walker Basin Trail—trail (2) AZ-5
Walker Basin Trail Number One Hundred Thirty Six—trail AZ-5
Walker Bay—bay MN-6
Walker Bay—bay NV-8
Walker Bay Campground—locale MN-6
Walker Bayou—bay FL-3
Walker Bend—bend (2) TN-4
Walker Bend—bend TX-5
Walker Bldg—hist pl MA-1
Walker Bldg—hist pl OK-5
Walker Bluff—cliff TX-5
Walker Branch GA-3
Walker Branch—stream (5) AL-4
Walker Branch—stream (2) AR-4
Walker Branch—stream (2) FL-3
Walker Branch—stream (5) GA-3
Walker Branch—stream IL-6
Walker Branch—stream IA-7
Walker Branch—stream KS-7
Walker Branch—stream (6) KY-4
Walker Branch—stream (3) LA-4
Walker Branch—stream MD-2
Walker Branch—stream (5) MS-4
Walker Branch—stream (3) MO-7
Walker Branch—stream (8) NC-3
Walker Branch—stream OK-5
Walker Branch—stream SC-3
Walker Branch—stream (17) TN-4
Walker Branch—stream (11) TX-5
Walker Branch—stream (3) VA-3
Walker Branch—stream (3) WV-2
Walker Branch Ch—church MO-7
Walker Bridge—bridge CA-9
Walker Bridge—bridge FL-3
Walker Bridge—bridge MS-4
Walker Bridge—bridge (2) TN-4
Walker-Broderick House—hist pl AK-9
Walker Brook—stream (2) CT-1
Walker Brook—stream IN-6
Walker Brook—stream (4) ME-1
Walker Brook—stream (5) MA-1
Walker Brook—stream MI-6
Walker Brook—stream MN-6
Walker Brook—stream (5) NH-1
Walker Brook—stream NY-2
Walker Brook Lake—lake MN-6
Walker Butte—summit (3) AZ-5
Walker Butte—summit CA-9
Walker Buttes CA-9
Walker Butte Spring—spring AZ-5
Walker Camp—locale FL-3
Walker Camp (abandoned)—locale FL-3
Walker Camp Prong—stream TN-4
Walker Canal—canal GA-3
Walker Canal—canal LA-4
Walker Canal—canal UT-8
Walker Canyon AZ-5
Walker Canyon ID-8
Walker Canyon UT-8
Walker Canyon—valley (2) AZ-5
Walker Canyon—valley (4) CA-9
Walker Canyon—valley CO-8
Walker Canyon—valley ID-8
Walker Canyon—valley NV-8
Walker Canyon—valley (5) NM-5
Walker Canyon—valley OR-9
Walker Canyon—valley TX-5
Walker Canyon—valley (2) WA-9
Walker Canyon—valley WY-8
Walker Canyon Windmill—locale TX-5
Walker Cave AL-4
Walker Cem—cemetery (10) AL-4
Walker Cem—cemetery (10) AR-4
Walker Cem—cemetery CA-9
Walker Cem—cemetery (3) FL-3
Walker Cem—cemetery (9) GA-3
Walker Cem—cemetery (8) IL-6
Walker Cem—cemetery (6) IN-6
Walker Cem—cemetery (3) IA-7
Walker Cem—cemetery (6) KY-4
Walker Cem—cemetery (4) LA-4
Walker Cem—cemetery ME-1
Walker Cem—cemetery MI-6
Walker Cem—cemetery (12) MS-4
Walker Cem—cemetery (8) MO-7
Walker Cem—cemetery NE-7
Walker Cem—cemetery NY-2
Walker Cem—cemetery (7) NC-3
Walker Cem—cemetery OH-6
Walker Cem—cemetery (3) OK-5
Walker Cem—cemetery (2) PA-2
Walker Cem—cemetery SC-3
Walker Cem—cemetery (42) TN-4

Walking Cane Ranch—locale NM-5
Walking Circle Ranch—locale NE-7
Walking Fern Pit—cave AL-4
Walking Fish Lake—lake ID-8
Walkinghood—locale KS-7
**Walkinghood**—pop pl KS-7
Walking Horse Cem—cemetery SD-7
Walking Horse Coulee—valley MT-8
Walking Horse Creek—stream MT-8
Walking Horse Hotel—hist pl TN-4
Walking H Windmill—locale NM-5
Walkingstick Cem—cemetery OK-5
Walkingstick Hollow—valley OK-5
Walkingstick Mtn—summit OK-5
Walking X Canyon—valley NM-5
Walking X Ranch—locale NM-5
Walkins Beam Wells—well NM-5
Walkinshaw—locale GA-3
Walkinshaw, Mount—summit WA-9
Walkins Rapids—rapids MN-6
Walk-in-the Water Lake FL-3
Walk Lake—lake TX-5
Walkley Hill—summit CT-1
**Walkleys Landing**—pop pl NY-2
Walk Moore Canyon—valley AZ-5
Walkover Mine—mine AZ-5
Walkover Tank—reservoir AZ-5
Walks Camp Cem—cemetery CO-8
Walks Camp Lutheran Cem—cemetery CO-8
Walks Camp Lutheran Ch—church CO-8
Walks Camp Park—park CO-8
Walk Sch—school IL-6
Walkters Harbor—bay MI-6
Walkton—locale PA-2
Walkup UT-8
Walkup Cem—cemetery MO-7
Walkup Cem—cemetery OH-6
Walkup Ch—church MO-7
Walkup City Lake MI-6
Walkup Country Club—other OH-6
Walkup Gulch—valley MT-8
Walkup Lake—lake MI-6
Walk-Up Lake—lake UT-8
Walk Upon Me Lake SD-7
Walkup Sch—school MO-7
Walkup Spring—spring UT-8
Walk-up-well—well NM-5
Walkyns Glen—locale IA-7
Wall AZ-5
Wall—locale AZ-5
**Wall**—pop pl PA-2
**Wall**—pop pl SD-7
**Wall**—pop pl TX-5
Wall, George W., House—hist pl NC-3
Wall, Joseph, Gristmill—hist pl UT-8
Wall, Judge T. B., House—hist pl KS-7
Wall, Mount—summit OK-5
Wall, The—cliff MT-8
Wall, The—cliff UT-8
Wall, The—cliff (2) WY-8
Wall, The—other AK-9
Wall, The—pillar UT-8
Wall, The—ridge NV-8
Wall, The—ridge NM-5
Wall, The—ridge WY-8
Wall, The (LA 55840)—hist pl NM-5
Wall, Thomas R., Residence—hist pl WI-6
Wallabout Bay—bay NY-2
Wallabout Channel—channel NY-2
Wallace ND-7
Wallace—locale AR-4
Wallace—locale FL-3
Wallace—locale GA-3
Wallace—locale KY-4
Wallace—locale MS-4
Wallace—locale OR-9
Wallace—locale (2) PA-2
Wallace—locale TX-5
Wallace—other WV-2
**Wallace**—pop pl AL-4
**Wallace**—pop pl AR-4
**Wallace**—pop pl CA-9
**Wallace**—pop pl ID-8
**Wallace**—pop pl IN-6
**Wallace**—pop pl IA-7
**Wallace**—pop pl KS-7
**Wallace** pop pl LA-4
**Wallace**—pop pl (2) MI-6
**Wallace**—pop pl MS-4
**Wallace**—pop pl MO-7
**Wallace**—pop pl NE-7
**Wallace**—pop pl NY-2
**Wallace**—pop pl NC-3
**Wallace**—pop pl (2) PA-2
**Wallace**—pop pl SC-3
**Wallace**—pop pl SD-7
**Wallace**—pop pl VA-3
**Wallace**—pop pl WV-2
Wallace, Charles, House—hist pl KY-4
Wallace, Charlton, House—hist pl OH-6
Wallace, Gen. Lew, Study—hist pl IN-6
Wallace, Henry C., House—hist pl IA-7
Wallace, J. M., Archeol Site—hist pl MO-7
Wallace, J. N., House—hist pl ID-8
Wallace, Lake—lake AR-4
Wallace, Lake—lake MI-6
Wallace, Lake—reservoir SC-3
Wallace, Michael, House—hist pl KY-4
Wallace, Mount—summit (2) CA-9
Wallace, Mount—summit MT-8
Wallace, Napoleon, House—hist pl KY-4
Wallace, Thomas, House—hist pl VA-3
**Wallace Acres**—pop pl TN-4
**Wallace Acres (subdivision)**—pop pl NC-3
Wallace Administrative City (USFS)—locale AZ-5
Wallace Airstrip—airport OR-9
Wallace Aylesworth Elem Sch—school IN-6
Wallace Bar (historical)—bar AL-4
Wallace Bay—swamp FL-3
Wallace Bayou—stream (4) LA-4
Wallace Block-Old Saline Village Hall—hist pl MI-6
Wallace Bluff—cliff AR-4
Wallace Bluffs—cliff KS-7
Wallace Branch—canal MI-6
Wallace Branch—stream (3) AL-4
Wallace Branch—stream GA-3
Wallace Branch—stream IL-6
Wallace Branch—stream IN-6
Wallace Branch—stream (3) KY-4
Wallace Branch—stream MS-4
Wallace Branch—stream (5) NC-3
Wallace Branch—stream (2) SC-3
Wallace Branch—stream (6) TN-4
Wallace Branch—stream (8) TX-5
Wallace Branch—stream VA-3
Wallace Branch—stream WV-2
Wallace Bridge—bridge AL-4
Wallace Bridge—bridge OR-9
Wallace Bridge—bridge TX-5
**Wallace Bridge**—pop pl OR-9
Wallace Bridge Cem—cemetery OR-9
Wallace Brook—stream ME-1
Wallace Brook—stream (2) NH-1
Wallace Brook—stream NJ-2
Wallace Brook—stream PA-2
Wallace Brook Reservoir MA-1
Wallaceburg—locale AR-4
Walloceburg (Township of)—fmr MCD AR-4
Wallace Butte—summit AZ-5
Wallace Cabin—locale WY-8
Wallace Canyon—valley AZ-5
Wallace Canyon—valley CA-9
Wallace Canyon—valley (2) NV-8
Wallace Canyon—valley (2) OR-9
Wallace Canyon—valley TX-5
Wallace Canyon—valley UT-8
Wallace Canyon—valley WA-9
Wallace Caraway Gut—gut NC-3
Wallace Carnegie Library—hist pl ID-8
Wallace Cave—cave PA-2
Wallace Cave Creek WY-8
Wallace (CCD)—cens area SC-3
Wallace Cem—cemetery (5) AL-4
Wallace Cem—cemetery (2) AR-4
Wallace Cem—cemetery (3) IL-6
Wallace Cem—cemetery IN-6
Wallace Cem—cemetery (2) KS-7
Wallace Cem—cemetery (6) KY-4
Wallace Cem—cemetery (2) LA-4
Wallace Cem—cemetery (6) MO-7
Wallace Cem—cemetery NC-3
Wallace Cem—cemetery OH-6
Wallace Cem—cemetery (2) SC-3
Wallace Cem—cemetery (14) TN-4
Wallace Cem—cemetery (3) TX-5
Wallace Cem—cemetery (2) VA-3
Wallace Cem—cemetery (2) WV-2
Wallace Cemeteries—cemetery AL-4
**Wallace Center**—pop pl CA-9
Wallace Ch—church (2) LA-4
Wallace Ch—church MS-4
Wallace Ch—church SC-3
Wallace Channel—channel NC-3
Wallace Channel Beacon—tower NC-3
Wallace Channel Light—tower NC-3
Wallace Chapel MS-4
Wallace Chapel—church AL-4
Wallace Chapel—church AR-4
Wallace Chapel—church IL-6
Wallace Chapel—church KY-4
Wallace Chapel—church MS-4
Wallace Chapel—church MO-7
Wallace Chapel—church TX-5
**Wallace Chapel**—pop pl TX-5
Wallace Chapel African Methodist Episcopal Zion Ch—church TN-4
Wallace Chapel Ch—church AL-4
Wallace Chapel (historical)—church MS-4
Wallace Church Cem—cemetery AL-4
Wallace Circus and American Circus Corporation Winter Quarters—hist pl IN-6
Wallace City—locale PA-2
**Wallace Corners**—pop pl PA-2
Wallace Coulee—valley MT-8
Wallace County—civil KS-7
Wallace County (historical)—civil ND-7
Wallace County HS—school KS-7
Wallace Cove—bay ME-1
Wallace Creek IN-6
Wallace Creek NV-8
Wallace Creek PA-2
Wallace Creek—locale MS-4
Wallace Creek—stream (4) AL-4
Wallace Creek—stream (2) AR-4
Wallace Creek—stream (4) CA-9
Wallace Creek—stream CO-8
Wallace Creek—stream (2) ID-8
Wallace Creek—stream LA-4
Wallace Creek—stream MD-2
Wallace Creek—stream MI-6
Wallace Creek—stream (2) MS-4
Wallace Creek—stream MO-7
Wallace Creek—stream (4) MT-8
Wallace Creek—stream NE-7
Wallace Creek—stream (2) NC-3
Wallace Creek—stream OK-5
Wallace Creek—stream (4) OR-9
Wallace Creek—stream SC-3
Wallace Creek—stream (2) TN-4
Wallace Creek—stream (5) TX-5
Wallace Creek—stream (2) VA-3
Wallace Creek—stream WA-9
Wallace Creek—stream WY-8
Wallace Creek Cem—cemetery TX-5
Wallace Creek Marsh—swamp MD-2
Wallace Creek Rec Area—park MS-4
Wallace Creek Sch—school TX-5
Wallace Creek Trail—trail MT-8
Wallace-Cross Mill—hist pl PA-2
Wallace Crossroads—locale NC-3
Wallace Ditch—canal (2) IN-6
Wallace Draft—valley VA-3
Wallace Drain—canal MI-6
Wallace Drain—stream MI-6
Wallace Draw—valley TX-5
Wallace Draw—valley (4) WY-8
Wallace Elem Sch—school IN-6
Wallace Elem Sch—school KS-7
Wallace Elem Sch—school NC-3
Wallace Epting Lake Dam—dam MS-4
Wallace Falls—falls IN-6
Wallace Falls—falls WA-9
Wallace Farm—hist pl OH-6
Wallace Ferry (historical)—locale AL-4
Wallace Field (airport)—airport AL-4
Wallace Fork KS-7
Wallace Fork—stream KY-4
Wallace Fork—stream OH-6
Wallace Fork—stream WV-2
Wallace Fry Ditch—canal IN-6
Wallace Gap—gap (2) NC-3
Wallace Grove Ch—church GA-3
Wallace Grove Ch—church NC-3
Wallace Gulch—valley (2) CO-8
Wallace Gulch—valley OR-9
Wallace Harrison Lake Dam—dam MS-4
Wallace Hathcock Dam—dam AL-4
Wallace Hathcock Lake—reservoir AL-4
Wallace Head—cape ME-1
**Wallace Heights**—pop pl OH-6
**Wallace Heights**—pop pl UT-8
Wallace Heights Sch—school WV-2
**Wallace Heights (Wallace)**—pop pl WV-2
Wallace Hill—summit AL-4
Wallace Hill—summit (2) NH-1
Wallace Hill—summit NM-5
Wallace Hill—summit OR-9
Wallace Hill—summit PA-2
Wallace Hill—summit TN-4
Wallace Hill—summit VT-1
Wallace Hill Sch—school PA-2
Wallace Hills Golf Course—locale TN-4
Wallace Hist Dist—hist pl ID-8
Wallace Hist Dist (Boundary Increase)—hist pl ID-8
**Wallace (historical)**—pop pl OR-9
Wallace Hollow—valley AR-4
Wallace Hollow—valley KY-4
Wallace Hollow—valley (2) MO-7
Wallace Hollow—valley (6) TN-4
Wallace Hollow—valley WV-2
Wallace House—hist pl MO-7
Wallace House—hist pl NJ-2
Wallace HS—school AL-4
Wallace Island—island MO-7
Wallace Island—island NH-1
Wallace Island—island OR-9
Wallace Island—island WI-6
Wallace Jewett Airstrip*—airport SD-7
Wallace JHS—school TX-5
**Wallace Junction**—pop pl IN-6
**Wallace Junction**—pop pl PA-2
Wallace Junction Station PA-2
Wallace Junior Coll—school (2) AL-4
Wallace Knob—summit (2) AR-4
Wallace Lake AK-9
Wallace Lake MN-6
Wallace Lake VT-1
Wallace Lake—lake AK-9
Wallace Lake—lake AZ-5
Wallace Lake—lake CA-9
Wallace Lake—lake ID-8
Wallace Lake—lake (2) LA-4
Wallace Lake—lake (3) MI-6
Wallace Lake—lake MN-6
Wallace Lake—lake NM-5
Wallace Lake—lake OH-6
Wallace Lake—lake TX-5
Wallace Lake—lake WA-9
Wallace Lake—lake (3) WI-6
Wallace Lake—reservoir LA-4
Wallace Lake—reservoir TX-5
Wallace Lake Dam—dam LA-4
Wallace Lake Recreation Site—locale ID-8
Wallace Lake Reservoir LA-4
Wallace Landing—locale LA-4
**Wallace Lane Condominium**—pop pl UT-8
Wallace Ledge—bar ME-1
Wallace Ledge—cliff VT-1
Wallace Lode Mine—mine MT-8
Wallace McAllister Bridge—bridge WI-6
Wallace McAllister Bridge—other MI-6
Wallace-McGee House—hist pl SC-3
Wallace Memorial Baptist Ch—church TN-4
Wallace Memorial Cem—cemetery WV-2
Wallace Memorial Presbyterian Ch—church FL-3
Wallace Mesa NM-5
Wallace Methodist Ch—church AL-4
Wallace Methodist Church MS-4
Wallace Mill—locale NJ-2
Wallace Mill—locale NC-3
Wallace Mill Branch—stream MS-4
Wallace Mill Dam—dam NJ-2
Wallace Mill Pond—reservoir NJ-2
Wallace Mills—locale OH-6
Wallace Mountain TX-5
Wallace Mountain Cem—cemetery TX-5
Wallace Mtn—summit AL-4
Wallace Mtn—summit GA-3
Wallace Mtn—summit NY-2
Wallace Mtn—summit (2) NC-3
Wallace Park—flat CO-8
Wallace Park—park CT-1
Wallace Park—park (2) IL-6
Wallace Park—park KS-7
Wallace Park—park (2) OR-9
Wallace Park—park WI-6
Wallace Peak—summit MT-8
Wallace Peak—summit VA-3
Wallace Peak—summit WA-9
Wallace Plaza—locale MA-1
Wallace Point—cape ME-1
Wallace Pond NJ-2
Wallace Pond—lake MA-1
Wallace Pond—lake NH-1
Wallace Pond—lake NJ-2
Wallace Pond—lake VT-1
Wallace Pond—reservoir MA-1
Wallace Pond—reservoir NY-2
Wallace Pond—reservoir NC-3
Wallace Pond—reservoir SC-3
Wallace Pond Dam—dam NC-3
Wallace Pond Dam (breeched)—dam MA-1
Wallace Pond Outlet Dam—dam MA-1
Wallace Post Office (historical)—building MS-4
Wallace Prong Creek SC-3
Wallace Prospect—mine TN-4
Wallace Ranch—locale CO-8
Wallace Ranch—locale MT-8
Wallace Ranch—locale (3) NM-5
Wallace Ranch Airstrip—airport OR-9
Wallace Reef—bar AK-9
Wallace Reservoir MA-1
**Wallace Ridge**—pop pl LA-4
Wallace Ridge—ridge (2) TN-4
Wallace Ridge Cave Number One—cave TN-4
Wallace Ridge Cave Number Two—cave TN-4
Wallace River SC-3
Wallace River—stream WA-9
Wallace Rock—island AK-9
Wallace Rsvr—reservoir CO-8
Wallace Run—stream (6) PA-2
Wallaces Bar—bar AL-4
Wallace Sch—school AL-4
Wallace Sch—school AZ-5
Wallace Sch—school AR-4
Wallace Sch—school CA-9
Wallace Sch—school (2) IA-7
Wallace Sch—school (2) MO-7
Wallace Sch—school NE-7
Wallace Sch—school NJ-2
Wallace Sch—school NC-3
Wallace Sch—school OR-9
Wallace Sch—school (2) PA-2
Wallace Sch—school SC-3
Wallace Sch—school (2) TX-5
Wallace Sch—school WA-9
Wallace Sch (abandoned)—school MO-7
Wallace Sch (abandoned)—school PA-2
Wallaces Channel NC-3
Wallaces Chapel Ch of Christ (historical)—church MS-4
Wallace Sch (historical)—school AL-4
Wallace Sch (historical)—school MS-4
Wallace Sch (historical)—school (2) PA-2
Wallace Sch (historical)—school (2) TN-4
Wallace School IN-6
Wallace School (Abandoned)—locale MO-7
Wallace School Number 107 IN-6
Wallaces Corner MS-4
Wallaces Cross Roads TN-4
Wallaces Cross Roads Post Office TN-4
Wallaces Island OR-9
Wallace Slough—gut WA-9
Wallace Slough—stream OR-9
**Wallaces Mill**—pop pl GA-3
Wallaces Mill (historical)—locale AL-4
Wallaces Peak—summit UT-8
Wallaces Pond—reservoir AL-4
Wallace Spring—spring AZ-5
Wallace Spring—spring CA-9
Wallace Spring—spring KY-4
Wallace Springs—spring AL-4
Wallace Springs—spring TX-5
Wallaces Run PA-2
Wallaces Store—locale VA-3
Wallace State Park—park MO-7
Wallace Station—building PA-2
Wallace Station—locale PA-2
Wallace Stool WA-9
Wallace Store (historical)—locale MS-4
**Wallace Store (historical)**—pop pl NC-3
Wallace Street United Presbyterian Ch—church IN-6
**Wallace Subdivision**—pop pl UT-8
Wallace Tank—reservoir (3) AZ-5
Wallace Tank—reservoir (2) NM-5
Wallace Tank—reservoir (2) TX-5
Wallaceton—locale VA-3
**Wallaceton**—pop pl KY-4
**Wallaceton**—pop pl PA-2
Wallaceton Boggs Elem Sch—school PA-2
Wallaceton Borough—civil PA-2
Wallacetown VA-3
Wallace Township—civil SD-7
**Wallace Township**—pop pl KS-7
**Wallace Township**—pop pl ND-7
Wallace (Township of)—fmr MCD (4) AR-4
**Wallace (Township of)**—pop pl IL-6
**Wallace (Township of)**—pop pl PA-2
Wallace Trail—trail CA-9
Wallace Trail—trail PA-2
Wallace Trough Canyon—valley NM-5
**Wallace Village**—pop pl CO-8
Wallaceville—locale PA-2
**Wallaceville**—pop pl GA-3
Wallaceville Ch—church PA-2
Wallaceville Post Office (historical)—building PA-2
Wallaceville Sch—school GA-3
Wallaceville Sch—school MI-6
Wallace Well—well NM-5
Wallace Well Draw—valley TX-5
Wallace Windmill—locale TX-5
Wallace Woods Area Residential Hist Dist—hist pl KY-4
Wallace 1910 Fire Memorial—hist pl ID-8
Walla Ch—church SD-7
Wallack Hollow—valley CA-9
Wallacks Branch—stream PA-2
Wallacut River—stream WA-9
**Wallagrass**—pop pl (2) ME-1
Wallagrass Lakes—lake ME-1
Wallagrass (Plantation of)—civ div ME-1
Wallagrass Station—locale ME-1
Wallagrass Stream—stream ME-1
Walla Gulch—valley CA-9
Walla Hatchee Creek AL-4
Wallahatchee Creek—stream AL-4
Wallalah Mtn—summit GA-3
Wallalute Falls—falls OR-9
Wallamanumps Falls—falls MA-1
Wallamat OR-9
Wallamatogus Mtn—summit ME-1
Walla Matte OR-9
Walla Matte River OR-9
Wal-lamt River OR-9
**Walland**—pop pl TN-4
Walland Elem Sch—school TN-4
Walland HS (historical)—school TN-4
Wallanding Creek—stream WA-9
Walland MS—school TN-4
Walland Post Office—building TN-4
Walland Quarry Cave—cave TN-4
Wallapai AZ-5
Wall Arch—arch UT-8
Wallashuck Campground Lake Red Rock—locale IA-7
Wallauer, Fred, Farmhouse—hist pl MN-6
Walla Valley—valley AZ-5
Walla Walla WA-9
Walla Walla—locale IL-6
**Walla Walla**—pop pl WA-9
Walla Walla City County Airp—airport WA-9
Walla Walla Coll—school WA-9
Walla Walla-College Place (CCD)—cens area WA-9
Walla Walla Country Club—other WA-9
**Walla Walla County**—pop pl WA-9
Walla Walla Creek—stream AK-9
Walla Walla Creek—stream CA-9
Walla Walla Creek—stream WI-6
Walla Walla East—CDP WA-9
Walla Walla Forest Camp—locale OR-9
Walla Walla General Hospital Heliport—airport WA-9
Walla Walla Gulch—valley ID-8
Walla Walla HS—school WA-9
Walla Walla Public Library—hist pl WA-9
Walla Walla Ridge—ridge CA-9
**Walla Walla River**—pop pl WA-9
Walla Walla River—stream OR-9
Walla Walla River—stream WA-9
Walla Walla Sch—school KS-7
Walla Walla Valley—valley OR-9
Walla Walla Valley—valley WA-9
Walla Walla Valley Acad—school WA-9
Walla Walla West—other WA-9
Walla Walls—locale AK-9
Walla Watta—locale NC-3
**Wallback**—pop pl (2) WV-2
Wall Bay—bay AK-9
Wall Bayou—stream LA-4
Wall Bluff Spring—spring MO-7
Wall Borough—civil PA-2
Wall Branch—stream DE-2
Wall Branch—stream TN-4
Wall Branch—stream TX-5
Wall Branch—stream VA-3
Wallbridge Tank—reservoir NM-5
**Wall (Br. P.O.)**—pop pl NJ-2
**Wallburg**—pop pl NC-3
Wallburg Sch—school (2) NC-3
Wall Canyon—valley MT-8
Wall Canyon—valley (2) NV-8
Wall Canyon—valley SD-7
Wall Canyon—valley TX-5
Wall Canyon—valley WA-9
Wall Canyon Creek—stream MT-8
Wall Canyon Creek—stream NV-8
Wall Canyon Mine—mine NV-8
Wall Canyon Ranch—locale NV-8
Wall Canyon Rsvr—reservoir NV-8
Wall Canyon Windmill—locale NV-8
Wall Canyon Windmill—locale TX-5
Wall Cave—cave TN-4
Wall Cem—cemetery AR-4
Wall Cem—cemetery CT-1
Wall Cem—cemetery (2) GA-3
Wall Cem—cemetery (2) IL-6
Wall Cem—cemetery IN-6
Wall Cem—cemetery IA-7
Wall Cem—cemetery (3) KY-4
Wall Cem—cemetery ME-1
Wall Cem—cemetery (3) MS-4
Wall Cem—cemetery MO-7
Wall Cem—cemetery (2) NC-3
Wall Cem—cemetery (6) TN-4
Wall Cem—cemetery (3) TX-5
Wall Cem—cemetery (2) WV-2
Wall Ch—church NJ-2
Wall City—locale MT-8
Wall Cove—bay MD-2
Wall Creek AL-4
Wall Creek MS-4
Wall Creek NC-3
Wall Creek TX-5
Wall Creek—stream AZ-5
Wall Creek—stream AR-4
Wall Creek—stream FL-3
Wall Creek—stream (4) ID-8
Wall Creek—stream LA-4
Wall Creek—stream (2) MT-8
Wall Creek—stream (2) NV-8
Wall Creek—stream OH-6
Wall Creek—stream (8) OR-9
Wall Creek—stream SC-3
Wall Creek—stream TN-4
Wall Creek—stream (2) WY-8
Wall Creek Cem—cemetery AR-4
Wall Creek Cliffs—cliff MT-8
Wall Creek Hot Springs OR-9
Wall Creek Lake—lake MT-8
Wall Creek Ranger Station—locale MT-8
Wall Creek Ridge—ridge OR-9
Wall Creek Trail—trail OR-9
Wallcutt Mtn—summit AK-9
Walldell Cem—cemetery KY-4
Walldens Ridge Post Office (historical)—building TN-4
Wall Doxey State Park—park MS-4
Wall Doxey State Park Lake Dam—dam MS-4
Walle Ch—church ND-7
Walled Lake—lake (2) MI-6
**Walled Lake**—pop pl MI-6
Walled Lake Branch—stream MI-6
Walled Lake Cem—cemetery MI-6
Walled Lake HS—school MI-6
Walled Lake Sch—school MI-6
Walled Sink—basin FL-3
Walled Spring—spring TN-4
Wallee Hatchee Creek AL-4
Walle (historical)—locale ND-7
Walle Lutheran Church Cem—cemetery ND-7
**Wallen**—pop pl IN-6
Wallen Cem—cemetery MO-7
Wallen Cem—cemetery OK-5
Wallen Cem—cemetery TN-4
Wallen Creek—stream MO-7
Wallen Creek—stream (2) VA-3
Wallen Fork—stream KY-4
Wallenmeyer Ditch—canal IN-6
Wallen Mill Reservoir VA-3
Wallen Park—park MI-6
Wallenpaupack, Lake—reservoir PA-2
Wallenpaupack Area HS—school PA-2
Wallenpaupack Area MS—school PA-2
Wallenpaupack Creek—stream PA-2
Wallenpaupack Dam—dam PA-2
Wallenpaupack Elem Sch—school PA-2
Wallenpaupack Lake PA-2
**Wallenpaupack Mills**—pop pl PA-2
Wallenpaupack North Elem Sch—school PA-2
Wallen Ridge—ridge TN-4
Wallen Ridge—ridge VA-3
Wallen Ridge Ch—church TN-4
Wallens Bend—bend TN-4
Wallens Bend Ch—church TN-4
Wallens Bend Sch (historical)—school TN-4
Wallens Hill—summit CT-1
Wal-Len Shop Ctr—locale MA-1
Wallens Pond—lake NJ-2
Wallen's Ridge VA-3
Wallentine Farmstead—hist pl ID-8
**Waller**—pop pl IA-7
**Waller**—pop pl PA-2
**Waller**—pop pl TX-5
**Waller**—pop pl VA-3
Waller, Mount—summit MO-7
Waller, William, House—hist pl IL-6
Waller Airp—airport PA-2
Waller Bayou—stream AR-4
Waller Branch—stream KY-4
Waller Bridge—bridge MS-4
Waller Cave—cave IN-6
Waller (CCD)—cens area TX-5
Waller Cem—cemetery KY-4
Waller Cem—cemetery LA-4
Waller Cem—cemetery MO-7
Waller Cem—cemetery (5) TN-4
Waller Cem—cemetery (4) TX-5
Waller Cem—cemetery VT-1
**Waller (County)**—pop pl TX-5
Waller Creek AL-4
Waller Creek—stream AL-4
Waller Creek—stream (2) CA-9
Waller Creek—stream (2) TX-5
Waller Elem Sch—school FL-3
Waller Ferry TN-4
Waller Gap—gap AR-4
Waller Gully—valley TX-5
Waller Hall, Willamette Univ—hist pl OR-9
Waller Hill CT-1
Waller Hill—summit CT-1
Waller Hill—summit KY-4
Waller Hollow—valley AR-4
Waller HS—school IL-6
Waller Lake—lake IA-7
Waller Lake—reservoir TX-5
Waller Lakes—lake WI-6
Waller Landing—locale LA-4
Waller Mill Rsvr—reservoir VA-3
Waller Park—park CA-9
Waller Pond VA-3
Waller Pond Dam—dam MS-4
Waller Ranch—locale (3) NM-5
Waller Ridge Cem—cemetery MS-4
Waller Ridge Ch—church MS-4
Waller Rsvr—reservoir CO-8
Waller Rsvr Number Four—reservoir OR-9
Waller Rsvr Number One—reservoir OR-9
Waller Rsvr 2—reservoir OR-9
Waller Rsvr 3—reservoir OR-9
Waller Rsvr 4—reservoir OR-9
Waller Rsvr 5—reservoir OR-9
Waller Rsvr 6—reservoir OR-9
Wallers Bar PA-2
Wallers Ch—church VA-3
Waller Sch—school CT-1
Waller Sch—school IL-6
Waller Sch—school LA-4
Waller Sch—school MI-6
Waller Sch—school WI-6
Wallers Chapel—church AR-4
Waller School (Abandoned)—locale IA-7
Wallers Corner—locale VA-3
Wallers Creek—stream AL-4
Wallers Ferry (historical)—locale TN-4
Wallers Mill (historical)—locale AL-4
Wallers Pond—lake GA-3
Wallers Shoals—bar TN-4
Wallersville MA-1
Wallersville Cem—cemetery MS-4
**Wallerville**—pop pl MS-4
Wallerville Baptist Ch—church MS-4
Wallerville Pond—lake PA-2
Wallerville Post Office (historical)—building MS-4
Waller Well—well NM-5
Waller Windmill—locale NM-5
Wallet Canyon—valley CA-9
Walle Town Hall—building ND-7
**Walle Township**—pop pl ND-7
Wallet Pond—lake FL-3
Wallet Spring ID-8
Walley—locale AL-4
Walley, Mount—summit MA-1
Walley Cem—cemetery (2) MS-4
Walley Cem—cemetery MO-7
Walley Cem—cemetery ND-7
Walley Chapel—church GA-3
Walleye Bay—swamp SC-3
Walleye Creek—stream TX-5
Walleye Lake—lake OH-6
Walley Hollow—valley AL-4
Walley Hollow—valley AR-4
Walley Mill—locale PA-2
Walley Mound—summit MO-7
Walley Run—stream IL-6
Walley Run—stream PA-2
Walley Sch—school IL-6
Walleys Hot Springs—locale NV-8
Walleys Mill PA-2
Wallface Mtn—summit NY-2
Wallface Ponds—lake NY-2
Wall Ferry (historical)—locale AL-4
Wallfield—locale MS-4
Wallfield Ch—church MS-4
Wallfield New Life Freewill Baptist Ch MS-4
Wallfield Sch (historical)—school MS-4
Wall Fork—stream WV-2
Wall Gulch—valley OR-9
Wall Highway Baptist Church AL-4
Wall Highway Ch—church AL-4
Wall Hill MS-4
Wallhill—locale MS-4
Wall Hill Cem—cemetery MS-4
Wall Hill Ch—church MS-4
Wallhill Post Office (historical)—building MS-4
Wallholla CA-9
Wallholla River CA-9
Wall Hollow—valley TN-4
Wall Hollow Branch—stream TN-4
Wall House—hist pl LA-4
Wall House—hist pl PA-2
Wallick Cem—cemetery OH-6
Wallick Creek—stream AK-9

Wallic Lake—*lake* MI-6
**Wallicut**—*pop pl* WA-9
*Wallicut River* WA-9
Wallila Coulee—*stream* MT-8
Walli Lake—*lake* MN-6
Wallin—*locale* IA-7
Wallin—*locale* MI-6
Wallin, Frank, House—*hist pl* MT-8
Wallin Branch—*stream* NC-3
Wallinch—*locale* OR-9
Wallin Coal Mine—*mine* AK-9
*Walling* FL-3
Walling—*locale* FL-3
**Walling**—*pop pl* TN-4
Walling, Ansel T., House—*hist pl* OH-6
Walling, Joseph Daniel, House—*hist pl* TN-4
Walling Bar—*bar* AR-4
Walling Bend—*bend* TX-5
Walling Bend Park—*locale* TX-5
Walling Brick Factory—*building* TX-5
Walling Canyon—*valley* WA-9
Walling Cave—*cave* TN-4
*Walling Cem* AL-4
Walling Cem—*cemetery* AL-4
Walling Cem—*cemetery* FL-3
Walling Cem—*cemetery* (2) TN-4
Walling Cem—*cemetery* (3) TX-5
Walling Ch—*church* FL-3
Walling Ch of Christ—*church* TN-4
Walling Ditch—*canal* IN-6
Wallingford—*CDP* CT-1
**Wallingford**—*pop pl* CT-1
**Wallingford**—*pop pl* IL-6
**Wallingford**—*pop pl* IA-7
**Wallingford**—*pop pl* KY-4
**Wallingford**—*pop pl* PA-2
**Wallingford**—*pop pl* VT-1
**Wallingford**—*pop pl* WA-9
Wallingford, Mount—*summit* NH-1
Wallingford Cem—*cemetery* IA-7
Wallingford Creek—*stream* MN-6
Wallingford Fire and Police Station—*hist pl* WA-9
**Wallingford Hills**—*pop pl* PA-2
Wallingford Main Street Hist Dist—*hist pl* VT-1
Wallingford Mills—*locale* PA-2
Wallingford Pond—*lake* ME-1
Wallingford Pond—*lake* VT-1
Wallingford Station—*building* PA-2
**Wallingford (Town of)**—*pop pl* VT-1
Walling (historical)—*locale* AL-4
Walling Lake—*lake* CA-9
Walling Landing (historical)—*locale* AL-4
Walling Mill Creek—*stream* TN-4
Walling Mtn—*summit* AL-4
Walling Mtn—*summit* MA-1
*Walling Pond* PA-2
Walling Post Office—*building* TN-4
Walling Post Office (historical)—*building* AL-4
Walling Reef—*cliff* MT-8
Walling Sch (historical)—*school* TN-4
Wallings Landing (historical)—*locale* AL-4
*Wallingslock Creek* IA-7
Wallingslock Creek—*stream* IA-7
*Wallings Pond* RI-1
Wallings Sch—*school* OH-6
**Wallington**—*pop pl* NJ-2
**Wallington**—*pop pl* NY-2
Wallington County Park—*park* NJ-2
Wallington Reach—*channel* NJ-2
Wallington Sch—*school* NJ-2
*Wallin Lake* MN-6
Wallin Lake—*lake* MI-6
Wallin Lake—*lake* WI-6
*Wallins* KY-4
Wallins—*other* KY-4
**Wallins Corner**—*pop pl* NY-2
**Wallins Corners**—*pop pl* NY-2
**Wallins Creek**—*pop pl* KY-4
Wallins Creek—*stream* KY-4
Wallins Creek (CCD)—*cens area* KY-4
**Wallins Creek (Wallins)**—*pop pl* KY-4
Wallins Store (historical)—*locale* AL-4
*Wallins Wallow* IN-6
Wallin Well—*locale* NM-5
**Wallis**—*pop pl* MO-7
**Wallis**—*pop pl* TX-5
Wallis Branch—*stream* WV-2
*Wallis Brook* ME-1
Wallis Brook—*stream* NH-1
Wallis Cabin—*locale* ID-8
Wallis (CCD)—*cens area* TX-5
Wallis Cem—*cemetery* MO-7
Wallis Cem—*cemetery* TN-4
Wallis Cem—*cemetery* TX-5
Wallis Chapel—*church* AL-4
Wallischeck Homestead—*hist pl* OH-6
*Wallis City* PA-2
*Wallis Cut* SC-3
Wallis-Estill-Hayden-March Cem—*cemetery* TN-4
*Wallis Lake* MI-6
Wallis Lake—*lake* TX-5
Wall Island—*island* DE-2
Wallis Mine—*mine* CA-9
*Wallis Pond* VT-1
Wallis Pond—*lake* MA-1
**Wallispond**—*pop pl* VT-1
Wallis Pond—*reservoir* MA-1
Wallis Pond Dam—*dam* MA-1
Wallis Ranch—*locale* WY-8
Wallis Rec Area—*park* WY-8
**Wallis (reduced Usage)**—*pop pl* (2) MS-4
*Wallis Reservoir* MA-1
*Wallis Run* PA-2
Wallis Run—*locale* PA-2
Wallis Run—*stream* PA-2
**Wallis Sands**—*pop pl* NH-1
*Wallis Sands Beach* NH-1
Wallis Sch—*school* MA-1
*Walliss Channel* NC-3
Wallis Street—*post sta* MA-1
Wallisville—*locale* TX-5
Wallisville Cem—*cemetery* TX-5
Wallisville Sch—*school* TX-5
**Wallkill**—*pop pl* NY-2
**Wallkill Camp**—*pop pl* NY-2
Wallkill Cem—*cemetery* NY-2
**Wallkill Lake**—*pop pl* NJ-2
Wallkill Lake—*reservoir* NJ-2
*Wallkill Mountains* NJ-2
*Wall Kill River* NJ-2
Wallkill River—*stream* NJ-2
Wallkill River—*stream* NY-2
Wallkill Sch Number 18—*school* NY-2
Wallkill State Prison—*other* NY-2
**Wallkill (Town of)**—*pop pl* NY-2
Wallkill Valley Cem—*cemetery* NY-2
Wall Knob—*summit* KY-4
*Wall Lake* AR-4
*Wall Lake* IA-7
*Wall Lake* MT-8
Wall Lake—*lake* AZ-5
Wall Lake—*lake* AR-4
Wall Lake—*lake* CO-8
Wall Lake—*lake* FL-3
Wall Lake—*lake* IN-6
Wall Lake—*lake* LA-4
Wall Lake—*lake* MI-6
Wall Lake—*lake* MN-6
Wall Lake—*lake* (2) MT-8
Wall Lake—*lake* OR-9
Wall Lake—*lake* (2) SD-7
Wall Lake—*lake* UT-8
Wall Lake—*lake* (3) WA-9
Wall Lake—*lake* (2) WY-8
Wall Lake—*locale* MN-6
**Wall Lake**—*pop pl* IN-6
**Wall Lake**—*pop pl* IA-7
**Wall Lake**—*pop pl* LA-4
**Wall Lake**—*pop pl* MI-6
Wall Lake—*reservoir* NM-5
Wall Lake—*reservoir* UT-8
Wall Lake Cem—*cemetery* IA-7
Wall Lake Dam—*dam* UT-8
Wall Lake (historical)—*lake* SD-7
Wall Lake Inlet—*canal* IA-7
Wall Lake Outlet—*canal* IA-7
Wall Lake State Public Shooting Area—*park* SD-7
**Wall Lake Station**—*pop pl* IA-7
Wall Lake Township—*fmr MCD* (2) IA-7
**Wall Lake Township**—*pop pl* SD-7
Wallman—*locale* MD-2
Wallman Park—*park* KS-7
Wallmark Lake—*lake* MN-6
Wall Mountain—*ridge* AR-4
Wall Mtn—*summit* CO-8
Wall Mtn—*summit* GA-3
Wall Mtn—*summit* ID-8
Wall Mtn—*summit* MT-8
Wall Mtn—*summit* WY-8
Wall Municipal Airp—*airport* SD-7
Wallner—*locale* WA-9
**Wallner (historical)**—*pop pl* PA-2
Walloand Bluff Cave—*cave* TN-4
Walloch Farmstead—*hist pl* SD-7
Wallock, Lake—*reservoir* AL-4
Wallock Dam—*dam* AL-4
Wall of China—*ridge* AK-9
Wall of Windows—*cliff* UT-8
Wallon Creek—*stream* OR-9
**Wallonia**—*pop pl* KY-4
**Walloomsac**—*pop pl* NY-2
*Walloomsack* NY-2
*Walloomsack River* VT-1
Walloomsac River—*stream* NY-2
Walloomsac River—*stream* VT-1
*Walloomshack River* NY-2
Walloon Lake—*lake* MI-6
**Walloon Lake**—*pop pl* (2) MI-6
Wallooskee River—*stream* OR-9
Wallop Butte—*summit* MT-8
Wallop Hollow—*valley* (2) TN-4
Wallops Beach—*beach* VA-3
Wallops Flight Center (NASA)—*building* VA-3
Wallops Island—*island* VA-3
Wallops Island—*post sta* VA-3
*Wallops Mill Pond* VA-3
Wallops Neck—*cape* MD-2
Wallops Neck—*cape* VA-3
Wallops Pond—*lake* VA-3
Wallory Bar—*bar* PA-2
Walloth School—*locale* MT-8
**Wallowa**—*pop pl* OR-9
Wallowa (CCD)—*cens area* OR-9
Wallowa Cem—*cemetery* OR-9
**Wallowa County**—*pop pl* OR-9
Wallowa Creek—*stream* (2) OR-9
Wallowa Falls—*falls* OR-9
Wallowa Lake—*reservoir* OR-9
Wallowa Lake Dam—*dam* OR-9
Wallowa Lake State Park—*park* OR-9
Wallowa Mountains—*range* OR-9
Wallowa Natl For—*forest* OR-9
Wallowa Ponds—*lake* OR-9
Wallowa River—*stream* OR-9
*Wallowa Valley Canal* OR-9
Wallowa Valley Improvement Canal—*canal* OR-9
Wallowa Whitman Natl For—*forest* OR-9
Wallow Creek—*stream* MN-6
Wallow Creek—*stream* OR-9
Wallow Draw—*valley* WY-8
Wallow Hole Ch—*church* KY-4
Wallow Hole Creek—*stream* KY-4
Wallowhole Fork—*stream* WV-2
Wallowhole Hollow—*valley* VA-3
Wallowhole Knob—*summit* WV-2
Wallowhole Mtn—*summit* WV-2
Wallowhole Ridge—*ridge* WV-2
Wallow Hole Sch—*school* KY-4
Wallow Hollow—*valley* VA-3
Wallowing Bull Cem—*cemetery* WY-8
Wallowing Hole—*bay* PA-2
Wallow Mtn—*summit* ID-8
Wallows, The—*basin* WY-8
Wallows Creek—*stream* WY-8
Wallow Spring—*spring* OR-9
*Wallow Wallows* WA-9
*Wallow Wallows River* OR-9
Wallpack Bend—*bend* NJ-2
Wallpack Bend—*bend* PA-2
Wallpack Cem—*cemetery* NJ-2
**Wallpack Center**—*pop pl* NJ-2
Wallpack Center Hist Dist—*hist pl* NJ-2
Wallpack Consolidated Sch—*school* NJ-2
Wall Park—*park* PA-2
Wall Peak—*summit* ID-8
Wall Point—*cape* FL-3
Wall Point—*cape* ME-1
Wall Point—*summit* CA-9
Wall Point—*summit* ID-8
Wall Pond—*lake* MA-1
Wall Pond—*reservoir* NC-3
Wall Pond Dam—*dam* NC-3
Wallrich Lake—*lake* IA-7
Wall Ridge—*ridge* WI-6
Wall Rock—*cliff* AR-4
Wallrock—*cliff* MT-8
Wall Rock—*gap* OR-9
Wall Rock—*summit* WY-8
Wallrock Basin—*basin* MT-8
*Wallrock Creek* WY-8
Wall Rock Creek—*stream* OR-9
Wallrock Creek—*stream* (2) WY-8
Wall Rock Ridge—*ridge* OR-9
Wall Rock Springs—*spring* OR-9
*Wallrose* PA-2
**Wall Rose**—*pop pl* PA-2
Wall Rsvr—*reservoir* OR-9
Wall Rsvr—*reservoir* WY-8
*Wall Run* OH-6
Wall Run—*stream* IN-6
*Walls* MS-4
Walls—*locale* LA-4
Walls—*locale* OK-5
Walls—*other* KY-4
**Walls**—*pop pl* MS-4
Walls, James A., House—*hist pl* AR-4
*Walls, The* MS-4
**Wallsboro**—*pop pl* AL-4
Wallsboro Community Club—*building* AL-4
Walls Bottom—*flat* AR-4
Walls Branch—*stream* AL-4
Walls Branch—*stream* VA-3
Walls Branch—*stream* WV-2
Walls Bridge—*locale* VA-3
*Wallsburg* AL-4
**Wallsburg**—*pop pl* AL-4
**Wallsburg**—*pop pl* UT-8
Wallsburg Cem—*cemetery* UT-8
Wallsburg Post Office—*building* UT-8
Wallsburg Ridge—*ridge* UT-8
Wallsburg Wildlife Mngmt Area—*park* UT-8
Walls Cave—*cave* AL-4
Walls Cem—*cemetery* GA-3
Walls Cem—*cemetery* IL-6
Walls Cem—*cemetery* IN-6
Walls Cem—*cemetery* (2) MS-4
Walls Cem—*cemetery* NC-3
Walls Cem—*cemetery* OH-6
Walls Cem—*cemetery* VA-3
Walls Ch—*church* NC-3
Wall Sch—*school* IL-6
Walls Chapel—*church* AL-4
Walls Chapel—*church* (2) AR-4
Walls Chapel—*church* NC-3
*Walls Chapel Ch* AL-4
Wall Sch (historical)—*school* (2) MS-4
**Walls Corners**—*pop pl* PA-2
*Walls Creek* GA-3
*Walls Creek* PA-2
Walls Creek—*stream* GA-3
Walls Creek—*stream* MS-4
Walls Crossing—*locale* GA-3
*Walls Cut* SC-3
Walls Cut—*channel* SC-3
Walls Dam—*dam* AL-4
Walls Elem Sch—*school* MS-4
**Wallsend**—*pop pl* KY-4
Wallsend Cem—*cemetery* KY-4
Wall-Seppanen House—*hist pl* MI-6
Walls Ferry—*locale* AR-4
Walls Flat—*flat* CA-9
Walls Gulch—*valley* CO-8
Walls Hill—*summit* ME-1
*Walls Hollow* TN-4
Walls Hollow—*valley* AR-4
Walls Hollow—*valley* (2) TN-4
Walls House—*hist pl* AR-4
Walls Island—*island* (2) PA-2
Walls Jericho—*cliff* TN-4
Walls Lake—*flat* OR-9
Walls Lake—*lake* AZ-5
Walls Lake—*reservoir* (2) AL-4
Walls Lake Canyon—*valley* OR-9
Walls Lake Dam—*dam* AL-4
Walls Lake Dam—*dam* MS-4
Walls Lakes—*reservoir* NC-3
Walls Lake Well—*well* OR-9
Walls Landing—*locale* NC-3
Walls Landing Creek—*stream* VA-3
Wall-Smethurst Mound Group—*hist pl* WI-6
Wallsmith Branch—*stream* TN-4
Wallsmith Canyon—*valley* NM-5
Walls of Jericho—*cliff* AL-4
Walls Pond—*lake* NY-2
Walls Post Office—*building* MS-4
Wall Spring—*spring* CA-9
Wall Spring—*spring* (2) NV-8
Wall Spring—*spring* WA-9
**Wall Springs**—*pop pl* FL-3
*Wall Springs Point* FL-3
*Walls Reservoir* MA-1
Walls Rsvr—*reservoir* OR-9
Walls Run—*stream* (2) VA-3
Walls Sch—*school* AR-4
Walls Sch—*school* NJ-2
Walls Schoolhouse (historical)—*school* MS-4
Walls Siding—*locale* IL-6
Walls Store (historical)—*locale* MS-4
Wallstown—*locale* AL-4
Walls Township—*civil* MO-7
Walls (Township of)—*fmr MCD* AR-4
**Walls (Township of)**—*pop pl* MN-6
*Wallstreet* AL-4
*Wall Street* UT-8
Wall Street—*locale* AL-4
**Wallstreet**—*pop pl* CO-8
**Wall Street**—*pop pl* MO-7
Wall Street—*uninc pl* NY-2
Wall Street Canyon—*valley* CA-9
Wall Street Ch—*church* KS-7
**Wall Street Condominium**—*pop pl* UT-8
Wall Street Creek—*stream* AK-9
Wall Street (historical)—*locale* KS-7
Wall Street Mill—*hist pl* CA-9
Wall Street Mill—*locale* CA-9
Wall Street Mine—*mine* CA-9
Wall Street Mine—*mine* NV-8
Wall Street Mine—*mine* NM-5
**Wallsville**—*pop pl* PA-2
Wallsville Cem—*cemetery* PA-2
*Walls Well* AZ-5
*Walls Wells* AZ-5
Walls Windmill—*locale* NM-5
Walltown—*locale* CA-9
Walltown—*locale* KY-4
**Walltown**—*pop pl* PA-2
Walltown Ch—*church* KY-4
Wall Town Drainage Ditch—*canal* IL-6
Walltown Recreation Center—*building* NC-3
Walltown Sch—*school* NC-3
**Wall Township**—*pop pl* SD-7
**Wall (Township of)**—*pop pl* IL-6
**Wall (Township of)**—*pop pl* NJ-2
Wall Trip Branch—*stream* OK-5
Wallula—*locale* KS-7
**Wallula**—*pop pl* WA-9
Wallula, Lake—*reservoir* OR-9
Wallula, Lake—*reservoir* WA-9
Wallula Gap—*channel* WA-9
Wallula Junction—*locale* WA-9
Wallula Station—*locale* WA-9
Wallum Lake—*lake* MA-1
Wallum Lake—*lake* RI-1
Wallum Lake—*reservoir* RI-1
Wallum Lake Dam—*dam* RI-1
**Wallum Lake (Zambarano Memorial Hospital)**—*pop pl* RI-1
*Wallum Pond* MA-1
*Wallum Pond* RI-1
Wallum Pond Hill—*summit* MA-1
*Wallumshack* NY-2
*Wallumshack River* NY-2
*Wallumshack River* VT-1
Wallum Siding—*locale* MT-8
*Wallupa Creek* OR-9
Wallupa Creek—*stream* OR-9
*Walluski River* OR-9
Wallville—*locale* MD-2
**Wallville**—*pop pl* OK-5
Wallwood Boy Scout Camp Reserve—*locale* FL-3
Wallworth Lake—*reservoir* NJ-2
**Wallworth Park**—*pop pl* NJ-2
**Wally**—*pop pl* MO-7
Wally Dresskell Lake—*reservoir* ND-7
Wally Hill—*summit* CA-9
Wally Holler Pond—*reservoir* AZ-5
Wally Lake—*lake* MN-6
*Wally Leg* GA-3
Wallyn Park—*park* MN-6
Wally Reservoir—*lake* ID-8
Wallys Leg—*channel* GA-3
Wally Spring—*spring* NV-8
Wallys Woods Lake—*reservoir* IN-6
Wallys Woods Lake Dam—*dam* IN-6
Walman Nichlos Hollow—*valley* PA-2
*Walmar* IL-6
Walmar Sch—*school* CA-9
Walmers Ch—*church* PA-2
*Walmington* DE-2
**Walmo**—*pop pl* PA-2
**Walmore**—*pop pl* NY-2
Walmore Mine (underground)—*mine* AL-4
Walmort—*locale* CA-9
*Walmouth Head* WA-9
Walmsey—*locale* VA-3
**Walmsley**—*pop pl* VA-3
Waln Creek—*stream* OR-9
*Walnee* HI-9
*Walness Hill* WI-6
Walnford—*hist pl* NJ-2
**Walnford**—*pop pl* NJ-2
Waln Run—*stream* PA-2
*Walnut* TX-5
Walnut—*locale* AR-4
Walnut—*locale* IL-6
Walnut—*locale* MS-4
Walnut—*locale* MO-7
Walnut—*locale* OH-6
Walnut—*locale* (2) WV-2
**Walnut**—*pop pl* CA-9
**Walnut**—*pop pl* IL-6
**Walnut**—*pop pl* IN-6
**Walnut**—*pop pl* IA-7
**Walnut**—*pop pl* KS-7
**Walnut**—*pop pl* MD-2
**Walnut**—*pop pl* MS-4
**Walnut**—*pop pl* NE-7
**Walnut**—*pop pl* NC-3
**Walnut**—*pop pl* (2) PA-2
**Walnut Acres**—*pop pl* TN-4
Walnut Acres Sch—*school* CA-9
**Walnut Acres (subdivision)**—*pop pl* PA-2
Walnut Ave Ch—*church* FL-3
Walnut Ave Sch—*school* CA-9
Walnut Baptist Ch—*church* (2) MS-4
*Walnut Bayou* LA-4
*Walnut Bayou* MS-4
*Walnut Bayou* OK-5
Walnut Bayou—*gut* LA-4
Walnut Bayou—*stream* AR-4
Walnut Bayou—*stream* LA-4
Walnut Bayou—*stream* MS-4
Walnut Bayou—*stream* (2) OK-5
Walnut Bayou—*stream* TX-5
*Walnut Beach* CT-1
**Walnut Beach**—*pop pl* CT-1
Walnut Beach Park—*park* OH-6
Walnut Bend—*bend* MS-4
Walnut Bend—*bend* PA-2
Walnut Bend—*bend* TX-5
**Walnut Bend**—*pop pl* PA-2
Walnut Bend—*uninc pl* TX-5
Walnut Bend Oil and Gas Field—*oilfield* KS-7
Walnut Bend Oil Field—*oilfield* TX-5
Walnut Bend Revet—*levee* AR-4
Walnut Bend Sch—*school* (2) TX-5
Walnut Bluff—*cliff* AL-4
Walnut Bottom—*bend* MD-2
Walnut Bottom—*locale* WV-2
**Walnut Bottom**—*pop pl* PA-2
Walnut Bottom—*valley* NC-3
Walnut Bottom Camp (historical)—*locale* PA-2
Walnut Bottom Cave—*cave* AL-4
Walnut Bottom Ch—*church* AR-4
Walnut Bottom Ch—*church* MD-2
Walnut Bottom Creek—*stream* NC-3
**Walnut Bottom (RR name Greythorne)**—*pop pl* PA-2
Walnut Bottom Run—*stream* PA-2
Walnut Bottom Run—*stream* WV-2
*Walnut Branch* MO-7
*Walnut Branch* WV-2
Walnut Branch—*stream* AL-4
Walnut Branch—*stream* AR-4
Walnut Branch—*stream* (2) GA-3
Walnut Branch—*stream* (2) KY-4
Walnut Branch—*stream* LA-4
Walnut Branch—*stream* MO-7
Walnut Branch—*stream* (2) NC-3
Walnut Branch—*stream* OK-5
Walnut Branch—*stream* (2) SC-3
Walnut Branch—*stream* TN-4
Walnut Branch—*stream* (5) TX-5
Walnut Branch—*stream* (5) VA-3
Walnut Branch Ch—*church* NC-3
Walnut Bridge—*bridge* PA-2
Walnut Brook—*stream* NJ-2
**Walnut Brook Subdivision**—*pop pl* UT-8
Walnutcamp Run—*stream* OH-6
Walnut Canal—*canal* CA-9
*Walnut Canyon* AZ-5
Walnut Canyon—*valley* (12) AZ-5
Walnut Canyon—*valley* (2) CA-9
Walnut Canyon—*valley* (5) NM-5
Walnut Canyon—*valley* TX-5
Walnut Canyon Bridge—*hist pl* AZ-5
Walnut Canyon Dam—*hist pl* AZ-5
Walnut Canyon Interchange—*crossing* AZ-5
Walnut Canyon Loop Trail—*trail* AZ-5
Walnut Canyon Natl—*park* AZ-5
Walnut Canyon Natl Monmt—*hist pl* AZ-5
Walnut Canyon Natl Monmt—*park* AZ-5
Walnut Canyon Natl Monument HQ—*building* AZ-5
Walnut Canyon Road Tank—*reservoir* AZ-5
Walnut Canyon Rsvr—*reservoir* CA-9
Walnut Canyon Spring—*spring* AZ-5
Walnut Cave—*cave* AL-4
Walnut (CCD)—*cens area* OK-5
Walnut Cem—*cemetery* GA-3
Walnut Cem—*cemetery* IL-6
Walnut Cem—*cemetery* (2) IA-7
Walnut Cem—*cemetery* KS-7
Walnut Cem—*cemetery* MA-1
Walnut Ch—*church* (2) IN-6
Walnut Ch—*church* OH-6
Walnut Ch—*church* TX-5
Walnut-Chancellor Hist Dist—*hist pl* PA-2
Walnut Chapel—*church* IL-6
Walnut Chapel—*church* IN-6
Walnut Chapel—*church* VA-3
*Walnut City* KS-7
Walnut City—*locale* IA-7
Walnut Corner—*locale* AR-4
**Walnut Corner**—*pop pl* AR-4
Walnut Corner Ch—*church* IL-6
Walnut Corner Ch—*church* IN-6
Walnut Corner Ch—*church* TN-4
**Walnut Corners**—*pop pl* IN-6
Walnut Corner (Township of)—*fmr MCD* AR-4
Walnut Cove—*basin* GA-3
Walnut Cove—*bay* (2) GA-3
Walnut Cove—*bay* TN-4
Walnut Cove—*bay* TX-5
**Walnut Cove**—*pop pl* NC-3
Walnut Cove—*valley* GA-3
Walnut Cove—*valley* (6) NC-3
Walnut Cove Creek—*stream* GA-3
Walnut Cove Creek—*stream* NC-3
Walnut Cove Elem Sch—*school* NC-3
Walnut Cove Mtn—*summit* NC-3
Walnut Cove Mtn—*summit* SC-3
Walnut Cove Rec Area—*park* MO-7
**Walnut Cove (subdivision)**—*pop pl* NC-3
*Walnut Creek* AL-4
*Walnut Creek* AZ-5
*Walnut Creek* IN-6
*Walnut Creek* KS-7
*Walnut Creek* NC-3
*Walnut Creek* OK-5
*Walnut Creek* TX-5
**Walnut Creek**—*pop pl* CA-9
**Walnut Creek**—*pop pl* MS-4
**Walnut Creek**—*pop pl* (2) NC-3
**Walnut Creek**—*pop pl* OH-6
Walnut Creek—*stream* (4) AL-4
Walnut Creek—*stream* AK-9
Walnut Creek—*stream* (8) AZ-5
Walnut Creek—*stream* (4) AR-4
Walnut Creek—*stream* (3) CA-9
Walnut Creek—*stream* CO-8
Walnut Creek—*stream* (7) GA-3
Walnut Creek—*stream* (6) IL-6
Walnut Creek—*stream* (5) IN-6
Walnut Creek—*stream* (15) IA-7
Walnut Creek—*stream* (27) KS-7
Walnut Creek—*stream* KY-4
Walnut Creek—*stream* (2) LA-4
Walnut Creek—*stream* (4) MS-4
Walnut Creek—*stream* (11) MO-7
Walnut Creek—*stream* (10) NE-7
Walnut Creek—*stream* (6) NM-5
Walnut Creek—*stream* NY-2
Walnut Creek—*stream* (6) NC-3
Walnut Creek—*stream* (6) OH-6
Walnut Creek—*stream* (11) OK-5
Walnut Creek—*stream* PA-2
Walnut Creek—*stream* SC-3
Walnut Creek—*stream* (31) TX-5
Walnut Creek—*stream* VA-3
Walnut Creek—*stream* WV-2
Walnut Creek Archeol District—*hist pl* TX-5
Walnut Creek Baptist Church—*hist pl* LA-4
Walnut Creek Boat Ramp—*locale* KY-4
Walnut Creek Bridge—*hist pl* KS-7
Walnut Creek Cem—*cemetery* AL-4
Walnut Creek Cem—*cemetery* IN-6
Walnut Creek Cem—*cemetery* (2) KS-7
Walnut Creek Cem—*cemetery* MS-4
Walnut Creek Cem—*cemetery* (2) NE-7
Walnut Creek Cem—*cemetery* OH-6
Walnut Creek Cem—*cemetery* (2) TX-5
Walnut Creek Ch—*church* AL-4
Walnut Creek Ch—*church* GA-3
Walnut Creek Ch—*church* IN-6
Walnut Creek Ch—*church* LA-4
Walnut Creek Ch—*church* MS-4
Walnut Creek Ch—*church* NC-3
Walnut Creek Ch—*church* OH-6
Walnut Creek Ch—*church* (2) TX-5
Walnut Creek Crossing—*hist pl* KS-7
Walnut Creek Ditch—*canal* IL-6
Walnut Creek Duck Marsh Dam—*dam* IA-7
Walnut Creek Gap—*gap* NC-3
Walnut Creek Golf Course—*locale* PA-2
Walnut Creek Lake—*reservoir* IA-7
*Walnut Creek Methodist Ch* AL-4
Walnut Creek Metropolitan Park—*park* TX-5
Walnut Creek Mine Spring—*spring* AZ-5
Walnut Creek Peninsula Park—*park* OK-5
Walnut Creek Peninsula Rec Area—*park* OK-5
*Walnut Creek Presbyterian Ch* MS-4
Walnut Creek Ranger Station—*locale* AZ-5
Walnut Creek Sch—*school* NE-7
Walnut Creek Sch—*school* NC-3
Walnut Creek Sch—*school* TX-5
Walnut Creek Settling Basin—*basin* IL-6
**Walnut Creek (subdivision)**—*pop pl* NC-3
Walnut Creek Tank—*reservoir* TX-5
Walnut Creek Township—*civil* MO-7
**Walnut Creek Township**—*pop pl* KS-7
Walnut Creek (Township of)—*civ div* OH-6
Walnut Creek Tributary Bridge—*hist pl* KS-7
Walnut Creek Tunnel—*tunnel* CA-9
*Walnut Creek Wash* CA-9
Walnut Creek West—*CDP* CA-9
Walnut Creek Work Center—*locale* AZ-5
Walnut Dell Sch—*school* IL-6
Walnut Ditch—*canal* CA-9
Walnut Draw—*valley* AZ-5
Walnut Draw—*valley* (3) NM-5
Walnut Draw—*valley* (3) TX-5
Walnut Eddy—*rapids* OR-9
Walnut Eddy—*rapids* WI-6
Walnut Elem Sch—*school* IN-6
Walnut Elem Sch—*school* KS-7
Walnut Elem Sch—*school* MS-4
Walnut Elem Sch—*school* NC-3
Walnut Farm—*hist pl* DE-2
Walnut Flat—*flat* AZ-5
Walnut Flat—*flat* CA-9
Walnut Flat—*locale* KY-4
Walnut Flat Creek—*stream* KY-4
Walnut Flats—*flat* VA-3
**Walnut Forest**—*pop pl* TX-5
*Walnut Fork* IN-6
Walnut Fork—*stream* GA-3
Walnut Fork—*stream* IL-6
Walnut Fork—*stream* (3) IN-6
Walnut Fork—*stream* (2) KY-4
Walnut Fork—*stream* MO-7
Walnut Fork—*stream* TX-5
Walnut Fork—*stream* (6) WV-2
Walnut Fork Ch—*church* GA-3
Walnut Fork Ch—*church* TN-4
Walnut Fork Ch—*church* WV-2
Walnut Fork Creek—*stream* TN-4
Walnut Fork Sugar Creek—*stream* IN-6
Walnut Gap—*gap* AL-4
Walnut Gap—*gap* AZ-5
Walnut Gap—*gap* GA-3
Walnut Gap—*gap* (5) NC-3
Walnut Gap—*gap* TN-4
Walnut Gap—*gap* WV-2
Walnut Gap Ch—*church* WV-2
Walnut Gap Sch—*school* KY-4
Walnut Gap Sch—*school* WV-2
**Walnut Gardens**—*pop pl* IN-6
**Walnut Gardens**—*pop pl* PA-2
Walnut Grange Hall—*building* KS-7
Walnut Green Airp—*airport* DE-2
*Walnut Grove* AL-4
*Walnut Grove* NJ-2
Walnut Grove—*hist pl* LA-4
Walnut Grove—*hist pl* NC-3
Walnut Grove—*hist pl* (2) TN-4
Walnut Grove—*hist pl* WV-2
Walnut Grove—*locale* AZ-5
Walnut Grove—*locale* (5) AR-4
Walnut Grove—*locale* GA-3
Walnut Grove—*locale* IL-6
Walnut Grove—*locale* KY-4
Walnut Grove—*locale* PA-2
Walnut Grove—*locale* (5) TN-4
Walnut Grove—*locale* (3) TX-5
Walnut Grove—*locale* VA-3
Walnut Grove—*locale* WV-2
**Walnut Grove**—*pop pl* (3) AL-4
**Walnut Grove**—*pop pl* (3) AR-4
**Walnut Grove**—*pop pl* CA-9
**Walnut Grove**—*pop pl* GA-3
**Walnut Grove**—*pop pl* IN-6
**Walnut Grove**—*pop pl* IA-7
**Walnut Grove**—*pop pl* KY-4
**Walnut Grove**—*pop pl* MN-6
**Walnut Grove**—*pop pl* (2) MS-4
**Walnut Grove**—*pop pl* MO-7
**Walnut Grove**—*pop pl* (2) OH-6
**Walnut Grove**—*pop pl* PA-2
**Walnut Grove**—*pop pl* SC-3
**Walnut Grove**—*pop pl* (10) TN-4
**Walnut Grove**—*pop pl* TX-5
**Walnut Grove**—*pop pl* WA-9
Walnut Grove Airp—*airport* PA-2
Walnut Grove Baptist Ch—*church* AL-4
Walnut Grove Baptist Ch—*church* MS-4
Walnut Grove Baptist Ch—*church* (3) TN-4
Walnut Grove Branch—*stream* AR-4
Walnut Grove Branch—*stream* (2) TN-4
Walnut Grove Bridge—*hist pl* AZ-5
Walnut Grove Camp—*park* IN-6
Walnut Grove Campground—*park* AZ-5
**Walnut Grove (Cartertown)**—*pop pl* KY-4
Walnut Grove Cem—*cemetery* (3) AL-4
Walnut Grove Cem—*cemetery* AZ-5
Walnut Grove Cem—*cemetery* (5) AR-4
Walnut Grove Cem—*cemetery* CT-1
Walnut Grove Cem—*cemetery* (4) IL-6
Walnut Grove Cem—*cemetery* (2) IN-6
Walnut Grove Cem—*cemetery* (3) IA-7
Walnut Grove Cem—*cemetery* (2) KS-7
Walnut Grove Cem—*cemetery* (3) MA-1
Walnut Grove Cem—*cemetery* MN-6
Walnut Grove Cem—*cemetery* MS-4
Walnut Grove Cem—*cemetery* (7) MO-7

Walnut Grove Cem—*cemetery* ... NE-7
Walnut Grove Cem—*cemetery* ... NY-2
Walnut Grove Cem—*cemetery* (5) ... OH-6
Walnut Grove Cem—*cemetery* ... OK-5
Walnut Grove Cem—*cemetery* ... SC-3
Walnut Grove Cem—*cemetery* (11) ... TN-4
Walnut Grove Cem—*cemetery* ... TX-5
Walnut Grove Cem—*cemetery* (3) ... WV-2
Walnut Grove Cem—*cemetery* ... WI-6
Walnut Grove Cemetary—*cemetery* ... AR-4
Walnut Grove Cemetary—*cemetery* ... TN-4
Walnut Grove Cemetery—*hist pl* ... MA-1
Walnut Grove Ch—*church* (6) ... AL-4
Walnut Grove Ch—*church* (14) ... AR-4
Walnut Grove Ch—*church* (3) ... GA-3
Walnut Grove Ch—*church* (6) ... IL-6
Walnut Grove Ch—*church* (3) ... IN-6
Walnut Grove Ch—*church* (13) ... KY-4
Walnut Grove Ch—*church* (5) ... LA-4
Walnut Grove Ch—*church* (4) ... MS-4
Walnut Grove Ch—*church* (6) ... MO-7
Walnut Grove Ch—*church* ... NH-1
Walnut Grove Ch—*church* (7) ... NC-3
Walnut Grove Ch—*church* (3) ... OH-6
Walnut Grove Ch—*church* ... PA-2
Walnut Grove Ch—*church* (4) ... SC-3
Walnut Grove Ch—*church* (18) ... TN-4
Walnut Grove Ch—*church* (3) ... TX-5
Walnut Grove Ch—*church* (5) ... VA-3
Walnut Grove Ch—*church* (6) ... WV-2
Walnut Grove Chapel—*church* ... WV-2
Walnut Grove Ch (historical)—*church* ... MS-4
Walnut Grove Ch (historical)—*church* ... MO-7
Walnut Grove Ch (historical)—*church* ... TN-4
Walnut Grove Christian Acad—*school* ... PA-2
Walnut Grove Church (historical)—*locale* ... MO-7
**Walnut Grove Corner**—*pop pl* ... AR-4
**Walnut Grove (corporate name for Walnutgrove)**—*pop pl* ... GA-3
*Walnutgrove (corporate name Walnut Grove)* ... GA-3
Walnut Grove Country Club—*other* ... OH-6
*Walnut Grove Creek* ... IA-7
Walnut Grove Creek—*stream* ... NE-7
Walnut Grove Creek—*stream* ... OK-5
Walnut Grove Cumberland Presbyterian Ch—*church* ... MS-4
Walnut Grove Cumberland Presbyterian Ch—*church* ... TN-4
Walnut Grove Gakuen Hall—*hist pl* ... CA-9
Walnut Grove Hill—*summit* ... MA-1
Walnut Grove (historical)—*locale* ... KS-7
Walnut Grove (historical P.O.)—*locale* ... IA-7
Walnut Grove Hollow—*valley* ... KY-4
Walnut Grove Hollow—*valley* ... MO-7
Walnut Grove Lake—*reservoir* ... IN-6
Walnut Grove Lake—*reservoir* ... TN-4
Walnut Grove Lake Dam—*dam* ... TN-4
Walnut Grove Methodist Ch—*church* ... MS-4
Walnut Grove Methodist Church—*hist pl* ... AR-4
*Walnut Grove Middle School* ... AL-4
Walnut Grove Mills—*locale* ... MD-2
Walnut Grove Mission—*church* ... OK-5
Walnut Grove Plantation—*hist pl* ... SC-3
Walnut Grove Plantation (historical)—*locale* ... AL-4
Walnut Grove Post Office (historical)—*building* ... TN-4
Walnut Grove Ranch—*locale* ... CA-9
Walnut Grove Sch—*hist pl* ... KY-4
Walnut Grove Sch—*school* ... AL-4
Walnut Grove Sch—*school* ... AZ-5
Walnut Grove Sch—*school* ... AR-4
Walnut Grove Sch—*school* (2) ... CA-9
Walnut Grove Sch—*school* (12) ... IL-6
Walnut Grove Sch—*school* (2) ... IN-6
Walnut Grove Sch—*school* (3) ... IA-7
Walnut Grove Sch—*school* (2) ... KY-4
Walnut Grove Sch—*school* ... MI-6
Walnut Grove Sch—*school* (8) ... MO-7
Walnut Grove Sch—*school* ... NE-7
Walnut Grove Sch—*school* ... OH-6
Walnut Grove Sch—*school* (2) ... OK-5
Walnut Grove Sch—*school* ... SC-3
Walnut Grove Sch—*school* ... SD-7
Walnut Grove Sch—*school* (4) ... TN-4
Walnut Grove Sch—*school* ... VA-3
Walnut Grove Sch—*school* (2) ... WV-2
Walnut Grove Sch (abandoned)—*school* (4) ... MO-7
Walnut Grove Sch (abandoned)—*school* ... PA-2
Walnut Grove Sch (historical)—*school* (2) ... AL-4
Walnut Grove Sch (historical)—*school* ... MS-4
Walnut Grove Sch (historical)—*school* (6) ... MO-7
Walnut Grove Sch (historical)—*school* ... PA-2
Walnut Grove Sch (historical)—*school* (9) ... TN-4
Walnut Grove School (Abandoned)—*locale* ... NE-7
Walnut Grove School (Abandoned)—*locale* ... WI-6
Walnut Grove Spring—*spring* ... TN-4
**Walnut Grove Subdivision**—*pop pl* ... UT-8
Walnut Grove Township—*civil* ... MO-7
**Walnut Grove Township**—*pop pl* ... KS-7
**Walnut Grove Township**—*pop pl* ... NE-7
**Walnut Grove Township**—*pop pl* ... SD-7
Walnut Grove (Township of)—*civ div* (2) ... IL-6
Walnut Grove (Township of)—*fmr MCD* (2) ... NC-3
Walnut Grove United Methodist Ch—*church* ... TN-4
Walnut Gulch—*valley* (2) ... AZ-5
**Walnut Heights**—*pop pl* ... CA-9
**Walnut Heights**—*pop pl* ... IN-6
Walnut Heights Sch—*school* ... CA-9
*Walnut Hill* ... MA-1
Walnut Hill—*locale* ... AL-4
Walnut Hill—*locale* (3) ... KY-4
Walnut Hill—*locale* (2) ... PA-2
**Walnut Hill**—*pop pl* ... AL-4
**Walnut Hill**—*pop pl* ... AR-4
**Walnut Hill**—*pop pl* ... CT-1
**Walnut Hill**—*pop pl* ... DE-2
**Walnut Hill**—*pop pl* ... FL-3
**Walnut Hill**—*pop pl* ... IL-6
**Walnut Hill**—*pop pl* ... LA-4
**Walnut Hill**—*pop pl* (2) ... ME-1
**Walnut Hill**—*pop pl* ... MD-2
**Walnut Hill**—*pop pl* ... MA-1
**Walnut Hill**—*pop pl* ... OH-6
**Walnut Hill**—*pop pl* (2) ... PA-2
**Walnut Hill**—*pop pl* (3) ... TN-4
**Walnut Hill**—*pop pl* ... VA-3
**Walnut Hill**—*pop pl* ... WV-2
Walnut Hill—*post sta* ... RI-1
Walnut Hill—*post sta* ... TX-5
Walnut Hill—*summit* (4) ... CT-1
Walnut Hill—*summit* ... IL-6
Walnut Hill—*summit* ... KY-4
Walnut Hill—*summit* ... ME-1
Walnut Hill—*summit* ... MD-2
Walnut Hill—*summit* (13) ... MA-1
Walnut Hill—*summit* (3) ... NH-1
Walnut Hill—*summit* ... NY-2
Walnut Hill—*summit* ... OR-9
Walnut Hill—*summit* (2) ... VT-1
Walnut Hill—*summit* ... VA-3
Walnut Hill—*summit* ... WV-2
**Walnut Hill Addition (subdivision)**—*pop pl* ... UT-8
Walnut Hill Baptist Ch—*church* (2) ... TN-4
Walnut Hill Brook—*stream* ... CT-1
Walnut Hill Cem—*cemetery* ... AR-4
Walnut Hill Cem—*cemetery* (2) ... IL-6
Walnut Hill Cem—*cemetery* (6) ... IN-6
Walnut Hill Cem—*cemetery* (2) ... IA-7
Walnut Hill Cem—*cemetery* (3) ... KS-7
Walnut Hill Cem—*cemetery* (2) ... KY-4
Walnut Hill Cem—*cemetery* ... MA-1
Walnut Hill Cem—*cemetery* ... OH-6
Walnut Hill Cem—*cemetery* ... TN-4
Walnut Hill Cem—*cemetery* ... WI-6
Walnut Hill Ch—*church* ... AR-4
Walnut Hill Ch—*church* ... FL-3
Walnut Hill Ch—*church* ... IL-6
Walnut Hill Ch—*church* (3) ... KY-4
Walnut Hill Ch—*church* (2) ... LA-4
Walnut Hill Ch—*church* ... MO-7
Walnut Hill Ch—*church* (2) ... OH-6
Walnut Hill Ch—*church* ... PA-2
Walnut Hill Ch—*church* ... SC-3
Walnut Hill Ch—*church* ... TN-4
Walnut Hill Ch—*church* ... TX-5
Walnut Hill Ch—*church* (2) ... VA-3
Walnut Hill Chapel—*church* ... AR-4
Walnut Hill Christian Sch—*school* ... FL-3
**Walnut Hill (Continental No.2)**—*pop pl* ... PA-2
Walnut Hill Cotton Gin—*hist pl* ... NC-3
Walnut Hill Country Club—*other* ... MO-7
Walnut Hill District—*hist pl* ... CT-1
Walnut Hill Elem Sch—*school* ... TN-4
**Walnut Hill Estates**—*pop pl* ... TN-4
Walnut Hill Golf Club—*other* ... OH-6
Walnut Hill HS—*school* ... OH-6
Walnut Hill Lookout Tower—*tower* ... FL-3
Walnut Hill Park—*hist pl* ... CT-1
Walnut Hill Park—*park* ... CT-1
Walnut Hill Park Site—*park* ... TX-5
Walnut Hill Plantation (historical)—*locale* ... TN-4
Walnut Hill Post Office (historical)—*building* ... TN-4
Walnut Hill Presbyterian Church—*hist pl* ... KY-4
Walnut Hill Run—*stream* ... VA-3
*Walnut Hills* ... MS-4
*Walnut Hills* (3) ... OH-6
Walnut Hills—*hist pl* ... MS-4
**Walnut Hills**—*pop pl* ... CO-8
**Walnut Hills**—*pop pl* (2) ... OH-6
**Walnut Hills**—*pop pl* ... VA-3
Walnut Hills—*range* (2) ... MS-4
Walnut Hills Cemetery—*hist pl* ... MA-1
Walnut Hill Sch—*school* (2) ... IL-6
Walnut Hill Sch—*school* ... IA-7
Walnut Hill Sch—*school* (2) ... KY-4
Walnut Hill Sch—*school* ... MA-1
Walnut Hill Sch—*school* (2) ... NE-7
Walnut Hill Sch—*school* (2) ... TX-5
Walnut Hill Sch—*school* ... VA-3
Walnut Hill Sch (historical)—*school* ... PA-2
Walnut Hill Sch (historical)—*school* ... TN-4
Walnut Hill School (Abandoned)—*locale* ... NE-7
Walnut Hills Country Club—*other* ... MI-6
**Walnut Hills Estates (subdivision)**—*pop pl* ... TN-4
Walnut Hills Park—*park* ... OH-6
Walnut Hills Sch—*school* ... LA-4
**Walnut Hills (subdivision)**—*pop pl* (2) ... NC-3
**Walnut Hills (subdivision)**—*pop pl* ... TN-4
**Walnut Hills Subdivision**—*pop pl* ... UT-8
Walnut Hill Station—*locale* ... PA-2
Walnut Hills United Presbyterian Church—*hist pl* ... OH-6
Walnut Hill (Township of)—*fmr MCD* ... NC-3
Walnut Hollow—*valley* ... AR-4
Walnut Hollow—*valley* ... KY-4
Walnut Hollow—*valley* (7) ... MO-7
Walnut Hollow—*valley* (2) ... NC-3
Walnut Hollow—*valley* (3) ... VA-3
Walnut Hollow—*valley* (2) ... WV-2
Walnut Hollow—*valley* ... WI-6
Walnut Hollow Gap—*gap* ... NC-3
Walnut Hollow Run—*stream* ... WV-2
Walnut HS—*school* ... MS-4
Walnut Inn—*hist pl* ... MO-7
**Walnut Island**—*pop pl* ... NC-3
Walnut JHS—*school* ... NE-7
Walnut Knob—*summit* ... AR-4
Walnut Knob—*summit* ... GA-3
Walnut Knob—*summit* (2) ... NC-3
Walnut Knob—*summit* (2) ... TN-4
Walnut Knob—*summit* ... VA-3
Walnut Knob—*summit* (3) ... WV-2
*Walnut Lake* ... AR-4
Walnut Lake—*lake* (2) ... AR-4
Walnut Lake—*lake* ... MI-6
Walnut Lake—*lake* (2) ... MS-4
**Walnut Lake**—*pop pl* ... MI-6
Walnut Lake—*reservoir* ... MN-6
Walnut Lake—*reservoir* ... MS-4
Walnut Lake Cem—*cemetery* ... AR-4
*Walnut Lake Church* ... MS-4
Walnut Lake Sch—*school* ... MI-6
Walnut Lake (Township of)—*fmr MCD* ... AR-4
**Walnut Lake (Township of)**—*pop pl* ... MN-6
Walnut Landing—*locale* (2) ... MD-2
Walnut Lane—*hist pl* ... DE-2
Walnut Lane Bridge—*bridge* ... PA-2
Walnut Lane (historical)—*locale* ... AL-4
Walnut Lawn—*hist pl* ... KY-4
**Walnut Ledge**—*pop pl* ... VT-1
**Walnut Level**—*pop pl* ... IN-6
**Walnut Log**—*pop pl* ... TN-4
Walnut Log Baptist Ch—*church* ... TN-4
Walnut Log Ditch—*canal* ... TN-4
Walnutlog Post Office (historical)—*building* ... TN-4
Walnut Meadow Branch—*stream* ... KY-4
Walnut Meadows—*hist pl* ... KY-4
Walnut Methodist Ch—*church* ... MS-4
Walnut Mound Cem—*cemetery* ... WI-6
Walnut Mountain Ch—*church* ... TN-4
Walnut Mountain Lookout Tower—*locale* ... TN-4
Walnut Mountains—*range* ... NC-3
Walnut Mountain Trail—*trail* ... TN-4
Walnut Mtn—*summit* ... AZ-5
Walnut Mtn—*summit* ... CT-1
Walnut Mtn—*summit* ... GA-3
Walnut Mtn—*summit* ... NY-2
Walnut Mtn—*summit* ... OK-5
Walnut Mtn—*summit* ... SC-3
Walnut Mtn—*summit* (3) ... TN-4
Walnut Mtn—*summit* ... VA-3
Walnut Neck—*cape* ... NY-2
Walnut Park—*park* ... NJ-2
**Walnut Park**—*pop pl* ... AL-4
**Walnut Park**—*pop pl* ... CA-9
Walnut Park Advent Christian Ch—*church* ... AL-4
Walnut Park Baptist Ch—*church* ... AL-4
Walnut Park Ch of Christ—*church* ... AL-4
*Walnut Park Elementary School* ... AL-4
Walnut Park Hist Dist—*hist pl* ... NY-2
Walnut Park Methodist Ch—*church* ... AL-4
Walnut Park Presbyterian Ch—*church* ... AL-4
Walnut Park Sch—*school* ... AL-4
Walnut Park Sch—*school* ... MO-7
*Walnut Place Landing* ... MS-4
Walnut Place (Shop Ctr)—*locale* ... MA-1
Walnut Pocosin—*swamp* ... NC-3
Walnut Point—*cape* (4) ... MD-2
Walnut Point—*cape* ... MS-4
Walnut Point—*cape* ... NY-2
Walnut Point—*cape* (2) ... VA-3
Walnut Point—*locale* ... MI-6
**Walnut Point**—*pop pl* ... VA-3
**Walnutport**—*pop pl* ... PA-2
**Walnutport Acres (subdivision)**—*pop pl* ... PA-2
Walnutport Borough—*civil* ... PA-2
Walnutport Elem Sch—*school* ... PA-2
Walnut Powell Sch—*school* ... OH-6
**Walnut Prairie**—*pop pl* ... IL-6
Walnut Prairie Cem—*cemetery* ... IL-6
Walnut Ranch—*locale* ... AZ-5
Walnut Ranch Well—*locale* ... NM-5
*Walnut Ridge* ... TN-4
Walnut Ridge—*locale* ... AR-4
Walnut Ridge—*locale* ... TX-5
**Walnut Ridge**—*pop pl* ... AR-4
**Walnut Ridge**—*pop pl* ... DE-2
**Walnut Ridge**—*pop pl* (2) ... IN-6
**Walnut Ridge**—*pop pl* ... MD-2
Walnut Ridge—*ridge* (3) ... AR-4
Walnut Ridge—*ridge* (2) ... IN-6
Walnut Ridge—*ridge* ... MD-2
Walnut Ridge—*ridge* ... MI-6
Walnut Ridge—*ridge* ... MO-7
Walnut Ridge—*ridge* ... NY-2
Walnut Ridge—*ridge* ... WV-2
Walnut Ridge Cem—*cemetery* ... AR-4
Walnut Ridge Cem—*cemetery* ... IL-6
Walnut Ridge Cem—*cemetery* ... IN-6
Walnut Ridge Cem—*cemetery* ... MO-7
Walnut Ridge Ch—*church* (2) ... IN-6
Walnut Ridge Ch—*church* ... LA-4
Walnut Ridge Ch—*church* ... OH-6
Walnut Ridge Ch (historical)—*church* ... TN-4
Walnut Ridge Friends Meetinghouse—*hist pl* ... IN-6
Walnut Ridge Park—*park* ... MN-6
Walnut Ridge Sch—*school* ... AR-4
Walnut Ridge Sch—*school* ... KS-7
Walnut Ridge Sch—*school* ... MO-7
Walnut Ridge Sch—*school* ... OH-6
**Walnut Ridge (subdivision)**—*pop pl* ... NC-3
Walnut River—*stream* ... KS 7
Walnut Row Sch—*school* ... IL-6
Walnut Row Sch—*school* ... MO-7
*Walnut Run* ... VA-3
Walnut Run—*stream* ... NE-7
Walnut Run—*stream* (3) ... OH-6
Walnut Run—*stream* (5) ... PA-2
Walnut Run—*stream* (2) ... TX-5
Walnut Run—*stream* (2) ... WV-2
**Walnutrun (Newport)**—*pop pl* ... OH-6
Walnut Run Sch—*school* ... PA-2
Walnut Sch—*school* (4) ... CA-9
Walnut Sch—*school* ... IL-6
Walnut Sch—*school* ... IN-6
Walnut Sch—*school* ... IA-7
Walnut Sch—*school* (2) ... KS-7
Walnut Sch—*school* ... MI-6
Walnut Sch—*school* ... MO-7
Walnut Sch (historical)—*school* (2) ... MS-4
Walnut Sch (historical)—*school* ... MO-7
**Walnut Shade**—*pop pl* ... MO-7
**Walnut Shade**—*pop pl* ... TN-4
Walnut Shade Cem—*cemetery* ... MO-7
Walnut Shade Community Hall—*building* ... MO-7
*Walnut Shade Post Office* ... TN-4
Walnut Shade Post Office—*building* ... MO-7
Walnutshade Post Office (historical)—*building* ... TN-4
Walnut Shade Sch—*school* ... MO-7
Walnut Shop Ctr—*locale* ... NC-3
Walnut Siding—*locale* ... CA-9
Walnut Sink Hollow—*valley* ... MO-7
Walnut Slough—*stream* ... NE-7
Walnut Special Ditch—*canal* ... IL-6
Walnut Spring—*spring* (34) ... AZ-5
Walnut Spring—*spring* ... CA-9
Walnut Spring—*spring* ... MO-7
Walnut Spring—*spring* (2) ... NM-5
Walnut Spring—*spring* ... OK-5
Walnut Spring—*spring* ... OR-9
Walnut Spring—*spring* ... TN-4
Walnut Spring—*spring* (10) ... TX-5
Walnut Spring Canyon—*valley* ... AZ-5
Walnut Spring Ch—*church* ... TX-5
Walnut Spring Ch—*church* ... VA-3
Walnut Spring Creek—*stream* (2) ... TX-5
Walnut Spring Hollow—*valley* ... TX-5
*Walnut Springs* ... AL-4
Walnut Springs—*locale* ... TX-5
**Walnut Springs**—*pop pl* ... AR-4
**Walnut Springs**—*pop pl* ... TX-5
Walnut Springs—*spring* (4) ... AZ-5
Walnut Springs—*spring* ... NM-5
Walnut Springs—*spring* ... TX-5
Walnut Springs Baptist Ch (historical)—*church* ... AL-4
Walnut Springs Cem—*cemetery* ... TX-5
Walnut Springs Ch—*church* (2) ... TX-5
Walnut Springs Ch—*church* ... VA-3
Walnut Springs Creek—*stream* ... AR-4
Walnut Square Sch—*school* ... MA-1
*Walnut Station* ... KS-7
Walnut Street Bridge—*bridge* ... TN-4
Walnut Street Bridge—*hist pl* ... PA-2
Walnut Street Elem Sch—*school* ... PA-2
Walnut Street Hist Dist—*hist pl* ... AL-4
Walnut Street Hist Dist—*hist pl* ... AR-4
Walnut Street Hist Dist—*hist pl* ... MN-6
Walnut Street Hist Dist—*hist pl* ... MO-7
Walnut Street Hist Dist—*hist pl* ... NY-2
Walnut Street Hosp (historical)—*hospital* ... AL-4
Walnut Street Sch—*hist pl* ... MA-1
Walnut Street Sch—*hist pl* ... OH-6
Walnut Street Sch—*school* ... MI-6
Walnut Street Sch—*school* (2) ... NJ-2
Walnut Street Sch—*school* ... NY-2
Walnut Street Sch—*school* ... NC-3
Walnut Street Sch—*school* (3) ... OH-6
Walnut Street Sch—*school* ... PA-2
Walnut Street Sch—*school* ... WI-6
Walnut Street Station—*locale* ... NJ-2
Walnut Street Theater—*hist pl* ... KY-4
Walnut Street Theatre—*hist pl* ... PA-2
Walnutta, Lake—*reservoir* ... AL-4
Walnut Tank—*reservoir* (2) ... AZ-5
**Walnut Terrace (subdivision)**—*pop pl* ... NC-3
Walnut Timber Lake—*lake* ... AR-4
Walnut Top—*summit* ... VA-3
**Walnuttown**—*pop pl* ... PA-2
Walnut Township—*civil* ... MO-7
Walnut Township—*fmr MCD* (9) ... IA-7
**Walnut Township**—*pop pl* (13) ... KS-7
**Walnut Township**—*pop pl* ... MO-7
Walnut (Township of)—*fmr MCD* (4) ... AR-4
**Walnut (Township of)**—*pop pl* ... IL-6
**Walnut (Township of)**—*pop pl* (2) ... IN-6
**Walnut (Township of)**—*pop pl* (3) ... OH-6
Walnut Trail—*trail* ... PA-2
**Walnut Tree Hill**—*pop pl* ... CT-1
Walnut Tree Hill—*summit* ... CT-1
Walnut Tree Hill—*summit* ... KY-4
Walnut Tree Hill—*summit* ... MA-1
Walnut Tree Hollow—*valley* ... VA-3
**Walnut Valley**—*pop pl* ... NJ-2
**Walnut Valley Acres**—*pop pl* ... WV-2
Walnut Valley Branch—*stream* ... MO-7
Walnut Valley Cem—*cemetery* ... KS-7
Walnut Valley Ch—*church* ... AR-4
Walnut Valley Ch—*church* ... KS-7
Walnut Valley Ch—*church* ... OH-6
Walnut Valley Memorial Park—*cemetery* ... KS-7
Walnut Valley Post Offce (historical)—*building* ... TN-4
Walnut Valley Post Office (historical)—*building* ... TN-4
Walnut Valley Sch—*school* ... KS-7
Walnut View Sch—*school* ... KS-7
Walnut Wash—*stream* ... AZ-5
Walnut Well—*well* (2) ... AZ-5
Walnut Well—*well* ... NM-5
Walnut Well—*well* ... TX-5
Walnut Wells—*well* ... NM-5
**Walnut Woods**—*pop pl* ... MD-2
Walnutwood Sch—*school* ... CA-9
Walnut Woods State Park—*park* ... IA-7
Walo Creek—*stream* ... ID-8
Walong—*locale* ... CA-9
Waloope Creek—*stream* ... TX-5
Walo Point—*summit* ... ID-8
Waloven Creek—*stream* ... MT-8
*Waloy* ... FM-9
*Walpack* ... NJ-2
Walpack Fish and Wildlife Mngmt Area—*park* ... NJ-2
**Walpack (Township of)**—*pop pl* ... NJ-2
Walpert Ridge—*ridge* ... CA-9
Walpi—*locale* ... AZ-5
*Walpole* ... IN-6
Walpole—*locale* ... ME-1
**Walpole**—*pop pl* ... IL-6
**Walpole**—*pop pl* ... MA-1
**Walpole**—*pop pl* ... NH-1
Walpole Acad—*hist pl* ... NH-1
Walpole Cem—*cemetery* ... NE-7
Walpole Creek—*stream* ... OR-9
Walpole East JHS—*school* ... MA-1
**Walpole Heights**—*pop pl* ... MA-1
Walpole HS—*school* ... MA-1
*Walpole Junction* ... MA-1
Walpole Mall, The—*locale* ... MA-1
Walpole Meetinghouse—*hist pl* ... ME-1
Walpole Mine—*mine* ... MI-6
Walpole Rsvr—*reservoir* ... NH-1
Walpole Shopping Plaza—*locale* ... MA-1
Walpole Tank—*reservoir* ... NM-5
Walpole Town Hall—*hist pl* ... MA-1
**Walpole (Town of)**—*pop pl* ... MA-1
**Walpole (Town of)**—*pop pl* ... NH-1
**Walport**—*pop pl* ... AR-4
*Walquist Junior High School* ... UT-8
Walradt Street Sch—*school* ... NY-2
Walrath, Arthur, House—*hist pl* ... NY-2
Walrath Cem—*cemetery* (2) ... NY-2
Walrath Draw—*valley* (2) ... NE-7
Walrath-Van Horne House—*hist pl* ... NY-2
WALR-FM (Union City)—*tower* ... TN-4
Walridge Ch—*church* ... TN-4
Walrod Gulch—*valley* ... CO-8
Walroy—*locale* ... LA-4
*Walrus Glacier* ... WA-9
Walrus Island—*island* ... AK-9
Walrus Islands—*island* ... AK-9
Walrus Islands State Game Sanctuary—*park* ... AK-9
Walrus Island State Game Sanctuary—*park* ... AK-9
Walrus Rocks—*island* ... OR-9
Walruth Cem—*cemetery* ... NY-2
**Walsall**—*pop pl* ... PA-2
Walsburg—*locale* ... KS-7
*Walsen* ... CO-8
Walsen Arroyo—*stream* ... CO-8
**Walsenburg**—*pop pl* ... CO-8
Walsenburg Rsvr—*reservoir* ... CO-8
Walsen Crag—*summit* ... CO-8
Walsen Robinson Mines—*mine* ... CO-8
*Walsen Springs Draw* ... CO-8
Walser—*locale* ... NC-3
Walser—*locale* ... OH-6
Walser, Ulrich, House—*hist pl* ... WI-6
Walser Bridge—*bridge* ... MO-7
Walser Creek—*stream* ... IL-6
Walser Crossing—*locale* ... ND-7
Walser Ranch—*locale* ... ND-7
*Walsfeld Lake* ... MN-6
Walsh—*locale* ... KY-4
Walsh—*locale* ... LA-4
Walsh—*locale* ... MI-6
Walsh—*locale* ... PA-2
**Walsh**—*pop pl* ... CO-8
**Walsh**—*pop pl* ... IL-6
**Walsh**—*pop pl* ... MS-4
**Walsh**—*pop pl* ... NC-3
**Walsh**—*pop pl* ... WI-6
Walsh, Johnnie, Homestead—*hist pl* ... MT-8
Walsh Airp—*airport* ... PA-2
Walsh Archeol District—*hist pl* ... KS-7
Walsh Bog—*swamp* ... MA-1
**Walsh Centre Township**—*pop pl* ... ND-7
Walsh Coll—*school* ... OH-6
Walsh County—*civil* ... ND-7
Walsh County Courthouse—*hist pl* ... ND-7
Walsh Creek—*stream* ... AK-9
Walsh Creek—*stream* ... MI-6
Walsh Creek—*stream* ... MT-8
Walsh Creek—*stream* ... TX-5
Walsh Creek—*stream* ... WA-9
Walsh Ditch—*canal* ... IN-6
Walsh Ditch—*canal* ... MI-6
Walsh Draw—*valley* ... WY-8
Walsh (Election Precinct)—*fmr MCD* ... IL-6
Walsh Fishing Lake—*reservoir* ... NC-3
Walsh Fishing Lake Dam—*dam* ... NC-3
Walsh Flats/Langworth Bldg—*hist pl* ... IA-7
Walsh Glacier—*glacier* ... AK-9
Walsh Hill—*summit* ... CA-9
Walsh Home Ranch (historical)—*locale* ... NV-8
Walsh HS—*school* ... IA-7
Walsh HS—*school* ... NJ-2
Walsh Knolls—*summit* ... UT-8
Walsh Lake—*lake* ... ID-8
Walsh Lake—*lake* ... LA-4
Walsh Lake—*lake* ... MI-6
Walsh Lake—*lake* ... WA-9
Walsh Lake—*lake* ... WI-6
Walsh Lake Diversion Ditch—*canal* ... WA-9
Walsh Lake Nursery—*other* ... WA-9
**Walsh Landing**—*pop pl* ... CA-9
Walsh Mansion (Resettlement Administration Building)—*building* ... DC-2
Walsh Mica Prospect Mine—*mine* ... SD-7
Walsh Mtn—*summit* ... OK-5
Walsh Park—*park* ... MI-6
Walsh Park—*park* ... PA-2
Walsh Point—*cape* ... ND-7
Walsh Pond—*lake* ... MA-1
Walsh Ranch—*locale* ... WY-8
*Walsh Run* ... VA-3
Walsh's, Johnnie, Guest Lodge—*hist pl* ... MT-8
Walsh Sch—*school* ... CA-9
Walsh Sch—*school* ... CT-1
Walsh Sch—*school* (2) ... IL-6
Walshs Pocket—*valley* ... CA-9
Walsh Stable—*hist pl* ... DC-2
**Walsh Station**—*pop pl* ... CA-9
Walshtown Cem—*cemetery* ... SD-7
Walshtown (historical)—*locale* ... SD-7
Walshtown Sch—*hist pl* ... SD-7
Walshtown Sch—*school* ... SD-7
**Walshtown Township**—*pop pl* ... SD-7
**Walshville**—*pop pl* ... IL-6
Walshville (historical)—*locale* ... ND-7
Walshville Town Hall—*building* ... ND-7
**Walshville Township**—*pop pl* ... ND-7
**Walshville (Township of)**—*pop pl* ... IL-6
Walsh Well—*well* ... SD-7
Walsh Windmill—*locale* ... NM-5
**Walsingham**—*pop pl* ... FL-3
Walsingham Acad—*school* ... VA-3
Walsingham Elem Sch—*school* ... FL-3
Walsingham Plaza (Shop Ctr)—*locale* ... FL-3
Walsingham Rsvr—*reservoir* ... FL-3
Walsingham Sch (abandoned)—*school* ... PA-2
Walson Gap—*gap* ... NM-5
Walsonham Point—*cape* ... FL-3
Walson Lake—*lake* ... LA-4
Walson Well—*well* ... NM-5
Walstead Park—*park* ... MT-8
Walston—*locale* ... MD-2
**Walston**—*pop pl* ... PA-2
Walston Branch—*stream* ... MD-2
Walston Bridge—*bridge* ... AL-4
Walston-Bulluck House—*hist pl* ... NC-3
**Walstonburg**—*pop pl* ... NC-3
**Walstonburg (Fieldsboro)**—*pop pl* ... NC-3
Walston Cem—*cemetery* ... AL-4
Walston Ch—*church* ... AL-4
Walston Creek—*stream* ... VA-3
Walstone Ch—*church* ... NC-3
Walston Junction—*uninc pl* ... PA-2
**Walston Springs**—*pop pl* ... TX-5
Walston Springs Ch—*church* ... TX-5
*Walt* ... MP-9
WALT-AM (Meridian)—*tower* ... MS-4
Waltanna, Lake—*reservoir* ... KS-7
Walta Oil Field—*oilfield* ... KS-7
Walt Bailey Peak—*summit* ... WY-8
Walt Bench—*bench* ... UT-8
Walt Brown Gulch—*valley* ... OR-9
Walt Canyon—*valley* ... NM-5
Walt Canyon Hills—*range* ... NM-5
Walt Crawford Dam—*dam* ... SD-7
Walt Creek—*stream* ... CO-8
Walt Davis Spring Branch—*stream* ... AL-4
*Walt Disney Elementary School* ... PA-2
Walt Disney Sch—*school* ... NY-2
Walt Disney Sch—*school* ... PA-2
Walt Disney World—*park* ... FL-3
*Waltenburg Canyon* ... AZ-5
*Waltenburg Rapids* ... AZ-5
Walte Park—*park* ... OH-6
*Walter* ... OK-5
*Walter* ... TX-5
**Walter**—*pop pl* ... AL-4
**Walter**—*pop pl* ... LA-4
Walter, Henry, House—*hist pl* ... PA-2
Walter, Lake—*reservoir* ... NC-3
Walter, Lowell E., House—*hist pl* ... IA-7
Walter, Martin, House—*hist pl* ... CO-8
Walter, Mount—*summit* ... NM-5
Walter Ahern Spring—*spring* ... UT-8
Walter A Hurst Elem Sch—*school* ... FL-3
Walter Airp—*airport* ... KS-7
Walter A Kynoch Sch—*school* ... CA-9
*Walter Allen Cemetery* ... MS-4
Walter A Swalley Airpark—*airport* ... KS-7
Walter Bass Dam—*dam* ... AL-4
Walter Bass Pond—*reservoir* ... AL-4
Walter Bickett Sch—*school* ... NC-3
Walter Bickett Stadium—*park* ... NC-3
**Walterboro**—*pop pl* ... SC-3
Walterboro (CCD)—*cens area* ... SC-3
Walterboro Hist Dist—*hist pl* ... SC-3
Walterboro Library Society Bldg—*hist pl* ... SC-3
Walter Bouldin Dam—*dam* ... AL-4
Walter Branch—*stream* ... KY-4
Walter Canyon—*valley* ... CO-8
Walter Cem—*cemetery* ... AL-4
Walter Cem—*cemetery* ... IL-6
Walter Cem—*cemetery* ... OH-6
Walter Cem—*cemetery* ... TN-4
Walter C Givhan Bridge—*bridge* ... AL-4
*Walter Ch* ... AL-4
Walter Ch—*church* ... AL-4
Walter Chapel—*church* ... AL-4
**Walter Chapel**—*pop pl* ... PA-2
Walter Colton JHS—*school* ... CA-9
Walter Community Center—*building* ... AL-4
Walter Coon Brook—*stream* ... NY-2
Walter Creek—*stream* ... ID-8
Walter Creek—*stream* ... KY-4
Walter Creek—*stream* ... MI-6
Walter Creek—*stream* ... MN-6
Walter Creek—*stream* ... OR-9
Walter Creek—*stream* ... TX-5
**Walter Crossroad**—*pop pl* ... TN-4
Walter Curtis Memorial Park—*park* ... TN-4
Walter Dennis Irrigation Dam—*dam* ... SD-7
Walter Dike Number One—*dam* ... PA-2
Walter Dike Number Two—*dam* ... PA-2
Walter D Miller Dam Number 1—*dam* ... SD-7
Walter Douglas Sch—*school* ... AZ-5
Walter Dunagan—*locale* ... NM-5
Walter E. Long Lake—*reservoir* ... TX-5
Walter Family Cem—*cemetery* ... AL-4
*Walter F. George Lake* ... GA-3
Walter F George Lock and Dam—*dam* ... AL-4
Walter F George Lock And Dam—*dam* ... GA-3
Walter F George Rsvr—*reservoir* ... AL-4
Walter F George Rsvr—*reservoir* ... GA-3
Walter Flat—*flat* ... CA-9
Walter Flat—*flat* ... WA-9
Walter F Pratt Memorial Forest—*park* ... NY-2
Walter-Gimble House—*hist pl* ... IA-7
Walter Hamilton Place—*locale* ... FL-3
Walter Harvey Sch—*school* ... VT-1
**Walter Heights**—*pop pl* ... MD-2
**Walter Heights**—*pop pl* ... VA-3
Walter-Heins House—*hist pl* ... WI-6
**Walterhill**—*pop pl* ... TN-4
Walter Hill—*summit* ... GA-3
Walter Hill Ch—*church* ... TN-4
Walter Hill Dam—*dam* ... TN-4
Walter Hill Lake—*reservoir* ... TN-4
Walter Hollow—*valley* ... OH-6
Walter Hosp—*hospital* ... IN-6
**Walteria**—*pop pl* ... CA-9
Walteria Park—*park* ... CA-9
Walter Island—*island* ... AK-9
Walter Island—*island* ... NY-2
*Walter Jackson Elementary School* ... AL-4
Walter Jackson Sch—*school* ... AL-4
*Walter J Baird Junior High School* ... TN-4
Walter J Baird MS—*school* ... TN-4
Walter J Meyer Sch—*school* ... AZ-5
Walter Johnson HS—*school* ... MD-2
Walter Johnson Sch—*school* ... KS-7
Walter Korpela Ranch—*locale* ... MT-8
*Walter Lake* ... ID-8
*Walter Lake* ... NE-7
*Walter Lake* ... OR-9
Walter Lake—*lake* ... MN-6
Walter Lake—*lake* ... WA-9
Walter Landing Strip—*airport* ... KS-7
*Walter Lott Cemetery* ... MS-4
Walter May Lake Dam—*dam* ... MS-4
Walter Miller Number 1 Dam—*dam* ... SD-7
Walter Miller Sch—*school* ... PA-2
Waltermire Sch—*school* ... NY-2
*Walter Missionary Baptist Church* ... AL-4
Walter Mitchell Ch—*church* ... AL-4
*Walter M Thompson Elementary School* ... NC-3
Walter Mtn—*summit* ... NH-1
Walter Oldland Ranch—*locale* ... CO-8
Walter Park—*park* ... NJ-2
Walter Point—*cape* ... DE-2
Walter Post Office (historical)—*building* ... AL-4
Walter Power Dam—*dam* ... PA-2
Walter Ranch—*locale* ... MT-8
Walter Reed Army Med Ctr—*hospital* ... DC-2
Walter Reed JHS—*school* ... CA-9
Walter Reed Med Ctr Farm—*locale* ... MD-2
Walter Reed Sch—*school* (2) ... VA-3
Walter Richards, Lake—*reservoir* ... GA-3
*Walters* ... MD-2
*Walters* ... NE-7
Walters—*locale* ... LA-4
Walters—*locale* ... WA-9
**Walters**—*pop pl* ... AR-4
**Walters**—*pop pl* ... MI-6
**Walters**—*pop pl* ... MN-6
**Walters**—*pop pl* ... MS-4
**Walters**—*pop pl* ... OK-5
**Walters**—*pop pl* ... PA-2

**Walters**—*pop pl* TX-5
**Walters**—*pop pl* VA-3
Walters, Dr. Jefferson A., House—*hist pl* OH-6
Walters, Solomon, House—*hist pl* SD-7
Walters Arv Ultralight—*airport* WA-9
Walters Bath No. 2—*hist pl* MD-2
Walters Bay—*stream* GA-3
Walters Bend—*bend* TX-5
Walters Bluff—*cliff* AR-4
Walters Branch—*stream* AL-4
Walters Branch—*stream* KY-4
Walters Branch—*stream* MS-4
Walters Bridge—*bridge* TN-4
Waltersburg—*locale* IL-6
**Waltersburg**—*pop pl* PA-2
Waltersburg Ch—*church* IL-6
Walters Butte—*summit* ID-8
Walters Butte Lateral—*canal* ID-8
Walters Camp—*locale* (2) CA-9
Walters Canyon—*valley* (2) CA-9
Walters Canyon—*valley* NV-8
Walter S Carpenter State Park—*park* DE-2
Walters (CCD)—*cens area* OK-5
Walters Cem—*cemetery* (2) AR-4
Walters Cem—*cemetery* FL-3
Walters Cem—*cemetery* (2) GA-3
Walters Cem—*cemetery* IL-6
Walters Cem—*cemetery* (2) IN-6
Walters Cem—*cemetery* (4) KY-4
Walters Cem—*cemetery* (6) MS-4
Walters Cem—*cemetery* (3) NC-3
Walters Cem—*cemetery* OH-6
Walters Cem—*cemetery* OK-5
Walters Cem—*cemetery* (3) TN-4
Walters Cem—*cemetery* VA-3
Walters Cem—*cemetery* WV-2
Walter Sch—*school* CA-9
Walters Chapel—*church* AR-4
Walters Chapel—*church* IN-6
Walters Chapel—*church* MS-4
Walters Chapel—*church* NC-3
Walter Sch (historical)—*school* AL-4
Walter Schlomer Dam—*dam* SD-7
Walters Coulee—*valley* MT-8
*Walters Creek* KY-4
Walters Creek—*stream* (2) CA-9
Walters Creek—*stream* ID-8
Walters Creek—*stream* IL-6
Walters Creek—*stream* KY-4
Walters Creek—*stream* (2) MS-4
Walters Creek—*stream* VA-3
Walters Dam—*dam* NC-3
Walters-Davis House—*hist pl* GA-3
*Walters Ditch* IN-6
Walters Ditch—*canal* (2) IN-6
Walters Ditch—*canal* OH-6
Walters Drain—*canal* MI-6
Walters Draw—*valley* WY-8
**Walters Ferry**—*pop pl* ID-8
*Walters Flat* CA-9
Walters Fork—*stream* KY-4
Walters Gap—*gap* VA-3
Walters Grove Cem—*cemetery* MS-4
Walters Grove Ch—*church* NC-3
Walters Gulch—*valley* CA-9
Walter Shelley Rsvr—*reservoir* AZ-5
*Walter Shelly Rsvr* AZ-5
Walters Hill—*summit* MA-1
Walters Hill—*summit* OR-9
Walters Hollow—*valley* MO-7
Walters Hollow—*valley* TN-4
Walters House—*hist pl* WV-2
*Walter Silers Coliseum* MS-4
Walter Sillers Memorial Park—*park* MS-4
Walters Jail—*hist pl* MN-6
Walters JHS—*school* CA-9
*Walters Lake* NC-3
*Walters Lake* OK-5
Walters Lake—*lake* CO-8
Walters Lake—*lake* IN-6
Walters Lake—*lake* MI-6
Walters Lake—*lake* MN-6
Walters Lake—*lake* NE-7
Walters Lake—*lake* NM-5
Walters Lake—*lake* (2) WI-6
Walters Landing—*locale* MS-4
Walters Landing (historical)—*locale* TN-4
Walter Slough—*channel* NC-3
Walters Lower Landing
(historical)—*locale* AL-4
*Walters Lower Mill* PA-2
**Walters (Lower Mill)**—*pop pl* PA-2
*Walters Mill* PA-2
Walter's Mill Bridge—*hist pl* PA-2
Walters Mill (historical P.O.)—*locale* IA-7
Walters Millpond—*reservoir* NC-3
Walters Mill Pond—*reservoir* PA-2
Walters Millpond Dam—*dam* NC-3
Walters Mine—*mine* CA-9
Walters Mine—*mine* ND-7
Walters Mine (surface)—*mine* TN-4
Walters Mule Trail—*trail* OK-5
Walters Oil Field—*oilfield* OK-5
Walters Point—*cape* MN-6
Walters Pond—*reservoir* AL-4
Walters Pond—*reservoir* GA-3
Walters Post Office—*locale* NV-8
Walter Spreader Tank—*reservoir* AZ-5
Walter Spring—*spring* UT-8
Walter Spring—*spring* WA-9
**Walter Springs**—*pop pl* CA-9
Walters Ranch—*hist pl* CA-9
Walters Ranch—*locale* ID-8
Walters Ranch—*locale* MT-8
Walters Ranch—*locale* NV-8
Walters Ranch—*locale* NM-5
Walters Ranch—*locale* TX-5
Walters Ridge—*ridge* CA-9
Walters Rsvr—*reservoir* OR-9
Walters Rsvr—*reservoir* WY-8
Walters Run—*stream* PA-2
Walters Run Trail—*trail* PA-2
Walters Sch—*school* FL-3
Walters Sch—*school* IL-6
Walters Sch—*school* LA-4
Walters Sch—*school* NY-2
Walters Sch—*school* NC-3
Walters Sch (abandoned)—*school* PA-2
Walters Sch (historical)—*school* MS-4
Walters Sch (historical)—*school* MO-7
Walters Sch Number 1—*school* ND-7
Walters Sch Number 2—*school* ND-7
Walters Sch Number 3—*school* ND-7
Walters Sch Number 4—*school* ND-7
Walters Spring—*spring* CO-8
Walters Spring—*spring* ID-8
Walters Spring—*spring* MO-7
Walters Spring—*spring* MT-8
Walters Spring—*spring* OR-9
Walters State Community Coll—*school* TN-4
Walters Store—*locale* SC-3
Walters Store (historical)—*locale* TN-4
Walters Supply Ditch—*canal* WY-8
Walter Stol Strip—*airport* KS-7
**Walters Township**—*pop pl* ND-7
Walters Trail—*trail* PA-2
Walters Upper Landing (historical)—*locale* AL-4
Walter Sutton's Private Strip
Airp—*airport* WA-9
Walters Valley—*valley* WI-6
**Waltersville**—*pop pl* KY-4
**Waltersville**—*pop pl* MS-4
Waltersville Sch—*school* CT-1
Walters Well—*well* AZ-5
Walters Wiggles—*trail* UT-8
**Walters Woods**—*pop pl* VA-3
Walter Thompson Dam—*dam* SD-7
Walter T Moore Junior Elem Sch—*school* FL-3
Waltertown—*locale* GA-3
**Walter (Township of)**—*pop pl* MN-6
*Walterville* PA-2
**Walterville**—*pop pl* OR-9
Walterville Bridge—*bridge* OR-9
Walterville Canal—*canal* OR-9
Walterville Dam—*dam* OR-9
Walterville Powerplant—*other* OR-9
Walterville Rsvr—*reservoir* OR-9
Walterville Sch—*school* OR-9
Walter Vinson Lake Dam—*dam* MS-4
*Walter Wellborn High School* AL-4
Walter W Fondren JHS—*school* TX-5
*Walter Williams Lake* GA-3
Walter Windmill—*locale* (2) TX-5
Walter Wisler Ditch—*canal* IN-6
*Walthal* VA-3
Walthal—*locale* CA-9
*Walthall* MS-4
Walthall—*locale* VA-3
**Walthall**—*pop pl* CA-9
**Walthall**—*pop pl* MS-4
Walthall, Lake—*reservoir* MS-4
Walthall, Sen. Edward C., House—*hist pl* MS-4
Walthall Baptist Ch—*church* MS-4
Walthall Branch—*stream* AL-4
Walthall Cem—*cemetery* KY-4
Walthall Cem—*cemetery* TX-5
**Walthall County**—*pop pl* MS-4
Walthall County Courthouse—*building* MS-4
Walthall County Hosp—*hospital* MS-4
Walthall County Library—*building* MS-4
Walthall Creek—*stream* TX-5
*Walthall Elementary School* MS-4
Walthall HS (historical)—*school* MS-4
Walthall Lake—*reservoir* AL-4
Walthall Lake Dam—*dam* AL-4
Walthall Mill—*locale* VA-3
Walthall Normal Sch (historical)—*school* MS-4
Walthall Sch—*school* MS-4
Walthall Sch—*school* SD-7
Walthall Sch (historical)—*school* MS-4
Walthall Slough—*stream* CA-9
Walthalls Post Office (historical)—*building* AL-4
Walthall United Methodist Ch—*church* MS-4
Waltham—*locale* IL-6
Waltham—*locale* IA-7
Waltham—*locale* ME-1
Waltham—*locale* MT-8
**Waltham**—*pop pl* MA-1
**Waltham**—*pop pl* MN-6
Waltham, City of—*civil* MA-1
Waltham Cem—*cemetery* MN-6
Waltham City Hall—*building* MA-1
*Waltham Creek* CA-9
**Waltham Highlands
(subdivision)**—*pop pl* MA-1
Waltham HS (North)—*school* MA-1
Waltham HS (South)—*school* MA-1
Waltham JHS—*school* MA-1
Waltham Mine—*mine* CO-8
**Waltham North**—*pop pl* MA-1
Waltham Plaza—*locale* MA-1
Waltham Ridge—*ridge* ME-1
Waltham Sch—*school* IL-6
**Waltham (Town of)**—*pop pl* ME-1
**Waltham (Town of)**—*pop pl* VT-1
**Waltham (Township of)**—*pop pl* IL-6
**Waltham (Township of)**—*pop pl* MN-6
Waltham Vocational HS—*school* MA-1
Walthausen Lake—*lake* MN-6
Walth Bay Rec Area—*park* SD-7
Walthenberg Canyon—*valley* AZ-5
Walthenberg Rapids—*rapids* AZ-5
*Walthenburg Canyon* AZ-5
*Walthenburg Rapids* AZ-5
Walthen Ditch—*canal* CO-8
**Walther**—*pop pl* PA-2
Walther Drain—*canal* MI-6
Walther Hosp—*hospital* IL-6
Walther Park—*park* MO-7
Walther Sch—*school* IL-6
Walther Sch—*school* NJ-2
Walther Slough—*lake* ND-7
**Walthill**—*pop pl* NE-7
Walthill Cem—*cemetery* AL-4
Walt Hoffman Number 1 Dam—*dam* SD-7
Walthom Cem—*cemetery* IA-7
Walthour Swamp—*swamp* (2) GA-3
**Walthourville**—*pop pl* GA-3
Walthourville Cem—*cemetery* GA-3
Walthourville Ch—*church* GA-3
Walthourville Presbyterian
Church—*hist pl* GA-3
Walti Hot Springs—*spring* NV-8
Walti Ranch—*locale* NV-8
*Walt Josenhans* MD-2
Walt Kimble Ditch—*canal* IN-6
Waltman—*locale* WY-8
Waltman Airp—*airport* PA-2
Waltman Draw—*valley* WY-8
Waltman Ford—*locale* TN-4
Waltman Ford Bridge—*bridge* TN-4
Waltman Pond—*lake* AR-4
Waltman Spring—*spring* WY-8
Walt Mills—*locale* PA-2
Waltner and Richards Airfield—*airport* SD-7
Waltoffer Sch—*school* NY-2
*Walton* PA-2
Walton—*locale* KY-4
Walton—*locale* (2) PA-2
Walton—*locale* (2) TX-5
Walton—*locale* VA-3
**Walton**—*pop pl* FL-3
**Walton**—*pop pl* IL-6
**Walton**—*pop pl* IN-6
**Walton**—*pop pl* KS-7
**Walton**—*pop pl* KY-4
**Walton**—*pop pl* MI-6
**Walton**—*pop pl* NE-7
**Walton**—*pop pl* NY-2
**Walton**—*pop pl* OH-6
**Walton**—*pop pl* OR-9
**Walton**—*pop pl* TX-5
**Walton**—*pop pl* UT-8
**Walton**—*pop pl* WV-2
Walton, Asa, House—*hist pl* PA-2
Walton, Dr. James Wyatt, House—*hist pl* AR-4
Walton, James A., House—*hist pl* GA-3
Walton, Lake—*lake* IL-6
Walton, Lake—*lake* NY-2
Walton, Lake—*reservoir* SD-7
Walton, Rudolph, Sch—*hist pl* PA-2
Walton and Willett Stone Store—*hist pl* NY-2
Walton Basin—*basin* NY-2
Walton Bend Landing (historical)—*locale* MS-4
Walton Branch—*stream* (2) AL-4
Walton Branch—*stream* AR-4
Walton Branch—*stream* (2) GA-3
Walton Brook—*stream* ME-1
Walton Brook—*stream* NY-2
Walton Cabin Spring—*spring* CA-9
Walton Canyon—*valley* UT-8
Walton (CCD)—*cens area* KY-4
Walton Cem—*cemetery* (3) AL-4
Walton Cem—*cemetery* AR-4
Walton Cem—*cemetery* (2) IN-6
Walton Cem—*cemetery* IA-7
Walton Cem—*cemetery* KS-7
Walton Cem—*cemetery* (3) KY-4
Walton Cem—*cemetery* (5) MS-4
Walton Cem—*cemetery* (2) NY-2
Walton Cem—*cemetery* NC-3
Walton Cem—*cemetery* OR-9
Walton Cem—*cemetery* (6) TN-4
Walton Cem—*cemetery* (2) TX-5
*Walton Ch* MS-4
Walton Ch—*church* MS-4
Walton Chapel—*church* MS-4
Walton Chapel—*church* MO-7
**Walton County**—*pop pl* FL-3
**Walton (County)**—*pop pl* GA-3
Walton County Courthouse—*hist pl* GA-3
Walton County Jail—*hist pl* GA-3
Walton County Vocational Technical
Sch—*school* FL-3
Walton Court—*building* TN-4
Walton Cove—*cove* MA-1
Walton Crawley Branch—*stream* NC-3
*Walton Creek* MT-8
*Walton Creek* WA-9
Walton Creek—*stream* AZ-5
Walton Creek—*stream* CO-8
Walton Creek—*stream* (5) GA-3
Walton Creek—*stream* ID-8
Walton Creek—*stream* IL-6
Walton Creek—*stream* IN-6
Walton Creek—*stream* IA-7
Walton Creek—*stream* KY-4
Walton Creek—*stream* MI-6
Walton Creek—*stream* (2) MT-8
Walton Creek—*stream* TX-5
Walton Creek—*stream* UT-8
Walton Creek—*stream* VA-3
Walton Creek Campground—*locale* CO-8
Walton Creek Ch—*church* KY-4
Walton Creek Ditch—*canal* CO-8
**Walton Crossroads**—*pop pl* NC-3
Walton Drain—*canal* (2) MI-6
Walton Draw—*valley* (2) TX-5
*Walton Elementary School* MS-4
Walton Ferry Access Area—*park* TN-4
Walton Ferry Elem Sch—*school* TN-4
Walton Fork—*stream* VA-3
Walton Furnace—*locale* VA-3
Walton Grove Ch—*church* GA-3
Walton Guard Station—*locale* OR-9
Walton Gulch—*valley* UT-8
**Walton Heights**—*pop pl* AR-4
Walton Hill—*summit* NY-2
**Walton Hills**—*pop pl* OH-6
Walton (historical)—*locale* MS-4
**Walton (historical)**—*pop pl* IN-6
Walton Hollow—*valley* KY-4
Walton Hotel—*hist pl* GA-3
Walton-Howry House—*hist pl* MS-4
Walton HS—*school* FL-3
Walton HS—*school* NY-2
**Waltonia**—*pop pl* CO-8
**Waltonia**—*pop pl* TX-5
**Waltonia (historical)**—*pop pl* MS-4
Waltonian Island—*island* NY-2
Waltonian Park—*park* PA-2
Waltonian Pond—*reservoir* VA-3
Waltonia Sch (historical)—*school* MS-4
*Walton Island* NY-2
Walton Island—*island* TX-5
Walton JHS—*school* CA-9
Walton Junction—*locale* MI-6
*Walton Lake* IN-6
*Walton Lake* MI-6
Walton Lake—*lake* CA-9
Walton Lake—*lake* (2) MI-6
Walton Lake—*lake* OH-6
Walton Lake—*lake* OR-9
**Walton Lake**—*pop pl* NY-2
Walton Lake—*reservoir* IL-6
Walton Lake—*reservoir* (2) IN-6
Walton Lake—*reservoir* IA-7
Walton Lake—*reservoir* NY-2
Walton Lake—*reservoir* OR-9
Walton Lake—*reservoir* VA-3
Walton Lake Dam—*dam* IN-6
Walton Lake No 1—*reservoir* CO-8
Walton Lake No 2—*reservoir* CO-8
Walton Lake No 3—*reservoir* CO-8
Walton Lake No 4—*lake* CO-8
Walton Lakes—*lake* ID-8
Walton Lake Sch—*school* NY-2
Walton Landing—*locale* NH-1
Walton Landing Strip—*airport* KS-7
Walton Lateral—*canal* AZ-5
Walton Lookout Tower—*locale* GA-3
Walton (Magisterial District)—*fmr MCD* VA-3
Walton (Magisterial District)—*fmr MCD* WV-2
Walton Manor Cottage—*hist pl* KY-4
Walton Marsh—*lake* MI-6
Walton Memorial Ch—*church* VA-3
Walton Mine—*mine* ID-8
Walton MS—*school* FL-3
Walton Mtn—*summit* MT-8
Walton Mtn—*summit* (2) NY-2
Walton Outlet—*stream* MI-6
Walton Park—*park* GA-3
Walton Park—*park* TX-5
**Walton Park**—*pop pl* NY-2
Walton Peak—*summit* CO-8
Walton Picnic Area—*park* IA-7
Walton Point—*cape* NY-2
Walton Pond—*lake* CT-1
Walton Pond—*lake* FL-3
Walton Pond—*lake* MI-6
Walton Pond—*lake* VT-1
Walton Quarters—*locale* AL-4
Walton Ranch—*locale* NM-5
Walton Ranch—*locale* TX-5
Walton Ranger Station—*locale* MT-8
Walton Ranger Station Hist Dist—*hist pl* MT-8
Walton Ridge—*ridge* AZ-5
Walton Ridge—*ridge* WV-2
Walton River—*stream* MI-6
Walton Road Ford—*locale* AL-4
Walton Run—*stream* PA-2
Walton Run—*stream* WV-2
Walton Sch—*school* AL-4
Walton Sch—*school* CA-9
Walton Sch—*school* ME-1
Walton Sch—*school* MA-1
Walton Sch—*school* MI-6
Walton Sch—*school* (2) MS-4
Walton Sch—*school* OH-6
Walton Sch—*school* PA-2
Walton Sch—*school* (2) TX-5
Walton Sch—*school* VA-3
Waltons Chapel—*church* MS-4
Waltons Chapel—*church* TN-4
Walton Sch (historical)—*school* MS-4
Walton Sch (historical)—*school* MO-7
*Waltons Creek* GA-3
*Waltons Creek* MS-4
Waltons Ferry (historical)—*locale* MS-4
Waltons Islands (historical)—*island* TN-4
*Waltons Landing* AL-4
Waltons Landing—*locale* NC-3
Walton Slough—*stream* OR-9
Waltons Mill—*locale* ME-1
Waltons Mill (historical)—*locale* AL-4
Walton Spring—*spring* AZ-5
Walton Spring—*spring* GA-3
Walton Spring—*spring* TX-5
Waltons Shoals—*bar* TN-4
*Waltons Store* NC-3
Waltons Store—*locale* VA-3
**Waltons Store**—*pop pl* NC-3
Walton State Fish Hatchery—*other* GA-3
Walton Street-Church Street Hist
Dist—*hist pl* GA-3
Walton Street Park—*park* NC-3
Walton Technical Sch—*school* GA-3
**Walton (Town of)**—*pop pl* NY-2
Walton Township—*civil* MO-7
**Walton Township**—*pop pl* (3) KS-7
**Walton (Township of)**—*pop pl* MI-6
Waltonville—*locale* PA-2
**Waltonville**—*pop pl* IL-6
Waltonville Public Use Area—*area* IL-6
*Walt Ranch* NV-8
**Waltreak**—*pop pl* AR-4
Waltrip HS—*school* TX-5
**Waltrous**—*pop pl* PA-2
Walts Air Service Landing Strip—*airport* ND-7
Walts Bay—*bay* ID-8
Walts Chapel—*church* NC-3
Walts Corner—*locale* CO-8
Walts Flat—*flat* UT-8
Walts Gulch—*valley* CA-9
Walts Landing—*locale* AL-4
Walts Landing—*locale* TN-4
*Walts Mill* PA-2
Walt Smith Canyon—*valley* SD-7
*Walts Number One* NV-8
Walts Post Office (historical)—*building* TN-4
Walt Spring—*spring* NM-5
Walts Sch—*school* NY-2
Walts Tank—*reservoir* (2) AZ-5
Walt Whitman Birthplace—*building* NY-2
Walt Whitman Bridge—*bridge* PA-2
**Walt Whitman Homes**—*pop pl* NJ-2
Walt Whitman HS—*school* MD-2
Walt Whitman HS—*school* NY-2
Walt Whitman Sch—*school* (2) NY-2
Walty Creek—*stream* AK-9
Waltz—*locale* KY-4
**Waltz**—*pop pl* MI-6
**Waltz**—*pop pl* PA-2
Waltz Airp—*airport* PA-2
Waltz Cem—*cemetery* KY-4
Waltz Ch—*church* OH-6
Waltz Creek—*stream* PA-2
Waltz Key—*island* FL-3
Waltz Key Basin—*bay* FL-3
*Waltzmill* PA-2
**Waltz Mill**—*pop pl* PA-2
*Waltz Point* ME-1
Waltz Ranch—*locale* CA-9
**Waltz (Township of)**—*pop pl* IN-6
Waltzvale—*locale* PA-2
Waluga Park—*park* OR-9
Waluga Sch—*school* OR-9
**Walum**—*pop pl* ND-7
Walunga, Inya—*channel* FM-9
Walung (Municipality)—*civ div* FM-9
Walupt Creek—*stream* WA-9
Walupt Lake—*lake* WA-9
Walupt Lake Campground—*locale* WA-9
Walupt Lake Guard Station—*locale* WA-9
*Waluska* GA-3
Walverine Creek—*stream* WA-9
Walville—*locale* WA-9
Walville Peak—*summit* WA-9
Walworth—*locale* NE-7
**Walworth**—*pop pl* NY-2
**Walworth**—*pop pl* WI-6
Walworth Cem—*cemetery* NE-7
Walworth Cem—*cemetery* NY-2
Walworth Center Cem—*cemetery* NY-2
Walworth Ch—*church* MN-6
Walworth County—*civil* SD-7
**Walworth (County)**—*pop pl* WI-6
Walworth (historical)—*locale* SD-7
Walworth Sch—*school* NE-7
Walworth Station—*locale* NY-2
**Walworth (Town of)**—*pop pl* NY-2
**Walworth (Town of)**—*pop pl* WI-6
Walworth Township—*civil* SD-7
**Walworth (Township of)**—*pop pl* MN-6
WALX-FM (Selma)—*tower* AL-4
Walz—*locale* IL-6
Walz Cem—*cemetery* SD-7
*Walz Creek* PA-2
Walzem Creek—*stream* TX-5
Walzem Sch—*school* TX-5
*Walzer Creek* IL-6
Walz Sch—*school* SD-7
Wam, Mount—*summit* MT-8
**Wamac**—*pop pl* IL-6
*Wamack* AL-4
Wamac Point—*cape* AR-4
Wamac West Oil Field—*other* IL-6
Wamaduze Valley—*valley* NE-7
**Wamar**—*pop pl* ID-8
**Wamba**—*pop pl* TX-5
Wambach Lake—*lake* MN-6
Wambach Ranch—*locale* ND-7
Wambach State Wildlife Mngmt
Area—*park* MN-6
Wambacker Mine—*mine* AZ-5
WAMB-AM (Donelson)—*tower* TN-4
Wambaugh Run—*stream* PA-2
Wambaw Corner—*locale* SC-3
Wambaw Creek—*stream* SC-3
*Wambaw River* SC-3
Wambaw Swamp—*swamp* (2) SC-3
Wambel Cem—*cemetery* MO-7
Wamble Cem—*cemetery* TN-4
Wamble Creek—*stream* GA-3
**Wamblee Park**—*pop pl* CO-8
**Wamblee Valley**—*pop pl* CO-8
Wamble Mtn—*summit* IL-6
Wambo Bar—*bar* CA-9
Wambold Hollow—*valley* PA-2
Wamboldt Cem—*cemetery* MI-6
Wambolt Creek—*stream* NV-8
Wambolt Springs—*spring* NV-8
*Wambraw Creek* SC-3
W A McCrary Lake—*reservoir* NC-3
W A McCrary Lake Dam—*dam* NC-3
Wam Creek—*stream* MT-8
**Wamduska (historical)**—*pop pl* ND-7
Wamduska Town Hall—*building* ND-7
**Wamduska Township**—*pop pl* ND-7
WAME-AM (Charlotte)—*tower* NC-3
**Wamego**—*pop pl* KS-7
Wamego Municpal Airp—*airport* KS-7
**Wamego Township**—*pop pl* KS-7
Wamel Canal—*canal* NM-5
Wamel Ranch—*locale* NM-5
Wamels Draw—*valley* NM-5
Wamels Lower Well—*well* NM-5
Wamels Pond—*reservoir* NM-5
Wamels Upper Well—*well* NM-5
*Wamesit* MA-1
**Wamesit**—*pop pl* MA-1
Wamesit Canal-Whipple Mill Industrial
Complex—*hist pl* MA-1
Wamesit Power Company Dam—*dam* MA-1
WAMG-AM (Gallatin)—*tower* TN-4
*Wamgumbaug Lake* CT-1
Wami, Lake—*reservoir* FL-3
WAMI-AM (Opp)—*tower* AL-4
**Wamic**—*pop pl* OR-9
Wamic Cem—*cemetery* OR-9
Wamic Elem Sch—*school* OR-9
WAMI-FM (Opp)—*tower* AL-4
Wamin Lake—*lake* WI-6
W A Minus—*locale* TX-5
WAMJ-AM (South Bend)—*tower* IN-6
*Wamkeag Hill* RI-1
WAML-AM (Laurel)—*tower* MS-4
Wammen Spring—*spring* SD-7
WAMN-AM (Washington)—*tower* IN-6
WAMO-AM (Pittsburgh)—*tower* PA-2
Wamogo HS—*school* CT-1
*Wamoma* CA-9
Wamoset Hill—*summit* MA-1
Wampanoag, Lake—*reservoir* MA-1
Wampanoag Country Club—*other* CT-1
Wampanoag Ind Res—*reserve* MA-1
Wampanoag Mills—*hist pl* MA-1
Wampanoag Royal Cemetery—*hist pl* MA-1
Wampanucket Site—*hist pl* MA-1
Wampatuck Bogs—*swamp* MA-1
Wampatuck Country Club—*locale* MA-1
Wampatuck Hill—*summit* MA-1
Wampatuck Pond—*lake* MA-1
Wampatuck Pond—*reservoir* MA-1
Wampatuck Pond Dam—*dam* MA-1
Wampatuck Sch—*school* MA-1
Wamp Ditch—*canal* OH-6
Wampecack Creek—*stream* NY-2
**Wampee**—*pop pl* (2) SC-3
Wampee Bay—*swamp* FL-3
Wampee Fire Lookout Tower—*locale* SC-3
Wampee Pond—*reservoir* CT-1
Wampee Ponds—*swamp* FL-3
Wampee Strand—*swamp* FL-3
Wampenum Brook—*stream* MA-1
*Wampetuck Pond* MA-1
*Wamphassuck Neck* CT-1
*Wamphassuck Point* CT-1
Wamphassuc Neck—*cape* CT-1
Wamphassuc Point—*cape* CT-1
**Wamphassuc Point**—*pop pl* CT-1
*Wamphassue Point* CT-1
Wamp Lake—*lake* MN-6
Wampler—*locale* TX-5
Wampler Cem—*cemetery* MO-7
Wampler Cem—*cemetery* TX-5
Wampler Cem—*cemetery* (5) VA-3
Wampler Hill—*summit* TX-5
Wampler Hollow—*valley* VA-3
*Wampler Lake* MI-6
Wampler Marsh—*swamp* OR-9
Wampler Ridge—*ridge* VA-3
Wamplers Lake—*lake* MI-6
Wamplers Lake Sch—*school* MI-6
Wampler Spring—*spring* OR-9
Wampler Spur—*uninc pl* AR-4
Wampole Run—*stream* PA-2
**Wampoo**—*pop pl* AR-4
Wampoo Creek—*stream* MT-8
Wampoo Wash—*stream* AZ-5
Wampoo Wash—*stream* NM-5
Wamp Spring—*spring* NV-8
**Wampsville**—*pop pl* NY-2
*Wampum* MA-1
**Wampum**—*pop pl* PA-2
Wampum Borough—*civil* PA-2
Wampum Brook—*stream* NJ-2
**Wampum Corner**—*pop pl* MA-1
Wampum Creek—*stream* ID-8
*Wampum Dam* NJ-2
Wampum Lake—*lake* CA-9
Wampum Lake—*lake* IL-6
**Wampum Rock**—*pop pl* MA-1
Wampum Run—*stream* PA-2
*Wampum's Rock* MA-1
Wampum Swamp—*swamp* MA-1
Wampus Ave Sch—*school* NY-2
Wampus Butte—*summit* OR-9
Wampus Cat Canyon—*valley* OR-9
Wampus Creek—*stream* ID-8
**Wampus (historical)**—*pop pl* OR-9
Wampus Lake—*lake* (2) MN-6
Wampus Lake Rsvr—*reservoir* NY-2
Wampus River—*stream* NY-2
Wampus Springs—*spring* OR-9
WAMQ-AM (Loretto)—*tower* PA-2
WAMS-AM (Wilmington)—*tower* DE-2
*Wamser Island* NY-2
**Wamsley**—*pop pl* OH-6
Wamsley, Other C., House—*hist pl* MT-8
Wamsley Cattle Ranch—*locale* CO-8
Wamsley Cem—*cemetery* MO-7
Wamsley Ch—*church* OH-6
Wamsley Ch (historical)—*church* MO-7
Wamsley Creek—*stream* MO-7
Wamsley Creek—*stream* OK-5
Wamsley Field—*airport* KS-7
Wamsley Mine—*mine* NV-8
Wamsley Run—*stream* (4) WV-2
Wamsley Sch—*school* MT-8
Wamsley Sch (historical)—*school* MO-7
Wamsley Village Site—*hist pl* OH-6
Wam Squam Bay—*swamp* NC-3
Wamsutta Trail—*trail* NH-1
**Wamsutter**—*pop pl* WY-8
Wamsutter Gas Field—*oilfield* WY-8
Wamsutter Rim—*cliff* WY-8
W A Mtn Howard—*summit* OR-9
Wamul Tank—*reservoir* AZ-5
WAMY-AM (Amory)—*tower* MS-4
Wan—*locale* VA-3
**Wana**—*pop pl* WV-2
WANA-AM (Anniston)—*tower* AL-4
*Wanacott Lake* WA-9
Wanacut Creek—*stream* WA-9
Wanadoga Creek—*stream* MI-6
*Wanagan Creek* ND-7
Wanagan Creek—*stream* MI-6
*Wanaissa Peak* VA-3
**Wanakah**—*pop pl* NY-2
Wanakah Country Club—*other* NY-2
Wanakah Mine—*mine* CO-8
*Wanake Creek* WA-9
**Wanakena**—*pop pl* NY-2
Wanaki Campground—*locale* MN-6
Wanaksink Lake—*reservoir* NY-2
Wanalain, Lake—*reservoir* SD-7
Wanalain Lake Dam—*dam* SD-7
*Wanalaw Cemetery* MS-4
**Wanamake**—*pop pl* FL-3
*Wanamaker* MS-4
*Wanamaker* PA-2
Wanamaker—*locale* KY-4
**Wanamaker**—*pop pl* IN-6
**Wanamaker**—*pop pl* IA-7
**Wanamaker**—*pop pl* MO-7
Wanamaker, John, Store—*hist pl* PA-2
Wanamaker Cave—*cave* TN-4
Wanamaker Cem—*cemetery* OK-5
Wanamaker Ch—*church* OK-5
Wanamaker Ch—*church* SC-3
Wanamaker Cove—*valley* TN-4
*Wanamaker Creek* CO-8
Wanamaker Elem Sch—*school* KS-7
Wanamaker (historical)—*locale* SD-7
Wanamaker JHS—*school* PA-2
Wanamaker Lake—*lake* MA-1
Wanamaker Lake—*lake* MI-6
*Wanamaker (New Bethel)* IN-6
Wanamaker Pit—*cave* TN-4
**Wanamakers**—*pop pl* PA-2
Wanamaker State Special Use
Area—*park* NE-7
**Wanamassa**—*pop pl* NJ-2
Wanamassa Sch—*school* NJ-2
**Wanamie**—*pop pl* PA-2
Wanamie Dam—*dam* PA-2
Wanamie Number 19 Colliery—*building* PA-2
**Wanamingo**—*pop pl* MN-6
Wanamingo Cem—*cemetery* MN-6
Wanamingo Township Hall—*hist pl* MN-6
**Wanamingo (Township of)**—*pop pl* MN-6
Wananalua—*civil* HI-9
Wananalua Congregational
Church—*hist pl* HI-9
Wananapaoa Islands—*island* HI-9
Wanango Country Club—*other* PA-2
**Wananish**—*pop pl* NC-3
Wanapanaquin Hill—*summit* MA-1
*Wanapuka* HI-9

Ward Creek—*stream* ... ID-8
Ward Creek—*stream* ... KS-7
Ward Creek—*stream* ... KY-4
Ward Creek—*stream* ... LA-4
Ward Creek—*stream* (4) ... MT-8
Ward Creek—*stream* ... NC-3
Ward Creek—*stream* ... OK-5
Ward Creek—*stream* (7) ... OR-9
Ward Creek—*stream* ... SC-3
Ward Creek—*stream* ... TN-4
Ward Creek—*stream* (3) ... TX-5
Ward Creek—*stream* ... WA-9
Ward Creek—*stream* ... WI-6
Ward Creek—*stream* ... WY-8
Ward Creek Ch—*church* ... TX-5
Ward Cut—*canal* ... CA-9
Ward Dam—*dam* ... AZ-5
Ward District No. 3 Schoolhouse—*hist pl* ... WI-6
Ward Ditch—*canal* ... CO-8
Ward Ditch—*canal* ... IN-6
Ward Ditch—*canal* ... MD-2
Ward Ditch—*canal* (2) ... MT-8
Ward Ditch—*canal* ... OH-6
Ward D (Police Jury Ward)—*fmr MCD* ... LA-4
Ward Drainage Canal—*canal* ... CA-9
Ward Draw—*valley* ... SD-7
Warde, J. C. B., House—*hist pl* ... IA-7
Ward Earth Lodge Village Site (32BL3)—*hist pl* ... ND-7
Wardeberg Lake—*lake* ... MN-6
Warde HS—*school* ... CT-1
*Ward Elementary School* ... MS-4
Wardell—*locale* ... VA-3
**Wardell**—*pop pl* ... AR-4
**Wardell**—*pop pl* ... MO-7
Wardell Buffalo Trap—*hist pl* ... WY-8
Wardell Cem—*cemetery* ... KS-7
Wardell Ch—*church* ... AR-4
Wardell Chapell—*church* ... NC-3
Wardell Ditch—*canal* ... WY-8
Wardell House—*hist pl* ... MO-7
Wardell House—*hist pl* ... NJ-2
Wardell Memorial Cem—*cemetery* ... MO-7
Wardell Ranch—*locale* ... MT-8
Wardell Rsvr—*reservoir* ... WY-8
Wardell Rsvr No 1—*reservoir* ... WY-8
Wardell Rsvr No 2—*reservoir* ... WY-8
Wardell Rsvr No 3—*reservoir* ... WY-8
Wardell Rsvr No 5—*reservoir* ... WY-8
Wardell Rsvr No 6—*reservoir* ... WY-8
Wardell Rsvr No 7—*reservoir* ... WY-8
Wardells Corner (historical)—*locale* ... MA-1
Wardells Neck—*cape* ... NJ-2
Wardel Rsvr—*reservoir* ... WY-8
**Warden**—*pop pl* ... LA-4
**Warden**—*pop pl* ... WA-9
**Warden**—*pop pl* ... WV-2
Warden, William Gray, House—*hist pl* ... FL-3
Warden Branch—*stream* ... AR-4
Warden Branch—*stream* ... MO-7
Warden Branch—*stream* ... TN-4
Warden Cabin—*locale* ... AZ-5
Warden-Carden Sch—*school* ... MS-4
Warden (CCD)—*cens area* ... WA-9
Warden Cem—*cemetery* ... IN-6
Warden Cem—*cemetery* ... MO-7
Warden Cem—*cemetery* ... TN-4
Warden Cem—*cemetery* ... TX-5
Warden Cem—*cemetery* ... WI-6
Warden Chapel—*church* ... MO-7
Warden Creek—*stream* ... CA-9
Warden Creek—*stream* ... OR-9
Warden Creek—*stream* ... PA-2
Warden Ditch—*canal* ... OH-6
*Wardendorf Pasture* ... NV-8
Warden Draw—*valley* ... CO-8
Warden Grove Ch—*church* ... NC-3
Warden Gulch—*valley* ... CO-8
Warden Gulch—*valley* ... ID-8
Wardenhoff Creek—*stream* ... ID-8
Wardenhoff Meadows—*flat* ... ID-8
Warden Hollow—*valley* (2) ... TN-4
*Warden-Keith Cemetery* ... TN-4
*Warden Lake* ... MT-8
Warden Lake—*lake* ... TX-5
Warden Lake—*reservoir* ... WV-2
Warden Lake—*swamp* ... CA-9
Warden Lake Public Fishing Area—*park* ... WV-2
Warden Locomotive Shop—*other* ... TX-5
*Warden Mountain* ... MT-8
*Wardenot Pasture* ... NV-8
Warden Park—*park* ... MT-8
*Warden Peak* ... TX-5
*Warden Pond* ... VT-1
Warden Pond—*lake* ... NY-2
Warden Pond—*lake* ... RI-1
Warden Ranch—*locale* ... NE-7
Warden Ridge—*ridge* ... WV-2
Warden Rsvr—*reservoir* ... OR-9
Warden Run—*stream* ... PA-2
Warden Run—*stream* ... WV-2
Warden Sch—*school* ... WI-6
Wardens Forge (historical)—*locale* ... TN-4
Warden's House-Old Louisiana State Penitentiary—*hist pl* ... LA-4
Wardens Pond—*lake* ... VT-1
Warden Spring—*spring* ... UT-8
Wardens Slough—*stream* ... KY-4
**Wardensville**—*pop pl* ... WV-2
Ward E (Police Jury Ward)—*fmr MCD* ... LA-4
Warder, John Aston, House—*hist pl* ... OH-6
*Warder Creek* ... PA-2
*Warder Lake* ... WI-6
Warder Park—*park* ... OH-6
Warder Park Sch—*school* ... OH-6
Warder Public Library—*hist pl* ... OH-6
Warder-Totten House—*hist pl* ... DC-2
Ward Estate Dam—*dam* ... AL-4
Ward Estes North Oil Field—*oilfield* ... TX-5
Ward Ferry (abandoned)—*locale* ... AR-4
Ward Field—*flat* ... NC-3
Ward Field Tank—*reservoir* ... TX-5
**Ward Five School**—*pop pl* ... LA-4
Ward-Force House and Condit Family Cook House—*hist pl* ... NJ-2
Ward Forge Number 1 (historical)—*locale* ... TN-4
Ward Forge Number 2 (historical)—*locale* ... TN-4
Ward Fork—*stream* ... TN-4
*Ward Fork Creek* ... TN-4
Ward F (Police Jury Ward)—*fmr MCD* ... LA-4
*Ward Gap* ... AL-4
Ward Gap—*gap* ... AL-4
Ward Gap—*gap* ... GA-3
Ward Gap—*gap* (2) ... NC-3
Ward Gap—*gap* ... TN-4
Ward G (Police Jury Ward)—*fmr MCD* ... LA-4
Ward Grundy Sch—*school* ... IL-6
Ward Gulch—*valley* (2) ... CO-8
Ward Gulch—*valley* ... MT-8
Ward Gulch—*valley* ... NV-8
Ward Gulch—*valley* ... SD-7
Ward Gulch—*valley* ... WY-8
Ward Hall—*hist pl* ... KY-4
Ward Hall (Boundary Increase)—*hist pl* ... KY-4
Ward-Hays House—*hist pl* ... AR-4
*Ward Hill* ... MA-1
**Ward Hill**—*pop pl* ... MA-1
Ward Hill—*summit* ... AR-4
Ward Hill—*summit* (2) ... ME-1
Ward Hill—*summit* (3) ... MA-1
Ward Hill—*summit* (2) ... NY-2
Ward Hill—*summit* ... ND-7
Ward Hill—*summit* (3) ... TN-4
Ward Hill Lookout Tower—*locale* ... MI-6
Ward (historical)—*locale* ... KS-7
**Ward (historical)**—*pop pl* ... TN-4
Ward-Holland House—*hist pl* ... MI-6
Ward Hollow—*valley* ... AL-4
Ward Hollow—*valley* (2) ... AR-4
Ward Hollow—*valley* ... NY-2
Ward Hollow—*valley* (2) ... NC-3
Ward Hollow—*valley* (3) ... TN-4
Ward Hollow—*valley* (2) ... WV-2
Ward Homestead—*locale* ... NJ-2
Ward Hotel—*hist pl* ... MT-8
Ward House—*hist pl* ... MS-4
Ward House—*hist pl* ... NY-2
Ward House—*hist pl* ... OH-6
Ward House—*hist pl* ... TX-5
Ward House—*hist pl* ... WA-9
Ward H (Police Jury Ward)—*fmr MCD* ... LA-4
Ward HS—*school* ... FL-3
Ward HS—*school* ... KS-7
Ward HS—*school* ... TN-4
Ward I (Police Jury Ward)—*fmr MCD* ... LA-4
*Ward Island* ... RI-1
*Ward Island* ... TX-5
Ward Island—*island* ... CA-9
Ward Island—*island* (3) ... FL-3
Ward Island—*island* ... IL-6
Ward Island—*island* ... MI-6
Ward Island—*island* ... NY-2
Ward Island—*island* ... RI-1
Ward Island—*island* ... TX-5
Ward-Jackson Sch—*school* ... IN-6
Ward J (Police Jury Ward)—*fmr MCD* ... LA-4
Ward Knob—*summit* ... VA-3
Ward Knob—*summit* ... WV-2
Ward K (Police Jury Ward)—*fmr MCD* ... LA-4
*Ward Lake* ... MI-6
*Ward Lake* ... TX-5
*Ward Lake* ... WA-9
Ward Lake—*lake* ... AK-9
Ward Lake—*lake* (2) ... CA-9
Ward Lake—*lake* ... FL-3
Ward Lake—*lake* (4) ... MI-6
Ward Lake—*lake* (3) ... MN-6
Ward Lake—*lake* ... MS-4
Ward Lake—*lake* ... NE-7
Ward Lake—*lake* ... ND-7
Ward Lake—*lake* ... OR-9
Ward Lake—*lake* (2) ... TX-5
Ward Lake—*lake* (2) ... WA-9
Ward Lake—*lake* ... WI-6
Ward Lake—*reservoir* ... AR-4
Ward Lake—*reservoir* ... FL-3
Ward Lake—*reservoir* (2) ... GA-3
Ward Lake—*reservoir* ... NJ-2
Ward Lake—*reservoir* (2) ... OK-5
Ward Lake Campground—*locale* ... CO-8
Ward Lake Dam—*dam* ... MS-4
Ward Lake Ranger Station—*locale* ... CO-8
Ward Lakes—*lake* ... CA-9
Ward Lateral—*canal* ... CO-8
Ward Lateral—*canal* ... WI-6
Wardlaw—*locale* ... TX-5
Wardlaw, Andrew James, House—*hist pl* ... KY-4
Wardlaw, Dr. Herbert A., House—*hist pl* ... TX-5
Wardlaw Creek—*stream* ... AL-4
Wardlaw JHS—*hist pl* ... SC-3
Wardlaw JHS—*school* ... SC-3
Wardlaw Ranch—*locale* (3) ... TX-5
Wardlaw-Smith House—*hist pl* ... FL-3
Wardlaw-Steele House—*hist pl* ... TN-4
Wardlaw-Swango House—*hist pl* ... MS-4
Ward Lode Mine—*mine* ... MT-8
Wardlow Branch—*stream* ... MS-4
Wardlow Canyon—*valley* ... CA-9
Wardlow Cem—*cemetery* ... MS-4
Wardlow Cem—*cemetery* (2) ... OH-6
Wardlow Creek—*stream* ... MS-4
Wardlow Creek—*stream* ... TN-4
Wardlow Park—*park* ... CA-9
Wardlow Rock—*pillar* ... CA-9
Wardlow Sch—*school* ... CA-9
Wardlow Sch—*school* ... MS-4
Wardlows Pocket—*lake* ... TN-4
Wardlows Pocket Landing—*locale* ... TN-4
Wardlow Wash—*stream* ... CA-9
Wardman Park Annex and Arcade—*hist pl* ... DC-2
Wardman Row—*hist pl* ... DC-2
Ward Marsh—*swamp* ... NY-2
Ward-Meade House—*hist pl* ... KS-7
Ward Memorial Cem—*cemetery* ... OR-9
Ward Memorial Cem—*cemetery* ... TN-4
Ward Memorial Ch—*church* ... NC-3
Ward Memorial Hall—*hist pl* ... WI-6
Ward Memorial Presbyterian Ch—*church* ... AL-4
Ward Memorial State Park—*park* ... ID-8
Ward Mesa—*summit* ... NM-5
Ward Mill Branch—*stream* ... SC-3
*Ward Mill Creek* ... AL-4
Ward Mill Creek—*stream* ... FL-3
Ward Mine—*mine* ... CO-8
Ward Mine—*mine* ... NV-8
Ward Mine—*mine* ... NM-5
Ward Mine—*mine* ... OR-9
Ward Mine—*mine* ... TN-4
Ward Mountain Ch—*church* ... TX-5
Ward Mountain Division—*forest* ... NV-8
Ward Mountain Lake—*lake* ... CA-9
Ward Mountain Rec Area—*park* ... NV-8
Ward Mountain Ski Hill—*locale* ... NV-8
Ward Mountain Trail—*trail* ... MT-8
*Ward Mtn* ... TN-4
Ward Mtn—*summit* ... AL-4
Ward Mtn—*summit* ... AK-9
Ward Mtn—*summit* (4) ... CA-9
Ward Mtn—*summit* ... GA-3
Ward Mtn—*summit* ... MT-8
Ward Mtn—*summit* ... NV-8
Ward Mtn—*summit* (3) ... NC-3
Ward Mtn—*summit* ... TN-4
Ward Mtn—*summit* (2) ... TX-5
**Wardner**—*pop pl* ... ID-8
Wardner, James F., House—*hist pl* ... WA-9
Wardner Hill—*summit* ... VT-1
Wardner Peak—*summit* ... ID-8
Wardner Pond—*lake* ... VT-1
Wardner Ranch—*locale* (2) ... TX-5
Ward Nicholson Corner Store—*hist pl* ... AL-4
Ward No 2 Sch—*school* ... IL-6
War Dog Cem—*cemetery* ... GU-9
**Wardour**—*pop pl* ... MD-2
**Wardour Bluffs**—*pop pl* ... MD-2
Ward Park—*park* ... AL-4
Ward Park—*park* ... AZ-5
Ward Park—*park* ... MA-1
Ward Park—*park* ... MN-6
Ward Park—*park* ... TX-5
Ward Peak—*summit* ... CA-9
Ward Peak—*summit* ... ID-8
Ward Peak—*summit* (2) ... MT-8
Ward Pocket—*valley* ... AZ-5
Ward Point—*cape* ... NY-2
Ward Point—*cape* ... NC-3
Ward Point Bend (West)—*bend* ... NY-2
Ward Pond—*lake* ... ME-1
Ward Pond—*lake* (5) ... MA-1
Ward Pond—*lake* (2) ... NY-2
Ward Pond—*swamp* ... TX-5
Ward Post Office (historical)—*building* ... TN-4
Ward Pound Ridge Reservation—*park* ... NY-2
Ward Prairie—*locale* ... TX-5
Ward Prairie Lakes—*lake* ... TX-5
Ward Ranch—*locale* ... CO-8
Ward Ranch—*locale* (2) ... MT-8
Ward Ranch—*locale* (2) ... NV-8
Ward Ranch—*locale* ... NM-5
Ward Ranch—*locale* (2) ... TX-5
**Ward Ridge**—*pop pl* ... FL-3
Ward Ridge—*ridge* ... ID-8
Ward Ridge—*ridge* (2) ... TN-4
Ward Ridge—*ridge* ... VA-3
Ward Ridge—*ridge* (2) ... WI-6
Ward Road Cem—*cemetery* ... WV-2
Ward Road Ch—*church* ... WV-2
Wardrop Creek—*stream* ... ID-8
**Ward (RR name Concordville (sta.))**—*pop pl* ... PA-2
Ward Rsvr—*reservoir* ... AR-4
Ward Rsvr—*reservoir* ... SD-7
Ward Rsvr No 1—*reservoir* ... CO-8
Ward Rsvr No 2—*reservoir* ... CO-8
Ward Rsvr No 5—*reservoir* ... CO-8
*Ward Run* ... MD-2
Ward Run—*stream* ... NC-3
Ward Run—*stream* (2) ... PA-2
Ward Run—*stream* (2) ... WV-2
*Wards* ... PA-2
*Wards* ... SC-3
Wards—*locale* ... KY-4
**Wards**—*pop pl* ... NC-3
Wards and Reynolds Ditch—*canal* ... CO-8
Wards Bank—*levee* ... FL-3
Wards Bayou—*stream* ... AR-4
Wards Bayou—*stream* ... LA-4
**Wardsboro**—*pop pl* ... VT-1
Wardsboro Brook—*stream* (2) ... VT-1
Wardsboro Cem—*cemetery* ... NY-2
**Wardsboro Center**—*pop pl* ... VT-1
**Wardsboro (Town of)**—*pop pl* ... VT-1
Wards Branch—*stream* ... DE-2
Wards Branch—*stream* ... KY-4
Wards Bridge—*bridge* ... AL-4
Wards Bridge—*bridge* (3) ... NC-3
Wards Brook—*stream* ... NY-2
*Wardsburg* ... PA-2
**Wardsburg**—*pop pl* ... PA-2
Wards Butte—*summit* ... ID-8
Wards Butte—*summit* ... OR-9
Wards Cache—*basin* ... UT-8
Wards Camp (historical)—*locale* ... MS-4
Wards Canal—*canal* ... OH-6
Wards Canyon—*valley* ... SD-7
Wards Cem—*cemetery* ... FL-3
Wards Cem—*cemetery* ... IN-6
Wards Cem—*cemetery* (2) ... OK-5
*Ward Sch* ... PA-2
Wards Ch—*church* ... PA-2
Wards Ch—*church* ... TN-4
Ward Sch—*school* ... AZ-5
Ward Sch—*school* ... CA-9
Ward Sch—*school* ... FL-3
Ward Sch—*school* (6) ... IL-6
Ward Sch—*school* ... LA-4
Ward Sch—*school* ... ME-1
Ward Sch—*school* ... MA-1
Ward Sch—*school* ... MS-4
Ward Sch—*school* (2) ... NE-7
Ward Sch—*school* ... NY-2
Ward Sch—*school* ... ND-7
Ward Sch—*school* ... OK-5
Ward Sch—*school* ... OR-9
Ward Sch—*school* ... PA-2
Ward Sch—*school* (5) ... TX-5
Ward Sch—*school* ... VT-1
Ward Sch—*school* ... WA-9
Ward Sch—*school* ... WV-2
Ward Sch (abandoned)—*school* (2) ... PA-2
Wards Channel—*channel* ... NC-3
Wards Chapekl—*church* ... TN-4
Wards Chapel—*church* ... AR-4
Wards Chapel—*church* ... LA-4
Wards Chapel—*church* ... MD-2
Wards Chapel—*church* ... NC-3
Wards Chapel—*church* ... OK-5
Wards Chapel—*church* ... VA-3
**Wards Chapel**—*pop pl* ... MD-2
Wards Chapel Cem—*cemetery* ... OK-5
Wards Chapel Sch (historical)—*school* ... TN-4
Ward Sch (historical)—*school* ... MO-7
*Ward School* ... IN-6
*Ward School* ... KS-7
*Wards Church* ... AL-4
Wards Corner—*locale* ... NC-3
Wards Corner—*locale* ... VA-3
Wards Corners—*locale* (2) ... NY-2
Wards Corners—*locale* ... WI-6
Wards Corners (historical P.O.)—*locale* ... IA-7
Wards Corner Shop Ctr—*locale* ... VA-3
Wards Corral—*locale* ... ID-8
*Wards Cove* ... ME-1
**Wards Cove**—*pop pl* ... ME-1
Wards Cove Rapids—*rapids* ... AZ-5
Wards Cove Sch—*school* ... ME-1
*Wards Creek* ... CA-9
*Wards Creek* ... GA-3
*Wards Creek* ... OK-5
**Wards Creek**—*pop pl* ... TX-5
Wards Creek—*stream* ... AR-4
Wards Creek—*stream* ... FL-3
Wards Creek—*stream* (2) ... GA-3
Wards Creek—*stream* (3) ... NC-3
Wards Creek—*stream* ... SC-3
Wards Creek—*stream* (2) ... TX-5
Wards Creek—*stream* ... VT-1
Wards Creek—*stream* (2) ... VA-3
Wards Crossing—*locale* ... AR-4
Wards Crossroads—*locale* ... NC-3
*Wards Cut* ... CA-9
Wards Draw—*valley* ... NM-5
Wards Draw—*valley* ... TX-5
*Wardsesson* ... NJ-2
Wards Ferry Bridge—*bridge* ... CA-9
Wards Ferry (historical)—*locale* ... MS-4
Wards Ferry (historical)—*locale* ... TN-4
Wards Ferry Sch—*school* ... CA-9
Wards Forge (historical)—*locale* ... TN-4
Wards Forge Post Office (historical)—*building* ... TN-4
Wards Fork—*stream* ... CA-9
Wards Fork Creek—*stream* ... VA-3
Wards Fork Mill—*locale* ... VA-3
Wards Gap—*gap* ... VA-3
Wards Gap Ch—*church* ... VA-3
Wards Grove Cem—*cemetery* ... OK-5
Wards Grove Ch—*church* ... GA-3
Wards Grove Ch—*church* (3) ... TN-4
Wards Grove Sch (historical)—*school* ... TN-4
**Wards Grove (Township of)**—*pop pl* ... IL-6
Wards Gulch—*valley* ... ID-8
Ward Shaft—*mine* ... NV-8
Wards Hill—*summit* ... MO-7
Wards Hill—*summit* ... NY-2
Wards (historical)—*locale* ... AZ-5
*Ward Shoal* ... AL-4
*Ward Shoals* ... AL-4
Wards Hollow—*valley* ... WV-2
*Wards Island* ... CA-9
*Wards Island* ... RI-1
Wards Island—*island* ... NY-2
Wards Island—*post sta* ... NY-2
Wards Island Park—*park* ... NY-2
Ward (Site)—*locale* ... NV-8
Wards Lake—*lake* ... CA-9
Wards Lake—*lake* ... LA-4
Wards Lake—*lake* ... MN-6
Wards Lake—*lake* ... TX-5
Wards Lakes—*reservoir* ... GA-3
*Wards Landing* ... TN-4
Wards Landing (historical)—*locale* ... MS-4
Ward Slough—*stream* ... AR-4
Wards Meadow—*swamp* ... OR-9
Wards Mill—*locale* ... AL-4
**Wards Mill**—*pop pl* ... VA-3
Wards Mill Branch—*stream* ... GA-3
Wards Mill Branch—*stream* ... VA-3
*Wards Mill Bridge* ... AL-4
*Wards Mill Creek* ... AL-4
Wards Mill Creek—*stream* ... AL-4
Wards Mill (historical)—*locale* (2) ... AL-4
Wards Millpond—*reservoir* ... CT-1
*Wards Mills* ... IN-6
Wards Park—*park* ... MN-6
Wards Pass—*gap* ... WA-9
*Ward's Point* ... NY-2
Wards Point—*cape* ... MI-6
Wards Point—*cape* ... NY-2
Ward's Point Conservation Area—*hist pl* ... NY-2
Wards Pond—*dam* ... MA-1
Wards Pond—*lake* ... ME-1
Wards Pond—*reservoir* ... AL-4
Wards Pond—*reservoir* ... GA-3
Wards Pond—*reservoir* ... ME-1
Wards Pond—*reservoir* ... MA-1
Ward Spring—*locale* ... TX-5
Ward Spring—*spring* ... AL-4
Ward Spring—*spring* ... AZ-5
Ward Spring—*spring* (2) ... CA-9
Ward Spring—*spring* ... NV-8
Ward Spring—*spring* (3) ... TN-4
Ward Spring—*spring* (2) ... TX-5
Ward Springs—*locale* ... OK-5
**Ward Springs**—*pop pl* ... MN-6
Ward Springs Cem—*cemetery* ... OK-5
Wards Rock—*rock* ... MA-1
*Wards Run* ... MD-2
Wards Run—*stream* ... MD-2
Wards Run—*stream* ... OH-6
Wards Sch (historical)—*school* ... MS-4
Wards Sch (historical)—*school* ... TN-4
Wards Shoal (historical)—*bar* ... AL-4
Wards Stand (historical)—*locale* ... MS-4
Wards Store—*locale* (2) ... NC-3
Wards Stream—*stream* ... MA-1
Ward Station—*locale* ... NC-3
*Wards Town* ... IN-6
Ward Stream—*stream* ... ME-1
Ward Street School-Millbury Street—*hist pl* ... MA-1
Ward's Variety Store—*hist pl* ... AZ-5
**Wardsville**—*pop pl* ... MO-7
**Wardsville (Bosley)**—*pop pl* ... NC-3
Wardsville Sch—*school* ... WI-6
Ward Swamp—*stream* ... NC-3
Wardswell Draw—*valley* ... NM-5
Wardswell Draw—*valley* ... TX-5
Wardsworth Creek—*stream* ... UT-8
Wardsworth Mtn—*summit* ... ME-1
Wardsworth Peak—*summit* ... UT-8
Ward Tank—*reservoir* (2) ... AZ-5
Ward Tank—*reservoir* ... NM-5
Ward Tank—*reservoir* (2) ... TX-5
Ward Terrace—*bench* ... AZ-5
Ward-Thomas House—*hist pl* ... OH-6
**Wardton (historical)**—*pop pl* ... OR-9
*Ward Town* ... OH-6
**Wardtown**—*pop pl* ... ME-1
**Wardtown**—*pop pl* ... VA-3
Wardtown—*summit* ... ME-1
**Ward (Town of)**—*pop pl* ... NY-2
Ward Township—*fmr MCD* ... IA-7
**Ward Township**—*pop pl* ... ND-7
**Ward Township**—*pop pl* ... SD-7
Ward (Township of)—*fmr MCD* (3) ... AR-4
**Ward (Township of)**—*pop pl* ... IN-6
**Ward (Township of)**—*pop pl* ... MN-6
**Ward (Township of)**—*pop pl* ... OH-6
**Ward (Township of)**—*pop pl* ... PA-2
Ward Tunnel—*tunnel* ... CA-9
Ward Valley—*valley* (2) ... CA-9
Ward Vanhorn Dam—*dam* ... SD-7
**Wardview**—*pop pl* ... LA-4
Wardville—*locale* ... LA-4
Wardville—*locale* ... NC-3
**Wardville**—*pop pl* ... LA-4
**Wardville**—*pop pl* ... NC-3
**Wardville**—*pop pl* ... OK-5
**Wardville**—*pop pl* ... PA-2
Wardville Cem—*cemetery* ... PA-2
Wardville Ch—*church* ... LA-4
**Ward (Wards)**—*pop pl* ... SC-3
Ward Waterhole—*reservoir* ... NM-5
Wardwell—*locale* ... MS-4
Ward Well—*locale* ... NM-5
Wardwell—*locale* ... NY-2
**Wardwell**—*pop pl* ... MS-4
**Wardwell**—*pop pl* ... OH-6
Ward Well—*well* ... AZ-5
Ward Well—*well* ... NM-5
Wardwell Island—*island* ... ME-1
Wardwell Island—*island* ... PA-2
Wardwell Point—*cape* ... ME-1
Wardwell Pond—*lake* ... CT-1
Wardwell Run—*stream* ... WV-2
*Wardwell Settlement* ... NY-2
**Wardwell Settlement**—*pop pl* ... NY-2
Ward Windmill—*locale* ... NM-5
Ward Windmill—*locale* ... TX-5
**Wardwood Acres**—*pop pl* ... OH-6
Wardy Hedgecock Dam—*dam* ... NM-5
Ward 1, Alexandria (Police Jury Ward)—*fmr MCD* ... LA-4
Ward 1, Cow Island (Police Jury Ward)—*fmr MCD* ... LA-4
Ward 1 (Police Jury Ward)—*fmr MCD* (60) ... LA-4
Ward 1 Sch—*school* ... NY-2
Ward 10, Rigolette (Police Jury Ward)—*fmr MCD* ... LA-4
Ward 10 (Police Jury Ward)—*fmr MCD* (15) ... LA-4
Ward 11, Buckeye (Police Jury Ward)—*fmr MCD* ... LA-4
Ward 11 (Police Jury Ward)—*fmr MCD* (3) ... LA-4
Ward 2, Grand Chenier (Police Jury Ward)—*fmr MCD* ... LA-4
Ward 2, Lamourie (Police Jury Ward)—*fmr MCD* ... LA-4
Ward 2 (Police Jury Ward)—*fmr MCD* (60) ... LA-4
Ward 3, Cameron (Police Jury Ward)—*fmr MCD* ... LA-4
Ward 3, Cheneyville (Police Jury Ward)—*fmr MCD* ... LA-4
Ward 3 (Police Jury Ward)—*fmr MCD* (59) ... LA-4
Ward 3 Sch—*school* ... LA-4
Ward 4, Grand Lake (Police Jury Ward)—*fmr MCD* ... LA-4
Ward 4, Spring Hill (Police Jury Ward)—*fmr MCD* ... LA-4
Ward 4 (Police Jury Ward)—*fmr MCD* (58) ... LA-4
Ward 5, Hineston (Police Jury Ward)—*fmr MCD* ... LA-4
Ward 5, Johnsons Bayou (Police Jury Ward)—*fmr MCD* ... LA-4
Ward 5 Ch—*church* ... LA-4
Ward 5 (Police Jury Ward)—*fmr MCD* (55) ... LA-4
Ward 5 Sch—*school* ... LA-4
Ward 6, Calcasieu (Police Jury Ward)—*fmr MCD* ... LA-4
Ward 6, Hackberry (Police Jury Ward)—*fmr MCD* ... LA-4
Ward 6 (Police Jury Ward)—*fmr MCD* (45) ... LA-4
Ward 7, Cotile (Police Jury Ward)—*fmr MCD* ... LA-4
Ward 7 (Police Jury Ward)—*fmr MCD* (43) ... LA-4
Ward 8, Rapides (Police Jury Ward)—*fmr MCD* ... LA-4
Ward 8 (Police Jury Ward)—*fmr MCD* (35) ... LA-4
Ward 9, Pineville (Police Jury Ward)—*fmr MCD* ... LA-4
Ward 9 (Police Jury Ward)—*fmr MCD* (26) ... LA-4
Ware—*locale* ... AL-4
Ware—*locale* ... AR-4
Ware—*locale* ... KY-4
Ware—*locale* ... MT-8
Ware—*locale* ... TX-5
**Ware**—*pop pl* ... AL-4
**Ware**—*pop pl* ... IL-6
**Ware**—*pop pl* ... IA-7
**Ware**—*pop pl* ... MA-1
**Ware**—*pop pl* ... MO-7
Ware, Charles, House—*hist pl* ... KY-4
Ware, Clarence R., House—*hist pl* ... GA-3
Ware, Dr. John Christie, Bungalow—*hist pl* ... NJ-2
Ware, Edwin L., House—*hist pl* ... OH-6
Ware, Jasper A., House—*hist pl* ... NE-7
Ware, John M., Sr., House—*hist pl* ... GA-3
Ware, Lake—*lake* ... FL-3
Ware, Shelby D., House—*hist pl* ... KY-4
Wareaf—*locale* ... FM-9
*Wareagle* ... AR-4
War Eagle—*locale* ... WV-2
**War Eagle**—*pop pl* ... AR-4
War Eagle Bridge—*hist pl* ... AR-4
War Eagle Canyon—*valley* ... NV-8
War Eagle Cave—*cave* ... AL-4
War Eagle Ch—*church* ... AR-4
War Eagle Creek—*stream* ... AR-4
*War Eagle Fork Kings River* ... AR-4
War Eagle Grave—*cemetery* ... IA-7
War Eagle Hill—*summit* ... MT-8
War Eagle Hill—*summit* ... SD-7
War Eagle Mine—*mine* ... AZ-5
War Eagle Mine—*mine* (2) ... CA-9
War Eagle Mine—*mine* ... ID-8
War Eagle Mine—*mine* ... NV-8
War Eagle Mine—*mine* ... SD-7
War Eagle Mine—*mine* ... UT-8
*War Eagle Mountain* ... ID-8
War Eagle Mtn—*summit* (2) ... ID-8
War Eagle Mtn—*summit* ... MT-8
War Eagle Number One Mine—*mine* ... CA-9
War Eagle Park*—*park* ... IA-7
War Eagle Peak—*summit* ... ID-8
War Eagle Public Use Area—*park* ... AR-4
War Eagle (Township of)—*fmr MCD* (2) ... AR-4
Ware and Hinds Ditch—*canal* ... CO-8
Ware Bayou—*stream* ... MS-4
Ware Bogs—*swamp* ... MA-1
**Ware Branch**—*pop pl* ... TN-4
Ware Branch—*stream* ... GA-3
Ware Branch—*stream* ... MS-4
Ware Branch—*stream* ... TN-4
Ware Branch—*stream* ... TX-5
Ware Branch—*stream* ... VA-3
Ware Branch Ch—*church* ... TN-4
Ware Bridge (historical)—*locale* ... NC-3
Ware Brook—*stream* ... VT-1
*Ware Cem* ... AL-4
Ware Cem—*cemetery* ... AL-4
Ware Cem—*cemetery* ... GA-3
Ware Cem—*cemetery* ... KY-4
Ware Cem—*cemetery* (3) ... MS-4
Ware Cem—*cemetery* ... NE-7
Ware Cem—*cemetery* ... OH-6
Ware Cem—*cemetery* (2) ... OK-5
Ware Cem—*cemetery* (2) ... TN-4
Ware Cem—*cemetery* (2) ... TX-5
Ware Cem—*cemetery* (2) ... WV-2
Ware (census name for Ware Center)—*CDP* ... MA-1
**Ware Center**—*pop pl* ... MA-1
Ware Center (census name Ware)—*other* ... MA-1
Ware Center Hist Dist—*hist pl* ... MA-1
*Ware Centre* ... MA-1
Ware Ch—*church* ... VA-3
Ware Chapel—*church* ... OK-5
**Wareco**—*pop pl* ... GA-3
Ware Correctional Institute—*building* ... GA-3
**Ware (County)**—*pop pl* ... GA-3
*Ware Cove* ... ME-1
Ware Cove—*bay* ... DE-2
*Ware Creek* ... AL-4
*Ware Creek* ... FL-3
*Ware Creek* ... MA-1
Ware Creek—*bay* ... NC-3
Ware Creek—*stream* ... AR-4
Ware Creek—*stream* (2) ... NJ-2
Ware Creek—*stream* ... NC-3
Ware Creek—*stream* ... SC-3
Ware Creek—*stream* (2) ... VA-3
Ware Creek—*stream* ... WA-9
Ware Creek Ch—*church* ... NC-3
Ware Creek Sch—*school* ... NC-3
*Waref* ... FM-9
Ware Ferry (historical)—*locale* ... AL-4
Ware Gap—*gap* ... AL-4
Ware Grove Ch—*church* ... GA-3
Ware Hall—*hist pl* ... MA-1
**Wareham**—*pop pl* ... MA-1
**Wareham Center**—*pop pl* ... MA-1
Wareham (historical P.O.)—*locale* ... MA-1
Wareham HS—*school* ... MA-1
Wareham Narrows—*area* ... MA-1
Wareham Neck—*cape* ... MA-1
Wareham Plaza (Shop Ctr)—*locale* ... MA-1
Wareham River—*stream* ... MA-1
Wareham Station (historical)—*locale* ... MA-1
**Wareham (Town of)**—*pop pl* ... MA-1
Ware-Hardwick Covered Bridge—*hist pl* ... MA-1
Ware Hill—*summit* ... MS-4
Ware Hill—*summit* ... WA-9
Ware Hill Cem—*cemetery* ... MS-4
Ware Hollow—*valley* ... MO-7
Warehouse Bayou—*gut* ... LA-4
Warehouse Bayou—*stream* ... AR-4
Warehouse Bluff—*other* ... AK-9
Warehouse Canyon—*valley* ... UT-8
Warehouse Channel—*channel* ... AK-9
Warehouse Cove—*bay* ... VA-3
*Warehouse Creek* ... VA-3
Warehouse Creek—*stream* ... AK-9
Warehouse Creek—*stream* ... MD-2
Warehouse Creek—*stream* (2) ... VA-3
Warehouse District—*hist pl* ... KY-4
Warehouse District—*hist pl* ... UT-8
*Warehouse Landing* ... MD-2
Warehouse Landing—*locale* ... GA-3
Warehouse Point—*cape* (2) ... MD-2
Warehouse Point—*cape* (2) ... VA-3
**Warehouse Point**—*pop pl* (2) ... CT-1
Warehouse Point Elem Sch—*school* ... CT-1
Warehouse Prong—*stream* ... VA-3
Warehouse Riffle—*rapids* ... IN-6
Warehouse Rock—*summit* ... UT-8
Warehouse Row—*hist pl* ... CA-9
Warehouse Run—*stream* ... MD-2
Ware HS—*school* ... MA-1
Ware Industries Main Upper Dam—*dam* ... MA-1
**Wareingwood (subdivision)**—*pop pl* ... AL-4
*Wareiock* ... NC-3
Ware Island—*island* ... AL-4
Ware Island—*island* ... ID-8
Ware Island Airp—*airport* ... AL-4
Ware Knob—*summit* ... KY-4
Ware Lake—*lake* ... MI-6
Ware Lake—*lake* ... MS-4

Ware Lake—reservoir MO-7
Wareland—locale CO-8
Warelands—hist pl MA-1
Ware-Lyndon House—hist pl GA-3
Ware (Magisterial District)—fmr MCD VA-3
Ware Millyard Hist Dist—hist pl MA-1
Ware Mine—mine CA-9
Ware Mounds and Village Site—hist pl IL-6
Ware Mtn—summit WV-2
Ware Neck—cape VA-3
**Ware Neck**—pop pl VA-3
Ware Neck Point—cape VA-3
Ware Oil Field—oilfield KS-7
Warep FM-9
Ware Paper Mill—hist pl MA-1
Ware Parish Church—hist pl VA-3
**Ware Place**—pop pl SC-3
Ware Point MD-2
Ware Point—cape (2) MD-2
Ware Point—cape NC-3
Ware Point—cape (2) VA-3
Ware Point—summit KY-4
Ware Point Cove—bay MD-2
Ware Point Marsh—swamp MD-2
Ware Pond—lake GA-3
Ware Pond—lake MA-1
Ware Pond—reservoir AL-4
Ware Ridge—ridge KY-4
Ware Ridge—ridge WV-2
Ware River MA-1
Ware River—stream MA-1
Ware River—stream VA-3
Ware River Dam—dam MA-1
Ware River Point—cape VA-3
Ware River Rsvr—reservoir (2) MA-1
Ware Run—stream PA-2
Wares AL-4
**Waresboro**—pop pl GA-3
Waresboro (CCD)—cens area GA-3
Waresboro Cem—cemetery GA-3
Wares Bridge—bridge VA-3
Wares Bridge (historical)—bridge MS-4
Wares Buff MS-4
Wares Cem—cemetery VA-3
Wares Sch—school GA-3
Wares Sch—school KS-7
Wares Sch—school TX-5
Wares Chapel—church AR-4
Wares Chapel—church (2) NC-3
Wares Chapel—church OH-6
Wares Chapel—locale AR-4
Ware Sch (historical)—school MO-7
Ware School KS-7
Wares Creek MO-7
Wares Creek—stream FL-3
Wares Crossroads—locale GA-3
Wares Crossroads—locale VA-3
Wares Ferry Elem Sch—school AL-4
Wares Furnace (historical)—locale AL-4
Wares Grove Ch—church IL-6
Wares Grove (historical)—locale AL-4
Waresha Creek—stream OK-5
**Ware Shoals**—pop pl SC-3
Ware Shoals-Hodges (CCD)—cens area SC-3
Wares Island AL-4
Wares Lake—lake IL-6
Wares Machias Flight Park
Ultralight—airport WA-9
Ware Spring—spring UT-8
Wares Quarter Cem—cemetery AL-4
Ware's Tavern—hist pl MA-1
Wares Temple Holiness Ch—church AL-4
Ware Stick Point—cape VA-3
**Ware Subdivision**—pop pl UT-8
Waresville—locale GA-3
Waresville—locale TX-5
Waresville Cem—cemetery TX-5
**Wares Wharf**—pop pl VA-3
Ware Thorofare—channel NJ-2
**Waretown**—pop pl NJ-2
Waretown Creek—stream NJ-2
Ware Town Hall—hist pl MA-1
Waretown Harbor—bay NJ-2
**Waretown Junction**—pop pl NJ-2
Waretown Mill Branch NJ-2
**Ware (Town of)**—pop pl MA-1
Ware Village MA-1
Warf Airp—airport NC-3
WARF-AM (Jasper)—tower AL-4
Warf Branch—stream TN-4
Warf Cem—cemetery KY-4
Warf Cem—cemetery TN-4
Warfel Sch (abandoned)—school MO-7
Warfield MD-2
Warfield—locale GA-3
Warfield—locale TX-5
Warfield—locale VA-3
Warfield—locale WV-2
**Warfield**—pop pl KY-4
Warfield, Dr. Walter, Bldg—hist pl KY-4
Warfield, Pratt and Howell Company
Warehouse—hist pl IA-7
Warfield, William S., House—hist pl IL-6
**Warfieldburg**—pop pl MD-2
Warfield (CCD)—cens area KY-4
Warfield Cem—cemetery KY-4
Warfield Cem—cemetery MA-1
Warfield Cem—cemetery MO-7
Warfield Cem—cemetery TN-4
Warfield Creek—stream ID-8
Warfield Creek—stream OR-9
Warfield Creek—stream WY-8
Warfield Elem Sch—school FL-3
Warfield Hot Spring—spring ID-8
Warfield Landing—locale MS-4
Warfield Meadow—flat OR-9
Warfield Mtn—summit MA-1
Warfield Oil Field—oilfield TX-5
Warfield Park—park FL-3
Warfield Point—cape MS-4
Warfield Post Office (historical)—building TN-4
Warfield Revetment—levee MS-4
Warfield Run—stream WV-2
**Warfieldsburg**—pop pl MD-2
Warfield Sch—school TN-4
Warfield Sch—school VA-3
Warfields Point MS-4
Warfield Springs—spring WY-8
Warford Creek—stream NJ-2
**Warfordsburg**—pop pl PA-2
Warford Sch—school MO-7
War Fork—stream KY-4
War Fork—stream VA-3
War Fork Sch—school VA-3
War Gap TN-4
War Gap—gap (2) TN-4
War Gap Post Office (historical)—building TN-4
Warge Kijhlen DE-2
Wargelin, Nickolai, Homestead—hist pl ID-8
War God Spring—spring UT-8
Wargo Landing—locale AR-4
War Hill—summit GA-3
War Hill Church AL-4
War Hill Park—locale GA-3
War Horse Lake—reservoir MT-8
War Horse Natl Wildlife Ref—park MT-8
Warhouse Creek—stream WY-8
Warhouse Hollow—valley AR-4
Warhouse Trail—trail WY-8
WARI-AM (Abbeville)—tower AL-4
Warick—post sta OK-5
Warick Creek—stream NC-3
Warier Brook—stream NH-1
Wariets Creek NC-3
Warila Boarding House and
Sauna—hist pl MT-8
Warinanco Park—park NJ-2
Wariners Ledges—bench ME-1
**Waring**—pop pl GA-3
**Waring**—pop pl MD-2
**Waring**—pop pl PA-2
**Waring**—pop pl TX-5
Waring, Guy, Cabin—hist pl WA-9
Waring, Orville, T., House—hist pl NJ-2
Waring Canyon—valley UT-8
Waring Cem—cemetery KY-4
Waring Cem—cemetery MS-4
Waring Ch—church SC-3
Waring Creek WA-9
Waring Creek—stream WA-9
Waringer Bayou LA-4
Waring House—hist pl OH-6
Waring Mountains—other AK-9
Waring Ranch—locale AZ-5
Waring Sch—school OH-6
Waring Sch—school PA-2
Waring-Sinleheagan Creek WA-9
**Warington Hills**—pop pl MD-2
Warington Lake—lake WI-6
**Waring Township**—pop pl KS-7
War in the Pacific Natl Historical
Park—park GU-9
Warix Run KY-4
Warix Run—stream KY-4
Warkentin, Bernhard, Homestead—hist pl KS-7
Warkentin House—hist pl KS-7
Warkentin Mill—hist pl KS-7
Warkum Creek—stream WA-9
**Warland**—pop pl MT-8
Warland Creek—stream MT-8
Warland Peak—summit MT-8
Warland Sch—school MT-8
Warley—locale AL-4
Warley Creek—stream SC-3
Warleys AL-4
Warlick Cem—cemetery NC-3
Warlick Ch—church NC-3
Warlick Sch—school NC-3
Warlicks Chapel—church NC-3
**Warlinda**—pop pl MD-2
Warlings Ranch—locale CO-8
Warloch Creek AL-4
Warlock—locale TX-5
Warlock Mine—mine NV-8
Warlock Mine Group—mine CA-9
Warlock Spring—spring NV-8
Warloop Creek—stream AR-4
Warloup Reach—channel TX-5
Warlow, Mount—summit CA-9
Warmack Cem—cemetery AL-4
Warmack Cem—cemetery MO-7
Warmacks Landing (historical)—locale MS-4
Warmack Spring—spring AL-4
WARM-AM (Scranton)—tower PA-2
**Warman**—pop pl MN-6
War Man Creek—stream MT-8
War Man Mtn—summit MT-8
**Warm Beach**—pop pl WA-9
Warm Brook—stream (2) ME-1
Warm Brook—stream NY-2
Warm Brook—stream VT-1
Warm Brook Flow—lake NY-2
Warm Chuck Inlet—bay AK-9
Warm Corners Cem—cemetery MO-7
Warm Cove—valley UT-8
Warm Cove Branch—stream NC-3
Warm Cove Ridge—ridge UT-8
Warm Creek AR-4
Warm Creek ID-8
Warm Creek MO-7
Warm Creek NV-8
Warm Creek UT-8
Warm Creek—stream AK-9
Warm Creek—stream AZ-5
Warm Creek—stream (3) CA-9
Warm Creek—stream (13) ID-8
Warm Creek—stream (4) NV-8
Warm Creek—stream OR-9
Warm Creek—stream (3) UT-8
Warm Creek—stream WA-9
Warm Creek Bay—bay UT-8
Warm Creek Cabins (inundated)—locale UT-8
Warm Creek Golf Course—other CA-9
Warm Creek Meadow—flat CA-9
Warm Creek Ranch—locale ID-8
Warm Creek Ranch—locale NV-8
Warm Ditch Spring—spring UT-8
War Memorial Hosp—hospital LA-4
War Memorial Natatorium—hist pl HI-9
War Memorial Park—park AR-4
War Memorial Park—park MS-4
War Memorial Park—park (2) OK-5
War Memorial Park—park WV-2
War Memorial Stadium—other NY-2
Warmer Gulch—valley CO-8
Warm Fork—stream AR-4
Warm Fork—stream KY-4
Warm Fork—stream MO-7
Warm Fork Creek AR-4
Warm Fork Spring—spring MO-7
Warm Fork Spring River—stream AR-4
Warm Gulch—valley CA-9
Warm Hollow—valley KY-4
Warminster—locale PA-2
Warminster—locale VA-3
Warminster Ch—church VA-3
Warminster Gardens Cem—cemetery PA-2
**Warminster Heights**—pop pl PA-2
Warminster NADC Airp—airport PA-2
Warminster Naval Air Station PA-2
Warminster Sch—school PA-2
**Warminster (Township of)**—pop pl PA-2
**Warminster Village**—pop pl PA-2
Warm Lake—lake CA-9
Warm Lake—lake ID-8
Warm Lake—lake OR-9
Warm Lake—lake WA-9
**Warm Lake**—pop pl ID-8
Warm Lake Creek—stream ID-8
Warm Lake Lodge Campground—locale ID-8
Warm Lake Summit—summit ID-8
Warm Mineral Spring—spring OR-9
Warm Mineral Springs—hist pl FL-3
**Warm Mineral Springs**—pop pl FL-3
Warmouth Lake—lake FL-3
Warmouth Pond FL-3
Warm Owl Spring NV-8
Warm Pass Valley—valley AK-9
Warm Pit—cave AL-4
Warm Point—cliff (2) UT-8
Warm Pond NY-2
**Warm River**—pop pl ID-8
Warm River—stream ID-8
Warm River Butte—summit ID-8
Warm River Campground—locale ID-8
Warm River Spring—spring ID-8
Warm Run—stream IN-6
Warm Run—stream PA-2
Warm Run—stream VA-3
Warmsley Oil Field—oilfield TX-5
Warm Slough—gut MT-8
Warm Slough—stream ID-8
Warm Slough—stream NE-7
Warm Slough Sch—school NE-7
Warm Spring AZ-5
Warm Spring NV-8
Warmspring OR-9
Warm Spring—locale PA-2
Warm Spring—spring AK-9
Warm Spring—spring (7) AZ-5
Warm Spring—spring (7) CA-9
Warm Spring—spring CO-8
Warm Spring—spring (10) ID-8
Warm Spring—spring (2) MT-8
Warm Spring—spring (14) NV-8
Warm Spring—spring (3) NM-5
Warm Spring—spring (6) OR-9
Warm Spring—spring PA-2
Warm Spring—spring (5) UT-8
Warm Spring—spring WY-8
Warm Spring Butte—summit OR-9
Warm Spring Canyon AZ-5
Warm Spring Canyon CA-9
Warm Spring Canyon NM-5
Warm Spring Canyon OR-9
Warm Spring Canyon—valley AZ-5
Warm Spring Canyon—valley CA-9
Warm Spring Canyon—valley NV-8
Warm Spring Canyon—valley WY-8
Warm Spring Creek ID-8
Warm Spring Creek MT-8
Warm Spring Creek NV-8
Warmspring Creek OR-9
Warm Spring Creek—stream AZ-5
Warm Spring Creek—stream (10) ID-8
Warm Spring Creek—stream (2) MT-8
Warm Spring Creek—stream NV-8
Warm Spring Creek—stream (4) OR-9
Warm Spring Creek—stream WY-8
Warm Spring Creek Sch—school MT-8
Warm Spring Flat CA-9
Warm Spring Gulch—valley (2) ID-8
Warm Spring Hammock—island FL-3
Warm Spring Hills—summit UT-8
Warm Spring Mine—mine CA-9
Warm Spring Mountain UT-8
Warm Spring Mtn—summit WY-8
Warm Spring Point—cape AZ-5
Warm Spring Ranger Cabin—locale ID-8
Warm Spring Ridge—ridge WV-2
Warm Spring Rsvr—reservoir UT-8
Warm Spring Run—stream WV-2
Warm Springs ID-8
Warm Springs MT-8
Warm Springs NV-8
Warm Springs—locale (2) NV-8
**Warm Springs**—pop pl AL-4
**Warm Springs**—pop pl AR-4
**Warm Springs**—pop pl GA-3
**Warmsprings**—pop pl MT-8
**Warm Springs**—pop pl MT-8
**Warm Springs**—pop pl NV-8
**Warm Springs**—pop pl OR-9
**Warm Springs**—pop pl VA-3
Warm Springs—spring AK-9
Warm Springs—spring (4) AZ-5
Warm Springs—spring (2) CA-9
Warm Springs—spring CO-8
Warm Springs—spring GA-3
Warm Springs—spring (7) ID-8
Warm Springs—spring (2) MT-8
Warm Springs—spring (8) NV-8
Warm Springs—spring (4) NM-5
Warm Springs—spring (4) OR-9
Warm Springs—spring PA-2
Warm Springs—spring (6) UT-8
Warm Springs—spring WA-9
Warm Springs—spring (3) WY-8
Warm Springs—stream ID-8
Warm Springs—uninc pl CA-9
Warm Springs Ave Hist Dist—hist pl ID-8
Warm Springs Bar—bar ID-8
Warm Springs Bathhouses—hist pl VA-3
Warm Springs Bay—bay AK-9
Warm Springs Branch—stream GA-3
Warm Springs Branch—stream OR-9
Warm Springs Butte—summit OR-9
Warm Springs Cabin—locale OR-9
Warm Springs Camp—locale CA-9
Warm Springs Campground—locale GA-3
Warm Springs Campground—locale (2) ID-8
Warm Springs Campground—locale MT-8
Warm Springs Canal—canal ID-8
Warm Springs Canal—canal MT-8
Warm Springs Canal—canal OR-9
Warm Springs Canyon—valley (2) AZ-5
Warm Springs Canyon—valley (2) CA-9
Warm Springs Canyon—valley NV-8
Warm Springs Canyon—valley (2) NM-5
Warm Springs Canyon—valley OR-9
Warm Springs Canyon—valley UT-8
Warm Springs Canyon—valley (2) WA-9
Warm Springs Canyon—valley WY-8
Warm Springs (CCD)—cens area GA-3
Warm Springs (CCD)—cens area (2) OR-9
Warm Springs Cedars—area CO-8
Warm Springs Cem—cemetery VA-3
Warm Springs Ch—church MS-4
Warm Springs Cow Camp—locale MT-8
Warm Springs Creek ID-8
Warm Springs Creek MT-8
Warm Springs Creek NV-8
Warm Springs Creek OR-9
Warm Springs Creek WY-8
Warm Springs Creek—stream AR-4
Warm Springs Creek—stream (2) CA-9
Warm Springs Creek—stream (15) ID-8
Warm Springs Creek—stream MO-7
Warm Springs Creek—stream (12) MT-8
Warm Springs Creek—stream (8) OR-9
Warm Springs Creek—stream (2) UT-8
Warm Springs Creek—stream (3) WY-8
Warm Springs Dam—dam CA-9
Warmsprings Dam—dam OR-9
**Warm Springs District**—pop pl CA-9
Warm Springs Ditch—canal CO-8
Warm Springs Ditch—canal MT-8
Warm Springs Ditch—canal UT-8
Warm Springs Divide Truck Trail—trail CA-9
Warm Springs Draw—valley CO-8
Warm Springs Fish Canyon Truck
Trail—trail CA-9
Warm Springs Flat—flat AZ-5
Warm Springs Forest Service
Station—locale ID-8
Warm Springs Foundation—building GA-3
Warm Springs Gulch—valley ID-8
Warm Springs Hill—summit WY-8
Warm Springs Hist Dist—hist pl GA-3
**Warm Springs (historical)**—pop pl OR-9
Warm Springs Hollow—valley VA-3
**Warm Springs Ind Res**—pop pl OR-9
Warm Springs Junction—locale OR-9
Warm Springs Lake—lake AZ-5
Warm Springs (Magisterial
District)—fmr MCD VA-3
Warm Springs Meadow—swamp OR-9
Warm Springs Meadows—swamp OR-9
Warm Springs Meadow Trail—trail OR-9
Warm Springs Mountain—ridge NV-8
Warm Springs Mountain Trail—trail VA-3
Warm Springs Mtn—summit CA-9
Warm Springs Mtn—summit UT-8
Warm Springs Mtn—summit VA-3
Warm Springs Natl Fish Hatchery—other GA-3
Warm Springs Necktie Trail—trail CA-9
Warm Springs Park—park UT-8
Warm Springs Pass—gap ID-8
Warm Springs Point—cliff AZ-5
Warm Springs Point—summit (2) ID-8
Warm Springs Pump Canal—canal OR-9
Warm Springs Ranch NV-8
Warm Springs Ranch—locale (2) NV-8
Warm Springs Ranch—locale WY-8
Warm Springs Rapids—rapids ID-8
Warm Springs Rapids—rapids OR-9
Warm Springs River—stream OR-9
Warm Springs Rsvr—reservoir ID-8
Warm Springs Rsvr—reservoir NV-8
Warm Springs Rsvr—reservoir (2) OR-9
Warm Springs Run—stream VA-3
Warm Springs Saddle—gap ID-8
Warm Springs Sch—school (2) CA-9
Warm Springs Sch—school OR-9
Warm Springs Slough—stream UT-8
Warm Springs State Hosp—hospital MT-8
Warm Springs Summit—gap NV-8
Warm Springs (Township of)—fmr MCD AR-4
Warm Springs Trail—trail CA-9
Warm Springs Valley—basin NV-8
Warm Springs Valley—valley (2) CA-9
Warm Springs Valley—valley (2) OR-9
Warm Springs Valley—valley VA-3
Warm Springs Wash—stream AZ-5
Warm Spring Valley CA-9
Warm Spring Valley NV-8
Warm Spring Wash—valley UT-8
Warm Srings Ridge—ridge WV-2
Warm Spring Cliff—cliff CO-8
Warms Springs Creek—stream OR-9
Warm Sulphur Spring—spring CA-9
Warm Sulphur Springs—spring CA-9
Warm Swamp—stream NE-7
Warm Water Canyon—valley UT-8
Warm Well—well NM-5
Warnack Coral OR-9
Warne—locale NC-3
Warnecke Post Office
(historical)—building SD-7
Warneke Coulee—valley MT-8
Warneke Flat—flat MT-8
Warneke Hollow—valley OH-6
Warneke Spring—spring MT-8
Warneke Valley—basin NE-7
Warner AL-4
Warner NY-2
Warner—locale AR-4
Warner—locale CA-9
Warner—locale IL-6
Warner—locale OR-9
Warner—locale VA-3
Warner—locale WA-9
Warner—other KY-4
Warner—other NY-2
**Warner**—pop pl MI-6
**Warner**—pop pl NH-1
**Warner**—pop pl OH-6
**Warner**—pop pl (2) OK-5
**Warner**—pop pl (2) PA-2
**Warner**—pop pl SD-7
**Warner**—pop pl UT-8
Warner, Andrew J., House—hist pl UT-8
Warner, Capt. John T., House—hist pl AR-4
Warner, H. H., Bldg—hist pl NY-2
Warner, Jonathon, House—hist pl CT-1
Warner, J. W., House—hist pl FL-3
Warner, Lake—reservoir AL-4
Warner, Lake—reservoir MA-1
Warner, Maj. William, House—hist pl MO-7
Warner, Mount—summit MA-1
Warner, Oliver, Farmstead—hist pl NY-2
Warner, Orlando W., House—hist pl UT-8
Warner, P. C., First House—hist pl AZ-5
Warner, Samuel Adams, House—hist pl NY-2
Warner, Seth, House—hist pl IL-6
Warner, Solomon, House and
Mill—hist pl AZ-5
Warner Apartment Bldg—hist pl IA-7
Warner Ave Sch—school CA-9
Warner Bay—bay AK-9
Warner Bay—bay (2) NY-2
Warner Bayou—swamp MI-6
Warner Bay Spring—spring MO-7
Warner Branch—stream TN-4
Warner Branch—stream VA-3
Warner Branch—stream WV-2
Warner Branch—stream WI-6
Warner Bridge—bridge NE-7
Warner Bridge—bridge TN-4
Warner Bridge—other IL-6
Warner Brook—stream NY-2
Warner Brook—stream PA-2
Warner Brook—stream RI-1
Warner Brothers Studios—other CA-9
Warner Campground—park UT-8
Warner Canyon ID-8
Warner Canyon—valley CA-9
Warner Canyon—valley ID-8
Warner Canyon—valley OR-9
Warner Canyon—valley WA-9
Warner Canyon Ski Area—locale OR-9
Warner-Cather House—hist pl NE-7
Warner (CCD)—cens area OK-5
Warner Cem—cemetery AR-4
Warner Cem—cemetery CT-1
Warner Cem—cemetery IN-6
Warner Cem—cemetery KY-4
Warner Cem—cemetery LA-4
Warner Cem—cemetery MD-2
Warner Cem—cemetery MI-6
Warner Cem—cemetery MS-4
Warner Cem—cemetery NE-7
Warner Cem—cemetery (3) OH-6
Warner Cem—cemetery (2) OR-9
Warner Cem—cemetery SD-7
Warner Cem—cemetery (2) TN-4
Warner Cem—cemetery VT-1
Warner Cem—cemetery WV-2
Warner Cem Number One—cemetery TN-4
Warner Cem Number Two—cemetery TN-4
Warner Ch—church OH-6
Warner Ch—church WV-2
Warner Chapel—church AL-4
Warner Corners—locale NY-2
Warner Corral Spring—spring NV-8
Warner Cove—bay FL-3
Warner Cove—valley TN-4
Warner Creek AR-4
Warner Creek NY-2
Warner Creek OR-9
Warner Creek WI-6
Warner Creek—stream (2) AK-9
Warner Creek—stream AR-4
Warner Creek—stream CA-9
Warner Creek—stream FL-3
Warner Creek—stream LA-4
Warner Creek—stream (2) MI-6
Warner Creek—stream MT-8
Warner Creek—stream (2) NY-2
Warner Creek—stream (2) NC-3
Warner Creek—stream (5) OR-9
Warner Creek—stream (2) WI-6
Warner Creek Campground—locale CA-9
Warner Dam—dam PA-2
Warner Ditch—canal (2) IN-6
Warner Drain—canal MI-6
Warner Drain—stream MI-6
Warner Draw—valley WY-8
Warner Draw Debris Basin Dam—dam UT-8
Warner Draw Debris Basin Rsvr—reservoir UT-8
Warner East Bayou—gut FL-3
Warner Elem Sch—school DE-2
Warner Flat—flat ID-8
Warner Furnace TN-4
Warner Gap—gap MD-2
Warner Gap Hollow—valley MD-2
Warner Grade Rsvr—reservoir CA-9
Warner Grove Church MS-4
Warner Gulch—valley CA-9
Warner Gulch—valley NM-5
Warner Gulch—valley WA-9
Warner Gulch—valley WY-8
Warner Hall—hist pl VA-3
Warner Hill—summit (2) MA-1
Warner Hill—summit MI-6
Warner Hill—summit (2) MT-8
Warner Hill—summit NH-1
Warner Hill—summit NY-2
Warner Hill—summit PA-2
Warner Hill—summit (3) VT-1
Warner (historical)—locale AL-4
Warner Hollow—valley AR-4
Warner Hollow—valley MO-7
Warner Hollow—valley NY-2
Warner Hollow—valley PA-2
Warner Hollow—valley UT-8
Warner Hollow—valley WY-8
Warner Home—hist pl VT-1
Warner Hospital Airp—airport PA-2
Warner Hot Spring—spring CA-9
Warner House—hist pl CT-1
Warner Islands—island NY-2
**Warner Junction**—pop pl TX-5
Warner Lake—lake CA-9
Warner Lake—lake (2) IN-6
Warner Lake—lake LA-4
Warner Lake—lake (3) MI-6
Warner Lake—lake MN-6
Warner Lake—lake NY-2
Warner Lake—lake ND-7
Warner Lake—lake OR-9
Warner Lake—lake SD-7
Warner Lake—lake (3) WI-6
Warner Lake—reservoir AL-4
Warner Lake—reservoir OK-5
Warner Lake—reservoir UT-8
**Warner Lake (historical)**—pop pl OR-9
Warner Lakes—lake OR-9
Warner Lake State Public Shooting
Area—park SD-7
Warner-Lambert—airport NJ-2
Warner-Lambert Airp—airport PA-2
Warner Lambert Parking Lot—airport NJ-2
Warner Meadows Cross Roads AL-4
Warner Memorial Cem—cemetery OK-5
Warner Mine—mine MI-6
Warner Mine—mine NV-8
**Warner Mine Junction**—pop pl MI-6
Warner Mine (underground)—mine AL-4
Warner Mine (underground)—mine TN-4
Warner Mountain AR-4
Warner Mountains—range CA-9
Warner Mtn OR-9
Warner Mtn—summit MA-1
Warner Mtn—summit OK-5
Warner Mtn—summit OR-9
Warner Oil Field—oilfield KS-7
Warner Oil Field—oilfield TX-5
Warner Pacific Coll—school OR-9
Warner Park—park TN-4
Warner Park—park WI-6
Warner Park Historic Park—hist pl TN-4
**Warner Park (subdivision)**—pop pl (2) AZ-5
Warner Peak—summit OR-9
Warner Point—cape FL-3
Warner Point—cliff CO-8
Warner Point—summit CO-8
Warner Pond—lake CT-1
Warner Pond—lake ID-8
Warner Pond—lake (2) MA-1
Warner Pond—lake NY-2
Warner Pond—reservoir CT-1
Warner Pond—reservoir GA-3
Warner Pond—reservoir PA-2
Warner Post Office (historical)—building TN-4
Warner Prairie—flat WA-9
Warner Ranch—locale CA-9
Warner Ranch—locale WY-8
**Warner Ranch**—pop pl CA-9
Warner Ranger Station—locale UT-8
Warner Ravine—valley CA-9
Warner Reservoir AZ-5
Warner Reservoir MA-1
Warner Ridge—ridge UT-8
Warner River—stream NH-1
**Warner Robins**—pop pl GA-3
Warner Robins (CCD)—cens area GA-3
Warner Robins JHS—school GA-3
Warner Rsvr—reservoir WY-8
Warner Run WV-2
Warner Run—stream PA-2
Warner Run—stream (2) WV-2
Warners AL-4
Warner's NY-2
**Warners**—pop pl NY-2
Warners—uninc pl NJ-2
Warners Airp—airport PA-2
Warners Brook RI-1
Warnersburgh KS-7
Warner Sch DE-2
Warners Ch—church NC-3
Warner Sch—school CA-9
Warner Sch—school GA-3
Warner Sch—school ID-8
Warner Sch—school IN-6
Warner Sch—school MA-1
Warner Sch—school (3) MI-6
Warner Sch—school MO-7
Warner Sch—school (2) NE-7
Warner Sch—school NV-8
Warner Sch—school OH-6
Warner Sch—school PA-2
Warner Sch—school TN-4
Warner Sch (abandoned)—school MO-7
Warners-Congress Cem—cemetery OH-6
Warners Cove—bay MI-6
Warner's Creek MI-6
Warners Creek OR-9
Warners Creek Ch (historical)—church TN-4
Warner's Grant—fmr MCD VT-1
Warner's Island NY-2
Warners Lake MI-6
Warners Lake NY-2
Warners Landing Campgrounds—locale TX-5
Warners Mill—locale NJ-2
Warners Mill (historical)—locale TN-4
Warners Mill Pond—reservoir NJ-2
Warners Mill Stream—stream NJ-2
Warners Mountain AZ-5
Warner Southern Coll—school FL-3
Warners Point RI-1
Warners Point—cape MD-2
Warners Pond—reservoir MA-1
Warners Pond Dam—dam MA-1
Warners Post Office (historical)—building AL-4
Warner Spring—spring (2) NV-8
Warner Spring—spring (2) UT-8
Warner Spring—spring WA-9
**Warner Springs**—pop pl CA-9
Warner Springs Creek—stream WY-8
Warner's Ranch—hist pl CA-9
Warners Ranch—locale CA-9
Warners Station—locale NJ-2
Warner Station—locale PA-2
Warner Station—locale UT-8
Warner Storage Tank—reservoir AZ-5
Warnersville CA-9
**Warnersville (subdivision)**—pop pl NC-3
Warner Swamp—swamp AL-4
Warner Swamp—swamp CT-1
Warner Tank—reservoir AZ-5
Warner Theater—hist pl OH-6
Warner Theater—hist pl (2) PA-2
Warner Theatre—hist pl CT-1
Warnerton KS-7
**Warnerton**—pop pl LA-4
Warnertown—locale PA-2
**Warner (Town of)**—pop pl NH-1
**Warner (Town of)**—pop pl WI-6
**Warner Township**—pop pl SD-7

Warner (Township of)—pop pl ... MI-6
Warner Trail ... PA-2
Warner Union Sch—school ... CA-9
Warner Valley—basin ... UT-8
Warner Valley—pop pl ... OR-9
Warner Valley—valley ... CA-9
Warner Valley—valley ... OR-9
Warner Valley Campground—locale ... CA-9
Warner Valley (CCD)—cens area ... OR-9
Warner Valley Ranger Station—hist pl ... CA-9
Warner Valley Rim—cliff ... CA-9
Warner Valley Spring—spring ... UT-8
Warner Village—pop pl ... NJ-2
Warnerville—locale ... CA-9
Warnerville—locale ... NE-7
Warnerville—pop pl ... NY-2
Warnerville Hill—summit ... NY-2
Warnerville (historical P.O.)—locale ... MA-1
Warner West Bayou—gut ... FL-3
Warner Work Center—locale ... OR-9
Warner YMCA Camp—locale ... MS-4
Warnes Brook—stream ... NJ-2
Warnes Slough—lake ... SD-7
Warnett Lateral—canal ... ID-8
Warn Hill—summit ... PA-2
Warnica Springs—spring ... AZ-5
Warnick—locale ... WA-9
Warnick Campground—park ... UT-8
Warnick Canyon—valley ... CA-9
Warnick Creek ... OR-9
Warnicke Creek—stream ... OR-9
Warnick Gulch—valley ... UT-8
Warnick Point—cape ... MD-2
Warnick Run—stream ... MD-2
Warnicott Oil Field—oilfield ... LA-4
Warniho River ... HI-9
Warnimont Park—park ... WI-6
Warnimont Sch—school ... WI-6
Warnke Covered Bridge—hist pl ... OH-6
Warnke Hill—summit ... ND-7
Warn Lake—lake ... NY-2
Warnnersburgh ... KS-7
Warnnersburg (historical)—locale ... KS-7
Warnock—locale ... IL-6
Warnock—locale ... KY-4
Warnock—pop pl ... OH-6
Warnock, Dr. Francis B., House—hist pl ... IA-7
Warnock, William P., House—hist pl ... OR-9
Warnock And Barrow Pond—reservoir ... GA-3
Warnock Branch—stream ... KY-4
Warnock Cave—cave ... AL-4
Warnock Cem—cemetery ... IN-6
Warnock Cem—cemetery ... KY-4
Warnock Cem—cemetery ... OH-6
Warnock Corral—locale ... OR-9
Warnock Gulch—valley ... OR-9
Warnock House—hist pl ... KY-4
Warnock Mountain ... AL-4
Warnock Park—park ... GA-3
Warnock Po—locale ... KY-4
Warnock Pond—lake ... GA-3
Warnock Post Office (historical)—building ... TN-4
Warnock Ridge—ridge ... ID-8
Warnocks—locale ... WV-2
Warnock Spring—spring ... OR-9
Warnock Springs—locale ... AR-4
Warnock Station ... IN-6
Warnstaff Lake—lake ... IA-7
Warn Swamp*—stream ... NE-7
WARO-AM (Canonsburg)—tower ... PA-2
War Office—hist pl ... CT-1
War Of 1812 Battle Site—hist pl ... OH-6
War of 1812 Cem—cemetery ... NY-2
War Of 1812 Memorial Cem—cemetery ... PA-2
Waromontogus Pond ... ME-1
Warpaint Lake—lake ... MN-6
Warpath Hollow—valley ... PA-2
Warpath Valley—valley ... AZ-5
War Point—cape ... NC-3
Warpole Creek—stream ... OH-6
Warr—pop pl ... ID-8
War ra can he River ... ND-7
Warr Acres—pop pl ... OK-5
WARR-AM (Warrenton)—tower ... NC-3
Warranty Subdivision Five—pop pl ... UT-8
Warranty Subdivision Three—pop pl ... UT-8
Warrasketuck Creek ... NY-2
Warr Canyon—valley ... CO-8
Warr Cem—cemetery ... MS-4
Warr Cem—cemetery ... SC-3
Warr Cem—cemetery ... TN-4
Warren ... PA-2
Warren ... WI-6
Warren ... WY-8
Warren—locale ... CO-8
Warren—locale ... CT-1
Warren—locale ... MT-8
Warren—locale ... NM-5
Warren—locale ... NY-2
Warren—locale ... ND-7
Warren—locale ... PA-2
Warren—locale ... VA-3
Warren—locale ... WA-9
Warren—mine ... AZ-5
Warren—pop pl ... AZ-5
Warren—pop pl ... AR-4
Warren—pop pl ... CA-9
Warren—pop pl ... GA-3
Warren—pop pl ... ID-8
Warren—pop pl ... IL-6
Warren—pop pl ... IN-6
Warren—pop pl (2) ... KY-4
Warren—pop pl (2) ... ME-1
Warren—pop pl ... MD-2
Warren—pop pl ... MA-1
Warren—pop pl ... MI-6
Warren—pop pl ... MN-6
Warren—pop pl ... MO-7
Warren—pop pl ... NH-1
Warren—pop pl ... NY-2
Warren—pop pl ... OH-6
Warren—pop pl (2) ... OK-5
Warren—pop pl ... OR-9
Warren—pop pl ... PA-2
Warren—pop pl ... RI-1
Warren—pop pl ... TN-4
Warren—pop pl ... TX-5
Warren—pop pl ... UT-8
Warren—pop pl ... VT-1
Warren, Daniel Knight, House—hist pl ... OR-9
Warren, David, House—hist pl ... ME-1
Warren, Dr. Samuel, House—hist pl ... MA-1
Warren, Edward Kirk, House and Garage—hist pl ... IL-6
Warren, Lake—lake ... FL-3
Warren, Lake—lake ... NH-1
Warren, Lake—reservoir ... AL-4
Warren, Lake—reservoir ... PA-2
Warren, Langford H., House—hist pl ... MA-1
Warren, Moses, House—hist pl ... OH-6
Warren, Mount—summit ... AZ-5
Warren, Mount—summit ... CA-9
Warren, Mount—summit ... CO-8
Warren, Mount—summit ... NY-2
Warren, Mount—summit ... WY-8
Warren, Russell, House—hist pl ... CA-9
Warren, Stephen, House—hist pl ... WI-6
Warren, William, Two Rivers House Site and McDougall, Peter, Farmstead—hist pl ... MN-6
Warren Acad—school ... NC-3
Warren Acad (historical)—school ... AL-4
Warren and Ouachita Valley Railway Station—hist pl ... AR-4
Warren Ave Playfield—park ... WA-9
Warren Bayou—bay ... FL-3
Warren Bench—bench ... CA-9
Warren Block—hist pl ... ME-1
Warren Block—hist pl ... MA-1
Warren Borough—civil ... PA-2
Warren Bottom—bend ... CO-8
Warren Branch—stream (3) ... AL-4
Warren Branch—stream (2) ... AR-4
Warren Branch—stream ... IL-6
Warren Branch—stream (2) ... KY-4
Warren Branch—stream (2) ... MO-7
Warren Branch—stream ... OK-5
Warren Branch—stream ... SC-3
Warren Branch—stream (3) ... TN-4
Warren Branch—stream ... TX-5
Warren Branch—stream ... VA-3
Warren Branch—swamp ... SC-3
Warren Branch Sch—school ... MO-7
Warren Bridge—bridge ... WY-8
Warren Brook—stream (2) ... CT-1
Warren Brook—stream (3) ... ME-1
Warren Brook—stream ... MA-1
Warren Brook—stream (2) ... NH-1
Warrenburg—pop pl ... TN-4
Warren Canal—canal ... LA-4
Warren Canal—canal (2) ... UT-8
Warren Canyon—valley ... AZ-5
Warren Canyon—valley ... CA-9
Warren Canyon—valley ... OR-9
Warren Canyon—valley (2) ... UT-8
Warren Cave—cave ... FL-3
Warren Cave—cave ... TN-4
Warren (CCD)—cens area ... TX-5
Warren Cem—cemetery (5) ... AL-4
Warren Cem—cemetery (2) ... AR-4
Warren Cem—cemetery (3) ... GA-3
Warren Cem—cemetery (2) ... IL-6
Warren Cem—cemetery ... IN-6
Warren Cem—cemetery ... IA-7
Warren Cem—cemetery ... KY-4
Warren Cem—cemetery (2) ... LA-4
Warren Cem—cemetery ... MN-6
Warren Cem—cemetery (4) ... MS-4
Warren Cem—cemetery (2) ... MO-7
Warren Cem—cemetery (4) ... NY-2
Warren Cem—cemetery (2) ... OH-6
Warren Cem—cemetery ... OK-5
Warren Cem—cemetery (3) ... SC-3
Warren Cem—cemetery (10) ... TN-4
Warren Cem—cemetery ... TX-5
Warren Cem—cemetery ... UT-8
Warren Cem—cemetery ... VT-1
Warren Cem—cemetery ... VA-3
Warren Cem—cemetery ... WI-6
Warren (census name for Warren Center)—CDP ... MA-1
Warren Center ... IN-6
Warren Center—locale ... PA-2
Warren Center (census name Warren)—other ... MA-1
Warren Center Sch—school ... IA-7
Warren Central Elem Sch—school ... IN-6
Warren Central HS—school ... IN-6
Warren Central Sch—school ... MS-4
Warren Centre ... MA-1
Warren Centre ... PA-2
Warren Ch—church ... GA-3
Warren Ch—church ... IA-7
Warren Ch—church ... LA-4
Warren Ch—church ... MD-2
Warren Ch—church ... MO-7
Warren Ch—church ... OH-6
Warren Ch—church (2) ... TN-4
Warren Ch—church ... TX-5
Warren Channel—channel ... AK-9
Warren Chapel—church ... AR-4
Warren Chapel—church ... GA-3
Warren Chapel—church ... KY-4
Warren Chapel—church (3) ... NC-3
Warren Chapel—church ... TN-4
Warren Chapel—church ... WV-2
Warren Chapel African Methodist Episcopal Ch—church ... TN-4
Warren Chapel Branch—stream ... KY-4
Warren Chapel Cem—cemetery ... MS-4
Warren Church ... AL-4
Warren City—pop pl ... TX-5
Warren Clyde Park—park ... IL-6
Warren Commercial Hist Dist—hist pl ... OH-6
Warren Country Club—other ... AR-4
Warren County—civil ... MO-7
Warren County—civil ... NC-3
Warren (County)—pop pl ... GA-3
Warren (County)—pop pl ... IL-6
Warren County—pop pl ... IN-6
Warren (County)—pop pl ... KY-4
Warren County—pop pl ... MS-4
Warren (County)—pop pl ... MO-7
Warren County—pop pl ... NJ-2
Warren (County)—pop pl ... NY-2
Warren (County)—pop pl ... OH-6
Warren County—pop pl ... PA-2
Warren County—pop pl ... TN-4
Warren (County)—pop pl ... VA-3
Warren County Airp—airport ... NC-3
Warren County Branch—stream ... TN-4
Warren County Courthouse—building ... IA-7
Warren County Courthouse—building ... MS-4
Warren County Courthouse—building ... PA-2
Warren County Courthouse—building ... TN-4
Warren County Courthouse—hist pl ... GA-3
Warren County Courthouse—hist pl ... KY-4
Warren County Courthouse—hist pl ... PA-2
Warren County Courthouse and Circuit Court Bldg—hist pl ... MO-7
Warren County Fairgrounds—locale ... TN-4
Warren County Farm (historical)—locale ... MS-4
Warren County Farm (historical)—locale ... TN-4
Warren County General Hosp—hospital ... TN-4
Warren County Home—building ... IA-7
Warren County Home (historical)—locale ... TN-4
Warren County HS—school ... NC-3
Warren County HS—school ... TN-4
Warren County JHS—school ... TN-4
Warren County Memorial Airp—airport ... TN-4
Warren County Recreational Complex—park ... MS-4
Warren County Shop Ctr, The—locale ... MO-7
Warren Cove—bay ... AK-9
Warren Cove—cove ... MA-1
Warren Covered Bridge—hist pl ... VT-1
Warren Creek ... AR-4
Warren Creek ... OR-9
Warren Creek—pop pl ... CA-9
Warren Creek—stream ... AL-4
Warren Creek—stream (3) ... AK-9
Warren Creek—stream (3) ... CA-9
Warren Creek—stream ... GA-3
Warren Creek—stream (2) ... ID-8
Warren Creek—stream ... IN-6
Warren Creek—stream ... MI-6
Warren Creek—stream (3) ... MT-8
Warren Creek—stream ... NJ-2
Warren Creek—stream ... NC-3
Warren Creek—stream ... OK-5
Warren Creek—stream (4) ... OR-9
Warren Creek—stream ... SD-7
Warren Creek—stream ... TX-5
Warren Creek—stream ... VA-3
Warren Creek Ch—church ... TX-5
Warren Creek Falls—falls ... OR-9
Warren Creek Sch—school ... CA-9
Warren Crossroads—locale ... SC-3
Warren Crossroads—pop pl ... SC-3
Warren-Crowell House—hist pl ... TX-5
Warrendale—pop pl ... OR-9
Warrendale—pop pl ... PA-2
Warren Dale Cem—cemetery ... NC-3
Warrendale (historical)—locale ... KS-7
Warrendale Lower Range Channel—channel ... OR-9
Warrendale Sch—school ... KS-7
Warrendale Sch—school ... MA-1
Warrendale Sch—school ... MI-6
Warren Ditch—canal (2) ... CO-8
Warren Ditch—canal ... TN-4
Warren Ditch—stream ... MD-2
Warren Drain—canal ... CA-9
Warren Drain—canal ... WY-8
Warren Drain—stream ... MI-6
Warren Drain One—canal ... CA-9
Warren Drain Two—canal ... CA-9
Warren Drain Two B—canal ... CA-9
Warren Drain Two C—canal ... CA-9
Warren Drain Two C Number One—canal ... CA-9
Warren Drain Two E—canal ... CA-9
Warren Drain Two F—canal ... CA-9
Warren Draw—valley ... CO-8
Warren Draw—valley ... UT-8
Warren Draw Mine—mine ... SD-7
Warren Draw Wildlife Mngmt Area—park ... UT-8
Warren Dunes State Park—park ... MI-6
Warren E Hearnes Sch—school ... MO-7
Warren Elem Sch—school ... IN-6
Warren-Erwin House—hist pl ... MS-4
Warren Falls—falls ... ME-1
Warren Featherbone Company Office Bldg—hist pl ... MI-6
Warren Field—airport ... NC-3
Warren-Forbes Cemetery ... MS-4
Warren Fork—stream ... CA-9
Warren Franklin Pond—reservoir ... GA-3
Warren Gap—gap ... WA-9
Warren Gas Plant—oilfield ... TX-5
Warren G Harding Elem Sch—school ... IN-6
Warren Gilgos Creek—gut ... NC-3
Warren Glen—pop pl ... NJ-2
Warren Glen (Sta.)—pop pl ... NJ-2
Warren Grove—church ... NC-3
Warren Grove—pop pl ... NJ-2
Warren Grove Creek—stream ... IA-7
Warren Grove Sch—school ... IA-7
Warren Grove Target Area—military ... NJ-2
Warren-Guild-Simmons House—hist pl ... MS-4
Warren Gulch—valley (2) ... CO-8
Warren Gulch—valley ... SD-7
Warren Gulch Spring—spring ... SD-7
Warren Hall Chapel (historical)—church ... TN-4
Warrenham—locale ... PA-2
Warren Harding Sch—school ... NY-2
Warren Hill ... MA-1
Warren Hill—ridge ... AZ-5
Warren Hill—summit ... IN-6
Warren Hill—summit (3) ... ME-1
Warren Hill—summit ... MA-1
Warren Hill—summit ... MN-6
Warren Hill Cem—cemetery ... ME-1
Warren Hill Ch—church ... AR-4
Warren Hill Ch—church ... MS-4
Warren Hills ... IN-6
Warren Hills—pop pl ... IN-6
Warren H Manning State Park—park ... MA-1
Warren H Ohl Dam—dam ... PA-2
Warren H. Ohl Rsvr—reservoir ... PA-2
Warren Hollow—valley ... AR-4
Warren Hollow—valley (3) ... MO-7
Warren Hollow—valley ... NC-3
Warren Hollow—valley (8) ... TN-4
Warren Hood Lake Dam—dam ... MS-4
Warren House—hist pl ... VA-3
Warren House and Warren's Store—hist pl ... NC-3
Warren HS—school ... CA-9
Warren HS—school (2) ... OH-6
Warren Hughey Cem—cemetery ... MS-4
Warrenhurst—pop pl ... IL-6
Warren Investment Company Housing Group—hist pl ... OR-9
Warren Island ... NJ-2
Warren Island ... NY-2
Warren Island ... WY-8
Warren Island—island ... AK-9
Warren Island—island ... GA-3
Warren Island—island ... ID-8
Warren Island—island ... ME-1
Warren Island—island ... SC-3
Warren JHS—school ... MA-1
Warren Knob—summit (2) ... KY-4
Warren Lake ... MI-6
Warren Lake—lake (2) ... CA-9
Warren Lake—lake ... CO-8
Warren Lake—lake ... LA-4
Warren Lake—lake (5) ... MN-6
Warren Lake—lake ... MS-4
Warren Lake—lake ... MT-8
Warren Lake—lake ... OR-9
Warren Lake—lake ... WA-9
Warren Lake—reservoir ... CO-8
Warren Lake—reservoir ... IN-6
Warren Lake—reservoir ... NC-3
Warren Lake—reservoir ... TX-5
Warren Lake Dam—dam ... IN-6
Warren Lake Dam—dam ... NC-3
Warren Lakes—lake ... CO-8
Warren Lake State Wildlife Mngmt Area—park ... MN-6
Warren Landing—locale ... DE-2
Warren Landing—pop pl ... MA-1
Warren Lane Sch—school ... CA-9
Warren Levis Lake—reservoir ... IL-6
Warren Livestock Summer Camp—locale ... WY-8
Warren (Magisterial District)—fmr MCD ... WV-2
Warren Meadow—flat ... ID-8
Warren Meadows—flat ... ME-1
Warren Mill—locale ... VA-3
Warren Mill Creek ... NC-3
Warren Millpond—lake ... CT-1
Warren Millpond—reservoir ... NC-3
Warren Mountain Tank—reservoir ... AZ-5
Warren Mtn—summit ... AR-4
Warren Mtn—summit ... ID-8
Warren Neck ... RI-1
Warren Neck Creek—stream ... NC-3
Warren North (CCD)—cens area ... KY-4
Warren North Sch—school ... MI-6
Warren-Oak Sch—school ... MA-1
Warren Opera House Block and Hetherington Block—hist pl ... IA-7
Warren Park ... IL-6
Warren Park—park ... TX-5
Warren Park—pop pl ... IN-6
Warren Park—pop pl ... VA-3
Warren Park Wesleyan Ch—church ... IN-6
Warren Pass—gap ... MT-8
Warren Peak—summit ... AL-4
Warren Peak—summit ... AK-9
Warren Peak—summit ... CA-9
Warren Peak—summit ... CO-8
Warren Peak—summit ... MT-8
Warren Peaks—summit ... WY-8
Warren Pigott Cem—cemetery ... MS-4
Warren Pinnacle—pillar ... VT-1
Warren Place ... NJ-2
Warren Place (subdivision)—pop pl ... MS-4
Warren Plains—pop pl ... NC-3
Warren Plains Cem—cemetery ... NC-3
Warren Point—cape ... ME-1
Warren Point—cape ... MA-1
Warren Point—cape ... NJ-2
Warren Point—cape ... NY-2
Warren Point—cape ... RI-1
Warrenpoint—hist pl ... PA-2
Warren Point—pop pl ... NJ-2
Warren Point—pop pl ... RI-1
Warren Point Cave—cave ... PA-2
Warren Pond ... MA-1
Warren Pond ... NH-1
Warren Pond ... PA-2
Warren Pond ... VA-3
Warren Pond—lake ... ME-1
Warren Pond—lake ... NY-2
Warren Pond—reservoir ... CT-1
Warren Post Office (historical)—building ... TN-4
Warren Prospect—mine ... TN-4
Warren Public Library—hist pl ... OH-6
Warren Ranch—locale ... NE-7
Warren Ranch—locale ... NM-5
Warren Ranch—locale (2) ... TX-5
Warren Ranch (historical)—locale ... SD-7
Warren Refinery—other ... TX-5
Warren Reservoir Dam—dam ... MA-1
Warren Reservoir Lower Dam—dam ... RI-1
Warren Reservoir Upper Dam—dam ... RI-1
Warren Ridge—ridge ... NC-3
Warren Ridge—ridge ... OH-6
Warren River ... MA-1
Warren River ... RI-1
Warren River—stream ... RI-1
Warren Rocks—summit ... PA-2
Warren (RR name for Warrens)—other ... WI-6
Warren RR Station—building ... AZ-5
Warren Rsvr—reservoir ... MA-1
Warren Rsvr—reservoir ... PA-2
Warren Rsvr—reservoir ... RI-1
Warren Rsvr Upper—reservoir ... RI-1
Warren Run—stream ... OH-6
Warrens ... CA-9
Warrens—locale ... ID-8
Warrens—pop pl ... ID-8
Warrens—pop pl ... WI-6
Warrens Bend—bend ... TX-5
Warrens Bluff—cliff ... FL-3
Warrens Bluff—pop pl ... TN-4
Warrens Bluff Post Office (historical)—building ... TN-4
Warrensburg—pop pl ... IL-6
Warrensburg—pop pl ... MO-7
Warrensburg—pop pl ... NY-2
Warrensburg—pop pl ... OH-6
Warrensburg—pop pl ... TN-4
Warrensburg Airp—airport ... TN-4
Warrensburg Baptist Ch—church ... TN-4
Warrensburg (census name for Warrenburg Center)—CDP ... NY-2
Warrensburg Center (census name Warrensburg)—other ... NY-2
Warrensburgh Post Office ... TN-4
Warrensburg Mills Hist Dist—hist pl ... NY-2
Warrensburg Post Office (historical)—building ... TN-4
Warrensburg Sch—school ... TN-4
Warrensburg (Town of)—pop pl ... NY-2
Warrensburg Township—civil ... MO-7
Warrensburg United Methodist Ch—church ... TN-4
Warren Sch ... TN-4
Warren Sch—school ... AZ-5
Warren Sch—school (2) ... CA-9
Warren Sch—school (3) ... IL-6
Warren Sch—school ... KS-7
Warren Sch—school (3) ... MA-1
Warren Sch—school (2) ... MI-6
Warren Sch—school ... MO-7
Warren Sch—school ... MT-8
Warren Sch—school ... NE-7
Warren Sch—school ... NV-8
Warren Sch—school ... NY-2
Warren Sch—school (2) ... OH-6
Warren Sch—school ... OR-9
Warren Sch—school ... TN-4
Warren Sch—school ... TX-5
Warren Sch (abandoned)—school ... PA-2
Warrens Chapel—church ... MS-4
Warrens Chapel—church ... NC-3
Warren Sch (historical)—school ... AL-4
Warren Sch (historical)—school ... TN-4
Warrens Corners—pop pl ... NY-2
Warrens Cove ... MA-1
Warrens Crag ... CO-8
Warrens Creek—stream ... OR-9
Warrensdale ... OH-6
Warrens Fork—stream ... KY-4
Warren's Gore—fmr MCD ... VT-1
Warrens Grove Ch—church ... KY-4
Warrens Grove Sch (historical)—school ... TN-4
Warren Sheep Camp—locale ... WY-8
Warrens Hollow—valley ... UT-8
Warrens Lake—lake ... IN-6
Warrens Lake Dam—dam ... MS-4
Warren Slough—gut ... OR-9
Warren Slough—stream ... OR-9
Warren's Mill—hist pl ... DE-2
Warrens Mill—pop pl ... PA-2
Warrens Mill (historical)—locale ... MS-4
Warren Smith Cem—cemetery ... FL-3
Warren Smith Creek—stream ... AL-4
Warren Smith Hill—summit ... AL-4
Warren's Opera House—hist pl ... NE-7
Warren South—CDP ... PA-2
Warren South Sch—school ... MI-6
Warren Space Center Industrial Park—facility ... OH-6
Warrens Point ... MA-1
Warrens Point ... RI-1
Warrens Point—ridge ... PA-2
Warrens Pond—lake ... NY-2
Warrens Pond—reservoir (2) ... NC-3
Warrens Pond Dam—dam ... NC-3
Warren Spring ... AL-4
Warren Spring—spring ... AL-4
Warren Spring—spring ... OR-9
Warren Spring—spring ... TN-4
Warren Springs—locale ... TX-5
Warren Springs—spring ... AL-4
Warrens Ranch (historical)—locale ... SD-7
Warrens Savanna—swamp ... SC-3
Warrens Spring—spring ... UT-8
Warrens Station ... NC-3
Warrens Store—locale ... VA-3
Warren State Hosp—hospital ... PA-2
Warren State Hosp Farm Colony—hospital ... PA-2
Warren Station—locale ... ME-1
Warren Stephens Homestead—locale ... OR-9
Warren Stewart Cem—cemetery ... AL-4
Warrens Trailer Park—pop pl ... NC-3
Warren Street Methodist Ch—church ... AL-4
Warren Street Methodist Episcopal Ch ... AL-4
Warren Street Sch—school ... NY-2
Warren Summit—gap ... ID-8
Warrensville ... OH-6
Warrensville ... VA-3
Warrensville—pop pl ... NC-3
Warrensville—pop pl ... OH-6
Warrensville—pop pl ... PA-2
Warrensville Cem—cemetery ... OH-6
Warrensville Heights—pop pl ... OH-6
Warrensville (Township of)—civ div ... OH-6
Warrensville West Cem—cemetery ... OH-6
Warren Swamp—stream ... VA-3
Warren Swamp—swamp ... NY-2
Warren Swamp—swamp ... TX-5
Warrens Well (Dry)—well ... CA-9
Warren Tannery Brook—stream ... MA-1
Warren Tavern—locale ... PA-2
Warren Tavern Complex—hist pl ... OH-6
Warren Tavern Post Office (historical)—building ... PA-2
Warren Terrace—pop pl ... GA-3
Warren Terrace—pop pl ... MA-1
Warren Tison Ranch—locale ... OR-9
Warrenton ... AL-4
Warrenton—pop pl ... AL-4
Warrenton—pop pl ... GA-3
Warrenton—pop pl ... IN-6
Warrenton—pop pl ... KY-4
Warrenton—pop pl ... MS-4
Warrenton—pop pl ... MO-7
Warrenton—pop pl ... NC-3
Warrenton—pop pl ... OH-6
Warrenton—pop pl ... OR-9
Warrenton—pop pl ... TX-5
Warrenton—pop pl ... VA-3
Warrenton, Lake—lake ... MO-7
Warrenton Cave—cave ... AL-4
Warrenton (CCD)—cens area ... GA-3
Warrenton Cem—cemetery ... AL-4
Warrenton Ch—church ... AL-4
Warrenton Ch—church ... NC-3
Warrenton Ch—church ... SC-3
Warrenton City Pond—reservoir ... GA-3
Warrenton Country Club—locale ... NC-3
Warrenton Dam—dam ... OR-9
Warrenton Elem Sch—school ... MS-4
Warrenton Estates (subdivision)—pop pl ... AL-4
Warrenton Heights Recreation Lake Dam—dam ... MS-4
Warrenton Heights (subdivision)—pop pl ... MS-4
Warrenton Hist Dist—hist pl ... NC-3
Warrenton Hist Dist—hist pl ... VA-3
Warrenton HS—school ... OR-9
Warrenton Rsvr—reservoir ... OR-9
Warrenton Rsvr—reservoir ... VA-3
Warrenton Sch—school ... GA-3
Warrenton Sch—school ... OR-9
Warrenton Sch (historical)—school ... AL-4
Warrenton State Wildlife Area—park ... MO-7
Warrenton Station ... NC-3
Warrenton Subdivision (subdivision)—pop pl ... AL-4
Warrenton (Township of)—fmr MCD ... NC-3
Warrenton (Township of)—pop pl ... MN-6
Warrenton Training Center—school ... VA-3
Warrenton Upper Range Channel—channel ... OR-9
Warrenton Woolen Mill—hist pl ... CT-1
Warrentown ... IN-6
Warrentown—pop pl ... MA-1
Warrentown—pop pl ... OH-6
Warrentown—pop pl ... WI-6
Warrentown Coulee—valley ... WI-6
Warren Town Hall—building ... ND-7
Warren (Town of)—pop pl ... CT-1
Warren (Town of)—pop pl ... ME-1
Warren (Town of)—pop pl ... MA-1
Warren (Town of)—pop pl ... NH-1
Warren (Town of)—pop pl ... NY-2
Warren (Town of)—pop pl ... RI-1
Warren (Town of)—pop pl ... VT-1
Warren (Town of)—pop pl (2) ... WI-6
Warrentown Ridge—ridge ... WI-6
Warren Townsend Park—park ... MI-6
Warren Township—civil (2) ... MO-7
Warren Township—fmr MCD (6) ... IA-7
Warren Township—pop pl ... ND-7
Warren Township—pop pl (2) ... SD-7
Warren Township Hall—building ... SD-7
Warren (Township of)—pop pl (2) ... IL-6
Warren (Township of)—pop pl (6) ... IN-6
Warren (Township of)—pop pl ... MI-6
Warren (Township of)—pop pl ... MN-6
Warren (Township of)—pop pl ... NJ-2
Warren (Township of)—pop pl (5) ... OH-6
Warren (Township of)—pop pl (2) ... PA-2
Warren United Methodist Church and Parsonage—hist pl ... RI-1
Warren Upper Reservoir Dam—dam ... MA-1
Warren Upper Rsvr—reservoir ... MA-1
Warren Valley—valley ... MO-7
Warren Valley Sch—school ... MI-6
Warrenville ... NJ-2
Warrenville—locale ... WA-9
Warrenville—pop pl ... CT-1
Warrenville—pop pl ... IL-6
Warrenville—pop pl ... NJ-2
Warrenville—pop pl ... SC-3
Warrenville Sch—school ... CT-1
Warren (Warrenville)—pop pl ... NJ-2
Warren Waterfront Hist Dist—hist pl ... RI-1
Warren Well—well ... AZ-5
Warren Well—well ... WY-8
Warren West Well—well ... NM-5
Warren Wilson Coll—school ... NC-3
Warrenwood Elem Sch—school ... NC-3
Warren Woods ... SD-7
Warren Woods—pop pl ... VA-3
Warren Woods—uninc pl ... VA-3
Warren Woods HS—school ... MI-6
Warren Woods State Park—park ... MI-6
Warrenwood (subdivision)—pop pl ... NC-3
Warreruza River ... KS-7
Warrick—locale ... MT-8
Warrick (Alcoa Plant)—pop pl ... IN-6
Warrick Branch—stream ... NC-3
Warrick County—pop pl ... IN-6
Warrick Creek—stream ... AL-4
Warrick Hollow—valley ... AR-4
Warrick Mountain ... VA-3
Warrick Ranch—locale ... CO-8
Warricott ... PA-2
War Ridge ... WV-2
War Ridge—ridge ... TN-4
Warrigue Branch ... VA-3
Warrigus Branch ... VA-3
Warriner Draw—valley ... WY-8
Warriner Pond—lake ... PA-2
Warring Canyon—valley ... CA-9
Warring Park—park ... CA-9
Warring Sch—school ... NY-2
Warrington ... SD-7
Warrington—locale ... NJ-2
Warrington—pop pl ... FL-3
Warrington—pop pl ... IL-6
Warrington—pop pl ... IN-6
Warrington—pop pl ... PA-2
Warrington Airp—airport ... PA-2
Warrington Assembly of God Ch—church ... FL-3
Warrington Baptist Ch—church ... FL-3
Warrington Branch—stream ... VA-3
Warrington Cem—cemetery ... AR-4
Warrington Cem—cemetery ... TN-4
Warrington Field (airport)—airport ... DE-2
Warrington JHS—school ... FL-3
Warrington Lake—reservoir ... PA-2
Warrington Manor (subdivision)—pop pl ... DE-2
Warrington Meetinghouse—hist pl ... PA-2
Warrington Mill Dam—dam ... NJ-2
Warrington Millpond—reservoir ... NJ-2
Warrington Neck—cape ... DE-2
Warrington Sch—school ... FL-3
Warrington Sch—school ... PA-2
Warrington Site—hist pl ... DE-2
Warrington Stone Bridge—hist pl ... NJ-2
Warrington (Township of)—pop pl (2) ... PA-2
Warrington Township Retention Basin Dam—dam ... PA-2
Warrington Village (Shop Ctr)—locale ... FL-3
Warrior—pop pl ... AL-4
Warrior—pop pl ... NC-3
Warrior Acad—school ... AL-4
Warrior Bottom—flat ... AR-4
Warrior Branch ... OR-9
Warrior Bridge ... AL-4

Warrior Canal—canal CO-8
Warrior Canal—canal MS-4
Warrior Canyon—valley AZ-5
Warrior (CCD)—cens area AL-4
Warrior Cem—cemetery AL-4
Warrior Ch—church AL-4
Warrior Chapel (historical)—church AL-4
Warrior Ch (historical)—church AL-4
*Warrior Creek* NC-3
Warrior Creek—stream AL-4
Warrior Creek—stream AR-4
Warrior Creek—stream GA-3
Warrior Creek—stream MS-4
Warrior Creek—stream MT-8
Warrior Creek—stream (2) NC-3
Warrior Creek—stream OR-9
Warrior Creek—stream PA-2
Warrior Creek—stream SC-3
Warrior Creek Boat Ramp—locale NC-3
Warrior Creek Ch—church SC-3
Warrior Creek Mtn—summit NC-3
Warrior-Creek Stand (CCD)—cens area AL-4
Warrior-Creek Stand Division—civil AL-4
Warrior Division—civil AL-4
Warrior Elem Sch—school AL-4
*Warrior Fork* NC-3
Warrior Fork—stream NC-3
Warrior Fork—stream WV-2
Warrior Gap—gap NC-3
Warrior Gap—gap PA-2
**Warrior Heights (subdivision)**—pop pl AL-4
Warrior Hill Ch—church AL-4
Warrior Hollow—valley TX-5
Warrior Hotel—hist pl IA-7
Warrior HS—school AL-4
*Warrior Lake* CA-9
Warrior Lake—lake AL-4
Warrior Lake—lake CA-9
Warrior Lake—lake WI-6
Warrior Lake—reservoir AL-4
Warrior Lake—reservoir NC-3
Warrior Lake Dam—dam NC-3
Warrior Lakes—lake ID-8
Warrior Lock and Dam—dam AL-4
Warrior Lock and Dam Public Use Area—park AL-4
*Warriormark* PA-2
*Warrior Mine* WV-2
Warrior Mine—mine NV-8
**Warriormine**—pop pl WV-2
Warrior Mountain Ch—church NC-3
Warrior Mountain Lake—reservoir NC-3
Warrior Mountains—range NC-3
Warrior MS—school AL-4
*Warrior Mtn* NC-3
Warrior Mtn—summit CO-8
Warrior Mtn—summit MD-2
Warrior Mtn—summit MT-8
Warrior Mtn—summit (2) NC-3
Warrior Number One Mine (underground)—mine AL-4
Warrior Peak—summit WA-9
Warrior Peaks—summit WY-8
Warrior P.O. (historical)—locale AL-4
Warrior Point—cape NV-8
Warrior Point—cape OR-9
**Warrior Ridge**—pop pl PA-2
Warrior Ridge—ridge MD-2
Warrior Ridge—ridge (2) PA-2
Warrior Ridge Dam—dam PA-2
Warrior Ridge Sch (historical)—school PA-2
*Warrior River* AL-4
Warrior River Ch—church AL-4
Warrior River Mine (underground)—mine AL-4
*Warrior River Missionary Baptist Church* AL-4
Warrior Rock—pillar OR-9
Warrior Rock Range—channel OR-9
Warrior Rock Range—range WA-9
*Warrior Run* PA-2
Warrior Run—locale PA-2
**Warrior Run**—pop pl PA-2
Warrior Run—stream MD-2
Warrior Run—stream PA-2
Warrior Run Borough—civil PA-2
Warrior Run Ch—church PA-2
Warrior Run HS—school PA-2
**Warrior Run (Peely)**—pop pl PA-2
Warrior Run Presbyterian Church—hist pl PA-2
Warrior Sch—school IL-6
Warrior Sch—school OK-5
Warrior Sch (abandoned)—school PA-2
Warrior Sch (historical)—school AL-4
Warrior Shaft Mine (underground)—mine AL-4
*Warrior Siding* AL-4
*Warrior's Mark* PA-2
**Warriors Mark**—pop pl PA-2
*Warriorsmark Creek* PA-2
Warriors Mark Elem Sch—school PA-2
Warriors Mark Mine—mine CO-8
Warriors Mark Run—stream (2) PA-2
**Warriors Mark (Township of)**—pop pl PA-2
Warriors Passage Trail—trail TN-4
Warriors Path State Park—park PA-2
Warriors Path State Park—park TN-4
Warriors Point—cliff PA-2
*Warriors Rock* OR-9
*Warriors Run* PA-2
*Warrior Stand* AL-4
**Warriorstand**—pop pl AL-4
Warrior Stand Cem—cemetery AL-4
*Warrior Stand Post Office* AL-4
Warriorstand Post Office (historical)—building AL-4
Warriorstand Sch—school AL-4
*Warrior Station* AL-4
Warrior Swamp—swamp FL-3
Warrior Trail—trail PA-2
Warrior Valley—valley AL-4
Warrior View Mine (underground)—mine AL-4
Warriorville Post Office (historical)—locale AL-4
**Warrior Woods (subdivision)**—pop pl NC-3
**Warroad**—pop pl MN-6
*Warroad River* MN-6
Warroad River—stream MN-6
Warrock Mine—mine NM-5
*Warronoco* MA-1
Warrs Lake—lake AL-4
Warrs Lake—reservoir AL-4
War Run—stream IN-6
**Warrwood Subdivision**—pop pl UT-8
*Warsaw* GA-3
Warsaw—fmr MCD NE-7
Warsaw—locale (2) GA-3
Warsaw—locale IA-7
Warsaw—locale MS-4
**Warsaw**—pop pl AL-4
**Warsaw**—pop pl AR-4
**Warsaw**—pop pl IL-6
**Warsaw**—pop pl IN-6
**Warsaw**—pop pl KY-4
**Warsaw**—pop pl (2) MN-6
**Warsaw**—pop pl MS-4
**Warsaw**—pop pl MO-7
**Warsaw**—pop pl NY-2
**Warsaw**—pop pl NC-3
**Warsaw**—pop pl ND-7
**Warsaw**—pop pl OH-6
**Warsaw**—pop pl (3) PA-2
**Warsaw**—pop pl SC-3
**Warsaw**—pop pl TX-5
**Warsaw**—pop pl VA-3
Warsaw Acad—hist pl NY-2
Warsaw and Florence Ferry—locale IN-6
*Warsaw Baptist Church* MS-4
Warsaw Bar—bar AL-4
Warsaw Branch—stream KY-4
Warsaw Branch—stream TX-5
Warsaw Canyon—valley AZ-5
Warsaw (CCD)—cens area KY-4
Warsaw Cem—cemetery GA-3
Warsaw Cem—cemetery NE-7
Warsaw Cem—cemetery NY-2
Warsaw Cem—cemetery SC-3
*Warsaw Cemetery* MS-4
Warsaw Center—locale TX-5
Warsaw Ch—church LA-4
Warsaw Ch—church SC-3
Warsaw Courthouse and Jail Hist Dist—hist pl IN-6
*Warsaw Creek* TX-5
Warsaw Creek—stream TX-5
Warsaw Cut Glass Company—hist pl IN-6
Warsaw Cut Off—channel AL-4
Warsaw Elem Sch—school NC-3
Warsaw Ferry (historical)—locale AL-4
Warsaw Flats—flat SC-3
Warsaw Freshman HS—school IN-6
*Warsaw Gulch* AZ-5
Warsaw Hist Dist—hist pl IL-6
Warsaw Hist Dist—hist pl KY-4
Warsaw (historical)—locale IA-7
Warsaw (historical)—locale MS-4
Warsaw (historical)—locale TX-5
Warsaw HS—school IN-6
*Warsaw Island* GA-3
Warsaw Island—island SC-3
*Warsaw JHS* NC-3
Warsaw JHS (historical)—school NC-3
**Warsaw Junction**—pop pl OH-6
Warsaw Landing—locale LA-4
**Warsaw Landing**—pop pl LA-4
Warsaw MS—school IN-6
Warsaw Municipal Airp—airport IN-6
Warsaw Oil Field—oilfield TX-5
Warsaw Run—stream IL-6
Warsaw Sch—school PA-2
Warsaw Sch—school SC-3
Warsaw Sch—school WA-9
*Warsaw Sound* GA-3
Warsaw Spring—spring AZ-5
Warsaw Tank—reservoir AZ-5
**Warsaw (Town of)**—pop pl NY-2
Warsaw Township—civil PA-2
Warsaw (Township of)—fmr MCD NC-3
**Warsaw (Township of)**—pop pl IL-6
**Warsaw (Township of)**—pop pl (2) MN-6
**Warsaw (Township of)**—pop pl PA-2
Warsaw Windmill—locale TX-5
Wars Branch—stream TN-4
Warsham Creek—stream OK-5
Warshauer Mansion—hist pl CO-8
Warshaver Cem—cemetery CO-8
War Shoal Branch—stream KY-4
Warsing Dam—dam ND-7
Warsing Sch (historical)—school PA-2
Warson Cem—cemetery NC-3
Warson Sch—school MI-6
**Warson Woods**—pop pl MO-7
War Spur—ridge VA-3
War Spur Branch—stream VA-3
Warstler Sch—school OH-6
Warszawa Neighborhood District—hist pl OH-6
Wart, The—summit WA-9
**Wartburg**—pop pl IL-6
**Wartburg**—pop pl TN-4
Wartburg Acad (historical)—school TN-4
Wartburg Blue Gem Mine (surface)—mine TN-4
Wartburg (CCD)—cens area TN-4
Wartburg Cem—cemetery TN-4
Wartburg Coll—school (2) IA-7
Wartburg Division—civil TN-4
Wartburg First Baptist Ch—church TN-4
*Wartburgh Post Office* TN-4
Wartburg Post Office—building TN-4
Wartburg School, The—school NY-2
Wartburg Seminary—school IA-7
Wartburg Swiss Reformed Ch—church TN-4
Wartburg Teachers' Seminary—hist pl IA-7
Wart Creek—stream ID-8
Wartenbe Cem—cemetery IN-6
Warter Cem—cemetery TN-4
Warters Mtn—summit TX-5
*Wartham Creek* CA-9
Wartham Cem—cemetery CA-9
Warthan Cem—cemetery TX-5
Warthan Creek—stream CA-9
Warth Cem—cemetery IN-6
*Warthem Creek* CA-9
**Warthen**—pop pl GA-3
Warthen (CCD)—cens area GA-3
*Warthen Creek* CA-9
*Warthen's Store* GA-3
Wart Lake—lake MN-6
*Warton's* AR-4
Wart on Tree Tank—reservoir CA-9
Wart Peak—summit OR-9
Wart Point—cape AK-9
Wartrace—locale IL-6
**Wartrace**—pop pl TN-4
Wartrace Baptist Ch—church TN-4
Wartrace (CCD)—cens area TN-4
Wartrace Cem—cemetery (2) TN-4
Wartrace Ch—church TN-4
Wartrace Creek—stream (3) TN-4
Wartrace Creek Cave—cave TN-4
*Wartrace Depot Post Office* TN-4
Wartrace Division—civil TN-4
Wartrace Lake—lake TN-4
Wartrace Lake—reservoir TN-4
Wartrace Lake Dam—dam TN-4
Wartrace Post Office—building TN-4
Wartrace Sch—school (2) TN-4
Wartrace United Methodist Ch—church TN-4
WARU-AM (Peru)—tower IN-6
WARU-FM (Peru)—tower IN-6
*Waruku River* HI-9
War Valley—valley TN-4
WARV-AM (Warwick)—tower RI-1
WARV-AM (Warwick-East Greenwich)—tower RI-1
Warvel Park—park IN-6
War Veterans Park—park NY-2
Warvet Lake—lake WI-6
Warwarofsky Cem—cemetery TX-5
Warwhoop Springs—spring MT-8
*Warwick* OH-6
*Warwick* VA-3
Warwick—locale CO-8
Warwick—locale DE-2
Warwick—locale KS-7
Warwick—locale PA-2
Warwick—locale TX-5
Warwick—locale WA-9
Warwick—locale WV-2
Warwick—other KY-4
**Warwick**—pop pl GA-3
**Warwick**—pop pl MD-2
**Warwick**—pop pl MA-1
**Warwick**—pop pl NY-2
**Warwick**—pop pl ND-7
**Warwick**—pop pl OK-5
**Warwick**—pop pl PA-2
**Warwick**—pop pl RI-1
Warwick—uninc pl VA-3
Warwick, The—hist pl PA-2
*Warwick Bay* NC-3
Warwick Branch—stream VA-3
Warwick Brook—stream NY-2
Warwick Brook—stream RI-1
Warwick (CCD)—cens area GA-3
Warwick Cem—cemetery MA-1
Warwick Cem—cemetery MO-7
Warwick Cem—cemetery NY-2
Warwick Cem—cemetery NC-3
Warwick Cem—cemetery ND-7
Warwick Cem—cemetery TN-4
*Warwick Centre* MA-1
Warwick Channel—channel VA-3
Warwick Civic Center Hist Dist—hist pl RI-1
Warwick Corner—locale VA-3
Warwick County Courthouses—hist pl VA-3
*Warwick Court House* VA-3
Warwick Cove—bay DE-2
Warwick Cove—bay RI-1
Warwick Dam—dam ND-7
Warwick Ditch—canal IN-6
Warwick Drain—stream MI-6
Warwick Elem Sch—school PA-2
Warwick Furnace/Forms—hist pl PA-2
**Warwick Gardens**—pop pl VA-3
Warwick Gut—stream DE-2
Warwick Hills—summit TX-5
Warwick Hills Golf Course—other MI-6
Warwick HS—school PA-2
Warwick HS—school VA-3
Warwick Lake—reservoir GA-3
Warwick Lake Dam—dam MS-4
**Warwick Lawns**—pop pl VA-3
*Warwick Light* RI-1
Warwick Lighthouse—hist pl RI-1
*Warwick Manufacturing Company Dam* MA-1
Warwick Mill Bay (Carolina Bay)—swamp NC-3
Warwick Mill Pond—reservoir NC-3
Warwick Mills—hist pl PA-2
Warwick MS—school PA-2
Warwick Mtn—summit NY-2
Warwick Mtn—summit VA-3
*Warwick Neck* RI-1
Warwick Neck—cape RI-1
Warwick on the James—unic pl VA-3
**Warwick Park (subdivision)**—pop pl DE-2
Warwick Point—cape DE-2
Warwick Point—cape RI-1
*Warwick Pond* NC-3
Warwick Pond—lake RI-1
Warwick-Rhodes Cem—cemetery OH-6
*Warwick River* VA-3
Warwick River—stream MD-2
Warwick River—stream VA-3
Warwick River Sch—school VA-3
*Warwick Rsvr* GA-3
Warwick Rsvr—reservoir NY-2
*Warwick Run* VA-3
Warwick Run—stream WV-2
Warwick Sch—school NJ-2
Warwick Sch—school PA-2
Warwick Sch—school TX-5
Warwicks Cross Roads Post Office (historical)—building TN-4
*Warwick Senior HS* PA-2
Warwick State For—forest MA-1
Warwick State Training School for Boys—other NY-2
**Warwick (St. Marys)**—pop pl PA-2
*Warwicks Tripoli Cave* AL-4
Warwick Swamp—stream VA-3
Warwicktown—locale TN-4
**Warwick (Town of)**—pop pl MA-1
**Warwick (Town of)**—pop pl NY-2
**Warwick Township**—pop pl ND-7
**Warwick (Township of)**—pop pl OH-6
**Warwick (Township of)**—pop pl (3) PA-2
Warwick Valley HS—school NY-2
**Warwick Village**—pop pl VA-3
Warwick Village—unic pl AZ-5
Warwick Village Hist Dist—hist pl NY-2
Warwick Yacht Club—other VA-3
Warwir—locale MP-9
Warwoman Creek—stream GA-3
*Warwoman Dell* GA-3
**Warwoman Dell**—pop pl GA-3
Warwoman Dell Picnic Grounds—locale GA-3
Warwoman Ford—locale GA-3
Warwoman Wildlife Mngmt Area—park GA-3
**Warwood**—pop pl WV-2
*Warwor* MP-9
Wary Lake—reservoir KS-7
Warzecha Ranch—locale TX-5
Wasa (historical)—locale ND-7
Wasai, Baie de—bay MI-6
*Wasa Mill* PA-2
W A Sanders Pond Dam—dam MS-4
**Wasas**—pop pl MI-6
*Wasatch* UT-8
Wasatch—cens area UT-8
Wasatch—mine UT-8
Wasatch Acad—hist pl UT-8
Wasatch Baptist Ch—church UT-8
Wasatch-Cache Natl For—forest UT-8
Wasatch Camp—locale CO-8
Wasatch Canal—canal UT-8
Wasatch Canyons Hosp—hospital UT-8
Wasatch Ch of Christ—church UT-8
Wasatch County—civil UT-8
Wasatch County Hosp—hospital UT-8
Wasatch County Hospital Heliport—airport UT-8
Wasatch County HS—school UT-8
Wasatch Creek—stream UT-8
Wasatch Creek—stream WY-8
Wasatch Ditch—canal UT-8
Wasatch Division—civil UT-8
Wasatch Drain Tunnel—mine UT-8
Wasatch Front Industrial Park—locale UT-8
**Wasatch Gardens Subdivision**—pop pl UT-8
Wasatch Gulch—valley UT-8
**Wasatch Heights Subdivision**—pop pl UT-8
**Wasatch Hills Addition (subdivision)**—pop pl UT-8
Wasatch Hills Seventh Day Adventist Ch—church UT-8
Wasatch HS—school UT-8
Wasatch JHS—school UT-8
*Wasatch Lawn Cemetery* UT-8
Wasatch Lawn Memorial Park—cemetery UT-8
Wasatch Mine—mine CO-8
Wasatch Mine—mine UT-8
Wasatch Mountain Club Lodge—hist pl UT-8
*Wasatch Mountains* UT-8
Wasatch Mountain State Park—park UT-8
Wasatch MS—school UT-8
Wasatch Mtn—summit CO-8
*Wasatch Natl Forest* UT-8
Wasatch Natl Forest-Vernon Division—forest UT-8
**Wasatch Oaks Condominium**—pop pl UT-8
*Wasatch Peak* CO-8
Wasatch Plateau—plateau UT-8
Wasatch Presbyterian Ch—church UT-8
Wasatch Rampart—cliff UT-8
*Wasatch Range* ID-8
*Wasatch Range* UT-8
Wasatch Range—range ID-8
Wasatch Range—range UT-8
**Wasatch Resort**—pop pl UT-8
Wasatch Ridge—ridge UT-8
Wasatch Saloon—hist pl UT-8
Wasatch Sch—school (4) UT-8
*Wasatch Springs Plunge* UT-8
Wasatch Springs Plunge—hist pl UT-8
Wasatch Stake Tabernacle and Heber Amusement Hall—hist pl UT-8
**Wasatch View Acres Subdivision**—pop pl UT-8
**Wasatch Village Subdivision**—pop pl UT-8
**Wasatch Village Subdivisions 2 & 3**—pop pl UT-8
Wasatch Wave Publishing Company Bldg—hist pl UT-8
Wasburn Ranch—locale ND-7
**Wasco**—pop pl CA-9
**Wasco**—pop pl IL-6
**Wasco**—pop pl OR-9
Wasco Butte—summit OR-9
Wasco (CCD)—cens area CA-9
Wasco (CCD)—cens area OR-9
**Wasco County**—pop pl OR-9
Wasco County HS—school OR-9
Wasco Dam—dam OR-9
Wasco Guard Station—locale OR-9
Wasco Lake—lake CA-9
Wasco Lake—lake OR-9
Wasco Light—locale OR-9
Wasco Lookout—locale OR-9
Wascomb Tank—reservoir TX-5
Wasco Methodist Cem—cemetery OR-9
*Wasco Oil Field* CA-9
*Wasco Rsvr* OR-9
Wasco Sewage Disposal—other CA-9
Wasco State Airp—airport OR-9
**Wascott**—pop pl WI-6
Wascott Cem—cemetery WI-6
Wascott Lake—lake WI-6
**Wascott (Town of)**—pop pl WI-6
*Wascue Bluff* MA-1
Wasden Site (Owl Cave)—hist pl ID-8
WASD-FM (Exeter)—tower PA-2
*Waseca* KS-7
**Waseca**—pop pl MN-6
**Waseca (County)**—pop pl MN-6
Waseca County Courthouse—hist pl MN-6
Waseck—locale CA-9
**Waseka Acres (subdivision)**—pop pl PA-2
Wasel Rsvr—reservoir CT-1
Wasena Park—park VA-3
Wasena Sch—school VA-3
**Wasepi**—pop pl MI-6
Wasepka Ranch—locale ND-7
*Waser River* ID-8
*Wasetihoge River* KS-7
WASG-AM (Atmore)—tower AL-4
Wasgott Playground—park MA-1
**Wash**—pop pl UT-8
Wash, Cape—cape ME-1
Wash, Lake—lake FL-3
*Wash, The* NV-8
Wash, The—stream CA-9
Washa, Lake—lake LA-4
Washabaugh County (historical)—civil SD-7
*Washacum Brook* MA-1
*Washacum Pond* MA-1
*Washakamaug Farm Pond* MA-1
**Washakie**—pop pl UT-8
Washakie Cem—cemetery UT-8
Washakie Creek—stream (2) WY-8
Washakie Glacier—glacier WY-8
Washakie Ind Res—reserve UT-8
Washakie Lake—lake WY-8
Washakie Memorial Hosp—hospital WY-8
Washakie Mineral Hot Springs—spring WY-8
*Washakie Mountain* WY-8
Washakie Needles—pillar WY-8
Washakie Park—flat (2) WY-8
Washakie Pass—gap WY-8
Washakie Peak—summit WY-8
Washakie Rsvr—reservoir WY-8
Washakie Station (Historical Ruins)—locale WY-8
Washakie Station Site—hist pl WY-8
Washakie Trail—trail WY-8
Washakie Wilderness—park WY-8
*Washa Lake* LA-4
Washam Cem—cemetery KS-7
Washam Cem—cemetery MS-4
Washam Cem—cemetery TX-5
Washam Ditch—canal IN-6
Washam Spring—spring WY-8
Washam Wash—valley WY-8
Washapie Mtn—summit CA-9
Washaqua Hill—summit MA-1
*Washaqua Point* MA-1
Washaw Creek—stream SC-3
Washbasin Lake—lake CA-9
*Washboard* OR-9
Washboard—area UT-8
*Washboard, The* OR-9
Washboard, The—flat CA-9
Washboard, The—flat UT-8
Washboard Canyon—valley TX-5
*Washboard Creek* AZ-5
Washboard Creek—stream ID-8
Washboard Creek—stream TN-4
Washboard Creek—stream TX-5
Washboard Falls—falls WA-9
Washboard Flat—flat UT-8
Washboard Rapids—rapids OR-9
Washboard Reef—ridge MT-8
Washboard Ridge—ridge (2) OR-9
Washboard Rock—cliff CO-8
Washboard Rsvr—reservoir (2) OR-9
Washboards—area ID-8
Washboards—flat UT-8
Washboard Tank—reservoir NM-5
Washboard Trail (pack)—trail OR-9
Washboard Wash—stream AZ-5
Washboard Wash—valley UT-8
Washboard Well—well AZ-5
*Washbord Canyon* TX-5
Washbourn Brook—stream NY-2
Washbowl—lake NY-2
Washbowl Basin—basin AK-9
Wash Bowl Butte—summit MT-8
Wash Branch—stream (3) AL-4
Wash Branch—stream GA-3
Wash Branch—stream IL-6
Wash Branch—stream IN-6
Wash Branch—stream KY-4
Wash Branch—stream LA-4
Wash Branch—stream NC-3
Wash Branch—stream (2) SC-3
Wash Branch—stream TN-4
Wash Branch—stream TX-5
Wash Branch—stream VA-3
Wash Branch—stream (2) WV-2
Wash Branson Cem—cemetery MO-7
Wash Brook—stream CT-1
Wash Brook—stream MA-1
Wash Broomfield Branch—stream KY-4
Washburn—locale WV-2
**Washburn**—pop pl AR-4
**Washburn**—pop pl IL-6
**Washburn**—pop pl IA-7
**Washburn**—pop pl LA-4
**Washburn**—pop pl ME-1
**Washburn**—pop pl MO-7
**Washburn**—pop pl (2) NC-3
**Washburn**—pop pl ND-7
**Washburn**—pop pl TN-4
**Washburn**—pop pl TX-5
**Washburn**—pop pl WI-6
Washburn, Benjamin, House—hist pl KY-4
Washburn, C.P., Grain Mill—hist pl MA-1
Washburn, George, House—hist pl ME-1
Washburn, Gov. Israel, House—hist pl ME-1
Washburn, Mount—summit WY-8
Washburn, Rev. Ebenezer, House—hist pl OH-6
Washburn, Samuel, House—hist pl MA-1
Washburn A Mill Complex—hist pl MN-6
Washburn and Moen North Works District—hist pl MA-1
Washburn Arroyo—valley TX-5
Washburn Baptist Ch—church TN-4
Washburn Basin—basin NV-8
Washburn Branch—stream TN-4
Washburn Bridge—bridge NC-3
Washburn Brook—stream MA-1
Washburn Brook—stream MN-6
Washburn Brook—stream (2) VT-1
Washburn Butte—summit OR-9
Washburncamp Run—stream WV-2
Washburn (CCD)—cens area TN-4
Washburn Cem—cemetery AR-4
Washburn Cem—cemetery (2) MO-7
Washburn Cem—cemetery NY-2
Washburn Cem—cemetery NC-3
Washburn Cem—cemetery OH-6
Washburn Cem—cemetery (2) TN-4
Washburn Cem—cemetery (2) TX-5
Washburn Center (census name Washburn)—other ME-1
Washburn Corner—locale NH-1
Washburn Corners—locale NY-2
**Washburn (County)**—pop pl WI-6
Washburn Cove—basin CA-9
Washburn Cove—bay FL-3
*Washburn Creek* WI-6
Washburn Creek—stream AR-4
Washburn Creek—stream NV-8
Washburn Ditch—canal IN-6
Washburn Division—civil TN-4
Washburn Dock—locale NY-2
Washburn Draw—valley TX-5
Washburne, Elihu Benjamin, House—hist pl IL-6
Washburne Hist Dist—hist pl OR-9
Washburne HS—school IL-6
Washburne Park—park (2) OR-9
Washburne Wayside—locale OR-9
Washburn Fair Oaks—park MN-6
Washburn-Fair Oaks Mansion District—hist pl MN-6
Washburn Farm Creek—stream WI-6
Washburn Ford—locale KY-4
Washburn Hill—ridge OH-6
Washburn Hill—summit WA-9
Washburn (historical)—locale KS-7
Washburn Hollow—valley MO-7
Washburn Hot Springs—spring WY-8
Washburn HS—school MN-6
Washburn Island—island MA-1
*Washburn Junction* ME-1
Washburn Junction—locale ME-1
Washburn Lake—lake CA-9
Washburn Lake—lake MI-6
Washburn Lake—lake (2) MN-6
Washburn Lake—lake WA-9
Washburn Lake—lake (2) WI-6
Washburn Lake Campground—locale MN-6
Washburn Lateral—canal IN-6
Washburn Lookout Tower—locale WI-6
Washburn Memorial Park—cemetery OH-6
Washburn Mine—mine CA-9
Washburn Mountains—ridge AR-4
Washburn Mtn—summit MT-8
Washburn Mtn—summit NY-2
Washburn Mtn—summit TX-5
Washburn Municipal Airp—airport ND-7
Washburn Observatory and Observatory Director's Residence—hist pl WI-6
*Washburn Park* MN-6
Washburn Park—park KS-7
Washburn Park Water Tower—hist pl MN-6
Washburn Peak—summit AK-9
Washburn Point—cape MO-7
Washburn Point—locale CA-9
Washburn Pond—lake ME-1
Washburn Post Office—building TN-4
Washburn Prairie Cem—cemetery MO-7
Washburn Prairie Church (historical)—locale MO-7
Washburn Prairie School (historical)—locale MO-7
Washburn Public Library—hist pl WI-6
Washburn Ranch—locale CA-9
Washburn Ranch—locale NV-8
Washburn Ranch—locale NM-5
Washburn Ranch—locale WA-9
Washburn Range—range WY-8
Washburn Ridge—ridge NY-2
Washburn Ridge—ridge SD-7
Washburn Rsvr—reservoir UT-8
Washburn Run—stream OH-6
Washburn Run—stream PA-2
Washburn Run—stream (2) WV-2
Washburn Sch—school ME-1
Washburn Sch—school (2) MN-6
Washburn Sch—school OH-6
Washburn Sch—school TN-4
Washburn Sch—school WI-6
Washburns Lake—reservoir NC-3
Washburns Lake Dam—dam NC-3
Washburn Slide—cliff CA-9
Washburn Slough—stream AK-9
*Washburns Pond* MA-1
Washburn Spring—spring OR-9
Washburn Spring—spring TX-5
Washburn Spring—spring UT-8
**Washburn Store**—pop pl NC-3
Washburn Street Cem—cemetery PA-2
Washburn Street Ch—church TN-4
Washburn Tank—reservoir TX-5
Washburn Tower Site State Public Hunting Grounds—park MO-7
Washburn Town Hall—building ND-7
**Washburn (Town of)**—pop pl ME-1
**Washburn (Town of)**—pop pl (2) WI-6
Washburn Township—civil MO-7
**Washburn Township**—pop pl ND-7
Washburn (Township of)—fmr MCD (2) AR-4
Washburn Univ—school KS-7
Washburn Univ Carnegie Library Bldg—hist pl KS-7
Washburn University—unic pl KS-7
Washburn View Shop Ctr—locale KS-7
Wash Canyon—valley ID-8
Wash Canyon—valley (4) UT-8
Wash Cem—cemetery AR-4
Wash Clark Well—well CA-9
Wash Creek—stream AL-4
Wash Creek—stream (3) ID-8
Wash Creek—stream KY-4
Wash Creek—stream MS-4
Wash Creek—stream MO-7
Wash Creek—stream (2) NC-3
Wash Creek—stream OR-9
Wash Creek—stream PA-2
Wash Creek—stream (2) WA-9
Wash Creek Butte—summit OR-9
Wash Creek Sch—school PA-2
*Wash de Flag* AZ-5
Washdown Point—cape AK-9
Wash Dug Well—well AZ-5
Washe Creek—stream AK-9
Washedout Tank—reservoir AZ-5
Washelli Cem—cemetery WA-9
Washer—locale TX-5
Washer Cove—bay NH-1
Washer Gulf—bay GA-3
Washer Hill—summit AL-4
Washer Hollow—valley (2) TN-4
Washer Hollow—valley VA-3
Washer Hollow Tunnel Mine—mine TN-4
Washers, The—bar ME-1
Washers Branch—stream KY-4
*Washer Woman* UT-8
Washer Woman—arch UT-8
Washer Woman—pillar UT-8

Washington Plaza (Shop Ctr)—*locale* PA-2
*Washington Point* WI-6
Washington Point Neck—*cape* NJ-2
*Washington Pond* MA-1
Washington Pond—*bay* LA-4
Washington Pond—*lake* ME-1
Washington Pond—*reservoir* NJ-2
Washington Ponds—*lake* OR-9
Washington Pond Upper Dam—*dam* RI-1
Washington Post Office—*building* UT-8
Washington Pot Office (historical)—*building* TN-4
**Washington Prairie**—*pop pl* IA-7
Washington Prairie Cem—*cemetery* IA-7
Washington Prairie Cem—*cemetery* ND-7
Washington Prairie Ch—*church* IA-7
Washington Prairie Ch—*church* ND-7
Washington Prairie Methodist Church—*hist pl* IA-7
Washington Presbyterian Church—*hist pl* GA-3
Washington Reformed Ch—*church* IA-7
Washington Relief Society Hall—*hist pl* UT-8
*Washington Reservoir Number Three* PA-2
*Washington Reservoir Number 4* PA-2
Washington Ridge—*ridge* CA-9
Washington Road—*uninc pl* MD-2
Washington Rock—*pillar* CA-9
Washington Rock—*pillar* NJ-2
Washington Rock—*summit* WA-9
Washington Rock Outlook—*locale* NJ-2
*Washington Rocks* PA-2
Washington Rock State Park—*park* NJ-2
Washington-Rose Sch—*school* NY-2
Washington (RR name Kearney)—*uninc pl* CA-9
Washington RR Station—*hist pl* NJ-2
Washington Run—*stream* PA-2
Washington Run—*stream* WV-2
Washington Sailing Marina—*other* VA-3
Washington Sanitarium—*hospital* MD-2
**Washingtons Birthplace**—*pop pl* VA-3
Washingtons Boyhood Home—*building* VA-3
*Washington Sch* IN-6
*Washington Sch* PA-2
Washington Sch—*hist pl* CT-1
Washington Sch—*hist pl* (2) MA-1
Washington Sch—*hist pl* NY-2
Washington Sch—*hist pl* OK-5
Washington Sch—*hist pl* (2) UT-8
Washington Sch—*hist pl* WI-6
Washington Sch—*school* (3) AL-4
Washington Sch—*school* (4) AZ-5
Washington Sch—*school* (2) AR-4
Washington Sch—*school* (37) CA-9
Washington Sch—*school* (7) CO-8
Washington Sch—*school* (4) CT-1
Washington Sch—*school* GA-3
Washington Sch—*school* HI-9
Washington Sch—*school* (9) ID-8
Washington Sch—*school* (60) IL-6
Washington Sch—*school* (8) IN-6
Washington Sch—*school* (14) IA-7
Washington Sch—*school* (7) KS-7
Washington Sch—*school* (4) KY-4
Washington Sch—*school* (5) LA-4
Washington Sch—*school* (8) ME-1
Washington Sch—*school* MD-2
Washington Sch—*school* (10) MA-1
Washington Sch—*school* (22) MI-6
Washington Sch—*school* (18) MN-6
Washington Sch—*school* (2) MS-4
Washington Sch—*school* (13) MO-7
Washington Sch—*school* (7) MT-8
Washington Sch—*school* (7) NE-7
Washington Sch—*school* (21) NJ-2
Washington Sch—*school* (3) NM-5
Washington Sch—*school* (11) NY-2
Washington Sch—*school* (4) NC-3
Washington Sch—*school* (6) ND-7
Washington Sch—*school* (28) OH-6
Washington Sch—*school* (22) OK-5
Washington Sch—*school* (9) OR-9
Washington Sch—*school* (16) PA-2
Washington Sch—*school* SC-3
Washington Sch—*school* (7) SD-7
Washington Sch—*school* (2) TN-4
Washington Sch—*school* (17) TX-5
Washington Sch—*school* (2) UT-8
Washington Sch—*school* (14) WA-9
Washington Sch—*school* (5) WV-2
Washington Sch—*school* (25) WI-6
Washington Sch—*school* (3) WY-8
Washington Sch (abandoned)—*school* (3) MO-7
Washington Sch (abandoned)—*school* (3) PA-2
Washington Sch For The Blind—*school* WA-9
Washington Sch For The Deaf—*school* WA-9
Washington Sch (historical)—*school* (2) MS-4
Washington Sch (historical)—*school* (2) MO-7
Washington Sch (historical)—*school* (3) PA-2
Washington Sch (historical)—*school* TN-4
Washington Sch Number 17—*school* IN-6
Washington School—*locale* CO-8
Washington School (Abandoned)—*locale* (2) IA-7
Washington Shoal—*bar* NY-2
Washington Shoppes—*locale* IN-6
Washington Shores—*uninc pl* FL-3
Washington Shores Elem Sch—*school* FL-3
Washington Shores Presbyterian Ch—*church* FL-3
Washington's HQ—*hist pl* NY-2
Washington's HQ—*hist pl* PA-2
Washington (Site)—*locale* NV-8
Washington Spring—*spring* AZ-5
Washington Spring—*spring* NM-5
Washington Spring—*spring* VA-3
Washington Springs—*spring* PA-2
Washington Springs Ch—*church* VA-3
*Washington Square* CT-1
*Washington Square* PA-2
Washington Square—*hist pl* PA-2
Washington Square—*locale* KS-7
Washington Square—*locale* MA-1
Washington Square—*other* CA-9
Washington Square—*park* AL-4
Washington Square—*park* CA-9
Washington Square—*park* IL-6
Washington Square—*park* MN-6
Washington Square—*park* PA-2
**Washington Square**—*pop pl* PA-2
Washington Square—*post sta* DC-2
**Washington Square Gardens**—*pop pl* PA-2
Washington Square Hist Dist—*hist pl* MA-1
Washington Square Mall—*locale* NC-3
Washington Square Park—*park* NY-2
Washington Square Shop Ctr—*locale* (2) IN-6
**Washington Square (subdivision)**—*pop pl* AL-4
**Washington Square (subdivision)**—*pop pl* NC-3
**Washington Square Subdivision**—*pop pl* UT-8
Washington Square West Hist Dist—*hist pl* PA-2
Washington State Capitol Hist Dist—*hist pl* WA-9
Washington State For—*forest* VT-1
Washington State Normal Sch—*school* ME-1
Washington State Normal Sch Bldg—*hist pl* WA-9
Washington State Park—*park* MO-7
Washington State Park—*park* TX-5
Washington State Park CCC Hist Dist—*hist pl* MO-7
Washington State Park Petroglyph Archeol Site—*hist pl* MO-7
Washington State Univ—*school* WA-9
Washington State Univ Experimental Station—*school* WA-9
Washington Station (historical)—*locale* MS-4
Washington Statue—*other* HI-9
Washington Statue—*park* DC-2
Washington Street—*uninc pl* KS-7
Washington Street—*uninc pl* NJ-2
Washington Street Bridge—*hist pl* WA-9
Washington Street Ch—*church* AL-4
Washington Street Elem Sch—*school* NC-3
Washington Street Hist Dist—*hist pl* CT-1
Washington Street Hist Dist—*hist pl* MD-2
Washington Street Hist Dist—*hist pl* MA-1
Washington Street Hist Dist—*hist pl* MS-4
Washington Street Hist Dist—*hist pl* WA-9
Washington Street Hist Dist—*hist pl* WI-6
Washington Street Methodist Church—*hist pl* VA-3
Washington Street Park—*park* AL-4
Washington Street Presbyterian Ch—*church* IN-6
Washington Street Public Boat Landing Facility—*hist pl* WA-9
Washington Street Rowhouses—*hist pl* NY-2
Washington Street Sch—*hist pl* CT-1
Washington Street Sch—*school* (2) CT-1
Washington Street Sch—*school* GA-3
Washington Street Sch—*school* ME-1
Washington Street Sch—*school* MA-1
Washington Street Sch—*school* NJ-2
Washington Street Sch—*school* (2) NY-2
Washington Street Sch—*school* NC-3
Washington Street Shoe District—*hist pl* MA-1
Washington Street Station (historical)—*locale* MA-1
Washington Street Theatre District—*hist pl* MA-1
Washington Street United Methodist Ch—*church* IN-6
Washington Street United Methodist Church—*hist pl* SC-3
Washington Tank—*reservoir* NM-5
Washington Tank—*reservoir* TX-5
Washington Technical HS—*school* MO-7
Washington Temple—*church* AL-4
Washington Temple—*church* SC-3
Washington Temple—*church* TN-4
*Washington Temple Ch of God in Christ* AL-4
**Washington Terrace**—*pop pl* UT-8
Washington Terrace Apartments—*hist pl* OH-6
**Washington Terrace Parcel H**—*pop pl* UT-8
Washington Terrace Sch—*school* UT-8
**Washington Theological Coalition**—*pop pl* MD-2
Washington Tourist Center Bldg—*building* DC-2
Washington Townhall—*building* IA-7
**Washington (Town of)**—*pop pl* CT-1
**Washington (Town of)**—*pop pl* ME-1
**Washington (Town of)**—*pop pl* MA-1
**Washington (Town of)**—*pop pl* NH-1
**Washington (Town of)**—*pop pl* NY-2
**Washington (Town of)**—*pop pl* VT-1
**Washington (Town of)**—*pop pl* (7) WI-6
Washington Township—*CDP* NJ-2
Washington Township—*civ div* NE-7
Washington Township—*civil* (2) KS-7
Washington Township—*civil* (19) MO-7
Washington Township—*civil* (2) PA-2
Washington Township—*civil* (4) SD-7
Washington Township—*fmr MCD* (49) IA-7
**Washington Township**—*pop pl* (12) KS-7
**Washington Township**—*pop pl* (9) MO-7
**Washington Township**—*pop pl* (4) NE-7
**Washington Township**—*pop pl* ND-7
**Washington Township**—*pop pl* (3) SD-7
Washington Township Cem—*cemetery* (3) IA-7
Washington Township Center HS—*hist pl* IA-7
Washington Township Ditch—*canal* IN-6
Washington Township Elem Sch—*school* (2) PA-2
Washington Township (historical)—*civil* SD-7
Washington Township Hosp—*hospital* CA-9
Washington Township HS—*school* (2) PA-2
Washington (Township of)—*fmr MCD* (12) AR-4
Washington (Township of)—*fmr MCD* (2) NC-3
Washington (Township of)—*other* OH-6
**Washington (Township of)**—*pop pl* (3) IL-6
**Washington (Township of)**—*pop pl* (46) IN-6
**Washington (Township of)**—*pop pl* (3) MI-6
**Washington (Township of)**—*pop pl* MN-6
**Washington (Township of)**—*pop pl* (6) NJ-2
**Washington (Township of)**—*pop pl* (43) OH-6
**Washington (Township of)**—*pop pl* (22) PA-2
Washington (Township of)—*unorg* ME-1
Washington Township Sch—*hist pl* OH-6
Washington Township Sch—*school* (2) IN-6
Washington Township Sch—*school* IA-7
Washington Township Voting Hall—*hist pl* OH-6
Washington Trail—*trail* CT-1
Washington Trailer Park—*locale* AZ-5
Washington Union HS—*hist pl* CA-9
Washington Union HS—*school* (2) CA-9
Washington Union Sch—*school* CA-9
*Washington United Methodist Ch* MS-4
Washington United Methodist Ch—*church* MS-4
Washington Univ—*school* MO-7
Washington Univ Hilltop Campus Hist Dist—*hist pl* MO-7
Washington Univ Research Center—*school* MO-7
Washington Valley—*basin* NJ-2
Washington Valley—*locale* NJ-2
Washington Valley Ch—*church* PA-2
Washington Valley Rsvr—*reservoir* NJ-2
Washington Valley Schoolhouse—*hist pl* NJ-2
*Washington Village* DE-2
*Washington Village* RI-1
Washingtonville—*locale* NJ-2
**Washingtonville**—*pop pl* NY-2
**Washingtonville**—*pop pl* OH-6
**Washingtonville**—*pop pl* PA-2
Washingtonville—*uninc pl* NJ-2
Washingtonville Borough—*civil* PA-2
Washingtonville Cem—*cemetery* OH-6
Washington Vocational Sch—*hist pl* PA-2
Washington Wash—*stream* CA-9
Washington Water Reservoir Dam—*dam* KS-7
Washington Waterworks—*other* IN-6
Washington Well—*well* AZ-5
**Washington West**—*pop pl* PA-2
Washington-Wilkes Historical Museum—*hist pl* GA-3
Washington-Willow Hist Dist—*hist pl* AR-4
Washington Windmill—*locale* NM-5
Washington Windmill—*locale* TX-5
Washington Yacht And Country Club—*locale* NC-3
Washining Lake—*lake* CT-1
Washinton Gulch—*valley* OR-9
Washinton Sch—*school* NY-2
Wash Island—*island* FL-3
Washita—*locale* OK-5
**Washita**—*pop pl* AR-4
**Washita**—*pop pl* OK-5
Washita Battlefield—*hist pl* OK-5
Washita Cem—*cemetery* TX-5
**Washita (County)**—*pop pl* OK-5
Washita County Courthouse—*hist pl* OK-5
Washita Creek—*stream* AR-4
Washita Indian Cem—*cemetery* OK-5
Washita Natl Wildlife Ref—*park* OK-5
Washita Point—*cape* OK-5
*Washita River* LA-4
Washita River—*stream* OK-5
Washita River—*stream* TX-5
Wash Lake—*lake* FL-3
Wash Lake—*lake* LA-4
Wash Lake—*lake* TX-5
Wash Lake—*swamp* AR-4
Wash Lake Slough—*canal* IL-6
Wash Ledge—*bar* ME-1
Washley Creek—*stream* LA-4
Washman Lookout—*locale* KY-4
Washman Rock—*bar* ME-1
Wash Mason Run—*stream* PA-2
Wash Morgan Hollow—*valley* TN-4
*Washoe* NV-8
Washoe—*locale* ID-8
Washoe—*locale* MT-8
**Washoe**—*pop pl* NV-8
Washoe Cem—*cemetery* CA-9
Washoe Cem—*cemetery* ID-8
Washoe Cem—*cemetery* NV-8
**Washoe City**—*pop pl* NV-8
Washoe County—*civil* NV-8
Washoe County Courthouse—*hist pl* NV-8
Washoe Creek—*stream* CA-9
Washoe Creek—*stream* (2) MT-8
Washoe Ditch—*canal* ID-8
Washoe Fish Rearing Station—*locale* NV-8
Washoe Gulch—*valley* CO-8
Washoe Hill—*summit* NV-8
Washoe Ind Res—*reserve* NV-8
Washoe Lake—*lake* NV-8
Washoe Med Ctr Heliport—*airport* NV-8
*Washoe Mountains* NV-8
Washoe Park—*park* MT-8
Washoe Ranches—*reserve* NV-8
**Washoe Spur**—*pop pl* ID-8
Washoe Station Nevada Department of Wildlife Heliport—*airport* NV-8
Washoe Theater—*hist pl* MT-8
Washoe Valley—*basin* NV-8
Washoke Canyon—*valley* NV-8
Wash O'Neal Creek—*stream* NV-8
Wash O'Neal Ranch—*locale* NV-8
Washonis Creek—*stream* IN-6
**Washougal**—*pop pl* WA-9
Washougal HS—*school* WA-9
Washougal Lower Range—*channel* OR-9
Washougal Memorial Cem—*cemetery* WA-9
Washougal Radio Fan Marker Beacon—*other* WA-9
Washougal Ranger Station—*locale* WA-9
Washougal River—*stream* WA-9
Washougal Trail—*trail* WA-9
Washougal Upper Range Channel—*channel* OR-9
*Washouset Point Neck* RI-1
Washout—*stream* WA-9
Washout Bayou—*stream* MS-4
Washout Bayou Oil Field—*oilfield* MS-4
Washout Branch—*stream* NC-3
*Washout Creek* WA-9
Washout Creek—*stream* CO-8
Washout Creek—*stream* (2) ID-8
Washout Creek—*stream* MT-8
Washout Creek—*stream* NY-2
Washout Creek—*stream* (3) OR-9
Washout Creek—*stream* TX-5
Wash-Out Creek—*stream* WY-8
Washout Dam—*dam* SD-7
Washout Draw—*valley* WY-8
Washout Gulch—*valley* CO-8
Washout Gulch—*valley* MT-8
Washout Gulch—*valley* UT-8
Washout Gulch—*valley* WA-9
Washout Mtn—*summit* TX-5
Washout Point—*summit* ID-8
Washout Rsvr—*reservoir* WY-8
Washout Spring—*spring* NV-8
Washout Spring—*spring* OR-9
Washout Spring—*spring* WA-9
Wash Out Tank—*reservoir* AZ-5
Washovia Bank and Trust Company Bldg—*hist pl* NC-3
Wash Pan Creek—*stream* ID-8
*Washpan Lake* OR-9
Washpan Lake—*lake* KY-4
Washpan Lake Waterhole—*lake* OR-9
Washpan Tank—*reservoir* NM-5
Washplace Ford—*locale* TN-4
*Washplace Mountain* AL-4
Wash Point—*cape* MD-2
Wash Pond—*lake* (7) FL-3
Wash Pond—*lake* NH-1
Wash Pond—*lake* (2) RI-1
Wash Pond—*reservoir* GA-3
Washpot Cave—*cave* AL-4
*Washqua Bluff* MA-1
*Washqua Point* MA-1
Wash Reef—*bar* AK-9
Wash Ridge—*ridge* NC-3
Wash Ridge—*ridge* TN-4
Wash Rock—*bar* CA-9
Wash Rock—*island* OR-9
Wash Rock Canyon—*valley* UT-8
Wash Run—*stream* PA-2
Wash Run—*stream* (3) WV-2
Wash Sch—*school* CA-9
Washs Nipple—*summit* UT-8
Wash Spring—*spring* CO-8
Washspring Mtn—*summit* AL-4
Wash Supply Ditch—*canal* WY-8
**Washta**—*pop pl* IA-7
Wash Tank—*reservoir* AZ-5
Washte Lake—*lake* MN-6
Washtenaw Community Coll—*school* MI-6
**Washtenaw (County)**—*pop pl* MI-6
Washtenong Memorial Park—*cemetery* MI-6
Washtub Cave—*cave* AL-4
Washtub Falls—*falls* CA-9
Washtub Gulch—*valley* CO-8
Wash Tub Rsvr—*reservoir* CO-8
Wash Tub Tank—*reservoir* AZ-5
**Washtucna**—*pop pl* WA-9
Washtucna Coulee—*valley* WA-9
*Washtucna Lake* WA-9
Washtucna Lake—*lake* WA-9
Washtucna Spring—*spring* WA-9
*Washtuena* WA-9
**Washunga**—*pop pl* OK-5
Washunga Cem—*cemetery* OK-5
*Washungo* OK-5
Washusk Lake Number One—*lake* MN-6
Washusk Lake Number Three—*lake* MN-6
Washusk Lake Number Two—*lake* MN-6
Washwater Run—*stream* PA-2
Washwomen, Lake—*lake* MI-6
Wash Wood—*woods* NC-3
Washwood Pond—*reservoir* WI-6
Washy Hollow—*valley* AR-4
Wasigan, Lake—*reservoir* NJ-2
Wasigan Camp—*locale* NJ-2
**Wasilla**—*pop pl* AK-9
Wasilla Community Hall—*hist pl* AK-9
Wasilla Creek—*stream* AK-9
Wasilla Depot—*hist pl* AK-9
Wasilla Elem Sch—*hist pl* AK-9
Wasilla Lake—*lake* AK-9
**Wasioja**—*pop pl* MN-6
Wasioja Hist Dist—*hist pl* MN-6
**Wasioja (Township of)**—*pop pl* MN-6
Wasioto—*locale* KY-4
Wasioto Ch—*church* KY-4
Waskanareska Bay—*bay* AK-9
*Waske River* MI-6
Waskey, Mount—*summit* AK-9
WASK-FM (Lafayette)—*tower* IN-6
**Waskish**—*pop pl* (2) MN-6
**Waskish (Township of)**—*pop pl* MN-6
**Waskom**—*pop pl* TX-5
Waskom (CCD)—*cens area* TX-5
Waskom Cem—*cemetery* IN-6
Waskom Gas And Oil Field—*oilfield* TX-5
Wasky Cabins—*locale* AK-9
WASL-FM (Dyersburg)—*tower* TN-4
Wasmer Draw—*valley* WY-8
Wasmer Sch—*school* NE-7
**Wasola**—*pop pl* MO-7
Wason Barranca—*valley* CA-9
Wason Draw—*valley* TX-5
Wason Park—*flat* CO-8
Wason Ranch—*locale* CO-8
Wason-Springfield Steam Power Blocks—*hist pl* MA-1
Wason Stock Driveway—*trail* CO-8
*Wasp* NC-3
Wasp—*locale* TN-4
Wasp—*locale* WV-2
**Wasp**—*pop pl* NC-3
WASP-AM (Brownsville)—*tower* PA-2
Wasp Branch—*stream* PA-2
Wasp Canyon—*valley* AZ-5
Wasp Cove—*bay* AK-9
Wasp Creek—*stream* AK-9
Wasp Creek—*stream* GA-3
Wasp Creek—*stream* NE-7
Wasp Creek—*stream* (2) TX-5
Wasp Hollow—*valley* PA-2
*Wasp Island* WA-9
Wasp Islands—*island* WA-9
Wasp Lake—*lake* MS-4
Wasp Lake Landing (historical)—*locale* MS-4
Wasp Passage—*channel* WA-9
Wasp Passage Light—*locale* WA-9
Wasp Point—*cape* AK-9
Wasp Post Office (historical)—*building* TN-4
Wasp Rsvr—*reservoir* OR-9
Wasp Spring—*spring* AZ-5
Wasp Tank—*reservoir* NM-5
Wasque Point—*cliff* MA-1
Wasque Shoal—*bar* MA-1
*Wasquiatucket River* RI-1
*Wasquodomesit Brook* RI-1
Wassaic—*locale* ND-7
**Wassaic**—*pop pl* NY-2
Wassaic Creek—*stream* NY-2
Wassaic State Sch—*school* NY-2
Wassaic State Sch (RR name State School)—*school* NY-2
Wassamassaw Ch—*church* SC-3
Wassamassaw Swamp—*swamp* (2) SC-3
Wassataquoik Lake—*lake* ME-1
*Wassataquoik Mtn* ME-1
Wassataquoik Mtn—*summit* (2) ME-1
Wassataquoik Stream—*stream* ME-1
Wassataquoik Tote Road—*trail* ME-1
*Wassaw* GA-3
Wassaw Breaker—*bar* GA-3
Wassaw Creek—*stream* GA-3
Wassaw Island—*island* GA-3
Wassaw Natl Wildlife Ref—*park* GA-3
Wassaw Sound—*bay* GA-3
Wasseman Farms Airp—*airport* KS-7
*Wassen Creek* OR-9
Wassen Hollow—*valley* AR-4
*Wassen Lake* OR-9
Wassen Meadows—*flat* OR-9
Wassen Pond—*lake* OR-9
Wasserburger Pond—*reservoir* SD-7
Wasserburger Pond Dam—*dam* SD-7
*Wassergas* PA-2
Wassergass—*locale* PA-2
Wassergass Sch (abandoned)—*school* PA-2
Wasserman Creek—*stream* MI-6
Wasserman House—*hist pl* CA-9
*Wasserman Lake* MN-6
Wassermann Lake—*lake* MN-6
Wasseta—*locale* OK-5
Wasset Creek—*stream* ID-8
Wasset Peak—*summit* ID-8
Wassin Canyon—*valley* MT-8
W Assmessen Dam—*dam* SD-7
Wassom Cem—*cemetery* TN-4
Wassom Ridge—*ridge* TN-4
Wasson—*locale* TX-5
**Wasson**—*pop pl* CO-8
**Wasson**—*pop pl* IL-6
Wasson, Alberry, Homeplace—*hist pl* LA-4
Wasson Bluff—*cliff* MO-7
Wasson Branch—*stream* TX-5
Wasson Canyon—*valley* OR-9
Wasson Cem—*cemetery* IN-6
Wasson Cem—*cemetery* (2) TN-4
Wasson Cem—*cemetery* TX-5
Wasson Cove—*bay* ME-1
Wasson Creek—*stream* MT-8
Wasson Creek—*stream* (2) OR-9
Wasson Creek—*stream* WY-8
Wasson Draw—*valley* CO-8
Wasson House—*hist pl* AR-4
Wasson HS—*school* CO-8
Wasson Lake—*lake* MI-6
Wasson Lake—*lake* MN-6
Wasson Lake—*lake* OR-9
Wasson Lake Trail—*trail* MN-6
Wasson Lateral—*canal* CO-8
Wasson Oil Field—*oilfield* TX-5
Wasson Peak—*summit* (2) AZ-5
Wasson Ridge—*ridge* OR-9
Wasson Sch—*school* AR-4
Wasson Sch (historical)—*school* TN-4
*Wassons Peak* AZ-5
Wasson Spring—*spring* MO-7
Wassonville Cem—*cemetery* IA-7
**Wassonville (historical)**—*pop pl* IA-7
Wassookeag, Lake—*lake* ME-1
Wassookeag Camp—*locale* ME-1
*Wass Point* ME-1
Wass Point—*cape* ME-1
Wass Run—*stream* WV-2
Wassuc Cem—*cemetery* CT-1
*Wassuk Mountains* NV-8
Wassuk Range—*range* NV-8
Wassum—*other* VA-3
Wassum Cem—*cemetery* VA-3
Wassum Valley—*valley* VA-3
Wassum Valley Ch—*church* VA-3
Wassweiler Hotel and Bath Houses—*hist pl* MT-8
**Wasta**—*pop pl* SD-7
Wasta Creek—*stream* AK-9
Wasta No. 2 Township—*civ div* SD-7
Wasta Township—*civil* SD-7
Waste Canyon—*valley* UT-8
Waste Creek—*stream* CO-8
*Wastecunk Creek* NJ-2
Waste Ditch—*canal* CO-8
Waste Ditch—*canal* ID-8
Wastedo—*locale* MN-6
Wastedo Sch—*school* MN-6
Waste Gate—*locale* MD-2
Waste Gate Creek—*stream* MD-2
Waste Hill—*summit* VT-1
Wastehouse Bayou—*stream* LA-4
Waste House Dam Number One—*dam* PA-2
Waste House Run Dam Number Three—*dam* PA-2
Waste House Run Reservoirs—*reservoir* PA-2
Waste House Run Rsvr—*reservoir* PA-2
Waste House Run Rsvr Number Three—*reservoir* PA-2
Waste Lagoon—*reservoir* TN-4
Waste Lagoon Dam—*dam* TN-4
*Waste Lake* SD-7
Wastella—*locale* TX-5
Wastell Mine—*mine* MO-7
Wastena, Lake—*lake* FL-3
Waste Treatment Dam—*dam* NC-3
Waste Valley—*valley* WI-6
Wasteway Branch—*stream* FL-3
Wasteway Coulee—*valley* MT-8
Wasteway Number Three—*canal* CA-9
Wasteway Number Two—*canal* CA-9
Wasteway Pond—*lake* SC-3
Wasteway 3—*canal* WA-9
Wastina Butte—*summit* OR-9
**Wastina (historical)**—*pop pl* OR-9
WASU-FM (Boone)—*tower* NC-3
Wasulu Ridge—*ridge* NC-3
*Wasunca* ID-8
**Wasupa (historical)**—*pop pl* FL-3
WASZ-FM (Ashland)—*tower* AL-4
WATA-AM (Boone)—*tower* NC-3
Watab—*locale* MN-6
Wataba Lake—*reservoir* CT-1
*Watab Lake* MN-6
Watab Lake—*lake* MN-6
Watab River—*stream* MN-6
**Watab (Township of)**—*pop pl* MN-6
**Wataga**—*pop pl* IL-6
Watahomigie Point—*cliff* AZ-5
Watahomigie Tank—*reservoir* AZ-5
*Watahomigi Point* AZ-5
*Watahomiji Tank* AZ-5
Watakma Butte—*summit* CA-9
Watalula—*locale* AR-4
Watalula (Township of)—*fmr MCD* AR-4
Watana, Mount—*summit* AK-9
Watana Creek—*stream* AK-9
Watana Lake—*lake* AK-9
Watanama Post Office (historical)—*building* AL-4
Watanga Creek—*stream* CO-8
Watanga Lake—*lake* CO-8
Watanga Mtn—*summit* CO-8
W A Tank—*reservoir* AZ-5
*Watap Lake* MN-6
Watap Lake—*lake* MN-6
Wataquadock Hill—*summit* MA-1
Wata Ridges, The—*ridge* AZ-5
Wata Spring—*spring* AZ-5
Watassa Lake—*lake* MI-6
Watatic, Lake—*reservoir* MA-1
Watatic, Mount—*summit* MA-1
*Watatick Pond* MA-1
*Watatic Lake* MA-1
*Watatic Mtn* MA-1
Watatic Pond—*lake* MA-1
Watauga—*locale* KY-4
Watauga—*locale* TN-4
Watauga—*locale* VA-3
**Watauga**—*pop pl* NC-3
**Watauga**—*pop pl* SD-7
**Watauga**—*pop pl* TN-4
**Watauga**—*pop pl* TX-5
Watauga Acad (historical)—*school* (2) TN-4
Watauga Area Mental Health Center—*hospital* TN-4
Watauga Ave Fire Station—*building* TN-4
Watauga Ave Presbyterian Ch—*church* TN-4
Watauga Ch—*church* NC-3
Watauga County—*civil* NC-3
Watauga County HS—*school* NC-3
Watauga County Industrial Fields Complex—*park* NC-3
Watauga Creek—*stream* NC-3
Watauga Dam—*dam* TN-4
Watauga Falls—*falls* NY-2
Watauga Falls—*falls* NC-3
Watauga First Baptist Ch—*church* TN-4
Watauga Flats—*locale* TN-4
Watauga Flats Sch (historical)—*school* TN-4
Watauga HS—*school* TN-4
Watauga Lake—*reservoir* TN-4
Watauga Mine—*mine* TN-4
Watauga Old Fields—*area* TN-4
**Watauga Point**—*pop pl* TN-4
Watauga Point Rec Area—*park* TN-4
Watauga Post Office—*building* TN-4
Watauga Powerhouse—*building* TN-4
Watauga River—*stream* NC-3
Watauga River—*stream* TN-4
Watauga River Mine—*mine* TN-4
Watauga Sch—*school* NC-3
Watauga Sch—*school* TN-4
Watauga Sch (historical)—*school* TN-4
Watauga Steam Plant—*building* TN-4
**Watauga Township**—*pop pl* SD-7
Watauga (Township of)—*fmr MCD* NC-3
Watauga Valley—*basin* VA-3
**Watauga Valley**—*pop pl* TN-4
Watauga Valley—*valley* TN-4
Watauga Valley Ch—*church* TN-4
Watauga Valley Post Office—*building* TN-4
Watauga Village Shop Ctr—*locale* NC-3
Watauga Vista Dam—*dam* NC-3
Watauga Vista Lake—*reservoir* NC-3
*Watawago Lake* PA-2
Watawah, Lake—*lake* PA-2
Watawga, Lake—*reservoir* PA-2
W A Taylor Camp Dam—*dam* AL-4
Wat Buddharangsi Buddhist Temple—*church* FL-3
Watch—*locale* KY-4
Watchabob Springs—*spring* ID-8
*Watchage Brook* MA-1
*Watchange Brook* MA-1
Watcha Pond—*lake* MA-1
Watchaug Brook—*stream* CT-1
Watchaug Brook—*stream* MA-1
Watchaug Pond—*lake* RI-1
*Watch Call Branch* SC-3
Watch Canyon—*valley* UT-8
*Watchcaw Creek* SC-3
Watch Chain Slough—*stream* FL-3
Watch Creek—*stream* KY-4
Watch Creek—*stream* WA-9
Watchdog Butte—*summit* OR-9
Watchemoket Cove—*bay* RI-1
*Watcher Creek* AL-4
Watches Butte—*summit* OR-9
Watches Creek—*stream* AL-4
Watches Fork—*stream* KY-4
**Watch Farm Acres**—*pop pl* OH-6
**Watch Hill**—*pop pl* OH-6
**Watch Hill**—*pop pl* RI-1
Watch Hill—*summit* MA-1
Watch Hill—*summit* NY-2
Watch Hill—*summit* RI-1
Watch Hill Cove—*bay* RI-1
Watch Hill Hist Dist—*hist pl* RI-1
Watch Hill Passage—*channel* RI-1
Watch Hill Point—*cape* RI-1
*Watch Hill Pond* RI-1
Watch Hill Reef—*bar* RI-1
Watch (historical P.O.)—*locale* AL-4
Watch House Pond—*lake* RI-1
Watchic Pond—*lake* ME-1
Watch Island—*island* (6) NY-2
Watch Knob—*summit* NC-3
Watch Lake—*lake* (2) WA-9
Watchman, The—*summit* ID-8
Watchman, The—*summit* OR-9
Watchman, The—*summit* UT-8

Watchman Campground—*park* ... UT-8
Watchman Ch—*church* ... AL-4
Watchman Ch—*church* ... KY-4
Watchman Lookout Station No. 68—*hist pl* ... OR-9
**Watchman Residential Area**—*pop pl* ... UT-8
Watchman Trail—*trail* ... UT-8
*Watchmocket Square* ... RI-1
Watch Mtn—*summit* ... TX-5
Watch Mtn—*summit* ... WA-9
Watchogue Creek—*stream* ... NY-2
Watchorn—*locale* ... OK-5
Watchorn Basin—*harbor* ... CA-9
Watch Point—*cape* ... AK-9
Watch Point—*cape* ... NY-2
Watch Point—*cape* ... NC-3
Watch Rock—*cape* ... NY-2
Watch Run—*stream* ... VA-3
Watch Tower—*pillar* ... WY-8
Watchtower Ch—*church* ... VA-3
Watchtower Creek—*stream* ... MT-8
Watchtower Inn—*locale* ... AK-9
Watchtower Lake—*lake* ... MT-8
*Watch Tower Peak* ... ID-8
Watchtower Peak—*summit* ... ID-8
Watchtower Peak—*summit* ... MT-8
**Watchung**—*pop pl* ... NJ-2
Watchung Ave Station—*hist pl* ... NJ-2
Watchung Ave Station—*locale* ... NJ-2
Watchung Lake—*reservoir* ... NJ-2
Watchung Lake Dam—*dam* ... NJ-2
Watchung Reservation—*park* ... NJ-2
Watchung Sch—*school* (3) ... NJ-2
**Watchwood**—*pop pl* ... UT-8
Wateland Cem—*cemetery* ... PA-2
Wately (Town of)—*civil* ... MA-1
Watensaw (Township of)—*fmr MCD* ... AR-4
*Watepquin* ... MD-2
*Watepquin Creek* ... MD-2
Water, Wall, and Pine Streets Lenticular Truss Bridges—*hist pl* ... NY-2
*Water Anaric Brook* ... VT-1
Water Andric—*stream* ... VT-1
*Water Andric Brook* ... VT-1
*Waterandrick Brook* ... VT-1
Water Ave Hist Dist—*hist pl* ... AL-4
Water Bag Spring—*spring* ... AZ-5
Water Baptist Cem—*cemetery* ... CT-1
Water Barge Cove—*bay* ... NV-8
Water Barrel Mtn—*summit* ... NY-2
Waterbarrel Opening—*flat* ... CA-9
Water Bay—*bay* ... VI-3
Water Bay—*lake* ... FL-3
Water Bay—*lake* ... GA-3
Waterbirch Spring—*spring* ... OR-9
Waterbird Lake—*lake* ... NM-5
Waterboard Park—*park* ... OR-9
Water Board Park—*park* ... OR-9
Waterboot Creek—*stream* ... AK-9
*Waterboro* ... SC-3
Waterboro—*locale* ... NY-2
**Waterboro**—*pop pl* ... ME-1
**Waterboro Center**—*pop pl* ... ME-1
**Waterboro (Town of)**—*pop pl* ... ME-1
Waterbox Canyon—*valley* ... CA-9
Waterbox Canyon—*valley* ... TX-5
*Water Branch* ... FL-3
*Water Branch* ... WV-2
Water Branch—*stream* ... AL-4
Water Branch—*stream* ... FL-3
Water Branch—*stream* (2) ... KY-4
Water Branch—*stream* (2) ... MO-7
Water Branch—*stream* (3) ... NC-3
Water Branch—*stream* ... OR-9
Water Branch Ch—*church* ... GA-3
Water Branch Hollow—*valley* ... TN-4
Water Branch Sch—*school* ... NC-3
Waterbug Hill—*summit* ... MA-1
Water Bug Rsvr—*reservoir* ... CO-8
**Waterburg**—*pop pl* ... NY-2
Waterbury—*locale* ... FL-3
Waterbury—*locale* ... WI-6
**Waterbury**—*pop pl* ... CT-1
**Waterbury**—*pop pl* ... MD-2
**Waterbury**—*pop pl* ... NE-7
**Waterbury**—*pop pl* ... VT-1
Waterbury Brass Mill—*hist pl* ... CT-1
Waterbury Cem—*cemetery* ... CT-1
Waterbury Cem—*cemetery* ... NY-2
**Waterbury Center**—*pop pl* ... VT-1
Waterbury Center Methodist Church—*hist pl* ... VT-1
Waterbury Ch—*church* ... MD-2
Waterbury Clock Company—*hist pl* ... CT-1
**Waterbury Condominium**—*pop pl* ... UT-8
Waterbury Country Club—*other* ... CT-1
Waterbury Creek—*stream* ... CO-8
Waterbury Ditch—*canal* ... OR-9
Waterbury Draw—*valley* ... NM-5
Waterbury Gulch—*valley* ... OR-9
Waterbury Hill—*summit* ... NY-2
Waterbury (historical)—*locale* ... SD-7
*Waterbury Lake* ... VT-1
Waterbury Lake—*lake* ... MI-6
Waterbury Mill—*locale* ... OR-9
Waterbury Municipal Center Complex—*hist pl* ... CT-1
Waterbury Post Office (historical)—*building* ... SD-7
*Waterbury River* ... VT-1
Waterbury Rsvr—*reservoir* ... VT-1
Waterbury Rsvr No 2—*reservoir* ... CT-1
Waterbury Sch Number 3 (historical)—*school* ... SD-7
Waterbury State Technical Institute—*school* ... CT-1
Waterbury State Wildlife Mngmt Area—*park* ... MN-6
Waterbury (Town of)—*civ div* ... CT-1
**Waterbury (Town of)**—*pop pl* ... VT-1
**Waterbury (Township of)**—*pop pl* ... MN-6
Waterbury Union Station—*hist pl* ... CT-1
Waterbury Village Hist Dist—*hist pl* ... VT-1
*Water Bush Island* ... NC-3
Waterbush Point—*cape* ... NC-3
Water Can Crossing—*locale* ... AR-4
Water Can Rsvr—*reservoir* ... WY-8
*Water Canyon* ... UT-8
*Water Canyon* ... WY-8
Water Canyon—*locale* ... NM-5
Water Canyon—*valley* (7) ... AZ-5
Water Canyon—*valley* (20) ... CA-9
Water Canyon—*valley* (2) ... CO-8
Water Canyon—*valley* (7) ... ID-8
Water Canyon—*valley* ... MT-8
Water Canyon—*valley* (30) ... NV-8
Water Canyon—*valley* (18) ... NM-5
Water Canyon—*valley* ... OK-5
Water Canyon—*valley* ... OR-9
Water Canyon—*valley* (6) ... TX-5
Water Canyon—*valley* (32) ... UT-8
Water Canyon—*valley* ... WA-9
Water Canyon—*valley* (2) ... WY-8
Water Canyon Campground—*locale* ... CA-9
*Water Canyon Creek* ... UT-8
*water Canyon Creek* ... WY-8
Water Canyon Creek—*stream* ... AZ-5
Water Canyon Creek—*stream* ... CA-9
Water Canyon Lodge—*locale* ... NM-5
Water Canyon Peak—*summit* ... UT-8
Water Canyon Point—*cliff* ... AZ-5
Water Canyon Ranger Station—*other* ... AZ-5
Water Canyon Rsvr—*reservoir* ... AZ-5
Water Canyon Rsvr—*reservoir* ... CO-8
Water Canyon Spring—*spring* ... CA-9
Water Canyon Spring—*spring* ... ID-8
Water Canyon Spring—*spring* (5) ... NV-8
Water Canyon Spring—*spring* (2) ... NM-5
Water Canyon Windmill—*locale* ... TX-5
Water Cave—*cave* (3) ... AL-4
Water Chief Bay—*bay* ... ND-7
*Waterchuichi River* ... VT-1
*Watercomet* ... MA-1
Water Company Dam Number Four—*dam* ... PA-2
Water Company of Tonapah Bldg—*hist pl* ... NV-8
*Water Company Pond* ... PA-2
Water Company Pond No 1—*lake* ... CT-1
*Water Coulee* ... MT-8
Water Coulee—*valley* ... MT-8
Watercourse Drain—*canal* ... MI-6
Water Cove—*bay* ... ME-1
Watercrease Branch—*stream* ... TN-4
Water Creek—*bay* ... VI-3
Water Creek—*stream* (2) ... AR-4
Water Creek—*stream* ... CA-9
Water Creek—*stream* ... ID-8
Water Creek—*stream* ... NC-3
Water Creek—*stream* (2) ... TX-5
Water Creek—*stream* ... UT-8
Water Creek—*stream* ... WA-9
Water Creek—*stream* ... WY-8
Water Creek Canyon—*valley* ... UT-8
Water Creek Ch—*church* ... AR-4
Water Creek Mtn—*summit* ... AK-9
Water Creek (Township of)—*fmr MCD* (2) ... AR-4
*Water Cress* ... UT-8
Watercress Canyon—*valley* ... WY-8
Watercress Creek—*stream* ... WI-6
Watercress Darter Natl Wildlife Ref—*park* ... AL-4
Watercress Gulch—*valley* ... CA-9
Watercress Marsh—*swamp* ... OH-6
*Watercress Park* ... MO-7
Watercress Pond—*lake* ... TN-4
Watercress (site)—*locale* ... UT-8
Water Cress Spring—*spring* ... ID-8
Watercress Spring—*spring* ... ID-8
Watercress Spring—*spring* ... UT-8
Water Cress Spring—*spring* ... WY-8
Watercress Spring Camp—*park* ... MO-7
Watercress Spring Picnic Grounds—*park* ... MO-7
Watercress Springs—*spring* ... WA-9
Water Crest Spring—*spring* ... ID-8
Watercrest Spring—*spring* (2) ... UT-8
Water Cure Creek—*stream* ... TN-4
Water Cure Springs—*spring* ... TN-4
Waterdog Basin—*basin* ... CO-8
Waterdog Branch—*stream* ... TN-4
Waterdog Creek—*stream* ... CA-9
Waterdog Creek—*stream* ... OR-9
Waterdog Lake—*lake* ... CA-9
Waterdog Lake—*lake* (2) ... CO-8
Waterdog Lake—*lake* ... ID-8
Waterdog Lake—*lake* ... OR-9
Waterdog Lake—*lake* ... WY-8
Waterdog Lake—*reservoir* ... CO-8
Water Dog Lakes—*lake* ... CA-9
Waterdog Lakes—*lake* ... CO-8
Water Dog Lakes—*lake* ... WY-8
Waterdog Peak—*summit* ... CO-8
Waterdog Recreational Site—*park* ... AZ-5
Water Dog Rsvr—*reservoir* ... CO-8
Water Dog Tank—*reservoir* ... AZ-5
Water Drain—*stream* ... IN-6
Water Draw—*valley* ... ID-8
Water Draw—*valley* ... SD-7
Water Draw Spring—*spring* ... SD-7
Watered Fork—*stream* ... MO-7
Watered Fork Creek—*stream* ... AR-4
Wateredge Ch—*church* ... MD-2
*Watered Hollow* ... MO-7
Watered Hollow—*valley* (5) ... MO-7
Watered Hollow Branch—*stream* ... MO-7
Watered Rock Hollow—*valley* ... MO-7
**Wateree**—*pop pl* ... SC-3
Wateree Ch—*church* (2) ... SC-3
*Wateree Creek* ... SC-3
Wateree Creek—*stream* ... NC-3
Wateree Creek—*stream* ... SC-3
Wateree Dam—*dam* ... SC-3
Wateree Lake—*reservoir* ... SC-3
*Wateree Pond* ... SC-3
**Wateree River**—*pop pl* ... SC-3
Wateree River—*stream* ... SC-3
Wateree River State Correctional Institution—*other* ... SC-3
*Wateree Rsvr* ... SC-3
Wateree Sch—*school* ... SC-3
Wateree Swamp—*swamp* ... SC-3
Wateree Swamp Hunting Club—*other* ... SC-3
Waterfall—*locale* ... VA-3
Waterfall—*locale* (2) ... WY-8
**Waterfall**—*pop pl* ... AK-9
**Waterfall**—*pop pl* ... NM-5
**Waterfall**—*pop pl* ... PA-2
Waterfall Bay—*bay* ... AK-9
Waterfall Bayou—*stream* ... LA-4
Waterfall Branch—*stream* ... AL-4
Waterfall Branch—*stream* ... AR-4
Waterfall Branch—*stream* (3) ... GA-3
Waterfall Branch—*stream* ... KY-4
Waterfall Branch—*stream* ... NC-3
Waterfall Branch—*stream* ... TN-4
Waterfall Branch—*stream* (3) ... VA-3
Waterfall Canyon—*valley* ... AZ-5
Waterfall Canyon—*valley* ... CA-9
Waterfall Canyon—*valley* ... ID-8
Waterfall Canyon—*valley* (2) ... NV-8
Waterfall Canyon—*valley* ... OR-9
Waterfall Canyon—*valley* (2) ... UT-8
Waterfall Cave—*cave* (2) ... AL-4
Waterfall Cove—*bay* ... AK-9
Waterfall Cove—*valley* ... GA-3
Water Fall Cove—*valley* ... TN-4
Waterfall Creek—*stream* (3) ... AK-9
Waterfall Creek—*stream* (3) ... CO-8
Waterfall Creek—*stream* (2) ... ID-8
Waterfall Creek—*stream* ... NC-3
Waterfall Creek—*stream* ... OK-5
Waterfall Creek—*stream* (2) ... OR-9
Waterfall Creek—*stream* ... TN-4
Waterfall Dam—*dam* ... AZ-5
Waterfall Gulch—*valley* ... CA-9
Waterfall Gulch—*valley* ... CO-8
Waterfall Hollow—*valley* (5) ... AR-4
Waterfall Hollow—*valley* ... KY-4
Waterfall Hollow—*valley* ... MO-7
Waterfall Hollow—*valley* ... TN-4
Waterfall Hollow—*valley* ... VA-3
Waterfall Hollow Cave—*cave* ... TN-4
Waterfall Lake—*lake* (3) ... AK-9
Waterfall Lake—*lake* ... OH-6
Waterfall Mtn—*summit* ... VA-3
Waterfall Park—*park* ... TN-4
Waterfall Peak—*summit* ... AK-9
Waterfall Point—*cape* ... AK-9
Waterfall Post Office (historical)—*building* ... AL-4
Waterfall Rapids—*rapids* ... AZ-5
Waterfall Run—*stream* (2) ... WV-2
Waterfalls Branch—*stream* ... AL-4
Waterfalls Canyon—*valley* ... WY-8
Water Falls Ch—*church* ... NC-3
Waterfall Sch (historical)—*school* ... PA-2
*Waterfalls Creek* ... ID-8
Waterfalls Creek—*stream* ... NC-3
Waterfalls Hollow—*valley* ... OR-9
Waterfalls Hollow—*valley* ... PA-2
Waterfalls Hollow—*valley* ... TN-4
Waterfall (Site)—*locale* ... NM-5
Waterfall Spring—*spring* (4) ... AZ-5
Waterfall Spring Canyon—*valley* ... AZ-5
Water Falls Spring—*spring* ... WA-9
Waterfall Trail—*trail* (2) ... ID-8
Waterfall Valley Conservation Club—*locale* ... AL-4
Waterfall Well—*well* ... AZ-5
Waterfence Landing—*locale* ... VA-3
Waterfield, William, House—*hist pl* ... IA-7
Waterfield Cem—*cemetery* ... KY-4
Water Flat—*flat* (2) ... UT-8
Waterflat Trail—*trail* ... PA-2
Waterflow—*locale* ... NM-5
*Waterford* ... CT-1
*Waterford* ... IN-6
*Waterford* ... NJ-2
*Waterford* ... PA-2
Waterford—*CDP* ... CT-1
Waterford—*locale* ... AL-4
**Waterford**—*pop pl* ... CA-9
**Waterford**—*pop pl* ... IN-6
**Waterford**—*pop pl* ... KY-4
**Waterford**—*pop pl* ... LA-4
**Waterford**—*pop pl* ... ME-1
**Waterford**—*pop pl* ... MD-2
**Waterford**—*pop pl* (2) ... MI-6
**Waterford**—*pop pl* (2) ... MN-6
**Waterford**—*pop pl* ... MS-4
**Waterford**—*pop pl* ... NY-2
**Waterford**—*pop pl* (2) ... OH-6
**Waterford**—*pop pl* (3) ... PA-2
**Waterford**—*pop pl* ... RI-1
**Waterford**—*pop pl* ... VA-3
**Waterford**—*pop pl* ... WI-6
Waterford, Lake—*reservoir* ... MD-2
Waterford Borough—*civil* ... PA-2
Waterford (CCD)—*cens area* ... CA-9
Waterford Cem—*cemetery* ... IA-7
Waterford Cem—*cemetery* ... MI-6
Waterford Cem—*cemetery* ... MS-4
Waterford Ch—*church* ... CT-1
Waterford Country Sch—*school* ... CT-1
Waterford Covered Bridge—*hist pl* ... PA-2
*Waterford Creek* ... IN-6
Waterford Creek—*stream* ... IN-6
Waterford Hill—*summit* ... MI-6
Waterford Hist Dist—*hist pl* ... ME-1
Waterford Hist Dist—*hist pl* ... VA-3
Waterford (historical)—*locale* ... SD-7
Waterford HS—*school* ... MI-6
Waterford Inn Country Club—*other* ... MI-6
Waterford Island—*island* ... CT-1
Waterford Kettering HS—*school* ... MI-6
Waterford Lower Main Canal—*canal* ... CA-9
**Waterford Mills**—*pop pl* ... IN-6
Waterford Park—*park* ... WV-2
Waterford Point—*cape* ... VA-3
Waterford Pond—*reservoir* ... MI-6
Waterford Run—*stream* ... VA-3
Waterford Rural Cem—*cemetery* ... NY-2
Waterford Sch—*school* ... CT-1
Waterford Sch—*school* ... VT-1
Waterford Sch—*school* ... VA-3
**Waterford Spur**—*pop pl* ... LA-4
Waterford (station)—*locale* ... MI-6
Waterford Station—*locale* ... PA-2
**Waterford (subdivision)**—*pop pl* (2) ... NC-3
**Waterford (Town of)**—*pop pl* ... CT-1
**Waterford (Town of)**—*pop pl* ... ME-1
**Waterford (Town of)**—*pop pl* ... NY-2
**Waterford (Town of)**—*pop pl* ... VT-1
**Waterford (Town of)**—*pop pl* ... WI-6
Waterford Township—*fmr MCD* (2) ... IA-7
**Waterford Township**—*pop pl* ... ND-7
**Waterford (Township of)**—*pop pl* ... IL-6
**Waterford (Township of)**—*pop pl* ... MI-6
**Waterford (Township of)**—*pop pl* ... MN-6
**Waterford (Township of)**—*pop pl* ... NJ-2
**Waterford (Township of)**—*pop pl* ... OH-6
**Waterford (Township of)**—*pop pl* ... PA-2
Waterford Union Ch—*church* ... IL-6
Waterford Village Hist Dist—*hist pl* ... MI-6
Waterford Village Hist Dist—*hist pl* ... NY-2
*Waterford (Waterford Works)* ... NJ-2
**Waterford Woods**—*pop pl* ... WI-6
**Waterford Works**—*pop pl* ... NJ-2
**Waterford Works (Waterford)**—*pop pl* ... NJ-2
*Water Fork* ... UT-8
Water Fork—*stream* ... GA-3
Water Fork—*stream* ... ID-8
Water Fork—*stream* ... NC-3
Water Fork—*stream* (2) ... TN-4
Water Fork—*valley* ... UT-8
Water Fork Branch—*stream* ... AR-4
Waterfork Branch—*stream* ... MS-4
Water Fork Branch—*stream* ... MO-7
Water Fork Community Bldg—*building* ... MO-7
Waterfork Creek—*stream* ... AR-4
Water Fork Creek—*stream* ... MO-7
Water Fork Hollow—*valley* ... MO-7
*Water Fork Mike Spencer Canyon* ... ID-8
Water Fork Mill—*locale* ... TN-4
*Water Fork Of Buffalo Creek* ... GA-3
Water Fork Sch (abandoned)—*school* ... MO-7
Water Fork Settlement Canyon—*valley* ... UT-8
Waterfowl Flowage—*reservoir* ... WI-6
Waterfowl Lake—*lake* ... AK-9
Waterfowl Marsh—*swamp* ... ME-1
*Waterfowl Pond* ... MA-1
Waterfront Cave—*cave* ... AL-4
**Waterfront Estates (subdivision)**—*pop pl* ... MS-4
Water Front Landing (historical)—*locale* ... MS-4
Water Front Memorial Park—*cemetery* ... CA-9
Waterfront Park—*park* ... NY-2
Waterfull Creek—*stream* ... UT-8
*Water Gap* ... PA-2
Water Gap—*gap* ... NV-8
Water Gap—*gap* ... NC-3
Water Gap—*gap* ... OR-9
Watergap—*locale* ... KY-4
Water Gap—*other* ... PA-2
Water Gap Creek—*stream* ... OR-9
Watergap Creek—*stream* ... WY-8
Water Gap Draw—*valley* ... WY-8
Water Gap Golf Course—*locale* ... PA-2
Water Gap Observation Tower—*tower* ... PA-2
Water Gap Rsvr—*reservoir* ... MT-8
Water Gap Slough—*stream* ... TX-5
Water Gap Spring—*spring* ... CA-9
Water Gap Wash—*valley* ... WY-8
Water Gate—*locale* ... DC-2
Watergate—*post sta* ... DC-2
Watergate Complex—*building* ... DC-2
Watergate Spring—*spring* ... AZ-5
Water Grove Ch—*church* ... MS-4
Water Gulch—*valley* (6) ... CA-9
Water Gulch—*valley* (3) ... CO-8
Water Gulch—*valley* ... ID-8
Water Gulch—*valley* (5) ... MT-8
Water Gulch—*valley* (8) ... OR-9
Water Gulch—*valley* (2) ... WY-8
Water Haul Tank—*reservoir* (2) ... AZ-5
Waterhaul Tank—*reservoir* ... AZ-5
**Waterhaven**—*pop pl* ... TN-4
Water Hen Creek—*stream* ... MN-6
Water Hill—*summit* ... MT-8
Water Hill Trail—*trail* ... MT-8
*Water Hole* ... AZ-5
Water Hole—*lake* ... FL-3
Waterhole—*lake* ... GA-3
Water Hole—*lake* ... TX-5
Waterhole—*reservoir* ... OR-9
Waterhole—*swamp* ... FL-3
Waterhole Bay—*basin* ... SC-3
Water Hole Bay—*swamp* ... NC-3
Waterhole Brake—*stream* ... MS-4
Waterhole Branch—*stream* (3) ... AL-4
Waterhole Branch—*stream* ... GA-3
Waterhole Branch—*stream* (4) ... LA-4
Waterhole Branch—*stream* ... MS-4
Waterhole Branch—*stream* ... TX-5
Water Hole Branch—*stream* (2) ... TX-5
Waterhole Branch—*stream* ... TX-5
Waterhole Brook—*stream* ... NH-1
Water Hole Butte—*summit* ... OR-9
*Waterhole Canyon* ... UT-8
Waterhole Canyon—*valley* ... AZ-5
Water Hole Canyon—*valley* ... NV-8
Water Hole Canyon—*valley* ... NM-5
Waterhole Canyon—*valley* ... NM-5
Waterhole Canyon—*valley* ... OR-9
Waterhole Canyon—*valley* ... UT-8
Waterhole Cemetery—*hist pl* ... OK-5
Waterhole Ch—*church* ... OK-5
Waterhole Cove—*bay* ... MD-2
*Water Hole Creek* ... AL-4
*Waterhole Creek* ... OK-5
*Waterhole Creek* ... TX-5
Water Hole Creek—*stream* ... FL-3
Water Hole Creek—*stream* ... GA-3
Waterhole Creek—*stream* ... ID-8
Waterhole Creek—*stream* ... MI-6
Waterhole Creek—*stream* ... MT-8
Waterhole Creek—*stream* ... OK-5
Waterhole Creek—*stream* (2) ... SD-7
Waterhole Creek—*stream* ... TX-5
Water Hole Creek—*stream* ... TX-5
Waterhole Creek—*stream* ... TX-5
Water Hole Creek—*stream* ... TX-5
Waterhole Creek—*stream* ... TX-5
Waterhole Creek—*stream* ... VA-3
Waterhole Creek—*stream* ... WA-9
Waterhole Draw—*valley* ... NM-5
Waterhole Draw—*valley* ... WY-8
Water Hole Draw—*valley* ... WY-8
Waterhole Flat—*flat* ... UT-8
Waterhole Fork—*stream* ... LA-4
Waterhole Hollow—*valley* ... MO-7
Waterhole Mine Spring—*spring* ... CA-9
Water Hole Rsvr—*reservoir* ... OR-9
Water Holes—*area* ... ID-8
*Waterholes Creek* ... SD-7
Water Holes Creek—*stream* ... MT-8
Waterhole Slide—*valley* ... CO-8
Waterhole Spring—*spring* ... AZ-5
Waterhole Spring—*spring* ... HI-9
Waterhole Spring—*spring* (2) ... OR-9
Water Holes Trail—*trail* ... OR-9
Water Hole Tank—*reservoir* ... AZ-5
Waterhole Tank—*reservoir* ... NM-5
Water Hole Well—*well* ... NM-5
*Water Hollow* ... UT-8
Water Hollow—*valley* ... CA-9
Water Hollow—*valley* ... LA-4
Water Hollow—*valley* (4) ... MO-7
Water Hollow—*valley* (5) ... TN-4
Water Hollow—*valley* ... TX-5
Water Hollow—*valley* (18) ... UT-8
Water Hollow Benches—*bench* ... UT-8
Water Hollow Branch—*stream* ... TN-4
Water Hollow Ridge—*ridge* ... UT-8
Water Hollow Tunnel—*canal* ... UT-8
**Waterhouse**—*pop pl* ... AL-4
Waterhouse, William H., House—*hist pl* ... FL-3
Waterhouse Brook—*stream* ... CT-1
Waterhouse Brook—*stream* ... ME-1
Waterhouse Cem—*cemetery* ... AL-4
Waterhouse Cem—*cemetery* ... TN-4
Waterhouse Ch—*church* ... OH-6
Waterhouse Cove—*bay* ... AL-4
Waterhouse Creek—*stream* ... NY-2
Waterhouse Ditch—*canal* ... IN-6
Waterhouse Field—*park* ... ME-1
Waterhouse Gap—*gap* ... PA-2
Waterhouse Gulch—*valley* ... ID-8
Waterhouse Lake—*lake* ... CA-9
Waterhouse Peak—*summit* ... CA-9
Waterhouse Pond—*lake* ... CT-1
Waterhouse Post Office (historical)—*building* ... AL-4
Waterhouse Slough—*stream* ... OR-9
Waterhouse Spring—*spring* ... ID-8
Watering Branch—*stream* ... TX-5
Watering Creek—*stream* ... FL-3
Watering Head—*valley* ... FL-3
Watering Hole Branch—*stream* ... GA-3
Watering Hole Swamp—*stream* (2) ... NC-3
Watering Lake—*lake* ... FL-3
Watering Place Branch—*stream* ... NJ-2
*Watering Pond* ... FL-3
Watering Pond—*lake* ... FL-3
Watering Pond Knob—*summit* ... WV-2
Watering Race Branch—*stream* ... NJ-2
Watering Run—*stream* ... PA-2
Watering Trough Canyon—*valley* ... WA-9
Watering Trough Creek—*stream* ... OR-9
Watering Trough Draw—*valley* ... OR-9
Watering Trough Gulch—*valley* ... CO-8
Water Island—*island* ... ME-1
Water Island—*island* ... VI-3
**Water Island**—*pop pl* ... NY-2
Water Island (Census Subdistrict)—*cens area* ... VI-3
*Water Jar Cave* ... UT-8
Water Key—*island* (2) ... FL-3
Water Key Mangroves—*island* ... FL-3
Water Keys—*island* ... FL-3
Water Lake—*lake* ... AK-9
Water Lake—*lake* ... LA-4
Water Lake—*lake* ... TX-5
Water Lake—*reservoir* ... NC-3
Waterlemon Bay—*bay* ... VI-3
Waterlemon Cay—*island* ... VI-3
Water Level Cave—*cave* ... AL-4
Waterlick—*locale* ... VA-3
Waterlick Run—*stream* ... WV-2
**Waterlilly**—*pop pl* ... NC-3
Water Lily—*mine* ... UT-8
**Waterlily**—*pop pl* ... NC-3
Waterlily Bay—*bay* ... MN-6
Water Lily Lake—*lake* ... UT-8
Water Lily Lake—*reservoir* ... UT-8
Water Lily Lake Dam—*dam* ... UT-8
Water Lily Shaft—*hist pl* ... UT-8
Waterlode Mine—*mine* ... MT-8
Water Log Cave—*cave* ... AL-4
Waterlog Gulch—*valley* ... OR-9
*Waterlog Run* ... IN-6
Waterlog Summit—*summit* ... NV-8
*Waterloo* ... DE-2
*Waterloo* ... NY-2
*Waterloo* ... OH-6
*Waterloo* ... PA-2
*Waterloo* ... TX-5
Waterloo—*hist pl* ... MD-2
Waterloo—*hist pl* ... NJ-2
Waterloo—*hist pl* ... NC-3
Waterloo—*locale* ... AR-4
Waterloo—*locale* ... KY-4
Waterloo—*locale* ... LA-4
Waterloo—*locale* ... MT-8
Waterloo—*locale* ... NJ-2
Waterloo—*locale* ... NM-5
Waterloo—*locale* ... TN-4
Waterloo—*locale* ... TX-5
Waterloo—*locale* (2) ... VA-3
Waterloo—*locale* ... WV-2
**Waterloo**—*pop pl* ... AL-4
**Waterloo**—*pop pl* ... CA-9
**Waterloo**—*pop pl* ... GA-3
**Waterloo**—*pop pl* ... IL-6
**Waterloo**—*pop pl* (3) ... IN-6
**Waterloo**—*pop pl* ... IA-7
**Waterloo**—*pop pl* ... KS-7
**Waterloo**—*pop pl* ... MD-2
**Waterloo**—*pop pl* ... MI-6
**Waterloo**—*pop pl* ... MO-7
**Waterloo**—*pop pl* ... NE-7
**Waterloo**—*pop pl* ... NH-1
**Waterloo**—*pop pl* ... NJ-2
**Waterloo**—*pop pl* ... NY-2
**Waterloo**—*pop pl* (4) ... OH-6
**Waterloo**—*pop pl* (2) ... OK-5
**Waterloo**—*pop pl* ... OR-9
**Waterloo**—*pop pl* (3) ... PA-2
**Waterloo**—*pop pl* ... SC-3
**Waterloo**—*pop pl* ... VA-3
**Waterloo**—*pop pl* ... WI-6
Waterloo—*uninc pl* ... TX-5
**Waterloo Addition (subdivision)**—*pop pl* ... UT-8
Waterloo Bayou—*stream* ... AR-4
Waterloo Branch—*stream* ... NC-3
Waterloo Bridge—*bridge* ... PA-2
Waterloo Bridge—*other* ... MO-7
Waterloo (CCD)—*cens area* ... AL-4
Waterloo Cem—*cemetery* ... IA-7
Waterloo Cem—*cemetery* ... KS-7
Waterloo Cem—*cemetery* ... MS-4
Waterloo Cem—*cemetery* ... MO-7
Waterloo Cem—*cemetery* (2) ... OH-6
Waterloo Cem—*cemetery* ... OK-5
Waterloo Ch—*church* ... KY-4
Waterloo Ch—*church* ... MI-6
Waterloo Ch—*church* ... MS-4
Waterloo Ch—*church* ... WV-2
Waterloo City Park—*park* ... AL-4
Waterloo Covered Bridge—*hist pl* ... NH-1
*Waterloo Creek* ... MN-6
*Waterloo Creek* ... WI-6
Waterloo Creek—*stream* ... IA-7
Waterloo Creek—*stream* ... VA-3
Waterloo Division—*civil* ... AL-4
Waterloo Drainage Ditch—*canal* (2) ... AR-4
Waterloo Elem Sch—*school* ... IN-6
*Waterloo Ferry* ... AL-4
Waterloo Forge (historical)—*locale* ... TN-4
Waterloo Golf Course—*other* ... MI-6
Waterloo Gulch—*valley* ... CO-8
Waterloo Hist Dist—*hist pl* ... IL-6
Waterloo HS—*school* ... AL-4
Waterloo Island (historical)—*island* ... AL-4
Waterloo JHS—*school* ... IA-7
Waterloo JHS—*school* ... MD-2
Waterloo Lake—*lake* ... ND-7
Waterloo Lake—*reservoir* ... TX-5
Waterloo Lakes—*reservoir* ... NJ-2
Waterloo Landing (inundated)—*locale* ... AL-4
Waterloo Lookout Tower—*locale* ... OH-6
Waterloo Marsh—*swamp* ... WA-9
Waterloo Memorial Park—*cemetery* ... IA-7
Waterloo Mills—*locale* ... NY-2
Waterloo Mills—*locale* ... PA-2
Water Loom Pond—*lake* ... NH-1
Waterloo Municipal Airp—*airport* ... IA-7
Waterloo Number 1 Ch—*church* ... LA-4
Waterloo Park—*park* ... OR-9
Waterloo Plantation (historical)—*locale* ... MS-4
Waterloo Point—*cape* ... MD-2
Waterloo Post Office (historical)—*building* ... TN-4
Waterloo Public Library-East Side Branch—*hist pl* ... IA-7
Waterloo Public Library (West Branch)—*hist pl* ... IA-7
Waterloo Ridge Ch—*church* ... IA-7
*Waterloo Run* ... MD-2
Waterloo Run—*stream* ... IN-6
Waterloo Sch—*school* ... CA-9
Waterloo Sch—*school* ... MI-6
Waterloo Sch—*school* ... NE-7
Waterloo Sch—*school* ... PA-2
Waterloo Sch—*school* ... WA-9
Waterloo Sch—*school* ... WI-6
Waterloo Sch (historical)—*school* ... MO-7
*Waterloo Shoals* ... AL-4
Waterloo Spring—*spring* ... AL-4
Waterloo Springs—*locale* ... AL-4
Waterloo State Forest—*park* ... OH-6
Waterloo State Rec Area—*park* ... MI-6
**Waterloo (Town of)**—*pop pl* ... NY-2
**Waterloo (Town of)**—*pop pl* (2) ... WI-6
Waterloo Township—*fmr MCD* ... IA-7
**Waterloo Township**—*pop pl* ... KS-7
**Waterloo Township**—*pop pl* ... ND-7
**Waterloo (Township of)**—*pop pl* ... IN-6
**Waterloo (Township of)**—*pop pl* ... MI-6
**Waterloo (Township of)**—*pop pl* ... OH-6
Waterloo Valley—*basin* ... KY-4
Waterloo Wildlife Area—*locale* ... OH-6
Water Madden Sch—*school* ... IN-6
*Waterman* ... CA-9
*Waterman* (2) ... IN-6
Waterman—*locale* ... IA-7
Waterman—*locale* (2) ... OR-9
**Waterman**—*pop pl* ... IL-6
**Waterman**—*pop pl* ... IA-7
**Waterman**—*pop pl* ... PA-2
**Waterman**—*pop pl* ... TX-5
**Waterman**—*pop pl* ... WA-9
Waterman, John R., House—*hist pl* ... RI-1
Waterman, William, House—*hist pl* ... RI-1
Waterman Beach—*locale* ... ME-1
Waterman Branch—*stream* ... SC-3
Waterman Brook—*stream* ... CT-1
Waterman Brook—*stream* ... ME-1
Waterman Brook—*stream* ... NH-1
Waterman Brook—*stream* ... NY-2
Waterman Brook—*stream* ... VT-1
Waterman Canyon—*valley* ... AK-9
Waterman Canyon—*valley* ... CA-9
Waterman Canyon Station—*locale* ... CA-9
Waterman Cem—*cemetery* ... IA-7
Waterman Cem—*cemetery* ... TN-4
Waterman Ch—*church* ... IN-6
Waterman Corner—*locale* ... NY-2
Waterman Cove—*bay* ... ME-1
Waterman Covered Bridge—*hist pl* ... VT-1
Waterman Creek—*stream* ... AZ-5
Waterman Creek—*stream* (2) ... CA-9
Waterman Creek—*stream* ... IA-7
Waterman Ditch—*canal* ... MT-8
Waterman Flat—*flat* ... OR-9
Waterman Four Corners—*locale* ... RI-1
Waterman Gap—*gap* ... CA-9
Waterman Gardens—*uninc pl* ... CA-9
Waterman-Gramps House—*hist pl* ... NY-2
Waterman Gulch—*valley* ... OR-9
Waterman Gulch—*valley* ... WA-9
Waterman Hill—*summit* ... NY-2
Waterman Hill—*summit* ... RI-1
Waterman Hills—*range* ... CA-9
Waterman (historical P.O.)—*locale* ... IA-7
*Waterman Junction* ... CA-9
*Waterman Lake* ... MN-6
Waterman Lakes—*lake* ... FL-3
Waterman Ledge—*bar* ... ME-1
Waterman Med Ctr—*hospital* ... FL-3
Waterman Mine—*mine* ... CA-9
Waterman Mine—*mine* ... OR-9
*Waterman Mountains* ... AZ-5
Waterman Mountains—*summit* ... AZ-5
Waterman Mtn—*summit* ... CA-9
*Watermann Lake* ... MN-6
*Watermann's Lake* ... MN-6
Waterman Pass—*gap* ... AZ-5
Waterman Peak—*summit* ... AZ-5
Waterman Peak—*summit* ... NY-2
Waterman Point—*cape* ... ME-1
**Waterman Point**—*pop pl* ... WA-9
Waterman Pond—*lake* ... RI-1

Waterman Pond—lake VT-1
Waterman Pond—reservoir RI-1
Waterman Pond Dam—dam RI-1
Waterman Ranch—locale CO-8
Waterman Reservoir Dam—dam RI-1
Waterman Ridge—ridge CA-9
Waterman Rsvr—reservoir RI-1
Watermans Brook—stream CT-1
Waterman Sch—school CA-9
Waterman Sch—school IL-6
Waterman Sch—school MI-6
Waterman Sch—school MT-8
Waterman Sch—school NY-2
Waterman Sch—school VA-3
Waterman Sch—school WI-6
Waterman Sch (abandoned)—school MO-7
Watermans Corner—locale CA-9
Watermans Four Corners RI-1
Watermans Hill RI-1
Watermans Lake MN-6
Waterman Street Sch—school GA-3
Waterman Swamp—swamp NY-2
Waterman Tavern—hist pl RI-1
Waterman Township—fmr MCD IA-7
Waterman Wash—stream AZ-5
Waterman-Winsor Farm—hist pl RI-1
Watermaster HQ—building WA-9
Watermelon Bay—bay LA-4
Watermelon Bluff—cliff SC-3
Watermelon Branch—stream NC-3
Watermelon Branch—stream SC-3
Watermelon Branch—stream TX-5
Watermelon Ch—church GA-3
Watermelon Creek—stream AL-4
Watermelon Creek—stream GA-3
Watermelon Creek—stream OR-9
Watermelon Creek—stream (2) SC-3
Watermelon Gulch WA-9
Watermelon Hill—summit NY-2
Watermelon Island (historical)—island TN-4
Watermelon Lake—lake AK-9
Watermelon Lake—lake LA-4
Watermelon Lake—swamp LA-4
Watermelon Point—cape (2) MD-2
Watermelon Pond—lake FL-3
Watermelon Road County Park—park AL-4
Watermelon Run—stream NC-3
Watermelon Shoal—bar MO-7
Watermelon Spring—spring NV-8
Watermelon Tank—reservoir AZ-5
Watermelon Town FL-3
Watermelon Trail—trail OR-9
Watermelon Water Tank—reservoir TX-5
Watermelon Well—well NM-5
Water Mill—hist pl NY-2
**Watermill**—pop pl NY-2
Watermill Beach—beach NY-2
Watermill Beach Club—other NY-2
Watermill Bridge—other MO-7
Watermill Ch—church OK-5
Water Mill Creek—stream GA-3
Watermill Creek—stream MS-4
Water Mill Creek—stream WA-9
Water Mill (historical)—locale AL-4
**Watermill Lake**—pop pl MI-6
Water Mill Pond—reservoir WI-6
Water Mill Run PA-2
Watermill Run—stream PA-2
**Water Mill (Watermill Station)**—pop pl NY-2
Waternomee, Mount—summit NH-1
Waternomee Falls—falls NH-1
Water Oak—locale MS-4
**Wateroak**—pop pl AL-4
Water Oak Creek—stream FL-3
Water Oak Creek—stream GA-3
Wateroak Creek—stream NC-3
Wateroak Gap—gap NC-3
Water Oak Gap—gap NC-3
Water Oak Gully—valley TX-5
Wateroak Point—cape FL-3
Water Oak Point—cape MD-2
**Wateroak Point**—pop pl MD-2
Water Oak Sch—school FL-3
Water Oak Sch—school IL-6
Wateroak Sch—school IL-6
**Wateroaks (subdivision)**—pop pl MS-4
**Water Oak (subdivision)**—pop pl NC-3
Water of Life Lutheran Ch—church UT-8
Water on the Rock Spring—spring AZ-5
Water Ouzel Trail—trail MT-8
Water Pipe Butte—summit NV-8
Water Pipe Canyon—valley NV-8
Waterpipe Cave—cave AL-4
Waterpipe Creek—stream OR-9
Water Pipe Gulch—valley OR-9
Water Plant Park—park FL-3
Water Plug—locale PA-2
Water Plug Hollow—valley PA-2
Waterpocket Canyon—valley UT-8
Waterpocket Creek—stream UT-8
Water Pocket Flexure UT-8
Waterpocket Fold UT-8
Waterpocket Fold—cliff UT-8
Water Pocket Fold—ridge UT-8
Water Pockets—basin AZ-5
Water Pockets Tank—reservoir AZ-5
Water Point—cape VI-3
Water Pond—lake (3) FL-3
Water Pond Sch (abandoned)—school PA-2
**Waterport**—pop pl GA-3
**Waterport**—pop pl NY-2
Waterport Pond—reservoir NY-2
**Waterport Station**—pop pl NY-2
Water Power Lake—lake WI-6
Water Prong—stream GA-3
Water Prong—stream TN-4
Water Prong Creek—stream MS-4
**Waterproof**—pop pl (2) LA-4
Water Proof Cutoff—channel MS-4
Waterqueechy River VT-1
Water Reclamation Plant—hist pl AZ-5
Water Reed Tank—reservoir TX-5
Water River MA-1
Water Rock House Mtn—summit KY-4
Waterrock Knob—summit NC-3
Waterrock Knob Overlook—locale NC-3
Waterrock Mountain NC-3
Water Rocks Draw—valley WY-8
Water Rsvr—reservoir ID-8
Water Run—stream (3) IN-6
Water Run—stream KY-4
Water Run—stream MO-7
**Waters**—pop pl MI-6
**Waters**—pop pl MS-4
**Waters**—pop pl SC-3
Waters, Asa, Mansion—hist pl MA-1
Waters, Charles Clary, House—hist pl AR-4
Waters, Mount—summit AK-9
Waters and Nash Drain—canal MI-6
Waters Bay—bay NC-3
Waters Bayou—gut AR-4
Waters Bayou—stream LA-4
Waters Bldg—hist pl AL-4
Waters Bluff—locale TX-5
Waters Bluff Cem—cemetery TX-5
Waters Bluff Ch—church TX-5
Waters Branch—stream AL-4
Waters Branch—stream NC-3
Waters Branch—stream SC-3
Waters Branch—stream (2) TN-4
Waters Branch—stream (2) TX-5
Waters Branch Prospects—mine TN-4
Waters Camp—locale CA-9
Waters Canyon—valley CO-8
Waters Canyon—valley TX-5
Waters Cem TN-4
Waters Cem—cemetery AL-4
Waters Cem—cemetery (7) GA-3
Waters Cem—cemetery (2) IL-6
Waters Cem—cemetery (3) KY-4
Waters Cem—cemetery (2) MO-7
Waters Cem—cemetery NY-2
Waters Cem—cemetery NC-3
Waters Cem—cemetery OH-6
Waters Cem—cemetery SC-3
Waters Cem—cemetery (2) TN-4
Waters Ch—church (2) MD-2
Waters Chapel—church NY-2
Waters Chapel—church TX-5
Waters Chapel Church AL-4
Waters Coll—school FL-3
Waters Creek MD-2
**Waters Creek**—pop pl OR-9
Waters Creek—stream AL-4
Waters Creek—stream AR-4
Waters Creek—stream GA-3
Waters Creek—stream ID-8
Waters Creek—stream MS-4
Waters Creek—stream (2) OR-9
Waters Creek—stream TX-5
Waters Creek—stream VA-3
Waters Creek Campground (historical)—park OR-9
Waters Defeat—stream WV-2
Waters Ditch—canal IN-6
Waters Drain IN-6
Waters Draw—valley AZ-5
Waters Draw Spring—spring AZ-5
**Waters Edge (subdivision)**—pop pl NC-3
Waters Estate Dam—dam TN-4
Waters Estate Lake—reservoir TN-4
Waters Farm—hist pl MA-1
Waters Grove Ch—church GA-3
Waters Grove Ch—church MS-4
Waters Gulch—valley CA-9
Waters Gulch—valley OR-9
Waters/Hanley Plaza (Shop Ctr)—locale FL-3
**Watershaw**—pop pl TN-4
Watershed Mtn—summit NC-3
Watershed Ridge—summit NC-3
Watershed Structure Number Eleven—reservoir AL-4
Watershed Structure Number Twelve—reservoir AL-4
Watershed Study Plot—area UT-8
Watershed Trail—trail PA-2
Waters Hill—summit SD-7
Waters Hill Cem—cemetery ME-1
Water Shiloh Cem—cemetery GA-3
**Watership Downs (subdivision)**—pop pl NC-3
Watershop Pond MA-1
Water Shops Armory—hist pl MA-1
Watershops Pond—reservoir MA-1
Watershops Pond Dam—dam MA-1
Waters House—hist pl AR-4
Waters House—hist pl TN-4
Waterside CT-1
**Waterside**—pop pl PA-2
Waterside Cem—cemetery MA-1
Waterside Ch—church NC-3
**Waterside Park**—pop pl NY-2
Water Sign Meadows—flat MT-8
Water Sinks—basin VA-3
Waters Island—island MN-6
Waters Lake AL-4
Waters Lake MN-6
Waters Lake—lake FL-3
**Waters Lake**—pop pl FL-3
Waters Lake—reservoir MS-4
Waters Lake—reservoir NC-3
Waters Lake Bayou—gut TX-5
Waters Lake Dam—dam NC-3
Waters Landing—locale AL-4
Waters Landing—locale MS-4
Water Slough—gut TX-5
Waters Lower Landing AL-4
**Watersmeet**—pop pl MI-6
Watersmeet Lake—lake WI-6
Watersmeet Lookout Tower—locale MI-6
**Watersmeet (Township of)**—pop pl MI-6
Waters Millpond—lake NY-2
Waters Mtn—summit TX-5
Waters Mtn—summit VA-3
Watersnake Creek—stream NY-2
**Waterson**—pop pl PA-2
Waterson Creek MD-2
Waterson Point Park—park NY-2
**Waters Park**—pop pl TX-5
Waters Peak—summit AZ-5
Waters Peak—summit CA-9
Waters-Pierce Oil Company Bldg—hist pl AR-4
Waters Pierce Oil Company Stable Bldg—hist pl LA-4
Waters Pond—lake FL-3
Waters Post Office (historical)—building TN-4
Water Spout CA-9
Waterspout—spring CA-9
Water Spout Branch—stream NC-3
Waterspout Creek—stream ID-8
Waterspout Creek—stream (3) OR-9
Waterspout Draw—valley ID-8
Waterspout Draw—valley OR-9
Waterspout Gulch—valley (2) OR-9
Waterspout Rapids—rapids OR-9
Waterspout Run—stream MD-2
Waterspout Spring CA-9
Waterspout Spring—spring NV-8
Water Spring—spring AZ-5
Waters River—bay MA-1
Waters' River—hist pl MD-2
Waters Rsvr—reservoir PA-2
Waters Run—stream MD-2
Waters Sch—school IL-6
Waters Sch—school MI-6
Waters Sch—school NJ-2
Waters Sch—school OH-6
Waters Sch—school WI-6
Waters Ski Club—locale MI-6
Waters Spring Branch—stream TX-5
Waters Stadium—other NJ-2
Waters Store (historical)—locale AL-4
Water Storage Rsvr Number-Four—reservoir UT-8
**Waterstown**—pop pl TN-4
Water Street ME-1
Waterstreet NJ-2
**Water Street**—pop pl PA-2
Water Street Commercial Buildings—hist pl OH-6
Water Street/Darden Road Bridge—hist pl IN-6
Water Street District—hist pl PA-2
Water Street Hist Dist—hist pl KY-4
Waterstreet Hist Dist—hist pl OH-6
Waters Upper Landing AL-4
Water Supply and Storage Rsvr No. 3—reservoir CO-8
Water Supply and Storage Rsvr No. 4—reservoir CO-8
Water Supply Caves—cave TN-4
Water Supply Dam—dam (2) PA-2
Waters Valley—valley WI-6
**Watersville**—pop pl (2) MD-2
**Watersville Junction**—pop pl MD-2
Waters Wash—stream AZ-5
**Waterswolde**—pop pl IN-6
Water System Canyon—valley UT-8
Water Tank—reservoir TN-4
Water Tank—reservoir TX-5
Water Tank Branch—stream KY-4
Watertank Branch—stream NC-3
Watertank Branch—stream (4) TN-4
Watertank Canyon—valley CO-8
Water Tank Canyon—valley UT-8
Watertank Creek—stream OR-9
Water Tank Creek—stream OR-9
Water Tank Gulch—valley CO-8
Water Tank Gulch—valley MT-8
Water Tank Gulch—valley OR-9
Water Tank Hill—summit AL-4
Water Tank Hill—summit NM-5
Water Tank Hill—summit WY-8
Water Tank Hollow—valley KY-4
Water Tank Hollow—valley PA-2
Watertank Hollow—valley TN-4
Water Tank Hollow—valley (2) TN-4
Watertank Hollow—valley WV-2
Water Tank Hollow Trail—trail PA-2
Water Tank Lake—lake MI-6
Water Tank Lake—lake MN-6
Water Tank Lakes—lake MI-6
Water Tank Mine—mine NV-8
Water Tank No 8—locale WY-8
Water Tank Number Eight—reservoir AZ-5
Water Tank Number One—reservoir AZ-5
Water Tank Number One and One-Half—reservoir AZ-5
Water Tank Number Seven—reservoir AZ-5
Water Tank Number Six—reservoir AZ-5
Water Tank Number Two—reservoir AZ-5
Water Tank Run—stream (2) PA-2
Water Tank Spring—spring NV-8
Water Tank Spring—spring OR-9
Water Tank Trail PA-2
Water Tank Trail—trail (2) PA-2
Water Terrace—bench UT-8
Water Thief Canyon—valley AZ-5
Waterton CO-8
Waterton—locale CO-8
Waterton—locale PA-2
Waterton Creek MD-2
Waterton Lake—lake MT-8
Waterton Ranger Station—locale MT-8
Waterton River—stream MT-8
Waterton Sch—school PA-2
Waterton Substation—locale CO-8
Waterton Valley—valley MT-8
Waterton Valley Trail—trail MT-8
Water Tower—hist pl AL-4
Water Tower—hist pl WI-6
Water Tower, Bldg 49—hist pl IL-6
Water Tower Mtn—summit OR-9
Water Tower Park—park OH-6
Water Tower Peak ID-8
Watertown IL-6
Watertown—locale IL-6
**Watertown**—pop pl CT-1
**Watertown**—pop pl FL-3
**Watertown**—pop pl MA-1
**Watertown**—pop pl MI-6
**Watertown**—pop pl MN-6
**Watertown**—pop pl NY-2
**Watertown**—pop pl OH-6
**Watertown**—pop pl SD-7
**Watertown**—pop pl (2) TN-4
**Watertown**—pop pl WI-6
Watertown Air Force Station—military NY-2
Watertown (CCD)—cens area TN-4
Watertown Cem—cemetery MI-6
**Watertown Center**—pop pl NY-2
Watertown Center Sch—school MI-6
Watertown Ch—church FL-3
Watertown Ch of Christ—church TN-4
Watertown Country Club—locale SD-7
Watertown Division—civil TN-4
Watertown Elem Sch—school TN-4
Watertown Golf Club—other NY-2
Watertown Hist Dist—hist pl OH-6
Watertown (historical)—locale IA-7
Watertown HS—school CT-1
Watertown HS—school MA-1
Watertown HS—school TN-4
Watertown JHS—school TN-4
Watertown Junction—uninc pl NY-2
Watertown Lake—reservoir FL-3
Watertown Mall (Shop Ctr)—locale SD-7
Watertown Masonic Temple—hist pl NY-2
Watertown Municipal Airp—airport SD-7
Watertown New York International Airp—airport NY-2
Watertown Post Office—building TN-4
Watertown Post Office—hist pl SD-7
Watertown Pumping Station—locale CT-1
Watertown Rsvr—reservoir CT-1
Watertown Sch—school IL-6
Watertown Sch—school NE-7
Watertown State Drain—canal MI-6
Watertown Townhall—building MA-1
**Watertown (Town of)**—pop pl CT-1
**Watertown (Town of)**—pop pl MA-1
**Watertown (Town of)**—pop pl NY-2
**Watertown (Town of)**—pop pl WI-6
**Watertown (Township of)**—pop pl (3) MI-6
**Watertown (Township of)**—pop pl MN-6
**Watertown (Township of)**—pop pl OH-6
Water Treece Cem—cemetery TN-4
Watertrough Camp—locale CA-9
Water Trough Canyon—valley AZ-5
Water Trough Canyon—valley OR-9
Water Trough Draw—valley MT-8
Water Trough Draw—valley OR-9
Water Trough Hollow—valley (2) PA-2
Watertrough Hollow—valley TN-4
Water Trough Spring—spring AZ-5
Water Trough Spring—spring CA-9
Water Trough Springs—spring CA-9
Water Trough Trail—trail (3) PA-2
Water Trough Well—well AZ-5
Water Tunnel—tunnel NV-8
Water Tunnels Mine—mine NV-8
Water Turkey Bayou—bay FL-3
Water under the Rock Pond—lake AZ-5
Water Users Camp Ten—locale AZ-5
Water Users Yaqui Camp—locale AZ-5
Watervale—locale MD-2
**Watervale**—pop pl MI-6
**Watervale**—pop pl NY-2
Watervale Butte—summit CO-8
Water Valley—locale AL-4
Water Valley—locale IL-6
**Watervalley**—pop pl IL-6
**Water Valley**—pop pl KY-4
**Water Valley**—pop pl MS-4
**Water Valley**—pop pl NY-2
**Water Valley**—pop pl TN-4
**Water Valley**—pop pl TX-5
Water Valley—valley CA-9
Water Valley Cem—cemetery TX-5
Water Valley Ch—church IL-6
Water Valley Ch—church LA-4
Watervalley Ch—church MS-4
Water Valley Ch—church (2) TN-4
Water Valley Ch (historical)—church MS-4
Water Valley Elem Sch—school MS-4
Water Valley HS—school MS-4
Water Valley Landing—locale MS-4
Water Valley Landing Rec Area—park MS-4
Water Valley Lookout Tower—locale IL-6
Water Valley Municipal Airp—airport MS-4
Water Valley Oil Field—oilfield TX-5
Water Valley Pentecostal Holiness Church MS-4
Water Valley Ranch—locale WY-8
Water Valley Sch (historical)—school MS-4
Water Valley Sewage Lagoon Dam—dam MS-4
Water Valley (Township of)—fmr MCD AR-4
Waterview VA-3
Waterview—locale OR-9
**Waterview**—pop pl KY-4
**Waterview**—pop pl MD-2
**Waterview**—pop pl VA-3
**Water View**—pop pl VA-3
**Waterview Acres**—pop pl DE-2
Waterview Creek—stream VA-3
Waterview Lake—lake FL-3
Waterview Recreation Center—park PA-2
Waterview Station (historical)—locale AL-4
**Water Village**—pop pl NH-1
Waterville CT-1
Waterville KS-7
Waterville NH-1
Waterville—locale (3) NY-2
Waterville—locale PA-2
**Waterville**—pop pl CT-1
**Waterville**—pop pl IA-7
**Waterville**—pop pl KS-7
**Waterville**—pop pl ME-1
**Waterville**—pop pl (2) MA-1
**Waterville**—pop pl MN-6
**Waterville**—pop pl NY-2
**Waterville**—pop pl NC-3
**Waterville**—pop pl OH-6
**Waterville**—pop pl (3) PA-2
**Waterville**—pop pl TN-4
**Waterville**—pop pl VT-1
**Waterville**—pop pl WA-9
**Waterville**—pop pl WI-6
Waterville Airp—airport WA-9
Waterville Baptist Ch—church TN-4
Waterville Bridge—hist pl PA-2
Waterville (CCD)—cens area WA-9
Waterville Ch—church GA-3
Waterville Commercial District—hist pl OH-6
Waterville Creek—stream MN-6
Waterville Cutoff Trail—trail NH-1
Waterville Dam—dam KS-7
Waterville Dam—dam MA-1
Waterville Elem Sch—school TN-4
**Waterville Estates**—pop pl NH-1
Waterville Forest Camp—locale NH-1
Waterville Golf Course—locale TN-4
Waterville Golf Course—other KS-7
Waterville Hotel—hist pl WA-9
Waterville Lake—lake WI-6
Waterville Lake—reservoir NC-3
Waterville Lookout Tower—tower PA-2
Waterville Opera House and City Hall—hist pl ME-1
Waterville Plateau—plain WA-9
Waterville Pond WI-6
Waterville Pond—reservoir MA-1
Waterville Post Office—hist pl ME-1
Waterville Post Office (historical)—building TN-4
Waterville Robert Lafleur Airp—airport ME-1
Waterville Sch—school OR-9
Waterville Sch (historical)—school TN-4
**Waterville (Town of)**—pop pl VT-1
**Waterville (Town of)**—pop pl WI-6
**Waterville Township**—pop pl KS-7
**Waterville (Township of)**—pop pl MN-6
**Waterville (Township of)**—pop pl OH-6
Waterville Triangle Hist Dist—hist pl NY-2
**Waterville Valley**—pop pl NH-1
**Waterville Valley (Town of)**—pop pl NH-1
**Watervliet**—pop pl MI-6
**Watervliet**—pop pl NY-2
Watervliet Arsenal—hist pl NY-2
Watervliet Arsenal—military NY-2
Watervliet Arsenal (U.S. Army)—military NY-2
Watervliet Fish And Game Club—other NY-2
Watervliet Paper Company—facility MI-6
Watervliet Rsvr—reservoir NY-2
Watervliet Shaker Hist Dist—hist pl NY-2
Watervliet Shaker Hist Dist (Boundary Increase)—hist pl NY-2
Watervliet Side Cut Locks—hist pl NY-2
**Watervliet (Township of)**—pop pl MI-6
**Waterway Estates**—pop pl FL-3
Waterway Park—park KS-7
Waterways Experiment Station Dam—dam MS-4
Waterway Spring—spring TN-4
Waterwheel—hist pl CO-8
Water Wheel Camp—locale CA-9
Waterwheel Falls—falls CA-9
**Waterwitch**—pop pl NJ-2
**Waterwood**—pop pl TX-5
**Waterwood (subdivision)**—pop pl MS-4
Waterwork Park—park MI-6
**Water Works**—pop pl KY-4
Waterworks Bldg—hist pl WI-6
**Water Works Branch**—pop pl VA-3
Waterworks Brook—stream (2) CT-1
Waterworks Canyon—valley WA-9
Waterworks Creek—stream IN-6
Waterworks Creek—stream MD-2
Waterworks Creek—stream MI-6
Waterworks Creek—stream OR-9
Water Works Dam PA-2
Water Works Dam—dam PA-2
Waterworks Hill—summit MT-8
Water Works Lake NC-3
Waterworks Lake TX-5
Water Works Lake—lake IA-7
Water Works Lake—reservoir IN-6
Water Works Lake Dam—dam IN-6
Waterworks Park—park (3) IA-7
Waterworks Park—park MI-6
Waterworks Park—park MO-7
Waterworks Park—park (3) OH-6
Waterworks Picnic Area—locale OK-5
Water Works Sch (historical)—school AL-4
Waterworks Spring—spring NV-8
Waterworth Memorial Park—cemetery OH-6
Watery Bay—swamp SC-3
**Watery Branch**—pop pl NC-3
Watery Branch—stream GA-3
Watery Branch—stream KY-4
Watery Branch—stream (5) NC-3
Watery Branch—stream TN-4
Watery Creek—stream TX-5
Watery Fork—stream NC-3
Watery Hollow—valley (2) PA-2
Watery Mountains—range VA-3
Watery Prong Creek MS-4
Wates Cem—cemetery AL-4
Wates Ch—church AR-4
WATE-TV (Knoxville)—tower TN-4
Watford Branch—stream AL-4
**Watford City**—pop pl ND-7
Watford City Golf Course—locale ND-7
Watford City Municipal Airp—airport ND-7
**Watha**—pop pl NC-3
Wathaga River NC-3
Watha Gulch—valley CO-8
Watha (historical)—locale AL-4
**Wathena**—pop pl KS-7
Wathena HS—school KS-7
Wathen Ditch—canal KY-4
**Wathen Heights**—pop pl IN-6
Wathen Park—park IN-6
Watheys—locale OH-6
Wathier Landing—locale CA-9
Wathir—summit FM-9
Watia Creek—stream NC-3
WATI-AM (Indianapolis)—tower IN-6
Watie Sch—school OK-5
Watipquin MD-2
Watipquin Creek MD-2
Wat Island—island FM-9
Watkin Cem—cemetery LA-4
Watkins—locale AL-4
Watkins—locale CO-8
Watkins—locale IL-6
Watkins—locale MO-7
Watkins—locale (2) MT-8
Watkins—locale OK-5
Watkins—locale TN-4
Watkins—locale TX-5
**Watkins**—pop pl AR-4
**Watkins**—pop pl IL-6
**Watkins**—pop pl IA-7
**Watkins**—pop pl MN-6
**Watkins**—pop pl NC-3
**Watkins**—pop pl OH-6
**Watkins**—pop pl OR-9
**Watkins**—pop pl PA-2
Watkins, John and Margaret, House—hist pl UT-8
Watkins, Lake—lake FL-3
Watkins, Mount—summit CA-9
Watkins, Paul, House—hist pl MN-6
Watkins, Thomas B., House—hist pl KY-4
Watkins, William, House—hist pl TN-4
**Watkins Addition (subdivision)**—pop pl UT-8
Watkins Bend—bend KY-4
Watkins Bluff—cliff AL-4
Watkins Brake—swamp AR-4
Watkins Branch AR-4
Watkins Branch—stream AL-4
Watkins Branch—stream AR-4
Watkins Branch—stream GA-3
Watkins Branch—stream (3) KY-4
Watkins Branch—stream MS-4
Watkins Branch—stream MO-7
Watkins Branch—stream NC-3
Watkins Branch—stream TN-4
Watkins Branch—stream TX-5
Watkins Branch—stream (2) VA-3
Watkins Bridge—bridge VA-3
Watkins Bridge—locale AL-4
Watkins Brook—stream AL-4
Watkins Butte—summit OR-9
Watkins-Cartan House—hist pl CA-9
Watkins Cem—cemetery (5) AL-4
Watkins Cem—cemetery (4) AR-4
Watkins Cem—cemetery GA-3
Watkins Cem—cemetery (2) IL-6
Watkins Cem—cemetery (3) IA-7
Watkins Cem—cemetery KY-4
Watkins Cem—cemetery (3) MS-4
Watkins Cem—cemetery (4) MO-7
Watkins Cem—cemetery MT-8
Watkins Cem—cemetery (2) NC-3
Watkins Cem—cemetery (3) OH-6
Watkins Cem—cemetery (3) TN-4
Watkins Cem—cemetery (2) VA-3
Watkins Cem—cemetery WV-2
Watkins Ch—church MT-8
Watkins Chapel—church AR-4
Watkins Chapel—church NC-3
Watkins Chapel—church (2) TN-4
Watkins Chapel—church TX-5
Watkins-Coleman House—hist pl UT-8
Watkins Corner—locale (2) VA-3
**Watkins Corner**—pop pl AR-4
Watkins Creek—stream AL-4
Watkins Creek—stream CA-9
Watkins Creek—stream IN-6
Watkins Creek—stream MO-7
Watkins Creek—stream (3) MT-8
Watkins Creek—stream (2) NC-3
Watkins Creek—stream OR-9
Watkins Creek—stream SC-3
Watkins Creek—stream TN-4
Watkins Creek—stream WY-8
Watkins Creek Ranch—locale MT-8
Watkins Cut—gap AL-4
Watkins Dam`—dam AL-4
Watkins Dam—dam (2) AL-4
Watkins Ditch—canal ID-8
Watkins Ditch—canal WY-8
Watkins Draw—valley (2) WY-8
Watkins Elementary School MS-4
Watkins Ferry Toll House—hist pl WV-2
Watkins Field Airp—airport WA-9
Watkins Flat—flat OR-9
Watkins Ford—locale IL-6
Watkins Fork—stream OH-6
Watkins Gate—locale CA-9
**Watkins Glen**—pop pl MD-2
**Watkins Glen**—pop pl NY-2
Watkins Glen—valley NY-2
Watkins Glen State Park—park NY-2
Watkins Glen Station—locale NY-2
Watkins Grove Ch—church GA-3
Watkins Gulch—valley (2) CO-8
Watkins Hill—summit NH-1
Watkins Hill—summit NY-2
Watkins Hollow—valley OR-9
Watkins Hollow—valley VA-3
Watkins House—hist pl MO-7
Watkins House—hist pl OH-6
Watkins HS—school MS-4
Watkins HS—school MO-7
Watkins-Ingram Cemetery MS-4
Watkins Island—island KY-4
Watkins Island—island MD-2
Watkins Island—island MO-7
Watkins Knob—summit NC-3
Watkins Lake IA-7
Watkins Lake—lake (2) MI-6
Watkins Lake—lake MN-6
Watkins Lake—lake UT-8
Watkins Lake—reservoir (3) AL-4
Watkins Lake—reservoir MN-6
Watkins Lake Dam—dam AL-4
Watkins Lake Dam—dam (5) MS-4
Watkins Lakes—lake WY-8
Watkins Landing (historical)—locale AL-4
Watkins Lateral Ditch—canal WY-8
Watkins Memorial HS—school OH-6
Watkins Mill—hist pl MO-7
Watkins Mill—locale NC-3
Watkins Mill (historical)—locale AL-4
Watkins Mill State Park—park MO-7
Watkinson Brook—stream NH-1
Watkinson Sch—school CT-1
Watkins-Overton HS—school TN-4
Watkins Park—park IN-6
Watkins Park—park TN-4
Watkins Point—cape AK-9
Watkins Point—cape MD-2
Watkins Pond—reservoir AR-4
Watkins Pond—reservoir GA-3
Watkins Pond—reservoir NC-3
Watkins Pond Dam—dam NC-3
Watkins Ranch—locale AZ-5
Watkins Ranch—locale WY-8
Watkins Run—stream OH-6
Watkins Run—stream PA-2
Watkins Sch—school DC-2
Watkins Sch—school FL-3
Watkins Sch—school MS-4
Watkins Sch—school MO-7
Watkins Sch—school OH-6
Watkins Sch—school (2) SC-3
Watkins Sch—school TN-4
Watkins Sch—school VA-3
Watkins Site (15LO12)—hist pl KY-4
Watkins Spring—spring IN-6
Watkins Spring—spring (2) OR-9
Watkins Spring—spring TN-4
Watkins Stadium—park MS-4
**Watkins Store**—pop pl SC-3
Watkins Store (historical)—locale (2) AL-4
Watkins Store (historical)—locale (2) MS-4

**Watkins Subdivision**—*pop pl* MS-4
Watkins Tank—*reservoir* NM-5
Watkins Township—*civil* MO-7
Watkins (Township of)—*fmr MCD* NC-3
**Watkins Village**—*pop pl* NC-3
Watkinsville—*locale* KY-4
**Watkinsville**—*pop pl* GA-3
Watkinsville (CCD)—*cens area* GA-3
Watkins Water Mill (historical)—*locale* AL-4
Watkins Well—*well* TX-5
Watkinville Ch—*church* GA-3
Watleg Branch—*stream* VA-3
*Watlins* NY-2
WATM-AM (Atmore)—*tower* AL-4
Watmough Bay—*bay* WA-9
*Watmough Bight* WA-9
Watmough Head—*summit* WA-9
Watnong Mtn—*summit* NJ-2
WATO-AM (Oak Ridge)—*tower* TN-4
Watoga—*locale* WV-2
*Watoga River* NC-3
*Watoga River* TN-4
Watoga State Park—*park* WV-2
*Wa Toh Sah Lake* WI-6
Watona Park—*park* MN-6
**Watonga**—*pop pl* OK-5
Watonga (CCD)—*cens area* OK-5
Watonga Indian Cem—*cemetery* OK-5
Watonga Lake—*reservoir* OK-5
**Watonwan (County)**—*pop pl* MN-6
Watonwan County Country Club—*other* MN-6
Watonwan County Courthouse—*hist pl* MN-6
Watonwan Lake—*lake* MN-6
Watonwan River—*stream* MN-6
Watoola Cem—*cemetery* AL-4
Watoola Ch—*church* AL-4
*Watoola Creek* AL-4
*Watoola Methodist Ch* AL-4
*Watoolee Ch* AL-4
*Watoolee Creek* AL-4
**Watopa (Township of)**—*pop pl* MN-6
*Watoquodoc Hill* MA-1
Watosah, Lake—*lake* WI-6
*Watourikku-to* MP-9
Watova—*locale* OK-5
Watres Armory—*building* PA-2
Watres Dam—*dam* PA-2
Watres Rsvr—*reservoir* PA-2
Watrous—*hist pl* NM-5
Watrous—*locale* ND-7
**Watrous**—*pop pl* NM-5
**Watrous**—*pop pl* PA-2
Watrous, Lake—*reservoir* CT-1
Watrous Cem—*cemetery* NM-5
*Watrous Corner* PA-2
Watrous Corners—*locale* PA-2
Watrous Creek—*stream* NM-5
Watrous General Store—*hist pl* MI-6
Watrous Gulch—*valley* (2) CO-8
Watrous Hill—*summit* NY-2
Watrous Island—*island* MN-6
Watrous Point—*cape* CT-1
*Watrous Pond* CT-1
Watrous Run—*stream* PA-2
Watrous Sch—*school* IA-7
Watrous Tank—*reservoir* NM-5
**Watrousville**—*pop pl* MI-6
Watrousville Cem—*cemetery* MI-6
Watrous Windmill—*locale* NM-5
*Watsack Point* WA-9
*Watsak Point* WA-9
WATS-AM (Sayre)—*tower* PA-2
*Watsaping* NJ-2
Watseca Mine—*mine* MT-8
**Watseco**—*pop pl* OR-9
Watseco Creek—*stream* OR-9
**Watseka**—*pop pl* IL-6
*Watsessing* NJ-2
**Watsessing**—*pop pl* NJ-2
Watsessing Park—*park* NJ-2
Watsh Field—*park* MI-6
*Watson* KS-7
*Watson* PA-2
Watson—*locale* AL-4
Watson—*locale* AR-4
Watson—*locale* CA-9
Watson—*locale* FL-3
Watson—*locale* IA-7
Watson—*locale* MI-6
Watson—*locale* MT-8
Watson—*locale* (2) TN-4
Watson—*locale* (2) TX-5
Watson—*locale* UT-8
Watson—*locale* VA-3
**Watson**—*pop pl* AL-4
**Watson**—*pop pl* AR-4
**Watson**—*pop pl* FL-3
**Watson**—*pop pl* IL-6
**Watson**—*pop pl* IN-6
**Watson**—*pop pl* KS-7
**Watson**—*pop pl* LA-4
**Watson**—*pop pl* ME-1
**Watson**—*pop pl* MA-1
**Watson**—*pop pl* MI-6
**Watson**—*pop pl* MN-6
**Watson**—*pop pl* MS-4
**Watson**—*pop pl* MO-7
**Watson**—*pop pl* NY-2
**Watson**—*pop pl* NC-3
**Watson**—*pop pl* OH-6
**Watson**—*pop pl* OK-5
**Watson**—*pop pl* OR-9
**Watson**—*pop pl* TN-4
**Watson**—*pop pl* WV-2
Watson, Abraham, House—*hist pl* MA-1
Watson, Elkanah, House—*hist pl* NY-2
Watson, Gov. William T., Mansion—*hist pl* DE-2
Watson, H. C., House—*hist pl* NC-3
Watson, Henry R., House—*hist pl* MI-6
Watson, Irinda, House—*hist pl* UT-8
Watson, Isaac, House—*hist pl* NJ-2
Watson, James, House—*hist pl* NY-2
Watson, John, House—*hist pl* ME-1
Watson, Lake—*reservoir* AL-4
Watson, Laura, House—*hist pl* AL-4
Watson, Mount—*summit* AK-9
Watson, Mount—*summit* CA-9
Watson, Mount—*summit* UT-8
Watson, Mount—*summit* WA-9
Watson, Sally, House—*hist pl* PA-2
Watson, Samuel Stewart, House—*hist pl* MO-7
Watson, Thomas E., House—*hist pl* GA-3
Watson, William H. and Sabrina, House—*hist pl* MI-6
Watson Acad—*hist pl* NH-1
Watson Acad—*school* NH-1
Watson Airp—*airport* MO-7
Watson Airp—*airport* PA-2
Watson Airp—*airport* WA-9
Watson and Summers Drain—*canal* MI-6
Watson Basin—*basin* WY-8
Watson Bay—*swamp* FL-3
*Watson Bayou* LA-4
Watson Bayou—*bay* FL-3
Watson Bayou—*gut* LA-4
Watson Bayou—*stream* (3) LA-4
Watson Bayou—*stream* MS-4
Watson Bayou—*stream* TX-5
Watson Bluff—*cliff* AR-4
Watson Bluff—*cliff* KY-4
Watson Brake—*swamp* LA-4
*Watson Branch* KY-4
*Watson Branch* TX-5
Watson Branch—*church* OK-5
Watson Branch—*locale* TX-5
Watson Branch—*stream* (2) AL-4
Watson Branch—*stream* (2) AR-4
Watson Branch—*stream* FL-3
Watson Branch—*stream* GA-3
Watson Branch—*stream* KS-7
Watson Branch—*stream* KY-4
Watson Branch—*stream* LA-4
Watson Branch—*stream* MS-4
Watson Branch—*stream* MO-7
Watson Branch—*stream* (2) NC-3
Watson Branch—*stream* PA-2
Watson Branch—*stream* (5) TN-4
Watson Branch—*stream* (5) TX-5
Watson Branch—*stream* WV-2
Watson Bridge—*bridge* KY-4
Watson Bridge Mine (Active)—*mine* KY-4
Watson Brook—*stream* ME-1
Watson Brook—*stream* (2) MA-1
Watson Brook—*stream* (2) NH-1
Watson Brook—*stream* NY-2
Watson Butte—*summit* OR-9
Watson Cabin—*locale* OR-9
Watson Canyon—*valley* CA-9
Watson Canyon—*valley* NM-5
Watson Canyon—*valley* OR-9
Watson Canyon—*valley* UT-8
Watson Cave—*cave* MO-7
*Watson Cem* AL-4
*Watson Cem* TX-5
Watson Cem—*cemetery* (2) AL-4
Watson Cem—*cemetery* (5) AR-4
Watson Cem—*cemetery* (2) IN-6
Watson Cem—*cemetery* (3) KY-4
Watson Cem—*cemetery* (5) LA-4
Watson Cem—*cemetery* (2) ME-1
Watson Cem—*cemetery* (2) MN-6
Watson Cem—*cemetery* (3) MS-4
Watson Cem—*cemetery* (2) MO-7
Watson Cem—*cemetery* (6) NC-3
Watson Cem—*cemetery* ND-7
Watson Cem—*cemetery* (2) OH-6
Watson Cem—*cemetery* OR-9
Watson Cem—*cemetery* (3) SC-3
Watson Cem—*cemetery* (13) TN-4
Watson Cem—*cemetery* (3) TX-5
Watson Cem—*cemetery* (4) VA-3
Watson Cem—*cemetery* (2) WV-2
Watson Center—*locale* MS-4
Watson Chapel—*church* (2) AL-4
Watson Chapel—*church* AR-4
Watson Chapel—*church* KY-4
Watson Chapel—*church* (2) MS-4
Watson Chapel—*church* (3) TN-4
Watson Chapel—*church* (2) TX-5
**Watson Chapel**—*pop pl* AR-4
Watson Chapel Cem—*cemetery* AL-4
Watson Community Chapel—*church* MS-4
Watson Corner—*locale* NJ-2
*Watson Corners* MI-6
Watson Coulee—*valley* (2) MT-8
Watson Cove—*valley* NC-3
*Watson Creek* CO-8
Watson Creek—*stream* (5) AL-4
Watson Creek—*stream* (2) AK-9
Watson Creek—*stream* (2) AR-4
Watson Creek—*stream* (4) CA-9
Watson Creek—*stream* (2) CO-8
Watson Creek—*stream* (5) GA-3
Watson Creek—*stream* (2) IL-6
Watson Creek—*stream* KY-4
Watson Creek—*stream* MD-2
Watson Creek—*stream* MI-6
Watson Creek—*stream* MN-6
Watson Creek—*stream* MO-7
Watson Creek—*stream* MT-8
Watson Creek—*stream* NJ-2
Watson Creek—*stream* NY-2
Watson Creek—*stream* NC-3
Watson Creek—*stream* (2) OH-6
Watson Creek—*stream* (2) OK-5
Watson Creek—*stream* (4) OR-9
Watson Creek—*stream* PA-2
Watson Creek—*stream* TN-4
Watson Creek—*stream* (3) TX-5
Watson Creek—*stream* VA-3
Watson Creek—*stream* (2) WA-9
*Watson Creek Reservoir* MA-1
**Watson Crossing (Weldbank)**—*pop pl* PA-2
Watson Crossroads—*locale* GA-3
Watson Crossroads—*locale* NC-3
Watson-Curtze Mansion—*hist pl* PA-2
**Watsondale (historical)**—*pop pl* PA-2
Watson Dam—*dam* OR-9
Watson Ditch—*canal* CA-9
Watson Divide—*gap* CO-8
Watson Drain—*canal* (3) MI-6
Watson Draw—*valley* (2) CO-8
Watson Draw—*valley* MT-8
Watson Draw—*valley* SD-7
Watson Draw—*valley* WA-9
Watson Draw—*valley* WY-8
Watson Falls—*falls* OR-9
Watson Family Cem—*cemetery* GA-3
**Watson Farm**—*pop pl* PA-2
*Watson Ferry* TN-4
Watson Flats—*flat* CO-8
Watson Flats—*flat* MT-8
Watson Ford—*locale* AL-4
Watson Fork—*stream* AK-9
Watson Fork—*stream* PA-2
*Watson Furnace* TN-4
Watson Gap—*gap* AL-4
Watson Gap—*gap* (2) GA-3
Watson Gap—*gap* NC-3
Watson Gap—*gap* VA-3
Watson Gap Branch—*stream* VA-3
Watson Gap Ch—*church* VA-3
*Watson Ghost Town* UT-8
Watson Glacier—*glacier* AK-9
Watson Grave—*cemetery* CA-9
Watson Grove Ch—*church* NC-3
Watson Gulch—*valley* CA-9
Watson Gulch—*valley* (2) CO-8
Watson Gulch—*valley* ID-8
Watson Gulch—*valley* (2) MT-8
Watson Gulch—*valley* OR-9
Watson Hill—*summit* AR-4
Watson Hill—*summit* GA-3
Watson Hill—*summit* (2) ME-1
Watson Hill—*summit* MA-1
Watson Hill—*summit* (2) NH-1
Watson Hill—*summit* NY-2
Watson Hill—*summit* TX-5
Watson Hills—*summit* MI-6
Watson (historical)—*locale* AL-4
Watson (historical)—*locale* ND-7
Watson (historical)—*locale* SD-7
**Watson (historical)**—*pop pl* OR-9
Watson Hollow—*valley* AR-4
Watson Hollow—*valley* CA-9
Watson Hollow—*valley* KY-4
Watson Hollow—*valley* NY-2
Watson Hollow—*valley* (4) TN-4
Watson Hollow Cove—*bay* (2) MO-7
Watson Hosp (historical)—*hospital* AL-4
Watson House—*hist pl* AR-4
Watson House—*hist pl* IN-6
Watson HS—*school* VA-3
*Watsonia* MS-4
Watsonia—*locale* AL-4
**Watsonia**—*pop pl* SC-3
*Watson Island* MD-2
Watson Island—*island* (2) FL-3
Watson Island—*island* NM-5
Watson Island—*island* TN-4
Watson Island Park—*park* FL-3
Watson Junction—*locale* CA-9
Watson Knob—*summit* (2) KY-4
Watson Lake—*lake* AK-9
Watson Lake—*lake* AZ-5
Watson Lake—*lake* AR-4
Watson Lake—*lake* CA-9
Watson Lake—*lake* (2) CO-8
Watson Lake—*lake* IL-6
Watson Lake—*lake* KY-4
Watson Lake—*lake* (2) MI-6
Watson Lake—*lake* NE-7
Watson Lake—*lake* NJ-2
Watson Lake—*lake* UT-8
Watson Lake—*lake* WA-9
Watson Lake—*lake* WI-6
Watson Lake—*reservoir* AL-4
Watson Lake—*reservoir* AZ-5
Watson Lake—*reservoir* (3) NC-3
Watson Lake Dam—*dam* MS-4
Watson Lake Dam—*dam* (3) NC-3
Watson Lake Park—*park* AZ-5
Watson Lakes—*lake* WA-9
Watson Landing Field—*airport* KS-7
Watson Lane Sch—*school* KY-4
Watson Lateral—*canal* CA-9
Watson Lateral—*canal* ID-8
Watson Lateral—*canal* IN-6
Watson Ledge—*bench* NH-1
Watson Level Ch—*church* VA-3
Watson Log Cabin—*hist pl* CA-9
Watson Mall Shop Ctr—*locale* TN-4
Watson Memorial Ch—*church* KY-4
Watson-Miller Tank—*reservoir* TX-5
Watson Millpond—*lake* GA-3
Watson Millpond—*reservoir* MA-1
Watson Mill State Park—*park* GA-3
Watson Mine—*mine* SD-7
**Watson (Mineral Springs)**—*pop pl* AL-4
Watson Mine (surface)—*mine* TN-4
Watson Mine (underground)—*mine* AL-4
Watson Monument Emigrant Pass Marker—*locale* CA-9
Watson Mtn—*summit* CO-8
Watson Mtn—*summit* GA-3
Watson Mtn—*summit* ID-8
Watson Mtn—*summit* NM-5
Watson Mtn—*summit* OR-9
Watson Mtn—*summit* SC-3
Watson Mtn—*summit* TX-5
*Watson Park* FL-3
Watson Park—*flat* CO-8
Watson Park—*park* KS-7
Watson Park—*park* (2) MA-1
Watson Park Creek—*stream* CO-8
Watson Pasture—*flat* KS-7
Watson Path—*trail* NH-1
Watson Peak—*summit* AK-9
Watson Peak—*summit* (2) ID-8
Watson Place—*locale* CO-8
Watson Place, The—*locale* FL-3
Watson Playground—*park* MI-6
Watson Point—*cape* AK-9
Watson Point—*cape* KY-4
Watson Point Dike—*levee* TN-4
Watson Pond—*lake* FL-3
Watson Pond—*lake* ME-1
Watson Pond—*lake* MA-1
Watson Pond—*lake* OH-6
Watson Pond—*lake* VT-1
Watson Pond—*reservoir* GA-3
Watson Pond—*reservoir* MA-1
Watson Pond Dam—*dam* MA-1
Watson Pond State Park—*park* MA-1
Watson Post Office (historical)—*building* TN-4
Watson Prairie—*swamp* FL-3
Watson Private Airstrip—*airport* ND-7
Watson Ranch—*locale* AZ-5
Watson Ranch—*locale* MT-8
Watson Ranch—*locale* (2) NM-5
Watson Ranch—*locale* (2) TX-5
Watson Range—*summit* CA-9
Watson Reefs—*bar* MI-6
Watson Ridge—*ridge* AR-4
Watson Ridge—*ridge* CA-9
Watson Ridge—*ridge* OH-6
Watson Ridge—*ridge* (3) TN-4
Watson Ridge—*ridge* WA-9
Watson Riffle—*rapids* (2) OR-9
Watson River—*stream* FL-3
Watson Road Cem—*cemetery* MI-6
Watson Road Dam—*dam* MA-1
Watson Rsvr—*reservoir* CO-8
Watson Rsvr—*reservoir* OR-9
Watson Rsvr—*reservoir* RI-1
Watson Run—*locale* PA-2
**Watson Run**—*pop pl* PA-2
Watson Run—*stream* KY-4
Watson Run—*stream* (4) PA-2
Watson Run—*stream* VA-3
Watson Run Ch—*church* PA-2
*Watsons* AL-4
*Watsons* OH-6
**Watsons**—*pop pl* OH-6
Watson Sag—*stream* MN-6
Watson-Sawyer House—*hist pl* AR-4
Watson Sch—*hist pl* CA-9
Watson Sch—*school* AR-4
Watson Sch—*school* CA-9
Watson Sch—*school* GA-3
Watson Sch—*school* IL-6
Watson Sch—*school* IA-7
Watson Sch—*school* KY-4
Watson Sch—*school* LA-4
Watson Sch—*school* (2) MA-1
Watson Sch—*school* MI-6
Watson Sch—*school* MO-7
Watson Sch—*school* (2) NY-2
Watson Sch—*school* (2) OH-6
Watson Sch—*school* OK-5
Watson Sch—*school* SC-3
Watson Sch—*school* SD-7
Watson Sch—*school* TX-5
Watson Sch—*school* VA-3
Watson Sch—*school* WV-2
Watson Sch—*school* WI-6
Watson Sch (abandoned)—*school* MO-7
Watson Sch (abandoned)—*school* PA-2
Watson Sch (historical)—*school* (2) AL-4
Watson Sch (historical)—*school* MS-4
Watson Sch (historical)—*school* (2) PA-2
Watson Sch (historical)—*school* (2) TN-4
Watsons Corner—*locale* (2) NJ-2
Watsons Cow Pond—*lake* UT-8
*Watsons Creek* MD-2
*Watsons Creek* PA-2
Watsons Creek—*stream* IA-7
*Watsons Crossing* AL-4
Watson Settlement Bridge—*hist pl* ME-1
Watsons Ferry (historical)—*locale* TN-4
Watsons Field Spring—*spring* AL-4
Watsons House Spring—*spring* AL-4
Watsons Landing (historical)—*locale* MS-4
Watson Slough—*stream* ID-8
Watsons Mill (historical)—*locale* AL-4
Watsons Mill (historical)—*locale* MS-4
Watsons Mill Pond—*reservoir* MS-4
Watsons Mill Pond—*reservoir* NJ-2
Watsons Point—*cape* NY-2
Watsons Point—*cape* VA-3
*Watsons Pond* MA-1
Watson Spring—*spring* AL-4
Watson Spring—*spring* AZ-5
Watson Spring—*spring* CA-9
Watson Spring—*spring* (2) MO-7
Watson Spring—*spring* OR-9
Watson Spring Branch—*stream* AL-4
Watson Spur—*locale* ID-8
*Watsons Run* PA-2
*Watsons Store* TN-4
Watsons Store (historical)—*locale* MS-4
Watson Station (historical P.O.)—*locale* IA-7
Watson Store—*hist pl* KY-4
**Watson Subdivision**—*pop pl* UT-8
Watson Swamp—*swamp* MI-6
Watson Tank—*reservoir* AZ-5
Watson Tank—*reservoir* TX-5
Watson Temple—*church* MS-4
Watson Temple Ch of God in Christ—*church* FL-3
**Watsontown**—*pop pl* PA-2
Watsontown—*uninc pl* NJ-2
Watsontown Borough—*civil* PA-2
**Watson (Town of)**—*pop pl* NY-2
Watsontown River Bridge—*hist pl* PA-2
Watsontown Run—*stream* PA-2
Watson Township—*civil* PA-2
**Watson Township**—*pop pl* ND-7
**Watson (Township of)**—*pop pl* IL-6
**Watson (Township of)**—*pop pl* MI-6
**Watson (Township of)**—*pop pl* (2) PA-2
**Watson Village**—*pop pl* NC-3
Watsonville—*locale* AL-4
**Watsonville**—*pop pl* CA-9
**Watsonville**—*pop pl* NY-2
**Watsonville**—*pop pl* TX-5
Watsonville (CCD)—*cens area* CA-9
Watsonville City Place—*hist pl* CA-9
Watsonville Golf Course—*other* CA-9
**Watsonville (historical)**—*pop pl* OR-9
Watsonville Junction—*locale* CA-9
Watsonville-Lee Road Site—*hist pl* CA-9
Watsonville Slough—*stream* CA-9
Watson Wash—*stream* AZ-5
Watson Wash—*stream* CA-9
Watson Williams Park—*park* NY-2
Watson Windmill—*locale* AZ-5
Watson Windmill—*locale* NM-5
Watson Windmill—*locale* TX-5
*Watstine Lake* WA-9
**Watt**—*pop pl* TX-5
Watt, Henry, House—*hist pl* KY-4
Watt, W. H., Bldg—*hist pl* ID-8
Watt, William, House—*hist pl* WA-9
Wattacoo Creek—*stream* SC-3
Wattamuse Creek—*stream* AK-9
*Wattaquottock Hill* MA-1
Watt Branch—*stream* KY-4
Watt Canyon—*valley* WA-9
Watt Cem—*cemetery* AL-4
Watt Cem—*cemetery* AR-4
Watt Cem—*cemetery* IL-6
Watt Creek—*stream* MT-8
Watt Draw—*valley* MT-8
Watt Draw—*valley* WY-8
Watt Draw Spring—*spring* MT-8
Watt Draw Spring Number One—*spring* MT-8
Wattenbarger Branch—*stream* TN-4
Wattenbarger Cave—*cave* TN-4
Wattenbarger Cem—*cemetery* TN-4
Wattenbarger Gap—*gap* TN-4
**Wattenberg**—*pop pl* CO-8
Wattenberger Mine—*mine* TN-4
Wattenberg Ranch—*locale* CO-8
Wattenberg Sch—*school* CO-8
**Wattensaw**—*pop pl* AR-4
Wattensaw Bayou—*stream* AR-4
Wattensaw Ch—*church* AR-4
Wattensaw State Game Area—*park* AR-4
**Watterfern Hills**—*pop pl* KY-4
Watterman Branch—*stream* TN-4
*Watters* MI-6
**Watters**—*pop pl* PA-2
Watters, William, House—*hist pl* AL-4
*Watters Branch* AL-4
Watters Ch—*church* MD-2
Watters Lake—*reservoir* AL-4
*Watterson* PA-2
Watterson—*locale* TX-5
**Watterson**—*pop pl* IA-7
Watterson Canyon—*valley* CA-9
Watterson Cem—*cemetery* IN-6
Watterson Cem—*cemetery* MO-7
Watterson Ditch—*canal* IN-6
Watterson Meadow—*flat* CA-9
**Watterson Park**—*pop pl* KY-4
Watterson Sch—*school* (2) KY-4
Watterson Sch—*school* OH-6
Watterson Troughs—*spring* CA-9
**Wattersonville**—*pop pl* PA-2
Watters Sch (historical)—*school* AL-4
Watters Smith Memorial State Park—*park* WV-2
Watters Tank—*reservoir* AZ-5
**Watterstown (Town of)**—*pop pl* WI-6
Watterworth Park—*park* TX-5
Watt Glen—*valley* UT-8
Watt-Groce-Fickhardt House—*hist pl* OH-6
Watt Gulch—*valley* MT-8
Watt Hardison Elem Sch—*school* TN-4
**Watt Heights**—*pop pl* TN-4
Watt Hollow—*valley* (2) PA-2
Watt House—*building* VA-3
*Wattie Lake* MI-6
Wattington Cem—*cemetery* TN-4
Wattis—*locale* UT-8
Wattis Junction—*locale* UT-8
Wattis Siding—*locale* UT-8
Watt Lake—*lake* WY-8
Watt Lake—*reservoir* NC-3
Watt Lateral—*canal* CA-9
Wattlebury Island—*island* ME-1
Wattle Duck Pond—*reservoir* TX-5
Wattle Hollow— *valley* AR-4
Wattle Landing Strip—*airport* MO-7
*Wattle Pond* MA-1
Wattles Brook—*stream* CT-1
**Wattlesburg**—*pop pl* NY-2
Wattles Creek—*stream* NV-8
Wattles Ditch—*canal* IN-6
Wattles Lake—*reservoir* KS-7
**Wattles Park**—*pop pl* MI-6
*Wattles Pond* CT-1
Wattles Pond—*lake* MA-1
*Wattles Pond Brook* CT-1
Wattles Run—*stream* PA-2
Wattles Sch—*school* MI-6
*Wattless Pond* MA-1
Watt Mine (underground)—*mine* AL-4
Watt Number 1 Tunnel—*tunnel* HI-9
Watt Number 2 Tunnel—*tunnel* HI-9
Watt Oliver Branch—*stream* WV-2
**Watton**—*pop pl* MI-6
*Watton Canyon* UT-8
Watton Cem—*cemetery* KS-7
Watton Hill—*summit* IN-6
Watton Labor Camp—*other* CA-9
Wattons Mill—*locale* ME-1
*Wattoogee River* NC-3
*Wattoogee River* TN-4
*Wattoquottoc Hill Wattoquottock Hill* MA-1
Watt Powell Stadium—*other* WV-2
*Watts* KY-4
Watts—*locale* AR-4
Watts—*locale* KY-4
Watts—*locale* OR-9
Watts—*locale* SC-3
Watts—*locale* TX-5
Watts—*locale* VA-3
**Watts**—*pop pl* CA-9
**Watts**—*pop pl* LA-4
**Watts**—*pop pl* MS-4
**Watts**—*pop pl* OK-5
**Watts**—*pop pl* OR-9
**Watts**—*pop pl* WV-2
Watts, George T., House—*hist pl* GA-3
Watts, James Grant, House—*hist pl* OR-9
Watts, Lake—*reservoir* MS-4
Watts, M. L., House—*hist pl* OR-9
Watts Airp—*airport* AZ-5
Watts and Perry Cem—*cemetery* WV-2
Watts and Yuille Warehouses—*hist pl* NC-3
Watts Bar—*bar* AL-4
Watts Bar—*bar* TN-4
Watts Bar (dam)—*dam* TN-4
Watts Bar Dam—*dam* TN-4
Watts Bar Dam (Post Office)—*locale* TN-4
Watts Bar Dam Rec Area—*park* TN-4
**Watts Bar Estates**—*pop pl* TN-4
*Watts Bar Ferry* TN-4
Watts Bar Lake—*reservoir* TN-4
Watts Bar Nuclear Plant—*building* TN-4
Watts Bar Resort—*locale* TN-4
Watts Bar Steam Plant—*building* TN-4
*Watts Bay* VT-1
Watts Bay—*bay* VA-3
Watts Bay—*swamp* SC-3
Watts Bayou—*stream* MS-4
Watts Bldg—*hist pl* AL-4
Watts Bldg—*hist pl* CA-9
Watts Bluff—*cliff* AR-4
Wattsboro—*locale* VA-3
Watts Box (historical)—*locale* MS-4
Watts Branch—*stream* DC-2
Watts Branch—*stream* (2) GA-3
Watts Branch—*stream* (2) KY-4
Watts Branch—*stream* LA-4
Watts Branch—*stream* (2) MD-2
Watts Branch—*stream* SC-3
Watts Branch—*stream* TN-4
Watts Branch—*stream* (3) VA-3
Watts Branch Parkway—*park* DC-2
Watts Brook—*stream* NH-1
**Wattsburg**—*pop pl* PA-2
Wattsburg Borough—*civil* PA-2
Watts Canyon—*valley* MT-8
Watts (CCD)—*cens area* OK-5
Watts Cem—*cemetery* (2) AL-4
Watts Cem—*cemetery* (2) AR-4
Watts Cem—*cemetery* (2) IN-6
Watts Cem—*cemetery* LA-4
Watts Cem—*cemetery* (4) MS-4
Watts Cem—*cemetery* (3) MO-7
Watts Cem—*cemetery* OK-5
Watts Cem—*cemetery* PA-2
Watts Cem—*cemetery* TN-4
Watts Cem—*cemetery* (2) VA-3
Watts Ch—*church* OK-5
Watts Ch—*church* TX-5
Watts Chapel—*church* KY-4
Watts Chapel—*church* NC-3
Watts Chapel—*church* TX-5
Watts Chapel Cem—*cemetery* WV-2
Watts Cove—*bay* (2) ME-1
*Watts Creek* VA-3
**Watts Creek**—*pop pl* KY-4
Watts Creek—*stream* (2) AL-4
Watts Creek—*stream* AZ-5
Watts Creek—*stream* CA-9
Watts Creek—*stream* GA-3
Watts Creek—*stream* (3) KY-4
Watts Creek—*stream* MD-2
Watts Creek—*stream* MS-4
Watts Creek—*stream* NC-3
Watts Creek—*stream* PA-2
Watts Creek—*stream* TN-4
Watts Creek—*stream* (2) TX-5
Watts Creek—*stream* VA-3
Watts Crossroads—*locale* AL-4
**Watts Crossroads**—*pop pl* NC-3
Watts Cut—*channel* SC-3
Watts Dam—*dam* NC-3
Watts Ditch—*canal* IN-6
Watts Draw—*valley* CO-8
Watts Field (airport)—*airport* MS-4
**Watts Flat**—*pop pl* NY-2
Watts Fork—*stream* KY-4
Watts Fork Sch—*school* KY-4
Watts-Fuller Cem—*cemetery* TX-5
Watts Gin Branch—*stream* GA-3
Watts Grove Ch—*church* NC-3
Watt Shaft—*mine* NV-8
Watts Hill—*summit* ME-1
Watts Hill—*summit* NM-5
Watts Hill—*summit* (2) PA-2
Watts Hill—*summit* TN-4
**Watts (historical)**—*pop pl* NC-3
Watt Shoals—*bar* TX-5
Watts Hollow—*valley* AL-4
Watts Hollow—*valley* (2) AR-4
Watts Hollow—*valley* MS-4
Watts Hollow—*valley* MO-7
Watts Home—*school* NY-2
Watts Homestead—*locale* CO-8
Watts Hosp—*hist pl* NC-3
Watts Hosp—*hospital* NC-3
Watts House—*hist pl* KY-4
*Watts Island* OR-9
Watts Island—*island* CT-1
Watts Island—*island* TX-5
Watts Island—*island* VA-3
Watts Lake—*lake* CA-9
Watts Lake—*lake* MS-4
Watts Lake—*lake* NE-7
Watts Lake—*lake* PA-2
Watts Lake—*reservoir* AL-4
Watts Lake—*reservoir* NC-3
Watts Lakes—*reservoir* GA-3
**Watts Landing**—*pop pl* NC-3
Watts Landing (historical)—*locale* AL-4
Watts Lateral—*canal* ID-8
Watts Ledge—*bar* ME-1
Watts Mill (historical)—*locale* AL-4
Watts Mills (census name for Wattsville)—*CDP* SC-3
*Watts Mine* AL-4
Watts Mine—*mine* OR-9
Watts Mtn—*summit* KY-4
Watts Park—*park* IL-6
Watts Park—*park* NC-3
Watts Point—*cape* (2) ME-1
Watts Point—*cape* VA-3
Watts Pond—*lake* FL-3
Watt Spring—*spring* CO-8
Watt Spring—*spring* MT-8
Watts Ranch—*locale* CA-9
Watts Ranch—*locale* TX-5
Watts Ridge—*ridge* WV-2
*Watts Run* OH-6
Watts Run—*stream* KY-4
Watts Run—*stream* MA-1
Watts Sch—*school* CA-9
Watts Sch—*school* NC-3
Watts Sch—*school* (2) TX-5
Watts Sch—*school* VA-3
Watts Sch—*school* WV-2
Watts Sch (abandoned)—*school* PA-2
Watts Sch (historical)—*school* MS-4
Watts-Smith Airp—*airport* MO-7
*Watts Spring* UT-8
Watts Spring—*spring* AZ-5
Watts Spring—*spring* NM-5
Watts Station—*hist pl* CA-9
Watts Station—*locale* KY-4
Watts Stream—*stream* MA-1
Watts Tank—*reservoir* NM-5
Watts Tower—*other* CA-9
Watts Towers of Simon Rodia—*hist pl* CA-9
**Watts (Township of)**—*pop pl* PA-2

**Watts Transfer**—*pop pl* ... PA-2
Watts Union Ch—*church* ... AL-4
Watts Valley—*basin* ... CA-9
**Watts Valley**—*pop pl* ... CA-9
Watts Valley Cem—*cemetery* ... CA-9
Wattsville—*locale* ... AL-4
Wattsville—*locale* ... WV-2
**Wattsville**—*pop pl* ... OH-6
**Wattsville**—*pop pl* ... SC-3
**Wattsville**—*pop pl* ... VA-3
Wattsville Branch—*stream* ... VA-3
Wattsville (census name Watts Mills)—*uninc pl* ... SC-3
Wattsville Ch—*church* ... AL-4
Wattsville Sch—*school* ... NE-7
Watts Well—*well* (2) ... NM-5
Watt Windmill—*locale* ... AZ-5
Wattwood Branch—*stream* ... TN-4
Watuaga Valley—*other* ... TN-4
Watula Creek—*stream* ... AL-4
Watuppa—*uninc pl* ... MA-1
*Watuppa Pond* ... RI-1
Watuppa Pond—*lake* ... MA-1
*Watuppa Ponds* ... MA-1
Watuppa Res—*reserve* ... MA-1
Watuppa Reservation—*park* ... MA-1
WATV-AM (Birmingham)—*tower* ... AL-4
*Watwerok Island* ... MP-9
Watwood Cem—*cemetery* ... KY-4
Watwood Sch—*school* ... AL-4
Watzek, Aubrey R., House—*hist pl* ... OR-9
Watznauer Sch (historical)—*school* ... SD-7
Wau—*island* ... MP-9
**Wauban Beach**—*pop pl* ... MI-6
Wauban Pond—*reservoir* ... MA-1
Waubansee Creek—*stream* ... IL-6
**Waubay**—*pop pl* ... SD-7
Waubay Lake—*lake* ... SD-7
Waubay Natl Wildlife Ref—*park* ... SD-7
**Waubay Township**—*pop pl* ... SD-7
Waubedonia Park—*park* ... WI-6
**Waubeek**—*pop pl* ... IA-7
Waubeeka Lake—*lake* ... CT-1
Waubeek Cem—*cemetery* ... WI-6
Waubeek Mound—*summit* ... WI-6
**Waubeek (Town of)**—*pop pl* ... WI-6
Waubee Lake—*lake* ... WI-6
**Waubeesee**—*pop pl* ... WI-6
Waubeesee Lake—*lake* ... WI-6
**Waubeka**—*pop pl* ... WI-6
Waubeka Union Cem—*cemetery* ... WI-6
Wauberg Lake—*lake* ... FL-3
Waubesa, Lake—*lake* ... WI-6
Waubesa Sch—*school* ... WI-6
Waubonsie Ch—*church* ... IA-7
Waubonsie Creek—*stream* ... IA-7
Waubonsie Creek Ditch—*canal* ... IA-7
Waubonsie Sch—*school* ... IL-6
Waubonsie State Park—*park* ... IA-7
Waubonsie Township—*fmr MCD* ... IA-7
**Waubun**—*pop pl* ... MN-6
Waubun Cem—*cemetery* ... MN-6
Waubun Lake—*lake* ... MN-6
Waubun State Wildlife Mngmt Area—*park* ... MN-6
Waucantuck Mill Complex—*hist pl* ... MA-1
*Waucausta* ... WI-6
**Waucedah**—*pop pl* ... MI-6
**Waucedah (Township of)**—*pop pl* ... MI-6
Wauchecha Bald—*summit* ... NC-3
Waucheesi—*locale* ... TN-4
Waucheesi Creek—*stream* ... TN-4
Waucheesi Mtn—*summit* ... TN-4
Wauchessi Fire Tower—*tower* ... TN-4
*Wauchessi Lookout Tower* ... TN-4
Wauchessi Sch (historical)—*school* ... TN-4
*Wauchimoquit* ... MA-1
*Wauch Lake* ... CA-9
**Wauchula**—*pop pl* ... FL-3
Wauchula (CCD)—*cens area* ... FL-3
Wauchula Cem—*cemetery* ... FL-3
Wauchula Elem Sch—*school* ... FL-3
**Wauchula Hills (subdivision)**—*pop pl* ... FL-3
Wauchula Plaza (Shop Ctr)—*locale* ... FL-3
*Waucimaw River* ... NC-3
Waucoba Canyon—*valley* ... CA-9
Waucoba Mtn—*summit* ... CA-9
Waucoba Spring—*spring* ... CA-9
Waucoba Tungsten Mine—*mine* ... CA-9
Waucoba Wash—*stream* ... CA-9
*Waucob Mountain* ... CA-9
**Waucoma**—*pop pl* ... IA-7
Waucoma Cem—*cemetery* ... IA-7
Waucoma Hotel—*hist pl* ... OR-9
Waucoma Ridge—*ridge* ... OR-9
Wauconda—*locale* ... WA-9
**Wauconda**—*pop pl* ... IL-6
Wauconda Summit—*summit* ... WA-9
**Wauconda (Township of)**—*pop pl* ... IL-6
**Waucousta**—*pop pl* ... WI-6
Waucup Creek—*stream* ... OR-9
WAUD-AM (Auburn)—*tower* ... AL-4
Waud Bluff—*cliff* ... OR-9
*Waugan* ... MT-8
Waugh—*locale* ... VA-3
Waugh—*other* ... MS-4
**Waugh**—*pop pl* ... AL-4
**Waugh**—*pop pl* ... IN-6
Waugh, Robert, House—*hist pl* ... IL-6
Waughan Arroyo—*stream* ... NM-5
Waughaw Mtn—*summit* ... NJ-2
Waugh Branch—*stream* ... IA-7
Waugh Branch—*stream* ... WV-2
Waugh Cem—*cemetery* ... AL-4
Waugh Cem—*cemetery* ... MD-2
Waugh Cem—*cemetery* ... NC-3
Waugh Cem—*cemetery* (2) ... OH-6
Waugh Cem—*cemetery* ... WV-2
Waugh Ch—*church* ... MD-2
Waugh Creek—*stream* ... MT-8
Waugh Gulch—*valley* ... CO-8
Waugh Gulch—*valley* ... ID-8
Waugh Hollow—*valley* ... OH-6
Waugh House—*hist pl* ... TX-5
Waugh Lake—*lake* ... CA-9
Waugh Mtn—*summit* ... AR-4
Waugh Mtn—*summit* ... CO-8
Waugh Mtn—*summit* ... ID-8
Waughn Cem—*cemetery* ... ME-1
Waughop Lake—*lake* ... WA-9
Waugh Point—*cape* ... VA-3
Waugh Pond—*lake* ... AR-4
Waugh Post Office (historical)—*building* ... MS-4
Waugh Ridge—*ridge* ... ID-8
Waugh Run—*stream* ... OH-6
Waugh Sch—*school* ... CA-9
Waughtal Spring—*spring* ... AZ-5
**Waughtown**—*pop pl* ... NC-3
Waugoshance Island—*island* ... MI-6
Waugoshance Light Station—*hist pl* ... MI-6
Waugoshance Point—*cape* ... MI-6
*Waugum Lake* ... CT-1
*Waugwoosh* ... MN-6
Wauhab Ridge—*ridge* ... CA-9
Wauhatchie—*locale* ... TN-4
Wauhatchie Branch—*stream* ... GA-3
Wauhatchie Post Office (historical)—*building* ... TN-4
Wauhatchie Yards—*locale* ... TN-4
Wauhaukaupauken Falls—*falls* ... WA-9
Wauhillau—*locale* ... OK-5
**Wauhillau (Bidding Springs)**—*pop pl* ... OK-5
Wauhob Lake—*lake* ... IN-6
**Wauhob Lake**—*pop pl* ... IN-6
*Waukarusa Creek* ... IL-6
*Waukarusa River* ... IL-6
*Waukarusa River Township* ... KS-7
**Waukau**—*pop pl* ... WI-6
Waukau Creek—*stream* ... WI-6
Waukau Lake—*lake* ... WI-6
Waukaway, Lake—*reservoir* ... MS-4
Waukazoo Sch—*school* ... MI-6
**Waukeag**—*pop pl* ... ME-1
Waukeag Neck—*cape* ... ME-1
**Waukechon (Town of)**—*pop pl* ... WI-6
**Waukee**—*pop pl* ... IA-7
Waukee Cem—*cemetery* ... IA-7
Waukeefriskee Creek—*stream* ... GA-3
**Waukeenah**—*pop pl* ... FL-3
Waukeena Lake—*lake* ... NH-1
Waukegan—*locale* ... TX-5
**Waukegan**—*pop pl* ... IL-6
Waukegan River—*stream* ... IL-6
**Waukegan (Township of)**—*pop pl* ... IL-6
Waukell Creek—*stream* (2) ... CA-9
Waukell Flat—*flat* ... CA-9
**Waukena**—*pop pl* ... CA-9
**Waukenabo**—*pop pl* ... MN-6
Waukenabo Cem—*cemetery* ... MN-6
Waukenabo Lake—*lake* ... MN-6
**Waukenabo (Township of)**—*pop pl* ... MN-6
Waukena Lake—*lake* ... MT-8
*Waukesa* ... PA-2
*Waukesha* ... PA-2
**Waukesha**—*pop pl* ... WI-6
**Waukesha (County)**—*pop pl* ... WI-6
Waukesha Post Office—*hist pl* ... WI-6
Waukesha Pure Food Company—*hist pl* ... WI-6
Waukesha Spring—*spring* ... WA-9
**Waukesha (Town of)**—*pop pl* ... WI-6
Waukewan, Lake—*lake* ... NH-1
*Waukewan Lake* ... NH-1
Waukiki Creek—*stream* ... MD-2
Waukokee Cem—*cemetery* ... MN-6
*Waukoma Creek* ... WI-6
**Waukomis**—*pop pl* ... OK-5
Waukomis Cem—*cemetery* ... OK-5
**Waukomis Lake**—*pop pl* ... MO-7
Waukomis Lake—*reservoir* ... MS-4
Waukomis Lake—*reservoir* ... MO-7
Waukomis Spring—*spring* ... MS-4
Waukon—*locale* ... MN-6
Waukon—*locale* ... WA-9
**Waukon**—*pop pl* ... IA-7
Waukon City Park—*park* ... IA-7
Waukon Junction—*locale* ... IA-7
**Waukon (Township of)**—*pop pl* ... MN-6
*Wauk Point* ... VA-3
Wauksha, Bayou—*stream* ... LA-4
**Waukuzoo**—*pop pl* ... MI-6
*Wauld Bluff* ... OR-9
**Waumandee**—*pop pl* ... WI-6
Waumandee Cem—*cemetery* ... WI-6
Waumandee Creek—*stream* ... WI-6
Waumandee Sch—*school* ... WI-6
**Waumandee (Town of)**—*pop pl* ... WI-6
Waumandee Valley—*valley* ... WI-6
Waumanona Mound—*summit* ... AL-4
Waumbeck Junction—*locale* ... NH-1
Waumbek, Mount—*summit* ... NH-1
Wau-Me-Gah Lake—*lake* ... MI-6
*Waumgumbaug Lake* ... CT-1
Waumilla Lodge—*locale* ... WA-9
**Wauna**—*pop pl* ... OR-9
**Wauna**—*pop pl* ... WA-9
**Waunakee**—*pop pl* ... WI-6
Waunakee Marsh—*swamp* ... WI-6
Waunakee RR Depot—*hist pl* ... WI-6
Wauna Lake—*lake* ... WA-9
Wauna Point—*cape* ... OR-9
Wauna Range—*channel* ... OR-9
Waunatta, Lake—*lake* ... FL-3
Wauncher Gulch—*valley* ... ID-8
Waunch Prairie—*flat* ... WA-9
Waunch Prairie—*uninc pl* ... WA-9
Waun Drain—*canal* ... MI-6
Wauneka Point—*summit* ... OR-9
Wauneta—*locale* ... CO-8
Wauneta—*locale* ... KS-7
**Wauneta**—*pop pl* ... NE-7
Wauneta Trading Post—*locale* ... AZ-5
*Waungumbaug Lake* ... CT-1
Waunita Hot Springs—*locale* ... CO-8
Waunita Park—*flat* ... CO-8
Waunita Pass—*gap* ... CO-8
**Waupaca**—*pop pl* ... WI-6
Waupaca Boys Camp—*locale* ... WI-6
Waupaca Country Club—*other* ... WI-6
**Waupaca (County)**—*pop pl* ... WI-6
Waupaca River—*stream* ... WI-6
**Waupaca (Town of)**—*pop pl* ... WI-6
Waupace County Park—*park* ... WI-6
Waupan Valley—*basin* ... NE-7
Waupecan Creek—*stream* ... IL-6
*Waupecan Island* ... IL-6
*Waupecon Creek* ... IL-6
Waupee Creek—*stream* ... WI-6
Waupee Flowage—*channel* ... WI-6
*Waupee Lake* ... WI-6
Waupee Lake—*lake* ... WI-6
Waupeton—*locale* ... IA-7
Waupeton (historical P.O.)—*locale* ... IA-7
Waupeton School(Abandoned)—*locale* ... IA-7
*Waupe-um Brook* ... MA-1
**Wauponsee**—*pop pl* ... IL-6
**Wauponsee (Township of)**—*pop pl* ... IL-6
Waupopin Creek—*stream* ... NC-3
**Waupun**—*pop pl* ... WI-6
Waupun Public Library—*hist pl* ... WI-6
**Waupun (Town of)**—*pop pl* ... WI-6
**Wauregan**—*pop pl* ... CT-1
Wauregan Hist Dist—*hist pl* ... CT-1
Wauregan Pond—*lake* ... CT-1
**Wauregan Station**—*pop pl* ... CT-1
**Waurika**—*pop pl* ... OK-5
Waurika, Lake—*reservoir* ... OK-5
Waurika (CCD)—*cens area* ... OK-5
Waurika Cem—*cemetery* ... OK-5
*Waurika Reservoir* ... OK-5
**Wausa**—*pop pl* ... NE-7
*Wausau* ... MS-4
**Wausau**—*pop pl* ... FL-3
**Wausau**—*pop pl* ... WI-6
Wausau, Lake—*reservoir* ... WI-6
**Wausau Junction**—*pop pl* ... WI-6
**Wausaukee**—*pop pl* ... WI-6
Wausaukee River—*stream* ... WI-6
**Wausaukee (Town of)**—*pop pl* ... WI-6
Wausau Lookout Tower—*locale* ... MS-4
Wausau Oil Field—*oilfield* ... MS-4
**Wausau (Town of)**—*pop pl* ... WI-6
Wausau West—*uninc pl* ... WI-6
Wausau West-Rib Mountain—*CDP* ... WI-6
Wausau Work Center—*locale* ... MS-4
Wausaw Sch (historical)—*school* ... MS-4
Wauseca Mine—*mine* ... MI-6
**Wauseon**—*pop pl* ... OH-6
Wauseon Bay—*bay* ... FL-3
Wauseon Rsvr—*reservoir* ... OH-6
*Waushaccum Brook* ... MA-1
*Waushaccum Ponds* ... MA-1
Waushacum Brook—*stream* ... MA-1
*Waushacum Pond* ... MA-1
Waushakum Pond—*lake* ... MA-1
**Waushara (County)**—*pop pl* ... WI-6
Waushara County Courthouse, Waushara County Sheriff's Residence and Jail—*hist pl* ... WI-6
Waushara (historical)—*locale* ... KS-7
Wauswaugoning Bay—*bay* ... MN-6
**Wautauga Beach**—*pop pl* ... WA-9
Wautauga Spring—*spring* ... AR-4
*Wau-To* ... MP-9
**Wautoma**—*pop pl* ... WI-6
Wautoma, Lake—*lake* ... WI-6
**Wautoma Beach**—*pop pl* ... NY-2
Wautoma Cem—*cemetery* ... WI-6
Wautoma Pond—*lake* ... WI-6
Wautoma Shoals—*bar* ... NY-2
Wautoma Swamp—*swamp* ... WI-6
**Wautoma (Town of)**—*pop pl* ... WI-6
Wautubbee—*locale* ... MS-4
**Wauwatosa**—*pop pl* ... WI-6
Wauwatosa Cem—*cemetery* ... WI-6
Wauwatosa (Town of)—*civ div* ... WI-6
*Wauwecus Hill* ... CT-1
Wauwinel Island—*island* ... NY-2
**Wauwinet**—*pop pl* ... MA-1
Wauxamaka Creek—*stream* ... AL-4
**Wauzeka**—*pop pl* ... WI-6
Wauzeka Ridge—*ridge* ... WI-6
**Wauzeka (Town of)**—*pop pl* ... WI-6
*Wavaco* ... WV-2
Wave—*locale* ... AR-4
Wave—*locale* ... CA-9
Wave Creek—*gut* ... NJ-2
Wave Creek—*stream* ... WA-9
**Wave Crest**—*pop pl* ... NY-2
Wave Hill—*hist pl* ... NY-2
*Waveland* ... AL-4
Waveland—*hist pl* (2) ... KY-4
Waveland—*locale* ... IA-7
Waveland—*locale* ... MI-6
**Waveland**—*pop pl* ... AR-4
**Waveland**—*pop pl* ... FL-3
**Waveland**—*pop pl* ... IN-6
**Waveland**—*pop pl* ... MS-4
Waveland, Lake—*reservoir* ... IN-6
Waveland Cem—*cemetery* ... IA-7
Waveland Ch—*church* ... IL-6
Waveland City Hall—*building* ... MS-4
Waveland Civic Center—*building* ... MS-4
Waveland Conservation Club—*other* ... IN-6
Waveland Creek—*stream* ... IL-6
Waveland Elem Sch—*school* ... IN-6
Waveland Elem Sch—*school* ... MS-4
Waveland (historical)—*locale* ... KS-7
Waveland (historical P.O.)—*locale* ... IA-7
Waveland Library—*building* ... MS-4
Waveland Mine—*mine* ... UT-8
Waveland Museum—*building* ... KY-4
Waveland Park—*park* ... MN-6
Waveland Park Rec Area—*locale* ... AR-4
Waveland Post Office—*building* ... MS-4
Waveland Round Barn—*hist pl* ... IA-7
**Waveland (subdivision)**—*pop pl* ... MA-1
Waveland Township—*fmr MCD* ... IA-7
Waveland (Township of)—*fmr MCD* ... AR-4
Waveland United Methodist Ch—*church* ... MS-4
Wavering Park—*park* ... IL-6
**Waverland Beach**—*pop pl* ... MI-6
*Waverland Creek* ... IL-6
*Waverley* ... MS-4
Waverley—*hist pl* (2) ... MD-2
Waverley—*hist pl* ... MS-4
**Waverley**—*pop pl* ... ME-1
Waverley Cem—*cemetery* ... MS-4
*Waverley Plantation* ... MS-4
Waverley Post Office (historical)—*building* ... MS-4
**Waverley (subdivision)**—*pop pl* ... MA-1
*Waverly* ... FL-3
*Waverly* ... MA-1
Waverly—*hist pl* ... MD-2
Waverly—*hist pl* ... TX-5
Waverly—*hist pl* (2) ... VA-3
Waverly—*locale* ... CO-8
Waverly—*locale* ... MI-6
Waverly—*locale* ... NC-3
**Waverly**—*pop pl* ... AL-4
**Waverly**—*pop pl* ... AR-4
**Waverly**—*pop pl* ... CO-8
**Waverly**—*pop pl* ... FL-3
**Waverly**—*pop pl* ... GA-3
**Waverly**—*pop pl* ... IL-6
**Waverly**—*pop pl* ... IN-6
**Waverly**—*pop pl* ... IA-7
**Waverly**—*pop pl* ... KS-7
**Waverly**—*pop pl* ... KY-4
**Waverly**—*pop pl* ... LA-4
**Waverly**—*pop pl* ... ME-1
**Waverly**—*pop pl* ... MD-2
**Waverly**—*pop pl* ... MI-6
**Waverly**—*pop pl* ... MN-6
**Waverly**—*pop pl* ... MS-4
**Waverly**—*pop pl* ... MO-7
**Waverly**—*pop pl* ... NE-7
**Waverly**—*pop pl* (2) ... NY-2
**Waverly**—*pop pl* ... OH-6
**Waverly**—*pop pl* ... PA-2
**Waverly**—*pop pl* ... SD-7
**Waverly**—*pop pl* ... TN-4
**Waverly**—*pop pl* ... TX-5
**Waverly**—*pop pl* ... VA-3
**Waverly**—*pop pl* ... WA-9
**Waverly**—*pop pl* ... WV-2
**Waverly**—*pop pl* ... WI-6
Waverly Baby Home—*building* ... OR-9
**Waverly Beach**—*pop pl* ... WI-6
Waverly-Belmont Sch—*school* ... TN-4
*Waverly Boro* ... PA-2
*Waverly Branch* ... VA-3
Waverly Branch—*stream* ... VA-3
Waverly Campground—*locale* ... WI-6
Waverly Canal Hist Dist—*hist pl* ... OH-6
Waverly (CCD)—*cens area* ... AL-4
Waverly (CCD)—*cens area* ... TN-4
Waverly Cem—*cemetery* ... AL-4
Waverly Cem—*cemetery* ... KS-7
Waverly Cem—*cemetery* ... LA-4
Waverly Cem—*cemetery* ... MI-6
Waverly Cem—*cemetery* ... NY-2
Waverly Cem—*cemetery* ... TN-4
Waverly Central HS—*school* ... TN-4
*Waverly Central Sch* ... TN-4
Waverly Ch—*church* ... LA-4
Waverly Ch—*church* ... MN-6
**Waverly City**—*pop pl* ... OH-6
Waverly City Hall—*building* ... TN-4
Waverly City Park—*park* ... TN-4
Waverly Country Club—*locale* ... TN-4
Waverly Country Club—*other* ... OR-9
Waverly Creek—*stream* ... GA-3
Waverly Creek—*stream* ... MD-2
Waverly Creek—*stream* ... SC-3
Waverly Cutoff—*channel* ... MS-4
Waverly Division—*civil* ... AL-4
Waverly Division—*civil* ... TN-4
Waverly Drain Ditch—*canal* ... CO-8
Waverly (Election Precinct)—*fmr MCD* ... IL-6
Waverly Elem Sch—*school* ... IN-6
Waverly Elem Sch—*school* ... PA-2
Waverly Elem Sch—*school* ... TN-4
Waverly Ferry—*locale* ... MS-4
Waverly Ferry Access Area—*park* ... MS-4
Waverly Ferry Cutoff—*channel* ... MS-4
Waverly First Baptist Ch—*church* ... TN-4
Waverly Gables—*locale* ... OH-6
Waverly Gulch—*valley* ... CO-8
**Waverly Hall**—*pop pl* ... GA-3
Waverly Hall (CCD)—*cens area* ... GA-3
Waverly Hall Cem—*cemetery* ... GA-3
**Waverly Hall (subdivision)**—*pop pl* ... NC-3
Waverly Heights—*locale* ... PA-2
**Waverly Heights**—*pop pl* ... OR-9
**Waverly Heights**—*pop pl* ... PA-2
Waverly Hill—*hist pl* ... VA-3
**Waverly Hills**—*pop pl* ... KY-4
**Waverly Hills**—*pop pl* ... VA-3
Waverly Hills—*uninc pl* ... FL-3
**Waverly Hills (Geriatrics Center)**—*pop pl* ... KY-4
Waverly Hills Municipal Golf Course—*other* ... MI-6
Waverly Hills Park—*park* ... KY-4
Waverly Hills Sanatorium—*hospital* ... KY-4
Waverly Hills Tuberculosis Sanitarium Hist Bldgs—*hist pl* ... KY-4
Waverly Hollow—*valley* ... TN-4
Waverly Hosp—*hospital* ... TN-4
Waverly House—*hist pl* ... IA-7
Waverly HS—*school* ... IA-7
Waverly HS—*school* ... MI-6
Waverly Industrial Park—*locale* ... TN-4
Waverly JHS—*school* ... MI-6
Waverly JHS—*school* ... TN-4
Waverly Junction—*locale* ... IA-7
Waverly Junction Cem—*cemetery* ... IA-7
Waverly Lake—*lake* ... IL-6
Waverly Lake—*lake* ... MN-6
Waverly Lake—*lake* ... OR-9
Waverly Lake—*reservoir* ... NC-3
Waverly Lake Dam—*dam* ... NC-3
Waverly Landing (historical)—*locale* ... TN-4
Waverly (Magisterial District)—*fmr MCD* ... VA-3
**Waverly Manor**—*pop pl* ... PA-2
Waverly Mansion Cutoff—*channel* ... MS-4
Waverly Memorial Cem—*cemetery* ... OR-9
Waverly Mills—*locale* ... SC-3
Waverly Mine—*mine* ... ID-8
Waverly Mtn—*summit* ... CO-8
Waverly Park—*park* ... MN-6
**Waverly Park**—*pop pl* ... GA-3
Waverly Park—*uninc pl* ... CA-9
Waverly Park Sch—*school* ... NY-2
Waverly Place Hist Dist—*hist pl* ... TN-4
Waverly Place Landing—*locale* ... MS-4
**Waverly Place (subdivision)**—*pop pl* ... NC-3
Waverly Plantation—*hist pl* ... NC-3
Waverly Plaza Shop Ctr—*locale* ... TN-4
Waverly Point—*cape* ... LA-4
Waverly Point—*cape* ... MD-2
Waverly Point—*cape* ... VA-3
Waverly Point Oil Field—*oilfield* ... LA-4
Waverly Post Office—*building* ... TN-4
Waverly Public Sch—*school* ... AL-4
Waverly Reservoirs—*reservoir* ... NY-2
Waverly Sanitarium—*locale* ... SC-3
Waverly Sch—*school* ... CA-9
Waverly Sch—*school* ... CO-8
Waverly Sch—*school* ... KY-4
Waverly Sch—*school* ... LA-4
Waverly Sch—*school* ... MD-2
Waverly Sch—*school* ... NY-2
Waverly Sch—*school* ... OH-6
Waverly Sch—*school* ... OR-9
Waverly Sch—*school* ... PA-2
Waverly Sch—*school* ... SC-3
Waverly Shoal—*bar* ... WI-6
Waverly Street Bridge—*hist pl* ... MD-2
**Waverly Subdivision**—*pop pl* ... UT-8
Waverly Swamp—*swamp* ... GA-3
Waverly Terrace—*hist pl* ... GA-3
Waverly Terrace JHS—*school* ... GA-3
**Waverly (Town of)**—*pop pl* ... NY-2
Waverly Township—*civil* ... MO-7
**Waverly Township**—*pop pl* (2) ... SD-7
Waverly Township (historical)—*civil* ... SD-7
**Waverly (Township of)**—*pop pl* (2) ... MI-6
**Waverly (Township of)**—*pop pl* ... MN-6
**Waverly Village**—*pop pl* ... VA-3
**Waverly Woods**—*pop pl* ... IN-6
WAVERTREE—*hist pl* ... NY-2
Waver Tree Branch—*stream* ... SD-7
Wavertree Plantation—*locale* ... LA-4
**Waves**—*pop pl* ... NC-3
Waves Landing—*locale* ... NC-3
WAVL-AM (Apollo)—*tower* ... PA-2
Wavrick Cem—*cemetery* ... AR-4
WAVT-FM (Pottsville)—*tower* ... PA-2
WAVU-AM (Albertville)—*tower* ... AL-4
*Wavuer Mountain* ... AZ-5
WAVV-FM (Vevay)—*tower* ... IN-6
Waw, Mount—*summit* ... AK-9
Wawa—*locale* ... PA-2
Wawa Creek—*stream* ... ID-8
Wawa Creek—*stream* ... OR-9
Wawaeku—*summit* ... HI-9
Wawaeolepe—*civil* ... HI-9
Wawah (historical)—*locale* ... AL-4
Wawahiwaa Point—*cape* ... HI-9
Wawaia—*civil* ... HI-9
Wawaia Gulch—*valley* ... HI-9
Wawaionu Bay—*bay* ... HI-9
**Wawaka**—*pop pl* ... IN-6
Wawaka Elem Sch—*school* ... IN-6
Wawaka Lake—*lake* ... NY-2
Wawa Lake—*lake* ... MN-6
Wawaloli Beach—*beach* ... HI-9
Wawamalu Beach Park—*park* ... HI-9
Wawa Point—*cape* ... WA-9
**Wawa (P.O.) (Wawa Dairy)**—*pop pl* ... PA-2
**Wawarsing**—*pop pl* ... NY-2
**Wawarsing (Town of)**—*pop pl* ... NY-2
**Wawasee**—*pop pl* ... IN-6
Wawasee, Lake—*lake* ... IN-6
Wawasee Airp—*airport* ... IN-6
Wawasee Golf Club—*other* ... IN-6
Wawasee HS—*school* ... IN-6
*Wawasee Lake* ... IN-6
Wawasee Public Fishing Area—*park* ... IN-6
Wawasee State Fish Hatchery—*other* ... IN-6
*Wawasee State Fishing Area* ... IN-6
**Wawasee Village**—*pop pl* ... IN-6
**Wawaset**—*pop pl* ... PA-2
**Wawaset Park**—*pop pl* ... DE-2
Wawaset Park Hist Dist—*hist pl* ... DE-2
W A Wash—*stream* ... AZ-5
Wawaswi Lake—*lake* ... MN-6
*Wawatam Beach* ... MI-6
**Wawatam (Township of)**—*pop pl* ... MI-6
Wawatosa Island—*island* ... MN-6
Wawau—*cape* ... HI-9
**Wawawai**—*pop pl* ... WA-9
Wawawai Bay—*bay* ... WA-9
Wawawai Canyon—*valley* ... WA-9
Wawawai Landing—*locale* ... WA-9
Wawayanda—*locale* (2) ... NJ-2
Wawayanda Channel—*channel* ... NY-2
Wawayanda Creek—*stream* ... NJ-2
Wawayanda Creek—*stream* ... NY-2
*Wawayanda Furnace* ... NJ-2
Wawayanda Lake—*reservoir* ... NJ-2
Wawayanda Lake Dam—*dam* ... NJ-2
Wawayanda Mtn—*summit* ... NJ-2
Wawayanda State Park—*park* ... NJ-2
**Wawayanda (Town of)**—*pop pl* ... NY-2
*Wawayontat* ... MA 1
*Wawayontat River* ... MA-1
*Wawaytick Creek* ... MA-1
Wawbeek—*locale* ... AL-4
**Wawbeek**—*pop pl* ... NH-1
**Wawbeek**—*pop pl* ... NY-2
Wawbeek-Horace A.J. Upham House—*hist pl* ... WI-6
Wawecus Hill—*summit* ... CT-1
**Wawela Park**—*pop pl* ... MA-1
W A Well—*well* ... AZ-5
Wawenock Country Club—*other* ... ME-1
WAWF-FM (Kendallville)—*tower* ... IN-6
**Wa-Will-Away Park**—*pop pl* ... IN-6
W A Williamson Dam—*dam* ... AL-4
**Wawina**—*pop pl* ... MN-6
Wawina Ch—*church* ... MN-6
**Wawina (Township of)**—*pop pl* ... MN-6
WAWK-AM (Kendallville)—*tower* ... IN-6
*Wawkasawsa* ... FL-3
*Wawk Hudunik* ... AZ-5
**Wawona**—*pop pl* ... CA-9
Wawona Campground—*locale* ... CA-9
Wawona Dome—*summit* ... CA-9
Wawona Hotel and Pavilion—*hist pl* ... CA-9
Wawona JHS—*school* ... CA-9
Wawona Point—*summit* ... CA-9
WAWONA (schooner)—*hist pl* ... WA-9
Wawona Tunnel—*tunnel* ... CA-9
W A Woodward Lumber Company Log Dam—*dam* ... OR-9
W A Woodward Lumber Company Log Pond—*reservoir* ... OR-9
**Wawpecong**—*pop pl* ... IN-6
Wawwanoka, Lake—*reservoir* ... MO-7
Wax—*locale* ... GA-3
Wax—*locale* ... KY-4
*Waxa Creek* ... NC-3
**Waxahachie**—*pop pl* ... TX-5
Waxahachie, Lake—*reservoir* ... TX-5
Waxahachie (CCD)—*cens area* ... TX-5
Waxahachie Chautauqua Bldg—*hist pl* ... TX-5
Waxahachie Creek—*stream* ... TX-5
Waxahachie Lumber Company—*hist pl* ... TX-5
Waxahachie Slough—*gut* ... TX-5
Waxahatchee Camp—*locale* ... AL-4
Waxahatchee Creek—*stream* ... AL-4
Waxahatchee (historical)—*locale* ... AL-4
*Wax Bayou* ... LA-4
Wax Bayou—*gut* ... LA-4
Wax Branch—*stream* ... KY-4
**Waxdale**—*pop pl* ... WI-6
Waxell Ridge—*ridge* ... AK-9
Wax Factory Laccolith—*summit* ... TX-5
Wax Factory Pond—*reservoir* ... MA-1
Wax Factory Pond Dam—*dam* ... MA-1
Waxhaw—*locale* ... MS-4
**Waxhaw**—*pop pl* ... NC-3
Waxhaw Branch—*stream* ... NC-3
Waxhaw Ch—*church* ... MS-4
Waxhaw Ch—*church* ... NC-3
*Wax Haw Creek* ... NC-3
Waxhaw Creek—*stream* ... NC-3
Waxhaw Creek—*stream* ... SC-3
*Waxhaw Landing* ... MS-4
*Waxhaw Plantation* ... MS-4
Waxhaw Post Office (historical)—*building* ... MS-4
Waxhaw Presbyterian Church Cemetery—*hist pl* ... SC-3
Waxhaw-Weddington Roads Hist Dist—*hist pl* ... NC-3
Waxhoma, Lake—*reservoir* ... OK-5
**Waxia**—*pop pl* ... LA-4
WAXI-FM (Rockville)—*tower* ... IN-6
Wax Lake—*lake* ... GA-3
Wax Lake—*lake* ... LA-4
Wax Lake—*lake* ... MN-6
Wax Lake Outlet—*channel* ... LA-4
Wax Lake Pass—*channel* ... LA-4
Waxler Ch—*church* ... OH-6
Wax North Channel—*channel* ... LA-4
WAXO-AM (Lewisburg)—*tower* ... TN-4
Wax Orchards Airp—*airport* ... WA-9
Waxpool—*locale* ... VA-3
Wax South Channel—*channel* ... LA-4
Wax Spring Branch—*stream* ... AL-4
Waxter Hollow—*valley* ... WV-2
WAXT-FM (Alexandria)—*tower* ... IN-6
Waxtree Hollow—*valley* ... AL-4
Waxtree Hollow—*valley* ... TN-4
Waxweed Run—*stream* ... AR-4
Way—*locale* ... OH-6
Way—*locale* ... TN-4
Way—*locale* ... WI-6
**Way**—*pop pl* ... KS-7
**Way**—*pop pl* ... MS-4
Way, Dr. J. Howell, House—*hist pl* ... NC-3
Way, Nicholas, House—*hist pl* ... PA-2
Wayah Bald—*summit* ... NC-3
Wayah Branch—*stream* ... NC-3
*Wayah Creek* ... NC-3
Wayah Creek—*stream* ... NC-3
Wayah Crest Camp Ground—*locale* ... NC-3
**Wayah Depot**—*pop pl* ... NC-3
Wayah Gap—*gap* ... NC-3
Wayan Creek—*stream* ... ID-8
Wayan Sch—*school* ... ID-8
**Wayan (Unincorp)**—*pop pl* ... ID-8
*Wayauwega* ... WI-6
**Wayback**—*pop pl* ... GA-3
Way Back Trail—*trail* ... WV-2
Waybourn Windmill—*locale* ... TX-5
Waybright Cem—*cemetery* ... WV-2
Waybright Run—*stream* ... WV-2
Waybright Sch—*school* ... MA-1
Wayburn Windmill—*locale* ... TX-5
Waybury Inn—*hist pl* ... VT-1
*Waycake Creek* ... NJ-2
WAYC-AM (Bedford)—*tower* ... PA-2
Way Cem—*cemetery* ... CT-1
Way Cem—*cemetery* ... OR-9
Way Cem—*cemetery* ... WV-2
**Waycinden Park**—*pop pl* ... IL-6
**Wayco**—*pop pl* ... OH-6
Waycoster Spring—*spring* ... TN-4
Way Creek—*stream* ... OR-9
Way Creek—*stream* ... WA-9
Way Creek—*stream* ... WY-8
Waycross—*locale* ... NC-3
Waycross—*locale* ... TN-4
**Waycross**—*pop pl* ... GA-3
**Waycross**—*pop pl* ... IN-6
Waycross (CCD)—*cens area* ... GA-3
*Way Cross Ch* ... AL-4
Waycross Ch—*church* ... AL-4
Waycross Ch—*church* ... SC-3
Waycrosse-Ware County Airp—*airport* ... GA-3
Waycross Gospel Tabernacle—*church* ... GA-3
Waycross Hist Dist—*hist pl* ... GA-3
Waycross State For—*forest* ... GA-3
Waycross State Forest—*park* ... GA-3
Waycross Vocational Sch—*school* ... GA-3
Waycross Ware Technical Sch—*school* ... GA-3
Way Dam—*dam* ... MI-6
WAYD-AM (Ozark)—*tower* ... AL-4
Waydelich Creek—*stream* ... AK-9
*Way Ditch* ... IN-6
Waydown Rsvr—*reservoir* ... MT-8
*Wayeh River* ... TN-4
Wayehutta Creek—*stream* ... NC-3
Wayfair Ch—*church* ... FL-3
Wayfare Cem—*cemetery* ... FL-3
Wayfarer Ch—*church* (2) ... GA-3
Wayfarers Chapel—*church* ... CA-9
Wayfares Chapel—*locale* ... WY-8
Wayfaring Ch of God—*church* ... AL-4
*Wayfield* ... KY-4
**Wayfield (subdivision)**—*pop pl* ... TN-4
Wayfound Ch—*church* ... NC-3
Waygadt—*locale* ... PA-2
Way Hill—*summit* ... CA-9
Way Hollow—*valley* ... IN-6
Way Hollow—*valley* ... MO-7
Way House—*hist pl* ... OK-5
Wayka Creek—*stream* ... WI-6
Wayka Falls—*falls* ... WI-6
Way Key—*island* ... FL-3
*Way Lake* ... CA-9
Way Lake—*lake* ... CA-9
Way Lake Oil Field—*oilfield* ... TX-5
Wayland—*locale* ... ID-8
Wayland—*locale* ... IL-6
Wayland—*locale* ... MN-6

Wayland—locale OR-9
Wayland—locale TX-5
Wayland—pop pl IA-7
Wayland—pop pl KY-4
Wayland—pop pl MA-1
Wayland—pop pl MI-6
Wayland—pop pl MO-7
Wayland—pop pl NY-2
Wayland—pop pl OH-6
Wayland—pop pl PA-2
Wayland—pop pl RI-1
Wayland—pop pl (2) VA-3
Wayland, Julius A., House—hist pl KS-7
Wayland Acad—school WI-6
Wayland Ampitheater—building TX-5
Wayland Arbor Cem—cemetery AR-4
Wayland Canyon—valley (2) NM-5
Wayland (CCD)—cens area KY-4
Wayland Cem—cemetery IL-6
Wayland Cem—cemetery OK-5
Wayland Center—pop pl MA-1
Wayland Center Hist Dist—hist pl MA-1
Wayland Centre MA-1
Wayland Ch—church NE-7
Wayland Ch—church (2) VA-3
Wayland Coll—school TX-5
Wayland Country Club—locale MA-1
Wayland Creek—stream AR-4
Wayland Creek—stream CA-9
Wayland Hot Springs—spring ID-8
Wayland HS—school (2) MA-1
Wayland Island—island CT-1
Wayland JHS—school MA-1
Wayland Lake—reservoir TN-4
Wayland Lake Dam—dam TN-4
Waylands Mill—locale VA-3
Wayland Spring—spring AR-4
Wayland Spring Camp—locale AR-4
Wayland Springs—pop pl TN-4
Wayland Springs Cem—cemetery TN-4
Wayland Springs Methodist Ch—church TN-4
Wayland Springs Post Office (historical)—building TN-4
Wayland Station at Old Farm Condo—pop pl UT-8
Wayland (Town of)—pop pl MA-1
Wayland (Town of)—pop pl NY-2
Wayland Township—pop pl MO-7
Wayland (Township of)—pop pl MI-6
Wayle Creek—stream ID-8
Waylee Sch—school MI-6
Waylett Canyon—valley ID-8
Waylett Mine—mine MT-8
Waylett Spring—spring ID-8
Waylonzo—pop pl FL-3
Waylyn—pop pl SC-3
Wayman MD-2
Wayman, Lake—lake FL-3
Wayman Branch—stream KY-4
Wayman Branch—stream NY-2
Wayman Cem—cemetery IL-6
Wayman Cem—cemetery (2) IN-6
Wayman Cem—cemetery KY-4
Wayman Ch—church MD-2
Wayman Ch—church NC-3
Wayman Chapel—church AL-4
Wayman Chapel—church SC-3
Wayman Chapel—church TN-4
Wayman Chapel AME Ch—church AL-4
Wayman Creek—stream IA-7
Wayman Ditch—canal IN-6
Wayman Draw CA-9
Wayman Hill—summit NY-2
Wayman Lakes (historical)—lake MO-7
Wayman Ranch—locale CA-9
Wayman Ranch—locale MT-8
Wayman Sch (abandoned)—school MO-7
Waymans Chapel AL-4
Waymans Chapel AME Ch—church AL-4
Wayman Sch (historical)—school MO-7
Waymans Creek NC-3
Wayman Spring—spring CA-9
Waymans Ridge—ridge WV-2
Waymans Ridge Ch—church WV-2
Waymansville—pop pl IN-6
Waymans Wharf MD-2
Wayman Wharf—locale MD-2
Waymark Subdivision—pop pl UT-8
Waymart—pop pl PA-2
Waymart Borough—civil PA-2
Waymeir Creek—stream MT-8
Waymeyer Chute—channel MO-7
Waymier Lake—lake MN-6
Waymire, C. H., Bldg—hist pl ID-8
Waymire Cem—cemetery IN-6
Waymire Creek—stream OR-9
Waymire Creek—stream WA-9
Waymire Sch—school NE-7
Waymires Lake—reservoir IN-6
Waymires Lake Dam—dam IN-6
Waymon Chapel—church NC-3
Waymon Chapel—church TX-5
Waymon Chapel Sch—school NC-3
Waymond Cem—cemetery TN-4
Way-Morr County Park—park WI-6
WAYN-AM (Rockingham)—tower NC-3
Wayne TN-4
Wayne—locale AZ-5
Wayne—locale CA-9
Wayne—locale MT-8
Wayne—locale WA-9
Wayne—pop pl AL-4
Wayne—pop pl IL-6
Wayne—pop pl IN-6
Wayne—pop pl KS-7
Wayne—pop pl ME-1
Wayne—pop pl MI-6
Wayne—pop pl MO-7
Wayne—pop pl NE-7
Wayne—pop pl NJ-2
Wayne—pop pl (2) NY-2
Wayne—pop pl (2) OH-6
Wayne—pop pl OK-5
Wayne—pop pl PA-2
Wayne—pop pl WV-2
Wayne—pop pl WI-6
Wayne, Anthony, Sch—hist pl PA-2
Wayne, Lake—reservoir TX-5
Wayne Acad—school MS-4
Wayne Ave Park—park OH-6
Wayne Ave Sch—school NC-3
Wayne Ave Shop Ctr—locale NC-3
Wayne Besler Dam—dam SD-7
Wayne Blockhouse—building PA-2
Wayne Branch—stream MS-4
Wayne Branch—stream TN-4
Wayne Butte—summit OR-9
Wayne Canyon—valley (2) NM-5
Wayne Canyon—valley UT-8
Waynecastle—pop pl PA-2
Waynecastle Cave—cave PA-2
Wayne Cem—cemetery IA-7
Wayne Cem—cemetery KS-7
Wayne Cem—cemetery MI-6
Wayne Cem—cemetery (2) WV-2
Wayne Cem—cemetery (2) WI-6
Wayne Center—pop pl IL-6
Wayne Center—pop pl IN-6
Wayne Center—pop pl NY-2
Wayne Center Cem—cemetery IL-6
Wayne Center Elem Sch—school IN-6
Wayne Center Sch—school IA-7
Wayne Center Sch—school WI-6
Wayne Central Sch—school NY-2
Wayne Ch—church OH-6
Wayne Ch—church PA-2
Wayne Chapel—church AR-4
Wayne Chapel—church MI-6
Wayne Chapel—church NC-3
Wayne City—pop pl IL-6
Wayne Company Wildlife Club Pond—reservoir NC-3
Wayne Cooper Subdivision—pop pl UT-8
Wayne County—civil MO-7
Wayne County—civil NC-3
Wayne County—civil UT-8
Wayne (County)—pop pl GA-3
Wayne (County)—pop pl IL-6
Wayne County—pop pl IN-6
Wayne (County)—pop pl KY-4
Wayne (County)—pop pl MI-6
Wayne County—pop pl MS-4
Wayne (County)—pop pl MO-7
Wayne (County)—pop pl NY-2
Wayne (County)—pop pl OH-6
Wayne County—pop pl PA-2
Wayne County—pop pl TN-4
Wayne (County)—pop pl WV-2
Wayne County Child Development Center—building MI-6
Wayne County Courthouse—building MS-4
Wayne County Courthouse—building TN-4
Wayne County Courthouse—hist pl GA-3
Wayne County Courthouse—hist pl IN-6
Wayne County Courthouse—hist pl MI-6
Wayne County Courthouse—hist pl NE-7
Wayne County Courthouse District—hist pl OH-6
Wayne County Day Sch—school NC-3
Wayne County Dixie Baseball Complex—park MS-4
Wayne County Farm (historical)—locale MS-4
Wayne County Farm (historical)—locale TN-4
Wayne County General Hosp—hospital TN-4
Wayne County Hosp—hospital IA-7
Wayne County HS—hist pl UT-8
Wayne County HS—school TN-4
Wayne County Memorial Gardens—cemetery TN-4
Wayne County Memory Gardens—cemetery TN-4
Wayne County Vocational Center—school TN-4
Wayne County Vocational Complex—school MS-4
Wayne County Wildlife Pond Dam—dam NC-3
Wayne Creek—stream MT-8
Wayne Creek—stream TX-5
Wayne Creek—stream VA-3
Wayne Creek—stream WI-6
Waynedale IN-6
Waynedale—pop pl IN-6
Waynedale Memorial Park—park IN-6
Waynedale Sch—school OH-6
Wayne E Kirch Wildlife Mngmt Area—park NV-8
Wayne Elem Sch (abandoned)—school PA-2
Wayne Fitzgerrell State Park—park IL-6
Wayne Four Corners—locale NY-2
Wayne Furnace (historical)—locale TN-4
Wayne General Hosp—hospital MS-4
Wayne Golf Course—other WA-9
Wayne Grove For Preserve—forest IL-6
Wayne Haven United Methodist Ch—church MS-4
Wayne Heights—pop pl PA-2
Wayne Highlands MS—school PA-2
Wayne Hills Sch—school VA-3
Wayne (historical P.O.)—locale IA-7
Wayne Hollow—valley MO-7
Wayne Hotel—hist pl PA-2
Wayne HS—school UT-8
Wayne HS—school WV-2
Wayne Isley Dam—dam NC-3
Wayne Isley Lake—reservoir NC-3
Wayne Junction MI-6
Wayne Junction—pop pl PA-2
Wayne Kennedy Dam—dam SD-7
Wayne Kjos Dam—dam SD-7
Wayne Kopp Lake—reservoir IN-6
Wayne Kopp Lake Dam—dam IN-6
Wayne Lakes Park—pop pl OH-6
Wayne Lakes Parke—pop pl OH-6
Wayne Lookout Tower—locale MS-4
Wayne (Magisterial District)—fmr MCD VA-3
Wayne Marsh—swamp WI-6
Wayne Memorial Ch—church AL-4
Wayne Memorial Hosp—hospital GA-3
Wayne Memorial Park—cemetery NC-3
Wayne MS—school PA-2
Wayne MS—school UT-8
Wayne N Aspinall Unit, The—reservoir CO-8
Wayne Natl For—forest OH-6
Wayne Office Helistop—airport NJ-2
Wayne Park—park PA-2
Wayne P. O. AL-4
Wayneport—pop pl NY-2
Wayne Ranch—locale TX-5
Wayner Cem—cemetery IL-6
Wayne Ridge—ridge WV-2
Wayne Ridge (subdivision)—pop pl NC-3
Waynes Air Service Airp—airport OR-9
Waynesboro—pop pl GA-3
Waynesboro—pop pl MS-4
Waynesboro—pop pl (2) PA-2
Waynesboro—pop pl TN-4
Waynesboro Borough—civil PA-2
Waynesboro Bridge—hist pl MS-4
Waynesboro (CCD)—cens area GA-3
Waynesboro (CCD)—cens area TN-4
Waynesboro Cem—cemetery MS-4
Waynesboro City Hall—building MS-4
Waynesboro Country Club—locale MS-4
Waynesboro Country Club—other PA-2
Waynesboro Cumberland Presbyterian Church—hist pl TN-4
Waynesboro Dam PA-2
Waynesboro Dam—dam PA-2
Waynesboro Division—civil TN-4
Waynesboro Elem Sch—school MS-4
Waynesboro Elem Sch—school TN-4
Waynesboro First Baptist Ch—church TN-4
Waynesboro First United Methodist Ch—church MS-4
Waynesboro High School MS-4
Waynesboro Hospital Airp—airport PA-2
Waynesboro (ind. city)—pop pl VA-3
Waynesboro Industrial Park—locale MS-4
Waynesboro Industrial Park—locale TN-4
Waynesboro JHS—school MS-4
Waynesboro Junction—locale PA-2
Waynesboro Lagoon Dam—dam MS-4
Waynesboro Lake—reservoir MS-4
Waynesboro Lake Dam—dam MS-4
Waynesboro Memorial Library—building MS-4
Waynesboro MS—school TN-4
Waynesboro Municipal Airp—airport MS-4
Waynesboro Post Office—building TN-4
Waynesboro Presbyterian Ch—church MS-4
Waynesboro Ridge—ridge TN-4
Waynesboro Rsvr—reservoir (2) PA-2
Waynesboro Spring—spring TN-4
Waynesborough—hist pl PA-2
Waynesborough Post Office TN-4
Waynesburg PA-2
Waynesburg—pop pl IN-6
Waynesburg—pop pl KY-4
Waynesburg—pop pl (2) OH-6
Waynesburg—pop pl PA-2
Waynesburg Borough—civil PA-2
Waynesburg (CCD)—cens area KY-4
Waynesburg Coll—school PA-2
Waynesburgh IN-6
Waynesburg Hist Dist—hist pl PA-2
Waynesburg Sch—school PA-2
Waynesburg Water Company Dam—dam PA-2
Waynesburg Water Company Rsvr—reservoir PA-2
Wayne Sch PA-2
Wayne Sch—school IA-7
Wayne Sch—school MI-6
Wayne Sch—school (6) OH-6
Wayne Sch—school PA-2
Wayne Sch (abandoned)—school MO-7
Wayne Sch (abandoned)—school PA-2
Wayne Sch (historical)—school PA-2
Wayne Sch Number 2 PA-2
Wayne School (Abondoned)—locale CA-9
Waynes Corner DE-2
Waynes Corner—pop pl DE-2
Waynes Creek—stream WY-8
Waynes Creek Range Experiment Station—locale WY-8
Waynesfield—pop pl OH-6
Waynesfield (Township of)—civ div OH-6
Waynes Hole—flat WY-8
Wayne State Univ—school MI-6
Wayne State Univ Buildings—hist pl MI-6
Wayne State Univ Med Ctr—school MI-6
Wayne State Univ Sch of Medicine—school MI-6
Wayne Station—building PA-2
Wayne Station—locale NJ-2
Wayne Station (historical)—locale TN-4
Waynesville—pop pl GA-3
Waynesville—pop pl IL-6
Waynesville—pop pl IN-6
Waynesville—pop pl MO-7
Waynesville—pop pl NC-3
Waynesville—pop pl OH-6
Waynesville—pop pl PA-2
Waynesville (CCD)—cens area GA-3
Waynesville General Hosp—hospital MO-7
Waynesville Golf and Country Club—locale NC-3
Waynesville Greek Revival Houses—hist pl OH-6
Waynesville JHS—school NC-3
Waynesville Memorial Airfield (historical)—locale MO-7
Waynesville Plaza (Shop Ctr)—locale NC-3
Waynesville Rsvr—reservoir (2) NC-3
Waynesville (sta.) (RR name for Corwin)—other OH-6
Waynesville (Township of)—fmr MCD NC-3
Waynesville (Township of)—pop pl IL-6
Waynesville Water Supply Dam—dam NC-3
Waynesville Water Supply Lake—reservoir NC-3
Waynes Well—well AZ-5
Wayne Taylor Peak—summit AK-9
Wayne Thomas Sch—school IL-6
Waynetown—pop pl IN-6
Waynetown Elementary and JHS—school IN-6
Wayne Town House—hist pl ME-1
Wayne (Town of)—pop pl ME-1
Wayne (Town of)—pop pl NY-2
Wayne (Town of)—pop pl (2) WI-6
Wayne Township—civil (2) MO-7
Wayne Township—civil PA-2
Wayne Township—fmr MCD (4) IA-7
Wayne Township—pop pl (2) KS-7
Wayne Township—pop pl NE-7
Wayne Township—pop pl ND-7
Wayne Township—pop pl (3) SD-7
Wayne (Township of)—fmr MCD OH-6
Wayne (Township of)—other OH-6
Wayne (Township of)—pop pl IL-6
Wayne (Township of)—pop pl (16) IN-6
Wayne (Township of)—pop pl MI-6
Wayne (Township of)—pop pl NJ-2
Wayne (Township of)—pop pl (20) OH-6
Wayne (Township of)—pop pl (9) PA-2
Wayne Trace Ridge—ridge TN-4
Wayne Trail Sch—school OH-6
Wayne Tunnel—tunnel MT-8
Wayne Tunnel—tunnel PA-2
Wayne Valley Ch—church PA-2
Wayne Village Hist Dist—hist pl IL-6
Wayne Village Shop Ctr—locale MS-4
Wayne Wallace, Lake—reservoir OK-5
Wayne West Ranch—locale TX-5
Wayne Wonderland Airp—airport UT-8
Waynewood—pop pl VA-3
Waynewood Lake—reservoir PA-2
Waynewood Sch—school VA-3
Wayne Zion Cem—cemetery IA-7
Wayne Zion Ch—church IA-7
Waynick Hollow—valley TN-4
Waynick Lake—reservoir NC-3
Waynick Lake Dam—dam NC-3
Waynoka—pop pl OK-5
Waynoka, Lake—reservoir OH-6
Waynoka Municipal Cem—cemetery OK-5
Waynsboro PA-2
Way of Florida, The—church FL-3
Way of Grace Baptist Ch—church MS-4
Way of Life Assembly of God Ch—church FL-3
Way of Life Baptist Ch—church FL-3
Way of Life Chapel—church MO-7
Way of the Cross Ch—church MN-6
Way of the Cross Church, The—church AL-4
Wayomink PA-2
Way Park—park OK-5
Way Park Museum—hist pl SD-7
Way Point—cape AK-9
Way Pond—lake FL-3
Wayport—pop pl IN-6
Way Post Office (historical)—building TN-4
Way Ranch—locale OR-9
Way River MA-1
Ways GA-3
WAYS-AM (Charlotte)—tower NC-3
Ways Bluff MS-4
Ways Brook—stream NH-1
Ways Ch—church GA-3
Way Sch—school IL-6
Way Sch—school MI-6
Ways Corner—pop pl DE-2
Ways Garden Park—park PA-2
Ways Grove Ch—church GA-3
Ways Gulch—valley CO-8
Wayside MS-4
Wayside—hist pl TN-4
Wayside—locale IL-6
Wayside—locale IA-7
Wayside—locale KY-4
Wayside—locale LA-4
Wayside—locale MD-2
Wayside—locale NE-7
Wayside—locale NC-3
Wayside—locale (2) TN-4
Wayside—locale TX-5
Wayside—locale WA-9
Wayside—pop pl AL-4
Wayside—pop pl GA-3
Wayside—pop pl KS-7
Wayside—pop pl MA-1
Wayside—pop pl MS-4
Wayside—pop pl NJ-2
Wayside—pop pl TX-5
Wayside—pop pl VA-3
Wayside—pop pl WV-2
Wayside—pop pl WI-6
Wayside, The—building MA-1
Wayside, The—hist pl MA-1
Wayside Baptist Ch AL-4
Wayside Baptist Ch—church (2) AL-4
Wayside Baptist Church MS-4
Wayside Baptist Preschool—school FL-3
Wayside Butte—summit NE-7
Wayside Canyon—valley CA-9
Wayside Canyon Oil Field CA-9
Wayside Cem—cemetery AL-4
Way Side Cem—cemetery IA-7
Wayside Cem—cemetery ME-1
Wayside Cem—cemetery NY-2
Wayside Cem—cemetery ND-7
Wayside Cem—cemetery TX-5
Wayside Cem—cemetery WA-9
Wayside Cem—cemetery WI-6
Wayside Ch—church (3) AL-4
Wayside Ch—church (2) FL-3
Wayside Ch—church (3) GA-3
Wayside Ch—church IN-6
Wayside Ch—church KY-4
Wayside Ch—church (3) LA-4
Wayside Ch—church MI-6
Wayside Ch—church (4) MS-4
Wayside Ch—church NJ-2
Wayside Ch—church (8) NC-3
Wayside Ch—church OK-5
Wayside Ch—church PA-2
Wayside Ch—church (2) SC-3
Wayside Ch—church (3) TN-4
Wayside Ch—church (3) TX-5
Wayside Ch—church (2) VA-3
Wayside Ch—church (2) WV-2
Wayside Chapel—church (2) MI-6
Wayside Chapel—church NH-1
Wayside Chapel—church OH-6
Wayside Chapel—church PA-2
Wayside Chapel—church SC-3
Wayside Chapel—church TN-4
Wayside Chapel—church TX-5
Wayside Chapel—church WI-6
Wayside Chaple—church CO-8
Wayside Ch of Deliverance MS-4
Wayside Community Center—locale TX-5
Wayside Community Ch AL-4
Wayside Cottage—hist pl NY-2
Wayside Creek OK-5
Wayside Creek—stream OK-5
Wayside Holt School AL-4
Wayside Honor Rancho—civil CA-9
Wayside House—hist pl WI-6
Wayside Inn—building MA-1
Wayside Inn—hist pl LA-4
Wayside Inn—hist pl MA-1
Wayside Inn Hist Dist—hist pl MA-1
Wayside Junior High School AL-4
Wayside Lode Mine—mine SD-7
Wayside Manor—pop pl VA-3
Wayside Memorial State For Picnic Area—area PA-2
Wayside Methodist Ch AL-4
Wayside Mine—mine WA-9
Wayside Mission—church WI-6
Wayside Mission Ch—church PA-2
Wayside Oil Field—oilfield MS-4
Wayside Park—park CA-9
Wayside Park—park FL-3
Wayside Park—park IL-6
Wayside Park—park KS-7
Wayside Park—park (3) MN-6
Wayside Park—park NE-7
Wayside Park—park (2) WI-6
Wayside Plaza—locale MA-1
Wayside Sch—school AL-4
Wayside Sch—school CA-9
Wayside Sch—school MD-2
Wayside Sch—school (3) NE-7
Wayside Sch—school NY-2
Wayside Sch—school NC-3
Wayside Sch—school OK-5
Wayside Sch—school SC-3
Wayside Sch—school (2) SD-7
Wayside Sch—school (2) WI-6
Wayside Sch (historical)—school MS-4
Wayside Sch (historical)—school TN-4
Wayside School—locale WA-9
Wayside Shop Ctr—locale FL-3
Wayside Springs Forest Camp—park OR-9
Wayside State Park—park OR-9
Wayside (subdivision)—pop pl AL-4
Wayside Temple—church OH-6
Wayside Well—cave TN-4
Wayside Woods—park IL-6
Ways Lake—lake MN-6
Wayson Pond—lake MD-2
Ways Run—stream PA-2
Way's Station GA-3
WAYT-AM (Wabash)—tower IN-6
Wayte, Mount—summit MA-1
Wayton—locale AR-4
Wayunckeke Hill RI-1
Wayunckeko Hill RI-1
Wayunkeak Hill RI-1
Wayup Mine—mine MT-8
Way-Up Mtn—summit NM-5
Wayville—locale NY-2
Way Way Cem—cemetery LA-4
WAYZ-AM (Waynesboro)—tower PA-2
Wayzata—pop pl MN-6
Wayzata Bay—bay MN-6
Wayzata Boulevard MN-6
Wayzata Country Club—other MN-6
Wayzata HS—school MN-6
Wayzetta Township—pop pl ND-7
WAYZ-FM (Waynesboro)—tower PA-2
Wazeecha Lake—reservoir WI-6
Waze River ID-8
Wazer River ID-8
WAZF-AM (Yazoo City)—tower MS-4
WAZI-FM (Morristown)—tower TN-4
WAZL-AM (Hazelton)—tower PA-2
WAZY-FM (Lafayette)—tower IN-6
WAZZ-FM (New Bern)—tower NC-3
WBAA-AM (West Lafayette)—tower IN-6
WBAC-AM (Cleveland)—tower TN-4
WBAD-FM (Leland)—tower MS-4
WBAG-FM (Burlington-Graham)—tower NC-3
WBAK-TV (Terre Haute)—tower IN-6
WBAM-AM (Montgomery)—tower AL-4
WBAM-FM (Montgomery)—tower AL-4
WBAQ-FM (Greenville)—tower MS-4
W Bar K Ranch—locale NM-5
W-Bar Tank—reservoir TX-5
WBAT-AM (Marion)—tower IN-6
WBAX-AM (Wilkes-Barre)—tower PA-2
WBBB-AM (Burlington-Graham)—tower NC-3
WBBJ-TV (Jackson)—tower TN-4
WBBO-AM (Forest City)—tower NC-3
WBBO-FM (Forest City)—tower NC-3
W B Boutwell Pond Dam—dam MS-4
WBCA-AM (Bay Minette)—tower AL-4
WBCB-AM (Lancaster)—tower PA-2
WBCF-AM (Florence)—tower AL-4
WBCL-FM (Fort Wayne)—tower IN-6
W B Cogdell Dam—dam AL-4
WBCV-AM (Bristol)—tower (2) TN-4
WBCW-AM (Jeannette)—tower PA-2
WBCY-FM (Charlotte)—tower NC-3
WBDC-FM (Huntingburg)—tower IN-6
WBDG-FM (Indianapolis)—tower IN-6
WBDJ-FM (Brazil)—tower IN-6
W B D Oil Field—oilfield TX-5
W B Donovan Lake Dam—dam MS-4
WBDX-AM (White Bluff)—tower TN-4
WBEJ-AM (Elizabethton)—tower TN-4
WBFD-AM (Bedford)—tower PA-2
WBFJ-AM (Winston-Salem)—tower NC-3
W B Flats—flat TX-5
WBFN-AM (Quitman)—tower MS-4
WBGY-AM (Tullahoma)—tower TN-4
WBGY-FM (Tullahoma)—tower TN-4
WBHM-FM (Birmingham)—tower AL-4
WBHN-AM (Bryson City)—tower NC-3
WBHP-AM (Huntsville)—tower AL-4
WBHT-AM (Brownsville)—tower TN-4
WBIB-AM (Centreville)—tower AL-4
WBIC-AM (New Bern)—tower NC-3
WBIC-AM (New Bern-James City)—tower NC-3
WBIC-AM (Trent Woods)—tower NC-3
WBIF-FM (Bedford)—tower IN-6
WBIG-AM (Greensboro)—tower NC-3
WBIL-AM (Tuskegee)—tower AL-4
WBIL-FM (Tuskegee)—tower AL-4
WBIN-AM (Benton)—tower TN-4
WBIP-AM (Booneville)—tower MS-4
WBIP-FM (Booneville)—tower MS-4
WBIQ-TV (Birmingham)—tower AL-4
WBIR-TV (Knoxville)—tower TN-4
WBIW-AM (Bedford)—tower IN-6
W B Jordon Pond—lake FL-3
W B J Spring—spring OR-9
W B Junction—locale MO-7
WBKE-FM (North Manchester)—tower IN-6
WBKH-AM (Hattiesburg)—tower MS-4
WBLA-AM (Elizabethtown)—tower NC-3
WBLC-AM (Lenoir City)—tower TN-4
WBLE-FM (Batesville)—tower MS-4
WBLF-AM (Bellefonte)—tower PA-2
WBLP-AM (Fairview)—tower TN-4
WBLX-FM (Mobile)—tower (2) AL-4
WBMA-AM (Beaufort)—tower NC-3
WBMC-AM (McMinnville)—tower TN-4
WBMC-FM (McMinnville)—tower TN-4
WBMG-TV (Birmingham)—tower AL-4
WBMK-AM (Knoxville)—tower TN-4
WBMP-FM (Elwood)—tower IN-6
WBMR-FM (Telford)—tower PA-2
WBMU-FM (Asheville)—tower NC-3
WBNI-FM (Fort Wayne)—tower IN-6
WBNL-AM (Boonville)—tower IN-6
WBNL-FM (Boonville)—tower IN-6
WBNT-AM (Oneida)—tower TN-4
WBNT-FM (Oneida)—tower TN-4
WBOL-AM (Bolivar)—tower TN-4
W Bounds Pond Dam—dam MS-4
WBOW-AM (Terre Haute)—tower IN-6
WBPZ-AM (Lock Haven)—tower PA-2
WBPZ-FM (Lock Haven)—tower PA-2
WBQM-FM (Decatur)—tower AL-4
WBQW-AM (Scranton)—tower PA-2
WBRC-TV (Birmingham)—tower AL-4
WBRE-TV (Wilkes-Barre)—tower PA-2
WBRI-AM (Indianapolis)—tower IN-6
W Briggs Ranch—locale SD-7
WBRM-AM (Marion)—tower (2) NC-3
W B Royse Farm Airp—airport KS-7
WBRU-FM (Providence)—tower RI-1
WBRX-AM (Berwick)—tower PA-2
WBRY-AM (Woodbury)—tower TN-4
WBSA-AM (Boaz)—tower AL-4
WBSJ-FM (Ellisville)—tower MS-4
W.B. Spring House—hist pl KY-4
WBS Sch—school TX-5
WBST-FM (Muncie)—tower IN-6
WBT-AM (Charlotte)—tower NC-3
WBTE-AM (Windsor)—tower NC-3
WBTG-FM (Sheffield)—tower AL-4
WBTO-AM (Linton)—tower IN-6
WBTS-AM (Bridgeport)—tower AL-4
WBTV Airp—airport NC-3
WBTV-TV (Charlotte)—tower (2) NC-3
WBTZ-AM (Oliver Springs)—tower TN-4
WBUL-AM (Birmingham)—tower AL-4
WBUT-AM (Butler)—tower PA-2
WBUX-AM (Doylestown)—tower PA-2
WBUY-AM (Lexington)—tower (2) NC-3
WBVP-AM (Beaver Falls)—tower PA-2
WBWB-FM (Bloomington)—tower IN-6
W B Wicker Elem Sch—school NC-3
W B Woodall Lake—reservoir AL-4
W B Woodall Lake Dam—dam AL-4
WBXB-FM (Edenton)—tower NC-3
WBXQ-FM (Cresson)—tower PA-2
WBYE-AM (Calera)—tower AL-4
WBYO-FM (Boyertown)—tower PA-2
WBZB-AM (Selma)—tower NC-3
WBZQ-AM (Greenville)—tower NC-3
WBZT-AM (Waynesboro)—tower PA-2
WBZY-AM (New Castle)—tower PA-2
WBZZ-FM (Pittsburgh)—tower PA-2
WCAB-AM (Rutherfordton)—tower NC-3
W C A Boarding House—hist pl MA-1
WCAE-TV (Saint John)—tower IN-6
W C Allen Dam—dam AL-4
W Canal—canal ID-8
W Cantrell Dam—dam NC-3
W Cantrell Lake—reservoir NC-3
WCAU Airp—airport PA-2
WCAU-AM (Philadelphia)—tower PA-2
WCAU-FM (Philadelphia)—tower PA-2
WCAU Studios—hist pl PA-2
WCAU-TV (Philadelphia)—tower PA-2
WCBG-AM (Chambersburg)—tower PA-2
WCBI-AM (Columbus)—tower MS-4
WCBI-TV (Columbus)—tower (2) MS-4
WCBK-FM (Martinsville)—tower IN-6
WCBQ-AM (Oxford)—tower NC-3
WCBT-AM (Roanoke Rapids)—tower NC-3
WCCA-FM (Mccomb)—tower (2) MS-4
WCCB-TV (Charlotte)—tower (2) NC-3
WCCE-FM (Buies Creek)—tower (2) NC-3
WCCK-FM (Erie)—tower PA-2
WCCL-AM (Jackson)—tower MS-4
W C Culbertson Mansion—park IN-6
W C Devinney Lake Dam—dam MS-4
WCDJ-AM (Edenton)—tower NC-3
WCDL-AM (Carbondale)—tower PA-2
WCDT-AM (Winchester)—tower TN-4
WCEC-AM (Rocky Mount)—tower NC-3
WCED-AM (Du Bois)—tower PA-2
WCEL-AM (Southern Pines)—tower NC-3
WCFT-TV (Tuscaloosa)—tower AL-4
WCGC-AM (Belmont)—tower NC-3
W C Gibson Dam—dam AL-4
W C Gibson Lake—reservoir AL-4
W C Gray Dam—dam AL-4
W C Griggs Elem Sch—school AL-4
WCGS-FM (Goshen)—tower IN-6
WCHA-AM (Chambersburg)—tower PA-2
WCHE-AM (West Chester)—tower PA-2
W Childress Ranch—locale TX-5
W C Hines Dam—dam AL-4
W C Hines Lake—reservoir AL-4
WCHJ-AM (Brookhaven)—tower MS-4
WCHL-AM (Chapel Hill)—tower NC-3
WCHU-AM (Soddy-Daisy)—tower TN-4
WCHU-FM (Soddy-Daisy)—tower TN-4
W C Huggins Dam—dam AL-4
WCIQ-TV (Mount Cheaha)—tower AL-4
WCIS Bank—hist pl MA-1
WCJC-FM (Madison)—tower IN-6
WCJU-AM (Columbia)—tower MS-4
WCKB-AM (Dunn)—tower NC-3
W/C Lake IL-6
WCLC-AM (Jamestown)—tower TN-4
WCLD-AM (Cleveland)—tower MS-4
WCLD-FM (Cleveland)—tower MS-4
WCLE-AM (Cleveland)—tower TN-4
WCLH-FM (Wilkes-Barre)—tower PA-2
WCLN-AM (Clinton)—tower NC-3
WCLY-AM (Columbia)—tower PA-2
W Clyde Lucas Lake—reservoir NC-3
W C Majors Pond Dam—dam MS-4
WCMB-AM (Harrisburg)—tower PA-2
WCMG-AM (Lawrenceburg)—tower TN-4
W C Mills Elem Sch—school IN-6

WCMR-AM (Elkhart)—tower IN-6
WCMS-AM (Norfolk)—tower VA-3
WCMS-FM (Norfolk)—tower VA-3
WCMT-AM (Martin)—tower TN-4
WCMT-FM (Martin)—tower TN-4
WCNB-AM (Connersville)—tower IN-6
WCNB-FM—tower IN-6
WCNC-AM (Elizabeth City)—tower NC-3
WCNR-AM (Bloomsburg)—tower PA-2
WCNS-AM (Latrobe)—tower PA-2
WCOG-AM (Greensboro)—tower NC-3
WCOJ-AM (Coatesville)—tower PA-2
WCOK-AM (Sparta)—tower NC-3
W Combellick Dam—dam SD-7
WCOR-AM (Lebanon)—tower TN-4
W Coupland Ranch—locale NM-5
WCOV-AM (Montgomery)—tower AL-4
W C Overby Lake Dam—dam MS-4
WCOV-TV (Montgomery)—tower AL-4
WCOX-AM (Camden)—tower AL-4
WCPA-AM (Clearfield)—tower PA-2
WCPC-AM (Houston)—tower MS-4
WCPC-FM (Houston)—tower MS-4
WCPE-FM (Raleigh)—tower NC-3
WCPH-AM (Etowah)—tower TN-4
WCPK-AM (Chesapeake)—tower VA-3
W C P Peak—summit AZ-5
WCPQ-AM (Havelock)—tower NC-3
WCPS-AM (Tarboro)—tower NC-3
WCPT-TV (Crossville)—tower (2) TN-4
WCQO-FM (Blairsville)—tower PA-2
WCRD-FM (Bluffton)—tower IN-6
WCRK-AM (Morristown)—tower TN-4
WCRL-AM (Oneonta)—tower AL-4
WCRO-AM (Johnstown)—tower PA-2
WCRQ-FM (Arab)—tower AL-4
WCRT-AM (Birmingham)—tower AL-4
WCRT-AM (Vestavia Hills)—tower AL-4
WCSA-AM (Ripley)—tower MS-4
WCSD-FM (Warminster)—tower PA-2
WCSE-FM (Asheboro)—tower NC-3
WCSI-AM (Columbus)—tower IN-6
WCSI-FM (Colombus)—tower IN-6
WCSK-FM (Kingsport)—tower TN-4
WCSL-AM (Cherryville)—tower NC-3
WCSO-FM (Signal Mountain)—tower TN-4
WCSP-AM (Crystal Springs)—tower MS-4
WCSP-AM (Port Gibson)—tower MS-4
W C Steinback Dam—dam NC-3
WCSV-AM (Crossville)—tower TN-4
WCTA-AM (Alamo)—tower TN-4
WCTE-TV (Cookeville)—tower TN-4
WCTI-TV (New Bern)—tower NC-3
WCTL-FM (Union City)—tower PA-2
WCTU Childrens Home—school OR-9
WCTU Home—building CA-9
WCTW-AM (New Castle)—tower IN-6
WCTX-FM (Palmyra)—tower PA-2
WCUC-FM (Clarion)—tower PA-2
WCVI-AM (Connellsville)—tower PA-2
WCVL-AM (Crawfordsville)—tower IN-6
WCVP-AM (Murphy)—tower NC-3
WCVY-FM (Coventry)—tower RI-1
W C Wills Dam—dam AL-4
WCYJ-FM (Waynesburg)—tower PA-2
WDAC-FM (Lancaster)—tower PA-2
WDAD-AM (Indiana)—tower PA-2
WDAF-AM (Kansas City)—tower MO-7
WDAF-TV (Kansas City)—tower MO-7
WDAI-TV (Gary)—tower IN-6
WDAM-TV (Laurel)—tower MS-4
WDAS-AM (Philadelphia)—tower PA-2
WDAS-FM (Philadelphia)—tower PA-2
WDAU-TV (Scranton)—tower PA-2
WDAV-FM (Davidson)—tower NC-3
WDAY-AM (Fargo)—tower ND-7
W Day Dam—dam SD-7
WDAY-FM (Fargo)—tower ND-7
WDAY-TV (Fargo)—tower ND-7
WDAZ-TV (Devils Lake)—tower ND-7
WDBA-FM (Dubois)—tower PA-2
WDBL-AM (Springfield)—tower TN-4
WDBL-FM (Springfield)—tower TN-4
WDBS-FM (Durham)—tower NC-3
WDCC-FM (Sanford)—tower NC-3
WDCG-FM (Durham)—tower (2) NC-3
W D Cheney Dam—dam MA-1
WDCN-TV (Nashville)—tower TN-4
W D Crockett Dam—dam SD-7
WDCV-FM (Carlisle)—tower PA-2
WDDT-AM (Greenville)—tower MS-4
WDEB-AM (Jamestown)—tower TN-4
WDEB-FM (Jamestown)—tower TN-4
WDEF-AM (Chattanooga)—tower TN-4
WDEF-FM (Chattanooga)—tower TN-4
WDEF-TV (Chattanooga)—tower TN-4
WDEH-AM (Sweetwater)—tower TN-4
WDEH-FM (Sweetwater)—tower TN-4
WDEL-AM (Wilmington)—tower DE-2
WDEX-AM (Monroe)—tower NC-3
W D Farrior Junior Lake—reservoir AL-4
W D Farrior Junior Lake Dam—dam AL-4
WDFM-FM (State College)—tower PA-2
WDGM-FM (Canton)—tower MS-4
WDGM-FM (Madison)—tower MS-4
WDGS-AM (New Albany)—tower IN-6
W D Harrigan And Eunice H Woods Dam—dam AL-4
W D Harrigan And Eunice Woods Lak—reservoir AL-4
W D Harrigan Dam—dam AL-4
WDHB-AM (Harriman)—tower TN-4
WDHN-TV (Dothan)—tower AL-4
WDIA-AM (Memphis)—tower TN-4
WDIQ-TV (Dozier)—tower AL-4
WDJB-FM (Windsor)—tower NC-3
WDJC-FM (Birmingham)—tower AL-4
W D Johnston Dam—dam AL-4
W D Johnston Dams—dam (2) AL-4
W D Johnston Lake Number 1—reservoir AL-4
W D Johnston Lake Number 2—reservoir AL-4
WDJS-AM (Mount Olive)—tower NC-3
WDKN-AM (Dickson)—tower TN-4
WDLK-AM (Dadeville)—tower AL-4
W D Luckie Pond AL-4
WDLV-AM (Pinehurst)—tower NC-3
W.D. McKinney Cotton Gin (historical)—building TX-5
WDMS-FM (Greenville)—tower MS-4
WDNC-AM (Durham)—tower NC-3
WDNG-AM (Anniston)—tower AL-4
WDNH-AM (Honesdale)—tower PA-2
WDNH-FM (Honesdale)—tower PA-2
WDNR-FM (Chester)—tower PA-2
WDNT-AM (Dayton)—tower TN-4
WDNX-FM (Olive Hill)—tower TN-4
WDOD-AM (Chattanooga)—tower TN-4
WDOD-FM (Chattanooga)—tower TN-4
WDOM-FM (Providence)—tower RI-1
W Douglas Hartley Elem Sch—school FL-3
WDOV-AM (Dover)—tower DE-2
WDPB-TV (Seaford)—tower DE-2
W D Reynolds Lake Dam—dam MS-4
WDRM-FM (Decatur)—tower AL-4
WDRV-AM (Statesville)—tower NC-3
WDSD-FM (Dover)—tower DE-2
WDSG-AM (Dyersburg)—tower TN-4
WDSL-AM (Mocksville)—tower NC-3
W D Sugg MS—school FL-3
WDSY-FM (Pittsburgh)—tower PA-2
W D Tank—reservoir TX-5
W D Thompson Sch—school GA-3
WDTM-AM (Selmer)—tower TN-4
WDUQ-FM (Pittsburgh)—tower PA-2
WDUR-AM (Durham)—tower NC-3
W D Valliant Ranch—locale TX-5
WDVE-FM (Pittsburgh)—tower PA-2
W D Webb Dam—dam MS-4
WDXB-AM (Chattanooga)—tower TN-4
WDXE-AM (Lawrenceburg)—tower TN-4
WDXE-FM (Lawrenceburg)—tower TN-4
WDXI-AM (Jackson)—tower TN-4
WDXL-AM (Lexington)—tower TN-4
WDXN-AM (Clarksville)—tower TN-4
WDYN-FM (Chattanooga)—tower TN-4
WDZD-FM (Shallotte)—tower NC-3
**Wea**—pop pl KS-7
Wea Cem—cemetery KS-7
Weach—summit FM-9
Weachong—well FM-9
Wea Creek KS-7
Wea Creek—stream IN-6
Weader, Lake—lake FL-3
**Weadlock**—pop pl MI-6
Weadock—locale MI-6
Wead Run—stream IN-6
WEAG-AM (Alcoa)—tower TN-4
Weahawk NJ-2
Weak Cem—cemetery ND-7
Weakeyever Lake FL-3
Weakeyever River FL-3
Weakfish Creek—stream NJ-2
Weakfish Island—island NJ-2
Weakfish Thorofare—channel NJ-2
Weak Legged Pitch—cave TN-4
Weakley—locale TN-4
Weakley, Thomas, House—hist pl KY-4
Weakley Cem—cemetery KS-7
Weakley Cem—cemetery TN-4
**Weakley County**—pop pl TN-4
Weakley County Courthouse—building TN-4
Weakley County Farm (historical)—locale TN-4
Weakley County Library—building TN-4
Weakley County Training Sch (historical)—school TN-4
Weakley Creek TN-4
Weakley Creek—stream TN-4
Weakley Hollow—valley VA-3
Weakley Horn Hollow—valley TN-4
Weakleys Creek TN-4
Weakly TN-4
**Weakly**—pop pl TN-4
Weakly Branch—stream TX-5
Weakly Creek TN-4
Weakly Creek—stream TN-4
Weakly Post Office (historical)—building TN-4
Weakly Sch (historical)—school TN-4
Weaks Cem—cemetery (2) TN-4
Weaks Hollow—valley TN-4
Weaks Lake—reservoir TN-4
Weaks Lake Dam—dam TN-4
Weak Wells Tank—reservoir NM-5
Weak Windmill—locale (3) TX-5
**Weal**—pop pl VA-3
WEAL-AM (Greensboro)—tower NC-3
Wealand—uninc pl OK-5
Weale—locale MI-6
We-al-hus AZ-5
Wealing Airp—airport IN-6
Weallup Lake—lake WA-9
Wealtha VA-3
Wealthia VA-3
**Wealthwood**—pop pl MN-6
Wealthwood State For—forest MN-6
**Wealthwood (Township of)**—pop pl MN-6
**Wealthy**—pop pl MI-6
**Wealthy**—pop pl TX-5
Wealthy Street Sch—school MI-6
Weamaconk, Lake—reservoir NJ-2
Weamaconk Creek—stream NJ-2
Weamaconk Dam NJ-2
WEAN-AM (Providence)—tower RI-1
We and Our Neighbors Clubhouse—hist pl CA-9
Weaner Creek MS-4
Weaners Creek MS-4
Weaner Spring—spring ID-8
Weaning Corral Spring—spring MT-8
Weaning Pasture Windmill—locale NM-5
Weaning Pen Tank—reservoir AZ-5
Weapon Lake—lake MN-6
Weaquabsqua Cliffs MA-1
Wear Cem—cemetery AL-4
Wear Cem—cemetery TN-4
Wear Chapel—church AL-4
Wear Cove—valley TN-4
Wear Cove Gap—gap TN-4
Wear Creek MO-7
Weare—locale MI-6
**Weare**—pop pl NH-1
Weare, Gov. Meshech, House—hist pl NH-1
Weare Cem—cemetery NH-1
**Weare Corner**—pop pl NH-1
Weare Dike—dam AK-9
Weare Point—cape ME-1
Weare Reservoir—lake NH-1
Weare River MA-1
Weares Cove TN-4
**Weares Mill**—pop pl NH-1
Weare Town House—hist pl NH-1
**Weare (Town of)**—pop pl NH-1
**Weare (Township of)**—pop pl MI-6
Wearied Rest Ch—church AR-4
Wearin Sch—school IA-7
Wearley Branch—stream MS-4
Wearley Ditch—canal IN-6
Wear Park—flat CO-8
Wear Point—cape MD-2
Wear Ranch—locale AZ-5
Wearren Place—hist pl KY-4
Wears Chapel Ch AL-4
Wears Chapel Presbyterian Church TN-4
Wears Cove TN-4
Wears Creek—stream MO-7
Wears Ferry TN-4
Wears Mill (historical)—locale TN-4
Wear Tank—reservoir AZ-5
Wearts Corner NJ-2
**Wear Valley**—pop pl TN-4
Wear Valley (CCD)—cens area TN-4
Wear Valley Ch—church TN-4
Wear Valley Division—civil TN-4
Weary Creek—stream MI-6
Weary Flat—flat NV-8
Weary Lake—lake MI-6
Wearyman Creek—stream CO-8
Weary Pond—lake ME-1
Wearyrick Ditch—canal ID-8
Weary River—stream AK-9
Weasau Creek IN-6
Weasaw Ch—church IN-6
Wea Sch—school IN-6
Wease Knob—summit NC-3
Weasel NJ-2
Weasel Bend AR-4
Weasel Branch—stream TN-4
Weasel Brook—stream MA-1
Weasel Brook—stream NJ-2
Weasel Brook Park—park NJ-2
Weasel Butte—summit OR-9
Weasel Cabin—locale MT-8
Weasel Collar Glacier—glacier MT-8
Weasel Cove—bay (2) AK-9
Weasel Creek MT-8
Weasel Creek—stream (2) AK-9
Weasel Creek—stream (3) ID-8
Weasel Creek—stream (2) IN-6
Weasel Creek—stream IA-7
Weasel Creek—stream (8) MT-8
Weasel Creek—stream NJ-2
Weasel Creek—stream WA-9
Weasel Creek—stream (2) WI-6
Weasel Creek—stream (2) WY-8
Weasel Creek Trail (pack)—trail MT-8
Weasel Draw—valley WY-8
Weasel Gulch—valley ID-8
Weasel Gulch—valley (4) MT-8
Weasel Hollow—valley KY-4
Weasel Lake—lake AK-9
Weasel Lake—lake MI-6
Weasel Lake—lake (2) MN-6
Weasel Lake—lake MT-8
Weasel Meadow—flat MT-8
Weasel Mtn—summit AK-9
Weasel Point—cape ME-1
Weasel Point—cape UT-8
Weasel Point—summit (2) ID-8
Weasel Run PA-2
Weasel Run—stream OH-6
Weaselskin Bridge—bridge CO-8
Weasel Skin Creek—stream CO-8
Weasel Spring—spring OR-9
Weasel Spring—spring UT-8
Weasel Spring—spring WA-9
Weasel Spring—spring WY-8
Weasel Trail—trail FL-3
Weaser Cem—cemetery WV-2
Weasner Ditch—canal IN-6
**Weather**—pop pl PA-2
Weather, Mount—summit VA-3
Weatherall Cem—cemetery MS-4
Weatherall Creek—stream VA-3
Weatherbee Canyon—valley CO-8
Weatherbee Canyon—valley UT-8
Weatherbee Cem—cemetery AL-4
Weatherbee Hill—summit ME-1
Weatherbee Lake—lake CA-9
Weatherby AR-4
Weatherby—locale OR-9
**Weatherby**—pop pl MO-7
Weatherby Brook—stream VT-1
Weatherby Canyon—valley NM-5
Weatherby Cem—cemetery OH-6
Weatherby Cem—cemetery PA-2
Weatherby Hill—summit PA-2
**Weatherby Lake**—pop pl MO-7
Weatherby Lake—reservoir MO-7
Weatherby Mtn—summit OR-9
Weatherby Pond—reservoir NY-2
Weatherby Ranch—locale NM-5
Weatherby Ranch—locale (2) TX-5
Weatherby Sch—school (2) MI-6
Weatherby Sch—school OR-9
Weatherby Spring—spring OR-9
Weatherby Sprs—ridge ID-8
Weather Cem—cemetery KY-4
Weather Creek—stream IL-6
Weatherd Windmill—locale TX-5
Weathered Oil Field—oilfield KS-7
Weatherfield VT-1
Weatherfoot Ch—church VA-3
**Weatherford**—pop pl KY-4
**Weatherford**—pop pl OK-5
**Weatherford**—pop pl TX-5
Weatherford, Lake—reservoir TX-5
Weatherford-Bear Creek Dam Number Two—dam TN-4
Weatherford-Bear Creek Lake Number Two—reservoir TN-4
Weatherford-Bear Dam Number One B—dam TN-4
Weatherford-Bear Lake Number One B—reservoir TN-4
Weatherford Branch—stream GA-3
Weatherford Canyon—valley AZ-5
Weatherford (CCD)—cens area OK-5
Weatherford (CCD)—cens area TX-5
Weatherford Cem—cemetery KY-4
Weatherford Coll—school TX-5
Weatherford Creek—stream TN-4
**Weatherford (historical)**—pop pl TN-4
Weatherford Historical Mon—other OR-9
Weatherford Hotel—hist pl AZ-5
Weatherford House—hist pl TX-5
**Weatherford Junction**—pop pl TX-5
Weatherford Knob—summit KY-4
Weatherford Lake Dam—dam (2) MS-4
Weatherford Mill (historical)—locale AL-4
Weatherford-Mineral Wells and Northwestern RR Depot—hist pl TX-5
Weatherford Northwest (CCD)—cens area TX-5
Weatherford Post Office (historical)—building TN-4
Weatherford Southeast (CCD)—cens area TX-5
Weatherford Spring—spring TX-5
Weatherhead Creek—stream NY-2
Weatherhead Hollow—valley VT-1
Weatherhead Hollow Sch—school VT-1
Weatherhead Ranch—locale AZ-5
**Weatherhill Farms**—pop pl DE-2
**Weatherhill (subdivision)**—pop pl NC-3
Weatherhogs Creek—stream MI-6
Weatherhogs Lake—lake MI-6
Weatherholt Sch—school IL-6
Weatherington Camp—locale GA-3
Weatherley Branch—stream AL-4
Weatherley Hollow—valley AL-4
**Weatherly**—pop pl PA-2
Weatherly Borough—civil PA-2
Weatherly Branch—stream GA-3
Weatherly Branch—stream MO-7
Weatherly Branch—stream TN-4
Weatherly Cave—cave AL-4
Weatherly Cem—cemetery AL-4
Weatherly Cem—cemetery TN-4
Weatherly Cove—valley AL-4
Weatherly Cove Branch—stream AL-4
Weatherly Creek—stream OR-9
**Weatherly Heights**—pop pl AL-4
Weatherly Heights Baptist Ch—church AL-4
Weatherly Heights Ch of Christ—church AL-4
Weatherly Heights Elementary School AL-4
Weatherly Heights Sch—school AL-4
Weatherly Lake—reservoir TX-5
Weatherly Lake Number One NC-3
Weatherly Lookout Tower—locale TN-4
Weatherly Mtn—summit AL-4
Weatherly Spring—spring OR-9
Weatherly Spring—spring WA-9
Weatherly Switch—locale TN-4
Weatherman Bald—summit NC-3
Weatherman Draw—valley MT-8
Weatherman Sch—school MO-7
Weather Ridge—summit AK-9
Weathers—locale AL-4
Weathers—locale AR-4
Weathers—locale OK-5
Weathers Branch—stream GA-3
Weathers Branch—stream KY-4
**Weathersby**—pop pl MS-4
Weathersby Cem—cemetery (2) MS-4
Weathersby-Clairborne Cem—cemetery MS-4
Weathersby Hollow—valley TX-5
Weathersby Ranch TX-5
Weathersbys Box (historical)—locale MS-4
Weathers Cem—cemetery (2) IN-6
Weathers Cem—cemetery (2) KY-4
Weathers Cem—cemetery MS-4
Weathers Creek—stream NC-3
Weather Service Bldg—hist pl OK-5
Weathersfield IL-6
Weathersfield VT-1
**Weathersfield**—pop pl FL-3
**Weathersfield Bow**—pop pl VT-1
Weathersfield Center—locale VT-1
Weathersfield Center Hist Dist—hist pl VT-1
**Weathersfield (Town of)**—pop pl VT-1
Weathersfield (Township of)—civ div OH-6
Weathers Hosp—hospital TN-4
**Weatherspon (historical)**—pop pl NC-3
Weatherspoon Branch—stream MO-7
Weatherspoon Cem—cemetery TN-4
Weatherspoon Ditch—canal OR-9
Weatherspoon Hollow—valley TN-4
Weatherspoon Island (historical)—island TN-4
Weatherspoon Spring—spring MO-7
Weatherspoon Spring—spring TN-4
Weather Station—other NM-5
Weather Station Rsvr—reservoir ID-8
**Weatherstone (subdivision)**—pop pl NC-3
Weather Tower Number 6-280—tower NV-8
Weather Tower Station 14—tower NV-8
Weatherwax Basin—basin WA-9
Weatherwax Cem—cemetery NY-2
Weatherwax Coulee—valley MT-8
Weatherwax Creek—stream MT-8
Weatherwax HS—school WA-9
Weatherwax Ridge—ridge WA-9
**Weathington Heights (subdivision)**—pop pl NC-3
**Weatogue**—pop pl CT-1
**Wea Township**—pop pl KS-7
**Wea (Township of)**—pop pl IN-6
**Weaubleau**—pop pl MO-7
Weaubleau Creek—stream MO-7
Weaubleau Township—civil MO-7
Weaver AZ-5
Weaver—fmr MCD NE-7
Weaver—locale CO-8
Weaver—locale IL-6
Weaver—locale KS-7
Weaver—locale ND-7
Weaver—locale OR-9
Weaver—locale WV-2
Weaver—other LA-4
**Weaver**—pop pl AL-4
**Weaver**—pop pl GA-3
**Weaver**—pop pl IN-6
**Weaver**—pop pl MN-6
**Weaver**—pop pl NC-3
**Weaver**—pop pl TN-4
**Weaver**—pop pl TX-5
Weaver, Henry, Farmstead—hist pl PA-2
Weaver, James B., House—hist pl IA-7
Weaver, Julian A., House—hist pl MN-6
Weaver, Lake—lake AL-4
Weaver, Valentine, House—hist pl PA-2
Weaver, William, House—hist pl NC-3
Weaver Airp—airport IN-6
Weaver and Waddell Cem—cemetery PA-2
Weaver Bally Mtn CA-9
Weaver Bally Mtn—summit CA-9
Weaver Bayou—stream AR-4
Weaver Bend KS-7
Weaver Bend—bend TN-4
Weaver Bottom—bend TN-4
Weaver Branch TN-4
Weaver Branch TX-5
Weaver Branch—stream (2) AL-4
Weaver Branch—stream GA-3
Weaver Branch—stream IL-6
Weaver Branch—stream KY-4
Weaver Branch—stream MO-7
Weaver Branch—stream (2) NC-3
Weaver Branch—stream (6) TN-4
Weaver Branch—stream TX-5
Weaver Branch Library—building AL-4
Weaver Bridge—bridge PA-2
Weaver Brook—stream VT-1
Weaver Bully CA-9
Weaver Cabin—locale OR-9
Weaver Canyon—valley AZ-5
Weaver Canyon—valley (2) CO-8
Weaver Canyon—valley (2) NV-8
Weaver Canyon—valley OR-9
Weaver Canyon—valley UT-8
Weaver Cave—cave AL-4
Weaver Cem TN-4
Weaver Cem—cemetery (6) AL-4
Weaver Cem—cemetery CO-8
Weaver Cem—cemetery (2) GA-3
Weaver Cem—cemetery (2) IL-6
Weaver Cem—cemetery (3) IN-6
Weaver Cem—cemetery KY-4
Weaver Cem—cemetery (2) LA-4
Weaver Cem—cemetery (2) MI-6
Weaver Cem—cemetery (3) MS-4
Weaver Cem—cemetery (4) MO-7
Weaver Cem—cemetery NY-2
Weaver Cem—cemetery (2) NC-3
Weaver Cem—cemetery (5) OH-6
Weaver Cem—cemetery (11) TN-4
Weaver Cem—cemetery (5) TX-5
Weaver Cem—cemetery VA-3
Weaver Cem—cemetery WV-2
Weaver Ch—church MO-7
Weaver Ch—church TX-5
Weaver Ch—church VA-3
Weaver Chapel—church AR-4
Weaver Chapel—church IL-6
Weaver Chapel—church IN-6
Weaver Chapel—church NC-3
Weaver Chapel—church OH-6
Weaver Chapel Cem—cemetery OK-5
Weaver Chapel Cem—cemetery TX-5
Weaver City IN-6
Weaver Community House—locale AL-4
Weaver Congregational Methodist Ch—church AL-4
Weaver Corner—locale NY-2
Weaver Corners OH-6
Weaver Cove—bay RI-1
Weaver Creek AL-4
Weaver Creek AZ-5
Weaver Creek CA-9
Weaver Creek KY-4
Weaver Creek MT-8
Weaver Creek TN-4
Weaver Creek—stream AL-4
Weaver Creek—stream AZ-5
Weaver Creek—stream (4) AR-4
Weaver Creek—stream (3) CA-9
Weaver Creek—stream CO-8
Weaver Creek—stream FL-3
Weaver Creek—stream (4) GA-3
Weaver Creek—stream ID-8
Weaver Creek—stream (2) IL-6
Weaver Creek—stream IN-6
Weaver Creek—stream MI-6
Weaver Creek—stream MS-4
Weaver Creek—stream MO-7
Weaver Creek—stream (2) NV-8
Weaver Creek—stream (2) NC-3
Weaver Creek—stream (7) OR-9
Weaver Creek—stream SC-3
Weaver Creek—stream (2) TN-4
Weaver Creek—stream TX-5
Weaver Creek—stream (2) VA-3
Weaver Creek—stream WA-9
Weaver Creek Ch—church IL-6
Weaver Creek Ch—church VA-3
Weaver Creek Cutoff—channel MS-4
Weaver Creek Lookout Tower—tower FL-3
Weaver Creek Sch—school VA-3
Weaver Dam—dam OR-9
Weaver Dam—dam UT-8
Weaver Davis Ditch—canal IN-6
Weaver Ditch—canal (3) IN-6
Weaver Ditch—canal MT-8
Weaver Dock—locale TN-4
Weaver Drain—canal (3) MI-6
Weaver Draw—valley WY-8
Weaver Elem Sch—school AL-4
Weaver Falls—falls AL-4
Weaver Falls Access Area—park PA-2
Weaver Falls Boat Launch PA-2
Weaver First United Methodist Ch—church AL-4
Weaver-Fox House—hist pl MD-2
Weaver Gap—gap (2) PA-2
Weaver Gulch—valley (2) CO-8
Weaver Gulch—valley MT-8
Weaver Gulch—valley OR-9
Weaver Hill—summit AR-4
Weaver Hill—summit FL-3
Weaver Hill—summit ME-1
Weaver Hill—summit NV-8
Weaver Hill—summit NY-2
Weaver Hill—summit OH-6
Weaver Hill—summit RI-1
Weaver Hill—summit VT-1
Weaver Hill—summit WI-6
Weaver (historical)—locale KS-7
Weaver (historical)—locale PA-2
Weaver Hole Slough—gut FL-3
Weaver Hollow—valley AR-4
Weaver Hollow—valley KY-4
Weaver Hollow—valley MO-7
Weaver Hollow—valley (2) NY-2
Weaver Hollow—valley PA-2
Weaver Hollow—valley (2) TN-4
Weaver Hollow—valley VA-3
Weaver Homestead—locale WY-8
Weaver Hotel—hist pl KS-7
Weaver House—hist pl VA-3
Weaver HS—school AL-4
Weaver HS—school CT-1
Weavering Spit—cape WA-9
Weaver Island (inundated)—island AL-4
Weaver JHS—school AL-4
Weaver Knob—summit TN-4
Weaver Knob—summit VA-3
Weaver Knob—summit WV-2
Weaver Lake—lake (2) CA-9
Weaver Lake—lake MI-6
Weaver Lake—lake MN-6
Weaver Lake—lake NY-2
Weaver Lake—lake OR-9
Weaver Lake Cem—cemetery MN-6
Weaver Lake Park—park MN-6
Weaverland—locale PA-2
Weaverland Sch—school PA-2
Weaver Ledge—bar ME-1
Weaverly Sch—school KS-7
Weaver Memorial Ch—church SC-3
Weaver Mercantile Bldg—hist pl MN-6
Weaver Mill Creek—stream AL-4
**Weaver Mill (Crisp)**—pop pl PA-2
Weaver Mill (historical)—locale AL-4
Weaver Mine—mine NM-5
Weaver Mountains—range AZ-5
Weaver Mtn—summit AZ-5
Weaver Mtn—summit CA-9
Weaver Mtn—summit OR-9
Weaver Mtn—summit VA-3
Weaver Park—park GA-3
Weaver Park—park MI-6
Weaver Park—park NC-3
Weaver Pass—gap AZ-5
Weaver Peak—summit AZ-5
Weaver Pike Industrial Park—locale TN-4
Weaver Place—hist pl MS-4
Weaver Place—locale OR-9
Weaver Placer—mine OR-9
Weaver Plantation (historical)—locale AL-4
Weaver Point—cape WA-9
Weaver Pond VA-3
Weaver Pond—lake AL-4
Weaver Pond—lake GA-3
Weaver Pond—reservoir AL-4
Weaver Pond—swamp IN-6
Weaver Ranch—locale AZ-5
Weaver Ranch—locale CO-8
Weaver Ranch—locale NM-5
Weaver Ranch—locale (3) WY-8
Weaver Ranch Airp—airport KS-7
Weaver Ranch (historical)—locale OR-9
Weaver Ridge—ridge CO-8
Weaver Ridge—ridge ME-1
Weaver Ridge—ridge MO-7
Weaver Ridge—ridge TN-4
Weaver Ridge—ridge UT-8
Weaver River—stream FL-3
Weaver Rsvr—reservoir (2) OR-9
Weaver Rsvr—reservoir UT-8
Weaver Run—stream KY-4
Weaver Run—stream OH-6
Weaver Run—stream PA-2
Weavers AL-4
**Weavers**—pop pl OH-6
Weaver Saddle—gap NV-8
Weavers Arm Hollow—valley TN-4
Weavers Arm Prospect—mine TN-4
Weavers Ave Park—park NC-3
Weavers Bend—bend KS-7
Weavers Branch—stream TN-4
Weaversburg PA-2
Weaver's Cem—cemetery AR-4
Weavers Ch—church VA-3
Weaver Sch—school AL-4
Weaver Sch—school AR-4
Weaver Sch—school (2) CA-9
Weaver Sch—school IL-6
Weaver Sch—school MI-6
Weaver Sch—school MN-6
Weaver Sch—school MO-7
Weaver Sch—school (2) OH-6
Weaver Sch—school OK-5
Weaver Sch—school WY-8
Weaver Sch (abandoned)—school (3) PA-2
Weavers Chapel—church TX-5
Weaver School TN-4
Weaver Schoolhouse (abandoned)—school PA-2
**Weavers Corners**—pop pl OH-6
Weavers Cove—bay MA-1
Weavers Creek AR-4
Weavers Creek KY-4
Weavers Creek TN-4
Weavers Creek—stream AL-4
Weavers Creek—stream KY-4
Weavers Creek—stream OK-5
Weavers Creek—stream TN-4
Weavers Elem Sch—school TN-4
Weaver Settlement Cem—cemetery NY-2
Weavers Ford—locale NC-3
**Weaversford**—pop pl NC-3
Weavers Hole—locale ID-8
Weaver Short Mill Creek AL-4
Weavers Knob—summit TN-4
Weavers Knob—summit VA-3
Weavers Landing—locale NC-3
Weaver's Mill Covered Bridge—hist pl PA-2
Weavers Mill (historical)—locale AL-4
Weavers Millpond—reservoir VA-3
Weavers Mill Post Office (historical)—building PA-2
Weavers Needle—pillar AZ-5
Weavers Old Stand PA-2
**Weavers Old Stand**—pop pl PA-2
Weaver Spring—spring OR-9
Weaver Spring—spring (2) TN-4
Weaver Spring—spring WY-8
Weaver Spring Branch AL-4
Weaver Springs—spring FL-3
Weaver Springs Creek—stream TX-5
Weavers Station AL-4
Weavers Station—locale FL-3
Weavers Store (historical)—locale TN-4
Weavers Store Post Office (historical)—building TN-4

**Webster Chapel**—pop pl AL-4
Webster Chapel Ch—church AL-4
Webster Chapel Methodist Ch AL-4
Webster Chapel United Methodist Church—hist pl TX-5
**Webster City**—pop pl IA-7
Webster City Post Office—hist pl IA-7
Webster Cliff Trail—trail NH-1
Webster Coll—school MO-7
Webster College-Eden Theological Seminary Collegiate District—hist pl MO-7
Webster Congregational Church—hist pl NH-1
**Webster Corner**—pop pl ME-1
**Webster Corners**—pop pl NY-2
Webster County—civil MO-7
**Webster (County)**—pop pl GA-3
**Webster (County)**—pop pl KY-4
**Webster County**—pop pl MS-4
**Webster (County)**—pop pl MO-7
**Webster (County)**—pop pl WV-2
Webster County Agricultural HS (historical)—school MS-4
Webster County Courthouse—building IA-7
Webster County Courthouse—building MS-4
Webster County Courthouse—hist pl GA-3
Webster County Courthouse—hist pl IA-7
Webster County Courthouse—hist pl NE-7
Webster County Hosp—hospital IA-7
Webster County Training Sch—school MS-4
Webster County Vocational Technical Sch—school MS-4
Webster Cove—bay MD-2
webster Creek KS-7
Webster Creek—gut FL-3
Webster Creek—stream GA-3
Webster Creek—stream ID-8
Webster Creek—stream IL-6
Webster Creek—stream (2) IN-6
Webster Creek—stream KS-7
Webster Creek—stream MI-6
Webster Creek—stream MN-6
Webster Creek—stream MS-4
Webster Creek—stream (2) NC-3
Webster Creek—stream PA-2
Webster Creek—stream TX-5
Webster Creek—stream WA-9
Webster Creek—stream WI-6
Webster Creek—stream WY-8
Webster Creek Pool—reservoir MN-6
**Webster Crossing**—pop pl NY-2
Webster Dam—dam KS-7
Webster Dam—dam NE-7
Webster Ditch OH-6
Webster Ditch—canal OH-6
Webster Donora Bridge—hist pl PA-2
Webster Drain—canal MI-6
Webster Dugway—locale WY-8
Webster Elem Sch—school AL-4
Webster Elem Sch—school AZ-5
Webster Elem Sch—school (2) FL-3
Webster Elem Sch—school IN-6
Webster Elem Sch—school MS-4
**Webster Farm**—pop pl DE-2
Webster Flat—flat CA-9
Webster Flat—flat OR-9
Webster Flat—flat UT-8
Webster Gap—gap GA-3
Webster-Garfield Sch—school MT-8
Webster General Hosp—hospital MS-4
**Webster Grove**—pop pl SD-7
**Webster Grove Addition (subdivision)**—pop pl SD-7
Webster Grove Ch—church MO-7
**Webster Groves**—pop pl MO-7
Webster Gulch—valley AZ-5
Webster Gulch—valley CO-8
Webster Head—cape ME-1
Webster Hill—summit CO-8
Webster Hill—summit NH-1
Webster Hill—summit NY-2
Webster Hills—locale MI-6
Webster Hill Sch—school CT-1
Webster (historical)—locale AL-4
Webster Hole—cave TN-4
Webster Hole Tank—reservoir AZ-5
Webster Hollow—valley (2) AL-4
Webster Hollow—valley (2) TN-4
Webster Hotel—hist pl NY-2
Webster HS—school OK-5
Webster Intermediate Sch—school MA-1
Webster JHS—school (2) CA-9
Webster JHS—school ME-1
Webster JHS—school NJ-2
Webster JHS—school NY-2
Webster JHS—school OK-5
**Webster Junction**—pop pl MA-1
**Webster Junction**—pop pl NC-3
Webster Junior Coll—school NH-1
Webster Knob—summit NC-3
Webster Knob—summit TN-4
Webster Lake NH-1
Webster Lake—lake AK-9
Webster Lake—lake IN-6
Webster Lake—lake ME-1
Webster Lake—lake MI-6
Webster Lake—lake (2) MN-6
Webster Lake—lake NE-7
Webster Lake—lake NH-1
Webster Lake—lake WA-9
**Webster Lake**—pop pl NH-1
Webster Lake—reservoir CO-8
Webster Lake—reservoir GA-3
Webster Lake—swamp MI-6
Webster Lake Campground—locale MN-6
Webster Lake Dam-East—dam IN-6
Webster Lookout Tower—locale MS-4
Webster Manufacturing—hist pl OH-6
Webster Memorial Baptist Ch—church FL-3
Webster Memorial Bldg—hist pl CT-1
Webster Memorial Gardens—cemetery MS-4
Webster Mesa—bench NM-5
Webster Mesa—summit CO-8
Webster Mills PA-2
**Webster Mills**—pop pl PA-2
Webster Mtn—summit (2) AZ-5
Webster Municipal Airp—airport SD-7
Webster No. 5 (Election Precinct)—fmr MCD IL-6
Webster Number One Spring—spring AZ-5
Webster Oil Field—oilfield KS-7
Webster Overlook—locale GA-3
**Webster Parish**—pop pl LA-4
Webster Parish Library Bldg—hist pl LA-4
Webster Park CO-8
Webster Park IL-6
Webster Park MO-7
Webster Park—flat (2) CO-8
Webster Park—park IN-6
Webster Park—park NY-2
Webster Park—park OH-6
Webster Park—park (2) WA-9
Webster Park—park WI-6
Webster Park Hist Dist—hist pl MA-1
Webster Pass—gap CO-8
Webster Pass—gap NM-5
Webster Peak AZ-5
Webster Peak—summit AK-9
Webster Place NH-1
**Webster Place**—pop pl NH-1
**Webster Place**—pop pl NM-5
Webster Plantation—locale LA-4
Webster (Plantation of)—civ div ME-1
Webster Point—cape AL-4
Webster Point—cape CT-1
Webster Point—cape MD-2
Webster Point—cape NY-2
Webster Point—cape WA-9
Webster Point Station (historical)—locale MA-1
Webster Pond—lake ME-1
Webster Pond—lake NH-1
Webster Pond—lake (2) NY-2
Webster Ponds—lake MD-2
Webster Post Office (historical)—building TN-4
Webster Poultry Company Pond—reservoir NC-3
Webster Poultry Company Pond Dam—dam NC-3
Webster Prairie Cem—cemetery WI-6
Webster Ranch—locale ID-8
Webster Ranch—locale TX-5
Webster Range—range ID-8
Webster Reservoir Airstrip—airport KS-7
Webster Road Cem—cemetery NY-2
Webster Rock—bar ME-1
Webster Rsvr—reservoir KS-7
Webster Rsvr—reservoir NM-5
Webster Run—stream OH-6
Webster Run—stream PA-2
Webster Run—stream (2) WV-2
Webster Rural Cem—cemetery NY-2
Websters AL-4
Webster Sch—hist pl CT-1
Webster Sch—hist pl MO-7
Webster Sch—school AZ-5
Webster Sch—school (8) CA-9
Webster Sch—school (3) CT-1
Webster Sch—school DC-2
Webster Sch—school FL-3
Webster Sch—school ID-8
Webster Sch—school (10) IL-6
Webster Sch—school (4) IA-7
Webster Sch—school KS-7
Webster Sch—school (3) ME-1
Webster Sch—school MA-1
Webster Sch—school (8) MI-6
Webster Sch—school (3) MN-6
Webster Sch—school (3) MO-7
Webster Sch—school NH-1
Webster Sch—school (2) NY-2
Webster Sch—school ND-7
Webster Sch—school (3) OH-6
Webster Sch—school (2) OK-5
Webster Sch—school (4) PA-2
Webster Sch—school SD-7
Webster Sch—school TX-5
Webster Sch—school UT-8
Webster Sch—school (2) VT-1
Webster Sch—school WA-9
Webster Sch—school WV-2
Webster Sch—school (5) WI-6
Websters Chapel-Alexandria Valley (CCD)—cens area AL-4
Websters Chapel-Alexandria Valley Division—civil AL-4
Websters Chapel JHS—school AL-4
Webster Sch (historical)—school AL-4
Webster Sch (historical)—school MS-4
Webster School IN-6
Webster School UT-8
Webster School (abandoned)—locale MT-8
Webster School Number 46 IN-6
**Websters Corners**—pop pl NY-2
**Websters Crossing**—pop pl NY-2
Websters Ferry TN-4
Webster's Forest—hist pl MD-2
Webster Shopping Plaza—locale MA-1
Webster Siding—locale IL-6
Websters Knolls—summit UT-8
Webster Slide Mtn—summit NH-1
Webster Slough—lake MN-6
**Websters Mill**—pop pl NH-1
**Websters Mill**—pop pl PA-2
Websters Mills NH-1
Webster's Point MA-1
Websters Pond—reservoir AL-4
Webster Spring—spring (4) AZ-5
Webster Spring—spring MO-7
**Webster Springs**—pop pl WV-2
Webster Springs (corporate name Addison) WV-2
**Webster Spur**—pop pl MN-6
**Webster Square (subdivision)**—pop pl MA-1
Webster Stanley JHS—school WI-6
Webster State Park—park KS-7
Webster Statue—park DC-2
Webster Stream—stream NH-1
Webster Street—uninc pl CA-9
Webster Street Cem—cemetery NY-2
Webster Street Elem Sch MS-4
Webster Street Firehouse—hist pl MA-1
Websters Well—well UT-8
Webster Tank—reservoir (2) AZ-5
Webster Tank—reservoir NM-5
Webster Tank—reservoir TX-5
Webster Telephone Exchange Bldg—hist pl NE-7
Webster Townhall—building IA-7
Webster (Town Of)—other ME-1
**Webster (Town of)**—pop pl MA-1
**Webster (Town of)**—pop pl NH-1
**Webster (Town of)**—pop pl NY-2
**Webster (Town of)**—pop pl WI-6
Webster Township—civ div NE-7
Webster Township—civil SD-7
Webster Township—fmr MCD (4) IA-7
**Webster Township**—pop pl (2) KS-7
**Webster Township**—pop pl NE-7
**Webster Township**—pop pl ND-7
**Webster Township**—pop pl SD-7
Webster Township (historical)—civil SD-7
Webster (Township of)—fmr MCD NC-3
**Webster (Township of)**—pop pl (2) IN-6
**Webster (Township of)**—pop pl MI-6
**Webster (Township of)**—pop pl MN-6
**Webster (Township of)**—pop pl OH-6
Webster Trail—trail (2) PA-2
Webster Valley—valley TN-4
**Webster Village (Webster)**—pop pl MD-2
**Websterville**—pop pl VT-1
Webster Wildlife Area—park KS-7
Web Tank—reservoir AZ-5
**Webtown**—pop pl NC-3
Weburg Spring—spring OR-9
Web Water—reservoir AZ-5
W-E Camp Shelter—locale WA-9
Wecas Corners—locale PA-2
Wech FM-9
**Wech Corners**—pop pl PA-2
Wechech Basin—basin NV-8
Wecheech Basin NV-8
Wechekemmipihquiau MA-1
Wechepemepquah MA-1
Weches—locale TX-5
Weches Cem—cemetery TX-5
Wechotookme FL-3
Wechsler Sch—school MS-4
WECI-FM (Richmond)—tower IN-6
Weckbaugh House—hist pl CO-8
**Weco**—pop pl NE-7
WECO-AM (Wartburg)—tower TN-4
**Wecoma Beach (Post Office)**—pop pl OR-9
**Wecota**—pop pl SD-7
WECP-AM (Carthage)—tower MS-4
WECT-TV (Wilmington)—tower NC-3
WEDA-FM (Grove City)—tower PA-2
Wedboo Creek—stream SC-3
Wedde Creek WI-6
Wedde Creek—stream WI-6
**Weddell**—pop pl SC-3
Weddell Cem—cemetery IN-6
Weddell Creek—stream IN-6
**Wedderburn**—pop pl OR-9
Wedderspoon Hollow—valley NY-2
Weddige Ranch—locale NM-5
Wedding Bell Camp—locale CO-8
Wedding Bell Mtn—summit CO-8
Wedding Cake—summit CA-9
Wedding Cake Butte—summit NM-5
Wedding Canyon—valley CO-8
Wedding Cem—cemetery KY-4
Wedding Of The Waters—locale WY-8
Wedding Ring Arch UT-8
Wedding Ring Arch—arch UT-8
Wedding Rock—island CA-9
Wedding Rock Petroglyphs—hist pl WA-9
Wedding Tank—reservoir AZ-5
Wedding Tank—reservoir NM-5
Weddington—locale AR-4
**Weddington**—pop pl NC-3
Weddington, Lake—reservoir AR-4
Weddington Branch—stream KY-4
Weddington Cem—cemetery KY-4
Weddington Cem—cemetery OH-6
Weddington Ch—church AR-4
Weddington Creek—stream AR-4
Weddington Elementary School MS-4
Weddington Fork—stream KY-4
Weddington Gap—gap AR-4
Weddington Hill—summit OH-6
Weddington Lookout Tower—locale AR-4
Weddington Mtn—summit AR-4
Weddington Park—park CA-9
Weddington Sch—school MS-4
Weddle, Callahill and Priscilla, House—hist pl OH-6
Weddle Canyon—valley WA-9
Weddle Cem—cemetery KY-4
Weddle Creek—stream CO-8
Weddle Creek—stream OR-9
Weddle Hollow—valley IN-6
Weddlesville IN-6
**Weddleville**—pop pl IN-6
Wedean Number 1 Dam—dam SD-7
Wedean Number 2 Dam—dam SD-7
Wedean Number 3 Dam—dam SD-7
Wedean Ranch—locale SD-7
Wede Branch—stream KY-4
Wedeburg (site)—locale OR-9
Wedekind Creek—stream WA-9
Wedekind House and Servant's Quarters—hist pl KY-4
Wedelburg Ditch—canal IN-6
Wedel Cem—cemetery TX-5
Wedelco Industrial Subdivision—locale UT-8
Wedel Lake—lake MN-6
**Wedells Five Point Addition (subdivision)**—pop pl UT-8
Wedemeyer Ranch—locale (2) WY-8
Wedemeyer Sch—school WY-8
Weden Creek WA-9
Weden Lake WA-9
Wedens Bay—bay MI-6
Wederspahn Lake—lake WA-9
Wedertz Canyon—valley NV-8
Wedertz Flat—flat CA-9
Wedertz Spring—spring NV-8
WEDG-AM (Soddy-Daisy)—tower TN-4
Wedge IL-6
Wedge, Cape—cape AK-9
Wedge, Dr. Albert C., House—hist pl MN-6
Wedge, The MT-8
Wedge, The—area DE-2
Wedge, The—cape MT-8
Wedge, The—cape UT-8
Wedge, The—hist pl SC-3
Wedge, The—plateau UT-8
Wedge, The—ridge WA-9
Wedge, The—spring MT-8
Wedge, The—summit AK-9
Wedge Brook—stream NY-2
Wedge Camp—locale ID-8
Wedge Canyon—valley MT-8
Wedge Cape—cape AK-9
Wedge Creek—stream MT-8
**Wedgefield**—pop pl SC-3
Wedge Glacier—glacier AK-9
**Wedge Hills**—pop pl DE-2
Wedge Hill Tank—reservoir NM-5
Wedge Hollow—valley PA-2
Wedge Hollow—valley UT-8
Wedge Island—island AK-9
Wedge Lake—lake CA-9
Wedge Lake—lake MI-6
Wedge Lake—lake MN-6
**Wedgemere**—pop pl MA-1
Wedgemere Station MA-1
Wedgemere Station—locale MA-1
Wedge Mine—mine (2) CO-8
Wedge Mtn—summit AK-9
Wedge Mtn—summit MT-8
Wedge Mtn—summit WA-9
Wedge Overlook—locale UT-8
Wedge Overlook, The—locale UT-8
Wedge Peak—summit AK-9
Wedge Plantation—locale SC-3
Wedge Point—cape (2) AK-9
Wedge Point—cape FL-3
Wedge Pond—reservoir MA-1
Wedge Pond Dam—dam MA-1
Wedge Pond No 1—lake UT-8
Wedge Pond No. 2—lake UT-8
Wedge Pond No. 4—lake UT-8
Wedge Prairie Cem—cemetery WI-6
Wedge Ridge—ridge TN-4
Wedge Rock Pit—cave AL-4
**Wedges Corner**—pop pl IL-6
Wedges Creek—stream WI-6
Wedgewood—locale NY-2
**Wedgewood**—pop pl (2) DE-2
**Wedgewood**—pop pl MO-7
**Wedgewood**—pop pl VA-3
**Wedgewood**—pop pl WA-9
Wedgewood—uninc pl TX-5
Wedgewood, Dr. Milton, House—hist pl ME-1
**Wedgewood Acres**—pop pl DE-2
Wedgewood Airp—airport NC-3
Wedgewood Cem—cemetery NH-1
Wedgewood Country Club—locale NC-3
Wedgewood Country Club—other NJ-2
Wedgewood Creek—stream AK-9
**Wedgewood Estates (subdivision)**—pop pl TN-4
Wedgewood Golf Course—locale PA-2
**Wedgewood Green**—pop pl MO-7
**Wedgewood Hills**—pop pl (2) TN-4
**Wedgewood Lakes**—pop pl NC-3
Wedgewood MS—school FL-3
Wedgewood Sch—school WA-9
Wedgewood Shop Ctr—locale MO-7
**Wedgewood (subdivision)**—pop pl NC-3
**Wedgewood West (subdivision)**—pop pl NC-3
**Wedgewood Willows Condo**—pop pl UT-8
**Wedgeworth**—pop pl AL-4
Wedgeworth Cem—cemetery MS-4
Wedgeworth Creek—stream MS-4
Wedgeworth Creek—stream TX-5
Wedgeworth Lake—lake MS-4
Wedgeworth Point—cape NY-2
Wedgeworth (Wedgworth)—other AL-4
**Wedgwood**—pop pl VA-3
Wedgwood—uninc pl WA-9
Wedgwood Brook—stream ME-1
**Wedgworth (Wedgeworth)**—pop pl AL-4
**Wedington**—pop pl AR-4
Wedington Creek AR-4
Wedington Creek—stream TX-5
Wedington Gap AR-4
Wedington Lake AR-4
Wedington Mountain AR-4
Wedington (Township of)—fmr MCD AR-4
Wedin Lehpe—unknown FM-9
Wedkeng—swamp FM-9
Wedkeng, Dauen—bay FM-9
Wedlers Pond—reservoir WI-6
WEDM-FM (Indianapolis)—tower IN-6
W Edmiston Ranch—locale TX-5
Wednesday Bay—bay MN-6
Wednesday Hill—summit NH-1
Wednesday Island FM-9
Wednesday Point—cape FL-3
Wednesday Rsvr—reservoir OR-9
WEDO-AM (Mckeesport)—tower PA-2
**Wedonia**—pop pl KY-4
**Wedowee**—pop pl AL-4
Wedowee (CCD)—cens area AL-4
Wedowee Ch—church AL-4
Wedowee Club Lake—reservoir AL-4
Wedowee Club Lake Dam—dam AL-4
Wedowee Creek—stream AL-4
Wedowee Division—civil AL-4
Wedowee HS—school AL-4
**Wedron**—pop pl IL-6
Wee Burn Country Club—other CT-1
Wee Care Center—school FL-3
Wee Care of Plantation Learning Center—school FL-3
Weece Ranch—locale NE-7
Weechaaw—summit FM-9
Weechatookame River FL-3
Weechatookame Spring FL-3
Weechatooka River FL-3
Weechatooka Spring FL-3
Weechotomakee River FL-3
Weechotomakee Sp FL-3
Wee Creek—stream ID-8
Wee Creek—stream OR-9
Weed—locale KY-4
Weed—locale MT-8
**Weed**—pop pl CA-9
**Weed**—pop pl NM-5
Weed, Justin, House—hist pl WI-6
WEED-AM (Rocky Mount)—tower NC-3
Weeda Post Office (historical)—building AL-4
Weed Basin—basin UT-8
Weed Bench—bench AZ-5
Weed Bight—bay AK-9
Weed Bluff—cliff TX-5
Weed Branch—stream AL-4
Weed Branch—stream GA-3
Weed Bridge—bridge OR-9
Weed Brook NY-2
Weed Brook—stream NH-1
Weed Brook—stream NY-2
Weed Brook—stream VT-1
Weed Canyon—valley AZ-5
Weed (CCD)—cens area CA-9
Weed Cem—cemetery CT-1
Weed Cem—cemetery KY-4
Weed Cem—cemetery VT-1
Weed Ch—church AL-4
Weed Circle—locale HI-9
Weed Creek NE-7
Weed Creek WY-8
Weed Creek—stream MI-6
Weed Creek—stream MT-8
Weed Creek—stream (2) OR-9
Weed Creek—stream PA-2
Weed Creek—stream WY-8
Weed Crossroad—locale AL-4
Weed Draw—valley WY-8
Weeden AL-4
Weeden Creek—stream (2) WA-9
**Weeden Heights**—pop pl AL-4
Weeden Heights Baptist Ch—church AL-4
Weeden Heights Pentecostal Ch—church AL-4
Weeden Heights United Methodist Ch—church AL-4
Weeden Hill—summit VT-1
Weeden Island Site—hist pl FL-3
Weeden Lake—lake WA-9
Weeden Mtn—summit AL-4
Weedens—locale WI-6
Weeden Sch—school AL-4
Weedens Island FL-3
Weedens Sch—school WI-6
Weede Sch—school MT-8
Weed Field Airp—airport IN-6
Weedhaven—locale TX-5
**Weed Heights**—pop pl NV-8
Weed Hill—summit CT-1
Weed Hollow—valley OK-5
Weed Hollow—valley PA-2
Weed Island—island GA-3
Weed Island—island OK-5
Weed Island—island OR-9
Weed Island Ditch—canal CA-9
Weed Knob WV-2
Weed Knob—summit WV-2
Weed Lake—lake AK-9
Weed Lake—lake MN-6
Weed Lake—lake MT-8
Weed Lake—lake NE-7
Weed Lake—lake OR-9
Weed Lake—lake TX-5
Weed Lake—reservoir OR-9
Weed Lake Butte—summit OR-9
Weed Lake Butte Waterhole OR-9
Weed Lake Butte Waterhole—well OR-9
Weed Lake Dam—dam OR-9
Weed Lake Flat—flat OR-9
Weed Lookout Tower—hist pl NM-5
Weed Lookout Tower—other NM-5
Weedman—locale IL-6
Weedman Sch (abandoned)—school SD-7
Weed Meadow—flat CA-9
Weed Mines—locale NY-2
Weed Mtn—summit CO-8
Weedon Field (airport)—airport AL-4
Weedon Hammock—island FL-3
Weedonia—locale KY-4
Weedon Island—island FL-3
Weedon Island State Preserve—park FL-3
Weedon Lake—reservoir MS-4
Weedons Fork—locale VA-3
Weedonville—locale VA-3
Weed Park—park IA-7
**Weed Patch**—pop pl CA-9
Weed Patch Hill—summit IN-6
Weed Patch Knob IN-6
Weed Patch Mtn—summit NC-3
Weed Point—locale CA-9
Weed Pond—lake AZ-5
Weed Pond—lake ME-1
Weed Pond—lake NH-1
Weed Pond—reservoir AL-4
Weed Ranch—locale MT 8
Weed Rsvr—reservoir AZ-5
Weed Run—stream IN-6
Weed Run—stream PA-2
Weeds Bay—bay NY-2
Weeds Brook—stream NY-2
Weed Sch—school GA-3
**Weeds Corners**—pop pl PA-2
Weeds Lake—swamp MI-6
Weeds Point—locale CA-9
**Weedsport**—pop pl NY-2
Weedsport Canal Terminal—locale NY-2
Weedsport Rsvr—reservoir NY-2
Weedsport Rural Cem—cemetery NY-2
Weed Spring—spring OR-9
Weed Valley—basin TX-5
Weed Valley—valley CA-9
Weed Valley Ranch—locale CA-9
**Weedville**—pop pl AZ-5
**Weedville**—pop pl PA-2
Weedweeder Ponds MA-1
Weedy Cove Knob—summit NC-3
Weedy Creek—stream TX-5
Weedy Flat—flat NM-5
Weedy Gap—gap NC-3
Weedy Knob—summit NC-3
Weedy Knob—summit WV-2
Weedy Rough Mtn—summit AR-4
Weedy Run—stream WV-2
Weedy Shoals—bar AK-9
Wee Folks School-Tanner Acad—school FL-3
Wee Folks School-Tanner Academy—school FL-3
Wee Grimmet—hist pl PA-2
Wee Haven Sch—school IN-6
**Weehawken**—pop pl NJ-2
Weehawken Cem—cemetery NJ-2
Weehawken Cove—bay NJ-2
Weehawken Creek—stream CO-8
Weehawken Edgewater Channel—channel NJ-2
Weehawken Pack Trail—trail CO-8
**Weehawken (Township of)**—pop pl NJ-2
Weehaw Rice Mill Chimney—hist pl SC-3
Weehinkle Divide—ridge WY-8
Weehunt Branch—stream AR-4
Weehunt Mtn—summit AR-4
Weeint Hollow—valley UT-8
**Weekapaug**—pop pl RI-1
Weekapaug Beach—locale RI-1
Weekapaug Point—cape RI-1
Week Creek AL-4
Week Creek—stream FL-3
**Weekeempee**—pop pl CT-1
Weekeepeemee River—stream CT-1
Weekend Island—island CA-9
Weekes Cem—cemetery NY-2
Weekes Corner—locale NY-2
Weekes Wash—stream AZ-5
Weekewah Creek FL-3
Weeki-Wachee FL-3
Weeki Wachee—locale FL-3
Weeki Wachee Acres—CDP FL-3
Weeki Wachee (CCD)—cens area FL-3
**Weekiwachee Gardens (subdivision)**—pop pl FL-3
Weekiwachee Prairie Lake—lake FL-3
Weekiwachee River FL-3
Weeki Wachee River—stream FL-3
Weeki Wachee Spring—spring FL-3
Weekiwachee Springs FL-3
Weeki Wachee Springs—other FL-3
Weekiwachee Swamp FL-3
Weeki Wachee Swamp—swamp FL-3
Weekiwachee Tower—tower FL-3
**Weeki Wachee (Weeki Wachee Springs)**—pop pl FL-3
**Weekiwachee Woodlands (subdivision)**—pop pl FL-3
Weeki-Wackee FL-3
Weeklakatchee FL-3
Week Landing—locale FL-3
Weekley, John M., House—hist pl TX-5
Weekley Bayou—bay FL-3
Weekly Bayou FL-3
Weekly Creek—stream OR-9
Weekly Run—stream WV-2
Week Mills ME-1
Weeks KS-7
Weeks—locale (2) AR-4
Weeks—locale OK-5
**Weeks**—pop pl AL-4
**Weeks**—pop pl (2) LA-4
**Weeks**—pop pl NV-8
**Weeks**—pop pl SC-3
Weeks, Barzillai, House—hist pl MA-1
Weeks, Charles H., House—hist pl UT-8
Weeks, Charles M., House—hist pl NY-2
Weeks, Lake—lake FL-3
Weeks, Mount—summit NH-1
Weeks Assembly Church AL-4
Weeks Basin—basin ME-1
Weeks Bay—bay AL-4
Weeks Bay—bay LA-4
Weeks Bay Channel—channel LA-4
Weeks Bayou—gut LA-4
Weeks Bayou—stream MS-4
Weeks Bench—bench UT-8
Weeksboro—locale ME-1
Weeksboro Ridge—ridge ME-1
Weeks Branch AL-4
Weeks Branch—stream AL-4
Weeks Branch—stream GA-3
Weeks Branch—stream LA-4
Weeks Branch—stream TX-5
Weeks Bridge—bridge AL-4
Weeks Brook—stream (4) ME-1
Weeks Brook—stream (2) NH-1
Weeks Brook—stream NY-2
Weeks Brook Trail—trail NH-1
Weeksburg KY-4
Weeksbury—locale KY-4
Weeks Canal—canal LA-4
Weeks Canyon UT-8
Weeks Canyon—valley NV-8
Weeks Cem—cemetery (2) AL-4
Weeks Cem—cemetery AR-4
Weeks Cem—cemetery FL-3
Weeks Cem—cemetery ME-1
Weeks Cem—cemetery MA-1
Weeks Cem—cemetery MS-4
Weeks Cem—cemetery OH-6
Weeks Cem—cemetery SC-3
Weeks Cem—cemetery TX-5
Weeks Ch AL-4
Weeks Ch—church AL-4
Weeks Chapel—church GA-3
Weeks Chapel—church TX-5
Weeks Chapel Ch—church AL-4
Weeks Community Center—locale MO-7
Weeks Corner—locale ME-1
Weeks Creek—stream AL-4
Weeks Creek—stream (2) CA-9
Weeks Creek—stream GA-3
Weeks Creek—stream NV-8
Weeks Creek—stream VA-3
Weeks Ditch—canal IN-6
Weeks Drain—canal ID-8
Weeks Drain—canal MI-6
Weeks Estate—hist pl NH-1
Weeks Family Cem—cemetery AL-4
Weeks Fisher Creek—stream FL-3
Weeks Fishpond—reservoir AL-4
Weeks Gulch—valley ID-8
Weeks Hill—summit RI-1
Weeks (historical)—locale MS-4
Weeks Hollow—valley MO-7
Weeks Hollow—valley VA-3
Weeks House—hist pl NH-1
Weeks House—hist pl TX-5
Weeks Island LA-4
Weeks Island—island LA-4
Weeks Island Oil and Gas Field—oilfield LA-4
Weeks JHS—hist pl MA-1
Weeks JHS—school IA-7
Weeks JHS—school MA-1
Weeks-Kimbrough House—hist pl GA-3
Weeks Lake—lake FL-3
Weeks Lake—reservoir MS-4
Weeks Lake Dam—dam MS-4
Weeks Lakes—lake FL-3
Weeks Lakes—lake WI-6
Weeks Landing—locale NJ-2
Weeks Landing—locale SC-3
Weeks Memorial Church AL-4

Weeks Mill Creek—*stream* ... MS-4
Weeks Mills—*locale* ... ME-1
**Weeks Mills**—*pop pl* ... ME-1
Weeks Mtn—*summit* ... GA-3
*Weeks Neck* ... MA-1
Weeks Neck—*cape* ... MA-1
Weeks Park—*park* ... TX-5
Weeks Point—*cape* ... NH-1
Weeks Point—*cape* (2) ... NY-2
Weeks Point—*cape* ... VA-3
*Weeks Pond* ... ME-1
Weeks Pond—*lake* ... ME-1
Weeks Pond—*lake* (3) ... MA-1
Weeks Pond—*lake* (2) ... NH-1
Weeks Pond—*reservoir* ... NY-2
Weeks Pond—*reservoir* ... NC-3
Weeks Pond—*reservoir* ... SC-3
Weeks Pond—*swamp* ... FL-3
Weeks Pond Dam—*dam* ... NC-3
Weeks Post Office (historical)—*building* ... MS-4
Weeks Road Sch—*school* ... NY-2
Weeks Sch—*school* ... AL-4
Weeks Sch—*school* ... IL-6
Weeks Sch—*school* ... MI-6
Weeks Sch—*school* ... NY-2
Weeks Settlement—*locale* ... TX-5
Weeks Spring—*spring* ... SD-7
**Weekstown**—*pop pl* ... NJ-2
Weeksville—*locale* ... MT-8
**Weeksville**—*pop pl* ... NC-3
Weeksville Creek—*stream* ... MT-8
Weeksville Elem Sch—*school* ... NC-3
Weeks Waterhole—*lake* ... FL-3
Weeks Well—*well* ... NV-8
Weeks Windmill—*locale* ... NM-5
Wee Laddie Pond—*reservoir* ... MA-1
Wee Lads and Lassies Preschool—*school* ... FL-3
Wee Lake—*lake* ... FL-3
We-E Lake—*lake* ... MI-6
Wee Lake—*lake* ... MN-6
Wee Lake—*lake* ... MT-8
Wee Lambie Spring—*spring* ... OR-9
*Weelanee River* ... FL-3
*Weeloay* ... FM-9
Weeloey—*civil* ... FM-9
Weelung Creek—*stream* ... AK-9
Weeman Bridge—*bridge* ... WA-9
Weeman Cem—*cemetery* ... ME-1
Weemasoul Creek—*stream* ... CA-9
Weemasoul Spring—*spring* ... CA-9
Wee-Ma-Tuk, Lake—*lake* ... IL-6
**Wee-ma-tuk Hills**—*pop pl* ... IL-6
Wee-Ma-Tuk Hills Country Club—*other* ... IL-6
WEEM-FM (Pendleton)—*tower* ... IN-6
*Weems* ... OH-6
Weems—*locale* ... AL-4
**Weems**—*pop pl* ... VA-3
Weems-Botts House—*hist pl* ... VA-3
Weems Cem—*cemetery* ... MO-7
Weems Cem—*cemetery* (5) ... TN-4
Weems Cem—*cemetery* ... TX-5
Weems Chapel—*church* ... TN-4
Weems Chapel United Methodist Ch—*church* ... MS-4
**Weems Creek**—*pop pl* ... MD-2
Weems Creek—*stream* ... MD-2
Weems Creek—*stream* ... SC-3
Weems Gap—*gap* ... AL-4
**Weems (historical)**—*pop pl* ... MS-4
Weems Hollow—*valley* ... TN-4
Weems House—*hist pl* ... AL-4
Weems Island—*island* ... LA-4
Weems Lake—*lake* ... LA-4
*Weems Landing* ... AL-4
Weems Memorial Hosp—*hospital* ... FL-3
Weems Pond—*lake* ... GA-3
Weems Post Office (historical)—*building* ... MS-4
Weems Sch—*school* ... AL-4
Weems Sch—*school* ... MS-4
*Weems Sch Community* ... MS-4
Weems Sch (historical)—*school* ... MS-4
**Weems (Smithfield Station)**—*pop pl* ... OH-6
Weems Spring—*spring* ... NM-5
WEEN-AM (Lafayette)—*tower* ... TN-4
Weenan Creek—*stream* ... WA-9
*Weenausabuck* ... PA-2
*We-en-de-quint Creek* ... UT-8
Wee Nee Plantation—*locale* ... SC-3
Wee Nee Sch—*school* ... SC-3
Weenfaraq—*locale* ... FM-9
*Weenly Creek* ... TX-5
*Weenomset* ... MA-1
*Weenomsit* ... MA-1
Weeny Lake—*lake* ... MN-6
*Weeowoka Creek* ... AL-4
Weepah—*locale* ... NV-8
Weepah Hills—*summit* ... NV-8
Weepah Mine—*mine* ... NV-8
Weepah Spring—*spring* ... NV-8
WEEP-AM (Hampton Township)—*tower* ... PA-2
WEEP-AM (Pittsburgh)—*tower* ... PA-2
Wee Peak—*summit* ... MT-8
Weepecket Island—*island* ... MA-1
Weepecket Islands—*island* ... MA-1
Weepecket Rock—*rock* ... MA-1
*Weepecket Shoal* ... MA-1
*Weeping Child Creek* ... MT-8
*Weeping Cliff* ... AZ-5
Weeping Cliffs—*cliff* ... AZ-5
Weeping Ledge Lake—*lake* ... UT-8
**Weeping Mary**—*pop pl* ... TX-5
Weeping Mary AME Zion Ch—*church* ... AL-4
Weeping Mary Baptist Ch—*church* ... AL-4
Weeping Mary Ch—*church* (3) ... AL-4
Weeping Mary Ch—*church* (6) ... NC-3
Weeping Mary Ch—*church* (4) ... SC-3
Weeping Mary Sch—*school* (2) ... SC-3
Weeping Mary Zion Methodist Ch—*church* ... AL-4
Weeping Rachel Ch—*church* ... NC-3
Weeping Rock—*pillar* ... UT-8
Weeping Rock Campground—*park* ... OR-9
Weeping Rock Springs—*spring* ... CO-8
Weeping Wall—*area* ... AK-9
Weeping Wall—*cliff* ... MT-8
**Weeping Water**—*pop pl* ... NE-7
Weeping Water Creek—*stream* ... NE-7
Weeping Water Hist Dist—*hist pl* ... NE-7
Weeping Willow Baptist Ch—*church* ... AL-4
Weeping Willow Cem—*cemetery* ... KY-4
Weeping Willow Ch—*church* (2) ... AL-4
*Weeping Willow Plantation* ... MS-4
Weeping Willow Sch—*school* ... SC-3
Weeping Willow Spring—*spring* ... MO-7
*Weepo Spring* ... AZ-5
Weequahic—*uninc pl* ... NJ-2
Weequahic HS—*school* ... NJ-2
Weequahic Lake—*lake* ... NJ-2
Weequahic Park—*park* ... NJ-2
Weequakut (historical)—*locale* ... MA-1
Wee Riffle—*rapids* ... OR-9
*Weesatch Cove* ... TX-5
*Weesatch Creek* ... TX-5
**Weesatche**—*pop pl* ... TX-5
Weesatche-Ander (CCD)—*cens area* ... TX-5
Weesatche Gas Field—*oilfield* ... TX-5
Weesau Creek—*stream* ... IN-6
**Weesaw (Township of)**—*pop pl* ... MI-6
Weese—*locale* (2) ... WV-2
**Weese Addition (subdivision)**—*pop pl* ... UT-8
Weese Cem—*cemetery* ... IL-6
Weese Cem—*cemetery* ... MO-7
Weese Run—*stream* ... WV-2
**Weeset**—*pop pl* ... MA-1
Weeset Point—*cape* ... MA-1
*Weesett* ... MA-1
*Weesett Point* ... MA-1
Weesha Club—*other* ... CA-9
Weesquamsett—*locale* ... MA-1
*Weesquobs* ... MA-1
Wees Run—*stream* ... WV-2
Weess, Frank J., House—*hist pl* ... IA-7
Weesuck Creek—*stream* ... NY-2
Weetamoo, Mount—*summit* ... NH-1
Weetamoo Cliff—*summit* ... MA-1
Weetamoo Rock—*pillar* ... NH-1
Weetamoo Trail—*trail* ... NH-1
Weetches Canyon—*valley* ... UT-8
*Wee Tee Bay* ... SC-3
*Wee Tee Branch* ... SC-3
*Wee Tee Island* ... SC-3
*Wee Tee Lake* ... SC-3
*Weethatookamee Village* ... FL-3
Weethee Hist Dist—*hist pl* ... OH-6
Weeth Ranch—*locale* ... CA-9
Weeting Lake—*lake* ... WI-6
Wee Town—*locale* ... NE-7
WEEU-AM (Reading)—*tower* ... PA-2
WEEW-AM (Washington)—*tower* ... NC-3
*Weeweder Ponds* ... MA-1
Wee Wee Hill—*summit* ... IN-6
WeeWisdom and Unity Elem Sch—*school* ... FL-3
Wee Wisdom Montessori/Unity Sch—*school* ... FL-3
Weewoka Creek—*stream* ... AL-4
WEEX-AM (Easton)—*tower* ... PA-2
Weey—*summit* ... FM-9
*Wee-Yot* ... CA-9
WEEZ-FM (Heidelberg)—*tower* ... MS-4
**Wefanie**—*pop pl* ... GA-3
Weferling Canyon—*valley* ... CA-9
WE Four Ranch—*locale* ... TX-5
Wegal Lake—*lake* ... MI-6
Wegaman Sch—*school* ... OH-6
**Wegan**—*pop pl* ... IN-6
**Wegatchie**—*pop pl* ... NY-2
*Wegathiy* ... FM-9
**Wegdahl**—*pop pl* ... MN-6
**Wegee**—*pop pl* ... OH-6
Wegee Creek—*stream* ... OH-6
Wegeforth Sch—*school* ... CA-9
Wegenast Cem—*cemetery* ... IN-6
Wegens Point—*cape* ... MN-6
Weger Oil Field—*oilfield* ... TX-5
Wegert Rsvr—*reservoir* ... AR-4
WEGG-AM (Rose Hill)—*tower* ... NC-3
Weggland Ditch—*canal* ... ID-8
Weggum Mine—*mine* ... MN-6
Weglein Sch—*school* ... MD-2
**Wegley**—*pop pl* ... PA-2
Wegley Mtn—*summit* ... NY-2
WEGL-FM (Auburn)—*tower* ... AL-4
WEGN-AM (Evergreen)—*tower* ... AL-4
Wegner, C. H., House—*hist pl* ... WI-6
Wegner Cem—*cemetery* ... TX-5
Wegner Creek—*stream* ... MT-8
Wegner Creek—*stream* (2) ... OR-9
Wegner Lake—*lake* ... CA-9
Wegner Ranch—*locale* ... TX-5
WEGO-AM (Concord)—*tower* ... NC-3
**Wegoe**—*pop pl* ... WA-9
**Wego-Waco**—*pop pl* ... KS-7
*Wegowaie Creek* ... AL-4
**Wegra**—*pop pl* ... AL-4
Wegra Ch—*church* ... AL-4
Wegra Mine (underground)—*mine* ... AL-4
*Wegwaas Lake* ... MI-6
Wegwaas Lake—*lake* ... MI-6
*Wegwass Lake* ... MI-6
Wegwos Lake—*lake* ... MN-6
Weha—*civil* ... HI-9
Wehadkee—*locale* ... AL-4
Wehadkee Ch—*church* ... AL-4
Wehadkee Ch—*church* ... GA-3
Wehadkee Creek—*stream* ... AL-4
Wehadkee Creek—*stream* ... GA-3
We Ha Kee Church Camp—*locale* ... WI-6
*Wehapa Dam* ... AL-4
Wehapa Lake—*reservoir* ... AL-4
W E Harbor Pond Dam—*dam* (2) ... MS-4
*Wehbers Pond* ... MA-1
Wehdem—*locale* ... TX-5
Wehe Cem—*cemetery* ... TX-5
We-Hi Lake—*lake* ... IN-6
Wehle Lake—*reservoir* ... AL-4
Wehle Lake Dam—*dam* ... AL-4
Wehmer House—*hist pl* ... IA-7
Wehmeyer Creek—*stream* ... OR-9
Wehmeyer Ranch—*locale* ... TX-5
Wehmhoff Mound (47KN15)—*hist pl* ... WI-6
**Wehnwood**—*pop pl* ... PA-2
*Wehowgee Creek* ... AL-4
*Wehr* ... PA-2
Wehr Covered Bridge—*bridge* ... PA-2
Wehr Covered Bridge—*hist pl* ... PA-2
Wehrli Canyon—*valley* ... OR-9
Wehrman Landing Strip—*airport* ... MO-7
Wehrman Oil Field—*oilfield* ... KS-7
Wehrs Sch (abandoned)—*school* ... PA-2
Wehrum—*locale* ... PA-2
WEHT-TV (Evansville)—*tower* ... IN-6
Wehunt Creek—*stream* ... AR-4
Wehutty—*locale* ... NC-3
Wehutty Ch—*church* ... NC-3
Wehutty Mtn—*summit* ... NC-3
**Weiant**—*pop pl* ... OH-6
Weible Cem—*cemetery* ... MO-7
Weible Peak—*summit* ... CO-8
Weicher Creek—*stream* ... KY-4
Weicht Ditch—*canal* ... IN-6
Weidas Mill Bridge—*bridge* ... PA-2
Weidasville—*locale* ... PA-2
Weide Creek—*stream* ... TX-5
Weidel—*airport* ... NJ-2
Weideman Creek—*stream* ... TX-5
Weidemann Creek—*stream* ... MO-7
Weidenmaier Lakes—*reservoir* ... OK-5
Weidensaul Hollow—*valley* ... MO-7
Weiden School—*locale* ... NE-7
Weiderich Cem—*cemetery* ... ND-7
Weidernoch Point—*cape* ... FL-3
Weiders Crossing—*locale* ... PA-2
Weidman—*locale* ... MD-2
**Weidman**—*pop pl* ... MI-6
Weidman Ch—*church* ... MI-6
Weidman Gulch—*valley* ... WA-9
Weidman Lake—*lake* ... MI-6
Weidman Run—*stream* ... WV-2
Weidmanville—*locale* ... PA-2
Weidner Cem—*cemetery* (2) ... TX-5
Weidner Ranch—*locale* ... WY-8
Weidner Rock House—*hist pl* ... NC-3
*Weid Run* ... PA-2
Weiferich Ranch—*locale* ... MT-8
Weigand Ave Sch—*school* ... CA-9
*Weigand Cave* ... AL-4
Weigand Creek—*stream* ... MO-7
Weigand Creek—*stream* ... NE-7
Weigand Lake—*lake* ... MN-6
Weigand Pit—*cave* ... AL-4
Weigand Rec Area—*park* ... NE-7
Weigand Rsvr—*reservoir* ... MT-8
Weigands Cem—*cemetery* ... DE-2
Weigang Oil Field—*oilfield* ... TX-5
Weigel Creek—*stream* ... MI-6
Weigel Creek—*stream* ... MT-8
Weigel Mtn—*summit* ... MT-8
**Weigelstown**—*pop pl* ... PA-2
Weigelt Pond—*lake* ... NY-2
Weiger Slough State Public Shooting Area—*park* ... SD-7
Weigert Cem—*cemetery* ... NE-7
Weighlock Bldg—*hist pl* ... NY-2
*Weighman Chapel* ... AL-4
*Weighman Chapel AME Zion Church* ... AL-4
*Weighman Church* ... AL-4
**Weigh Scale**—*pop pl* ... PA-2
Weigh Scales—*locale* ... PA-2
Weigh Scale Tipple Station—*locale* ... PA-2
Weightman Creek—*stream* ... NC-3
Weightman Drain—*stream* ... MI-6
Weigle, William, House and Water Tank—*hist pl* ... ID-8
Weigle Hill—*summit* ... WA-9
Weigles Butte—*summit* ... AZ-5
**Weigletown**—*pop pl* ... PA-2
Weihermiller Sch—*school* ... IL-6
*Weihnachts Hafen* ... MP-9
Weikel—*locale* ... WA-9
Weikel Sch—*school* ... PA-2
Weikels Run (historical)—*stream* ... PA-2
*Weiker Run* ... PA-2
*Weiker Station* ... PA-2
**Weikert**—*pop pl* ... PA-2
Weikert Run—*stream* ... PA-2
Weikswood—*locale* ... WA-9
Weil—*locale* ... LA-4
Weil, Lake—*reservoir* ... AL-4
Weil, Solomon and Henry, Houses—*hist pl* ... NC-3
Weiland—*locale* ... TX-5
Weiland Cem—*cemetery* ... TX-5
Weiland Ch—*church* ... TX-5
*Weiland Gulch* ... CO-8
Weiland Oil Field—*oilfield* ... TX-5
Weiland Valley—*valley* ... WI-6
Weil Dam—*dam* ... AL-4
Weilder Camp—*locale* ... PA-2
Weil Ditch—*canal* ... IN-6
Weiler Cave—*cave* ... AL-4
Weiler Dam Rsvr—*reservoir* ... ND-7
Weilermann, Gus, House—*hist pl* ... ID-8
Weiler State Wildlife Mngmt Area—*park* ... MN-6
**Weilersville**—*pop pl* ... OH-6
**Weilersville**—*pop pl* ... PA-2
Weil Lake—*lake* ... CA-9
Weill Park—*park* ... CA-9
Weil Point—*cape* ... NC-3
Weil Ranch—*locale* ... TX-5
*Weilsboro* ... PA-2
Weimann Community Cem—*cemetery* ... MN-6
Weimann Lake—*lake* ... MN-6
**Weimar**—*pop pl* ... CA-9
**Weimar**—*pop pl* ... TX-5
Weimar (CCD)—*cens area* ... TX-5
*Weimar City* ... KS-7
Weimar (historical)—*locale* ... KS-7
**Weimar (New England Mills)**—*pop pl* ... CA-9
*Weimen* ... PA-2
**Weimer**—*pop pl* ... MI-6
**Weimer**—*pop pl* ... PA-2
Weimer Black Dam—*dam* ... IN-6
Weimer Camp—*locale* ... CO-8
Weimer Canyon—*valley* ... AZ-5
Weimer Cem—*cemetery* ... OH-6
Weimer Creek—*stream* ... MT-8
Weimer Creek—*stream* ... WA-9
Weimer Lake—*reservoir* ... IN-6
Weimer Lake Dam—*dam* ... IN-6
Weimer Point—*cliff* ... AZ-5
Weimer Run—*stream* (2) ... PA-2
Weimer Sch—*school* ... PA-2
Weimer Sch (abandoned)—*school* (2) ... PA-2
Weimer Spring—*spring* ... AZ-5
Weimer Tank—*reservoir* (4) ... AZ-5
**Weimer Township**—*pop pl* ... ND-7
**Weimer (Township of)**—*pop pl* ... MN-6
Weinacht Draw—*valley* ... TX-5
*Weinals Crossroads* ... PA-2
Weinbach Shop Ctr—*locale* ... IN-6
Wein-bahi Spring—*spring* ... AZ-5
*Weinberg Cross Roads* ... SC-3
Weinberger Lake—*lake* ... MN-6
Weinberger Sch—*school* ... CA-9
Weinegar Windmill—*locale* ... CO-8
*Weinel Cross Roads* ... PA-2
**Weinel Crossroads**—*pop pl* ... PA-2
**Weinel Cross Roads**—*pop pl* ... PA-2
**Weiner**—*pop pl* ... AR-4
Weiner Creek—*stream* ... LA-4
Weiner Creek—*stream* ... WY-8
Weiners Caves—*cave* ... TN-4
Weiner Swale—*lake* ... IL-6
**Weinert**—*pop pl* (2) ... TX-5
Weinert (CCD)—*cens area* ... TX-5
Weinert Cem—*cemetery* ... TX-5
Weinert Oil Field—*area* ... TX-5
Weinert Ranch—*locale* ... TX-5
Weinert Rsvr—*reservoir* ... TX-5
Weinert Sch—*school* ... TX-5
**Weingarten**—*pop pl* ... MO-7
Weinhard, Jacob, House—*hist pl* ... WA-9
Weinheimer Gulch—*valley* ... ID-8
Weinheimer Ranch—*locale* ... TX-5
*Weinhimer Gulch* ... ID-8
Weinie Lake—*lake* ... AK-9
Weinland Park Sch—*school* ... OH-6
Weinmann Block—*hist pl* ... MI-6
Weino Creek—*stream* ... MT-8
Weins, Jacob, House-Barn—*hist pl* ... SD-7
Wein Schlucht—*valley* ... TX-5
Weinsheimer Ditch—*canal* ... IN-6
**Weintz**—*pop pl* ... PA-2
Weintz Cem—*cemetery* ... IL-6
Weintz Draw—*valley* ... WY-8
Weipowe—*locale* ... FM-9
**Weippe**—*pop pl* ... ID-8
Weippe Cem—*cemetery* ... ID-8
Weippe Prairie—*flat* ... ID-8
Weippe Prairie—*hist pl* ... ID-8
WEIQ-TV (Mobile)—*tower* ... AL-4
*Weir* ... MA-1
Weir—*locale* ... CO-8
Weir—*locale* ... NE-7
Weir—*locale* ... TX-5
Weir—*locale* ... WV-2
**Weir**—*pop pl* ... KS-7
**Weir**—*pop pl* ... KY-4
**Weir**—*pop pl* ... MS-4
**Weir**—*pop pl* ... TX-5
Weir, Dr. David P., House—*hist pl* ... NC-3
Weir, J. Alden, Farm (District)—*hist pl* ... CT-1
Weir, John, House—*hist pl* ... IL-6
Weir, Lake—*lake* ... FL-3
*Weir, The* ... MA-1
Weir and Johnson Campground—*locale* ... CO-8
Weir and Johnson Rsvr—*reservoir* ... CO-8
Weir Attendance Center—*school* ... MS-4
Weir Blair Cem (historical)—*cemetery* ... AL-4
Weir Branch—*stream* ... TX-5
Weirbush Ranch—*locale* ... TX-5
Weir Canyon—*valley* ... CA-9
Weir Cave—*cave* ... AL-4
Weir Cem—*cemetery* ... AL-4
Weir Cem—*cemetery* ... AR-4
Weir Cem—*cemetery* ... IN-6
Weir Cem—*cemetery* ... MS-4
Weir Cem—*cemetery* (3) ... TN-4
Weir Chapel Cem—*cemetery* ... MS-4
*Weir City* ... KS-7
*Weir Cove* ... ME-1
Weir Cove—*bay* (2) ... ME-1
Weir Cove—*bay* ... MD-2
Weir-Crawford Ditch—*canal* ... MT-8
*Weir Creek* ... KY-4
*Weir Creek* ... MO-7
Weir Creek—*stream* ... CA-9
Weir Creek—*stream* ... ID-8
Weir Creek—*stream* ... MD-2
Weir Creek—*stream* ... MA-1
Weir Creek—*stream* ... MI-6
Weir Creek—*stream* ... MS-4
Weir Creek—*stream* ... NJ-2
Weir Creek—*stream* ... PA-2
Weir Creek—*stream* ... SC-3
Weir Creek—*stream* ... TX-5
Weir Creek Hot Springs—*spring* ... ID-8
Weir Creek (Magisterial District)—*fmr MCD* ... VA-3
**Weircrest**—*pop pl* ... WV-2
Weir Dam—*dam* ... UT-8
Weird Cem—*cemetery* ... KY-4
Weird Lake—*lake* ... MN-6
Weir Drain—*canal* ... MI-6
Weir Elem Sch—*school* ... MS-4
Weir Engine House—*hist pl* ... MA-1
Weir Gap—*gap* ... VA-3
**Weirgor**—*pop pl* ... WI-6
*Weirgor Creek* ... WI-6
Weirgor Lake—*lake* ... WI-6
Weirgor Springs—*spring* ... WI-6
Weirgor Springs State Public Hunting Grounds—*park* ... WI-6
Weirgor Springs State Wildlife Area—*park* ... WI-6
**Weirgor (Town of)**—*pop pl* ... WI-6
Weir Greenhouse—*hist pl* ... NY-2
Weir Gulch—*valley* ... CO-8
Weir Gulch—*valley* ... ID-8
Weir Gulch Park—*lake* ... CO-8
Weir Hill—*summit* ... MA-1
**Weir (historical)**—*pop pl* ... TN-4
Weir HS—*school* ... WV-2
Weirich Cem—*cemetery* ... IA-7
*Weirickstown* ... PA-2
Weir Island—*island* ... AK-9
Weir Junction Station—*building* ... MA-1
Weir Lagoon Dam—*dam* ... MS-4
*Weir Lake* ... UT-8
Weir Lake—*lake* ... CA-9
Weir Lake—*lake* ... IN-6
Weir Lake—*lake* ... MN-6
**Weir Lake**—*pop pl* ... PA-2
Weir Lake—*reservoir* ... PA-2
Weir Ledges—*bar* ... ME-1
Weir Lookout Tower—*locale* ... MS-4
Weir Mill Brook—*stream* ... VT-1
Weir Mountain—*ridge* ... PA-2
Weir Number Eight—*dam* ... AZ-5
Weir Number Eleven—*dam* ... AZ-5
Weir Number Nine—*dam* ... AZ-5
Weir Number Seven—*dam* ... AZ-5
Weir Park—*uninc pl* ... WA-9
Weir Park Rsvr—*reservoir* ... CO-8
Weir Peak—*summit* ... MT-8
Weir Place—*locale* ... CO-8
*Weir Point* ... VA-3
Weir Point—*cape* ... MD-2
Weir Point—*cape* ... NC-3
Weir Point—*cape* ... VA-3
Weir Point—*summit* ... MT-8
*Weir Pond* ... MA-1
Weir Pond—*lake* ... ME-1
Weir Post Office (historical)—*building* ... TN-4
*Weir Prairie* ... WA-9
Weir Ranch—*locale* ... OR-9
*Weir River* ... VA-3
Weir River—*stream* ... MA-1
Weir River Marshes—*swamp* ... MA-1
Weir Rsvr—*reservoir* ... UT-8
Weirs—*lake* ... IN-6
*Weirs, The* (2) ... NH-1
Weirs, The—*hist pl* ... NH-1
**Weirs Beach**—*pop pl* ... NH-1
*Weirs Beach (The Weirs)* ... NH-1
Weir Sch—*school* ... CA-9
Weir Sch—*school* ... IN-6
Weir Sch—*school* ... MA-1
Weir Sch Number 71—*school* ... IN-6
*Weirs Creek* ... MO-7
*Weirs Creek* ... TX-5
Weirs Creek—*stream* ... KY-4
Weirs Creek—*stream* ... TX-5
**Weirsdale**—*pop pl* ... FL-3
Weirs Lake—*lake* ... IN-6
*Weirs Mill* ... MS-4
Weirs Pond—*lake* ... PA-2
*Weir Spring* ... PA-2
Weirs Run—*stream* ... PA-2
**Weirton**—*pop pl* ... WV-2
Weirton General Hosp—*hospital* ... WV-2
**Weirton Heights**—*pop pl* ... WV-2
Weirton Heights Sch—*school* ... WV-2
Weirton Junction—*locale* ... WV-2
**Weirton Junction**—*pop pl* ... WV-2
Weirton (Magisterial District)—*fmr MCD* ... WV-2
Weirton Mine—*mine* ... WV-2
Weirton Yards—*locale* ... WV-2
Weir Tower—*locale* ... SC-3
**Weirtown**—*pop pl* ... NJ-2
Weir Valley—*valley* ... AZ-5
**Weir Village**—*pop pl* ... MA-1
**Weirville**—*pop pl* ... TX-5
Weir Wash—*stream* ... AZ-5
Weirwood—*locale* ... WV-2
**Weirwood**—*pop pl* ... VA-3
Weirwood Fairgrounds—*locale* ... VA-3
**Weirwood (RR name Wierwood)**—*pop pl* ... VA-3
WEIS-AM (Centre)—*tower* ... AL-4
Weisbach Ch—*church* ... IN-6
Weisbrook Sch—*school* ... IL-6
**Weisburg**—*pop pl* ... IN-6
**Weisburg**—*pop pl* ... MD-2
Weisdorfer Draw—*valley* ... NM-5
Weise Island—*island* ... PA-2
Weisel—*locale* ... CA-9
Weisel—*locale* ... PA-2
Weisel, Andrew, House—*hist pl* ... IL-6
Weisel Youth Hoslel—*building* ... PA-2
Weisenbeck Valley—*valley* ... WI-6
*Weisenberg* ... PA-2
Weisenberg Ch—*church* ... PA-2
Weisenberg Elem Sch—*school* ... PA-2
Weisenberger Mills and Related Buildings—*hist pl* ... KY-4
*Weisenberg Sch* ... PA-2
**Weisenberg (Township of)**—*pop pl* ... PA-2
*Weisenberg Valley* ... WI-6
Weise Pond—*lake* ... NY-2
**Weiser**—*pop pl* ... ID-8
Weiser, Conrad, House—*hist pl* ... PA-2
Weiser Cem—*cemetery* ... ND-7
Weiser Cove—*basin* ... ID-8
Weiser Creek—*stream* ... CA-9
Weiser Creek—*stream* ... WY-8
Weiser Draw—*valley* ... WY-8
**Weiser Junction**—*pop pl* ... OR-9
Weiser Knoll—*summit* ... WY-8
Weiser Lake—*lake* ... PA-2
Weiser Pass—*gap* ... WY-8
Weiser Post Office—*hist pl* ... ID-8
Weiser Ranch—*locale* ... WY-8
Weiser Ridge—*ridge* ... NV-8
Weiser River—*stream* ... ID-8
Weiser Run—*stream* ... PA-2
Weiser Sch—*school* ... IL-6
Weiser Sch—*school* ... PA-2
Weiser State Forest—*park* ... PA-2
**Weiser Township**—*pop pl* ... ND-7
Weiser Valley—*valley* ... NV-8
Weiser Warm Springs—*spring* ... ID-8
Weiser Wash—*stream* ... NV-8
Weishample—*locale* ... PA-2
Weisingel Branch—*stream* ... AL-4
Weisinger (historical)—*locale* ... AL-4
Weisinger Sch (historical)—*school* ... AL-4
Weisjahn Ditch—*canal* ... IN-6
*Weis-Jann-Tyler Ditch* ... IN-6
Weiskittel-Roehle Burial Vault—*hist pl* ... MD-2
Weiskopf Sch—*school* ... WI-6
Weis Lake—*lake* ... IL-6
Weisler Creek—*stream* ... MI-6
**Weis Library**—*pop pl* ... PA-2
Weislocker Cem—*cemetery* ... MO-7
**Weisman Acres**—*pop pl* ... DE-2
Weisman-Hirsch House—*hist pl* ... TX-5
Weisman Lake—*lake* ... CO-8
Weis Manufacturing Company—*hist pl* ... MI-6
*Weisner* ... NC-3
Weisner, Lake—*reservoir* ... AL-4
Weisner Cem—*cemetery* ... MO-7
Weisner Creek—*stream* ... IN-6
*Weisner Dam* ... SD-7
Weisner Dam—*dam* ... AL-4
Weisner Dam—*dam* ... SD-7
Weisner Dam 1—*dam* ... SD-7
Weisner Ditch—*canal* ... WI-6
Weisner Mtn—*summit* ... AL-4
Weisner Ranch—*locale* ... MT-8
*Weisners Branch* ... IN-6
Weiss—*locale* ... LA-4
Weiss, Lake—*reservoir* ... PA-2
Weiss Airp—*airport* ... KS-7
Weiss Airp—*airport* ... MO-7
Weiss Airp—*airport* ... PA-2
Weiss Branch—*stream* ... VA-3
Weiss Bridge—*bridge* ... OR-9
Weiss Canal—*canal* ... TX-5
Weiss Canyon—*valley* ... CA-9
Weiss Cem—*cemetery* ... IN-6
Weiss Cem—*cemetery* ... IA-7
Weiss Cem—*cemetery* ... TX-5
Weiss Creek—*stream* ... MN-6
Weiss Dam—*dam* ... AL-4
**Weiss Dam**—*pop pl* ... AL-4
Weiss Dam Powerhouse—*building* ... AL-4
Weiss Ditch—*canal* ... IN-6
Weiss Drain—*canal* ... MI-6
*Weissenberg* ... PA-2
Weissenfels Ridge—*ridge* ... WA-9
Weissenfluh Rsvr—*reservoir* ... OR-9
Weisser Dam—*dam* ... ND-7
Weisser Dam—*reservoir* ... ND-7
Weisser Park—*park* ... IN-6
**Weissert**—*pop pl* ... NE-7
Weissert Sch—*school* ... NE-7
Weiss Field—*park* ... IL-6
Weiss Field (Park)—*park* ... OH-6
Weiss Hall—*hist pl* ... PA-2
Weiss Hill—*summit* ... CA-9
Weiss Hosp—*hospital* ... IL-6
Weissinger-Gaulbert Apartments—*hist pl* ... KY-4
Weissinger Lakes—*reservoir* ... AL-4
Weissinger Mule Barn—*hist pl* ... KY-4
Weiss Knob—*summit* ... WV-2
Weiss Lake—*lake* ... WI-6
Weiss Lake—*reservoir* (2) ... AL-4
Weiss Lake—*reservoir* ... GA-3
Weiss Lake Dike—*levee* ... AL-4
Weissman Mine—*mine* ... CA-9
Weiss Playground—*park* ... MI-6
*Weiss Port* ... PA-2
**Weissport**—*pop pl* ... PA-2
Weissport Borough—*civil* ... PA-2
Weissport East—*CDP* ... PA-2
Weiss Ranch—*locale* ... MT-8
Weiss Ranch—*locale* ... OR-9
Weiss Ranch—*locale* ... WY-8
*Weiss Reservoir* ... AL-4
Weiss Roadside Park—*park* ... MO-7
*Weiss Rsvr* ... GA-3
Weiss Sch—*school* ... FL-3
Weiss Sch—*school* ... MI-6
Weiss Sch—*school* ... SD-7
Weiss Spring—*spring* ... AZ-5
Weiss West Ranch—*locale* ... MT-8
Weiss Windmill—*locale* ... CO-8
Weist Cem—*cemetery* ... IN-6
Weist Creek—*stream* ... OR-9
*Weister* ... PA-2
Weister Creek—*stream* ... WI-6
Weisz Ranch—*locale* ... ND-7
*Weitas-beaver Creek* ... ID-8
Weitas Butte—*summit* ... ID-8
Weitas Creek—*stream* (2) ... ID-8
Weitas Meadows—*flat* ... ID-8
Weitas Ridge—*ridge* ... ID-8
Weitas Station—*locale* ... ID-8
**Weitchpec**—*pop pl* ... CA-9
Weitchpec Creek—*stream* ... CA-9
Weitemier Cem—*cemetery* ... MN-6
Weitz—*locale* ... ID-8
Weitzel—*fmr MCD* ... NE-7
Weitzel Cem—*cemetery* ... IL-6
Weitzel Sch—*school* ... AZ-5
Weitzig Drain—*canal* ... MI-6
Weizer Bldg—*hist pl* ... OH-6
WEIZ-FM (Phenix City)—*tower* ... AL-4
WEJL-AM (Scranton)—*tower* ... PA-2
*Wekabaug* ... MA-1
Wekea Point—*cape* ... HI-9
Wekepeke Brook—*stream* ... MA-1
Wekepeke Hill—*summit* ... MA-1
*Wekewa Creek* ... FL-3
Wekiu—*summit* ... HI-9
Wekiva—*locale* ... FL-3
Wekiva, Lake—*lake* ... FL-3
Wekiva Assembly of God—*church* ... FL-3
Wekiva Beach—*channel* ... FL-3
Wekiva Cutoff—*bend* ... FL-3
Wekiva Elem Sch—*school* ... FL-3
*Wekiva Lake* ... FL-3
Wekiva Presbyterian Ch—*church* ... FL-3
*Wekiva River* ... FL-3
Wekiva River—*stream* (2) ... FL-3
Wekiva Springs—*CDP* ... FL-3
Wekiva Springs—*spring* ... FL-3
Wekiva Square (Shop Ctr)—*locale* ... FL-3
Wekiva Swamp—*swamp* ... FL-3
Wekiwa—*locale* ... OK-5
*Wekiwachee* ... FL-3
*Wekiwachee River* ... FL-3
*Wekiwa Creek* ... FL-3
**Wekiwa Manor**—*pop pl* ... FL-3
*Wekiwa Springs* ... FL-3
Wekiwa Springs Baptist Ch—*church* ... FL-3
Wekiwa Springs State Park—*park* ... FL-3
**Wekiwa Springs (Wekiva Springs)**—*pop pl* ... FL-3
*Wekiway River* ... FL-3
*Wekiwoochee* ... FL-3
*Wekiwoochee River* ... FL-3
Weko Beach Rec Area—*park* ... MI-6
WEKR-AM (Fayetteville)—*tower* ... TN-4
*Wela* ... FM-9
**Welagamika (historical)**—*pop pl* ... PA-2
*Welagesn* ... PA-2
*Welagesniko* ... PA-2
*Wela Insel* ... FM-9
*Welaka* ... FL-3
**Welaka**—*pop pl* ... FL-3
Welaka Springs—*spring* ... FL-3
Welaka Tower—*tower* ... FL-3
**Wela Park**—*pop pl* ... MO-7
*Wela-Tolos* ... FM-9
Welaton Cem—*cemetery* ... TX-5
Welaunee Ch—*church* ... FL-3
Welaunee Creek—*stream* ... FL-3
Welaunee Plantation—*locale* ... FL-3

Welaunee Sch—school ... FL-3
Welaunee Sink—basin ... FL-3
**Wela (Wela Park)**—pop pl ... MO-7
Welba ... CO-8
Welba, Mount—summit ... CO-8
WELB-AM (Elba)—tower ... AL-4
Welba Peak ... CO-8
Welborn ... IN-6
Welborn—locale ... KY-4
**Welborn**—pop pl ... KS-7
Welborn—uninc pl ... KS-7
Welborn, John Henry, House—hist pl ... NC-3
Welborn, Lake—reservoir ... KS-7
Welborn Cem—cemetery ... MS-4
Welborn Ch—church ... IN-6
Welborne Ch—church ... VA-3
Welborn Elementary School—locale ... KS-7
Welborn Memorial Baptist Hospital Airp—airport ... IN-6
Welborn Sch—school ... KS-7
**Welborn Switch**—pop pl ... IN-6
Welborn (Township of)—fmr MCD ... AR-4
Welbourn Airp—airport ... NC-3
Welbourne—hist pl ... VA-3
Welbourne—locale ... MD-2
Welbourne Ave Nursery and Kindergarten—school ... FL-3
Welbrook Lake—reservoir ... GA-3
Welburn Ridge—ridge ... KY-4
Welby—locale ... CA-9
Welby—locale ... UT-8
**Welby**—pop pl ... CO-8
**Welby Ave Subdivision**—pop pl ... UT-8
Welby Ranch—locale ... WY-8
Welby Sch—school ... SD-7
Welby Sch—school ... UT-8
Welcek Farmstead—hist pl ... LA-4
Welch—locale ... MT-8
Welch—locale ... PA-2
Welch—locale ... TN-4
Welch—locale ... WY-8
**Welch**—pop pl ... AL-4
**Welch**—pop pl ... CA-9
**Welch**—pop pl ... MN-6
**Welch**—pop pl ... NC-3
**Welch**—pop pl ... OK-5
**Welch**—pop pl ... PA-2
**Welch**—pop pl ... TX-5
**Welch**—pop pl ... WV-2
Welch, C. A., House—hist pl ... WI-6
Welch, David, House—hist pl ... CT-1
Welch, Edward, House—hist pl ... ID-8
Welch, J. C., House—hist pl ... OK-5
Welch, Jenkins H., House—hist pl ... MS-4
Welch, Lake—reservoir ... NY-2
Welch, William, House—hist pl ... AR-4
Welch, William H., House—hist pl ... MD-2
Welch and Peabody Ditch—canal ... CO-8
Welch Apartments—hist pl ... IA-7
Welch Ave—post sta ... IA-7
Welch-Averiett House—hist pl ... AL-4
Welch Bald—summit ... NC-3
Welch Bay—swamp ... FL-3
Welch-Bornholdt Oil Field—oilfield ... KS-7
Welch Branch—stream ... MS-4
Welch Branch—stream (4) ... NC-3
Welch Branch—stream (3) ... TN-4
Welch Branch—stream ... TX-5
Welch Branch—stream ... WV-2
Welch Brook ... MA-1
Welch Brook—stream ... ME-1
Welch Brook—stream ... NH-1
Welch Brook—stream ... NY-2
Welchburg—locale ... KY-4
Welchburg Sch—school ... KY-4
Welch Butte—summit ... OR-9
Welch Camp—locale ... NY-2
**Welch Camp**—pop pl ... TN-4
Welch Canyon—valley ... UT-8
Welch Cem—cemetery ... AL-4
Welch Cem—cemetery (2) ... IL-6
Welch Cem—cemetery (2) ... KY-4
Welch Cem—cemetery ... LA-4
Welch Cem—cemetery ... MI-6
Welch Cem—cemetery (2) ... MS-4
Welch Cem—cemetery (3) ... MO-7
Welch Cem—cemetery ... NY-2
Welch Cem—cemetery ... NC-3
Welch Cem—cemetery ... OK-5
Welch Cem—cemetery (6) ... TN-4
Welch Cem—cemetery (3) ... TX-5
Welch Cem—cemetery ... WV-2
Welch Center (Shop Ctr)—locale ... FL-3
Welch Ch—church ... MN-6
Welch Ch—church ... NY-2
Welch Ch—church ... OK-5
Welch Ch—church ... PA-2
Welch Ch—church ... WI-6
Welch Chapel—church ... TN-4
Welch Chapel Cem—cemetery ... TN-4
Welch Chapel (historical)—church ... MO-7
Welch Corners—locale (2) ... NY-2
Welch Coulee—valley ... WI-6
Welch Cove ... NC-3
Welch Cove—other ... NC-3
Welch Cove Branch—stream ... NC-3
Welch Cove Cem—cemetery ... NC-3
Welch Creek ... AL-4
Welch Creek ... WA-9
Welch Creek—stream ... CA-9
Welch Creek—stream ... IL-6
Welch Creek—stream ... KY-4
Welch Creek—stream (2) ... MI-6
Welch Creek—stream ... NV-8
Welch Creek—stream ... NY-2
Welch Creek—stream (2) ... NC-3
Welch Creek—stream ... OR-9
Welch Creek—stream (2) ... SC-3
Welch Creek—stream ... TX-5
Welch Creek—stream ... UT-8
Welch Creek Camp—locale ... OR-9
Welch Creek Ch—church ... NC-3
Welch Creek Cove ... WA-9
Welch Creek Mine—mine ... OR-9
Welch Creek (Township of)—fmr MCD ... NC-3
Welch Creek Trail—trail ... OR-9
Welch Crossroad—locale ... TN-4
Welch Dam—dam ... AL-4
Welch Ditch—canal (2) ... CO-8
Welch Ditch—canal ... ID-8
Welch Ditch—canal ... IN-6
Welch Drain—canal ... MI-6
Welch Drain—canal ... OR-9
Welchel Branch—stream ... IN-6
Welche Point ... CT-1
Welcher Cem—cemetery ... TN-4
Welcher Hollow—valley ... MO-7
**Welches**—pop pl ... OR-9
Welches Butte ... OR-9
Welches Canyon—valley ... NV-8
Welches Creek—stream ... NV-8
Welches Creek—stream ... OR-9
Welches Flat—flat ... UT-8
Welches Hollow—valley ... UT-8
Welches Point—cape ... CT-1
Welches Pond—lake ... DE-2
Welches Pond—lake ... OR-9
Welches Run ... VA-3
Welches Sch—school ... OR-9
Welches Spring Branch—stream ... AL-4
Welchester Sch—school ... CO-8
Welch Factory Bldg No. 1—hist pl ... NY-2
Welch Ferry (historical)—locale ... AL-4
Welch Fork—stream ... KY-4
Welch-Gillispie Saddle—gap ... MT-8
Welch Glade—locale ... WV-2
Welch Gulch—valley (3) ... MT-8
Welch Hill—locale ... NY-2
Welch Hill—summit ... ME-1
Welch Hill—summit (2) ... NY-2
Welch Hill—summit ... PA-2
Welch Hill—summit (2) ... TN-4
Welch Hill Ch—church ... PA-2
Welch Hill Sch—school ... PA-2
Welch (historical P.O.)—locale ... MS-4
Welch Hollow—valley (2) ... PA-2
Welch Hollow—valley (3) ... TN-4
Welch Hollow—valley ... WY-8
Welch Hollow Cem—cemetery ... NY-2
Welch Hosp (historical)—hospital ... MO-7
Welch-Hurst—hist pl ... CA-9
Welch Interchange—crossing ... AZ-5
Welch Island—island ... NH-1
Welch Island—island (2) ... OR-9
Welch JHS—school ... IA-7
Welch Knob—summit ... KY-4
Welch Knob—summit ... TN-4
Welch Lake—lake ... MI-6
Welch Lake—lake ... MN-6
Welch Lake—reservoir ... AL-4
**Welchland**—pop pl ... TN-4
Welchland Baptist Ch—church ... TN-4
Welchland (CCD)—cens area ... TN-4
Welchland Division—civil ... TN-4
Welch Landing—locale ... MO-7
Welchland Sch—school ... TN-4
Welch Memorial Cem—cemetery ... TN-4
Welch Memorial Ch—church ... GA-3
Welch Mill Creek—stream ... NC-3
Welch Mill (historical)—locale ... AL-4
Welch Mill (historical)—locale ... TN-4
Welch Mountain ... PA-2
Welch Mountains—summit ... OK-5
Welch Mtn—summit ... KY-4
Welch Mtn—summit ... NH-1
Welch Mtn—summit ... OK-5
Welch-Nicholson House and Mill Site—hist pl ... NC-3
Welch Oil Field—oilfield ... TX-5
Welch Park—park ... CA-9
Welch Park—park ... TX-5
Welch Plantation Cem—cemetery ... MS-4
Welch Plantation (historical)—locale ... MS-4
Welch Plaza (Shop Ctr)—locale ... FL-3
Welch Point—cape ... ME-1
Welch Point—cape ... MD-2
Welch Pond ... DE-2
Welch Pond—lake (2) ... MA-1
Welch Pottery Works—hist pl ... AR-4
Welch Quarry—mine ... MT-8
Welch Ranch—locale ... MT-8
Welch Ranch—locale (2) ... NV-8
Welch Ranch—locale ... NM-5
Welch Ridge ... WA-9
Welch Ridge—ridge ... CA-9
Welch Ridge—ridge ... NC-3
Welch Ridge—ridge ... TN-4
Welch Ridge—ridge ... WA-9
Welch Ridge Trail—trail ... PA-2
Welch Rsvr—reservoir ... CO-8
Welch Rsvr—reservoir ... OR-9
Welch Run—stream (2) ... PA-2
Welch Run—stream ... WV-2
Welchs—locale ... VA-3
Welch Sawmill—locale ... CO-8
**Welch's Camp**—pop pl ... TN-4
Welchs Camp Landing (historical)—locale ... MS-4
Welch Sch—school ... CT-1
Welch Sch—school ... IL-6
Welchs Creek—locale ... KY-4
Welchs Creek—stream ... KY-4
Welchs Creek (CCD)—cens area ... KY-4
Welchs Creek Ch—church ... KY-4
Welchs Depot ... AL-4
Welch-Sherman House—hist pl ... UT-8
Welch Siding ... TN-4
Welch Sinks—basin ... MO-7
Welch's Island ... ME-1
Welchs Island ... OR-9
Welchs Lake Youth Lake ... MA-1
Welch's Point ... CT-1
Welchs Pond—lake ... ME-1
Welch Spring—spring ... AZ-5
Welch Spring—spring ... MO-7
Welch Springs Branch—stream ... TX-5
Welchs Spring ... AL-4
Welchs Spring Branch ... AL-4
Welch Station—locale ... PA-2
Welch Store—locale ... OK-5
Welch Tank—reservoir ... AZ-5
Welch Top—summit ... NH-1
Welch Top—summit ... NC-3
Welchtown ... NJ-2
Welchtown ... PA-2
Welch Township—civil ... MO-7
**Welch (Township of)**—pop pl ... MN-6
Welch Training Sch—hist pl ... CT-1
Welch Valley—valley ... WI-6
**Welchville**—pop pl ... ME-1
**Welchville**—pop pl ... NJ-2
Welch Vly—swamp ... NY-2
Welch Zion Ch—church ... SC-3
Welckers Forge (historical)—locale ... TN-4
**Welco**—pop pl ... KY-4
**Welco Corners**—pop pl ... IL-6
Welcome—locale ... AR-4
Welcome—locale ... KY-4
Welcome—locale ... MD-2
Welcome—locale ... MO-7
Welcome—locale ... TX-5
Welcome—locale ... WY-8
**Welcome**—pop pl ... AR-4
**Welcome**—pop pl ... FL-3
**Welcome**—pop pl ... GA-3
**Welcome**—pop pl ... LA-4
**Welcome**—pop pl ... MN-6
**Welcome**—pop pl ... NV-8
**Welcome**—pop pl ... NY-2
**Welcome**—pop pl ... NC-3
**Welcome**—pop pl ... OH-6
**Welcome**—pop pl (2) ... SC-3
**Welcome**—pop pl ... VA-3
**Welcome**—pop pl ... WA-9
Welcome, Lake—lake ... AK-9
Welcome, Point—cape ... MN-6
Welcome Acres—hist pl ... NH-1
Welcome All Ch—church (2) ... GA-3
Welcome Ave Ch—church ... GA-3
Welcome Baptist Church ... MS-4
Welcome Basin—basin ... WA-9
Welcome Bethel Ch—church ... AL-4
Welcome Cem ... AL-4
Welcome Cem—cemetery ... AL-4
Welcome Cem—cemetery ... FL-3
Welcome Cem—cemetery ... KS-7
Welcome Cem—cemetery ... LA-4
Welcome Cem—cemetery ... MN-6
Welcome Cem—cemetery ... NY-2
Welcome Ch ... AL-4
Welcome Ch—church (8) ... AL-4
Welcome Ch—church (5) ... FL-3
Welcome Ch—church (9) ... GA-3
Welcome Ch—church ... LA-4
Welcome Ch—church (3) ... MS-4
Welcome Ch—church (3) ... NC-3
Welcome Ch—church ... OH-6
Welcome Ch—church (5) ... SC-3
Welcome Ch—church ... TX-5
Welcome Ch—church ... VA-3
Welcome Ch—church ... WV-2
Welcome Chapel—church ... MS-4
Welcome Chapel—church ... NC-3
Welcome Chapel—church (2) ... OH-6
Welcome Chapel Ch—church ... AL-4
Welcome Ch (historical)—church ... AL-4
**Welcome Corner**—pop pl ... MI-6
Welcome Cove—bay ... AK-9
Welcome Cove—bay ... RI-1
Welcome Creek ... PA-2
Welcome Creek—stream ... AK-9
Welcome Creek—stream ... MN-6
Welcome Creek—stream (2) ... MT-8
Welcome Creek—stream ... OR-9
Welcome Creek—stream ... UT-8
Welcome Creek Guard Station—locale ... MT-8
Welcome Creek Wilderness—park ... MT-8
Welcome Falls—falls ... AL-4
Welcome Friend Ch—church ... GA-3
Welcome Gap Ch—church ... GA-3
Welcome Grange Hall—locale ... WA-9
Welcome Grove Ch—church (2) ... GA-3
Welcome Grove Ch—church ... VA-3
Welcome Grove Sch—school ... TN-4
Welcome Hall—hist pl ... KY-4
Welcome Hill—locale ... GA-3
Welcome Hill—summit ... ME-1
Welcome Hill—summit ... MT-8
Welcome Hill Baptist Church ... AL-4
Welcome Hill Cem—cemetery ... AL-4
Welcome Hill Cem—cemetery ... MS-4
Welcome Hill Ch—church (3) ... AL-4
Welcome Hill Ch—church ... AR-4
Welcome Hill Ch—church (4) ... GA-3
Welcome Hill Ch—church ... NC-3
Welcome Hill Ch—church ... TN-4
Welcome Hill Ch Number 2—church ... GA-3
Welcome (historical)—locale ... AL-4
Welcome (historical)—locale ... KS-7
Welcome (historical)—locale ... SD-7
Welcome Home Cem—cemetery ... LA-4
Welcome Home Ch ... NC-3
Welcome Home Ch—church (3) ... AL-4
Welcome Home Ch—church (4) ... AR-4
Welcome Home Ch—church ... MS-4
Welcome Home Ch—church (5) ... NC-3
Welcome Home Ch—church ... WV-2
Welcome Home Mobile Park—locale ... AZ-5
Welcome Home Sch—school ... AR-4
Welcome Hope Ch—church ... GA-3
Welcome Island—island ... NY-2
Welcome Lake—lake ... ID-8
Welcome Lake—lake ... MI-6
Welcome Lake—lake ... MN-6
Welcome Lake—lake ... PA-2
Welcome Lake—lake ... WA-9
Welcome Lakes—lake ... OR-9
Welcome Lakes Ridge Trail—trail ... OR-9
Welcome Lakes Trail—trail ... OR-9
Welcome Mine—mine ... CA-9
Welcome Mission, The—church ... MD-2
Welcome Missionary Baptist Ch ... AL-4
Welcome Mission Ch—church ... WV-2
Welcome Number One Ch ... AL-4
Welcome Park—park ... MN-6
Welcome Park—park ... OH-6
Welcome Pass—gap ... MT-8
Welcome Pass—gap ... WA-9
Welcome Point—cape ... AK-9
Welcome Ridge Ch—church ... AR-4
Welcome Sch—school ... NC-3
Welcome Sch—school ... SC-3
Welcome Sch—school ... TX-5
Welcome Sch (historical)—school ... AL-4
Welcome School ... PA-2
Welcomes Cove ... RI-1
Welcome Slough—stream ... WA-9
Welcome Spiritual True Holiness Ch of Christ—church ... AL-4
Welcome Spring—spring ... ID-8
Welcome Spring—spring (2) ... MT-8
Welcome Spring—spring ... UT-8
Welcome Springs Ch—church ... AL-4
Welcome Springs Methodist Ch ... AL-4
Welcome Springs Sch (historical)—school ... AL-4
Welcome (Station)—locale ... FL-3
Welcome Stranger Baptist Ch—church ... FL-3
Welcometon ... MS-4
Welcome Township—fmr MCD ... IA-7
Welcome Traveler Ch—church ... SC-3
Welcome Ussery Creek—stream ... TN-4
Welcome Valley—basin ... CA-9
**Welcome Valley**—pop pl ... TX-5
Welcome Valley Ch—church ... GA-3
Welcome Valley Ch—church (3) ... TN-4
Welcome View Ch—church ... AL-4
**Welco Station**—pop pl ... KY-4
**Weld**—pop pl ... ME-1
**Welda**—pop pl ... KS-7
Welda, Lake—reservoir ... KS-7
Welda Cem—cemetery ... KS-7
**Welda Township**—pop pl ... KS-7
**Weldbank**—pop pl ... PA-2
Weldbank PO (historical)—building ... PA-2
Weld Cem—cemetery ... PA-2
Weld Corner—locale ... ME-1
Weld County Courthouse—hist pl ... CO-8
Weld County Municipal Airp—airport ... CO-8
Weld County Public Hosp—hospital ... CO-8
Weldele, Simon, House—hist pl ... MN-6
Welden ... IA-7
Welden Ch—church ... AL-4
Welden River ... MO-7
**Welder**—pop pl ... TX-5
Welder Brook—stream ... VT-1
Welder Dobie Ranch—locale ... TX-5
Welder Park—park ... TX-5
Welder Point—cape ... TX-5
Welder Ranch—locale ... TX-5
Welder Sch—school ... TX-5
**Weldin Farms (subdivision)**—pop pl ... DE-2
**Weldin Park (subdivision)**—pop pl ... DE-2
**Weldin Woods (subdivision)**—pop pl ... DE-2
Weld Memorial Park—park ... IL-6
Weldon—locale ... LA-4
Weldon—locale ... MI-6
Weldon—locale ... MO-7
Weldon—locale ... NJ-2
**Weldon**—pop pl ... AR-4
**Weldon**—pop pl ... CA-9
**Weldon**—pop pl ... IL-6
**Weldon**—pop pl ... IA-7
**Weldon**—pop pl ... KY-4
**Weldon**—pop pl ... MD-2
**Weldon**—pop pl ... MT-8
**Weldon**—pop pl ... NC-3
**Weldon**—pop pl ... PA-2
**Weldon**—pop pl ... TX-5
**Weldon**—pop pl ... VA-3
Weldon, James, House—hist pl ... KY-4
**Weldona**—pop pl ... CO-8
Weldona, Lake—lake ... FL-3
Weldon Branch—stream ... AL-4
Weldon Branch—stream ... MO-7
Weldon Brook—stream ... NJ-2
Weldon Brook Lake—reservoir ... NJ-2
Weldon Burris Homestead—locale ... NM-5
Weldon Canyon—valley (2) ... CA-9
Weldon Cem—cemetery (2) ... AL-4
Weldon Cem—cemetery ... MI-6
Weldon Cem—cemetery ... TX-5
Weldon Ch—church ... KY-4
Weldon Ch—church ... SC-3
Weldon Creek ... IA-7
Weldon Creek ... MO-7
Weldon Creek—stream ... AL-4
Weldon Creek—stream ... IA-7
Weldon Creek—stream ... MD-2
Weldon Creek—stream ... MI-6
Weldon Elem Sch—school ... NC-3
Weldon Fork ... IA-7
Weldon Fork ... MO-7
Weldon Fork of Grand River ... MO-7
Weldon Grand River ... IA-7
Weldon Grand River ... MO-7
Weldon Gulch—valley ... CO-8
Weldon Hill—summit ... AZ-5
Weldon (historical)—locale ... AL-4
Weldon Hotel—hist pl ... MA-1
Weldon HS—school ... NC-3
Weldon Lake—reservoir ... GA-3
Weldon Landing (historical)—locale ... TN-4
Weldon Meadow ... CA-9
Weldon Meadow—flat ... CA-9
Weldon Methodist Ch (historical)—church ... TX-5
Weldon Mine—mine ... AZ-5
Weldon Peak—summit ... CA-9
Weldon Pond—reservoir ... CA-9
Weldon Pond—reservoir ... GA-3
Weldon Post Office (historical)—building ... MS-4
Weldon Post Office (historical)—building ... TX-5
Weldon River—stream ... IA-7
Weldon River—stream ... MO-7
Weldons—locale ... CA-9
Weldons Airp—airport ... PA-2
Weldons Branch—stream ... MO-7
Weldon Sch—school ... CA-9
Weldon Sch—school (2) ... TX-5
**Weldons Mill**—pop pl ... NC-3
Weldons Pond—reservoir ... NC-3
Weldons Pond Dam—dam ... NC-3
**Weldon Spring**—pop pl ... MO-7
Weldon Spring Ch—church ... GA-3
Weldon Spring Ch—church ... MO-7
**Weldon Spring Heights**—pop pl ... MO-7
Weldon Spring Ordnance Works—other ... MO-7
Weldon Springs Park—park ... IL-6
Weldon Spring Township—civil ... MO-7
Weldon Spring (Township of)—fmr MCD ... MO-7
Weldon (Township of)—fmr MCD ... NC-3
**Weldon (Township of)**—pop pl ... MI-6
Weldon Valley Ditch—canal ... CO-8
Weld Oregon Church ... AL-4
Weld Park—park ... NY-2
Weld Pond—lake ... MA-1
Weld Tank—reservoir ... NM-5
**Weld (Town of)**—pop pl ... ME-1
**Weld Township**—pop pl ... ND-7
Weldwood—hist pl ... NH-1
**Weldwood**—pop pl ... OR-9
Weldwood Park—park ... OR-9
Weldy Amish Sch—school ... IN-6
Weldy Canyon—valley ... NM-5
Weldy Cem—cemetery ... AL-4
Weldy Creek—stream (2) ... MS-4
Weldy Sch ... IN-6
Weldy Well—well ... NM-5
Weldy Windmill—locale ... AZ-5
**Weleetka**—pop pl ... OK-5
Weleetka (CCD)—cens area ... OK-5
Weleetka Lake—reservoir ... OK-5
Weleetka Oil Field—oilfield ... OK-5
Welen ... FM-9
Welfare—locale ... TX-5
Welfare Ch—church ... AL-4
Welfare Ch—church ... KY-4
Welfare Ch—church ... SC-3
Welfare Island ... NY-2
**Welfleet**—pop pl ... VA-3
Welford ... SC-3
Welford ... WV-2
Welford Hurt Park—park ... VA-3
Welford Sch—school ... TX-5
**Welge**—pop pl ... IL-6
Welge Cem—cemetery ... TX-5
Welge Creek—stream ... IL-6
Welgehausen Cem—cemetery ... TX-5
Welge Poing—cliff ... TX-5
Welham Plantation—locale ... LA-4
**Welhams**—pop pl ... MD-2
Welhern Pond ... ME-1
Welhurn Pond ... ME-1
Weli ... HI-9
Welias—unknown ... FM-9
Welik, Dolen—summit ... FM-9
**Welika (historical)**—pop pl ... FL-3
Welikee Lake—reservoir ... AL-4
Weli Point—cape ... HI-9
Weliweli—civil ... HI-9
Weliweli—locale ... HI-9
Weliweli Point—cape ... HI-9
Welka—locale ... AL-4
Welk Dam—dam ... ND-7
Welker, James R., House—hist pl ... AZ-5
Welker, Mount—summit ... AK-9
Welker Branch—stream ... TN-4
Welker Cem—cemetery ... TN-4
Welker Creek—stream ... OR-9
Welker Creek—stream ... WA-9
Welker Hollow—valley ... WI-6
Welker Lake—lake ... SD-7
Welker Lateral—canal ... OH-6
Welker Peak—summit ... WA-9
Welker Post Office (historical)—building ... TN-4
Welker Sch—school ... MN-6
Welker Spring—spring ... OR-9
Welker Well—locale ... NM-5
Welk Rocks—island ... VI-3
Well—fmr MCD ... NE-7
Well—well ... NM-5
Well, B,—well ... NV-8
Well, The—hist pl ... MS-4
Well, The—locale ... NM-5
Well, The—well ... AZ-5
Welland—locale ... WA-9
**Welland**—pop pl (2) ... IL-6
Wellbacher Cem—cemetery ... TX-5
Wellborn—hist pl ... AL-4
**Wellborn**—pop pl ... AL-4
**Wellborn**—pop pl ... FL-3
**Wellborn**—pop pl ... TX-5
Wellborn Cem—cemetery ... AL-4
Wellborn Cem—cemetery ... FL-3
Wellborn Creek—stream ... GA-3
Wellborne Ferry (historical)—locale ... AL-4
Wellborn Elem Sch—school ... AL-4
Wellborn (historical)—locale ... AL-4
Wellborn Lake—lake ... FL-3
Wellborn Mtn—summit ... GA-3
Wellborn P.O. ... AL-4
Wellborn Sch—school ... AL-4
**Wellborn Subdivision**—pop pl ... MS-4
Well Branch ... AL-4
Well Branch—stream ... GA-3
Well Branch—stream ... KY-4
Well Branch—stream ... TN-4
Well Brook—stream ... IN-6
Well Camp—locale ... NM-5
Well Camp Canyon—valley ... AZ-5
Well Camp Tank—reservoir ... AZ-5
Well Canyon—valley (2) ... AZ-5
Well Canyon—valley ... ID-8
Well Canyon—valley ... NE-7
Well Canyon—valley (2) ... NV-8
Well Canyon—valley (3) ... NM-5
Well Canyon Tank—reservoir ... AZ-5
Well Canyon Tank Number One—reservoir ... AZ-5
Well Canyon Tank Number Three—reservoir ... AZ-5
Well Canyon Tank Number Two—reservoir ... AZ-5
Well Cave—cave ... AL-4
Well Cave—cave ... MO-7
Wellcave Hollow—valley ... AR-4
Well Cem—cemetery ... NY-2
Well Cem—cemetery ... TN-4
Well Cement Tank—reservoir ... AZ-5
Wellcome Middle School ... NC-3
Wellcome Sch—school ... NC-3
Well Creek ... MA-1
Well Creek—stream ... AK-9
Well Creek—stream ... MT-8
Well Creek—stream ... TX-5
Well Creek—stream ... WY-8
Well Creek Siding ... TX-5
Well Ditch—canal ... NM-5
Well Draw—valley ... UT-8
Well Draw—valley (2) ... WY-8
Well Drill Draw—valley ... TX-5
Well Drilled Canyon—valley ... NM-5
Well Drill Tank—reservoir ... TX-5
Welleby Plaza (Shop Ctr)—locale ... FL-3
Well Eightmile Windmill—locale ... NM-5
Wellenbrock Spring—spring ... WA-9
Wellendorf Branch—stream ... PA-2
Wellendorf Station—locale ... PA-2
Wellen Peak—summit ... MT-8
Wellenstein Sch—school ... NE-7
Weller—locale ... AL-4
Weller—locale ... CO-8
Weller—locale ... IA-7
Weller—locale ... VA-3
Weller Baker Sch—school ... VA-3
Weller Branch—stream ... TN-4
Weller Brook—stream ... CT-1
Weller Butte—summit ... WA-9
Weller Canyon—valley ... WA-9
Weller Canyon Airp—airport ... WA-9
Weller Cem—cemetery ... IL-6
Weller Cem—cemetery ... OH-6
Weller Cem—cemetery (2) ... PA-2
Weller County ... KS-7
Weller Creek—stream ... ID-8
Weller Creek—stream ... IL-6
Weller Creek—stream (2) ... OR-9
Weller Creek—stream ... WA-9
Weller Draw—valley ... CO-8
Weller Gap—valley ... PA-2
Weller (historical P.O.)—locale ... IA-7
Weller Hollow—valley ... PA-2
Weller House—hist pl ... CA-9
Weller House—hist pl ... IN-6
Weller Lake—lake ... CO-8
Weller Lake Campground—locale ... CO-8
Weller Mtn—summit ... NY-2
Weller Number 1 Dam—dam ... SD-7
Weller Number 1 Mine (underground)—mine ... AL-4
Weller Number 2 Mine (underground)—mine ... AL-4
Weller Playground—park ... OH-6
Weller Pond—lake (2) ... NY-2
Weller Pond Outlet—stream ... NY-2
Weller Road Sch—school ... MD-2
Wellers—other ... PA-2
**Wellersburg**—pop pl ... PA-2
Wellersburg Borough—civil ... PA-2
Weller Sch—school ... CA-9
Weller Sch—school ... MO-7
Weller Sch—school (2) ... OH-6
Weller Sch (historical)—school ... MO-7
Wellers Ditch ... IL-6
Wellers Drainage ... IL-6
Weller Slough—lake ... ND-7
**Weller (Township of)**—pop pl ... IL-6
**Weller (Township of)**—pop pl ... OH-6
Wellerwood Sch—school ... MI-6
Welles, Gideon, House—hist pl ... CT-1
Welles Block—building ... MA-1
Welles Cem—cemetery ... ME-1
Welles Lake—lake ... MI-6
**Wellesley**—pop pl ... MA-1
**Wellesley**—pop pl ... VA-3
Wellesley Air Natl Guard Station—building ... MA-1
Wellesley Coll—school ... MA-1
Wellesley Farms RR Station—hist pl ... MA-1
Wellesley Farms Station (historical)—locale ... MA-1
**Wellesley Farms (subdivision)**—pop pl ... MA-1
**Wellesley Fells (subdivision)**—pop pl ... MA-1
Wellesley Glacier—glacier ... AK-9
Wellesley Hills (historical P.O.)—locale ... MA-1
**Wellesley Hills (subdivision)**—pop pl ... MA-1
Wellesley (historical P.O.)—locale ... MA-1
Wellesley HS—school ... MA-1
Wellesley Island—island ... NY-2
Wellesley Island State Park—park ... NY-2
Wellesley JHS—school ... MA-1
Wellesley Lakes—lake ... AK-9
Wellesley Mtn—summit ... AK-9
Wellesley Park—park ... CA-9
Wellesley Park—park ... NM-5
Wellesley Peak—summit ... WA-9
Wellesley Shop Ctr—locale ... MA-1
Wellesley Station (historical)—locale ... MA-1
Wellesley Town Hall—hist pl ... MA-1
**Wellesley (Town of)**—pop pl ... MA-1
Welles Park—park ... IL-6
Welles Park—park ... MN-6
Welles Pond—lake ... CT-1
Welles-Shipman-Ward House—hist pl ... CT-1
**Welles Village**—pop pl ... CT-1
Wellet Cem—cemetery ... OH-6
Wellever Sch—school ... MI-6
Welloyo Lake ... MN-6
Well Flat—flat ... AL-4
**Wellfleet**—pop pl ... MA-1
**Wellfleet**—pop pl ... NE-7
Wellfleet Bay ... MA-1
Wellfleet Bay Sanctuary ... MA-1
Wellfleet Bay Wildlife Sanctuary ... MA-1
**Wellfleet by the Sea**—pop pl ... MA-1
Wellfleet Cem—cemetery ... NE-7
Wellfleet Harbor—bay ... MA-1
Wellfleet Harbor Breakwater Light—locale ... MA-1
Wellfleet Historical Society Museum—building ... MA-1
Wellfleet Lake—reservoir ... NE-7
Wellfleet Town Hall—building ... MA-1
**Wellfleet (Town of)**—pop pl ... MA-1
Wellfleet Town Pier—locale ... MA-1
Wellford—locale ... WV-2
**Wellford**—pop pl ... SC-3
**Wellford**—pop pl ... VA-3
Wellford (CCD)—cens area ... SC-3
Well Gulch—valley (2) ... CO-8
Well Gulch—valley ... MT-8
Well Hill—summit ... VA-3
Well Hollow—valley ... AR-4
Well Hollow—valley (5) ... MO-7
Well Hollow—valley ... OK-5
Well Hollow—valley (4) ... TN-4
Well Hollow—valley ... TX-5
Well Hollow—valley ... UT-8
Wellhope—locale ... KY-4
Wellhope Ch—church ... KY-4
Wellhope Sch—school ... KY-4
Wellie Peak—summit ... WA-9
**Welling**—pop pl ... OK-5
Welling, John, House—hist pl ... NJ-2
**Welling Beach**—pop pl ... WI-6
Welling-Everly Horse Barn—hist pl ... IL-6
Welling Rsvr—reservoir ... OR-9
Wellingsly ... MA-1
Wellington ... MS-4
Wellington ... NV-8
Wellington ... UT-8

Wellington—*CDP* ... FL-3
Wellington—*locale* ... KY-4
Wellington—*locale* ... MD-2
Wellington—*locale* ... MI-6
Wellington—*locale* ... VA-3
**Wellington**—*pop pl* ... AL-4
**Wellington**—*pop pl* ... CO-8
**Wellington**—*pop pl* ... IL-6
**Wellington**—*pop pl* ... IN-6
**Wellington**—*pop pl* ... KS-7
**Wellington**—*pop pl* ... KY-4
**Wellington**—*pop pl* ... ME-1
**Wellington**—*pop pl* ... MO-7
**Wellington**—*pop pl* ... NV-8
**Wellington**—*pop pl* ... OH-6
**Wellington**—*pop pl* ... PA-2
**Wellington**—*pop pl* ... TX-5
**Wellington**—*pop pl* ... UT-8
**Wellington**—*pop pl* ... VA-3
Wellington, Mount—*summit* ... NY-2
Wellington Acad (historical)—*school* ... AL-4
**Wellington Addition (subdivision)**—*pop pl* ... UT-8
*Wellington Airport* ... KS-7
*Wellington Baptist Church* ... AL-4
**Wellington Beach**—*pop pl* ... MD-2
Wellington Bog—*swamp* ... ME-1
Wellington Bridge—*bridge* ... MA-1
Wellington Brook—*stream* ... MA-1
Wellington Butte—*summit* ... OR-9
Wellington Canal—*canal* ... UT-8
Wellington Carnegie Library—*hist pl* ... KS-7
Wellington (CCD)—*cens area* ... TX-5
Wellington Cem—*cemetery* ... NC-3
Wellington Cem—*cemetery* ... SD-7
Wellington Center Hist Dist—*hist pl* ... OH-6
Wellington Ch—*church* ... AL-4
Wellington Circle Plaza (Shop Ctr)—*locale* ... MA-1
Wellington Circle Shop Ctr—*locale* ... MA-1
**Wellington Circle Subdivision**—*pop pl* ... UT-8
Wellington City Cem—*cemetery* ... UT-8
Wellington City Dam—*dam* ... KS-7
Wellington City Park—*park* ... KS-7
Wellington Community Elem Sch—*school* ... FL-3
**Wellington Corner**—*pop pl* ... NY-2
Wellington County Plaza (Shop Ctr)—*locale* ... FL-3
**Wellington Court (subdivision)**—*pop pl* (2) ... AZ-5
*Wellington Cove* ... TN-4
Wellington Creek—*stream* ... ID-8
Wellington Creek—*stream* ... MI-6
Wellington Creek—*stream* ... OH-6
**Wellington Estates**—*pop pl* ... MD-2
Wellington Farm Hist Dist—*hist pl* ... MA-1
Wellington Gulch—*valley* ... CO-8
*Wellington Heights* ... IN-6
**Wellington Heights**—*pop pl* ... CA-9
**Wellington Heights**—*pop pl* ... IL-6
**Wellington Heights**—*pop pl* ... IN-6
**Wellington Heights**—*pop pl* ... VA-3
**Wellington Heights**—*pop pl* ... WV-2
Wellington Hill—*summit* (2) ... MA-1
Wellington Hill—*summit* ... VT-1
**Wellington Hills**—*pop pl* ... DE-2
Wellington Hills—*range* ... NV-8
Wellington Hills—*summit* ... NV-8
Wellington Hills Golf Course—*other* ... WA-9
Wellington Hist Dist—*hist pl* ... OH-6
Wellington (historical)—*locale* ... SD-7
Wellington HS—*school* ... KS-7
Wellington JHS—*school* ... KS-7
Wellington Lake—*lake* ... MI-6
Wellington Lake—*lake* ... WI-6
Wellington Lake—*reservoir* ... CO-8
Wellington Lake—*reservoir* ... KS-7
Wellington Marsh—*swamp* ... MA-1
Wellington Mepham HS—*school* ... NY-2
Wellington Mill—*other* ... SC-3
Wellington Mine—*mine* ... CO-8
Wellington Municipal Airp—*airport* ... KS-7
Wellington Neck—*cape* ... VA-3
Wellington Northeast Oil Field—*oilfield* ... KS-7
Wellington Oil Field—*oilfield* ... CO-8
Wellington Oil Field—*oilfield* ... KS-7
Wellington Park—*park* ... OR-9
**Wellington Park**—*pop pl* ... NJ-2
**Wellington Park**—*pop pl* ... OH-6
**Wellington Park (subdivision)**—*pop pl* ... NC-3
**Wellington Park (subdivision)**—*pop pl* ... TN-4
Wellington Peak—*summit* ... WA-9
Wellington Piano Case Company Bldg—*hist pl* ... MA-1
Wellington Place Baptist Ch—*church* ... KS-7
Wellington Playground—*park* ... MI-6
Wellington Reservoirs—*reservoir* ... OH-6
Wellington Ridge—*ridge* ... ME-1
Wellington Sch—*school* ... MI-6
Wellington Sch—*school* ... MN-6
Wellington Sch—*school* ... UT-8
Wellington Service Area—*locale* ... KS-7
Wellington Siding—*locale* ... CO-8
Wellington (site)—*locale* ... NV-8
Wellington Spring—*spring* ... NV-8
Wellington Springs—*spring* ... NV-8
Wellington State Park—*park* ... NH-1
Wellington State Wildlife Mngmt Area—*park* ... MD-2
*Wellington Station* ... MI-6
Wellington Street Apartment House District—*hist pl* ... MA-1
Wellington Street Missionary Baptist Ch—*church* ... AL-4
**Wellington (subdivision)**—*pop pl* ... MA-1
**Wellington (Town of)**—*pop pl* ... ME-1
**Wellington (Town of)**—*pop pl* ... WI-6
**Wellington Township**—*pop pl* ... KS-7
**Wellington Township**—*pop pl* ... ND-7
**Wellington Township**—*pop pl* ... SD-7
**Wellington (Township of)**—*pop pl* ... MI-6
**Wellington (Township of)**—*pop pl* ... MN-6
**Wellington (Township of)**—*pop pl* ... OH-6
**Wellington Way (subdivision)**—*pop pl* ... NC-3
**Wellington Woods (subdivision)**—*pop pl* ... DE-2
**Wellington Woods (subdivision)**—*pop pl* ... NC-3
Welling Tunnel—*locale* ... WV-2
Wellin Lake—*lake* ... WA-9
Wellin Neout—*well* ... FM-9
Well Island—*island* ... GA-3
Well Island—*island* ... MA-1
Welliversville—*locale* ... PA-2
Well Lake—*lake* ... LA-4
Well Madison Sch—*school* ... CA-9
*Wellman* ... CA-9
Wellman—*locale* ... MS-4
Wellman—*locale* ... OH-6
**Wellman**—*pop pl* ... IA-7
**Wellman**—*pop pl* ... TX-5
Wellman Apartments—*hist pl* ... ID-8
Wellman Baptist Ch—*church* ... MS-4
Wellman Basin—*basin* ... WA-9
Wellman Brook—*stream* ... MA-1
Wellman Canyon—*valley* ... CA-9
Wellman Cem—*cemetery* ... IA-7
Wellman Cem—*cemetery* (3) ... WV-2
Wellman Ch—*church* ... SD-7
Wellman Creek—*stream* ... CA-9
Wellman Creek—*stream* ... MT-8
Wellman Divide—*gap* ... CA-9
Wellman Field—*park* ... FL-3
Wellman Hall—*hist pl* ... CA-9
Wellman House—*hist pl* ... NY-2
Wellman Ledge—*bar* ... MA-1
Wellman Mine—*mine* ... MT-8
Wellman Pond—*lake* ... ME-1
Wellman Pond—*lake* ... NH-1
Wellman Post Office (historical)—*building* ... MS-4
Wellman Road Cem—*cemetery* ... NY-2
Wellman Sch—*school* ... KS-7
Wellman Sch—*school* ... SD-7
Wellman Sch—*school* ... VT-1
Wellman Sch (abandoned)—*school* ... PA-2
Wellmans Cienaga—*swamp* ... CA-9
Wellmans Corners—*locale* ... PA-2
Wellmans Creek—*stream* ... PA-2
Wellmans Hill—*summit* ... NH-1
Wellmanville (historical)—*locale* ... KS-7
Well No 1—*well* ... ID-8
Well No 2—*well* ... NM-5
Well No 2 Rsvr—*reservoir* ... ID-8
Well No 28—*well* ... UT-8
Well No 3—*locale* ... NM-5
Well No 3—*well* (2) ... ID-8
Well No 4—*well* ... ID-8
Well No 4—*well* (2) ... NM-5
Well No. 4, Pico Canyon Oil Field—*hist pl* ... CA-9
Well No 5—*well* ... ID-8
Well No 5—*well* (2) ... NM-5
Well No 5—*well* ... GU-9
Well No 6—*well* ... NM-5
Well No 6 (abandoned)—*well* ... NM-5
Well No 7—*well* ... NM-5
Well No 8—*well* ... NM-5
Well Number Five—*well* ... OR-9
Well Number Four—*well* ... OR-9
Well Number Seven—*well* ... OR-9
Well Number Six—*well* ... OR-9
Well Number Three—*well* ... OR-9
Well Number Two—*well* ... OR-9
Well of the Eight Echoes—*well* ... CA-9
Well Old Price Ranch—*locale* ... NM-5
Wellon Creek—*stream* ... TX-5
Wellongate Shopping Plaza—*locale* ... NC-3
Wellons Village—*uninc pl* ... NC-3
Well-on-the-Hill—*well* ... NM-5
Well Park—*flat* ... SD-7
Well Pass—*gap* ... UT-8
**Wellpinit**—*pop pl* ... WA-9
Wellpinit Creek—*stream* ... WA-9
Wellpinit Mtn—*summit* ... WA-9
Well Point—*cape* ... TX-5
Well Pole Creek—*stream* ... SD-7
Well Pond—*lake* ... CA-9
Well Pond—*swamp* ... FL-3
Wellridge Creek—*bay* ... MD-2
Well Riley Ranch—*locale* ... WY-8
Well River Graded Sch—*hist pl* ... VT-1
Well Rock—*rock* ... MA-1
Well Rsvr—*reservoir* ... MT-8
Well Rsvr—*reservoir* ... WY-8
Well Run—*stream* (2) ... IN-6
*Wells* ... AL-4
*Wells* ... MS-4
*Wells* ... WV-2
Wells—*fmr MCD* ... NE-7
Wells—*locale* ... KY-4
Wells—*locale* ... PA-2
Wells—*locale* ... TN-4
Wells—*locale* ... TX-5
Wells—*locale* ... WI-6
**Wells**—*pop pl* ... AK-9
**Wells**—*pop pl* ... IL-6
**Wells**—*pop pl* ... IN-6
**Wells**—*pop pl* ... KS-7
**Wells**—*pop pl* ... KY-4
**Wells**—*pop pl* ... ME-1
**Wells**—*pop pl* (2) ... MI-6
**Wells**—*pop pl* ... MN-6
**Wells**—*pop pl* (2) ... MS-4
**Wells**—*pop pl* ... NV-8
**Wells**—*pop pl* ... NY-2
**Wells**—*pop pl* ... SC-3
**Wells**—*pop pl* ... TX-5
**Wells**—*pop pl* ... VT-1
**Wells**—*pop pl* ... VA-3
**Wells**—*pop pl* ... WA-9
Wells, Charles, House—*hist pl* ... MA-1
Wells, Edward, House—*hist pl* ... VT-1
Wells, George A., House—*hist pl* ... IA-7
Wells, George A., Jr., House—*hist pl* ... OR-9
Wells, Hannah, House—*hist pl* ... UT-8
Wells, J. M., House—*hist pl* ... MI-6
Wells, John, Jr., House—*hist pl* ... CT-1
Wells, Osborne, House—*hist pl* ... SC-3
Wells, Point—*cape* ... WA-9
Wells, The—*locale* ... WY-8
Wells, William, House—*hist pl* ... WV-2
Wells, William H., House—*hist pl* ... MI-6
Wells-Bagley House—*hist pl* ... GA-3
Wells Baptist Church—*hist pl* ... NY-2
Wells Baptist Church Parsonage—*hist pl* ... ME-1
Wells-Barnett, Ida B., House—*hist pl* ... IL-6
Wells Basin—*basin* ... CO-8
Wells Bay—*bay* ... AK-9
Wells Bay—*bay* ... NC-3
Wells Bayou—*gut* ... AR-4
Wells Bayou Sch—*school* (2) ... AR-4
Wells Bayou (Township of)—*fmr MCD* ... AR-4
Wells Beach—*beach* ... ME-1
**Wells Beach**—*pop pl* ... ME-1
Wells Beach (sta.) (RR name for Wells)—*other* ... ME-1
**Wells Beach Station**—*pop pl* ... ME-1
Wells Bench—*bench* ... ID-8
*Wells Bend* ... TN-4
Wells Bldg—*hist pl* ... OH-6
Wells Block—*hist pl* ... MA-1
Wells Bluff—*cliff* ... WY-8
**Wellsboro**—*pop pl* ... IN-6
**Wellsboro**—*pop pl* ... PA-2
Wellsboro Borough—*civil* ... PA-2
Wellsboro Country Club—*other* ... PA-2
Wellsboro Junction—*locale* ... PA-2
*Wellsboro Junction Station* ... PA-2
*Wellsborough* ... PA-2
Wells Bottom—*bend* ... AR-4
Wells Bottom—*bend* ... KY-4
Wells Bottom—*bend* (2) ... WV-2
**Wells Branch**—*pop pl* ... ME-1
Wells Branch—*stream* ... AL-4
Wells Branch—*stream* (3) ... KY-4
Wells Branch—*stream* (2) ... MO-7
Wells Branch—*stream* ... SC-3
Wells Branch—*stream* (4) ... TN-4
Wells Branch—*stream* (3) ... TX-5
Wells Branch—*stream* ... VA-3
Wells Branch—*stream* ... WV-2
Wells Branch Hollow—*valley* ... MO-7
Wells Bridge—*locale* ... NY-2
**Wells Bridge**—*pop pl* ... NY-2
Wells Bridge (historical)—*bridge* ... AL-4
Wells Brook—*stream* ... CT-1
Wells Brook—*stream* ... ME-1
Wells Brook—*stream* ... NH-1
Wells Brook—*stream* ... NJ-2
Wells Brook—*stream* (2) ... NY-2
Wells Brook—*stream* (3) ... VT-1
*Wellsburg* ... AL-4
*Wellsburg* ... PA-2
Wellsburg—*locale* ... KY-4
Wellsburg—*other* ... PA-2
**Wellsburg**—*pop pl* ... IN-6
**Wellsburg**—*pop pl* ... IA-7
**Wellsburg**—*pop pl* ... NY-2
**Wellsburg**—*pop pl* ... ND-7
**Wellsburg**—*pop pl* ... WV-2
Wellsburg Hist Dist—*hist pl* ... WV-2
Wellsburg (Magisterial District)—*fmr MCD* ... WV-2
Wellsburg Wharf—*hist pl* ... WV-2
Wells Cabin Campground—*locale* ... CA-9
Wells Camp—*locale* ... NE-7
Wells Canyon—*valley* ... CA-9
Wells Canyon—*valley* ... ID-8
Wells Canyon—*valley* ... UT-8
Wells-Carey Sch—*school* ... IA-7
Wells (CCD)—*cens area* ... TX-5
Wells Cem—*cemetery* (4) ... AR-4
Wells Cem—*cemetery* (2) ... GA-3
Wells Cem—*cemetery* ... ID-8
Wells Cem—*cemetery* (5) ... IL-6
Wells Cem—*cemetery* ... IN-6
Wells Cem—*cemetery* ... KS-7
Wells Cem—*cemetery* (4) ... KY-4
Wells Cem—*cemetery* ... LA-4
Wells Cem—*cemetery* ... MI-6
Wells Cem—*cemetery* (3) ... MS-4
Wells Cem—*cemetery* ... NH-1
Wells Cem—*cemetery* (2) ... NY-2
Wells Cem—*cemetery* (3) ... NC-3
Wells Cem—*cemetery* (2) ... OH-6
Wells Cem—*cemetery* ... OK-5
Wells Cem—*cemetery* ... OR-9
Wells Cem—*cemetery* (10) ... TN-4
Wells Cem—*cemetery* (3) ... TX-5
Wells Cem—*cemetery* (4) ... VA-3
Wells Cem—*cemetery* (2) ... WV-2
*Wells Ch* ... TN-4
Wells Ch—*church* ... MS-4
Wells Ch—*church* (2) ... TX-5
Wells Chapel—*church* ... AR-4
Wells Chapel—*church* ... IL-6
Wells Chapel—*church* ... KY-4
Wells Chapel—*church* ... MS-4
Wells Chapel—*church* (2) ... NC-3
Wells Chapel—*church* (2) ... VA-3
Wells Chapel Cem—*cemetery* ... MS-4
Wells Chapel United Methodist Ch—*church* ... TN-4
Wells Coll—*school* ... NY-2
Wells Corner—*locale* ... NY-2
**Wells Corner**—*pop pl* ... MD-2
*Wells Corners* ... PA-2
Wells Corners—*locale* ... PA-2
*Wellscott Creek* ... GA-3
*Wellscott Mountain* ... GA-3
Wells Coulee—*valley* ... MT-8
Wells Coulee—*valley* ... WI-6
Wells County—*civil* ... ND-7
**Wells County**—*pop pl* ... IN-6
Wells County Courthouse—*hist pl* ... IN-6
Wells County Courthouse—*hist pl* ... ND-7
Wells Cove—*bay* (2) ... MD-2
Wells Cow Camp—*locale* ... CO-8
*Wells Creek* ... AL-4
*Wells Creek* ... CA-9
*Wells Creek* ... TX-5
Wells Creek—*bay* ... NY-2
Wells Creek—*bay* ... NC-3
Wells Creek—*locale* ... TX-5
**Wells Creek**—*pop pl* ... PA-2
**Wellscreek**—*pop pl* ... PA-2
Wells Creek—*stream* (3) ... AL-4
Wells Creek—*stream* ... AK-9
Wells Creek—*stream* (3) ... AR-4
Wells Creek—*stream* (3) ... CA-9
Wells Creek—*stream* ... GA-3
Wells Creek—*stream* ... KS-7
Wells Creek—*stream* (3) ... KY-4
Wells Creek—*stream* ... MA-1
Wells Creek—*stream* ... MI-6
Wells Creek—*stream* ... MN-6
Wells Creek—*stream* ... MS-4
Wells Creek—*stream* (2) ... MO-7
Wells Creek—*stream* ... NE-7
Wells Creek—*stream* (2) ... NY-2
Wells Creek—*stream* ... NC-3
Wells Creek—*stream* ... OH-6
Wells Creek—*stream* ... OK-5
Wells Creek—*stream* (3) ... OR-9
Wells Creek—*stream* ... PA-2
Wells Creek—*stream* (2) ... TN-4
Wells Creek—*stream* ... TX-5
Wells Creek—*stream* ... VA-3
Wells Creek—*stream* (2) ... WA-9
Wells Creek—*stream* ... WY-8
Wells Creek Basin—*basin* ... TN-4
*Wells Creek Camp Ground School* ... TN-4
Wells Creek Cave—*cave* ... TN-4
Wells Creek Cem—*cemetery* ... MN-6
Wells Creek Ch—*church* ... KS-7
*Wells Creek Glacier* ... WA-9
*Wells Creek Island* ... TN-4
Wells Creek Oil Field—*oilfield* ... MS-4
Wells Creek Peak—*summit* ... CA-9
Wells Creek Sch—*school* ... KS-7
Wells Creek Sch (historical)—*school* ... MO-7
*Wells Creek Siding* ... TX-5
Wells Crossroads—*locale* ... SC-3
Wellsdale—*locale* ... OR-9
Wells Dam—*dam* ... SD-7
Wells Dam—*dam* ... WA-9
*Wells Depot* ... ME-1
Wells District Ranger Office—*locale* ... NV-8
*Wells Ditch* ... IN-6
Wells Ditch—*canal* (3) ... IN-6
Wells Drain—*canal* ... CA-9
Wells Drain—*canal* (2) ... TX-5
Wells Draw—*valley* ... UT-8
Wells Elem Sch—*school* ... KS-7
*Wellseley Fells* ... MA-1
Wells Fargo and Company Express Bldg—*hist pl* ... UT-8
Wells Fargo and Company Livery Stable—*hist pl* ... OK-5
Wells Fargo Bldg—*hist pl* ... OR-9
Wells Fargo Mine—*mine* ... WA-9
Wells Fargo Mine (historical)—*mine* ... SD-7
*Wells Farm Lake* ... TN-4
*Wells Ferry* ... PA-2
Wells Flat—*summit* ... WY-8
Wells Ford—*locale* ... AL-4
**Wellsford**—*pop pl* ... KS-7
Wellsford Cem—*cemetery* ... KS-7
Wellsford Township—*civil* ... KS-7
Wells Fork—*locale* ... KY-4
Wells Fork—*stream* ... IL-6
Wells Fork—*stream* ... KY-4
Wells Fork—*stream* ... WV-2
Wells Fork Rock Creek—*stream* ... MT-8
Wells Fort (historical)—*locale* ... TN-4
Wells Grove Ch—*church* ... MS-4
Wells Grove Ch—*church* ... NC-3
Wells Gulch—*valley* (2) ... CO-8
Wells Gulch—*valley* ... ID-8
Wells Gulch Spring—*spring* ... CO-8
**Wells Hill**—*pop pl* ... KY-4
Wells Hill—*summit* ... GA-3
Wells Hill—*summit* ... NY-2
Wells Hill—*summit* ... TX-5
Wells Hill Cem—*cemetery* ... TN-4
**Wells Hill (historical)**—*pop pl* ... TN-4
*Wellshire* ... CO-8
Wellshire Municipal Golf Course—*other* ... CO-8
**Wells (historical)**—*pop pl* ... OR-9
Wells (historical P.O.)—*locale* ... IA-7
Wells Hollow—*locale* ... PA-2
Wells Hollow—*valley* ... AR-4
Wells Hollow—*valley* ... KY-4
Wells Hollow—*valley* (3) ... MO-7
Wells Hollow—*valley* ... OK-5
Wells Hollow—*valley* (4) ... TN-4
Wells Hollow—*valley* ... VA-3
Wells Hollow—*valley* ... WV-2
Wells Homestead—*hist pl* ... ME-1
Wells House—*hist pl* ... AZ-5
Wells House—*hist pl* ... MA-1
Wells House—*hist pl* ... WA-9
Wells HS—*school* ... IL-6
Wells HS—*school* ... IN-6
Wells HS—*school* ... WV-2
Wells Indian Colony—*reserve* ... NV-8
Wells Inn—*hist pl* ... WV-2
*Wells Island* ... NY-2
*Wells Island* ... TN-4
Wells Island—*island* ... NJ-2
Wells Island—*island* (2) ... OR-9
Wells Island—*island* ... WV-2
Wells Island (historical)—*island* ... TN-4
Wells-Jackson Carriage House Complex—*hist pl* ... VT-1
Wells Japanese Garden—*hist pl* ... SC-3
Wells JHS—*school* ... MA-1
Wells-Keith House—*hist pl* ... KY-4
Wells Key—*island* ... FL-3
Wells Knob—*summit* ... NC-3
*Wells Lake* ... WA-9
Wells Lake—*lake* (2) ... MI-6
Wells Lake—*lake* ... MN-6
Wells Lake—*lake* ... MS-4
Wells Lake—*lake* ... TX-5
Wells Land Company Lake—*reservoir* ... TN-4
Wells Land Company Lake Dam—*dam* ... TN-4
Wells Landing—*locale* ... FL-3
Wells Landing—*locale* ... OR-9
**Wells Landing**—*pop pl* ... KY-4
Wells Meadow—*flat* ... CA-9
*Wells Mill* ... NJ-2
*Wells Mill* ... TN-4
Wells Mill Creek—*stream* ... FL-3
Wells Mill Creek—*stream* ... GA-3
Wells Mill (historical)—*locale* ... TN-4
Wells Millpond—*reservoir* ... GA-3
**Wells Mills**—*pop pl* ... GA-3
**Wells Mills**—*pop pl* ... NJ-2
Wells Mills Pond—*reservoir* ... NJ-2
Wells Mills Reservoir Dam—*dam* ... NJ-2
Wells Mills Rsvr—*reservoir* ... NJ-2
Wells Mineral Spring—*spring* ... NC-3
Wells Mountain, The—*summit* ... PA-2
Wells Mtn—*summit* ... AK-9
Wells Mtn—*summit* ... CA-9
Wells Mtn—*summit* ... GA-3
Wells Mtn—*summit* ... NC-3
Wells Mtn—*summit* ... SC-3
Wells Mtn—*summit* ... WV-2
**Wellsona**—*pop pl* ... CA-9
Wellson Slough—*gut* ... MO-7
Wells Park—*park* ... CA-9
Wells Park—*park* ... HI-9
Wells Park—*park* ... KS-7
Wells Park—*park* ... MI-6
Wells Park—*park* ... MN-6
Wells Park—*park* ... NM-5
Wells Park—*park* ... SC-3
Wells Park—*park* ... TX-5
Wells Passage—*channel* ... AK-9
Wells Peak—*summit* (2) ... CA-9
Wells Peak—*summit* ... NV-8
*Wells Pit* ... WV-2
Wells Place (Site)—*locale* ... CA-9
Wells Point—*cape* ... AR-4
Wells Point—*cape* ... FL-3
Wells Point—*cape* ... MD-2
*Wells Pond* ... MA-1
*Wells Pond* ... VT-1
Wells Pond—*lake* ... CT-1
Wells Pond—*lake* ... FL-3
Wells Pond—*lake* ... ME-1
Wells Pond—*lake* ... NY-2
Wells Pond—*lake* ... RI-1
Wells Pond—*lake* ... TX-5
Wells Pond—*reservoir* ... GA-3
Wells Pond—*reservoir* ... MA-1
Wells Post Office (historical)—*building* ... MS-4
Well Spring—*locale* ... TN-4
Well Spring—*spring* ... AZ-5
Well Spring—*spring* ... OR-9
*Well Spring Butte* ... OR-9
Well Spring Canyon—*valley* ... OR-9
Well Spring Cem—*cemetery* ... TN-4
Well Spring Ch—*church* ... TN-4
*Well Spring Post Office* ... TN-4
Wellspring Post Office (historical)—*building* ... TN-4
Well Springs Sch (historical)—*school* ... TN-4
**Wells Quarter Village**—*pop pl* ... CT-1
Wells Ranch—*locale* ... AZ-5
Wells Ranch—*locale* ... CA-9
Wells Ranch—*locale* ... NM-5
Wells Ranch—*locale* (2) ... TX-5
Wells Ranch—*locale* ... WY-8
*Wells Reservoir* ... WA-9
Wells-Richardson District—*hist pl* ... VT-1
Wells Ridge—*ridge* ... CO-8
Wells Ridge—*ridge* ... KY-4
**Wells River**—*pop pl* ... VT-1
Wells River—*stream* ... VT-1
Wells River Village Hist Dist—*hist pl* ... VT-1
Wells Road Sch—*school* ... CT-1
Wells Rsvr—*reservoir* ... KS-7
*Wells Run* ... PA-2
*Wells Run* ... WV-2
Wells Run—*stream* ... KY-4
Wells Run—*stream* (3) ... OH-6
Wells Run—*stream* (2) ... WV-2
Wells Sch—*school* (3) ... CA-9
Wells Sch—*school* ... IL-6
Wells Sch—*school* (2) ... KY-4
Wells Sch—*school* ... MI-6
Wells Sch—*school* ... MO-7
Wells Sch—*school* ... NE-7
Wells Sch—*school* ... NC-3
Wells Sch—*school* (3) ... OH-6
Wells Sch—*school* ... SD-7
Wells Sch—*school* ... TN-4
Wells Sch—*school* ... TX-5
Wells Sch—*school* ... WI-6
Wells Sch (abandoned)—*school* ... MO-7
Wells-Schaff House—*hist pl* ... WV-2
Wells Sch (historical)—*school* ... MS-4
Wells Sch Number 1—*school* ... ND-7
Wells Shoals—*bar* ... TN-4
Wells Slough—*gut* ... CA-9
*Wells Spring* ... CA-9
*Wells Spring* ... OR-9
Wells Spring—*spring* (2) ... AZ-5
Wells Spring—*spring* ... CA-9
Wells Spring—*spring* (2) ... NM-5
Wells Spring—*spring* (2) ... OR-9
Wells Spring—*spring* ... SD-7
Wells Spring—*spring* ... TN-4
Wells Spring Cem—*cemetery* ... OR-9
Wells Spring Landing—*locale* ... GA-3
Wells State Park—*park* ... MA-1
*Wells Station* ... AL-4
*Wells Station* ... TN-4
Wells Station—*locale* ... KY-4
Wells Station—*locale* ... NV-8
Wells Station—*uninc pl* ... TN-4
Wells Station Sch—*school* ... TN-4
Wells Station Summit—*gap* ... NV-8
Wells Street Bridge—*hist pl* ... IN-6
Wells Street JHS—*school* ... WI-6
Wells–Stubbs House—*hist pl* ... IA-7
**Wells Subdivision**—*pop pl* ... UT-8
Wells Summit—*gap* ... NV-8
Wells Summit—*summit* ... ID-8
Wells Tank—*reservoir* (2) ... AZ-5
Wells Tank—*reservoir* ... NM-5
**Wells Tannery**—*pop pl* ... PA-2
Wells Theatre—*hist pl* ... VA-3
*Wellston* ... GA-3
**Wellston**—*pop pl* ... MI-6
**Wellston**—*pop pl* ... MO-7
**Wellston**—*pop pl* ... OH-6
**Wellston**—*pop pl* ... OK-5
Wellston (CCD)—*cens area* ... OK-5
Wellston Cem—*cemetery* ... OK-5
Wellston Oil And Gas Field—*oilfield* ... OK-5
*Wellston (P.O.)* ... MO-7
Wellston (Township of)—*other* ... OH-6
**Wells Town**—*pop pl* (2) ... MS-4
Wells Town Hall—*locale* ... WI-6
**Wells (Town of)**—*pop pl* ... ME-1
**Wells (Town of)**—*pop pl* ... NY-2
**Wells (Town of)**—*pop pl* ... VT-1
**Wells (Town of)**—*pop pl* ... WI-6
Wellstown Sch—*school* ... PA-2
Wells Township—*fmr MCD* ... IA-7
Wells Township—*inact MCD* ... NV-8
**Wells Township**—*pop pl* ... KS-7
**Wells Township**—*pop pl* ... ND-7
**Wells Township**—*pop pl* ... SD-7
**Wells (Township of)**—*pop pl* (3) ... MI-6
**Wells (Township of)**—*pop pl* ... MN-6
**Wells (Township of)**—*pop pl* ... OH-6
**Wells (Township of)**—*pop pl* (2) ... PA-2
Wells United Methodist Ch—*church* ... MS-4
Wells Valley Cem—*cemetery* ... OK-5
Wells Valley Ch—*church* ... PA-2
*Wellsview* ... TN-4
Wellsview Sch (historical)—*school* ... TN-4
*Wellsville* ... KS-7
Wellsville—*locale* ... CO-8
Wellsville—*locale* ... CT-1
Wellsville—*locale* ... MI-6
**Wellsville**—*pop pl* ... KS-7
**Wellsville**—*pop pl* ... MO-7
**Wellsville**—*pop pl* (2) ... NY-2
**Wellsville**—*pop pl* ... OH-6
**Wellsville**—*pop pl* ... PA-2
**Wellsville**—*pop pl* ... TN-4
**Wellsville**—*pop pl* ... UT-8
Wellsville Borough—*civil* ... PA-2
Wellsville Canal—*canal* ... UT-8
Wellsville Canyon—*valley* ... UT-8
Wellsville Cem—*cemetery* ... KS-7
Wellsville Cem—*cemetery* ... UT-8
Wellsville City Rsvr—*reservoir* ... OH-6
Wellsville Cone—*summit* ... UT-8
Wellsville Creek—*stream* ... UT-8
Wellsville Division—*civil* ... UT-8
Wellsville Erie Depot—*hist pl* ... NY-2
Wellsville Hist Dist—*hist pl* ... PA-2
Wellsville HS—*school* ... KS-7
Wellsville Lake—*lake* ... MO-7
Wellsville Lake State Wildlife Mngmt Ar—*park* ... MO-7
Wellsville-Mendon Lower Canal—*canal* ... UT-8
Wellsville-Mendon Upper Canal—*canal* ... UT-8
Wellsville Mill (historical)—*locale* ... TN-4
Wellsville Mtns—*range* ... UT-8
Wellsville Oil Field—*oilfield* ... KS-7
Wellsville-Paola Oil Field—*oilfield* ... KS-7
Wellsville Post Office—*building* ... UT-8
Wellsville Post Office (historical)—*building* ... TN-4
Wellsville Rsvr—*reservoir* ... UT-8
Wellsville Sch—*school* ... UT-8
Wellsville Tabernacle—*hist pl* ... UT-8
**Wellsville (Town of)**—*pop pl* ... NY-2
Wellsville (Township of)—*other* ... OH-6
Wells Vly—*swamp* ... NY-2
Wellswood—*uninc pl* ... FL-3
Wells Woods—*locale* ... CT-1
Well Tank—*reservoir* (2) ... AZ-5
Well Tank—*reservoir* ... TX-5
Well that Johnny Dug—*well* ... AZ-5
**Wellton**—*pop pl* ... AZ-5
Wellton Airp—*airport* ... AZ-5
Wellton Canal—*canal* ... AZ-5
Wellton (CCD)—*cens area* ... AZ-5
Wellton Elem Sch—*school* ... AZ-5
Wellton Hills—*ridge* ... AZ-5
Wellton Lateral 7.7—*canal* ... AZ-5
Wellton Mesa—*summit* ... AZ-5
Wellton Mohawk Canal—*canal* ... AZ-5
Wellton Mohawk Main Channel—*canal* ... AZ-5
Wellton Overpass—*crossing* ... AZ-5
Wellton Underpass—*crossing* ... AZ-5
Wellton 4.2 Lateral—*canal* ... AZ-5
Welltown—*locale* ... VA-3
Well under the Rock—*spring* ... AZ-5
Well Valley—*basin* ... NE-7
Well Valley Sch—*school* ... NE-7
Wellville—*locale* ... VA-3
**Wellville**—*pop pl* ... MA-1
Well Water—*locale* ... VA-3
**Wellwood**—*pop pl* ... MD-2
**Wellwood**—*pop pl* ... NJ-2
**Wellwood**—*pop pl* ... NY-2
**Wellwood**—*pop pl* ... TN-4
Wellwood Cem—*cemetery* (2) ... NY-2
Wellwood Post Office (historical)—*building* ... TN-4
Wellwood Sch (historical)—*school* ... TN-4
Wellworth Park—*park* ... MI-6
Welman Pond—*lake* ... ME-1
**Welmar Heights**—*pop pl* ... NC-3
Welmet Camps—*locale* ... NY-2
Welmet Lake—*lake* ... NY-2
Welnack Drain—*canal* ... MI-6
WELO-AM (Tupelo)—*tower* ... MS-4
Weloka—*civil* ... HI-9
**Weloka**—*pop pl* ... HI-9
Weloka Heiau—*locale* ... HI-9
*Welokeuebacook Lake* ... ME-1
Welon—*locale* ... OK-5
Welona—*locale* ... AL-4
Welona Creek—*stream* ... AL-4
Weloy (Municipality)—*civ div* ... FM-9
*Welport Oil* ... CA-9
WELR-AM (Roanoke)—*tower* ... AL-4
WELR-FM (Roanoke)—*tower* ... AL-4
WELS-AM (Kinston)—*tower* ... NC-3
Welsbach Bldg—*hist pl* ... OH-6
Welser Cem—*cemetery* ... IL-6
*Welsh* ... AL-4
Welsh—*locale* ... AR-4
**Welsh**—*pop pl* ... LA-4
**Welsh**—*pop pl* ... OH-6
**Welsh**—*pop pl* ... TX-5
Welsh, William L., Terrace—*hist pl* ... MI-6
Welshans Trail—*trail* ... PA-2
Welsh Branch—*stream* ... DE-2
Welsh Brook—*stream* ... MA-1
Welsh Calvinistic Methodist Church—*hist pl* ... NY-2
Welsh Canal—*canal* ... LA-4
Welsh Canyon—*valley* ... CO-8
Welsh Cem—*cemetery* ... IN-6
Welsh Cem—*cemetery* ... MO-7
Welsh Cem—*cemetery* ... NY-2
Welsh Cem—*cemetery* ... OH-6
Welsh Cem—*cemetery* ... OK-5
Welsh Cem—*cemetery* ... WA-9
Welsh Cem—*cemetery* (2) ... WI-6
Welsh Ch—*church* ... IA-7
Welsh Ch—*church* ... NY-2
Welsh Ch—*church* ... OH-6
Welsh Congregational Church—*hist pl* ... OH-6
Welsh Cove—*bay* ... NH-1
Welsh Creek—*stream* (2) ... IN-6
Welsh Creek—*stream* ... IA-7

Welsh Creek—*stream* ... WA-9
Welsh Creek Cove—*bay* ... WA-9
Welshes Bay—*bay* ... MN-6
**Welshfield**—*pop pl* ... OH-6
*Welsh Gulch* ... MT-8
Welsh Gulch—*valley* ... OR-9
Welsh Gully—*stream* ... LA-4
**Welsh Heights (subdivision)**—*pop pl* ... NC-3
**Welsh Hill**—*pop pl* ... PA-2
Welsh Hill—*summit* ... OK-5
Welsh Hills Cem—*cemetery* ... OH-6
Welsh Hills Ch—*church* ... OH-6
Welsh Hill Sch—*school* ... WI-6
Welsh Hollow—*valley* ... IL-6
Welsh Hollow—*valley* ... WI-6
Welsh House—*hist pl* ... ND-7
**Welshire**—*pop pl* ... DE-2
Welsh Lake—*lake* ... IA-7
Welsh Lake—*lake* ... LA-4
Welsh Lake—*lake* ... MN-6
Welsh Lake—*lake* (2) ... NE-7
Welsh Lake—*lake* ... WI-6
Welsh Lake State For—*forest* ... MN-6
Welsh Lake State Game Mngmt
Area—*park* ... IA-7
Welshman Gut—*stream* ... NC-3
Welsh Mtn—*summit* ... PA-2
Welsh Mtn—*summit* ... VA-3
Welsh Neck—*cape* ... SC-3
Welsh Neck-Long Bluff-Society Hill Hist
Dist—*hist pl* ... SC-3
Welsh Oil and Gas Field—*oilfield* ... LA-4
Welsh Park—*park* ... MD-2
*Welsh Pond* ... MA-1
Welsh Pond—*lake* ... MA-1
Welsh Pond—*reservoir* ... NC-3
Welsh Prairie Sch—*school* ... WI-6
Welsh Presbyterian Church—*hist pl* ... OH-6
Welsh Ranch—*locale* ... WA-9
Welsh Rsvr—*reservoir* ... CO-8
*Welsh Run* ... PA-2
**Welsh Run**—*pop pl* ... PA-2
Welsh Run—*stream* ... OH-6
Welsh Run—*stream* ... PA-2
Welsh Run—*stream* ... VA-3
Welsh Run Cave—*cave* ... PA-2
Welsh Sch—*school* ... IL-6
Welsh Sch—*school* ... PA-2
Welsh Sch—*school* ... TN-4
Welshs Corner—*locale* ... NH-1
Welsh Settlement Cem—*cemetery* ... PA-2
Welsh Settlement Ch—*church* ... PA-2
Welsh Spring—*spring* ... OR-9
Welshs Slough—*stream* ... IA-7
**Welshtown**—*pop pl* ... OH-6
**Welshtown**—*pop pl* ... PA-2
Welsh Tract Baptist Church—*hist pl* ... DE-2
Welsh Tract Ch—*church* ... DE-2
Welsh Valley—*valley* ... WI-6
*Welsh Valley Middle School* ... PA-2
Welsh Valley Sch—*school* ... PA-2
Welsh Valley Sch—*school* ... WI-6
Wels Lutheran—*church* ... FL-3
*Welso* ... TX-5
Welta Tank—*reservoir* ... TX-5
Weltbote (historical)—*locale* ... KS-7
Welter Creek—*stream* ... OR-9
Welter Sch—*school* ... OH-6
**Welti**—*pop pl* ... AL-4
Welti (CCD)—*cens area* ... AL-4
Welti Ch—*church* ... AL-4
*Welti Cumberland Presbyterian Ch* ... AL-4
Welti Division—*civil* ... AL-4
Welti Sch—*school* ... AL-4
Weltner Draw—*valley* ... WY-8
Weltner Prong Waddle Creek—*stream* ... WY-8
**Welton**—*pop pl* ... IA-7
**Welton**—*pop pl* (2) ... WV-2
Welton, Allen, House—*hist pl* ... OH-6
Welton Brook—*stream* ... CT-1
Welton Cem—*cemetery* ... MO-7
Welton Cem—*cemetery* ... OH-6
Welton Chapel—*church* ... IN-6
Welton Coal Mine—*mine* ... WY-8
Welton Ditch—*canal* ... CO-8
Welton Falls—*falls* ... NH-1
Welton Fish Pond—*lake* ... WY-8
Welton Glade—*flat* ... CA-9
Welton Lake—*lake* ... WY-8
Welton (Magisterial District)—*fmr MCD* ... WV-2
Welton Pond—*lake* ... CT-1
Welton Township—*fmr MCD* ... IA-7
Welton Tunnel—*tunnel* ... WV-2
**Weltonville**—*pop pl* ... NY-2
Weltot Island—*island* ... FM-9
Welty—*locale* ... CO-8
**Welty**—*pop pl* ... OK-5
Welty Cem—*cemetery* (2) ... OH-6
Welty Cem—*cemetery* ... OK-5
Welty Hill—*summit* ... NM-5
Welty Park—*park* ... MO-7
Welty Ranch—*locale* ... WY-8
Welty Run—*stream* ... PA-2
**Weltys**—*pop pl* ... PA-2
Weltys Ch—*church* ... MD-2
Welty's General Store—*hist pl* ... WY-8
Welty's Mill Bridge—*hist pl* ... PA-2
**Weltytown**—*pop pl* ... PA-2
**Welty (Weltytown)**—*pop pl* ... PA-2
Weltzin Ditch—*canal* ... IN-6
*Welustee Creek* ... AL-4
**Welwyn (historical)**—*pop pl* ... TN-4
WELZ-AM (Belzoni)—*tower* ... MS-4
Wemac Oil Field—*oilfield* ... TX-5
WEMB-AM (Erwin)—*tower* ... TN-4
Wembly Island—*island* ... LA-4
**Wembly (subdivision)**—*pop pl* ... DE-2
Weme—*locale* ... MN-6
Wemette Brook—*stream* ... NY-2
*Wemiamik* ... IN-6
Weminuche Creek—*stream* ... CO-8
Weminuche Pass—*gap* ... CO-8
Weminuche Valley—*valley* ... CO-8
W E Mitchell JHS—*school* ... CA-9
**Wemme**—*pop pl* ... OR-9
W E Morse Lake Dam—*dam* ... MS-4
*We Mountain* ... WA-9
Wemple—*locale* ... LA-4
Wemple—*locale* ... NY-2
Wemple Cabin—*locale* ... CA-9
**Wempleton**—*pop pl* ... IL-6
**Wempletown**—*pop pl* ... IL-6
*Wemrock Branch Matchaponix Brook* ... NJ-2
*Wemrock Brook* ... NJ-2
Wemrock Brook—*stream* ... NJ-2
Wemrock Pond—*reservoir* ... NJ-2
Wemrock Pond Dam—*dam* ... NJ-2
Wemyss Bldg—*hist pl* ... WI-6
*Wenache* ... WA-9
*Wenache Lake* ... WA-9
*Wenache Mountains* ... WA-9
*Wenache River* ... WA-9
Wenaha Forks—*locale* ... OR-9
**Wenaha (historical)**—*pop pl* ... OR-9
Wenaha River—*stream* ... OR-9
Wenaha-Tucannon Wilderness
Area—*reserve* ... OR-9
Wenande Rsvr No 1—*reservoir* ... WY-8
Wenas—*locale* ... WA-9
Wenas Camp—*locale* ... WA-9
Wenas Cem—*cemetery* ... WA-9
Wenas Creek—*stream* ... WA-9
Wenas Lake—*lake* ... WA-9
**Wenasoga**—*pop pl* ... MS-4
Wenasoga Ch of Christ—*church* ... MS-4
Wenasr—*reef* ... FM-9
Wenas Valley—*valley* ... WA-9
Wenas Valley Grange—*locale* ... WA-9
*Wenatche* ... WA-9
**Wenatchee**—*pop pl* ... WA-9
Wenatchee, Lake—*lake* ... WA-9
Wenatchee Carnegie Library—*hist pl* ... WA-9
Wenatchee (CCD)—*cens area* ... WA-9
Wenatchee Cem—*cemetery* ... WA-9
*Wenatchee Creek* ... WA-9
Wenatchee Flat Site—*hist pl* ... WA-9
Wenatchee Guard Station—*locale* ... WA-9
Wenatchee Heights—*locale* ... WA-9
Wenatchee Heights Rsvr No 1—*reservoir* ... WA-9
Wenatchee Heights Rsvr No 2—*reservoir* ... WA-9
Wenatchee HS—*school* ... WA-9
Wenatchee Junior Acad—*school* ... WA-9
*Wenatchee Lake* ... WA-9
Wenatchee Mountains—*range* ... WA-9
Wenatchee Mtn—*summit* ... WA-9
Wenatchee Pass—*gap* ... WA-9
Wenatchee Reclamation Ditch—*canal* ... WA-9
Wenatchee Ridge—*ridge* ... WA-9
*Wenatchee River* ... WA-9
Wenatchee River—*stream* ... WA-9
Wenatchee Spring—*spring* ... WA-9
Wenatchee Valley Junior Coll—*school* ... WA-9
*Wenatche Lake* ... WA-9
*Wenatche Mountains* ... WA-9
*Wenatche River* ... WA-9
*Wenatuckset River* ... MA-1
*Wenatuxet* ... MA-1
*Wenatuxet River* ... MA-1
*Wenatuxet Village* ... MA-1
*Wenaumet Neck* ... MA-1
Wenaumet Station (historical)—*building* ... MA-1
Wenban Spring—*spring* ... NV-8
Wenberg Hill—*summit* ... CT-1
Wenberg State Park—*park* ... WA-9
WENC-AM (Whiteville)—*tower* ... NC-3
*Wenchaw* ... FM-9
*Wencher Ditch* ... TX-5
Wench Flat—*flat* ... CA-9
Wench Lake—*lake* ... MN-6
**Wenco Acres Subdivision**—*pop pl* ... UT-8
**Wenco Condominium**—*pop pl* ... UT-8
**Wen Dale Park Subdivision**—*pop pl* ... UT-8
Wende—*locale* ... AL-4
**Wende**—*pop pl* ... NY-2
**Wende (County Institutions)**—*pop pl* ... NY-2
*Wendel* ... NC-3
Wendel—*locale* ... IL-6
**Wendel**—*pop pl* ... CA-9
**Wendel**—*pop pl* ... PA-2
**Wendel**—*pop pl* ... WV-2
Wendel Canyon—*valley* ... CA-9
Wendel Canyon—*valley* ... MT-8
Wendel Cem—*cemetery* ... TX-5
**Wendel (Edna Mine No.2)**—*pop pl* ... PA-2
Wendel Hot Springs—*spring* ... CA-9
**Wendelin**—*pop pl* ... IL-6
**Wendelin**—*pop pl* ... OH-6
**Wendell**—*pop pl* ... ID-8
**Wendell**—*pop pl* ... MA-1
**Wendell**—*pop pl* ... MN-6
**Wendell**—*pop pl* ... NH-1
**Wendell**—*pop pl* ... NC-3
Wendell, Lake—*reservoir* ... NC-3
Wendell Branch—*stream* ... IL-6
Wendell Cem—*cemetery* ... MA-1
*Wendell Center* ... MA-1
**Wendell Circle Subdivision**—*pop pl* ... UT-8
**Wendell Depot**—*pop pl* ... MA-1
Wendell Elem Sch—*school* ... NC-3
Wendell Gilman Dam—*dam* ... SD-7
Wendell Hill Cem—*cemetery* ... MN-6
Wendell (historical)—*locale* ... IA-7
Wendell (historical)—*locale* ... KS-7
**Wendell (historical)**—*pop pl* ... OR-9
Wendell-Knightdale Airp—*airport* ... NC-3
Wendell Kreder Dam—*dam* ... OR-9
Wendell Kreder Rsvr—*reservoir* ... OR-9
Wendell Lake—*reservoir* ... NC-3
Wendell Phillips Sch—*school* ... MA-1
Wendell Phillips Sch—*school* ... WA-9
Wendell Playground—*park* ... CA-9
Wendell Post Office—*building* ... MT-8
*Wendell R. ladue Reservoir* ... OH-6
Wendell Run—*stream* ... PA-2
Wendell State For—*forest* ... MA-1
*Wendells Town* ... MA-1
Wendell Town Hall—*building* ... MA-1
**Wendell (Town of)**—*pop pl* ... MA-1
**Wendell Township**—*pop pl* ... KS-7
**Wendell Way Subdivision**—*pop pl* ... UT-8
Wendell Well—*well* ... ID-8
**Wendelville**—*pop pl* ... NY-2
**Wenden**—*pop pl* (2) ... AZ-5
Wenden Airfield—*airport* ... AZ-5
*Wendendale* ... AZ-5
Wenden Elem Sch—*school* ... AZ-5
Wendi, Lake—*reservoir* ... GA-3
Wendigo Arm Bay—*bay* ... MN-6
Wendigo Island—*island* ... MN-6
Wendigo Mines—*mine* ... MI-6
Wendigo Sch—*school* ... MN-6
Wending Glade—*flat* ... OR-9
Wending Lake—*lake* ... MN-6
Wendland Lake—*lake* ... ND-7
Wendland Oil Field—*oilfield* ... TX-5
Wendle Creek—*stream* ... ID-8
Wendler Bldg—*hist pl* ... AK-9
**Wendling**—*pop pl* ... OR-9
Wendling Bridge—*hist pl* ... OR-9
Wendling Picnic Area—*area* ... OR-9
Wendona Cem—*cemetery* ... IL-6
*Wendover* ... NV-8
Wendover—*hist pl* ... KY-4
Wendover—*locale* ... KY-4
**Wendover**—*pop pl* ... NV-8
**Wendover**—*pop pl* ... UT-8
**Wendover**—*pop pl* ... WY-8
Wendover Air Force Auxiliary
Field—*military* ... UT-8
Wendover Air Force Base—*hist pl* ... UT-8
Wendover Airp—*airport* ... UT-8
Wendover Bend Ranch—*locale* ... WY-8
Wendover Campground—*locale* ... ID-8
Wendover Canyon—*valley* ... WY-8
Wendover Cem—*cemetery* ... UT-8
*Wendover Creek* ... ID-8
Wendover Creek—*stream* ... ID-8
Wendover Heliport—*airport* ... UT-8
Wendover HS—*school* ... UT-8
Wendover Peak—*summit* ... UT-8
Wendover Ridge—*ridge* ... ID-8
Wendover Well—*well* ... NV-8
Wend Public Sch (historical)—*school* ... AL-4
Wendson—*locale* ... OR-9
Wendt—*locale* ... TX-5
Wendt Butte—*summit* ... OR-9
Wendt Cem—*cemetery* ... TX-5
Wendt Ditch—*canal* ... OR-9
Wendt Drain—*canal* ... MI-6
Wendte—*locale* ... SD-7
Wendte Township—*civil* ... SD-7
Wendt Gulch—*valley* ... OR-9
Wendt Lake—*lake* ... MN-6
Wendtland Park—*park* ... MI-6
Wendt Rsvr—*reservoir* ... OR-9
*Wendts Island* ... OR-9
Wendts Lake—*lake* ... NE-7
Wendt Spring—*spring* ... CA-9
Wendts Siding—*locale* ... WI-6
Wendy Creek—*stream* ... OR-9
**Wendy Wood (subdivision)**—*pop pl* ... AL-4
Wenee Ditch—*canal* ... ID-8
Wenen—*island* ... FM-9
*Wenfara'* ... FM-9
*Wenfra'* ... FM-9
Wenger Cem—*cemetery* ... IL-6
Wenger Cem—*cemetery* ... IN-6
Wenger Ch—*church* ... PA-2
Wenger Ditch—*canal* ... IN-6
Wenger Gulch—*valley* ... MT-8
**Wengerlawn**—*pop pl* ... OH-6
Wenger Sch—*school* ... PA-2
Wengers Ditch—*canal* ... MT-8
Wengert Ch—*church* ... PA-2
Wengert Sch—*school* ... PA-2
*Wengerts Sch* ... PA-2
Wengler—*locale* ... CA-9
Wengler Ave Sch—*school* ... PA-2
Wenglikowski Drain—*canal* ... MI-6
*Wenham* ... MA-1
**Wenham**—*pop pl* (2) ... MA-1
*Wenham and Hamilton Station* ... MA-1
*Wenham Brook* ... MA-1
Wenham Cem—*cemetery* ... MA-1
*Wenham Centre* ... MA-1
Wenham Ch—*church* ... MA-1
*Wenham Depot* ... MA-1
Wenham Hist Dist—*hist pl* ... MA-1
Wenham Lake—*lake* ... MA-1
**Wenham Neck**—*pop pl* ... MA-1
*Wenham Pond* ... MA-1
Wenham Pond—*lake* ... MA-1
*Wenham Station* ... MA-1
Wenham Swamp—*swamp* ... MA-1
Wenham Townhall—*building* ... MA-1
**Wenham (Town of)**—*pop pl* ... MA-1
Wenho Creek—*stream* ... MN-6
Weniger Island—*island* ... WI-6
Wenik—*civil* ... FM-9
Wenik, Dolen—*summit* ... FM-9
*Wenimesset* ... MA-1
*Wenimisset* ... MA-1
*W E Nitraver Elem Sch* ... PA-2
WENK-AM (Union City)—*tower* ... TN-4
Wenke, John G., House—*hist pl* ... SD-7
Wenks Post Office—*building* ... PA-2
**Wenksville**—*pop pl* ... PA-2
**Wenks (Wenksville)**—*pop pl* ... PA-2
Wenlock—*locale* ... VT-1
**Wenmeir**—*pop pl* ... IN-6
*Wennacutt Lake* ... WA-9
WENN-AM (Birmingham)—*tower* ... AL-4
*Wenne* ... FM-9
Wenner, Charles, House—*hist pl* ... IL-6
Wenner Bay—*bay* ... UT-8
Wenner Creek—*stream* ... OR-9
Wenner Lakes—*lake* (2) ... WA-9
**Wennersville**—*pop pl* ... PA-2
Wenner Swamp—*swamp* ... PA-2
*Wennerville* ... PA-2
Wennesborg Cem—*cemetery* ... MN-6
WENN-FM (Birmingham)—*tower* ... AL-4
*Wennuchus Lake* ... MA-1
Wenny Lake—*lake* ... MS-4
Wenona—*locale* ... GA-3
Wenona—*locale* ... NC-3
**Wenona**—*pop pl* ... IL-6
**Wenona**—*pop pl* ... MD-2
**Wenona**—*pop pl* ... MI-6
*Wenona Beach* ... MI-6
**Wenona Beach**—*pop pl* ... MI-6
Wenona Ch—*church* ... NC-3
**Wenonah**—*pop pl* ... AL-4
**Wenonah**—*pop pl* ... IL-6
**Wenonah**—*pop pl* ... NJ-2
**Wenonah**—*pop pl* ... WV-2
Wenona Hall and Wecota Hall—*hist pl* ... SD-7
*Wenonah Elementary School* ... AL-4
Wenonah HS—*school* ... AL-4
Wenonah (RR name for Dott)—*other* ... WV-2
Wenonah Sch—*school* ... AL-4
Wenonah Sch—*school* ... MN-6
Wenonah Sch—*school* ... VA-3
Wenonan Falls—*falls* ... PA-2
Wenona Sch—*school* ... MI-6
WENR-AM (Englewood)—*tower* ... TN-4
*Wenrich Church* ... PA-2
Wenrich Islands—*island* ... AK-9
**Wensa Place (subdivision)**—*pop pl* ... AL-4
Wenscott Reservoir Dam—*dam* ... RI-1
Wenscott Rsvr—*reservoir* ... RI-1
*Wensel Run* ... PA-2
WENS-FM (Shelbyville)—*tower* ... IN-6
**Went (historical)**—*pop pl* ... OR-9
Wenth Ranch—*locale* ... MT-8
Wenthworth Sch—*school* ... NC-3
*Wentling Corners* ... PA-2
**Wentling Corners**—*pop pl* ... PA-2
Wentling Hollow—*valley* ... PA-2
*Wentlings Corner* ... PA-2
**Wentlings Corners**—*pop pl* ... PA-2
Went Ridge—*ridge* ... UT-8
Wentworth—*locale* ... TX-5
**Wentworth**—*pop pl* ... KY-4
**Wentworth**—*pop pl* ... MI-6
**Wentworth**—*pop pl* ... MO-7
**Wentworth**—*pop pl* ... NH-1
**Wentworth**—*pop pl* ... NC-3
**Wentworth**—*pop pl* ... SD-7
**Wentworth**—*pop pl* ... WI-6
Wentworth, George W., House—*hist pl* ... MN-6
Wentworth, Gov. John, House—*hist pl* ... NH-1
Wentworth, Lake—*lake* ... NH-1
*Wentworth Acres* ... NH-1
**Wentworth Acres**—*pop pl* ... NH-1
Wentworth Ave—*post sta* ... IL-6
Wentworth Brook—*stream* ... NH-1
Wentworth Brook—*stream* ... NY-2
**Wentworth By The Sea**—*pop pl* ... NH-1
Wentworth Canyon—*valley* ... CA-9
Wentworth Cem—*cemetery* (2) ... ME-1
Wentworth Cem—*cemetery* ... MS-4
Wentworth Ch—*church* ... NH-1
Wentworth Ch—*church* ... NC-3
Wentworth-Coolidge Mansion—*hist pl* ... NH-1
Wentworth Corners—*locale* ... ME-1
Wentworth Country Club—*other* ... MO-7
*Wentworth Creek* ... KS-7
Wentworth Creek—*stream* ... NE-7
Wentworth Ditch—*canal* ... IN-6
Wentworth Ditch—*canal* ... MT-8
Wentworth-Dover Hosp—*hospital* ... NH-1
Wentworth Elem Sch—*school* ... NC-3
Wentworth-Gardner and Tobias Lear
Houses—*hist pl* ... NH-1
Wentworth-Gardner House—*hist pl* ... NH-1
Wentworth Golf Club—*other* ... NH-1
Wentworth Gulch—*valley* ... ID-8
Wentworth Halcomb Drain—*canal* ... MI-6
**Wentworth Hill**—*pop pl* ... NH-1
Wentworth (historical)—*locale* ... MS-4
Wentworth (historical P.O.)—*locale* ... IA-7
Wentworth Institute—*school* ... MA-1
Wentworth Island—*island* ... NH-1
Wentworth JHS—*school* ... IL-6
Wentworth Lake—*lake* ... WA-9
**Wentworth Location**—*pop pl* ... NH-1
Wentworth Methodist Episcopal Church and
Cemetery—*hist pl* ... NC-3
Wentworth Military Acad—*hist pl* ... MO-7
Wentworth Military Acad—*school* ... MO-7
Wentworth Mine—*mine* ... MN-6
Wentworth Mtn—*summit* ... ME-1
Wentworth Park—*park* ... IL-6
Wentworth Point—*cape* (2) ... ME-1
*Wentworth Pond* ... ME-1
Wentworth Roadside Park—*park* ... SD-7
Wentworth Sch—*school* ... IL-6
Wentworth Sch—*school* ... NH-1
Wentworth Springs—*spring* ... CA-9
Wentworth Springs Campground—*locale* ... CA-9
Wentworth State Park—*park* ... NH-1
**Wentworth Terrace**—*pop pl* ... NH-1
Wentworth (Town of)—*civ div* ... NH-1
**Wentworth (Town of)**—*pop pl* ... NH-1
**Wentworth Township**—*pop pl* ... SD-7
Wentworth Township (historical)—*civil* ... SD-7
Wentworth (Township of)—*fmr MCD* ... NC-3
Wentworth Trail—*trail* ... NH-1
Wentworth Woods—*woods* ... IL-6
Wentz—*locale* ... KY-4
**Wentz**—*pop pl* ... KY-4
**Wentz**—*pop pl* ... MD-2
**Wentz**—*pop pl* ... VA-3
Wentz, Harry F., Studio—*hist pl* ... OR-9
Wentz, Jacob, House—*hist pl* ... IA-7
Wentz, John, House—*hist pl* ... PA-2
Wentz, Peter, Homestead—*hist pl* ... PA-2
Wentz, Peter, House—*hist pl* ... UT-8
Wentz Bend—*bend* ... TX-5
Wentz Camp—*locale* ... OK-5
*Wentz Cave* ... PA-2
Wentz Cem—*cemetery* ... IN-6
Wentz Cem—*cemetery* ... OH-6
Wentz Ch—*church* ... PA-2
Wentz Ditch—*canal* ... IN-6
Wentzel Lake—*lake* ... WI-6
Wentzell-Wilson Dam—*dam* ... NJ-2
Wentzell-Wilson Pond—*reservoir* ... NJ-2
Wentzel Trail—*trail* ... PA-2
Wentz Lake—*reservoir* ... OK-5
Wentz Lakes—*reservoir* ... VA-3
Wentz Oil And Gas Field—*oilfield* ... TX-5
**Wentzville**—*pop pl* ... MO-7
Wentzville Airp—*airport* ... MO-7
Wentzville Township—*civil* ... MO-7
*Wenuchus Lake* ... MA-1
Wenworth Farm Dam—*dam* ... MA-1
Wenzel Creek—*stream* ... TX-5
Wenzel Hollow—*valley* ... PA-2
Wenzel House—*hist pl* ... MI-6
Wenzel Mound—*summit* ... IL-6
Wenzel Post Office (historical)—*building* ... AL-4
Wenzel Sch (historical)—*school* ... SD-7
Wenzel Spring—*spring* ... TX-5
Wenzel Springs Pumping Station—*other* ... WA-9
Wenzel Street Sch—*school* ... MI-6
Wenzel Windmill—*locale* ... CO-8
Wenz Graves—*cemetery* ... NE-7
Wenz Sch—*school* ... IL-6
Weobiji Island—*island* ... MP-9
*Weobiji-To* ... MP-9
**Weogufka**—*pop pl* ... AL-4
Weogufka Cem—*cemetery* ... AL-4
*Weogufka Ch* ... AL-4
Weogufka Ch—*church* ... AL-4
Weogufka Creek—*stream* ... AL-4
*Weogufka First Baptist Church* ... AL-4
Weogufka HS—*school* ... AL-4
Weogufka-Marble Valley
(CCD)—*cens area* ... AL-4
Weogufka-Marble Valley Division—*civil* ... AL-4
*Weogufka Mountain* ... AL-4
Weogufka State For—*forest* ... AL-4
Weogufkee Ch—*church* ... OK-5
Weohyakapka, Lake—*lake* ... FL-3
Weohyakapka Creek—*stream* ... FL-3
*Weoh-ya-kapka Lake* ... FL-3
Weok—*reef* ... FM-9
**Weoka**—*pop pl* ... AL-4
*Weoka Creek* ... AL-4
Weoka Creek—*stream* ... AL-4
Weoka Mills—*locale* ... AL-4
*Weoke Creek* ... AL-4
*Weoky Creek* ... AL-4
Weolustee Creek—*stream* ... AL-4
**Weona**—*pop pl* ... AR-4
Weona, Lake—*reservoir* ... TN-4
**Weona Junction**—*pop pl* ... AR-4
Weona Park—*park* ... PA-2
Weonme Flat—*flat* ... CA-9
Weos Lagoon—*swamp* ... NE-7
Weot Ditch—*canal* ... OH-6
**Weott**—*pop pl* ... CA-9
Weoweopilau Stream—*stream* ... HI-9
Weowlet Spring—*spring* ... CA-9
Weowna Yacht Club—*other* ... NY-2
*Weown Lake* ... NJ-2
WEPA-AM (Eupora)—*tower* ... MS-4
Wepah Creek—*stream* ... ID-8
Wepawaug, Lake—*lake* ... CT-1
Wepawaug River—*stream* ... CT-1
Wepawaug Rsvr—*reservoir* ... CT-1
**Wepco**—*pop pl* ... WI-6
*Wepecket Island* ... MA-1
*Wepecket Islands* ... MA-1
*Wepecket Shoal* ... MA-1
WEPG-AM (South Pittsburg)—*tower* ... TN-4
Wepler Cabin—*locale* ... MT-8
Wepo Spring—*spring* ... AZ-5
*Wepo Springs* ... AZ-5
Wepo Valley—*valley* ... AZ-5
Wepo Village—*locale* ... AZ-5
Wepo Wash—*stream* ... AZ-5
W E Pritchett Lake Dam Number
One—*dam* ... AL-4
W E Pritchett Lake Dam Number
Two—*dam* ... AL-4
W E Pritchett Lake Number
One—*reservoir* ... AL-4
W E Pritchett Lake Number
Two—*reservoir* ... AL-4
**Wepua Point**—*pop pl* ... MA-1
WEQR-FM (Goldsboro)—*tower* ... NC-3
*Wequapaugset Pond* ... RI-1
Wequapauset, Lake—*lake* ... CT-1
Wequaquet Lake—*lake* ... MA-1
*Wequaquet Pond* ... MA-1
**Wequetequock**—*pop pl* ... CT-1
Wequetequock Cove—*bay* ... CT-1
Wequetequock Pond—*lake* ... CT-1
**Wequetonsing**—*pop pl* ... MI-6
**Wequiock**—*pop pl* ... WI-6
Wequiock Ch—*church* ... WI-6
*Wequobsket Cliffs* ... MA-1
Wequobsque Cliffs—*cliff* ... MA-1
Wequos, Lake—*lake* ... MI-6
**Weracoba Heights**—*pop pl* ... GA-3
Weracoba Park—*park* ... GA-3
*Weraxshuck* ... CT-1
WERC-AM (Birmingham)—*tower* ... AL-4
Werckman Sch—*school* ... SD-7
Werdenhoff Mine—*mine* ... ID-8
Werdenhoff Pasture—*flat* ... NV-8
*Wereleys* ... PA-2
*Wereleys Corners* ... PA-2
Worfiold Hollow—*valley* ... MO-7
WERF-TV (Hazleton)—*tower* ... PA-2
Wergeland Cem—*cemetery* ... MN-6
**Wergeland (Township of)**—*pop pl* ... MN-6
WERG-FM (Erie)—*tower* ... PA-2
Wergman Run—*stream* ... WV-2
WERH-AM (Hamilton)—*tower* ... AL-4
WERH-FM (Hamilton)—*tower* ... AL-4
WERI-AM (Westerly)—*tower* ... RI-1
WERI-FM (Westerly)—*tower* ... RI-1
Werito-Martin Well—*well* ... NM-5
Weritos Rincon—*valley* ... NM-5
WERK-AM (Muncie)—*tower* ... IN-6
Werkheiser—*locale* ... PA-2
Werk Lake—*lake* (2) ... MN-6
Werland Draw—*valley* ... WY-8
Werley—*locale* ... WI-6
Werleys Corner—*locale* ... PA-2
*Werleysville* ... PA-2
Werlick Island—*island* ... AK-9
Werling Ditch—*canal* ... IN-6
Werling Joint Ditch—*canal* ... IN-6
Werling Myers Ditch—*canal* ... IN-6
*Wernecke Lake* ... WA-9
*Werner* ... PA-2
Werner—*airport* ... NJ-2
Werner—*locale* ... CA-9
Werner—*locale* ... MN-6
Werner—*locale* ... WV-2
Werner—*other* ... TN-4
**Werner**—*pop pl* ... ND-7
Werner, Mount—*summit* ... CO-8
Werner, Mount—*summit* ... MT-8
Werner, William, House—*hist pl* ... PA-2
Werner Arroyo—*stream* ... CO-8
Werner Camp—*locale* ... CA-9
**Werner Camp**—*pop pl* ... OR-9
Werner Ch—*church* ... OH-6
Werner Company Bldg—*hist pl* ... OH-6
Werner Creek—*stream* ... MT-8
Werner Creek—*stream* ... TX-5
Werner Dam—*dam* ... OR-9
Werner Ditch—*canal* ... IN-6
Werner Dredger Cut—*canal* ... CA-9
Werner-Gilchrist House—*hist pl* ... NM-5
Werner Inn—*hist pl* ... OH-6
Werner Oil Field—*oilfield* ... KS-7
Werner Park—*uninc pl* ... LA-4
Werner Park Sch—*school* ... LA-4
Werner Peak—*summit* ... MT-8
Werner Ranch—*locale* (2) ... WY-8
Werner Rsvr—*reservoir* ... OR-9
Werners Creek—*stream* ... MI-6
Werners Hotel—*building* ... MI-6
*Werners Lake* ... NY-2
*Wernersville* ... PA-2
**Wernersville**—*pop pl* ... PA-2
Wernersville Borough—*civil* ... PA-2
Wernersville State Hosp—*hospital* ... PA-2
Wernert Sch—*school* ... OH-6
Wernerts Corners—*other* ... OH-6
*Wernert (Wernerts Corners)* ... OH-6
Wernette Mtn—*summit* ... TX-5
Wernetts Pond—*reservoir* ... PA-2
Werney Flat—*flat* ... NM-5
Werney Hill—*summit* ... NM-5
Werney Mine—*mine* ... NM-5
Wernicke Glacier—*glacier* ... AK-9
Wernicke River—*stream* ... AK-9
Werning Sch—*school* ... SD-7
Wernle Cem—*cemetery* ... IN-6
Wernli Cem—*cemetery* ... TX-5
Wern Siding—*locale* ... MO-7
Werntz Ditch—*canal* ... IN-6
Wernwag Hollow—*valley* ... PA-2
*Weroi* ... FM-9
Werre Landing Strip—*airport* ... ND-7
Werriats Island—*island* ... GA-3
Werr Sch—*school* ... GA-3
Werry Lake—*lake* ... PA-2
Werry Lake Dam—*dam* ... PA-2
*Werrys Lake* ... PA-2
Werschky Drain—*canal* ... MI-6
Werson Lake—*lake* ... MN-6
Wertenbaker Hill—*summit* ... MD-2
**Wertenberg**—*pop pl* ... IL-6
**Werth**—*pop pl* ... WV-2
*Werthan Lake* ... TN-4
*Werthan Lake Dam* ... TN-4
Wertheim Natl Wildlife Ref—*park* ... NY-2
**Wertheins Corner**—*pop pl* ... NJ-2
Werthheimer Bldg—*hist pl* ... ID-8
Werthman Grocery—*hist pl* ... IA-7
Wertland Street Hist Dist—*hist pl* ... VA-3
Werts Bridge—*bridge* ... PA-2
Werts Cem—*cemetery* ... SC-3
Wert Sch (historical)—*school* ... PA-2
Werts Hollow—*valley* ... PA-2
Werts Path—*trail* ... PA-2
**Wertsville**—*pop pl* ... NJ-2
**Wertz**—*pop pl* ... PA-2
Wertz And Viall Pond—*reservoir* ... RI-1
Wertz And Viall Pond Dam—*dam* ... RI-1
Wertz Camp—*locale* ... WY-8
Wertz Chapel—*church* ... WV-2
**Wertz Crossroads**—*pop pl* ... SC-3
Wertz Ditch—*canal* ... IN-6
Wertz Draw—*stream* ... OR-9
Wertz Draw—*valley* ... WY-8
Wertz Hollow—*valley* ... PA-2
Wertzner Creek—*stream* ... TX-5
Wertz Oil Field—*oilfield* ... WY-8
Wertz Rsvr—*reservoir* ... MT-8
Wertz Run—*stream* ... PA-2
*Wertz Sch* ... IN-6
Wertz Sch—*school* ... IN-6
Wertz Sch (abandoned)—*school* ... PA-2
Wertz Sch (historical)—*school* ... PA-2
Wertz Sch (historical)—*school* ... SD-7
Wertz's Covered Bridge—*hist pl* ... PA-2
Wertz Spring—*spring* ... OR-9
**Wertzville**—*pop pl* ... PA-2
**Wes**—*pop pl* ... OK-5
WESA-AM (Charleroi)—*tower* ... PA-2
WESA-FM (Charleroi)—*tower* ... PA-2
*Wesatch Cove* ... TX-5
*Wesatch Creek* ... TX-5
Wesauking, Lake—*lake* ... PA-2
WESB-AM (Bradford)—*tower* ... PA-2
Wes Bradley Branch—*stream* ... KY-4
*Weshy Creek* ... MS-4
**Wescall (subdivision)**—*pop pl* ... UT-8
Wesch, Phillip, House—*hist pl* ... SD-7
*Wesch-Ach-Ach-Apochka* ... PA-2
W E Schmidt Dam—*dam* ... AL-4
**Wescliff (subdivision)**—*pop pl* ... NC-3
*Wesco* ... MA-1
Wesco—*locale* ... TX-5
**Wesco**—*pop pl* ... KY-4
**Wesco**—*pop pl* ... MO-7
**Wesco**—*pop pl* ... WA-9
*Wescoat Corners* ... DE-2
Wescoat Cove—*bay* ... VA-3
Wescoat Point—*cape* ... VA-3
**Wescoats Corner**—*pop pl* ... DE-2
*Wescoats Corners* ... DE-2
Wescoatville—*locale* ... NJ-2
Wesco Cem—*cemetery* ... MO-7
*Wesco Creek* ... TX-5
*Wescoesville* ... PA-2
*Wescoeville* ... PA-2
Wescogame Point—*cliff* ... AZ-5
*Wesconnet* ... FL-3
**Wesconnett**—*pop pl* ... FL-3
Wesconnett Christian Acad—*school* ... FL-3
Wesconnett Elem Sch—*school* ... FL-3
*Wesco Pond* ... MA-1
Wesco Spring—*spring* ... MT-8
**Wescosville**—*pop pl* ... PA-2
Wescosville Elem Sch—*school* ... PA-2
Wescosville Memorial Park—*park* ... PA-2
Wescot Stream—*stream* ... ME-1
**Wescott**—*pop pl* ... MN-6
**Wescott**—*pop pl* ... NE-7
**Wescott**—*pop pl* ... RI-1
Wescott, Gibbons & Bragg Store—*hist pl* ... NE-7
Wescott, Mount—*summit* ... CO-8
**Wescott Beach**—*pop pl* ... RI-1
Wescott Cem—*cemetery* ... AL-4
Wescott Coulee—*valley* ... MT-8
*Wescott Cove* ... VA-3
Wescott Cove—*bay* ... VA-3
Wescott Creek—*stream* ... CA-9
Wescott Island—*island* ... MA-1

Wescott Lake—*lake* WI-6
Wescott Oil Field—*oilfield* TX-5
Wescott Park—*park* IA-7
*Wescott Point* VA-3
Wescott Road—*hist pl* SC-3
Wescott Sch—*school* IL-6
Wescott Sch—*school* NE-7
*Wescott's Point* VA-3
**Wescott (Town of)**—*pop pl* WI-6
Wes Cove—*bay* TX-5
Wescove Sch—*school* CA-9
Wescutogo Hill—*summit* ME-1
Wes-Del MS—*school* IN-6
Wes-Del Senior HS—*school* IN-6
WESE-FM (Baldwyn)—*tower* MS-4
*Wesel Creek* OR-9
Wesel Creek—*stream* WA-9
*Wesel Reservoir* CT-1
Wesely, Joseph, House and Barn—*hist pl* OR-9
Weseman Cem—*cemetery* ID-8
Wesen Lake—*lake* MN-6
Weser—*locale* TX-5
*Weserly Chapel* AL-4
*Weset* MA-1
*Weset Point* MA-1
Wesgum Oil and Gas Field—*oilfield* AR-4
*Weshakim* MA-1
Wes Hicks Cem—*cemetery* TX-5
Weshrinarin Creek—*stream* AK-9
Wesickaman Creek—*stream* NJ-2
**Weskan**—*pop pl* KS-7
Weskan Cem—*cemetery* KS-7
Weskan Elem Sch—*school* KS-7
Weskan HS—*school* KS-7
**Weskan Township**—*pop pl* KS-7
Weskeag River—*stream* ME-1
*Weskit* PA-2
*Wesko* MA-1
**Weslaco**—*pop pl* TX-5
Weslaco Cem—*cemetery* TX-5
**Weslaco Farm Labor Center**—*pop pl* TX-5
Weslayan—*post sta* TX-5
Wesler Canyon—*valley* OR-9
*Wesley* GA-3
*Wesley* IL-6
Wesley—*locale* GA-3
Wesley—*locale* (2) MD-2
Wesley—*locale* OH-6
Wesley—*locale* OK-5
**Wesley**—*pop pl* AR-4
**Wesley**—*pop pl* GA-3
**Wesley**—*pop pl* IL-6
**Wesley**—*pop pl* IN-6
**Wesley**—*pop pl* IA-7
**Wesley**—*pop pl* ME-1
**Wesley**—*pop pl* NY-2
**Wesley**—*pop pl* PA-2
**Wesley**—*pop pl* TX-5
Wesley, John, Methodist Episcopal Church—*hist pl* SC-3
Wesley, Lake—*lake* TX-5
Wesley, Lake—*lake* VA-3
Wesley, Lake—*reservoir* NJ-2
Wesley Acres Camp—*locale* ND-7
*Wesley Acres United Methodist Camp* ND-7
Wesley AME Zion Church—*hist pl* PA-2
*Wesleyan* CT-1
**Wesleyan**—*pop pl* SC-3
Wesleyan Ave Hist Dist—*hist pl* RI-1
Wesleyan Camp—*locale* KY-4
Wesleyan Camp—*locale* WI-6
Wesleyan Campground—*locale* GA-3
Wesleyan Campground—*locale* NE-7
Wesleyan Campground—*locale* PA-2
Wesleyan Cem—*cemetery* KS-7
Wesleyan Cem—*cemetery* MA-1
Wesleyan Cem—*cemetery* NY-2
Wesleyan Cem—*cemetery* OH-6
Wesleyan Cem—*cemetery* PA-2
*Wesleyan Ch* TN-4
Wesleyan Ch—*church* AL-4
Wesleyan Ch—*church* AR-4
Wesleyan Ch—*church* (2) DE-2
Wesleyan Ch—*church* (4) FL-3
Wesleyan Ch—*church* (3) IN-6
Wesleyan Ch—*church* (2) KS-7
Wesleyan Ch—*church* MD-2
Wesleyan Ch—*church* (3) MI-6
Wesleyan Ch—*church* MO-7
Wesleyan Ch—*church* (5) NY-2
Wesleyan Ch—*church* (4) NC-3
Wesleyan Ch—*church* (4) OH-6
Wesleyan Ch—*church* (7) PA-2
Wesleyan Ch—*church* (3) SC-3
Wesleyan Ch—*church* (3) TN-4
Wesleyan Ch—*church* (4) VA-3
Wesleyan Ch—*church* (2) WI-6
Wesleyan Chapel—*church* AR-4
Wesleyan Chapel—*church* OK-5
Wesleyan Chapel—*church* PA-2
Wesleyan Chapel—*church* VA-3
Wesleyan Chapel—*church* WV-2
Wesleyan Ch First—*church* FL-3
Wesleyan Ch of Newark—*church* DE-2
Wesleyan Ch of Prattville—*church* AL-4
Wesleyan Coll—*school* GA-3
Wesleyan Coll—*school* IA-7
Wesleyan Coll—*school* OK-5
**Wesleyan College**—*pop pl* NC-3
**Wesleyan Estates**—*pop pl* GA-3
Wesleyan Hall—*hist pl* AL-4
Wesleyan Holiness Ch—*church* AL-4
Wesleyan Hope Ch—*church* FL-3
Wesleyan (Kansas Wesleyan University)—*uninc pl* KS-7
Wesleyan Methodist Chapel—*church* TN-4
Wesleyan Methodist Church—*hist pl* NY-2
Wesleyan Methodist Coll—*school* SC-3
Wesleyan Methodist Protestant Ch—*church* AL-4
Wesleyanna—*locale* TN-4
Wesleyanna Cem—*cemetery* MS-4
Wesley Anna Ch—*church* GA-3
Wesleyanna Ch (historical)—*church* MS-4
Wesleyanna Methodist Ch—*church* TN-4
Wesleyanna Sch (historical)—*school* TN-4
Wesley Ann Cem—*cemetery* (2) TN-4
Wesleyann Ch—*church* TN-4
Wesley Ann Methodist Ch (historical)—*church* TN-4
**Wesleyan Park**—*pop pl* KY-4
Wesleyan Sch—*school* TN-4
Wesleyan Uniuersity—*school* CT-1
Wesleyan (Wesleyan College)—*uninc pl* GA-3
Wesleyan Woods—*uninc pl* GA-3
Wesleyan Youth Camp Lake—*reservoir* NC-3
Wesleyan Youth Camp Lake Dam—*dam* NC-3
Wesley Ave Sch—*school* GA-3
Wesley Bailey Catfish Pond Dam—*dam* MS-4
Wesley Beaman Dam—*dam* SD-7
Wesley Bend—*bend* KY-4
Wesley Bldg—*hist pl* PA-2
Wesley Branch—*stream* AL-4
Wesley Branch—*stream* GA-3
Wesley Branch—*stream* (2) KY-4
Wesley Branch—*stream* MD-2
Wesley Branch—*stream* MS-4
Wesley Brethren Church—*hist pl* TX-5
Wesley Brook—*stream* ME-1
Wesleybury Ch—*church* VA-3
Wesley Cem—*cemetery* AL-4
Wesley Cem—*cemetery* AR-4
Wesley Cem—*cemetery* (3) IL-6
Wesley Cem—*cemetery* (3) IN-6
Wesley Cem—*cemetery* (2) KY-4
Wesley Cem—*cemetery* (2) MS-4
Wesley Cem—*cemetery* MO-7
Wesley Cem—*cemetery* NC-3
Wesley Cem—*cemetery* (3) OH-6
Wesley Cem—*cemetery* SC-3
Wesley Cem—*cemetery* (3) TN-4
Wesley Cem—*cemetery* TX-5
Wesley Center—*locale* KS-7
*Wesley Ch* AL-4
*Wesley Ch* DE-2
*Wesley Ch* MS-4
Wesley Ch—*church* (5) AL-4
Wesley Ch—*church* AR-4
Wesley Ch—*church* (2) DE-2
Wesley Ch—*church* DC-2
Wesley Ch—*church* (5) GA-3
Wesley Ch—*church* IL-6
Wesley Ch—*church* (2) KY-4
Wesley Ch—*church* LA-4
Wesley Ch—*church* (10) MD-2
Wesley Ch—*church* MA-1
Wesley Ch—*church* (2) MS-4
Wesley Ch—*church* (4) MO-7
Wesley Ch—*church* NH-1
Wesley Ch—*church* (2) NJ-2
Wesley Ch—*church* NY-2
Wesley Ch—*church* (3) NC-3
Wesley Ch—*church* (2) OH-6
Wesley Ch—*church* (4) PA-2
Wesley Ch—*church* (5) SC-3
Wesley Ch—*church* TN-4
Wesley Ch—*church* (3) TX-5
Wesley Ch—*church* (5) VA-3
Wesley Ch—*church* (2) WV-2
Wesley Ch—*church* WI-6
*Wesley Chapel* AL-4
*Wesley Chapel* MS-4
*Wesley Chapel* TN-4
Wesley Chapel—*church* (15) AL-4
Wesley Chapel—*church* (8) AR-4
Wesley Chapel—*church* DE-2
Wesley Chapel—*church* FL-3
Wesley Chapel—*church* (27) GA-3
Wesley Chapel—*church* (6) IL-6
Wesley Chapel—*church* (12) IN-6
Wesley Chapel—*church* IA-7
Wesley Chapel—*church* (4) KS-7
Wesley Chapel—*church* (7) KY-4
Wesley Chapel—*church* (3) LA-4
Wesley Chapel—*church* (6) MD-2
Wesley Chapel—*church* MN-6
Wesley Chapel—*church* (14) MS-4
Wesley Chapel—*church* (8) MO-7
Wesley Chapel—*church* NY-2
Wesley Chapel—*church* (12) NC-3
Wesley Chapel—*church* (10) OH-6
Wesley Chapel—*church* OK-5
Wesley Chapel—*church* (6) PA-2
Wesley Chapel—*church* (9) SC-3
Wesley Chapel—*church* (11) TN-4
Wesley Chapel—*church* (6) TX-5
Wesley Chapel—*church* (14) VA-3
Wesley Chapel—*church* (8) WV-2
Wesley Chapel—*hist pl* (2) OH-6
Wesley Chapel—*locale* AR-4
Wesley Chapel—*locale* FL-3
**Wesley Chapel**—*pop pl* NY-2
**Wesley Chapel**—*pop pl* NC-3
**Wesley Chapel**—*pop pl* PA-2
Wesley Chapel A.M.E Church—*hist pl* TX-5
Wesley Chapel Cem—*cemetery* (6) AL-4
Wesley Chapel Cem—*cemetery* AR-4
Wesley Chapel Cem—*cemetery* CO-8
Wesley Chapel Cem—*cemetery* GA-3
Wesley Chapel Cem—*cemetery* (2) IL-6
Wesley Chapel Cem—*cemetery* (4) IN-6
Wesley Chapel Cem—*cemetery* (2) IA-7
Wesley Chapel Cem—*cemetery* (6) MS-4
Wesley Chapel Cem—*cemetery* (2) MO-7
Wesley Chapel Cem—*cemetery* (2) NE-7
Wesley Chapel Cem—*cemetery* NC-3
Wesley Chapel Cem—*cemetery* (5) OH-6
Wesley Chapel Cem—*cemetery* PA-2
Wesley Chapel Cem—*cemetery* (2) TN-4
Wesley Chapel Cem—*cemetery* (4) TX-5
Wesley Chapel Cem—*cemetery* VA-3
Wesley Chapel Ch—*church* LA-4
Wesley Chapel Ch—*church* SC-3
Wesley Chapel Christian Methodist Episcopal Ch—*church* TN-4
*Wesley Chapel Church* AL-4
Wesley Chapel Community Christian Ch—*church* TN-4
Wesley Chapel (historical)—*church* AL-4
Wesley Chapel (historical)—*church* (3) MS-4
*Wesley Chapel Methodist Ch* AL-4
*Wesley Chapel Methodist Ch* MS-4
Wesley Chapel Methodist Ch—*church* (2) AL-4
Wesley Chapel Methodist Episcopal Church—*hist pl* MD-2
Wesley Chapel Oil Field—*oilfield* MS-4
Wesley Chapel Sch—*school* AL-4
Wesley Chapel Sch—*school* MS-4
Wesley Chapel Sch—*school* NC-3
Wesley Chapel Sch—*school* TN-4
Wesley Chapel Sch (historical)—*school* AL-4
Wesley Chapel Sch (historical)—*school* (2) MS-4
Wesley Chapel Sch (historical)—*school* TN-4
Wesley Chapel Sch (historical)—*school* TX-5
Wesley Chapel United Methodist Ch—*church* TN-4
*Wesley Chapel United Methodist Church* AL-4
Wesley Ch (historical)—*church* TN-4
*Wesley Church* IN-6
Wesley Church—*locale* MD-2
Wesley Church Cem—*cemetery* TX-5
Wesley Churh—*church* TN-4
Wesley Chute—*channel* TN-4
Wesley Chute Shoals—*bar* TN-4
Wesley Coll—*school* DE-2
Wesley Coll—*school* MS-4
Wesley Coll—*school* ND-7
Wesley Community Center—*building* TN-4
Wesley Creek—*bay* MD-2
Wesley Creek—*stream* (2) AK-9
Wesley Creek—*stream* ID-8
Wesley Creek—*stream* IN-6
Wesley Creek—*stream* (2) NC-3
Wesley Creek—*stream* WA-9
Wesley Dairy—*locale* TX-5
Wesley Dean Branch—*stream* NC-3
Wesley Drain—*stream* IN-6
Wesley E Seale Dam—*dam* TX-5
Wesley Evergreen Cem—*cemetery* IA-7
Wesley Falls Creek—*stream* AK-9
Wesley Fellowship Ch—*church* MI-6
Wesley Forest Camp—*locale* PA-2
Wesley Fork—*stream* KY-4
Wesley Gap—*gap* TN-4
Wesley Grey Pond—*swamp* TX-5
**Wesley Grove**—*pop pl* MD-2
**Wesley Grove**—*pop pl* TX-5
Wesley Grove Ch—*church* MD-2
Wesley Grove Ch—*church* SC-3
Wesley Grove Ch—*church* TX-5
Wesley Grove Sch—*school* TX-5
**Wesley Heights**—*pop pl* DC-2
Wesley Heights Ch—*church* TN-4
Wesley Heights Sch—*school* NC-3
**Wesley Heights (subdivision)**—*pop pl* NC-3
Wesley Hill Ch—*church* AL-4
**Wesley Hills**—*pop pl* NY-2
Wesley (historical)—*locale* SD-7
**Wesley (historical)**—*pop pl* MS-4
Wesley Horn—*bend* GA-3
Wesley Hosp—*hospital* IL-6
Wesley Hosp—*hospital* KS-7
Wesley House—*hist pl* LA-4
Wesley House Child Care Center—*school* FL-3
Wesley Independent Methodist Ch—*church* MS-4
Wesley Ives Creek—*stream* CA-9
*Wesley Junction* IL-6
*Wesley Junior Coll* DE-2
Wesley Lake—*lake* GA-3
Wesley Lake—*lake* WI-6
Wesley Lakes—*lake* TN-4
**Wesley Manor**—*pop pl* FL-3
**Wesley Manor**—*pop pl* IN-6
**Wesley Manor Retirement Village**—*pop pl* FL-3
Wesley Martin Branch—*stream* NC-3
Wesley M.E. Church—*hist pl* DE-2
Wesley Med Ctr Airp—*airport* KS-7
Wesley Memorial Ch—*church* AL-4
Wesley Memorial Ch—*church* FL-3
Wesley Memorial Ch—*church* (2) NC-3
Wesley Memorial Ch—*church* (2) SC-3
Wesley Memorial Ch—*church* TN-4
Wesley Memorial Ch—*church* TX-5
Wesley Memorial Methodist Ch—*church* TN-4
Wesley Memorial Methodist Episcopal—*hist pl* MS-4
Wesley Memorial United Methodist Ch—*church* FL-3
Wesley Methodist Ch—*church* AL-4
Wesley Methodist Ch—*church* TN-4
Wesley Methodist Chapel Ch (historical)—*church* TX-5
Wesley Methodist Church—*hist pl* KY-4
Wesley Methodist Church—*hist pl* MA-1
Wesley Methodist Episcopal Church—*hist pl* MN-6
Wesley Park—*park* MN-6
**Wesley Park (subdivision)**—*pop pl* NC-3
Wesley Point—*cape* TX-5
Wesley Post Office (historical)—*building* AL-4
Wesley Post Office (historical)—*building* PA-2
Wesley Post Office (historical)—*building* TN-4
Wesley Ray Sch—*school* LA-4
Wesley Rsvr—*reservoir* CO-8
Wesleys Cem—*cemetery* NC-3
Wesley Sch—*school* IL-6
Wesley Sch—*school* SC-3
Wesley Sch—*school* TX-5
*Wesleys Chapel* MS-4
Wesleys Chapel—*church* AL-4
Wesleys Chapel—*church* GA-3
Wesleys Chapel—*church* (3) NC-3
Wesleys Chapel—*church* TN-4
Wesleys Chapel Cem—*cemetery* (2) TN-4
Wesleys Chapel Cemetary—*cemetery* AR-4
Wesleys Chapel Sch (historical)—*school* TN-4
Wesley Sch (historical)—*school* TN-4
Wesley Seminary—*school* DC-2
Wesley Southern Methodist Ch—*church* MS-4
Wesley Tank—*reservoir* AZ-5
Wesley Tank—*reservoir* NM-5
**Wesley (Town of)**—*pop pl* ME-1
Wesley Township—*fmr MCD* IA-7
**Wesley Township**—*pop pl* SD-7
**Wesley (Township of)**—*pop pl* IL-6
**Wesley (Township of)**—*pop pl* OH-6
Wesley Union Cem—*cemetery* OH-6
Wesley United Ch—*church* MO-7
Wesley United Methodist Ch—*church* DE-2
Wesley United Methodist Ch—*church* (3) FL-3
Wesley United Methodist Ch—*church* IN-6
Wesley United Methodist Ch—*church* (6) MS-4
Wesley United Methodist Church—*hist pl* TX-5
*Wesleyville* PA-2
Wesleyville—*locale* KY-4
**Wesleyville**—*pop pl* PA-2
Wesleyville Borough—*civil* PA-2
Weslyan Cem—*cemetery* SD-7
Weslyan Independent Methodist Ch—*church* AL-4
Wesmond—*uninc pl* MD-2
Wes-Mor Shop Ctr—*locale* NC-3
Wesner Bald—*summit* NC-3
Wesner Ditch—*canal* IN-6
Weso—*locale* NV-8
We-So-Braska Camp—*locale* NE-7
Wesobulga Creek—*stream* AL-4
Weso Creek—*stream* WI-6
**Wesoda**—*pop pl* AL-4
Weso Lake—*lake* WI-6
Wesoller Cem—*cemetery* OH-6
Weson Island—*island* IL-6
Wesp Gulch—*valley* ID-8
Wes Pile Tank—*reservoir* TX-5
Wes-Port Equipment Park Airp—*airport* PA-2
*Wesquabsqu Cliffs* MA-1
*Wesquabsque Cliffs* MA-1
Wesquage Pond—*lake* RI-1
*Wesr Fork Drake Creek* KY-4
Wes Rsvr—*reservoir* UT-8
Wes Run—*stream* OH-6
*Wessacucon Plantation* MA-1
*Wessaguscus* MA-1
*Wessaguscus Plantation* MA-1
*Wessaguscusset* MA-1
*Wessagusset* MA-1
Wessagusset Beach—*beach* MA-1
*Wessaquscus* MA-1
*Wessawakeag River* ME-1
*Wessaweskeag River* ME-1
Wess Chapel—*church* MS-4
*Wess Chapel Baptist Ch* MS-4
*Wessel Creek* OR-9
Wessel Creek—*stream* OR-9
Wesseler Ranch—*locale* WA-9
Wessel Hill—*summit* NY-2
**Wessell**—*pop pl* KY-4
Wessells Cem—*cemetery* VA-3
Wessells Root Cellar—*hist pl* VA-3
Wesselman Park Golf Course—*other* IN-6
Wesselman Park Nature Center—*park* IN-6
Wesseln Cut—*channel* IL-6
Wessel Ranch—*locale* WY-8
*Wessel Slough* OR-9
Wessels Reef—*bar* AK-9
Wessels Sch—*school* IL-6
*Wessen* MS-4
Wessendonck Ch—*church* VA-3
Wessendorf Canyon—*valley* WA-9
Wesser—*locale* NC-3
Wesser Bald—*summit* NC-3
Wesser Cem—*cemetery* NC-3
Wesser Creek—*stream* (2) NC-3
Wesser Creek Shelter—*locale* NC-3
Wesser Gap—*gap* NC-3
Wesserlauf Pond—*reservoir* NY-2
*Wesserrunsett Lake* ME-1
*Wesserrunsett Stream* ME-1
Wesserunsett Lake—*lake* ME-1
Wesserunsett Stream—*stream* ME-1
*Wesses Canyon* UT-8
Wesses Canyon—*valley* UT-8
Wesses Cove—*basin* UT-8
WESS-FM (East Stroudsburgh)—*tower* PA-2
Wess Hollow—*valley* MO-7
Wessinger, Vastine, House—*hist pl* SC-3
Wessington—*locale* AL-4
**Wessington**—*pop pl* SD-7
Wessington Cem—*cemetery* SD-7
Wessington Hills—*summit* SD-7
Wessington House—*building* NC-3
Wessington House—*hist pl* NC-3
*Wessington Place Elem Sch* TN-4
Wessington Place Sch—*school* TN-4
**Wessington Springs**—*pop pl* SD-7
Wessington Springs Opera House—*hist pl* SD-7
**Wessington Springs Township**—*pop pl* SD-7
**Wessington Township**—*pop pl* SD-7
Wessling Sch—*school* IL-6
Wessly Well—*well* NM-5
*Wessnerville* PA-2
*Wessnesville* PA-2
**Wesson**—*pop pl* AR-4
**Wesson**—*pop pl* MS-4
Wesson, Franklin, House—*hist pl* MA-1
Wesson Attendance Center—*school* MS-4
Wesson Branch—*stream* MS-4
Wesson Cem—*cemetery* AL-4
Wesson Cem—*cemetery* AR-4
Wesson Cem—*cemetery* MS-4
Wesson Cem—*cemetery* TN-4
Wesson Cem—*cemetery* TX-5
Wesson Chapel Cumberland Presbyterian Ch—*church* TN-4
Wesson Dam—*dam* AL-4
Wesson Gap—*gap* (2) AL-4
Wesson Hill—*summit* VT-1
Wesson Hollow—*valley* AL-4
Wesson Hosp—*hospital* MA-1
Wesson Lake—*reservoir* MS-4
Wesson Lake Dam—*dam* (2) MS-4
Wesson Mill (historical)—*locale* AL-4
Wesson North Oil And Gas Field—*oilfield* AR-4
Wesson Oil And Gas Field—*oilfield* AR-4
Wesson Park—*park* MA-1
Wesson Sch—*school* FL-3
Wessons Lake—*reservoir* AL-4
Wessons Lake—*reservoir* SC-3
Wesson (Township of)—*fmr MCD* AR-4
**Wessonville**—*pop pl* MA-1
Wess Sch—*school* KY-4
Wessyngton—*hist pl* TN-4
**Wessyngton (historical)**—*pop pl* TN-4
Wessyngton Post Office (historical)—*building* TN-4
*West* MA-1
*West* NC-3
West—*locale* MD-2
West—*locale* NM-5
West—*locale* WV-2
**West**—*pop pl* AL-4
**West**—*pop pl* IA-7
**West**—*pop pl* MS-4
**West**—*pop pl* NC-3
**West**—*pop pl* OR-9
**West**—*pop pl* TN-4
**West**—*pop pl* TX-5
West—*uninc pl* AL-4
West—*uninc pl* MS-4
West—*uninc pl* NJ-2
West—*uninc pl* TN-4
West, Benjamin, Birthplace—*hist pl* PA-2
West, Deacon, Octagon House—*hist pl* WI-6
West, Dr. Edmond, House—*hist pl* WA-9
West, Fisher, Farm—*hist pl* IN-6
West, Gen. Francis H., House—*hist pl* WI-6
West, Lake—*lake* MT-8
West, Lake—*lake* (2) WA-9
West, Nathaniel, Buildings—*hist pl* OR-9
*West, The* MA-1
West, Theophilus, House—*hist pl* FL-3
West, Wesley, House—*hist pl* IA-7
**West Abington**—*pop pl* MA-1
**West Abington (Township of)**—*pop pl* PA-2
West Abutment Rec Area—*park* TX-5
West Academy—*locale* TX-5
West Access Area—*locale* IL-6
**West Acres**—*pop pl* AR-4
**West Acres**—*pop pl* CA-9
**Westacres**—*pop pl* IN-6
**Westacres**—*pop pl* MI-6
**West Acres**—*pop pl* PA-2
**West Acres Development (subdivision)**—*pop pl* SD-7
West Acres Sch—*school* CA-9
West Acres Shop Ctr—*locale* ND-7
**West Acton**—*pop pl* MA-1
West Adair Cem—*cemetery* OK-5
West Adamana Tank—*reservoir* AZ-5
West Adams—*cens area* CO-8
West Adams—*uninc pl* CA-9
West Adams Cem—*cemetery* ND-7
**West Addison**—*pop pl* VT-1
West Admah Cem—*cemetery* NE-7
West Adrian Sch—*school* MI-6
West Adrian Windmill—*locale* TX-5
West Aero Ranch Airp—*airport* MO-7
West Aetna Cem—*cemetery* MI-6
**West Agawam**—*pop pl* MA-1
West Agawam HS—*school* MA-1
West Agua Fria Creek—*stream* NM-5
West Airp—*airport* DE-2
West Akers Ch—*church* WI-6
Westakre Ch—*church* MN-6
*West Akron* OH-6
**West Akron**—*pop pl* OH-6
West Alabama—*locale* NY-2
West Alabama Crippled Childrens Clinic—*hospital* AL-4
West Alabama General Hosp—*hospital* AL-4
West Alabama Oil Field—*oilfield* OK-5
West Alamo Canyon—*valley* CO-8
West Alamocitos Windmill—*locale* TX-5
West Alamosa Creek—*stream* TX-5
West Alapah Glacier—*glacier* AK-9
West Alaska Lake—*lake* WI-6
West Albany—*locale* MN-6
**West Albany**—*pop pl* NY-2
West Albany Cem—*cemetery* MN-6
**West Albany (Township of)**—*pop pl* MN-6
West Albee Cem—*cemetery* MI-6
**West Albion**—*pop pl* MN-6
**West Alden**—*pop pl* NY-2
West Alder Creek—*stream* CO-8
**West Alexander**—*pop pl* PA-2
West Alexander Borough—*civil* PA-2
West Alexander Elem Sch—*school* PA-2
West Alexander Hist Dist—*hist pl* PA-2
*West Alexandria* AL-4
**West Alexandria**—*pop pl* AL-4
**West Alexandria**—*pop pl* OH-6
West Aliquippa—*uninc pl* PA-2
West Alkali Creek—*stream* MT-8
West Alkali Creek—*stream* WY-8
West Alkali Gulch—*valley* CO-8
West Alkali Rsvr—*reservoir* MT-8
Westall Cem—*cemetery* NC-3
West Allegheny Cem—*cemetery* PA-2
West Allegheny HS—*school* PA-2
*West Allegheny Joint Sch* PA-2
West Allegheny MS—*school* PA-2
West Allen—*locale* NY-2
*West Allen Creek* WI-6
West Allen Creek—*stream* WI-6
**West Allenhurst**—*pop pl* NJ-2
**West Alliance**—*pop pl* OH-6
West Alliance (RR name for Alliance)—*other* NC-3
**West Allis**—*pop pl* WI-6
West Allis Memorial Hosp—*hospital* WI-6
Westall Sch—*school* MA-1
Westall Swamp—*swamp* TN-4
West Almond—*locale* WI-6
**West Almond**—*pop pl* NY-2
**West Almond (Town of)**—*pop pl* NY-2
West Alto Cem—*cemetery* WI-6
**West Alton**—*pop pl* MO-7
**West Alton**—*pop pl* NH-1
West Alton Access Area—*locale* MO-7
West Alton Brook—*stream* NH-1
**Westalton (RR name West Alton)**—*pop pl* MO-7
West Alto Sch—*school* WI-6
**West Amana**—*pop pl* IA-7
West Amarillo Creek—*stream* TX-5
West Amatuli Island—*island* AK-9
**West Ambler**—*pop pl* PA-2
**West Amboy**—*pop pl* NY-2
WEST-AM (Easton)—*tower* PA-2
*West Amesbury* MA-1
West Amite Creek Prong—*stream* LA-4
West Amity—*locale* PA-2
West Amityville—*CDP* NY-2
West Amory Ch of Christ—*church* MS-4
West Amory Community Center—*building* MS-4
**Westampton (Township of)**—*pop pl* NJ-2
West Amwell Sch—*school* NJ-2
**West Amwell (Township of)**—*pop pl* NJ-2
West Anacoco Creek—*stream* LA-4
West Anadarche Arm—*bay* OK-5
West Anadarche Creek—*stream* OK-5
**West Anaheim**—*pop pl* CA-9
West Anchor Cove—*bay* AK-9
**West Anderson**—*pop pl* SC-3
West Anderson Oil Field—*other* NM-5
**West Andover**—*pop pl* MA-1
**West Andover**—*pop pl* NH-1
**West Andover**—*pop pl* OH-6
West Andover HS—*school* MA-1
West and Pyle Ranch—*locale* NM-5
*West Andrew Nelson Lake* MN-6
**West Andrews**—*pop pl* SC-3
West Andrews—*uninc pl* SC-3
West Annalaide Lake—*lake* MN-6
**West Annapolis**—*pop pl* MD-2
West Annex—*post sta* VA-3
West Anniston—*uninc pl* AL-4
West Anniston Baptist Ch—*church* AL-4
West Anniston Ch of Christ—*church* AL-4
West Anniston Ch of God—*church* AL-4
West Anniston Methodist Ch—*church* AL-4
West Anniston Park—*park* AL-4
West Anniston Presbyterian Ch—*church* AL-4
**West Annville**—*pop pl* PA-2
West Ansonville Sch—*school* NC-3
*West Antelope Creek* NE-7
*West Antelope Creek* WY-8
West Antelope Creek—*stream* CO-8
West Antelope Creek—*stream* MT-8
West Antelope Draw—*valley* NM-5
West Antelope Mtn—*summit* CO-8
West Antelope Station—*locale* CA-9
**West Antelope Township**—*pop pl* ND-7
West Antioch Cem—*cemetery* MO-7
West Antioch Ch Number 1—*church* MS-4
West Antioch Elem Sch—*school* KS-7
West Ant Tank—*reservoir* NM-5
West Anvil Point—*cliff* CO-8
West Apollo—*uninc pl* PA-2
*West Applegate (Applegate)* CA-9
West Apple Lake—*lake* WI-6
West Appleton—*locale* ME-1
**Westarado**—*pop pl* OH-6
*West Aransas Creek* TX-5
West Arapahoe Creek—*stream* WY-8
West Arapaho Rsvr—*reservoir* CO-8
**West Arcadia**—*pop pl* CA-9
**Westarea**—*pop pl* NC-3
Westarea Ch—*church* NC-3
Westarea Elem Sch—*school* NC-3
West Arkansas Ch—*church* AR-4
West Arkansas Community Coll—*school* AR-4
*West Arkansas Junior Coll* AR-4
West Arkansas Regional Park—*park* AR-4
West Arkdale Cem—*cemetery* WI-6
**West Arlington**—*pop pl* MD-2
**West Arlington**—*pop pl* VT-1
**West Arlington**—*pop pl* VA-3
West Arlington—*uninc pl* NJ-2
West Arlington Station—*locale* NJ-2
West Arm—*bay* MN-6
West Arm—*bay* OR-9
West Arm—*gut* AK-9
West Arm Bay of Isles—*bay* AK-9
West Arm Bridge—*bridge* FL-3
West Arm Bull Ditch—*canal* IN-6
West Arm Cholmondeley Sound—*bay* AK-9
West Arm Clifford Lake—*bay* ME-1
West Arm Ditch—*canal* IN-6
West Arm Grand Traverse Bay—*bay* MI-6
West Arm Grube Ditch—*canal* IN-6
West Arm Holtz Bay—*bay* AK-9
West Arm Kendrick Bay—*bay* AK-9
West Arm Lake Itasca—*lake* MN-6
West Arm Moira Sound—*bay* AK-9
West Arm Nevidiskov Bay—*bay* AK-9
West Arm Nuka Bay—*bay* AK-9
*West Arm of Grand Traverse Bay* MI-6
West Arm Port Dick—*bay* AK-9
West Arm Scholtz—*canal* IN-6
*West Armuchee Creek* GA-3
West Armuchee Creek—*stream* GA-3
West Armuchee Sch—*school* GA-3
West Armuchee Valley—*valley* GA-3
West Arm Uncompahgre River—*channel* CO-8
West Arm Upper Richardson Lake—*bay* ME-1
*West Arsenicker* FL-3
West Arsenicker Key—*island* FL-3
West Art Cem—*cemetery* TX-5
West Ash Creek—*stream* NE-7
West Asher Cem—*cemetery* KS-7
West Asher Creek—*stream* KS-7
West Asher (historical)—*locale* KS-7
West Asher Oil Field—*oilfield* OK-5
*West Asheville* NC-3
**West Asheville**—*pop pl* NC-3
**West Ashford**—*pop pl* CT-1
West Ash Fork Interchange—*crossing* AZ-5
West Aspetuck River—*stream* CT-1
*West Asphalt Canyon* UT-8
West A Street Ch—*church* NC-3
West Atate—*hist pl* GU-9
West Atchafalaya Floodway—*flat* LA-4
West Atchison Mall—*locale* KS-7
**West Atco**—*pop pl* NJ-2
West Athens—*CDP* CA-9
West Athens—*locale* NY-2
West Athens—*locale* PA-2
**West Athens**—*pop pl* ME-1
West Athens Hill Site—*hist pl* NY-2
West Athens Sch—*school* AL-4
West Athens Sch—*school* CA-9
**West Atherton**—*pop pl* IN-6
West Atkinson Creek—*stream* CO-8
**West Atlantic City**—*pop pl* NJ-2
West Atlantic Peak—*summit* WY-8
West Atoka (CCD)—*cens area* OK-5
*West Auburn* ME-1
West Auburn—*locale* IA-7
**West Auburn**—*pop pl* ME-1
**West Auburn**—*pop pl* MA-1
**West Auburn**—*pop pl* PA-2
**West Auburndale**—*pop pl* FL-3
West Augusta—*CDP* GA-3
West Augusta—*locale* VA-3
West Augusta Cem—*cemetery* VA-3
West Augusta Trail—*trail* VA-3
West August Ch—*church* VA-3
West Augustine—*uninc pl* FL-3
West Aurelius Drain—*canal* MI-6
**West Aurora**—*pop pl* IL-6
**West Aurora**—*pop pl* MO-7
West Aurora Cem—*cemetery* IL-6
*West Ausdale* OH-6
West Austin—*uninc pl* TX-5
West Austin Park—*park* TX-5

West Austintown—pop pl ... OH-6
West Autwine Oil Field—oilfield ... OK-5
West Aux Sable Creek—stream ... IL-6
West Avant Oil Field—oilfield ... OK-5
West Ave Cem—cemetery ... NY-2
West Avenue-Roberts Street Residential Hist Dist—hist pl ... GA-3
West Ave Sch—school ... NY-2
West Ave Sch—school ... TX-5
Westavia Woods—pop pl ... TN-4
West Avon—locale ... CT-1
West Avondale Gas Field—oilfield ... LA-4
West Avondale School ... KS-7
Westaway—pop pl ... IL-6
Westaway—pop pl ... PA-2
West Babcock Canyon—valley ... AZ-5
West Babylon—pop pl ... NY-2
West Babylon Creek—stream ... NY-2
West Babylon HS—school ... NY-2
West Babylon JHS—school ... NY-2
West Babylon Sch—school ... NY-2
West Bacon Creek—stream ... WY-8
West Bacon Waterhole—reservoir ... OR-9
West Baden ... IN-6
West Baden (corporate name West Baden Springs) ... IN-6
West Baden Springs—pop pl ... IN-6
West Baden Springs Hotel—hist pl ... IN-6
West Badger Creek—stream ... KS-7
West Badger Lateral—canal ... WA-9
West Badin Hist Dist—hist pl ... NC-3
West Badlands Creek—stream ... SD-7
West Bahia Honda Key—island ... FL-3
West Bailey Creek—stream ... WY-8
West Bailey Run—stream ... OH-6
West Bainbridge—locale ... NY-2
West Bainbridge—pop pl ... GA-3
West Bainbridge Cem—cemetery ... NY-2
West Baker Canal—canal ... FL-3
West Baker Slough—stream ... MT-8
West Baker Well—well ... NM-5
West Bald Peak Lateral—canal ... NE-7
West Baldwin—pop pl ... ME-1
West Baldy—summit (2) ... CO-8
West Baldy—summit ... NM-5
West Baldy Basin—basin ... MT-8
West Baltimore—locale ... MD-2
West Bancroft—locale ... WI-6
West Bangor—locale ... MI-6
West Bangor—locale ... PA-2
West Bangor—pop pl ... ME-1
West Bangor—pop pl ... NY-2
West Bangor—pop pl ... PA-2
West Bangs Canyon—valley ... CO-8
West Bank—bar ... AL-4
West Bank—bar ... FL-3
West Bank—bar ... MS-4
West Bank—bar ... NY-2
West Bank—bar ... WA-9
West Bank Ch—church ... MN-6
Westbank Creek—stream ... SC-3
West Bank Lighthouse—locale ... NY-2
West Bank Overlook—locale ... AL-4
West Bank Park—park ... MS-4
West Bank Public Use Area—park ... GA-3
West Bank Sch—school ... PA-2
West Bank Township—pop pl ... ND-7
West Bank (Township of)—pop pl ... MN-6
West Bantam—pop pl ... CT-1
West Baptist Church ... SD-7
West Baptist Church—hist pl ... OH-6
West Baptist Hollow Mine—mine ... TN-4
West Bar—bar ... WA-9
West Baraboo—pop pl ... WI-6
West Barataria Oil and Gas Field—oilfield ... LA-4
West Barge—island ... ME-1
West Barnet—pop pl ... VT-1
West Barnitz Creek—stream ... OK-5
West Barnsdall Oil Field—oilfield ... OK-5
West Barnstable—pop pl ... MA-1
West Barnstable Sch—school ... MA-1
West Barnstable Station—building ... MA-1
West Barnstable Village-Meetinghouse Way Hist Dist—hist pl ... MA-1
West Barre—pop pl ... NY-2
Westbarre Cem—cemetery ... OH-6
West Barrens—flat ... ME-1
West Barrington—pop pl ... NH-1
West Barrington—pop pl ... RI-1
West Barron Creek ... AR-4
West-Bar-Val Wood Park—park ... CO-8
West Base Windmill—locale ... NM-5
West Basin—basin ... FL-3
West Basin—basin ... NV-8
West Basin—basin ... OH-6
West Basin—basin ... TX-5
West Basin—basin ... UT-8
West Basin—harbor (3) ... CA-9
West Basin—harbor ... NY-2
West Basin—harbor ... OR-9
West Basin Canyon—valley ... OR-9
West Basin Draw—valley ... ID-8
West Basin Draw—valley ... NV-8
West Basin Well—well ... OR-9
West Bass Creek—stream ... AR-4
West Basset Slough ... MN-6
West Bassett—pop pl ... VA-3
West Bassett Creek ... AL-4
West Bassetts Creek ... AL-4
West Bass Lake—lake ... MN-6
West Bass Lake—lake ... WI-6
West Bass Lake—pop pl ... OH-6
West Basswood Creek—stream ... IA-7
West Bastian Bay Oil and Gas Field—oilfield ... LA-4
West Batavia—pop pl ... NY-2
West Batavia Cem—cemetery ... IL-6
West Bates Camp Lake—reservoir ... OR-9
West Bates Drain—stream ... MI-6
West Batesville HS—school ... AR-4
West Bath—locale ... NH-1
West Bath Ch—church ... ME-1
West Bath (Town of)—pop pl ... ME-1
West Baton Rouge Parish—pop pl ... LA-4
West Battle Lake—lake ... MN-6
West Bauxite—pop pl ... AR-4
Westbay ... FL-3
West Bay ... ME-1
West Bay ... MA-1
West Bay ... TX-5
West Bay—bay ... AK-9
West Bay—bay ... FL-3
West Bay—bay ... LA-4
West Bay—bay ... ME-1
West Bay—bay ... MD-2
West Bay—bay ... MA-1
West Bay—bay ... MI-6
West Bay—bay (2) ... MN-6
West Bay—bay ... NY-2
West Bay—bay ... NC-3
West Bay—bay ... OK-5
West Bay—bay (2) ... OR-9
West Bay—bay ... TX-5
West Bay—bay (2) ... WA-9
West Bay—bay ... WI-6
West Bay—flat ... ND-7
West Bay—pop pl ... FL-3
West Bay—swamp ... FL-3
West Bay—uninc pl ... FL-3
West Bayard—fmr MCD ... NE-7
West Bay Bridge—bridge ... FL-3
West Bay Center (Shop Ctr)—locale ... FL-3
West Bay City—pop pl ... MI-6
West Bay Creek—stream ... FL-3
West Bay Creek—stream ... OR-9
West Bay Elem Sch—school ... FL-3
West Bay Entrance Light—locale ... MA-1
West Bay Lake—lake ... MI-6
West Bay Lake—lake ... WI-6
West Bay Little Saint Germain Lake—lake ... WI-6
West Bay Oil and Gas Field—oilfield ... LA-4
West Bayou—bay ... FL-3
West Bayou—gut ... AR-4
West Bayou—stream ... FL-3
West Bayou—stream ... LA-4
West Bayou Cocodrie Oil Field—oilfield ... LA-4
West Bayou Grand Marais—stream ... LA-4
West Bayou Lacassine—stream ... LA-4
West Bay Park (trailer park)—pop pl ... DE-2
West Bay Point ... FL-3
West Bay Point ... TX-5
West Bay Point—cape ... FL-3
West Bay Pond—lake ... ME-1
West Bays Fork—stream ... KY-4
West Bay Shore—pop pl ... NY-2
West Baytown—uninc pl ... TX-5
West Bay Township—pop pl ... ND-7
West Bay Tump—island ... MD-2
West Beach ... NY-2
West Beach—beach ... CA-9
West Beach—beach ... CT-1
West Beach—beach (2) ... MA-1
West Beach—beach (2) ... NY-2
West Beach—beach ... TX-5
West Beach—beach (2) ... WA-9
West Beach—locale ... DE-2
West Beach—pop pl ... MD-2
West Beach—pop pl ... WA-9
West Beach Cove—bay ... TX-5
West Beach Hist Dist—hist pl ... MS-4
West Bear Canyon—valley ... AZ-5
West Bear Creek—stream (2) ... CO-8
West Bear Creek—stream ... GA-3
West Bear Creek—stream ... ID-8
West Bear Creek—stream ... MO-7
West Bear Creek—stream ... MT-8
West Bear Creek—stream ... NC-3
West Bear Creek—stream ... OR-9
West Bear Creek—stream ... TX-5
West Bear Creek—stream ... WA-9
West Bear Lake—lake ... MI-6
West Bearskin Lake ... MN-6
West Bear Springs Arroyo—stream ... CO-8
West Bear Wallow Gulch—valley ... CO-8
West Beaumont Oil Field—oilfield ... TX-5
West Beaver Brook—stream ... NY-2
West Beaver Ch—church ... OH-6
West Beaver Ch—church ... WI-6
West Beaver Charlie Rsvr—reservoir ... OR-9
West Beaver Creek ... CA-9
West Beaver Creek ... OH-6
West Beaver Creek ... WY-8
West Beaver Creek—stream (3) ... CO-8
West Beaver Creek—stream ... ID-8
West Beaver Creek—stream ... IA-7
West Beaver Creek—stream ... KS-7
West Beaver Creek—stream (2) ... OK-5
West Beaver Creek—stream (2) ... OR-9
West Beaver Creek—stream ... UT-8
West Beaver Creek—stream ... WI-6
West Beaver Creek—stream ... WY-8
West Beaver Creek Canal—canal ... TN-4
West Beaverdam Creek—stream ... TX-5
West Beaver Highline Ditch—canal ... CO-8
West Beaver Lake—lake ... AK-9
West Beaver River ... MN-6
West Beaver Sch—school ... WI-6
West Beaver Sch (historical)—school ... IA-7
West Beaverton Oil Field—other ... MI-6
West Beaver (Township of)—pop pl ... PA-2
West Beaver Trap Creek—stream ... SD-7
West Becket—pop pl ... MA-1
West Beckley—pop pl ... WV-2
West Beckwith Mtn—summit ... CO-8
West Beckwith Peak ... CO-8
West Bedford—pop pl ... MA-1
West Bedford—pop pl ... OH-6
West Bedford Cem—cemetery ... OH-6
West Bee Branch—stream ... MO-7
West Beech—locale ... PA-2
West Beecher Hill—summit ... NY-2
West Beech Woods—woods ... PA-2
West Beef River Cem—cemetery ... WI-6
West Beekmantown—locale ... NY-2
West Bee Rock—other ... AK-9
West Belews Creek—stream ... NC-3
West Belfast Cem—cemetery ... ME-1
West Belknap Creek—stream ... TX-5
West Bellaire ... OH-6
West Bellemont Oil Field—oilfield ... OK-5
West Belle Vernon—other ... PA-2
West Bellevue—pop pl ... PA-2
West Bellows Creek—stream ... CO-8
West Belmar—pop pl (2) ... NJ-2
West Belmont Cem—cemetery ... MN-6
West Belmore Cem—cemetery ... OH-6
West Belt Junction—uninc pl ... PA-2
West Belt Junction Station—building ... PA-2
West Bemis Sch—school ... TN-4
West Bench—bench ... CO-8
West Bench—bench (2) ... MT-8
West Bench—bench ... OR-9
West Bench—bench ... UT-8
West Bench Canal—canal ... MT-8
West Bench Canal Lateral—canal ... MT-8
West Bench Ditch—canal ... UT-8
West Bend—locale ... PA-2
West Bend—pop pl ... AL-4
West Bend—pop pl ... IA-7
Westbend—pop pl ... KY-4
West Bend—pop pl ... NC-3
West Bend—pop pl ... WI-6
West Bend Ch—church ... AL-4
Westbend Ch—church ... KY-4
West Bend Ch—church ... PA-2
West Bend Creek—stream ... AL-4
West Bend(historical P.O.)—locale ... IA-7
West Bend Rec Area—park ... SD-7
West Bend Sch (historical)—school ... PA-2
West Bend (Town of)—pop pl ... WI-6
West Bend Township—fmr MCD ... IA-7
West Bennett—unorg reg ... SD-7
West Bennett Well—well ... TX-5
West Benson ... NE-7
West Benson Interchange—crossing ... AZ-5
West Benton Ch—church ... MI-6
West Benton Ditch—canal ... IA-7
West Benton Township—civil (3) ... MO-7
West Berdoo Canyon—valley ... CA-9
West Bergen—pop pl ... NJ-2
West Bergen—pop pl ... NY-2
West Berkley ... MA-1
West Berkshire—pop pl ... VT-1
West Berlin—pop pl ... MA-1
West Berlin—pop pl ... NJ-2
West Berlin—pop pl ... OH-6
West Berlin—pop pl ... VT-1
West Berlin Cem—cemetery ... OH-6
West Berlin Ch—church (2) ... MI-6
West Berlin Sch—school ... VT-1
West Bernard Creek—stream ... TX-5
West Berne—pop pl ... NY-2
West Berrien Sch—school ... GA-3
Westberry Cem—cemetery ... MS-4
West Berryhill Windmill—locale ... NM-5
Westberry Sch—school ... SC-3
West Bertie Sch—school ... NC-3
West Berwick—uninc pl ... PA-2
West Bessemer Church ... AL-4
West Bethany—pop pl ... NY-2
West Bethany—pop pl ... PA-2
West Bethany Cem—cemetery ... KS-7
West Bethany Ch—church ... KS-7
West Bethany Ch—church ... SD-7
West Bethel—pop pl ... ME-1
West Bethel Ch—church ... MN-6
West Bethel Community Hall—building ... KS-7
West Bethesda—pop pl ... MD-2
West Bethesda Ch—church ... OH-6
West Bethlehem Ch—church ... TX-5
West Bethlehem HS—school ... PA-2
West Bethlehem (Township of)—pop pl ... PA-2
West Bexar (CCD)—cens area ... TX-5
West B F Windmill—locale ... TX-5
West Bicknell Pond—reservoir ... UT-8
West Big Creek—stream ... KS-7
West Big Foot Gas Field—oilfield ... TX-5
West Big Rock Cem—cemetery ... IL-6
West Bijou Creek—stream ... CO-8
West Billerica—pop pl ... MA-1
West Bills Creek—stream ... OK-5
West Biloxi—uninc pl ... MS-4
West Biloxi Community Center—building ... MS-4
West Biloxi Library—building ... MS-4
West Bingham—locale ... PA-2
West Birch Creek—stream (2) ... OR-9
Westbird Center (Shop Ctr)—locale ... FL-3
West Birdville Sch—school ... TX-5
West Birdwood Creek—stream ... NE-7
West Birmingham—pop pl ... AL-4
West Bitter Creek ... CO-8
West Bitter Creek ... UT-8
West Bitter Creek—stream ... OK-5
West Bitter Creek—stream ... TX-5
West Black Bay Oil and Gas Field—oilfield ... LA-4
West Blackburn Fork—stream ... TN-4
West Black Butte Rsvr—reservoir ... OR-9
West Black Creek Ch—church ... MS-4
West Black Hollow Mine—mine ... TN-4
West Black Ledge—bar ... ME-1
West Black Oak ... AR-4
West Black Ridge—ridge ... UT-8
West Black Rock—island ... ME-1
West Black Rock Rsvr—reservoir ... CA-9
West Blacktail Creek—stream ... MT-8
West Bladenboro Ch—church ... NC-3
West Blakely—pop pl ... WA-9
West Bliss Sch—school ... MI-6
West Blocton—pop pl ... AL-4
West Blocton (CCD)—cens area ... AL-4
West Blocton Division—civil ... AL-4
West Blocton Elem Sch—school ... AL-4
West Blocton HS—school ... AL-4
West Blocton Water Works—building ... AL-4
West Bloomfield—pop pl ... NY-2
West Bloomfield—pop pl ... WI-6
West Bloomfield HS—school ... MI-6
West Bloomfield-Orchard Lake—pop pl ... MI-6
West Bloomfield (Town of)—pop pl ... NY-2
West Bloomfield (Township of)—civ div ... MI-6
West Blossburg (historical)—locale ... AL-4
West Blossburg Mine (underground)—mine ... AL-4
West Blue—fmr MCD ... NE-7
West Blue Ch—church ... NE-7
West Blue Creek ... IA-7
West Bluegrass Creek—stream ... WY-8
West Blue Lake—lake ... AZ-5
West Blue Mounds Creek ... WI-6
West Blue Mtn—summit ... NM-5
West Blue River ... NE-7
West Blue Township—pop pl (2) ... NE-7
West Bluff—cliff ... MI-6
West Bluff—cliff ... WI-6
West Bluff—pop pl ... TX-5
West Bluff—ridge ... WI-6
West Bluff Bay—bay ... NC-3
West Bluff Hist Dist—hist pl ... IL-6
West Bluff Windmill—locale ... TX-5
West Blvd Interchange—crossing ... AZ-5
West Blvd Sch—school ... MO-7
West Blvd Sch—school ... OH-6
West Blvd Subdivision—pop pl ... UT-8
West Blyville Sch—school ... NE-7
West Bob Smith Creek—stream ... ID-8
West Boca Place (Shop Ctr)—locale ... FL-3
West Boettcher Ditch—canal ... CO-8
West Boggs Creek—stream ... IN-6
West Boggs Creek Dam—dam ... IN-6
West Boggs Creek Lake ... IN-6
West Boggs Lake—reservoir ... IN-6
West Boggs Park—park ... IN-6
West Boggy Bayou—stream ... AR-4
West Boggy Creek—stream ... OK-5
West Boggy Hollow ... MS-4
West Boggy Hollow Creek—stream ... MS-4
West Bogue Chitto—stream ... LA-4
West Bogue Chitto—stream ... MS-4
West Bogue Chitto River ... MS-4
West Bogue Hasty—stream ... MS-4
West Boise JHS—school ... ID-8
West Bolivar—pop pl ... PA-2
West Bologna Canyon—valley ... OR-9
West Bolton—pop pl ... VT-1
West Bona Site—hist pl ... GU-9
West Bonetraill—pop pl ... ND-7
West Boone Draw ... CO-8
West Boone Draw—valley ... CO-8
West Boone Prairie Ch—church ... TX-5
West Boone Township—pop pl ... MO-7
West Booneville Ch of Christ—church ... MS-4
West Boone Windmill—locale ... TX-5
West Boothbay ... ME-1
West Boothbay Harbor—pop pl ... ME-1
West Boot Lake—lake ... MN-6
West Boro—hospital ... MA-1
Westboro ... MA-1
Westboro—pop pl ... MD-2
Westboro—pop pl ... MO-7
Westboro—pop pl ... OH-6
Westboro—pop pl ... WI-6
Westboro—uninc pl ... KS-7
Westboro—uninc pl ... NJ-2
Westboro, Town of ... MA-1
Westboro Country Club—locale ... MA-1
West Boron Sch—school ... CA-9
Westboro Park—park ... KS-7
Westboro (RR name for Westborough)—other ... MA-1
Westboro Rsvr—reservoir ... MA-1
Westboro Shop Ctr—locale ... KS-7
Westboro Shopping Plaza—locale ... MA-1
Westboro (Town of)—pop pl ... WI-6
Westborough—pop pl ... MA-1
Westborough—pop pl ... TN-4
Westborough, Town of ... MA-1
Westborough Centre ... MA-1
Westborough Country Club—other ... MO-7
Westborough JHS—school ... MA-1
Westborough Reservoir ... MA-1
Westborough (RR name Westboro)—CDP ... MA-1
Westborough (Town of)—pop pl ... MA-1
Westboro (West Lebanon)—pop pl ... NH-1
West Bosshart Coulee—valley ... MT-8
West Bottom—pop pl ... VA-3
West Boulder Canyon—valley ... AZ-5
West Boulder Creek ... ID-8
West Boulder Creek—stream ... CA-9
West Boulder Divide—ridge ... MT-8
West Boulder Draw—valley ... UT-8
West Boulder Lake—lake ... CA-9
West Boulder Lake—lake ... MT-8
West Boulder Meadows—flat ... MT-8
West Boulder Plateau—plain ... MT-8
West Boulder Point—cliff ... UT-8
West Boulder Ranger Station—locale ... MT-8
West Boulder River—stream ... MT-8
West Boulder Sch—school ... MT-8
West Boulder Trail—trail ... AZ-5
West Bouldin Creek—stream ... TX-5
West Boundary Street Hist Dist—hist pl ... SC-3
West Boundary Trail—trail ... ID-8
West Boundary Truck Trail—trail ... CA-9
West Bountiful—pop pl ... UT-8
West Bourbon Elem Sch—school ... KS-7
West Bourland Mtn—summit ... TX-5
Westbourne ... OH-6
Westbourne—locale ... TN-4
Westbourne—pop pl ... VA-3
Westbourne Post Office (historical)—building ... TN-4
Westbourne Sch (historical)—school ... TN-4
Westbourne (subdivision)—pop pl ... NC-3
West Bow Creek—stream ... NE-7
West Bowdoin—pop pl ... ME-1
West Bowie—uninc pl ... MD-2
West Bowie Creek—stream ... MS-4
West Bowie Interchange—crossing ... AZ-5
West Bowie Union Ch—church ... TX-5
West Bowman—unorg reg ... ND-7
West Bowmans—pop pl ... PA-2
West Bowmanstown ... PA-2
West Bowmanstown—other ... PA-2
West Box Elder—cens area ... UT-8
West Box Elder Creek—stream ... NE-7
West Box Elder Division—civil ... UT-8
West Boxford—pop pl ... MA-1
West Boylston—pop pl ... AL-4
West Boylston—pop pl ... MA-1
West Boylston HS—school ... MA-1
West Boylston Sch—school ... MA-1
West Boylston (Town of)—pop pl ... MA-1
West Br ... DE-2
West Bradenton Baptist Ch—church ... FL-3
West Bradenton Ch—church ... FL-3
West Bradenton (Rosedale)—CDP ... FL-3
West Bradford—pop pl ... PA-2
West Bradford Cem—cemetery ... VT-1
West Bradford Elem Sch—school ... PA-2
West Bradford (Township of)—pop pl ... PA-2
West Bradley Brook—stream ... CT-1
West Bradley (CCD)—cens area ... TN-4
West Bradley Division—civil ... TN-4
West Bradley Well—well ... NM-5
West Braintree—pop pl ... VT-1
West Branch ... AR-4
West Branch ... CO-8
West Branch ... HI-9
West Branch ... ME-1
West Branch ... MA-1
West Branch ... MI-6
West Branch ... MN-6
West Branch ... MS-4
West Branch ... PA-2
West Branch—canal (2) ... MI-6
West Branch—channel ... CT-1
West Branch—channel ... ME-1
West Branch—pop pl ... IA-7
West Branch—pop pl ... MI-6
West Branch—pop pl ... NY-2
West Branch—pop pl ... PA-2
West Branch—pop pl ... VT-1
West Branch—stream ... AR-4
West Branch—stream ... MA-1
West Branch—stream ... MO-7
West Branch—stream ... NE-7
West Branch—stream ... NH-1
West Branch—stream (2) ... NC-3
West Branch—stream (2) ... TN-4
West Branch Abbott Brook—stream ... NH-1
West Branch Acoaksett River ... MA-1
West Branch Alamo Creek—stream ... CA-9
West Branch Alder Stream—stream ... ME-1
West Branch Allagash Stream—stream ... ME-1
West Branch Alum Creek—stream ... OH-6
West Branch Amazon Brook—stream ... ME-1
West Branch Anderson Creek—stream ... MI-6
West Branch Antelope Creek—stream ... ND-7
West Branch Antietam Creek—stream ... PA-2
West Branch Apple Creek—stream ... ND-7
West Branch Armstrong Creek—stream ... MI-6
West Branch Armstrong Creek—stream ... WI-6
West Branch Ash Creek ... NE-7
West Branch Ash Creek—stream ... SD-7
West Branch Ash Swale—stream ... OR-9
West Branch Ashtabula River—stream ... OH-6
West Branch Atkins Brook—stream ... ME-1
West Branch Ausable River—stream ... NY-2
West Branch Bantam River—stream ... CT-1
West Branch Baptism River—stream ... MN-6
West Branch Baraboo River—stream ... WI-6
West Branch Barnetts Creek—stream ... GA-3
West Branch Barney Creek—stream ... OK-5
West Branch Baron Fork—stream ... OK-5
West Branch Bass River—stream ... NJ-2
West Branch Batten Kill—stream ... VT-1
West Branch Bear Creek—stream ... KS-7
West Branch Bear Creek—stream ... NC-3
West Branch Bear Creek—stream ... TN-4
West Branch Beaver Brook—stream ... ME-1
West Branch Beaver Brook—stream ... NH-1
West Branch Beaver Creek ... MN-6
West Branch Beaver Creek—stream ... WI-6
West Branch Beaver Dam Creek ... IA-7
West Branch Beaverdam Creek—stream ... IA-7
West Branch Beaver Dam Creek—stream ... SD-7
West Branch Beaver Riv ... MN-6
West Branch Beaver River—stream ... MN-6
West Branch Beaver River—stream ... NY-2
West Branch Beech Creek ... PA-2
West Branch Beer Kill—stream ... NY-2
West Branch Ben Glazier Brook—stream ... ME-1
West Branch Big Canyon—valley ... CO-8
West Branch Big Creek—stream (2) ... MI-6
West Branch Big Creek—stream ... WI-6
West Branch Big Eau Pleine River—stream ... WI-6
West Branch Big Elk Creek—stream ... PA-2
West Branch Big Lost River ... ID-8
West Branch Big Musquash Stream—stream ... ME-1
West Branch Big Rock Creek—stream ... IL-6
West Branch Big Run—stream ... PA-2
West Branch Biloxi River ... MS-4
West Branch Black Creek—stream ... LA-4
West Branch Black Creek—stream (2) ... NY-2
West Branch Blackfoot Canal—canal ... ID-8
West Branch Black River—stream ... OH-6
West Branch Black Stream—stream ... ME-1
West Branch Blockhouse Creek—stream ... FL-3
West Branch Blue Creek—stream ... IA-7
West Branch Blue Earth River—stream ... IA-7
West Branch Blue Earth River—stream ... MN-6
West Branch Blue Jay Creek ... PA-2
West Branch Bluejay Creek—stream ... PA-2
West Branch Bluelick Run—stream ... MD-2
West Branch Blue Mounds Creek—stream ... WI-6
West Branch Bluff Creek—stream ... KS-7
West Branch Bog Brook—stream ... ME-1
West Branch Boone Creek—stream ... OK-5
West Branch Boyd Creek—stream ... SC-3
West Branch Brandy Brook—stream ... ME-1
West Branch Brandywine Creek—stream ... PA-2
West Branch Briar Creek—stream ... PA-2
West Branch Bridge—bridge ... CA-9
West Branch Bridge Creek—stream ... OR-9
West Branch Brighton Canal—canal ... UT-8
West Branch Brook ... RI-1
West Branch Brook—stream ... MA-1
West Branch Brook—stream ... NH-1
West Branch Bruce Lake Trail—trail ... PA-2
West Branch Brush Creek—stream ... TN-4
West Branch Bucktooth Run—stream ... NY-2
West Branch Buffalo Creek—stream ... IA-7
West Branch Buffalo Creek—stream ... TN-4
West Branch Bug Creek—stream ... MN-6
West Branch Bull Creek—stream ... SD-7
West Branch Bull Run Creek—stream ... TN-4
West Branch Bullskin Creek—stream ... OH-6
West Branch Bunch Ditch ... IN-6
West Branch Bunch Ditch—canal ... IN-6
West Branch Buttahatchee River—stream ... AL-4
West Branch Butte Creek—stream ... CA-9
West Branch Butternut Brook—stream ... CT-1
West Branch Buttrick Creek ... IA-7
West Branch Cahoochie Creek—stream ... MO-7
West Branch Caldwell Creek—stream ... PA-2
West Branch California Aqueduct—canal ... CA-9
West Branch Camas Creek ... ID-8
West Branch Camp—locale ... CA-9
West Branch Campground—locale ... MI-6
West Branch Canal—canal ... ID-8
West Branch Caney Creek—stream ... OK-5
West Branch Canopus Creek—stream ... NY-2
West Branch Canyon Creek—stream ... CA-9
West Branch Carrabassett River—stream ... ME-1
West Branch Carry Brook—stream ... ME-1
West Branch Carter Creek—stream ... OR-9
West Branch Cascade Creek—stream ... PA-2
West Branch Caulks Creek—stream ... MO-7
West Branch Cayuga Inlet—stream ... NY-2
West Branch Cazenovia Creek—stream ... NY-2
West Branch Cedar Creek—stream ... AR-4
West Branch Cedar Creek—stream ... MI-6
West Branch Cedar River ... MI-6
West Branch Cedar River—stream (2) ... MI-6
West Branch Cedar Run—stream ... PA-2
West Branch Cedar Stream—stream ... NH-1
West Branch Cem—cemetery ... IA-7
West Branch Cem—cemetery ... KS-7
West Branch Cem—cemetery (2) ... MI-6
West Branch Cem—cemetery ... MN-6
West Branch Cem—cemetery (2) ... OH-6
West Branch Cem—cemetery ... OR-9
West Branch Cem—cemetery ... PA-2
West Branch Cem—cemetery ... WI-6
West Branch Ch—church ... MN-6
West Branch Ch—church ... NC-3
West Branch Chapman Creek ... KS-7
West Branch Charbonneau Creek—stream ... ND-7
West Branch Chase Brook—stream ... ME-1
West Branch Chester Creek—stream ... MN-6
West Branch Chester Creek—stream ... PA-2
West Branch Chigley Sandy Creek—stream ... OK-5
West Branch Chillisquaque Creek—stream ... PA-2
West Branch Chippewa River—stream ... MI-6
West Branch Chocolay River—stream ... MI-6
West Branch Christina River—stream ... DE-2
West Branch Christina River—stream ... MD-2
West Branch Clam River—stream ... MI-6
West Branch Clarion Creek ... PA-2
West Branch Clarion River—stream ... PA-2
West Branch Clark Fork—stream ... MO-7
West Branch Clay Creek—stream ... NE-7
West Branch Clear Creek—stream ... CA-9
West Branch Clear Creek—stream ... IN-6
West Branch Clear Creek—stream ... TX-5
West Branch Clear Gulch—valley ... CA-9
West Branch Clear Stream—stream ... NH-1
West Branch Clearwater Brook—stream ... ME-1
West Branch Cloquet River—stream ... MN-6
West Branch Clovis Ditch—canal ... CA-9
West Branch Codorus Creek ... PA-2
West Branch Codorus Creek—stream ... PA-2
West Branch Cohansey River—stream ... NJ-2
West Branch Cold Brook—stream ... ME-1
West Branch Colorado River—stream ... TX-5
West Branch Commercial Hist Dist—hist pl ... IA-7
West Branch Conestoga River—stream ... PA-2
West Branch Conewango Creek—stream ... NY-2
West Branch Conneaut Creek—stream ... PA-2
West Branch Conococheague Creek—stream ... PA-2
West Branch Coon Creek—stream ... MO-7
West Branch Cooper River—stream ... SC-3
West Branch Copperas Creek—stream ... IL-6
West Branch Coral Creek—stream ... FL-3
West Branch Corrotoman ... VA-3
West Branch Coulee—valley ... MT-8
West Branch County Line Brook—stream ... NY-2
West Branch Cow Creek—stream ... CO-8
West Branch Cowley Run—stream ... PA-2
West Branch Coxes Creek—stream ... PA-2
West Branch Crabgrass Creek—stream ... FL-3
West Branch Crawford Creek—stream ... MO-7
West Branch Creek ... KS-7
West Branch Creek ... OK-5
West Branch Creek ... OR-9
West Branch Creek ... WI-6
West Branch Creek—stream ... NY-2
West Branch Creek—stream ... OH-6
West Branch Crooked Arroyo—stream ... CO-8
West Branch Crooked Creek ... MN-6
West Branch Crooked Creek—stream ... IN-6
West Branch Cross Creek—stream ... CA-9
West Branch Croton River—stream ... NY-2
West Branch Crow Creek—stream ... CA-9
West Branch Cussewago Creek—stream ... PA-2
West Branch Cuyahoga River—stream ... OH-6
West Branch Daily Creek—stream ... MT-8
West Branch Davis Creek—stream ... KS-7
West Branch Davis Stream—stream ... ME-1
West Branch Days River—stream ... MI-6
West Branch Dayton Lateral—canal ... CO-8
West Branch Dead Creek—stream ... VT-1
West Branch Dead Diamond—stream ... NH-1
West Branch Dead Stream—stream ... ME-1
West Branch Deer Creek—stream ... ID-8
West Branch Deer Creek—stream ... MI-6
West Branch Deer Creek—stream ... NY-2
West Branch Deer Creek—stream ... PA-2
West Branch Deerfield River—stream ... VT-1
West Branch Deer River—stream ... NY-2
West Branch Delaware River—stream ... NY-2
West Branch Delaware River—stream ... PA-2
West Branch Denham Stream—stream ... ME-1
West Branch Denomie Creek—stream ... WI-6
West Branch Des Moines River ... IA-7
West Branch Des Moines River ... MN-6
West Branch Des Moines River ... MO-7
West Branch Devers Canal—canal ... TX-5
West Branch Dingman Run—stream ... PA-2
West Branch Ditch ... DE-2
West Branch Dobbins Creek—stream ... CA-9
West Branch Dolet Bayou—stream ... LA-4
West Branch Douglas Creek—stream ... ND-7
West Branch Downie River—stream ... CA-9
West Branch Dragoon Creek—stream ... WA-9
West Branch Drake Brook—stream ... ME-1
West Branch Drummer Creek—stream ... IL-6
West Branch Dry Creek—stream ... KS-7
West Branch Dry Creek—stream ... VA-3
West Branch Dry Fork La Prele Creek ... WY-8
West Branch Dry Hollow—valley ... CO-8
West Branch Duck Creek ... MI-6
West Branch Duck Creek—stream ... MI-6
West Branch Duck River ... MI-6
West Branch Du Page River—stream ... IL-6
West Branch Dyberry Creek—stream ... PA-2
West Branch Eagle River—stream ... MI-6
West Branch East Canada Creek—stream ... NY-2
West Branch Eastern River—stream ... ME-1
West Branch East Fork Pond River ... KY-4

West Branch Eau Claire River—*stream* WI-6
*West Branch Eau Pleine River* WI-6
West Branch Egypt Stream—*stream* ME-1
West Branch El Dorado Canyon—*valley* CA-9
West Branch Elem Sch—*school* (2) PA-2
West Branch Elizabeth River—*stream* NJ-2
West Branch Elk Creek—*stream* OR-9
West Branch Elk River—*stream* WA-9
West Branch Ellis River—*stream* ME-1
West Branch Elm Creek—*stream* KS-7
West Branch English River—*stream* NY-2
West Branch Enoch Brook—*stream* ME-1
West Branch Escanaba River—*stream* MI-6
*West Branch Evergreen River* WI-6
West Branch Extension—*canal* MI-6
West Branch Fall Creek—*stream* TN-4
West Branch Fall River—*stream* KS-7
West Branch Falls—*falls* MI-6
West Branch Falls Creek—*stream* OR-9
West Branch Farmington River—*stream* CT-1
West Branch Farmington River—*stream* MA-1
West Branch Fawn Brook—*stream* CT-1
West Branch Feather River—*stream* CA-9
West Branch Fence River—*stream* MI-6
West Branch Fever Brook—*stream* MA-1
West Branch Fife Creek—*stream* CA-9
West Branch Finn Ditch—*canal* MT-8
West Branch Firesteel Creek—*stream* SD-7
West Branch Firesteel River—*stream* MI-6
West Branch Fish Creek—*stream* IN-6
West Branch Fish Creek—*stream* (2) MI-6
West Branch Fish Creek—*stream* NY-2
*West Branch Fishing Creek* PA-2
West Branch Fishing Creek—*stream* AL-4
West Branch Fishing Creek—*stream* (2) PA-2
West Branch Flat Creek—*stream* AR-4
West Branch Floodwood River—*stream* MN-6
West Branch Floyd River—*stream* IA-7
West Branch Fond Du Lac River—*stream* WI-6
West Branch Ford River—*stream* MI-6
West Branch Fortythree Creek—*stream* MN-6
West Branch Fourmile Creek—*stream* NY-2
West Branch Fox River—*stream* MI-6
West Branch Freeman Run—*stream* PA-2
West Branch French Creek—*stream* CA-9
West Branch French Creek—*stream* NY-2
West Branch French Creek—*stream* PA-2
West Branch Furlong Creek—*stream* MI-6
West Branch Galloway Creek—*stream* MO-7
West Branch Galls Creek—*stream* OR-9
West Branch Genesee River—*stream* PA-2
West Branch Georges Creek—*stream* PA-2
West Branch Gillman Creek—*stream* NY-2
West Branch Gogomain River—*stream* MI-6
*West Branch Gold Creek* CO-8
West Branch Goodnow River—*stream* NY-2
West Branch Goose Creek—*stream* ID-8
*West Branch Grannys Creek* VA-3
West Branch Grannys Creek—*stream* VA-3
West Branch Grant Creek—*stream* KS-7
West Branch Great Brook—*stream* NY-2
West Branch Green River—*stream* MA-1
West Branch Greenville Creek—*stream* OH-6
West Branch Guard Station—*locale* CA-9
West Branch Gulf Stream—*stream* ME-1
West Branch Gulliver Brook—*stream* ME-1
*West Branch Gulpha Creek* AR-4
West Branch Gum Branch—*stream* DE-2
West Branch Gypsum Creek—*stream* KS-7
West Branch Gypsy Creek—*stream* WA-9
West Branch Halfaday Creek—*stream* MI-6
*West Branch Hams Fork* WY-8
West Branch Handsome Brook—*stream* NY-2
*West Branch Harraseeket River* ME-1
West Branch Hathaway Creek—*stream* CA-9
West Branch Hay Creek—*stream* MN-6
West Branch Hay Creek—*stream* WI-6
West Branch Heald Creek—*stream* MI-6
*West Branch Held Creek* MI-6
West Branch Helm Colonial Ditch—*canal* CA-9
West Branch Hemlock River—*stream* MI-6
West Branch Hendrie River—*stream* MI-6
West Branch Herbert Run—*stream* MD-2
West Branch Hickey Creek—*stream* MI-6
West Branch Hickory Creek—*stream* MS-4
West Branch Hicks Run—*stream* PA-2
West Branch Highway—*channel* MI-6
West Branch Hog Creek—*stream* OK-5
West Branch Honey Creek—*stream* IL-6
West Branch Honokane Iki Stream—*stream* HI-9
West Branch Honokane Nui Stream—*stream* HI-9
West Branch Hopkins Creek—*stream* CA-9
West Branch Horse Creek—*stream* (2) IL-6
West Branch Horse Creek—*stream* SD-7
West Branch Hot Brook—*stream* ME-1
*West Branch Housatonic River* MA-1
West Branch Housatonic River—*stream* MA-1
West Branch Housatonic River Rsvr—*reservoir* MA-1
West Branch HS—*school* OH-6
West Branch HS—*school* PA-2
West Branch HS (abandoned)—*school* PA-2
West Branch Huerhuero Creek—*stream* CA-9
West Branch Humboldt Creek—*stream* KS-7
West Branch Humbug Creek—*stream* CA-9
West Branch Huntley Brook—*stream* ME-1
West Branch Huron River—*stream* MI-6
West Branch Huron River—*stream* OH-6
West Branch Hurricane Creek—*stream* IL-6
West Branch Hurricane Creek—*stream* TN-4
*West Branch Indian Creek* CA-9
*West Branch Indian Creek* IA-7
West Branch Indian Creek—*stream* (3) CA-9
West Branch Indian Creek—*stream* IL-6
West Branch Indian Creek—*stream* PA-2
West Branch Indian Stream—*stream* NH-1
West Branch Iowa River—*stream* IA-7
West Branch Iron River—*stream* MI-6
West Branch Jasper Creek—*stream* MS-4
West Branch JHS—*school* OH-6
West Branch Jumbo River—*stream* MI-6
*West Branch Kersey Run* PA-2
West Branch Kettle River—*stream* MN-6
West Branch Keuka Lake—*lake* NY-2
West Branch Key Creek—*stream* AK-9
West Branch Knife River—*stream* MN-6
West Branch Knights Creek—*stream* WI-6
West Branch Knob Creek—*stream* MO-7
West Branch Knoll And Kneale Drain—*canal* MI-6
West Branch Lackawanna River—*stream* PA-2
West Branch Lackawaxen River—*stream* PA-2
West Branch Lac qui Parle River—*stream* MN-6
West Branch Lac qui Parle River—*stream* SD-7
West Branch Lake—*lake* MI-6
West Branch Lakeland Canal—*canal* CA-9
West Branch Lakes—*lake* (3) MI-6
West Branch Lamarsh Creek—*stream* IL-6
West Branch Lampee Canal—*canal* CA-9
West Branch Laramie River—*stream* CO-8
West Branch Last Chance Ditch—*canal* CA-9
West Branch Lateral—*canal* CA-9
West Branch Laughing Water Creek—*stream* NE-7
West Branch Laughing Whitefish River—*stream* MI-6
West Branch Laurel Run—*stream* MD-2
West Branch Leadmine Brook—*stream* CT-1
*West Branch LeClerc Creek* WA-9
West Branch LeClerc Creek—*stream* WA-9
West Branch Lick Creek—*stream* NC-3
West Branch Lick Run—*stream* PA-2
West Branch Lick Run Trail—*trail* PA-2
West Branch Lights Creek—*stream* CA-9
West Branch Lightwood Knot Creek—*stream* FL-3
*West Branch Lime Creek* NE-7
West Branch Limestone Creek—*stream* NY-2
*West Branch Little Antietam Creek* PA-2
West Branch Little Black River—*stream* ME-1
West Branch Little Black River—*stream* WI-6
West Branch Little Conestoga Creek—*stream* PA-2
West Branch Little Dead Diamond River—*stream* NH-1
West Branch Little Hocking River—*stream* OH-6
West Branch Little Kennebec Bay—*bay* ME-1
West Branch Little Magalloway River—*stream* ME-1
West Branch Little Magalloway River—*stream* NH-1
West Branch Little Molunkus Stream—*stream* ME-1
West Branch Little Muncy Creek—*stream* PA-2
West Branch Little Muskegon River—*stream* MI-6
West Branch Little Neshannock Creek—*stream* PA-2
West Branch Little Northeast Creek—*stream* MD-2
West Branch Little Pine Creek—*stream* WI-6
West Branch Little River—*stream* NY-2
West Branch Little River—*stream* VT-1
*West Branch Little Rock River* MN-6
West Branch Little Sandy Creek—*stream* KS-7
West Branch Little Sioux River—*stream* IA-7
West Branch Little Spokane River—*stream* WA-9
*West Branch Little Sugar River* WI-6
West Branch Little Sugar River—*stream* WI-6
West Branch Little Wabash River—*stream* IL-6
West Branch Little Walnut Creek—*stream* OH-6
West Branch Little Yellow River—*stream* WI-6
West Branch Little Youngs Creek—*stream* WY-8
West Branch Live Oak Creek—*stream* TX-5
*West Branch Lizard Creek* IA-7
West Branch Llagas Creek—*stream* CA-9
West Branch Lockes Creek—*stream* MS-4
West Branch Long John Creek—*stream* OR-9
West Branch Long Lake Creek—*stream* ND-7
*West Branch Long Pine Creek* NE-7
*West Branch Lost Creek* AL-4
West Branch Lost Creek—*stream* MO-7
West Branch Lost Creek—*stream* OH-6
West Branch Louse Creek—*stream* NE-7
West Branch Lowney Creek—*stream* MI-6
*West Branch Lynnhaven River* VA-3
West Branch Lyon Creek—*stream* KS-7
West Branch Machias River—*stream* ME-1
West Branch Mad Island Slough—*stream* TX-5
West Branch Mad River—*stream* NH-1
West Branch Magalloway River—*stream* ME-1
West Branch Magalloway River—*stream* NH-1
West Branch Mahantango Creek—*stream* PA-2
West Branch Mahoning River—*stream* OH-6
West Branch Mall Creek—*stream* KS-7
West Branch Mamaroneck River—*stream* NY-2
West Branch Manistique River—*stream* MI-6
*West Branch Maple River* MI-6
West Branch Maple River—*stream* MI-6
West Branch Mare Creek—*stream* FL-3
West Branch Marshall Creek—*stream* WI-6
West Branch Marsh Run—*stream* MD-2
West Branch Martin Canal—*canal* ID-8
West Branch Mattagodus Stream—*stream* ME-1
West Branch Mattawamkeag River—*stream* ME-1
West Branch McCutcheon Creek—*stream* MI-6
*West Branch McGowers Creek* MS-4
West Branch Meander Creek—*stream* OH-6
West Branch Meshoppen Creek—*stream* PA-2
West Branch Middle Branch Escanaba River—*stream* MI-6
West Branch Middle Branch River—*stream* MI-6
West Branch Middle Brook—*stream* NJ-2
West Branch Middle Creek—*stream* MD-2
West Branch Millard Canyon—*valley* CA-9
West Branch Millberry Brook—*stream* ME-1
West Branch Mill Brook—*stream* ME-1
West Branch Mill Brook—*stream* NH-1
West Branch Mill Creek—*stream* (2) CA-9
West Branch Mill Creek—*stream* IA-7
West Branch Mill Creek—*stream* KS-7
West Branch Mill Creek—*stream* MO-7
West Branch Mill Creek—*stream* PA-2
West Branch Mill Creek—*stream* WI-6
West Branch Mill Pond—*reservoir* WI-6
West Branch Mill River—*stream* MA-1
West Branch Millstone Creek—*stream* PA-2
West Branch Milwaukee River—*stream* WI-6
West Branch Minnehaha Creek—*stream* MI-6
West Branch Misery Stream—*stream* ME-1
West Branch Missisquoi River—*stream* VT-1
*West Branch Mitchigan Creek* MI-6
West Branch Mitchigan River—*stream* MI-6
West Branch Mohawk River—*stream* NH-1
West Branch Mohawk River—*stream* NY-2
West Branch Molunkus Stream—*stream* ME-1
West Branch Mongaup River—*stream* NY-2
West Branch Montgomery Creek—*stream* PA-2
*West Branch Moose Creek* PA-2
*West Branch Moose River* MN-6
West Branch Moose River—*stream* ME-1
West Branch Moose River—*stream* VT-1
West Branch Mosquito Creek—*stream* IN-6
West Branch Mosquito Creek—*stream* KS-7
*West Branch Mounds Creek* WI-6
West Branch Mountain Creek—*stream* NC-3
West Branch Mount Creek—*stream* VA-3
West Branch Mud Brook—*stream* ME-1
*West Branch Mud Creek* IN-6
*West Branch Murphy Creek* MI-6
West Branch Murray Run—*stream* PA-2
West Branch Muskegon River—*stream* MI-6
*West Branch Musquash River* ME-1
*West Branch Musquash Stream* ME-1
*West Branch Mustinka River* MN-6
West Branch Naaman Creek—*stream* PA-2
West Branch Naked Creek—*stream* VA-3
West Branch Naked Creek Trail—*trail* VA-3
West Branch Narcelle Creek—*stream* SD-7
West Branch Narraguagus River—*stream* (2) ME-1
West Branch Nash Stream—*stream* ME-1
West Branch Naugatuck River—*stream* CT-1
West Branch Nelson Creek—*stream* CA-9
West Branch Nelson Creek—*stream* MI-6
*West Branch Nelson Run* PA-2
West Branch Nescatunga Creek—*stream* KS-7
West Branch Neshaminy Creek—*stream* PA-2
West Branch Net River—*stream* MI-6
*West Branch Neversink Creek* NY-2
West Branch Neversink River—*stream* NY-2
West Branch Newman Creek—*stream* WA-9
West Branch New Stream—*stream* ME-1
West Branch Nezinscot River—*stream* ME-1
West Branch Nimishillen Creek—*stream* OH-6
West Branch North Branch Nippersink Creek—*stream* WI-6
West Branch North Branch Patapsco River—*stream* MD-2
*West Branch North Carrizo Creek* CO-8
West Branch North Fork Elkhorn River—*stream* NE-7
West Branch North Fork Indian Creek—*stream* CA-9
West Branch North Fork Little Snake River—*stream* WY-8
West Branch North Fork Smith River—*stream* OR-9
West Branch North River—*stream* MA-1
*West Branch Nuckolls Creek* CO-8
West Branch Oak Creek—*stream* KS-7
West Branch Octoraro Creek—*stream* PA-2
*West Branch of Apple Creek* ND-7
*West Branch Of Big Blue River* NE-7
*West Branch of Big West Branch Escanaba River* MI-6
*West Branch of Fish Creek* MI-6
*West Branch of Martins Creek* PA-2
*West Branch Of Miami River* OH-6
*West Branch Of The Farmington River* CT-1
*West Branch of the South Branch of the Paw Paw River* MI-6
*West Branch of West River* VT-1
West Branch Ogontz River—*stream* MI-6
*West Branch Oil Creek - in part* PA-2
West Branch Oil Field—*other* MI-6
West Branch Okannatie Creek—*stream* MS-4
West Branch Ompompanoosuc River—*stream* VT-1
West Branch One Hundred and Two River—*stream* IA-7
West Branch Onion River—*stream* MN-6
West Branch Onondaga Creek—*stream* NY-2
West Branch Ontonagon River—*stream* MI-6
*West Branch Oswegatchie River* NY-2
West Branch Oswegatchie River—*stream* NY-2
West Branch Otego Creek—*stream* NY-2
West Branch Otsdawa Creek—*stream* NY-2
*West Branch Otter Creek* IA-7
West Branch Otter River—*stream* MI-6
*West Branch Overpeck Creek* NJ-2
West Branch Owego Creek—*stream* NY-2
West Branch Owl Creek—*stream* IN-6
West Branch Oyster Bayou—*gut* LA-4
West Branch Oyster River—*stream* ME-1
West Branch Pack River—*stream* ID-8
West Branch Paint Creek—*stream* MI-6
West Branch Painter Creek—*stream* KY-4
West Branch Painter Run—*stream* PA-2
West Branch Palmer River—*stream* MA-1
West Branch Panther Creek—*stream* IL-6
West Branch Panther Creek—*stream* IA-7
West Branch Papakating Creek—*stream* NJ-2
*West Branch Papillion Creek* NE-7
West Branch Park—*locale* OH-6
West Branch Parks Creek—*stream* PA-2
West Branch Passadumkeag River—*stream* ME-1
West Branch Passumpsic River—*stream* VT-1
*West Branch Paw Paw River* MI-6
West Branch Peabody River—*stream* NH-1
West Branch Penobscot River—*stream* ME-1
West Branch Pequonnock River—*stream* CT-1
West Branch Perkiomen Creek—*stream* PA-2
West Branch Perry Creek—*stream* IA-7
West Branch Peshekee River—*stream* MI-6
West Branch Peshtigo Brook—*stream* WI-6
West Branch Peshtigo River—*stream* WI-6
West Branch Pete Creek—*stream* WY-8
West Branch Phillips Brook—*stream* NH-1
West Branch Phillips Creek—*stream* TN-4
West Branch Picnic Area—*locale* MI-6
*West Branch Pigeon River* MI-6
West Branch Pine Arroyo—*valley* CO-8
West Branch Pine Creek—*stream* IL-6
West Branch Pine Creek—*stream* IA-7
West Branch Pine Creek—*stream* (2) PA-2
West Branch Pine Creek—*stream* UT-8
*West Branch Pine River* MI-6
West Branch Pine River—*stream* MI-6
West Branch Pine River—*stream* WI-6
*West Branch Pine Run* PA-2
West Branch Pinos Creek—*stream* CO-8
West Branch Piscasaw Creek—*stream* IL-6
West Branch Piscasaw Creek—*stream* WI-6
West Branch Piscataquis River—*stream* ME-1
*West Branch Pleasant River* ME-1
West Branch Pleasant River—*stream* (3) ME-1
West Branch Plum Creek—*stream* WI-6
West Branch Pocwock Stream—*stream* ME-1
*West Branch Pond River* KY-4
West Branch Potato Creek—*stream* PA-2
West Branch Potter Ravine—*valley* CA-9
*West Branch Prairie Creek* KS-7
*West Branch Prairie Creek* OH-6
West Branch Prairie Creek—*stream* OH-6
*West Branch Presque Isle River* WI-6
West Branch Presque Isle River—*stream* MI-6
West Branch Presque Isle Stream—*stream* ME-1
West Branch Price Creek—*stream* NC-3
*West Branch Priest River* ID-8
West Branch Queens Run—*stream* PA-2
West Branch Raccoon Creek—*stream* OH-6
West Branch Rainey Brook—*stream* ME-1
West Branch Ranch Creek—*stream* OK-5
West Branch Rattlesnake Creek—*stream* OH-6
West Branch Rattlesnake Creek—*stream* WA-9
West Branch Rattling Creek—*stream* PA-2
West Branch Rausch Creek—*stream* PA-2
West Branch Raven Stream—*stream* MN-6
West Branch Red Brook—*stream* CT-1
West Branch Red Brook—*stream* ME-1
West Branch Red Cedar River—*stream* MI-6
West Branch Red Clay Creek—*stream* PA-2
West Branch Red Dirt Creek—*stream* CO-8
West Branch Red River—*stream* WI-6
*West Branch Reservoir* MA-1
*West Branch Reservoir* OH-6
West Branch Richards Run—*stream* PA-2
West Branch Richfield Canal—*canal* CO-8
*West Branch Rifle River* MI-6
West Branch Rifle River—*stream* MI-6
West Branch Ripogenus Stream—*stream* ME-1
*West Branch River* MN-6
West Branch River—*stream* MI-6
West Branch Roaring Run—*stream* PA-2
West Branch Roberts Creek—*stream* IA-7
West Branch Rock Creek—*stream* KS-7
West Branch Rock Creek—*stream* OR-9
*West Branch Rock River* NC-3
West Branch Rock River—*stream* WI-6
West Branch Rocky River—*stream* NC-3
West Branch Rocky River—*stream* OH-6
West Branch Root River Canal—*canal* WI-6
West Branch Rosebud Creek—*stream* SD-7
West Branch Rousseau Creek—*stream* SD-7
*West Branch Rsvr* CT-1
West Branch Rsvr—*reservoir* CT-1
West Branch Rsvr—*reservoir* NY-2
West Branch Rum River—*stream* MN-6
West Branch Run—*stream* PA-2
West Branch Russian Gulch—*valley* CA-9
West Branch Sacandaga River—*stream* NY-2
West Branch Saddle River—*stream* NJ-2
West Branch Sage Creek Drain—*canal* ID-8
West Branch Sage River—*stream* MI-6
West Branch Saint Francis River—*stream* MN-6
West Branch Saint Joseph River—*stream* MI-6
West Branch Saint Joseph River—*stream* OH-6
West Branch Saint Regis River—*stream* NY-2
West Branch Salmon Brook—*stream* CT-1
West Branch Salmon Brook—*stream* ME-1
West Branch Salmon Trout River—*stream* MI-6
West Branch Salt Creek—*stream* IL-6
*West Branch Salt Fork* IL-6
West Branch Salvia Wash—*stream* CA-9
West Branch Sam Creek—*stream* OR-9
West Branch Sandy Creek—*stream* IL-6
West Branch Sandy Creek—*stream* NY-2
*West Branch Sandy Hook Ditch* IN-6
West Branch Sandy Stream—*stream* ME-1
West Branch Santa Cruz River—*stream* AZ-5
West Branch Sante River—*stream* MI-6
West Branch San Vicente Creek—*stream* CA-9
West Branch Saugatuck River—*stream* CT-1
West Branch Sawtelle Brook—*stream* ME-1
West Branch Sawyer Drain—*canal* MI-6
West Branch Sch—*school* IL-6
West Branch Sch—*school* KS-7
West Branch Sch—*school* (2) MI-6
West Branch Sch—*school* NE-7
*West Branch Schuylkill River* PA-2
West Branch Schuylkill River—*stream* PA-2
West Branch Scribner Creek—*stream* KS-7
West Branch Seboeis Stream—*stream* ME-1
*West Branch Sebois Stream* ME-1
West Branch Sees Creek—*stream* MO-7
West Branch Shabakunk Creek—*stream* NJ-2
*West Branch Shade River* OH-6
West Branch Shade River—*stream* OH-6
West Branch Sheepscot River—*stream* ME-1
*West Branch Shepaug River* CT-1
West Branch Shepaug River—*stream* CT-1
West Branch Sherrette Creek—*stream* AK-9
West Branch Shioc River—*stream* WI-6
*West Branch Shonkin Creek* MT-8
West Branch Short Creek—*stream* KS-7
West Branch Short Creek*—*stream* ND-7
West Branch Sideling Hill Creek—*stream* PA-2
West Branch Sidnaw Creek—*stream* MI-6
West Branch Silver Creek—*stream* MN-6
West Branch Silvermine River—*stream* NY-2
West Branch Simms Stream—*stream* NH-1
West Branch Simpson Creek—*stream* WV-2
West Branch Sippican River—*stream* MA-1
*West Branch Sippican River* MA-1
West Branch Skippack Creek—*stream* PA-2
West Branch Skunk Creek—*stream* SD-7
West Branch Smith Ferry Canal—*canal* CA-9
*West Branch Snake Creek* SD-7
West Branch Snake River Valley Canal—*canal* ID-8
West Branch Soda Creek—*stream* CA-9
West Branch Soldier Creek—*stream* SD-7
West Branch Sopchoppy River—*stream* FL-3
West Branch Soquel Creek—*stream* CA-9
West Branch Souadabscook Stream—*stream* ME-1
West Branch South Cedar Creek—*stream* IA-7
West Branch South Elm Creek—*stream* KS-7
West Branch South Fork Big Creek—*stream* MT-8
West Branch South Fork Clear Creek—*stream* ID-8
West Branch South Fork South Eden Canyon—*valley* UT-8
*West Branch South Fork Zumbro River* MN-6
West Branch South Prong Alafia River—*stream* FL-3
West Branch Southwest Prong Slocum Creek—*stream* NC-3
West Branch Spencer Stream—*stream* ME-1
West Branch Spring Creek—*stream* NE-7
West Branch Spruce Run—*stream* PA-2
West Branch Squaconning Creek—*stream* MI-6
West Branch Squa Pan Inlet—*stream* ME-1
West Branch Squaw Creek—*stream* MO-7
West Branch Squaw Creek—*stream* OR-9
West Branch Squeak Brook—*stream* NY-2
West Branch Steels Fork Horse Creek—*stream* CO-8
West Branch Stevenson Drain—*canal* MI-6
West Branch Stony Creek—*stream* MI-6
West Branch Stony Fork—*stream* PA-2
West Branch Struve Slough—*stream* CA-9
West Branch Sturgeon River—*stream* (4) MI-6
West Branch Suamico River—*stream* WI-6
West Branch Sucker River—*stream* MI-6
West Branch Sugar Creek—*stream* IL-6
West Branch Sugar Creek—*stream* IA-7
West Branch Sugar Creek—*stream* KY-4
West Branch Sugar Creek—*stream* (2) PA-2
West Branch Sugar River—*stream* NY-2
West Branch Sugar River—*stream* WI-6
West Branch Sunday Creek—*stream* OH-6
West Branch Sunrise River—*stream* MN-6
West Branch Susquehanna River—*stream* PA-2
West Branch Swartz Creek—*stream* MI-6
West Branch Swift Brook—*stream* ME-1
West Branch Swift River—*stream* ME-1
West Branch Swift River—*stream* MA-1
West Branch Taku Glacier—*glacier* AK-9
West Branch Teaspoon Creek—*stream* MI-6
West Branch Tenmile River—*stream* ME-1
West Branch Third Creek—*stream* KS-7
West Branch Thirtytwo Mile Creek—*stream* NE-7
West Branch Thompson Brook—*stream* ME-1
West Branch Thompson Creek—*stream* NE-7
West Branch Thoroughfare Brook—*stream* ME-1
*West Branch Thoroughfare Stream* ME-1
West Branch Threemile Creek—*stream* MO-7
West Branch Thumb Run—*stream* VA-3
West Branch Tickfaw River—*stream* MS-4
West Branch Tinklepaugh Creek—*stream* PA-2
West Branch Tionesta Creek—*stream* PA-2
West Branch Tioughnioga Creek—*stream* NY-2
West Branch Tioughnioga River—*stream* NY-2
West Branch Tittabawassee River—*stream* MI-6
West Branch Tomjack Creek—*stream* PA-2
West Branch Toms Run—*stream* PA-2
West Branch Tontogany Creek—*stream* OH-6
West Branch Township—*fmr MCD* IA-7
**West Branch Township**—*pop pl* KS-7
**West Branch (Township of)**—*pop pl* (4) MI-6
**West Branch (Township of)**—*pop pl* PA-2
West Branch Trail—*trail* CO-8
West Branch Trail—*trail* PA-2
West Branch Trail Creek—*stream* IN-6
West Branch Troublesome Creek—*stream* KS-7
West Branch Trout Brook—*stream* NY-2
West Branch Trout Creek—*stream* NY-2
West Branch Trout River—*stream* NY-2
West Branch Tully River—*stream* MA-1
West Branch Tunungwant Creek—*stream* PA-2
*West Branch Turkey Creek* KS-7
West Branch Turkey Creek—*stream* KS-7
West Branch Turkey Creek*—*stream* NE-7
West Branch Turkey Creek—*stream* NE-7
West Branch Turkey Creek*—*stream* NE-7
West Branch Turkey Creek—*stream* NE-7
West Branch Turkey River—*stream* IA-7
*West Branch Tweed River* VT-1
West Branch Tweed River—*stream* VT-1
West Branch Twelve Mile Creek—*stream* IN-6
West Branch Twelvemile Creek—*stream* KS-7
West Branch Twelvemile Creek—*stream* MN-6
West Branch Twentyfour Mile Creek—*stream* MI-6
*West Branch Twin Creek* MI-6
West Branch Two Hearted River—*stream* MI-6
West Branch Twomile Run—*stream* PA-2
West Branch Umcolcus Stream—*stream* ME-1
West Branch Unadilla River—*stream* NY-2
West Branch Union River—*stream* ME-1
West Branch Upper Ammonoosuc River—*stream* NH-1
West Branch Upper Rainy River—*stream* MI-6
West Branch Ute Creek—*stream* CO-8
West Branch Van Campen Creek—*stream* NY-2
*West Branch Vermilion River* IL-6
*West Branch Vermillion River* IL-6
West Branch Vernooy Kill—*stream* NY-2
West Branch Victoria Canal—*canal* CA-9
West Branch Village Brook—*stream* NH-1
West Branch Wading River—*stream* NJ-2
West Branch Waiska River—*stream* MI-6
West Branch Walburn Run—*stream* PA-2
West Branch Walker Brook—*stream* MA-1
West Branch Wallenpaupack Creek—*stream* PA-2
West Branch Wallis Run—*stream* PA-2
West Branch Walnut Creek—*stream* NC-3
West Branch Walnut River—*stream* KS-7
West Branch Wapsinonoc Creek—*stream* IA-7
West Branch War Creek—*stream* SD-7
West Branch Wards Fork Creek—*stream* VA-3
West Branch Ware River—*stream* MA-1
West Branch Warner River—*stream* NH-1
*West Branch Warroad River* MN-6
West Branch Warroad River—*stream* MN-6
West Branch Weiser River—*stream* ID-8
West Branch Wesserunsett Stream—*stream* ME-1
West Branch West Crockett Branch—*stream* OR-9
*West Branch Westfield River* MA-1
West Branch Westfield River—*stream* MA-1
West Branch Westport River—*stream* MA-1
*West Branch West River* VT-1
West Branch West Salt Creek—*stream* CO-8
West Branch Wheelock Brook—*stream* ME-1
West Branch Whistle Creek—*stream* WY-8
West Branch White Clay Creek—*stream* PA-2
West Branch White Creek—*stream* IN-6
West Branch Whitefish River—*stream* MI-6
West Branch White Oak Creek—*stream* TX-5
*West Branch White River* IN-6
*West Branch White River* VT-1
West Branch White River—*stream* VT-1
West Branch White River—*stream* WI-6
West Branch Whitewater Creek—*stream* KS-7
*West Branch Whitewater River* IN-6
West Branch Whitewater River—*stream* KS-7
West Branch Whitney Creek—*stream* PA-2
West Branch Wild Horse Creek—*stream* KS-7
West Branch Willard Stream—*stream* VT-1
*West Branch Williams Creek* IN-6
West Branch Willow Creek—*stream* MI-6
West Branch Willow Creek—*stream* OR-9
West Branch Willow Creek—*stream* (2) SD-7
West Branch Willow Creek—*stream* WY-8
West Branch Winters Run—*stream* MD-2
*West Branch Wolf* OH-6
West Branch Wolf Creek—*stream* KS-7
West Branch Wolf Creek—*stream* OH-6
West Branch Wolf Creek—*stream* OK-5
West Branch Wolfe Creek—*stream* AL-4
*West Branch Wolf River* WI-6
West Branch Wolf River—*stream* WI-6
West Branch Wormley Creek—*stream* VA-3
West Branch Wynoochee River—*stream* WA-9
*West Branch Yellow Creek* PA-2
West Branch Zippel Creek—*stream* MN-6
*West Branch Zipple Creek* MN-6
**West Brandywine (Township of)**—*pop pl* PA-2
**West Brattleboro**—*pop pl* VT-1
West Brazos (CCD)—*cens area* TX-5
West Breakwater—*other* CT-1
West Breedlove Well—*well* NM-5
West Bremen—*locale* GA-3
**West Brentwood**—*pop pl* NH-1
**West Brentwood (Pilgrim State Hospital)**—*pop pl* NY-2
West Brevard (CCD)—*cens area* FL-3
**West Brewster**—*pop pl* MA-1
*Westbriar* IN-6
**Westbriar**—*pop pl* VA-3
Westbriar Sch—*school* VA-3
**Westbriar (subdivision)**—*pop pl* (2) AZ-5
West Brick Sch—*school* MI-6
West Brick Sch—*school* WI-6
West Bridge—*bridge* FL-3
West Bridge—*bridge* NH-1
Westbridge—*locale* MO-7
West Bridge Creek—*stream* KS-7
**West Bridge Junction**—*pop pl* LA-4
West Bridger Basin—*basin* WY-8
West Bridger Creek—*stream* MT-8
West Bridger Creek—*stream* WY-8
West Bridger Station—*locale* MT-8
**Westbridge (subdivision)**—*pop pl* NC-3
*West Bridgewater* PA-2
**West Bridgewater**—*pop pl* MA-1
**West Bridgewater**—*pop pl* VT-1
*West Bridgewater Centre* MA-1
**West Bridgewater (corporate and RR name Bridgewater)**—*pop pl* PA-2
West Bridgewater (historical P.O.)—*locale* MA-1
West Bridgewater HS—*school* MA-1
West Bridgewater Post Office—*building* PA-2
West Bridgewater Station (historical)—*locale* MA-1
**West Bridgewater (Town of)**—*pop pl* MA-1
West Bridgton—*locale* ME-1
West Bridport—*locale* VT-1
**West Brighton**—*pop pl* NY-2
**West Brimfield**—*pop pl* MA-1
West Bristol—*locale* ME-1
**West Bristol**—*pop pl* PA-2
West Bristol Cem—*cemetery* ME-1
West Britton—*locale* SD-7
*West Britton Station* SD-7
West Britts Landing—*locale* TN-4
West Broad Channel—*channel* NY-2
*West Broad Church* TN-4
West Broad Street Hist Dist—*hist pl* SC-3
West Broad Street Sch—*school* GA-3
West Broad Street Sch—*school* OH-6
*West Broadway* IA-7
West Broadway Baptist Ch—*church* TN-4
*West Broadway Ch* TN-4
Westbrock Funeral Home—*hist pl* OH-6
West Bronc Tank—*reservoir* NM-5
West Bronc Windmill—*locale* NM-5
*West Brook* CT-1
*West Brook* MA-1
Westbrook—*locale* AL-4
West Brook—*locale* KY-4
Westbrook—*locale* NC-3
Westbrook—*locale* (2) TX-5
**Westbrook**—*pop pl* CT-1
**Westbrook**—*pop pl* GA-3
**Westbrook**—*pop pl* ME-1
**Westbrook**—*pop pl* MA-1
**Westbrook**—*pop pl* MN-6
**West Brook**—*pop pl* NC-3
**Westbrook**—*pop pl* TN-4
**Westbrook**—*pop pl* TX-5
**Westbrook**—*pop pl* WA-9
West Brook—*stream* (4) CT-1
West Brook—*stream* IN-6
West Brook—*stream* (5) ME-1
West Brook—*stream* (8) MA-1
West Brook—*stream* (2) NJ-2
West Brook—*stream* (8) NY-2
West Brook—*stream* VT-1
Westbrook, John C., House—*hist pl* TX-5
*West Brook Acres* IN-6
*Westbrook Beach* CT-1
Westbrook Bridge—*bridge* VA-3
Westbrook (CCD)—*cens area* TX-5
Westbrook Cem—*cemetery* MS-4
Westbrook Cem—*cemetery* NY-2
Westbrook Cem—*cemetery* NC-3

Westbrook Cem—*cemetery* ... PA-2
Westbrook Cem—*cemetery* ... TN-4
Westbrook Cem—*cemetery* (3) ... TX-5
**Westbrook Center (census name Westbrook)**—*pop pl* ... CT-1
Westbrook Ch—*church* ... TN-4
Westbrook College Hist Dist—*hist pl* ... ME-1
Westbrook Country Club—*other* ... KS-7
Westbrook Creek—*stream* ... GA-3
Westbrook Creek—*stream* ... KY-4
Westbrook Creek—*stream* ... MS-4
West Brook Creek—*stream* ... TX-5
Westbrook Creek—*stream* ... TX-5
**Westbrook Crossroads**—*pop pl* ... NC-3
*West Brook Deer Creek* ... MI-6
**West Brook Downs**—*pop pl* ... IN-6
Westbrook Draw—*valley* ... SD-7
*Westbrook Estates* ... IL-6
**Westbrook Estates (subdivision)**—*pop pl* ... UT-8
*West Brookfield* ... OH-6
**West Brookfield**—*pop pl* ... MA-1
**West Brookfield**—*pop pl* ... NY-2
**West Brookfield**—*pop pl* ... OH-6
**West Brookfield**—*pop pl* ... VT-1
West Brookfield State For—*forest* ... MA-1
**West Brookfield (Town of)**—*pop pl* ... MA-1
West Brookfield Windmill—*locale* ... TX-5
**Westbrook Forest (subdivision)**—*pop pl* ... NC-3
Westbrook Glacier—*glacier* ... AK-9
Westbrook Harbor—*bay* ... CT-1
Westbrook HS—*hist pl* ... ME-1
Westbrook HS—*school* ... GA-3
West Brook JHS—*school* ... NJ-2
Westbrook Junior Coll—*school* ... ME-1
**West Brooklin**—*pop pl* ... ME-1
**West Brookline**—*pop pl* ... NH-1
**West Brooklyn**—*pop pl* ... IL-6
West Brooklyn (Election Precinct)—*fmr MCD* ... IL-6
Westbrook Mart Shop Ctr—*locale* ... MS-4
Westbrook Memorial Cem—*cemetery* ... MS-4
Westbrook Mtn—*summit* ... KY-4
Westbrook Nazarene Ch—*church* ... IN-6
Westbrook Park—*park* (2) ... FL-3
Westbrook Park—*park* ... OH-6
**Westbrook Park**—*pop pl* (2) ... PA-2
Westbrook Park Elem Sch—*school* ... PA-2
**Westbrook Park Subdivision**—*pop pl* ... UT-8
West Brook Pond—*reservoir* ... NY-2
Westbrook Psychiatric Hosp—*hospital* ... VA-3
West Brook Rsvr—*reservoir* ... CT-1
West Brook Rsvr—*reservoir* ... MA-1
Westbrook Run—*stream* ... VA-3
Westbrook Sch—*school* (2) ... IL-6
Westbrook Sch—*school* ... MD-2
Westbrook Sch—*school* ... MI-6
Westbrook Sch—*school* ... MS-4
Westbrook Sch—*school* ... NY-2
Westbrook Sch—*school* ... TN-4
Westbrook Sch—*school* ... UT-8
*West Brooks Lake* ... PA-2
Westbrooks (Township of)—*fmr MCD* ... NC-3
**Westbrook (subdivision)**—*pop pl* ... NC-3
**Westbrook Subdivision**—*pop pl* (3) ... UT-8
**West Brooksville**—*pop pl* ... ME-1
**Westbrook (Town of)**—*pop pl* ... CT-1
**Westbrook (Township of)**—*pop pl* ... MN-6
Westbrook Valley—*airport* ... NJ-2
*West Brook Village* ... IL-6
**Westbrook Village (subdivision)**—*pop pl* (2) ... AZ-5
**Westbrookville**—*pop pl* (2) ... NY-2
West Brookwood True Gospel Ch—*church* ... AL-4
West Broomy Valley Tank—*reservoir* ... AZ-5
West Brother Island—*island* ... AK-9
West Brothers Mine—*mine* ... TN-4
**West Brow**—*pop pl* ... GA-3
West Broward Hosp—*hospital* ... FL-3
West Broward Shop Ctr—*locale* ... FL-3
West Brow Chapel—*church* ... GA-3
West Brow Lake—*reservoir* ... GA-3
West Brown Cow—*island* ... ME-1
West Brownfield—*locale* ... ME-1
West Brownlee Creek—*stream* ... ID-8
*West Brownsville* ... PA-2
**West Brownsville**—*pop pl* ... PA-2
West Brownsville Borough—*civil* ... PA-2
**West Brownsville Junction**—*pop pl* ... PA-2
West Brown Tank—*reservoir* (2) ... AZ-5
*West (Br. P.O.name for West Hollywood)* ... CA-9
West Brule Creek—*stream* ... SD-7
**West Brunswick**—*pop pl* ... NJ-2
**West Brunswick (Township of)**—*pop pl* ... PA-2
West Brush Creek—*stream* (3) ... CO-8
West Brush Creek—*stream* ... KS-7
West Brush Creek—*stream* ... MO-7
West Brush Creek—*stream* ... NV-8
West Brush Creek—*stream* ... OK-5
West Brush Creek—*stream* ... OR-9
West Brush Lateral—*canal* ... CO-8
West Brushy Branch—*stream* ... TX-5
West Brushy Canyon—*valley* ... AZ-5
West Brushy Canyon Tank—*reservoir* ... AZ-5
West Brushy Creek—*stream* ... MO-7
West Brushy Sch—*school* ... IL-6
West Buchanan Well—*well* ... TX-5
West Buck Creek—*stream* ... IA-7
West Buck Creek—*stream* ... OK-5
West Buckeye Creek—*stream* ... MT-8
West Buckhorn Draw—*valley* ... WY-8
*West Buck Island* ... MA-1
West Buck Rsvr—*reservoir* ... CO-8
West Buckskin Tank—*reservoir* ... AZ-5
West Buckskin Trail—*trail* ... AZ-5
West Buck Trap Windmill—*locale* ... NM-5
West Bude Oil Field—*oilfield* ... MS-4
**West Buechel**—*pop pl* ... KY-4
West Buena Vista Park—*park* ... FL-3
West Buffalo Cem—*cemetery* ... NC-3
West Buffalo Cem—*cemetery* ... OH-6
West Buffalo Creek—*stream* (2) ... KS-7
West Buffalo Creek—*stream* ... MT-8
West Buffalo Creek—*stream* (2) ... NE-7
West Buffalo Creek—*stream* ... NC-3
West Buffalo Creek—*stream* ... OK-5
West Buffalo Creek—*stream* ... TX-5
West Buffalo Ditch—*canal* ... CO-8
West Buffalo Peak—*summit* ... CO-8
**West Buffalo (Township of)**—*pop pl* ... PA-2
West Buhach Lateral—*canal* ... CA-9
West Buies Creek—*stream* ... NC-3
West Buker Spring—*spring* ... OR-9
West Bull Canyon—*valley* ... CA-9
West Bull Creek—*stream* ... SD-7
West Bull Creek—*stream* ... TX-5
West Bull Creek—*stream* (2) ... WY-8
West Bull Gulch—*valley* ... CO-8
West Bull Pasture Windmill—*locale* ... TX-5
West Bull Spring Tank—*reservoir* ... TX-5
West Buncombe Sch—*school* ... NC-3
West Bunker Peak Wash—*stream* ... NV-8
West Burbank Creek—*stream* ... ID-8
West Burbank Creek—*stream* ... WY-8
West Bureau Consolidated Sch—*school* ... IL-6
West Bureau Creek—*stream* ... IL-6
Westburg Townhall—*building* ... IA-7
Westburg Township—*fmr MCD* ... IA-7
**West Burke**—*pop pl* ... VT-1
West Burkett Windmill—*locale* ... TX-5
West Burleigh—*unorg reg* ... ND-7
West Burlington—*locale* ... CO-8
West Burlington—*locale* ... PA-2
**West Burlington**—*pop pl* ... IA-7
**West Burlington**—*pop pl* ... NY-2
**West Burlington**—*pop pl* ... NC-3
West Burlington Cem—*cemetery* ... MI-6
West Burlington Extension Ditch—*canal* ... CO-8
**West Burlington (Township of)**—*pop pl* ... PA-2
West Burns Valley—*valley* ... MN-6
West Burnsville Ch—*church* ... NC-3
West Burn Tank—*reservoir* ... AZ-5
West Burnt Creek—*stream* ... MT-8
West Burnt Log Spring—*spring* ... OR-9
West Burr Oak Creek—*stream* ... IA-7
*Westbury* ... IL-6
Westbury—*locale* ... TX-5
**Westbury**—*pop pl* ... MN-6
**Westbury**—*pop pl* (2) ... NY-2
**Westbury**—*pop pl* ... PA-2
Westbury Hosp—*hospital* ... TX-5
Westbury HS—*school* ... NY-2
Westbury HS—*school* ... TX-5
Westbury Lake—*lake* ... SC-3
Westbury Park—*park* ... TX-5
Westbury Sch—*school* ... NY-2
Westbury Shop Ctr—*locale* ... AL-4
**Westbury South**—*pop pl* ... NY-2
*Westbury Station* ... NY-2
**Westbury (subdivision)**—*pop pl* ... AL-4
**Westbury (subdivision)**—*pop pl* ... NC-3
Westbury Temple—*church* ... NY-2
**West Bush**—*pop pl* ... NY-2
*West Bush Lake* ... WI-6
West Butler—*locale* ... AL-4
**West Butler**—*pop pl* ... NY-2
**West Butte**—*pop pl* (2) ... CA-9
West Butte—*summit* (2) ... CA-9
West Butte—*summit* ... ID-8
West Butte—*summit* (3) ... MT-8
West Butte—*summit* (2) ... OR-9
West Butte—*summit* ... WA-9
West Butte—*unorg reg* ... SD-7
West Butte Dam—*dam* ... SD-7
West Buttercreek Airp—*airport* ... OR-9
West Butte Ridge—*ridge* ... WA-9
West Butte Rsvr—*reservoir* ... OR-9
West Buttes—*summit* ... NV-8
West Butte Well Number 1—*well* ... NV-8
West Butte Well Number 2—*well* ... NV-8
West Buttons—*other* ... AK-9
West Buttress—*ridge* ... AK-9
West Buttrick Creek—*stream* ... IA-7
**West Buxton**—*pop pl* ... ME-1
West Buzzard Point—*cliff* ... AZ-5
**Westby**—*pop pl* ... MT-8
**Westby**—*pop pl* (2) ... ND-7
**Westby**—*pop pl* ... WI-6
Westby Lake—*lake* ... ND-7
West Byron Cem—*cemetery* ... ME-1
Westby Sch—*school* ... WI-6
Westby Sch Center—*school* ... MT-8
**Westby Township**—*pop pl* ... ND-7
West Cabanne Place Hist Dist—*hist pl* ... MO-7
West Cabin Community Center—*locale* ... OK-5
West Cabin Creek—*stream* ... MT-8
West Cache Canal—*canal* ... ID-8
West Cache Canal—*canal* ... UT-8
West Cache Creek—*stream* ... OK-5
West Cache Creek Oil Field—*oilfield* ... OK-5
*West Cache Ditch* ... AR-4
West Cache River Ditch—*canal* ... AR-4
West Cache River Slough—*stream* ... AR-4
West Cactus Flat—*flat* ... CO-8
*West Caddo Butte* ... TX-5
West Caddo Creek—*stream* ... TX-5
West Caddo Peak—*summit* ... TX-5
West Cady Creek—*stream* ... WA-9
West Cady Ridge—*ridge* ... WA-9
**West Caldwell**—*pop pl* ... NJ-2
West Caldwell HS—*school* ... NC-3
West Caldwell Industrial Park—*locale* ... NJ-2
**West Caldwell (Township of)**—*pop pl* ... NJ-2
*West Calico* ... MS-4
**West Caln (Township of)**—*pop pl* ... PA-2
West Calvary Baptist Ch—*church* ... MS-4
West Calvary Ch—*church* ... NC-3
West Calvert Ch—*church* ... AL-4
West Camas—*cens area* ... ID-8
West Camas Creek—*stream* ... ID-8
West Cambridge—*locale* ... NY-2
West Cambridge—*uninc pl* ... MA-1
*West Cambridge, Town of* ... MA-1
*West Camden* ... DE-2
West Camden Creek—*stream* ... NY-2
West Camden Heights—*uninc pl* ... AR-4
**West Cameron**—*pop pl* ... NY-2
**West Cameron**—*pop pl* ... PA-2
**West Cameron (Township of)**—*pop pl* ... PA-2
**West Camilla**—*pop pl* ... GA-3
West Camp—*locale* ... AZ-5
West Camp—*locale* ... CA-9
West Camp—*locale* (3) ... NM-5
West Camp—*locale* (4) ... TX-5
**West Camp**—*pop pl* ... NY-2
West Campbell Branch—*stream* ... TX-5
West Campbell Creek—*stream* ... CO-8
West Campbell Ditch—*canal* ... NV-8
West Campbell Draw—*valley* ... WY-8
West Campbell Sch—*school* ... MO-7
West Campbell Sch—*school* ... SD-7
West Camp Bend—*bend* ... TX-5
West Camp Branch—*stream* ... NC-3
West Camp Cem—*cemetery* ... TX-5
West Camp Ch—*church* ... MS-4
West Camp Clarke—*fmr MCD* ... NE-7
West Camp Creek—*stream* ... OR-9
West Camp Lake—*lake* ... TX-5
*West Camp Missionary Baptist Ch* ... MS-4
West Camp Tank No 1—*reservoir* ... NM-5
West Camp Tank No 3—*reservoir* ... NM-5
**West Campton**—*pop pl* ... NH-1
West Campus HS—*school* ... CA-9
West Camp Well—*well* ... NV-8
West Camp Well—*well* ... NM-5
West Camp Windmill—*locale* ... TX-5
**West Canaan**—*pop pl* ... NH-1
**West Canaan**—*pop pl* ... OH-6
West Canaan Ch—*church* ... TN-4
West Canada Creek—*stream* ... NY-2
West Canada Lakes—*lake* ... NY-2
West Canada Mtn—*summit* ... NY-2
West Canadian (CCD)—*cens area* ... OK-5
**West Canadice Corners**—*pop pl* ... NY-2
West Canal—*canal* (4) ... CA-9
West Canal—*canal* ... CO-8
West Canal—*canal* (2) ... ID-8
West Canal—*canal* ... KS-7
West Canal—*canal* ... NV-8
West Canal—*canal* ... NJ-2
West Canal—*canal* ... NY-2
West Canal—*canal* ... OK-5
West Canal—*canal* (3) ... OR-9
West Canal—*canal* ... TX-5
West Canal—*canal* (2) ... UT-8
West Canal—*canal* ... WA-9
West Canal Ancho (historical)—*canal* ... AZ-5
West Canal Park—*park* ... NY-2
West Candor—*locale* ... NY-2
West Cane Creek—*stream* ... GA-3
West Cane Creek—*stream* ... TN-4
West Cane Island—*island* ... TX-5
West Caney Branch—*stream* ... LA-4
West Caney Creek—*stream* (2) ... TX-5
West Canfield Butte—*summit* ... ID-8
West Canfield Hist Dist—*hist pl* ... MI-6
*West Canon* ... UT-8
**West Canton**—*pop pl* ... NC-3
West Canyon—*valley* (2) ... CA-9
West Canyon—*valley* (2) ... CO-8
West Canyon—*valley* (3) ... NM-5
West Canyon—*valley* (6) ... UT-8
West Canyon—*valley* ... WY-8
West Canyon Canal—*canal* ... ID-8
West Canyon Creek—*stream* ... AZ-5
West Canyon Creek—*stream* ... WY-8
West Canyon Picnic Grounds—*park* ... AZ-5
West Canyon Wash—*valley* ... UT-8
West Cape—*cape* ... AK-9
West Cape—*cape* ... FM-9
**West Cape May**—*pop pl* ... NJ-2
West Capitol Street Hist Dist—*hist pl* ... MS-4
West Captain Creek—*stream* ... OK-5
West Carancahua Creek—*stream* ... TX-5
West Carbon (RR name for Winifrede)—*other* ... WV-2
West Caribou Island—*island* ... MI-6
**West Carlisle**—*pop pl* ... MI-6
**West Carlisle**—*pop pl* (2) ... OH-6
**West Carlisle**—*pop pl* ... TX-5
**West Carlisle (Carlisle)**—*pop pl* ... TX-5
West Carlisle Sch—*school* ... OH-6
**West Carlsbad**—*pop pl* ... NM-5
West Caroga Lake—*lake* ... NY-2
West Carolina Creek—*stream* ... TX-5
West Carpenter Canyon—*valley* ... WY-8
West Carrizo Creek—*stream* ... CO-8
West Carroll Lake—*lake* ... WY-8
**West Carroll Parish**—*pop pl* ... LA-4
*West Carrollton* ... OH-6
**West Carrollton**—*pop pl* ... OH-6
**West Carrollton City**—*pop pl* ... OH-6
West Carrollton HS—*school* ... OH-6
West Carrollton (Township of)—*other* ... OH-6
**West Carroll (Township of)**—*pop pl* ... PA-2
West Carrol Township Water Sewer Authority Dam—*dam* ... PA-2
West Carry Camp—*locale* ... ME-1
West Carrying Place Cove—*bay* ... ME-1
West Carry Pond—*lake* ... ME-1
West Carson—*CDP* ... CA-9
West Carson Canyon—*valley* ... CA-9
*West Carson River* ... NV-8
**West Carteret**—*pop pl* ... NJ-2
West Carteret HS—*school* ... NC-3
West Carteret (West Carteret-Woodbridge)—*uninc pl* ... NJ-2
West Carteret-Woodbridge (West Carteret)—*uninc pl* ... NJ-2
West Carter Lake—*lake* ... MS-4
**West Carthage**—*pop pl* ... NY-2
West Carthage Point Oil Field—*oilfield* ... MS-4
West Cary JHS—*school* ... NC-3
West Casitas Pass—*gap* ... CA-9
West Castine—*locale* ... ME-1
Westcastle Sch—*school* ... IA-7
**West Castleton**—*pop pl* ... VT-1
West Catahoula Lake Oil Field—*oilfield* ... LA-4
West Cataract Creek—*stream* ... AZ-5
West Cataract Creek Dam—*dam* ... AZ-5
**West Catasauqua**—*pop pl* ... PA-2
West Cat Canyon—*valley* ... NV-8
West Cathance Stream—*stream* ... ME-1
West Catnip Spring—*spring* ... NV-8
**West Caton**—*pop pl* ... NY-2
West Catskill—*uninc pl* ... NY-2
West Cattle Creek—*stream* ... OK-5
West Cave—*cave* ... TN-4
West Cay—*island* ... VI-3
West (CCD)—*cens area* ... TX-5
West Cedar Cem—*cemetery* ... KS-7
*West Cedar Creek* ... NE-7
West Cedar Creek—*stream* ... AZ-5
West Cedar Creek—*stream* ... AR-4
West Cedar Creek—*stream* ... IA-7
West Cedar Creek—*stream* (3) ... KS-7
West Cedar Grove Rsvr—*reservoir* ... UT-8
West Cedar (historical)—*locale* ... KS-7
West Cedar Mountain Tank—*reservoir* ... AZ-5
West Cedar Mtn—*summit* ... AZ-5
**West Cedar Rapids**—*pop pl* ... IA-7
West Cedar Sch—*school* ... IA-7
**West Cedartown**—*pop pl* ... GA-3
West Cedar Valley Cem—*cemetery* ... NE-7
West Cem—*cemetery* (2) ... AL-4
West Cem—*cemetery* (2) ... AR-4
West Cem—*cemetery* ... CA-9
West Cem—*cemetery* (6) ... CT-1
West Cem—*cemetery* (2) ... GA-3
West Cem—*cemetery* (3) ... IL-6
West Cem—*cemetery* ... IN-6
West Cem—*cemetery* (3) ... IA-7
West Cem—*cemetery* ... KY-4
West Cem—*cemetery* (2) ... LA-4
West Cem—*cemetery* (8) ... MA-1
West Cem—*cemetery* (2) ... MI-6
West Cem—*cemetery* ... MN-6
West Cem—*cemetery* ... MS-4
West Cem—*cemetery* ... NH-1
West Cem—*cemetery* ... NM-5
West Cem—*cemetery* ... NY-2
West Cem—*cemetery* ... NC-3
West Cem—*cemetery* (3) ... OH-6
West Cem—*cemetery* (4) ... OK-5
West Cem—*cemetery* (2) ... SD-7
West Cem—*cemetery* (12) ... TN-4
West Cem—*cemetery* ... TX-5
West Cem—*cemetery* ... VT-1
West Cem—*cemetery* (2) ... VA-3
West Cem—*cemetery* ... WV-2
*West Cemetery* ... SD-7
West Cemetery, The—*cemetery* ... NY-2
West Center Canal—*canal* ... ID-8
West Center Cem—*cemetery* (2) ... MA-1
West Center City Day Care Nursery, Incorporated—*school* ... DE-2
West Center Harbor—*harbor* ... NH-1
**West Center Harbor**—*pop pl* ... NH-1
West Center Sch—*school* ... ID-8
West Center Sch—*school* ... IL-6
West Center Sch (abandoned)—*school* ... MO-7
*West Center Street Elementary School* ... AL-4
West Center Street Sch—*school* ... AL-4
West Center Tank—*reservoir* ... NM-5
West Center Township—*civil* ... KS-7
West Central Elem Sch—*school* ... IN-6
West Central Franklin (Unorganized Territory of)—*unorg* ... ME-1
West Central Hist Dist—*hist pl* ... IN-6
West Central Hist Dist—*hist pl* ... MS-4
West Central HS—*school* ... IA-7
West Central JHS—*school* ... IN-6
West Central Perkins—*unorg reg* ... SD-7
West Central Sch—*school* (2) ... FL-3
West Central Sch—*school* ... MO-7
West Central Senior HS—*school* ... IN-6
West Central Shop Ctr—*locale* ... FL-3
West Ch—*church* ... IL-6
West Ch—*church* ... SC-3
West Ch—*church* ... SD-7
West Chain Lake—*lake* ... OR-9
West Chairback Pond—*lake* ... ME-1
West Champagne Bay—*bay* ... LA-4
West Champoeg Creek—*stream* ... OR-9
West Chandler—*locale* ... AZ-5
West Chandler RR Station—*building* ... AZ-5
West Channel—*canal* ... WY-8
West Channel—*channel* (4) ... AK-9
West Channel—*channel* ... CA-9
West Channel—*channel* (2) ... FL-3
West Channel—*channel* (2) ... NY-2
West Channel—*channel* ... NC-3
West Channel—*channel* (2) ... WI-6
West Channel—*channel* (2) ... FM-9
West Channel Hayward Strait—*channel* ... AK-9
West Channel Island—*island* ... AK-9
West Channel Uinta River—*stream* ... UT-8
West Chapel—*church* ... KY-4
West Chapel—*church* ... MS-4
West Chapel—*church* ... NC-3
West Chapel—*church* ... SC-3
West Chapel—*church* ... TX-5
West Chapel Cem—*cemetery* ... NC-3
West Chapel Cem—*cemetery* ... OH-6
*West Chapel Ch of Christ* ... MS-4
West Chapin Mine—*mine* ... MI-6
West Chapman Canyon—*valley* ... CA-9
West Chapman Creek—*stream* ... KS-7
**West Charles City**—*pop pl* ... IA-7
West Charleston—*locale* ... ME-1
**West Charleston**—*pop pl* ... OH-6
**West Charleston**—*pop pl* ... VT-1
West Charleston—*uninc pl* ... WV-2
West Charleston Sch—*school* ... NV-8
*West Charley Creek* ... MT-8
West Charlie Creek—*stream* ... MT-8
West Charlie Young Canyon—*valley* ... NV-8
*West Charlotte HS* ... NC-3
West Charlotte HS—*school* ... NC-3
West Charlotte Oil Field—*oilfield* ... TX-5
**West Charlton**—*pop pl* ... NY-2
West Charlton Cem—*cemetery* ... NY-2
West Charter Oak School (historical)—*locale* ... MO-7
Westchase—*post sta* ... TX-5
**West Chatham**—*pop pl* ... MA-1
West Chatham Park—*park* ... IL-6
West Chavez Windmill—*locale* ... NM-5
West Chavez Windmill—*locale* ... TX-5
**West Chazy**—*pop pl* ... NY-2
West Chazy Rural Cem—*cemetery* ... NY-2
West Cheatham Elem Sch—*school* ... TN-4
**West Chehalem (historical)**—*pop pl* ... OR-9
**West Chelmsford**—*pop pl* ... MA-1
West Chelsea Cem—*cemetery* ... IL-6
West Chemsford Junior Sch—*school* ... MA-1
**West Chenango**—*pop pl* ... NY-2
West Cheniere Au Tigre Canal—*canal* ... LA-4
West Cherry Creek—*stream* ... CO-8
West Cherry Creek—*stream* (2) ... ID-8
**West Cherry Township**—*pop pl* ... KS-7
West Cherry Well—*well* ... NM-5
**West Chesapeake**—*pop pl* ... OH-6
West Chesapeake—*uninc pl* ... VA-3
**West Cheshire**—*pop pl* (2) ... CT-1
*Westchester* ... IN-6
West Chester—*hist pl* ... IA-7
Westchester—*locale* ... CT-1
**Westchester**—*pop pl* ... CA-9
**Westchester**—*pop pl* ... FL-3
**Westchester**—*pop pl* ... IL-6
**Westchester**—*pop pl* (2) ... IN-6
**West Chester**—*pop pl* ... IA-7
**Westchester**—*pop pl* ... MD-2
**Westchester**—*pop pl* ... NY-2
**West Chester**—*pop pl* (2) ... OH-6
**West Chester**—*pop pl* ... PA-2
**Westchester**—*pop pl* (2) ... VA-3
**Westchester**—*pop pl* ... WV-2
Westchester—*uninc pl* ... WI-6
Westchester Acad—*school* ... NC-3
West Chester Borough—*civil* ... PA-2
West Chester (CCD)—*cens area* ... TN-4
Westchester Cem—*cemetery* ... CT-1
West Chester Cem—*cemetery* ... IA-7
Westchester Community Coll—*school* ... NY-2
*Westchester Corner* ... CT-1
Westchester Country Club—*other* ... NY-2
**Westchester (County)**—*pop pl* ... NY-2
Westchester County Airp—*airport* ... NY-2
West Chester County Elem Sch—*school* ... TN-4
Westchester Creek—*stream* ... NY-2
Westchester Day Sch—*school* ... NY-2
West Chester Division—*civil* ... TN-4
West Chester Downtown Hist Dist—*hist pl* ... PA-2
Westchester Elem Sch—*school* ... FL-3
**Westchester Estates**—*pop pl* ... IN-6
**Westchester Estates**—*pop pl* ... MD-2
**West Chesterfield**—*pop pl* ... MA-1
**West Chesterfield**—*pop pl* ... NH-1
Westchester General Hosp—*hospital* ... FL-3
Westchester Heights—*locale* ... MI-6
Westchester Heights—*uninc pl* ... NY-2
Westchester Hills Golf Club—*other* ... NY-2
**Westchester Hills (subdivision)**—*pop pl* ... MS-4
Westchester House—*hist pl* ... NY-2
Westchester HS—*school* ... CA-9
Westchester HS—*school* ... TX-5
Westchester Mall—*locale* ... FL-3
Westchester MS—*school* ... IN-6
*Westchester Park* ... OH-6
Westchester Park—*park* ... TX-5
Westchester Park—*uninc pl* ... MD-2
Westchester Penitentiary—*other* ... NY-2
Westchester Playground—*park* ... CA-9
Westchester Sch—*school* ... MI-6
West Chester Sch—*school* ... SC-3
Westchester Shop Ctr—*locale* ... FL-3
*West Chester State College* ... PA-2
West Chester State College Quadrangle Hist Dist—*hist pl* ... PA-2
*West Chester State Teachers College* ... PA-2
West Chester Station—*locale* ... OH-6
**Westchester (subdivision)**—*pop pl* ... MA-1
**Westchester (subdivision)**—*pop pl* (3) ... NC-3
Westchester Temple—*church* ... NY-2
**Westchester (Township of)**—*pop pl* ... IN-6
West Chester Univ—*school* ... PA-2
**Westchester Village**—*pop pl* ... MI-6
Westchester Village (Shop Ctr)—*locale* ... MO-7
West Chevelon Canyon—*valley* ... AZ-5
*West Chevelon Creek* ... AZ-5
West Chevelon Creek—*stream* ... AZ-5
West Chevelon Crossing—*locale* ... AZ-5
**West Chevy Chase Heights**—*pop pl* ... MD-2
West Cheyenne Creek—*stream* ... TX-5
**West Chicago**—*pop pl* ... IL-6
West Chicago Creek—*stream* ... CO-8
West Chickamauga Creek—*stream* ... GA-3
West Chickamauga Creek—*stream* ... TN-4
West Chickasaw Baptist Ch—*church* ... AL-4
West Chickasawhatchee Creek—*stream* ... GA-3
West Chicken Creek—*stream* ... OR-9
West Chico Oil Field—*oilfield* ... TX-5
West Chicos Rsvr—*reservoir* ... CO-8
West Chihuahua Well—*well* ... NM-5
**West Chili**—*pop pl* ... NY-2
**West Chillisquaque (Township of)**—*pop pl* ... PA-2
West Chimney—*pillar* ... CO-8
West Chimney Rock Draw—*valley* ... CO-8
West China Gulch—*valley* ... MT-8
West Chin Creek Rsvr—*reservoir* ... NV-8
West Chippy Creek—*stream* ... MT-8
West Choctaw (CCD)—*cens area* ... OK-5
West Chokecherry Spring—*spring* ... UT-8
West Chop—*cape* ... MA-1
**West Chop**—*pop pl* ... MA-1
West Chop Light—*locale* ... MA-1
West Chop Light Station—*hist pl* ... MA-1
West Chops Point—*cape* ... ME-1
West Christiania Cem—*cemetery* ... MN-6
West Chub Lake—*lake* ... MN-6
West Chunu Point—*cape* ... AK-9
West Church Ridge—*ridge* ... WA-9
West Chute—*stream* ... NE-7
West Circle Community Center—*building* ... AL-4
**West Circle (subdivision)**—*pop pl* ... AL-4
West Citrus County Landing Field—*airport* ... FL-3
**West City**—*pop pl* (2) ... IL-6
West City Creek Truck Trail—*trail* ... CA-9
West City Park—*park* ... IN-6
*West C Lake* ... IL-6
West Clara Oil Field—*oilfield* ... MS-4
*West Claremont* ... NH-1
**West Claremont**—*pop pl* ... NH-1
West Clarendon Cem—*cemetery* ... MI-6
West Clarendon Cem—*cemetery* ... VT-1
*West Clarion Creek* ... PA-2
*West Clarion River* ... PA-2
*West Clark* ... UT-8
West Clark—*cens area* ... ID-8
West Clark Bench—*bench* ... UT-8
**West Clarksfield**—*pop pl* ... OH-6
West Clarkson Cem—*cemetery* ... NY-2
West Clarkston—*uninc pl* ... WA-9
West Clarkston-Highland—*CDP* ... WA-9
**West Clarksville**—*pop pl* ... NY-2
West Clarno Sch—*school* ... WI-6
West Clawson Rsvr—*reservoir* ... UT-8
*West Clay County Elementary School* ... MS-4
West Clay County HS—*school* ... MS-4
West Clay County Sch—*school* ... MS-4
West Clay Creek—*stream* ... CO-8
West Clay Creek—*stream* ... OK-5
West Clay Knoll Rsvr—*reservoir* ... UT-8
West Clayton Cem—*cemetery* ... WI-6
West Clear Creek—*stream* ... AZ-5
West Clear Creek—*stream* ... TX-5
West Clear Creek Canyon—*valley* ... AZ-5
*West Clear Water Creek* ... AL-4
West Clearwater Creek—*stream* ... AL-4
West Clearwater Lake—*lake* ... FL-3
West Cleo—*locale* ... OK-5
West Cleveland Elem Sch—*school* ... NC-3
West Cleveland Sch—*school* ... IL-6
West Cliff—*cliff* ... MA-1
**Westcliff**—*pop pl* ... SC-3
**West Cliff**—*pop pl* ... TX-5
**Westcliffe**—*pop pl* ... CO-8
**West Clifford**—*pop pl* ... PA-2
**Westcliff Park (subdivision)**—*pop pl* (2) ... AZ-5
Westcliff Sch—*school* ... TX-5
**Westcliff (subdivision)**—*pop pl* ... NC-3
West Clifty—*locale* ... KY-4
**West Clinton**—*pop pl* ... IN-6
**West Clinton**—*pop pl* ... IA-7
**West Clinton**—*pop pl* ... SC-3
West Clinton Ch—*church* ... OH-6
*West Clinton Junction* ... IN-6
West Clinton Junction—*other* ... IN-6
West Clinton Sch—*school* ... MI-6
West Clinton Sch—*school* ... UT-8
*West Clump* ... MD-2
West Clump—*bar* ... NY-2
West Clyde Sch—*school* ... IL-6
West Coal (CCD)—*cens area* ... OK-5
West Coal Creek—*stream* ... CO-8
West Coast Bible Coll—*school* ... CA-9
West Coast Junior Acad—*school* ... FL-3
West Coast Mine—*mine* ... CA-9
West Coast Seminary—*school* ... CA-9
West Coast Tank—*reservoir* ... AZ-5
West Coast the Center for Human Development—*church* ... FL-3
West Cobb—*locale* ... AR-4
West Cobb Windmill—*locale* ... TX-5
**West Cocalico (Township of)**—*pop pl* ... PA-2
*West Cocopah Reservation* ... AZ-5
West Cod Ledge—*bar* ... ME-1
West Cod Ledge Rock—*bar* ... ME-1
West Cody Lake—*lake* ... NE-7
West Coffee Creek—*stream* ... TX-5
**West Coffeyville**—*pop pl* ... KS-7
West Cogswell House—*hist pl* ... MA-1
West Cohasset Chapel—*church* ... MN-6
Westcolang—*locale* ... PA-2
Westcolang Creek—*stream* ... PA-2
*Westcolang Lake* ... PA-2
Westcolang Lake Dam—*dam* ... PA-2
**Westcolang Park**—*pop pl* (2) ... PA-2
Westcolang Pond—*reservoir* ... PA-2
West Colbert Sportsman Club—*locale* ... AL-4
West Cole Oil Field—*oilfield* ... TX-5
West Colerain Sch—*school* ... NC-3
**West Colesville**—*pop pl* ... NY-2
**West College Corner**—*pop pl* ... IN-6
**West Collingswood**—*pop pl* ... NJ-2
**West Collingswood Heights**—*pop pl* ... NJ-2
West Colonias Tank—*reservoir* ... NM-5
West Colton—*locale* ... CA-9
*West Columbia* ... MS-4
West Columbia—*other* ... MS-4
**West Columbia**—*pop pl* ... SC-3
**West Columbia**—*pop pl* ... TX-5
**West Columbia**—*pop pl* ... WV-2
West Columbia-Cayce (CCD)—*cens area* ... SC-3
West Columbia Ch—*church* ... MI-6
West Columbia Ch of God—*church* ... MS-4
West Columbia Oil Field—*oilfield* ... TX-5
West Columbia Street District—*hist pl* ... KY-4
West Columbia Substation—*locale* ... TN-4
West Columbine Gulch—*valley* ... CO-8
*West Columbus* ... OH-6
West Columbus Gas Field—*other* ... MI-6
West Columbus HS—*school* ... NC-3
West Columbus Sch—*school* ... WI-6
West Colusa (CCD)—*cens area* ... CA-9
West Colyell Creek—*stream* ... LA-4
West Comanche Creek—*stream* ... TX-5
West Commerce Street Hist Dist—*hist pl* ... AL-4
West Commerce Street Hist Dist—*hist pl* ... MS-4
West Community Ch—*church* ... PA-2
West Company Airp—*airport* ... PA-2
West Compton (census name for Compton West)—*CDP* ... CA-9
West Compton Hollow—*valley* ... OK-5
*West Concord* ... NH-1
**West Concord**—*pop pl* ... MA-1
**West Concord**—*pop pl* ... MN-6
**West Concord**—*pop pl* ... NH-1
**West Concord**—*pop pl* ... NC-3
West Concord (Brown and Norcott Mills)—*CDP* ... NC-3
West Concord Ch—*church* ... AL-4
West Concord Ch—*church* ... MO-7
West Concord Sch—*school* ... NC-3
West Concord Sch—*school* ... OR-9
**West Conesville**—*pop pl* ... NY-2
West Congregaion Jehovahs Witnesses—*church* ... KS-7
West Conical Rock—*island* ... OR-9
Westconnaug Brook—*stream* ... RI-1
Westconnaug Reservoir Dam—*dam* ... RI-1
Westconnaug Rsvr—*reservoir* ... RI-1
*Westconnauq Brook* ... RI-1
Westconnett Baptist Weekday Ministry—*school* ... FL-3
West Conroe Oil Field—*oilfield* ... TX-5
**West Conshohocken**—*pop pl* ... PA-2
West Conshohocken Borough—*civil* ... PA-2
West Constable—*other* ... NY-2
West Contra Costa (CCD)—*cens area* ... CA-9
West Cook (Unorganized Territory of)—*unorg* ... MN-6
West Coon Creek—*stream* ... OR-9
**West Coon Rapids**—*pop pl* ... MN-6
West Cooper Creek—*stream* ... AR-4
West Cooper Sch—*school* ... SD-7
**West Cooper Township**—*pop pl* ... KS-7
**West Copake**—*pop pl* ... NY-2
West Copake Ch—*church* ... NY-2
*West Coplay* ... PA-2
West Coplay—*other* ... PA-2
West Coplay Sch—*school* ... PA-2

West Copperas Creek—*stream* TX-5
West Copper Creek—*stream* UT-8
West Copper Mountain Tank—*reservoir* AZ-5
West Corazones Draw—*valley* TX-5
West Corbett Oil Field—*oilfield* OK-5
West Corcoran Ditch—*canal* CA-9
**West Cordele**—*pop pl* GA-3
Westcor Heliport (Paradise Valley Mall)—*airport* AZ-5
West Corinth—*locale* ME-1
**West Corinth**—*pop pl* VT-1
West Corinth Baptist Ch—*church* MS-4
West Corinth Ch—*church* NC-3
West Corinth Ch of Christ—*church* MS-4
*West Corinth Elementary School* MS-4
West Corinth Pentecostal Ch—*church* MS-4
*West Corn Creek* UT-8
West Cornell Creek—*stream* WA-9
**West Corners**—*pop pl* (2) NY-2
**West Corners (historical)**—*pop pl* MA-1
West Cornfield Tank—*reservoir* NM-5
West Cornwall—*locale* NY-2
**West Cornwall**—*pop pl* CT-1
**West Cornwall**—*pop pl* VT-1
West Cornwall Bridge—*hist pl* CT-1
West Cornwall Sch—*school* PA-2
**West Cornwall (Township of)**—*pop pl* PA-2
West Corona—*locale* AL-4
West Corona Mine (underground)—*mine* AL-4
West Corral Creek—*stream* MT-8
West Corral de Piedra Creek—*stream* CA-9
West Corral Windmill—*locale* NM-5
West Corson—*unorg reg* SD-7
*Westcosville* PA-2
Westcote—*hist pl* RI-1
West Coteau Lake (historical)—*lake* SD-7
West Cote Blanche Bay—*bay* LA-4
West Cote Blanche Bay Oil and Gas Field—*oilfield* LA-4
*Westcott* RI-1
Westcott—*locale* TX-5
**Westcott**—*pop pl* RI-1
Westcott Bay—*bay* WA-9
**Westcott Beach**—*pop pl* RI-1
Westcott Beach State Park—*park* NY-2
Westcott Brook—*stream* (2) ME-1
Westcott Cem—*cemetery* AL-4
Westcott Cem—*cemetery* ME-1
Westcott Cem—*cemetery* NY-2
Westcott Cem—*cemetery* TX-5
Westcott Cove—*bay* CT-1
Westcott Hills—*range* WA-9
Westcott House—*hist pl* OH-6
Westcott HS—*school* IL-6
West Cottonwood Canyon—*valley* NV-8
West Cottonwood Creek—*stream* CA-9
West Cottonwood Creek—*stream* (2) SD-7
West Cottonwood Creek—*stream* (2) WY-8
West Cottonwood Lake—*lake* NE-7
West Cottonwood Ridge—*ridge* AZ-5
West Cottonwood Sch—*school* CA-9
West Cottonwood Spring—*spring* NV-8
West Cottonwood Spring—*spring* NM-5
Westcott Reservoir—*lake* NY-2
**Westcotville**—*pop pl* NJ-2
West Coulee—*uninc pl* WA-9
West Coulter Creek—*stream* CO-8
**West County**—*pop pl* MO-7
West County Center (Shop Ctr)—*locale* MO-7
*West County Line Baptist Church* AL-4
West County Line Ch—*church* AL-4
West County Line Ch—*church* MS-4
West Court Cem—*cemetery* NC-3
*West Cove* ME-1
*West Cove* NY-2
*West Cove* TN-4
West Cove—*basin* UT-8
West Cove—*bay* AK-9
West Cove—*bay* CA-9
West Cove—*bay* CT-1
West Cove—*bay* (2) ME-1
West Cove—*bay* NY-2
West Cove—*bay* RI-1
**Westcove**—*pop pl* UT-8
West Cove—*valley* NC-3
West Cove Camp—*locale* LA-4
West Cove Point—*cape* ME-1
**West Covina**—*pop pl* CA-9
West Covina Christian Sch—*school* CA-9
West Covina HS—*school* CA-9
**West Covington**—*pop pl* KY-4
**West Covington**—*pop pl* OH-6
**West Covington**—*pop pl* PA-2
*West Cow Creek* CO-8
West Cow Creek—*stream* MO-7
West Cow Creek—*stream* OR-9
West Cow Creek Ranch Rsvr—*reservoir* WY-8
West Cow Pasture Windmill—*locale* TX-5
West Cox Pond—*reservoir* AZ-5
**West Coxsackie**—*pop pl* NY-2
West Coyle Hollow—*valley* MO-7
*West Coyote Creek* UT-8
West Coyote Creek—*stream* MT-8
West Coyote Creek—*stream* UT-8
West Coyote Hills—*range* CA-9
West Coyote Wash—*valley* UT-8
West Craggy—*cliff* WA-9
**West Cramerton**—*pop pl* NC-3
West Cranberry Lake—*lake* MN-6
West Crane Bayou—*gut* TX-5
West Crater—*crater* OR-9
West Crater—*crater* WA-9
West Craven HS—*school* NC-3
West Craven JHS—*school* NC-3
West Crawfish Inlet—*bay* AK-9
West Crawford Island—*island* NY-2
West Crazy Mountains—*other* AK-9
*West Creek* CA-9
*West Creek* ID-8
*West Creek* IN-6
*West Creek* MD-2
*West Creek* MI-6
*West Creek* NV-8
*West Creek* NJ-2
*West Creek* NY-2
*West Creek* TX-5
*West Creek* UT-8
*West Creek* WA-9
**West Creek**—*pop pl* CO-8
**West Creek**—*pop pl* NJ-2
**West Creek**—*pop pl* PA-2
West Creek—*stream* (5) AK-9
West Creek—*stream* (4) AR-4
West Creek—*stream* (5) CO-8
West Creek—*stream* FL-3
West Creek—*stream* (2) ID-8
West Creek—*stream* (2) IL-6
West Creek—*stream* IN-6
West Creek—*stream* (3) KS-7
West Creek—*stream* KY-4
West Creek—*stream* MD-2
West Creek—*stream* MA-1
West Creek—*stream* MN-6
West Creek—*stream* (2) MS-4
West Creek—*stream* (5) MT-8
West Creek—*stream* NE-7
West Creek—*stream* NV-8
West Creek—*stream* NJ-2
West Creek—*stream* (7) NY-2
West Creek—*stream* (2) OH-6
West Creek—*stream* (3) OK-5
West Creek—*stream* (6) OR-9
West Creek—*stream* (5) PA-2
West Creek—*stream* SC-3
West Creek—*stream* TN-4
West Creek—*stream* (3) TX-5
West Creek—*stream* UT-8
West Creek—*stream* (2) VA-3
West Creek—*stream* (2) WA-9
West Creek—*stream* WV-2
West Creek—*stream* WI-6
West Creek Cem—*cemetery* (2) IN-6
West Creek Cem—*cemetery* OK-5
West Creek Ch—*church* NY-2
West Creek Ch—*church* OH-6
West Creek Ch—*church* SC-3
*West Creek Ditch* IN-6
West Creek Draw—*valley* TX-5
West Creek Hills Sch—*school* PA-2
**West Creek Hills (subdivision)**—*pop pl* PA-2
West Creek (historical)—*locale* KS-7
West Creek Industrial Park—*locale* NJ-2
West Creek Lake—*lake* CO-8
West Creek Lake—*lake* NY-2
Westcreek Lake—*reservoir* CO-8
West Creek Marsh—*swamp* MD-2
West Creek Marshes—*swamp* MA-1
West Creek Mtn—*summit* NY-2
West Creek Point—*cape* MD-2
**West Creek (subdivision)**—*pop pl* TN-4
**West Creek (Township of)**—*pop pl* IN-6
West Creek Well—*well* TX-5
West Creek Windmill—*locale* TX-5
West Cressona—*uninc pl* PA-2
West Crocker Lake—*reservoir* UT-8
West Crockett Branch—*stream* OR-9
West Crockett Camp—*locale* CA-9
West Crockett (CCD)—*cens area* TX-5
**Westcroft (subdivision)**—*pop pl* NC-3
West Cromo Creek—*stream* MT-8
*West Cronese Lake* CA-9
West Cronise Lake—*flat* CA-9
West Crooked Creek—*stream* IL-6
West Crooked Lake—*lake* FL-3
West Crooked Lake—*lake* MI-6
West Crooked Lake—*lake* MN-6
West Cross Canyon—*valley* CO-8
West Cross Creek—*stream* (2) CO-8
**West Crossett**—*pop pl* AR-4
West Crossing—*locale* GA-3
*West Crossroads* NC-3
West Crossroads—*other* NC-3
West Crow Creek—*stream* KS-7
West Crow Flat Well—*well* NM-5
West Crow Island—*island* NY-2
West Crow Wing (Unorganized Territory of)—*unorg* MN-6
West C Streamline Lake—*lake* IL-6
West Cuba Landing—*locale* TN-4
West Cucamonga Truck Trail—*trail* CA-9
West Cuivre Ch—*church* MO-7
*West Cullman Methodist Episcopal Ch* AL-4
West Cultus Lake Campground—*park* OR-9
**West Cumberland**—*pop pl* ME-1
**West Cummington**—*pop pl* MA-1
West Cundy Point—*cape* ME-1
West Curran Coulee—*valley* WI-6
West Curtis Canyon—*valley* NM-5
West Custer—*unorg reg* SD-7
West Custom House—*building* NC-3
West Cut Bank Creek—*stream* ND-7
Westcut Lake—*lake* LA-4
West Cutoff—*channel* FL-3
West Cutoff Trail—*trail* WY-8
*West Cypress* KY-4
West Cypress Creek—*stream* MS-4
**West Cyruston**—*pop pl* TN-4
West Daggett—*cens area* UT-8
West Daggett Division—*civil* UT-8
Westdahi Rock—*bar* CA-9
Westdahl Cove—*bay* AK-9
Westdahl Peak—*summit* AK-9
Westdahl Point—*cape* AK-9
Westdahl Rock—*bar* AK-9
Westdale—*locale* LA-4
**Westdale**—*pop pl* IL-6
**Westdale**—*pop pl* MA-1
**Westdale**—*pop pl* NY-2
**Westdale**—*pop pl* VA-3
Westdale—*uninc pl* LA-4
Westdale Baptist Ch—*church* AL-4
**Westdale Gardens**—*pop pl* IL-6
Westdale (historical P.O.)—*locale* MA-1
Westdale JHS—*school* LA-4
Westdale Park—*park* IL-6
Westdale Sch—*school* IL-6
Westdale Sch—*school* LA-4
Westdale Sch—*school* MI-6
Westdale Shop Ctr—*locale* AZ-5
Westdale Station (historical)—*locale* MA-1
West Dallas—*uninc pl* TX-5
West Dallas Township—*civil* MO-7
West Dam—*dam* AL-4
West Damascus—*locale* PA-2
West Dam Creek—*stream* TX-5
West Dam Tank—*reservoir* TX-5
West Dam Windmill—*locale* TX-5
**West Dana**—*pop pl* IN-6
**West Danby**—*pop pl* NY-2
*West Danger Island* MP-9
West Danish Cem—*cemetery* WI-6
**West Dante**—*pop pl* VA-3
*West Danvers* MA-1
*West Danvers Station* MA-1
**West Danville**—*pop pl* KY-4
**West Danville**—*pop pl* VT-1
West Darian Run—*stream* PA-2
**West Darlington**—*pop pl* PA-2
*West Davenport* IA-7
**West Davenport**—*pop pl* NY-2
West Davidson Senior HS—*school* NC-3
West Davis Draw—*valley* WY-8
West Davis Lake—*lake* WI-6
West Davis Lake Campground—*park* OR-9
West Davis Sch—*school* CA-9
West Davis Street-Fountain Place Hist Dist—*hist pl* NC-3
**West Dawson**—*pop pl* GA-3
West Dawson Pass Trail—*trail* MT-8
West Dawson Tank—*reservoir* TX-5
**West Day**—*pop pl* NY-2
**West Days**—*pop pl* MS-4
West Days Creek—*stream* OK-5
West Dayton Cem—*cemetery* MI-6
West Dayton Sch—*school* MI-6
*West Dead Lake* MN-6
**West Deal**—*pop pl* NJ-2
West Deaton Windmill—*locale* TX-5
West De Baca (CCD)—*cens area* NM-5
*West Decatur* PA-2
**West Decatur**—*pop pl* AL-4
**West Decatur**—*pop pl* PA-2
West Decatur Ch—*church* MS-4
*West Decatur Elementary School* AL-4
**West Decatur (RR name Blue Ball)**—*pop pl* PA-2
West Decatur Sch—*school* AL-4
West Deception Canyon—*valley* CA-9
*West Dedham* MA-1
West Deep Creek—*stream* NV-8
West Deep Creek—*stream* TX-5
West Deep Creek—*stream* UT-8
West Deep Creek Ch—*church* NC-3
West Deep Creek Sch—*school* NC-3
West Deep Creek Sch—*school* SD-7
*West Deer Creek* MO-7
West Deer Creek—*stream* UT-8
West Deer Creek—*stream* WA-9
*West Deer Creek Irrigation System* UT-8
**West Deerfield**—*pop pl* MA-1
**West Deerfield Beach**—*pop pl* FL-3
West Deerfield Cem—*cemetery* MA-1
West Deerfield Ch—*church* MI-6
West Deerfield Oil Field—*oilfield* MS-4
West Deerfield (Township of)—*civ div* IL-6
West Deer HS—*school* PA-2
**West Deering**—*pop pl* NH-1
West Deer Island Oil Field—*oilfield* LA-4
*West Deer Isle* ME-1
West Deer Lake—*reservoir* PA-2
West Deer Sch—*school* PA-2
**West Deer (Township of)**—*pop pl* PA-2
West DeFuniak Sch—*school* FL-3
West De Land—*CDP* FL-3
West Delaware Aqueduct—*canal* NY-2
West Delaware Cem—*cemetery* MI-6
West Delaware HS—*school* IA-7
West Delaware Junoir HS—*school* IA-7
West Delhi—*locale* NY-2
West Delhi Oil and Gas Field—*oilfield* LA-4
West Dell Creek—*stream* WY-8
West Dell Falls—*falls* WY-8
West Delta—*locale* TX-5
**West Delta**—*pop pl* OH-6
West Delta Canal—*canal* CA-9
West Delta Drain—*canal* CA-9
West Delta Farms Oil and Gas Field—*oilfield* LA-4
West Dempsey Creek—*stream* ID-8
West Dempsey Gulch—*valley* CO-8
West Denmark—*locale* ME-1
**West Denmark**—*pop pl* WI-6
**West Dennis**—*pop pl* MA-1
West Dennis—*summit* ID-8
**West Denton**—*pop pl* MD-2
**West De Pere**—*pop pl* WI-6
West De Pere—*uninc pl* WI-6
**West Deptford (Br. P.O.)**—*pop pl* NJ-2
West Deptford HS—*school* NJ-2
**West Deptford (Township of)**—*pop pl* NJ-2
*West Derby* VT-1
*West Derry* NH-1
**West Derry**—*pop pl* NH-1
**West Derry**—*pop pl* PA-2
West Derry Grade Sch (historical)—*school* PA-2
West Desert Sch—*school* UT-8
**West Des Moines**—*pop pl* IA-7
West Des Moines City Hall—*building* IA-7
*West Des Moines River* IA-7
*West Des Moines River* MN-6
*West Des Moines River* MO-7
West Des Moines Township—*fmr MCD* IA-7
*West Detroit* MI-6
West Devils Playground Windmill—*locale* TX-5
West Diamond Ranch—*locale* WY-8
West Diamond Spring—*spring* WY-8
West Diamond Springs Draw—*valley* WY-8
West Dietz Creek—*arroyo* TX-5
**West Dighton**—*pop pl* MA-1
West Dike—*levee* SC-3
West Dinwiddie Tank—*reservoir* NM-5
West Dip Gulch—*valley* UT-8
West Dipping Vat Coulee—*valley* MT-8
West District Elem Sch—*school* MS-4
West District HS—*school* MS-4
West District Sch—*school* CT-1
West Ditch—*canal* CO-8
West Ditch—*canal* (2) MS-4
West Ditch—*canal* (2) MO-7
West Ditch—*canal* NY-2
West Ditch—*canal* UT-8
West Ditch, The—*canal* WY-8
West Divide Creek—*stream* CO-8
West Divide Creek Ditch—*canal* CO-8
West Divide Two Hundred Eighty-nine—*trail* AZ-5
West Divide Windmill—*locale* TX-5
West Division HS—*school* WI-6
**West Dixie Bend**—*pop pl* FL-3
West Dixie Landing—*locale* TN-4
West Dixon Creek—*stream* TX-5
West Dixon Sch—*school* CA-9
West Dobbin Creek—*stream* NV-8
*West Dodge* NE-7
West Dodson Sch (abandoned)—*school* MO-7
West Dog Canyon—*valley* NM-5
West Dog Canyon—*valley* TX-5
West Dog Creek—*stream* FL-3
West Dog Creek—*stream* OK-5
West Dog Lake—*lake* MN-6
West Dolan Creek—*stream* TX-5
West Dolan Township—*civil* MO-7
West Dolores Campground—*locale* CO-8
West Dolores River—*stream* CO-8
West Dome Cat Creek Oil Field—*oilfield* MT-8
**West Donegal (Township of)**—*pop pl* PA-2
West Donica Creek—*stream* IL-6
West Donica Sch—*school* IL-6
West Doniphan Township—*civil* MO-7
West Donner Windmill—*locale* CO-8
West Double Bayou—*gut* LA-4
West Double Canyon—*valley* CA-9
West Double Creek—*stream* NC-3
West Double Dam—*dam* AZ-5
West Doubtful Canyon—*valley* AZ-5
West Doubtful Detention Dam—*dam* AZ-5
West Dougherty (CCD)—*cens area* GA-3
West Dougherty Community House—*building* GA-3
West Douglas Ch—*church* IA-7
West Douglas Ch of Christ—*church* KS-7
West Douglas Creek—*stream* CO-8
West Douglas Park—*park* KS-7
West Douglas Tanks—*reservoir* NM-5
West Douglas Well—*well* NM-5
West Dover—*locale* ME-1
**West Dover**—*pop pl* OH-6
**West Dover**—*pop pl* VT-1
West Dover Hundred—*civil* DE-2
West Dover Village Hist Dist—*hist pl* VT-1
West Dragoo Hollow—*valley* TX-5
West Drain—*canal* AZ-5
West Drain—*canal* NM-5
West Drain—*canal* TX-5
West Drainage Canal—*canal* CA-9
West Drake Ditch—*canal* IN-6
West Draw—*valley* NM-5
West Draw—*valley* (2) TX-5
West Draw—*valley* (3) WY-8
West Draw Waterhole—*reservoir* OR-9
West Drenthe Sch—*school* MI-6
**West Dresden**—*pop pl* ME-1
West Drew Ch—*church* MS-4
West Dripping Rock—*spring* CO-8
**West Drive Subdivision**—*pop pl* UT-8
**West Drummer**—*pop pl* NH-1
West Dry Branch—*stream* TX-5
West Dry Branch—*stream* VA-3
West Dry Canyon—*valley* ID-8
West Dry Canyon Spring—*spring* ID-8
*West Dry Creek* FL-3
*West Dry Creek* ID-8
West Dry Creek—*stream* AR-4
West Dry Creek—*stream* CO-8
West Dry Creek—*stream* (2) ID-8
West Dry Creek—*stream* (2) KS-7
West Dry Creek—*stream* OR-9
West Dry Creek—*stream* WY-8
West Dry Creek Rsvr—*reservoir* OR-9
**West Dryden**—*pop pl* NY-2
West Dry Fork Coulee—*valley* MT-8
West Dry Fork Creek—*stream* MT-8
West Dry Gulch—*valley* CO-8
West Dry Lake Canyon—*valley* CO-8
West Dry Lake Tank—*reservoir* NM-5
West Dry Run Fork—*stream* VA-3
West Dublin—*uninc pl* GA-3
West Dublin Windmill—*locale* NM-5
West Dubuque Sch—*school* IA-7
West Duck Creek—*stream* MT-8
**West Dudley**—*pop pl* MA-1
West Dugout Creek—*stream* TX-5
*West Duluth* MN-6
**West Duluth**—*pop pl* MN-6
*West Duluth Junction* MN-6
*West Duluth Yard* MN-6
**West Dummerston**—*pop pl* VT-1
West Dummerston Covered Bridge—*hist pl* VT-1
West Dummerston Dam—*dam* VT-1
**West Dunbar**—*pop pl* WV-2
West Dunbar Sch—*school* WV-2
West Dunbury (historical P.O.)—*locale* MA-1
West Duncan Oil And Gas Field—*oilfield* OK-5
**West Dundee (Dundee PO)**—*pop pl* IL-6
West Dunklin Sch—*school* SC-3
West DuNoir Creek—*stream* WY-8
**West DuPage Park**—*pop pl* IL-6
West Duplin Ch—*church* NC-3
West Durant Gulch—*valley* CO-8
**West Durham**—*pop pl* ME-1
**West Durham**—*pop pl* NY-2
West Durham—*uninc pl* NC-3
West Durham Hist Dist—*hist pl* NC-3
West Durham Well—*well* NM-5
West Durrance Island—*island* FL-3
West Dustin Oil Field—*oilfield* OK-5
West Dutchman Tank—*reservoir* AZ-5
West Dutch Woman Draw—*valley* TX-5
**West Duwamish**—*pop pl* WA-9
**West Duxbury**—*pop pl* MA-1
West Dyer Creek—*stream* CO-8
West Dyer Mtn—*summit* CO-8
West Eagle Creek—*stream* OR-9
West Eagle Creek Ch—*church* OH-6
West Eagle Head Ranch—*locale* KS-7
West Eagle Meadow—*flat* OR-9
West Eagle Meadow Campground—*park* OR-9
West Eagle Mountain Tunnel—*tunnel* CA-9
West Eagle Trail—*trail* OR-9
West Earl Community Park—*park* PA-2
West Earl Post Office (historical)—*building* PA-2
**West Earl (Township of)**—*pop pl* PA-2
**West Easton**—*pop pl* PA-2
West Easton Borough—*civil* PA-2
West Easy Canal—*canal* FL-3
**West Eaton**—*pop pl* NY-2
West Eaton Canyon—*valley* AZ-5
**West Eau Gallie**—*pop pl* FL-3
West Eau Gallie Shop Ctr—*locale* FL-3
West Echo Lake—*lake* WY-8
West Echols (CCD)—*cens area* GA-3
West Eckford Cem—*cemetery* MI-6
West Eckford Ch—*church* MI-6
*Westeconk Creek* NJ-2
West Economy—*locale* PA-2
West Economy Station (historical)—*locale* PA-2
*Westecung Creek* NJ-2
*Westecunk* NJ-2
Westecunk Creek—*stream* NJ-2
*Westecunk Forge* NJ-2
*Westecunk Mills* NJ-2
*West Eden* ME-1
West Eden Cem—*cemetery* IL-6
West Eden Ch—*church* IL-6
West Edgecombe JHS—*school* NC-3
**West Edmeston**—*pop pl* NY-2
**West Edmondale**—*pop pl* MD-2
West Edmond Oil And Gas Field—*oilfield* OK-5
West Edmond Oil Field—*oilfield* OK-5
West Eel River Ch—*church* IN-6
**West Egg Harbor**—*pop pl* NJ-2
West Eighth Street Hist Dist—*hist pl* IN-6
*West Eightmile Lake* WI-6
West Eightmile Lake—*lake* WI-6
West Eight Section Windmill—*locale* TX-5
**Westel**—*pop pl* TN-4
Westel Baptist Ch—*church* TN-4
West Elba Sch—*school* IL-6
West Elbow Ditch—*canal* MT-8
West Elbow Hollow—*valley* ID-8
West Elbow Lake Ch—*church* MN-6
Westel Community Center—*building* TN-4
**West Eldred**—*pop pl* PA-2
*West Elementary School* MS-4
*West Elem Sch* TN-4
West Elem Sch—*school* AL-4
West Elem Sch—*school* DE-2
West Elem Sch—*school* FL-3
West Elem Sch—*school* IN-6
West Elem Sch—*school* (2) KS-7
West Elem Sch—*school* MO-7
West Elem Sch—*school* NC-3
West Elem Sch—*school* OH-6
West Elem Sch—*school* (2) TN-4
West Elem Sch—*school* TX-5
West Eleventh Street Hist Dist—*hist pl* MO-7
West Elim Cem—*cemetery* MN-6
**West Elizabeth**—*pop pl* PA-2
West Elizabeth Borough—*civil* PA-2
West Elk Basin—*basin* CO-8
*West Elk Creek* CO-8
West Elk Creek—*stream* (3) CO-8
West Elk Creek—*stream* ID-8
West Elk Creek—*stream* OK-5
West Elk Fork—*stream* MO-7
West Elkhorn Canyon—*valley* ID-8
West Elkhorn Creek—*stream* (2) KS-7
West Elk HS—*school* KS-7
West Elkin—*other* NC-3
*West Elk Mountain* CO-8
West Elk Mtns—*range* CO-8
West Elk Peak—*summit* CO-8
West Elk Peak—*summit* ID-8
**West Elkridge**—*pop pl* MD-2
West Elk Rsvr—*reservoir* CO-8
West Elk Spring—*spring* AZ-5
West Elk Stock Driveway—*trail* CO-8
**West Elkton**—*pop pl* OH-6
West Elk Wilderness—*park* CO-8
Westella (historical)—*locale* KS-7
West Ellerson Lake—*lake* WI-6
**West Ellery**—*pop pl* NY-2
**West Ellicott (census name Jamestown West)**—*pop pl* NY-2
West Ellisville Baptist Ch—*church* MS-4
*West Ellsworth* ME-1
West Ellsworth—*locale* ME-1
*West Ellwood Junction* PA-2
West Ellwood Junction—*uninc pl* PA-2
West Elma Sch—*school* NY-2
West Elm Branch—*stream* MO-7
*West Elm Creek* TX-5
West Elm Creek—*stream* OK-5
West Elm Creek—*stream* SD-7
West Elm Creek—*stream* TX-5
**West Elmira**—*pop pl* NY-2
West Elm Street Park—*park* IL-6
Westel Post Office—*building* TN-4
**West Elwood**—*pop pl* IN-6
West Elwood Creek—*stream* MI-6
**West Ely**—*pop pl* MO-7
West Emerald—*summit* ID-8
West Emerick Sch—*school* NE-7
**West Eminence**—*pop pl* MO-7
West Emma Creek—*stream* KS-7
West Emmaus Cem—*cemetery* MN-6
West Emmons—*unorg reg* ND-7
West Emory—*locale* TN-4
West Emory Ch—*church* TN-4
Westenage Hill—*summit* MI-6
Westenberg Spring—*spring* WI-6
*West End* CT-1
*West End* ME-1
*West End* MA-1
*West End* MN-6
*West End* NJ-2
*West End* OH-6
West End—*cape* CA-9
West End—*cape* NY-2
West End—*cape* NC-3
West End—*CDP* NY-2
West End—*cens area* MT-8
Westend—*hist pl* VA-3
West End—*locale* AZ-5
West End—*locale* MT-8
West End—*locale* VA-3
West End—*locale* WV-2
West End—*other* WV-2
**West End**—*pop pl* (2) AL-4
**West End**—*pop pl* AR-4
**Westend**—*pop pl* CA-9
**West End**—*pop pl* GA-3
**West End**—*pop pl* (2) IL-6
**West End**—*pop pl* ME-1
**West End**—*pop pl* (2) NJ-2
**West End**—*pop pl* NC-3
**West End**—*pop pl* (2) PA-2
**West End**—*pop pl* (2) TN-4
**West End**—*pop pl* (2) TX-5
**West End**—*pop pl* VA-3
**West End**—*pop pl* WV-2
West End—*post sta* DC-2
West End—*uninc pl* CO-8
West End—*uninc pl* FL-3
West End—*uninc pl* GA-3
West End—*uninc pl* LA-4
West End—*uninc pl* NJ-2
Westend—*uninc pl* NC-3
West End—*uninc pl* PA-2
West End Acad—*school* TN-4
**West End Anniston**—*pop pl* AL-4
West End Baptist Ch—*church* (5) AL-4
West End Baptist Ch—*church* (2) MS-4
West End Baptist Ch—*church* (3) TN-4
West End Bridge—*bridge* PA-2
West End Canyon—*valley* CO-8
West End Canyon—*valley* UT-8
West End (CCD)—*cens area* TX-5
West End (CCD)—*cens area* WA-9
West End Cem—*cemetery* GA-3
West End Cem—*cemetery* KY-4
West End Cem—*cemetery* ME-1
West End Cem—*cemetery* (2) PA-2
West End Cem—*cemetery* (2) SC-3
West End Cem—*cemetery* (2) TX-5
West End Cem—*cemetery* VA-3
West End (census name Ocala West)—*other* FL-3
West End (Census Subdistrict)—*cens area* VI-3
*West End Ch* AL-4
West End Ch—*church* (2) AL-4
West End Ch—*church* NC-3
West End Ch—*church* (3) TN-4
West End Ch—*church* TX-5
Westend Ch—*church* VA-3
West End Ch—*church* (2) VA-3
West End Ch—*church* WA-9
Westend Ch (historical)—*church* TN-4
Westend Circle—*locale* NC-3
*West End Cobb Town* AL-4
West End-Cobb Town—*CDP* AL-4
West End Collegiate Church and Collegiate Sch—*hist pl* NY-2
West End Creek—*stream* AK-9
West End Creek—*stream* ID-8
West End Cumberland Presbyterian Ch—*church* AL-4
West End Drain—*canal* ID-8
West End Early Childhood Education Center—*school* AL-4
*West End Elementary School* PA-2
*West End Elem Sch* MS-4
West End Elem Sch—*hist pl* OH-6
West End Elem Sch—*hist pl* SC-3
West End Elem Sch—*school* AL-4
West End Elem Sch—*school* MS-4
West End Elem Sch—*school* TN-4
West End Gospel Tabernacle—*church* AL-4
**Westend Hampton**—*pop pl* NJ-2
**West End Heights**—*pop pl* TN-4
West End Hist Dist—*hist pl* IN-6
West End Hist Dist—*hist pl* MS-4
West End Hist Dist—*hist pl* NC-3
Westend Hist Dist—*hist pl* TX-5
West End Hist Dist—*hist pl* TX-5
West End Hotel—*hist pl* AZ-5
West End HS—*school* (2) AL-4
West End HS—*school* TN-4
West End HS—*school* VA-3
**West Endicott**—*pop pl* NY-2
**West End (Industrial Area)**—*pop pl* VA-3
West End JHS—*school* TN-4
West End Land Club—*other* CA-9
**West End Manor**—*pop pl* VA-3
West End Masonic Temple—*hist pl* AL-4
West End Methodist Ch—*church* (2) AL-4
West End North Hist Dist—*hist pl* CT-1
West End-North Side Bridge—*hist pl* PA-2
West End Number 1 Colliery—*building* PA-2
West End Number 2 Colliery—*building* PA-2
West End Park—*locale* TX-5
West End Park—*park* AL-4
West End Park—*park* FL-3
West End Park—*park* LA-4
West End Park—*park* MO-7
West End Park—*park* PA-2
West End Park—*park* TX-5
West End Park—*park* VA-3
**West End Park**—*pop pl* MD-2
West End Picnic Area—*park* WI-6
**West End Place**—*pop pl* TX-5
West End Point—*cape* UT-8
*West End Pond* MA-1
*West End Pond* PA-2
Westend Pond—*lake* (2) MA-1
Westend Pond—*reservoir* PA-2
West End Post Office (historical)—*building* PA-2
West End Presbyterian Ch (historical)—*church* AL-4
Westend Saltpond—*lake* VI-3
West End Sch—*school* AL-4
West End Sch—*school* CA-9
West End Sch—*school* (2) GA-3
West End Sch—*school* IN-6
West End Sch—*school* KY-4
West End Sch—*school* MI-6
West End Sch—*school* MS-4
West End Sch—*school* MO-7
West End Sch—*school* NE-7
West End Sch—*school* NJ-2
West End Sch—*school* (3) NY-2
West End Sch—*school* (2) NC-3
West End Sch—*school* (2) OH-6
West End Sch—*school* (4) PA-2
West End Sch—*school* (4) SC-3
West End Sch—*school* (3) TX-5
West End Sch—*school* (4) VA-3
West End Sch (historical)—*school* MS-4
West End Sch (historical)—*school* PA-2
West End Sch (historical)—*school* TN-4
West End Shop Ctr—*locale* AL-4
West-End Shop Ctr—*locale* FL-3
West End Shop Ctr—*locale* FL-3
West End Shop Ctr—*locale* PA-2
West End Shop Ctr—*locale* TN-4
West End Slough—*stream* TX-5
West End South Hist Dist—*hist pl* CT-1

Westfield Whip Manufacturing Company—hist pl ... MA-1
West Field Windmill—locale ... TX-5
West Fifteenth Street Hist Dist—hist pl ... KY-4
West Fifth Ave Apartments Hist Dist—hist pl ... IN-6
West Fifth Street Bridge—hist pl ... OH-6
West Finger Inlet—bay ... AK-9
**West Finley**—pop pl ... PA-2
**West Finley (Burnsville)**—pop pl ... PA-2
West Finley Cem—cemetery ... PA-2
West Finley Ch—church ... MO-7
**West Finley (Township of)**—pop pl ... PA-2
West Finn Valley—basin ... NE-7
**Westfir**—pop pl ... OR-9
West Fire Island—island ... NY-2
West Fire Prairie Creek—stream ... MO-7
Westfir HS—school ... OR-9
West Fish Creek—stream ... CO-8
West Fisher Creek ... MT-8
West Fisher Creek—stream ... MO-7
West Fisher Creek—stream ... MT-8
West Fisher Lake—lake ... OR-9
West Fish Lake—lake ... MI-6
West Fishtail Creek—stream ... MT-8
**West Fitchburg (subdivision)**—pop pl ... MA-1
West Fitts Oil Field—oilfield ... OK-5
West Five Points ... MI-6
West Flagler Day Care—school ... FL-3
West Flagler Kennel Club ... FL-3
West Flagstaff Interchange—crossing ... AZ-5
West Flank Island—island ... AK-9
West Flat—flat ... NM-5
West Flat Creek—stream ... AR-4
West Flat Fork Creek—stream ... AR-4
West Flathead Mine—mine ... MT-8
West Flatiron—summit ... CO-8
West Flatiron Mesa ... CO-8
West Flats—flat ... NY-2
West Flattop Mtn—summit ... MT-8
West Flat Top Mtn—summit ... WY-8
West Flat Top Rsvr No 1—reservoir ... UT-8
West Flat Top Rsvr No 2—reservoir ... UT-8
West Fleming Creek ... AR-4
West Fleming Creek—stream ... AR-4
**West Fletcher**—pop pl ... VT-1
West Flint Ch—church ... MI-6
West Flint Creek—stream ... AL-4
West Flint Creek Oil Field—oilfield ... OK-5
**West Florence**—pop pl ... OH-6
**West Florence**—pop pl ... SC-3
West Florence Cem—cemetery ... MN-6
West Florence Immanuel Ch—church ... MN-6
West Florence Ridge—ridge ... MN-6
West Florida Community Care Center—hospital ... FL-3
West Florida Regional Med Ctr—hospital ... FL-3
West Flow—bay ... NY-2
West Fly-By Tower—other ... CA-9
**Westfold Subdivision**—pop pl ... UT-8
**Westford**—pop pl ... CT-1
**Westford**—pop pl ... MA-1
**Westford**—pop pl ... NY-2
**Westford**—pop pl ... PA-2
**Westford**—pop pl ... VT-1
West Ford—stream ... OR-9
Westford Acad—school ... MA-1
Westford Cem—cemetery ... MN-6
Westford Centre ... MA-1
**West Ford City**—pop pl ... PA-2
Westford Depot Dam—dam ... MA-1
Westford Hill—summit ... CT-1
Westford Hill—summit ... ME-1
Westford Hill—summit ... MA-1
Westford Hill Ch—church ... CT-1
Westford Plains Cem—cemetery ... VT-1
Westford Pond—lake ... VT-1
West Ford River Cem—cemetery ... MI-6
Westford Sch—school ... VT-1
**Westford Station**—pop pl ... MA-1
**Westford (Town of)**—pop pl ... MA-1
**Westford (Town of)**—pop pl ... NY-2
**Westford (Town of)**—pop pl ... VT-1
**Westford (Town of)**—pop pl (2) ... WI-6
**Westford Township**—pop pl ... ND-7
**Westford (Township of)**—pop pl ... MN-6
Westford Village Cem—cemetery ... CT-1
West Foreland—cape ... AK-9
**West Forest**—pop pl ... TN-4
West Forest Cem—cemetery ... ND-7
West Forest Ch—church ... MI-6
West Forestdale Tank—reservoir ... AZ-5
West Forest Elementary School ... PA-2
West Forest Junior Senior High School ... PA-2
**West Forest Park**—pop pl ... MD-2
West Forgey Creek—stream ... MT-8
West Fork ... AZ-5
West Fork ... AR-4
West Fork ... CA-9
West Fork ... CO-8
West Fork ... GA-3
West Fork ... ID-8
West Fork ... IN-6
West Fork ... KS-7
West Fork ... KY-4
West Fork ... MN-6
West Fork ... MO-7
West Fork ... MT-8
West Fork ... NC-3
West Fork ... OH-6
West Fork ... OK-5
West Fork ... OR-9
West Fork ... TN-4
West Fork ... TX-5
West Fork ... VA-3
West Fork ... WA-9
West Fork ... WY-8
West Fork—gut ... AK-9
West Fork—locale ... AK-9
West Fork—locale ... KY-4
West Fork—locale ... MT-8
West Fork—locale ... OR-9
West Fork—locale ... VA-3
**West Fork**—pop pl ... AR-4
**West Fork**—pop pl ... IN-6
**Westfork**—pop pl ... KY-4
**West Fork**—pop pl ... MO-7
**West Fork**—pop pl ... SD-7
**West Fork**—pop pl ... TN-4
**West Fork**—pop pl ... WA-9
West Fork—stream ... AK-9
West Fork—stream ... AR-4
West Fork—stream ... MS-4
West Fork—stream (2) ... NM-5
West Fork—stream ... OK-5
West Fork—stream ... TX-5
West Fork—stream (4) ... WY-8
West Fork—valley ... NM-5
West Fork Abbott Creek—stream ... OR-9
West Fork Adams Creek—stream ... WA-9
West Fork Adams Fork—stream ... KY-4
West Fork Adobe Creek—stream ... CA-9
West Fork Aenon Creek—stream ... TN-4
West Fork Agency Creek—stream ... OR-9
West Fork Agnes Creek—stream ... WA-9
West Fork Ahtell Creek—stream ... AK-9
West Fork Albion Creek—stream ... WA-9
West Fork Alder Creek ... CO-8
West Fork Alder Creek—stream ... CA-9
West Fork Alder Creek—stream ... CO-8
West Fork Alder Creek—stream ... ID-8
West Fork Alder Creek—stream ... MT-8
West Fork Aliso Spring—spring ... AZ-5
West Fork Alkali Creek—stream ... WY-8
West Fork Allen Canyon—valley ... UT-8
West Fork Alligator Creek—stream ... KY-4
West Fork Allison Creek—stream ... ID-8
West Fork Althouse Creek—stream ... CA-9
West Fork Althouse Creek—stream ... OR-9
West Fork American Creek ... ID-8
West Fork American River—stream ... ID-8
West Fork Amite River—stream ... LA-4
West Fork Amite River—stream ... MS-4
West Fork Anderson Creek—stream ... AL-4
West Fork Anderson Creek—stream (2) ... ID-8
West Fork Anderson Creek—stream ... OK-5
West Fork Andrews Creek—stream ... WA-9
West Fork Angostura Trail (Pack)—trail ... NM-5
West Fork Animas River—stream ... CO-8
West Fork Antelope Creek—stream ... MT-8
West Fork Antelope Creek—stream ... TX-5
West Fork Antelope Creek—stream ... WY-8
West Fork Anthill Draw—valley ... WY-8
West Fork Apple Creek—stream ... TX-5
West Fork Applegate Creek—stream ... OR-9
West Fork Apple River—stream ... IL-6
West Fork Apple River—stream ... WI-6
West Fork Armells Creek—stream ... MT-8
West Fork Armstrong Creek—stream ... TX-5
West Fork Armuchee Creek ... GA-3
West Fork Arroyo Sequit—stream ... CA-9
West Fork Asay Creek—stream ... UT-8
West Fork Asbill Creek—stream ... CA-9
West Fork Ashburn Creek—stream ... TN-4
West Fork Ash Creek ... UT-8
West Fork Ash Creek—stream ... MT-8
West Fork Ash Creek—stream ... OR-9
West Fork Ashland Creek—stream ... OR-9
West Fork Asphalt Wash—valley ... UT-8
West Fork Austin Creek—stream ... OR-9
West Fork Avalanche Creek—stream ... CO-8
West Fork A VAR Crooked Creek ... MN-6
West Fork Avintaquin Creek—stream ... UT-8
West Fork Bachatna Creek—stream ... AK-9
West Fork Back Creek—stream ... KY-4
West Fork Badlands Draw—valley ... ND-7
West Fork Bad Route Creek—stream ... MT-8
West Fork Baldy Creek—stream ... CO-8
West Fork Bannock Creek—stream (2) ... ID-8
West Fork Bare Creek—stream ... WY-8
West Fork Bare Mountain Canyon—valley ... CA-9
West Fork Barkers Creek—stream ... NC-3
West Fork Barley Creek ... NV-8
West Fork Barton Creek—stream ... CA-9
West Fork Bartons Creek—stream ... TN-4
West Fork Basin—basin ... ID-8
West Fork Basin Creek—stream (2) ... MT-8
West Fork Basin Creek—stream ... OR-9
West Fork Bass Canyon—valley ... AZ-5
West Fork Battle Butte Creek—stream ... MT-8
West Fork Battle Creek—stream ... IA-7
West Fork Battle Creek—stream ... WY-8
West Fork Baudette River—stream ... MN-6
West Fork Bayou Darrow ... LA-4
West Fork Bayou Long—stream ... LA-4
West Fork Bayou L'Ours—gut ... LA-4
West Fork Bayou Nezpique—stream ... LA-4
West Fork Bayou Pigeon—stream ... LA-4
West Fork Bayou Plaquemine Brule—stream ... LA-4
West Fork Bear Canyon—valley ... CA-9
West Fork Bear Creek ... WA-9
West Fork Bear Creek—stream (3) ... CA-9
West Fork Bear Creek—stream ... IL-6
West Fork Bear Creek—stream ... IN-6
West Fork Bear Creek—stream (2) ... MO-7
West Fork Bear Creek—stream ... MT-8
West Fork Bear Creek—stream ... TX-5
West Fork Bear Creek—stream ... WA-9
West Fork Bear Creek—stream ... WY-8
West Fork Bear River—stream ... UT-8
West Fork Beaver Brook—stream ... ME-1
West Fork Beaver Creek—stream (2) ... CA-9
West Fork Beaver Creek—stream (2) ... CO-8
West Fork Beaver Creek—stream (3) ... ID-8
West Fork Beaver Creek—stream ... KY-4
West Fork Beaver Creek—stream ... MN-6
West Fork Beaver Creek—stream (4) ... MT-8
West Fork Beaver Creek—stream ... NV-8
West Fork Beaver Creek—stream (2) ... OR-9
West Fork Beaver Creek—stream (2) ... UT-8
West Fork Beaver Creek—stream (2) ... WY-8
West Fork Beaverdam Creek—stream ... TN-4
West Fork Beaverdam Creek—stream ... VA-3
West Fork Beaver Wash ... AZ-5
West Fork Beaver Wash ... NV-8
West Fork Beaver Wash ... UT-8
West Fork Beckwith Creek—stream ... WY-8
West Fork Beech Creek—stream ... AL-4
West Fork Beech Creek—stream ... AR-4
West Fork Beech Creek—stream ... GA-3
West Fork Beech Creek—stream ... TN-4
West Fork Beecher Creek—stream ... MT-8
West Fork Bee Creek—stream ... KY-4
West Fork Bell Mare Creek—stream ... ID-8
West Fork Bendire Creek—stream ... OR-9
West Fork Bengis Creek—stream ... AL-4
West Fork Benton Creek—stream ... MO-7
West Fork Benton Creek—stream ... WY-8
West Fork Ben Williams Canyon—valley ... NM-5
West Fork Bergher Creek—stream ... TX-5
West Fork Big Bear Creek—stream ... ID-8
West Fork Big Beaver Creek—stream ... MT-8
West Fork Big Bigby Creek—stream ... TN-4
West Fork Big Blue River—stream ... NE-7
West Fork Big Cabin Creek—stream ... OK-5
West Fork Big Cedar Creek—stream ... AR-4
West Fork Big Coldwater Creek—stream ... FL-3
West Fork Big Creek—stream ... AR-4
West Fork Big Creek—stream ... CA-9
West Fork Big Creek—stream (4) ... ID-8
West Fork Big Creek—stream ... IL-6
West Fork Big Creek—stream ... IA-7
West Fork Big Creek—stream (3) ... MO-7
West Fork Big Creek—stream ... MT-8
West Fork Big Creek—stream ... VA-3
West Fork Big Creek—stream ... WA-9
West Fork Big Elk Creek—stream ... ID-8
West Fork Big Elm Creek—stream ... TX-5
West Fork Big Goose Creek—stream ... WY-8
West Fork Big Harts Creek—stream ... WV-2
West Fork Big Indian Creek—stream ... VA-3
West Fork Big Lost River ... ID-8
West Fork Big Muddy Creek ... UT-8
West Fork Big Muddy Creek ... WY-8
West Fork Big Muddy Creek—stream ... MO-7
West Fork Big Pasture Creek—stream ... OR-9
West Fork Big Peak Creek—stream ... ID-8
West Fork Big Pine Creek—stream ... ID-8
West Fork Big Piney Creek—stream ... AR-4
West Fork Big Ramey Creek—stream ... ID-8
West Fork Big Reedy Creek—stream ... KY-4
West Fork Big Rock Creek—stream ... MT-8
West Fork Big Sand Coulee—valley ... WY-8
West Fork Big Smoky Creek—stream ... ID-8
West Fork Big Walnut Creek ... IN-6
West Fork Big Water Canyon—valley ... UT-8
West Fork Big Witch Creek—stream ... ID-8
West Fork Big Wood River ... ID-8
West Fork Big Woody Creek—stream ... MT-8
West Fork Birch Creek ... OR-9
West Fork Birch Creek—stream ... ID-8
West Fork Birch Creek—stream ... MT-8
West Fork Birch Creek—stream ... OR-9
West Fork Birch Creek—stream ... UT-8
West Fork Birdsong Creek—stream ... TN-4
West Fork Bitter Creek ... OK-5
West Fork Bitter Creek ... TX-5
West Fork Bitter Creek—stream ... MT-8
West Fork Bitter Creek—stream ... UT-8
West Fork Bitterroot River—stream ... MT-8
West Fork Blackbird Creek—stream ... ID-8
West Fork Black Canyon—valley (2) ... AZ-5
West Fork Black Coulee—valley ... MT-8
West Fork Black Creek ... WA-9
West Fork Black Creek—stream ... AZ-5
West Fork Black River—stream ... AZ-5
West Fork Black River—stream ... MN-6
West Fork Black River—stream ... MO-7
West Fork Blacks Creek ... UT-8
West Fork Blacks Creek ... WY-8
West Fork Blacks Fork—stream ... UT-8
West Fork Blacktail Creek—stream ... MT-8
West Fork Blacktail Deer Creek—stream ... MT-8
West Fork Blackwater Creek—stream ... WY-8
West Fork Blake Creek—stream ... MT-8
West Fork Blue Creek—stream ... CA-9
West Fork Blue Creek—stream ... ID-8
West Fork Blue Creek—stream ... MT-8
West Fork Blue Earth River ... IA-7
West Fork Blue Earth River ... MN-6
West Fork Blue River ... IN-6
West Fork Blue River—stream ... AK-9
West Fork Blue River—stream ... IN-6
West Fork Bluff Creek—stream ... ID-8
West Fork Bluff Creek—stream ... NV-8
West Fork Bluff Creek—stream ... TX-5
West Fork Boggy Creek—stream ... FL-3
West Fork Bois Brule River—stream ... WI-6
West Fork Bonita Surface Creek—stream ... CO-8
West Fork Bonito creek ... AZ-5
West Fork Booneville Channel—channel ... OR-9
West Fork Boulder Canyon ... AZ-5
West Fork Boulder Creek ... ID-8
West Fork Boulder Creek—stream ... ID-8
West Fork Boulder Creek—stream ... NV-8
West Fork Boulder Creek—stream ... UT-8
West Fork Boulder River—stream ... MT-8
West Fork Boundary Creek—stream ... OR-9
West Fork Boundary Gulch—valley ... WY-8
West Fork Box Canyon Creek—stream ... WA-9
West Fork Boxelder Creek—stream ... MT-8
West Fork Brackett Creek—stream ... MT-8
West Fork Bradburn Creek—stream ... CA-9
West Fork Bradley Branch—stream ... AL-4
West Fork Bradshaw Creek—stream ... TN-4
West Fork Braffits Creek—stream ... UT-8
West Fork Brant Coulee—valley ... MT-8
West Fork Brave Bull Creek—stream ... SD-7
West Fork Bridge Creek—stream ... CA-9
West Fork Bridge Creek—stream ... OR-9
West Fork Bright Angel Creek ... AZ-5
West Fork Brisbois Creek—stream ... OR-9
West Fork Britt Creek—stream ... OR-9
West Fork Broady Creek—stream ... OR-9
West Fork Brookbank Canyon ... AZ-5
West Fork Brookbank Canyon—valley ... AZ-5
West Fork Brownlee Creek ... ID-8
West Fork Browns Creek ... ID-8
West Fork Browns Creek—stream ... TN-4
West Fork Brummit Creek—stream ... OR-9
West Fork Bruneau River ... ID-8
West Fork Bruneau River ... NV-8
West Fork Brush Creek—stream ... CA-9
West Fork Brush Creek—stream ... CO-8
West Fork Brush Creek—stream (2) ... MO-7
West Fork Brush Creek—stream ... TN-4
West Fork Brushy Creek—stream ... NC-3
West Fork Brushy Creek—stream ... TX-5
West Fork Buckatunna Creek ... MS-4
West Fork Buck Creek ... CO-8
West Fork Buck Creek—stream ... ID-8
West Fork Buck Creek—stream ... KY-4
West Fork Buck Creek—stream ... NV-8
West Fork Buck Creek—stream ... OR-9
West Fork Buckhorn Canyon—valley ... WY-8
West Fork Buckhorn Creek—stream ... ID-8
West Fork Buckhorn Creek—stream ... OH-6
West Fork Buckland River—stream ... AK-9
West Fork Buck Park Creek—stream ... CO-8
West Fork Buckskin Draw—valley ... AZ-5
West Fork Buffalo Creek—stream ... NV-8
West Fork Buffalo Creek—stream (2) ... WY-8
West Fork Buffalo Fork—stream ... MT-8
West Fork Bufford Creek—stream ... TX-5
West Fork Bull Creek ... MT-8
West Fork Bull Creek—stream ... ID-8
West Fork Bull Creek—stream ... MO-7
West Fork Bull Creek—stream ... NC-3
West Fork Bull Flat Canyon—stream ... AZ-5
West Fork Bullwhacker Creek ... MT-8
West Fork Bullwhacker Creek—stream ... WY-8
West Fork Burch Creek—stream ... LA-4
West Fork Burnett Creek—stream ... CA-9
West Fork Burnt Cane Creek—stream ... AL-4
West Fork Burnt Creek—stream ... ID-8
West Fork Burnt Fork Creek—stream ... MT-8
West Fork Burnt River—stream ... OR-9
West Fork Burntwood Creek—stream ... KS-7
West Fork Burton Creek ... LA-4
West Fork Busseron Creek—stream ... IN-6
West Fork Buster Creek—stream ... MT-8
West Fork Butcher Creek—stream ... MT-8
West Fork Butler Branch—stream ... TN-4
West Fork Butte—summit ... MT-8
West Fork Butte Creek—stream ... ID-8
West Fork Butte Creek—stream ... MT-8
West Fork Butte Creek—stream (2) ... OR-9
West Fork Butte Creek—stream ... WA-9
West Fork Butte Creek Rsvr—reservoir ... OR-9
West Fork Buttermilk Branch—stream ... TN-4
West Fork Buttermilk Creek—stream ... WA-9
West Fork Buttes—summit ... MT-8
West Fork Butts Creek—stream ... ID-8
West Fork Cabin—locale ... ID-8
West Fork Cabin Gulch—valley ... MT-8
West Fork Cable Canyon—valley ... CA-9
West Fork Cache Creek ... MT-8
West Fork Cahokia Creek—stream ... IL-6
West Fork Calcasieu Pass—channel ... LA-4
West Fork Calcasieu River—stream ... LA-4
West Fork Calf Creek—stream ... MT-8
West Fork Camas Creek—stream ... ID-8
West Fork Cameron Creek—stream ... ID-8
West Fork Campbell Creek—stream ... NC-3
West Fork Camp Branch—stream ... FL-3
West Fork Camp Creek ... MT-8
West Fork Camp Creek—stream ... IA-7
West Fork Camp Creek—stream (2) ... MT-8
West Fork Camp Creek—stream ... OR-9
West Fork Camp Creek—stream ... TX-5
West Fork Campground—locale ... CO-8
West Fork Campground—locale ... ID-8
West Fork Campground—locale ... WA-9
West Fork Campground—park ... AZ-5
West Fork Camp Sixtyone D Creek—stream ... CA-9
West Fork Cane Creek—stream ... AR-4
West Fork Cane Creek—stream ... TN-4
West Fork Caney Creek—stream ... AL-4
West Fork Caney Creek—stream ... LA-4
West Fork Caney Creek—stream ... TN-4
West Fork Caney Creek—stream ... TX-5
West Fork Canoe Creek—stream ... KY-4
West Fork Canyon—valley ... ID-8
West Fork Canyon—valley ... NV-8
West Fork Canyon—valley ... WY-8
West Fork Canyon Creek—stream ... AZ-5
West Fork Canyon Creek—stream ... MT-8
West Fork Canyon Creek—stream ... OR-9
West Fork Carbon Creek—stream ... AZ-5
West Fork Carcus Creek—stream ... OR-9
West Fork Caribou Creek ... ID-8
West Fork Carman Creek—stream ... CA-9
West Fork Carmen Creek ... CA-9
West Fork Carr Creek—stream ... CA-9
West Fork Carrol Creek—stream ... OR-9
West Fork Carson River—stream ... CA-9
West Fork Carson River—stream ... NV-8
West Fork Carter Creek—stream ... UT-8
West Fork Cash Creek—stream ... MT-8
West Fork Cassi Creek—stream ... TN-4
West Fork Cataract Creek—stream ... MT-8
West Fork Caton Creek—stream ... ID-8
West Fork Cave Creek—stream ... ID-8
West Fork Cebolla Creek—stream ... CO-8
West Fork Cedar Creek—stream ... ID-8
West Fork Cedar Creek—stream ... VA-3
West Fork Cedar Creek—stream (2) ... WA-9
West Fork Cedar Peak Draw—valley ... UT-8
West Fork Cedar River—stream ... IA-7
West Fork Cem—cemetery ... AR-4
West Fork Cem—cemetery ... IN-6
West Fork Cem—cemetery ... IA-7
West Fork Cem—cemetery ... LA-4
West Fork Cem—cemetery ... MO-7
West Fork Cem—cemetery (2) ... TX-5
West Fork Cem—cemetery ... WI-6
West Fork Centerfire Creek—stream ... NM-5
Westfork Ch—church ... IN-6
West Fork Ch—church ... IA-7
West Fork Ch—church ... KY-4
West Fork Ch—church ... OH-6
West Fork Ch—church ... TX-5
West Fork Chadron Creek—stream ... NE-7
West Fork Chakina River—stream ... AK-9
West Fork Chalk Creek—stream ... TX-5
West Fork Chamberlain Creek—stream ... ID-8
West Fork Chamberlain Creek—stream ... MT-8
West Fork Chambers Creek—stream ... NC-3
West Fork Chambers Creek—stream ... TX-5
West Fork Chandalar River—stream ... AK-9
West Fork Charley Creek—stream ... MT-8
West Fork Chattooga River—stream ... GA-3
West Fork Chaves Creek ... NM-5
West Fork Chavez Creek—stream ... NM-5
West Fork Checkerboard Creek—stream ... MT-8
West Fork Chehalis River—stream ... WA-9
West Fork Chena River—stream ... AK-9
West Fork Cherokee Creek—stream ... CO-8
West Fork Cherokee Creek—stream (2) ... WY-8
West Fork Cherry Creek—stream ... CA-9
West Fork Cherry Creek—stream ... MT-8
West Fork Chestnut Creek—stream ... NC-3
West Fork Chevelon Creek ... AZ-5
West Fork Chicken Creek—stream ... OR-9
West Fork Chicot Pass ... LA-4
West Fork Chicot Pass—channel ... LA-4
West Fork Chignik River—stream ... AK-9
West Fork Chimney Canyon—valley ... NM-5
West Fork Chippewa River—stream ... WI-6
West Fork Chiquito Creek—stream ... CA-9
West Fork Chisholm Creek—stream ... KS-7
West Fork Chistochina River—stream ... AK-9
West Fork Chochetopa Creek ... CO-8
West Fork Chocolate Bayou—stream ... TX-5
West Fork Choctawhatchee River ... AL-4
West Fork Choctawhatchee River—stream ... AL-4
West Fork Chowchilla River—stream ... CA-9
West Fork Chubby Creek—stream ... MS-4
West Fork Chulitna River—stream ... AK-9
West Fork Cibolo Creek—stream ... TX-5
West Fork Cimarron Creek ... CO-8
West Fork Cimarron River—stream ... CO-8
West Fork Circle Bar Draw—valley ... AZ-5
West Fork Citico Creek ... TN-4
West Fork City Creek—stream ... CA-9
West Fork Clarks Creek—stream ... CA-9
West Fork Clarks Fork ... MT-8
West Fork Clarks Fork—stream ... MT-8
West Fork Clarks Fork yellowstone River ... WY-8
West Fork Clarks River—stream (2) ... KY-4
West Fork Clay Hill Creek—stream ... OR-9
West Fork Clear Creek ... IN-6
West Fork Clear Creek—stream ... AR-4
West Fork Clear Creek—stream ... CA-9
West Fork Clear Creek—stream ... CO-8
West Fork Clear Creek—stream (2) ... ID-8
West Fork Clear Creek—stream ... IN-6
West Fork Clear Creek—stream ... MO-7
West Fork Clear Creek—stream ... MT-8
West Fork Clear Creek—stream (4) ... OR-9
West Fork Clear Creek—stream (2) ... TX-5
West Fork Clearwater River—stream ... MT-8
West Fork Clifty Creek—stream ... AL-4
West Fork Clover Creek ... UT-8
West Fork Clover Creek—stream ... CA-9
West Fork Clover Gulch—valley ... CO-8
West Fork Coal Bed Canyon ... CO-8
West Fork Coal Bed Canyon ... UT-8
West Fork Coal Canyon ... CO-8
West Fork Coal Canyon ... UT-8
West Fork Coal Creek—stream ... AK-9
West Fork Coal Creek—stream ... OR-9
West Fork Coal Creek—stream ... WY-8
West Fork Coal Creek Canyon—valley ... CO-8
West Fork Cochetopa Creek ... CO-8
West Fork Cochran Creek—stream ... OR-9
West Fork Cold Spring Canyon—valley ... CA-9
West Fork Cold Springs Creek—stream ... ID-8
West Fork Coldwater Creek—stream ... CO-8
West Fork Cole Mill Branch—stream ... AL-4
West Fork Coleto Creek ... TX-5
West Fork Collahan Creek—stream ... VA-3
West Fork Comb Creek ... MT-8
West Fork Comb Creek—stream ... MT-8
West Fork Combest Creek—stream ... MT-8
West Fork Coon Creek—stream ... WY-8
West Fork Cooper Canyon—valley ... AZ-5
West Fork Cooper Creek—stream ... MT-8
West Fork Coosa Creek—stream ... GA-3
West Fork Copperas Canyon—valley ... AZ-5
West Fork Copper Canyon—valley ... UT-8
West Fork Corn Creek—stream ... UT-8
West Fork Corral—locale ... NM-5
West Fork Corral Creek—stream (2) ... ID-8
West Fork Corral De Piedra Creek ... CA-9
West Fork Costilla Creek—stream ... CO-8
West Fork Costilla Creek—stream ... NM-5
West Fork Cotaco Creek ... AL-4
West Fork Cotaco Creek—stream ... AL-4
West Fork Cottonwood Creek—stream (3) ... CO-8
West Fork Cottonwood Creek—stream ... ID-8
West Fork Cottonwood Creek—stream (5) ... MT-8
West Fork Cottonwood Creek—stream (2) ... OR-9
West Fork Cottonwood Creek—stream (2) ... TX-5
West Fork Cottonwood Creek—stream ... UT-8
West Fork Cottonwood Creek—stream (2) ... WY-8
West Fork Cottonwood Gulch—valley ... CO-8
West Fork Cottonwood Wash—stream ... AZ-5
West Fork Cottonwood Wash—valley ... UT-8
West Fork Cougar Canyon—valley ... ID-8
West Fork Cougar Creek—stream ... ID-8
West Fork Cougar Creek—stream ... WA-9
West Fork Cougar Gulch—valley ... ID-8
West Fork County Park—park ... IA-7
West Fork Cove Creek—stream ... NC-3
West Fork Cove Creek—stream (2) ... VA-3
West Fork Cow Camp—locale ... MT-8
West Fork Cow Creek—stream ... OR-9
West Fork Cow Creek—stream ... TX-5
West Fork Cow Creek—stream ... WY-8
West Fork Cox Creek—stream ... KY-4
West Fork Coyle Branch—stream ... TN-4
West Fork Coyote Creek—stream (2) ... CA-9
West Fork Coyote Creek—stream (2) ... OR-9
West Fork Cramer Creek—stream ... MT-8
West Fork Cranberry River—stream ... WI-6
West Fork Crane Creek—stream ... SC-3
West Fork Crawford Creek—stream ... CA-9
West Fork Crazy Creek—stream ... OR-9
West Fork Cream Creek—stream ... MT-8
West Fork Creek ... AR-4
West Fork Creek ... CA-9
West Fork Creek ... CO-8
West Fork Creek ... ID-8
West Fork Creek ... OH-6
West Fork Creek ... OK-5
West Fork Creek ... TN-4
West Fork Creek ... WA-9
West Fork Creek ... WY-8
West Fork Creek—stream (4) ... ID-8
West Fork Creek—stream ... IL-6
West Fork Creek—stream ... IN-6
West Fork Creek—stream ... LA-4
West Fork Creek—stream (3) ... TN-4
West Fork Creek—stream ... WA-9
West Fork Creek—stream ... WV-2
West Fork Crevice Creek—stream ... MT-8
West Fork Cripple Creek—stream ... AL-4
West Fork Crocus Creek—stream ... KY-4
West Fork Crooked Creek ... MN-6
West Fork Crooked Creek—stream ... AR-4
West Fork Crooked Creek—stream (3) ... ID-8
West Fork Crooked Creek—stream ... IA-7
West Fork Crooked Creek—stream ... MN-6
West Fork Crooked River ... MN-6
West Fork Crooked River—stream ... ID-8
West Fork Crooked River—stream ... MO-7
West Fork Crooks Creek—stream ... WY-8
West Fork Crow Creek—stream ... MT-8
West Fork Crow Gulch—valley ... CA-9
West Fork Crown Creek—stream ... WA-9
West Fork Crystal Creek—stream ... TX-5
West Fork Crystal Creek—stream ... WY-8
West Fork Cub Creek—stream ... TN-4
West Fork Cuivre Creek ... MO-7
West Fork Cuivre River—stream ... MO-7
West Fork Cummins Creek—stream ... TX-5
West Fork Cunniff Creek—stream ... OR-9
West Fork Currant Creek—stream ... CO-8
West Fork Currant Creek—stream ... WY-8
West Fork Curtis Creek ... CO-8
West Fork Dairy Creek—stream ... OR-9
West Fork Dale Creek—stream ... WY-8
West Fork Dallas Creek—stream ... CO-8
West Fork Dall River—stream ... AK-9
West Fork Dam—dam ... MT-8
West Fork Dam—dam ... OH-6
West Fork Dark Canyon—valley ... CO-8
West Fork Davis Creek—stream ... WY-8
West Fork Dayton Creek—stream ... MT-8
West Fork Deadhorse Creek ... CO-8
West Fork Dead Horse Creek—stream ... CO-8
West Fork Deadwood Creek—stream (2) ... OR-9
West Fork Deep Canyon—stream ... UT-8
West Fork Deep Creek ... TX-5
West Fork Deep Creek—stream ... GA-3
West Fork Deep Creek—stream ... ID-8
West Fork Deep Creek—stream ... ND-7
West Fork Deep Creek—stream ... OR-9
West Fork Deep Red Creek—stream ... OK-5
West Fork Deep River—stream ... NC-3
West Fork Deer Creek ... UT-8
West Fork Deer Creek—stream ... ID-8
West Fork Deer Creek—stream ... MT-8
West Fork Deer Creek—stream ... NV-8
West Fork Deer Creek—stream (2) ... OR-9
West Fork Deer Creek—stream (2) ... TX-5
West Fork Deer Creek—stream (3) ... WY-8
West Fork Defeated Creek—stream ... TN-4
West Fork Delaware Creek—stream ... OK-5
West Fork DeLisle Creek—stream ... AR-4
West Fork Dempsey Creek—stream ... WY-8
West Fork Dennison Fork—stream ... AK-9
West Fork Denny Creek ... MT-8
West Fork Denny Creek—stream ... MT-8
West Fork Deschutes River—stream ... WA-9
West Fork Des Moines River ... IA-7
west Fork des Moines River ... MN-6
West Fork Des Moines River ... MO-7
West Fork Devil Canyon—valley ... CA-9
West Fork Devil Creek—stream ... CO-8
West Fork Devils Gate Creek—stream ... WY-8
West Fork Devore Creek—stream ... WA-9
West Fork Dickey Brook—stream ... ME-1
West Fork Dickey River—stream ... WA-9
West Fork Dick Hooten Branch—stream ... TX-5
West Fork Dicks Creek—stream ... NC-3
West Fork Didallas Creek—stream ... CA-9
West Fork Dinner Creek—stream ... TX-5
West Fork Dismal Creek—stream (2) ... OR-9
West Fork Ditch ... IN-6
West Fork Ditch—canal ... CO-8
West Fork Ditch—canal ... IA-7
West Fork Ditch—canal ... OH-6
West Fork Ditch Creek—stream ... WY-8
West Fork Ditch Of Brownlee System ... IN-6
West Fork Dodd Creek—stream ... VA-3
West Fork Doga Creek—stream ... OK-5
West Fork Doling Branch—stream ... MO-7
West Fork Donaldson Creek—stream ... KY-4
West Fork Dosewallips River—stream ... WA-9
West Fork Double Bayou—stream ... TX-5
West Fork Double Branch—stream ... TX-5
West Fork Dougherty Creek—stream ... CA-9
West Fork Doughspoon Creek—stream ... CO-8
West Fork Douglas Creek ... CO-8
West Fork Dove Creek—stream ... TX-5
West Fork Downey Coulee—valley ... MT-8
West Fork Downey Creek—stream ... ID-8
West Fork Drake Creek ... TN-4
West Fork Drakes Creek—stream ... KY-4
West Fork Drakes Creek—stream ... TN-4
West Fork Drift Creek—stream ... OR-9
West Fork Dry Canyon—valley (2) ... CA-9
West Fork Dry Comal Creek—stream ... TX-5
West Fork Dry Creek ... WY-8
West Fork Dry Creek—stream (3) ... CO-8
West Fork Dry Creek—stream ... ID-8
West Fork Dry Creek—stream (3) ... MT-8
West Fork Dry Creek—stream (3) ... OR-9
West Fork Dry Creek—stream ... TN-4
West Fork Dry Creek—stream ... TX-5
West Fork Dry Creek—stream ... WY-8
West Fork Dry Fork—stream ... MO-7
West Fork Dry Fork Creek—stream ... MT-8
West Fork Dry Gulch Creek—stream ... UT-8
West Fork Dry Hollow ... CO-8
West Fork Drywood Creek ... KS-7
West Fork Dry Wood Creek—stream ... KS-7
West Fork Dry Wood Creek—stream ... MO-7
West Fork Duchesne River—stream ... UT-8
West Fork Duck Creek ... OH-6
West Fork Duck Creek—stream ... MT-8
West Fork Duck Creek—stream ... OH-6
West Fork Duck Creek—stream ... OR-9
West Fork Duck Creek—stream ... TN-4
West Fork Duck Creek—stream ... WY-8
West Fork Dugger Branch—stream ... TN-4
West Fork Dugout Gulch—valley ... WY-8
West Fork Dungeness River ... WA-9
West Fork Durozano Bayou ... TX-5
West Fork Dutch Creek—stream ... CA-9
West Fork Dutton Creek—stream ... WY-8
West Fork Dyce Creek—stream ... MT-8
West Fork Dyer Creek ... CO-8
West Fork Eagle Creek ... KY-4
West Fork Eagle Creek—stream ... ID-8
West Fork Eagle Creek—stream ... KY-4
West Fork Eagle Creek—stream ... OH-6
West Fork Eagle Creek—stream ... UT-8
West Fork Early Gulch—valley ... CO-8
West Fork East Bosque River—stream ... TX-5
West Fork East Branch Black River—stream ... OH-6

West Fork East Cheyenne Creek—stream ... TX-5
West Fork East Creek—stream ... MO-7
West Fork East Fork Duck Creek—stream .. OH-6
West Fork East Fork Little Miami River—stream ... OH-6
West Fork East Fork Salmon River—stream ... ID-8
West Fork East Fork Whitewater River—stream ... IN-6
West Fork East Fork Williams Fork—stream ... CO-8
West Fork East Gulch—valley ... OR-9
West Fork East Muddy Creek ... IL-6
West Fork East Pass Creek—stream ... WY-8
West Fork Ecola Creek—stream ... OR-9
West Fork Eddy Gulch—valley ... CA-9
West Forked Gulch—valley ... CO-8
West Fork Eightmile Creek—stream ... KS-7
West Fork Eightmile Creek—stream ... UT-8
West Fork Elk Creek ... OR-9
West Fork Elk Creek—stream (6) ... ID-8
West Fork Elk Creek—stream ... KS-7
West Fork Elk Creek—stream ... MT-8
West Fork Elk Creek—stream ... OR-9
West Fork Elkhorn Creek—stream ... IL-6
West Fork Elkhorn Creek—stream ... WA-9
West Fork Elk River—stream ... CO-8
West Fork Ellis Branch—stream ... TX-5
West Fork Ellis Canyon ... MT-8
West Fork Ellis Canyon—valley ... MT-8
West Fork Ellis Creek ... MT-8
West Fork Ellis Creek—stream ... WA-9
West Fork Elm Creek—stream ... NE-7
West Fork Elm Creek—stream ... SD-7
West Fork Elochoman River—stream ... WA-9
West Fork Emerald Creek—stream ... ID-8
West Fork Encampment River—stream ... CO-8
West Fork Englebaugh Creek—stream ... MT-8
West Fork English Bayou—stream ... LA-4
West Fork Eno River—stream ... NC-3
West Fork Enos Creek—stream ... ID-8
West Fork Espenberg River—stream ... AK-9
West Fork Estes Creek—stream ... SD-7
West Fork Evans Creek—stream ... OR-9
West Fork Evans Gulch—valley ... OR-9
West Fork Fall Branch—stream ... TN-4
West Fork Fall Creek—stream ... CO-8
West Fork Fall Creek—stream ... ID-8
West Fork Falls—falls ... CO-8
West Fork Falls Creek—stream ... MT-8
West Fork Farm Creek—stream (2) ... UT-8
West Fork Farmers Creek—stream ... NE-7
West Fork Fawn Creek—stream ... CO-8
West Fork Fawn Creek—stream ... WA-9
West Fork Feather River ... CA-9
West Fork Ferguson Creek—stream ... CA-9
West Fork Fern Creek—stream ... CA-9
West Fork Fiddler Creek ... WY-8
West Fork Fiddler Creek—stream ... WY-8
West Fork Finney Creek—stream ... MO-7
West Fork First Creek—stream ... OR-9
West Fork First Creek—stream ... WA-9
West Fork Fish Creek—stream (2) ... ID-8
West Fork Fish Creek—stream ... IN-6
West Fork Fish Creek—stream ... MT-8
West Fork Fishhook Creek—stream ... ID-8
West Fork Fishtrap Creek—stream (2) ... MT-8
West Fork Fishtrap Trail—trail ... MT-8
West Fork Fivemile Draw—valley ... NM-5
West Fork Flagstaff Creek—stream ... MT-8
West Fork Flannigan Creek—stream ... ID-8
West Fork Flat Creek—stream ... AK-9
West Fork Flat Creek—stream (2) ... MT-8
West Fork Flat Creek—stream ... WA-9
West Fork Flint Creek ... AL-4
West Fork Flint River—stream ... AL-4
West Fork Floodwood Creek—stream ... ID-8
West Fork Floras Creek—stream ... OR-9
West Fork Floyd River ... IA-7
West Fork Foote Creek—stream ... WY-8
West Fork Forest Camp—locale ... AZ-5
West Fork Fork Run—stream ... PA-2
West Fork Fort Goff Creek—stream ... CA-9
West Fork Fortier Creek—stream ... ID-8
West Fork Fortyeight Creek—stream ... TN-4
West Fork Fortysix Creek—stream ... MT-8
West Fork Foss River—stream ... WA-9
West Fork Fourche Creek—stream ... MO-7
West Fork Fourmile Creek—stream ... WY-8
West Fork Four Mile Run—stream ... IN-6
West Fork Fourmile Wash—stream ... NM-5
West Fork Fourteenmile Creek—stream ... IN-6
West Fork Fox Creek—stream ... CA-9
West Fork Fox Creek—stream ... OR-9
West Fork Free Creek ... AR-4
West Fork Freeman Draw—valley ... WY-8
West Fork French Broad River—stream ... NC-3
West Fork French Cabin Creek—stream ... WA-9
West Fork Frozen Creek ... OR-9
West Fork Froze To Death Creek—stream . MT-8
West Fork Gale Creek—stream ... WA-9
West Fork Gallatin River—stream ... MT-8
West Fork Gallegos Canyon—valley ... NM-5
West Fork Gap Draw—valley ... NM-5
West Fork Garden Creek—stream ... WY-8
West Fork Gedney Creek—stream ... ID-8
West Fork Genito Creek—stream ... VA-3
West Fork Gila River—stream ... NM-5
West Fork Gilbert Creek—stream ... OR-9
West Fork Gists Creek—stream ... TN-4
West Fork Glacier—glacier (3) ... AK-9
West Fork Glady Fork—stream ... WV-2
West Fork Glen Annie Canyon—valley ... CA-9
West Fork Glen Creek—stream ... AK-9
West Fork Glenn Creek—stream ... OR-9
West Fork Glover Creek ... OK-5
West Fork Glover River—stream ... OK-5
West Fork Gold Creek—stream ... MT-8
West Fork Golden Gulch Drain—canal ... ID-8
West Fork Gonzales Creek ... TX-5
West Fork Goodeve Creek—stream ... WA-9
West Fork Good Spring Creek—stream ... CO-8
West Fork Goose Creek ... TN-4
West Fork Goose Creek ... WY-8
West Fork Goose Creek—stream ... ID-8
West Fork Goose Creek—stream (2) ... NC-3
West Fork Goose Creek—stream ... OR-9
West Fork Goose Creek—stream ... TX-5
West Fork Gospel Creek—stream ... ID-8
West Forkgraham Creek ... AR-4
West Fork Graham Draw—valley ... WY-8
West Fork Grand ... MO-7
West Fork Grand Central River—stream ... AK-9
West Fork Grand River ... IA-7
West Fork Granite Boulder Creek—stream ... OR-9
West Fork Granite Creek—stream ... AK-9
West Fork Granite Creek—stream ... CA-9
West Fork Granite Creek—stream ... ID-8
West Fork Granite Creek—stream ... MT-8
West Fork Granite Creek—stream ... NV-8
West Fork Granite Creek—stream ... WA-9
West Fork Grant Canyon—valley ... NV-8
West Fork Grants Bayou—stream ... LA-4
West Fork Grape Creek—stream ... TX-5
West Fork Grave Creek ... ID-8
West Fork Gravelly Creek—stream ... TX-5
West Fork Gray Creek—stream ... CA-9
West Fork Gray Creek—stream ... WY-8
West Fork Grays River—stream ... WA-9
West Fork Greasewood Creek—stream ... OR-9
West Fork Greasy Creek ... AR-4
West Fork Greenbrier River—stream ... WV-2
West Fork Green Creek—stream ... CA-9
West Fork Greens Creek—stream ... MS-4
West Fork Gregory Creek—stream ... SC-3
West Fork Greys River—stream ... WY-8
West Fork Griffith Draw—valley ... WY-8
West Fork Grindstone Creek—stream ... ID-8
West Fork Groat Creek—stream ... MT-8
West Fork Groundhog Creek—stream ... NV-8
West Fork Groundhouse River—stream ... MN-6
West Fork Grouse Creek—stream ... ID-8
West Fork Grouse Creek—stream ... WA-9
West Fork Grub Creek—stream ... OR-9
West Fork Guess Creek ... TN-4
West Fork Gulch ... CO-8
West Fork Gulkana River—stream ... AK-9
West Fork Gunsolus Creek—stream ... TX-5
West Fork Gunstocker Creek—stream ... TN-4
West Fork Hall Creek—stream ... WA-9
West Fork Halls Creek ... WI-6
West Fork Hamilton Creek—stream ... TN-4
West Fork Hams Fork—stream ... WY-8
West Fork Hanging Woman Creek ... WY-8
West Fork Hanley Creek—stream ... MT-8
West Fork Harts Creek ... WV-2
West Fork Hatcher Creek—stream ... KY-4
West Fork Hatchet Creek—stream ... AL-4
West Fork Hatchie River ... MS-4
West Fork Hat Creek—stream ... CA-9
West Fork Hawkins Creek ... ID-8
West Fork Hawkwright Creek—stream ... SD-7
West Fork Hay Creek ... MN-6
West Fork Hay Creek ... WY-8
West Fork Hay Creek—stream ... OR-9
West Fork Hay Creek—stream ... SD-7
West Fork Hay Creek—stream (2) ... WY-8
West Fork Hayden Creek—stream ... ID-8
West Fork Hellroaring Creek ... MT-8
West Fork Hellroaring Creek ... WY-8
West Fork Hendricks Creek—stream ... IN-6
West Fork Henshaw Creek—stream ... AK-9
West Fork Henshaw (Sozhekla) Creek—stream ... AK-9
West Fork Herd Creek—stream ... ID-8
West Fork Hermaphrodite Creek—stream .. SD-7
West Fork Hickory Creek—stream ... TN-4
West Fork Hicks Creek—stream ... TN-4
West Fork High Prairie Creek—stream ... OR-9
West Fork Hill Creek—stream ... UT-8
**West Fork Hills (subdivision)**—pop pl ... TN-4
West Fork Hines Branch—stream ... TX-5
Westfork (historical)—locale ... SD-7
**Westfork (historical)**—pop pl ... TN-4
West Fork Hiwassee River—stream ... TN-4
West Fork Hobo Creek—stream ... ID-8
West Fork Hodson Creek—stream ... ID-8
West Fork Hollow—valley ... MO-7
West Fork Hollow—valley ... WV-2
West Fork Homochitto River—stream ... MS-4
West Fork Honey Creek ... MO-7
West Fork Honey Creek—stream ... OH-6
West Fork Honeydew Creek—stream ... CA-9
West Fork Hood River—stream ... OR-9
West Fork Hoop Creek—stream ... TN-4
West Fork Hopkins Branch—stream ... VA-3
West Fork Hopley Creek—stream ... MT-8
West Fork Hoquiam River ... WA-9
West Fork Hoquiam River—stream ... WA-9
West Fork Horn Creek—stream ... ID-8
West Fork Horse Canyon—valley ... CO-8
West Fork Horse Creek—stream ... CA-9
West Fork Horse Creek—stream ... FL-3
West Fork Horse Creek—stream (2) ... MT-8
West Fork Horse Creek—stream ... OK-5
West Fork Horse Creek—stream ... OR-9
West Fork Horse Creek—stream ... TX-5
West Fork Horse Creek—stream ... WY-8
West Fork Horsefly Creek—stream ... CO-8
West Fork Horsehead Creek—stream ... AR-4
West Fork Horse Heaven Creek ... OR-9
West Fork Horseshoe Draw—valley ... WY-8
West Fork Horsetail Creek—stream ... WY-8
West Fork Hospital Canyon—valley ... CA-9
West Fork Hot Air Canyon—valley ... AZ-5
West Fork Hotel Creek—stream ... ID-8
West Fork Hound Creek—stream ... MT-8
West Fork Howard Creek—stream ... OR-9
West Fork Hudlow Creek—stream ... ID-8
West Fork Hughes Creek—stream ... CA-9
West Fork Hughes Creek—stream ... ID-8
West Fork Hugus Creek—stream ... ID-8
West Fork Hull Creek—stream ... ID-8
West Fork Humptulips River—stream ... WA-9
West Fork Hundred And Two River ... IA-7
West Fork Hundred and Two Rivers ... MO-7
West Fork Hungry Creek ... ID-8
West Fork Hungry Creek—stream ... MT-8
West Fork Hunt Creek—stream ... UT-8
West Fork Hunter Creek—stream ... CA-9
West Fork Hunters Creek—stream ... TX-5
West Fork Hunton Creek—stream ... WY-8
West Fork Huzzah Creek—stream ... MO-7
West Fork Hyalite Creek ... MT-8
West Fork Ichawaynochaway Creek—stream ... GA-3
West Fork Illinois River—stream ... OR-9
West Fork Immells Creek ... MT-8
West Fork Indian Creek—stream ... AK-9
West Fork Indian Creek—stream ... CO-8
West Fork Indian Creek—stream (2) ... ID-8
West Fork Indian Creek—stream ... IN-6
West Fork Indian Creek—stream ... KY-4
West Fork Indian Creek—stream (3) ... MT-8
West Fork Indian Creek—stream (2) ... OR-9
West Fork Indian Creek—stream ... TN-4
West Fork Indian Creek—stream ... TX-5
West Fork Indian Kentucky Creek—stream . IN-6
West Fork Indigo Creek—stream ... OR-9
West Fork Iron Creek—stream ... ID-8
West Fork Iron Mountain Creek—stream .. WY-8
West Fork Iron Spring Creek—stream ... WY-8
West Fork Jack Creek—stream ... MT-8
West Fork Jacks River—stream ... GA-3
West Fork James Creek—stream ... ID-8
West Fork Jenkins Creek—stream ... MO-7
West Fork Jenkins Creek—stream ... NC-3
West Fork Jenkins Draw—valley ... WY-8
West Fork Jernigan Creek—stream ... TX-5
West Fork Jester Creek—stream ... KS-7
West Fork Jimmie New Creek—stream ... MT-8
West Fork Joe Branch—stream ... TN-4
West Fork Joe Lott Creek—stream ... UT-8
West Fork Johns Creek—stream ... TX-5
West Fork Johnson Creek—stream ... OR-9
West Fork Jones Creek—stream ... MO-7
West Fork Jones Creek—stream ... OR-9
West Fork Jordan Branch—stream ... MO-7
West Fork Jordan Creek—stream ... CA-9
West Fork Jordan Creek—stream ... WY-8
West Fork Jubb Creek—stream ... CO-8
West Fork Junetta Creek—stream ... OR-9
West Fork Juniper Creek—stream ... FL-3
West Fork Juniper Creek Rsvr—reservoir ... OR-9
West Fork Kalaloch Creek—stream ... WA-9
West Fork Kaskaskia River—stream ... IL-6
West Fork Katete River—stream ... AK-9
West Fork Kawela Gulch—valley ... HI-9
West Fork Keechi Creek ... TX-5
West Fork Keechi Creek—stream ... TX-5
West Fork Keeler Creek—stream ... ID-8
West Fork Keeler Creek—stream ... MT-8
West Fork Keg Creek—stream ... IN-6
West Fork Kelley Creek—stream ... ID-8
West Fork Kelly Bayou—stream ... AR-4
West Fork Kennedy Creek—stream ... CA-9
West Fork Kent Branch—stream ... VA-3
West Fork Kettle River ... MN-6
West Fork Kickapoo Creek—stream ... IL-6
West Fork Kickapoo Creek—stream ... IN-6
West Fork Kickapoo River—stream ... WI-6
West Fork Kimball Creek—stream ... CO-8
West Fork King Creek—stream ... CA-9
West Fork King Hill Creek—stream ... ID-8
West Fork Klickitat River—stream ... WA-9
West Fork Knapp Creek—stream ... WI-6
West Fork Knoblick Creek—stream ... KY-4
West Fork Knownothing Creek—stream ... CA-9
West Fork Koontz Creek—stream ... OR-9
West Fork Kutz Canyon—valley ... NM-5
West Fork Kuyukutuk River—stream ... AK-9
West Fork La Bonte Creek—stream (2) ... WY-8
West Fork Ladd Canyon—valley ... CA-9
West Fork Ladue River—stream ... AK-9
West Fork Lagunitas Creek—stream ... CA-9
West Fork Lake—lake ... CO-8
West Fork Lake—lake ... ID-8
West Fork Lake Creek—stream ... ID-8
West Fork Lake Creek—stream ... MT-8
West Fork Lake Creek—stream (2) ... OR-9
West Fork Lake Greeson—bay ... AR-4
West Fork Lakes—lake (2) ... ID-8
West Fork La Marche Creek—stream ... MT-8
West Fork Lanahassee Creek—stream ... GA-3
West Fork Langford Creek—stream ... MD-2
West Fork Laura Furnace Creek—stream .. KY-4
West Fork Laurel Branch—stream ... TN-4
West Fork Lavender Creek—stream ... UT-8
West Fork Lawrence Creek—stream ... LA-4
West Fork Lazy Creek—stream ... MT-8
West Fork Leatherwood Creek—stream ... PA-2
West Fork Leatherwood Creek—stream ... TN-4
West Fork Leatherwood Creek—stream ... VA-3
West Fork Lehigh River—stream ... PA-2
West Fork Lehman Creek—stream ... ID-8
West Fork Leopard Creek—stream ... CO-8
West Fork Lewis Creek—stream ... KY-4
West Fork Lewis Creek—stream ... MS-4
West Fork Lewis Fork ... NC-3
West Fork Libby Creek—stream ... AK-9
West Fork Lick Creek—stream ... IN-6
West Fork Lick Creek—stream ... OR-9
West Fork Lick Creek—stream ... TN-4
West Fork Licks—locale ... MT-8
West Fork Liebre Gulch—valley ... CA-9
West Fork Lilly Creek ... TX-5
West Fork Lime Creek—stream ... UT-8
West Fork Lime Creek—stream ... WA-9
West Fork Limekiln Creek—stream ... CA-9
West Fork Limestone Creek—stream ... MO-7
West Fork Lincoln Creek ... CO-8
West Fork Lindley Creek—stream ... ID-8
West Fork Linville Creek—stream ... VA-3
West Fork Linville River—stream ... NC-3
West Fork Lion Canyon—valley ... CO-8
West Fork Listle Creek—stream ... MT-8
West Fork Little Badger Creek—stream ... WY-8
West Fork Little Bear Creek—stream ... ID-8
West Fork Little Bear Creek—stream ... OR-9
West Fork Little Bear River—stream ... UT-8
West Fork Little Beaver Creek—stream ... OH-6
West Fork Little Bridge Creek—stream ... WA-9
West Fork Little Cane Creek—stream ... TN-4
West Fork Little Colorado River—stream ... AZ-5
West Fork Little Comite Creek—stream ... LA-4
West Fork Little Comite Creek—stream (2) ... MS-4
West Fork Little Creek—stream ... MO-7
West Fork Little Creek—stream ... NC-3
West Fork Little Creek—stream ... TN-4
West Fork Little Delta River—stream ... AK-9
West Fork Little Eightmile Creek—stream .. ID-8
West Fork Little Goose Creek—stream ... WY-8
West Fork Little Indian Creek—stream ... OR-9
West Fork Little Kanawha River—stream .. WV-2
West Fork Little Kiokee Creek ... GA-3
West Fork Little Loon Creek—stream ... ID-8
West Fork Little McKittrick Draw—valley .. NM-5
West Fork Little Meramec River ... MO-7
West Fork Little Mud River—stream ... AK-9
West Fork Little Nisqually River—stream ... WA-9
West Fork Little Pigeon River ... TN-4
West Fork Little Porcupine Creek—stream ... MT-8
West Fork Little Pudding River—stream ... OR-9
West Fork Little Pumpkin Creek—stream ... MT-8
West Fork Little Reed Island Creek—stream ... VA-3
West Fork Little Rib River—stream ... WI-6
West Fork Little River ... SC-3
West Fork Little River—stream ... AL-4
West Fork Little River—stream (2) ... GA-3
West Fork Little River—stream ... NC-3
West Fork Little River—stream ... SC-3
West Fork Little River—stream ... VA-3
West Fork Little Roanoke Creek ... VA-3
West Fork Little Sand Creek—stream ... UT-8
West Fork Little Sheep Creek—stream ... MT-8
West Fork Little Sioux River—stream (2) ... IA-7
West Fork Little Sioux River—stream ... MN-6
West Fork Little Snake Creek—stream ... NY-2
West Fork Little Soda Canyon—valley ... CO-8
West Fork Little Soldier Creek—stream ... ID-8
West Fork Little South Fork Indian Creek—stream ... CA-9
West Fork Little Springs Canyon—valley ... AZ-5
West Fork Little Thompson River ... CO-8
West Fork Little Thompson River—stream . CO-8
West Fork Little Timber Creek—stream ... MT-8
West Fork Little Wildcat Creek—stream ... IN-6
West Fork Lizard Canyon—valley ... CA-9
West Fork Loco Creek—stream ... WY-8
West Fork Locust Creek—stream ... IA-7
West Fork Lolo Creek—stream ... MT-8
West Fork Lone Tree Creek—stream ... MT-8
West Fork Long Branch—locale ... CO-8
West Fork Long Branch Tomichi Creek—stream ... CO-8
West Fork Long Canyon—valley ... CO-8
West Fork Long Creek—stream ... MT-8
West Fork Long Creek—stream ... TN-4
West Fork Long Creek—stream ... WA-9
West Fork Long Creek—stream (2) ... WY-8
West Fork Long Meadow Creek—stream ... CA-9
West Fork Long Tom Creek—stream ... ID-8
West Fork Lookout Creek—stream ... AL-4
West Fork Lookout Tower—locale ... WI-6
West Fork Lookout Tower—tower ... IN-6
West Fork Loop Loop Creek ... WA-9
West Fork Lost Creek—stream (2) ... AL-4
West Fork Lost Creek—stream (2) ... MO-7
West Fork Lost Creek—stream ... MT-8
West Fork Lost Fork—stream ... MT-8
West Fork Lost Man Creek—stream ... ID-8
West Fork Lost Mine Creek ... ID-8
West Fork Lower Bowman Run—stream ... WV-2
West Fork Lower Deer Creek—stream ... MT-8
West Fork Lower Howard Creek—stream ... KY-4
West Fork Lower Willow Creek—stream ... MT-8
West Fork Luffenholtz Creek ... CA-9
West Fork Lukfata Creek—stream ... OK-5
West Fork Luna Creek—stream ... NM-5
West Fork Lunt Branch—stream ... TN-4
West Fork Lynn Creek ... TN-4
West Fork Lyons Gulch—valley ... MT-8
West Fork Maclaren River—stream ... AK-9
West Fork Madison River—stream ... MT-8
West Fork Magpie Canyon—valley ... UT-8
West Fork Major Creek—stream ... WA-9
West Fork Maloney Creek—stream ... ID-8
West Fork Mancos River ... CO-8
West Fork Maple Creek—stream ... NE-7
West Fork Markham Wash ... AZ-5
West Fork Marsh Bog Brook—stream ... NJ-2
West Fork Martins Creek—stream ... PA-2
West Fork Marys Creek—stream ... WY-8
West Fork Marys Lake Creek ... WY-8
West Fork Marys River ... OR-9
West Fork Marys River—stream ... OR-9
West Fork Massac Creek—stream ... KY-4
West Fork Matilija Creek ... CA-9
West Fork Mayfield Creek—stream ... ID-8
West Fork Mayfield Creek—stream ... KY-4
West Fork Maynard Creek—stream ... TX-5
West Fork Mazon River—stream ... IL-6
West Fork McFarren Gulch—valley ... ID-8
West Fork McGraw Creek—stream ... OR-9
West Fork McKinney Creek—stream ... CA-9
West Fork McLean Brook—stream ... ME-1
West Fork McQuade Creek—stream ... OR-9
West Fork Meadow Brook—stream ... OR-9
West Fork Meadow Creek—stream ... ID-8
West Fork Meadow Creek—stream ... WY-8
West Fork Meadows—flat ... CO-8
West Fork Medicine Creek ... MO-7
West Fork Medicine Creek*—stream ... IA-7
West Fork Medicine Creek—stream ... MO-7
West Fork Menatchee Creek—stream ... WA-9
West Fork Mendenhall Creek—stream ... MT-8
West Fork Merchant Creek—stream ... UT-8
West Fork Merry Creek—stream ... ID-8
West Fork Methow River ... WA-9
West Fork Methow River—stream ... WA-9
West Fork Methow Trail—trail ... WA-9
West Fork Mica Creek—stream ... ID-8
West Fork Middle Blue Creek—stream ... CO-8
West Fork Middle Cottonwood Creek—stream ... WY-8
West Fork Middle Creek—stream ... CA-9
West Fork Middle Creek—stream ... MT-8
West Fork Middle Fork Big Creek—stream ... MT-8
West Fork Middle Fork Stewart Gulch—valley ... CO-8
West Fork Middle Fork Ute Canyon—valley ... CO-8
West Fork Middle Nodaway River—stream . IA-7
West Fork Middle Rock Creek—stream ... OK-5
West Fork Middle Sandy Creek—stream ... TX-5
West Fork Milk River ... MT-8
West Fork Mill Creek ... IN-6
West Fork Mill Creek ... TX-5
West Fork Mill Creek—stream ... AL-4
West Fork Mill Creek—stream (2) ... AR-4
West Fork Mill Creek—stream ... CA-9
West Fork Mill Creek—stream ... KY-4
West Fork Mill Creek—stream (2) ... MT-8
West Fork Mill Creek—stream (3) ... OH-6
West Fork Mill Creek—stream (2) ... OR-9
West Fork Mill Creek—stream ... TX-5
West Fork Miller Creek—stream (2) ... MT-8
West Fork Miller Creek—stream ... VA-3
West Fork Miller Creek—stream ... WY-8
West Fork Miller River—stream ... WA-9
West Fork Millicoma River—stream ... OR-9
West Fork Mimbres River—stream ... NM-5
West Fork Minagamahone Brook—stream .. NJ-2
West Fork Miners Creek—stream ... CA-9
West Fork Mink Creek—stream ... ID-8
West Fork Minneconjou Creek—stream ... SD-7
West Fork Mission Creek—stream ... CA-9
West Fork Mission Creek—stream ... ID-8
West Fork Moccasin Creek—stream ... AR-4
West Fork Mogollon Creek—stream ... NM-5
West Fork Mojave River—stream ... CA-9
West Fork Montana Creek—stream ... ID-8
West Fork Montgomery Creek—stream ... GA-3
West Fork Montgomery Creek—stream ... ID-8
West Fork Montreal River—stream ... WI-6
West Fork Monumental Creek—stream ... ID-8
West Fork Moon Creek—stream ... ID-8
West Fork Moon Creek—stream ... MT-8
West Fork Moores Creek—stream ... ID-8
West Fork Moorman Creek—stream ... NY-2
West Fork Moose Creek—stream (2) ... AK-9
West Fork Moose Horn River—stream ... MN-6
West Fork Moose River—stream ... AK-9
West Fork Morgan Creek—stream ... ID-8
West Fork Morgan Gulch ... CO-8
West Fork Mosby Creek—stream ... OR-9
West Fork Moses Creek—stream ... NC-3
West Fork Mosier Creek—stream ... OR-9
West Fork Mtn—summit ... ID-8
West Fork Mtn—summit ... OK-5
West Fork Mud Creek—stream ... CO-8
West Fork Mud Creek—stream (2) ... MT-8
West Fork Mudd Creek—stream ... MT-8
West Fork Muddy Creek—stream ... KS-7
West Fork Muddy Creek—stream ... MT-8
West Fork Muir Creek—stream ... OR-9
West Fork Mukewater Creek ... TX-5
West Fork Mulberry Creek ... AL-4
West Fork Mulberry Creek—stream ... TN-4
West Fork Mulberry River ... AL-4
West Fork Mule Creek—stream ... OR-9
West Fork Mule Creek—stream ... SD-7
West Fork Murray Draw—valley ... WY-8
West Fork Mustang Creek ... TX-5
West Fork Mustang Creek—stream ... TX-5
West Fork Myers Creek—stream ... WA-9
West Fork Naches River ... WA-9
West Fork Naneum Creek ... WA-9
West Fork Naneum Creek—stream ... WA-9
West Fork Nara Visa Arroyo—stream ... NM-5
West Fork Navajo Canyon—valley ... CO-8
West Fork Navarre Creek—stream ... ID-8
West Fork Navarro Creek ... ID-8
West Fork Neal Creek—stream ... OR-9
West Fork Nehouse Creek—stream ... CA-9
West Fork Neosho River—stream ... KS-7
West Fork Nevada Creek—stream ... MT-8
West Fork Newsome Creek—stream ... ID-8
West Fork Nez Perce Creek—stream ... ID-8
West Fork Niangua River—stream ... MO-7
West Fork Ninemile Creek—stream ... CO-8
West Fork Nixon Fork—stream ... AK-9
West Fork Nixon River—stream ... AK-9
West Fork Nizina River—stream ... AK-9
West Fork Nolan River—stream ... TX-5
West Fork No Mouth Creek—stream ... SD-7
West Fork Nordaway River ... IA-7
West Fork North Branch Chicago River—stream ... IL-6
West Fork North Canyon—valley ... UT-8
West Fork North Creek—stream ... UT-8
West Fork North Creek Draw—valley ... TX-5
West Fork North Elk Creek—stream ... CO-8
West Fork North Fork Big Wood River—stream ... ID-8
West Fork North Fork Embarrass River ... IL-6
West Fork North Fork Innoko River—stream ... AK-9
West Fork North Fork Purgatoire River—stream ... CO-8
West Fork North Fork Salmon River—stream ... ID-8
West Fork North Fork Teton River—stream ... MT-8
West Fork North Fork Wilson River—stream ... OR-9
West Fork North Honcut Creek—stream ... CA-9
West Fork North Sunday Creek—stream ... MT-8
West Fork O,Hara Creek—stream ... ID-8
West Fork Oak Creek—stream (2) ... AZ-5
West Fork Oaks Creek—stream ... TX-5
West Fork Obey River—stream ... TN-4
West Fork Obia Creek ... ID-8
West Fork of Beaver Dam Creek ... SD-7
West Fork Of Big Blue River ... NE-7
West Fork Of Calcasieu River ... LA-4
West Fork of Deep Creek ... ND-7
West Fork of East Fork Salmon River ... ID-8
West Fork of Fishhook Creek ... ID-8
West Fork of Kickapoo River ... WI-6
West Fork of Lake Fork ... UT-8
West Fork of Monongahela River ... WV-2
West Fork of North Fork Desolation Creek—stream ... OR-9
West Fork of North Fork Eel River ... CA-9
West Fork of Point Remove Creek ... AR-4
West Fork of South Fork of St. Joe River ... ID-8
West Fork Of Ten-mile Creek ... CO-8
West Fork of The Forks—stream ... AK-9
West Fork of the San Jacinto River ... TX-5
West Fork of the Trinity River ... TX-5
West Fork of the West Fork of Mill Creek ... MT-8
West Fork Of Watermelon ... GA-3
West Fork Of White River ... IN-6
West Fork Ohio Brush Creek—stream ... OH-6
West Fork Oil Field—oilfield ... CO-8
West Fork Olallie Creek ... OR-9
West Fork Oldman Creek—gut ... NJ-2
West Fork Old Mans Gulch—valley ... CO-8
West Fork Olsen Bay Creek—stream ... AK-9
West Fork One Hundred and Two River—stream ... IA-7
West Fork One Hundred and Two River—stream ... MO-7
West Fork Onion Creek—stream ... WA-9
West Fork Oraibi Wash—valley ... AZ-5
West Fork Osier Creek—stream ... ID-8
West Fork Otter Creek—stream ... IL-6
West Fork Otter Creek—stream (2) ... KY-4
West Fork Overalls Creek—stream ... KY-4
West Fork Overflow Creek—stream ... NC-3
West Fork Packer Creek—stream ... ID-8
West Fork Packer Creek—stream ... MT-8
West Fork Pahsimeroi River—stream ... ID-8
West Fork Paint Creek—stream ... TN-4
West Fork Palm Canyon—valley ... CA-9
West Fork Palmer Canyon—valley ... CA-9
West Fork Palmer Creek—stream ... OR-9
West Fork Palo Pinto Creek—stream ... TX-5
West Fork Panther Creek—stream ... FL-3
West Fork Panther Creek—stream ... OR-9
West Fork Panther Creek—stream ... TN-4
West Fork Panther Creek—stream ... TX-5
West Fork Papoose Creek—stream ... ID-8
West Fork Parachute Creek—stream ... CO-8
West Fork Parashant Wash—valley ... AZ-5
West Fork Park Creek—stream ... CO-8
West Fork Park Creek—stream ... OR-9
West Fork Parks Creek—stream ... CA-9
West Fork Pasayten River—stream ... WA-9
West Fork Pass—gap ... WY-8
West Fork Pasture Creek—stream ... MT-8
West Fork Pat Canyon—valley ... CO-8
West Fork Patrick Creek—stream ... CA-9
West Fork Pea Creek—stream ... AL-4
West Fork Peasley Creek—stream ... ID-8
West Fork Peavine Creek—stream ... OR-9
West Fork Pebble Creek—stream ... OR-9
West Fork Pecwan Creek—stream ... CA-9
West Fork Pen Creek—stream ... TX-5
West Fork Perreau Creek—stream ... ID-8
West Fork Petite Saline Creek—stream ... MO-7
West Fork Petty Creek—stream ... MT-8
West Fork Phantom Creek ... AZ-5
West Fork Phipps Creek—stream ... OR-9
West Fork Phoenix Park Canyon—valley ... AZ-5
West Fork Physic Creek—stream ... MT-8
West Fork Pigeon Creek—stream ... IN-6
West Fork Pigeon River—stream ... NC-3
West Fork Pigeon Roost Branch—stream ... KY-4
West Fork Pilgrim Creek—stream ... MT-8
West Fork Pilot Grove Creek—stream ... TX-5
West Fork Pine Creek ... ID-8
West Fork Pine Creek ... UT-8
West Fork Pine Creek—stream ... ID-8
West Fork Pine Creek—stream ... NV-8
West Fork Pine Creek—stream (6) ... OR-9
West Fork Pine Swamp Creek—stream ... NC-3
West Fork Pinhook Creek—stream ... AL-4
West Fork Pinkham Creek—stream ... MT-8
West Fork Pinos Creek—stream ... CO-8
West Fork Pinto Creek—stream ... AZ-5
West Fork Placer Creek—stream ... ID-8
West Fork Platte River ... CO-8
West Fork Plattin Creek—stream ... MO-7
West Fork Plum Bush Creek—stream ... CO-8
West Fork Plum Creek—stream ... CA-9
West Fork Plum Creek—stream ... TX-5
West Fork Plum Creek—stream ... VA-3
West Fork Plummer Creek—stream ... CA-9
West Fork Point—cliff ... ID-8
West Fork Point—summit ... MT-8
West Fork Point Remove Creek ... AR-4
West Fork Point Remove Creek—stream ... AR-4
West Fork Pole Creek ... NV-8
West Fork Pole Creek—stream ... CO-8
West Fork Pole Creek—stream (2) ... MT-8
West Fork Pollock Canyon—valley ... CO-8
West Fork Pond Creek—stream ... TN-4
West Fork Pond Creek—stream ... TX-5
West Fork Pond Fork—stream ... WV-2
West Fork Pond River—stream ... KY-4
West Fork Pony Creek ... KS-7
West Fork Poplar River—stream ... MT-8
West Fork Porcupine Creek—stream ... MT-8
West Fork Porphyry Creek—stream ... ID-8
West Fork Portage Creek—stream ... MI-6
West Fork Porter Creek—stream ... WA-9
West Fork Post Oak Creek ... MO-7
West Fork Post Oak Creek—stream ... MO-7
Westfork Post Office ... TN-4
West Fork Postoffice Creek—stream ... ID-8
West Fork Post Office (historical)—building ... TN-4
West Fork Potlatch Creek ... ID-8
West Fork Potlatch River—stream ... ID-8
West Fork Powderhorn Creek—stream ... CO-8
West Fork Prairie Creek—stream ... AR-4
West Fork Prairie Creek—stream ... ID-8
West Fork Prairie Creek—stream ... LA-4
West Fork Prairie Creek—stream ... OR-9
West Fork Prairie Dog Town Fork Red River—stream ... TX-5
West Fork Prairie River—stream ... MN-6
West Fork Prather Creek—stream ... OR-9
West Fork Preuss Creek ... ID-8
West Fork Price Creek—stream ... MT-8
West Fork Price River ... UT-8
West Fork Prichard Creek—stream ... ID-8
West Fork Pryor Cove Branch—stream ... TN-4
West Fork Pryor Creek—stream ... MO-7
West Fork Ptarmigan Creek—stream ... WA-9
West Fork Pueblo Creek—stream ... NM-5
West Fork Pumpkin Creek—stream ... TX-5
West Fork Pumpkinvine Creek ... GA-3
West Fork Pumpkinvine Creek—stream ... GA-3
West Fork Pushepatapa Creek—stream ... LA-4
West Fork Pushepatapa Creek—stream ... MS-4
West Fork Quanah Creek—stream ... OK-5
West Fork Quartz Creek—stream ... MT-8
West Fork Quartzville Creek—stream ... OR-9
West Fork Quilceda Creek—stream ... WA-9
West Fork Race Creek—stream ... ID-8
West Fork Rainy Creek—stream ... AK-9
West Fork Ranch—locale ... CO-8
West Fork Ranch Creek—stream ... MT-8
West Fork Rancherie Creek—stream ... OR-9
West Fork Ranger Station—locale (3) ... MT-8
West Fork Rapid Creek—stream ... ID-8
West Fork Rapid River—stream ... ID-8
West Fork Rat Root River ... MN-6
West Fork Rattlesnake Creek ... KS-7
West Fork Rattlesnake Creek—stream ... CA-9
West Fork Rattlesnake Creek—stream (2) .. ID-8
West Fork Rattlesnake Creek—stream ... OR-9

West Fork Rattlesnake Creek (distributary)—stream ... OR-9
West Fork Rattlesnake Draw—valley ... WY-8
West Fork Razor Creek—stream ... MT-8
West Fork Red Canyon—valley ... ID-8
West Fork Red Canyon—valley ... UT-8
West Fork Red Creek—stream ... CO-8
West Fork Red Dirt Creek—stream ... CO-8
West Fork Red River ... ID-8
West Fork Red River—stream ... ID-8
West Fork Red River—stream ... KY-4
West Fork Red River—stream ... NM-5
West Fork Red River—stream ... TN-4
West Fork Remuda Creek—stream ... MT-8
West Fork Reservoir Creek—stream ... ID-8
West Fork Rest Area—locale (2) ... MT-8
West Fork Revais Creek—stream ... MT-8
West Fork Reynolds Creek—stream ... ID-8
West Fork Reynolds Creek—stream ... TX-5
West Fork Richardson Creek—stream ... AL-4
West Fork Richland Creek—stream ... IL-6
West Fork Ridge ... WY-8
West Fork Ridge—ridge ... VA-3
West Fork Ridge Creek—stream ... NJ-2
West Fork Riley Creek—stream ... TN-4
West Fork Riley Creek - in part ... TN-4
West Fork Rio Brazos—stream ... NM-5
West Fork Rio Chama—stream ... CO-8
West Fork Rio Santa Barbara—stream ... NM-5
West Fork River—stream ... WV-2
West Fork Road Spring—spring ... OR-9
West Fork Roaring Run—stream ... PA-2
West Fork Roark Creek—stream ... MO-7
West Fork Robbins Creek—stream ... ID-8
West Fork Robertson Creek—stream ... MT-8
West Fork Robertson River—stream ... AK-9
West Fork Robinson Creek—stream ... TN-4
West Fork Rock Canyon—valley ... CO-8
West Fork Rock Creek ... ID-8
West Fork Rock Creek—stream ... CA-9
West Fork Rock Creek—stream (3) ... ID-8
West Fork Rock Creek—stream (4) ... MT-8
West Fork Rock Creek—stream ... NV-8
West Fork Rock Creek—stream ... OK-5
West Fork Rock Creek—stream ... OR-9
West Fork Rock Creek—stream ... TN-4
West Fork Rock Creek—stream ... UT-8
West Fork Rock Creek—stream ... WA-9
West Fork Rock Creek—stream ... WY-8
West Fork Rockhouse Creek—stream ... KY-4
West Fork Rocky Creek—stream ... TX-5
West Fork Rocky River ... NC-3
West Fork Rogers Coulee—valley ... MT-8
West Fork Rollins Creek—stream ... MO-7
West Fork Romero Creek—stream ... TX-5
West Fork Roubidoux Creek—stream ... MO-7
West Fork Rough Creek—stream ... TN-4
West Fork Rough Creek—stream ... TX-5
West Fork Rsvr—reservoir (2) ... OR-9
West Fork Rsvr—reservoir (2) ... UT-8
West Fork Rube Creek—stream ... NC-3
West Fork Ruby Creek—stream ... MT-8
West Fork Ruby Creek—stream ... OR-9
West Fork Ruby River—stream ... MT-8
West Fork Rue Creek—stream ... WA-9
West Fork Ruff Creek—stream ... KY-4
West Fork Run—stream ... PA-2
West Fork Rush Creek—stream ... ID-8
West Fork Rush Creek—stream ... IN-6
West Fork Russel Creek—stream ... OR-9
West Fork Ruth Glacier—glacier ... AK-9
West Fork Ryegrass Creek—stream ... MT-8
West Forks—locale ... ME-1
West Fork Sabinal River ... TX-5
West Fork Sabino Canyon—valley ... AZ-5
West Fork Sable Creek—stream ... ID-8
West Fork Saddle—gap ... NM-5
West Fork Saddletree Draw—valley ... UT-8
West Fork Sage Creek—stream ... ID-8
West Fork Sage Creek—stream ... MT-8
West Fork Sage Valley—valley ... UT-8
West Fork Saint Maries River—stream ... ID-8
West Fork Salmon Creek—stream ... WA-9
West Fork Salmon River ... WA-9
West Fork Salmon River—stream ... NY-2
West Fork Salmon River—stream (2) ... OR-9
West Fork Sals Creek—stream ... MO-7
West Fork Salt Creek ... KS-7
West Fork Salt Creek ... MT-8
West Fork Salt Creek ... OR-9
West Fork Salt Creek—stream (2) ... CA-9
West Fork Salt Creek—stream ... ID-8
West Fork Salt Creek—stream ... IL-6
West Fork Salt Creek—stream ... MT-8
West Fork Salt Creek—stream ... OK-5
West Fork Salt Creek—stream ... TX-5
West Fork Salt Creek—stream ... UT-8
West Fork Sampson Creek—stream ... MO-7
West Fork San Arroyo Creek—stream ... CO-8
West Fork Sand Arroyo—valley ... MT-8
West Fork Sand Canyon—valley ... CA-9
West Fork Sand Creek—stream ... CO-8
West Fork Sand Creek—stream ... KS-7
West Fork Sand Creek—stream (3) ... MT-8
West Fork Sand Creek—stream ... WY-8
West Fork San Dimas Canyon—valley ... CA-9
West Fork Sandy Creek—stream ... ID-8
West Fork Sandy Creek—stream (2) ... OK-5
West Fork Sandy Creek—stream ... TX-5
West Fork Sandy River—stream ... VA-3
West Fork Sandy Run—stream ... NC-3
West Fork San Francisco Creek—stream ... CO-8
West Fork San Gabriel River—stream ... CA-9
West Fork San Jacinto River—stream ... TX-5
West Fork San Juan River—stream ... CO-8
West Fork San Luis Rey River—stream ... CA-9
West Fork Sanpoil River—stream ... WA-9
West Fork Santa Ana Creek—stream ... CA-9
West Fork Santa Cruz Creek—stream ... CA-9
West Fork Satsop River—stream ... WA-9
West Fork Savoy Creek ... MT-8
West Fork Sawmill Canyon—valley ... NM-5
West Fork Sawmill Creek—stream ... AK-9
West Fork Sawmill Gulch—valley ... CO-8
West Fork Scarp Canyon - in part ... NV-8
West Fork Schafer Creek—stream ... MT-8
West Fork Schoolhouse Canyon—valley ... NM-5
West Fork School Section Canyon—valley ... CO-8
West Fork Schwartz Creek—stream ... MT-8
West Fork Scott Creek—stream ... OR-9
West Fork Scouter Branch—stream ... SC-3
West Fork Scriver Creek—stream ... ID-8
West Fork Second Creek—stream ... MT-8
West Fork Seepay Creek—stream ... MT-8
West Fork Seiad Creek—stream ... CA-9
West Fork Separation Canyon—valley ... AZ-5
West Fork Sespe Creek—stream ... CA-9
West Fork Seventysix Creek—stream ... NV-8
West Fork Shadow Creek—stream ... CA-9
West Fork Shake Creek—stream ... ID-8
West Fork Shane Creek—stream ... MT-8
West Fork Shaw Creek—stream ... CO-8
West Fork Shawnee Creek—stream ... WY-8
West Fork Shearer Creek—stream ... CO-8
West Fork Sheep Creek—stream (2) ... CO-8
West Fork Sheep Creek—stream (2) ... ID-8
West Fork Sheep Creek—stream ... MT-8
West Fork Sheep Creek—stream (2) ... WY-8
West Fork Shellman Creek—stream ... AK-9
West Fork Shelter—locale ... WA-9
West Fork Shelving Rock Creek—stream ... CA-9
West Fork Sheridan Creek—stream ... ID-8
West Fork Shoal Creek—stream ... IL-6
West Fork Shoal Creek—stream ... TN-4
West Fork Shockaloo Creek—stream ... MS-4
West Fork Shoestring Creek—stream ... OR-9
West Fork Shonkin Creek ... MT-8
West Fork Shoofly Creek—stream ... ID-8
West Fork Shop Creek—stream ... AR-4
West Fork Shotbag Creek—stream ... AL-4
West Fork Shut-In Creek—stream ... NC-3
West Fork Shutler Creek—stream ... OR-9
West Fork Siebert Creek—stream ... WA-9
West Fork Silesia Creek—stream ... WA-9
West Fork Silver Creek—stream ... IN-6
West Fork Silver Creek—stream ... KY-4
West Fork Silver Creek—stream (2) ... OR-9
West Fork Silver Creek—stream ... WA-9
West Fork Silvies River—stream ... OR-9
West Fork Simpson Creek—stream ... KY-4
West Fork Simpson Draw—valley ... WY-8
West Fork Sinker Creek—stream ... ID-8
West Fork Sinking Fork—stream ... KY-4
West Fork Sister Creek ... TX-5
West Fork Situk River—stream ... AK-9
West Fork Sixmile Coulee—valley ... MT-8
West Fork Sixmile Creek—stream ... AL-4
West Fork Sixmile Creek—stream ... ID-8
West Fork Sixmile Creek—stream ... LA-4
West Fork Sixmile Creek—stream ... WY-8
West Fork Skamokawa Creek—stream ... WA-9
West Fork Skegg Creek—stream ... KY-4
West Fork Skeleton Creek—stream ... ID-8
West Fork Skimmerhorn Creek—stream ... OR-9
West Fork Skull Creek ... NV-8
West Fork Skull Creek—stream ... WY-8
West Fork Skyland Creek—stream ... MT-8
West Fork Slabtown Branch—stream ... TN-4
West Fork Slate Creek—stream ... ID-8
West Fork Slate Divide Trail—trail ... ID-8
West Fork Slater Creek—stream ... ID-8
West Fork Slaughterhouse Creek—stream ... NV-8
West Fork Sly Run—stream ... IN-6
West Fork Smay Creek—stream ... WA-9
West Fork Smith Branch—stream ... TX-5
West Fork Smith Creek ... TX-5
West Fork Smith Creek—stream ... GA-3
West Fork Smith Creek—stream ... ID-8
West Fork Smith Fork ... UT-8
West Fork Smith River—stream ... OR-9
West Fork Smiths Creek ... TX-5
West Fork Smiths Fork—stream ... UT-8
West Fork Smiths Fork—stream (2) ... WY-8
West Fork Smoky Creek ... ID-8
West Fork Sni-A-Bar Creek—stream ... MO-7
West Fork Snipe Creek—stream ... OR-9
West Fork Snow Creek—stream ... CA-9
West Fork Snow Creek—stream ... NM-5
West Fork Soap Creek ... CO-8
West Fork Socagee Creek—stream ... TX-5
West Fork Soldier Creek—stream ... WY-8
West Fork Solitaire Creek—stream ... ID-8
West Fork Sombrero Canyon—valley ... CA-9
West Fork Somer Creek—stream ... OR-9
West Fork South Fork Goodpaster River—stream ... AK-9
West Fork South Fork Sun River—stream ... MT-8
West Fork South Prong Spotted Horse Creek—stream ... WY-8
West Fork South River—stream ... NC-3
West Fork South Tongue River—stream ... WY-8
West Fork Spanish Creek—stream ... CA-9
West Fork Speelyai Creek—stream ... WA-9
West Forks (Plantation of)—civ div ... ME-1
West Fork Spoon River—stream ... IL-6
West Fork Spotted Bear Creek—stream ... SD-7
West Fork Spotted Dog Creek—stream ... MT-8
West Fork Spring—spring ... MT-8
West Fork Spring—spring ... UT-8
West Fork Spring Branch—stream ... MO-7
West Fork Spring Branch—stream ... TX-5
West Fork Spring Creek—stream (2) ... CO-8
West Fork Spring Creek—stream ... MO-7
West Fork Spring Creek—stream ... MT-8
West Fork Spring Creek—stream ... NV-8
West Fork Spring Creek—stream (3) ... TN-4
West Fork Spring Creek—stream (2) ... TX-5
West Fork Springfield Creek—stream ... ID-8
West Fork Spring Hollow Creek—stream ... OR-9
West Fork Spring River—stream ... MO-7
West Fork Springs—spring ... ID-8
West Fork Sproul Creek—stream ... CA-9
West Fork Squaw Creek—stream ... CA-9
West Fork Squaw Creek—stream (4) ... ID-8
West Fork Squaw Creek—stream (2) ... OR-9
West Fork Squaw Creek—stream ... WY-8
West Fork Stack Creek—stream ... OR-9
West Fork Station—locale ... CA-9
West Fork Steamboat Creek—stream ... ID-8
West Fork Stearns Creek—stream ... WA-9
West Fork Stevens Creek—stream ... WA-9
West Fork Stevenson Creek—stream ... MT-8
West Fork Stewart Gulch—valley ... CO-8
West Fork Stillwater Creek—stream ... CA-9
West Fork Stillwater River—stream ... MT-8
West Fork Stiner Creek—stream ... MT-8
West Fork Stinking River—stream ... VA-3
West Fork Stone River ... TN-4
West Fork Stones River—stream ... TN-4
West Fork Stony Creek—stream ... ID-8
West Fork Stony Flat Creek ... TN-4
West Fork Story Gulch—valley ... CO-8
West Fork Straight Creek—stream ... OH-6
West Fork Stratton Creek—stream ... ID-8
West Fork Sugar Creek ... IL-6
West Fork Sugar Creek ... IN-6
West Fork Sugar Creek ... KS-7
West Fork Sugar Creek—stream ... IL-6
West Fork Sugar Creek—stream ... IN-6
West Fork Sugar Creek—stream ... KY-4
West Fork Sugar Creek—stream ... TN-4
West Fork Sulphur Creek—stream ... CA-9
West Fork Sulphur Creek—stream ... MO-7
West Fork Summit Creek—stream ... UT-8
West Fork Sunbean Creek—stream ... ID-8
West Fork Sunday Gulch—valley ... CA-9
West Fork Sunflower Creek—stream ... TX-5
West Fork Sunset Canyon—valley ... AZ-5
West Fork Susitna River—stream ... AK-9
West Fork Sutton Creek ... OR-9
West Fork Sutton Creek—stream ... OR-9
West Fork Swamp Creek—stream ... MT-8
West Fork Swan Creek ... OH-6
West Fork Swan Creek ... TN-4
West Fork Swede George Creek—stream ... CA-9
West Fork Sweetwater Creek ... ID-8
West Fork Sweetwater Creek—stream ... ID-8
West Fork Swift Creek—stream ... MT-8
West Fork Swift Creek—stream ... WA-9
West Fork Sycamore Creek ... TX-5
West Fork Sycamore Creek—stream (2) ... AZ-5
West Fork Sycamore Creek—stream ... CA-9
West Fork Sycamore Creek—stream ... TX-5
West Fork Sylvia Creek—stream ... WA-9
West Fork Taffner Creek—stream ... WY-8
West Fork Tana River—stream ... AK-9
West Fork Tank—reservoir ... AZ-5
West Fork Tanners Creek—stream ... IN-6
West Fork Tanyard Branch—stream ... AL-4
West Fork Tarkio creek ... IA-7
West Fork Tarkio Creek ... MO-7
West Fork Tauy Creek—stream ... KS-7
West Fork Taylor Creek—stream ... OR-9
West Fork Teanaway River—stream ... WA-9
West Fork Tebo Creek—stream ... MO-7
West Fork Tenmile Creek ... CO-8
West Fork Tenmile Swamp—stream ... FL-3
West Fork Tepee Creek—stream ... ID-8
West Fork Terrapin Creek—stream ... AR-4
West Fork Terrapin Creek—stream ... KY-4
West Fork Terror Creek—stream ... CO-8
West Fork Texas Creek—stream ... AK-9
West Fork Third Creek—stream ... TN-4
West Fork Thirsty Canyon—valley ... NV-8
West Fork Thomas Creek ... ID-8
West Fork Thomas Creek—stream ... ID-8
West Fork Thomason Creek—stream ... OR-9
West Fork Thompson Creek—stream ... LA-4
West Fork Thompson Creek—stream ... MS-4
West Fork Thompson Creek—stream ... MT-8
West Fork Thompson River—stream ... MT-8
West Fork Thorobred Creek ... ID-8
West Fork Thoroughbred Creek—stream ... ID-8
West Fork Three Lakes Canyon—valley ... UT-8
West Fork Three Links Creek—stream ... ID-8
West Fork Threemile Creek—stream ... ID-8
West Fork Threemile Creek—stream ... TX-5
West Fork Thunder Creek—stream ... WA-9
West Fork Tilseys Creek—stream ... MS-4
West Fork Tilton River—stream ... WA-9
West Fork Timber Canyon ... OR-9
West Fork Timber Creek—stream (2) ... MT-8
West Fork Timber Creek—stream (2) ... WY-8
West Fork Tinaja Creek—stream ... NM-5
West Fork T L Creek—stream ... MT-8
West Fork Tolovana River—stream ... AK-9
West Fork Tombigbee River ... MS-4
West Fork Toms Canyon—valley ... ID-8
West Fork Tonk Creek—stream ... TX-5
West Fork Torch River ... WI-6
West Fork Torry Creek ... WY-8
West Fork Totagatic River—stream ... WI-6
West Fork Touchet River ... WA-9
West Fork Township—fmr MCD (3) ... IA-7
West Fork (Township of)—fmr MCD ... AR-4
West Fork Trabing Dry Creek—stream ... WY-8
West Fork Trail—trail ... CA-9
West Fork Trail—trail (2) ... CO-8
West Fork Trail—trail ... MT-8
West Fork Trail Creek—stream ... AK-9
West Fork Trail Creek—stream ... GA-3
West Fork Trail Creek—stream ... ID-8
West Fork Trail Creek—stream ... OR-9
West Fork Trail (Pack)—trail ... NM-5
West Fork Traleika Glacier—glacier ... AK-9
West Fork Trapper Creek—stream ... MT-8
West Fork Trinity River ... TX-5
West Fork Trinity River—stream ... TX-5
West Fork Troublesome Creek—stream ... WA-9
West Fork Trout Creek—stream ... ID-8
West Fork Trout Creek—stream ... MT-8
West Fork Trout Creek—stream ... OR-9
West Fork Trout Creek—stream ... WA-9
West Fork Trout Creek—stream ... WY-8
West Fork Tsivat River—stream ... AK-9
West Fork Tuckasegee River—stream ... NC-3
West Fork Tuckaseigee River ... NC-3
West Fork Tucker Creek—stream ... OR-9
West Fork Tule Creek—stream ... MT-8
West Fork Tulip Creek—stream ... AR-4
West Fork Tullock Creek—stream ... MT-8
West Fork Tuluga River—stream ... AK-9
West Fork Turkey Creek—stream ... CO-8
West Fork Turkey Creek—stream ... TN-4
West Fork Turkey Creek—stream (3) ... TX-5
West Fork Turman Creek—stream ... IN-6
West Fork Turtle Brook—stream ... NJ-2
West Fork Twelve Mile Creek ... NC-3
West Fork Twelvemile Creek—stream ... MN-6
West Fork Twelvemile Creek—stream ... MT-8
West Fork Twelvemile Creek—stream ... NC-3
West Fork Twelvepole Creek—stream ... WV-2
West Fork Twentymile Creek ... WA-9
West Fork Twentymile Creek—stream ... ID-8
West Fork Twentymile Creek—stream ... WA-9
West Fork Twentymile Creek—stream ... WY-8
West Fork Twentyone Creek—stream ... WY-8
West Fork Twentytwo Gulch—valley ... AK-9
West Fork Twin Canyon—valley ... UT-8
West Fork Twin Canyon - in part ... UT-8
West Fork Twin Creek—stream ... AK-9
West Fork Twin Creek—stream ... ID-8
West Fork Twin Creek—stream ... WY-8
West Fork Two Leggin Creek ... MT-8
West Fork Two Leggins Creek ... MT-8
West Fork Ty Hatch Creek ... UT-8
West Fork Tyler Creek—stream (2) ... MT-8
West Fork Tyler Saddle—gap ... MT-8
West Fork Upper Deer Creek—stream ... MT-8
West Fork Upper Timber Canyon—valley ... OR-9
West Fork Ute Canyon—valley ... CO-8
West Fork Van Duzen Creek ... CA-9
West Fork Van Duzen River—stream ... CA-9
West Fork Vermillion River—stream ... SD-7
West Fork Vesta Creek—stream ... WA-9
West Fork Volney Creek—stream ... MT-8
West Fork Wager Gulch—valley ... CO-8
West Fork Waggoner Creek—stream ... MS-4
West Fork Wagner Creek ... MS-4
West Fork Wagoner Creek ... MS-4
West Fork Wagonhound Creek—stream ... WY-8
West Fork Wakenda Creek—stream ... MO-7
West Fork Walker Creek—stream ... VA-3
West Fork Walker Creek—stream ... WY-8
West Fork Wall Creek—stream ... MT-8
West Fork Wallowa River—stream ... OR-9
West Fork Walnut Run—stream ... OH-6
West Fork Warm Spring Creek ... WY-8
West Fork Warm Springs Canyon—valley ... AZ-5
West Fork Warm Springs Creek—stream ... ID-8
West Fork Warm Springs Creek—stream (2) ... MT-8
West Fork Warrens Creek—stream ... OR-9
West Fork Washougal River—stream ... WA-9
West Fork Water Canyon—valley ... ID-8
West Fork Water Canyon—valley ... WY-8
West Fork Watkins Creek—stream ... MT-8
West Fork Wattacoo Creek—stream ... SC-3
West Fork Wayne Creek—stream ... MT-8
West Fork Weakly Branch—stream ... TX-5
West Fork Weaver Creek ... CA-9
West Fork Weaver Draw—valley ... WY-8
West Fork Weiser River—stream ... ID-8
West Fork Wendover Creek—stream ... ID-8
West Fork West Beaver Creek—stream ... CO-8
West Fork West Boulder River—stream ... MT-8
West Fork West Branch Potato Creek—stream ... PA-2
West Fork West Branch Saint Joseph River—stream ... MI-6
West Fork West Canyon—valley ... CO-8
West Fork West Creek—stream ... ID-8
West Fork West Dallas Creek—stream ... CO-8
West Fork West Nishnabotna River—stream ... IA-7
West Fork West Walker River—stream ... CA-9
West Fork Wet Cottonwood Creek—stream ... MT-8
West Fork Wet Prong Creek ... AZ-5
West Fork Wetweather Creek—stream ... IL-6
West Fork Wheatridge Lateral—canal ... CO-8
West Fork Whimpey Creek ... ID-8
West Fork Whimstick Creek—stream ... ID-8
West Fork Whisky Creek—stream ... OR-9
West Fork White Creek—stream ... WA-9
West Fork White Eyes Creek—stream ... OH-6
West Fork White Lick Creek—stream (2) ... IN-6
West Fork White Oak Creek—stream ... TX-5
West Fork White River ... IN-6
West Fork White River—stream ... AR-4
West Fork White River—stream ... WA-9
West Fork White River—stream ... WI-6
West Fork Whiterocks River—stream ... UT-8
West Fork Whites Gulch—valley ... CA-9
West Fork Whitewater River ... IN-6
West Fork Whitewater River ... OH-6
West Fork Wickiup Canyon—valley ... CO-8
West Fork Wickiup Creek—stream ... ID-8
West Fork Wickiup Creek—stream ... OR-9
West Fork Widow Woman Canyon ... CO-8
West Fork Widow Woman Canyon—valley ... CO-8
West Fork Wildcat Creek—stream ... WA-9
West Fork Wildcat Creek—stream ... WY-8
West Fork Wildhorse Creek—stream ... OK-5
West Fork Willame Creek ... WA-9
West Fork Willard Creek—stream ... CA-9
West Fork Willard Creek—stream ... UT-8
West Fork Williams Creek—stream ... OR-9
West Fork Williams Creek—stream ... TX-5
West Fork Williamson Creek ... TX-5
West Fork Willow Creek—stream ... CA-9
West Fork Willow Creek—stream ... CO-8
West Fork Willow Creek—stream (2) ... ID-8
West Fork Willow Creek—stream (3) ... MT-8
West Fork Willow Creek—stream ... NV-8
West Fork Willow Creek—stream ... SD-7
West Fork Willow Creek—stream ... UT-8
West Fork Willow Creek—stream ... WY-8
West Fork Wilson Creek—stream ... MT-8
West Fork Wimpey Creek—stream ... ID-8
West Fork Wind Creek—stream ... WY-8
West Fork Windham Canyon—valley ... NM-5
West Fork Winding Gulf—stream ... WV-2
West Fork Windy Creek—stream ... AK-9
West Fork Winnemucca Creek ... CO-8
West Fork Wise River ... MT-8
West Fork Wishkah River—stream ... WA-9
West Fork Wolf Creek ... CO-8
West Fork Wolf Creek—stream ... AK-9
West Fork Wolf Creek—stream ... GA-3
West Fork Wolf Creek—stream ... KS-7
West Fork Wolf Creek—stream ... MO-7
West Fork Wolf Creek—stream (2) ... MT-8
West Fork Wolf Creek—stream (2) ... OR-9
West Fork Wolf Creek—stream (3) ... TN-4
West Fork Wolf Creek—stream ... VA-3
West Fork Wood River—stream ... IL-6
West Fork Woods Creek—stream ... WA-9
West Fork Work Center—locale ... MT-8
West Fork Wrights Creek—stream ... OR-9
West Fork Yaak River—stream ... MT-8
West Fork Yankee Creek—stream ... CO-8
West Fork Yankee Fork—stream ... ID-8
West Fork Yankee Run ... OR-9
West Fork Yanubbee Creek—stream ... OK-5
West Fork Yellow Brook—stream ... NJ-2
West Fork Yellowjacket Creek—stream ... ID-8
West Fork Yellowstone Creek ... UT-8
West Fork Yentna River—stream ... AK-9
West Fork Yoncalla Creek—stream ... OR-9
West Fork Young Creek—stream ... AK-9
West Fork Younts Creek—stream ... WY-8
West Fork Yuma Wash—stream ... AZ-5
West Fork Zapato Creek ... CA-9
West Fork Zena Creek—stream ... ID-8
West Forsyth HS—school ... NC-3
**West Fort Ann**—pop pl ... NY-2
**West Fort Dodge (historical)**—pop pl ... IA-7
West Fort Lee—uninc pl ... NJ-2
West Fort Smith—locale ... OK-5
**West Fort Towson**—pop pl ... OK-5
West Forty Creek—stream ... MT-8
West Forty-sixth Ave Parkway—hist pl ... CO-8
West Foster Creek—stream ... WA-9
West Four Legged Lake—lake ... MN-6
West Fourmile Creek—stream ... CO-8
West Fourmile Draw—valley ... CO-8
West Fourmile Rsvr—reservoir ... CO-8
West Fourth Street District—hist pl ... KY-4
West Fourth Street Hist Dist—hist pl ... OH-6
West Fourth Street Hist Dist (Amendment)—hist pl ... OH-6
West Fowler—locale ... NY-2
West Fowler Cem—cemetery ... NY-2
West Fowl River ... AL-4
West Fowl River—stream ... AL-4
**West Foxboro**—pop pl ... MA-1
West Foxborough ... MA-1
West Fox Creek—channel ... NY-2
West Fox Lake ... FL-3
West Fox Lake—lake ... MN-6
West France Cem—cemetery ... IL-6
**West Frankfort**—pop pl ... IL-6
**West Frankfort**—pop pl ... NY-2
West Frankfort—uninc pl ... KY-4
West Frankfort City Lake—lake ... IL-6
**West Frankfort Lake**—pop pl ... IL-6
West Frankfort Oil Field—other ... IL-6
West Frankfort Rsvr—reservoir ... IL-6
West Frankfort South Oil Field—other ... IL-6
West Franklin ... NH-1
**West Franklin**—pop pl ... IN-6
**West Franklin**—pop pl ... ME-1
**West Franklin**—pop pl ... PA-2
West Franklin Ch—church (2) ... OH-6
West Franklin HS—school ... IL-6
West Franklin Sch—school ... OH-6
West Franklin Street Hist Dist—hist pl ... VA-3
**West Franklin (Township of)**—pop pl ... PA-2
West Frayser Ch—church ... TN-4
West Frazor Windmill—locale ... NM-5
West Fredericksburg—uninc pl ... VA-3
West Fredlund Sch—school ... SD-7
West Freeborn Cem—cemetery ... MN-6
West Freeborn Ch—church ... MN-6
**West Freedom**—pop pl ... PA-2
**West Freehold**—pop pl ... NJ-2
West Freemason Street Area Hist Dist—hist pl ... VA-3
**West Friendship**—pop pl ... MD-2
West Friendship Baptist Ch—church ... FL-3
West Friesland Ch—church ... IA-7
West Frio River—stream ... TX-5
**West Frostproof**—pop pl ... FL-3
West Frostproof (RR name for West Frost Proof)—other ... FL-3
**West Frost Proof (RR name West Frostproof)**—pop pl ... FL-3
**West Fryeburg**—pop pl ... ME-1
West Fryeburg Cem—cemetery ... ME-1
**West Fulton**—pop pl ... MS-4
**West Fulton**—pop pl ... NY-2
West Fulton Beach Gas And Oil Field—oilfield ... TX-5
West Fulton Ch—church ... OH-6
West Fulton HS—school ... GA-3
West Fulton Township—civil ... MO-7
West Furnace Ridge—ridge ... TN-4
West Furnace Ridge Mine—mine ... TN-4
**West Future City**—pop pl ... KY-4
Westgaard Cem—cemetery ... ND-7
West Gadsden Methodist Episcopal Ch (historical)—church ... AL-4
West Gadsden Sch—school ... AL-4
West Gafford Creek—stream ... AR-4
West Gaffords Creek ... AR-4
West Gage Windmill—locale ... TX-5
**West Gaines**—pop pl ... NY-2
West Gaines Street Ch of Christ—church ... TN-4
**West Galax**—pop pl ... VA-3
**West Galena (Township of)**—pop pl ... IL-6
West Gallatin—locale ... MT-8
West Gallatin Canal—canal ... MT-8
West Gallatin River ... MT-8
West Gallatin River ... WY-8
**West Galway**—pop pl ... NY-2
**West Gantt**—pop pl ... SC-3
West Gap ... FL-3
West Gap—channel ... FL-3
West Gap—gap ... CO-8
West Garden Grove—uninc pl ... CA-9
West Garden Valley Ch—church ... WI-6
West Gardiner ... ME-1
**West Gardiner (Town of)**—pop pl ... ME-1
West Gardner ... MA-1
West Gardner Square Hist Dist—hist pl ... MA-1
Westgard Pass—gap ... CA-9
West Garland Pond—lake ... ME-1
West Garland Sch—school ... ME-1
**West Garrett**—pop pl ... KY-4
West Garrison Ave Hist Dist—hist pl ... AR-4
West Gary ... IN-6
**West Gastonia**—pop pl ... NC-3
West Gastonia Industrial Park—locale ... NC-3
Westgate ... NV-8
West Gate—CDP ... VA-3
West Gate—gap ... NV-8
West Gate—locale ... NV-8
**Westgate**—pop pl ... AK-9
**Westgate**—pop pl ... CA-9
**West Gate**—pop pl ... FL-3
**Westgate**—pop pl ... FL-3
**Westgate**—pop pl ... IL-6
**Westgate**—pop pl ... IA-7
**Westgate**—pop pl ... LA-4
**Westgate**—pop pl (2) ... MD-2
**Westgate**—pop pl ... MI-6
**Westgate**—pop pl (2) ... TN-4
**Westgate**—pop pl ... TX-5
Westgate—post sta ... CA-9
Westgate—post sta ... FL-3
Westgate—post sta ... NY-2
Westgate—uninc pl ... CA-9
Westgate—uninc pl ... GA-3
Westgate Acres ... ID-8
**West Gate Addition Subdivision**—pop pl ... UT-8
Westgate Baptist Ch—church (2) ... AL-4
Westgate Baptist Ch—church ... FL-3
Westgate Baptist Ch—church ... MS-4
West Gate Basin—harbor ... WI-6
Westgate Ch—church ... AL-4
Westgate Ch—church ... MS-4
West Gate Ch of Christ—church ... AL-4
West Gate Christian Sch—school ... FL-3
Westgate Country Club—other ... IL-6
Westgate Drain—stream ... MI-6
West Gate Elem Sch—school ... FL-3
Westgate Elem Sch—school ... FL-3
**Westgate Farms**—pop pl ... DE-2
Westgate Gulch—valley ... ID-8
Westgate Heights—uninc pl ... NM-5
**West Gate Hills**—pop pl ... PA-2
**Westgate Hills**—pop pl (2) ... PA-2
**Westgate Lake Manor**—pop pl ... FL-3
Westgate Mall—building ... ME-1
Westgate Mall—locale ... PA-2
Westgate Mall (Shop Ctr)—locale ... MA-1
Westgate Memorial Park—park ... AL-4
West Gate Mill (Site)—locale ... NV-8
Westgate New Testament Ch—church ... FL-3
**West Gate Of Lomond**—pop pl ... VA-3
Westgate Park—park ... OH-6
**Westgate Park**—pop pl ... GA-3
**Westgate Park**—pop pl ... MA-1
Westgate-Peterson Cem—cemetery ... NH-1
Westgate Plaza—locale ... MA-1
Westgate Plaza—locale ... VA-3
West Gate Plaza Shop Ctr—locale ... AL-4
Westgate Plaza (Shop Ctr)—locale ... FL-3
West Gate Plaza (Shop Ctr)—locale ... FL-3
West Gate Rest Area—park ... IA-7
West Gates Ave Sch—school ... NY-2
Westgate Sch—school ... IL-6
Westgate Sch—school ... MI-6
West Gate Sch—school ... MI-6
Westgate Sch—school (2) ... OH-6
West Gate Sch—school ... VA-3
Westgate Sch—school (2) ... WA-9
Westgate Shop Ctr—locale ... AL-4
Westgate Shop Ctr—locale (5) ... FL-3
Westgate Shop Ctr—locale ... KS-7
Westgate Shop Ctr—locale ... MA-1
Westgate Shop Ctr—locale ... MS-4
Westgate Shop Ctr—locale ... MO-7
Westgate Shop Ctr—locale ... NC-3
Westgate Shop Ctr—locale ... OH-6
West Gate Shop Ctr—locale ... TN-4
Westgate Shop Ctr—locale ... TN-4
Westgate Square Shop Ctr—locale ... FL-3
Westgate Square (Shop Ctr)—locale ... FL-3
West Gate Station ... NV-8
**Westgate (subdivision)**—pop pl ... AL-4
**Westgate (subdivision)**—pop pl ... FL-3
**Westgate (subdivision)**—pop pl ... MS-4
**Westgate (subdivision)**—pop pl ... NC-3
**Westgate (subdivision)**—pop pl ... TN-4
**Westgate Subdivision**—pop pl ... UT-8
**Westgate Terrace (subdivision)**—pop pl ... NC-3
Westgate Village Shop Ctr—locale ... AL-4
**West Gate Woods**—pop pl ... MD-2
West Geauga HS—school ... OH-6
West Geauga JHS—school ... OH-6
West Genesee Cem—cemetery ... NY-2
West Genesee Central Sch—school ... NY-2
**West Genesee Terrace**—pop pl ... NY-2
West Geneva Creek ... CO-8
West Genoa Cem—cemetery ... NY-2
**West Georgetown**—pop pl ... ME-1
West Georgetown Hill—summit ... ME-1
West George West Oil Field—oilfield ... TX-5
**West Georgia**—pop pl ... VT-1
West Georgia Coll—school ... GA-3
West Georgia Temple—church ... GA-3
West Gervais Street Hist Dist—hist pl ... SC-3
West Gethsemane Cem—cemetery ... TX-5
West Ghent—locale ... NY-2
**West Ghent**—pop pl ... VA-3
West Gibraltar Peak—summit ... CO-8
West Gibson Ditch—canal ... IL-6
West Gilbert—uninc pl ... WV-2
West Gilbertsville Station—locale ... KY-4
West Gilgo ... NY-2
**West Gilgo Beach**—pop pl ... NY-2
West Gilgo Heading ... NY-2
West Gilkey Lake—lake ... MI-6
West Gillum Windmill—locale ... NM-5
West Gin (historical)—locale ... AL-4
West Girl Windmill—locale ... NM-5
West Gismo Creek—stream ... CO-8
West Glacier—glacier ... AK-9
**West Glacier**—pop pl ... MT-8
West Glacier Creek—stream ... AK-9
West Glade Run Ch—church ... PA-2
**West Gladstone**—pop pl ... MI-6
West Glasgow—locale ... MO-7
West Glaveston—uninc pl ... TX-5
West Glen ... IL-6
**West Glenburn**—pop pl ... ME-1
**West Glendale**—pop pl ... CA-9
West Glen Park (alternate name for Glen Park West) ... IN-6
**West Glens Falls**—pop pl ... NY-2
**West Glenview**—pop pl ... IL-6
**Westglen Village Condominium**—pop pl ... UT-8
**West Glenville**—pop pl ... NY-2
West Gloucester—locale ... RI-1
**West Gloucester**—pop pl ... MA-1
West Gloucester Ch—church ... MA-1
West Gloucester (historical P.O.)—locale ... MA-1
West Gloucester Station—locale ... MA-1
**West Glover**—pop pl ... VT-1
Westglow—hist pl ... NC-3
West Goat Creek—stream ... TX-5
West Goat Peak—summit ... MT-8
West Goat Windmill—locale ... NM-5
West Goens Creek—stream ... TX-5

West Gold Brook—*stream* OR-9
West Gold Creek—*stream* ID-8
West Golden Ch—*church* MI-6
*West Gonic* NH-1
**West Gonic**—*pop pl* NH-1
*West Goodenough Creek* ID-8
*West Gooseberry Creek* WY-8
West Gooseberry Creek—*stream* WY-8
*West Goose Creek* WY-8
West Goose Creek—*stream* FL-3
West Goose Creek Seine Yard—*locale* FL-3
*West Goosefare Rocks* ME-1
West Goose Lake—*lake* IA-7
West Goose Rocks—*island* ME-1
West Goose Valley—*valley* MS-4
West Goosewing Creek—*stream* WY-8
West Gopher Pond—*lake* OR-9
West Gordon—*fmr MCD* NE-7
West Gordon Gulch—*valley* CO-8
**West Gorham**—*pop pl* ME-1
**West Gorham**—*pop pl* NY-2
Westgorough HS—*school* MA-1
West Goshen—*CDP* PA-2
**West Goshen**—*pop pl* CT-1
West Goshen Cem—*cemetery* CT-1
West Goshen Ch—*church* IN-6
West Goshen Elem Sch—*school* IN-6
**West Goshen Hills**—*pop pl* PA-2
West Goshen Hist Dist—*hist pl* CT-1
**West Goshen Park**—*pop pl* PA-2
**West Goshen (Township of)**—*pop pl* PA-2
West Gould Ditch—*canal* CA-9
**West Gouldsboro**—*pop pl* ME-1
West Government Creek—*stream* UT-8
West Government Mtn—*summit* OK-5
West Gowder Branch—*stream* AL-4
West Grace Cem—*cemetery* MN-6
West Grade Sch—*school* MT-8
**West Grafton**—*pop pl* WV-2
West Graham—*other* VA-3
West Graham Lake—*lake* MN-6
**West Granby**—*pop pl* CT-1
West Grandaddy Mtn—*summit* UT-8
West Grand Lake—*reservoir* ME-1
*West Grand Marais Ditch* LA-4
West Grand Marais Ditch—*canal* LA-4
*West Grand River* IA-7
*West Grand River* MO-7
West Grand Sch—*school* IL-6
**West Grand View Subdivision**—*pop pl* UT-8
West Granite Mtn—*summit* AZ-5
West Grant—*unorg reg* ND-7
West Grant Ch—*church* MI-6
West Grant HS—*school* WI-6
West Grants Ridge—*ridge* NM-5
**West Granville**—*pop pl* MA-1
**West Granville**—*pop pl* NY-2
**West Granville**—*pop pl* WI-6
West Granville—*uninc pl* WI-6
**West Granville Corners**—*pop pl* NY-2
West Grapevine Ditch—*canal* CO-8
West Grassy Rsvr—*reservoir* OR-9
West Graveyard Windmill—*locale* NM-5
**West Gray**—*pop pl* ME-1
West Greasy Creek—*stream* AR-4
West Greasy Creek—*stream* TX-5
West Greasy Sch—*school* IL-6
**West Greece**—*pop pl* NY-2
West Greeley—*post sta* CO-8
West Greeley—*reservoir* CO-8
**West Green**—*pop pl* GA-3
West Green Bay—*uninc pl* WI-6
West Greenbush Cem—*cemetery* WI-6
West Green (CCD)—*cens area* GA-3
West Green Ch—*church* GA-3
West Greene—*locale* AL-4
**West Greene**—*pop pl* PA-2
West Greene—*uninc pl* TN-4
West Greene Ch—*church* AL-4
West Greene Ch—*church* PA-2
West Greene HS—*school* PA-2
West Greene HS—*school* TN-4
West Greene Post Office—*building* TN-4
West Greene Sch—*school* NC-3
West Greene Shop Ctr—*locale* TN-4
**West Greene (sta.)**—*pop pl* AL-4
**Westgreen Estates (subdivision)**—*pop pl* (2) AZ-5
West Green Lake Cem—*cemetery* MN-6
West Green Mine—*mine* IL-6
West Greentree Ch—*church* PA-2
West Greenville—*locale* RI-1
**West Greenville**—*pop pl* NY-2
**West Greenville**—*pop pl* SC-3
West Greenwich Baptist Church and Cemetery—*hist pl* RI-1
West Greenwich Center—*locale* RI-1
*West Greenwich Centre* RI-1
**West Greenwich (Town of)**—*pop pl* RI-1
West Greenwood—*CDP* SC-3
West Greenwood—*locale* NY-2
West Greenwood Cem—*cemetery* WA-9
West Gregerie Channel—*channel* VI-3
West Gregory—*unorg reg* SD-7
West Gresham Sch—*school* OR-9
West Greynolds Park—*park* FL-3
West Grider Creek—*stream* CA-9
West Griffin Creek—*stream* FL-3
West Griffin Sch—*school* GA-3
West Griffith Lake—*reservoir* CO-8
West Grinnell Creek—*stream* WY-8
West Gros Ventre Butte—*summit* WY-8
**West Groton**—*pop pl* MA-1
**West Groton**—*pop pl* NY-2
**West Groton**—*pop pl* VT-1
West Grouse Creek—*stream* CO-8
West Grouse Peak—*summit* ID-8
West Grout Ch—*church* MI-6
**West Grove**—*pop pl* IN-6
**West Grove**—*pop pl* IA-7
**West Grove**—*pop pl* NJ-2
**West Grove**—*pop pl* PA-2
**Westgrove**—*pop pl* VA-3
West Grove Borough—*civil* PA-2
West Grove Cem—*cemetery* (3) IN-6
West Grove Cem—*cemetery* IA-7
West Grove Cem—*cemetery* MS-4
West Grove Cem—*cemetery* (2) OH-6
West Grove Ch—*church* AL-4
West Grove Ch—*church* IL-6
West Grove Ch—*church* (2) MS-4
West Grove Ch—*church* NC-3
West Grove Ch—*church* OH-6
West Grove Sch—*school* IL-6
West Grove Sch—*school* TX-5
West Grove Township—*fmr MCD* IA-7
West Guard Lock—*other* NY-2
**West Guernewood**—*pop pl* CA-9
West Gueydan Oil and Gas Field—*oilfield* LA-4
**West Guilford**—*pop pl* VT-1
West Gulch—*valley* CO-8
West Gulch—*valley* ID-8
West Gulch—*valley* (2) MT-8
West Gulch—*valley* OR-9
West Gulf Brook—*stream* MA-1
**West Gulfport**—*pop pl* MS-4
West Gulfport (census name North Gulfport)—*other* MS-4
West Gulkana Glacier—*glacier* AK-9
*West Gulpha creek* AR-4
*West Gum Creek* OR-9
West Gum Creek—*stream* TX-5
West Gumlog Creek—*stream* GA-3
**West Gum Springs**—*pop pl* AR-4
West Gum Springs—*spring* AR-4
West Gunsight Mtn—*summit* TX-5
West Gut—*gut* MA-1
West Guth Park—*park* TX-5
West Gutter—*gut* MA-1
West Gypsum Bay—*bay* AZ-5
West Gypsum Creek—*stream* AZ-5
West Gypsum Creek—*stream* UT-8
West Haakon—*unorg reg* SD-7
West Hackberry Creek—*stream* OK-5
West Hackberry Oil Field—*oilfield* LA-4
**West Haddam**—*pop pl* CT-1
**West Haddonfield**—*pop pl* NJ-2
West Haight Mtn—*summit* CA-9
West Halbert Windmill—*locale* TX-5
**West Hale Township**—*pop pl* KS-7
West Halibut Ledges—*bar* ME-1
**West Halifax**—*pop pl* VT-1
West Hall—*hist pl* KY-4
West Hall—*hist pl* OR-9
West Hallock—*locale* IL-6
**Westham**—*pop pl* VA-3
**West Hamburg**—*pop pl* PA-2
Westham Creek—*stream* VA-3
West Hamilton—*civil* KS-7
West Hamilton Ch—*church* (2) TX-5
**West Hamilton Heights**—*pop pl* PA-2
West Hamilton Oil And Gas Field—*other* MI-6
West Hamlet—*uninc pl* NC-3
**West Hamlin**—*pop pl* WV-2
West Hammond Creek—*stream* MT-8
West Hampden—*locale* ME-1
**West Hampstead**—*pop pl* NH-1
*West Hampton* KS-7
**Westhampton**—*pop pl* MA-1
**Westhampton**—*pop pl* NY-2
**Westhampton**—*pop pl* VA-3
**West Hampton**—*pop pl* VA-3
**Westhampton**—*pop pl* VA-3
Westhampton—*uninc pl* VA-3
*West Hampton Beach* NY-2
**Westhampton Beach**—*pop pl* NY-2
Westhampton Ch—*church* NY-2
Westhampton Ch—*church* VA-3
Westhampton Country Club—*other* NY-2
Westhampton Lake—*reservoir* VA-3
Westhampton Memorial Park (Cemetery)—*cemetery* VA-3
**Westhampton Park**—*pop pl* VA-3
**Westhampton PUD (subdivision)**—*pop pl* UT-8
Westhampton Sch—*school* VA-3
**Westhampton (Town of)**—*pop pl* MA-1
West Hanawana—*civil* HI-9
West Hancock Ave Hist Dist—*hist pl* GA-3
West Handley Sch—*school* TX-5
West Hanks Lake—*lake* OR-9
West Hanna Mtn—*summit* AR-4
*West Hanover* NJ-2
*West Hanover* PA-2
**West Hanover**—*pop pl* MA-1
West Hanover Sch—*school* PA-2
**West Hanover (Township of)**—*pop pl* PA-2
**West Hanson Township**—*pop pl* SD-7
West Haralson Sch—*school* GA-3
*West Harbor* NY-2
*West Harbor* WI-6
West Harbor—*bay* MI-6
West Harbor—*bay* (2) NY-2
West Harbor—*bay* OH-6
West Harbor—*bay* WI-6
West Harbor Arm—*harbor* IN-6
West Harbor Key—*island* FL-3
West Harbor Key Channel—*channel* FL-3
West Harbor Pond—*bay* ME-1
West Harbor Reef—*bar* OH-6
West Hardin HS—*school* KY-4
West Harmony Ch—*church* AR-4
West Harmony Creek—*stream* AR-4
West Harney Creek—*stream* WY-8
West Harper Ch—*church* MS-4
**West Harpersfield**—*pop pl* NY-2
West Harpeth—*locale* TN-4
West Harpeth Ch—*church* TN-4
West Harpeth Post Office (historical)—*building* TN-4
West Harpeth River—*stream* TN-4
West Harpeth Sch—*school* TN-4
**West Harpswell**—*pop pl* ME-1
**West Harrington**—*pop pl* ME-1
*West Harrison* NY-2
**West Harrison**—*pop pl* IN-6
West Hartford—*CDP* CT-1
**West Hartford**—*pop pl* AR-4
**West Hartford**—*pop pl* CT-1
**West Hartford**—*pop pl* VT-1
West Hartland—*locale* CT-1
West Hartland Ch—*church* OH-6
West Hartley—*locale* CA-9
West Hartley Gulch—*valley* ID-8
**West Hartsville**—*pop pl* SC-3
West Hartsville Sch—*school* SC-3
**West Harwich**—*pop pl* MA-1
West Haskell (CCD)—*cens area* OK-5
West Hastings Brook—*stream* ME-1
West Hatchie Structure 29 Dam—*dam* MS-4
West Hatchie Structure 37 Dam—*dam* MS-4
West Hatchie Structure 38 Dam—*dam* MS-4
West Hatchie Watershed 25 Dam—*dam* MS-4
West Hatchie Watershed 36 Dam—*dam* MS-4
West Hatchie Watershed 9 Dam—*dam* MS-4
West Hat Creek—*stream* NE-7
**West Hatfield**—*pop pl* MA-1
**West Hatfield (RR name Hatfield (sta.))**—*pop pl* MA-1
West Hatton Point—*cape* MD-2
*West Hauxhurst Creek* CO-8
*Westhaven* IL-6
*West Haven* NC-3
*Westhaven* OH-6
**Westhaven**—*pop pl* (2) CA-9
**West Haven**—*pop pl* CT-1
**West Haven**—*pop pl* DE-2
**Westhaven**—*pop pl* IL-6
**West Haven**—*pop pl* NC-3
**West Haven**—*pop pl* OR-9
**West Haven**—*pop pl* (2) TN-4
**Westhaven**—*pop pl* TX-5
**West Haven**—*pop pl* VT-1
**Westhaven**—*pop pl* VA-3
**Westhaven**—*pop pl* WA-9
**West Haven (Avery Creek)**—*pop pl* NC-3
Westhaven Baptist Ch—*church* MS-4
West Haven Cem—*cemetery* IN-6
West Haven Cem—*cemetery* MI-6
West Haven Ch—*church* MI-6
West Haven Ch of God—*church* MS-4
West Haven Elem Sch—*school* TN-4
West Haven Green Cem—*cemetery* CT-1
Westhaven Lake—*reservoir* VA-3
Westhaven Park—*park* IN-6
Westhaven Park—*park* TX-5
**Westhaven Park**—*pop pl* VA-3
Westhaven Park—*uninc pl* TX-5
**West Haven Park (subdivision)**—*pop pl* NC-3
Westhaven Sch—*school* TN-4
Westhaven Sch—*school* VA-3
West Haven Shop Ctr—*locale* TN-4
Westhaven Siding—*locale* CA-9
**West Haven (subdivision)**—*pop pl* AL-4
**Westhaven (subdivision)**—*pop pl* NC-3
**West haven (subdivision)**—*pop pl* NC-3
**West Haven Subdivision**—*pop pl* UT-8
West Haven (Town of)—*civ div* CT-1
**West Haven (Town of)**—*pop pl* VT-1
**West Haven (Trailer Park)**—*pop pl* IN-6
Westhaven Village—*uninc pl* TN-4
**West Haverstraw**—*pop pl* NY-2
*West Hawkhurst Creek* CO-8
**West Hawley**—*pop pl* MA-1
**West Hawley**—*pop pl* PA-2
West Hawxhurst Creek—*stream* CO-8
West Hay Draw Creek—*stream* ND-7
West Hay Hollow Draw—*valley* AZ-5
West Hayshed Creek—*stream* CA-9
West Haystack Wash—*valley* WY-8
*West Hazelton* PA-2
**West Hazleton**—*pop pl* PA-2
West Hazleton Borough—*civil* PA-2
West Head—*cape* AK-9
West Head—*cape* MS-4
West Head—*cliff* MA-1
West Head—*valley* FL-3
West Hearn Lateral—*canal* AZ-5
**West Hebron**—*pop pl* NY-2
West Heidelberg Oil Field—*oilfield* MS-4
Westheight Manor Hist Dist (Boundary Increase)—*hist pl* KS-7
Westheight Park—*park* KS-7
*West Heights Baptist Church* MS-4
West Heights Ch—*church* MS-4
West Heights Sch—*school* IN-6
Westheim Cem—*cemetery* ND-7
Westheimer—*uninc pl* TX-5
Westheimer Site—*hist pl* NY-2
**West Helena**—*pop pl* AR-4
West Hell Canyon—*valley* SD-7
West Hemlock Creek—*stream* PA-2
**West Hemlock (Township of)**—*pop pl* PA-2
**West Hempfield (Township of)**—*pop pl* PA-2
West Hempfield Township Park—*park* PA-2
**West Hempstead**—*pop pl* NY-2
West Hempstead HS—*school* NY-2
**West Henderson**—*pop pl* KY-4
West Henderson HS—*school* NC-3
West Hendersonville—*uninc pl* NC-3
**West Henniker**—*pop pl* NH-1
**West Henniker Emerson Station**—*pop pl* NH-1
**West Henrietta**—*pop pl* NY-2
West Henshaw Oil Field—*other* NM-5
West Hensley Ch—*church* AR-4
West Hermon Cem—*cemetery* NY-2
**West Hermondale**—*pop pl* MO-7
West Hernando JHS—*school* FL-3
West Heron Lake (Township of)—*civ div* MN-6
West Hess Hills—*range* NM-5
West Hialeah Baptist Church Kindergarten—*school* FL-3
**West Hibbard Township**—*pop pl* KS-7
West Hickman Creek—*stream* KY-4
**West Hickory**—*pop pl* PA-2
West Hickory Bridge—*hist pl* PA-2
West Hickory Creek—*stream* (2) KS-7
West Hickory Creek—*stream* OK-5
West Hickory Creek—*stream* PA-2
West Hickory Sch—*school* IL-6
West High Creek*—*stream* IA-7
West High Creek—*stream* MO-7
**West Highland**—*pop pl* MI-6
*West Highland Baptist Ch* AL-4
West Highland Baptist Ch—*church* (2) AL-4
West Highland Ch—*church* AL-4
West Highland Ch—*church* MI-6
West Highland Elem Sch—*school* TN-4
West Highland HS—*school* AL-4
West Highland Memorial Cem—*cemetery* AL-4
**West Highlands**—*pop pl* AL-4
**West Highlands**—*pop pl* CA-9
**West Highlands**—*pop pl* NC-3
**West Highlands**—*pop pl* WA-9
West Highlands—*uninc pl* GA-3
West Highlands Baptist Ch—*church* AL-4
West Highlands Ch—*church* AL-4
West Highland Sch—*school* AL-4
*West Highlands Elementary School* AL-4
West High Peak—*summit* OK-5
West High Point Sch (abandoned)—*school* MO-7
*West High School* KS-7
West High Street Hist Dist—*hist pl* KY-4
*West Hill* NY-2
West Hill—*hist pl* GA-3
Westhill—*hist pl* TX-5
**West Hill**—*pop pl* AL-4
**Westhill**—*pop pl* IN-6
**West Hill**—*pop pl* IN-6
**West Hill**—*pop pl* MS-4
**West Hill**—*pop pl* NY-2
**West Hill**—*pop pl* PA-2
**West Hill**—*pop pl* VT-1
West Hill—*ridge* MA-1
West Hill—*summit* AK-9
West Hill—*summit* CT-1
West Hill—*summit* GA-3
West Hill—*summit* (7) MA-1
West Hill—*summit* (2) NH-1
West Hill—*summit* (11) NY-2
West Hill—*summit* OR-9
West Hill—*summit* (2) PA-2
West Hill—*summit* (5) VT-1
West Hill—*summit* WI-6
West Hill Brook—*stream* VT-1
West Hill Cem—*cemetery* FL-3
West Hill Cem—*cemetery* (2) GA-3
West Hill Cem—*cemetery* NE-7
West Hill Cem—*cemetery* (5) NY-2
West Hill Cem—*cemetery* OK-5
West Hill Cem—*cemetery* TN-4
West Hill Cem—*cemetery* TX-5
West Hill Cem—*cemetery* (2) VT-1
Westhill Cem—*cemetery* VT-1
West Hill Cem—*cemetery* VT-1
Westhill Cem—*cemetery* VA-3
Westhill Central HS—*school* NY-2
West Hill Ch—*church* MS-4
Westhill Ch—*church* VA-3
West Hill Ch—*church* VA-3
West Hill Ch—*church* WV-2
West Hill Covered Bridge—*hist pl* VT-1
West Hill Creek—*stream* TX-5
West Hill Dam—*dam* MA-1
*West Hill Elementary School* PA-2
*West Hillery* IL-6
**Westhill Heights**—*pop pl* OH-6
West Hill Lake—*lake* NE-7
West Hill Mine—*mine* MN-6
West Hill Park—*park* MT-8
West Hill Park—*park* TX-5
West Hill Pond—*lake* VT-1
West Hill Pond—*reservoir* CT-1
*West Hills* ID-8
West Hills—*CDP* NY-2
West Hills—*locale* FL-3
**West Hills**—*pop pl* CA-9
**West Hills**—*pop pl* (2) MD-2
**West Hills**—*pop pl* PA-2
**West Hills**—*pop pl* (3) TN-4
West Hills—*range* UT-8
West Hills—*summit* NY-2
West Hills—*summit* UT-8
West Hills, The—*range* UT-8
West Hills Arroyo—*stream* NM-5
**West Hillsborough**—*pop pl* NC-3
West Hillsborough Baptist Sch—*school* FL-3
West Hills Ch—*church* TN-4
West Hill Sch—*school* MO-7
West Hill Sch—*school* NE-7
West Hill Sch—*school* NY-2
West Hill Sch—*school* OH-6
West Hill Sch—*school* PA-2
West Hill Sch—*school* TN-4
West Hill Sch—*school* VT-1
*West Hills Elementary School* MS-4
West Hills Elem Sch—*school* PA-2
West Hills Elem Sch—*school* TN-4
**West Hills Estates**—*pop pl* PA-2
West Hill Shop Ctr—*locale* IN-6
West Hills HS—*school* MI-6
West Hills Memorial Gardens—*cemetery* FL-3
West Hills Memorial Gardens (cemetery)—*cemetery* WA-9
West Hills Park—*park* TN-4
West Hills Par 3 Golf Course—*locale* PA-2
West Hills Presbyterian Ch—*church* (2) TN-4
West Hills Sch—*school* CT-1
West Hills Sch—*school* MS-4
West Hills Sch—*school* NY-2
West Hills Sch—*school* (2) OR-9
**West Hills (subdivision)**—*pop pl* MS-4
**West Hills (subdivision)**—*pop pl* NC-3
**West Hills (subdivision)**—*pop pl* (2) TN-4
**West Hills Subdivision**—*pop pl* (2) UT-8
**West Hills Subdivision - Number 2**—*pop pl* UT-8
**West Hima**—*pop pl* TN-4
West Hingham (historical P.O.)—*locale* MA-1
West Hingham Station (historical)—*locale* MA-1
**West Hingham (subdivision)**—*pop pl* MA-1
*West Hinsdale* IL-6
West Hinson Lake—*lake* FL-3
West Hitchen Creek—*stream* KS-7
West Hobbs Street Ch of Christ—*church* AL-4
West Hoboken—*uninc pl* NJ-2
West Hoboken (Sta.)—*uninc pl* NJ-2
West Hobolochitto Creek—*stream* MS-4
West Hodges Creek—*stream* UT-8
**Westhoff**—*pop pl* TX-5
Westhoff-Arneckville (CCD)—*cens area* TX-5
Westhoff Cem—*cemetery* TX-5
**West Hoffman**—*pop pl* PA-2
West Hogback—*ridge* MT-8
West Hog Branch—*stream* LA-4
West Hog Creek—*stream* OK-5
West Hogshead Rock—*rock* MA-1
*West Hogup Mountains* UT-8
West Hoke Elem Sch—*school* NC-3
West Holbrook Interchange—*crossing* AZ-5
West Holcomb Trail—*trail* AZ-5
West Holden Ch—*church* WI-6
West Holland Creek—*stream* KS-7
**West Hollis**—*pop pl* ME-1
**West Hollis**—*pop pl* NH-1
*West Hollow* TN-4
West Hollow—*valley* AR-4
West Hollow—*valley* (2) KY-4
West Hollow—*valley* MO-7
West Hollow—*valley* NY-2
West Hollow—*valley* NC-3
West Hollow—*valley* TN-4
West Hollow—*valley* (2) TX-5
West Hollow—*valley* WV-2
West Holloway Creek—*stream* TX-5
*West Hollow Brook* MA-1
West Hollow Cave—*cave* (2) TN-4
**West Holly Hill**—*pop pl* FL-3
**West Holly Hills (subdivision)**—*pop pl* NC-3
**West Hollywood**—*pop pl* CA-9
**West Hollywood (Br. P.O. name West)**—*pop pl* CA-9
West Hollywood Park—*park* CA-9
West Hollywood Private Sch—*school* FL-3
West Hollywood Sch—*school* CA-9
West Hollywood Sch—*school* FL-3
West Hollywood Shopping Plaza—*locale* FL-3
West Hollywood Stores (Shop Ctr)—*locale* FL-3
**West Hollywood (subdivision)**—*pop pl* FL-3
West Holy Hill Ch—*church* MS-4
West Home Ch—*church* PA-2
West Home Ranch—*locale* CO-8
West Homer Ch—*church* OH-6
**West Homestead**—*pop pl* PA-2
West Homestead Borough—*civil* PA-2
West Homestead Elem Sch—*school* FL-3
West Homestead Yard Station—*building* PA-2
*West Honey Creek* OH-6
West Honey Creek—*stream* IN-6
West Honey Creek—*stream* MO-7
West Honey Island Flowage—*reservoir* WI-6
West Honomaele—*civil* HI-9
**West Hoosick**—*pop pl* NY-2
West Hoosier Creek—*stream* IA-7
*West Hoosuck Plantation* MA-1
Westhope—*hist pl* OK-5
West Hope—*locale* VA-3
**Westhope**—*pop pl* ND-7
**Westhope**—*pop pl* OH-6
West Hope Cem—*cemetery* (2) KS-7
Westhope Cem—*cemetery* ND-7
Westhope Municipal Airp—*airport* ND-7
West Hope Sch—*school* KS-7
**West Hope Township**—*pop pl* ND-7
**West Hopewell**—*pop pl* VA-3
**West Hopkinsville**—*pop pl* KY-4
**West Hopkinton**—*pop pl* NH-1
West Hopley Spring—*spring* MT-8
West Horn—*summit* WY-8
West Horse Basin Rsvr—*reservoir* ID-8
West Horse Creek—*stream* CO-8
West Horse Creek—*stream* ID-8
West Horse Creek—*stream* SD-7
West Horse Creek—*stream* TX-5
West Horsehead Lake—*lake* WI-6
West Horse Pasture Windmill—*locale* TX-5
West Horse Point—*summit* ID-8
West House—*hist pl* AR-4
West House—*hist pl* OH-6
*West House Creek* VA-3
West Howellsville (Township of)—*fmr MCD* NC-3
West HQ Pasture—*flat* KS-7
West HQ Well—*well* NM-5
West HQ Windmill—*locale* TX-5
West HS—*school* AL-4
West HS—*school* (2) CA-9
West HS—*school* CO-8
West HS—*school* (2) IL-6
West HS—*school* (2) IA-7
West HS—*school* (2) KS-7
West HS—*school* (2) MI-6
West HS—*school* MN-6
West HS—*school* NH-1
West HS—*school* (2) NY-2
West HS—*school* NC-3
West HS—*school* (2) OH-6
West HS—*school* (2) PA-2
West HS—*school* SD-7
West HS—*school* (3) TN-4
West HS—*school* WI-6
West Hubbard Creek—*stream* CO-8
West Hubbell Tank—*reservoir* NM-5
West Hubbell Well—*well* NM-5
West Hudson—*uninc pl* NJ-2
West Hudson Hosp—*hospital* NJ-2
West Hudson Park—*park* NJ-2
West Hudson Sch—*school* IL-6
West Hue and Cry—*bar* ME-1
*West Huffman Creek* TX-5
West Hughes—*unorg reg* SD-7
West Humboldt Range—*range* NV-8
West Humbug Creek—*stream* OR-9
West Hume Sch—*school* IL-6
West Humphrey Tank—*reservoir* TX-5
West Hunt Creek—*stream* CA-9
West Hunter Creek—*stream* CO-8
West Hunter Lake—*lake* MN-6
**West Hunter Subdivision**—*pop pl* UT-8
**West Huntington**—*pop pl* NY-2
**West Huntington**—*pop pl* WV-2
**West Huntsville**—*pop pl* AL-4
West Huntsville AME Ch (historical)—*church* AL-4
West Huntsville Baptist Ch—*church* AL-4
West Huntsville Ch of Christ—*church* AL-4
West Huntsville Elem Sch—*school* AL-4
West Huntsville Public Sch (historical)—*school* AL-4
West Hurlburt Camp—*locale* OR-9
**West Hurley**—*pop pl* NY-2
West Hurley District Sch Number 6—*school* NY-2
West Hurricane Creek—*stream* MO-7
*West Huttonsville* WV-2
*West Hyannis Port* MA-1
**West Hyannisport**—*pop pl* MA-1
West Hyattsville—*uninc pl* MD-2
West Hyland Ditch—*canal* NV-8
West Hy Pond—*reservoir* AZ-5
West Ike Tank—*reservoir* AZ-5
Westimber—*locale* OR-9
West Immanuel Cem—*cemetery* ND-7
West Immanuel Ch—*church* WI-6
West Imongalasha (historical)—*locale* MS-4
West Imperial (CCD)—*cens area* CA-9
West Independence—*locale* MO-7
**West Independence**—*pop pl* OH-6
West Independent Sch—*school* IA-7
*West Index Mountain* WA-9
*West Indianapolis* IN-6
West Indian Bayou—*stream* LA-4
West Indian Creek—*stream* CO-8
West Indian Creek—*stream* IA-7
West Indian Creek—*stream* KS-7
West Indian Creek—*stream* MN-6
West Indian Creek—*stream* (2) TX-5
West Indian Creek Sch—*school* SD-7
West Indianola Elem Sch—*school* KS-7
West Indian Pine Tank—*reservoir* AZ-5
*West Indian River* MN-6
West Indian Tank—*reservoir* AZ-5
Westing Branch—*stream* MO-7
Westinghouse—*other* PA-2
Westinghouse, George, Jr., Birthplace and Boyhood Home—*hist pl* NY-2
Westinghouse, George, Memorial Bridge—*hist pl* PA-2
Westinghouse Air Brake Company General Office Bldg—*hist pl* PA-2
Westinghouse Bridge—*bridge* PA-2
Westinghouse Electric Corporation—*facility* VA-3
Westinghouse Elem Sch—*school* PA-2
Westinghouse E Pittsburgh Airp—*airport* PA-2
Westinghouse Hill—*summit* VT-1
Westinghouse HS—*hist pl* PA-2
Westinghouse Lamp Division—*facility* KY-4
Westinghouse Nuclear Turbine Plant—*facility* NC-3
Westinghouse Park—*park* PA-2
*Westinghouse School* PA-2
**Westinghouse Village**—*pop pl* PA-2
West Inlet—*stream* ME-1
West Inlet—*stream* (2) NH-1
West Inlet—*stream* NY-2
West Interception Canal—*canal* CA-9
West Ionine Creek—*stream* OK-5
West Iredell HS—*school* NC-3
West Iredell MS—*school* NC-3
**West Iron Hills**—*pop pl* IA-7
West Ironhills Cem—*cemetery* IA-7
West Iron Portal—*gap* CA-9
**West Irvine**—*pop pl* KY-4
West Irving Acres Park—*park* TX-5
**West Irvington**—*pop pl* VA-3
**West Ishpeming**—*pop pl* MI-6
*West Island* NY-2
*West Island* FM-9
West Island—*island* AK-9
West Island—*island* CA-9
West Island—*island* FL-3
West Island—*island* MA-1
West Island—*island* NJ-2
West Island—*island* NY-2
West Island—*island* RI-1
West Island—*island* VA-3
West Island—*island* MH-9
West Island Lateral—*canal* WA-9
West Island Ledge—*rock* MA-1
West Island Marshes—*swamp* MA-1
**West Islip**—*pop pl* NY-2
West Italian Rsvr—*reservoir* CO-8
West Italy Hill—*summit* NY-2
**West Iva**—*pop pl* SC-3
**Westivew Woods (subdivision)**—*pop pl* TN-4
West Jack Hollow Creek—*stream* OK-5
**West Jackson**—*pop pl* OH-6
West Jackson—*uninc pl* MS-4
West Jackson Baptist Ch—*church* (2) MS-4
West Jackson Blvd District—*hist pl* IL-6
West Jackson (CCD)—*cens area* GA-3
West Jackson (CCD)—*cens area* OK-5
West Jackson Ch—*church* PA-2
West Jackson Ch of Christ—*church* MS-4
West Jackson Creek—*stream* IA-7
West Jackson HS—*school* TX-5
**West Jacksonport**—*pop pl* WI-6
West Jackson Sch—*school* TN-4
**West Jacksonville**—*pop pl* FL-3
West Jacksonville Advent Christian Ch—*church* FL-3
West Jacksonville Ch of God in Christ—*church* FL-3
West Jacksonville Christian Center—*church* FL-3
West Jacksonville Elem Sch—*school* FL-3
West Jack Tank—*reservoir* AZ-5
West Jakeman Creek—*stream* CO-8
**West Jamaica**—*pop pl* VT-1
*West Jamestown* RI-1
West Jasper Ch—*church* NY-2
West Jasper Elem Sch—*school* AL-4
*West Jasper Grammar Sch* AL-4
West Jeannette—*uninc pl* PA-2
**West Jefferson**—*pop pl* AL-4
**West Jefferson**—*pop pl* NY-2
**West Jefferson**—*pop pl* NC-3
**West Jefferson**—*pop pl* (2) OH-6
West Jefferson (CCD)—*cens area* AL-4
West Jefferson Cem—*cemetery* OH-6
*West Jefferson (corporate name Jefferson)* OH-6
West Jefferson Division—*civil* AL-4
West Jefferson Elem Sch—*school* NC-3
West Jefferson Sch—*school* AL-4
West Jefferson Sch—*school* CO-8
West Jefferson (Township of)—*fmr MCD* NC-3
West Jemtland Cem—*cemetery* ME-1
West Jennings Creek—*stream* OH-6
West Jericho—*other* VA-3
**West Jersey**—*pop pl* IL-6
West Jersey Cranberry Meadow—*swamp* NJ-2
West Jersey Hosp—*hospital* (2) NJ-2
**West Jersey (Township of)**—*pop pl* IL-6
West Jett Windmill—*locale* NM-5
West Jetty—*dam* LA-4
West Jetty—*locale* TX-5
West Jewett—*locale* NY-2
West JHS—*school* AR-4
West JHS—*school* CA-9
West JHS—*school* (2) CO-8
West JHS—*school* ID-8
West JHS—*school* (2) IL-6
West JHS—*school* (3) IA-7

West JHS—*school* (3) KS-7
West JHS—*school* MD-2
West JHS—*school* (3) MA-1
West JHS—*school* (4) MI-6
West JHS—*school* (2) MN-6
West JHS—*school* MS-4
West JHS—*school* (3) MO-7
West JHS—*school* (2) MT-8
West JHS—*school* (2) NY-2
West JHS—*school* NC-3
West JHS—*school* (5) OH-6
West JHS—*school* (3) OK-5
West JHS—*school* SC-3
West JHS—*school* SD-7
West JHS—*school* TN-4
West JHS—*school* UT-8
West Jiggs Well—*well* NV-8
West Jim Creek—*stream* NE-7
West Jim Windmill—*locale* NM-5
West Job Canyon—*valley* NV-8
West Joe Windmill—*locale* NM-5
West Jog Windmills—*locale* NM-5
West Johnson City—*CDP* TN-4
West Johnson Creek—*stream* ID-8
*West Johnston* KS-7
West Johnston (CCD)—*cens area* OK-5
West Jones HS—*school* MS-4
**West Jonesport**—*pop pl* ME-1
**West Jonestown**—*pop pl* PA-2
**West Jordan**—*pop pl* UT-8
West Jordan Ch—*church* IL-6
West Jordan City Cem—*cemetery* UT-8
West Jordan Gulch—*valley* CO-8
*West Jordan High School* UT-8
West Jordan MS—*school* UT-8
West Jordan Park—*park* UT-8
West Jordan Post Office—*building* UT-8
West Jordan Sch—*school* UT-8
*West Joslin Branch* MO-7
West Juab—*cens area* UT-8
West Juab Division—*civil* UT-8
*West Junction* DE-2
West Junction—*locale* IL-6
West Junction—*locale* OH-6
West Junction—*locale* TN-4
**West Junction**—*pop pl* WV-2
West Junction—*uninc pl* TX-5
**West Juneau**—*pop pl* AK-9
West Juniper Creek—*stream* CA-9
West Junius—*locale* NY-2
West Junius Ch—*church* NY-2
West Junk Creek—*stream* WY-8
**West Jupiter**—*pop pl* FL-3
**West Jutts Creek**—*pop pl* NC-3
West Kaiser Campground—*locale* CA-9
West Kaiser Creek—*stream* CA-9
West Kammerdiner Run—*stream* PA-2
*West Kankakee* IL-6
**West Kankakee**—*pop pl* IL-6
*Westkap* MP-9
West Karako Bay—*bay* LA-4
*West Karankawa River* TX-5
West Kate Creek Spring—*spring* MT-8
West Kaupakulua—*civil* HI-9
West Kaysville—*locale* UT-8
West Kaysville Marshes—*swamp* UT-8
*westkeag River* ME-1
**West Keansburg**—*pop pl* NJ-2
West Keansburg Sch—*school* NJ-2
West Kearns Canyon—*valley* CO-8
West Kearns Sch—*school* UT-8
**West Keating (Township of)**—*pop pl* PA-2
West Keen Well—*well* NM-5
West Keggy Coulee—*valley* MT-8
West Keg Springs Waterhole—*lake* OR-9
West Kehl Canyon—*valley* AZ-5
**West Keithsburg**—*pop pl* IA-7
West Kellehan Creek—*stream* WY-8
**West Kelso**—*pop pl* WA-9
*West Kemper Baptist Church* MS-4
West Kemper Cem—*cemetery* MS-4
West Kemper Ch—*church* MS-4
West Kemper Elem Sch—*school* MS-4
West Kemper HS—*school* MS-4
West Kemper P.O. (historical)—*building* MS-4
**West Kendall**—*pop pl* NY-2
West Kennebago Mtn—*summit* ME-1
**West Kennebunk**—*pop pl* ME-1
West Kennedy Lake—*lake* CA-9
West Kennett—*locale* AR-4
West Kenney JHS—*school* NJ-2
West Kent Creek—*stream* NY-2
West Kentucky Creek—*stream* KS-7
West Kentucky Sch—*school* KY-4
West Kentucky State Wildlife Mngmt
Area—*park* KY-4
West Kettle Falls—*locale* WA-9
West Kewaunee Ch—*church* WI-6
**West Kewaunee (Town of)**—*pop pl* WI-6
West Key—*island* FL-3
**West Keystone**—*pop pl* MO-7
West Key Well—*well* NM-5
West Kickapoo Creek—*stream* TX-5
**West Kill**—*pop pl* NY-2
West Kill—*stream* (2) NY-2
*West Killingly* CT-1
West Kill Mtn—*summit* NY-2
West Kilns—*locale* NY-2
West Kinderhook—*locale* MI-6
West King—*locale* MS-4
West King Ch—*church* MS-4
West King Junction (historical)—*locale* MS-4
**West Kingston**—*pop pl* NH-1
**West Kingston**—*pop pl* RI-1
West Kingston Cem—*cemetery* MN-6
West Kiowa—*unorg reg* KS-7
West Kiowa Creek—*stream* CO-8
West Kiowa Creek—*stream* KS-7
West Kirby Creek—*stream* WY-8
West Kiska Lake—*lake* AK-9
**West Kittanning**—*pop pl* PA-2
West Kittanning Borough—*civil* PA-2
West Kitty Creek—*stream* IA-7
**West Klamath (historical)**—*pop pl* OR-9
West Knee—*summit* MT-8
West Kneebone Draw—*arroyo* SD-7
West Knob—*summit* NC-3
**West Knoxville**—*pop pl* TN-4
West Knoxville Ch—*church* TN-4
West Knoxville Post Office—*building* TN-4
West Knuckey Creek—*stream* MN-6
*West Kopiliula Stream* HI-9
West Kortright—*locale* NY-2
**West Kraft**—*pop pl* WI-6
West Kuparuk State No 1—*well* AK-9
**West Labadie**—*pop pl* MO-7
West Laberdie Creek—*stream* KS-7
West Lacey Creek—*stream* AR-4
**West La Crosse**—*pop pl* WI-6
West Lacy Fork—*valley* AZ-5
**West Lafayette**—*pop pl* IN-6
**West Lafayette**—*pop pl* OH-6
West Lafayette Baptist Church—*hist pl* IN-6
West Lafayette Senior HS—*school* IN-6
West Lafferty Creek—*stream* AR-4
West Lagoon—*bay* FM-9
West Lagoon—*lake* IL-6
West La Jolla Canyon—*valley* NM-5
*West Lake* FL-3
*Westlake* IL-6
*West Lake* ME-1
*West Lake* MA-1
*Westlake* OK-5
*Westlake* OR-9
*West Lake* UT-8
West Lake—*lake* AK-9
West Lake—*lake* AZ-5
West Lake—*lake* (2) CA-9
West Lake—*lake* CO-8
West Lake—*lake* CT-1
West Lake—*lake* (7) FL-3
West Lake—*lake* IN-6
West Lake—*lake* IA-7
West Lake—*lake* (2) ME-1
West Lake—*lake* (13) MI-6
West Lake—*lake* (5) MN-6
West Lake—*lake* NE-7
West Lake—*lake* NV-8
West Lake—*lake* (4) NY-2
West Lake—*lake* (2) ND-7
West Lake—*lake* (2) OR-9
West Lake—*lake* TX-5
West Lake—*lake* (8) WI-6
West Lake—*locale* FL-3
Westlake—*locale* GA-3
Westlake—*locale* ID-8
Westlake—*locale* MT-8
**West Lake**—*pop pl* IL-6
**Westlake**—*pop pl* LA-4
**Westlake**—*pop pl* MD-2
**Westlake**—*pop pl* OH-6
**West Lake**—*pop pl* OR-9
**Westlake**—*pop pl* OR-9
**Westlake**—*pop pl* TX-5
**Westlake**—*pop pl* WA-9
Westlake—*post sta* CA-9
West Lake—*reservoir* AL-4
West Lake—*reservoir* (2) CO-8
West Lake—*reservoir* (2) GA-3
West Lake—*reservoir* (2) IL-6
West Lake—*reservoir* (2) IA-7
West Lake—*reservoir* KS-7
West Lake—*reservoir* MA-1
West Lake—*reservoir* NJ-2
West Lake—*reservoir* NY-2
West Lake—*reservoir* NC-3
West Lake—*reservoir* OK-5
West Lake—*reservoir* OR-9
West Lake—*reservoir* TX-5
West Lake—*reservoir* UT-8
West Lake Amelia Cem—*cemetery* MN-6
West Lake Andes Cem—*cemetery* SD-7
West Lake Arthur Oil Field—*oilfield* LA-4
West Lakebed—*flat* MN-6
**Westlake Business Park**
**(subdivision)**—*pop pl* UT-8
Westlake Butte—*summit* CA-9
West Lake Cem—*cemetery* FL-3
West Lake Cem—*cemetery* IA-7
West Lake Cem—*cemetery* SD-7
West Lake Ch—*church* FL-3
West Lake Ch—*church* MN-6
Westlake Ch—*church* MS-4
West Lake Ch—*church* TX-5
**West Lake Charles**—*pop pl* LA-4
Westlake Ch of Christ—*church* IN-6
*West Lake Creek* ID-8
Westlake Creek—*stream* CA-9
West Lake Creek—*stream* CO-8
West Lake Creek—*stream* ID-8
West Lake Creek—*stream* WA-9
West Lake Dam—*dam* IA-7
West Lake Dam—*dam* MA-1
West Lake Dam—*dam* (2) MS-4
West Lake Dam—*dam* NJ-2
West Lake Dam—*dam* NC-3
*West Lake Ditch* IN-6
Westlake Ditch—*canal* IN-6
Westlake Elem Sch—*school* IN-6
West Lake Ellis—*lake* FL-3
**West Lake Estates**—*pop pl* TN-4
West Lake Farms—*locale* CA-9
West Lakefield Cem—*cemetery* MI-6
*West Lake Forest* IL-6
**West Lake Forest**—*pop pl* IL-6
West Lake Fork—*stream* UT-8
**West Lake Francis Shores**—*pop pl* MN-6
Westlake Golf Course—*other* TX-5
**West Lake Highlands**—*pop pl* AL-4
**West Lake Hills**—*pop pl* TX-5
West Lake Hosp—*hospital* FL-3
Westlake Hotel—*hist pl* OH-6
Westlake HS—*school* NY-2
Westlake Island—*island* OR-9
*Westlake Islands* OR-9
Westlake JHS—*school* CA-9
West Lake JHS—*school* UT-8
West Lake Johanna Ch—*church* MN-6
West Lakeland (Township of)—*civ div* MN-6
West Lake Mall Shop Ctr—*locale* AL-4
**West Lake Manor**
**(subdivision)**—*pop pl* MS-4
West Lake Marsh State Public Shooting
Area—*park* SD-7
Westlake Mine—*mine* AZ-5
Westlake MS—*school* PA-2
West Lake Mtn—*summit* NY-2
*West Lake Okahumpka* FL-3
West Lake Park—*park* FL-3
West Lake Park—*park* OH-6
Westlake Park—*park* OR-9
West Lake Park—*park* TX-5
West Lake Point—*cliff* AZ-5
West Lake Ponca—*reservoir* OK-5
West Lake Rec Area—*park* AL-4
West Lake Ridge—*ridge* ME-1
West Lake Road Cem—*cemetery* NY-2
*West Lake RR Dam* SD-7
West Lake (RR name for
Westlake)—*other* LA-4
**Westlake (RR name West**
**Lake)**—*pop pl* LA-4
West Lake Rsvr—*reservoir* CT-1
West Lake Rsvr—*reservoir* MA-1
West Lakes—*lake* IN-6
**West Lakes**—*pop pl* CT-1
**West Lakes**—*pop pl* FL-3
West Lakes—*reservoir* TX-5
Westlake Sch—*school* (3) CA-9
Westlake Sch—*school* CO-8
Westlake Sch—*school* MI-6
*Westlake School Number 5* IN-6
West Lakes (historical)—*locale* AL-4
West Lakeside Park—*park* WI-6
West Lakes Trail—*trail* MT-8
West Lake Tank—*reservoir* TX-5
West Lake (Unorganized Territory
of)—*unorg* MN-6
**West Lake Valley**
**(subdivision)**—*pop pl* NC-3
West Lake Verret Oil and Gas
Field—*oilfield* LA-4
**Westlake Village**—*pop pl* CA-9
Westlake Village—*uninc pl* CA-9
**Westlake Village Subdivision**—*pop pl*
(2) UT-8
*West Lakeville* OH-6
West Lakeville Cem—*cemetery* OH-6
**West Lake Wales**—*pop pl* FL-3
West Lake Windmill—*locale* TX-5
West Lakewood Sch—*school* CO-8
**West Lamont**—*pop pl* CA-9
**West Lampeter**—*pop pl* PA-2
**West Lampeter (Township of)**—*pop pl* PA-2
**West Lancaster**—*pop pl* OH-6
**West Lancaster**—*pop pl* PA-2
West Lancaster Township—*fmr MCD* IA-7
**West Lance Creek**—*pop pl* WY-8
*Westland* NC-3
Westland—*locale* OH-6
Westland—*locale* OR-9
**Westland**—*pop pl* (3) IN-6
**Westland**—*pop pl* MI-6
**Westland**—*pop pl* PA-2
**Westland**—*pop pl* TX-5
**Westland**—*pop pl* VA-3
Westland—*uninc pl* MS-4
Westland A Canal—*canal* OR-9
*Westland Acres* ID-8
*Westland B Canal* OR-9
Westland Cem—*cemetery* ND-7
Westland Cem—*cemetery* OH-6
Westland Cem—*cemetery* PA-2
Westland Ch—*church* OH-6
Westland Dam—*dam* OR-9
West Landergin Well—*well* TX-5
**Westland Estates**—*pop pl* MO-7
Westland F Canal—*canal* OR-9
Westland Flats—*flat* MT-8
**Westland Forest (subdivision)**—*pop pl* NC-3
Westland Friends Ch—*church* IN-6
**Westland Heights**
**(subdivision)**—*pop pl* MS-4
Westland Hill—*summit* MT-8
West Landing—*lake* MP-9
West Landing—*locale* FL-3
West Landing—*locale* NC-3
West Landing—*locale* (2) VA-3
West Landing Creek—*stream* VA-3
*Westland Main Canal* OR-9
*Westland Main Ditch* OR-9
Westland Mall—*locale* FL-3
Westland Oil Filling Station—*hist pl* ND-7
Westland Plaza Shop Ctr—*locale* AL-4
Westland Plaza Shop Ctr—*locale* MS-4
Westland Run—*stream* PA-2
**Westlands**—*pop pl* MA-1
Westland Sch—*school* CA-9
Westland Sch—*school* MI-6
Westland Sch—*school* OH-6
Westland Sch—*school* PA-2
Westland Sch—*school* UT-8
Westland Shop Ctr—*locale* MS-4
Westland Shop Ctr—*locale* NC-3
Westland Shop Ctr—*other* CO-8
Westlands Sch—*school* MA-1
**Westland Subdivision**—*pop pl* UT-8
**Westland (Township of)**—*pop pl* OH-6
Westlane JHS—*school* IN-6
Westlane Shop Ctr—*locale* IN-6
**West Langley**—*pop pl* VA-3
West Langsdale Oil Field—*oilfield* MS-4
**West Lanham Hills**—*pop pl* MD-2
West Lanham Hills Sch—*school* MD-2
West Lantana—*uninc pl* FL-3
**West Laramie**—*pop pl* WY-8
West Largoeta Well—*well* NM-5
West Larimore Tank—*reservoir* AZ-5
West Las Moras Creek—*stream* TX-5
West Last Resort Creek—*stream* CO-8
West Las Vegas—*uninc pl* NM-5
West Las Vegas HS—*school* NM-5
West Lateral—*canal* (2) CO-8
West Lateral—*canal* ID-8
West Lateral—*canal* OR-9
West Lateral—*canal* UT-8
West Lateral—*canal* WA-9
West Lateral Spring Creek Extension
Ditch—*canal* CO-8
West Lathham—*post sta* NY-2
West Latigo Tank—*reservoir* NM-5
**West Latrobe (subdivision)**—*pop pl* PA-2
West Lauderdale Baptist Ch—*church* FL-3
West Lauderdale Elem Sch—*school* MS-4
West Lauderdale HS—*school* MS-4
West Lauderdale JHS—*school* MS-4
**West Laurel**—*pop pl* MD-2
**West Laurel Acres**—*pop pl* MD-2
West Laurel Baptist Ch—*church* MS-4
West Laurel Ch of God—*church* MS-4
West Laurel Elem Sch—*school* DE-2
West Laurel Hill Cem—*cemetery* PA-2
**West Laurens**—*pop pl* NY-2
West Laurens HS—*school* GA-3
West Laurens JHS—*school* GA-3
West Lava Creek—*stream* OR-9
West Lava Forest Camp—*locale* OR-9
Westlawn—*hist pl* NC-3
Westlawn—*hist pl* PA-2
West Lawn—*hist pl* PA-2
**Westlawn**—*pop pl* AL-4
**Westlawn**—*pop pl* IN-6
**Westlawn**—*pop pl* NY-2
**West Lawn**—*pop pl* (2) PA-2
**Westlawn**—*pop pl* TX-5
**West Lawn**—*pop pl* VA-3
**Westlawn**—*pop pl* VA-3
Westlawn Baptist Ch—*church* (2) AL-4
Westlawn Baptist Ch—*church* MS-4
West Lawn Borough—*civil* PA-2
Westlawn Cem—*cemetery* AR-4
Westlawn Cem—*cemetery* IL-6
West Lawn Cem—*cemetery* IN-6
Westlawn Cem—*cemetery* IN-6
West Lawn Cem—*cemetery* IN-6
Westlawn Cem—*cemetery* (2) IN-6
West Lawn Cem—*cemetery* (2) IA-7
Westlawn Cem—*cemetery* KS-7
West Lawn Cem—*cemetery* KY-4
Westlawn Cem—*cemetery* (2) MA-1
Westlawn Cem—*cemetery* (3) MI-6
West Lawn Cem—*cemetery* MO-7
West Lawn Cem—*cemetery* (2) NE-7
Westlawn Cem—*cemetery* NH-1
West Lawn Cem—*cemetery* NC-3
West Lawn Cem—*cemetery* (2) OH-6
Westlawn Cem—*cemetery* (2) OH-6
West Lawn Cem—*cemetery* (2) OH-6
Westlawn Cem—*cemetery* OH-6
West Lawn Cem—*cemetery* OH-6
West Lawn Cem—*cemetery* OK-5
Westlawn Cem—*cemetery* PA-2
West Lawn Cem—*cemetery* SD-7
Westlawn Cem—*cemetery* TX-5
Westlawn Cemetery—*cape* MA-1
West Lawn Ch—*church* GA-3
Westlawn Ch of God—*church* AL-4
*Westlawn Elementary School* AL-4
Westlawn JHS—*school* AL-4
Westlawn JHS—*school* TX-5
Westlawn Memorial Cem—*cemetery* GA-3
Westlawn Memorial Cem—*cemetery* LA-4
Westlawn Memorial Cem—*cemetery* NE-7
West Lawn Memorial Cem—*cemetery* WI-6
Westlawn Memorial Gardens—*cemetery* FL-3
*Westlawn Memorial Park* NC-3
West Lawn Memorial Park—*cemetery* NC-3
Westlawn Memorial Park
(Cem)—*cemetery* TX-5
West Lawn Memorial Park
(cemetery)—*cemetery* OR-9
*Westlawn MS* AL-4
Westlawn MS—*school* AL-4
West Lawn Park—*park* IL-6
West Lawn Park—*park* TX-5
Westlawn Playground—*park* WI-6
West Lawn Run—*stream* IN-6
Westlawn Sch—*school* (2) AL-4
West Lawn Sch—*school* IL-6
West Lawn Sch—*school* NE-7
Westlawn Sch—*school* VA-3
Westlawn South Cem—*cemetery* LA-4
West Lawrie Oil Field—*oilfield* OK-5
West Layton—*locale* UT-8
West Layton Marshes—*swamp* UT-8
West Lazy Creek Oil Field—*oilfield* MS-4
*Westlea* IN-6
West Leach Park—*park* IA-7
West Lead—*bay* MI-6
West Leaf Lake—*reservoir* MN-6
Westlea Park—*park* IN-6
West Leatherwood Creek—*stream* AR-4
**West Lebanon**—*pop pl* IN-6
**West Lebanon**—*pop pl* ME-1
**West Lebanon**—*pop pl* MO-7
**West Lebanon**—*pop pl* NH-1
**West Lebanon**—*pop pl* NY-2
**West Lebanon**—*pop pl* OH-6
**West Lebanon**—*pop pl* (2) PA-2
West Lebanon Cem—*cemetery* IN-6
West Lebanon Cem—*cemetery* PA-2
West Lebanon Hist Dist—*hist pl* ME-1
**West Lebanon Station**—*pop pl* PA-2
**West Lebanon (Township of)**—*pop pl* PA-2
*West Lebanon (Westboro)* NH-1
West Leck Windmill—*locale* TX-5
West Ledge—*bar* ME-1
West Ledge—*summit* CT-1
**West Lee**—*pop pl* NY-2
West Lee Canyon—*valley* NV-8
**West Leechburg**—*pop pl* (2) PA-2
West Leechburg Borough—*civil* PA-2
West Leechburg Elem Sch—*school* PA-2
*West Leechburg Reservoir Dam* PA-2
**West Leeds**—*pop pl* ME-1
West Lee Fork—*stream* VA-3
West Lee JHS—*school* NC-3
**West Leesburg**—*pop pl* MS-4
West Lee Sch—*school* SC-3
**West Leesport**—*pop pl* PA-2
West Lee Well—*well* NV-8
West Leg Westwood Run—*stream* IN-6
West Lehman Windmill—*locale* TX-5
**West Leigh**—*pop pl* VA-3
Westleigh Cove—*cove* AL-4
**West Leipsic**—*pop pl* OH-6
**West Leisenring**—*pop pl* PA-2
West Lelia Lake Creek—*stream* TX-5
West Le Mars—*locale* IA-7
West Lemonweir Cem—*cemetery* WI-6
West Lenoir Elem Sch—*school* NC-3
**West Lenox**—*pop pl* PA-2
West Lenox Cem—*cemetery* OH-6
West Lenox Ch—*church* PA-2
**West Leominster**—*pop pl* MA-1
West Leonard Canyon—*valley* AZ-5
*West Leonard Cemetery* MS-4
West Leonard Sch—*school* MI-6
West Leon Creek—*stream* CO-8
Westler Lake—*lake* IN-6
West Leroux Creek—*stream* CO-8
West Leroy—*locale* MI-6
West Leroy—*locale* PA-2
Westlers Branch—*stream* IA-7
West Levant—*locale* ME-1
West Levee—*levee* CA-9
**West Lewinsville Heights**—*pop pl* VA-3
**West Lewistown**—*pop pl* MT-8
West Lexington—*uninc pl* VA-3
**Westley**—*pop pl* CA-9
Westley Cem—*cemetery* AR-4
Westley Cem—*cemetery* OH-6
**West Leyden**—*pop pl* MA-1
**West Leyden**—*pop pl* NY-2
West Leyden Cem—*cemetery* MA-1
West Leyden Cem—*cemetery* NY-2
*West Leydon* MA-1
Westley Wasteway—*canal* CA-9
*West Liberty* IN-6
*West Liberty* OH-6
*West Liberty* TX-5
West Liberty—*locale* AR-4
West Liberty—*locale* OH-6
**West Liberty**—*pop pl* IL-6
**West Liberty**—*pop pl* (2) IN-6
**West Liberty**—*pop pl* IA-7
**West Liberty**—*pop pl* KY-4
**West Liberty**—*pop pl* MD-2
**West Liberty**—*pop pl* (2) OH-6
**West Liberty**—*pop pl* (3) PA-2
**West Liberty**—*pop pl* WV-2
West Liberty Borough—*civil* PA-2
West Liberty (CCD)—*cens area* FL-3
West Liberty (CCD)—*cens area* KY-4
West Liberty Cem—*cemetery* IL-6
West Liberty Cem—*cemetery* IA-7
West Liberty Cem—*cemetery* (2) KS-7
West Liberty Cem—*cemetery* PA-2
West Liberty Ch—*church* IN-6
West Liberty Ch—*church* KS-7
West Liberty Ch—*church* MD-2
West Liberty Ch—*church* MO-7
West Liberty Ch—*church* OK-5
West Liberty Ch—*church* VA-3
West Liberty Country Club—*other* IA-7
**West Liberty (Eriton)**—*pop pl* PA-2
West Liberty Esker—*ridge* PA-2
West Liberty Presbyterian
Church—*hist pl* WV-2
West Liberty Sch—*school* CA-9
West Liberty Sch—*school* (3) IL-6
West Liberty Sch—*school* KS-7
West Liberty Sch (abandoned)—*school* MO-7
West Liberty Sch (historical)—*school* (2) MO-7
West Liberty Sch No 1—*school* IA-7
West Liberty Sch No 2—*school* IA-7
West Liberty Sch No 3—*school* IA-7
West Liberty State Coll—*school* WV-2
West Liberty Station—*building* PA-2
**West Library**—*pop pl* PA-2
*Westlichen Gefahr Island* MP-9
West Lick Creek—*stream* MO-7
West Licking Creek—*stream* PA-2
West Liddell Creek—*stream* CA-9
*West Liebre Gulch* CA-9
West Liebre Lookout—*locale* CA-9
West Light—*locale* OR-9
Westlight Ch—*church* GA-3
West Lightning Creek—*stream* MT-8
**West Lima**—*pop pl* WI-6
West Limb Mine—*mine* MT-8
*West Lime Creek* CO-8
West Lime Creek—*stream* CO-8
West Lime Hills—*other* NM-5
West Limestone Creek—*stream* CO-8
West Limestone Creek—*stream* KS-7
West Limestone Sch—*school* AL-4
**West Lincoln**—*pop pl* MS-4
**West Lincoln**—*pop pl* NE-7
**West Lincoln**—*pop pl* VT-1
West Lincoln Attendance Center—*school* MS-4
*West Lincoln Consolidated Sch* MS-4
*West Lincoln HS* NC-3
West Lincoln JHS—*school* NC-3
West Lincolnton Ch—*church* NC-3
West Lincolnton Sch—*school* NC-3
West Lincoln Township—*fmr MCD* IA-7
West Lincoln (Township of)—*civ div* IL-6
West Lincoln Trail—*trail* AZ-5
West Line—*locale* AR-4
**West Line**—*pop pl* MO-7
**Westline**—*pop pl* PA-2
West Line Camp—*locale* TX-5
West Line Cem—*cemetery* AR-4
*West Line Creek* TX-5
Westline State Wildlife Mngmt
Area—*park* MN-6
**Westline (Township of)**—*pop pl* MN-6
West Line Trap Windmill—*locale* TX-5
West Line Well—*well* NM-5
Westlink Baptist Ch—*church* KS-7
Westlink Ch of Christ—*church* KS-7
Westlink Christian Ch—*church* KS-7
Westlink Shop Ctr—*locale* KS-7
**Westlink Village**—*pop pl* KS-7
Westlink Village—*uninc pl* KS-7
**West Linn**—*pop pl* OR-9
West Linn Cem—*cemetery* IA-7
*West Linton* IN-6
*West Little Horn River* WY-8
West Little Owyhee River—*stream* OR-9
West Little Pine Hollow—*valley* OR-9
*West Little Postoak Creek* TX-5
West Little Post Oak Creek—*stream* TX-5
West Little River—*CDP* FL-3
West Little River Sch—*school* FL-3
West Little Seneca Creek—*stream* VA-3
West Little Sugar Creek—*stream* IL-6
West Little Sugar Creek—*stream* (2) IN-6
*West Little Sunflower River* MS-4
West Little Thompson Creek—*stream* MS-4
*West Little Thompsons Creek* MS-4
West Littleton Cem—*cemetery* NH-1
*West Little Walla Walla River* OR-9
West Little Walla Walla River—*stream* WA-9
West Livingston Creek—*stream* AR-4
*Westlo* KS-7
West Loch—*bay* HI-9
West Locke Ch—*church* MI-6
West Locomotive Slough—*stream* UT-8
West Locomotive Spring—*spring* UT-8
West Locust Creek*—*stream* IA-7
West Locust Creek—*stream* (2) MO-7
West Locust Hill Oil Field—*oilfield* MS-4
West Lodge Creek—*stream* WA-9
**West Lodi**—*pop pl* OH-6
West Lodi Cem—*cemetery* NY-2
Westlog Airstrip—*airport* OR-9
**West Logan**—*pop pl* OH-6
**West Logan**—*pop pl* WV-2
West Logan—*unorg reg* ND-7
West Logan Draw—*valley* WY-8
West Log House—*hist pl* TX-5
West Londo Lake—*lake* MI-6
*West London* OH-6
West London Ch—*church* KY-4
West Lone Star Lateral—*canal* CO-8
**West Long Branch**—*pop pl* NJ-2
West Long Branch—*stream* VA-3
West Long Creek—*stream* (2) IA-7
West Longfellow Sch—*school* IN-6
West Long Hill—*summit* CT-1
West Long Hollow Tank—*reservoir* AZ-5
West Long Lake—*lake* MI-6
*West Long Pond* VT-1
West Longwell Ridge—*ridge* NV-8
West Lonsdale Baptist Ch—*church* TN-4
West Look Cem—*cemetery* VT-1
West Lookout Tower—*locale* GU-9
West Looney Township—*civil* MO-7
West Loop Ch—*church* PA-2
West Loop Shop Ctr—*locale* KS-7
West Loraleno Windmill—*locale* TX-5
**West Los Angeles**—*pop pl* CA-9
West Los Angeles Junior Coll—*school* CA-9
West Lost Creek—*stream* WI-6
West Lost Lake—*lake* CO-8
West Lost Lake—*lake* MI-6
West Lost Lake—*lake* MN-6
West Lost Trail Creek—*stream* CO-8
West Lost Valley Tank—*reservoir* TX-5
**West Louisville**—*pop pl* KY-4
West Love (CCD)—*cens area* OK-5
**West Lovell**—*pop pl* ME-1
West Lovington Oil Field—*other* NM-5
West Low Gap—*gap* CA-9
*West Lowndes Elementary School* MS-4
West Lowndes Sch—*school* MS-4
**West Lowville**—*pop pl* NY-2
West L Tank—*reservoir* TX-5
West Lubec—*locale* ME-1
West Lubec Cem—*cemetery* ME-1
West Lucas Creek—*stream* TX-5
West Lucas Township—*fmr MCD* IA-7
West Lumberton—*uninc pl* NC-3
West Lumberton Elem Sch—*school* NC-3
West Lump Reef—*bar* MI-6
Westlund Creek—*stream* CA-9
Westlund Place—*locale* CA-9
West Lunenburg Sch—*school* VT-1
West Lutheran Cem—*cemetery* IA-7
West Luther Oil And Gas Field—*oilfield* OK-5
West Luther Valley Ch—*church* WI-6
West Luther Valley Lutheran
Church—*hist pl* WI-6
West Luxen Draw—*valley* CO-8
**Westlyn**—*pop pl* TN-4
**West Lynchburg**—*pop pl* VA-3
West Lynn Station (historical)—*locale* MA-1
**West Lynn (subdivision)**—*pop pl* MA-1
West Lyons Cem—*cemetery* MN-6
West Lyon Sch—*school* IA-7
West Lytle Creek—*stream* WY-8
**Westma**—*pop pl* ID-8
West Madden Lateral—*canal* ID-8
West Madison Canal—*canal* (2) MT-8
West Madison Cem—*cemetery* MI-6
West Madison Depot, Chicago, Milwaukee, and
St. Paul Railway—*hist pl* WI-6
West Madison Rec Area—*locale* MT-8
West Madison Sch—*school* AL-4
West Madison Township—*civil* MO-7
West (Magisterial District)—*fmr MCD* WV-2
West Magnolia Cem—*cemetery* WI-6
West Magpie Creek—*stream* MT-8
**West Mahanoy (Township of)**—*pop pl* PA-2
*West Mahantango Creek* PA-2
West Maher Landing—*locale* AL-4
**West Mahoning (Township of)**—*pop pl* PA-2
**West Mahopac**—*pop pl* NY-2
**West Mahwah**—*pop pl* NJ-2
West Maiden Spring—*spring* WA-9
**West Main**—*pop pl* OR-9
West Main Baptist Ch—*church* TN-4
*West Main Canal* CA-9
West Main Canal—*canal* (2) AZ-5
West Main Canal—*canal* CA-9
West Main Canal—*canal* ID-8
West Main Ch of Christ—*church* MS-4
West Main Drain—*canal* TX-5
West Main-North Chesnutt Streets Hist
Dist—*hist pl* NC-3
West Main Sch—*school* MI-6
West Main Sch—*school* OH-6
West Main Street Cem—*cemetery* NY-2
West Main Street Cem—*cemetery* OH-6
West Main Street Dam—*dam* MA-1
West Main Street District—*hist pl* KY-4
West Main Street District—*hist pl* (2) OH-6
West Main Street Hist Dist—*hist pl* (2) KY-4
West Main Street Hist Dist—*hist pl* MA-1
West Main Street Hist Dist—*hist pl* SC-3
West Main Street Hist Dist—*hist pl* WI-6
West Main Street Hist Dist,
Expanded—*hist pl* KY-4
West Main Street Houses—*hist pl* MN-6
West Main Street Residential
District—*hist pl* GA-3
West Makaiwa—*civil* HI-9
West Mall Shop Ctr—*locale* FL-3
*West Mam Creek* CO-8
West Mamm Creek—*stream* CO-8
**West Manayunk**—*pop pl* PA-2
**West Manayunk (Belmont**
**Hills)**—*pop pl* PA-2
*West Manchester* PA-2
**West Manchester**—*pop pl* MA-1
**West Manchester**—*pop pl* OH-6
West Manchester Ch—*church* IN-6

West Niles Rural Cem—*cemetery* ... NY-2
West Nimishillen Ch—*church* ... OH-6
West Ninemile Point—*cape* ... NY-2
West Ninemile Tank—*reservoir* ... TX-5
West Ninemile Well—*well* ... AZ-5
West Nine Section Tank—*reservoir* ... AZ-5
West Nine Section Windmill—*locale* ... TX-5
West Nine Tank—*reservoir* ... AZ-5
West Ninth Ave Park—*park* ... NC-3
*West Nishnabotna River* ... IA-7
West Nishnabotna River—*stream* ... IA-7
West Nobel Mission—*church* ... TX-5
West Noble HS—*school* (2) ... IN-6
West Noble MS—*school* ... IN-6
*West Noblesville* ... IN-6
**West Noblesville**—*pop pl* ... IN-6
West Nodaway River—*stream* ... IA-7
West Nolan Creek—*stream* ... TX-5
West Nooksack Glacier—*glacier* ... WA-9
West Norden Cem—*cemetery* ... SD-7
*West Norden Lutheran Church* ... SD-7
West Norden Lutheran Church (historical)—*locale* ... SD-7
**West Norfolk**—*pop pl* ... CT-1
**West Norfolk**—*pop pl* ... VA-3
West Norfolk Bridge—*bridge* ... VA-3
West Norristown Hist Dist—*hist pl* ... PA-2
West Norriton—*CDP* ... PA-2
**West Norriton (Township of)**—*pop pl* ... PA-2
**West Northfield**—*pop pl* ... MA-1
West Northfield Cem—*cemetery* ... MA-1
West Northfield Sch—*school* ... IL-6
West North Immanuel Cem—*cemetery* ... MN-6
West North Main Canal—*canal* ... CA-9
West Northumberland Canyon—*valley* ... NV-8
*West Norwalk* ... CT-1
West Norwalk—*locale* ... CT-1
West Norway Lake Ch—*church* ... MN-6
**West Norway Township**—*pop pl* ... ND-7
**West Norwich**—*pop pl* ... VT-1
West Norwood—*uninc pl* ... NJ-2
West Notaway Mine—*mine* ... CO-8
West Notch—*gap* ... NY-2
West Notch—*locale* ... NY-2
West Notch Mtn—*summit* ... NY-2
**West Nottingham**—*pop pl* ... MD-2
**West Nottingham**—*pop pl* ... NH-1
West Nottingham Meetinghouse—*hist pl* ... MD-2
**West Nottingham (Township of)**—*pop pl* ... PA-2
West Novato Sch—*school* ... CA-9
*West Novi* ... MI-6
West Novillos Tank—*reservoir* ... TX-5
West Nueces River—*stream* ... TX-5
West Nugget Gulch—*valley* ... SD-7
West Numa Lateral—*canal* ... CO-8
West Nunatak Glacier—*glacier* ... AK-9
West Nutgrass—*reservoir* ... NV-8
**West Nyack**—*pop pl* ... NY-2
West Oak—*fmr MCD* ... NE-7
**Westoak**—*pop pl* ... GA-3
West Oak—*uninc pl* ... OR-9
West Oakboro Ch—*church* ... NC-3
West Oak Brush Creek—*stream* ... UT-8
*West Oakchia* ... AL-4
West Oak Creek—*stream* (2) ... KS-7
West Oak Creek—*stream* ... NE-7
West Oak Grove Cem—*cemetery* ... MN-6
**West Oakland**—*pop pl* ... CA-9
**West Oakland**—*pop pl* ... TX-5
West Oakland Branch—*stream* ... TX-5
**West Oakland Park (subdivision)**—*pop pl* ... TN-4
West Oakley Sch—*school* ... OH-6
**West Oaks**—*pop pl* ... NC-3
West Oak Spring—*spring* ... NV-8
West Oakview Sch—*school* ... MI-6
West Oakwood Cem—*cemetery* ... MO-7
*West Oberlin* ... OH-6
Westobulga Ch—*church* ... AL-4
Westobulga (historical)—*locale* ... AL-4
**West Occidental**—*pop pl* ... FL-3
**West Ocean City**—*pop pl* ... MD-2
**West Ocean City**—*pop pl* ... NJ-2
**West Ocean Grove**—*pop pl* ... NJ-2
**West Odessa**—*pop pl* ... TX-5
West of Frazier Park—*other* ... CA-9
West of Pecos RR Camps District—*hist pl* ... TX-5
**West Ogden**—*pop pl* ... UT-8
**West Ogden Addition (subdivision)**—*pop pl* ... UT-8
**West Ogden Heights (subdivision)**—*pop pl* ... UT-8
W E Stogner Lake Dam—*dam* ... MS-4
West Ohia—*civil* ... HI-9
West Oil Field—*oilfield* ... KS-7
West Oil Field—*oilfield* (3) ... TX-5
West Okaw River—*stream* ... IL-6
*West Okchai* ... AL-4
**West Okoboji**—*pop pl* ... IA-7
West Okoboji Lake—*lake* ... IA-7
West Okoboji Lake State Game Mngmt Area—*park* ... IA-7
Westola (historical)—*locale* ... KS-7
West Olalla Creek—*stream* ... OR-9
*West Olallie Creek* ... OR-9
Westola Township—*civil* ... KS-7
*West Old Town* ... ME-1
**West Old Town**—*pop pl* ... ME-1
**West Olive**—*pop pl* ... MI-6
West Olive Cem—*cemetery* ... MI-6
West Oliver—*unorg reg* ... ND-7
West Olive Sch—*school* ... NE-7
West Olmos Creek—*stream* ... TX-5
West Olson Lake—*lake* ... MN-6
*West Omaha* ... NE-7
Weston—*CDP* ... WI-6
Weston—*hist pl* ... DE-2
Weston—*locale* ... AL-4
Weston—*locale* (2) ... KY-4
Weston—*locale* ... ME-1
Weston—*locale* ... PA-2
Weston—*locale* ... SC-3
Weston—*locale* ... WY-8
**Weston**—*pop pl* ... AL-4
**Weston**—*pop pl* ... CO-8
**Weston**—*pop pl* ... CT-1
**Weston**—*pop pl* ... GA-3
**Weston**—*pop pl* ... ID-8
**Weston**—*pop pl* (2) ... IL-6
**Weston**—*pop pl* ... IA-7
**Weston**—*pop pl* ... LA-4
**Weston**—*pop pl* ... MA-1
**Weston**—*pop pl* ... MI-6
**Weston**—*pop pl* ... MN-6
**Weston**—*pop pl* ... MO-7
**Weston**—*pop pl* ... NE-7
**Weston**—*pop pl* ... NJ-2
**Weston**—*pop pl* ... NY-2
**Weston**—*pop pl* ... OH-6
**Weston**—*pop pl* ... OR-9
**Weston**—*pop pl* ... PA-2
**Weston**—*pop pl* ... TX-5
**Weston**—*pop pl* ... VT-1
**Weston**—*pop pl* ... WV-2
**Weston**—*pop pl* ... WI-6
Weston—*uninc pl* ... WA-9
Weston, Daniel, Homestead—*hist pl* ... ME-1
Weston, Ephrain, House—*hist pl* ... MA-1
Weston, Jabez, House—*hist pl* ... MA-1
Weston, Lake—*lake* ... FL-3
Weston, Samuel, Homestead—*hist pl* ... ME-1
Weston Airp—*airport* ... ND-7
Weston-Babcock House—*hist pl* ... WI-6
Weston Baptist Ch—*church* ... AL-4
Weston Bar—*bar* ... OR-9
Weston Bend—*bend* ... KS-7
Weston Bend—*bend* ... OR-9
Weston Bend State Park—*park* ... MO-7
Weston Branch—*stream* ... NC-3
Weston Brook—*stream* (2) ... MA-1
Weston Brook—*stream* ... PA-2
Weston Canyon—*valley* ... ID-8
Weston Canyon—*valley* ... MT-8
Weston Canyon Rock Shelter—*hist pl* ... ID-8
Weston (CCD)—*cens area* ... GA-3
Weston (CCD)—*cens area* ... OR-9
Weston Cem—*cemetery* ... IL-6
Weston Cem—*cemetery* (3) ... IN-6
Weston Cem—*cemetery* ... NE-7
Weston Cem—*cemetery* ... OH-6
Weston Cem—*cemetery* ... OR-9
Weston Cem—*cemetery* ... TN-4
Weston Cem—*cemetery* ... WI-6
Weston Central Cem—*cemetery* ... MA-1
*Weston Centre* ... MA-1
Weston Ch—*church* ... AL-4
Weston Ch—*church* ... IN-6
Weston Ch—*church* ... MA-1
Weston Chapel Cem—*cemetery* ... IN-6
Weston Coll—*school* ... MA-1
Weston Commercial Hist Dist—*hist pl* ... OR-9
Weston Creek—*stream* ... ID-8
Weston Creek—*stream* ... MT-8
Weston Creek—*stream* ... VA-3
Weston Creek Rsvr—*reservoir* ... ID-8
Weston Ditch—*canal* ... CO-8
Weston Downtown Hist Dist—*hist pl* ... WV-2
Weston Drain—*canal* (2) ... MI-6
Weston Drain—*stream* ... MI-6
*West One Hundred And Two River* ... IA-7
*West One Hundred and Two River* ... MO-7
**West Oneida**—*pop pl* ... TN-4
**West Oneonta**—*pop pl* ... NY-2
Weston Field—*park* ... MA-1
Weston Flat—*swamp* ... SC-3
*Weston Gardens* ... OH-6
Weston Golf Club—*locale* ... MA-1
Weston Gulch—*valley* ... CA-9
Weston Hill—*summit* ... KS-7
Weston Hist Dist—*hist pl* ... MO-7
Weston (historical)—*locale* ... KS-7
Weston (historical)—*locale* ... ND-7
**Weston (historical)**—*pop pl* ... OR-9
Weston Homestead—*hist pl* ... ME-1
Weston HS—*school* ... MA-1
Weston HS—*school* ... MS-4
Weston HS—*school* ... WI-6
**Westonia (historical)**—*pop pl* ... MS-4
Westonia Lookout—*locale* ... MS-4
Westonia Playground—*park* ... KY-4
Weston Island—*island* ... ME-1
Weston JHS—*school* ... CT-1
Weston JHS—*school* ... MA-1
Weston Junoir HS—*school* ... MA-1
Weston Knob—*summit* ... NC-3
Weston Lake—*lake* ... OR-9
Weston Lake—*lake* ... SC-3
Weston Lake—*reservoir* ... AL-4
Weston Lake Dam—*dam* ... AL-4
Weston Landing—*locale* ... OR-9
Weston Manor—*hist pl* ... VA-3
**Weston-Manville**—*pop pl* ... NJ-2
Weston Meadow—*flat* ... CA-9
Weston Meadow—*swamp* ... ME-1
*Weston Mills* ... NY-2
Weston Mills—*CDP* ... NY-2
Weston Mills—*uninc pl* ... NJ-2
Weston Mountains—*other* ... AK-9
Weston Mtn—*summit* ... MA-1
Weston Mtn—*summit* (2) ... NY-2
Weston Mtn—*summit* (2) ... OR-9
Weston Observatory—*hist pl* ... NH-1
Weston Park—*park* ... MA-1
Weston Pass—*gap* ... CO-8
Weston Pass Ranch—*locale* ... CO-8
Weston Peak—*summit* ... CO-8
Weston Peak—*summit* ... ID-8
**Weston Place**—*pop pl* ... PA-2
*Weston Point* ... ME-1
Weston Point—*cliff* ... WY-8
*Weston Pond* ... NH-1
Weston Pond—*lake* ... OR-9
Weston Pond—*reservoir* ... MA-1
Weston Pond—*reservoir* ... OR-9
*Weston Pond Brook* ... MA-1
*Weston Ponds* ... SC-3
Weston Post Office (historical)—*building* ... AL-4
Weston Priory—*church* ... VT-1
**Weston Priory**—*pop pl* ... VT-1
Weston Ranch—*locale* ... CA-9
Weston Ranch—*locale* ... NE-7
Weston Ranch—*locale* ... NM-5
Weston Ranch—*locale* ... WY-8
Weston Ridge—*ridge* ... OR-9
Weston Rsvr—*reservoir* ... MA-1
Weston Rsvr—*reservoir* ... WY-8
*Westons* ... NY-2
Weston Sch—*school* ... IL-6
Weston Sch—*school* (2) ... IN-6
Weston Sch—*school* ... IA-7
Weston Sch—*school* ... MI-6
Weston Sch—*school* ... NH-1
Weston Sch—*school* ... WI-6
Weston Sch (abandoned)—*school* ... PA-2
Weston Sch (abandoned)—*school* ... SD-7
**Westons Iroquois Beach**—*pop pl* ... MI-6
**West Onslow Beach**—*pop pl* ... NC-3
Westons Mill Pond—*reservoir* ... NJ-2
Westons Mill Pond Dam—*dam* ... NJ-2
**Westons Mills**—*pop pl* ... NJ-2
**Westons Mills**—*pop pl* ... NY-2
Westons Mill Sch—*school* ... NJ-2
Westons Pond—*reservoir* ... SC-3
Weston Spring—*spring* ... UT-8
**Weston (Sta.)**—*pop pl* ... WI-6
Weston State Hosp—*hist pl* ... WV-2
Weston State Hosp—*hospital* ... WV-2
Weston Station—*locale* ... IA-7
Weston Station—*locale* ... OR-9
**Weston Station**—*pop pl* ... MA-1
**Weston (subdivision)**—*pop pl* ... NC-3
**West Ontario**—*pop pl* ... ND-7
**Weston (Town of)**—*pop pl* ... CT-1
**Weston (Town of)**—*pop pl* ... ME-1
**Weston (Town of)**—*pop pl* ... MA-1
**Weston (Town of)**—*pop pl* ... VT-1
**Weston (Town of)**—*pop pl* (3) ... WI-6
Weston Township—*civil* ... MO-7
**Weston Township**—*pop pl* ... SD-7
Weston Township (historical)—*civil* ... ND-7
**Weston (Township of)**—*pop pl* ... OH-6
Weston Trail—*trail* ... NY-2
Weston Village Hist Dist—*hist pl* ... VT-1
*Westonville* ... NY-2
West Onward Landing (historical)—*locale* ... TN-4
West Opdal Ch—*church* ... ND-7
West Opening—*channel* ... MP-9
**West Opening**—*pop pl* ... MA-1
**Westor**—*pop pl* ... AR-4
**West Orange**—*pop pl* ... CA-9
**West Orange**—*pop pl* ... MA-1
**West Orange**—*pop pl* ... NJ-2
**West Orange**—*pop pl* ... TX-5
West Orange Armory—*building* ... NJ-2
West Orangeburg—*CDP* ... SC-3
West Orange HS—*school* ... FL-3
West Orange Memorial Gardens—*cemetery* ... FL-3
West Orange Memorial Hosp—*hospital* ... FL-3
West Orange Memorial Park—*cemetery* ... FL-3
West Orange Sch—*school* ... CA-9
West Orange Station—*locale* ... NJ-2
**West Orange (Township of)**—*pop pl* ... NJ-2
West Ord Mtn—*summit* ... CA-9
West Ore Bank Hollow—*valley* ... TN-4
West Ore Bank Mine—*mine* ... TN-4
West Orient Sch—*school* ... OR-9
West Orlando Christian Elem Sch—*school* ... FL-3
**West Ormond Beach**—*pop pl* ... FL-3
West Osborne Lake—*lake* ... NE-7
West Oso Creek—*stream* ... TX-5
West Oso HS—*school* ... TX-5
**West Ossipee**—*pop pl* ... NH-1
West Otis—*fmr MCD* ... NE-7
West Otis—*locale* ... AR-4
**West Otis**—*pop pl* ... MA-1
West Otis Ch—*church* ... AR-4
West Ottawa Center Sch—*school* ... MI-6
West Ottawa HS—*school* ... MI-6
West Otter Creek—*stream* (2) ... IA-7
West Otter Creek—*stream* ... OK-5
West Otterson Wash—*valley* ... WY-8
West Outer Channel—*channel* ... MI-6
West Outlet—*stream* (2) ... ME-1
West Oval Lake—*lake* ... WA-9
Westover—*CDP* ... VA-3
Westover—*hist pl* ... GA-3
Westover—*hist pl* (2) ... VA-3
Westover—*locale* ... AL-4
Westover—*locale* ... GA-3
Westover—*locale* ... NC-3
Westover—*locale* ... SD-7
Westover—*locale* ... TX-5
Westover—*locale* ... VA-3
**Westover**—*pop pl* ... AR-4
**Westover**—*pop pl* ... IN-6
**Westover**—*pop pl* ... LA-4
**Westover**—*pop pl* ... MD-2
**Westover**—*pop pl* ... MO-7
**Westover**—*pop pl* ... NY-2
**Westover**—*pop pl* ... NC-3
**Westover**—*pop pl* ... PA-2
**Westover**—*pop pl* ... TN-4
**Westover**—*pop pl* ... TX-5
**Westover**—*pop pl* (3) ... VA-3
**Westover**—*pop pl* ... WV-2
**Westover Acres**—*pop pl* ... SC-3
Westover AFB (Westover Field)—*military* ... MA-1
Westover Baptist Ch—*church* ... MS-4
Westover Baptist Ch—*church* ... TN-4
West Over Bayou—*stream* ... LA-4
Westover Borough—*civil* ... PA-2
Westover Brook—*stream* ... NY-2
Westover Cem—*cemetery* ... CT-1
Westover Cem—*cemetery* ... MO-7
Westover Ch—*church* ... AL-4
Westover Ch—*church* ... NC-3
Westover Ch—*church* ... VA-3
Westover Church—*hist pl* ... VA-3
Westover City Park—*park* ... WV-2
Westover Creek—*stream* ... AK-9
Westover Elem Sch—*school* ... TN-4
Westover Field—*other* ... MA-1
Westover Golf Course—*locale* ... PA-2
Westover Gulch—*valley* ... MT-8
**Westover Heights**—*pop pl* ... VA-3
*Westover Hill* ... DE-2
**Westover Hills**—*pop pl* ... DE-2
**Westover Hills**—*pop pl* ... TX-5
**Westover Hills**—*pop pl* (5) ... VA-3
Westover Hills Ch—*church* ... VA-3
Westover Hills Park—*park* ... TX-5
Westover Hills Sch—*school* ... VA-3
**Westover Hills (subdivision)**—*pop pl* ... TN-4
**Westover II (subdivision)**—*pop pl* ... NC-3
Westover Island—*island* ... MT-8
Westover JHS—*school* ... NC-3
Westover Junction—*locale* ... AL-4
West Over Landing (historical)—*locale* ... MS-4
West Overlook—*locale* ... TN-4
**West Overlook**—*pop pl* ... IN-6
West Over Look Area—*park* ... AL-4
Westover Lookout Tower—*locale* ... MO-7
*West Overlook Park* ... AL-4
Westover (Magisterial District)—*fmr MCD* ... VA-3
Westover Manor—*hist pl* ... TX-5
Westover Memorial Cem—*cemetery* ... GA-3
*Westover Park* ... TN-4
**Westover (Phillipps Crossroads)**—*pop pl* ... AL-4
Westover P. O. (historical)—*locale* ... AL-4
Westover Pond—*lake* ... PA-2
Westover Ranch—*locale* ... NE-7
Westover Sch—*school* (2) ... CT-1
Westover Sch—*school* ... MD-2
Westover Sch—*school* ... MO-7
Westover Sch (historical)—*school* ... TN-4
Westover School (historical)—*locale* ... MO-7
Westover Senior HS—*school* ... NC-3
Westover Spring—*spring* ... AZ-5
Westover Spring—*spring* ... MO-7
**Westover (subdivision)**—*pop pl* ... MS-4
**Westover (subdivision)**—*pop pl* (2) ... NC-3
**Westover (subdivision)**—*pop pl* ... TN-4
**West Overton**—*pop pl* ... PA-2
West Overton Hist Dist—*hist pl* ... PA-2
**West Overton (sta.)**—*pop pl* ... PA-2
**Westover Township**—*pop pl* ... SD-7
**Westover West (subdivision)**—*pop pl* ... MS-4
**Westover Woods**—*pop pl* ... PA-2
West Owl Creek—*stream* ... OK-5
**Westowne**—*pop pl* ... MD-2
Westowne Sch—*school* ... MD-2
Westown II Shop Ctr—*locale* ... AZ-5
Westown Park—*park* ... AZ-5
Westown Shop Ctr—*locale* ... AZ-5
**West Oxford**—*pop pl* ... MA-1
West Oxford Cem—*cemetery* ... OH-6
West Oxford Ch—*church* ... NC-3
West Oxford Sch—*school* ... NC-3
*West Oyster Reef* ... FL-3
West Ozark Sch—*school* ... MO-7
West Pacific Creek—*stream* ... WY-8
**West Paducah**—*pop pl* ... KY-4
West Paducah Ch—*church* ... KY-4
**West Paducah (RR name Maxon)**—*pop pl* ... KY-4
West Paducah Sch—*school* ... KY-4
West Page Cabin Spring—*spring* ... OR-9
West Paint Creek Ch—*church* ... IA-7
West Painterhood Creek—*stream* ... KS-7
West Paint Sch (historical)—*school* ... SD-7
West Palisades Cem—*cemetery* ... MN-6
West Palm Acres—*locale* ... NC-3
**West Palm Beach**—*pop pl* ... FL-3
West Palm Beach Canal—*canal* ... FL-3
West Palm Beach (CCD)—*cens area* ... FL-3
**West Palm Beach Farms**—*pop pl* ... FL-3
West Palm Beach Junior Acad—*school* ... FL-3
West Palm Beach Plaza (Shop Ctr)—*locale* ... FL-3
West Palm Beach Public Library—*building* ... FL-3
West Palm Beach Winter Club—*locale* ... FL-3
West Palmer Gulch—*valley* ... CO-8
West Palmetto Park—*uninc pl* ... FL-3
West Palm Run—*stream* ... FL-3
**West Palm Springs**—*pop pl* ... CA-9
West Palmyra—*locale* ... ME-1
*West Panama City Beach* ... FL-3
**West Panama City Beach**—*pop pl* ... FL-3
**West Pangburn**—*pop pl* ... AR-4
West Panola Acad—*school* ... MS-4
West Panther Creek—*stream* ... CA-9
West Panther Creek—*stream* ... IL-6
West Panton Sch—*school* ... VT-1
West Papillion Creek—*stream* ... NE-7
West Paradox Creek—*stream* ... CO-8
West Par Golf Course—*other* ... MO-7
**West Paris**—*pop pl* ... ME-1
West Paris—*uninc pl* ... KY-4
*West Parish* ... MA-1
**West Parish**—*pop pl* (2) ... MA-1
West Parish Cem—*cemetery* ... MA-1
West Parish Center District—*hist pl* ... MA-1
West Parish Filter Number Three Rsvr—*reservoir* ... MA-1
West Parish Filter Number 1 Dam—*dam* ... MA-1
West Parish Filter Number 2 Dam—*dam* ... MA-1
West Parish Filter Number 3 Dam—*dam* ... MA-1
West Parish (historical)—*locale* ... MA-1
West Paris Hist Dist—*hist pl* ... TN-4
*West Parish of Lynn* ... MA-1
West Parishville—*locale* ... NY-2
**West Paris (Town of)**—*pop pl* ... ME-1
*West Park* ... AL-4
*West Park* (3) ... OH-6
West Park—*flat* (2) ... UT-8
West Park—*hist pl* ... AL-4
West Park—*park* ... AZ-5
West Park—*park* ... CA-9
West Park—*park* ... ID-8
West Park—*park* (5) ... IL-6
West Park—*park* ... IA-7
West Park—*park* ... KS-7
West Park—*park* ... MI-6
West Park—*park* ... MN-6
West Park—*park* ... OH-6
West Park—*park* (2) ... PA-2
West Park—*park* ... TN-4
West Park—*park* (2) ... WI-6
**West Park**—*pop pl* ... CA-9
**West Park**—*pop pl* ... DE-2
**West Park**—*pop pl* ... NY-2
**West Park**—*pop pl* (3) ... OH-6
**West Park**—*pop pl* ... PA-2
**West Park**—*pop pl* ... WA-9
West Park—*post sta* ... OK-5
West Park—*uninc pl* ... PA-2
West Park—*uninc pl* ... TX-5
West Park Cem—*cemetery* ... OH-6
West Park Cem—*cemetery* ... TX-5
West Park Ch—*church* ... NC-3
West Park Ch—*church* ... TX-5
West Park Creek—*stream* ... CO-8
West Park Dam—*dam* ... AZ-5
West Park Draw—*valley* ... AZ-5
West Parker Spring—*spring* ... NV-8
*West Park Heights Baptist Church* ... AL-4
West Park Heights Ch—*church* ... AL-4
West Park Hosp—*hospital* ... PA-2
West Park Lakes—*lake* ... CA-9
**West Parkland**—*pop pl* ... NC-3
West Park Mall—*locale* ... MO-7
West Park Place—*hist pl* ... PA-2
**Westpark Place (subdivision)**—*pop pl* ... NC-3
West Park Sch—*school* (3) ... CA-9
West Park Sch—*school* ... CO-8
West Park Sch—*school* ... LA-4
West Park Sch—*school* ... MO-7
West Park Sch—*school* ... OR-9
West Parks Creek—*stream* ... ID-8
West Park Shop Ctr—*locale* ... KS-7
West Park Shop Ctr—*locale* ... NC-3
Westpark Shop Ctr—*locale* ... NC-3
West Park Shop Ctr—*locale* ... NC-3
West Park Spring—*spring* ... UT-8
West Park Street Ch of God—*church* ... FL-3
**West Park (subdivision)**—*pop pl* ... FL-3
West Park Tank—*reservoir* ... AZ-5
West Park United Methodist Ch—*church* ... MS-4
West Parkview Baptist Ch—*church* ... IN-6
*West Park View Ch* ... IN-6
West Parlier—*CDP* ... CA-9
West Parrish Ch—*church* ... MA-1
West Parrish Sch—*school* ... MA-1
West Parrot Creek—*stream* ... MT-8
West Parsons Rsvr—*reservoir* ... CO-8
*West Pascagoula* ... MS-4
West Pascagoula River—*stream* ... MS-4
West Pasco—*CDP* ... WA-9
West Pasco Ch—*church* ... FL-3
*West Pass* ... FM-9
*West Pass* ... MP-9
West Pass—*channel* (4) ... FL-3
West Pass—*channel* ... TX-5
West Pass—*channel* ... WA-9
West Pass—*channel* ... MP-9
West Pass—*gap* ... NM-5
West Pass—*gap* ... TX-5
West Pass—*gap* ... UT-8
West Pass—*gap* ... WY-8
West Passage—*channel* ... FM-9
West Passage, Narragansett Bay—*channel* ... RI-1
West Pass Bay—*bay* ... FL-3
West Pass Calcasieu River—*channel* ... LA-4
West Pass Creek—*stream* ... CO-8
West Pass Creek—*stream* ... ID-8
West Pass Creek—*stream* ... MT-8
West Pass Creek—*stream* ... SD-7
West Pass Creek—*stream* ... WY-8
West Pass Creek Way—*trail* ... OR-9
West Pasture Rsvr No 1—*reservoir* ... CO-8
West Pasture Rsvr No 2—*reservoir* ... CO-8
West Pasture Tank—*reservoir* (2) ... AZ-5
West Pasture Tank—*reservoir* ... NM-5
West Pasture Well—*well* ... AZ-5
West Pasture Well—*well* ... NM-5
West Pasture Well—*well* ... TX-5
West Pasture Windmill—*locale* ... CO-8
West Pasture Windmill—*locale* (2) ... NM-5
West Pasture Windmill—*locale* (3) ... TX-5
**West Paterson**—*pop pl* ... NJ-2
West Patit Creek—*stream* ... WA-9
West Patrick Mine—*mine* ... MN-6
West Patterson—*locale* ... NY-2
West Patuk Creek—*stream* ... AK-9
West Pauls Valley Oil Field—*oilfield* ... OK-5
**West Pawlet**—*pop pl* ... VT-1
West Pawling—*locale* ... NY-2
**West Pawling (Stonehouse)**—*pop pl* ... NY-2
**West Payne**—*pop pl* ... TX-5
**West Peabody**—*pop pl* ... MA-1
*West Peak* ... NV-8
West Peak—*summit* (4) ... AK-9
West Peak—*summit* ... AZ-5
West Peak—*summit* (2) ... CA-9
West Peak—*summit* ... CO-8
West Peak—*summit* ... CT-1
West Peak—*summit* (4) ... ME-1
West Peak—*summit* ... MT-8
West Peak—*summit* (2) ... NH-1
West Peak—*summit* (3) ... WA-9
West Peak Burke Mtn—*summit* ... VT-1
West Peak Lookout Tower—*hist pl* ... AZ-5
West Peak State Park—*park* ... CT-1
West Peak Tank—*reservoir* ... NM-5
West Peak Trail—*trail* ... CO-8
**West Pea Ridge**—*pop pl* ... WV-2
West Pearl Creek—*stream* ... SD-7
West Pearl River—*stream* ... LA-4
West Pearson Branch—*stream* ... MO-7
West Pearson Rsvr—*reservoir* ... WY-8
West Peavine Sch—*school* ... OK-5
West Pecos Sch—*school* ... TX-5
West Peculiar Township—*civil* ... MO-7
**West Pelham**—*pop pl* ... MA-1
**West Pelzer**—*pop pl* ... SC-3
**West Pembroke**—*pop pl* ... ME-1
**West Pen Argyl**—*pop pl* ... PA-2
*West Pender Primary School* ... NC-3
West Pender Sch—*school* ... NC-3
**West Penn**—*pop pl* ... PA-2
West Penn Airp—*airport* ... PA-2
West Penn Ch—*church* ... PA-2
West Pennfield Cem—*cemetery* ... MI-6
West Penn Hospital Airp—*airport* ... PA-2
West Pennington—*unorg reg* ... SD-7
West Penn Recreation Center—*park* ... PA-2
West Pennsboro Sch (abandoned)—*school* ... PA-2
**West Pennsboro (Township of)**—*pop pl* ... PA-2
West Penn Township Elem Sch—*school* ... PA-2
**West Penn (Township of)**—*pop pl* ... PA-2
West Penny Creek—*stream* ... KS-7
West Penny Creek—*stream* ... NE-7
**West Penobscot**—*pop pl* ... ME-1
West Penobscot Bay—*bay* ... ME-1
**West Pensacola**—*pop pl* ... FL-3
West Pensacola Baptist Ch—*church* ... FL-3
West Pensacola Sch—*school* ... FL-3
**West Peoria**—*pop pl* ... IL-6
**West Peoria (Township of)**—*pop pl* ... IL-6
West Peotone Cem—*cemetery* ... IL-6
West Peotone Ch—*church* ... IL-6
West Pepper Creek—*stream* ... FL-3
West Perkins—*unorg reg* ... SD-7
West Perrin Canal—*canal* ... CA-9
West Perrine Park—*park* ... FL-3
**West Perry**—*pop pl* ... NY-2
**West Perry Center**—*pop pl* ... NY-2
West Perrysburg—*locale* ... NY-2
West Perry Sch (historical)—*school* ... AL-4
*West Perry School* ... PA-2
**West Perry (Township of)**—*pop pl* ... PA-2
**West Pershing Plaza**—*pop pl* ... AZ-5
**West Perth**—*pop pl* ... NY-2
*West Peru* ... IN-6
**West Peru**—*pop pl* ... ME-1
**West Petaluma**—*pop pl* ... CA-9
West Petenwell Ditch—*canal* ... WI-6
**West Peterborough**—*pop pl* ... NH-1
*West Petersburg* ... IN-6
**West Petersburg**—*pop pl* ... AK-9
**West Petersburg**—*pop pl* ... IN-6
**West Petersburg**—*pop pl* ... VA-3
West Petersburg (Kupreanof)—*other* ... AK-9
West Peterson Creek—*stream* ... MT-8
Westphal, August, Farmstead—*hist pl* ... MI-6
Westphal Cem—*cemetery* ... AR-4
Westphal Gulch—*valley* ... WA-9
Westphalia—*locale* ... MD-2
**Westphalia**—*pop pl* ... IN-6
**Westphalia**—*pop pl* ... IA-7
**Westphalia**—*pop pl* ... KS-7
**Westphalia**—*pop pl* ... MI-6
**Westphalia**—*pop pl* ... MO-7
**Westphalia**—*pop pl* ... TX-5
Westphalia And Riley Drain—*canal* ... MI-6
Westphalia Elem Sch—*school* ... KS-7
**Westphalia Estates**—*pop pl* ... MD-2
Westphalia Township—*fmr MCD* ... IA-7
**Westphalia Township**—*pop pl* ... KS-7
**Westphalia (Township of)**—*pop pl* ... MI-6
**Westphalia Woods**—*pop pl* ... MD-2
Westphall Lake—*lake* ... WI-6
Westphal-Schmidt House—*hist pl* ... IA-7
Westphal Spring—*spring* ... MT-8
West Phelan Creek—*stream* ... AK-9
**West Philadelphia**—*pop pl* ... NC-3
West Philadelphia—*uninc pl* ... PA-2
West Philadelphia Boys Catholic HS—*school* ... PA-2
West Philadelphia Girls Catholic HS—*school* ... PA-2
West Philadelphia HS—*hist pl* ... PA-2
*West Philadelphia Senior HS* ... PA-2
**West Phoenix**—*pop pl* ... NY-2
West Phoenix HS—*school* ... AZ-5
West Pickerel Pond—*lake* ... WI-6
West Pierce Gulch—*valley* ... CO-8
West Pierrepont—*locale* ... NY-2
West Pie Town Tank—*reservoir* ... NM-5
West Pigpen Creek—*stream* ... NM-5
**West Pike**—*pop pl* ... PA-2
West Pike Cem—*cemetery* ... MN-6
West Pike Lake—*lake* ... MN-6
**West Pikeland**—*pop pl* ... PA-2
**West Pikeland (Township of)**—*pop pl* ... PA-2
West Pike Run Grange—*locale* ... PA-2
**West Pike Run (Township of)**—*pop pl* ... PA-2
West Pine Barren Creek—*stream* ... AL-4
West Pine Cem—*cemetery* ... MI-6
West Pine Creek—*stream* ... CO-8
West Pine Creek—*stream* (2) ... ID-8
West Pine Creek Girls Camp—*locale* ... ID-8
*West Pine Elementary School* ... TN-4
West Pine Flat—*flat* ... CA-9
*West Pine Lake* ... MN-6
West Pine Pond—*lake* (2) ... NY-2
West Pine Ridge Oil Field—*oilfield* ... MS-4
West Pine Sch (abandoned)—*school* ... MO-7
West Pines Elem Sch—*school* ... TN-4
West Pines Park—*park* ... FL-3
**West Piney**—*pop pl* ... VA-3
West Piney Creek—*stream* ... MO-7
West Piney River—*stream* ... TN-4
West Pinhead Butte—*summit* ... OR-9
West Pinnacle—*pillar* ... KY-4
West Pinnacles Creek—*stream* ... CA-9
West Pin Oak Creek—*stream* ... MO-7
*West Pinos Creek* ... CO-8
West Pintler Peak—*summit* ... MT-8
West Pinto Creek—*stream* ... TX-5
West Pioche Mine—*mine* ... UT-8
West Pioneer Sch—*school* ... WA-9
West Pipe Creek—*stream* ... KS-7
West Pipe Lake—*lake* ... MN-6
West Pipestone Creek—*stream* ... SD-7
West Pit—*lake* ... AZ-5
West Pithole Creek—*stream* ... PA-2
West Pittman Ch—*church* ... FL-3
West Pittman Creek—*stream* ... FL-3
**West Pittsburg**—*pop pl* ... CA-9
**West Pittsburg**—*pop pl* ... PA-2
**West Pittsfield**—*pop pl* ... MA-1
West Pittsfield Cem—*cemetery* ... ME-1
**West Pittston**—*pop pl* ... PA-2
West Pittston Borough—*civil* ... PA-2
West Pittston Junction—*uninc pl* ... PA-2
West Pittston Junction Station—*locale* ... PA-2
West Pittston Station—*locale* ... PA-2
West Place Branch—*stream* ... GA-3
West Plain Cem—*cemetery* ... CT-1
**West Plainfield**—*pop pl* ... WI-6
*West Plains* (2) ... KS-7
*West Plains* ... MI-6
Westplains—*locale* ... CO-8
Westplains—*locale* ... KY-4
**West Plains**—*pop pl* ... MO-7
West Plains Cem—*cemetery* ... KS-7
West Plains Ch—*church* ... TN-4
West Plains HS—*school* ... MO-7
West Plains JHS—*school* ... MO-7
West Plains Municipal Airp—*airport* ... MO-7
West Plains Sch—*school* ... KS-7
**West Plains Township**—*pop pl* ... KS-7
West Plains Voc-Tech Sch—*school* ... MO-7
West Plano Substation—*other* ... TX-5
*West Planter Brook* ... NY-2
West Platner Brook—*stream* ... NY-2
West Platner Brook Sch—*school* ... NY-2
West Platte—*locale* ... MO-7
West Platte River—*stream* ... IA-7
**West Plattsburg**—*pop pl* ... NY-2
**West Plattsburgh**—*pop pl* ... NY-2
West Plaza—*locale* ... MO-7
West Plaza Park—*park* ... AZ-5
West Plaza Shop Ctr—*locale* ... AZ-5
West Plaza (Shop Ctr)—*locale* ... MO-7

West Pleasant Grove Ch—*church* MS-4
West Pleasant Hill Ch—*church* OH-6
West Pleasant Ridge Sch—*school* WI-6
*West Plowboy Mountain* ID-8
West Plumbago Draw—*valley* WY-8
West Plum Creek—*stream* CO-8
West Plum Creek—*stream* KS-7
West Plum Creek—*stream* SD-7
West Plum Creek—*stream* WY-8
**West Plymouth**—*pop pl* NH-1
*West Poamoho Stream* HI-9
West Pocket—*valley* WY-8
*West Point* CO-8
*West Point* IN-6
*Westpoint* NE-7
West Point—*cape* AL-4
West Point—*cape* (6) AK-9
West Point—*cape* CA-9
West Point—*cape* FL-3
West Point—*cape* GA-3
West Point—*cape* (6) ME-1
West Point—*cape* MD-2
West Point—*cape* MA-1
West Point—*cape* (3) MS-4
West Point—*cape* NH-1
West Point—*cape* NY-2
West Point—*cape* OR-9
West Point—*cape* TX-5
West Point—*cape* UT-8
West Point—*cape* (4) VA-3
West Point—*cape* (2) WA-9
West Point—*cape* MP-9
West Point—*cliff* AZ-5
West Point—*cliff* OR-9
West Point—*cliff* WA-9
West Point—*locale* AL-4
West Point—*locale* AR-4
West Point—*locale* LA-4
West Point—*locale* MN-6
West Point—*locale* OK-5
West Point—*locale* TX-5
**West Point**—*pop pl* (2) AL-4
**West Point**—*pop pl* AR-4
**West Point**—*pop pl* CA-9
**West Point**—*pop pl* GA-3
**West Point**—*pop pl* IL-6
**Westpoint**—*pop pl* IN-6
**West Point**—*pop pl* IA-7
**West Point**—*pop pl* KY-4
**West Point**—*pop pl* ME-1
**Westpoint**—*pop pl* ME-1
**West Point**—*pop pl* MS-4
**West Point**—*pop pl* NE-7
**West Point**—*pop pl* NY-2
**West Point**—*pop pl* (2) OH-6
**West Point**—*pop pl* (2) PA-2
**Westpoint**—*pop pl* TN-4
**West Point**—*pop pl* TX-5
**West Point**—*pop pl* UT-8
**West Point**—*pop pl* VA-3
West Point—*ridge* MP-9
West Point—*summit* AK-9
West Point—*summit* (2) CA-9
West Point—*summit* TN-4
West Point—*summit* TX-5
West Point—*summit* WA-9
West Point Airfield—*airport* OR-9
West Point Airp—*airport* OR-9
*West Point Baptist Church* AL-4
West Point Campground—*locale* WI-6
West Point (CCD)—*cens area* GA-3
West Point (CCD)—*cens area* KY-4
West Point Cem—*cemetery* AL-4
West Point Cem—*cemetery* IL-6
West Point Cem—*cemetery* (2) IN-6
West Point Cem—*cemetery* IA-7
West Point Cem—*cemetery* KS-7
West Point Cem—*cemetery* ME-1
West Point Cem—*cemetery* MO-7
West Point Cem—*cemetery* NV-8
West Point Cem—*cemetery* ND-7
West Point Cem—*cemetery* (2) OH-6
West Point Cem—*cemetery* OK-5
West Point Cem—*cemetery* OR-9
West Point Cem—*cemetery* TN-4
West Point Cem—*cemetery* TX-5
West Point Cem—*cemetery* UT-8
West Point Central City Hist Dist—*hist pl* MS-4
*West Point Ch* AL-4
West Point Ch—*church* (2) AL-4
West Point Ch—*church* IL-6
West Point Ch—*church* (2) IN-6
West Point Ch—*church* KY-4
West Point Ch—*church* ME-1
West Point Ch—*church* MO-7
West Point Ch—*church* NC-3
West Point Ch—*church* OK-5
West Point Ch—*church* (2) TN-4
West Point Ch—*church* TX-5
Westpoint Ch—*church* WV-2
West Point Ch (historical)—*church* AL-4
West Point Christian Church—*hist pl* OK-5
West Point City Hall—*building* MS-4
West Point City Park—*park* MS-4
West Point Country Club—*other* VA-3
West Point Creek—*stream* IL-6
West Point Creek—*stream* VA-3
**West Pointe A La Hache**—*pop pl* LA-4
**Westpointe Subdivision**—*pop pl* UT-8
West Point Ferry—*locale* IL-6
West Point Ferry—*locale* MO-7
West Point First Christian Ch—*church* AL-4
West Point Foundry—*hist pl* NY-2
West Point Gas Field—*oilfield* MS-4
West Point Girls Camp—*locale* NY-2
West Point Grade Sch—*hist pl* ID-8
West Point Hill—*summit* CO-8
West Point Hill—*summit* OR-9
West Point (historical)—*locale* KS-7
West Point (historical)—*locale* SD-7
West Point Hotel—*hist pl* KY-4
West Point HS—*school* AL-4
West Point HS—*school* MS-4
West Point HS—*school* VA-3
West Point Island—*island* NJ-2
**West Point Island**—*pop pl* NJ-2
West Point Lake—*reservoir* AL-4
West Point Lake—*reservoir* GA-3
West Point Landing—*locale* IL-6
West Point Landing (historical)—*locale* MS-4
West Point Light—*locale* WA-9
West Point Light Station—*hist pl* WA-9
West Point (Magisterial District)—*fmr MCD* VA-3
**West Point Marion**—*pop pl* PA-2
West Point Memorial Gardens—*cemetery* MS-4
*West Point Mennonite Church* MS-4
Westpoint Methodist Ch—*church* TN-4
West Point Milit Reservation—*military* NY-2
*West Point Mine* TN-4
West Point Missionary Baptist Ch—*church* AL-4
Westpoint Missionary Baptist Ch—*church* TN-4
West Point on the Eno—*hist pl* NC-3
West Point Pleasant—*uninc pl* NJ-2
*West Point Post Office* TN-4
West Point Post Office—*building* MS-4
Westpoint Post Office—*building* TN-4
West Point Power House—*other* CA-9
*West Point Reservoir* AL-4
*West Point Rsvr* GA-3
West Point Rsvr—*reservoir* UT-8
West Point Sch—*school* (6) IL-6
West Point Sch—*school* IA-7
West Point Sch—*school* KY-4
West Point Sch—*school* (3) MO-7
West Point Sch—*school* PA-2
West Point Sch—*school* UT-8
West Point Sch (abandoned)—*school* (2) MO-7
West Point Sch (abandoned)—*school* (2) PA-2
West Point Sch (historical)—*school* (2) AL-4
West Point Sch (historical)—*school* MS-4
West Point Sch (historical)—*school* (2) TN-4
West Point Seventh Day Adventist Ch—*church* MS-4
West Point Sewage Lagoon Dam—*dam* MS-4
West Point Shoal—*bar* AK-9
West Point Shop Ctr—*locale* MS-4
Westpoint Slough—*gut* CA-9
**West Point (Town of)**—*pop pl* WI-6
West Point Township—*fmr MCD* (2) IA-7
**West Point Township**—*pop pl* MO-7
**West Point Township**—*pop pl* SD-7
**West Point (Township of)**—*pop pl* IL-6
**West Point (Township of)**—*pop pl* IN-6
West Point Tunnel—*tunnel* CA-9
*West Point (Westpoint)* IN-6
West Point-Wilseyville (CCD)—*cens area* CA-9
**West Poison Spider**—*pop pl* WY-8
West Poison Spider Camp—*locale* WY-8
West Poker Mtn—*summit* AZ-5
**West Poland**—*pop pl* ME-1
West Polecat Canyon—*valley* AZ-5
West Pole Creek—*stream* UT-8
**West Polk**—*pop pl* FL-3
West Polk RR Station—*locale* FL-3
West Polles Tank Number One—*reservoir* AZ-5
West Pollock Rec Area—*park* SD-7
*west Pond* CT-1
*West Pond* MA-1
*West Pond* VT-1
West Pond—*bay* ME-1
West Pond—*lake* (2) ME-1
West Pond—*lake* MA-1
West Pond—*lake* MO-7
West Pond—*lake* NJ-2
West Pond—*lake* (6) NY-2
West Pond—*lake* TN-4
West Pond—*reservoir* CO-8
West Pond—*reservoir* MA-1
West Pond—*reservoir* NC-3
West Pond—*swamp* DE-2
*West Pond Creek* CO-8
West Pond Dam—*dam* MS-4
West Pond Dam—*dam* NC-3
*West Pond Mtn* VT-1
West Pond Outlet Dam—*dam* MA-1
West Ponds—*lake* NY-2
*West Pontiac* MI-6
West Pontotoc Ch—*church* MS-4
West Pope Lake—*lake* MN-6
**West Poplarville**—*pop pl* MS-4
West Poplarville Baptist Ch—*church* MS-4
*Westport* (2) IN-6
*Westport* MA-1
*Westport* MO-7
Westport—*CDP* CT-1
Westport—*locale* IL-6
Westport—*locale* ME-1
Westport—*locale* WI-6
**Westport**—*pop pl* CA-9
**Westport**—*pop pl* CT-1
**Westport**—*pop pl* IL-6
**Westport**—*pop pl* IN-6
**Westport**—*pop pl* KY-4
**Westport**—*pop pl* LA-4
**Westport**—*pop pl* MD-2
**Westport**—*pop pl* MN-6
**Westport**—*pop pl* NH-1
**Westport**—*pop pl* NY-2
**Westport**—*pop pl* NC-3
**Westport**—*pop pl* OK-5
**Westport**—*pop pl* OR-9
**Westport**—*pop pl* PA-2
**Westport**—*pop pl* SD-7
**Westport**—*pop pl* TN-4
**Westport**—*pop pl* WA-9
Westport—*post sta* MA-1
Westport—*uninc pl* KS-7
**Westport Addition**—*pop pl* IN-6
Westport Airp—*airport* KS-7
Westport Airp—*airport* WA-9
*West Portal* CO-8
West Portal—*flat* CA-9
West Portal—*locale* CA-9
West Portal—*locale* CO-8
West Portal—*locale* (2) UT-8
West Portal—*other* CO-8
**West Portal**—*pop pl* NJ-2
West Portal—*uninc pl* CA-9
West Portal Duchesne Tunnel—*tunnel* UT-8
West Portal Fisherman Access (proposed)—*locale* UT-8
West Portal Sch—*school* CA-9
West Portal Water Hollow Tunnel—*tunnel* UT-8
**West Port Arthur**—*pop pl* TX-5
Westport Auxiliary Airp—*airport* KS-7
West Port Bar—*bar* MS-4
Westport Branch—*stream* MO-7
Westport (CCD)—*cens area* CA-9
Westport Cem—*cemetery* IN-6
Westport Cem—*cemetery* IA-7
Westport Cem—*cemetery* SD-7
*West Port Cemetery* MS-4
Westport Ch—*church* ME-1
Westport Ch—*church* NC-3
Westport Chute—*stream* MO-7
Westport Covered Bridge—*hist pl* IN-6
Westport Drain—*canal* CA-9
West Porter Cow Camp—*locale* WY-8
West Porter Creek—*stream* CO-8
**Westport Factory**—*pop pl* MA-1
Westport Golf Course—*locale* NC-3
*Westport Harbor* MA-1
Westport Harbor—*harbor* MA-1
Westport Harbor Entrance Light—*locale* MA-1
Westport Heights Sch—*school* CA-9
Westport (historical)—*locale* KS-7
**West Port (historical)**—*pop pl* MS-4
Westport HS—*school* MA-1
Westport HS—*school* MO-7
Westport Island—*island* ME-1
Westport Island—*island* MO-7
*Westport Lake* WA-9
Westport Lake—*lake* MN-6
**West Portland**—*pop pl* NY-2
**West Portland**—*pop pl* OR-9
Westport Landing Field—*airport* KS-7
**West Portland Park**—*pop pl* OR-9
West Portland Ridge—*ridge* WI-6
West Portland Sch—*school* WI-6
Westport Light—*locale* MA-1
Westport Longshore Club Park—*park* CT-1
West Port Madison—*locale* WA-9
*Westport Mills* MA-1
Westport MS—*school* MA-1
Westport Park—*park* MO-7
West Port Plaza (Shop Ctr)—*locale* MO-7
Westport Point—*cape* MA-1
**Westport Point**—*pop pl* MA-1
Westport Post Office—*building* TN-4
Westport Range—*channel* OR-9
*Westport River* MA-1
Westport River—*gut* MA-1
*Westport River-East Branch* MA-1
Westport River East Branch Marshes—*swamp* MA-1
*Westport River West Branch* MA-1
Westport River West Branch Marshes—*swamp* MA-1
Westport Road HS—*school* KY-4
Westport Sch—*school* MO-7
Westport Sch (historical)—*school* TN-4
Westport Shop Ctr—*locale* MO-7
Westport Slough—*stream* OR-9
**West Portsmouth**—*pop pl* OH-6
Westport Station—*locale* CT-1
Westport Town For—*forest* MA-1
Westport Townhall—*building* MA-1
**Westport (Town of)**—*pop pl* ME-1
**Westport (Town of)**—*pop pl* MA-1
**Westport (Town of)**—*pop pl* NY-2
**Westport (Town of)**—*pop pl* WI-6
Westport Township—*fmr MCD* IA-7
**Westport Township**—*pop pl* SD-7
Westport Township (historical)—*civil* SD-7
**Westport (Township of)**—*pop pl* MN-6
Westport-Union Landing State Beach—*park* CA-9
Westport Union Sch—*school* CA-9
*Westport Village* MA-1
Westport Yacht Club—*locale* MA-1
West Post Office (historical)—*building* TN-4
West Potomac Park—*park* DC-2
West Potrillo Mountains—*range* NM-5
**West Potsdam**—*pop pl* NY-2
West Potsdam Cem—*cemetery* NY-2
West Potter—*unorg reg* SD-7
**West Pottsgrove**—*pop pl* PA-2
**West Pottsgrove (Township of)**—*pop pl* PA-2
West Pottstown Elem Sch—*school* PA-2
*West Powderhorn Creek* CO-8
**West Powellhurst**—*pop pl* OR-9
West Powellhurst Sch—*school* OR-9
*West Powhatan* OH-6
**West Pownal**—*pop pl* ME-1
West Prague Oil Field—*oilfield* OK-5
West Prairie—*flat* FL-3
West Prairie—*flat* TX-5
West Prairie—*locale* IA-7
West Prairie—*locale* WI-6
**West Prairie**—*pop pl* WI-6
West Prairie Cem—*cemetery* IA-7
West Prairie Cem—*cemetery* MI-6
West Prairie Cem—*cemetery* ND-7
West Prairie Cem—*cemetery* OH-6
West Prairie Ch—*church* IL-6
West Prairie Ch—*church* MO-7
West Prairie Ch—*church* (2) ND-7
West Prairie Ch—*church* SD-7
West Prairie Ch—*church* WI-6
West Prairie Church—*dam* IA-7
West Prairie Creek—*stream* KS-7
West Prairie Creek Cem—*cemetery* IN-6
West Prairie Grove Sch (historical)—*school* MO-7
West Prairie (historical P.O.)—*locale* IA-7
West Prairie Sch—*school* (2) IL-6
West Prairie Sch—*school* MO-7
West Prairie Sch—*school* SD-7
West Prairie Sch—*school* WI-6
West Prairie (Township of)—*fmr MCD* AR-4
West Prairie View Cem—*cemetery* IA-7
**West Pratt**—*pop pl* AL-4
*West Pratt Island* CT-1
*West Precinct of Chelmsford* MA-1
*West Precinct of Watertown* MA-1
West Presbyterian Ch—*church* DE-2
West President Ch of Christ—*church* MS-4
West Presley Windmill—*locale* NM-5
West Presley Windmill—*locale* TX-5
**West Prestonsburg**—*pop pl* KY-4
West Prestonsburg (Middlecreek)—*uninc pl* KY-4
West Priewe Well—*locale* NM-5
West Primrose Cem—*cemetery* WI-6
**West Princeton**—*pop pl* ME-1
*West Proctor Creek* MO-7
*West Prong* FL-3
*West Prong* NC-3
*West Prong* TX-5
West Prong—*bay* FL-3
*West Prong Abalochitto Creek* MS-4
*West Prong AbolochittoRiver* MS-4
West Prong Alamocitos Creek—*stream* TX-5
West Prong Alkali Creek—*stream* CO-8
West Prong Arminto Draw—*valley* WY-8
West Prong Ash Creek—*stream* NM-5
West Prong Atascosa River—*stream* TX-5
West Prong Barron Creek—*stream* AR-4
West Prong Bayou Casotte—*stream* MS-4
West Prong Big Creek—*stream* TX-5
West Prong Bird Creek—*stream* TN-4
West Prong Blackwater Creek—*stream* AL-4
West Prong Bogue Falaya—*stream* LA-4
West Prong Brice Creek—*stream* NC-3
West Prong Broad Creek—*stream* NC-3
West Prong Burnt Branch—*stream* TX-5
West Prong Calf Creek—*stream* TX-5
West Prong Caney Fork Creek—*stream* TN-4
West Prong Catfish Creek—*stream* TX-5
West Prong Cem—*cemetery* TX-5
West Prong Chaparrosa Creek—*stream* TX-5
*West Prong Clear Fork* TN-4
West Prong Clifty Creek—*stream* MO-7
West Prong Cole Draw—*valley* WY-8
West Prong Contrary Creek—*stream* TX-5
West Prong Cox Creek—*stream* NC-3
*West Prong Coxs Creek* NC-3
*West Prong Creek* AZ-5
*West Prong Creek* NC-3
West Prong Davids Creek—*stream* TN-4
West Prong Dearborn River—*stream* MT-8
West Prong Doe Creek—*stream* TN-4
West Prong Duck Creek—*stream* TX-5
*West Prong Fleming Creek* AR-4
West Prong Flush Creek—*stream* TX-5
West Prong Fort Ewell Creek—*stream* TX-5
West Prong Fowler Branch—*stream* MO-7
West Prong Franks Drain—*stream* IN-6
West Prong Furnace Creek—*stream* VA-3
West Prong Gentry Creek—*stream* AZ-5
West Prong Glade Creek—*stream* NC-3
West Prong Glady Fork—*stream* NC-3
West Prong Glens Fork—*stream* KY-4
West Prong Goff Creek—*stream* MO-7
West Prong Grape Creek—*stream* NC-3
West Prong Green Canyon—*valley* WY-8
West Prong Green Creek—*stream* IN-6
West Prong Hamer Creek—*stream* NC-3
West Prong Hanging Woman Creek—*stream* MT-8
West Prong Hanging Woman Creek—*stream* WY-8
West Prong Hemphill Creek—*stream* LA-4
West Prong Hickey Fork—*stream* NC-3
West Prong Hill Creek—*stream* TN-4
West Prong Hoghead Creek—*stream* AR-4
West Prong Indian Bayou—*stream* MS-4
West Prong Indian Camp Creek—*stream* KY-4
West Prong Indian Creek—*stream* (2) MO-7
West Prong Indian Creek—*stream* TX-5
West Prong Jennings Fork—*stream* TN-4
West Prong Juniper Creek—*stream* NC-3
West Prong Lavaca River—*stream* TX-5
West Prong Leoncita Creek—*stream* TX-5
West Prong Little Klickitat River—*stream* WA-9
West Prong Little Pigeon River—*stream* TN-4
West Prong Little River—*stream* TN-4
*West Prong Little Walla Walla River* WA-9
West Prong Little Walla Walla River—*stream* OR-9
West Prong Little Yadkin River—*stream* NC-3
West Prong Locust Creek—*stream* KY-4
West Prong Lynn Branch—*stream* MO-7
West Prong McKim Creek—*stream* TX-5
West Prong Medina River—*stream* TX-5
West Prong Mill Creek—*stream* MS-4
West Prong Moon Creek—*stream* NC-3
West Prong Moravian Creek—*stream* NC-3
West Prong Mortons Mill Pond—*stream* NC-3
West Prong Muddy Creek—*stream* MS-4
West Prong Murfrees Fork—*stream* TN-4
West Prong New Light Creek—*stream* NC-3
West Prong New River—*stream* FL-3
West Prong Nicks Creek—*stream* TN-4
West Prong of Osgood Branch—*stream* NC-3
West Prong Old River—*stream* TX-5
West Prong Osburn Creek—*stream* AR-4
West Prong Pursley Creek—*stream* AL-4
West Prong Quapaw Creek—*stream* OK-5
West Prong Raccoon Creek—*stream* NC-3
West Prong Red Creek—*stream* CO-8
West Prong Roaring River—*stream* NC-3
West Prong Rock Creek—*stream* AL-4
*West Prong Rocky River* NC-3
*West Prong San Geronimo Creek* TX-5
West Prong Seventysix Creek—*stream* WY-8
West Prong Silas Creek—*stream* AL-4
West Prong Silver Creek—*stream* MS-4
West Prong Simpson Canyon—*valley* TX-5
West Prong Sister Grove Creek—*stream* TX-5
West Prong Sons Creek—*stream* MO-7
West Prong South Fork Slater Creek—*stream* CO-8
West Prong Spring Creek—*stream* CO-8
West Prong Spring Creek—*stream* WY-8
West Prong Waterman Wash—*stream* AZ-5
West Prong West Spring Draw—*valley* WY-8
West Prong Whites Creek—*stream* TX-5
West Prong Windmill—*locale* TX-5
West Prong Youngs Bayou—*stream* LA-4
**West Property Subdivision**—*pop pl* UT-8
West Prospect Peak—*summit* CA-9
West Protection Levee—*levee* (2) LA-4
West Providence Ch—*church* KY-4
West Providence Sch—*school* PA-2
**West Providence (Township of)**—*pop pl* PA-2
West Pryor Mtn—*summit* MT-8
West Puddin Lake—*lake* ID-8
West Pueblo—*uninc pl* CO-8
West Pueblo Ditch—*canal* CO-8
West Puente Valley—*CDP* CA-9
West Puerto De Luna Ditch—*canal* NM-5
*West Pullman* IL-6
**West Pullman**—*pop pl* IL-6
West Pullman Branch Sch—*school* IL-6
West Pullman Park—*park* IL-6
West Pullman Sch—*school* IL-6
West Pump Canal—*canal* UT-8
West Pump Lateral—*canal* CA-9
West Purdum Sch—*school* NE-7
West Purebred Windmill—*locale* TX-5
**West Putnam Ave**—*pop pl* CT-1
West Putnam Sch—*school* CA-9
West Putnam Sch—*school* MO-7
West Pyramid Peak—*summit* AK-9
*Westquadomesit Brook* RI-1
West Quartz Creek—*stream* WA-9
West Quartz Creek Falls—*falls* WA-9
West Quartzsite Interchange—*crossing* AZ-5
West Queen Canyon—*valley* NV-8
West Quincy—*locale* MO-7
**West Quincy (subdivision)**—*pop pl* MA-1
West Quito Oil Field—*oilfield* TX-5
West Quoddy Head—*cape* ME-1
West Quoddy Head Light Station—*hist pl* ME-1
West Rabbit Creek—*stream* ID-8
West Rabbit Creek Oil Field—*oilfield* OK-5
West Rabbit Mtn—*summit* WY-8
West Racine—*uninc pl* WI-6
West Rader Windmill—*locale* TX-5
West Ragged Brook—*stream* ME-1
West Ragged Top Well—*well* NV-8
West Ragsdale Creek—*stream* TX-5
West Rainbow Creek—*stream* KS-7
West Rainbow Sch—*school* KS-7
**West Rainier**—*pop pl* OR-9
West Rainy Butte—*summit* ND-7
*West Raleigh* WV-2
**West Raleigh**—*pop pl* WV-2
West Ramsey—*summit* TN-4
West Ranch—*locale* (2) AZ-5
West Ranch—*locale* OR-9
West Ranch—*locale* SD-7
West Ranch—*locale* (3) TX-5
West Ranch—*locale* (2) WY-8
West Ranch Branch—*stream* TX-5
West Randall Lake—*lake* WI-6
West Randall Sch—*school* CA-9
West Range—*ridge* NV-8
Westrap—*uninc pl* WI-6
Westra Rapids—*rapids* MN-6
West Rat Creek—*stream* IA-7
*West Rattlesnake Branch* MS-4
West Rattlesnake Branch—*stream* MS-4
**West Raven**—*pop pl* VA-3
West Ravine—*valley* CA-9
Westray Cem—*cemetery* NC-3
**West Reading**—*pop pl* PA-2
West Reading Borough—*civil* PA-2
West Reading Ch—*church* MI-6
West Recreation Field—*park* OH-6
West Red Bench Windmill—*locale* CO-8
West Red Bluff Creek—*stream* OK-5
West Red Canyon—*valley* NM-5
West Redcliff Island—*island* AK-9
West Red Creek—*stream* CO-8
West Redding—*locale* CT-1
West Redding Brook—*stream* CT-1
West Red Hill Oil And Gas Field—*oilfield* OK-5
West Redlands School—*locale* CO-8
West Red Lodge Creek—*stream* MT-8
*West Red Mtn* AL-4
West Red Mtn—*summit* (2) AL-4
West Red Pasture—*area* NM-5
West Redstone Creek—*stream* SD-7
West Red Wash—*stream* CO-8
West Red Windmill—*locale* TX-5
*West Red Wing* MN-6
West Reedley Ditch—*canal* CA-9
West Reedy Creek—*stream* MS-4
West Reef—*bar* OH-6
*West Refuge Trail* PA-2
**West Rehoboth (subdivision)**—*pop pl* DE-2
Westren Brook—*stream* MI-6
**West Reno**—*pop pl* NV-8
**West Renovo**—*pop pl* PA-2
West Republic Township—*civil* MO-7
*West Reservoir* CO-8
Westreville—*locale* SD-7
West Rhudes Creek—*stream* KY-4
*West Richardson Ditch* IN-6
*West Richfield* OH-6
**West Richfield**—*pop pl* OH-6
West Richfield Cem—*cemetery* OH-6
**West Richland**—*pop pl* WA-9
**West Richland (Enterprise)**—*pop pl* WA-9
*West richmond Gulch* ID-8
West Richmond Hist Dist—*hist pl* KY-4
**West Richmondville**—*pop pl* NY-2
**West Richwoods**—*pop pl* AR-4
West Richwoods Church & Sch—*hist pl* AR-4
*Westridge* IL-6
West Ridge—*locale* IL-6
**West Ridge**—*pop pl* AR-4
**Westridge**—*pop pl* CA-9
**Westridge**—*pop pl* NC-3
**West Ridge**—*pop pl* (2) PA-2
**West Ridge**—*pop pl* TN-4
Westridge—*post sta* AZ-5
West Ridge—*ridge* CA-9
West Ridge—*ridge* ME-1
West Ridge—*ridge* MA-1
West Ridge—*ridge* OR-9
West Ridge—*ridge* UT-8
West Ridge—*ridge* VT-1
West Ridge—*ridge* VA-3
West Ridge—*ridge* WI-6
West Ridge—*uninc pl* NY-2
West Ridge Branch—*stream* NC-3
West Ridge Camp—*locale* OR-9
Westridge Cem—*cemetery* MA-1
Westridge Ch—*church* (3) TX-5
Westridge Country Club—*other* AR-4
Westridge Country Club—*other* TX-5
West Ridge Creek—*stream* VA-3
**Westridge Heights (subdivision)**—*pop pl* NC-3
Westridge JHS—*school* FL-3
Westridge Mall—*locale* AZ-5
Westridge MS—*school* UT-8
**Westridge Park (subdivision)**—*pop pl* (2) AZ-5
Westridge Sch—*school* CA-9
West Ridge Sch—*school* CT-1
West Ridge Sch—*school* IL-6
West Ridge Sch—*school* IA-7
West Ridge Sch—*school* ME-1
Westridge Sch—*school* (2) MO-7
West Ridge Sch—*school* NY-2
Westridge Sch—*school* UT-8
**Westridge (subdivision)**—*pop pl* AL-4
**West Ridge (subdivision)**—*pop pl* AL-4
**Westridge (subdivision)**—*pop pl* (2) NC-3
**West Ridge (subdivision)**—*pop pl* TN-4
**Westridge Subdivision**—*pop pl* (2) UT-8
West Ridge Trail—*trail* CA-9
West Ridge Trail—*trail* NH-1
**West Ridgeway**—*pop pl* NY-2
**West Riding**—*pop pl* DE-2
**West Ridley Park (subdivision)**—*pop pl* PA-2
West Rifle Creek—*stream* CO-8
West Rim Rsvr No 1—*reservoir* ID-8
West Rim Trail—*trail* UT-8
**West Rindge**—*pop pl* NH-1
*West Ripley* ME-1
**West Ripley**—*pop pl* ME-1
West Ripley Baptist Ch—*church* MS-4
West Ripley Ch—*church* MS-4
*West Ripley Ch of Christ* MS-4
West Rita Blanca Creek—*stream* TX-5
*West River* CT-1
*West River* IN-6
*West River* MD-2
*West River* RI-1
West River—*gut* IL-6
**West River**—*pop pl* MD-2
West River—*stream* AL-4
West River—*stream* (2) CT-1
West River—*stream* IN-6
West River—*stream* ME-1
West River—*stream* MD-2
West River—*stream* MA-1
West River—*stream* MS-4
West River—*stream* NY-2
West River—*stream* RI-1
West River—*stream* VT-1
West River Ch—*church* IN-6
**West Riverdale**—*pop pl* MD-2
**West River Estates (subdivision)**—*pop pl* UT-8
West River Front Park—*park* IA-7
West River Memorial Park—*cemetery* CT-1
**West River (Owensville)**—*pop pl* MD-2
West River Park—*park* IL-6
West River Pond—*reservoir* MA-1
West River Pond Dam—*dam* MA-1
West River Rsvr—*reservoir* (2) MA-1
*West Riverside* (2) CA-9
**West Riverside**—*pop pl* MT-8
**West Riverside**—*pop pl* TN-4
West Riverside Canal—*canal* CA-9
West Riverside Canal Lateral Number Two—*canal* CA-9
West Riverside Ch of Christ—*church* TN-4
West Riverside Lateral Number One—*canal* CA-9
West Riverside Lateral Number Three—*canal* CA-9
West Riverside Mountains—*range* CA-9
West Riverside Sch—*hist pl* MN-6
West Riverside Sch—*school* CA-9
West Riverside Sch—*school* FL-3
West Riverside Sch—*school* MN-6
West Riverside Sch—*school* SD-7
West Riverside Slide—*valley* CO-8
West Riverton Cem—*cemetery* MI-6
West Riverview Sch—*school* CO-8
West River Windmill—*locale* NM-5
West Riviera Elem Sch—*school* FL-3
West Road Ch—*church* MI-6
West Road Gulch—*valley* OR-9
West Road Sch—*school* ME-1
West Roanoke Rapids—*other* NC-3
West Roaring Creek—*stream* MS-4
West Roatcap Creek—*stream* CO-8
*West Roatcap Gulch* CO-8
**West Robbin**—*pop pl* TN-4
**West Robbins**—*pop pl* TN-4
West Robbins Baptist Ch—*church* TN-4
West Robbins Sch (historical)—*school* TN-4
West Roberts Canyon—*valley* CO-8
West Robert Toombs District—*hist pl* GA-3
West Robeson Senior HS—*school* NC-3
*West Rock* FL-3
West Rock—*island* AK-9
West Rock—*island* CT-1
West Rock—*locale* MN-6
West Rock—*other* AK-9
West Rock—*summit* WA-9
West Rock Bluff—*fmr MCD* NE-7
West Rock Cem—*cemetery* MN-6
*West Rock Creek* KS-7
West Rock Creek—*stream* CA-9
West Rock Creek—*stream* IA-7
West Rock Creek—*stream* KS-7
West Rock Creek—*stream* OK-5
West Rock Creek—*stream* TX-5
West Rock Creek Sch—*school* MO-7
West Rockhill Elem Sch—*school* PA-2
**West Rockhill (Township of)**—*pop pl* PA-2
**West Rockingham**—*pop pl* NC-3
West Rockingham Elem Sch—*school* NC-3
West Rock Mtn—*summit* AL-4
West Rock Park—*park* CT-1
**West Rockport**—*pop pl* ME-1
West Rock Ridge—*ridge* CT-1
West Rocks JHS—*school* CT-1
West Rock Tunnel—*tunnel* CT-1
West Rockville Sch—*school* MD-2
West Rocky Bayou—*stream* AR-4
*West Rocky Branch* TX-5
West Rocky Branch—*stream* TX-5
West Rocky Creek—*stream* TX-5
West Rocky Ford Ch—*church* NC-3
West Rocky Gutter Brook—*stream* MA-1
West Rocky Mount—*uninc pl* NC-3
West Rogersville Ch—*church* AL-4
West Rolinda Ditch—*canal* CA-9
West Rome—*locale* GA-3
West Rome Cem—*cemetery* MI-6
West Rome Ch—*church* MI-6
West Rome HS—*school* GA-3
West Romney (RR name for Vanderlip)—*other* WV-2
**West Rondell Township**—*pop pl* SD-7

West Rondell Township Hall—*building* SD-7
**West Ronkonkoma**—*pop pl* NY-2
West Roodhouse—*locale* IL-6
*West Roodmont* MI-6
West Ropes Oil Field—*oilfield* TX-5
West Rosebud Creek—*stream* (2) MT-8
West Rosebud Ditch—*canal* MT-8
West Rosebud Lake—*lake* MT-8
West Rosebud Park—*park* MT-8
West Rose Draw—*valley* TX-5
West Rosendale—*locale* WI-6
West Rosiclare (Election Precinct)—*fmr MCD* IL-6
West Round Hill Brook—*stream* CT-1
West Round Lake—*lake* MN-6
*West Round Rock* MA-1
West Rowan HS—*school* NC-3
West Rowan JHS—*school* NC-3
West Rowlett Creek—*stream* TX-5
West Roxbury Station (historical)—*locale* MA-1
**West Roxbury (subdivision)**—*pop pl* MA-1
**West Royalston**—*pop pl* MA-1
**West Royalton**—*pop pl* KY-4
West Royce Mtn—*summit* NH-1
West RR Canyon—*valley* NM-5
West Rsvr—*reservoir* OH-6
West Rsvr—*reservoir* WY-8
West Rsvr No 1—*reservoir* CO-8
West Ruark Oil Field—*other* IL-6
**West Rumney**—*pop pl* NH-1
*West Run* OH-6
West Run—*stream* (3) PA-2
West Run—*stream* (2) VA-3
West Run—*stream* (2) WV-2
*West Run Brook* NH-1
West Run Cracker Branch—*stream* FL-3
West Running Brook—*stream* NH-1
**West Rupert**—*pop pl* VT-1
West Rural Hill—*locale* IL-6
**West Rush**—*pop pl* NY-2
**West Rushville**—*pop pl* OH-6
West Rusk HS—*school* TX-5
West Rusk Sch—*school* TX-5
**West Russell**—*pop pl* KY-4
West Rustler Spring—*spring* AZ-5
West Rustlers Spring—*spring* AZ-5
West Rutland—*CDP* VT-1
**West Rutland**—*pop pl* MA-1
**West Rutland**—*pop pl* VT-1
West Rutland Cem—*cemetery* MA-1
**West Rutland Center**—*pop pl* VT-1
West Rutland Town Hall—*hist pl* VT-1
**Westry**—*pop pl* NC-3
**West Rye**—*pop pl* NH-1
West Ryman Draw—*valley* CO-8
West Sabinal River—*stream* TX-5
**West Sabraton**—*pop pl* WV-2
**West Sacramento**—*pop pl* CA-9
West Sacramento Sch—*school* CA-9
**West Sadsbury (Township of)**—*pop pl* PA-2
West Sage Hen Creek—*stream* WY-8
West Sage Hen Rocks—*summit* WY-8
West Sager Sch (abandoned)—*school* MO-7
West Sageville Sch—*school* IA-7
*West Saginaw* MI-6
*West Saint* LA-4
West Saint Clair Street Hist Dist—*hist pl* MI-6
**West Saint Clair (Township of)**—*pop pl* PA-2
West Saint George Spring—*spring* UT-8
*West Saint George Springs* UT-8
**West Saint Helens**—*pop pl* OR-9
**West Saint Johnsville**—*pop pl* NY-2
West Saint Louis Creek—*stream* CO-8
West Saint Lucie (CCD)—*cens area* FL-3
West Saint Marys—*locale* IA-7
West Saint Marys Peak—*summit* MT-8
West Saint Olaf Ch—*church* MN-6
West Saint Olaf Ch—*church* ND-7
West Saint Paul—*locale* TX-5
**West Saint Paul**—*pop pl* MN-6
West Saint Paul Cem—*cemetery* MN-6
West Salamanca—*uninc pl* NY-2
**West Salem**—*pop pl* IL-6
**West Salem**—*pop pl* NC-3
**West Salem**—*pop pl* OH-6
**West Salem**—*pop pl* OR-9
**West Salem**—*pop pl* WI-6
*West Salem Baptist Church* MS-4
West Salem Cem—*cemetery* IN-6
West Salem Cem—*cemetery* MN-6
West Salem Ch—*church* KS-7
West Salem Ch—*church* MI-6
West Salem Ch—*church* MS-4
*West Salem Elementary School* PA-2
West Salem Rsvr—*reservoir* IL-6
West Salem Sch—*school* (2) IL-6
West Salem Sch—*school* PA-2
West Salem Shop Ctr—*locale* NC-3
**West Salem (Township of)**—*pop pl* PA-2
West Saline Lake Oil Field—*oilfield* LA-4
**West Saline Township**—*pop pl* KS-7
**West Salisbury**—*pop pl* NH-1
**West Salisbury**—*pop pl* NC-3
**West Salisbury**—*pop pl* PA-2
**West Salisbury**—*pop pl* VT-1
*West Salisbury School* PA-2
West Salmon Falls—*cens area* ID-8
*West Salt Creek* KS-7
*West Salt Creek* TX-5
West Salt Creek—*stream* (2) CO-8
West Salt Creek—*stream* KS-7
West Salt Creek—*stream* TX-5
*West Salt Draw* TX-5
West Salt Fork Oil Field—*oilfield* OK-5
**West Salt Lake Subdivision**—*pop pl* UT-8
West San Antonio Heights Sch—*school* TX-5
West Sand Canyon—*valley* CO-8
*West Sand Creek* MS-4
West Sand Creek—*stream* CO-8
West Sand Creek—*stream* OK-5
West Sand Creek Trail—*trail* WA-9
West Sanders Windmill—*locale* TX-5
**West Sandgate**—*pop pl* VT-1
West Sand Hills Oil Field—*oilfield* TX-5
*West Sandies Creek* TX-5
*West Sand Island* AL-4
*West Sandlake* NY-2
**West Sand Lake**—*pop pl* NY-2
*West Sandpoint Creek* ID-8
West Sand Springs—*spring* NM-5
West Sand Springs Windmill—*locale* NM-5
*West Sandwich* MA-1
West Sand Windmill—*locale* NM-5
*West Sandy Creek* OK-5
West Sandy Creek—*stream* FL-3
West Sandy Creek—*stream* KS-7
West Sandy Creek—*stream* OK-5
West Sandy Creek—*stream* TN-4
West Sandy Creek—*stream* (3) TX-5
West Sandy Creek Dewatering Area—*basin* TN-4
*West Sandy Creek Drainage Canal* TN-4
West Sandy Creek Drainage Ditch—*canal* TN-4
West Sandy Dike—*dam* TN-4
West Sandy Landing—*locale* TN-4
West Sandy Wash—*arroyo* NV-8
*West San Jacinto River* TX-5
West San Jose Sch—*school* NM-5
West San Juan Drain—*canal* CA-9
West San Juan Drain Number One—*canal* CA-9
West San Simon Interchange—*crossing* AZ-5
**West Santa Ana**—*pop pl* CA-9
West Santa Barbara—*uninc pl* CA-9
West Santa Clara (CCD)—*cens area* CA-9
West Santa Rita Drain—*canal* CA-9
**West Saticoy**—*pop pl* CA-9
West Sattes Sch—*school* WV-2
West Sauer (historical)—*locale* MS-4
**West Saugerties**—*pop pl* NY-2
West Savannah—*uninc pl* GA-3
West Savannah Sch—*school* GA-3
West Savanna River—*stream* MN-6
West Saviors Cem—*cemetery* SD-7
West Savoy Creek—*stream* MT-8
West Sawmill Canyon—*valley* AZ-5
West Sawtelle Pond—*lake* ME-1
**West Saxonburg**—*pop pl* PA-2
*West Saxton* PA-2
**West Sayre**—*pop pl* AL-4
**West Sayville**—*pop pl* NY-2
West's Block—*hist pl* OR-9
Wests Branch—*stream* NC-3
Wests Butte—*summit* OR-9
West Scalp Creek—*stream* TX-5
West Scandia Cem—*cemetery* ND-7
*West Scarboro* ME-1
West Scarboro Cem—*cemetery* ME-1
**West Scarborough**—*pop pl* ME-1
**West Scenic Park**—*pop pl* FL-3
West Sch—*hist pl* OH-6
West Sch—*school* AZ-5
West Sch—*school* CA-9
West Sch—*school* (2) CO-8
West Sch—*school* DC-2
West Sch—*school* GA-3
West Sch—*school* (9) IL-6
West Sch—*school* (3) IA-7
West Sch—*school* KS-7
West Sch—*school* KY-4
West Sch—*school* (4) MA-1
West Sch—*school* (6) MI-6
West Sch—*school* (2) MN-6
West Sch—*school* (2) MS-4
West Sch—*school* (3) MO-7
West Sch—*school* (2) NE-7
West Sch—*school* NH-1
West Sch—*school* NY-2
West Sch—*school* (2) NC-3
West Sch—*school* (5) OH-6
West Sch—*school* (3) OK-5
West Sch—*school* PA-2
West Sch—*school* (2) SD-7
West Sch—*school* (2) TN-4
West Sch—*school* (6) TX-5
West Sch—*school* UT-8
West Sch—*school* VA-3
West Sch—*school* (2) WV-2
West Sch—*school* (2) WI-6
West Sch (abandoned)—*school* PA-2
Wests Chapel (historical)—*church* AL-4
West Sch (historical)—*school* MS-4
West Sch (historical)—*school* TN-4
West Sch No 44—*school* NE-7
West Sch No 7—*school* NE-7
West Sch No 8—*school* NE-7
*West School* IN-6
*West School* KS-7
West School (historical)—*locale* MO-7
West Schoolhouse—*hist pl* MA-1
**West Schuyler**—*pop pl* NY-2
West Schuyler Cem—*cemetery* NY-2
West Science Ridge Ch—*church* IL-6
West Science Ridge Sch—*school* IL-6
West Scio—*locale* OR-9
West Scipio Cem—*cemetery* KS-7
*West Scituate* MA-1
West Scituate (historical P.O.)—*locale* MA-1
West Scott—*locale* IA-7
West Scott Baptist Hosp—*hospital* MS-4
West Scottsville Ch—*church* AL-4
West Scottville Cem—*cemetery* IL-6
Wests Cove—*valley* NC-3
West Scranton—*uninc pl* PA-2
West Scranton HS—*school* PA-2
West Sdie Baptist Ch—*church* MS-4
West Seabolt Creek—*stream* GA-3
West Seaford Elem Sch—*school* DE-2
West Searsmont—*locale* ME-1
**West Seattle**—*pop pl* WA-9
West Seattle Golf Course—*other* WA-9
West Seattle HS—*school* WA-9
West Seattle Rsvr—*reservoir* WA-9
**West Sebago**—*pop pl* ME-1
West Sebewa—*locale* MI-6
West Sebewa Ch—*church* MI-6
**West Seboeis**—*pop pl* ME-1
West Seboeis Stream—*stream* ME-1
*West Seboois* ME-1
**West Seboois**—*pop pl* ME-1
*West Seboois Stream* ME-1
West Second Street Hist Dist—*hist pl* WI-6
West Second Street Residential Hist Dist—*hist pl* MN-6
West Section Well—*well* NM-5
West Section Windmill—*locale* TX-5
West Sedge—*island* NJ-2
West Sedona Elem Sch—*school* AZ-5
**West Sedona (Grasshopper Flats)**—*pop pl* AZ-5
West Seelye Bay—*bay* MN-6
West Seligman Interchange—*crossing* AZ-5
Westselline Ch—*church* OK-5
West Selma Trinity Baptist Ch (historical)—*church* AL-4
**West Selmont**—*pop pl* AL-4
*West Selser Canal* LA-4
West Seminary Oil Field—*other* IL-6
West Seminole Oil Field—*oilfield* TX-5
**West Seneca**—*pop pl* NY-2
**West Seneca**—*pop pl* OK-5
West Seneca State Sch—*school* NY-2
**West Seneca (Town of)**—*pop pl* NY-2
*West Senix Creek* NY-2
West Sentinel—*summit* WY-8
West Sentinel Island—*island* AK-9
West Sentinel Oil Field—*oilfield* OK-5
West Sepulga River—*stream* AL-4
West Serviceberry Draw—*valley* CO-8
West Servilleta Tank—*reservoir* NM-5
West Settlement—*locale* (2) NY-2
West Settlement—*locale* VT-1
West Settlement Creek—*stream* NY-2
West Sevenmile Creek—*stream* CO-8
West Sevenmile Tank—*reservoir* AZ-5
**West Severna Park**—*pop pl* MD-2
*West Sewartstown* NH-1
West Shadley Creek—*stream* AR-4
*West Shady Grove Baptist Ch* MS-4
West Shady Grove Cem—*cemetery* TX-5
*West Shady Grove Cemetery* MS-4
West Shady Grove Ch—*church* MS-4
West Shady Grove Ch—*church* (2) TX-5
West Shady Grove Sch—*school* MO-7
**West Shadyside**—*pop pl* MD-2
West Shag Rock—*rock* MA-1
West Shannon—*unorg reg* SD-7
West Shed Lake—*lake* MI-6
West Sheep Creek—*stream* MO-7
West Sheep Creek—*stream* (3) MT-8
West Sheep Island—*island* ME-1
**West Sheffield**—*pop pl* PA-2
**West Shelby**—*pop pl* NY-2
**West Shelby**—*pop pl* NC-3
West Shelbyville District—*hist pl* KY-4
**West Shenango (Township of)**—*pop pl* PA-2
West Sheridan—*summit* CO-8
West Shilie Windmill—*locale* TX-5
**West Shiloh**—*pop pl* TN-4
West Shiloh Baptist Ch—*church* TN-4
West Shiloh Cem—*cemetery* TN-4
West Shingle Creek Lake—*lake* UT-8
West Shinnery Windmill—*locale* TX-5
West Shipps Landing—*locale* TN-4
West Shirley Bog—*lake* ME-1
West Shoal Creek—*stream* WY-8
West Shoals Creek—*stream* AL-4
**West Shokan**—*pop pl* NY-2
West Shoo Fly Creek—*stream* KS-7
*West Shore* CT-1
West Shore—*locale* KS-7
**West Shore**—*pop pl* CT-1
West Shore Airp—*airport* PA-2
West Shore Ch—*church* TX-5
West Shore Country Club—*other* MI-6
West Shore Country Club—*other* PA-2
Westshore County Park—*park* CA-9
West Shore Elem Sch—*school* FL-3
**Westshore Estates**—*pop pl* TN-4
West Shore Golf Course—*locale* PA-2
West Shore Gulch—*valley* CA-9
**West Shoreham**—*pop pl* MD-2
West Shore JHS—*school* PA-2
West Shore Plaza—*locale* PA-2
West Shore Plaza (Shop Ctr)—*locale* FL-3
West Shore Ponds—*lake* NY-2
West Shore Rec Area—*park* SD-7
West Shore Sandy Beach—*beach* ME-1
West Shores Baptist Ch—*church* FL-3
West Shore State Park—*park* MT-8
West Shore Terminal—*locale* NJ-2
West Shore YMCA Camp—*locale* PA-2
West Short Pine Hills—*range* SD-7
West Shotgun Creek—*stream* MT-8
West Shotgun Spring—*spring* OR-9
West Shreveport—*uninc pl* LA-4
West Shreveport Sch—*school* LA-4
West Shreve Run—*stream* PA-2
**West Shrewsbury**—*pop pl* NJ-2
West Shumway Ditch—*canal* AZ-5
*West Side* AL-4
*West Side* CT-1
*Westside* IN-6
*West Side* (2) IA-7
*West Side* (2) OH-6
*West Side* PA-2
Westside—*CDP* GA-3
Westside—*locale* MS-4
Westside—*locale* TN-4
**Westside**—*pop pl* CA-9
**Westside**—*pop pl* GA-3
**Westside**—*pop pl* IN-6
**Westside**—*pop pl* IA-7
**Westside**—*pop pl* NC-3
**West Side**—*pop pl* OH-6
**West Side**—*pop pl* (2) OR-9
**West Side**—*pop pl* PA-2
**West Side**—*pop pl* TX-5
**West Side**—*pop pl* WV-2
Westside—*post sta* LA-4
Westside—*post sta* OK-5
West Side—*uninc pl* (2) AL-4
Westside—*uninc pl* (2) CA-9
Westside—*uninc pl* FL-3
West Side—*uninc pl* MA-1
West Side—*uninc pl* NJ-2
West Side—*uninc pl* NY-2
West Side—*uninc pl* PA-2
West Side—*uninc pl* WA-9
Westside Airlines Terminal—*building* NY-2
Westside Alliance Ch—*church* FL-3
West Side Assembly of God Ch—*church* AL-4
West Side Bank—*hist pl* CA-9
*West Side Baptist Ch* AL-4
Westside Baptist Ch—*church* AL-4
West Side Baptist Ch—*church* AL-4
Westside Baptist Ch—*church* AL-4
West Side Baptist Ch—*church* AL-4
Westside Baptist Ch—*church* (2) AL-4
West Side Baptist Ch—*church* (2) AL-4
Westside Baptist Ch—*church* (3) FL-3
West Side Baptist Ch—*church* (2) KS-7
West Side Baptist Ch—*church* MS-4
Westside Baptist Ch—*church* MS-4
Westside Baptist Ch—*church* (4) TN-4
Westside Baptist Ch of Jacksonville—*church* FL-3
Westside Baptist Church Sch—*school* FL-3
*West Side Canal* CA-9
West Side Canal—*canal* (2) CA-9
Westside Canal—*canal* CA-9
West Side Canal—*canal* CO-8
West Side Canal—*canal* (2) MT-8
West Side Canal—*canal* NV-8
West Side Canal—*canal* (2) NM-5
West Side Canal—*canal* UT-8
West Side Canal—*canal* WA-9
West Side Canal—*canal* WY-8
Westside (CCD)—*cens area* CA-9
Westside (CCD)—*cens area* GA-3
West Side Cem—*cemetery* AL-4
West Side Cem—*cemetery* (2) CT-1
Westside Cem—*cemetery* CT-1
West Side Cem—*cemetery* CT-1
West Side Cem—*cemetery* IN-6
Westside Cem—*cemetery* (2) IA-7
Westside Cem—*cemetery* MA-1
West Side Cem—*cemetery* (2) MI-6
Westside Cem—*cemetery* MN-6
West Side Cem—*cemetery* NE-7
Westside Cem—*cemetery* OH-6
West Side Cem—*cemetery* OR-9
West Side Cem—*cemetery* PA-2
West Side Cem—*cemetery* SC-3
West Side Cem—*cemetery* TN-4
Westside Cem—*cemetery* TX-5
Westside Ch—*church* AL-4
West Side Ch—*church* AL-4
Westside Ch—*church* (4) AL-4
West Side Ch—*church* AL-4
Westside Ch—*church* AR-4
West Side Ch—*church* AR-4
Westside Ch—*church* AR-4
Westside Ch—*church* (2) FL-3
West Side Ch—*church* FL-3
Westside Ch—*church* FL-3
West Side Ch—*church* (2) FL-3
Westside Ch—*church* GA-3
West Side Ch—*church* IL-6
Westside Ch—*church* IL-6
Westside Ch—*church* IN-6
West Side Ch—*church* KY-4
West Side Ch—*church* MN-6
West Side Ch—*church* NE-7
West Side Ch—*church* NY-2
Westside Ch—*church* (3) NC-3
West Side Ch—*church* NC-3
Westside Ch—*church* OH-6
West Side Ch—*church* OH-6
Westside Ch—*church* (2) SC-3
Westside Ch—*church* TN-4
Westside Ch—*church* TX-5
Westside Ch—*church* VA-3
Westside Ch (historical)—*church* MS-4
Westside Ch of Christ—*church* (2) AL-4
Westside Ch of Christ—*church* FL-3
West Side Ch of Christ—*church* KS-7
West Side Ch of God—*church* KS-7
Westside Ch of the Nazarene—*church* KS-7
Westside Ch of the Nazarene—*church* TN-4
Westside Christian Ch—*church* (2) FL-3
Westside Christian Ch—*church* KS-7
West Side Christian Ch—*church* KS-7
Westside Christian Ch—*church* TN-4
Westside Christian Sch—*school* MI-6
West Side City Park—*park* OH-6
West Side Community Center—*building* MS-4
Westside Community Center—*locale* KS-7
West Side Community Center—*locale* SC-3
Westside Community Center—*park* FL-3
West Side Community Ch—*church* GA-3
Westside Community Park—*park* NC-3
West Side Cotton Gin—*locale* TX-5
West Side Cow Camp—*locale* CO-8
West Side Creek—*stream* CA-9
Westside Ditch—*canal* CO-8
West Side Ditch—*canal* MT-8
Westside Ditch—*canal* NV-8
Westside Ditch—*canal* OR-9
West Side Ditch—*canal* OR-9
Westside Ditch—*canal* UT-8
West Side Ditch—*canal* (2) WY-8
West Side Diversion Ditch—*canal* IL-6
Westside Drain—*canal* CA-9
West Side Drain—*canal* CA-9
Westside Drain—*canal* NV-8
*West Side Drainage Ditch* OK-5
*Westside Elementary School* OR-9
*West Side Elem Sch* MS-4
Westside Elem Sch—*school* AL-4
Westside Elem Sch—*school* (3) FL-3
Westside Elem Sch—*school* KS-7
Westside Elem Sch—*school* MS-4
Westside Elem Sch—*school* NJ-2
Westside Elem Sch—*school* (2) TN-4
West Side Elem Sch—*school* TN-4
Westside Elem Sch—*school* TN-4
**West Side Estates Subdivision**—*pop pl* UT-8
West Side Feed and Sale Stable—*hist pl* OR-9
West Side Field Park—*park* CT-1
Westside Free Will Baptist Ch—*church* KS-7
**West Side Heights**—*pop pl* KY-4
**Westside Heights**—*pop pl* TN-4
Westside Heights—*uninc pl* TN-4
West Side Highland Ditch—*canal* CO-8
*West Side Hill* CT-1
**West Side Hill**—*pop pl* CT-1
West Side Hist Dist—*hist pl* CO-8
West Side Hist Dist—*hist pl* IL-6
West Side Historic Residential District—*hist pl* MI-6
Westside Holiness Ch—*church* GA-3
Westside Hosp—*hospital* CA-9
West Side Hosp—*hospital* CA-9
*Westside HS* AL-4
*West Side HS* IN-6
Westside HS—*school* GA-3
West Side HS—*school* GA-3
Westside HS—*school* ID-8
Westside HS—*school* IN-6
Westside HS—*school* NE-7
West Side HS—*school* NJ-2
Westside HS—*school* SC-3
Westside HS—*school* TN-4
Westside HS—*school* VA-3
Westside Independent Ch—*church* FL-3
*Westside JHS* IN-6
West Side JHS—*school* AR-4
West Side JHS—*school* CT-1
Westside JHS—*school* GA-3
West Side JHS—*school* IN-6
Westside Lake Fork Ditch—*canal* ID-8
West Side Lateral—*canal* NM-5
West Side Lateral—*canal* WY-8
Westside Main Canal—*canal* CA-9
West Side-Main Strasse Hist Dist—*hist pl* KY-4
West Side Market—*hist pl* OH-6
*West Side Memorial Cem* PA-2
*Westside Methodist Church* AL-4
Westside Mine—*mine* UT-8
Westside Mission—*church* FL-3
Westside Missionary Baptist Ch—*church* IN-6
Westside Missionary Ch—*church* TX-5
West Side MS—*school* IN-6
Westside Neighborhood—*hist pl* CO-8
Westside Neighborhood Center—*building* AL-4
Westside Neighborhood Hist Dist—*hist pl* MI-6
Westside Park—*hist pl* NJ-2
West Side Park—*park* AL-4
Westside Park—*park* AL-4
West Side Park—*park* AZ-5
West Side Park—*park* CA-9
Westside Park—*park* (3) FL-3
Westside Park—*park* GA-3
West Side Park—*park* IL-6
Westside Park—*park* IN-6
West Side Park—*park* IN-6
Westside Park—*park* IA-7
West Side Park—*park* MI-6
Westside Park—*park* (2) MS-4
West Side Park—*park* MT-8
West Side Park—*park* (2) NJ-2
West Side Park—*park* OH-6
Westside Park—*park* (3) OK-5
Westside Park—*park* SD-7
West Side Park—*park* (2) WA-9
West Side Planing Mill (rear)—*hist pl* OH-6
*West Side Pond* CT-1
West Side Pond—*reservoir* CT-1
West Side Pond Brook—*stream* CT-1
Westside Post Office (historical)—*building* MS-4
West Side Residential District—*hist pl* MT-8
West Side Rsvr—*reservoir* ID-8
West Side Rsvr—*reservoir* MT-8
*West Side Sch* MS-4
*Westside Sch* TN-4
Westside Sch—*school* AR-4
West Side Sch—*school* AR-4
Westside Sch—*school* (3) AR-4
West Side Sch—*school* AR-4
Westside Sch—*school* (4) CA-9
Westside Sch—*school* (2) FL-3
West Side Sch—*school* FL-3
Westside Sch—*school* FL-3
Westside Sch—*school* GA-3
West Side Sch—*school* (2) GA-3
Westside Sch—*school* GA-3
West Side Sch—*school* (3) GA-3
Westside Sch—*school* GA-3
Westside Sch—*school* ID-8
West Side Sch—*school* ID-8
West Side Sch—*school* (2) IL-6
West Side Sch—*school* IN-6
Westside Sch—*school* KY-4
West Side Sch—*school* LA-4
Westside Sch—*school* MA-1
Westside Sch—*school* MI-6
West Side Sch—*school* MN-6
West Side Sch—*school* MS-4
Westside Sch—*school* (4) MS-4
Westside Sch—*school* MO-7
Westside Sch—*school* MT-8
Westside Sch—*school* NE-7
West Side Sch—*school* (2) NE-7
Westside Sch—*school* NV-8
West Side Sch—*school* (2) NY-2
West Side Sch—*school* (2) OH-6
West Side Sch—*school* OK-5
Westside Sch—*school* OK-5
West Side Sch—*school* OR-9
West Side Sch—*school* (2) PA-2
Westside Sch—*school* (2) TN-4
Westside Sch—*school* (2) TX-5
West Side Sch—*school* (4) TX-5
Westside Sch—*school* UT-8
Westside Sch—*school* (2) VA-3
West Side Sch—*school* WA-9
West Side Sch—*school* WV-2
West Side Sch—*school* (6) WI-6
West Side Sch—*school* WY-8
West Side Sch (abandoned)—*school* PA-2
Westside Sch (historical)—*school* AL-4
West Side Sch (historical)—*school* PA-2
Westside Sch (historical)—*school* TN-4
West Side Sch No 1—*school* MI-6
West Side Sch No 2—*school* MI-6
*West Side School* AL-4
Westside School—*locale* CO-8
West Side School (historical)—*building* TN-4
West Side Shaft—*mine* WA-9
Westside Shop Ctr—*locale* KS-7
West Side Shop Ctr—*locale* LA-4
Westside Skills Center—*school* FL-3
Westside Spring—*spring* (2) NV-8
Westside Spring—*spring* UT-8
**Westside (subdivision)**—*pop pl* AL-4
*West Side Tamarack Canal* CA-9
West Side Tank—*reservoir* AZ-5
Westside Tank—*reservoir* AZ-5
West Side Tank—*reservoir* TX-5
West Side Township—*fmr MCD* IA-7
**Westside Township**—*pop pl* NE-7
**Westside (Township of)**—*pop pl* MN-6
Westside Trail—*trail* NH-1
West Side Union HS—*school* CA-9
West Side Union Sch—*school* CA-9
Westside United Pentacostal Ch—*church* TN-4
Westside Village—*locale* KS-7
Westside Vocational-Technical Center—*school* FL-3
Westside Waterhole—*lake* OR-9
West Side Windmill—*locale* AZ-5
West Side YMCA—*building* TN-4
West Sidney—*locale* ME-1
West Sierra (CCD)—*cens area* CA-9
West Signal Trail—*trail* OK-5
West Sign Camp Canyon—*valley* NM-5
West Silent Lake—*lake* MN-6
**West Siloam Springs**—*pop pl* OK-5
West Silsbee Oil Field—*oilfield* TX-5
*West Silverbell Mountains* AZ-5
West Silver Bell Mountains—*summit* AZ-5
West Silver Lake—*reservoir* WI-6
West Silver Mesa—*summit* CO-8
West Silver Sands Beach—*beach* CT-1
*West Simons Creek* IN-6
West Simpson Well—*well* CO-8
West Simsbury—*locale* CT-1
West Singer Windmill—*locale* NM-5
**West Sinton**—*pop pl* TX-5
West Sioux HS—*school* IA-7
West Sippo Creek—*stream* OH-6
West Sister—*bar* ME-1
West Sister—*summit* ID-8
West Sister Creek—*stream* TX-5
*West Sister Island* ME-1
West Sister Island—*island* ME-1
West Sister Island—*island* OH-6
West Sister Island Light—*hist pl* OH-6
West Sister Island Natl Wildlife Refuge—*area* OH-6
West Sister Peak—*summit* ID-8
West Sister Reef—*bar* OH-6
West Sister Rock—*island* FL-3
*West Sit Down Bench* UT-8
West Sit Down Bench—*bench* UT-8
West Six Tank—*reservoir* AZ-5
West Sixth Street and Mayes Place Hist Dist—*hist pl* TN-4
West Sixth Street Hist Dist—*hist pl* PA-2
West Skate Canyon—*valley* NM-5
*West Skinner Tank* AZ-5
West Skinner Tank—*reservoir* AZ-5
Wests Landing (historical)—*locale* MS-4
West Slash—*lake* MO-7
**West Slaterville**—*pop pl* NY-2
West Slaughter Canyon—*valley* NM-5
West Sleeping River—*stream* MI-6
West Slope—*flat* WY-8
**West Slope**—*pop pl* OR-9
West Slope—*unorg reg* ND-7
West Slope, The—*slope* UT-8
West Slough Windmill—*locale* TX-5
West Slovan Cem—*cemetery* WI-6
**Wests Mill (Post Office)**—*pop pl* NC-3
Wests Mine—*mine* OR-9
West Smith Canyon—*valley* NE-7
**West Smithfield**—*pop pl* NC-3
West Smithfield Ch—*church* NC-3
**West Smithtown**—*pop pl* NY-2
West Sneech Brook—*stream* RI-1
*West Sneech Pond Brook* RI-1
West Snider Creek—*stream* MT-8
West Snowflake Creek*—*stream* ND-7
West Snowflake Ditch—*canal* AZ-5
West Snowmass Creek—*stream* CO-8
West Snow Windmill—*locale* TX-5
West Snyder HS—*school* PA-2
West Soap Creek—*stream* CO-8
West Soap Creek—*stream* MT-8
West Soap Creek—*stream* TX-5
West Soldier Ditch—*canal* IA-7
West Solomon Lake—*lake* MN-6
**West Somerset**—*pop pl* NY-2
West Somerset—*uninc pl* KY-4
**West Somerville (subdivision)**—*pop pl* MA-1
*West Sonora* (2) IN-6
**West Sonora**—*pop pl* OH-6
West Sopchoppy Cem—*cemetery* FL-3
West Sopris Creek—*stream* CO-8
West Souhegan River—*stream* NH-1
West Sound—*bay* WA-9
**West Sound**—*pop pl* WA-9
**West Southport**—*pop pl* ME-1
West South Town Windmill—*locale* TX-5
West South West Ledge—*rock* MA-1
West Spaniard Creek—*stream* OK-5
West Spanish Peak—*summit* CO-8
West Sparta—*locale* NY-2
*West Sparta Elem Sch* TN-4
West Sparta Station—*locale* NY-2
**West Sparta (Town of)**—*pop pl* NY-2
Wests Peak—*summit* AK-9
West Spear Windmill—*locale* NM-5
West Spencer Cem—*cemetery* WI-6
West Spider Lake—*lake* WI-6
West Spiller Creek—*stream* AR-4
West Spirit Lake—*lake* MN-6
West Spit—*bar* AK-9
West Spit—*bar* MP-9
West Spit—*ridge* MP-9
*West-Spitze* MP-9
West Split Rock River—*stream* MN-6
West Split Tank—*reservoir* AZ-5
**West Spokane**—*pop pl* WA-9
*Wests Pond* MA-1
Wests Pond—*lake* NC-3
Wests Pond—*reservoir* VA-3
West Spraberry Oil Field—*oilfield* TX-5
*West Spring* AL-4
*West Spring* NV-8
West Spring—*locale* NV-8
West Spring—*spring* (3) AZ-5
West Spring—*spring* AR-4
West Spring—*spring* CA-9
West Spring—*spring* (2) ID-8
West Spring—*spring* (3) NV-8
West Spring—*spring* OR-9
West Spring—*spring* SD-7
West Spring—*spring* TX-5
West Spring—*spring* (3) UT-8
West Spring—*spring* WY-8
West Spring Branch—*stream* AL-4
West Spring Branch—*stream* AR-4
West Spring Branch—*stream* LA-4

West Spring Branch—*stream* TX-5
**West Springbrook**—*pop pl* MD-2
**West Springbrook**—*pop pl* TN-4
West Spring Coulee—*valley* MT-8
**West Spring Creek**—*pop pl* PA-2
West Spring Creek—*stream* ID-8
West Spring Creek—*stream* (3) KS-7
West Spring Creek—*stream* (2) OK-5
West Spring Creek—*stream* WY-8
West Spring Draw—*valley* WY-8
**West Springfield**—*pop pl* MA-1
**West Springfield**—*pop pl* NH-1
**West Springfield**—*pop pl* PA-2
**West Springfield**—*pop pl* VT-1
**West Springfield**—*pop pl* VA-3
West Springfield Fish and Game Club Dam—*dam* MA-1
West Springfield JHS—*school* MA-1
West Springfield Sch—*school* VA-3
West Springfield Station—*locale* PA-2
West Springfield Town Hall—*building* MA-1
**West Springfield (Town of)**—*pop pl* MA-1
West Spring Green Sch—*school* WI-6
West Spring Hollow—*valley* AR-4
*West Spring Lake* MI-6
**West Spring Mills**—*pop pl* PA-2
**West Springs**—*pop pl* SC-3
West Springs—*spring* NV-8
West Springs—*spring* UT-8
West Springs Branch—*stream* SC-3
West Springs (CCD)—*cens area* SC-3
West Spring Seep Gulch—*valley* ID-8
West Spring Street Sch—*school* IN-6
West Spring Street Sch—*school* NY-2
West Springtown Sch (abandoned)—*school* PA-2
West Spruce Brook—*stream* CT-1
West Spruce Mtn—*summit* AZ-5
*West Spruce Pond* PA-2
West Spur—*ridge* CA-9
West Spur Whiteface—*ridge* NH-1
West Squaw Canyon—*valley* CO-8
*West Squaw Creek* UT-8
West Squaw Creek*—*stream* NE-7
West Squaw Creek—*stream* NV-8
West Squaw Creek—*stream* SD-7
West Squaw Draw—*valley* UT-8
*West Squirrel Creek* TX-5
West Squirrel Creek—*stream* TX-5
West's Ranch—*locale* MT-8
Wests Rsvr—*reservoir* UT-8
*Wests Station* MS-4
Wests Store—*locale* VA-3
**West Stafford**—*pop pl* CT-1
West Stancel Corral—*locale* NM-5
West Stanfield Sch—*school* OR-9
West Stanislaus Main Canal—*canal* CA-9
West Stanly HS—*school* NC-3
West Star Ch—*church* IA-7
West Stark—*unorg reg* ND-7
West Star Sch (historical)—*school* (2) MO-7
*West State Line Creek* TX-5
West Statesville (census name Statesville West)—*other* NC-3
West Statesville (P.O.)—*uninc pl* NC-3
**West Statesville (subdivision)**—*pop pl* NC-3
**West Stayton**—*pop pl* OR-9
West Steadman Ranch—*locale* ID-8
West Steel Creek—*stream* ID-8
**West Steels Corners**—*pop pl* OH-6
West Steep Hill Valley—*valley* AZ-5
**West Stephentown**—*pop pl* NY-2
**West Sterling**—*pop pl* IL-6
**West Sterling**—*pop pl* MA-1
West Sterling Cem—*cemetery* MA-1
West Steuben Creek—*stream* CO-8
*West Steubenville* OH-6
**West Stewartstown**—*pop pl* NH-1
**West St. James**—*pop pl* NY-2
West St. Mary's Manor—*hist pl* MD-2
*West Stockbridge* MA-1
**West Stockbridge**—*pop pl* MA-1
West Stockbridge Cem—*cemetery* MA-1
**West Stockbridge Center**—*pop pl* MA-1
*West Stockbridge Centre* MA-1
West Stockbridge Hill—*summit* NY-2
West Stockbridge Mtn—*summit* MA-1
**West Stockbridge (Town of)**—*pop pl* MA-1
**West Stockholm**—*pop pl* NY-2
West Stockholm Hist Dist—*hist pl* NY-2
West Stone Cabin Valley—*valley* NV-8
West Stone Hill Sch—*school* IA-7
Weststone Hollow—*valley* TN-4
West Stone House Creek—*stream* KS-7
**West Stonington**—*pop pl* ME-1
*West Stony Creek* ID-8
*West Stony Creek* NY-2
West Stony Creek—*stream* NY-2
*West Stooping Bush Island* CT-1
**West Store Crossroads**—*pop pl* SC-3
West Store (historical)—*locale* AL-4
**West Storm Lake**—*pop pl* IA-7
**West Stoughton**—*pop pl* MA-1
**West St. Paul**—*pop pl* MN-6
West Strait Creek—*stream* VA-3
West Strand Hist Dist—*hist pl* NY-2
**West Strang Junction**—*pop pl* NE-7
West Stratton Oil Field—*oilfield* TX-5
West Strawberry Creek—*stream* SD-7
West Strawberry Sch (historical)—*school* MO-7
West Street Cem—*cemetery* MA-1
West Street Cem—*cemetery* OH-6
West Street District—*hist pl* MA-1
West Street Hist Dist—*hist pl* ME-1
West Street Sch—*hist pl* CT-1
West Street Sch—*school* (2) MA-1
West Street Sch—*school* NY-2
West Street Sch—*school* VT-1
West Stringer—*stream* CA-9
West Stringer Saddle—*gap* CA-9
West Strip East Fork Mujares Creek—*stream* TX-5
West Sturgeon Lake—*lake* MN-6
**West Suffield**—*pop pl* CT-1
West Suffield Cem—*cemetery* CT-1
West Suffield Mtn—*summit* CT-1
West Sugar Creek—*stream* OK-5
West Sugarloaf—*summit* CT-1
*West Sugarloaf Creek* AR-4
West Sugarloaf Creek—*stream* AR-4
*West Sugar Orchard Creek* AR-4
**West Sullivan**—*pop pl* ME-1
West Sullivan (Township of)—*fmr MCD* AR-4
West Sully—*unorg reg* SD-7
West Sulphur Branch—*stream* TX-5
West Sulphur Creek—*stream* CA-9
West Sulphur Creek—*stream* MO-7
*West Summerland Key* FL-3
West Summerland Key—*island* FL-3
*West Summerland Keys* FL-3
**West Summerville**—*pop pl* GA-3
**West Summit**—*pop pl* MA-1
West Summit—*summit* UT-8
West Summit Cem—*cemetery* KS-7
West Summit Sch—*school* UT-8
**West Sumner**—*pop pl* ME-1
**West Sumpter**—*pop pl* MI-6
West Sunburg Lake—*lake* MN-6
**West Sunbury**—*pop pl* PA-2
West Sunbury Borough—*civil* PA-2
West Sunbury Cem—*cemetery* PA-2
West Sunflower Windmill—*locale* TX-5
West Sunny Hill Ch—*church* MS-4
West Sunny Side Ch—*church* GA-3
West Sunset Mtn—*summit* AZ-5
**West Sunset View Estates Subdivision**—*pop pl* UT-8
West Surry Cem—*cemetery* ME-1
West Sussex—*uninc pl* WI-6
West Sussex-Dugout Oil Field—*oilfield* WY-8
**West Sutton**—*pop pl* MA-1
West Swag—*basin* UT-8
West Swale—*valley* UT-8
West Swamp Brook—*stream* CT-1
West Swamp Ch—*church* PA-2
*West Swamp Creek* PA-2
West Swan Creek—*stream* NC-3
West Swan River—*stream* MN-6
West Swansea Mine—*mine* UT-8
**West Swanton**—*pop pl* VT-1
West Swanzey—*CDP* NH-1
West Swanzey Covered Bridge—*hist pl* NH-1
West Sweden—*locale* TX-5
**West Sweden**—*pop pl* NY-2
**West Sweden**—*pop pl* WI-6
West Sweden Cem—*cemetery* NY-2
**West Sweden (Town of)**—*pop pl* WI-6
*West Sweetwater Creek* ID-8
West Sweetwater Gulch—*valley* WY-8
West Swift Run—*stream* VA-3
West Sycamore Canyon—*valley* CA-9
West Sycamore Creek—*stream* TX-5
West Sycamore Landing—*locale* TN-4
West Sylvan Sch—*school* OR-9
West Table—*summit* (2) NE-7
West Table Creek—*stream* WY-8
West Tabor Well—*well* NV-8
West Tabyago Canyon—*valley* UT-8
**West Tacoma**—*pop pl* WA-9
**West Taghkanic**—*pop pl* NY-2
West Tallahala Creek—*stream* MS-4
West Tallahatchie HS—*school* MS-4
*West Talla HS* MS-4
West Tamarack—*locale* MI-6
**West Tampa**—*pop pl* FL-3
West Tampa Hist Dist—*hist pl* FL-3
West Tampa JHS—*school* FL-3
West Tank—*reservoir* (13) AZ-5
West Tank—*reservoir* (13) NM-5
West Tank—*reservoir* (7) TX-5
West Tank Hollow Prospect—*mine* TN-4
West Tanks—*reservoir* (2) NM-5
West Tank 16—*reservoir* NM-5
West Tappan—*locale* MI-6
West Tap Sublateral—*canal* ID-8
*West Tarboro* NC-3
**West Tarboro**—*pop pl* NC-3
**West Tarboro (subdivision)**—*pop pl* NC-3
**West Tarentum**—*pop pl* PA-2
West Targhee Creek—*stream* ID-8
West Tarkio Creek—*stream* IA-7
West Tarkio Creek—*stream* MO-7
West Tarter Gulch—*valley* OR-9
*West Tate Elem Sch* MS-4
West Tate Sch—*school* MS-4
**West Tatnuck (subdivision)**—*pop pl* MA-1
West Tavaputs Plateau—*flat* UT-8
**West Tawakoni**—*pop pl* TX-5
West Taylor Ditch—*canal* AZ-5
**West Taylor (Township of)**—*pop pl* PA-2
West Technical Education Center—*school* FL-3
West Technical HS—*school* OH-6
West Tehama (CCD)—*cens area* CA-9
West Tehuacana Creek—*stream* TX-5
West Telephone Canyon—*valley* NM-5
West Telfair Acad—*school* GA-3
West Telford—*uninc pl* PA-2
West Tellico School—*locale* OK-5
West Tempe—*locale* TX-5
West Tempe Creek—*stream* TX-5
**West Temple**—*pop pl* TX-5
West Temple, The—*summit* UT-8
**West Temple Addition (subdivision)**—*pop pl* UT-8
*West Temple Creek* TX-5
*West Tencent Creek* OR-9
West Ten Cent Creek—*stream* OR-9
**West Tenino**—*pop pl* WA-9
West Tenmile Creek—*stream* CO-8
West Tenmile Creek—*stream* TX-5
West Tennessee Coll (historical)—*school* TN-4
West Tennessee Creek—*stream* CO-8
West Tennessee Fairgrounds—*locale* TN-4
West Tennessee Lakes—*lake* CO-8
*West Tennessee State Normal School* TN-4
*West Tennessee State Teachers'College* TN-4
West Tensleep Creek—*stream* WY-8
West Tensleep Lake—*lake* WY-8
West Tent Canyon—*valley* UT-8
West Tepee Canyon—*valley* SD-7
West Tepetate Oil and Gas Field—*oilfield* LA-4
West Terrace Elementary and JHS—*school* IN-6
West Terrace Park—*park* MO-7
*West Terrace Sch* IN-6
West Terrapin Creek—*stream* OK-5
**West Terre Haute**—*pop pl* IN-6
West Terre Hill Sch—*school* PA-2
West Terrell (CCD)—*cens area* TX-5
West Terrell Creek—*stream* MT-8
**West Texarkana**—*pop pl* TX-5
West Texarkana Ch—*church* TX-5
West Texas (CCD)—*cens area* OK-5
West Texas Childrens Home—*building* TX-5
West Texas Fairground—*locale* TX-5
West Texas Hosp—*hospital* TX-5
West Texas State Coll—*school* TX-5
*West Texas State College* TX-5
West Texas Street Park—*park* CA-9
West Texas Utilities Office—*hist pl* TX-5
West Texas (West Texas State College)—*uninc pl* TX-5
West Third Street Hist Dist—*hist pl* IA-7
West Thirteen Ditch—*canal* NM-5
West Thompson—*locale* CT-1
West Thompson Cem—*cemetery* CT-1
West Thompson Lake—*reservoir* CT-1
*West Thompson Rsvr* CT-1
**West Thornton**—*pop pl* NH-1
West Thornton Creek—*stream* OR-9
*West Thornton-Walnut Grove Gas Field* CA-9
West Thorofare Bay—*bay* NC-3
West Three Creeks—*stream* AR-4
West Threemile Creek—*stream* ID-8
*West Thrumb* WY-8
West Thumb—*bay* WY-8
West Thumb—*locale* WY-8
West Thumb Geyser Basin—*basin* WY-8
*West Thumb Junction* WY-8
West Thunder Creek—*stream* WI-6
West Thurmon Creek—*stream* ID-8
**West Tiana**—*pop pl* NY-2
West Tidwell Canyon—*valley* UT-8
West Tidwell Spring—*spring* UT-8
West Tiger Creek—*stream* MS-4
West Tiger Mtn—*summit* WA-9
West Timber Canyon—*valley* CO-8
West Timber Creek—*stream* WY-8
West Timberlake Creek—*stream* CO-8
West Timothy Lake—*lake* UT-8
West Tin House Tank—*reservoir* AZ-5
West Tinmouth—*locale* VT-1
*West Tintic Mountain Range* UT-8
West Tintic Mtns—*range* UT-8
**West Tisbury**—*pop pl* MA-1
**West Tisbury (Town of)**—*pop pl* MA-1
West Tocoi—*locale* FL-3
West Todd—*unorg reg* SD-7
West Toe—*summit* CO-8
West Togiak Lake—*lake* AK-9
*West Toledo* OH-6
West Toledo Yard—*locale* OH-6
West Toll Gate Creek—*stream* CO-8
West Tom Green (CCD)—*cens area* TX-5
West Tom Patterson Canyon—*valley* UT-8
West Topisaw Creek—*stream* MS-4
**West Topsham**—*pop pl* VT-1
West Toqua Lake—*lake* MN-6
West Torch River—*stream* WI-6
West Toro Creek—*stream* LA-4
**West Torresdale**—*pop pl* PA-2
West Torrey Creek—*stream* WY-8
*West Torrington* CT-1
**West Torrington**—*pop pl* CT-1
West Torrington Cem—*cemetery* CT-1
West Tower Mine—*mine* CA-9
*West Town* OH-6
Westtown—*locale* PA-2
**Westtown**—*pop pl* NY-2
**Westtown Acres**—*pop pl* PA-2
West Town Corner Lake—*lake* MI-6
Westtown Dam—*dam* PA-2
West Town Drain—*canal* MI-6
West Towne Ch—*church* TN-4
West Towne Plaza Shop Ctr—*locale* (2) TN-4
West Town Historic Commercial and Industrial District—*hist pl* MI-6
Westtown Lake—*reservoir* PA-2
**West Town Landing**—*pop pl* MA-1
West Town Mall—*locale* TN-4
West Townsand Windmill—*locale* NM-5
Westtown Sch—*school* PA-2
**West Townsend**—*pop pl* MA-1
**West Townsend**—*pop pl* VT-1
**West Townshend**—*pop pl* VT-1
West Townshend Stone Arch Bridge—*hist pl* VT-1
West Townshend Village Hist Dist—*hist pl* VT-1
West Township—*civil* MO-7
West Township—*fmr MCD* IA-7
West Township—*locale* NY-2
**West (Township of)**—*pop pl* (2) IL-6
**West (Township of)**—*pop pl* IN-6
**West (Township of)**—*pop pl* OH-6
**West (Township of)**—*pop pl* PA-2
*West Township School* IN-6
Westtown Shop Ctr—*locale* OH-6
*Westtown Thornburg School* PA-2
Westtown-Thornbury Sch—*school* PA-2
**Westtown (Township of)**—*pop pl* PA-2
West Toxaway Creek—*stream* SC-3
West Trace Creek—*stream* AR-4
West Tract Ch—*church* AR-4
West Trade Sch—*school* OH-6
West Trade Street—*uninc pl* NC-3
West Trail—*trail* MD-2
West Trail Draw—*valley* MT-8
West Trail Draw Spring—*spring* MT-8
West Trail Lake—*lake* NM-5
West Trap Tank—*reservoir* TX-5
West Traverse (Township of)—*civ div* MI-6
West Tremont—*locale* ME-1
**West Trenton**—*pop pl* ME-1
**West Trenton**—*pop pl* NJ-2
West Trenton Station—*hist pl* NJ-2
West Trenton Station—*locale* NJ-2
West Triangle Tank—*reservoir* AZ-5
West Triangle Windmill—*locale* WY-8
West Trinity Ch—*church* IN-6
West Trinity Creek—*stream* OR-9
West Tritt Lake—*lake* WA-9
West Trout Brook—*stream* NY-2
West Trout Creek—*stream* CO-8
West Trout Lake—*lake* MI-6
West Troy—*locale* IA-7
West Truro Sch—*school* IL-6
West Tschuddi Gulch—*valley* CO-8
West Tualatin View Sch—*school* OR-9
West Tub—*well* NM-5
West Tub Mountain Rsvr—*reservoir* OR-9
**West Tuckerton**—*pop pl* NJ-2
**West Tuckerton Landing**—*pop pl* NJ-2
West Tulare Lands Ranch—*locale* CA-9
West Tule Creek—*stream* CA-9
West Tuleta Oil Field—*oilfield* TX-5
West Tuley Springs—*spring* CA-9
West Tulip Creek—*stream* MS-4
**West Tulsa**—*pop pl* OK-5
West Turbine Lateral—*canal* WA-9
**West Turin (Town of)**—*pop pl* NY-2
West Turkey Canyon—*valley* CO-8
*West Turkey Creek* LA-4
West Turkey Creek—*stream* AL-4
West Turkey Creek—*stream* AZ-5
West Turkey Creek—*stream* KS-7
West Turkey Creek—*stream* LA-4
West Turkey Creek—*stream* (2) TX-5
West Turkey Creek Campground—*park* AZ-5
West Turtle Shoal—*bar* FL-3
West Twelfth Sch—*school* NE-7
West Twin—*summit* ID-8
West Twin Bay—*bay* AK-9
West Twin Brook—*stream* ME-1
West Twin Butte—*summit* ND-7
West Twin Butte—*summit* WA-9
West Twin Creek—*stream* AR-4
West Twin Creek—*stream* CA-9
West Twin Creek—*stream* KS-7
West Twin Creek—*stream* (2) MT-8
West Twin Creek—*stream* UT-8
West Twin Creek—*stream* (2) WA-9
West Twin Creek—*stream* WY-8
West Twin Glacier—*glacier* AK-9
West Twin Grove Ch—*church* IL-6
West Twin Gulch—*valley* CO-8
*West Twin Lake* MI-6
West Twin Lake—*lake* (2) AK-9
West Twin Lake—*lake* IA-7
West Twin Lake—*lake* (2) MI-6
West Twin Lake—*lake* (5) MN-6
West Twin Lake—*lake* (2) NE-7
West Twin Lake—*lake* (2) WI-6
West Twin Lake State Game Mngmt Area—*park* IA-7
*West Twin Peak* AZ-5
West Twin Peak—*summit* AK-9
West Twin Peak—*summit* AZ-5
*West Twin Pup Lake* MI-6
*West Twin River* WI-6
**West Twin River**—*pop pl* MD-2
West Twin River—*stream* WA-9
West Twin River—*stream* WI-6
**West Twin River Beach**—*pop pl* MD-2
West Twin River County Park—*park* WI-6
West Twin Sisters Creek—*stream* NM-5
West Twin Wash—*stream* AZ-5
West Twin Wash—*stream* CO-8
West Two Creek—*stream* CO-8
West Two River—*stream* (2) MN-6
West Two River Rsvr—*reservoir* MN-6
West Two Tank—*reservoir* AZ-5
West Ullensvang Cem—*cemetery* IA-7
West Underwood Windmill—*locale* TX-5
*West Union* IN-6
*West Union* KS-7
West Union—*hist pl* MN-6
West Union—*locale* NY-2
West Union—*locale* OR-9
West Union—*locale* (2) TN-4
**West Union**—*pop pl* IL-6
**West Union**—*pop pl* IN-6
**West Union**—*pop pl* IA-7
**West Union**—*pop pl* MN-6
**West Union**—*pop pl* MS-4
**West Union**—*pop pl* OH-6
**West Union**—*pop pl* PA-2
**West Union**—*pop pl* SC-3
**West Union**—*pop pl* WV-2
West Union Baptist Ch—*church* TN-4
*West Union Baptist Church* MS-4
West Union Baptist Church—*hist pl* OR-9
West Union Bridge—*hist pl* IN-6
West Union Canal—*canal* UT-8
West Union Canyon—*valley* NV-8
West Union Cem—*cemetery* (2) IN-6
West Union Cem—*cemetery* (3) IA-7
West Union Cem—*cemetery* KS-7
West Union Cem—*cemetery* MS-4
West Union Cem—*cemetery* (2) NE-7
West Union Cem—*cemetery* ND-7
West Union Cem—*cemetery* (2) OH-6
West Union Cem—*cemetery* OR-9
West Union Cem—*cemetery* PA-2
West Union Cem—*cemetery* TN-4
West Union Ch—*church* AL-4
West Union Ch—*church* AR-4
West Union Ch—*church* (2) GA-3
West Union Ch—*church* (2) IL-6
West Union Ch—*church* (2) IN-6
West Union Ch—*church* IA-7
West Union Ch—*church* KS-7
West Union Ch—*church* (2) KY-4
West Union Ch—*church* MN-6
West Union Ch—*church* (2) MS-4
West Union Ch—*church* (4) MO-7
West Union Ch—*church* NY-2
West Union Ch—*church* ND-7
West Union Ch—*church* (4) OH-6
West Union Ch—*church* (2) PA-2
West Union Ch—*church* (2) WV-2
West Union Creek—*stream* SD-7
West Union Elem Sch—*school* MS-4
West Union Hill—*summit* WV-2
**West Union (historical)**—*pop pl* IA-7
West Union Lake—*lake* MN-6
West Union (Magisterial District)—*fmr MCD* WV-2
West Union Park—*park* IL-6
West Union Presbyterian Church—*hist pl* OH-6
West Union Sch—*hist pl* OH-6
West Union Sch—*school* (6) IL-6
West Union Sch—*school* KS-7
West Union Sch—*school* MS-4
West Union Sch—*school* (2) MO-7
West Union Sch—*school* (2) NE-7
West Union Sch—*school* OR-9
West Union Sch (historical)—*school* TN-4
*West Union Station* IN-6
West Union Street Hist Dist—*hist pl* NC-3
**West Union (Town of)**—*pop pl* NY-2
*West Union Township* KS-7
**West Union Township**—*pop pl* NE-7
**West Union (Township of)**—*pop pl* MN-6
*West United Methodist Ch* AL-4
West Unit Highline Canal—*canal* WA-9
West Unity—*locale* NH-1
**West Unity**—*pop pl* OH-6
**West University Place**—*pop pl* TX-5
West Univ Hist Dist—*hist pl* AZ-5
**West Upton**—*pop pl* MA-1
West Ute Canyon—*valley* CO-8
West Ute Creek—*stream* CO-8
West Ute Lake—*lake* CO-8
West Ute Mesa—*summit* CO-8
West Utica—*uninc pl* NY-2
West Utica Sch—*school* MI-6
Westvaco—*locale* WY-8
**Westvaco**—*pop pl* KY-4
**Westvaco**—*pop pl* WY-8
*Westvaco Chlorine Products Company* CA-9
Westvaco Corporation—*facility* KY-4
Westvaco Mine—*mine* ID-8
Westvaco Mine—*mine* NM-5
**Westvaco Section**—*pop pl* WY-8
Westvaco Shaft No 3—*locale* WY-8
Westvaco Siding—*locale* ID-8
**West Vail**—*pop pl* CO-8
West Valdor Gulch—*valley* CA-9
**West Valdosta**—*pop pl* GA-3
**Westvale**—*pop pl* NY-2
West Vale (CCD)—*cens area* OR-9
Westvale Elem Sch—*school* IN-6
Westvale (historical P.O.)—*locale* MA-1
Westvale Presbyterian Ch—*church* UT-8
Westvale Sch—*school* UT-8
West Valle Cem—*cemetery* MN-6
**West Valley**—*pop pl* MT-8
**West Valley**—*pop pl* NY-2
**West Valley**—*pop pl* PA-2
**West Valley**—*pop pl* UT-8
West Valley—*valley* UT-8
West Valley—*valley* WA-9
West Valley Branch—*stream* TX-5
West Valley (CCD)—*cens area* CA-9
West Valley Ch—*church* AR-4
**West Valley City**—*pop pl* UT-8
West Valley City Interchange—*crossing* ND-7
West Valley Creek—*stream* CA-9
West Valley Creek—*stream* WA-9
West Valley Dam—*dam* CA-9
West Valley Falls—*uninc pl* NY-2
West Valley HS—*school* AK-9
West Valley HS—*school* (2) WA-9
West Valley Junior Coll—*school* CA-9
West Valley Ranch—*locale* CA-9
West Valley Rsvr—*reservoir* CA-9
West Valley Sch—*school* CA-9
West Valley Sch—*school* MI-6
West Valley Sch (historical)—*school* MO-7
West Valley Sch (historical)—*school* PA-2
West Valley Seventh Day Adventist Ch—*church* UT-8
West Valley Spring—*spring* CA-9
**West Valley (Township of)**—*pop pl* MN-6
West Valley Windmill—*locale* TX-5
West Vance Creek—*stream* MT-8
West Vancorum—*locale* CO-8
**West Vandergrift**—*pop pl* PA-2
**West Van Hooris**—*pop pl* WV-2
West Van Lear—*locale* KY-4
**West Van Lear (RR name Van Lear Junction)**—*pop pl* KY-4
**West Vanvoorhis**—*pop pl* WV-2
West Van Zandt Sch—*school* TX-5
West Vat Windmill—*locale* TX-5
West Vaya Dam—*dam* CO-8
West Velma Oil Field—*oilfield* OK-5
West Venida—*locale* CA-9
West Verde Creek—*stream* TX-5
West Vermillion Cem—*cemetery* SD-7
Westvern—*uninc pl* CA-9
*West Vernon* NJ-2
West Vernon—*locale* PA-2
West Vernon—*uninc pl* TX-5
West Vernon Ave Sch—*school* CA-9
West Vernon Cem—*cemetery* SD-7
**West Vero Beach**—*pop pl* FL-3
West Verona Cem—*cemetery* MN-6
West Vidalia—*uninc pl* GA-3
West Vidauri Oil Field—*oilfield* TX-5
West Vidler Creek—*stream* OR-9
West Vienna—*other* NY-2
**West Vienna**—*pop pl* IL-6
West Vienna Ch—*church* MI-6
West Vienna United Methodist Church—*hist pl* MI-6
*West View* OH-6
*Westview* OH-6
Westview—*CDP* FL-3
Westview—*CDP* SC-3
Westview—*hist pl* AL-4
West View—*hist pl* OH-6
Westview—*locale* NY-2
West View—*locale* VA-3
**Westview**—*pop pl* IL-6
**Westview**—*pop pl* IA-7
**Westview**—*pop pl* KY-4
**Westview**—*pop pl* MA-1
**West View**—*pop pl* MS-4
**Westview**—*pop pl* MO-7
**West View**—*pop pl* NJ-2
**Westview**—*pop pl* NC-3
**West View**—*pop pl* OH-6
**Westview**—*pop pl* OH-6
**West View**—*pop pl* PA-2
**West View**—*pop pl* SC-3
**West View**—*pop pl* (2) TN-4
**West View**—*pop pl* VT-1
**Westview**—*pop pl* VA-3
**West View**—*pop pl* VA-3
Westview—*uninc pl* NY-2
Westview—*uninc pl* TX-5
**Westview Acres**—*pop pl* CT-1
*Westview Baptist Ch* AL-4
Westview Baptist Ch—*church* (2) AL-4
Westview Baptist Ch—*church* FL-3
Westview Baptist Ch—*church* KS-7
Westview Baptist Ch—*church* MS-4
West View Baptist Ch—*church* (2) TN-4
West View Borough—*civil* PA-2
Westview Boys Home—*building* OK-5
West View Camp—*locale* PA-2
West View Canal—*canal* UT-8
Westview Cem—*cemetery* (2) AL-4
Westview Cem—*cemetery* AR-4
West View Cem—*cemetery* FL-3
Westview Cem—*cemetery* FL-3
West View Cem—*cemetery* (2) GA-3
Westview Cem—*cemetery* (2) GA-3
West View Cem—*cemetery* (2) GA-3
Westview Cem—*cemetery* GA-3
West View Cem—*cemetery* (2) GA-3
Westview Cem—*cemetery* (2) IA-7
Westview Cem—*cemetery* MA-1
Westview Cem—*cemetery* (2) NH-1
Westview Cem—*cemetery* (2) NY-2
Westview Cem—*cemetery* NC-3
Westview Cem—*cemetery* ND-7
Westview Cem—*cemetery* OH-6
West View Cem—*cemetery* OH-6
Westview Cem—*cemetery* (3) PA-2
West View Cem—*cemetery* (2) PA-2
Westview Cem—*cemetery* (2) SC-3
West View Cem—*cemetery* SC-3
Westview Cem—*cemetery* (2) SC-3
Westview Cem—*cemetery* TN-4
West View Cem—*cemetery* TN-4
West View Cem—*cemetery* TX-5
West View Cem—*cemetery* (2) VA-3
Westview Cem—*cemetery* VA-3
West View Cem—*cemetery* VA-3
**Westview Cemetery**—*pop pl* GA-3
*Westview Ch* IN-6
Westview Ch—*church* AL-4
Westview Ch—*church* AR-4
Westview Ch—*church* FL-3
West View Ch—*church* GA-3
Westview Ch—*church* GA-3
Westview Ch—*church* KS-7
Westview Ch—*church* KY-4
Westview Ch—*church* LA-4
Westview Ch—*church* (4) NC-3
Westview Ch—*church* OK-5
West View Ch—*church* PA-2
Westview Ch—*church* (2) TN-4
Westview Ch—*church* TX-5
West View Ch—*church* VA-3
Westview Chapel—*church* GA-3
Westview Chapel—*church* TN-4
Westview Christian Ch—*church* IN-6
Westview Christian Sch—*school* FL-3
Westview Country Club—*locale* FL-3
Westview Country Club—*other* WI-6
Westview County Home—*locale* NE-7
West View Elem Sch—*school* IN-6
Westview Elem Sch—*school* IN-6
Westview Elem Sch—*school* KS-7
West View Elem Sch—*school* PA-2
West View Elem Sch—*school* (2) TN-4
Westview Elem Sch—*school* TN-4
West View Elem Sch—*school* TN-4
Westview Gardens—*cemetery* NC-3
Westview Gardens Cem—*cemetery* AL-4
Westview Gardens Ch of Christ—*church* AL-4
**Westview Gardens (subdivision)**—*pop pl* AL-4
West View Golf Course—*locale* PA-2
**Westview Heights**—*pop pl* CT-1
**Westview Heights**—*pop pl* PA-2
**Westview Heights**—*pop pl* TN-4
West View Heights Chapel—*church* AL-4
**Westview Hills**—*pop pl* VA-3
Westview HS—*school* TN-4
Westview JHS—*school* FL-3
Westview Junior-Senior HS—*school* IN-6
**Westview Manor**—*pop pl* NY-2
Westview Memorial Gardens—*cemetery* NC-3
Westview Park—*park* IL-6
Westview Park—*park* IA-7
Westview Park—*park* MN-6
West View Park—*park* PA-2
Westview Park—*park* TN-4
**Westview Park**—*pop pl* MD-2
**West View Park**—*pop pl* TN-4
**Westview Park (subdivision)**—*pop pl* MA-1
**West View Park Subdivision**—*pop pl* UT-8
*West View Sch* TN-4
West View Sch—*school* AL-4
West View Sch—*school* CA-9
Westview Sch—*school* CA-9
Westview Sch—*school* FL-3
Westview Sch—*school* IL-6
West View Sch—*school* IL-6
West View Sch—*school* IA-7
Westview Sch—*school* MI-6
Westview Sch—*school* (2) MN-6
West View Sch—*school* MO-7
Westview Sch—*school* (2) MO-7
Westview Sch—*school* MT-8
Westview Sch—*school* (3) OH-6
Westview Sch—*school* (2) TN-4
Westview Sch—*school* VA-3
Westview Sch—*school* (2) WA-9
Westview Sch (abandoned)—*school* PA-2
West View Schoolhouse—*hist pl* VA-3
**West View Shores**—*pop pl* MD-2
West View Station—*locale* NJ-2
**Westview (subdivision)**—*pop pl* AL-4
**Westview (subdivision)**—*pop pl* DE-2
**Westview (subdivision)**—*pop pl* (2) NC-3
**Westview (subdivision)**—*pop pl* TN-4
**Westview Subdivision**—*pop pl* UT-8
**Westview Terrace (subdivision)**—*pop pl* NC-3
**Westview Terrace Subdivision**—*pop pl* UT-8
West View United Methodist Ch—*church* TN-4
West Village—*locale* NJ-2
West Village—*locale* NM-5
**West Village**—*pop pl* CO-8
**West Village**—*pop pl* (2) MA-1
**West Village**—*pop pl* NM-5
West Village—*post sta* NY-2
West Village Ch—*church* IL-6
West Village Commons (Shop Ctr)—*locale* FL-3
West Village Creek—*stream* IL-6
West Village Creek—*stream* SC-3
West Village District—*hist pl* MI-6
West Village Green—*park* NY-2
West Village Hist Dist—*hist pl* NY-2
West Village Mills Oil Field—*oilfield* TX-5
West Village Plaza (Shop Ctr)—*locale* MO-7

Westville ... CT-1
Westville ... IN-6
Westville ... NJ-2
Westville—locale ... AR-4
Westville—locale ... CA-9
Westville—locale ... MO-7
Westville—locale ... TX-5
**Westville**—pop pl ... CT-1
**Westville**—pop pl ... FL-3
**Westville**—pop pl ... IL-6
**Westville**—pop pl ... IN-6
**Westville**—pop pl (2) ... MA-1
**Westville**—pop pl ... MI-6
**Westville**—pop pl (2) ... MS-4
**Westville**—pop pl ... NH-1
**Westville**—pop pl (2) ... NJ-2
**Westville**—pop pl (2) ... NY-2
**Westville**—pop pl (2) ... OH-6
**Westville**—pop pl ... OK-5
**Westville**—pop pl ... PA-2
**Westville**—pop pl (2) ... SC-3
Westville (CCD)—cens area ... OK-5
Westville (CCD)—cens area ... SC-3
Westville Cem—cemetery ... CT-1
Westville Cem—cemetery ... FL-3
Westville Cem—cemetery ... MA-1
Westville Cem—cemetery ... MS-4
Westville Cem—cemetery ... OH-6
Westville Cem—cemetery ... OK-5
Westville Cem—cemetery ... TX-5
Westville Cem—cemetery ... VT-1
Westville Cem—cemetery ... WI-6
**Westville Center**—pop pl ... NY-2
Westville Ch—church ... IL-6
Westville Ch—church ... VA-3
Westville Congregational Church—hist pl ... MA-1
Westville Creek—stream ... MS-4
Westville Dam—dam ... MA-1
Westville Elem Sch—school ... IN-6
**Westville Grove**—pop pl ... NJ-2
Westville HS—school ... IN-6
**Westville Lake**—pop pl ... OH-6
Westville Lake—reservoir ... IL-6
Westville Lake—reservoir ... MA-1
Westville Lake—reservoir ... OH-6
Westville Landmark Ch—church ... OK-5
Westville (Magisterial District)—fmr MCD ... VA-3
**Westville Oaks (Woodbury Terrace)**—pop pl ... NJ-2
Westville Post Office (historical)—building ... MS-4
Westville Rsvr ... MA-1
Westville Rsvr—reservoir ... OK-5
**Westville (Town of)**—pop pl ... NY-2
**Westville (West Constable)**—pop pl ... NY-2
West Vincent ... PA-2
West Vincent Post Office (historical)—building ... PA-2
**West Vincent (Township of)**—pop pl ... PA-2
**West Vindex**—pop pl ... MD-2
**West Viola**—pop pl ... KY-4
**West Virginia**—pop pl ... MN-6
West Virginia Capitol Complex—hist pl ... WV-2
West Virginia Central Junction—locale ... WV-2
West Virginia Fork Dunkard Creek—stream ... WV-2
West Virginia Fork Fish Creek—stream ... WV-2
West Virginia Gulch—valley ... CO-8
West Virginia Industrial Sch for Boys—school ... WV-2
West Virginia Institute of Technology—school ... WV-2
**West Virginia No. 2**—pop pl ... WV-2
West Virginia State Capitol—building ... WV-2
West Virginia State Coll—school ... WV-2
West Virginia State Prison For Women—other ... WV-2
West Virginia Univ—school ... WV-2
West Virginia Univ Agronomy Farm—school ... WV-2
West Virginia Univ Dairy Farm—school ... WV-2
West Virginia University Med Ctr—hospital ... WV-2
West Virginia Univ Experimental Farm—school ... WV-2
West Virginia Univ Experimental Station—school ... WV-2
West Virginia Univ Horticultural Farm—school ... WV-2
West Virginia Univ Parkerburg Branch—school ... WV-2
West Virginia Univ Poultry Farm—school ... WV-2
West Virginia Westeyan Coll—school ... WV-2
West Virgin Peak ... NV-8
West Vly Creek—stream ... NY-2
West Volusia Memorial Hosp—hospital ... FL-3
West Vulcan Mine—mine ... MI-6
West Wachusett Brook—stream ... MA-1
West Waco JHS—school ... TX-5
West Waddaquadduck Mountain Mountain ... MA-1
West Waddaquodduck ... MA-1
West Waddell Creek—stream ... CA-9
West Waha Oil Field—oilfield ... TX-5
West Wailuaiki Stream—stream ... HI-9
West Wailuanui Stream—stream ... HI-9
West Wait Brook—stream ... MA-1
West Wakulla (CCD)—cens area ... FL-3
West Walakalua—civil ... HI-9
**West Waldoboro**—pop pl ... ME-1
West Walker Ch—church ... AL-4
West Walker Ch of Christ ... AL-4
West Walker River—stream ... CA-9
West Walker River—stream ... NV-8
West Walkers Reservoir ... CT-1
West Walker Tank—reservoir ... AZ-5
West Walnut Creek ... NE-7
West Walnut Creek—stream ... IA-7
West Walnut Creek—stream ... NE-7
West Walnut Creek—stream ... TX-5
West Walnut Street Hist Dist—hist pl ... IL-6
**West Walpole**—pop pl ... MA-1
West Walton Sch—school ... GA-3
**West Walworth**—pop pl ... NY-2
West Walworth—unorg reg ... SD-7
West Wanette Oil Field—oilfield ... OK-5
**West Wapole**—pop pl ... MA-1
Westward—post sta ... FL-3
Westward Beach—beach ... CA-9
Westward Bridge—bridge ... VA-3
West Ward Cem—cemetery ... NE-7
Westward Creek—stream ... MD-2
Westward Elem Sch—school ... FL-3
West Ward Elem Sch—school ... IA-7
West Ward Elem Sch—school ... MS-4
West Warden—locale ... WA-9
Westward Ho Country Club—locale ... SD-7
Westward Point—cape ... MD-2
Westward Point—cape ... NC-3
**Westward Quest (Trailer Park)**—pop pl ... AZ-5
**West Wardsboro**—pop pl ... VT-1
West Ward Sch ... IN-6
West Ward Sch—hist pl ... IN-6
Westward Sch—school ... AR-4
West Ward Sch—school ... IN-6
West Ward Sch—school ... MA-1
West Ward Sch—school ... MO-7
West Ward Sch—school (3) ... NE-7
West Ward Sch—school (5) ... TX-5
Westward Siding—locale ... WA-9
**Westward Terrace Subdivision**—pop pl ... UT-8
**West Ware**—pop pl ... MA-1
**West Wareham**—pop pl ... MA-1
West Wareham (historical P.O.)—locale ... MA-1
West Wareham (RR name Tremont)—CDP ... MA-1
**West Warm Springs**—pop pl ... VA-3
West Warm Springs Hist Dist—hist pl ... ID-8
West Warm Springs Oil Field—oilfield ... WY-8
West Warren ... OH-6
West Warren—locale ... PA-2
West Warren—other ... ME-1
**West Warren**—pop pl ... MA-1
**West Warren**—pop pl ... UT-8
West Warren Cem—cemetery ... UT-8
West Warren Ch—church ... WV-2
West Warren Creek—stream ... OK-5
West Warren Mill Pond Dam—dam ... MA-1
West Warrior Creek—stream ... ID-8
West Warrior Peak—summit ... ID-8
**West Warwick**—pop pl ... RI-1
**West Warwick (Town of)**—pop pl ... RI-1
West Wash—stream (2) ... AZ-5
West Washabaugh—unorg reg ... SD-7
West Washacum Pond ... MA-1
West Washerwoman Shoal—bar ... FL-3
West Washington—locale ... ME-1
West Washington Ave Hist Dist—hist pl ... AR-4
West Washington Elem Sch—school ... IN-6
West Washington Hist Dist—hist pl ... IN-6
West Washington Junior-Senior HS—school ... IN-6
West Washington Oil Field—oilfield ... OK-5
West Washington Sch—school ... MO-7
West Washington Street Pumping Station—hist pl ... IN-6
**West Washington Township**—pop pl ... KS-7
Westwater—locale ... UT-8
Westwater Arroyo—stream ... NM-5
West Waterbury Island ... CT-1
West Water Canyon ... NE-7
West Water Canyon—valley ... AZ-5
West Water Canyon—valley ... ID-8
Westwater Canyon—valley ... UT-8
Westwater Canyon Archeol District—hist pl ... UT-8
West Water Creek ... MS-4
West Water Creek—stream ... NE-7
Westwater Creek—stream (2) ... UT-8
Westwater Ditch—canal ... OH-6
West Waterford—locale ... VT-1
West Waterford—uninc pl ... NY-2
West Waterford Sch—school ... IL-6
Westwater Gas Field—oilfield ... UT-8
Westwater Inn Heliport—airport ... WA-9
Westwater Point—cape ... UT-8
Westwater River Ranger Station and Put In Site—locale ... UT-8
Westwater Ruins—locale ... UT-8
West Water Spring—spring ... AZ-5
Westwater Spring—spring ... NM-5
**West Watertown**—pop pl ... MA-1
Westwater Wash ... UT-8
Westwater Wash—stream ... AZ-5
West Waugh Creek—stream ... CO-8
**West Wauregan**—pop pl ... CT-1
West Waushaccum Pond ... MA-1
West Waushacum Pond—lake ... MA-1
Westway—locale ... TX-5
**Westway**—pop pl ... TX-5
Westway Bight—bay ... AK-9
Westway Community Center ... TX-5
**West Wayne**—pop pl ... PA-2
**West Waynesburg**—pop pl ... PA-2
West Wayne Sch—school ... WI-6
Westway Shop Ctr—locale ... KS-7
West Wayside Sch—school ... MT-8
West Weaver Bally ... CA-9
West Weaver Baptist Ch—church ... AL-4
West Weaver Creek—stream ... AR-4
West Weaver Creek—stream ... CA-9
West Webber Creek—stream ... AZ-5
**West Weber**—pop pl ... UT-8
West Weber Canal—canal ... UT-8
West Weber Cem—cemetery ... UT-8
West Weber Fort—locale ... UT-8
West Weber Sch—school ... UT-8
West Weber-Taylor Cemetery ... UT-8
**West Webster**—pop pl ... NY-2
West Webster Lake—lake ... MI-6
West Weed Lake Butte Waterhole—lake ... OR-9
West Weedy Creek—stream ... TX-5
**Westwego**—pop pl ... LA-4
Westwego Drainage Canal—canal ... LA-4
Westwego Oil and Gas Field—oilfield ... LA-4
West Weiser Flat—flat ... ID-8
West Weleetka Oil Field—oilfield ... OK-5
West Well—locale (2) ... NM-5
West Well—oilfield ... TX-5
West Well—well (9) ... AZ-5
West Well—well ... CA-9
West Well—well ... CO-8
West Well—well (20) ... NM-5
West Well—well ... OR-9
West Well—well (8) ... TX-5
West Well Canyon—valley ... TX-5
West Well Corral—locale ... AZ-5
West Well Detention Dam—dam ... AZ-5
**West Wellington**—pop pl ... AL-4
West Wells ... AZ-5
West Wells—well ... AZ-5
West Wells Interchange—crossing ... NV-8
West Wellston Oil And Gas Field—oilfield ... OK-5
West Wenatchee—CDP ... WA-9
West Wendover ... NV-8
West West Branch Schuylkill River—stream ... PA-2
West Weta 91 Dam—dam ... SD-7
West Weta 91 Rsvr—reservoir ... SD-7
West Wets Creek—stream ... MT-8
West Wharf—locale ... CT-1
**West Whately**—pop pl ... MA-1
West Whately Upper Reservoir ... MA-1
**West Wheatcroft**—pop pl ... KY-4
**West Wheatfield (Township of)**—pop pl ... PA-2
**West Wheeling**—pop pl ... OH-6
West Whetstone Creek—stream ... WY-8
West White Beaver Creek—stream ... MT-8
West Whitehorse Rsvr—reservoir ... OR-9
West White Lake Oil and Gas Field—oilfield ... LA-4
West Whiteland Inn—hist pl ... PA-2
West Whiteland Post Office (historical)—building ... PA-2
**West Whiteland (subdivision)**—pop pl ... IN-6
**West Whiteland (Township of)**—pop pl ... PA-2
West Whiteoak Sch (abandoned)—school ... MO-7
West White Pine Mtn—summit ... CO-8
West White Sch (historical)—school ... MO-7
West Whitetail Creek—stream ... AZ-5
West Whiteville Ch—church ... NC-3
**West Whittier**—pop pl ... CA-9
West Whittier-Los Nietos—CDP ... CA-9
West Whittier Sch—school ... CA-9
**Westwick**—pop pl ... GA-3
West Wide Canyon—valley ... CA-9
West Wildcat Creek—stream ... KS-7
West Wildcat Creek—stream ... MO-7
West Wildcat Gap—gap ... GA-3
West Wildcat Knob—summit ... GA-3
West Wild Horse Creek—stream ... CO-8
West Wild Rice Cem—cemetery (2) ... MN-6
**West Wildwood**—pop pl ... NJ-2
West Wiley Spring—spring ... CO-8
West Willcox Interchange—crossing ... AZ-5
**West William Penn**—pop pl ... PA-2
**West Williamsfield**—pop pl ... OH-6
**West Williamson**—pop pl ... WV-2
West Williams Windmill—locale ... TX-5
West Willies—rock ... MA-1
**West Willington**—pop pl ... CT-1
West Willis Creek—stream ... OR-9
West Willisville Oil Field—oilfield ... AR-4
**West Willow**—pop pl ... MI-6
**West Willow**—pop pl ... PA-2
West Willow Creek—stream (6) ... CO-8
West Willow Creek—stream ... ID-8
West Willow Creek—stream ... OK-5
West Willow Creek—stream ... OR-9
West Willow Creek—stream ... UT-8
West Willow Creek—stream (2) ... WY-8
West Willow Creek Rsvr—reservoir ... OR-9
West Willowdale Cem—cemetery ... NE-7
West Willow Peak—summit ... ID-8
West Willow Sch—school ... MI-6
West Willow Spring—spring ... NV-8
West Willow Well—well ... TX-5
**West Wilmerding**—pop pl ... PA-2
West Wilshire Recreation Center—park ... CA-9
West Wilson Elementary School ... TN-4
West Wilson Oil Field—other ... NM-5
West Wilson Plaza Shop Ctr—locale ... TN-4
**West Wilton**—pop pl ... NH-1
West Wind Airp—airport ... NC-3
**West Windham**—pop pl ... NH-1
West Windham Cem—cemetery ... VT-1
West Wind Lake—lake ... MI-6
West Windmill—locale ... AZ-5
West Windmill—locale (22) ... NM-5
West Windmill—locale (43) ... TX-5
West Windmill—well ... AZ-5
West Windmill—well ... NM-5
West Windmills—locale ... NM-5
**West Wind Park**—pop pl ... KY-4
Westwinds Campground—locale ... MI-6
**West Wind Shores**—pop pl ... MA-1
West Windsor—locale ... ME-1
**West Windsor**—pop pl ... MI-6
**West Windsor**—pop pl ... NY-2
**West Windsor (Town of)**—pop pl ... VT-1
**West Windsor (Township of)**—pop pl ... NJ-2
West Winds Trailer Court, The—locale ... AZ-5
**Westwind (subdivision)**—pop pl (2) ... AZ-5
West Windy Prairie—flat ... OK-5
West Windy Sch—school ... KS-7
**West Winfield**—pop pl ... NY-2
**West Winfield**—pop pl ... PA-2
West Wing Mtn—summit ... AZ-5
**West Winslow**—pop pl ... AZ-5
West Winter Creek—stream ... OK-5
West Winter Haven (census name Inwood)—other ... FL-3
West Winterport—locale ... ME-1
West Winterport Ch—church ... ME-1
West Winters Creek—fmr MCD ... NE-7
West Wiota Ch—church ... WI-6
West Woburn—uninc pl ... MA-1
West Wolf Creek ... KS-7
West Wolf Creek—stream ... IA-7
West Wolf Ditch—canal ... WY-8
Westwood ... CO-8
Westwood ... IL-6
Westwood ... MI-6
Westwood (4) ... OH-6
Westwood—CDP ... PA-2
Westwood—hist pl ... AL-4
Westwood—hist pl ... TN-4
Westwood—locale ... MI-6
Westwood—locale ... PA-2
Westwood—locale ... VA-3
Westwood—locale ... WA-9
Westwood—other ... MI-6
**Westwood**—pop pl ... AL-4
**Westwood**—pop pl ... AR-4
**Westwood**—pop pl (2) ... CA-9
**Westwood**—pop pl (2) ... FL-3
**Westwood**—pop pl ... GA-3
**Westwood**—pop pl (2) ... IN-6
**Westwood**—pop pl ... IA-7
**Westwood**—pop pl ... KS-7
**Westwood**—pop pl (2) ... KY-4
**Westwood**—pop pl ... LA-4
**Westwood**—pop pl (2) ... MD-2
**Westwood**—pop pl ... MA-1
**Westwood**—pop pl ... MI-6
**Westwood**—pop pl ... MO-7
**Westwood**—pop pl ... NE-7
**Westwood**—pop pl ... NJ-2
**Westwood**—pop pl ... NY-2
**Westwood**—pop pl (2) ... OH-6
**Westwood**—pop pl ... OR-9
**Westwood**—pop pl (2) ... PA-2
**Westwood**—pop pl (3) ... TN-4
**Westwood**—pop pl ... VA-3
Westwood—post sta ... WA-9
Westwood—uninc pl ... SC-3
Westwood—uninc pl ... TN-4
**Westwood Acres**—pop pl ... CA-9
**Westwood Acres (subdivision)**—pop pl ... FL-3
**Westwood Acres Subdivision**—pop pl ... UT-8
Westwood Baptist Ch ... AL-4
Westwood Baptist Ch—church ... AL-4
Westwood Baptist Ch—church ... IN-6
Westwood Baptist Ch—church ... MS-4
Westwood Baptist Ch—church ... TN-4
Westwood (Boundary Increase)—hist pl ... AL-4
Westwood Branch—stream ... IN-6
West Woodbridge Cem—cemetery ... MI-6
West Woodbridge Ch—church ... MI-6
**West Woodburn**—pop pl ... OR-9
Westwood Camp—locale ... RI-1
Westwood (CCD)—cens area ... CA-9
Westwood Cem—cemetery ... CT-1
Westwood Cem—cemetery ... GA-3
Westwood Cem—cemetery ... IL-6
Westwood Cem—cemetery ... MI-6
Westwood Cem—cemetery ... NJ-2
Westwood Cem—cemetery (2) ... OH-6
Westwood Cem—cemetery ... OK-5
Westwood Ch—church ... AL-4
Westwood Ch—church ... AR-4
Westwood Ch—church ... DE-2
Westwood Ch—church ... FL-3
Westwood Ch—church ... MD-2
Westwood Ch—church ... MN-6
Westwood Ch—church (2) ... NC-3
Westwood Ch—church ... OH-6
West Wood Ch—church ... OH-6
Westwood Ch—church ... SC-3
Westwood Ch—church (3) ... TN-4
Westwood Ch—church ... TX-5
Westwood Ch—church ... VA-3
Westwood Ch of Christ—church ... TN-4
Westwood Christian Day Sch—school ... FL-3
Westwood Christian Sch—school ... AZ-5
Westwood Christian Sch—school (3) ... FL-3
Westwood Common—park ... OH-6
Westwood Corners—locale ... NY-2
Westwood Country Club—other ... MO-7
Westwood Country Club—other ... NY-2
Westwood Country Club—other ... OH-6
Westwood Country Club—other ... TX-5
Westwood Country Club—other ... VA-3
Westwood Creek—stream ... OR-9
Westwood Drive Cem—cemetery ... AL-4
Westwood Elem Sch—school ... PA-2
Westwood Elem Sch—school ... TN-4
Westwood Estates ... OH-6
**Westwood Estates**—pop pl ... MD-2
**Westwood Estates**—pop pl ... TN-4
**Westwood Estates**—pop pl ... VA-3
**Westwood Estates Subdivision**—pop pl (2) ... UT-8
Westwood Farm—hist pl ... KY-4
**Westwood Forest (subdivision)**—pop pl ... NC-3
**Westwood Gardens**—pop pl ... TN-4
**Westwood-Gray Subdivision**—pop pl ... TN-4
**Westwood Heights**—pop pl ... PA-2
Westwood Heights Sch—school ... FL-3
Westwood Heights Sch—school ... MI-6
**Westwood Heights (subdivision)**—pop pl (2) ... NC-3
**Westwood Heights (subdivision)**—pop pl ... TN-4
**Westwood Hills**—pop pl ... KS-7
**Westwood Hills**—pop pl ... PA-2
**Westwood Hills**—pop pl ... TN-4
Westwood Hills Christian Acad—school ... FL-3
Westwood Hills Park—park ... OK-5
Westwood Hills Sch—school ... VA-3
**Westwood Hills (subdivision)**—pop pl ... MA-1
**Westwood Hills (subdivision)**—pop pl ... NC-3
**Westwood Homes**—pop pl ... TN-4
Westwood HS—school ... AZ-5
Westwood HS—school ... MA-1
Westwood HS—school ... OH-6
West Wood Island—locale ... MA-1
Westwood JHS—school (2) ... FL-3
Westwood JHS—school ... MA-1
Westwood JHS—school ... MN-6
Westwood JHS—school ... TN-4
Westwood Junction—locale ... CA-9
Westwood Lake—lake ... FL-3
West Wood Lake—lake ... MN-6
**Westwood Lake**—pop pl ... CO-8
**Westwood Lake**—pop pl ... FL-3
Westwood Lake First Baptist Ch—church ... FL-3
Westwood Lakes ... FL-3
Westwood Lakes—CDP ... FL-3
Westwood Lake South—lake ... FL-3
Westwood Library—building ... MA-1
**Westwood Manor**—pop pl ... DE-2
**Westwood Manor Plat One**—pop pl ... UT-8
**Westwood Manor Plat Two**—pop pl ... UT-8
Westwood Memorial Park—cemetery ... CA-9
Westwood Park ... CT-1
Westwood Park—park (2) ... CA-9
Westwood Park—park ... FL-3
Westwood Park—park (2) ... IA-7
Westwood Park—park ... MI-6
Westwood Park—park ... MN-6
Westwood Park—park ... MO-7
Westwood Park—park (2) ... NC-3
Westwood Park—park ... OH-6
Westwood Park—park ... TX-5
Westwood Park—park ... WA-9
Westwood Park—park ... WY-8
**Westwood Park**—pop pl ... PA-2
**Westwood Park**—pop pl (2) ... TX-5
**Westwood Park**—pop pl ... VA-3
Westwood Park Rsvr—reservoir ... IN-6
**Westwood Park Subdivision**—pop pl ... UT-8
**Westwood Place**—pop pl ... VA-3
Westwood Plantation(Boundary Increase)—hist pl ... AL-4
Westwood Plantation (historical)—locale ... AL-4
Westwood Plaza Shop Ctr—locale ... AZ-5
Westwood Plaza (Shop Ctr)—locale ... FL-3
Westwood Point—cape ... MD-2
**Westwood Ranchettes (subdivision)**—pop pl ... UT-8
Westwood Range—locale ... MD-2
West Woodrock Campground—locale ... WY-8
Westwood-Ross Park—park ... MI-6
Westwood Run—stream ... IN-6
West Woods—locale ... CT-1
Westwoods—locale ... DE-2
West Woods Brook ... CT-1
West Woods (CCD)—cens area ... OK-5
Westwood Sch ... PA-2
Westwood Sch—school ... AL-4
Westwood Sch—school ... AZ-5
Westwood Sch—school ... AR-4
Westwood Sch—school (4) ... CA-9
Westwood Sch—school ... CO-8
Westwood Sch—school ... CT-1
Westwood Sch—school ... IL-6
Westwood Sch—school ... IN-6
Westwood Sch—school (3) ... MI-6
Westwood Sch—school (4) ... MN-6
Westwood Sch—school ... MO-7
Westwood Sch—school (7) ... OH-6
Westwood Sch—school (4) ... OK-5
Westwood Sch—school ... PA-2
Westwood Sch—school (2) ... TN-4
Westwood Sch—school ... TX-5
Westwood Sch—school ... WI-6
Westwood Sch—school ... WY-8
West Woods Creek ... WA-9
Westwood Shop Ctr—locale (2) ... FL-3
Westwood Shop Ctr—locale (3) ... NC-3
Westwood Shops—locale ... KS-7
Westwood Shops—locale ... MO-7
Westwood Siding ... CA-9
**West Woods Mobile Homes PUD**—pop pl ... UT-8
**Westwood Square**—pop pl ... IN-6
**Westwood (sta.)**—pop pl ... MA-1
West Woodstock—locale ... NY-2
**West Woodstock**—pop pl ... CT-1
**West Woodstock**—pop pl ... VT-1
**Westwood (subdivision)**—pop pl (2) ... MS-4
**Westwood (subdivision)**—pop pl (10) ... NC-3
**Westwood Subdivision**—pop pl (2) ... UT-8
**Westwood (Teabury Flats)**—pop pl ... VA-3
Westwood Terrace Sch—school ... TX-5
Westwood Town Center Hist Dist—hist pl ... OH-6
**Westwood (Town of)**—pop pl ... MA-1
Westwood United Methodist Church—hist pl ... OH-6
Westwood View Elem Sch—school ... KS-7
Westwood Village ... NC-3
**Westwood Village**—pop pl ... CA-9
**Westwood Village**—pop pl ... TX-5
Westwood Village—uninc pl ... CA-9
Westwood Village Park—park ... TX-5
**Westwood Village (subdivision)**—pop pl ... PA-2
**Westwood Village Subdivision**—pop pl ... UT-8
Westwood Village (Westwood Siding)—uninc pl ... CA-9
West Woodville ... OH-6
**West Woodville**—pop pl ... OH-6
Westwood/128 Plaza—locale ... MA-1
West Woolwich ... ME-1
**Westworth**—pop pl ... TX-5
**Westworth (corporate name for Westworth Village)**—pop pl ... TX-5
**West Worthington**—pop pl ... MA-1
Westworth Village ... TX-5
Westworth Village (corporate name Westworth) ... TX-5
**West Wrentham**—pop pl ... MA-1
**West Wyoming**—pop pl ... PA-2
West Wyoming Borough—civil ... PA-2
**West Wyomissing**—pop pl ... PA-2
West Wyomissing Elem Sch—school ... PA-2
West Wytheville (Magisterial District)—fmr MCD ... VA-3
West Xenia Oil Field—oilfield ... CO-8
West Yadkin Sch—school ... NC-3
**West Yanceyville**—pop pl ... NC-3
West Yankton—unorg reg ... SD-7
**West Yaphank**—pop pl ... NY-2
West Yard—locale ... DE-2
**West Yards**—pop pl ... IA-7
**West Yarmouth**—pop pl ... MA-1
West Yarmouth Village ... MA-1
West Yaso ... MS-4
West Yeager Tank—reservoir ... TX-5
West Yegua Creek—stream ... TX-5
West Yellow Creek—stream ... MO-7
West Yellow Creek Oil Field—oilfield ... MS-4
West Yellowhouse Well—well ... TX-5
**West Yellowstone**—pop pl ... MT-8
West Yellowstone Basin ... MT-8
West Yellowstone Basin ... WY-8
West Yellowstone Oregon Shortline Terminus Hist Dist—hist pl ... MT-8
West Yeocomico River—stream ... VA-3
**West Yermo**—pop pl ... CA-9
**West York**—pop pl ... IL-6
**West York**—pop pl ... PA-2
West York Borough—civil ... PA-2
West York Cave—cave ... PA-2
West York JHS—school ... PA-2
West York Senior HS—school ... PA-2
**West Ysleta**—pop pl ... TX-5
West Yucca Interchange—crossing ... AZ-5
**West Yuma**—pop pl ... AZ-5
West Zephyrhills Elem Sch—school ... FL-3
West Zephyrhills Sch—school ... FL-3
West Zephyr Plaza (Shop Ctr)—locale ... FL-3
West Zigzag Lookout—summit ... OR-9
West Zigzag Mountain Trail—trail ... OR-9
West Zion Cem—cemetery ... KS-7
West Zion Cem—cemetery ... ND-7
West Zion Ch—church ... MN-6
West Zion Ch—church ... OH-6
**West Zollarsville**—pop pl ... PA-2
West Zuni Windmill—well ... AZ-5
West 22d Street Sch—school ... SD-7
West 22nd Street (Chicago) ... IL-6
West 5th Sch—school ... NE-7
West 5th Street Sch—school ... OH-6
West 67th Street Artists' Colony Hist Dist—hist pl ... NY-2
West 73rd-74th Street Hist Dist—hist pl ... NY-2
West 76th Street Hist Dist—hist pl ... NY-2
West 9th Street-Baltimore Ave Hist Dist—hist pl ... MO-7
Wesumkee Camp—locale ... FL-3
Wes White Canyon—valley ... AZ-5
WESY-AM (Leland)—tower (2) ... MS-4
Weta—locale ... SD-7
Wet And Dry Branch—stream ... VA-3
Wet Anglais Creek ... MO-7
**Wetappo**—pop pl (2) ... FL-3
Wetappo Cem ... FL-3
Wetappo Cem—cemetery ... FL-3
Wetappo Creek—stream ... FL-3
Wetappo Forest Ranger Station ... FL-3
Wetappo Forest Ranger Station—locale ... FL-3
Wetappo Side Camp—locale ... FL-3
Wetappo Swamp—swamp ... FL-3
Wetappo Tower (fire tower)—tower ... FL-3
We tar hoo River ... SD-7
Wet Ash Bridge—bridge ... NC-3
Wet Ash Swamp—stream ... NC-3
Weta Station ... SD-7
**Weta Township**—pop pl ... SD-7
Wetaug ... CT-1
**Wetaug**—pop pl ... IL-6
Wetaug (Election Precinct)—fmr MCD ... IL-6
Wetauwanchu Brook—stream ... CT-1
Wetauwanchu Mtn—summit ... CT-1
Wetback Cave—cave ... AL-4
WETB-AM (Johnson City)—tower ... TN-4
Wetbank Tank—reservoir ... NM-5
Wet Beaver Creek ... AZ-5
Wet Beaver Creek—stream ... AZ-5
Wet Bottom Creek—stream ... AZ-5
Wet Bottom Mesa—summit ... AZ-5
Wet Branch—stream ... VA-3
Wet Branch—stream ... WV-2
Wet Branch Ch—church ... WV-2
Wet Branch Sch—school ... WV-2
Wet Burnt Canyon—valley ... NM-5
Wetbutt Creek—stream ... AK-9
Wet Camp Gap—gap ... NC-3
WETC-AM (Wendell-Zebulon)—tower ... NC-3
Wet Canyon—valley (2) ... AZ-5
Wet Canyon—valley ... CA-9
Wet Canyon—valley ... CO-8
Wet Canyon—valley ... NM-5
Wet Canyon Campground—park ... AZ-5
Wet Cave—cave ... TN-4
Wet Choteau Creek ... SD-7
Wet Cottonwood Creek—stream ... MT-8
Wet Coulee—valley ... WI-6
Wet Creek ... IA-7
Wet Creek—stream ... ID-8
Wet Creek—stream ... MT-8
Wet Creek—stream ... NC-3
Wet Creek—stream (2) ... OR-9
Wet Creek Basin—basin ... ID-8
Wet Draw—valley ... WY-8
Wet Flats—flat ... VA-3
Wet Foot Creek—stream ... ID-8
Wetfoot Hammocks—island ... LA-4
Wet Fork—stream ... CA-9
Wet Fork—stream ... KY-4
Wet Fork—stream (2) ... MO-7
Wet Fork—stream ... MT-8
Wet Fork Blackwater Wash—stream ... CA-9
Wet Fork Creek ... CA-9
Wet Fork Mill Creek—stream ... UT-8
Wet Fork Schuster Creek—stream ... UT-8
Wet Fork Ty Hatch Creek—stream ... UT-8
Wet Fork West Fork Parachute Creek—stream ... CO-8
Wet Georgia Gulch—valley ... MT-8
Wet Glaise ... MO-7
**Wet Glaize**—pop pl ... MO-7
Wet Glaize Creek ... MO-7
Wet Glaize Creek—stream ... MO-7
Wet Grounds Ch—church ... VA-3
Wet Gulch—valley (2) ... AK-9
Wet Gulch—valley (3) ... CA-9
Wet Gulch—valley (2) ... CO-8
Wet Gulch—valley (5) ... ID-8
Wet Gulch—valley ... OR-9
Wethea Lake—lake ... MI-6
Wetheral Lake—lake ... MI-6
Wetherbee House—hist pl ... MS-4
Wetherbee Pond—lake ... CT-1
Wetherbee Sch—school ... MA-1
Wetherby-Hampton-Snyder-Wilson-Erdman Log House—hist pl ... PA-2
Wetherby Point—cape ... MD-2
Wetherby Trail, The—trail ... KY-4
**Wetheredsville**—pop pl ... MD-2
Wetherell Pond—lake ... CT-1
Wetherells Pond—lake ... MA-1
Wetherill ... PA-2
Wetherill Arch ... UT-8
Wetherill Canyon—valley ... AZ-5
Wetherill Canyon—valley ... UT-8
Wetherill Cem—cemetery ... IN-6
Wetherill Junction—locale ... PA-2
Wetherill Mesa—summit ... AZ-5
Wetherill Mesa—summit ... CO-8
Wetherills Cem—cemetery ... PA-2
Wetherill Sch—school ... PA-2
**Wetherills Corner**—pop pl ... PA-2
Wetherills Dam—dam ... PA-2
Wetherill Trail—trail ... UT-8
Wetherington Cem—cemetery ... GA-3
Wetherly Lake—reservoir ... NM-5
Wethern Pond—lake ... ME-1
Wethero Mtn—summit ... NC-3
Wether Ridge—ridge ... CA-9
Wethersfield—CDP ... CT-1
**Wethersfield**—pop pl ... MA-1
Wethersfield Ave Car Barn—hist pl ... CT-1

Wethersfield Cem—*cemetery* NY-2
Wethersfield Country Club—*other* CT-1
Wethersfield Cove—*bay* CT-1
Wethersfield Green—*park* CT-1
**Wethersfield Springs**—*pop pl* NY-2
**Wethersfield (Town of)**—*pop pl* CT-1
**Wethersfield (Town of)**—*pop pl* NY-2
Wethersfield (Township of)—*civ div* IL-6
Wetherspoon Hollow—*valley* TN-4
Wetherspoon Hollow Cem—*cemetery* TN-4
Wethey Creek—*stream* WA-9
Wethington Slough—*stream* GA-3
**Wethocouchy (historical)**—*pop pl* FL-3
*Wethoecuchytalofa* FL-3
Wet Hollow—*valley* (10) MO-7
Wet Hollow—*valley* NC-3
Wet Hollow—*valley* TX-5
Wet Hollow—*valley* (2) UT-8
Wet Hurricane Creek—*stream* TX-5
Wetiak, Dauen—*gut* FM-9
**Wetico**—*pop pl* WA-9
Wetikitik En Rohleng—*valley* FM-9
**Wetipquin**—*pop pl* MD-2
Wetipquin Creek—*stream* MD-2
Wetipquin Ferry—*locale* MD-2
Wetipquin Neck—*cape* MD-2
Wet Joplin Creek—*stream* TX-5
Wet Knob—*summit* WV-2
Wet Lacy Fork—*stream* TX-5
Wet Lake—*lake* MN-6
Wet Lake—*swamp* MN-6
Wetland (historical P.O.)—*locale* IN-6
Wetland Hollow—*valley* AR-4
Wetland Spring—*spring* OR-9
Wet Leggett Canyon—*valley* NM-5
Wet Leggett Spring—*spring* NM-5
Wet Leggett Tank—*reservoir* NM-5
Wetlegs Creek—*stream* MN-6
Wetle Spring—*spring* OR-9
Wet Lost Creek—*stream* AR-4
Wet Marsh Pond—*lake* TX-5
*Wet Meadow* CA-9
Wet Meadow—*flat* (3) CA-9
Wet Meadow Hill—*summit* CA-9
Wet Meadows—*flat* CA-9
Wet Meadows—*flat* (3) ID-8
Wet Meadows Rsvr—*reservoir* CA-9
Wet Meadows Springs—*spring* CA-9
Wet Mills Trail—*trail* NM-5
Wetmor Brook—*stream* NY-2
Wetmore—*locale* NY-2
**Wetmore**—*pop pl* CO-8
**Wetmore**—*pop pl* KS-7
**Wetmore**—*pop pl* MI-6
**Wetmore**—*pop pl* OR-9
**Wetmore**—*pop pl* PA-2
**Wetmore**—*pop pl* TN-4
**Wetmore**—*pop pl* TX-5
Wetmore, Seth, House—*hist pl* CT-1
Wetmore Baptist Ch—*church* TN-4
Wetmore Campground—*park* OR-9
Wetmore Cem—*cemetery* LA-4
Wetmore Cem—*cemetery* (2) NY-2
Wetmore Cem—*cemetery* TX-5
Wetmore Cem—*cemetery* VT-1
Wetmore Creek—*stream* OH-6
Wetmore Elem Sch—*school* KS-7
Wetmore Gap—*gap* VT-1
Wetmore Gap Trail—*trail* VT-1
Wetmore House—*building* PA-2
Wetmore House—*hist pl* CA-9
Wetmore House—*hist pl* PA-2
Wetmore HS—*school* KS-7
Wetmore Lake—*lake* (2) MI-6
Wetmore Landing—*locale* MI-6
Wetmore Lookout Tower—*locale* MI-6
Wetmore Park—*park* AZ-5
Wetmore Pond—*lake* MI-6
Wetmore Pond—*reservoir* MA-1
Wetmore Pond Dam—*dam* MA-1
Wetmore Post Office (historical)—*building*. TN-4
Wetmore Run—*stream* (2) PA-2
Wetmore Sch—*school* AZ-5
Wetmore Sch—*school* MI-6
**Wetmore Township**—*pop pl* KS-7
**Wetmore (Township of)**—*pop pl* PA-2
Wetmore Trail—*trail* PA-2
Wet Mountain Valley—*basin* CO-8
Wet Mtn—*summit* GA-3
Wet Mtns—*range* CO-8
Wet Mulkey Gulch—*valley* MT-8
Wetnight Ditch—*canal* IN-6
Wet Nothing Cave—*cave* AL-4
*Wetoerakku* MP-9
Wetona—*locale* PA-2
Wetona Cem—*cemetery* PA-2
**Wetonka**—*pop pl* SD-7
Wetonka Cem—*cemetery* SD-7
*Wetowerakke* MP-9
*Wetowerakke-to* MP-9
*Wetowerakku* MP-9
*Wetowerakku*—*island* MP-9
*Wetowerakku-To* MP-9
*Wetowerok* MP-9
Wet Park—*flat* MT-8
Wet Parmlee Canyon—*valley* SD-7
Wet Parmlee Canyon—*valley* WY-8
Wet Pit—*cave* AL-4
Wet Prairie—*flat* AR-4
Wet Prairie—*flat* OK-5
Wet Prairie Cem—*cemetery* AR-4
Wet Prong Buffalo Creek—*stream* KY-4
Wet Prong Creek—*stream* AZ-5
Wet Prong Farris Creek—*stream* TN-4
Wet Prong Leatherwood Creek—*stream* TN-4
Wet Prong Salamander Creek—*stream* CA-9
Wet Prong Spring—*spring* AZ-5
WETQ-FM (Oak Ridge)—*tower* TN-4
Wet Rat Cave—*cave* AL-4
Wet Ravine—*valley* (2) CA-9
Wet Rock Hammock—*island* FL-3
Wet Rock Marsh—*swamp* FL-3
Wet Rock Trail—*trail* PA-2
Wet Salt Creek—*stream* TX-5
Wet Sandy—*stream* UT-8
Wet Sandy Trail—*trail* UT-8
Wetsel—*locale* TX-5
**Wetsel**—*pop pl* OH-6
WETS-FM (Johnson City)—*tower* (2) TN-4
Wet Slash Hollow—*valley* MO-7
Wet Sleeve Creek—*stream* VA-3
Wet Stone Branch—*stream* MD-2
Wetstone Tobacco Company Dam Number 3—*dam* MA-1
Wet Swizer Creek—*stream* CO-8
Wettengel Junction—*locale* GU-9
Wettergren Ranch—*locale* SD-7
Wetterhorn Basin—*basin* CO-8
*Wetterhorn Creek* CO-8
Wetterhorn Creek—*stream* CO-8
Wetterhorn Peak—*summit* CO-8
Wettersten Lake—*lake* MN-6
Wettick—*locale* KS-7
*Wettington* AL-4
Wettles Lake—*lake* MN-6
Wet Tobacco Creek—*stream* TX-5
Wetton Cem—*cemetery* IL-6
WETU-AM (Wetumpka)—*tower* AL-4
*We-tum-cau Falls* AL-4
*Wetumka* AL-4
**Wetumka**—*pop pl* OK-5
Wetumka, Lake—*reservoir* OK-5
Wetumka Armory—*hist pl* OK-5
Wetumka (CCD)—*cens area* OK-5
Wetumka Cem—*cemetery* OK-5
Wetumka Cemetery Pavilion and Fence—*hist pl* OK-5
Wetumka Ch—*church* OK-5
Wetumka Oil Field—*oilfield* OK-5
*Wetumpka* OK-5
Wetumpka—*locale* FL-3
**Wetumpka**—*pop pl* AL-4
Wetumpka (CCD)—*cens area* AL-4
*Wetumpka Church* AL-4
Wetumpka Council House (historical)—*locale* AL-4
*Wetumpka Creek* AL-4
Wetumpka Division—*civil* AL-4
Wetumpka Elem Sch—*school* AL-4
Wetumpka Falls—*falls* AL-4
Wetumpka HS—*school* AL-4
Wetumpka Industrial Park—*locale* AL-4
Wetumpka Institute (historical)—*school* AL-4
Wetumpka JHS—*school* AL-4
Wetumpka L & N Depot—*hist pl* AL-4
*Wetumpka MS* AL-4
Wetumpka Municipal Airp—*airport* AL-4
Wetumpka Municipal Park—*park* AL-4
Wetumpka Prison (historical)—*building* AL-4
*Wetview Middle School* TN-4
*Wet Walnut Creek* KS-7
Wet Water Creek—*stream* MS-4
Wetwater Post Office (historical)—*building* MS-4
Wet Weakley Creek—*stream* TN-4
Wet Weather Creek—*stream* AL-4
Wet Weather Creek—*stream* IL-6
Wet Weather Creek—*stream* KY-4
Wet Weather Creek—*stream* WA-9
Wet Weather Gulch—*valley* CO-8
Wet Weather Lake—*lake* CA-9
Wet Weather Pond—*lake* AL-4
Wet Weather Pond—*lake* NM-5
Wet Weather Rsvr—*reservoir* ID-8
Wet Weather Spring—*spring* NV-8
Wetzel—*locale* IL-6
Wetzel—*locale* MI-6
Wetzel—*locale* MT-8
Wetzel, Christian, Cabin—*hist pl* KS-7
Wetzel Branch—*stream* MO-7
Wetzel Cem—*cemetery* KS-7
Wetzel Cem—*cemetery* MO-7
Wetzel Cem—*cemetery* WV-2
**Wetzel (County)**—*pop pl* WV-2
Wetzel Creek—*stream* CO-8
Wetzel Creek—*stream* PA-2
Wetzel Field—*park* NJ-2
Wetzel Hollow—*valley* WV-2
Wetzel Knob—*summit* VA-3
Wetzel Lake—*lake* MI-6
Wetzell Sch (abandoned)—*school* PA-2
Wetzel Road Sch—*school* NY-2
*Wetzel Run* WV-2
Wetzel Run—*stream* PA-2
Wetzel Run—*stream* WV-2
**Wetzels Corner**—*pop pl* OR-9
Wetzlar, Julius, House—*hist pl* CA-9
Wetzler Cove—*bay* NY-2
Wetzler Lake—*lake* IL-6
Wetz Sch—*school* SD-7
WEUP-AM (Huntsville)—*tower* AL-4
**Weurtsburg**—*pop pl* WI-6
**Wevaco**—*pop pl* WV-2
**Wever**—*pop pl* IA-7
Wever Sch—*school* MI-6
**Weverton**—*pop pl* MD-2
**Wevertown**—*pop pl* NY-2
WEVL-FM (Memphis)—*tower* (2) TN-4
**Wevok**—*pop pl* AK-9
**Wewahitchka**—*pop pl* FL-3
Wewahitchka (CCD)—*cens area* FL-3
Wewahitchka Elem Sch—*school* FL-3
Wewahitchka Junior-Senior HS—*school* FL-3
We-Wah Lake—*reservoir* NY-2
**Wewahotee**—*pop pl* FL-3
Wewaka Brook—*stream* CT-1
WEW-AM (St Louis)—*tower* MO-7
*Weweantet River* MA-1
*Weweanth River* MA-1
Weweantic River—*stream* MA-1
Weweantic River Rsvr—*reservoir* MA-1
*Weweantit River* MA-1
*Weweantitt River* MA-1
*Wewe Creek* MI-6
Weweeder Ponds—*swamp* MA-1
Wewe Hills—*summit* MI-6
**Wewela**—*pop pl* SD-7
W E Wilson Elem Sch—*school* IN-6
WEWO-AM (Laurinburg)—*tower* NC-3
*Wewoka* AL-4
**Wewoka**—*pop pl* OK-5
*Wewoka Assembly of God Church* AL-4
Wewoka Camp Ground (historical)—*locale* AL-4
Wewoka (CCD)—*cens area* OK-5
Wewoka Ch—*church* AL-4
Wewoka Ch—*church* OK-5
*Wewoka Creek* AL-4
Wewoka Creek—*stream* OK-5
Wewoka Junction (historical)—*locale* AL-4
Wewoka Lake—*reservoir* OK-5
*Wewoka Mountain* AL-4
*Wewoka River* CT-1
Wewoka Switch and Side Tracks—*hist pl* OK-5
*Wewokee* AL-4
*We-wo-kee Creek* AL-4
*Wewokee River* CT-1
Wew Post Office (historical)—*building* AL-4
WEXA-FM (Eupora)—*tower* MS-4
Wexford—*locale* MO-7
**Wexford**—*pop pl* MD-2
**Wexford**—*pop pl* PA-2
**Wexford**—*pop pl* SC-3
Wexford Ch—*church* PA-2
Wexford Corner—*locale* MI-6
**Wexford (County)**—*pop pl* MI-6
Wexford Creek—*stream* IA-7
Wexford District Sch (historical)—*school* IA-7
**Wexford Downs**—*pop pl* TN-4
**Wexford East**—*pop pl* NJ-2
Wexford Elem Sch—*school* PA-2
Wexford Run—*stream* PA-2
*Wexford School* PA-2
**Wexford (Township of)**—*pop pl* MI-6
Wexler Bend—*bend* TN-4
Wexler Islands—*island* TN-4
WEXP-FM (Gadsden)—*tower* AL-4
*Wey* FM-9
Weyand Cem—*cemetery* TX-5
Weyand Ditch—*canal* IN-6
Weyanoke—*hist pl* VA-3
Weyanoke—*locale* LA-4
Weyanoke—*locale* VA-3
**Weyanoke**—*pop pl* VA-3
**Weyanoke**—*pop pl* WV-2
Weyanoke Point—*cape* VA-3
Weyanoke Sch—*school* VA-3
**Weyant**—*pop pl* PA-2
Weyant Post Office (historical)—*building* PA-2
Weyants Pond—*lake* NY-2
**Weyauwega**—*pop pl* WI-6
Weyauwega Lake—*reservoir* WI-6
**Weyauwega (Town of)**—*pop pl* WI-6
Weyble Pond—*reservoir* NJ-2
*Weybosset Hill* RI-1
**Weybridge**—*pop pl* VT-1
**Weybridge Hill**—*pop pl* VT-1
**Weybridge (Town of)**—*pop pl* VT-1
Weybright Cem—*cemetery* IN-6
Weybright Sch—*school* KS-7
Weydhal Field—*airport* ND-7
WEYE-FM (Thomasville)—*tower* NC-3
Weyer—*locale* NY-2
Weyer Creek—*stream* KS-7
Weyer Gulch—*valley* (2) ID-8
**Weyerhaeuser**—*pop pl* WI-6
Weyerhaeuser, Charles A., and Musser, Richard Drew, Houses—*hist pl* MN-6
*Weyerhaeuser Camp Six* OR-9
Weyerhaeuser Company Dam—*dam* NC-3
Weyerhaeuser Creek—*stream* OR-9
Weyerhaeuser Ditch—*canal* NC-3
Weyerhaeuser Heliport—*airport* WA-9
Weyerhaeuser House—*hist pl* IL-6
Weyerhaeuser Lumber Company Lake Dam—*dam* MS-4
Weyerhaeuser Pe Ell Bridge—*hist pl* WA-9
Weyerhaeuser Sch—*school* WA-9
**Weyerhaeuser Townsite**—*pop pl* OR-9
Weyerhauser—*facility* MS-4
**Weyerhauser**—*pop pl* WA-9
**Weyerhauser**—*pop pl* WI-6
*Weyerhauser Ditch* NC-3
Weyerhauser Lumber Company Lake Dam—*dam* MS-4
Weyerhauser Lumber Company Pond Dam—*dam* (2) MS-4
*Weyerhauser Mountain* WA-9
Weyerhouser Office Bldg—*hist pl* WA-9
Weyer Pond—*lake* NY-2
**Weyers**—*pop pl* OH-6
**Weyers Cave**—*pop pl* VA-3
**Weyers Cave (Cave)**—*pop pl* VA-3
Weyers Cave Sch—*hist pl* VA-3
Weyers Lake—*lake* WI-6
Weyers Point—*cape* NY-2
**Weyerts**—*pop pl* NE-7
Weyert Sch—*school* NE-7
Weygandt Canyon—*valley* OR-9
**Wey Lake**—*pop pl* IN-6
Weyland Camp—*locale* CA-9
Weyland Cem—*cemetery* TN-4
Weyland Ch—*church* VA-3
Weyland Missionary Baptist Ch—*church* TN-4
Weyler Lake—*reservoir* AL-4
Weyman Chapel—*church* NC-3
Weyman Creek—*stream* NC-3
Weyman Creek—*stream* UT-8
*Weyman Lake* UT-8
Weyman Lakes—*lake* UT-8
Weyman Park—*flat* UT-8
Weymiller Butte—*summit* TX-5
**Weymouth**—*pop pl* KY-4
**Weymouth**—*pop pl* MA-1
**Weymouth**—*pop pl* NJ-2
**Weymouth**—*pop pl* OH-6
Weymouth Back River—*bay* MA-1
Weymouth Back River—*stream* MA-1
Weymouth Back River Marshes—*swamp* MA-1
Weymouth Branch—*stream* KY-4
Weymouth Brook—*stream* ME-1
Weymouth Cem—*cemetery* ME-1
Weymouth Central JHS—*school* MA-1
*Weymouth Centre* MA-1
Weymouth Flat—*flat* AZ-5
Weymouth Fore River—*bay* MA-1
Weymouth Fore River Marshes—*swamp* MA-1
Weymouth Great Hill—*summit* MA-1
Weymouth Great Pond—*reservoir* MA-1
Weymouth Great Pond Dam—*dam* MA-1
Weymouth Hall—*hist pl* MS-4
**Weymouth Heights (subdivision)**—*pop pl* MA-1
Weymouth Hill—*summit* ME-1
Weymouth Hill—*summit* NH-1
Weymouth HS (east)—*school* MA-1
Weymouth HS (west)—*school* MA-1
Weymouth Inn—*locale* CA-9
Weymouth Lake—*lake* WI-6
**Weymouth Landing**—*pop pl* MA-1
Weymouth Lateral—*canal* ID-8
Weymouth Point—*cape* (2) ME-1
Weymouth Pond—*lake* (2) ME-1
Weymouth Ranch—*locale* TX-5
WEYMOUTH (schooner)—*hist pl* NJ-2
*Weymouth Station* NJ-2
Weymouth Townhall—*building* MA-1
**Weymouth (Town of)**—*pop pl* MA-1
**Weymouth (Township of)**—*pop pl* NJ-2
Weymouth Village—*locale* MA-1
Weynant Spring—*spring* PA-2
*Weyo* CA-9
Weys Corners—*locale* NY-2
Weythman Gulch—*valley* MT-8
WEYY-AM (Talladega)—*tower* AL-4
WEZC-FM (Charlotte)—*tower* NC-3
Wezel—*locale* CO-8
WEZI-FM (Memphis)—*tower* TN-4
WEZK-FM (Knoxville)—*tower* TN-4
WEZQ-AM (Winfield)—*tower* AL-4
WEZV-FM (Fort Wayne)—*tower* IN-6
WEZX-FM (Scranton)—*tower* PA-2
WEZZ-FM (Clanton)—*tower* AL-4
WFAE-FM (Charlotte)—*tower* NC-3
WFAI-AM (Fayetteville)—*tower* NC-3
W Fayette Ch—*church* NY-2
W F Baker Lake—*reservoir* TN-4
W F Baker Lake Dam—*dam* TN-4
WFBG-AM (Altoona)—*tower* PA-2
WFBG-FM (Altoona)—*tower* PA-2
WFBM-AM (Noblesville)—*tower* IN-6
WFBQ-FM (Indianapolis)—*tower* IN-6
WFBS-AM (Spring Lake)—*tower* NC-3
W F Burns Oak Hill Elem Sch—*school* FL-3
W F Cattle Company Dam—*dam* AZ-5
WFCI-FM (Franklin)—*tower* IN-6
W F Collins Dam—*dam* SD-7
WFCT-TV (Fayetteville)—*tower* NC-3
WFCV-AM (New Haven)—*tower* IN-6
WFDD-FM (Winston-Salem)—*tower* NC-3
WFEB-AM (Sylacauga)—*tower* AL-4
WFEC-AM (Harrisburg)—*tower* PA-2
WFEM-FM (Ellwood City)—*tower* PA-2
WFEZ-AM (Meridian)—*tower* MS-4
WFFF-AM (Columbia)—*tower* MS-4
WFFF-FM (Columbia)—*tower* MS-4
W F Fiddyment Ranch—*locale* CA-9
WFFT-TV (Fort Wayne)—*tower* IN-6
WF George—*locale* TX-5
WFGW-AM (Black Mountain)—*tower* NC-3
WFHC-FM (Henderson)—*tower* TN-4
WFHK-AM (Peel City)—*tower* AL-4
WFHK-AM (Pell City)—*tower* AL-4
W Fields Ranch—*locale* TX-5
WFIE-TV (Evansville)—*tower* IN-6
WFIL-AM (Philadelphia)—*tower* PA-2
WFIL Studio—*hist pl* PA-2
WFIQ-TV (Florence)—*tower* AL-4
WFIU-FM (Bloomington)—*tower* IN-6
WFIX-AM (Huntsville)—*tower* AL-4
WFJA-FM (Sanford)—*tower* NC-3
WFLB-AM (Fayetteville)—*tower* NC-3
WFLI-AM (Lookout Mountain)—*tower* TN-4
WFLN-AM (Philadelphia)—*tower* PA-2
WFLN-FM (Philadelphia)—*tower* PA-2
WFLQ-FM (French Lick)—*tower* IN-6
WFMA-FM (Rocky Mount)—*tower* NC-3
WFMC-AM (Goldsboro)—*tower* NC-3
WFMH-AM (Cullman)—*tower* AL-4
WFMH-FM (Cullman)—*tower* AL-4
WFML-FM (Washington)—*tower* IN-6
WFMO-AM (Fairmont)—*tower* NC-3
WFMQ-FM (Lebanon)—*tower* TN-4
WFMS-FM (Indianapolis)—*tower* IN-6
WFMX-FM (Statesville)—*tower* NC-3
WFMY-TV (Greensboro)—*tower* NC-3
WFMZ-FM (Allentown)—*tower* PA-2
WFMZ-TV (Allentown)—*tower* PA-2
WFNC-AM (Fayetteville)—*tower* NC-3
WFNM-FM (Lancaster)—*tower* PA-2
WFOG-FM (Suffolk)—*tower* VA-3
WFOR-AM (Hattiesburg)—*tower* MS-4
WFOS-FM (Chesapeake)—*tower* VA-3
WFPA-AM (Fort Payne)—*tower* AL-4
*W F Parkers Landing* MS-4
WFRA-AM (Franklin)—*tower* PA-2
W Francis Rock—*other* AK-9
WFRI-FM (Auburn)—*tower* AL-4
WFRM-AM (Coudersport)—*tower* PA-2
WFRN-FM (Elkhart)—*tower* IN-6
W F Rover—*locale* TX-5
WFSC-AM (Franklin)—*tower* NC-3
WFSE-FM (Edinboro)—*tower* PA-2
*W F Simmons Cemetery* MS-4
WFSS-FM (Fayetteville)—*tower* NC-3
WFTA-FM (Fulton)—*tower* MS-4
WFTC-AM (Kinston)—*tower* NC-3
WFTE-AM (Lafayette)—*tower* IN-6
WFTO-AM (Fulton)—*tower* MS-4
WFWL-AM (Camden)—*tower* TN-4
WFWQ-FM (Fort Wayne)—*tower* IN-6
WFYI-TV (Indianapolis)—*tower* IN-6
WGAD-AM (Gadsden)—*tower* AL-4
WGAE-FM (Girard)—*tower* PA-2
WGAI-AM (Elizabeth City)—*tower* NC-3
WGAL-TV (Lancaster)—*tower* PA-2
WGAP-AM (Maryville)—*tower* TN-4
W Gardner Ranch—*locale* NV-8
WGAS-AM (South Gastonia)—*tower* NC-3
W G Barnes Dam—*dam* AL-4
W G Barnes Lake—*reservoir* AL-4
WGBI-AM (Scranton)—*tower* PA-2
WGBI-FM (Scranton)—*tower* PA-2
WGBR-AM (Goldsboro)—*tower* NC-3
WGBU-AM (Farrell)—*tower* PA-2
WGCA-AM (Chattanooga)—*tower* TN-4
WGCB-AM (Red Lion)—*tower* PA-2
WGCB-FM (Red Lion)—*tower* PA-2
WGCB-TV (Red Lion)—*tower* PA-2
WGCM-FM (Gulfport)—*tower* MS-4
WGCR-FM (Wellsboro)—*tower* PA-2
W G Draw—*valley* SD-7
WGEA-AM (Geneva)—*tower* AL-4
WGEA-FM (Geneva)—*tower* AL-4
*Wgem* FM-9
WGET-AM (Gettysburg)—*tower* PA-2
WGEV-FM (Beaver Falls)—*tower* PA-2
W G Flat—*flat* SD-7
W G Flat Sch—*school* SD-7
W G Flat Township—*civil* SD-7
WGGF-TV (Lebanon)—*tower* PA-2
WGGT-TV (Greensboro)—*tower* NC-3
WGH-AM (Newport News)—*tower* VA-3
WGHB-AM (Farmville)—*tower* NC-3
WGHF-FM (Newport News)—*tower* VA-3
WGHP-TV (High Point)—*tower* NC-3
WGIB-FM (Birmingham)—*tower* AL-4
WGIQ-TV (Louisville)—*tower* AL-4
WGIV-AM (Charlotte)—*tower* NC-3
W G Jones State Forest—*park* TX-5
WGLD-FM (High Point)—*tower* NC-3
*W G L Rice Memorial Park* TN-4
WGLU-FM (Johnstown)—*tower* PA-2
WGMA-AM (Spindale)—*tower* NC-3
WGMD-FM (Rehoboth Beach)—*tower* DE-2
WGMR-FM (Tyrone)—*tower* PA-2
WGN, Lake—*lake* WY-8
WGNC-AM (Gastonia)—*tower* NC-3
WGNG Airp—*airport* RI-1
WGNG-AM (Pawtucket)—*tower* RI-1
WGNI-FM (Wilmington)—*tower* NC-3
WGNS-AM (Murfreesboro)—*tower* TN-4
WGOC-AM (Kingsport)—*tower* TN-4
WGOK-AM (Mobile)—*tower* AL-4
WGOM-AM (Marion)—*tower* IN-6
WGOS-AM (High Point)—*tower* NC-3
WGOW-AM (Chattanooga)—*tower* TN-4
WGPA-AM (Bethlehem)—*tower* PA-2
WGRE-FM (Greencastle)—*tower* IN-6
WGRM-AM (Greenwood)—*tower* MS-4
WGRP-AM (Greenville)—*tower* PA-2
WGRP-FM (Greenville)—*tower* PA-2
WGRT-FM (Danville)—*tower* IN-6
W Grueb Dam—*dam* SD-7
WGRV-AM (Greeneville)—*tower* TN-4
WGSA-AM (Ephrata)—*tower* PA-2
WGSF-AM (Arlington)—*tower* TN-4
WGSQ-FM (Cookeville)—*tower* (2) TN-4
WGSS-FM (Lumberton)—*tower* NC-3
WGSV-AM (Guntersville)—*tower* AL-4
WG Taylor Ranch—*locale* WY-8
WGTC-FM (Bloomington)—*tower* IN-6
WGTL-AM (Kannapolis)—*tower* NC-3
WGTM-AM (Wilson)—*tower* NC-3
WGTY-FM (Gettysburg)—*tower* PA-2
WGUD-FM (Pascagoula)—*tower* MS-4
W Gudgel Ranch—*locale* NE-7
WGUF-AM (Gulfport)—*tower* MS-4
WGUF-FM (Gulfport)—*tower* MS-4
WGVM-AM (Greenville)—*tower* MS-4
W G Williams Pond Dam—*dam* MS-4
W G Wilson Ditch—*canal* OH-6
WGWR-AM (Asheboro)—*tower* NC-3
WGYV-AM (Greenville)—*tower* AL-4
*Whackenbush Drain* MI-6
Whackers Pond—*lake* NY-2
Whack Lake—*lake* MN-6
Whackoff Creek—*stream* WY-8
Whackup Creek—*stream* FL-3
WHAL-AM (Shelbyville)—*tower* TN-4
**Whalan**—*pop pl* MN-6
Whalan Station—*locale* CA-9
*Whaleback* ME-1
Whale Back—*bar* DE-2
Whale Back—*bar* ME-1
Whaleback—*bar* (2) ME-1
Whaleback—*cape* ME-1
Whaleback—*locale* PA-2
Whaleback—*ridge* CA-9
Whaleback—*ridge* ME-1
Whaleback—*rock* MA-1
Whaleback—*summit* AZ-5
Whaleback—*summit* NY-2
Whaleback—*summit* OR-9
Whaleback, The—*island* AK-9
Whaleback, The—*ridge* MA-1
Whaleback, The—*summit* CA-9
Whaleback Cove—*bay* ME-1
Whaleback Island—*island* NH-1
Whaleback Island—*island* NY-2
Whaleback Key—*island* FL-3
Whaleback Ledge—*bar* ME-1
Whaleback Light Station—*hist pl* ME-1
*Whaleback Mtn* CA-9
*Whale Back Mtn* ME-1
Whaleback Mtn—*summit* CA-9
Whale Back Mtn—*summit* ME-1
Whaleback Mtn—*summit* NH-1
Whaleback Pond—*lake* NH-1
Whaleback Reef—*bar* ME-1
Whaleback Ridge—*ridge* ME-1
Whaleback Rock—*island* CT-1
Whaleback Rock—*island* ME-1
Whaleback Shoal—*bar* MI-6
Whale Bay—*bay* (3) AK-9
Whale Bay—*bay* LA-4
Whale Beach—*beach* NJ-2
**Whale Beach**—*pop pl* NJ-2
Whaleboat Island—*island* ME-1
Whaleboat Ledge—*bar* ME-1
Whaleboat Point—*cape* RI-1
*Whale Bone* NC-3
Whalebone—*area* NC-3
**Whalebone**—*pop pl* NC-3
Whalebone Branch—*stream* NC-3
Whalebone Cape—*cape* AK-9
Whalebone Creek—*stream* CT-1
Whalebone Inlet—*gut* NC-3
Whalebone Island—*island* NC-3
Whalebone Island—*island* VA-3
*Whalebone Junction* NC-3
Whalebone Junction Information Center—*park* NC-3
*Whalebone Point* RI-1
Whalebone Point—*cape* NJ-2
Whale Branch—*stream* SC-3
Whale Buttes—*summit* MT-8
Whale Cove—*bay* OR-9
Whale Cove—*cove* MA-1
Whale Creek—*bay* NC-3
Whale Creek—*gut* NJ-2
Whale Creek—*harbor* NY-2
Whale Creek—*stream* CO-8
Whale Creek—*stream* MN-6
Whale Creek—*stream* MT-8
Whale Creek—*stream* NJ-2
Whale Creek—*stream* OR-9
Whale Creek—*stream* SC-3
Whale Creek—*stream* WA-9
Whale Creek Falls—*falls* MT-8
Whale Gulch—*valley* CA-9
Whale Harbor—*bay* FL-3
Whale Harbor—*harbor* NJ-2
Whale Harbor Channel—*channel* FL-3
Whalehead—*cape* OR-9
Whale Head—*summit* AK-9
Whale Head—*summit* OR-9
Whale Head Bay—*bay* NC-3
Whalehead Club—*hist pl* NC-3
Whalehead Creek—*stream* OR-9
Whale Head Hill—*summit* NC-3
Whale Head Island—*island* AK-9
Whalehead Island—*island* OR-9
Whalehead Ridge—*ridge* WA-9
Whale Hill—*summit* CO-8
Whale Hill—*summit* NY-2
Whalehouse Point—*cape* NY-2
Whale Island—*island* (4) AK-9
Whale Island—*island* CA-9
Whale Island—*island* FL-3
Whale Island—*island* MA-1
Whale Island Light—*locale* AK-9
Whale Key—*island* FL-3
Whale Lake—*lake* AK-9
Whale Lake—*lake* CO-8
Whale Lake—*lake* MN-6
Whale Lake—*lake* MT-8
Whale Lake—*lake* WA-9
Whale Ledge—*bar* ME-1
Whale Mine—*mine* (2) CO-8
Whale Mine—*mine* NV-8
Whale Mountain—*ridge* AK-9
Whale Mtn—*summit* AK-9
Whale Mtn—*summit* (2) CA-9
*Whalen* KY-4
Whalen Bay—*bay* AK-9
Whalen Bay—*bay* WI-6
Whalen Bottom—*bend* WY-8
Whalen Butte—*summit* WY-8
Whalen Canyon—*valley* UT-8
Whalen Canyon—*valley* WY-8
Whalen Cem—*cemetery* AZ-5
Whalen Cem—*cemetery* KY-4
Whalen Creek—*stream* CO-8
Whalen Creek—*stream* (2) MO-7
Whalen Creek—*stream* WI-6
Whalen Diversion Dam—*dam* WY-8
Whaleneck Point—*cape* NY-2
*Whaleneck River* NY-2
Whalen Island County Park—*park* OR-9
Whalen JHS—*school* CT-1
*Whalen Lake* CA-9
Whalen Lake—*lake* (2) MI-6
Whalen Lake—*lake* TX-5
Whalen Lake—*lake* WI-6
Whalen Site (125-Ly-48)—*hist pl* KY-4
Whalen Slough—*gut* MO-7
Whalen Spring—*spring* CA-9
Whalen Springs—*spring* WI-6
Whalen Tank—*reservoir* AZ-5
Whale Oil Row—*hist pl* CT-1
Whale Passage—*channel* (2) AK-9
Whale Peak—*summit* CA-9
Whale Peak—*summit* CO-8
*Whale Point* AK-9
Whale Point—*cape* (2) AK-9
Whale Point—*cape* MD-2
Whale Point—*cape* VA-3
Whale Pond—*lake* TN-4
Whale Pond Brook—*stream* NJ-2
Whaler Creek—*stream* CA-9
Whaler Island—*island* CA-9
Whale Rock—*bar* CA-9
Whale Rock—*island* AK-9
Whale Rock—*island* CA-9
Whale Rock—*island* CT-1
Whale Rock—*island* ME-1
Whale Rock—*island* AS-9
Whale Rock—*other* AK-9
Whale Rock—*pillar* RI-1
Whale Rock—*pillar* UT-8
Whale Rock—*rock* (4) MA-1
Whale Rock Ledge—*bar* ME-1
**Whale Rock Light (historical)**—*pop pl* RI-1
Whale Rock Rsvr—*reservoir* CA-9
Whale Rocks—*island* WA-9
Whalers Creek—*stream* AK-9
Whalers Island—*island* CA-9
Whalers Knoll—*summit* CA-9
*Whalers Rock* CA-9
*Whalers Rocks* CA-9
*Whales Back* MA-1
*Whale's Back* MI-6
Whalesback—*summit* ME-1
Whales Back—*summit* ME-1
Whales Back—*summit* NH-1
Whalesback, The—*ridge* ME-1
Whales Back Cem—*cemetery* ME-1
*Whales Back Mountain* ME-1
Whales Beach—*beach* MA-1
Whales Creek—*stream* MO-7
Whales Gizzard Shoals—*bar* MD-2
Whales Head—*summit* MA-1
*Whaleshead Creek* OR-9
**Whales Jaw**—*pop pl* MA-1
Whales Tail Mtn—*summit* NY-2
Whaletail Cove—*bay* AK-9
*whale Tail Lake* MN-6
Whaletail Lake—*lake* MN-6
Whaletail Point—*cape* AK-9
Whale View Point—*cape* CA-9
Whaley—*locale* SC-3
Whaley—*locale* VA-3
**Whaley**—*pop pl* MS-4
**Whaley**—*pop pl* NC-3
**Whaley**—*pop pl* TX-5
Whaley, Robert J., House—*hist pl* MI-6
Whaley, W. B. Smith, House—*hist pl* SC-3
Whaley Archeol Site—*hist pl* MS-4
Whaley Branch—*stream* NC-3
Whaley Branch—*stream* (2) TN-4
Whaley Brook—*stream* RI-1
Whaley Canyon—*valley* SD-7
Whaley Cave—*cave* MO-7
Whaley Cem—*cemetery* AL-4
Whaley Cem—*cemetery* IN-6
Whaley Cem—*cemetery* MO-7
Whaley Cem—*cemetery* (2) TN-4
Whaley Cem—*cemetery* TX-5
Whaley Cem—*cemetery* WY-8

Wheeler Draw—valley (2) CO-8
**Wheeler Estates—pop pl** NY-2
Wheeler Farms CT-1
Wheeler Field—hist pl HI-9
Wheeler Field—park MN-6
**Wheeler Field—pop pl** HI-9
Wheeler Fire Tower—tower PA-2
Wheeler Flat—flat CA-9
Wheeler Flat—flat OR-9
Wheeler Flat—flat WY-8
Wheeler Flats—flat CO-8
Wheeler Flats Cem—cemetery OK-5
Wheeler Flowage WI-6
Wheeler Fork—stream UT-8
Wheeler Fork—stream WV-2
Wheeler Gap—gap AR-4
Wheeler Gap—gap TN-4
Wheeler Gorge—gap CA-9
Wheeler Gorge Guard Station—locale CA-9
Wheeler Grove Baptist Church MS-4
Wheeler Grove Cem—cemetery IN-6
Wheeler Grove Ch—church (2) AL-4
Wheeler Grove Ch—church IA-7
Wheeler Grove Ch—church MS-4
Wheeler Grove Ch of Christ AL-4
Wheeler Grove (historical P.O.)—locale IA-7
Wheeler Guard Station—locale CA-9
Wheeler Guard Station—locale CO-8
Wheeler Gulch—valley CA-9
Wheeler Gulch—valley (2) CO-8
Wheeler Gulch—valley MT-8
Wheeler Gulch—valley SD-7
Wheeler Gut—stream NC-3
Wheeler Hall—hist pl CA-9
Wheeler Hall, Northland College—hist pl WI-6
**Wheeler Heights—pop pl** GA-3
**Wheeler Heights—pop pl** OR-9
Wheeler Hill—summit (2) AL-4
Wheeler Hill—summit CT-1
Wheeler Hill—summit ME-1
Wheeler Hill—summit (2) MA-1
Wheeler Hill—summit (2) NH-1
Wheeler Hill—summit (2) NY-2
Wheeler Hill—summit PA-2
Wheeler Hill—summit WA-9
Wheeler Hill Cem—cemetery NH-1
Wheeler Hill Ch—church (2) NY-2
Wheeler Hill Ch—church TN-4
Wheeler Hill Reservoir WA-9
Wheeler Hills—range ND-7
Wheeler Hills—summit WA-9
Wheeler (historical)—locale SD-7
**Wheeler (historical)—pop pl** SD-7
Wheeler Hollow—valley AL-4
Wheeler Hollow—valley (2) AR-4
Wheeler Hollow—valley IN-6
Wheeler Hollow—valley KY-4
Wheeler Hollow—valley MO-7
Wheeler Hollow—valley NY-2
Wheeler Hollow—valley OK-5
Wheeler Hollow—valley PA-2
Wheeler Hollow—valley (3) TN-4
Wheeler Hollow—valley VA-3
Wheeler Home—hist pl NY-2
Wheeler Hotel—hist pl SD-7
Wheeler House—hist pl AL-4
Wheeler House—hist pl FL-3
Wheeler House Complex—hist pl NY-2
Wheeler HS—school CT-1
Wheeler HS—school TX-5
Wheeler-Ingalls House—hist pl MA-1
Wheeler Island—island CA-9
Wheeler Island—island CT-1
Wheeler Island—island ME-1
Wheeler Islands—island WV-2
Wheeler Junction—locale CO-8
Wheeler Knob—summit AR-4
Wheeler Knob—summit GA-3
Wheeler Knob—summit VA-3
Wheeler Knob—summit WV-2
Wheeler Lake AR-4
Wheeler Lake—lake AR-4
Wheeler Lake—lake CA-9
Wheeler Lake—lake (2) CO-8
Wheeler Lake—lake (3) MI-6
Wheeler Lake—lake (3) MN-6
Wheeler Lake—lake NM-5
Wheeler Lake—lake NC-3
Wheeler Lake—lake (2) WA-9
Wheeler Lake—lake (2) WI-6
Wheeler Lake—lake WY-8
Wheeler Lake—reservoir (2) AL-4
Wheeler Lake—reservoir GA-3
Wheeler Lake—reservoir TX-5
Wheeler Lakes—lake CO-8
Wheeler Lakes—lake MI-6
Wheeler Landing—locale MN-6
Wheeler Landing Field—airport AZ-5
Wheeler Location IN-6
Wheeler Marsh—swamp NY-2
Wheeler Memorial Sch (historical)—school AL-4
Wheeler-Merriam House—hist pl MA-1
Wheeler Mill Branch—stream AL-4
Wheeler Mine—mine NV-8
Wheeler Mine—mine WA-9
Wheeler Mine, Mount—mine NV-8
Wheeler Mine (underground)—mine AL-4
Wheeler Mission Campground—park IN-6
Wheeler Monmt—park NV-8
Wheeler Monument—summit CO-8
Wheeler MS—school NY-2
Wheeler Mtn—summit AL-4
Wheeler Mtn—summit AR-4
Wheeler Mtn—summit CO-8
Wheeler Mtn—summit ID-8
Wheeler Mtn—summit ME-1
Wheeler Mtn—summit MT-8
Wheeler Mtn—summit NV-8
Wheeler Mtn—summit NH-1
Wheeler Mtn—summit (2) NY-2
Wheeler Mtn—summit VT-1
Wheeler Mtn—summit WA-9
Wheeler Natl Wildlife Ref—park AL-4
Wheeler Natl Wildlife Refuge Headquarter—locale AL-4
Wheeler No. 1 Oil Well—hist pl OK-5
Wheeler Oil Field—oilfield TX-5
Wheeler Opera House—hist pl CO-8
Wheeler Park—park (2) CA-9
Wheeler Park—park IL-6
Wheeler Park—park MI-6
Wheeler Park—park MN-6
Wheeler Park—park NJ-2
Wheeler Park—park OK-5
Wheeler Park Pit—cave AL-4
Wheeler Pass—gap (2) NV-8
Wheeler Peak—summit AK-9
Wheeler Peak—summit (3) CA-9
Wheeler Peak—summit NV-8
Wheeler Peak Campground—locale NV-8
Wheeler Peak Forest Service Recreation Site NV-8
Wheeler Peak (Highest Point In New Mexico)—summit NM-5
Wheeler Peak Scenic Area—area NV-8
Wheeler Peak Wilderness—park NM-5
Wheeler Place—locale AZ-5
Wheeler Point MN-6
Wheeler Point—cape CA-9
Wheeler Point—cape CT-1
Wheeler Point—cape FL-3
Wheeler Point—cape MA-1
Wheeler Point—cape OR-9
Wheeler Point—cape WI-6
Wheeler Point—cliff AZ-5
Wheeler Pond MA-1
Wheeler Pond NH-1
Wheeler Pond WI-6
Wheeler Pond—lake (3) NH-1
Wheeler Pond—lake (2) NY-2
Wheeler Pond—lake (3) VT-1
Wheeler Pond—reservoir (3) MA-1
Wheeler Pond Dam—dam MA-1
Wheeler Post Office (historical)—building AL-4
Wheeler Prairie—flat IN-6
Wheeler Prairie Cem—cemetery WI-6
Wheeler Primitive Baptist Ch—church MS-4
Wheeler Quarter Cem—cemetery AL-4
Wheeler Ranch—locale (2) CA-9
Wheeler Ranch—locale ID-8
Wheeler Ranch—locale MT-8
Wheeler Ranch—locale NV-8
Wheeler Ranch—locale TX-5
Wheeler Ranch—locale WY-8
Wheeler Ranch Prospect—mine NV-8
Wheeler Ranch Trail—trail WY-8
Wheeler Reservoir WA-9
Wheeler Ridge—locale CA-9
Wheeler Ridge—ridge AZ-5
Wheeler Ridge—ridge CA-9
Wheeler Ridge—ridge IL-6
Wheeler Ridge—ridge IN-6
Wheeler Ridge—ridge OR-9
Wheeler Ridge Oil Field CA-9
Wheeler Road Sch—school NY-2
Wheeler Rock—bar ME-1
Wheeler Rock—island CT-1
**Wheeler (RR name for Wheelers)—pop pl** MS-4
Wheeler Rsvr—reservoir AL-4
Wheeler Rsvr—reservoir (2) NV-8
Wheeler Run—stream OH-6
Wheeler Run—stream WV-2
**Wheelers—pop pl** NY-2
Wheelersburg—locale KY-4
**Wheelersburg—pop pl** OH-6
Wheelers Cem—cemetery AR-4
Wheelers Ch—church NC-3
Wheeler Sch—school AL-4
Wheeler Sch—school AZ-5
Wheeler Sch—school (2) CT-1
Wheeler Sch—school (3) IL-6
Wheeler Sch—school IN-6
Wheeler Sch—school KS-7
Wheeler Sch—school KY-4
Wheeler Sch—school (2) MI-6
Wheeler Sch—school MN-6
Wheeler Sch—school MS-4
Wheeler Sch—school NH-1
Wheeler Sch—school NY-2
Wheeler Sch—school OK-5
Wheeler Sch (abandoned)—school MO-7
Wheeler Sch (historical)—school PA-2
Wheeler Sch Number Four IN-6
Wheelers Creek—stream NY-2
Wheelers Gap TN-4
Wheelers Gully—valley NY-2
Wheeler Shaft—mine UT-8
Wheelers Hill—summit NY-2
Wheelers Mill NC-3
Wheelers Mill—locale KY-4
Wheelers Mill—locale MO-7
Wheelers Mill—locale OH-6
Wheelers Point MA-1
Wheelers Point—cape MA-1
**Wheelers Point—pop pl** MN-6
Wheelers Pond MA-1
Wheelers Pond—reservoir MA-1
Wheelers Pond—reservoir NY-2
Wheelers Pond—reservoir VA-3
Wheelers Pond Dam—dam MA-1
Wheelers Pond (historical)—lake MA-1
Wheeler Spring—spring AR-4
Wheeler Spring—spring (2) NV-8
Wheeler Spring—spring OR-9
Wheeler Spring—spring (2) TN-4
Wheeler Spring—spring (3) UT-8
Wheeler Springs AL-4
Wheeler Springs—locale TX-5
**Wheeler Springs—pop pl** CA-9
Wheeler Springs—spring NV-8
Wheeler Springs—spring NM-5
Wheeler Springs—spring TX-5
Wheeler Springs—spring UT-8
Wheeler Springs Cem—cemetery AR-4
Wheeler Springs Ch—church AR-4
Wheeler Spur—ridge TN-4
Wheelers Ranch—locale IA-7
Wheeler's Rock CT-1
Wheelers (RR name for Wheeler)—other MS-4
Wheelers Run—stream KY-4
Wheelers Run—stream VA-3
Wheelers Sheep Camp—locale CA-9
Wheelers Siding OH-6
Wheelers Station AL-4
Wheeler-Stallard House—hist pl CO-8
Wheeler Station AL-4
Wheeler Station Post Office AL-4
Wheeler Stream—stream ME-1
Wheeler Stream—stream VT-1
Wheeler Tank—reservoir (2) AZ-5
**Wheelerton—pop pl** TN-4
Wheelerton Baptist Ch—church TN-4
Wheelerton Post Office (historical)—building TN-4
**Wheelertown—pop pl** NY-2
Wheelertown Cem—cemetery NY-2
Wheeler (Town Of)—other WI-6
**Wheeler (Town of)—pop pl** NY-2
Wheeler Township—fmr MCD (2) IA-7
Wheeler Township (historical)—civil SD-7
Wheeler (Township of)—fmr MCD AR-4
**Wheeler (Township of)—pop pl** MI-6
Wheeler Trail—trail (2) CO-8
Wheeler Trail—trail PA-2
Wheeler Tunnel—tunnel NV-8
**Wheeler Village Subdivision Unit One—pop pl** UT-8
**Wheeler Village Subdivision Unit Two—pop pl** UT-8
Wheelerville AL-4
**Wheelerville—pop pl** AL-4
**Wheelerville—pop pl** MO-7
**Wheelerville—pop pl** NY-2
**Wheelerville—pop pl** PA-2
Wheelerville (historical)—locale MA-1
Wheelerville Sch (historical)—school MS-4
Wheeler Wash—stream AZ-5
Wheeler Wash—stream NV-8
Wheeler Well—locale NV-8
Wheeler Well—well AZ-5
Wheeler Well—well (2) TX-5
Wheeler Windmill—locale (2) TX-5
Wheeler Windmills—locale TX-5
**Wheelerwood—pop pl** IA-7
Wheeles OK-5
Wheeless—locale OK-5
Wheeless Lake Dam—dam AL-4
Wheeless Pond—reservoir AL-4
Wheel Gulch—valley (3) CA-9
Wheel Gulch—valley OR-9
Wheel Gulch Basin—basin OR-9
Wheel Gulch Basin Spring—spring OR-9
Wheelhouse Cem—cemetery TN-4
Wheelhouse Pond—lake WA-9
Wheeling AL-4
Wheeling TN-4
**Wheeling—pop pl** AR-4
**Wheeling—pop pl** IL-6
**Wheeling—pop pl (3)** IN-6
**Wheeling—pop pl** LA-4
**Wheeling—pop pl** MO-7
**Wheeling—pop pl** WV-2
Wheeling Ave Hist Dist—hist pl OH-6
Wheeling Baltimore and Ohio RR Passenger Station—hist pl WV-2
Wheeling Branch—stream DE-2
Wheeling Cem—cemetery IN-6
Wheeling Cem—cemetery IA-7
Wheeling Cemetery MS-4
Wheeling Coll—school WV-2
Wheeling Country Club—other WV-2
Wheeling Creek PA-2
Wheeling Creek WV-2
**Wheeling Creek—pop pl** OH-6
Wheeling Creek—stream OH-6
Wheeling Creek—stream WV-2
Wheeling Crossroad—locale AL-4
Wheeling Downs—other WV-2
Wheeling Drainage Ditch—canal IL-6
Wheeling-Hatter Ranch—locale ND-7
Wheeling Hill Ch—church PA-2
Wheeling Hist Dist—hist pl WV-2
Wheeling (historical)—locale MS-4
Wheeling Hollow—valley VA-3
Wheeling HS—school IL-6
Wheeling Island—island WV-2
Wheeling Island—uninc pl WV-2
Wheeling Mine—mine MN-6
Wheeling Park—park WV-2
Wheeling Pike Addition IN-6
Wheeling Sch—school MN-6
Wheeling Sch—school OH-6
Wheeling Slope Mine (underground)—mine AL-4
Wheeling Suspension Bridge—hist pl WV-2
**Wheeling Township—pop pl** MO-7
**Wheeling (Township of)—pop pl** IL-6
**Wheeling (Township of)—pop pl** MN-6
**Wheeling (Township of)—pop pl (2)** OH-6
Wheeling Valley—valley OH-6
Wheeling Valley Cem—cemetery OH-6
Wheel Inn Ranch (trailer park)—locale AZ-5
**Wheel Inn Ranch (trailer park)—pop pl** AZ-5
Wheel Leasing, Incorporated—facility KY-4
Wheelless Airp—airport AL-4
Wheelless Lake—reservoir AL-4
**Wheelman—pop pl** CO-8
Wheelmeadow Brook MA-1
Wheel Meadow Brook—stream MA-1
Wheel Meadow Grove—woods CA-9
Wheel Mtn—summit CA-9
Wheelock—locale ME-1
Wheelock—locale PA-2
Wheelock—locale TX-5
**Wheelock—pop pl** ND-7
**Wheelock—pop pl** VT-1
Wheelock, Cyrus, House—hist pl UT-8
Wheelock Acad—hist pl OK-5
Wheelock Acad—school OK-5
Wheelock Brook—stream ME-1
Wheelock Brook—stream NH-1
Wheelock Cem—cemetery ND-7
Wheelock Cem—cemetery OH-6
Wheelock Cem—cemetery PA-2
Wheelock Cem—cemetery (2) TX-5
Wheelock Church—hist pl OK-5
Wheelock Corners—locale PA-2
Wheelock Creek—stream OK-5
Wheelock Creek—stream OR-9
Wheelock Creek—stream TX-5
Wheelock Hill—summit MA-1
Wheelock Hill—summit NY-2
Wheelock Hollow—valley TN-4
Wheelock House—hist pl VT-1
Wheelock Island—island ME-1
Wheelock Lake—lake ME-1
Wheelock Law Office—hist pl VT-1
Wheelock Memorial Hosp—hospital MI-6
Wheelock Mill—locale ME-1
Wheelock Mtn—summit VT-1
Wheelock Pond VT-1
Wheelock Pond—lake (2) NY-2
Wheelock Sch—school MA-1
Wheelock Sch—school MN-6
Wheelock Sch—school TX-5
Wheelock Sch (abandoned)—school PA-2
Wheelock School SD-7
Wheelock Siding—locale ME-1
Wheelock Spring—spring TN-4
**Wheelocktown (historical)—pop pl** TN-4
**Wheelock (Town of)—pop pl** VT-1
**Wheelock Township—pop pl** ND-7
**Wheelockville—pop pl** MA-1
Wheelockville District—hist pl MA-1
Wheel of Fortune—hist pl DE-2
Wheel of Fortune—park DE-2
**Wheel of Fortune—pop pl** VI-3
Wheel of Fortune Island—island GA-3
Wheelon—locale UT-8
Wheel Ravine MH-9
Wheel Rim—locale KY-4
Wheel Rim Fork—stream KY-4
Wheel Rim Hollow—valley AR-4
Wheel Run—stream IN-6
Wheel Run—stream WV-2
Wheels Canyon—valley AZ-5
Wheel Sch (historical)—school TN-4
Wheel Store, The—hist pl AR-4
Wheelus Branch—stream TX-5
**Wheelwright—pop pl** KY-4
**Wheelwright—pop pl** MA-1
**Wheelwright—pop pl** VA-3
Wheelwright Block—hist pl ME-1
Wheelwright Commercial District—hist pl KY-4
Wheelwright Creek—stream NH-1
**Wheelwright Junction—pop pl** KY-4
Wheelwright Park—park MA-1
Wheelwright Pond—lake NH-1
Wheelwright (sta.)—other KY-4
Wheelwright-Weeksbury (CCD)—cens area KY-4
Wheetip Creek—stream ID-8
Wheir Lake PA-2
Whelan—locale WA-9
Whelan Bridge—bridge WY-8
Whelan Creek—stream AK-9
Whelan Gas Field—area TX-5
Whelan Hill—summit NY-2
Whelan Lake—lake (2) MI-6
Whelan Lake—reservoir CA-9
Whelan Sch—school CA-9
Whelan Sch—school MA-1
Whelchel, Lake—reservoir SC-3
Whelden Mtn—summit NY-2
Whelen AR-4
Whelenaughwemack River NY-2
**Whelen Springs—pop pl** AR-4
Wheless—locale GA-3
Wheless Branch—stream LA-4
Wheless Road Sch—school GA-3
Whelin Cem—cemetery MS-4
Wheling—locale IA-7
Whell Lake MN-6
Whelock Lake—lake (2) MI-6
Whelp Creek—stream MI-6
Whelp Creek—stream MN-6
Whelp Creek—stream MT-8
Whelp Lake—lake MN-6
Whelp Lake—lake MT-8
WHEP-AM (Foley)—tower AL-4
Where the Hills End Windmill—locale AZ-5
WHER-FM (Hattiesburg)—tower MS-4
Wher-Rena Marina—locale NC-3
Wherritt House—hist pl KY-4
Wherritts Pond—lake MD-2
Wherry Cem—cemetery OH-6
Wherry Housing CA-9
Wherry Oil Field—oilfield KS-7
Wherry Run—stream WV-2
Wherry Sch—school NM-5
**Wherrys Crossroads—pop pl** OH-6
Wherrys Store TN-4
Whery Lake—lake TN-4
Whestphal Basin—basin MT-8
Whestphal Creek—stream MT-8
Whetham—locale PA-2
Whetham Fire Tower—locale PA-2
Whetham Tower Trail—trail PA-2
Whetly AL-4
Whetmiller Knob—summit WV-2
Whetner Branch—stream SC-3
Whetrock Canyon—valley AZ-5
Whetrock Canyon—valley UT-8
**Whetsell—pop pl** SC-3
Whetsett Sch (historical)—school MO-7
Whetstone—locale AZ-5
Whetstone—locale KY-4
Whetstone—locale SC-3
Whetstone—locale WA-9
**Whetstone—pop pl** KY-4
**Whetstone—pop pl** WV-2
Whetstone Agency (historical)—locale SD-7
Whetstone Airstrip—airport AZ-5
Whetstone Bay—bay SD-7
Whetstone Bay Rec Area—park SD-7
Whetstone Bluff—cliff VT-1
Whetstone Branch—stream (2) AL-4
Whetstone Branch—stream GA-3
Whetstone Branch—stream (4) KY-4
Whetstone Branch—stream (3) MS-4
Whetstone Branch—stream PA-2
Whetstone Branch—stream (4) TN-4
Whetstone Branch—stream TX-5
Whetstone Branch—stream (3) VA-3
Whetstone Branch—stream WV-2
Whetstone Brook VT-1
Whetstone Brook—stream CT-1
Whetstone Brook—stream (2) NH-1
Whetstone Brook—stream (2) MA-1
Whetstone Brook—stream MI-6
Whetstone Brook—stream NY-2
Whetstone Brook—stream (4) VT-1
Whetstone Butte—summit OR-9
Whetstone Buttes—ridge ND-7
Whetstone Camp—locale MT-8
Whetstone Cem—cemetery MS-4
Whetstone Cem—cemetery ND-7
Whetstone Ch—church IN-6
Whetstone Ch—church (2) MO-7
Whetstone Ch—church NC-3
Whetstone Creek WY-8
Whetstone Creek—stream AL-4
Whetstone Creek—stream AR-4
Whetstone Creek—stream GA-3
Whetstone Creek—stream IL-6
Whetstone Creek—stream KS-7
Whetstone Creek—stream (5) KY-4
Whetstone Creek—stream MI-6
Whetstone Creek—stream MS-4
Whetstone Creek—stream (2) MO-7
Whetstone Creek—stream MT-8
Whetstone Creek—stream NY-2
Whetstone Creek—stream NC-3
Whetstone Creek—stream (3) OH-6
Whetstone Creek—stream (2) OR-9
Whetstone Creek—stream (3) SC-3
Whetstone Creek—stream SD-7
Whetstone Creek—stream TN-4
Whetstone Creek—stream UT-8
Whetstone Creek—stream VA-3
Whetstone Creek—stream (2) WV-2
Whetstone Creek—stream WY-8
Whetstone Creek State Wildlife Area—park MO-7
Whetstone Creek Trail—trail WY-8
Whetstone Dam—dam AL-4
Whetstone Falls—falls ME-1
Whetstone Gap—gap GA-3
Whetstone Gap—gap NC-3
Whetstone Gap—gap PA-2
Whetstone Gap—gap WV-2
Whetstone Gulch ID-8
Whetstone Gulf—valley NY-2
Whetstone Gulf State Park—park NY-2
Whetstone Hill—summit VT-1
Whetstone (historical)—locale ND-7
**Whetstone (historical)—pop pl** TN-4
Whetstone Hollow—valley MO-7
Whetstone Hollow—valley VA-3
Whetstone Hollow—valley WA-9
Whetstone HS—school OH-6
Whetstone Interchange—crossing AZ-5
Whetstone Island (historical)—island SD-7
Whetstone Lake—lake MT-8
Whetstone Mountains—summit AZ-5
Whetstone Mtn—summit AR-4
Whetstone Mtn—summit CO-8
Whetstone Mtn—summit ME-1
Whetstone Mtn—summit NC-3
Whetstone Mtn—summit OR-9
Whetstone Mtn—summit SC-3
Whetstone Mtn—summit TN-4
Whetstone Mtn—summit WY-8
Whetstone Park—park OH-6
Whetstone Point—cape (2) FL-3
Whetstone Point—cape MD-2
Whetstone Point—cape OR-9
Whetstone Pond—lake ME-1
Whetstone Pond—lake OR-9
Whetstone Post Office (historical)—building AL-4
Whetstone Post Office (historical)—building TN-4
Whetstone Ridge—ridge (2) MT-8
Whetstone Ridge—ridge TN-4
Whetstone Ridge—ridge (3) VA-3
Whetstone River OH-6
Whetstone River—stream SD-7
Whetstone Rsvr—reservoir CO-8
Whetstone Rsvr No. 3—reservoir CO-8
Whetstone Run PA-2
Whetstone Run WV-2
Whetstone Run—stream MD-2
Whetstone Run—stream OH-6
Whetstone Run—stream (3) PA-2
Whetstone Run—stream VA-3
Whetstone Run—stream (4) WV-2
Whetstone Sch—school (2) KY-4
Whetstone Sch—school WV-2
Whetstone Spring—spring AZ-5
Whetstone Spring—spring TX-5
**Whetstone Township—pop pl** ND-7
**Whetstone Township—pop pl** SD-7
Whetstone Township (historical)—civil SD-7
**Whetstone (Township of)—pop pl** OH-6
Whetstone Trail—trail OR-9
Whetstone Water Tank—reservoir TX-5
Whetten Ditch—canal IN-6
Whetzel Hollow—valley WV-2
Whetzell Spring VA-3
Whetzel Spring—spring VA-3
WHEX-AM (Columbia)—tower PA-2
Whey Hollow—valley TX-5
Whe-Yol-Do-Sah Wash AZ-5
Whe-yol-do-sah Wash—arroyo AZ-5
Whey Pond—lake NY-2
WHGM-FM (Bellwood)—tower PA-2
WHHM-AM (Henderson)—tower TN-4
W H Hodnett Catfish Ponds Dam—dam MS-4
WHHS-FM (Havertown)—tower PA-2
W H Hughes Lake Dam—dam MS-4
WHHY-AM (Montgomery)—tower AL-4
WHHY-FM (Montgomery)—tower AL-4
Whichard—locale NC-3
**Whichard Beach—pop pl** NC-3
Whichards Beach NC-3
Which Church Hollow—valley MO-7
Whick—locale KY-4
Whick Ch—church KY-4
Whicker Cem—cemetery IN-6
Whickerville—locale KY-4
Whickney Tree Rsvr—reservoir ID-8
Whidbey Air Park Airp—airport WA-9
Whidbey Bay—bay AK-9
Whidbey Island—island WA-9
Whidbey Island Nas (Ault Field) Airp—airport WA-9
Whidbey Island Naval Air Station—military WA-9
Whidbey Passage—channel AK-9
Whidby Island WA-9
Whidby Sch—school TX-5
Whidby Structure 20 Dam—dam SD-7
Whidden Bay—bay FL-3
Whidden Branch—stream FL-3
Whidden Corner—locale FL-3
**Whidden Corner—pop pl** MA-1
Whidden Creek—stream (2) FL-3
Whidden Ditch—canal OH-6
Whidden-Kerr House and Garden—hist pl OR-9
Whidden Key—island FL-3
Whidden Lake—lake FL-3
Whidden Memorial Hosp—hospital MA-1
Whidden Pond—swamp FL-3
Whidden Ponds—lake ME-1
Whiddens Pass—channel FL-3
Whidden-Ward House—hist pl NH-1
Whiddon Cem—cemetery FL-3
Whiddon Lake—lake FL-3
Whiddon Lake Ch—church FL-3
Whiddons Mill Creek—stream GA-3
Whiddons Millpond—reservoir GA-3
Whifford Hill—summit CT-1
Whig TN-4
Whig Branch—stream WI-6
Whig Cem—cemetery WI-6
Whig Center Sch—school MI-6
Whig Ch—church WI-6
**Whig Corners—pop pl** NY-2
Whig Creek—stream AR-4
Whig Creek—stream MO-7
Whigg Branch—stream NC-3
Whigg Cabin—locale TN-4
Whigg Lead TN-4
Whigg Meadow—flat TN-4
Whigg Placer Mine—mine AK-9
Whigg Ridge—ridge TN-4
Whigg Ridge Trail—trail TN-4
**Whigham—pop pl** GA-3
Whigham (CCD)—cens area GA-3
Whig Hill—locale PA-2
**Whig Hill—pop pl** NY-2
Whig Hill and Dependencies—hist pl NY-2
Whig Hill Cem—cemetery PA-2
Whig Hill Cem—cemetery SC-3
Whig Hill Sch—school IL-6
Whig Inlet—channel NY-2
Whig Lake—lake OR-9
Whiglane NJ-2
Whig Lane—locale NJ-2
**Whiglane—pop pl** NJ-2
Whig Post Office (historical)—building TN-4
Whig Ridge TN-4
Whig Sch—school MI-6
Whig Street Ch—church NY-2
Whig Street Creek—stream NY-2
Whig Swamp—swamp SC-3
Whig Valley—valley MO-7
Whigville—locale DE-2
**Whigville—pop pl** CT-1
**Whigville—pop pl (2)** OH-6
Whigville Brook—stream CT-1
Whigville Cem—cemetery MI-6
Whigville Chapel—church CT-1
Whigville Creek—stream MI-6
Whigville Lake—lake MI-6
WHII-AM (Bay Springs)—tower MS-4
Whilden Cem—cemetery SC-3
Whilden Mine AL-4
While Brant Creek SD-7
Whiley Chapel Cem—cemetery IN-6
WHIL-FM (Mobile)—tower AL-4
Whilldin Bldg—hist pl AL-4
Whilt Creek PA-2
**Whilton (subdivision)—pop pl** DE-2
Whim—hist pl VI-3
**Whim—pop pl** VI-3
WHIM-AM (East Providence)—tower RI-1
WHIM-AM (Providence)—tower RI-1
Whim Drift Mine (underground)—mine AL-4
Whim Hill—summit GA-3
Whim Knob—summit NC-3
Whimmer Whammer Draw—valley SD-7
Whimpey Creek ID-8
Whims Cem—cemetery TN-4
Whimstick Creek—stream ID-8
WHIN-AM (Gallatin)—tower TN-4
Whindling Ridge—ridge NC-3
Whinokie NJ-2
Whinokie River NJ-2
WHIP-AM (Mooresville)—tower NC-3
Whipany River NJ-2
Whipfast Lake WI-6
Whip Gap—gap WV-2
Whip Hill summit MA-1
**Whipholt—pop pl** MN-6
Whipholt Creek—stream MN-6
Whipholt Lookout Tower—locale MN-6
Whip Island—island AK-9
Whipkey Dam—dam PA-2
Whipkey Run—stream PA-2
**Whipkeys-Dam—pop pl** PA-2
Whip Lake—lake MN-6
Whiplash Lake—lake (2) WI-6
Whipoorwill Island PA-2
Whiporwill Creek AL-4
Whiporwil Sch—school NY-2
Whip-O-Will Farms Number One Dam—dam NC-3
Whip-O-Will Farms Number One Lake—reservoir NC-3
**Whippany—pop pl** NJ-2
Whippany Farm—hist pl NJ-2
Whippany River—stream NJ-2
Whipped Lake—lake MN-6
**Whipper-Barnoy—pop pl** SC-3
Whipper Barony—uninc pl SC-3
Whipperwill Creek KS-7
Whippie—locale AR-4
Whippie Canyon—valley CO-8
Whippie Cave—cave NV-8
Whippie Mtn—summit NY-2
Whipping Creek—stream NC-3
Whipping Creek—stream VA-3
Whipping Creek Lake—lake NC-3
Whip Pit—cave AL-4
Whipple MN-6
Whipple—locale AZ-5
**Whipple—pop pl** AR-4
**Whipple—pop pl** OH-6
**Whipple—pop pl** RI-1
**Whipple—pop pl** WV-2
Whipple, A., House—hist pl MA-1
Whipple, Dr. Solomon M., House—hist pl NH-1
Whipple, John, House—hist pl MA-1
Whipple, Lake—lake SD-7
Whipple, Mount—summit AK-9
Whipple, Nelson Wheeler, House—hist pl UT-8

*Whipple Barracks* ... AZ-5
Whipple Barracks Target Range—*military* ... AZ-5
Whipple Bay—*bay* ... CA-9
Whipple Bog—*swamp* ... ME-1
Whipple Brook—*stream* (3) ... NH-1
Whipple Brook—*stream* ... NY-2
Whipple Camp—*locale* ... ME-1
Whipple Canyon—*valley* ... NE-7
Whipple Cast and Wrought Iron Bowstring Truss Bridge—*hist pl* ... NY-2
Whipple Cem—*cemetery* ... IA-7
Whipple Cem—*cemetery* ... MI-6
Whipple Cem—*cemetery* ... NY-2
Whipple Cem—*cemetery* ... PA-2
Whipple Ch—*church* ... KY-4
Whipple Corner—*locale* ... NY-2
Whipple Creek—*stream* ... AK-9
Whipple Creek—*stream* ... CO-8
Whipple Creek—*stream* ... MI-6
Whipple Creek—*stream* ... UT-8
Whipple Creek—*stream* ... WA-9
Whipple Dam—*dam* ... PA-2
Whipple Dam State Park—*park* ... PA-2
Whipple Dam State Park Day Use District—*hist pl* ... PA-2
Whipple Ditch—*canal* (2) ... IN-6
Whipple Farm—*locale* ... ME-1
Whipple Fork—*stream* ... UT-8
Whipple Gulch—*valley* ... CO-8
Whipple Gulch—*valley* ... OR-9
**Whipple Heights**—*pop pl* ... OH-6
Whipple Heights Sch—*school* ... OH-6
Whipple Hill—*summit* ... ME-1
Whipple Hill—*summit* (2) ... MA-1
Whipple Hill—*summit* ... NH-1
Whipple Hill—*summit* ... NY-2
Whipple Hill—*summit* ... RI-1
Whipple Hollow—*locale* ... WY-8
Whipple Hollow—*valley* ... VT-1
Whipple Hollow Sch—*school* ... VT-1
Whipple House—*hist pl* ... NH-1
Whipple Junction—*locale* ... WV-2
Whipple-Lacey House—*hist pl* ... WY-8
Whipple Lake—*lake* ... AZ-5
Whipple Lake—*lake* (2) ... MI-6
Whipple Lake—*lake* ... MN-6
Whipple Lake—*lake* ... NE-7
*Whipple Lakes* ... MN-6
Whipple Lane Sch—*school* ... NY-2
Whipple Memorial Park—*cemetery* ... AZ-5
Whipple Mission—*church* ... MN-6
Whipple Mountain Adit—*tunnel* ... CA-9
Whipple Mountains—*range* ... CA-9
Whipple Mountain Tunnel—*tunnel* ... CA-9
Whipple Mtn—*summit* ... CO-8
Whipple Park—*park* ... AZ-5
*Whipple plateau* ... AZ-5
Whipple Point—*cape* ... CA-9
Whipple Point—*cape* ... MI-6
Whipple Point—*cape* ... VT-1
Whipple Point—*cliff* ... AZ-5
Whipple Pond—*lake* ... ME-1
Whipple Pond—*lake* ... NY-2
Whipple Pond—*reservoir* ... TX-5
Whipple Ranch—*locale* ... CA-9
Whipple Ranch Strip (airport)—*airport* ... SD-7
*Whipple Reservoir* ... AZ-5
Whipple Reservoir Dam—*dam* ... MA-1
Whipple Ridge—*ridge* ... AR-4
Whipple Ridge—*ridge* ... CA-9
Whipple Ridge—*ridge* ... NH-1
Whipple Rsvr—*reservoir* ... MA-1
Whipple Rsvr—*reservoir* ... NV-8
Whipple Run—*stream* ... OH-6
**Whipples**—*pop pl* ... MA-1
Whipple Sch—*school* ... NY-2
Whipple Sch—*school* ... SD-7
Whipples Crossing—*locale* ... AZ-5
Whipples Crossing—*locale* ... GA-3
*Whipples Hill* ... MA-1
*Whipple's Point* ... VT-1
Whipple Springs—*spring* ... CA-9
**Whipple (Tejay)**—*pop pl* ... KY-4
Whipple Trail—*trail* ... UT-8
Whipple Valley—*basin* ... UT-8
**Whippleville**—*pop pl* ... NY-2
Whipple Wash—*valley* ... CA-9
Whipple Well—*well* ... AZ-5
Whipple Well—*well* ... NV-8
Whipple Well (Dry)—*well* ... CA-9
*Whipplewill Island* ... PA-2
Whipponock Creek—*stream* ... VA-3
*Whipponong* ... NJ-2
Whippoorwill—*locale* ... KY-4
**Whippoorwill**—*pop pl* ... NY-2
**Whippoorwill**—*pop pl* ... OK-5
Whippoorwill Branch—*stream* ... AR-4
Whippoorwill Branch—*stream* ... IL-6
Whippoorwill Branch—*stream* ... IN-6
Whippoorwill Branch—*stream* ... IA-7
Whippoorwill Branch—*stream* (3) ... KY-4
Whippoorwill Branch—*stream* ... TN-4
Whip-Poor-Will Camp—*locale* ... OH-6
Whippoorwill Camp—*locale* ... PA-2
Whippoorwill Canyon—*valley* ... CA-9
Whippoorwill Cem—*cemetery* ... AR-4
Whippoorwill Cem—*cemetery* ... OH-6
Whippoorwill Ch—*church* ... AR-4
Whippoorwill Ch—*church* ... KY-4
Whip Poor Will Colliery (historical)—*mine* ... PA-2
Whippoorwill Corners—*locale* ... NY-2
Whippoorwill Corners State For—*forest* ... NY-2
Whippoorwill Country Club—*other* ... NY-2
*Whippoorwill Creek* ... AL-4
*Whippoorwill Creek* ... IA-7
Whippoorwill Creek—*stream* (2) ... AL-4
Whippoorwill Creek—*stream* ... AR-4
Whippoorwill Creek—*stream* ... IA-7
Whippoorwill Creek—*stream* (4) ... KY-4
Whippoorwill Creek—*stream* ... MO-7
Whippoorwill Creek—*stream* ... MT-8
Whippoorwill Creek—*stream* ... WI-6
Whippoorwill Flat—*flat* ... CA-9
Whippoorwill Hollow—*valley* ... IL-6
Whippoorwill Hollow—*valley* ... OH-6
Whippoorwill Hollow—*valley* (2) ... PA-2
*Whip-poor-will Island* ... PA-2
Whippoorwill Island—*island* ... PA-2
Whippoorwill Lake—*lake* ... GA-3
Whippoorwill Lake—*reservoir* (2) ... IN-6
Whippoorwill Lake—*reservoir* ... NY-2
Whippoorwill Lake—*reservoir* ... NC-3
Whippoorwill Lake Dam—*dam* (2) ... IN-6
Whippoorwill Lake Dam—*dam* ... NC-3
Whippoorwill Marina—*harbor* ... FL-3
Whippoorwill Mtn—*summit* ... MA-1
Whippoorwill Mtn—*summit* ... NY-2
Whippoorwill Rsvr—*reservoir* ... CO-8
Whippoorwill Sch—*school* ... AZ-5
Whippoorwill Sch—*school* ... IL-6
Whippoorwill Sch—*school* ... NY-2
Whippoorwill Spring—*spring* ... AZ-5
Whippoorwill Spring Mesa—*summit* ... AZ-5
Whippoorwill Swamp—*swamp* ... ME-1
*Whippoorwill Valley Mill Pond* ... NJ-2
*Whippor* ... PA-2
**Whipporrwill Hills (subdivision)**—*pop pl* ... NC-3
Whipporwill Cem—*cemetery* ... KY-4
**Whipporwill Estates (subdivision)**—*pop pl* ... AL-4
**Whipps Millgate**—*pop pl* ... KY-4
**Whipps Mill Village**—*pop pl* ... KY-4
Whipps Run—*stream* ... WV-2
Whippy Swamp—*stream* ... SC-3
Whipray Basin—*bay* ... FL-3
Whipray Channel—*channel* ... FL-3
Whipray Keys—*island* ... FL-3
Whip Run—*stream* ... WV-2
Whipsawasons Point—*cape* ... VA-3
Whipsaw Creek—*stream* ... AZ-5
Whipsaw Flat—*flat* ... UT-8
Whipsaw Mine—*mine* ... AZ-5
Whipsaw Saddle—*locale* ... ID-8
Whipsaw Spring—*spring* ... AZ-5
*Whips Cove* ... PA-2
Whips Cove—*valley* ... PA-2
**Whipstick**—*pop pl* ... CT-1
Whipstock Branch—*stream* ... AL-4
Whipstock Creek—*stream* ... UT-8
Whipstock Draw—*valley* ... UT-8
Whipstock Hill—*summit* ... VT-1
Whiptown Ch—*church* ... OH-6
Whipup—*locale* ... UT-8
WHIQ-TV (Huntsville)—*tower* ... AL-4
Whirl, The—*bend* ... TN-4
Whirl, The—*rapids* ... TX-5
Whirl Bar—*island* ... TN-4
*Whirl Creek* ... AR-4
Whirl Creek—*stream* ... AL-4
Whirl Creek—*stream* ... AR-4
Whirledge Lake—*lake* ... IN-6
Whirley Basin Tank Number One—*reservoir* ... AZ-5
Whirley Basin Tank Number Two—*reservoir* ... AZ-5
Whirleys Pond—*reservoir* ... AL-4
Whirligig Point—*cape* ... GA-3
Whirling Eddy Brook—*stream* ... NY-2
Whirl Point—*cape* ... AK-9
Whirlpool, The—*rapids* ... NH-1
Whirlpool Canyon—*valley* ... CO-8
Whirlpool Canyon—*valley* ... UT-8
Whirlpool Canyon Falls—*falls* ... PA-2
Whirlpool Channel—*channel* ... NJ-2
Whirlpool Creek—*stream* ... MT-8
Whirlpool Island—*island* ... AK-9
Whirlpool Island—*island* ... NJ-2
Whirlpool Park—*park* ... OH-6
Whirlpool Point—*cape* (2) ... AK-9
Whirlpool Point—*cape* ... NJ-2
Whirlpool Point—*cape* ... NY-2
*Whirlpool Rapids* ... WA-9
Whirlpool Rapids—*rapids* ... WI-6
Whirlpool Rock—*summit* ... AZ-5
Whirlpool Rock (historical)—*summit* ... AZ-5
Whirlpool Slough—*stream* ... AK-9
*Whirl's End* ... PA-2
*Whirl's End State Park* ... PA-2
**Whirlwind**—*pop pl* ... WV-2
Whirlwind Cem—*cemetery* ... OK-5
Whirlwind Creek—*stream* ... AK-9
Whirlwind Creek—*stream* ... SC-3
Whirlwind Draw—*valley* ... UT-8
*Whirlwind Lake* ... MT-8
Whirlwind Mesa—*summit* ... TX-5
Whirlwind Mine—*mine* ... UT-8
Whirlwind Peak—*summit* ... WY-8
Whirlwind Ridge—*ridge* ... AK-9
Whirlwind Rock—*summit* ... AZ-5
Whirlwind Rsvr—*reservoir* ... UT-8
Whirlwind Spring—*spring* ... TX-5
Whirlwind Valley—*valley* ... NV-8
Whirlwind Valley—*valley* ... UT-8
Whirly Brook—*stream* ... ME-1
Whir Spring—*spring* ... ID-8
**Whisconier**—*pop pl* ... CT-1
Whisenant Cem—*cemetery* ... AL-4
Whisenant Hollow—*valley* ... AR-4
Whisenant Junior Cave—*cave* ... AL-4
Whisenant Post Office (historical)—*building* ... AL-4
Whisenant Sch (historical)—*school* ... AL-4
Whisenhunt Cem—*cemetery* ... AR-4
Whishler Ditch—*canal* ... IN-6
*Whishman Slough* ... CA-9
Whisker Lake—*lake* ... MN-6
Whisker Lake—*lake* ... WI-6
Whisker Point—*cape* ... AK-9
Whiskers Campground—*locale* ... CA-9
Whiskers Creek—*stream* ... AK-9
Whiskers Creek—*stream* ... MI-6
Whiskers Draw—*valley* ... UT-8
Whiskers Peak—*summit* ... OR-9
Whiskers Pond—*lake* ... CO-8
Whiskerville—*locale* ... AR-4
**Whiskerville**—*pop pl* ... PA-2
**Whiskerville (Ridgeville)**—*pop pl* ... PA-2
*Whiskey* ... IL-6
Whiskey Bar—*bar* ... TN-4
*Whiskey Barrel Run* ... VA-3
Whiskey Basin—*basin* ... AZ-5
Whiskey Basin—*basin* (2) ... WY-8
*Whiskey Bay* ... MI-6
Whiskey Bay—*bay* ... LA-4
Whiskey Bayou Lakes—*lake* ... LA-4
Whiskey Beach—*beach* ... DE-2
Whiskey Bend—*bend* ... WY-8
Whiskey Bend—*locale* ... WA-9
Whiskey Bottle Creek—*stream* ... OR-9
Whiskey Bottle Rock—*summit* ... AZ-5
**Whiskey Bottom**—*pop pl* ... MD-2
Whiskey Branch—*stream* ... AL-4
Whiskey Branch—*stream* ... OK-5
Whiskey Brook—*stream* ... ME-1
Whiskey Brook—*stream* ... NY-2
Whiskey Brook—*stream* ... VT-1
*Whiskey Butte* ... CA-9
*Whiskey Butte* ... OR-9
Whiskey Butte—*summit* (3) ... ID-8
Whiskey Butte—*summit* ... MT-8
Whiskey Buttes—*summit* ... WY-8
Whiskey Cabin—*locale* ... ID-8
Whiskey Canyon—*valley* ... AZ-5
Whiskey Canyon—*valley* (2) ... CA-9
Whiskey Canyon—*valley* ... OR-9
Whiskey Canyon—*valley* ... UT-8
Whiskey Canyon—*valley* ... WA-9
*Whiskey Chitto* ... LA-4
*Whiskey Chitto Creek* ... LA-4
Whiskey Chute—*gut* ... MS-4
Whiskey Chute—*lake* ... AR-4
Whiskey Chute—*stream* ... MS-4
Whiskey Chute—*swamp* ... MS-4
**Whiskey Corners**—*pop pl* ... IL-6
Whiskey Coulee—*valley* (4) ... MT-8
Whiskey Coulee Spring—*spring* ... MT-8
Whiskey Cove—*bay* ... AK-9
*Whiskey Creek* ... CA-9
*Whiskey Creek* ... IA-7
*Whiskey Creek* ... MI-6
*Whiskey Creek* ... MN-6
*Whiskey Creek* ... NM-5
*Whiskey Creek* ... OK-5
*Whiskey Creek* ... OR-9
*Whiskey Creek* ... WI-6
Whiskey Creek—*channel* (2) ... FL-3
Whiskey Creek—*locale* ... AK-9
Whiskey Creek—*stream* ... AL-4
Whiskey Creek—*stream* (2) ... AK-9
Whiskey Creek—*stream* ... AZ-5
Whiskey Creek—*stream* (3) ... CA-9
Whiskey Creek—*stream* (4) ... CO-8
Whiskey Creek—*stream* ... FL-3
Whiskey Creek—*stream* (11) ... ID-8
Whiskey Creek—*stream* (3) ... IA-7
Whiskey Creek—*stream* ... KS-7
Whiskey Creek—*stream* ... MN-6
Whiskey Creek—*stream* ... MS-4
Whiskey Creek—*stream* (3) ... MT-8
Whiskey Creek—*stream* (4) ... NM-5
Whiskey Creek—*stream* ... NC-3
Whiskey Creek—*stream* ... OK-5
Whiskey Creek—*stream* (20) ... OR-9
Whiskey Creek—*stream* (2) ... TX-5
Whiskey Creek—*stream* (2) ... UT-8
Whiskey Creek—*stream* ... WA-9
Whiskey Creek—*stream* ... WI-6
Whiskey Creek—*stream* (6) ... WY-8
Whiskey Creek Cabin—*park* ... OR-9
Whiskey Creek Hills—*summit* ... MS-4
*Whiskey Creek Pass* ... CO-8
Whiskey Creek Picnic Area—*locale* ... CA-9
Whiskey Dick—*locale* ... OR-9
*Whiskey Dick Creek* ... WA-9
Whiskey Dick Creek—*stream* (2) ... WA-9
Whiskey Dick Flat—*flat* ... ID-8
Whiskey Dick Mtn—*summit* ... WA-9
Whiskey Diggings—*mine* ... CA-9
Whiskey Draw—*valley* (2) ... CO-8
Whiskey Draw—*valley* ... ID-8
Whiskey Draw—*valley* ... MT-8
Whiskey Draw—*valley* ... WY-8
*Whiskey Flat* ... NV-8
Whiskey Flat—*flat* ... CA-9
Whiskey Flat—*flat* ... ID-8
Whiskey Flat—*flat* (3) ... OR-9
Whiskey Flat—*flat* ... UT-8
Whiskey Ford—*locale* ... TX-5
Whiskey Gap—*gap* ... OK-5
Whiskey Gap—*gap* ... WY-8
Whiskey George Creek—*stream* ... FL-3
Whiskey Grove Campground—*locale* ... WY-8
*Whiskey Gulch* ... OR-9
Whiskey Gulch—*valley* (2) ... AK-9
Whiskey Gulch—*valley* (4) ... CO-8
Whiskey Gulch—*valley* ... ID-8
Whiskey Gulch—*valley* (9) ... MT-8
Whiskey Gulch—*valley* (2) ... OR-9
Whiskey Gulch—*valley* (2) ... SD-7
Whiskey Gulch—*valley* ... WA-9
Whiskey Gulch—*valley* (2) ... WY-8
Whiskey Harbor—*bay* ... MI-6
**Whiskey Hill**—*pop pl* ... OR-9
Whiskey Hill—*summit* (2) ... CA-9
Whiskey Hill—*summit* ... MN-6
Whiskey Hill—*summit* ... NM-5
Whiskey Hill—*summit* ... NY-2
Whiskey Hill Glacier—*glacier* ... AK-9
Whiskey Hollow—*valley* ... IN-6
Whiskey Hollow—*valley* ... KY-4
Whiskey Hollow—*valley* ... MD-2
Whiskey Hollow—*valley* ... NY-2
Whiskey Hollow—*valley* ... OH-6
Whiskey Hollow—*valley* ... OK-5
Whiskey Hollow—*valley* ... TX-5
Whiskey Hollow—*valley* ... UT-8
Whiskey Hollow—*valley* ... WV-2
Whiskey Hollow Hill—*summit* ... PA-2
Whiskey Island—*island* ... AK-9
Whiskey Island—*island* ... GA-3
Whiskey Island—*island* ... ME-1
Whiskey Island—*island* ... MS-4
Whiskey Island—*island* (2) ... NY-2
Whiskey Island—*island* ... TN-4
Whiskey Island (historical)—*locale* ... SD-7
Whiskey Island Lake—*lake* ... UT-8
Whiskey Jack Creek—*stream* ... ID-8
Whiskey Jack Slough—*stream* ... AK-9
Whiskey Jack Spring—*spring* ... OR-9
Whiskey Jim Creek—*stream* ... WA-9
Whiskey Jim Flat—*flat* ... WA-9
Whiskey John Flat—*flat* ... OR-9
Whiskey Key—*island* ... FL-3
Whiskey Knob—*summit* ... OK-5
Whiskey Knoll—*summit* ... UT-8
Whiskey Lake—*lake* ... AK-9
Whiskey Lake—*lake* ... KS-7
Whiskey Lake—*lake* (3) ... MN-6
Whiskey Lake—*lake* ... NM-5
Whiskey Lake—*lake* ... OR-9
*Whiskey Mountain* ... WA-9
Whiskey Mountain Trail—*trail* ... WY-8
Whiskey Mtn—*summit* ... ID-8
Whiskey Mtn—*summit* ... OR-9
Whiskey Mtn—*summit* ... WY-8
Whiskey Park—*flat* ... CO-8
Whiskey Pass—*channel* ... AK-9
Whiskey Pass—*channel* ... LA-4
Whiskey Pass—*gap* ... CO-8
Whiskey Peak—*summit* ... AR-4
Whiskey Peak—*summit* ... OR-9
Whiskey Peak—*summit* ... WY-8
Whiskey Point—*cape* ... MI-6
Whiskey Point—*cape* ... NY-2
Whiskey Pup—*stream* ... AK-9
Whiskey Ridge—*ridge* ... AZ-5
Whiskey Ridge—*ridge* ... MT-8
Whiskey Ridge—*ridge* ... WY-8
Whiskey Ridge Tank—*reservoir* ... AZ-5
Whiskey Rock—*pillar* ... ID-8
Whiskey Rock—*pillar* ... WA-9
Whiskey Rock Bay—*bay* ... ID-8
Whiskey Rock Recreation Site—*locale* ... ID-8
Whiskey Rsvr—*reservoir* ... AZ-5
*Whiskey Run* ... IN-6
*Whiskey Run* ... PA-2
Whiskey Run—*stream* (2) ... IN-6
Whiskey Run—*stream* ... IA-7
Whiskey Run—*stream* ... KY-4
Whiskey Run—*stream* ... OH-6
Whiskey Run—*stream* (3) ... PA-2
Whiskey Run—*stream* ... WV-2
*Whiskey Run Creek* ... IN-6
**Whiskey Run (Township of)**—*pop pl* ... IN-6
Whiskey Saddle—*gap* ... CA-9
Whiskey Slough—*gut* (3) ... CA-9
Whiskey Slough—*stream* ... AK-9
Whiskey Slough—*stream* ... ID-8
Whiskey Slough Landing (historical)—*locale* ... MS-4
*Whiskey Spring* ... NV-8
*Whiskey Spring* ... OR-9
*Whiskey Spring* ... WA-9
Whiskey Spring—*spring* (11) ... AZ-5
Whiskey Spring—*spring* ... AR-4
Whiskey Spring—*spring* (3) ... CA-9
Whiskey Spring—*spring* ... CO-8
Whiskey Spring—*spring* ... ID-8
Whiskey Spring—*spring* (2) ... MT-8
Whiskey Spring—*spring* (4) ... NV-8
Whiskey Spring—*spring* ... NM-5
Whiskey Spring—*spring* (7) ... OR-9
Whiskey Spring—*spring* ... TX-5
Whiskey Spring—*spring* (3) ... UT-8
Whiskey Spring—*spring* ... WY-8
Whiskey Spring Canyon—*valley* ... AZ-5
Whiskey Spring Canyon—*valley* ... NM-5
Whiskey Spring Coulee—*valley* ... MT-8
Whiskey Spring Creek—*stream* ... ID-8
Whiskey Spring Creek—*stream* ... UT-8
Whiskey Spring Number Two—*spring* ... OR-9
Whiskey Spring Picnic Area—*locale* ... UT-8
*Whiskey Spring Picnic Ground* ... UT-8
Whiskey Springs—*locale* ... CA-9
Whiskey Springs—*spring* ... CA-9
Whiskey Springs—*spring* ... CO-8
Whiskey Springs—*spring* (2) ... NV-8
Whiskey Springs—*spring* (3) ... OR-9
Whiskey Springs—*spring* ... WY-8
Whiskey Springs Canyon—*valley* ... NV-8
Whiskey Springs Ranch—*locale* ... CO-8
Whiskey Spring Trail—*trail* ... AZ-5
Whiskey Spring Vly—*swamp* ... NY-2
Whiskey Still Pond—*swamp* ... TX-5
Whiskey Stump Key—*island* ... FL-3
*Whiskey Swamp* ... NC-3
Whiskey Swamp—*stream* ... NC-3
*Whiskey Tank* ... NM-5
Whiskey Tank—*reservoir* (2) ... AZ-5
**Whiskeytown**—*pop pl* ... CA-9
Whiskeytown Lake—*reservoir* ... CA-9
Whiskeytown-Shasta-Trinity Natl Rec Area—*park* ... CA-9
Whiskey Trail—*trail* ... AZ-5
Whiskey Trail—*trail* ... NM-5
Whiskey Wash—*valley* ... UT-8
Whiskey Well—*well* ... AZ-5
Whiskey Well—*well* ... NM-5
Whiskey Well Tank—*reservoir* ... NM-5
Whiskey Windmill—*locale* ... NM-5
Whiskinboo Creek—*stream* ... SC-3
Whisky Bay—*bay* ... LA-4
Whisky Bayou—*stream* (2) ... LA-4
Whisky Bay Pilot Channel—*channel* ... LA-4
Whisky Bill Peak—*summit* ... CA-9
Whisky Bob Creek—*stream* ... ID-8
Whisky Branch—*stream* (2) ... AL-4
Whisky Branch—*stream* ... MS-4
Whisky Branch—*stream* (2) ... OK-5
Whisky Branch—*stream* ... TX-5
*Whisky Butte* ... ID-8
Whisky Butte—*summit* ... CA-9
Whisky Butte—*summit* ... OR-9
Whisky Cache Creek—*stream* ... WA-9
Whisky Camp—*locale* ... CA-9
Whisky Camp—*locale* ... OR-9
Whisky Canyon—*valley* ... CA-9
Whisky Canyon—*valley* ... NV-8
Whisky Canyon—*valley* ... WA-9
Whisky Chitto Creek—*stream* ... LA-4
Whisky Cove—*bay* ... AK-9
*Whisky Creek* ... CA-9
*Whisky Creek* ... CO-8
*Whisky Creek* ... ID-8
*Whisky Creek* ... KS-7
*Whisky Creek* ... MN-6
*Whisky Creek* ... OR-9
Whisky Creek—*stream* (2) ... AR-4
Whisky Creek—*stream* (11) ... CA-9
Whisky Creek—*stream* ... IL-6
Whisky Creek—*stream* ... IA-7
Whisky Creek—*stream* ... KS-7
Whisky Creek—*stream* (5) ... MI-6
Whisky Creek—*stream* (3) ... MN-6
Whisky Creek—*stream* ... MS-4
Whisky Creek—*stream* ... MO-7
Whisky Creek—*stream* ... NE-7
Whisky Creek—*stream* ... NY-2
Whisky Creek—*stream* (2) ... ND-7
Whisky Creek—*stream* (5) ... OK-5
Whisky Creek—*stream* (12) ... OR-9
Whisky Creek—*stream* ... TX-5
Whisky Creek—*stream* ... UT-8
Whisky Creek—*stream* ... VA-3
Whisky Creek—*stream* (2) ... WA-9
Whisky Creek—*stream* (4) ... WI-6
Whisky Creek—*stream* ... WY-8
Whisky Creek Cabin—*hist pl* ... OR-9
Whisky Creek Camp—*locale* ... CA-9
Whisky Creek Spring—*spring* ... OR-9
*Whisky Dick Creek* ... WA-9
Whisky Diggins Canal—*canal* ... CA-9
Whisky Ditch—*canal* ... MN-6
Whisky Draw—*valley* ... WY-8
Whisky Falls—*locale* ... CA-9
Whisky Flat—*flat* (2) ... CA-9
Whisky Flat—*flat* ... NV-8
Whisky Flat—*flat* ... OR-9
Whisky Flats—*flat* ... WA-9
*Whisky George Creek* ... FL-3
Whisky Gulch—*valley* ... CA-9
Whisky Gulch—*valley* ... MT-8
Whisky Gulch—*valley* (4) ... OR-9
Whisky Gulch Mine—*mine* ... MT-8
Whisky Gulch Springs—*spring* ... OR-9
Whisky Hill—*summit* (2) ... CA-9
Whisky Hill—*summit* ... OR-9
Whisky Hill—*summit* ... TN-4
Whisky Hollow—*valley* ... IL-6
Whisky Hollow—*valley* ... NY-2
Whisky Hollow—*valley* (3) ... OK-5
Whisky Hollow Creek—*stream* ... MI-6
*Whisky Island* ... NY-2
Whisky Island—*island* ... GA-3
Whisky Island—*island* (2) ... LA-4
Whisky Island—*island* ... MI-6
Whisky Island—*island* ... MN-6
Whisky Jack Lake—*lake* ... MN-6
*Whisky Lake* ... MN-6
*Whisky Lake* ... OR-9
Whisky Lake—*lake* ... AR-4
Whisky Lake—*lake* ... CA-9
Whisky Lake—*lake* (2) ... MN-6
Whisky Lake—*lake* ... WI-6
*Whisky Mountain* ... WY-8
Whisky Mtn—*summit* ... WA-9
*Whisky Peak* ... OR-9
Whisky Peak—*summit* ... UT-8
Whisky Point—*cape* ... IL-6
Whisky Point—*summit* ... NV-8
Whisky Ridge—*ridge* (3) ... CA-9
Whisky Ridge—*ridge* ... OR-9
*Whisky Rock* ... ID-8
*Whisky Rock Bay* ... ID-8
Whisky Rsvr—*reservoir* ... WY-8
*Whisky Run* ... IN-6
*Whisky Run* ... PA-2
Whisky Run—*stream* ... CA-9
Whisky Run—*stream* ... IA-7
Whisky Run—*stream* (3) ... NE-7
Whisky Run—*stream* ... OH-6
Whisky Run—*stream* ... OR-9
Whisky Run—*stream* (5) ... PA-2
Whisky Run Beach—*beach* ... OR-9
Whisky Run Sch—*school* ... PA-2
*Whisky Slough* ... CA-9
Whisky Slough—*stream* (2) ... NE-7
Whisky Spring—*spring* (2) ... AZ-5
Whisky Spring—*spring* ... CA-9
Whisky Spring—*spring* (2) ... ID-8
Whisky Spring—*spring* (4) ... NV-8
Whisky Spring—*spring* (4) ... OR-9
Whisky Spring—*spring* ... PA-2
Whisky Spring—*spring* ... UT-8
Whisky Spring Forest Camp—*locale* ... OR-9
Whisky Spring Lean-to—*building* ... PA-2
*Whisky Springs* ... CA-9
Whisky Springs—*spring* ... OR-9
Whisky Springs—*spring* ... UT-8
Whisky Springs Draw—*valley* ... UT-8
Whisky Spring Trail—*trail* ... OR-9
**Whisler**—*pop pl* ... OH-6
Whisler Cem—*cemetery* ... TN-4
Whisler Number 1 Dam—*dam* ... SD-7
Whisler Run—*stream* ... WV-2
Whislers Branch—*stream* ... IA-7
Whisman—*airport* ... NJ-2
Whisman Cem—*cemetery* (2) ... KY-4
Whisman Cem—*cemetery* ... VA-3
Whisman Hollow—*valley* ... VA-3
Whisman Sch—*school* ... CA-9
*Whisman Slough* ... CA-9
Whisnant Old River—*stream* ... AR-4
Whisners Run—*stream* ... WV-2
**Whisp**—*pop pl* ... AR-4
Whispering Cave—*cave* ... CO-8
Whispering Cedars—*woods* ... TX-5
Whispering Creek—*stream* ... VA-3
Whispering Hill—*summit* ... MA-1
**Whispering Hills**—*pop pl* ... IL-6
**Whispering Hills**—*pop pl* ... KY-4
**Whispering Hills**—*pop pl* ... MO-7
**Whispering Hills**—*pop pl* ... TN-4
Whispering Hills—*uninc pl* ... AZ-5
Whispering Hills—*uninc pl* ... FL-3
Whispering Hills Ch—*church* ... TN-4
**Whispering Hills Golf Estates**—*pop pl* ... FL-3
**Whispering Hills (subdivision)**—*pop pl* ... AL-4
**Whispering Hills (subdivision)**—*pop pl* ... TN-4
Whispering Hollow—*valley* ... AR-4
Whispering Lake—*lake* ... MN-6
Whispering Lake—*lake* ... WI-6
*Whispering Oaks* ... IL-6
**Whispering Oaks**—*pop pl* ... TX-5
Whispering Oaks—*uninc pl* (2) ... TX-5
Whispering Oaks Dam Number One—*dam* ... KS-7
**Whispering Oaks PRUD (subdivision)**—*pop pl* ... UT-8
**Whispering Oaks (subdivision)**—*pop pl* ... NC-3
Whispering Palms—*uninc pl* ... FL-3
Whispering Pines—*locale* ... AZ-5
Whispering Pines—*locale* ... GA-3
Whispering Pines—*locale* ... TX-5
Whispering Pines—*locale* ... VA-3
**Whispering Pines**—*pop pl* (2) ... CA-9
**Whispering Pines**—*pop pl* ... FL-3
**Whispering Pines**—*pop pl* ... NC-3
**Whispering Pines**—*pop pl* ... TN-4
**Whispering Pines**—*pop pl* ... WI-6
Whispering Pines Cabins—*locale* ... MI-6
Whispering Pines Camp—*locale* ... GA-3
Whispering Pines Camp—*locale* ... NY-2
Whispering Pines Cem—*cemetery* ... AL-4
Whispering Pines Cem—*cemetery* ... CA-9
Whispering Pines Cem—*cemetery* ... NV-8
Whispering Pines Ch—*church* ... LA-4
Whispering Pines Ch—*church* (2) ... NC-3
Whispering Pines Ch—*church* ... SC-3
Whispering Pine Sch—*school* ... SD-7
Whispering Pines Elem Sch—*school* (2) ... FL-3
Whispering Pines Forest Camp—*locale* ... OR-9
Whispering Pines Golf Course—*locale* ... PA-2
Whispering Pines Hammock Park—*park* ... FL-3
*Whispering Pines Lake* ... WI-6
Whispering Pines Lake—*reservoir* ... AL-4
Whispering Pines Lake—*reservoir* ... GA-3
**Whispering Pines Number Two (subdivision)**—*pop pl* ... NC-3
Whispering Pines Park—*park* ... FL-3
Whispering Pines Pond—*reservoir* ... IN-6
Whispering Pines Sch—*school* ... TN-4
**Whispering Pines (subdivision)**—*pop pl* ... AL-4
**Whispering Pines (subdivision)**—*pop pl* ... MS-4
**Whispering Pines (subdivision)**—*pop pl* (3) ... NC-3
**Whispering Pines (trailer park)**—*pop pl* ... DE-2
Whispering Spring Campground—*locale* ... AL-4
**Whispering Springs**—*pop pl* ... AR-4
Whispering Willows Golf Course—*other* ... MI-6
Whispering Wind Lake—*reservoir* ... IN-6
Whispering Wind Lake Dam—*dam* ... IN-6
Whispering Winds Ch—*church* ... MO-7
Whispering Winds Dam—*dam* ... OR-9
Whispering Winds Rsvr—*reservoir* ... OR-9
Whispering Woods—*woods* ... NY-2
Whisper Lake—*lake* ... AK-9
Whisper Lake—*lake* ... MI-6
Whisper Lake—*lake* ... MN-6
Whisper Pines Airp—*airport* ... PA-2
**Whisperwood**—*pop pl* ... TN-4
Whisperwood—*post sta* ... TX-5
**Whisperwood Subdivision**—*pop pl* ... UT-8
Whissenhunt Mtn—*summit* ... GA-3
Whisson Ridge—*ridge* ... VA-3
Whisting Cave—*cave* ... NM-5
*Whist Island* ... MI-6
Whist Landing—*locale* ... MO-7
**Whistle**—*pop pl* ... MS-4
Whistle Berry Hill—*summit* ... WY-8
Whistleberry Slough—*gut* ... TX-5
Whistle Creek—*fmr MCD* ... NE-7
Whistle Creek—*stream* (2) ... IN-6
Whistle Creek—*stream* (2) ... MT-8
Whistle Creek—*stream* ... NE-7
Whistle Creek—*stream* ... OR-9
Whistle Creek—*stream* ... SD-7
Whistle Creek—*stream* ... TN-4
Whistle Creek—*stream* ... VA-3
Whistle Creek—*stream* ... WA-9
Whistle Creek—*stream* ... WY-8
Whistle Creek Mine—*mine* ... TN-4
Whistle Creek Ridge—*ridge* ... TN-4
Whistle Creek Rsvr—*reservoir* ... WY-8
Whistle Geyser—*geyser* ... WY-8
Whistle Lake—*lake* ... WA-9
Whistle Mtn—*summit* ... KY-4
Whistle Peak—*summit* ... OK-5
Whistlepig Branch—*stream* ... TN-4
Whistle Point—*summit* ... OR-9
Whistle Pond—*lake* ... NY-2
*Whistler* ... OH-6
**Whistler**—*pop pl* ... AL-4
**Whistler**—*pop pl* ... MS-4
**Whistler**—*pop pl* ... OH-6
Whistler, Lake—*lake* ... FL-3
Whistler Baptist Ch—*church* ... AL-4
Whistler Basin—*basin* (2) ... WA-9
Whistler Bend County Park—*park* ... OR-9
Whistler Canal—*canal* ... UT-8
Whistler Cem—*cemetery* ... AL-4
Whistler Cem—*cemetery* ... IN-6
Whistler Cem—*cemetery* ... KS-7
Whistler Cem—*cemetery* ... OK-5
Whistler Creek—*stream* (3) ... AK-9
Whistler Creek—*stream* ... MT-8
Whistler Creek—*stream* (2) ... WA-9
Whistler Creek—*stream* ... WY-8
Whistler Gulch—*valley* ... SD-7
Whistle Ridge—*ridge* ... AK-9
*Whistler Lake* ... MI-6
Whistler Lake—*lake* ... WA-9
Whistler Lookout Tower—*locale* ... MS-4
Whistler Methodist Ch—*church* ... AL-4
Whistler Mine—*mine* ... WA-9
Whistler Mtn—*summit* ... NV-8
Whistler Mtn—*summit* ... WA-9
Whistler Pass—*gap* (2) ... WA-9
Whistler Pentecostal Holiness Ch—*church* ... AL-4
Whistler Point—*cape* ... MA-1
Whistler Point—*summit* ... OR-9
Whistler Preserve—*park* ... IL-6
Whistler Range—*range* ... NV-8
Whistlers Bend—*bend* ... OR-9
Whistlers Bend—*bend* ... UT-8
Whistlers Bend Dam—*dam* ... OR-9
Whistlers Bend Rsvr—*reservoir* ... OR-9
Whistler Sch—*school* ... AL-4
Whistler Sch—*school* ... IL-6
Whistlers Cove—*bay* ... NY-2
Whistlers Landing (historical)—*locale* ... AL-4
*Whistlers Mother* ... UT-8
*Whistlers Pass* ... WA-9
Whistle Spring—*spring* ... OR-9
Whistle Stop Mall (Shop Ctr)—*locale* ... AZ-5
Whistle Tank—*reservoir* ... AZ-5
**Whistletown**—*pop pl* ... PA-2
Whistletown Cem—*cemetery* ... CT-1
Whistle Valley—*valley* ... TN-4
Whistleville—*locale* ... GA-3
**Whistleville**—*pop pl* ... AR-4
Whistlewing Bay—*bay* ... AK-9
Whistling Branch—*stream* ... TN-4
Whistling Cay—*island* ... VI-3
Whistling Creek—*stream* ... ID-8

Whistling Creek—*stream* WA-9
Whistling Gap—*gap* NC-3
Whistling Gap—*gap* TN-4
Whistling Gap Branch—*stream* NC-3
Whistling Gulch—*valley* AK-9
Whistling Jim Hollow—*valley* KY-4
Whistling Lake—*lake* AR-4
Whistling Lamp Cave—*cave* AL-4
Whistling Peak—*summit* ID-8
Whistling Pig Canyon—*valley* ID-8
Whistling Pig Creek—*stream* ID-8
Whistling Pig Creek—*stream* WA-9
Whistling Pig Meadow—*flat* WA-9
Whistling Ridge—*ridge* WA-9
Whistling Spring—*spring* AZ-5
Whist Pond—*reservoir* CT-1
*Whists Landing* MO-7
**Whit**—*pop pl* TX-5
Whitabee Lake—*lake* MI-6
*Whitackerville* MO-7
Whitacre—*locale* VA-3
Whitacre Ditch—*canal* IN-6
Whitacre Point—*cape* TN-4
**Whitacres**—*pop pl* CT-1
*Whitaker* NC-3
*Whitaker* WV-2
Whitaker—*locale* KY-4
Whitaker—*locale* MS-4
Whitaker—*locale* OR-9
**Whitaker**—*pop pl* AR-4
**Whitaker**—*pop pl* IL-6
**Whitaker**—*pop pl* IN-6
**Whitaker**—*pop pl* KY-4
**Whitaker**—*pop pl* PA-2
**Whitaker**—*pop pl* TN-4
Whitaker, Charles, House—*hist pl* IA-7
Whitaker, Charles, House—*hist pl* KY-4
Whitaker, James, House—*hist pl* UT-8
Whitaker, John M., House—*hist pl* UT-8
Whitaker Bayou—*gut* FL-3
Whitaker Bend—*bend* TN-4
Whitaker Bend Cut Off—*bend* TX-5
Whitaker Bluff—*cliff* TN-4
Whitaker Borough—*civil* PA-2
*Whitaker Branch* TN-4
Whitaker Branch—*stream* (2) KY-4
Whitaker Branch—*stream* (2) NC-3
Whitaker Branch—*stream* TN-4
Whitaker Bridge—*bridge* MT-8
Whitaker Brook—*stream* ME-1
Whitaker Brook—*stream* NY-2
Whitaker Cem—*cemetery* GA-3
Whitaker Cem—*cemetery* (3) KY-4
Whitaker Cem—*cemetery* LA-4
Whitaker Cem—*cemetery* ME-1
Whitaker Cem—*cemetery* MS-4
Whitaker Cem—*cemetery* (2) MO-7
Whitaker Cem—*cemetery* (2) NC-3
Whitaker Cem—*cemetery* (4) TN-4
Whitaker Cem—*cemetery* TX-5
*Whitaker Cemetery* AL-4
Whitaker Ch—*church* AL-4
Whitaker Ch—*church* MO-7
Whitaker Chapel—*church* NC-3
Whitaker-Clary House—*hist pl* MA-1
*Whitaker Columbia Middle School* OR-9
*Whitaker Cove* TN-4
Whitaker Cove—*valley* NC-3
Whitaker Creek—*stream* AR-4
Whitaker Creek—*stream* ID-8
Whitaker Creek—*stream* IL-6
Whitaker Creek—*stream* IN-6
Whitaker Creek—*stream* MS-4
Whitaker Creek—*stream* TX-5
Whitaker Draw—*valley* WY-8
Whitaker Elem Sch—*school* NC-3
**Whitaker Estates (subdivision)**—*pop pl* UT-8
Whitaker Falls—*falls* WV-2
Whitaker Field Tank—*reservoir* TX-5
Whitaker Flat—*flat* MT-8
Whitaker Fork—*stream* KY-4
Whitaker For (university of California)—*forest* CA-9
Whitaker Grove Ch—*church* KY-4
Whitaker Hill—*summit* MO-7
Whitaker Hill Cem—*cemetery* GA-3
**Whitakor (historical)** *pop pl* OR 9
Whitaker Holes—*basin* OR-9
Whitaker Hollow—*valley* (3) TN-4
Whitaker Hollow—*valley* WI-6
Whitaker House—*hist pl* TX-5
Whitaker Lake—*lake* MN-6
Whitaker Lake—*lake* NY-2
Whitaker Lake—*lake* OR-9
Whitaker Lake—*reservoir* NC-3
Whitaker Lake—*reservoir* TN-4
Whitaker Lake Dam—*dam* NC-3
Whitaker Lake Dam—*dam* TN-4
Whitaker Lake Outlet—*stream* NY-2
Whitaker-McClendon House—*hist pl* TX-5
Whitaker Mtn—*summit* SC-3
Whitaker Park—*building* NC-3
Whitaker Park—*park* NV-8
Whitaker Park—*park* OK-5
Whitaker Park—*park* TN-4
**Whitaker Park (subdivision)**—*pop pl* NC-3
Whitaker-Patrick Cem—*cemetery* IN-6
Whitaker Peak—*summit* CA-9
Whitaker Peak Lookout—*locale* CA-9
Whitaker Pond—*lake* TX-5
Whitaker Post Office (historical)—*building* MS-4
Whitaker Post Office (historical)—*building*. TN-4
Whitaker Ranch—*locale* CA-9
Whitaker Ranch—*locale* CO-8
Whitaker Ranch—*locale* (2) WY-8
Whitaker Ridge—*ridge* VA-3
Whitaker (RR name for Whittaker)—*other* WV-2
Whitaker Run—*stream* PA-2
**Whitakers**—*pop pl* NC-3
Whitaker Saint Sch—*school* TX-5
Whitakers Bayou—*bay* TX-5
Whitakers Boat Dock—*locale* TN-4
Whitaker Sch—*school* AR-4
Whitaker Sch—*school* CA-9
Whitaker Sch—*school* (2) IL-6
Whitaker Sch—*school* (2) KY-4
Whitaker Sch—*school* OR-9
Whitakers Chapel—*church* NC-3
*Whitakers Cut* TX-5
*Whitakers Forest* CA-9
*Whitakers Mill* NC-3
Whitakers Mill (historical)—*locale* AL-4
Whitaker Spring—*spring* TN-4
Whitaker Springs—*spring* UT-8
Whitakers Run—*stream* OH-6
Whitakers Sch (historical)—*school* TN-4
Whitaker State Childrens Home—*other* OK-5
Whitaker Station—*locale* WV-2
**Whitaker Subdivision**—*pop pl* UT-8
Whitaker Summit—*gap* CA-9
Whitaker Swamp—*swamp* NY-2
**Whitakerville**—*pop pl* MO-7
Whitaker Well—*well* NM-5
Whitall, James, Jr., House—*hist pl* NJ-2
Whitamore Cem—*cemetery* AL-4
*Whitback Rock* UT-8
Whitbeck, Mount—*summit* MA-1
Whitbeck Rock—*summit* UT-8
Whit Branch—*stream* VA-3
Whitbread Springs—*spring* MT-8
Whit Brook—*stream* ME-1
**Whitbury**—*pop pl* MS-4
**Whitby**—*pop pl* WV-2
Whitby Canyon—*valley* CO-8
Whitby Ditch—*canal* OR-9
Whitby Mansion—*hist pl* OH-6
Whitby Rsvr—*reservoir* ID-8
Whitby Sch Number 1—*school* ND-7
Whitby Sch Number 3—*school* ND-7
Whitby Sch Number 4—*school* ND-7
**Whitby Township**—*pop pl* ND-7
Whit Cem—*cemetery* GA-3
Whitcher Brook—*stream* NH-1
Whitcher Creek—*stream* OR-9
*Whitcher Hill* MA-1
Whitcher Hill—*summit* NH-1
Whitcher Mtn—*summit* VT-1
Whitchurch Cem—*cemetery* IL-6
**Whitcliff**—*pop pl* KY-4
**Whitco**—*pop pl* KY-4
**Whitco**—*pop pl* TN-4
*Whitcoal Branch* WV-2
Whitcomb—*locale* WA-9
**Whitcomb**—*pop pl* (2) IN-6
**Whitcomb**—*pop pl* WV-2
**Whitcomb**—*pop pl* WI-6
Whitcomb, Harlie, Farm—*hist pl* VT-1
Whitcomb, Lake—*lake* (2) FL-3
Whitcomb Bayou—*bay* FL-3
Whitcomb Branch—*stream* MO-7
Whitcomb Brook—*stream* MA-1
Whitcomb Butte—*summit* MT-8
Whitcomb Cabin—*hist pl* WA-9
Whitcomb Canal—*canal* CA-9
Whitcomb Cem—*cemetery* IN-6
Whitcomb Cem—*cemetery* TX-5
Whitcomb Coulee—*valley* MT-8
Whitcomb Court Sch—*school* VA-3
Whitcomb Creek—*stream* MT-8
Whitcomb Creek—*stream* OR-9
Whitcomb Creek—*stream* WA-9
Whitcomb Creek—*stream* WI-6
Whitcomb Drain Two A—*canal* CA-9
Whitcombe Brook—*stream* ME-1
Whitcomb Farm—*hist pl* RI-1
Whitcomb Flats—*bar* WA-9
**Whitcomb Heights**—*pop pl* IN-6
**Whitcomb Hill**—*pop pl* CT-1
Whitcomb Hill—*summit* AZ-5
Whitcomb Hill—*summit* CT-1
Whitcomb Hill—*summit* MA-1
Whitcomb Hill—*summit* NH-1
Whitcomb Hill—*summit* VT-1
Whitcomb Hill—*summit* WY-8
*Whitcomb Hills* MA-1
Whitcomb Hollow—*valley* NY-2
Whitcomb House—*hist pl* MA-1
Whitcomb HS—*school* VT-1
Whitcomb Island—*island* OR-9
Whitcomb Lake—*lake* MI-6
Whitcomb Lake—*lake* MT-8
Whitcomb Lake—*lake* WI-6
Whitcomb Ledge—*bar* MA-1
Whitcomb Mansion—*hist pl* MA-1
Whitcomb Mountain—*ridge* NH-1
Whitcomb Peak—*summit* MT-8
Whitcomb Peak—*summit* NH-1
Whitcomb Pond—*lake* NH-1
Whitcomb Ranch—*locale* WY-8
*Whitcomb River* MA-1
Whitcomb Sch—*school* CA-9
Whitcomb Sch—*school* IL-6
Whitcomb Sch—*school* OR-9
Whitcomb Sch—*school* WI-6
Whitcombs Corner—*locale* ME-1
*Whitcomb Spring* AZ-5
**Whitcomb Summit**—*pop pl* MA-1
Whitcomb Swamp—*swamp* MA-1
Whitcomb Three Drain—*canal* CA-9
Whitcomb Two Drain—*canal* CA-9
Whitcomb View Sch—*school* PA-2
Whitcomb Warehouse—*hist pl* MA-1
Whitcom Spring—*spring* AZ-5
Whitcox Branch—*stream* TN-4
Whitcraft Gulch—*valley* MT-8
Whit Creek—*stream* WY-8
*White* AL-4
*White* CA-9
*White* KS-7
*White* MS-4
*White* PA-2
White—*locale* AR-4
White—*locale* CA-9
White—*locale* MI-6
White—*locale* MT-8
White—*locale* ND-7
White—*locale* PA-2
White—*locale* WV-2
White—*mine* NV-8
**White**—*pop pl* AL-4
**White**—*pop pl* CO-8
**White**—*pop pl* GA-3
**White**—*pop pl* LA-4
**White**—*pop pl* PA-2
**White**—*pop pl* SD-7
**White**—*pop pl* TX-5
**White**—*pop pl* WA-9
White—*uninc pl* TN-4
White, Almond A., House—*hist pl* MN-6
White, Andrew Dickson, House—*hist pl* NY-2
White, Asa, House—*hist pl* AL-4
White, Asbury, House—*hist pl* CO-8
White, Bayou—*stream* LA-4
White, Benjamin, House—*hist pl* MA-1
White, Catherine, House—*hist pl* OR-9
White, Charles Dennis, House—*hist pl* UT-8
White, Charles M., House—*hist pl* TN-4
White, David, House—*hist pl* DC-2
White, Dr. James, House—*hist pl* PA-2
White, Dr. Toler R., House—*hist pl* AZ-5
White, E. B., House—*hist pl* ME-1
White, Edward Douglass, House—*hist pl* LA-4
White, Elisha, House—*hist pl* TN-4
White, Elizabeth, House—*hist pl* SC-3
White, E. M., Dairy Barn—*hist pl* AZ-5
White, Ethelbert and Stewart, William M., Ranch House—*hist pl* UT-8
White, F. F., Block—*hist pl* WI-6
White, Francis, Homestead—*hist pl* MN-6
White, Frank, House—*hist pl* TN-4
White, H. A., General Store and House—*hist pl* IA-7
White, Hamilton, House—*hist pl* NY-2
White, Hannah, Log House—*hist pl* PA-2
White, Henry P., House—*hist pl* OH-6
White, Isaac, House—*hist pl* NC-3
White, Island—*island* CA-9
White, Jacob Hanmer, House—*hist pl* UT-8
White, James P., House—*hist pl* ME-1
White, James Phelps, House—*hist pl* NM-5
White, Jay, House—*hist pl* MI-6
White, Jeff, House—*hist pl* NC-3
White, Jesse and Simon, House—*hist pl* KY-4
White, John, House—*hist pl* NJ-2
White, John M., House—*hist pl* SC-3
White, John W., House—*hist pl* AR-4
White, Joseph and Minnie, House—*hist pl* NJ-2
White, Josephine, Block—*hist pl* RI-1
White, Judge P. W., House—*hist pl* FL-3
White, Lake—*lake* MN-6
White, Lake—*lake* OH-6
White, Louise, Sch—*hist pl* IL-6
White, Maggie Gillies, House—*hist pl* UT-8
White, Milo, House—*hist pl* MN-6
White, Mount—*summit* CO-8
White, Munger and Company, Store—*hist pl* IA-7
White, Newton, House—*hist pl* TN-4
White, Orrin, House—*hist pl* MI-6
White, Point—*cape* WA-9
White, Samuel, House—*hist pl* UT-8
White, Samuel M., house—*hist pl* OH-6
White, Theodore, House—*hist pl* IA-7
White, T. L., Barn—*hist pl* KS-7
White, Walter C., Estate—*hist pl* OH-6
White, William Allen, Cabins—*hist pl* CO-8
White, William Allen, House—*hist pl* KS-7
White, William Elliott, House—*hist pl* SC-3
White, William H., House—*hist pl* UT-8
White, William L., Jr., House—*hist pl* MA-1
White, W. J., House—*hist pl* AR-4
White Acorn Ranch—*locale* WY-8
Whiteacre Peak—*summit* CA-9
Whiteacre Peak Trail—*trail* CA-9
**White Acres**—*pop pl* TN-4
White Acres—*uninc pl* FL-3
Whiteacres Mill (historical)—*locale* TN-4
**White Addition (subdivision)**—*pop pl* UT-8
White-Aiken House—*hist pl* TX-5
Whiteaker Cem—*cemetery* VA-3
**Whiteaker (historical)**—*pop pl* OR-9
Whiteaker Number 1 Sch—*school* ND-7
Whiteaker Number 2 Sch—*school* ND-7
Whiteaker Number 3 Sch—*school* ND-7
Whiteaker Number 4 Sch—*school* ND-7
Whiteaker Ranch—*locale* TX-5
Whiteaker Sch—*school* OR-9
White-Alford House—*hist pl* MS-4
White and Blain Drain—*canal* MI-6
White and Brown Ditch—*canal* IL-6
White And Burney Hollow—*valley* PA-2
White And Francis Cem—*cemetery* KY-4
White and Moffatt Drain—*canal* MI-6
White and Rowley Ditch—*canal* IL-6
White and Shelby Cem—*cemetery* AR-4
*Whiteapple* MS-4
**White Apple**—*pop pl* MS-4
White Apple Cem—*cemetery* MS-4
White Apple Oil Field—*oilfield* MS-4
Whiteapple Post Office (historical)—*building* MS-4
White Arches—*building* MS-4
White Area Canyon—*valley* AZ-5
White Area Spring—*spring* AZ-5
White Arm—*swamp* GA-3
White Arm Bay—*swamp* GA-3
White Arm Swamp—*swamp* GA-3
White around the Mountain Spring—*spring* AZ-5
White Arrow Hot Spring—*spring* ID-8
White Arrow Trail—*trail* NH-1
White Ash—*locale* IA-7
White Ash—*locale* KY-4
**White Ash**—*pop pl* IL-6
**Whiteash**—*pop pl* IL-6
White Ash Branch—*stream* IA-7
White Ash Lake—*lake* WI-6
White Ash Mine—*mine* CO-8
White Ash Peak—*summit* AZ-5
White Ash Sch—*school* ND-7
*Whiteash Swamp* MA-1
White Ash Swamp—*swamp* MA-1
**White Ash Township**—*pop pl* ND-7
White Ave Hist Dist—*hist pl* AL-4
White Azalea Campground—*locale* CA-9
*Whiteback Rock* UT-8
White Baker Oil Field—*oilfield* TX-5
White Baldy—*summit* UT-8
*White Ball Park* UT-8
Whitebank—*locale* VA-3
White Bank Dry Rocks—*bar* FL-3
White Bank Landing—*locale* NC-3
*Whitebanks* MA-1
White Banks—*bar* SC-3
White Banks—*cliff* MD-2
White Banks—*cliff* MA-1
Whitebank Spring—*spring* AZ-5
*White Barn* PA-2
*White Barn Country Club Condominium* UT-8
**White Barn Country Club PRUD Subdivision**—*pop pl* UT-8
White Basin—*basin* NV-8
White Basin Tank—*reservoir* AZ-5
White Bass Lake—*lake* WI-6
White Battery—*locale* VA-3
White-Baucum House—*hist pl* AR-4
White Bay—*bay* VT-1
White Bay Branch—*stream* TX-5
*White Bayou* LA-4
White Bayou—*stream* (2) LA-4
*White Beach* MH-9
White Beach—*beach* MA-1
White Beach—*beach* NY-2
White Beach—*beach* WA-9
**White Beach**—*pop pl* FL-3
White Beach Bay—*bay* WA-9
*White Bead* OK-5
**White Bead**—*pop pl* OK-5
Whitebead Cem—*cemetery* OK-5
*White Bear* PA-2
White Bear—*locale* MO-7
**White Bear Beach**—*pop pl* MN-6
White Bear Cliff (historical)—*cliff* SD-7
*White Bear Creek* ID-8
White Bear Creek—*stream* (3) MT-8
White Bear Creek—*stream* PA-2
*White Bear Lake* MN-6
White Bear Lake—*lake* CA-9
White Bear Lake—*lake* (2) MN-6
**White Bear Lake**—*pop pl* MN-6
White Bear Lake (Township of)—*civ div* MN-6
White Bear Mine—*mine* CA-9
White Bear Mine (Site)—*locale* CA-9
White Bear Ranch—*locale* CO-8
White Bear Rsvr—*reservoir* MT-8
**White Bear (Scarlets Mill)**—*pop pl* PA-2
White Bear Spring—*spring* MT-8
White Bear Spring—*spring* UT-8
White Bear State Wildlife Mngmt Area—*park* MN-6
**White Bear (Township of)**—*pop pl* MN-6
White Beaver Creek—*stream* MT-8
White Beaver Sch—*school* MT-8
Whitebeck Knoll—*summit* UT-8
White Bedground Camp—*locale* UT-8
White Bedground Spring—*spring* UT-8
White Beeches Golf Club—*other* NJ-2
White Beech Hollow—*valley* WV-2
*White Bee Lake* WI-6
White Bell Sch—*school* SD-7
Whitebelly Wash—*valley* UT-8
White Bend—*bend* TN-4
White Birch Creek—*stream* (2) WI-6
**White Birches**—*pop pl* NY-2
White Birch Hill—*summit* NH-1
White Birch Island—*island* ME-1
White Birch Lake—*lake* (2) NY-2
White Birch Lake—*lake* (2) WI-6
White Birch Pond—*lake* NY-2
White Birch Ridge—*ridge* NY-2
White Birch Swamp—*swamp* PA-2
White Birch Trail—*trail* PA-2
**White Bird**—*pop pl* ID-8
White Bird Battlefield—*hist pl* ID-8
White Bird Canyon—*valley* ID-8
White Bird Cem—*cemetery* ID-8
*Whitebird Creek* ID-8
White Bird Creek—*stream* (2) ID-8
Whitebird Creek—*stream* MT-8
Whitebird Ditch—*canal* MT-8
White Bird Grade—*hist pl* ID-8
White Bird Hill—*ridge* ID-8
White Bird Hill Summit—*summit* ID-8
White Bird Meadow—*flat* ID-8
*Whitebird Ridge* ID-8
White Bird Ridge—*ridge* (2) ID-8
Whitebird Sch—*school* MT-8
White Bird Station—*locale* ID-8
White Blotch Springs—*spring* NV-8
*White Blowout Mine* SD-7
*White Bluff* AL-4
*White Bluff* WA-9
White Bluff—*cliff* AK-9
White Bluff—*cliff* (3) AR-4
White Bluff—*cliff* MS-4
White Bluff—*cliff* TN-4
White Bluff—*cliff* (4) TX-5
White Bluff—*hist pl* AL-4
White Bluff—*locale* GA-3
White Bluff—*locale* MS-4
**White Bluff**—*pop pl* (2) AR-4
**Whitebluff**—*pop pl* MS-4
**White Bluff**—*pop pl* SC-3
**White Bluff**—*pop pl* TN-4
White Bluff—*summit* AZ-5
White Bluff—*summit* TX-5
White Bluff Bar—*bar* AL-4
White Bluff Cem—*cemetery* AR-4
White Bluff Ch—*church* AR-4
White Bluff Ch—*church* MS-4
**White Bluff Corssroads**—*pop pl* SC-3
White Bluff Creek—*stream* TX-5
White Bluff Forge (40DS27)—*hist pl* TN-4
White Bluff Mtn—*summit* AR-4
*White Bluff River* GA-3
*White Bluffs* AL-4
White Bluffs—*cliff* (2) AZ-5
White Bluffs—*cliff* NM-5
White Bluffs—*cliff* TX-5
White Bluffs—*cliff* WA-9
White Bluffs—*locale* WA-9
White Bluff Tank—*reservoir* AZ-5
White Bluff Well—*well* NM-5
Whitebody Coulee—*valley* ND-7
White Bottom—*flat* GA-3
White Bottom Creek—*stream* NY-2
White Bottoms—*bend* AL-4
White Bottoms—*bend* MT-8
White Bottom Spring—*spring* WY-8
White Bottom Tank—*reservoir* NM-5
White Brake—*swamp* LA-4
*White Branch* AR-4
*White Branch* IN-6
*White Branch* LA-4
*White Branch* VA-3
White Branch—*canal* IN-6
**White Branch**—*pop pl* MO-7
White Branch—*stream* (7) AL-4
White Branch—*stream* (2) AR-4
White Branch—*stream* (3) FL-3
White Branch—*stream* GA-3
White Branch—*stream* IL-6
White Branch—*stream* IN-6
White Branch—*stream* (2) KY-4
White Branch—*stream* (2) LA-4
White Branch—*stream* (2) MS-4
White Branch—*stream* (3) MO-7
White Branch—*stream* NY-2
White Branch—*stream* (4) NC-3
White Branch—*stream* OK-5
White Branch—*stream* OR-9
White Branch—*stream* SC-3
White Branch—*stream* (7) TN-4
White Branch—*stream* (6) TX-5
White Branch—*stream* VT-1
White Branch—*stream* (5) VA-3
White Branch Ch—*church* IN-6
*White Branch Creek* OR-9
White Branch North Fork Cowanesque River—*stream* PA-2
White Branch Youth Camp—*locale* OR-9
*White Bread* OK-5
White Bread Creek—*stream* OK-5
White Bread Reach—*channel* TX-5
White Breaks—*cliff* NM-5
**Whitebreast**—*pop pl* IA-7
*Whitebreast Creek* IA-7
White Breast Creek—*stream* IA-7
Whitebreast Sch—*school* IA-7
White Breast Township—*fmr MCD* IA-7
Whitebreast Township—*fmr MCD* IA-7
**White Briar**—*pop pl* DE-2
White Bridge—*bridge* AL-4
White Bridge—*bridge* ID-8
White Bridge—*bridge* NJ-2
White Bridge—*bridge* PA-2
White Bridge—*hist pl* OH-6
White Bridge—*locale* NJ-2
White Bridge—*locale* NY-2
White Bridge—*locale* PA-2
White Bridge—*uninc pl* TN-4
White Bridge Campground—*park* UT-8
White Bridge Tunnel—*tunnel* PA-2
White Brook—*stream* CT-1
White Brook—*stream* (4) ME-1
White Brook—*stream* (5) MA-1
White Brook—*stream* (7) NH-1
White Brook—*stream* NJ-2
White Brook—*stream* (3) NY-2
White Brook—*stream* PA-2
White Brook—*stream* RI-1
White Buck Branch—*stream* FL-3
White Buck Knob—*summit* WV-2
White Buffalo Creek—*stream* MT-8
White Bull—*island* ME-1
White Bull Mtn—*summit* OR-9
White Bull Tank—*reservoir* TX-5
Whiteburg—*locale* MD-2
**Whitebury**—*pop pl* MS-4
White Bush—*hist pl* WV-2
**White Butte**—*pop pl* SD-7
White Butte—*summit* AZ-5
White Butte—*summit* CO-8
White Butte—*summit* ID-8
White Butte—*summit* (3) ND-7
White Butte—*summit* (2) OR-9
White Butte—*summit* (2) SD-7
White Butte Creek—*stream* OR-9
White Butte Rsvr—*reservoir* ND-7
White Butte Rsvr—*reservoir* SD-7
White Buttes—*summit* MT-8
**White Butte Township**—*pop pl* SD-7
White Cabin—*locale* MT-8
Whitecabin Branch—*stream* (2) KY-4
White Cabin Creek—*stream* CA-9
White Cafe—*hist pl* NM-5
White Cairn Trail—*trail* ME-1
Whitecalf Coulee—*valley* MT-8
White Calf Mtn—*summit* MT-8
White Camp—*locale* TX-5
*White Camp Fork* WV-2
*White Canyon* NV-8
White Canyon—*locale* UT-8
White Canyon—*valley* AZ-5
White Canyon—*valley* (4) CA-9
White Canyon—*valley* CO-8
White Canyon—*valley* (2) ID-8
White Canyon—*valley* KS-7
White Canyon—*valley* NM-5
White Canyon—*valley* OK-5
White Canyon—*valley* OR-9
White Canyon—*valley* TX-5
White Canyon—*valley* (4) UT-8
White Canyon Creek—*stream* UT-8
White Canyon Flat—*flat* UT-8
White Canyon Spring—*spring* UT-8
**White Cap**—*pop pl* MS-4
White Cap—*summit* CA-9
White Cap—*summit* CO-8
White Cap—*summit* SD-7
Whitecap, Mount—*summit* WY-8
Whitecap, The—*summit* ME-1
*White Cap Arch* UT-8
Whitecap Brook—*stream* ME-1
Whitecap Canyon—*valley* NM-5
Whitecap Creek—*stream* ID-8
White Cap Creek—*stream* ID-8
White Cap Hill—*summit* NE-7
White Cap Lakes—*lake* ID-8
*White Cap Mine* SD-7
*Whitecap Mount* ME-1
White Cap Mtn—*summit* AK-9
Whitecap Mtn—*summit* CO-8
White Cap Mtn—*summit* ME-1
Whitecap Mtn—*summit* ME-1
White Cap Mtn—*summit* ME-1
Whitecap Peak—*summit* AZ-5
White Cap Pond—*lake* ME-1
White Cap Rapids—*rapids* WA-9
White Caps Mine—*mine* CA-9
White Caps Mine—*mine* NV-8
White Cascade—*falls* CA-9
**White Castle**—*pop pl* LA-4
White Castle Bldg No. 8—*hist pl* MN-6
White Castle Ch—*church* MS-4
White Castle Oil Field—*oilfield* LA-4
Whitecat Mine—*mine* CA-9
White Cat Point—*cape* NE-7
White Cave—*cave* AL-4
White Cave Spring—*spring* AZ-5
*White Cem* MS-4
White Cem—*cemetery* (7) AL-4
White Cem—*cemetery* (6) AR-4
White Cem—*cemetery* (10) GA-3
White Cem—*cemetery* (4) IL-6
White Cem—*cemetery* (4) IN-6
White Cem—*cemetery* (3) IA-7
White Cem—*cemetery* (2) KS-7
White Cem—*cemetery* (3) KY-4
White Cem—*cemetery* (3) LA-4
White Cem—*cemetery* ME-1
White Cem—*cemetery* (2) MD-2
White Cem—*cemetery* MA-1
White Cem—*cemetery* MI-6
White Cem—*cemetery* (14) MS-4
White Cem—*cemetery* (17) MO-7
White Cem—*cemetery* (3) NY-2
White Cem—*cemetery* (3) NC-3
White Cem—*cemetery* (3) OH-6
White Cem—*cemetery* OK-5
White Cem—*cemetery* (2) PA-2
White Cem—*cemetery* (2) SC-3
White Cem—*cemetery* (30) TN-4
White Cem—*cemetery* (8) TX-5
White Cem—*cemetery* (3) VA-3
White Cem—*cemetery* (8) WV-2
White Cem—*cemetery* (2) WI-6
**White Center**—*pop pl* WA-9
White Center-Shorewood—*CDP* WA-9
White Ch—*church* AL-4
White Ch—*church* (2) AR-4
White Ch—*church* GA-3
White Ch—*church* (2) IN-6
White Ch—*church* (2) KY-4
White Ch—*church* MD-2
White Ch—*church* NH-1
White Ch—*church* (3) NY-2
White Ch—*church* NC-3
White Ch—*church* OH-6
White Ch—*church* OK-5
White Ch—*church* (5) PA-2
White Ch—*church* SC-3
White Ch—*church* TX-5
White Ch—*church* VA-3
White Ch—*church* WV-2
Whitechair Bridge—*bridge* KS-7
White Channel Creek—*stream* AK-9
White Chapel—*church* (2) AL-4
White Chapel—*church* GA-3
White Chapel—*church* (2) IL-6
White Chapel—*church* IN-6
White Chapel—*church* KY-4
White Chapel—*church* LA-4
White Chapel—*church* (3) MS-4
White Chapel—*church* NC-3
White Chapel—*church* (2) OH-6
White Chapel—*church* OK-5
White Chapel—*church* PA-2
White Chapel—*church* TN-4
White Chapel—*church* (2) TX-5
White Chapel—*church* VT-1
White Chapel—*church* VA-3
White Chapel—*church* WV-2
White Chapel—*hist pl* TN-4
**White Chapel**—*pop pl* WV-2
*White Chapel Baptist Ch* AL-4
White Chapel Cem—*cemetery* GA-3
White Chapel Cem—*cemetery* IL-6
White Chapel Cem—*cemetery* IN-6
White Chapel Cem—*cemetery* IA-7
White Chapel Cem—*cemetery* KS-7
White Chapel Cem—*cemetery* MI-6
White Chapel Cem—*cemetery* PA-2
White Chapel Cem—*cemetery* WV-2
White Chapel Ch—*church* PA-2
*White Chapel Ch of God* MS-4
White Chapel Ch of God—*church* FL-3
White Chapel Gardens (Cemetery)—*cemetery* PA-2
White Chapel (historical)—*church* PA-2
White Chapel (historical)—*church* TN-4
White Chapel (Magisterial District)—*fmr MCD* VA-3
White Chapel Memorial Cem—*cemetery* NY-2
*White Chapel Memorial Cemetery* TN-4
White Chapel Memorial Garden—*cemetery* TX-5
White Chapel Memorial Gardens—*cemetery* KY-4
White Chapel Memorial Gardens—*cemetery* MO-7
White Chapel Memorial Gardens Cem—*cemetery* MO-7
White Chapel Memory Gardens—*cemetery* NY-2
White Chapel Sch—*school* KY-4
White Chapel Sch (historical)—*school* MO-7
*White Chapel School* TN-4
White Ch (historical)—*church* TN-4
White Chief Branch—*stream* CA-9
White Chief Lake—*lake* CA-9
White Chief Mine—*mine* AZ-5
White Chief Mtn—*summit* CA-9
White Chief Peak—*summit* CA-9
White Chimney Cem—*cemetery* FL-3
White Chimney Cem—*cemetery* OK-5
White Chimney River—*stream* GA-3
White Chimneys—*hist pl* PA-2
White Chuck Campground—*locale* WA-9
White Chuck Cinder Cone—*summit* WA-9
White Chuck Glacier—*glacier* WA-9
White Chuck Lakes—*lake* WA-9
White Chuck Mtn—*summit* WA-9
White Chuck River—*stream* WA-9
*White Church* PA-2
White Church—*hist pl* SC-3
White Church—*locale* KS-7
White Church—*locale* PA-2
**White Church**—*pop pl* MO-7
**White Church**—*pop pl* NY-2
White Church—*uninc pl* KS-7
White Church Cem—*cemetery* (3) AR-4
White Church Cem—*cemetery* NY-2
White Church Cem—*cemetery* OK-5
White Church Cem—*cemetery* PA-2
White Church Cem—*cemetery* TX-5

Whitehall Farm—*hist pl* OH-6
*White Hall Fields* MO-7
Whitehall Flats—*flat* MD-2
White Hall Foundry—*hist pl* IL-6
**Whitehall (High Point)**—*pop pl* LA-4
White Hall Hist Dist—*hist pl* IL-6
Whitehall (historical)—*locale* KS-7
**White Hall (historical)**—*pop pl* NC-3
Whitehall HS—*school* PA-2
*Whitehall Intermediate HS* PA-2
Whitehall Lake—*lake* LA-4
Whitehall Landing—*locale* DE-2
Whitehall Landing—*locale* MS-4
Whitehall Landing—*locale* NC-3
White Hall (Magisterial District)—*fmr MCD* VA-3
Whitehall Mall—*locale* PA-2
**Whitehall Manor**—*pop pl* MD-2
Whitehall Mansion—*hist pl* CT-1
*Whitehall Methodist Church* MS-4
Whitehall Neck—*cape* DE-2
White Hall of Bristol College—*hist pl* PA-2
**Whitehall Park**—*pop pl* PA-2
Whitehall Plantation—*locale* LA-4
White Hall Plantation (historical)—*locale* MS-4
Whitehall Plantation (historical)—*locale* MS-4
Whitehall Plantation House—*hist pl* LA-4
White Hall Plantation House—*hist pl* LA-4
Whitehall Point—*cape* SC-3
*White Hall Pond* MA-1
*Whitehall Pond* RI-1
Whitehall Pond—*lake* MA-1
White Hall Pond—*reservoir* SC-3
Whitehall Ranch—*locale* MT-8
White Hall Ranch—*locale* TX-5
Whitehall Ravine—*valley* CA-9
Whitehall Reservoir Dam—*dam* MA-1
*Whitehall River* MD-2
Whitehall (RR name for White Hall)—*other* IL-6
Whitehall Rsvr—*reservoir* MA-1
Whitehall Rsvr—*reservoir* NY-2
White Hall Sch—*school* AL-4
White Hall Sch—*school* AR-4
Whitehall Sch—*school* IL-6
White Hall Sch—*school* IL-6
White Hall Sch—*school* (2) KY-4
White Hall Sch—*school* LA-4
White Hall Sch—*school* (2) MO-7
Whitehall Sch—*school* (3) PA-2
White Hall Sch—*school* PA-2
White Hall Sch—*school* SC-3
Whitehall Sch—*school* TN-4
White Hall Sch—*school* WV-2
Whitehall Sch (abandoned)—*school* (2) PA-2
White Hall Sch (historical)—*school* MO-7
White Hall Sch (historical)—*school* TN-4
Whitehall Sch (historical)—*school* TN-4
**Whitehall Shores**—*pop pl* NC-3
Whitehall State Childrens Home—*locale* NE-7
Whitehall State Park—*park* MA-1
*Whitehall Station* NJ-2
**Whitehall Terrace**—*pop pl* SC-3
**Whitehall (Town of)**—*pop pl* NY-2
Whitehall (Township of)—*other* OH-6
**White Hall (Township of)**—*pop pl* IL-6
**Whitehall (Township of)**—*pop pl* MI-6
**Whitehall (Township of)**—*pop pl* PA-2
*Whitehallville* PA-2
Whitehall (White Hall)—*other* GA-3
**White Hall (Whitehall)**—*pop pl* GA-3
**White Hall (Whitehall)**—*pop pl* VA-3
White Hammock—*island* FL-3
**White Harbor**—*pop pl* MS-4
Whitehard Cem—*cemetery* NC-3
White Hardee Cem—*cemetery* SC-3
White Hat Landing—*locale* NC-3
White Haven—*hist pl* MO-7
**Whitehaven**—*pop pl* MD-2
**White Haven**—*pop pl* MT-8
**White Haven**—*pop pl* PA-2
**Whitehaven**—*pop pl* TN-4
White Haven Borough—*civil* PA-2
White Haven Cem—*cemetery* NY-2
**White Haven Center**—*pop pl* PA-2
Whitehaven Ch (historical)—*church* MS-4
Whitehaven Country Club—*locale* TN-4
Whitehaven Hist Dist—*hist pl* MD-2
Whitehaven HS—*school* TN-4
Whitehaven Memorial Park—*flat* OH-6
White Haven Memorial Park—*park* NY-2
Whitehaven Parkway—*park* DC-2
White Haven Road Cem—*cemetery* NY-2
**White Hawk**—*pop pl* MN-6
Whitehawk Basin—*basin* ID-8
Whitehawk Basin Trail—*trail* ID-8
*White Hawk Canyon* AZ-5
*Whitehawk Creek* ID-8
White Hawk Creek—*stream* CA-9
Whitehawk Creek—*stream* ID-8
Whitehawk Mtn—*summit* ID-8
White Hawk Ranch—*locale* MS-4
Whitehawk Trail—*trail* ID-8
*White Head* MA-1
Whitehead—*cape* ME-1
White Head—*cliff* MA-1
Whitehead—*locale* MS-4
Whitehead—*locale* TX-5
**Whitehead**—*pop pl* AL-4
**Whitehead**—*pop pl* MA-1
**Whitehead**—*pop pl* NJ-2
**Whitehead**—*pop pl* NC-3
**Whitehead**—*pop pl* SC-3
**Whitehead**—*pop pl* TN-4
White Head—*summit* ME-1
White Head—*summit* MA-1
Whitehead, C. H., House—*hist pl* IA-7
Whitehead, Charles C., House—*hist pl* UT-8
Whitehead, Lake—*reservoir* CA-9
Whitehead, Stephen R., House—*hist pl* NV-8
Whitehead Bay—*swamp* GA-3
Whitehead Bluff—*cliff* AR-4
Whitehead Branch—*stream* KY-4
Whitehead Branch—*stream* TN-4
Whitehead Brothers Ranch—*locale* TX-5
Whitehead Cem—*cemetery* (2) AL-4
Whitehead Cem—*cemetery* AR-4
Whitehead Cem—*cemetery* GA-3
Whitehead Cem—*cemetery* IL-6
Whitehead Cem—*cemetery* KY-4
Whitehead Cem—*cemetery* LA-4
Whitehead Cem—*cemetery* (2) MS-4
Whitehead Cem—*cemetery* MO-7
Whitehead Cem—*cemetery* NC-3
Whitehead Cem—*cemetery* (9) TN-4
Whitehead Cem—*cemetery* (2) TX-5
Whitehead Cem—*cemetery* (2) VA-3
Whitehead Ch—*church* AL-4
Whitehead Ch—*church* MS-4
Whitehead Corners—*locale* PA-2
*Whitehead Creek* AL-4
Whitehead Creek—*stream* AL-4
Whitehead Creek—*stream* (3) GA-3
Whitehead Creek—*stream* MS-4
Whitehead Creek—*stream* (2) MO-7
Whitehead Creek—*stream* NE-7
Whitehead Creek—*stream* NC-3
Whitehead Creek—*stream* OR-9
Whitehead Creek—*stream* WI-6
Whitehead Crossroads—*locale* FL-3
**Whitehead Cross Roads**—*pop pl* FL-3
White Head Flats—*flat* MA-1
Whitehead-Fogleman Farm—*hist pl* NC-3
Whitehead Ford—*locale* AR-4
Whitehead Gulch—*valley* CO-8
White Head Hall—*locale* VA-3
Whitehead Hill—*locale* TN-4
Whitehead Hill—*summit* NY-2
**Whitehead Hills**—*pop pl* TN-4
Whitehead (historical)—*locale* KS-7
Whitehead Hollow—*valley* AL-4
Whitehead Hollow—*valley* AR-4
Whitehead Hollow—*valley* TN-4
*Whitehead Island* IL-6
Whitehead Island—*island* ME-1
Whitehead Lake—*lake* FL-3
Whitehead Lake—*lake* LA-4
Whitehead Lake—*lake* ME-1
Whitehead Lake—*lake* (2) MI-6
Whitehead Lake—*lake* (2) NE-7
Whitehead Lake—*reservoir* GA-3
Whitehead Lake Dam—*dam* (2) MS-4
Whitehead Landing—*locale* MS-4
Whitehead Lifesaving Station—*hist pl* ME-1
White Head Light—*locale* MA-1
Whitehead Light Station—*hist pl* ME-1
Whitehead Passage—*channel* ME-1
Whitehead Peak—*summit* CO-8
Whitehead Pond—*reservoir* NJ-2
Whitehead Pond Dam—*dam* NJ-2
Whitehead Prairie—*flat* TX-5
Whitehead Ranch—*locale* (2) AZ-5
Whitehead Ranch—*locale* CA-9
Whitehead Ranch—*locale* MT-8
Whitehead Ranch—*locale* (3) TX-5
Whitehead Ranch—*locale* WY-8
Whitehead Ridge—*ridge* AZ-5
Whitehead Ridge—*ridge* TN-4
Whitehead Run—*stream* PA-2
Whitehead Run—*stream* WV-2
Whitehead Sch—*school* AL-4
Whitehead Sch (historical)—*school* AL-4
Whiteheads Grove Ch—*church* VA-3
Whiteheads Landing—*locale* AL-4
Whitehead Slough—*stream* CA-9
**Whiteheads Mill (historical)**—*pop pl* NC-3
Whitehead Spit—*cape* FL-3
Whiteheads Pond—*reservoir* AL-4
Whitehead Spring—*spring* TN-4
Whitehead Spring Branch—*stream* AL-4
White Head Spring Branch—*stream* FL-3
Whitehead Station—*locale* NJ-2
**Whitehead Subdivision**—*pop pl* UT-8
Whitehead Swamp—*swamp* FL-3
Whitehead (Township of)—*fmr MCD* NC-3
Whitehead Trail—*trail* CO-8
Whitehead Well—*well* AZ-5
White Heart Cem—*cemetery* IN-6
**White Heath**—*pop pl* IL-6
White Heather—*locale* CA-9
White Heifer Springs—*spring* NV-8
White Heron Dam—*dam* PA-2
*White Heron Lake* PA-2
White Highland Hills—*spring* MT-8
*White Hill* HI-9
*White Hill* MA-1
White Hill—*locale* GA-3
Whitehill—*other* IL-6
**Whitehill**—*pop pl* GA-3
**White Hill**—*pop pl* NC-3
**White Hill**—*pop pl* PA-2
**White Hill**—*pop pl* (2) TN-4
**White Hill**—*pop pl* VA-3
White Hill—*summit* AK-9
White Hill—*summit* (3) AZ-5
White Hill—*summit* AR-4
White Hill—*summit* CA-9
White Hill—*summit* CO-8
White Hill—*summit* KY-4
White Hill—*summit* (3) MA-1
White Hill—*summit* (4) NV-8
White Hill—*summit* (2) NM-5
White Hill—*summit* (2) NY-2
White Hill—*summit* OH-6
White Hill—*summit* (3) UT-8
White Hill—*summit* VT-1
White Hill—*summit* (2) VA-3
White Hill—*summit* WV-2
White Hill—*summit* WI-6
White Hill—*summit* WY-8
*White Hill Baptist Church* MS-4
Whitehill Cem—*cemetery* GA-3
White Hill Cem—*cemetery* GA-3
White Hill Cem—*cemetery* NE-7
White Hill Cem—*cemetery* TN-4
White Hill Cem—*cemetery* TX-5
White Hill Ch—*church* GA-3
White Hill Ch—*church* (2) KY-4
White Hill Ch—*church* MS-4
White Hill Ch—*church* NC-3
Whitehill Ch—*church* NC-3
Whitehill Ch—*church* SC-3
White Hill Ch—*church* SC-3
**White Hill (Chasco)**—*pop pl* IL-6
White Hill Creek—*stream* OR-9
White Hill Dam—*dam* NM-5
**White Hill Estates Subdivision**—*pop pl* UT-8
**Whitehill (historical)**—*pop pl* OR-9
Whitehill House—*hist pl* VT-1
Whitehill Lake—*lake* AR-4
White Hill Lake—*reservoir* VA-3
White Hill Lake Trail—*trail* VA-3
White Hill Missionary Ch—*church* TX-5
Whitehill Range—*channel* NJ-2
Whitehill Range—*channel* PA-2
White Hills—*locale* AZ-5
White Hills—*other* AK-9
White Hills—*other* CA-9
**White Hills**—*pop pl* CA-9
**White Hills**—*pop pl* LA-4
White Hills—*range* (2) AZ-5
White Hills—*range* CA-9
White Hills—*range* ID-8
White Hills—*range* UT-8
White Hills—*spring* MT-8
White Hills—*summit* (4) AZ-5
White Hills—*summit* CO-8
White Hills—*summit* MN-6
White Hills—*summit* NM-5
White Hills—*summit* (2) UT-8
White Hills—*summit* WY-8
White Hills Ch—*church* CT-1
White Hill Sch—*school* AL-4
White Hill Sch—*school* SD-7
White Hill Sch (historical)—*school* (2) TN-4
White Hills Community Brook—*stream* CT-1
White Hills Junction—*uninc pl* CA-9
Whitehills Park—*park* MI-6
White Hills Sch—*school* LA-4
Whitehills Sch—*school* MI-6
White Hills Siding—*locale* CA-9
White Hills Tank—*reservoir* (3) AZ-5
White Hill Station—*locale* PA-2
White Hills Well—*well* NV-8
White Hill Tank—*reservoir* AZ-5
White Hill Tank—*reservoir* TX-5
**White Hill Township**—*pop pl* SD-7
*White Hollow* AR-4
White Hollow—*locale* TN-4
White Hollow—*valley* (2) AL-4
White Hollow—*valley* (2) AR-4
White Hollow—*valley* ID-8
White Hollow—*valley* IN-6
White Hollow—*valley* (2) KY-4
White Hollow—*valley* (4) MO-7
White Hollow—*valley* NY-2
White Hollow—*valley* (2) OH-6
White Hollow—*valley* (3) PA-2
White Hollow—*valley* (11) TN-4
White Hollow—*valley* UT-8
White Hollow—*valley* (2) WV-2
White Hollow—*valley* (2) WI-6
White Hollow Brook—*stream* CT-1
White Hollow Ch—*church* MO-7
White Hollow Pack Trail—*trail* UT-8
White Hollow Sch—*school* MO-7
White-Holman House—*hist pl* NC-3
White Homestead—*locale* ID-8
White Hoover Ditch—*canal* IN-6
Whitehorn—*locale* CO-8
White Horn—*locale* TN-4
Whitehorn, Point—*cape* WA-9
White Horn Brook—*stream* RI-1
Whitehorn Cem—*cemetery* OK-5
White Horn Ch—*church* TN-4
Whitehorn Cove Public Use Area—*park* OK-5
*Whitehorn Creek* VA-3
Whitehorn Creek—*stream* KY-4
Whitehorn Creek—*stream* TN-4
Whitehorn Creek—*stream* VA-3
Whitehorn Creek—*stream* WV-2
Whitehorne, Samuel, House—*hist pl* RI-1
*Whitehorn Post Office* TN-4
White Horn Post Office (historical)—*building* TN-4
*Whitehorn Run* PA-2
Whitehorn Spring—*spring* AZ-5
*Whitehorse* MI-6
*Whitehorse* NJ-2
*White Horse* PA-2
White Horse—*locale* CA-9
Whitehorse—*locale* PA-2
**White Horse**—*pop pl* NJ-2
**White Horse**—*pop pl* NM-5
**Whitehorse**—*pop pl* NM-5
**White Horse**—*pop pl* (3) PA-2
**White Horse**—*pop pl* SC-3
**Whitehorse**—*pop pl* SD-7
**White Horse**—*pop pl* WA-9
Whitehorse Access Public Hunting Area—*area* IA-7
White Horse Basin—*basin* ID-8
White Horse Bay—*bay* MI-6
**White Horse Beach**—*pop pl* MA-1
White Horse Bench—*bench* MT-8
Whitehorse Bluff—*cliff* OR-9
White Horse Branch—*stream* TN-4
White Horse Butte—*summit* AZ-5
Whitehorse Butte—*summit* ID-8
Whitehorse Butte—*summit* (2) OR-9
Whitehorse Butte—*summit* WY-8
Whitehorse Butte Rsvr—*reservoir* OR-9
White Horse Canal—*canal* MT-8
White Horse Canyon—*valley* AZ-5
Whitehorse Canyon—*valley* AZ-5
White Horse Canyon—*valley* CA-9
White Horse Canyon—*valley* MT-8
White Horse Canyon—*valley* (2) NV-8
White Horse Canyon—*valley* NM-5
White Horse Canyon—*valley* UT-8
White Horse Canyon—*valley* WA-9
Whitehorse Canyon—*valley* WY-8
Whitehorse Catholic Ch—*church* SD-7
White Horse Cem—*cemetery* MA-1
Whitehorse Cem—*cemetery* OK-5
White Horse Cem—*cemetery* SD-7
White Horse Ch—*church* SC-3
White Horse Coulee—*valley* (2) MT-8
*Whitehorse Creek* KY-4
*Whitehorse Creek* NE-7
*White Horse Creek* OK-5
Whitehorse Creek—*stream* AK-9
White Horse Creek—*stream* CA-9
Whitehorse Creek—*stream* CA-9
White Horse Creek—*stream* ID-8
Whitehorse Creek—*stream* MT-8
White Horse Creek—*stream* (2) MT-8
White Horse Creek—*stream* NE-7
Whitehorse Creek—*stream* OK-5
Whitehorse Creek—*stream* (3) OR-9
White Horse Creek—*stream* OR-9
Whitehorse Creek—*stream* OR-9
White Horse Creek—*stream* (3) SD-7
Whitehorse Creek—*stream* SD-7
Whitehorse Creek—*stream* WA-9
Whitehorse Creek—*stream* WY-8
White Horse Creek—*valley* SD-7
White Horse Divide—*ridge* MT-8
*White Horse Draw* AZ-5
*White Horse Draw* SD-7
White Horse Draw—*valley* NM-5
White Horse Draw—*valley* WY-8
Whitehorse Falls Campground—*park* OR-9
White Horse Farm—*hist pl* PA-2
**White Horse Farm (subdivision)**—*pop pl* DE-2
White Horse Flat—*flat* NV-8
Whitehorse Flat Rsvr—*reservoir* CA-9
*Whitehorse Gulch* SD-7
Whitehorse Gulch—*valley* MT-8
**White Horse Heights**—*pop pl* SC-3
White Horse Hills—*summit* AZ-5
White Horse Hollow—*valley* PA-2
White Horse Hotel (historical)—*building* PA-2
Whitehorse HS—*school* UT-8
Whitehorse Island—*island* ME-1
White Horse Island—*island* ME-1
White Horse Key—*island* FL-3
White Horse Knoll—*summit* AZ-5
*White Horse Lake* AZ-5
White Horse Lake—*lake* AZ-5
White Horse Lake—*lake* ME-1
White Horse Lake—*lake* MT-8
Whitehorse Lake—*reservoir* SD-7
White Horse Lake Campground—*park* AZ-5
*Whitehorse Landing* MI-6
Whitehorse Ledge—*bar* ME-1
White Horse Ledge—*bench* NH-1
Whitehorse Mine—*mine* UT-8
White Horse Mine—*mine* WA-9
White Horse Mountains—*range* CA-9
White Horse Mountains—*range* OR-9
Whitehorse Mountains—*summit* CA-9
*Whitehorse Mtn* OR-9
White Horse Mtn—*summit* NV-8
Whitehorse Mtn—*summit* NM-5
Whitehorse Mtn—*summit* NY-2
Whitehorse Mtn—*summit* OR-9
Whitehorse Mtn—*summit* WA-9
White Horse Pass—*gap* AZ-5
White Horse Pass—*gap* NV-8
White Horse Pasture—*flat* NV-8
White Horse Pike Hist Dist—*hist pl* NJ-2
White Horse Point—*cape* AL-4
Whitehorse Point—*cape* ME-1
Whitehorse Pond—*lake* OR-9
White Horse Ranch—*locale* NE-7
Whitehorse Ranch—*locale* OR-9
White Horse Ranch Airstrip—*airport* OR-9
White Horse Ranger Station—*locale* AZ-5
Whitehorse Rapids—*rapids* (2) ID-8
Whitehorse Rapids—*rapids* OR-9
White Horse Rapids—*rapids* OR-9
White Horse Rec Area—*park* AZ-5
Whitehorse Reef—*bar* ME-1
Whitehorse Ridge—*ridge* OR-9
White Horse Ridge—*ridge* OR-9
Whitehorse Ridge—*ridge* WA-9
Whitehorse Riffle—*rapids* OR-9
Whitehorse Rincon—*valley* NM-5
White Horse Rips—*rapids* ME-1
*White Horse Rock* MA-1
White Horse Rock—*summit* VA-3
White Horse Rocks—*rock* MA-1
*Whitehorse Rsvr* OR-9
White Horse Rsvr—*reservoir* CA-9
White Horse Rsvr—*reservoir* ID-8
White Horse Run—*stream* PA-2
White Horse Sch—*school* MT-8
White Horse Sch—*school* PA-2
*White Horse Spring* OR-9
*White Horse Spring* WA-9
White Horse Spring—*spring* AZ-5
White Horse Spring—*spring* MT-8
White Horse Spring—*spring* (2) NV-8
White Horse Spring—*spring* NM-5
White Horse Spring—*spring* OR-9
Whitehorse Spring—*spring* OR-9
White Horse Spring—*spring* TX-5
*White Horse Springs* NV-8
White Horse Springs—*spring* NV-8
White Horse Springs—*spring* SD-7
*White Horse Tank* AZ-5
White Horse Tank—*reservoir* (2) AZ-5
White Horse Tank—*reservoir* TX-5
White Horse Tavern—*hist pl* (2) PA-2
White Horse Tavern—*hist pl* RI-1
*Whitehorse Trail* DC-2
White Horse Village—*locale* UT-8
Whitehorse Well—*well* NM-5
White Hound Canyon—*valley* WY-8
*White House* AL-4
*White House* MD-2
*Whitehouse* MI-6
*White House* NJ-2
White House—*hist pl* AZ-5
White House—*hist pl* AR-4
White House—*hist pl* KY-4
White House—*hist pl* NC-3
White House—*hist pl* SC-3
White House—*hist pl* TX-5
White House—*locale* AZ-5
Whitehouse—*locale* GA-3
White House—*locale* GA-3
Whitehouse—*locale* MD-2
Whitehouse—*locale* NY-2
Whitehouse—*locale* TN-4
White House—*locale* UT-8
White House—*locale* (2) VA-3
**Whitehouse**—*pop pl* AL-4
**Whitehouse**—*pop pl* FL-3
**Whitehouse**—*pop pl* KY-4
**Whitehouse**—*pop pl* MD-2
**White House**—*pop pl* MO-7
**Whitehouse**—*pop pl* NJ-2
**Whitehouse**—*pop pl* NC-3
**Whitehouse**—*pop pl* OH-6
**White House**—*pop pl* PA-2
**White House**—*pop pl* TN-4
**Whitehouse**—*pop pl* TX-5
White House, The—*locale* DC-2
Whitehouse Baptist Ch—*church* FL-3
White House Bar—*bar* ID-8
Whitehouse Bay—*bay* NY-2
Whitehouse Bayou—*stream* AL-4
**White House Beach (trailer park)**—*pop pl* DE-2
Whitehouse Bend—*bend* AL-4
Whitehouse Block—*hist pl* ME-1
*Whitehouse Branch* VA-3
White House Branch—*stream* AL-4
Whitehouse Branch—*stream* GA-3
White House Branch—*stream* LA-4
Whitehouse Branch—*stream* TN-4
*White House Brook* NH-1
Whitehouse Brook—*stream* ME-1
Whitehouse Brook—*stream* NH-1
Whitehouse Campground—*locale* ID-8
*White House Canon* NM-5
White House Canyon—*valley* CA-9
White House Canyon—*valley* NM-5
White House (CCD)—*cens area* TN-4
Whitehouse (CCD)—*cens area* TX-5
Whitehouse Cem—*cemetery* AL-4
Whitehouse Cem—*cemetery* AR-4
Whitehouse Cem—*cemetery* IN-6
Whitehouse Cem—*cemetery* (2) KY-4
Whitehouse Cem—*cemetery* ME-1
Whitehouse Cem—*cemetery* NH-1
Whitehouse Cem—*cemetery* TX-5
Whitehouse Ch—*church* AL-4
Whitehouse Ch—*church* TX-5
Whitehouse Ch of Christ—*church* AL-4
White House Ch of Christ—*church* TN-4
White House City Hall—*building* TN-4
White House City Park—*park* TN-4
White House Cove—*bay* DE-2
Whitehouse Cove—*bay* FL-3
White House Cove—*bay* VA-3
*White House Creek* AL-4
*Whitehouse Creek* NY-2
Whitehouse Creek—*stream* AL-4
Whitehouse Creek—*stream* (2) CA-9
Whitehouse Creek—*stream* CO-8
Whitehouse Creek—*stream* GA-3
White House Creek—*stream* MI-6
White House Creek—*stream* VA-3
Whitehouse Creek—*stream* VA-3
Whitehouse Crossing—*locale* NY-2
White House Dam—*dam* AZ-5
White House Dam—*dam* NV-8
White House Department Store and Hotel McCoy—*hist pl* TX-5
White House Ditch—*canal* NV-8
White House Division—*civil* TN-4
White House Elem Sch—*school* TN-4
White House Farm—*hist pl* WV-2
White House Farm Airp—*airport* DE-2
Whitehouse Flat—*flat* OR-9
Whitehouse Ford (Abandoned)—*locale* MO-7
Whitehouse Ford Boat Access—*locale* MO-7
Whitehouse Fork Ch—*church* AL-4
*White House Fork Pentecostal Ch* AL-4
Whitehouse Forks—*locale* AL-4
Whitehouse Forks—*locale* NC-3
*Whitehouse Fork School* AL-4
White House Gulch—*valley* SD-7
**White House Heights**—*pop pl* MD-2
Whitehouse Hill—*summit* GA-3
Whitehouse Hill—*summit* ME-1
**White House (historical)**—*pop pl* MS-4
Whitehouse Hollow—*valley* AR-4
Whitehouse Hollow—*valley* (2) KY-4
Whitehouse Hollow—*valley* PA-2
White House HS—*school* TN-4
White House Inn—*hist pl* PA-2
White House Inn Museum—*building* TN-4
*White House Lake* AZ-5
*White House Lake* ME-1
Whitehouse Lake—*lake* IL-6
White House Landing—*locale* DE-2
Whitehouse Landing—*locale* MI-6
White House Landing—*locale* MS-4
Whitehouse Landing—*locale* VA-3
*White House Landing, The* MI-6
Whito Houso Landing (historical) *locale* MS 4
White House Library—*building* TN-4
*White House Marsh* NY-2
Whitehouse Marsh—*swamp* NY-2
Whitehouse Meadows—*flat* OR-9
White House MS—*school* TN-4
Whitehouse Mtn—*summit* (2) CO-8
White House Mtn—*summit* MS-4
Whitehouse Mtn—*summit* NH-1
Whitehouse Mtn—*summit* TX-5
White House of the Chickasaws—*hist pl* OK-5
White House of the Confederacy—*hist pl* VA-3
White House Overlook—*locale* AZ-5
Whitehouse Park—*park* FL-3
Whitehouse Picnic Ground—*locale* MT-8
Whitehouse Place—*locale* OR-9
White House Plantation—*locale* SC-3
White House Point—*cape* DE-2
Whitehouse Pond—*lake* ID-8
White House Pool—*other* CA-9
White House Post Office—*building* TN-4
White House Ranch—*locale* NE-7
White House Ranch—*locale* (2) NV-8
White House Ranch—*locale* (3) NM-5
White House Ridge—*ridge* TX-5
White House (RR name for Whitehouse)—*other* KY-4
**Whitehouse (RR name White House)**—*pop pl* KY-4
White House Ruins—*locale* AZ-5
Whitehouse Ruins—*locale* AZ-5
White House (Ruins)—*locale* UT-8
White House Run—*stream* PA-2
Whitehouse Sch—*school* AL-4
White House Sch—*school* AR-4
Whitehouse Sch—*school* FL-3
Whitehouse Sch—*school* NE-7
Whitehouse Sch—*school* NY-2
White House Sch (historical)—*school* AL-4
Whitehouse Sch (historical)—*school* TN-4
White House Spring—*spring* AL-4
White House Spring—*spring* NV-8
White House Spring—*spring* NM-5
White House Spring—*spring* OR-9
White House Spring—*spring* UT-8
**White House Springs**—*pop pl* AL-4
*White House Station* UT-8
White House Station—*hist pl* NJ-2
**Whitehouse Station**—*pop pl* NJ-2
**White House Station (White Station)**—*pop pl* NJ-2
White House Tank—*reservoir* AZ-5
Whitehouse Trail—*trail* NH-1
Whitehouse Trailhead—*locale* UT-8
White House United Methodist Church—*hist pl* SC-3
White House Valley—*valley* AZ-5
Whitehouse Well—*well* AZ-5
White House Well—*well* NM-5
Whitehouse Well—*well* TX-5
*White House (Whitehouse)* FL-3
Whitehouse (White House)—*uninc pl* FL-3
*White House (White House Station)* NJ-2
White House Windmill—*locale* TX-5
White House Woods—*woods* SC-3
Whitehurse Point—*cape* NC-3
**Whitehurst**—*pop pl* NC-3
Whitehurst, Lake—*reservoir* VA-3
Whitehurst Airp—*airport* NC-3
Whitehurst Airp—*airport* TN-4
Whitehurst Branch—*stream* MS-4
Whitehurst Cem—*cemetery* MS-4
Whitehurst Creek—*bay* NC-3
Whitehurst Creek—*canal* NC-3
Whitehurst Creek—*stream* (3) NC-3
Whitehurst Island—*island* NC-3
Whitehurst Lake—*reservoir* TX-5
**Whitehurst Landing**—*pop pl* VA-3
Whitehurst Point—*cape* NC-3
Whitehurst Pond—*lake* FL-3
Whitehurst Pond—*reservoir* GA-3
Whitehurst Spring—*spring* MS-4
White Ibis Pond—*swamp* SC-3
White-Indian Contact Site—*hist pl* CO-8
*Whiteings Pond* CT-1
White Institute—*school* IN-6
**White Iron**—*pop pl* MN-6
White Iron Canyon—*valley* AZ-5
White Iron Lake—*lake* MN-6
*White Island* PA-2
White Island—*island* IL-6
White Island—*island* KY-4
White Island—*island* LA-4
White Island—*island* (5) ME-1
White Island—*island* NH-1
White Island—*island* NJ-2
White Island—*island* SC-3
White Island Bogs—*swamp* MA-1
White Island Ledge—*bar* ME-1
White Island Ledge—*bar* NH-1
White Island Point—*cape* NJ-2
White Island Pond—*reservoir* MA-1
White Island Pond Dam—*dam* MA-1
White Island Reef—*bar* ME-1
White Islands—*island* ME-1
**White Island Shores**—*pop pl* MA-1
White JHS—*school* CA-9
White John B., House—*hist pl* OR-9
White Key—*island* FL-3
White King Mine—*mine* OR-9
**White Kitchen**—*pop pl* LA-4
White Kitchen, The—*locale* TX-5
White Knob—*summit* MT-8
White Knob Creek—*stream* MT-8
White Knob Mtns—*range* ID-8
White Knob Mtns—*summit* ID-8
*White Knobs* UT-8
White Knob Summit—*summit* ID-8
White Knob Windmill—*locale* TX-5
White Knoll—*summit* NV-8
White Knoll—*summit* PA-2
White Knoll—*summit* (2) UT-8
White Knoll Rsvr—*reservoir* NV-8
White Knolls—*summit* AZ-5
Whitelace Creek—*stream* NC-3
*White Lake* AZ-5
*White Lake* IN-6
*White Lake* LA-4
*White Lake* MI-6
*White Lake* OH-6
*White Lake* SC-3
*White Lake* TN-4
*White Lake* TX-5
*White Lake* WI-6
White Lake—*basin* NM-5
White Lake—*flat* NV-8
White Lake—*lake* (3) AK-9
White Lake—*lake* AZ-5
White Lake—*lake* (4) AR-4
White Lake—*lake* (2) CA-9
White Lake—*lake* (3) FL-3
White Lake—*lake* GA-3
White Lake—*lake* ID-8
White Lake—*lake* IN-6
White Lake—*lake* LA-4
White Lake—*lake* ME-1
White Lake—*lake* (5) MI-6
White Lake—*lake* (3) MN-6
White Lake—*lake* (4) MS-4
White Lake—*lake* (2) MT-8
White Lake—*lake* NE-7
White Lake—*lake* (2) NJ-2
White Lake—*lake* (3) NM-5
White Lake—*lake* (4) NY-2
White Lake—*lake* NC-3
White Lake—*lake* (3) ND-7
White Lake—*lake* OK-5
White Lake—*lake* (2) OR-9
White Lake—*lake* SC-3
White Lake—*lake* (3) SD-7
White Lake—*lake* (3) TX-5
White Lake—*lake* UT-8
White Lake—*lake* WA-9
White Lake—*lake* (5) WI-6
White Lake—*lake* WY-8
**White Lake**—*pop pl* MI-6
**White Lake**—*pop pl* (2) NY-2
**White Lake**—*pop pl* NC-3
**White Lake**—*pop pl* SD-7
**White Lake**—*pop pl* WI-6
White Lake—*reservoir* (2) AL-4
White Lake—*reservoir* (2) GA-3
White Lake—*reservoir* MS-4
White Lake—*reservoir* NM-5

White Lake—*reservoir* ... NC-3
White Lake—*reservoir* ... ND-7
White Lake—*reservoir* ... OH-6
White Lake—*reservoir* ... SD-7
White Lake—*reservoir* ... TN-4
White Lake—*reservoir* ... TX-5
White Lake—*reservoir* ... VA-3
White Lake Airp—*airport* ... NC-3
White Lake Brook—*stream* ... NY-2
White Lake Cem—*cemetery* ... MI-6
White Lake Cem—*cemetery* ... NM-5
**White Lake Center**—*pop pl* ... MI-6
White Lake Ch—*church* ... AR-4
White Lake Ch—*church* ... MS-4
White Lake Ch—*church* ... NY-2
White Lake Ch—*church* ... NC-3
**White Lake City (historical)**—*pop pl* ... OR-9
White Lake Creek—*stream* ... WI-6
White Lake Cut -Off—*bend* ... MS-4
White Lake Dam—*dam* ... AL-4
White Lake Dam—*dam* (3) ... MS-4
White Lake Dam—*dam* ... NC-3
White Lake Dam—*dam* ... ND-7
White Lake Divide—*ridge* ... AZ-5
White Lake Drain—*stream* ... NC-3
White Lake Grange—*locale* ... WA-9
White Lake Mtn—*summit* ... NY-2
White Lake Natl Wildlife Ref—*park* ... ND-7
White Lake Number 1—*reservoir* ... AL-4
White Lake Number 2—*reservoir* ... AL-4
White Lake Oil Field—*oilfield* ... TX-5
White Lake Outlet—*stream* ... NY-2
White Lake Public Sch—*school* ... SD-7
White Lakes—*lake* ... NM-5
White Lakes—*lake* (2) ... WA-9
White Lakes—*locale* ... NM-5
White Lakes Basin—*basin* ... AZ-5
Whitelake Sch—*school* ... MI-6
White Lake Sch Number 1—*school* ... ND-7
White Lake School—*locale* ... WA-9
White Lake-Seven Harbors—*CDP* ... MI-6
White Lakes Plaza—*locale* ... KS-7
White Lakes Shop Ctr—*locale* ... KS-7
White Lakes Tank—*reservoir* ... NM-5
White Lake State Game Ref—*park* ... SD-7
White Lake State Park—*park* ... NH-1
White Lake Tank—*reservoir* ... NM-5
**White Lake Township**—*pop pl* ... ND-7
**White Lake Township**—*pop pl* ... SD-7
**White Lake (Township of)**—*pop pl* ... MI-6
White Lake Well—*well* ... NM-5
*Whiteland* ... PA-2
Whiteland—*locale* ... TX-5
**Whiteland**—*pop pl* ... IN-6
Whiteland Ch—*church* ... PA-2
Whiteland Community HS—*school* ... IN-6
**Whiteland Crest (Whiteland Station)**—*pop pl* ... PA-2
**Whiteland Farms**—*pop pl* ... PA-2
White Landing—*locale* ... MD-2
White Landing—*locale* ... NC-3
White Landing—*locale* ... VA-3
*White Landing Field* ... KS-7
White Lateral—*canal* ... AZ-5
Whitelaw—*locale* ... KS-7
**Whitelaw**—*pop pl* ... KS-7
**Whitelaw**—*pop pl* ... NY-2
**Whitelaw**—*pop pl* ... WI-6
Whitelaw Cem—*cemetery* ... NY-2
Whitelaw Creek—*stream* ... WA-9
Whitelaw Creek—*stream* ... WY-8
White Lawn Cem—*cemetery* ... NJ-2
Whitelawn Cem—*cemetery* ... TN-4
White Lead Lake—*lake* ... NY-2
*White Ledge* ... NH-1
White Ledge—*bar* ... ME-1
White Ledge—*bench* ... NH-1
White Ledge—*bench* ... UT-8
White Ledge—*cliff* ... UT-8
White Ledge—*cliff* ... VT-1
White Ledge—*island* ... ME-1
White Ledge—*rock* ... MA-1
White Ledge Camping Area—*locale* ... NH-1
White Ledge Canyon—*valley* ... CA-9
White Ledge Fork—*stream* ... UT-8
White Ledge Peak—*summit* ... CA-9
White Ledges—*cliff* ... AZ-5
White Ledges—*cliff* ... UT-8
White Ledge Spring—*spring* ... UT-8
White Ledges Spring—*spring* ... AZ-5
White Ledge Tank—*reservoir* ... AZ-5
**White Level**—*pop pl* ... NC-3
White Level Airfield—*airport* ... NC-3
White Level Ch—*church* ... NC-3
*Whiteley* ... PA-2
**Whiteley**—*pop pl* ... MD-2
**Whiteley**—*pop pl* ... TX-5
Whiteley Cem—*cemetery* ... PA-2
Whiteley Creek—*stream* ... AR-4
Whiteley Creek—*stream* ... MN-6
Whiteley Creek—*stream* ... PA-2
Whiteley Creek—*stream* ... TX-5
Whiteley Peak—*summit* ... CO-8
Whiteley Peak Rsvr—*reservoir* ... CO-8
Whiteleysburg—*locale* ... DE-2
Whiteleysburg—*locale* ... MD-2
**Whiteley (Township of)**—*pop pl* ... PA-2
**Whiteleyville**—*pop pl* ... TN-4
White Liberty Cem—*cemetery* ... MS-4
*White Lick Branch* ... IN-6
White Lick Cem—*cemetery* ... IN-6
White Lick Ch—*church* ... IN-6
White Lick Ch—*church* ... KY-4
*Whitelick Creek* ... IN-6
White Lick Creek—*stream* ... IN-6
White Lick Creek—*stream* ... KY-4
Whitelick Creek—*stream* ... KY-4
White Lick Creek—*stream* ... LA-4
White Lick Golf Course—*other* ... IN-6
*White Lick River* ... IN-6
White Licks—*cliff* ... ID-8
White Lily Brook—*stream* ... NY-2
White Lily Ch—*church* ... AL-4
**White Lily (Grade)**—*pop pl* ... KY-4
White Lily Lake—*lake* ... MN-6
White Lily Pond—*lake* (3) ... NY-2
White Lily Pond—*reservoir* ... MA-1
White Lily Pond Dam—*dam* ... MA-1
White Lily Ridge—*ridge* ... KY-4
White Lily Sch—*school* ... IL-6
White Lily Sch—*school* ... KY-4
White Lily Sch (historical)—*school* ... MO-7
Whitelime Sch—*school* ... WI-6
White Limestone Sch—*hist pl* ... WI-6
Whiteline Dam—*dam* ... OR-9
Whiteline Ditch—*canal* ... OR-9
Whiteline Rsvr—*reservoir* ... OR-9
Whiteline Spring—*spring* ... OR-9
White Line Trail—*trail* ... PA-2
*Whitelink* ... IN-6
*White-Littrell Mine* ... TN-4
*White Loaf Mtn* ... MA-1
Whiteloaf Mtn—*summit* ... MA-1
Whitelock, Henry F., House and Farm—*hist pl* ... IN-6
Whitelock Cem—*cemetery* ... VA-3
Whitelock Creek—*stream* ... PA-2
Whitelock Ditch—*canal* ... IN-6
Whitelock Lake—*reservoir* ... GA-3
White Log Branch—*stream* ... TN-4
White Log Lake—*lake* ... LA-4
White Loon Island—*island* ... MI-6
White Lot Brook—*stream* ... NH-1
Whitelow Ferry—*locale* ... AR-4
Whitely Bridge—*bridge* ... AR-4
Whitely Canyon—*valley* ... TX-5
Whitely Cem—*cemetery* ... VA-3
*Whitely Creek* ... DE-2
*Whitely Creek* ... TX-5
Whitely Landing County Park—*locale* ... OR-9
White Mallard Hunting Club—*other* ... CA-9
Whiteman, Benjamin, House—*hist pl* ... OH-6
Whiteman Afb Airp—*airport* ... MO-7
Whiteman Air Force Base—*other* (2) ... MO-7
Whiteman Bar—*bar* ... OR-9
Whiteman Bench—*bench* ... UT-8
*Whiteman Brook* ... MA-1
Whiteman Brook—*stream* ... VT-1
Whiteman Canyon—*valley* ... CA-9
Whiteman Cave—*cave* ... UT-8
Whiteman Cem—*cemetery* (2) ... IN-6
Whiteman Cem—*cemetery* ... OH-6
Whiteman Connecting Trail—*trail* ... UT-8
White Man Coulee—*valley* ... MT-8
Whiteman Cove—*bay* ... WA-9
Whiteman Creek—*stream* ... NV-8
White Man Creek—*stream* ... WA-9
Whiteman Ditch—*canal* ... IN-6
Whiteman Draw—*valley* ... ID-8
*Whiteman Flats* ... WV-2
Whiteman Fork—*stream* ... WV-2
Whiteman Gulch—*valley* ... MT-8
Whiteman Gully—*valley* ... NY-2
*Whiteman Hollow* ... NY-2
White Man Mtn—*summit* ... NY-2
Whiteman Ranch—*locale* ... CA-9
White Man Ravine—*valley* ... CA-9
Whiteman Run—*stream* ... VA-3
White Man Runs Him Creek—*stream* ... MT-8
*Whitemans Brook* ... MA-1
Whitemans Brook—*stream* ... MA-1
Whiteman Sch—*school* ... CO-8
Whitemans Chapel Cem—*cemetery* ... TX-5
*Whiteman's Creek* ... CO-8
Whitemans Creek—*stream* ... AR-4
*White Mans Fork* ... CO-8
White Mans Glory Creek—*stream* ... NC-3
White Mansion—*hist pl* ... CA-9
White Mansion—*summit* ... SD-7
White Man Spring—*spring* ... OK-5
Whiteman Spring—*spring* ... UT-8
*Whiteman Swamp* ... VA-3
Whiteman Swamp—*stream* ... VA-3
Whiteman Vega—*area* ... NM-5
White Marble Mine—*mine* ... AZ-5
White Mare Run—*stream* ... WV-2
White Marl Bluff—*cliff* ... UT-8
*White Marsh* ... DE-2
*Whitemarsh* ... VA-3
**White Marsh**—*pop pl* ... MD-2
**Whitemarsh**—*pop pl* ... PA-2
**White Marsh**—*pop pl* ... VA-3
White Marsh—*stream* ... NC-3
White Marsh—*stream* ... VA-3
White Marsh—*swamp* ... MD-2
White Marsh—*swamp* (2) ... VA-3
White Marsh Branch—*stream* (2) ... DE-2
White Marsh Branch—*stream* (2) ... MD-2
White Marsh Branch—*stream* ... VA-3
White Marsh Ch—*church* (2) ... NC-3
*Whitemarsh Creek* ... DE-2
White Marsh Creek—*bay* ... MD-2
Whitemarsh Creek—*stream* ... MD-2
White Marsh Creek—*stream* ... MD-2
*White Marsh Ditch* ... DE-2
**Whitemarsh Downs**—*pop pl* ... PA-2
*Whitemarsh Elementary School* ... PA-2
**Whitemarsh Estates**—*pop pl* ... PA-2
**Whitemarsh Greens**—*pop pl* ... PA-2
**Whitemarsh Hills**—*pop pl* ... PA-2
Whitemarsh Island—*island* ... GA-3
**Whitemarsh Island**—*pop pl* ... GA-3
Whitemarsh JHS—*school* (2) ... PA-2
**White Marsh Junction**—*pop pl* ... PA-2
Whitemarsh Junction Station—*locale* ... PA-2
Whitemarsh Memorial Park (Cemetery)—*cemetery* ... PA-2
White Marsh Park—*park* ... MD-2
Whitemarsh Research Lab—*building* ... PA-2
Whitemarsh Run—*stream* ... MD-2
White Marsh Run—*stream* ... NJ-2
White Marsh Run—*stream* ... NC-3
White Marsh Sch—*school* ... MD-2
Whitemarsh Sch—*school* ... PA-2
**White Marsh Station**—*pop pl* ... MD-2
White Marsh Swamp—*swamp* ... SC-3
Whitemarsh Township—*CDP* ... PA-2
**Whitemarsh (Township of)**—*pop pl* ... PA-2
Whitemarsh Valley Country Club—*other* ... PA-2
**Whitemarsh Valley Farms**—*pop pl* ... PA-2
**White Marsh Village**—*pop pl* ... PA-2
White Meadow—*flat* (2) ... CA-9
White Meadow Branch—*stream* ... NC-3
White Meadow Brook—*stream* ... NJ-2
White Meadow Lake—*CDP* ... NJ-2
White Meadow Lake—*reservoir* ... NJ-2
White Meadow Lake Dam—*dam* ... NJ-2
White Meadow Run—*stream* ... MD-2
White Meeting Cem—*cemetery* ... SC-3
White Meetinghouse—*hist pl* ... NH-1
Whitemeir Ditch—*canal* ... OH-6
White Memorial Bldg—*hist pl* ... ME-1
White Memorial Bldg—*hist pl* ... NY-2
White Memorial Camp—*locale* ... KS-7
White Memorial Ch—*church* ... NC-3
White Memorial Ch—*church* ... TN-4
White Memorial Hosp—*hospital* ... CA-9
White Memorial Presbyterian Ch—*church* ... MS-4
White Memorial Sch—*school* ... CA-9
White Memorial State Game Farm—*park* ... NY-2
White Memorial State Wildlife Area—*park* ... MO-7
White Mesa—*summit* (5) ... AZ-5
White Mesa—*summit* (4) ... NM-5
White Mesa—*summit* (2) ... UT-8
White Mesa Arch—*arch* ... AZ-5
White Mesa Mtn—*summit* ... UT-8
*White Mesa Natural Bridge* ... AZ-5
White Mesa Overlook—*locale* ... UT-8
White Mesa Tank—*reservoir* ... AZ-5
White Mesa Tank—*reservoir* ... NM-5
White Mesa Valley—*valley* ... UT-8
White Mesa Village—*locale* ... UT-8
White-Meyer House—*hist pl* ... DC-2
White Mill—*hist pl* ... KY-4
White Mill—*locale* ... VA-3
**White Mill**—*pop pl* ... PA-2
White Mill Cem—*cemetery* ... MO-7
White Mill Creek—*stream* ... NC-3
**White Mill Crossing**—*pop pl* ... PA-2
White Miller Lake—*lake* ... UT-8
White Mill (historical)—*locale* (2) ... MS-4
**White Mill (Lowland)**—*pop pl* ... VA-3
White Millpond—*lake* ... NC-3
**White Mills**—*pop pl* ... KY-4
**White Mills**—*pop pl* ... PA-2
White Mills Distillery Company—*hist pl* ... KY-4
White Mills Junction—*locale* ... KY-4
White Mills Station—*locale* ... PA-2
*White Mills Wells* ... NM-5
White Mine—*mine* (2) ... CA-9
White Mine—*mine* ... CO-8
White Mine—*mine* ... NM-5
White Mine—*mine* ... UT-8
White Mine Peak—*mine* ... NM-5
White Mine Peak—*summit* ... NM-5
White Mine (underground)—*mine* ... AL-4
White Monument—*ridge* ... ID-8
*Whitemore Canyon* ... UT-8
White Motor Corporation—*facility* ... VA-3
*Whitemound* ... TX-5
**White Mound**—*pop pl* ... TX-5
White Mound—*summit* ... OK-5
White Mound Cem—*cemetery* ... TX-5
Whitemound Cem—*cemetery* ... WI-6
White Mound Ch—*church* ... TX-5
**White Mound Township**—*pop pl* ... KS-7
*White Mountain* ... HI-9
*White Mountain* ... MT-8
**White Mountain**—*pop pl* ... AK-9
White Mountain Boys Ranch—*locale* ... AZ-5
White Mountain Cabin—*locale* ... UT-8
White Mountain Camp—*locale* ... NH-1
White Mountain City (Ruin)—*locale* ... CA-9
*White Mountain Communities Hospital* ... AZ-5
White Mountain Community Hosp—*hospital* ... AZ-5
White Mountain Creek—*stream* ... AK-9
White Mountain Dam—*dam* ... AZ-5
White Mountain Draw—*valley* ... TX-5
White Mountain Gulch—*valley* ... WY-8
*White Mountain Ind Res* ... AZ-5
White Mountain Kettle—*basin* ... PA-2
White Mountain Lake—*locale* ... AZ-5
White Mountain Lake—*reservoir* ... AZ-5
White Mountain Lake Airp—*airport* ... AZ-5
White Mountain Lake Post Office—*building* ... AZ-5
**White Mountain Lakes Estates**—*pop pl* ... AZ-5
White Mountain Lodge Cem—*cemetery* ... NE-7
White Mountain Mine—*mine* ... AZ-5
*White Mountain Notch* ... NH-1
White Mountain Research Station Barcroft Laboratory—*other* ... CA-9
White Mountain Research Station Crooked Creek—*other* ... CA-9
White Mountain Research Station Summit Laboratory—*school* ... CA-9
White Mountain Ridge Irail—*trail* ... PA-2
White Mountain Rsvr—*reservoir* ... AZ-5
*White Mountains* ... UT-8
White Mountains—*other* ... AK-9
White Mountains—*range* ... AZ-5
White Mountains—*range* ... CA-9
White Mountains—*range* (2) ... NH-1
White Mountains—*range* ... WA-9
White Mountain Ski Area—*other* ... PA-2
White Mountain Tank—*reservoir* ... AZ-5
White Mountain Tanks—*reservoir* ... TX-5
White Mountain Trail—*trail* ... CA-9
White Mountain Trail—*trail* ... ID-8
White Mountain Trail—*trail* ... WA-9
White Mountain Wild Area—*area* ... PA-2
White Mtn—*summit* (2) ... AK-9
White Mtn—*summit* (3) ... AZ-5
White Mtn—*summit* ... AR-4
White Mtn—*summit* (9) ... CA-9
White Mtn—*summit* ... CT-1
White Mtn—*summit* ... GA-3
White Mtn—*summit* (3) ... ID-8
White Mtn—*summit* ... ME-1
White Mtn—*summit* ... MT-8
White Mtn—*summit* (2) ... NV-8
White Mtn—*summit* ... NY-2
White Mtn—*summit* ... NC-3
White Mtn—*summit* ... OR-9
White Mtn—*summit* ... PA-2
White Mtn—*summit* (2) ... TX-5
White Mtn—*summit* (5) ... UT-8
White Mtn—*summit* ... VA-3
White Mtn—*summit* (3) ... WA-9
White Mtn—*summit* (2) ... WY-8
White Mtn Peak—*summit* ... CA-9
White Mtns—*range* ... ID-8
White Mtns—*range* ... NV-8
White Mud Branch—*stream* ... NC-3
White Mud Branch—*stream* ... VA-3
White Mud Lake—*lake* ... WA-9
White Mule Canyon—*valley* ... NM-5
White Mule Creek—*stream* ... AZ-5
White Mule Creek—*stream* ... OR-9
White Mule Flat—*flat* ... OR-9
White Mule Ridge—*ridge* (2) ... NM-5
White Mule Spring—*spring* ... UT-8
White Mule Well—*well* ... TX-5
White Mule Windmill—*well* ... AZ-5
Whiten—*locale* ... AL-4
White Narrows—*gap* ... NV-8
Whitenberger Eiler Ditch—*canal* ... IN-6
Whitenburg, The—*stream* ... OR-9
Whiten Cem—*cemetery* ... MS-4
Whiten Creek—*stream* ... GA-3
*White Neck* ... MA-1
*White Neck* ... VA-3
White Neck—*cape* (2) ... DE-2
*White Neck Creek* ... MD-2
White Neck Valley—*valley* ... AZ-5
Whitener—*locale* ... AR-4
Whitener Branch—*stream* ... AR-4
Whitener Cem—*cemetery* (2) ... MO-7
Whitener Creek—*stream* ... MO-7
Whitener Creek—*stream* ... NC-3
Whitener Ford—*locale* ... MO-7
Whitener Hill—*summit* ... TN-4
Whitener Hunting Lodge—*locale* ... SC-3
Whiten Pond—*reservoir* ... GA-3
Whitens Creek—*stream* ... MS-4
*White Number Two Beach* ... MH-9
*White Number 1 Beach* ... MH-9
White Number 1 Cem—*cemetery* ... MS-4
White Number 1 Dam—*dam* ... AL-4
White Number 2 Cem—*cemetery* ... MS-4
White Number 2 Dam—*dam* ... AL-4
*Whiteoak* ... AR-4
*Whiteoak* ... OH-6
*Whiteoak* ... OK-5
*Whiteoak* ... PA-2
*Whiteoak* ... SC-3
*White Oak* ... TX-5
White Oak—*locale* (2) ... AL-4
White Oak—*locale* (2) ... AR-4
White Oak—*locale* ... IL-6
White Oak—*locale* ... IA-7
White Oak—*locale* ... KY-4
White Oak—*locale* ... MI-6
White Oak—*locale* ... MS-4
White Oak—*locale* ... OH-6
White Oak—*locale* ... OK-5
White Oak—*locale* ... TN-4
Whiteoak—*locale* ... TN-4
White Oak—*locale* (2) ... TX-5
White Oak—*locale* (2) ... VA-3
White Oak—*locale* ... WI-6
Whiteoak—*other* ... MS-4
**Whiteoak**—*pop pl* ... AL-4
**White Oak**—*pop pl* (2) ... AL-4
**Whiteoak**—*pop pl* ... AL-4
**Whiteoak**—*pop pl* ... AR-4
**White Oak**—*pop pl* ... GA-3
**Whiteoak**—*pop pl* ... IN-6
**White Oak**—*pop pl* ... IA-7
**White Oak**—*pop pl* ... KY-4
**White Oak**—*pop pl* ... MD-2
**White Oak**—*pop pl* (3) ... MS-4
**White Oak**—*pop pl* ... MO-7
**White Oak**—*pop pl* (4) ... NC-3
**Whiteoak**—*pop pl* ... NC-3
**White Oak**—*pop pl* ... NC-3
**White Oak**—*pop pl* ... OH-6
**Whiteoak**—*pop pl* ... OH-6
**White Oak**—*pop pl* ... OH-6
**White Oak**—*pop pl* ... OK-5
**White Oak**—*pop pl* (2) ... PA-2
**White Oak**—*pop pl* (2) ... SC-3
**White Oak**—*pop pl* (2) ... TN-4
**Whiteoak**—*pop pl* ... TN-4
**White Oak**—*pop pl* ... TN-4
**White Oak**—*pop pl* ... TX-5
**White Oak**—*pop pl* ... VA-3
**White Oak**—*pop pl* ... WV-2
White Oak Acres—*uninc pl* ... TX-5
White Oak Attendance Center—*school* ... MS-4
White Oak Baptist Ch—*church* ... TN-4
*White Oak Baptist Church* ... MS-4
White Oak Bar—*bar* ... TN-4
Whiteoak Bay—*basin* ... SC-3
White Oak Bay—*swamp* ... SC-3
*Whiteoak Bayou* ... MS-4
*White Oak Bayou* ... TX-5
White Oak Bayou—*stream* ... AR-4
Whiteoak Bayou—*stream* ... FL-3
White Oak Bayou—*stream* ... LA-4
White Oak Bayou—*stream* ... MS-4
Whiteoak Bayou—*stream* ... TX-5
White Oak Bayou—*stream* ... TX-5
**White Oak Bluff**—*pop pl* ... AR-4
Whiteoak Boat Dock—*locale* ... TN-4
White Oak Borough—*civil* ... PA-2
**White Oak Bottom**—*pop pl* ... NJ-2
White Oak Bottom—*valley* ... MS-4
Whiteoak Bottoms—*bend* ... TN-4
Whiteoak Bottoms—*flat* ... NC-3
*Whiteoak Branch* ... GA-3
*White Oak Branch* ... IN-6
*Whiteoak Branch* ... WV-2
Whiteoak Branch—*stream* ... AL-4
White Oak Branch—*stream* (4) ... AR-4
White Oak Branch—*stream* (2) ... GA-3
White Oak Branch—*stream* ... IL-6
White Oak Branch—*stream* ... IN-6
White Oak Branch—*stream* (9) ... KY-4
Whiteoak Branch—*stream* ... KY-4
White Oak Branch—*stream* ... KY-4
White Oak Branch—*stream* ... LA-4
White Oak Branch—*stream* ... MS-4
White Oak Branch—*stream* (2) ... MO-7
White Oak Branch—*stream* (2) ... NJ-2
Whiteoak Branch—*stream* (3) ... NC-3
White Oak Branch—*stream* (2) ... NC-3
Whiteoak Branch—*stream* ... NC-3
White Oak Branch—*stream* (3) ... NC-3
Whiteoak Branch—*stream* ... NC-3
White Oak Branch—*stream* ... OK-5
White Oak Branch—*stream* (3) ... SC-3
White Oak Branch—*stream* (2) ... TN-4
Whiteoak Branch—*stream* (5) ... TN-4
White Oak Branch—*stream* ... TN-4
White Oak Branch—*stream* (9) ... TX-5
Whiteoak Branch—*stream* ... VA-3
White Oak Branch—*stream* ... VA-3
Whiteoak Branch—*stream* ... VA-3
White Oak Branch—*stream* (3) ... VA-3
White Oak Branch—*stream* (11) ... WV-2
White Oak Branch—*swamp* ... FL-3
White Oak Breaker—*building* ... PA-2
White Oak Bridge—*bridge* ... TN-4
Whiteoak Bridge—*bridge* ... TN-4
*White Oak Brook* ... IN-6
White Oak Brook—*stream* ... MA-1
White Oak Camp Branch—*stream* ... VA-3
White Oak Campground—*locale* ... GA-3
White Oak Canal—*canal* ... NC-3
White Oak Canyon—*valley* ... CA-9
Whiteoak Canyon—*valley* ... VA-3
White Oak Canyon Trail—*trail* ... VA-3
White Oak Cave—*cave* ... TN-4
White Oak (CCD)—*cens area* ... KY-4
White Oak Cem—*cemetery* ... AL-4
White Oak Cem—*cemetery* (3) ... AR-4
White Oak Cem—*cemetery* ... FL-3
White Oak Cem—*cemetery* ... GA-3
White Oak Cem—*cemetery* (2) ... IL-6
White Oak Cem—*cemetery* (3) ... IA-7
White Oak Cem—*cemetery* ... KY-4
White Oak Cem—*cemetery* ... MN-6
White Oak Cem—*cemetery* (3) ... MS-4
White Oak Cem—*cemetery* (2) ... MO-7
Whiteoak Cem—*cemetery* ... MO-7
White Oak Cem—*cemetery* (2) ... OH-6
White Oak Cem—*cemetery* ... OK-5
White Oak Cem—*cemetery* ... PA-2
White Oak Cem—*cemetery* (2) ... TN-4
White Oak Cem—*cemetery* ... TX-5
White Oak Cem—*cemetery* (2) ... WV-2
White Oak Cem—*cemetery* ... WI-6
*White Oak Ch* ... AL-4
White Oak Ch—*church* (4) ... AL-4
White Oak Ch—*church* (9) ... AR-4
White Oak Ch—*church* ... FL-3
White Oak Ch—*church* (2) ... GA-3
Whiteoak Ch—*church* ... GA-3
White Oak Ch—*church* ... GA-3
White Oak Ch—*church* ... IL-6
White Oak Ch—*church* (2) ... IN-6
White Oak Ch—*church* (4) ... IA-7
White Oak Ch—*church* (9) ... KY-4
Whiteoak Ch—*church* ... LA-4
White Oak Ch—*church* ... LA-4
White Oak Ch—*church* (7) ... MS-4
White Oak Ch—*church* (6) ... MO-7
Whiteoak Ch—*church* ... NC-3
White Oak Ch—*church* (14) ... NC-3
White Oak Ch—*church* ... OH-6
White Oak Ch—*church* (5) ... PA-2
Whiteoak Ch—*church* ... SC-3
White Oak Ch—*church* (6) ... SC-3
Whiteoak Ch—*church* ... TN-4
White Oak Ch—*church* ... TN-4
Whiteoak Ch—*church* (2) ... TN-4
White Oak Ch—*church* ... TN-4
White Oak Ch—*church* (2) ... TX-5
White Oak Ch—*church* (2) ... VA-3
White Oak Ch—*church* (4) ... WV-2
White Oak Chapel—*church* (2) ... KY-4
White Oak Chapel—*church* ... OH-6
Whiteoak Chapel—*church* ... TN-4
Whiteoak Ch (historical)—*church* (2) ... TN-4
*White Oak Churches* ... PA-2
White Oak Community Center—*locale* ... NC-3
**White Oak Corner**—*pop pl* ... ME-1
White Oak Country Club—*other* ... WV-2
White Oak Cove—*valley* ... VA-3
*White Oak Creek* ... AL-4
*Whiteoak Creek* ... AR-4
*Whiteoak Creek* ... DE-2
*White Oak Creek* ... IN-6
*Whiteoak Creek* ... KY-4
*Whiteoak Creek* ... MS-4
*Whiteoak Creek* ... MO-7
*Whiteoak Creek* ... NC-3
*Whiteoak Creek* ... SC-3
*White Oak Creek* ... TN-4
*White Oak Creek* ... TX-5
*White Oak Creek* ... VA-3
*Whiteoak Creek* ... WV-2
Whiteoak Creek—*stream* ... AL-4
White Oak Creek—*stream* ... AL-4
Whiteoak Creek—*stream* ... AL-4
White Oak Creek—*stream* (4) ... AL-4
White Oak Creek—*stream* (23) ... AR-4
White Oak Creek—*stream* (3) ... CA-9
White Oak Creek—*stream* ... DE-2
White Oak Creek—*stream* ... FL-3
White Oak Creek—*stream* (6) ... GA-3
Whiteoak Creek—*stream* ... IL-6
White Oak Creek—*stream* (4) ... IL-6
White Oak Creek—*stream* ... IN-6
White Oak Creek—*stream* (3) ... IA-7
White Oak Creek—*stream* (27) ... KY-4
White Oak Creek—*stream* (4) ... LA-4
White Oak Creek—*stream* (5) ... MS-4
White Oak Creek—*stream* (9) ... MO-7
White Oak Creek—*stream* ... NC-3
Whiteoak Creek—*stream* (2) ... NC-3
White Oak Creek—*stream* (3) ... NC-3
Whiteoak Creek—*stream* (2) ... NC-3
White Oak Creek—*stream* (2) ... NC-3
Whiteoak Creek—*stream* (2) ... NC-3
White Oak Creek—*stream* (2) ... NC-3
Whiteoak Creek—*stream* (2) ... NC-3
White Oak Creek—*stream* ... NC-3
Whiteoak Creek—*stream* ... NC-3
White Oak Creek—*stream* (2) ... OH-6
White Oak Creek—*stream* (3) ... OK-5
White Oak Creek—*stream* (5) ... SC-3
Whiteoak Creek—*stream* ... TN-4
White Oak Creek—*stream* ... TN-4
Whiteoak Creek—*stream* (4) ... TN-4
White Oak Creek—*stream* (3) ... TN-4
Whiteoak Creek—*stream* ... TN-4
White Oak Creek—*stream* ... TN-4
White Oak Creek—*stream* (20) ... TX-5
White Oak Creek—*stream* (9) ... VA-3
White Oak Creek—*stream* (7) ... WV-2
White Oak Creek Cabin Site Area—*locale* ... TN-4
Whiteoak Creek Ch—*church* ... NC-3
White Oak Creek Covered Bridge—*hist pl* ... GA-3
*White Oak Creek Park* ... AL-4
White Oak Creek Rec Area—*park* ... AL-4
White Oak Creek Rsvr—*reservoir* ... TX-5
**Whiteoak Creek Subdivision**—*pop pl* ... TN-4
White Oak Creek Swamp—*swamp* ... FL-3
*Whiteoak Crossing* ... TN-4
White Oak Dam—*dam* ... NC-3
Whiteoak Dam—*dam* ... NC-3
White Oak Dam—*dam* ... PA-2
Whiteoak Dam—*dam* ... TN-4
White Oak Ditch—*gut* ... DE-2
White Oak Draft—*valley* ... PA-2
White Oak Draft—*valley* (2) ... VA-3
White Oak Draft Trail—*trail* ... VA-3
White Oak Elem Sch—*school* ... NC-3
White Oak Elem Sch—*school* ... PA-2
White Oak Elem Sch—*school* ... TN-4
**White Oak Estates (subdivision)**—*pop pl* ... NC-3
**White Oak Farms**—*pop pl* ... DE-2
White Oak Flat—*flat* ... CA-9
Whiteoak Flat—*flat* ... TN-4
White Oak Flat—*flat* (2) ... VA-3
White Oak Flat—*flat* ... WV-2
**White Oak Flat**—*pop pl* ... TN-4
White Oak Flat Branch—*stream* ... KY-4
Whiteoak Flat Branch—*stream* ... TN-4
*White Oak Flats* ... TN-4
Whiteoak Flats—*flat* (2) ... GA-3
Whiteoak Flats—*flat* (2) ... NC-3
Whiteoak Flats—*flat* (2) ... TN-4
White Oak Flats—*flat* ... VA-3
Whiteoak Flats—*gap* ... NC-3
Whiteoak Flats—*locale* ... NC-3
White Oak Flats Branch—*stream* ... NC-3
Whiteoak Flats Branch—*stream* ... NC-3
Whiteoak Flats Branch—*stream* ... TN-4
Whiteoak Flats Ch—*church* ... NC-3
Whiteoak Flats Trail—*trail* ... NC-3
White Oak Flatt Sch—*school* ... TN-4
White Oak For—*woods* ... MO-7
**White Oak Forest**—*pop pl* ... TN-4
*Whiteoak Fork* ... VA-3
White Oak Fork—*stream* (5) ... KY-4
Whiteoak Fork—*stream* ... TN-4
White Oak Fork—*stream* ... WV-2
Whiteoak Fork—*stream* ... WV-2
White Oak Fork—*stream* (3) ... WV-2
White Oak Fork Ch—*church* ... VA-3
White Oak Gap—*gap* ... GA-3
Whiteoak Gap—*gap* ... GA-3
Whiteoak Gap—*gap* ... TN-4
Whiteoak Gap—*gap* ... VA-3
White Oak Gap—*gap* ... WV-2
Whiteoak Gap—*locale* ... AL-4
Whiteoak Gap Cem—*cemetery* ... VA-3
Whiteoak Gap Spring—*spring* ... GA-3
White Oak Gas Field—*oilfield* (2) ... AR-4
Whiteoak Grove—*locale* ... WV-2
White Oak Grove Cem—*cemetery* ... LA-4
White Oak Grove Ch—*church* (2) ... GA-3
White Oak Grove Ch—*church* ... IA-7
White Oak Grove Ch—*church* (2) ... MO-7
White Oak Grove Ch—*church* (4) ... NC-3
White Oak Grove Ch—*church* ... OH-6
White Oak Grove Ch—*church* (3) ... VA-3
White Oak Grove Ch of God—*church* ... TN-4
Whiteoak Grove Sch—*school* ... IL-6
White Oak Grove Sch—*school* ... LA-4
White Oak Grove Sch—*school* ... WV-2
White Oak Grove Sch (historical)—*school* ... AL-4
White Oak Hammock—*island* ... GA-3
**White Oak Heights**—*pop pl* ... NC-3
White Oak Hill—*summit* ... ME-1
White Oak Hill—*summit* ... NH-1
White Oak Hill—*summit* ... PA-2
Whiteoak Hill Ch—*church* ... NC-3
White Oak Hills Ch—*church* ... GA-3
White Oak Hist Dist—*hist pl* ... SC-3
White Oak (historical P.O.)—*locale* ... IA-7
*Whiteoak Hollow* ... MO-7
*Whiteoak Hollow* ... PA-2
Whiteoak Hollow—*valley* (2) ... AL-4
White Oak Hollow—*valley* (2) ... AL-4
White Oak Hollow—*valley* (6) ... AR-4
White Oak Hollow—*valley* ... MD-2
White Oak Hollow—*valley* ... MS-4
Whiteoak Hollow—*valley* ... MO-7
White Oak Hollow—*valley* (6) ... MO-7
Whiteoak Hollow—*valley* ... MO-7
Whlte Oak Hollow—*valley* (2) ... MO-7
White Oak Hollow—*valley* (2) ... PA-2
Whiteoak Hollow—*valley* (2) ... TN-4
White Oak Hollow—*valley* ... WV-2
White Oak HS—*school* ... NC-3
*White Oak Island* ... TN-4
White Oak Island—*summit* ... MA-1
White Oak Island Brook—*stream* ... MA-1
Whiteoak Island (historical)—*island* ... TN-4
White Oak JHS—*school* ... MD-2
White Oak JHS—*school* ... OH-6
White Oak Junction—*locale* ... TX-5
White Oak Junction—*locale* ... WV-2
**White Oak Junction**—*pop pl* ... KY-4
*Whiteoak Knob* ... GA-3
Whiteoak Knob—*summit* (2) ... NC-3
Whiteoak Knoll—*summit* ... TX-5
White Oak Lake—*lake* (2) ... AR-4
White Oak Lake—*lake* ... GA-3
White Oak Lake—*lake* ... LA-4
White Oak Lake—*lake* (2) ... MN-6
White Oak Lake—*lake* ... NC-3
White Oak Lake—*lake* (2) ... SC-3
White Oak Lake—*reservoir* ... AR-4
White Oak Lake—*reservoir* ... IL-6
White Oak Lake—*reservoir* ... IN-6
White Oak Lake—*reservoir* (2) ... NC-3
Whiteoak Lake—*reservoir* ... TN-4
White Oak Lake—*reservoir* ... TX-5
White Oak Lake—*reservoir* ... VA-3
White Oak Lake Dam—*dam* ... IN-6
White Oak Lake Dam—*dam* ... NC-3
White Oak Lake Number One—*reservoir* ... AL-4
White Oak Lake Number Two—*reservoir* ... AL-4
White Oak Lakes—*reservoir* ... AL-4
White Oak Lake State Park—*park* ... AR-4
White Oak Landing—*locale* ... FL-3
White Oak Landing—*locale* ... NC-3
White Oak Landing—*locale* ... VA-3
Whiteoak Landing (historical)—*locale* ... TN-4
White Oak Level—*flat* ... VA-3

White Oak Lick Run—*stream* ... WV-2
Whiteoak Limb Ridge—*ridge* ... NC-3
White Oak Lookout Tower—*locale* ... AR-4
White Oak Lookout Tower—*locale* ... SC-3
**White Oak Manor**—*pop pl* ... MD-2
**White Oak Manor**—*pop pl* ... PA-2
**White Oak Meadows**—*pop pl* ... OH-6
White Oak Mine—*mine* ... AZ-5
Whiteoak Missionary Baptist Ch—*church* ... MS-4
*White Oak Missionary Baptist Church* ... AL-4
White Oak Mound—*summit* ... IL-6
White Oak Mountain—*ridge* (2) ... AR-4
White Oak Mountains—*ridge* ... AR-4
*White Oak Mtn* ... NC-3
*Whiteoak Mtn* ... TN-4
White Oak Mtn—*range* ... TN-4
White Oak Mtn—*summit* ... AL-4
White Oak Mtn—*summit* (5) ... AR-4
White Oak Mtn—*summit* (2) ... GA-3
White Oak Mtn—*summit* (2) ... NC-3
Whiteoak Mtn—*summit* ... NC-3
White Oak Mtn—*summit* ... OK-5
White Oak Mtn—*summit* ... TN-4
White Oak Mtn—*summit* ... VA-3
White Oak Mtn—*summit* ... WV-2
White Oak Naval Surface Weapons
Center—*military* ... MD-2
White Oak Nook—*swamp* ... SC-3
White Oak Number One Dam—*dam* ... AL-4
White Oak Number Two Dam—*dam* ... AL-4
White Oak Opening—*flat* ... CA-9
White Oak Park—*park* ... PA-2
White Oak Park—*park* ... TX-5
**White Oak Park (subdivision)**—*pop pl* ... NC-3
White Oak Plantation—*hist pl* ... NC-3
White Oak Plats Overlook—*locale* ... VA-3
Whiteoak Pocosin—*swamp* ... NC-3
White Oak Pocosin—*swamp* ... NC-3
*Whiteoak Pocoson* ... NC-3
*Whiteoak Point* ... DE-2
White Oak Point—*cape* ... AR-4
White Oak Point—*cape* ... DE-2
White Oak Point—*cape* ... MD-2
White Oak Point—*cape* ... MN-6
White Oak Point—*cape* ... VA-3
White Oak Point—*summit* ... CA-9
White Oak Point Site—*hist pl* ... MN-6
White Oak Pond—*lake* ... ME-1
White Oak Pond—*lake* ... NH-1
White Oak Pond—*reservoir* ... PA-2
White Oak Pond Ch—*church* ... MO-7
White Oak Pond Dam—*dam* ... PA-2
*White Oak Post Office* ... TN-4
White Oak Post Office
(historical)—*building* ... PA-2
Whiteoak Post Office
(historical)—*building* ... TN-4
White Oak Prairie—*area* ... MO-7
White Oak Public Fishing Area—*park* ... IN-6
White Oak Ranger Station—*locale* ... VA-3
White Oak Regional park—*park* ... PA-2
*White Oak Ridge* ... LA-4
**Whiteoak Ridge**—*pop pl* ... NJ-2
**White Oak Ridge**—*pop pl* ... NJ-2
White Oak Ridge—*ridge* (2) ... AR-4
White Oak Ridge—*ridge* ... IN-6
White Oak Ridge—*ridge* ... KY-4
White Oak Ridge—*ridge* ... MO-7
Whiteoak Ridge—*ridge* ... NC-3
White Oak Ridge—*ridge* ... NC-3
Whiteoak Ridge—*ridge* (2) ... TN-4
White Oak Ridge—*ridge* ... TX-5
White Oak Ridge—*ridge* (2) ... VA-3
White Oak Ridge Ch—*church* ... KY-4
White Oak Ridge Ch—*church* ... NJ-2
White Oak Ridge Ch—*church* ... TX-5
White Oak Ridge Lake—*lake* ... LA-4
White Oak River—*stream* ... NC-3
Whiteoak (RR name White
Oak)—*inactive* ... MO-7
White Oak Rsvr—*reservoir* (2) ... PA-2
*Whiteoak Run* ... PA-2
White Oak Run—*stream* ... MD-2
White Oak Run—*stream* (6) ... PA-2
Whiteoak Run—*stream* ... VA-3
White Oak Run—*stream* ... VA-3
Whiteoak Run—*stream* ... VA-3
White Oak Run—*stream* (3) ... VA-3
White Oak Run—*stream* (4) ... WV-2
Whiteoak Run—*stream* ... WV-2
White Oak Run—*stream* ... WV-2
Whiteoak Run—*stream* ... WV-2
White Oak Run—*stream* ... WV-2
White Oak Run Ch—*church* ... VA-3
*White Oaks* ... OH-6
White Oaks—*locale* ... CT-1
White Oaks—*locale* ... NM-5
**White Oaks**—*pop pl* ... MA-1
**White Oaks**—*pop pl* ... NC-3
**White Oaks**—*pop pl* ... TN-4
**White Oaks**—*pop pl* ... TX-5
**White Oaks**—*pop pl* ... VA-3
Whiteoak Saltpeter Cave—*cave* ... TN-4
**White Oaks Bay**—*pop pl* ... IL-6
White Oaks Camp—*locale* ... CA-9
White Oaks Canyon—*valley* (2) ... NM-5
*White Oak Sch* ... PA-2
*White Oak Sch* ... TN-4
Whiteoak Sch—*school* ... AR-4
White Oak Sch—*school* (2) ... AR-4
White Oak Sch—*school* ... IL-6
Whiteoak Sch—*school* ... IL-6
White Oak Sch—*school* (3) ... IL-6
Whiteoak Sch—*school* (2) ... IL-6
White Oak Sch—*school* ... IL-6
Whiteoak Sch—*school* (2) ... IL-6
White Oak Sch—*school* ... IL-6
White Oak Sch—*school* ... IA-7
Whiteoak Sch—*school* ... IA-7
White Oak Sch—*school* ... IA-7
White Oak Sch—*school* (3) ... KY-4
White Oak Sch—*school* ... MI-6
White Oak Sch—*school* ... MN-6
White Oak Sch—*school* (2) ... MO-7
Whiteoak Sch—*school* ... NH-1
White Oak Sch—*school* (3) ... NC-3
White Oak Sch—*school* (3) ... PA-2
White Oak Sch—*school* ... SC-3
Whiteoak Sch—*school* ... SC-3
Whiteoak Sch—*school* ... TN-4
White Oak Sch—*school* ... TN-4
White Oak Sch—*school* ... WV-2
Whiteoak Sch (abandoned)—*school* ... MO-7
White Oak Sch (abandoned)—*school* ... MO-7
Whiteoak Sch (abandoned)—*school* (3) ... PA-2
Whiteoak Sch (historical)—*school* (2) ... AL-4
Whiteoak Sch (historical)—*school* ... MS-4
White Oak Sch (historical)—*school* ... MS-4
Whiteoak Sch (historical)—*school* ... MO-7
White Oak Sch (historical)—*school* ... MO-7
Whiteoak Sch (historical)—*school* (2) ... MO-7
White Oak Sch (historical)—*school* ... PA-2
Whiteoak Sch (historical)—*school* (3) ... TN-4
*White Oak School* ... AL-4
White Oak School (abandoned)—*locale* ... MO-7
White Oak School (Abandoned)—*locale* ... WI-6
White Oaks Draw—*valley* (2) ... NM-5
White Oaks Guard Station—*locale* ... CA-9
White Oaks Hist Dist—*hist pl* ... NM-5
Whiteoak Sink—*basin* ... TN-4
Whiteoak Slash—*basin* ... TN-4
White Oak Slash Lake—*reservoir* ... SC-3
White Oak Slope Mine—*mine* ... PA-2
*White Oak Slough* ... LA-4
White Oak Slough—*stream* (3) ... AR-4
White Oak Slough—*stream* ... IL-6
White Oak Slough—*stream* ... LA-4
White Oak Slough—*stream* ... TX-5
White Oaks Park—*park* ... CA-9
*White Oak Spring* ... AL-4
Whiteoak Spring—*spring* ... AL-4
White Oak Spring—*spring* ... AZ-5
White Oak Spring—*spring* (2) ... AR-4
Whiteoak Spring—*spring* ... GA-3
White Oak Spring—*spring* (2) ... MO-7
White Oak Spring—*spring* ... NM-5
Whiteoak Spring—*spring* ... NC-3
White Oak Spring—*spring* ... TN-4
White Oak Spring—*spring* ... TX-5
White Oak Spring Branch—*stream* ... GA-3
White Oak Spring Branch—*stream* ... VA-3
*Whiteoak Springs* ... WV-2
White Oak Springs—*locale* ... TX-5
**White Oak Springs**—*pop pl* ... WV-2
White Oak Springs—*spring* ... CA-9
White Oak Springs Branch—*stream* ... MO-7
White Oak Springs Ch—*church* ... GA-3
White Oak Springs Ch—*church* (2) ... NC-3
White Oak Springs Ch—*church* ... PA-2
White Oak Springs Ch—*church* ... VA-3
White Oak Springs Run—*stream* ... MD-2
White Oak Springs Run—*stream* ... WV-2
**White Oak Springs (Town of)**—*pop pl* ... WI-6
White Oak Spur—*ridge* ... KY-4
White Oaks Ranch—*locale* ... MS-4
White Oaks Sch—*school* ... CA-9
Whiteoaks Sch—*school* ... NC-3
White Oaks Spring—*spring* (2) ... NM-5
**White Oaks (subdivision)**—*pop pl* ... NC-3
White Oak Stamp—*gap* ... GA-3
Whiteoak Stamp—*summit* ... NC-3
White Oak Stamp Branch—*stream* ... GA-3
White Oak Stamp Gap—*gap* ... GA-3
White Oak State Fishing Area—*park* ... IN-6
Whiteoak Stomp—*gap* ... GA-3
Whiteoak Stomp—*summit* ... GA-3
**White Oak (subdivision)**—*pop pl* (2) ... NC-3
*Whiteoak Swamp* ... GA-3
**Whiteoak Swamp**—*pop pl* ... VA-3
**White Oak Swamp**—*pop pl* ... VA-3
Whiteoak Swamp—*stream* (2) ... NC-3
White Oak Swamp—*stream* ... NC-3
Whiteoak Swamp—*stream* ... NC-3
White Oak Swamp—*stream* (2) ... NC-3
Whiteoak Swamp—*stream* ... NC-3
White Oak Swamp—*stream* ... NC-3
Whiteoak Swamp—*stream* ... NC-3
White Oak Swamp—*stream* ... SC-3
Whiteoak Swamp—*stream* ... SC-3
White Oak Swamp—*stream* ... VA-3
White Oak Swamp—*swamp* (3) ... FL-3
White Oak Swamp—*swamp* (3) ... GA-3
White Oak Swamp—*swamp* ... MD-2
White Oak Swamp—*swamp* ... NC-3
Whiteoak Swamp—*swamp* ... TN-4
White Oak Swamp Creek—*stream* ... VA-3
White Oak Swamp Ditch—*canal* ... DE-2
White Oak Swamp Ditch—*stream* ... DE-2
Whiteoak Swamps—*swamp* ... TN-4
White Oak Tank—*reservoir* ... AZ-5
White Oak Township—*fmr MCD* (2) ... IA-7
**White Oak Township**—*pop pl* (2) ... MO-7
White Oak (Township of)—*fmr MCD* (3) ... AR-4
White Oak (Township of)—*fmr MCD* (6) ... NC-3
**White Oak (Township of)**—*pop pl* ... IL-6
**White Oak (Township of)**—*pop pl* ... MI-6
**White Oak (Township of)**—*pop pl* ... MN-6
**White Oak (Township of)**—*pop pl* ... OH-6
**White Oak (trailer park)**—*pop pl* ... DE-2
White Oak United Methodist Ch—*church* ... TN-4
*Whiteoak Valley* ... TN-4
**White Oak Valley**—*pop pl* ... OH-6
Whiteoak Valley—*valley* ... AR-4
White Oak Valley—*valley* (2) ... TN-4
White Oak Woods—*woods* ... IL-6
White Oil Field—*oilfield* ... TX-5
Whiteout Glacier—*glacier* ... AK-9
**White Owl**—*pop pl* ... SD-7
White Owl Butte—*summit* ... ID-8
White Owl Creek—*stream* ... CO-8
White Owl Creek—*stream* ... SD-7
White Owl (historical)—*locale* ... SD-7
White Owl Lake—*lake* ... CO-8
White Panther Creek—*stream* ... FL-3
White Panther Ditch—*canal* ... WY-8
White Park—*hist pl* ... NH-1
White Park—*park* ... CA-9
White Park—*park* ... MI-6
White Park—*park* ... MO-7
White Park—*park* ... NH-1
White Park—*park* ... UT-8
White Park—*park* ... WA-9
White Park—*park* ... WI-6
White Park Ch—*church* ... LA-4
White Parker Cem—*cemetery* ... AR-4
White Pass—*gap* ... AK-9
White Pass—*gap* ... ID-8
White Pass—*gap* (2) ... WA-9
White Pass—*gap* ... WY-8
White Pass Campground—*locale* ... WA-9
White Pass Fork—*stream* ... AK-9
White Pass HS—*school* ... WA-9
**White Pass (Recreational
Area)**—*pop pl* ... WA-9
White Patch Draw—*valley* ... NV-8
White Patch Hollow—*valley* ... MO-7
White Path—*locale* ... GA-3
Whitepath Creek—*stream* ... GA-3
White Peak—*summit* ... AZ-5
White Peak—*summit* ... ID-8
White Peak—*summit* ... MT-8
White Peak—*summit* (2) ... NM-5
White Peak Mine—*mine* ... AZ-5
*White Peaks* ... NV-8
White Peaks—*summit* ... AZ-5
White Peaks—*summit* (2) ... NV-8
White Peaks—*summit* ... WY-8
White Peaks Mine—*mine* ... NV-8
White-Penick House—*hist pl* ... KY-4
White Perch Bay—*bay* ... NC-3
White Perch Channel—*gut* ... VA-3
White Perch Cove—*bay* ... VA-3
White Perch Creek—*stream* ... VA-3
White Perch Paradise Site
(22MD641)—*hist pl* ... MS-4
White Picacho—*summit* ... AZ-5
**White Pidgeon**—*pop pl* ... IL-6
White Pigeon—*locale* ... IL-6
White Pigeon—*locale* ... IA-7
**White Pigeon**—*pop pl* (2) ... MI-6
White Pigeon Cem—*cemetery* ... IA-7
White Pigeon (historical P.O.)—*locale* ... IA-7
*White Pigeon River* ... IN-6
*White Pigeon River* ... MI-6
White Pigeon Sch—*school* ... WI-6
White Pigeon (Township of)—*civ div* ... MI-6
White Pilgrim Ch—*church* ... WV-2
White Pilgrim Sch—*school* ... IL-6
*White Pine* ... CO-8
White Pine—*locale* ... MT-8
White Pine—*locale* ... WV-2
Whitepine—*other* ... PA-2
**White Pine**—*pop pl* ... CO-8
**Whitepine**—*pop pl* ... CO-8
**White Pine**—*pop pl* ... MI-6
**White Pine**—*pop pl* ... PA-2
**White Pine**—*pop pl* ... TN-4
White Pine Branch—*stream* ... KY-4
White Pine Branch—*stream* ... NC-3
Whitepine Branch—*stream* ... TN-4
White Pine Branch—*stream* ... VA-3
White Pine Buttes—*summit* ... WA-9
White Pine Cabins—*locale* ... UT-8
White Pine Campground—*locale* ... WA-9
White Pine Campground—*park* ... OR-9
White Pine Camping Area—*locale* ... NC-3
White Pine Canyon—*valley* (3) ... ID-8
White Pine Canyon—*valley* ... MT-8
White Pine Canyon—*valley* (3) ... UT-8
White Pine (CCD)—*cens area* ... TN-4
Whitepine Cem—*cemetery* ... MT-8
White Pine Cem—*cemetery* ... WV-2
White Pine Ch—*church* ... TN-4
White Pine Ch—*church* ... WV-2
White Pine Chrome Mine
(Inactive)—*mine* ... CA-9
White Pine Cliffs—*cliff* ... NC-3
White Pine County—*civil* ... NV-8
White Pine County Courthouse—*hist pl* ... NV-8
*White Pine Creek* ... MT-8
White Pine Creek—*stream* (2) ... ID-8
Whitepine Creek—*stream* ... MT-8
White Pine Creek—*stream* ... MT-8
White Pine Creek—*stream* ... NC-3
White Pine Creek—*stream* (4) ... UT-8
Whitepine Creek—*stream* ... WA-9
White Pine Creek—*stream* ... WV-2
White Pine Creek—*stream* ... WY-8
White Pine Dam—*dam* ... UT-8
White Pine Division—*civil* ... TN-4
White Pine Division—*forest* ... NV-8
White Pine Elem Sch—*school* ... TN-4
White Pine Extension Mine—*mine* ... MI-6
White Pine First Baptist Ch—*church* ... TN-4
White Pine Flat—*flat* ... UT-8
White Pine Ford—*locale* ... TN-4
White Pine Fork—*stream* (3) ... UT-8
White Pine Golf Course—*locale* ... NV-8
White Pine Golf Course—*locale* ... TN-4
White Pine Gulch—*valley* ... ID-8
**White Pine (historical)**—*pop pl* ... OR-9
White Pine Hollow—*valley* ... IA-7
White Pine Hollow—*valley* ... KY-4
White Pine Hollow—*valley* (2) ... UT-8
White Pine Hollow State Park—*park* ... IA-7
White Pine Knob—*summit* ... OR-9
White Pine Lake—*lake* ... MN-6
White Pine Lake—*lake* (2) ... UT-8
White Pine Lake—*reservoir* ... UT-8
**White Pine Lodge**—*pop pl* ... VA-3
White-Pine Log (CCD)—*cens area* ... GA-3
White Pine Lookout Tower—*locale* ... MN-6
White Pine Marsh—*swamp* ... OR-9
White Pine Mine—*mine* (2) ... MI-6
White Pine Mine—*mine* ... NV-8
*White Pine Mountains* ... NV-8
White Pine Park—*park* ... MI-6
White Pine Peak—*summit* ... NV-8
White Pine Peak—*summit* ... UT-8
White Pine Picnic Area—*locale* ... MI-6
White Pine Point—*summit* ... TN-4
*Whitepine Post Office* ... TN-4
White Pine Post Office
(historical)—*building* ... TN-4
White Pine Quarry Cave—*cave* ... TN-4
White Pine Range—*range* ... NV-8
White Pine Ranger District—*forest* ... NV-8
*White Pine Ranger District, subdivision of* ... NV-8
*White Pine Ridge* ... WA-9
White Pine Ridge—*ridge* (2) ... MT-8
White Pine Ridge—*ridge* ... VA-3
White Pine Ridge Trail—*trail* ... MT-8
*White Pines* ... TN-4
**White Pines**—*pop pl* ... CA-9
**White Pines**—*pop pl* ... IL-6
White Pine Sch—*school* ... MI-6
White Pine Sch—*school* ... PA-2
White Pine Sch—*school* ... WV-2
White Pine Sch—*school* (2) ... WI-6
White Pines Coll—*school* ... NH-1
White Pines Golf Club—*other* ... IL-6
White Pine Shoal—*bar* ... NC-3
White Pines Lake—*reservoir* ... SC-3
White Pine Spring—*spring* ... MT-8
White Pine Spring—*spring* ... PA-2
*White Pines Recreation Site* ... NC-3
White Pines State Park Lodge and
Cabins—*hist pl* ... IL-6
**White Pines (subdivision)**—*pop pl* ... NC-3
White Pine State Park—*park* ... IL-6
White Pine Station—*locale* ... MT-8
White Pine Swamp—*swamp* ... NH-1
**White Pine (Township of)**—*pop pl* ... MN-6
White Pine Trough Spring—*spring* ... OR-9
White Pine Well—*well* ... NV-8
**White Pine (Whitepine)**—*pop pl* ... PA-2
White Pinnacle—*summit* ... NM-5
**White Place**—*pop pl* ... NM-5
White Place Hist Dist—*hist pl* ... IL-6
White Place Hist Dist—*hist pl* ... MA-1
Whiteplace Ridge—*ridge* ... VA-3
*White Place Spring* ... OR-9
White Plain Ch—*church* ... GA-3
White Plain Ch—*church* ... MS-4
*White Plains* ... NC-3
White Plains—*hist pl* ... SC-3
White Plains—*locale* ... AL-4
White Plains—*locale* ... VA-3
White Plains—*plain* ... NV-8
**White Plains**—*pop pl* ... AL-4
**White Plains**—*pop pl* ... GA-3
**White Plains**—*pop pl* ... KY-4
**White Plains**—*pop pl* ... MD-2
**White Plains**—*pop pl* ... MS-4
**White Plains**—*pop pl* ... NY-2
**White Plains**—*pop pl* (2) ... NC-3
**White Plains**—*pop pl* (2) ... SC-3
**White Plains**—*pop pl* ... TN-4
White Plains—*uninc pl* ... KY-4
White Plains Armory—*hist pl* ... NY-2
*White Plains Baptist Church* ... MS-4
White Plains (CCD)—*cens area* ... GA-3
White Plains Cem—*cemetery* ... MS-4
White Plains Cem—*cemetery* ... TN-4
White Plains Ch—*church* (2) ... GA-3
White Plains Ch—*church* (3) ... MS-4
White Plains Ch—*church* (4) ... NC-3
White Plains Ch—*church* (2) ... SC-3
White Plains Christian Acad—*school* ... NC-3
White Plains Crossroad—*locale* ... SC-3
White Plains Elem Sch—*school* ... NC-3
White Plains (historical)—*locale* ... NV-8
White Plains HS—*school* ... AL-4
White Plains (Indian Head
Junction)—*CDP* ... MD-2
White Plains Missionary Baptist
Ch—*church* ... AL-4
White Plains Rsvr Number One—*reservoir* ... NY-2
White Plains Rsvr Number Two—*reservoir* ... NY-2
White Plains Sch—*school* ... KY-4
White Plains Sch (historical)—*school* ... MS-4
White Plains United Methodist
Ch—*church* ... AL-4
White Plan Ch—*church* ... NC-3
**White Plantation**—*pop pl* ... LA-4
White Plume Cem—*cemetery* ... WY-8
White Pocket—*basin* (2) ... AZ-5
White Pockets Canyon—*valley* ... AZ-5
White Pockets Tank—*reservoir* ... AZ-5
White Pockets Water Catchment—*dam* ... AZ-5
White Pockets Windmill—*locale* ... AZ-5
*White Point* ... AL-4
*White Point* ... MD-2
*White Point* ... VA-3
*White Point* ... WA-9
White Point—*cape* (2) ... AK-9
White Point—*cape* (2) ... CA-9
White Point—*cape* ... CT-1
White Point—*cape* (2) ... FL-3
White Point—*cape* (2) ... ME-1
White Point—*cape* (2) ... MD-2
White Point—*cape* (2) ... NY-2
White Point—*cape* (2) ... NC-3
White Point—*cape* (2) ... OR-9
White Point—*cape* (3) ... SC-3
White Point—*cape* ... TX-5
White Point—*cape* ... UT-8
White Point—*cape* (3) ... VA-3
White Point—*cape* (2) ... WA-9
White Point—*cape* ... VI-3
White Point—*cliff* (3) ... AZ-5
White Point—*cliff* ... CA-9
White Point—*cliff* ... WY-8
White Point—*ridge* ... AZ-5
White Point—*summit* ... UT-8
**White Point Beach**—*pop pl* ... MD-2
White Point Causeway—*bridge* ... TX-5
White Point Ch—*church* ... TX-5
White Point Creek—*stream* ... VA-3
White Point Gardens—*park* ... SC-3
**White Point (historical)**—*pop pl* ... OR-9
White Point Island—*island* ... MD-2
White Point Landing—*locale* ... SC-3
White Point Oil Field—*oilfield* ... TX-5
White Point Swash—*beach* ... SC-3
White Point Well—*well* ... NM-5
White Point Windmill—*locale* ... TX-5
*White Pond* ... FL-3
*White Pond* ... GA-3
*White Pond* ... MA-1
*White Pond* ... MS-4
*White Pond* ... NJ-2
White Pond—*lake* ... AL-4
White Pond—*lake* ... AR-4
White Pond—*lake* (4) ... FL-3
White Pond—*lake* (2) ... GA-3
White Pond—*lake* ... ME-1
White Pond—*lake* ... MD-2
White Pond—*lake* (3) ... MA-1
White Pond—*lake* ... MS-4
White Pond—*lake* (3) ... NH-1
White Pond—*lake* ... NY-2
White Pond—*lake* ... RI-1
White Pond—*lake* (2) ... SC-3
White Pond—*locale* ... SC-3
**White Pond**—*pop pl* ... NC-3
**White Pond**—*pop pl* ... OH-6
**White Pond**—*pop pl* ... SC-3
White Pond—*reservoir* ... GA-3
White Pond—*reservoir* (2) ... MA-1
White Pond—*reservoir* ... OH-6
White Pond—*reservoir* ... PA-2
White Pond—*swamp* ... SC-3
*White Pond Bay* ... NC-3
White Pond Bay—*swamp* (2) ... NC-3
White Pond Bay (Carolina Bay)—*swamp* ... NC-3
White Pond Brook—*stream* ... NH-1
White Pond Ch—*church* ... AL-4
White Pond Ch—*church* ... FL-3
White Pond Ch—*church* ... GA-3
White Pond Creek—*stream* ... MS-4
White Pond Dam—*dam* (2) ... MA-1
White Pond Dam—*dam* ... MS-4
White Pond (historical)—*lake* ... AL-4
White Pond Number 1 Dam—*dam* ... SD-7
White Pond Post Office
(historical)—*building* ... AL-4
White Pond Sch—*school* ... SC-3
White-Pool House—*hist pl* ... TX-5
White Porky Lake—*lake* ... MN-6
**Whiteport**—*pop pl* ... NY-2
*White Post* ... NC-3
**Whitepost**—*pop pl* ... NC-3
**White Post**—*pop pl* ... NC-3
**White Post**—*pop pl* ... VA-3
White Post Hist Dist—*hist pl* ... VA-3
White Post Sch—*school* ... KS-7
Whitepost Sch—*school* ... KY-4
**White Post (Township of)**—*pop pl* ... IN-6
White Potato Lake—*lake* ... WI-6
White Prairie Sch—*school* ... IA-7
White Princess—*summit* ... AK-9
White Prospect—*mine* (2) ... TN-4
White Quail Gulch—*valley* ... CO-8
White Quartz Mtn—*summit* ... ID-8
White Quartz Ridge—*ridge* ... ID-8
*White Quick Creek* ... IN-6
White Quiver Falls—*falls* ... MT-8
White Rabbit Swamp—*swamp* ... MA-1
White Rag Gulch—*valley* ... ID-8
*White Ramon Church* ... AL-4
White Ranch—*locale* (3) ... CA-9
White Ranch—*locale* ... CO-8
White Ranch—*locale* ... MT-8
White Ranch—*locale* ... NE-7
White Ranch—*locale* (7) ... NM-5
White Ranch—*locale* (2) ... SD-7
White Ranch—*locale* (6) ... TX-5
White Ranch—*locale* (2) ... UT-8
White Ranch—*locale* (4) ... WY-8
White Ranch Dam—*dam* ... SD-7
White Ranch Glades—*flat* ... CA-9
White Rancho Cem—*cemetery* ... TX-5
White Rapids—*rapids* ... UT-8
White Rapids—*rapids* ... WI-6
White Rapids Ch—*church* ... WI-6
White Rapids Dam—*dam* ... MI-6
White Rapids Dam—*dam* ... WI-6
White Reef—*bar* ... AK-9
White Reef—*ridge* ... UT-8
*White Reservoir* ... CO-8
White Reservoir Dam—*dam* ... MA-1
**White Ridge**—*pop pl* ... IN-6
White Ridge—*ridge* ... AZ-5
White Ridge—*ridge* ... CA-9
White Ridge—*ridge* ... CO-8
White Ridge—*ridge* ... IN-6
White Ridge—*ridge* ... KY-4
White Ridge—*ridge* ... MO-7
White Ridge—*ridge* ... MT-8
White Ridge—*ridge* (3) ... NV-8
White Ridge—*ridge* ... NM-5
White Ridge—*ridge* ... TN-4
White Ridge—*ridge* ... WV-2
White Ridge Cem—*cemetery* ... NJ-2
White Ridge Ch—*church* ... KY-4
White Ridge Ch—*church* ... WV-2
White Ridge Sch—*school* ... WV-2
White Ridge Tank—*reservoir* ... AZ-5
White Rim—*cliff* ... UT-8
White Rim Mtn—*summit* ... TX-5
White Rim Trail—*trail* ... UT-8
White Rincon—*basin* ... AZ-5
*White River* ... AZ-5
*White River* ... CO-8
*White River* ... MA-1
*White River* ... MI-6
*White River* ... UT-8
*White River* ... WA-9
White River—*locale* ... CA-9
White River—*locale* ... WI-6
**Whiteriver**—*pop pl* ... AZ-5
**White River**—*pop pl* ... IN-6
**White River**—*pop pl* ... SD-7
White River—*stream* (4) ... AK-9
White River—*stream* ... AZ-5
White River—*stream* ... AR-4
White River—*stream* ... CA-9
White River—*stream* ... CO-8
White River—*stream* ... FL-3
White River—*stream* ... IN-6
White River—*stream* (2) ... MI-6
White River—*stream* (3) ... MO-7
White River—*stream* ... MT-8
White River*—*stream* ... NE-7
White River—*stream* ... NV-8
White River—*stream* ... NY-2
White River—*stream* ... OR-9
White River—*stream* ... SD-7
White River—*stream* ... TX-5
White River—*stream* (2) ... UT-8
White River—*stream* ... VT-1
White River—*stream* (2) ... WA-9
White River—*stream* (3) ... WI-6
Whiteriver Airfield—*airport* ... IN-6
Whiteriver Airp—*airport* ... AZ-5
White River Association Church
Camp—*locale* ... MO-7
*White River Badlands* ... SD-7
White River Badlands—*area* ... SD-7
White River Bluff—*cliff* ... IN-6
*White River Bluffs* ... IN-6
White River Boy Scout Camp—*locale* ... AK-9
White River Butte—*summit* ... MT-8
White River Campground—*locale* ... WA-9
*White River Canyon* ... AZ-5
White River Cave—*cave* ... GA-3
Whiteriver Cem—*cemetery* ... AZ-5
White River Cem—*cemetery* ... IN-6
White River Ch—*church* (2) ... IN-6
White River City—*locale* ... CO-8
Whiteriver City Hall—*building* ... AZ-5
White River Community House—*locale* ... CO-8
White River Crossing Camp—*locale* ... OR-9
White River Dam—*dam* ... TX-5
Whiteriver Elem Sch—*school* ... AZ-5
White River Elem Sch—*school* ... IN-6
**White River Estates**—*pop pl* ... DE-2
White River Falls—*falls* ... WA-9
White River Falls Campground—*locale* ... WA-9
Whiteriver Fire Station—*building* ... AZ-5
White River Flowage—*reservoir* (2) ... WI-6
White River Forest Camp—*locale* ... OR-9
White River Forest Service Recreation
Site—*locale* ... NV-8
*White River Glacier* ... WA-9
White River Glacier—*glacier* ... AK-9
White River Glacier—*glacier* ... OR-9
White River Glacier—*glacier* ... WA-9
White River Grazing Association Number 2
Dam—*dam* ... SD-7
White River Grazing Association Number 3
Dam—*dam* ... SD-7
**White River Junction**—*pop pl* ... VT-1
White River Junction Hist Dist—*hist pl* ... VT-1
*White River Lake* ... TX-5
White River Med Ctr—*hospital* ... AR-4
White River Municipal Airp—*airport* ... SD-7
White River Narrows—*gap* ... NV-8
White River Narrows Archeol
District—*hist pl* ... NV-8
White River Natl For—*forest* ... CO-8
White River Natl Wildlife Ref—*park* ... AR-4
White River Oil and Gas Field—*oilfield* ... UT-8
White River Park—*flat* ... MT-8
White River Park—*flat* ... WA-9
White River Park Campground—*park* ... OR-9
White River Pass—*gap* ... MT-8
White River Pass Canyon—*valley* ... NV-8
White River Plateau—*summit* ... CO-8
Whiteriver Post Office—*building* ... AZ-5
White River Power Plant—*other* ... WA-9
*White River Project Dam* ... SD-7
White River Ranger Station—*locale* ... WA-9
White River Rsvr—*reservoir* ... TX-5
White River Sch—*school* ... IN-6
White River Sink—*basin* ... NV-8
White River State For—*forest* ... MO-7
**White River Summer Home
Tract**—*pop pl* ... CA-9
**White River (Town of)**—*pop pl* ... WI-6
White River Township—*civil* ... MO-7
White River Township—*civil* ... SD-7
White River (Township of)—*fmr MCD* (7) ... AR-4
**White River (Township of)**—*pop pl* (4) ... IN-6
**White River (Township of)**—*pop pl* ... MI-6
White River Trail—*trail* ... MT-8
White River Valley—*valley* ... NV-8
**White River Village**—*pop pl* ... WI-6
White River Wash—*stream* ... NV-8
White River Well—*well* ... NV-8
White Road Ch—*church* ... NC-3
**White Road (historical)**—*pop pl* ... NC-3
*White Rock* ... CT-1
*White Rock* ... FL-3
*Whiterock* ... KS-7
*White Rock* ... NV-8
*Whiterock* ... TN-4
White Rock—*bar* ... MD-2
White Rock—*bar* ... NC-3
White Rock—*cliff* ... CA-9
White Rock—*cliff* ... CO-8
White Rock—*cliff* ... WY-8
White Rock—*island* (3) ... AK-9
White Rock—*island* (8) ... CA-9
White Rock—*island* (4) ... CT-1
White Rock—*island* ... MI-6
White Rock—*island* ... OR-9
White Rock—*island* ... UT-8
White Rock—*island* ... WA-9
White Rock—*locale* ... AR-4
White Rock—*locale* ... CA-9
Whiterock—*locale* ... CO-8
White Rock—*locale* ... MI-6
White Rock—*locale* ... NM-5
White Rock—*locale* ... PA-2
White Rock—*locale* ... TN-4
White Rock—*locale* (3) ... TX-5
White Rock—*locale* ... VA-3
White Rock—*other* ... AK-9
White Rock—*other* ... CA-9
White Rock—*pillar* ... AZ-5
White Rock—*pillar* (4) ... CA-9
White Rock—*pillar* (2) ... OR-9
White Rock—*pillar* ... TN-4
White Rock—*pillar* ... UT-8
White Rock—*pillar* ... WA-9
**Whiterock**—*pop pl* ... AR-4
**White Rock**—*pop pl* ... AR-4
**White Rock**—*pop pl* ... IL-6
**White Rock**—*pop pl* ... KS-7
**White Rock**—*pop pl* ... ME-1
**White Rock**—*pop pl* ... MD-2
**White Rock**—*pop pl* ... MI-6
**White Rock**—*pop pl* ... MN-6
**White Rock**—*pop pl* ... MO-7
**White Rock**—*pop pl* ... NM-5
**Whiterock**—*pop pl* ... NC-3
**White Rock**—*pop pl* (2) ... NC-3
**White Rock**—*pop pl* ... RI-1
**White Rock**—*pop pl* ... SC-3
**White Rock**—*pop pl* ... SD-7
**White Rock**—*pop pl* ... TN-4
**White Rock**—*pop pl* (3) ... TX-5
**White Rock**—*pop pl* ... WV-2
White Rock—*rock* (4) ... MA-1
White Rock—*summit* (2) ... AZ-5
White Rock—*summit* ... CO-8
White Rock—*summit* (2) ... CT-1
White Rock—*summit* ... ID-8
White Rock—*summit* (2) ... NM-5
White Rock—*summit* (2) ... NY-2
White Rock—*summit* ... NC-3
White Rock—*summit* (2) ... UT-8
White Rock—*summit* (2) ... VA-3
White Rock—*summit* ... WA-9
**White Rock Acres
(subdivision)**—*pop pl* ... PA-2
White Rock-Bailey Spring—*spring* ... NV-8
White Rock Bay—*bay* ... UT-8

White Rock Bluff AL-4
Whiterock Bluff—cliff CA-9
White Rock Bluff—cliff MO-7
Whiterock Bluff—cliff MO-7
White Rock Bluff—cliff MO-7
White Rock Bluffs Archeol Pictograph Site—hist pl MO-7
White Rock Branch VA-3
Whiterock Branch—stream NC-3
White Rock Branch—stream NC-3
Whiterock Branch—stream NC-3
White Rock Branch—stream TX-5
White Rock Branch—stream VA-3
Whiterock Branch—stream VA-3
White Rock Branch—stream (2) VA-3
White Rock Branch—stream WV-2
White Rock Cabin Springs—spring NV-8
White Rock Canal—canal KS-7
White Rock Canyon—valley (2) AZ-5
Whiterock Canyon—valley AZ-5
White Rock Canyon—valley (3) CA-9
White Rock Canyon—valley (6) NV-8
Whiterock Canyon—valley NV-8
White Rock Canyon—valley NV-8
White Rock Canyon—valley (2) NM-5
Whiterock Canyon—valley NM-5
White Rock Canyon—valley (6) NM-5
White Rock Canyon—valley WA-9
White Rock Canyon—valley WY-8
White Rock (CCD)—cens area NM-5
White Rock Cem—cemetery AR-4
White Rock Cem—cemetery CA-9
White Rock Cem—cemetery (2) KS-7
White Rock Cem—cemetery ME-1
White Rock Cem—cemetery MI-6
White Rock Cem—cemetery (4) TX-5
Whiterock Cem—cemetery TX-5
White Rock Cem—cemetery (2) VA-3
White Rock Center—locale IL-6
White Rock Ch TX-5
White Rock Ch—church (2) AL-4
White Rock Ch—church AR-4
White Rock Ch—church (2) GA-3
White Rock Ch—church (2) MD-2
White Rock Ch—church MS-4
White Rock Ch—church (9) NC-3
White Rock Ch—church (2) SC-3
White Rock Ch—church TN-4
White Rock Ch—church (5) TX-5
White Rock Ch—church (2) VA-3
Whiterock Ch—church VA-3
White Rock Ch—church (2) VA-3
White Rock Ch (historical)—church AL-4
White Rock City (Site)—locale CA-9
Whiterock Cliff—cliff KY-4
Whiterock Cliff—cliff NC-3
White Rock Cliff—cliff VA-3
Whiterock Corral—locale AZ-5
White Rock Coulee—valley (2) MT-8
Whiterock Cove—valley (2) VA-3
White Rock Creek CA-9
White Rock Creek NV-8
White Rock Creek UT-8
Whiterock Creek—stream AL-4
White Rock Creek—stream AR-4
White Rock Creek—stream (3) CA-9
Whiterock Creek—stream CA-9
White Rock Creek—stream ID-8
White Rock Creek—stream KS-7
White Rock Creek—stream MI-6
Whiterock Creek—stream MT-8
White Rock Creek—stream (5) NV-8
Whiterock Creek—stream NC-3
White Rock Creek—stream OR-9
Whiterock Creek—stream OR-9
White Rock Creek—stream (2) OR-9
Whiterock Creek—stream OR-9
White Rock Creek—stream (2) OR-9
White Rock Creek—stream SC-3
White Rock Creek—stream (7) TX-5
Whiterock Creek—stream TX-5
White Rock Creek—stream TX-5
White Rock Creek—stream UT-8
White Rock Creek—stream (3) VA-3
White Rock Creek Overlook—locale AR-4
**White Rock Curve Village**—pop pl UT-8
White Rock Dam—dam AZ-5
White Rock Dam—dam MN-6
White Rock Dam—dam OR-9
White Rock Dam—dam RI-1
White Rock Dam—dam SD-7
White Rock Dam State Wildlife Mngmt Area—park MN-6
Whiterock Ditch—canal CO-8
White Rock Draw—valley NM-5
White Rock Draw—valley (2) WY-8
White Rock Extension Canal—canal KS-7
White Rock Fire Control Station—locale CA-9
White Rock Forest Camp—locale OR-9
White Rock Forge Covered Bridge—hist pl PA-2
Whiterock Gap—gap NC-3
White Rock Gap—gap (3) VA-3
White Rock Gap Trail—trail VA-3
White Rock Glade—flat WV-2
White Rock Glade—stream MD-2
White Rock Guard Station—locale CA-9
White Rock Gulch—valley CA-9
Whiterock Gulch—valley ID-8
White Rock Gulch—valley (2) OR-9
White Rock Gun Club—other CA-9
**White Rock Hill**—pop pl VA-3
White Rock Hill—summit MA-1
White Rock Hill Ch—church WV-2
White Rock Hills—summit NV-8
Whiterock Hills—summit TX-5
White Rock Hollow—valley PA-2
White Rock Hollow—valley TN-4
White Rock Hollow - in part TN-4
Whiterock Hollow Mine TN-4
White Rock Hollow Mine—mine TN-4
Whiterock Hump—ridge UT-8
Whiterock Island—island AK-9
White Rock Knob—summit SC-3
White Rock Lake—lake CA-9
White Rock Lake—lake MN-6
White Rock Lake—lake TX-5
White Rock Lake—reservoir CA-9
White Rock Lake—reservoir MO-7
White Rock Lake—reservoir NJ-2
White Rock Lakes—lake WA-9
White Rock Landing—locale NC-3
White Rock Lateral—canal ID-8
White Rock Lateral—canal NV-8
White Rock Light—locale WV-2
White Rock Lookout Tower—locale TN-4
White Rock Mesa AZ-5
White Rock Mesa—summit AZ-5
Whiterock Mesa—summit AZ-5
White Rock Mesa—summit NM-5
White Rock Mesa Windmill—locale AZ-5
White Rock Mine—mine (4) CA-9
White Rock Mine—mine NV-8
White Rock Mission—church AR-4
White Rock Mountain—ridge WV-2
White Rock Mountain Rec Area—park AR-4
White Rock Mtn MA-1
White Rock Mtn—summit (2) AR-4
White Rock Mtn—summit CA-9
White Rock Mtn—summit CO-8
White Rock Mtn—summit KY-4
White Rock Mtn—summit (2) NV-8
Whiterock Mtn—summit NM-5
White Rock Mtn—summit (2) NC-3
Whiterock Mtn—summit NC-3
White Rock Mtn—summit (2) OK-5
White Rock Mtn—summit OR-9
White Rock Mtn—summit VT-1
White Rock Mtn—summit (4) VA-3
Whiterock Mtn—summit VA-3
White Rock Mtns—range NV-8
White Rock Peak—summit ID-8
White Rock Peak—summit NV-8
White Rock Peak Trail—trail ID-8
White Rock Pit Rsvr—reservoir WY-8
White Rock Plantation—hist pl NC-3
White Rock Point—cliff UT-8
White Rock Point—summit AZ-5
White Rock Quarry—mine KY-4
White Rock Ranch—locale MT-8
White Rock Ranch—locale NM-5
White Rock Ranch—locale OR-9
White Rock Rec Area—park VA-3
White Rock Ridge TN-4
White Rock Ridge—ridge CA-9
White Rock Ridge—ridge (2) NC-3
Whiterock Ridge—ridge NC-3
White Rock Ridge—ridge OR-9
Whiterock Ridge—ridge TN-4
White Rock Rsvr—reservoir ID-8
White Rock Rsvr—reservoir MT-8
White Rock Rsvr—reservoir NV-8
White Rock Rsvr—reservoir OR-9
White Rock Rsvr—reservoir UT-8
White Rock Rsvrs—reservoir OR-9
White Rock Run—stream MD-2
White Rocks VA-3
White Rocks—area UT-8
White Rocks—bar MA-1
White Rocks—bench UT-8
White Rocks—cliff WY-8
White Rocks—island MD-2
White Rocks—locale PA-2
White Rocks—other AK-9
White Rocks—other MT-8
White Rocks—pillar UT-8
White Rocks—pillar (2) VA-3
**Whiterocks**—pop pl UT-8
White Rocks—rock ID-8
White Rocks—summit KY-4
Whiterocks—summit NM-5
White Rocks—summit NY-2
White Rocks—summit NC-3
White Rocks—summit OK-5
White Rocks—summit PA-2
White Rocks—summit SD-7
White Rocks—summit (3) UT-8
Whiterocks—summit UT-8
White Rocks—summit UT-8
White Rocks—summit (2) VT-1
White Rocks—summit (2) VA-3
Whiterocks and Ouray Valley Canal—canal UT-8
White Rocks Cabin—locale AZ-5
Whiterocks Campground—park UT-8
Whiterocks Canal—canal UT-8
White Rocks Canyon—valley NM-5
White Rocks Canyon—valley UT-8
Whiterocks Cave—cave UT-8
White Rocks Cem—cemetery UT-8
White Rock Sch—school CA-9
White Rock Sch—school ME-1
White Rock Sch—school (2) MO-7
White Rock Sch—school NC-3
Whiterock Sch—school NC-3
White Rock Sch—school ND-7
White Rock Sch—school OK-5
White Rock Sch—school PA-2
White Rock Sch—school WI-6
White Rock Sch (historical)—school MO-7
Whiterocks Creek UT-8
White Rocks Draw—valley UT-8
White Rock Seeding Well—well NV-8
Whiterocks Fish Hatchery—other UT-8
White Rock Shoal—bar FL-3
White Rock (Site)—locale NV-8
Whiterocks Lake—reservoir UT-8
Whiterocks Lake Dam—dam UT-8
White Rocks Light—locale MA-1
White Rocks Mtn VT-1
White Rocks Mtn—summit MT-8
Whiterocks Mtn—summit NM-5
White Rocks Mtn—summit TN-4
Whiterock Soapstone Rsvr—reservoir AZ-5
White Rock Spring—spring (2) AZ-5
Whiterock Spring—spring AZ-5
White Rock Spring—spring (6) AZ-5
White Rock Spring—spring (2) CA-9
White Rock Spring—spring ID-8
White Rock Spring—spring (3) NV-8
Whiterock Spring—spring NV-8
White Rock Spring—spring (4) NV-8
Whiterock Spring—spring NV-8
White Rock Spring—spring (3) NV-8
White Rock Spring—spring (2) NM-5
White Rock Spring—spring (4) OR-9
White Rock Spring—spring (3) UT-8
White Rock Spring—spring VA-3
White Rock Spring—spring WY-8
White Rock Spring Loop Trail Number Thirty Eight—trail AZ-5
White Rock Springs NV-8
White Rock Springs—spring ID-8
White Rock Springs—spring (3) NV-8
White Rock Springs—spring OR-9
Whiterock Springs—spring WY-8
Whiterocks River UT-8
Whiterocks River—stream UT-8
White Rocks Rsvr—reservoir UT-8
Whiterocks Trail—trail UT-8
White Rocks Trail—trail VA-3
Whiterocks Village Site—hist pl UT-8
White Rocks Wash—valley UT-8
White Rock Tank TX-5
White Rock Tank—reservoir AZ-5
White Rock Tank—reservoir (2) NM-5
Whiterock Tank—reservoir TX-5
White Rock Tanks—reservoir AZ-5
White Rock Tower Trail—trail VA-3
White Rock Township—civil KS-7
White Rock Township—civil MO-7
**White Rock Township**—pop pl (2) KS-7
**White Rock Township**—pop pl SD-7
White Rock (Township of)—civ div IL-6
White Rock (Township of)—fmr MCD AR-4
**White Rock (Township of)**—pop pl IL-6
White Rock Trail—trail OR-9
White Rock United Methodist Ch—church TX-5
White Rock Wash—stream (2) NV-8
White Rock Wash—valley (2) AZ-5
White Rock Water—spring AZ-5
White Rock Well—well AZ-5
Whiterock Well—well ID-8
White Rock Well—well NV-8
White Rock Well—well NM-5
Whiterock 1 Drill Hole—well NV-8
Whiterock 2 Drill Hole—well NV-8
Whiterock 4 Drill Hole—well NV-8
White Roe Lake—lake NY-2
White Roost Canyon—valley UT-8
White Rose—locale KY-4
**White Rose**—pop pl IN-6
White Rose Cem—cemetery (2) OK-5
White Rose Cem—cemetery TN-4
White Rose Cem—cemetery TX-5
White Rose Ch—church LA-4
White Roselake—lake TX-5
White Rose Sch—school IL-6
White Ross Cem—cemetery OK-5
White Row Branch—stream KY-4
Whiterow Creek NC-3
Whiter Rocks Canyon—valley NV-8
Whiter Rock Well Number One—well NV-8
Whiter Sch—school IA-7
Whiterspoon Creek WY-8
Whiterspoon Ridge WY-8
White Rsvr—reservoir CA-9
White Rsvr—reservoir MA-1
White Rsvr—reservoir (2) OR-9
White Rsvr—reservoir (2) WY-8
White Ruin Canyon—valley AZ-5
White Run WV-2
White Run—locale KY-4
White Run—stream (4) PA-2
White Run—stream (4) VA-3
White Run—stream (2) WV-2
White Run Sch (historical)—school PA-2
Whites PA-2
Whites—locale KY-4
Whites—locale MS-4
Whites—locale NY-2
Whites—locale WA-9
Whites—other PA-2
**Whites**—pop pl MS-4
**Whites**—pop pl OH-6
**Whites Addition**—pop pl IL-6
**Whites Addition**—pop pl WV-2
**Whites Additon**—pop pl WV-2
White Saddle—gap CA-9
White Saddle—gap WY-8
White Saddle Pass—gap NV-8
White Saddle Spring—spring AZ-5
White Sage Canyon NV-8
White Sage Canyon—valley (2) NV-8
White Sage Canyon Well—well NV-8
White Sage Draw—valley CO-8
White Sage Flat—flat AZ-5
White Sage Flat—flat CA-9
White Sage Flat—flat (4) NV-8
White Sage Flat—flat (3) UT-8
White Sage Flats UT-8
White Sage Flats, The—flat UT-8
White Sage Flat Well—well NV-8
White Sage Gap—valley NV-8
White Sage Guzzler—reservoir NV-8
White Sage Rsvr—reservoir (2) NV-8
White Sage Spring—spring NV-8
White Sage Valley—basin UT-8
White Sage Wash—stream AZ-5
White Sage Wash—stream CA-9
White Sage Wash—stream (2) NV-8
White Sage Wash—valley UT-8
White Sage Well—well NV-8
White Sage Well—well OR-9
**White Salmon**—pop pl WA-9
White Salmon (CCD)—cens area WA-9
White Salmon Creek—stream WA-9
White Salmon Glacier—glacier (2) WA-9
White Salmon River—stream WA-9
**White Salmon (RR name Bingen-White Salmon)**—pop pl WA-9
Whitesand—locale MS-4
Whitesand—locale MO-7
Whitesand—locale TN-4
**White Sand**—pop pl MS-4
White Sand Baptist Ch—church MS-4
White Sand Beach HI-9
White Sand Campground—locale ID-8
Whitesand Ch—church MS-4
Whitesand Ch—church OK-5
White Sand Creek ID-8
White Sand Creek—stream AK-9
White Sand Creek—stream ID-8
White Sand Creek—stream MI-6
White Sand Creek—stream (2) MS-4
Whitesand Creek—stream OK-5
White Sand Creek—stream WI-6
White Sand Dunes—area UT-8
White Sand Island FM-9
White Sand Islet FM-9
White Sand Lake ID-8
White Sand Lake—lake ID-8
White Sand Lake—lake MI-6
White Sand Lake—lake MN-6
White Sand Lake—lake (2) WI-6
White Sand Landing—locale FL-3
White Sand Landing—locale GA-3
White Sand Ruins—locale AZ-5
White Sands—area NM-5
White Sands—flat UT-8
**White Sands**—pop pl MD-2
**White Sands**—pop pl NM-5
**White Sands Beach**—pop pl CT-1
White Sands Campground—park UT-8
White Sands (CCD)—cens area NM-5
White Sands Ch—church OK-5
White Sand Sch—school (2) MS-4
White Sand Sch (historical)—school MS-4
White Sands Draws—valley CO-8
White Sands Gate—other NM-5
White Sands Lake—lake NM-5
White Sands Missile Range—military NM-5
White Sands Natl Monmt—park NM-5
White Sands Natl Monmt Hist Dist—hist pl NM-5
White Sands Ranch—locale NM-5
White Sands Rsvr—reservoir CO-8
White Sands Spring—spring CO-8
**White Sands Subdivision**—pop pl UT-8
White Sand Well—well AZ-5
Whites Bar—bar AL-4
Whites Bar Creek—stream CA-9
Whites Bar Landing TN-4
Whites Basin—basin UT-8
Whites Bay—basin (2) SC-3
Whites Bay—bay NY-2
Whites Bay—locale VI-3
Whites Bay—swamp SC-3
Whites Bayou—stream LA-4
Whites Bayou—stream MS-4
Whites Bayou—stream TX-5
**Whites Beach**—pop pl MI-6
**Whites Beach**—pop pl NC-3
Whites Bend—bend (2) TN-4
Whites Bend Ch—church TN-4
Whites Bend Sch (historical)—school TN-4
Whites Bluff—cliff (3) AL-4
Whites Bluff—cliff TN-4
Whites Bluff—cliff WI-6
**Whites Bluff**—pop pl AL-4
Whites Bog NJ-2
**Whitesbog**—pop pl NJ-2
Whitesbog Hist Dist—hist pl NJ-2
Whitesboro TX-5
Whitesboro—locale CA-9
Whitesboro—locale IA-7
**Whitesboro**—pop pl AL-4
**Whitesboro**—pop pl NJ-2
**Whitesboro**—pop pl NY-2
**Whitesboro**—pop pl OK-5
**Whitesboro**—pop pl TX-5
Whitesboro Baptist Ch—church AL-4
Whitesboro Bay CA-9
Whitesboro-Burleigh—CDP NJ-2
Whitesboro Cem—cemetery AL-4
Whitesboro Cem—cemetery TX-5
Whitesboro Cove—bay CA-9
Whitesboro Elem Sch—school AL-4
Whitesboro Oil Field—oilfield TX-5
Whites Bottom—bend KY-4
Whites Branch DE-2
Whites Branch—stream (2) AL-4
Whites Branch—stream (4) KY-4
Whites Branch—stream (2) MO-7
Whites Branch—stream SC-3
Whites Branch—stream (5) TX-5
Whites Branch—stream VA-3
Whites Branch—stream WV-2
Whites Branch Arch—arch KY-4
Whites Branch Sch—school KY-4
Whites Bridge NJ-2
Whites Bridge PA-2
Whites Bridge—bridge CA-9
Whites Bridge—bridge ME-1
Whites Bridge—other MI-6
Whites Brook CT-1
Whites Brook—stream (2) ME-1
Whites Brook—stream MA-1
Whitesburg MD-2
Whitesburg—locale AL-4
**Whitesburg**—pop pl GA-3
**Whitesburg**—pop pl KY-4
**Whitesburg**—pop pl PA-2
**Whitesburg**—pop pl TN-4
Whitesburg Baptist Church AL-4
Whitesburg Bar (historical)—bar AL-4
Whitesburg Branch—stream TN-4
Whitesburg Bridge AL-4
Whitesburg (CCD)—cens area GA-3
Whitesburg (CCD)—cens area KY-4
Whitesburg (CCD)—cens area TN-4
Whitesburg Ch—church AL-4
Whitesburg Ch of God—church AL-4
Whitesburg Division—civil TN-4
Whitesburg Elem Sch—school TN-4
**Whitesburg Estates**—pop pl AL-4
Whitesburg Ferry (historical)—locale AL-4
Whitesburgh Post Office TN-4
Whitesburg Junior High School AL-4
Whitesburg Middle School AL-4
Whitesburg Mtn—summit AL-4
Whitesburg Park—park AL-4
Whitesburg Plaza Shop Ctr—locale AL-4
Whitesburg Post Office—building TN-4
Whitesburg Post Office (historical)—building AL-4
Whitesburg Sch—school AL-4
Whitesburg Sch (historical)—school TN-4
Whitesbury Branch—stream KY-4
Whites Butte—summit AZ-5
Whites Cabin—locale CA-9
Whites Camp Dock—locale TN-4
Whites Camp Fork—stream WV-2
Whites Camp Lake—lake AR-4
Whites Canyon—valley CO-8
Whites Canyon—valley NV-8
Whites Cave—cave KY-4
Whites Cem—cemetery AR-4
Whites Cem—cemetery CO-8
Whites Cem—cemetery LA-4
Whites Cem—cemetery (2) MS-4
Whites Cem—cemetery TX-5
Whites Cem—cemetery VA-3
Whites Ch—church DE-2
Whites Ch—church KY-4
Whites Ch—church (2) MS-4
Whites Ch—church TN-4
Whites Ch—church VA-3
White Sch—school AZ-5
White Sch—school (5) CA-9
White Sch—school (12) IL-6
White Sch—school (3) IA-7
White Sch—school KY-4
White Sch—school LA-4
White Sch—school (2) ME-1
White Sch—school (4) MA-1
White Sch—school (11) MI-6
White Sch—school (5) MO-7
White Sch—school (2) NY-2
White Sch—school (2) NC-3
White Sch—school ND-7
White Sch—school OH-6
White Sch—school (2) PA-2
White Sch—school SD-7
White Sch—school (3) TN-4
White Sch—school TX-5
White Sch—school VT-1
White Sch—school (5) WI-6
White Sch—school WY-8
White Sch (abandoned)—school (3) MO-7
White Sch (abandoned)—school (4) PA-2
Whites Chapel AL-4
Whites Chapel—church (4) AL-4
Whites Chapel—church (2) AR-4
Whites Chapel—church DE-2
Whites Chapel—church (2) GA-3
Whites Chapel—church (4) KY-4
Whites Chapel—church (2) MS-4
Whites Chapel—church (3) TN-4
Whites Chapel—church TX-5
Whites Chapel—church VA-3
Whites Chapel—church WV-2
Whites Chapel—locale NC-3
**Whites Chapel**—pop pl (2) AL-4
Whites Chapel Baptist Church AL-4
Whites Chapel Cem—cemetery MS-4
Whites Chapel Cem—cemetery VA-3
Whites Chapel Ch—church AL-4
Whites Chapel Ch—church MS-4
Whites Chapel Ch of Christ AL-4
**Whites Chapel Church**—pop pl NC-3
Whites Chapel (historical)—church MS-4
Whites Chapel (historical)—church TN-4
Whites Chapel Sch—school MS-4
Whites Chapel Sch—school TN-4
Whites Chapel Sch (historical)—school TN-4
White's Chapel United Methodist Church—hist pl LA-4
Whites Cheaha Lake—reservoir AL-4
White Sch (historical)—school (2) AL-4
White Sch (historical)—school (2) PA-2
White Sch (historical)—school (2) TN-4
White Sch Number 2—school MI-6
White School KS-7
White School—locale KS-7
White School (Abandoned)—locale ID-8
White School Corner—locale ME-1
White Schoolhouse Corners—locale NY-2
White Schoolhouse Corners—locale TN-4
Whites City—locale MT-8
**Whites City**—pop pl NM-5
Whites Corner—locale ME-1
Whites Corner—locale OH-6
Whites Corner—locale VA-3
**Whites Corner**—pop pl (2) ME-1
**Whites Corner**—pop pl VT-1
Whites Corners—locale NY-2
Whites Corners—locale PA-2
Whites Cove—bay MD-2
Whites Cove—valley UT-8
Whites Creek AL-4
Whites Creek DE-2
Whites Creek MS-4
Whites Creek TN-4
White's Creek VA-3
Whites Creek WY-8
Whites Creek—bay VA-3
**Whites Creek**—pop pl TN-4
**Whites Creek**—pop pl WV-2
Whites Creek—stream (4) AL-4
Whites Creek—stream CA-9
Whites Creek—stream (2) GA-3
Whites Creek—stream IA-7
Whites Creek—stream KS-7
Whites Creek—stream (2) KY-4
Whites Creek—stream MI-6
Whites Creek—stream (6) MS-4
Whites Creek—stream (3) MO-7
Whites Creek—stream MT-8
Whites Creek—stream NV-8
Whites Creek—stream (3) NC-3
Whites Creek—stream OR-9
Whites Creek—stream PA-2
Whites Creek—stream (2) SC-3
Whites Creek—stream (5) TN-4
Whites Creek—stream (4) TX-5
Whites Creek—stream UT-8
Whites Creek—stream (2) VA-3
Whites Creek—stream WV-2
Whites Creek Boat Dock—locale TN-4
Whites Creek Cave—cave MO-7
Whites Creek Cem—cemetery MO-7
Whites Creek Cem—cemetery TN-4
Whites Creek Ch—church NC-3
Whites Creek Ch—church SC-3
Whites Creek Ch—church (3) TN-4
**Whites Creek East (subdivision)**—pop pl MS-4
Whites Creek Hist Dist—hist pl TN-4
Whites Creek Lake—lake CA-9
Whites Creek Oil Field—oilfield MS-4
**White's Creek (Reids Camp)**—pop pl TN-4
Whites Creek Sch—school KY-4
Whites Creek Sch—school TX-5
Whites Creek Sch (historical)—school MO-7
Whites Creek Shoals TN-4
Whites Creek Small Wildlife Area—park TN-4
Whites Creek (Township of)—fmr MCD NC-3
**Whites Creek West (subdivision)**—pop pl MS-4
Whites Crossing IN-6
Whites Crossing NC-3
Whites Crossing—locale MS-4
Whites Crossing—locale NC-3
Whites Crossing—locale UT-8
**Whites Crossing**—pop pl PA-2
**Whites Crossing (White Rose)**—pop pl IN-6
**Whites Crossing (Whites)**—pop pl PA-2
**Whites Crossroads**—pop pl NC-3
**Whites Crossroads**—pop pl SC-3
Whites Cut—gap GA-3
Whites Cut Ridge—ridge (2) GA-3
Whites Cut Ridge—ridge TN-4
Whites Dam—dam AL-4
Whites Draft—valley WV-2
Whites Draw—valley NM-5
Whites East Pit—lake TX-5
Whitesell, Jesse, House—hist pl KY-4
Whitesell Lake Lower Dam—dam NC-3
Whitesell Lake Number One—reservoir NC-3
Whitesell Lake Number Two—reservoir NC-3
Whitesell Lake Upper Dam—dam NC-3
Whitesell Sch—school PA-2
Whitesell-Wilhoite Cem—cemetery TN-4
Whitesels Ch—church VA-3
White Seminary (historical)—school TN-4
**White Settlement**—pop pl OR-9
**White Settlement**—pop pl TX-5
White Settlement Sch—school IL-6
Whites Ferry AL-4
Whites Ferry MA-1
Whites Ferry TN-4
Whites Ferry—locale MD-2
Whites Ferry—locale PA-2
Whites Ferry—locale VA-3
Whites Ferry (historical)—locale (2) AL-4
Whites Ferry (historical)—locale MS-4
Whites Flat—flat MA-1
Whites Flat—flat UT-8
Whites Flat Bay—swamp GA-3
Whites Ford TN-4
Whites Ford—locale FL-3
Whites Fork NC-3
Whites Gap—gap AL-4
Whites Gap—gap TN-4
Whites Gap—gap VA-3
Whites Gap—gap WV-2
Whites Gap—locale AL-4
Whites Gap Baptist Ch—church AL-4
Whites Gap Cem—cemetery AL-4
Whites Gap Overlook—locale VA-3
Whites Gap Sch (historical)—school AL-4
Whites Gap Spring—spring AL-4
**Whites Garage (Covington Store)**—pop pl NC-3
Whites Grove Cem—cemetery NC-3
Whites Grove Ch—church NC-3
Whites Grove Sch—school IL-6
Whites Gulch—valley (6) CA-9
Whites Gulch—valley (2) CO-8
White's Gulch Arrastra—hist pl CA-9
Whites Head—summit ME-1
White Shed—locale TX-5
White Sheep Creek WA-9
White Shell Bar—bar FL-3
White Shell Bar Gap—gap FL-3
White Sheperd Church, The AL-4
White Shepherd Church, The—church AL-4
**White Shield**—pop pl ND-7
White Shield Creek—stream OK-5
White Shield Home—building OR-9
White Shield Island—island MT-8
White Shield Sch—school ND-7
**Whites Hill**—pop pl PA-2
Whites Hill—summit CO-8
Whites Hill—summit CT-1
Whites Hill—summit IN-6
Whites Hill—summit ME-1
Whites Hill—summit (2) MA-1
Whites Hill—summit NY-2
Whites Hill—summit RI-1
Whites Hill—summit VT-1
Whites Hill—summit VA-3
White Shirt Creek—stream SD-7
White Shoal—bar FL-3
White Shoal—bar VA-3
White Shoal Light Station—hist pl MI-6
White Shoal Marsh—swamp NC-3
White Shoals AL-4
White Shoals—bar GA-3
White Shoals—bar VA-3
White Shoals Ch—church VA-3
White Shoals (Magisterial District)—fmr MCD VA-3
Whites Hollow—valley VA-3
Whites Hollow—valley (2) WV-2
White Shop—locale VA-3
**White Shop**—pop pl VA-3
Whites House (ruins)—locale ID-8
Whiteside—locale AL-4
Whiteside—locale KS-7
**Whiteside**—pop pl MO-7
**Whiteside**—pop pl PA-2
**Whiteside**—pop pl TN-4
Whiteside, Lake—reservoir MS-4
Whiteside Bakery—hist pl KY-4
Whiteside Baptist Ch—church TN-4
Whiteside Branch—stream IL-6
Whiteside Branch—stream TN-4
Whiteside Branch—stream VA-3
Whiteside Branch—stream WI-6
Whiteside Bridge—bridge KS-7
Whiteside Bridge—bridge NC-3
Whiteside Canyon—valley NM-5
Whiteside Cave—cave TN-4
Whiteside (CCD)—cens area TN-4
Whiteside Cem—cemetery AR-4
Whiteside Cem—cemetery (2) IL-6
Whiteside Cem—cemetery MS-4
Whiteside Cem—cemetery (2) MO-7
Whiteside Cem—cemetery (4) TN-4
Whiteside Ch—church NC-3
Whiteside Ch—church TN-4
**Whiteside Corners**—pop pl NY-2
**Whiteside (County)**—pop pl IL-6
Whiteside Cove—valley NC-3
Whiteside Cove Cem—cemetery NC-3
Whiteside Creek—stream AR-4

White Water Tank—*reservoir* ... AZ-5
**Whitewater (Town of)**—*pop pl* ... WI-6
Whitewater Township—*civil* (2) ... MO-7
Whitewater Township—*fmr MCD* ... IA-7
**Whitewater (Township of)**—*pop pl* ... IN-6
**Whitewater (Township of)**—*pop pl* ... MI-6
**Whitewater (Township of)**—*pop pl* ... MN-6
**Whitewater (Township of)**—*pop pl* ... OH-6
*Whitewater Township School* ... IN-6
Whitewater Trail (Pack)—*trail* ... NM-5
Whitewater Trout Farm—*locale* ... CA-9
White Water Wash—*stream* ... AZ-5
White Water Wash—*valley* ... AZ-5
Whitewater Wells—*well* ... NM-5
**Whitewater (White Water Park)**—*pop pl* ... OH-6
*Whiteway* ... TN-4
Whiteway—*locale* ... TX-5
Whiteway Farms Lake Dam—*dam* ... MS-4
Whiteway Shop Ctr—*locale* ... TN-4
*White Welch Branch* ... MS-4
White Well—*locale* ... AZ-5
White Well—*well* (2) ... AZ-5
White Well—*well* ... CA-9
White Well—*well* (7) ... NM-5
White Well—*well* (3) ... TX-5
Whitewell Ch of God—*church* ... TN-4
White Well (dry)—*well* ... AZ-5
White Well Post Office (historical)—*building* ... TN-4
White Western Lake—*lake* ... FL-3
White Whale Mine—*mine* ... SD-7
White (White Spur)—*uninc pl* ... TX-5
White Willow—*locale* ... MN-6
White Willow Creek—*stream* ... SD-7
White Willow Lake—*lake* ... NE-7
White Willow Sch—*school* ... IL-6
White Willow Sch—*school* ... SD-7
White Willow Spring—*spring* ... AL-4
White Windmill—*locale* (2) ... NM-5
White Windmill—*locale* (6) ... TX-5
White Windmills—*locale* ... TX-5
White Wine Brook—*stream* ... RI-1
White Wing Artesian Well—*well* ... TX-5
White Wing Ch—*church* ... TN-4
*Whitewing Ferry* ... TN-4
White Wing Ferry (historical)—*locale* ... TN-4
White Wing Ranch—*locale* ... AZ-5
Whitewing Valley—*valley* ... AK-9
White Wolf—*locale* ... CA-9
White Wolf Bridge—*bridge* ... OK-5
White Wolf Canyon—*valley* ... NV-8
*Whitewoman Basin* ... KS-7
White Woman Basin—*basin* ... KS-7
White Woman Bottoms—*basin* ... KS-7
*White Woman Creek* ... CO-8
*Whitewoman Creek* ... KS-7
White Woman Creek—*stream* ... CO-8
White Woman Creek—*stream* (2) ... KS-7
White Woman Creek—*stream* ... TX-5
*White Woman River* ... OH-6
*White Woman's Creek* ... OH-6
White Womans Grave—*cemetery* ... KS-7
White Womans Point—*cape* ... GA-3
White Womans Rock—*pillar* ... OH-6
*Whitewoman Township* ... KS-7
Whitewood—*locale* ... KY-4
Whitewood—*locale* ... VA-3
**Whitewood**—*pop pl* ... PA-2
**Whitewood**—*pop pl* ... SD-7
Whitewood, Lake—*lake* ... SD-7
Whitewood Cove—*bay* ... MD-2
Whitewood Creek—*stream* ... MI-6
Whitewood Creek—*stream* ... SD-7
**Whitewood Estates (subdivision)**—*pop pl* ... UT-8
Whitewood Gut—*gut* ... MD-2
Whitewood Lakes—*lake* ... MI-6
Whitewood Peak—*summit* ... SD-7
Whitewood Point—*cape* ... NY-2
Whitewood Sch—*school* ... VA-3
**Whitewood Township**—*pop pl* ... SD-7
White Worm Cave—*cave* ... AL-4
**Whitewright**—*pop pl* ... TX-5
*Whitey Cove* ... ME-1
Whitey Davis Spring—*spring* ... ID-8
Whiteye Lake—*lake* ... WI-6
Whitey Hollow—*valley* ... TN-4
Whitey Lake—*lake* ... WI-6
*Whitey Point* ... ME-1
Whiteys Gulch—*valley* ... CA-9
*White Zion Presbyterian Church* ... MS-4
White Zion Sch (historical)—*school* ... MS-4
*Whitfield* ... KS-7
Whitfield—*locale* ... GA-3
Whitfield—*locale* ... KY-4
Whitfield—*locale* ... MS-4
Whitfield—*locale* ... TN-4
Whitfield—*locale* ... VA-3
**Whitfield**—*pop pl* ... AL-4
**Whitfield**—*pop pl* ... FL-3
**Whitfield**—*pop pl* ... IN-6
**Whitfield**—*pop pl* ... MS-4
**Whitfield**—*pop pl* ... NY-2
**Whitfield**—*pop pl* ... OH-6
**Whitfield**—*pop pl* ... PA-2
**Whitfield**—*pop pl* ... VA-3
Whitfield, Copeland, House—*hist pl* ... TN-4
Whitfield, Henry, House—*hist pl* ... CT-1
Whitfield, J. G., Estate—*hist pl* ... FL-3
Whitfield Baptist Ch—*church* ... MS-4
*Whitfield-Bates Foundry* ... TN-4
Whitfield Bight—*bay* ... MS-4
Whitfield Branch—*stream* ... AL-4
Whitfield Canal—*canal* ... AL-4
Whitfield Canal Extension—*canal* ... AL-4
Whitfield Cem—*cemetery* ... AL-4
Whitfield Cem—*cemetery* ... GA-3
Whitfield Cem—*cemetery* ... KS-7
Whitfield Cem—*cemetery* ... KY-4
Whitfield Cem—*cemetery* ... NY-2
Whitfield Cem—*cemetery* ... NC-3
Whitfield Cem—*cemetery* (2) ... TN-4
Whitfield Cem—*cemetery* (2) ... TX-5
Whitfield Cem (historical)—*cemetery* ... MS-4
Whitfield Ch—*church* ... AL-4
Whitfield Ch—*church* ... FL-3
Whitfield Ch—*church* ... MS-4
**Whitfield (County)**—*pop pl* ... GA-3
Whitfield Creek—*stream* ... TN-4
*Whitfield Crossroads* ... NC-3
**Whitfield Crossroads**—*pop pl* ... NC-3
*Whitfield Elementary School* ... MS-4
**Whitfield Estates**—*pop pl* ... FL-3
Whitfield Farms Airp—*airport* ... NC-3
Whitfield (historical)—*locale* ... KS-7
**Whitfield Homes (subdivision)**—*pop pl* ... NC-3
Whitfield Island—*island* ... TN-4
Whitfield Lake Dam—*dam* ... MS-4
Whitfield Line Sch—*school* ... MS-4
Whitfield Memorial Baptist Ch—*church* (2) ... FL-3
Whitfield Memorial Gardens—*cemetery* ... GA-3
Whitfield Memorial Methodist Ch—*church* ... AL-4
Whitfield (Mississippi State Hospital)—*hospital* ... MS-4
Whitfield Plantation (historical)—*locale* ... MS-4
Whitfield Plaza (Shop Ctr)—*locale* ... FL-3
Whitfield Pond—*reservoir* ... NC-3
Whitfield Pond Dam—*dam* ... NC-3
Whitfield Post Office (historical)—*building* ... TN-4
Whitfield Sch—*school* ... IL-6
Whitfield Sch—*school* ... MI-6
Whitfield Sch—*school* ... MS-4
Whitfield Sch—*school* ... NC-3
*Whitfields Landing* ... AL-4
Whitfield Slough—*swamp* ... FL-3
Whitfields Pond—*reservoir* ... NC-3
Whitfield Spring—*spring* ... CA-9
**Whitfield (subdivision)**—*pop pl* ... AL-4
*Whitfild* ... KS-7
Whit Flat—*flat* ... CA-9
Whitford—*locale* ... NC-3
Whitford—*locale* ... PA-2
**Whitford**—*pop pl* ... OR-9
Whitford Brook—*stream* ... CT-1
Whitford Canyon—*valley* ... AZ-5
Whitford Cem—*cemetery* ... TN-4
Whitford Corners—*locale* ... NY-2
Whitford Garne—*hist pl* ... PA-2
Whitford Hall—*hist pl* ... PA-2
Whitford Hollow—*valley* ... TN-4
Whitford JHS—*school* ... OR-9
Whitford Lake—*lake* ... MI-6
Whitford Landing—*locale* ... NC-3
Whitford Park—*park* ... PA-2
**Whitford Place**—*pop pl* ... IL-6
Whitford Pond—*lake* ... CT-1
Whitford Pond—*reservoir* ... RI-1
Whitford Post Office (historical)—*building* ... PA-2
Whitford's Ranch—*locale* ... MT-8
Whitford Station—*locale* ... PA-2
Whitford Station House—*hist pl* ... PA-2
Whitham—*locale* ... MO-7
Whitham Cem—*cemetery* ... IN-6
Whitham Ditch—*canal* ... IN-6
Whitham Lake—*lake* ... AK-9
**Whitharral**—*pop pl* ... TX-5
Whitharral Cem—*cemetery* ... TX-5
Whitherup Island—*island* ... PA-2
Whitherup Run—*stream* ... PA-2
Whithier Sch—*school* ... IL-6
Whit Hollow—*valley* ... TN-4
Whities Canyon—*valley* ... UT-8
Whitin Brook—*stream* ... NH-1
Whitin Brook Trail—*trail* ... NH-1
*Whiting* ... AL-4
Whiting—*locale* ... WY-8
**Whiting**—*pop pl* ... IN-6
**Whiting**—*pop pl* ... IA-7
**Whiting**—*pop pl* ... KS-7
**Whiting**—*pop pl* ... ME-1
**Whiting**—*pop pl* ... MO-7
**Whiting**—*pop pl* ... NJ-2
**Whiting**—*pop pl* ... VT-1
**Whiting**—*pop pl* ... WI-6
Whiting, Oliver, Homestead—*hist pl* ... NH-1
Whiting, Samuel Kidder, House—*hist pl* ... ME-1
Whiting, Timothy A., House—*hist pl* ... MN-6
Whiting Bay—*bay* ... ME-1
*Whiting Bayou* ... MS-4
Whiting Bayou—*stream* ... MS-4
Whiting Brake—*swamp* ... MS-4
Whiting Brook—*stream* ... CT-1
Whiting Brook—*stream* ... NH-1
Whiting Camp—*locale* ... UT-8
Whiting Cem—*cemetery* ... IL-6
Whiting Cem—*cemetery* ... IA-7
Whiting Chapel (historical)—*church* ... MS-4
Whiting Chute—*stream* ... MS-4
Whiting City Dam—*dam* ... KS-7
Whiting Corners—*locale* ... NY-2
Whiting Corners—*locale* ... PA-2
Whiting Cove—*bay* ... ME-1
Whiting Creek—*stream* ... PA-2
Whiting Creek—*stream* ... VA-3
Whiting Creek—*stream* ... WI-6
Whitinger Mtn—*summit* ... CA-9
Whiting Falls—*falls* ... AK-9
Whiting Field—*park* ... WI-6
Whiting Field Naval Air Station—*military* ... FL-3
Whiting Field U S Naval Reservation—*military* ... FL-3
**Whitingham**—*pop pl* ... VT-1
*Whitingham reservoir* ... VT-1
**Whitingham (Town of)**—*pop pl* ... VT-1
Whiting Harbor—*bay* ... AK-9
Whiting Hill—*summit* ... ME-1
Whiting Hill—*summit* ... MA-1
Whiting Hill—*summit* ... NH-1
**Whiting (historical)**—*pop pl* ... TN-4
Whiting Hollow—*valley* ... NY-2
Whiting Homestead—*hist pl* ... CT-1
Whiting Homestead—*locale* ... AZ-5
Whiting Junior-Senior HS—*school* ... IN-6
Whiting Key—*island* ... FL-3
Whiting Knoll—*summit* ... AZ-5
Whiting Lake—*lake* ... MN-6
Whiting Lake—*lake* ... MS-4
Whiting Lane Sch—*school* ... CT-1
Whiting Memorial Community House—*hist pl* ... IN-6
Whiting Mtn—*summit* (2) ... AR-4
Whiting Park—*park* ... IN-6
Whiting Park—*park* ... MI-6
*Whiting Passage* ... ME-1
Whiting Peak—*summit* ... MA-1
*Whiting Place* ... AL-4
Whiting Point—*cape* ... AK-9
*Whiting Pond* ... MA-1
Whiting Pond—*reservoir* ... MA-1
Whiting Pond Dam—*dam* ... MA-1
Whiting Ranch—*locale* ... OR-9
Whiting Ranch—*locale* ... WY-8
Whiting Ridge—*ridge* (2) ... CA-9
Whiting River—*stream* ... AK-9
Whiting River—*stream* ... CT-1
Whiting River—*stream* ... MA-1
Whiting Robertsdale Boat Club—*locale* ... IN-6
Whiting Rock—*bar* ... CA-9
Whiting Run—*stream* ... PA-2
*Whitings* ... NJ-2
Whiting Sch—*school* ... WY-8
Whiting Sch (historical)—*school* (2) ... MS-4
Whitings Corner—*locale* ... CT-1
Whitings Fish and Wildlife Mngmt Area—*park* ... NJ-2
*Whiting's Lake* ... NY-2
Whitings Ledge—*rock* ... MA-1
Whiting Slough—*stream* ... OR-9
Whitings Neck—*cape* ... WV-2
*Whitings Pond* ... MA-1
Whiting Spring—*spring* ... CA-9
Whiting Spring—*spring* ... OR-9
Whiting Street Pond Dam—*dam* ... MA-1
Whiting Street Rsvr—*reservoir* ... MA-1
Whiting Swamp—*stream* ... VA-3
Whiting Swamp—*swamp* ... VT-1
*Whitings (Whing)* ... NJ-2
Whiting Tank—*reservoir* (4) ... AZ-5
Whitington Cem—*cemetery* ... LA-4
Whitington Roadside Park—*park* ... MS-4
**Whiting (Town of)**—*pop pl* ... ME-1
**Whiting (Town of)**—*pop pl* ... VT-1
**Whiting Township**—*pop pl* ... KS-7
**Whiting Township**—*pop pl* ... ND-7
Whiting Wash—*valley* ... AZ-5
Whiting Woods Rec Area—*park* ... IA-7
*Whitin Pond* ... MA-1
Whitin Pond—*reservoir* ... MA-1
Whitin Pond Dam—*dam* ... MA-1
Whitin Reservoir Dam—*dam* ... MA-1
Whitin Ridge—*ridge* ... NH-1
Whitin Rsvr—*reservoir* ... MA-1
*Whitins* ... MA-1
*Whitins Machine Works Pond* ... MA-1
*Whitins Pond* ... MA-1
Whitins Pond—*reservoir* ... MA-1
*Whitins Pond Rsvr* ... MA-1
Whitins (RR name for Linwood)—*other* ... MA-1
*Whitins Station* ... MA-1
**Whitinsville**—*pop pl* ... MA-1
Whitinsville Hist Dist—*hist pl* ... MA-1
*Whitinsville Pond* ... MA-1
*Whitinville* ... MA-1
*Whitiw Pond* ... MA-1
Whitkowski Ponds—*lake* ... CT-1
Whit Lake—*lake* ... MI-6
Whitlash—*locale* ... MT-8
Whitlash Cem—*cemetery* ... MT-8
Whitlash Gas and Oil Field—*oilfield* ... MT-8
Whitlatch Sch—*school* ... IL-6
*Whitley* ... KY-4
*Whitley* ... MA-1
Whitley—*locale* ... VA-3
Whitley, William, House State Shrine—*hist pl* ... KY-4
Whitley Bend—*bend* ... TX-5
Whitley Bottom—*bend* ... ID-8
Whitley Branch—*stream* ... AL-4
Whitley Branch—*stream* ... GA-3
Whitley Branch—*stream* (4) ... KY-4
Whitley Branch—*stream* ... LA-4
Whitley Branch—*stream* ... NC-3
Whitley Branch—*stream* (2) ... VA-3
Whitley Canyon—*valley* ... OR-9
Whitley Cem—*cemetery* ... AL-4
Whitley Cem—*cemetery* ... GA-3
Whitley Cem—*cemetery* ... LA-4
Whitley Cem—*cemetery* (3) ... NC-3
Whitley Cem—*cemetery* ... TN-4
Whitley Cem—*cemetery* ... TX-5
Whitley Ch—*church* ... NC-3
Whitley Ch—*church* ... TN-4
**Whitley City**—*pop pl* ... KY-4
Whitley City (RR name Whitley)—*CDP* ... KY-4
**Whitley County**—*pop pl* ... IN-6
**Whitley (County)**—*pop pl* ... KY-4
Whitley County Courthouse—*hist pl* ... IN-6
Whitley Creek—*stream* ... AL-4
Whitley Creek—*stream* ... IL-6
Whitley Creek—*stream* ... OR-9
*Whitley Crossroads* ... VA-3
Whitley Dam—*dam* ... AL-4
Whitley Fork—*stream* ... VA-3
Whitley Gap—*gap* ... KY-4
**Whitley Gardens**—*pop pl* ... CA-9
**Whitley Heights**—*pop pl* ... NC-3
Whitley Heights Hist Dist—*hist pl* ... CA-9
Whitley Hollow—*valley* ... MO-7
Whitley Hollow—*valley* ... TN-4
Whitley HS—*school* ... NC-3
*Whitley Intermediate Sch* ... NC-3
Whitley Knob—*summit* ... KY-4
Whitley Lake—*reservoir* ... AL-4
Whitley Lake—*reservoir* ... IN-6
Whitley Lake Dam—*dam* ... IN-6
Whitley Memorial Gardens—*cemetery* ... KY-4
Whitley Mill—*locale* ... NC-3
Whitley MS—*school* ... NC-3
Whitley Place—*locale* ... NC-3
*Whitley Pond* ... MA-1
Whitley Pond Dam Number One—*dam* ... NC-3
Whitley Pond Number One—*reservoir* ... NC-3
Whitley Ridge—*ridge* ... VA-3
Whitley (RR name for Whitley City)—*other* ... KY-4
Whitleys Bluff—*cliff* ... TN-4
Whitleys Branch—*stream* ... VA-3
*Whitleysburg* ... DE-2
Whitleys Cem—*cemetery* ... GA-3
Whitley Sch—*school* ... AL-4
Whitley Sch (historical)—*school* ... MS-4
Whitleys Creek—*stream* ... NC-3
Whitleys Crossroads—*locale* ... NC-3
Whitleys Island—*island* ... TN-4
Whitleys Peak—*summit* ... CA-9
Whitley (Township of)—*fmr MCD* ... AR-4
**Whitley (Township of)**—*pop pl* ... IL-6
**Whitleyville**—*pop pl* ... TN-4
Whitleyville Post Office—*building* ... TN-4
Whitleyville Sch (historical)—*school* ... TN-4
Whitley Windmill—*locale* ... NM-5
**Whitlock**—*pop pl* ... TN-4
**Whitlock**—*pop pl* ... VA-3
Whitlock Branch—*stream* ... AL-4
Whitlock Branch—*stream* ... AR-4
Whitlock Branch—*stream* ... GA-3
Whitlock Butte—*summit* ... CA-9
Whitlock Cabin—*locale* ... UT-8
Whitlock Campground—*locale* ... CA-9
Whitlock Cem—*cemetery* (2) ... IL-6
Whitlock Cem—*cemetery* ... KY-4
Whitlock Cem—*cemetery* ... TN-4
Whitlock Cem—*cemetery* ... VA-3
Whitlock Cienega—*locale* ... AZ-5
Whitlock Creek—*stream* (2) ... CA-9
Whitlock Creek—*stream* ... LA-4
Whitlock Detention Dam—*dam* ... AZ-5
Whitlock Ford (historical)—*locale* ... TN-4
*Whitlock Forks* ... VA-3
Whitlock Gulch—*valley* ... ID-8
Whitlock Hollow—*valley* ... AR-4
Whitlock Hollow—*valley* ... TX-5
Whitlock Lake—*lake* ... MI-6
Whitlock Lakes—*reservoir* ... SC-3
Whitlock Log Cabin—*hist pl* ... KY-4
Whitlock Millpond—*lake* ... VA-3
Whitlock Mountains—*range* ... AZ-5
Whitlock Park—*park* ... OK-5
Whitlock Peak—*summit* ... AZ-5
Whitlock Place—*locale* ... CA-9
Whitlock Post Office (historical)—*building* ... TN-4
Whitlock Ravine—*valley* ... CA-9
Whitlocks Bay Rec Area—*park* ... SD-7
Whitlocks Bay Rec Area(West Unit)—*park* ... SD-7
Whitlock Sch (Abandoned)—*school* ... MO-7
Whitlock Sch (abandoned)—*school* ... MO-7
Whitlock Sch (historical)—*school* ... TN-4
Whitlocks Crossing (historical)—*locale* ... SD-7
**Whitlocks Mill**—*pop pl* ... ME-1
Whitlocks Mill Light Station—*hist pl* ... ME-1
Whitlock Valley—*basin* ... AZ-5
Whitlock Wash—*stream* (2) ... AZ-5
Whitlook Pond—*reservoir* ... NC-3
*Whitlow* ... MO-7
Whitlow—*locale* ... AR-4
Whitlow—*locale* ... CA-9
Whitlow—*locale* ... WA-9
Whitlow Branch—*stream* (2) ... TN-4
Whitlow Canyon—*valley* ... AZ-5
Whitlow Cave—*cave* (2) ... AL-4
Whitlow Cem—*cemetery* ... AL-4
Whitlow Cem—*cemetery* ... AR-4
Whitlow Cem—*cemetery* ... KY-4
Whitlow Corral—*locale* ... AZ-5
Whitlow Creek—*stream* ... CA-9
Whitlow Creek—*stream* ... GA-3
Whitlow Junction—*locale* ... AR-4
Whitlow Mine (underground)—*mine* ... TN-4
Whitlow Ranch Dam—*dam* ... AZ-5
Whitlow Ranch Flood Control Basin—*reservoir* ... AZ-5
*Whitlow Ranch Rsvr* ... AZ-5
Whitlow Ridge—*ridge* ... CA-9
*Whitlow Rsvr* ... AZ-5
Whitly Gap—*gap* ... GA-3
*Whitman* ... MD-2
Whitman—*locale* ... KS-7
Whitman—*locale* ... MN-6
Whitman—*locale* ... NY-2
Whitman—*locale* ... WY-8
**Whitman**—*pop pl* ... LA-4
**Whitman**—*pop pl* ... MA-1
**Whitman**—*pop pl* ... NE-7
**Whitman**—*pop pl* ... ND-7
**Whitman**—*pop pl* ... TX-5
**Whitman**—*pop pl* ... WA-9
**Whitman**—*pop pl* ... WV-2
Whitman, Joseph, House—*hist pl* ... NY-2
Whitman, Josiah B., House—*hist pl* ... MA-1
Whitman, Lake—*lake* ... WA-9
Whitman, Walt, House—*hist pl* ... NJ-2
Whitman, Walt, House—*hist pl* ... NY-2
Whitman, Walt, Neighborhood—*hist pl* ... NJ-2
Whitman-Anderson House—*hist pl* ... GA-3
Whitman-Belden House—*hist pl* ... WI-6
Whitman Bog—*swamp* ... ME-1
Whitman Branch—*stream* ... AL-4
Whitman Branch—*stream* ... KY-4
Whitman Branch—*stream* ... MO-7
Whitman Branch—*stream* ... PA-2
Whitman Branch—*stream* (2) ... TX-5
*Whitman Bridge* ... PA-2
Whitman Bridge—*bridge* ... NJ-2
Whitman Brook—*stream* ... CT-1
Whitman Brook—*stream* (2) ... MA-1
Whitman Brook—*stream* ... VT-1
Whitman Camp—*locale* ... NH-1
Whitman Canyon—*valley* ... CA-9
Whitman Canyon—*valley* ... NM-5
Whitman Cem—*cemetery* ... AL-4
Whitman Cem—*cemetery* ... TX-5
Whitman Cem—*cemetery* ... WV-2
Whitman Cem—*cemetery* ... WY-8
Whitman Ch—*church* ... WV-2
Whitman-Cobb House—*hist pl* ... AL-4
Whitman Coll—*school* ... WA-9
Whitman Co Memorial Airp—*airport* ... WA-9
Whitman Community Hospital Heliport—*airport* ... WA-9
Whitman Corners—*locale* ... PA-2
Whitman Coulee—*valley* ... MT-8
**Whitman County**—*pop pl* ... WA-9
Whitman Creek—*stream* ... AL-4
Whitman Creek—*stream* ... AK-9
Whitman Creek—*stream* ... CA-9
Whitman Creek—*stream* ... ID-8
Whitman Creek—*stream* (2) ... OR-9
Whitman Creek—*stream* ... WV-2
Whitman Crest—*summit* ... WA-9
Whitman Dam—*dam* ... ND-7
*Whitman Ditch* ... IN-6
Whitman Ditch—*canal* ... OH-6
Whitman Ditch—*canal* ... WA-9
Whitman Elem Sch—*school* ... AZ-5
Whitman Flats—*flat* ... WV-2
Whitman Flow—*stream* ... NY-2
Whitman Glacier—*glacier* ... WA-9
Whitman-Gregory Cem—*cemetery* ... TN-4
Whitman-Hanson Regional HS—*school* ... MA-1
Whitman Hill—*summit* ... ME-1
Whitman (historical)—*locale* ... KS-7
**Whitman (historical)**—*pop pl* ... TN-4
Whitman (historical P.O.)—*locale* ... MA-1
Whitman Hollow—*valley* ... ID-8
Whitman Hollow—*valley* ... PA-2
Whitman Hollow—*valley* ... TN-4
Whitman Hollow Boat Dock—*locale* ... TN-4
Whitman Hollow Campground—*locale* ... ID-8
Whitman Hollow Ch—*church* ... TN-4
Whitman Hollow Park—*park* ... NY-2
Whitman House—*hist pl* ... CT-1
Whitman HS—*school* ... MA-1
Whitman JHS—*school* ... MI-6
**Whitman Junction**—*pop pl* ... WV-2
Whitman Knob—*summit* ... WV-2
Whitman Lake—*lake* ... AK-9
Whitman Lake—*lake* (2) ... MI-6
Whitman Lakebed—*lake* ... MN-6
Whitman Memorial—*park* ... WA-9
Whitman Mission Natl Historic Site—*locale* ... WA-9
Whitman Mtn—*summit* (2) ... ME-1
Whitman Natl For—*forest* ... OR-9
Whitman Park—*park* ... NJ-2
Whitman Park—*park* ... NY-2
**Whitman Park**—*pop pl* ... NJ-2
Whitman-Place House—*hist pl* ... NY-2
*Whitman Pond* ... MA-1
Whitman Pond—*reservoir* ... AL-4
Whitman Pond Dam—*dam* ... AL-4
Whitman Post Office (historical)—*building* ... TN-4
Whitman River—*stream* ... MA-1
Whitman Rock—*pillar* ... OR-9
*Whitman Rsvr* ... MA-1
Whitman Rsvr—*reservoir* ... MA-1
Whitman Run—*stream* (2) ... WV-2
*Whitmans* ... WV-2
Whitmans Cabin—*locale* ... MT-8
Whitman Sch—*school* ... CA-9
Whitman Sch—*school* (2) ... CO-8
Whitman Sch—*school* ... CT-1
Whitman Sch—*school* ... ID-8
Whitman Sch—*school* ... IL-6
Whitman Sch—*school* ... IA-7
Whitman Sch—*school* ... MA-1
Whitman Sch—*school* ... MI-6
Whitman Sch—*school* ... NJ-2
Whitman Sch—*school* ... OK-5
Whitman Sch—*school* ... OR-9
Whitman Sch—*school* ... VA-3
Whitman Sch—*school* (5) ... WA-9
Whitman Sch—*school* ... WV-2
Whitman Sch—*school* ... WI-6
Whitman Sch (abandoned)—*school* ... PA-2
Whitmans Draft—*valley* ... WV-2
*Whitmans Island* ... ME-1
Whitmans Pond—*lake* ... CT-1
Whitmans Pond—*reservoir* ... MA-1
Whitmans Pond Dam—*dam* ... MA-1
Whitman Spring—*spring* ... OR-9
**Whitman Square**—*pop pl* ... NJ-2
*Whitmans River* ... MA-1
*Whitmans Run* ... WV-2
*Whitmans Swamp* ... RI-1
Whitman Street Area Hist Dist—*hist pl* ... SC-3
Whitman Street HS—*school* ... GA-3
*Whitman'S Village* ... MA-1
Whitman Townhall—*building* ... MA-1
**Whitman (Town of)**—*pop pl* ... MA-1
Whitman Trail—*trail* ... WV-2
**Whitmanville**—*pop pl* ... MA-1
**Whitmarsh**—*pop pl* ... WA-9
Whitmarsh, Alvah Horace, House—*hist pl* ... AR-4
Whitmarsh, Col. Micah, House—*hist pl* ... RI-1
Whitmarsh Brook—*stream* ... MA-1
Whitmarsh Gulch—*valley* ... MT-8
Whitmarsh Junction—*locale* ... WA-9
Whitmarsh Lake—*lake* ... MI-6
Whitmeadow Run—*stream* ... WV-2
Whitmel Canal—*canal* ... LA-4
Whitmell—*locale* ... VA-3
Whitmell Ch—*church* ... VA-3
**Whitmer**—*pop pl* ... WV-2
Whitmer, Frieda, House—*hist pl* ... OH-6
Whitmer, Solaman, House—*hist pl* ... OH-6
Whitmer Cem—*cemetery* ... IA-7
Whitmer HS—*school* ... OH-6
*Whitmer Lake* ... WA-9
*Whitmer Run* ... PA-2
Whitmeyer Creek—*stream* ... WY-8
Whitmeyer Sch—*school* ... MI-6
Whitmier Island—*island* ... FL-3
Whitmire—*locale* ... OK-5
**Whitmire**—*pop pl* ... SC-3
Whitmire Branch—*stream* ... SC-3
Whitmire Canyon—*valley* ... NM-5
Whitmire (CCD)—*cens area* ... SC-3
Whitmire Cem—*cemetery* ... FL-3
Whitmire Cem—*cemetery* ... NC-3
Whitmire Cem—*cemetery* ... PA-2
Whitmire Ch—*church* ... SC-3
*Whitmire Creek* ... WY-8
Whitmire Dam Lower—*dam* ... NC-3
Whitmire Dam Upper—*dam* ... NC-3
Whitmire Lake Dam—*dam* ... AL-4
Whitmire Lake Lower—*reservoir* ... NC-3
Whitmire Lake Upper—*reservoir* ... NC-3
Whitmire Pass—*gap* ... NM-5
Whitmire Ponds—*reservoir* ... AL-4
Whitmire Ranch—*locale* ... NM-5
Whitmire Sch (historical)—*school* ... PA-2
*Whitmore* (2) ... HI-9
**Whitmore**—*pop pl* ... AR-4
**Whitmore**—*pop pl* ... CA-9
Whitmore, George Carter, Mansion—*hist pl* ... UT-8
Whitmore, John T., House—*hist pl* ... NY-2
Whitmore Arch—*arch* ... UT-8
Whitmore Bight—*bay* ... FL-3
Whitmore Branch—*stream* ... TX-5
Whitmore Brook—*stream* ... VT-1
Whitmore Cabin—*locale* ... NM-5
*Whitmore Canyon* ... AZ-5
*Whitmore Canyon* ... UT-8
Whitmore Canyon—*valley* ... AZ-5
Whitmore Canyon—*valley* ... NM-5
Whitmore Canyon—*valley* ... OR-9
Whitmore Canyon—*valley* (3) ... UT-8
*Whitmore Canyon Dam* ... UT-8
Whitmore Cem—*cemetery* ... AR-4
Whitmore Cem—*cemetery* ... IL-6
Whitmore Cem—*cemetery* ... MO-7
Whitmore Cem—*cemetery* ... OH-6
Whitmore Cem—*cemetery* ... TX-5
Whitmore Cem—*cemetery* ... UT-8
*Whitmore City* ... HI-9
Whitmore Creek—*stream* ... CA-9
Whitmore Creek—*stream* ... ND-7
Whitmore Ditch—*canal* ... IN-6
Whitmore Drain—*canal* ... MI-6
**Whitmore (historical)**—*pop pl* ... OR-9
Whitmore Hot Springs—*locale* ... CA-9
Whitmore Lake—*lake* ... FL-3
Whitmore Lake—*lake* (2) ... MI-6
**Whitmore Lake**—*pop pl* ... MI-6
Whitmore Meadow—*flat* ... CA-9
Whitmore Mine—*mine* ... NV-8
Whitmore Mtn—*summit* ... AR-4
Whitmore Mtn—*summit* ... WA-9
Whitmore Neck—*island* ... ME-1
Whitmore Park—*flat* ... UT-8
Whitmore Park—*park* ... CA-9
Whitmore Park—*park* ... WV-2
Whitmore Point—*cliff* ... AZ-5
Whitmore Point Pond—*lake* ... AZ-5
Whitmore Pond—*reservoir* ... MA-1
Whitmore Pond—*swamp* ... MI-6
Whitmore Pond Dam—*dam* ... MA-1
*Whitmore Ponds* ... MI-6
Whitmore Ranch—*locale* ... WA-9
Whitmore Rapids—*falls* ... AZ-5
Whitmore Rsvr—*reservoir* ... OR-9
Whitmore Sch—*school* ... AZ-5
Whitmore Sch—*school* ... CA-9
Whitmore Sch—*school* ... ID-8
Whitmore Sch—*school* ... KS-7
*Whitmore Spring* ... AZ-5
Whitmore Spring—*spring* ... TN-4
Whitmore Spring (historical)—*spring* ... AZ-5
Whitmore's Ranch—*locale* ... MT-8
**Whitmore Terrace Subdivision**—*pop pl* ... UT-8
**Whitmore (Township of)**—*pop pl* ... IL-6
**Whitmore Village**—*pop pl* ... HI-9
Whitmore Village (Whitmore)—*CDP* ... HI-9
*Whitmore Wash* ... AZ-5
Whitmore Wash—*stream* ... AZ-5
Whitmore Wash—*stream* ... NV-8
Whitmore Yard—*locale* ... OH-6
Whit Mtn—*summit* ... TX-5
Whitnach Falls—*falls* ... CO-8
Whitnall HS—*school* ... WI-6
Whitnall Park—*park* ... WI-6
**Whitnel**—*pop pl* ... NC-3
Whitnel Sch—*school* ... NC-3
*Whitner* ... WV-2
**Whitner**—*pop pl* ... KY-4
Whitner Creek—*stream* ... SC-3
**Whitner Heights**—*pop pl* ... CA-9
Whitner HS—*school* ... OH-6
*Whitney* ... NV-8
Whitney—*locale* ... AK-9
Whitney—*locale* ... CA-9
Whitney—*locale* ... GA-3
Whitney—*locale* ... ID-8
Whitney—*locale* ... MI-6
Whitney—*locale* ... NC-3
Whitney—*locale* ... OH-6
Whitney—*locale* ... OR-9
Whitney—*locale* ... TX-5
Whitney—*locale* ... WA-9
**Whitney**—*pop pl* ... AL-4
**Whitney**—*pop pl* ... FL-3
**Whitney**—*pop pl* ... ID-8
**Whitney**—*pop pl* ... MS-4
**Whitney**—*pop pl* ... NE-7
**Whitney**—*pop pl* ... PA-2
**Whitney**—*pop pl* ... SC-3
**Whitney**—*pop pl* ... TX-5
Whitney, David, House—*hist pl* ... MI-6
Whitney, Eli, Gun Factory—*hist pl* ... CT-1
Whitney, F. A., Carriage Company Complex Hist Dist—*hist pl* ... MA-1
Whitney, George W., House—*hist pl* ... OH-6
Whitney, Grant, House—*hist pl* ... ID-8
Whitney, Israel, House—*hist pl* ... MA-1
Whitney, J. T., Funeral Home—*hist pl* ... AZ-5
Whitney, Lake—*lake* ... FL-3
Whitney, Lake—*lake* ... MN-6
Whitney, Lake—*reservoir* ... CT-1
Whitney, Lake—*reservoir* ... TX-5
Whitney, Mount—*summit* (2) ... CA-9
Whitney, Mount—*summit* ... NY-2
Whitney, Newel K., Store—*hist pl* ... OH-6
Whitney and Gray Bldg and Jake's Famous Crawfish Restaurant—*hist pl* ... OR-9
Whitney Ave Sch—*school* ... NY-2
Whitney Bay—*bay* ... MI-6
Whitney Bay—*bay* ... NY-2
*Whitney Beach* ... ID-8
Whitney Beach—*locale* ... FL-3
Whitney Bog—*swamp* ... ME-1
Whitney Branch—*stream* ... TX-5
Whitney Bridge—*bridge* ... OR-9
**Whitney Brook**—*pop pl* ... ME-1
Whitney Brook—*stream* (5) ... ME-1
Whitney Brook—*stream* ... MN-6
Whitney Brook—*stream* (2) ... NH-1
Whitney Brook—*stream* (2) ... NY-2
Whitney Brook—*stream* (2) ... VT-1
Whitney Brook Sch—*school* ... MN-6
Whitney Butte—*summit* ... CA-9
Whitney Canyon—*valley* (2) ... CA-9
Whitney Canyon—*valley* ... UT-8
Whitney Canyon—*valley* (2) ... WA-9
Whitney Canyon—*valley* ... WY-8
Whitney Canyon Creek—*stream* ... WY-8
Whitney (CCD)—*cens area* ... TX-5
Whitney Cem—*cemetery* ... ID-8
Whitney Cem—*cemetery* ... IL-6
Whitney Cem—*cemetery* ... MI-6
Whitney Cem—*cemetery* ... MN-6
Whitney Cem—*cemetery* ... NE-7
Whitney Cem—*cemetery* (2) ... NY-2
Whitney Cem—*cemetery* ... PA-2
Whitney Cem—*cemetery* ... TX-5
Whitney Cem—*cemetery* ... WI-6

Whortleberry Pond—*lake* MA-1
Whortleberry Pond—*lake* (2) NY-2
Whortlekill Creek—*stream* NY-2
*Whorton* AR-4
**Whorton**—*pop pl* AL-4
Whorton, John Hart, House—*hist pl* WI-6
Whorton Bend—*bend* AL-4
*Whorton Bend Baptist Church* AL-4
Whorton Bend Ch—*church* AL-4
*Whorton Bend Methodist Ch* AL-4
*Whorton Branch* TN-4
Whorton Cem—*cemetery* IA-7
Whorton Cem—*cemetery* MO-7
*Whorton Gap* AL-4
Whortons Creek—*stream* AL-4
Whorton Springs Ch—*church* TN-4
**Whortonsville**—*pop pl* NC-3
*Whortonville* NC-3
**Whortonville**—*pop pl* NC-3
WHOS-AM (Decatur)—*tower* AL-4
Who Who Creek—*stream* CA-9
Who Who Lake—*lake* CA-9
WHPA-FM (Hollidaysburg)—*tower* PA-2
WHP-AM (Harrisburg)—*tower* PA-2
W H Peeples Pond One—*lake* FL-3
W H Peeples Pond Three—*lake* FL-3
W H Peeples Pond Two—*lake* FL-3
WHPE-FM (High Point)—*tower* NC-3
WHPF-FM (Harrisburg)—*tower* PA-2
WHPT-TV (Harrisburg)—*tower* PA-2
WHPY-AM (Clayton)—*tower* NC-3
W H Rhodes Elem Sch—*school* FL-3
WHRK-FM (Memphis)—*tower* TN-4
WHRT-AM (Hartselle)—*tower* AL-4
W H Shrum Tank—*reservoir* NM-5
WHSK-FM (Kokomo)—*tower* IN-6
WHSL-FM (Wilmington)—*tower* NC-3
WHSP-FM (Fairhope)—*tower* AL-4
W H Swain Dam—*dam* TN-4
W H Swain Lake—*reservoir* TN-4
WHSY-AM (Hattiesburg)—*tower* MS-4
WHSY-FM (Hattiesburg)—*tower* (2) MS-4
W H Tank—*reservoir* NM-5
WHTB-FM (Talladega)—*tower* AL-4
Whteman Lake—*swamp* MS-4
WHTM-TV (Harrisburg)—*tower* PA-2
WHTV-TV (Meridian)—*tower* MS-4
WHUB-AM (Cookeville)—*tower* TN-4
WHUB-FM (Cookeville)—*tower* TN-4
WHUM-AM (Reading)—*tower* PA-2
WHUN-AM (Huntingdon)—*tower* PA-2
WHUT-AM (Anderson)—*tower* IN-6
WHUZ-FM (Huntington)—*tower* IN-6
WHVL-AM (Hendersonville)—*tower* NC-3
WHVN-AM (Charlotte)—*tower* NC-3
WHVR-AM (Hanover)—*tower* PA-2
W H Walker—*dam* PA-2
W H Williams Junior Dam—*dam* AL-4
*W H Williams Lake* AL-4
**Why**—*pop pl* AZ-5
WHYC-FM (Swan Quarter)—*tower* NC-3
*Whycott* PA-2
*Whyhehine* HI-9
Why Lake—*lake* AK-9
WHYL-AM (Carlisle)—*tower* PA-2
Whyland Lake—*lake* IN-6
WHYL-FM (Carlisle)—*tower* PA-2
Whyman House—*hist pl* NJ-2
Whymper Creek—*stream* AK-9
*Why Not* MS-4
Whynot—*locale* MS-4
Whynot—*locale* NC-3
Whynot Ch (historical)—*church* MS-4
Why Not Hunting Club—*locale* AL-4
Whynot Post Office (historical)—*building* MS-4
Whynot Raceway—*other* MS-4
Why Not Sch (historical)—*school* MS-4
WHYP-AM (North East)—*tower* PA-2
Why Pond—*lake* NY-2
**Why (Rocky Point Junction)**—*pop pl* AZ-5
Whyte—*locale* WV-2
**Whyte**—*pop pl* MN-6
Whyte Creek—*stream* MN-6
Whyte Park Rest Area—*park* OR-9
WHYW-AM (Braddock)—*tower* PA-2
WHYW-FM (Braddock)—*tower* PA-2
WHYY-TV (Wilmington)—*tower* DE-2
WHZN-AM (Hazelton)—*tower* PA-2
WIAM-AM (Williamston)—*tower* NC-3
*Wiandot Creek* IN-6
WIAN-FM (Indianapolis)—*tower* IN-6
**Wianno**—*pop pl* MA-1
Wianno Beach—*beach* MA-1
Wianno Club—*hist pl* MA-1
Wianno Head—*cape* MA-1
Wianno Hist Dist—*hist pl* MA-1
*Wiano* MA-1
Wiant And Highline Ditch—*canal* WY-8
Wiant Ditch—*canal* (2) WY-8
Wiant Highland Ditch—*canal* WY-8
Wiant Ranch—*locale* WY-8
Wiant Supply Ditch—*canal* WY-8
*Wiapa River* HI-9
Wiard, John, House—*hist pl* CT-1
Wiard Park—*park* OR-9
**Wibaux**—*pop pl* MT-8
Wibaux, Pierre, House—*hist pl* MT-8
Wibaux Park—*park* MT-8
WIBC-AM (Indianapolis)—*tower* IN-6
Wibel—*locale* AK-9
Wibert Sch—*school* NY-2
WIBF-FM (Jenkintown)—*tower* PA-2
Wible Corner—*locale* PA-2
Wible Lake—*lake* IN-6
**Wible Orchard**—*pop pl* CA-9
Wible Spring—*spring* CA-9
**Wiborg**—*pop pl* KY-4
WIBW-AM (Topeka)—*tower* KS-7
WIBW-FM (Topeka)—*tower* KS-7
WIBW-TV (Topeka)—*tower* KS-7
*Wicabaug Pond* MA-1
*Wicadaug Pond* MA-1
Wicasset Park—*park* NC-3
Wicassic Falls—*falls* MA-1
*Wicasuck Island* MA-1
**Wic-a-te-wah**—*pop pl* MI-6
Wiccacanee Lake—*reservoir* NC-3
Wiccacanee Lake Dam—*dam* NC-3
Wiccacanee Pond—*lake* NC-3
Wiccacanee Swamp—*stream* NC-3
Wiccacanee (Township of)—*fmr MCD* NC-3
Wiccacon Creek—*stream* NC-3
*Wiccomic Cove* DE-2
*Wiccomis Branch* DE-2
**Wiccopee**—*pop pl* NY-2
Wiccopee Brook—*stream* NY-2
Wiccopee Creek—*stream* NY-2
Wiccopee Pass—*gap* NY-2
Wiccopee Rsvr—*reservoir* NY-2
**Wiccopee (Wicopee)**—*pop pl* NY-2
WICE-AM (Providence)—*tower* RI-1
Wice Ch—*church* KY-4
Wicham—*summit* FM-9
Wichap—*gut* FM-9
**Wichap**—*pop pl* FM-9
Wichap—*summit* FM-9
Wichen—*stream* FM-9
Wichendon Shop Ctr—*locale* MA-1
**Wichert**—*pop pl* IL-6
Wichert Ch—*church* IL-6
Wiches Spring—*spring* AL-4
**Wichita**—*pop pl* IA-7
**Wichita**—*pop pl* KS-7
**Wichita**—*pop pl* OR-9
Wichita, Lake—*reservoir* TX-5
Wichita Ave Ch—*church* TX-5
Wichita Baptist Tabernacle—*church* KS-7
Wichita Bay—*bay* TX-5
Wichita Cem—*cemetery* IA-7
Wichita City Carnegie Library Bldg—*hist pl* KS-7
Wichita City Hall—*hist pl* KS-7
Wichita Country Club—*other* KS-7
Wichita County—*civil* KS-7
**Wichita (County)**—*pop pl* TX-5
Wichita County HS—*school* KS-7
**Wichita Falls**—*pop pl* TX-5
Wichita Falls (CCD)—*cens area* TX-5
Wichita Falls Dam—*dam* TX-5
Wichita Falls Route Bldg—*hist pl* TX-5
Wichita Falls State Hosp—*hospital* TX-5
**Wichita Heights**—*pop pl* KS-7
Wichita Heights HS—*school* KS-7
Wichita Hollow—*valley* MO-7
Wichita Lake—*lake* MN-6
Wichita Mall—*locale* KS-7
Wichita Mid-Continent Airp—*airport* KS-7
Wichita Mission—*church* OK-5
Wichita Mountains—*range* OK-5
Wichita Mountains Wildlife Ref—*park* OK-5
Wichita Mtn—*summit* CO-8
*Wichita Municipal Airport* KS-7
Wichita North Junior-Senior HS—*school* KS-7
Wichita Park—*park* OK-5
Wichita Park Cem—*cemetery* KS-7
Wichita Plaza—*locale* KS-7
Wichita Prairies—*plain* KS-7
Wichita River—*stream* TX-5
Wichita Sch—*school* OR-9
Wichita Southeast High School—*stream* KS-7
Wichita South HS—*school* KS-7
**Wichita (sta)**—*pop pl* OR-9
Wichita State Univ—*school* KS-7
**Wichita Station**—*pop pl* OR-9
Wichita Street Ch—*church* TX-5
Wichita Tank—*reservoir* TX-5
Wichita University—*uninc pl* KS-7
*Wichita Valley Center Flood Control* KS-7
Wichita-Valley Center Floodway—*canal* KS-7
Wichita Valley Community House—*building* TX-5
**Wichita Valley Farms**—*pop pl* TX-5
Wichita West HS—*school* KS-7
Wichita Wholesale Grocery Company—*hist pl* KS-7
Wichiup Rsvr—*reservoir* MT-8
Wichman Canyon—*valley* NV-8
Wichman's Grocery—*hist pl* OH-6
Wichopi, Nom En—*bay* FM-9
Wichou—*bar* FM-9
Wichser Lake—*lake* WI-6
*Wichuk* FM-9
Wichuk—*summit* FM-9
*Wichukuna* FM-9
Wichukuno—*locale* FM-9
Wichukuno—*summit* FM-9
**Wick**—*pop pl* IA-7
**Wick**—*pop pl* OH-6
**Wick**—*pop pl* PA-2
**Wick**—*pop pl* WV-2
Wick, Michael, Farmhouse and Barn—*hist pl* WI-6
Wick, Mount—*summit* AK-9
*Wickaboag Lake* MA-1
Wickaboag Pond—*lake* MA-1
Wickaboxet Pond—*lake* RI-1
Wickadahl Ranch—*locale* MT-8
Wickahoney—*locale* ID-8
*Wickahoney Creek* ID-8
Wickahoney Creek—*stream* ID-8
Wickahoney Crossing—*locale* ID-8
Wickahoney Point—*cape* ID-8
Wickahoney Post Office and Stage Station—*hist pl* ID-8
WICK-AM (Scranton)—*tower* PA-2
*Wickapeket Hill* MA-1
Wickapogue Pond—*lake* NY-2
Wickapogue Road Hist Dist—*hist pl* NY-2
*Wickataquay Pond* MA-1
**Wickatunk**—*pop pl* NJ-2
Wick Ave Hist Dist—*hist pl* OH-6
Wick Ave Hist Dist (Boundary Decrease)—*hist pl* OH-6
Wick Bldg—*hist pl* OH-6
*Wickboag Pond* MA-1
*Wickboro* PA-2
Wick Brothers Ranch—*locale* WY-8
Wick Brothers Sheep Camp—*locale* WY-8
Wickchoupai—*locale* AZ-5
**Wick City (subdivision)**—*pop pl* PA-2
Wickcliffe Presbyterian Church—*hist pl* NJ-2
Wickcliffe (Township of)—*other* OH-6
Wick Creek—*stream* OR-9
*Wickechecoke Creek* NJ-2
Wickecheoke Creek—*stream* NJ-2
Wicked Creek—*stream* AR-4
Wicked Creek—*stream* MT-8
**Wickenburg**—*pop pl* AZ-5
Wickenburg (CCD)—*cens area* AZ-5
Wickenburg Community Hosp—*hospital* AZ-5
Wickenburg Country Club—*other* AZ-5
Wickenburg HS—*school* AZ-5
Wickenburg HS and Annex—*hist pl* AZ-5
Wickenburg HS Gymnasium—*hist pl* AZ-5
Wickenburg Ice and Cold Storage—*hist pl* AZ-5
Wickenburg Massacre Historical Monmt—*park* AZ-5
Wickenburg Mountains—*range* AZ-5
Wickenburg Municipal Airp—*airport* AZ-5
Wickenburg Post Office—*building* AZ-5
*Wickenburg Ranch* AZ-5
Wickenburg RR Station—*building* AZ-5
Wickenburg Substation—*locale* AZ-5
Wickenburg Town Hall—*building* AZ-5
Wickenson Gulch—*valley* CO-8
Wickenson Mtn—*summit* CO-8
Wicker—*locale* TX-5
**Wicker**—*pop pl* (2) MS-4
Wicker Branch—*stream* MS-4
Wicker Branch—*stream* NC-3
Wicker Branch—*stream* TN-4
Wicker Cem—*cemetery* AR-4
Wicker Cem—*cemetery* IA-7
Wicker Cem—*cemetery* (2) MS-4
Wicker Cem—*cemetery* (2) SC-3
Wicker Corner—*locale* VA-3
Wicker Ditch—*canal* IN-6
Wickerham Hill—*summit* OH-6
Wickerham Inn—*hist pl* OH-6
**Wickerham Manor**—*pop pl* PA-2
*Wicker Hill* RI-1
Wicker Lake Dam—*dam* MS-4
Wicker Lakes—*lake* FL-3
Wicker Mtn—*summit* MS-4
*Wicker Park* IL-6
Wicker Park—*park* IL-6
Wicker Park—*park* IN-6
Wicker Park Hist Dist—*hist pl* IL-6
Wicker Park Sch—*school* IL-6
Wicker Run—*stream* IN-6
Wicker Sch—*school* LA-4
*Wickers Creek* GA-3
Wickers Creek—*stream* NY-2
**Wickersham**—*pop pl* WA-9
Wickersham, David, House—*hist pl* AZ-5
Wickersham, Gideon, Farmstead—*hist pl* PA-2
Wickersham, Mount—*summit* AK-9
Wickersham Apartments—*hist pl* OR-9
Wickersham Basin—*basin* WA-9
Wickersham Bridge—*bridge* WA-9
Wickersham Cem—*cemetery* AR-4
Wickersham Creek—*stream* (3) AK-9
Wickersham Dome—*summit* AK-9
Wickersham Draw—*valley* WY-8
*Wickersham Elem Sch* PA-2
Wickersham Hill—*summit* PA-2
Wickersham House—*hist pl* (2) AK-9
*Wickersham Mountain* WA-9
Wickersham Ranch—*locale* CA-9
Wickersham Sch—*school* KS-7
Wickersham Sch—*school* PA-2
Wickersham Wall—*area* AK-9
Wickers Memorial Ch—*church* NJ-2
Wickers Pond—*lake* FL-3
Wicker Spring—*spring* CO-8
*Wickersville* AL-4
Wicker Tank—*reservoir* (2) TX-5
Wickerton—*locale* PA-2
Wickerts Lake—*lake* WI-6
*Wickerville* AL-4
Wickes—*locale* MO-7
**Wickes**—*pop pl* AR-4
**Wickes**—*pop pl* MT-8
Wickes, Oliver A., House—*hist pl* RI-1
Wickes Beach—*beach* MD-2
**Wickes Spur**—*pop pl* TX-5
Wickes Tunnel—*tunnel* MT-8
*Wicketequock Cove* CT-1
*Wicket Island* MA-1
*Wicket Pond* MA-1
Wickets Island—*island* MA-1
**Wickett**—*pop pl* TX-5
*Wickett Brook* MA-1
Wickett Brook—*stream* MA-1
Wickett Creek—*stream* AL-4
Wickett Pond—*lake* MA-1
Wickett South Oil Field—*oilfield* TX-5
Wickey Branch—*stream* TX-5
Wickey Canal—*canal* LA-4
Wickfield Round Barn—*hist pl* IA-7
**Wickford**—*pop pl* MD-2
**Wickford**—*pop pl* RI-1
Wickford Cove—*bay* RI-1
Wickford Harbor—*bay* RI-1
Wickford Hist Dist—*hist pl* RI-1
**Wickford Junction**—*pop pl* RI-1
Wickford Junction—*summit* RI-1
Wickham—*locale* WV-2
**Wickham**—*pop pl* WV-2
Wickham, Mount—*summit* MN-6
Wickham, O. P., House—*hist pl* IA-7
Wickham Canyon—*valley* CA-9
Wickham Cem—*cemetery* TN-4
*Wickham Creek* MT-8
Wickham Creek—*stream* AR-4
Wickham Creek—*stream* IL-6
Wickham Creek—*stream* MT-8
Wickham Creek—*stream* NY-2
Wickham Crossing—*locale* VA-3
Wickham Drain—*canal* MI-6
Wickham Hall Pratt Museum—*building* TN-4
Wickham Hollow—*valley* TN-4
**Wickham Knolls**—*pop pl* NY-2
Wickham Lake—*lake* NY-2
Wickham Marsh State Game Mngmt Area—*park* NY-2
Wickham Park—*park* CT-1
Wickham Rsvr—*reservoir* CT-1
*Wickham Spur* IA-7
Wickham Valley—*valley* WI-6
**Wickham Village**—*pop pl* NY-2
**Wickham Village**—*pop pl* PA-2
Wickham Waterhole—*lake* TX-5
**Wickhaven**—*pop pl* PA-2
**Wick Haven (sta.)**—*pop pl* PA-2
Wickheiser Spring—*spring* OR-9
Wick Hollow—*valley* MO-7
Wick House—*building* NJ-2
*Wickieup* AZ-5
Wickiser Slough—*stream* OR-9
Wickiser Spring—*spring* OR-9
Wickiup, The—*summit* UT-8
Wickiup Butte—*summit* ID-8
Wickiup Butte—*summit* (2) OR-9
*Wickiup Camp* OR-9
Wickiup Camp—*locale* OR-9
Wickiup Campground—*locale* CA-9
Wickiup Campground—*locale* OR-9
Wickiup Campground—*locale* WA-9
Wickiup Canyon—*valley* AZ-5
Wickiup Canyon—*valley* CA-9
Wickiup Canyon—*valley* CO-8
Wickiup Canyon—*valley* UT-8
*Wickiup Creek* CA-9
Wickiup Creek—*stream* AZ-5
Wickiup Creek—*stream* (8) ID-8
Wickiup Creek—*stream* (5) MT-8
Wickiup Creek—*stream* NV-8
Wickiup Creek—*stream* (8) OR-9
Wickiup Creek—*stream* WA-9
Wickiup Dam—*dam* OR-9
Wickiup Forest Camp—*locale* OR-9
Wickiup Gulch—*valley* OR-9
Wickiup Knoll—*summit* WY-8
Wickiup Lake—*lake* OR-9
Wickiup Lake Dam—*dam* OR-9
Wickiup Meadow—*flat* OR-9
Wickiup Mtn—*summit* MT-8
Wickiup Pass—*gap* UT-8
Wickiup Pit Tank—*reservoir* AZ-5
Wickiup Plain—*flat* OR-9
Wickiup Plain Trail—*trail* OR-9
Wickiup Ridge—*ridge* OR-9
Wickiup Ridge—*ridge* UT-8
Wickiup Rsvr—*reservoir* (2) OR-9
Wickiup Shelter—*locale* OR-9
Wickiup Spring—*spring* (6) OR-9
Wickiup Spring—*spring* WA-9
Wickiup Springs—*spring* OR-9
*Wickiup Tank* AZ-5
Wickiup Tank Number One—*reservoir* AZ-5
Wickiup Tank Number Two—*reservoir* AZ-5
Wickiup Trail—*trail* OR-9
Wickizer Pond—*swamp* TX-5
Wickland—*hist pl* (2) KY-4
**Wickland**—*pop pl* KY-4
Wickland Ch—*church* KY-4
**Wickland Terrace**—*pop pl* LA-4
Wickliff Cem—*cemetery* OH-6
Wickliffe—*locale* VA-3
**Wickliffe**—*pop pl* IN-6
**Wickliffe**—*pop pl* KY-4
**Wickliffe**—*pop pl* LA-4
**Wickliffe**—*pop pl* (2) OH-6
Wickliffe (CCD)—*cens area* KY-4
Wickliffe Cem—*cemetery* KY-4
*Wickliffe Creek* LA-4
Wickliffe Creek—*stream* LA-4
Wickliffe Creek—*stream* OK-5
Wickliffe Road Sch—*school* OH-6
Wickliffe Sch—*school* OH-6
Wickliffe Sch—*school* OK-5
Wickliffe Site 15 BA 4—*hist pl* KY-4
Wickline Canyon—*valley* CA-9
*Wicklittle Creek* OK-5
Wick Lower Ranch—*locale* WY-8
Wicklow Hall Plantation—*hist pl* SC-3
Wickman Millpond—*lake* NY-2
**Wickman Park**—*pop pl* NY-2
**Wick Mill**—*pop pl* AR-4
**Wickmore**—*pop pl* IL-6
*Wickomis Branch* DE-2
Wickopee Hill—*summit* VT-1
Wick Park—*park* OH-6
Wick Playground—*park* WI-6
Wick Point—*cape* MI-6
Wick Road Ch—*church* MI-6
**Wicks**—*pop pl* UT-8
Wicks Bldg—*hist pl* IN-6
Wicks Branch—*stream* KY-4
**Wicksburg**—*pop pl* AL-4
Wicksburg Ch—*church* AL-4
*Wicksburg High School* AL-4
Wicksburg Post Office (historical)—*building* AL-4
Wicksburg Sch—*school* AL-4
Wicks Cave—*cave* MO-7
Wicks Cem—*cemetery* KY-4
Wicks Cem—*cemetery* MS-4
Wicks Cem—*cemetery* TN-4
Wicks Chapel—*church* AL-4
Wicks Corner—*locale* CA-9
**Wicks Corners**—*pop pl* NY-2
Wicks Dam—*dam* PA-2
*Wickser Lake* WI-6
Wicks Gulch—*valley* NM-5
Wickshire Sch—*school* NY-2
Wicks Hollow—*valley* AL-4
Wicks Island—*island* MA-1
Wicks Knob—*summit* WV-2
Wicks Lake—*lake* CA-9
Wicks Lake—*lake* WA-9
Wickson Creek—*stream* TX-5
Wickson Draw—*valley* CO-8
Wickson Lake—*lake* NE-7
Wickson Lake—*lake* TX-5
Wicks Rsvr—*reservoir* OR-9
Wickstrom Coulee—*valley* MT-8
**Wicksville**—*pop pl* SD-7
Wicksville Community Sch—*school* SD-7
Wicksville 1 Dam—*dam* SD-7
Wicks Well—*locale* KY-4
Wickum Sch—*school* MT-8
Wickup Creek—*stream* OR-9
Wickup Hill County Park—*park* IA-7
**Wickville**—*pop pl* IN-6
**Wickward (historical)**—*pop pl* MS-4
Wickware—*locale* MI-6
**Wickware**—*pop pl* MS-4
**Wickware**—*pop pl* WI-6
Wickware Pond—*reservoir* MS-4
Wickwas Lake—*lake* NH-1
*Wickwas Pond* NH-1
Wickwire Brook—*stream* NY-2
Wickwire Corners—*locale* NY-2
Wickwire Hill—*summit* NY-2
Wickwire Run—*stream* WV-2
**Wickwood (subdivision)**—*pop pl* DE-2
*Wicky Creek* WA-9
Wicky Creek—*stream* WA-9
Wicky Creek Shelter—*locale* WA-9
**Wico**—*pop pl* MI-6
**Wicomico**—*pop pl* MD-2
**Wicomico**—*pop pl* VA-3
Wicomico Beach—*beach* MD-2
**Wicomico Beach**—*pop pl* MD-2
Wicomico Ch—*church* VA-3
**Wicomico Church**—*pop pl* VA-3
**Wicomico (County)**—*pop pl* MD-2
Wicomico Creek—*stream* MD-2
Wicomico (Magisterial District)—*fmr MCD* VA-3
Wicomico Memorial Park—*cemetery* MD-2
Wicomico Orphanage—*locale* MD-2
Wicomico River—*stream* (2) MD-2
**Wiconisco**—*pop pl* PA-2
Wiconisco (census name Wiconisco Center)—*CDP* PA-2
Wiconisco Center (census name for Wiconisco)—*other* PA-2
Wiconisco Creek—*stream* PA-2
**Wiconisco (Township of)**—*pop pl* PA-2
Wicopee—*locale* OR-9
Wicopee—*other* NY-2
Wicopesset Island—*island* NY-2
Wicopesset Passage—*channel* NY-2
*Wicota* SD-7
WICR-FM (Indianapolis)—*tower* IN-6
WICU-TV (Erie)—*tower* PA-2
*Wicwas Lake* NH-1
Wida—*locale* VA-3
Widcat Creek—*stream* OR-9
Widco Mine—*mine* CA-9
WIDD-AM (Elizabethton)—*tower* TN-4
Widden Brook—*stream* ME-1
WIDD-FM (Elizabethton)—*tower* TN-4
Widdlefield Run—*stream* PA-2
Widdons Cem—*cemetery* GA-3
Widdop Cem—*cemetery* WY-8
Widdop Mtn—*summit* UT-8
Widdowfield—*locale* WY-8
Widdows Island—*island* CA-9
Wideawake—*locale* CO-8
Wide Awake Grocery Bldg—*hist pl* SD-7
Wide-awake Gulch—*valley* CO-8
Wide Awake Mine—*mine* CA-9
Wideawake Mine—*mine* CA-9
Wide Awake Ranch—*locale* CA-9
Wide Awake Sch—*school* MN-6
Wide Awake Sch—*school* WI-6
Wide Awake School (historical)—*locale* MO-7
Wide Bay—*bay* (2) AK-9
Wide Bay—*swamp* NC-3
Wide Beach—*beach* NY-2
Wide Branch—*stream* AL-4
Wide Branch—*stream* GA-3
*Wide Butte* UT-8
Wide Butte—*summit* AZ-5
Wide Canyon—*valley* NV-8
Wide Canyon—*valley* (9) UT-8
Wide Canyon Spring—*spring* UT-8
*Wide Creek* WI-6
Widecreek—*locale* KY-4
Wide Crossing Waterhole—*lake* TX-5
Wide Cut Highway—*channel* MI-6
Wide Cypress Branch—*gut* FL-3
Wide Cypress Swamp—*swamp* FL-3
Wide Divide Ridge—*ridge* WY-8
Wide Draft—*valley* VA-3
Wide Draft Hollow—*valley* VA-3
**Widefield**—*pop pl* CO-8
Widefield HS—*school* CO-8
Wide Ford—*crossing* TN-4
Wide Ford—*locale* MO-7
Wide Ford Bridge—*bridge* TN-4
Wideford Hollow Cove—*bay* MO-7
Wide Gap—*gap* GA-3
Widegeon Point—*cape* MA-1
Widehall—*hist pl* MD-2
*Wide Hollow* UT-8
*Wide Hollow* VA-3
Wide Hollow—*valley* AZ-5
Wide Hollow—*valley* ID-8
Wide Hollow—*valley* (16) UT-8
Wide Hollow—*valley* (3) VA-3
Wide Hollow—*valley* WA-9
Wide Hollow Creek—*stream* (2) WA-9
Wide Hollow Dam—*dam* UT-8
Wide Hollow Rsvr—*reservoir* (2) UT-8
Wide Hollow Sch—*school* PA-2
Wide Hollow Sch—*school* WA-9
Wide Hollow Spring—*spring* UT-8
Wide Horizon Sanatorium—*other* CO-8
Wide Lick—*stream* KY-4
Widel Lake—*lake* MO-7
**Wideman**—*pop pl* AR-4
Wideman Creek—*stream* AR-4
Wideman Mtn—*summit* AR-4
Wide Mesa—*summit* AZ-5
*Widemouth* WV-2
Wide Mouth Branch—*stream* NC-3
Wide Mouth Canyon—*valley* AZ-5
Widemouth Canyon—*valley* UT-8
Widemouth Creek—*stream* VA-3
Widemouth Creek—*stream* WV-2
*Widemouth Gulch* MT-8
Widemouth Gulch—*valley* MT-8
*Widemouth Hollow* VA-3
**Widemouth (Piedmont)**—*pop pl* WV-2
Widemouth Run—*stream* WV-2
Wide Mouth Shoal Sluice—*hist pl* NC-3
Wide Mouth Tank—*reservoir* AZ-5
Wide Mouth Wash—*valley* UT-8
**Widen**—*pop pl* WV-2
Wide Narrows—*channel* MN-6
**Widener**—*pop pl* AR-4
Widener Cave—*cave* AL-4
Widener Cem—*cemetery* KS-7
Widener College—*uninc pl* PA-2
Widener Cove—*valley* AL-4
Widener Home—*building* PA-2
Widener Sch—*school* PA-2
Widener Spring—*spring* VA-3
Widener Valley—*basin* VA-3
Widen Well—*locale* NM-5
Wide Pass—*channel* MP-9
*Wide Passage* MP-9
Wide Passage—*island* MP-9
*Wide Range* KS-7
Widerange (historical)—*locale* KS-7
Wide Reeds Ruins—*locale* AZ-5
Wide Ridge—*ridge* UT-8
*Wide Ruin* AZ-5
**Wide Ruins**—*pop pl* AZ-5
Wide Ruin Valley—*valley* AZ-5
*Wide Ruin Wash* AZ-5
Wide Ruin Wash—*stream* AZ-5
Wide Sky Canyon—*valley* WA-9
Wide Slough—*gut* GA-3
Wide Springs—*spring* OK-5
Wide Springs Branch—*stream* OK-5
Wide Valley—*valley* UT-8
Wideview Trail—*trail* PA-2
Widewake—*locale* VA-3
Widewater—*channel* MD-2
Widewater—*locale* VA-3
Wide Water—*other* VA-3
**Widewater Beach**—*pop pl* VA-3
Widewater Lake—*lake* MT-8
Wide Waters—*lake* MI-6
Wide Waters, The—*channel* NY-2
Widewaters, The—*lake* MI-6
**Widewater (Wide Water)**—*pop pl* VA-3
Wide West Gulch—*valley* ID-8
Wide West Mine—*mine* CO-8
Wide West Mine—*mine* NV-8
Wide West Peak—*summit* NV-8
Widforss Point—*cliff* AZ-5
**Widgen Woods (subdivision)**—*pop pl* NC-3
Widgeon—*locale* MD-2
Widgeon Bay—*bay* FL-3
Widgeon Bay—*bay* NJ-2
Widgeon Bay—*bay* UT-8
Widgeon Cove—*bay* ME-1
Widgeon Creek—*stream* AK-9
Widgeon Creek—*stream* MI-6
Widgeon Creek—*stream* VA-3
Widgeon Gun Club—*other* CA-9
*Widgeon Hole Pond* MA-1
*Widgeon Lake* WI-6
Widgeon Lake—*lake* AK-9
Widgeon Lake—*lake* OR-9
Widgeon Lake—*lake* (2) WA-9
Widgeon Lake—*reservoir* UT-8
Widgeon Marsh—*swamp* UT-8
Widgeon Pond—*lake* LA-4
Widgeon Pond—*lake* MA-1
Widgeon Pond—*lake* MT-8
Widgeon Pond—*reservoir* OH-6
Widgeon Ponds—*lake* NJ-2
Widgeon Spring—*spring* UT-8
Widgeon Wharf—*locale* MD-2
Widger Hill—*summit* NY-2
Widger Hole—*lake* MA-1
Widgit Lake—*lake* WY-8
Widick Cem—*cemetery* (2) TN-4
Widicus Cem—*cemetery* IL-6
Widincamp Cem—*cemetery* GA-3
Wid Legg Cem—*cemetery* AL-4
Widman Dam—*dam* OR-9
Widman Rsvr—*reservoir* OR-9
Widmark Airp—*airport* MO-7
Widmer Sch—*school* WI-6
Widmer Strip—*airport* ND-7
Widmeyer Creek—*stream* NY-2
Widner Creek—*stream* AL-4
Widner Creek—*stream* MI-6
Widners Cem—*cemetery* AL-4
**Widner (Township of)**—*pop pl* IN-6
Widney HS—*school* CA-9
**Widnoon**—*pop pl* PA-2
Widnoon Station—*locale* PA-2
WIDO-FM (Dunn)—*tower* NC-3
*Widow Ansons Place* AL-4
Widow Bar—*bar* ID-8
*Widow Bay* WI-6
*Widow Bayou* MS-4
Widow Bayou—*stream* (2) MS-4
Widow Branch—*stream* KY-4
Widow Branch—*stream* VA-3
Widow B Spring—*spring* OR-9
*Widow Cave* TN-4
Widow Coulee—*valley* (3) MT-8
*Widow Creek* AL-4
*Widow Creek* IN-6
Widow Creek—*stream* AR-4
Widow Creek—*stream* CA-9
Widow Creek—*stream* IN-6
Widow Creek—*stream* KS-7
Widow Creek—*stream* MO-7
Widow Creek—*stream* MT-8
Widow Creek—*stream* (2) OR-9
Widow Creek—*stream* TN-4
Widow Flats—*flat* CA-9
*Widow Green Creek* WI-6
Widow Harding Pond—*lake* MA-1
Widow Harris Brook—*stream* NH-1
Widow Hawkins Branch—*stream* MD-2
Widow Hill—*summit* VT-1
Widow Hollow—*valley* TN-4
Widow Island—*island* ME-1
Widow Jones Spring—*spring* AL-4
Widow Lake—*lake* CA-9
Widow Lake—*lake* GA-3
Widow Lake—*lake* LA-4
Widow Lake—*lake* MN-6
Widow Lake—*lake* NM-5
Widow Lake—*lake* SC-3
Widow Maker Rapids—*rapids* TN-4
Widow Maloby's Tavern—*hist pl* PA-2
Widow McDowell House—*hist pl* KY-4
Widow Mine—*mine* CA-9
Widow Mine—*mine* NV-8
Widow Moore Creek—*stream* OK-5
Widow Morin Claim—*civil* MS-4
Widow Mtn—*summit* CA-9
Widow Mtn—*summit* ID-8
Widow Mtn—*summit* NC-3
Widow North Ladner Claim—*civil* MS-4
Widow Piper's Tavern—*hist pl* PA-2
*Widow's* AL-4
Widows Bar—*bar* AL-4
Widows Branch—*stream* KY-4
Widows Cove, The—*cove* MA-1
*Widows Creek* TN-4
Widows Creek—*stream* (2) AL-4
Widows Creek—*stream* MS-4
Widows Creek—*stream* NY-2
Widows Creek—*stream* NC-3
Widows Creek—*stream* OR-9

Widows Creek Bridge—*bridge* MS-4
Widow's Creek Bridge—*hist pl* MS-4
Widows Creek Burn—*area* OR-9
Widows Creek Spring—*spring* AL-4
**Widows Creek Station**—*pop pl* AL-4
Widows Creek Steam Plant—*other* AL-4
Widows' Home—*hist pl* CT-1
*Widows Island* ME-1
Widows Ledge—*bar* ME-1
Widows Mite (historical)—*civil* DC-2
Widows Mite (historical)—*locale* DC-2
Widows Point—*cape* MA-1
Widow Spring—*spring* CA-9
Widow Spring—*spring* CO-8
Widow Spring—*spring* (2) OR-9
Widow Spring—*spring* TX-5
*Widows Tears* CA-9
Widow Tapp Spring Drain—*stream* VA-3
**Widow Town**—*pop pl* TN-4
Widow Valley—*stream* CA-9
Widow Valley—*valley* CA-9
Widow Valley Creek—*stream* CA-9
Widow Valley Mountains—*range* CA-9
**Widowville**—*pop pl* OH-6
Widow Well—*well* NM-5
Widow White Creek—*stream* CA-9
*Widow Whites Peak* MA-1
Widow Whites Peak—*summit* MA-1
Widow Wilson Field—*area* CA-9
Widow Woman Canyon—*valley* CO-8
*Widow Wood Ponds* MA-1
Widrick, George, House—*hist pl* MD-2
Wids Tank—*reservoir* AZ-5
Widtsoe—*locale* UT-8
Widtsoe Cem—*cemetery* UT-8
Widtsoe Junction—*locale* UT-8
WIDU-AM (Fayetteville)—*tower* NC-3
Wieber Drain—*canal* MI-6
Wieberg Creek—*stream* WA-9
Wieber Wash—*stream* NV-8
**Wiechert Estates Subdivision**—*pop pl* UT-8
Wiechman Well—*well* MT-8
Wied—*locale* TX-5
Wiedeman Hollow—*valley* IL-6
Wiedemann, Charles, House—*hist pl* KY-4
Wiedemann Hill—*summit* CA-9
Wiedenbeck-Dobelin Warehouse—*hist pl* WI-6
**Wiederkehr Village**—*pop pl* AR-4
Wiederkehr Wine Cellar—*hist pl* AR-4
Wiederrick Ranch—*locale* MT-8
Wiedersphan Ranch—*locale* CO-8
Wiedeville—*locale* TX-5
Wiedman Memorial Park—*park* WI-6
Wiedower Cem—*cemetery* AR-4
Wiedower Mtn—*summit* AR-4
*Wief* FM-9
Wiegand Cem—*cemetery* NE-7
Wiegand Lake—*lake* OH-6
Wiegand Park—*park* MI-6
Wiegands Bay—*bay* WI-6
Wiegands Lake—*lake* MI-6
Wiegel Mine—*mine* CA-9
*Wiegletown* PA-2
**Wiegletown**—*pop pl* PA-2
*Wiehachen* NJ-2
**Wiehe**—*pop pl* MS-4
Wiehl Mtn—*summit* AK-9
Wieker State Wildlife Mngmt
Area—*park* MN-6
Wiek Ranch—*locale* AZ-5
**Wieland**—*pop pl* TX-5
Wieland Branch—*stream* MO-7
Wieland Brewery Bldg—*hist pl* NV-8
Wieland Flat—*flat* NV-8
Wieland Gulch—*valley* CO-8
Wieland North Oil Field—*oilfield* KS-7
Wieland Ranch—*locale* NM-5
Wieland West Oil Field—*oilfield* KS-7
Wieler Dam—*dam* ND-7
*Wiel Lake* CA-9
Wielock Pond—*reservoir* MA-1
Wielock Pond Dam—*dam* MA-1
*Wiemer Creek* MO-7
Wiemer Creek—*stream* MO-7
Wiemer Dam—*dam* WI-6
Wiemer Hollow—*valley* PA-2
**Wien**—*pop pl* MO-7
**Wien**—*pop pl* WI-6
Wieneke Branch—*stream* MO-7
Wiener Lake—*lake* AK-9
Wiener Mesa—*summit* NM-5
Wienger Hollow—*valley* KY-4
Wienges Lake—*lake* SC-3
Wien Lake—*lake* AK-9
Wien Mtn—*summit* AK-9
Wientjes Brothers Number 1 Dam—*dam* SD-7
Wientjes Brothers Number 2 Dam—*dam* SD-7
Wier, James, House,—*hist pl* TN-4
Wier Cem—*cemetery* AR-4
Wier Cem—*cemetery* TN-4
Wier Chapel—*church* MS-4
*Wier Creek* MS-4
**Wiergate**—*pop pl* TX-5
Wier Gut—*gut* DE-2
Wierlong Run—*stream* WV-2
Wier Neck Cem—*cemetery* VA-3
Wier Number Five—*dam* AZ-5
Wier Number One—*dam* AZ-5
Wier Number Six—*dam* AZ-5
Wier Number Three—*dam* AZ-5
Wier Number Two—*dam* AZ-5
Wiers Chapel Cem—*cemetery* MS-4
*Wiers Chapel Methodist Church* MS-4
Wiers Chapel Sch (historical)—*school* MS-4
Wier Sch (historical)—*school* MS-4
Wierwood (RR name for
Wierwood)—*other* VA-3
Wiese Cem—*cemetery* MO-7
Wiese Field—*park* SD-7
Wieseman Windmill—*locale* TX-5
**Wieser**—*pop pl* WA-9
Wieser Branch—*stream* KY-4
Wiese Slough—*reservoir* IA-7
Wiese Slough State Game Mngmt
Area—*park* IA-7
Wiese Upper Ditch—*canal* CO-8
Wiesman Spring—*spring* CA-9
Wies Mtn—*summit* TN-4
Wiesner Cem—*cemetery* (2) WI-6
Wiess Bluff—*cliff* TX-5
Wiess Canal—*canal* TX-5
Wiess Cem—*cemetery* MO-7
Wiesse Creek—*stream* CO-8
Wiessengarber Sch (historical)—*school* MO-7
Wiessner, Mount—*summit* ID-8
*Wiessner's Peak* ID-8
Wiess Park—*park* TX-5
**Wiest**—*pop pl* CA-9
Wiest Creek—*stream* WA-9
**Wiester**—*pop pl* (2) PA-2
Wiest Lake—*lake* CA-9
**Wieston**—*pop pl* IA-7
Wietbrock Airp—*airport* IN-6
Wieting Theater—*hist pl* IA-7
Wife, The—*summit* OR-9
WIFE-AM (Indianapolis)—*tower* IN-6
Wife Canyon—*valley* UT-8
Wife Creek—*stream* UT-8
Wife Lead—*channel* NY-2
WIFF-AM (Auburn)—*tower* IN-6
WIFF-FM (Auburn)—*tower* IN-6
Wiffin Cem—*cemetery* NY-2
Wiffs Pasture—*flat* UT-8
WIFI-FM (Philadelphia)—*tower* (2) PA-2
WIFM-AM (Elkin)—*tower* NC-3
WIFM-FM (Elkin)—*tower* NC-3
WIFN-FM (Franklin)—*tower* IN-6
Wigal Cem—*cemetery* IN-6
Wigal Cem—*cemetery* WV-2
Wigand Creek—*stream* AK-9
Wigand Park—*flat* MT-8
Wigand Ranch—*locale* MT-8
WIGC-FM (Troy)—*tower* (2) AL-4
Wig Creek—*stream* MT-8
Wigdale Lake—*lake* SD-7
Wigent Cem—*cemetery* IN-6
Wigfield Trail—*trail* PA-2
Wiggam Branch—*stream* GA-3
Wiggam Branch Lake—*lake* GA-3
WIGG-AM (Wiggins)—*tower* MS-4
**Wiggans**—*pop pl* PA-2
Wiggan Well—*well* NM-5
Wiggens Arm—*bay* LA-4
Wiggens Cem—*cemetery* (2) GA-3
Wiggers Hollow—*valley* MO-7
Wiggin, Cornet Thomas, House—*hist pl* NH-1
Wiggin Brook—*stream* CT-1
Wiggin Cem—*cemetery* NH-1
Wiggin Cem—*cemetery* NC-3
Wiggington Cem—*cemetery* MS-4
Wiggington Creek—*stream* KY-4
Wiggington Knob—*summit* VA-3
Wiggington Progressive—*school* FL-3
Wiggin Mtn—*summit* ME-1
*Wiggin Pond* MA-1
*Wiggins* PA-2
Wiggins—*locale* TX-5
Wiggins—*locale* WV-2
**Wiggins**—*pop pl* AL-4
**Wiggins**—*pop pl* CO-8
**Wiggins**—*pop pl* FL-3
**Wiggins**—*pop pl* GA-3
**Wiggins**—*pop pl* (2) MS-4
**Wiggins**—*pop pl* SC-3
**Wiggins**—*pop pl* TX-5
Wiggins Baptist Ch—*church* MS-4
Wiggins Bayou—*stream* LA-4
Wiggins Bluff—*cliff* TX-5
Wiggins Branch—*stream* (2) AL-4
Wiggins Branch—*stream* FL-3
Wiggins Branch—*stream* NC-3
Wiggins Branch—*stream* TN-4
Wiggins Branch—*stream* VA-3
Wiggins Bridge—*bridge* FL-3
Wiggins Bridge—*bridge* SC-3
Wiggins Brook—*stream* (3) ME-1
Wiggins Cabin—*hist pl* AR-4
Wiggins Cem—*cemetery* (2) AL-4
Wiggins Cem—*cemetery* MS-4
Wiggins Cem—*cemetery* (2) NC-3
Wiggins Cem—*cemetery* (2) TN-4
Wiggins Cem—*cemetery* (3) TX-5
Wiggins Cem—*cemetery* VT-1
Wiggins Ch—*church* MS-4
Wiggin Sch—*school* CA-9
Wiggin Sch—*school* IL-6
Wiggin Sch—*school* SD-7
Wiggins City Hall—*building* MS-4
*Wiggins Cove* AL-4
Wiggins Cove—*valley* NC-3
Wiggins Creek—*stream* (3) AL-4
Wiggins Creek—*stream* AR-4
Wiggins Creek—*stream* GA-3
Wiggins Creek—*stream* KS-7
Wiggins Creek—*stream* NC-3
Wiggins Creek—*stream* TN-4
Wiggins Creek—*stream* TX-5
Wiggins Crossing—*locale* AZ-5
Wiggins Crossroads—*locale* NC-3
**Wiggins Crossroads**—*pop pl* NC-3
Wiggins Dam—*dam* TN-4
*Wiggins Elementary School* MS-4
Wiggins Fork—*stream* WY-8
*Wiggins Fork River* WY-8
Wiggins Fork Trail—*trail* WY-8
Wiggins-Hadley House—*building* NC-3
Wiggins Head—*cape* WA-9
Wiggins Hill—*summit* CA-9
Wiggins Hill—*summit* MO-7
Wiggins Hill—*summit* TN-4
Wiggins Hollow—*valley* AL-4
Wiggins Hollow Cave Number One—*cave* AL-4
Wiggins Hollow Cave Number Two—*cave* AL-4
Wiggins Junction (railroad
station)—*locale* FL-3
Wiggins Lake—*lake* AL-4
Wiggins Lake—*lake* AR-4
Wiggins Lake—*lake* GA-3
Wiggins Lake—*lake* MI-6
Wiggins Lake—*lake* WI-6
Wiggins Lake—*reservoir* NC-3
Wiggins Lake—*reservoir* TN-4
Wiggins Lake Dam—*dam* AL-4
Wiggins Lake Dam—*dam* NC-3
Wiggins Methodist Ch—*church* MS-4
Wiggins Mill—*locale* DE-2
**Wiggins Mill**—*pop pl* NC-3
Wiggins Mill Branch—*stream* NC-3
Wiggins Mill Park—*park* DE-2
Wiggins Mill Pond—*reservoir* DE-2
Wiggins Millpond—*reservoir* NC-3
Wiggins Mill Pond Dam—*dam* DE-2
Wiggins Millpond Dam—*dam* NC-3
Wiggins Mill Rsvr—*reservoir* NC-3
Wiggins Mine—*mine* MT-8
*Wiggins Moundville Dam* AL-4
*Wiggins Mountain* ME-1
Wiggins Oil Field—*oilfield* KS-7
Wiggins Park—*park* TX-5
Wiggins Pass—*channel* FL-3
Wiggins Peak—*summit* WY-8
*Wiggins Plantation* SC-3
Wiggins Point—*cape* MI-6
Wiggins Point—*cape* NC-3
Wiggins Point Shoal—*bar* MI-6
*Wiggins Pond* MA-1
Wiggins Post Office—*building* MS-4
Wiggins Prairie—*swamp* FL-3
Wiggins Ralley Ditch No 1—*canal* NM-5
Wiggins Ranch—*locale* AZ-5
Wiggins Ranch—*locale* NM-5
Wiggins Ridge—*ridge* NC-3
Wiggins Rock—*bar* ME-1
Wiggins-Rolph House—*hist pl* NY-2
Wiggins Run—*stream* WV-2
Wiggins Sch—*school* CA-9
Wiggins Sch—*school* VT-1
Wiggins Sch (abandoned)—*school* MO-7
Wiggins Sch (historical)—*school* (2) AL-4
Wiggins Spring Shelter—*locale* VA-3
**Wiggins Subdivision**—*pop pl* UT-8
Wiggins Swamp—*swamp* SC-3
Wiggins Tank—*reservoir* AZ-5
Wiggins Top—*summit* NC-3
Wigginsville—*locale* TX-5
**Wigginsville**—*pop pl* AL-4
Wigginsville—*uninc pl* MA-1
Wigginsville Ch—*church* FL-3
Wiggins-Watson Cem—*cemetery* NC-3
Wiggle Brook—*stream* ME-1
Wiggle Creek—*stream* AK-9
Wiggle Creek—*stream* MI-6
Wiggle Creek—*stream* NE-7
Wiggle Creek Sch—*school* NE-7
Wiggler Bench—*bench* UT-8
Wiggler Lake—*lake* ID-8
Wiggle Rock Pit—*cave* AL-4
Wiggler Spring—*spring* OR-9
Wiggler Wash—*valley* UT-8
Wigglesworth Bldg—*hist pl* MA-1
Wigglesworth Spring—*spring* OR-9
Wiggletail Creek—*stream* MT-8
Wiggleton Hollow—*valley* ID-8
Wiggleton Hollow—*valley* WY-8
Wiggleton Tank—*reservoir* TX-5
Wiggly Creek—*stream* AK-9
**Wiggonsville**—*pop pl* OH-6
*Wiggs Branch* TN-4
Wiggs Ford—*locale* MO-7
Wigg Trail—*trail* NH-1
Wigham Creek—*stream* CA-9
*Wighcocomoco* DE-2
Wig Hill—*summit* CT-1
Wight, Allyn, House—*hist pl* NJ-2
Wight, Oliver, House—*hist pl* MA-1
Wight Brook—*stream* ME-1
Wight Cem—*cemetery* IA-7
Wight Cem—*cemetery* MO-7
Wight Corner—*island* ME-1
Wight Heath—*swamp* ME-1
Wightman—*locale* IA-7
Wightman—*locale* VA-3
**Wightman**—*pop pl* MO-7
Wightman, Dr. W. C., House—*hist pl* NE-7
Wightman Cem—*cemetery* NY-2
Wightman Ch—*church* NC-3
Wightman Drain—*canal* MI-6
Wightman Fork—*stream* CO-8
Wightman Hollow—*valley* NY-2
Wightman Lake—*lake* IL-6
Wightman Sch—*hist pl* PA-2
Wightman Sch—*school* PA-2
Wightmans Corner—*locale* RI-1
**Wightmans Grove**—*pop pl* OH-6
Wightman Well—*well* NV-8
Wight Playground—*locale* MA-1
Wight Point—*cape* MD-2
Wight Pond—*lake* ME-1
Wight Pond—*lake* NH-1
Wight Ranch—*locale* WY-8
Wight Sch—*school* IL-6
*Wights Fort Cemetery* UT-8
Wights Pond—*lake* MA-1
Wightwood Sch—*school* FL-3
W I Gibson Coll (historical)—*school* MS-4
Wigington Cem—*cemetery* KY-4
**Wiginton**—*pop pl* AL-4
Wig Lake—*lake* GA-3
Wigle Creek—*stream* NE-7
Wigleeva—*cliff* AZ-5
Wigle Memorial Playground—*park* MI-6
Wiglesworth Spring—*spring* OR-9
Wig Mtn—*summit* UT-8
Wignal Flat—*flat* UT-8
Wignal Spring—*spring* UT-8
Wigner Run—*stream* WV-2
Wigrich—*locale* OR-9
Wigrich Airfield—*airport* OR-9
Wigrich Landing—*locale* OR-9
Wigrich Spur—*locale* OR-9
Wigton—*other* PA-2
Wigtop Butte—*summit* OR-9
**Wigul**—*pop pl* WV-2
Wigwam—*hist pl* VA-3
Wigwam—*locale* CO-8
**Wigwam**—*pop pl* PA-2
Wigwam Bay—*bay* MI-6
Wigwam Bay—*bay* MN-6
**Wig Wam Bay**—*pop pl* MN-6
**Wigwam Beach**—*pop pl* MA-1
Wigwam Brook—*stream* (2) CT-1
Wigwam Brook—*stream* (2) MA-1
Wigwam Campground—*locale* CO-8
Wigwam Club—*locale* CO-8
Wigwam Country Club—*other* AZ-5
Wigwam Creek—*stream* AK-9
Wigwam Creek—*stream* CO-8
Wigwam Creek—*stream* FL-3
Wigwam Creek—*stream* ID-8
Wigwam Creek—*stream* (2) MT-8
Wigwam Creek—*stream* NJ-2
Wigwam Creek—*stream* NY-2
Wigwam Creek—*stream* SD-7
Wigwam Creek—*stream* VA-3
Wigwam Dam—*dam* UT-8
Wigwam Fish Rearing Station—*locale* WY-8
*Wigwam Hill* MA-1
Wigwam Hill—*summit* (3) MA-1
Wigwam Hill—*summit* PA-2
Wigwam Hollow—*valley* IL-6
Wigwam Hollow—*valley* MO-7
Wigwam Island—*island* MN-6
*Wigwam Lake* UT-8
Wigwam Lake—*lake* (2) MN-6
Wigwam Lake—*lake* UT-8
Wigwam Lake—*reservoir* PA-2
Wigwam Lake Dam—*dam* PA-2
**Wigwam Lake Estates**—*pop pl* PA-2
*Wigwam Mtn* VA-3
Wigwam Mtn—*summit* VA-3
Wigwam Park—*flat* CO-8
*Wigwam Peak* MT-8
Wigwam Picnic Area—*locale* MI-6
Wigwam Point—*cape* MA-1
Wigwam Point—*cape* NY-2
Wigwam Pond—*lake* (3) MA-1
Wigwam Ponds—*lake* MA-1
*Wigwam Rapids* ME-1
Wigwam Riffles—*rapids* ME-1
Wigwam River—*stream* MT-8
Wigwam Rock—*island* CT-1
Wigwam Rsvr—*reservoir* CT-1
Wigwam Rsvr—*reservoir* (2) OR-9
Wigwam Rsvr—*reservoir* UT-8
Wigwam Run—*stream* (2) PA-2
Wigwams, The—*summit* ID-8
Wigwams, The—*summit* WY-8
Wigwam Sch—*school* CO-8
Wigwam Slough—*gut* WI-6
Wigwam Spring—*spring* AZ-5
Wigwam Spring—*spring* OR-9
Wigwam Spring—*spring* UT-8
Wigwam Valley—*valley* MA-1
Wigwam Village No. 2—*hist pl* KY-4
Wigwam Villa Mobile Home Park—*locale* AZ-5
**Wihiteoak**—*pop pl* WV-2
Wiichen Men's Meetinghouse—*hist pl* FM-9
*Wiicukuno* FM-9
Wiig Spring—*spring* MT-8
WIIQ-TV (Demopolis)—*tower* AL-4
*Wiisas* FM-9
*Wiises* FM-9
*Wiisopw* FM-9
*Wiiton* FM-9
*Wiitonomo* FM-9
WIIZ-AM (Jacksonville)—*tower* NC-3
Wijiji Ruins—*locale* NM-5
*Wijndrufwe Udden* DE-2
*W. I. Junction* IL-6
Wikahlap—*island* FM-9
Wike Branch—*stream* GA-3
Wike Gap—*gap* GA-3
Wike Knob—*summit* GA-3
**Wikel**—*pop pl* WV-2
Wikel Ditch—*canal* IN-6
*Wikes County* NC-3
Wikieup—*locale* AZ-5
Wikieup Post Office—*building* AZ-5
Wikieup Spring—*spring* UT-8
Wikieup Tank—*reservoir* AZ-5
Wiki Peak—*summit* AK-9
W I Kitchens Lake Dam—*dam* MS-4
*Wikiup Butte* OR-9
*Wikiup Creek* ID-8
Wikle Branch—*stream* NC-3
Wikle Drug Company—*hist pl* AL-4
Wikoff, Bayou—*stream* LA-4
Wikoff Ditch—*canal* IN-6
Wikoff Hill—*summit* AL-4
Wikoff Run—*stream* OH-6
WIKQ-FM (Greeneville)—*tower* TN-4
WIKS-FM (Greenfield)—*tower* IN-6
Wik Spring—*spring* CA-9
WIKU-FM (Pikeville)—*tower* TN-4
WIKY-FM (Evansville)—*tower* IN-6
WIKZ-FM (Chambersburg)—*tower* PA-2
*Wil* PA-2
**Wila**—*pop pl* PA-2
Wiladel—*locale* CO-8
*Wilaers Creek* IN-6
*Wilam Branch* AL-4
**Wila (Milford)**—*pop pl* PA-2
WIL-AM (St Louis)—*tower* MO-7
*Wilapiro Lake* WI-6
**Wilark**—*pop pl* OR-9
Wilawana—*locale* PA-2
**Wilbanks**—*pop pl* NC-3
Wilbanks Cabin—*locale* AZ-5
Wilbanks Cem—*cemetery* IL-6
Wilbanks Cem—*cemetery* LA-4
Wilbanks Lake Dam—*dam* MS-4
Wilbanks Lookout Tower—*locale* GA-3
Wilbanks Mesa—*summit* CO-8
Wilbanks Pond—*reservoir* GA-3
Wilbanks Well—*well* AZ-5
Wilbar—*locale* (2) NC-3
Wilbar, Lake—*lake* FL-3
**Wilbarger (County)**—*pop pl* TX-5
Wilbarger Creek—*stream* (2) TX-5
Wilbarger Memorial Park—*cemetery* TX-5
Wilbargers Bend—*bend* TX-5
*Wilbargers Creek* TX-5
Wilbar Mtn—*summit* TX-5
Wilbe Fire Tower—*locale* MS-4
*Wilber* KS-7
**Wilber**—*pop pl* MI-6
**Wilber**—*pop pl* NE-7
Wilber, J. B., House—*hist pl* OH-6
Wilber Allen Memorial State Wildlife
Area—*park* MO-7
Wilber Brook—*stream* (2) ME-1
*Wilber-by-the-Sea* FL-3
Wilber Cem—*cemetery* MI-6
Wilber Ch—*church* MI-6
Wilber Creek—*stream* AK-9
*Wilberforce* KS-7
**Wilberforce**—*pop pl* OH-6
Wilberforce Univ—*school* OH-6
Wilberg Flat—*flat* UT-8
Wilberg Memorial—*park* UT-8
Wilberg Mine—*mine* UT-8
Wilberg Wash—*valley* UT-8
Wilber Lake—*lake* NY-2
Wilbern—*locale* IL-6
Wilberns Glen—*valley* TX-5
Wilber Point—*cape* ME-1
Wilbers Creek—*stream* AL-4
Wilber Stephens Pond Dam—*dam* MS-4
**Wilbert**—*pop pl* MN-6
Wilbert Canal—*canal* (2) LA-4
Wilberton Sch—*school* IL-6
**Wilberton (Township of)**—*pop pl* IL-6
*Wilbertown* PA-2
**Wilber (Township of)**—*pop pl* MI-6
Wilberts Corner—*locale* VA-3
**Wilbeth**—*pop pl* AR-4
Wilbeth Arlington Park—*park* OH-6
**Wilbon**—*pop pl* NC-3
*Wilborn* KY-4
Wilborn—*locale* MT-8
Wilborn Brake—*swamp* AR-4
Wilborn Branch—*stream* AL-4
Wilborn Branch—*stream* TN-4
Wilborn Cem—*cemetery* AL-4
*Wilborn Creek* MS-4
Wilborn Creek—*stream* IL-6
Wilborn Creek—*stream* MS-4
Wilborn Lake—*lake* AL-4
Wilborn Lake—*reservoir* AL-4
Wilborn Lake Dam—*dam* AL-4
Wilborn-Steinberg Site—*hist pl* MO-7
Wilbourn Cem—*cemetery* AR-4
Wilbourn Cem—*cemetery* MS-4
*Wilbourne Island* MO-7
Wilbourne Lake—*reservoir* AL-4
**Wilbourns**—*pop pl* NC-3
*Wilbourns Island* MO-7
**Wilbourns Store**—*pop pl* NC-3
Wilbour Woods—*area* RI-1
**Wilbraham**—*pop pl* MA-1
Wilbraham Acad—*school* MA-1
Wilbraham (census name for Wilbraham
Center)—*CDP* MA-1
Wilbraham Center (census name
Wilbraham)—*other* MA-1
*Wilbraham Centre* MA-1
Wilbraham Country Club—*locale* MA-1
Wilbraham JHS—*school* MA-1
Wilbraham Mountains—*range* MA-1
Wilbraham Regional HS—*school* MA-1
**Wilbraham (Town of)**—*pop pl* MA-1
Wilbren—*locale* OH-6
Wilbur—*fmr MCD* NE-7
Wilbur—*locale* KY-4
Wilbur—*locale* TN-4
**Wilbur**—*pop pl* IN-6
**Wilbur**—*pop pl* NY-2
**Wilbur**—*pop pl* OR-9
**Wilbur**—*pop pl* PA-2
**Wilbur**—*pop pl* WA-9
**Wilbur**—*pop pl* (2) WV-2
Wilbur, Frank, House—*hist pl* RI-1
Wilbur, Mount—*summit* AK-9
Wilbur, Mount—*summit* MT-8
Wilbur Airp—*airport* WA-9
Wilbur Bay—*bay* FL-3
Wilbur Bench—*bench* UT-8
Wilbur Brook—*stream* MN-6
**Wilbur-by-the-Sea**—*pop pl* FL-3
Wilbur Canyon—*valley* (3) AZ-5
Wilbur Canyon—*valley* UT-8
Wilbur (CCD)—*cens area* WA-9
Wilbur Cem—*cemetery* OR-9
Wilbur Center Sch—*school* SD-7
Wilbur Ch—*church* OH-6
*Wilbur Creek* MN-6
Wilbur Creek—*stream* CO-8
Wilbur Creek—*stream* MI-6
Wilbur Creek—*stream* MN-6
Wilbur Creek—*stream* (2) MT-8
Wilbur Creek—*stream* WA-9
Wilbur Crossing—*locale* PA-2
**Wilburdale**—*pop pl* VA-3
Wilbur Dam—*dam* TN-4
Wilbur Ditch—*canal* CA-9
Wilbur Ditch—*canal* IN-6
Wilbur Drain—*canal* (2) MI-6
Wilbur Drain—*stream* MI-6
Wilbur Grave—*cemetery* CA-9
Wilbur Gulch—*valley* MT-8
**Wilbur Heights**—*pop pl* IL-6
Wilbur Hill—*summit* NY-2
Wilbur Hill—*summit* PA-2
Wilbur Hill—*summit* RI-1
Wilbur Hollow Brook—*stream* RI-1
Wilbur House—*hist pl* NY-2
**Wilburite Corner**—*pop pl* MA-1
Wilbur JHS—*school* CA-9
Wilbur Lake—*lake* CO-8
Wilbur Lake—*lake* MI-6
Wilbur Lake—*lake* (2) MN-6
Wilbur Lake—*reservoir* TN-4
Wilbur Lateral—*canal* WA-9
Wilbur Lynch HS—*school* NY-2
Wilbur May Lake—*lake* CA-9
Wilbur McKnight Ranch—*locale* NM-5
Wilbur Mtn—*summit* ME-1
Wilbur Mtn—*summit* OR-9
Wilburn—*locale* VA-3
**Wilburn**—*pop pl* AL-4
**Wilburn**—*pop pl* AR-4
**Wilburn**—*pop pl* FL-3
Wilburn Bar—*bar* KY-4
*Wilburn Branch* TN-4
Wilburn Branch—*stream* FL-3
Wilburn Branch—*stream* MO-7
Wilburn Branch—*stream* TN-4
Wilburn Branch—*stream* TX-5
Wilburn Branch—*stream* VA-3
Wilburn Butte—*summit* ID-8
Wilburn Cem—*cemetery* AL-4
Wilburn Cem—*cemetery* KS-7
Wilburn Cem—*cemetery* MO-7
Wilburn Cem—*cemetery* (2) TN-4
Wilburn Cem—*cemetery* VA-3
Wilburn Ch—*church* VA-3
Wilburn Chapel—*church* AL-4
Wilburn Chapel—*church* TN-4
Wilburn Creek—*stream* AL-4
Wilburn Creek—*stream* AR-4
Wilburn Creek—*stream* SD-7
Wilburn Creek—*stream* TN-4
Wilburn Creek—*stream* TX-5
Wilbur Neck—*cape* ME-1
**Wilburn Estates**—*pop pl* MD-2
Wilburne Station—*locale* PA-2
Wilburn Hill—*summit* AR-4
Wilburn (historical)—*locale* KS-7
Wilburn Hollow—*valley* TN-4
Wilburn Island—*island* NE-7
Wilburn Kilgore Mine
(underground)—*mine* TN-4
Wilburn Knob—*summit* AR-4
Wilburn Lake—*lake* TX-5
Wilburn Post Office (historical)—*building* AL-4
Wilburn Ranch—*locale* CA-9
Wilburn Ranch—*locale* MT-8
Wilburn Ridge—*ridge* VA-3
Wilburn Sch—*school* NC-3
Wilburn Sch (historical)—*school* AL-4
*Wilburns Island* MO-7
Wilburn Tank—*reservoir* NM-5
**Wilburn Township**—*pop pl* KS-7
Wilburn (Township of)—*fmr MCD* AR-4
Wilburn Valley—*valley* VA-3
Wilburn Valley Cem—*cemetery* VA-3
Wilbur Park—*park* NY-2
**Wilbur Park**—*pop pl* (2) MO-7
Wilbur Point—*cape* MA-1
*Wilbur Pond* MA-1
Wilbur Pond—*lake* MD-2
Wilbur Pond—*lake* MA-1
Wilbur Pond—*lake* NY-2
Wilbur Pond—*lake* RI-1
Wilbur Pond—*reservoir* RI-1
Wilbur Pond Dam—*dam* RI-1
Wilbur Ridge—*ridge* WV-2
Wilbur Run—*stream* KY-4
Wilbur Russell Dam—*dam* SD-7
Wilbur Sch—*school* ME-1
Wilbur Sch—*school* MA-1
Wilburs Place—*locale* AK-9
*Wilburs Pond* MA-1
Wilbur Spring—*spring* MT-8
Wilbur Spring—*spring* UT-8
Wilbur Springs—*locale* CA-9
Wilbur Springs Station California
Division—*locale* CA-9
**Wilbur (subdivision)**—*pop pl* PA-2
Wilbur Tank Number One—*reservoir* AZ-5
Wilbur Tank Number Two—*reservoir* AZ-5
**Wilburtha**—*pop pl* NJ-2
**Wilburtha Manor**—*pop pl* NJ-2
Wilbur Theatre—*building* MA-1
Wilbur Theatre—*hist pl* MA-1
*Wilburton* PA-2
Wilburton—*locale* KS-7
Wilburton—*locale* WA-9
**Wilburton**—*pop pl* OK-5
**Wilburton**—*pop pl* PA-2
Wilburton (CCD)—*cens area* OK-5
Wilburton Cem—*cemetery* KS-7
Wilburton Cem—*cemetery* OK-5
**Wilburton Number One (Wilburton
Po)**—*pop pl* (2) PA-2
Wilburton Oil and Gas Field—*oilfield* KS-7
Wilburton Sch—*school* WA-9
**Wilbur Township**—*pop pl* ND-7
**Wilbur Township**—*pop pl* SD-7
Wilbur Wadley Draw—*valley* NM-5
Wilbur Wash—*arroyo* AZ-5
Wilbur Wash—*stream* CA-9
Wilbur Watts HS—*school* NJ-2
Wilbur Weems Pond Dam—*dam* MS-4
Wilbur Well—*well* AZ-5
Wilbur Womble Mine—*mine* CA-9
*Wilbur Wright Birthplace* IN-6
Wilbur Wright Creek—*stream* IN-6
Wilbur Wright Elem Sch—*school* IN-6
Wilbur Wright HS—*school* OH-6
Wilbur Wright Memorial—*park* IN-6
Wilbur Wright MS—*school* IN-6
Wilby—*locale* MO-7
Wilby HS—*hist pl* CT-1
Wilby HS—*school* CT-1
Wilby Island—*island* AK-9
Wilcat Branch—*stream* NC-3
Wilcher Cem—*cemetery* KY-4
Wilchester—*uninc pl* TX-5
Wilchester Sch—*school* TX-5
Wilco—*locale* TX-5
**Wilco**—*pop pl* TN-4
Wilcocks, Walter and Ann, House—*hist pl* UT-8
*Wilcockson* AR-4
**Wilcoe**—*pop pl* WV-2
**Wilco Estates**—*pop pl* MS-4
**Wilco Hill**—*pop pl* PA-2
Wilco Industrial Park—*locale* NC-3
Wilcok Cem—*cemetery* NY-2
**Wilco Manor Mobile Home Park
(subdivision)**—*pop pl* NC-3
*Wilcox* AZ-5
Wilcox—*locale* AL-4
Wilcox—*locale* OR-9
Wilcox—*locale* TN-4
Wilcox—*locale* TX-5
Wilcox—*locale* WA-9
Wilcox—*locale* WI-6
Wilcox—*locale* WY-8
**Wilcox**—*pop pl* FL-3
**Wilcox**—*pop pl* IL-6
**Wilcox**—*pop pl* MO-7
**Wilcox**—*pop pl* NE-7
**Wilcox**—*pop pl* NY-2
**Wilcox**—*pop pl* PA-2
Wilcox—*uninc pl* CA-9
Wilcox, Albert Spencer, Bldg—*hist pl* HI-9
Wilcox, Andrew, House—*hist pl* MI-6
Wilcox, Benjamin, House—*hist pl* CA-9
Wilcox, Charles, House—*hist pl* WA-9
Wilcox, Crittenden Mill—*hist pl* CT-1
Wilcox, D. K. and Inez, House—*hist pl* TX-5
Wilcox, Hiram, House—*hist pl* OH-6
Wilcox, Jacob, Farm—*hist pl* OH-6
Wilcox, James, House—*hist pl* OH-6
Wilcox, James D., House—*hist pl* UT-8
Wilcox, Josiah, House—*hist pl* CT-1
Wilcox, Lake—*lake* SD-7
Wilcox, Mount—*summit* CO-8
Wilcox, Mount—*summit* MA-1

Wilcox, Roy, House—*hist pl* WI-6
Wilcox, W. G., House—*hist pl* NY-2
Wilcox Acad—*school* AL-4
Wilcox Airstrip—*airport* IN-6
Wilcox andHall Cem—*cemetery* GA-3
Wilcox Bar—*bar* AL-4
Wilcox Bay—*bay* VT-1
Wilcox Bend—*bend* MO-7
*Wilcox Branch* TN-4
Wilcox Branch—*stream* OK-5
Wilcox Branch—*stream* PA-2
Wilcox Branch—*stream* (2) TX-5
Wilcox Branch and Chinquapin Merge—*bend* TX-5
Wilcox Bridge—*bridge* NC-3
Wilcox Camping and Boating Resort—*locale* UT-8
Wilcox Canyon—*valley* (2) CA-9
Wilcox Canyon—*valley* MT-8
Wilcox Canyon—*valley* (2) NV-8
Wilcox Canyon—*valley* OR-9
Wilcox Canyon—*valley* UT-8
Wilcox Canyon—*valley* WA-9
Wilcox Cem—*cemetery* AR-4
Wilcox Cem—*cemetery* CO-8
Wilcox Cem—*cemetery* (2) CT-1
Wilcox Cem—*cemetery* (2) FL-3
Wilcox Cem—*cemetery* (3) GA-3
Wilcox Cem—*cemetery* IA-7
Wilcox Cem—*cemetery* KS-7
Wilcox Cem—*cemetery* KY-4
Wilcox Cem—*cemetery* ME-1
Wilcox Cem—*cemetery* (2) MO-7
Wilcox Cem—*cemetery* NE-7
Wilcox Cem—*cemetery* (2) NY-2
Wilcox Cem—*cemetery* OR-9
Wilcox Cem—*cemetery* TN-4
Wilcox Cem—*cemetery* VA-3
Wilcox Community Hall—*locale* MO-7
Wilcox Corners—*locale* NY-2
**Wilcox County**—*pop pl* AL-4
**Wilcox (County)**—*pop pl* GA-3
Wilcox County Courthouse—*building* AL-4
Wilcox County Courthouse—*hist pl* GA-3
Wilcox County Courthouse Hist Dist—*hist pl* AL-4
Wilcox County HS—*school* AL-4
Wilcox Creek—*stream* CA-9
Wilcox Creek—*stream* GA-3
Wilcox Creek—*stream* NY-2
Wilcox Creek—*stream* PA-2
Wilcox-Cutts House—*hist pl* VT-1
Wilcox Dam—*dam* UT-8
Wilcox Ditch—*canal* HI-9
Wilcox Ditch—*canal* (3) OR-9
Wilcox Drain—*canal* MI-6
Wilcox Drain—*stream* MI-6
Wilcox Draw—*valley* MT-8
Wilcox Draw—*valley* NM-5
Wilcoxen Knob—*summit* MO-7
Wilcox Farm Airstrip—*airport* ND-7
Wilcox Female Institute—*hist pl* AL-4
Wilcox Field—*airport* KS-7
Wilcox Flat—*flat* CA-9
Wilcox Flat—*flat* UT-8
*Wilcox Furnace* TN-4
Wilcox Grange—*locale* WA-9
Wilcox-Graves House—*hist pl* TX-5
Wilcox Gulch—*valley* CO-8
Wilcox Hill—*summit* ME-1
Wilcox Hill—*summit* NH-1
Wilcox Hill—*summit* RI-1
Wilcox Hill—*summit* (3) VT-1
Wilcox Hills—*summit* TX-5
Wilcox (historical)—*locale* KS-7
Wilcox (historical)—*locale* MS-4
Wilcox Hollow—*valley* AR-4
Wilcox Hollow—*valley* MA-1
Wilcox Hollow—*valley* (2) MO-7
Wilcox Hollow—*valley* (2) TN-4
Wilcox Hollow—*valley* VT-1
Wilcox Homestead—*locale* MT-8
Wilcox HS—*school* AZ-5
Wilcox HS—*school* CA-9
Wilcox Island—*island* CT-1
Wilcox Island—*island* WI-6
Wilcox Junction—*locale* FL-3
Wilcox Lake—*lake* IL-6
Wilcox Lake—*lake* MI-6
Wilcox Lake—*lake* MN-6
Wilcox Lake—*lake* NY-2
Wilcox Lake—*lake* (2) WI-6
Wilcox Lake—*reservoir* KY-4
Wilcox Lake—*reservoir* MI-6
Wilcox Lake—*reservoir* VA-3
*Wilcox Landing Field* KS-7
Wilcox Memorial Hosp—*hospital* HI-9
Wilcox-Mills House—*hist pl* OH-6
Wilcox Mtn—*summit* MO-7
Wilcox Mtn—*summit* NY-2
Wilcox Mtn—*summit* WA-9
Wilcox Neck—*cape* VA-3
Wilcox Oaks Golf Course—*other* CA-9
Wilcox Octagon House—*hist pl* NY-2
Wilcox Outlet—*stream* NY-2
Wilcox Park—*park* CT-1
Wilcox Park—*park* MI-6
Wilcox Park Hist Dist—*hist pl* RI-1
Wilcox Peak—*locale* NM-5
Wilcox Peak—*summit* CA-9
Wilcox Peak—*summit* OR-9
Wilcox Peak—*summit* VT-1
*Wilcox Point* VT-1
Wilcox Point—*cape* VT-1
Wilcox Point—*cliff* WY-8
Wilcox Point—*summit* UT-8
Wilcox Pond—*lake* (2) CT-1
Wilcox Pond—*lake* ME-1
Wilcox Pond—*lake* NY-2
Wilcox Pond—*reservoir* CT-1
Wilcox Prospect—*mine* TN-4
Wilcox Ranch—*locale* AZ-5
Wilcox Ranch—*locale* CA-9
Wilcox Ranch—*locale* NE-7
Wilcox Ranch—*locale* NV-8
Wilcox Ranch—*locale* UT-8
Wilcox Refinery—*other* TX-5
Wilcox Ridge—*ridge* (2) CA-9
Wilcox Road Cem—*cemetery* NY-2
*Wilcox Rsvr* CT-1
Wilcox Rsvr—*reservoir* UT-8
Wilcox Run—*stream* PA-2
Wilcox Sch—*school* (3) CA-9
Wilcox Sch—*school* HI-9
Wilcox Sch—*school* IL-6
Wilcox Sch—*school* ME-1
Wilcox Sch—*school* MI-6
Wilcox Sch—*school* (2) OH-6
Wilcox Sch—*school* OR-9
Wilcox Sch—*school* WI-6
Wilcox Sch (historical)—*school* MO-7
Wilcox Settlement—*locale* ME-1
Wilcoxson and Company Bank—*hist pl* MO-7
Wilcoxson Ranch—*locale* NM-5
Wilcoxson Sch—*school* CT-1
Wilcox Spring—*spring* (2) CA-9
Wilcox Spring—*spring* CO-8
Wilcox Spring—*spring* NV-8
Wilcox Spring—*spring* UT-8
Wilcox Tanks—*reservoir* NM-5
Wilcox Technical Sch—*school* CT-1
**Wilcox Township**—*pop pl* KS-7
Wilcox (Township of)—*other* OH-6
**Wilcox (Township of)**—*pop pl* IL-6
**Wilcox (Township of)**—*pop pl* MI-6
Wilcox Trail—*trail* CA-9
Wilcox Training Sch—*school* AL-4
Wilcox Tunnel—*tunnel* TN-4
Wilcox Valley—*valley* CA-9
Wilcox Wells—*well* NM-5
*Wilcox Wharf* VA-3
Wilcut Creek—*stream* OR-9
*Wilczinski* MS-4
*Wilda* TX-5
**Wilda**—*pop pl* LA-4
**Wilda**—*pop pl* VA-3
Wilda, Lake—*reservoir* VA-3
Wild Ace Lake—*lake* OR-9
Wilda Ch—*church* LA-4
**Wildacres**—*pop pl* NC-3
**Wild Acres**—*pop pl* PA-2
Wild Acres Lake—*reservoir* AL-4
Wild Acres Lake—*reservoir* PA-2
Wild Acres Lake Dam—*dam* AL-4
Wild Acres Lake Dam—*dam* PA-2
Wildacres Tunnel—*tunnel* NC-3
Wild Ammonoosuc River—*stream* NH-1
Wild Apple Trail—*trail* PA-2
Wildare—*locale* OH-6
**Wildasin**—*pop pl* CA-9
Wildasin Chapel—*church* PA-2
Wildason Animal Cem—*cemetery* OH-6
*Wildat Shoals* TN-4
Wildband Canyon—*valley* AZ-5
Wild Band Pockets—*basin* AZ-5
Wild Band Rsvr—*reservoir* AZ-5
Wildband Spring—*spring* AZ-5
Wild Band Valley—*valley* AZ-5
Wild Basin—*basin* CO-8
Wild Basin House—*hist pl* CO-8
Wild Basin Ranger Station—*locale* CO-8
Wild Basin Ranger Station and House—*hist pl* CO-8
*Wild Bee Canyon* AZ-5
Wild Beef Trap—*cliff* AZ-5
Wild Bee Spring—*spring* AZ-5
Wild Bend—*bend* TX-5
Wild Berry Canyon—*valley* NM-5
Wild Berry Lake—*lake* WA-9
Wild Bill Bayou—*stream* MS-4
*Wild Bill Canyon* CO-8
Wild Bill Canyon—*valley* CO-8
Wild Bill Creek—*stream* CA-9
Wild Bill Creek—*stream* (2) MT-8
Wild Bill Flat—*flat* MT-8
Wild Bill Gulch—*valley* CA-9
Wild Bill Gulch—*valley* CO-8
Wild Bill Hill—*summit* AZ-5
Wild Bill Lake—*lake* MT-8
Wild Bill Mine—*mine* UT-8
Wild Bill Mtn—*summit* MT-8
Wild Bill Place—*locale* CA-9
Wild Bill Ridge—*ridge* CA-9
Wild Bills Flat—*flat* NV-8
Wild Bill Spring—*spring* CO-8
Wild Bill Tank—*reservoir* (2) AZ-5
Wild Billy Lake—*lake* OR-9
Wildblood Branch—*stream* LA-4
Wild Boar Bluff—*cliff* TN-4
Wild Boar Creek—*stream* TX-5
Wild Boar Lake—*lake* LA-4
Wild Boar Point—*cape* NC-3
Wild Boy Canyon—*valley* NM-5
Wildboy Creek—*stream* WA-9
Wild Boy Lake—*lake* CO-8
Wild Boy Run—*stream* PA-2
Wild Branch—*stream* (2) AL-4
Wild Branch—*stream* KY-4
Wild Branch—*stream* (2) NC-3
Wild Branch—*stream* VT-1
*Wild Brier* PA-2
Wild Brook—*stream* (2) ME-1
Wild Brook—*stream* VT-1
**Wildbrook Acres**—*pop pl* OH-6
Wild Buck Bayou—*stream* LA-4
Wild Buck Creek—*stream* ID-8
Wild Buck Peak—*summit* ID-8
Wild Buck Trail—*trail* ID-8
Wild Bull Canyon—*valley* NM-5
Wild Bull Spring—*spring* AZ-5
Wild Bunch Canyon—*valley* AZ-5
Wild Bunch Tank—*reservoir* AZ-5
Wild Burro Bay—*bay* NV-8
Wild Burro Canyon—*valley* AZ-5
Wild Burro Mesa—*summit* AZ-5
Wild Calf Canyon—*valley* OR-9
Wild Canyon—*valley* CO-8
Wild Canyon—*valley* OR-9
Wild Carrot Spring—*spring* NV-8
*Wild Cat* KS-7
*Wildcat* OK-5
Wildcat—*island* PA-2
Wildcat—*locale* CO-8
Wild Cat—*locale* KY-4
Wildcat—*locale* LA-4
Wildcat—*locale* UT-8
Wildcat—*locale* WV-2
Wildcat—*locale* WY-8
Wildcat—*other* OK-5
**Wild Cat**—*pop pl* CO-8
**Wildcat**—*pop pl* PA-2
Wildcat—*post sta* TX-5
Wildcat, The—*rock* MA-1
Wildcat Air Landing Area—*airport* IN-6
Wildcat Airp—*airport* PA-2
Wild Cat Aqueduct—*canal* MA-1
Wildcat Basin—*basin* OR-9
Wildcat Battlefield Site—*hist pl* KY-4
Wildcat Bay—*swamp* FL-3
Wildcat Bay—*swamp* (2) NC-3
*Wild Cat Bayou* MS-4
Wildcat Bayou—*gut* (2) LA-4
Wildcat Bayou—*stream* AR-4
Wildcat Bayou—*stream* (2) LA-4
Wildcat Bayou—*stream* (2) MS-4
Wildcat Beach—*beach* CA-9
Wildcat Bend—*bend* LA-4
Wildcat Bend—*bend* MS-4
Wildcat Bend—*bend* (2) TX-5
Wildcat Bluff—*cliff* (2) AR-4
Wildcat Bluff—*cliff* IL-6
Wildcat Bluff—*cliff* IA-7
Wildcat Bluff—*cliff* MN-6
Wildcat Bluff—*cliff* NM-5
Wildcat Bluff—*summit* WI-6
Wildcat Bluff Rec Area—*park* IA-7
*Wildcat Branch* AL-4
*Wildcat Branch* KY-4
*Wildcat Branch* VA-3
Wildcat Branch—*stream* (5) AL-4
Wildcat Branch—*stream* AR-4
Wildcat Branch—*stream* DE-2
Wildcat Branch—*stream* (2) FL-3
Wildcat Branch—*stream* (6) GA-3
Wildcat Branch—*stream* IN-6
Wildcat Branch—*stream* (6) KY-4
Wildcat Branch—*stream* (2) LA-4
Wildcat Branch—*stream* (4) MD-2
Wildcat Branch—*stream* (3) MO-7
Wildcat Branch—*stream* (2) NJ-2
Wildcat Branch—*stream* (13) NC-3
Wildcat Branch—*stream* (3) SC-3
Wildcat Branch—*stream* (9) TN-4
Wildcat Branch—*stream* TX-5
Wildcat Branch—*stream* (2) VA-3
Wildcat Branch—*stream* WV-2
Wildcat Branch Petroglyphs—*hist pl* WV-2
Wildcat Bridge—*bridge* NC-3
*Wild Cat Brook* MA-1
Wildcat Brook—*stream* (2) CT-1
Wildcat Brook—*stream* IN-6
Wildcat Brook—*stream* ME-1
Wildcat Brook—*stream* MA-1
Wildcat Brook—*stream* NH-1
Wildcat Butte—*summit* (2) CA-9
Wildcat Butte—*summit* UT-8
Wildcat Butte—*summit* (2) WY-8
Wildcat Camp—*locale* (2) OR-9
Wildcat Camp—*locale* PA-2
Wildcat Campground—*park* UT-8
*Wildcat Canyon* UT-8
Wildcat Canyon—*uninc pl* CA-9
Wildcat Canyon—*valley* (8) AZ-5
Wildcat Canyon—*valley* (16) CA-9
Wildcat Canyon—*valley* (7) CO-8
Wildcat Canyon—*valley* (3) ID-8
Wildcat Canyon—*valley* IL-6
Wildcat Canyon—*valley* KS-7
Wildcat Canyon—*valley* MT-8
Wildcat Canyon—*valley* (5) NV-8
Wildcat Canyon—*valley* (6) NM-5
Wildcat Canyon—*valley* OK-5
Wildcat Canyon—*valley* OR-9
Wildcat Canyon—*valley* (2) SD-7
Wildcat Canyon—*valley* (6) TX-5
Wildcat Canyon—*valley* (7) UT-8
Wildcat Canyon—*valley* (2) WY-8
Wildcat Canyon Creek—*stream* MI-6
Wildcat Canyon Rsvr—*reservoir* OR-9
*Wildcat Canyon Trail* UT-8
Wildcat Cave—*cave* AZ-5
Wildcat Cave—*cave* KY-4
Wildcat Cave—*cave* MO-7
Wildcat Cave—*cave* PA-2
Wildcat Cave—*cave* SD-7
Wildcat Cave—*cave* (2) TN-4
Wildcat Cave Access—*park* IA-7
Wildcat Cave Hollow—*valley* KY-4
Wildcat Cem—*cemetery* IL-6
Wildcat Cem—*cemetery* IN-6
Wildcat Cem—*cemetery* OK-5
Wildcat Ch—*church* NC-3
Wildcat Ch—*church* TX-5
Wildcat Cliff—*cliff* KY-4
Wildcat Cliffs—*cliff* NC-3
Wildcat Conservation Club—*other* IN-6
Wildcat Corner—*locale* VA-3
Wildcat Coulee—*valley* (4) MT-8
Wildcat Coulee—*valley* WI-6
Wildcat Cove—*bay* AK-9
Wildcat Cove—*bay* FL-3
Wildcat Cove—*bay* (2) WA-9
Wildcat Cove—*valley* NC-3
Wildcat Cove—*valley* TN-4
Wildcat Cove Branch—*stream* TN-4
Wildcat Cove Cave—*cave* TN-4
*Wildcat Creek* CA-9
*Wildcat Creek* GA-3
*Wild Cat Creek* IN-6
*Wildcat Creek* IA-7
*Wildcat Creek* KS-7
*Wildcat Creek* ME-1
*Wild Cat Creek* MS-4
*Wildcat Creek* NV-8
*Wildcat Creek* OR-9
*Wild Cat Creek* PA-2
*Wild Cat Creek* SC-3
*Wild Cat Creek* TX-5
*Wildcat Creek* WA-9
*Wild Cat Creek* WY-8
Wildcat Creek—*stream* (4) AL-4
Wildcat Creek—*stream* AK-9
Wildcat Creek—*stream* (3) AZ-5
Wildcat Creek—*stream* (2) AR-4
Wildcat Creek—*stream* (19) CA-9
Wildcat Creek—*stream* (6) CO-8
Wildcat Creek—*stream* (3) FL-3
Wildcat Creek—*stream* (12) GA-3
Wildcat Creek—*stream* (6) ID-8
Wildcat Creek—*stream* (4) IL-6
Wildcat Creek—*stream* IN-6
Wildcat Creek—*stream* (5) IA-7
Wildcat Creek—*stream* (14) KS-7
Wildcat Creek—*stream* KY-4
Wild Cat Creek—*stream* KY-4
Wildcat Creek—*stream* (2) KY-4
Wildcat Creek—*stream* MA-1
Wildcat Creek—*stream* (4) MI-6
Wildcat Creek—*stream* MN-6
Wildcat Creek—*stream* (4) MS-4
Wildcat Creek—*stream* (9) MO-7
Wildcat Creek—*stream* (3) MT-8
Wildcat Creek—*stream* NE-7
Wildcat Creek*—*stream* NE-7
Wildcat Creek—*stream* NE-7
Wildcat Creek*—*stream* NE-7
Wildcat Creek—*stream* (3) NE-7
Wildcat Creek—*stream* (2) NV-8
Wildcat Creek—*stream* NC-3
Wild Cat Creek—*stream* NC-3
Wildcat Creek—*stream* (2) NC-3
Wildcat Creek—*stream* (2) OH-6
Wildcat Creek—*stream* (10) OK-5
Wildcat Creek—*stream* (25) OR-9
Wildcat Creek—*stream* (2) PA-2
Wild Cat Creek—*stream* PA-2
Wildcat Creek—*stream* (5) SC-3
Wildcat Creek—*stream* SD-7
Wildcat Creek—*stream* (5) TN-4
Wildcat Creek—*stream* (10) TX-5
Wildcat Creek—*stream* (4) UT-8
Wildcat Creek—*stream* (2) VA-3
Wildcat Creek—*stream* (9) WA-9
Wildcat Creek—*stream* WV-2
Wildcat Creek—*stream* (5) WI-6
Wildcat Creek—*stream* (7) WY-8
Wildcat Creek Access Point—*locale* GA-3
Wildcat Creek Bridge—*hist pl* OR-9
Wildcat Creek Cem—*cemetery* AL-4
Wildcat Creek Cove—*bay* GA-3
Wildcat Creek Rsvr—*reservoir* OR-9
Wildcat Creek Workings—*mine* TN-4
Wildcat Cut—*channel* GA-3
Wildcat Cutoff—*trail* NH-1
Wildcat Dam—*dam* CA-9
Wildcat Den State Park—*park* IA-7
Wildcat Ditch—*canal* AR-4
Wildcat Ditch—*canal* CA-9
Wildcat Ditch—*canal* (2) IL-6
Wildcat Drain—*canal* CA-9
*Wildcat Draw* TX-5
Wildcat Draw—*valley* AZ-5
Wildcat Draw—*valley* CO-8
Wildcat Draw—*valley* MT-8
Wildcat Draw—*valley* NM-5
Wildcat Draw—*valley* SD-7
Wildcat Draw—*valley* (6) TX-5
Wildcat Draw—*valley* UT-8
Wildcat Draw—*valley* (3) WY-8
Wildcat Falls—*falls* CA-9
Wildcat Falls—*falls* NH-1
Wildcat Falls—*falls* WA-9
Wildcat Fields—*flat* UT-8
Wildcat Flowage—*lake* WI-6
*Wildcat Forest Service Station* UT-8
Wildcat Freight Station ( Ruins)—*locale* NV-8
*Wildcat Gap* GA-3
Wildcat Gap—*gap* (2) GA-3
Wildcat Gap—*gap* (4) NC-3
Wildcat Gap—*gap* PA-2
Wildcat Glades—*flat* OR-9
Wildcat Gorge—*valley* CT-1
Wildcat Gorge—*valley* NV-8
Wildcat Guard Station—*locale* NV-8
Wildcat Gulch—*valley* (3) CA-9
Wildcat Gulch—*valley* (4) CO-8
Wildcat Gulch—*valley* ID-8
Wildcat Gulch—*valley* (2) MT-8
Wildcat Gulch—*valley* (3) OR-9
Wildcat Gulch—*valley* SD-7
Wildcat Gulch—*valley* UT-8
Wildcat Gulch—*valley* (2) WY-8
Wildcat Gully—*valley* NY-2
Wildcat Gut—*gut* VA-3
Wildcat Hammock—*island* FL-3
*Wildcat Harbor* WA-9
*Wild Cat Hill* MA-1
*Wildcat Hill* WI-6
Wildcat Hill—*summit* AL-4
Wildcat Hill—*summit* (3) AZ-5
Wildcat Hill—*summit* AR-4
Wildcat Hill—*summit* CO-8
Wildcat Hill—*summit* (2) MA-1
Wildcat Hill—*summit* (2) NV-8
Wildcat Hill—*summit* NH-1
Wildcat Hill—*summit* NM-5
Wildcat Hill—*summit* NY-2
Wildcat Hill—*summit* PA-2
*Wild Cat Hills* UT-8
Wildcat Hills—*range* WY-8
Wildcat Hills—*summit* IL-6
Wildcat Hills—*summit* UT-8
Wildcat Hill Waste Water Treatment Plant—*locale* AZ-5
Wildcat Hollow—*valley* (2) AL-4
Wildcat Hollow—*valley* (14) AR-4
Wildcat Hollow—*valley* CT-1
Wildcat Hollow—*valley* IL-6
Wildcat Hollow—*valley* KS-7
Wildcat Hollow—*valley* (7) KY-4
Wildcat Hollow—*valley* (2) MD-2
Wildcat Hollow—*valley* (16) MO-7
Wildcat Hollow—*valley* NH-1
Wildcat Hollow—*valley* (2) NY-2
Wildcat Hollow—*valley* (2) NC-3
Wildcat Hollow—*valley* (10) OH-6
Wildcat Hollow—*valley* (2) OK-5
Wildcat Hollow—*valley* (4) PA-2
Wild Cat Hollow—*valley* PA-2
Wildcat Hollow—*valley* (8) PA-2
Wildcat Hollow—*valley* (20) TN-4
Wild Cat Hollow—*valley* TN-4
Wildcat Hollow—*valley* TN-4
Wildcat Hollow—*valley* TX-5
Wildcat Hollow—*valley* (3) UT-8
Wildcat Hollow—*valley* (8) VA-3
Wildcat Hollow—*valley* (2) WV-2
Wildcat Island—*island* (2) GA-3
Wildcat Island—*island* ID-8
Wildcat Island—*island* MN-6
*Wildcat Knob* GA-3
*Wild Cat Knob* PA-2
Wildcat Knob—*summit* AR-4
Wildcat Knob—*summit* GA-3
Wildcat Knob—*summit* IN-6
Wildcat Knob—*summit* (2) KY-4
Wildcat Knob—*summit* (5) NC-3
Wildcat Knob—*summit* PA-2
Wildcat Knob—*summit* TN-4
Wildcat Knob—*summit* (3) VA-3
Wildcat Knob—*summit* (2) WV-2
Wildcat Knolls—*summit* UT-8
*Wildcat Lake* WA-9
Wildcat Lake—*lake* AR-4
Wildcat Lake—*lake* (2) CA-9
Wildcat Lake—*lake* FL-3
Wildcat Lake—*lake* (2) IL-6
Wildcat Lake—*lake* (3) MI-6
Wildcat Lake—*lake* MN-6
Wildcat Lake—*lake* MT-8
Wildcat Lake—*lake* WA-9
Wild Cat Lake—*lake* WA-9
Wildcat Lake—*lake* WA-9
Wildcat Lake—*lake* (2) WI-6
**Wildcat Lake**—*pop pl* WA-9
Wildcat Lake—*reservoir* (2) NC-3
Wild Cat Lake—*swamp* NC-3
Wildcat Lake Dam—*dam* NC-3
Wildcat Landing—*locale* AL-4
Wildcat Landing—*locale* (2) NC-3
Wildcat Landing (historical)—*locale* NC-3
Wildcat Landing Public Access—*locale* MN-6
Wildcat Lead—*ridge* GA-3
Wildcat Ledge—*bench* CT-1
Wildcat Marsh—*swamp* VA-3
Wildcat Mesa—*summit* UT-8
Wildcat Mine—*mine* AZ-5
Wildcat Mine—*mine* NV-8
Wildcat Mine—*mine* TN-4
Wildcat Mine—*mine* WA-9
Wildcat Mound—*summit* CO-8
Wildcat Mound—*summit* (2) WI-6
Wildcat Mountain Research Area—*area* OR-9
Wildcat Mountains—*range* TX-5
Wildcat Mountain Ski Area—*other* NH-1
Wildcat Mountain State Park—*park* WI-6
*Wild Cat Mtn* MA-1
*Wildcat Mtn* OR-9
Wildcat Mtn—*summit* AL-4
Wildcat Mtn—*summit* (3) AR-4
Wildcat Mtn—*summit* (4) CA-9
Wildcat Mtn—*summit* (2) CO-8
Wildcat Mtn—*summit* CT-1
Wildcat Mtn—*summit* GA-3
Wildcat Mtn—*summit* (2) KY-4
Wildcat Mtn—*summit* MA-1
Wildcat Mtn—*summit* (2) MO-7
Wildcat Mtn—*summit* (2) MT-8
Wildcat Mtn—*summit* NE-7
Wildcat Mtn—*summit* NH-1
Wildcat Mtn—*summit* (2) NY-2
Wildcat Mtn—*summit* (3) NC-3
Wildcat Mtn—*summit* OK-5
Wildcat Mtn—*summit* (4) OR-9
Wildcat Mtn—*summit* PA-2
Wildcat Mtn—*summit* (4) TX-5
Wildcat Mtn—*summit* UT-8
Wildcat Mtn—*summit* (3) VA-3
Wildcat Mtn—*summit* (2) WA-9
Wildcat Mtn—*summit* WI-6
Wildcat Notch—*gap* MA-1
Wildcat No 3 Mine—*mine* CO-8
Wildcat No 8 Mine—*mine* CO-8
Wildcat Pass—*channel* AK-9
Wildcat Pasture—*flat* UT-8
Wildcat Peak—*summit* (3) AZ-5
Wildcat Peak—*summit* (2) CA-9
Wildcat Peak—*summit* (5) NV-8
Wildcat Peak—*summit* NM-5
Wildcat Peak—*summit* SD-7
Wildcat Peak—*summit* WY-8
Wildcat Point—*cape* (2) CA-9
Wildcat Point—*cape* SC-3
Wildcat Point—*cape* VA-3
Wildcat Point—*cliff* CO-8
Wildcat Point—*cliff* MD-2
**Wildcat Point**—*pop pl* OK-5
Wildcat Point—*summit* AZ-5
Wildcat Point—*summit* CA-9
Wildcat Point—*summit* OR-9
Wildcat Pond—*reservoir* MA-1
Wildcat Pond—*swamp* TX-5
Wildcat Ranch—*locale* AZ-5
Wildcat Ranger Station—*locale* UT-8
Wildcat Rapids—*rapids* OR-9
Wildcat Ravine—*valley* CA-9
Wildcat Ravine—*valley* NY-2
*Wild Cat Ridge* PA-2
Wildcat Ridge—*ridge* (3) CA-9
Wildcat Ridge—*ridge* (3) GA-3
Wildcat Ridge—*ridge* (3) KY-4
Wildcat Ridge—*ridge* LA-4
Wildcat Ridge—*ridge* NH-1
Wildcat Ridge—*ridge* (2) OR-9
Wildcat Ridge—*ridge* (2) PA-2
Wildcat Ridge—*ridge* TN-4
Wildcat Ridge—*ridge* TX-5
Wildcat Ridge—*ridge* (4) VA-3
Wildcat Ridge—*ridge* (3) WV-2
Wildcat Ridge—*ridge* WY-8
Wildcat Ridge Trail—*trail* NH-1
Wildcat Ridge Trail—*trail* VA-3
*Wild Cat River* IN-6
*Wildcat River* ME-1
Wildcat River Trail—*trail* NH-1
Wildcat Rock—*cliff* NC-3
Wildcat Rock—*pillar* CA-9
Wildcat Rock—*pillar* RI-1
Wildcat Rock—*pillar* TN-4
Wildcat Rock—*rock* WV-2
Wildcat Rocks—*summit* PA-2
Wildcat Rsvr—*reservoir* CO-8
Wildcat Rsvr—*reservoir* ID-8
Wildcat Rsvr—*reservoir* (2) UT-8
*Wildcat Run* PA-2
Wildcat Run—*slope* UT-8
Wildcat Run—*stream* IN-6
Wildcat Run—*stream* (3) OH-6
Wildcat Run—*stream* (10) PA-2
Wildcat Run—*stream* (8) WV-2
Wildcat Run East Fork—*stream* PA-2
Wildcat Scarp—*ridge* NV-8
Wildcat Sch—*school* IL-6
Wild Cat Sch—*school* KY-4
Wildcat Sch—*school* TX-5
Wildcat Sch (abandoned)—*school* MO-7
Wildcat Sch (abandoned)—*school* PA-2
Wildcat School (abandoned)—*locale* OR-9
Wildcat Seep—*spring* AZ-5
Wildcat Shoal—*other* MO-7
Wildcat Siding (historical)—*locale* UT-8
Wildcat Slough—*gut* LA-4
Wildcat Slough—*stream* FL-3
Wildcat Slough—*stream* IL-6
Wildcat Slough—*stream* LA-4
Wildcat Slough—*stream* MS-4
Wildcat Slough—*stream* TX-5
Wildcat Spring—*spring* (4) AZ-5
Wildcat Spring—*spring* AR-4
Wildcat Spring—*spring* (2) CA-9
Wildcat Spring—*spring* CO-8
Wildcat Spring—*spring* GA-3
Wildcat Spring—*spring* (2) ID-8
Wildcat Spring—*spring* (8) NV-8
Wildcat Spring—*spring* NM-5
Wildcat Spring—*spring* NC-3
Wildcat Spring—*spring* (4) OR-9
Wildcat Spring—*spring* TN-4
Wildcat Spring—*spring* (3) UT-8
Wildcat Spring—*spring* WA-9
Wildcat Spring Number One—*spring* MT-8
Wildcat Spring Number Two—*spring* MT-8
Wildcat Springs—*spring* OK-5
Wildcat Springs—*spring* WY-8
Wildcat Springs Hollow—*valley* MO-7
Wildcat Springs Park—*park* IL-6
Wildcat Spur—*ridge* NC-3
Wildcat Spur—*ridge* (2) TN-4
Wildcat Spur—*ridge* VA-3
Wildcat Summit—*gap* VA-3
*Wild Cat Swamp* NC-3
Wildcat Swamp—*stream* (2) NC-3
Wildcat Swamp—*stream* VA-3
Wildcat Swamp—*swamp* CT-1
Wildcat Swamp—*swamp* (2) FL-3
Wildcat Swamp—*swamp* MI-6
Wildcat Swamp—*swamp* OR-9
Wildcat Swamp—*swamp* PA-2
Wildcat Swamp—*swamp* SC-3
Wildcat Tank—*reservoir* (3) AZ-5
Wildcat Tank—*reservoir* (2) NM-5
Wildcat Tank—*reservoir* (4) TX-5
Wildcat Tanks—*reservoir* TX-5
Wild Cattle Canyon—*valley* CA-9
Wild Cattle Creek—*stream* (2) CA-9
Wild Cattle Hollow—*valley* UT-8
Wild Cattle Mtn—*summit* CA-9
Wild Cattle Ridge—*ridge* UT-8
Wild Cattle Swamp—*swamp* NC-3
Wildcat Top—*summit* NC-3
Wildcat Top—*summit* TN-4
Wildcat Top—*summit* WY-8
Wild Cat Township—*civil* KS-7
**Wild Cat Township**—*pop pl* KS-7
**Wildcat Township**—*pop pl* KS-7
**Wildcat (Township of)**—*pop pl* IN-6
Wildcat Trail—*trail* CA-9
Wildcat Trail—*trail* KY-4
Wild Cat Trail—*trail* MA-1
Wildcat Trail—*trail* OK-5
Wildcat Trail—*trail* OR-9
Wildcat Trail—*trail* (4) PA-2
*Wildcat Un* PA-2
*Wild Cat Valley* PA-2
Wildcat Wash—*stream* AZ-5
Wildcat Wash—*stream* (2) NV-8
Wildcat Wash—*valley* UT-8
Wildcat Waterhole—*lake* OR-9
Wildcat Well—*well* (3) AZ-5
Wildcat Well—*well* TX-5
Wildcat Wildlife Mngmt Area—*park* UT-8
Wildcat Windmill—*locale* (2) NM-5
Wildcat Windmill—*locale* (8) TX-5
Wild Celery Creek—*stream* NM-5
Wild Cem—*cemetery* NC-3
Wild Cheat Meadow—*flat* OR-9
**Wild Cherry**—*pop pl* AR-4
Wild Cherry Branch—*stream* NC-3
*Wild Cherry Canyon* AZ-5
*Wild Cherry Canyon* TX-5
Wild Cherry Canyon—*valley* AZ-5
Wild Cherry Canyon—*valley* CA-9
Wild Cherry Cem—*cemetery* MI-6
*Wildcherry Creek* CO-8
Wild Cherry Creek—*stream* CO-8
Wild Cherry Ridge—*ridge* NC-3
Wild Cherry Ruins—*locale* AZ-5
Wild Cherry (Township of)—*fmr MCD* AR-4
Wild Cow Bay—*bay* ND-7
Wild Cow Bayou—*stream* LA-4
Wild Cow Branch—*stream* LA-4
Wild Cow Branch—*stream* TX-5
Wild Cow Campground—*park* AZ-5
Wild Cow Canyon—*valley* AZ-5
Wild Cow Canyon—*valley* CA-9
Wild Cow Canyon—*valley* CO-8
Wild Cow Canyon—*valley* NM-5
Wildcow Canyon—*valley* UT-8
Wild Cow Cem—*cemetery* FL-3
Wild Cow Creek—*stream* ID-8
Wild Cow Creek—*stream* LA-4
Wild Cow Creek—*stream* ND-7
Wild Cow Creek—*stream* WY-8
Wild Cow Island—*island* (2) FL-3
Wild Cow Island—*island* TX-5
Wild Cow Lake—*lake* AZ-5
Wild Cow Marsh—*swamp* TX-5
Wild Cow Mesa—*summit* CO-8
Wild Cow Mesa—*summit* NM-5
Wild Cow Mtn—*summit* (2) CA-9
Wild Cow Park—*flat* CO-8
Wild Cow Point—*cape* UT-8
Wild Cow Prairie—*swamp* FL-3
Wild Cow Ravine—*valley* AZ-5
Wild Cow Spring—*spring* (4) AZ-5
Wild Cow Spring—*spring* NM-5
Wild Cow Spring—*spring* UT-8
Wild Cow Tank—*reservoir* (2) AZ-5
Wild Cow Tank—*reservoir* NM-5
Wild Cow Wash—*stream* AZ-5

Wild Cow Wash—*valley* ..... UT-8
*Wild Creek* ..... CA-9
*Wild Creek* ..... GA-3
Wild Creek—*stream* ..... AK-9
Wild Creek—*stream* ..... IL-6
Wild Creek—*stream* (2) ..... MT-8
Wild Creek—*stream* ..... OK-5
Wild Creek—*stream* ..... PA-2
Wild Creek—*stream* ..... WI-6
Wild Creek Dam—*dam* ..... PA-2
Wild Creek Rsvr—*reservoir* ..... PA-2
Wild Crossing—*locale* ..... CA-9
Wild Deer Spring—*spring* ..... AZ-5
Wild Dog Creek—*stream* ..... CO-8
Wild Dog Creek—*stream* ..... KY-4
Wild Dog Creek—*stream* ..... LA-4
Wild Dove Butte—*summit* ..... AZ-5
Wild Duck Branch—*stream* ..... OH-6
**Wild Duck Dunes (subdivision)**—*pop pl* ..... NC-3
Wild Duck Pond—*lake* ..... NJ-2
Wilde, Lake—*lake* ..... UT-8
**Wilde Acres**—*pop pl* ..... VA-3
Wilde Canyon—*valley* ..... ID-8
Wilde Hill—*summit* ..... ME-1
Wilde Hill—*summit* ..... NY-2
Wilde Lake—*lake* ..... ND-7
**Wilde Lake**—*pop pl* ..... MD-2
Wildell—*locale* ..... WV-2
Wildell Shelter—*locale* ..... WV-2
*Wildemere Beach* ..... CT-1
Wilden—*other* ..... PA-2
**Wilden Acres**—*pop pl* ..... PA-2
Wilde Park—*park* ..... FL-3
Wilder—*locale* ..... NH-1
**Wilder**—*pop pl* ..... ID-8
**Wilder**—*pop pl* ..... KS-7
**Wilder**—*pop pl* ..... KY-4
**Wilder**—*pop pl* ..... MN-6
**Wilder**—*pop pl* ..... SC-3
**Wilder**—*pop pl* ..... TN-4
**Wilder**—*pop pl* ..... VT-1
**Wilder**—*pop pl* ..... VA-3
Wilder, Benjamin C., House—*hist pl* ..... ME-1
Wilder, John, House—*hist pl* ..... VT-1
Wilder, John T., House—*hist pl* ..... TN-4
Wilder, Laura Ingalls, House—*hist pl* ..... MO-7
Wilder, Mount—*summit* ..... WA-9
Wilder Bay—*swamp* ..... FL-3
Wilder Bend—*bend* ..... VA-3
Wilder Bldg—*hist pl* ..... NY-2
*Wilder Branch* ..... NC-3
Wilder Branch—*stream* ..... AR-4
Wilder Branch—*stream* ..... FL-3
Wilder Branch—*stream* (4) ..... KY-4
Wilder Branch—*stream* ..... MS-4
Wilder Branch—*stream* ..... TN-4
Wilder Bridge—*bridge* ..... ME-1
Wilder Bridge—*bridge* ..... NC-3
Wilder Brook—*stream* ..... ME-1
Wilder Brook—*stream* (3) ..... MA-1
Wilder Brook—*stream* ..... NY-2
Wilder Brook—*stream* ..... VT-1
Wilder Camp—*locale* ..... ME-1
Wilder Cave—*cave* ..... AL-4
Wilder Cem—*cemetery* ..... ID-8
Wilder Cem—*cemetery* (2) ..... KY-4
Wilder Cem—*cemetery* ..... LA-4
Wilder Cem—*cemetery* ..... MO-7
Wilder Cem—*cemetery* ..... NH-1
Wilder Cem—*cemetery* (4) ..... TN-4
Wilder Cem—*cemetery* ..... TX-5
Wilder Cem—*cemetery* ..... VT-1
Wilder Center—*building* ..... MN-6
**Wilder Center**—*pop pl* ..... MI-6
Wilder Ch—*church* ..... GA-3
Wilder Chapel—*church* (2) ..... TN-4
**Wilder Chapel**—*pop pl* ..... TN-4
*Wilder Chapel School* ..... TN-4
Wilder Coulee—*valley* ..... MT-8
*Wilder Creek* ..... IN-6
*Wilder Creek* ..... WA-9
Wilder Creek—*stream* ..... AZ-5
Wilder Creek—*stream* (2) ..... CA-9
Wilder Creek—*stream* ..... FL-3
Wilder Creek—*stream* ..... MI-6
Wilder Creek—*stream* (2) ..... NV-8
Wilder Creek—*stream* ..... OR-9
Wilder Creek—*stream* ..... TN-4
Wilder Creek—*stream* ..... WA-9
Wilder Creek Ranch—*locale* ..... NV-8
**Wildercroft**—*pop pl* ..... MD-2
Wildercroft Sch—*school* ..... MD-2
Wilder Dam—*dam* ..... NH-1
Wilder Dam—*dam* ..... VT-1
Wilder Flat—*flat* ..... MA-1
Wilder Gulch—*valley* ..... CA-9
Wilder Gulch—*valley* ..... CO-8
Wilder Gulch—*valley* ..... MT-8
Wilder Hill—*summit* (2) ..... ME-1
Wilder Hill (historical)—*locale* ..... AL-4
Wilder Hollow—*valley* ..... TN-4
Wilder Hollow Branch—*stream* ..... TN-4
Wilder-Holton House—*hist pl* ..... NH-1
Wilder House—*hist pl* ..... AZ-5
Wilder House—*hist pl* ..... LA-4
Wilder Island—*island* ..... MN-6
Wilder JHS—*school* ..... OH-6
Wilder Lake—*lake* ..... MI-6
Wilder Lake—*lake* ..... UT-8
Wilder Lake—*reservoir* ..... AL-4
Wilder Lake—*reservoir* ..... TN-4
Wilder Lake Dam—*dam* ..... AL-4
Wilder Lake Dam—*dam* ..... TN-4
*Wilder Lakes* ..... MN-6
Wilder Landing—*locale* ..... NC-3
Wilder Landing Strip—*airport* ..... SD-7
Wilderman—*locale* ..... IL-6
*Wildermere* ..... CT-1
**Wildermere Beach**—*pop pl* ..... CT-1
*Wilder Mesa* ..... AZ-5
Wilder Mesa—*summit* (2) ..... AZ-5
Wilder Mine Hollow—*valley* ..... TN-4
Wilder Mtn—*summit* ..... VT-1
Wildermuth Memorial Ch—*church* ..... OH-6
Wildermuth Sch—*school* ..... IL-6
Wildermuth Strebe Ditch—*canal* ..... IN-6
Wilderness—*locale* ..... VA-3
Wilderness—*locale* ..... WA-9
Wilderness—*locale* ..... WY-8
**Wilderness**—*pop pl* ..... MO-7
**Wilderness**—*pop pl* ..... VA-3
Wilderness, Lake—*lake* ..... WA-9
Wilderness, The—*area* ..... TN-4
Wilderness, The—*area* ..... UT-8
Wilderness, The—*hist pl* (2) ..... MD-2
**Wilderness Acres**—*pop pl* ..... NJ-2
**Wilderness Acres**—*pop pl* ..... PA-2
Wilderness Area Overlook—*locale* ..... UT-8
Wilderness Battlefield—*locale* ..... VA-3
Wilderness Bay—*bay* ..... MI-6
Wilderness Branch—*stream* ..... VA-3
Wilderness Camp Area—*locale* ..... KY-4
Wilderness Campground—*locale* ..... IL-6
Wilderness Campground—*park* ..... AL-4
Wilderness Ch—*church* ..... AR-4
Wilderness Ch—*church* ..... GA-3
Wilderness Ch—*church* (2) ..... MS-4
Wilderness Ch—*church* ..... NC-3
Wilderness Ch—*church* ..... TX-5
Wilderness Ch—*church* ..... VA-3
Wilderness Ch—*church* ..... WI-6
Wilderness Corner—*locale* ..... VA-3
Wilderness Coulee—*valley* ..... MT-8
*Wilderness Creek* ..... VA-3
Wilderness Creek—*stream* ..... CA-9
Wilderness Creek—*stream* (2) ..... VA-3
Wilderness Creek—*stream* ..... WY-8
Wilderness Falls—*falls* ..... WY-8
Wilderness Field Airp—*airport* ..... IN-6
*Wilderness Fork* ..... WV-2
Wilderness Fork—*stream* ..... WV-2
**Wilderness Garden**—*pop pl* ..... AL-4
Wilderness Gateway Pack Bridge—*locale* ..... ID-8
Wilderness Hill—*summit* ..... MA-1
Wilderness Hollow—*valley* ..... MO-7
*Wilderness Lake* ..... MN-6
Wilderness Lake—*lake* ..... AK-9
Wilderness Lake—*lake* ..... MN-6
Wilderness Lake—*lake* ..... UT-8
Wilderness Lake—*lake* ..... WI-6
Wilderness Landing (historical)—*locale* ..... MS-4
Wilderness Lodge—*locale* ..... CA-9
Wilderness Lodge—*locale* ..... NY-2
Wilderness (Magisterial District)—*fmr MCD* ..... WV-2
Wilderness of Rocks—*area* ..... AZ-5
Wilderness Park—*park* ..... MI-6
Wilderness Peak—*summit* ..... ID-8
Wilderness Plantation (historical)—*locale* ..... MS-4
Wilderness Point—*cape* ..... MN-6
Wilderness Point—*cape* ..... NY-2
Wilderness Ranch—*locale* ..... WY-8
Wilderness Road—*locale* ..... KY-4
Wilderness Rsvr—*reservoir* (2) ..... MT-8
*Wilderness Run* ..... VA-3
Wilderness Run Lake—*reservoir* ..... VA-3
**Wilderness Shores**—*pop pl* ..... TN-4
Wilderness State Park—*park* ..... MI-6
Wilderness Swamp—*swamp* ..... AL-4
Wilderness Tank—*reservoir* ..... AZ-5
Wilderness Trail—*trail* ..... NH-1
Wilderness Trail—*trail* ..... TX-5
Wilderness Trail—*trail* ..... VA-3
Wilderness Trail—*trail* ..... WV-2
*Wilderness Trailhead Campground* ..... UT-8
Wilderness Trails Ranch—*locale* ..... CO-8
**Wilderness Village**—*pop pl* ..... WA-9
Wilderness Waterway—*channel* ..... FL-3
Wilder Park—*park* (2) ..... IL-6
**Wilder Park**—*pop pl* ..... KY-4
Wilder Place—*locale* ..... CA-9
Wilder Playground—*park* ..... MN-6
Wilder Point—*cliff* ..... AZ-5
Wilder Point—*cliff* ..... TN-4
Wilder Pond—*lake* ..... NH-1
Wilder Pond—*lake* ..... NY-2
Wilder Post Office—*building* ..... TN-4
Wilder Quarters—*locale* ..... AL-4
Wilder Radar Bomb Scoring Site—*military* ..... ID-8
Wilder Ridge—*ridge* ..... CA-9
Wilder Ridge—*ridge* ..... MT-8
**Wilders**—*pop pl* ..... IN-6
**Wilders**—*pop pl* ..... KY-4
*Wilders Brook* ..... MA-1
Wilders Cem—*cemetery* ..... MS-4
Wilder Sch—*school* (2) ..... KY-4
Wilder Sch—*school* ..... MA-1
Wilder Sch—*school* ..... MI-6
Wilder Sch—*school* ..... MO-7
Wilder Sch—*school* ..... ND-7
Wilder Sch—*school* ..... SC-3
Wilder Sch—*school* ..... SD-7
Wilder Sch (historical)—*school* ..... TN-4
*Wilders Creek* ..... IN-6
Wilders Creek—*stream* ..... LA-4
**Wilders Grove**—*pop pl* ..... NC-3
Wilderson, John, House—*hist pl* ..... IN-6
Wilderson Cem—*cemetery* ..... OH-6
Wilders Pond—*lake* ..... MI-6
Wilders Pond—*reservoir* ..... GA-3
Wilder Spring—*spring* ..... AZ-5
Wilder Spring—*spring* ..... MO-7
Wilder Spring—*spring* ..... OR-9
Wilder Springs—*spring* ..... AZ-5
Wilders (Township of)—*fmr MCD* ..... NC-3
**Wildersville**—*pop pl* ..... TN-4
Wildersville Baptist Ch—*church* ..... TN-4
Wildersville (CCD)—*cens area* ..... TN-4
Wildersville Division—*civil* ..... TN-4
Wildersville Post Office—*building* ..... TN-4
Wildersville Sch (historical)—*school* ..... TN-4
Wilder-Swaim House—*hist pl* ..... OH-6
Wilder Swamp—*swamp* ..... FL-3
Wilder Swamp—*swamp* ..... MA-1
Wilder Swamp—*swamp* ..... PA-2
Wilder Tower—*pillar* ..... GA-3
Wilder Trail—*trail* ..... MT-8
Wilderville—*locale* ..... TX-5
**Wilderville**—*pop pl* ..... OR-9
Wilderville (CCD)—*cens area* ..... OR-9
Wilderville Cem—*cemetery* ..... OR-9
Wilderville Sch—*school* ..... OR-9
Wilder Vly—*swamp* ..... NY-2
Wilderwood Dam—*dam* ..... TN-4
Wilderwood Lake—*reservoir* ..... TN-4
Wilde Sch—*school* ..... MI-6
*Wilde Sch Number 79* ..... IN-6
*Wildes Corner* ..... RI-1
Wildes Corner—*locale* ..... RI-1
**Wildes Corner**—*pop pl* ..... ME-1
Wildes Creek—*stream* ..... NC-3
Wildes Creek—*stream* ..... WA-9
**Wildes District**—*pop pl* ..... ME-1
Wildes Knob—*summit* ..... NC-3
Wilde Tank—*reservoir* ..... NM-5
Wildey Cem—*cemetery* ..... MI-6
Wildey Cem—*cemetery* ..... MO-7
Wildey Sch—*school* ..... MI-6
**Wildeys (Lake Cora)**—*pop pl* ..... MI-6
Wildfell—*hist pl* ..... MD-2
Wildflower—*locale* ..... CA-9
Wild Flower and Bird Sanctuary in Mahoney Park—*hist pl* ..... IL-6
Wildflower Ditch—*canal* ..... CA-9
Wild Flower Gulch—*valley* ..... AZ-5
Wild Flower Mine—*mine* ..... AZ-5
Wild Flower Saddle—*gap* ..... AZ-5
**Wild Flower (subdivision)**—*pop pl* (2) ..... AZ-5
**Wildflower Subdivision**—*pop pl* ..... UT-8
Wild Fork Creek—*stream* ..... AL-4
*Wild Fork Fire Tower* ..... AL-4
Wildfork (historical)—*locale* ..... AL-4
Wild Fork Lookout Tower—*locale* ..... AL-4
*Wildfowl Bay* ..... MI-6
Wild Fowl Bay—*bay* ..... MI-6
Wild Fowl Bay State Park—*park* ..... MI-6
Wildfowl Lake—*lake* ..... MI-6
*Wildfowl Point* ..... MI-6
Wild Fowl Point—*cape* ..... MI-6
*Wild Fowl Pond* ..... PA-2
Wild Fowl Pond—*reservoir* ..... PA-2
Wild Gal Spring—*spring* ..... OR-9
Wild Geese Nest Spring—*spring* ..... AZ-5
Wild Glen—*flat* ..... KS-7
Wild Goat Canyon—*valley* ..... NM-5
Wild Goat Cave—*cave* ..... AL-4
Wild Goat Cove—*basin* ..... AL-4
Wild Goat Creek—*stream* ..... ID-8
*Wild Goose* ..... TN-4
Wild Goose—*locale* ..... WA-9
Wild Goose Branch—*stream* ..... AR-4
Wild Goose Campground—*locale* ..... ID-8
Wild Goose Canyon—*valley* ..... UT-8
Wild Goose Club—*other* ..... ME-1
Wild Goose Country Club—*other* ..... CA-9
*Wildgoose Creek* ..... AL-4
Wild Goose Creek—*stream* ..... AL-4
Wild Goose Creek—*stream* ..... AK-9
Wild Goose Creek—*stream* ..... AR-4
Wild Goose Creek—*stream* ..... UT-8
Wild Goose Gulch—*valley* ..... CA-9
Wild Goose Island—*island* ..... LA-4
Wild Goose Island—*island* ..... MT-8
Wild Goose Lagoon—*lake* ..... FL-3
Wild Goose Lake—*lake* ..... MI-6
Wild Goose Lake—*lake* ..... UT-8
Wild Goose Lake—*lake* ..... WI-6
Wild Goose Ledge—*bench* ..... RI-1
Wild Goose Pipeline—*canal* ..... AK-9
Wild Goose Point—*cape* ..... RI-1
**Wild Goose Point**—*pop pl* ..... RI-1
Wild Goose Pond—*lake* ..... NH-1
*Wild Goose Post Office* ..... TN-4
*Wild Goose Rapids* ..... ID-8
Wild Goose Rapids—*rapids* ..... ID-8
Wild Goose Rapids—*rapids* ..... WA-9
Wild Goose Sch—*school* ..... IL-6
Wild Goose Spring—*spring* (2) ..... UT-8
Wild Gulch—*valley* ..... CA-9
Wildhack's Grocery Store-Post Office—*hist pl* ..... CO-8
*Wildham* ..... TN-4
Wildham Post Office (historical)—*building* ..... TN-4
Wild Harbor—*cove* ..... MA-1
Wild Harbor River—*stream* ..... MA-1
Wild Heron—*hist pl* ..... GA-3
Wildhide Gulch—*valley* ..... CA-9
Wild Hog Basin—*basin* ..... AZ-5
Wild Hog Basin—*basin* ..... MT-8
Wild Hog Bluff—*cliff* ..... MO-7
Wild Hog Butte—*summit* ..... MT-8
Wild Hog Canyon—*valley* ..... AZ-5
Wild Hog Canyon—*valley* (3) ..... CA-9
Wild Hog Canyon—*valley* ..... TX-5
Wild Hog Coulee—*valley* ..... MT-8
Wild Hog Creek—*stream* ..... CA-9
Wildhog Creek—*stream* ..... GA-3
Wild Hog Creek—*stream* ..... MT-8
Wild Hog Creek—*stream* ..... NC-3
Wild Hog Creek—*stream* ..... OK-5
Wild Hog Creek—*stream* ..... SC-3
Wild Hog Hill—*summit* ..... CA-9
Wild Hog Hollow—*valley* ..... AL-4
Wild Hog Hollow—*valley* ..... AR-4
Wild Hog Hollow—*valley* ..... TN-4
Wild Hog Lake—*lake* ..... TX-5
Wild Hog Mtn—*summit* ..... AZ-5
Wild Hog Mtn—*summit* ..... AR-4
Wild Hog Ridge—*ridge* ..... GA-3
Wild Hog Ridge—*ridge* ..... KY-4
Wild Hog Spring—*spring* ..... MT-8
Wild Hog Swamp—*swamp* ..... AL-4
Wild Hollow—*valley* ..... KY-4
Wild Homestead—*locale* ..... MT-8
Wild Homestead (abandoned)—*stream* ..... MT-8
Wild Hope Mine—*mine* ..... ID-8
Wild Horn Cem—*cemetery* ..... GA-3
Wildhorn Ranch—*locale* ..... CO-8
*Wild Horse* ..... KS-7
Wild Horse—*locale* ..... NV-8
Wildhorse—*locale* ..... OK-5
Wild Horse—*locale* ..... TX-5
**Wild Horse**—*pop pl* (2) ..... CO-8
**Wild Horse**—*pop pl* ..... OK-5
Wild Horse—*summit* ..... OR-9
Wild Horse, The—*area* ..... SC-3
Wild Horse Airp—*airport* ..... NV-8
Wild Horse Arroyo—*stream* ..... CO-8
Wild Horse Arroyo—*stream* ..... NM-5
Wild Horse Bar—*bar* ..... AL-4
Wild Horse Bar (historical)—*bar* ..... UT-8
Wild Horse Bar (inundated)—*bar* ..... UT-8
Wildhorse Basin—*basin* ..... AZ-5
Wild Horse Basin—*basin* (3) ..... NV-8
Wildhorse Basin—*basin* ..... OR-9
Wildhorse Basin—*basin* ..... OR-9
Wild Horse Basin—*basin* ..... UT-8
Wildhorse Basin—*basin* ..... WY-8
Wild Horse Basin—*basin* ..... WY-8
Wildhorse Basin Rsvr—*reservoir* ..... OR-9
Wildhorse Bayou—*gut* ..... LA-4
Wildhorse Bayou—*stream* ..... AR-4
Wild Horse Bench—*bench* ..... UT-8
*Wildhorse Bill Spring* ..... NV-8
Wildhorse Branch—*stream* ..... SC-3
Wild Horse Branch—*stream* ..... TX-5
Wild Horse Butte—*summit* ..... ID-8
Wildhorse Butte—*summit* ..... ID-8
Wild Horse Butte—*summit* ..... ID-8
Wild Horse Butte—*summit* (3) ..... MT-8
Wild Horse Butte—*summit* ..... NE-7
Wild Horse Butte—*summit* (2) ..... OR-9
Wild Horse Butte—*summit* ..... UT-8
Wild Horse Butte—*summit* (4) ..... WY-8
Wild Horse Butte Oil Field—*oilfield* ..... WY-8
Wildhorse Campground—*locale* ..... ID-8
Wildhorse Campground—*locale* ..... OR-9
*Wild Horse Canyon* ..... AZ-5
*Wild Horse Canyon* ..... NV-8
Wild Horse Canyon—*valley* (2) ..... AZ-5
Wildhorse Canyon—*valley* ..... AZ-5
Wildhorse Canyon—*valley* ..... CA-9
Wild Horse Canyon—*valley* ..... CA-9
Wildhorse Canyon—*valley* ..... CA-9
Wild Horse Canyon—*valley* ..... CA-9
Wildhorse Canyon—*valley* (4) ..... CA-9
Wild Horse Canyon—*valley* (2) ..... CA-9
Wildhorse Canyon—*valley* ..... CO-8
Wild Horse Canyon—*valley* ..... CO-8
Wildhorse Canyon—*valley* ..... KS-7
Wild Horse Canyon—*valley* ..... NE-7
Wildhorse Canyon—*valley* (2) ..... NE-7
Wild Horse Canyon—*valley* ..... NE-7
Wildhorse Canyon—*valley* (3) ..... NV-8
Wild Horse Canyon—*valley* (3) ..... NV-8
Wildhorse Canyon—*valley* ..... NV-8
Wild Horse Canyon—*valley* ..... NM-5
Wildhorse Canyon—*valley* ..... NM-5
Wild Horse Canyon—*valley* (4) ..... NM-5
Wildhorse Canyon—*valley* ..... NM-5
Wild Horse Canyon—*valley* ..... NM-5
Wild Horse Canyon—*valley* ..... OK-5
Wildhorse Canyon—*valley* (2) ..... OR-9
Wild Horse Canyon—*valley* ..... TX-5
Wildhorse Canyon—*valley* ..... UT-8
Wild Horse Canyon—*valley* ..... UT-8
Wildhorse Canyon—*valley* ..... UT-8
Wild Horse Canyon—*valley* ..... UT-8
Wildhorse Canyon—*valley* ..... UT-8
Wild Horse Canyon—*valley* ..... UT-8
Wildhorse Canyon—*valley* ..... WY-8
Wild Horse Canyon Mine—*mine* ..... NV-8
Wildhorse Canyon Obsidian Quarry—*hist pl* ..... UT-8
Wild Horse Canyon Spring—*spring* ..... NV-8
Wild Horse Cem—*cemetery* ..... KS-7
Wildhorse Ch—*church* ..... NE-7
Wild Horse Cienega—*flat* ..... AZ-5
Wild Horse Corral—*locale* ..... AZ-5
Wild Horse Corral—*locale* ..... CA-9
Wild Horse Corral—*locale* ..... UT-8
Wild Horse Corral—*locale* ..... WA-9
Wild Horse Corral—*locale* ..... WY-8
Wild Horse Corrals—*locale* ..... ID-8
Wild Horse Coulee—*valley* ..... MT-8
*Wildhorse Creek* ..... CA-9
*Wild Horse Creek* ..... CO-8
*Wildhorse Creek* ..... ID-8
*Wild Horse Creek* ..... KS-7
*Wildhorse Creek* ..... MS-4
*Wild Horse Creek* ..... MT-8
*Wildhorse Creek* ..... NE-7
*Wildhorse Creek* ..... OK-5
*Wild Horse Creek* ..... OR-9
*Wild Horse Creek* ..... WA-9
Wildhorse Creek—*stream* (3) ..... AK-9
Wild Horse Creek—*stream* ..... AR-4
Wildhorse Creek—*stream* ..... CA-9
Wild Horse Creek—*stream* ..... CA-9
Wildhorse Creek—*stream* ..... CA-9
Wild Horse Creek—*stream* ..... CA-9
Wildhorse Creek—*stream* ..... CA-9
Wild Horse Creek—*stream* (3) ..... CO-8
Wildhorse Creek—*stream* (2) ..... CO-8
Wild Horse Creek—*stream* (2) ..... CO-8
Wildhorse Creek—*stream* (4) ..... ID-8
Wildhorse Creek—*stream* (2) ..... ID-8
Wild Horse Creek—*stream* (7) ..... KS-7
Wildhorse Creek—*stream* ..... MS-4
Wildhorse Creek—*stream* ..... MO-7
Wild Horse Creek—*stream* (3) ..... MT-8
Wild Horse Creek—*stream* ..... NE-7
Wildhorse Creek—*stream* ..... NV-8
Wild Horse Creek—*stream* (2) ..... NV-8
Wild Horse Creek—*stream* (2) ..... NM-5
Wildhorse Creek—*stream* ..... OK-5
Wild Horse Creek—*stream* (3) ..... OK-5
Wildhorse Creek—*stream* ..... OK-5
Wild Horse Creek—*stream* ..... OK-5
Wildhorse Creek—*stream* (4) ..... OK-5
Wild Horse Creek—*stream* ..... OK-5
Wildhorse Creek—*stream* (2) ..... OK-5
Wild Horse Creek—*stream* ..... OK-5
Wildhorse Creek—*stream* (5) ..... OK-5
Wild Horse Creek—*stream* (2) ..... OR-9
Wildhorse Creek—*stream* (2) ..... OR-9
Wild Horse Creek—*stream* ..... OR-9
Wildhorse Creek—*stream* (2) ..... OR-9
Wild Horse Creek—*stream* ..... SD-7
Wild Horse Creek—*stream* (2) ..... TX-5
Wildhorse Creek—*stream* ..... TX-5
Wild Horse Creek—*stream* ..... TX-5
Wildhorse Creek—*stream* (2) ..... UT-8
Wild Horse Creek—*stream* ..... UT-8
Wildhorse Creek—*stream* (2) ..... WA-9
Wild Horse Creek—*stream* ..... WA-9
Wild Horse Creek—*stream* (4) ..... WY-8
Wild Horse Crossing—*locale* ..... NV-8
Wild Horse Crossing Natl Forest Campground—*locale* ..... NV-8
Wildhorse Dam—*dam* ..... NE-7
Wild Horse Dam—*dam* ..... NV-8
Wild Horse Ditch—*canal* ..... CO-8
Wild Horse Divide—*gap* ..... ID-8
Wildhorse Drain—*canal* ..... NE-7
*Wildhorse Draw* ..... TX-5
Wild Horse Draw—*valley* (2) ..... CO-8
Wildhorse Draw—*valley* ..... CO-8
Wild Horse Draw—*valley* ..... KS-7
Wild Horse Draw—*valley* ..... NE-7
Wild Horse Draw—*valley* ..... NV-8
Wildhorse Draw—*valley* ..... TX-5
Wild Horse Draw—*valley* ..... TX-5
Wild Horse Draw—*valley* (2) ..... UT-8
Wild Horse Draw—*valley* (3) ..... WY-8
Wildhorse Draw—*valley* ..... WY-8
Wild Horse Draw—*valley* ..... WY-8
Wildhorse Falls—*falls* ..... ID-8
Wildhorse Falls Rsvr—*reservoir* ..... OR-9
Wild Horse Flat—*flat* ..... CA-9
Wildhorse Flat—*flat* ..... NV-8
Wild Horse Flats—*flat* (2) ..... NE-7
Wild Horse Flats—*flat* ..... WY-8
Wildhorse Flats—*flat* ..... WY-8
Wild Horse Gap—*gap* ..... OK-5
Wildhorse Guard Station—*locale* ..... ID-8
Wild Horse Heaven—*summit* ..... WY-8
Wild Horse Hill—*summit* ..... AZ-5
Wild Horse Hill—*summit* ..... NE-7
Wildhorse Hill—*summit* ..... NE-7
Wild Horse Hill—*summit* ..... WA-9
Wild Horse Hill—*summit* ..... WY-8
Wild Horse (historical)—*locale* ..... KS-7
Wildhorse Hollow—*valley* ..... MO-7
Wildhorse Hollow—*valley* ..... OK-5
Wild Horse Island—*island* ..... MT-8
*Wild Horse Lake* ..... MT-8
*Wildhorse Lake* ..... NE-7
Wild Horse Lake—*cens area* ..... MT-8
Wildhorse Lake—*flat* ..... OR-9
Wildhorse Lake—*lake* ..... AZ-5
Wild Horse Lake—*lake* ..... CO-8
Wildhorse Lake—*lake* (2) ..... ID-8
Wild Horse Lake—*lake* ..... ID-8
Wildhorse Lake—*lake* ..... KS-7
Wild Horse Lake—*lake* ..... KS-7
Wildhorse Lake—*lake* ..... KS-7
Wild Horse Lake—*lake* (2) ..... MT-8
Wild Horse Lake—*lake* ..... NE-7
Wild Horse Lake—*lake* ..... OK-5
Wildhorse Lake—*lake* ..... OR-9
Wildhorse Lake—*lake* ..... SC-3
Wild Horse Lake—*lake* ..... WY-8
Wild Horse Lake—*reservoir* ..... KS-7
Wildhorse Lake Campground—*locale* ..... ID-8
Wildhorse Lake Campground—*park* ..... AZ-5
Wildhorse Lake Rsvr—*reservoir* ..... OR-9
Wildhorse Lakes—*lake* ..... ID-8
Wildhorse Lookout—*locale* ..... OR-9
Wild Horse Meadow—*flat* ..... CA-9
Wildhorse Meadow—*flat* ..... OR-9
Wild Horse Meadow—*flat* ..... WY-8
Wildhorse Meadows—*flat* ..... CA-9
*Wild Horse Mesa* ..... UT-8
Wild Horse Mesa—*bench* ..... NM-5
Wild Horse Mesa—*summit* (2) ..... AZ-5
Wild Horse Mesa—*summit* ..... CA-9
Wildhorse Mesa—*summit* ..... CO-8
Wild Horse Mesa—*summit* (2) ..... NM-5
Wildhorse Mesa—*summit* ..... NM-5
Wild Horse Mesa—*summit* ..... NM-5
Wildhorse Mine—*mine* ..... AZ-5
Wild Horse Mine—*mine* ..... CO-8
Wildhorse Mine—*mine* (2) ..... NV-8
Wildhorse Mines—*mine* ..... ID-8
Wildhorse Mtn—*summit* ..... AZ-5
Wild Horse Mtn—*summit* (2) ..... CA-9
Wild Horse Mtn—*summit* ..... ID-8
Wild Horse Mtn—*summit* (3) ..... MT-8
Wild Horse Mtn—*summit* ..... NV-8
Wildhorse Mtn—*summit* (4) ..... OK-5
Wildhorse Mtn—*summit* ..... OR-9
Wildhorse Mtn—*summit* (2) ..... TX-5
Wild Horse Mtn—*summit* ..... TX-5
Wildhorse Mtn—*summit* ..... TX-5
Wildhorse Mtn—*summit* ..... UT-8
Wild Horse Mtn—*summit* ..... WY-8
Wild Horse NE Oil Field—*oilfield* ..... OK-5
Wild Horse Oil Field—*oilfield* ..... OK-5
Wild Horse Opening—*flat* ..... CA-9
Wildhorse Park—*flat* ..... AZ-5
Wild Horse Park—*flat* ..... CO-8
Wild Horse Park—*flat* ..... NM-5
Wild Horse Parks—*flat* ..... MT-8
Wild Horse Pass—*gap* (2) ..... MT-8
Wild Horse Pass—*gap* ..... NV-8
Wildhorse Pass—*gap* (2) ..... NV-8
Wild Horse Pass—*gap* ..... UT-8
Wild Horse Pasture—*flat* ..... NV-8
Wildhorse Peak—*summit* ..... CA-9
Wild Horse Peak—*summit* (2) ..... CA-9
Wildhorse Peak—*summit* ..... CO-8
Wild Horse Peak—*summit* ..... UT-8
Wild Horse Pete Coulee—*valley* ..... MT-8
Wild Horse Point—*cliff* (2) ..... CO-8
Wild Horse Point—*summit* ..... MT-8
Wild Horse Port of Entry—*locale* ..... MT-8
Wild Horse Prairie—*area* ..... MS-4
Wildhorse Prairie—*flat* ..... OK-5
Wild Horse Prairie—*flat* ..... OK-5
Wildhorse Prairie—*flat* ..... OR-9
Wild Horse Ranch—*locale* ..... AZ-5
Wild Horse Ranch—*locale* ..... NV-8
Wild Horse Range—*range* ..... NV-8
Wildhorse Rapids—*rapids* ..... ID-8
Wildhorse Rapids—*rapids* ..... OR-9
Wild Horse Rapids—*rapids* ..... UT-8
Wild Horse Ridge—*ridge* (2) ..... CA-9
Wild Horse Ridge—*ridge* ..... CO-8
Wild Horse Ridge—*ridge* ..... ID-8
Wild Horse Ridge—*ridge* (2) ..... MT-8
Wildhorse Ridge—*ridge* (2) ..... OR-9
Wild Horse Ridge—*ridge* (2) ..... UT-8
Wildhorse River—*stream* ..... ID-8
Wild Horse Rsvr—*reservoir* (2) ..... CA-9
Wild Horse Rsvr—*reservoir* (2) ..... CO-8
Wild Horse Rsvr—*reservoir* ..... MT-8
Wildhorse Rsvr—*reservoir* ..... NV-8
Wildhorse Rsvr—*reservoir* (2) ..... OR-9
Wild Horse Rsvr—*reservoir* (2) ..... WY-8
Wildhorse Saddle—*gap* ..... ID-8
Wild Horse Sch—*school* ..... KS-7
Wild Horse Sch—*school* (2) ..... NE-7
*Wild Horse Siding* ..... TX-5
Wild Horse Slope—*summit* ..... WY-8
Wild Horse Slough—*gut* ..... TX-5
*Wildhorse Spring* ..... AZ-5
*Wild Horse Spring* ..... NV-8
Wild Horse Spring—*spring* (2) ..... AZ-5
Wildhorse Spring—*spring* ..... AZ-5
Wild Horse Spring—*spring* (2) ..... AZ-5
Wildhorse Spring—*spring* ..... AZ-5
Wild Horse Spring—*spring* (2) ..... AZ-5
Wild Horse Spring—*spring* ..... CA-9
Wildhorse Spring—*spring* ..... CA-9
Wild Horse Spring—*spring* (2) ..... CA-9
Wild Horse Spring—*spring* ..... CO-8
Wild Horse Spring—*spring* ..... ID-8
Wildhorse Spring—*spring* ..... ID-8
Wild Horse Spring—*spring* ..... ID-8
Wild Horse Spring—*spring* ..... MT-8
Wild Horse Spring—*spring* ..... NV-8
Wildhorse Spring—*spring* (2) ..... NV-8
Wild Horse Spring—*spring* (2) ..... NV-8
Wildhorse Spring—*spring* ..... NV-8
Wild Horse Spring—*spring* (3) ..... NV-8
Wildhorse Spring—*spring* (7) ..... OR-9
Wildhorse Spring—*spring* ..... TX-5
Wildhorse Spring—*spring* (2) ..... UT-8
Wild Horse Spring—*spring* ..... UT-8
Wildhorse Spring—*spring* ..... UT-8
Wild Horse Spring—*spring* (2) ..... UT-8
Wildhorse Spring—*spring* ..... UT-8
Wildhorse Spring—*spring* ..... WA-9
Wild Horse Spring—*spring* (2) ..... WA-9
Wild Horse Spring—*spring* (2) ..... WY-8
Wild Horse Spring Ruins—*locale* ..... ID-8
Wildhorse Springs—*spring* ..... ID-8
Wild Horse Springs—*spring* ..... WY-8
Wild Horse Spring (Site)—*other* ..... NE-7
*Wild Horse State Park* ..... NV-8
Wild Horse State Rec Area—*park* ..... NV-8
Wild Horse Table—*summit* ..... ID-8
*Wildhorse Tank* ..... TX-5
Wildhorse Tank—*reservoir* (3) ..... AZ-5
Wild Horse Tank—*reservoir* ..... AZ-5
Wildhorse Tank—*reservoir* ..... AZ-5
Wild Horse Tank—*reservoir* (4) ..... AZ-5
Wildhorse Tank—*reservoir* ..... AZ-5
Wild Horse Tank—*reservoir* ..... AZ-5
Wildhorse Tank—*reservoir* ..... NM-5
Wild Horse Tank—*reservoir* ..... NM-5
Wildhorse Tank—*reservoir* ..... TX-5
Wild Horse Tank—*reservoir* ..... TX-5
Wildhorse Tit—*summit* ..... CO-8
**Wildhorse Township**—*pop pl* ..... KS-7
Wildhorse Trail—*trail* ..... OK-5
Wild Horse Trap Mesa—*summit* ..... AZ-5
Wild Horse Valley—*valley* (2) ..... CA-9
Wildhorse Valley—*valley* ..... NE-7
Wild Horse Valley—*valley* (2) ..... NE-7
Wild Horse Valley—*valley* ..... NV-8
Wildhorse Valley—*valley* ..... OR-9
Wild Horse Valley Ranch*—*locale* ..... NE-7
Wild Horse Valley Sch—*school* ..... NE-7
*Wild Horse Wash* ..... AZ-5
Wildhorse Wash—*stream* ..... AZ-5
Wildhorse Well—*well* ..... NV-8
Wildhorse Well—*well* ..... NM-5
Wild Horse Windmill—*locale* (2) ..... NM-5
*Wildhurst* ..... TX-5
Wild Hurst—*locale* ..... TX-5
**Wildie**—*pop pl* ..... KY-4
Wild Indian Spring—*spring* ..... NV-8
**Wilding**—*pop pl* ..... WV-2
Wild Irishman Bend—*bend* ..... CA-9
Wild Irishman Gulch—*valley* ..... SD-7
Wild Irishman Mine—*mine* ..... CO-8
Wild Irish Rsvr—*reservoir* ..... WY-8
Wild Island—*island* ..... LA-4
Wild Island—*locale* ..... FL-3
Wild Lake—*lake* (2) ..... AK-9
Wild Lake—*lake* ..... CA-9
Wild Lake—*reservoir* ..... CA-9
Wildlick Branch—*stream* ..... KY-4
Wildlife Cabin—*locale* ..... VA-3
**Wildlife Cove Village**—*pop pl* ..... TN-4
Wildlife (historical P.O.)—*locale* ..... IA-7
Wildlife Lake—*lake* ..... GA-3
Wildlife Lake—*lake* ..... MI-6
Wildlife Landing—*locale* ..... NC-3
Wildlife Marsh Pond—*reservoir* ..... NY-2
Wildlife Pond—*reservoir* ..... GA-3
Wildlife Rsvr—*reservoir* ..... MT-8
Wildlife Tank Number Two—*reservoir* ..... AZ-5
Wildman, E. A., & Co. Tobacco Warehouse—*hist pl* ..... CT-1
Wildman Cave—*cave* ..... TN-4
Wildman Cove—*valley* ..... TN-4
Wildman Lake—*lake* ..... AK-9
Wildman Meadow—*flat* ..... CA-9
Wild Man Mesa—*summit* ..... AZ-5
Wild Mans Canyon—*valley* ..... CA-9
*Wild Mans Island* ..... AL-4
Wildmans Island—*island* ..... AL-4
Wildmans Landing—*locale* ..... CT-1
Wildman Tank—*reservoir* ..... AZ-5
Wild Mare Lake—*lake* ..... NE-7
Wildmead Cem—*cemetery* ..... KS-7
**Wild Meadow**—*pop pl* ..... WV-2
Wild Meadow Brook—*stream* ..... NH-1
Wild Meadow Ch—*church* ..... WV-2
Wild Meadow Run—*stream* ..... WV-2
Wild Meadows—*flat* ..... PA-2
Wildmere, Lake—*lake* ..... FL-3
Wildmere House—*locale* ..... NY-2
Wild Monkey Trap—*cliff* ..... AZ-5
Wild Mtn—*summit* (2) ..... CO-8
Wild Mtn—*summit* ..... MN-6
Wild Mtn—*summit* ..... UT-8
*Wildmule Peak* ..... UT-8
Wild Mule Spring—*spring* ..... NM-5
Wild Neck—*cape* ..... GA-3
Wildness, Lake—*lake* ..... MT-8
Wild Nut Spring—*spring* ..... AZ-5
Wild Oat Canyon—*valley* (2) ..... CA-9
Wild Oat Creek—*stream* ..... CA-9
Wild Oat Dam—*dam* ..... CA-9
Wild Oat Mesa—*summit* ..... CO-8
Wild Oat Mountain—*ridge* ..... NV-8
Wild Oat Peak—*summit* ..... CA-9
Wild Oat Springs—*spring* ..... CA-9
Wild Olive Spring—*spring* ..... NM-5
**Wildomar**—*pop pl* ..... CA-9
Wildomar Truck Trail—*trail* ..... CA-9
Wildon Draw—*valley* ..... KS-7
Wildon Grove Ch—*church* ..... VA-3
*Wild Onion Creek* ..... ND-7
Wild Onion Hollow—*valley* ..... MO-7

Wilkes Area Poultry Association Laboratory—*building* NC-3
Wilkes Art Gallery—*building* NC-3
**Wilkes-Barre**—*pop pl* PA-2
Wilkes-Barre City—*civil* PA-2
Wilkes-Barre Day Sch—*school* PA-2
Wilkes Barre Filtration Plant—*other* PA-2
Wilkes-Barre General Hosp—*hospital* PA-2
Wilkes-Barre Golf Course—*locale* PA-2
*Wilkes-Barre Interchange* PA-2
Wilkes-Barre Mtn—*summit* PA-2
Wilkes-Barre/Scranton International Airp—*airport* PA-2
Wilkes-Barre Township—*CDP* PA-2
Wilkes Barre Township Elem Sch—*school* PA-2
**Wilkes-Barre (Township of)**—*pop pl* PA-2
Wilkes Barre Tunnels—*mine* CO-8
Wilkes-Barre Wyoming Valley Airp—*airport* PA-2
Wilkes Bayou—*stream* MS-4
**Wilkesboro**—*pop pl* NC-3
**Wilkesboro**—*pop pl* OR-9
Wilkesboro Community Coll—*school* NC-3
*Wilkesboro Elem Sch* NC-3
Wilkesboro Presbyterian Church—*hist pl* NC-3
*Wilkesboro Reservoir* NC-3
Wilkesboro Sch—*school* NC-3
Wilkesboro-Smithey Hotel—*hist pl* NC-3
Wilkesboro (Township of)—*fmr MCD* NC-3
Wilkes Branch—*stream* NC-3
Wilkes Branch—*stream* SC-3
Wilkes Branch—*stream* TX-5
*Wilkesburg* SC-3
Wilkesburg Post Office (historical)—*building* TN-4
Wilkes Cabin—*locale* WY-8
Wilkes Campsite—*hist pl* HI-9
Wilkes Camp (Site)—*locale* HI-9
*Wilkes Career Education Center* NC-3
Wilkes Cem—*cemetery* (3) GA-3
Wilkes Cem—*cemetery* TN-4
Wilkes Cem—*cemetery* TX-5
Wilkes Central HS—*school* NC-3
Wilkes Chapel—*church* SC-3
Wilkes County—*civil* NC-3
**Wilkes (County)**—*pop pl* GA-3
Wilkes County Airp—*airport* NC-3
Wilkes County Courthouse—*hist pl* GA-3
Wilkes County Courthouse—*hist pl* NC-3
Wilkes County Jaycees Clubhouse—*building* NC-3
Wilkes Cove—*valley* NC-3
Wilkes Creek—*stream* AL-4
Wilkes Creek—*stream* MI-6
Wilkes Creek—*stream* MO-7
Wilkes Creek—*stream* MT-8
Wilkes Crossroads—*locale* SC-3
*Wilkes Elementary School* AL-4
Wilkes General Hosp—*hospital* NC-3
Wilkes Hills—*range* WA-9
Wilkes Hollow—*valley* TN-4
Wilkes Island—*island* MP-9
Wilkes Knob—*summit* NC-3
Wilkes Lake—*lake* MI-6
Wilkes Lake—*reservoir* NC-3
Wilkes Landing—*locale* (2) NC-3
Wilkes Ledge—*rock* MA-1
Wilkes Mall—*locale* NC-3
Wilkes Mill (historical)—*locale* MS-4
Wilkes Millpond—*reservoir* SC-3
**Wilkeson**—*pop pl* WA-9
*Wilkeson Creek* AL-4
Wilkeson Creek—*stream* WA-9
Wilkeson Sch—*hist pl* WA-9
**Wilkes Park (subdivision)**—*pop pl* AL-4
Wilkes Peak—*summit* AK-9
*Wilkes Pond* CT-1
Wilkes Powerplant—*other* TX-5
Wilkes Range—*range* AK-9
Wilkes-Rockwood—*CDP* OR-9
Wilkes Sch—*school* AL-4
Wilkes Sch—*school* OR-9
Wilkes Spring—*spring* MT-8
**Wilkes Spur**—*pop pl* TX-5
Wilkes Store—*locale* AL-4
**Wilkes Subdivision**—*pop pl* UT-8
Wilkes Tank—*reservoir* AZ-5
Wilkes Temple—*church* NC-3
Wilkes T Thrasher Bridge—*bridge* TN-4
Wilkes T Thrasher Sch—*school* TN-4
**Wilkesville**—*pop pl* OH-6
**Wilkesville (Township of)**—*pop pl* OH-6
Wilkes Windmill—*locale* NM-5
Wilkey Cem—*cemetery* IA-7
Wilkey Ch—*church* NC-3
Wilkey Creek—*stream* GA-3
Wilkey Creek—*stream* MO-7
Wilkey Ranch—*locale* TX-5
Wilk Gulch—*valley* CA-9
Wilkie—*locale* MO-7
**Wilkie**—*pop pl* MO-7
Wilkie Branch—*stream* TN-4
Wilkie Bridge—*bridge* GA-3
*Wilkie Creek* VA-3
Wilkie Drain—*canal* MI-6
*Wilkie High School* IN-6
Wilkie Intake Rsvr—*reservoir* NY-2
Wilkie Lake Dam—*dam* MS-4
Wilkie Post Office (historical)—*building* AL-4
*Wilkie Ranch* TX-5
Wilkie Ridge—*ridge* VA-3
Wilkie Rsvr—*reservoir* NY-2
Wilkies Ch—*church* NC-3
Wilkie Slough—*gut* SD-7
Wilkies Point—*cape* FL-3
Wilkie Well—*well* TX-5
Wilkin Cem—*cemetery* OH-6
**Wilkin (County)**—*pop pl* MN-6
Wilkin County Courthouse—*hist pl* MN-6
Wilkin Ranch—*locale* TX-5
Wilkin Ridge—*ridge* UT-8
*Wilkins* (2) AR-4
Wilkins—*locale* AR-4
Wilkins—*locale* IA-7
Wilkins—*locale* OH-6
Wilkins—*locale* TX-5
**Wilkins**—*pop pl* NV-8
**Wilkins**—*pop pl* OR-9
**Wilkins**—*pop pl* SC-3
Wilkins, Lake—*lake* FL-3
Wilkins Air Force Station—*locale* OH-6
**Wilkins Beach**—*pop pl* VA-3
Wilkins Bluff—*cliff* NC-3
Wilkins Branch—*stream* MS-4
Wilkins Branch—*stream* TN-4
Wilkins Bridge—*bridge* NC-3
*Wilkins Bridge Creek* VA-3
Wilkins Brook—*stream* NY-2
Wilkins Brook—*stream* VT-1
**Wilkinsburg**—*pop pl* PA-2
Wilkinsburg Borough—*civil* PA-2
Wilkinsburg Junior-Senior HS—*school* PA-2
Wilkins Cabin—*locale* UT-8
*Wilkins Canal* LA-4
Wilkins Canal—*canal* ID-8
Wilkins Canyon—*valley* AZ-5
Wilkins Canyon—*valley* CA-9
*Wilkins Cem* MS-4
Wilkins Cem—*cemetery* (2) AL-4
Wilkins Cem—*cemetery* GA-3
Wilkins Cem—*cemetery* (2) IL-6
Wilkins Cem—*cemetery* KY-4
Wilkins Cem—*cemetery* (7) MS-4
Wilkins Cem—*cemetery* NE-7
Wilkins Cem—*cemetery* (2) TN-4
Wilkins Ch—*church* (2) MS-4
Wilkins Ch—*church* PA-2
Wilkins Chapel—*church* MS-4
Wilkins Chapel (historical)—*church* MS-4
**Wilkins Corners**—*pop pl* OH-6
Wilkins Creek—*stream* AL-4
Wilkins Creek—*stream* AK-9
Wilkins Creek—*stream* CO-8
Wilkins Creek—*stream* KY-4
Wilkins Creek—*stream* MI-6
Wilkins Creek—*stream* (2) MS-4
Wilkins Creek—*stream* NY-2
Wilkins Creek—*stream* NC-3
Wilkins Creek—*stream* (3) OR-9
Wilkins Creek—*stream* TX-5
Wilkins Creek—*stream* (2) VA-3
Wilkins Drain—*canal* MI-6
*Wilkins Elementary School* MS-4
*Wilkins Ferry* NC-3
**Wilkins Four Corners**—*pop pl* MA-1
Wilkins Gulch—*valley* CA-9
Wilkins Gulch—*valley* (2) ID-8
Wilkins Hill—*summit* NC-3
Wilkins House—*hist pl* GA-3
Wilkins House—*hist pl* TX-5
*Wilkins Island* WA-9
Wilkins Island—*area* MO-7
Wilkins Island—*island* ID-8
Wilkins Lagoon Natl Mngmt Area—*swamp* NE-7
Wilkins Lake—*lake* AR-4
Wilkins Lake—*lake* IL-6
Wilkins Lake—*lake* MN-6
Wilkins Mill Bridge—*hist pl* IN-6
Wilkins Mill Covered Bridge—*bridge* IN-6
Wilkins MS—*school* PA-2
Wilkins Mtn—*summit* AR-4
Wilkinson—*locale* IL-6
Wilkinson—*locale* MN-6
Wilkinson—*locale* MS-4
**Wilkinson**—*pop pl* IN-6
**Wilkinson**—*pop pl* MS-4
**Wilkinson**—*pop pl* NC-3
**Wilkinson**—*pop pl* TX-5
**Wilkinson**—*pop pl* WV-2
Wilkinson, Clyde, House—*hist pl* ID-8
Wilkinson, Thomas C., House—*hist pl* IA-7
Wilkinson, Winston, House—*hist pl* MS-4
Wilkinson Acad (historical)—*school* MS-4
Wilkinson Bar—*bar* AL-4
Wilkinson Bay—*bay* LA-4
Wilkinson Bayou—*gut* LA-4
Wilkinson Bluff—*cliff* FL-3
Wilkinson Branch—*stream* AL-4
Wilkinson Branch—*stream* MO-7
Wilkinson Brook—*stream* NH-1
Wilkinson Canal—*canal* LA-4
Wilkinson Canyon—*valley* CA-9
Wilkinson Canyon—*valley* WA-9
Wilkinson Cem—*cemetery* (2) GA-3
Wilkinson Cem—*cemetery* KY-4
Wilkinson Cem—*cemetery* MI-6
Wilkinson Cem—*cemetery* (3) MS-4
Wilkinson Cem—*cemetery* (3) MO-7
Wilkinson Cem—*cemetery* NC-3
Wilkinson Cem—*cemetery* (3) TN-4
Wilkinson Cem—*cemetery* (2) TX-5
Wilkinson Cem—*cemetery* VA-3
Wilkinson Community Airp—*airport* MS-4
Wilkinson Corner—*locale* TN-4
Wilkinson Coulee—*valley* MT-8
**Wilkinson (County)**—*pop pl* GA-3
**Wilkinson County**—*pop pl* MS-4
Wilkinson County Elem Sch—*school* MS-4
Wilkinson County Farm (historical)—*locale* MS-4
Wilkinson County HS—*school* MS-4
*Wilkinson Creek* NC-3
*Wilkinson Creek* TN-4
Wilkinson Creek—*stream* (2) CA-9
Wilkinson Creek—*stream* FL-3
Wilkinson Creek—*stream* MI-6
Wilkinson Creek—*stream* MO-7
Wilkinson Creek—*stream* (3) NC-3
Wilkinson Creek—*stream* OR-9
Wilkinson Creek—*stream* WY-8
Wilkinson Ditch—*canal* CO-8
Wilkinson Ditch—*canal* IN-6
Wilkinson-Dozier House—*hist pl* NC-3
Wilkinson Elem Sch—*school* FL-3
Wilkinson Female Acad (historical)—*school* MS-4
*Wilkinson Gap* VA-3
Wilkinson Garden Sch—*school* GA-3
Wilkinson Gun Club—*other* CA-9
Wilkinson-Hawkinson House—*hist pl* UT-8
Wilkinson Heights—*CDP* SC-3
Wilkinson Hollow—*valley* TN-4
Wilkinson Hollow—*valley* WV-2
Wilkinson House—*hist pl* PA-2
Wilkinson Island—*island* IL-6
Wilkinson Island—*island* MO-7
Wilkinson JHS—*school* MI-6
Wilkinson Knob—*summit* MO-7
Wilkinson Lake—*lake* GA-3
Wilkinson Lake—*lake* MI-6
Wilkinson Lake—*lake* MN-6
Wilkinson Lake—*lake* NE-7
Wilkinson Lake—*lake* PA-2
Wilkinson Lakes—*lake* NE-7
Wilkinson Lookout Tower—*locale* GA-3
Wilkinson Memorial Ch—*church* MS-4
**Wilkinson (Monitor)**—*pop pl* WV-2
Wilkinson Mtn—*summit* AL-4
Wilkinson Park—*park* NV-8
Wilkinson Place—*locale* WY-8
*Wilkinson Point* LA-4
Wilkinson Point—*cape* NC-3
Wilkinson Pond—*lake* AL-4
Wilkinson Pond—*reservoir* VA-3
Wilkinson Pond Slough—*stream* TN-4
Wilkinson Post Office (historical)—*building* MS-4
Wilkinson Ranch—*locale* CA-9
Wilkinson Ranch—*locale* NV-8
Wilkinson Ranch—*locale* NM-5
Wilkinson Ranch—*locale* WY-8
Wilkinson Ridge—*ridge* TN-4
Wilkinson Rsvr—*reservoir* UT-8
Wilkinson Saddle—*gap* WA-9
Wilkinson Saint Sch—*school* KY-4
Wilkinson Sch—*school* NC-3
Wilkinson Sch (historical)—*school* PA-2
Wilkinson School—*locale* WY-8
Wilkinson Seep—*spring* AZ-5
Wilkinson Sheep Sheds—*locale* WY-8
*Wilkinson's Island* IL-6
*Wilkinsons Landing* MS-4
Wilkinsons Pond—*reservoir* GA-3
Wilkinsons Store—*locale* VA-3
**Wilkinsons Subdivision**—*pop pl* UT-8
*Wilkinsons Ta* PA-2
Wilkinson-Swem Bldg—*hist pl* OR-9
Wilkinson Tank—*reservoir* NM-5
**Wilkinson Terrace**—*pop pl* VA-3
**Wilkinson (Town of)**—*pop pl* WI-6
**Wilkinson (Township of)**—*pop pl* MN-6
**Wilkinsonville**—*pop pl* MA-1
Wilkinson Wildlife Area—*park* IA-7
Wilkins Peak—*summit* WY-8
Wilkins Point—*cape* DE-2
Wilkins Point—*cape* NC-3
Wilkins Pond—*reservoir* VA-3
Wilkins Ranch—*locale* MT-8
Wilkins Ranch—*locale* (2) TX-5
Wilkins Ranch—*locale* WY-8
**Wilkins Run**—*pop pl* OH-6
Wilkins Run—*stream* OH-6
*Wilkins Sch* PA-2
Wilkins Sch—*school* IL-6
Wilkins Sch—*school* IA-7
Wilkins Sch—*school* KY-4
Wilkins Sch—*school* MI-6
Wilkins Sch—*school* MS-4
Wilkins Sch—*school* NH-1
Wilkins Sch—*school* TX-5
Wilkins Sch (historical)—*school* MS-4
Wilkins (Siding)—*locale* NV-8
Wilkins Slough—*gut* CA-9
Wilkins Slough Main Irrigation Canal—*canal* (2) CA-9
Wilkins Spring—*spring* MO-7
Wilkins Spring Branch—*stream* TN-4
Wilkins Station—*locale* NJ-2
Wilkins Strip Airp—*airport* IN-6
Wilkins Tank—*reservoir* TX-5
**Wilkinstown**—*pop pl* AL-4
**Wilkinstown**—*pop pl* TN-4
Wilkins Township—*CDP* PA-2
**Wilkins (Township of)**—*pop pl* PA-2
Wilkins Township Sch—*school* PA-2
Wilkins Trick Tank—*reservoir* AZ-5
**Wilkinsville**—*pop pl* SC-3
**Wilkinsville**—*pop pl* TN-4
Wilkins-Walston House—*building* NC-3
**Wilko Hill**—*pop pl* PA-2
Wilks Airp (historical)—*airport* TN-4
**Wilksburg**—*pop pl* SC-3
Wilks Cem—*cemetery* GA-3
Wilks Cem—*cemetery* (3) MS-4
Wilks Cem—*cemetery* TX-5
Wilks Cemeteries—*cemetery* TN-4
*Wilks Creek* KS-7
Wilks Creek—*stream* GA-3
Wilks Gulch—*valley* MT-8
Wilkshire Sch—*school* MI-6
Wilks Mtn—*summit* TX-5
Wilkson Cem—*cemetery* IA-7
Wilkson Cem—*cemetery* OH-6
Wilkson Creek—*stream* NJ-2
Wilkson Hollow—*valley* TN-4
Wilk Spring—*spring* AZ-5
*Will* OH-6
**Will**—*pop pl* VA-3
Will, Lake—*reservoir* AL-4
Will, Mount—*summit* ME-1
Willa—*locale* WA-9
**Willabet**—*pop pl* WV-2
Willaby Creek—*stream* WA-9
Willaby Creek Forest Camp—*locale* WA-9
Willa Cather Memorial Prairie—*hist pl* NE-7
**Willacoochee**—*pop pl* GA-3
Willacoochee (CCD)—*cens area* GA-3
Willacoochee Creek—*stream* FL-3
Willacoochee Creek—*stream* (2) GA-3
Willacoochee River—*stream* GA-3
Willacy Canal (elevated)—*canal* TX-5
**Willacy (County)**—*pop pl* TX-5
Willacy County Housing Authority—*other* TX-5
Willacy Park—*park* TX-5
*Willada* WA-9
**Willada (Lancaster)**—*pop pl* WA-9
Willadsen Ranch—*locale* WY-8
Willadsen Sch—*school* WY-8
Willagillespie Sch—*school* OR-9
Willaha—*locale* AZ-5
Willaha RR Station—*building* AZ-5
Willaha Tank—*reservoir* AZ-5
Willailla—*locale* KY-4
*Willaims Ridge* OR-9
Willakenzie—*uninc pl* OR-9
Willakenzie Sch—*school* OR-9
Willa Lake—*reservoir* OR-9
Willamalane Park—*park* OR-9
Willamar—*locale* TX-5
Willamar Camp—*locale* TX-5
Willamar Oil Field—*oilfield* TX-5
Willamaud Creek—*stream* WA-9
*Willame Creek* WA-9
Willame Creek—*stream* WA-9
Willame Lake—*lake* WA-9
Willame Trail—*trail* WA-9
**Willamette**—*pop pl* OR-9
Willamette Center Heliport—*airport* OR-9
**Willamette City**—*pop pl* OR-9
Willamette Divide Trail—*trail* OR-9
Willamette Falls—*falls* OR-9
Willamette Falls Community Hospital Heliport—*airport* OR-9
Willamette Falls Dam—*dam* OR-9
Willamette Falls Hydroelectric Power Rsvr—*reservoir* OR-9
Willamette Falls Locks—*hist pl* OR-9
**Willamette Forks (historical)**—*pop pl* OR-9
**Willamette Heights**—*pop pl* OR-9
Willamette Heights Park—*park* OR-9
Willamette HS—*school* OR-9
Willamette Log Pond—*lake* OR-9
Willamette Log Pond—*reservoir* OR-9
Willamette Memorial Park (cemetery)—*cemetery* OR-9
Willamette Natl Cem—*cemetery* OR-9
Willamette Natl For—*forest* OR-9
Willamette Natl Lumber Company Dam—*dam* OR-9
Willamette Nat. Lumber Co. Rsvr—*reservoir* OR-9
Willamette Park—*park* (2) OR-9
*Willamette Pass* OR-9
Willamette Pass—*gap* OR-9
Willamette Pass Ski Area—*locale* OR-9
*Willamette River* OR-9
Willamette River—*stream* OR-9
Willamette River Airstrip—*airport* OR-9
Willamette Slough—*stream* OR-9
Willamette Stone State Park—*park* OR-9
*Willamette Summit* OR-9
Willamette Univ—*school* OR-9
Willamette Valley—*valley* OR-9
**Willamina**—*pop pl* OR-9
Willamina (CCD)—*cens area* OR-9
Willamina Cem—*cemetery* OR-9
Willamina Creek—*stream* OR-9
Willamina Rsvr—*reservoir* OR-9
Willams Ditch—*canal* OR-9
*Willanauchee Talofa* FL-3
Willanch Creek—*stream* OR-9
Willanch Inlet—*bay* OR-9
Willanch Slough—*stream* OR-9
Willand Pond—*lake* NH-1
**Willanocha (historical)**—*pop pl* FL-3
**Willapa**—*pop pl* WA-9
Willapa Bay—*bay* WA-9
Willapa Bay Boathouse—*hist pl* WA-9
Willapa Camp—*locale* WA-9
Willapa Falls—*falls* WA-9
Willapa Harbor Airp—*airport* WA-9
Willapa Harbor Heliport—*airport* WA-9
Willapa Natl Wildlife Ref—*park* WA-9
Willapa River—*stream* WA-9
Willapa Valley (CCD)—*cens area* WA-9
*Willapirol Lake* WI-6
*Willard* ME-1
Willard—*locale* GA-3
Willard—*locale* ID-8
Willard—*locale* OK-5
Willard—*locale* WA-9
**Willard**—*pop pl* CO-8
**Willard**—*pop pl* (2) IL-6
**Willard**—*pop pl* IA-7
**Willard**—*pop pl* KS-7
**Willard**—*pop pl* KY-4
**Willard**—*pop pl* MI-6
**Willard**—*pop pl* MO-7
**Willard**—*pop pl* MT-8
**Willard**—*pop pl* NM-5
**Willard**—*pop pl* NY-2
**Willard**—*pop pl* NC-3
**Willard**—*pop pl* OH-6
**Willard**—*pop pl* TN-4
**Willard**—*pop pl* UT-8
**Willard**—*pop pl* WA-9
**Willard**—*pop pl* WV-2
**Willard**—*pop pl* WI-6
Willard, Emma, House—*hist pl* VT-1
Willard, Emma, Sch—*hist pl* NY-2
Willard, Frances, House—*hist pl* IL-6
Willard, Frances, House—*hist pl* TN-4
Willard, Frances, Schoolhouse—*hist pl* WI-6
Willard, Francis E., Sch—*hist pl* PA-2
Willard, Leroy R., House—*hist pl* IA-7
Willard, Mount—*summit* ID-8
Willard, Mount—*summit* NH-1
**Willard Addition (subdivision)**—*pop pl.* TN-4
Willard Asylum for the Chronic Insane—*hist pl* NY-2
Willard Basin—*basin* UT-8
Willard Basin Campground—*park* UT-8
*Willard Bay* UT-8
Willard Bay—*bay* CT-1
Willard Bay—*bay* UT-8
*Willard Bay Dike* UT-8
Willard Bay (North Marina) Campground—*park* UT-8
Willard Bay Rsvr—*reservoir* UT-8
Willard Bay (South Marina) Campground—*park* UT-8
Willard Bay State Park—*park* UT-8
*Willard Bay State Rec Area* UT-8
Willard Bay Upland Game Mngmt Area—*park* UT-8
Willard Beach—*beach* ME-1
Willard Bldg—*hist pl* WA-9
Willard Branch—*stream* KY-4
Willard Branch—*stream* TN-4
Willard Brook—*stream* (3) ME-1
Willard Brook—*stream* (2) MA-1
Willard Brook—*stream* NH-1
Willard Brook Quarry—*hist pl* ME-1
Willard Brook State For—*forest* MA-1
Willard Canal—*canal* UT-8
Willard Canyon—*valley* CA-9
Willard Canyon—*valley* NV-8
Willard Canyon—*valley* (2) UT-8
Willard (CCD)—*cens area* KY-4
Willard Cem—*cemetery* IA-7
Willard Cem—*cemetery* MO-7
Willard Cem—*cemetery* NM-5
Willard Cem—*cemetery* NY-2
Willard Cem—*cemetery* OK-5
Willard Cem—*cemetery* (3) TN-4
Willard Cem—*cemetery* TX-5
Willard Cem—*cemetery* WI-6
Willard Ch—*church* SD-7
Willard City Spring—*spring* UT-8
Willard Covered Bridge—*hist pl* VT-1
Willard Creek—*stream* CA-9
Willard Creek—*stream* ID-8
Willard Creek—*stream* KS-7
Willard Creek—*stream* NV-8
Willard Creek—*stream* UT-8
Willard Creek—*stream* WA-9
*Willard Dam* UT-8
Willard Drain—*stream* MI-6
Willard Elem Sch—*school* IN-6
Willard Field Airp—*airport* WA-9
Willard Gap—*gap* SD-7
Willard Gap—*gap* VT-1
Willard George Hill—*summit* AR-4
Willard Glacier—*glacier* AK-9
Willard Grove Cem—*cemetery* IL-6
Willard Grove (historical)—*locale* AL-4
*Willard Hill* ME-1
Willard Hill—*summit* NV-8
Willard Hill—*summit* NH-1
Willard Hist Dist—*hist pl* UT-8
**Willard (historical)**—*pop pl* (2) OR-9
Willard Homestead—*hist pl* CT-1
Willard Homestead—*hist pl* NH-1
Willard Hotel—*hist pl* DC-2
Willard House—*hist pl* AZ-5
Willard House and Clock Museum—*hist pl* MA-1
Willard Inlet—*bay* AK-9
Willard Island—*island* AK-9
Willard Island—*island* CT-1
Willard Island—*island* NY-2
Willard J Gambold JHS—*school* IN-6
Willard JHS—*school* (2) CA-9
Willard JHS—*school* VA-3
Willard Lake—*lake* MN-6
Willard Lake—*lake* ND-7
Willard Lake—*lake* TX-5
Willard Lake—*reservoir* OH-6
Willard Landing—*locale* IL-6
Willard Lateral—*canal* ID-8
Willard Ledge—*bench* NH-1
Willard Library—*hist pl* IN-6
Willard-McDonald Mine—*mine* NV-8
Willard Mine (historical)—*mine* NV-8
Willard Mtn—*summit* ME-1
Willard Mtn—*summit* (2) NH-1
Willard Mtn—*summit* NY-2
Willard Mtn—*summit* UT-8
Willard Mtn—*summit* (2) VT-1
Willard Mtn—*summit* VA-3
Willard Notch—*gap* NH-1
Willard Orphanage Country Home—*building* PA-2
Willard Park—*park* (2) IN-6
Willard Park—*park* MI-6
Willard Park—*park* NY-2
**Willard Park**—*pop pl* VA-3
Willard Park Cem—*cemetery* TN-4
Willard Peak—*summit* UT-8
Willard Point—*cape* ME-1
Willard Point—*cape* MI-6
Willard Point—*cape* NY-2
Willard Pond—*lake* NH-1
Willard Precinct Cem—*cemetery* UT-8
Willard Primary Sch—*school* NC-3
Willard Pumping Station No 1—*other* UT-8
Willard Ranch—*locale* WY-8
*Willard Reservoir* UT-8
Willard Ridge—*ridge* ME-1
Willard Road Canyon—*valley* UT-8
Willard Rock—*bar* ME-1
*Willard's* MD-2
**Willards**—*pop pl* MD-2
*Willards Brook* MA-1
Willards Camp—*locale* CA-9
Willard Sch—*school* AL-4
Willard Sch—*school* (4) CA-9
Willard Sch—*school* CT-1
Willard Sch—*school* (5) IL-6
Willard Sch—*school* IA-7
Willard Sch—*school* (2) KS-7
Willard Sch—*school* KY-4
Willard Sch—*school* (2) ME-1
Willard Sch—*school* (2) MA-1
Willard Sch—*school* MI-6
Willard Sch—*school* MN-6
Willard Sch—*school* (2) MO-7
Willard Sch—*school* MT-8
Willard Sch—*school* (2) NE-7
Willard Sch—*school* NJ-2
Willard Sch—*school* (2) OH-6
Willard Sch—*school* (3) OK-5
Willard Sch—*school* OR-9
Willard Sch—*school* PA-2
Willard Sch—*school* UT-8
Willard Sch—*school* VA-3
Willard Sch—*school* (2) WA-9
Willard Sch—*school* WI-6
Willard Sch—*school* WY-8
Willard Sch (abandoned)—*school* PA-2
Willard Sch Number 80—*school* IN-6
*Willard School* KS-7
Willards Dam—*dam* OR-9
Willard Shambaugh Elem Sch—*school* IN-6
Willard Slough—*stream* MT-8
Willard Slough—*swamp* MT-8
*Willards Peak* UT-8
Willards Pool—*lake* OR-9
*Willard Spring* NV-8
Willard Spring—*spring* AZ-5
Willard Spring—*spring* CO-8
Willard Spring—*spring* WA-9
Willard Springs—*spring* NV-8
Willard Springs Interchange—*crossing* AZ-5
Willard Spur—*channel* UT-8
Willard Square—*park* ME-1
Willards Sch (historical)—*school* MS-4
Willard State Hosp—*hospital* (2) NY-2
*Willard Stream* MA-1
Willard Street Sch—*school* NY-2
**Willard Subdivision**—*pop pl* UT-8
Willard Substation—*other* NM-5
**Willardtown**—*pop pl* TN-4
**Willard (Town of)**—*pop pl* WI-6
Willard (Township of)—*other* OH-6
**Willardville**—*pop pl* NC-3
Willar Well—*well* NM-5
Willa Springs Village (Shop Ctr)—*locale* FL-3
**Willaura Estates**—*pop pl* CA-9
Willawalla Creek—*stream* TX-5
Willa Zhinni Toh—*spring* AZ-5
Willbanks Branch—*stream* GA-3
Willbanks Cem—*cemetery* TN-4
Willbanks Hollow—*valley* TN-4
Willborg Lake—*lake* MN-6
Willborn Cem—*cemetery* TX-5
Will Branch—*stream* KY-4
Will Branch—*stream* NC-3
Will Branch—*stream* TN-4
**Willbridge**—*pop pl* OR-9
*Willbur Mountain* OR-9
Will Christy Park—*park* OH-6
*Willcockson* AR-4
Will Cone Pond—*reservoir* CT-1
**Will (County)**—*pop pl* IL-6
Will County Historical Society HQ—*hist pl* IL-6
**Willcox**—*pop pl* AZ-5
Willcox Airp—*airport* IN-6
Willcox (CCD)—*cens area* AZ-5
Willcox City Hall—*building* AZ-5
Willcox Community Center Park—*park* AZ-5
*Willcox Dry Lake* AZ-5
Willcox Dry Lake Bombing Range—*military* AZ-5
Willcox Elem Sch—*school* AZ-5
*Willcox Flat* AZ-5
**Willcox (historical)**—*pop pl* MS-4
Willcox JHS—*school* AZ-5
Willcox Playa—*flat* AZ-5
Willcox Post Office—*building* AZ-5
Willcox's—*hist pl* SC-3
Willcoxson Ranch—*locale* NM-5
Willcox Tank—*reservoir* AZ-5
Willcox Wharf—*locale* VA-3
Willcox Women's Club—*hist pl* AZ-5
Willcraft Lake Lower Dam—*dam* IN-6
*Will Creek* AL-4
Will Creek—*stream* GA-3
Will Creek—*stream* IN-6
Will Creek—*stream* NC-3
Willcutt Ranch—*locale* MT-8
Will Dam—*dam* SD-7
Will Davis Canyon—*valley* TX-5
Willden, Charles, House—*hist pl* UT-8
Willden, Elliot, House—*hist pl* UT-8
Willden, Feargus O'Connor, House—*hist pl* UT-8
Willden, John, House—*hist pl* UT-8
*Willden Hills* UT-8
*Willees Creek* AL-4
Willeford Pond—*reservoir* GA-3
Willeke, John, Jr., House—*hist pl* TX-5
Willeke, John, Sr., House—*hist pl* TX-5
Willeke, John and Anton, House—*hist pl* TX-5
Willeke Site—*hist pl* TX-5
Willene, Lake—*lake* NY-2
Willen Gap—*gap* NC-3
Willen Gap—*gap* TN-4
**Willen Gap**—*pop pl* TN-4
Will Engle Dam—*dam* AL-4
Will Engle Lake—*reservoir* AL-4
Willen Mtn—*summit* NC-3
Willen Mtn—*summit* TN-4
Willeo Cem—*cemetery* GA-3
Willeo Ch—*church* GA-3
Willeo Creek—*stream* GA-3
**Willerburn Acres**—*pop pl* MD-2
*Willer Lake* SC-3
**Willernie**—*pop pl* MN-6
Willers Lake—*reservoir* MO-7
Willer Tank—*reservoir* TX-5
Willerth Creek—*stream* WI-6
**Willes Subdivision**—*pop pl* UT-8
Willet—*locale* MS-4
**Willet**—*pop pl* NY-2
**Willet**—*pop pl* PA-2
Willet Branch—*stream* NC-3
Willet Cem—*cemetery* IN-6
*Willet Creek* NY-2
Willet Creek—*stream* NY-2
Willet Eddy—*rapids* ME-1
Willet Gulch—*valley* MT-8
Willet Hollow—*valley* TN-4
Willet Lake—*lake* MI-6
Willet Mtn—*summit* (2) TN-4
Willeto Well—*well* NM-5
Willet Point—*cape* AL-4
Willet Post Office (historical)—*building* MS-4
**Willets**—*pop pl* NY-2
Willets Bottom—*bend* KY-4
*Willets Creek* NY-2
*Willets Lake* MI-6
Willets Lake—*swamp* IN-6
*Willet's Point* NY-2
Willets Point—*cape* NY-2
Willets Road Sch—*school* NY-2
Willets Siding—*locale* AZ-5
*Willets Station* NY-2
*Willets Station* PA-2
**Willetsville**—*pop pl* OH-6
*Willett* NY-2
**Willett**—*pop pl* GA-3
**Willett**—*pop pl* IA-7
Willett Ave Sch—*school* NY-2
Willett Branch—*stream* MD-2
Willett Brook—*stream* (2) ME-1
Willett Cem—*cemetery* OH-6
Willett Cove—*bay* VA-3
Willett Creek—*stream* WY-8
Willett Ditch—*canal* KY-4
Willett Ditch—*canal* NM-5
**Willette**—*pop pl* TN-4
Willette Drain—*stream* MI-6
Willette Lake Dam—*dam* NC-3
Willette Post Office (historical)—*building* TN-4
Willette Sch (historical)—*school* TN-4
Willett Hill—*summit* ME-1
Willett (historical)—*locale* SD-7
Willett Lake—*lake* WY-8

Willett Lake—*reservoir* NC-3
**Willet (Town of)**—*pop pl* NY-2
Willett Park—*park* PA-2
Willett Pond—*reservoir* MA-1
Willett Pond—*reservoir* RI-1
Willett Pond Dam—*dam* MA-1
Willett Run—*stream* WV-2
**Willetts**—*pop pl* LA-4
Willett Sch—*school* (2) MA-1
Willett Sch—*school* NY-2
Willett Sch (historical)—*school* TN-4
Willetts Creek—*stream* NY-2
Willetts Creek—*stream* VA-3
Willetts Point—*cape* NY-2
*Willetts Pond* MA-1
Willett Spring—*spring* AL-4
Willettsville—*locale* OH-6
*Willettville* OH-6
*Willettville* RI-1
Willever Lake—*reservoir* NJ-2
Willever Lake Dam—*dam* NJ-2
**Willey**—*pop pl* IA-7
Willey, E. H., House—*hist pl* SD-7
Willey, Malcolm, House—*hist pl* MN-6
Willey, Mount—*summit* NH-1
Willey, Waitman T., House—*hist pl* WV-2
Willey Branch—*stream* IA-7
*Willey Brook* NH-1
Willey Brook—*stream* NH-1
Willey Brook—*stream* NY-2
Willey Cem—*cemetery* IL-6
Willey Cem—*cemetery* NC-3
Willey Cem—*cemetery* OK-5
Willey Cem—*cemetery* VA-3
Willey Creek—*stream* ID-8
Willey Creek—*stream* OH-6
Willey Creek—*stream* WY-8
Willey Drain—*canal* MI-6
Willey Fork—*stream* WV-2
Willey Granite Quarry—*mine* VT-1
Willey Gulch—*valley* ID-8
Willey Hill—*summit* (2) VT-1
Willey Hollow—*valley* UT-8
Willey House—*locale* NH-1
Willey House Camps—*locale* NH-1
Willey House Post Office—*locale* NH-1
Willey Lake—*lake* WA-9
**Willey Lumber Camp**—*pop pl* CO-8
Willey Neck—*cape* MD-2
Willey Point—*cape* FL-3
*Willey Pond* NH-1
Willey Ponds—*lake* NH-1
Willey Ranch—*locale* NE-7
Willeys—*locale* IL-6
**Willeys**—*pop pl* OH-6
Willey Sch (historical)—*school* PA-2
*Willeys Island* MD-2
Willeys Lake—*lake* MN-6
**Willeyton**—*pop pl* NC-3
**Willey Township**—*pop pl* ND-7
Willey Use Spring—*spring* MT-8
Will Field Gap—*gap* GA-3
*Willford Pond* CT-1
Willford Ranch—*locale* WY-8
Will Fork—*stream* KY-4
Will Gap—*gap* NC-3
Willgo Creek—*stream* MS-4
Will Hall Creek—*stream* TN-4
Will Hamilton Sch—*school* KY-4
Will Hay Branch—*stream* IN-6
*Willhide Hollow* MO-7
*Will Hill* MA-1
*Willhite* LA-4
**Willhite**—*pop pl* LA-4
Willhite Airp—*airport* MO-7
Willhite Cem—*cemetery* IN-6
Willhite Cem—*cemetery* TN-4
Willhite Sch (historical)—*school* MO-7
Willhoit—*locale* MO-7
Willhoit Hollow—*valley* MO-7
Will Hole, The—*channel* VA-3
Willholm Run—*stream* PA-2
Willhoyt Cem—*cemetery* KY-4
*William* MN-6
*William* PA-2
William—*locale* WV-2
William—*locale* VI-3
William, H.B., House—*hist pl* FL-3
William, Lake—*lake* AK-9
William, Lake—*lake* (2) MN-6
William, Lake—*reservoir* IN-6
William, Lake—*reservoir* NC-3
William, Mount—*summit* NH-1
William A Bell Elem Sch—*school* IN-6
William A Chapman Elem Sch—*school* FL-3
*William Aches Canyon* CA-9
William Adams HS—*school* TX-5
William A Jameson Lake—*reservoir* TN-4
William A Jameson Lake Dam—*dam* TN-4
William Alexander Percy Library—*building* MS-4
William Allen Senior HS—*school* PA-2
William Allen White Elem Sch—*school* KS-7
William Allen White Sch—*school* KS-7
William Anderson Pond Dam—*dam* MS-4
Williamantic (Norton's Corners)—*other* ME-1
Williamantic (Town of)—*other* ME-1
William Arm of Tuesburg Ditch—*canal* IN-6
William Arnold Lake—*reservoir* NC-3
William Arnold Lake Dam—*dam* NC-3
*Williamasett* MA-1
William A Wirt Senior HS—*school* IN-6
William Bacon Oliver Lake—*reservoir* AL-4
*William Bacon Oliver Lock and Dam* AL-4
William Baker Ditch—*canal* IN-6
William Baxter Dam—*dam* SD-7
*William Bayou* FL-3
William B Bankhead Natl Forest—*park* AL-4
William B Crumpton Bridge—*bridge* AL-4
William Beaumont Army Med Ctr—*uninc pl* TX-5
William Berrie Grant—*civil* FL-3
William B Ide Adobe State Historical Monument—*park* CA-9
William "Bill" Dannelly Lake—*reservoir* AL-4
William "Bill" Dannelly Rsvr—*reservoir* AL-4
William Blount HS—*school* TN-4
William Boyd Ranch—*locale* WY-8
William Boyles Bayou—*gut* LA-4
*William Branch* MO-7
William Branch—*stream* GA-3
William Branch—*stream* KY-4
William Branch—*stream* VA-3
William Brinton House—*building* PA-2
William Browder Dam—*dam* TN-4
William Browder Lake—*reservoir* TN-4
William B Umstead Memorial Bridge—*bridge* NC-3
William B Umstead State Park—*park* NC-3
William Byrd HS—*school* VA-3
William Byrd Park—*park* VA-3
William Canal—*canal* (2) LA-4
William Carey Coll—*school* MS-4
William Carey Coll on the Coast—*school* MS-4
William Carmichael Sch—*school* AZ-5
William Carr Sch—*school* IL-6
William Carter Cem—*cemetery* AL-4
William Cathcart Ditch—*canal* OH-6
William C Bowen, Lake—*reservoir* SC-3
William C. Davol, Jr. House—*building* MA-1
William Cem—*cemetery* AL-4
William Cem—*cemetery* (3) KY-4
William Cem—*cemetery* LA-4
William Cem—*cemetery* (2) WV-2
William C Friday JHS—*school* NC-3
William Chapel—*church* AL-4
William Chapel—*church* GA-3
William Chapel—*church* LA-4
William Chapel—*church* (2) NC-3
William Chapel AME Zion Ch—*church* AL-4
William Chapel Baptist Ch—*church* FL-3
*William Clapp Lake* WA-9
William Clark Ditch—*canal* IN-6
*William Clark Lake* ID-8
*William Clark Lake* WA-9
*William Colmer JHS* MS-4
*William Cooper Junior High School* NC-3
William Cove—*bay* AK-9
William Craig Historical Monmt—*park* ID-8
*William Creek* MO-7
William Creek—*stream* AL-4
William Creek—*stream* AK-9
William Creek—*stream* CA-9
William Creek—*stream* IL-6
William Creek—*stream* IN-6
William Creek—*stream* (2) OR-9
William Creek—*stream* TX-5
William Creuse Dam—*dam* NC-3
William Cullen Bryant Intermediate Sch—*school* VA-3
William Dale Dam—*dam* AL-4
William Dale Lake—*reservoir* AL-4
*William D Baird Municipal Park* TN-4
William D Boyce Regional Park—*park* PA-2
William Doan Drain—*canal* MI-6
*William Doyls Tavern* PA-2
William D Robbins Elem Sch—*school* AL-4
William Drummond Grant—*civil* FL-3
William E Lewis Sch—*school* MA-1
*Williamette Natl Forest* OR-9
Williamette Station Site, Methodist Mission in Oregon—*hist pl* OR-9
William Eubanks Grant—*civil* FL-3
William F. Cody Museum and Grave—*locale* CO-8
William Fegely MS—*school* IN-6
William Field—*park* NJ-2
*Williamfield P O* OH-6
William Finley Natl Wildlife Ref—*park* OR-9
William Fitzpatrick Grant—*civil* FL-3
William F James Boys Ranch—*locale* CA-9
William Fleming HS—*school* VA-3
William F Loper Elem Sch—*school* IN-6
William Forsythe Ditch—*canal* IN-6
William Freise Dam—*dam* SD-7
William Frith Cem—*cemetery* MS-4
William Gardner Grant—*civil* FL-3
William Garvin Grant—*civil* (2) FL-3
William Gibson and Others Grant—*civil* FL-3
William Gibson and Others or C Seton Grant—*civil* FL-3
William G Paden Sch—*school* CA-9
William Grace Sch—*school* MI-6
William Grady Stembridge Bridge—*bridge* AL-4
William Grove Ch—*church* GA-3
William Grove Ch—*church* VA-3
William Hambley Grant—*civil* FL-3
William Hamilton Browder Bridge—*bridge*. TN-4
*William Hamilton Hall* SD-7
William Hamilton Lake—*reservoir* IN-6
William Hamilton Lake Dam—*dam* IN-6
**William Hamilton Township**—*pop pl* SD-7
William Hartley Grant—*civil* FL-3
William H Bashaw Elem Sch—*school* FL-3
William Head—*summit* VI-3
William Hendricks Grant—*civil* FL-3
William Henry Bay—*bay* AK-9
William Henry Burkhart Elem Sch—*school* IN-6
William Henry Creek—*stream* AK-9
William Henry MS—*school* DE-2
William Hershman Lateral—*canal* IN-6
William H Harsha Lake—*reservoir* OH-6
William Hill—*summit* MA-1
William H Miner Agricultural Research Institute—*other* NY-2
William H Newton Ditch—*stream* DE-2
William Hollingsworth Grant—*civil* FL-3
William Hollow—*valley* TN-4
William Howard Taft HS—*school* TX-5
William Howard Taft Natl Historic Site—*hist pl* OH-6
William Howard Taft Natl Historic Site—*park* OH-6
William H Pouch Boy Scout Camp—*locale* NY-2
William H. Taft—*uninc pl* CA-9
William H Taft Sch—*school* OH-6
William Huether Dam—*dam* SD-7
William Huff Cem—*cemetery* MS-4
William Island—*island* FL-3
William Jackson Cem—*cemetery* MS-4
*William Jason High School* DE-2
William Jennings Bryan Sch—*school* FL-3
William Jennings Bryan Univ—*school* TN-4
William Jewell Coll—*school* MO-7
William J Kelly Park—*park* FL-3
William Jones Reservation—*park* AL-4
William J Owen Elem Sch—*school* NC-3
William Kent Guard Station—*locale* CA-9
William Kerr Ditch—*canal* CO-8
William Key Reservation—*park* AL-4
William King HS—*school* VA-3
William K Newton Memorial Park—*park* NC-3
William Knight Sch—*school* OR-9
William K. Wrigley Company—*facility* GA-3
*William Lake* MN-6
William Lake—*lake* (2) MN-6
William Lake Dam—*dam* MS-4
William Land Park—*park* CA-9
William Land Sch—*school* CA-9
William Lane Grant—*civil* FL-3
William Latham Dam—*dam* AL-4
William Latham Lake—*reservoir* AL-4
William L Bork Memorial Hosp—*hospital* TN-4
William Lehr Ditch—*canal* IN-6
William Lenoir MS—*school* NC-3
William Lewis Elem Sch—*school* DE-2
William L. Finley Natl Wildlife Ref—*park* OR-9
William Logan State Wildlife Area—*park* MO-7
William L Radney Sch—*school* AL-4
William L Walker Dam—*dam* NC-3
*William L Yancey State Junior Coll* AL-4
*William M Allen Cemetery* MS-4
William M. Black (dredge)—*hist pl* IA-7
William M. Black Museum—*building* IA-7
*William M Chick* MO-7
William McKinley Elem Sch—*school* (2) IN-6
William McKinley Osceola Seminole Village—*locale* FL-3
William Merritt Chase Elem Sch—*school* IN-6
*William Mesa* AZ-5
*William Mill Creek* GA-3
William Miller Chapel—*church* NY-2
William Miller Ditch—*canal* MT-8
William Millpond—*lake* GA-3
William Mitchell State Park—*park* MI-6
William M Powell Bridge—*bridge* FL-3
William M Raines Senior HS—*school* FL-3
William O'Brien State Park—*park* MN-6
William O Huske Lock and Dam—*dam* NC-3
William Olson Dam—*dam* SD-7
William Panton Grant—*civil* FL-3
William Panton (Heirs) Grant—*civil* FL-3
William Patterson Dam—*dam* SD-7
*William Penn* PA-2
William Penn—*locale* TX-5
William Penn—*other* PA-2
William Penn Annex—*uninc pl* PA-2
William Penn Camp (historical)—*locale* PA-2
William Penn Cem—*cemetery* PA-2
William Penn Coll—*school* IA-7
*William Penn College* IA-7
William Penn Dam—*dam* PA-2
William Penn Elem Sch—*school* IN-6
William Penn Elem Sch—*school* (2) PA-2
William Penn Gardens Of Remembrance—*cemetery* PA-2
William Penn Hotel—*hist pl* PA-2
*William Penn HS* PA-2
William Penn HS—*school* DE-2
William Penn HS—*school* NC-3
William Penn HS—*school* PA-2
**William Penn Manor**—*pop pl* PA-2
*William Penn Middle School* PA-2
William Penn P. O. (historical)—*building* PA-2
*William Penn Sch* PA-2
William Penn Sch—*school* PA-2
William Penn Sch—*school* TX-5
William Penn Sch—*school* UT-8
William Penn Sch (abandoned)—*school* PA-2
William Penn Senior HS—*school* PA-2
William Penns Landing Site—*airport* PA-2
William P Harrell Bridge—*bridge* TN-4
William Phillips Dam At Bedford—*dam* AL-4
William Phillips Lake—*reservoir* AL-4
William P. Hobby Airp—*airport* TX-5
William P. Keady Wayside—*locale* OR-9
William Point—*cape* WA-9
William P Ransch Dam—*dam* SD-7
William Preston Lane Junior Memorial Bridge—*other* MD-2
William Putnam Memorial Bridge—*bridge* CT-1
William Rainey Harper Coll—*school* IL-6
William Rall Sch—*school* NY-2
William Raws Monmt—*park* NJ-2
William R Davie Elem Sch—*school* NC-3
*William R Davie MS* NC-3
William R Day Sch—*school* OH-6
William Reed Elem Sch—*school* IN-6
William R Fairchild Intl Airp—*airport* WA-9
William Rice (Rice University)—*uninc pl* TX-5
William Riley Cem—*cemetery* TN-4
**William Ritter Manor (subdivision)**—*pop pl* DE-2
*William R King Female College* AL-4
William Ross Hollow—*valley* OK-5
**William R Patterson Subdivision**—*pop pl* UT-8
William Rsvr—*reservoir* WY-8
*William Run* PA-2
William Rust Summit—*summit* CA-9
*Williams* AZ-5
*Williams* ME-1
*Williams* NJ-2
*Williams* VA-3
Williams—*cemetery* MO-7
Williams—*locale* (2) AL-4
Williams—*locale* KY-4
Williams—*locale* LA-4
Williams—*locale* MS-4
Williams—*locale* PA-2
Williams—*locale* (2) TX-5
Williams—*locale* VA-3
**Williams**—*pop pl* AL-4
**Williams**—*pop pl* AZ-5
**Williams**—*pop pl* CA-9
**Williams**—*pop pl* FL-3
**Williams**—*pop pl* GA-3
**Williams**—*pop pl* (2) IN-6
**Williams**—*pop pl* IA-7
**Williams**—*pop pl* (2) KY-4
**Williams**—*pop pl* LA-4
**Williams**—*pop pl* MN-6
**Williams**—*pop pl* MS-4
**Williams**—*pop pl* MT-8
**Williams**—*pop pl* (2) NC-3
**Williams**—*pop pl* (2) OK-5
**Williams**—*pop pl* OR-9
**Williams**—*pop pl* (4) PA-2
**Williams**—*pop pl* SC-3
**Williams**—*pop pl* (2) TN-4
**Williams**—*pop pl* (2) TX-5
**Williams**—*pop pl* WV-2
Williams, Abiathar King, House—*hist pl* MA-1
Williams, Abner, Log House—*hist pl* OH-6
Williams, Abraham L., L & N Guest House—*hist pl* KY-4
Williams, Alex, House—*hist pl* MS-4
Williams, Alfred, House—*hist pl* MI-6
Williams, Benjamin, House—*hist pl* MI-6
Williams, B. F., House—*hist pl* TX-5
Williams, C. C., House—*hist pl* MO-7
Williams, C. E., House—*hist pl* MN-6
Williams, Col. John, House—*hist pl* TN-4
Williams, C. S., House—*hist pl* OR-9
Williams, Dan, House—*hist pl* AZ-5
Williams, Daniel Motley, House—*hist pl* KY-4
Williams, Dr. Daniel Hale, House—*hist pl* IL-6
Williams, Dr. Edward H., House—*hist pl* NJ-2
Williams, Dr. Issac Elmer, House And Office—*hist pl* OH-6
Williams, Dr. Robert George, House—*hist pl* AR-4
Williams, E. B., House—*hist pl* AZ-5
Williams, Eleazer, House—*hist pl* CT-1
Williams, Elias, House—*hist pl* OH-6
Williams, Enoch, House—*hist pl* MA-1
Williams, Eustace, House—*hist pl* KY-4
Williams, Francis D., House—*hist pl* MA-1
Williams, Frank J., House—*hist pl* WI-6
Williams, Gen. John, House—*hist pl* ME-1
Williams, George H., Townhouses—*hist pl* OR-9
Williams, Hattie, House—*hist pl* WA-9
Williams, Henry, House—*hist pl* NY-2
Williams, Henry Harrison, House—*hist pl* OH-6
Williams, Herbert, House—*hist pl* WA-9
Williams, Hubbard, House—*hist pl* KY-4
Williams, Isaac, House—*hist pl* NC-3
Williams, James, House—*hist pl* DE-2
Williams, James Robert, House—*hist pl* IL-6
Williams, J. B., Co. Hist Dist—*hist pl* CT-1
Williams, J. K., House—*hist pl* DE-2
Williams, Johann, Farm—*hist pl* NY-2
Williams, John, Farm—*hist pl* PA-2
Williams, John, House—*hist pl* KY-4
Williams, John, House—*hist pl* ME-1
Williams, John, House—*hist pl* PA-2
Williams, John C., House—*hist pl* FL-3
Williams, John Siddle, House—*hist pl* MO-7
Williams, Judge Henry, House—*hist pl* OH-6
Williams, Lake—*lake* (2) MN-6
Williams, Lake—*lake* (2) ND-7
Williams, Lake—*reservoir* GA-3
Williams, Lake—*reservoir* (3) NC-3
Williams, Lake—*reservoir* TN-4
Williams, M. D. L., Barn—*hist pl* KS-7
Williams, Merritt, House—*hist pl* KY-4
Williams, Micah, House—*hist pl* MA-1
Williams, Mount—*summit* AK-9
Williams, Mount—*summit* MA-1
Williams, N., House—*hist pl* MA-1
Williams, Nathaniel J., House—*hist pl* UT-8
Williams, N.S., House—*hist pl* MA-1
Williams, Olzie Whitehead, House—*hist pl* NC-3
Williams, Porter L., House—*hist pl* TX-5
Williams, Reese, House—*hist pl* UT-8
Williams, Robert, House—*hist pl* NC-3
Williams, Robert Lee, Public Library—*hist pl* OK-5
Williams, Samuel May, House—*hist pl* TX-5
Williams, Samuel P., House—*hist pl* IN-6
Williams, Seneca, Mill—*hist pl* IA-7
Williams, Sidney, House—*hist pl* WA-9
Williams, Silas, House—*hist pl* IL-6
Williams, Spafford, Hotel—*hist pl* MN-6
Williams, T.E., Block—*hist pl* WI-6
Williams, Tom, House—*hist pl* SC-3
Williams, Warham, House—*hist pl* CT-1
Williams, William, House—*hist pl* CT-1
Williams, William Carlos, House—*hist pl* NJ-2
Williams, W. L., House—*hist pl* OH-6
Williams Acad—*school* IL-6
Williams Acres—*locale* (2) NM-5
Williams AFB—*military* AZ-5
Williams Air Force Base Golf Course—*other* AZ-5
Williams and Chesser Ranch—*locale* NM-5
Williams and Cook Drain—*canal* MI-6
Williams and Dorf Mine (Inactive)—*mine* CA-9
Williams and Reynolds Mine—*mine* NM-5
Williams and Stancliff Octagon Houses—*hist pl* CT-1
Williams and Tavenner Ranch—*locale* MT-8
Williams Arm Ditch—*canal* IN-6
Williams Arroyo—*stream* NM-5
Williams Auxiliary Field Six—*military* AZ-5
Williams Ave Athletic Facilities—*park* AL-4
Williams Ave JHS—*school* AL-4
Williams Ave Sch—*school* OH-6
Williams-Ball-Copeland House—*hist pl* SC-3
Williams-Barneveld Creek—*stream* WI-6
Williams Basin—*basin* NV-8
Williams Bay—*bay* (2) WI-6
**Williams Bay**—*pop pl* WI-6
Williams Bay—*swamp* (5) FL-3
Williams Bayou—*bay* (2) FL-3
Williams Bayou—*stream* MS-4
Williams Bays—*swamp* NC-3
Williams Bend—*bend* KY-4
Williams Bend—*bend* MO-7
Williams Bend—*bend* TN-4
Williams Block—*hist pl* ME-1
Williams Bluff—*cliff* GA-3
**Williamsboro**—*pop pl* NC-3
Williamsboro (Township of)—*fmr MCD* NC-3
**Williamsborough (subdivision)**—*pop pl* NC-3
Williams Bottom—*bend* UT-8
*Williams Branch* AR-4
*Williams Branch* GA-3
*Williams Branch* KY-4
*Williams Branch* WI-6
Williams Branch—*stream* AL-4
Williams Branch—*stream* (4) AR-4
Williams Branch—*stream* (2) FL-3
Williams Branch—*stream* (2) GA-3
Williams Branch—*stream* (11) KY-4
Williams Branch—*stream* (2) LA-4
Williams Branch—*stream* (2) MS-4
Williams Branch—*stream* (5) MO-7
Williams Branch—*stream* (6) NC-3
Williams Branch—*stream* (4) SC-3
Williams Branch—*stream* (13) TN-4
Williams Branch—*stream* (5) TX-5
Williams Branch—*stream* (3) VA-3
Williams Branch—*stream* WV-2
Williams Branch Sch—*school* KY-4
*Williamsbridge* NY-2
Williams Bridge—*bridge* AL-4
Williams Bridge—*bridge* GA-3
Williams Bridge—*bridge* IN-6
Williams Bridge—*bridge* MT-8
Williams Bridge—*bridge* NC-3
Williams Bridge—*hist pl* IN-6
**Williams Bridge**—*pop pl* NY-2
Williams Bridge Dam—*dam* PA-2
Williams Bridge Rsvr—*reservoir* PA-2
*Williams Brook* MA-1
Williams Brook—*stream* CT-1
Williams Brook—*stream* (4) ME-1
Williams Brook—*stream* MA-1
Williams Brook—*stream* NH-1
Williams Brook—*stream* NY-2
Williams Brook—*stream* PA-2
Williams-Brown House and Store—*hist pl* VA-3
Williams-Brueder House—*hist pl* TX-5
*Williamsburg* IN-6
*Williamsburg* MD-2
*Williamsburg* NJ-2
*Williamsburg* NC-3
*Williamsburg* PA-2
Williamsburg—*locale* DE-2
Williamsburg—*locale* (2) GA-3
Williamsburg—*locale* (2) IL-6
Williamsburg—*locale* ME-1
Williamsburg—*locale* TN-4
Williamsburg—*locale* TX-5
**Williamsburg**—*pop pl* AL-4
**Williamsburg**—*pop pl* CO-8
**Williamsburg**—*pop pl* GA-3
**Williamsburg**—*pop pl* IN-6
**Williamsburg**—*pop pl* IA-7
**Williamsburg**—*pop pl* KS-7
**Williamsburg**—*pop pl* KY-4
**Williamsburg**—*pop pl* (2) MD-2
**Williamsburg**—*pop pl* MA-1
**Williamsburg**—*pop pl* MI-6
**Williamsburg**—*pop pl* MS-4
**Williamsburg**—*pop pl* MO-7
**Williamsburg**—*pop pl* MT-8
**Williamsburg**—*pop pl* NM-5
**Williamsburg**—*pop pl* NY-2
**Williamsburg**—*pop pl* (2) NC-3
**Williamsburg**—*pop pl* OH-6
**Williamsburg**—*pop pl* (3) PA-2
**Williamsburg**—*pop pl* WV-2
Williamsburg—*post sta* FL-3
Williamsburg—*uninc pl* TX-5
Williamsburg Baptist Ch—*church* MS-4
Williamsburg Battlefield—*locale* VA-3
Williamsburg Borough—*civil* PA-2
Williamsburg Bridge—*bridge* NY-2
Williamsburg Catholic Ch (historical)—*church* MS-4
Williamsburg (CCD)—*cens area* KY-4
Williamsburg Cem—*cemetery* IN-6
Williamsburg Cem—*cemetery* MS-4
Williamsburg Cem—*cemetery* NY-2
Williamsburg Cem—*cemetery* TN-4
Williamsburg Center Hist Dist—*hist pl* MA-1
Williamsburg Ch—*church* AL-4
Williamsburg Ch—*church* GA-3
Williamsburg Ch—*church* NE-7
Williamsburg Ch—*church* (2) TN-4
Williamsburg Ch (historical)—*church* AL-4
Williamsburg Colored Sch (historical)—*school* MS-4
Williamsburg Country Club—*other* VA-3
**Williamsburg (County)**—*pop pl* SC-3
Williamsburg Creek—*stream* IN-6
Williamsburg Creek—*stream* MI-6
*Williamsburg Crossroads* GA-3
*Williamsburg Depot* MS-4
Williamsburg Elem Sch—*school* IN-6
**Williamsburg Estates**—*pop pl* (2) MD-2
**Williamsburg Estates**—*pop pl* TN-4
**Williamsburg Estates (subdivision)**—*pop pl* (2) TN-4
**Williamsburg Estates Subdivision**—*pop pl* UT-8
Williamsburg General Cem—*cemetery* MS-4
Williamsburg Golf Club—*locale* MA-1
*Williamsburgh* KS-7
*Williamsburgh* MS-4
Williamsburg Hill—*locale* IL-6
Williamsburg Hist Dist—*hist pl* VA-3
Williamsburg (historical)—*locale* MS-4
*Williamsburgh Post Office* TN-4
Williamsburgh Savings Bank—*hist pl* NY-2
**Williamsburgh Subdivision**—*pop pl* UT-8
**Williamsburg (ind. city)**—*pop pl* VA-3
Williamsburg JHS—*school* VA-3
Williamsburg (Magisterial District)—*fmr MCD* WV-2
Williamsburg Male and Female Coll (historical)—*school* MS-4
**Williamsburg Manor**—*pop pl* VA-3
**Williamsburg Manor North (subdivision)**—*pop pl* NC-3
**Williamsburg Manor (subdivision)**—*pop pl* NC-3
Williamsburg Memorial Park—*cemetery* VA-3
Williamsburg Methodist Ch—*church* MS-4
**Williamsburg Park Condo**—*pop pl* UT-8
Williamsburg Post Office (historical)—*building* MS-4
Williamsburg Post Office (historical)—*building* TN-4
Williamsburg Rod and Gun Club—*locale* MA-1
Williamsburg Rsvr—*reservoir* PA-2
Williamsburg Sch—*school* ME-1
Williamsburg Sch—*school* NC-3
Williamsburg Sch (historical)—*school* MS-4
Williamsburg Sportsmens Park—*park* PA-2
**Williamsburg Square (subdivision)**—*pop pl* NC-3
**Williamsburg Station**—*pop pl* MA-1
Williamsburg Station Dam—*dam* PA-2
Williamsburg Station Lake—*reservoir* PA-2
**Williamsburg Subdivision**—*pop pl* UT-8
Williamsburg Tank—*reservoir* TX-5
**Williamsburg (Thompsonville)**—*pop pl* NC-3
**Williamsburg (Town of)**—*pop pl* MA-1
**Williamsburg Township**—*pop pl* KS-7
**Williamsburg Township**—*pop pl* NE-7
Williamsburg (Township of)—*civ div* OH-6
Williamsburg (Township of)—*fmr MCD* NC-3
Williamsburg (Township of)—*unorg* ME-1
**Williamsburg Village**—*pop pl* MD-2
**Williamsburg Village**—*pop pl* VA-3
Williamsburg Wildlife Club Lake—*reservoir* NC-3
Williamsburg Wildlife Club Lake Dam—*dam* NC-3
Williamsburg Wildlife Lake—*reservoir* NC-3
Williams Butte—*summit* (2) CA-9
Williams Butte—*summit* KS-7
Williams Butte—*summit* OR-9
Williams Butte—*summit* WA-9
Williams Cabin—*locale* (2) CO-8
Williams Cabin—*locale* NV-8
Williams Camp—*locale* AL-4
Williams Camp—*locale* AZ-5
Williams Camp—*locale* CA-9
Williams Camp—*locale* FL-3
Williams Camp—*locale* IL-6
Williams Camp—*locale* MT-8
Williams Camp—*locale* WI-6
Williams Camp Run—*stream* (2) WV-2
*Williams Canal* DE-2
Williams Canal—*canal* (2) LA-4
Williams Canal Ditch—*canal* DE-2
*Williams Canyon* ID-8
Williams Canyon—*valley* AZ-5
Williams Canyon—*valley* (8) CA-9
Williams Canyon—*valley* (2) CO-8
Williams Canyon—*valley* ID-8
Williams Canyon—*valley* (3) NV-8
Williams Canyon—*valley* (3) NM-5
Williams Canyon—*valley* (3) OR-9
Williams Canyon—*valley* UT-8
Williams Canyon—*valley* WA-9
Williams Canyon Well—*well* NV-8
Williams Catfish Ponds Dam—*dam* MS-4
Williams Cave—*cave* TN-4
Williams (CCD)—*cens area* AZ-5
Williams (CCD)—*cens area* OR-9
*Williams Cem* AL-4
Williams Cem—*cemetery* (21) AL-4
Williams Cem—*cemetery* (14) AR-4
Williams Cem—*cemetery* (4) FL-3
Williams Cem—*cemetery* (18) GA-3
Williams Cem—*cemetery* (9) IL-6
Williams Cem—*cemetery* (11) IN-6
Williams Cem—*cemetery* (2) IA-7
Williams Cem—*cemetery* KS-7
Williams Cem—*cemetery* (18) KY-4
Williams Cem—*cemetery* (7) LA-4
Williams Cem—*cemetery* (2) ME-1
Williams Cem—*cemetery* MA-1
Williams Cem—*cemetery* MI-6
Williams Cem—*cemetery* (22) MS-4
Williams Cem—*cemetery* (15) MO-7
Williams Cem—*cemetery* NE-7
Williams Cem—*cemetery* (3) NY-2
Williams Cem—*cemetery* (13) NC-3
Williams Cem—*cemetery* (6) OH-6
Williams Cem—*cemetery* (2) OK-5
Williams Cem—*cemetery* OR-9
Williams Cem—*cemetery* (4) PA-2
Williams Cem—*cemetery* (6) SC-3
Williams Cem—*cemetery* (55) TN-4
Williams Cem—*cemetery* (19) TX-5
Williams Cem—*cemetery* VT-1
Williams Cem—*cemetery* (12) VA-3
Williams Cem—*cemetery* (9) WV-2
Williams Cem—*cemetery* WI-6
Williams Cem Number One—*cemetery* MS-4
**Williams Center**—*pop pl* OH-6
*Williams Ch* AL-4
Williams Ch—*church* AR-4
Williams Ch—*church* IL-6
Williams Ch—*church* (2) NC-3
Williams Ch—*church* TN-4
Williams Ch—*church* VA-3
*Williams Chapel* TN-4
Williams Chapel—*church* (4) AL-4
Williams Chapel—*church* (8) GA-3
Williams Chapel—*church* IL-6
Williams Chapel—*church* KY-4
Williams Chapel—*church* (3) LA-4
Williams Chapel—*church* (3) MS-4
Williams Chapel—*church* (5) NC-3
Williams Chapel—*church* (7) TN-4
Williams Chapel—*church* (4) TX-5
Williams Chapel—*church* (2) VA-3
Williams Chapel A.M.E. Church—*hist pl* SC-3
Williams Chapel AME Zion Ch—*church* AL-4
Williams Chapel Cem—*cemetery* AL-4
Williams Chapel Cem—*cemetery* MS-4
Williams Chapel Cem—*cemetery* OH-6
Williams Chapel Cem—*cemetery* TN-4
Williams Chapel Cem—*cemetery* TX-5
*Williams Chapel Church* AL-4
Williams Chapel (historical)—*church* (4) AL-4
Williams Chapel (historical)—*church* (3) MS-4
*Williams Chapel Methodist Ch* AL-4
Williams Chapel Sch—*school* AR-4
Williams Charco—*lake* OR-9
*Williams Church* PA-2
Williams Chute—*lake* MO-7
Williams Coal Bed Mine (underground)—*mine* AL-4
Williams-Cole House—*hist pl* MI-6
Williams Coll—*school* IL-6
Williams Coll—*school* MA-1
Williams College Ski Area—*locale* MA-1
Williams' Conquest—*hist pl* MD-2
*Williams Corner* AL-4
Williams Corner—*locale* NY-2
Williams Corner—*locale* (2) PA-2
Williams Corner—*locale* VA-3
**Williams Corner**—*pop pl* OH-6
*Williams Corners* PA-2
Williams Corners—*locale* NY-2
**Williams Corners**—*pop pl* NY-2
**Williams Corners**—*pop pl* OH-6

William Scott Memorial Monmt—*pillar* VT-1
Williams Coulee—*valley* (4) MT-8
Williams Coulee Rsvr—*reservoir* MT-8
Williams Country Club—*other* AZ-5
Williams Country Club—*other* WV-2
Williams County—*civil* ND-7
**Williams (County)**—*pop pl* OH-6
Williams County Courthouse—*hist pl* OH-6
**Williams Court**—*pop pl* VA-3
Williams Cove—*basin* NC-3
Williams Cove—*valley* (2) AL-4
Williams Cove—*valley* TN-4
Williams Cove—*valley* VA-3
Williams Cove Cave—*cave* AL-4
Williams Cove Cem—*cemetery* AL-4
Williams Cove Ch—*church* AL-4
Williams Cove Spring—*spring* AL-4
Williams Crater—*summit* OR-9
Williams Creek AZ-5
Williams Creek AR-4
Williams Creek CA-9
Williams Creek ID-8
Williams Creek IN-6
Williams Creek NV-8
Williams Creek OR-9
Williams Creek PA-2
Williams Creek TN-4
Williams Creek VA-3
Williams Creek WI-6
Williams Creek—*gut* SC-3
Williams Creek—*locale* KY-4
**Williams Creek**—*pop pl* IN-6
Williams Creek—*stream* (9) AL-4
Williams Creek—*stream* (3) AK-9
Williams Creek—*stream* AZ-5
Williams Creek—*stream* (6) AR-4
Williams Creek—*stream* (10) CA-9
Williams Creek—*stream* (6) CO-8
Williams Creek—*stream* DE-2
Williams Creek—*stream* (4) FL-3
Williams Creek—*stream* (7) GA-3
Williams Creek—*stream* (16) ID-8
Williams Creek—*stream* (2) IL-6
Williams Creek—*stream* (4) IN-6
Williams Creek—*stream* (4) IA-7
Williams Creek—*stream* (8) KY-4
Williams Creek—*stream* (3) LA-4
Williams Creek—*stream* MD-2
Williams Creek—*stream* (2) MI-6
Williams Creek—*stream* (2) MN-6
Williams Creek—*stream* (3) MS-4
Williams Creek—*stream* (9) MO-7
Williams Creek—*stream* (7) MT-8
Williams Creek—*stream* (3) NV-8
Williams Creek—*stream* (3) NC-3
Williams Creek—*stream* ND-7
Williams Creek—*stream* (3) OH-6
Williams Creek—*stream* (10) OR-9
Williams Creek—*stream* PA-2
Williams Creek—*stream* (2) SC-3
Williams Creek—*stream* SD-7
Williams Creek—*stream* (6) TN-4
Williams Creek—*stream* (17) TX-5
Williams Creek—*stream* (6) VA-3
Williams Creek—*stream* (6) WA-9
Williams Creek—*stream* WV-2
Williams Creek—*stream* WY-8
Williams Creek Archeol District—*hist pl* MO-7
Williams Creek Campground—*locale* CO-8
Williams Creek Campground—*park* OR-9
Williams Creek Cem—*cemetery* TX-5
Williams Creek Ch—*church* GA-3
Williams Creek Ch—*church* IN-6
Williams Creek Ch—*church* (2) KY-4
Williams Creek Dam NC-3
Williams Creek Dam—*dam* ND-7
Williams Creek Guard Station ID-8
Williams Creek Lake Number One AL-4
Williams Creek Lake Number Three AL-4
Williams Creek Lake Number Two AL-4
Williams Creek Natl Fish Hatchery—*park* AZ-5
Williams Creek Ranger Station—*locale* ID-8
Williams Creek Ridge—*ridge* ID-8
Williams Creek Rsvr—*reservoir* CO-8
Williams Creek Sch—*school* TN-4
Williams Creek Spring—*spring* ID-8
Williams Creek Summit—*gap* ID-8
**Williams Creek Township**—*pop pl* SD-7
Williams Creek Trail—*trail* OR-9
Williams Crossing GA-3
Williams Crossing—*locale* CT-1
Williams Crossing—*locale* MI-6
Williams Crossroads MS-4
Williams Crossroads NC-3
Williams Cross Roads—*locale* NC-3
Williams Crossroads—*locale* TN-4
**Williams Cross Roads**—*pop pl* NC-3
**Williams Crossroads**—*pop pl* NC-3
Williams Crossroads (historical)—*locale* AL-4
Williams Dairy—*locale* AZ-5
**Williamsdale**—*pop pl* OH-6
Williams Dale Sch (historical)—*school* PA-2
Williams Dam—*dam* AL-4
Williams Dam—*dam* IN-6
Williams Dam—*dam* ND-7
Williams Dam—*dam* PA-2
Williams Dam—*dam* SD-7
Williams Dam Public Fishing Area—*park* IN-6
Williams Day Care and Kindergarten—*school* FL-3
Williams Delight—*locale* VI-3
Williams Deluxe Cabins—*hist pl* PA-2
Williams District Ranger Station—*locale* AZ-5
Williams Ditch—*canal* CA-9
Williams Ditch—*canal* CO-8
Williams Ditch—*canal* IL-6
Williams Ditch—*canal* (5) IN-6
Williams Ditch—*canal* KY-4
Williams Ditch—*canal* (4) MT-8
Williams Ditch—*canal* (2) OH-6
Williams Ditch—*canal* (3) OR-9
Williams Ditch—*canal* WA-9
Williams Ditch Landing—*locale* FL-3
Williams Ditch No. 2—*canal* CO-8
Williams Divide—*ridge* WY-8
Williams Dock—*locale* TN-4
Williams Drain—*canal* OR-9
Williams Drain—*stream* (2) MI-6
Williams Draw—*valley* (2) CO-8
Williams Draw—*valley* ID-8
Williams Draw—*valley* MT-8
Williams Draw—*valley* SD-7
Williams Draw—*valley* TX-5
Williams Draw—*valley* UT-8
Williams Draw—*valley* (5) WY-8
Williams-Duckworth Cem—*cemetery* CA-9
Williams Dudley Cem—*cemetery* AL-4
Williams Seale Cem—*cemetery* AL-4
Williams-Earle House—*hist pl* SC-3
Williams Elementary School MS-4
Williams Elem Sch—*school* FL-3
Williams-Erwin House—*hist pl* TX-5
**Williams Estate**—*pop pl* SC-3
Williams Estate Pond Dam—*dam* MS-4
Williamsett MA-1
Williams Fall Ch—*church* TN-4
Williams Farm—*hist pl* NY-2
Williams Ferry Access Point—*locale* GA-3
Williams Ferry (historical)—*locale* MS-4
Williams Ferry (historical)—*locale* TN-4
Williams Ferry Post Office MS-4
Williamsfield OH-6
Williams Field—*flat* OR-9
**Williamsfield**—*pop pl* IL-6
**Williamsfield**—*pop pl* OH-6
Williamsfield Cem—*cemetery* OH-6
Williamsfield P O OH-6
Williamsfield (Township of)—*civ div* OH-6
Williams Flat—*flat* CA-9
Williams Flying Service Airp—*airport* MS-4
Williams Fork AZ-5
Williams Fork CO-8
Williams Fork WV-2
Williams Fork—*stream* (2) CO-8
Williams Fork—*stream* (3) KY-4
Williams Fork—*stream* OH-6
Williams Fork—*stream* WV-2
Williams Fork Lake CO-8
Williams Fork Lakes CO-8
Williams Fork Mtns—*range* (2) CO-8
Williams Fork River CO-8
Williams Fork Rsvr—*reservoir* CO-8
Williams Free Library—*hist pl* WI-6
Williams Gap—*gap* GA-3
Williams Gap—*gap* NE-7
Williams Gap—*gap* TN-4
Williams Glacier—*glacier* AK-9
Williams Grade Sch—*school* AZ-5
Williams Graveyard Hill—*summit* MS-4
Williams Grove PA-2
**Williams Grove**—*pop pl* NY-2
**Williams Grove**—*pop pl* PA-2
Williams Grove—*woods* CA-9
Williams Grove Airp—*airport* PA-2
Williams Grove Caves—*cave* PA-2
Williams Grove Cem—*cemetery* GA-3
Williams Grove Cem—*cemetery* TN-4
Williams Grove Ch—*church* (5) GA-3
Williams Grove Ch—*church* NC-3
Williams Grove Ch—*church* TN-4
Williams Grove Park—*park* PA-2
Williams Grove Park Airport PA-2
Williams Grove Sch—*school* GA-3
Williams Grove Sch (historical)—*school* TN-4
Williams Guard Station—*locale* OR-9
Williams Gulch—*valley* (2) CA-9
Williams Gulch—*valley* (2) CO-8
Williams Gulch—*valley* (2) MT-8
Williams Gulch—*valley* WY-8
Williams Gully—*stream* TX-5
Williams Gut—*stream* MD-2
Williams-Hamm Ditch—*canal* CO-8
Williams-Hamm Diversion Ditch CO-8
Williams-Hamm Diversion Ditch—*canal* CO-8
Williams Hammock—*island* FL-3
Williams-Harrison House—*hist pl* NJ-2
Williams-Hays Cem—*cemetery* MO-7
Williams Heights Sch—*school* GA-3
**Williams Heights (subdivision)**—*pop pl* AL-4
Williams-Henson Boys Home—*building* TN-4
William'S Hill MA-1
Williams Hill—*locale* SC-3
Williams Hill—*ridge* AZ-5
Williams Hill—*summit* AK-9
Williams Hill—*summit* CA-9
Williams Hill—*summit* CT-1
Williams Hill—*summit* IL-6
Williams Hill—*summit* KY-4
Williams Hill—*summit* ME-1
Williams Hill—*summit* (2) MA-1
Williams Hill—*summit* NH-1
Williams Hill—*summit* PA-2
Williams Hill—*summit* (2) VT-1
Williams Hill Ch—*church* NC-3
Williams-Hill Family Cem—*cemetery* MS-4
Williams (historical)—*locale* KS-7
Williams Historic Business District—*hist pl* AZ-5
Williams Hole—*cave* NV-8
Williams Hole—*lake* WA-9
Williams Hollow TX-5
Williams Hollow—*basin* NM-5
Williams Hollow—*valley* (3) AL-4
Williams Hollow—*valley* (6) AR-4
Williams Hollow—*valley* CA-9
Williams Hollow—*valley* IL-6
Williams Hollow—*valley* (3) KY-4
Williams Hollow—*valley* MD-2
Williams Hollow—*valley* (2) MO-7
Williams Hollow—*valley* (4) PA-2
Williams Hollow—*valley* (14) TN-4
Williams Hollow—*valley* (2) TX-5
Williams Hollow—*valley* UT-8
Williams Hollow—*valley* VA-3
Williams Hollow—*valley* (5) WV-2
Williams Hosp—*hospital* AZ-5
Williams House—*hist pl* DE-2
Williams House—*hist pl* VA-3
Williams House Sch (historical)—*school* TN-4
Williams HS—*school* AZ-5
Williams HS—*school* NC-3
Williams HS—*school* (2) TX-5
William Shugart Lake—*reservoir* NC-3
William Shugart Lake Dam—*dam* NC-3
William Silcox Grant—*civil* FL-3
Williams Island—*hist pl* TN-4
Williams Island—*island* (3) ME-1
Williams Island—*island* MI-6
Williams Island—*island* MN-6
Williams Island—*island* NJ-2
Williams Island—*island* (2) TN-4
Williams Island—*island* VA-3
Williams Island—*island* WA-9
Williams Island—*island* WI-6
Williams Island (historical)—*island* TN-4
Williams JHS—*school* AZ-5
Williams JHS—*school* IA-7
Williams JHS—*school* NY-2
Williams JHS—*school* NC-3
Williams JHS—*school* SD-7
Williams Junction—*locale* AZ-5
Williams Junction—*locale* AR-4
Williams Junior High School AL-4
Williams Knob—*summit* IN-6
Williams Lake MI-6
Williams Lake MN-6
Williams Lake OR-9
Williams Lake—*lake* AK-9
Williams Lake—*lake* CO-8
Williams Lake—*lake* (3) FL-3
Williams Lake—*lake* GA-3
Williams Lake—*lake* (3) ID-8
Williams Lake—*lake* IN-6
Williams Lake—*lake* IA-7
Williams Lake—*lake* (3) LA-4
Williams Lake—*lake* (7) MI-6
Williams Lake—*lake* (6) MN-6
Williams Lake—*lake* (3) NM-5
Williams Lake—*lake* OH-6
Williams Lake—*lake* (2) OR-9
Williams Lake—*lake* PA-2
Williams Lake—*lake* (2) TX-5
Williams Lake—*lake* (6) WA-9
Williams Lake—*lake* (4) WI-6
**Williams Lake**—*pop pl* NY-2
Williams Lake—*reservoir* (6) AL-4
Williams Lake—*reservoir* AR-4
Williams Lake—*reservoir* CO-8
Williams Lake—*reservoir* (4) GA-3
Williams Lake—*reservoir* MA-1
Williams Lake—*reservoir* (2) MS-4
Williams Lake—*reservoir* (2) NC-3
Williams Lake—*reservoir* OH-6
Williams Lake—*reservoir* TN-4
Williams Lake—*stream* FL-3
Williams Lake Dam AL-4
Williams Lake Dam—*dam* (2) AL-4
Williams Lake Dam—*dam* MA-1
Williams Lake Dam—*dam* (9) MS-4
Williams Lake Dam—*dam* NC-3
Williams Lake Recreation Site—*locale* ID-8
Williams Lakes—*lake* CO-8
Williams Lakes—*reservoir* TX-5
Williams Lake Sch—*school* MI-6
Williams Landing MS-4
Williams Landing—*locale* AL-4
Williams Landing—*locale* FL-3
Williams Landing—*locale* GA-3
Williams Landing—*locale* MI-6
Williams Landing and Eastern Downtown Residential Hist Dist—*hist pl* MS-4
Williams Landing (historical)—*locale* (2) AL-4
Williams Landing (historical)—*locale* TN-4
Williams Landing Strip—*airport* CO-8
Williams-Linscott House—*hist pl* MA-1
Williams Little League Park and Municipal Swimming Pool—*park* AZ-5
Williams Lodge—*other* CA-9
Williams (Magisterial District)—*fmr MCD* WV-2
Williams Marina—*locale* AL-4
Williams Meadow—*flat* CA-9
Williams Memorial Cem—*cemetery* FL-3
Williams Memorial Ch—*church* AL-4
Williams Memorial Ch—*church* GA-3
Williams Memorial Ch—*church* NC-3
Williams Memorial Institute—*hist pl* CT-1
Williams Memorial Park—*cemetery* VA-3
Williams Memorial Park—*park* CT-1
Williams Memorial Park—*park* OH-6
Williams Memorial Park Hist Dist—*hist pl* CT-1
Williams Memorial Presbyterian Ch AL-4
Williams Mesa—*summit* AZ-5
Williams Microwave Relay Station—*tower* AZ-5
Williams Mill—*locale* TN-4
Williams Mill—*locale* VA-3
Williams Mill—*locale* WY-8
Williams Mill Branch NC-3
Williams Mill Branch—*stream* AL-4
Williams Mill Creek NC-3
Williams Mill Creek—*stream* GA-3
Williams Mill (historical)—*locale* MS-4
Williams Mill (historical)—*locale* PA-2
Williams Mill (historical)—*locale* (2) TN-4
**Williams Mill (historical)**—*pop pl* OR-9
Williams Mill P. O. (historical)—*locale* AL-4
Williams Mill Pond—*lake* FL-3
Williams Millpond—*reservoir* (2) AL-4
Williams Millpond—*reservoir* MA-1
Williams Millpond—*reservoir* NC-3
Williams Millpond Creek—*stream* AL-4
Williams Millpond Dam—*dam* NC-3
**Williams Mills**—*pop pl* VA-3
Williams Mills (historical)—*locale* AL-4
Williams Mills Post Office (historical)—*building* TN-4
Williams Mine—*mine* AK-9
Williams Mine—*mine* CO-8
Williams Mine—*mine* NV-8
Williams Mine—*mine* TN-4
Williams Mine—*mine* WA-9
Williams Mine—*mine* WV-2
Williams Mine—*mine* WY-8
Williams Mine (underground)—*mine* (2) AL-4
WILLIAM S. MITCHELL (dredge)—*hist pl* MO-7
William Smith Dam—*dam* SD-7
William Smith House—*building* MA-1
William Smith Spring—*spring* UT-8
**Williams Mountain**—*pop pl* WV-2
Williams Mountains AZ-5
Williams Mtn—*summit* AK-9
Williams Mtn—*summit* CA-9
Williams Mtn—*summit* GA-3
Williams Mtn—*summit* ME-1
Williams Mtn—*summit* MO-7
Williams Mtn—*summit* MT-8
Williams Mtn—*summit* NC-3
Williams Mtn—*summit* OK-5
Williams Mtn—*summit* TN-4
Williams Mtns—*range* CO-8
Williams Municipal Airp—*airport* AZ-5
Williams Municipal Golf Course—*other* AZ-5
Williams Narrows MN-6
Williams Number 3 Dam—*dam* SD-7
Williams Number 3 Rsvr—*reservoir* SD-7
Williams Oil Field—*oilfield* TX-5
Williams Old Mill Branch—*stream* NC-3
Williamson IN-6
Williamson MS-4
Williamson—*locale* IA-7
**Williamson**—*pop pl* AR-4
**Williamson**—*pop pl* GA-3
**Williamson**—*pop pl* IL-6
**Williamson**—*pop pl* IA-7
**Williamson**—*pop pl* NY-2
**Williamson**—*pop pl* PA-2
**Williamson**—*pop pl* TX-5
**Williamson**—*pop pl* WV-2
Williamson, Lake—*reservoir* IL-6
Williamson, Mount—*summit* (2) CA-9
Williamson, Mrs. B. F., House—*hist pl* SC-3
Williamson Airp—*airport* IN-6
Williamson and Adams Carriage Factory—*hist pl* TN-4
Williamson Archeol Site—*hist pl* KS-7
Williamson Bayou—*gut* MS-4
Williamson Branch TN-4
Williamson Branch—*stream* GA-3
Williamson Branch—*stream* (3) KY-4
Williamson Branch—*stream* (2) LA-4
Williamson Branch—*stream* MD-2
Williamson Branch—*stream* MO-7
Williamson Branch—*stream* NC-3
Williamson Branch—*stream* (4) TN-4
Williamson Branch—*stream* (2) TX-5
Williamson Branch—*stream* (2) WV-2
Williamson Butte—*summit* MT-8
Williamson Campground OR-9
Williamson Canyon—*valley* AZ-5
Williamson (CCD)—*cens area* GA-3
Williamson Cem—*cemetery* (3) AL-4
Williamson Cem—*cemetery* AR-4
Williamson Cem—*cemetery* (5) GA-3
Williamson Cem—*cemetery* (2) IL-6
Williamson Cem—*cemetery* (2) KY-4
Williamson Cem—*cemetery* LA-4
Williamson Cem—*cemetery* (3) MS-4
Williamson Cem—*cemetery* MO-7
Williamson Cem—*cemetery* (3) NC-3
Williamson Cem—*cemetery* (3) OH-6
Williamson Cem—*cemetery* PA-2
Williamson Cem—*cemetery* SC-3
Williamson Cem—*cemetery* (4) TN-4
Williamson Cem—*cemetery* (2) TX-5
Williamson Cem—*cemetery* (3) WV-2
Williamson Cem Number One—*cemetery* MS-4
Williamson Cem Number Two—*cemetery* MS-4
Williamson (census name for Williamson Center)—*CDP* NY-2
Williamson Center (census name Williamson)—*other* NY-2
Williamson Ch—*church* AR-4
Williamson Ch—*church* OH-6
Williamson Ch—*church* OK-5
Williamson Ch—*church* TN-4
Williamson Ch—*church* TX-5
Williamson Chapel TN-4
Williamson Chapel—*church* AR-4
Williamson Chapel—*church* GA-3
Williamson Chapel—*church* (2) NC-3
Williamson Chapel—*church* TN-4
Williamson Corrals—*locale* WY-8
**Williamson (County)**—*pop pl* IL-6
**Williamson County**—*pop pl* TN-4
**Williamson (County)**—*pop pl* TX-5
Williamson County Airp—*airport* IL-6
Williamson County Courthouse Hist Dist (Boundary Increase)—*hist pl* TX-5
Williamson County Courthouse Historical District—*hist pl* TX-5
Williamson County Memorial Hospital TN-4
Williamson Cove—*valley* GA-3
Williamson Creek TX-5
Williamson Creek—*stream* AR-4
Williamson Creek—*stream* (2) CA-9
Williamson Creek—*stream* FL-3
Williamson Creek—*stream* (2) GA-3
Williamson Creek—*stream* ID-8
Williamson Creek—*stream* (2) LA-4
Williamson Creek—*stream* MI-6
Williamson Creek—*stream* (2) NC-3
Williamson Creek—*stream* (3) OR-9
Williamson Creek—*stream* (2) TX-5
Williamson Creek—*stream* WA-9
Williamson Creek—*stream* WV-2
Williamson Creek—*stream* WI-6
Williamson Creek Cem—*cemetery* TX-5
Williamson Crossroad NC-3
**Williamson Crossroads**—*pop pl* NC-3
Williamson Ditch—*canal* (3) IN-6
Williamson Ditch—*canal* VA-3
Williamson Draw—*valley* WY-8
**Williamson Estates**—*pop pl* TN-4
Williamson Forest Camp—*locale* OR-9
Williamson Grove Sch—*school* TN-4
Williamson Gulch—*valley* SD-7
Williamson Hollow TN-4
Williamson Hollow—*valley* ID-8
Williamson Hollow—*valley* KY-4
Williamson Hollow—*valley* (2) OH-6
Williamson House—*hist pl* AR-4
Williamson House—*hist pl* GA-3
Williamson House—*hist pl* NH-1
Williamson House—*hist pl* NC-3
Williamson Island—*island* GA-3
Williamson Island—*island* MN-6
Williamson Island—*island* WV-2
Williamson-Johnson Cem—*cemetery* PA-2
Williamson-Johnson-Walker Cem AL-4
Williamson-Jones Cem AL-4
Williamson Lake NE-7
Williamson Lake—*lake* GA-3
Williamson Lake—*lake* TX-5
Williamson Lake Dam—*dam* MS-4
Williamson-Little Cem—*cemetery* AL-4
Williamson (Magisterial District)—*fmr MCD* WV-2
Williamson Med Ctr—*hospital* TN-4
Williamson Memorial Ch—*church* VA-3
Williamson Mine (Open Pit)—*mine* CA-9
Williamson Mine (underground)—*mine* TN-4
Williamson Mound Archeol District—*hist pl* OH-6
Williamson Mound State Memorial—*hist pl* OH-6
Williamson Mtn—*summit* OR-9
Williamson Mtn—*summit* TX-5
Williamson Park—*park* MT-8
Williamson Park—*park* ND-7
Williamson Park—*park* PA-2
Williamson Park—*park* SC-3
Williamson Park—*park* TN-4
Williamson Park—*park* TX-5
Williamson Pond—*lake* FL-3
Williamson Pond—*reservoir* NC-3
Williamson Pond Dam—*dam* NC-3
Williamson Ranch—*locale* NM-5
Williamson Ridge—*ridge* TN-4
Williamson River—*stream* OR-9
Williamson River Campground—*park* OR-9
Williamson River Ditch—*canal* OR-9
Williamson River Mission—*church* OR-9
Williamson River Pumping Plant—*other* OR-9
Williamson River Spring—*spring* OR-9
Williamson Road—*uninc pl* VA-3
Williamson Rocks—*island* WA-9
Williamson Run PA-2
Williamson Run—*stream* OH-6
Williamson-Russell-Rahilly House—*hist pl* MN-6
Williamson Sch—*school* AL-4
Williamson Sch—*school* CA-9
Williamson Sch—*school* PA-2
Williamson Sch—*school* SD-7
Williamson Sch—*school* WI-6
Williamsons Chapel Cem—*cemetery* TN-4
Williamson Sch (historical)—*school* (2) TN-4
Williamson School PA-2
**Williamson School (Trade School)**—*pop pl* PA-2
Williamsons Cribs (historical)—*locale* TN-4
Williamson Site—*hist pl* VA-3
Williamsons Lake—*reservoir* AL-4
Williamson Spring—*spring* CA-9
Williamson Spring—*spring* MT-8
Williamsons Sch (historical)—*school* TN-4
Williamsons Store (historical)—*locale* AL-4
Williamsons Township—*civil* NC-3
Williamsons Valley AZ-5
Williamson Swamp—*stream* NC-3
Williamson Swamp Creek GA-3
Williamson Swamp Creek—*stream* GA-3
Williamson Tank—*reservoir* AZ-5
**Williamson (Town of)**—*pop pl* NY-2
Williamson Trade Sch—*school* PA-2
Williamson Valley—*valley* AZ-5
Williamson Valley—*valley* CA-9
Williamson Valley Sch—*school* AZ-5
Williamson Valley Tank—*reservoir* AZ-5
Williamson Valley Wash—*stream* AZ-5
Williamson Well—*locale* NM-5
Williamson Wood Canyon—*valley* MT-8
Williams Overpass (historical)—*crossing* AZ-5
Williams Park—*flat* (2) CO-8
Williams Park—*flat* MT-8
Williams Park—*park* CT-1
Williams Park—*park* FL-3
Williams Park—*park* GA-3
Williams Park—*park* IN-6
Williams Park—*park* (2) IA-7
Williams Park—*park* MI-6
Williams Park—*park* NY-2
Williams Park—*park* OK-5
Williams Park—*park* TN-4
Williams Park—*park* (2) TX-5
**Williams Park**—*pop pl* IL-6
Williams Park Ditch—*canal* CO-8
Williams Pass CO-8
Williams Pass—*gap* CO-8
Williams Pass—*gap* MT-8
Williams Pass—*gut* (2) LA-4
Williams Peak—*summit* AK-9
Williams Peak—*summit* AZ-5
Williams Peak—*summit* (2) CA-9
Williams Peak—*summit* CO-8
Williams Peak—*summit* (3) ID-8
Williams Peak—*summit* MT-8
Williams Peak—*summit* OK-5
Williams Peak—*summit* UT-8
**William Spear Addition**—*pop pl* TX-5
Williams Place—*hist pl* SC-3
Williams Place—*locale* NV-8
**Williams Place**—*pop pl* IL-6
Williams Plains—*hist pl* MD-2
Williams Plantation—*locale* MS-4
Williams Playground—*park* ME-1
Williams Plaza—*post sta* GA-3
Williams Point—*cape* AL-4
Williams Point—*cape* (2) CA-9
Williams Point—*cape* (2) MD-2
Williams Point—*cape* (2) MO-7
Williams Point—*cape* TX-5
Williams Point—*cape* VA-3
Williams Point—*cape* WA-9
Williams Point—*cape* WI-6
Williams Point—*cliff* TN-4
**Williams Point**—*pop pl* FL-3
Williams Pond MA-1
Williams Pond—*lake* (3) AL-4
Williams Pond—*lake* CT-1
Williams Pond—*lake* (2) FL-3
Williams Pond—*lake* (4) ME-1
Williams Pond—*lake* MD-2
Williams Pond—*lake* MO-7
Williams Pond—*lake* NH-1
Williams Pond—*lake* RI-1
Williams Pond—*lake* SC-3
Williams Pond—*reservoir* AL-4
Williams Pond—*reservoir* CT-1
Williams Pond—*reservoir* DE-2
Williams Pond—*reservoir* MA-1
Williams Pond—*reservoir* (5) NC-3
Williams Pond—*reservoir* (2) PA-2
Williams Pond—*swamp* (2) FL-3
Williams Pond—*swamp* MA-1
Williams Pond Cem—*cemetery* PA-2
Williams Pond Dam—*dam* DE-2
Williams Pond Dam—*dam* (3) NC-3
Williams Pond Dam—*dam* (2) PA-2
Williamsport IN-6
Williamsport KS-7
Williams Port PA-2
Williamsport—*locale* AK-9
Williamsport—*locale* WV-2
**Williamsport**—*pop pl* IN-6
**Williamsport**—*pop pl* KY-4
**Williamsport**—*pop pl* LA-4
**Williamsport**—*pop pl* MD-2
**Williamsport**—*pop pl* (3) OH-6
**Williamsport**—*pop pl* PA-2
**Williamsport**—*pop pl* TN-4
Williamsport Area Community Coll—*school* PA-2
Williamsport Ch—*church* OH-6
Williamsport City—*civil* PA-2
Williamsport City Hall—*hist pl* PA-2
Williamsport Elem Sch—*school* IN-6
Williamsport (historical)—*locale* KS-7
Williamsport Hospital Airp—*airport* PA-2
Williamsport-Lycoming County Airp—*airport* PA-2
Williamsport Station—*locale* MD-2
**Williamsport (subdivision)**—*pop pl* PA-2
**Williamsport Township**—*pop pl* KS-7
Williams-Powell House—*hist pl* NC-3
Williams Prairie—*flat* OR-9
Williams Prairie Ch—*church* IL-6
Williams Precinct MS-4
Williams Preston Hovet Ditch—*canal* MT-8
William Spring—*spring* UT-8
William Spring Branch AL-4
Williams Private Sch—*school* FL-3
Williams Prong Indian Coulee—*valley* MT-8
Williams Quarry—*mine* PA-2
Williams Ranch CO-8
Williams Ranch—*locale* AZ-5
Williams Ranch—*locale* (5) CA-9
Williams Ranch—*locale* (2) CO-8
Williams Ranch—*locale* MT-8
Williams Ranch—*locale* (2) NE-7
Williams Ranch—*locale* NV-8
Williams Ranch—*locale* (7) NM-5
Williams Ranch—*locale* SD-7
Williams Ranch—*locale* (8) TX-5
Williams Ranch—*locale* (3) WY-8
Williams Ranch Cem—*cemetery* TX-5
Williams Ranch HQ—*locale* NM-5
Williams Range—*range* ID-8
Williams Ravine—*valley* CA-9
Williams Reef—*bar* AK-9
Williams Reservoir MA-1
Williams-rewey Branch—*stream* WI-6
Williams Ridge WA-9
Williams Ridge—*ridge* CA-9
Williams Ridge—*ridge* NV-8
Williams Ridge—*ridge* OH-6
Williams Ridge (historical)—*ridge* OR-9
Williams River AZ-5
Williams River CO-8
Williams River—*stream* MA-1
Williams River—*stream* OR-9
Williams River—*stream* VT-1
Williams River—*stream* WV-2
Williams River Mountains CO-8
Williams River State For—*forest* VT-1
Williams River Trail—*trail* WV-2
Williams Rock—*rock* MA-1
Williams Rocks—*rock* AR-4
Williams RR Station—*building* AZ-5
Williams RR Station—*locale* FL-3
Williams Rsvr—*reservoir* (3) CA-9
Williams Rsvr—*reservoir* (2) CO-8
Williams Rsvr—*reservoir* ID-8
Williams Rsvr—*reservoir* MT-8
Williams Rsvr—*reservoir* ND-7
Williams Rsvr—*reservoir* OR-9
Williams Rsvr—*reservoir* (2) WY-8
Williams Rsvr No 2—*reservoir* WY-8
Williams Run OH-6
Williams Run—*stream* OH-6
Williams Run—*stream* (6) PA-2
Williams Run—*stream* VA-3
Williams Run—*stream* (3) WV-2
Williams Run Dam—*dam* PA-2
Williams Run Rsvr—*reservoir* PA-2
Williams Saltpeter Cave—*cave* AL-4
Williams Saltpeter Cave—*cave* TN-4
Williams Sanctuary Ch—*church* AL-4
Williams Sch IN-6
Williams Sch TN-4
Williams Sch—*hist pl* OK-5
Williams Sch—*school* AL-4
Williams Sch—*school* AR-4
Williams Sch—*school* (8) CA-9
Williams Sch—*school* (2) CT-1
Williams Sch—*school* DE-2
Williams Sch—*school* FL-3
Williams Sch—*school* GA-3
Williams Sch—*school* (6) IL-6
Williams Sch—*school* IN-6
Williams Sch—*school* (2) KS-7
Williams Sch—*school* KY-4
Williams Sch—*school* LA-4
Williams Sch—*school* (2) ME-1
Williams Sch—*school* (5) MA-1
Williams Sch—*school* (3) MI-6
Williams Sch—*school* MN-6
Williams Sch—*school* (2) MS-4
Williams Sch—*school* MO-7
Williams Sch—*school* NE-7
Williams Sch—*school* NV-8
Williams Sch—*school* (2) NY-2
Williams Sch—*school* (2) NC-3
Williams Sch—*school* OH-6
Williams Sch—*school* (2) PA-2
Williams Sch—*school* SC-3
Williams Sch—*school* (2) TN-4
Williams Sch—*school* (6) TX-5
Williams Sch—*school* (2) VA-3
Williams Sch—*school* WV-2
Williams Sch (abandoned)—*school* (2) MO-7
Williams Sch (historical)—*school* (3) AL-4
Williams Sch (historical)—*school* (3) MS-4
Williams Sch (historical)—*school* MO-7
Williams Sch (historical)—*school* (2) PA-2
Williams Sch (historical)—*school* TN-4
Williams Shaft—*mine* AZ-5
Williams Shearing Pens—*locale* WY-8
Williams Shoals—*bar* TN-4
Williams Sink—*basin* NM-5

Williamss Island ... TN-4
Williams Site (22-Ha-585)—hist pl ... MS-4
Williams Ski Area—park ... AZ-5
Williams Ski Run—other ... AZ-5
Williams Slope Mine (underground)—mine ... AL-4
Williams Slough—stream ... AK-9
Williams Slough—stream ... FL-3
Williams Slough—stream ... NV-8
Williams Spring ... MO-7
Williams Spring—spring (4) ... AL-4
Williams Spring—spring (2) ... AZ-5
Williams Spring—spring ... GA-3
Williams Spring—spring ... MS-4
Williams Spring—spring (2) ... MO-7
Williams Spring—spring (2) ... NV-8
Williams Spring—spring ... OR-9
Williams Spring—spring ... TN-4
Williams Spring—spring ... TX-5
Williams Spring—spring ... WA-9
Williams Spring—spring ... WY-8
Williams Spring Branch—stream (2) ... AL-4
Williams Spring Branch—stream ... MO-7
Williams Spring Number Three—spring ... OR-9
Williams Spring Number Two—spring ... OR-9
Williams Springs ... NV-8
Williams Springs—locale ... TN-4
Williams Springs—spring ... OR-9
Williams Spur ... AL-4
Williamss Shoals ... TN-4
Williams Stadium—other ... TX-5
Williams Station ... AL-4
Williams Station ... PA-2
**Williams Station**—pop pl ... KY-4
Williams Station Cem—cemetery ... AL-4
Williams Storage Canal—canal ... LA-4
Williams Store—locale ... KY-4
Williams Store—locale ... MO-7
Williams Store—locale ... TN-4
Williams Store (historical)—locale (2) ... AL-4
Williams Store (historical)—locale (4) ... MS-4
Williams Store (historical)—locale (2) ... TN-4
Williams Stream ... ME-1
Williams Street Parkway—hist pl ... CO-8
Williams Street Sch—school ... MA-1
**Williams Subdivision)**—pop pl ... TN-4
**Williams Subdivision**—pop pl (2) ... UT-8
**Williams Subdivision (subdivision)**—pop pl ... NC-3
**Williams Subdivision (subdivision)**—pop pl ... SD-7
Williams Sullivan High Schol ... MS-4
William S Sutton Sch—school ... TX-5
Williams Swamp—stream ... NC-3
Williams Swamp—swamp ... FL-3
William S Talbot Elem Sch—school ... FL-3
Williams Tank—reservoir (2) ... AZ-5
Williams Tank—reservoir (2) ... NM-5
Williams Tank—reservoir (2) ... TX-5
Williams Tanks—reservoir ... AZ-5
Williams-Tarbutton House—hist pl ... TX-5
**Williamston**—pop pl ... MI-6
**Williamston**—pop pl ... NC-3
**Williamston**—pop pl ... SC-3
Williamston City Hall—building ... NC-3
Williamston Gencral Hosp—hospital ... NC-3
Williamston HS—school ... NC-3
Williamston JHS—school ... NC-3
Williamston-Pelzer (CCD)—cens area ... SC-3
Williamston Post Office—building ... NC-3
Williamston Primary Sch—school ... NC-3
Williamston (Township of)—fmr MCD ... NC-3
**Williamston (Township of)**—pop pl ... MI-6
Williamstown (2) ... IN-6
Williamstown ... NJ-2
Williamstown ... PA-2
Williamstown—locale ... IA-7
Williamstown—locale ... PA-2
**Williamstown**—pop pl ... AL-4
**Williamstown**—pop pl ... GA-3
**Williamstown**—pop pl ... IN-6
**Williamstown**—pop pl (2) ... IA-7
**Williamstown**—pop pl ... KS-7
**Williamstown**—pop pl ... KY-4
**Williamstown**—pop pl ... MA-1
**Williamstown**—pop pl ... MO-7
**Williamstown**—pop pl ... NJ-2
**Williamstown**—pop pl ... NY-2
**Williamstown**—pop pl ... OH-6
**Williamstown**—pop pl (3) ... PA-2
**Williamstown**—pop pl ... VT-1
**Williamstown**—pop pl ... WV-2
Williamstown Borough—civil ... PA-2
Williamstown Cem—cemetery ... MO-7
Williamstown (census name for Williamstown Center)—CDP ... MA-1
Williamstown Center (census name Williamstown)—other ... MA-1
Williamstown Ch—church ... GA-3
Williamstown Ch—church ... IA-7
Williamstown Creek—stream ... KY-4
Williamstown-Dry Ridge (CCD)—cens area ... KY-4
Williamstown Gulf—valley ... VT-1
Williamstown (historical)—locale ... MS-4
Williamstown House of Local History—building ... MA-1
Williamstown HS—school ... NJ-2
**Williamstown Junction**—pop pl ... NJ-2
Williamstown Lake—reservoir ... KY-4
Williamstown Reservoir Dam—dam ... MA-1
Williamstown Rsvr—reservoir ... MA-1
Williams Township—civil (3) ... MO-7
Williams Township—fmr MCD (2) ... IA-7
**Williams Township**—pop pl (2) ... ND-7
Williams Township Elem Sch—school ... PA-2
Williams Township Hall—locale ... IA-7
Williams Township HS—school ... NC-3
Williams (Township of)—fmr MCD ... AR-4
Williams (Township of)—fmr MCD (2) ... NC-3
**Williams (Township of)**—pop pl ... IL-6
**Williams (Township of)**—pop pl ... MI-6
**Williams (Township of)**—pop pl ... MN-6
**Williams (Township of)**—pop pl (2) ... PA-2
**Williamstown (Town of)**—pop pl ... MA-1
**Williamstown (Town of)**—pop pl ... NY-2
**Williamstown (Town of)**—pop pl ... VT-1
**Williamstown (Town of)**—pop pl ... WI-6
Williamstown Tunnel—tunnel ... PA-2
Williams Trail—trail ... PA-2
William Street Hist Dist—hist pl ... MA-1
William Street Sch—hist pl ... IN-6
Williams Truax Ditch—canal ... CO-8
Williams Valley—basin ... CA-9
Williams Valley—flat ... CA-9
Williams Valley—stream ... CA-9
Williams Valley—valley ... AZ-5
Williams Valley—valley ... WA-9
Williams Valley Hillside Cem—cemetery ... WA-9
Williams Valley HS—school ... PA-2
Williams Valley Junction—locale ... PA-2
Williams Valley Sch—school ... PA-2
Williams Valley Tank—reservoir ... CA-9
**Williams Village**—pop pl ... NC-3
Williamsville ... GA-3
Williamsville—hist pl ... VA-3
Williamsville—locale (2) ... DE-2
Williamsville—locale ... PA-2
Williamsville—locale (2) ... VA-3
**Williamsville**—pop pl ... IL-6
**Williamsville**—pop pl (2) ... MA-1
**Williamsville**—pop pl (2) ... MI-6
**Williamsville**—pop pl (2) ... MS-4
**Williamsville**—pop pl ... MO-7
**Williamsville**—pop pl ... NY-2
**Williamsville**—pop pl ... VT-1
Williamsville Baptist Ch—church ... MS-4
Williamsville Cem—cemetery ... MS-4
Williamsville Cem—cemetery ... OH-6
Williamsville Ch—church ... MS-4
Williamsville Ch—church ... SC-3
Williamsville Covered Bridge—hist pl ... VT-1
Williamsville (historical)—locale ... MS-4
Williamsville Lake—lake ... MI-6
Williamsville Lookout Tower—tower ... MO-7
Williamsville (Magisterial District)—fmr MCD ... VA-3
Williamsville Pond—reservoir ... MA-1
Williamsville Pond Dam—dam ... MA-1
Williamsville Post Office (historical)—building ... MS-4
Williamsville Sch—school ... NE-7
Williamsville Sch—school ... NY-2
**Williamsville Station**—pop pl ... VT-1
Williamsville Water Mill Complex—hist pl ... NY-2
Williams-Walker Cemetery ... MS-4
Williams-Warren-Zimmerman House—hist pl ... IN-6
Williams Waterhole—lake ... FL-3
Williams Well—locale ... NM-5
Williams Well—well (2) ... AZ-5
Williams Well—well ... CA-9
Williams Well—well ... NM-5
Williams Well—well (2) ... TX-5
Williams Wells—well ... WA-9
**Williams West Subdivision**—pop pl ... UT-8
Williams Wharf—locale ... MD-2
Williams Wharf—locale ... VA-3
Williams-Wilson Cem—cemetery ... MS-4
Williams Windmill—locale ... CO-8
Williams Windmill—locale (4) ... TX-5
Williams-Wootton House—hist pl ... AR-4
William Symington, Lake—lake ... WA-9
Williams 783 Dam—dam ... SD-7
Williams 783 Rsvr—reservoir ... SD-7
William Teague Cem—cemetery ... AR-4
William Tell Mine—mine ... CA-9
William Tell Saloon and Hotel—hist pl ... CA-9
William Thomas Cem—cemetery ... MS-4
William T McFather Vocational Technical Center—school ... FL-3
Williamtown ... IN-6
William (Township of)—fmr MCD ... NC-3
William T Piper Memorial Airport ... PA-2
William Traverse Grant—civil ... FL-3
William Troup Ditch—canal ... IN-6
William Vogus Ditch—canal ... IN-6
William Watson Woolen Elem Sch—school ... IN-6
William W Borden Elem Sch—school ... IN-6
William W Borden HS—school ... IN-6
William W Estes Elem Sch—school ... NC-3
William Whitley House State Shrine—park ... KY-4
William Winans Attendance Center—school ... MS-4
William Wise Oil Field—oilfield ... TX-5
William Woods Coll—school ... MO-7
William Wren Sch (historical)—school ... MO-7
William Wyatt Bibb Bridge ... AL-4
**Williana**—pop pl ... LA-4
Willian Creek ... ID-8
Willian Lock Ditch—canal ... IN-6
Williard—locale ... PA-2
Williard Hall—hist pl ... OH-6
Williard Run—stream ... OH-6
Williards ... MD-2
Williard School ... IN-6
Williard Ward Ch—church ... WY-8
Willia Wilson Elem Sch—school ... MS-4
Williba—locale ... KY-4
Willibert, Mount—summit ... AK-9
Willibet—locale ... WV-2
Willie—locale ... GA-3
Willie, James G., House—hist pl ... UT-8
Willie, Point—cape ... FL-3
Willie Bluff—cliff ... TN-4
Willie Branch—stream ... KY-4
Willie Branch—stream ... TN-4
Willie Branch—stream ... TX-5
Willie Brook—stream ... VT-1
Willie Bull Prong—stream ... MT-8
Willie B Whitehead Ranch—locale ... TX-5
Willie Canyon—valley ... NM-5
Willie Cem—cemetery ... FL-3
Willie Cem—cemetery ... LA-4
Willie Chapel—church ... VA-3
Willie Cockran Estate Lake Dam—dam ... MS-4
Willie Creek—stream ... TX-5
Willie Creek—stream ... WA-9
Willie Dumas Pond Dam—dam ... MS-4
Willie Fortenberry Lake Dam—dam ... MS-4
Willie Hoaglin Place—locale ... CA-9
Willie Holcomb Lake Dam—dam ... MS-4
Willie Knob—summit ... NC-3
Willie Knob—summit ... VA-3
Willie Lake—lake ... MN-6
Willie Lee Creek—stream ... AL-4
Willie Mae Mine (underground)—mine ... AL-4
Willie May Mine ... AL-4
Willie Metcalf Creek—stream ... NC-3
Willie Moore Prospect—mine ... TN-4
Willieo Ch—church ... OK-5
Willie Park—park ... AZ-5
Willie Parker Lake Dam—dam ... MS-4
Willie Patch Creek ... UT-8
Willie Petes—locale ... AK-9
Willie Pond—lake ... FL-3
Willie Rose Mine—mine ... AZ-5
Willie Rsvr—reservoir ... MT-8
Willies Bayou—gut ... LA-4
Willies Canyon—valley ... ID-8
Willies Creek—stream ... ID-8
Willies Flat—flat ... UT-8
Willies Flat Rsvr—reservoir ... UT-8
Willie's Hill ... MA-1
Willies Hollow—valley ... UT-8
Willie Slough Gully—gut ... TX-5
Willies Necktie Rapids—rapids ... AZ-5
Willies Point—cape ... ID-8
Willies Pond ... MA-1
Willies Pond—lake ... WI-6
Willie Spring—spring ... UT-8
Willies Rsvr—reservoir ... ID-8
Willies Tank—reservoir ... NM-5
Willie Tank—reservoir ... NM-5
Willie Tank—reservoir ... TX-5
Willie Well—well ... NM-5
Willie White Canyon—valley ... NM-5
Willie Wilbourne Dam—dam ... AL-4
Willie Wilbourne Lake ... AL-4
Willie Woods Dam Number 1—dam ... AL-4
Willie Woods Dam Number 2—dam ... AL-4
Willie Woods Dam Number 3—dam ... AL-4
Willie Woods Lake—reservoir ... AL-4
Williford—locale ... FL-3
**Williford**—pop pl ... AR-4
Williford Bend ... AL-4
Williford Branch—stream ... GA-3
Williford Branch—stream ... TN-4
Williford Sch—school ... NC-3
Willifords Landing—locale ... AL-4
Willifords Landing—locale ... NC-3
Willifordtown—uninc pl ... NC-3
Willigs Point—cape ... NY-2
Willima Lake—swamp ... MN-6
Williman Creek—stream ... SC-3
Williman Island ... SC-3
Williman Islands—island ... SC-3
**Willimansett (subdivision)**—pop pl ... MA-1
Willimantic ... CT-1
**Willimantic**—pop pl ... CT-1
**Willimantic**—pop pl ... ME-1
Willimantic Armory—hist pl ... CT-1
Willimantic Camp Ground—locale ... CT-1
Willimantic Country Club—other ... CT-1
Willimantic Footbridge—hist pl ... CT-1
Willimantic Freight House and Office—hist pl ... CT-1
Willimantic River—stream ... CT-1
Willimantic Rsvr ... CT-1
Willimantic Rsvr—reservoir ... CT-1
**Willimantic (Town of)**—pop pl ... ME-1
Willim Branch—stream ... KY-4
Willimson Cem—cemetery ... KY-4
Willimson Spring—spring ... KY-4
Willimston ... MA-1
Willincham Cem—cemetery ... TX-5
Willing—locale ... MS-4
Willing, Dr. George M., House—hist pl ... MO-7
**Willingboro**—pop pl ... NJ-2
Willingboro (Levittown)—CDP ... NJ-2
Willingboro Plaza—locale ... NJ-2
**Willingboro (Township of)**—pop pl ... NJ-2
Willinger Spring—spring ... ID-8
**Willingham**—pop pl ... GA-3
Willingham Bay—bay ... TX-5
Willingham Bayou—stream ... LA-4
Willingham Branch—stream ... AL-4
Willingham Branch—stream ... TX-5
Willingham Cem—cemetery (2) ... AL-4
Willingham Creek—stream ... OR-9
**Willingham Estates**—pop pl ... AL-4
Willingham-Hill-O'Neal Cottage—hist pl ... GA-3
Willingham Methodist Church ... AL-4
Willingham Sch (historical)—school ... AL-4
Willinghams Dock ... AL-4
Willinghams Ferry (historical)—locale ... AL-4
Willingham Site—hist pl ... TX-5
Willingham Spring—spring ... GA-3
Willingham Spring Creek—stream ... GA-3
Willingham Springs Ch—church ... TX-5
Willinghams Traps (historical)—locale ... AL-4
Willing Lake—lake ... MI-6
Willing Lake—lake ... MN-6
Willing Post Office (historical)—building ... MS-4
Willings Bayou ... MS-4
Willings Creek—stream ... MD-2
Willington ... DE-2
**Willington**—pop pl ... SC-3
Willington Cem—cemetery ... SC-3
Willington Grove—locale ... MN-6
**Willington Hill**—pop pl ... CT-1
Willington's Point ... MD 2
**Willington (Town of)**—pop pl ... CT-1
Willingtown ... DE-2
**Willing (Town of)**—pop pl ... NY-2
Willing Worker Cem—cemetery ... MS-4
Willing Worker Ch—church ... NC-3
Willinicker Spring—spring ... ID-8
Willin Village Archeol Site—hist pl ... MD-2
Willis ... OH-6
Willis ... VA-3
Willis—locale ... AR-4
Willis—locale ... FL-3
Willis—locale ... LA-4
Willis—locale ... NE-7
Willis—locale ... TN-4
**Willis**—pop pl ... IN-6
**Willis**—pop pl ... KS-7
**Willis**—pop pl ... MI-6
**Willis**—pop pl ... MS-4
**Willis**—pop pl ... MT-8
**Willis**—pop pl ... OK-5
**Willis**—pop pl ... TN-4
**Willis**—pop pl ... TX-5
**Willis**—pop pl (2) ... VA-3
Willis, Henry, House—hist pl ... NC-3
Willis, Joseph, House—hist pl ... MA-1
Willis, Joseph S., House—hist pl ... UT-8
Willis, Judge William R., House—hist pl ... OR-9
Willis, Lake—lake ... FL-3
Willis, Mathias, Store House—hist pl ... KY-4
Willis, Stillman, House—hist pl ... MA-1
Willisara, Lake—lake ... FL-3
Willis Ave Sch—school ... NY-2
Willis Bald—summit ... AR-4
Willis Barber Hollow—valley ... TN-4
Willis Bayou—stream ... LA-4
Willis Bayou—stream ... MS-4
Willis Bottom (historical)—flat ... TN-4
**Willis Branch**—pop pl ... WV-2
Willis Branch—stream (3) ... AL-4
Willis Branch—stream (2) ... AR-4
Willis Branch—stream ... DE-2
Willis Branch—stream ... IL-6
Willis Branch—stream (4) ... KY-4
Willis Branch—stream (2) ... MS-4
Willis Branch—stream (2) ... MO-7
Willis Branch—stream ... NC-3
Willis Branch—stream (4) ... TN-4
Willis Branch—stream (3) ... VA-3
Willis Branch—stream (2) ... WV-2
Willis Branch Oil Field—oilfield ... MS-4
Willis Brook ... CT-1
Willis Brook ... NJ-2
Willis Brook ... NY-2
Willis Brook—stream ... MA-1
Willis Brook—stream (2) ... NY-2
**Willisburg**—pop pl ... KY-4
Willisburg (CCD)—cens area ... KY-4
Willisburg Ch—church ... KY-4
Willisburg Lake—reservoir ... KY-4
Willis Buttes—summit ... MT-8
Willis Campbells Cem—cemetery ... VA-3
Willis Canyon—valley ... AZ-5
Willis Canyon—valley ... UT-8
Willis Canyon—valley ... WA-9
Willis Cave—cave ... AL-4
Willis (CCD)—cens area ... TX-5
Willis Cem—cemetery (4) ... AL-4
Willis Cem—cemetery (2) ... AR-4
Willis Cem—cemetery (4) ... GA-3
Willis Cem—cemetery (2) ... IN-6
Willis Cem—cemetery (2) ... KY-4
Willis Cem—cemetery ... LA-4
Willis Cem—cemetery ... MS-4
Willis Cem—cemetery (4) ... MO-7
Willis Cem—cemetery (2) ... NY-2
Willis Cem—cemetery ... OH-6
Willis Cem—cemetery ... SC-3
Willis Cem—cemetery (4) ... TN-4
Willis Cem—cemetery ... TX-5
Willis Cem—cemetery ... VT-1
Willis Cem—cemetery (3) ... VA-3
Willis Ch—church ... VA-3
Willis Chapel—church ... AL-4
Willis Chapel—church ... GA-3
Willis Chapel—church ... IL-6
Willis Chapel—church ... MO-7
Willis Chapel—church ... SC-3
Willis Chapel—church (2) ... TN-4
Willis Chapel—church (3) ... VA-3
Willis Chapel Cem—cemetery ... MO-7
Willis Chapel Ch ... AL-4
Willis Corner—locale ... NJ-2
**Willis Corners**—pop pl ... ME-1
Willis Coulee—valley (2) ... MT-8
Willis Cove—valley (2) ... NC-3
Williscraft Dam—dam ... AZ-5
Williscraft Tank—reservoir ... AZ-5
Willis Creek ... NJ-2
Willis Creek ... NY-2
Willis Creek ... NC-3
Willis Creek ... TX-5
Willis Creek ... VA-3
Willis Creek—bay (2) ... NC-3
Willis Creek—locale ... KY-4
Willis Creek—stream (2) ... AK-9
Willis Creek—stream ... AR-4
Willis Creek—stream ... GA-3
Willis Creek—stream ... MD-2
Willis Creek—stream (2) ... MS-4
Willis Creek—stream ... MT-8
Willis Creek—stream ... NV-8
Willis Creek—stream ... NJ-2
Willis Creek—stream ... NY-2
Willis Creek—stream ... NC-3
Willis Creek—stream ... OK-5
Willis Creek—stream (4) ... OR-9
Willis Creek—stream ... PA-2
Willis Creek—stream ... SC-3
Willis Creek—stream ... TN-4
Willis Creek—stream (3) ... TX-5
Willis Creek—stream (3) ... UT-8
Willis Creek—stream (2) ... VA-3
Willis Creek Cem—cemetery ... OR-9
Willis Creek Ch—church ... NC-3
Willis Day Industrial Park—facility ... OH-6
Willis Dickerson Tank—reservoir ... NM-5
Willis Ditch ... IN-6
Willis Ditch—canal ... TX-5
Willis Ditch—canal ... UT-8
Willis Drain canal ... MI-6
Willis Draw—valley ... WY-8
Willis Folks Cem—cemetery ... MS-4
Willis Gap—gap ... NC-3
Willis Gap—gap ... VA-3
Willis Gap Ch—church ... VA-3
Willis Glacier ... WA-9
Willis Grove Ch—church ... GA-3
Willis Gulch—valley (2) ... CO-8
Willis Gulch—valley ... ID-8
Willis Gulf—valley ... NY-2
Willis Hall-Carlton College—hist pl ... MN-6
Willis-Hare Elementary School ... NC-3
Willis Heights—uninc pl ... MS-4
Willis Heights Primitive Baptist Ch—church ... MS-4
Willis Hill ... MA-1
Willis Hill—summit (2) ... MA-1
Willis Hill—summit ... OH-6
Willis Hill—summit ... TN-4
Willis Hole—lake ... CA-9
Willis Hollow—valley (4) ... AL-4
Willis Hollow—valley ... TN-4
Willis Hollow—valley ... VA-3
Willis House—hist pl ... PA-2
Willis HS—school ... OH-6
Willis Island—island ... ME-1
Willis Jepson Hole ... CA-9
Willis JHS—school ... AZ-5
Willis Knob—summit ... GA-3
Willis Knob—summit ... KY-4
Willis Lake ... GA-3
Willis Lake ... MA-1
Willis Lake—lake ... CO-8
Willis Lake—lake ... GA-3
Willis Lake—lake ... LA-4
Willis Lake—lake ... MI-6
Willis Lake—lake ... MN-6
Willis Lake—lake ... NY-2
Willis Lake—lake ... NC-3
Willis Lake—lake ... PA-2
Willis Lake—lake ... TX-5
Willis Lake—reservoir (2) ... GA-3
Willis Lake—reservoir (2) ... NC-3
Willis Lake—swamp ... MN-6
Willis Lake Bridge (historical)—bridge ... TN-4
Willis Lake Cove—valley ... TN-4
Willis Lake Dam—dam (2) ... NC-3
Willis Lake Mission—church ... GA-3
Willis Landing—locale ... FL-3
Willis Landing—locale (3) ... NC-3
Willis Line Well—well ... NM-5
Willis Lookout—locale ... TX-5
Willis (Magisterial District)—fmr MCD ... VA-3
Willis Marsh—swamp ... TX-5
Willis Marsh—swamp ... VA-3
Willis Meadow—flat ... NV-8
Willis Meadows—flat ... NV-8
Willis Mill ... AL-4
Willis Mill—locale ... ME-1
Willis Millpond—reservoir ... SC-3
Willis Mountain ... TX-5
Willisms Point—cape ... ME-1
Willis Mtn—summit ... NH-1
Willis Mtn—summit ... NY-2
Willis Mtn—summit ... VA-3
Willis Oil Field—oilfield ... TX-5
Willison Branch—stream ... KY-4
Willison Cem—cemetery ... IA-7
Willison Run—stream ... OH-6
Willis Palms—locale ... CA-9
Willis Park Sch—school ... OH-6
**Willis Park (subdivision)**—pop pl ... PA-2
**Willis Plaza**—pop pl ... GA-3
Willis Point—cape ... FL-3
Willis Point—cape ... ME-1
Willis Point—cape ... NC-3
Willis Point—cape ... VA-3
Willis Pond—lake ... CT-1
Willis Pond—lake ... LA-4
Willis Pond—lake ... MA-1
Willis Pond—lake ... NY-2
Willis Pond—reservoir ... MA-1
Willis Pond—reservoir ... SC-3
Willis Pond—swamp ... FL-3
Willis Pond Rsvr ... MA-1
Willis Prospect—mine ... TN-4
Willis Ranch—locale ... AZ-5
Willis Ranch—locale ... NM-5
Willis Ranch—locale ... TX-5
Willis Ranch—locale ... UT-8
Willis Ranch (reduced usage)—locale ... TX-5
Willis Ridge ... VA-3
Willis Ridge—ridge ... CA-9
Willis River—stream ... VA-3
Willis Ross Camp—locale ... VT-1
Willis Rsvr—reservoir ... UT-8
Willis Run ... NJ-2
Willis Run—stream ... OH-6
Willis Run—stream ... PA-2
Willis Run Pit—cave ... PA-2
Willis-Sale-Stennett House—hist pl ... GA-3
Willis Sch—school ... CT-1
Willis Sch—school ... KS-7
Willis Sch—school ... KY-4
Willis Sch—school ... MI-6
Willis Sch—school ... NH-1
Willis Sch—school ... NJ-2
Willis Sch—school ... OH-6
Willis Sch—school ... TN-4
Willis Sch—school (2) ... VA-3
Willis Sch (abandoned)—school ... PA-2
Willis Sch (historical)—school ... PA-2
Willis Sch (historical)—school (2) ... TN-4
Willis-Scott Cem—cemetery ... AL-4
Willis Sink—basin ... UT-8
Willis Slough—gut ... MS-4
**Willis Spring**—pop pl ... TN-4
Willis Spring—spring ... ID-8
Willis Spring—spring ... UT-8
Willis Spring Cave—cave ... AL-4
**Willis Springs**—pop pl ... TN-4
Willis Station Post Office ... TN-4
Willis Store—locale ... TN-4
Willis Store—locale ... VA-3
**Willis Store**—pop pl ... VA-3
Willis Store (historical)—locale ... MS-4
**Willis Subdivision)**—pop pl ... TN-4
Willis Tank—reservoir ... AZ-5
Willis Tank—reservoir ... TX-5
Willis Thorofare—channel ... NJ-2
Williston—locale ... PA-2
**Williston**—pop pl ... FL-3
**Williston**—pop pl ... MD-2
**Williston**—pop pl ... MS-4
**Williston**—pop pl ... NY-2
**Williston**—pop pl ... NC-3
**Williston**—pop pl ... ND-7
**Williston**—pop pl ... OH-6
**Williston**—pop pl ... PA-2
**Williston**—pop pl ... SC-3
**Williston**—pop pl ... TN-4
**Williston**—pop pl ... VT-1
Williston Acad—school ... MA-1
Williston Baptist Ch—church ... TN-4
Williston Basin—basin ... SD-7
Williston Branch—stream ... VA-3
Williston-Bronson (CCD)—cens area ... FL-3
Williston (CCD)—cens area ... SC-3
Williston Cem—cemetery ... ND-7
Williston Cem—cemetery ... OH-6
Williston Ch—church ... MD-2
Williston City Hall—building ... TN-4
Williston Congregational Church—hist pl ... VT-1
Williston Creek—stream ... NC-3
Williston Highlands (subdivision)—locale ... FL-3
Williston HS—school ... FL-3
Williston Intermediate Sch—school ... FL-3
Williston JHS—school ... NC-3
Williston Lake—lake ... MD-2
Williston Memorial Hosp—hospital ... FL-3
Williston Mill Pond ... MA-1
**Williston Park**—pop pl ... NY-2
Williston Plaza (Shop Ctr)—locale ... FL-3
Williston Point—cliff ... KS-7
Williston Pond ... MA-1
Williston Post Office—building ... TN-4
Williston Road Section ... VT-1
Williston Sch (historical)—school ... TN-4
Willistons Pond ... MA-1
**Williston (Town of)**—pop pl ... VT-1
**Williston Township**—pop pl ... ND-7
Williston Village Hist Dist—hist pl ... VT-1
Williston-West Church and Parish House—hist pl ... ME-1
Willistown—locale ... PA-2
Willistown Post Office (historical)—building ... PA-2
**Willis Township**—pop pl ... ND-7
Willis (Township of)—fmr MCD ... AR-4
**Willistown (Township of)**—pop pl ... PA-2
Willisville—locale ... NY-2
Willisville—locale ... VA-3
**Willisville**—pop pl ... AR-4
**Willisville**—pop pl ... IL-6
**Willisville**—pop pl ... IN-6
Willisville Cem—cemetery ... NY-2
Willisville (Election Precinct)—fmr MCD ... IL-6
Willisville Oil Field—oilfield ... AR-4
Willis Vly—swamp ... NY-2
Willis Wall—cliff ... WA-9
Willis Well—well ... CA-9
Willis Well—well (2) ... NM-5
**Willis Wharf**—pop pl ... VA-3
Willis Windmill—locale ... NM-5
Willit Creek ... WY-8
Willit Ridge—ridge ... MT-8
Willits ... NC-3
**Willits**—pop pl ... CA-9
**Willits**—pop pl ... NC-3
Willits, Ward Winfield, House—hist pl ... IL-6
Willits (CCD)—cens area ... CA-9
Willits Cem—cemetery ... CA-9
Willits Cem—cemetery ... MI-6
Willits Creek—stream ... CA-9
**Willits-Ochre Hill**—pop pl ... NC-3
Willits Ravine—valley ... CA-9
Willits Ridge—ridge ... OR-9
Williwakas Creek—stream ... WA-9
Williwakas Glacier—glacier ... WA-9
Williwaw, Mount—summit ... AK-9
Williwaw Cove—bay ... AK-9
Williwaw Point—cape ... AK-9
Williw Creek—stream ... CO-8
Will Johns Gap—gap ... PA-2
Will Johnson Tank—reservoir ... NM-5
Willke Cem—cemetery ... TX-5
Willkie, Wendell L., Sch—hist pl ... IN-6
Will King Gap—gap ... NC-3
Will Knob—summit ... NC-3
Will Lindon Branch—stream ... KY-4
Willman—locale ... TX-5
Willman Cem—cemetery ... IN-6
Willmansett (historical P.O.)—locale ... MA-1
**Willmar**—pop pl ... MN-6
Willmar Cem—cemetery ... MN-6
Willmar Hosp Farm for Inebriates Hist Dist—hist pl ... MN-6
Willmar Lake—lake ... MN-6
Willmar State Hosp—hospital ... MN-6
Willmarth Sch—school ... VT-1
**Willmar (Township of)**—pop pl ... MN-6
Will Mason Branch—stream ... NC-3
Willmathe Gulch—valley ... ID-8
**Willmathsville**—pop pl ... MO-7
**Willmay**—pop pl ... AL-4
Will May Branch—stream ... KY-4
Willmen Sch—school ... ND-7
Willmer Creek—stream ... MD-2
Willmeth Airp—airport ... KS-7
Willmeth Tank—reservoir ... NM-5
Willmeth Windmill—locale ... NM-5
Willmont Canyon—valley ... CA-9
Willmont Saddle—gap ... CA-9
Will-Moore Sch—school ... ND-7
Willmore Creek ... MO-7
Will-More Mine (underground)—mine ... AL-4
Willmore Park—park ... MO-7
Willmore Post Office (historical)—building ... MS-4
Willmo Sand Creek—stream ... TX-5
Willmuth Cem—cemetery ... AR-4
Willmuth Hill—summit ... AR-4
Will M Whittington Auxiliary Channel—canal (2) ... MS-4
Willobee ... OH-6
**Willock**—pop pl ... PA-2
Willocoochee Creek ... FL-3
Willocoochee Creek ... GA-3
**Will-O-Dean Acres (subdivision)**—pop pl ... NC-3
Willola—locale ... ID-8
Willon Springs—spring ... WA-9
**Willopenn**—pop pl ... PA-2
Will-o-point ... CA-9
Willo Spring ... CA-9
Willota—locale ... CA-9
**Will-O-The-Wisp**—pop pl ... CO-8
Willouby Lake ... WA-9
Willoughby—locale ... MD-2
**Willoughby**—pop pl ... MS-4
**Willoughby**—pop pl ... NY-2
**Willoughby**—pop pl ... OH-6
Willoughby, Lake—lake ... VT-1
**Willoughby Acres (subdivision)**—pop pl ... FL-3
Willoughby Bank—bar ... VA-3
Willoughby Bay—bay ... VA-3
Willoughby-Baylor House—hist pl ... VA-3
Willoughby Beach—beach ... VA-3
**Willoughby Beach**—pop pl ... MD-2
**Willoughby Beach**—pop pl ... VA-3
Willoughby Branch—stream ... AL-4
Willoughby Branch—stream ... MI-6
Willoughby Brook—stream ... NJ-2
Willoughby Brook—stream ... VT-1
Willoughby Canal—canal ... NC-3
Willoughby Cem—cemetery ... GA-3
Willoughby Cem—cemetery ... KS-7

Willoughby Cem—cemetery KY-4
Willoughby Cem—cemetery NC-3
Willoughby Cem—cemetery (2) TN-4
Willoughby Ch—church AR-4
**Willoughby Condominiums (subdivision)**—pop pl NC-3
Willoughby Coulee—valley MT-8
Willoughby Cove—bay AK-9
Willoughby Creek PA-2
Willoughby Creek—gut FL-3
Willoughby Creek—stream KY-4
Willoughby Creek—stream MT-8
Willoughby Creek—stream NY-2
Willoughby Creek—stream TX-5
Willoughby Creek—stream WA-9
Willoughby Drain—canal MI-6
Willoughby Fork—stream KY-4
Willoughby Hill—summit VA-3
**Willoughby Hills**—pop pl OH-6
Willoughby (historical P.O.)—locale IA-7
Willoughby Hollow—valley TN-4
Willoughby Industrial Park—facility OH-6
Willoughby Island—island AK-9
Willoughby Island—island MI-6
Willoughby Lake—lake WA-9
Willoughby Landing Field—airport ND-7
Willoughby Landing (historical)—locale AL-4
Willoughby Mine—mine CA-9
Willoughby Mtn—summit NH-1
Willoughby Mtn—summit VA-3
**Willoughby Place (subdivision)**—pop pl NC-3
Willoughby Point—cape VA-3
Willoughby Ranch—locale (2) TX-5
Willoughby River—stream VT-1
Willoughby Rock—island WA-9
Willoughby Run—stream PA-2
Willoughby Sch—school IL-6
Willoughby Sch—school VT-1
Willoughby School TN-4
Willoughby Spit—cape VA-3
Willoughby Spring—spring OR-9
Willoughby Spring—spring TN-4
Willoughbys Sch (historical)—school TN-4
Willoughby-Suydam Hist Dist—hist pl NY-2
**Willoughby Terrace**—pop pl VA-3
Willoughby (Township of)—other OH-6
Willow CA-9
Willow NE-7
Willow OH-6
Willow WV-2
Willow—CDP AK-9
Willow—locale AZ-5
Willow—locale FL-3
Willow—locale IL-6
Willow—locale IA-7
Willow—locale KY-4
Willow—locale TX-5
Willow—locale VA-3
**Willow**—pop pl AR-4
**Willow**—pop pl KY-4
**Willow**—pop pl MI-6
**Willow**—pop pl NY-2
**Willow**—pop pl NC-3
**Willow**—pop pl OK-5
**Willow Addition**—pop pl WY-8
Willow and Owl Ditch—canal CO-8
Willow Arroyo—valley (2) TX-5
Willoway IL-6
Willowbank Point DE-2
**Willowbank Township**—pop pl ND-7
Willow Bar—bar CA-9
Willow Bar—bar (2) IL-6
Willow Bar—bar (2) MO-7
Willow Bar—bar NE-7
Willow Bar Cem—cemetery OK-5
Willow Bar Cutoff—channel TN-4
Willow Bar Island—island IL-6
Willow Bar Islands—island OR-9
Willow Bar Lake—lake OK-5
Willow Bar Landing—locale IL-6
Willow Basin NV-8
Willow Basin—basin CA-9
Willow Basin—basin NV-8
Willow Basin—basin (2) OR-9
Willow Basin—basin (3) UT-8
Willow Basin—basin WY-8
Willow Basin Creek—stream CA-9
Willow Basin Creek—stream CO-8
Willow Basin Creek—stream OR-9
Willow Basin Creek—stream UT-8
Willow Basin Rsvr—reservoir OR-9
Willow Basin Spring—spring OR-9
Willow Basket Creek—stream ID-8
Willow Bay—bay AK-9
Willow Bay—bay KY-4
Willow Bay—bay PA-2
Willow Bay—bay WA-9
Willow Bay Bayou—gut LA-4
Willow Bayou TX-5
Willow Bayou—gut LA-4
Willow Bayou—stream (4) LA-4
Willow Bayou—stream MS-4
Willow Bayou—stream TX-5
Willow Bayou—swamp MS-4
Willow Bayou Canal—canal LA-4
Willow Bayou Ch—church (2) LA-4
**Willow Bay Subdivision - Numbers 3 and 4**—pop pl UT-8
**Willow Bay Subdivision - Plat 1-4**—pop pl UT-8
Willow Beach—locale AZ-5
**Willow Beach**—pop pl NV-8
**Willow Beach**—pop pl NY-2
**Willow Beach Colony**—pop pl MD-2
**Willow Beach Colony (Willows)**—pop pl MD-2
Willow Beach Gauging Station—hist pl AZ-5
Willow Beach Gauging Station—hist pl NV-8
Willow Beach Lake—lake AR-4
Willow Beach Public Use Area—park AR-4
Willow Beach Sub-District Ranger Station—locale AZ-5
Willow Belle—locale AR-4
Willow Bend—bend AR-4
Willow Bend—bend UT-8
Willow Bend—locale WV-2
**Willowbend**—pop pl NC-3
Willow Bend—uninc pl TX-5
Willow Bend Ch—church AR-4
Willow Bend Sch—school AR-4
Willow Bend Sch—school MT-8
Willow Bend Sch—school NE-7
Willow Bend Sch—school SD-7
**Willow Bend (subdivision)**—pop pl AL-4
**Willow Bend (subdivision)**—pop pl NC-3
**Willow Bend (subdivision)**—pop pl TN-4
Willow Bluff—cliff TX-5
Willow Bog Spring—spring CO-8
Willow Bottom—flat UT-8
Willow Branch AZ-5
Willow Branch TX-5
**Willow Branch**—pop pl IN-6
Willow Branch—stream AK-9
Willow Branch—stream GA-3
Willow Branch—stream (7) IL-6
Willow Branch—stream IN-6
Willow Branch—stream (5) KY-4
Willow Branch—stream MA-1
Willow Branch—stream (19) MO-7
Willow Branch—stream NC-3
Willow Branch—stream (2) OK-5
Willow Branch—stream OR-9
Willow Branch—stream (5) TN-4
Willow Branch—stream (12) TX-5
Willow Branch—stream VA-3
Willow Branch—stream (2) WV-2
Willow Branch—stream WI-6
Willow Branch—stream WY-8
Willow Branch Cem—cemetery IL-6
Willow Branch Cem—cemetery OH-6
Willow Branch Cem—cemetery VA-3
Willow Branch Ch—church IL-6
Willow Branch Ch—church VA-3
Willow Branch Creek—stream OK-5
Willow Branch (historical)—stream TN-4
Willow Branch Hollow—valley VA-3
Willow Branch Landing—locale NC-3
Willow Branch Park—park FL-3
Willow Branch Sch—school (3) MO-7
Willow Branch Sch—school WI-6
Willow Branch School (historical)—locale MO-7
Willow Branch Spring—spring OR-9
Willow Branch (Township of)—civ div IL-6
Willow Bridge Windmill—locale TX-5
Willow Brook MA-1
Willow Brook—locale NJ-2
Willow Brook—locale NY-2
Willowbrook—locale VA-3
**Willowbrook**—pop pl AL-4
**Willow Brook**—pop pl CA-9
**Willowbrook**—pop pl CO-8
**Willowbrook**—pop pl (3) IL-6
**Willowbrook**—pop pl KS-7
**Willowbrook**—pop pl MD-2
**Willow Brook**—pop pl MO-7
**Willow Brook**—pop pl NY-2
**Willowbrook**—pop pl NY-2
**Willowbrook**—pop pl PA-2
**Willowbrook**—pop pl VA-3
Willow Brook—stream (2) CA-9
Willow Brook—stream (4) CT-1
Willow Brook—stream IN-6
Willow Brook—stream (2) IA-7
Willow Brook—stream KS-7
Willow Brook—stream (3) ME-1
Willow Brook—stream MD-2
Willow Brook—stream (6) MA-1
Willow Brook—stream (2) NH-1
Willow Brook—stream NJ-2
Willow Brook—stream (6) NY-2
Willow Brook—stream PA-2
Willow Brook—stream (2) TX-5
Willow Brook—stream (2) VT-1
Willow Brook—stream VA-3
Willow Brook—stream WV-2
Willowbrook Arena—other CO-8
Willowbrook Baptist Ch—church AL-4
Willowbrook Cem—cemetery CT-1
Willow Brook Cem—cemetery IL-6
Willowbrook Ch—church MI-6
Willow Brook Ch—church TN-4
Willow Brook Ch—church WV-2
**Willowbrook Condominium, The**—pop pl UT-8
Willowbrook Country Club—other NY-2
Willow Brook Country Club—other TX-5
**Willow Brooke**—pop pl IL-6
**Willowbrook Estates**—pop pl AL-4
**Willowbrook Estates**—pop pl IN-6
**Willowbrook Estates**—pop pl UT-8
**Willowbrook Farm Subdivision**—pop pl UT-8
Willowbrook Golf Course—other PA-2
Willowbrook Golf Course—locale PA-2
Willow Brook Golf Course—other AZ-5
Willow Brook Golf Course—other NY-2
**Willow Brook Heights**—pop pl OH-6
Willowbrook HS—school IL-6
**WillowBrook II (subdivision)**—pop pl (2) AZ-5
Willowbrook JHS—school CA-9
Willowbrook Lake—reservoir NC-3
Willowbrook Mill (historical)—locale TN-4
Willow Brook Park—park CT-1
Willowbrook Park—park NY-2
**Willow Brook Park**—pop pl NY-2
Willowbrook Park Cem—cemetery NY-2
Willowbrook Park Sch—school CT-1
Willowbrook (RR Name Willowbrook)—CDP CA-9
Willow Brook Sch—school CA-9
Willow Brook Sch—school OK-5
Willow Brook Sch—school TN-4
Willow Brook Sch—school VT-1
Willow Brook Sch (historical)—school MO-7
Willowbrook Square Shop Ctr—locale AL-4
Willowbrook State Sch—school NY-2
**Willowbrook (subdivision)**—pop pl AL-4
**Willow Brook (subdivision)**—pop pl NC-3
**Willowbrook Subdivision**—pop pl UT-8
Willowbrook Village Shop Ctr—locale AL-4
Willow Bunch—woods UT-8
Willow Bunch Rsvr—reservoir WI-6
**Willowburn**—pop pl PA-2
Willow Bush Spring—spring NM-5
Willow Butte—summit (2) OR-9
Willowby Presbyterian Ch (historical)—church AL-4
Willowbys Bay VA-3
Willowbys Point VA-3
Willow Campground—locale (2) CA-9
Willow Campground—locale MT-8
Willow Campground—park OR-9
Willow Camp Spring—spring OR-9
Willow Canal—canal CA-9
Willow Canyon AZ-5
Willow Canyon NV-8
Willow Canyon OR-9
**Willow Canyon**—pop pl AZ-5
Willow Canyon—valley (4) AZ-5
Willow Canyon—valley (3) CA-9
Willow Canyon—valley (9) NV-8
Willow Canyon—valley (5) NM-5
Willow Canyon—valley (2) OR-9
Willow Canyon—valley (2) TX-5
Willow Canyon—valley (5) UT-8
Willow Canyon Sch—school UT-8
Willow Cave—cave AL-4
Willow Cem—cemetery (2) IA-7
Willow Cem—cemetery MA-1
Willow Cem—cemetery NH-1
Willow Cem—cemetery OH-6
Willow Cem—cemetery (2) OK-5
Willow Cem—cemetery TN-4
Willow Cem—cemetery TX-5
Willow Cem—cemetery WY-8
**Willow Cereek Road Terrace Subdivision**—pop pl UT-8
Willow Ch—church GA-3
Willow Ch—church OH-6
Willow Chapel—church NC-3
Willow Chute—locale LA-4
Willow Chute—stream (2) LA-4
Willow Cienega—flat AZ-5
Willow City—locale TX-5
**Willow City**—pop pl ND-7
Willow City Cem—cemetery TX-5
Willow Corral Pass—gap NV-8
Willow Coulee—valley (2) MT-8
Willow Cove CA-9
Willow Cove—basin TX-5
Willow Cove—bay (2) FL-3
Willow Cove—bay LA-4
Willow Cove—bay MS-4
Willow Cove—bay TX-5
Willow Cove Branch—stream FL-3
Willow Cove Public Use Area—park MS-4
**Willow Cove Subdivision**—pop pl UT-8
Willow Creek AZ-5
Willow Creek AR-4
Willow Creek CA-9
Willow Creek CO-8
Willow Creek ID-8
Willow Creek (2) IN-6
Willow Creek KY-4
Willow Creek MI-6
Willow Creek MN-6
Willow Creek MS-4
Willow Creek MO-7
Willow Creek MT-8
Willow Creek NE-7
Willow Creek NV-8
Willow Creek NY-2
Willow Creek ND-7
Willow Creek OH-6
Willow Creek OR-9
Willow Creek SD-7
Willow Creek TX-5
Willow Creek UT-8
Willow Creek WA-9
Willow Creek WY-8
Willow Creek—bay NC-3
Willow Creek—fmr MCD NE-7
Willow Creek—locale (2) AK-9
Willow Creek—locale MN-6
Willow Creek—locale NM-5
Willow Creek—locale NY-2
Willow Creek—locale NC-3
Willowcreek—locale OR-9
Willow Creek—locale TX-5
Willow Creek—locale WY-8
Willow Creek—park IA-7
**Willow Creek**—pop pl AR-4
**Willow Creek**—pop pl CA-9
**Willow Creek**—pop pl CO-8
**Willow Creek**—pop pl IN-6
**Willow Creek**—pop pl MT-8
**Willow Creek**—pop pl SC-3
**Willow Creek**—pop pl WI-6
Willow Creek—stream (11) AK-9
Willow Creek—stream (19) AZ-5
Willow Creek—stream AR-4
Willow Creek—stream (64) CA-9
Willow Creek—stream (36) CO-8
Willow Creek—stream (34) ID-8
Willow Creek—stream (10) IL-6
Willow Creek—stream (6) IN-6
Willow Creek—stream (17) IA-7
Willow Creek—stream (6) KS-7
Willow Creek—stream (7) KY-4
Willow Creek—stream LA-4
Willow Creek—stream MA-1
Willow Creek—stream (8) MI-6
Willow Creek—stream (12) MN-6
Willow Creek—stream (5) MO-7
Willow Creek—stream (41) MT-8
Willow Creek—stream (11) NE-7
Willow Creek—stream (48) NV-8
Willow Creek—stream (9) NM-5
Willow Creek—stream (5) NY-2
Willow Creek—stream NC-3
Willow Creek—stream (6) ND-7
Willow Creek—stream (6) OH-6
Willow Creek—stream (10) OK-5
Willow Creek—stream (31) OR-9
Willow Creek—stream (2) PA-2
Willow Creek—stream SC-3
Willow Creek—stream (14) SD-7
Willow Creek—stream (2) TN-4
Willow Creek—stream (48) TX-5
Willow Creek—stream (29) UT-8
Willow Creek—stream (9) WA-9
Willow Creek—stream (8) WI-6
Willow Creek—stream (52) WY-8
Willow Creek Basin—basin NV-8
Willow Creek Bay—bay SD-7
Willow Creek Branch—stream IN-6
Willow Creek Butte—summit (2) OR-9
Willow Creek Butte—summit SD-7
Willow Creek Butte—summit UT-8
Willow Creek Buttes SD-7
Willow Creek Butte Township—civil SD-7
Willow Creek Cabin—locale MT-8
Willow Creek Cabin—locale OR-9
Willow Creek Camp—locale (2) CA-9
Willow Creek Camp—locale WY-8
Willow Creek Campground—locale (3) ID-8
Willow Creek Campground—locale NV-8
Willow Creek Campground—locale NM-5
Willow Creek Campground—park OR-9
Willow Creek Canal—canal WY-8
Willow Creek Canyon UT-8
Willow Creek Canyon—valley AZ-5
Willow Creek Canyon—valley CO-8
Willow Creek Canyon—valley (2) NV-8
Willow Creek Canyon—valley OR-9
Willow Creek Canyon—valley UT-8
Willow Creek Cem—cemetery CA-9
Willow Creek Cem—cemetery IA-7
Willow Creek Cem—cemetery MT-8
Willow Creek Cem—cemetery NE-7
Willow Creek Cem—cemetery ND-7
Willow Creek Cem—cemetery OK-5
Willow Creek Cem—cemetery (2) TX-5
Willow Creek Ch—church (2) IL-6
Willow Creek Ch—church IN-6
Willow Creek Ch—church NE-7
Willow Creek Ch—church SC-3
Willow Creek Ch—church SD-7
Willow Creek Corral—locale OR-9
Willow Creek Country Club—locale NC-3
Willow Creek Country Club—other MN-6
Willow Creek Country Club—other UT-8
Willow Creek Country Club Estates UT-8
Willow Creek Crossing—locale CA-9
Willow Creek Dam—dam AZ-5
Willow Creek Dam—dam MT-8
Willow Creek Dam—dam (2) OR-9
Willow Creek Dam—dam SD-7
Willow Creek Dam—dam UT-8
Willow Creek Ditch—canal IN-6
Willow Creek Ditch—canal MT-8
Willow Creek Ditch—canal OR-9
**Willowcreek East Subdivision**—pop pl UT-8
**Willow Creek Estates Subdivision**—pop pl UT-8
**Willow Creek Farms (subdivision)**—pop pl AL-4
Willow Creek Feeder Canal—canal MT-8
Willow Creek Flat Rsvr—reservoir MT-8
Willow Creek Flats—flat OR-9
Willow Creek Flowage Number One—reservoir WI-6
Willow Creek Flowage Number Three—reservoir WI-6
Willow Creek Flowage Number Two—reservoir WI-6
Willow Creek Forest Service Facility—locale NV-8
Willow Creek For Preserve—forest IL-6
Willow Creek Golf Course—other AZ-5
Willow Creek Golf Course—other IA-7
Willow Creek Guard Station—locale ID-8
Willow Creek Guard Station—locale NM-5
Willow Creek Guard Station—locale OR-9
Willow Creek Guard Station—locale UT-8
Willow Creek Guard Station—locale WY-8
Willow Creek Gun Club—other CA-9
**Willow Creek Heights Subdivision**—pop pl UT-8
**Willow Creek Hills**—pop pl UT-8
Willow Creek Hills—summit OR-9
**Willow Creek Hill Subdivision**—pop pl UT-8
Willow Creek (historical P.O.)—locale IA-7
Willow Creek Homesite—locale CA-9
Willow Creek - in part UT-8
Willow Creek Jeep Trail—trail CA-9
Willow Creek Lake OR-9
Willow Creek Lake—lake CO-8
Willow Creek Lake—lake OR-9
Willow Creek Lake—reservoir SD-7
Willow Creek Lakes—lake CO-8
Willow Creek Lateral—canal (2) SD-7
Willow Creek Lava Field—lava ID-8
Willow Creek Lodge—locale NM-5
Willow Creek Lookout—locale WY-8
**Willow Creek Meadows**—pop pl UT-8
Willow Creek Mesa—summit CO-8
Willow Creek Mesa Ditch—canal NM-5
**Willow Creek Mesa Subdivision**—pop pl UT-8
Willow Creek Mine—mine AK-9
Willow Creek Mine—mine CO-8
Willow Creek Mountain Trail—trail CA-9
Willow Creek Mtn—summit CA-9
Willow Creek Natl Wildlife Ref—park MT-8
**Willowcreek Oaks Subdivision**—pop pl UT-8
Willow Creek Park—flat CO-8
Willow Creek Park—flat MT-8
Willow Creek Park—locale CO-8
Willow Creek Park—park AZ-5
Willow Creek-Park River Dam Number 1—dam ND-7
Willow Creek Pass—gap CO-8
Willow Creek Pass—gap MT-8
Willow Creek Peak—summit CA-9
Willow Creek Peak—summit ID-8
Willow Creek Peak—summit UT-8
Willow Creek Point—cape NY-2
Willow Creek Port of Entry—locale MT-8
Willow Creek Pump Canal—canal CO-8
Willow Creek Pumping Station No 7—other WY-8
Willow Creek Pump Lateral—canal ID-8
Willow Creek Ranch NV-8
Willow Creek Ranch—locale (2) CA-9
Willow Creek Ranch—locale (2) CO-8
Willow Creek Ranch—locale (2) MT-8
Willow Creek Ranch—locale (7) NV-8
Willow Creek Ranch—locale OK-5
Willow Creek Ranch—locale UT-8
Willow Creek Ranch—locale WY-8
Willow Creek Reservoir SD-7
Willow Creek Resort—locale OR-9
Willow Creek Ridge—ridge NV-8
Willow Creek Ridge—ridge (2) UT-8
Willow Creek Rim—cliff WY-8
Willow Creek Rim Archeol District—hist pl CA-9
Willow Creek Rsvr OR-9
Willow Creek Rsvr—reservoir AZ-5
Willow Creek Rsvr—reservoir (2) CO-8
Willow Creek Rsvr—reservoir ID-8
Willow Creek Rsvr—reservoir (4) MT-8
Willow Creek Rsvr—reservoir (3) NV-8
Willow Creek Rsvr—reservoir (3) OR-9
Willow Creek Rsvr—reservoir (2) UT-8
Willow Creek Rsvr—reservoir WY-8
Willow Creek Rsvr Four—reservoir OR-9
Willow Creek Rsvr Number Three OR-9
Willow Creek Rsvr Two—reservoir OR-9
Willow Creek Rsvr 1—reservoir OR-9
Willow Creek Sch—school CA-9
Willow Creek Sch—school ID-8
Willow Creek Sch—school NE-7
Willowcreek Sch—school OR-9
Willow Creek Sch—school SC-3
Willow Creek Sch—school SD-7
Willow Creek Sch—school (2) WI-6
Willow Creek Sch—school WY-8
Willow Creek Shopping Plaza—locale SD-7
**Willow Creek Siding**—pop pl SC-3
Willow Creek Spring—spring (2) NV-8
Willow Creek Station—locale CA-9
**Willow Creek (subdivision)**—pop pl NC-3
**Willowcreek Subdivision**—pop pl (2) UT-8
**Willow Creek Subdivision**—pop pl UT-8
Willow Creek Summit—summit ID-8
**Willow Creek Terrace Subdivision**—pop pl UT-8
**Willow Creek Township**—pop pl ND-7
**Willow Creek Township**—pop pl SD-7
Willow Creek (Township of)—civ div IL-6
Willow Creek Trail—trail CA-9
Willow Creek Trail—trail ID-8
Willow Creek Valley—valley CA-9
Willow Creek Valley—valley OR-9
**Willow Creek View Subdivision**—pop pl UT-8
Willow Creek Waterhole—reservoir OR-9
Willow Creek Weir—dam AZ-5
Willow Creek Well—well OR-9
Willow Creek Wildlife Mngmt Area—park UT-8
**Willowcrest**—pop pl OH-6
**Willow Crest**—pop pl OH-6
Willow Crest—uninc pl KY-4
Willow Crest Dam—dam NJ-2
Willow Crest Lake—reservoir GA-3
Willow Crest Lake—reservoir NJ-2
Willowcrest Sch—school IL-6
**Willowcrest Subdivision**—pop pl UT-8
Willow Crossing—locale MT-8
Willow Crossing Cem—cemetery MT-8
Willow Cut Off—bend LA-4
Willow Cutoff—channel LA-4
Willowdale—locale OR-9
Willowdale—locale WV-2
**Willowdale**—pop pl KS-7
**Willowdale**—pop pl LA-4
**Willowdale**—pop pl MA-1
**Willowdale**—pop pl NJ-2
**Willowdale**—pop pl PA-2
Willow Dale—valley NY-2
Willowdale Cem—cemetery NE-7
Willow Dale Cem—cemetery NC-3
Willow Dale Cem—cemetery PA-2
Willowdale Ch—church KS-7
Willow Dale Chapel—church WV-2
Willowdale Creek—stream ID-8
Willowdale Golf Course—other ME-1
Willowdale Hill MA-1
Willow Dale (historical P.O.)—locale IA-7
Willowdale Lake—lake OH-6
Willowdale Landing—locale MS-4
Willowdale Oil and Gas Field—oilfield KS-7
Willowdale Reservoir MA-1
Willowdale Sch—school IN-6
Willowdale Sch—school (3) NE-7
Willowdale Sch—school SD-7
Willowdale State For—forest MA-1
**Willowdale Township**—pop pl KS-7
**Willowdale Township**—pop pl NE-7
Willow Dam Slough—stream TX-5
Willow Dam Tank—dam AZ-5
**Willowdell**—pop pl OH-6
Willow Dell Cem—cemetery NY-2
Willowdell Cem—cemetery OH-6
Willowdell Park Site—park TX-5
Willow Dell Sch—school NE-7
Willow Dell Sch—school WY-8
Willow Dike—dam WY-8
Willow Ditch—canal AR-4
Willow Ditch—canal WY-8
Willow Divide—ridge CO-8
Willow Draw—valley (2) CO-8
Willow Draw—valley (3) NM-5
Willow Draw—valley (3) TX-5
Willow Draw—valley (2) UT-8
Willow Draw—valley (3) WY-8
Willow Draw Creek—stream CA-9
Willow Drive Ch—church TX-5
Willow Drive Sch—school SC-3
Willow Edge Park—park NJ-2
Willow Edge Sch—school WI-6
**Willowemac**—pop pl NY-2
**Willowemoc**—pop pl NY-2
Willowemoc Campsite—locale NY-2
Willowemoc Creek—stream NY-2
Willowemock River NY-2
**Willow Estates**—pop pl (2) IL-6
Willow Farm—locale OH-6
**Willow Farm Estates (subdivision)**—pop pl UT-8
**Willow Farms Mobile Home Park**—pop pl PA-2
Willow Fields—flat UT-8
Willow Flat MT-8
Willow Flat—flat (7) CA-9
Willow Flat—flat (2) ID-8
Willow Flat—flat (4) OR-9
Willow Flat—flat UT-8
Willow Flat Campground—park UT-8
Willow Flat Creek—stream CA-9
Willow Flat Diversion Dam—dam MT-8
Willow Flat Rsvr—reservoir MT-8
Willow Flat Rsvr—reservoir OR-9
Willow Flats—flat OR-9
Willow Flats—flat TX-5
Willow Flats—flat (2) UT-8
Willow Flats—flat WY-8
Willow Flats Overlook—locale WY-8
Willow Flat Spring—spring ID-8
Willow Fork—stream ID-8
Willow Fork—stream MO-7
Willow Fork—stream TN-4
Willow Fork—stream TX-5
Willow Fork—stream WV-2
**Willow Forks (historical)**—pop pl OR-9
Willow Fork Township—civil MO-7
Willow Gap—gap UT-8
Willow Gardens—other MI-6
Willow Glen—locale LA-4
**Willow Glen**—pop pl CA-9
**Willow Glen**—pop pl (3) NY-2
Willow Glen Acad Sch—school WI-6
Willow Glen Cem—cemetery NY-2
Willow Glen Ch—church OK-5
Willow Glen Creek—stream CA-9
Willow Glen Creek—stream NY-2
Willow Glen HS—school CA-9
Willow Glenn—hist pl MD-2
Willow Glen Oil Field—oilfield MS-4
Willow Glen Park—park CA-9
Willow Glen Plantation (historical)—locale AL-4
Willow Glen Ranch—locale CA-9
Willow Glen Ranch—locale MT-8
Willow Glen Ranch—locale WY-8
Willow Glen Ridge—ridge CA-9
Willow Glen Rsvr—reservoir WY-8
**Willow Glen South Subdivision**—pop pl UT-8
**Willow Glen (subdivision)**—pop pl AL-4
**Willow Glen Subdivision**—pop pl UT-8
**Willow Green**—pop pl NC-3
Willow Green Country Club—other MN-6
**Willow Green Subdivision**—pop pl UT-8
Willowgrove DE-2
Willowgrove NJ-2
Willow Grove WV-2
Willow Grove—fmr MCD NE-7
Willow Grove—hist pl MD-2
Willow Grove—hist pl VA-3
Willow Grove—locale KY-4
Willow Grove—locale NV-8
Willow Grove—locale NJ-2
Willow Grove—locale PA-2
Willow Grove—locale (2) TN-4
**Willow Grove**—pop pl DE-2
**Willow Grove**—pop pl MD-2
**Willow Grove**—pop pl NJ-2
**Willow Grove**—pop pl (3) NY-2
**Willow Grove**—pop pl (2) OH-6
**Willow Grove**—pop pl (2) PA-2
**Willow Grove**—pop pl TN-4
**Willow Grove**—pop pl (3) TX-5
**Willow Grove**—pop pl (2) VA-3
Willow Grove—woods WA-9
Willow Grove Acad (historical)—school TN-4
Willow Grove Baptist Church MS-4
Willow Grove Cem—cemetery IN-6
Willow Grove Cem—cemetery MI-6
Willow Grove Cem—cemetery MS-4
Willow Grove Cem—cemetery NH-1
Willow Grove Cem—cemetery NJ-2
Willow Grove Cem—cemetery OH-6
Willow Grove Cem—cemetery PA-2
Willow Grove Cem—cemetery SC-3
Willow Grove Cem—cemetery TN-4
Willow Grove Cem—cemetery (2) TX-5
Willow Grove Cem—cemetery WY-8
Willow Grove Ch—church IN-6
Willow Grove Ch—church LA-4
Willow Grove Ch—church (2) MS-4
Willow Grove Ch—church PA-2
Willow Grove Ch—church SC-3
Willow Grove Ch—church (3) TN-4
Willow Grove Ch—church (2) TX-5
Willow Grove Ch—church (2) VA-3
Willow Grove Chapel—church KY-4
Willow Grove Ch (historical)—church AL-4
Willow Grove Ch of God—church DE-2
Willow Grove Church DE-2
Willow Grove Country Club—other VA-3
Willow Grove Creek—stream MD-2
Willow Grove Dam—dam NJ-2
Willow Grove Day Camp—locale PA-2
Willow Grove Dock—locale TN-4
Willow Grove Golf Course—other OH-6
Willow Grove (historical P.O.)—locale IA-7
Willow Grove Interchange PA-2
Willow Grove Lake—reservoir NJ-2
**Willow Grove Mine No. 10**—pop pl OH-6
Willow Grove NAS Airp—airport PA-2
Willow Grove Naval Air Station—military PA-2
Willow Grove Park—park OH-6
Willow Grove Park Mall—locale PA-2
Willow Grove Point—cape NY-2
Willowgrove Post Office TN-4
Willow Grove Post Office (historical)—building TN-4
Willow Grove Prong—stream DE-2
Willow Grove Ranch—locale NE-7
Willow Grove Rec Area—park TN-4
Willow Grove Sch—school CA-9
Willow Grove Sch—school (2) IL-6
Willow Grove Sch—school (3) IA-7
Willow Grove Sch—school KY-4
Willow Grove Sch—school MO-7
Willow Grove Sch—school NC-3
Willow Grove Sch—school PA-2
Willow Grove Sch—school SC-3
Willow Grove Sch—school TN-4
Willow Grove Sch—school WV-2
Willow Grove Sch—school WI-6
Willow Grove Sch (abandoned)—school MO-7
Willow Grove Sch (abandoned)—school PA-2
Willow Grove Sch (historical)—school AL-4
Willow Grove Sch (historical)—school MS-4
Willow Grove Sch (historical)—school (4) TN-4
Willow Grove School (Abandoned)—locale CA-9
Willow Grove Shop Ctr—locale PA-2
Willow Grove Station—building (2) PA-2
**Willow Gulch**—pop pl CO-8
Willow Gulch—valley (5) CA-9
Willow Gulch—valley (5) CO-8
Willow Gulch—valley MT-8

Willow Gulch—*valley* ... NM-5
Willow Gulch—*valley* (2) ... UT-8
Willow Gulch—*valley* (2) ... WA-9
Willow Gulch—*valley* ... WY-8
Willow Gulch Canyon—*valley* ... AZ-5
Willow Hall Swamp—*swamp* ... SC-3
Willow Harbor—*bay* ... WI-6
Willow Harvey Divide Trail—*trail* ... MT-8
Willowhaven Country Club—*locale* ... NC-3
Willowhaven Lake Number One—*reservoir* ... NC-3
Willowhaven Lake Number One Dam—*dam* ... NC-3
Willowhaven Lake Number Two—*reservoir* ... NC-3
Willowhaven Lake Number Two Dam—*dam* ... NC-3
Willow Heights—*summit* ... UT-8
Willow Hill—*hist pl* ... KY-4
Willow Hill—*locale* ... VA-3
**Willow Hill**—*pop pl* ... IL-6
**Willow Hill**—*pop pl* ... PA-2
Willow Hill—*summit* ... MA-1
Willow Hill—*summit* ... NH-1
Willow Hill—*summit* ... NM-5
Willow Hill—*summit* ... WY-8
Willow Hill Cem—*cemetery* ... NY-2
Willow Hill Ch—*church* ... VA-3
Willow Hill Creek—*stream* ... MI-6
*Willow Hill Interchange* ... PA-2
Willow Hill Rsvr—*reservoir* ... CA-9
Willow Hill Sch—*school* ... GA-3
Willow Hill Sch—*school* ... IL-6
Willow Hill Sch—*school* ... PA-2
**Willow Hills Estates (subdivision)**—*pop pl* ... AL-4
**Willow Hill Subdivision**—*pop pl* ... UT-8
**Willow Hill (Township of)**—*pop pl* ... IL-6
Willow (historical)—*locale* ... ND-7
Willow Hole—*flat* ... CA-9
Willow Hole—*lake* ... OR-9
Willow Hole—*other* ... CA-9
Willow Hole Ch—*church* ... TX-5
Willow Hole Tank—*reservoir* ... TX-5
Willow Hollow—*valley* ... TX-5
Willow Hollow—*valley* ... UT-8
Willow Hollow Golf Course—*locale* ... PA-2
Willow Hollow Tank—*reservoir* ... TX-5
**Willowick**—*pop pl* ... OH-6
Willowick (Township of)—*other* ... OH-6
*Willow Island* ... CT-1
*Willow Island* ... MS-4
Willow Island—*island* ... AK-9
Willow Island—*island* ... CA-9
Willow Island—*island* (7) ... IL-6
Willow Island—*island* ... IA-7
Willow Island—*island* (3) ... LA-4
Willow Island—*island* ... NE-7
Willow Island—*island* ... OR-9
Willow Island—*island* ... TX-5
Willow Island—*island* ... WA-9
Willow Island—*island* (3) ... WI-6
Willow Island—*island* ... WY-8
Willow Island—*locale* ... WV-2
**Willow Island**—*pop pl* ... NE-7
Willow Island Cem—*cemetery* ... NE-7
Willow Island Creek—*stream* ... WV-2
Willow Island (historical)—*island* ... SD-7
Willow Island Locks And Dam—*dam* ... WV-2
Willow Islands—*area* ... AK-9
Willow Island Sch—*school* ... NE-7
Willowisp Country Club—*other* ... TX-5
*Willow Lake* ... AZ-5
*Willow Lake* ... MN-6
*Willow Lake* ... MT-8
Willow Lake—*area* ... NV-8
Willow Lake—*flat* ... NV-8
Willow Lake—*hist pl* ... GA-3
Willow Lake—*lake* (5) ... AK-9
Willow Lake—*lake* (2) ... AZ-5
Willow Lake—*lake* (7) ... AR-4
Willow Lake—*lake* (5) ... CA-9
Willow Lake—*lake* (3) ... CO-8
Willow Lake—*lake* ... GA-3
Willow Lake—*lake* ... ID-8
Willow Lake—*lake* ... IA-7
Willow Lake*—*lake* ... IA-7
Willow Lake—*lake* (13) ... LA-4
Willow Lake—*lake* ... MI-6
Willow Lake—*lake* (6) ... MN-6
Willow Lake—*lake* ... MS-4
Willow Lake—*lake* (4) ... NE-7
Willow Lake—*lake* ... NM-5
Willow Lake—*lake* (2) ... NY-2
Willow Lake—*lake* (4) ... ND-7
Willow Lake—*lake* (2) ... OH-6
Willow Lake—*lake* ... OR-9
Willow Lake—*lake* ... SD-7
Willow Lake—*lake* (2) ... TN-4
Willow Lake—*lake* (5) ... TX-5
Willow Lake—*lake* (2) ... UT-8
Willow Lake—*lake* (5) ... WA-9
Willow Lake—*lake* ... WI-6
Willow Lake—*lake* (2) ... WY-8
**Willow Lake**—*pop pl* ... AK-9
**Willow Lake**—*pop pl* ... PA-2
**Willow Lake**—*pop pl* ... SD-7
Willow Lake—*reservoir* ... AL-4
Willow Lake—*reservoir* ... AR-4
Willow Lake—*reservoir* (2) ... CO-8
Willow Lake—*reservoir* ... IL-6
Willow Lake—*reservoir* ... NV-8
Willow Lake—*reservoir* ... NY-2
Willow Lake—*reservoir* (2) ... OR-9
Willow Lake—*reservoir* (2) ... TN-4
Willow Lake—*reservoir* (3) ... TX-5
Willow Lake—*reservoir* ... UT-8
Willow Lake—*reservoir* (2) ... VA-3
Willow Lake—*swamp* (2) ... AR-4
Willow Lake—*swamp* ... LA-4
Willow Lake—*swamp* ... MN-6
Willow Lake—*swamp* ... MS-4
Willow Lake Airp—*airport* ... SD-7
Willow Lake Campground—*locale* ... WY-8
Willow Lake Campground—*park* ... UT-8
Willow Lake Cem—*cemetery* ... GA-3
Willow Lake Ch—*church* ... MN-6
Willow Lake Cut-Off—*bend* ... MS-4
Willow Lake Dam—*dam* ... AL-4
Willow Lake Dam—*dam* (2) ... MS-4
Willow Lake Dam—*dam* ... NC-3
Willow Lake Dam—*dam* ... TN-4
Willow Lake Dam—*dam* ... UT-8
Willow Lake Natl Wildlife Ref—*park* ... ND-7
Willow Lake Oil Field—*oilfield* ... LA-4
Willow Lake Park—*park* ... AZ-5
Willow Lakes—*lake* ... CO-8
**Willow Lakes**—*pop pl* ... OH-6
**Willow Lakes**—*pop pl* ... VA-3
Willow Lake Sch—*school* (2) ... NE-7
Willow Lake Sch—*school* ... SD-7
Willow Lakes Dam—*dam* ... MS-4
Willow Lake State Public Shooting Area—*park* ... SD-7
Willow Lake State Wildlife Mngmt Area—*park* ... MN-6
Willow Lake Tank—*reservoir* ... TX-5
**Willow Lake Township**—*pop pl* ... ND-7
**Willow Lake Township**—*pop pl* ... SD-7
**Willow Lake (Township of)**—*pop pl* ... MN-6
Willow Lake Trail—*trail* ... WY-8
Willow Landing—*locale* ... VA-3
Willow Lane Farm—*hist pl* ... OH-6
Willow Lane Park—*park* ... MN-6
Willow Lane Sch—*school* (2) ... MN-6
**Willow Lawn**—*pop pl* ... VA-3
Willow Lawn Cem—*cemetery* ... IA-7
Willow Lawn Shop Ctr—*locale* ... VA-3
Willow Lower Range—*channel* ... WA-9
Willow Lower Range Channel—*channel* ... OR-9
Willow Manor Sch—*school* ... CA-9
Willow Marsh—*swamp* ... LA-4
Willow Marsh—*swamp* ... TX-5
Willow Marsh—*swamp* ... WY-8
Willow Marsh Bayou—*stream* ... TX-5
*Willow Marsh Creek* ... TX-5
Willow Marsh (historical)—*swamp* ... IA-7
Willow Meadow—*flat* (5) ... CA-9
Willow Meadow—*flat* ... ID-8
Willow Meadows Campground—*locale* ... CA-9
**Willowmere**—*pop pl* ... PA-2
Willow Mesa—*summit* ... CO-8
Willow Metro Park—*park* ... MI-6
Willow Mill - Hurlbut Dam—*dam* ... MA-1
Willow Mill Park—*park* ... PA-2
Willow Mountain—*locale* ... NM-5
Willow Mountain Tank—*reservoir* ... AZ-5
Willowmount Cem—*cemetery* ... TN-4
Willow Mtn—*summit* (2) ... AK-9
Willow Mtn—*summit* ... AZ-5
Willow Mtn—*summit* ... CO-8
Willow Mtn—*summit* (2) ... MT-8
Willow Mtn—*summit* ... TX-5
Willow Net Tank—*reservoir* ... TX-5
*Willow Number Two Spring* ... AZ-5
**Willow Oak**—*pop pl* ... FL-3
**Willow Oak**—*pop pl* ... TX-5
Willow Oak Cem—*cemetery* ... FL-3
Willow Oak Ch—*church* ... FL-3
Willow Oak Ch—*church* ... NC-3
Willow Oak Ch—*church* ... TX-5
Willow Oak Creek—*stream* ... TX-5
Willow Oak Point—*cape* ... SC-3
**Willow Oaks**—*pop pl* ... VA-3
Willow Oak Sch—*school* ... CA-9
Willow Oak Sch—*school* ... MO-7
Willow Oaks Sch—*school* ... TN-4
Willow Oaks Shop Ctr—*locale* ... NC-3
**Will-O-Wood**—*pop pl* ... PA-2
**Will O Wood**—*pop pl* ... PA-2
Willowood Bridge—*other* ... WV-2
Willowood Center—*school* ... MS-4
Willowood Country Club—*other* ... MI-6
Willowood Sch—*school* ... CA-9
Willowood Shop Ctr—*locale* ... VA-3
**Willowood (subdivision)**—*pop pl* ... MS-4
Willow Outside Pond—*lake* ... LA-4
Willow Park—*flat* (7) ... CO-8
Willow Park—*flat* ... MT-8
Willow Park—*flat* ... UT-8
Willow Park—*flat* ... WY-8
Willow Park—*locale* ... WY-8
Willow Park—*park* ... AL-4
Willow Park—*park* ... AZ-5
Willow Park—*park* ... CA-9
Willow Park—*park* ... IL-6
Willow Park—*park* ... IN-6
Willow Park—*park* ... IA-7
Willow Park—*park* ... KS-7
Willow Park—*park* (2) ... OH-6
Willow Park—*park* ... PA-2
Willow Park—*park* ... TN-4
Willow Park—*park* ... TX-5
Willow Park—*park* ... UT-8
Willow Park—*park* (3) ... WY-8
**Willow Park**—*pop pl* ... TX-5
Willow Park Cem—*cemetery* ... MS-4
Willow Park Golf Course—*other* ... CA-9
Willow Park Patrol Cabin—*hist pl* ... CO-8
Willow Park Rsvr—*reservoir* ... WY-8
Willow Park Sch—*school* ... WI-6
Willow Park South—*park* ... IL-6
Willow Park Stable—*hist pl* ... CO-8
Willow Pass—*channel* (2) ... LA-4
Willow Pass—*gap* ... CO-8
Willow Pass Trail—*trail* ... CO-8
Willow Patch—*bar* (2) ... UT-8
Willow Patch—*basin* ... ID-8
Willow Patch Creek—*stream* ... UT-8
Willow Patch Draw—*valley* ... AZ-5
Willow Patch (historical P.O.), The—*locale* ... IA-7
Willow Patch Spring—*spring* ... ID-8
Willow Patch Spring—*spring* (2) ... NV-8
Willow Patch Spring—*spring* (2) ... UT-8
Willow Peak—*summit* ... ID-8
Willow Peak—*summit* ... MT-8
Willow Peak—*summit* ... NV-8
Willowpeg Cem—*cemetery* ... GA-3
Willowpeg Creek—*stream* ... GA-3
Willow Place—*post sta* ... TX-5
**Willow Place Subdivision**—*pop pl* ... UT-8
Willow Plant Cem—*cemetery* ... FL-3
Willow Plant Ch—*church* ... FL-3
Willow Plaza Shop Ctr—*locale* ... TN-4
Willow Point—*cape* ... AL-4
Willow Point—*cape* ... AK-9
Willow Point—*cape* (2) ... CA-9
Willow Point—*cape* (2) ... CT-1
Willow Point—*cape* ... FL-3
Willow Point—*cape* ... ID-8
Willow Point—*cape* (3) ... LA-4
Willow Point—*cape* ... MA-1
Willow Point—*cape* ... MI-6
Willow Point—*cape* (2) ... MN-6
Willow Point—*cape* (4) ... NY-2
Willow Point—*cape* ... NC-3
Willow Point—*cape* (2) ... OR-9
Willow Point—*cape* ... WA-9
Willow Point—*cliff* ... AZ-5
Willow Point—*cliff* ... OH-6
Willow Point—*locale* ... TX-5
Willow Point—*locale* ... VT-1
**Willow Point**—*pop pl* ... CA-9
**Willow Point**—*pop pl* ... CT-1
**Willow Point**—*pop pl* ... NY-2
Willow Point—*summit* ... OR-9
Willow Point Cem—*cemetery* ... TX-5
Willow Point Country Club—*locale* ... AL-4
Willow Point Landing—*locale* ... MS-4
Willow Point (Old Stage Station)—*locale* ... NV-8
**Willow Point (subdivision)**—*pop pl* ... AL-4
Willow Pond—*bay* ... LA-4
Willow Pond—*lake* ... AR-4
Willow Pond—*lake* ... GA-3
Willow Pond—*lake* ... ID-8
Willow Pond—*lake* ... IL-6
Willow Pond—*lake* ... KY-4
Willow Pond—*lake* (2) ... LA-4
Willow Pond—*lake* (3) ... MO-7
Willow Pond—*lake* (2) ... NY-2
Willow Pond—*lake* ... NC-3
Willow Pond—*lake* ... SC-3
Willow Pond—*lake* ... TX-5
Willow Pond—*reservoir* ... GA-3
Willow Pond—*reservoir* ... OR-9
Willow Pond Bed—*flat* ... IN-6
Willow Pond Cem—*cemetery* ... TX-5
Willow Pond Ch—*church* ... TX-5
Willow Pond Creek—*stream* ... IL-6
Willow Pond Creek—*stream* ... TX-5
*Willow Pond Ditch* ... IN-6
Willow Pond Ditch—*canal* ... IN-6
Willow Pond Sch—*school* ... MI-6
*Willow Pond Slough* ... IL-6
Willow Pond Slough—*swamp* ... IL-6
*Willow Prairie* ... IN-6
Willow Prairie—*flat* ... OR-9
Willow Prairie Ch—*church* ... IL-6
Willow Prairie Forest Camp—*locale* ... OR-9
Willow Prairie Lake—*lake* ... FL-3
Willow Prong—*stream* ... TX-5
Willow Ranch—*locale* ... ID-8
Willow Ranch—*locale* ... MT-8
**Willow Ranch**—*pop pl* ... CA-9
Willow Ranch Cem—*cemetery* ... CA-9
Willow Ranch Creek—*stream* ... CA-9
Willow Ranch Sch—*school* ... TX-5
Willow Ranger Station—*locale* ... AZ-5
Willow Rapids—*rapids* ... WI-6
Willow Reed Spring—*spring* ... NM-5
**Willow Ridge**—*pop pl* ... NJ-2
Willow Ridge—*ridge* (2) ... CA-9
Willow Ridge—*ridge* ... CO-8
Willow Ridge—*ridge* (2) ... ID-8
Willow Ridge Cave—*cave* ... PA-2
Willow Ridge Country Club—*other* ... NY-2
**Willow Ridge Estates**—*pop pl* ... NY-2
**Willow Ridge (subdivision)**—*pop pl* ... NC-3
*Willow River* ... IA-7
*Willow River* ... MI-6
*Willow River* ... MN-6
**Willow River**—*pop pl* ... MN-6
Willow River—*stream* (3) ... MN-6
Willow River—*stream* (2) ... WI-6
Willow River Cem—*cemetery* ... WI-6
Willow River Ditch—*canal* ... MN-6
Willow River Lookout Tower—*locale* ... MN-6
Willow River Pool—*reservoir* ... MN-6
Willow River State Park—*park* ... WI-6
Willow Road Dam—*dam* ... IL-6
Willow Road Sch—*school* ... NY-2
*Willow Rock Creek* ... NV-8
Willow Rounds—*locale* ... MT-8
Willow Row Ch—*church* ... MO-7
Willow Row Sch (historical)—*school* ... SD-7
*Willow Rsvr* ... OR-9
Willow Rsvr—*reservoir* ... CO-8
Willow Rsvr—*reservoir* ... OR-9
Willow Rsvr—*reservoir* ... WI-6
Willow Rsvr—*reservoir* (3) ... WY-8
*Willow Run* ... PA-2
**Willow Run**—*pop pl* ... DE-2
**Willow Run**—*pop pl* (2) ... MI-6
**Willow Run**—*pop pl* ... VA-3
Willow Run—*stream* ... DE-2
Willow Run—*stream* ... IN-6
Willow Run—*stream* (3) ... MI-6
Willow Run—*stream* ... NJ-2
Willow Run—*stream* ... NY-2
Willow Run—*stream* (2) ... OH-6
Willow Run—*stream* (4) ... PA-2
Willow Run—*stream* (2) ... WV-2
Willow Run Airp—*airport* ... MI-6
Willow Run Inn Golf Course—*locale* ... PA-2
*Willow Run Lake* ... AL-4
**Willow Run Park Subdivision**—*pop pl* ... UT-8
Willow Run Ridge—*ridge* ... PA-2
Willows—*locale* ... MD-2
Willows—*locale* ... MS-4
Willows—*locale* ... OR-9
Willows—*locale* ... WA-9
**Willows**—*pop pl* ... CA-9
**Willows**—*pop pl* ... MA-1
Willows, The—*basin* ... WY-8
Willows, The—*hist pl* ... MD-2
Willows, The—*hist pl* ... WV-2
Willows, The—*locale* ... NV-8
Willows, The—*locale* ... SC-3
Willows, The—*locale* ... WA-9
Willows, The—*locale* ... WY-8
**Willows, The**—*pop pl* (2) ... CA-9
**Willows, The**—*pop pl* ... NH-1
Willows, The—*swamp* ... FL-3
Willows Airp—*airport* ... PA-2
Willows Anchorage—*bay* ... CA-9
Willow Sandy Creek—*stream* ... OK-5
Willowsburg Cem—*cemetery* ... TX-5
Willows Camp—*locale* ... AZ-5
Willows Campground—*locale* ... WA-9
Willows (CCD)—*cens area* ... CA-9
Willow Sch—*school* (7) ... CA-9
Willow Sch—*school* (3) ... IL-6
Willow Sch—*school* ... IA-7
Willow Sch—*school* ... NH-1
Willow Sch—*school* ... OR-9
Willows Chapel—*church* ... VA-3
Willow Sch Number 2—*school* ... ND-7
Willow Sch Number 3—*school* ... ND-7
**Willows Condominium**—*pop pl* ... UT-8
*Willow's East* ... IL-6
Willow Seep—*spring* (2) ... UT-8
*Willow Seep Spring* ... NV-8
Willow Shade—*locale* ... KY-4
Willow Sink—*basin* ... FL-3
**Willow Sink**—*pop pl* ... FL-3
Willow Sink Spring—*spring* ... UT-8
Willow Siphon—*canal* ... CA-9
*Willow Slough* ... IA-7
*Willow Slough* ... MS-4
*Willow Slough* ... NE-7
Willow Slough—*bay* ... TX-5
Willow Slough—*gut* ... KY-4
Willow Slough—*gut* ... LA-4
Willow Slough—*gut* ... MN-6
Willow Slough—*gut* (2) ... MS-4
Willow Slough—*lake* ... TX-5
Willow Slough—*stream* (2) ... AR-4
Willow Slough—*stream* ... CA-9
Willow Slough—*stream* ... IL-6
Willow Slough—*stream* ... IN-6
Willow Slough—*stream* ... TX-5
Willow Slough—*swamp* ... FL-3
*Willow Slough By Pasa* ... CA-9
Willow Slough Bypass—*canal* ... CA-9
Willow Slough Dam—*dam* ... IA-7
Willow Slough Marsh—*swamp* ... TX-5
Willow Slough Oil Field—*oilfield* ... TX-5
*Willow Slough State Fish and Game Reservation* ... IN-6
Willow Slough State Game Mngmt Area—*park* ... IA-7
Willow Slough State Game Preserve—*park* ... IN-6
**Willows of Riverbend**—*pop pl* ... MD-2
Willows Park Picnic Ground—*locale* ... UT-8
Willow-Spence Streets Hist Dist—*hist pl* ... TX-5
Willows Pond—*swamp* ... GA-3
*Willow Spring* ... CA-9
*Willow Spring* ... KS-7
*Willow Spring* ... NV-8
*Willow Spring* ... OR-9
Willow Spring—*locale* ... AZ-5
**Willow Spring**—*pop pl* ... VA-3
Willow Spring—*spring* ... AL-4
Willow Spring—*spring* (56) ... AZ-5
Willow Spring—*spring* (50) ... CA-9
Willow Spring—*spring* (11) ... CO-8
Willow Spring—*spring* (9) ... ID-8
Willow Spring—*spring* (2) ... MT-8
Willow Spring—*spring* (61) ... NV-8
Willow Spring—*spring* (7) ... NM-5
Willow Spring—*spring* (31) ... OR-9
Willow Spring—*spring* (9) ... TX-5
Willow Spring—*spring* (41) ... UT-8
Willow Spring—*spring* (7) ... WA-9
Willow Spring—*spring* (10) ... WY-8
Willow Spring Basin—*basin* ... AZ-5
Willow Spring Basin—*basin* ... CA-9
Willow Spring Brook—*stream* ... OR-9
*Willowspring Canyon* ... AZ-5
Willow Spring Canyon—*valley* (7) ... AZ-5
Willow Spring Canyon—*valley* (4) ... CA-9
Willow Spring Canyon—*valley* ... NV-8
Willow Spring Canyon—*valley* ... NM-5
Willow Spring Canyon—*valley* (3) ... OR-9
Willow Spring Canyon—*valley* ... UT-8
Willow Spring Cem—*cemetery* ... TN-4
Willow Spring Ch—*church* ... AL-4
Willow Spring Ch—*church* ... GA-3
Willow Spring Ch—*church* ... MS-4
Willow Spring Ch—*church* ... OK-5
Willow Spring Ch—*church* (2) ... TN-4
Willow Spring Ch—*church* ... TX-5
Willow Spring Corral—*other* ... NM-5
Willow Spring Cow Camp—*locale* ... UT-8
*Willow Spring Creek* ... UT-8
Willow Spring Creek—*stream* (4) ... CA-9
Willow Spring Creek—*stream* ... CO-8
Willow Spring Creek—*stream* ... ID-8
Willow Spring Creek—*stream* ... MT-8
Willow Spring Creek—*stream* (3) ... OR-9
Willow Spring Creek—*stream* (2) ... UT-8
Willow Spring Creek—*stream* ... WY-8
Willow Spring Draw—*valley* ... NM-5
Willow Spring Draw—*valley* (3) ... UT-8
Willow Spring Draw—*valley* ... WY-8
Willow Spring Elem Sch—*school* ... NC-3
Willow Spring Girl Scout Camp—*locale* ... AZ-5
Willow Spring Guard Station—*locale* ... CO-8
Willow Spring Gulch—*valley* (2) ... AZ-5
Willow Spring Gulch—*valley* ... CA-9
Willow Spring Hollow—*valley* ... AR-4
Willow Spring Lake Recreation Site—*park* ... AZ-5
Willow Spring Lakes—*lake* ... OH-6
*Willow Spring Lodge* ... CA-9
Willow Spring Mountain—*ridge* ... NM-5
Willow Spring Mtn—*summit* ... AZ-5
Willow Spring Number Two—*spring* ... AZ-5
**Willow Spring (RR name Willow Springs)**—*pop pl* ... NC-3
Willow Spring Rsvr—*reservoir* ... CO-8
*Willow Springs* ... CA-9
*Willow Springs* ... ID-8
*Willow Springs* ... KS-7
*Willow Springs* ... MS-4
*Willow Springs* ... NV-8
*Willow Springs* ... NC-3
*Willow Springs* ... UT-8
*Willow Springs* ... WI-6
Willow Springs—*fmr MCD* ... NE-7
Willow Springs—*hist pl* ... AZ-5
Willow Springs—*locale* ... AL-4
Willow Springs—*locale* ... AZ-5
Willow Springs—*locale* ... CA-9
Willow Springs—*locale* ... PA-2
Willow Springs—*locale* (3) ... TX-5
Willow Springs—*locale* (2) ... VA-3
Willow Springs—*locale* ... WY-8
**Willow Springs**—*pop pl* (3) ... CA-9
**Willow Springs**—*pop pl* ... IL-6
**Willow Springs**—*pop pl* ... MO-7
**Willow Springs**—*pop pl* (2) ... NC-3
**Willow Springs**—*pop pl* ... PA-2
**Willow Springs**—*pop pl* ... TN-4
**Willow Springs**—*pop pl* ... WI-6
Willow Springs—*spring* (2) ... AZ-5
Willow Springs—*spring* (2) ... CA-9
Willow Springs—*spring* ... CO-8
Willow Springs—*spring* (2) ... ID-8
Willow Springs—*spring* (2) ... MT-8
Willow Springs—*spring* (13) ... NV-8
Willow Springs—*spring* (2) ... NM-5
Willow Springs—*spring* (3) ... OR-9
Willow Springs—*spring* (5) ... UT-8
Willow Springs—*spring* (3) ... WA-9
Willow Springs—*spring* (2) ... WI-6
Willow Springs—*spring* (4) ... WY-8
Willow Springs—*springs* ... CO-8
Willow Springs—*stream* ... UT-8
Willow Springs—*stream* ... WY-8
Willow Springs—*uninc pl* ... OK-5
Willow Spring Saddle—*gap* ... WA-9
*Willow Springs Baptist Church* ... AL-4
Willow Springs Basin Tank—*reservoir* ... AZ-5
Willow Springs Bayou—*stream* ... TX-5
Willow Springs Branch—*stream* ... AR-4
Willow Springs Branch—*stream* ... SC-3
Willow Springs Branch—*stream* (2) ... TX-5
Willow Springs Branch—*stream* ... VA-3
Willow Springs Butte—*summit* ... CA-9
Willow Springs Camp—*locale* ... OR-9
Willow Springs Canyon—*valley* (3) ... AZ-5
Willow Springs Canyon—*valley* (6) ... CA-9
Willow Springs Canyon—*valley* ... NV-8
Willow Springs Canyon—*valley* (2) ... NM-5
Willow Springs Cem—*cemetery* ... MO-7
Willow Springs Cem—*cemetery* (2) ... TX-5
Willow Springs Cem—*cemetery* ... WI-6
Willow Springs Ch—*church* (2) ... GA-3
Willow Springs Ch—*church* ... IL-6
Willow Springs Ch—*church* ... MO-7
Willow Springs Ch—*church* ... NC-3
Willow Springs Ch—*church* (2) ... SC-3
Willow Springs Ch—*church* ... TN-4
Willow Springs Ch—*church* (7) ... TX-5
Willow Springs Ch—*church* ... WI-6
Willow Spring Sch—*school* ... CA-9
Willow Spring Sch—*school* ... LA-4
*Willow Springs Church* ... AL-4
Willow Springs Community Center—*locale* ... TX-5
Willow Springs Creek—*stream* (2) ... CA-9
Willow Springs Creek—*stream* ... ID-8
Willow Springs Creek—*stream* ... OR-9
Willow Springs Creek—*stream* ... TX-5
Willow Springs Creek—*stream* ... WY-8
Willow Springs Dam—*dam* ... AZ-5
*Willow Springs Draw* ... WA-9
Willow Springs Draw—*valley* ... WY-8
Willow Springs Gap—*gap* ... TN-4
Willow Springs Golf Course—*other* ... TX-5
*Willow Springs Gulch* ... CA-9
Willow Springs (historical)—*locale* ... KS-7
Willow Springs Hollow—*valley* ... MO-7
*Willow Springs Lake* ... AZ-5
Willow Springs Lake—*lake* ... AZ-5
Willow Springs Lake—*reservoir* ... AR-4
Willow Springs Lake—*reservoir* ... GA-3
Willow Springs Lookout—*locale* ... TX-5
Willow Springs Memorial Airp—*airport* (2) ... MO-7
Willow Springs Methodist Ch—*church* ... MS-4
**Willow Springs Park**—*pop pl* ... SC-3
*Willow Springs Pony Express and Stage Station-Site* ... UT-8
*Willow Spring Spring Creek* ... WI-6
Willow Springs Raceway—*other* ... CA-9
Willow Springs Ranch—*locale* (2) ... AZ-5
Willow Springs Ranch—*locale* ... CO-8
Willow Springs (RR name for Willow Spring)—*other* ... NC-3
Willow Springs Rsvr—*reservoir* ... WY-8
Willow Springs Sch—*school* ... CA-9
Willow Springs Sch—*school* ... KS-7
Willow Springs Sch—*school* ... KY-4
Willow Springs Sch—*school* (2) ... MO-7
Willow Springs Sch—*school* ... NE-7
Willow Springs Sch—*school* ... TX-5
Willow Springs Sch—*school* ... WI-6
Willow Springs Sch (abandoned)—*school* ... MO-7
Willow Springs Sch (historical)—*school* (2) ... TN-4
Willow Springs School—*locale* ... OR-9
Willow Springs Station—*locale* ... UT-8
Willow Springs Tank—*reservoir* ... NM-5
**Willow Springs (Town of)**—*pop pl* ... WI-6
Willow Springs Township—*civil* ... MO-7
**Willow Springs Township**—*pop pl* ... KS-7
Willow Springs Valley—*basin* ... CA-9
Willow Springs Wash—*stream* ... AZ-5
Willow Springs Wash—*valley* ... UT-8
Willow Springs Well—*well* (2) ... AZ-5
Willow Springs Woods—*woods* ... IL-6
Willow Spring Tank—*reservoir* (3) ... AZ-5
Willow Spring Trail—*trail* (2) ... AZ-5
Willow Spring Trail (Pack)—*trail* ... CA-9
Willow Spring Union Sch—*school* ... CA-9
Willow Spring Wash—*stream* (2) ... AZ-5
Willow Spring Wash—*stream* (2) ... CA-9
Willow Spring Wash—*valley* ... UT-8
Willow Spring Wash Tank—*reservoir* ... AZ-5
Willow Spring Well—*well* ... CA-9
Willows Ranch—*locale* ... NV-8
Willows Resort Airp—*airport* ... RI-1
*Willows Rock Creek* ... NV-8
Willows Sch (historical)—*school* ... MS-4
Willows Spring—*spring* ... OR-9
**Willows (subdivision), The**—*pop pl* ... DE-2
*Willow (sta.)* ... OH-6
Willows Tank—*reservoir* ... AZ-5
Willows Tanks—*reservoir* ... AZ-5
Willowstone Park—*park* ... MN-6
**Willow Stream Estates Subdivision**—*pop pl* ... UT-8
**Willow Street**—*pop pl* ... PA-2
Willow Street Ch—*church* ... PA-2
Willow Street Elem Sch—*school* ... PA-2
Willow Street HS—*school* ... LA-4
Willow Street Post Office (historical)—*building* ... PA-2
Willow Street Sch—*school* (2) ... MI-6
Willow Street Sch—*school* ... PA-2
Willow Street Vocational Technical Sch—*school* ... PA-2
Willows Trick Tank—*reservoir* ... AZ-5
*Willow Stump Branch* ... AL-4
Willowstump Branch—*stream* ... AL-4
Willow Swamp—*stream* ... OH-6
Willow Swamp—*stream* (2) ... SC-3
Willow Swamp—*swamp* ... CO-8
Willow Swamp—*swamp* ... FL-3
Willow Swamp—*swamp* ... MS-4
Willow Swamp—*swamp* ... MT-8
Willow Swamp Branch—*stream* ... SC-3
Willow Swamp Ch—*church* ... SC-3
*Willow Swamp Creek* ... SC-3
Willow Swamp Creek—*stream* ... AL-4
Willow Swamp Creek—*stream* ... MT-8
Willow Swamp Sch (historical)—*school* ... TN-4
**Willows West (subdivision)**—*pop pl* (2) ... AZ-5
*Willow Tank* ... TX-5
Willow Tank—*reservoir* (10) ... AZ-5
Willow Tank—*reservoir* (2) ... NM-5
Willow Tank—*reservoir* (21) ... TX-5
Willow Tank Dam—*dam* ... AZ-5
*Willow Tanks* ... AZ-5
Willow Tanks—*reservoir* ... AZ-5
Willow Tanks—*reservoir* ... TX-5
Willow Tanks—*reservoir* ... UT-8
Willow Tank Slide—*valley* ... UT-8
Willow Thicket Hollow—*valley* ... TN-4
**Willowton**—*pop pl* ... WV-2
Willowton Sch—*school* ... WV-2
Willow Towhead—*island* ... TN-4
*Willowtown* ... WV-2
Willowtown—*locale* ... KY-4
**Willowtown**—*pop pl* ... MS-4
Willowtown Creek—*stream* ... KY-4
Willow Town Hall—*building* ... ND-7
**Willow (Town of)**—*pop pl* ... WI-6
Willow Township—*civil* ... SD-7
Willow Township—*fmr MCD* (5) ... IA-7
**Willow Township**—*pop pl* ... NE-7
**Willow Township**—*pop pl* ... ND-7
Willow (Township of)—*fmr MCD* ... AR-4
Willow Trail—*trail* ... NY-2
Willow Trail—*trail* ... UT-8
Willow Trap—*valley* ... AZ-5
Willow Trap Springs—*spring* ... AZ-5
Willow Trap Tank—*reservoir* ... AZ-5
**Willow Tree**—*pop pl* ... KY-4
**Willow Tree**—*pop pl* ... PA-2
**Willow Tree**—*pop pl* ... VA-3
Willow Tree Bottom—*valley* ... MA-1
Willow Tree Ch—*church* ... NC-3
Willow Tree Ch—*church* ... WV-2
Willow Tree Dam—*dam* ... CA-9
Willow Tree Ditch—*canal* ... CA-9
Willow Tree Private Sch—*school* ... FL-3
Willow Tree Sch—*school* ... NC-3
Willow Tree Shop Ctr—*locale* ... TN-4
Willow Tree Springs—*spring* ... WY-8
Willow Tub Peak—*summit* ... NV-8
Willow Tub Spring—*spring* ... NV-8
Willow Tunnel—*tunnel* ... IN-6
Willow Upper Range—*channel* ... OR-9
Willow Upper Range—*channel* ... WA-9
Willow Upper Range Channel—*channel* ... OR-9
Willow Vale Sch—*school* ... IL-6
Willowvale Sch (historical)—*school* ... MO-7
**Willow Vale Township**—*pop pl* ... ND-7
*Willow Valley* ... CA-9
Willow Valley—*basin* ... NE-7
Willow Valley—*flat* ... OR-9
**Willow Valley**—*pop pl* ... CA-9
**Willow Valley**—*pop pl* ... IN-6
Willow Valley—*valley* ... AZ-5
Willow Valley—*valley* (2) ... CA-9
Willow Valley—*valley* ... NE-7
Willow Valley Campground—*park* ... OR-9
Willow Valley Canal—*canal* ... OR-9
Willow Valley Cem—*cemetery* ... MN-6
Willow Valley Cem—*cemetery* ... NC-3
Willow Valley Cem—*cemetery* ... WI-6
Willow Valley Ch—*church* ... NC-3
Willow Valley Creek—*stream* ... CA-9
Willow Valley Dam—*dam* ... AZ-5
Willow Valley Dam—*dam* ... OR-9
**Willow Valley Estates**—*pop pl* ... AZ-5
Willow Valley Farm—*locale* ... TX-5
Willow Valley Golf Course—*locale* ... PA-2
Willow Valley (historical)—*locale* ... KS-7
Willow Valley Lake—*reservoir* ... AZ-5
Willow Valley Lake Dam—*dam* ... NC-3
Willow Valley Rsvr—*reservoir* ... OR-9
Willow Valley Sch—*school* ... NE-7
Willow Valley Square Shop Ctr—*locale* ... PA-2
Willow Valley Tank—*reservoir* ... AZ-5
Willow Valley (Township of)—*civ div* ... MN-6
Willow View—*locale* ... OK-5
Willowview—*locale* ... TX-5
Willow View Cem—*cemetery* ... OH-6
Willow View Cem—*cemetery* ... OK-5
Willow View Cem—*cemetery* ... PA-2
**Willow View Estates**—*pop pl* ... UT-8
**Willow View Heights**—*pop pl* ... PA-2
Willow View Lakes—*reservoir* ... NC-3
Willow View Sch—*school* ... CO-8
Willowview Sch—*school* ... IL-6
Willow View Sch—*school* ... OK-5
**Willow View Subdivision**—*pop pl* (2) ... UT-8
**Willowville**—*pop pl* ... MO-7
**Willowville**—*pop pl* ... OH-6
Willow Wall—*hist pl* ... WV-2
Willow Wash—*stream* (3) ... AZ-5
Willow Wash—*stream* (3) ... CA-9
Willow Wash—*stream* (2) ... NV-8
Willow Wash—*stream* (2) ... NM-5
Willow Wash Spring—*spring* ... AZ-5
Willow Waterhole—*lake* ... TX-5
Willow Waterhole Bayou—*stream* ... TX-5
Willow Water Lake—*lake* ... MN-6
Willow Well—*locale* ... NM-5
Willow Well—*well* ... ID-8
Willow Well—*well* ... NM-5
Willow Well—*well* (3) ... TX-5
Willow Wells—*well* ... NM-5
Willow Wells Ranch—*locale* ... TX-5
**Willow Wew (subdivision)**—*pop pl* ... NC-3

**Willow Wick Estates**—*pop pl* UT-8
Willow Wild Cem—*cemetery* TX-5
Willow Windmill—*locale* (2) TX-5
Willow Witch Well—*well* NV-8
*Willow Wood* IL-6
**Willow Wood**—*pop pl* OH-6
**Willow Wood Estates**—*pop pl* TX-5
Willowwood Park—*park* AL-4
Willow Wood Pond—*reservoir* AL-4
**Willow Woods**—*pop pl* VA-3
**Willow Woods (subdivision)**—*pop pl* NC-3
**Willow Wood Subdivision**—*pop pl* UT-8
Willowwood Subdivision Lake Dam—*dam* MS-4
Willox Park—*flat* WY-8
Willox Ranch—*locale* WY-8
Will Puett Cove—*valley* NC-3
Will Redden Branch—*stream* AL-4
Will Rice Eddy—*rapids* TN-4
Will Risk Memorial Park—*park* WA-9
Willrode Oil Field—*oilfield* TX-5
Will Rodgers Sch—*school* KS-7
Will Rogers—*uninc pl* CA-9
Will Rogers and Wiley Post Memorial—*other* AK-9
Will Rogers Beach State Park—*park* CA-9
Will Rogers Camp—*locale* OK-5
*Will Rogers Dam* OK-5
Will Rogers Home—*building* OK-5
Will Rogers JHS—*school* CA-9
Will Rogers JHS—*school* OK-5
Will Rogers Memorial—*other* TX-5
Will Rogers Memorial Hosp—*hist pl* NY-2
Will Rogers Memorial Hosp—*hospital* NY-2
Will Rogers Memorial Park—*cemetery* CA-9
Will Rogers Memorial Park—*park* CA-9
Will Rogers Park—*park* OK-5
Will Rogers Park—*park* TX-5
Will Rogers Sch—*school* (6) CA-9
Will Rogers Sch—*school* CO-8
Will Rogers Sch—*school* (2) MI-6
Will Rogers Sch—*school* NM-5
Will Rogers Sch—*school* (11) OK-5
Will Rogers Sch—*school* (3) TX-5
Will Rogers Shrine of the Sun—*other* CO-8
Will Rogers Spring—*spring* OR-9
Will Rogers State Park—*park* CA-9
Will Rogers State Park—*park* OK-5
Will Rogers Theatre and Commercial Block—*hist pl* IL-6
Will Rogers Wiley Post Meml Seaplane Base—*airport* WA-9
Will Rogers World Airp—*airport* OK-5
Will Ruben Canal—*canal* UT-8
*Wills* IN-6
*Will's* OH-6
*Wills* WV-2
Wills—*locale* TN-4
Wills—*locale* WV-2
Wills—*locale* WI-6
Wills, William B., House—*hist pl* AL-4
Wills Bay—*swamp* SC-3
**Willsboro**—*pop pl* NY-2
Willsboro Bay—*bay* NY-2
Willsboro Congregational Church—*hist pl* NY-2
Willsboro Point—*cape* NY-2
**Willsboro Point**—*pop pl* NY-2
**Willsboro (Town of)**—*pop pl* NY-2
Wills Branch—*stream* FL-3
Wills Branch—*stream* KY-4
Wills Branch—*stream* MD-2
Wills Branch—*stream* MO-7
Wills Branch—*stream* TN-4
*Will's Brook* MA-1
Wills Brook—*stream* MA-1
Wills Brook—*stream* NJ-2
**Willsburg (historical)**—*pop pl* IA-7
Willsburg Junction—*uninc pl* OR-9
Wills Canyon—*valley* CA-9
Wills Canyon—*valley* ID-8
Wills Canyon—*valley* NM-5
Wills Canyon—*valley* OR-9
Wills Cem—*cemetery* (3) TN-4
Wills Cem—*cemetery* (2) WV-2
Wills Ch—*church* PA-2
Will Sch—*school* IL-6
Will Sch—*school* MN-6
Wills Chapel—*church* MS-4
Wills Chapel—*church* TN-4
Wills Chapel Sch (historical)—*school* TN-4
Wills Corner—*locale* VA-3
*Willscot Creek* GA-3
*Willscot Mountain* GA-3
Will Scott Ch—*church* NC-3
Will Scott Creek—*stream* NC-3
Will Scott Mtn—*summit* NC-3
Wills Cove—*bay* VA-3
Wills Cove—*valley* VA-3
*Wills Creek* AL-4
*Wills Creek* NJ-2
*Wills Creek* OH-6
*Will's Creek* PA-2
*Wills Creek* TX-5
**Wills Creek**—*pop pl* OH-6
**Wills Creek**—*pop pl* PA-2
Wills Creek—*stream* (2) AL-4
Wills Creek—*stream* IL-6
Wills Creek—*stream* MT-8
Wills Creek—*stream* NY-2
Wills Creek—*stream* (2) OH-6
Wills Creek—*stream* OR-9
Wills Creek—*stream* PA-2
Wills Creek—*stream* (3) TX-5
Wills Creek—*stream* WV-2
Wills Creek Ch—*church* PA-2
Wills Creek Dam—*dam* OH-6
Wills Creek Lake—*reservoir* OH-6
*Wills Creek Rsvr* OH-6
**Wills Crossroads**—*pop pl* AL-4
Wills-Dickey Stone House—*hist pl* TN-4
Wills Ditch—*canal* IN-6
Wills Ditch—*canal* MT-8
Willsdorf Branch—*stream* TN-4
Wills Drain—*canal* CA-9
Wills Drain One—*canal* CA-9
Wills Drain Two—*canal* CA-9
Willse Four Corners—*locale* NY-2
Willse Hill—*summit* NY-2
Willse Hill Cem—*cemetery* NY-2
Willsey Brook—*stream* NY-2
Willsey Cem—*cemetery* OH-6
Willsey Creek—*stream* CA-9
**Willseyville**—*pop pl* NY-2
Willseyville Creek—*stream* NY-2
*Will S. Green Canal* CA-9
Wills Gut—*gut* ME-1
Wills Gut—*gut* VA-3
Will Shadows Pond Dam—*dam* MS-4
Willshaw Flats—*flat* MT-8
Willshaw Sch—*school* MT-8
Wills Hill—*summit* (3) MA-1
**Willshire**—*pop pl* OH-6
**Willshire Heights**—*pop pl* OH-6
Willshire Sch—*hist pl* OH-6
**Willshire (Township of)**—*pop pl* OH-6
Wills (historical)—*locale* AL-4
**Wills (historical)**—*pop pl* TN-4
Wills Hole—*basin* UT-8
Wills Hole Thoroughfare—*channel* NJ-2
Wills Hollow—*valley* KY-4
Wills Hollow—*valley* PA-2
Wills-Hopwood Cem—*cemetery* TN-4
Wills Hosp—*hist pl* PA-2
Wills Hosp—*hospital* PA-2
Willsie Branch—*stream* TX-5
Wills Island—*island* MA-1
Wills Island—*island* VA-3
Wills Lake—*lake* MN-6
Wills Lake—*lake* WA-9
Wills Lake—*reservoir* AL-4
Wills Lake—*reservoir* OK-5
Wills Lateral—*canal* CA-9
Wills Memorial Ch—*church* (2) VA-3
Wills Memorial Hosp—*hospital* GA-3
Wills Mine—*mine* TN-4
*Wills Mountai* VA-3
*Will's Mountain* PA-2
Wills Mountain—*ridge* PA-2
Wills Mtn—*summit* AR-4
Wills Mtn—*summit* MD-2
Willson Cem—*cemetery* IL-6
Willson Cem—*cemetery* MS-4
Willson Cem—*cemetery* PA-2
Willson Cem—*cemetery* VT-1
Willson Creek—*stream* TX-5
**Willson Hills**—*pop pl* MD-2
Willson Peak—*summit* ID-8
Willson Sch—*school* NY-2
Willson Sch—*school* OH-6
*Willsons Siding* ND-7
Willsons Woods Park—*park* NY-2
Willson Windmill—*locale* NM-5
Wills Point—*cape* FL-3
**Wills Point**—*pop pl* LA-4
**Wills Point**—*pop pl* TX-5
Wills Point (CCD)—*cens area* TX-5
Wills Point Landing (historical)—*locale* TN-4
Wills Point Post Office (historical)—*building* TN-4
Wills Point Rsvr—*reservoir* TX-5
*Wills Pond* MA-1
Wills Post Office (historical)—*building* TN-4
Wills Reservoir—*spring* UT-8
Wills Ridge—*ridge* VA-3
Wills Rsvr—*reservoir* CO-8
Wills Run—*stream* PA-2
Wills Sch—*school* TN-4
Wills Sch—*school* TX-5
Wills Sch (historical)—*school* AL-4
Wills Sch (historical)—*school* PA-2
Wills Shanty—*locale* TN-4
*Wills Station* WV-2
Wills Store (historical)—*locale* AL-4
*Wills Strait* ME-1
*Wills Straits* ME-1
*Wills Sulpher Springs* AL-4
Will Stafford Canyon—*valley* KS-7
Will Stanfford Canyon—*valley* NE-7
Wills Thorofare—*channel* NJ-2
**Willston**—*pop pl* VA-3
Will Stone Cave—*cave* TN-4
Willstown (historical)—*locale* AL-4
Willstown Mission (historical)—*church* AL-4
**Wills (Township of)**—*pop pl* IN-6
**Wills (Township of)**—*pop pl* OH-6
*Will Straits* ME-1
Wills Valley—*locale* AL-4
Wills Valley (CCD)—*cens area* AL-4
Wills Valley Ch (historical)—*church* AL-4
Wills Valley Division—*civil* AL-4
Wills Valley Sch—*school* AL-4
Willswood—*locale* LA-4
Willswood Pond—*swamp* LA-4
Will Tank—*reservoir* NM-5
Will Tank—*reservoir* TX-5
Will-'-the-Wisp Camp—*locale* AL-4
Will Thrall Peak—*summit* CA-9
Willtown Bluff—*hist pl* SC-3
**Will (Township of)**—*pop pl* IL-6
Will Unit Sch—*school* IL-6
Willuweit Dam Number 10 Rsvr—*reservoir* SD-7
Will Valley—*valley* CA-9
Will-Vera Camp—*locale* KY-4
**Willwalk**—*pop pl* MI-6
Will Wet Hollow—*valley* MO-7
Will White Neck—*bay* GA-3
**Willwood**—*pop pl* WY-8
Willwood Cem—*cemetery* IL-6
Willwood Draw—*valley* WY-8
Will Woods Branch—*stream* VA-3
Willy Billy Spring—*spring* NV-8
Willy Branch—*stream* TX-5
Willy Canyon—*valley* AZ-5
Willy Cox Pocosin—*swamp* VA-3
Willy Dick Canyon—*valley* WA-9
Willy Dick Crossing—*locale* WA-9
Willy Drain—*canal* MI-6
Willy Draw—*valley* WY-8
Willy Grubb Cem—*cemetery* TX-5
Willy Hollow—*valley* KY-4
*Willy Island* MD-2
Willy Island—*island* NY-2
Willy Lake—*lake* NE-7
*Willy Mtn* OR-9
Willy Mtn—*summit* OR-9
Willy-O Lake—*lake* WA-9
Will Young Cem—*cemetery* NC-3
Willy Pittman Pond Dam—*dam* MS-4
*Willy Ponds* NH-1
Willy Ranch—*locale* TX-5
Willy Rock—*locale* OR-9
Willys Chapel—*church* IN-6
Willys Creek—*stream* GA-3
Willys Lake—*lake* NY-2
Willy Smith Cave—*cave* AL-4
Willy's Overland Block—*hist pl* MA-1
Willys Park—*park* OH-6
Willys Tip—*ridge* NM-5
*Willzetta* OK-5
*Wilma* MP-9
**Wilma**—*pop pl* FL-3
**Wilma**—*pop pl* WA-9
Wilma Chapel—*church* OH-6
*Wilma Creek* MT-8
Wilma Creek—*stream* WA-9
Wilma Fire Tower—*tower* FL-3
Wilma Lake—*lake* CA-9
Wilma Lake—*lake* FL-3
Wilma Magee Sch—*school* TX-5
WILM-AM (Wilmington)—*tower* DE-2
Wilmans Peaks—*summit* WA-9
*Wilmans Swamp* RI-1
Wilmar—*locale* IA-7
**Wilmar**—*pop pl* AR-4
**Wilmar**—*pop pl* NC-3
Wilmar—*uninc pl* CA-9
Wilmar Cem—*cemetery* AR-4
Wilmar Cem—*cemetery* IA-7
Wilmar Creek—*stream* MI-6
Wilmar Lookout Tower—*locale* AR-4
**Wil-Mar Park**—*pop pl* NC-3
*Wilmarth* PA-2
Wilmarth, Martin L. C., House—*hist pl* NY-2
Wilmarth Dam—*dam* SD-7
Wilmarth Lake—*reservoir* SD-7
Wilmarth Sch—*hist pl* WI-6
Wilmarth Sch—*school* WI-6
Wilma Sch (historical)—*school* AL-4
Wilmas Pond—*lake* NJ-2
Wilma Theatre—*hist pl* MT-8
*Wilmathsville* MO-7
**Wilma (Township of)**—*pop pl* MN-6
Wilmer—*locale* PA-2
**Wilmer**—*pop pl* AL-4
**Wilmer**—*pop pl* LA-4
**Wilmer**—*pop pl* OH-6
**Wilmer**—*pop pl* PA-2
**Wilmer**—*pop pl* TX-5
Wilmer Ave Baptist Ch—*church* AL-4
Wilmer Ave Sch (historical)—*school* AL-4
Wilmer Bridge—*bridge* TX-5
Wilmer Canyon—*valley* NM-5
Wilmer Cem—*cemetery* AL-4
Wilmer Ch—*church* AL-4
Wilmer Ch—*church* LA-4
**Wilmerding**—*pop pl* PA-2
Wilmerding Borough—*civil* PA-2
Wilmer Elem Sch—*school* AL-4
Wilmer E. Shue MS—*school* DE-2
Wilmer F Loomis Elem Sch—*school* PA-2
Wilmer Gulch—*valley* CO-8
**Wilmer (Harveysville)**—*pop pl* PA-2
*Wilmer Lake* CA-9
Wilmer Memorial Cem—*cemetery* LA-4
Wilmer Neck—*cape* MD-2
Wilmer Owl Gulch—*valley* ID-8
Wilmer Point—*cape* MD-2
Wilmers—*locale* MD-2
Wilmers Park—*park* FL-3
Wilmerth Cem—*cemetery* ND-7
Wilmert Lake—*lake* MN-6
Wilmes Lake—*lake* MN-6
Wilmes Rsvr—*reservoir* OR-9
**Wilmeth**—*pop pl* TX-5
Wilmeth Canyon—*valley* NM-5
Wilmeth Cem—*cemetery* TX-5
**Wilmette**—*pop pl* IL-6
Wilmette Harbor—*bay* IL-6
*Wilmington* IN-6
Wilmington—*locale* KS-7
Wilmington—*locale* MN-6
Wilmington—*locale* VA-3
Wilmington—*other* GA-3
**Wilmington**—*pop pl* CA-9
**Wilmington**—*pop pl* DE-2
**Wilmington**—*pop pl* IL-6
**Wilmington**—*pop pl* IN-6
**Wilmington**—*pop pl* MA-1
**Wilmington**—*pop pl* NY-2
**Wilmington**—*pop pl* NC-3
**Wilmington**—*pop pl* OH-6
**Wilmington**—*pop pl* VT-1
Wilmington Amtrak Station—*hist pl* DE-2
Wilmington and Western RR—*hist pl* DE-2
**Wilmington Beach**—*pop pl* NC-3
Wilmington Branch—*hist pl* CA-9
Wilmington (CCD)—*cens area* DE-2
Wilmington Cem—*cemetery* KS-7
Wilmington Cem—*cemetery* ND-7
*Wilmington Center* MA-1
Wilmington Ch—*church* MN-6
Wilmington Christian Sch—*school* DE-2
*Wilmington City* DE-2
Wilmington Coll—*school* DE-2
Wilmington Commercial Hist Dist—*hist pl* OH-6
**Wilmington (corporate name for Patterson)**—*pop pl* IL-6
Wilmington Country Club—*other* DE-2
Wilmington Country Club Airp—*airport* DE-2
Wilmington Friends Sch—*school* DE-2
Wilmington (historical)—*locale* AL-4
Wilmington Historic and Archeol District—*hist pl* NC-3
Wilmington HS—*school* DE-2
Wilmington HS—*school* MA-1
Wilmington Hundred—*civil* DE-2
Wilmington Industrial Park—*locale* DE-2
Wilmington Intermediate Sch—*school* MA-1
Wilmington Island—*CDP* GA-3
Wilmington Island—*island* GA-3
Wilmington JHS—*school* CA-9
Wilmington JHS—*school* MA-1
Wilmington Junction—*locale* PA-2
**Wilmington Junction**—*pop pl* MA-1
Wilmington Junior Acad—*school* DE-2
Wilmington Junior Camp—*locale* MA-1
Wilmington Junior-Senior HS—*school* PA-2
Wilmington Landing—*locale* AR-4
**Wilmington Manor**—*pop pl* DE-2
**Wilmington Manor-Chelsea-Leedom**—*pop pl* DE-2
Wilmington Manor Elem Sch—*school* DE-2
**Wilmington Manor Gardens**—*pop pl* DE-2
*Wilmington Manor School* DE-2
Wilmington Marine Terminal—*locale* DE-2
Wilmington Market (Shop Ctr)—*locale* NC-3
Wilmington Merchandise Mart—*locale* DE-2
Wilmington Notch—*gap* NY-2
**Wilmington Park**—*pop pl* GA-3
Wilmington Park—*uninc pl* CA-9
Wilmington Park Sch—*school* CA-9
Wilmington Plaza—*locale* MA-1
Wilmington Post Office (historical)—*building* AL-4
Wilmington Range—*range* NY-2
*Wilmington Reservoir* DE-2
Wilmington River—*stream* GA-3
Wilmington Rsvr—*reservoir* VT-1
Wilmington Savings Fund Society—*hist pl* DE-2
Wilmington Skill Center—*school* DE-2
**Wilmington Subdivision**—*pop pl* UT-8
**Wilmington (Town of)**—*pop pl* MA-1
**Wilmington (Town of)**—*pop pl* NY-2
**Wilmington (Town of)**—*pop pl* VT-1
**Wilmington Township**—*pop pl* KS-7
Wilmington (Township of)—*fmr MCD* AR-4
Wilmington (Township of)—*fmr MCD* NC-3
**Wilmington (Township of)**—*pop pl* IL-6
**Wilmington (Township of)**—*pop pl* IN-6
**Wilmington (Township of)**—*pop pl* MN-6
**Wilmington (Township of)**—*pop pl* (2) PA-2
Wilmington Trust Company Bank—*hist pl* DE-2
Wilmington Village Hist Dist—*hist pl* VT-1
*Wilmington Water Company Reservoir* DE-2
Wilmoe Lake—*lake* MN-6
*Wilmon Peak* WA-9
*Wilmon Peaks* WA-9
*Wilmont* NC-3
*Wilmont* VA-3
**Wilmont**—*pop pl* DE-2
**Wilmont**—*pop pl* MN-6
Wilmont Brook—*stream* NH-1
Wilmont Cem—*cemetery* MN-6
Wilmont Creek—*stream* WA-9
Wilmonts Pond—*reservoir* AZ-5
**Wilmont (Township of)**—*pop pl* MN-6
Wilmont Wharf—*locale* VA-3
**Wilmoore Heights**—*pop pl* WI-6
Wilmor—*locale* CO-8
**Wilmore**—*pop pl* KS-7
**Wilmore**—*pop pl* KY-4
**Wilmore**—*pop pl* PA-2
**Wilmore**—*pop pl* WV-2
Wilmore, Lake—*reservoir* AL-4
Wilmore Borough—*civil* PA-2
Wilmore (CCD)—*cens area* KY-4
Wilmore Cem—*cemetery* IL-6
Wilmore Cem—*cemetery* TN-4
Wilmore Creek—*stream* MO-7
Wilmore Dam—*dam* AL-4
Wilmore Dam—*dam* PA-2
Wilmore Davis Sch—*school* CO-8
Wilmore Farm—*locale* TX-5
**Wilmore Heights**—*pop pl* PA-2
Wilmore Hollow—*valley* (2) TN-4
Wilmore Sch—*school* NC-3
**Wilmore (subdivision)**—*pop pl* NC-3
Wilmor Lake—*lake* CO-8
*Wilmot* VA-3
Wilmot—*locale* AZ-5
Wilmot—*locale* KS-7
Wilmot—*locale* MS-4
Wilmot—*locale* PA-2
**Wilmot**—*pop pl* AR-4
**Wilmot**—*pop pl* IN-6
**Wilmot**—*pop pl* MI-6
**Wilmot**—*pop pl* NH-1
**Wilmot**—*pop pl* NC-3
**Wilmot**—*pop pl* OH-6
**Wilmot**—*pop pl* SD-7
**Wilmot**—*pop pl* WI-6
Wilmot, David, Sch—*hist pl* PA-2
Wilmot Brook—*stream* CT-1
Wilmot Brook—*stream* ME-1
Wilmot Cem—*cemetery* AR-4
Wilmot Cem—*cemetery* GA-3
Wilmot Cem—*cemetery* KY-4
Wilmot Cem—*cemetery* SD-7
*Wilmot Center* NH-1
Wilmot Ch—*church* KY-4
Wilmot Cove—*bay* ME-1
Wilmot Creek—*stream* CO-8
**Wilmot Flat**—*pop pl* NH-1
Wilmot Floral Oil Field—*oilfield* KS-7
Wilmot Gulch—*valley* ID-8
**Wilmoth**—*pop pl* WV-2
Wilmoth Branch—*stream* VA-3
Wilmoth Cave—*cave* TN-4
Wilmoth Cem—*cemetery* TN-4
Wilmoth Hill—*summit* KY-4
Wilmoth Hollow—*valley* VA-3
Wilmot Hills Raceway—*other* WI-6
Wilmot House—*hist pl* PA-2
Wilmoth Run—*stream* WV-2
Wilmot Interchange—*crossing* AZ-5
Wilmot JHS—*school* IL-6
*Wilmot Lake* IN-6
Wilmot Mansion—*hist pl* PA-2
Wilmot Mtn—*summit* VT-1
Wilmot Plaza Shop Ctr—*locale* AZ-5
Wilmot Pond—*lake* IN-6
*Wilmot Pond Dam* IN-6
Wilmot Ranch—*locale* CO-8
Wilmot RR Station—*building* AZ-5
Wilmot Sch—*school* CO-8
Wilmot Sch—*school* MI-6
**Wilmot (Town of)**—*pop pl* NH-1
Wilmot (Township of)—*fmr MCD* AR-4
**Wilmot (Township of)**—*pop pl* MI-6
**Wilmot (Township of)**—*pop pl* PA-2
Wilmot Trail—*trail* NH-1
Wilmot United Brethren Church—*hist pl* OH-6
**Wilmot Woods**—*pop pl* NY-2
Wilmount Cem—*cemetery* MS-4
Wilmount Ch—*church* MS-4
*Wilmouth Branch* VA-3
*Wilmouth Creek* TN-4
Wilmouth Creek—*stream* TN-4
Wilmouth Hill—*summit* VT-1
Wilmouth Sch (historical)—*school* TN-4
*Wilmouth School* TN-4
Wilmsen Sch—*school* SD-7
*Wilmur Creek* MI-6
Wilmurt Corners—*locale* NY-2
Wilmurt Lake—*lake* NY-2
Wilmurt Lake Outlet—*stream* NY-2
Wilmurt Mtn—*summit* NY-2
Wilmurt Sch—*school* NY-2
Wilna—*locale* NM-5
**Wilna**—*pop pl* MD-2
Wilna Creek—*stream* VA-3
Wilna Point—*cape* VA-3
Wilna Range—*locale* NY-2
**Wilna (Town of)**—*pop pl* NY-2
*Wilnets Hill* NC-3
**Wilno**—*pop pl* MN-6
*Wilnot Ch* MS-4
Wilnot Chapel (historical)—*church* MS-4
WILO-AM (New Albany)—*tower* IN-6
Wiloma—*hist pl* VA-3
Wilow Spring Basin—*basin* OR-9
Wilpen—*locale* MN-6
**Wilpen**—*pop pl* PA-2
Wilpitz Cem—*cemetery* TX-5
WILQ-FM (Williamsport)—*tower* PA-2
Wilroads—*locale* KS-7
*Wilroads Garden* KS-7
**Wilroads Gardens**—*pop pl* KS-7
Wilroads Gardens Airp—*airport* KS-7
Wilroy—*locale* VA-3
Wilroy Ch—*church* VA-3
Wilroy Cove—*bay* VA-3
Wilroy Iron Furnace, The—*locale* PA-2
Wilroy Swamp—*swamp* VA-3
**Wilsall**—*pop pl* MT-8
Wilsall Cem—*cemetery* MT-8
**Wilscot**—*pop pl* GA-3
Wilscot Cem—*cemetery* GA-3
Wilscot Creek—*stream* GA-3
Wilscot Gap—*gap* GA-3
Wilscot Mtn—*summit* GA-3
Wilsdorf Hollow—*valley* TN-4
Wilse, Mount—*summit* MT-8
Wilset Creek—*stream* CO-8
Wilsey—*locale* TX-5
**Wilsey**—*pop pl* KS-7
Wilsey Bay—*bay* MI-6
Wilsey Bay Creek—*stream* MI-6
Wilsey Bay Point—*cape* MI-6
Wilsey Cem—*cemetery* MI-6
Wilsey Creek—*stream* NY-2
Wilsey Hollow—*valley* UT-8
Wilsey Ranch—*locale* SD-7
Wilsey Rsvr—*reservoir* OR-9
*Wilseyville* NY-2
**Wilseyville**—*pop pl* CA-9
Wilsford—*hist pl* MS-4
Wilsford Cem—*cemetery* TN-4
*Wilshire* IN-6
**Wilshire**—*pop pl* GA-3
**Wilshire**—*pop pl* IN-6
Wilshire Branch—*hist pl* CA-9
**Wilshire Condo, The**—*pop pl* UT-8
*Wilshire Condominium* UT-8
**Wilshire Condominium**—*pop pl* UT-8
Wilshire Country Club—*other* CA-9
Wilshire Crest Sch—*school* CA-9
**Wilshire Estates**—*pop pl* GA-3
Wilshire Golf Club—*locale* NC-3
Wilshire Heights Park—*park* AZ-5
**Wilshire Hills**—*pop pl* (2) PA-2
Wilshire JHS—*school* CA-9
**Wilshire-La Brea**—*pop pl* CA-9
Wilshire Oil Field—*oilfield* TX-5
Wilshire Park—*park* OR-9
**Wilshire Park**—*pop pl* LA-4
**Wilshire Park**—*pop pl* NC-3
**Wilshire Park Subdivision**—*pop pl* UT-8
Wilshire Peak—*summit* CA-9
Wilshire Peak Trail (Jeep)—*trail* CA-9
Wilshire Pond—*reservoir* CT-1
Wilshire Pond Brook—*stream* CT-1
Wilshire Pond Brook—*stream* NY-2
Wilshire Sch—*school* TX-5
**Wilshire (subdivision)**—*pop pl* NC-3
Wilshire Terrace Park—*park* TX-5
Wilsie—*locale* CA-9
**Wilsie**—*pop pl* WV-2
Wilsie Canyon—*valley* CA-9
Wilsman—*locale* IL-6
**Wilsmere**—*pop pl* DE-2
Wilsmere Yards—*locale* DE-2
*Wilson* (2) IN-6
*Wilson* NC-3
*Wilson* PA-2
*Wilson* TN-4
*Wilson* VA-3
Wilson—*fmr MCD* NE-7
Wilson—*hist pl* IN-6
Wilson—*locale* AR-4
Wilson—*locale* CA-9
Wilson—*locale* DE-2
Wilson—*locale* FL-3
Wilson—*locale* KY-4
Wilson—*locale* (3) MD-2
Wilson—*locale* MN-6
Wilson—*locale* OK-5
Wilson—*locale* (3) TX-5
Wilson—*locale* VA-3
Wilson—*locale* WA-9
Wilson—*locale* (2) WV-2
Wilson—*locale* WI-6
Wilson—*other* PA-2
**Wilson**—*pop pl* (2) AL-4
**Wilson**—*pop pl* AR-4
**Wilson**—*pop pl* CT-1
**Wilson**—*pop pl* GA-3
**Wilson**—*pop pl* (2) IL-6
**Wilson**—*pop pl* (2) IN-6
**Wilson**—*pop pl* KS-7
**Wilson**—*pop pl* LA-4
**Wilson**—*pop pl* MD-2
**Wilson**—*pop pl* MI-6
**Wilson**—*pop pl* NH-1
**Wilson**—*pop pl* NY-2
**Wilson**—*pop pl* (2) NC-3
**Wilson**—*pop pl* OH-6
**Wilson**—*pop pl* (2) OK-5
**Wilson**—*pop pl* OR-9
**Wilson**—*pop pl* (2) PA-2
**Wilson**—*pop pl* SC-3
**Wilson**—*pop pl* TX-5
**Wilson**—*pop pl* UT-8
**Wilson**—*pop pl* WV-2
**Wilson**—*pop pl* WI-6
**Wilson**—*pop pl* (2) WY-8
Wilson—*uninc pl* MA-1
Wilson, A. G., House—*hist pl* TX-5
Wilson, Ammie, House—*hist pl* TX-5
Wilson, Anson, House—*hist pl* IA-7
Wilson, Asa, House—*hist pl* IA-7
Wilson, Bay—*lake* LA-4
Wilson, Benjamin, House—*hist pl* KY-4
Wilson, Catlin, House—*hist pl* AL-4
Wilson, Charles, Jr., House—*hist pl* AZ-5
Wilson, C. J. (Blinky), House—*hist pl* AZ-5
Wilson, David, House—*hist pl* KY-4
Wilson, Dr. C. B., House—*hist pl* FL-3
Wilson, Edmund, House—*hist pl* NY-2
Wilson, Edward R., House—*hist pl* DE-2
Wilson, Ephraim J., Farm Complex—*hist pl* MO-7
Wilson, George, Homestead—*hist pl* PA-2
Wilson, George D., House—*hist pl* OH-6
Wilson, Gordon, Hall—*hist pl* KY-4
Wilson, Homer, Ranch—*hist pl* TX-5
Wilson, Hudson, House—*hist pl* MN-6
Wilson, James O., House—*hist pl* OR-9
Wilson, J. C., House—*hist pl* AZ-5
Wilson, J. L., Bldg—*hist pl* OK-5
Wilson, J. Mark, House—*hist pl* AZ-5
Wilson, John, House—*hist pl* CT-1
Wilson, John, House—*hist pl* IA-7
Wilson, John Calvin, House—*hist pl* SC-3
Wilson, John E., House—*hist pl* NC-3
Wilson, John T., Homestead—*hist pl* OH-6
Wilson, Joseph, House—*hist pl* TN-4
Wilson, Judge Isaac, House—*hist pl* IL-6
Wilson, Judge Robert S., House—*hist pl* MI-6
Wilson, Judge William, House—*hist pl* GA-3
Wilson, J. Woodrow, House—*hist pl* IN-6
Wilson, Lake—*lake* AR-4
Wilson, Lake—*lake* (3) FL-3
Wilson, Lake—*lake* LA-4
Wilson, Lake—*lake* (2) MI-6
Wilson, Lake—*lake* MN-6
Wilson, Lake—*reservoir* NC-3
Wilson, Lake—*reservoir* VA-3
Wilson, Mary Park, House—*hist pl* WV-2
Wilson, Monroe, House—*hist pl* SC-3
Wilson, Mount—*summit* AK-9
Wilson, Mount—*summit* AZ-5
Wilson, Mount—*summit* CA-9
Wilson, Mount—*summit* CO-8
Wilson, Mount—*summit* (4) NV-8
Wilson, Mount—*summit* OR-9
Wilson, Mount—*summit* VT-1
Wilson, Mount—*summit* WA-9
Wilson, Orme, and Company Storehouse—*hist pl* TN-4
Wilson, Paul, Place—*hist pl* KY-4
Wilson, Point—*cape* WA-9
Wilson, R. H., House—*hist pl* KY-4
Wilson, Robert, House—*hist pl* PA-2
Wilson, Sanford, House—*hist pl* TN-4
Wilson, Seth and Elizabeth, House—*hist pl* IA-7
Wilson, Shoreborne, House—*hist pl* MA-1
Wilson, Solomon, Bldg—*hist pl* IN-6
Wilson, Thomas Woodrow, Boyhood Home—*hist pl* SC-3
Wilson, Valentine, House—*hist pl* OH-6
Wilson, Victor E., House—*hist pl* NE-7
Wilson, Warren, Beach House—*hist pl* CA-9
Wilson, Warren, House—*hist pl* NY-2
Wilson, William, House—*hist pl* KY-4
Wilson, William, House—*hist pl* WV-2
Wilson, William J., House—*hist pl* NC-3
Wilson, Willie W., House—*hist pl* OK-5
Wilson, Woodrow, Birthplace—*hist pl* VA-3
Wilson, Woodrow, Boyhood Home—*hist pl* GA-3
Wilson, Woodrow, Bridge—*hist pl* MS-4
Wilson, Woodrow, House—*hist pl* DC-2
Wilson, Woodrow, JHS—*hist pl* PA-2
**Wilsona**—*pop pl* CA-9
**Wilsona**—*pop pl* LA-4
**Wilson Acres (subdivision)**—*pop pl* NC-3
**Wilson Addition Subdivision**—*pop pl* UT-8
**Wilsona Gardens**—*pop pl* CA-9
Wilson Airfield—*airport* OR-9
Wilson Airp—*airport* IN-6
Wilson Airp—*airport* KS-7
Wilson Airp—*airport* PA-2
Wilson Airport—*other* GA-3
Wilson and Company—*facility* IN-6
Wilson and Screws Landing—*locale* MS-4
Wilsona Ranch—*locale* CA-9
Wilson Arch—*arch* UT-8
Wilson Area HS—*school* PA-2
Wilson Arm—*bay* AK-9
Wilson Arroyo—*stream* CO-8
Wilson Arroyo—*stream* NM-5
Wilson Arroyo—*valley* TX-5
Wilsona Sch—*school* CA-9
Wilson Attendance Center—*school* MS-4
Wilson Ave Baptist Ch—*church* AL-4
Wilson Ave Ch—*church* OH-6
Wilson Ave Ch of Christ—*church* TN-4
Wilson Ave Ch of God—*church* AL-4
Wilson Ave Sch—*school* NJ-2
Wilson Ave Sch—*school* WI-6
Wilson Barn—*hist pl* MI-6
Wilson Basin—*basin* OR-9
Wilson Bay—*bay* AK-9
Wilson Bay—*bay* MN-6
Wilson Bay—*bay* NY-2
Wilson Bay—*bay* NC-3
*Wilson Bayou* LA-4
Wilson Bayou—*gut* MS-4
Wilson Bayou—*stream* (3) LA-4
Wilson Bayou—*stream* MO-7
Wilson Bay Park—*park* NC-3
Wilson Beach—*beach* FL-3
Wilson Beach—*beach* OR-9
**Wilson Beach**—*pop pl* OR-9
Wilson Bend—*bend* MO-7

Wilson Bend—*bend* (2) TN-4
Wilson Bend—*bend* TX-5
Wilson Bend—*locale* AL-4
Wilson Bend Mine (surface)—*mine* AL-4
Wilson Bldg—*hist pl* TX-5
Wilson Block—*hist pl* TX-5
Wilson Blue Spring—*spring* GA-3
Wilson Bluff—*cliff* AL-4
Wilson Bluff—*cliff* ID-8
Wilson Bluff—*cliff* KY-4
Wilson Bluff—*cliff* TX-5
Wilson Boat Dock—*locale* TN-4
Wilson Borough—*civil* PA-2
Wilson Borough Elem Sch—*school* PA-2
Wilson Bottom—*valley* MS-4
Wilson Brake—*lake* AR-4
Wilson Brake—*swamp* LA-4
*Wilson Branch* AR-4
*Wilson Branch* KS-7
*Wilson Branch* TN-4
*Wilson Branch* TX-5
Wilson Branch—*stream* (5) AL-4
Wilson Branch—*stream* (5) AR-4
Wilson Branch—*stream* (2) FL-3
Wilson Branch—*stream* (5) GA-3
Wilson Branch—*stream* (6) KY-4
Wilson Branch—*stream* (4) LA-4
Wilson Branch—*stream* (2) MS-4
Wilson Branch—*stream* MO-7
Wilson Branch—*stream* (7) NC-3
Wilson Branch—*stream* OK-5
Wilson Branch—*stream* (3) SC-3
Wilson Branch—*stream* (15) TN-4
Wilson Branch—*stream* (7) TX-5
Wilson Branch—*stream* (2) VA-3
Wilson Branch—*stream* (3) WV-2
Wilson Branch - Cade Branch Prospect—*mine* TN-4
Wilson Branch Sch (historical)—*school* MS-4
Wilson Bridge—*bridge* KY-4
Wilson Bridge—*bridge* MS-4
Wilson Bridge—*bridge* NC-3
Wilson Bridge—*bridge* OH-6
Wilson Bridge—*bridge* OR-9
Wilson Bridge—*bridge* VA-3
Wilson Brook—*stream* CT-1
Wilson Brook—*stream* IN-6
Wilson Brook—*stream* (2) ME-1
Wilson Brook—*stream* MA-1
Wilson Brook—*stream* NH-1
Wilson Brook—*stream* (2) NY-2
Wilson Brothers Dam Number One—*dam* NC-3
Wilson Brothers Dam Number Two—*dam* NC-3
Wilson Brothers Lake Number One—*reservoir* NC-3
Wilson Brothers Lake Number Two—*reservoir* NC-3
*Wilsonburg* WV-2
**Wilsonburg**—*pop pl* WV-2
Wilson Butte—*summit* CA-9
Wilson Butte—*summit* ID-8
Wilson Butte—*summit* MT-8
Wilson Butte—*summit* OR-9
Wilson Butte—*summit* WA-9
Wilson Butte Cave—*cave* ID-8
Wilson Butte Cave—*hist pl* ID-8
*Wilson Cabin* ID-8
Wilson Cabin—*locale* CA-9
Wilson Cabin—*locale* ID-8
Wilson Cabin—*locale* NC-3
Wilson Cabin—*locale* OR-9
Wilson Cager Sch (historical)—*school* TN-4
Wilson Camp—*locale* CA-9
Wilson Camp—*locale* NM-5
Wilson Camp State Wildlife Area—*park* MO-7
Wilson Campus Sch—*school* MN-6
Wilson Canal—*canal* TX-5
Wilson Canal—*canal* (2) UT-8
*Wilson Canyon* UT-8
Wilson Canyon—*valley* AZ-5
Wilson Canyon—*valley* (4) CA-9
Wilson Canyon—*valley* KS-7
Wilson Canyon—*valley* NE-7
Wilson Canyon—*valley* (5) NV-8
Wilson Canyon—*valley* (4) NM-5
Wilson Canyon—*valley* OR-9
Wilson Canyon—*valley* (2) TX-5
Wilson Canyon—*valley* (3) UT-8
Wilson Canyon—*valley* WA-9
Wilson Canyon Saddle—*gap* CA-9
Wilson Canyon Tank—*reservoir* NM-5
Wilson Canyon Tank No 1—*reservoir* NM-5
Wilson Canyon Tank No 2—*reservoir* NM-5
Wilson Castle Park—*park* TN-4
Wilson Cave—*cave* AL-4
Wilson Cave—*cave* IN-6
Wilson Cave—*cave* KY-4
Wilson Cave Hollow—*valley* KY-4
Wilson (CCD)—*cens area* OK-5
Wilson (CCD)—*cens area* TX-5
*Wilson Cem* AL-4
*Wilson Cem* MO-7
*Wilson Cem* TN-4
Wilson Cem—*cemetery* (15) AL-4
Wilson Cem—*cemetery* (10) AR-4
Wilson Cem—*cemetery* CO-8
Wilson Cem—*cemetery* (6) GA-3
Wilson Cem—*cemetery* (5) IL-6
Wilson Cem—*cemetery* (9) IN-6
Wilson Cem—*cemetery* (5) IA-7
Wilson Cem—*cemetery* (3) KS-7
Wilson Cem—*cemetery* (15) KY-4
Wilson Cem—*cemetery* (5) LA-4
Wilson Cem—*cemetery* (2) ME-1
Wilson Cem—*cemetery* (5) MI-6
Wilson Cem—*cemetery* (2) MN-6
Wilson Cem—*cemetery* (14) MS-4
Wilson Cem—*cemetery* (13) MO-7
Wilson Cem—*cemetery* NM-5
Wilson Cem—*cemetery* (10) NC-3
Wilson Cem—*cemetery* (8) OH-6
Wilson Cem—*cemetery* (7) OK-5
Wilson Cem—*cemetery* OR-9
Wilson Cem—*cemetery* PA-2
Wilson Cem—*cemetery* (2) SC-3
Wilson Cem—*cemetery* SD-7
Wilson Cem—*cemetery* (36) TN-4
Wilson Cem—*cemetery* (4) TX-5
Wilson Cem—*cemetery* VT-1
Wilson Cem—*cemetery* (10) VA-3
Wilson Cem—*cemetery* WA-9
Wilson Cem—*cemetery* (9) WV-2
Wilson Cemetary—*cemetery* TN-4
Wilson Cem No 1—*cemetery* GA-3
Wilson Cem No 2—*cemetery* GA-3
Wilson Central Business-Tobacco Warehouse Hist Dist—*hist pl* NC-3
*Wilson Ch* MS-4
Wilson Ch—*church* AL-4
Wilson Ch—*church* (2) GA-3
Wilson Ch—*church* KY-4
Wilson Ch—*church* (2) MD-2
Wilson Ch—*church* MI-6
Wilson Ch—*church* MO-7
Wilson Ch—*church* NE-7
Wilson Ch—*church* NJ-2
Wilson Ch—*church* (3) NC-3
Wilson Ch—*church* OH-6
Wilson Ch—*church* (2) OK-5
Wilson Ch—*church* (2) TX-5
Wilson Ch—*church* VA-3
Wilson Ch—*church* WV-2
Wilson Ch—*church* WI-6
Wilson Chapel—*church* (2) AL-4
Wilson Chapel—*church* (2) GA-3
Wilson Chapel—*church* IN-6
Wilson Chapel—*church* LA-4
Wilson Chapel—*church* (3) NC-3
Wilson Chapel—*church* (3) OH-6
Wilson Chapel—*church* (2) OK-5
Wilson Chapel—*church* TN-4
Wilson Chapel—*church* (3) TX-5
Wilson Chapel—*church* (2) VA-3
Wilson Chapel—*church* (3) WV-2
Wilson Chapel—*church* WI-6
Wilson Chapel Baptist Ch—*church* AL-4
Wilson Chapel Cem—*cemetery* (2) OK-5
*Wilson Chapel Ch* AL-4
Wilson Chapel Ch—*church* TX-5
Wilson Chapel (historical)—*church* (2) MS-4
Wilson Chapel (historical)—*church* (2) TN-4
Wilson Chapel Sch (historical)—*school* TN-4
Wilson Charley Canyon—*valley* WA-9
Wilson Christian Sch—*school* NC-3
*Wilson City* KS-7
**Wilson City**—*pop pl* MO-7
Wilson-Clary House—*hist pl* SC-3
Wilson-Clements House—*hist pl* AL-4
Wilson Coll—*school* IL-6
Wilson Common—*park* OH-6
**Wilson Community Center**—*pop pl* IN-6
Wilson Community Hall—*building* WV-2
*Wilson Corner* ME-1
Wilson Corner—*locale* CA-9
Wilson Corner—*locale* FL-3
Wilson Corner—*locale* ME-1
**Wilson Corner**—*pop pl* IN-6
**Wilson Corner**—*pop pl* OR-9
Wilson Corners—*locale* FL-3
Wilson Corners—*locale* (2) NY-2
**Wilson Corners**—*pop pl* NH-1
**Wilson Corners**—*pop pl* NY-2
Wilson Corrals Trail—*trail* ID-8
Wilson Coulee—*valley* (6) MT-8
Wilson Country Club—*locale* NC-3
Wilson County—*civil* KS-7
Wilson County—*civil* NC-3
**Wilson County**—*pop pl* TN-4
**Wilson (County)**—*pop pl* TX-5
Wilson County Courthouse—*building* TN-4
Wilson County Courthouse—*hist pl* NC-3
Wilson County Courthouse and Jail—*hist pl* TX-5
Wilson County Farm (historical)—*locale* TN-4
Wilson County Park—*park* OR-9
Wilson County State Lake—*reservoir* KS-7
Wilson County State Lake Dam—*dam* KS-7
Wilson County State Park—*park* KS-7
Wilson County Training Sch (historical)—*school* TN-4
Wilson County Vocational Center—*school* TN-4
Wilson-Courtney House—*hist pl* IN-6
Wilson Cove—*basin* WV-2
Wilson Cove—*bay* AK-9
Wilson Cove—*bay* CA-9
Wilson Cove—*bay* CT-1
Wilson Cove—*bay* FL-3
Wilson Cove—*bay* (2) ME-1
Wilson Cove—*bay* NC-3
Wilson Cove—*valley* CA-9
Wilson Cove—*valley* GA-3
Wilson Cove—*valley* (2) NC-3
Wilson Cove Creek—*stream* GA-3
Wilson Cove Trail—*trail* OR-9
Wilson Cow Camp—*locale* ID-8
*Wilson Creek* CA-9
*Wilson Creek* CO-8
*Wilson Creek* GA-3
*Wilson Creek* ID-8
*Wilson Creek* MS-4
*Wilson Creek* MO-7
*Wilson Creek* MT-8
*Wilson Creek* NV-8
*Wilson Creek* OR-9
*Wilson Creek* WA-9
*Wilson Creek* WI-6
Wilson Creek—*locale* NY-2
Wilsoncreek—*other* WA-9
**Wilson Creek**—*pop pl* PA-2
**Wilson Creek**—*pop pl* WA-9
Wilson Creek—*stream* (6) AL-4
Wilson Creek—*stream* (6) AK-9
Wilson Creek—*stream* AZ-5
Wilson Creek—*stream* (7) AR-4
Wilson Creek—*stream* (21) CA-9
Wilson Creek—*stream* (8) CO-8
Wilson Creek—*stream* DE-2
Wilson Creek—*stream* (4) GA-3
Wilson Creek—*stream* (15) ID-8
Wilson Creek—*stream* (3) IL-6
Wilson Creek—*stream* (4) IN-6
Wilson Creek—*stream* (3) KS-7
Wilson Creek—*stream* (8) KY-4
Wilson Creek—*stream* LA-4
Wilson Creek—*stream* ME-1
Wilson Creek—*stream* (5) MI-6
Wilson Creek—*stream* (2) MN-6
Wilson Creek—*stream* (5) MS-4
Wilson Creek—*stream* (4) MO-7
Wilson Creek—*stream* (8) MT-8
Wilson Creek—*stream* (3) NE-7
Wilson Creek—*stream* (6) NV-8
Wilson Creek—*stream* (2) NM-5
Wilson Creek—*stream* (2) NY-2
Wilson Creek—*stream* (6) NC-3
Wilson Creek—*stream* (3) ND-7
Wilson Creek—*stream* (2) OH-6
Wilson Creek—*stream* (5) OK-5
Wilson Creek—*stream* (25) OR-9
Wilson Creek—*stream* (5) PA-2
Wilson Creek—*stream* (4) SC-3
Wilson Creek—*stream* SD-7
Wilson Creek—*stream* (3) TN-4
Wilson Creek—*stream* (9) TX-5
Wilson Creek—*stream* (4) UT-8
Wilson Creek—*stream* (7) VA-3
Wilson Creek—*stream* (13) WA-9
Wilson Creek—*stream* WV-2
Wilson Creek—*stream* (8) WI-6
Wilson Creek—*stream* (2) WY-8
Wilson Creek Airp—*airport* WA-9
Wilson Creek Camp—*locale* CO-8
Wilson Creek Campground—*locale* CO-8
Wilson Creek Campground—*locale* ID-8
Wilson Creek Canyon—*valley* NV-8
Wilson Creek (CCD)—*cens area* WA-9
Wilson Creek Cem—*cemetery* KY-4
Wilson Creek Ch—*church* IN-6
Wilson Creek Ch—*church* KY-4
Wilson Creek Dam—*dam* PA-2
Wilson Creek Driveway—*trail* OR-9
Wilson Creek Falls—*falls* WA-9
*Wilson Creek Flowage* WI-6
**Wilson Creek Heights (subdivision)**—*pop pl* NC-3
Wilson Creek Lake—*reservoir* PA-2
Wilson Creek Lakes—*lake* WY-8
Wilson Creek (Magisterial District)—*fmr MCD* VA-3
Wilson Creek Mines—*mine* PA-2
Wilson Creek Number 1 Ch—*church* SC-3
Wilson Creek Number 2 Ch—*church* SC-3
Wilson Creek Oil Field—*oilfield* CO-8
Wilson Creek Range—*range* NV-8
Wilson Creek Sch—*school* CO-8
Wilson Creek Slough—*stream* AK-9
Wilson Creek Spring—*spring* ID-8
Wilson Creek Spring—*spring* OR-9
Wilson Creek State Bank—*hist pl* WA-9
Wilson Creek Station—*locale* PA-2
Wilson Creek (Township of)—*fmr MCD* NC-3
Wilson Creek Trail—*trail* ID-8
Wilson Creek Trail—*trail* VA-3
Wilson Creek VORTAC Station—*locale* NV-8
**Wilson Creek (Wilsoncreek)**—*pop pl* WA-9
*Wilson Crossing* NH-1
Wilson Crossing—*locale* CO-8
*Wilson Crossroads* SC-3
**Wilson Crossroads**—*pop pl* SC-3
Wilson Curtis Cem—*cemetery* TX-5
Wilson Cut—*channel* FL-3
Wilson Cypress—*swamp* FL-3
Wilsondale—*locale* WV-2
*Wilson Dam* ND-7
Wilson Dam—*dam* AL-4
Wilson Dam—*dam* KS-7
Wilson Dam—*dam* ND-7
Wilson Dam—*dam* OR-9
Wilson Dam—*dam* SD-7
Wilson Dam—*hist pl* AL-4
**Wilson Dam**—*pop pl* AL-4
Wilson Dam—*reservoir* ND-7
Wilson Dam P.O. (historical)—*locale* AL-4
Wilson Dam Village Number Three (historical)—*locale* AL-4
Wilson Dam Village Number Two (historical)—*locale* AL-4
Wilson Debris Basin—*basin* CA-9
Wilson Desert—*plain* MT-8
*Wilson Ditch* IN-6
*Wilson Ditch* OR-9
Wilson Ditch—*canal* (2) CA-9
Wilson Ditch—*canal* (2) CO-8
Wilson Ditch—*canal* HI-9
Wilson Ditch—*canal* (5) IN-6
Wilson Ditch—*canal* IA-7
Wilson Ditch—*canal* LA-4
Wilson Ditch—*canal* MT-8
Wilson Ditch—*canal* OH-6
Wilson Ditch—*canal* OR-9
Wilson Ditch—*canal* WY-8
Wilson Ditch—*stream* IN-6
Wilson Ditch Arm Number Two—*canal* IN-6
Wilson-Donaldson Site—*hist pl* TX-5
Wilson Drain—*canal* ID-8
Wilson Drain—*canal* (9) MI-6
Wilson Drain—*stream* MI-6
Wilson Draw—*valley* AZ-5
Wilson Draw—*valley* CO-8
Wilson Draw—*valley* MT-8
Wilson Draw—*valley* OR-9
Wilson Draw—*valley* SD-7
Wilson Draw—*valley* (2) TX-5
Wilson Draw—*valley* (2) WY-8
Wilson-Durbin House—*hist pl* OR-9
Wilson Elem Sch—*school* KS-7
Wilson Elem Sch—*school* (2) TN-4
Wilson Elem Sch (abandoned)—*school* PA-2
Wilson Falls—*falls* GA-3
Wilson Falls—*falls* OR-9
Wilson Falls—*falls* TN-4
**Wilson Farm (subdivision), The**—*pop pl* NC-3
Wilson Feed Mill—*hist pl* OH-6
Wilson Field—*area* CA-9
Wilson Field (airport)—*airport* AL-4
Wilson-Finlay House—*hist pl* AL-4
Wilson Flat—*flat* CA-9
Wilson Flat—*flat* ID-8
Wilson Flats—*flat* OR-9
Wilson Flowage—*lake* WI-6
Wilson Ford—*locale* IL-6
Wilson Ford (historical)—*locale* MO-7
Wilson Fork—*stream* IN-6
Wilson Fork—*stream* (4) KY-4
Wilson Fork—*stream* UT-8
Wilson Fork—*stream* (3) WV-2
Wilson Friedrick Ditch—*canal* IN-6
Wilson Fruit Lateral—*canal* ID-8
*Wilson Gap* TN-4
Wilson Gap—*gap* (2) GA-3
Wilson Gap—*gap* NC-3
Wilson Gap—*gap* (2) TN-4
Wilson Gap—*gap* VA-3
Wilson Gap—*gap* WV-2
Wilson Gap—*gap* WY-8
**Wilson Gap**—*pop pl* TN-4
Wilson Gap Hollow—*valley* TN-4
Wilson-Gibson House—*hist pl* OH-6
Wilson Glacier—*glacier* (2) WA-9
Wilson Glade—*flat* CA-9
Wilson Glade Canyon—*valley* CA-9
Wilson Godfrey Dam—*dam* NC-3
Wilson Golf Course—*other* CA-9
Wilson-Gomez Mine (Inactive)—*mine* CA-9
Wilson Grade Sch—*school* KS-7
Wilson Grove—*locale* CA-9
**Wilson Grove**—*pop pl* VA-3
*Wilson Grove Baptist Church* MS-4
Wilson Grove Cem—*cemetery* IA-7
Wilson Grove Ch—*church* MS-4
Wilson Grove Ch—*church* NC-3
Wilson Grove Ch—*church* VA-3
Wilson Grove (historical)—*locale* IA-7
*Wilson Gulch* CO-8
Wilson Gulch—*valley* AK-9
Wilson Gulch—*valley* (3) CA-9
Wilson Gulch—*valley* (2) CO-8
Wilson Gulch—*valley* (2) ID-8
Wilson Gulch—*valley* MT-8
Wilson Gulch—*valley* WY-8
Wilson Gut—*stream* NC-3
Wilson Hall—*hist pl* ME-1
Wilson Hammock—*island* GA-3
*Wilson-Hardy Cemetery* AL-4
**Wilson Haven**—*pop pl* FL-3
Wilson Head—*cape* ME-1
Wilson Head—*island* CT-1
Wilson Health Springs—*spring* UT-8
**Wilson Heights**—*pop pl* IL-6
**Wilson Heights**—*pop pl* TN-4
Wilson Heights Ch—*church* NC-3
**Wilson Heights (subdivision)**—*pop pl* AL-4
Wilson Heliport—*airport* WA-9
Wilson Hill—*locale* TN-4
Wilson Hill—*locale* VA-3
Wilson Hill—*summit* (2) AR-4
Wilson Hill—*summit* CT-1
Wilson Hill—*summit* DE-2
Wilson Hill—*summit* IN-6
Wilson Hill—*summit* (3) KY-4
Wilson Hill—*summit* (2) ME-1
Wilson Hill—*summit* (2) MA-1
Wilson Hill—*summit* MI-6
Wilson Hill—*summit* MO-7
Wilson Hill—*summit* (4) NH-1
Wilson Hill—*summit* NM-5
Wilson Hill—*summit* (2) NY-2
Wilson Hill—*summit* PA-2
Wilson Hill—*summit* (2) TX-5
Wilson Hill—*summit* UT-8
Wilson Hill Ch—*church* TN-4
Wilson Hill Hollow—*valley* TN-4
Wilson Hill Island—*island* NY-2
Wilson Hill Mine—*mine* TN-4
Wilson Hill Mine (underground)—*mine* AL-4
Wilson Hill Pond—*lake* ME-1
**Wilson Hills**—*pop pl* MD-2
Wilson Hill State Fish And Game Mngmt Area—*park* NY-2
Wilson (historical)—*locale* AL-4
Wilson (historical)—*locale* KS-7
Wilson (historical)—*locale* SD-7
**Wilson (historical)**—*pop pl* IA-7
**Wilson (historical)**—*pop pl* MS-4
**Wilson (historical)**—*pop pl* NC-3
**Wilson (historical)**—*pop pl* OR-9
Wilson (historical P.O.)—*locale* AL-4
Wilson Hole—*basin* UT-8
Wilson Hole—*bay* WV-2
Wilson Hollow—*valley* AL-4
Wilson Hollow—*valley* (4) AR-4
Wilson Hollow—*valley* IN-6
Wilson Hollow—*valley* (5) KY-4
Wilson Hollow—*valley* (11) MO-7
Wilson Hollow—*valley* (3) NY-2
Wilson Hollow—*valley* NC-3
Wilson Hollow—*valley* OK-5
Wilson Hollow—*valley* (9) TN-4
Wilson Hollow—*valley* (3) TX-5
Wilson Hollow—*valley* (2) VA-3
Wilson Hollow—*valley* WV-2
Wilson Hollow Brook—*stream* NY-2
Wilson Hollow Cem—*cemetery* NY-2
Wilson Homesite—*hist pl* TX-5
Wilson Hosp—*hospital* NY-2
Wilson Hosp—*hospital* OH-6
Wilson Hosp—*hospital* TX-5
Wilson Hot Spring—*spring* NV-8
Wilson House—*hist pl* AR-4
Wilson House—*hist pl* CA-9
Wilson House—*hist pl* MS-4
Wilson House—*hist pl* NY-2
Wilson House—*hist pl* SC-3
Wilson House—*hist pl* TX-5
Wilson HS—*school* (2) CA-9
Wilson HS—*school* CT-1
Wilson HS—*school* DC-2
Wilson HS—*school* KS-7
Wilson HS—*school* OH-6
Wilson HS—*school* PA-2
Wilson HS—*school* TX-5
Wilson HS—*school* (2) WV-2
Wilson HS—*school* WI-6
Wilson Hunter Ditch—*canal* CA-9
Wilsonia—*locale* AL-4
Wilsonia—*locale* LA-4
Wilsonia—*locale* WV-2
**Wilsonia**—*pop pl* CA-9
**Wilsonia**—*pop pl* OR-9
*Wilson Island* ME-1
Wilson Island—*island* FL-3
Wilson Island—*island* IA-7
Wilson Island—*island* LA-4
Wilson Island—*island* (2) MI-6
Wilson Island—*island* NC-3
Wilson Island—*island* (2) TN-4
Wilson Island—*island* WV-2
Wilson Island—*swamp* MO-7
Wilson Islands—*area* AK-9
Wilson Islands—*island* FL-3
Wilson Island Shoals—*bar* TN-4
Wilson Island State Park—*park* IA-7
Wilson JHS—*school* (5) CA-9
Wilson JHS—*school* (2) CO-8
Wilson JHS—*school* FL-3
Wilson JHS—*school* (2) IL-6
Wilson JHS—*school* (4) IA-7
Wilson JHS—*school* MA-1
Wilson JHS—*school* MI-6
Wilson JHS—*school* MN-6
Wilson JHS—*school* NJ-2
Wilson JHS—*school* NM-5
Wilson JHS—*school* (2) NC-3
Wilson JHS—*school* (2) OH-6
Wilson JHS—*school* OK-5
Wilson JHS—*school* OR-9
Wilson JHS—*school* (2) PA-2
Wilson JHS—*school* (3) TX-5
Wilson JHS—*school* WI-6
**Wilson Junction**—*pop pl* AR-4
**Wilson Junction**—*pop pl* CO-8
**Wilson Junction**—*pop pl* IL-6
Wilson Key—*island* FL-3
Wilson Killen Cem—*cemetery* IN-6
Wilson Knob—*summit* AR-4
Wilson Knob—*summit* GA-3
Wilson Knob—*summit* NC-3
Wilson Knob—*summit* (2) TN-4
Wilson Knob—*summit* VA-3
Wilson Knob—*summit* WV-2
Wilson-Kuykendall Farm—*hist pl* WV-2
*Wilson Lake* IA-7
*Wilson Lake* MI-6
*Wilson Lake* MN-6
*Wilson Lake* WI-6
Wilson Lake—*lake* (2) AK-9
Wilson Lake—*lake* (2) AR-4
Wilson Lake—*lake* CA-9
Wilson Lake—*lake* (2) FL-3
Wilson Lake—*lake* ID-8
Wilson Lake—*lake* IN-6
Wilson Lake—*lake* (2) IA-7
Wilson Lake—*lake* KS-7
Wilson Lake—*lake* (5) LA-4
Wilson Lake—*lake* ME-1
Wilson Lake—*lake* (7) MI-6
Wilson Lake—*lake* (13) MN-6
Wilson Lake—*lake* (5) MS-4
Wilson Lake—*lake* MO-7
Wilson Lake—*lake* MT-8
Wilson Lake—*lake* NJ-2
Wilson Lake—*lake* (2) NM-5
Wilson Lake—*lake* (2) OR-9
Wilson Lake—*lake* SC-3
Wilson Lake—*lake* (3) TX-5
Wilson Lake—*lake* WA-9
Wilson Lake—*lake* (8) WI-6
**Wilson Lake**—*pop pl* IN-6
Wilson Lake—*reservoir* (2) AL-4
Wilson Lake—*reservoir* CA-9
Wilson Lake—*reservoir* KS-7
Wilson Lake—*reservoir* MS-4
Wilson Lake—*reservoir* NC-3
Wilson Lake—*reservoir* OR-9
Wilson Lake—*reservoir* TX-5
Wilson Lake—*reservoir* VA-3
Wilson Lake Dam—*dam* IA-7
Wilson Lake Dam—*dam* MS-4
Wilson Lake Dam—*dam* NC-3
Wilson Lake Dam—*dam* OR-9
**Wilson Lake Estates**—*pop pl* CO-8
Wilson Lake Rsvr—*reservoir* ID-8
**Wilson Lake Shores**—*pop pl* AL-4
Wilson Lake Trail—*trail* MN-6
*Wilson Landing* SC-3
Wilson Landing—*locale* IL-6
Wilson Landing—*locale* SC-3
Wilson Landing (historical)—*locale* AL-4
Wilson Landing (historical)—*locale* TN-4
Wilson Landing (Site)—*locale* CA-9
Wilson Lateral—*canal* SD-7
Wilson Ledges—*bar* (2) ME-1
Wilson-Lenox House—*hist pl* OH-6
Wilson Lick Ranger Station—*locale* NC-3
Wilson Line Ch—*church* TN-4
Wilson Lodge—*locale* AR-4
Wilson Lookout Tower—*locale* LA-4
Wilson Lookout Tower—*locale* WI-6
Wilson Lower—*dam* NC-3
Wilson Lower—*reservoir* NC-3
Wilson (Magisterial District)—*fmr MCD* VA-3
Wilson Marsh—*swamp* DE-2
Wilson Marsh—*swamp* FL-3
Wilson Marsh Flowage—*reservoir* WI-6
Wilson-McKissack Ditch—*canal* WY-8
Wilson Meadow—*flat* (2) CA-9
Wilson Meadows—*flat* CO-8
Wilson Meadows—*flat* ID-8
Wilson Meadows—*flat* NV-8
Wilson Meadows—*flat* WY-8
Wilson Memorial Ch—*church* (2) FL 3
Wilson Memorial HS—*school* VA-3
Wilson Memorial Sch—*school* VA-3
Wilson Mesa—*summit* (2) CO-8
Wilson Mesa—*summit* (2) NM-5
Wilson Mesa—*summit* (2) UT-8
Wilson Mesa Trail—*trail* CO-8
*Wilson Middle School* NC-3
Wilson Mill—*locale* GA-3
Wilson Mill—*locale* MD-2
Wilson Mill Branch—*stream* AL-4
Wilson Mill Creek—*stream* FL-3
Wilson Mill Creek—*stream* NC-3
Wilson-Miller Farm—*hist pl* MD-2
Wilson Mill (historical)—*locale* PA-2
Wilson Mill (historical)—*locale* (2) TN-4
Wilson Mill Pond—*reservoir* SC-3
Wilson Mills—*locale* PA-2
Wilson Mills Ch—*church* NC-3
Wilson Mills (Township of)—*fmr MCD* NC-3
Wilson Mine—*mine* CA-9
Wilson Mine—*mine* ID-8
Wilson Mine—*mine* NM-5
Wilson Mine—*mine* (2) UT-8
Wilson Mine (Abandoned)—*mine* AL-4
Wilson Mines—*mine* NV-8
Wilson Mine (underground)—*mine* (2) AL-4
Wilson Mounds and Village Site—*hist pl* IL-6
*Wilson Mountain* CO-8
Wilson Mountain Trail—*trail* AZ-5
Wilson Mountain Trail—*trail* ID-8
*Wilson MS* PA-2
Wilson MS—*school* AL-4
Wilson MS—*school* IN-6
Wilson MS—*school* PA-2
Wilson Mtn—*summit* (2) AL-4
Wilson Mtn—*summit* AZ-5
Wilson Mtn—*summit* AR-4
Wilson Mtn—*summit* (2) GA-3
Wilson Mtn—*summit* (2) ID-8
Wilson Mtn—*summit* KY-4
Wilson Mtn—*summit* MA-1
Wilson Mtn—*summit* (2) NM-5
Wilson Mtn—*summit* NY-2
Wilson Mtn—*summit* NC-3
Wilson Mtn—*summit* (2) TN-4
Wilson Mtn—*summit* TX-5
Wilson Mtn—*summit* (3) VA-3
Wilson Mtn—*summit* WA-9
Wilson Municipal Airp—*airport* NC-3
Wilson Neck—*cape* VA-3
Wilson Nicholson Ditch—*canal* OH-6
Wilson-Nooe Cem—*cemetery* AL-4
Wilson Number 1 Dam—*dam* (2) SD-7
Wilson Number 1 Mine (underground)—*mine* AL-4
Wilson Number 2 Dam—*dam* SD-7
Wilson Oil Field—*other* NM-5
Wilson Owens Branch—*stream* MD-2
*Wilson Park* CO-8
Wilson Park—*flat* CO-8
Wilson Park—*flat* (3) MT-8
Wilson Park—*park* AL-4
Wilson Park—*park* (3) CA-9
Wilson Park—*park* FL-3
Wilson Park—*park* (2) IL-6
Wilson Park—*park* (3) IN-6
Wilson Park—*park* KS-7
Wilson Park—*park* (2) MI-6
Wilson Park—*park* (4) MN-6
Wilson Park—*park* MS-4
Wilson Park—*park* (2) NJ-2
Wilson Park—*park* NY-2
Wilson Park—*park* OH-6
Wilson Park—*park* (2) PA-2
Wilson Park—*park* (2) TN-4
Wilson Park—*park* VA-3
Wilson Park—*park* (2) WI-6
Wilson Park—*uninc pl* NY-2
Wilson Park Houses—*hist pl* AL-4
Wilson Park Municipal Golf Course—*other* MI-6
Wilson Park Sch—*school* OR-9
Wilson Park Sch—*school* WI-6
Wilson Park Spring—*spring* MT-8
Wilson Pass—*gap* (2) NV-8
Wilson Pasture—*flat* (2) ID-8
Wilson Pasture Windmill—*locale* TX-5
Wilson Patch Ranch—*locale* CA-9
*Wilson Peak* ID-8
Wilson Peak—*summit* CA-9
Wilson Peak—*summit* CO-8
Wilson Peak—*summit* (2) ID-8
Wilson Peak—*summit* MT-8
Wilson Peak—*summit* NV-8
Wilson Peak—*summit* (2) UT-8
Wilson Pen Branch—*stream* TN-4
Wilson Pewee Mine (surface)—*mine* TN-4
Wilson Pigott Bridge—*bridge* FL-3
Wilson-Pittman-Campbell-Gregory House—*hist pl* AR-4
Wilson Place—*locale* CA-9
Wilson Place—*locale* CO-8
Wilson Place—*locale* FL-3
Wilson Place—*locale* TX-5
Wilson Place—*uninc pl* LA-4
Wilson Playground—*park* IL-6
Wilson Playground—*park* MI-6
Wilson Plaza Shop Ctr—*locale* AL-4
Wilson Point—*cape* AL-4
Wilson Point—*cape* (2) CA-9
Wilson Point—*cape* CT-1
Wilson Point—*cape* (2) FL-3
Wilson Point—*cape* LA-4
Wilson Point—*cape* ME-1
Wilson Point—*cape* (4) MD-2
Wilson Point—*cape* MI-6
Wilson Point—*cape* MO-7
Wilson Point—*cape* (2) NY-2
Wilson Point—*cape* OK-5
Wilson Point—*cape* (2) TX-5
Wilson Point—*cape* (2) WA-9
**Wilson Point**—*pop pl* LA-4
**Wilson Point**—*pop pl* MD-2
Wilson Point—*summit* AL-4
Wilson Point—*summit* OR-9
Wilson Point Ch—*church* TX-5
*Wilson Pond* ME-1
Wilson Pond—*lake* AR-4
Wilson Pond—*lake* DE-2
Wilson Pond—*lake* ME-1
Wilson Pond—*lake* MD-2
Wilson Pond—*lake* MA-1
Wilson Pond—*lake* NH-1
Wilson Pond—*lake* (2) NY-2
Wilson Pond—*reservoir* AL-4
Wilson Pond—*reservoir* CT-1
Wilson Pond—*reservoir* FL-3
Wilson Pond—*reservoir* ME-1
Wilson Pond—*reservoir* (2) SC-3
Wilson Pond Dam—*dam* AL-4
Wilson Pond Dam—*dam* MS-4
Wilson Ponds—*lake* GA-3
Wilson Pool, The—*oilfield* TX-5
Wilson Prairie—*flat* (2) OR-9
Wilson Prairie Ch—*church* TX-5
Wilson Primitive Baptist Ch—*church* NC-3
*Wilson Prong* DE-2
Wilson Prospect—*mine* (2) TN-4
Wilson Quarry—*mine* KY-4
Wilson Quarry—*mine* MD-2
**Wilson Quarters**—*pop pl* AL-4
Wilson Ranch—*locale* AZ-5
Wilson Ranch—*locale* (7) CA-9
Wilson Ranch—*locale* (3) CO-8
Wilson Ranch—*locale* (2) MT-8
Wilson Ranch—*locale* (4) NE-7
Wilson Ranch—*locale* (2) NV-8
Wilson Ranch—*locale* (6) NM-5
Wilson Ranch—*locale* SD-7

Wilson Ranch—*locale* (4) TX-5
Wilson Ranch—*locale* UT-8
Wilson Ranch—*locale* WA-9
Wilson Ranch—*locale* (2) WY-8
**Wilson Ranch**—*pop pl* NE-7
Wilson Ranch Dam—*dam* (2) SD-7
Wilson Rapids—*rapids* WI-6
Wilson Reservation—*reserve* (2) AL-4
*Wilson Reservoir* AL-4
*Wilson Reservoir* KS-7
Wilson Reservoir Dam—*dam* RI-1
Wilson Rhodes Ditch—*canal* IN-6
Wilson Ridge—*ridge* (2) AL-4
Wilson Ridge—*ridge* AZ-5
Wilson Ridge—*ridge* ID-8
Wilson Ridge—*ridge* (3) KY-4
Wilson Ridge—*ridge* (2) NY-2
Wilson Ridge—*ridge* (4) NC-3
Wilson Ridge—*ridge* OH-6
Wilson Ridge—*ridge* OR-9
Wilson Ridge—*ridge* (3) TN-4
Wilson Ridge—*ridge* (4) WV-2
Wilson Ridge—*ridge* WY-8
Wilson Ridge Ch—*church* KY-4
Wilson Ridge Well—*well* ID-8
Wilson River—*stream* (2) AK-9
Wilson River—*stream* OR-9
Wilson River Picnic Ground—*park* OR-9
**Wilson Road**—*pop pl* IL-6
Wilson Rock—*island* CA-9
Wilson Rock—*summit* OK-5
Wilson Rozier Park—*park* MO-7
Wilson (RR name for Wilsons)—*other* VA-3
*Wilson Rsvr* OR-9
Wilson Rsvr—*reservoir* (2) CA-9
Wilson Rsvr—*reservoir* (3) CO-8
Wilson Rsvr—*reservoir* (2) MT-8
Wilson Rsvr—*reservoir* NV-8
Wilson Rsvr—*reservoir* NM-5
Wilson Rsvr—*reservoir* (3) OR-9
Wilson Rsvr—*reservoir* RI-1
Wilson Rsvr—*reservoir* WY-8
Wilson Rsvr Number Two—*reservoir* OR-9
*Wilson Rsvr Number 1* OR-9
*Wilson Run* VA-3
Wilson Run—*stream* DE-2
Wilson Run—*stream* IN-6
Wilson Run—*stream* KY-4
Wilson Run—*stream* MD-2
Wilson Run—*stream* MO-7
Wilson Run—*stream* (2) OH-6
Wilson Run—*stream* (11) PA-2
Wilson Run—*stream* VA-3
Wilson Run—*stream* (4) WV-2
*Wilsons* NC-3
*Wilsons* TN-4
*Wilsons* WV-2
Wilsons—*locale* VA-3
**Wilsons**—*pop pl* SC-3
Wilsons Bluff—*cliff* NC-3
Wilson's Bridge—*hist pl* MD-2
Wilsons Camp—*locale* NV-8
Wilsons Cem—*cemetery* AL-4
*Wilson Sch* IN-6
Wilson Sch—*hist pl* OK-5
Wilson Sch—*school* (2) AL-4
Wilson Sch—*school* AZ-5
Wilson Sch—*school* (2) AR-4
Wilson Sch—*school* (21) CA-9
Wilson Sch—*school* (2) DC-2
Wilson Sch—*school* (2) FL-3
Wilson Sch—*school* GA-3
Wilson Sch—*school* HI-9
Wilson Sch—*school* (10) IL-6
Wilson Sch—*school* (2) IN-6
Wilson Sch—*school* (5) IA-7
Wilson Sch—*school* KY-4
Wilson Sch—*school* LA-4
Wilson Sch—*school* ME-1
Wilson Sch—*school* MD-2
Wilson Sch—*school* (2) MA-1
Wilson Sch—*school* (16) MI-6
Wilson Sch—*school* (4) MN-6
Wilson Sch—*school* MS-4
Wilson Sch—*school* (2) MO-7
Wilson Sch—*school* (3) MT-8
Wilson Sch—*school* NE-7
Wilson Sch—*school* NH-1
Wilson Sch—*school* (6) NJ-2
Wilson Sch—*school* (2) NM-5
Wilson Sch—*school* (3) NY-2
Wilson Sch—*school* (3) NC-3
Wilson Sch—*school* ND-7
Wilson Sch—*school* (6) OH-6
Wilson Sch—*school* (10) OK-5
Wilson Sch—*school* OR-9
Wilson Sch—*school* (7) PA-2
Wilson Sch—*school* (4) SD-7
Wilson Sch—*school* TN-4
Wilson Sch—*school* (9) TX-5
Wilson Sch—*school* (2) UT-8
Wilson Sch—*school* VA-3
Wilson Sch—*school* (2) WA-9
Wilson Sch—*school* WV-2
Wilson Sch—*school* (9) WI-6
Wilson Sch—*school* (2) WY-8
Wilson Sch (abandoned)—*school* MO-7
Wilson Sch (abandoned)—*school* PA-2
Wilsons Chapel—*church* SC-3
Wilson Sch (historical)—*school* (3) AL-4
Wilson Sch (historical)—*school* (3) MO-7
Wilson Sch (historical)—*school* PA-2
Wilson Sch (historical)—*school* (2) TN-4
Wilson Sch Number 5—*school* NJ-2
*Wilson School* KS-7
Wilson School (abandoned)—*locale* MO-7
Wilson School (Abandoned)—*locale* WI-6
Wilson Schoolhouse (historical)—*school* PA-2
**Wilsons Church**—*pop pl* GA-3
Wilsons Corner—*locale* PA-2
Wilsons Corner—*locale* VA-3
**Wilsons Corners**—*pop pl* PA-2
Wilson Scout Reservation—*locale* VA-3
*Wilsons Creek* AL-4
*Wilsons Creek* IN-6
*Wilsons Creek* KS-7
*Wilsons Creek* NC-3
Wilsons Creek—*locale* MO-7
Wilsons Creek Ch—*church* MO-7
Wilsons Creek (historical)—*locale* IA-7
*Wilsons Creek - in* NV-8
Wilson's Creek Natl Battlefield—*hist pl* MO-7
Wilson's Creek Natl Battlefield—*park* MO-7
Wilsons Creek (Township of)—*fmr MCD* NC-3
**Wilsons Cross Roads**—*pop pl* SC-3
Wilsons Cut—*channel* TX-5
*Wilson's Depot* VA-3
Wilson Seep—*spring* AZ-5
Wilsons Ferry (historical)—*locale* MS-4
*Wilsons Field* AL-4
Wilsons Field—*flat* CA-9
*Wilsons Fork Creek* IN-6
Wilsons Grove—*locale* IA-7
Wilson Shepard Dam—*dam* NC-3
Wilson Shepard Lake—*reservoir* NC-3
Wilson Shepherd Pond—*lake* FL-3
Wilson-Shields House—*hist pl* UT-8
*Wilsons Hill* AL-4
Wilsons (historical)—*locale* AL-4
Wilson Shoals—*locale* GA-3
Wilson Siding—*locale* WV-2
Wilson's Inheritance—*hist pl* MD-2
*Wilsons Island* MO-7
*Wilsons Lake* MI-6
Wilsons Lake—*lake* MS-4
Wilsons Lake—*reservoir* AL-4
*Wilsons Landing* LA-4
Wilsons Landing—*locale* MS-4
Wilsons Landing—*locale* NJ-2
Wilsons Landing—*locale* SC-3
Wilsons Landing—*locale* TN-4
**Wilsons Landing**—*pop pl* LA-4
Wilson Slough—*gut* AR-4
Wilson Slough—*stream* KS-7
Wilson Slough—*stream* LA-4
*Wilsons Mill* AL-4
*Wilsons Mill* ME-1
Wilson's Mill Covered Bridge—*hist pl* PA-2
*Wilsons Mill Creek* AL-4
Wilsons Mill (historical)—*locale* (5) AL-4
Wilson's Mill (RR name for Wilsons Mill)—*other* NC-3
**Wilsons Mill (RR name Wilson's Mill)**—*pop pl* NC-3
*Wilsons Mills* ME-1
Wilsons Mills—*locale* ME-1
**Wilsons Mills**—*pop pl* NC-3
Wilsons Mills Elem Sch—*school* NC-3
Wilson's Mills Settlement District—*hist pl* OH-6
*Wilson's Point* CT-1
*Wilsons Point* ME-1
*Wilsons Point* MD-2
*Wilsons Pond* DE-2
*Wilsons Pond* RI-1
Wilsons Pond—*lake* GA-3
Wilsons Pond—*reservoir* (2) AL-4
Wilsons Post Office (historical)—*building* TN-4
*Wilson Spring* OK-5
Wilson Spring—*spring* AL-4
Wilson Spring—*spring* AZ-5
Wilson Spring—*spring* AR-4
Wilson Spring—*spring* CA-9
Wilson Spring—*spring* CO-8
Wilson Spring—*spring* ID-8
Wilson Spring—*spring* (2) MO-7
Wilson Spring—*spring* NV-8
Wilson Spring—*spring* (2) NM-5
Wilson Spring—*spring* (4) OR-9
Wilson Spring—*spring* TX-5
Wilson Spring—*spring* (2) UT-8
Wilson Spring—*spring* WA-9
Wilson Spring—*spring* WY-8
Wilson Spring Creek—*stream* SC-3
*Wilson Springs* CA-9
Wilson Springs—*lake* MI-6
Wilson Springs—*locale* VA-3
Wilson Springs—*spring* NV-8
Wilson Square—*locale* MA-1
Wilsons Ranch—*locale* CO-8
Wilsons Ranch—*locale* TX-5
**Wilsons (RR name Wilson)**—*pop pl* VA-3
*Wilsons Run* PA-2
Wilsons Run—*stream* NJ-2
Wilsons Sch (historical)—*school* AL-4
Wilsons Shoals—*bar* TN-4
*Wilsons Spring* IN-6
*Wilson's Spring* MI-6
*Wilson's Springs* MI-6
Wilsons Station—*locale* NJ-2
Wilsons Store—*locale* NC-3
Wilsons Store—*locale* SC-3
Wilsons Store—*locale* VA-3
*Wilson's Stream* ME-1
Wilsons Swamp Pond—*lake* PA-2
*Wilson Stand* AL-4
Wilson State Fishing Lake—*park* KS-7
Wilson State Park—*park* KS-7
Wilson State Park—*park* MI-6
Wilson State Wildlife Area—*park* KS-7
Wilson State Wildlife Mngmt Area—*park* MN-6
Wilson Station—*locale* TN-4
Wilson Station Post Office (historical)—*building* TN-4
Wilson Store—*locale* MS-4
*Wilson Stream* ME-1
Wilson Stream—*stream* (4) ME-1
Wilson Street Cem—*cemetery* MA-1
*Wilson Street Elem Sch* AL-4
Wilson Street Park—*park* AL-4
Wilson Street Sch—*school* AL-4
Wilson Street Sch—*school* CT-1
**Wilson Subdivision**—*pop pl* (3) UT-8
Wilson Substation—*other* CA-9
*Wilsonsville Post Office* TN-4
Wilson Swamp—*swamp* PA-2
Wilsons Wharf—*locale* MD-2
Wilson Tank—*reservoir* (3) AZ-5
Wilson Tank—*reservoir* NV-8
Wilson Tank—*reservoir* (2) NM-5
Wilson Tank—*reservoir* TX-5
Wilson Tanks—*reservoir* NM-5
Wilson Terrace Sch—*school* PA-2
Wilson Theatre—*building* NC-3
Wilson Theatre—*hist pl* MI-6
Wilsonton Cem—*cemetery* KS-7
Wilsonton (historical)—*locale* KS-7
Wilson Top—*summit* AL-4
Wilsontown—*locale* WV-2
Wilsontown Ch—*church* MO-7
Wilson Townhall—*building* IA-7
**Wilson (Town of)**—*pop pl* NY-2
**Wilson (Town of)**—*pop pl* (5) WI-6
Wilson Township—*civil* (4) MO-7
Wilson Township—*fmr MCD* IA-7
**Wilson Township**—*pop pl* (4) KS-7
**Wilson Township**—*pop pl* (3) MO-7
**Wilson Township**—*pop pl* ND-7
**Wilson Township**—*pop pl* (2) SD-7
Wilson Township Cem—*cemetery* IA-7
Wilson (Township of)—*civ div* MI-6
Wilson (Township of)—*fmr MCD* (6) AR-4
Wilson (Township of)—*fmr MCD* NC-3
**Wilson (Township of)**—*pop pl* IL-6
**Wilson (Township of)**—*pop pl* (2) MI-6
**Wilson (Township of)**—*pop pl* (2) MN-6
**Wilson (Township of)**—*pop pl* OH-6
Wilson Tunnel—*tunnel* HI-9
Wilson Upper Elem Sch—*school* KS-7
Wilson Utility Pottery Kilns Archeol District—*hist pl* TX-5
*Wilson Valley* CA-9
Wilson Valley—*basin* NE-7
Wilson Valley—*stream* CA-9
Wilson Valley—*valley* (3) CA-9
Wilsonvile Sch—*school* OR-9
**Wilson Village**—*pop pl* AK-9
*Wilsonville* AL-4
*Wilsonville* KS-7
*Wilsonville* TN-4
Wilsonville—*locale* GA-3
**Wilsonville**—*pop pl* AL-4
**Wilsonville**—*pop pl* CT-1
**Wilsonville**—*pop pl* IL-6
**Wilsonville**—*pop pl* (3) KY-4
**Wilsonville**—*pop pl* NE-7
**Wilsonville**—*pop pl* NC-3
**Wilsonville**—*pop pl* OR-9
**Wilsonville**—*pop pl* PA-2
**Wilsonville**—*pop pl* TN-4
Wilsonville (CCD)—*cens area* AL-4
Wilsonville (CCD)—*cens area* OR-9
Wilsonville Cem—*cemetery* AL-4
Wilsonville Ch—*church* AL-4
Wilsonville Division—*civil* AL-4
Wilsonville Elem Sch—*school* AL-4
**Wilsonville (historical)**—*pop pl* NC-3
*Wilsonville Post Office* TN-4
Wilsonville Post Office (historical)—*building* TN-4
Wilsonville Rec Areaand Boat Launch—*locale* PA-2
Wilsonville Sch (historical)—*school* TN-4
Wilson Warehouse—*hist pl* VA-3
Wilson Wash—*stream* AZ-5
Wilson Well—*well* (3) NM-5
Wilson-Wentworth Sch—*school* IL-6
Wilson White HS—*school* TX-5
Wilson Wildlife Area—*park* KS-7
Wilson-Willie Cem—*cemetery* LA-4
**Wilson (Wilson Corner)**—*pop pl* IN-6
**Wilson (Wilson Station)**—*pop pl* KY-4
Wilson Windmill—*locale* AZ-5
Wilson Windmill—*locale* CO-8
Wilson Windmill—*locale* NM-5
Wilson Windmill—*locale* (3) TX-5
Wilson Wiseley Ditch—*canal* IN-6
Wilson-Wodrow-Mytinger House—*hist pl* WV-2
Wilson Woods—*woods* IL-6
**Wilson Wood (subdivision)**—*pop pl* NC-3
Wilson-Young House—*hist pl* TN-4
Wilsor Cem—*cemetery* AL-4
*Wilsor Point* MD-2
Wilstacy—*locale* KY-4
Wiltbank Landing—*locale* DE-2
Wiltbank Spring—*spring* AZ-5
Wilt Brook—*stream* NY-2
Wilt Cem—*cemetery* OH-6
*Wilton* NJ-2
Wilton—*hist pl* MD-2
Wilton—*hist pl* (2) VA-3
Wilton—*locale* IL-6
Wilton—*locale* KY-4
Wilton—*locale* MN-6
Wilton—*locale* NC-3
Wilton—*locale* VA-3
**Wilton**—*pop pl* AL-4
**Wilton**—*pop pl* AR-4
**Wilton**—*pop pl* CA-9
**Wilton**—*pop pl* CT-1
**Wilton**—*pop pl* IA-7
**Wilton**—*pop pl* ME-1
**Wilton**—*pop pl* MN-6
**Wilton**—*pop pl* MO-7
**Wilton**—*pop pl* NH-1
**Wilton**—*pop pl* NY-2
**Wilton**—*pop pl* ND-7
**Wilton**—*pop pl* WI-6
Wilton, Joshua, House—*hist pl* VA-3
Wilton Airp—*airport* PA-2
Wilton Bayou—*swamp* MS-4
Wilton Brook—*stream* MA-1
Wilton Cem—*cemetery* IL-6
Wilton Cem—*cemetery* MN-6
Wilton Cem—*cemetery* NC-3
**Wilton Center**—*pop pl* IL-6
**Wilton Center**—*pop pl* NH-1
Wilton Center (census name Wilton)—*other* ME-1
**Wilton Compact (census name Wilton)**—*pop pl* NH-1
*Wilton Creek* VA-3
Wilton Creek—*stream* MT-8
Wilton Creek—*stream* VA-3
**Wiltondale**—*pop pl* MD-2
**Wiltondale**—*pop pl* OH-6
Wilton Elem Sch—*school* NC-3
**Wilton Farm Acres**—*pop pl* MD-2
Wilton Hist Dist—*hist pl* CA-9
**Wilton Intervale**—*pop pl* ME-1
Wilton JHS—*school* CT-1
*Wilton Junction* (2) IA-7
Wilton Lake—*reservoir* KY-4
*Wilton Manor* FL-3
*Wilton Manor (corporate name Wilton Manors)* FL-3
**Wilton Manors**—*pop pl* FL-3
**Wilton Manors (corporate name for Wilton Manor)**—*pop pl* FL-3
Wilton Manors Elem Sch—*school* FL-3
Wilton Mine State Game Mngmt Area—*park* ND-7
Wilton Mtn—*summit* OK-5
Wilton Oil Field—*oilfield* TX-5
Wilton Place Sch—*school* CA-9
Wilton Plaza (Shop Ctr)—*locale* FL-3
Wilton Point—*cape* VA-3
Wilton Pond—*reservoir* CT-1
Wilton Public and Gregg Free Library—*hist pl* NH-1
Wilton Sch—*school* IA-7
Wilton Sch—*school* MO-7
Wilton Sch—*school* OH-6
Wilton Sch—*school* VA-3
Wiltons Landing—*locale* MS-4
Wilton Springs—*locale* MO-7
Wilton Springs—*locale* TN-4
Wilton Springs—*spring* TN-4
Wilton Springs Post Office (historical)—*building* TN-4
*Wiltons Springs Post Office* TN-4
Wilton (sta.) (RR name for Dryden)—*other* ME-1
Wilton State School—*other* NY-2
**Wilton Subdivision**—*pop pl* LA-4
**Wilton (Town of)**—*pop pl* CT-1
**Wilton (Town of)**—*pop pl* ME-1
**Wilton (Town of)**—*pop pl* NH-1
**Wilton (Town of)**—*pop pl* NY-2
**Wilton (Town of)**—*pop pl* WI-6
Wilton Township—*fmr MCD* IA-7
**Wilton (Township of)**—*pop pl* IL-6
**Wilton (Township of)**—*pop pl* MN-6
**Wilton Woods**—*pop pl* VA-3
Wilton Woods Sch—*school* VA-3
*Wiltor Creek* VA-3
Wilt Sch—*school* KY-4
Wilt Sch (abandoned)—*school* PA-2
Wilts Creek—*stream* OR-9
**Wiltshire**—*pop pl* MS-4
**Wiltshire**—*pop pl* TN-4
Wiltshire and Versailles Historic Buildings—*hist pl* MO-7
Wiltshire Hollow—*valley* TN-4
Wiltshire-king Cem—*cemetery* MS-4
Wiltsie Cem—*cemetery* OH-6
Wiltsie Corners—*locale* PA-2
Wiltsie Run—*stream* NY-2
Wiltsie Run—*stream* PA-2
Wiltsie Sch (abandoned)—*school* PA-2
Wilts Sch (abandoned)—*school* PA-2
Wilts State Wildlife Mngmt Area—*park* MN-6
Wiltwyck Cem—*cemetery* NY-2
Wiltwyck Sch—*school* (2) NY-2
*Wiltzin Ditch* IN-6
Wiltz Lake—*lake* MI-6
Wiltz Pass—*gut* LA-4
Wily Wake (reduced usage)—*lake* IL-6
Wilzetta—*locale* OK-5
**Wilzone**—*pop pl* MS-4
Wimar Lake—*lake* MN-6
**Wimauma**—*pop pl* FL-3
Wimauma, Lake—*lake* FL-3
Wimauma Elem Sch—*school* FL-3
Wimauma-Lithia (CCD)—*cens area* FL-3
Wimbee Creek—*stream* SC-3
Wimbeldon Municipal Airp—*airport* ND-7
**Wimberley**—*pop pl* TX-5
Wimberley Cem—*cemetery* AL-4
Wimberley Cem—*cemetery* LA-4
*Wimberley Creek* AL-4
Wimberley Well—*well* TX-5
*Wimberly* AL-4
**Wimberly**—*pop pl* AL-4
Wimberly Branch—*stream* AL-4
Wimberly Branch—*stream* KY-4
Wimberly Branch—*stream* LA-4
Wimberly Cem—*cemetery* (2) GA-3
Wimberly Cem—*cemetery* LA-4
Wimberly Cem—*cemetery* TX-5
**Wimberly Estates**—*pop pl* FL-3
Wimberly Hill Ch—*church* GA-3
Wimberly House—*hist pl* TX-5
Wimberly Methodist Protestant Ch—*church* AL-4
Wimberly Mill Branch—*stream* GA-3
Wimberly Oil Field—*oilfield* TX 5
Wimberly Place—*locale* TX-5
Wimberly Plantation—*hist pl* GA-3
Wimberly Preschool and Kindergarden—*school* FL-3
Wimberly Ranch—*locale* NM-5
Wimberly-Thomas Warehouse—*hist pl* AL-4
Wimberry Lake—*lake* TX-5
*Wimbesocom Branch* DE-2
Wimbish, Lewis, Plantation—*hist pl* NC-3
Wimbish Hollow—*valley* MS-4
Wimbish Lake—*reservoir* NC-3
Wimbish Lake Dam—*dam* NC-3
Wimbish Wood—*uninc pl* GA-3
**Wimbledon**—*pop pl* MA-1
**Wimbledon**—*pop pl* ND-7
**Wimbledon (subdivision)**—*pop pl* NC-3
**Wimbledon (subdivision)**—*pop pl* TN-4
Wimble Shoals—*bar* NC-3
Wimbley Cem—*cemetery* AL-4
Wimbly—*locale* AL-4
**Wimer**—*pop pl* OK-5
**Wimer**—*pop pl* OR-9
Wimer, James, Octagonal Barn—*hist pl* OR-9
Wimer Bridge—*hist pl* OR-9
Wimer Community Ch—*church* OK-5
Wimer Creek—*stream* (2) OR-9
Wimer Place—*locale* NV-8
*Wimer Ridge* UT-8
Wimico, Lake—*lake* FL-3
*Wiminain Brook* CT-1
*Wiminam Brook* CT-1
Wimisink Brook—*stream* CT-1
Wimmer—*locale* MO-7
Wimmer Cem—*cemetery* IL-6
Wimmer Cem—*cemetery* VA-3
Wimmer Cem—*cemetery* (2) WV-2
Wimmer Ditch—*canal* IN-6
Wimmer Flat—*flat* UT-8
Wimmer Gap—*gap* VA-3
Wimmer Gap—*gap* WV-2
Wimmer Knoll—*summit* UT-8
*Wimmer Lake* WI-6
Wimmer Ranch Creek—*stream* UT-8
Wimmers—*locale* PA-2
Wimmers Cem—*cemetery* VA-3
Wimmer Spring—*spring* UT-8
Wimmers Spur—*ridge* VA-3
Wimp—*locale* CA-9
Wimpey Creek—*stream* ID-8
Wimpy Branch—*stream* (2) GA-3
WIMS-AM (Michigan City)—*tower* IN-6
**Wimsatt**—*pop pl* NM-5
Wimsatt Sch—*school* KY-4
**Wimsattville**—*pop pl* NM-5
Wims Cem—*cemetery* TX-5
Wimsett Cem—*cemetery* IN-6
Wimsett Point—*cape* MT-8
Wim Wigor Spring—*spring* OK-5
WIMZ-AM (Knoxville)—*tower* TN-4
WIMZ-FM (Knoxville)—*tower* TN-4
*Win* FM-9
**Win**—*pop pl* KY-4
Win—*spring* FM-9
*Winakapi* FM-9
Winaker Cem—*cemetery* CT-1
Winall Creek—*stream* VA-3
Winall Point—*cape* VA-3
**Winamac**—*pop pl* IN-6
Winamac Community HS—*school* IN-6
Winamac Community JHS—*school* IN-6
*Winamac State Fish and Game Area* IN-6
Winamac State Fish and Wildlife Area—*park* IN-6
**Winameg**—*pop pl* OH-6
Winameg Mounds—*hist pl* OH-6
Winam Spring—*spring* OR-9
Winan—*island* FM-9
Winans—*locale* SD-7
Winans, Dr. J. C., House—*hist pl* OH-6
Winans Cem—*cemetery* MS-4
Winans Cove—*bay* MD-2
Winans Creek—*stream* IA-7
Winans Creek—*stream* TX-5
Winans Elem Sch—*school* KS-7
Winans Lake—*lake* MI-6
Winans Park—*park* OK-5
Winans Sch—*school* IL-6
Winans Sch—*school* MI-6
Winans Sch—*school* MT-8
Winans Sch—*school* SD-7
Winans Spring—*spring* TX-5
Winant—*locale* OR-9
Winape, Lake—*lake* NY-2
Winapi Wash—*arroyo* NV-8
*Winatuxet River* MA-1
Winawan—*bar* FM-9
**Winberry**—*pop pl* LA-4
**Winberry**—*pop pl* OR-9
Winberry Creek—*stream* OR-9
Winberry Mtn—*summit* OR-9
**Winbon Acres (subdivision)**—*pop pl* NC-3
**Winborn**—*pop pl* MS-4
Winborne, W. H., House—*hist pl* SC-3
*Winborn Lookout Fire Tower* MS-4
Winborn Lookout Tower—*locale* MS-4
Winborn Spring—*spring* OK-5
Winbourn Cem—*cemetery* AL-4
Winbourn Cem—*cemetery* MS-4
Winbourne Sch—*school* LA-4
Win Branch—*stream* KY-4
Winburn—*locale* AL-4
Winburn Camp—*locale* OR-9
Winburn Cem—*cemetery* FL-3
**Winburn (Dunavant)**—*pop pl* AL-4
**Winburne**—*pop pl* PA-2
Winburn JHS—*school* KY-4
Winburn Lake—*lake* FL-3
Winburn Pond—*lake* FL-3
Winbush Ridge—*ridge* MS-4
Wince Lake—*lake* MN-6
*Wincel Valley* WI-6
Winch—*locale* OR-9
Winch Creek—*stream* MO-7
*Wincheck Pond* RI-1
Wincheck Pond—*lake* RI-1
Wincheck Pond—*reservoir* RI-1
Wincheck Pond Dam—*dam* RI-1
Winchell—*locale* NY-2
Winchell—*locale* TX-5
Winchell, Mount summit CA 9
*Winchel Lake* MA-1
Winchell Arm—*canal* IN-6
Winchell Bay—*bay* CA-9
Winchell Brook—*stream* MA-1
Winchell Brothers Number 1 Dam—*dam* SD-7
Winchell Cem—*cemetery* TX-5
Winchell Cove Campground—*locale* CA-9
Winchell Creek—*stream* CA-9
Winchell Creek—*stream* NV-8
Winchell Creek—*stream* NY-2
Winchell Hill—*summit* NY-2
*Winchell Lake* MA-1
Winchell Lake—*lake* MN-6
Winchell Lake—*lake* NV-8
Winchell Lakes—*lake* CO-8
Winchell Mtn—*summit* MA-1
Winchell Mtn—*summit* NY-2
Winchell Rsvr—*reservoir* MA-1
Winchell Sch—*school* CA-9
Winchell Sch—*school* MI-6
Winchell Valley—*valley* WI-6
Winchelsea—*airport* NJ-2
*Winchels Mountain* MA-1
*Winchel Valley* WI-6
Winche Mtn—*summit* ME-1
**Winchendon**—*pop pl* MA-1
Winchendon (census name for Winchendon Center)—*CDP* MA-1
**Winchendon Center**—*pop pl* MA-1
Winchendon Center (census name Winchendon)—*other* MA-1
*Winchendon Centre* MA-1
Winchendon Sch—*school* MA-1
**Winchendon Springs**—*pop pl* MA-1
Winchendon State For—*forest* MA-1
Winchendon Town Hall—*building* MA-1
**Winchendon (Town of)**—*pop pl* MA-1
*Winchester* MD-2
*Winchester* OH-6
*Winchester* TN-4
Winchester—*locale* GA-3
Winchester—*locale* MD-2
Winchester—*locale* OK-5
Winchester—*locale* WA-9
**Winchester**—*pop pl* AR-4
**Winchester**—*pop pl* CA-9
**Winchester**—*pop pl* ID-8
**Winchester**—*pop pl* IL-6
**Winchester**—*pop pl* IN-6
**Winchester**—*pop pl* IA-7
**Winchester**—*pop pl* KS-7
**Winchester**—*pop pl* KY-4
**Winchester**—*pop pl* MD-2
**Winchester**—*pop pl* MA-1
**Winchester**—*pop pl* MS-4
**Winchester**—*pop pl* (2) MO-7
**Winchester**—*pop pl* NV-8
**Winchester**—*pop pl* NH-1
**Winchester**—*pop pl* NY-2
**Winchester**—*pop pl* (2) OH-6
**Winchester**—*pop pl* OK-5
**Winchester**—*pop pl* OR-9
**Winchester**—*pop pl* (2) TN-4
**Winchester**—*pop pl* (2) TX-5
**Winchester**—*pop pl* (2) WI-6
**Winchester**—*pop pl* WY-8
Winchester, Lake—*reservoir* CT-1
**Winchester And Western Junction**—*pop pl* VA-3
Winchester Ave Community Facility Center—*park* NC-3
Winchester Baldy—*summit* OR-9
*Winchester Bay* OR-9
Winchester Bay—*bay* OR-9
**Winchester Bay**—*pop pl* OR-9
Winchester Branch—*stream* TN-4
Winchester Butte—*summit* ND-7
Winchester Butte—*summit* WY-8
Winchester Camp—*locale* VA-3
Winchester Canyon—*valley* AZ-5
Winchester Canyon—*valley* CA-9
Winchester Canyon—*valley* NM-5
Winchester Cave—*cave* AL-4
Winchester (CCD)—*cens area* KY-4
Winchester (CCD)—*cens area* TN-4
Winchester Cem—*cemetery* CT-1
Winchester Cem—*cemetery* (2) KY-4
Winchester Cem—*cemetery* MI-6
Winchester Cem—*cemetery* MN-6
Winchester Cem—*cemetery* MS-4
Winchester Cem—*cemetery* ND-7
Winchester Cem—*cemetery* SC-3
Winchester Cem—*cemetery* VT-1
Winchester Cem—*cemetery* WI-6
*Winchester Cemetery* AL-4
**Winchester Center**—*pop pl* CT-1
Winchester Center Hist Dist—*hist pl* MA-1
Winchester Ch—*church* (2) IN-6
Winchester Chatham Station—*locale* WY-8
Winchester Ch of Christ—*church* TN-4
Winchester Chute—*stream* MO-7
Winchester City Cem—*cemetery* TN-4
Winchester City Hall—*building* TN-4
Winchester City Park—*park* TN-4
Winchester Club Pond—*reservoir* CT-1
Winchester Community HS—*school* IN-6
Winchester Country Club—*locale* MA-1
Winchester Country Club—*other* VA-3
Winchester Cove—*valley* NC-3
*Winchester Creek* WA-9
Winchester Creek—*bay* MD-2
Winchester Creek—*stream* GA-3
Winchester Creek—*stream* ID-8
Winchester Creek—*stream* (2) NC-3
Winchester Creek—*stream* (2) OR-9
Winchester Creek—*stream* (2) WA-9
Winchester Creek—*stream* WY-8
Winchester Dam—*dam* MI-6
Winchester Dam—*dam* (2) OR-9
Winchester Ditch—*canal* WY-8
Winchester Division—*civil* TN-4
Winchester Downtown Commercial District—*hist pl* KY-4
Winchester Draw—*valley* WY-8
Winchester Flat—*flat* UT-8
Winchester Forest Camp—*locale* OR-9
**Winchester Gap**—*pop pl* MO-7
Winchester Gulch—*valley* ID-8
Winchester Gun Club—*other* CA-9
Winchoster Hoad swamp FL 3
**Winchester Highlands (subdivision)**—*pop pl* MA-1
Winchester Hill—*summit* MA-1
Winchester Hist Dist—*hist pl* IL-6
Winchester Hist Dist—*hist pl* VA-3
Winchester Hollow—*valley* TN-4
Winchester Hosp—*hospital* MA-1
Winchester Hosp—*hospital* MI-6
Winchester House—*hist pl* CA-9
Winchester House—*hist pl* KY-4
Winchester House—*hist pl* MS-4
Winchester HS—*school* MA-1
**Winchester (ind. city)**—*pop pl* VA-3
Winchester Lake—*lake* CA-9
Winchester Lake—*lake* MN-6
Winchester Lake—*lake* OR-9
Winchester Lake—*lake* TX-5
Winchester Lake—*reservoir* OH-6
Winchester Memorial Cem—*cemetery* VA-3
Winchester Mesa—*summit* OK-5
Winchester Mine—*mine* CA-9
Winchester Mountain Lookout—*hist pl* WA-9
Winchester Mountains—*ridge* AZ-5
Winchester Mtn—*summit* WA-9
Winchester Municipal Airp—*airport* TN-4
Winchester No. 1 (Election Precinct)—*fmr MCD* IL-6
Winchester No. 2 (Election Precinct)—*fmr MCD* IL-6
Winchester No. 3 (Election Precinct)—*fmr MCD* IL-6
Winchester Oil Field—*oilfield* MS-4
**Winchester on the Severn**—*pop pl* MD-2
**Winchester-on-the-Severn**—*pop pl* MD-2
Winchester Park—*park* TN-4
**Winchester Park**—*pop pl* MD-2
Winchester Peak—*summit* (2) AZ-5
Winchester Peak—*summit* NM-5
Winchester Peak—*summit* WA-9
Winchester Pit Number One—*cave* AL-4
Winchester Pit Number Two—*cave* AL-4
Winchester Plaza—*locale* MA-1
Winchester Point—*cape* OR-9

Winchester Pond—*lake* ... MD-2
Winchester Post Office—*building* ... MA-1
Winchester Post Office—*building* ... TN-4
Winchester Recreation Park—*park* ... VA-3
Winchester Repeating Arms Company Hist Dist—*hist pl* ... CT-1
*Winchester Reservoir* ... MA-1
Winchester Ridge—*ridge* ... CA-9
Winchester Rsvr—*reservoir* ... AZ-5
Winchester Rsvr—*reservoir* ... KY-4
Winchester Rsvr—*reservoir* ... OR-9
Winchester Savings Bank—*hist pl* ... MA-1
Winchester Sch—*school* ... CT-1
Winchester Sch—*school* ... NY-2
Winchester Sch—*school* ... TN-4
Winchester Sch (historical)—*school* ... TN-4
Winchester Shop Ctr—*locale* ... MA-1
Winchester Soldiers' Monmt—*hist pl* ... CT-1
Winchester Speedway—*other* ... IN-6
**Winchester Springs**—*pop pl* ... TN-4
Winchester Springs—*spring* ... TN-4
Winchester Springs Branch—*stream* ... TN-4
Winchester Springs Cem—*cemetery* ... TN-4
Winchester Springs Sch—*school* ... TN-4
Winchester Square—*park* ... MA-1
Winchester Square Hist Dist—*hist pl* ... MA-1
Winchester (sta.)—*uninc pl* ... NY-2
Winchester State Park—*park* ... ID-8
Winchester Strand—*swamp* ... FL-3
Winchester Swamp—*swamp* ... WA-9
Winchester Towhead—*area* ... MO-7
Winchester Town Hall—*hist pl* ... MA-1
Winchester Town Hall—*hist pl* ... NH-1
*Winchester (Town name for Winchester Center)* ... CT-1
**Winchester (Town of)**—*pop pl* ... CT-1
**Winchester (Town of)**—*pop pl* ... MA-1
**Winchester (Town of)**—*pop pl* ... NH-1
**Winchester (Town of)**—*pop pl* (2) ... WI-6
**Winchester (Township of)**—*pop pl* ... MN-6
**Winchester (Township of)**—*pop pl* ... OH-6
Winchester Trail—*trail* ... OR-9
Winchester United Methodist Ch—*church* ... MS-4
*Winchester United Methodist Church* ... TN-4
*Winchester Village* ... MI-6
Winchester Wasteway—*canal* ... WA-9
Winchester Waterworks—*locale* ... MA-1
*Winchey Branch* ... MO-7
Winch Hill—*summit* ... NH-1
Winch Mtn—*summit* (2) ... NY-2
Winch Park JHS—*school* ... MA-1
Winch Pond—*lake* ... NY-2
Winchuck Forest Camp—*locale* ... OR-9
Winchuck River—*stream* ... CA-9
Winchuck River—*stream* ... OR-9
Winchuck Wayside—*park* ... OR-9
**Winco**—*pop pl* ... CA-9
Winco Block Sch—*school* ... KY-4
**Wincoma**—*pop pl* ... NY-2
Wincoma Point—*cape* ... NY-2
Win Creek—*bay* ... NC-3
Windaga, Lake—*reservoir* ... MI-6
Windall Ditch—*canal* ... WY-8
Windam Coll—*school* ... VT-1
Windamere—*uninc pl* ... AR-4
Wind around the Rock Well—*well* ... AZ-5
Wind Bay—*bay* ... MN-6
Wind Bayou—*stream* ... LA-4
*Wind Beach* ... MH-9
**Windber**—*pop pl* ... PA-2
Windber Borough—*civil* ... PA-2
Windber Country Club—*other* ... PA-2
Windberg—*locale* ... VI-3
Windber Rsvr—*reservoir* ... PA-2
**Wind Blow**—*pop pl* ... NC-3
Windbound Bay—*bay* ... AK-9
Windbourne Millpond—*reservoir* ... VA-3
Windbreak Windmill—*locale* ... CO-8
**Windbrook**—*pop pl* ... MD-2
Windbrook Recreation Center—*locale* ... MD-2
Windburn Ch—*church* ... MS-4
Windburn Chapel Cem—*cemetery* ... MS-4
Windbush Branch—*stream* ... TX-5
*Windbush Hollow* ... MS-4
Wind Butte—*summit* ... ID-8
Wind Butte Lakes—*lake* ... ID-8
Wind Canyon—*valley* (2) ... NM-5
Wind Cave—*cave* ... KY-4
Wind Cave—*cave* ... PA-2
Wind Cave—*cave* ... SD-7
Wind Cave—*cave* ... UT-8
Wind Cave—*locale* ... KY-4
Wind Cave Branch—*stream* ... KY-4
Wind Cave Canyon—*valley* ... SD-7
Wind Cave Hollow—*valley* ... KY-4
Wind Cave Natl Park—*park* ... SD-7
Wind Cave Natl Park Hist Dist—*hist pl* ... SD-7
**Windchester Hills**—*pop pl* ... OH-6
**Windcliff**—*pop pl* ... VA-3
Wind Cow Draw—*valley* ... CO-8
*Wind Creek* ... OR-9
Wind Creek—*stream* (2) ... AL-4
Wind Creek—*stream* (2) ... AK-9
Wind Creek—*stream* ... KS-7
Wind Creek—*stream* ... MT-8
Wind Creek—*stream* (6) ... OR-9
Wind Creek—*stream* ... SD-7
Wind Creek—*stream* ... WV-2
Wind Creek—*stream* (2) ... WY-8
Wind Creek Basin—*basin* ... OR-9
**Wind Creek Farms**—*pop pl* ... AL-4
Wind Creek Mtn—*summit* ... WV-2
Wind Creek Peak—*summit* ... OR-9
Wind Creek State Park—*park* ... AL-4
Wind Creek Trail—*trail* ... OR-9
**Windcrest**—*pop pl* ... TX-5
Windcrest Golf Club—*other* ... MN-6
**Windcrest Park**—*pop pl* ... NY-2
**Windcrest (subdivision)**—*pop pl* (2) ... AL-4
Winde—*locale* ... MI-6
Windealt Sch—*school* ... MI-6
Windecker—*locale* ... NY-2
Windego Park Auditorium/Open Air Theater—*hist pl* ... MN-6
Windell Hill—*summit* ... IN-6
**Win Del Subdivision**—*pop pl* ... UT-8
Windem Creek—*stream* ... CA-9
*Windemere* ... CT-1
**Windemere**—*pop pl* ... ME-1
**Windemere**—*pop pl* ... MI-6
Windemere, Lake—*reservoir* ... CO-8
Windemere Ch—*church* ... MN-6
**Windemere Lake**—*pop pl* ... IN-6
Windemere Lake—*reservoir* ... IN-6
Windemere Lake Dam—*dam* ... MA-1
Windemere Lake Rsvr—*reservoir* ... MA-1
**Windemere Mobile Homes (subdivision)**—*pop pl* ... NC-3
Windemere Park Sch—*school* ... MI-6
Windemere Sch—*school* ... OH-6
**Windemere (subdivision)**—*pop pl* (2) ... AZ-5
**Windemere (subdivision)**—*pop pl* ... MA-1
**Windemere (subdivision)**—*pop pl* ... NC-3
**Windemere (Township of)**—*pop pl* ... MN-6
Windemere View Sch—*school* ... MI-6
**Winden Oak**—*pop pl* ... IL-6
Winden Ranch—*locale* ... NM-5
Winden Tank—*reservoir* ... AZ-5
**Winder**—*pop pl* ... GA-3
**Winder**—*pop pl* ... ID-8
Winder, Lake—*lake* ... FL-3
Winder Bldg—*hist pl* ... DC-2
Winder (CCD)—*cens area* ... GA-3
Winder Creek—*stream* ... VA-3
Winder Depot—*hist pl* ... GA-3
**Winderest Park**—*pop pl* ... NY-2
Winder Hollow—*valley* ... TN-4
**Winder Meadows Subdivision**—*pop pl* ... UT-8
**Windermer**—*pop pl* ... DE-2
*Windermere* ... ME-1
Windermere—*hist pl* ... NH-1
Windermere—*locale* ... CT-1
**Windermere**—*pop pl* ... FL-3
**Windermere**—*pop pl* ... MD-2
**Windermere**—*pop pl* ... TN-4
Windermere, Lake—*reservoir* ... NC-3
Windermere, Lake—*reservoir* ... TN-4
Windermere Blvd Sch—*school* ... NY-2
Windermere Church Camp—*locale* ... MO-7
Windermere Elem Sch—*school* ... FL-3
Windermere Hills—*summit* ... NV-8
Windermere Lake Dam—*dam* ... NC-3
Windermere Park—*park* ... CA-9
Windermere Park—*park* ... WA-9
Windermere Point—*cape* ... CA-9
Windermere Sch—*school* ... OH-6
*Windermere Village* ... CT-1
Winder Rsvr—*reservoir* ... GA-3
Winder Rsvr—*reservoir* ... ID-8
**Winders Cross Roads**—*pop pl* ... NC-3
Winders Neck—*cape* ... VA-3
Winders Ranch—*locale* ... UT-8
**Winder Village**—*pop pl* ... PA-2
Windes Creek—*stream* ... MO-7
Windes Hill—*summit* ... MO-7
Windes Sch (historical)—*school* ... AL-4
Windey Pitch—*cliff* ... ME-1
Windfall—*locale* (2) ... NY-2
Windfall—*locale* ... PA-2
**Windfall**—*pop pl* ... IN-6
**Windfall**—*pop pl* ... OH-6
Windfall Adverse—*trail* ... OR-9
Windfall Branch—*stream* ... NC-3
Windfall Brook—*stream* (4) ... NY-2
Windfall Brook—*stream* ... PA-2
Windfall Brook—*stream* ... VT-1
Windfall Canyon—*valley* ... ID-8
Windfall Canyon—*valley* ... NV-8
Windfall Canyon—*valley* ... NM-5
Windfall Cem—*cemetery* (3) ... OH-6
Windfall Cem—*cemetery* ... WI-6
Windfall Ch—*church* ... IN-6
*Windfall City* ... IN-6
**Windfall City (corporate name for Windfall)**—*pop pl* ... IN-6
*Windfall (corporate name Windfall City)* ... IN-6
*Windfall Creek* ... NY-2
*Windfall Creek* ... OR-9
Windfall Creek—*stream* ... AK-9
Windfall Creek—*stream* (2) ... ID-8
Windfall Creek—*stream* ... IL-6
Windfall Creek—*stream* (3) ... MT-8
Windfall Creek—*stream* (3) ... NY-2
Windfall Creek—*stream* (3) ... OR-9
Windfall Creek—*stream* (2) ... WA-9
Windfall Elem Sch—*school* ... IN-6
Windfall Harbor—*bay* (2) ... AK-9
Windfall Hill—*summit* ... NY-2
Windfall Hill—*summit* ... PA-2
Windfall Hollow—*valley* ... NY-2
Windfall Hollow—*valley* (3) ... PA-2
Windfall Island—*island* ... AK-9
Windfall Islands—*area* ... AK-9
Windfall Lake—*lake* ... AK-9
Windfall Lake—*lake* ... MT-8
Windfall Lake—*lake* (2) ... WI-6
Windfall Lake—*reservoir* ... IL-6
Windfall Mesa Well—*well* ... NM-5
Windfall Mine—*mine* ... NV-8
Windfall Mine—*mine* ... WA-9
Windfall Mtn—*summit* ... AK-9
Windfall Mtn—*summit* (2) ... NY-2
Windfall Pass—*gap* ... ID-8
Windfall Peak—*summit* ... ID-8
Windfall Peak—*summit* ... MT-8
Windfall Peak—*summit* ... WA-9
Windfall Peak Trail—*trail* ... MT-8
*Windfall Pond* ... PA-2
Windfall Pond—*lake* (3) ... NY-2
*Windfall Run* ... PA-2
Windfall Run—*stream* (10) ... PA-2
Windfall Sch—*school* ... MI-6
Windfall Sch (historical)—*school* ... PA-2
Windfall Spring—*spring* ... AZ-5
Windfall Spring—*spring* ... OR-9
Windfall Tank—*reservoir* ... NM-5
Windfall Tanks—*reservoir* ... NM-5
Wind Flat—*flat* ... CA-9
*Windford* ... KY-4
Wind Gap—*gap* ... PA-2
Wind Gap—*gap* ... VT-1
**Wind Gap**—*pop pl* ... PA-2
Wind Gap Borough—*civil* ... PA-2
**Wind Gap (corporate name for Windgap)**—*pop pl* ... PA-2
*Windgap (corporate name Wind Gap)* ... PA-2
Windgap Post Office (historical)—*building* ... PA-2
*Wind Gap Pumping Plant* ... CA-9
*Wind Gap Quarries* ... PA-2
Windgate, The—*summit* ... UT-8
Windgate Oaks Center—*school* ... FL-3
Windgate Ridge—*ridge* ... AR-4
Windger Flats—*flat* ... CO-8
*Windham* ... ME-1
Windham—*locale* ... PA-2
**Windham**—*pop pl* ... CT-1
**Windham**—*pop pl* ... IA-7
**Windham**—*pop pl* ... MT-8
**Windham**—*pop pl* ... NH-1
**Windham**—*pop pl* ... NY-2
**Windham**—*pop pl* ... OH-6
**Windham**—*pop pl* ... VT-1
Windham, Point—*cape* ... AK-9
Windham Bay—*bay* ... AK-9
Windham Bay Trail—*trail* ... AK-9
Windham Canyon—*valley* ... NM-5
Windham Cem—*cemetery* ... CT-1
Windham Cem—*cemetery* ... IA-7
Windham Cem—*cemetery* (2) ... MS-4
Windham Cem—*cemetery* ... OH-6
Windham Cem—*cemetery* ... PA-2
Windham Cem—*cemetery* ... TX-5
*Windham Center* ... VT-1
Windham Center—*locale* ... PA-2
**Windham Center**—*pop pl* ... ME-1
Windham Center Hist Dist—*hist pl* ... CT-1
*Windham Centre* ... PA-2
Windham Ch—*church* ... IA-7
Windham Construction Office Bldg—*hist pl* ... AL-4
**Windham County**—*pop pl* ... CT-1
**Windham County**—*pop pl* ... VT-1
Windham Creek—*stream* ... LA-4
Windham Dam—*dam* ... MS-4
**Windham Depot**—*pop pl* ... NH-1
Windham Ferry (historical)—*locale* ... MS-4
Windham High Peak—*summit* ... NY-2
**Windham Hill**—*pop pl* ... ME-1
Windham Hill—*summit* ... ME-1
*Windham Manor* ... IL-6
**Windham Manor**—*pop pl* ... MD-2
Windham Plains Chapel—*church* ... ME-1
**Windham Post Office**—*pop pl* ... AK-9
**Windham (P.O.) (Windham Depot)**—*pop pl* ... NH-1
Windham Ranch—*locale* ... NM-5
Windham Ranch—*locale* (2) ... TX-5
Windhams Bar—*bar* ... AL-4
Windham Sch—*school* ... MS-4
Windham Sch—*school* ... NY-2
Windham Sch—*school* ... PA-2
Windham Sch (historical)—*school* ... AL-4
Windhams Creek—*stream* ... MS-4
Windhams Crossroads—*locale* ... SC-3
Windhams Landing—*locale* ... AL-4
**Windham Springs**—*pop pl* ... AL-4
Windham Springs Baptist Ch—*church* ... AL-4
Windham Springs (CCD)—*cens area* ... AL-4
Windham Springs Division—*civil* ... AL-4
*Windhams Springs* ... AL-4
Windhams Store (historical)—*locale* ... AL-4
Windham Summit—*locale* ... PA-2
**Windham (Town of)**—*pop pl* ... CT-1
**Windham (Town of)**—*pop pl* ... ME-1
**Windham (Town of)**—*pop pl* ... NH-1
**Windham (Town of)**—*pop pl* ... NY-2
**Windham (Town of)**—*pop pl* ... VT-1
**Windham (Township of)**—*pop pl* ... OH-6
**Windham (Township of)**—*pop pl* (2) ... PA-2
Windham Village Hist Dist—*hist pl* ... VT-1
Wind Hill—*summit* ... VA-3
**Wind Hill (historical)**—*pop pl* ... NC-3
**Windhorst**—*pop pl* ... KS-7
Windhouse Hollow—*valley* ... MO-7
Windiate Playground—*park* ... MI-6
**Windiate (Windiate Park)**—*pop pl* ... MI-6
Windigo—*locale* ... MI-6
Windigo, Lake—*lake* ... MN-6
Windigo Butte—*summit* ... OR-9
Windigo Creek—*stream* ... MN-6
*Windigo Inn* ... MI-6
Windigo Lake—*lake* ... WI-6
Windigo Lakes—*lake* ... OR-9
Windigo Pass—*gap* ... OR-9
Windigo Way—*trail* ... OR-9
Winding Blade Chapel—*church* ... KY-4
Winding Branch—*stream* ... IN-6
Winding Branch—*stream* ... KY-4
Winding Branch—*stream* ... TX-5
Winding Branch—*swamp* ... GA-3
Winding Brook—*stream* ... CT-1
**Winding Brook Village**—*pop pl* ... MD-2
Winding Chapel—*church* ... LA-4
Winding Creek—*stream* (2) ... AK-9
Winding Creek—*stream* ... WI-6
Winding Creek Lake—*reservoir* ... NC-3
**Winding Creek Village (trailer park)**—*pop pl* ... DE-2
**Winding Falls**—*pop pl* ... KY-4
Winding Fork—*stream* ... OH-6
Winding Gap—*gap* ... VA-3
Winding Gap—*locale* ... KY-4
**Winding Gulf**—*pop pl* ... WV-2
Winding Gulf—*stream* ... WV-2
**Winding Heights**—*pop pl* ... PA-2
Winding Highway—*channel* ... MI-6
**Winding Hill**—*pop pl* ... PA-2
Winding Hill—*summit* ... NY-2
Winding Hill Brook—*stream* ... NH-1
*Winding Hill Heights* ... PA-2
**Winding Hill Heights**—*pop pl* ... PA-2
Winding Hollow Country Club—*other* ... OH-6
**Winding Lanes**—*pop pl* ... CT-1
Winding Ridge—*locale* ... MD-2
Winding Ridge—*ridge* ... MD-2
Winding Ridge—*ridge* ... PA-2
Winding Ridge—*ridge* ... TN-4
Winding Ridge—*ridge* (3) ... VA-3
Winding Ridge Cem—*cemetery* ... TN-4
Winding River Ranch—*locale* ... CO-8
Windings Cem—*cemetery* ... KY-4
Winding Sch—*school* ... WV-2
Winding Shoals—*bar* ... TN-4
Winding Shoals Branch—*stream* ... WV-2
Winding Slough—*stream* (2) ... AR-4
Winding Stair Bluff—*cliff* ... AL-4
Winding Stair Bluff—*cliff* ... TN-4
Winding Stair Branch—*stream* ... NC-3
Winding Staircase Hollow—*valley* ... AR-4
Winding Stair Cave—*cave* ... CA-9
Winding Stair Gap—*gap* ... GA-3
Winding Stair Gap—*gap* ... NC-3
*Winding Stair Mountains* ... OK-5
*Windingstair Mtn* ... OK-5
Winding Stair Mtn—*summit* ... OK-5
Winding Stairs—*cliff* ... AL-4
Winding Stairs—*cliff* ... NC-3
Winding Stairs—*trail* ... TN-4
Winding Stairs Hollow—*valley* ... MO-7
Winding Stairs Mtn—*summit* ... NC-3
Winding Stairs Trail—*trail* ... CO-8
Winding Stairs Trail—*trail* ... SC-3
Winding Star Hollow—*valley* ... AR-4
Winding Star Hollow—*valley* ... KY-4
Winding Trail—*trail* ... VA-3
Winding Wash—*arroyo* ... NV-8
Winding Way—*uninc pl* ... KY-4
**Winding Ways**—*pop pl* ... NY-2
Windischar's General Blacksmith Shop—*hist pl* ... OR-9
*Wind Lake* ... MN-6
*Wind Lake* ... WA-9
Wind Lake—*lake* ... FL-3
Wind Lake—*lake* ... MN-6
Wind Lake—*lake* (2) ... OR-9
Wind Lake—*lake* ... WI-6
**Wind Lake**—*pop pl* ... WI-6
Wind Lake—*reservoir* ... WI-6
Wind Lake Drainage Canal—*canal* ... WI-6
Wind Lakes—*lake* ... ID-8
Wind Lakes Creek—*stream* ... ID-8
Windlass Bridge—*bridge* ... MT-8
Windlass Cave—*cave* ... TN-4
Windlass Creek—*stream* ... OR-9
*Windlass Gulch* ... MT-8
Windlass Gulch—*valley* ... MT-8
Windlass Hill—*summit* ... NE-7
Windlass Hollow—*valley* ... KY-4
Windlass Run—*stream* ... MD-2
Windlass Spring—*spring* ... NV-8
Windle—*locale* ... TN-4
Windle Cem—*cemetery* ... AL-4
*Windle Municipal Field* ... KS-7
Windle Pond—*lake* ... MA-1
Windle Post Office (historical)—*building* ... TN-4
Windler Gulch—*valley* ... CA-9
Windle Sch (historical)—*school* ... TN-4
Windles Lake—*reservoir* ... AL-4
Windles Lake Dam—*dam* ... AL-4
Windless Gulch—*valley* ... OR-9
Windless Point—*cape* ... MD-2
Windless Ridge—*ridge* ... CA-9
Windless Rsvr—*reservoir* ... OR-9
**Windletown**—*pop pl* ... TN-4
Windley Harbor—*bay* ... FL-3
Windley Key—*island* ... FL-3
Windling Stair Knob—*summit* ... NC-3
*Windlumis Creek* ... AL-4
Windmaker Lake—*lake* ... MT-8
*Windman Creek* ... TN-4
**Windmaster Corner**—*pop pl* ... OR-9
**Windmere**—*pop pl* ... MA-1
**Windmere Acres**—*pop pl* ... MD-2
*Windmere Lake* ... FL-3
Windmere Lake Dam—*dam* ... IN-6
**Windmere (subdivision)**—*pop pl* ... NC-3
**Windmere (subdivision)**—*pop pl* ... TN-4
Wind Mesa—*summit* ... NM-5
Windmill—*locale* ... CA-9
Windmill—*locale* ... NM-5
Windmill, Lake—*lake* (2) ... TX-5
Windmill, The—*locale* ... CA-9
Windmill at Water Mill—*hist pl* ... NY-2
Windmill Bluff—*cliff* ... ID-8
Windmill Branch—*stream* ... FL-3
Windmill Bremmer Camp—*locale* ... NM-5
Windmill Canyon—*valley* (6) ... CA-9
Windmill Canyon—*valley* (2) ... NM-5
Windmill Canyon—*valley* (2) ... OR-9
Windmill Canyon—*valley* ... TX-5
Windmill Ch—*church* ... AR-4
Windmill Cottage—*hist pl* ... RI-1
Windmill Coulee—*valley* ... MT-8
Windmill Cove—*bay* (2) ... MD-2
Windmill Creek—*stream* ... CA-9
Windmill Creek—*stream* (2) ... MD-2
Windmill Creek—*stream* ... MT-8
Windmill Creek—*stream* (2) ... TX-5
Windmill Creek—*stream* ... WY-8
Windmill Draw—*valley* ... AZ-5
Windmill Draw—*valley* ... CA-9
Windmill Draw—*valley* ... NM-5
Windmill Draw—*valley* (2) ... SD-7
Windmill Draw—*valley* (4) ... TX-5
Windmill Draw—*valley* (9) ... WY-8
Windmiller Cabin—*locale* ... CA-9
Windmiller Ravine—*valley* ... CA-9
Windmiller Trail—*trail* ... CA-9
**Windmill Farm**—*pop pl* ... NY-2
**Windmill Farms**—*pop pl* ... NY-2
Windmill Flat—*flat* (2) ... CA-9
Windmill Flat—*flat* ... ID-8
Windmill Gap—*gap* ... WV-2
Windmill Gap Branch—*stream* ... WV-2
Windmill Gate Shop Ctr—*locale* ... FL-3
Windmill Gulch—*valley* ... CA-9
*Windmill Hill* ... RI-1
Windmill Hill—*hist pl* ... NH-1
Windmill Hill—*summit* ... CT-1
Windmill Hill—*summit* (3) ... RI-1
Windmill Hill—*summit* ... SC-3
Windmill Hill—*summit* ... TX-5
Windmill Hill Hist Dist—*hist pl* ... RI-1
Windmill Hollow—*valley* (2) ... TX-5
Windmill Hollow—*valley* ... WY-8
Windmill in the Flat—*locale* ... TX-5
*Windmill Island* ... MI-6
Windmill Island—*island* ... MI-6
Wind Mill Island (historical)—*island* ... PA-2
Windmill Lake—*lake* ... CO-8
Windmill Lake—*lake* (2) ... NE-7
Windmill Lake—*lake* ... WA-9
Windmill Lake—*reservoir* ... CA-9
Windmill Lake—*reservoir* ... IA-7
Windmill Lake—*reservoir* ... NY-2
Windmill Lake Dam—*dam* ... IA-7
Windmill Mine—*mine* ... NV-8
Windmill Mtn—*summit* ... AZ-5
Windmill Mtn—*summit* ... VT-1
Windmill No A-11—*locale* ... NM-5
Windmill No A-12—*locale* ... NM-5
Windmill No 1—*locale* ... ID-8
Windmill No 1—*locale* (3) ... NM-5
Windmill No 10—*locale* (2) ... NM-5
Windmill No 2—*locale* ... ID-8
Windmill No 2—*locale* (4) ... NM-5
Windmill No 3—*locale* ... ID-8
Windmill No 3—*locale* (4) ... NM-5
Windmill No 4—*locale* (4) ... NM-5
Windmill No 5—*locale* (3) ... NM-5
Windmill No 6—*locale* (2) ... NM-5
Windmill No 7—*locale* ... NM-5
Windmill No 8—*locale* ... NM-5
Windmill No 9—*locale* (2) ... NM-5
Windmill Number Eight—*locale* (5) ... TX-5
Windmill Number Eighteen—*locale* (2) ... TX-5
Windmill Number Eightyfive—*locale* ... TX-5
Windmill Number Eightyfour—*locale* ... TX-5
Windmill Number Eightyone—*locale* ... TX-5
Windmill Number Eightyseven—*locale* ... TX-5
Windmill Number Eightysix—*locale* ... TX-5
Windmill Number Eleven—*locale* ... TX-5
Windmill Number Fifteen—*locale* (3) ... TX-5
Windmill Number Fiftyeight—*locale* ... TX-5
Windmill Number Fiftynine—*locale* ... TX-5
Windmill Number Fiftyseven—*locale* ... TX-5
Windmill Number Fiftysix—*locale* ... TX-5
Windmill Number Fiftythree—*locale* ... TX-5
Windmill Number Five—*locale* (6) ... TX-5
Windmill Number Four—*locale* (12) ... TX-5
Windmill Number Fourteen—*locale* (4) ... TX-5
Windmill Number Nine—*locale* (5) ... TX-5
Windmill Number Nineteen—*locale* (3) ... TX-5
Windmill Number One—*locale* (8) ... TX-5
Windmill Number Seven—*locale* (6) ... TX-5
Windmill Number Seventeen—*locale* (2) ... TX-5
Windmill Number Seventy—*locale* ... TX-5
Windmill Number Seventynine—*locale* ... TX-5
Windmill Number Six—*locale* (8) ... TX-5
Windmill Number Sixteen—*locale* (3) ... TX-5
Windmill Number Sixtyeight—*locale* ... TX-5
Windmill Number Sixtyfive—*locale* ... TX-5
Windmill Number Sixtynine—*locale* ... TX-5
Windmill Number Ten—*locale* (4) ... TX-5
Windmill Number Thirteen—*locale* (2) ... TX-5
Windmill Number Thirty—*locale* ... TX-5
Windmill Number Thirtyfive—*locale* ... TX-5
Windmill Number Thirtyfour—*locale* (3) ... TX-5
Windmill Number Thirtyone—*locale* ... TX-5
Windmill Number Thirtysix—*locale* ... TX-5
Windmill Number Thirtythree—*locale* (2) ... TX-5
Windmill Number Three—*locale* (14) ... TX-5
Windmill Number Twelve—*locale* (5) ... TX-5
Windmill Number Twenty—*locale* ... TX-5
Windmill Number Twentyeight—*locale* ... TX-5
Windmill Number Twentyfour—*locale* ... TX-5
Windmill Number Twentyone—*locale* ... TX-5
Windmill Number Twentyseven—*locale* ... TX-5
Windmill Number Twentythree—*locale* ... TX-5
Windmill Number Twentytwo—*locale* (2) ... TX-5
Windmill Number Two—*locale* (10) ... TX-5
Windmill Number Two—*well* ... AZ-5
Windmill on the Hill—*locale* (2) ... TX-5
Windmill On The Hill—*locale* ... TX-5
Windmill Park—*park* ... MA-1
Windmill Pictographs—*other* ... UT-8
Windmill Pit Tank—*reservoir* ... TX-5
Windmill Point—*cape* ... ME-1
Windmill Point—*cape* (8) ... MD-2
Windmill Point—*cape* (2) ... MA-1
Windmill Point—*cape* ... MI-6
Windmill Point—*cape* ... NY-2
Windmill Point—*cape* (4) ... NC-3
Windmill Point—*cape* ... VT-1
Windmill Point—*cape* (4) ... VA-3
Windmill Point—*cliff* ... WA-9
**Windmill Point**—*pop pl* ... VA-3
Windmill Point Creek—*stream* ... VA-3
*Windmill Pointe* ... MI-6
Windmill Point Light—*locale* ... MA-1
Windmill Point Reef—*bar* ... VT-1
Windmill Pond—*lake* ... GA-3
Windmill Prairie—*flat* ... FL-3
Windmill Quaker State—*hist pl* ... WV-2
Windmill Ranch—*locale* (2) ... AZ-5
Windmill Ranch—*locale* ... WY-8
Windmill Ridge—*ridge* ... UT-8
Windmill Rock—*bar* ... MN-6
Windmill Sch—*school* ... IL-6
Windmill Spring—*spring* ... CA-9
Windmill Square—*locale* ... KS-7
**Windmill (subdivision)**—*pop pl* (2) ... AZ-5
Windmill Tank—*reservoir* (4) ... AZ-5
Windmill Tank—*reservoir* (7) ... TX-5
Windmill Tree Peak—*summit* ... CA-9
**Windmill Village Trailer Park**—*pop pl* ... FL-3
Windmill 16—*locale* ... NM-5
*Wind Mountain* ... ME-1
Wind Mountain Draw—*valley* ... NM-5
Wind Mountain Lower Range Channel—*channel* ... OR-9
Wind Mountain Upper Range Channel—*channel* ... OR-9
Wind Mountain Well—*locale* ... NM-5
Wind Mtn—*summit* ... MT-8
Wind Mtn—*summit* (3) ... NM-5
Wind Mtn—*summit* ... WA-9
Wind-N-Wave—*locale* ... KS-7
**Wind Oaks Town Homes (subdivision)**—*pop pl* ... NC-3
Windom—*locale* ... PA-2
Windom—*locale* ... WV-2
**Windom**—*pop pl* ... IN-6
**Windom**—*pop pl* ... KS-7
**Windom**—*pop pl* ... MN-6
**Windom**—*pop pl* ... NY-2
**Windom**—*pop pl* ... NC-3
**Windom**—*pop pl* ... TX-5
Windom Ball Field—*park* ... AL-4
Windom Cem—*cemetery* ... KS-7
Windom Corner—*locale* ... SC-3
*Windom Creek* ... AL-4
Windom (historical)—*locale* ... SD-7
Windom Lake—*swamp* ... FL-3
Windom Mine—*mine* ... WA-9
*Windom Mountain* ... CO-8
Windom Park—*park* ... MN-6
Windom Peak—*summit* ... CO-8
Windom Sch—*school* ... MN-6
Windom Sch—*school* ... NY-2
**Windom (Township of)**—*pop pl* ... MN-6
Windon Lake—*lake* ... WA-9
**Windor Hills (subdivision)**—*pop pl* ... NC-3
**Windor Park**—*pop pl* ... NJ-2
Windover Archeol Site (8BR246)—*hist pl* ... FL-3
Windover Lake—*lake* ... MI-6
Windover Lake—*lake* ... NY-2
Windover Sch—*school* ... MI-6
**Windover (subdivision)**—*pop pl* ... AL-4
Window, The—*arch* ... AZ-5
Window, The—*cliff* ... TX-5
Window, The—*gap* ... CO-8
*Window Arch* ... UT-8
Window Blind Peak—*summit* ... UT-8
Window Canyon—*valley* ... UT-8
Windowcliffe Post Office (historical)—*building* ... TN-4
**Window Cliff Estates**—*pop pl* ... TN-4
Window Cliffs—*cliff* ... CA-9
*Window Cliffs Post Office* ... TN-4
Window Cliffs Post Office (historical)—*building* ... TN-4
Window Falls—*falls* ... NC-3
Windowfield Ditch—*canal* ... CO-8
Window in Rock—*pillar* ... NV-8
Window Lake—*lake* ... CO-8
Window Lake—*lake* ... ID-8
*Window Mount* ... AZ-5
*Window Mountains* ... AZ-5
Window Mountain Well—*well* ... AZ-5
Window Mtn—*summit* ... AZ-5
Windowpane Lake—*lake* ... WI-6
Window Peak—*summit* ... CA-9
Window Peak—*summit* ... WY-8
*Window Rock* ... AZ-5
Window Rock—*arch* (3) ... AZ-5
Window Rock—*other* ... NM-5
Window Rock—*other* ... GU-9
Window Rock—*park* ... UT-8
Window Rock—*pillar* (3) ... AZ-5
Window Rock—*pillar* ... CO-8
Window Rock—*pillar* ... MT-8
Window Rock—*pillar* ... NV-8
Window Rock—*pillar* ... SD-7
**Window Rock**—*pop pl* ... AZ-5
Window Rock—*rock* ... UT-8
Window Rock—*summit* ... AZ-5
Window Rock—*summit* ... UT-8
Window Rock Airp—*airport* ... AZ-5
*Window Rock Arch* ... UT-8
Window Rock Canyon—*valley* (2) ... NM-5
Window Rock Canyon—*valley* ... UT-8
Window Rock Coal Mine—*mine* ... NM-5
Window Rock Elem Sch—*school* ... AZ-5
Window Rock HS—*school* ... AZ-5
Window Rock Interchange—*crossing* ... AZ-5
*Window Rock Junction (Yah-Ta-Hey)* ... NM-5
Window Rock (Navajo Agency)—*CDP* ... AZ-5
Window Rock Post Office—*building* ... AZ-5
Window Rock Pumping Station—*locale* ... AZ-5
Window Rock Spring—*spring* ... UT-8
Window Rock Station—*locale* ... MT-8
Window Sash Bench—*bench* ... UT-8
Windows Section, The—*area* ... UT-8
Window Valley—*valley* ... AZ-5
Window Wind Arch—*arch* ... UT-8
Wind Point—*cape* ... AK-9
Wind Point—*cape* ... TX-5
Wind Point—*cape* ... WI-6
**Wind Point**—*pop pl* ... WI-6
Windpoint Light Station—*hist pl* ... WI-6
Wind Point Park—*park* ... TX-5
Wind Point Sch—*school* ... WI-6
Wind Pudding Lake—*lake* ... WI-6
Windrem House—*hist pl* ... IA-7
**Wind Ridge**—*pop pl* ... PA-2
Wind Ridge—*ridge* ... ID-8
Windridge Country Club—*other* ... KY-4
Windridge Shop Ctr—*locale* ... IN-6
Windrift Ranch—*locale* ... CO-8
*Wind River* ... WY-8
Wind River—*cens area* ... WY-8
Wind River—*locale* ... WY-8
**Wind River**—*pop pl* ... WY-8
Wind River—*stream* (2) ... AK-9
Wind River—*stream* ... CO-8
Wind River—*stream* ... ID-8
Wind River—*stream* ... OR-9
Wind River—*stream* ... TX-5
Wind River—*stream* ... WA-9
Wind River—*stream* ... WI-6
Wind River—*stream* ... WY-8
Wind River Camp—*locale* ... TX-5
Wind River Canal—*canal* (2) ... WY-8
Wind River Canyon—*valley* ... WY-8
Wind River (CCD)—*cens area* ... WA-9
Wind River Day Sch—*school* ... WY-8
Wind River Experimental For—*forest* ... WA-9
**Wind River Indian Reservation**—*pop pl* ... WY-8
Wind River Lake—*lake* ... WY-8
Wind River Meadows—*flat* ... ID-8
*Wind River Mountains* ... WY-8
Wind River Natural Area—*park* ... WA-9
Wind River Pass—*gap* ... CO-8
Wind River Peak—*summit* ... WY-8
Wind River Ranch—*locale* ... WY-8
Wind River Range—*range* ... WY-8
Wind River Trail—*trail* (2) ... WY-8
*Wind Rock* ... TN-4
Wind Rock—*locale* ... OR-9
Windrock—*locale* ... TN-4
Wind Rock—*pillar* ... AZ-5
Wind Rock—*summit* ... AZ-5
Wind Rock—*summit* ... VA-3
Windrock Fields—*flat* ... TN-4
Windrock Mine Number 1—*mine* ... TN-4
Windrock Mtn—*summit* ... TN-4
Wind Rock Point—*cliff* ... AZ-5
Windrock Post Office (historical)—*building* ... TN-4
Wind Rock Ridge—*ridge* ... UT-8
Wind Rock Valley—*valley* ... AZ-5
Windrow—*locale* ... TN-4
Windrow Bluff—*cliff* ... WI-6
Windrow Branch—*stream* ... TN-4
**Windrow Estates (subdivision)**—*pop pl* ... NC-3
*Wind Run* ... PA-2
Wind Run—*stream* (2) ... IN-6

**Winfield**—*pop pl* TN-4
**Winfield**—*pop pl* TX-5
**Winfield**—*pop pl* (2) WV-2
Winfield Campsites—*locale* GA-3
Winfield Carraway Hosp—*hospital* AL-4
Winfield (CCD)—*cens area* AL-4
Winfield (CCD)—*cens area* TN-4
Winfield (CCD)—*cens area* TX-5
Winfield Cem—*cemetery* AL-4
Winfield Cem—*cemetery* MN-6
Winfield Cem—*cemetery* WI-6
Winfield Ch—*church* IN-6
Winfield Ch of Christ—*church* AL-4
Winfield City Cem—*cemetery* AL-4
*Winfield-Clinton School* PA-2
Winfield Creek—*stream* GA-3
Winfield Creek—*stream* NY-2
Winfield Creek—*stream* PA-2
Winfield Creek—*stream* WA-9
Winfield Division—*civil* AL-4
Winfield Division—*civil* TN-4
Winfield Elem Sch—*school* AL-4
Winfield Elem Sch—*school* PA-2
Winfield Elem Sch—*school* TN-4
Winfield Freewill Baptist Ch—*church* AL-4
Winfield Heights Ch—*church* SC-3
**Winfield Hill**—*pop pl* GA-3
Winfield HS—*school* AL-4
Winfield HS—*school* KS-7
Winfield Junction—*locale* PA-2
Winfield Lake—*lake* MI-6
Winfield Lock Dam No 1—*dam* WV-2
Winfield (Magisterial District)—*fmr MCD* WV-2
Winfield Manor Heliport—*airport* MO-7
Winfield Methodist Church—*hist pl* AR-4
Winfield Mining Camp—*hist pl* CO-8
Winfield Oil Field—*oilfield* KS-7
Winfield Park Sch—*school* NJ-2
*Winfield Peak* CO-8
Winfield Peak—*summit* CO-8
Winfield Plaza—*locale* KS-7
Winfield Post Office—*building* TN-4
Winfield Public Carnegie Library—*hist pl* KS-7
Winfield Sanitarium—*hospital* IL-6
Winfield Sch—*school* MI-6
Winfield Sch—*school* NE-7
Winfield Sch—*school* TN-4
Winfield Sch—*school* WV-2
Winfield Scott, Lake—*reservoir* GA-3
Winfield Scott Sch—*school* AZ-5
Winfield Scott Sch—*school* CA-9
Winfields Ford (historical)—*locale* NC-3
Winfield Shop Ctr—*locale* FL-3
Winfields Mill—*locale* VA-3
Winfields Millpond—*reservoir* VA-3
Winfield South Oil Field—*oilfield* KS-7
Winfield State Hosp—*hospital* (2) KS-7
Winfield Street Sch—*school* NY-2
**Winfield Subdivision**—*pop pl* UT-8
Winfield Town Hall—*building* ND-7
**Winfield (Town of)**—*pop pl* NY-2
**Winfield (Town of)**—*pop pl* WI-6
Winfield Township—*fmr MCD* IA-7
**Winfield Township**—*pop pl* KS-7
**Winfield Township**—*pop pl* ND-7
**Winfield (Township of)**—*pop pl* IL-6
**Winfield (Township of)**—*pop pl* IN-6
**Winfield (Township of)**—*pop pl* MI-6
**Winfield (Township of)**—*pop pl* MN-6
**Winfield (Township of)**—*pop pl* NJ-2
**Winfield (Township of)**—*pop pl* PA-2
*Winfield United Methodist Church* AL-4
Winford—*locale* KY-4
Winford Brake—*swamp* AR-4
Winford Hollow—*valley* TN-4
*Winford Junction* KY-4
Winford Pond—*lake* KY-4
**Winfred**—*pop pl* SD-7
Winfred, Lake—*lake* SD-7
Winfred Cem—*cemetery* SD-7
Winfred Mine—*mine* AZ-5
Winfred Owens Mine
(underground)—*mine* AL-4
**Winfred Township**—*pop pl* SD-7
Winfred Township (historical)—*civil* SD-7
Winfree—*locale* (2) TX-5
**Winfree**—*pop pl* TX-5
Winfree Cem—*cemetery* TN-4
Winfree Cem—*cemetery* (2) TX-5
Winfree Ch—*church* (2) TX-5
Winfree Ch—*church* VA-3
Winfree Knob—*summit* TN-4
Winfree Sch—*school* TX-5
Winfrees Nose—*cliff* TX-5
Winfrey—*locale* AR-4
Winfrey Branch—*stream* TX-5
Winfrey Cem—*cemetery* AR-4
Winfrey Cem—*cemetery* MO-7
Winfrey Cem—*cemetery* TN-4
Winfrey Cem—*cemetery* TX-5
Winfrey Cem—*cemetery* WV-2
Winfrey Chapel—*church* KY-4
Winfrey Creek—*stream* LA-4
Winfrey Lake—*reservoir* TN-4
Winfrey Lake Dam—*dam* TN-4
Winfreys Ferry—*locale* KY-4
Winfreys Rocks—*summit* KY-4
Winfrey (Township of)—*fmr MCD* AR-4
Winfried Creek—*stream* TX-5
*Wing* AL-4
*Wing* UT-8
Wing—*locale* NY-2
Wing—*locale* NC-3
Wing—*locale* OR-9
Wing—*locale* (2) PA-2
Wing—*locale* UT-8
**Wing**—*pop pl* AL-4
**Wing**—*pop pl* AR-4
**Wing**—*pop pl* IL-6
**Wing**—*pop pl* ND-7
Wing, Helen, House—*hist pl* NY-2
Wing, Joseph, Farm Complex—*hist pl* NY-2
Wing, William R., Farm Complex—*hist pl* NY-2
*Wingaersheek* MA-1
*Wingaersheek Beach* MA-1
Wingaersheek Beach—*beach* MA-1
**Wingaersheek (historical)**—*pop pl* MA-1
Winganon—*locale* OK-5
Winganon Cem—*cemetery* OK-5
Winganon Ch—*church* OK-5
**Wingard**—*pop pl* AL-4
Wingard Bridge—*bridge* AL-4
Wingard Cem—*cemetery* AL-4
Wingard Cem—*cemetery* IN-6
Wingard Ditch—*canal* IN-6
Wingard Hollow—*valley* PA-2
Wingard Lake—*reservoir* AL-4
Wingard Lake Dam—*dam* AL-4
Wingard Pond—*reservoir* AL-4
Wingard Sch—*school* IL-6
Wingard Trail—*trail* PA-2
**Wingaro**—*pop pl* AL-4
Wingart Sch (historical)—*school* PA-2
Wingate—*locale* KS-7
Wingate—*locale* NM-5
**Wingate**—*pop pl* IN-6
**Wingate**—*pop pl* MD-2
**Wingate**—*pop pl* MS-4
**Wingate**—*pop pl* MO-7
**Wingate**—*pop pl* NC-3
**Wingate**—*pop pl* PA-2
**Wingate**—*pop pl* TX-5
Wingate Arm—*bay* SD-7
Wingate Baptist Ch—*church* NC-3
Wingate Bar—*bar* CA-9
Wingate Bridge—*bridge* MS-4
Wingate Brook—*stream* NH-1
Wingate Canyon—*valley* OR-9
Wingate Cem—*cemetery* NC-3
Wingate Ch—*church* TN-4
Wingate Coll—*school* NC-3
Wingate College Alumni Hall—*building* NC-3
Wingate Cove—*bay* DE-2
Wingate Cove—*bay* MD-2
Wingate Cove—*bay* NH-1
Wingate Creek—*bay* MD-2
Wingate Creek—*stream* CA-9
Wingate Creek—*stream* FL-3
Wingate Creek—*stream* NC-3
Wingate Ford—*locale* MO-7
Wingate Hill—*summit* WA-9
Wingate House—*hist pl* LA-4
Wingate HS—*school* NM-5
Wingate HS—*school* NY-2
Wingate Mesa—*area* UT-8
Wingate Mesa—*summit* UT-8
Wingate Park—*park* FL-3
Wingate Pass—*gap* CA-9
Wingate Point—*cape* (2) MD-2
**Wingates Point**—*pop pl* MD-2
Wingate Spring—*spring* OR-9
**Wingate (subdivision)**—*pop pl* TN-4
Wingate Swamp—*swamp* NY-2
Wingate Wash—*stream* CA-9
**Wingate West (subdivision)**—*pop pl* TN-4
*Wing Beach* MH-9
Wing Branch—*stream* IN-6
Wing Branch—*stream* NC-3
Wing Brook—*stream* ME-1
Wing Brook—*stream* VT-1
Wing Butte—*summit* OR-9
Wing Butte Cabin—*locale* OR-9
Wing Canyon—*valley* CA-9
Wing Cem—*cemetery* (3) ME-1
Wing Cem—*cemetery* ND-7
Wing Cem—*cemetery* OH-6
Wing Ch—*church* AL-4
*Wing Chapel* AL-4
*Wing Cove* MA-1
*Wing Creek* ID-8
Wing Creek—*stream* ID-8
Wing Creek—*stream* MT-8
Wing Creek—*stream* NY-2
Wing Creek—*stream* OR-9
**Wingdale**—*pop pl* NY-2
Wingdam Gulch—*valley* OR-9
Wingdam Island—*island* ME-1
Wing Ditch—*canal* TN-4
Winged Foot Golf Club—*other* NY-2
*Winge Draw* MT-8
Winge Draw—*valley* MT-8
**Winger**—*pop pl* MN-6
*Winger Canyon* UT-8
Winger Cem—*cemetery* MN-6
Winger Ranch—*locale* CO-8
Winger Spring—*spring* AZ-5
Wingerter Run—*stream* PA-2
Wingerton—*locale* PA-2
**Winger (Township of)**—*pop pl* MN-6
Wingert Sch—*school* MI-6
Winget Canyon—*valley* UT-8
Wingett Run—*locale* OH-6
Wingett Run—*stream* OH-6
Wing Family House—*building* MA-1
Wingfield—*locale* AZ-5
Wingfield, George, House—*hist pl* NV-8
Wingfield, Robert W., House—*hist pl* AZ-5
Wingfield Branch—*stream* VA-3
Wingfield Cem—*cemetery* AR-4
Wingfield Ch—*church* AR-4
Wingfield Ch—*church* KY-4
Wingfield Corral—*locale* AZ-5
*Wingfield Creek* AR-4
Wingfield Creek—*stream* AR-4
Wingfield Gap—*gap* VA-3
Wingfield HS—*school* MS-4
Wingfield Lake—*reservoir* AR-4
Wingfield Lake Dam—*dam* MS-4
Wingfield Mesa—*summit* AZ-5
Wingfield Mtn—*summit* VA-3
Wingfield Pines Golf Course—*locale* PA-2
**Wingfield Place (subdivision)**—*pop pl* MS-4
Wingfield Ranch—*locale* CO-8
Wingfield Run—*stream* PA-2
Wingfield Shop Ctr—*locale* MS-4
Wingfield Tank—*reservoir* AZ-5
**Wingfield Township**—*pop pl* KS-7
Wing Flat—*flat* (2) UT-8
**Wingfoot**—*pop pl* CA-9
Wingfoot Lake—*reservoir* OH-6
Wingfoot Lake Outlet—*stream* OH-6
Wingfoot Pens—*other* WY-8
Wing Fort House—*hist pl* MA-1
Wing Gully—*stream* LA-4
Wing Hall—*hist pl* NY-2
Wingham Island—*island* AK-9
Wing Hill—*summit* MA-1
Wing Hollow—*valley* NY-2
Wing Hollow—*valley* WI-6
Wing House—*hist pl* MI-6
Wingina—*locale* VA-3
Winginaw Coulee—*valley* MT-8
Winginaw Valley—*flat* MT-8
Winginaw Valley Sch—*school* MT-8
Wing Island—*island* IL-6
Wing Lake—*lake* (2) MI-6
Wing Lake—*lake* (2) MN-6
Wing Lake—*lake* WA-9
Wing Lake—*reservoir* MO-7
Wing Lake Sch—*school* MI-6
**Wing Lake Shores**—*pop pl* MI-6
Wingland Sch—*school* CA-9
Wing Lane Sch—*school* CA-9
Wingler Creek—*stream* NC-3
Wingleton Lake—*lake* MI-6
Wing Memorial Hosp—*hospital* MA-1
Wing Mine—*mine* AZ-5
Wing Mtn—*summit* AZ-5
Wingo—*locale* CA-9
Wingo—*locale* CO-8
**Wingo**—*pop pl* KY-4
**Wingo**—*pop pl* TN-4
Wingo Branch—*stream* MS-4
Wingo Cem—*cemetery* AL-4
Wingo Cem—*cemetery* (2) MS-4
Wingo Ch—*church* TN-4
Wingo Creek—*stream* KY-4
Wingo Heights Ch—*church* SC-3
Wingohocking Creek (historical)—*stream* PA-2
Wingos Lake—*reservoir* SC-3
Wingo Slough—*stream* MO-7
Wing-Over Farm Airp—*airport* RI-1
Wingo-Water Valley (CCD)—*cens area* KY-4
Wing Park—*park* IL-6
Wing Point—*cape* WA-9
Wing Point Golf Club—*other* WA-9
Wing Pond—*lake* ME-1
Wing Pond—*lake* (2) NY-2
Wingra, Lake—*lake* WI-6
Wing Ridge—*ridge* (2) OR-9
Wing River—*stream* (2) MN-6
Wing River Lake—*lake* MN-6
Wing River Tabernacle—*church* MN-6
**Wing River (Township of)**—*pop pl* MN-6
Wing River Union Cem—*cemetery* MN-6
Wing Road—*locale* NH-1
**Wingrove**—*pop pl* WV-2
Wingrove Branch—*stream* WV-2
Wing Rsvr—*reservoir* CA-9
Wing Sch—*school* IL-6
Wing Sch—*school* MA-1
Wings Cove—*cove* (2) MA-1
Wings Cove Marshes—*swamp* MA-1
Wings Field—*airport* PA-2
*Wings Flat* MA-1
Wings Flats—*flat* MA-1
Wings Hole—*basin* MA-1
*Wings Hollow* NY-2
Wings Landing—*locale* MD-2
Wings Lower Landing (historical)—*locale* AL-4
Wings Mills—*locale* ME-1
Wings Neck—*cape* MA-1
Wing's Neck Light—*hist pl* MA-1
Wings Neck Light (historical)—*building* MA-1
Wings of Deliverance Faith Temple Number
One—*church* MS-4
Wings of Joy—*church* FL-3
Wings Over Jordan Baptist Ch—*church* AL-4
Wings Point—*cape* VT-1
*Wing's Pond* ME-1
Wings Pond—*lake* MA-1
Wing Spring—*spring* CO-8
Wing Spring—*spring* (2) UT-8
*Wings Station* NY-2
*Wing Station* NY-2
**Wingston**—*pop pl* OH-6
Wingston Cem—*cemetery* OH-6
Wing Street Sch—*school* NY-2
Wings Upper Landing (historical)—*locale* AL-4
**Wing Township**—*pop pl* ND-7
Wingville—*locale* OR-9
Wingville (CCD)—*cens area* OR-9
Wingville Cem—*cemetery* OR-9
**Wingville (Town of)**—*pop pl* WI-6
Wingy Cove—*valley* UT-8
*Winhall Brook* VT-1
Winhall Hollow Cem—*cemetery* VT-1
Winhall River—*stream* VT-1
Winhall Station—*locale* VT-1
**Winhall (Town of)**—*pop pl* VT-1
Winham Lake—*lake* AR-4
Winhold Montessori Sch—*school* FL-3
Winhole Channel—*channel* NY-2
Winhole Hassock—*island* NY-2
Winhole Point—*cape* NY-2
Winian, Unen En—*bar* FM-9
Winichon—*spring* FM-9
Winifanaf—*bar* FM-9
Winifanai—*well* FM-9
*Winifauwach* FM-9
*Winifauwach, Mount* FM-9
**Winifei**—*pop pl* FM-9
*Winifewuno* FM-9
*Winifewureer, Mount* FM-9
Winifirer—*island* FM-9
Winifouch—*gap* FM-9
Winifoun—*cape* FM-9
Winifouno—*summit* FM-9
Winifoup—*spring* FM-9
*Winifourer* FM-9
Winifouror—*ridge* FM-9
Winifouror—*summit* FM-9
Winifred—*locale* KY-4
**Winifred**—*pop pl* KS-7
**Winifred**—*pop pl* MT-8
Winifred, Lake—*lake* CA-9
Winifred, Lake—*lake* ID-8
**Winifrede**—*pop pl* WV-2
*Winifrede Branch* WV-2
Winifrede Junction—*locale* WV-2
**Winifrede (RR name West
Carbon)**—*pop pl* WV-2
*Winifredes Junction* WV-2
*Winifred Harelson Elementary School* AZ-5
Winifred Island—*island* AK-9
Winifred Lake—*lake* WI-6
Winifred Peak—*summit* WY-8
Winifree Creek—*stream* AR-4
**Winigan**—*pop pl* MO-7
Winigan Creek—*stream* MO-7
Winiger Gulch—*valley* CO-8
Winiger Ridge—*ridge* CO-8
Wini Gulch—*valley* HI-9
*Winiinis* FM-9
*Winiitiw* FM-9
Winikai—*spring* FM-9
*Winikap* FM-9
Winikap—*summit* FM-9
**Winikei, Oror En**—*pop pl* FM-9
Winikeikei—*cape* FM-9
Winikep—*cape* FM-9
*Winikeyikey* FM-9
Winikon—*summit* FM-9
*Winikopos* FM-9
Winikot, Unun En—*bar* FM-9
Winiku—*summit* FM-9
Winimas—*summit* FM-9
*Winimekur* FM-9
*Winimisset* MA-1
*Winimisset Brook* MA-1
*Winimogomog* FM-9
Winimon—*summit* FM-9
Winimong—*summit* FM-9
Winimor—*ridge* FM-9
Winimor—*summit* FM-9
Winimusset Brook—*stream* MA-1
*Winimwer* FM-9
Wininen—*island* FM-9
Wininen, Mochun—*channel* FM-9
Winingar Cabin—*locale* WY-8
Wininger—*locale* AL-4
**Wininger**—*pop pl* VA-3
Wininger Cave—*cave* AL-4
Wininger Cem—*cemetery* IN-6
Wininger Cem—*cemetery* VA-3
Wininger Hollow—*valley* AL-4
Wininger Sch—*school* AL-4
Wininger Spring Branch—*stream* TN-4
Winingham Cem—*cemetery* MO-7
Winings, Jacob, House and Clover
Mill—*hist pl* PA-2
Winington—*locale* AR-4
Wininin—*summit* FM-9
**Wininis**—*pop pl* FM-9
*Wininni Lake* MN-6
Wininon—*bar* FM-9
*Winino Springs* OR-9
Wininuk—*cape* FM-9
Winioch—*swamp* FM-9
Winion—*bar* FM-9
Winion, Mochun—*channel* FM-9
Winipi, Unun En—*bar* FM-9
*Winipirea* FM-9
Winipiru—*bar* FM-9
Winipiru, Mochun—*channel* FM-9
**Winipis**—*pop pl* FM-9
Winipochokun—*bar* FM-9
Winipot—*summit* FM-9
Winipou—*summit* FM-9
Winipur—*bar* FM-9
Winipwou—*cape* FM-9
Winirom—*spring* FM-9
**Winisi**—*pop pl* FM-9
**Winisi, Oror En**—*pop pl* FM-9
Winisinen—*bar* FM-9
Winito—*bar* FM-9
**Wink**—*pop pl* TX-5
Winkai, Ununen—*cape* FM-9
Wink (CCD)—*cens area* TX-5
Wink Cem—*cemetery* PA-2
Wink Ditch—*canal* IN-6
Winkedoodle Point—*cape* VA-3
Winkel—*locale* IL-6
Winkelblech Gap—*gap* PA-2
Winkelblech Mtn—*summit* PA-2
*Winkelbleck Mtn* PA-2
**Winkelman**—*pop pl* AZ-5
Winkelman Bridge—*hist pl* AZ-5
Winkelman (CCD)—*cens area* AZ-5
Winkelman Elem Sch—*school* AZ-5
Winkelman Post Office—*building* AZ-5
Winkelmans—*locale* IA-7
Winkelman Sch (historical)—*school* MO-7
Winkelmeyer Bldg—*hist pl* MO-7
Winkey Branch—*stream* OK-5
*Winkheigres Hill* RI-1
Winkie Flat—*flat* CA-9
Winkle—*locale* IL-6
**Winkle**—*pop pl* OH-6
Winkle, Jacob W., House—*hist pl* NJ-2
Winkle Bar—*bar* OR-9
Winkle Bar Airstrip—*airport* OR-9
Winkle Bar Riffle—*rapids* OR-9
Winkleblack Sch—*school* IL-6
*Winklebleck Run* PA-2
Winkle Bluff—*cliff* MO-7
Winkle Butte—*summit* OR-9
Winkle Cem—*cemetery* AR-4
Winkle Cem—*cemetery* OR-9
Winkle Creek—*stream* MO-7
Winkle Drain—*canal* MI-6
Winkle Flat Rsvr—*reservoir* OR-9
Winkle Hollow—*valley* MO-7
Winkle Island—*island* NJ-2
Winkle Lake—*lake* MN-6
Winkle Lake—*lake* OR-9
*Winkleman* AZ-5
Winkleman Cem—*cemetery* IL-6
Winkleman Dome—*summit* WY-8
Winkleman Dome Oil Field—*oilfield* WY-8
Winkleman Dome Sch—*school* WY-8
Winkleman Windmill—*locale* TX-5
Winklepleck Grove—*locale* OH-6
Winkle Point—*cape* NY-2
Winkler—*locale* KS-7
Winkler—*locale* MO-7
Winkler—*locale* TX-5
Winkler Bakery—*building* NC-3
Winkler Canal—*canal* ID-8
Winkler Cem—*cemetery* ID-8
Winkler Cem—*cemetery* IL-6
Winkler Cem—*cemetery* IN-6
Winkler Cem—*cemetery* (2) KY-4
Winkler Cem—*cemetery* NC-3
Winkler Cem—*cemetery* SC-3
Winkler Cem—*cemetery* (2) TN-4
**Winkler (County)**—*pop pl* TX-5
Winkler County Oil Field—*oilfield* TX-5
Winkler Creek—*stream* MO-7
Winkler Creek—*stream* NC-3
*Winkler Crossroads* TN-4
Winkler Gulch—*valley* MT-8
Winkler Hills—*summit* WI-6
Winkler Hollow—*valley* OH-6
Winkler Lake—*lake* MN-6
Winkler Middle Windmill—*locale* NM-5
*Winkler Mill* OH-6
Winkler Park—*park* TX-5
Winkler Point—*summit* UT-8
Winkler Pond—*reservoir* MI-6
Winkler Ranch—*locale* AZ-5
Winkler Ranch—*locale* (2) NM-5
Winkler Ranch—*locale* SD-7
Winkler Road Baptist Ch—*church* FL-3
Winkler Rsvr—*reservoir* CO-8
*Winklers* TN-4
**Winklers**—*pop pl* TN-4
Winkler Sch—*school* IL-6
Winkler Sch—*school* MI-6
Winkler Sch—*school* MT-8
Winkler Sch—*school* SD-7
Winkler Sch—*school* WI-6
*Winklers Creek* NC-3
**Winklers Crossroads**—*pop pl* TN-4
*Winklers Lake* MN-6
Winklers Mill—*locale* OH-6
*Winklers Mills* KS-7
Winkler South Windmill—*locale* NM-5
Winkler State Wildlife Mngmt
Area—*park* MN-6
Winkler Tank—*reservoir* AZ-5
*Winkle School* TN-4
Winkle Windmill—*locale* NM-5
Winkley Branch—*stream* FL-3
Winkley Branch—*stream* (2) GA-3
Winkley Bridge—*bridge* AR-4
Winkley Bridge—*hist pl* AR-4
Winkley Brook—*stream* NH-1
Winkley Camp—*locale* MT-8
Winkley Pond—*lake* NH-1
Winkonley Ranch—*locale* NV-8
Wink Pond—*reservoir* OR-9
Winks Canyon—*valley* UT-8
Winks Creek—*stream* WI-6
Winks Panorama—*hist pl* CO-8
Wink Tank—*reservoir* NM-5
Winkum Creek—*stream* MT-8
Winkumpaugh Brook—*stream* ME-1
*Winkumpaugh Corners* ME-1
Winkumpaugh Corners—*locale* ME-1
Winkworth—*hist pl* KY-4
Winky Branch—*stream* GA-3
Winlack Run—*stream* PA-2
Winland Cem—*cemetery* IL-6
Winlock—*locale* OR-9
**Winlock**—*pop pl* WA-9
Winlock Cem—*cemetery* OR-9
Winlock Knob—*summit* KY-4
Winlow Creek—*stream* KY-4
Winlow Park—*locale* KY-4
**Winmere**—*pop pl* MA-1
**Winmill (subdivision)**—*pop pl* DE-2
*Winn* GA-3
Winn—*locale* AL-4
**Winn**—*pop pl* ME-1
**Winn**—*pop pl* MI-6
Winn, Elisha, House—*hist pl* GA-3
**Winnabow**—*pop pl* NC-3
Winnabow Airp—*airport* NC-3
Winn Airfield—*airport* OR-9
*Winnamucca Valley* NV-8
Winnapaug Pond—*lake* RI-1
*Winnatuxet River* MA-1
Winn Bay—*bay* NC-3
Winn Branch—*stream* GA-3
Winn Branch—*stream* IA-7
Winn Branch—*stream* KY-4
Winn Branch—*stream* LA-4
Winn Branch—*stream* MO-7
Winn Brook—*stream* MA-1
Winn Brook Sch—*school* MA-1
Winn Campground—*park* AZ-5
Winn Canyon—*valley* (2) NM-5
Winn Cem—*cemetery* AL-4
Winn Cem—*cemetery* IL-6
Winn Cem—*cemetery* IA-7
Winn Cem—*cemetery* LA-4
Winn Cem—*cemetery* MO-7
Winn Cem—*cemetery* OH-6
Winn Cem—*cemetery* (4) TN-4
Winn Cem—*cemetery* TX-5
Winn Cem—*cemetery* VA-3
Winn Center—*building* AZ-5
Winn Chapel—*church* NC-3
*Winn Cove* TN-4
*Winn Creek* MO-7
*Winn Creek* TN-4
Winn Creek—*stream* AL-4
Winn Creek—*stream* AR-4
Winn Creek—*stream* LA-4
Winn Creek—*stream* VA-3
Winn Creek—*stream* WI-6
Winn Creek Ch—*church* VA-3
Winn Crossing—*locale* TN-4
Winn Crossroads—*locale* AL-4
Winn Drain—*canal* MI-6
Winnebago—*locale* WI-6
**Winnebago**—*pop pl* IL-6
**Winnebago**—*pop pl* (2) MN-6
**Winnebago**—*pop pl* NE-7
Winnebago, Lake—*lake* WI-6
Winnebago, Lake—*reservoir* MO-7
Winnebago Acad—*school* WI-6
Winnebago Bend—*bend* NE-7
Winnebago Brook—*stream* NY-2
Winnebago Cem—*cemetery* IL-6
Winnebago Cem—*cemetery* MN-6
Winnebago Cem—*cemetery* NE-7
Winnebago Ch—*church* IA-7
Winnebago City (Township of)—*civ div* MN-6
**Winnebago (County)**—*pop pl* IL-6
**Winnebago (County)**—*pop pl* WI-6
Winnebago County Courthouse—*hist pl* IA-7
Winnebago County Courthouse—*hist pl* WI-6
Winnebago Creek—*stream* MN-6
Winnebago Creek—*stream* NE-7
Winnebago Ditch—*canal* IL-6
**Winnebago Heights**—*pop pl* IA-7
**Winnebago Heights**—*pop pl* WI-6
Winnebago Hill—*summit* CO-8
Winnebago Indian Agency—*locale* NE-7
Winnebago Indian Reservation—*other* WI-6
Winnebago Ind Res—*reserve* NE-7
Winnebago Ind Res (historical)—*reserve* SD-7
Winnebago Island—*island* IL-6
**Winnebago Mission**—*pop pl* WI-6
Winnebago Park—*park* IL-6
**Winnebago Park**—*pop pl* WI-6
Winnebago Point—*cape* WI-6
Winnebago Pond—*lake* NY-2
*Winnebago River* MN-6
Winnebago River—*stream* IA-7
Winnebago Sch—*school* (2) WI-6
Winnebago State Hosp—*hospital* WI-6
Winnebago State Prison Farm—*other* WI-6
**Winnebago Subdivision**—*pop pl* TN-4
**Winnebago (Township of)**—*pop pl* IL-6
**Winnebago (Township of)**—*pop pl* MN-6
Winnebago Valley—*valley* SD-7
Winneberger—*locale* IL-6
*Winnebigoshish Lake* MN-6
Winneboujou—*locale* WI-6
Winne Cem—*cemetery* NY-2
*Winnecomac Win-Ne-Co-Mack* NY-2
**Winneconne**—*pop pl* WI-6
Winneconne, Lake—*lake* WI-6
*Winneconnet* MA-1
**Winneconne (Town of)**—*pop pl* WI-6
*Winneconnet Pond* MA-1
Winnecook—*locale* ME-1
**Winnecook**—*pop pl* MT-8
*Winnecook Lake* ME-1
Winnecook Siding—*locale* MT-8
*Winnecum Creek* VA-3
**Winnecunnet**—*pop pl* MA-1
Winnecunnet Pond—*lake* MA-1
Winne Dam—*dam* SD-7
Winnedumah Paiute Monmt—*pillar* CA-9
*Winnegance* ME-1
**Winnegance**—*pop pl* ME-1
Winnegance Bay—*bay* ME-1
Winnegance Creek—*stream* ME-1
*Winnegan Creek* MO-7
Winnegar Canyon—*valley* NE-7
*Winneissimet, Town of* MA-1
Winnekeag Lake—*reservoir* MA-1
Winnekeag Lake Dam—*dam* MA-1
Winnekenni Park—*park* MA-1
Winnemac Park—*park* IL-6
Winnemanna Lodge—*locale* MD-2
Winnemaug, Lake—*reservoir* CT-1
Winnemisett, Lake—*lake* FL-3
*Winnemoiset* MA-1
**Winnemucca**—*pop pl* NV-8
Winnemucca—*summit* NV-8
Winnemucca Air Force Station—*military* NV-8
Winnemucca Colony—*reserve* NV-8
Winnemucca Creek—*stream* ID-8
Winnemucca Creek—*stream* OR-9
Winnemucca Flat—*flat* UT-8
**Winnemucca Indian Colony**—*pop pl* NV-8
Winnemucca Lake—*lake* CA-9
Winnemucca Lake—*lake* NV-8
Winnemucca Municipal Airp—*airport* NV-8
Winnemucca Spring—*spring* UT-8
Winnemucca Valley—*valley* NV-8
Winnepesaug Creek—*stream* MI-6
Winnepesaug Lake—*lake* MI-6
Winnepesauka, Lake—*reservoir* GA-3
Winnepocket, Lake—*lake* NH-1
*Winnepocket Pond* NH-1
*Winneposaug Lake* MI-6
Winner—*locale* MN-6
Winner—*locale* MO-7
Winner—*locale* TN-4
**Winner**—*pop pl* SD-7
*Winnerburg Campground* OR-9
Winner Creek—*stream* AK-9
Winner Creek—*stream* CA-9
Winner Post Office (historical)—*building* TN-4
Winner Sch—*school* TN-4
**Winner Township**—*pop pl* ND-7
Winnesheik (historical)—*locale* KS-7
*Winneshick* IL-6
Winneshiek—*locale* IL-6
Winneshiek, Lake—*lake* WI-6
Winneshiek Bluff—*cliff* WI-6
Winneshiek Bottoms—*swamp* WI-6
Winneshiek County Courthouse—*building* IA-7
Winneshiek County Fairground—*locale* IA-7
Winneshiek County Hosp—*hospital* IA-7
Winneshiek Creek—*stream* IL-6
Winneshiek Slough—*gut* WI-6
Winnesoka, Mount—*summit* TN-4
Winnesuket Golf Club—*locale* MA-1
**Winnetka**—*pop pl* CA-9
**Winnetka**—*pop pl* IL-6
Winnetka Ave Sch—*school* CA-9
Winnetka Heights Hist Dist—*hist pl* TX-5
Winnetka Park—*park* IL-6
Winnetka Sch—*school* MN-6
Winnetka Sch—*school* TX-5
Winnetonka Lake—*reservoir* MO-7
**Winnetoon**—*pop pl* NE-7
**Winnett**—*pop pl* MT-8
Winnett Canyon—*valley* WA-9
Winnett Ch—*church* PA-2
Winnett Irrigation County Ditch—*canal* MT-8
Winnett North—*cens area* MT-8
Winnett South—*cens area* MT-8
*Winnetukeset River* MA-1
Winnetuxet River—*stream* MA-1
Winnewana Impoundment—*reservoir* MI-6
Winnewana Lake—*lake* MI-6
Winnewauken Island—*island* OH-6
Winnewissa Falls—*falls* MN-6
Winney Hollow—*valley* VA-3
Winn Falls—*falls* AZ-5
Winn Farm—*hist pl* MA-1
**Winnfield**—*pop pl* LA-4
Winnfield Hotel—*hist pl* LA-4
Winn Gap—*gap* UT-8
*Winn Gap Trail* PA-2
Winn Gully—*stream* LA-4
Winn Hill—*summit* MA-1
Winn Hill Cem—*cemetery* TX-5
Winn Hollow—*valley* UT-8
Winn House—*hist pl* ME-1
Winnibigoshish, Lake—*reservoir* MN-6
Winnibigoshish Lake Dam—*hist pl* MN-6

Winnibigoshish Lake Reservoir ... MN-6
Winnibigoshish Resort—hist pl ... MN-6
Winnibulli Creek—stream ... CA-9
Winnibulli Mtn—summit ... CA-9
**Winnick Spur**—pop pl ... MN-6
Winnicomac Sch—school ... NY-2
**Winniconic**—pop pl ... NH-1
Winniconic Brook—stream ... NH-1
Winnicunnet Pond ... MA-1
**Winnicut Mills**—pop pl ... NH-1
Winnicut Mills Pond—reservoir ... NH-1
Winnicut River—stream ... NH-1
Winnie—CDP ... TX-5
Winnie—locale ... VA-3
**Winnie**—pop pl ... TX-5
Winnie, Lake—lake ... WY-8
Winnie Branch—stream ... KY-4
Winnie Branch—stream ... SC-3
Winnie Campground—locale ... MN-6
Winnie Cem—cemetery (2) ... TN-4
Winnie Comac ... NY-2
Winnie Creek—stream ... AK-9
Winnie Creek—stream ... WA-9
Winnie Hill—summit ... NY-2
Winnie Hollow—valley ... NY-2
Winnie Hollow—valley ... PA-2
Winnie Knob—summit ... TN-4
Winnie Lookout Tower—locale ... MN-6
Winnie Moore Bay—swamp ... NC-3
Winniemuck Creek—stream ... MT-8
Winniemuck Lake—lake ... MT-8
Winnie Pond—lake ... AL-4
Winnie Sch—school ... NY-2
Winnie Smith Mill (Ruins)—locale ... CA-9
Winnie's Point ... NY-2
Winnies Slide—cliff ... WA-9
Winnie-Stowell (CCD)—cens area ... TX-5
Winnie Valley—basin ... NE-7
**Winniford (historical)**—pop pl ... OR-9
Winnifred Creek—stream ... KS-7
Winnigan ... MO-7
Winnigan Creek ... MO-7
Winnimisset Brook ... MA-1
Winning Ch—church ... MO-7
Winning Cove—bay ... AK-9
**Winninger**—pop pl ... AL-4
Winninger Ranch—locale ... WY-8
Winningham Branch—stream ... TN-4
Winningham Cem—cemetery ... TN-4
Winningham Creek—stream ... AR-4
Winningham Creek—stream ... VA-3
**Winningham Farm (subdivision)**—pop pl ... NC-3
Winningham (Magisterial District)—fmr MCD ... VA-3
Winningham Rsvr—reservoir ... OR-9
Winningkoff—locale ... TX-5
Winning Pond—reservoir ... MA-1
Winning Pond Dam—dam ... MA-1
Winnings Pond ... MA-1
Winnipauk ... CT-1
**Winnipauk**—pop pl ... CT-1
Winnipauk Millpond—lake ... CT-1
Winnipauk Sch—school ... CT-1
Winnipeg—locale ... MO-7
Winnipeg Cem—cemetery ... MO-7
Winnipeg Creek—stream ... MT-8
Winnipeg Junction—locale ... MN-6
**Winnipeg Junction**—pop pl ... MN-6
Winnipeglake ... MN-6
Winnipeg Lake—lake ... MI-6
**Winnipesaukee**—pop pl ... NH-1
Winnipesaukee, Lake—lake ... NH-1
Winnipesaukee River—stream ... NH-1
Winnisemit ... MA-1
Winnisheik ... KS-7
Winnisimmet ... MA-1
Winnisook Club—other ... NY-2
Winnisook Lake—reservoir ... NY-2
**Winnisquam**—pop pl ... NH-1
Winnisquam Lake—lake ... NH-1
Winnisquam Orchard—locale ... VT-1
Winnissimmet ... MA-1
Winniweta Falls—falls ... NH-1
Winn Lake—lake ... WA-9
Winn Lake Slue—stream ... TX-5
Winn Mtn—summit ... AR-4
Winn Mtn—summit ... ME-1
Winn Mtn—summit ... NH-1
Winnocks Neck—cape ... ME-1
Winnogar Canyon ... NE-7
Winnogene, Lake—lake ... MI-6
Winnona Park Sch—school ... GA-3
Winnott, Lake—lake ... FL-3
**Winn Parish**—pop pl ... LA-4
Winn Park—park ... CA-9
Winn Ranch—locale (2) ... TX-5
Winn Road Sch—hist pl ... ME-1
**Winnsboro**—pop pl ... LA-4
**Winnsboro**—pop pl ... SC-3
**Winnsboro**—pop pl ... TX-5
Winnsboro Branch—stream ... SC-3
Winnsboro (CCD)—cens area (2) ... TX-5
Winnsboro Commercial Hist Dist—hist pl ... LA-4
Winnsboro Hist Dist—hist pl ... SC-3
Winnsboro HS—school ... SC-3
**Winnsboro Mills**—pop pl ... SC-3
Winnsboro Mills Cem—cemetery ... SC-3
Winnsboro North (CCD)—cens area ... SC-3
Winnsboro Oil Field—oilfield ... TX-5
Winnsboro South (CCD)—cens area ... SC-3
Winns Brook ... MA-1
Winns Ch—church ... VA-3
Winn Sch—school ... AZ-5
Winn Sch—school ... CA-9
Winn Sch—school ... IL-6
Winn Sch—school ... SC-3
Winn Sch (abandoned)—school ... MO-7
Winns Creek—stream ... NC-3
Winns Creek—stream ... VA-3
Winns Gap—gap ... PA-2
Winns Gap Trail—trail ... PA-2
Winns Hill—summit ... ME-1
Winns Landing—locale ... FL-3
Winns Landing—locale ... VA-3
**Winn Springs**—pop pl ... TN-4
Winn Springs Branch—stream ... TN-4
Winn Street Sch—school ... GA-3
**Winn (Town of)**—pop pl ... ME-1
Winn Trail—trail ... CO-8
Winn View Cem—cemetery ... OK-5
Winnwood ... MO-7
Winnwood Gardens ... MO-7
**Winnwood Gardens**—pop pl ... MO-7
**Winnwood Homes (subdivision)**—pop pl (2) ... AZ-5
Winnwood Lake ... MO-7
Winnwood Park—park ... MO-7
Winnwood Sch—school ... MO-7
Winnytuckett River ... MA-1
Wino—gut ... FM-9
Wino Basin—basin ... ID-8
Winofall Creek—stream ... MT-8
Winokee River ... NJ-2
Win-O-Ki Camp—locale ... MT-8
**Winokur**—pop pl ... GA-3
Winokur Lookout Tower—locale ... GA-3
Winola, Lake—reservoir ... PA-2
Winola Mill Pond ... PA-2
Winola Mill Pond Dam—dam ... PA-2
Winom—bar ... FM-9
Winom Butte—summit ... OR-9
Winom Creek—stream ... OR-9
Winom Meadows—flat ... OR-9
Winona ... IN-6
Winona—hist pl ... AZ-5
Winona—hist pl ... VA-3
Winona—locale ... AZ-5
Winona—locale ... ID-8
Winona—locale ... NH-1
Winona—locale ... NY-2
Winona—locale ... OR-9
**Winona**—pop pl ... IN-6
**Winona**—pop pl ... KS-7
**Winona**—pop pl ... MI-6
**Winona**—pop pl ... MN-6
**Winona**—pop pl ... MS-4
**Winona**—pop pl ... MO-7
**Winona**—pop pl ... OH-6
**Winona**—pop pl ... OR-9
**Winona**—pop pl ... SC-3
**Winona**—pop pl (2) ... TN-4
**Winona**—pop pl ... TX-5
**Winona**—pop pl ... VA-3
**Winona**—pop pl ... WA-9
**Winona**—pop pl ... WV-2
Winona, Lake—lake (2) ... FL-3
Winona, Lake—lake (2) ... MN-6
Winona, Lake—lake ... NJ-2
Winona, Lake—lake ... WY-8
Winona, Lake—reservoir ... AR-4
Winona and St. Peter Engine House—hist pl ... MN-6
Winona and St. Peter Freight Depot—hist pl ... MN-6
Winona and St. Peter RR Freight House—hist pl ... MN-6
Winona Area Technical Sch—school ... MN-6
Winona Baptist Ch—church ... MS-4
Winona Baptist Temple—church ... MS-4
Winona Camp—locale ... WY-8
Winona (CCD)—cens area ... TX-5
Winona Cem—cemetery ... ID-8
Winona Cem—cemetery ... KS-7
Winona Cem—cemetery ... OR-9
Winona Country Club—other ... MN-6
Winona Country Club—other ... MS-4
Winona Country Club Dam—dam ... MS-4
**Winona (County)**—pop pl ... MN-6
Winona County Courthouse—hist pl ... MN-6
Winona Creek—stream ... AK-9
Winona Falls—falls ... PA-2
Winona Flats—flat ... ND-7
Winona Free Public Library—hist pl ... MN-6
Winona (historical)—locale ... KS-7
Winona (historical)—locale ... ND-7
Winona (historical P.O.)—locale ... IA-7
Winona Hollow—valley ... AR-4
Winona Homes—uninc pl ... PA-2
Winona Hotel—hist pl ... MN-6
Winona HS—school ... MS-4
Winona Industrial HS—school ... TX-5
Winona Interchange—crossing ... AZ-5
Winona Island—island ... ND-7
Winona JHS—school ... MS-4
**Winona Junction**—pop pl ... WI-6
Winona Lake ... AR-4
Winona Lake ... PA-2
Winona Lake—lake ... GA-3
Winona Lake—lake ... MI-6
Winona Lake—lake ... MT-8
Winona Lake—lake ... NH-1
Winona Lake—lake ... NY-2
Winona Lake—lake ... VT-1
**Winona Lake**—pop pl ... IN-6
**Winona Lake**—pop pl ... NY-2
Winona Lake—swamp ... MI-6
**Winona Lakes**—pop pl ... PA-2
Winona Lookout Tower—locale ... LA-4
Winona Memorial Hosp—hospital ... IN-6
Winona Mine—mine ... MI-6
Winona-Montgomery County Airp—airport ... MS-4
Winona Park—park ... GA-3
**Winona Park**—pop pl ... GA-3
**Winona Park (Wanon Park)**—pop pl ... GA-3
Winona Plantation—locale ... LA-4
Winona Pond—reservoir ... MA-1
Winona Pond Dam—dam ... MA-1
Winona Post Office—building ... MS-4
Winona Post Office—building ... TN-4
Winona Ridge—ridge ... MT-8
Winona Savings Bank Bldg—hist pl ... MN-6
Winona Sch (historical)—school ... TN-4
Winona Sewage Lagoon Dam—dam ... MS-4
Winona Springs—spring ... AR-4
Winona Springs Ch—church ... AR-4
Winona State Coll—school ... MN-6
Winona Substation—locale ... AZ-5
Winona Tank—reservoir ... AZ-5
Winona Township—civil ... MO-7
**Winona Township**—pop pl ... KS-7
**Winona Township**—pop pl ... ND-7
Winona (Township of)—fmr MCD ... AR-4
**Winona (Township of)**—pop pl ... MN-6
**Winooski**—pop pl ... VT-1
Winooski Archeol Site—hist pl ... VT-1
Winooski Block—hist pl ... VT-1
Winooski Cem—cemetery ... WI-6
Winooski Falls Mill District—hist pl ... VT-1
Winooski Gorge—valley ... VT-1
**Winooski Park**—pop pl ... VT-1
Winooski River—stream ... VT-1
Winopee Lake—lake ... OR-9
Winopee Lake Trail—trail ... OR-9
Winos Corner ... CA-9
Winoski—locale ... AL-4
Wino Tank—reservoir (3) ... AZ-5
Winous Point—cliff ... OH-6
Winpis ... FM-9
Win Post Office—locale ... KY-4
Winquepin Cem—cemetery ... FL-3
Winquepin Pond—lake ... FL-3
Winquipin Lake—reservoir ... FL-3
Win Ridge—ridge ... OR-9
Winrock—locale ... AR-4
Winrock Farms—locale ... OK-5
Winrod Mine—mine ... CA-9
Winscott—locale ... TX-5
Winscut River ... RI-1
**Winsegansett Heights**—pop pl ... MA-1
Winsel Branch—stream ... MO-7
Winsel Cem—cemetery ... MO-7
Winsel Creek—stream ... MO-7
Winsell Cem—cemetery ... IA-7
Winser Creek—stream ... KS-7
Winset Hollow—valley ... OK-5
Winset Mtn—summit ... AR-4
Winsett Cem—cemetery (2) ... TN-4
Winsett Drain ... NV-8
Winsett Drain—canal ... NV-8
Winsett Spring—spring ... TX-5
Winsey, Bayou—gut ... LA-4
Winship—locale ... SD-7
Winship Branch—stream ... OK-5
Winship Brook ... MA-1
Winship Brook ... NH-1
Winship Brook—stream ... ME-1
Winship Post Office (historical)—building ... SD-7
Winship Prairie—flat ... OK-5
Winship Sch—school ... CA-9
Winship Sch—school ... GA-3
Winship Sch—school ... ME-1
Winship Sch—school ... MA-1
Winship Sch—school ... MI-6
Winship Sch—school ... ND-7
Winship-Smernes Bldg—hist pl ... CA-9
Winship Stream—stream ... ME-1
**Winside**—pop pl ... NE-7
Winskeag Harbor ... ME-1
Winslett Cemetery ... AL-4
Winslette Chapel ... AL-4
Winslette Chapel Ch—church ... AL-4
Winsletts Cem—cemetery ... AL-4
Winslow ... GA-3
Winslow ... MA-1
Winslow—locale ... AL-4
Winslow—locale ... MO-7
Winslow—locale ... NC-3
Winslow—locale ... PA-2
Winslow—locale ... TN-4
Winslow—locale ... TX-5
**Winslow**—pop pl ... AZ-5
**Winslow**—pop pl ... AR-4
**Winslow**—pop pl ... IL-6
**Winslow**—pop pl ... IN-6
**Winslow**—pop pl ... KY-4
**Winslow**—pop pl ... ME-1
**Winslow**—pop pl (2) ... NE-7
**Winslow**—pop pl ... NJ-2
**Winslow**—pop pl ... WA-9
**Winslow**—pop pl ... WV-2
Winslow, George F., House—hist pl ... WI-6
Winslow, Luther, Jr., House—hist pl ... MA-1
Winslow, Point—cape ... AK-9
Winslow, William H., House And Stable—hist pl ... IL-6
**Winslow Acres (subdivision)**—pop pl ... NC-3
**Winslow Beach**—pop pl ... FL-3
Winslow Brook—stream ... ME-1
Winslow Brook—stream ... NY-2
**Winslow (Br. P.O. name Bainbridge Island-Winslow)**—pop pl ... WA-9
Winslow Cabin Spring—spring ... OR-9
Winslow Canyon—valley ... AZ-5
Winslow (CCD)—cens area ... WA-9
Winslow Cem—cemetery ... IN-6
Winslow Cem—cemetery ... IA-7
Winslow Cem—cemetery ... ME-1
Winslow Cem—cemetery (2) ... MA-1
Winslow Cem—cemetery ... MN-6
Winslow Cem—cemetery ... NC-3
Winslow Center (census name Winslow)—other ... ME-1
Winslow City Hall—building ... AZ-5
Winslow City Park—park ... AZ-5
Winslow Civic Center—building ... AZ-5
Winslow Congregational Church—hist pl ... MA-1
Winslow Cove—bay ... CA-9
Winslow Creek ... UT-8
Winslow Creek—stream (2) ... GA-3
Winslow Creek—stream ... MI-6
Winslow Creek—stream ... MT-8
Winslow Creek—stream ... OK-5
Winslow Creek—stream ... OR-9
Winslow-Crocker House—building ... MA-1
Winslow Ditch—canal ... IN-6
Winslow Elem Sch—school ... IN-6
Winslow Fish and Wildlife Mngmt Area—park ... NJ-2
Winslow Gulch—valley ... OR-9
Winslow Hallock And Capen Ditch—canal ... WY-8
Winslow-Haskell Mansion—hist pl ... MA-1
Winslow Hill—locale ... ME-1
Winslow Hill—summit ... PA-2
**Winslow Hills**—pop pl ... VA-3
**Winslow (historical)**—pop pl ... OR-9
Winslow Hollow—valley ... IN-6
Winslow Hosp—hospital ... VA-3
Winslow HS—school ... AZ-5
Winslow Island—island ... ME-1
Winslow JHS—school ... AZ-5
Winslow Job Corps Civilian Conservation Center—school ... AZ-5
Winslow Junction—locale ... NJ-2
Winslow Lake—lake ... ME-1
Winslow Lake—lake ... MI-6
Winslow Lake—lake ... NE-7
Winslow Lake—lake ... WA-9
Winslow Lake—lake ... WI-6
Winslow Ledge—bench ... NH-1
Winslow Memorial Hospital—building ... AZ-5
Winslow Mills ... ME-1
Winslow Municipal Airp—airport ... AZ-5
Winslow Municipal Well Field—locale ... AZ-5
**Winslow Park**—pop pl ... KY-4
Winslow Park Ch—church ... OH-6
**Winslow Park PUD (subdivision)**—pop pl ... UT-8
Winslow Point—cape ... MA-1
Winslow Pond—lake ... ME-1
Winslow Pond—lake ... NY-2
Winslow Pond—lake ... TX-5
Winslow Post Office—building ... AZ-5
Winslow Public Library—building ... AZ-5
Winslow Rocks—bar ... ME-1
Winslow RR Bridge—hist pl ... WA-9
Winslow RR Station—building ... AZ-5
**Winslows**—pop pl ... MA-1
Winslow Sch—school (5) ... MA-1
Winslow Sch—school ... NY-2
Winslow Sch—school ... WI-6
**Winslows Crossing**—pop pl ... MA-1
Winslows Mill ... MA-1
Winslows Mills—locale ... ME-1
Winslows Narrows—isthmus ... MA-1
Winslows Pond—reservoir ... NC-3
Winslows Pond Dam—dam ... NC-3
Winslow Spring—spring ... WA-9
Winslow Stream—stream ... ME-1
**Winslow (subdivision)**—pop pl ... AL-4
Winslow Tank—reservoir ... AZ-5
**Winslow (Town of)**—pop pl ... ME-1
Winslow (Township of)—fmr MCD ... AR-4
**Winslow (Township of)**—pop pl ... IL-6
**Winslow (Township of)**—pop pl ... NJ-2
**Winslow (Township of)**—pop pl ... PA-2
Winslow-Turner Carriage House—hist pl ... NY-2
Winslow Underpass—hist pl ... AZ-5
Winslow Valley—basin ... NE-7
Winsom Cem—cemetery ... LA-4
Winsor, Stephen, House—hist pl ... RI-1
Winsor and Snover Bank Bldg—hist pl ... MI-6
Winsor Bldg—hist pl ... NJ-2
Winsor Brook—stream ... RI-1
Winsor Cove—valley ... UT-8
Winsor Creek—stream ... NM-5
Winsor Dam—dam ... MA-1
Winsor Ditch—canal ... WY-8
Winsor Lateral—canal ... AZ-5
Winsor Memorial Cem—cemetery ... UT-8
Winsor-Swan-Whitman Farm—hist pl ... RI-1
Winsor Tank—reservoir ... AZ-5
**Winsor Township**—pop pl ... SD-7
**Winsor (Township of)**—pop pl ... MI-6
**Winsor (Township of)**—pop pl ... MN-6
Winsor Trail—trail ... NM-5
Winsor Wash—stream ... AZ-5
Winsper—locale ... ID-8
Winstanley Creek—stream ... AK-9
Winstanley Island—island ... AK-9
Winstanley Lakes—lake ... AK-9
**Winstead**—pop pl ... PA-2
Winstead, John M., Houses—hist pl ... TN-4
Winstead Branch—stream ... MS-4
Winstead Bridge—bridge ... NC-3
Winstead Cem—cemetery (2) ... KY-4
Winstead Cem—cemetery (2) ... TN-4
Winstead Crossroads—locale ... NC-3
Winstead Hill—hist pl ... TN-4
Winstead Hill—summit ... GA-3
Winstead Hill—summit ... TN-4
Winstead House—hist pl ... TN-4
Winstead Pond—reservoir ... NC-3
Winstead Pond Dam—dam ... NC-3
Winstead Sch—school ... NC-3
**Winsteadville**—pop pl ... NC-3
Winstead '76' Airp—airport ... NC-3
Winsted—hist pl ... MD-2
**Winsted**—pop pl ... CT-1
**Winsted**—pop pl ... MN-6
Winsted City Hall—hist pl ... MN-6
Winsted Green Hist Dist—hist pl ... CT-1
Winsted Green Natl Register Hist Dist (Boundary Increase)—hist pl ... CT-1
Winsted Hosiery Mill—hist pl ... CT-1
Winsted Lake—lake ... MN-6
Winsted Pond ... CT-1
**Winsted (Township of)**—pop pl ... MN-6
Winston ... NC-3
Winston—locale ... IL-6
Winston—locale ... VA-3
Winston—locale ... WA-9
**Winston**—pop pl ... FL-3
**Winston**—pop pl ... GA-3
**Winston**—pop pl ... KY-4
**Winston**—pop pl ... MS-4
**Winston**—pop pl ... MO-7
**Winston**—pop pl ... MT-8
**Winston**—pop pl ... NM-5
**Winston**—pop pl ... OR-9
Winston, Joseph P., House—hist pl ... VA-3
Winston, Lake—lake ... FL-3
Winston, Obediah, Farm—hist pl ... NC-3
Winston, William, House—hist pl ... AL-4
Winston, William C. and Agnes, House—hist pl ... OR-9
Winston Acad—school ... MS-4
Winston Baptist Ch—church ... FL-3
Winston Basin—basin ... CA-9
Winston Branch—stream ... KY-4
Winston Cave—cave ... AL-4
Winston (CCD)—cens area ... GA-3
Winston Cem—cemetery ... AR-4
Winston Cem—cemetery ... ID-8
Winston Cem—cemetery ... MS-4
Winston Cem—cemetery ... MT-8
Winston Cem—cemetery ... TN-4
Winston Cem—cemetery ... TX-5
Winston Ch—church ... AL-4
Winston Ch—church ... MS-4
Winston Churchill Apartments—hist pl ... MO-7
Winston Churchill HS—school ... MD-2
Winston Churchill Memorial—hist pl ... MO-7
Winston Churchill Sch—school ... TX-5
Winston Community Hall—locale ... ID-8
**Winston County**—pop pl ... AL-4
**Winston County**—pop pl ... MS-4
Winston County Community Hosp—hospital ... MS-4
Winston County Courthouse—building ... MS-4
Winston County Courthouse—hist pl ... AL-4
Winston County Drag Strip—locale ... AL-4
Winston County HS—school ... AL-4
Winston County Med Ctr ... MS-4
Winston County Vocational Center—school ... AL-4
Winston Creek—stream ... AK-9
Winston Creek—stream ... OR-9
Winston Creek—stream ... VA-3
Winston Creek—stream (2) ... WA-9
Winston Dillard County Park—park ... OR-9
Winston Gap—gap (2) ... AL-4
Winston Gate (historical)—locale ... MS-4
Winston Gulch—valley ... CA-9
Winston Hill—summit ... ME-1
Winston Hills ... IL-6
Winston (historical)—locale ... AL-4
Winston Junction—uninc pl ... NC-3
Winston Lake—lake ... FL-3
Winston Lake—lake ... TX-5
Winston Lake—reservoir ... NC-3
Winston Lake—reservoir ... VA-3
Winston Lake Dam—dam ... NC-3
Winston Lake Golf Course—locale ... NC-3
Winston Landing (historical)—locale ... ND-7
Winston Memorial Cem—cemetery ... AL-4
Winston Park ... IL-6
Winston Park—park ... FL-3
Winston Park—park ... KS-7
**Winston Park**—pop pl ... KY-4
**Winston Park**—pop pl ... NJ-2
Winston Park—uninc pl ... KY-4
Winston Park Elem Sch—school ... FL-3
Winston Park Northwest ... IL-6
Winston Park Sch—school ... IL-6
Winston Park Shop Ctr—locale ... IL-6
Winston Park South ... IL-6
Winston Peak—summit ... CA-9
Winston Peak—summit ... ID-8
Winston Place—hist pl ... AL-4
Winston P.O. (historical)—locale ... AL-4
Winston Quarters—locale ... AL-4
Winston Quarters Pond—lake ... AL-4
Winston Ranch—locale ... NE-7
Winston Ridge—ridge ... CA-9
Winston's, Dr., House—hist pl ... KY-4
**Winston-Salem**—pop pl ... NC-3
Winston-Salem City Hall—building ... NC-3
Winston-Salem Post Office—building ... NC-3
Winston-Salem Shop Ctr—locale ... NC-3
Winston-Salem State Univ—school ... NC-3
Winston Sch—school ... FL-3
Winston Sch—school ... GA-3
Winston Sch—school ... MS-4
Winston Sch—school ... TX-5
Winston Spring—spring ... AL-4
Winston Spring—spring ... CA-9
Winston Springs—spring ... AL-4
**Winston Terrace**—pop pl ... AR-4
**Winston Terrace**—pop pl ... VA-3
Winston (Township of)—fmr MCD ... NC-3
Winston Village ... IL-6
Winstonville ... MS-4
**Winstonville**—pop pl ... MS-4
Winston Wash—stream ... CA-9
Winston Wash—valley ... CA-9
Winston Woods ... IL-6
**Wint**—pop pl ... KY-4
Wintberg Peak—summit ... VI-3
Wintch Dam—dam ... UT-8
Wintch Rsvr—reservoir ... UT-8
Wintechog Hill—summit ... CT-1
**Wintel (historical)**—pop pl ... OR-9
Winter—locale ... MN-6
**Winter**—pop pl ... WV-2
**Winter**—pop pl ... WI-6
Winter, Amos G., House—hist pl ... ME-1
Winter, Lake—reservoir ... WI-6
Winter, William, Stone House—hist pl ... OH-6
Wintera Trail—trail ... HI-9
Winter Bar—bar ... CA-9
Winter Bay—bay ... AK-9
**Winter Beach**—pop pl ... FL-3
Winter Beach Ch of God—church ... FL-3
Winter Bldg—hist pl ... AL-4
**Wintorboro**—pop pl ... AL 4
Winterboro Baptist Ch—church ... AL-4
Winterboro HS—school ... AL-4
Winterbotham Estate—hist pl ... VT-1
Winterbottom Riffle—rapids ... OR-9
Winterbows Branch—stream ... MO-7
Winter Brook—stream ... ME-1
Winter Brook—stream ... NH-1
Winterburn—locale ... PA-2
Winterburne ... PA-2
**Winterburne**—pop pl ... PA-2
**Winterbury**—pop pl ... DE-2
Winter Butte—summit ... OR-9
Winter Cabin—locale ... AZ-5
Winter Cabin Spring—spring ... AZ-5
Winter Cabin Tank—reservoir (2) ... AZ-5
Winter Camp—locale (2) ... AZ-5
Winter Camp—locale ... CO-8
Winter Camp—locale ... ID-8
Winter Camp—locale ... OR-9
Winter Camp Butte—summit ... ID-8
Winter Camp Canyon—valley ... UT-8
Winter Camp Coulee—valley ... MT-8
Winter Camp Draw—valley ... UT-8
Winter Camp Ridge—ridge ... UT-8
Winter Camp Tank—reservoir (5) ... AZ-5
Winter Camp Wash—valley ... UT-8
Winter Camp Well—well ... AZ-5
Winter Canal ... NE-7
Winter Canyon ... NE-7
Winter Canyon—valley ... CA-9
Winter Canyon—valley ... OR-9
Winter Canyon—valley ... UT-8
Winter Canyon Spring—spring ... OR-9
Winter Cem—cemetery ... PA-2
Winter Cem—cemetery ... WI-6
Winter Clove—valley ... NY-2
Wintercone Park (trailer park)—locale ... AZ-5
**Wintercone Park (trailer park)**—pop pl ... AZ-5
Winter Cove—cove ... MA-1
Winter Cove Picnic Area—locale ... MI-6
Winter Creek ... NE-7
Winter Creek ... TX-5
Winter Creek—stream (2) ... AK-9
Winter Creek—stream (2) ... CA-9
Winter Creek—stream ... ID-8
Winter Creek—stream (3) ... MT-8
Winter Creek—stream ... NV-8
Winter Creek—stream ... NJ-2
Winter Creek—stream ... ND-7
Winter Creek—stream ... OK-5
Winter Creek—stream ... OR-9
Winter Creek—stream ... WA-9
Winter Creek—stream ... WY-8
Winter Creek Trail—trail ... CA-9
Winter Creek Well—well ... NV-8
Winter Crossing—locale ... WY-8
Winterdale ... OH-6
Winterdale—locale ... PA-2
Winter Dam—dam ... WI-6
Winter Draw—valley ... ID-8
Winter Draw—valley ... SD-7
Winter Draw—valley ... WY-8
Winter Falls—falls ... OR-9
Winter Fat Rsvr—reservoir ... WY-8
Winter Fat Tank—reservoir ... AZ-5
Winterfield—locale ... TX-5
Winter Field Airp—airport ... MO-7
Winterfield Cem—cemetery ... MI-6
Winterfield Ch—church ... TX-5
Winterfield Elem Sch—school ... GA-3
Winterfield Hollow—valley ... WV-2
Winterfield Oil And Gas Storage Field—other ... MI-6
Winterfield Park—park ... OH-6
Winterfield Sch—school ... NC-3
**Winterfield (subdivision)**—pop pl ... NC-3
**Winterfield (Township of)**—pop pl ... MI-6
Winter Flat—flat ... NE-7
Winter Flats—flat ... CO-8
**Winter Garden**—pop pl ... FL-3
**Winter Garden**—pop pl ... TX-5
Winter Garden Cem—cemetery ... FL-3
Winter Garden-Ocoee (CCD)—cens area ... FL-3
Winter Garden Rodeo Ground—locale ... TX-5
**Winter Gardens**—pop pl ... CA-9
Winter Gardens—uninc pl ... LA-4
Winter Gardens Sch—school (2) ... CA-9
Wintergreen—locale ... VA-3
**Wintergreen**—pop pl ... NC-3
Wintergreen, Lake—lake ... CT-1
Wintergreen Brook—stream (2) ... CT-1
Winter Green Canal ... NE-7
Wintergreen Cem—cemetery ... MS-4
Wintergreen Cem—cemetery ... NY-2
Wintergreen Cem—cemetery ... VA-3
Wintergreen Cemetery—hist pl ... MS-4
Wintergreen Ch—church ... NC-3
Wintergreen Elem Sch—school ... NC-3
Wintergreen Flats—flat ... NY-2
Wintergreen Gorge Cem—cemetery ... PA-2
Wintergreen Hollow—valley ... WI-6
Wintergreen Island ... NY-2
Wintergreen Island—island ... CT-1
Wintergreen Island—island ... NY-2
Wintergreen Lake ... CT-1
Wintergreen Lake ... PA-2
Wintergreen Lake—lake ... MI-6
Wintergreen Lake—lake ... MN-6
Wintergreen Lake—lake ... NY-2
Wintergreen Lake—lake (2) ... WI-6
Wintergreen Ledges Ch—church ... OH-6
Wintergreen Mink Ranch—locale ... AZ-5
Wintergreen Missionary Ch—church ... TX-5
Wintergreen Mtn—summit ... VT-1
Wintergreen Run—stream ... OH-6
Wintergreen Run—stream ... PA-2
Wintergreen Sch—school ... CT-1
Wintergreen Sch (abandoned)—school ... PA-2
**Wintergreen (Slaughter)**—pop pl ... VA-3
Winter Gulch—valley ... MT-8
Winterhalter Sch—school ... MI-6
Winterham—locale ... VA-3
Winter Harbor ... ME-1
Winter Harbor—bay (3) ... ME-1
Winter Harbor—bay ... NH-1
Winter Harbor—bay ... VA-3
**Winter Harbor**—pop pl ... ME-1
Winter Harbor Cove—bay ... CA-9
Wintor Harbor Light Station hist pl ... ME 1
Winter Harbor Naval Security Group Activity—military ... ME-1
**Winter Harbor (Town of)**—pop pl ... ME-1
Winter Haven—locale ... TX-5
**Winterhaven**—pop pl ... CA-9
**Winter Haven**—pop pl ... FL-3
Winterhaven Anthropomorph and Bowknot, L-9—hist pl ... CA-9
Winterhaven Anthropomorph (L-8)—hist pl ... CA-9
Winter Haven-Auburndale (CCD)—cens area ... FL-3
Winterhaven-Bard (CCD)—cens area ... CA-9
Winter Haven Country Club—locale ... FL-3
Winter Haven Mall—locale ... FL-3
Winter Haven Motor Speedway—locale ... FL-3
Winter Haven Public Library—building ... FL-3
Winter Haven Senior HS—school ... FL-3
Winter Hill ... CO-8
Winter Hill—ridge ... WY-8
Winter Hill—summit ... ME-1
Winter Hill—summit (3) ... MA-1
Winter Hills—summit ... CO-8
Winter Hill Sch—school ... TX-5
**Winter Hill (subdivision)**—pop pl ... MA-1
Winterhoff Park—park ... IL-6
Winter Hollow—valley ... AR-4
Winter Hollow—valley ... NY-2
Winter Hollow—valley ... TN-4
Winter Horse Pasture Windmill—locale ... NM-5
Winter Hotel—hist pl ... MN-6
Winter House—hist pl ... ND-7
Wintering River—stream ... ND-7
Wintering River Flats—flat ... ND-7
Wintering River Natl Wildlife Ref—park ... ND-7
Wintering Sch Number 1—school ... ND-7
Wintering Sch Number 2—school ... ND-7
Winter Inn—hist pl ... MI-6
Winter Island ... FM-9
Winter Island—island ... CA-9
Winter Island—island ... MA-1
Winter Island—island ... NY-2
Winter Jacob Broils Shoals—bar ... TN-4

*Winter Lake* ... WI-6
Winter Lake—*lake* ... AK-9
Winter Lake—*lake* ... MI-6
Winter Lake—*lake* ... NY-2
Winter Lake—*lake* ... WA-9
Winter Lookout Tower—*locale* ... WI-6
Winter Mesa—*summit* ... CO-8
Winter Mesa Trail—*trail* ... CO-8
Winter Mine—*mine* ... TN-4
Wintermoot Island—*island* ... PA-2
Wintermute Lake—*lake* ... MN-6
Wintermute Memorial Hosp—*hospital* ... TX-5
Wintermutes Corner—*locale* ... WA-9
Wintermutes Foundry—*locale* ... NJ-2
Wintermuth Lake—*lake* ... NE-7
Winter Night Camp—*locale* ... OR-9
Winter Park—*park* ... FL-3
**Winter Park**—*pop pl* ... CO-8
**Winter Park**—*pop pl* ... FL-3
**Winter Park**—*pop pl* ... NC-3
Winter Park Adult Vocational Center—*school* ... FL-3
Winter Park Ch of Religious Science—*church* ... FL-3
Winter Park Ch of the Nazarene—*church* ... FL-3
Winter Park Day Nursery—*school* ... FL-3
Winter Park Elem Sch—*school* ... NC-3
Winter Park Gardens—*uninc pl* ... NC-3
Winter Park HS—*school* ... FL-3
Winter Park JHS—*school* ... FL-3
Winter Park Mall—*locale* ... FL-3
Winter Park Memorial Hosp—*hospital* ... FL-3
Winter Park Memorial Hospital, Medical Staff Library—*building* ... FL-3
Winter Park Presbyterian Ch—*church* ... FL-3
Winter Park Public Library—*building* ... FL-3
**Winter Park (subdivision)**—*pop pl* (2) ... NC-3
Winter Pasture Tank—*reservoir* ... AZ-5
Winter Pasture Windmill—*locale* ... WY-8
Winter Playground—*park* ... PA-2
Winterpock—*locale* ... VA-3
Winterpock Creek—*stream* ... VA-3
Winterpock Sch—*school* ... VA-3
Winter Point—*cape* ... FL-3
Winter Point—*cape* ... MI-6
Winter Points—*summit* ... MT-8
Winter Pond—*lake* ... MA-1
Winterport—*CDP* ... ME-1
**Winterport**—*pop pl* ... ME-1
Winterport Congregational Church—*hist pl* ... ME-1
Winterport Hist Dist—*hist pl* ... ME-1
Winterport Station—*locale* ... ME-1
**Winterport (Town of)**—*pop pl* ... ME-1
Winter Quarters—*hist pl* ... LA-4
Winter Quarters—*other* ... UT-8
**Winter Quarters**—*pop pl* ... UT-8
Winter Quarters Canyon—*valley* ... UT-8
Winter Quarters Landing (historical)—*locale* ... MS-4
Winterquarters Ridge—*ridge* ... UT-8
Winter Range Well—*well* ... OR-9
Winter Ridge—*ridge* ... CO-8
Winter Ridge—*ridge* ... NV-8
Winter Ridge—*ridge* (2) ... OR-9
Winter Ridge—*ridge* ... UT-8
*Winter Rim* ... OR-9
Winterringer Bldg and House—*hist pl* ... OH-6
Winter Road Catchment—*reservoir* ... AZ-5
Winter Road Lake—*lake* ... MN-6
Winter Road River—*stream* ... MN-6
**Winterrowd**—*pop pl* ... IL-6
Winterrow (historical P.O.)—*locale* ... IN-6
Winter Run—*stream* ... IN-6
*Winters* ... TN-4
**Winters**—*pop pl* ... CA-9
**Winters**—*pop pl* ... MI-6
**Winters**—*pop pl* ... TX-5
Winters, Aaron, House—*hist pl* ... NJ-2
Winters, Lake—*reservoir* ... TX-5
Winter Saloon—*hist pl* ... MN-6
Winters Bayou—*stream* ... LA-4
Winters Bayou—*stream* ... TX-5
Winters Blowout—*crater* ... ID-8
Winters Branch—*stream* ... MS-4
Winters Branch—*stream* ... NC-3
Wintersburg—*locale* ... AZ-5
**Wintersburg**—*pop pl* ... CA-9
Winters Camp—*locale* ... AL-4
Winters Camp—*locale* ... MT-8
Winters Canal—*canal* ... CA-9
Winters Canyon—*valley* ... CA-9
Winters (CCD)—*cens area* ... CA-9
Winters (CCD)—*cens area* ... TX-5
Winters Cem—*cemetery* (2) ... AL-4
Winters Cem—*cemetery* ... AR-4
Winters Cem—*cemetery* (2) ... IN-6
Winters Cem—*cemetery* ... IA-7
Winters Cem—*cemetery* ... KY-4
Winters Cem—*cemetery* ... MS-4
Winters Cem—*cemetery* ... MO-7
Winters Cem—*cemetery* ... NJ-2
Winters Cem—*cemetery* ... NC-3
Winters Cem—*cemetery* ... OH-6
Winters Cem—*cemetery* (2) ... TN-4
Winters Ch—*church* ... OH-6
Winter Sch—*school* ... MD-2
Winters Chapel—*church* ... GA-3
Winters Chapel African Methodist Episcopal Ch—*church* ... TN-4
Winterscheid Oil Field—*oilfield* ... KS-7
Winter Sch (historical)—*school* ... TN-4
**Winters Corner**—*pop pl* ... MA-1
Winters Country Club—*other* ... TX-5
Winters-Courter House—*hist pl* ... NJ-2
*Winters Creek* ... OR-9
*Winters Creek* ... TX-5
Winters Creek—*stream* ... AR-4
Winters Creek—*stream* (2) ... CA-9
Winters Creek—*stream* ... FL-3
Winters Creek—*stream* ... IL-6
Winters Creek—*stream* (2) ... MI-6
Winters Creek—*stream* ... MT-8
Winters Creek—*stream* ... NE-7
Winters Creek—*stream* (5) ... NV-8
Winters Creek—*stream* ... OK-5
Winters Creek—*stream* ... OR-9
Winters Creek Canal—*canal* ... NE-7
Winters Creek Lake—*lake* ... NE-7
Winters Creek Sch—*school* ... IL-6
Winters Ditch—*canal* (2) ... IN-6
Winters Ditch—*canal* ... OH-6
Winters Drain—*canal* ... MI-6
Winters Drain—*stream* ... MI-6
Winterseat—*locale* ... SC-3
Winterset—*locale* ... PA-2
**Winterset**—*pop pl* ... IA-7
**Winterset**—*pop pl* ... OH-6
Winterset, Lake—*lake* ... FL-3
Winterset Cem—*cemetery* ... KS-7
Winterset Cem—*cemetery* ... OH-6
Winterset City Hall—*building* ... IA-7
Winterset City Park—*park* ... IA-7
Winterset (historical)—*locale* ... KS-7
**Winterset Township**—*pop pl* ... KS-7
Winters Ferry (historical)—*locale* ... AL-4
Winters Flat—*flat* ... CA-9
*Winters Gap* ... TN-4
Winters Gap—*gap* ... TN-4
Winters Gulch—*valley* ... CA-9
Winters Gulch—*valley* ... OR-9
Winters Hollow—*valley* ... OK-5
Winters Hollow—*valley* (3) ... TN-4
Winter Site—*hist pl* ... MI-6
Winters Lake—*lake* ... IN-6
Winters Lake—*lake* ... MI-6
Winters Lake—*lake* ... WA-9
Winters Mine—*mine* ... NV-8
Wintersmith, Horatio, House—*hist pl* ... KY-4
Wintersmith Park—*park* ... OK-5
Winters Mtn—*summit* ... WA-9
Winters Park—*park* ... MI-6
Winters Pass—*gap* ... CA-9
Winters Peak—*summit* ... CA-9
Winters Pond—*reservoir* ... NJ-2
Winters Pond—*reservoir* ... SC-3
Winters Post Office (historical)—*building* ... AL-4
Winter Spring—*spring* ... NV-8
Winter Spring—*spring* ... OR-9
Winter Spring—*spring* ... WY-8
Winter Spring Picnic Area—*locale* ... ID-8
**Winter Springs**—*pop pl* ... FL-3
Winter Springs—*spring* ... UT-8
Winter Springs Elem Sch—*school* ... FL-3
Winter Springs Seventh Day Adventist Ch—*church* ... FL-3
Winters Ranch—*locale* (2) ... AZ-5
Winters Ranch—*locale* ... NV-8
Winters Ranch—*locale* ... SD-7
Winters Ranch Rsvr—*reservoir* ... NV-8
Winters Ridge—*ridge* ... CA-9
Winters Ridge—*ridge* ... NV-8
Winters Run—*stream* ... MD-2
Winters Sch—*school* ... GA-3
Winters Sch—*school* ... KS-7
Winters Sch—*school* ... MO-7
Winters Sch—*school* ... PA-2
Winters Spring—*spring* ... OR-9
Winter Star Mtn—*summit* ... NC-3
*Winter Star Ridge* ... NC-3
Winter Star Ridge—*ridge* ... NC-3
Wintersteen Park—*flat* ... CO-8
Wintersteen Trail—*trail* ... CO-8
Winterstein Cem—*cemetery* ... OH-6
Winterstein Run—*stream* ... OH-6
Winterstein Sch—*school* ... CA-9
Winter Store—*building* ... MO-7
**Winterstown**—*pop pl* ... PA-2
Winterstown Borough—*civil* ... PA-2
Winters Trail—*trail* ... PA-2
Winter Street Chruch—*hist pl* ... ME-1
*Winter Street Dam* ... MA-1
Winter Street Hist Dist—*hist pl* ... MA-1
Wintersville—*locale* ... MO-7
Wintersville—*locale* ... PA-2
**Wintersville**—*pop pl* ... OH-6
Wintersville Cem—*cemetery* ... MO-7
Winters Wash—*stream* ... AZ-5
Winters Well—*locale* ... AZ-5
Winters Well—*well* ... AZ-5
Winter Tank—*reservoir* (2) ... AZ-5
Winterthur—*locale* ... DE-2
Winterthur Museum and Gardens—*hist pl* ... DE-2
Winterthur Museum and Gardens—*locale* ... DE-2
**Winterton**—*pop pl* ... NY-2
**Winter (Town of)**—*pop pl* ... WI-6
Winter Trail—*trail* ... CO-8
Winter Trail—*trail* ... PA-2
Winter Valley—*valley* ... CO-8
Winter Valley—*valley* ... OK-5
**Winter Valley Estates**—*pop pl* ... TX-5
Winter Valley Gulch—*valley* ... CO-8
Winter Veterans Administration Hosp—*hospital* ... KS-7
*Winterville* ... IN-6
Winterville—*locale* ... ME-1
Winterville—*locale* ... VA-3
**Winterville**—*pop pl* ... GA-3
**Winterville**—*pop pl* ... MS-4
**Winterville**—*pop pl* ... NC-3
**Winterville**—*pop pl* ... OR-9
Winterville (CCD)—*cens area* ... GA-3
Winterville Ch—*church* ... FL-3
Winterville Creek—*stream* ... OR-9
Winterville Fire Station—*building* ... NC-3
*Winterville Mounds State Park* ... MS-4
Winterville (Plantation of)—*civ div* ... ME-1
Winterville Sch—*school* ... MS-4
Winterville Site—*hist pl* ... MS-4
Winterville (sta.) (RR name for Quimby)—*other* ... ME-1
Winterville State Park—*park* ... MS-4
*Winterville Station* ... ME-1
Winterville Station—*locale* ... ME-1
Winterville Town Hall—*building* ... NC-3
Winterville (Township of)—*fmr MCD* ... NC-3
**Winterwarm**—*pop pl* ... CA-9
Winter Water Creek—*stream* ... OR-9
Winter Well—*well* ... TX-5
Winter Wells Sch—*school* ... AZ-5
Winter Windmill—*locale* ... TX-5
Winterwood Golf Course—*locale* ... NV-8
Winterwood Park—*park* ... NV-8
Winther Sch—*school* ... SD-7
*Wintherthrup* ... DE-2
**Winthrop**—*pop pl* ... AR-4
**Winthrop**—*pop pl* ... CT-1
**Winthrop**—*pop pl* ... IN-6
**Winthrop**—*pop pl* ... IA-7
**Winthrop**—*pop pl* ... ME-1
**Winthrop**—*pop pl* ... MA-1
**Winthrop**—*pop pl* ... MN-6
**Winthrop**—*pop pl* ... MO-7
**Winthrop**—*pop pl* ... NY-2
**Winthrop**—*pop pl* ... WA-9
Winthrop, John, Jr., Iron Furnace Site—*hist pl* ... MA-1
Winthrop, Lake—*lake* ... MA-1
Winthrop, Mount—*summit* ... NH-1
Winthrop, Mount—*summit* ... WA-9
Winthrop Ave Sch—*school* ... NY-2
Winthrop Beach—*beach* ... MA-1
**Winthrop Beach**—*pop pl* ... MA-1
Winthrop Beach Station (historical)—*locale* ... MA-1
Winthrop Bldg—*hist pl* ... MA-1
*Winthrop Brook* ... CT-1
Winthrop Canal—*stream* ... MA-1
**Winthrop Center**—*pop pl* ... ME-1
Winthrop Ch—*church* ... NC-3
Winthrop Coll—*school* ... SC-3
Winthrop College Hist Dist—*hist pl* ... SC-3
Winthrop Creek—*stream* (2) ... WA-9
*Winthrop Glacier* ... WA-9
Winthrop Glacier—*glacier* ... WA-9
**Winthrop Harbor**—*pop pl* ... IL-6
**Winthrop Harbor Station**—*pop pl* ... IL-6
Winthrop Head—*cliff* ... MA-1
**Winthrop Highlands (subdivision)**—*pop pl* ... MA-1
Winthrop Hill—*summit* ... MA-1
Winthrop HS—*school* ... WA-9
*Winthrop Junction* ... MI-6
**Winthrop Junction**—*pop pl* ... MI-6
*Winthrop Lake* ... MA-1
Winthrop Light—*locale* ... MA-1
Winthrop Mill—*hist pl* ... CT-1
Winthrop Natl Fish Hatchery—*other* ... WA-9
Winthrop Park—*park* ... FL-3
Winthrop Point—*cape* ... AK-9
Winthrop Point—*cape* ... CT-1
Winthrop Point—*cape* ... NC-3
*Winthrop Pond* ... MA-1
Winthrop Sch—*school* (4) ... MA-1
*Winthrops Pond* ... MA-1
Winthrop Square—*park* (3) ... MA-1
**Winthrop Square (subdivision)**—*pop pl* ... AL-4
Winthrop Street Baptist Church—*hist pl* ... MA-1
Winthrop Townhall—*building* ... MA-1
**Winthrop (Town of)**—*pop pl* ... ME-1
**Winthrop (Town of)**—*pop pl* ... MA-1
Winthrop Yacht Club—*locale* ... MA-1
Winthrow-Melhase Block—*hist pl* ... OR-9
*Winticomack Creek* ... VA-3
Winticomack Creek—*stream* ... VA-3
Wint New Ground—*island* ... FL-3
*Winton* ... GA-3
*Winton* ... SD-7
Winton—*hist pl* ... VA-3
Winton—*locale* ... AL-4
Winton—*locale* ... WA-9
Winton—*locale* ... WY-8
**Winton**—*pop pl* ... CA-9
**Winton**—*pop pl* (2) ... MN-6
**Winton**—*pop pl* ... NC-3
**Winton**—*pop pl* ... PA-2
Winton Branch—*stream* ... AL-4
Wintonbury Sch—*school* ... CT-1
Winton Canyon—*valley* ... CA-9
Winton Cave—*cave* ... AL-4
Winton Cem—*cemetery* ... AL-4
Winton Cem—*cemetery* ... CA-9
Winton Cem—*cemetery* (2) ... TN-4
Winton Chapel—*church* ... TN-4
Winton Corners—*locale* ... CA-9
Winton Cove—*valley* ... AL-4
Winton Creek—*stream* ... ID-8
**Wintondale**—*pop pl* ... OH-6
Winton Grove Sch—*school* ... CA-9
*Winton Junction* ... OH-6
*Winton Junction* ... WY-8
Winton Junction—*locale* ... WY-8
Winton Lake—*reservoir* ... OH-6
Winton Lateral—*canal* ... CA-9
Winton Park—*park* ... CA-9
*Winton Place* ... OH-6
**Winton Place**—*pop pl* ... OH-6
Winton Place Methodist Episcopal Church—*hist pl* ... OH-6
Winton Post Office (historical)—*building* ... AL-4
Winton Run—*stream* ... PA-2
Winton Sch—*school* (2) ... CA-9
Winton Sch—*school* ... WA-9
Winton Sch (historical)—*school* ... AL-4
Winton Sch (historical)—*school* ... TN-4
*Wintons Island* ... TN-4
Winton Spring—*spring* ... AR-4
Wintons Ripples—*rapids* ... TN-4
Winton Station—*building* ... PA-2
**Winton Terrace**—*pop pl* ... OH-6
Winton Town—*locale* ... TN-4
Winton (Township of)—*fmr MCD* ... NC-3
Winton Well—*well* ... AZ-5
Winton Woods—*woods* ... OH-6
*Wintoon Butte* ... CA-9
Wintoon Campground—*locale* ... CA-9
Wintoon Flat—*flat* ... CA-9
*Wintoon Glacier* ... CA-9
**Wintringham Park**—*pop pl* ... NJ-2
Wintucket Cove—*bay* ... MA-1
Wintun Glacier—*glacier* ... CA-9
*Winwalasta Creek* ... AL-4
Win Wan Flat—*flat* ... NV-8
Win Wan Valley—*valley* ... NV-8
Winway—*uninc pl* ... KS-7
Winway Park—*park* ... KS-7
**Winwood**—*pop pl* ... AZ-5
Winwood Shop Ctr—*locale* ... MO-7
**Winwood (subdivision)**—*pop pl* ... NC-3
Winwright Station—*locale* ... KY-4
Winyah, Lake—*lake* ... FL-3
Winyah, Lake—*reservoir* ... MI-6
Winyah Bay—*bay* ... SC-3
Winyah Bay Entrance—*channel* ... SC-3
Winyah Bay West Channel Light Two—*locale* ... SC-3
Winyah Fire Tower—*locale* ... SC-3
Winyah Indigo Sch—*hist pl* ... SC-3
*Winyaw Bay* ... SC-3
Winz Creek—*stream* ... NV-8
Winzeler Cem—*cemetery* ... IL-6
Winzy Creek—*stream* ... FL-3
*Wionkeake Hill* ... RI-1
Wionkhiege Hill—*summit* ... RI-1
*Wionkhiege River* ... RI-1
Wion Ranch—*locale* ... NE-7
WIOO-AM (Carlisle)—*tower* ... PA-2
WIOQ-FM (Philadelphia)—*tower* ... PA-2
*Wiorickheag* ... RI-1
**Wiota**—*pop pl* ... IA-7
**Wiota**—*pop pl* ... WI-6
Wiota Cem—*cemetery* ... IA-7
**Wiota (Town of)**—*pop pl* ... WI-6
WIOU-AM (Kokomo)—*tower* ... IN-6
WIOV-FM (Ephrata)—*tower* ... PA-2
WIOZ-FM (South Pines)—*tower* ... NC-3
*Wip* ... UT-8
Wipala Wiki Ranch—*locale* ... AZ-5
WIP-AM (Philadelphia)—*tower* ... PA-2
*Wiparo Lake* ... WI-6
WIPB-TV (Muncie)—*tower* ... IN-6
*Wiper Loop* ... WV-2
*Wiper Loop Creek* ... WV-2
Wiper Memorial Ch—*church* ... OH-6
Wipf, J. & C., Mills—*hist pl* ... WI-6
Wipff Farm—*locale* ... TX-5
*Wipho* ... AZ-5
*Wipo Spring* ... AZ-5
*Wippany* ... NJ-2
Wippel Creek—*stream* ... WA-9
Wipple Sch—*school* ... WI-6
Wipple Wasteway—*canal* ... WA-9
WIQR-AM (Prattville)—*tower* ... AL-4
WIRB-AM (Enterprise)—*tower* ... AL-4
WIRC-AM (Hickory)—*tower* ... NC-3
Wirch—*locale* ... ND-7
Wirch Cem—*cemetery* ... ND-7
*Wircher Creek* ... GA-3
*Wire* ... MA-1
Wire, Lake—*lake* ... FL-3
Wire, Mount—*summit* ... UT-8
WIRE-AM (Indianapolis)—*tower* ... IN-6
*Wire Branch* ... TX-5
Wire Branch—*stream* ... OK-5
Wire Branch—*stream* ... WV-2
Wire Bridge—*bridge* ... TX-5
Wire Bridge—*locale* ... GA-3
Wire Bridge—*other* ... MO-7
Wire Corral—*locale* ... AZ-5
Wire Corral—*locale* ... OR-9
*Wire Corral Draw* ... AZ-5
Wire Corral Draw—*valley* ... AZ-5
Wire Corral Mesa—*summit* (2) ... AZ-5
Wire Corral Ranch—*locale* ... NV-8
Wire-Corral Spring—*spring* ... AZ-5
Wire Corral Spring—*spring* ... CA-9
Wire Corral Spring—*spring* ... OR-9
Wire Corral Springs—*spring* ... OR-9
Wire Corral Tank—*reservoir* (3) ... AZ-5
Wire Corral Tank—*reservoir* (2) ... NM-5
Wire Corret Canyon—*valley* ... OR-9
Wire Creek—*stream* ... TX-5
Wire Creek—*stream* ... VA-3
Wire Draw—*valley* ... CO-8
Wire Fence Canyon—*valley* (3) ... UT-8
Wire Fence Opening—*flat* ... CA-9
Wire Fence Point—*summit* ... UT-8
Wire Gap—*gap* ... TX-5
Wire Gate Saddle—*gap* ... CA-9
Wire Gold Tank—*reservoir* ... AZ-5
Wiregrass Bench—*bench* ... UT-8
Wiregrass Branch—*stream* ... GA-3
Wiregrass Canyon—*valley* ... UT-8
Wiregrass Comprehensive Mental Health Center—*hospital* ... AL-4
Wire Grass Coulee—*valley* ... MT-8
Wiregrass Ditch—*canal* ... OH-6
**Wiregrass Hills (subdivision)**—*pop pl* ... AL-4
Wiregrass Hospital Airp—*airport* ... AL-4
Wiregrass Lake—*lake* ... AZ-5
Wire Grass Lake—*lake* ... MI-6
Wiregrass Mall Shop Ctr—*locale* ... AL-4
Wiregrass Marsh—*swamp* ... MN-6
Wire Grass Meadow—*flat* ... MN-6
Wiregrass Memorial Park—*park* ... AL-4
Wiregrass Prairie—*area* ... CA-9
Wiregrass Ridge—*ridge* ... CA-9
Wiregrass Rsvr—*reservoir* ... ID-8
Wiregrass Sch (historical)—*school* ... TN-4
*Wire Grass Spring* ... NV-8
Wiregrass Spring—*spring* ... CA-9
Wiregrass Spring—*spring* (3) ... NV-8
Wiregrass Spring—*spring* (2) ... UT-8
Wire Grass Spring—*spring* ... UT-8
Wiregrass Spring—*spring* ... UT-8
Wiregrass Springs—*spring* ... CA-9
Wiregrass Stadium—*other* ... AL-4
Wire Gulch—*valley* ... ID-8
Wire Gut—*gut* ... DE-2
*Wire Hill* ... MA-1
Wire Hill—*ridge* ... NM-5
Wire Hollow—*valley* ... WI-6
Wire Hollow Creek—*stream* ... TX-5
Wire Knob—*summit* ... TN-4
Wirekraft, Incorporated—*facility* ... IN-6
Wire Lake—*area* ... CA-9
Wire Lake—*lake* ... AR-4
Wire Lake—*lake* ... IA-7
Wire Lake—*lake* (2) ... NM-5
Wire Lakes—*lake* ... CA-9
Wireman Cem—*cemetery* (2) ... KY-4
*Wireman Fork* ... KY-4
Wireman Fork—*stream* ... KY-4
Wire Meadow—*flat* ... OR-9
Wire Mesa—*summit* ... UT-8
Wire Mtn—*summit* ... CA-9
Wire Narrows—*gut* ... VA-3
Wire Narrows Marsh—*swamp* ... VA-3
Wire Pass—*gap* ... UT-8
Wire Passage—*gut* ... VA-3
Wire Pen Windmill—*locale* ... TX-5
*Wire Point* ... VA-3
Wire Point—*cape* ... NC-3
*Wire Ridge* ... PA-2
Wire Rsvr—*reservoir* ... OR-9
Wire Run—*stream* ... IN-6
Wire Sch—*school* ... CA-9
Wires Corners—*locale* ... IA-7
*Wires Creek* ... NJ-2
Wires Ditch—*canal* ... IN-6
*Wire Spring* ... PA-2
Wire Spring—*spring* (2) ... AZ-5
Wire Spring—*spring* (2) ... CA-9
Wire Spring—*spring* ... CO-8
Wire Spring—*spring* ... MT-8
Wire Springs Canyon—*valley* ... CA-9
*Wireton* ... IL-6
**Wireton**—*pop pl* ... PA-2
**Wireton (RR name Anderson Road)**—*pop pl* ... PA-2
*Wiretown* ... NJ-2
*Wiretown Branch* ... NJ-2
Wire Trail—*trail* ... MT-8
Wire valley Knoll—*summit* ... UT-8
Wire Valley Wash—*valley* ... UT-8
*Wire Village* ... MA-1
Wirick Cem—*cemetery* ... SC-3
Wirick-Simmons House—*hist pl* ... FL-3
*Wirilee* ... FM-9
WIRJ-AM (Humboldt)—*tower* ... TN-4
Wirkkala Airp—*airport* ... WA-9
*Wirlidge Lake* ... IN-6
Wirmingham—*locale* ... TN-4
Wirmingham Cem—*cemetery* ... TN-4
Wirmingham Post Office (historical)—*building* ... TN-4
**Wirock**—*pop pl* ... MN-6
Wirong, Oror En—*locale* ... FM-9
W I Rowland Pond—*reservoir* ... NC-3
W I Rowland Pond Dam—*dam* ... NC-3
Wirsing—*locale* ... PA-2
Wirsing Sch (historical)—*school* ... PA-2
Wirt—*locale* ... NY-2
**Wirt**—*pop pl* ... IN-6
**Wirt**—*pop pl* ... MN-6
**Wirt**—*pop pl* ... OK-5
*Wirt Auxiliary Landing Field* ... KS-7
Wirt Canyon—*valley* ... NM-5
Wirt Cem—*cemetery* ... MN-6
Wirt Cem—*cemetery* ... NM-5
**Wirt (County)**—*pop pl* ... WV-2
*Wirtemburg* ... PA-2
**Wirth**—*pop pl* ... AR-4
Wirth, Jacob, Buildings—*hist pl* ... MA-1
Wirth Dam—*dam* ... OR-9
Wirth Haven Cove—*bay* ... TX-5
Wirth Island—*island* ... IL-6
Wirth Lake—*lake* ... MN-6
Wirth Lake—*lake* ... OR-9
Wirth Park—*park* ... IN-6
Wirth Park—*park* ... MN-6
Wirth Park—*park* ... WI-6
Wirth Rsvr—*reservoir* ... OR-9
Wirt JHS—*school* ... MD-2
Wirt Lake—*lake* ... MN-6
Wirtland—*hist pl* ... VA-3
*Wirtonia* ... KS-7
Wirtonia Cem—*cemetery* ... KS-7
Wirtonia Sch—*school* ... KS-7
Wirt Park—*park* ... PA-2
Wirt Sch—*school* ... TN-4
*Wirt School* ... IN-6
Wirt Seminary (historical)—*school* ... TN-4
**Wirt Station**—*pop pl* ... IN-6
**Wirt (Town of)**—*pop pl* ... NY-2
**Wirt (Township of)**—*pop pl* ... MN-6
Wirt Wharf—*locale* ... VA-3
Wirtz—*locale* ... VA-3
*Wirtzboro* ... NY-2
Wirtz Branch—*stream* ... OR-9
Wirtz Sch—*school* ... CA-9
Wirz Ranch—*locale* ... WY-8
*Wisacasset Dam* ... PA-2
Wisacco Cipus (historical)—*stream* ... DE-2
*Wisachi Cove* ... TX-5
*Wisachi Creek* ... TX-5
**Wisacky**—*pop pl* ... SC-3
*Wisacode* ... MN-6
*wisacode River* ... MN-6
Wisapan Ch—*church* ... FM-9
Wisas—*island* ... FM-9
Wisbey Cem—*cemetery* ... TX-5
Wisby Memorial Ch—*church* ... LA-4
Wisby Oil Field—*oilfield* ... KS-7
**Wiscasset**—*pop pl* ... ME-1
**Wiscasset**—*pop pl* ... PA-2
Wiscasset Ball Park—*park* ... NC-3
Wiscasset Hist Dist—*hist pl* ... ME-1
Wiscasset HS—*school* ... ME-1
Wiscasset Jail and Museum—*hist pl* ... ME-1
**Wiscasset (Town of)**—*pop pl* ... ME-1
Wiscassett Park—*park* ... NC-3
Wiscaya County Park—*park* ... FL-3
Wiscoal—*locale* ... KY-4
Wiscoble Lake—*lake* ... WI-6
*Wiscoggin Creek* ... MI-6
Wiscoggin Drain—*stream* ... MI-6
*Wiscoggin River* ... MI-6
*Wiscogosis* ... ME-1
Wiscon—*locale* ... FL-3
Wiscona—*uninc pl* ... WI-6
**Wisconsin**—*pop pl* ... KY-4
Wisconsin, Lake—*reservoir* ... WI-6
Wisconsin Acad—*school* ... WI-6
Wisconsin Acad Grade Sch—*school* ... WI-6
Wisconsin Ave Hist Dist—*hist pl* (2) ... WI-6
Wisconsin Ave Park—*park* ... WI-6
Wisconsin Bay—*bay* ... WI-6
Wisconsin Canyon—*valley* ... AZ-5
Wisconsin Channel—*channel* ... WI-6
Wisconsin Correctional Institution—*building* ... WI-6
Wisconsin Creek—*stream* (2) ... MT-8
Wisconsin Creek—*stream* ... NV-8
Wisconsin Creek—*stream* ... WA-9
Wisconsin Creek—*stream* ... WI-6
**Wisconsin Dam**—*pop pl* ... WI-6
**Wisconsin Dells**—*pop pl* ... WI-6
Wisconsin Dells Speedway—*other* ... WI-6
Wisconsin Ditch—*canal* (2) ... CO-8
Wisconsin Electric Company—*facility* ... WI-6
Wisconsin Gulch—*valley* ... CA-9
Wisconsin Industrial Sch—*school* ... WI-6
Wisconsin Industrial Sch for Boys—*hist pl* ... WI-6
Wisconsin Institute of Technology—*school* ... WI-6
Wisconsin International Raceway—*other* ... WI-6
Wisconsin Junction—*locale* ... WI-6
Wisconsin Lutheran HS—*school* ... WI-6
Wisconsin Memorial Hosp Hist Dist—*hist pl* ... WI-6
Wisconsin Memorial Park Cem—*cemetery* ... WI-6
Wisconsin Mine—*mine* (2) ... AZ-5
Wisconsin Mine—*mine* ... CO-8
Wisconsin Natl Life Insurance Bldg—*hist pl* ... WI-6
Wisconsin Point—*cape* ... WI-6
**Wisconsin Rapids**—*pop pl* ... WI-6
Wisconsin Ravine—*valley* ... CA-9
Wisconsin River—*stream* ... WI-6
Wisconsin River Country Club—*other* ... WI-6
Wisconsin River Flowage—*reservoir* ... WI-6
Wisconsin Sch—*school* ... TN-4
Wisconsin Sch—*school* ... WI-6
Wisconsin Sch for Boys—*school* ... WI-6
Wisconsin Sch for Girls—*school* ... WI-6
Wisconsin Slough—*gut* ... WI-6
Wisconsin State Capitol—*building* ... WI-6
Wisconsin State Capitol—*hist pl* ... WI-6
Wisconsin State Coll—*school* (2) ... WI-6
Wisconsin State Reformatory—*other* ... WI-6
Wisconsin State Univ—*school* (2) ... WI-6
Wisconsin Street Hist Dist—*hist pl* ... KS-7
Wisconsin Telephone Company Bldg—*hist pl* ... WI-6
**Wisconsin (Township of)**—*pop pl* ... MN-6
Wisconsin Truck Trail—*trail* ... WA-9
*Wisconsin Veterans Home* ... WI-6
**Wisconsin Village**—*pop pl* ... FL-3
**Wisconsin Winnebago Ind Res**—*pop pl* ... WI-6
**Wiscotta**—*pop pl* ... IA-7
Wiscotta Cem—*cemetery* ... IA-7
**Wiscoy**—*pop pl* ... NY-2
Wiscoy Creek—*stream* ... NY-2
**Wiscoy (Township of)**—*pop pl* ... MN-6
Wiscoy Valley—*valley* ... MN-6
Wisdom—*locale* ... KY-4
Wisdom—*locale* ... MO-7
**Wisdom**—*pop pl* ... MT-8
Wisdom Branch—*stream* ... TN-4
Wisdom Canyon—*valley* ... OK-5
Wisdom Cave—*cave* ... TN-4
Wisdom Cem—*cemetery* ... KY-4
Wisdom Cem—*cemetery* ... MO-7
Wisdom Cem—*cemetery* ... MT-8
Wisdom Cem—*cemetery* ... TN-4
Wisdom Ch—*church* ... KY-4
*Wisdom County* ... TN-4
Wisdom Creek—*stream* (2) ... ID-8
Wisdom Creek—*stream* ... KY-4
Wisdom Creek—*stream* ... OR-9
Wisdom Dock—*locale* ... KY-4
Wisdom Ferry (historical)—*locale* ... AL-4
Wisdom Hollow—*valley* ... MO-7
Wisdom Hollow—*valley* ... PA-2
Wisdom House—*hist pl* ... AZ-5
Wisdom Lane JHS—*school* ... NY-2
Wisdom Lane Sch Annex—*school* ... NY-2
Wisdom Mine—*mine* ... TN-4
Wisdom Peak—*summit* ... ID-8
Wisdom Sch—*school* ... PA-2
Wisdom Tank—*reservoir* ... AZ-5
Wisdom Temple—*locale* ... TX-5
*Wisdon River* ... MT-8
Wise—*locale* ... KS-7
Wise—*locale* ... MI-6
Wise—*locale* ... TX-5
**Wise**—*pop pl* ... IA-7
**Wise**—*pop pl* ... NC-3
**Wise**—*pop pl* ... VA-3
Wise—*uninc pl* ... CA-9
Wise, J. E., Bldg—*hist pl* ... AZ-5
Wise, Peter, House—*hist pl* ... OH-6
WISE-AM (Asheville)—*tower* ... NC-3
Wiseboy Creek—*stream* ... ID-8
Wiseboy Lakes—*lake* ... ID-8
Wiseboy Mine—*mine* ... ID-8
Wise Branch—*stream* ... AL-4
Wise Branch—*stream* ... NC-3
Wise Branch—*stream* ... TX-5
Wise Brook—*stream* ... NH-1
Wiseburg—*locale* ... WV-2
**Wiseburg**—*pop pl* ... MD-2
Wiseburg Cem—*cemetery* ... MD-2
Wiseburn—*uninc pl* ... CA-9
Wise Camp—*locale* ... FL-3
Wise Canal—*canal* ... CA-9
Wisecarver Cem—*cemetery* (2) ... TN-4
Wisecarver Cem—*cemetery* ... VA-3
Wisecarver Gap—*gap* ... VA-3
Wisecarver Run—*stream* ... PA-2
Wisecarver Truck Trail—*trail* ... CA-9
Wise Cem—*cemetery* (2) ... AL-4
Wise Cem—*cemetery* ... AR-4
Wise Cem—*cemetery* ... GA-3
Wise Cem—*cemetery* (2) ... IN-6
Wise Cem—*cemetery* ... KS-7
Wise Cem—*cemetery* ... KY-4
Wise Cem—*cemetery* (2) ... LA-4
Wise Cem—*cemetery* ... MI-6
Wise Cem—*cemetery* ... MO-7
Wise Cem—*cemetery* ... NC-3
Wise Cem—*cemetery* ... OK-5
Wise Cem—*cemetery* ... SC-3
Wise Cem—*cemetery* ... TN-4
Wise Cem—*cemetery* ... TX-5
*Wise Ch* ... AL-4
Wise Chapel—*church* ... AL-4
Wise Chapel—*church* ... SC-3
Wise Chapel—*church* ... VA-3
Wise Chapel Cem—*cemetery* ... AL-4
*Wise Chapel Ch* ... AL-4
Wise Chapel Ch—*church* ... AL-4
*Wise County* ... KS-7
**Wise (County)**—*pop pl* ... TX-5
**Wise (County)**—*pop pl* ... VA-3
Wise County Courthouse—*hist pl* ... TX-5
Wise County Courthouse—*hist pl* ... VA-3
Wise County Industrial Sch—*school* ... VA-3
Wise County Memorial Hosp—*hospital* ... VA-3
Wise Creek—*stream* ... CO-8
Wise Creek—*stream* ... FL-3
Wise Creek—*stream* ... GA-3
Wise Creek—*stream* ... ID-8
Wise Creek—*stream* ... MI-6
Wise Creek—*stream* (2) ... OR-9
Wise Ditch—*canal* ... IN-6
Wise Ditch—*canal* ... WY-8
Wise Dugout Draw—*valley* ... WY-8

Wise-Fielding House and Carriage House—hist pl ... TX-5
Wise Flat—flat ... WY-8
Wise Forebay—reservoir ... CA-9
Wise Fork ... NC-3
**Wise Forks**—pop pl ... NC-3
Wise Gap—gap ... WV-2
Wise Gap—locale ... MS-4
**Wise (Gladeville)**—pop pl ... VA-3
Wise Gulch—valley ... CA-9
Wise Gulch—valley ... CO-8
Wise Hammock Pond—swamp ... FL-3
Wisehart Creek—stream ... OR-9
Wise Hill—summit ... TN-4
Wise Hill—summit ... VA-3
Wise Hill Cem—cemetery ... MO-7
Wise (historical)—locale ... AL-4
Wise Hollow—valley ... IN-6
Wise Hollow—valley ... SC-3
Wise Hollow—valley ... TN-4
Wise Hollow—valley ... VA-3
Wise-Holloway Cem—cemetery ... TN-4
Wise House—hist pl ... KY-4
Wise Island ... PA-2
Wise Knob—summit ... NC-3
Wise Lake ... MI-6
Wise Lake—lake ... IL-6
Wise Lake—lake ... LA-4
Wise Lake—lake ... MI-6
Wise Lake—lake ... MN-6
Wise Lake—lake ... MS-4
Wise Lake—lake ... SC-3
Wise Lake—lake ... WI-6
Wise Lake—reservoir ... KS-7
Wisel Creek—stream ... MN-6
Wiselka Draw—valley ... WY-8
Wisely Cem—cemetery ... AR-4
Wisely Cem—cemetery (2) ... OH-6
**Wiseman**—pop pl (2) ... AK-9
**Wiseman**—pop pl ... AR-4
**Wiseman**—pop pl ... MS-4
Wiseman, Lake—lake ... WA-9
Wiseman Archeol Site—hist pl ... NE-7
Wiseman Bend—bend ... TN-4
Wiseman Branch—stream ... TN-4
Wiseman Branch—stream ... WV-2
Wiseman Brook—stream ... NH-1
Wiseman Cem—cemetery ... IN-6
Wiseman Cem—cemetery ... KY-4
Wiseman Cem—cemetery ... NC-3
Wiseman Cem—cemetery (3) ... OH-6
Wiseman Cem—cemetery ... TN-4
Wiseman Cem—cemetery ... WV-2
Wiseman Ch—church ... MO-7
Wiseman Creek—stream ... AK-9
Wise Man Creek—stream ... MI-6
Wiseman Creek—stream (2) ... NV-8
Wiseman Creek—stream ... WA-9
Wiseman Ditch—canal ... LA-4
Wiseman Flat ... CA-9
Wiseman Hollow—valley (2) ... TN-4
Wiseman Island—island ... OR-9
Wiseman Lake—lake ... TX-5
Wiseman Run—stream (2) ... WV-2
Wisemans Creek ... NV-8
Wiseman Spring—spring ... TN-4
Wisemans View—locale ... NC-3
**Wisemantown**—pop pl ... KY-4
Wise Marsh—swamp (2) ... MD-2
Wise Marsh—swamp ... SC-3
Wise Meadow—flat ... OR-9
Wise Memorial Ch—church ... LA-4
Wise Mesa—summit ... AZ-5
Wise Mill Cem—cemetery ... AL-4
Wise Mill Ch—church ... AL-4
Wise Mountain Lookout Tower—locale ... VA-3
Wise Mtn—summit ... CO-8
Wisenachen—tunnel ... FM-9
Wisenbaker Lake—lake ... TX-5
Wisener Cem—cemetery ... TN-4
Wisener Hollow—valley ... MO-7
Wisenet—summit ... FM-9
Wisenif, Oror En—locale ... FM-9
Wisenor Flat—flat ... CA-9
Wise Oil Field—other ... MI-6
Wise Penstock—canal ... CA-9
Wise Point—cape ... NC-3
Wise Point—cape ... VA-3
Wise Pond—reservoir (2) ... AL-4
**Wiser**—pop pl ... IN-6
Wiser Cem—cemetery ... TN-4
Wiser Creek—stream ... MT-8
Wiser Creek—stream (2) ... OR-9
Wiser Hollow—valley ... TN-4
Wise Ridge—ridge ... IL-6
**Wise River**—pop pl ... MT-8
Wise River—stream ... MT-8
Wise River Ditch—canal ... MT-8
Wise River Sch—school ... MT-8
Wiser Lake—lake ... WA-9
Wisers Bluff Cem—cemetery ... TN-4
Wisers Branch—stream ... TN-4
Wisers Buff Sch (historical)—school ... TN-4
wisers River ... ID-8
**Wiser Township**—pop pl ... ND-7
Wise Run—stream ... KY-4
Wise Run—stream ... OH-6
Wise Run—stream ... PA-2
Wise Run—stream ... WV-2
Wise Sch—school ... IL-6
Wise Sch—school ... OH-6
Wise Sch (historical)—school ... AL-4
Wise Sch (historical)—school ... PA-2
Wises Gap ... MS-4
Wises Lake ... MI-6
Wises Landing—locale ... KY-4
Wises Mill Creek—stream ... AL-4
Wises Mill (historical)—locale ... AL-4
Wise Spirit Lake—lake ... SD-7
Wise Spring—spring ... MO-7
Wise Spring—spring ... TN-4
Wise Station—locale ... CA-9
Wise Store ... MS-4
Wisetown ... IL-6
Wisetown—other ... IL-6
Wisetown Cem—cemetery ... IL-6
**Wise Township**—pop pl ... ND-7
**Wise (Township of)**—pop pl ... MI-6
Wiseville Post Office (historical)—building ... AL-4
Wise Well—well ... NM-5
Wisgapolla River ... KS-7
Wishard Creek—stream ... MT-8
Wishard Peak—summit ... ID-8
**Wishart**—pop pl ... MO-7
**Wishart**—pop pl ... VA-3
Wishart-Boush House—hist pl ... VA-3
Wishart Cem—cemetery ... NC-3
Wishart Creek ... OR-9
Wishart Hill—summit ... NV-8
Wishart Point ... VA-3
Wishart Point—cape ... VA-3
Wisharts Point ... VA-3
**Wisharts Point**—pop pl ... VA-3
Wishart Swamp—swamp ... PA-2
Wishart Township—civil ... MO-7
Wishart (Township of)—fmr MCD ... NC-3
**Wishaw**—pop pl ... PA-2
Wishbone Creek—stream ... ID-8
Wishbone Glacier—glacier ... WA-9
Wishbone Hill—summit ... AK-9
Wishbone Island—island ... NJ-2
Wishbone Lake—lake ... AK-9
Wishbone Lake—lake ... MT-8
Wishbone Lake—lake ... WI-6
Wishbone Loop—bend ... CA-9
Wishbone Mtn—summit ... AZ-5
Wish Cem—cemetery ... TX-5
**Wishek**—pop pl ... ND-7
Wishek Municipal Airp—airport ... ND-7
**Wisher**—pop pl ... ND-7
Wisher Cem—cemetery ... IL-6
Wisher Creek—stream ... FL-3
Wisherd Bridge—bridge ... MT-8
Wisherd Gulch—valley ... MT-8
Wisherd Ridge—ridge ... MT-8
Wishert Point ... VA-3
Wish-Ham Cem—cemetery ... WA-9
Wish-I-Ah Sanatorium—hospital ... CA-9
Wishing Shrine—church ... AZ-5
Wishing Spring—spring ... MO-7
Wishing Well Cave—cave ... AL-4
Wishing Well Cove—bay ... AZ-5
**Wishing Well (subdivision)**—pop pl ... NC-3
Wishing Well Trailer Park—locale ... AZ-5
**Wishkah**—pop pl ... WA-9
Wishkah (CCD)—cens area ... WA-9
Wishkah Pipeline—other ... WA-9
Wishkah River—stream ... WA-9
Wishkah River Bridge—hist pl ... WA-9
Wishkah River Ranch Airp—airport ... WA-9
Wishkah Valley Sch—school ... WA-9
Wish Lake—lake ... MN-6
**Wishon**—pop pl ... CA-9
Wishon Campground—locale ... CA-9
Wishon Cem—cemetery ... MO-7
Wishon Cove—bay ... CA-9
Wishon Powerhouse—other ... CA-9
Wishon Rsvr—reservoir ... CA-9
Wishon Sch—school ... CA-9
Wishow Lake—lake ... WI-6
**Wishram**—pop pl ... WA-9
**Wishram Heights**—pop pl ... WA-9
Wishram Indian Village Site—hist pl ... WA-9
Wish Sch—school ... CT-1
Wishtenatan C ... OR-9
WISH-TV (Indianapolis)—tower ... IN-6
Wishwell Sch—school ... SC-3
Wish Woods ... NC-3
Wisineno—spring ... FM-9
Wisini Lake—lake ... MN-6
Wisino—bar ... FM-9
Wiskapalla River ... KS-7
Wiskapella ... KS-7
Wiskeag Creek—stream ... ME-1
Wiskers Draw ... UT-8
WISL-AM (Shamokin)—tower ... PA-2
Wisler Ch—church (2) ... IN-6
Wisler Ditch ... IN-6
Wisler Ditch—canal ... IN-6
Wislow Island—island ... AK-9
Wismer—locale ... PA-2
Wismer, Mount—summit ... PA-2
Wismer Cem—cemetery ... PA-2
Wismer Drain—canal ... MI-6
Wismer PO—locale ... PA-2
**Wismer Township**—pop pl ... SD-7
Wisnaint Mtn summit ... GA 3
**Wisner**—locale ... MN-6
Wisner—locale ... MS-4
Wisner—locale ... NY-2
**Wisner**—pop pl ... LA-4
**Wisner**—pop pl ... MI-6
**Wisner**—pop pl ... NE-7
Wisner, Jacob, House—hist pl ... PA-2
Wisner Cem—cemetery ... MI-6
Wisner Cem—cemetery ... MO-7
Wisner Cem—cemetery ... NE-7
Wisner Cem—cemetery ... NY-2
Wisner Cem—cemetery ... OK-5
Wisner Cem—cemetery ... OR-9
Wisner Cem—cemetery ... TN-4
Wisner Cem—cemetery ... TX-5
Wisner Ch—church ... MI-6
Wisner Creek—stream ... WA-9
Wisner Crossing—locale ... MT-8
Wisner-Gilbert Sch—school ... LA-4
Wisner Gulch—valley ... MT-8
Wisner Hill—summit ... TN-4
**Wisner (historical)**—pop pl ... ND-7
Wisner House—hist pl ... MI-6
Wisner HS—school ... MS-4
Wisner Oil Field—oilfield ... MS-4
Wisner Oil Field—other ... MI-6
Wisner Point—cape ... MI-6
Wisner Ranch—locale ... NE-7
Wisner's ... MI-6
Wisner Sch—school ... MI-6
Wisners Point ... MI-6
Wisner Township—fmr MCD ... IA-7
**Wisner Township**—pop pl ... NE-7
**Wisner (Township of)**—pop pl ... MI-6
Wisner Trail—trail ... MN-6
Wisneski State Wildlife Mngmt Area—park ... MN-6
Wisniewski Pond—lake ... IA-7
Wisnoski House—hist pl ... TX-5
Wison—spring ... FM-9
Wisop—summit ... FM-9
Wiso Sch (historical)—school ... SD-7
WISP-AM (Kinston)—tower ... NC-3
Wisp Creek—stream ... CO-8
Wispering Winds Dam—dam ... TN-4
Wispering Winds Lake—reservoir ... TN-4
Wisp Lake—lake ... MN-6
WISR-AM (Butler)—tower ... PA-2
Wisroth Rsvr—reservoir ... WY-8
Wissahackon Senior High School ... PA-2
Wissahicken Brook—stream ... NJ-2
Wissahickon—hist pl ... PA-2
**Wissahickon**—pop pl ... PA-2
Wissahickon Creek—stream ... PA-2
Wissahickon Heights ... PA-2
Wissahickon HS—school ... PA-2
Wissahickon Inn—hist pl ... PA-2
Wissahickon Memorial Bridge—hist pl ... PA-2
Wissahickon Sch—school ... PA-2
Wissahickon Valley Park—park ... PA-2
**Wissahickon Village**—pop pl ... PA-2
Wissahissic ... MA-1
Wissahissic Pond ... MA-1
Wissakode Zibi ... MN-6
Wissalohican Camp—locale ... OH-6
**Wisseman Acres**—pop pl ... DE-2
Wissenhunt Mtn ... GA-3
Wiss Hollow—valley ... TN-4
Wissikihon Creek—stream ... MT-8
**Wissingers**—pop pl ... PA-2
**Wissingertown**—pop pl ... PA-2
Wissinoming—locale ... PA-2
Wissinoming Creek (historical)—stream ... PA-2
Wissinoming Park—park ... PA-2
Wissiup Ditch—canal ... UT-8
Wissler ... OH-6
Wissler, Susan, House—hist pl ... WY-8
Wissler Ranch—locale ... CO-8
Wissler Run—stream ... PA-2
Wissler's Airp—airport ... WA-9
Wisslers Run—stream ... PA-2
Wissmath Craters—locale ... NM-5
Wisson Hunt Mtn ... GA-3
Wissota, Lake—reservoir ... WI-6
**Wissota Dam**—pop pl ... WI-6
WIST-AM (Charlotte)—tower ... NC-3
**Wistar Farms**—pop pl ... VA-3
Wistaria Canal—canal ... CA-9
Wistaria Drain—canal ... CA-9
Wistaria Drain Five—canal ... CA-9
Wistariahurst—hist pl ... MA-1
Wistaria Island ... FM-9
Wistaria Lake—lake ... FL-3
Wistaria Lateral Eight—canal ... CA-9
Wistaria Lateral Five—canal ... CA-9
Wistaria Lateral Four—canal ... CA-9
Wistaria Lateral One—canal ... CA-9
Wistaria Lateral P Two—canal ... CA-9
Wistaria Lateral Seven—canal ... CA-9
Wistaria Lateral Six—canal ... CA-9
Wistaria Lateral Three—canal ... CA-9
Wistaria Lateral Two—canal ... CA-9
Wistar Run—stream ... PA-2
**Wister**—pop pl ... CA-9
**Wister**—pop pl ... OK-5
**Wister**—pop pl ... PA-2
Wister, Mary Channing, Sch—hist pl ... PA-2
Wister, Mount—summit ... WY-8
Wister (CCD)—cens area ... OK-5
Wister Dam—dam ... OK-5
Wisteria Cem—cemetery ... GA-3
Wisteria Hotel—hist pl ... MS-4
Wisteria Island—island ... FL-3
Wisteria Lodge—hist pl ... MA-1
Wisteria Place—building ... MS-4
Wister Island ... PA-2
Wister Lake—reservoir ... OK-5
**Wisterman**—pop pl ... OH-6
Wister Sch—school ... PA-2
Wister Waterfowl Mngmt Area—park ... CA-9
Wister Woods Park—park ... PA-2
**Wistful Vista**—pop pl ... OR-9
Wist Hollow—valley ... AR-4
Wistie—locale ... PA-2
Wistrand Lake—lake ... MI-6
WISU-FM (Terre Haute)—tower ... IN-6
WISU-TV (Terre Haute)—tower ... IN-6
Wiswall, Oliver, House—hist pl ... NY-2
Wiswall Ditch—canal ... CO-8
Wiswall Falls Mills Site hist pl ... NH 1
Wiswall Hill—summit ... VT-1
Wiswalls Pond ... MA-1
Wiswell—locale ... KY-4
Wiswell—uninc pl ... WI-6
Wiswell Cem—cemetery ... ME-1
Wiswell Cem—cemetery ... VT-1
Wiswell Hill ... VT-1
Wiswell Road Covered Bridge—hist pl ... OH-6
WITA-AM (Knoxville)—tower (2) ... TN-4
Witachek Mound—summit ... IL-6
Wita Lake—lake ... MN-6
Witan—bar ... FM-9
Witbeck—locale ... MI-6
Witch Brook ... MA-1
Witch Brook—stream (2) ... MA-1
Witch Canyon ... AZ-5
Witch Canyon Trail Two Hundred Sixty—trail ... AZ-5
Witchcoate Point ... MD-2
Witchcoat Point—cape ... MD-2
Witchcraft Point—cape ... AK-9
Witch Creek—locale ... CA-9
Witch Creek—stream ... AL-4
Witch Creek—stream ... AZ-5
Witch Creek—stream (2) ... CA-9
Witch Creek—stream ... NH-1
Witch Creek—stream ... WY-8
Witch Creek Ch—church ... AL-4
Witch Creek Fire Control Station—locale ... CA-9
Witch Creek Mtn—summit ... CA-9
Witch Dance Hill—summit ... MS-4
Witch Dance Lookout Tower—tower ... MS-4
Witch Dance Picnic Area—park ... MS-4
Witch Drain Pond—lake ... OR-9
Witch Duck—unince pl ... VA-3
Witch Duck Bay—bay ... VA-3
Witch Duck Point—cape ... VA-3
**Witch Duck Point**—pop pl ... VA-3
Withce Creek—stream ... LA-4
Witcher—locale ... OK-5
**Witcher**—pop pl ... WV-2
Witcher Brook—stream ... ME-1
Witcher Cem—cemetery ... MO-7
Witcher Cem—cemetery ... WV-2
Witcher Creek ... GA-3
Witcher Creek—stream (2) ... CA-9
Witcher Creek—stream ... TX-5
Witcher Creek—stream ... VA-3
Witcher Creek—stream ... WV-2
Witcher Fork—stream ... WV-2
Witcher Hill ... MA-1
Witcher Holes Creek—stream ... SD-7
Witcher Hollow—valley ... TN-4
Witcher Hollow Branch—stream ... TN-4
Witcher Knob—summit ... VA-3
Witcher Meadow—flat ... CA-9
Witcher Mtn—summit ... CO-8
Witcher Ranch—locale ... CO-8
Witcher Rsvr—reservoir ... MT-8
Witcher Sch—school ... OK-5
Witchers Creek ... WV-2
Witcher Swamp—swamp ... ME-1
Witcher Tank—reservoir ... TX-5
Witcher Unit ... CO-8
**Witcherville**—pop pl ... AR-4
Witches, The—bar ... NH-1
Witches Brook—stream ... NH-1
Witches Cauldron—glacier ... AK-9
Witches Glen—valley ... MA-1
Witches Gulch—valley ... WI-6
Witches Knoll—summit ... UT-8
Witches Lake—lake ... WI-6
Witches Pool ... AZ-5
Witches Spring—spring ... NH-1
**Witch Hazel**—pop pl ... OR-9
Witch Hazel Millpond—lake ... CT-1
Witch Hazel Pond—lake ... OH-6
Witch Hazel Sch—school ... OR-9
Witch Hill—summit ... MA-1
Witch Hill—summit ... RI-1
Witchhobble Bay—bay ... NY-2
Witchhobble Point—cape ... NY-2
Witch Hole—lake ... OK-5
Witch Hole Pond—lake ... ME-1
Witch Hollow—valley ... KY-4
Witch Hollow—valley ... UT-8
Witchhopple Lake—lake ... NY-2
Witchie Coulee—valley ... MT-8
Witch Island ... NH-1
Witch Island—island ... ME-1
Witch Lake—lake ... MI-6
Witch Lake—locale ... MI-6
Witch Meadow Brook—stream ... CT-1
Witchmere Harbor ... MA-1
Witchopple Mountain ... NY-2
Witch P ... MA-1
Witchpond ... MA-1
Witch Pond—lake (2) ... MA-1
Witch Pond Swamp—swamp ... MA-1
Witch Pool—lake ... AZ-5
Witch Pool (historical)—lake ... AZ-5
Witch Rock—bar ... ME-1
Witch Rocks—cliff ... UT-8
Witchrot Hill ... ME-1
Witchs Head ... PA-2
Witch Spring ... NH-1
Witch Spring—spring ... NM-5
Witch Spring—spring ... SD-7
Witchs Walk—cliff ... NY-2
Witchtrot Hill—summit ... ME-1
Witch Well—well ... NM-5
Witch Well—well ... TX-5
Witch Well Ranch—locale ... AZ-5
Witch Well Trading Post—locale ... AZ-5
Witco—locale ... TX-5
**Witco**—pop pl ... NM-5
Witcox Flat ... UT-8
Wite Fort Cem—cemetery ... UT-8
Witek Junction—locale ... GU-9
Witeside Creek ... MO-7
WITF-FM (Harrisburg)—tower ... PA-2
WITF-TV (Harrisburg)—tower ... PA-2
Witham ... TN-4
Witham, Stuart, House—hist pl ... GA-3
Witham Bog—lake ... ME-1
Witham Brook—stream (3) ... ME-1
Witham Cem—cemetery ... IN-6
Witham Corner—locale ... ME-1
Witham Cotton Mills Village Hist Dist—hist pl ... GA-3
Witham Coulee—valley ... MT-8
Witham Creek—stream ... OR-9
Witham Ditch—canal ... IN-6
W I Thames Junior High School ... MS-4
Witham Hill—summit ... OR-9
Witham Hosp—hospital ... IN-6
Witham Mtn—summit ... ME-1
Witham Pond—lake ... ME-1
Witham Post Office (historical)—building ... TN-4
**Withams**—pop pl ... VA-3
**Withamsville**—pop pl ... OH-6
Withamtown—locale ... TN-4
Withcoate Point ... MD-2
Withe Creek—stream ... IN-6
**Withee**—pop pl ... WI-6
Withee Brook—stream ... ME-1
Withee Pond—lake ... ME-1
**Withee (Town of)**—pop pl ... WI-6
**Witherbee**—pop pl ... NY-2
**Witherbee**—pop pl ... SC-3
Witherby, Constance, Park—hist pl ... RI-1
Wither Ditch—canal ... CO-8
Withered Run—stream ... OH-6
Witherel Hosp—hospital ... CT-1
Witherell Creek—stream ... CA-9
Witherell Island—island ... ME-1
Witherington, Lake—lake ... FL-3
Witherington Cem—cemetery ... AL-4
Witherington Dam—dam ... TN-4
Witherington Lake—reservoir ... TN-4
Witheringtons Pond—reservoir ... AL-4
Witherington Spring—spring ... FL-3
Witherle Ravine—valley ... ME-1
Witherow Dam—dam ... NC-3
Witherow Lake—reservoir ... NC-3
Witherow Ranch—locale ... CA-9
Withers—locale ... GA-3
Withers—locale ... TX-5
Withers—locale ... VA-3
Withers—locale ... WV-2
Withers—other ... KY-4
Withers, Horace, House—hist pl ... KY-4
Withers, M. A., House—hist pl ... TX-5
Withers Bldg—hist pl ... SC-3
Withers Brake—swamp ... MS-4
Withers Brook—stream ... VT-1
Withers Canyon—valley ... CO-8
Withers Cem—cemetery ... AL-4
Withers Cem—cemetery ... KY-4
Withers Cem—cemetery ... TX-5
Withers Ch—church ... MS-4
Withers Chapel—church ... NC-3
Withers-Chapman House—hist pl ... AL-4
Withers Creek ... NC-3
Withers Creek—stream ... OR-9
Withers Creek Access Area—park ... NC-3
Withers Dam—dam ... OR-9
Withers Hollow—valley ... TX-5
Withers House—hist pl ... KY-4
Withers Lake—reservoir ... OR-9
Withers Landing—locale ... AL-4
Withers-Maguire House—hist pl ... FL-3
**Withers Mill**—pop pl ... MO-7
Withers Mills ... MO-7
Witherspoon—locale ... AR-4
Witherspoon, Mount—summit ... AK-9
Witherspoon Bldg—hist pl ... PA-2
Witherspoon Branch—stream ... TX-5
Witherspoon Brook—stream ... NY-2
Witherspoon Cem—cemetery ... AR-4
Witherspoon Cem—cemetery ... KY-4
Witherspoon Creek—stream ... WY-8
**Witherspoon Crossroad**—pop pl ... NC-3
Witherspoon Draw—valley ... TX-5
Witherspoon Elementary School ... MS-4
Witherspoon-Hunter House—hist pl ... SC-3
Witherspoon Island—island ... SC-3
Witherspoon Ridge—ridge ... WY-8
Witherspoon Sch—school ... MS-4
Witherspoon Sch—school ... NJ-2
Witherspoon Sch—school ... SC-3
Witherspoons Spring—spring ... AL-4
Witherspoon Statue—park ... DC-2
Withers Ranch—locale (2) ... NM-5
Withers Sch—school ... MS-4
Withers Sch—school ... SC-3
Withers Spring—spring ... AL-4
Withers Spring Branch—stream ... AL-4
**Withers Subdivision**—pop pl ... TN-4
Withers Swamp—swamp ... SC-3
Withers Swash—beach ... SC-3
Withers Tank—reservoir ... NM-5
Witherup Bridge—hist pl ... PA-2
Withey—locale ... NY-2
Withey, S. B., House—hist pl ... MA-1
Withey Bog—swamp ... ME-1
Withey Brook—stream ... ME-1
Withey Hill—summit ... CT-1
Withey Lake—lake ... MI-6
Withey Sch—school ... MI-6
Withey Wood Canal—stream ... SC-3
Withington, Mount—summit ... NM-5
Withington Basin—basin ... NV-8
Withington Creek—stream ... ID-8
Withington Creek—stream ... NV-8
Withington Estate—hist pl ... NJ-2
Withington House—hist pl ... MO-7
Withington Lake—lake ... MI-6
Withir ... FM-9
Withla—locale ... FL-3
**Withla**—pop pl ... FL-3
Withlacoochee ... FL-3
Withlacoochee Area Vocational-Technical Center—school ... FL-3
Withlacoochee Bay—bay ... FL-3
Withlacoochee Cem—cemetery ... FL-3
Withlacoochee Creek ... FL-3
Withlacoochee Creek ... GA-3
Withlacoochee Reefs—bar ... FL-3
Withlacoochee River—stream (2) ... FL-3
Withlacoochee River—stream ... GA-3
Withlacoochee River Swamp—swamp ... FL-3
Withlacoochee State For—forest ... FL-3
Withro Bottoms—bend ... MT-8
Withrow—locale ... KY-4
**Withrow**—pop pl ... MN-6
**Withrow**—pop pl ... WA-9
Withrow, James, House—hist pl ... WV-2
Withrow Cem—cemetery ... MN-6
Withrow Cem—cemetery ... WV-2
Withrow Creek—stream ... KY-4
Withrow Creek—stream ... NC-3
Withrow Creek—stream ... OR-9
Withrow HS—hist pl ... OH-6
Withrow HS—school ... OH-6
Withrow Lake—lake ... WI-6
Withrow Sch—school ... IL-6
Withrow Sch—school ... MN-6
Withrows Creek ... NC-3
Withrow Spring—spring ... WA-9
Withrow Spring—spring ... WY-8
Withrow Springs—spring ... AR-4
Withrow Springs State Park—park ... AR-4
**Witinski Villa**—pop pl ... PA-2
Witipon ... FM-9
Witipon, Mount ... FM-9
Witipwon—summit ... FM-9
**Witmer**—pop pl ... PA-2
Witmer Dam—dam ... PA-2
Witmer Ditch—canal ... IN-6
Witmer Drain—canal ... MI-6
Witmer Lake—lake ... IN-6
**Witmer Manor**—pop pl ... IN-6
Witmer Park—park ... IA-7
Witmer Run—stream ... PA-2
Witmers Lake—reservoir ... PA-2
Witmers Run—stream ... PA-2
Witmer's Tavern—hist pl ... PA-2
WITN-AM (Washington)—tower ... NC-3
Witners Ranch—locale ... NE-7
Witness Corner Rsvr—reservoir ... WY-8
Witnesses, The—area ... AK-9
Witness Lake—lake ... MN-6
Witness Rock Ridge—ridge ... NC-3
Witness Rocks—area ... AK-9
Witney Gulch—valley ... CO-8
WITN-FM (Washington)—tower ... NC-3
WITN-TV (Washington)—tower ... NC-3
**Witoka**—pop pl ... MN-6
Witoka Cem—cemetery ... MN-6
Witolap ... FM-9
Witon ... FM-9
Witon—summit ... FM-9
Witonap—summit ... FM-9
Wits End—summit ... OR-9
Wits End Ranch—locale ... CO-8
Witsher Creek—stream ... ID-8
Wit-So-Nah-Pah, Lake—lake ... CA-9
Witt—locale ... KY-4
Witt—locale ... NM-5
Witt—locale ... VA-3
**Witt**—pop pl ... IL-6
**Witt**—pop pl ... TN-4
Witt, Michael, Fachwerkbau—hist pl ... NE-7
**Witt Acres**—pop pl ... TN-4
Wittawaket Creek—stream ... CA-9
Witt Branch—stream ... TN-4
Wittbuish Cem—cemetery ... VA-3
Witt Butte—summit ... OR-9
Witt Cem—cemetery ... IA-7
Witt Cem—cemetery (3) ... KY-4
Witt Cem—cemetery ... TN-4
Witt Creek—stream ... AL-4
Witt Creek—stream (2) ... MS-4
Witt Creek—stream ... TN-4
Witt Creek—stream ... VA-3
Wittee Bay—swamp ... SC-3
Wittee Branch—stream ... SC-3
Wittee Island—island ... SC-3
Wittee Lake—lake (2) ... SC-3
Wittee Sch—school ... SC-3
Witte Ford (historical)—locale ... MO-7
Witte Museum—building ... TX-5
Witten ... OH-6
**Witten**—pop pl ... SD-7
Witten, Pat, House—hist pl ... TX-5
Wittenberg ... WI-6
**Wittenberg**—pop pl ... MO-7
**Wittenberg**—pop pl ... NY-2
**Wittenberg**—pop pl ... PA-2
**Wittenberg**—pop pl ... WI-6
Wittenberg, Mount—summit ... CA-9
Wittenberg Brook—stream ... NY-2
Wittenberg Cem—cemetery ... IA-7
Wittenberg Cem—cemetery ... NC-3
Wittenberg Ch—church ... SC-3
Wittenberg Ch—church ... SD-7
Wittenberg Creek—stream ... CA-9
Wittenberg Grange Hall—locale ... IA-7
Wittenberg (historical)—locale ... SD-7
Wittenberg Mtn—summit ... NY-2
Wittenberg Post Office (historical)—building ... PA-2
Wittenberg Post Office (historical)—building ... SD-7
Wittenberg Sch—school ... SD-7
**Wittenberg (Town of)**—pop pl ... WI-6
**Wittenberg Township**—pop pl ... SD-7
Wittenberg (Township of)—fmr MCD ... NC-3
Wittenberg Univ—school ... OH-6
Wittenbert, Dane, House—hist pl ... TX-5
Wittenbery Rock ... MO-7
Wittenburg ... MO-7
Wittenburg ... PA-2
Wittenburg ... WI-6
**Wittenburg**—pop pl ... NY-2
Wittenburg Draw—valley ... ID-8
Wittenburg Draw—valley ... TX-5
Wittenburg Sch—school ... NC-3
Witten Cem—cemetery ... OH-6
Witten Cem—cemetery ... VA-3
Witten Cem—cemetery ... WV-2
Witten Dam ... SD-7
Witten Dam Rsvr—reservoir ... SD-7
Witten Fork—stream ... OH-6
Wittenmeyer Lake ... WA-9
Witten Run—stream ... OH-6
Wittens—locale ... OH-6
Wittens Fort—locale ... VA-3
Wittens Mills—locale ... VA-3
Wittensville—locale ... KY-4
Witten Towhead—island ... WV-2
**Witten Township**—pop pl ... SD-7
Witten Valley—valley ... VA-3
Witter—locale ... AR-4
Witte Ranch—locale ... NM-5
Witter Creek—stream ... ID-8
Witter Elem Sch—school ... FL-3
Witter Gulch—valley ... CO-8
Witter Hill—summit ... NY-7
Witter House—hist pl ... CT-1
Witter Lake ... SC-3
Witter Lake ... WI-6
Witter Peak—summit ... CO-8
Witter Point—summit ... ID-8
Witter Ridge—ridge ... ID-8
Witter Ridge Campsite—locale ... ID-8
Witter Sch—school ... CA-9
Witters Lake—lake ... WI-6
**Witter Springs**—pop pl ... CA-9
Witter Springs—spring ... CA-9
Witter Springs Post Office—locale ... CA-9
wittes Lake ... SC-3
Witte Tank—reservoir ... NM-5
Witteville—locale ... OK-5
Witt Flowage—reservoir ... WI-6
Witt Hill—summit ... ME-1
Witt Hollow—valley (2) ... TN-4
Wittich (Township of)—fmr MCD ... AR-4
Wittie Lake ... SC-3
Wittigton ... IN-6
**Witting**—pop pl ... TX-5
Wittington ... IN-6
Wittington Cem—cemetery ... MS-4
Wittington Creek—stream ... TX-5
Wittis Creek—stream ... MS-4
Wittkop Drain—stream ... MI-6
Wittkop Park—park ... FL-3
Witt Lake ... UT-8
Witt Lake Dam ... UT-8
Wittle Cem—cemetery ... IN-6
Wittling Swamp—swamp ... NY-2
Wittman ... AZ-5
**Wittman**—pop pl ... MD-2
Wittman Cem—cemetery ... IL-6
Wittman Field (Airport)—airport ... WI-6
**Wittmann**—pop pl ... AZ-5
Wittman Sch—school ... MD-2
Wittmayer, Peter, House-Barn—hist pl ... SD-7
Wittmayer Ranch—locale ... MT-8
**Wittmer**—pop pl ... PA-2
Wittmer, Charles, House—hist pl ... TX-5
Wittmer Cem—cemetery ... IL-6

Wittmer Number One Ditch—*canal* ... IN-6
Wittmer Number Two Ditch—*canal* ... IN-6
Wittombona Peak—*summit* ... WY-8
Wittona, Lake—*reservoir* ... MO-7
Witt Park—*flat* ... NM-5
Witt Ranch—*locale* ... MT-8
Wittrup (historical)—*locale* ... KS-7
*Witts* ... TN-4
**Witts**—*pop pl* ... IN-6
*Witts Branch* ... MS-4
**Wittsburg**—*pop pl* ... AR-4
Wittsburg Island—*flat* ... AR-4
Wittsburg Lake—*lake* ... AR-4
Witts Cem—*cemetery* ... MO-7
Witt Sch—*school* ... MO-7
Witt Sch—*school* ... TN-4
Witt Sch (abandoned)—*school* ... PA-2
*Witts Foundry* ... TN-4
Witts Foundry Post Office (historical)—*building* ... TN-4
Witt Site—*hist pl* ... CA-9
Witts Lake—*reservoir* ... UT-8
Witts Lake Dam—*dam* ... UT-8
Witts Ledge—*beach* ... MA-1
Wittson Bridge—*bridge* ... AL-4
Witts Pond—*lake* ... MA-1
Witts Pond (historical)—*lake* ... TN-4
Witt Spring—*spring* ... TN-4
*Witt Springs* ... AR-4
Witt Springs—*locale* ... KY-4
Witt Springs Sch—*school* ... KY-4
Witts Run—*stream* ... IN-6
Witts Sch (historical)—*school* ... MS-4
**Witts Springs**—*pop pl* ... AR-4
**Witts Station**—*pop pl* ... IN-6
Wittstruck Creek—*stream* ... NE-7
*Wittsville Post Office* ... TN-4
Witt Swamp—*swamp* ... ME-1
**Witt (Township of)**—*pop pl* ... IL-6
Wittwer, Dr. William Frederick, House—*hist pl* ... NM-5
Wittwer Canyon—*valley* ... UT-8
Wittwer Hill—*summit* ... UT-8
Wittwer Lateral—*canal* ... NM-5
Witty Branch—*stream* ... AL-4
Witty Cem—*cemetery* ... AL-4
Witty Creek—*stream* ... AL-4
Witty Creek—*stream* ... TN-4
Witty Hollow—*valley* ... TN-4
Wittys Crossroads—*locale* ... NC-3
Witty Tom Tank—*reservoir* ... AZ-5
*Witumka* ... AL-4
*Witumpka* ... AL-4
Witun—*summit* ... FM-9
Witunukis—*gap* ... FM-9
Witunumo—*summit* ... FM-9
Witwell Park—*park* ... OH-6
**Witwen**—*pop pl* ... WI-6
*Witynokis* ... FM-9
WITZ-AM (Jasper)—*tower* ... IN-6
Witzel, Robert, House—*hist pl* ... OR-9
Witzel Ranch—*locale* ... OR-9
Witzel Rsvr—*reservoir* ... OR-9
Witzel Spring—*spring* ... OR-9
Witzel Well—*well* ... OR-9
WITZ-FM (Jasper)—*tower* ... IN-6
Witzgall Ditch—*canal* ... IN-6
WIUP-FM (Indiana)—*tower* ... PA-2
Wives of Charles C. Rich Hist Dist—*hist pl* ... ID-8
**Wiville**—*pop pl* ... AR-4
WIVK-AM (Knoxville)—*tower* ... TN-4
WIVK-FM (Knoxville)—*tower* ... TN-4
W I Walker Dam—*dam* ... AL-4
Wiwi Bay—*swamp* ... MN-6
*Wiwi Lake* ... MN-6
*Wiwoka* ... AL-4
*Wiwoka River* ... CT-1
Wix Branch—*stream* ... TN-4
WIXC-AM (Fayetteville)—*tower* ... TN-4
WIXE-AM (Monroe)—*tower* ... NC-3
*Wixerboxet Pond* ... RI-1
WIXO-AM (Mobile)—*tower* ... AL-4
**Wixom**—*pop pl* ... MI-6
Wixom Cem—*cemetery* ... MI-6
Wixom Drain—*canal* ... CA-9
Wixom Lake—*reservoir* ... MI-6
Wixon Cem—*cemetery* ... TX-5
Wixon Drain—*stream* ... MI-6
*Wixon Lake* ... MI-6
Wixon MS—*school* ... MA-1
Wixon Pond—*lake* ... NY-2
Wixon Sch—*school* ... MA-1
Wixon Slough—*stream* ... MS-4
WIXQ-FM (Millersville)—*tower* ... PA-2
Wixson Cem—*cemetery* ... MI-6
Wixson Divide—*gap* ... CO-8
Wixson Mtn—*summit* ... CO-8
Wixted Airp—*airport* ... MO-7
**Wixtown**—*pop pl* ... TN-4
WIXZ-AM (Mckeesport)—*tower* (2) ... PA-2
**Wiya**—*pop pl* ... FM-9
Wiyapka Lake—*lake* ... MN-6
*Wiyapko Lake* ... MN-6
*Wiyarka Lake* ... MN-6
*Wiyeast Basin* ... OR-9
Wiyef—*cape* ... FM-9
Wiyef—*summit* ... FM-9
Wiygul Cem—*cemetery* ... MS-4
*Wiyot* ... CA-9
WIYQ-FM (Ebensburg)—*tower* ... PA-2
Wiyu—*locale* ... FM-9
Wiyu, Infal—*stream* ... FM-9
Wizard Creek—*stream* ... OR-9
Wizard Falls—*falls* ... OR-9
Wizard Falls Campground—*park* ... OR-9
Wizard Gulch—*valley* ... CA-9
Wizard Island—*island* ... OR-9
Wizardism Run—*stream* ... WV-2
*Wizard Lake* ... OR-9
Wizard Pond—*lake* ... ME-1
Wizards Beach—*beach* ... NV-8
Wizards Cove—*bay* ... NV-8
Wizard's Roost—*hist pl* ... NM-5
**Wizard Wells**—*pop pl* ... TX-5
Wizard Wells Cem—*cemetery* ... TX-5
WIZO-AM (Franklin)—*tower* (2) ... TN-4
WIZS-AM (Henderson)—*tower* ... NC-3
*Wizsinski Coulee* ... MT-8
Wizzard Falls Spring—*spring* ... OR-9
Wizzard Lake—*lake* ... OR-9
WJAC-AM (Johnstown)—*tower* ... PA-2
WJAC-FM (Johnstown)—*tower* ... PA-2
W. Jacob Burrus House—*hist pl* ... GA-3
WJAC-TV (Johnstown)—*tower* ... PA-2
WJAK-AM (Jackson)—*tower* ... TN-4
WJAM-AM (Marion)—*tower* ... AL-4
WJAR-TV (Providence)—*tower* ... RI-1
WJAS-AM (Pittsburgh)—*tower* ... PA-2
W J Asmussen Dam—*dam* ... SD-7
WJBB-AM (Haleyville)—*tower* ... AL-4
WJBB-FM (Haleyville)—*tower* ... AL-4
WJBI-FM (Clarksdale)—*tower* ... MS-4
WJBR-AM (Wilmington)—*tower* ... DE-2
WJBR-FM (Wilmington)—*tower* ... DE-2
WJCD-AM (Seymour)—*tower* ... IN-6
WJCD-FM (Seymour)—*tower* ... IN-6
WJCK-FM (Rensselaer)—*tower* ... IN-6
WJCR-FM (Washington)—*tower* ... PA-2
WJCW-AM (Johnson City)—*tower* ... TN-4
WJDB-AM (Thomasville)—*tower* ... AL-4
WJDB-FM (Thomasville)—*tower* ... AL-4
WJD Ditch—*canal* ... WY-8
WJDQ-AM (Marion)—*tower* ... MS-4
WJDQ-AM (Meridian)—*tower* ... MS-4
WJDQ-FM (Meridian)—*tower* ... MS-4
WJDR-FM (Prentiss)—*tower* ... MS-4
WJDW-AM (Corydon)—*tower* ... IN-6
WJDX-AM (Jackson)—*tower* ... MS-4
WJED-AM (Somerville)—*tower* ... TN-4
WJEF-FM (Lafayette)—*tower* ... IN-6
WJEL-FM (Indianapolis)—*tower* ... IN-6
W J Ellis Dam—*dam* ... AL-4
W J Ellis Lake—*reservoir* ... AL-4
WJET-AM (Erie)—*tower* ... PA-2
WJET-TV (Erie)—*tower* ... PA-2
WJFC-AM (Jefferson City)—*tower* ... TN-4
WJFL-AM (Vicksburg)—*tower* ... MS-4
W J Four Lateral—*canal* ... TX-5
W J Gooding Bridge—*bridge* ... SC-3
W J Hale Sch—*school* ... TN-4
WJHD-FM (Portsmouth)—*tower* ... RI-1
WJHL-TV (Johnson City)—*tower* ... TN-4
WJHO-AM (Opelika)—*tower* ... AL-4
WJHR-FM (Jackson)—*tower* ... TN-4
WJIK-AM (Camp Lejeune)—*tower* (2) ... NC-3
WJJM-AM (Lewisburg)—*tower* ... TN-4
WJJM-FM (Lewisburg)—*tower* ... TN-4
W J Johnson Ranch—*locale* ... SD-7
*W J Jones High School* ... AL-4
WJJT-AM (Jellico)—*tower* ... TN-4
WJKA-TV (Wilmington)—*tower* ... NC-3
WJKM-AM (Hartsville)—*tower* ... TN-4
WJKX-AM (Moss Point)—*tower* ... MS-4
WJKZ-FM (Franklin)—*tower* (2) ... TN-4
W J Lateral—*canal* ... TX-5
WJLD-AM (Fairfield)—*tower* ... AL-4
WJLE-AM (Smithville)—*tower* ... TN-4
WJLE-FM (Smithville)—*tower* ... TN-4
W J Linn Lake Dam—*dam* ... MS-4
WJMB-AM (Brookhaven)—*tower* ... MS-4
WJMF-FM (Smithfield)—*tower* ... RI-1
WJMG-FM (Hattiesburg)—*tower* ... MS-4
WJMI-FM (Jackson)—*tower* ... MS-4
W J Morris Pond Dam—*dam* ... MS-4
W J Murphy Park—*park* ... AZ-5
WJMW-AM (Athens)—*tower* ... AL-4
WJNC-AM (Jacksonville)—*tower* ... NC-3
WJNL-AM (Johnstown)—*tower* ... PA-2
WJNL-FM (Johnstown)—*tower* ... PA-2
WJNL-TV (Johnstown)—*tower* (2) ... PA-2
WJNS-FM (Yazoo City)—*tower* ... MS-4
WJNZ-FM (Greencastle)—*tower* ... IN-6
WJOB-AM (Hammond)—*tower* ... IN-6
WJOJ-FM (Picayune)—*tower* ... MS-4
W Jordan Dam—*dam* ... SD-7
WJOZ-AM (Troy)—*tower* ... PA-2
WJPA-AM (Washington)—*tower* ... PA-2
WJPJ-AM (Huntingdon)—*tower* ... TN-4
WJQI-AM (New Bern)—*tower* ... NC-3
WJQS-AM (Jackson)—*tower* ... MS-4
WJQY-FM (Chickasaw)—*tower* ... AL-4
WJRD-AM (Tuscaloosa)—*tower* ... AL-4
WJRH-FM (Easton)—*tower* ... PA-2
WJRI-AM (Lenoir)—*tower* ... NC-3
WJRL-AM (Calhoun City)—*tower* ... MS-4
WJRM-AM (Troy)—*tower* ... NC-3
WJSA-AM (Jersey Shore)—*tower* ... PA-2
WJSK-FM (Lumberton)—*tower* ... NC-3
WJSM-AM (Martinsburg)—*tower* ... PA-2
WJSM-FM (Martinsburg)—*tower* ... PA-2
WJSO-AM (Jonesboro)—*tower* ... TN-4
W J Sorrell Dam—*dam* ... AL-4
WJSQ-FM (Athens)—*tower* ... TN-4
WJSR-FM (Birmingham)—*tower* ... AL-4
WJSU-FM (Jackson)—*tower* ... MS-4
W J Sumrall Lake Dam—*dam* ... MS-4
WJTM-TV (Winston-Salem)—*tower* ... NC-3
WJTP-AM (Newland)—*tower* ... NC-3
WJTT-FM (Red Bank)—*tower* ... TN-4
WJTV-TV (Jackson)—*tower* ... MS-4
WJUN-AM (Mexico)—*tower* ... PA-2
WJWF-FM (Columbus)—*tower* ... MS-4
WJWL-AM (Georgetown)—*tower* ... DE-2
WJXL-AM (Jacksonville)—*tower* ... AL-4
WJXN-AM (Jackson)—*tower* ... MS-4
WJYN-FM (Nashville)—*tower* (2) ... TN-4
WJYV-AM (Forest)—*tower* ... MS-4
WJZM-AM (Clarksville)—*tower* ... TN-4
WJZR-FM (Kannapolis)—*tower* ... NC-3
WKAB-TV (Montgomery)—*tower* ... AL-4
WKAC-AM (Athens)—*tower* ... AL-4
WKAD-FM (Canton)—*tower* ... PA-2
*Wkahigua* ... FL-3
WKAM-AM (Goshen)—*tower* ... IN-6
WKAP-AM (Allentown)—*tower* ... PA-2
WKAX-AM (Russellville)—*tower* ... AL-4
WKBB-FM (West Point)—*tower* ... MS-4
WKBC-AM (North Wilkesboro)—*tower* ... NC-3
WKBC-FM (North Wilkesboro)—*tower* ... NC-3
WKBI-AM (Saint Marys)—*tower* ... PA-2
WKBI-FM (Ridgeway)—*tower* ... PA-2
WKBJ-AM (Milan)—*tower* ... TN-4
WKBJ-FM (Milan)—*tower* ... TN-4
WKBL-AM (Covington)—*tower* ... TN-4
WKBL-FM (Covington)—*tower* ... TN-4
WKBO-AM (Harrisburg)—*tower* ... PA-2
WKBQ-AM (Garner)—*tower* ... NC-3
WKBV-AM (Richmond)—*tower* ... IN-6
WKCD-FM (Mechanicsburg)—*tower* (2) ... PA-2
WKCE-AM (Harriman)—*tower* ... TN-4
WKCS-FM (Knoxville)—*tower* ... TN-4
WKDA-AM (Nashville)—*tower* ... TN-4
WKDF-FM (Nashville)—*tower* (2) ... TN-4
WKDU-FM (Philadelphia)—*tower* ... PA-2
WKDX-AM (Hamlet)—*tower* ... NC-3
WKEA-AM (Scottsboro)—*tower* ... AL-4
WKEA-FM (Scottsboro)—*tower* (2) ... AL-4
WKEG-AM (Washington)—*tower* ... PA-2
WKEN-AM (Dover)—*tower* ... DE-2
W Kerr Scott Dam—*dam* ... NC-3
W Kerr Scott Rsvr—*reservoir* ... NC-3
WKEW-AM (Greensboro)—*tower* ... NC-3
WKFT-TV (Fayetteville)—*tower* ... NC-3
WKFX-AM (Gadsden)—*tower* ... AL-4
WKFX-AM (Rainbow City)—*tower* ... AL-4
WKGN-AM (Knoxville)—*tower* ... TN-4
WKGX-AM (Lenoir)—*tower* ... NC-3
W K Hill—*summit* ... CA-9
WKIN-AM (Kingsport)—*tower* (2) ... TN-4
WKIR-FM (Jackson)—*tower* ... TN-4
WKIT-FM (Hendersonville)—*tower* ... NC-3
WKIX-AM (Raleigh)—*tower* (2) ... NC-3
WKJA-FM (Belhaven)—*tower* ... NC-3
WKJG-TV (Fort Wayne)—*tower* ... IN-6
WKJK-AM (Granite Falls)—*tower* ... NC-3
WKJS-FM (Harriman)—*tower* ... TN-4
WKKE-AM (Pearl)—*tower* (2) ... MS-4
W. K. Kellogg Regional Airp—*airport* ... MI-6
WKKR-AM (Evansville)—*tower* ... IN-6
WKKX-AM (Paoli)—*tower* ... IN-6
WKKY-FM (Moss Point)—*tower* ... MS-4
WKLD-FM (Oneonta)—*tower* ... AL-4
WKLF-AM (Clanton)—*tower* ... AL-4
WKLM-AM (Leland)—*tower* ... NC-3
WKLM-AM (Wilmington)—*tower* ... NC-3
WKLN-FM (Cullman)—*tower* ... AL-4
WKLX-FM (Plymouth)—*tower* ... NC-3
WKMC-AM (Roaring Spring)—*tower* ... PA-2
WKMT-AM (Kings Mountain)—*tower* ... NC-3
WKMX-FM (Enterprise)—*tower* ... AL-4
WKNC-FM (Raleigh)—*tower* ... NC-3
WKNO-FM (Memphis)—*tower* ... TN-4
WKNO-TV (Memphis)—*tower* ... TN-4
W Knox Dam—*dam* ... SD-7
WKNS-FM (Kinston)—*tower* ... NC-3
WKNU-FM (Brewton)—*tower* ... AL-4
WKNZ-FM (Collins)—*tower* ... MS-4
WKOE-AM (Dayton)—*tower* ... TN-4
WKOI-TV (Richmond)—*tower* ... IN-6
WKOK-AM (Sunbury)—*tower* ... PA-2
WKOM-FM (Columbia)—*tower* ... TN-4
WKOR-AM (Starkville)—*tower* ... MS-4
WKOR-FM (Starkville)—*tower* ... MS-4
WKOS-FM (Murfreesboro)—*tower* ... TN-4
WKOZ-AM (Kosciusko)—*tower* ... MS-4
WKOZ-FM (Kosciusko)—*tower* ... MS-4
WKPA-AM (New Kensington)—*tower* ... PA-2
WKPG-AM (Port Gibson)—*tower* ... MS-4
WKPO-AM (Prentiss)—*tower* ... MS-4
WKPT-AM (Kingsport)—*tower* ... TN-4
WKPT-TV (Kingsport)—*tower* ... TN-4
WKQK-FM (Eufaula)—*tower* ... AL-4
WKRA-AM (Holly Springs)—*tower* ... MS-4
WKRA-FM (Holly Springs)—*tower* ... MS-4
WKRG-AM (Mobile)—*tower* ... AL-4
WKRG-FM (Mobile)—*tower* ... AL-4
WKRG-TV (Mobile)—*tower* ... AL-4
WKRI-AM (West Warwick)—*tower* ... RI-1
WKRK-AM (Murphy)—*tower* ... NC-3
WKRM-AM (Columbia)—*tower* ... TN-4
WKRX-FM (Roxboro)—*tower* ... NC-3
WKRZ-AM (Wilkes-Barre)—*tower* ... PA-2
WKRZ-FM (Wilkes-Barre)—*tower* ... PA-2
WKSB-FM (Williamsport)—*tower* ... PA-2
WKSJ-FM (Mobile)—*tower* ... AL-4
WKSK-AM (West Jefferson)—*tower* ... NC-3
WKSL-FM (Greencastle-West)—*tower* ... PA-2
WKSM-FM (Tabor City)—*tower* ... NC-3
WKSR-AM (Pulaski)—*tower* ... TN-4
WKST-AM (New Castle)—*tower* ... PA-2
WKSY-FM (Columbia City)—*tower* ... IN-6
WKSZ-FM (Media)—*tower* ... PA-2
WKTA-FM (McKenzie)—*tower* ... TN-4
WKTC-FM (Tarboro)—*tower* ... NC-3
WKTE-AM (King)—*tower* ... NC-3
WKUZ-FM (Wabash)—*tower* ... IN-6
WKVA-AM (Lewistown)—*tower* ... PA-2
WKVI-AM (Knox)—*tower* ... IN-6
WKVL-AM (Clarksville)—*tower* ... TN-4
WKVR-FM (Huntingdon)—*tower* ... PA-2
W-K-W County Park—*park* ... IA-7
W K Wilson Lake—*reservoir* ... AL-4
W K Wilson Lake Dam—*dam* ... AL-4
WKWL-AM (Florala)—*tower* ... AL-4
WKWR-TV (Cookeville)—*tower* ... TN-4
WKWX-FM (Savannah)—*tower* ... TN-4
WKXI-AM (Jackson)—*tower* ... MS-4
WKXN-FM (Greenville)—*tower* ... AL-4
WKXQ-AM (Reidsville)—*tower* ... NC-3
WKXV-AM (Knoxville)—*tower* ... TN-4
WKXX-FM (Birmingham)—*tower* ... AL-4
WKYD-AM (Andalusia)—*tower* ... AL-4
WKYD-FM (Andalusia)—*tower* ... AL-4
WKYK-AM (Burnsville)—*tower* ... NC-3
WKYV-FM (Vicksburg)—*tower* (2) ... MS-4
WKZA-AM (Kane)—*tower* ... PA-2
WKZB-FM (Drew)—*tower* ... MS-4
WKZL-FM (Winston-Salem)—*tower* ... NC-3
WLAC-AM (Nashville)—*tower* ... TN-4
*Wladiminif Lake* ... MN-6
WLAF-AM (La Follette)—*tower* ... TN-4
W Lake—*lake* ... CA-9
WLAN-AM (Lancaster)—*tower* ... PA-2
WLAN-FM (Lancaster)—*tower* (2) ... PA-2
WLAR-AM (Athens)—*tower* ... TN-4
WLAS-AM (Jacksonville)—*tower* ... NC-3
W Lassey Ranch—*locale* ... ND-7
W Lateral—*canal* ... CA-9
WLAU-AM (Laurel)—*tower* ... MS-4
WLAY-AM (Muscle Shoals)—*tower* ... AL-4
WLAY-FM (Muscle Shoals)—*tower* ... AL-4
W L Baker Ditch—*canal* ... KY-4
WLBC-AM (Muncie)—*tower* ... IN-6
WLBC-FM (Muncie)—*tower* ... IN-6
WLBM-TV (Meridian)—*tower* ... MS-4
WLBR-AM (Lebanon)—*tower* ... PA-2
WLBT-TV (Jackson)—*tower* ... MS-4
W L Butte—*summit* ... MT-8
WLCF-FM (Southport)—*tower* ... NC-3
W L Childress Lake Dam—*dam* ... MS-4
W L Crawford Ranch—*locale* ... CA-9
W L Creek—*stream* ... MT-8
WLCY-FM (Cleveland)—*tower* ... TN-4
W L Draw—*valley* ... MT-8
W. & L. E. Gurley Bldg—*hist pl* ... NY-2
WLEM-AM (Emporium)—*tower* ... PA-2
WLER-FM (Butler)—*tower* ... PA-2
WLEV-FM (Easton)—*tower* ... PA-2
W Lewis Ranch—*locale* ... ND-7
WLFI-TV (Lafayette)—*tower* ... IN-6
WLFL-TV (Raleigh)—*tower* ... NC-3
WLFQ-FM (Crawfordsville)—*tower* ... IN-6
W L Golden Dam—*dam* ... AL-4
*W L Golden Lake* ... AL-4
WLHI-FM (Fort Wayne)—*tower* ... IN-6
WLHN-FM (Anderson)—*tower* ... IN-6
WLHQ-FM (Enterprise)—*tower* ... AL-4
WLHT-TV (Hattiesburg)—*tower* ... MS-4
WLIC-AM (Adamsville)—*tower* (2) ... TN-4
WLIJ-AM (Shelbyville)—*tower* ... TN-4
WLIK-AM (Newport)—*tower* ... TN-4
WLIL-AM (Lenoir City)—*tower* ... TN-4
WLIL-FM (Lenoir City)—*tower* ... TN-4
WLIN-FM (Jackson)—*tower* ... MS-4
*Wlitonnap* ... FM-9
WLIU-FM (Lincoln University)—*tower* ... PA-2
WLIV-AM (Livingston)—*tower* ... TN-4
W L Johns Sch—*school* ... MO-7
WLJS-FM (Jacksonville)—*tower* ... AL-4
WLJT-TV (Lexington)—*tower* ... TN-4
WLKK-AM (Erie)—*tower* ... PA-2
WLKW-AM (Providence)—*tower* ... RI-1
WLKW-FM (Providence)—*tower* ... RI-1
WLLE-AM (Raleigh)—*tower* ... NC-3
WLLF-AM (Prichard)—*tower* ... AL-4
Wlliam T Malloy Dam—*dam* ... SD-7
WLLN-AM (Lillington)—*tower* ... NC-3
WLLY-AM (Wilson)—*tower* (2) ... NC-3
*W L Manning Elementary School* ... NC-3
WLNC-AM (Laurinburg)—*tower* (2) ... NC-3
WLNK-FM (Columbus)—*tower* ... MS-4
WLNT-AM (Loudon)—*tower* ... TN-4
WLOI-AM (La Porte)—*tower* ... IN-6
WLOK-AM (Memphis)—*tower* (2) ... TN-4
WLON-AM (Lincolnton)—*tower* ... NC-3
WLOS-FM (Asheville)—*tower* ... NC-3
WLOS-TV (Asheville)—*tower* ... NC-3
WLOX-AM (Biloxi)—*tower* ... MS-4
WLOX-TV (Biloxi)—*tower* ... MS-4
WLPA-AM (Lancaster)—*tower* ... PA-2
WLPH-AM (Irondale)—*tower* ... AL-4
WLPR-FM (Mobile)—*tower* ... AL-4
WLRH-FM (Huntsville)—*tower* ... AL-4
WLSB-AM (Copperhill)—*tower* ... TN-4
WLSE-AM (Wallace)—*tower* ... NC-3
WLSH-AM (Lansford)—*tower* ... PA-2
WLSM-AM (Louisville)—*tower* ... MS-4
WLSM-FM (Louisville)—*tower* ... MS-4
W L Smith Ditch—*canal* ... WY-8
*W L Smith Elementary School* ... MS-4
WLSP-FM (Carbondale)—*tower* ... PA-2
WLSQ-AM (Montgomery)—*tower* (2) ... AL-4
WLSW-FM (Scottdale)—*tower* ... PA-2
WLTC-AM (Gastonia)—*tower* ... NC-3
WLTD-FM (Lexington)—*tower* ... MS-4
WLTH-AM (Gary)—*tower* ... IN-6
WLTM-AM (Franklin)—*tower* ... NC-3
WLTY-FM (Norfolk)—*tower* ... VA-3
WLUY-AM (Nashville)—*tower* ... TN-4
WLVN-AM (Luverne)—*tower* ... AL-4
WLVR-FM (Bethlehem)—*tower* ... PA-2
WLVS-FM (Germantown)—*tower* ... TN-4
WLVT-TV (Allentown)—*tower* ... PA-2
WLVU-FM (Erie)—*tower* ... PA-2
WLVV-FM (Statesville)—*tower* ... NC-3
WLWI-FM (Montgomery)—*tower* ... AL-4
Wl Williams Ranch—*locale* ... NM-5
WLWL-AM (Rockingham)—*tower* ... NC-3
WLXI-TV (Greensboro)—*tower* (2) ... NC-3
WLXN-FM (Lexington)—*tower* ... NC-3
WLYC-AM (Williamsport)—*tower* (2) ... PA-2
WLYH-TV (Lancaster)—*tower* ... PA-2
WLYX-FM (Memphis)—*tower* ... TN-4
WLZN-FM (Hazleton)—*tower* ... PA-2
WMAA-TV (Jackson)—*tower* ... MS-4
WMAB-TV (State College)—*tower* ... MS-4
W Madison Ranch (historical)—*locale* ... SD-7
WMAE-TV (Booneville)—*tower* ... MS-4
WMAG-FM (High Point)—*tower* (2) ... NC-3
WMAH-TV (Biloxi)—*tower* ... MS-4
WMAJ-AM (State College)—*tower* ... PA-2
WMAK-FM (Hendersonville)—*tower* ... TN-4
W Mann Number 1 Dam—*dam* ... SD-7
W Mann Number 2 Dam—*dam* ... SD-7
W Mann Number 3 Dam—*dam* ... SD-7
WMAO-TV (Greenwood)—*tower* ... MS-4
WMAP-AM (Monroe)—*tower* ... NC-3
W Marshall Ranch—*locale* ... NE-7
WMAU-TV (Bude)—*tower* ... MS-4
WMAV-TV (Oxford)—*tower* ... MS-4
WMAW-TV (Meridian)—*tower* ... MS-4
WMBA-AM (Ambridge)—*tower* ... PA-2
WMBC-AM (Columbus)—*tower* ... MS-4
WMBH-AM (Joplin)—*tower* ... MO-7
WMBJ-FM (Morehead City)—*tower* ... NC-3
WMBL-AM (Morehead City)—*tower* ... NC-3
WMBS-AM (Uniontown)—*tower* ... PA-2
WMBT-AM (Shenandoah)—*tower* ... PA-2
WMC-AM (Memphis)—*tower* ... TN-4
WMCC-FM (Etowah)—*tower* ... TN-4
WMCF-FM (Memphis)—*tower* ... TN-4
WMCF-TV (Montgomery)—*tower* ... AL-4
WMCH-AM (Church Hill)—*tower* ... TN-4
WMCP-AM (Columbia)—*tower* ... TN-4
WMCT-AM (Mountain City)—*tower* ... TN-4
WMCT-TV (Memphis)—*tower* ... TN-4
WMDC-FM (Hazlehurst)—*tower* (2) ... MS-4
WMDH-FM (New Castle)—*tower* ... IN-6
WMEE-FM (Fort Wayne)—*tower* ... IN-6
WMFC-AM (Monroeville)—*tower* ... AL-4
WMFC-FM (Monroeville)—*tower* ... AL-4
WMFD-AM (Wilmington)—*tower* ... NC-3
WMFR-AM (High Point)—*tower* ... NC-3
WMGK-FM (Philadelphia)—*tower* ... PA-2
WMGL-FM (Pulaski)—*tower* ... TN-4
WMGO-AM (Canton)—*tower* ... MS-4
WMGW-AM (Meadville)—*tower* ... PA-2
WMGW (Radio Tower)—*tower* ... PA-2
WMGY-AM (Montgomery)—*tower* ... AL-4
WMGZ-FM (Sharpsville)—*tower* ... PA-2
WMHD-FM (Terre Haute)—*tower* ... IN-6
*W Mills* ... ME-1
WMIM-AM (Mt. Carmel)—*tower* ... PA-2
WMIS-AM (Natchez)—*tower* ... MS-4
WMIT-FM (Black Mountain)—*tower* ... NC-3
WMJT-AM (Mount Juliet)—*tower* ... TN-4
WMJW-FM (Nanticoke)—*tower* ... PA-2
WMKW-TV (Memphis)—*tower* ... TN-4
WMKX-FM (Brookville)—*tower* (2) ... PA-2
WMLC-AM (Monticello)—*tower* ... MS-4
W M Leek Breaker—*building* ... PA-2
W M Lott Pond Dam—*dam* ... MS-4
WMLP-AM (Milton)—*tower* ... PA-2
WMLR-AM (Hohenwald)—*tower* ... TN-4
WMLS-FM (Sylacauga)—*tower* ... AL-4
**Wm Lunds Lynne Addition (subdivision)**—*pop pl* ... UT-8
WMMH-AM (Marshall)—*tower* ... NC-3
W & M Mine—*mine* ... CO-8
WMMR-FM (Philadelphia)—*tower* ... PA-2
WMNC-AM (Morganton)—*tower* ... NC-3
WMOB-AM (Chickasaw)—*tower* ... AL-4
WMOC-AM (Chattanooga)—*tower* ... TN-4
WMOO-AM (Fairhope)—*tower* ... AL-4
WMOO-AM (Mobile)—*tower* ... AL-4
WMOT-FM (Murfreesboro)—*tower* ... TN-4
WMOX-AM (Meridian)—*tower* ... MS-4
WMOZ-AM (Mobile)—*tower* (2) ... AL-4
WMPA-AM (Aberdeen)—*tower* ... MS-4
WMPH-FM (Wilmington)—*tower* ... DE-2
WMPI-FM (Scottsburg)—*tower* ... IN-6
WMPM-AM (Smithfield)—*tower* ... NC-3
WMPR-FM (Jackson)—*tower* ... MS-4
WMPS-AM (Memphis)—*tower* ... TN-4
WMPT-AM (South Williamsport)—*tower* ... PA-2
WMPT-FM (South Williamsport)—*tower* ... PA-2
WMPV-TV (Mobile)—*tower* ... AL-4
WMQM-AM (Memphis)—*tower* ... TN-4
WMRF-AM (Lewistown)—*tower* ... PA-2
WMRF Holes—*cave* ... PA-2
WMRI-FM (Marion)—*tower* ... IN-6
WMRK-AM (Selma)—*tower* ... AL-4
WMRL-AM (Portland)—*tower* ... TN-4
WMRQ-FM (Brookhaven)—*tower* ... MS-4
W M Russell Junior Dam—*dam* ... AL-4
WMSB-FM (Mississippi State)—*tower* ... MS-4
WMSI-FM (Jackson)—*tower* ... MS-4
WMSL-AM (Decatur)—*tower* ... AL-4
WMSO-AM (Collierville)—*tower* (2) ... TN-4
WMSP-FM (Harrisburg)—*tower* ... PA-2
WMSQ-FM (Havelock)—*tower* ... NC-3
WMSR-AM (Manchester)—*tower* ... TN-4
WMSR-FM (Manchester)—*tower* ... TN-4
WMSS-FM (Middletown)—*tower* ... PA-2
WMSU-FM (Hattiesburg)—*tower* ... MS-4
W m Taft JHS—*school* ... NM-5
WMT-FM (Cedar Rapids)—*tower* ... IA-7
W Mtn—*summit* ... AZ-5
W Mtn—*summit* ... CO-8
W Mtn—*summit* ... NY-2
WMTN-AM (Morristown)—*tower* ... TN-4
WMTS-AM (Murfreesboro)—*tower* ... TN-4
WMUF-AM (Paris)—*tower* ... TN-4
WMUH-FM (Allentown)—*tower* ... PA-2
WMUW-FM (Columbus)—*tower* ... MS-4
W M Wilkinson Dam—*dam* ... NC-3
Wm W Powers Conservation Area—*park* ... IL-6
WMYD-AM (Wickford)—*tower* ... RI-1
W Myers Ranch—*locale* ... ND-7
WMYN-AM (Mayodan)—*tower* ... NC-3
WMYQ-AM (Newton)—*tower* ... MS-4
WMYQ-FM (Newton)—*tower* ... MS-4
WMYU-FM (Sevierville)—*tower* ... TN-4
WNAA-FM (Greensboro)—*tower* ... NC-3
WNAE-AM (Warren)—*tower* ... PA-2
WNAH-AM (Nashville)—*tower* ... TN-4
WNAK-AM (Nanticoke)—*tower* ... PA-2
WNAN-FM (Demopolis)—*tower* ... AL-4
WNAP-FM (Indianapolis)—*tower* ... IN-6
WNAR-AM (Norristown)—*tower* ... PA-2
WNAS-FM (New Albany)—*tower* ... IN-6
WNAT-AM (Natchez)—*tower* ... MS-4
WNAU-AM (New Albany)—*tower* ... MS-4
WNAX-AM (Yankton)—*tower* ... SD-7
WNAZ-FM (Nashville)—*tower* ... TN-4
W N Barrick Estate Dam—*dam* ... SD-7
WNBB-FM (Grifton)—*tower* ... NC-3
WNBG-AM (Waynesboro)—*tower* ... TN-4
WNBT-AM (Wellsboro)—*tower* ... PA-2
WNCA-AM (Siler City)—*tower* ... NC-3
WNCC-AM (Barnesboro)—*tower* ... PA-2
WNCE-FM (Lancaster)—*tower* ... PA-2
WNCR-AM (Saint Pauls)—*tower* ... NC-3
WNCT-AM (Greenville)—*tower* ... NC-3
WNCT-FM (Greenville)—*tower* ... NC-3
WNCT-TV (Greenville)—*tower* ... NC-3
WNDA-FM (Huntsville)—*tower* ... AL-4
WNDE-AM (Indianapolis)—*tower* ... IN-6
WNDI-AM (Sullivan)—*tower* ... IN-6
WNDI-FM (Sullivan)—*tower* ... IN-6
WNDN-FM (Salisbury)—*tower* ... NC-3
WNDU-AM (South Bend)—*tower* ... IN-6
WNDU-TV (South Bend)—*tower* ... IN-6
WNDY-FM (Crawfordsville)—*tower* ... IN-6
WNEP-TV (Scranton)—*tower* ... PA-2
WNFM-FM (Dayton)—*tower* ... TN-4
WNGE-TV (Nashville)—*tower* ... TN-4
W N Henderson Ditch—*canal* ... IN-6
WNHS-FM (Portsmouth)—*tower* ... VA-3
WNIN-TV (Evansville)—*tower* ... IN-6
WNIS-AM (Portsmouth)—*tower* ... VA-3
WNIX-AM (Greenville)—*tower* ... MS-4
WNJC-FM (Senatobia)—*tower* ... MS-4
**W. N. Jct.**—*pop pl* ... KS-7
WNKX-FM (Clinton)—*tower* ... TN-4
WNKZ-AM (Madison)—*tower* ... TN-4
WNLA-AM (Indianola)—*tower* ... MS-4
WNLA-FM (Indianola)—*tower* ... MS-4
WNNC-AM (Newton)—*tower* ... NC-3
WNON-FM (Lebanon)—*tower* ... IN-6
WNOO-AM (Chattanooga)—*tower* ... TN-4
WNOR-AM (Norfolk)—*tower* ... VA-3
WNOR-FM (Norfolk)—*tower* ... VA-3
WNOW-AM (York)—*tower* ... PA-2
WNOX-AM (Knoxville)—*tower* ... TN-4
WNPC-AM (Newport)—*tower* ... TN-4
*W N Phillips Dam* ... AL-4
WNPT-AM (Tuscaloosa)—*tower* ... AL-4
WNPV-AM (Lansdale)—*tower* ... PA-2
Wnp-2 Plant Support Facility Heliport—*airport* ... WA-9
WNRK-AM (Newark)—*tower* ... DE-2
WNRN-FM (Virginia Beach)—*tower* ... VA-3
WNSB-FM (Norfolk)—*tower* ... VA-3
WNSL-FM (Laurel)—*tower* (2) ... MS-4
WNTE-FM (Mansfield)—*tower* ... PA-2
WNTS-AM (Beech Grove)—*tower* ... IN-6
WNTT-AM (Tazewell)—*tower* ... TN-4
WNUF-FM (Tarentum)—*tower* ... PA-2
WNUZ-AM (Talladega)—*tower* ... AL-4
WNWI-AM (Valparaiso)—*tower* ... IN-6
*Wo* ... FM-9
WOAB-FM (Ozark)—*tower* ... AL-4
Woahink Creek—*stream* ... OR-9
Woahink Lake—*lake* ... OR-9
Woaplanne, Lake—*reservoir* ... MO-7
*Woarowoq* ... FM-9
Woaten Cem—*cemetery* ... TX-5
Wobbly Creek—*stream* ... WA-9
Wobbly Lake—*lake* ... WA-9
*Wobel Canyon* ... CA-9
*Wobel Lake* ... CA-9
Wobic—*locale* ... MI-6
W O Blackmon Dam—*dam* ... AL-4
WOBR-AM (Wanchese)—*tower* ... NC-3
WOBR-FM (Wanchese)—*tower* ... NC-3
WOBS-AM (New Albany)—*tower* ... IN-6
Wob Tank—*reservoir* ... AZ-5
Woburn—*locale* ... IL-6
**Woburn**—*pop pl* ... MA-1
**Woburn**—*pop pl* ... ND-7
*Woburn Centre* ... MA-1
Woburn City Hall—*building* ... MA-1
Woburn Consolidated Oil Field—*other* ... IL-6
*Woburn Highland* ... MA-1
**Woburn Highlands (subdivision)**—*pop pl* ... MA-1
Woburn HS—*school* ... MA-1
Woburn Mall—*locale* ... MA-1
Woburn Public Library—*hist pl* ... MA-1
Woburn Rsvr—*reservoir* ... MA-1
Woburn Sch—*school* ... ND-7
Woburn Street Hist Dist—*hist pl* ... MA-1
Woburn Street Sch—*school* ... MA-1
Woburn (Town of)—*civil* ... MA-1
*Wocaaney* ... FM-9
*Wocca* ... FM-9
*Woc-coo-che Creek* ... AL-4
WOCG-FM (Huntsville)—*tower* ... AL-4
WOCH-AM (North Vernon)—*tower* ... IN-6
*Woche'* ... FM-9
*Woche* ... MP-9
WOCH-FM (North Vernon)—*tower* ... IN-6
*Wochgal* ... FM-9
*Wochngal* ... FM-9
*Wocholab* ... FM-9
Wocket Ledge—*summit* ... NH-1
*Wococon Inlet* ... NC-3
*Woconap* ... FM-9
*Woconuuk* ... FM-9
*Wocopeges* ... FM-9
*Wocus* ... OR-9
**Wocus**—*pop pl* ... OR-9
*Wocus Bay* ... OR-9
Wocus Bay—*bay* ... OR-9
Wocus Bay Guard Station—*locale* ... OR-9
Wocus Butte—*summit* ... OR-9
Wocus Butte Spring—*spring* ... OR-9
Wocus Drainage Canal—*canal* ... OR-9
Wocus Marsh—*swamp* ... OR-9
**Woddale**—*pop pl* ... PA-2
Wodd Cem—*cemetery* ... NC-3
*Woddo Inseln* ... MP-9
*Wodds Canyon* ... UT-8
Woden—*locale* ... TX-5
**Woden**—*pop pl* ... IA-7
Wodena—*island* ... MP-9
Woden Ch—*church* ... IA-7
*Wodes Canyon* ... UT-8
*Wodmeej* ... MP-9
Wodo, Mount—*summit* ... AZ-5
Wodward Creek—*stream* ... KY-4
Woe Cave—*cave* ... AL-4
Woelfel Lake—*lake* ... WA-9
Woelfel Slough—*gut* ... MN-6
Woempner Lake—*lake* ... WI-6
*Woepecket Island* ... MA-1
Woerdeman Lake—*lake* ... NE-7
Woerner Cem—*cemetery* ... MI-6
Woerner JHS—*school* ... KY-4
Woerner Sch—*school* ... MO-7
Woertz Creek—*stream* ... IN-6
Woesner Lake—*lake* ... MI-6
Woestina Cem—*cemetery* ... NY-2
Woestina Sch—*school* ... NY-2
Woewodski Island—*island* ... AK-9
WOEZ-FM (Milton)—*tower* ... PA-2
WOFE-AM (Rockwood)—*tower* ... TN-4
Wofed Cem—*cemetery* ... LA-4
Woffard Chapel—*church* ... AR-4
*Woff Island Bar* ... KY-4
**Wofford**—*pop pl* ... KY-4
Wofford Airp—*airport* ... NV-8
Wofford Branch—*stream* ... MS-4
Wofford Branch—*stream* ... MO-7
Wofford Branch—*stream* (3) ... SC-3
Wofford Cem—*cemetery* ... MO-7
Wofford Cem—*cemetery* ... OK-5
Wofford Cem—*cemetery* ... TX-5
Wofford Ch—*church* ... AL-4
Wofford Chapel—*church* ... SC-3
Wofford Coll—*school* ... SC-3
Wofford College Hist Dist—*hist pl* ... SC-3
Wofford Creek—*stream* ... GA-3
**Wofford Crossroads**—*pop pl* ... GA-3
**Wofford Heights**—*pop pl* ... CA-9
Wofford Hollow—*valley* ... TN-4
Wofford Lake—*lake* ... OK-5
Wofford Lake—*reservoir* ... AR-4
Wofford Lookout Complex—*hist pl* ... NM-5
Wofford Lookout Tower—*locale* ... NM-5
*Wofford Mill* ... AL-4
Wofford Mtn—*summit* ... SC-3
Wofford Post Office (historical)—*building* ... AL-4
Woffords Chapel Cem—*cemetery* ... AR-4
Wofford Sch (historical)—*school* ... MO-7
Woffords Crossroads Ch—*church* ... GA-3
Wofford Shoals—*bar* ... GA-3
Wofford Shoals—*rapids* ... SC-3

Wofford Spring ... TN-4
**Woftoka (historical)**—pop pl ... FL-3
Wogansport—locale ... ND-7
Wogmech ... FM-9
Wogolikad ... FM-9
Wogolkad ... FM-9
Wogolk'aed—summit ... FM-9
Wogoyol ... FM-9
Wogyol ... FM-9
Woheld Falls—falls ... WY-8
Wohelo Lake Dam—dam ... PA-2
Wo He Lo Woods Camp—locale ... MO-7
Wo Hing Society Bldg—hist pl ... HI-9
Wohlenberg Draw—valley ... AZ-5
Wohlford, Lake—reservoir ... CA-9
Wohlford Gap—gap ... PA-2
Wohlford Rsvr ... CA-9
Wohlford Run—stream ... PA-2
Wohlheter, George, House—hist pl ... MN-6
Wohl Lake—lake ... NY-2
Wohlys Pass—gap ... CA-9
Wohoa Bay—bay ... ME-1
Wohrer Cem—cemetery ... IN-6
WOHS-AM (Shelby)—tower ... NC-3
Wohseepee Park—park ... NY-2
Woino—bar ... FM-9
Woinona ... IN-6
Woito—cape ... FM-9
Woitzel Field—airport ... ND-7
Woiwode (historical)—locale ... ND-7
WOIX-AM (Blowing Rock)—tower ... NC-3
Woja ... MP-9
Woja—locale ... MP-9
**Wojciechowski**—pop pl ... MI-6
Wojcjecha Cem—cemetery ... NY-2
Wojeiaion (not verified)—island ... MP-9
Wojejaion ... MP-9
Wojejaiong—island ... MP-9
Wojejaiong Island ... MP-9
Wojejairok—island ... MP-9
Wojejairok Pass—channel ... MP-9
Wojejalong ... MP-9
Wojia Islet ... MP-9
Wojja ... MP-9
Wojje-to ... MP-9
W O Johnson Ranch—locale ... SD-7
Wokas Bay ... OR-9
Wokeley Hollow—valley ... PA-2
WOKI-FM (Oak Ridge)—tower ... TN-4
WOKJ-AM (Jackson)—tower (2) ... MS-4
WOKK-FM (Meridian)—tower ... MS-4
WOKM-FM (New Albany)—tower (2) ... MS-4
WOKN-FM (Goldsboro)—tower ... NC-3
Woksapiwi Creek—stream ... MN-6
Woksapiwi Lake—lake ... MN-6
WOKU-FM (Greensburg)—tower ... PA-2
WOKX-AM (High Point)—tower ... NC-3
Wola ... FM-9
Wolauna Island—island ... FM-9
**Wolbach**—pop pl (2) ... NE-7
Wol'barach—summit ... FM-9
Wolbert Run—stream ... PA-2
Wolco—locale ... OK-5
Wolcot Mountain ... CO-8
**Wolcott**—pop pl ... CO-8
**Wolcott**—pop pl ... CT-1
**Wolcott**—pop pl ... IN-6
**Wolcott**—pop pl ... KS-7
**Wolcott**—pop pl ... NY-2
**Wolcott**—pop pl ... VT-1
Wolcott, Oliver, House—hist pl ... CT-1
Wolcott Bldg—hist pl ... OK-5
Wolcott Cem—cemetery ... IN-6
Wolcott Community Airp—airport ... IN-6
Wolcott Creek—stream ... NY-2
Wolcott Creek—stream ... PA-2
Wolcott Hill—summit ... MA-1
Wolcott Hollow—valley ... OH-6
Wolcott House—hist pl ... IN-6
Wolcott House—hist pl ... OH-6
Wolcott Island—island ... MA-1
Wolcott Lake—lake ... CO-8
Wolcott Lake—lake ... MI-6
**Wolcott Mills**—pop pl ... MI-6
Wolcott Mtn—summit ... CO-8
Wolcott Peak—summit ... AZ-5
Wolcott Pond—lake ... VT 1
Wolcott Pond Brook—stream ... VT-1
Wolcott Ranch—locale ... TX-5
Wolcott Ranch—locale ... WY-8
Wolcott Reef—bar ... AK-9
Wolcott Run—stream ... PA-2
**Wolcottsburg**—pop pl ... NY-2
Wolcott Sch—school (2) ... CT-1
Wolcott Sch—school ... MI-6
Wolcott Stage Station—hist pl ... CO-8
**Wolcottsville**—pop pl ... NY-2
**Wolcott (Town of)**—pop pl ... CT-1
**Wolcott (Town of)**—pop pl ... NY-2
**Wolcott (Town of)**—pop pl ... VT-1
**Wolcottville**—pop pl ... IN-6
Wolcottville Elem Sch—school ... IN-6
Wold, Lake—lake ... MN-6
Woldale Sch—school ... WA-9
Wold Creek ... KS-7
Wolden County Park—park ... IA-7
Woldert Park—park ... TX-5
Wold Lake—lake ... MN-6
Wold Slough—swamp ... ND-7
Wold Town Hall—building ... ND-7
**Wold Township**—pop pl ... ND-7
Woleai—island ... FM-9
Woleai Atoll—island ... FM-9
Woleai (Municipality)—civ div ... FM-9
Wol'eamaqut—bay ... FM-9
Wol'eburach ... FM-9
Wolem ... AR-4
Wolemaut ... FM-9
Woleott Sch—school ... MA-1
Woleran—bay ... FM-9
Woles ... FM-9
Wolesy Creek ... OR-9
Wolf ... IL-6
Wolf—island ... PA-2
Wolf—locale (2) ... CA-9
Wolf—locale ... IA-7
Wolf—locale ... KS-7
Wolf—locale ... KY-4
Wolf—locale ... MN-6
**Wolf**—pop pl ... MS-4
**Wolf**—pop pl ... OH-6
**Wolf**—pop pl ... OK-5
**Wolf**—pop pl ... WY-8
Wolf, Charles, House—hist pl ... IA-7
Wolf, George, Sch—hist pl ... PA-2
Wolf, Jacob, House—hist pl ... AR-4
Wolf, Mier, House—hist pl ... IA-7
Wolf, Mount—summit ... NH-1
Wolf, William R., House—hist pl ... MN-6
Wolf Acad—school ... PA-2
**Wolf Acres**—pop pl ... MD-2
**Wolf Acres**—pop pl ... TN-4
Wolfall Hollow ... AR-4
Wolf and Neerland Ditch—canal ... CO-8
Wolfangol ... FM-9
Wol'fangol—summit ... FM-9
Wolf Arm—canal ... IN-6
Wolf Arroyo—valley ... CO-8
Wolf Bald—summit ... NC-3
Wolf Bar Shelter—locale ... WA-9
Wolf Bay—bay ... MN-6
Wolf Bay—bay ... WA-9
Wolf Bay—lake ... AL-4
Wolf Bay—swamp (4) ... FL-3
Wolf Bay—swamp (3) ... GA-3
Wolf Bay—swamp ... NC-3
Wolf Bay Drain—stream ... GA-3
Wolf Bayou—gut ... AR-4
Wolf Bayou—gut ... LA-4
Wolf Bayou—locale ... AR-4
Wolf Bayou—stream ... AR-4
Wolf Bayou—stream ... MO-7
Wolf Bend Island—island ... FL-3
Wolf Bluff—cliff ... AL-4
Wolfborough ... NH-1
Wolf Branch ... DE-2
Wolf Branch ... MS-4
Wolf Branch ... TX-5
Wolf Branch ... WV-2
Wolf Branch—stream (9) ... AL-4
Wolf Branch—stream (4) ... AR-4
Wolf Branch—stream (4) ... FL-3
Wolf Branch—stream (7) ... GA-3
Wolf Branch—stream (2) ... IL-6
Wolf Branch—stream ... IA-7
Wolf Branch—stream (13) ... KY-4
Wolf Branch—stream ... LA-4
Wolf Branch—stream (7) ... MS-4
Wolf Branch—stream (8) ... MO-7
Wolf Branch—stream (11) ... NC-3
Wolf Branch—stream ... PA-2
Wolf Branch—stream ... SC-3
Wolf Branch—stream (10) ... TN-4
Wolf Branch—stream (12) ... TX-5
Wolf Branch—stream (3) ... VA-3
Wolf Branch—stream ... WV-2
Wolf Branch Ditch—canal ... KY-4
Wolf Branch Hollow—valley ... MO-7
Wolf Branch Sch—school ... IL-6
Wolf Branch Trail—trail ... PA-2
Wolf Bridge—other ... IL-6
Wolf Brook ... MO-7
Wolf Brook—stream ... CT-1
Wolf Brook—stream (2) ... MA-1
Wolf Butte—summit ... MT-8
Wolf Butte—summit ... NE-7
Wolf Butte—summit (2) ... ND-7
Wolf Butte—summit ... OR-9
Wolf Butte*—summit ... SD-7
Wolf Butte Ch—church ... ND-7
Wolf Butte Coulee—valley ... MT-8
Wolf Butte Creek—stream ... ND-7
Wolf Butte Dam—dam ... ND-7
Wolf Buttes ... ND-7
**Wolf Butte Township**—pop pl ... ND-7
Wolf Cabin—locale ... AK-9
Wolf Cabin—locale ... TX-5
**Wolfcale**—pop pl ... OH-6
Wolf Camp Butte—summit ... OR-9
Wolf Camp Hills—summit ... TX-5
Wolf Camp Run—stream ... PA-2
Wolfcamp Run—stream ... WV-2
Wolf Canyon ... ID-8
Wolf Canyon ... NM-5
Wolf Canyon—valley ... AZ-5
Wolf Canyon—valley (2) ... CA-9
Wolf Canyon—valley (2) ... CO 8
Wolf Canyon—valley ... ID-8
Wolf Canyon—valley (2) ... KS-7
Wolf Canyon—valley ... MT-8
Wolf Canyon—valley ... NE-7
Wolf Canyon—valley (2) ... NM-5
Wolf Canyon—valley (2) ... SD-7
Wolf Canyon—valley ... WA-9
Wolf Canyon—valley ... WY-8
Wolf Canyon Tank—reservoir ... AZ-5
Wolf Cave—cave ... AL-4
Wolf Cave—cave ... IN-6
Wolf Cave—cave (2) ... TN-4
Wolf Cave Hollow—valley ... MO-7
Wolf Cave Mtn—summit ... GA-3
Wolf Ceek ... MS-4
Wolf Cem—cemetery ... IL-6
Wolf Cem—cemetery ... KY-4
Wolf Cem—cemetery (4) ... MO-7
Wolf Cem—cemetery ... MT-8
Wolf Cem—cemetery (3) ... OH-6
Wolf Cem—cemetery (2) ... OK-5
Wolf Cem—cemetery ... PA-2
Wolf Cem—cemetery ... TX-5
Wolf Cem—cemetery ... VA-3
Wolf Ch—church ... PA-2
Wolf Chief Bay—bay ... ND-7
Wolf Cliff—cliff ... KY-4
Wolf Coal—locale ... KY-4
Wolfcoal (RR name for Wolf Coal)—other ... KY-4
**Wolf Coal (RR name Wolfcoal)**—pop pl ... KY-4
Wolf Corners—locale ... OH-6
Wolf Coulee—valley (5) ... MT-8
Wolf Coulee—valley ... ND-7
Wolf Cove—basin ... TN-4
Wolf Cove—bay ... TX-5
Wolf Cove—valley ... NC-3
Wolf Cove Creek—stream ... NC-3
Wolf Covered Bridge—hist pl ... IL-6
Wolf Creek ... AL-4
Wolf Creek ... AR-4
Wolf Creek ... DE-2
Wolf Creek ... GA-3
Wolf Creek ... ID-8
Wolf Creek ... IN-6
Wolf Creek ... KS-7
Wolf Creek ... MN-6
Wolf Creek ... MT-8
Wolf Creek ... NV-8
Wolf Creek ... NC-3
Wolf Creek ... OH-6
Wolf Creek ... OK-5
Wolf Creek ... PA-2
Wolf Creek ... SC-3
Wolf Creek ... SD-7
Wolf Creek ... TN-4
Wolf Creek ... TX-5
Wolf Creek ... VA-3
Wolf Creek ... WA-9
Wolf Creek ... WV-2
Wolf Creek—channel ... GA-3
Wolf Creek—locale ... AL-4
Wolf Creek—locale ... IL-6
Wolf Creek—locale ... KS-7
Wolf Creek—locale ... OH-6
Wolf Creek—locale ... SD-7
Wolf Creek—locale (2) ... TN-4
Wolf Creek—locale ... TX-5
Wolfcreek—other ... KY-4
**Wolf Creek**—pop pl ... KY-4
**Wolf Creek**—pop pl ... MT-8
**Wolf Creek**—pop pl ... NC-3
**Wolf Creek**—pop pl (2) ... OR-9
**Wolf Creek**—pop pl ... TN-4
**Wolfcreek**—pop pl ... WV-2
**Wolf Creek**—pop pl ... WI-6
**Wolfcreek**—pop pl ... WI-6
Wolf Creek—stream (21) ... AL-4
Wolf Creek—stream (10) ... AK-9
Wolf Creek—stream (2) ... AZ-5
Wolf Creek—stream (13) ... AR-4
Wolf Creek—stream (9) ... CA-9
Wolf Creek—stream (12) ... CO-8
Wolf Creek—stream (10) ... FL-3
Wolf Creek—stream (26) ... GA-3
Wolf Creek—stream (8) ... ID-8
Wolf Creek—stream (19) ... IL-6
Wolf Creek—stream (14) ... IN-6
Wolf Creek—stream (16) ... IA-7
Wolf Creek—stream (28) ... KS-7
Wolf Creek—stream (17) ... KY-4
Wolf Creek—stream (4) ... LA-4
Wolf Creek—stream (12) ... MI-6
Wolf Creek—stream (7) ... MN-6
Wolf Creek—stream (15) ... MS-4
Wolf Creek—stream (24) ... MO-7
Wolf Creek—stream (25) ... MT-8
Wolf Creek—stream (6) ... NE-7
Wolf Creek—stream ... NV-8
Wolf Creek—stream ... NJ-2
Wolf Creek—stream (2) ... NM-5
Wolf Creek—stream (7) ... NY-2
Wolf Creek—stream (8) ... NC-3
Wolf Creek—stream (3) ... ND-7
Wolf Creek—stream (14) ... OH-6
Wolf Creek—stream (24) ... OK-5
Wolf Creek—stream (24) ... OR-9
Wolf Creek—stream (4) ... PA-2
Wolf Creek—stream (5) ... SC-3
Wolf Creek—stream (6) ... SD-7
Wolf Creek—stream (17) ... TN-4
Wolf Creek—stream (31) ... TX-5
Wolf Creek—stream (2) ... UT-8
Wolf Creek—stream (7) ... VA-3
Wolf Creek—stream (6) ... WA-9
Wolf Creek—stream (9) ... WV-2
Wolf Creek—stream (7) ... WI-6
Wolf Creek—stream (7) ... WY-8
**Wolf Creek Acres (subdivision)**—pop pl ... NC-3
Wolf Creek Airp—airport ... KS-7
Wolf Creek Boat Dock—locale ... VA-3
Wolf Creek Bridge—bridge ... TN-4
Wolf Creek Camp—locale ... AR-4
Wolf Creek Camp—locale ... NY-2
Wolf Creek Campground—locale ... CO-8
Wolf Creek Campground—locale ... WY-8
Wolf Creek Campground—park (2) ... OR-9
Wolf Creek Campground—park ... UT-8
Wolf Crook Canyon—valloy ... CO-8
Wolf Creek Cem—cemetery (3) ... IL-6
Wolf Creek Cem—cemetery ... IN-6
Wolf Creek Cem—cemetery ... MI-6
Wolf Creek Cem—cemetery ... MS-4
Wolf Creek Cem—cemetery ... OH-6
Wolf Creek Cem—cemetery (2) ... OK-5
Wolf Creek Cem—cemetery ... OR-9
Wolf Creek Cem—cemetery (3) ... TN-4
Wolf Creek Ch—church (2) ... GA-3
Wolf Creek Ch—church ... IN-6
Wolf Creek Ch—church (3) ... KY-4
Wolf Creek Ch—church (2) ... MS-4
Wolf Creek Ch—church (2) ... MO-7
Wolf Creek Ch—church (3) ... OH-6
Wolf Creek Ch—church (4) ... TN-4
Wolf Creek Ch (historical)—church ... TN-4
Wolf Creek Colony ... SD-7
**Wolf Creek Colony**—pop pl ... SD-7
Wolf Creek County Park—park ... TX-5
Wolf Creek Dam—building ... KY-4
Wolf Creek Dam—dam ... KY-4
Wolf Creek Dam—dam ... NC-3
Wolf Creek Dam—dam ... OR-9
Wolf Creek Dam—dam (2) ... PA-2
Wolf Creek Ditch—canal ... MT-8
Wolf Creek Drain—canal ... IL-6
Wolf Creek Drainage Ditch—canal ... IA-7
Wolf Creek Falls—falls ... MT-8
Wolf Creek Falls—falls ... OR-9
Wolf Creek Falls Recreation Site—park ... OR-9
Wolf Creek Gaging Station—other ... MT-8
Wolf Creek Gap—gap ... NC-3
Wolf Creek Guard Station—locale ... OR-9
Wolf Creek Hall—building ... MT-8
Wolf Creek Hill—summit ... MT-8
Wolf Creek (historical)—locale ... MS-4
Wolf Creek Hot Spring—spring ... MT-8
Wolf Creek Island—island ... TN-4
Wolf Creek junction ... OR-9
Wolf Creek Lake—lake (2) ... CA-9
Wolf Creek Lake—reservoir ... NC-3
Wolf Creek Lake—reservoir ... SD-7
Wolf Creek Lake—reservoir ... TX-5
Wolf Creek Lake Dam—dam ... SD-7
Wolf Creek Landing—locale ... MS-4
**Wolf Creek (Laurel Hill)**—pop pl ... TN-4
Wolf Creek (Magisterial District)—fmr MCD ... WV-2
Wolf Creek Meadow—flat ... CA-9
Wolf Creek Meadow—flat ... OR-9
Wolf Creek Mill (historical)—locale ... TN-4
Wolf Creek Mound—hist pl ... OH-6
Wolf Creek Mountian—summit ... AL-4
Wolf Creek Mtn—summit ... AK-9
Wolf Creek Mtn—summit ... VA-3
Wolf Creek Mtn—summit (2) ... WV-2
Wolf Creek Nuclear Plant—building ... KS-7
Wolf Creek Oil Field—oilfield ... MS-4
Wolf Creek Pass—gap ... CA-9
Wolf Creek Pass—gap ... CO-8
Wolf Creek Peak—summit ... UT-8
Wolf Creek Pond—reservoir ... OH-6
Wolfcreek Post Office ... TN-4
Wolf Creek Post Office (historical)—building ... TN-4
Wolf Creek Public Use Area—park ... MS-4
Wolf Creek Public Use Area—park ... ND-7
Wolf Creek Ranch—locale ... MT-8
Wolf Creek Rapids—rapids ... ID-8
Wolf Creek Rapids—rapids ... OR-9
Wolf Creek Rec Area—park ... KS-7
Wolf Creek Rec Area—park ... KY-4
Wolf Creek Reservoir ... KY-4
Wolf Creek Ridge—ridge ... CA-9
Wolf Creek Rsvr—reservoir ... CO-8
Wolf Creek Rsvr—reservoir ... OR-9
Wolf Creek Rsvr—reservoir ... PA-2
Wolf Creek Rsvr No. 2—reservoir ... CO-8
Wolf Creek Sch—school (2) ... IL-6
Wolf Creek Sch—school (2) ... KY-4
Wolf Creek Sch—school ... SC-3
Wolf Creek Sch—school ... TN-4
Wolf Creek Sch—school ... WY-8
Wolf Creek Sch (historical)—school ... AL-4
Wolf Creek Sch (historical)—school ... TN-4
Wolf Creek Spring—spring ... CO-8
Wolf Creek State Game Mngmt Area—park ... ND-7
Wolf Creek Station—locale ... WV-2
Wolf Creek Stock Driveway—trail ... CO-8
Wolf Creek Store—locale ... OR-9
**Wolf Creek Subdivision**—pop pl ... UT-8
Wolf Creek Summit—summit ... UT-8
Wolf Creek Tank—reservoir ... AZ-5
Wolf Creek Tank—reservoir ... TX-5
Wolf Creek Tavern—hist pl ... OR-9
Wolf Creek Test Wells—well ... AK-9
Wolf Creek Township—fmr MCD ... IA-7
**Wolf Creek Township**—pop pl ... SD-7
Wolf Creek (Township of)—fmr MCD ... AR-4
**Wolf Creek (Township of)**—pop pl ... PA-2
Wolf Creek Trail—trail ... MT-8
**Wolf Creek Village Subdivision**—pop pl ... UT-8
Wolf Creek Wildlife Area—park ... OH-6
Wolf Creek Wildlife Mngmt Area—park ... AL-4
Wolf Crossing—locale ... AZ-5
Wolf Crossing—locale ... MI-6
Wolf Crossing Cem—cemetery ... TX-5
Wolf Dale—locale ... IA-7
**Wolfdale**—pop pl ... PA-2
Wolf Dam ... PA-2
Wolf Dam—dam ... NV-8
Wolf Den—locale ... UT-8
Wolf Den Airport, The—airport ... IN-6
Wolf Den Branch—stream ... AL-4
Wolfden Branch—stream ... GA-3
Wolfden Branch—stream ... IL-6
Wolf Den Branch—stream ... MD-2
Wolf Den Branch—stream ... MO-7
Wolfden Branch—stream ... MO-7
Wolfden Branch—stream ... NC-3
Wolfden Branch—stream ... TN-4
Wolf Den Branch—stream ... TX-5
Wolf Den Brook—stream ... CT-1
Wolf Den Canyon ... CO-8
Wolf Den Canyon ... UT-8
Wolf Den Canyon—valley ... CO-8
Wolf Den Canyon—valley ... TX-5
Wolf Den Canyon—valley ... UT-8
Wolf Den Cave—cave ... AL-4
Wolf Den Dam—dam ... NJ-2
Wolf Den Draw—valley ... WY-8
Wolfden Flats—flat ... AL-4
Wolfden Hill—summit ... MA-1
Wolf Den Hollow—valley ... AL-4
Wolfden Hollow—valley ... AL-4
Wolf Den Hollow—valley (3) ... AR-4
Wolfden Hollow—valley ... IL-6
Wolfden Hollow—valley ... MO-7
Wolf Den Hollow—valley ... MO-7
Wolf Den Hollow—valley ... UT-8
Wolfden Hollow—valley ... WV-2
Wolf Den Hollow Drift Mine (underground)—mine ... AL-4
Wolfden Knob—summit ... NC-3
Wolfden Lake—reservoir ... OH-6
Wolf Den Mine—mine ... MO-7
Wolfden Mtn—summit ... AL-4
Wolf Den Mtn—summit ... AR-4
Wolfden Ridge—ridge ... NC-3
Wolf Den Rsvr—reservoir ... CO-8
Wolfden Run—stream ... MD-2
Wolfden Run—stream ... OH-6
Wolf Den Spring—spring ... CO-8
Wolf Den Spring—spring ... MT-8
Wolf Den Tank—reservoir ... TX-5
Wolf Den Trail—trail ... MD-2
Wolf Ditch—canal ... CA-9
Wolf Ditch—canal ... CO-8
Wolf Ditch—canal ... IN-6
Wolf Ditch—canal ... OH-6
Wolf Divide—gap ... AR-4
Wolf Drain—canal ... MI-6
Wolf Drain—stream ... SD-7
Wolf Draw—valley ... ID-8
Wolf Draw—valley ... MT-8
Wolf Draw—valley ... NM-5
Wolf Draw—valley ... ND-7
Wolf Draw—valley ... SD-7
Wolf Draw—valley (2) ... TX-5
Wolf Draw—valley ... WA-9
Wolf Draw—valley (2) ... WY-8
**Wolfe**—pop pl ... WV-2
Wolfe, Mary A., House—hist pl ... OH-6
Wolfe, Thomas, House—hist pl ... NC-3
Wolfe Archeol Site—hist pl ... NE-7
**Wolfeboro**—pop pl ... NH-1
Wolfeboro Bay—bay ... NH-1
**Wolfeboro Center**—pop pl ... NH-1
Wolfeboro Centre Community Church—hist pl ... NH-1
**Wolfeboro Compact**—pop pl ... NH-1
**Wolfeboro Falls**—pop pl ... NH-1
Wolfeboro Neck—cape ... NH-1
**Wolfeboro (Town of)**—pop pl ... NH-1
Wolfe Branch ... DE-2
Wolfe Branch—stream ... NC-3
Wolfe Branch—stream (3) ... TN-4
Wolfe Cabin ... UT-8
Wolfe Cabin—bay ... AK-9
Wolfe Canyon—valley ... KS-7
Wolfe Cave—cave ... TN-4
Wolfe Cem—cemetery ... AR-4
Wolfe Cem—cemetery (2) ... IL-6
Wolfe Cem—cemetery ... IN-6
Wolfe Cem—cemetery ... IA-7
Wolfe Cem—cemetery ... KY-4
Wolfe Cem—cemetery ... ND-7
Wolfe Cem—cemetery ... OK-5
Wolfe Cem—cemetery (2) ... TN-4
Wolfe Cem—cemetery (5) ... VA-3
Wolfe Cem—cemetery (2) ... WV-2
**Wolfe City**—pop pl ... TX-5
Wolfe City (CCD)—cens area ... TX-5
Wolfe City Reservoirs—reservoir ... TX-5
Wolfe Coulee—valley (2) ... MT-8
**Wolfe (County)**—pop pl ... KY-4
Wolfe Cow Camp—locale ... WY-8
Wolfe Creek ... IN-6
Wolfe Creek ... MS-4
Wolfe Creek—stream ... FL-3
Wolfe Creek—stream ... GA-3
Wolfe Creek—stream ... IN-6
Wolfe Creek—stream ... NC-3
Wolfe Creek—stream (2) ... OK-5
Wolfe Creek—stream ... OR-9
Wolfe Creek—stream ... PA-2
Wolfe Creek—stream ... SC-3
Wolfe Creek—stream ... VA-3
Wolfe Creek—stream ... WA-9
Wolfe Creek—stream ... WV-2
**Wolfe Creek (historical)**—pop pl ... MS-4
Wolfe Dam—dam ... TN-4
Wolfe Draft—valley ... VA-3
Wolfe Draw—valley ... WY-8
Wolfe Field Airp—airport ... IN-6
Wolfe Gap—gap ... PA-2
Wolfe Gap Trail—trail ... PA-2
Wolfe Glade—stream ... DE-2
Wolfe Hill—summit ... IN-6
Wolfe Hollow—valley ... PA-2
Wolfe HS—school ... AL-4
Wolfe Lake—reservoir ... TN-4
Wolfe Lake—swamp ... MN-6
Wolf Elem Sch—school ... PA-2
Wolfe Marsh Run—stream ... VA-3
Wolfe Mill—locale ... MD-2
Wolfenbarger Cave—cave ... TN-4
Wolfenbarger Cem—cemetery ... TN-4
Wolfenbarger Ch—church ... TN-4
Wolfenbarger Lakes ... NE-7
Wolfenbarger Site—hist pl ... WA-9
Wolfenberger Cem—cemetery ... TX-5
Wolfenberger Lakes—lake ... NE-7
Wolfender Ranch—locale ... NE-7
Wolfe Neck—cape ... DE-2
Wolfe Park—park ... IL-6
Wolfe Park—park ... MN-6
Wolfe Park—park ... OH-6
Wolfe Pen Branch—stream ... KY-4
Wolfe Place ... ID-8
Wolfe Pond ... NY-2
Wolfe Ranch—locale (2) ... MT-8
Wolfe Ranch—locale ... WY-8
Wolfe Ranch Historical District—hist pl ... UT-8
Wolfer Creek—stream ... OR-9
Wolfer Ditch—canal ... CO-8
Wolferd Sch—school ... PA-2
Wolfert—locale ... NJ-2
Wolfert Creek ... NC-3
Wolfert Sch (abandoned)—school ... PA-2
Wolfe Run—stream ... PA-2
Wolfes Branch—stream ... VA-3
Wolfe Sch—school ... IL-6
Wolfe Sch—school ... MN-6
Wolfe Sch—school (2) ... MO-7
Wolfe Sch (abandoned)—school ... PA-2
Wolfe Sch (historical)—school ... PA-2
Wolfe-Shorter HS ... AL-4
Wolfe's Neck Site—hist pl ... DE-2
Wolfes Pond—lake ... NY-2
Wolfes Pond Park—park ... NY-2
Wolfe Spring—spring ... TN-4
Wolfe Spring Ch—church ... AL-4
Wolfes Store ... PA-2
Wolfe Well—well ... CA-9
Wolfey Gulch—valley ... CA-9
Wolff ... AL-4
**Wolff**—pop pl ... IN-6
Wolff, Philip A., House and Carriage House—hist pl ... IA-7
Wolf Fall Hollow—valley ... AR-4
Wolf Fang Creek—stream ... ID-8
Wolf Fang Peak—summit ... ID-8
Wolf Fangs—ridge ... ID-8
Wolffarth Sch—school ... TX-5
Wolff Cem—cemetery ... SD-7
Wolff Creek ... LA-4
Wolff Dam—dam ... ND-7
Wolff Farm Dam—dam ... PA-2
Wolff Lake—reservoir ... SD-7
Wolff Lake Dam—dam ... SD-7
Wolf Flat—flat ... ID-8
Wolf Flat—flat ... OR-9
Wolf Flat—flat ... TX-5
Wolf Flat—flat ... UT-8
**Wolf Flat**—pop pl ... TX-5
Wolf Fly Creek—stream ... NY-2
Wolf Ford—locale ... NC-3
Wolf Fork—stream (2) ... KY-4
Wolf Fork—stream ... WA-9
Wolf Fork—stream ... WV-2
Wolf Fork Ch—church ... GA-3
Wolf Fork Hollow—valley ... TN-4
**Wolfforth**—pop pl ... TX-5
Wolff Post Office (historical)—building ... AL-4
Wolff Project Sch—school ... AR-4
Wolff Ranch—locale ... OR-9
Wolff Ranch—locale ... WY-8
Wolff Rsvr—reservoir ... MT-8
Wolff Sch—school ... SD-7
Wolff Springs Church ... AL-4
Wolffs Run—stream ... PA-2
Wolfgang Sch (abandoned)—school ... PA-2
Wolfgangs Sch—school ... PA-2
Wolf Gap—gap ... KY-4
Wolf Gap—gap ... MD-2
Wolf Gap—gap (2) ... NC-3
Wolf Gap—gap ... OR-9
Wolf Gap—gap ... PA-2
Wolf Gap—gap (3) ... TN-4
Wolf Gap—gap ... VA-3
Wolf Gap—gap (2) ... WV-2
Wolf Gap—gap ... WY-8
Wolf Gap Mtn—summit ... KY-4
Wolf Gap Rec Area—park ... VA-3
Wolf Gap Rec Area—park ... WV-2
Wolf Glade ... DE-2
Wolf Glade—flat ... CA-9
**Wolf Glade**—pop pl ... VA-3
**Wolfglade**—pop pl ... VA-3
Wolfgram Cem—cemetery ... WI-6
Wolf Grove Creek—stream ... MO-7
Wolf Grove Sch (historical)—school ... MO-7
Wolfgrum Ranch—locale ... ND-7
Wolf Gulch—valley ... CA-9
Wolf Gulch—valley ... OR-9
Wolf Gulch—valley ... WA-9
Wolf Gulch—valley ... WY-8
Wolf Gulf—bay ... GA-3
Wolf Gully—valley ... TX-5
Wolf Gun Mtn—summit ... MT-8
Wolf Gut—gut ... AL-4
Wolf Hammock—island ... FL-3
Wolfharbor Branch—stream ... NC-3
Wolf Harbor Branch—stream ... VA-3
Wolf Head Pond—swamp ... FL-3
Wolf Head Spring—spring ... TX-5
Wolf Hill—locale ... NY-2
Wolf Hill—summit ... CA-9
Wolf Hill—summit ... CO-8
Wolf Hill—summit ... CT-1
Wolf Hill—summit ... IN-6
Wolf Hill—summit ... IA-7
Wolf Hill—summit ... KY-4
Wolf Hill—summit (2) ... MA-1
Wolf Hill—summit ... MS-4
Wolf Hill—summit ... MT-8
Wolf Hill—summit ... NH-1
Wolf Hill—summit (2) ... NY-2
Wolf Hill—summit ... NC-3
Wolf Hill—summit (3) ... PA-2
Wolf Hill—summit (2) ... RI-1
Wolf Hill—summit ... SD-7
Wolf Hill—summit (2) ... TN-4
Wolf Hill—summit (3) ... TX-5
Wolf Hill—summit ... VT-1
Wolf Hill—summit ... VA-3
Wolf Hill—summit ... WV-2
Wolf Hill Cem—cemetery ... IA-7
Wolf Hill Cem—cemetery ... TN-4
Wolf Hill Lookout Tower—locale ... TX-5
Wolf Hills—range ... KY-4
Wolf Hills—summit ... WV-2
Wolf Hole ... AZ-5
Wolf Hole—bay ... NY-2
Wolf Hole—canal ... MO-7
Wolf Hole—locale ... AZ-5
Wolf Hole Lake—lake ... AZ-5
Wolf Hole Lateral—canal ... MO-7
Wolf Hole Mtn—summit ... AZ-5
Wolf Hole Pass—gap ... AZ-5
Wolf Hole Spring—spring ... AZ-5
Wolf Hole Spring (Dry)—spring ... NV-8
Wolf Hole Tank—reservoir ... AZ-5
Wolf Hole Valley—valley ... AZ-5
Wolf Hole Valley Pond—reservoir ... AZ-5
Wolf Hole Wildlife Rsvr—reservoir ... AZ-5
Wolf Hollow ... AR-4
Wolf Hollow ... TX-5
Wolf Hollow—stream ... KY-4
Wolf Hollow—valley ... AL-4
Wolf Hollow—valley (4) ... AR-4
Wolf Hollow—valley ... GA-3
Wolf Hollow—valley ... IL-6
Wolf Hollow—valley (3) ... KY-4
Wolf Hollow—valley (14) ... MO-7
Wolf Hollow—valley (2) ... NY-2
Wolf Hollow—valley (2) ... OK-5
Wolf Hollow—valley (2) ... OR-9
Wolf Hollow—valley (3) ... PA-2
Wolf Hollow—valley (4) ... TN-4
Wolf Hollow—valley (12) ... TX-5
Wolf Hollow—valley (4) ... UT-8
Wolf Hollow—valley ... VA-3
Wolf Hollow—valley (2) ... WV-2
Wolf Hollow Canyon—valley ... NM-5
Wolf Hollow Creek ... NY-2
Wolf Hollow Creek ... TX-5
Wolf Hollow Creek—stream ... OK-5
Wolf Hollow Falls—falls ... OR-9
Wolf Hollow Golf Course—locale ... PA-2
Wolfhook, The—valley ... TN-4
Wolf House Point—cape ... NC-3
Wolfhouse Run—stream ... PA-2
Wolf HS—school ... GA-3
**Wolfhurst**—pop pl ... OH-6
Wolfinger Butte—summit ... OR-9
Wolfinger Cem—cemetery (2) ... OH-6
**Wolfington**—pop pl ... IN-6
Wolfington (historical)—locale ... NC-3
Wolfin Meadow—flat ... CA-9
Wolfin Sch—school ... TX-5
Wolf Island ... MN-6
Wolf Island—island (2) ... GA-3
Wolf Island—island ... ME-1
Wolf Island—island ... MN-6
Wolf Island—island ... MT-8
Wolf Island—island ... OH-6
Wolf Island—island ... TN-4
Wolf Island—island ... WI-6
**Wolf Island**—pop pl ... MO-7

Wolf Island Branch—*stream* MS-4
Wolf Island Cem—*cemetery* MO-7
Wolf Island Ch—*church* (2) NC-3
Wolf Island Ch (abandoned)—*church* MO-7
Wolf Island Creek—*stream* NC-3
Wolf Island Natl Wildlife Ref—*park* GA-3
Wolf Island No 5—*island* KY-4
Wolf Island Racetrack—*locale* NC-3
Wolf Island Slash—*stream* AR-4
Wolf Island Spit—*bar* GA-3
Wolf Island Township—*civil* MO-7
Wolfjaw Brook—*stream* NY-2
Wolf JHS—*school* MI-6
Wolfjump Post Office (historical)—*building* TN-4
Wolfkiln Run—*stream* OH-6
Wolf Knob—*summit* AR-4
Wolf Knob—*summit* GA-3
Wolf Knob—*summit* (2) KY-4
Wolf Knob—*summit* (6) NC-3
Wolf Knob—*summit* TN-4
Wolf Knob—*summit* VA-3
Wolf Knob Ch—*church* VA-3
Wolf Knoll—*summit* AZ-5
Wolf Knoll—*summit* UT-8
*Wolf Lake* AR-4
*Wolf Lake* (2) IN-6
*Wolf Lake* MI-6
*Wolf Lake* MN-6
*Wolf Lake* OR-9
*Wolf Lake* WI-6
Wolf Lake—*lake* (4) AK-9
Wolf Lake—*lake* (2) AR-4
Wolf Lake—*lake* CA-9
Wolf Lake—*lake* CO-8
Wolf Lake—*lake* (2) FL-3
Wolf Lake—*lake* (3) IL-6
Wolf Lake—*lake* (3) IN-6
Wolf Lake—*lake* (19) MI-6
Wolf Lake—*lake* (23) MN-6
Wolf Lake—*lake* (3) MS-4
Wolf Lake—*lake* MO-7
Wolf Lake—*lake* (3) NE-7
Wolf Lake—*lake* NJ-2
Wolf Lake—*lake* (3) NY-2
Wolf Lake—*lake* ND-7
Wolf Lake—*lake* (2) OR-9
Wolf Lake—*lake* PA-2
Wolf Lake—*lake* SC-3
Wolf Lake—*lake* SD-7
Wolf Lake—*lake* (2) TX-5
Wolf Lake—*lake* (14) WI-6
Wolf Lake—*lake* (2) WY-8
**Wolf Lake**—*pop pl* IL-6
**Wolflake**—*pop pl* (2) IN-6
**Wolf Lake**—*pop pl* MA-1
**Wolf Lake**—*pop pl* (3) MI-6
**Wolf Lake**—*pop pl* MN-6
**Wolf Lake**—*pop pl* WI-6
Wolf Lake—*reservoir* IA-7
Wolf Lake—*reservoir* NC-3
Wolf Lake—*reservoir* PA-2
Wolf Lake Addition—*locale* IA-7
Wolflake Cem—*cemetery* IN-6
Wolf Lake Ch—*church* MI-6
Wolf Lake Ch—*church* MN-6
Wolf Lake Ch—*church* MS-4
*Wolf Lake Creek* MI-6
Wolf Lake Dam—*dam* NC-3
Wolf Lake Dam—*dam* PA-2
Wolf Lake Elem Sch—*school* IN-6
Wolf Lake Fish Hatchery—*other* MI-6
Wolf Lake Landing—*locale* MS-4
Wolf Lake Landing—*locale* NY-2
Wolf Lake Lookout Tower—*locale* MI-6
Wolf Lake Lookout Tower—*locale* MN-6
Wolf Lake Park—*park* IN-6
Wolf Lake Park—*park* WI-6
Wolf Lake (reduced usage)—*locale* IL-6
Wolf Lake Run—*stream* PA-2
Wolf Lakes—*area* AK-9
Wolf Lakes—*lake* NE-7
*Wolf Lake Saints Church* MS-4
Wolf Lake State Wildlife Mngmt Area—*park* MN-6
**Wolf Lake (Township of)**—*pop pl* MN-6
Wolf Lake Trail—*trail* WY-8
Wolf Lateral—*canal* SD-7
Wolf Laurel Basin—*basin* NC-3
Wolf Laurel Branch—*stream* (3) NC-3
Wolf Laurel Gap—*gap* NC-3
Wolf Laurel Top—*summit* GA-3
Wolfle Sch—*school* WA-9
Wolfley Creek—*stream* KS-7
Wolfley Hill—*summit* AZ-5
*Wolfleys Hill* AZ-5
Wolf Lick—*locale* KY-4
Wolf Lick Creek—*stream* KY-4
Wolf Lick Rsvr—*reservoir* PA-2
Wolf Lick Run—*stream* PA-2
**Wolf Lodge**—*pop pl* ID-8
Wolf Lodge Bay—*bay* ID-8
**Wolf Lodge Condominium**—*pop pl* UT-8
Wolf Lodge Creek—*stream* ID-8
Wolf Lodge Mtn—*summit* ID-8
Wolflok Well—*well* AZ-5
Wolf Meadow—*flat* OR-9
Wolf Meadow Branch—*stream* NC-3
*Wolf Mill* MD-2
Wolf Mine—*mine* AZ-5
Wolf Mountain—*locale* NC-3
Wolf Mountain Ch—*church* NC-3
Wolf Mountain Creek—*stream* MI-6
Wolf Mountain Lookout Tower—*locale* MT-8
Wolf Mountain Mine (surface)—*mine* AL-4
Wolf Mountain Trail—*trail* OR-9
*Wolf Mtn* TX-5
Wolf Mtn—*summit* AL-4
Wolf Mtn—*summit* AK-9
Wolf Mtn—*summit* AZ-5
Wolf Mtn—*summit* (3) AR-4
Wolf Mtn—*summit* CA-9
Wolf Mtn—*summit* (2) CO-8
Wolf Mtn—*summit* (2) ID-8
Wolf Mtn—*summit* MI-6
Wolf Mtn—*summit* (2) MO-7
Wolf Mtn—*summit* (2) MT-8
Wolf Mtn—*summit* NY-2
Wolf Mtn—*summit* (5) NC-3
Wolf Mtn—*summit* (5) OK-5
Wolf Mtn—*summit* (4) OR-9
Wolf Mtn—*summit* (6) TX-5
Wolf Mtn—*summit* (2) VA-3
Wolf Mtn—*summit* WY-8
Wolf Mtns—*range* MT-8
Wolf Mtns—*range* WY-8
*Wolf Neck* DE-2
Wolf Neck—*cape* ME-1
*Wolfnite Mountain* WA-9
Wolfolk—*locale* FL-3
**Wolford**—*pop pl* MN-6
**Wolford**—*pop pl* ND-7
**Wolford**—*pop pl* VA-3
Wolford Cabin—*locale* CA-9
Wolford Canyon—*valley* OR-9
Wolford Cem—*cemetery* IN-6
Wolford Cem—*cemetery* TN-4
Wolford Ch—*church* WV-2
Wolford Ditch—*canal* (2) WY-8
*Wolford Gap* PA-2
*Wolford Gap Run* PA-2
Wolford Gulch—*valley* CA-9
Wolford Mtn—*summit* CO-8
Wolford Run—*stream* PA-2
Wolford Sch—*school* MI-6
*Wolford's Creek* MD-2
Wolfords Gap—*gap* PA-2
*Wolford's Neck* MD-2
Wolford Spring—*spring* TN-4
**Wolford (Township of)**—*pop pl* MN-6
Wolford Valley—*basin* NE-7
Wolford Well—*well* TX-5
Wolfpack Creek—*stream* MN-6
Wolf Pack Islands—*island* MN-6
Wolfpack Lake—*lake* MN-6
Wolf Park—*flat* (2) CO-8
Wolf Park—*flat* MT-8
Wolf Pass—*gap* UT-8
Wolf Pass Well—*well* AZ-5
Wolf Path—*trail* PA-2
Wolf Peak—*summit* (2) OR-9
Wolf Pen—*locale* WV-2
**Wolfpen**—*pop pl* OH-6
Wolf Pen Bay—*swamp* NC-3
*Wolfpen Branch* KY-4
*Wolfpen Branch* WV-2
Wolf Pen Branch—*stream* AL-4
Wolfpen Branch—*stream* AL-4
Wolfpen Branch—*stream* AR-4
Wolfpen Branch—*stream* (6) GA-3
Wolfpen Branch—*stream* IN-6
Wolf Pen Branch—*stream* KY-4
Wolfpen Branch—*stream* (3) KY-4
Wolf Pen Branch—*stream* KY-4
Wolfpen Branch—*stream* (2) KY-4
Wolf Pen Branch—*stream* KY-4
Wolfpen Branch—*stream* (2) KY-4
Wolf Pen Branch—*stream* KY-4
Wolfpen Branch—*stream* (9) KY-4
Wolf Pen Branch—*stream* (6) KY-4
Wolfpen Branch—*stream* (2) KY-4
Wolf Pen Branch—*stream* KY-4
Wolfpen Branch—*stream* (3) KY-4
Wolf Pen Branch—*stream* KY-4
Wolfpen Branch—*stream* (11) KY-4
Wolf Pen Branch—*stream* MS-4
Wolfpen Branch—*stream* (2) MS-4
Wolf Pen Branch—*stream* MO-7
Wolfpen Branch—*stream* (4) NC-3
Wolfpen Branch—*stream* (6) TN-4
Wolf Pen Branch—*stream* TN-4
Wolfpen Branch—*stream* TN-4
Wolf Pen Branch—*stream* TN-4
Wolfpen Branch—*stream* (11) VA-3
Wolfpen Branch—*stream* (4) WV-2
Wolf Pen Branch—*stream* WV-2
Wolfpen Branch—*stream* (10) WV-2
*Wolf Pen Branch Banklick Branch* KY-4
Wolf Pen Branch Mill—*hist pl* KY-4
Wolfpen Cem—*cemetery* AL-4
Wolfpen Ch—*church* WV-2
Wolf Pen Ch—*church* WV-2
Wolfpen Cove—*valley* NC-3
Wolfpen Creek—*stream* AL-4
Wolfpen Creek—*stream* IN-6
Wolf Pen Creek—*stream* KS-7
Wolfpen Creek—*stream* KS-7
Wolfpen Creek—*stream* (3) KY-4
Wolf Pen Creek—*stream* KY-4
Wolfpen Creek—*stream* KY-4
Wolfpen Creek—*stream* (2) MO-7
Wolfpen Creek—*stream* (3) NC-3
Wolfpen Creek—*stream* OH-6
Wolfpen Creek—*stream* TN-4
Wolf Pen Creek—*stream* TX-5
Wolfpen Creek—*stream* (2) TX-5
Wolf Pen Creek—*stream* TX-5
Wolfpen Creek—*stream* TX-5
Wolfpen Creek—*stream* WV-2
Wolfpen Draft—*valley* VA-3
Wolfpen Fork—*stream* KY-4
Wolfpen Fork—*stream* WV-2
*Wolfpen Gap* GA-3
Wolf Pen Gap—*gap* AR-4
Wolfpen Gap—*gap* (8) GA-3
Wolfpen Gap—*gap* MO-7
Wolfpen Gap—*gap* (2) NC-3
Wolf Pen Gap—*gap* NC-3
Wolfpen Gap—*gap* (6) NC-3
Wolf Pen Gap—*gap* TN-4
Wolfpen Gap—*gap* TN-4
*Wolf Pen Hill* MA-1
Wolfpen Hill—*summit* MA-1
*Wolf Pen Hollow* MO-7
Wolfpen Hollow—*valley* AL-4
Wolf Pen Hollow—*valley* (4) AR-4
Wolfpen Hollow—*valley* IN-6
Wolf Pen Hollow—*valley* KY-4
Wolfpen Hollow—*valley* (5) KY-4
Wolfpen Hollow—*valley* MO-7
Wolf Pen Hollow—*valley* MO-7
Wolfpen Hollow—*valley* (4) MO-7
Wolf Pen Hollow—*valley* MO-7
Wolfpen Hollow—*valley* MO-7
Wolf Pen Hollow—*valley* MO-7
Wolf Pen Hollow—*valley* OH-6
Wolf Pen Hollow—*valley* TN-4
Wolfpen Hollow—*valley* (2) TN-4
Wolfpen Hollow—*valley* VA-3
Wolfpen Hollow—*valley* (6) WV-2
Wolfpen Knob—*summit* GA-3
Wolfpen Knob—*summit* VA-3
Wolf Pen Mountain—*ridge* NC-3
*Wolfpen Mtn* GA-3
*Wolf Pen Mtn* NC-3
Wolfpen Mtn—*summit* GA-3
Wolf Pen Mtn—*summit* NC-3
Wolfpen Mtn—*summit* NC-3
Wolfpen Mtn—*summit* TN-4
Wolfpen Point—*cape* TN-4
Wolf Pen Rec Area—*locale* AR-4
Wolf Pen Ridge—*ridge* (2) AL-4
Wolfpen Ridge—*ridge* (2) GA-3
Wolfpen Ridge—*ridge* IN-6
Wolfpen Ridge—*ridge* MO-7
Wolfpen Ridge—*ridge* TN-4
Wolfpen Ridge—*ridge* (2) VA-3
Wolfpen Ridge—*ridge* (2) WV-2
*Wolfpen Run* WV-2
Wolfpen Run—*stream* KY-4
Wolfpen Run—*stream* (6) OH-6
Wolfpen Run—*stream* (22) WV-2
Wolf Pen Run—*stream* WV-2
Wolfpen Run—*stream* (5) WV-2
Wolfpen Sch—*school* KY-4
Wolfpen Sch—*school* WV-2
Wolf Pen Slough—*stream* AR-4
Wolfpen Stamp—*summit* GA-3
Wolfpin Branch—*stream* SC-3
Wolfpin Gully—*valley* TX-5
Wolf Pinnacle—*summit* (2) AR-4
Wolf Pit—*locale* TN-4
**Wolfpit**—*pop pl* KY-4
Wolf Pit Bay—*swamp* (2) SC-3
*Wolfpit Branch* DE-2
Wolf Pit Branch—*stream* AL-4
Wolf Pit Branch—*stream* GA-3
Wolfpit Branch—*stream* KY-4
Wolfpit Branch—*stream* MD-2
Wolf Pit Branch—*stream* MD-2
Wolfpit Branch—*stream* NC-3
Wolf Pit Branch—*stream* (2) NC-3
Wolfpit Branch—*stream* NC-3
Wolf Pit Branch—*stream* SC-3
Wolf Pit Brook—*stream* CT-1
Wolf Pit Cem—*cemetery* SC-3
Wolfpit Creek—*stream* AL-4
Wolf Pit Creek—*stream* NC-3
Wolf Pit Gap—*gap* NC-3
Wolfpit Gap—*gap* (2) NC-3
*Wolf Pit Hill* PA-2
Wolfpit Hill—*summit* AL-4
Wolf Pit Hill—*summit* CT-1
Wolfpit Hill—*summit* PA-2
Wolf Pit Lake—*lake* NY-2
Wolfpit Marsh—*swamp* DE-2
Wolfpit Marsh—*swamp* MD-2
Wolfpit Meadows—*flat* MA-1
Wolf Pit Mtn—*summit* CT-1
Wolfpit Mtn—*summit* VA-3
Wolfpit Pond—*lake* DE-2
Wolf Pit Pond—*lake* GA-3
Wolfpit Pond—*lake* MD-2
Wolfpit Ridge—*ridge* NC-3
Wolfpit Ridge—*ridge* TN-4
Wolf Pit Ridge—*ridge* TN-4
Wolfpit Run—*stream* NC-3
Wolfpit Run—*stream* SC-3
Wolfpit Run—*stream* VA-3
Wolfpit Run—*stream* WV-2
Wolf Pit (Township of)—*fmr MCD* NC-3
*Wolfplain Brook* MA-1
Wolf Plain Brook—*stream* MA-1
Wolf Plains—*hist pl* OH-6
*Wolf Point* MI-6
Wolf Point—*cape* (2) AK-9
Wolf Point—*cape* MN-6
Wolf Point—*cape* (2) MT-8
Wolf Point—*cape* NY-2
Wolf Point—*cape* OK-5
Wolf Point—*cape* (2) TX-5
Wolf Point—*cape* UT-8
Wolf Point—*cape* WA-9
Wolf Point—*cliff* AZ-5
Wolf Point—*cliff* ID-8
Wolf Point—*cliff* (2) WY-8
**Wolf Point**—*pop pl* MT-8
Wolf Point—*summit* MT-8
Wolf Point—*summit* (2) OR-9
*Wolf Pond* PA-2
Wolf Pond—*lake* AL-4
Wolf Pond—*lake* (3) FL-3
Wolf Pond—*lake* GA-3
Wolf Pond—*lake* ME-1
Wolf Pond—*lake* MA-1
Wolf Pond—*lake* (15) NY-2
Wolf Pond—*lake* PA-2
Wolf Pond—*lake* WI-6
Wolf Pond—*locale* NY-2
Wolf Pond—*reservoir* TN-4
Wolf Pond—*swamp* FL-3
Wolf Pond Brook—*stream* (2) NY-2
Wolf Pond Camp—*locale* NY-2
Wolf Pond Ch—*church* SC-3
Wolf Pond Creek—*swamp* FL-3
Wolf Pond Mtn—*summit* (4) NY-2
Wolf Pond Outlet—*stream* (2) NY-2
*Wolf Pond Run* PA-2
Wolf Pond Trail—*trail* PA-2
Wolf Post Office—*locale* KY-4
Wolf Post Office (historical)—*building* AL-4
Wolf Prairie—*flat* LA-4
Wolf Prairie—*flat* MT-8
Wolf Prairie—*flat* OR-9
**Wolf Prairie**—*pop pl* MT-8
Wolf Prairie—*swamp* FL-3
Wolf Prairie Cem—*cemetery* IL-6
Wolf Prong Branch—*stream* LA-4
Wolf Prong Creek—*stream* TX-5
Wolf Proof Ranch—*locale* TX-5
Wolf Pup—*stream* AK-9
Wolfram Arm—*canal* IN-6
Wolframite Mtn—*summit* WA-9
Wolfram Lode—*mine* SD-7
Wolf Ranch—*locale* (2) CO-8
Wolf Ranch—*locale* MT-8
Wolf Ranch—*locale* NV-8
Wolf Ranch—*locale* ND-7
Wolf Ranch—*locale* SD-7
Wolf Ranch Lake—*reservoir* AL-4
Wolf Rapids—*rapids* WI-6
*Wolf Reservoir* NY-2
Wolf Ridge—*ridge* AL-4
Wolf Ridge—*ridge* AR-4
Wolf Ridge—*ridge* CA-9
Wolf Ridge—*ridge* CO-8
Wolf Ridge—*ridge* GA-3
Wolf Ridge—*ridge* KY-4
Wolf Ridge—*ridge* MO-7
Wolf Ridge—*ridge* NY-2
Wolf Ridge—*ridge* (6) NC-3
Wolf Ridge—*ridge* OK-5
Wolf Ridge—*ridge* (2) OR-9
Wolf Ridge—*ridge* (4) TN-4
Wolf Ridge—*ridge* (3) TX-5
Wolf Ridge—*ridge* (2) VA-3
Wolf Ridge Cem—*cemetery* AL-4
Wolf Ridge Cem—*cemetery* MS-4
Wolf Ridge Ch—*church* KY-4
Wolf Ridge Lookover—*locale* KY-4
Wolf Ridge Sch—*school* KY-4
**Wolf Ridge (subdivision)**—*pop pl* NC-3
Wolf Ridge Trail—*trail* TN-4
*Wolf River* WI-6
Wolf River—*locale* TN-4
Wolf River—*stream* KS-7
Wolf River—*stream* KY-4
Wolf River—*stream* (2) MS-4
Wolf River—*stream* (3) TN-4
Wolf River—*stream* (2) WI-6
Wolf River Cem—*cemetery* KS-7
Wolf River Cem—*cemetery* MS-4
Wolf River Cem—*cemetery* TN-4
Wolf River Cem—*cemetery* WI-6
Wolf River Ch—*church* TN-4
**Wolf River Dock**—*pop pl* KY-4
Wolf River Game Mngmt Area—*park* MS-4
Wolf River Lagoon—*lake* TN-4
Wolf River Lookout Tower—*locale* WI-6
Wolf River Post Office (historical)—*building* TN-4
Wolf River Ranch Airp—*airport* MS-4
Wolf River Ranch Lake—*reservoir* MS-4
Wolf River Rapids—*rapids* WI-6
Wolf River Sch—*school* WI-6
Wolf River State Fishery Area—*park* WI-6
**Wolf River (Town of)**—*pop pl* (2) WI-6
**Wolf River Township**—*pop pl* KS-7
Wolf Road Woods—*woods* IL-6
Wolf Rock—*pillar* MD-2
Wolf Rock—*pillar* OR-9
Wolf Rock—*pillar* (2) PA-2
Wolf Rock—*summit* CT-1
Wolf Rock—*summit* MD-2
Wolf Rock—*summit* (3) NC-3
Wolf Rock Cave—*cave* PA-2
Wolf Rock Hill—*summit* PA-2
Wolf Rock Hill—*valley* PA-2
Wolf Rock Hollow—*valley* VA-3
Wolf Rocks—*cliff* PA-2
Wolf Rocks—*range* PA-2
Wolf Rocks—*summit* RI-1
Wolf Rocks Cave—*cave* PA-2
Wolf Rocks Trail—*trail* (2) PA-2
Wolfrom Drain—*stream* MI-6
Wolf Rsvr—*reservoir* CO-8
Wolf-Ruebeling House—*hist pl* MO-7
Wolfrum Cem—*cemetery* MO-7
*Wolf Run* NE-7
*Wolf Run* PA-2
Wolf Run—*locale* OR-9
Wolf Run—*locale* WV-2
Wolfrun—*other* VA-3
**Wolf Run**—*pop pl* OH-6
**Wolf Run**—*pop pl* PA-2
Wolf Run—*stream* (2) IL-6
Wolf Run—*stream* (3) IN-6
Wolf Run—*stream* (2) IA-7
Wolf Run—*stream* (3) KY-4
Wolf Run—*stream* MO-7
Wolf Run—*stream* NJ-2
Wolf Run—*stream* (3) NY-2
Wolf Run—*stream* (14) OH-6
Wolf Run—*stream* OR-9
Wolf Run—*stream* (38) PA-2
Wolf Run—*stream* (5) VA-3
Wolf Run—*stream* (26) WV-2
Wolf Run—*stream* WI-6
Wolf Run Community Hall—*locale* OR-9
Wolf Run Creek—*stream* TX-5
Wolf Run Creek—*stream* VA-3
Wolf Run Ditch—*canal* OR-9
Wolf Run Hollow—*valley* VA-3
Wolf Run Lake—*reservoir* OH-6
Wolf Run Sch (historical)—*school* PA-2
Wolf Run Spring—*spring* PA-2
Wolf Run Trail—*trail* PA-2
Wolf Run Wild Area—*area* PA-2
**Wolfs**—*pop pl* (2) IL-6
Wolf Sawgrass Pond—*swamp* FL-3
Wolfs Bay—*swamp* NC-3
**Wolfsburg**—*pop pl* PA-2
Wolfs Cem—*cemetery* MD-2
Wolfs Cem—*cemetery* PA-2
Wolf Sch—*school* AR-4
Wolf Sch—*school* (2) IL-6
Wolf Sch—*school* KY-4
Wolf Sch—*school* (2) MO-7
Wolf Sch—*school* MT-8
Wolf Sch—*school* (2) PA-2
Wolf Sch—*school* VA-3
Wolf Sch (abandoned)—*school* PA-2
Wolfs Chapel (abandoned)—*church* PA-2
*Wolf School* FL-3
**Wolfs Corner**—*pop pl* PA-2
**Wolfs Corners**—*pop pl* PA-2
Wolfscrape Branch—*stream* NC-3
Wolfscrape (Township of)—*fmr MCD* NC-3
*Wolfs Crossing* IL-6
**Wolfs Crossroads**—*pop pl* PA-2
Wolf Shaft—*mine* WY-8
Wolfs Head—*summit* WY-8
Wolfs Head Lake—*lake* FL-3
Wolf Shelter—*locale* OR-9
Wolf Shoals—*bar* NC-3
*Wolf Siding* KS-7
Wolf Sink—*basin* AL-4
Wolf Sink—*basin* FL-3
Wolfskill Canyon—*valley* CA-9
*Wolfskill Creek* AL-4
Wolfskill Falls—*falls* CA-9
Wolfskill Sch—*school* CA-9
Wolfskull Creek—*stream* AL-4
Wolf Slough—*gut* AR-4
Wolf Slough—*gut* FL-3
Wolf Slough—*stream* AR-4
Wolf Slough—*stream* FL-3
Wolf Slough—*swamp* SD-7
Wolfs Mill—*locale* MD-2
Wolfsnare Creek—*stream* VA-3
**Wolfsnare Plantation**—*pop pl* VA-3
Wolfsnare Point—*cape* VA-3
*Wolfs Neck* ME-1
Wolfson Printing and Paper Co.—*hist pl* GA-3
Wolfson Ranch—*locale* CA-9
Wolfs Park—*park* NH-1
Wolfs Pond—*reservoir* WI-6
Wolf Spring—*spring* (3) AZ-5
Wolf Spring—*spring* CO-8
Wolf Spring—*spring* NM-5
Wolf Spring—*spring* OK-5
Wolf Spring—*spring* (4) OR-9
Wolf Spring—*spring* SD-7
Wolf Spring—*spring* TX-5
Wolf Spring—*spring* UT-8
Wolf Spring—*spring* WA-9
Wolf Spring—*spring* WY-8
Wolf Spring, The—*spring* CO-8
Wolf Spring Branch—*stream* VA-3
Wolf Spring Creek—*stream* MT-8
Wolf Spring Run—*stream* VA-3
**Wolf Springs**—*pop pl* AL-4
**Wolf Springs**—*pop pl* MS-4
Wolf Springs—*spring* MT-8
Wolf Springs—*spring* WY-8
*Wolf Springs Creek* MT-8
Wolf Spring Slough—*stream* TX-5
Wolf Springs Sch (historical)—*school* AL-4
*Wolf Springs Wash* UT-8
Wolf Springs Wash—*valley* UT-8
Wolf Spring Trail—*trail* OR-9
Wolf Spring Wash—*valley* UT-8
Wolfspur Branch—*stream* KY-4
Wolfs Spring Run—*stream* PA-2
Wolfs Stake Ch—*church* SC-3
**Wolfs Store**—*pop pl* PA-2
Wolfs Store Gap—*gap* PA-2
Wolf Stake Gap—*gap* GA-3
Wolfstake Knob—*summit* GA-3
Wolf Stand—*summit* NM-5
**Wolf Star Subdivision**—*pop pl* UT-8
Wolf State Public Shooting Area—*park* SD-7
**Wolf Summit**—*pop pl* WV-2
**Wolfsville**—*pop pl* MD-2
Wolfsville Crossing—*locale* MD-2
*Wolf Swamp* NC-3
Wolf Swamp—*stream* (2) NC-3
Wolf Swamp—*stream* VA-3
Wolf Swamp—*swamp* (2) CT-1
Wolf Swamp—*swamp* MD-2
Wolf Swamp—*swamp* (4) MA-1
Wolf Swamp—*swamp* (3) PA-2
Wolf Swamp Run—*stream* PA-2
Wolftail Mtn—*summit* MT-8
Wolf Tank—*reservoir* AZ-5
Wolf Tank—*reservoir* NM-5
Wolf Tank—*reservoir* (2) TX-5
Wolftever Bridge—*bridge* TN-4
Wolftever Creek—*stream* TN-4
Wolftever Fishing Club—*locale* TN-4
Wolf Thicket Bay—*swamp* AL-4
**Wolfton**—*pop pl* SC-3
Wolftone Campground—*locale* ID-8
Wolftone Creek—*stream* ID-8
Wolftone Point—*cape* NV-8
Wolfton Sch—*school* SC-3
*Wolftown* MS-4
*Wolftown* PA-2
Wolftown—*locale* AL-4
Wolftown—*locale* VA-3
Wolftown—*uninc pl* PA-2
Wolf Township—*civil* PA-2
**Wolf (Township of)**—*pop pl* PA-2
Wolf Trail—*trail* PA-2
Wolf Trail—*trail* WY-8
Wolf Trail Bay—*swamp* FL-3
Wolf Trail Lodge—*locale* AK-9
Wolf Trap—*CDP* VA-3
Wolf Trap—*locale* VA-3
Wolf Trap Bay—*swamp* FL-3
Wolftrap Branch—*stream* FL-3
Wolf Trap Branch—*stream* NC-3
Wolftrap Branch—*stream* (2) VA-3
Wolftrap Creek—*stream* MD-2
Wolftrap Creek—*stream* VA-3
Wolf Trap Creek—*stream* VA-3
Wolftrap Farm—*hist pl* VA-3
Wolf Trap Farm Park—*park* VA-3
Wolf Trap Farm Park For The Performing Arts—*park* VA-3
Wolftrap Stream Valley Park—*park* VA-3
Wolf Valley—*valley* (2) CA-9
Wolf Valley—*valley* TN-4
Wolf Valley—*valley* (2) WI-6
Wolf Valley Ch—*church* TN-4
Wolf Valley Ch—*church* TX-5
Wolf Valley Ch—*church* WV-2
**Wolfville (historical)**—*pop pl* NC-3
Wolf Wallow Ridge—*ridge* AR-4
Wolf Waterhole Draw—*valley* TX-5
Wolf Well—*well* NM-5
Wolf Windmill—*locale* CO-8
Wolf Windmill—*locale* NM-5
Wolf Windmill—*locale* TX-5
**Wolhurst**—*pop pl* CO-8
Wolhurst Lake—*lake* CO-8
Wolkenburg—*summit* TX-5
Wolken 2 Dam—*dam* SD-7
Wolk Harbor—*bay* AK-9
Wolk Point—*cape* AK-9
*Wollah Wollah* WA-9
*Wollah Wollah River* OR-9
Wollan Lake—*lake* MN-6
Wollard Cem—*cemetery* MO-7
*Wollard Creek* WA-9
Wollaston, Mount—*summit* MA-1
Wollaston Beach—*beach* MA-1
Wollaston Channel—*channel* MA-1
*Wollaston Heights* MA-1
Wollaston Heights—*summit* MA-1
Wollaston Heights Station (historical)—*locale* MA-1
Wollaston (historical P.O.)—*locale* MA-1
**Wollaston (subdivision)**—*pop pl* MA-1
*Wollaw Wollah* WA-9
Wollenson-Nacewonder Bldg—*hist pl* OK-5
Woller—*island* MP-9
Woller Cem—*cemetery* WI-6
*Woller Island* MP-9
*Woller Woller* WA-9
*Woller Woller River* OR-9
Wolley Stille—*hist pl* PA-2
**Wollingtown**—*pop pl* KY-4
Wollison-Shipton Bldg—*hist pl* MA-1
Wollman, Joseph, House—*hist pl* SD-7
Wollmon Spring—*spring* NV-8
Wollner Bldg—*hist pl* PA-2
Wollochet—*locale* WA-9
Wollochet Bay—*bay* WA-9
Wollochet-Point Fosdick Sch—*hist pl* WA-9
Wollum Branch—*stream* KY-4
Wollum Cem—*cemetery* KY-4
*Wolly Horn Ridge* OR-9
*Wolmad* FM-9
Wol'maed—*summit* FM-9
*Wolmat* FM-9
Woloke—*locale* FM-9
Woloki Slough—*stream* CA-9
Wolomolopoag Pond—*lake* MA-1
Wolomwin Island—*island* FM-9
*Wolopeconek Pond* RI-1
Wolosz Pond—*lake* WI-6
Wolpen Branch—*stream* WV-2
Wolphen Hollow—*valley* TX-5
*Wolpi* AZ-5
Wolquarry—*locale* AR-4
**Wolram (Walls)**—*pop pl* KY-4
Wolseth—*locale* ND-7
**Wolsey**—*pop pl* SD-7
Wolsey Branch—*stream* KY-4
Wolsey Cem—*cemetery* SD-7
Wolsey Creek—*stream* MT-8
Wolsey Creek—*stream* OR-9
**Wolsey Township**—*pop pl* SD-7
Wolsfeld Lake—*lake* MN-6
Wolsgrover Island—*island* ME-1
Wolstad Ranch—*locale* MT-8
*Wolte Creek* PA-2
Wolter Lake—*lake* OR-9
Wolters Colony Ditch—*canal* CA-9
Wolters Double Houses—*hist pl* ID-8
Wolters Filling Station—*hist pl* IA-7
Wolters Park—*park* TX-5
Wolters Sch—*school* CA-9
**Wolters Village**—*pop pl* TX-5
Wolton Rsvr—*reservoir* WY-8
Woltz Hollow—*valley* OH-6
Woltz Point—*cape* ME-1
*Woltz's Point* ME-1
Wolven Cem—*cemetery* NY-2
Wolverine—*locale* ID-8
Wolverine—*locale* KY-4
Wolverine—*locale* TN-4
**Wolverine**—*pop pl* (2) MI-6
Wolverine, Lake—*lake* WA-9
Wolverine, Mount—*summit* UT-8
Wolverine Basin—*basin* (2) CO-8
Wolverine Basin—*basin* MT-8
Wolverine Bench—*bench* UT-8
Wolverine Canyon—*valley* UT-8
Wolverine Crags—*summit* AK-9
*Wolverine Creek* MT-8
Wolverine Creek—*stream* (8) AK-9
Wolverine Creek—*stream* (2) CO-8
Wolverine Creek—*stream* (3) ID-8
Wolverine Creek—*stream* KS-7
Wolverine Creek—*stream* (4) MT-8
Wolverine Creek—*stream* OR-9
Wolverine Creek—*stream* UT-8
Wolverine Creek—*stream* WA-9
Wolverine Creek—*stream* (2) WY-8
Wolverine Drain—*canal* MI-6
Wolverine Falls—*falls* MI-6
Wolverine Flat—*flat* MT-8
Wolverine Fork—*stream* AK-9
Wolverine Glacier—*glacier* AK-9
Wolverine Gulch—*valley* AK-9
Wolverine Gulch—*valley* CO-8
Wolverine Gulch—*valley* MT-8
Wolverine Hollow—*valley* KY-4
Wolverine Hotel—*hist pl* MI-6
Wolverine Lake—*lake* (2) AK-9
Wolverine Lake—*lake* CA-9
Wolverine Lake—*lake* (2) CO-8
Wolverine Lake—*lake* (2) MI-6
Wolverine Lake—*lake* MN-6
**Wolverine Lake**—*pop pl* MI-6
Wolverine Lakes—*lake* MT-8
Wolverine Lookout Tower—*locale* MI-6
Wolverine Meadow—*flat* OR-9
Wolverine Mine—*mine* CA-9
Wolverine Mine—*mine* (2) CO-8
Wolverine Mines—*mine* AZ-5
Wolverine Mtn—*summit* (2) AK-9
Wolverine Pass—*gap* MT-8
Wolverine Peak—*summit* AK-9
Wolverine Peak—*summit* (2) MT-8
Wolverine Peak—*summit* WY-8
Wolverine Petrified Wood Area—*area* UT-8
*Wolverine Petrified Wood Natural Area* UT-8
**Wolverine (Riverside)**—*pop pl* KY-4
Wolverine Sch—*school* IL-6
Wolverine Trail—*trail* CO-8
Wolverton—*locale* CA-9
Wolverton—*locale* PA-2
**Wolverton**—*pop pl* MN-6
Wolverton Brook—*stream* ME-1
Wolverton Cem—*cemetery* MN-6
Wolverton Cem—*cemetery* MS-4
Wolverton Cem—*cemetery* TN-4
Wolverton Cem—*cemetery* (2) WV-2
Wolverton Corrals—*locale* CA-9
*Wolverton Creek* NV-8
Wolverton Creek—*stream* CA-9
Wolverton Creek—*stream* MN-6
Wolverton Gulch—*valley* CA-9
*Wolverton Meadow* CA-9
*Wolverton Mountain* AR-4
Wolverton Mtn—*summit* (2) AZ-5
Wolverton Plains Cem—*cemetery* MI-6

Woodbury Sch Number 5—*school* ND-7
Woodbury Shell Midden (15BT67)—*hist pl* KY-4
*Woodburys Point* MA-1
**Woodbury (subdivision)**—*pop pl* DE-2
**Woodbury Subdivision**—*pop pl* UT-8
Woodbury Terrace—*other* NJ-2
Woodbury Town Hall—*building* ND-7
**Woodbury (Town of)**—*pop pl* CT-1
**Woodbury (Town of)**—*pop pl* NY-2
**Woodbury (Town of)**—*pop pl* VT-1
Woodbury Township—*fmr MCD* IA-7
**Woodbury Township**—*pop pl* ND-7
**Woodbury (Township of)**—*pop pl* IL-6
**Woodbury (Township of)**—*pop pl* (2) PA-2
**Woodbury Village (subdivision)**—*pop pl* NC-3
Woodbury Waterworks—*other* GA-3
Woodbury Wildlife Area—*park* OH-6
Woodbush Sch—*school* PA-2
Wood Butte—*summit* OR-9
Woodby Cem—*cemetery* TN-4
Woodby Drain—*canal* MI-6
Woodby Hill—*locale* TN-4
Woodby Mtn—*summit* OR-9
Wood Cabin Creek—*stream* ID-8
Wood Camp—*locale* NV-8
Wood Camp Cabin—*locale* AZ-5
Wood Camp Campground—*locale* UT-8
Wood Camp Canyon—*valley* AZ-5
Woodcamp Canyon—*valley* WA-9
Woodcamp Creek—*stream* AK-9
Woodcamp Creek—*stream* CA-9
Wood Camp Creek—*stream* OR-9
Wood Camp Hollow—*valley* UT-8
Woodcamp Lake—*lake* MN-6
Wood Camp Rsvr—*reservoir* OR-9
Woodcamp Spring—*spring* AZ-5
Woodcamp Spring—*spring* (3) NV-8
Wood Camp Spring—*spring* OR-9
Woodcamp Springs—*spring* NV-8
Wood Camp Tank—*reservoir* AZ-5
*Wood Canyon* AZ-5
*Wood Canyon* ID-8
Wood Canyon—*valley* AK-9
Wood Canyon—*valley* (13) AZ-5
Wood Canyon—*valley* (14) CA-9
Wood Canyon—*valley* (9) ID-8
Wood Canyon—*valley* MT-8
Wood Canyon—*valley* NE-7
Wood Canyon—*valley* (14) NV-8
Wood Canyon—*valley* (7) NM-5
Wood Canyon—*valley* (6) TX-5
Wood Canyon—*valley* (7) UT-8
Wood Canyon—*valley* (3) WY-8
Wood Canyon Creek—*stream* NV-8
Wood Canyon Park—*flat* AZ-5
Wood Canyon Spring—*spring* AZ-5
Wood Canyon Spring—*spring* ID-8
Wood Canyon Spring—*spring* NV-8
Wood Canyon Spring—*spring* TX-5
Wood Canyon Wash—*stream* AZ-5
Wood Canyon Well—*well* TX-5
Woodcastle Sch—*school* NJ-2
*Wood Cem* MS-4
Wood Cem—*cemetery* (2) AR-4
Wood Cem—*cemetery* FL-3
Wood Cem—*cemetery* (2) GA-3
Wood Cem—*cemetery* IL-6
Wood Cem—*cemetery* (2) IN-6
Wood Cem—*cemetery* KS-7
Wood Cem—*cemetery* (2) KY-4
Wood Cem—*cemetery* MI-6
Wood Cem—*cemetery* (2) MS-4
Wood Cem—*cemetery* (2) MO-7
Wood Cem—*cemetery* NE-7
Wood Cem—*cemetery* (4) NY-2
Wood Cem—*cemetery* (2) NC-3
Wood Cem—*cemetery* OH-6
Wood Cem—*cemetery* OK-5
Wood Cem—*cemetery* (9) TN-4
Wood Cem—*cemetery* (5) TX-5
Wood Cem—*cemetery* (5) VA-3
Wood Cem—*cemetery* (2) WI-6
Wood Central Ditch—*canal* CA-9
Wood Ch—*church* AR-4
Wood Ch—*church* KY-4
Wood Ch—*church* TN-4
Wood Chapel—*church* LA-4
Wood Chapel—*church* MS-4
Wood Chapel—*church* OH-6
Wood Chapel Cem—*cemetery* SC-3
**Woodchase**—*pop pl* TN-4
Wood Chop Mesa—*summit* AZ-5
Woodchopper (Abandoned)—*locale* AK-9
Woodchopper Canyon—*valley* CA-9
Woodchopper Canyon—*valley* NV-8
Woodchopper Creek—*locale* AK-9
Woodchopper Creek—*stream* (2) AK-9
Woodchopper Creek—*stream* WY-8
Woodchopper Gulch—*valley* (2) CA-9
Woodchopper Gulch—*valley* MT-8
Woodchopper Ridge—*ridge* MT-8
Woodchopper Roadhouse—*hist pl* AK-9
Woodchopper Roadhouse (Aban'd)—*locale* AK-9
Woodchoppers Canyon—*valley* CA-9
Woodchoppers Canyon—*valley* WA-9
Woodchoppers Pond—*lake* NY-2
Woodchopper Spring—*spring* AZ-5
Woodchopper Spring—*spring* CA-9
Woodchopper Spring—*spring* (2) OR-9
Woodchoppers Spring—*spring* CA-9
Woodchoppers Spring—*spring* NM-5
Woodchoppertown—*locale* PA-2
Woodchopper Wash—*stream* AZ-5
Woodchopping Branch—*stream* TN-4
Woodchopping Ridge—*ridge* ME-1
Wood Chromite Mine—*mine* PA-2
Woodchuck—*locale* LA-4
Woodchuck Basin—*basin* CA-9
Woodchuck Basin—*basin* CO-8
Woodchuck Branch—*stream* TN-4
Woodchuck Canyon—*valley* MT-8
Woodchuck Canyon—*valley* UT-8
Woodchuck Cave—*cave* PA-2
Woodchuck Country—*area* CA-9
Woodchuck Creek—*stream* CA-9
Woodchuck Creek—*stream* MI-6
Woodchuck Creek—*stream* (2) MT-8
Woodchuck Creek—*stream* WY-8
Woodchuck Diich—*canal* CO-8
Woodchuck Flat—*flat* CA-9
Woodchuck Hill—*summit* CO-8
Woodchuck Hill—*summit* CT-1
Woodchuck Hill—*summit* ME-1
Woodchuck Hill—*summit* (3) MA-1
Woodchuck Hill—*summit* (6) NY-2
Woodchuck Hill—*summit* VT-1
Woodchuck Hole—*basin* NY-2
*Woodchuck Hollow* NY-2
Woodchuck Hollow—*basin* NY-2
Woodchuck Hollow—*valley* NY-2
Woodchuck Lake—*lake* CA-9
Woodchuck Lake—*lake* (2) MN-6
Woodchuck Ledge—*bench* NH-1
Woodchuck Mine—*mine* SD-7
*Woodchuck Mountain* CO-8
Woodchuck Mountian—*summit* MT-8
Woodchuck Mtn—*summit* VT-1
Woodchuck Pass—*gap* WY-8
Woodchuck Peak—*summit* CO-8
Woodchuck Peak—*summit* MT-8
Woodchuck Ridge—*ridge* MT-8
Woodchuck Run—*stream* PA-2
Woodchuck Sch—*school* WI-6
Woodchuck Spring—*spring* (2) NV-8
Woodchuck Spring—*spring* OR-9
Woodchuck Spring—*spring* UT-8
Wood Chute Gulch—*valley* MT-8
Woodchute Mtn—*summit* AZ-5
Woodchute Tank—*reservoir* AZ-5
Woodchute Trail—*trail* AZ-5
**Woodcliff**—*pop pl* GA-3
**Woodcliff**—*pop pl* NE-7
**Woodcliff**—*pop pl* NJ-2
**Woodcliff**—*pop pl* TN-4
**Woodcliff Acres**—*pop pl* WV-2
Woodcliff Burials—*hist pl* NE-7
Woodcliff Ch—*church* TN-4
**Woodcliffe**—*pop pl* MO-7
**Woodcliff Lake**—*pop pl* NJ-2
Woodcliff Lake—*reservoir* NJ-2
Woodcliff Lake Dam—*dam* NJ-2
**Woodcliff Park**—*pop pl* NY-2
Woodcliff Sch—*school* MI-6
Woodclift Canal—*canal* NY-2
Woodclinch Brook—*stream* IN-6
**Woodcock**—*pop pl* PA-2
Woodcock Bar—*bar* NJ-2
Woodcock Borough—*civil* PA-2
Woodcock Branch—*stream* GA-3
Woodcock Brook—*stream* ME-1
Woodcock Brook—*stream* NJ-2
Woodcock Cem—*cemetery* MO-7
Woodcock Cem—*cemetery* NC-3
Woodcock Coulee—*valley* MT-8
*Woodcock Creek* OR-9
Woodcock Creek—*stream* (2) OR-9
Woodcock Creek—*stream* (2) PA-2
Woodcock Creek—*stream* TN-4
Woodcock Creek Dam—*dam* PA-2
Woodcock Creek Lake—*reservoir* PA-2
*Woodcock Creek Rsvr* PA-2
**Woodcock Grange**—*pop pl* PA-2
Woodcock Gulf—*valley* TN-4
Woodcock Hill—*summit* NY-2
Woodcock Hill—*summit* PA-2
Woodcock Island—*island* OH-6
Woodcock Knob—*summit* NC-3
*Woodcock Lake* MN-6
Woodcock Lake—*lake* FL-3
Woodcock Lake—*lake* (2) MN-6
Woodcock Lake—*lake* WI-6
Woodcock Meadow—*flat* CA-9
Woodcock Mtn—*summit* NY-2
Woodcock Mtn—*summit* OR-9
*Woodcock Reservoir* PA-2
Woodcock Run—*stream* PA-2
Woodcocks Branch—*stream* KY-4
Woodcock Sch—*school* AL-4
Woodcock Sch—*school* (2) MA-1
Woodcock Spring—*spring* SD-7
**Woodcock (Township of)**—*pop pl* PA-2
Woodcock Trail—*trail* PA-2
Woodcock Valley—*valley* (2) PA-2
Woodcock Valley Elem Sch—*school* PA-2
Woodcolony Cem—*cemetery* CA-9
Wood Commercial Bldg—*hist pl* OH-6
Wood Cone Peak—*summit* NV-8
Wood Corners—*locale* NY-2
Wood Corners Sch—*school* PA-2
Wood Cottage Bar—*bar* MS-4
**Wood (County)**—*pop pl* OH-6
**Wood (County)**—*pop pl* TX-5
**Wood (County)**—*pop pl* WV-2
**Wood (County)**—*pop pl* WI-6
Wood County Airp (Gill Robb Wilson Field)—*airport* WV-2
Wood County Courthouse—*hist pl* WV-2
Wood County Courthouse And Jail—*hist pl* OH-6
Wood County Home and Infirmary—*hist pl* OH-6
Wood Cove—*bay* AK-9
Wood Cove—*bay* ME-1
**Woodcove Subdivision**—*pop pl* UT-8
*Wood Creek* CA-9
*Wood Creek* IA-7
*Wood Creek* MT-8
*Wood Creek* NV-8
*Wood Creek* TX-5
*Wood Creek* VA-3
*Wood Creek* WI-6
Wood Creek—*gut* NY-2
Wood Creek—*gut* SC-3
**Woodcreek**—*pop pl* DE-2
**Wood Creek**—*pop pl* MD-2
**Woodcreek**—*pop pl* TX-5
Wood Creek—*stream* (4) AK-9
Wood Creek—*stream* (2) AZ-5
Wood Creek—*stream* AR-4
Wood Creek—*stream* CA-9
Wood Creek—*stream* (2) CT-1
Wood Creek—*stream* GA-3
Wood Creek—*stream* (6) ID-8
Wood Creek—*stream* KY-4
Wood Creek—*stream* MD-2
Wood Creek—*stream* MO-7
Wood Creek—*stream* (4) MT-8
Wood Creek—*stream* NE-7
Wood Creek—*stream* (4) NY-2
Wood Creek—*stream* NC-3
Wood Creek—*stream* (7) OR-9
Wood Creek—*stream* (2) TX-5
Wood Creek—*stream* VA-3
Wood Creek—*stream* (2) WA-9
Wood Creek—*stream* (2) WI-6
Wood Creek—*stream* (2) WY-8
**Woodcreek Condo**—*pop pl* UT-8
*Wood Creek Farms* MI-6
**Wood Creek Farms**—*pop pl* MI-6
**Woodcreek Glen Condo**—*pop pl* UT-8
**Wood Creek Glen Condominium**—*pop pl* UT-8
Wood Creek Hogback—*ridge* MT-8
Wood Creek Lake—*reservoir* KY-4
Wood Creek Mtn—*summit* ID-8
Wood Creek Pond—*lake* CT-1
Wood Creek Slough—*stream* WI-6
Wood Creek Spring—*spring* AZ-5
**Woodcreek (subdivision)**—*pop pl* (2) AZ-5
**Wood Creek West**—*pop pl* TN-4
**Woodcrest**—*pop pl* AL-4
**Woodcrest**—*pop pl* CA-9
**Woodcrest**—*pop pl* (2) DE-2
**Woodcrest**—*pop pl* IL-6
**Woodcrest**—*pop pl* IN-6
**Woodcrest**—*pop pl* MD-2
**Woodcrest**—*pop pl* NJ-2
**Woodcrest**—*pop pl* PA-2
**Woodcrest Acres**—*pop pl* NJ-2
**Woodcrest Acres**—*pop pl* TX-5
Woodcrest Ch—*church* TX-5
Woodcrest Country Club—*other* NJ-2
Woodcrest Country Club—*other* NY-2
Woodcrest Dam—*dam* CA-9
**Woodcrest Estates**—*pop pl* DE-2
**Woodcrest Estates (subdivision)**—*pop pl* AL-4
**Woodcrest Hills**—*pop pl* TN-4
Woodcrest (OPlaza (Shop Ctr)—*locale* MO-7
Woodcrest Park—*park* (2) AL-4
Woodcrest Park—*park* (2) MN-6
**Woodcrest Park (subdivision)**—*pop pl* NC-3
Woodcrest Plaza—*locale* MO-7
Woodcrest Sch—*school* (2) CA-9
Woodcrest Sch—*school* MI-6
Woodcrest Sch—*school* MN-6
Woodcrest Sch—*school* NJ-2
Woodcrest Sch—*school* NY-2
Woodcrest Sch—*school* OH-6
Woodcrest Sch—*school* TX-5
**Woodcrest (subdivision)**—*pop pl* MS-4
**Woodcrest (subdivision)**—*pop pl* (2) NC-3
**Woodcroft**—*pop pl* MD-2
Woodcroft—*uninc pl* CO-8
Woodcroft Park—*park* WA-9
Woodcroft Sanatorium—*hist pl* CO-8
Woodcroft Sch—*school* NJ-2
Wood Curt Lake—*lake* WI-6
Wood Cut—*channel* GA-3
Woodcut Hollow—*valley* TN-4
Woodcutters Canyon—*valley* AZ-5
Wood-Cutting Sch (abandoned)—*school* PA-2
Wooddale—*locale* DE-2
Wooddale—*locale* PA-2
**Wood Dale**—*pop pl* IL-6
**Wooddale**—*pop pl* IL-6
**Wood Dale**—*pop pl* NC-3
**Wooddale**—*pop pl* PA-2
**Wooddale**—*pop pl* TN-4
**Wooddale**—*pop pl* WI-6
Wooddale Bridge—*hist pl* DE-2
Wooddale Ch—*church* TN-4
Wood Dale Grove—*woods* IL-6
Wooddale Hist Dist—*hist pl* DE-2
Wooddale Post Office (historical)—*building* AL-4
Wooddale Sch—*school* MI-6
Wooddale Sch—*school* MN-6
Wood Dale Sch—*school* TN-4
**Wooddale (sta.)**—*pop pl* DE-2
**Wooddale (subdivision)**—*pop pl* AL-4
**Wood Dale (subdivision)**—*pop pl* MS-4
Wood Dam—*dam* MA-1
Wood Dam—*dam* NC-3
Wood Ditch—*canal* (2) OH-6
Wood Draft—*valley* VA-3
Wood Drain—*canal* ID-8
Wood Draw—*valley* NM-5
Wood Draw—*valley* WY-8
Wood Duck Creek—*stream* VT-1
Wood Duck Island—*island* MN-6
Wood Duck Island—*island* TN-4
Wood Duck Lake—*reservoir* MS-4
Wood Duck Slough—*gut* IA-7
**Wooded Acres**—*pop pl* TN-4
**Wooded Acres (subdivision)**—*pop pl* DE-2
**Wooded Acres Subdivision**—*pop pl* UT-8
**Woodedge**—*pop pl* WY-8
Wooded Hill—*summit* CA-9
**Wooded Hills**—*pop pl* TX-5
**Wooded Hills Subdivision**—*pop pl* UT-8
Wooded Hollow—*valley* OK-5
Wooded Island—*island* AK-9
Wooded Island—*island* WA-9
Wooded Island Archeol District—*hist pl* WA-9
Wooded Islands—*island* AK-9
Wooded Lake—*reservoir* NC-3
Wooded Mtn—*summit* NC-3
Wooded Peak—*summit* WA-9
*Wooded Pond* LA-4
**Wooded Shores**—*pop pl* IL-6
Wooded Tank—*reservoir* AZ-5
*Woodell* PA-2
Woodell Branch—*stream* FL-3
Woodell Mine (underground)—*mine* AL-4
Wooden Baggage Express No. 6—*hist pl* PA-2
Wooden Ball Island—*island* ME-1
Wooden Branch—*stream* AL-4
Wooden Bridge Creek—*stream* PA-2
Wooden Bridge Run—*stream* PA-2
**Wooden Bridge (subdivision)**—*pop pl* DE-2
Wooden Canoe Lake—*lake* AK-9
Wooden Cem—*cemetery* KS-7
Wooden Cem—*cemetery* KY-4
Wooden Cem—*cemetery* WI-6
Wooden Chapel—*church* PA-2
Wooden Creek—*stream* OR-9
*Woodend* MA-1
Woodend—*hist pl* MD-2
**Wood End**—*pop pl* MA-1
Wood End Bar—*bar* MA-1
Wood End Light—*locale* MA-1
Wood End Lighthouse—*locale* MA-1
Wood End Light Lookout Station—*hist pl*. MA-1
Wooden Express Baggage No. 6076—*hist pl* PA-2
Woodenhawk—*locale* DE-2
Woodenhawk Bridge—*bridge* DE-2
Wooden Hills—*locale* AR-4
Wooden Hopper Gondola No. 1818—*hist pl* PA-2
Wooden Island—*island* AK-9
Wooden Leg Lake—*lake* MN-6
*Wooden Rock Creek* OR-9
Wooden Rock Creek—*stream* OR-9
Wooden Rock Guard Station—*locale* OR-9
Wooden Run—*stream* VA-3
**Woodensburg**—*pop pl* MD-2
Wooden Sch—*school* MI-6
Wooden Sch (historical)—*school* MO-7
Wooden Shoe—*pillar* UT-8
Wooden Shoe Annies Ranch (Ruins)—*locale* CA-9
Woodenshoe Arch—*arch* UT-8
Wooden Shoe Butte—*summit* ID-8
Woodenshoe Buttes—*summit* UT-8
Wooden Shoe Camp—*locale* MT-8
Woodenshoe Canyon—*valley* UT-8
Wooden Shoe Creek—*stream* ID-8
Wooden Shoe Creek—*stream* MT-8
*Wooden Shoe Peak* ID-8
Wooden Shoe Spring—*spring* ID-8
**Wooden Shoe Village**—*pop pl* MI-6
Wooden Tank—*reservoir* AZ-5
Wooden Tank—*reservoir* TX-5
Woodenthigh Creek—*stream* MT-8
Wooden Tower Tank—*reservoir* AZ-5
Wooden Tower Windmill—*locale* (2) TX-5
Wooden Trough Spring—*spring* AZ-5
Wooden Trough Spring—*spring* OR-9
Wooden Valley—*valley* CA-9
Wooden Valley Creek—*stream* CA-9
Wooden Valley Sch—*school* CA-9
Wooden Wheel Cove—*bay* AK-9
Wooden Wheel Well—*locale* NM-5
Wooden Windmill—*locale* (2) TX-5
Wooderson Cem—*cemetery* MO-7
Wooderson Sch (historical)—*school* (2) MO-7
**Wood Estates**—*pop pl* RI-1
**Wood Estates (subdivision)**—*pop pl* AL-4
**Wood Estates Subdivision**—*pop pl* UT-8
Woodey (historical)—*locale* KS-7
Woodey Spring—*spring* CO-8
Woodfell Cem—*cemetery* ID-8
Woodfell Cem—*cemetery* WV-2
Woodfern—*locale* NJ-2
Woodfern Creek—*stream* CO-8
Wood Ferry (historical)—*locale* AL-4
Woodfield—*CDP* SC-3
**Woodfield**—*pop pl* MD-2
Woodfield Airp—*airport* MO-7
**Woodfield Estates Subdivision**—*pop pl* UT-8
Woodfield Lake Dam—*dam* MS-4
Woodfield Mall—*post sta* IL-6
**Woodfield Park**—*pop pl* TN-4
Woodfield Road Sch—*school* NY-2
**Woodfields**—*pop pl* SC-3
Woodfields Sch—*school* SC-3
**Woodfield (subdivision)**—*pop pl* AL-4
**Woodfield (subdivision)**—*pop pl* (2) NC-3
Woodfill Sch—*school* KY-4
**Woodfin**—*pop pl* NC-3
Woodfin Branch—*stream* TX-5
Woodfin Cem—*cemetery* TN-4
Woodfin Creek—*stream* NC-3
Woodfin Elem Sch—*school* NC-3
Woodfin Mill—*locale* AL-4
Woodfin Mill—*locale* GA-3
Woodfin Reservoir Dam—*dam* NC-3
Woodfin Rsvr—*reservoir* (2) NC-3
Woodfin Valley—*valley* TN-4
Woodfir Creek—*stream* MT-8
Wood Flat Rsvr—*reservoir* CA-9
*Woodford* AL-4
Woodford—*hist pl* PA-2
Woodford—*hist pl* VA-3
Woodford—*locale* AL-4
Woodford—*locale* CA-9
Woodford—*locale* IL-6
Woodford—*locale* VA-3
**Woodford**—*pop pl* MD-2
**Woodford**—*pop pl* NC-3
**Woodford**—*pop pl* OK-5
**Woodford**—*pop pl* SC-3
**Woodford**—*pop pl* VT-1
**Woodford**—*pop pl* WI-6
Woodford Cem—*cemetery* WV-2
Woodford Corner—*locale* VA-3
**Woodford (County)**—*pop pl* IL-6
**Woodford (County)**—*pop pl* KY-4
Woodford County State Conservation Area—*forest* IL-6
Woodford Creek—*stream* OR-9
**Woodford Green (subdivision)**—*pop pl* NC-3
Woodford Hills Country Club—*other* KY-4
**Woodford (historical)**—*pop pl* TN-4
**Woodford Hollow**—*pop pl* VT-1
Woodford Hollow Ch—*church* VT-1
Woodford Hollow Sch—*school* VT-1
**Woodford (Keene)**—*pop pl* CA-9
Woodford (Northfield Station)—*locale* NY-2
Woodford Post Office (historical)—*building* TN-4
Woodford Run—*stream* WV-2
*Woodfords* ME-1
**Woodfords**—*pop pl* CA-9
**Woodfords**—*pop pl* ME-1
Woodford Sch—*school* OH-6
Woodfords Community (Indian Reservation)—*reserve* CA-9
**Woodfords Corner**—*pop pl* ME-1
Woodford South (CCD)—*cens area* KY-4
**Woodford (Town of)**—*pop pl* VT-1
**Woodford Village**—*pop pl* KY-4
Wood Fork—*stream* NC-3
Woodfork Cem—*cemetery* TX-5
Woodforks Landing—*locale* TN-4
**Woodfort**—*pop pl* PA-2
Woodfred Sch—*school* AL-4
Wood Gap—*gap* TN-4
**Woodgate**—*pop pl* IN-6
**Woodgate**—*pop pl* NY-2
**Woodgate**—*pop pl* PA-2
Woodgate Cem—*cemetery* NY-2
**Woodgate East**—*pop pl* IN-6
**Woodglen**—*pop pl* CO-8
**Woodglen**—*pop pl* NJ-2
**Woodglen**—*pop pl* PA-2
**Woodglen (subdivision)**—*pop pl* (2) AZ-5
**Woodgreen (subdivision)**—*pop pl* (2) NC-3
Wood Grove—*hist pl* NC-3
Wood Gulch—*stream* CO-8
Wood Gulch—*valley* (3) CA-9
Wood Gulch—*valley* (2) CO-8
Wood Gulch—*valley* (3) ID-8
Wood Gulch—*valley* (7) MT-8
Wood Gulch—*valley* NV-8
Wood Gulch—*valley* (2) OR-9
Wood Gulch—*valley* (2) WA-9
Wood Hall—*hist pl* VA-3
Woodham Bridge—*bridge* AL-4
Woodham Cem—*cemetery* AL-4
Woodham Cem—*cemetery* CO-8
Woodham Ditch—*canal* IN-6
Woodham HS—*school* FL-3
Woodham Pond—*reservoir* AL-4
Woodhams Creek—*stream* CA-9
Wood-Harrison House—*hist pl* UT-8
Woodhaul Canyon—*valley* NM-5
Woodhaven—*CDP* LA-4
**Woodhaven**—*pop pl* AL-4
**Woodhaven**—*pop pl* MD-2
**Woodhaven**—*pop pl* MI-6
**Woodhaven**—*pop pl* NY-2
**Woodhaven**—*pop pl* VA-3
Woodhaven, Lake—*reservoir* TN-4
Woodhaven Baptist Ch—*church* FL-3
Woodhaven Camp—*locale* CA-9
Wood Haven Cem—*cemetery* IN-6
Wood Haven Center Sch—*school* MI-6
Woodhaven Ch—*church* FL-3
Wood Haven Ch—*church* FL-3
Woodhaven Ch—*church* LA-4
Woodhaven Ch—*church* SC-3
Woodhaven Ch—*church* TX-5
Woodhaven Childrens Home—*locale* MO-7
Woodhaven Ch of the Nazarene—*church* AL-4
Woodhaven Country Club—*other* KY-4
Wood Haven Creek—*stream* IN-6
Woodhaven Junction—*uninc pl* NY-2
Woodhaven Lake—*reservoir* AL-4
Woodhaven Lake Dam—*dam* AL-4
Woodhaven Lake Dam—*dam* TN-4
**Woodhaven Park**—*pop pl* MD-2
**Woodhaven Shores**—*pop pl* VA-3
**Woodhaven (subdivision)**—*pop pl* (2) MS-4
**Woodhaven (subdivision)**—*pop pl* NC-3
**Wood Haven Subdivision**—*pop pl* UT-8
**Woodhaven Village Subdivision**—*pop pl* UT-8
**Woodhaven Village Subdivision - Number 5**—*pop pl* UT-8
*Woodhaven (Wood Haven)* NY-2
Wood Haven (Woodhaven)—*uninc pl* NY-2
Wood Hawk Bend (historical)—*bend* ND-7
Woodhawk Creek—*stream* MT-8
**Wood Heights**—*pop pl* MO-7
Woodhiff Sch—*school* ND-7
*Wood Hill* IL-6
*Wood Hill* PA-2
Woodhill—*locale* PA-2
Wood Hill—*locale* UT-8
**Woodhill**—*pop pl* KY-4
**Woodhill**—*pop pl* MO-7
**Wood Hill**—*pop pl* MO-7
**Wood Hill**—*pop pl* PA-2
Wood Hill—*summit* (4) MA-1
Wood Hill—*summit* NH-1
Wood Hill—*summit* PA-2
Wood Hill—*summit* WI-6
Wood Hill—*summit* WY-8
**Woodhill Addition (subdivision)**—*pop pl* TN-4
Wood Hill Cem—*cemetery* MN-6
Wood Hill Cem—*cemetery* OH-6
Wood Hill Cem—*cemetery* TN-4
Woodhill Ch—*church* WV-2
Woodhill Country Club—*other* MN-6
**Woodhill (historical)**—*pop pl* TN-4
Woodhills—*hist pl* CA-9
**Wood Hills**—*pop pl* AZ-5
Wood Hills—*summit* NV-8
Woodhill Sch—*school* NC-3
Wood Hill Sch—*school* TN-4
**Woodhine Heights**—*pop pl* MO-7
Wood Hollow—*valley* ID-8
Wood Hollow—*valley* MO-7
Wood Hollow—*valley* OR-9
Wood Hollow—*valley* PA-2
Wood Hollow—*valley* TN-4
Wood Hollow—*valley* (2) TX-5
Wood Hollow—*valley* (5) UT-8
Wood Hollow—*valley* VA-3
Wood Hollow—*valley* WV-2
Wood Hollow—*valley* WY-8
**Wood Hollow Condo**—*pop pl* UT-8
Wood Hollow Creek—*stream* TX-5
Wood Hollow Mountains—*summit* TX-5
**Wood Hollow Ranchettes**—*pop pl* UT-8
Wood Hollow Rsvr—*reservoir* UT-8
**Wood Hollow (subdivision)**—*pop pl* NC-3
Wood Hollow Tank—*reservoir* TX-5
Woodholme Golf Course—*other* MD-2
Wood Home for Boys—*hist pl* MS-4
**Woodhome Heights**—*pop pl* MD-2
Wood House—*hist pl* KS-7
Wood House—*hist pl* NH-1
Woodhouse—*locale* PA-2
Woodhouse Branch—*stream* IN-6
Woodhouse Corner—*locale* VA-3
Woodhouse House—*hist pl* TX-5
Woodhouse Lake—*lake* ND-7
Woodhouse Mesa—*summit* AZ-5
Woodhouse Run—*stream* PA-2
Woodhouse Spring—*spring* NM-5
Woodhouse Spring—*spring* UT-8
Wood Howell Ch—*church* VA-3
Wood HS—*school* IN-6
Wood HS—*school* TX-5
Wood HS—*school* VA-3
Woodhull—*locale* WI-6
**Woodhull**—*pop pl* IL-6
**Woodhull**—*pop pl* (2) NY-2
Woodhull, Charles, House—*hist pl* NY-2
Woodhull Cem—*cemetery* MI-6
Woodhull Cem—*cemetery* NY-2
Woodhull Creek—*stream* NY-2
Woodhull Lake—*lake* MI-6
Woodhull Lake—*lake* NY-2
Woodhull Landing—*locale* NY-2
Woodhull Mtn—*summit* (2) NY-2
Woodhull Park—*park* IL-6
Woodhull Sch—*school* (3) NY-2
Woodhull (Station)—*locale* WI-6
**Woodhull Station**—*pop pl* WI-6
**Woodhull (Town of)**—*pop pl* NY-2
**Woodhull (Township of)**—*pop pl* MI-6
Wood Hump—*summit* ID-8
Woodhurst Mtn—*summit* MT-8
Woodiff Cem—*cemetery* MI-6
Woodin—*locale* AZ-5
Woodin—*locale* MT-8
Woodin Corners—*locale* NY-2
Wooding Branch—*stream* VA-3
Wooding Ditch—*canal* OH-6
Woodings Pond—*lake* CT-1
**Woodington**—*pop pl* NC-3
**Woodington**—*pop pl* OH-6
Woodington Run—*stream* OH-6
Woodington SchoolJ—*school* NC-3
Woodington (Township of)—*fmr MCD* NC-3
Woodin Lake—*lake* MI-6
Woodin Spring—*spring* OR-9
Woodin Street Cem—*cemetery* CT-1
**Woodinville**—*pop pl* NY-2
**Woodinville**—*pop pl* WA-9
Woodis Cem—*cemetery* GA-3
Wood Island—*cape* MA-1
Wood Island—*island* CA-9
Wood Island—*island* CT-1
Wood Island—*island* (6) ME-1
Wood Island—*island* MD-2
Wood Island—*island* (3) MA-1
Wood Island—*island* MI-6
Wood Island—*island* NY-2
Wood Island—*island* (2) NC-3
Wood Island—*island* TX-5
Wood Island—*island* VA-3
Wood Island Harbor—*bay* ME-1
Wood Island (historical)—*island* SD-7
*Wood Island Lake* LA-4
Wood Island Light Station—*hist pl* ME-1
Wood Island Park (historical)—*park* MA-1
Wood Islands—*area* AK-9
Wood Island South Ledge—*bar* ME-1
Wood Island Station (historical)—*locale* MA-1
Woodis Store (historical)—*locale* AL-4
Wood JHS—*school* CA-9
Wood Junction—*locale* LA-4
Wood Junior Coll—*school* MS-4
Wood Key—*island* (2) FL-3
Wood Key Cove—*bay* FL-3
Wood Key Hill—*summit* CT-1
Wood Knoll—*summit* UT-8
*Wood Lake* CA-9
*Wood Lake* MN-6
Wood Lake—*lake* AK-9
Wood Lake—*lake* (2) CA-9
Wood Lake—*lake* CO-8
Wood Lake—*lake* (2) FL-3
Wood Lake—*lake* ID-8
Wood Lake—*lake* IN-6
Wood Lake—*lake* (8) MI-6
Wood Lake—*lake* (6) MN-6
Wood Lake—*lake* MT-8
Wood Lake—*lake* NE-7
Wood Lake—*lake* (2) ND-7
Wood Lake—*lake* OR-9
Wood Lake—*lake* SC-3
Wood Lake—*lake* (4) TX-5
Wood Lake—*lake* UT-8
Wood Lake—*lake* (2) WA-9
Wood Lake—*lake* (5) WI-6
Woodlake—*locale* CA-9
**Woodlake**—*pop pl* CA-9
**Woodlake**—*pop pl* KY-4
**Wood Lake**—*pop pl* LA-4
**Wood Lake**—*pop pl* MN-6
**Wood Lake**—*pop pl* NE-7
**Woodlake**—*pop pl* TN-4
**Woodlake**—*pop pl* TX-5
Wood Lake—*reservoir* MN-6
Wood Lake—*reservoir* MO-7
Wood Lake—*reservoir* (3) NC-3
Wood Lake—*reservoir* OH-6
Wood Lake—*reservoir* (2) TX-5
Wood Lake Cem—*cemetery* SD-7
Wood Lake Cem—*cemetery* WI-6
Wood Lake Ch—*church* ND-7
Wood Lake Creek—*stream* MN-6
Wood Lake Dam—*dam* (3) NC-3
Woodlake Junction—*locale* CA-9
Wood Lake Marsh Dam—*dam* ND-7
Wood Lake Marsh Rsvr—*reservoir* ND-7
*Woodlake Mountain* CA-9
Wood Lake Park—*park* MN-6
**Woodlake Park**—*pop pl* TX-5
Wood Lake Plaza (Shop Ctr)—*locale* FL-3
Woodlake Sch—*school* CA-9
Wood Lake Sch—*school* MN-6
Wood Lake Sch—*school* WI-6
Woodlake Site—*hist pl* CA-9
Wood Lake State Monument—*other* MN-6
Wood Lake State Wildlife Mngmt Area—*park* MN-6
**Woodlake (subdivision)**—*pop pl* MS-4
Woodlake-Three Rivers (CCD)—*cens area* CA-9
**Wood Lake Township**—*pop pl* ND-7
**Wood Lake (Township of)**—*pop pl* MN-6
Wood Lake Trail—*trail* CO-8
*Woodland* AL-4
*Woodland* DE-2
*Woodland* IA-7
*Woodland* MN-6
*Woodland* MS-4

Woodland ... NJ-2
Woodland ... NC-3
Woodland—hist pl (2) ... GA-3
Woodland—hist pl (2) ... KY-4
Woodland—hist pl ... PA-2
Woodland—locale ... AL-4
Woodland—locale ... AR-4
Woodland—locale ... DE-2
Woodland—locale (2) ... ID-8
Woodland—locale ... IA-7
Woodland—locale (2) ... LA-4
Woodland—locale ... MD-2
Woodland—LOCALE ... MN-6
Woodland—locale ... OH-6
Woodland—locale ... SC-3
Woodland—locale ... TN-4
**Woodland**—pop pl (2) ... AL-4
**Woodland**—pop pl (2) ... CA-9
**Woodland**—pop pl ... DE-2
**Woodland**—pop pl ... GA-3
**Woodland**—pop pl (2) ... IL-6
**Woodland**—pop pl ... IN-6
**Woodland**—pop pl ... IA-7
**Woodland**—pop pl ... ME-1
**Woodland**—pop pl ... MD-2
**Woodland**—pop pl ... MA-1
**Woodland**—pop pl ... MI-6
**Woodland**—pop pl (2) ... MN-6
**Woodland**—pop pl (2) ... MS-4
**Woodland**—pop pl ... MO-7
**Woodland**—pop pl (2) ... NY-2
**Woodland**—pop pl ... NC-3
**Woodland**—pop pl (2) ... PA-2
**Woodland**—pop pl (2) ... TX-5
**Woodland**—pop pl ... UT-8
**Woodland**—pop pl (2) ... WA-9
**Woodland**—pop pl ... WI-6
Woodland—uninc pl ... MA-1
Woodland—uninc pl ... TN-4
Woodland, Lake—reservoir ... IN-6
Woodland, Newton Highlands, and Newton Centre RR Stations—hist pl ... MA-1
Woodland Acad (historical)—school ... MS-4
**Woodland Acres**—pop pl ... CA-9
**Woodland Acres**—pop pl ... CO-8
**Woodland Acres**—pop pl ... MD-2
**Woodland Acres**—pop pl ... NC-3
**Woodland Acres**—pop pl (2) ... TN-4
**Woodland Acres**—pop pl ... VA-3
Woodland Acres—uninc pl ... FL-3
Woodland Acres JHS—school ... TX-5
Woodland Acres Sch—school ... FL-3
**Woodland Addition**—pop pl ... IL-6
Woodland Addition Lake—reservoir ... IN-6
Woodland Addition Lake Dam—dam ... IN-6
Woodland Ave and West Side RR Powerhouse—hist pl ... OH-6
Woodland Ave Sch—school ... NJ-2
Woodland Ave Sch—school ... NY-2
Woodland Baptist Ch—church ... KS-7
Woodland Baptist Ch—church (2) ... MS-4
Woodland Baptist Ch—church ... TN-4
Woodland Beach—locale ... WA-9
**Woodland Beach**—pop pl ... DE-2
**Woodland Beach**—pop pl ... MD-2
**Woodland Beach**—pop pl (2) ... MI-6
Woodland Beach Wildlife Area—park ... DE-2
Woodland Branch—stream (2) ... MD-2
Woodland Brook—stream ... NY-2
Woodland Camp—locale ... GA-3
Woodland Camp—locale ... MI-6
Woodland Camp—locale ... MN-6
Woodland Campground—park ... AZ-5
Woodland (CCD)—cens area ... AL-4
Woodland (CCD)—cens area ... CA-9
Woodland (CCD)—cens area ... GA-3
Woodland (CCD)—cens area ... TN-4
Woodland (CCD)—cens area ... WA-9
Woodland Cem—cemetery (3) ... AL-4
Woodland Cem—cemetery (2) ... AR-4
Woodland Cem—cemetery ... CA-9
Woodland Cem—cemetery ... CT-1
Woodland Cem—cemetery ... DE-2
Woodland Cem—cemetery (2) ... FL-3
Woodland Cem—cemetery ... ID-8
Woodland Cem—cemetery (4) ... IL-6
Woodland Cem—cemetery (3) ... IA-7
Woodland Cem—cemetery ... KS-7
Woodland Cem—cemetery ... LA-4
Woodland Cem—cemetery ... ME-1
Woodland Cem—cemetery (4) ... MI-6
Woodland Cem—cemetery (3) ... MN-6
Woodland Cem—cemetery (2) ... MS-4
Woodland Cem—cemetery (3) ... MO-7
Woodland Cem—cemetery ... NE-7
Woodland Cem—cemetery (2) ... NJ-2
Woodland Cem—cemetery (4) ... NY-2
Woodland Cem—cemetery (2) ... NC-3
Woodland Cem—cemetery (5) ... OH-6
Woodland Cem—cemetery (2) ... OK-5
Woodland Cem—cemetery ... PA-2
Woodland Cem—cemetery ... SD-7
Woodland Cem—cemetery (5) ... TX-5
Woodland Cem—cemetery ... UT-8
Woodland Cem—cemetery (2) ... VA-3
Woodland Cem—cemetery ... WA-9
Woodland Cem—cemetery ... WV-2
Woodland Cem—cemetery ... WI-6
Woodland Cemetery—hist pl ... OH-6
Woodland Cemetery Gateway, Chapel And Office—hist pl ... OH-6
Woodland Center—locale ... ME-1
Wood Land Ch ... MS-4
Woodland Ch—church (4) ... AL-4
Woodland Ch—church (3) ... GA-3
Woodland Ch—church (3) ... IL-6
Woodland Ch—church (3) ... KY-4
Woodland Ch—church (2) ... LA-4
Woodland Ch—church (2) ... MS-4
Woodland Ch—church ... NJ-2
Woodland Ch—church (5) ... NC-3
Woodland Ch—church (2) ... TX-5
Woodland Ch—church (6) ... VA-3
Woodland Ch—church ... WI-6
Woodland Chapel—church ... MS-4
Woodland Ch (historical)—church ... AL-4
Woodland Ch (historical)—church ... MS-4
Woodland Christian Acad—school ... AL-4
Woodland Consolidated Sch—school ... ME-1
Woodland Corner—locale ... WI-6
**Woodland Corner**—pop pl ... AR-4
Woodland Country Club—other ... NE-7
Woodland Country Club—other ... OK-5
Woodland Country Club—other ... WV-2
Woodland County Club—locale ... MA-1
**Woodland Court (trailer park)**—pop pl ... DE-2
**Woodland Cove**—pop pl ... TN-4
Woodland creek ... CO-8
Woodland Creek—bay ... MD-2
Woodland Creek—gut ... SC-3
Woodland Creek—stream ... ID-8
Woodland Creek—stream ... IL-6
Woodland Creek—stream ... KY-4
Woodland Creek—stream ... LA-4
Woodland Creek—stream (2) ... MD-2
Woodland Creek—stream ... MI-6
Woodland Creek—stream ... NY-2
Woodland Creek—stream ... VA-3
Woodland Creek—stream ... WA-9
Woodland Creek—stream ... WI-6
Woodland Cumberland Presbyterian Ch (historical)—church ... MS-4
Woodland Dam—dam ... AZ-5
Woodland Dell Cem—cemetery ... MA-1
Woodland Division—civil ... AL-4
Woodland Division—civil ... TN-4
Woodland Drive Ch—church ... AL-4
Woodland Drives—uninc pl ... FL-3
Woodland Echo Creek—stream ... AK-9
Woodland Echo Pass—gap ... AK-9
Woodland Elem Sch—school ... FL-3
Woodland Elem Sch—school ... KS-7
Woodland Elem Sch—school ... PA-2
Woodland Elem Sch—school ... TN-4
**Woodland Estates**—pop pl ... TN-4
**Woodland Estates East (subdivision)**—pop pl ... UT-8
**Woodland Estates (subdivision)**—pop pl ... TN-4
**Woodland Estates Subdivision**—pop pl ... UT-8
Woodland Farm-Leland House—hist pl ... MA-1
Woodland Ferry—locale ... DE-2
Woodland Forest Country Club—locale ... AL-4
Woodland Forest Elem Sch—school ... AL-4
**Woodland Forest (subdivision)**—pop pl ... AL-4
Woodland Friends Ch—church ... NC-3
**Woodland Gardens Subdivision**—pop pl ... UT-8
Woodland Golf Club—locale ... AL-4
Woodland Golf Course—other ... MI-6
Woodland Golf Course—other ... OH-6
Woodland Grammar Sch—school ... MS-4
Woodland Grove Ch—church ... AL-4
Woodland Hall Acad—school ... FL-3
Woodland Heights ... IL-6
Woodland Heights—locale ... TN-4
**Woodland Heights**—pop pl ... AR-4
**Woodland Heights**—pop pl ... DE-2
**Woodland Heights**—pop pl ... IN-6
**Woodland Heights**—pop pl ... PA-2
**Woodland Heights**—pop pl (2) ... TN-4
**Woodland Heights**—pop pl ... TX-5
Woodland Heights—uninc pl ... WV-2
Woodland Heights Baptist Ch—church ... TN-4
Woodland Heights Ch—church ... KY-4
Woodland Heights Ch—church ... VA-3
Woodland Heights Elem Sch—school ... TX-5
Woodland Heights Sch—school ... AR-4
Woodland Heights Sch—school ... OH-6
Woodland Heights Sch (historical)—school . TN-4
**Woodland Heights (subdivision)**—pop pl ... AL-4
**Woodland Heights (subdivision)**—pop pl (2) ... AZ-5
**Woodland Heights (subdivision)**—pop pl (3) ... MS-4
Woodland Hill Ch—church ... WV-2
Woodland Hills ... IL-6
Woodland Hills ... TX-5
**Woodland Hills**—pop pl ... AR-4
**Woodland Hills**—pop pl ... CA-9
**Woodland Hills**—pop pl (2) ... GA-3
**Woodland Hills**—pop pl ... IL-6
**Woodland Hills**—pop pl ... IA-7
**Woodland Hills**—pop pl ... KY-4
**Woodland Hills**—pop pl ... NC-3
**Woodland Hills**—pop pl ... SC-3
**Woodland Hills**—pop pl (2) ... TX-5
**Woodland Hills**—pop pl ... UT-8
**Woodland Hills**—pop pl ... VA-3
Woodland Hills Baptist Church ... MS-4
Woodland Hills Cem—cemetery ... AL-4
Woodland Hills Ch—church ... GA-3
Woodland Hills Ch—church ... MS-4
Woodland Hills Ch—church ... OK-5
**Woodland Hills Estates (subdivision)**—pop pl ... MS-4
**Woodland Hills Estates (subdivision)**—pop pl ... UT-8
Woodland Hills Golf Course—locale ... PA-2
Woodland Hills Lake ... AL-4
Woodland Hills Lake Dam ... AL-4
Woodland Hills Park—park ... OH-6
Woodland Hills Sch—school ... OH-6
Woodland Hills Sch—school ... OK-5
**Woodland Hills (subdivision)**—pop pl (4) ... AL-4
**Woodland Hills (subdivision)**—pop pl ... MS-4
**Woodland Hills Subdivision (Number 1)**—pop pl ... UT-8
**Woodland Hills Subdivision (Number 2)**—pop pl ... UT-8
**Woodland (historical)**—pop pl ... NC-3
Woodland Hollow—valley ... MO-7
**Woodland Homes**—pop pl ... DE-2
Woodland HS—school ... AL-4
Woodland HS—school ... MS-4
Woodland HS—school ... TX-5
Wood Landing ... SC-3
Wood Landing—locale ... AL-4
Wood Landing—locale ... NC-3
Wood Landing Point—cape ... NC-3
Woodland in Waverly Hist Dist—hist pl ... TN-4
Woodland JHS—school ... IL-6
Woodland JHS—school ... NY-2
Woodland Junction—locale ... IL-6
Woodland Junction—locale ... ME-1
Woodland Lake—lake ... AL-4
Woodland Lake—lake ... CO-8
Woodland Lake—lake ... IL-6
Woodland Lake—lake (2) ... MI-6
Woodland Lake—lake ... NJ-2
Woodland Lake—lake ... NY-2
Woodland Lake—lake ... OH-6
Woodland Lake—lake ... TX-5
**Woodland Lake**—pop pl ... IL-6
**Woodland Lake**—pop pl ... IN-6
**Woodland Lake**—pop pl ... MS-4
Woodland Lake—reservoir (3) ... AL-4
Woodland Lake—reservoir ... GA-3
Woodland Lake—reservoir (2) ... IN-6
Woodland Lake—reservoir ... IA-7
Woodland Lake—reservoir ... MS-4
Woodland Lake—reservoir ... NJ-2
Woodland Lake Dam—dam (2) ... IN-6
Woodland Lake Dam—dam ... IA-7
Woodland Lake Dam—dam ... MS-4
Woodland Landing—locale ... SC-3
Woodland Landing (historical)—locale ... AL-4
Woodland Lookout Tower—locale ... GA-3
Woodland Lookout Tower—locale ... MS-4
Woodland Memorial Cem—cemetery ... AR-4
Woodland Memorial Park—park ... OH-6
Woodland Mills—locale ... TN-4
**Woodland Mills**—pop pl ... AL-4
**Woodland Mills**—pop pl ... TN-4
Woodland Mills Baptist Ch—church ... TN-4
Woodland Mills Creek—stream ... AL-4
Woodland Mills HS—school ... TN-4
Woodland Mills Post Office—building ... TN-4
Woodland Mills Post Office (historical)—building ... AL-4
Woodland Mills Sch—school ... AL-4
Woodland Mine—mine ... MT-8
Woodland Mound Archeol District—hist pl . TN-4
Woodland Mountain—ridge ... CO-8
Woodland-Olney Elem Sch—school ... NC-3
Woodland Opera House—hist pl ... CA-9
Woodland Park ... MN-6
Woodland Park—flat ... NM-5
Woodland Park—inactive ... MO-7
Woodland Park—locale ... MI-6
Woodland Park—park ... AR-4
Woodland Park—park ... FL-3
Woodland Park—park ... IL-6
Woodland Park—park ... IA-7
Woodland Park—park ... KS-7
Woodland Park—park (2) ... KY-4
Woodland Park—park ... MI-6
Woodland Park—park (2) ... MT-8
Woodland Park—park (2) ... NJ-2
Woodland Park—park ... OH-6
Woodland Park—park ... OK-5
Woodland Park—park ... TX-5
Woodland Park—park (2) ... VA-3
Woodland Park—park ... WA-9
**Woodland Park**—pop pl ... CO-8
**Woodland Park**—pop pl ... FL-3
**Woodland Park**—pop pl ... ID-8
**Woodland Park**—pop pl (2) ... IN-6
**Woodland Park**—pop pl ... KY-4
**Woodland Park**—pop pl ... MA-1
**Woodland Park**—pop pl (2) ... MI-6
**Woodland Park**—pop pl ... MN-6
**Woodland Park**—pop pl ... NH-1
**Woodland Park**—pop pl ... NJ-2
**Woodland Park**—pop pl ... OH-6
**Woodland Park**—pop pl ... PA-2
**Woodland Park**—pop pl (3) ... VA-3
**Woodland Park**—pop pl ... WA-9
**Woodland Park**—pop pl ... WV-2
Woodland Park—uninc pl ... CA-9
Woodland Park—uninc pl ... WV-2
Woodland Park Baptist Ch—church ... AL-4
Woodland Park Campground—locale ... SC-3
Woodland Park Campground—park ... OR-9
Woodland Park Cem—cemetery ... TX-5
Woodland Park District—hist pl ... MN-6
Woodland Park Elem Sch—school ... TN-4
Woodland Park Filtration Plant—other ... CO-8
Woodland Park Hospital Helipad—airport .. OR-9
Woodland Park Ranger Station—locale ... CO-8
Woodland Park Sch—school ... LA-4
Woodland Park Sch—school ... WY-8
**Woodland Park (subdivision)**—pop pl (2) ... AL-4
**Woodland Park (subdivision)**—pop pl ... DE-2
**Woodland Park (subdivision)**—pop pl ... NC-3
Woodland Park Tank—reservoir ... NM-5
Woodland Park Trail—trail ... NM-5
Woodland Parkway—park ... AZ-5
**Woodland Pines (subdivision)**—pop pl ... AL-4
Woodland Plantation—hist pl ... MS-4
Woodland Plantation (historical)—locale (2) ... AL-4
Woodland Plaza Shop Ctr—locale (2) ... AZ-5
Woodland Plaza (Shop Ctr)—locale ... FL-3
Woodland Point—cape ... MD-2
Woodland Point—cape (2) ... MN-6
**Woodland Point**—pop pl ... MD-2
Woodland Pond—reservoir ... NC-3
Woodland Pond Dam—dam ... NC-3
Woodland Pond Park—park ... OR-9
Woodland Post Office—building ... MS-4
Woodland Post Office (historical)—building ... MS-4
Woodland Public Library—hist pl ... CA-9
Woodland Reservoir—lake ... NY-2
Woodland Retreat Dam—dam ... IN-6
Woodland Retreat Lake—reservoir ... IN-6
Woodland Road Sch—school ... WI-6
Woodland Rsvr—reservoir ... AZ-5
Woodlands—hist pl ... AL-4
Woodlands—hist pl ... MD-2
Woodlands—hist pl ... SC-3
**Woodlands**—pop pl ... CA-9
**Woodlands**—pop pl ... NH-1
**Woodlands**—pop pl ... NY-2
**Woodlands**—pop pl ... TN-4
**Woodlands**—pop pl ... WV-2
Woodlands, The—CDP ... TX-5
Woodlands, The—hist pl ... PA-2
**Woodlands, The**—pop pl ... PA-2
Woodlands and Blythewood—hist pl ... GA-3
**Woodlands Business Park, The**—pop pl ... UT-8
Woodlands Cem—cemetery ... PA-2
Woodland Sch ... AL-4
Woodland Sch—school ... AR-4
Woodland Sch—school ... CA-9
Woodland Sch—school ... CT-1
Woodland Sch—school (7) ... IL-6
Woodland Sch—school ... IA-7
Woodland Sch—school ... LA-4
Woodland Sch—school ... MA-1
Woodland Sch—school (5) ... MI-6
Woodland Sch—school (3) ... MN-6
Woodland Sch—school (2) ... MS-4
Woodland Sch—school (3) ... MO-7
Woodland Sch—school (2) ... NE-7
Woodland Sch—school (3) ... NJ-2
Woodland Sch—school (3) ... NC-3
Woodland Sch—school (4) ... OH-6
Woodland Sch—school ... PA-2
Woodland Sch—school ... SC-3
Woodland Sch—school (3) ... TN-4
Woodland Sch—school ... WA-9
Woodland Sch—school ... WI-6
Woodland Sch (abandoned)—school (2) ... MO-7
Woodland Sch (historical)—school (2) ... AL-4
Woodland Sch (historical)—school ... MS-4
Woodland Sch (historical)—school ... MO-7
Woodland Sch Number Three—school ... MN-6
Woodland School—locale ... MN-6
Woodland School (Abandoned)—locale ... MO-7
Woodlands Elem Sch—school ... FL-3
Woodland Seminary ... MS-4
Woodland Sewage Farm—other ... CA-9
Woodlands Hist Dist—hist pl ... KY-4
Woodland Shop Ctr—locale ... AL-4
Woodland Shop Ctr—locale ... MI-6
Woodland Shop Ctr—locale ... TN-4
**Woodland Shores**—pop pl ... IL-6
Woodlands HS—school ... NY-2
Woodlands Lake—reservoir ... NY-2
Woodland Slough—stream ... AR-4
Woodlands Oil Field—oilfield ... MS-4
Woodland Spring ... AL-4
Woodland Spring—spring ... AL-4
**Woodland Springs Subdivision**—pop pl ... UT-8
Woodlands Sch—school ... CA-9
Woodlands Sch—school ... OK-5
Woodlands Station—locale ... CA-9
**Woodlands (subdivision), The**—pop pl ... AL-4
**Woodlands (subdivision), The**—pop pl .. NC-3
Woodland (sta.) (RR name for George)—other ... NC-3
Woodland State Airp—airport ... WA-9
Woodland Station—building ... PA-2
Woodland Station—hist pl ... PA-2
**Woodland Station (subdivision)**—pop pl ... DE-2
Woodland Street Firehouse—hist pl ... MA-1
Woodland Street Hist Dist—hist pl ... MA-1
Woodland Street Sch—school ... TN-4
**Woodland (subdivision)**—pop pl ... AL-4
**Woodland Subdivision**—pop pl (2) ... UT-8
Woodlands United Methodist Ch—church ... FL-3
Woodland Tank—reservoir ... AZ-5
Woodland Terrace—hist pl ... PA-2
Woodland Terrace Ch—church ... NC-3
**Woodland Terrace (subdivision)**—pop pl ... AL-4
**Woodland (Town of)**—pop pl ... ME-1
**Woodland (Town of)**—pop pl ... WI-6
Woodland Township—fmr MCD ... IA-7
**Woodland Township**—pop pl ... SD-7
**Woodland (Township of)**—pop pl (2) ... IL-6
**Woodland (Township of)**—pop pl ... MI-6
**Woodland (Township of)**—pop pl ... MN-6
**Woodland (Township of)**—pop pl ... NJ-2
Woodland Trace ... IN-6
**Woodland Trace (subdivision)**—pop pl .. NC-3
**Woodland Trace (subdivision)**—pop pl .. TN-4
Woodland Trails (Boy Scout Camp)—locale ... OH-6
Woodland Union Ch—church ... VA-3
Woodland United Methodist Ch—church ... DE-2
Woodland Valley—valley ... NY-2
**Woodland View**—pop pl ... PA-2
Woodland View—post sta ... OK-5
**Woodland Village**—pop pl ... MD-2
**Woodland Village (subdivision)**—pop pl ... AL-4
Woodlandville—locale ... MO-7
Woodland Way JHS—school ... MD-2
**Woodland (Woodlands)**—pop pl ... WV-2
Wood Lane ... NJ-2
Woodlane—locale ... NJ-2
**Wood Lane**—pop pl ... MD-2
**Woodlark**—pop pl ... MD-2
Wood Lateral—canal ... ID-8
Wood Lateral—canal ... NM-5
Wood Lateral—canal ... SD-7
Woodlaw Memorial Park ... PA-2
Woodlawn ... AL-4
Woodlawn ... IN-6
Woodlawn ... NC-3
Woodlawn ... RI-1
Woodlawn—hist pl ... DE-2
Woodlawn—hist pl (2) ... KY-4
Woodlawn—hist pl (2) ... MD-2
Wood Lawn—hist pl ... NJ-2
Woodlawn—hist pl ... NY-2
Wood Lawn—hist pl ... NC-3
Woodlawn—hist pl ... TN-4
Woodlawn—hist pl ... TX-5
Woodlawn—hist pl (2) ... VA-3
Woodlawn—locale ... GA-3
Woodlawn—locale ... LA-4
Woodlawn—locale ... MI-6
Woodlawn—locale ... NE-7
Woodlawn—locale ... SC-3
Woodlawn—locale (2) ... TN-4
Woodlawn—locale ... TX-5
Woodlawn—locale ... VA-3
Woodlawn—locale ... WA-9
Woodlawn—locale ... WI-6
Woodlawn—other ... IL-6
**Woodlawn**—pop pl (2) ... AL-4
**Woodlawn**—pop pl (2) ... FL-3
**Woodlawn**—pop pl ... HI-9
**Woodlawn**—pop pl ... IL-6
**Woodlawn**—pop pl ... KS-7
**Woodlawn**—pop pl (3) ... KY-4
**Woodlawn**—pop pl (2) ... LA-4
**Woodlawn**—pop pl (3) ... MD-2
**Woodlawn**—pop pl ... MA-1
**Woodlawn**—pop pl (3) ... MS-4
**Woodlawn**—pop pl ... MO-7
**Woodlawn**—pop pl (3) ... NY-2
**Woodlawn**—pop pl (2) ... NC-3
**Woodlawn**—pop pl ... OH-6
**Woodlawn**—pop pl (4) ... PA-2
**Woodlawn**—pop pl ... RI-1
**Woodlawn**—pop pl (4) ... TN-4
**Woodlawn**—pop pl ... TX-5
**Woodlawn**—pop pl (2) ... VA-3
Woodlawn—uninc pl ... NY-2
Woodlawn—uninc pl ... NC-3
Woodlawn—uninc pl ... VA-3
Woodlawn, Lake—lake ... SC-3
Woodlawn Ave Baptist Ch—church ... KS-7
Woodlawn Ave Row—hist pl ... NY-2
Woodlawn Ave Sch—school ... CA-9
Woodlawn Baptist Ch—church ... AL-4
Woodlawn Baptist Ch—church (3) ... MS-4
Woodlawn Bayou—stream ... LA-4
Woodlawn Beach ... NY-2
**Woodlawn Beach**—pop pl ... FL-3
**Woodlawn Beach**—pop pl ... MI-6
**Woodlawn Beach (Woodlawn)**—pop pl . NY-2
Woodlawn Cem—cemetery ... AR-4
Woodlawn Cem—cemetery (2) ... CA-9
Woodlawn Cem—cemetery ... CO-8
Woodlawn Cem—cemetery ... CT-1
Woodlawn Cem—cemetery ... DC-2
Woodlawn Cem—cemetery (7) ... FL-3
Woodlawn Cem—cemetery ... GA-3
Woodlawn Cem—cemetery (8) ... IL-6
Woodlawn Cem—cemetery (6) ... IN-6
Woodlawn Cem—cemetery (4) ... IA-7
Woodlawn Cem—cemetery (4) ... KS-7
Woodlawn Cem—cemetery (2) ... LA-4
Woodlawn Cem—cemetery (11) ... ME-1
Woodlawn Cem—cemetery ... MD-2
Woodlawn Cem—cemetery (7) ... MA-1
Woodlawn Cem—cemetery (8) ... MI-6
Woodlawn Cem—cemetery (7) ... MN-6
Woodlawn Cem—cemetery (7) ... MS-4
Woodlawn Cem—cemetery (6) ... MO-7
Woodlawn Cem—cemetery ... MT-8
Woodlawn Cem—cemetery (4) ... NE-7
Woodlawn Cem—cemetery ... NV-8
Woodlawn Cem—cemetery (2) ... NH-1
Woodlawn Cem—cemetery ... NJ-2
Woodlawn Cem—cemetery (13) ... NY-2
Woodlawn Cem—cemetery (3) ... NC-3
Woodlawn Cem—cemetery ... ND-7
Woodlawn Cem—cemetery (15) ... OH-6
Woodlawn Cem—cemetery (2) ... OK-5
Woodlawn Cem—cemetery (6) ... PA-2
Woodlawn Cem—cemetery ... SC-3
Woodlawn Cem—cemetery (2) ... SD-7
Woodlawn Cem—cemetery (9) ... TN-4
Woodlawn Cem—cemetery (7) ... TX-5
Woodlawn Cem—cemetery ... VT-1
Woodlawn Cem—cemetery (2) ... VA-3
Woodlawn Cem—cemetery (3) ... WA-9
Woodlawn Cem—cemetery (2) ... WV-2
Woodlawn Cem—cemetery (17) ... WI-6
Woodlawn Cemetery—hist pl ... IL-6
Woodlawn Ch ... TN-4
Woodlawn Ch—church (3) ... AL-4
Woodlawn Ch—church ... FL-3
Woodlawn Ch—church (7) ... GA-3
Woodlawn Ch—church ... IL-6
Woodlawn Ch—church ... IN-6
Woodlawn Ch—church ... KY-4
Woodlawn Ch—church (3) ... LA-4
Woodlawn Ch—church (3) ... MS-4
Woodlawn Ch—church (2) ... NC-3
Woodlawn Ch—church ... OH-6
Woodlawn Ch—church ... OK-5
Woodlawn Ch—church (2) ... SC-3
Woodlawn Ch—church (3) ... TN-4
Woodlawn Ch—church ... TX-5
Woodlawn Ch—church (3) ... VA-3
Woodlawn Chapel—church ... GA-3
Woodlawn Ch of God—church ... FL-3
Woodlawn Christian Ch—church ... TN-4
Woodlawn City Hall—hist pl ... AL-4
Woodlawn Community Center—building ... NC-3
Woodlawn Country Club—other ... AR-4
Woodlawn Country Club—other ... TX-5
Woodlawn Country Club—other ... VA-3
Woodlawn-Dotsonville (CCD)—cens area ... TN-4
Woodlawn-Dotsonville Division—civil ... TN-4
Woodlawn Elem Sch—school ... FL-3
Woodlawn Elem Sch—school ... IN-6
Woodlawn Elem Sch—school ... KS-7
Woodlawn Elem Sch—school ... TN-4
**Woodlawn Estates**—pop pl ... GA-3
**Woodlawn Estates**—pop pl ... NJ-2
**Woodlawn Estates (subdivision)**—pop pl ... TN-4
Woodlawn Farm—hist pl ... OH-6
Woodlawn First Baptist Ch—church ... TN-4
Woodlawn Gas Field—oilfield ... TX-5
Woodlawn Golf Course—locale ... PA-2
**Woodlawn Grove**—pop pl ... IN-6
**Woodlawn Heights**—pop pl (2) ... AL-4
**Woodlawn Heights**—pop pl ... IL-6
**Woodlawn Heights**—pop pl ... IN-6
**Woodlawn Heights**—pop pl ... MD-2
**Woodlawn Heights (subdivision)**—pop pl ... AL-4
**Woodlawn Hills**—pop pl ... TX-5
Woodlawn Hills Cem—cemetery ... KY-4
Woodlawn Hills Sch—school ... TX-5
Woodlawn Hist Dist—hist pl ... GA-3
Woodlawn Hist Dist—hist pl ... IA-7
Woodlawn (historical)—locale ... AL-4
Woodlawn (historical)—locale ... MS-4
Woodlawn Hosp—hospital ... IL-6
Woodlawn Hosp—hospital (2) ... TX-5
Woodlawn HS—school ... AL-4
Woodlawn HS—school ... LA-4
Woodlawn JHS—school ... NY-2
Woodlawn Junction—uninc pl ... AL-4
Woodlawn Lake—lake ... NY-2
Woodlawn Lake—reservoir ... TX-5
**Woodlawn (Linwood)**—pop pl ... LA-4
**Woodlawn Manor**—pop pl ... VA-3
**Woodlawn Mansion**—pop pl ... VA-3
Woodlawn Memorial Cem—cemetery ... SC-3
Woodlawn Memorial Gardens—cemetery ... GA-3
Woodlawn Memorial Gardens—cemetery ... PA-2
Woodlawn Memorial Gardens—cemetery ... VA-3
Woodlawn Memorial Gardens Cem—cemetery ... KY-4
Woodlawn Memorial Park—cemetery ... FL-3
Woodlawn Memorial Park—cemetery ... MO-7
Woodlawn Memorial Park—cemetery ... WA-9
Woodlawn Memorial Park—park ... PA-2
Woodlawn Memorial Park Cem—cemetery .. FL-3
Woodlawn Memorial Park (Cemetery)—cemetery ... IL-6
Woodlawn Memorial Park (Cemetery)—cemetery ... NC-3
Woodlawn Methodist Ch—church ... AL-4
**Woodlawn Middle School**—pop pl ... PA-2
Woodlawn Mine—mine ... UT-8
Woodlawn Mtn—summit ... VT-1
Woodlawn Natl Cem—cemetery ... NY-2
Woodlawn-Oakdale—CDP ... KY-4
Woodlawn Oil and Gas Field—oilfield ... LA-4
Woodlawn Oil Field—oilfield ... TX-5
Woodlawn Oil Field—other ... IL-6
Woodlawn Park—park ... DE-2
Woodlawn Park—park ... FL-3
Woodlawn Park—park ... MI-6
Wood Lawn Park—park ... MN-6
Woodlawn Park—park ... NC-3
Woodlawn Park—park ... PA-2
Woodlawn Park—park ... TN-4
Woodlawn Park—park (2) ... TX-5
**Woodlawn Park**—pop pl ... ID-8
**Woodlawn Park**—pop pl ... KY-4
**Woodlawn Park**—pop pl ... OK-5
**Woodlawn Park**—pop pl ... VA-3
Woodlawn Park Cem—cemetery ... FL-3
Woodlawn Park Cem—cemetery ... MS-4
Woodlawn Park Cem South—cemetery ... FL-3
Woodlawn Plantation—hist pl ... VA-3
Woodlawn Plantation—locale ... LA-4
Woodlawn Plantation—locale ... VA-3
Woodlawn Plantation (historical)—locale ... AL-4
Woodlawn Plantation (historical)—locale ... MS-4
Woodlawn Plaza—locale ... TX-5
Woodlawn Post Office—building ... TN-4
Woodlawn Post Office (historical)—building ... MS-4
Woodlawn Presbyterian Ch—church ... AL-4
Woodlawn Sch ... PA-2
Woodlawn Sch—school (2) ... AR-4
Woodlawn Sch—school ... FL-3
Woodlawn Sch—school (3) ... IL-6
Woodlawn Sch—school ... IN-6
Woodlawn Sch—school ... IA-7
Woodlawn Sch—school (3) ... LA-4
Woodlawn Sch—school (2) ... MA-1
Woodlawn Sch—school ... NE-7
Woodlawn Sch—school (2) ... NY-2
Woodlawn Sch—school ... NC-3
Woodlawn Sch—school (2) ... OK-5
Woodlawn Sch—school ... OR-9
Woodlawn Sch—school ... PA-2
Woodlawn Sch—school (3) ... TN-4
Woodlawn Sch—school (2) ... TX-5
Woodlawn Sch—school (3) ... VA-3
Wood Lawn Sch—school ... WI-6
Woodlawn Sch—school (3) ... WI-6
Woodlawn Sch (abandoned)—school ... MO-7
Woodlawn Sch (historical)—school ... MS-4
Woodlawn Sch (historical)—school ... NC-3
Woodlawn Sch (historical)—school ... PA-2
Woodlawn Sch (historical)—school (6) ... TN-4
Woodlawn School (Abandoned)—locale ... MO-7
Woodlawn Schools—school ... VA-3
Woodlawn Shop Ctr—other ... CO-8
Woodlawn Station—locale ... SC-3
**Woodlawn (subdivision)**—pop pl ... MS-4
**Woodlawn Subdivision**—pop pl ... TN-4
**Woodlawn Terrace**—pop pl ... GA-3
**Woodlawn Terrace**—pop pl (2) ... VA-3
Woodlawn Terrace Acad—school ... TN-4
Woodlawn Township—civil ... MO-7
**Woodlawn Township**—pop pl ... ND-7
Woodlawn (Township of)—other ... OH-6
**Woodlawn-Woodmoor**—pop pl ... MD-2
**Woodleaf**—pop pl ... CA-9
**Woodleaf**—pop pl ... NC-3
Woodleaf Creek—stream ... CA-9
Woodleaf Elem Sch—school ... NC-3
Woodleaf Hotel—hist pl ... CA-9
**Woodleaf II (subdivision)**—pop pl (2) ... AZ-5
**Woodleaf (subdivision)**—pop pl (2) ... AZ-5
Woodlea Lake ... NC-3
Woodlea Lake Dam ... NC-3
**Woodlea Lakes (subdivision)**—pop pl ... NC-3
**Woodlea (subdivision)**—pop pl (3) ... NC-3
Woodledge—hist pl ... PA-2
**Woodledge Subdivision**—pop pl ... UT-8
**Woodlee**—pop pl ... VA-3
Woodlee, L. V., House—hist pl ... TN-4
Woodlee Cave—cave ... TN-4
Woodlee Post Office (historical)—building . TN-4
**Wood Lee (subdivision)**—pop pl ... NC-3
Woodleigh—locale ... NC-3
Woodley ... NC-3
**Woodley**—pop pl ... NC-3
**Woodley**—pop pl ... TX-5
**Woodley**—pop pl ... VA-3
Woodley, Jonathan, House—hist pl ... DE-2
Woodley Baptist Ch—church ... AL-4
Woodley Cem—cemetery ... GA-3
Woodley Cem—cemetery ... TX-5
Woodley Chapel—church ... NC-3
Woodley Ditch—canal ... MT-8
Woodley Draft—valley ... PA-2
Woodley East Ch—church ... AL-4
**Woodley East Estates (subdivision)**—pop pl ... AL-4
Woodley Flat—flat ... NM-5
**Woodley Gardens**—pop pl ... MD-2
Woodley Gardens Sch—school ... MD-2
**Woodley Hills**—pop pl (2) ... VA-3
Woodley Hills Sch—school ... VA-3
**Woodley Hills (Trailer Court)**—pop pl ... VA-3
Woodley Island—island ... CA-9
Woodley Knolls Sch—school ... MD-2
**Woodley Meadows (subdivision)**—pop pl ... AL-4
**Woodley North**—pop pl ... VA-3
Woodley Park—park ... DE-2

Woodley Park—park DC-2
**Woodley Park**—pop pl DC-2
**Woodley Park (subdivision)**—pop pl AL-4
Woodley Playground—park DC-2
Woodley Road—post sta DC-2
Woodley Road Alliance Ch—church AL-4
Woodley Sch—school MS-4
Woodleys Chapel—church NC-3
Woodleys Wharf—locale NC-3
Woodley Wharf NC-3
Woodley Windmills—locale NM-5
Woodliff Airpark Airp—airport MO-7
**Woodlin**—pop pl MT-8
Woodlin Sch—school CO-8
Woodlin Sch—school MD-2
**Woodloch**—pop pl TX-5
Woodlock Cem—cemetery MO-7
Woodlock Spring—spring MO-7
Woodlot Ridge—ridge ME-1
Woodly Branch—stream TN-4
Woodlyn—locale OH-6
**Woodlyn**—pop pl (2) PA-2
Woodlyn Elem Sch—school PA-2
**Woodlyn Manor**—pop pl PA-2
**Woodlynne**—pop pl NJ-2
**Wood-Lynne**—pop pl NJ-2
**Woodlyn Park**—pop pl PA-2
**Woodlyn (RR name Eddystone (sta.))**—pop pl PA-2
Woodman—locale CA-9
Woodman—locale KY-4
**Woodman**—pop pl NH-1
**Woodman**—pop pl WV-2
**Woodman**—pop pl WI-6
Woodman Bldg—hist pl ME-1
Woodman Bog—swamp ME-1
Woodman Branch—stream MS-4
Woodman Brook—stream (2) ME-1
Woodman Brook—stream (2) NH-1
Woodman Cem—cemetery (2) MN-6
Woodman Cem—cemetery MO-7
Woodman Cem—cemetery OK-5
Woodman Cem—cemetery (3) TX-5
Woodman Circle Home—building TX-5
Woodman Creek NV-8
Woodman Creek—stream (2) CA-9
Woodman Creek—stream MT-8
Woodman Draw—valley NM-5
Woodman Elem Sch—school KS-7
Woodman Field—park NJ-2
Woodman Hall (historical)—building TX-5
Woodman Hill—summit CA-9
Woodman Hill—summit ME-1
Woodman Hill Ch—church MS-4
Woodman Institute—hist pl NH-1
Woodman Lake—lake WI-6
Woodman Mine—mine NV-8
Woodman of the World Lake Dam—dam MS-4
Woodman of the World Lodge (historical)—building TX-5
**Wood Manor (subdivision)**—pop pl AL-4
**Wood Manor (subdivision)**—pop pl MS-4
Woodman Park—park NH-1
Woodman Park Sch—school NH-1
Woodman Peak—summit CA-9
Woodman Peak—summit UT-8
Woodman Point—cape NH-1
Woodman Pond—lake (2) ME-1
Woodman Pond—lake NY-2
Woodman Pond—reservoir MA-1
Woodman Pond Dam—dam MA-1
Woodman Ravine—valley CA-9
Woodman Road Hist Dist—hist pl NH-1
**Woodmans**—pop pl WA-9
Woodmans Butte—summit CA-9
Woodmans Cem—cemetery AR-4
Woodmans Cem—cemetery MN-6
Woodman Sch—school MT-8
Woodman Sch—school WI-6
Woodmans Cove—bay NH-1
Woodmans Cove—bay NY-2
**Woodmansee Addition (subdivision)**—pop pl UT-8
Woodmansee Cem—cemetery IN-6
Woodmansee Johnson Canal—canal ID-8
**Woodmansee Main Street Subdivision**—pop pl UT-8
Woodmansee Park—park OR-9
**Woodmansee Subdivision**—pop pl UT-8
Woodmansey Ford—locale MO-7
Woodmans Hollow State Park—park IA-7
**Woodmansie**—pop pl NJ-2
Woodmans Mills—locale ME-1
Woodman Springs (historical)—locale MS-4
Woodman State For—forest NH-1
Woodmanston Site—hist pl GA-3
**Woodman Terrace**—pop pl VA-3
**Woodman (Town of)**—pop pl WI-6
**Woodmar**—pop pl IN-6
Woodmar Country Club—other IN-6
Wood-McCullough Creek—stream NV-8
Woodmead Elem Sch—school AL-4
Wood Meadow—flat CA-9
**Woodmeadow**—pop pl AL-4
Wood Memorial Cem—cemetery WA-9
**Wood Memorial Hospital (G. Pierce Wood Mem. Hosp.)**—pop pl FL-3
Wood Memorial Park (Cemetery)—cemetery SC-3
Woodmen of the World Youth Camp—locale GA-3
Woodmen Sch—school CO-8
Woodmen Valley—valley CO-8
Woodmere IL-6
Woodmere MS-4
Woodmere—locale FL-3
**Woodmere**—pop pl NH-1
**Woodmere**—pop pl (2) NJ-2
**Woodmere**—pop pl NY-2
**Woodmere**—pop pl OH-6
Woodmere Acad—school NY-2
Woodmere Cem—cemetery (3) MI-6
Woodmere Channel—channel NY-2
Woodmere Dam—dam NJ-2
Woodmere Lake—reservoir NJ-2
Woodmere Mall Shop Ctr—locale TN-4
Woodmere Memorial Park—cemetery WV-2
Woodmere North JHS—school NY-2
Woodmere Number One Lake—reservoir AL-4
Woodmere Number Two Dam—dam AL-4
Woodmere Number Two Lake—reservoir AL-4
Woodmere Park NC-3
**Woodmere Park**—pop pl PA-2
Woodmere Sch—school OR-9
**Woodmere Subdivision**—pop pl UT-8
**Wood Mill**—pop pl DE-2
Wood Mine—mine CA-9
Wood Mine—mine CO-8
Wood Mine—mine TN-4
Wood Mine (underground)—mine AL-4
Woodminster Amphitheatre—building CA-9
**Woodmohr (Town of)**—pop pl WI-6
Woodmont—locale MD-2
Woodmont—locale PA-2
Woodmont—locale WV-2
**Woodmont**—pop pl AL-4
**Woodmont**—pop pl (2) CT-1
**Woodmont**—pop pl MD-2
**Woodmont**—pop pl (2) VA-3
Woodmont—uninc pl TN-4
**Woodmont Addition (subdivision)**—pop pl TN-4
Woodmont Baptist Ch—church (2) AL-4
**Woodmont Beach**—pop pl WA-9
Woodmont Cem—cemetery VT-1
Woodmont Ch—church NC-3
Woodmont Ch—church TN-4
Woodmont Club—other MD-2
Woodmont Country Club—locale TN-4
Woodmont Country Club—other MD-2
Woodmont Plaza (Shop Ctr)—locale FL-3
Woodmont Sch—school TN-4
Woodmont Sch—school VA-3
Woodmont Sch—school WA-9
**Woodmont (subdivision)**—pop pl (2) AL-4
Woodmoor MD-2
Woodmoor—CDP CO-8
**Woodmoor**—pop pl (2) MD-2
**Woodmoor (subdivision)**—pop pl MS-4
**Woodmore**—pop pl MD-2
**Woodmore**—pop pl TN-4
Woodmore Ch of God—church TN-4
Woodmore Hollow—valley (2) TN-4
Woodmore Road Sch—school MD-2
Woodmore Sch—school TN-4
Wood-Morris-Bonfils House—hist pl CO-8
Wood Mount—summit MT-8
Wood Mtn—summit AZ-5
Wood Mtn—summit CO-8
Wood Mtn—summit KY-4
Wood Mtn—summit MT-8
Wood Mtn—summit WY-8
Woodneath—hist pl MO-7
Woodnorth Lake—lake WI-6
Wood Old Homestead—hist pl OH-6
Wood Outlet Drain—stream MI-6
Wood Park—hist pl LA-4
Wood Park—park CA-9
Wood Park—park NJ-2
Wood Park Sch—school NY-2
Wood Pass—gap UT-8
Wood Peak—summit VT-1
Woodpeck—locale WV-2
Woodpecker Canyon—valley CA-9
Woodpecker Canyon—valley ID-8
Woodpecker Cem—cemetery OH-6
Woodpecker Cove—bay AK-9
Woodpecker Creek—stream MI-6
Woodpecker Creek—stream OR-9
Woodpecker Creek—stream VA-3
Woodpecker Gulch—valley CA-9
Woodpecker Gulch—valley CO-8
Woodpecker Hill—summit OR-9
Woodpecker Knobs—summit TN-4
Woodpecker Lake—lake AK-9
Woodpecker Lake—lake MI-6
Woodpecker Lake—lake MN-6
Woodpecker Lake—lake OR-9
Woodpecker Lake—lake PA-2
Woodpecker Meadow—flat CA-9
Woodpecker Mine—mine AZ-5
Woodpecker Point—cape MD-2
Woodpecker Ravine—valley CA-9
Woodpecker Ridge—ridge NY-2
Woodpecker Ridge—ridge OR-9
Woodpeckers Peak—summit NV-8
Woodpecker Spring—spring OR-9
Woodpecker Swamp—swamp PA-2
Woodpecker Tank—reservoir TX-5
Woodpecker Trail—trail OR-9
Woodpile, The—woods UT-8
Woodpile Cabin—locale WA-9
Woodpile Coulee—valley MT-8
Woodpile Creek—stream MN-6
Woodpile Creek—stream WA-9
Woodpile Gulch—valley CA-9
Woodpile Hollow—valley VA-3
Woodpile Lake—lake MN-6
Woodpile Pond—reservoir UT-8
Woodpile Ridge—ridge WA-9
Wood Place—locale MT-8
Wood Point—cape (2) AK-9
Wood Point—cape MA-1
Wood Point—locale MD-2
**Wood Point**—pop pl MD-2
Wood Pond ME-1
Wood Pond—lake CT-1
Wood Pond—lake FL-3
Wood Pond—lake ME-1
Wood Pond—lake MA-1
Wood Pond—lake NH-1
Wood Pond—lake UT-8
Wood Pond—reservoir NC-3
Wood Pond Cove—bay ME-1
Wood Pond Dam—dam NC-3
Wood Pond Point—cape ME-1
**Woodport**—pop pl NJ-2
Woodraffe—locale OR-9
Woodrail Lake—lake MI-6
Woodramtown Branch—stream WV-2
Wood Ranch—locale AZ-5
Wood Ranch—locale (2) CA-9
Wood Ranch—locale CO-8
Wood Ranch—locale MT-8
Wood Ranch—locale NE-7
Wood Ranch—locale NV-8
Wood Ranch—locale (3) NM-5
Wood Ranch—locale (4) TX-5
Wood Ranch—locale UT-8
**Wood Ranch**—pop pl CA-9
Wood Ranch HQ—locale NM-5
Wood Ranch Rsvr—reservoir CA-9
Wood Ranch Well Number Fifty Three—well NV-8
Woodrat Bar—bar CA-9
Woodrat Knob Dam—dam OR-9
Woodrat Knob Rsvr—reservoir OR-9
Woodrat Mine—mine CA-9
Woodrat Mine—mine ID-8
Woodrat Mtn—summit ID-8
Woodrat Mtn—summit OR-9
Woodrest Creek—stream MD-2
Woodridge—locale VA-3
**Woodridge**—pop pl DE-2
**Woodridge**—pop pl DC-2
**Woodridge**—pop pl (2) IL-6
**Woodridge**—pop pl IN-6
**Woodridge**—pop pl MO-7
**Wood-Ridge**—pop pl NJ-2
**Woodridge**—pop pl NY-2
Wood Ridge—ridge OH-6
Wood Ridge Ch—church PA-2
Wood Ridge Ch—church SC-3
**Woodridge Country Estates**—pop pl UT-8
**Woodridge Country Estates Subdivision**—pop pl UT-8
**Woodridge Estates (subdivision)**—pop pl PA-2
**Woodridge Estates (subdivision)**—pop pl TN-4
**Woodridge Estates Subdivision**—pop pl UT-8
Woodridge Golf Club—other IL-6
Woodridge Hosp—hospital GA-3
Woodridge Hosp—hospital TN-4
Woodridge House—hist pl MA-1
Wood-Ridge HS—school NJ-2
Woodridge HS—school OH-6
Woodridge Lake—lake CT-1
Woodridge Lake—reservoir IN-6
**Woodridge Lakes (subdivision)**—pop pl (2) AZ-5
**Wood Ridge Manor (subdivision)**—pop pl PA-2
Woodridge Sch—school DC-2
Woodridge Sch—school MD-2
Woodridge Sch—school TX-5
Woodridge Sch—school WA-9
**Wood Ridge (subdivision)**—pop pl AL-4
**Woodridge (subdivision)**—pop pl AL-4
**Woodridge (subdivision)**—pop pl NC-3
**Woodridge Subdivision**—pop pl UT-8
Woodridge Swim Club—park PA-2
**Woodridge Terrace**—pop pl UT-8
**Woodridge Twin Homes (subdivision)**—pop pl UT-8
**Woodridge VI (subdivision)**—pop pl (2) AZ-5
Woodriff Ditch—canal LA-4
Woodriff Falls—falls LA-4
Woodring, Mount—summit WY-8
Woodring Branch—stream (2) GA-3
Woodring Canyon—valley WA-9
Woodring Cem—cemetery IL-6
Woodring Cem—cemetery KS-7
Woodring Cem—cemetery NC-3
Woodring Gap—gap GA-3
Woodring Hollow—valley WV-2
Woodrings PA-2
Woodrings Point—cape FL-3
Wood River CT-1
Wood River ID-8
Wood River MN-6
Wood River MO-7
Wood River ND-7
Wood River RI-1
Wood River SD-7
Wood River—fmr MCD NE-7
**Wood River**—pop pl AK-9
**Wood River**—pop pl IL-6
**Wood River**—pop pl NE-7
Wood River—stream (2) AK-9
Wood River—stream CT-1
Wood River—stream (2) FL-3
Wood River—stream IL-6
Wood River—stream NE-7
Wood River—stream OR-9
Wood River—stream RI-1
Wood River—stream WI-6
Wood River—stream WY-8
Wood River Buttes—other AK-9
Wood River Campground—locale ID-8
Wood River Campground—locale WY-8
Wood River Cem—cemetery NE-7
Wood River Cem—cemetery WI-6
Wood River Ch—church NE-7
Wood River Ch—church WI-6
Woodriver Elem Sch—school AK-9
Wood River Guard Station—locale WY-8
**Wood River Junction**—pop pl RI-1
Wood River Junction Dam—dam RI-1
Wood River Lakes—lake AK-9
Wood River Marsh—swamp OR-9
Wood River Mills RI-1
Wood River Mountains—range (2) AK-9
Wood River Picnic Ground—park OR-9
Wood River Pond RI-1
Wood River Sch—school WI-6
**Wood River (Town of)**—pop pl WI-6
**Wood River Township**—pop pl (2) NE-7
**Wood River (Township of)**—pop pl IL-6
Wood River Valley—valley ID-8
Wood Road Canyon—valley WY-8
Wood Road Draw—valley CO-8
Wood Road Gulch—valley (2) ID-8
Wood Road Lake—lake ID-8
Wood Road Reservoirs—reservoir NV-8
Wood Road Rsvr—reservoir OR-9
Wood Road Sch—school NY-2
Wood Road Sch—school WI-6
Wood Road Spring—spring ID-8
Woodroad Waterhole—lake OR-9
Wood Road Well—well AZ-5
Woodrock Guard Station—locale WY-8
Wood Rock Run PA-2
Woodrock Run—stream PA-2
Woodrough Pond (historical)—lake MA-1
Woodrow—locale AR-4
Woodrow—locale KY-4
Woodrow—locale TX-5
Woodrow—locale UT-8
Woodrow—locale WV-2
**Woodrow**—pop pl AK-9
**Woodrow**—pop pl CO-8
**Woodrow**—pop pl MN-6
**Woodrow**—pop pl NY-2
**Woodrow**—pop pl (2) NC-3
**Woodrow**—pop pl PA-2
**Woodrow**—pop pl SC-3
**Woodrow**—pop pl (3) TN-4
**Woodrow**—pop pl TX-5
Woodrow, William, House—hist pl OH-6
Woodrow Canyon—valley NM-5
Woodrow Cem—cemetery IL-6
Woodrow Cem—cemetery TX-5
Woodrow Ch—church (2) AR-4
Woodrow Consolidated Sch (historical)—school MS-4
Woodrow Hayes Dam—dam SD-7
Woodrow JHS—school MI-6
Woodrow Lake—lake TX-5
Woodrow Memorial Presbyterian Church—hist pl SC-3
Woodrow Methodist Church—hist pl NY-2
Woodrow Mine AL-4
Woodrow Mine—mine NM-5
Woodrow Ruin—hist pl NM-5
Woodrow Sch—school CA-9
Woodrow Sch—school TN-4
Woodrow Sch—school TX-5
Woodrow Sch (historical)—school AL-4
Woodrow Sch (historical)—school (2) TN-4
Woodrow Spring—spring TX-5
Woodrows Tank—reservoir AZ-5
**Woodrow (Township of)**—pop pl (2) MN-6
Woodrow Union Ch—church WV-2
Woodrow Wilson, Mount—summit WY-8
Woodrow Wilson Birthplace—building VA-3
Woodrow Wilson Educational Center—school VA-3
Woodrow Wilson Elem Sch—school IN-6
Woodrow Wilson Elem Sch—school KS-7
Woodrow Wilson HS—hist pl CT-1
Woodrow Wilson HS—school CT-1
Woodrow Wilson HS—school NJ-2
Woodrow Wilson HS—school OR-9
Woodrow Wilson HS—school VA-3
Woodrow Wilson HS—school WA-9
Woodrow Wilson JHS—school AR-4
Woodrow Wilson JHS—school CA-9
Woodrow Wilson JHS—school IL-6
Woodrow Wilson JHS—school IN-6
Woodrow Wilson JHS—school VA-3
Woodrow Wilson JHS—school WA-9
Woodrow Wilson Memorial Bridge—bridge MD-2
Woodrow Wilson Memorial Bridge—bridge VA-3
Woodrow Wilson Park—park AL-4
Woodrow Wilson Park—park OH-6
Woodrow Wilson Sch—school (5) CA-9
Woodrow Wilson Sch—school (2) CT-1
Woodrow Wilson Sch—school (3) IL-6
Woodrow Wilson Sch—school IN-6
Woodrow Wilson Sch—school KS-7
Woodrow Wilson Sch—school (2) NJ-2
Woodrow Wilson Sch—school (2) NY-2
Woodrow Wilson Sch—school NC-3
Woodrow Wilson Sch—school ND-7
Woodrow Wilson Sch—school (2) OK-5
Woodrow Wilson Sch—school (3) TX-5
Woodrow Wilson Sch—school UT-8
Woodrow Wilson Sch—school (2) VA-3
Woodrow Wilson Sch (historical)—school MS-4
**Woodrow Wilson (State Rehabilitation Center)**—pop pl VA-3
Woodrow Wilson Vocational HS—school NY-2
Woodrow Windmill—locale AZ-5
Wood Rsvr—reservoir CO-8
Wood Rsvr—reservoir (2) OR-9
Wood Rsvr—reservoir WA-9
Wood Rsvr—reservoir WY-8
Woodruff IN-6
Woodruff—locale ID-8
Woodruff—locale MO-7
Woodruff—locale NJ-2
Woodruff—locale PA-2
Woodruff—other IL-6
**Woodruff**—pop pl AZ-5
**Woodruff**—pop pl FL-3
**Woodruff**—pop pl ID-8
**Woodruff**—pop pl IN-6
**Woodruff**—pop pl KS-7
**Woodruff**—pop pl NJ-2
**Woodruff**—pop pl SC-3
**Woodruff**—pop pl UT-8
**Woodruff**—pop pl VT-1
**Woodruff**—pop pl WV-2
**Woodruff**—pop pl WI-6
Woodruff, Asahel Hart, House—hist pl UT-8
Woodruff, Charles, House—hist pl OH-6
Woodruff, Ernest, House—hist pl GA-3
Woodruff, Henry Lindsay, House—hist pl GA-3
Woodruff, Henry Lindsay, Second House—hist pl GA-3
Woodruff, Jacob, House—hist pl WI-6
Woodruff, Lake—lake FL-3
Woodruff, Wilford, Farm House—hist pl UT-8
Woodruff, William H., House—hist pl OH-6
Woodruff Ave—uninc pl CA-9
Woodruff Ave Sch—school CA-9
Woodruff Bay—bay NY-2
Woodruff Bottom UT-8
Woodruff Bottom—bend UT-8
Woodruff Branch—stream IN-6
Woodruff Branch—stream KS-7
Woodruff Branch—stream MS-4
Woodruff Branch—stream (2) NC-3
Woodruff Bridge—bridge AL-4
Woodruff Bridge—bridge OR-9
Woodruff Bridge—hist pl AZ-5
Woodruff Bridge Picnic Site—locale OR-9
Woodruff Brook—stream MI-6
Woodruff Butte—summit AZ-5
Woodruff Cabin Site—hist pl WY-8
Woodruff Camp—locale NV-8
Woodruff Canyon—valley UT-8
Woodruff Canyon—valley WA-9
Woodruff (CCD)—cens area SC-3
Woodruff Cem—cemetery IL-6
Woodruff Cem—cemetery IN-6
Woodruff Cem—cemetery KS-7
Woodruff Cem—cemetery (2) MS-4
Woodruff Cem—cemetery OH-6
Woodruff Cem—cemetery PA-2
Woodruff Cem—cemetery UT-8
Woodruff Ch—church NC-3
Woodruff Corners—locale IL-6
Woodruff Corners—locale PA-2
**Woodruff (County)**—pop pl AR-4
Woodruff County Courthouse—hist pl AR-4
Woodruff Cove—bay ME-1
Woodruff Creek—stream AR-4
Woodruff Creek—stream (2) CA-9
Woodruff Creek—stream FL-3
Woodruff Creek—stream KY-4
Woodruff Creek—stream MI-6
Woodruff Creek—stream MS-4
Woodruff Creek—stream NV-8
Woodruff Creek—stream (2) OR-9
Woodruff Creek—stream UT-8
Woodruff Creek Dam—dam UT-8
Woodruff Creek Reservoir UT-8
Woodruff Dam—dam AZ-5
Woodruff Dam—dam SD-7
Woodruff Ditch—canal AZ-5
Woodruff Ditch—canal OH-6
Woodruffe Creek MS-4
Woodruff Flat—flat ID-8
Woodruff Gap—gap NJ-2
Woodruff Gulch—valley ID-8
**Woodruff Heights**—pop pl NY-2
Woodruff Hill—summit CT-1
Woodruff (historical)—locale AL-4
Woodruff Hole—basin UT-8
Woodruff Hollow—valley PA-2
Woodruff House—hist pl NJ-2
Woodruff HS—school IL-6
Woodruff Island—island VA-3
Woodruff JHS—school CA-9
Woodruff Lake—lake AZ-5
Woodruff Lake—lake (5) MI-6
Woodruff Lake—reservoir SD-7
Woodruff Lake State Game Area—park SD-7
Woodruff Lower Narrows—gap WY-8
Woodruff Meadow—flat OR-9
**Woodruff Mill**—pop pl WA-9
Woodruff Mill Mine (underground)—mine AL-4
Woodruff Mtn—summit ME-1
Woodruff Mtn—summit MA-1
Woodruff Mtn—summit NC-3
Woodruff Mtn—summit OR-9
Woodruff Narrows Dam—dam WY-8
Woodruff Narrows Rsvr—reservoir WY-8
Woodruff Park—flat UT-8
Woodruff Park—locale MT-8
Woodruff Pastures—flat UT-8
Woodruff Place IN-6
Woodruff Place—hist pl IN-6
Woodruff Place Baptist Ch—church IN-6
**Woodruff Place (subdivision)**—pop pl IN-6
Woodruff Plaza—locale MA-1
Woodruff Pond—lake GA-3
Woodruff Pond—lake (2) NY-2
Woodruff Ridge—ridge NC-3
Woodruff-Riter House—hist pl UT-8
Woodruff RR Station—locale FL-3
Woodruff Rsvr—reservoir AZ-5
Woodruff Rsvr—reservoir UT-8
Woodruffs SC-3
**Woodruffs**—pop pl NJ-2
Woodruff Sch—school AR-4
Woodruff Sch—school CA-9
Woodruff Sch—school MI-6
Woodruff Sch—school UT-8
Woodruffs Gap—locale NJ-2
**Woodruff's Gap**—pop pl NJ-2
Woodruffs Island—island IL-6
Woodruffs Pond—lake CT-1
Woodruff Spring—spring (2) UT-8
**Woodruff Springs**—pop pl FL-3
**Woodruffs Subdivision**—pop pl FL-3
Woodruff Swamp—swamp NY-2
**Woodruff (Town of)**—pop pl WI-6
Woodruff Trail—trail PA-2
Woodruff Upper Narrows—gap WY-8
Woodruff Villa—hist pl UT-8
Woodruff Well—well NM-5
**Woodrum**—pop pl VA-3
Woodrum Branch—stream WV-2
Woodrum Ridge—ridge KY-4
Woodrum Sch—school KY-4
Wood Run—other PA-2
**Wood Run**—pop pl PA-2
Wood Run—stream NC-3
Wood Run—stream WV-2
Wood Run Hollow—valley PA-2
Woodrun Lake Number One—reservoir TN-4
Woodrun Lake Number Two—reservoir TN-4
Woodrun Lakes Dam TN-4
Woodrun Number One Dam West—dam TN-4
Woodrun Number Two Dam—dam TN-4
**Woodrun (subdivision)**—pop pl NC-3
Woods KY-4
Woods OH-6
Woods—island ME-1
Woods—locale CO-8
Woods—locale CT-1
Woods—locale FL-3
Woods—locale KY-4
Woods—locale MI-6
Woods—locale NY-2
Woods—locale NC-3
Woods—locale ND-7
Woods—locale PA-2
Woods—locale TX-5
**Woods**—pop pl FL-3
**Woods**—pop pl KS-7
**Woods**—pop pl (2) KY-4
**Woods**—pop pl OK-5
**Woods**—pop pl OR-9
**Woods**—pop pl TN-4
Woods, Alexander, House—hist pl AL-4
Woods, Archibald, House—hist pl KY-4
Woods, Lake—lake CO-8
Woods, Lake—lake NM-5
Woods, Lake—reservoir CO-8
Woods, Lake ff the—lake MN-6
Woods, Lake in the—lake FL-3
Woods, Lake in the—lake OR-9
Woods, Lake in the—lake SC-3
Woods, Lake in the—reservoir AL-4
Woods, Lake in the—reservoir IN-6
Woods, Lake of the—lake CA-9
Woods, Lake of The—lake (2) CA-9
Woods, Lake of the—lake (4) FL-3
Woods, Lake of the—lake IN-6
Woods, Lake of the—lake (8) MI-6
Woods, Lake of the—lake (3) MT-8
Woods, Lake of the—lake NY-2
Woods, Lake of the—lake (3) OR-9
Woods, Lake of the—lake (2) WA-9
Woods, Lake of the—lake (3) WI-6
Woods, Lake Of The—lake (3) WY-8
Woods, Lake of the—reservoir AZ-5
Woods, Lake Of The—reservoir IL-6
Woods, Lake of the—reservoir IN-6
Woods, Lake of the—reservoir (2) MO-7
Woods, Lake Of The—reservoir VA-3
Woods, Lake of the—swamp MN-6
Woods, Nettie, Covered Bridge—hist pl PA-2
Woods, Oscar C., House—hist pl IA-7
Woods, Perry M., House—hist pl TX-5
Woods, Tet, Bldg—hist pl OH-6
Woods, The—island FL-3
**Woods, The**—pop pl PA-2
Woods, The—woods MA-1
**Woods, The (subdivision)**—pop pl DE-2
Woods and Caples General Store—hist pl OR-9
**Woods and Lakes (subdivision)**—pop pl FL-3
**Woods At Laurel Hill (subdivision), The**—pop pl NC-3
Woods Backbone—ridge OR-9
Woods Bar—bar CA-9
Woods Basin—basin ID-8
Woods Basin—basin WY-8
Woods Bay—bay MN-6
Woods Bay—bay MT-8
Woods Bay—bay WI-6
**Woods Bay**—pop pl MT-8
Woods Bayou—channel AL-4
Woods Bayou—stream (2) LA-4
Woods Beach Rock—rock MA-1
Woods Bend AL-4
Woods Bend—bend AR-4
Woods Bend—bend TX-5
Woodsbend—locale KY-4
Woods Bluff—cliff TN-4
Woods Bluff—locale AL-4
Woods Bluff Public Use Area—park AL-4
Woods Bluff Shoal—bar AL-4
**Woodsboro**—pop pl MD-2
**Woodsboro**—pop pl TX-5
Woodsboro and Frederick Turnpike Company Tollhouse—hist pl MD-2
Woodsboro (CCD)—cens area TX-5
Woodsboro Community Center—locale IL-6
Woodsboro P.O. (historical)—locale AL-4
Woods Branch DE-2
Woods Branch—stream AL-4
Woods Branch—stream AR-4
Woods Branch—stream FL-3
Woods Branch—stream GA-3
Woods Branch—stream (2) IN-6
Woods Branch—stream (2) KY-4
Woods Branch—stream LA-4
Woods Branch—stream NC-3
Woods Branch—stream (3) TN-4
Woods Branch—stream VA-3
Woods Bridge—bridge NY-2
**Woodsbro**—pop pl CA-9
Woods Brook—stream MA-1
Woods Brook—stream NH-1
Woods Brook—stream NY-2
Woods Brothers Bldg—hist pl NE-7
Woodsburg NY-2
Woodsburg Channel NY-2
**Woodsburgh**—pop pl NY-2
Woodsburgh Channel—channel NY-2
Woods Camp OR-9
Woods Camp—locale CA-9
Woods Camp—locale OR-9
Woods Canyon ID-8
Woods Canyon—valley (4) AZ-5
Woods Canyon—valley CA-9
Woods Canyon—valley (2) CO-8
Woods Canyon—valley ID-8
Woods Canyon—valley NV-8
Woods Canyon—valley (2) NM-5
Woods Canyon—valley (2) UT-8
Woods Canyon—valley WY-8
Woods Canyon Bridge—bridge AZ-5
Woods Canyon Creek—stream AZ-5
Woods Canyon Dam—dam AZ-5
Woods Canyon Lake—reservoir AZ-5
Woods Canyon Lake Rec Area—park AZ-5
Woods Castle—cape RI-1
Woods Cave—cave AL-4
Woods Cem—cemetery (5) AL-4
Woods Cem—cemetery (6) AR-4
Woods Cem—cemetery FL-3
Woods Cem—cemetery (3) GA-3
Woods Cem—cemetery (5) IL-6
Woods Cem—cemetery IN-6
Woods Cem—cemetery IA-7
Woods Cem—cemetery (2) KS-7
Woods Cem—cemetery (4) KY-4
Woods Cem—cemetery MA-1
Woods Cem—cemetery MI-6
Woods Cem—cemetery (2) MS-4
Woods Cem—cemetery (6) MO-7
Woods Cem—cemetery (5) OH-6
Woods Cem—cemetery (2) PA-2
Woods Cem—cemetery SC-3
Woods Cem—cemetery (11) TN-4
Woods Cem—cemetery (6) TX-5
Woods Cem—cemetery (2) VA-3
Woods Cem—cemetery WV-2
Woods Cemetery, The—cemetery IA-7
Woods Ch—church AL-4
Woods Ch—church NC-3
Woods Ch—church VA-3
Wood Sch—school AL-4
Wood Sch—school AZ-5
Wood Sch—school (2) CA-9
Wood Sch—school FL-3
Wood Sch—school IL-6
Wood Sch—school MA-1
Wood Sch—school (2) MI-6

**Woodvale**—*pop pl* VA-3
Woodvale Cem—*cemetery* OH-6
Woodvale Ch—*church* SC-3
**Woodvale Heights**—*pop pl* PA-2
Woodvale Lake—*reservoir* TX-5
Wood Valley—*valley* CA-9
Wood Valley—*valley* HI-9
*Wood Valley Camp* HI-9
Wood Valley Camp—*locale* HI-9
Wood Valley Homesteads—*civil* HI-9
**Woodview**—*pop pl* PA-2
**Woodview Estates (subdivision)**—*pop pl* UT-8
**Woodview Heights Subdivision**—*pop pl* UT-8
Woodview JHS—*school* IN-6
*Woodview Manor* IL-6
Woodview Park—*park* MN-6
Woodview Park—*park* OH-6
**Woodview Park**—*pop pl* OH-6
Woodview Sch—*school* IL-6
Woodview Sch—*school* TX-5
Woodview Sch (historical)—*school* MO-7
**Wood Village**—*pop pl* OR-9
**Wood Village (subdivision)**—*pop pl* AL-4
**Wood Villas (subdivision)**—*pop pl* AL-4
*Woodville* AL-4
*Woodville* NC-3
Woodville—*CDP* FL-3
Woodville—*hist pl* (2) GA-3
Woodville—*locale* CA-9
Woodville—*locale* CT-1
Woodville—*locale* IL-6
Woodville—*locale* IA-7
Woodville—*locale* LA-4
Woodville—*locale* MD-2
Woodville—*locale* MI-6
Woodville—*locale* MT-8
Woodville—*locale* NC-3
Woodville—*locale* OH-6
Woodville—*locale* (2) PA-2
Woodville—*locale* SD-7
Woodville—*locale* TN-4
**Woodville**—*pop pl* AL-4
**Woodville**—*pop pl* CA-9
**Woodville**—*pop pl* (2) FL-3
**Woodville**—*pop pl* (2) GA-3
**Woodville**—*pop pl* ID-8
**Woodville**—*pop pl* (3) IN-6
**Woodville**—*pop pl* KY-4
**Woodville**—*pop pl* MA-1
**Woodville**—*pop pl* (2) MI-6
**Woodville**—*pop pl* MS-4
**Woodville**—*pop pl* MO-7
**Woodville**—*pop pl* NJ-2
**Woodville**—*pop pl* (2) NY-2
**Woodville**—*pop pl* (3) NC-3
**Woodville**—*pop pl* OH-6
**Woodville**—*pop pl* OK-5
**Woodville**—*pop pl* (2) RI-1
**Woodville**—*pop pl* (2) SC-3
**Woodville**—*pop pl* TN-4
**Woodville**—*pop pl* TX-5
**Woodville**—*pop pl* VA-3
**Woodville**—*pop pl* WV-2
**Woodville**—*pop pl* WI-6
Woodville Airp—*airport* NC-3
Woodville Attendance Center—*school* MS-4
Woodville Baptist Ch—*church* TN-4
Woodville Branch—*stream* IL-6
Woodville Branch—*stream* MD-2
Woodville Canal—*canal* ID-8
Woodville (CCD)—*cens area* GA-3
Woodville (CCD)—*cens area* SC-3
Woodville (CCD)—*cens area* TX-5
Woodville Cem—*cemetery* ID-8
Woodville Cem—*cemetery* IN-6
Woodville Cem—*cemetery* LA-4
Woodville Cem—*cemetery* MN-6
Woodville Cem—*cemetery* (2) OH-6
Woodville Cem—*cemetery* OK-5
Woodville Cem—*cemetery* OR-9
Woodville Cem—*cemetery* (3) TN-4
Woodville Cem—*cemetery* TX-5
Woodville Cem—*cemetery* WI-6
Woodville Ch—*church* AL-4
Woodville Ch—*church* (2) MO-7
Woodville Ch—*church* NC-3
Woodville Ch—*church* (2) TX-5
Woodville Chapel—*church* MN-6
Woodville Classical Sch for Boys (historical)—*school* MS-4
Woodville Community Center—*locale* TX-5
**Woodville (corporate name for New Woodville)**—*pop pl* OK-5
Woodville Creek—*stream* TN-4
Woodville Creek—*stream* VA-3
Woodville Elem Sch—*school* FL-3
Woodville Farm Labor Supply Center—*other* CA-9
Woodville Female Acad (historical)—*school* MS-4
*Woodville Female Seminary* MS-4
**Woodville Gardens**—*pop pl* OH-6
Woodville Heights Baptist Ch—*church* MS-4
*Woodville Heights Elementary School* MS-4
Woodville Heights Sch—*school* MS-4
**Woodville Heights (subdivision)**—*pop pl* MS-4
**Woodville Hills**—*pop pl* IN-6
Woodville Hills—*range* SD-7
Woodville Hist Dist—*hist pl* MS-4
Woodville (historical)—*locale* KS-7
Woodville (historical P.O.)—*locale* IA-7
Woodville HS—*school* AL-4
Woodville Island—*island* SC-3
Woodville Lookout—*locale* TX-5
Woodville Pond—*reservoir* RI-1
Woodville Pond Dam—*dam* RI-1
*Woodville Post Office* TN-4
Woodville Post Office (historical)—*building* TN-4
Woodville (RR name Lewiston (sta.))—*other* NC-3
Woodville Sch—*school* AL-4
Woodville Sch—*school* IL-6
Woodville Sch—*school* MA-1
Woodville Sch—*school* MI-6
Woodville Sch—*school* OH-6
Woodville Sch—*school* SC-3
Woodville Sch—*school* TN-4
Woodville Sch—*school* TX-5
Woodville Sch—*school* VA-3
Woodville Sch—*school* WV-2
Woodville Sch (abandoned)—*school* PA-2
Woodville Sch (historical)—*school* TN-4
Woodville Shaft—*mine* NV-8
Woodville Spring—*spring* VA-3
Woodville State Hosp—*hospital* PA-2
**Woodville (Town of)**—*pop pl* ME-1
**Woodville (Town of)**—*pop pl* WI-6
**Woodville Township**—*pop pl* NE-7
Woodville (Township of)—*fmr MCD* NC-3
**Woodville (Township of)**—*pop pl* IL-6
**Woodville (Township of)**—*pop pl* MN-6
**Woodville (Township of)**—*pop pl* OH-6
Woodvine Cem—*cemetery* LA-4
*Woodward* KS-7
Woodward—*locale* SC-3
Woodward—*locale* TX-5
**Woodward**—*pop pl* AL-4
**Woodward**—*pop pl* IA-7
**Woodward**—*pop pl* OK-5
**Woodward**—*pop pl* PA-2
Woodward, Dr. M. M., House—*hist pl* TX-5
Woodward, Elias, House—*hist pl* OR-9
Woodward, John, House—*hist pl* MA-1
Woodward, Lake—*lake* FL-3
Woodward, Rev. Samuel, House—*hist pl* MA-1
Woodward, Robert Simpson, House—*hist pl* DC-2
Woodward, William, House—*hist pl* MA-1
Woodward Ave—*uninc pl* FL-3
Woodward Ave Baptist Ch—*church* AL-4
Woodward Ave Elem Sch—*school* FL-3
Woodward Ave. Presbyterian Church—*hist pl* MI-6
Woodward-Baird House—*hist pl* CO-8
*Woodward Bay* WA-9
Woodward Bay—*swamp* SC-3
Woodward Bldg—*hist pl* AL-4
Woodward Bldg—*hist pl* ID-8
Woodward Bluff Sch—*school* IL-6
Woodward Branch—*stream* KY-4
Woodward Branch—*stream* NC-3
Woodward Branch—*stream* SC-3
Woodward Branch—*stream* (2) TN-4
Woodward Branch—*stream* TX-5
Woodward Branch—*stream* WV-2
Woodward Bridge—*bridge* MA-1
*Woodward Brook* CT-1
Woodward Brook—*locale* MN-6
Woodward Brook—*stream* NH-1
Woodward Cabin—*locale* NV-8
Woodward Canal—*canal* CA-9
Woodward Canyon—*valley* WA-9
Woodward Cave—*cave* PA-2
Woodward (CCD)—*cens area* OK-5
Woodward Cem—*cemetery* AL-4
Woodward Cem—*cemetery* GA-3
Woodward Cem—*cemetery* IN-6
Woodward Cem—*cemetery* IA-7
Woodward Cem—*cemetery* KY-4
Woodward Cem—*cemetery* MD-2
Woodward Cem—*cemetery* NY-2
Woodward Cem—*cemetery* TN-4
Woodward Cem—*cemetery* TX-5
Woodward Cem—*cemetery* (2) VA-3
Woodward Ch—*church* SC-3
Woodward Chapel—*church* TN-4
Woodward Country Club—*other* AL-4
**Woodward (County)**—*pop pl* OK-5
Woodward Cove—*bay* ME-1
Woodward Cove Branch—*stream* VA-3
*Woodward Creek* NV-8
*Woodward Creek* WA-9
Woodward Creek—*stream* AL-4
Woodward Creek—*stream* (2) CA-9
Woodward Creek—*stream* GA-3
Woodward Creek—*stream* KY-4
Woodward Creek—*stream* MS-4
Woodward Creek—*stream* MO-7
Woodward Creek—*stream* MT-8
Woodward Creek—*stream* OH-6
Woodward Creek—*stream* OK-5
Woodward Creek—*stream* (3) OR-9
Woodward Creek—*stream* TX-5
Woodward Creek—*stream* WA-9
Woodward Creek—*stream* WI-6
*Woodward Crossing* AL-4
Woodward Crystal Beach Park—*hist pl* OK-5
Woodward Dam Camp—*locale* PA-2
Woodward East Hist Dist—*hist pl* MI-6
Woodward Elem Sch (historical)—*school* AL-4
Woodward Elevator—*locale* WA-9
Woodward Field—*airport* SC-3
Woodward Field (Southern Aviation School) (Airport)—*airport* SC-3
Woodward Gap—*gap* PA-2
Woodward Glen—*valley* IA-7
Woodward Grove—*woods* TX-5
Woodward Heights Neighborhood Hist Dist—*hist pl* KY-4
Woodward Hill—*summit* GA-3
Woodward Hill—*summit* WA-9
Woodward Hill Cem—*cemetery* PA-2
*Woodward Hollow* NY-2
Woodward Hollow—*valley* MO-7
Woodward Hollow—*valley* NY-2
Woodward Hollow—*valley* OK-5
Woodward Hollow—*valley* VA-3
Woodward Hollow—*valley* WI-6
Woodward House—*hist pl* KY-4
Woodward House—*hist pl* TX-5
Woodward House—*hist pl* VA-3
Woodward Houses—*hist pl* DE-2
Woodward HS—*school* (2) OH-6
Woodwardia Canyon—*valley* CA-9
Woodwardia Pond—*lake* NY-2
Woodward Inn—*hist pl* PA-2
*Woodward Island* ME-1
Woodward Island—*island* CA-9
Woodward Island Ferry—*locale* CA-9
*Woodward JHS* NC-3
Woodward JHS—*school* AZ-5
Woodward JHS—*school* NC-3
Woodward Junction—*locale* AL-4
Woodward Knob—*summit* NC-3
*Woodward Lake* MI-6
Woodward Lake—*lake* LA-4
Woodward Lake—*lake* MI-6
Woodward Lake—*lake* MT-8
Woodward Lake—*lake* NY-2
Woodward Lake—*reservoir* AL-4
Woodward Lake Dam—*dam* AL-4
Woodward Lakes—*reservoir* AL-4
Woodward Meadows—*flat* WA-9
Woodward Meadows—*swamp* MT-8
Woodward Millpond—*reservoir* SC-3
Woodward Mines (underground)—*mine* AL-4
Woodward Mountain—*ridge* PA-2
Woodward Mtn—*summit* AL-4
Woodward Mtn—*summit* MT-8
Woodward Mtn—*summit* PA-2
Woodward Mtn—*summit* VT-1
Woodward Opera House—*hist pl* OH-6
Woodward Park—*park* AL-4
Woodward Park—*park* OH-6
Woodward Park—*park* OK-5
Woodward Parkway Sch—*school* NY-2
Woodward Peak—*summit* CA-9
Woodward Place—*locale* MT-8
Woodward Point—*cape* (2) ME-1
Woodward Point—*summit* MT-8
Woodward Pond—*lake* NH-1
Woodward Pond—*lake* TX-5
Woodward Pond—*reservoir* MD-2
Woodward Pond Dam—*dam* MS-4
Woodward Ranch—*locale* MT-8
Woodward Ranch—*locale* NV-8
Woodward Ranch—*locale* (2) NM-5
*Woodward Red Ore* AL-4
Woodward Rsvr—*reservoir* CA-9
Woodward Rsvr—*reservoir* VT-1
Woodward Rsvr Number One—*reservoir* OR-9
Woodward Rsvr Number Two—*reservoir* OR-9
Woodward Run—*stream* PA-2
Woodwards—*locale* MS-4
**Wood Wards Addition (subdivision)**—*pop pl* DE-2
Woodwards Branch—*stream* NC-3
Woodward Sch—*hist pl* UT-8
Woodward Sch—*school* IL-6
Woodward Sch—*school* MA-1
Woodward Sch—*school* (2) MI-6
Woodward Sch—*school* ND-7
Woodward Sch—*school* OH-6
Woodward Sch—*school* (2) PA-2
Woodward Sch—*school* UT-8
Woodward Sch—*school* VT-1
Woodwards Corner—*locale* PA-2
*Woodwards Creek* MS-4
Woodwards Creek—*stream* NV-8
*Woodwards Dam* OR-9
*Woodwards Hollow* NY-2
Woodward Sidehill—*cliff* NY-2
Woodwards Lake—*reservoir* SC-3
Woodwards Mill (historical)—*locale* NV-8
Woodwards Pond—*reservoir* GA-3
Woodwards Pond Ch—*church* NC-3
Woodward Springs—*spring* TX-5
Woodward State Hosp—*hospital* IA-7
*Woodwardsville* NJ-2
Woodward Swamp—*swamp* MA-1
Woodward Township—*civil* PA-2
**Woodward Township**—*pop pl* ND-7
**Woodward (Township of)**—*pop pl* (3) PA-2
Woodward Valley Ch—*church* KY-4
Woodward Valley Trail—*trail* CA-9
Woodward Woods Ch—*church* WV-2
Woodway—*locale* TX-5
**Woodway**—*pop pl* TX-5
**Woodway**—*pop pl* VA-3
**Woodway**—*pop pl* WA-9
Wood Well—*well* AZ-5
Wood Well—*well* (3) NM-5
Wood Windmill—*locale* NM-5
Woodworth—*locale* MT-8
Woodworth—*locale* NC-3
**Woodworth**—*pop pl* IL-6
**Woodworth**—*pop pl* LA-4
**Woodworth**—*pop pl* MT-8
**Woodworth**—*pop pl* ND-7
**Woodworth**—*pop pl* OH-6
**Woodworth**—*pop pl* WI-6
Woodworth, Mount—*summit* CA-9
Woodworth, Nathan A., House—*hist pl* CT-1
Woodworth Cem—*cemetery* NY-2
Woodworth Ch—*church* NC-3
Woodworth Corners—*locale* OH-6
Woodworth Glacier—*glacier* AK-9
Woodworth (historical)—*locale* OR-9
Woodworth Hollow—*valley* NY-2
Woodworth Lake—*lake* NY-2
*Woodworth Post Office* SD-7
Woodworth Ranch—*locale* SD-7
Woodworth Sch—*school* CA-9
Woodworth Sch—*school* (2) MI-6
Woodworth Sch—*school* WI-6
Woodworth Spring—*spring* WY-8
Woodworth Township (historical)—*civil* SD-7
Woody—*locale* CA-9
Woody—*locale* IL-6
**Woody**—*pop pl* NE-7
**Woody**—*pop pl* TN-4
Woody Acres—*locale* TX-5
**Woody Acres**—*pop pl* AL-4
Woodyard—*locale* IL-6
Woodyard—*locale* MD-2
*Wood Yard, The* MS-4
**Woodyard (Alderson)**—*pop pl* IL-6
Woodyard Archeol Site—*hist pl* MD-2
Woodyard Canyon—*valley* AZ-5
Woodyard Cem—*cemetery* OH-6
Woodyard Creek—*stream* AK-9
Woodyard Creek—*stream* GA-3
Woodyard Flat—*flat* (2) CA-9
Woodyard Gut—*gut* AL-4
Woodyard Hammock—*island* FL-3
Woodyard Landing (historical)—*locale* AL-4
Woodyard Pond—*bay* LA-4
Woodyard Slough—*gut* IL-6
Woodyards Run—*stream* WV-2
**Woodyardville**—*pop pl* AR-4
Wood Yard Windmill—*locale* NM-5
Woody Bayou—*gut* MS-4
Woody Branch—*stream* GA-3
Woody Branch—*stream* (3) NC-3
Woody Branch—*stream* TX-5
**Woodybrook**—*pop pl* NY-2
Woody Canyon—*valley* (3) NV-8
Woody Cave—*cave* AL-4
Woody Cave—*cave* MO-7
Woody Cem—*cemetery* (2) GA-3
Woody Cem—*cemetery* (5) NC-3
Woody Cem—*cemetery* (3) TN-4
Woody Cem—*cemetery* WV-2
Woody Chapel—*church* OK-5
*Woody Creek* MT-8
Woody Creek—*locale* CO-8
Woody Creek—*stream* CO-8
Woody Creek—*stream* GA-3
Woody Creek—*stream* ID-8
Woody Creek—*stream* (4) MT-8
Woody Creek—*stream* NC-3
Woody Creek—*stream* TX-5
Woody Creek—*stream* VA-3
Woody Creek—*stream* (2) WA-9
Woody Creek—*stream* (3) WY-8
Woody Creek Camp—*locale* MT-8
Woody Creek Trail—*trail* ID-8
**Woodycrest**—*pop pl* PA-2
Woody Draw—*valley* TX-5
Woody Gap—*gap* (2) GA-3
Woody Gap—*gap* NC-3
Woody Gap HS—*school* GA-3
Woody Hill—*summit* RI-1
Woody Hill Brook—*stream* RI-1
Woody Hollow—*valley* AR-4
Woody Island—*cape* MA-1
Woody Island—*island* (2) AK-9
Woody Island—*island* OR-9
Woody Island—*island* TN-4
Woody Island ANV993—*reserve* AK-9
Woody Island Channel—*channel* AK-9
Woody Island Channel—*channel* OR-9
Woody Island Coulee—*valley* MT-8
Woody Island Light—*locale* AK-9
Woody Island South Channel—*channel* OR-9
Woody Lake—*lake* AK-9
Woody Lake—*reservoir* GA-3
Woody Lake—*reservoir* VA-3
Woody Mountain Lookout Tower—*hist pl* AZ-5
Woody Mtn—*summit* AZ-5
Woody Mtn—*summit* GA-3
Woody Mtn—*summit* (3) MT-8
Woody Mtn—*summit* WA-9
Woody Pass—*gap* WA-9
*Woody Pines* AL-4
*Woody Pines* MS-4
Woody Point—*cape* AK-9
Woody Pond—*lake* FL-3
Woody Pond—*reservoir* AZ-5
Woody Post Office (historical)—*building* TN-4
Woody Ranch—*locale* CA-9
Woody Ridge—*ridge* AZ-5
Woody Ridge—*ridge* MT-8
Woody Ridge—*ridge* (2) NC-3
Woody Ridge—*ridge* WY-8
Woody Sch—*school* LA-4
Woody Sch—*school* TN-4
*Woodys Corner* IN-6
Woodys Field—*airport* PA-2
Woodys Knob—*summit* NC-3
Woodys Lake—*lake* NC-3
Woodys Mill (historical)—*locale* TN-4
Woodys Pond—*reservoir* VA-3
Woody Spring—*spring* AZ-5
Woody Spring—*spring* TN-4
Woody Springs—*spring* NV-8
Woodys Rsvr—*reservoir* UT-8
Woodys Tank—*reservoir* AZ-5
Woody Tank—*reservoir* AZ-5
Woody Tank—*reservoir* (2) NM-5
Woody Village Shop Ctr—*locale* NC-3
*Woodyville* TN-4
*Woodyville Post Office* TN-4
Woody Wash—*stream* AZ-5
Woody Well—*well* TX-5
Woodzell—*locale* WV-2
**Woodzell**—*pop pl* MD-2
WOOF-AM (Dothan)—*tower* AL-4
Woof Creek—*stream* ID-8
WOOF-FM (Dothan)—*tower* AL-4
Woofin Cem—*cemetery* MO-7
Woofter Cem—*cemetery* (2) WV-2
Woofter Ranch—*locale* NM-5
**Wooglin**—*pop pl* NY-2
**Woolam**—*pop pl* MO-7
Woolam Cem—*cemetery* TX-5
Wooland Siding—*locale* TX-5
Woolard, Mount—*summit* WA-9
Woolard Cem—*cemetery* (2) MO-7
Woolard Cem—*cemetery* OH-6
Woolard Creek—*stream* ID-8
*Woolard Crossroads* NC-3
*Woolards Crossroads* NC-3
Woolaroc—*locale* AZ-5
Woolaroc—*locale* OK-5
Woolaroc Museum—*building* OK-5
Woolbank Creek—*stream* AL-4
*Woolber Creek* KY-4
Woolbridge Creek—*stream* OR-9
*Woolbright Creek* AR-4
Wool Canyon—*valley* NM-5
Woolcot Cem—*cemetery* OH-6
Woolcott—*locale* KY-4
Woolcott Creek—*stream* MI-6
Wool Cutter Spring—*spring* AZ-5
Wooldridge—*locale* MT-8
**Wooldridge**—*pop pl* MO-7
**Wooldridge**—*pop pl* TN-4
Wooldridge Archeol Site—*hist pl* MO-7
Wooldridge Butte—*summit* OR-9
Wooldridge Creek—*stream* AR-4
Wooldridge Monuments—*hist pl* KY-4
Wooldridge Park—*hist pl* TX-5
Wooldridge Park—*park* TX-5
Wooldridge Post Office (historical)—*building* TN-4
Wooldridge Sch—*school* OH-6
Wooldridge Sch—*school* TX-5
Wooldridge Spring—*spring* AR-4
Wooldridge's Ranch—*locale* MT-8
Wooldrige Cem—*cemetery* LA-4
Wooledge Dam—*dam* SD-7
Woolen, Isaac, House—*hist pl* OR-9
Woolen Canyon—*valley* OR-9
Woolen Canyon Spring—*spring* OR-9
Woolen Lake—*lake* LA-4
Woolen Lake Ch—*church* LA-4
Woolen Mills Chapel—*hist pl* VA-3
*Woolen Woodland Lake* AL-4
Woolery Cem—*cemetery* MO-7
Woolery Ranch Spring—*spring* WY-8
Wooley—*locale* MT-8
Wooley Camp—*locale* CA-9
Wooley Cem—*cemetery* (2) AL-4
Wooley Cem—*cemetery* WV-2
**Wooley Corner**—*pop pl* IN-6
Wooley Creek—*stream* (2) CA-9
Wooley Creek—*stream* KY-4
Wooley Creek—*stream* OR-9
Wooley Creek Pocket—*basin* CA-9
Wooley Hill—*summit* NY-2
Wooley Lake—*lake* CA-9
Wooley Lakes—*lake* UT-8
Wooley Lot Hollow—*valley* PA-2
Wooley Mine—*mine* AZ-5
Wooley Mine (underground)—*mine* AL-4
Wooley Pond—*lake* CT-1
Wooley Pond—*lake* NY-2
Wooley Range—*range* ID-8
*Wooley Ridge* NC-3
Wooley RR Station—*building* AZ-5
Wooley Rsvr—*reservoir* UT-8
Wooley Sch—*school* IL-6
Wooleyshot Branch—*stream* NC-3
Wooleys Mill (historical)—*locale* AL-4
Wooley Spring—*spring* AL-4
Wooley Spring—*spring* AZ-5
*Wooley Springs* AL-4
Wooley Springs Ch—*church* AL-4
Wooley Springs (historical)—*locale* AL-4
Wooley Springs Post Office (historical)—*building* AL-4
Wooley Springs Sch—*school* AL-4
**Wooley Valley**—*pop pl* ID-8
Wooley Valley—*valley* ID-8
Wooleyville—*locale* KY-4
Woolf Hollow—*valley* UT-8
Woolfolk—*locale* AL-4
Woolfolk, John W., House—*hist pl* GA-3
Woolfolk, William, House—*hist pl* KY-4
Woolfolk Cem—*cemetery* TX-5
Woolfolk Ch—*church* MS-4
Woolfolk Dam—*dam* OR-9
Woolfolk Elem Sch—*school* MS-4
Woolfolk Lake—*lake* AR-4
Woolfolk Rsvr—*reservoir* OR-9
*Woolford* MD-2
Woolford—*locale* MD-2
*Woolford Cem* MO-7
Woolford Cem—*cemetery* MO-7
Woolford Creek—*stream* MD-2
Woolford Creek—*stream* WA-9
Woolford Island—*island* MD-2
Woolford Mace Cem—*cemetery* MD-2
Woolford Neck—*cape* MD-2
Woolford Sch (historical)—*school* PA-2
Woolforks Lake (historical)—*lake* AL-4
Woolf Point—*cape* WY-8
Woolf Ranch HQ—*locale* NM-5
Woolf Sch (historical)—*school* AL-4
Woolf Spring—*spring* NM-5
Wool Growers Windmill—*well* AZ-5
Woolhizer Dam—*dam* SD-7
Wool Hollow—*valley* CA-9
Wool Hollow—*valley* TN-4
Woolhouse Mtn—*summit* AZ-5
Woolhouse Tank—*reservoir* AZ-5
Woolie Swamp—*swamp* NC-3
Woolington Cem—*cemetery* IL-6
Wooliver Creek—*stream* CA-9
Wool Lake—*lake* OR-9
Wool Lake—*lake* WI-6
Woollen Run—*stream* IN-6
*Woollen School Number 45* IN-6
Woolley Apartments—*hist pl* ID-8
Woolley Canyon—*valley* CA-9
Woolley Ditch—*canal* MI-6
**Woolley (historical)**—*pop pl* OR-9
Woollomes, Lake—*reservoir* CA-9
Woolloomooloo Creek—*stream* WA-9
Woollum—*locale* KY-4
*Woollur* KY-4
*Woolly Branch* MO-7
Woolly Creek—*stream* MO-7
Woolly Creek Community Hall—*locale* MO-7
Woolly Creek Ford (historical)—*locale* MO-7
Woolly Hole—*basin* UT-8
Woolly Horn Ridge—*ridge* OR-9
Woolly Ridge—*ridge* NC-3
Woolly Ridge Branch—*stream* NC-3
Woolly Tommy Mine—*mine* NM-5
Woolly Tops Branch—*stream* TN-4
Woolly Tops Mtn—*summit* TN-4
Woolman Hill—*summit* MA-1
Woolman Lake—*lake* NJ-2
Woolman Lake Park—*park* NJ-2
Wool Market—*locale* MS-4
Wool Market Baptist Ch—*church* MS-4
*Woolmarket Elementary School* MS-4
Wool Market Sch—*school* MS-4
**Woolmarket (Wool Market)**—*pop pl* MS-4
Wool Mtn—*summit* CA-9
Woolner Ave Sch—*school* CA-9
Woolper Creek—*stream* KY-4
Wool Point—*cape* NY-2
Woolrey-Koehler Hop Kiln—*hist pl* WA-9
**Woolrich**—*pop pl* PA-2
Woolrich Cem—*cemetery* KY-4
Woolrich Park—*park* PA-2
*Woolridge* MO-7
Woolridge Airstrip—*airport* OR-9
Woolridge Cem—*cemetery* KY-4
Woolridge Ferry Bridge—*bridge* KY-4
Wool Ridge Landing (historical)—*locale* AL-4
Woolridge Sch (historical)—*school* TN-4
Woolsey—*locale* AR-4
Woolsey—*locale* VA-3
**Woolsey**—*pop pl* (2) GA-3
**Woolsey**—*pop pl* NV-8
Woolsey—*uninc pl* NY-2
Woolsey, Jeremiah, House—*hist pl* NJ-2
Woolsey, Mount—*summit* WY-8
Woolsey Arch—*arch* UT-8
Woolsey Branch—*stream* NC-3
Woolsey Brook—*stream* NJ-2
Woolsey Butte—*summit* AZ-5
*Woolsey Butte Peak* AZ-5
Woolsey Canyon—*valley* CA-9
Woolsey Cem—*cemetery* AR-4
Woolsey Cem—*cemetery* CO-8
Woolsey Cem—*cemetery* KY-4
Woolsey Cem—*cemetery* OK-5
Woolsey Cem—*cemetery* (2) TN-4
Woolsey Ch—*church* AR-4
Woolsey Coll (historical)—*school* TN-4
*Woolsey Creek* MT-8
Woolsey Creek—*stream* (2) AR-4
Woolsey Creek—*stream* GA-3
Woolsey Creek—*stream* KY-4
Woolsey Creek—*stream* MO-7
Woolsey Creek—*stream* OR-9
Woolsey Ditch—*canal* MT-8
*Woolseyes* AZ-5
Woolsey Finnell Bridge—*bridge* AL-4
Woolsey Flat—*flat* CA-9
Woolsey Flat—*locale* CA-9
Woolsey Gap—*gap* TN-4
*Woolsey Hollow* KY-4
Woolsey Hollow—*valley* TN-4
Woolsey Lake—*swamp* AZ-5
Woolsey Peak—*summit* AZ-5
Woolsey Point—*cliff* AZ-5
Woolsey Point Recreation Site (Historical)—*locale* AZ-5
Woolsey Ranch—*locale* UT-8
Woolsey Ranchhouse Ruins—*hist pl* AZ-5
Woolsey Ridge—*ridge* UT-8
Woolsey Rock—*island* CT-1
Woolseys Bluff Landing (historical)—*locale* AL-4
Woolsey Sch—*school* CT-1
Woolsey Sch (historical)—*school* MO-7
*Woolseys College* TN-4
Woolsey Spring—*spring* (2) AZ-5
**Woolsey (subdivision)**—*pop pl* NC-3
Woolsey Valley—*basin* KY-4
Woolsey Wash—*stream* (2) AZ-5
Woolshop Pond—*lake* MA-1
*Woolsie Valley* KY-4
Woolslair Elem Sch—*hist pl* PA-2
*Woolsleys College* TN-4
Woolsleys College Post Office (historical)—*building* TN-4
Woolson Friends Ch—*church* IA-7
*Wool's Point* NY-2
Woolstalf Creek—*stream* CA-9
Woolstalf Meadow—*flat* CA-9
**Woolstock**—*pop pl* IA-7
Woolstock Cem—*cemetery* IA-7
Wool Stock (historical P.O.)—*locale* IA-7
Woolstock Township—*fmr MCD* IA-7
*Wooltz* ME-1
*Woolum* KY-4
Woolum—*locale* (2) AR-4
Woolum Cem—*cemetery* AR-4
Woolums Cem—*cemetery* IN-6
Woolverton-Boyd House—*hist pl* MS-4
Woolverton Creek—*stream* NV-8
Woolverton Mountain Cem—*cemetery* AR-4
Woolverton Mtn—*summit* AR-4
Woolverton Spring—*spring* NV-8
Wool Warehouse—*hist pl* MT-8
**Woolwich**—*pop pl* ME-1
Woolwich Town House—*hist pl* ME-1
**Woolwich (Town of)**—*pop pl* ME-1
**Woolwich (Township of)**—*pop pl* NJ-2
Woolwich-Wiscasset Ch—*church* ME-1
**Woolwine**—*pop pl* VA-3
Woolwine Cem—*cemetery* VA-3
Woolwine Run—*stream* WV-2
Woolwine Sch (historical)—*school* TN-4
Woolworth—*locale* MS-4
**Woolworth**—*pop pl* TN-4
Woolworth, F. W., Company Bldg—*hist pl* DE-2
Woolworth Bldg—*hist pl* NY-2
Woolworth Estate—*hist pl* NY-2
Woolworth Post Office (historical)—*building* TN-4
Woolworth Sch (historical)—*school* TN-4
*Wooly Bayou* LA-4
Wooly Bayou—*stream* LA-4
Wooly Fork—*stream* KY-4
Wooly Head—*cliff* AK-9
*Wooly Hole* UT-8
*Wooly Tops Branch* TN-4
*Woomog* FM-9
*Woonachasset Island* RI-1
*Woonasquatucket Reservoir* RI-1
Woonasquatucket River—*reservoir* RI-1
Woonasquatucket River—*stream* RI-1
Woonasquatucket River Site (RI-163)—*hist pl* RI-1
*Woonipw* FM-9
*Woonkinko River* MA-1
**Woonsocket**—*pop pl* RI-1
**Woonsocket**—*pop pl* SD-7
Woonsocket City Hall—*hist pl* RI-1
Woonsocket Civil War Monmt—*hist pl* RI-1
Woonsocket Company Mill Complex—*hist pl* RI-1
Woonsocket District Courthouse—*hist pl* RI-1
Woonsocket Hill—*summit* RI-1
Woonsocket Reservoir Number 3 Dam—*dam* RI-1
Woonsocket Rsvr Number One—*reservoir* RI-1
Woonsocket Rsvr Number Three—*reservoir* RI-1
Woonsocket Rsvr Number Two—*reservoir* RI-1
Woonsocket Rsvr Number 1—*reservoir* RI-1
Woonsocket Rsvr Number 3—*reservoir* RI-1
**Woonsocket Township**—*pop pl* SD-7
Woo Ranch—*locale* CA-9
WOOR-FM (Oxford)—*tower* MS-4
Woosh Clo Dee Toh—*spring* AZ-5
Woosky Ch—*church* TX-5
**Woosley**—*pop pl* TX-5
**Woosley**—*pop pl* WV-2
Woosley Branch—*stream* VA-3
Woosley Cem—*cemetery* AL-4
Woosley Cem—*cemetery* IL-6
Woosley Cem—*cemetery* (2) KY-4
Woosley Cem—*cemetery* TX-5
Woosley Creek—*stream* KY-4
Woosley Creek—*stream* OR-9
Woosley Ditch—*canal* OH-6
Wooster—*locale* GA-3
**Wooster**—*pop pl* AR-4

**Wooster**—pop pl (2) ... IN-6
**Wooster**—pop pl (2) ... MI-6
**Wooster**—pop pl ... OH-6
Wooster—uninc pl ... TX-5
Wooster Block—hist pl ... OH-6
Wooster Brook—stream (2) ... CT-1
Wooster Cem—cemetery ... CT-1
Wooster Cem—cemetery ... KS-7
Wooster Cem—cemetery ... OH-6
Wooster Ch—church ... TX-5
Wooster Cove—bay ... ME-1
**Wooster Heights**—pop pl ... OH-6
Wooster HS—school ... NV-8
Wooster Island—island ... CT-1
Wooster JHS—school ... CT-1
Wooster Lake—lake ... IL-6
**Wooster Lake**—pop pl ... IL-6
Wooster Mound—summit ... OK-5
Wooster Mountain State Park—park ... CT-1
Wooster Mtn—summit ... CT-1
Wooster Park—park ... CT-1
Wooster Plaza Shop Ctr—locale ... OH-6
Wooster Public Square Hist Dist (Boundary Increase)—hist pl ... OH-6
Wooster Ranch—locale ... MT-8
Wooster Sch—school ... CT-1
Wooster Sch—school ... OH-6
Wooster Square Hist Dist—hist pl ... CT-1
Wooster Street Cem—cemetery ... CT-1
*Woostertown* ... IN-6
**Wooster (Township of)**—pop pl ... OH-6
**Woosung**—pop pl ... IL-6
**Woosung (Township of)**—pop pl ... IL-6
Wootan Spring—spring ... AZ-5
*Wooten* ... AL-4
Wooten, Goodall, House—hist pl ... TX-5
Wooten, Joseph, House—hist pl ... KY-4
Wooten, Lake—lake ... WA-9
Wooten, Lake—reservoir ... MS-4
Wootenaux Creek—stream ... MD-2
Wooten Branch—stream ... AL-4
Wooten Branch—stream (2) ... KY-4
Wooten Branch—stream ... MS-4
Wooten Canyon—valley (2) ... NM-5
Wooten Cem—cemetery ... AL-4
Wooten Cem—cemetery (2) ... GA-3
Wooten Cem—cemetery (4) ... TN-4
Wooten Cem—cemetery (3) ... TX-5
Wooten Chapel—church (2) ... AL-4
Wooten Chapel—church ... NC-3
Wooten Chapel—church ... TN-4
Wooten Chapel Cem—cemetery ... TN-4
Wooten Cove—valley ... NC-3
Wooten Creek—stream ... CA-9
Wooten Creek—stream ... MS-4
Wooten Creek—stream ... NC-3
Wooten Creek—stream (2) ... TX-5
*Wooten Crossroads* ... NC-3
Wooten Fork—stream ... KY-4
Wooten Gap—gap ... AL-4
Wooten Gap—gap (2) ... VA-3
Wooten Hill—summit ... AL-4
Wooten Hollow—valley ... AR-4
Wooten Lake—lake ... FL-3
Wooten Lake—lake ... TX-5
Wooten Lake—reservoir ... GA-3
Wooten Landing—locale ... NC-3
Wooten Mesa—summit ... CO-8
Wooten Mill Creek—stream ... AL-4
Wooten Mtn—summit ... NC-3
Wooten Number 1 Mine—mine ... TN-4
Wooten Park—park ... FL-3
Wooten Post Office (historical)—building ... MS-4
Wooten Ranch (Headquarters)—locale ... NM-5
Wooten Sch—school ... TX-5
Wooten Sch (historical)—school ... MO-7
Wooten Sch (historical)—school ... TN-4
*Wootens Crossroad* ... NC-3
**Wootens Crossroads**—pop pl (3) ... NC-3
Wootens Folly Rapids—rapids ... TN-4
Wootens Knob—summit ... KY-4
Wooten Spring Cem—cemetery ... TX-5
*Wootens School* ... TN-4
**Wootentown**—pop pl ... NC-3
**Wooton**—pop pl ... KY-4
Wooton Branch—stream ... KY-4
Wooton Creek—stream ... KY-4
Wooton Creek—stream (2) ... MS-4
Wooton Presbyterian Center—hist pl ... KY-4
Wooton Sch—school ... KY-4
Wootton—locale ... CO-8
Wootton, Attewall, Jr., House—hist pl ... UT-8
WOOW-AM (Greenville)—tower ... NC-3
WOPC-TV (Altoona)—tower ... PA-2
Wop Draw—valley ... WY-8
Wopeias—tunnel ... FM-9
*Wopogasset* ... WI-6
Wopowog—locale ... CT-1
WOPP-AM (Opp)—tower ... AL-4
**Wopsononock**—pop pl ... PA-2
Wopsononock Lookout—locale ... PA-2
*Woquagonsett Pond* ... RI-1
Woraayal—bay ... FM-9
*Worad* ... FM-9
Woraed—summit ... FM-9
Worbab—island ... MP-9
*Worbab Island* ... MP-9
*Worbois Creek* ... ID-8
Worcester—locale ... MO-7
Worcester—locale ... PA-2
Worcester—locale ... WI-6
**Worcester**—pop pl ... MA-1
**Worcester**—pop pl ... NY-2
**Worcester**—pop pl ... VT-1
Worcester, City of—civil ... MA-1
Worcester, Mount—summit ... VT-1
Worcester Acad—hist pl ... MA-1
Worcester Air Natl Guard Base—building ... MA-1
Worcester Airp—airport ... PA-2
Worcester Art Museum and School—building ... MA-1
Worcester Asylum and related buildings—hist pl ... MA-1
Worcester Brook—stream ... MA-1
Worcester Brook—stream ... VT-1
Worcester Center—locale ... MA-1
Worcester Center Galleria—locale ... MA-1
**Worcester (Center Point)**—pop pl ... PA-2
Worcester Centrum—building ... MA-1
Worcester City Hall—building ... MA-1
Worcester City Hall and Common—hist pl ... MA-1
Worcester City Hosp—hospital ... MA-1
Worcester Corset Company Factory—hist pl ... MA-1
Worcester Country Club—locale ... MA-1
**Worcester (County)**—pop pl ... MD-2
Worcester County Convention and Visitors Bureau—building ... MA-1
Worcester County Horticultural Society—building ... MA-1
Worcester County Hosp—hospital (2) ... MA-1
**Worcester County (in (P)MSA 1120,2600, 6060,9240)**—pop pl ... MA-1
Worcester Five Cents Savings Bank—hist pl ... MA-1
*Worcester Hahnemann Hosp* ... MA-1
Worcester Hist Dist—hist pl ... NY-2
Worcester Hosp—hospital ... MA-1
Worcester House—hist pl ... MA-1
Worcester HS—school ... MA-1
Worcester Island—island ... NH-1
Worcester JHS (east)—school ... MA-1
Worcester JHS (north)—school ... MA-1
Worcester JHS (south)—school ... MA-1
Worcester JHS (west)—school ... MA-1
Worcester Junior Coll—school ... MA-1
Worcester Lake—lake ... WI-6
Worcester Lodge—locale ... ME-1
Worcester Market Bldg—hist pl ... MA-1
Worcester Mechanics Hall—building ... MA-1
Worcester Memorial Auditorium—building ... MA-1
Worcester Memorial Hospital—hospital ... MA-1
Worcester Mine—mine ... CO-8
Worcester Mountains—range ... VT-1
Worcester Municipal Airp—airport ... MA-1
Worcester Police Department—building ... MA-1
Worcester Polytechnic Institute—school ... MA-1
Worcester Pond—lake ... NY-2
Worcester Ponds—lake ... VT-1
Worcester Public Library—building ... MA-1
*Worcester Reservoir* ... MA-1
Worcester Sch—school ... WI-6
Worcester Science Center—building ... MA-1
Worcesters Millpond—reservoir ... NH-1
Worcester State Coll—school ... MA-1
**Worcester (Town of)**—pop pl ... NY-2
**Worcester (Town of)**—pop pl ... VT-1
**Worcester (Town of)**—pop pl ... WI-6
**Worcester (Township of)**—pop pl ... PA-2
Worcester Union Station (railroad)—building ... MA-1
Worcester YMCA—building ... MA-1
Worchester Cem—cemetery ... TX-5
Worchester Lake—lake ... MI-6
*Word* ... MS-4
**Wordan Place**—pop pl ... PA-2
Word Cave—cave ... TX-5
Word Cem—cemetery ... GA-3
Word Cem—cemetery ... MS-4
Word Cem—cemetery (2) ... TN-4
Word Creek—stream ... MS-4
Word Dam—dam ... SD-7
Worden—fmr MCD ... NE-7
Worden—locale ... OR-9
**Worden**—pop pl ... AR-4
**Worden**—pop pl ... IL-6
**Worden**—pop pl ... KS-7
**Worden**—pop pl ... MI-6
**Worden**—pop pl ... MT-8
Worden Brook—stream ... CT-1
Worden Brook—stream ... VT-1
Worden Cem—cemetery (2) ... KS-7
Worden Cem—cemetery ... NY-2
Worden Cem—cemetery ... OH-6
Worden Cem—cemetery ... OR-9
Worden Cem—cemetery ... TX-5
Worden Cem—cemetery ... VT-1
Worden Creek—stream ... MT-8
Worden Dam Number Two—dam ... OR-9
Worden Hill—summit (2) ... NY-2
**Worden (historical)**—pop pl ... OR-9
Worden Lake—lake ... MI-6
Worden Lake—lake ... MT-8
Worden Lake—lake ... WI-6
Worden Place—uninc pl ... PA-2
Worden Pond—lake ... RI-1
Worden Ranch—locale ... CO-8
Worden Ranch—locale ... NE-7
Worden Road Sch—school ... OH-6
Worden Rsvr—reservoir ... OR-9
Worden Sch—school ... MI-6
Wordens Chapel—church ... VA-3
*Wordens Pond* ... RI-1
**Worden (Town of)**—pop pl ... WI-6
Worder Branch—stream ... KY-4
Word Gap—gap ... AL-4
Wordica Lateral—canal ... ID-8
Wordie, Mount—summit ... AK-9
Word Mound—hist pl ... MS-4
Word Number 1 Dam—dam ... SD-7
Word of Life Ch—church ... AL-4
Word of Life Ch—church ... FL-3
Word of Life Chapel—church ... PA-2
Word of Life Christian Center—church (2) ... FL-3
Word of Life Christian Fellowship Ch—church ... MS-4
Word of Life Foursquare Ch—church ... FL-3
Word of Life Full Gospel Ch—church ... FL-3
Word of Truth Ch—church ... FL-3
Word Oil Field—oilfield ... TX-5
Word Ranch—locale ... SD-7
Word Ranch—locale (2) ... TX-5
Word Rsvr—reservoir ... OR-9
Word Sch—school ... GA-3
Words Chapel—church ... KY-4
Words Creek—stream ... GA-3
Words of Life Fellowship Ch—church ... FL-3
Words of Life Temple—church ... FL-3
*Wordswell Draw* ... TX-5
*Wordsworth Creek* ... UT-8
Word Tank—reservoir ... NM-5
*Wored Creek* ... OR-9
*Woref* ... FM-9
Wores Drain—canal ... CA-9
Worford Ch—church ... MS-4
Worford Ridge—ridge ... CO-8
Worford Sch—school ... MS-4
Worham Creek—stream ... MI-6
Worhies Cem—cemetery ... IA-7
WORI-AM (Oak Ridge)—tower ... TN-4
**Woriilaq**—pop pl ... FM-9
*Worila'* ... FM-9
*Worillag* ... FM-9
WORJ-FM (Ozark)—tower ... AL-4
Work—other ... TN-4
Work, Col. John, House—hist pl ... PA-2
Work, Edna, Hall—hist pl ... NE-7
*Worka an* ... MP-9
Work and Dragman Ditch—canal ... CO-8
Work and Play Day Care Center—school ... FL-3
Work and Rest—locale ... VI-3
Work Cem—cemetery ... KS-7
Work Cem—cemetery ... KY-4
Work Circle Cem—cemetery ... AZ-5
Work Cove—bay ... ME-1
Work Creek—stream (2) ... MT-8
Work Creek—stream ... NC-3
Worker's House at Lower Laurel Iron Works—hist pl ... PA-2
Workers' Neighborhood Hist Dist—hist pl ... ID-8
**Workfield**—pop pl ... CA-9
Workfield Siding—locale ... CA-9
Workhorse Butte—summit ... NV-8
Workhouse Bayou—stream ... TN-4
Working Benevolent Temple and Professional Bldg—hist pl ... SC-3
Working Boys Home—hist pl ... MA-1
Workinger Bayou—stream ... LA-4
**Workman**—pop pl ... CA-9
**Workman**—pop pl ... SC-3
Workman Adobe—hist pl ... CA-9
Workman Air Park—airport ... OR-9
Workman Ave Sch—school ... CA-9
Workman Branch—stream ... KY-4
Workman Branch—stream ... MO-7
Workman Branch—stream ... TN-4
Workman Branch—stream (5) ... WV-2
Workman Brook—stream ... MA-1
Workman Cem—cemetery ... OH-6
Workman Cem—cemetery ... OR-9
Workman Cem—cemetery ... PA-2
Workman Cem—cemetery ... TN-4
Workman Cem—cemetery (10) ... WV-2
Workman Creek—stream ... AZ-5
Workman Creek—stream (2) ... CO-8
Workman Creek—stream ... MO-7
Workman Creek—stream ... WA-9
Workman Creek—stream ... WV-2
Workman Creek Ch—church ... WV-2
Workman Creek Falls—falls ... AZ-5
Workman Draw—valley ... MT-8
Workman Family Cemetery—hist pl ... CA-9
Workman Fork—stream ... WV-2
Workman Fork Ch—church ... WV-2
Workman Hill—summit ... CA-9
Workman Hollow—valley (3) ... KY-4
Workman Hollow—valley ... TN-4
Workman Island—island ... TN-4
Workman Knob—summit ... WV-2
*Workman Lake* ... UT-8
Workman Lake—lake ... FL-3
Workman Lake—lake ... UT-8
Workman Mine—mine ... UT-8
Workman MS—school ... FL-3
Workman Mtn—summit ... OK-5
Workman Pond—lake ... FL-3
Workman Ridge—ridge ... NM-5
Workman Run—stream ... PA-2
Workmans Bar—bar ... CA-9
*Workmans Bayou* ... LA-4
Workmans Cem—cemetery ... OH-6
Workman Sch—school ... CA-9
Workman Sch—school ... IL-6
Workman Sch—school ... WV-2
**Workmans Circle Camp**—pop pl ... MA-1
Workmans Circle Cem—cemetery ... VA-3
Workmans Corners—locale ... DE-2
**Workman (Township of)**—pop pl ... MN-6
Workman Union Chapel (abandoned)—church ... MO-7
Workman Wash—valley ... UT-8
Workman Works—hist pl ... OH-6
Work Memorial Park—park ... CA-9
Workmen Circle Cem—cemetery ... MI-6
Workmen Hollow Cove—bay ... MO-7
Workmore—locale ... GA-3
Work Point—cape ... ME-1
Work Run—stream ... PA-2
Works Branch—stream ... AL-4
Works Bridge—bridge ... TX-5
Works Cem—cemetery ... WV-2
Work Tank—reservoir ... NM-5
**Worland**—pop pl ... MO-7
**Worland**—pop pl ... WY-8
Worland Canyon—valley ... NV-8
Worland Cem—cemetery ... MO-7
Worland House—hist pl ... WY-8
Worland Municipal Airport—airport ... WY-8
Worland Nowood Draw No 4—valley ... WY-8
World Beater Mine—mine ... CA-9
World Bible Church—locale ... OK-5
World Ch of the Living God—church ... FL-3
World End Brook—stream ... MA-1
World End Brook—stream ... NH-1
World End Pond—lake ... NH-1
World End Trail—trail ... PA-2
World Harvest Tabernacle—church ... LA-4
World Museum of Mining—building ... MT-8
World of Clothing—locale ... NC-3
World of Life Alliance Ch—church ... MN-6
World on Fire Revivals—church ... FL-3
World Powell Oil Field—oilfield ... TX-5
Worldridge Sch—school ... KY-4
Worlds—locale ... VA-3
Worlds Bridge—other ... MI-6
Worlds Ch of the Living God—church ... TN-4
Worlds Edge—cliff ... NC-3
*World'S End* ... MA-1
*Worlds End* ... PA-2
Worlds End—cliff ... MA-1
Worlds End Creek—stream ... MD-2
Worlds End Creek—stream ... NJ-2
Worlds End State Park—park ... PA-2
Worlds End State Park Family Cabin District—hist pl ... PA-2
Worlds Fair Mine—mine ... AZ-5
Worlds Fair Prospect—mine ... CO-8
Worlds Of Fun—post sta ... MO-7
World Trade Center—building ... FL-3
World Trade Center—uninc pl ... TX-5
World University—facility ... PR-3
World War II Memorial—other ... MO-7
World War II Memorial—park ... VA-3
World War I Memorial—hist pl ... CT-1
World War I Memorial—hist pl ... NJ-2
Worldway Postal Center—uninc pl ... CA-9
World West Oil Field—oilfield ... TX-5
World Wide Ch—church ... WI-6
World Wide Christian Fellowship Ch—church ... FL-3
Worldwide Gospel Ch—church ... UT-8
World 600 Airp—airport ... NC-3
*Worle Creek* ... IA-7
Worley—locale ... KY-4
Worley—locale ... NC-3
Worley—locale ... TN-4
Worley—locale ... WV-2
**Worley**—pop pl ... ID-8
Worley, Allen, and Foushee Houses—hist pl ... KY-4
Worley, Philip, House—hist pl ... IA-7
Worley Bluff—cliff ... TN-4
Worley Branch—stream ... GA-3
Worley Branch—stream (2) ... KY-4
Worley Branch—stream ... NC-3
Worley Branch—stream ... TN-4
Worley Branch—stream ... TX-5
*Worley Cave* ... TN-4
Worley Cem—cemetery (2) ... AR-4
Worley Cem—cemetery ... ID-8
Worley Cem—cemetery ... IL-6
Worley Cem—cemetery (2) ... MO-7
Worley Cem—cemetery ... NC-3
Worley Cem—cemetery ... OK-5
Worley Cem—cemetery (5) ... TN-4
Worley Cem—cemetery (2) ... VA-3
Worley Cem—cemetery ... WV-2
Worley Ch—church ... TN-4
Worley Chapel Cem—cemetery ... NC-3
Worley Cove—valley (3) ... NC-3
Worley Creek—stream ... GA-3
Worley Creek—stream ... NC-3
Worley Creek—stream ... OK-5
Worley Creek—stream ... OR-9
Worley Crossroads—locale ... GA-3
Worley Ditch—canal ... IN-6
Worley Drain—canal ... MI-6
Worley Draw—valley ... ID-8
Worley Draw—valley ... WY-8
Worley Flat—flat ... CA-9
Worley Furnace Branch—stream ... TN-4
Worley Gap—gap ... GA-3
**Worley Heights**—pop pl ... NY-2
Worley Hill—summit ... FL-3
Worley Hollow—valley ... KY-4
Worley Hollow—valley ... TN-4
Worley Hosp—hospital ... TX-5
Worley Knob—summit ... NC-3
Worley Lake—lake (2) ... GA-3
Worley Lake—reservoir ... IL-6
Worley Lake—reservoir ... TX-5
Worley Lakes—lake ... FL-3
Worley Mill Ridge—ridge ... NC-3
Worley Mine (surface)—mine ... TN-4
Worley Mtn—summit ... AR-4
Worley Ridge—ridge ... GA-3
Worley Rock—other ... MO-7
Worley Run—stream ... OH-6
Worley Run Cem—cemetery ... OH-6
Worley Sch—school ... OH-6
Worley Spring—spring ... AL-4
Worley Spring—spring ... MO-7
Worley Spring—spring ... OR-9
**Worleytown**—pop pl ... PA-2
Worlow Creek—stream ... OR-9
Worlow Meadow—swamp ... OR-9
Worlow Rsvr—reservoir ... OR-9
Worly Cut—bend ... SC-3
WORM-AM (Savannah)—tower ... TN-4
**Worman**—pop pl ... PA-2
Worman Cem—cemetery ... OH-6
*Wormansville* ... PA-2
Worm Basin Spring—spring ... ID-8
Worm Bayou—gut ... LA-4
Worm Branch—stream ... AL-4
Worm Branch—stream ... VA-3
*Worm Complex, The* ... WA-9
Worm Corral Hollow—valley ... ID-8
Worm Corral Spring—spring ... ID-8
Worm Creek—stream (2) ... ID-8
Worm Creek—stream ... NC-3
Worm Creek—stream ... UT-8
Worm Creek—stream ... WY-8
*Worm Creek Reservoir* ... ID-8
Worm Creek Spring—spring ... ID-8
Wormeley Cottage—hist pl ... VA-3
Wormell Gulch—valley ... WA-9
Wormell Ledges—bar ... ME-1
Wormer Lake—lake ... MI-6
Wormers Cave—cave ... PA-2
Worm Fence Spring—spring ... UT-8
Worm Flows—lava ... WA-9
WORM-FM (Savannah)—tower ... TN-4
Wormhole Canyon—valley ... CA-9
*Wormington* ... CO-8
Worm Island—island ... TN-4
*Worm Lake* ... MN-6
Worm Lake—lake ... ID-8
Worm Lake—lake ... MI-6
Wormley, John, House—hist pl ... PA-2
Wormley Branch—stream ... TN-4
Wormley Creek—stream ... VA-3
Wormley Pond—reservoir ... VA-3
**Wormleysburg**—pop pl ... PA-2
Wormleysburg Borough—civil ... PA-2
Worm Ranch—locale ... NE-7
**Worms**—pop pl ... NE-7
Wormser Sch—school ... MT-8
**Wormsloe**—pop pl ... GA-3
Wormsloe Plantation—hist pl ... GA-3
Worms Township—civil ... SD-7
*Wormumetch* ... MP-9
Wormwood Brook—stream ... VT-1
Wormwood Canal—canal ... CA-9
Wormwood Drain—canal ... CA-9
**Wormwood Hill**—pop pl ... CT-1
Wormwood Hill—summit ... CT-1
Wormwood Hill—summit ... VT-1
Wormwood Hill Cem—cemetery ... CT-1
Wormwood Lateral Four—canal ... CA-9
Wormwood Lateral Nine—canal ... CA-9
Wormwood Lateral Seven—canal ... CA-9
Wormwood Lateral Three-A—canal ... CA-9
Wormwood Pond—lake ... ME-1
Wormwood Ranch—locale ... WY-8
*Wornall* ... MO-7
Wornall House—hist pl ... MO-7
*Worn Creek* ... WY-8
Worn Mill Canyon—valley ... CA-9
Wornock Mtn—summit ... AL-4
*Worometchi* ... MP-9
Woronkofski, Mount—summit ... AK-9
Woronkofski Island—island ... AK-9
Woronkofski Point—cape ... AK-9
**Woronoco**—pop pl ... MA-1
**Woronoco Heights**—pop pl ... MA-1
*Woronoco Island* ... NY-2
Woronoco Island—island ... NY-2
Woronoco Mills Dam—dam ... MA-1
Woronoco Mills 29 Ft Dam—dam ... MA-1
Woronzof Shoal—bar ... AK-9
*Worooren* ... FM-9
*Worooren Faasafag* ... FM-9
*Worooren Neepiitiw* ... FM-9
*Worooren Neewoomas* ... FM-9
*Worooren Pisamw* ... FM-9
*Worooren Rusin* ... FM-9
*Worowa'* ... FM-9
Worqing—summit ... FM-9
*Worral Creek* ... IA-7
Worrall Covered Bridge—hist pl ... VT-1
*Worrall School* ... PA-2
Worrbar Island—island ... MP-9
Worrell—locale ... VA-3
**Worrell**—pop pl ... PA-2
Worrell, Lake—lake ... FL-3
Worrell Cem—cemetery ... IN-6
Worrell Cem—cemetery ... NC-3
Worrell Ch—church ... VA-3
Worrell Creek—stream ... IA-7
Worrell Landing (historical)—locale ... NC-3
Worrell Millpond—reservoir ... NC-3
Worrell Mill Swamp—stream ... NC-3
Worrick Cem—cemetery ... NC-3
Worrier Sch (historical)—school ... MS-4
*Worring* ... FM-9
*Worronoco* ... MA-1
Worry—locale ... NC-3
*Worry Crossroads* ... NC-3
Worse Creek—stream ... GA-3
Worser Creek—stream ... TX-5
*Worsha* ... MS-4
*Worsham* ... TN-4
Worsham—locale ... TX-5
Worsham—locale ... VA-3
Worsham Butte—summit ... OR-9
Worsham Cem—cemetery ... TN-4
Worsham Cem—cemetery ... VA-3
*Worsham Cemetery* ... MS-4
Worsham Creek—stream ... CA-9
Worsham Cree!:—stream ... MS-4
Worsham Crossing—locale ... LA-4
Worsham Hollow—valley (2) ... TN-4
Worsham Oil Field—oilfield (2) ... TX-5
Worsham Post Office (historical)—building ... TN-4
Worsham Ranch—locale ... TX-5
**Worshams**—pop pl ... VA-3
Worshams Bluff—cliff ... AR-4
Worsham Spring—spring ... TN-4
Worship Cem—cemetery ... MS-4
Worship Lake—lake ... MS-4
Worship Point Ch—church ... NC-3
Worship Point Mission—church ... NC-3
Worsley Cem—cemetery ... IL-6
Worsley Ch—church ... MO-7
Worster Brook—stream ... ME-1
Worster Cem—cemetery ... OK-5
Worster Lake—reservoir ... IN-6
**Worstville**—pop pl ... OH-6
Worswick—locale ... CA-9
Worswick Creek—stream ... ID-8
Worswick Hot Springs—spring ... ID-8
**Wortendyke**—pop pl ... NJ-2
Wortendyke, Frederick, House—hist pl ... NJ-2
Wortendyke, Jacob, House—hist pl ... NJ-2
Wortendyke Barn—hist pl ... NJ-2
Wortendyke-Demund House—hist pl ... NJ-2
*Worth* ... DE-2
*Worth* ... KS-7
*Worth* ... NC-3
Worth—locale ... CA-9
Worth—locale ... GA-3
Worth—locale ... NY-2
**Worth**—pop pl ... IL-6
**Worth**—pop pl ... MI-6
**Worth**—pop pl ... MO-7
**Worth**—pop pl ... WV-2
Worth—uninc pl ... NC-3
Worth, Gorham A., House—hist pl ... OH-6
Worth, Lake—lake ... FL-3
Worth, Lake—lake ... GA-3
Worth, Lake—lake ... NJ-2
Worth, Lake—reservoir ... TX-5
Worth Acad—school ... GA-3
Worth Airp—airport ... MO-7
Wortham—locale ... MS-4
**Wortham**—pop pl ... MO-7
**Wortham**—pop pl ... TX-5
Wortham Bend—bend ... TX-5
Wortham Bend Cem—cemetery ... TX-5
Wortham Branch—stream ... TX-5
Wortham (CCD)—cens area ... TX-5
Wortham Cem—cemetery ... TN-4
Wortham Chapel—church ... TN-4
Wortham Chapel Cem—cemetery ... TN-4
Wortham Chapel Sch—school ... TN-4
Wortham Creek—stream ... KS-7
Wortham Creek—stream ... NE-7
Wortham Hill—summit ... AR-4
Wortham Lake—reservoir ... TX-5
Wortham Mill Island—island ... AL-4
Wortham Oil Field—oilfield ... TX-5
Wortham Post Office (historical)—building ... MS-4
Wortham Sch—school ... WY-8
**Worthams Ferry**—pop pl ... SC-3
Worth Canal—canal ... NC-3
Worth Cem—cemetery ... MN-6
Worth Center—locale ... NY-2
Worth Ch—church ... PA-2
Worth Count Courthouse—hist pl ... MO-7
Worth County—civil ... MO-7
**Worth (County)**—pop pl ... GA-3
**Worth (County)**—pop pl ... MO-7
Worth County Community Lake State Rec Area—locale ... MO-7
Worth County Courthouse—hist pl ... GA-3
Worth County Courthouse—hist pl ... IA-7
Worth County Local Bldg—hist pl ... GA-3
Worth Creek—stream ... OR-9
Worthdale Park—park ... NC-3
Worthen—locale ... AR-4
Worthen Bank Bldg—hist pl ... AR-4
Worthen Bayou—stream ... IL-6
Worthen Cem—cemetery ... IL-6
Worthen Cem—cemetery ... MO-7
Worthen Cem—cemetery ... OH-6
Worthen Creek—stream ... AR-4
Worthen Sch—school ... IL-6
**Worthen Township**—pop pl ... SD-7
Worthey Cem—cemetery ... IL-6
Worth Heights Sch—school ... TX-5
Worth Hills Golf Course—other ... TX-5
Worth Hotel—hist pl ... OK-5
Worthing—locale ... TX-5
**Worthing**—pop pl ... SD-7
Worthing Canyon—valley ... ID-8
Worthing Cem—cemetery ... IA-7
Worthing Cem—cemetery ... SD-7
Worthing HS—school ... TX-5
*Worthington* ... FL-3
*Worthington* ... ND-7
Worthington—locale ... KY-4
Worthington—other ... FL-3
**Worthington**—pop pl ... IN-6
**Worthington**—pop pl ... IA-7
**Worthington**—pop pl ... KY-4
**Worthington**—pop pl (2) ... MD-2
**Worthington**—pop pl ... MN-6
**Worthington**—pop pl ... MO-7
**Worthington**—pop pl ... NY-2
**Worthington**—pop pl ... OH-6
**Worthington**—pop pl ... PA-2
**Worthington**—pop pl ... WV-2
Worthington, Robert, House—hist pl ... WV-2
**Worthington Acres**—pop pl ... IA-7
Worthington and Sioux Falls Freight Depot—hist pl ... MN-6
Worthington Borough—civil ... PA-2
Worthington Branch—stream ... TN-4
Worthington Brook—stream ... MA-1
Worthington Canyon—valley ... NV-8
Worthington (CCD)—cens area ... FL-3
Worthington Cem—cemetery ... KY-4
Worthington Cem—cemetery (2) ... MO-7
Worthington Cem—cemetery (2) ... TN-4
**Worthington Center**—pop pl ... MA-1
Worthington Center Cem—cemetery ... MA-1
*Worthington Centre* ... MA-1
Worthington Ch—church ... IA-7
Worthington Chapel—church ... KY-4
**Worthington Corners**—pop pl ... MA-1
Worthington Country Club—other ... MN-6
Worthington Cove—valley ... TN-4
Worthington Creek—stream ... AR-4
Worthington Creek—stream ... WV-2
Worthington Cutoff—channel ... MS-4
*Worthington Dam* ... AL-4
Worthington Ditch—canal ... OH-6
Worthington Elem Sch—school ... IN-6
Worthington Glacier—glacier ... AK-9
**Worthington Hills**—pop pl ... KY-4
Worthington Historical Society Museum—hist pl ... OH-6
Worthington Hollow—valley ... MO-7
Worthington Homestead—locale ... WY-8
Worthington House—hist pl ... KY-4
Worthington Knob—summit ... TN-4
Worthington Lake—lake ... TX-5
Worthington Manufacturing Company Boardinghouse—hist pl ... OH-6
Worthington Mine—mine ... ID-8
Worthington Mountains—ridge ... NV-8
Worthington Municipal Airp airport ... MN 6
Worthington Peak—summit ... NV-8
Worthington Point—cape ... MS-4
*Worthington Pond* ... MA-1
Worthington Pond—reservoir ... CT-1
Worthington Ranch—locale ... NM-5
Worthington Sch—school ... CA-9
Worthington Sch—school ... OH-6
Worthington Sch—school ... WV-2
*Worthington Scranton Campus Pennsylvania State University* ... PA-2
Worthington Sherwood Ditch—canal ... OH-6
Worthington Spring—spring ... ID-8
Worthington Spring—spring ... OR-9
**Worthington Springs**—pop pl ... FL-3
**Worthington Springs (Worthington)**—pop pl ... FL-3
Worthington State For—forest ... MA-1
Worthington State For—forest ... NJ-2
Worthington Store (historical)—locale ... AL-4
**Worthington (Town of)**—pop pl ... MA-1
**Worthington (Township of)**—pop pl ... MN-6
**Worthington (Township of)**—pop pl ... OH-6
Worthington United Presbyterian Church—hist pl ... OH-6
**Worthington Valley**—pop pl ... MD-2
Worthington Valley—valley ... MD-2
Worthington Valley Hist Dist—hist pl ... MD-2
Worthington Village Green—hist pl ... OH-6
**Worthington (Worthington Corners)**—pop pl ... MA-1
*Worth Lake* ... MI-6
Worth Lake—lake ... WA-9
**Worthland**—pop pl ... DE-2
*Worthless Bay* ... AK-9
*Worthless Creek* ... SD-7
**Worthley**—pop pl ... ME-1
Worthley Brook—stream (2) ... ME-1
Worthley Pond—lake (2) ... ME-1
**Worthley Pond**—pop pl ... ME-1
*Worthly Brook* ... ME-1
*Worthly Pond* ... ME-1
Worth Mountain Lodge—locale ... VT-1
Worth Mtn—summit ... SC-3

Wright Cycle Company-Wright and Wright Printing Offices—hist pl ... OH-6
Wright Dam—dam ... NC-3
Wright Ditch—canal ... OR-9
Wright Ditch—canal ... WY-8
Wright Divide—gap ... WY-8
Wright Drain ... IN-6
Wright Drain—canal (2) ... MI-6
Wright Draw—valley ... CO-8
Wright Draw—valley ... UT-8
Wright Draw—valley ... WY-8
**Wright Efficiency Park (subdivision)**—pop pl ... UT-8
Wright Elem Sch—school ... KS-7
Wright Elem Sch—school ... PA-2
Wrighter Corner—locale ... PA-2
Wrighter Lake—lake ... PA-2
Wrighters Pond ... PA-2
Wright Family Cem—cemetery ... AL-4
Wright Family Cemetery ... MS-4
Wright Ferry ... TN-4
Wright Field—airport ... ND-7
Wright Field (airport)—airport ... AL-4
Wrightfield Cem—cemetery ... SC-3
Wright Fork—stream ... KY-4
Wright Glacier—glacier ... AK-9
Wright Gulch—valley ... MT-8
**Wright (Haire Station)**—pop pl ... LA-4
Wright-Henderson-Duncan House—hist pl ... TX-5
Wright High School ... IN-6
Wright Hill—summit ... AZ-5
Wright Hill—summit ... MA-1
Wright Hill—summit (2) ... NH-1
Wright Hill—summit (2) ... PA-2
**Wright Hills Subdivision**—pop pl ... UT-8
**Wright (historical)**—pop pl ... OR-9
Wright Hollow ... TN-4
Wright Hollow—valley (2) ... KY-4
Wright Hollow—valley (3) ... MO-7
Wright Hollow—valley (5) ... TN-4
Wright Hollow—valley ... VA-3
Wright Hosp—hospital ... NH-1
Wright Hotel—hist pl ... GA-3
Wright House—hist pl ... DE-2
Wright House—hist pl ... GA-3
Wright House—hist pl ... KY-4
Wright House—hist pl ... MS-4
Wright Hunter Cem—cemetery ... WV-2
Wright II Archeol Site—hist pl ... MO-7
Wright International Airp—airport ... KS-7
Wright Island—island ... AR-4
Wright Island—island ... LA-4
Wright Island—island ... MI-6
Wright Island—island ... NY-2
Wright Island—island ... TN-4
Wright Island—island ... VA-3
Wright JHS—school ... LA-4
Wright JHS—school ... OH-6
Wright JHS—school ... OK-5
Wright JHS—school ... SC-3
Wright JHS—school ... TN-4
Wright JHS—school (2) ... WI-6
Wright-Kilgore House—hist pl ... AL-4
Wright Kingery Bend—bend ... TX-5
Wright Knob—summit ... NC-3
Wright Knob—summit ... PA-2
Wright Knobs—summit ... TX-5
Wright Lake—lake (2) ... FL-3
Wright Lake—lake ... MI-6
Wright Lake—lake (2) ... MN-6
Wright Lake—lake ... MT-8
Wright Lake—lake ... ND-7
Wright Lake—lake ... TX-5
Wright Lake—lake ... WI-6
Wright Lake—reservoir ... CA-9
Wright Lake—reservoir ... NY-2
Wright Lake—reservoir ... NC-3
Wright Lakes—lake ... CA-9
**Wrightland**—pop pl ... AR-4
Wright Landing—locale ... FL-3
Wright Landing Field—airport ... MO-7
Wrightman Canyon—valley ... OR-9
Wrightman Lake ... IL-6
Wright Manor ... IN-6
Wright Meadow—flat ... WA-9
Wright Memorial Bridge—bridge ... NC-3
Wright Memorial Institute (historical)—school ... TN-4
Wright Memorial Monmt ... NC-3
Wright Memorial Monmt—park ... NC-3
Wright Mill—locale ... GA-3
Wright Mill Branch—stream ... GA-3
Wright Mine—mine ... CA-9
Wright Mine—mine (2) ... TN-4
Wright Mineral Spring—locale ... GA-3
Wright Mines—mine ... CO-8
Wright Mines—mine ... KY-4
Wright Monmt ... NC-3
Wright Monmt—park ... NC-3
Wright Mountain Oil Field—oilfield ... TX-5
Wright Mtn—range ... TX-5
Wright Mtn—summit ... AR-4
Wright Mtn—summit (2) ... CA-9
Wright Mtn—summit (4) ... TN-4
Wright Mtn—summit ... WA-9
Wright Neck—cape ... MD-2
Wright No. 1 Mine—mine ... CO-8
Wright No. 2 Mine—mine ... CO-8
Wright Park—park ... FL-3
Wright Park—park ... IL-6
Wright Park—park ... KS-7
Wright Park—park ... NY-2
Wright Park—park ... OH-6
Wright Park—park ... TX-5
Wright Park—park ... WA-9
Wright Park and Seymour Conservatory—hist pl ... WA-9
Wright Park Beach—beach ... NY-2
Wright Park Manor (Air City)—uninc pl ... NY-2
Wright Pass—gut ... LA-4
Wright Patman Lake—reservoir ... TX-5
Wright Patterson AFB—military ... OH-6
Wright-Patterson Air Force Base—other (2) ... OH-6
Wright-Patterson Air Force Base Mound—hist pl ... OH-6
Wright Peak—summit ... CA-9
Wright Peak—summit ... NY-2
Wright Peaks—summit ... AK-9
Wright Petty Catfish Ponds Dam—dam ... MS-4
Wright Place—locale ... NM-5
Wright Place—locale ... NC-3
Wright Place (Site)—locale ... CA-9
Wright Point—cape ... AL-4
Wright Point—cape ... AK-9
Wright Point—cape ... NJ-2
Wright Pond ... CT-1
Wright Pond ... MA-1
Wright Pond—lake ... CT-1
Wright Pond—lake ... FL-3
Wright Pond—lake ... MA-1
Wright Pond—lake ... NH-1
Wright Pond—reservoir ... NJ-2
Wright Ponds—lake ... MA-1
Wright Prospect—mine ... TN-4
Wright Ranch—locale ... NE-7
Wright Ranch—locale (2) ... NM-5
Wright Ranch—locale ... TX-5
Wright Ranch—locale ... UT-8
Wright Ranch—locale (3) ... WY-8
Wright Reservoir Dam—dam ... MA-1
Wright Ridge—ridge ... TN-4
Wright Ridge—ridge ... VA-3
Wright River—stream ... AK-9
Wright River—stream ... SC-3
Wright (RR name for Beech Creek)—other ... KY-4
Wright (RR name for Wright-Patterson Air Force Base)—other ... OH-6
Wright Rsvr—reservoir ... MA-1
Wright Rsvr—reservoir ... VT-1
Wright Run ... PA-2
Wright Run ... VA-3
Wrights ... DE-2
Wrights ... WA-9
Wrights—locale ... KY-4
Wrights—locale ... MD-2
Wrights—locale ... PA-2
**Wrights**—pop pl ... IL-6
Wrights—uninc pl ... NJ-2
Wrights Airfield—airport ... OR-9
Wrights Beach—other ... CA-9
Wrights Bend—bend ... AL-4
Wrightsboro—locale ... GA-3
**Wrightsboro**—pop pl ... NC-3
**Wrightsboro**—pop pl ... TX-5
**Wrightsboro Acres (subdivision)**—pop pl ... NC-3
Wrightsboro Elem Sch—school ... NC-3
Wrights Branch ... SC-3
Wrights Branch—stream ... GA-3
Wrights Branch—stream ... MD-2
Wrights Branch—stream ... VA-3
Wrights Branch Ch—church ... NC-3
Wrights Bridge—bridge ... VA-3
Wright's Bridge—hist pl ... NH-1
Wrights Brook ... MA-1
Wrights Brook—stream ... CT-1
Wrightsburg—locale ... KY-4
Wrights Canyon—valley ... NM-5
Wrights Cave—cave ... PA-2
Wrights Cem—cemetery ... KY-4
Wrights Cem—cemetery ... NC-3
Wrights Cem—cemetery (2) ... SC-3
Wrights Cem—cemetery ... TX-5
Wrights Cemetery ... MS-4
Wright Sch ... PA-2
Wrights Ch—church ... PA-2
Wrights Ch—church ... TN-4
Wright Sch—school ... AL-4
Wright Sch—school ... AZ-5
Wright Sch—school (5) ... CA-9
Wright Sch—school ... CT-1
Wright Sch—school ... FL-3
Wright Sch—school ... GA-3
Wright Sch—school (4) ... IL-6
Wright Sch—school ... IA-7
Wright Sch—school (2) ... LA-4
Wright Sch—school ... ME-1
Wright Sch—school (4) ... MI-6
Wright Sch—school (3) ... MO-7
Wright Sch—school ... NY-2
Wright Sch—school (2) ... NC-3
Wright Sch—school ... ND-7
Wright Sch—school (2) ... OH-6
Wright Sch—school ... OR-9
Wright Sch—school (3) ... PA-2
Wright Sch—school ... SC-3
Wright Sch—school ... TN-4
Wright Sch—school (2) ... TX-5
Wright Sch—school ... VT-1
Wright Sch—school (2) ... VA-3
Wright Sch—school ... WI-6
Wright Sch (abandoned)—school (3) ... MO-7
Wright Sch (abandoned)—school ... PA-2
Wrights Chapel—church (2) ... AL-4
Wrights Chapel—church ... AR-4
Wrights Chapel—church (2) ... GA-3
Wrights Chapel—church ... IL-6
Wrights Chapel—church ... KY-4
Wrights Chapel—church ... OK-5
Wrights Chapel—church ... TN-4
Wrights Chapel—church ... VA-3
Wrights Chapel Cem—cemetery ... TX-5
Wrights Chapel Ch of God and Christ—church ... MS-4
Wright Sch (historical)—school ... AL-4
Wright Sch (historical)—school ... MS-4
Wright Sch (historical)—school ... MO-7
Wright Sch (historical)—school (2) ... TN-4
Wright School ... MS-4
Wright School Cut-Off—bend ... MS-4
Wrights Church Creek—stream ... GA-3
Wrights Corner—locale ... AR-4
Wrights Corner—locale ... IL-6
Wrights Corner—locale (2) ... VA-3
**Wrights Corner**—pop pl ... IN-6
**Wrights Corner**—pop pl (2) ... NY-2
Wrights Corners ... IL-6
Wrights Corners—locale (2) ... NY-2
**Wrights Corners**—pop pl ... IN-6
**Wrights Corners**—pop pl ... MI-6
**Wrights Corners**—pop pl ... NY-2
**Wrights Corners**—pop pl ... PA-2
Wrights Corners Sch—school ... NY-2
Wright's Cove ... CT-1
Wrights Cove—bay ... ME-1
Wrights Cove—bay ... VA-3
Wrights Cove—valley ... AL-4
Wrights Creek ... NC-3
Wrights Creek ... TX-5
Wrights Creek—stream (3) ... AL-4
Wrights Creek—stream ... CA-9
Wrights Creek—stream ... FL-3
Wrights Creek—stream ... GA-3
Wrights Creek—stream ... KS-7
Wrights Creek—stream ... LA-4
Wrights Creek—stream ... MI-6
Wrights Creek—stream ... MS-4
Wrights Creek—stream ... MO-7
Wrights Creek—stream ... NY-2
Wrights Creek—stream ... NC-3
Wrights Creek—stream (2) ... OR-9
Wrights Creek—stream ... TX-5
Wrights Creek—stream ... WA-9
Wrights Creek Cem—cemetery ... TX-5
Wrights Creek Ch—church ... NC-3
Wrights Creek Lookout Tower—tower ... FL-3
**Wrights Crossing**—pop pl ... MD-2
Wrights Crossroads—locale ... DE-2
Wrightsdale—locale ... PA-2
Wrightsdale Post Office (historical)—building ... PA-2
Wrights Dam—dam ... NJ-2
Wright Seale Cem—cemetery ... MS-4
Wright Seminary—school ... WA-9
**Wright Settlement**—pop pl ... NY-2
Wrights Ferry Ch—church ... TN-4
Wrights Ferry (historical)—crossing ... TN-4
Wrights Ferry (historical)—locale ... IN-6
Wright's Ferry Mansion—hist pl ... PA-2
Wrights Fork—locale ... VA-3
Wrights Grove Ch—church ... GA-3
Wrights Hill—summit ... IN-6
Wrights Hill—summit ... WA-9
**Wright Shop**—pop pl ... VA-3
Wrights Island ... TN-4
Wrights Island—island (2) ... GA-3
Wrights Island—island ... MA-1
Wrights Island—island ... MO-7
Wrights Island—island ... NH-1
Wright Site—hist pl ... NE-7
Wrights Lake ... ID-8
Wrights Lake—lake ... CA-9
Wrights Lake—lake (2) ... MI-6
Wrights Lake—reservoir ... AL-4
Wrights Lake—reservoir (2) ... GA-3
Wrights Lake Park—park ... MN-6
Wrights Lakes—reservoir ... AL-4
Wrights Landing ... AL-4
Wrights Landing—locale ... AL-4
Wrights Landing—locale ... FL-3
Wrights Landing—locale ... MD-2
Wrights Landing (inundated)—locale ... AL-4
Wright Slough—gut ... OR-9
Wright Slough—gut ... WI-6
Wright Slough—stream ... OR-9
Wrights Meadows—flat ... OR-9
Wrights Mesa—summit ... CO-8
Wrights Methodist Church ... MS-4
**Wrights Mill**—pop pl ... NJ-2
Wrights Mill Dam—dam ... NJ-2
Wrights Millpond—reservoir ... MD-2
Wrights Millpond—reservoir ... NJ-2
Wrights Millpond—reservoir ... SC-3
Wrights Millpond—reservoir ... VA-3
Wrights Millpond Branch—stream ... MD-2
Wrights Mill Road Elementary School ... AL-4
Wrights Mills ... IN-6
Wrights Mill Sch—school ... AL-4
Wrights Mill Stream—stream ... ME-1
Wrights Mountain Trail—trail ... VT-1
Wrights Mtn—summit ... VT-1
Wrights Mtn—summit ... WA-9
Wrights Neck ... MD-2
Wrightson, Mount—summit ... AZ-5
Wrights Park—park ... MA-1
Wrights Pasture—flat ... VA-3
Wrights Point—cape ... AR-4
Wrights Point—cliff ... OR-9
Wrightspond ... CT-1
Wrights Pond ... MA-1
Wrights Pond—lake ... MD-2
Wrights Pond—reservoir ... CT-1
Wrights Pond—reservoir ... MA-1
Wrights Pond—reservoir (2) ... NC-3
Wrights Pond—reservoir ... VA-3
Wrights Pond Dam—dam ... MA-1
Wrights Pond Dam—dam (2) ... NC-3
Wright Spring ... CO-8
Wright Spring—spring ... AL-4
Wright Spring—spring (2) ... OR-9
Wright Spring—spring ... WA-9
Wright Springs Windmill—locale ... NM-5
Wright Square—uninc pl ... GA-3
Wrights Reservoir Dam—dam ... MA-1
Wrights Ridge—ridge ... AL-4
Wrights Ridge—ridge ... CA-9
Wrights Ridge—ridge ... KY-4
Wrights River ... MA-1
Wrights Rsvr—reservoir ... CO-8
Wrights Rsvr—reservoir ... MA-1
Wrights Rsvrs—reservoir ... OR-9
Wrights Run ... PA-2
Wrights Run—stream ... OH-6
Wrights Run—stream (2) ... PA-2
Wrights Run—stream (2) ... VA-3
Wrights Run—stream ... WV-2
Wrights Sch (historical)—school (2) ... AL-4
Wrights Shoals—bar ... TN-4
**Wrights Shop**—pop pl ... VA-3
Wrights Siding—locale ... SC-3
Wrights Siding (historical)—locale ... PA-2
Wrights (Site)—locale ... CA-9
Wrights Spring—spring ... CO-8
Wrights Spring—spring ... OR-9
Wrights Spring—spring ... TN-4
Wrights Spring Branch ... SC-3
Wright's Stone Store—hist pl ... NY-2
Wrights Store—locale ... MS-4
Wrights Store (historical)—locale ... TN-4
Wright State Univ—school ... OH-6
Wright Station ... OK-5
Wright's Tavern—hist pl ... MA-1
Wrightstown—locale ... OH-6
Wrightstown—locale ... PA-2
**Wrightstown**—pop pl ... MN-6
**Wrightstown**—pop pl ... NJ-2
**Wrightstown**—pop pl ... WI-6
Wrightstown Cem—cemetery ... MN-6
Wrightstown Cem—cemetery ... OH-6
Wrights Towne ... PA-2
Wrightstown Friends Meeting Complex—hist pl ... PA-2
Wrightstown Post Office (historical)—building ... PA-2
Wrightstown Sch—school ... AZ-5
Wrightstown Sch—school ... PA-2
**Wrights (Township of)**—pop pl ... IL-6
**Wrightstown (Town of)**—pop pl ... WI-6
**Wrightstown (Township of)**—pop pl ... PA-2
**Wright Subdivision**—pop pl ... MS-4
**Wright Subdivision**—pop pl ... UT-8
**Wright Subdivision 11**—pop pl ... UT-8
**Wright Subdivision 1-5**—pop pl ... UT-8
**Wright Subdivision 6, 8, 10**—pop pl ... UT-8
Wrights Valley—valley ... CA-9
Wrights Valley—valley ... VA-3
Wrights Valley—valley ... WA-9
Wrights Valley Ch—church ... VA-3
Wrights Valley Creek—stream ... VA-3
Wrights View—locale ... PA-2
Wrightsville ... VT-1
**Wrightsville**—pop pl ... AR-4
**Wrightsville**—pop pl ... GA-3
**Wrightsville**—pop pl (2) ... NJ-2
**Wrightsville**—pop pl ... NC-3
**Wrightsville**—pop pl ... OH-6
**Wrightsville**—pop pl (2) ... PA-2
**Wrightsville**—pop pl ... VT-1
**Wrightsville**—pop pl ... VA-3
**Wrightsville**—pop pl ... WI-6
**Wrightsville Beach**—pop pl ... NC-3
Wrightsville Beach Elem Sch—school ... NC-3
Wrightsville Borough—civil ... PA-2
Wrightsville (CCD)—cens area ... GA-3
Wrightsville Cem—cemetery ... PA-2
Wrightsville Cem—cemetery ... WV-2
Wrightsville Ch—church ... GA-3
Wrightsville Channel ... NC-3
Wrightsville Creek—stream ... WI-6
Wrightsville Dam ... VT-1
Wrightsville Dam—dam ... VT-1
Wrightsville Dam Rec Area ... VT-1
Wrightsville Hist Dist—hist pl ... PA-2
Wrightsville Public Use Area—park ... AR-4
Wrightsville Sound ... NC-3
Wrights Well—well ... NV-8
Wrights Wharf ... MD-2
Wright Tank—reservoir ... AZ-5
Wright Tank—reservoir ... NM-5
Wright Tavern—building ... MA-1
Wright Tavern—hist pl ... NC-3
**Wright Town**—pop pl ... AR-4
Wright Town Hall—building ... ND-7
**Wright (Town of)**—pop pl ... NY-2
Wright Township—fmr MCD (2) ... IA-7
**Wright Township**—pop pl ... ND-7
**Wright Township**—pop pl ... SD-7
**Wright (Township of)**—pop pl ... IN-6
**Wright (Township of)**—pop pl (2) ... MI-6
**Wright (Township of)**—pop pl ... MN-6
**Wright (Township of)**—pop pl ... PA-2
Wright Tract—civil ... CA-9
Wright Trade Sch—school ... CT-1
Wright Valley—basin ... NE-7
Wrightview ... OH-6
Wrightview Heights ... OH-6
**Wrightville**—pop pl ... CT-1
**Wrightville**—pop pl ... ME-1
**Wrightville**—pop pl ... OH-6
Wright Watson Sch—school ... KY-4
Wright Well—well (2) ... NM-5
Wright-West Cem—cemetery ... TN-4
Wright Wharf—locale ... MD-2
Wright Will Ch—church ... AL-4
Wright Windmill—locale (2) ... NM-5
**Wrightwood**—pop pl ... CA-9
Wrightwood Park—park ... IL-6
**Wright Woods**—pop pl ... VA-3
**Wrigley**—pop pl ... KY-4
**Wrigley**—pop pl ... TN-4
Wrigley, William, Jr., Summer Cottage—hist pl ... CA-9
Wrigley Baptist Ch—church ... TN-4
Wrigley Bldg—building ... IL-6
Wrigley (CCD)—cens area ... KY-4
Wrigley Creek—stream ... UT-8
Wrigley Field—locale ... IL-6
Wrigley Furnace (historical)—locale ... TN-4
Wrigley Hill—summit ... UT-8
Wrigley Hollow—valley ... PA-2
Wrigley Mesa—summit ... CO-8
Wrigley Mine—mine ... AZ-5
Wrigley Peak—summit ... AZ-5
Wrigley Prospect—mine ... TN-4
Wrigley Ranch—locale ... CA-9
Wrigley Rsvr—reservoir ... CA-9
Wrigley Sch—school ... TN-4
Wrigley Spring—spring ... UT-8
Wrigley Springs Dam—dam ... UT-8
Wrigley Springs Rsvr—reservoir (2) ... UT-8
Wriley—locale ... GA-3
WRIN-AM (Rensselaer)—tower ... IN-6
Wringer Canyon—valley ... UT-8
Wringer Lake—lake ... MN-6
Wrinkle Canyon—valley ... NM-5
Wrinkle Cem—cemetery ... MO-7
Wrinkle Hollow—valley ... PA-2
Wrinkle Point—cape ... MA-1
Wrinkles, The—cliff ... UT-8
Wrinkley Branch—stream ... TN-4
WRIP-TV (Chattanooga)—tower ... TN-4
Wrist Canyon ... CO-8
Wristen Canal—canal ... CA-9
Wriston—locale ... WV-2
Wriston Cem—cemetery ... WV-2
Wriston Fork—stream ... WV-2
Wriston Knob—summit ... WV-2
Wrist Point—cape ... TX-5
Wrist Spring—spring ... NV-8
Writht Hollow—valley ... VA-3
Writing Rock ... MA-1
Writing Rock Coulee—valley ... ND-7
**Writing Rock Township**—pop pl ... ND-7
Writsman Brook—stream ... OR-9
WRIU-FM (Kingston)—tower ... RI-1
WRJB-FM (Camden)—tower ... TN-4
WRJH-FM (Brandon)—tower ... MS-4
WRJS-FM (Oil City)—tower ... PA-2
WRJW-AM (Picayune)—tower ... MS-4
WRJZ-AM (Knoxville)—tower ... TN-4
WRKB-AM (Kannapolis)—tower ... NC-3
WRKC-FM (Wilkes-Barre)—tower ... PA-2
WRKK-FM (Birmingham)—tower ... AL-4
WRKM-AM (Carthage)—tower ... TN-4
WRKM-FM (Carthage)—tower ... TN-4
WRKN-AM (Brandon)—tower ... MS-4
WRKQ-AM (Madisonville)—tower ... TN-4
WRKZ-FM (Elizabethtown)—tower ... PA-2
W R Lateral—canal ... OR-9
WRLC-FM (Williamsport)—tower ... PA-2
WRLR-FM (Huntingdon)—tower ... PA-2
W R McKelvin Junior Dam—dam ... MS-4
W R McKnight Ranch—locale ... NM-5
WRMG-AM (Red Bay)—tower ... AL-4
WRML-AM (Portage)—tower ... PA-2
WRMT-AM (Rocky Mount)—tower ... NC-3
WRNA-AM (China Grove)—tower ... NC-3
WRNB-AM (New Bern)—tower ... NC-3
WRNS-FM (Kinston)—tower ... NC-3
WROA-AM (Gulfport)—tower ... MS-4
W Road Ch—church ... TN-4
WROB-AM (West Point)—tower ... MS-4
W R Odum Dam—dam ... AL-4
WROI-FM (Rochester)—tower ... IN-6
**WRO Junction (Dana Junction)**—pop pl ... IN-6
Wrong Branch—stream ... IN-6
Wrong Branch Trail Creek—stream ... AK-9
Wrong Creek—stream ... AK-9
Wrong Creek—stream ... MT-8
Wrong Creek—stream ... WA-9
Wrong Creek—stream ... WY-8
Wrong Creek Guard Station—locale ... MT-8
Wrong Mtn—summit ... AZ-5
Wrong Name Pass—channel ... LA-4
Wrong Prong—stream (2) ... MS-4
Wrong Ridge—ridge ... MT-8
Wrongtrail Creek—stream ... AK-9
Wrong Way Creek—stream ... OR-9
Wronk Cem—cemetery ... WV-2
WROQ-FM (Charlotte)—tower ... NC-3
W Ross Walker Cemetery ... MS-4
Wroten And Carraway Cem—cemetery ... MS-4
Wroten Island—island ... MD-2
Wroten Rsvr 1—reservoir (2) ... OR-9
Wroth Point—cape ... MD-2
Wroths Point ... MD-2
W Round Hole Draw—valley ... TX-5
WROX-AM (Clarksdale)—tower ... MS-4
WROZ-AM (Evansville)—tower ... IN-6
WRPM-AM (Poplarville)—tower ... MS-4
WRPM-FM (Poplarville)—tower ... MS-4
WRQK-FM (Greensboro)—tower ... NC-3
WRQR-FM (Farmville)—tower ... NC-3
WRRN-FM (Warren)—tower ... PA-2
WRRZ-AM (Clinton)—tower ... NC-3
WRRZ-FM (Clinton)—tower ... NC-3
WRSA-FM (Decatur)—tower ... AL-4
WRSC-AM (State College)—tower ... PA-2
WRSD-FM (Folsom)—tower ... PA-2
W R Sherrer Lake—reservoir ... AL-4
WRSH-FM (Rockingham)—tower ... NC-3
W R Simmons Cemetery ... MS-4
WRSM-AM (Sumiton)—tower ... AL-4
WRSV-FM (Rocky Mount)—tower ... NC-3
WRSW-AM (Warsaw)—tower ... IN-6
WRSW-FM (Warsaw)—tower ... IN-6
WRTA-AM (Altoona)—tower ... PA-2
WRTB-FM (Vincennes)—tower ... IN-6
W R Thomas JHS—school ... FL-3
WRTI-FM (Philadelphia)—tower ... PA-2
W R Turnipseed Dam—dam ... AL-4
W R Turnipseed Lake—reservoir ... AL-4
WRTV-TV (Indianapolis)—tower ... IN-6
WRUA-AM (Monroeville)—tower ... PA-2
Wruck Canyon—valley ... CA-9
Wrucke Cem—cemetery ... WI-6
WRVR-FM (Memphis)—tower ... TN-4
WRVU-FM (Nashville)—tower (2) ... TN-4
WRXO-AM (Roxboro)—tower ... NC-3
WRXZ-FM (Kane)—tower ... PA-2
Wrzesinski Coulee—valley ... MT-8
WRZK-AM (Algood)—tower ... TN-4
WRZR-AM (Raleigh)—tower ... NC-3
WSAJ-AM (Grove City)—tower ... PA-2
WSAJ-FM (Grove City)—tower ... PA-2
WSAL-AM (Logansport)—tower ... IN-6
WSAL-FM (Logansport)—tower ... IN-6
W Sam Carpenters Dam—dam ... AL-4
W Sam Carpenters Lake—reservoir ... AL-4
WSAN Airp—airport ... PA-2
WSAN-AM (Allentown)—tower ... PA-2
WSAO-AM (Senatobia)—tower ... MS-4
WSAT-AM (Salisbury)—tower ... NC-3
W Sawyer Ranch—locale ... TX-5
WSBA-AM (York)—tower ... PA-2
WSBA-FM (York)—tower ... PA-2
WSBA-TV (York)—tower (2) ... PA-2
WSBE-TV (Providence)—tower ... RI-1
W S Billingslea Lake Dam—dam ... MS-4
W S Billingsly Lake Dam—dam ... MS-4
WSBL-AM (Sanford)—tower ... NC-3
WSBM-FM (Jefferson City)—tower ... TN-4
WSBT-AM (South Bend)—tower ... IN-6
WSBT-TV (South Bend)—tower ... IN-6
**W S Butler Subdivision**—pop pl ... UT-8
WSCA-FM (Union Springs)—tower ... AL-4
WSCH-FM (Aurora)—tower ... IN-6
W Schlautmann Ranch—locale ... WY-8
W Scholl Dam—dam ... SD-7
W Schutte Dam—dam ... SD-7
WSCO-AM (Taylorsville)—tower ... MS-4
WS Corral—locale ... NM-5
W S Draw—valley ... WY-8
WSEA-FM (Georgetown)—tower ... DE-2
W Seboeis ... ME-1
WSEC-FM (Williamston)—tower ... NC-3
WSEE-TV (Erie)—tower ... PA-2
WSEG-FM (Mckean)—tower ... PA-2
WSEL-AM (Pontotoc)—tower ... MS-4
WSEL-FM (Pontotoc)—tower ... MS-4
WSEV-AM (Sevierville)—tower (2) ... TN-4
WSEZ-FM (Winston-Salem)—tower ... NC-3
WSFA-TV (Montgomery)—tower ... AL-4
WSFL-FM (Bridgeton)—tower ... NC-3
WSFL-FM (New Bern)—tower ... NC-3
WSFM-FM (Harrisburg)—tower ... PA-2
WSGE-FM (Dallas)—tower ... NC-3
WSGI-AM (Springfield)—tower ... TN-4
WSGN-AM (Birmingham)—tower ... AL-4
WSHA-FM (Raleigh)—tower ... NC-3
W S Harlan Junior High School ... AL-4
WSHB-AM (Raeford)—tower ... NC-3
WSHF-AM (Sheffield)—tower ... AL-4
WSHH-FM (Pittsburgh)—tower ... PA-2
WSHP-AM (Shippensburg)—tower ... PA-2
WSHW-FM (Frankfort)—tower ... IN-6
WSIC-AM (Statesville)—tower ... NC-3
WSIF-FM (Wilkesboro)—tower ... NC-3
WSIX-AM (Nashville)—tower ... TN-4
WSIX-FM (Nashville)—tower ... TN-4
WSJC-AM (Magee)—tower ... MS-4
WSJC-FM (Magee)—tower ... MS-4
WSJK-TV (Sneedville)—tower ... TN-4
WSJS-AM (Winston-Salem)—tower ... NC-3
WSJV-TV (Elkhart)—tower ... IN-6
WSKE-AM (Everett)—tower ... PA-2
WSKR-FM (Atmore)—tower (2) ... AL-4
WSKT-AM (Knoxville)—tower ... TN-4
WSKY-AM (Asheville)—tower ... NC-3
WSKZ-FM (Chattanooga)—tower ... TN-4
W S Lake—lake ... AZ-5
WSLA-TV (Selma)—tower (2) ... AL-4
WSLI-AM (Jackson)—tower ... MS-4
WSLL-AM (Centreville)—tower ... MS-4
WSLM-AM (Salem)—tower ... IN-6
WSLM-FM—tower ... IN-6
WSLV-AM (Ardmore)—tower ... TN-4
WSLV-AM (Shelbyville)—tower ... IN-6
WSLY-FM (York)—tower ... AL-4
WSM Airp—airport ... TN-4
WSM-AM (Nashville)—tower ... TN-4
WSMC-FM (Collegedale)—tower ... TN-4
WSMF-FM (Nashville)—tower ... TN-4
WSMG-AM (Greeneville)—tower ... TN-4
W Smith Ditch—canal ... IN-6
WSML-AM (Graham)—tower ... NC-3
WSMQ-AM (Bessemer)—tower ... AL-4
WSMQ-FM (Havelock)—tower ... NC-3
WSMS-FM (Memphis)—tower ... TN-4
WSMT-AM (Sparta)—tower ... TN-4
WSMT-FM (Sparta)—tower ... TN-4
W S Mtn—summit ... AZ-5
WSMU-FM (Starkville)—tower ... MS-4
WSMV-TV (Nashville)—tower ... TN-4
WSMX-AM (Winston-Salem)—tower ... NC-3
WSMY-AM (Weldon)—tower ... NC-3
W Snare Ranch—locale ... CO-8
WSNC-FM (Winston-Salem)—tower ... NC-3
W S Neal High School ... AL-4
WSNI-FM (Philadelphia)—tower ... PA-2
WSOC-AM (Charlotte)—tower ... NC-3
WSOC-FM (Charlotte)—tower ... NC-3
WSOC-TV (Charlotte)—tower (2) ... NC-3
WSOE-FM (Elon College)—tower ... NC-3
WSPF-AM (Hickory)—tower ... NC-3
WSPI-FM (Shamokin)—tower ... PA-2
W Spurgeon Ranch—locale ... NM-5
WSQV-FM (Jersey Shore)—tower ... PA-2
W S Ranch—locale ... NM-5
W S Ranch Camp—locale ... NM-5
WSRC-AM (Durham)—tower (2) ... NC-3
WSRN-FM (Swarthmore)—tower ... PA-2
WSRU-FM (Slippery Rock)—tower ... PA-2
W S Sagar Lake—reservoir ... NC-3
W S Sagar Lake Dam—dam ... NC-3
WSSG-AM (Goldsboro)—tower ... NC-3
WSSO-AM (Starkville)—tower ... MS-4
W S Taylor Junior Pond Dam—dam ... MS-4
WSTG-TV (Providence)—tower ... RI-1
WSTP-AM (Salisbury)—tower ... NC-3
WSTS-FM (Laurinburg)—tower ... NC-3
WSTW-FM (Wilmington)—tower ... DE-2
WSUH-AM (Oxford)—tower ... MS-4
WSUX-AM (Seaford)—tower ... DE-2
WSUX-FM (Seaford)—tower ... DE-2
W S Valley Junior Coll—school ... CA-9
WSVC-AM (Dunlap)—tower ... TN-4
WSVM-AM (Valdese)—tower ... NC-3
WSVQ-AM (Harrogate)—tower ... TN-4
WSVT-AM (Smyrna)—tower ... TN-4
WSWB-TV (Scranton)—tower ... PA-2
WSWG-AM (Greenwood)—tower ... MS-4
WSWG-FM (Greenwood)—tower ... MS-4
WSWI-AM (Evansville)—tower ... IN-6
WSWS TV (Opolika)—tower ... AL-4
WSYC-FM (Shippensburg)—tower ... PA-2
WTAB-AM (Tabor City)—tower ... NC-3
WTAE-AM (Pittsburgh)—tower ... PA-2
WTAE-TV (Pittsburgh)—tower ... PA-2
WTAF-TV (Philadelphia)—tower ... PA-2
WTAJ-TV (Altoona)—tower ... PA-2
WTAK-AM (Huntsville)—tower ... AL-4
WTAM-AM (Gulfport)—tower ... MS-4
W Tank—reservoir ... TX-5
WTAR-AM (Norfolk)—tower ... VA-3
WTBC-AM (Tuscaloosa)—tower ... AL-4
WTBF-AM (Troy)—tower ... AL-4
WTBG-FM (Brownsville)—tower ... TN-4
WTBN-AM (Brentwood)—tower ... TN-4
WTBP-AM (Parsons)—tower ... TN-4
WTCA-AM (Plymouth)—tower ... IN-6
WTC Battery Park City Airp—airport ... NY-2
W. T. Chipman Junior Sch—school ... DE-2
WTCI-TV (Chattanooga)—tower ... TN-4
WTCJ-AM (Tell City)—tower ... IN-6
W T Draw—valley ... TX-5
WTEB-FM (New Bern)—tower ... NC-3
WTEL-AM (Philadelphia)—tower ... PA-2
WTFM-FM (Kingsport)—tower ... TN-4
WTGC-AM (Lewisburg)—tower ... PA-2
WTGP-FM (Greenville)—tower ... PA-2
W T Hams Dining Hall—building ... NC-3
WTHD-FM (Columbia)—tower ... NC-3
W T Hendricks Pond Dam—dam ... MS-4
WTHI-FM (Terre Haute)—tower ... IN-6
WTHI-TV (Terre Haute)—tower ... IN-6
WTHR-TV (Indianapolis)—tower ... IN-6
WTIB-FM (Iuka)—tower ... MS-4
WTII-FM (Evergreen)—tower ... AL-4
WTIK-AM (Durham)—tower ... NC-3
WTIU-TV (Bloomington)—tower ... IN-6
WTIV-AM (Titusville)—tower ... PA-2
WTJS-AM (Jackson)—tower ... TN-4
WTJT-AM (Franklin)—tower ... TN-4
WTKN-AM (Pittsburgh)—tower ... PA-2
WTKR-TV (Norfolk)—tower ... VA-3
WTLC-FM (Indianapolis)—tower ... IN-6
W T Lewis Dam—dam ... NC-3

WTLK-AM (Taylorsville)—*tower* NC-3
WTLQ-FM (Pittston)—*tower* PA-2
WTLR-FM (State College)—*tower* PA-2
WTLS-AM (Tallassee)—*tower* AL-4
WT Maddox Park—*park* TX-5
*W T Medlin Elementary School* NC-3
WTMX-FM (St Marys)—*tower* PA-2
WTNC-AM (Thomasville)—*tower* NC-3
WTNE-AM (Trenton)—*tower* TN-4
WTNE-FM (Trenton)—*tower* TN-4
WTNN-AM (Millington)—*tower* TN-4
WTNQ-FM (Dickson)—*tower* TN-4
WTNR-AM (Kingston)—*tower* TN-4
WTNX-AM (Lynchburg)—*tower* TN-4
WTOB-AM (Winston-Salem)—*tower* NC-3
WTOE-AM (Spruce Pine)—*tower* NC-3
WTOH-FM (Mobile)—*tower* AL-4
WTOK-TV (Meridian)—*tower* MS-4
WTPA-FM (Harrisburg)—*tower* PA-2
W T Phillips Dam—*dam* AL-4
W T Piper Memorial Airp—*airport* PA-2
WTPR-AM (Paris)—*tower* TN-4
W. T. PRESTON (snagboat)—*hist pl* WA-9
WTPR-FM (Paris)—*tower* TN-4
WTQR-FM (Winston-Salem)—*tower* NC-3
WTQX-AM (Selma)—*tower* AL-4
W T Ranch—*locale* TX-5
WTRB-AM (Ripley)—*tower* TN-4
WTRC-AM (Elkhart)—*tower* IN-6
WTRE-AM (Evansville)—*tower* IN-6
WTRE-FM (Greensburg)—*tower* IN-6
W-Triangle Tank—*reservoir* AZ-5
WTRN-AM (Tyrone)—*tower* PA-2
WTRO-AM (Dyersburg)—*tower* TN-4
WTRQ-AM (Warsaw)—*tower* NC-3
WTSB-AM (Lumberton)—*tower* NC-3
W T Simmons Pond Dam—*dam* (2) MS-4
W T Sims Ranch—*locale* NM-5
WTSK-AM (Tuscaloosa)—*tower* AL-4
WTSU-FM (Troy)—*tower* AL-4
WTTC-AM (Towanda)—*tower* PA-2
WTTC-FM (Towanda)—*tower* PA-2
WTTO-TV (Homewood)—*tower* AL-4
WTTS-AM (Bloomington)—*tower* IN-6
WTTU-FM (Cookeville)—*tower* TN-4
WTTV-TV (Bloomington)—*tower* IN-6
WTUG-FM (Tuscaloosa)—*tower* AL-4
WTUK-TV (Florence)—*tower* AL-4
WTUN-FM (Selma)—*tower* AL-4
WTUP-AM (Tupelo)—*tower* MS-4
WTVA-TV (Tupelo)—*tower* (2) MS-4
WTVC-TV (Chattanooga)—*tower* TN-4
WTVD-TV (Durham)—*tower* NC-3
WTVE-TV (Reading)—*tower* PA-2
WTVF-TV (Nashville)—*tower* TN-4
WTVI-TV (Charlotte)—*tower* NC-3
WTVK-TV (Knoxville)—*tower* TN-4
WTVW-TV (Evansville)—*tower* IN-6
WTVY-FM (Dothan)—*tower* AL-4
W T Wadsworth Dam—*dam* AL-4
WTWO-TV (Terre Haute)—*tower* IN-6
WTWX-FM (Gunthersville)—*tower* AL-4
WTWZ-AM (Clinton)—*tower* MS-4
WTXI-FM (Ripley)—*tower* MS-4
WTXN-AM (Lafayette)—*tower* AL-4
WTXY-AM (Whiteville)—*tower* NC-3
WTYJ-FM (Fayette)—*tower* MS-4
WTYL-AM (Tylertown)—*tower* MS-4
WTYL-FM (Tylertown)—*tower* MS-4
WTYN-AM (Tryon)—*tower* NC-3
WTYX-FM (Jackson)—*tower* MS-4
WUAA-TV (Jackson)—*tower* TN-4
WUAG-FM (Greensboro)—*tower* NC-3
WUAL-FM (Tuscaloosa)—*tower* AL-4
*Wuap* FM-9
WUAT-AM (Pikeville)—*tower* TN-4
Wuchoo—*bar* FM-9
WUCR-AM (Sparta)—*tower* TN-4
Wudbung—*bar* FM-9
Wuerdeman Lakes—*reservoir* OH-6
Wuerkers New Acres Farm—*airport* NJ-2
Wuertsburg—*locale* WI-6
Wuesthoff Memorial Hosp—*hospital* FL-3
WUEV-FM (Evansville)—*tower* IN-6
WUFM-FM (Lebanon)—*tower* PA-2
Wugeem—*locale* FM-9
*Wugem* FM-9
Wuh, Mount—*summit* CO-8
WUHX-TV (Norfolk)—*tower* VA-3
WUHY-FM (Philadelphia)—*tower* PA-2
*Wuiluku River* HI-9
*Wuinn Dam* SD-7
WUIV-AM (Icard Township)—*tower* NC-3
Wukaf River—*stream* FM-9
Wukoki Ruin—*locale* AZ-5
*Wukopapabi* AZ-5
Wuksi Butte—*summit* OR-9
Wukuklook Creek—*stream* AK-9
Wul—*locale* FM-9
Wul—*summit* FM-9
WULA-AM (Eufaula)—*tower* AL-4
**Wulfert**—*pop pl* FL-3
Wulfert Channel—*channel* FL-3
Wulfert Keys—*island* FL-3
Wulff Airstrip—*airport* OR-9
Wulff Dam—*dam* SD-7
Wulff Harbor Airp—*airport* MO-7
Wulff Run—*stream* OH-6
*Wulfs Creek* DE-2
Wulfs Crossing—*locale* CA-9
Wulik Peaks—*summit* AK-9
Wulik River—*stream* AK-9
Wullum Gulch—*valley* MT-8
Wulsin Triangle—*park* OH-6
*Wulu'* FM-9
*Wuluu* FM-9
Wuluug—*locale* FM-9
*Wumuunen Spwuu* FM-9
WUNC-FM (Chapel Hill)—*tower* NC-3
WUNC-TV (Chapel Hill)—*tower* NC-3
Wunderlick Sch—*school* ND-7
Wunders Cem—*cemetery* IL-6
WUND-TV (Columbia)—*tower* NC-3
*Wuneedaay* FM-9
WUNE-TV (Linville)—*tower* NC-3
*Wuneyiro* FM-9
WUNF-FM (Asheville)—*tower* NC-3
WUNF-TV (Asheville)—*tower* NC-3
*Wungum Lake* CT-1
WUNI-AM (Mobile)—*tower* AL-4
WUNJ-TV (Wilmington)—*tower* NC-3
WUNK-TV (Greenville)—*tower* NC-3
WUNL-TV (Winston-Salem)—*tower* NC-3
WUNM-TV (Jacksonville)—*tower* NC-3
**Wunotoo**—*pop pl* NV-8
Wunpost—*locale* CA-9
Wunsche Bros. Saloon and Hotel—*hist pl* TX-5
Wunsche Cem—*cemetery* TX-5
Wunsche Ditch—*canal* TX-5
Wunsche HS—*school* TX-5
*Wunun* FM-9
*Wununno* FM-9
*Wununown* FM-9
Wunup—*bay* FM-9
*Wunuuen Kuumur* FM-9
*Wunuun'* FM-9
Wunuun—*summit* FM-9
*Wunuunen Cukusirip* FM-9
*Wunuunen Enin* FM-9
*Wunuunen Faan Mwono* FM-9
*Wunuunen Marop* FM-9
*Wunuunen Neefewuwao* FM-9
*Wunuunen Neemeyis* FM-9
*Wunuunen Neenimwokut* FM-9
*Wunuunen Neepwasuk* FM-9
*Wunuunen Nekkuk* FM-9
*Wunuunen Newunukow* FM-9
*Wunuunen Nonaareg* FM-9
*Wunuunen Nukun Aget* FM-9
*Wunuunen Nuukanap* FM-9
*Wunuunen Odjamu* FM-9
*Wunuunen Piyesic* FM-9
*Wunuunen Pwukuno* FM-9
*Wunuunen Sopwiiram* FM-9
*Wunuunen Sopwotiw* FM-9
*Wunuunen Toow* FM-9
*Wunuunen Winikey* FM-9
*Wunuunen Winikot* FM-9
*Wunuunen Wocamwu* FM-9
*Wunuunen Wunnufa* FM-9
*Wunuunen Wunnukopw* FM-9
*Wunuunen Wunuf* FM-9
*Wunuunen Wunumw* FM-9
WUOA-FM (Tuscaloosa)—*tower* AL-4
WUOT-FM (Knoxville)—*tower* TN-4
Wupatki Basin—*basin* AZ-5
Wupatki Natl Monmt—*hist pl* AZ-5
Wupatki Natl Monmt—*park* AZ-5
Wupatki Ruin—*locale* AZ-5
Wupatki Spring—*spring* AZ-5
Wupperman Block/I.O.O.F. Hall—*hist pl* IA-7
*Wupwen* FM-9
*Wuraanu* FM-9
Wurdeman, Lake—*lake* MT-8
Wurdeman-Lawson Archeol Site—*hist pl* NE-7
Wurgler Natl Wildlife Ref—*park* ND-7
*Wurila'* FM-9
Wurl Cabin—*locale* ID-8
Wurley Creek—*stream* GA-3
**Wurlitzer Park Village**—*pop pl* NY-2
Wurmington Branch—*stream* MO-7
Wurno—*locale* VA-3
Wurn Park—*park* FL-3
*Wurooras* FM-9
*Wuror* FM-9
Wursten Spring—*spring* ID-8
Wurster Lake—*reservoir* IN-6
Wurster Lake Dam—*dam* IN-6
Wurster Park—*park* MI-6
Wurst Spring—*spring* ID-8
*Wurtemberg* PA-2
Wurtemburg—*locale* NY-2
**Wurtemburg**—*pop pl* PA-2
*Wurtemburg Academy* TN-4
Wurtemburg Cem—*cemetery* PA-2
**Wurtland**—*pop pl* KY-4
Wurtland (CCD)—*cens area* KY-4
**Wurtsboro**—*pop pl* NY-2
**Wurtsboro Hills**—*pop pl* NY-2
Wurtsboro Hills—*range* NY-2
*Wurtsborough* NY-2
Wurts Ditch—*canal* CO-8
Wurtsmith—*other* MI-6
Wurtsmith AFB—*military* MI-6
Wurtsmith Air Force Range—*military* MI-6
Wurtz Hill—*locale* MT-8
*Wuru* FM-9
Wuruipa—*locale* FM-9
Wuruq—*summit* FM-9
*Wurur* FM-9
Wuruur—*summit* FM-9
*Wurwo'* FM-9
WUSL-FM (Philadelphia)—*tower* PA-2
Wusp Number 2 Mine—*mine* SD-7
*Wusser Creek* TX-5
WUTC-FM (Chattanooga)—*tower* TN-4
Wutchumna Ditch—*canal* CA-9
Wutchumna Hill—*summit* CA-9
*Wuteet* FM-9
Wuthrich Hill—*locale* TX-5
Wuthrich Hill Cem—*cemetery* TX-5
*Wutiej* MP-9
WUTK-FM (Knoxville)—*tower* TN-4
WUTM-FM (Martin)—*tower* TN-4
WUTS-FM (Sewanee)—*tower* TN-4
WUTZ-FM (Summertown)—*tower* TN-4
*Wuumaan* FM-9
*Wuupwut* FM-9
*Wuzer River* ID-8
WVAM-AM (Altoona)—*tower* PA-2
WVBS-AM (Burgaw)—*tower* NC-3
WVBS-FM (Burgaw)—*tower* NC-3
WVBS-FM (Burgaw-Wilmington)—*tower* NC-3
WVBU-FM (Lewisburg)—*tower* PA-2
WVCB-AM (Shallotte)—*tower* NC-3
WVCC-FM (Linesville)—*tower* PA-2
WVCH-AM (Chester)—*tower* PA-2
WVCP-FM (Gallatin)—*tower* TN-4
WVCS-FM (California)—*tower* PA-2
WVEC-TV (Hampton)—*tower* VA-3
WVEN-FM (Franklin)—*tower* PA-2
W Venjohn Dam—*dam* SD-7
WVFC-AM (Mcconnellsburg)—*tower* PA-2
WVIA-FM (Scranton)—*tower* PA-2
WVIA-TV (Scranton)—*tower* PA-2
WVIM-FM (Coldwater)—*tower* MS-4
**W. V. Junction**—*pop pl* MS-4
WVLV-AM (Lebanon)—*tower* PA-2
WVLY-AM (Water Valley)—*tower* MS-4
WVME-FM (Paoli)—*tower* IN-6
WVMH-FM (Mars Hill)—*tower* NC-3
WVMI-AM (Biloxi)—*tower* MS-4
WVMW-FM (Scranton)—*tower* PA-2
WVNA-AM (Tuscumbia)—*tower* AL-4
WVNA-FM (Tuscumbia)—*tower* AL-4
WVOE-AM (Chadbourn)—*tower* NC-3
WVOK-AM (Birmingham)—*tower* AL-4
WVOK-AM (Midfield)—*tower* (2) AL-4
WVOL-AM (Berry Hill)—*tower* TN-4
WVOM-AM (Iuka)—*tower* MS-4
WVOT-AM (Wilson)—*tower* NC-3
WVPE-FM (Elkhart)—*tower* IN-6
WVPO-AM (Stroudsburg)—*tower* PA-2
WVPO-FM (Stroudsburg)—*tower* PA-2
WVRT-FM (Reform)—*tower* AL-4
WVRY-FM (Waverly)—*tower* TN-4
WVSA-AM (Vernon)—*tower* AL-4
WVSC-AM (Somerset)—*tower* PA-2
WVSC-FM (Somerset)—*tower* PA-2
WVSH-FM (Huntington)—*tower* IN-6
WVSM-AM (Rainsville)—*tower* AL-4
WVSP-FM (Warrenton)—*tower* NC-3
WVST-FM (Bolivar)—*tower* TN-4
WVSU-FM (Birmingham)—*tower* AL-4
WVSV-FM (Stevenson)—*tower* AL-4
WVTH-FM (Goodman)—*tower* MS-4
WVTL-FM (Monticello)—*tower* IN-6
WVTM-TV (Birmingham)—*tower* AL-4
WVTN-FM (Gatlinburg)—*tower* TN-4
WVTS-FM (Terre Haute)—*tower* IN-6
WVU Aeronautical Engineering Lab—*school* WV-2
WVUA-FM (Tuscaloosa)—*tower* AL-4
WVU Animal Husbandry Farm—*school* WV-2
WVUB-FM (Vincennes)—*tower* IN-6
WVUR-FM (Valparaise)—*tower* IN-6
WVUT-TV (Vincennes)—*tower* IN-6
*W V Whitmore School* AZ-5
WVWV-FM (Covington)—*tower* IN-6
WVYC-FM (York)—*tower* PA-2
W Wallace—*locale* TX-5
WWAS-FM (Williamsport)—*tower* PA-2
W Water Hole—*bay* FL-3
WWAX-AM (Mobile)—*tower* AL-4
WWAY-TV (Wilmington)—*tower* NC-3
W W Billingsly Lake Dam—*dam* MS-4
W W Bobo Dam—*dam* AL-4
WWBR-AM (Windber)—*tower* PA-2
WWCA-AM (Gary)—*tower* IN-6
WWCB-AM (Corry)—*tower* PA-2
WWCH-AM (Clarion)—*tower* PA-2
WWCJ-FM (Jackson)—*tower* MS-4
W W Cloud Lake Dam—*dam* MS-4
WWCM-AM (Brazil)—*tower* IN-6
WWCU-FM (Cullowhee)—*tower* NC-3
WWDB-FM (Philadelphia)—*tower* PA-2
WWDL-FM (Scranton)—*tower* PA-2
WWDR-AM (Murfreesboro)—*tower* NC-3
WWDR-FM (Murfreesboro)—*tower* NC-3
WWEE-AM (Germantown)—*tower* (2) TN-4
WWEE-AM (Memphis)—*tower* TN-4
W W Evans Memorial Elem Sch—*school* PA-2
WWGM-AM (Nashville)—*tower* TN-4
WWGP-AM (Sanford)—*tower* NC-3
WWGR-AM (La Follette)—*tower* TN-4
W W Harral Ranch—*locale* TX-5
WWHC-FM (Hartford City)—*tower* IN-6
WWHI-FM (Muncie)—*tower* IN-6
WWIC-AM (Scottsboro)—*tower* AL-4
WWIH-FM (High Point)—*tower* NC-3
WWIL-AM (Wilmington)—*tower* NC-3
WWIT-AM (Canton)—*tower* NC-3
WWIZ-FM (Mercer)—*tower* PA-2
W W Jones Dam—*dam* NC-3
W W Jones Lake—*reservoir* NC-3
WWJY-FM (Crown Point)—*tower* IN-6
WWKC-AM (West Hazelton)—*tower* PA-2
WWKI-FM (Kokomo)—*tower* IN-6
WWKO-AM (Fair Bluff)—*tower* NC-3
WWKS-FM (Beaver Falls)—*tower* PA-2
WWKX-FM (Gallatin)—*tower* TN-4
*W W Lawler Cemetery* AL-4
WWLX-AM (Lexington)—*tower* AL-4
WWMC-FM (Mifflinburg)—*tower* PA-2
WWMO-FM (Reidsville)—*tower* NC-3
WWNC-AM (Asheville)—*tower* NC-3
WWNT-AM (Dothan)—*tower* AL-4
WWNW-FM (New Wilmington)—*tower* PA-2
WWON-AM (Woonsocket)—*tower* RI-1
WWON-FM (Woonsocket)—*tower* RI-1
WWPA-AM (Williamsport)—*tower* PA-2
WWQQ-FM (Wilmington)—*tower* NC-3
WWSG-TV (Philadelphia)—*tower* PA-2
WWSH-FM (Philadelphia)—*tower* PA-2
WWSL-FM (Philadelphia)—*tower* MS-4
WWSM-FM (Bay Minette)—*tower* AL-4
WWSW-FM (Pittsburgh)—*tower* PA-2
WWTR-FM (Bethany Beach)—*tower* DE-2
WWUN-AM (Batesville)—*tower* MS-4
WWVR-FM (West Terre Haute)—*tower* IN-6
WWWB-AM (Jasper)—*tower* AL-4
WWWB-FM (Jasper)—*tower* AL-4
WWWC-AM (Wilkesboro)—*tower* NC-3
W W Weissinger Lake Number 1—*reservoir* AL-4
W W Weissinger Number 2 Dam—*dam* AL-4
W W Weissinger Number 2 Lake—*reservoir* AL-4
W W Weissinger Number 4 Dam—*dam* AL-4
W W Weissinger Number 4 Lake—*reservoir* AL-4
W W Wesssinger Number 1 Dam—*dam* AL-4
WWWF-AM (Fayette)—*tower* AL-4
W W Wilder Dam—*dam* TN-4
W W Wilder Lake—*reservoir* TN-4
WWWR-AM (Russellville)—*tower* AL-4
WWWY-FM (Columbus)—*tower* IN-6
WWYN-FM (Carthage)—*tower* MS-4
WWZE-FM (Central City)—*tower* PA-2
WXAC-FM (Reading)—*tower* PA-2
WXAL-AM (Demopolis)—*tower* AL-4
WXBK-AM (Albertville)—*tower* AL-4
WXBQ-FM (Bristol (TN-VA))—*tower* TN-4
WXDR-FM (Newark)—*tower* DE-2
WXGR-AM (Bay St. Louis)—*tower* MS-4
WXII-TV (Winston-Salem)—*tower* NC-3
WXIK-FM (Shelby)—*tower* NC-3
WXIR-FM (Plainfield)—*tower* IN-6
WXIS-FM (Erwin)—*tower* TN-4
WXIY-FM (Bay Springs)—*tower* MS-4
WXJC-TV (Angola)—*tower* IN-6
WXKE-FM (Fort Wayne)—*tower* IN-6
WXKG-FM (Livingston)—*tower* TN-4
WXKW-FM (Allentown)—*tower* PA-2
WXKX-FM (Pittsburgh)—*tower* PA-2
WXKY-AM (Milan)—*tower* TN-4
WXLE-FM (Abbeville)—*tower* AL-4
WXLR-FM (State College)—*tower* PA-2
WXLW-AM (Speedway)—*tower* IN-6
WXLY-FM (Jackson)—*tower* MS-4
WXOQ-AM (Tupelo)—*tower* MS-4
WXOR-AM (Florence)—*tower* AL-4
WXPN-FM (Philadelphia)—*tower* PA-2
WXQK-AM (Spring City)—*tower* TN-4
WXQR-FM (Jacksonville)—*tower* NC-3
WXRC-FM (Hickory)—*tower* NC-3
WXRI-FM (Norfolk)—*tower* VA-3
WXRQ-AM (Mount Pleasant)—*tower* TN-4
WXTN-AM (Lexington)—*tower* MS-4
WXTZ-FM (Indianapolis)—*tower* IN-6
WXUR-AM (Media)—*tower* PA-2
WXUS-FM (Lafayette)—*tower* IN-6
WXVI-AM (Montgomery)—*tower* AL-4
WXVL-FM (Crossville)—*tower* TN-4
WXVT-TV (Greenville)—*tower* MS-4
WXVW-AM (Lafayette)—*tower* IN-6
WXXR-AM (Cullman)—*tower* AL-4
WXXX-AM (Hattiesburg)—*tower* MS-4
WXYC-FM (Chapel Hill)—*tower* NC-3
WXYY-FM (Wilson)—*tower* NC-3
Wyach Lake—*lake* TX-5
**Wyaconda**—*pop pl* MO-7
Wyaconda Ch—*church* MO-7
Wyacondah Township—*fmr MCD* IA-7
Wyaconda River—*stream* MO-7
Wyaconda Township—*civil* MO-7
WYAH-TV (Portsmouth)—*tower* VA-3
WYAL-AM (Scotland Neck)—*tower* NC-3
Wyaloosing Creek—*stream* IN-6
**Wyalusing**—*pop pl* PA-2
**Wyalusing**—*pop pl* WI-6
Wyalusing Borough—*civil* PA-2
Wyalusing Creek—*stream* PA-2
*Wyalusing Lake* PA-2
Wyalusing Rocks—*cliff* PA-2
Wyalusing Slough—*channel* IA-7
Wyalusing State Park—*park* WI-6
Wyalusing Station—*locale* PA-2
**Wyalusing (Town of)**—*pop pl* WI-6
**Wyalusing (Township of)**—*pop pl* PA-2
**Wyandale**—*pop pl* NY-2
**Wyandanch**—*pop pl* NY-2
Wyandock Lake—*lake* WI-6
**Wyandot**—*pop pl* IN-6
**Wyandot**—*pop pl* OH-6
Wyandot Cem—*cemetery* IN-6
**Wyandot (County)**—*pop pl* OH-6
Wyandot County Courthouse and Jail—*hist pl* OH-6
*Wyandot Creek* IN-6
Wyandot Falls—*falls* PA-2
Wyandot Mission Church—*hist pl* OH-6
*Wyandotte* MS-4
Wyandotte—*locale* KY-4
Wyandotte—*locale* MI-6
**Wyandotte**—*pop pl* CA-9
**Wyandotte**—*pop pl* IN-6
**Wyandotte**—*pop pl* LA-4
**Wyandotte**—*pop pl* MI-6
**Wyandotte**—*pop pl* MS-4
**Wyandotte**—*pop pl* OK-5
Wyandotte, Lake—*reservoir* CA-9
Wyandotte Bldg—*hist pl* OH-6
Wyandotte Cave—*cave* IN-6
Wyandotte Cave—*park* IN-6
*Wyandotte Caves* IN-6
Wyandotte (CCD)—*cens area* OK-5
Wyandotte Cem—*cemetery* OK-5
Wyandotte Ch—*church* IN-6
Wyandotte Ch—*church* KS-7
Wyandotte Ch—*church* MO-7
Wyandotte County—*civil* KS-7
Wyandotte County Lake—*reservoir* KS-7
Wyandotte County Park—*park* (2) KS-7
Wyandotte Creek—*stream* CA-9
*Wyandotte Hill* PA-2
Wyandotte HS—*hist pl* KS-7
Wyandotte HS—*school* KS-7
Wyandotte HS—*school* MI-6
Wyandotte Lake—*reservoir* IN-6
Wyandotte Lake Dam—*dam* IN-6
Wyandotte Natl Wildlife Ref—*park* MI-6
Wyandotte Plaza—*locale* KS-7
Wyandotte Sch—*school* KS-7
Wyandotte Sch—*school* LA-4
Wyandotte Substation—*other* CA-9
**Wyandotte Township**—*pop pl* SD-7
Wyandotte Township Hall—*building* SD-7
**Wyandotte (Township of)**—*pop pl* MN-6
Wyandotte West—*post sta* KS-7
Wyandotte Woods—*park* IN-6
Wyandot Wildlife Area—*park* OH-6
**Wyanet**—*pop pl* IL-6
Wyanett—*locale* MN-6
Wyanett Creek—*stream* MN-6
*Wyanette* MN-6
**Wyanet (Township of)**—*pop pl* IL-6
**Wyanett (Township of)**—*pop pl* MN-6
**Wyano**—*pop pl* PA-2
Wyanoke—*locale* AR-4
Wyanoke—*locale* NC-3
Wyanoke Island—*island* NY-2
Wyan Sch—*school* KY-4
Wyant Branch—*stream* NC-3
Wyant Camp—*locale* ID-8
Wyant Cem—*cemetery* LA-4
Wyant Cem—*cemetery* MO-7
Wyant Coulee—*valley* MT-8
Wyant Creek—*stream* ID-8
Wyant Creek—*stream* WA-9
Wyant Drain—*canal* MI-6
Wyantenock State For—*forest* CT-1
Wyant Fork—*stream* WV-2
Wyant Lake—*lake* MT-8
**Wyantskill**—*pop pl* NY-2
*Wyapumseat* RI-1
Wyard Dam—*dam* ND-7
**Wyard Township**—*pop pl* ND-7
Wyarno—*locale* WY-8
Wyarno Draw—*valley* WY-8
Wyasket Bottom—*bend* UT-8
Wyassup Brook—*stream* CT-1
Wyassup Lake—*lake* CT-1
Wyatt—*locale* AL-4
Wyatt—*locale* MS-4
**Wyatt**—*pop pl* IN-6
**Wyatt**—*pop pl* LA-4
**Wyatt**—*pop pl* MO-7
**Wyatt**—*pop pl* NC-3
**Wyatt**—*pop pl* WV-2
Wyatt, Samuel, House—*hist pl* NH-1
Wyatt Airp—*airport* PA-2
*Wyatt Branch* TN-4
Wyatt Branch—*stream* TN-4
Wyatt Bridge (historical)—*bridge* MS-4
Wyatt Cem—*cemetery* (2) AR-4
Wyatt Cem—*cemetery* IN-6
Wyatt Cem—*cemetery* (2) KY-4
Wyatt Cem—*cemetery* LA-4
Wyatt Cem—*cemetery* (3) MS-4
Wyatt Cem—*cemetery* MO-7
Wyatt Cem—*cemetery* NC-3
Wyatt Cem—*cemetery* OH-6
Wyatt Cem—*cemetery* (3) TN-4
Wyatt Cem—*cemetery* (2) VA-3
Wyatt Ch—*church* AL-4
Wyatt Chapel Cem—*cemetery* MS-4
Wyatt Coulee—*valley* MT-8
Wyatt Creek—*stream* AL-4
Wyatt Creek—*stream* LA-4
Wyatt Creek—*stream* OR-9
Wyatt Creek—*stream* TN-4
Wyatt Creek—*stream* TX-5
Wyatt Creek—*stream* VA-3
Wyatt Crossing Public Use Area—*park* MS-4
Wyatt Draw—*valley* WY-8
Wyatt Dr Ch—*church* FL-3
**Wyatte**—*pop pl* MS-4
Wyatte Baptist Ch—*church* MS-4
Wyatte Cem—*cemetery* AR-4
Wyatte Creek—*stream* WY-8
Wyatte Sch (historical)—*school* MS-4
Wyatt Fire Trail—*trail* TN-4
Wyatt Gulch—*valley* OR-9
Wyatt Hall—*hist pl* (2) TN-4
Wyatt-Hickie Ranch Complex—*hist pl* TX-5
Wyatt Hill—*summit* NH-1
Wyatt Hills, The—*summit* MS-4
Wyatt (historical)—*locale* MS-4
**Wyatt (historical)**—*pop pl* TN-4
Wyatt Hollow—*valley* TN-4
Wyatt HS—*school* VA-3
*Wyatt Junction* MO-7
Wyatt Lake—*lake* NM-5
Wyatt Lake—*reservoir* AL-4
Wyatt Lake Dam—*dam* AL-4
Wyatt Landing—*locale* TN-4
Wyatt Lateral—*canal* CA-9
Wyatt Memorial Ch—*church* AR-4
Wyatt Mountain—*ridge* VA-3
Wyatt Mountain Ch—*church* VA-3
*Wyatt Park* MO-7
Wyatt Park—*park* NH-1
Wyatt Petroglyphs—*hist pl* AR-4
Wyatt Ranch—*locale* (2) TX-5
Wyatt Ranch—*locale* WY-8
Wyatt Rsvr—*reservoir* CO-8
Wyatt Rsvr—*reservoir* OR-9
Wyatt Run—*stream* OH-6
Wyatt Run—*stream* (3) WV-2
**Wyatts**—*pop pl* NY-2
Wyatts Branch—*stream* GA-3
Wyatts Cem—*cemetery* AR-4
Wyatts Ch—*church* TN-4
Wyatt Sch—*school* (2) CO-8
Wyatt Sch—*school* OR-9
Wyatts Chapel—*church* KY-4
Wyatts Chapel—*church* SC-3
**Wyatts Chapel**—*pop pl* TN-4
Wyatts Chapel Sch—*school* KY-4
Wyatt Sch (historical)—*school* TN-4
*Wyatts Creek* GA-3
Wyatts Cross Roads—*locale* NC-3
Wyatts Gap—*gap* AL-4
Wyatts Grove Ch—*church* NC-3
Wyatt Spring—*spring* AR-4
Wyatt Spring—*spring* UT-8
Wyatts Run—*stream* WV-2
*Wyatt Station Baptist Church* AL-4
Wyatt's Tavern-Fort Morrow Site—*hist pl* OH-6
Wyatt Street Shotgun House Hist Dist—*hist pl* TX-5
Wyatt Swamp—*stream* VA-3
Wyatt Tank—*reservoir* AZ-5
**Wyatt Village**—*pop pl* TN-4
Wyattville—*locale* MN-6
**Wyattville**—*pop pl* PA-2
Wybark—*locale* OK-5
**Wyben**—*pop pl* MA-1
Wyben Chapel—*church* MA-1
Wyble Sch—*school* MI-6
Wyboo Swamp—*stream* SC-3
WYCA-FM (Hammond)—*tower* IN-6
**Wycamp**—*pop pl* AR-4
Wycamp Creek—*stream* MI-6
Wycamp Creek Site—*hist pl* MI-6
Wycamp Lake—*lake* MI-6
Wych Branch—*stream* GA-3
Wyche—*locale* VA-3
Wyche Arm—*bay* FL-3
Wyche Canyon—*valley* NM-5
Wyche Cem—*cemetery* LA-4
Wyche Cem—*cemetery* VA-3
Wyche Draw—*valley* NM-5
Wyche Ranch—*locale* TX-5
Wyches Bayou—*stream* LA-4
Wyche Tank—*reservoir* NM-5
Wychmere Harbor—*harbor* MA-1
Wychmere Harbor Jetty Light—*locale* MA-1
Wychoff Ditch—*canal* NE-7
Wychoff Ranch—*locale* NE-7
*Wyckham Creek* MT-8
Wyck House—*hist pl* PA-2
Wyckles—*locale* IL-6
*Wyckles Corner* IL-6
**Wyckles Corners**—*pop pl* IL-6
Wyckoff—*locale* NY-2
**Wyckoff**—*pop pl* NJ-2
Wyckoff, Pieter, House—*hist pl* NY-2
Wyckoff Airstrip—*airport* IN-6
Wyckoff-Bennett Homestead—*hist pl* NY-2
Wyckoff Cem—*cemetery* OH-6
Wyckoff Heights—*uninc pl* NY-2
Wyckoff (historical)—*locale* KS-7
Wyckoff Lake—*lake* (2) MI-6
Wyckoff Lake—*reservoir* NJ-2
**Wyckoff Mills**—*pop pl* NJ-2
Wyckoff Sch—*school* MO-7
*Wyckoffs Mills* NJ-2
Wyckoffs Mills—*locale* NJ-2
*Wyckoff Station* KS-7
*Wyckoff Station* NY-2
**Wyckoff (Township of)**—*pop pl* NJ-2
Wyckstrom Lake—*lake* MN-6
Wycle Fork—*stream* NC-3
**Wycliff (subdivision)**—*pop pl* DE-2
Wycliff West Shop Ctr—*locale* KS-7
**Wyco**—*pop pl* WV-2
**Wyco**—*pop pl* WY-8
Wyco Club—*locale* WY-8
Wyco Drive Sch—*school* CO-8
Wycoff—*uninc pl* WA-9
Wycoff Cem—*cemetery* NY-2
Wycoff Community Hall—*building* KS-7
Wycoff Creek—*stream* OR-9
Wycoff Hollow—*valley* OH-6
Wycoff Ranch—*locale* CA-9
Wycoff Sch—*school* KS-7
**Wycombe**—*pop pl* PA-2
Wycombe Post Office (historical)—*building* PA-2
Wycombe Village Hist Dist—*hist pl* PA-2
**Wycon**—*pop pl* WY-8
*Wycott* PA-2
Wycough Branch—*stream* AR-4
Wycough-Jones House—*hist pl* AR-4
Wycough (Township of)—*fmr MCD* AR-4
WYCQ-FM (Shelbyville)—*tower* TN-4
WYCR-FM (York-Hanover)—*tower* PA-2
Wycroff Run—*stream* WV-2
Wycroft Canyon—*valley* UT-8
Wycroft Spring—*spring* UT-8
Wycross—*locale* WY-8
Wycross Ditch—*canal* WY-8
Wycross Ranch—*locale* WY-8
*Wydasville* PA-2
Wyda Way Sch—*school* CA-9
WYDD-FM (Pittsburgh)—*tower* PA-2
WYDE-AM (Birmingham)—*tower* AL-4
WYDK-AM (Yadkinville)—*tower* NC-3
Wydner Hollow—*valley* VA-3
**Wydnor**—*pop pl* PA-2
Wydown-Forsyth District—*hist pl* MO-7
Wye—*locale* AR-4
**Wye**—*pop pl* AR-4
**Wye**—*pop pl* MS-4
Wye, The—*lake* FL-3
Wye, The—*locale* AL-4
Wye, The—*locale* CA-9
Wye, The—*locale* GA-3
**Wye, The**—*pop pl* TN-4
WYEA-AM (Sylacauga)—*tower* AL-4
Wy'east Basin—*basin* OR-9
Wye Barricade—*locale* WA-9
**Wyebrooke**—*pop pl* PA-2
Wye Cem—*cemetery* AR-4
Wye Ch—*church* MD-2
**Wye (Chisney)**—*pop pl* OK-5
Wyecott Lake—*reservoir* AL-4
Wyecott Lake Dam—*dam* AL-4
Wyecott Plantation—*locale* AL-4
Wye Creek—*stream* AK-9
Wye Creek—*stream* ID-8
Wye Creek—*stream* WA-9
Wye East River—*stream* MD-2
Wye Hollow—*valley* TN-4
Wye House—*hist pl* MD-2
Wye Island—*island* MD-2
Wye Lake—*lake* MN-6
Wye Lake—*lake* MS-4
Wye Lake—*lake* WA-9
**Wye Lake**—*pop pl* WA-9
Wye Landing—*locale* MD-2
Wyemaha Valley—*basin* NV-8
Wye Mill—*hist pl* MD-2
**Wye Mills**—*pop pl* MD-2
**Wye Mills (sta.)**—*pop pl* MD-2
Wye Mountain—*ridge* AR-4
Wye Narrows—*channel* MD-2
Wye Neck—*cape* MD-2
Wye Oak State Park—*park* MD-2
WYEP-FM (Pittsburgh)—*tower* PA-2
Wye Radioactive Waste Dump—*other* WA-9
Wyer Island—*island* ME-1
Wye River—*stream* MD-2
Wyerough Run—*stream* PA-2
Wyer-Pearce House—*hist pl* MN-6
Wyers Cem—*cemetery* OH-6
*Wyers Creek* MO-7
Wyers Point—*cape* MA-1
Wye (Siding)—*locale* CA-9
Wye Siding—*locale* TX-5
*Wyesocking* NC-3
Wyeth—*locale* CA-9
**Wyeth**—*pop pl* MO-7
**Wyeth**—*pop pl* OR-9
Wyeth, John, House—*hist pl* MA-1
Wyeth Brickyard Superintendent's House—*hist pl* MA-1
Wyeth Cave—*cave* PA-2
Wyeth Flats—*hist pl* MO-7
Wyeth Glacier—*glacier* WA-9
Wyethia Creek—*stream* MT-8
*Wyeth Isla* OR-9
Wyeth Rock—*pillar* AL-4
Wyeth-Smith House—*hist pl* MA-1
Wyeth Trail—*trail* OR-9
Wye Town Farm House—*hist pl* MD-2
Wyetown Point—*cape* MD-2
Wye (Township of)—*fmr MCD* AR-4
Wyett—*locale* KY-4
**Wyeville**—*pop pl* WI-6
WYFI-FM (Norfolk)—*tower* VA-3
WYFL-FM (Henderson)—*tower* (2) NC-3
WYFM-FM (Sharon)—*tower* PA-2
Wygal Spring—*spring* CA-9
Wygant Hill—*summit* AL-4
Wygant Sch—*school* NY-2
Wygant State Park—*park* OR-9
Wygant Trail—*trail* OR-9

Wygaret Terrace—bench ... UT-8
WYHY-FM (Lebanon)—tower ... TN-4
WYIS-AM (Phoenixville)—tower ... PA-2
Wyit Sprowls Covered Bridge—hist pl ... PA-2
**Wykagyl**—pop pl ... NY-2
Wykagyl Country Club—other ... NY-2
**Wykagyl Park**—pop pl ... NY-2
WYKC-AM (Grenada)—tower ... MS-4
Wyke Cem—cemetery ... NC-3
Wykee Lake—lake ... WY-8
Wykee Peak—summit ... WY-8
**Wykeham (Township of)**—pop pl ... MN-6
Wykers Island ... PA-2
Wykertown—locale ... NJ-2
WYKK-FM (Quitman)—tower ... MS-4
Wykle Hill—summit ... NC-3
Wykle Run—stream ... PA-2
Wykles Mill (historical)—locale ... AL-4
**Wykoff**—pop pl ... MN-6
Wykoff Branch—stream ... PA-2
Wykoff Hollow—valley ... PA-2
Wykoff Run—stream ... PA-2
Wykoff Run State For Natural Area—area ... PA-2
**Wylam**—pop pl ... AL-4
Wylam Mine (underground)—mine ... AL-4
Wylam Number 4 Mine (underground)—mine ... AL-4
Wylam Park—park ... AL-4
Wylam Sch—school ... AL-4
Wylandanch ... NY-2
Wyland Ditch—canal ... IN-6
Wyland Elem Sch—school ... PA-2
Wyland Lake—lake ... IN-6
Wyland Sch ... PA-2
**Wylandville**—pop pl ... PA-2
Wylandville Elem Sch—school ... PA-2
Wylaunee—locale ... AL-4
Wylaunee Creek ... AL-4
Wylaunee Creek—stream ... AL-4
Wyldes Village ... ME-1
Wyldewood Camp—locale ... AR-4
Wyle Cem—cemetery ... PA-2
Wyler Foods—facility ... IL-6
Wyles Brook—stream ... ME-1
Wyles Cem—cemetery ... AR-4
Wyles Pond Slough—stream ... AR-4
Wyleswood Lake—reservoir ... OH-6
Wylettie Flat—flat ... CA-9
Wyley Creek—stream ... ID-8
Wyley Ditch—canal ... IN-6
Wyley Glade—flat ... CA-9
Wyley Hollow—valley ... KY-4
Wyleys Knob—summit ... CA-9
Wylie—locale ... PA-2
**Wylie**—pop pl ... MN-6
**Wylie**—pop pl ... PA-2
**Wylie**—pop pl (2) ... TX-5
Wylie, Andrew, House—hist pl ... IN-6
Wylie, Lake—reservoir ... NC-3
Wylie, Lake—reservoir ... SC-3
Wylie Ave Sch (abandoned)—school ... PA-2
Wylie Bend—bend ... TN-4
Wylie Branch—stream ... AL-4
Wylie Brook—stream ... NY-2
Wylie Canyon—valley ... CA-9
Wylie Cem—cemetery ... MS-4
Wylie Cem—cemetery (2) ... NY-2
Wylie Cem—cemetery (2) ... TN-4
Wylie Chapel—church ... WV-2
Wylie Creek—stream ... ID-8
Wylie Dam—dam ... SC-3
Wylie Draw—valley ... NM-5
Wylie Falls—falls ... VA-3
Wylie Gulch ... OR-9
Wylie Gulch—valley ... CO-8
Wylie Gulch—valley ... ID-8
Wylie Gulch—valley ... OR-9
Wylie Half Windmill—locale ... TX-5
Wylie Hill Lake Number One—reservoir ... AL-4
Wylie Hill Number 1 Dam—dam ... AL-4
Wylie Hill Number 2 Dam—dam ... AL-4
Wylie Island ... GA-3
Wylie Island—island ... WV-2
Wylie Knob—summit ... ID-8
Wylie Lake—lake ... SD-7
Wylie Memorial Ch—church ... TX-5
Wylie Morgan Tank—reservoir ... NM-5
Wylie Mountains—range ... TX-5
Wylie Mtn—summit ... VA-3
Wylie Park—park ... SC-3
Wylie Park—park ... SD-7
Wylie Park Pavilion—hist pl ... SD-7
Wylie Picnic Area—park ... AR-4
Wylie Retreat—locale ... UT-8
Wylie Run—stream ... PA-2
Wylie Sch—school ... KY-4
Wylie Sch—school ... PA-2
Wylie Sch—school ... TN-4
Wylies Creek—stream ... NC-3
Wylies Creek—stream ... SC-3
Wylie Sewage Disposal—other ... TX-5
Wylies Landing—locale ... MS-4
Wylies Peak—summit ... ID-8
**Wylie Spur**—pop pl ... AR-4
Wylies Ridge—ridge ... ID-8
Wylies Run—stream ... VA-3
Wylie (sta.)—uninc pl ... PA-2
Wylie Tank—reservoir ... NM-5
**Wylie (Township of)**—pop pl ... MN-6
Wylliesburg—locale ... VA-3
Wyllis Lake ... MI-6
Wylly Island—island ... GA-3
Wyllys Park—park ... MI-6
Wylo—locale ... WV-2
WYLS-AM (York)—tower ... AL-4
**Wyly**—pop pl ... TN-4
Wyly Cem—cemetery ... MS-4
Wyly Cem—cemetery (3) ... TN-4
Wyly Hollow—valley ... TN-4
Wyly Spring—spring ... TN-4
Wyly Well—well ... NM-5
Wyman ... MN-6
Wyman—locale ... AR-4
Wyman—locale ... KY-4
Wyman—locale ... MN-6
**Wyman**—pop pl ... IA-7
**Wyman**—pop pl ... ME-1
**Wyman**—pop pl ... MI-6
Wyman, Francis, House—hist pl ... MA-1
Wyman, Lake—lake ... FL-3
Wyman Airfield ... ND-7
Wyman Bay—bay ... ME-1
Wyman Brook—stream (4) ... ME-1
Wyman Brook Ridge—ridge ... ME-1
Wyman Cem—cemetery ... ME-1
Wyman Ch—church ... MS-4
Wyman Ch—church ... MO-7
Wyman Corner—locale ... NY-2
Wyman Creek ... WY-8
Wyman Creek—stream (2) ... CA-9
Wyman Creek—stream ... MN-6
Wyman Creek—stream (4) ... MT-8
Wyman Creek—stream ... NE-7
Wyman Creek—stream ... OR-9
Wyman Creek—stream ... WA-9
Wyman Creek—stream ... WI-6
Wyman Creek—stream ... WY-8
Wyman Dam—dam ... ME-1
Wyman Drain—stream ... MI-6
Wyman Flat—flat ... CA-9
Wyman Glade—flat ... CA-9
Wyman Gulch—valley (2) ... MT-8
Wyman Hill—summit (4) ... MA-1
Wyman Hill—summit ... NY-2
Wyman Lake—lake ... KY-4
Wyman Lake—lake (2) ... MI-6
Wyman Lake—lake ... UT-8
Wyman Lake—lake ... WI-6
Wyman Lake—reservoir ... ME-1
Wyman Lake—reservoir ... WI-6
Wyman Ledge—bar ... ME-1
Wyman Mtn—summit ... ME-1
Wyman Mtn—summit ... NY-2
Wyman Park—park ... FL-3
Wyman Park—park ... MD-2
Wyman Point—cape ... WI-6
Wyman Pond—lake ... ME-1
Wyman Pond—reservoir ... MA-1
Wyman Pond Dam—dam ... MA-1
Wyman Ravine—valley ... CA-9
Wyman Rsvr—reservoir (2) ... CO-8
Wyman-Rye Farmstead—hist pl ... WI-6
Wyman Sch—school ... CO-8
Wyman Sch—school ... MA-1
Wyman Sch—school (2) ... MO-7
Wymans Falls—falls ... VT-1
Wymans Hill ... MA-1
Wyman Spring—spring ... CA-9
Wyman Spring—spring ... OR-9
Wyman Spring—spring ... WY-8
Wyman Spring Branch—stream ... WY-8
Wymans Sch—school ... SC-3
Wyman Tavern—hist pl ... NH-1
Wyman (Township of)—fmr MCD ... AR-4
Wyman (Township of)—unorg ... ME-1
Wyman (Unorganized Territory of)—unorg ... ME-1
**Wymberley**—pop pl ... GA-3
**Wymberly**—pop pl ... GA-3
Wymer—locale ... WA-9
Wymer—locale (2) ... WV-2
Wymer Creek—stream ... OR-9
Wymer Draw—valley ... WY-8
Wymer Flat—flat ... OR-9
Wymer Glade—flat ... OR-9
Wymer Lake ... MN-6
Wymer Meadow—flat ... OR-9
Wymers Branch—stream ... KY-4
Wymoa Bay ... HI-9
Wymola—locale ... AZ-5
Wymola RR Station—building ... AZ-5
Wymond ... AL-4
**Wymore**—pop pl ... NE-7
Wymore Career Education Center—school ... FL-3
Wymore Cem—cemetery ... IL-6
Wymore Cem—cemetery ... NE-7
Wymore Ch—church ... IA-7
Wymore Creek—stream ... KS-7
Wymore Gulch—valley ... CO-8
Wymore Lake—lake ... CO-8
Wymore Lake—lake ... MT-8
Wymore Ranch—locale ... NE-7
Wymore Township—civ div ... NE-7
Wymore Valley—basin ... NE-7
Wymps Gap—gap ... PA-2
Wymps Gap—locale ... WV-2
Wymps Gap Sch (historical)—school ... PA-2
**Wynantskill**—pop pl ... NY-2
Wynants Kill—stream ... NY-2
WYNC-AM (Yanceyville)—tower ... NC-3
Wynche Sch—school ... NC-3
Wyncoop ... IN-6
Wyncoop Run—stream ... PA-2
Wyncoop Sch—school ... NJ-2
Wyncote—park ... PA-2
**Wyncote**—pop pl ... PA-2
Wyncote Elementary School ... PA-2
Wyncote Hills ... PA-2
**Wyncote Hills**—pop pl ... PA-2
Wyncote Hist Dist—hist pl ... PA-2
Wyncote Sch—school ... PA-2
**Wyncroft**—pop pl ... PA-2
Wyndal—locale ... WV-2
**Wyndale**—pop pl ... VA-3
Wyndcroft Sch—school ... PA-2
Wyndehurst—hist pl ... KY-4
**Wyndemere Crossing (subdivision)**—pop pl ... NC-3
Wyndemere Park—park ... MI-6
Wyndham—hist pl ... IN-6
**Wyndham Hills**—pop pl ... PA-2
Wyndham Lawn Home—building ... NY-2
Wyndham Springs ... AL-4
Wyndhams Springs ... AL-4
Wynding Brook Country Club—other ... PA-2
**Wyndmere**—pop pl ... ND-7
Wyndmere Municipal Airp—airport ... ND-7
Wyndmere Town Hall—building ... ND-7
**Wyndmere Township**—pop pl ... ND-7
**Wyndmoor**—pop pl ... PA-2
Wyndmoor—uninc pl ... PA-2
**Wyndmoor Estates**—pop pl ... PA-2
Wyndmoor Sch—school ... PA-2
**Wyndmoor Valley**—pop pl ... PA-2
**Wyndom**—pop pl ... PA-2
Wynds, Lake—reservoir ... KS-7
Wyne ... IN-6
Wynes Ferry (historical)—crossing ... TN-4
**Wyne Spur**—pop pl ... MT-8
Wynette (historical)—locale ... AL-4
Wynette P.O. ... AL-4
**Wyngate**—pop pl ... MD-2
Wyngate Park—park ... NY-2
Wyngate Sch—school ... MD-2
WYNG-FM (Evansville)—tower ... IN-6
**Wynglade Park**—pop pl ... PA-2
Wynhoff Canyon—valley ... WA-9
Wynhurst—hist pl ... VA-3
Wynia Store (historical)—locale ... SD-7
Wynkoop Brook—stream ... NY-2
Wynkoop Creek—stream ... NY-2
Wynkoop Ditch—canal ... IN-6
Wynkoop House—hist pl ... NY-2
Wynkoop Rsvr—reservoir ... MT-8
Wynkoop SU Rsvr—reservoir ... MT-8
**Wynmere Downs**—pop pl ... PA-2
Wynn ... IN-6
Wynn—locale ... TN-4
**Wynn**—pop pl ... PA-2
Wynn and Harrell Number 1 Dam—dam ... AL-4
Wynn and Harrell Number 2 Dam—dam ... AL-4
Wynn And Harrell Pond—reservoir ... AL-4
Wynn and Harrell Ponds ... AL-4
Wynn Branch—stream (2) ... KY-4
Wynn Branch—stream ... LA-4
Wynn Branch Creek—stream ... FL-3
Wynn Brothers Lake—reservoir ... AL-4
Wynn Brothers Lake Dam—dam ... AL-4
**Wynnburg**—pop pl ... TN-4
Wynnburg Baptist Ch—church ... TN-4
Wynnburg Methodist Ch—church ... TN-4
Wynnburg Post Office—building ... TN-4
Wynnburg Sch (historical)—school ... TN-4
Wynn Cem—cemetery (2) ... AR-4
Wynn Cem—cemetery ... GA-3
Wynn Cem—cemetery (2) ... IN-6
Wynn Cem—cemetery (2) ... KY-4
Wynn Cem—cemetery ... LA-4
Wynn Cem—cemetery ... MS-4
Wynn Cem—cemetery ... MO-7
Wynn Cem—cemetery (2) ... TN-4
Wynn Cem—cemetery ... VA-3
Wynn Ch (historical)—church ... MO-7
Wynn County (historical)—civil ... ND-7
Wynn Creek—stream ... AR-4
Wynn Creek—stream ... GA-3
Wynn Creek—stream ... ID-8
Wynn Creek—stream ... NM-5
Wynndale, Lake—reservoir ... MS-4
Wynndale Ch—church ... MS-4
Wynn Ditch—canal ... KY-4
Wynne—locale ... MD-2
**Wynne**—pop pl ... AR-4
Wynne, Mount—summit ... CA-9
Wynne, Thomas, House—hist pl ... GA-3
Wynnebrook Elem Sch—school ... FL-3
**Wynnebrook Manor**—pop pl ... PA-2
Wynne Cave—cave ... AL-4
Wynne Cave Spring—spring ... AL-4
Wynne Cem—cemetery ... AR-4
Wynne Cem—cemetery ... GA-3
Wynne Cem—cemetery ... TN-4
**Wynnedale**—pop pl ... IN-6
**Wynnefield**—pop pl ... PA-2
Wynnefield Ave.—uninc pl ... PA-2
**Wynne Fork Housing Development (subdivision)**—pop pl ... NC-3
**Wynnehaven Beach**—pop pl ... FL-3
Wynne House—hist pl ... AR-4
Wynne Lake—reservoir ... MN-6
Wynne Lake Lookout Tower—locale ... MN-6
Wynne Peak—summit ... VA-3
Wynne Point—cape ... TN-4
Wynne Ranch—locale ... TX-5
Wynne's Folly—hist pl ... NC-3
Wynnes Pit—cave ... AL-4
Wynne Spring—spring ... TN-4
Wynne State Prison Farm—other ... TX-5
Wynne (Township of)—fmr MCD ... AR-4
Wynne Watts Sch—school ... OR-9
**Wynnewood**—pop pl ... DE-2
**Wynnewood**—pop pl ... MD-2
**Wynnewood**—pop pl ... NJ-2
**Wynnewood**—pop pl ... OK-5
**Wynnewood**—pop pl (2) ... PA-2
Wynnewood—uninc pl ... TX-5
Wynnewood Ch—church ... TX-5
Wynnewood Plaza—locale ... PA-2
Wynnewood Sch—school ... PA-2
Wynnewood Station—building ... PA-2
**Wynnewood (subdivision)**—pop pl ... NC-3
Wynnewood View Cem—cemetery ... OK-5
Wynn-Habersham HS—school ... TN-4
Wynnhaven ... FL-3
Wynn House—hist pl ... GA-3
Wynn Lake ... AL-4
Wynn Lake ... MN-6
Wynn Lake—lake ... FL-3
Wynn Lake—lake ... GA-3
Wynn Lake—reservoir ... GA-3
**Wynnlum**—pop pl ... FL-3
**Wynnmere**—pop pl ... MA-1
Wynn Mtn—summit ... MT-8
Wynn Mtn—summit ... TX-5
Wynn Ponds ... AL-4
Wynn Post Office (historical)—building ... TN-4
**Wynns**—pop pl ... KY-4
Wynns Bayou—stream ... TX-5
**Wynnsboro (historical)**—pop pl ... IN-6
Wynns Bridge—bridge ... GA-3
Wynns Cem—cemetery ... KY-4
Wynns Cem—cemetery (2) ... TN-4
Wynn Sch—school ... OH-6
Wynn Sch—school ... TX-5
Wynn Sch (abandoned)—school ... MO-7
Wynn Seale JHS—school ... TX-5
Wynn Seale Sch—school ... TX-5
Wynns Grove Ch—church ... NC-3
Wynn Store (historical)—locale ... AL-4
**Wynnton**—pop pl ... GA-3
Wynnton Acad—hist pl ... GA-3
Wynnton Ch—church ... GA-3
Wynnton Sch—school ... GA-3
**Wynnville**—pop pl ... AL-4
Wynnville Community Ch—church ... AL-4
Wynnville Creek—stream ... AL-4
Wynnwood—hist pl ... GA-3
**Wynn Wood Manor**—pop pl ... PA-2
Wynnwood Park—park ... TX-5
**Wynnwood (subdivision)**—pop pl ... NC-3
**Wynola**—pop pl ... CA-9
Wynomesett ... MA-1
**Wynona**—pop pl ... OK-5
Wynona Oil Field—oilfield ... OK-5
Wynoochee (CCD)—cens area ... WA-9
Wynoochee Grange—locale ... WA-9
Wynoochee Pass—gap ... WA-9
Wynoochee River—stream ... WA-9
Wynoochee Valley—valley ... WA-9
Wynooche River ... WA-9
**Wynoose**—pop pl ... IL-6
Wynooska Lake—reservoir ... PA-2
Wynootchee River ... WA-9
Wynopits Mtn—summit ... UT-8
**Wynot**—pop pl ... NE-7
Wyno Tank—reservoir ... AZ-5
WYNS-AM (Lehighton)—tower ... PA-2
**Wyntoon**—pop pl ... CA-9
**Wynwood**—pop pl ... FL-3
Wynwood Park ... FL-3
Wynyate—hist pl ... CA-9
Wyo—locale ... CA-9
Wyoanna—locale ... PA-2
**Wyocena**—pop pl ... WI-6
**Wyocena (Town of)**—pop pl ... WI-6
Wyo Chapel—church ... NC-3
**Wyocolo**—pop pl ... WY-8
Wyodaho, Lake—lake ... WY-8
Wyodaho Lake ... WY-8
**Wyodak**—pop pl ... WY-8
Wyodak Strip Mine—mine ... WY-8
Wyoga Lake—lake ... OH-6
Wyoga Lake Park (Cemetery)—cemetery ... OH-6
Wyo Hereford Ranch Rsvr No 1—reservoir ... WY-8
Wyola—locale ... AR-4
**Wyola**—pop pl ... MT-8
**Wyola**—pop pl ... PA-2
Wyola, Lake—lake ... MA-1
Wyola Creek—stream ... MT-8
Wyolah Plantation—hist pl ... MS-4
Wyoma—locale ... WV-2
Wyoma Creek—stream ... MT-8
Wyoma Lake ... MA-1
**Wyomanock**—pop pl ... NY-2
Wyomanock Creek—stream ... NY-2
**Wyoma (subdivision)**—pop pl ... MA-1
Wyomehatchee River ... FL-3
Wyomi Creek ... FL-3
Wyomina Park Baptist Ch—church ... FL-3
Wyomina Park Ch—church ... FL-3
Wyomina Park Sch—school ... FL-3
Wyoming ... MS-4
Wyoming—hist pl ... MD-2
Wyoming—hist pl ... VA-3
Wyoming—locale ... KY-4
Wyoming—locale ... NE-7
Wyoming—locale ... WI-6
Wyoming—locale ... WY-8
**Wyoming**—pop pl ... DE-2
**Wyoming**—pop pl ... IL-6
**Wyoming**—pop pl ... IA-7
**Wyoming**—pop pl ... MI-6
**Wyoming**—pop pl ... MN-6
**Wyoming**—pop pl ... NJ-2
**Wyoming**—pop pl ... NY-2
**Wyoming**—pop pl ... OH-6
**Wyoming**—pop pl ... PA-2
**Wyoming**—pop pl ... RI-1
**Wyoming**—pop pl ... WV-2
Wyoming Angus Ranch—locale ... WY-8
Wyoming Apartments—hist pl ... DC-2
Wyoming Borough—civil ... PA-2
Wyoming Camp Ground—locale ... PA-2
Wyoming Canal—canal ... WY-8
Wyoming Canyon—valley ... WY-8
Wyoming Cem—cemetery ... IL-6
Wyoming Cem—cemetery ... IA-7
Wyoming Cem—cemetery ... LA-4
Wyoming Cem—cemetery ... MA-1
Wyoming Cem—cemetery ... MI-6
Wyoming Cem—cemetery ... WI-6
Wyoming Central Canal—canal ... WY-8
**Wyoming City (Mohawk PO)**—pop pl ... WV-2
**Wyoming (County)**—pop pl ... NY-2
**Wyoming County**—pop pl ... PA-2
**Wyoming (County)**—pop pl ... WV-2
Wyoming County Courthouse and Jail—hist pl ... WV-2
Wyoming Creek ... FL-3
Wyoming Creek—stream ... AK-9
Wyoming Creek—stream (2) ... ID-8
Wyoming Creek—stream (2) ... MT-8
Wyoming Creek—stream (2) ... WY-8
Wyoming Development Company Canal (abandoned)—canal ... WY-8
Wyoming Golf Club—other ... OH-6
Wyoming Gulch—valley ... SD-7
Wyoming Gulch—valley ... WY-8
Wyoming Gulf—valley ... NY-2
Wyoming Hereford Ranch—locale ... WY-8
Wyoming Hereford Ranch Ditch No 1—canal ... WY-8
Wyoming Hereford Ranch Ditch No 2—canal ... WY-8
Wyoming Hereford Ranch Rsvr No 2—reservoir ... WY-8
Wyoming Hill—summit ... WY-8
Wyoming Hills—other ... AK-9
Wyoming Hist Dist—hist pl ... DE-2
Wyoming (historical)—locale ... KS-7
Wyoming Industrial Institute—school ... WY-8
Wyoming Lake—reservoir ... DE-2
Wyoming Lake Dam—dam ... DE-2
**Wyoming (Mada)**—pop pl ... WV-2
**Wyoming Meadows**—pop pl ... OH-6
Wyoming Mine—mine ... CA-9
Wyoming Monument—other ... PA-2
Wyoming Mtn—summit ... PA-2
Wyoming Park ... MI-6
Wyoming Park HS—school ... MI-6
Wyoming Peak—summit ... WY-8
Wyoming Penitentiary Farm—locale ... WY-8
**Wyoming (P.O. name Camden-Wyoming)**—pop pl ... DE-2
Wyoming Pond—reservoir ... RI-1
Wyoming Pond Upper Dam—dam ... RI-1
Wyoming Presbyterian Church—hist pl ... OH-6
Wyoming Range—range ... WY-8
Wyoming Range Trail—trail (2) ... WY-8
Wyoming RR Station—hist pl ... DE-2
Wyoming Sch—school ... MI-6
Wyoming Sch—school ... NJ-2
Wyoming Seminary—hist pl ... PA-2
Wyoming Seminary—school ... PA-2
Wyoming Slough—stream ... IA-7
Wyoming State Capitol and Grounds—hist pl ... WY-8
Wyoming State For—forest ... PA-2
Wyoming State Penitentiary District—hist pl ... WY-8
Wyoming Station—locale ... PA-2
**Wyoming (subdivision)**—pop pl ... MA-1
Wyoming Territorial Penitentiary—hist pl ... WY-8
**Wyoming (Town of)**—pop pl (2) ... WI-6
Wyoming Township—fmr MCD ... IA-7
**Wyoming Township**—pop pl ... NE-7
**Wyoming (Township of)**—pop pl ... IL-6
**Wyoming (Township of)**—pop pl ... MN-6
Wyoming Trail—trail ... CO-8
Wyoming Tunnel—mine ... UT-8
Wyoming United Methodist Ch—church ... DE-2
Wyoming Valley—valley ... NY-2
Wyoming Valley—valley ... OH-6
Wyoming Valley—valley ... PA-2
Wyoming Valley—valley ... WI-6
Wyoming Valley Interchange ... PA-2
Wyoming Village Hist Dist—hist pl ... NY-2
Wyoming Village Hist Dist—hist pl ... RI-1
**Wyomissing**—pop pl ... PA-2
Wyomissing Area Athletic Field—park ... PA-2
Wyomissing Borough—civil ... PA-2
Wyomissing Borough Pool—reservoir ... PA-2
Wyomissing Camp—locale ... PA-2
Wyomissing Creek—stream ... PA-2
**Wyomissing Hills**—pop pl ... PA-2
Wyomissing Hills Borough—civil ... PA-2
Wyomissing Hills Elem Sch—school ... PA-2
Wyomissing Junction—uninc pl ... PA-2
Wyomissing Park—park ... PA-2
Wyopo—locale ... WY-8
Wyper Arroyo—stream ... NM-5
Wyper Tank—reservoir ... NM-5
**Wypo**—pop pl ... WY-8
Wyre HQ—locale ... NM-5
Wyreka Cem—cemetery ... MO-7
Wyrick Branch—stream ... KY-4
Wyrick Branch—stream ... MO-7
Wyrick Cem—cemetery (3) ... TN-4
Wyrick Cem—cemetery ... VA-3
Wyrick Chapel—church ... TN-4
Wyrick Hollow—valley ... TN-4
Wyrick Ranch—locale ... AZ-5
Wyrick Spring—spring ... VA-3
Wyrick Tank—reservoir ... AZ-5
**Wyricktown**—pop pl ... TN-4
WYRN-AM (Louisburg)—tower ... NC-3
Wyrosdick Pond—reservoir ... AL-4
Wyrosdick Pond Dam—dam ... AL-4
WYRU-AM (Red Springs)—tower ... NC-3
Wyse Cem—cemetery ... MS-4
Wyse Forks ... NC-3
Wyser Bluff—cliff ... TX-5
Wyser Bottom—bend ... TX-5
Wyser Valley ... VA-3
WYSH-AM (Clinton)—tower ... TN-4
**Wyside**—pop pl ... PA-2
Wysocking ... NC-3
Wysocking Bay—bay ... NC-3
Wysong Ranch—locale ... NV-8
Wysong Run ... OH-6
Wysong Run—stream ... OH-6
Wysong Windmill—locale ... TX-5
**Wysor**—pop pl ... VA-3
Wysor Heights Hist Dist—hist pl ... IN-6
Wysor Valley—valley ... VA-3
Wysox—locale ... KY-4
Wysox—locale ... PA-2
Wysox Creek—stream ... PA-2
Wysox Elementary School ... PA-2
**Wysox (Township of)**—pop pl ... IL-6
**Wysox (Township of)**—pop pl ... PA-2
WYSP-FM (Philadelphia)—tower ... PA-2
Wysses HS—school ... KS-7
WYSS-FM (Saegertown)—tower ... PA-2
**Wythe**—pop pl ... VA-3
Wythe Cem—cemetery ... IL-6
**Wythe (County)**—pop pl ... VA-3
Wythe House—hist pl ... VA-3
Wythe HS—school ... VA-3
Wythe Sch—school ... VA-3
**Wythe (Township of)**—pop pl ... IL-6
**Wytheville**—pop pl ... VA-3
Wytheville Community Coll—school ... VA-3
Wytheville Golf Club—other ... VA-3
Wytheville Natl Fish Hatchery No 1—other ... VA-3
Wytheville Natl Fish Hatchery No 2—other ... VA-3
Wytheville Sanitarium and Hosp—hospital ... VA-3
Wythougan Park—park ... IN-6
WYTK-FM (Washington)—tower ... PA-2
WYTM-FM (Fayetteville)—tower ... TN-4
Wyton—locale ... IL-6
**Wytopitlock**—pop pl ... ME-1
Wytopitlock Lake—lake ... ME-1
Wytopitlock Stream—stream ... ME-1
Wyuka Cem—cemetery (2) ... NE-7
Wyuka Cemetery—hist pl ... NE-7
WYUS-AM (Milford)—tower ... DE-2
Wyuta—locale ... UT-8
**Wyuta**—pop pl ... WY-8
Wyvill Reef—bar ... AK-9
WYXI-AM (Athens)—tower ... TN-4
WYYD-FM (Raleigh)—tower ... NC-3
WYZD-AM (Dobson)—tower ... NC-3
WYZZ-FM (Wilkes-Barre)—tower ... PA-2
WZBO-FM (Edenton)—tower ... NC-3
WZBR-AM (Amory)—tower ... MS-4
WZBT-FM (Gettysburg)—tower ... PA-2
WZDQ-FM (Humboldt)—tower (2) ... TN-4
WZEZ-FM (Nashville)—tower ... TN-4
WZKB-FM (Wallace)—tower ... NC-3
WZKX-FM (Gulfport)—tower ... MS-4
WZKY-AM (Albemarle)—tower ... NC-3
WZLQ-FM (Tupelo)—tower ... MS-4
WZLT-FM (Lexington)—tower ... TN-4
WZMB-FM (Greenville)—tower (2) ... NC-3
WZOB-AM (Fort Payne)—tower ... AL-4
WZOO-AM (Asheboro)—tower ... NC-3
WZPR-FM (Meadville)—tower ... PA-2
WZTA-FM (Tamaqua)—tower ... PA-2
WZTN-AM (Montgomery)—tower ... AL-4
WZTV-TV (Nashville)—tower (2) ... TN-4
WZVN-FM (Lowell)—tower ... IN-6
WZWZ-FM (Kokomo)—tower ... IN-6
WZXI-FM (Gastonia)—tower ... NC-3
WZXR-FM (Memphis)—tower ... TN-4
WZXY-FM (Kingsport)—tower ... TN-4
WZYC-FM (Newport)—tower ... NC-3
WZYP-FM (Athens)—tower (2) ... AL-4
WZYX-AM (Cowan)—tower ... TN-4
WZYZ-FM (Fairmont)—tower ... NC-3
WZZA-AM (Tuscumbia)—tower ... AL-4
WZZB-FM (Centreville)—tower ... MS-4
WZZD-AM (Philadelphia)—tower ... PA-2
WZZE-FM (Hockessin)—tower ... DE-2
WZZK-FM (Birmingham)—tower ... AL-4
WZZO-FM (Bethlehem)—tower ... PA-2
WZZQ-FM (Terra Haute)—tower ... IN-6
WZZY-FM (Winchester)—tower ... IN-6
W03A-TV (Russellville)—tower ... AL-4
W09B-TV (D'Iberville)—tower ... MS-4
W 4 Ranch—locale ... WY-8
W45A-TV (Columbia)—tower ... MS-4
W68B-TV (Driver)—tower ... VA-3
W 9-B Canal—canal ... WA-9

# X

X, The—*lake* FL-3
**X, The**—*pop pl* MA-1
**Xanadu Subdivision**—*pop pl* UT-8
X A Tank—*reservoir* AZ-5
Xaverian HS—*school* NY-2
**Xavier**—*pop pl* KS-7
Xavier Dock—*locale* FM-9
Xavier HS—*school* AZ-5
Xavier HS—*school* FM-9
Xavier Preparatory Sch—*school* LA-4
Xavier Sch—*school* MA-1
Xavier Sch—*school* TX-5
Xavier Univ—*school* LA-4
Xavier Univ—*school* OH-6
*Xavier (Xavier University)* OH-6
X Bar One Ranch—*locale* AZ-5
X Bar One Ranch Airstrip—*airport* AZ-5
X Bar Ranch—*locale* NM-5
X Bar Tank—*reservoir* NM-5
X Bar U Windmill—*locale* NM-5
X Bar 7 Ranch—*locale* CO-8
X Branch—*stream* MO-7
X B Tank—*reservoir* AZ-5
X Canal—*canal* ID-8
X Canyon—*valley* AZ-5
X Crossing—*locale* MT-8
Xddox Run—*stream* WV-2
X Drain—*canal* CA-9
Xebec Industrial Park Heliport—*airport* NV-8
*Xenia* IN-6
Xenia—*locale* CO-8
**Xenia**—*pop pl* IL-6
**Xenia**—*pop pl* (2) IA-7
**Xenia**—*pop pl* KS-7
**Xenia**—*pop pl* OH-6
Xenia Cem—*cemetery* (2) IA-7
Xenia Oil Field—*oilfield* CO-8
Xenia Oil Field—*other* IL-6
Xenia Sch—*school* MO-7
Xenia Sch—*school* NE-7
**Xenia (Township of)**—*pop pl* IL-6
**Xenia (Township of)**—*pop pl* OH-6
**Xenophon**—*pop pl* TN-4
Xenophon Post Office (historical)—*building* TN-4
Xerxes Post Office (historical)—*building* TN-4
Xerxes Sch—*school* KY-4
X E Tank—*reservoir* AZ-5
XH Crossing—*locale* WY-8
XIL Tank—*reservoir* AZ-5
Ximanies Creek—*stream* FL-3
Ximenes Chapel—*hist pl* TX-5
Ximenez-Fatio House—*hist pl* FL-3
XI Ranch—*locale* KS-7
X Iron Duke—*mine* UT-8
XI Spring—*spring* OR-9
X I Tank—*reservoir* AZ-5
XIT Bennett Well—*well* TX-5
XIT General Office—*hist pl* TX-5
XIT Ranch—*locale* KS-7
XIT Thirtysix Well—*well* TX-5
X I Well—*well* AZ-5
XJ Ranch—*locale* NV-8
X Lateral—*canal* CA-9
X Lazy F Ranch—*locale* CO-8
X L Lake—*lake* FL-3
X L Mine—*mine* ID-8
XL Ranch Ind Res—*24 (1980)* CA-9
Xmas Canyon—*valley* UT-8
*Xmas Creek* OR-9
Xmas Mtn—*summit* UT-8
Xmas Tank—*reservoir* TX-5
**X-Prairie**—*pop pl* MS-4
X-Prairie Cem—*cemetery* MS-4
X-Prairie Methodist Ch—*church* MS-4
X-Prairie Post Office (historical)—*building* MS-4
XQZ Ranch—*locale* TX-5
X-Ray Cem—*cemetery* TX-5
X-Ray Gas Field—*oilfield* TX-5
X-Ray Mine—*mine* CA-9
X-Ray Tunnel—*mine* NV-8
X Rock—*pillar* CO-8
X Rock Campground—*locale* CO-8
XSX Corral—*locale* NM-5
X S X Corral—*other* NM-5
X S X Ranch—*locale* NM-5
X S X Tank—*reservoir* NM-5
XT Draw—*valley* NM-5
X T Ranch—*locale* NM-5
X-T Ranch—*locale* SD-7
XT Spring—*spring* NM-5
X T Tank—*reservoir* NM-5
X T Wells—*well* NM-5
*X-Way* NC-3
X Way Mill Pond—*reservoir* NC-3
X Way Mill Pond Dam—*dam* NC-3
X X Ranch—*locale* WY-8
X-Y Canal—*canal* CO-8
Xylon Park—*park* MN-6
X Ziltner Dam—*dam* SD-7
X-10 Reactor, Oak Ridge Natl Laboratory—*hist pl* TN-4
X 4 Windmill—*locale* NM-5
X-7 Ranch—*locale* NM-5
X 9 Ranch—*locale* AZ-5

*Y, The* LA-4
Y, The—*locale* AL-4
Y, The—*locale* CA-9
**Y, The**—*pop pl* TN-4
**Y, The**—*pop pl* WV-2
**Yaak**—*pop pl* MT-8
Yaak Campground—*locale* MT-8
Yaak Community Center—*locale* MT-8
Yaak Falls—*falls* MT-8
*Yaak Mountain* ID-8
Yaak Mtn—*summit* MT-8
Yaak River—*stream* MT-8
Yaak Sch—*school* MT-8
**Yaak Valley**—*pop pl* MT-8
Yaak Valley Ch—*church* MT-8
Yaam Cem—*cemetery* FM-9
*Yaamo* MP-9
Yaamo—*island* MP-9
*Yaamo-To* MP-9
Yaara Tsu—*bar* FM-9
Yabach—*locale* FM-9
**Yabai**—*pop pl* GU-9
Yabbenohr—*island* MP-9
Yablonski Ranch—*locale* MT-8
*Yaboch* FM-9
**Yabucoa**—*pop pl* PR-3
Yabucoa (Municipio)—*civil* PR-3
Yabucoa (Pueblo)—*fmr MCD* PR-3
Yabut Lake—*lake* MN-6
Yabut Pass—*gap* UT-8
*Yacca Island* TX-5
**Yachats**—*pop pl* OR-9
Yachats Grange—*locale* OR-9
Yachats Memorial Park—*cemetery* OR-9
*Yachats Mtn* OR-9
Yachats Mtn—*summit* OR-9
Yachats Ocean Road State Park—*park* OR-9
Yachats Ridge—*ridge* OR-9
Yachats River—*stream* OR-9
Yachats State Park—*park* OR-9
Yach Bridge—*bridge* OR-9
Yacherk (Site)—*locale* AK-9
**Yach (historical)**—*pop pl* OR-9
Yacht Basin—*bay* FL-3
Yacht Basin—*bay* NC-3
Yacht Basin—*harbor* FL-3
Yacht Channel—*channel* FL-3
Yacht Club Bay—*bay* CA-9
Yacht Club Bay Dam Number 15—*dam* AL-4
Yacht Club Bay Dam Number 8—*dam* AL-4
Yacht Club Bay Lake Number 15—*reservoir* AL-4
Yacht Club Bay Lake Number 8—*reservoir* AL-4
**Yacht Club Bay (subdivision)**—*pop pl* AL-4
Yacht Club Camp—*locale* AL-4
*Yacht Harbor* NV-8
Yacht Harbor—*bay* IL-6
Yacht Harbor—*harbor* (2) CA-9
Yacht Harbor—*uninc pl* FL-3
Yacht Haven—*locale* WA-9
**Yacht Haven**—*pop pl* VA-3
**Yacht Haven Estates**—*pop pl* VA-3
Yacko Creek—*stream* AK-9
*Yackson Canyon* WA-9
**Yacolt**—*pop pl* WA-9
Yacolt (CCD)—*cens area* WA-9
Yacolt Creek—*stream* WA-9
Yacolt Mtn—*summit* WA-9
Yacolt Rsvr—*reservoir* WA-9
Yacum Hill—*summit* NH-1
Yadco Lake Dam—*dam* NC-3
**Yaddo**—*pop pl* NY-2
Yaden—*locale* KY-4
Yaden Creek—*stream* OR-9
Yaden Flat—*flat* OR-9
Yadkin—*locale* VA-3
**Yadkin**—*pop pl* NC-3
Yadkin Branch—*stream* NC-3
Yadkin Ch—*church* AR-4
Yadkin Ch—*church* (3) NC-3
Yadkin Coll—*school* NC-3
Yadkin College Hist Dist—*hist pl* NC-3
Yadkin College (Township of)—*fmr MCD* NC-3
**Yadkin County**—*pop pl* NC-3
Yadkin County Airp—*airport* NC-3
Yadkin County Developmental Resource Center—*school* NC-3
Yadkin Creek—*stream* MO-7
Yadkin Falls Dam—*dam* NC-3
Yadkin Junction—*locale* NC-3
Yadkin Junction—*uninc pl* NC-3
Yadkin Recreation Park Lake—*reservoir* NC-3
Yadkin Recreation Park Lake Dam—*dam* NC-3
*Yadkin River* NC-3
Yadkin River—*stream* NC-3
**Yadkins Acres (subdivision)**—*pop pl* NC-3
Yadkin Star Ch—*church* NC-3
Yadkin (Township of)—*fmr MCD* NC-3
**Yadkin Trail (subdivision)**—*pop pl* NC-3
**Yadkin Valley**—*pop pl* NC-3
Yadkin Valley—*valley* NC-3
Yadkin Valley Ch—*church* (3) NC-3
Yadkin Valley (Township of)—*fmr MCD* NC-3
**Yadkinville**—*pop pl* NC-3
Yadkinville Country Club—*locale* NC-3
Yadkinville Elem Sch—*school* NC-3
Yadon Cem—*cemetery* TN-4
Yaeger Bly Tank—*reservoir* AZ-5
Yaeger Canyon—*valley* (2) AZ-5
Yaeger Canyon Ranger Station—*locale* AZ-5
Yaeger Cem—*cemetery* KY-4
Yaeger Lake—*lake* AZ-5
Yaeger Lake—*lake* MN-6
Yaeger Mesa—*summit* CA-9
Yaeger Mine—*mine* AZ-5
Yaeger Mine Spring—*spring* AZ-5
Yaeger RR Station—*building* AZ-5
Yaeger Spring—*spring* AZ-5
*Yaeger Tank* AZ-5
Yaeger Tank—*reservoir* AZ-5
Yaeger Valley—*valley* WI-6
Yaga Glacier—*glacier* AK-9
Yaga Peak—*summit* AK-9
Yagar Pond—*lake* MA-1
Yager—*locale* TN-4
Yager Butte—*summit* MT-8
Yager Camp—*locale* CA-9
Yager Cem—*cemetery* AR-4
Yager Cem—*cemetery* IL-6
Yager Creek—*stream* CA-9
Yager Creek—*stream* OR-9
*Yageregarairu* FM-9
Yager Gulch—*valley* MT-8
Yager House—*hist pl* (2) KY-4
Yager Junction—*locale* CA-9
Yager Lake—*lake* MN-6
Yager Mtn—*summit* VA-3
Yager Sch—*school* MO-7
Yagers Corner Sch—*school* WI-6
Yagers Gulch—*valley* CA-9
Yagers Hollow—*valley* WI-6
Yager Slough State Game Mngmt Area—*park* IA-7
Yager Valley—*valley* CA-9
Yagerville—*locale* NY-2
Yager Well—*well* MT-8
Yagger—*locale* ME-1
Yaggy—*locale* KS-7
Yaggy Cem—*cemetery* IN-6
Yaghmelngak Mtn—*summit* AK-9
Yago Creek—*stream* ID-8
Yaguina John Point—*cape* OR-9
Yagura Shoal—*bar* FM-9
Yahara Place Park—*park* WI-6
Yahara River—*stream* WI-6
Yahara Sch—*school* (2) WI-6
*Yahata-Jima* FM-9
Yahi Indian Camp ( Ishii Caves)—*locale* CA-9
Yahi Knob—*summit* NV-8
Yahmer Hill—*summit* PA-2
Yahne Canyon—*valley* WA-9
Yahney Ranch—*locale* NE-7
Yahnundasis Lake—*lake* NY-2
*Yahoe Creek* NV-8
*Yahola* FL-3
Yahola—*locale* OK-5
Yahola, Lake—*reservoir* OK-5
*Yahoney Inlet* SC-3
Yahoo Canyon—*valley* NV-8
Yahoo Creek—*stream* ID-8
Yahoo Creek—*stream* KY-4
**Yahoola**—*pop pl* GA-3
*Yahoola Creek* GA-3
Yahoola Creek—*stream* GA-3
Yahoo Lake—*lake* WA-9
Yahoola Sch—*school* GA-3
Yahoo Mtn—*summit* CO-8
Yahou Dam—*dam* AL-4
Yahou Lake—*reservoir* AL-4
Yahr Park (historical)—*locale* SD-7
*Yahshoo River* MS-4
Yah-ta-hey—*locale* NM-5
Yahta Indian Sch—*school* AZ-5
Yahtic Lake—*lake* WY-8
Yahtse Glacier—*glacier* AK-9
Yahtse River—*stream* AK-9
Yahuecas (Barrio)—*fmr MCD* PR-3
Yahweh Education Center—*school* FL-3
Yainax Agency (site)—*locale* OR-9
*Yainax Butte* OR-9
Yainax Butte—*summit* OR-9
Yainax Guard Station—*locale* OR-9
Yainax Ridge—*ridge* OR-9
Yajome—*civil* CA-9
Yakak Peninsula—*cape* AK-9
Yakala Creek—*stream* ID-8
*Yakama River* WA-9
Yakataga Glacier—*glacier* AK-9
Yakataga Ridge—*ridge* AK-9
Yakawawa Canyon—*valley* WA-9
Yake Cem—*cemetery* OK-5
Yakel House and Union Brewery—*hist pl* IL-6
Yake Ranch—*locale* TX-5
**Yakima**—*pop pl* WA-9
Yakima Air Terminal Airp—*airport* WA-9
Yakima (CCD)—*cens area* WA-9
*Yakima City* WA-9
**Yakima County**—*pop pl* WA-9
Yakima Creek—*stream* MT-8
Yakima Firing Center—*area* WA-9
Yakima Firing Center—*military* WA-9
Yakima Firing Center Aaf Airp—*airport* WA-9
Yakima Indian Agency Bldg—*hist pl* WA-9
Yakima Indian Christian Mission—*church* WA-9
**Yakima Ind Res**—*pop pl* WA-9
Yakima Ind Res HQ—*locale* WA-9
Yakima Lateral—*canal* CA-9
Yakima Mine—*mine* ID-8
Yakima Park—*flat* WA-9
Yakima Park Stockade Group—*hist pl* WA-9
Yakima Pass—*gap* WA-9
Yakima Peak—*summit* WA-9
Yakima Reservation (CCD)—*cens area* WA-9
Yakima Ridge—*ridge* WA-9
Yakima River—*stream* WA-9
Yakima Sportsmen State Park—*park* WA-9
Yakima Tieton Main Canal—*canal* WA-9
Yakima Town And Country Club—*other* WA-9
Yakima Valley Junior Coll—*school* WA-9
Yakima Valley Memorial Hospital Heliport—*airport* WA-9
Yakima Valley Sch—*school* WA-9
Yakinikak Creek—*stream* MT-8
Yaki Point—*cliff* AZ-5
Yakobi Island—*island* AK-9
Yakobi Peak—*summit* AK-9
Yakobi Rock—*other* AK-9
Yako Creek—*stream* AK-9
Yakso Falls—*falls* OR-9
Yaksum Canyon—*valley* WA-9
Yakt—*locale* MT-8
Yak Tunnel—*mine* CO-8
Yakus Creek—*stream* ID-8
Yakutania Point—*cape* AK-9
**Yakutat**—*pop pl* AK-9
Yakutat Airp—*airport* AK-9
Yakutat Bay—*bay* AK-9
Yakutat Foreland—*area* AK-9
Yakutat Glacier—*glacier* AK-9
Yakutat Roads—*channel* AK-9
*Yal* CA-9
*Yalabutch* MS-4
**Yalaha**—*pop pl* FL-3
*Yalaka Creek* NC-3
**Yalaka (historical)**—*pop pl* FL-3
*Yalaka Mountain* NC-3
*Yalaka Mountains* NC-3
*Yalap* PW-9
*Yale* AL-4
*Yale* CO-8
*Yale* MI-6
Yale—*locale* AR-4
Yale—*locale* (2) ID-8
Yale—*locale* KS-7
Yale—*locale* NY-2
Yale—*locale* VA-3
Yale—*locale* WA-9
**Yale**—*pop pl* IL-6
**Yale**—*pop pl* IA-7
**Yale**—*pop pl* (2) MI-6
**Yale**—*pop pl* (2) OH-6
**Yale**—*pop pl* OK-5
**Yale**—*pop pl* SD-7
**Yale**—*pop pl* TX-5
Yale—*post sta* CT-1
Yale—*uninc pl* CA-9
Yale, Darwin E., House—*hist pl* MN-6
Yale, Lake—*lake* FL-3
Yale, Mount—*summit* CO-8
Yale Arm—*bay* AK-9
Yale Boathouse—*other* CT-1
Yale Bowl—*hist pl* CT-1
Yale Bridge—*hist pl* WA-9
Yale Brook—*stream* NY-2
Yale Camp—*locale* AR-4
Yale (CCD)—*cens area* OK-5
Yale Cem—*cemetery* MO-7
Yale Cem—*cemetery* OH-6
Yale Ch—*church* OH-6
Yale Coll (historical)—*school* (2) MS-4
Yale Community Center—*locale* MS-4
Yale Corners—*locale* NY-2
Yale Creek—*stream* AK-9
Yale Creek—*stream* CA-9
Yale Creek—*stream* ID-8
Yale Creek—*stream* OR-9
**Yalecrest Heights Subdivision**—*pop pl* UT-8
**Yalecrest Park Subdivision**—*pop pl* UT-8
**Yalecroft Subdivision**—*pop pl* UT-8
Yale Crossing—*locale* UT-8
Yale Dam—*dam* WA-9
Yale Engineering Camp—*locale* CT-1
Yale Forest Sch (historical)—*school* PA-2
Yale Gardens Park—*park* MN-6
**Yale Gardens Subdivision**—*pop pl* UT-8
Yale Glacier—*glacier* AK-9
Yale Harbor—*harbor* NJ-2
Yale Hardware Store—*hist pl* MN-6
**Yale Heights Subdivision**—*pop pl* UT-8
Yale (historical)—*locale* MS-4
Yale Lake—*reservoir* WA-9
Yale-New Haven Med Ctr—*hospital* CT-1
Yale Park—*park* MI-6
Yale Park—*park* NM-5
**Yale Park Subdivision**—*pop pl* UT-8
Yale Point—*cliff* AZ-5
Yale Preschool—*school* FL-3
*Yale Rsvr* WA-9
Yale Sch—*school* FL-3
Yale Sch—*school* (2) IL-6
Yale Sch—*school* IA-7
Yale Sch—*school* MT-8
Yale Sch (historical)—*school* MO-7
Yale Siding—*locale* NE-7
Yale Street Baptist Ch—*church* MS-4
**Yale (subdivision)**—*pop pl* NC-3
**Yalesville**—*pop pl* CT-1
Yalesville Sch—*school* CT-1
Yale Township—*civ div* NE-7
Yale Univ—*school* CT-1
Yale Univ Forestry Sch—*school* CT-1
Yaleville—*locale* NY-2
**Yaleville**—*pop pl* NY-2
Yaleville Brook—*stream* NY-2
Yale Well—*well* AZ-5
Yale Yards—*locale* TN-4
Yalik Bay—*bay* AK-9
Yalik Glacier—*glacier* AK-9
Yalik Point—*cape* AK-9
*Yalla Balla* CA-9
*Yalla Balley* CA-9
*Yalla Bally* CA-9
*Yallabusha* MS-4
*Yallaha* FL-3
Yallaly Hill—*summit* ME-1
*Yally Bally* CA-9
Yalmar—*locale* MI-6
Yalmar Station—*locale* MI-6
*Yalmer* MI-6
Yalobousha Female Institute (historical)—*school* MS-4
Yalobusha Acad—*school* MS-4
**Yalobusha County**—*pop pl* MS-4
Yalobusha County Agricultural HS (historical)—*school* MS-4
Yalobusha County Courthouse—*building* MS-4
Yalobusha General Hosp—*hospital* MS-4
Yalobusha (historical)—*locale* MS-4
Yalobusha Lookout Tower—*tower* MS-4
Yalobusha River—*stream* MS-4
Yalobusha River Canal—*canal* MS-4
Yalton—*locale* IA-7
*Yam* MH-9
Yama—*locale* MO-7
Yamacraw—*locale* KY-4
**Yamacraw**—*pop pl* NC-3
**Yamacraw (historical)**—*pop pl* MS-4
Yamacrow Creek—*stream* MS-4
**Yamada (historical)**—*pop pl* OR-9
Yamani Cove—*bay* AK-9
Yamani Islets—*area* AK-9
Yama Sch (historical)—*school* MO-7
**Yamassee (historical)**—*pop pl* FL-3
Yamato—*locale* FL-3
Yamboya (historical)—*locale* SD-7
Yam Canyon—*valley* AZ-5
Yam Canyon—*valley* NM-5
*Yam Cliffs* MH-9
*Yam Grandee Creek* GA-3
*Yam Grandie Creek* GA-3
*Yamgrandy Creek* GA-3
Yam Grandy Creek—*stream* GA-3
Yam Grandy State Park—*park* GA-3
**Yamhill**—*pop pl* OR-9
Yamhill-Carlton Cem—*cemetery* OR-9
**Yamhill County**—*pop pl* OR-9
Yamhill Creek—*stream* OR-9
Yamhill Locks Park—*park* OR-9
*Yamhill River* OR-9
Yamhill River—*stream* OR-9
Yamhill Rsvr—*reservoir* OR-9
**Yamhill Station**—*pop pl* OR-9
Yamme (historical)—*locale* AL-4
*Yamme Station* AL-4
**Yampa**—*pop pl* CO-8
**Yampa**—*pop pl* IA-7
Yampa Cem—*cemetery* CO-8
**Yampai**—*pop pl* AZ-5
Yampai Canyon—*valley* AZ-5
Yampai Divide—*ridge* AZ-5
Yampai RR Station—*building* AZ-5
Yampai Tank—*reservoir* AZ-5
Yampalita Creek—*stream* TX-5
Yampa Plateau—*plateau* UT-8
Yampa Ranch—*locale* CA-9
*Yampa Reservoir* CO-8
*Yampa River* CO-8
Yampa River—*stream* CO-8
Yampa Sch—*school* CO-8
Yampas Village—*locale* AZ-5
Yampa Valley Airport—*airport* CO-8
**Yampertown**—*pop pl* AL-4
Yampo—*locale* OR-9
Yamsay—*locale* OR-9
*Yamsay Butte* OR-9
Yamsay Guard Station—*locale* OR-9
**Yamsay (historical)**—*pop pl* OR-9
Yamsay Land and Cattle Company Ditch—*canal* OR-9
*Yam Say Mtn* OR-9
Yamsay Mtn—*summit* OR-9
*Yam Say Peak* OR-9
Yamsay Ranch—*locale* OR-9
Yamsay Spring—*spring* OR-9
*Yamsey Mountain* OR-9
*Yamsi Mountain* OR-9
Yamsi Rsvr—*reservoir* OR-9
Yam Yankees Airp—*airport* NC-3
*Yanabee Creek* MS-4
*Yanabi* MS-4
Yanaby (historical)—*locale* MS-4
*Yanagi* FM-9
*Yanagi Island* FM-9
Yana Point—*summit* NV-8
Yana Stream—*stream* AK-9
Yanaway Sch—*school* IL-6
Yance Branch—*stream* AL-4

Yance Canyon—*valley* ... UT-8
*Yancey* ... AL-4
*Yancey* ... VA-3
**Yancey**—*pop pl* ... KY-4
**Yancey**—*pop pl* ... TX-5
Yancey, Bartlett, House—*hist pl* ... NC-3
Yancey, William Lowndes, Law Office—*hist pl* ... AL-4
Yancey Bay—*gut* ... AL-4
Yancey Branch—*stream* ... AL-4
Yancey Branch—*stream* ... TN-4
Yancey Cave—*cave* ... MO-7
Yancey Cem—*cemetery* ... KY-4
Yancey Cem—*cemetery* ... TX-5
Yancey County—*civil* ... NC-3
Yancey County Courthouse—*hist pl* ... NC-3
Yancey Creek—*stream* ... AR-4
Yancey Creek—*stream* ... NC-3
Yancey Creek—*stream* ... TX-5
Yancey Hill—*summit* ... MT-8
**Yancey (historical)**—*pop pl* ... TN-4
Yancey Hollow—*valley* ... VA-3
Yancey HS—*school* ... NC-3
**Yancey (Kellogg)**—*pop pl* ... TX-5
Yancey Knob—*summit* ... TN-4
**Yancey Mills**—*pop pl* ... VA-3
Yancey Park—*park* ... AL-4
Yancey Pond—*reservoir* ... GA-3
Yancey Pond—*reservoir* ... NC-3
Yancey Ranch—*locale* ... NE-7
Yancey Ridge—*ridge* ... NC-3
Yancey Rsvr—*reservoir* ... OR-9
Yanceys—*locale* ... WY-8
Yanceys Bend—*bend* ... AL-4
Yanceys Ferry (historical)—*locale* ... MS-4
*Yanceys Pond* ... GA-3
Yancey Spring—*spring* ... AL-4
Yanceys Store—*locale* ... VA-3
Yancey's Tavern—*hist pl* ... TN-4
Yanceyville—*locale* ... VA-3
**Yanceyville**—*pop pl* ... NC-3
Yanceyville Hist Dist—*hist pl* ... NC-3
Yanceyville (Township of)—*fmr MCD* ... NC-3
Yanco (historical)—*locale* ... MS-4
Yancopin—*locale* ... AR-4
Yancopin Lake—*lake* (2) ... AR-4
Yancopin Lake—*swamp* (2) ... AR-4
Yancy—*locale* ... AR-4
**Yancy**—*pop pl* ... AL-4
Yancy Cem—*cemetery* ... TN-4
Yancy Cem—*cemetery* ... TX-5
*Yancy Creek* ... AL-4
*Yancy Creek* ... TX-5
Yancy Creek—*stream* (2) ... KY-4
Yancy Creek—*stream* ... WY-8
Yancy Mills—*locale* ... MO-7
Yancy Mills Post Office—*building* ... MO-7
Yancy Mtn—*summit* ... OK-5
Yancy Sch—*school* ... VA-3
Yancy Sch (historical)—*school* ... MO-7
*Yandai Creek* ... NV-8
Yandall Spring—*spring* ... OR-9
Yandell Mtn—*summit* ... ID-8
Yandell Site—*hist pl* ... TX-5
Yandell Springs—*spring* ... ID-8
Yanert—*locale* ... AK-9
Yanert Fork—*stream* ... AK-9
Yanert Glacier—*glacier* ... AK-9
Yaney Canyon—*valley* ... CA-9
Yaney Mine—*mine* ... CA-9
Yaney Sch—*school* ... MN-6
*Yangey* ... FM-9
Yangey—*summit* ... FM-9
*Yangrandee Creek* ... GA-3
Yang Yang Lakes—*lake* ... WA-9
**Yani**—*pop pl* ... PR-3
*Yanillo Creek* ... AL-4
Yankapin Basin—*lake* ... TN-4
Yank Creek—*stream* ... CA-9
Yank Creek—*stream* ... CO-8
Yank Creek—*stream* (2) ... MT-8
Yank Creek—*stream* ... OR-9
Yank Creek Cow Camp—*locale* ... CO-8
Yanke, Louis, Saloon—*hist pl* ... WI-6
Yankee—*fmr MCD* ... NE-7
Yankee—*locale* ... CO-8
Yankee—*locale* ... NM-5
Yankee—*mine* ... UT-8
Yankee Atomic Powerplant—*building* ... MA-1
Yankee Bar—*bar* ... OR-9
Yankee Bar—*bar* ... TN-4
Yankee Bar Creek—*stream* ... ID-8
Yankee Bar Rapids—*rapids* ... OR-9
Yankee Basin—*basin* ... AK-9
Yankee Bill Flat—*flat* ... NV-8
Yankee Bill Gulch—*valley* ... NV-8
Yankee Bill Prairie—*flat* ... OK-5
Yankee Billy Ridge—*ridge* ... CA-9
Yankee Blade—*locale* ... NV-8
Yankee Blade—*valley* ... NV-8
*Yankee Blade Canyon* ... NV-8
Yankee Boy Basin—*basin* ... CO-8
Yankee Boy Mine—*mine* ... AZ-5
Yankee Branch—*stream* ... GA-3
Yankee Branch—*stream* (2) ... IL-6
Yankee Branch—*stream* ... MO-7
Yankee Branch—*stream* ... OR-9
Yankee Branch—*stream* ... SC-3
Yankee Branch—*stream* ... TX-5
Yankee Branch—*stream* ... VA-3
Yankeeburg—*locale* ... OH-6
Yankee Bush Cem—*cemetery* ... PA-2
Yankee Bush Hill—*ridge* ... PA-2
Yankee Bush Hill—*summit* ... PA-2
Yankeebush Sch (abandoned)—*school* ... PA-2
Yankee Canal—*canal* ... LA-4
Yankee Canyon—*valley* ... CA-9
Yankee Canyon—*valley* ... NM-5
Yan-Kee Canyon Oil Field—*oilfield* ... TX-5
Yankee Cem—*cemetery* ... IA-7
Yankee Cem—*cemetery* ... MN-6
Yankee Cem—*cemetery* ... TN-4
Yankee Channel—*channel* ... NY-2
Yankee Charlie Ridge—*ridge* ... MS-4
Yankee Cove—*bay* ... AK-9
*Yankee Creek* ... CO-8
*Yankee Creek* ... OH-6
*Yankee Creek* ... UT-8
Yankee Creek—*ridge* ... IL-6
Yankee Creek—*stream* (2) ... AK-9
Yankee Creek—*stream* (2) ... CO-8
Yankee Creek—*stream* ... IL-6
Yankee Creek—*stream* ... IN-6
Yankee Creek—*stream* ... MT-8
Yankee Creek—*stream* ... NE-7
Yankee Creek—*stream* (2) ... OR-9
Yankee Creek—*stream* (2) ... TX-5
Yankee Creek Dam—*dam* ... OR-9
Yankee Creek Rsvr—*reservoir* (2) ... OR-9
Yankee Creek Siphon—*other* ... OR-9
Yankee Crossing—*locale* ... OH-6
Yankee Ditch—*canal* ... MT-8
Yankee Ditch—*canal* ... WY-8
*Yankee Doodle Creek* ... UT-8
Yankee Doodle Creek—*stream* ... MT-8
Yankee Doodle Hollow—*valley* ... UT-8
Yankee Doodle Hollow Creek—*stream* ... UT-8
Yankee Doodle Lake—*lake* ... CO-8
Yankee Doodle Peak—*summit* ... AZ-5
Yankee Doodle Trail—*trail* ... AZ-5
Yankee Draw—*valley* ... WY-8
Yankee Flat—*flat* ... MT-8
Yankee Fork—*stream* ... ID-8
Yankee Girl Mine—*mine* ... AZ-5
Yankee Girl Mine—*mine* ... UT-8
Yankee Gulch—*valley* ... CA-9
Yankee Gulch—*valley* ... CO-8
Yankee Gulch—*valley* ... NM-5
Yankee Gulch—*valley* ... WY-8
Yankee Hall—*locale* ... NC-3
*Yankee Hall Landing* ... NC-3
Yankee Headframe—*hist pl* ... UT-8
Yankee Hill—*fmr MCD* ... NE-7
Yankee Hill—*locale* (2) ... CA-9
Yankee Hill—*ridge* ... CA-9
Yankee Hill—*ridge* ... OH-6
Yankee Hill—*summit* ... CA-9
Yankee Hill—*summit* (2) ... CO-8
Yankee Hill—*summit* ... SD-7
Yankee Hill—*summit* ... TN-4
Yankee Hill Cem—*cemetery* ... NE-7
Yankee Hill Cem—*cemetery* ... OH-6
Yankee Hill Cem—*cemetery* ... PA-2
Yankee Hill Ch—*church* ... OH-6
Yankee Hill Lake—*reservoir* ... NE-7
**Yankee Hills**—*pop pl* ... OH-6
Yankee Hill Sch—*school* ... NY-2
Yankee Hill Sch (abandoned)—*school* ... PA-2
Yankee Hill Sch (historical)—*school* ... PA-2
Yankee Hollow—*valley* (2) ... TN-4
Yankee Hollow—*valley* (2) ... WI-6
Yankee Horse Ridge—*ridge* ... VA-3
Yankee Horse Ridge Parking Area—*locale* . VA-3
Yankee Jim Campground and Picnic Area—*locale* ... MT-8
Yankee Jim Canyon—*valley* ... MT-8
Yankee Jim Gulch—*valley* ... CA-9
Yankee Jim Lake—*lake* ... MT-8
Yankee Jim Ranch—*locale* ... CA-9
Yankee Jim Ridge—*ridge* ... MT-8
**Yankee Jims**—*pop pl* ... CA-9
Yankee Joe Canyon—*valley* ... AZ-5
Yankee Joe Creek—*stream* ... WI-6
Yankee Joe Seep—*spring* ... AZ-5
Yankee Joe Spring—*spring* ... AZ-5
Yankee John Creek—*stream* ... CA-9
Yankee John Mine—*mine* ... CA-9
Yankee Lake—*lake* ... FL-3
Yankee Lake—*lake* ... NY-2
Yankee Lake—*lake* ... OH-6
Yankee Lake—*lake* ... WI-6
**Yankee Lake**—*pop pl* ... NY-2
**Yankee Lake**—*pop pl* ... OH-6
Yankee Landing—*locale* ... GA-3
Yankee Lane Cem—*cemetery* ... IL-6
Yankee Meadow—*flat* ... UT-8
*Yankee Meadow Dam* ... UT-8
*Yankee Meadow Reservoir* ... UT-8
Yankee Meadows—*flat* ... UT-8
Yankee Meadows Dam—*dam* ... UT-8
Yankee Meadows Rsvr—*reservoir* ... UT-8
Yankee Mines—*mine* ... UT-8
Yankee Mtn—*summit* ... OR-9
**Yankee Orchards**—*pop pl* ... MA-1
Yankee Park—*park* ... OH-6
Yankee Peak—*summit* ... ID-8
Yankee Point—*cape* ... AK-9
Yankee Point—*cape* ... CA-9
Yankee Point—*cape* ... PA-2
Yankee Point—*cape* ... VA-3
Yankee Point Breaker—*bar* ... CA-9
Yankee Point Cem—*cemetery* ... IL-6
Yankee Point Cem—*cemetery* ... IA-7
Yankee Point Cem—*cemetery* ... OH-6
Yankee Point Rock—*island* ... CA-9
Yankee Pond—*lake* ... LA-4
Yankee Reach—*channel* ... GA-3
*Yankee Reservoir* ... NY-2
Yankee Ridge—*ridge* ... AK-9
Yankee Ridge—*ridge* ... IL-6
Yankee Ridge—*ridge* ... MO-7
Yankee Ridge—*ridge* ... TN-4
Yankee Ridge Cem—*cemetery* ... MO-7
Yankee Ridge Sch—*school* ... IL-6
Yankee Ridge Sch—*school* ... MO-7
*Yankee River* ... OR-9
Yankee River—*stream* ... AK-9
Yankee Rsvr—*reservoir* ... MT-8
Yankee Rsvr—*reservoir* ... OR-9
*Yankeerun* ... OR-9
*Yankee Run* ... PA-2
**Yankee Run**—*pop pl* ... KS-7
Yankee Run—*stream* (3) ... OH-6
Yankee Run—*stream* ... OR-9
Yankee Run—*stream* (2) ... PA-2
Yankee Run Country Club—*other* ... OH-6
Yankee Run Point Public Use Area—*park* .. KS-7
Yankee Run Trail—*trail* ... PA-2
*Yankee Settlement* ... IN-6
Yankees Gap—*gap* ... PA-2
Yankee Slough—*stream* ... AK-9
Yankee Slough—*stream* ... CA-9
Yankee Spring—*spring* ... MT-8
Yankee Spring—*spring* ... NM-5
Yankee Springs Ch—*church* ... LA-4
Yankee Springs Ch—*church* ... MI-6
Yankee Springs Island—*island* ... MI-6
Yankee Springs Rec Area—*park* ... MI-6
Yankee Springs (Township of)—*civ div* ... MI-6
Yankee Stadium—*other* ... NY-2
Yankee Street Sch—*school* ... MI-6
Yankee Swamp—*swamp* ... FL-3
Yankee Tank Creek—*stream* ... KS-7
*Yankee Touladi Brook* ... ME-1
*Yankeetown* ... IN-6
Yankeetown—*locale* ... MN-6
Yankeetown—*locale* ... OH-6
Yankeetown—*locale* ... TN-4
Yankeetown—*locale* ... VA-3
**Yankeetown**—*pop pl* ... FL-3
**Yankee Town**—*pop pl* ... IN-6
**Yankeetown**—*pop pl* ... IN-6
**Yankeetown**—*pop pl* (2) ... OH-6
Yankeetown Archeol Site—*hist pl* ... IN-6
Yankee Town Cem—*cemetery* ... AL-4
Yankeetown Cem—*cemetery* ... IN-6
Yankeetown Cem—*cemetery* (2) ... OH-6
Yankeetown Elem Sch—*school* ... IN-6
Yankeetown Free Will Christian Baptist Ch—*church* ... TN-4
Yankeetown Sch—*school* ... FL-3
Yankeetown Sch (historical)—*school* ... TN-4
Yankeetuladi Brook—*stream* ... ME-1
Yankeetuladi Pond—*lake* ... ME-1
Yankee Woods—*woods* ... IL-6
Yanketown Pond—*reservoir* ... NY-2
Yankey Sawmill (site)—*locale* ... OR-9
Yank Gulch—*stream* ... OR-9
Yank Gulch—*valley* ... OR-9
*Yank Gulch Creek* ... OR-9
Yank Prairie—*flat* ... OR-9
Yanks Bayou—*gut* ... LA-4
Yanks Canyon—*valley* ... AZ-5
Yanks Gulch—*valley* ... CO-8
Yanks Pasture—*flat* ... MT-8
Yanks Spring—*spring* (2) ... AZ-5
Yank Swamp—*swamp* ... MT-8
Yank Tank—*reservoir* ... AZ-5
*Yankton* ... VA-3
**Yankton**—*pop pl* ... OR-9
**Yankton**—*pop pl* ... SD-7
Yankton, Lake—*lake* ... MN-6
Yankton, Lake—*reservoir* ... NE-7
Yankton, Lake—*reservoir* ... SD-7
*Yankton Agency* ... SD-7
Yanktonai Creek—*stream* ... ND-7
Yanktonai Dam—*dam* ... ND-7
Yanktonai Lake—*lake* ... ND-7
Yankton Carnegie Library—*hist pl* ... SD-7
*Yankton Clay Creek Ditch* ... SD-7
Yankton Clay Ditch—*canal* ... SD-7
Yankton Coll—*school* ... SD-7
Yankton College Conservatory—*hist pl* ... SD-7
Yankton College Hist Dist—*hist pl* ... SD-7
Yankton County—*civil* ... SD-7
Yankton County Courthouse—*hist pl* ... SD-7
Yankton County Poor Farm (historical)—*locale* ... SD-7
Yankton-Hillcrest Cem—*cemetery* ... OR-9
Yankton Hist Dist—*hist pl* ... SD-7
Yankton Historic Commercial District—*hist pl* ... SD-7
**Yankton Ind Res**—*pop pl* ... SD-7
Yankton Mall (Shop Ctr)—*locale* ... SD-7
Yankton Plaza (Shop Ctr)—*locale* ... SD-7
Yankton Slough—*stream* ... NE-7
Yankum Lake—*swamp* ... MS-4
Yanneichiki Island—*island* ... FM-9
*Yanno's* ... MA-1
*Yannubbee* ... MS-4
Yanovski, Mount—*summit* ... AK-9
Yantacaw Brook Park—*park* ... NJ-2
Yantacaw Park—*park* ... NJ-2
Yantacaw Pond—*reservoir* ... NJ-2
Yantacaw Sch—*school* ... NJ-2
Yanta Gas Field—*oilfield* ... TX-5
Yantarni Bay—*bay* ... AK-9
Yantarni Creek—*stream* ... AK-9
Yant Ditch—*canal* ... IN-6
*Yantecaw Pond* ... NJ-2
*Yantecaw River* ... NJ-2
Yant Flat—*flat* ... UT-8
*Yantic* ... CT-1
*Yantic* ... MT-8
**Yantic**—*pop pl* ... CT-1
*Yanticaw Brook Park* ... NJ-2
Yantic Cem—*cemetery* ... CT-1
Yantic Falls Hist Dist—*hist pl* ... CT-1
Yantic River—*stream* ... CT-1
**Yantis**—*pop pl* ... TX-5
Yantis Canyon—*valley* ... OR-9
Yantis Cem—*cemetery* ... TX-5
Yantis Ditch—*canal* ... ID-8
Yantis Gas And Oil Field—*oilfield* ... TX-5
Yantis Ranch—*locale* ... TX-5
Yantiss Ditch—*canal* ... IN-6
**Yantisville**—*pop pl* ... IL-6
**Yantley**—*pop pl* ... AL-4
*Yantley Church* ... AL-4
Yantley Creek—*stream* ... AL-4
Yantley Creek—*stream* ... MS-4
Yanty Creek—*stream* ... NY-2
Yanty Marsh—*swamp* ... NY-2
Yantz Branch—*stream* ... MO-7
Yantz Creek—*lake* ... MD-2
Yantz Hill—*summit* ... VT-1
*Yanubbe Creek* ... OK-5
*Yanubbee Creek* ... OK-5
Yanubbee Creek—*stream* ... OK-5
Yanu Branch—*stream* ... NC-3
Yanu Ridge—*ridge* ... NC-3
**Yanush**—*pop pl* ... OK-5
Yanz Drain—*canal* ... MI-6
Yap—*island* ... FM-9
*Yapa* ... FM-9
Yapahank Creek—*stream* ... NY-2
Yap Airp—*airport* ... FM-9
Yapa Park—*park* ... AZ-5
**Yap (County-equivalent)**—*pop pl* ... FM-9
**Yaphank**—*pop pl* ... NY-2
*Yap-Inseln* ... FM-9
*Yap Island* ... FM-9
Yap Islands—*island* ... FM-9
Yaple Canyon—*valley* ... NM-5
Yaple Corners—*locale* ... PA-2
Yapoah Crater—*crater* ... OR-9
Yapoah Lake—*lake* ... OR-9
Yapp Marsh—*swamp* ... MD-2
*Yappu* ... FM-9
*Yappui Island* ... MP-9
Yappui Island—*island* ... MP-9
*Yappui-To* ... MP-9
*Yappu Ko* ... FM-9
*Yappu To* ... FM-9
*Yaptown* ... FM-9
Yaqui Canyon—*valley* ... AZ-5
Yaqui Canyon—*valley* ... CA-9
Yaqui Flat—*flat* ... CA-9
Yaqui Gulch—*valley* ... CA-9
Yaqui Indian Settlement—*uninc pl* ... AZ-5
Yaqui Indian Village—*other* ... AZ-5
Yaqui Meadows—*flat* ... CA-9
Yaquina—*locale* ... OR-9
Yaquina Bay—*bay* ... OR-9
Yaquina Bay State Park—*park* ... OR-9
Yaquina Head—*cape* ... OR-9
Yaquina River—*stream* ... OR-9
Yaquina View Sch—*school* ... OR-9
*Yaquinna* ... OR-9
*Yaquinna Bay* ... OR-9
*Yaquinna Head* ... OR-9
*Yaquinna River* ... OR-9
Yaqui Pass—*gap* ... CA-9
*Yaqui Point* ... AZ-5
Yaqui Ridge—*ridge* ... CA-9
Yaqui Spring—*spring* ... AZ-5
Yaqui Tanks—*reservoir* ... AZ-5
Yaquitepec Site—*locale* ... CA-9
Yaqui Wash—*stream* ... AZ-5
Yaqui Well—*well* ... CA-9
Yaqui (Yaqui Indian Village)—*uninc pl* ... AZ-5
Yarabaru Island—*island* ... MP-9
*Yarabaru-To* ... MP-9
*Yarangachieku* ... FM-9
Yaratich Bayou—*gut* ... LA-4
Yaratich Bend—*gut* ... LA-4
Yarber Branch—*stream* ... MS-4
Yarber Pond—*reservoir* ... FL-3
Yarberry Peninsular Rec Area—*park* ... TN-4
Yarber Springs—*spring* ... AZ-5
Yarber Wash—*stream* ... AZ-5
Yarber Well—*well* ... AZ-5
**Yarbo**—*pop pl* ... AL-4
**Yarbo**—*pop pl* ... AR-4
Yarbo, Lake—*lake* ... FL-3
Yarbo Cem—*cemetery* ... AR-4
Yarbo Ch—*church* ... AL-4
Yarbo Mine—*mine* ... AZ-5
Yarbo Place—*locale* ... AR-4
Yarbor, Bayou—*stream* ... LA-4
Yarboro—*locale* ... TX-5
Yarboro Cem—*cemetery* ... TX-5
Yarboro Lake—*reservoir* ... TX-5
Yarboro Mill (historical)—*locale* ... AL-4
*Yarborough* ... AL-4
Yarborough, Rev. Frank, House—*hist pl* ... SC-3
Yarborough Branch—*stream* ... SC-3
Yarborough Branch—*stream* ... TN-4
Yarborough Chapel—*church* ... SC-3
Yarborough Crossroads—*locale* ... SC-3
Yarborough Gulf—*valley* ... TN-4
Yarborough Hollow—*valley* (2) ... TN-4
Yarborough Park—*park* ... MS-4
Yarborough Pass—*channel* ... TX-5
Yarborough Springs—*spring* ... TX-5
Yarbo Sch—*school* ... AZ-5
Yarbough Cem—*cemetery* ... NC-3
Yarbough Gap—*gap* ... AR-4
*Yarbo Wash* ... AZ-5
*Yarbo Well* ... AZ-5
Yarbro—*locale* ... NC-3
**Yarbro**—*pop pl* ... AR-4
Yarbro Cem—*cemetery* (2) ... TN-4
Yarbro Hill—*summit* ... KY-4
Yarbro Landing—*locale* ... TN-4
Yarbro Ranch (reduced usage)—*locale* ... TX-5
Yarbros Post Office (historical)—*building* ... TN-4
Yarbrough—*locale* ... AL-4
**Yarbrough**—*pop pl* ... MS-4
Yarbrough Allen Oil Field—*oilfield* ... TX-5
Yarbrough Branch—*stream* ... AL-4
Yarbrough Cave—*cave* ... GA-3
Yarbrough Cem—*cemetery* (2) ... AL-4
Yarbrough Cem—*cemetery* ... KY-4
Yarbrough Cem—*cemetery* ... MS-4
Yarbrough Cem—*cemetery* (2) ... MO-7
Yarbrough Cem—*cemetery* ... OK-5
Yarbrough Cem—*cemetery* (3) ... TN-4
Yarbrough Chapel—*church* ... MS-4
Yarbrough Ch (historical)—*church* ... MS-4
Yarbrough Dam—*dam* ... AL-4
Yarbrough Hollow—*valley* ... TN-4
Yarbrough Hotel—*hist pl* ... AL-4
Yarbrough Lake—*lake* ... TX-5
Yarbrough Lake—*reservoir* ... TN-4
Yarbrough Lake Dam—*dam* ... MS-4
Yarbrough Mine—*mine* ... KY-4
Yarbrough Place—*locale* ... NM-5
Yarbrough Pond—*reservoir* ... GA-3
Yarbrough Sch—*school* ... OK-5
Yarbrough Sch (historical)—*school* ... MS-4
Yarbroughs Ferry (historical)—*locale* ... AL-4
Yarbroughs Field (historical)—*locale* ... AL-4
Yarbroughs Lake—*reservoir* ... AL-4
Yarbroughs Mill—*locale* ... GA-3
Yarbrough Store (historical)—*locale* ... TN-4
Yarbrough Street Baptist Ch—*church* ... AL-4
Yarbro Well—*well* ... NM-5
Yarbro Well—*well* ... TX-5
Yard—*locale* ... TX-5
*Yard Center* ... IL-6
Yarde Ditch—*canal* ... IN-6
Yardeka Ch—*church* ... OK-5
Yardeka Sch—*school* ... OK-5
Yardelle—*locale* ... AR-4
Yardelle Branch—*stream* ... AR-4
Yardelle Cem—*cemetery* ... AR-4
Yard Hill—*summit* ... NY-2
Yard House—*locale* ... CA-9
Yard Island—*island* ... NH-1
Yardley—*locale* ... WA-9
**Yardley**—*pop pl* ... PA-2
Yardley, John, House—*hist pl* ... UT-8
Yardley, Thomas, House—*hist pl* ... UT-8
Yardley Borough—*civil* ... PA-2
**Yardley Farms**—*pop pl* ... PA-2
*Yardley Ferry* ... PA-2
Yardley Golf Club—*other* ... PA-2
Yardley Post Office (historical)—*building* ... PA-2
**Yardley Village**—*pop pl* ... NJ-2
*Yardleyville* ... PA-2
Yard Mtn—*summit* ... NY-2
Yard Peak—*summit* ... UT-8
Yard Pond—*lake* ... FL-3
Yard Pond—*lake* ... RI-1
**Yards**—*pop pl* ... WV-2
Yard Sch—*school* ... AL-4
Yard Sch—*school* ... TX-5
Yard Sch (abandoned)—*school* ... PA-2
Yards Creek—*stream* ... NJ-2
Yards Creek Rsvr—*reservoir* ... NJ-2
**Yards (RR name Flat Top)**—*pop pl* ... VA-3
**Yardville**—*pop pl* ... NJ-2
Yardville-Groveville—*CDP* ... NJ-2
**Yardville Heights**—*pop pl* ... NJ-2
Yardville Heights Sch—*school* ... NJ-2
Yarema Ditch—*canal* ... DE-2
Yarema Ditch—*canal* ... MD-2
Yarger Butte—*summit* ... MT-8
Yarger Cem—*cemetery* ... MT-8
Yarger Creek—*stream* ... MT-8
Yarger Ditch—*canal* ... IN-6
Yarger Drain—*canal* ... MI-6
Yarger Lake—*lake* ... AK-9
**Yargerville**—*pop pl* ... MI-6
Yarian Ditch—*canal* ... IN-6
Yarico—*locale* ... OH-6
Yarmony—*locale* ... CO-8
*Yarmony Creek* ... CO-8
Yarmony Mtn—*summit* ... CO-8
Yarmouth—*hist pl* ... MD-2
**Yarmouth**—*pop pl* ... CA-9
**Yarmouth**—*pop pl* ... IA-7
**Yarmouth**—*pop pl* ... ME-1
**Yarmouth**—*pop pl* ... MA-1
*Yarmouth, Town of* ... MA-1
Yarmouth Campgrounds—*locale* ... MA-1
Yarmouth Center (census name Yarmouth)—*other* ... ME-1
Yarmouth Creek—*stream* ... VA-3
Yarmouth Farms (historical P.O.)—*locale* ... MA-1
*Yarmouth Harbor* ... MA-1
Yarmouth Island—*island* ... ME-1
Yarmouth Island—*island* ... VA-3
Yarmouth Junction—*locale* ... ME-1
Yarmouth Ledges—*bar* ... ME-1
*Yarmouthport* ... MA-1
**Yarmouth Port**—*pop pl* ... MA-1
Yarmouth Port (RR name Yarmouth (sta.))—*CDP* ... MA-1
*Yarmouth River* ... ME-1
Yarmouth Rsvr—*reservoir* ... ME-1
Yarmouth (sta.) (RR name for Yarmouth Port)—*other* ... MA-1
**Yarmouth Station**—*pop pl* ... MA-1
**Yarmouth (Town of)**—*pop pl* ... ME-1
**Yarmouth (Town of)**—*pop pl* ... MA-1
*Yarmouth Village* ... MA-1
*Yarmouthville* ... ME-1
*Yarmoutville* ... ME-1
Yarna—*locale* ... MO-7
**Yarnaby**—*pop pl* ... OK-5
Yarnaby Cem—*cemetery* ... OK-5
Yarnall—*locale* ... TX-5
Yarnall Knob—*summit* ... NC-3
Yarnallton—*locale* ... KY-4
Yarnell—*locale* ... MT-8
Yarnell—*locale* ... WI-6
**Yarnell**—*pop pl* ... AZ-5
**Yarnell**—*pop pl* ... PA-2
Yarnell Branch—*stream* (2) ... MO-7
Yarnell Branch—*stream* ... TN-4
Yarnell Brook—*stream* ... PA-2
Yarnell Canyon—*valley* ... OR-9
Yarnell Cem—*cemetery* (2) ... TN-4
Yarnell Community Hall—*building* ... AZ-5
Yarnell Creek—*stream* ... AZ-5
Yarnell Creek—*stream* ... WI-6
Yarnell Elem Sch—*school* ... AZ-5
Yarnell Gap—*gap* ... TN-4
**Yarnell (historical)**—*pop pl* ... OR-9
Yarnell Lateral—*canal* (2) ... ID-8
Yarnell Mine—*mine* ... AZ-5
Yarnell Northeast Oil and Gas Field—*oilfield* ... KS-7
Yarnell Oil and Gas Field—*oilfield* ... KS-7
Yarnell Park—*park* ... PA-2
Yarnell Point—*cape* ... TN-4
Yarnell Post Office—*building* ... AZ-5
Yarnell Spring—*spring* ... AZ-5
Yarnell Spring—*spring* ... TN-4
Yarn Lake—*lake* ... MN-6
Yarnold Cem—*cemetery* ... MO-7
Yarnold Sch—*school* ... KS-7
Yarn Spring—*spring* ... OR-9
Yaro Creek—*stream* ... CA-9
*Yar Passage* ... PW-9
Yarprough Cliff—*cliff* ... TN-4
Yarrell Well Number Two—*well* ... TX-5
Yarrelton—*locale* ... TX-5
Yarrow—*locale* ... MO-7
Yarrow Airp—*airport* ... PA-2
Yarrow Bay—*bay* ... WA-9
Yarrow Branch—*stream* ... SC-3
Yarrow Creek—*stream* ... AK-9
Yarrow Creek—*stream* ... WA-9
Yarrow Point—*cape* ... WA-9
**Yarrow Point**—*pop pl* ... WA-9
**Yarrowsburg**—*pop pl* ... MD-2
Yarrow Spring—*spring* ... ID-8
*Yaruto* ... MP-9
*Yaruto-ko* ... MP-9
*Yaruto-to* ... MP-9
*Yaruuto Ko* ... MP-9
*Yaruuto To* ... MP-9
Yarwood Ditch—*canal* ... WY-8
Yarwood Lateral—*canal* ... AZ-5
Yaryan Ranch—*locale* ... NE-7
Yasha Island—*island* ... AK-9
Yashau Creek—*stream* ... OK-5
*Yashoo Creek* ... OK-5
*Yashti Landing* ... AL-4
*Yashu Iskitini* ... MS-4
*Yasous River* ... MS-4
Yasuda Mtn—*summit* ... AK-9
Yatahoney Creek—*stream* ... ID-8
Yatahoney Rsvr No 1—*reservoir* ... ID-8
Yatahoney Rsvr No 2—*reservoir* ... ID-8
Yatama Creek—*stream* ... WA-9
Yate Cem—*cemetery* ... TN-4
Yateman Mines (underground)—*mine* ... AL-4
*Yates* ... NY-2
*Yates* ... PA-2
Yates—*locale* ... GA-3
Yates—*locale* ... MI-6
Yates—*locale* ... NM-5
Yates—*locale* ... TX-5
**Yates**—*pop pl* ... MI-6
**Yates**—*pop pl* ... MO-7
**Yates**—*pop pl* ... MT-8
**Yates**—*pop pl* ... NC-3
**Yates**—*pop pl* ... WV-2
Yates, Florence, House—*hist pl* ... WI-6
Yates, Gov. Richard, House—*hist pl* ... IL-6
Yates Acad—*school* ... FL-3
Yates Bay—*swamp* (2) ... FL-3
Yates Bayou—*bay* ... TX-5
**Yatesboro**—*pop pl* ... PA-2
Yates Branch—*stream* ... KY-4
Yates Branch—*stream* ... MO-7
Yates Branch—*stream* (2) ... TX-5
Yates Cabin—*locale* ... MT-8
Yates Camp—*locale* ... FL-3
Yates Canyon—*valley* ... ID-8
Yates Canyon—*valley* ... TX-5
Yates Canyon—*valley* ... UT-8
Yates Cave—*cave* ... TN-4
Yates Cem—*cemetery* ... AL-4
Yates Cem—*cemetery* ... AR-4
Yates Cem—*cemetery* ... GA-3
Yates Cem—*cemetery* (2) ... KY-4
Yates Cem—*cemetery* (2) ... MS-4
Yates Cem—*cemetery* (2) ... MO-7
Yates Cem—*cemetery* ... NY-2
Yates Cem—*cemetery* ... NC-3
Yates Cem—*cemetery* (2) ... OH-6
Yates Cem—*cemetery* (7) ... TN-4
Yates Cem—*cemetery* (2) ... TX-5
Yates Cem—*cemetery* (3) ... VA-3
Yates Cem (historical)—*cemetery* ... MO-7
**Yates Center**—*pop pl* ... KS-7
**Yates Center**—*pop pl* ... NY-2
Yates Center Airp—*airport* ... KS-7
Yates Center Carnegie Library—*hist pl* ... KS-7
Yates Center City Dam—*dam* ... KS-7
*Yates Center City Reservoir* ... KS-7
Yates Center Courthouse Square Hist Dist—*hist pl* ... KS-7
Yates Center Elem Sch—*school* ... KS-7
Yates Center HS—*school* ... KS-7
Yates Center (local name for Yates)—*other* ... NY-2
Yates Center Oil Field—*oilfield* ... KS-7
Yates Center Rsvr—*reservoir* ... KS-7
Yates Chapel—*church* ... KY-4
Yates Chapel—*church* ... VA-3
**Yates City**—*pop pl* ... IL-6
**Yates Corners**—*pop pl* ... OH-6
**Yates (County)**—*pop pl* ... NY-2
Yates County Courthouse Park District—*hist pl* ... NY-2
Yates Cove—*bay* ... TX-5
Yates Cove—*valley* ... NC-3
Yates Creek—*stream* ... AL-4
Yates Creek—*stream* ... FL-3
Yates Creek—*stream* ... MS-4
Yates Creek—*stream* ... NC-3
Yates Creek—*stream* (2) ... TX-5
**Yates Crossing**—*pop pl* ... WV-2
Yates Crossroads—*locale* ... GA-3
Yates Dam—*dam* (2) ... AL-4
Yates Ditch—*canal* ... IN-6
Yates Ditch—*canal* ... MT-8
Yates Drain—*stream* ... MI-6
Yates Draw—*valley* ... TX-5
Yates Elem Sch—*school* ... FL-3
Yates-Flora House—*hist pl* ... MS-4
Yates Ford—*locale* ... VA-3
Yates Fork—*stream* ... KY-4
Yates Gulch—*valley* ... CO-8
Yates Gully—*valley* ... TX-5
**Yates Hill**—*pop pl* ... NC-3
Yates Hill—*summit* ... NY-2
Yates Hill—*summit* ... TX-5
Yates (historical)—*locale* ... SD-7
**Yates (historical)**—*pop pl* ... TN-4
Yates Hollow—*valley* ... MO-7
Yates Hollow—*valley* (2) ... TN-4
Yates Hollow—*valley* ... VA-3
Yates Hollow Mine—*mine* ... TN-4
*Yates Hot Spring* ... CA-9
Yates Hot Springs—*spring* ... CA-9
Yates HS—*school* ... TX-5
Yates Knob—*summit* ... NC-3
*Yates Lake* ... AL-4
Yates Lake—*lake* ... MN-6
Yates Lake—*reservoir* ... AL-4
*Yates Lake Dam* ... AL-4
Yates Lake Dam—*dam* ... AL-4
Yates Lake Dam—*dam* ... MS-4
**Yates (local name Yates Center)**—*pop pl* ... NY-2
Yates Lookout Tower—*locale* ... MI-6
Yates Marsh—*swamp* ... FL-3
Yates Memorial Tabernacle—*church* ... VA-3
*Yates Mesa* ... TX-5
Yates Mill—*hist pl* ... NC-3
Yates Mill Creek—*stream* ... FL-3
Yates Millpond—*reservoir* ... NC-3
Yates Millpond Dam—*dam* ... NC-3
*Yates Mountain* ... NC-3
Yates Mtn—*summit* ... AR-4
Yates Oil Field—*oilfield* ... TX-5
Yates Park—*park* ... NY-2
Yates Park—*park* ... TX-5
*Yates Peak* ... TX-5
Yates Point—*cape* ... ME-1
Yates Point—*cape* ... MN-6
Yates Ranch—*locale* ... NM-5
Yates Ridge—*ridge* ... AR-4
Yates Ridge—*ridge* ... KY-4
Yates Rsvr—*reservoir* ... AL-4
Yates Rsvr—*reservoir* ... CO-8
Yates Sch—*school* ... CA-9
Yates Sch—*school* ... IL-6
Yates Sch—*school* ... KY-4
Yates Sch—*school* ... MO-7
Yates Sch—*school* ... NE-7
Yates Sch—*school* ... NY-2
Yates Sch—*school* (2) ... VA-3

Yellow Hill—*summit* NV-8
Yellow Hill—*summit* (2) NM-5
Yellow Hill—*summit* OK-5
Yellow Hill—*summit* PA-2
Yellow Hill—*summit* TX-5
Yellow Hill—*summit* WA-9
Yellow Hill Ch—*church* (2) NC-3
Yellow Hill Ch (historical)—*church* MS-4
Yellow Hill Landing—*locale* NC-3
Yellow Hill Mine—*mine* TN-4
Yellow Hill Pond—*lake* AL-4
Yellow Hills—*summit* NV-8
Yellow Hills—*summit* UT-8
Yellow Hole Island—*island* TN-4
Yellow Hollow Creek—*stream* WY-8
Yellowhorn Mine—*mine* OR-9
Yellowhorse Flat—*flat* AZ-5
Yellowhorse Ford—*locale* SD-7
Yellow Hound Ridge—*ridge* CA-9
Yellow House—*locale* OH-6
**Yellow House**—*pop pl* PA-2
Yellowhouse Branch—*stream* AL-4
Yellowhouse Branch—*stream* KY-4
*Yellow House Canyon* TX-5
Yellow House Canyon—*valley* TX-5
Yellow House Creek—*gut* SC-3
Yellow House Draw—*valley* TX-5
Yellow House Landing—*locale* SC-3
Yellow House Oil Field—*oilfield* TX-5
Yellow House Peak—*summit* TX-5
Yellow House Ranch—*locale* TX-5
*Yellow Island* ME-1
Yellow Island—*island* AK-9
Yellow Island—*island* ME-1
Yellow Island—*island* WA-9
Yellowjacked Mine (Inactive)—*mine* CA-9
Yellowjacket—*locale* CA-9
Yellow Jacket—*locale* FL-3
**Yellow Jacket**—*pop pl* CO-8
**Yellowjacket**—*pop pl* ID-8
**Yellow Jacket**—*pop pl* MI-6
Yellow Jacket, The—*area* OR-9
Yellow Jacket Bar—*bar* AL-4
Yellow Jacket Basin—*basin* CA-9
Yellow Jacket Branch—*stream* LA-4
Yellow Jacket Branch—*stream* MS-4
Yellowjacket Branch—*stream* TX-5
Yellowjacket Butte—*summit* CA-9
Yellow Jacket Butte—*summit* CA-9
Yellowjacket Camp—*locale* CA-9
*Yellowjacket Canyon* CO-8
*Yellowjacket Canyon* UT-8
Yellow Jacket Canyon—*valley* AZ-5
Yellowjacket Canyon—*valley* AZ-5
Yellow Jacket Canyon—*valley* AZ-5
Yellow Jacket Canyon—*valley* CA-9
Yellowjacket Canyon—*valley* CA-9
Yellow Jacket Canyon—*valley* CA-9
Yellowjacket Canyon—*valley* CO-8
Yellow Jacket Canyon—*valley* CO-8
Yellowjacket Canyon—*valley* NV-8
Yellow Jacket Canyon—*valley* NM-5
Yellow Jacket Canyon—*valley* UT-8
Yellowjacket Canyon—*valley* UT-8
Yellow Jacket Cienega—*flat* AZ-5
*Yellow Jacket Creek* ID-8
*Yellowjacket Creek* UT-8
*Yellowjacket Creek* WY-8
Yellowjacket Creek—*stream* AK-9
Yellow Jacket Creek—*stream* AZ-5
Yellow Jacket Creek—*stream* CA-9
Yellowjacket Creek—*stream* (3) CA-9
Yellow Jacket Creek—*stream* CA-9
Yellowjacket Creek—*stream* CA-9
Yellow Jacket Creek—*stream* CA-9
Yellowjacket Creek—*stream* (2) CO-8
Yellowjacket Creek—*stream* GA-3
Yellow Jacket Creek—*stream* ID-8
Yellowjacket Creek—*stream* (2) ID-8
Yellow Jacket Creek—*stream* MS-4
Yellowjacket Creek—*stream* MT-8
Yellow Jacket Creek—*stream* OR-9
Yellowjacket Creek—*stream* OR-9
Yellow Jacket Creek—*stream* OR-9
Yellowjacket Creek—*stream* (2) OR-9
Yellow Jacket Creek—*stream* UT-8
Yellowjacket Creek—*stream* WA-9
Yellow Jacket Creek—*stream* WA-9
Yellowjacket Creek—*stream* WA-9
Yellowjacket Creek—*stream* WY-8
Yellow Jacket Dam—*dam* (2) AZ-5
Yellow Jacket Draw—*valley* AZ-5
Yellow Jacket Draw—*valley* CO-8
Yellow Jacket Flat—*flat* OR-9
Yellowjacket Flat—*flat* WY-8
Yellowjacket Gap—*gap* GA-3
Yellow Jacket Glade—*flat* CA-9
Yellow Jacket Glade—*flat* OR-9
Yellowjacket Guard Station—*locale* CO-8
*Yellowjacket Gulch* AZ-5
*Yellowjacket Gulch* CA-9
Yellow Jacket Gulch—*valley* AZ-5
Yellow Jacket Gulch—*valley* UT-8
Yellow Jacket Gun Club—*other* CA-9
Yellowjacket Hollow—*valley* OK-5
Yellowjacket Ice Cave—*cave* CA-9
Yellowjacket Island—*island* SC-3
Yellowjacket Lake—*lake* ID-8
Yellow Jacket Lake—*reservoir* NC-3
Yellow Jacket Lake Dam—*dam* NC-3
Yellow Jacket Mesa—*summit* (2) AZ-5
Yellow Jacket Mine—*mine* AZ-5
Yellow Jacket Mine—*mine* CA-9
Yellowjacket Mine—*mine* CA-9
Yellowjacket Mine—*mine* ID-8
Yellowjacket Mine—*mine* NV-8
Yellowjacket Mine No 1—*mine* NM-5
Yellowjacket Mine No 2—*mine* NM-5
Yellowjacket Mtn—*summit* CA-9
Yellow Jacket Mtn—*summit* GA-3
Yellowjacket Mtn—*summit* OR-9
Yellowjacket Mtns—*range* ID-8
Yellow Jacket Pass—*gap* CO-8
Yellowjacket Pass—*gap* (2) CO-8
Yellow Jacket Pass—*gap* WA-9
Yellowjacket Pass Stock Driveway—*trail* CO-8
Yellowjacket Peak—*summit* NM-5
Yellowjacket Picnic Site—*park* UT-8
Yellowjacket Place—*locale* CA-9
Yellow Jacket Point—*summit* OR-9
Yellowjacket Pueblo (5-MT-5)—*hist pl* CO-8
Yellowjacket Ranch—*locale* ID-8
Yellowjacket Ranger Station—*locale* ID-8
Yellow Jacket Ridge—*ridge* CA-9
Yellowjacket Ridge—*ridge* OR-9
Yellow Jacket Ridge—*ridge* OR-9
Yellowjacket Rsvr—*reservoir* (2) OR-9
Yellow Jacket Shaft—*mine* NV-8
Yellow Jacket Shoals—*bar* GA-3
*Yellow Jacket Spring* NV-8
Yellow Jacket Spring—*spring* (3) AZ-5
Yellowjacket Spring—*spring* AZ-5
Yellow Jacket Spring—*spring* AZ-5
Yellowjacket Spring—*spring* AZ-5
Yellow Jacket Spring—*spring* AZ-5
Yellowjacket Spring—*spring* AZ-5
Yellow Jacket Spring—*spring* (7) AZ-5
Yellowjacket Spring—*spring* AZ-5
Yellow Jacket Spring—*spring* AZ-5
Yellow Jacket Spring—*spring* CA-9
Yellowjacket Spring—*spring* CA-9
Yellow Jacket Spring—*spring* CA-9
Yellowjacket Spring—*spring* (3) CA-9
Yellow Jacket Spring—*spring* CA-9
Yellowjacket Spring—*spring* CA-9
Yellow Jacket Spring—*spring* (2) ID-8
Yellowjacket Spring—*spring* NV-8
Yellow Jacket Spring—*spring* NM-5
Yellow Jacket Spring—*spring* (3) OR-9
Yellowjacket Spring—*spring* OR-9
Yellow Jacket Spring—*spring* (2) OR-9
Yellowjacket Spring—*spring* (2) OR-9
Yellow Jacket Spring—*spring* (2) OR-9
Yellowjacket Spring—*spring* OR-9
Yellow Jacket Spring—*spring* SD-7
Yellow Jacket Spring—*spring* TX-5
Yellowjacket Spring—*spring* (3) UT-8
Yellowjacket Springs—*spring* CA-9
Yellow Jacket Tank—*reservoir* (3) AZ-5
Yellowjacket Tank—*reservoir* (3) AZ-5
Yellow Jacket Tank—*reservoir* AZ-5
Yellow Jacket Tank Number One—*reservoir* (2) AZ-5
Yellow Jacket Tank Number Two—*reservoir* (2) AZ-5
Yellowjacket Trail—*trail* (2) OR-9
*Yellow Jacket Wash* UT-8
Yellow Jacket Wash—*stream* AZ-5
Yellow Jacket Wash—*valley* AZ-5
Yellowjacket Waterhole—*lake* ID-8
Yellowjacket Well—*well* (2) AZ-5
Yellowjack Wash—*stream* AZ-5
Yellow John Mtn—*summit* AZ-5
Yellow Knob—*summit* NC-3
Yellow Knob—*summit* TN-4
Yellow Knolls—*summit* AZ-5
Yellow Knolls—*summit* UT-8
*Yellow Lake* TX-5
Yellow Lake—*lake* CO-8
Yellow Lake—*lake* FL-3
Yellow Lake—*lake* MI-6
Yellow Lake—*lake* MS-4
Yellow Lake—*lake* MT-8
Yellow Lake—*lake* NM-5
Yellow Lake—*lake* NY-2
Yellow Lake—*lake* OR-9
Yellow Lake—*lake* SC-3
Yellow Lake—*lake* (3) TX-5
Yellow Lake—*lake* (2) UT-8
Yellow Lake—*lake* WA-9
Yellow Lake—*lake* WI-6
**Yellow Lake**—*pop pl* MS-4
**Yellow Lake**—*pop pl* WI-6
Yellow Lake—*reservoir* AR-4
Yellow Lake Bayou—*lake* MS-4
Yellow Lake Bayou—*stream* LA-4
Yellow Lake Bayou—*stream* MS-4
Yellow Lake Sink—*basin* NM-5
Yellow Lead—*ridge* GA-3
**Yellowleaf**—*pop pl* AL-4
*Yellowleaf Baptist Church* MS-4
Yellow Leaf Cem—*cemetery* MS-4
Yellow Leaf Ch—*church* MS-4
Yellow Leaf Creek—*stream* (2) AL-4
Yellowleaf Creek—*stream* (2) AL-4
Yellow Leaf Creek—*stream* MS-4
**Yellowleaf Creek Estates**—*pop pl* AL-4
Yellowleaf Game Preserve—*park* AL-4
*Yellowleaf Narrows* AL-4
Yellowleaf Sch (historical)—*school* MS-4
Yellow Ledge—*bar* (2) ME-1
Yellow Ledges—*bar* UT-8
Yellow Ledges—*bench* UT-8
Yellowlick Branch—*stream* KY-4
Yellow Lookout—*locale* OR-9
Yellow Man Spring—*spring* AZ-5
Yellow Marsh Branch—*stream* NC-3
Yellow Meadow—*flat* AZ-5
Yellow Medicine Butte—*summit* AZ-5
Yellow Medicine (County)—*civil* MN-6
Yellow Medicine Hills—*summit* AZ-5
Yellow Medicine Mine—*mine* CO-8
Yellow Medicine River—*stream* MN-6
Yellow Medicine Tank—*reservoir* AZ-5
Yellow Medicine Wash—*stream* AZ-5
Yellow Metal Mine—*mine* CA-9
Yellow Mill Channel—*channel* CT-1
*Yellow Mill Pond* CT-1
**Yellow Mills**—*pop pl* NY-2
**Yellow Mound**—*pop pl* TX-5
Yellow Mountain—*locale* KY-4
Yellow Mountain—*ridge* GA-3
Yellow Mountain Ch—*church* (2) NC-3
Yellow Mountain Creek—*stream* VA-3
Yellow Mountain Gap—*gap* GA-3
Yellow Mountain Gap—*gap* (2) NC-3
Yellow Mountain Gap—*gap* TN-4
*Yellow Mtn* NC-3
*Yellow Mtn* VA-3
Yellow Mtn—*summit* CA-9
Yellow Mtn—*summit* CO-8
Yellow Mtn—*summit* CT-1
Yellow Mtn—*summit* (3) GA-3
Yellow Mtn—*summit* KY-4
Yellow Mtn—*summit* MT-8
Yellow Mtn—*summit* (2) NM-5
Yellow Mtn—*summit* (6) NC-3
Yellow Mtn—*summit* TN-4
Yellow Mtn—*summit* UT-8
Yellow Mtn—*summit* VA-3
Yellow Mtn—*summit* WY-8
Yellow Mule Ranger Station—*locale* MT-8
*Yellow One Beach* MH-9
**Yellowood**—*pop pl* PA-2
Yellow Orchard Bed (historical)—*locale* MA-1
*Yellow Paint Creek* KS-7
Yellow Patch Branch—*stream* (2) NC-3
Yellow Peak—*summit* (2) AZ-5
Yellow Peak—*summit* ID-8
Yellow Peak—*summit* NV-8
Yellow Pine—*locale* LA-4
Yellowpine—*locale* TX-5
**Yellow Pine**—*pop pl* AL-4
**Yellow Pine**—*pop pl* ID-8
Yellow Pine Bar—*bar* ID-8
Yellow Pine Campground—*locale* ID-8
Yellow Pine Campground—*locale* (2) UT-8
Yellow Pine Campground—*park* OR-9
Yellow Pine Cem—*cemetery* AL-4
Yellow Pine Creek—*stream* (2) ID-8
Yellow Pine Creek—*stream* UT-8
Yellow Pine Gulch—*valley* WA-9
Yellowpine Lake—*lake* TX-5
Yellowpine Lookout—*locale* TX-5
Yellow Pine Mine—*mine* ID-8
Yellow Pine Mine—*mine* NV-8
Yellow Pine Ridge—*ridge* CO-8
Yellow Pine Ridge—*ridge* PA-2
Yellow Pine Sch—*school* AL-4
Yellow Pine Spring—*spring* AZ-5
Yellow Pine Tank—*reservoir* AZ-5
Yellow Pine Trail—*trail* PA-2
Yellow Point—*cape* (2) AK-9
Yellow Point—*cape* FL-3
Yellow Point—*cliff* AZ-5
Yellow Point—*summit* OR-9
Yellow Point Fork Sevenmile Gulch—*valley* WY-8
Yellow Point Ridge—*ridge* WY-8
Yellow Point Valley—*valley* NM-5
Yellow Pond—*lake* AZ-5
Yellow Pond—*reservoir* OH-6
Yellow Poplar Hollow—*valley* VA-3
Yellow Pup Creek—*stream* AK-9
Yellow Rabbit Branch—*stream* TX-5
Yellow Rabbit Creek—*stream* MS-4
Yellow Rabbit (historical)—*locale* MS-4
Yellow Rabbit Lake—*reservoir* MS-4
Yellow Rabbit Post Office (historical)—*building* MS-4
Yellow Red Corners—*locale* NY-2
Yellow Ridge—*ridge* NC-3
Yellow Ridge—*ridge* OH-6
Yellow Ridge—*ridge* PA-2
Yellow Ridge—*ridge* WY-8
Yellow Ridge Ch—*church* TX-5
Yellow Ridge Island—*island* ME-1
*Yellow River* IN-6
**Yellow River**—*pop pl* IA-7
Yellow River—*stream* AL-4
Yellow River—*stream* AK-9
Yellow River—*stream* FL-3
Yellow River—*stream* GA-3
Yellow River—*stream* IN-6
Yellow River—*stream* IA-7
Yellow River—*stream* (4) WI-6
Yellow River (CCD)—*cens area* GA-3
Yellow River Cem—*cemetery* GA-3
Yellow River Cem—*cemetery* WI-6
Yellow River Ch—*church* FL-3
Yellow River Ch—*church* GA-3
Yellow River Drain—*canal* MI-6
Yellow River (historical)—*locale* AL-4
Yellow River Lookout Tower—*locale* AL-4
Yellow River Marsh Aquatic Preserve—*park* FL-3
Yellow River State Forest—*park* IA-7
Yellow River State Public Fishery Area—*park* WI-6
Yellow River State Wildlife Area—*park* WI-6
Yellow River Swamp Site 47-Bt-36—*hist pl* WI-6
Yellow Rock—*bar* (2) ME-1
Yellow Rock—*cliff* CA-9
Yellow Rock—*island* CT-1
Yellow Rock—*island* OR-9
Yellow Rock—*other* AK-9
Yellow Rock—*pillar* OR-9
**Yellow Rock**—*pop pl* KY-4
Yellow Rock—*summit* KY-4
Yellow Rock—*summit* NV-8
Yellow Rock—*summit* VA-3
Yellow Rock Canyon—*valley* NV-8
Yellowrock Canyon—*valley* NM-5
Yellow Rock Canyon—*valley* OR-9
Yellow Rock Creek—*stream* GA-3
Yellow Rock Hollow—*valley* MO-7
Yellow Rock Point—*ridge* UT-8
Yellow Rocks—*area* AK-9
Yellow Rocks—*island* CT-1
Yellow Rocks—*rock* WV-2
Yellow Rock Sch—*school* KY-4
Yellow Rock Spring—*spring* NV-8
Yellow Rock Spring—*spring* TN-4
*Yellow Rock Spring Natl Monument* AZ-5
*Yellow Rocksprings Natl Monument* AZ-5
Yellow Root Branch—*stream* FL-3
Yellow Rose Mine—*mine* CA-9
Yellow Rose Mine—*mine* CO-8
Yellow Rose Shelter—*locale* VA-3
Yellow Rose Spring—*spring* CA-9
Yellow Rose Springs—*spring* NV-8
Yellow Run—*stream* IN-6
Yellow Run—*stream* OH-6
Yellow Run—*stream* (3) PA-2
Yellow Sand Creek—*stream* MS-4
Yellows Banks—*cliff* MD-2
Yellow Seep—*spring* UT-8
Yellow Seep Wash—*valley* UT-8
Yellow Shark Channel—*channel* FL-3
Yellow Shoals Ford—*locale* TN-4
Yellow Shoulder Creek—*stream* SD-7
Yellow Slide Gulch—*valley* CO-8
Yellow Slides—*slope* CA-9
Yellow Slough—*gut* FL-3
Yellow Soda Spring—*spring* CO-8
Yellow Spot—*summit* NC-3
Yellow Spot Rsvr—*reservoir* OR-9
Yellow Spots Canyon—*valley* CA-9
Yellow Spot Well Dry—*well* OR-9
Yellow Spring—*locale* PA-2
**Yellow Spring**—*pop pl* WV-2
Yellow Spring—*spring* (2) AZ-5
Yellow Spring—*spring* (2) NV-8
Yellow Spring—*spring* NM-5
Yellow Spring—*spring* OK-5
Yellow Spring—*spring* TN-4
Yellow Spring—*spring* (2) TX-5
Yellow Spring—*spring* (2) UT-8
Yellow Spring Branch—*stream* KY-4
Yellow Spring Branch—*stream* TN-4
Yellow Spring Branch—*stream* VA-3
Yellow Spring Ch—*church* TN-4
Yellow Spring Creek—*stream* IA-7
Yellow Spring Gap—*gap* TN-4
Yellow Spring Gap—*gap* WV-2
Yellow Spring Hollow—*valley* OK-5
Yellow Spring Hollow—*valley* TN-4
Yellow Spring Hollow—*valley* VA-3
Yellow Spring Ridge—*ridge* OK-5
*Yellow Spring Run* PA-2
Yellow Spring Run—*stream* PA-2
Yellow Spring Run—*stream* VA-3
Yellow Spring Run—*stream* WV-2
Yellow Springs—*locale* TN-4
Yellow Springs—*other* PA-2
**Yellow Springs**—*pop pl* MD-2
**Yellow Springs**—*pop pl* OH-6
**Yellow Springs**—*pop pl* TN-4
**Yellow Springs**—*pop pl* VA-3
Yellow Springs—*spring* AL-4
Yellow Springs—*spring* PA-2
Yellow Springs—*spring* (2) TN-4
Yellow Springs—*spring* VA-3
Yellow Springs Branch—*stream* TN-4
Yellow Springs Ch—*church* IL-6
Yellow Springs Ch—*church* (2) TN-4
Yellow Springs Ch of Christ (historical)—*church* MS-4
Yellow Springs Creek—*stream* OH-6
Yellow Springs Hist Dist—*hist pl* OH-6
Yellow Springs Mtn—*summit* TN-4
Yellow Springs Post Office (historical)—*building* TN-4
Yellow Springs Sch (historical)—*school* (2) TN-4
Yellow Springs Township—*fmr MCD* IA-7
Yellow Stand Lead—*ridge* TN-4
*Yellow Stand Lead Trail* TN-4
Yellow Steer Slough—*gut* TX-5
Yellowstone—*locale* WI-6
**Yellowstone**—*pop pl* IN-6
Yellowstone Airport—*airport* MT-8
Yellowstone-Bighorn Research Camp—*locale* MT-8
Yellowstone Branch—*stream* VA-3
Yellowstone Bridge Campground—*locale* UT-8
Yellowstone Camp—*locale* MT-8
Yellowstone Campground—*locale* UT-8
Yellowstone Canal—*canal* ID-8
Yellowstone Canal—*canal* MT-8
Yellowstone Canyon—*valley* (4) AZ-5
Yellowstone Canyon—*valley* NV-8
Yellowstone Ch—*church* WI-6
Yellowstone Cliffs—*cliff* WA-9
Yellowstone Conservation Area—*park* WI-6
Yellowstone Corral—*locale* UT-8
Yellowstone Corral—*locale* WY-8
Yellowstone Cow Camp—*locale* WY-8
*Yellowstone Creek* CO-8
*Yellowstone Creek* UT-8
*Yellowstone Creek* VA-3
Yellowstone Creek—*stream* AK-9
Yellowstone Creek—*stream* CO-8
Yellowstone Creek—*stream* OK-5
Yellowstone Creek—*stream* OR-9
Yellowstone Creek—*stream* UT-8
Yellowstone Crossing, Bozeman Trail—*hist pl* MT-8
Yellowstone Extension Canal—*canal* UT-8
Yellowstone Fairground—*locale* MT-8
Yellowstone Falls—*falls* NC-3
Yellowstone Feeder Canal—*canal* UT-8
*Yellowstone Forest Service Station* UT-8
Yellowstone Guard Station—*locale* OR-9
Yellowstone Guard Station—*locale* UT-8
Yellowstone Gulch—*valley* CO-8
Yellowstone Lake—*lake* WY-8
Yellowstone Lake—*reservoir* WI-6
Yellowstone Mesa—*summit* AZ-5
Yellowstone Mine—*mine* (2) CA-9
Yellowstone Mine—*mine* MT-8
Yellow Stone Mine—*mine* NV-8
Yellowstone Mine—*mine* NV-8
Yellowstone Mine—*mine* OR-9
*Yellowstone Mountains* MT-8
*Yellowstone Mountains* WY-8
Yellowstone Mtn—*summit* OR-9
Yellowstone Natl Park—*cens area* ID-8
Yellowstone Natl Park—*cens area* WY-8
Yellowstone Natl Park—*inact count* MT-8
Yellowstone Natl Park—*park* WY-8
Yellowstone Park—*obs name* WY-8
Yellowstone Park—*park* TX-5
Yellowstone Point—*cape* ID-8
Yellowstone Point—*ridge* WY-8
Yellowstone Point—*summit* AZ-5
Yellowstone Point Cem—*cemetery* ND-7
Yellowstone Power Diversion Dam—*dam* UT-8
Yellowstone Power Diversion Rsvr—*reservoir* UT-8
Yellowstone Prong—*stream* NC-3
Yellowstone Ranch—*locale* UT-8
Yellowstone Ranch—*locale* WY-8
Yellowstone River—*stream* MT-8
Yellowstone River—*stream* ND-7
Yellowstone River—*stream* UT-8
Yellowstone River—*stream* WI-6
Yellowstone River—*stream* WY-8
Yellowstone River Trail—*trail* WY-8
Yellowstone Road, The—*hist pl* WA-9
Yellowstone Sch—*school* WY-8
Yellowstone Spring—*spring* (2) AZ-5
Yellowstone Spring—*spring* NV-8
Yellowstone Spring—*spring* UT-8
Yellowstone Tank—*reservoir* (4) AZ-5
**Yellowstone Township**—*pop pl* ND-7
Yellowstone Wash—*stream* AZ-5
Yellowstone Waterhole—*lake* OR-9
Yellow Store—*locale* TN-4
Yellow Store Post Office (historical)—*building* TN-4
Yellow Sulphur—*locale* VA-3
Yellow Sulphur Post Office (historical)—*building* TN-4
Yellow Sulphur Spring—*spring* TN-4
Yellow Sulphur Springs—*hist pl* VA-3
Yellow Sulphur Springs—*locale* VA-3
Yellow Swale—*stream* OH-6
**Yellowtail**—*pop pl* MT-8
Yellowtail Dam—*dam* MT-8
*Yellowtail Reservoir* MT-8
*Yellowtail Reservoir* WY-8
Yellow Tank—*reservoir* (2) AZ-5
Yellow Tank—*reservoir* NM-5
Yellow Tank—*reservoir* (2) TX-5
**Yellow Tavern**—*pop pl* VA-3
*Yellow Three Beach* MH-9
Yellow Thunder Park—*park* WI-6
Yellowtop Mtn—*summit* NC-3
Yellowtop Windmill—*locale* TX-5
*Yellowtown* OH-6
**Yellowtown**—*pop pl* OH-6
Yellow Trail—*trail* WY-8
Yellow Tree Cem—*cemetery* OK-5
*Yellow Two Beach* MH-9
Yellow Valley—*basin* NM-5
Yellow Water—*reservoir* MT-8
Yellow Water Branch—*stream* GA-3
Yellow Water Canyon—*valley* AZ-5
Yellow Water Ch—*church* LA-4
*Yellowwater Creek* AL-4
Yellow Water Creek—*stream* (3) AL-4
Yellow Water Creek—*stream* AK-9
Yellow Water Creek—*stream* (2) FL-3
Yellow Water Creek—*stream* GA-3
Yellow Water Creek—*stream* MT-8
Yellow Water Creek—*stream* OH-6
Yellow Water Ditch—*canal* OK-5
Yellow Waterhole—*lake* TX-5
*Yellow Water River* FL-3
Yellow Water River—*stream* LA-4
Yellow Willow Creek—*stream* KY-4
Yellow Windmill—*locale* NM-5
Yellow Wolf Creek—*stream* TX-5
**Yellowwood**—*pop pl* PA-2
Yellowwood Lake—*reservoir* IN-6
Yellowwood State For—*forest* IN-6
Yell Post Office (historical)—*building* TN-4
Yell Township—*fmr MCD* (2) IA-7
Yell (Township of)—*fmr MCD* AR-4
**Yellville**—*pop pl* AR-4
Yellville Cem—*cemetery* AR-4
*Yellville (sta.) (Summit)* AR-4
Yellville-Summit Sch—*school* AR-4
**Yelm**—*pop pl* WA-9
Yelm Airpark Airp—*airport* WA-9
Yelm Creek—*stream* WA-9
Yelm Ditch—*canal* WA-9
Yelm Prairie—*flat* WA-9
Yelnu Islets—*area* AK-9
Yelper Cove—*bay* AK-9
Yelping Hill—*locale* CT-1
Yelping Run—*stream* WV-2
Yelpong—*reef* FM-9
Yelrug Cave—*cave* AL-4
Yelton Ditch—*canal* CO-8
Yelton Ranch—*locale* NV-8
Yelton Sch—*school* MO-7
Yelton Spring—*spring* MO-7
Yelverton—*locale* OH-6
Yelverton, Anthony, House—*hist pl* NY-2
Yelverton Ch—*church* NC-3
Yelverton Grove Ch—*church* NC-3
Yelverton Inn and Store—*hist pl* NY-2
Yelverton Pond Dam—*dam* MS-4
Yelverton Sch (historical)—*school* AL-4
Yelvertons Lake Dam—*dam* MS-4
Yelvington—*locale* FL-3
**Yelvington**—*pop pl* FL-3
**Yelvington**—*pop pl* KY-4
Yelvington Cem—*cemetery* FL-3
**Yemassee**—*pop pl* SC-3
Yemassee (CCD)—*cens area* SC-3
*Yemassee Creek* AL-4
Y E Mesa—*summit* TX-5
Yemowat Cem—*cemetery* WA-9
Yemulil—*locale* FM-9
Yemulil, Infal—*stream* FM-9
Yenas Island—*island* FM-9
Yenasr—*island* FM-9
Yence Hollow—*valley* UT-8
Yenei Island—*island* FM-9
Yenfinger—*bar* FM-9
Yenituk Creek—*stream* AK-9
Yenlo, Mount—*summit* AK-9
Yenlo Creek—*stream* AK-9
Yenlo Hills—*other* AK-9
**Yenne**—*pop pl* IN-6
Yenome—*locale* SC-3
Yenowine, George B., House—*hist pl* KY-4
Yenowine-Kennedy House—*hist pl* KY-4
Yenowine-Nichols-Collins House—*hist pl* IN-6
Yenruogis, Lake—*lake* IA-7
Yens Peters Gap—*gap* UT-8
Yent Bayou—*gut* FL-3
Yenter Pool—*oilfield* CO-8
Yent Mound—*hist pl* FL-3
Yentna Glacier—*glacier* AK-9
Yentna River—*stream* AK-9
Yent Place—*locale* FL-3
*Yenwood Spring* OR-9
Yen Yen—*island* FM-9
Yeocomico Ch—*church* VA-3
Yeocomico Chapel—*church* VA-3
Yeocomico Church—*hist pl* VA-3
*Yeocomico River* VA-3
Yeocomico River—*stream* VA-3
Yeoho—*locale* MD-2
Yeo HS—*school* TX-5
Ye Old Cem—*cemetery* NH-1
**Ye Olde Farm Subdivision**—*pop pl* UT-8
*Ye Old Mans Creek* PA-2
**Yeomalt**—*pop pl* WA-9
Yeomalt Point—*cape* WA-9
**Yeoman**—*pop pl* IN-6
Yeoman Cem—*cemetery* GA-3
Yeoman Cem—*cemetery* (2) IN-6
Yeoman Creek—*stream* CO-8
Yeoman Ditch—*canal* IN-6
Yeoman Elem Sch—*school* IN-6
**Yeoman (historical)**—*pop pl* OR-9
Yeoman Park—*flat* CO-8
Yeoman Park—*park* IL-6
Yeomans—*locale* GA-3
Yeomans—*locale* IL-6
**Yeomans**—*pop pl* IA-7
Yeomans, Edward, House—*hist pl* CT-1
Yeomans Cem—*cemetery* GA-3
Yeomans Lake—*reservoir* GA-3
Yeomans Pond—*lake* MN-6
Yeomans Run—*stream* PA-2
Yeo Neck—*cape* VA-3
Yeon Mtn—*summit* OR-9
Yeopim—*locale* (2) NC-3
Yeopim Creek—*stream* NC-3
Yeopim River—*stream* NC-3
**Yeoward Addition**—*pop pl* IL-6
*Yeowardville* IL-6
Yeowardville—*other* IL-6
Yepan—*locale* FM-9
Yepan Point—*cape* FM-9
Yep Kanum Park—*park* WA-9
Yerba—*locale* NM-5
**Yerba**—*pop pl* WV-2
Yerba Anis Windmill—*locale* TX-5
*Yerba Buena* CA-9
Yerba Buena—*civil* CA-9
Yerba Buena Canyon—*valley* AZ-5
Yerba Buena Creek—*stream* (2) CA-9
Yerba Buena Island—*island* CA-9
Yerba Buena Island—*uninc pl* CA-9
Yerba Buena Ridge—*ridge* CA-9
Yerba Buena Sch—*school* CA-9
Yerba Buena Spring—*spring* CA-9
Yerba Buena Trail (Pack)—*trail* CA-9
Yerbabuena Windmill—*locale* TX-5
Yerba Canyon—*valley* NM-5
Yerba Senta Butte—*summit* AZ-5
Yerby—*locale* OK-5
Yerby Branch—*stream* OK-5
Yerbys Creek—*stream* VA-3
Yerding Cem—*cemetery* NY-2
Yereance-Berry House—*hist pl* NJ-2
Yergen Creek—*stream* OR-9
Yergenson Creek—*stream* ID-8
*Yerger* MS-4
Yerger Draw—*valley* WY-8
Yerger Lake—*lake* LA-4
Yerger Lake Dam—*dam* MS-4
*Yergy Flat* UT-8
Yerian Cem—*cemetery* MI-6
**Yerington**—*pop pl* NV-8
Yerington Cem—*cemetery* NV-8
Yerington Grammar Sch—*hist pl* NV-8
**Yerington Ind Res**—*pop pl* NV-8
Yerington Mine—*mine* NV-8
Yerington Municipal Airp—*airport* NV-8
**Yerkes**—*pop pl* KY-4
**Yerkes**—*pop pl* PA-2
Yerkes, Joseph D., House—*hist pl* MI-6
Yerkes, Robert, House—*hist pl* MI-6
Yerkes Cem—*cemetery* MI-6
*Yerkes Island* PA-2
Yerkes Observatory—*other* WI-6
Yerkes Station—*building* PA-2
Yerkes Tunnel—*tunnel* KY-4
*Yerkesville* PA-2
**Yerkwood**—*pop pl* AL-4
Yermak Lake—*lake* AK-9
**Yermo**—*pop pl* CA-9
Ye Royal Strip Airp—*airport* PA-2
Yerra Basin—*basin* AZ-5
Yerra Basin Spring—*spring* AZ-5
Yerrick Creek—*stream* AK-9
*Yersin Hills* UT-8
*Yersin Ridge* UT-8
Yerxa Brook—*stream* ME-1
Yerxa Cem—*cemetery* ME-1
Yerxa Ridge—*ridge* ME-1
Yes Bay—*bay* AK-9
**Yescas (Las Yescas)**—*pop pl* TX-5
*Yescocking* NC-3
Yeseng—*locale* FM-9
Yeseng, Foko—*reef* FM-9
Yeseng, Infal—*stream* FM-9
Yeshiva of Flatbush Sch—*school* NY-2
Yeshiva Sch—*school* NJ-2
Yeshiva Sch—*school* NY-2
Yeshiva Univ—*school* CA-9
Yeshiva Univ—*school* NY-2
Yeske Sch—*school* WI-6
**Yesler Terrace**—*pop pl* WA-9
Yesmowit Canyon—*valley* WA-9
Yesmowit Cem—*cemetery* WA-9
**Yeso**—*pop pl* NM-5
Yeso—*uninc pl* AZ-5
Yeso Camp Windmill—*locale* NM-5
Yeso Cem—*cemetery* NM-5
*Yesocking* NC-3
Yeso Creek—*stream* NM-5
Yeso Hills—*range* NM-5
Yeso Hills—*range* TX-5
Yeso Lateral—*canal* NM-5
Yeso Tank—*reservoir* NM-5
Y E Spring—*spring* TX-5
Yesron—*locale* FM-9
Yesse—*locale* KY-4
Yessler Well—*well* NM-5
Yester House—*hist pl* VT-1
Yesteryears Doll Museum—*building* MA-1
Yet—*island* MP-9
**Yetes**—*pop pl* TX-5
Yethonat—*locale* WA-9
*Yet Island* MP-9
Yetna Creek—*stream* AK-9
**Yetta**—*pop pl* CO-8
**Yett Addition**—*pop pl* TN-4
Yett Basin Pond—*lake* TX-5
Yett-Ellison House—*hist pl* TN-4
**Yettem**—*pop pl* CA-9
**Yetter**—*pop pl* IA-7
Yetter Cem—*cemetery* IL-6
Yetter Drain—*stream* MI-6
Yetter Sch (abandoned)—*school* PA-2
Yetter Swamp—*swamp* PA-2
**Yettland Park**—*pop pl* TN-4
Yevell Sch—*school* MA-1
*Yevotj* FM-9
Yewak, Foko—*reef* FM-9

Yewbush Islands—*island* MN-6
Yew Camp—*locale* OR-9
Yew Creek—*stream* (2) ID-8
Yew Creek—*stream* MT-8
Yew Creek—*stream* (4) OR-9
Yewed—*locale* OK-5
Yewell Branch—*stream* GA-3
*Yewell Cove* GA-3
Yewell House—*hist pl* KY-4
Yewell-Snyder House—*hist pl* KY-4
Yew Lane Sch—*school* OR-9
*Yew Mountain* WV-2
Yew Mountains—*range* WV-2
*Yew Pine Mountains* WV-2
Yew Ridge—*ridge* ID-8
Yew Ridge—*ridge* OR-9
Yew Spring—*spring* (2) OR-9
Yew Wood Camp—*locale* OR-9
*Yew Wood Creek* CA-9
Yew Wood Creek—*stream* CA-9
Yew Wood Creek—*stream* OR-9
Yew Wood Gulch—*valley* OR-9
*Yewwood Spring* OR-9
Yew Wood Spring—*spring* OR-9
*Yexgonnongoune River* MS-4
Ygnacio Canal—*canal* CA-9
Ygnacio Creek—*stream* TX-5
Ygnacio Relift Station—*other* CA-9
Ygnacio Valley—*uninc pl* CA-9
Ygnacio Valley—*valley* CA-9
Ygnacio Valley Sch—*school* CA-9
Yhola Creek—*stream* OK-5
Y Hollow—*valley* TN-4
Y H Tank—*reservoir* AZ-5
Yiddish Art Theatre—*hist pl* NY-2
Yielding Lake—*reservoir* AL-4
Yielding Lake Dam—*dam* AL-4
Yielding Mill Creek—*stream* AL-4
Yielding Zion Ch—*church* VA-3
**Yigo**—*pop pl* GU-9
Yigo (Election District)—*fmr MCD* GU-9
Yigo Sch—*school* GU-9
*Yiilbelau* PW-9
Yike Cem—*cemetery* IN-6
Yiluuy—*cape* FM-9
*Yiluy* FM-9
Yimuch—*cape* FM-9
Yimuch—*locale* FM-9
Yin—*locale* FM-9
Yinbinaew—*channel* FM-9
*Yinbinau* FM-9
*Yinbinaw* FM-9
Yindastuki Ind Res—*reserve* AK-9
Yindastuki (Site)—*locale* AK-9
**Yingling**—*pop pl* KY-4
Yingling Cem—*cemetery* MO-7
Yingst Cem—*cemetery* IL-6
*Yinuf* FM-9
**Yinuuf**—*pop pl* FM-9
Yip Yip Mine—*mine* CO-8
Yirrell Beach—*beach* MA-1
**Yistletaw**—*pop pl* AK-9
Y J Canal—*canal* OR-9
Y J Gap—*gap* GA-3
*Y J Ridge* GA-3
YKL Ranch—*locale* NV-8
Y Lake—*lake* AK-9
Y Lake—*lake* NE-7
Y Lateral—*canal* CA-9
Y L Canyon—*valley* NM-5
Y-L Ch—*church* TX-5
Yle Canyon—*valley* AZ-5
Yledigao—*area* GU-9
Yledigao River—*stream* GU-9
Y L E Ranch—*locale* AZ-5
YLE Tank—*reservoir* AZ-5
Ylig—*summit* GU-9
Ylig Bay—*bay* GU-9
Y-Lightning Ranch—*locale* AZ-5
Ylig Point—*cape* GU-9
Ylig River—*stream* GU-9
Yllota Slough—*stream* AK-9
Y L Ranch—*locale* AZ-5
Y L Ranch—*locale* TX-5
Ylvisaker Bridge—*bridge* ND-7
YMCA—*building* (3) MA-1
YMCA—*building* NC-3
Y.M.C.A.—*hist pl* GA-3
YMCA—*hist pl* IN-6
YMCA—*hist pl* MA-1
YMCA—*hist pl* OH-6
YMCA—*locale* NC-3
YMCA—*park* NC-3
YMCA Bldg—*hist pl* IA-7
Y.M.C.A. Bldg—*hist pl* IA-7
Y.M.C.A. Bldg—*hist pl* KY-4
Y.M.C.A. Bldg—*hist pl* WA-9
*YMCA Camp* PA-2
Y M C A Camp—*locale* CA-9
YMCA Camp—*locale* (4) MA-1
YMCA Camp—*locale* MN-6
YMCA Camp—*locale* NH-1
YMCA Camp—*locale* NY-2
YMCA Camp—*locale* (3) OH-6
YMCA Camp—*locale* PA-2
YMCA CAMP—*locale* PA-2
Y M C A Camp—*locale* VA-3
YMCA Camp—*park* UT-8
YMCA Camp Child—*locale* MT-8
YMCA Cave—*cave* AL-4
YMCA Dam—*dam* (2) PA-2
YMCA Dam—*reservoir* PA-2
YMCA Day Camp—*locale* MA-1
YMCA Hotel—*hist pl* CA-9
Y M C A Mtn—*summit* CO-8
YMCA Park—*park* NC-3
YMCA Pond—*lake* CT-1
YMCA Skyline Ranch—*locale* NM-5
Y Meadow Dam—*dam* CA-9
Y Mtn—*summit* UT-8
*Yn* FM-9
Ynez Sch—*school* CA-9
Yniestra—*locale* FL-3
Yniestra Sch—*school* FL-3
Ynveeghik River—*stream* AK-9
Yoakam Hill—*summit* OR-9
Yoakam Point—*cape* OR-9
Yoakley Ferry (historical)—*locale* TN-4
Yoakum—*locale* OR-9
**Yoakum**—*pop pl* TX-5
Yoakum Cave—*cave* TN-4
Yoakum (CCD)—*cens area* (2) TX-5
Yoakum Cem—*cemetery* OH-6
Yoakum Cem—*cemetery* (2) TN-4
**Yoakum (County)**—*pop pl* TX-5
Yoakum Creek—*stream* TX-5
Yoakum Crossroad—*locale* TN-4
Yoakum Run—*stream* WV-2
Yoakums Chapel Ch of God—*church* TN-4
Yoakum Spring—*spring* MT-8
Yoakumville (Site)—*locale* CA-9
Yoal—*locale* FM-9
Yoas Drain—*stream* MI-6
Yoas Mtn—*summit* AZ-5
Yoast Draw—*valley* NM-5
Yoast Gulch—*valley* CO-8
Yoast Windmill—*locale* NM-5
**Yocana**—*pop pl* AR-4
Yocana Cem—*cemetery* AR-4
Yocana Ch—*church* AR-4
Yocana Lake Dam—*dam* MS-4
Yocanoocana (historical)—*locale* MS-4
Yocemento—*locale* KS-7
*Yocham Run* PA-2
Yochum Hill—*summit* PA-2
Yochum Hill Cem—*cemetery* PA-2
Yochum Run—*stream* PA-2
Yochum Trail—*trail* PA-2
*Yockahockany River* MS-4
*Yockammockanna Creek* MS-4
*Yockanookany* MS-4
Yockanookany Baptist Ch—*church* MS-4
Yockanookany River—*stream* MS-4
Yockey—*fmr MCD* NE-7
**Yockey**—*pop pl* IN-6
Yockey Creek—*stream* KS-7
Yockey Creek—*stream* WA-9
*Yockhapatalfa River* MS-4
Yock Lake—*reservoir* IL-6
*Yockley Creek* KS-7
Yocks Pond—*swamp* MI-6
Yockum Creek—*stream* CO-8
Yockwah Creek—*stream* ID-8
**Yocona**—*pop pl* MS-4
Yocona HS (historical)—*school* MS-4
Yocona Lake—*reservoir* MS-4
Yocona Ridge—*ridge* MS-4
Yocona River—*stream* MS-4
Yocona River Canal—*canal* MS-4
Yocona River Structure Y-14-2 Dam—*dam* MS-4
Yocona River Watershed Y-14-11 Dam—*dam* MS-4
Yocona River Watershed Y-14-12 Dam—*dam* MS-4
Yocona River Watershed Y-14-13 Dam—*dam* MS-4
Yocona Watershed Y-14-1 Dam—*dam* MS-4
Yocona Watershed Y-14-14 Dam—*dam* MS-4
Yocona Watershed Y-14-15 Dam—*dam* MS-4
Yocona Watershed Y-14-16 Dam—*dam* MS-4
Yocona Watershed Y-14-17 Dam—*dam* MS-4
Yocona Watershed Y-14-5 Dam—*dam* MS-4
Yocona Watershed Y-14-6 Dam—*dam* MS-4
Yocona Watershed Y-14-7 Dam—*dam* MS-4
Yocony (historical)—*locale* MS-4
Yocum—*locale* AR-4
**Yocum**—*pop pl* KY-4
Yocum Branch—*stream* KY-4
Yocum Cem—*cemetery* (2) AR-4
Yocum Cem—*cemetery* KS-7
Yocum Cem—*cemetery* OR-9
Yocum Cem—*cemetery* PA-2
Yocum Cove—*stream* AR-4
**Yocum Creek**—*pop pl* KY-4
Yocum Creek—*stream* AR-4
Yocum Creek—*stream* (2) KY-4
Yocum Creek—*stream* LA-4
Yocum Creek—*stream* MO-7
**Yocum Estates**—*pop pl* PA-2
Yocum Falls—*falls* OR-9
**Yocum (historical)**—*pop pl* (2) OR-9
Yocum Hollow—*valley* MO-7
Yocum Lake—*lake* WA-9
Yocum Lateral—*canal* AZ-5
Yocum Pond—*lake* MO-7
Yocum Pond Cem—*cemetery* MO-7
Yocum Pond Ch—*church* MO-7
Yocum Ridge—*ridge* OR-9
Yocums Boat House—*locale* PA-2
Yocum Sch—*school* PA-2
Yocum Spring—*spring* CA-9
**Yocumtown**—*pop pl* PA-2
Yocum Valley—*basin* OR-9
Yoda Creek—*stream* MS-4
Yodeler Lake—*lake* MN-6
Yoder—*locale* AR-4
Yoder—*locale* CO-8
Yoder—*locale* KY-4
**Yoder**—*pop pl* IN-6
**Yoder**—*pop pl* KS-7
**Yoder**—*pop pl* OH-6
**Yoder**—*pop pl* OR-9
**Yoder**—*pop pl* WY-8
Yoder (CCD)—*cens area* OR-9
Yoder Cem—*cemetery* AR-4
Yoder Cem—*cemetery* IL-6
Yoder Cem—*cemetery* (6) OH-6
Yoder Cem—*cemetery* TN-4
Yoder Ch—*church* KS-7
Yoder Creek—*stream* MI-6
Yoder Ditch—*canal* OH-6
Yoder Elem Sch—*school* KS-7
Yoder Gulch—*valley* CO-8
Yoder Hollow—*valley* PA-2
Yoder Island—*island* MN-6
Yoder Lake—*lake* AK-9
Yoder Pasture—*flat* KS-7
Yoder Pond—*reservoir* VA-3
Yoder Quarry—*mine* OR-9
Yoder Ranch—*locale* NM-5
Yoder Sch—*school* IL-6
Yoder Sch—*school* IN-6
Yoder Sch—*school* MD-2
Yoder Sch—*school* NC-3
Yoder Sch—*school* VA-3
Yoder Sch (abandoned)—*school* PA-2
Yoder Seventh Day Adventist Sch—*school* OR-9
Yoder's Mills Hist Dist—*hist pl* NC-3
Yoders Pond—*reservoir* PA-2
Yoder Spring—*spring* PA-2
Yoder Tank—*reservoir* NM-5
**Yoder Township**—*pop pl* KS-7
Yodi Tank—*reservoir* AZ-5
Yodlin Creek—*stream* MT-8
**Yoe**—*pop pl* PA-2
Yoe Borough—*civil* PA-2
Yoeder Branch—*stream* TN-4
Yoekel Lake—*lake* WI-6
*Yoeket Lake* WI-6
Yoeman Canyon—*valley* CO-8
Yoeman Tank—*reservoir* CO-8
Yoes, Col. Jacob, Bldg—*hist pl* AR-4
Yoes Cem—*cemetery* TN-4
Yoestown—*locale* AR-4
Yogaay—*cape* FM-9
Yogi Bears Jellystone Park—*park* AL-4
Yogi Lake—*lake* MN-6
Yogo Creek—*stream* MT-8
Yogo Creek—*stream* UT-8
Yogo Crossing—*locale* MT-8
Yogo Peak—*summit* MT-8
Yogoroporapu—*island* FM-9
*Yogowots Creek* UT-8
*Yogoy* FM-9
*Yoha Ditch* IN-6
*Yohe Ditch* IN-6
Yohn Lake—*lake* AK-9
Yohn Trail—*trail* PA-2
Yoho Branch—*stream* IN-6
Yoho Cem—*cemetery* (2) WV-2
Yoho Creek—*bay* ME-1
**Yohoghany**—*pop pl* PA-2
Yoho Head—*summit* ME-1
Yoho Hollow—*valley* TX-5
Yohola, Lake—*reservoir* GA-3
Yoho Run—*stream* WV-2
Yoho Sch—*school* WV-2
Yo Island—*island* MP-9
*Yokahocany River* MS-4
*Yokahochany River* MS-4
*Yokahockana River* MS-4
*Yokahockany River* MS-4
*Yokam Point* OR-9
Yokaya—*civil* CA-9
Yokayo Ranch—*locale* CA-9
Yokayo Sch—*school* CA-9
Yoke Bay—*bay* AK-9
Yoke Branch—*stream* FL-3
Yoke Creek—*stream* LA-4
Yokeko Point—*cape* WA-9
**Yokeko Point**—*pop pl* WA-9
Yoke Lake—*lake* MN-6
Yokel Branch—*stream* VA-3
Yokel Ridge—*ridge* VA-3
Yokely Bayou—*stream* LA-4
**Yokena**—*pop pl* MS-4
Yokena Presbyterian Church—*hist pl* MS-4
*Yoken River* MA-1
*Yoken Seat* MA-1
*Yokens Seat* MA-1
Yoke Pass—*channel* AK-9
Yoke Ponds—*lake* ME-1
Yoker Creek—*stream* (2) OH-6
Yokle Windmill—*locale* TX-5
**Yokley**—*pop pl* TN-4
Yokley Cem—*cemetery* (2) TN-4
Yokley Creek—*stream* TN-4
Yokneda Lake—*lake* AK-9
**Yokohl**—*pop pl* CA-9
Yokohl Creek—*stream* CA-9
Yokohl Valley—*valley* CA-9
Yokoi's Cave—*hist pl* GU-9
Yokontoh Slough—*gut* AK-9
Yokum—*locale* TX-5
Yokum—*locale* WV-2
Yokum Bend—*bend* CA-9
Yokum Branch—*stream* KY-4
Yokum Branch—*stream* TN-4
Yokum Brook—*stream* MA-1
Yokum Corrals Camp—*locale* OR-9
Yokum Creek—*stream* ID-8
Yokum Creek—*stream* TX-5
Yokum Hollow—*valley* OK-5
Yokum Knob—*summit* WV-2
Yokum Lake—*lake* LA-4
Yokum Pond—*reservoir* MA-1
Yokum Pond Dam—*dam* MA-1
Yokum Prospect—*mine* TN-4
Yokum Rsvr—*reservoir* OR-9
Yokum Run—*stream* WV-2
Yokum Sch (abandoned)—*school* PA-2
Yokum School State Wildlife Area—*park* MO-7
Yokum Station (Magisterial District)—*fmr MCD* VA-3
*Yokum Town Plantation* MA-1
*Yokun* MA-1
Yokun Brook—*stream* MA-1
*Yokun River* MA-1
Yokun Seat—*summit* MA-1
*Yokun Seat Mtn* MA-1
*Yokun Town* MA-1
Yola—*locale* MN-6
Yolanda, Lake—*lake* WI-6
Yolanda Sch—*school* OR-9
Yolandas Garden Sch—*school* FL-3
Yolande—*locale* AL-4
Yolande Mine Number 2 (surface)—*mine* AL-4
Yolande Number 3 Mine (surface)—*mine* AL-4
Yolano—*locale* CA-9
Yoledigo Creek—*stream* TX-5
**Yolo**—*pop pl* CA-9
*Yolo By-pasa* CA-9
Yolo By-pass—*area* CA-9
Yolo Cabin—*locale* AZ-5
Yolo Cem—*cemetery* WI-6
Yolo Central Canal—*canal* CA-9
*Yolo City* CA-9
**Yolo (County)**—*pop pl* CA-9
Yolo County Boys Camp—*locale* CA-9
Yolo County General Hosp—*hospital* CA-9
Yolo Fliers Club and Golf Course—*other* CA-9
Yolo Ranch—*locale* (2) AZ-5
Yolo Ranch Airstrip—*airport* AZ-5
Yolts Draw—*valley* TX-5
**Yolyn**—*pop pl* WV-2
Yolyn Ch—*church* WV-2
**Yoman**—*pop pl* WA-9
**Yoman Ferry**—*pop pl* WA-9
Yoman Point—*cape* WA-9
**Yomba Ind Res**—*pop pl* NV-8
Yomba Sch—*school* NV-8
*Yome Jima* FM-9
*Yomelsin Creek* WA-9
*Yome Shima* FM-9
*Yomtunnock* RI-1
Yomyaran—*island* MP-9
Yona—*area* GU-9
**Yona**—*pop pl* GU-9
Yonaba Creek—*stream* MS-4
Yona (Election District)—*fmr MCD* GU-9
Yonah—*locale* GA-3
**Yonah**—*pop pl* GA-3
Yonah Ch—*church* GA-3
Yonah Lake—*reservoir* GA-3
Yonah Lake—*reservoir* SC-3
Yonah Memorial Gardens—*cemetery* GA-3
Yonah Mtn—*summit* GA-3
Yona Island—*island* GU-9
*Yona Valley* OR-9
*Yonbiji Island* MP-9
Yonbiji Island—*island* MP-9
**Yoncalla**—*pop pl* OR-9
Yoncalla, Mount—*summit* OR-9
Yoncalla Cem—*cemetery* OR-9
Yoncalla Creek—*stream* (2) OR-9
Yoncalla Lumber Company Log Pond—*reservoir* OR-9
Yoncalla Lumber Company Log Pond Dam—*dam* OR-9
Yon Cem—*cemetery* FL-3
Yonce Millpond—*reservoir* SC-3
Yoncopin Lake—*lake* AR-4
Yon Creek—*stream* (2) FL-3
Yonder Airfield—*airport* NC-3
Yondorf Block and Hall—*hist pl* IL-6
**Yondota**—*pop pl* OH-6
Yondota Falls—*falls* MI-6
Yon Dot Mountains—*summit* AZ-5
*Yonelsin Creek* WA-9
*Yongeborough* AL-4
Yonge Sch—*school* FL-3
**Yonges Island**—*pop pl* SC-3
Yonge Street Sch—*hist pl* GA-3
Yongs Bay Lumber Company Pond—*reservoir* OR-9
Yonka Gulch—*valley* CA-9
Yonkapin Lake—*lake* (2) MS-4
Yonk Canyon—*valley* UT-8
Yonkee Cow Camp—*locale* WY-8
Yonkee Cutoff—*locale* MT-8
Yonke Lake—*lake* WI-6
Yonker Cem—*cemetery* WV-2
Yonker Pin Slough—*gut* TX-5
Yonkers—*locale* MD-2
Yonkers—*locale* OK-5
**Yonkers**—*pop pl* GA-3
**Yonkers**—*pop pl* NY-2
Yonkers Drain—*stream* MI-6
Yonkers Lake—*lake* IL-6
Yonkers Lake—*lake* MI-6
Yonkers Raceway—*other* NY-2
Yonkers Water Works—*hist pl* NY-2
**Yonkerville**—*pop pl* (2) MO-7
Yonkey Pond—*swamp* TX-5
Yonkipin Lake—*reservoir* OK-5
Yonk Spring—*spring* UT-8
Yon Mound and Village Site—*hist pl* FL-3
Yonna—*locale* OR-9
Yonna Ditch—*canal* OR-9
Yonna Valley—*valley* OR-9
Yonn Island—*island* FL-3
**Yon's Lakeside Estates (Lakeside)**—*pop pl* FL-3
*Yons Subdivision* FL-3
**Yon's Subdivision**—*pop pl* FL-3
Yontocket—*locale* CA-9
Yontocket Hist Dist—*hist pl* CA-9
Yontocket Slough—*gut* CA-9
Yonts Branch—*stream* KY-4
Yonts Fork—*stream* KY-4
*Yoogoy* FM-9
*Yoo Passage* PW-9
Yoosa Creek—*stream* ID-8
Yopa Swale—*valley* UT-8
Yopp Branch—*stream* MS-4
Yopp Branch—*stream* TN-4
Yopps Ch—*church* NC-3
Yopps Cove—*bay* VA-3
*Yoran* MP-9
Yoran, Mount—*summit* OR-9
YO Ranch—*locale* TX-5
Yoran Lake—*lake* OR-9
Yoran Lake Trail—*trail* OR-9
Yorba—*locale* CA-9
Yorba—*uninc pl* CA-9
Yorba, Domingo Adobe and Casa Manuel Garcia—*hist pl* CA-9
Yorba Hacienda Historical Marker—*park* CA-9
Yorba JHS—*school* CA-9
**Yorba Linda**—*pop pl* CA-9
Yorba Linda Rsvr—*reservoir* CA-9
Yorba Sch—*school* CA-9
Yorba Slaughter Adobe—*hist pl* CA-9
**Yorba Village (Oyo Tungi)**—*pop pl* SC-3
Yorbita Sch—*school* CA-9
Yorde Aviation Airp—*airport* DE-2
**Yordy**—*pop pl* PA-2
Yordy (historical)—*locale* KS-7
Yorges Ranch—*locale* WY-8
Yorges Rsvr—*reservoir* WY-8
**Yorick**—*pop pl* NC-3
Yori Pass—*gap* AK-9
Yoris Grove—*woods* CA-9
*York* AL-4
*York* KS-7
*York* MI-6
*York* WV-2
York—*locale* AK-9
York—*locale* AZ-5
York—*locale* FL-3
York—*locale* GA-3
York—*locale* KY-4
York—*locale* (2) MN-6
York—*locale* NY-2
York—*locale* WA-9
York—*locale* WV-2
**York**—*pop pl* AL-4
**York**—*pop pl* IL-6
**York**—*pop pl* IN-6
**York**—*pop pl* IA-7
**York**—*pop pl* ME-1
**York**—*pop pl* MI-6
**York**—*pop pl* MO-7
**York**—*pop pl* MT-8
**York**—*pop pl* NE-7
**York**—*pop pl* NY-2
**York**—*pop pl* NC-3
**York**—*pop pl* ND-7
**York**—*pop pl* OH-6
**York**—*pop pl* PA-2
**York**—*pop pl* SC-3
**York**—*pop pl* WI-6
York—*uninc pl* CA-9
York, Alvin Cullom, Farm—*hist pl* TN-4
York, Lake—*reservoir* SC-3
York Acad—*school* VA-3
York Acad (historical)—*school* TN-4
York Airp—*airport* PA-2
**Yorkana**—*pop pl* PA-2
Yorkana Borough—*civil* PA-2
York and Rannels Mine—*mine* OR-9
*York Ave Elementary School* PA-2
York Ave Sch—*school* PA-2
**York Beach**—*pop pl* DE-2
**York Beach**—*pop pl* ME-1
York Bible Sch—*school* TN-4
*York Bluff* AL-4
York Bluff—*cliff* KY-4
York Bluffs—*cliff* AL-4
*Yorkborough* CO-8
York Bottom Creek—*stream* SC-3
York Branch—*stream* (2) AL-4
York Branch—*stream* FL-3
York Branch—*stream* GA-3
York Branch—*stream* (2) KY-4
York Branch—*stream* (6) TN-4
York Bridge—*bridge* NC-3
York Brook—*stream* ME-1
York Brook—*stream* MA-1
York Brook—*stream* NH-1
Yorkburg Sch (historical)—*school* AL-4
York Butte—*summit* OR-9
*York Canyon* UT-8
**York Canyon**—*pop pl* NM-5
York Canyon—*valley* NM-5
York Catholic HS—*school* PA-2
York Cave—*cave* MO-7
York Cave—*cave* TN-4
York (CCD)—*cens area* AL-4
York (CCD)—*cens area* SC-3
York Cem—*cemetery* AL-4
York Cem—*cemetery* (4) AR-4
York Cem—*cemetery* KY-4
York Cem—*cemetery* (2) MI-6
York Cem—*cemetery* MS-4
York Cem—*cemetery* OH-6
York Cem—*cemetery* (2) TN-4
York Cem—*cemetery* TX-5
York Cem—*cemetery* VA-3
*York Center* IN-6
York Center—*CDP* ME-1
York Center—*locale* (2) IA-7
**York Center**—*pop pl* IL-6
**York Center**—*pop pl* OH-6
**York Center**—*pop pl* WI-6
York Center Cem—*cemetery* (2) WI-6
York Center Ch—*church* WI-6
York Center Sch—*school* IL-6
York Center Sch—*school* IN-6
York Central Market—*hist pl* PA-2
York Central Sch—*school* NY-2
York Ch—*church* IL-6
York Ch—*church* MS-4
York Ch—*church* OH-6
York Ch—*church* VA-3
York Ch—*church* WI-6
York Chapel—*church* AL-4
York Chapel—*church* MO-7
York Chapel—*church* NC-3
York Chapel—*church* TN-4
York Chapel—*locale* AR-4
*York Christian Elem Sch* PA-2
York City—*civil* PA-2
York Cliffs—*cliff* ME-1
**York Cliffs**—*pop pl* ME-1
York Cliffs Hist Dist—*hist pl* ME-1
York Coal Bed Mine (underground)—*mine* AL-4
York Coll—*school* NE-7
York Coll of Pennsylvania—*school* PA-2
**York Corner**—*pop pl* ME-1
York Corners—*locale* NY-2
York Country Club—*other* NE-7
York Country Day Sch—*school* PA-2
**York County**—*pop pl* PA-2
**York (County)**—*pop pl* SC-3
**York (County)**—*pop pl* VA-3
York County Area Vocational-Technical Sch—*school* PA-2
York County Courthouse—*hist pl* SC-3
York County Hosp and Home—*hospital* PA-2
**York County (in MSA 6400, 6450)**—*pop pl* ME-1
York County Nature Museum—*building* SC-3
York County Shop Ctr—*locale* PA-2
*York Creek* AZ-5
York Creek—*stream* (2) AK-9
York Creek—*stream* (4) CA-9
York Creek—*stream* CO-8
York Creek—*stream* GA-3
York Creek—*stream* KY-4
York Creek—*stream* MI-6
York Creek—*stream* MS-4
York Creek—*stream* NJ-2
York Creek—*stream* NC-3
York Creek—*stream* OR-9
York Creek—*stream* PA-2
York Creek—*stream* TX-5
York Creek Cem—*cemetery* TX-5
York Creek Ch—*church* TX-5
*York Cross Roads* OH-6
York Cutoff—*channel* IL-6
Yorkdale Sch—*school* CA-9
*York Day School* PA-2
York Dispatch Newspaper Offices—*hist pl* PA-2
York Ditch—*canal* WY-8
York Division—*civil* AL-4
York Drain—*canal* MI-6
York Draw—*valley* MT-8
Yorke Creek—*stream* OR-9
*Yorke Lake* WA-9
York Electro-Panel Airp—*airport* PA-2
York Elem Sch—*school* IN-6
York Elem Sch—*school* TN-4
York Elem Sch (abandoned)—*school* PA-2
**Yorkely**—*pop pl* TN-4
Yorker Hill—*summit* RI-1
Yorker Mill Pond Dam—*dam* RI-1
Yorker Mill Pond / Yawgoo Mill Pond—*reservoir* RI-1
Yorkers Swamp—*stream* VA-3
**York Estates (Old York Estates)**—*pop pl* NJ-2
Yorketown—*CDP* NJ-2
York Farm Junction—*locale* PA-2
York Field—*park* CA-9
**Yorkfield**—*pop pl* IL-6
Yorkfield Sch—*school* IL-6
York Flat—*flat* TX-5
York Free Chapel—*church* OH-6
York Furnace—*locale* PA-2
York Gap—*gap* TN-4
**York Gardens**—*pop pl* PA-2
York-Gordon House—*hist pl* NC-3
York Gulch—*valley* CO-8
York Gulch—*valley* (2) MT-8
York Harbor—*bay* ME-1
**York Harbor**—*pop pl* ME-1
York Harbor Entrance—*bay* ME-1
**York Haven**—*pop pl* PA-2
**York Haven Anchorage**—*pop pl* VA-3
York Haven Borough—*civil* PA-2
York Haven Dam—*dam* (2) PA-2
York Haven-Newberry Sch—*school* PA-2
**York Heights**—*pop pl* ME-1
*York Hill* PA-2
York Hill—*summit* (4) ME-1
York Hill—*summit* NH-1
York Hill—*summit* (2) NY-2
York Hill Cem—*cemetery* ME-1
York Hist Dist—*hist pl* ME-1
York Hist Dist—*hist pl* PA-2
York Hist Dist—*hist pl* SC-3
York Hollow—*valley* MO-7
York Hollow—*valley* PA-2
York Hollow—*valley* (5) TN-4
York Hosp—*hospital* PA-2
York House—*hist pl* GA-3
York House—*hist pl* KY-4
York House Ch—*church* IL-6
York HS—*school* IL-6
York HS—*school* ME-1
York HS—*school* VA-3
York Indian Rock Dam—*dam* PA-2
York Iron Company Mine—*hist pl* PA-2
York Island—*island* AR-4
York Island—*island* FL-3
York Island—*island* ME-1
York Island—*island* MT-8
York Island—*island* WI-6
*York Island Shoal* WI-6
York Island Shoals—*bar* WI-6
York JHS—*school* CO-8
York JHS—*school* NC-3
*York Lake* IL-6
*York Lake* WA-9
York Lake—*lake* LA-4
York Lake—*lake* MN-6
York Lake—*lake* NY-2
York Lake—*reservoir* AL-4
York Lake—*reservoir* GA-3
York Lake—*reservoir* MA-1
York Lake Dam—*dam* MA-1
York Landing—*locale* ME-1
York Landing—*locale* TN-4
York Ledge—*bar* (2) ME-1
**Yorkleigh**—*pop pl* MD-2
Yorkley Creek—*stream* SC-3
York Little Theatre—*building* PA-2
York Lodge No. 563—*hist pl* OH-6
York Lutheran Home—*building* PA-2
Yorklyn—*locale* DE-2
**Yorklyn**—*pop pl* PA-2
**Yorklyn Ridge**—*pop pl* DE-2
York (Magisterial District)—*fmr MCD* VA-3
York Mall—*locale* PA-2
**York Manor**—*pop pl* VA-3
York Mansion—*hist pl* KY-4
York Meetinghouse—*hist pl* PA-2
York Memorial Cem—*cemetery* NC-3
York Memorial Ch—*church* WI-6
York Mine—*mine* MN-6
York Mine—*mine* NM-5
York Mine (underground)—*mine* AL-4
Yorkminister Ch—*church* VA-3
Yorkmont Park—*uninc pl* NC-3
**Yorkmont (subdivision)**—*pop pl* NC-3
**York Mountain**—*pop pl* AL-4
York Mountains—*other* AK-9
**Yorkmount Park (subdivision)**—*pop pl* NC-3
York Mtn—*summit* (2) AL-4
York Mtn—*summit* CA-9
York Mtn—*summit* PA-2
*York New Salem (corporate name New Salem)* PA-2
Yorknic Ch—*church* IL-6
York Number 2 Dam—*dam* AL-4
York Outlet Mall—*locale* PA-2
York Park—*park* MN-6
York Park—*park* OH-6
York Point—*cape* VA-3
*York Pond* MA-1
York Pond—*lake* (2) ME-1
York Pond—*lake* NH-1
York Pond—*lake* NY-2
York Pond—*lake* RI-1
York Ponds—*lake* ME-1
York Pond Trail—*trail* NH-1
*York Post Office* AL-4
York Prairie—*locale* IA-7
York Prairie Cem—*cemetery* IA-7
York Prairie Creek—*stream* IN-6
York Public Sch (historical)—*school* AL-4
York Ranch—*locale* (4) NM-5
York Ranch—*locale* (2) WY-8
*York Reef* OR-9
York Retreat—*other* IL-6
York Ridge—*ridge* (3) GA-3
York Ridge—*ridge* IN-6
York Ridge—*ridge* VA-3

York Ridge—*summit* ME-1
Yorkrite Ch—*church* FL-3
York River—*stream* ME-1
York River—*stream* VA-3
York River Cliffs—*cliff* VA-3
York Road—*locale* PA-2
York Road—*post sta* PA-2
York Road Cem—*cemetery* PA-2
York Road Community Park—*park* NC-3
*York Road Junior High School* NC-3
York Road Sch—*school* SC-3
York RR Station—*building* AZ-5
*York Rsvr* PA-2
York Rsvr—*reservoir* MT-8
York Rsvr—*reservoir* OR-9
York Rsvr—*reservoir* PA-2
**York Run**—*pop pl* PA-2
York Run—*stream* (2) IN-6
York Run—*stream* NY-2
York Run—*stream* (2) PA-2
York Run—*stream* WV-2
York Run Junction—*locale* PA-2
York Run Junction Station (historical)—*building* PA-2
*Yorks* AZ-5
York Sch—*school* (2) CA-9
York Sch—*school* ID-8
York Sch—*school* (2) IL-6
York Sch—*school* KS-7
York Sch—*school* (2) MO-7
York Sch—*school* NC-3
York Sch—*school* (4) OH-6
York Sch—*school* SD-7
York Sch (historical)—*school* TN-4
Yorks Corner—*locale* ME-1
*Yorks Creek* TX-5
Yorks Creek—*stream* TX-5
Yorks Dead River—*lake* GA-3
Yorks Field—*airport* NC-3
Yorkship Square—*locale* NJ-2
**Yorkshire**—*pop pl* DE-2
**Yorkshire**—*pop pl* IA-7
**Yorkshire**—*pop pl* NY-2
**Yorkshire**—*pop pl* OH-6
**Yorkshire**—*pop pl* PA-2
**Yorkshire**—*pop pl* VA-3
Yorkshire—*uninc pl* TX-5
**Yorkshire Acres**—*pop pl* VA-3
**Yorkshire Downs (subdivision)**—*pop pl* NC-3
Yorkshire Elem Sch (abandoned)—*school* PA-2
**Yorkshire Knolls**—*pop pl* MD-2
**Yorkshire Meadows Condominium**—*pop pl* UT-8
**Yorkshire Meadow Subdivision**—*pop pl* UT-8
**Yorkshire Park**—*pop pl* VA-3
**Yorkshire Place Subdivision**—*pop pl* UT-8
Yorkshire Sch—*school* VA-3
**Yorkshire (subdivision)**—*pop pl* AL-4
**Yorkshire (Town of)**—*pop pl* NY-2
Yorkshire Village—*locale* MO-7
Yorkshire Village (Shop Ctr)—*locale* MO-7
*Yorkshire Woods* IL-6
York-Skinner House—*hist pl* NY-2
York S Lake Dam—*dam* MS-4
Yorks Logan—*lake* ME-1
Yorks Mill—*locale* AL-4
York-Southern Industrial Park—*facility* SC-3
York Spit—*bar* VA-3
York Spit Channel—*channel* VA-3
York Spit Lighthouse—*locale* VA-3
York Spring—*spring* (2) NM-5
**York Springs**—*pop pl* PA-2
York Springs Borough—*civil* PA-2
*Yorks Run* PA-2
*York Station* AL-4
York Street Cem—*cemetery* (2) OH-6
York Street Ch—*church* OH-6
*York Suburban Junior High School* PA-2
York Suburban MS—*school* PA-2
York Suburban Senior HS—*school* PA-2
York Sulphur Springs—*spring* PA-2
**York Switch**—*pop pl* IN-6
York Tanks—*reservoir* TX-5
York Tavern—*locale* NC-3
York Temple Country Club—*other* OH-6
**York Terrace**—*pop pl* VA-3
York Terrace Baptist Ch—*church* AL-4
York Terrace Ch of God—*church* AL-4
York Terrace Park—*park* AL-4
*Yorktown* MN-6
*Yorktown* SD-7
Yorktown—*locale* OH-6
Yorktown—*locale* PA-2
**Yorktown**—*pop pl* AR-4
**Yorktown**—*pop pl* IL-6
**Yorktown**—*pop pl* IN-6
**Yorktown**—*pop pl* IA-7
**Yorktown**—*pop pl* KY-4
**Yorktown**—*pop pl* MD-2
**Yorktown**—*pop pl* NJ-2
**Yorktown**—*pop pl* NY-2
**Yorktown**—*pop pl* TX-5
**Yorktown**—*pop pl* VA-3
Yorktown Baptist Ch—*church* AL-4
Yorktown Brook—*stream* ME-1
Yorktown (CCD)—*cens area* TX-5
Yorktown Cem—*cemetery* IN-6
Yorktown Ch—*church* AR-4
Yorktown Collieries (historical)—*building* PA-2
Yorktown Country Club—*other* TX-5
Yorktown Creek—*stream* TX-5
Yorktown Creek—*stream* VA-3
**York Towne**—*pop pl* DE-2
Yorktowne Golf Club—*locale* PA-2
**Yorktowne Homes**—*pop pl* PA-2
*Yorktown Elementary School* PA-2
Yorktown Gas Field—*oilfield* TX-5
*Yorktown Golf Course* PA-2
**Yorktown Heights**—*pop pl* NY-2
Yorktown Heights RR Station—*hist pl* NY-2
Yorktown (historical)—*locale* KS-7
**Yorktown Homes (subdivision)**—*pop pl* PA-2
Yorktown HS—*school* IN-6
Yorktown HS—*school* VA-3
**Yorktown Manor**—*pop pl* RI-1
Yorktown Monmt—*park* VA-3
Yorktown MS—*school* IN-6

Yorktown Naval Weapons Station—*military* VA-3
**York (Town of)**—*pop pl* ME-1
**York (Town of)**—*pop pl* NY-2
**York (Town of)**—*pop pl* (3) WI-6
Yorktown Post Office (historical)—*building* ND-7
Yorktown Sch—*school* MD-2
York Township—*fmr MCD* (3) IA-7
**York Township**—*pop pl* KS-7
**York Township**—*pop pl* MO-7
**York Township**—*pop pl* ND-7
**York Township**—*pop pl* (2) SD-7
York Township Ditch—*canal* IN-6
York Township Elem Sch—*school* PA-2
York (Township of)—*fmr MCD* AR-4
**York (Township of)**—*pop pl* (3) IL-6
**York (Township of)**—*pop pl* (6) IN-6
**York (Township of)**—*pop pl* MI-6
**York (Township of)**—*pop pl* MN-6
**York (Township of)**—*pop pl* (10) OH-6
**York (Township of)**—*pop pl* PA-2
**Yorktown (subdivision)**—*pop pl* NC-3
Yorktown Town Hall—*building* ND-7
**Yorktown (Town of)**—*pop pl* NY-2
**Yorktown Township**—*pop pl* ND-7
**Yorktown (Township of)**—*pop pl* IL-6
**Yorktown Village**—*pop pl* MD-2
**Yorktown Woods**—*pop pl* TN-4
Yorktown Wrecks—*hist pl* VA-3
York United Methodist Church—*hist pl* OH-6
York Valley—*valley* AZ-5
York Valley—*valley* PA-2
**York Village**—*pop pl* ME-1
*Yorkville* SC-3
Yorkville—*locale* CO-8
**Yorkville**—*pop pl* CA-9
**Yorkville**—*pop pl* GA-3
**Yorkville**—*pop pl* IL-6
**Yorkville**—*pop pl* IN-6
**Yorkville**—*pop pl* MI-6
**Yorkville**—*pop pl* NY-2
**Yorkville**—*pop pl* OH-6
**Yorkville**—*pop pl* TN-4
**Yorkville**—*pop pl* WI-6
Yorkville—*post sta* NY-2
Yorkville Acad (historical)—*school* TN-4
Yorkville (CCD)—*cens area* GA-3
Yorkville (CCD)—*cens area* TN-4
Yorkville Cem—*cemetery* TN-4
Yorkville Ch of Christ—*church* TN-4
Yorkville Cumberland Presbyterian Ch—*church* TN-4
Yorkville Division—*civil* TN-4
Yorkville Elem Sch—*school* TN-4
Yorkville (historical)—*locale* SD-7
Yorkville HS (historical)—*school* TN-4
Yorkville Post Office—*building* TN-4
Yorkville Post Office (historical)—*building* SD-7
Yorkville Sch—*school* IL-6
Yorkville Sch—*school* WI-6
**Yorkville (Town of)**—*pop pl* WI-6
York Water Company Dam—*dam* PA-2
York West End JHS—*school* AL-4
York Windmill—*locale* TX-5
York Woods—*woods* ME-1
**Yorkwood (subdivision)**—*pop pl* (2) NC-3
York (York Indian Rock Dam)—*dam* PA-2
Yorty Creek—*stream* CA-9
*Yoruoppu* MP-9
*Yorupoppu Passage* MP-9
*Yoruroppu Passage* MP-9
*Yoruroppu-to* MP-9
*Yory Township* SD-7
YOS Canyon—*valley* WY-8
*Yos Creek* WY-8
Yose Canyon—*valley* WY-8
Yoseda Windmill—*locale* TX-5
*Yosemite* CA-9
**Yosemite**—*pop pl* KY-4
Yosemite (CCD)—*cens area* CA-9
Yosemite Creek—*stream* CA-9
Yosemite Creek Campgrounds—*locale* CA-9
Yosemite Forks—*locale* CA-9
Yosemite Gulch—*valley* UT-8
Yosemite JHS—*school* CA-9
Yosemite Junction—*locale* CA-9
Yosemite Lake—*lake* CA-9
Yosemite Lake—*reservoir* CA-9
Yosemite Lake (County Park)—*reservoir* CA-9
**Yosemite Lakes Park**—*pop pl* CA-9
Yosemite Lateral—*canal* CA-9
**Yosemite Lodge**—*pop pl* CA-9
*Yosemite Lower Falls* CA-9
*Yosemite Natl Park* CA-9
Yosemite Natl Park—*park* CA-9
**Yosemite Natl Park (Place)**—*pop pl* CA-9
Yosemite Point—*cliff* CA-9
Yosemite Sch—*school* CA-9
Yosemite Transportation Company Office—*hist pl* CA-9
Yosemite Valley—*CDP* CA-9
Yosemite Valley—*valley* CA-9
Yosemite Valley Archeol District—*hist pl* CA-9
Yosemite Valley Bridges—*hist pl* CA-9
Yosemite Valley Chapel—*hist pl* CA-9
Yosemite Valley RR Caboose No. 15—*hist pl* CA-9
**Yosemite Village**—*pop pl* CA-9
Yosemite Village Hist Dist—*hist pl* CA-9
Yosets Lake—*lake* PA-2
Yoss Creek—*stream* OR-9
Yoss Creek Meadow—*flat* OR-9
**Yossem's Paradise Valley**—*pop pl* NE-7
Yost—*locale* OH-6
Yost—*locale* VA-3
**Yost**—*pop pl* IL-6
**Yost**—*pop pl* OK-5
**Yost**—*pop pl* UT-8
Yost, Frank K., House—*hist pl* KY-4
Yost Airp—*airport* PA-2
Yost Branch—*stream* KY-4
Yost Cabin—*locale* CA-9
Yost Cem—*cemetery* (2) IL-6
Yost Cem—*cemetery* UT-8
Yost Cem—*cemetery* (3) WV-2
Yost Corners—*locale* NY-2
Yost Creek—*stream* CA-9
Yost Creek—*stream* NY-2
Yost Creek—*stream* SC-3

Yost Drain—*stream* MI-6
*Yost Draw* NM-5
Yost Francisco Drain—*canal* MI-6
Yost Lake—*lake* CA-9
Yost Ranch—*locale* CO-8
Yost Ranch—*locale* MT-8
Yost Rsvr—*reservoir* OK-5
Yost Run—*stream* OH-6
Yost Run Trail—*trail* PA-2
**Yosts**—*pop pl* NY-2
Yost Sch—*school* KY-4
Yost Sch—*school* MI-6
*Yost School* IN-6
Yost Swamp—*swamp* PA-2
Yost Swamp (historical)—*swamp* PA-2
Yost Theater-Ritz Hotel—*hist pl* CA-9
**Yostville**—*pop pl* PA-2
*Yo Suido* PW-9
Yo Tambien Tunnel—*mine* AZ-5
*Yo-to* MP-9
**Youba**—*pop pl* OH-6
Youba Ridge—*ridge* OH-6
Youbedamn Landing—*locale* VA-3
You-Be Hollow—*valley* IL-6
You Bet—*locale* CA-9
Youche Golf Club—*other* IN-6
You Creek—*stream* AK-9
Youctangee Park—*park* OH-6
Youderian Coulee—*valley* MT-8
Youd School (Abandoned)—*locale* CA-9
Youens—*locale* TX-5
Yougeen—*locale* TX-5
Yough—*locale* IA-7
Youghapotit Rocks—*bar* AK-9
*Youghiogeny River* MD-2
*Youghiogeny River* PA-2
*Youghiogeny River* WV-2
*Youghiogheny* PA-2
Youghiogheny Country Club—*other* PA-2
Youghiogheny Dam—*dam* PA-2
*Youghiogheny Reservoir* MD-2
*Youghiogheny Reservoir* PA-2
Youghiogheny River—*stream* MD-2
Youghiogheny River—*stream* PA-2
Youghiogheny River—*stream* WV-2
Youghiogheny River Lake—*reservoir* MD-2
Youghiogheny River Lake—*reservoir* PA-2
*Youghiogheny River Rsvr* MD-2
*Youghiogheny River Rsvr* PA-2
Yough Senior HS—*school* PA-2
Youimpa Point View Area—*locale* UT-8
Youker Buch Sch—*school* NY-2
Youle Sch (Abandoned)—*school* WI-6
Youley—*other* GA-3
Youman Chapel—*church* GA-3
Youman Ditch—*canal* CO-8
Youman Lake—*lake* MN-6
Youman Ranch—*locale* SD-7
**Youmans**—*pop pl* FL-3
Youmans Cem—*cemetery* (2) GA-3
Youmans Corner—*locale* NY-2
Youmans Ranch—*locale* (2) CO-8
Younce Creek—*stream* NC-3
Younce Prospect—*mine* TN-4
Younds Landing—*locale* AL-4
Younes Cem—*cemetery* AR-4
*Young* AL-4
*Young* AR-4
*Young* ND-7
*Young* OH-6
Young—*locale* AR-4
Young—*locale* TX-5
**Young**—*pop pl* AZ-5
**Young**—*pop pl* (3) IN-6
**Young**—*pop pl* MS-4
**Young**—*pop pl* OR-9
**Young**—*pop pl* WV-2
Young, Alexander, Bldg—*hist pl* HI-9
Young, Alexander, Cabin—*hist pl* IA-7
Young, A. M., House—*hist pl* KY-4
Young, Andrew, House—*hist pl* OR-9
Young, Asa E., House—*hist pl* KY-4
Young, Benjamin, House and Carriage House—*hist pl* OR-9
Young, Brigham, Acad—*hist pl* UT-8
Young, Brigham, Houses—*hist pl* UT-8
Young, Brigham, Oil Well—*hist pl* WY-8
Young, Brigham, Winter Home and Office—*hist pl* UT-8
Young, Brigham J., House—*hist pl* NM-5
Young, Col., House—*hist pl* AR-4
Young, Col. Charles, House—*hist pl* OH-6
Young, Col. Joseph, Block—*hist pl* IA-7
Young, Daniel, House—*hist pl* ME-1
Young, Gen. Mason J., House—*hist pl* NH-1
Young, James, House and Inn—*hist pl* KY-4
Young, John Eben, House—*hist pl* OR-9
Young, John W., Round Barn—*hist pl* IA-7
Young, Joseph, House—*hist pl* PA-2
Young, Joshua P., House—*hist pl* IL-6
Young, Mount—*summit* AK-9
Young, Mount—*summit* CA-9
Young, Mount—*summit* MT-8
Young, Robert, House—*hist pl* PA-2
Young, Solomon, Farm—*hist pl* MO-7
Young, Thomas F., House—*hist pl* OH-6
Young, Virginia Durant, House—*hist pl* SC-3
Young, Whitney M., Jr., Birthplace—*hist pl* KY-4
Young, William, Archeol Site—*hist pl* KS-7
Young, William, House—*hist pl* DE-2
Young, William Friend, House—*hist pl* UT-8
Young-Almas House—*hist pl* MT-8
**Young America**—*pop pl* IN-6
**Young America**—*pop pl* MN-6
**Young America**—*pop pl* WI-6
Young America Canyon—*valley* CA-9
Young America Cem—*cemetery* IL-6
Young America City Hall—*hist pl* MN-6
Young America Creek—*stream* CA-9
**Young America Homes (subdivision)**—*pop pl* (2) AZ-5
Young America Lake—*lake* CA-9
Young America Lake—*lake* MN-6
Young America Mine—*mine* CA-9
Young America Mine—*mine* OR-9
Young America Mine—*mine* WA-9
Young American Creek—*stream* NV-8
Young American Spring—*spring* NV-8
Young America Sch (historical)—*school* SD-7

**Young America (subdivision)**—*pop pl* AL-4
Young America (Township of)—*civ div* IL-6
Young America (Township of)—*civ div* MN-6
**Young America West (subdivision)**—*pop pl* (2) AZ-5
Young Basin—*basin* WY-8
Young Bay—*bay* AK-9
Young Bay—*bay* NY-2
Young Bayou—*gut* LA-4
Young Bayou—*stream* MS-4
Young Beach—*beach* AK-9
Young Bend—*bend* TN-4
Young Bend—*locale* TN-4
Young Bend Ch of Christ (historical)—*church* TN-4
Youngberg—*locale* AZ-5
Youngberg Ranch Airp—*airport* NV-8
Young Bldg—*hist pl* VA-3
Young Block—*hist pl* UT-8
**Youngblood**—*pop pl* AL-4
Youngblood, Tessa, House—*hist pl* IA-7
Youngblood Branch—*stream* TN-4
Youngblood Bridge—*bridge* AR-4
Youngblood Bridge—*hist pl* MS-4
Youngblood Canyon—*valley* NM-5
Youngblood Cem—*cemetery* AR-4
Youngblood Cem—*cemetery* (2) IL-6
Youngblood Cem—*cemetery* (2) LA-4
Youngblood Cem—*cemetery* TX-5
Youngblood Ch—*church* TX-5
Youngblood Chapel—*church* AL-4
*Youngblood Chapel Ch* AL-4
*Youngblood Creek* TN-4
Youngblood Creek—*stream* AL-4
Young Blood Creek—*stream* MS-4
Youngblood Creek—*stream* TN-4
Youngblood Creek—*stream* TX-5
Youngblood Dam—*dam* AL-4
Youngblood Gap—*gap* AL-4
Youngblood Hill—*summit* AZ-5
Youngblood Hills—*summit* TX-5
**Youngblood (historical)**—*pop pl* TN-4
Youngblood Hollow—*valley* IL-6
Youngblood Lake—*reservoir* (2) AL-4
Youngblood Lake Dam—*dam* AL-4
Youngblood Number 1 Mine (underground)—*mine* AL-4
Youngblood Place (reduced usage)—*locale* TX-5
Youngblood Post Office (historical)—*building* TN-4
Youngblood Site (15GV26)—*hist pl* KY-4
Youngblood Tank—*reservoir* TX-5
Youngblood Windmill—*locale* TX-5
Young-Bradfield House—*hist pl* MS-4
Young Brake—*swamp* LA-4
Young Branch—*stream* AR-4
Young Branch—*stream* LA-4
Young Branch—*stream* MS-4
Young Branch—*stream* NC-3
Young Branch—*stream* (6) TN-4
Young Branch—*stream* VA-3
Young Branch—*stream* WI-6
Young Bridge—*other* MO-7
Young Brook—*stream* ME-1
*Young Brother Island* FM-9
Young Callaway Ditch—*canal* CO-8
Young Canal—*canal* NV-8
**Youngcane**—*pop pl* GA-3
Youngcane Creek—*stream* GA-3
Youngcane Sch—*school* GA-3
*Young Canyon* AZ-5
Young Canyon—*valley* CA-9
Young Canyon—*valley* NV-8
Young Canyon—*valley* NM-5
Young Canyon—*valley* TX-5
Young Canyon—*valley* UT-8
Young Cem—*cemetery* (5) AL-4
Young Cem—*cemetery* (2) AR-4
Young Cem—*cemetery* (4) GA-3
Young Cem—*cemetery* (2) IL-6
Young Cem—*cemetery* IN-6
Young Cem—*cemetery* (2) IA-7
Young Cem—*cemetery* (9) KY-4
Young Cem—*cemetery* (5) LA-4
Young Cem—*cemetery* MN-6
Young Cem—*cemetery* (3) MS-4
Young Cem—*cemetery* (5) MO-7
Young Cem—*cemetery* (3) NC-3
Young Cem—*cemetery* (4) OH-6
Young Cem—*cemetery* OK-5
Young Cem—*cemetery* (15) TN-4
Young Cem—*cemetery* (4) TX-5
Young Cem—*cemetery* (4) VA-3
Young Cem—*cemetery* WV-2
*Young Ch* MS-4
Young Chapel—*church* IL-6
Young Chapel—*church* KY-4
Young Chapel—*church* NC-3
Young Chapel—*church* (2) TN-4
Young Chapel—*church* VA-3
Young Chapel (historical)—*church* MS-4
Young Circle—*locale* FL-3
*Young Community* TX-5
*Young Corner* ME-1
Young Corner—*locale* VA-3
Young Corners—*locale* NY-2
**Young (County)**—*pop pl* TX-5
Young Cove—*bay* WA-9
Young Cove—*valley* (2) NC-3
Young Cove Creek—*stream* NC-3
*Young Creek* AL-4
*Young Creek* IN-6
*Young Creek* UT-8
Young Creek—*stream* (3) AK-9
Young Creek—*stream* CA-9
Young Creek—*stream* GA-3
Young Creek—*stream* ID-8
Young Creek—*stream* KY-4
Young Creek—*stream* (2) MS-4
Young Creek—*stream* MO-7
Young Creek—*stream* (2) MT-8
Young Creek—*stream* NV-8
Young Creek—*stream* OK-5
Young Creek—*stream* (3) OR-9
Young Creek—*stream* (2) TN-4
Young Creek—*stream* TX-5
Young Creek—*stream* VA-3
Young Creek—*stream* WA-9
Young Creek Shelter—*locale* WA-9

Young-Cummings Cem—*cemetery* TN-4
**Youngdale**—*pop pl* PA-2
Young Dam—*dam* NV-8
Young Dam—*dam* ND-7
Young Deer Creek—*stream* GA-3
Young Deer Creek Access Point—*locale* GA-3
Young Ditch—*canal* (2) IN-6
Young Ditch—*canal* OR-9
Young Draw—*valley* WY-8
Younger Branch—*stream* WV-2
Younger Branch Cem—*cemetery* WV-2
*Younger Brother Island* FM-9
Younger Cem—*cemetery* AR-4
Younger Cem—*cemetery* TX-5
Younger Coulee—*valley* MN-6
**Younger Creek**—*pop pl* KY-4
Younger Creek—*stream* AK-9
Younger Creek—*stream* KY-4
Younger Creek—*stream* TN-4
Younger Hill—*summit* AR-4
Younger Knob—*summit* AR-4
Younger Mtn—*summit* AR-4
Younger Oil Field—*oilfield* KS-7
Youngers—*locale* MO-7
Youngers Cem—*cemetery* MO-7
Younger Sch—*school* IL-6
Youngers Creek—*stream* MI-6
Youngers Lookout—*locale* MO-7
Younger Slough—*gut* MO-7
Younger Spring—*spring* OR-9
**Youngers Store**—*pop pl* VA-3
Younger Well—*well* NM-5
Younge Site—*hist pl* MI-6
Young Falls—*falls* CA-9
Young Farm—*hist pl* SC-3
Young Farm Cem—*cemetery* OH-6
Young Farmers and Homemakers Camp—*locale* TN-4
Young Field Slough—*gut* FL-3
Young Field Wildlife Mngmt Area—*park* UT-8
Young Florio Spring—*spring* NV-8
Young Ford—*locale* AL-4
**Young Forte Village (subdivision)**—*pop pl* AL-4
Young Gap—*gap* NC-3
Young Gap—*gap* OR-9
Young-Garner Cem—*cemetery* MS-4
Young Goose Creek—*stream* AK-9
Young Gravelly—*locale* AR-4
Young Grove Ch—*church* AL-4
Young Grove Ch—*church* KY-4
Young Gulch—*valley* CA-9
Young Gulch—*valley* CO-8
**Young Harris**—*pop pl* GA-3
Young Harris (CCD)—*cens area* GA-3
Young Harris Coll—*school* GA-3
Young Harris College Hist Dist—*hist pl* GA-3
**Young Haven Circle Subdivision**—*pop pl* UT-8
Young Hickory—*locale* NY-2
**Young Hickory**—*pop pl* OH-6
Young Hickory Hollow—*valley* NY-2
Young Hickory (Township of)—*civ div* IL-6
Young High School Ch of Christ—*church* TN-4
Young Hill—*summit* AK-9
Young Hill—*summit* (2) ME-1
Young Hill—*summit* NY-2
Young Hill—*summit* OR-9
Young Hill—*summit* WA-9
Young Hill Sch (historical)—*school* PA-2
Young (historical)—*locale* DE-2
Young (historical)—*locale* ND-7
**Young (historical)**—*pop pl* TN-4
Young Hollow—*valley* AR-4
Young Hollow—*valley* CO-8
Young Hollow—*valley* (3) MO-7
Young Hollow—*valley* NC-3
Young Hollow—*valley* OH-6
Young Hollow—*valley* PA-2
Young Hollow—*valley* (3) TN-4
Young Hollow—*valley* WV-2
Young Hollow—*valley* WY-8
Young Hollow Branch—*stream* TN-4
Younghood Cem—*cemetery* TN-4
Young House—*hist pl* KY-4
Young HS—*school* NY-2
Young HS—*school* (2) TN-4
Younginer Pond—*reservoir* SC-3
Young Island—*island* (2) AK-9
Young Island—*island* MI-6
Young Island—*island* VT-1
Young Island—*island* WA-9
Young JHS—*school* AL-4
Young JHS—*school* FL-3
Young JHS—*school* IA-7
Young JHS—*school* NM-5
Young JHS—*school* NY-2
Young JHS—*school* OR-9
Youngker Tank—*reservoir* AZ-5
*Young Lake* CA-9
*Young Lake* MI-6
Young Lake—*lake* AK-9
Young Lake—*lake* AR-4
Young Lake—*lake* (5) MI-6
Young Lake—*lake* (3) MN-6
Young Lake—*lake* NY-2
Young Lake—*lake* OK-5
Young Lake—*lake* OR-9
Young Lake—*lake* UT-8
Young Lake—*lake* (2) WI-6
Young Lake—*reservoir* NM-5
Young Lake—*reservoir* NC-3
Young Lake Dam—*dam* MS-4
Young Lakes—*lake* CA-9
Young Landing—*locale* LA-4
Young Landing (historical)—*locale* AL-4
Younglands—*hist pl* WI-6
Young Lateral—*canal* CA-9
Young Lateral—*canal* SD-7
Young Lateral—*canal* TX-5
Young Lick—*summit* GA-3
Young Lookout Tower—*locale* NC-3
Young-Lyle-Strickland Cem—*cemetery* TN-4
Young Macedonia Cem—*cemetery* SC-3
Young Macedonia Ch—*church* SC-3
Youngman, Frederick, House—*hist pl* IN-6
Youngman Brook—*stream* VT-1
Young Man Lake—*lake* MT-8
Young Mans Butte—*summit* ND-7
*Young Mans Butte Siding* ND-7

Youngman Sch—*school* SD-7
Young Memorial Ch—*church* (2) NC-3
Young Memorial Chapel—*church* GA-3
Young Men's and Young Women's Hebrew Association Bldg—*hist pl* MD-2
*Young Mens Butte* ND-7
Young Men's Christian Association—*hist pl* NY-2
Young Men's Christian Association—*hist pl* PA-2
Young Men's Christian Association Bldg—*hist pl* NY-2
Young Men's Christian Association Bldg—*hist pl* WI-6
Young Mens Christian Association Camp—*park* (2) AZ-5
Young Men's Christian Association Central Bldg—*hist pl* NY-2
*Young Mens Christian Association Ramada* AZ-5
Young Men's Institute Bldg—*hist pl* NC-3
Young Mill (historical)—*locale* AL-4
Young Mine—*mine* TN-4
Young Monument—*other* WV-2
*Young Mountain* MT-8
Young Mountain Number Two Tank—*reservoir* AZ-5
Young Mtn—*summit* AZ-5
Young Mtn—*summit* (2) NH-1
Young Mtn—*summit* NC-3
Young Mtn—*summit* TN-4
Young Mtn—*summit* WY-8
Young Oil Field—*oilfield* KS-7
Young Oil Field—*other* NM-5
Young Park—*park* FL-3
Young Park—*park* KS-7
Young Park—*park* KY-4
Young Park—*park* (2) NM-5
Young Park—*park* OK-5
Young Park—*park* TX-5
**Young Park**—*pop pl* VA-3
Young Park Sch—*school* VA-3
*Young Peak* UT-8
Young Peak—*summit* UT-8
Young-Pickering Ditch—*canal* MT-8
Young Pisgah Mtn—*summit* NC-3
Young Pisgah Ridge Tunnel—*tunnel* NC-3
Young Place—*hist pl* SC-3
Young Place—*locale* (2) NM-5
**Young Place (subdivision)**—*pop pl* AL-4
Young Point—*cape* (3) ME-1
Young Point—*cape* VA-3
Young Post Office (historical)—*building* TN-4
Young Ranch—*locale* AZ-5
Young Ranch—*locale* (2) CO-8
Young Ranch—*locale* ID-8
Young Ranch—*locale* NE-7
Young Ranch—*locale* (2) NV-8
Young Ranch—*locale* SD-7
Young Ranch—*locale* TX-5
Young Ranch—*locale* UT-8
Young Ranch—*locale* WY-8
Young Ridge—*ridge* (2) AR-4
Young Ridge—*ridge* OR-9
Young Rock—*other* AK-9
Young Round Barn—*hist pl* NY-2
Young Rsvr—*reservoir* CO-8
*Youngs* NC-3
Youngs—*locale* LA-4
Youngs—*locale* NY-2
**Youngs**—*pop pl* GA-3
**Youngs**—*pop pl* MS-4
**Youngs**—*pop pl* NY-2
**Youngs**—*pop pl* OH-6
**Youngs**—*pop pl* SC-3
Youngs, Lake—*reservoir* WA-9
Youngs Acad—*school* AL-4
Youngs Bay—*bay* ME-1
Youngs Bay—*bay* MN-6
Youngs Bay—*bay* OR-9
Youngs Bay Bridge—*bridge* OR-9
Youngs Bay Entrance Light—*locale* OR-9
Youngs Bay Light—*locale* OR-9
Youngs Bay Lumber Company Dam—*dam* OR-9
Youngs Bayou—*stream* (2) LA-4
*Youngsberg* AZ-5
**Youngs Bottom**—*pop pl* WV-2
*Youngs Branch* KY-4
Youngs Branch—*stream* (2) KY-4
Youngs Branch—*stream* NC-3
Youngs Branch—*stream* OH-6
Youngs Branch—*stream* SC-3
Youngs Branch—*stream* TX-5
Youngs Branch—*stream* (2) VA-3
Youngs Branch—*stream* (2) WV-2
Youngs Bridge—*bridge* AL-4
Youngs Bridge (historical)—*bridge* MS-4
*Youngs Brook* NH-1
Youngs Brook—*stream* IN-6
Youngs Brook—*stream* ME-1
Youngs Brook—*stream* NH-1
Youngs Brook—*stream* NY-2
Youngsburg—*locale* PA-2
Youngs Butte—*summit* (2) OR-9
Youngs Camp—*locale* VA-3
Youngs Camp Branch—*stream* NC-3
Youngs Canal—*canal* LA-4
Youngs Canyon—*valley* AZ-5
Youngs Canyon—*valley* CO-8
Youngs Canyon—*valley* NM-5
Youngs Canyon—*valley* OR-9
Youngs Canyon—*valley* UT-8
Youngs Canyon Dam—*dam* AZ-5
Youngs Canyon Tank—*reservoir* AZ-5
Youngs Cem—*cemetery* GA-3
Youngs Cem—*cemetery* KY-4
Youngs Cem—*cemetery* MS-4
Youngs Cem—*cemetery* MO-7
Youngs Cem—*cemetery* NE-7
Youngs Ch—*church* AL-4
Youngs Ch—*church* (2) PA-2
Young Sch—*school* DC-2
Young Sch—*school* (4) IL-6
Young Sch—*school* KS-7
Young Sch—*school* KY-4
Young Sch—*school* LA-4
Young Sch—*school* MA-1
Young Sch—*school* (2) MS-4
Young Sch—*school* MO-7
Young Sch—*school* NH-1

Yuma Wash—*stream* (2) .......... AZ-5
Yuma Wash Rsvr—*reservoir* .......... AZ-5
*Yumersee* .......... FL-3
*Yumital Berg* .......... FM-9
*Yumitheska Mesa* .......... AZ-5
*Yu-mos-tos* .......... WA-9
*Yum Tank* .......... AZ-5
Yumtheska Mesa—*summit* .......... AZ-5
Yumtheska Point—*cliff* .......... AZ-5
*Yumuch* .......... FM-9
**Yum Yum**—*pop pl* .......... TN-4
Yum-Yum Mine—*mine* .......... AZ-5
*Yum Yum Post Office* .......... TN-4
Yumyum Post Office (historical)—*building* . TN-4
Yunaska Island—*island* .......... AK-9
Yuncker, John F., House—*hist pl* .......... WA-9
Yunearawey—*channel* .......... FM-9
*Yunerawey* .......... FM-9
*Yuneroway* .......... FM-9
*Yung Hee Camp* .......... HI-9
**Yung Hee Village**—*pop pl* .......... HI-9
Yung See San Fong House—*hist pl* .......... CA-9
*Yuniirikku* .......... MP-9
Yuniirikku Island—*island* .......... MP-9
Y Unit Draw—*valley* .......... NM-5
Yunker Ranch Well—*well* .......... AZ-5
Yunkers High Bridge—*bridge* .......... OR-9
Yunosi Canyon—*valley* .......... AZ-5
Yunosi Point—*cliff* .......... AZ-5
*Yunuf* .......... FM-9
Yunya Park—*park* .......... AZ-5
Yuonglik River—*stream* .......... AK-9
**Yupon**—*pop pl* .......... AL-4
Yupon Creek—*stream* .......... TX-5
**Yuquiyu**—*pop pl* (2) .......... PR-3
Y U Ranch—*locale* .......... WY-8
Yurochi—*island* .......... MP-9
*Yurochi Island* .......... MP-9
Yust, E. C., Homestead—*hist pl* .......... CO-8
Yust Ranch—*locale* .......... CO-8
Yutamark Hollow—*valley* .......... PA-2
**Yutan**—*pop pl* .......... NE-7
Yutan Site—*hist pl* .......... NE-7
Yutes Run—*stream* .......... PA-2
Yutokh Hill—*summit* .......... AK-9
Yuton—*locale* .......... IL-6
Yutzy Cem—*cemetery* .......... OH-6
Yutzy Ditch—*canal* .......... OH-6
Yuub—*bay* .......... FM-9
*Yuyuan* .......... MH-9
Yuyu'an—*slope* .......... MH-9
*Yuyuhan* .......... MH-9
Yuza Mini Brook—*stream* .......... CT-1
Yuzhni Point—*cape* .......... AK-9
Yuzugan Island—*island* .......... MP-9
Y-View—*other* .......... WA-9
*Yvonne* .......... MP-9
Yvonne, Lake—*lake* (2) .......... FL-3
Yvonne, Lake—*lake* .......... WA-9
Y.W.C.A.—*hist pl* .......... CO-8
YWCA—*hist pl* .......... IN-6
YWCA, Phyllis Weatley Branch—*hist pl* .......... MO-7
Y.W.C.A. Bldg—*hist pl* .......... CA-9
YWCA Bldg—*hist pl* .......... OH-6
YWCA Blue Triangle Residence Hall—*hist pl* .......... IN-6
YWCA Camp—*locale* .......... IA-7
YWCA Child Care Center—*school* .......... FL-3
YWCA Girls Camp—*locale* .......... IL-6
YWCA Site—*hist pl* .......... RI-1
*YWCO Camp Grandview* .......... AL-4
**Y-Worry Estates Subdivision**—*pop pl* .......... UT-8
*Ymuch* .......... FM-9
YY Ranch—*locale* .......... AZ-5
Yzaguirre Banco Number 58—*levee* .......... TX-5
Y Z Ditch—*canal* .......... WY-8
Y Z Post Office (historical)—*building* .......... TN-4
Y-14-3 Dam—*dam* .......... MS-4
Y-14-4 Dam—*dam* .......... MS-4
Y-19a-1 Dam—*dam* .......... MS-4
Y-19a-1 Lake—*reservoir* .......... MS-4
Y-19a-2 Dam—*dam* .......... MS-4
Y-19a-2 Lake—*reservoir* .......... MS-4
Y-19a-3 Dam—*dam* .......... MS-4
Y-19a-3 Lake—*reservoir* .......... MS-4
Y-19c-1 Dam—*dam* .......... MS-4
Y-19c-1 Lake—*reservoir* .......... MS-4
Y-19c-2 Dam—*dam* .......... MS-4
Y-19c-2 Lake—*reservoir* .......... MS-4
Y-19c-3 Dam—*dam* .......... MS-4
Y-19c-3 Lake—*reservoir* .......... MS-4
Y-4 Ranch—*locale* .......... SD-7
Y-4 Well—*well* .......... SD-7
Y 6 Ranch—*locale* .......... NM-5

# Z

**Zabcikville**—*pop pl* TX-5
**Zabcikville (Marekville)**—*pop pl* TX-5
Zabel Canyon—*valley* CO-8
*Zabez* FM-9
Zabolio Lake—*lake* MN-6
Zaborosky Ditch—*canal* IN-6
Zabriskie, Albert J., Farmhouse—*hist pl* NJ-2
Zabriskie, Edgar, House—*hist pl* NE-7
Zabriskie, Garret, House—*hist pl* NJ-2
Zabriskie, Henry, House—*hist pl* NJ-2
Zabriskie, Nicholas, House—*hist pl* NJ-2
Zabriskie Brook—*stream* NJ-2
Zabriskie-Christie House—*hist pl* NJ-2
Zabriskie House—*hist pl* NJ-2
Zabriskie-Kipp-Cadmus House—*hist pl* NJ-2
Zabriskie Point—*summit* CA-9
Zabriskies Pond—*reservoir* NJ-2
Zabriskie Tenant House—*hist pl* NJ-2
Zabriskie Von Steuben House—*building* NJ-2
Zabriskie Well—*well* NV-8
Zabusta (historical)—*locale* AL-4
Zaca Creek—*stream* CA-9
Zacahuistle Pasture—*flat* TX-5
Zacahuistle Well (Windmill)—*locale* TX-5
Zacahuistle Windmill—*locale* TX-5
Zaca Lake—*lake* CA-9
Zaca Mine—*mine* CA-9
*Zaca Oil Field* CA-9
Zaca Peak—*summit* CA-9
Zaca Ridge—*ridge* CA-9
Zaca Substation—*other* CA-9
Zacata—*locale* VA-3
Zacata Creek—*stream* TX-5
*Zacatone Camp* AZ-5
Zacatoso, Arroyo—*valley* TX-5
Zacatoso Tank—*reservoir* TX-5
Zacaweista Ranch—*locale* TX-5
*Zach* TN-4
Zacha Junction—*locale* TX-5
Zachar Bay—*bay* AK-9
Zachariae Tank—*reservoir* AZ-5
**Zachariah**—*pop pl* (2) KY-4
Zachariah Fork—*stream* KY-4
Zacharias Creek—*stream* PA-2
Zacharias Point—*cape* SC-3
Zacharias Site (14LV380)—*hist pl* KS-7
**Zachary**—*pop pl* LA-4
Zachary Bay—*bay* AK-9
Zachary Branch—*stream* TN-4
Zachary Canyon—*valley* OR-9
Zachary Cem—*cemetery* (2) AR-4
Zachary Cem—*cemetery* (2) TN-4
Zachary Gulch—*valley* CA-9
Zachary Hill—*summit* MA-1
Zachary MS—*school* TX-5
Zachary Pond—*lake* MA-1
Zachary RR Depot—*hist pl* LA-4
Zacharys Gap—*gap* NC-3
Zachary Taylor Natl Cem—*cemetery* KY-4
Zachary Taylor Sch—*school* KY-4
Zacharytown—*locale* TN-4
Zachau Canyon—*valley* CA-9
Zach Branch—*stream* KY-4
Zach Branch—*stream* TX-5
Zachery Ch—*church* LA-4
**Zachow**—*pop pl* WI-6
Zach Post Office (historical)—*building* TN-4
Zach Rice Hollow—*valley* KY-4
Zach Ridge—*ridge* NC-3
Zach Rsvr—*reservoir* OR-9
Zachry Creek—*stream* GA 3
Zachry-Kingston House—*hist pl* GA-3
Zachs Bay—*bay* NY-2
Zachs Branch—*stream* MO-7
Zach Sch (historical)—*school* TN-4
Zachs Knob—*summit* TN-4
Zachs Run—*stream* WV-2
Zachy Hollow—*valley* TN-4
*Zack* TX-5
**Zack**—*pop pl* AR-4
**Zack**—*pop pl* TN-4
**Zack**—*pop pl* VA-3
Zack Creek—*gut* NC-3
Zacke Cox Bridge—*hist pl* IN-6
Zackendorf Spring—*spring* AZ-5
Zack Fork—*stream* WV-2
Zack Hollow—*valley* AR-4
Zackmire Cem—*cemetery* IN-6
Zack Pond—*lake* NY-2
Zack Ridge—*ridge* TN-4
Zacks Branch—*stream* LA-4
Zacks Branch—*stream* WV-2
Zacks Cliffs—*cliff* MA-1
Zacks Fork Creek—*stream* NC-3
*Zack Smith Cemetery* MS-4
Zacks Ridge Sch (historical)—*school* PA-2
Zackville—*locale* WV-2
Zack Woods Pond—*lake* VT-1
Zada Rsvr—*reservoir* ID-8
Zaddach Creek—*stream* OR-9
Zade Knob—*summit* NC-3
Zade Mtn—*summit* MT-8
Zadie Creek—*stream* MO-7
*Zadletone Mountain* OK-5
Zadock—*locale* MO-7
Zafra—*locale* OK-5
Zafra Sch—*school* OK-5
Zag—*locale* KY-4
Zaga Ranch—*locale* NV-8
Zag Creek—*stream* OR-9
Zager Lake—*lake* MN-6
Zagoskin Lake—*lake* AK-9
Zagst Hill—*summit* PA-2
**Zahl**—*pop pl* ND-7
Zahl, Lake—*reservoir* ND-7
Zahn, Herman and Alvina, House—*hist pl* TX-5
Zahn Bay—*bay* UT-8
Zahn Camp (inundated)—*mine* UT-8
Zahn Cem—*cemetery* MO-7
Zahn Cem—*cemetery* TX-5
Zahn Creek—*stream* OR-9
Zahn Hollow—*valley* IL-6
Zahniser Cem—*cemetery* (2) PA-2
Zahniser Sch (abandoned)—*school* PA-2
Zahn Lake—*lake* TX-5
Zahn Sch—*school* IL-6
**Zahns Corners**—*pop pl* OH-6
*Zahnville* KS-7
Zahn Well—*well* NM-5
*Zahries Creek* WI-6
Zahrte Creek—*stream* WI-6
Zaicek Pond—*reservoir* CT-1
Zaidee—*locale* GA-3
Zaidee Ch—*church* GA-3
Zaikof Bay—*bay* AK-9
Zaikof Point—*cape* AK-9
Zaimka Island—*island* AK-9
Zaimka Ridge—*ridge* AK-9
Zaino Lake—*reservoir* TX-5
Zajic Lake—*reservoir* MO-7
Zalatores Hill—*summit* MA-1
Zale Cave—*cave* AL-4
**Zaleski**—*pop pl* OH-6
Zaleski Camp—*locale* OH-6
Zaleski Ditch—*canal* OH-6
Zaleski Methodist Church Mound—*hist pl* OH-6
Zaleski State For—*forest* OH-6
Zalesk Ranch—*locale* AZ-5
Zaliva Point—*cape* AK-9
**Zalma**—*pop pl* MO-7
Zalmona Ch—*church* IA-7
Zalud House—*hist pl* CA-9
**Zama**—*pop pl* MS-4
Zama Baptist Ch—*church* MS-4
**Zamara**—*pop pl* CO-8
Zamas (Barrio)—*fmr MCD* PR-3
Zambarano Memorial Hospital—*other* RI-1
Zambarmo Lake—*reservoir* NM-5
Zambee—*locale* VI-3
Zamboni Hot Springs—*spring* CA-9
*Zamora* KS-7
Zamora—*locale* AL-4
**Zamora**—*pop pl* CA-9
**Zamora**—*pop pl* NM-5
*Zamora Country Club* AL-4
Zamora Creek—*stream* CA-9
Zamora Lake—*lake* NM-5
Zamora Lake—*reservoir* AL-4
Zamora Lake Dam—*dam* AL-4
Zamora Park—*park* AL-4
*Zamora Park Lake* AL-4
Zamora Park Lake—*reservoir* AL-4
Zamora Spring—*spring* NM-5
Zana—*locale* AL-4
Zana—*locale* FL-3
Zana Canyon—*valley* AZ-5
Zana Training Sch—*school* AL-4
Zancudedo Well—*well* TX-5
**Zandale**—*pop pl* KY-4
Zander—*locale* WI-6
Zander Cem—*cemetery* NE-7
Zandor Drain stroam MI-6
Zander Lake—*lake* WI-6
*Zanders Lake* WI-6
Zanders Lake—*lake* MN-6
Z and S Mine—*mine* CA-9
Zane—*locale* UT-8
Zane Camp—*locale* OH-6
Zane Canyon—*valley* UT-8
Zane Caverns Park—*park* OH-6
Zane Grey Lodge—*building* AZ-5
Zane Hills—*range* AK-9
**Zaneis**—*pop pl* OK-5
Zaneis Sch Teacher's Dormitory—*hist pl* OK-5
Zane-North Sch—*school* NJ-2
Zaner—*locale* PA-2
Zaner Sch—*school* PA-2
Zane Sch—*school* OH-6
*Zanes Creek* IN-6
**Zanesfield**—*pop pl* OH-6
Zanesfield Cem—*cemetery* OH-6
*Zanes Island* WV-2
Zane Spring—*spring* OR-9
Zanes Run—*stream* VA-3
Zanesville—*locale* IL-6
**Zanesville**—*pop pl* IN-6
**Zanesville**—*pop pl* OH-6
Zanesville Honor Camp—*locale* OH-6
Zanesville Memorial Park—*cemetery* OH-6
**Zanesville Terrace**—*pop pl* OH-6
**Zanesville (Township of)**—*pop pl* IL-6
Zanesville YMCA—*hist pl* OH-6
Zanesville YWCA—*hist pl* OH-6
Zaneta—*locale* IA-7
**Zane (Township of)**—*pop pl* OH-6
Zanetti, Mount—*summit* AK-9
Zanewood Park—*park* MN-6
Zanewood Sch—*school* MN-6
Zang, Adolph, Mansion—*hist pl* CO-8
Zang, Adolph J., House—*hist pl* CO-8
Zangar Junction—*locale* WA-9
Zanger Ditch—*canal* IN-6
Zangle Cove—*bay* WA-9
Zanja, The—*stream* CA-9
Zanja Barra—*canal* PR-3
Zanja (Barrio)—*fmr MCD* PR-3
**Zanja Blanca**—*pop pl* PR-3
*Zanja Cota Creek* CA-9
Zanja de Cota Creek—*stream* CA-9
**Zanja Negra**—*pop pl* PR-3
Zanja Peak—*summit* CA-9
Zanja San Jose—*canal* PR-3
Zanjones—*civil* CA-9
Zanmore (historical)—*locale* PA-2
Zannaropolis Mine—*mine* AZ-5
Zannie White Bay—*swamp* FL-3
**Zann's Corners**—*pop pl* OH-6
Zanones Camp—*locale* AR-4
Zanoni—*locale* MO-7
Zanoni—*locale* VA-3
*Zanora* AL-4
Zante—*locale* CA-9
Zante Plantation—*hist pl* SC-3
Zantgraf Mine—*mine* CA-9
Zaowachiichi Channel—*channel* FM-9
**Zap**—*pop pl* ND-7
Zapad Head—*cliff* AK-9
Zapadni Bay—*bay* AK-9
Zapadni Point—*cape* (2) AK-9
**Zapata**—*pop pl* TX-5
Zapata (CCD)—*cens area* TX-5
Zapata Cem—*cemetery* TX-5
**Zapata (County)**—*pop pl* TX-5
Zapata Falls—*falls* CO-8
Zapata Lake—*lake* TX-5
Zapata Mtn—*summit* AZ-5
Zapata Ranch—*locale* CO-8
Zapata Wash—*stream* AZ-5
Zapata Well—*well* AZ-5
*Zapato Canyon* CA-9
Zapato Chino Canyon—*valley* CA-9
Zapato Chino Creek—*stream* CA-9
*Zapato Creek* CA-9
*Zapatos Canyon* CA-9
*Zapatos Creek* CA-9
Zap Cem—*cemetery* ND-7
Zapeda Tank—*reservoir* AZ-5
Zapeda Well—*well* AZ-5
Zapeta Windmill—*locale* TX-5
**Zaphyr Hill**—*pop pl* MS-4
Zapp Bldg—*hist pl* TX-5
*Zara* KS-7
**Zara**—*pop pl* NC-3
**Zarah**—*pop pl* KS-7
Zaraigh Ch—*church* GA-3
*Zarcillo Canyon* CO-8
Zarcillo Creek—*stream* NM-5
Zarecor Cem—*cemetery* TN-4
Zarembo Island—*island* AK-9
Zarembo Spring—*spring* AK-9
Zarepath Grove Ch—*church* NC-3
Zarephath—*locale* NJ-2
Zare Point—*cape* VA-3
*Zares Marsh Point* VA-3
Zargosa Park—*park* TX-5
Zaring Sch—*school* MO-7
Zarling Lake—*lake* WI-6
Zartman Ditch—*canal* IN-6
Zartuche Windmill—*locale* TX-5
Zarzal (Barrio)—*fmr MCD* PR-3
*Zarzamora Creek* TX-5
Zarzamora Creek—*stream* TX-5
Zastrow Cem—*cemetery* NE-7
*Zasu River* MS-4
Zau Channel—*channel* FM-9
Zauel Park—*park* MI-6
Zaugg Bank Barn—*hist pl* TN-4
Zauss Ditch—*canal* IN-6
Zavadil, Franz, Farmstead—*hist pl* NE-7
Zavala—*locale* TX-5
Zavala Cem—*cemetery* TX-5
**Zavala (County)**—*pop pl* TX-5
Zavala Sch—*school* (5) TX-5
*Zavalla* TX-5
**Zavalla**—*pop pl* TX-5
Zavalla (CCD)—*cens area* TX-5
Zaverton Airp—*airport* PA-2
*Zayala* TX-5
Zayanta—*civil* CA-9
**Zayante**—*pop pl* CA-9
Zayante Creek—*stream* CA-9
Zay Hollow—*valley* MO-7
Zay Prairie—*lake* FL-3
Zaza—*locale* ID-8
Zazios Pond—*lake* KY-4
Zazu Tank—*reservoir* NM-5
Z Bar L Windmill—*locale* NM-5
Z Bar T Ranch—*locale* WY-8
Z Bar U Ranch—*locale* WY-8
Z B Draw—*valley* AZ-5
Z B Tank—*reservoir* AZ-5
Z Canal—*canal* OR-9
ZCBJ Cem—*cemetery* SD-7
ZCBJ Hall—*hist pl* SD-7
ZCBJ Hall—*hist pl* WI-6
ZCBJ Lodge No. 46—*hist pl* OK-5
Z.C.B.J. Opera House—*hist pl* NE-7
Z.C.B.J. Rad Tabor No. 74—*hist pl* NE-7
Z.C.M.I. Cast Iron Front—*hist pl* UT-8
ZCMI Center—*locale* UT-8
*ZdRuby Valley PO* NV-8
Z Drum Dam—*dam* SD-7
Zeacliff Pond—*lake* NH-1
Zeagher Cabin—*locale* UT-8
Zeagler—*post sta* FL-3
Zeagler Cem—*cemetery* MS-4
Zeaks Cem—*cemetery* TN-4
**Zeal**—*pop pl* VA-3
*Zealand* NH-1
*Zealand Camp* NH-1
Zealand Falls—*falls* NH-1
Zealand Forest Camp—*locale* NH-1
Zealandia—*hist pl* NC-3
Zealand Notch—*valley* NH-1
Zealand Ridge—*ridge* NH-1
Zealand River—*stream* NH-1
Zealand Trail—*trail* NH-1
Zealand Valley Trail—*trail* NH-1
Zeal (historical)—*locale* SD-7
Zealia Chapel—*church* AR-4
Zeal Point—*cape* AK-9
Zealy Branch—*stream* TN-4
Zea Mays Airp—*airport* IN-6
**Zeandale**—*pop pl* KS-7
**Zeandale Township**—*pop pl* KS-7
**Zearing**—*pop pl* IL-6
**Zearing**—*pop pl* IA-7
Zeast, Bayou—*gut* AL-4
Zeb—*locale* OK-5
**Zeba**—*pop pl* MI-6
Zebade Post Office (historical)—*building* AL-4
Zeb Cove—*bay* ME-1
Zebe Creek—*stream* CA-9
**Zebedee**—*pop pl* LA-4
Zebedee Brook—*stream* VT-1
Zebedee Ch—*church* LA-4
Zebell Table—*summit* SD-7
**Zebina**—*pop pl* GA-3
Zeb Lake—*lake* OR-9
Zebley Flats—*flat* PA-2
**Zebleys Corner**—*pop pl* PA-2
*Zebly Corner* PA-2
*Zeblys Corner* PA-2
Zeb Mtn—*summit* TN-4
Zeb Post Office (historical)—*building* TN-4
Zebra Hills Dam—*dam* NM-5
Zebra Station—*locale* CA-9
Zebree Homestead—*hist pl* AR-4
Zebs Creek—*stream* WV-2
Zebuion Ch—*church* GA-3
Zebulah Ch—*church* KY-4
*Zebulon* AL-4
*Zebulon* MS-4
Zebulon—*locale* GA-3
**Zebulon**—*pop pl* GA-3
**Zebulon**—*pop pl* KY-4
**Zebulon**—*pop pl* NC-3
Zebulon Airp—*airport* NC-3
Zebulon (CCD)—*cens area* GA-3
Zebulon Ch—*church* AL-4
Zebulon Ch—*church* (2) GA-3
Zebulon Country Club—*locale* NC-3
Zebulon Pike Lake—*lake* MN-6
Zebulon Pike Sch—*school* CO-8
Zebulon Post Office (historical)—*building* MS-4
Zecharias Zion Ch—*church* NC-3
Zech Cem—*cemetery* TN-4
Zechiel Arm—*canal* IN-6
*Zechinder Creek* MT-8
Zed Creek—*stream* TX-5
Zedds Campground—*locale* UT-8
Zedds Meadows—*flat* UT-8
Zedds Mtn—*summit* UT-8
Zedeck Cem—*cemetery* PA-2
Zediker—*locale* CA-9
Zediker—*locale* PA-2
Zedol Lake—*lake* AL-4
**Zee**—*pop pl* CA-9
**Zee**—*pop pl* LA-4
Zeeb Sch—*school* SD-7
Zee Creek—*stream* ID-8
Zeek Lake—*lake* MI-6
Zeek Ridge—*ridge* TN-4
Zeeks Branch—*stream* SC-3
Zeeks Pond—*lake* NY-2
Zee Lake—*lake* WI-6
**Zeeland**—*pop pl* MI-6
**Zeeland**—*pop pl* ND-7
*Zeeland Dam* ND-7
**Zeeland (Township of)**—*pop pl* MI-6
Zeewick Branch—*stream* MO-7
Zegafuse Ditch—*canal* IN-6
*Zegler Mountain* AZ-5
Zeh Corners—*locale* NY-2
Zehender Drain—*stream* MI-6
*Zehner* PA-2
Zehner Cem—*cemetery* OH-6
Zehner Hill—*summit* MD-2
Zehner Millpond—*lake* IN-6
Zehner Millpond Dam—*dam* IN-6
Zehner Run—*stream* MD-2
Zehner Run—*stream* PA-2
**Zehners**—*pop pl* PA-2
Zehntner Ranch—*locale* MT-8
Zeh Sch—*school* MA-1
Zeibright Mine—*mine* (2) CA-9
Zeigels Sch (abandoned)—*school* PA-2
*Zeigenfuss Lake* MI-6
Zeiger, Charles, House—*hist pl* NM-5
Zeigler—*locale* GA-3
Zeigler—*locale* PA-2
**Zeigler**—*pop pl* IL-6
**Zeigler**—*pop pl* IN-6
Zeigler, Rev. Jesse R., House—*hist pl* KY-4
*Zeigler Basin* ID-8
*Zeigler Campground* ME-1
Zeigler Campsite—*locale* ME-1
Zeigler Cem—*cemetery* GA-3
Zeigler Cem—*cemetery* IL-6
Zeigler Cem—*cemetery* (2) LA-4
*Zeigler Cemetery* AL-4
Zeigler Ch—*church* PA-2
Zeigler Creek—*stream* MS-4
Zeigler Creek—*stream* WY-8
Zeigler Dead River—*stream* FL-3
Zeigler (historical)—*locale* SD-7
Zeigler Island—*island* PA-2
**Zeigler Junction**—*pop pl* IL-6
Zeigler Mill (historical)—*locale* PA-2
Zeigler Mine (underground)—*mine* AL-4
Zeigler Oil Field—*other* IL-6
Zeigler Park—*park* OK-5
Zeigler Point—*cape* CA-9
Zeigler Pond—*lake* GA-3
Zeigler Rsvr—*reservoir* IL-6
Zeiglers Pond—*lake* CT-1
Zeiglers Pond—*reservoir* SC-3
Zeigler Spring—*spring* CA-9
**Zeiglerville**—*pop pl* MS-4
Zeiglr Ch—*church* PA-2
Zeikle Cem—*cemetery* MO-7
Zeiner Pond—*lake* CT-1
Zeiss Houses—*hist pl* MO-7
Zeiter Cem—*cemetery* OH-6
Zeiterower Branch—*stream* GA-3
Zeitler Cem—*cemetery* AL-4
Zeits Canyon—*valley* AZ-5
Zeitz Buckhorn Exchange—*hist pl* CO-8
Zeke Allart Dam—*dam* SD-7
Zeke Branch—*stream* KY-4
Zeke Creek—*stream* VA-3
Zeke Hollow—*valley* UT-8
Zeke Hollow Camp Ground—*locale* AL-4
Zeke Hollow Corral—*locale* UT-8
Zeke Lake—*lake* TX-5
Zeke Point—*cape* ME-1
Zeke Run—*stream* WV-2
Zeke Run Cem—*cemetery* WV-2
Zekes Bay—*bay* NY-2
Zekes Branch—*stream* VA-3
Zekes Creek—*stream* KY-4
Zekes Hole—*basin* UT-8
Zekes Island—*island* NC-3
Zekes Lookout—*locale* ME-1
Zekes Meadows—*flat* MT-8
Zekes Mtn—*summit* ME-1
Zekes Point—*locale* KY-4
Zeketown Branch—*stream* KY-4
Zeketown Ridge—*ridge* KY-4
*Zekiah Swamp* MD-2
Zekiah Swamp—*swamp* MD-2
Zekial Creek—*stream* SC-3
Zekin Lake—*lake* NE-7
**Zela**—*pop pl* WV-2
Zela Point—*cape* MI-6
Zela Shoal—*bar* MI-6
Zelatched Point—*cape* WA-9
Zelda—*locale* KY-4
Zelenka Dam—*dam* MT-8
Zelezny Bay—*bay* MT-8
**Zelienople**—*pop pl* PA-2
Zelienople Airp—*airport* PA-2
Zelienople Borough—*civil* PA-2
Zelienople Municipal Airp—*airport* PA-2
Zeliff Pond—*reservoir* NJ-2
Zeliff Pond Dam—*dam* NJ-2
**Zell**—*pop pl* MO-7
**Zell**—*pop pl* SD-7
**Zella**—*pop pl* TX-5
Zella (historical)—*locale* KS-7
Zella Island—*island* ME-1
Zeller, Heinrich, House—*hist pl* PA-2
Zeller Creek—*stream* MT-8
Zeller Elevation County Airp—*airport* IN-6
Zelleria—*locale* MS-4
*Zelleria Plantation* MS-4
*Zellers Pond* IN-6
Zelleweger Wash—*stream* AZ-5
Zell Lake—*reservoir* SD-7
Zell Lake Dam—*dam* SD-7
Zellmer Cem—*cemetery* KS-7
Zellner Brake—*gut* AR-4
Zellner Island—*island* GA-3
Zellobee—*locale* GA-3
Zellors Pond—*lake* IN-6
Zell Pond—*reservoir* OR-9
Zell Sch—*school* SD-7
Zell Station (abandoned)—*locale* MO-7
**Zell Township**—*pop pl* SD-7
**Zellwood**—*pop pl* FL-3
Zellwood Cem—*cemetery* FL-3
Zellwood Sch—*school* FL-3
Zellwood United Methodist Ch—*church* FL-3
**Zelma**—*pop pl* IN-6
Zelma Cem—*cemetery* OK-5
**Zelobee (Zellobee)**—*pop pl* GA-3
*Zelock Run* PA-2
Zelph Calder Dam—*dam* UT-8
Zelph Calder Rsvr—*reservoir* UT-8
Zeltenriech Ch—*church* PA-2
Zembo Rsvr—*reservoir* WY-8
Zemke Branch—*canal* MI-6
Zemorra Creek—*stream* CA-9
Zemp—*locale* SC-3
Zempel Lake—*reservoir* MT-8
Zempel Ranch—*locale* MT-8
Zemp Field—*park* SC-3
**Zemple**—*pop pl* MN-6
**Zemuly**—*pop pl* MS-4
Zemuly Ch—*church* MS-4
Zemuly Post Office (historical)—*building* MS-4
Zemuly Sch (historical)—*school* MS-4
Zemurray Gardens Lodge Complex—*hist pl* LA-4
Zemurray Gardens Lodge Complex (Boundary Increase)—*hist pl* LA-4
Zemurray Lodge—*locale* LA-4
Zemurray Park—*park* LA-4
Zem Zem Hosp—*hospital* PA-2
Zena—*locale* OK-5
**Zena**—*pop pl* NY-2
**Zena**—*pop pl* OR-9
Zena Cem—*cemetery* OK-5
Zena Cem—*cemetery* OR-9
Zena Creek—*stream* ID-8
Zenar—*locale* MO-7
Zenar Springs—*spring* WY-8
**Zenas**—*pop pl* IN-6
Zenas Cem—*cemetery* IN-6
Zenas Elem Sch—*school* IN-6
Zenas Wash—*stream* CA-9
Zenda—*locale* ID-8
Zenda—*locale* VA-3
**Zenda**—*pop pl* KS-7
**Zenda**—*pop pl* WI-6
Zenda Mine—*mine* CA-9
Zendi Mine—*mine* NV-8
Zenender Sink—*basin* MO-7
Zener Cem—*cemetery* IN-6
Zenia—*locale* CA-9
Zenia Bluffs—*cliff* CA-9
Zenia Guard Station—*locale* CA-9
Zeniff—*locale* AZ-5
Zeniff Substation—*locale* AZ-5
Zeni Ridge—*ridge* CA-9
Zenith—*locale* GA-3
Zenith—*locale* ND-7
Zenith—*locale* PA-2
Zenith—*locale* TN-4
Zenith—*locale* WV-2
**Zenith**—*pop pl* IL-6
**Zenith**—*pop pl* KS-7
**Zenith**—*pop pl* WA-9
Zenith (CCD)—*cens area* GA-3
Zenith Ch—*church* GA-3
Zenith East Oil Field—*other* IL-6
Zenith Heights—*locale* MI-6
Zenith Lake—*lake* MN-6
Zenith Lookout Tower—*locale* WI-6
Zenith Mine—*mine* ID-8
Zenith North Oil Field—*other* IL-6
Zenith Park—*park* NM-5
Zenith-Saltwater—*CDP* WA-9
Zenithscah Creek—*stream* KS-7
Zenkner Valley—*valley* WA-9
Zenners—*locale* PA-2
**Zeno**—*pop pl* OH-6
**Zeno**—*pop pl* PA-2
Zenobia—*locale* IL-6
Zenobia—*locale* NV-8
Zenobia—*locale* VA-3
Zenobia Basin—*basin* CO-8
Zenobia Ch—*church* IL-6
Zenobia Creek—*stream* CO-8
Zenobia Peak—*summit* CO-8
Zenobia Rock—*other* AK-9
Zenobia Spring—*spring* NV-8
Zeno Canyon—*valley* ID-8
Zenor, Bayou—*gut* LA-4
**Zenora**—*pop pl* LA-4
Zenor Cem—*cemetery* (2) IN-6
**Zenoria**—*pop pl* LA-4
Zenorsville—*locale* IA-7
*Zenos* AZ-5
Zenser Cem—*cemetery* MO-7
**Zent**—*pop pl* AR-4
*Zenthsc Creek* KS-7
**Zentmyer**—*pop pl* PA-2
Zentner—*locale* CA-9
Zentner Lateral—*canal* CA-9
Zentz Hollow—*valley* AR-4
**Zenz City (Sharpsburg)**—*pop pl* OH-6
**Zeona**—*pop pl* SD-7
Zeorb Hollow—*valley* PA-2
Zepernick Lake—*reservoir* OH-6
Zepernick Lake Wildlife Area—*park* OH-6
Zephaniah Kingsley Grant—*civil* FL-3
Zephania Post Office (historical)—*building* TN-4
Zeph Creek—*stream* ID-8
**Zephyr**—*pop pl* NC-3
**Zephyr**—*pop pl* TX-5
Zephyr, Lake—*lake* FL-3
Zephyr Cem—*cemetery* TX-5
Zephyr Cove—*bay* NV-8
**Zephyr Cove**—*pop pl* NV-8
Zephyr Cove-Round Hill Village—*CDP* NV-8
*Zephyr Creek* SD-7
Zephyr Creek—*stream* AK-9
Zephyr Encampment—*locale* TX-5
*Zephyr Heights* NV-8
*Zephyr Hill* MS-4
*Zephyr Hills* FL-3
**Zephyrhills**—*pop pl* FL-3
Zephyrhills (CCD)—*cens area* FL-3
Zephyrhills HS—*school* FL-3

Zephyrhills MS—*school* ..... FL-3
Zephyrhills North—*CDP* ..... FL-3
Zephyrhills Public Library—*building* ..... FL-3
Zephyrhills South—*CDP* ..... FL-3
Zephyrhills West—*CDP* ..... FL-3
Zephyr Lake—*lake* ..... FL-3
Zephyr Lake—*lake* ..... MN-6
Zephyr Lake—*lake* ..... NH-1
Zephyr Ledges—*bar* ..... ME-1
Zephyr Park—*park* ..... LA-4
Zephyr Point—*summit* ..... NV-8
Zephyr Rock—*bar* ..... ME-1
Zephyr Shop Ctr—*locale* ..... FL-3
Zepp—*locale* ..... VA-3
Zeppenfeld, August, House—*hist pl* ..... IN-6
Zeppernick Cem—*cemetery* ..... OH-6
Zerbe—*locale* ..... PA-2
*Zerbe Creek* ..... PA-2
Zerbel Slough—*gut* ..... IA-7
Zerbert Branch—*stream* ..... MO-7
Zerbe Run—*stream* ..... PA-2
**Zerbe (Township of)**—*pop pl* ..... PA-2
Zerby—*locale* ..... PA-2
Zerby Cem—*cemetery* ..... OH-6
Zerby Gap—*gap* ..... PA-2
Zerby Hill—*summit* ..... IL-6
**Zerkel**—*pop pl* ..... MN-6
Zerkle Cem—*cemetery* ..... OH-6
Zero—*locale* ..... MS-4
Zero—*locale* ..... MT-8
**Zero**—*pop pl* ..... IA-7
Zero Bay—*swamp* ..... GA-3
Zero Butte—*summit* ..... OR-9
Zero Creek—*stream* ..... ID-8
Zero Creek—*stream* ..... MT-8
Zero Flat—*flat* ..... UT-8
Zero Gravity Research Facility (B-2)—*hist pl* ..... OH-6
Zero Lake—*lake* ..... ID-8
Zero Manufacturing Company Dam—*dam* ..... MA-1
Zero Milestone—*other* ..... DC-2
Zeruns Island—*island* ..... MI-6
Zero Post Office (historical)—*building* ..... TN-4
Zero Spring—*spring* ..... CA-9
Zero Spring—*spring* ..... MT-8
Zero Three Ranch—*locale* ..... TX-5
**Zero Township**—*pop pl* ..... NE-7
Zero Tunnel—*mine* ..... CO-8
Zero Waterhole—*lake* ..... OR-9
Zerrer Sch—*school* ..... PA-2
Zerr Gulch—*valley* ..... CA-9
**Zerus**—*pop pl* ..... CA-9
Zeta Cem—*cemetery* ..... GA-3
Zeta Pass—*gap* ..... NH-1
**Zetella**—*pop pl* ..... GA-3
**Zetner Kern**—*pop pl* ..... CA-9
Zeto Point—*cape* ..... AK-9
Zetsche Cem—*cemetery* ..... IL-6
Zetser Hammock—*island* ..... GA-3
Zetta Chapel—*church* ..... VA-3
Zetterberg Company—*hist pl* ..... MN-6
Zetterower Sch—*school* ..... GA-3
Zettle Cem—*cemetery* ..... TX-5
Zettlemoyer Airp—*airport* ..... PA-2
Zettlemoyers Bridge—*bridge* ..... PA-2
Zetto—*locale* ..... GA-3
Zetus—*locale* ..... MS-4
Zetus Post Office (historical)—*building* ..... MS-4
Zeufeldt Arroyo—*stream* ..... NM-5
Zeufle Hollow—*valley* ..... OH-6
Zeus—*locale* ..... VA-3
Zeus and Moses—*pillar* ..... UT-8
**Zevely**—*pop pl* ..... WV-2
Zevely House—*hist pl* ..... NC-3
Zewerk Drain—*canal* ..... MI-6
*Zeyakku-to* ..... MP-9
Zeyen Sch—*school* ..... CA-9
Z H Canyon—*valley* ..... TX-5
Zhilo Cove—*bay* ..... AK-9
Zhulkie Creek—*stream* ..... MI-6
Zia JHS—*school* ..... NM-5
Zia North Side Canal—*canal* ..... NM-5
Zia Pueblo—*hist pl* ..... NM-5
**Zia Pueblo**—*pop pl* ..... NM-5
Zia Pueblo Grant—*civil* ..... NM-5
**Zia Pueblo (Indian Reservation)**—*pop pl* ..... NM-5
**Zia Pueblo (Place)**—*pop pl* ..... NM-5
Zia Rsvr—*reservoir* ..... NM-5
Zia Sch—*school* (2) ..... NM-5
Zia South Side Canal—*canal* ..... NM-5
Zia Supply Canal—*canal* ..... NM-5
Zia Trading Post—*locale* ..... NM-5
Ziba Dimmick State Park—*park* ..... OR-9
**Zibilich**—*pop pl* ..... LA-4
Zich Hills—*range* ..... ND-7
Zich Sch—*school* ..... MT-8
Zickafoose Ch—*church* ..... WV-2
**Zickrick Township**—*pop pl* ..... SD-7
Zidon Ch—*church* ..... GA-3
*Zidonia* ..... AL-4
Ziebach County—*civil* ..... SD-7
Ziebell Sch—*school* ..... IL-6
Zieg Cem—*cemetery* ..... OH-6
Zieg Ditch—*canal* ..... OH-6
Ziegel Ch—*church* ..... PA-2
Ziegele Coulee—*valley* ..... MT-8
*Ziegenfuse Lake* ..... MI-6
Ziegenfuss Lake—*lake* ..... MI-6
*Ziegen-Insel* ..... MP-9
Zieger Hosp—*hospital* ..... MI-6
Ziegler, Wihelm, House-Barn—*hist pl* ..... SD-7
Ziegler Basin—*basin* ..... ID-8
Ziegler Cem—*cemetery* ..... IL-6
Ziegler Chute—*stream* ..... MO-7
Ziegler Cove—*bay* ..... AK-9
Ziegler Creek—*stream* ..... IN-6
Ziegler Creek—*stream* ..... NE-7
Ziegler Creek—*stream* ..... WA-9
Ziegler Ditch—*canal* ..... OH-6
Ziegler Ditch—*canal* ..... WY-8
Ziegler Ford—*locale* ..... VA-3
Ziegler Gulch—*valley* ..... MT-8
Ziegler House—*hist pl* ..... AK-9
Ziegler Island—*island* ..... MO-7
Ziegler Island (historical)—*island* ..... TN-4
*Ziegler Lake* ..... MI-6
Ziegler Lake—*lake* ..... MI-6
Ziegler Lake—*lake* ..... ND-7
Ziegler Mtn—*summit* ..... AZ-5
Ziegler Mtn—*summit* ..... MT-8
Ziegler No 4 Mine—*mine* ..... IL-6
Ziegler Park—*park* ..... WI-6
Ziegler Pond—*lake* ..... NJ-2
Ziegler Rsvr—*reservoir* ..... MT-8
Ziegler Sch—*school* ..... ND-7
Ziegler Slough—*gut* ..... TN-4
Ziegler Slough*—*stream* ..... IA-7
Zieglers Pond—*reservoir* ..... NY-2
**Zieglersville (sta.)**—*pop pl* ..... PA-2
Zieglers Wash—*stream* ..... WY-8
**Zieglerville**—*pop pl* ..... MS-4
**Zieglerville**—*pop pl* ..... PA-2
Ziegman Ditch—*canal* ..... OH-6
Zieler Spring—*spring* ..... WI-6
Zielke Ditch—*canal* ..... OH-6
Zielke Lake—*lake* ..... WI-6
Ziemann Park—*park* ..... WI-6
Ziemer, Arthur C., House—*hist pl* ..... NE-7
Ziemer, Charles, House—*hist pl* ..... AZ-5
Ziemet Ranch—*locale* ..... SD-7
*Zienfield Church* ..... MS-4
Zierath Cem—*cemetery* ..... MO-7
Zier Cors—*locale* ..... IL-6
Ziesman Canyon—*valley* ..... WY-8
Ziesman Wildlife Area—*park* ..... IA-7
Zif Cem—*cemetery* ..... IL-6
Zif Ch—*church* ..... IL-6
**Zif (Township of)**—*pop pl* ..... IL-6
Ziger Spring—*spring* ..... AZ-5
Ziger Tank—*reservoir* ..... AZ-5
Zigfield—*airport* ..... NJ-2
Ziggler Park—*park* ..... OH-6
Ziggurat, Mount—*summit* ..... NV-8
*Ziglag Creek* ..... SC-3
Zigler—*locale* ..... WV-2
Zigler Canal—*canal* ..... LA-4
*Zigler Lake* ..... MI-6
Zigler Lake—*lake* ..... MI-6
Zigler Sch—*school* ..... MD-2
**Zigman**—*pop pl* ..... WA-9
Zigweid Ranch—*locale* ..... WY-8
**Zigzag**—*pop pl* ..... OR-9
Zigzag Branch—*stream* ..... SC-3
Zigzag Canyon—*valley* (3) ..... OR-9
*Zigzag Creek* ..... SC-3
Zigzag Creek—*stream* ..... CA-9
Zigzag Creek—*stream* ..... ID-8
Zigzag Creek—*stream* ..... MI-6
Zigzag Creek—*stream* ..... OR-9
Zig Zag Creek—*stream* (2) ..... OR-9
Zigzag Creek—*stream* ..... OR-9
Zigzag Creek—*stream* ..... TX-5
Zigzag East Lookout—*locale* ..... OR-9
Zigzag Glacier—*glacier* ..... OR-9
Zig Zag Lake—*lake* ..... WA-9
Zigzag Marsh—*swamp* ..... DE-2
Zigzag Mtn—*summit* ..... OR-9
Zigzag Ranger Station—*hist pl* ..... OR-9
Zigzag Rapids—*rapids* ..... ID-8
Zigzag Rapids—*rapids* ..... OR-9
Zigzag River—*stream* ..... OR-9
Zigzag River Campground—*park* ..... OR-9
Zig Zag Rsvr—*reservoir* ..... CO-8
Zig Zag Spring—*spring* ..... AZ-5
Zigzag Spring—*spring* ..... OR-9
Zig Zag Tank—*reservoir* ..... AZ-5
Zigzag Trail—*trail* ..... CA-9
Zig Zag Trail—*trail* ..... CA-9
Zigzag Trail—*trail* ..... OR-9
Zig Zag Trail—*trail* ..... WA-9
Zig-Zag Trail—*trail* ..... WY-8
Zigzag Trail Three—*trail* ..... CA-9
Zigzag Trail Two—*trail* ..... CA-9
*Zihi-dush-jhimi Peak* ..... AZ-5
**Zihlman**—*pop pl* ..... MD-2
*Zihl Nez* ..... AZ-5
Zilbetod Peak—*summit* ..... AZ-5
Zilch Cave—*cave* ..... AL-4
*Zildassaani* ..... AZ-5
Zilditloi Mtn—*summit* ..... NM-5
Zilditloi Wash—*stream* ..... NM-5
Ziler—*locale* ..... TX-5
*Zilh-in-sah Mesa* ..... AZ-5
*Zilh-le-sah Mesa* ..... AZ-5
*Zilh-nez Mesa* ..... AZ-5
*Zilh-tah-jimi Peak* ..... AZ-5
*Zilh-tah-jini Peak* ..... AZ-5
*Zilh-Tusayan* ..... AZ-5
Zilker Park—*park* ..... TX-5
Zilker Sch—*school* ..... TX-5
*Zilla* ..... KS-7
**Zillah**—*pop pl* ..... WA-9
Zillah MS—*school* ..... KS-7
Zillah Peak—*summit* ..... WA-9
Zilla Park—*park* ..... IN-6
Ziller Ranch—*locale* ..... WY-8
*Zillesa Mesa* ..... AZ-5
*Zillesa Peak* ..... AZ-5
*Zillnez* ..... AZ-5
*Zillnez Mesa* ..... AZ-5
Zillo—*locale* ..... IA-7
*Zilner Mesa* ..... AZ-5
*Zilnez Mesa* ..... AZ-5
Zilnez Mesa—*summit* ..... AZ-5
*Zil-ni-tsai* ..... AZ-5
Zilpha Creek—*stream* ..... MS-4
Zilpha Post Office (historical)—*building* ..... MS-4
Zilpo—*locale* ..... KY-4
*Ziltahjimi Mesa* ..... AZ-5
*Ziltahjimi Peak* ..... AZ-5
*Ziltahjini Mesa* ..... AZ-5
Ziltahjini Peak—*summit* ..... AZ-5
*Zilth-dush-jhini* ..... AZ-5
*Zilth Dush Jimi* ..... AZ-5
*Zilth Nez Mesa* ..... AZ-5
*Zilth Tah Jimi Peak* ..... AZ-5
**Zilwaukee**—*pop pl* ..... MI-6
**Zilwaukee (Township of)**—*pop pl* ..... MI-6
*Zil-yazi* ..... AZ-5
Zim—*locale* ..... MN-6
Zimbleman Deer Camp—*park* ..... SD-7
Zimbrick Brook—*stream* ..... MN-6
Zim Cem—*cemetery* ..... MN-6
Zim Ch—*church* ..... MN-6
Zimco—*locale* ..... AL-4
Zim Elevator—*locale* ..... MT-8
Zimerman Cem—*cemetery* ..... OH-6
*Zimershed Canyon* ..... NV-8
Zim Lake—*lake* ..... MI-6
Zimmer—*fmr MCD* ..... NE-7
**Zimmer**—*pop pl* ..... OH-6
Zimmer, Johann, Farmhouse—*hist pl* ..... WI-6
Zimmer, Mount—*summit* ..... MT-8
Zimmer Cem—*cemetery* ..... IL-6
Zimmer Cem—*cemetery* ..... IN-6
Zimmer Cem—*cemetery* (2) ..... NY-2
Zimmer Creek—*stream* ..... ID-8
Zimmer Creek—*stream* ..... LA-4
Zimmer Creek—*stream* ..... MT-8
Zimmer Creek—*stream* ..... TX-5
**Zimmerdale**—*pop pl* ..... KS-7
Zimmer Ditch—*canal* ..... IN-6
Zimmer Hill—*summit* ..... NY-2
Zimmer Lake—*lake* ..... MN-6
Zimmer Lake—*lake* ..... MT-8
Zimmerly Cem—*cemetery* ..... IL-6
Zimmerly Sch—*school* ..... NM-5
Zimmerman—*locale* ..... AL-4
Zimmerman—*locale* ..... LA-4
**Zimmerman**—*pop pl* ..... OH-6
**Zimmerman**—*pop pl* ..... PA-2
Zimmerman, Ezekiel B., Octagon House—*hist pl* ..... OH-6
Zimmerman, Jacob, House—*hist pl* ..... OR-9
Zimmerman, Marie, Farm—*hist pl* ..... PA-2
Zimmerman, Minnie Zulch, House—*hist pl* ..... TX-5
Zimmerman, S. T., House—*hist pl* ..... KS-7
Zimmerman Branch—*stream* ..... MI-6
Zimmerman Burn—*area* ..... OR-9
Zimmerman Butte—*summit* ..... OR-9
Zimmerman Buttes—*summit* ..... WY-8
Zimmerman Camp—*locale* ..... LA-4
Zimmerman Cem—*cemetery* ..... IL-6
Zimmerman Cem—*cemetery* ..... IA-7
Zimmerman Cem—*cemetery* ..... KS-7
Zimmerman Cem—*cemetery* (2) ..... MO-7
Zimmerman Cem—*cemetery* (2) ..... OH-6
Zimmerman Cem—*cemetery* ..... TN-4
Zimmerman Ch—*church* ..... PA-2
Zimmerman Chapel—*church* ..... NC-3
Zimmerman Creek—*stream* ..... AK-9
Zimmerman Creek—*stream* ..... NY-2
Zimmerman Creek—*stream* ..... OR-9
Zimmerman Creek—*stream* ..... PA-2
Zimmerman Ditch—*canal* ..... OR-9
Zimmerman Drain—*canal* ..... MI-6
Zimmerman Draw—*valley* ..... WY-8
Zimmerman Fire Tower—*tower* ..... PA-2
Zimmerman Gun Club—*other* ..... CA-9
Zimmerman Hill—*summit* ..... MT-8
**Zimmerman (historical)**—*pop pl* ..... NC-3
Zimmerman Hollow—*valley* ..... PA-2
Zimmerman House—*hist pl* ..... NH-1
Zimmerman House—*hist pl* ..... NY-2
Zimmerman House—*hist pl* ..... SC-3
Zimmerman Island—*island* ..... PA-2
Zimmerman Island (historical)—*island* ..... TN-4
Zimmerman Kame—*hist pl* ..... OH-6
Zimmerman Lake—*lake* ..... CO-8
Zimmerman Lake—*lake* ..... MN-6
Zimmerman Lake—*lake* ..... NE-7
**Zimmerman (Lake Fremont)**—*pop pl* ..... MN-6
Zimmerman Mtn—*summit* ..... VA-3
Zimmermann Oil Field—*oilfield* ..... KS-7
Zimmerman Point—*summit* ..... AZ-5
Zimmerman Pond—*lake* ..... NY-2
Zimmerman Pond—*lake* ..... WA-9
Zimmerman Pond—*reservoir* ..... SC-3
Zimmerman Ranch—*locale* ..... NM-5
Zimmerman Ranch—*locale* ..... WY-8
Zimmerman Run—*stream* ..... PA-2
Zimmerman Sch—*hist pl* ..... SC-3
Zimmerman Sch—*school* ..... CA-9
Zimmerman Sch—*school* ..... KS-7
Zimmerman Sch—*school* (2) ..... MI-6
Zimmerman Sch (abandoned)—*school* (2) ..... MO-7
Zimmerman Slough—*gut* ..... SD-7
Zimmermans Pass—*channel* ..... MN-6
Zimmerman Springs—*spring* ..... WY-8
Zimmermans Ranch (historical)—*locale* ..... SD-7
Zimmermans Shoals—*bar* ..... TN-4
Zimmerman Trail—*trail* ..... CO-8
Zimmerman Wash—*valley* ..... UT-8
Zimmer Nuclear Power Plant—*facility* ..... OH-6
Zimmer Orphanage—*building* ..... AL-4
Zimmer Ridge—*ridge* ..... SD-7
Zimmerscheidt Community Center—*locale* ..... TX-5
Zimmershed Canyon—*valley* ..... NV-8
Zimmershed Creek—*stream* ..... CA-9
Zimmy Lake—*lake* ..... MN-6
Zimory Canyon—*valley* ..... CA-9
Zimovia Islets—*area* ..... AK-9
Zimovia Point—*cape* ..... AK-9
Zimovia Strait—*channel* ..... AK-9
Zims Point—*cape* ..... OR-9
Zim Zim Creek—*stream* ..... CA-9
**Zinc**—*pop pl* ..... AR-4
Zinc Creek—*stream* ..... CA-9
Zinc Creek—*stream* ..... OR-9
Zinc Dam—*dam* ..... PA-2
Zinc Dam Rsvr—*reservoir* ..... PA-2
Zinc Hill—*summit* ..... CA-9
Zinc Hill—*summit* ..... NM-5
Zinck Fork—*stream* ..... PA-2
*Zinckrick Township* ..... SD-7
Zinc (Township of)—*fmr MCD* ..... AR-4
Zincville—*locale* ..... OK-5
Zindorf Cem—*cemetery* ..... WI-6
Ziner Butte—*summit* ..... ND-7
**Zinfandel**—*pop pl* ..... CA-9
Zingara—*locale* ..... GA-3
Zinger Lateral—*canal* ..... ID-8
*Zinian* ..... MH-9
Zink and Nolan Drain—*stream* ..... MI-6
Zinkand Pond—*lake* ..... PA-2
Zink Cem—*cemetery* (2) ..... OH-6
Zink Ditch—*canal* ..... OH-6
Zink Drain—*stream* ..... MI-6
Zinke Creek—*stream* ..... TX-5
Zinke Lake—*lake* ..... WI-6
Zinker Canyon—*valley* ..... NM-5
Zink Hollow—*valley* ..... AR-4
Zink Lake—*lake* ..... IN-6
Zink Rsvr—*reservoir* ..... OR-9
Zink Sch—*school* ..... MI-6
Zink Spring—*spring* ..... OR-9
Zinnamon Ch—*church* ..... AR-4
*Zinn Branch* ..... WV-2
Zinn Chapel—*church* ..... WV-2
Zinn Hall Public Sch (historical)—*school* ..... AL-4
*Zinnia* ..... MP-9
Zinnia—*locale* ..... WV-2
Zinn Park—*park* ..... AL-4
Zinn Ridge—*ridge* ..... WV-2
Zinn Ridge Trail—*trail* ..... WV-2
Zinns Mill—*locale* ..... PA-2
Zinns Run—*stream* ..... OH-6
Zinser Sch—*school* ..... MI-6
Zinszer's Peter, Mammoth Furniture House—*hist pl* ..... AL-4
Zintel Canyon—*valley* ..... WA-9
Zinter Pond—*lake* ..... OR-9
Zinter Pond—*reservoir* ..... OR-9
Zinzer—*locale* ..... CO-8
Zinzin Bay—*bay* ..... LA-4
Zioe Brown Creek—*stream* ..... GA-3
Ziolkouski Beach Park—*park* ..... OR-9
*Zion* ..... KY-4
*Zion* ..... TN-4
Zion—*locale* ..... GA-3
Zion—*locale* ..... IA-7
Zion—*locale* (2) ..... KY-4
Zion—*locale* ..... LA-4
Zion—*locale* ..... OK-5
Zion—*locale* ..... TN-4
Zion—*locale* ..... UT-8
Zion—*locale* ..... VA-3
Zion—*locale* ..... WI-6
**Zion**—*pop pl* (2) ..... AL-4
**Zion**—*pop pl* ..... AR-4
**Zion**—*pop pl* (2) ..... IL-6
**Zion**—*pop pl* ..... KY-4
**Zion**—*pop pl* ..... MD-2
**Zion**—*pop pl* ..... MS-4
**Zion**—*pop pl* ..... MO-7
**Zion**—*pop pl* ..... NJ-2
**Zion**—*pop pl* ..... PA-2
**Zion**—*pop pl* ..... SC-3
**Zion**—*pop pl* ..... WV-2
Zion—*uninc pl* ..... PA-2
Zion, Lake—*reservoir* ..... AL-4
Zion, Mount—*summit* ..... AR-4
Zion, Mount—*summit* (3) ..... CA-9
Zion, Mount—*summit* (2) ..... CO-8
Zion, Mount—*summit* ..... MA-1
Zion, Mount—*summit* ..... MI-6
Zion, Mount—*summit* ..... NY-2
Zion, Mount—*summit* ..... OR-9
Zion, Mount—*summit* ..... PA-2
Zion, Mount—*summit* ..... UT-8
Zion, Mount—*summit* ..... WA-9
Zion, Mount—*summit* ..... WI-6
Zion, Mount—*summit* ..... VI-3
Zion Acres—*other* ..... TN-4
*Zion AME Ch* ..... AL-4
Zion AME Ch—*church* ..... AL-4
Zion American Bible Coll—*school* ..... TX-5
Zion and Saint Johns Cem—*cemetery* ..... MN-6
Zion Arrows—*pillar* ..... UT-8
Zion Baptist Ch—*church* ..... AL-4
Zion Baptist Ch—*church* (2) ..... MS-4
Zion Baptist Ch (historical)—*church* ..... TN-4
Zion Baptist Temple—*church* ..... UT-8
Zion Bloom Cem—*cemetery* ..... OH-6
Zion Branch—*stream* ..... AL-4
Zion Branch—*stream* ..... TN-4
Zion Branch—*stream* ..... VA-3
Zion Branch Ch—*church* ..... SC-3
Zion Branch Ch—*church* ..... VA-3
Zion Brick Missionary Church—*hist pl* ..... KY-4
Zion Brush Creek Ch—*church* ..... AL-4
Zion Campground Ch—*church* ..... AL-4
Zion Canaan Ch—*church* ..... SC-3
Zion Canyon—*valley* ..... UT-8
Zion Canyon View—*locale* ..... UT-8
Zion Canyon Visitor Center—*locale* ..... UT-8
*Zion Cem* ..... AL-4
*Zion Cem* ..... OR-9
*Zion Cem* ..... PA-2
Zion Cem—*cemetery* (7) ..... AL-4
Zion Cem—*cemetery* (3) ..... AR-4
Zion Cem—*cemetery* ..... GA-3
Zion Cem—*cemetery* ..... ID-8
Zion Cem—*cemetery* (16) ..... IL-6
Zion Cem—*cemetery* (7) ..... IN-6
Zion Cem—*cemetery* (8) ..... IA-7
Zion Cem—*cemetery* (16) ..... KS-7
Zion Cem—*cemetery* ..... KY-4
Zion Cem—*cemetery* ..... LA-4
Zion Cem—*cemetery* ..... MD-2
Zion Cem—*cemetery* (8) ..... MI-6
Zion Cem—*cemetery* (20) ..... MN-6
Zion Cem—*cemetery* (4) ..... MS-4
Zion Cem—*cemetery* (7) ..... MO-7
Zion Cem—*cemetery* (17) ..... NE-7
Zion Cem—*cemetery* (2) ..... NY-2
Zion Cem—*cemetery* (22) ..... ND-7
Zion Cem—*cemetery* (15) ..... OH-6
Zion Cem—*cemetery* (5) ..... OK-5
Zion Cem—*cemetery* ..... OR-9
Zion Cem—*cemetery* (8) ..... PA-2
Zion Cem—*cemetery* ..... SC-3
Zion Cem—*cemetery* (11) ..... SD-7
Zion Cem—*cemetery* (7) ..... TN-4
Zion Cem—*cemetery* (7) ..... TX-5
Zion Cem—*cemetery* ..... VA-3
Zion Cem—*cemetery* (23) ..... WI-6
*Zion Ch* ..... AL-4
*Zion Ch* ..... IN-6
*Zion Ch* ..... MS-4
*Zion Ch* ..... MO-7
*Zion Ch* ..... PA-2
Zion Ch—*church* (27) ..... AL-4
Zion Ch—*church* (7) ..... AR-4
Zion Ch—*church* ..... CO-8
Zion Ch—*church* ..... DE-2
Zion Ch—*church* ..... FL-3
Zion Ch—*church* (12) ..... GA-3
Zion Ch—*church* (27) ..... IL-6
Zion Ch—*church* (22) ..... IN-6
Zion Ch—*church* (11) ..... IA-7
Zion Ch—*church* (8) ..... KS-7
Zion Ch—*church* (18) ..... KY-4
Zion Ch—*church* (6) ..... LA-4
Zion Ch—*church* (8) ..... MD-2
Zion Ch—*church* (15) ..... MI-6
Zion Ch—*church* (29) ..... MN-6
Zion Ch—*church* (13) ..... MS-4
Zion Ch—*church* (20) ..... MO-7
Zion Ch—*church* (20) ..... NE-7
Zion Ch—*church* (3) ..... NJ-2
Zion Ch—*church* (6) ..... NY-2
Zion Ch—*church* (41) ..... NC-3
Zion Ch—*church* (19) ..... ND-7
Zion Ch—*church* (36) ..... OH-6
Zion Ch—*church* (7) ..... OK-5
Zion Ch—*church* (47) ..... PA-2
Zion Ch—*church* (28) ..... SC-3
Zion Ch—*church* (8) ..... SD-7
Zion Ch—*church* (20) ..... TN-4
Zion Ch—*church* (13) ..... TX-5
Zion Ch—*church* (37) ..... VA-3
Zion Ch—*church* (12) ..... WV-2
Zion Ch—*church* (19) ..... WI-6
Zion Ch—*church* ..... WY-8
Zion Ch—*church* ..... VI-3
Zion Ch (abandoned)—*church* ..... MO-7
*Zion Chapel* ..... AL-4
*Zion Chapel* ..... MS-4
Zion Chapel—*church* (5) ..... AL-4
Zion Chapel—*church* (3) ..... AR-4
Zion Chapel—*church* ..... GA-3
Zion Chapel—*church* (2) ..... IN-6
Zion Chapel—*church* (7) ..... MS-4
Zion Chapel—*church* (7) ..... NC-3
Zion Chapel—*church* (2) ..... SC-3
Zion Chapel—*church* (2) ..... TN-4
Zion Chapel—*church* (2) ..... TX-5
Zion Chapel—*church* ..... VT-1
Zion Chapel—*church* ..... VA-3
Zion Chapel—*church* ..... WV-2
Zion Chapel AME Ch—*church* (2) ..... MS-4
*Zion Chapel AME Zion Ch* ..... AL-4
Zion Chapel Cem—*cemetery* (3) ..... MS-4
*Zion Chapel Ch* ..... AL-4
Zion Chapel Ch—*church* ..... AL-4
Zion Chapel Ch—*church* ..... SC-3
Zion Chapel (historical)—*church* ..... MS-4
Zion Chapel Number 2—*church* ..... SC-3
Zion Chapel Sch—*school* ..... AL-4
Zion Chapter House—*hist pl* ..... IL-6
Zion Ch (historical)—*church* (7) ..... AL-4
Zion Ch (historical)—*church* (2) ..... TN-4
Zion Childrens Home—*locale* ..... TN-4
Zion Ch of Jesus Christ—*church* ..... FL-3
*Zion Church* ..... TN-4
Zion Church—*cemetery* ..... IN-6
Zion Church*—*church* ..... ND-7
Zion Church—*hist pl* ..... TN-4
Zion Church—*school* ..... ND-7
Zion Church Cem—*cemetery* ..... AL-4
**Zion City**—*pop pl* ..... AL-4
**Zion City**—*pop pl* ..... LA-4
Zion City Ch—*church* (2) ..... MS-4
Zion City Sch—*school* ..... LA-4
Zion Community Cem—*cemetery* ..... OK-5
Zion Community Ch—*church* ..... UT-8
Zion Covenant Cem—*cemetery* ..... WI-6
*Zion Creek* ..... AL-4
*Zion Creek* ..... SC-3
*Zion Creek* ..... TN-4
*Zion Creek* ..... UT-8
Zion Creek—*stream* ..... AR-4
Zion Creek—*stream* ..... ID-8
Zion Creek—*stream* ..... IN-6
Zion Creek—*stream* (2) ..... MS-4
Zion Creek—*stream* ..... TN-4
Zion Cross Ch—*church* ..... NC-3
Zion Crossroad Ch—*church* ..... NC-3
**Zion Crossroads**—*pop pl* ..... VA-3
Zion Cypress Ch—*church* ..... MS-4
*Zion Cypress Methodist Ch* ..... MS-4
Zion Dam—*dam* ..... AZ-5
Zion Elizabeth Cem—*cemetery* ..... MN-6
Zionell Ch—*church* ..... MS-4
Zion Episcopal Church—*hist pl* ..... GA-3
Zion Episcopal Church—*hist pl* ..... OH-6
Zion Evangelical Church—*hist pl* ..... IN-6
Zion Evangelical Lutheran Ch—*church* ..... FL-3
Zion Evangelical Lutheran Church—*hist pl* ..... MI-6
Zion Evangelical Lutheran Church—*hist pl* ..... WI-6
Zion Evangelical Lutheran Church Cemetery—*hist pl* ..... VA-3
Zion Evergreen Cem—*cemetery* ..... WI-6
Zion Fair Baptist Ch—*church* ..... FL-3
Zion Fair Ch—*church* ..... GA-3
Zionfair Ch—*church* ..... SC-3
Zion Field Ch—*church* ..... AR-4
Zion Field Ch—*church* (2) ..... MS-4
Zionfield Ch—*church* ..... SC-3
Zion Fountain AME Zion Ch—*church* ..... AL-4
*Zion Franklin United Methodist Ch* ..... MS-4
Zion Friendship Ch—*church* ..... AL-4
Zion Gate Missionary Baptist Ch—*church* ..... MS-4
Zion Grove—*locale* ..... PA-2
Zion Grove—*locale* ..... TX-5
**Zion Grove**—*pop pl* ..... NC-3
**Zion Grove**—*pop pl* ..... TN-4
Zion Grove Cem—*cemetery* ..... IL-6
Zion Grove Cem—*cemetery* ..... MS-4
Zion Grove Ch—*church* (2) ..... AL-4
Zion Grove Ch—*church* ..... AR-4
Zion Grove Ch—*church* ..... FL-3
Zion Grove Ch—*church* (5) ..... GA-3
Zion Grove Ch—*church* ..... KY-4
Zion Grove Ch—*church* (2) ..... MS-4
Zion Grove Ch—*church* (2) ..... NC-3
Zion Grove Ch—*church* ..... SC-3
Zion Grove Ch—*church* ..... TN-4
Zion Grove Ch—*church* (3) ..... VA-3
Zion Gummere Cem—*cemetery* ..... IN-6
Zion Harmony Ch—*church* ..... KY-4
Zion Heights—*locale* ..... PA-2
**Zion Heights**—*pop pl* ..... AL-4
Zion Heights Pond—*lake* ..... PA-2
*Zion Hill* ..... PA-2
Zion Hill—*locale* ..... MS-4
Zion Hill—*locale* ..... PA-2
Zion Hill—*locale* ..... TN-4
Zion Hill—*locale* ..... TX-5
**Zion Hill**—*pop pl* ..... FL-3
**Zion Hill**—*pop pl* (2) ..... KY-4
**Zion Hill**—*pop pl* (2) ..... MS-4
**Zion Hill**—*pop pl* ..... MO-7
**Zionhill**—*pop pl* ..... PA-2
**Zion Hill**—*pop pl* ..... SC-3
**Zion Hill**—*pop pl* ..... TN-4
Zion Hill—*summit* ..... CA-9
Zion Hill—*summit* ..... IN-6
Zion Hill—*summit* (2) ..... KY-4
Zion Hill—*summit* ..... ME-1
Zion Hill—*summit* (2) ..... MA-1
Zion Hill—*summit* (2) ..... NH-1
Zion Hill—*summit* ..... TN-4
Zion Hill—*summit* ..... VT-1
Zion Hill Acad (historical)—*school* ..... MS-4
Zion Hill Acad (historical)—*school* ..... TN-4
*Zion Hill Baptist Ch* ..... AL-4
Zion Hill Baptist Ch—*church* ..... AL-4
Zion Hill Baptist Ch—*church* ..... TN-4
*Zion Hill Baptist Church* ..... MS-4
Zion Hill Cem—*cemetery* (2) ..... AL-4
Zion Hill Cem—*cemetery* (2) ..... AR-4
Zion Hill Cem—*cemetery* ..... CT-1
Zion Hill Cem—*cemetery* ..... FL-3
Zion Hill Cem—*cemetery* ..... GA-3
Zion Hill Cem—*cemetery* (2) ..... KY-4
Zion Hill Cem—*cemetery* (2) ..... LA-4
Zion Hill Cem—*cemetery* ..... ME-1
Zion Hill Cem—*cemetery* (13) ..... MS-4
Zion Hill Cem—*cemetery* ..... NE-7
Zion Hill Cem—*cemetery* ..... NY-2
Zion Hill Cem—*cemetery* ..... NC-3
Zion Hill Cem—*cemetery* ..... SC-3
Zion Hill Cem—*cemetery* (2) ..... TN-4
Zion Hill Cem—*cemetery* (4) ..... TX-5
Zion Hill Cem—*cemetery* ..... WA-9
*Zion Hill Ch* ..... MS-4
*Zion Hill Ch* ..... TN-4
Zion Hill Ch—*church* (15) ..... AL-4
Zion Hill Ch—*church* (10) ..... AR-4
Zion Hill Ch—*church* ..... CT-1
Zion Hill Ch—*church* (2) ..... FL-3
Zion Hill Ch—*church* (21) ..... GA-3
Zion Hill Ch—*church* (2) ..... IL-6
Zion Hill Ch—*church* ..... IN-6
Zion Hill Ch—*church* ..... KS-7
Zion Hill Ch—*church* (9) ..... LA-4
Zion Hill Ch—*church* (23) ..... MS-4
Zion Hill Ch—*church* (2) ..... MO-7
Zion Hill Ch—*church* (19) ..... NC-3
Zion Hill Ch—*church* ..... OH-6
Zion Hill Ch—*church* ..... OK-5
Zion Hill Ch—*church* (2) ..... PA-2
Zion Hill Ch—*church* (4) ..... SC-3
Zion Hill Ch—*church* (11) ..... TN-4
Zion Hill Ch—*church* (15) ..... TX-5
Zion Hill Ch—*church* (12) ..... VA-3
Zionhill Ch—*church* ..... VA-3
Zion Hill Ch—*church* ..... VA-3
Zion Hill Ch—*church* ..... WV-2
Zion Hill Ch (historical)—*church* ..... AL-4
Zion Hill Ch (historical)—*church* (2) ..... MS-4
Zion Hill Ch (historical)—*church* ..... SC-3
Zion Hill Ch (historical)—*church* ..... TN-4
Zion Hill Creek—*stream* ..... MS-4
*Zion Hill Free Will Baptist Church* ..... MS-4
Zion Hill Methodist Ch—*church* ..... MS-4
Zion Hill Mission—*church* ..... KY-4
Zion Hill Missionary Baptist Ch—*church* ..... IN-6
Zion Hill Post Office (historical)—*building* ..... MS-4
Zion Hill Post Office (historical)—*building* ..... PA-2
Zion Hill Primitive Baptist Ch—*church* ..... FL-3
Zion Hill Primitive Baptist Ch—*church* ..... MS-4
Zion Hills Ch—*church* ..... GA-3
Zion Hill Sch—*school* ..... AL-4
Zion Hill Sch—*school* ..... AR-4
Zion Hill Sch—*school* (2) ..... KY-4
Zion Hill Sch—*school* (2) ..... MS-4
Zion Hill Sch—*school* (2) ..... NE-7
Zion Hill Sch—*school* ..... TN-4
Zion Hill Sch—*school* ..... VA-3
Zion Hill Sch (historical)—*school* ..... AL-4
Zion Hill Sch (historical)—*school* (2) ..... MS-4
Zion Hill Sch (historical)—*school* (5) ..... TN-4
Zion Hill Tunnel—*tunnel* ..... CA-9
Zion Hirl Ch—*church* ..... AR-4
Zion (historical)—*locale* (2) ..... MS-4
**Zion (historical)**—*pop pl* ..... NC-3
**Zion (historical)**—*pop pl* ..... OR-9
Zion Hollow—*valley* ..... TN-4
Zion Hope Baptist Ch—*church* ..... FL-3
Zion Hope Cem—*cemetery* ..... GA-3
Zion Hope Ch—*church* ..... AL-4
Zion Hope Ch—*church* (2) ..... FL-3
Zion Hope Ch—*church* (7) ..... GA-3
Zion Hope Ch—*church* ..... KY-4
Zion Hope Ch (historical)—*church* ..... MO-7
Zion Hope Independent Baptist Ch—*church* ..... IN-6
Zion Hope Missionary Baptist Ch—*church* ..... FL-3
Zion Hope Missionary Ch—*church* ..... FL-3
Zion Hopewell Ch—*church* ..... SC-3
*Zion in Grove Ch* ..... AL-4
*Zion Inn* ..... UT-8
Zion Kindergarten/Preschool—*school* ..... DE-2
Zion Langedahl Cem—*cemetery* ..... ND-7
Zion Level Ch—*church* ..... NC-3
Zion Lodge—*locale* ..... UT-8
**Zion Lodge**—*pop pl* ..... UT-8
Zion Lodge-Birch Creek Hist Dist (Boundary Increase)—*hist pl* ..... UT-8
Zion Lodge Hist Dist—*hist pl* ..... UT-8
Zion Lookout—*locale* ..... TX-5
Zion Lutheran Cem—*cemetery* ..... IA-7
Zion Lutheran Cem—*cemetery* ..... KS-7
Zion Lutheran Cem—*cemetery* ..... MN-6
Zion Lutheran Ch—*church* ..... FL-3
Zion Lutheran Ch—*church* ..... IA-7
Zion Lutheran Ch—*church* ..... UT-8
*Zion Lutheran Church* ..... SD-7
Zion Lutheran Church—*hist pl* ..... CT-1
Zion Lutheran Church—*hist pl* ..... NY-2
Zion Lutheran Church—*hist pl* ..... NC-3
Zion Lutheran Church—*hist pl* (2) ..... OH-6
Zion Lutheran Church—*hist pl* ..... PA-2
Zion Lutheran Church—*hist pl* ..... SD-7
Zion Lutheran Church—*hist pl* ..... WI-6
Zion Lutheran Church and Graveyard—*hist pl* ..... PA-2
Zion Lutheran Church and Sch—*school* ..... FL-3
Zion Lutheran Church-LCA—*church* ..... FL-3
Zion Lutheran Sch—*hist pl* ..... OH-6
Zion Lutheran Sch—*school* ..... FL-3
Zion Lutheran Sch—*school* (3) ..... IN-6

Zumbrum Sch—*school* ....PA-2
Zummo—*locale* ....TX-5
Zumpf Lake—*lake* ....ND-7
Zumwait Detention Dam—*dam* ....AZ-5
Zumwalles Lake—*lake* ....MN-6
Zumwalt—*locale* ....OR-9
Zumwalt—*locale* ....WA-9
Zumwalt Coulee—*valley* ....MT-8
Zumwalt County Park—*park* ....OR-9
Zumwalt Creek—*stream* ....CA-9
Zumwalt Flat—*flat* ....CA-9
Zumwalt Meadows—*flat* ....CA-9
Zumwalt Ranch—*locale* ....NM-5
Zumwalt School (abandoned)—*locale* ....OR-9
Zumwalt Station Park—*park* ....IA-7
Zundel Hollow—*valley* ....PA-2
Zundelowitz JHS—*school* ....TX-5
*Zuni* ....CO-8
Zuni—*locale* ....CO-8
Zuni—*locale* ....NM-5
**Zuni**—*pop pl* ....NM-5
**Zuni**—*pop pl* ....VA-3
Zuni Basin—*basin* ....AZ-5
Zuni Buttes—*summit* ....NM-5
Zuni Canal—*canal* ....NM-5
Zuni Canyon—*valley* (2) ....NM-5
Zuni (CCD)—*cens area* ....NM-5
Zuni-Cibola Complex—*hist pl* ....NM-5
Zuni Creek—*stream* ....ID-8
Zuniga Point —*cape* ....CA-9
Zuniga Shoal —*bar* ....CA-9
Zuni (historical)—*locale* ....AL-4
*Zuni Mesas* ....AZ-5
Zuni Mountains—*other* ....NM-5
*Zuninga Point* ....CA-9
*Zuninga Shoal* ....CA-9
Zunino Ranch—*locale* ....NV-8
Zunino Rsvr—*reservoir* ....NV-8
Zuni Park—*park* (2) ....AZ-5
Zuni Plateau—*area* ....NM-5
*Zuni P.O.* ....AL-4
Zuni Point—*cliff* ....AZ-5
Zuni Pueblo—*civil* ....NM-5
**Zuni Pueblo (Indian Reservation)**—*pop pl* ....NM-5
Zuni-Ramah Navajo (CCD)—*cens area* ....NM-5
Zuni River—*stream* ....AZ-5
Zuni River—*stream* ....NM-5
Zuni Salt Lake—*lake* ....NM-5
Zuni Sch—*school* ....NM-5
Zuni Sch (historical)—*school* ....AL-4
Zuni Spring—*spring* ....AZ-5
Zuni Spring—*spring* ....NM-5
**Zuni (Sta)**—*pop pl* ....NM-5
Zuni Trail—*trail* ....AZ-5
Zuni Wash Bridge—*bridge* ....AZ-5
Zuni Well—*well* (2) ....AZ-5
Zunkerville—*locale* ....TX-5
Zurbrugg Memorial Hosp—*hospital* ....NJ-2
Zurcher Apartments—*hist pl* ....ID-8
Zurcher Draw—*valley* ....SD-7
*Zurcher Reservoir* ....CO-8
Zurhellen Bayou—*stream* ....MS-4
Zurhorst House—*hist pl* ....AL-4
Zurich—*locale* ....CA-9
Zurich—*locale* ....NY-2
**Zurich**—*pop pl* ....KS-7
**Zurich**—*pop pl* ....MT-8
Zurich, Lake—*lake* ....IL-6
Zurich Cem—*cemetery* ....KS-7
*Zurich Heights* ....IL-6
Zurich Park—*park* ....MT-8
Zurick Ranch—*locale* ....NM-5
**Zurkow Development (subdivision)**—*pop pl* ....DE-2
*Zurksville* ....PA-2
Zur Ruhe Cem—*cemetery* ....WI-6
*Zurukan* ....FM-9
Zuspan Cem—*cemetery* ....WV-2
Zussman Playground—*park* ....MI-6
Zuta—*locale* ....GA-3
Zuta Branch—*swamp* ....GA-3
Zutavern Cem—*cemetery* ....OH-6
**Zutphen**—*pop pl* ....MI-6
Zutphen Cem—*cemetery* ....MI-6
Zutphen Sch—*school* ....MI-6
Zuver—*locale* ....CA-9
Zuver Mine—*mine* ....CA-9
Zuver Sch (abandoned)—*school* ....PA-2
*Zuyder Zee* ....MA-1
*Zuydt Revier* ....NJ-2
*Zuydt Tevier* ....NY-2
**Zu Zu**—*pop pl* ....TN-4
*Zuzume* ....FM-9
Z V Creek—*stream* ....WY-8
*Zwaanendael* ....DE-2
Zwagg Island—*island* ....OR-9
Zwahlen Ditch—*canal* ....UT-8
Zwahlen Wash—*valley* ....UT-8
Zwahlen Wash Debris Basin Rsvr—*reservoir* ....UT-8
Zwang Peak—*summit* ....CA-9
Zweigel Hardware Store Bldg—*hist pl* ....OK-5
Zwemer Hall, Northwestern College—*hist pl* ....IA-7
Zwick Cem—*cemetery* ....OH-6
Zwicker Cem—*cemetery* ....TN-4
Zwicker Rsvr—*reservoir* ....CO-8
Zwicker Rsvr No. 2—*reservoir* ....CO-8
Zwick Point—*cape* ....CT-1
Zwicky Creek—*stream* ....TX-5
*Zwiefel Creek* ....OR-9
Zwinggi Lake—*swamp* ....MN-6
**Zwingle**—*pop pl* ....IA-7
Zwingley Cem—*cemetery* ....OH-6
Zwischen, Mount—*summit* ....CO-8
**Zwolle**—*pop pl* ....LA-4
ZX Brattain Ditch—*canal* ....OR-9
Z X Canyon—*valley* ....NM-5
ZX Ranch—*locale* (2) ....OR-9
Z X Ranch—*locale* ....OR-9
ZX Ranch Grain Camp—*locale* ....OR-9
Z-X Ranch (historical)—*locale* ....SD-7
ZX Ranch Red House—*locale* ....OR-9
*Zyabatto To* ....MP-9
*Zyaritto* ....MP-9
Zyba—*locale* ....KS-7
**Zybach**—*pop pl* ....TX-5
Zybach Cem—*cemetery* ....TX-5
Zyba Oil Field—*oilfield* ....KS-7
**Zylks**—*pop pl* ....LA-4
**Zylonite (subdivision)**—*pop pl* ....MA-1
Zymns Butte—*summit* ....NV-8
Zzyzx—*locale* ....CA-9
*Zzyzx Mineral Spring Resort* ....CA-9
*Zzyzx Mineral Springs* ....CA-9
Zzyzx Spring—*spring* ....CA-9
*Zzyzx Springs* ....CA-9


# 0-9


*00/1987)* ....PA-2
*2-Buttes Creek* ....WA-9
2\c No 1 Drain—*canal* ....CA-9
2D Northwest Ditch—*canal* ....UT-8
2 Lake—*lake* ....MI-6
*2 Little River* ....NC-3
2 Schali Drain—*canal* ....CA-9
*2 V Creek* ....WY-8
2 1/2 Beacon Street—*hist pl* ....NH-1
*2 1/2 Mile Creek* ....ID-8
3 Lake—*lake* ....MI-6
3 Lakes Plaza (Shop Ctr)—*locale* ....FL-3
*3 Little River* ....NC-3
3-M Airp—*airport* ....PA-2
*3 Mountain* ....CO-8
3SE33—*hist pl* ....AR-4
4A Point—*cliff* ....CO-8
4A Ridge—*ridge* ....CO-8
4 A-2020 Dam—*dam* ....MS-4
4 A-2020 Lake—*reservoir* ....MS-4
4H Camp—*locale* ....OR-9
4-H Club Camp—*locale* ....MA-1
4-H Park—*park* ....IN-6
4 J Canyon—*valley* ....WY-8
*4 Mile Creek* ....IA-7
4th Street Sch—*school* ....NY-2
4 Winds Aerodrome Airp—*airport* ....IN-6
5 Points West (Shop Ctr)—*locale* ....FL-3
6 and 50 Rsvr—*reservoir* ....CO-8
6 A Ranch—*locale* ....NM-5
6 Street Haitian Mission in Pompano—*church* ....FL-3
6th Ave Hotel-Windsor Hotel—*hist pl* ....AZ-5
7 Bays Airp—*airport* ....WA-9
7 - B Dam—*dam* ....AZ-5
7 L Bar Ranch—*locale* ....CO-8
7 Mile Corral—*locale* ....WY-8
7 N Mesa—*summit* ....CO-8
7th Ward Sch—*school* ....OH-6
7xv Ranch—*locale* ....NM-5
8 Dollar Mountain Creek—*stream* ....OR-9
8 Lake—*lake* ....MI-6
10 Cottages on Short Street—*hist pl* ....AZ-5
12 Mile Saddle—*gap* ....ID-8
12th Ave Drain—*stream* ....ID-8
12th Ave South Bridge—*hist pl* ....WA-9
*13 Mile Mountain* ....WA-9
*13 Mile Pond* ....FL-3
14—*channel* ....PR-3
14th Ave South Bridge—*hist pl* ....WA-9
*14th Street Bridge* ....DC-2
14th Street Viaduct—*hist pl* ....CO-8
16 Altamont Terrace—*hist pl* ....MD-2
16th Street Shop Ctr—*locale* ....FL-3
*17 Mile Creek* ....IN-6
18th Separate Company Armory—*hist pl* ....NY-2
19th Place Park—*park* ....FL-3
19th Street Bridge—*hist pl* ....CO-8
19th Ward Meetinghouse and Relief Society Hall—*hist pl* ....UT-8
20th Century Club—*hist pl* ....NV-8
20th Street Shop Ctr—*locale* ....FL-3
20th Street Viaduct—*hist pl* ....CO-8
21st Street Recreation Center—*locale* ....FL-3
22 Mesa—*summit* ....AZ-5
25 Mesa—*summit* ....CO-8
25 Mesa Guard Station—*locale* ....CO-8
25th Street Shop Ctr—*locale* ....IN-6
26th District Police and Patrol Station—*hist pl* ....PA-2
27th Ave Farmers Market (Shop Ctr)—*locale* ....FL-3
*29 Gulch* ....MT-8
*29 Mile Lake* ....AZ-5
33–61 Emerson Place Row—*hist pl* ....NY-2
34 Creek—*stream* ....ID-8
*34 Lakes* ....MI-6
34th Street Ch of God—*church* ....FL-3
36th Street Park—*park* ....FL-3
41 Cow Camp—*locale* ....CO-8
42 Lateral—*canal* ....WY-8
*44 Lake* ....OR-9
44 Ranch—*locale* ....WY-8
45 Hill—*summit* ....ID-8
45 Ranch—*locale* ....ID-8
45th Street Mental Health Center—*hospital* ....FL-3
45 Windmill—*locale* ....ID-8
48th Police Precinct Station—*hist pl* ....NY-2
52nd Police Precinct Station House and Stable—*hist pl* ....NY-2
53rd Street Park—*park* ....FL-3
54th Street Mini Park—*park* ....FL-3
56 Signers of the Declaration of Independence, The—*park* ....DC-2
63 Ranch—*locale* ....CO-8
64th Street Park—*park* ....FL-3
68th Avenue-64th Place Hist Dist—*hist pl* ....NY-2
68th Police Precinct Station House and Stable—*hist pl* ....NY-2
74 Ranch—*locale* ....CO-8
75 Murray Street Bldg—*hist pl* ....NY-2
75th and Metcalf Shop Ctr—*locale* ....KS-7
75th Avenue-61st Street Hist Dist—*hist pl* ....NY-2
*76 Gulch* ....AZ-5
83rd Precinct Police Station and Stable—*hist pl* ....NY-2
84 Ranch—*locale* ....CO-8
86th Ave Ch of Christ in Seminole—*church* ....FL-3
98th Ave Shop Ctr—*locale* ....FL-3
*101 Creek* ....ND-7
101 Ranch—*locale* ....CA-9
103rd Ohio Volunteer Infantry Association Barracks—*hist pl* ....OH-6
109 Community Hall—*building* ....SD-7
127th Street Shop Ctr—*locale* ....FL-3
136th Street Plaza, SW (Shop Ctr)—*locale* ....FL-3
163rd Street Mall—*locale* ....FL-3
170th Street Shop Ctr—*locale* ....FL-3
196 Mile Creek—*stream* ....AK-9
197 1/2 Mile Creek—*stream* ....AK-9
200–208 Decatur Street—*hist pl* ....MD-2
**214 North Temple Condominium**—*pop pl* ....UT-8
310 West Church Street Apartments—*hist pl* ....FL-3
*311 Canyon* ....NV-8
*380* ....PA-2
420 Main Ave Commercial Bldg—*hist pl* ....MN-6
500 Airp—*airport* ....IN-6
500 Shop Ctr—*locale* ....IN-6
500 Varas Square-Government Reserve—*hist pl* ....CA-9
*540* ....TN-4
601 Industrial Park—*locale* ....NC-3
706 Bridge—*bridge* ....FL-3
969 Ditch—*canal* ....CO-8
1000 Island Lake—*lake* ....WY-8
1001 Fourth Ave Plaza Heliport—*airport* ....WA-9
1300 Grove Street House—*hist pl* ....MS-4
*1500* ....TN-4
1616 Bldg—*hist pl* ....PA-2
1724 Chester Courthouse—*hist pl* ....PA-2
1761 Milestone—*hist pl* ....RI-1
1767 Milestones—*hist pl* ....MA-1
1790 Footprints—*hist pl* ....HI-9
1790 House—*hist pl* ....MA-1
1800's Mexican Consulate—*hist pl* ....TX-5
1841 Goshen Courthouse—*hist pl* ....NY-2
1862 Overland—*trail* ....NV-8
1872 California-Nevada State Boundary Marker—*hist pl* ....CA-9
1872 California-Nevada State Boundary Marker—*hist pl* ....NV-8
1879 Houston Waterworks—*hist pl* ....TX-5
1884 Houston Cotton Exchange Bldg—*hist pl* ....TX-5
1900 Rittenhouse Square Apartments—*hist pl* ....PA-2
1907 House—*hist pl* ....MS-4
1908 Clovis City Hall and Fire Station—*hist pl* ....NM-5
*1911* ....MN-6
1918 Creek—*stream* ....WA-9
1927 Cut-off Lake—*lake* ....AR-4
1931 Tempe Bridge—*hist pl* ....AZ-5
*1938 Dam* ....MA-1
1940 Cone—*summit* ....HI-9
1949 Cone—*summit* ....HI-9
*1950 Dam* ....MA-1
*1980 Breach* ....WA-9
1980 Crater—*crater* ....WA-9
2000 Block Of Eye Street, NW—*hist pl* ....DC-2
2345—*spring* ....CA-9
2900 Block Grove Ave Hist Dist—*hist pl* ....VA-3
3222 Center (Shop Ctr)—*locale* ....FL-3
3670, Point—*cliff* ....WA-9
*8760* ....ID-8
12346—*valley* ....TX-5